AN

ANGLO-SAXON DICTIONARY

BASED ON THE MANUSCRIPT COLLECTIONS

OF THE LATE

JOSEPH BOSWORTH, D.D., F.R.S.

RAWLINSONIAN PROFESSOR OF ANGLO-SAXON
IN THE UNIVERSITY OF OXFORD.

EDITED AND ENLARGED

BY

T. NORTHCOTE TOLLER, M.A.

LATE FELLOW OF CHRIST'S COLLEGE, CAMBRIDGE;
AND SMITH PROFESSOR OF ENGLISH IN THE OWENS COLLEGE, MANCHESTER.

OXFORD UNIVERSITY PRESS

Oxford University Press, Ely House, London W.1

GLASGOW NEW YORK TORONTO MELBOURNE WELLINGTON
CAPE TOWN IBADAN NAIROBI DAR ES SALAAM LUSAKA ADDIS ABABA
DELHI BOMBAY CALCUTTA MADRAS KARACHI LAHORE DACCA
KUALA LUMPUR SINGAPORE HONG KONG TOKYO

ISBN 0 19 863101 4

FIRST EDITION 1898
REPRINTED 1929, 1954, 1972
1973

REPRODUCED AND PRINTED BY PHOTOLITHOGRAPHY AND BOUND IN
GREAT BRITAIN AT THE PITMAN PRESS, BATH

PREFACE.

WITH the issue of the last part of this work comes the necessity for some additions to the Preliminary Notice that accompanied Parts I and II. In that Notice it was mentioned that Dr. Bosworth's MS. for so much of the Dictionary as was contained in Part II was incomplete, and a similar remark applies with more force to the succeeding parts: little, indeed, was added in the MS. to what was already contained in the previous edition. If with corresponding parts of this previous edition the later part of the present one be compared, it will be seen that much had to be done in order to get together the additional material that finds its place in the new work. As the editor could not devote his time exclusively to the Dictionary, the length of the interval between the date of appearance of Part II and that of Part IV may seem not inexcusably great. It has, however, been so great that in some respects alterations have occurred in matters with which the Dictionary is concerned. Fresh material has been brought to light, or old material has been brought forth in more accessible form; the views on many points connected with the language that are now held, are not those of fifteen years ago, and there will be certainly some points in work done fifteen years ago that now will need revision. There will also be other points that need revision, but which cannot plead this excuse: mistakes and omissions, to some extent, are almost inevitable. Revision required under one or other head will be attempted in a supplement, which will be prepared as soon as possible.

In the course of the work some alterations have been made in the plan adopted by Dr. Bosworth. One of the difficulties connected with the cataloguing of English words preserved in works written before 1100 is due to the variety of forms which a word may take according to the time at which, or the locality in which, the MS. where it occurs was written. The Old-English specimens are scattered over centuries, and belong to different parts of England; naturally the form of a word is not always the same in the earlier and in the later specimen of the same locality, or in the contemporary specimens of different localities. In the earlier part of the Dictionary the different forms of a word are given separately, in the later part they are collected under a single form; e.g. in the former case words having the mutation of *eá* may appear under each of the forms which the varieties of that mutation (*ȇ*, *ié*, *ȋ*, *ȳ*) admit of, in the latter one form alone (*ȋ*) is given. Slight alterations, too, will be found noted in the list of references.

With regard to the marks used to distinguish difference in the vowels it may be noticed that *eá*, *eó* are employed in all cases where the short *ea*, *eo* are not meant, e.g. *sceóp*, Goth. *skóp*, has the same symbols as *leóf*, Goth. *liubs*, etc.

My thanks are due to Professor Skeat for the readiness which he has always shown to answer an appeal for help in a difficulty; to Professor Kluge and to Professor Heyne for very helpful criticism of the earlier parts of the Dictionary. To the former I am indebted not only for pointing out omissions, but for the assistance he has given in remedying them. He very kindly sent me a copy of the glosses cited under the abbreviation Germ., and further gave the Delegates of the University Press the opportunity, which they accepted of acquiring a collection of Anglo-Saxon words that he had made. These words were drawn for the most part from sources already utilized for the Dictionary, but it was an advantage to have even the same material noted by another. As an example of this it may be remarked that between thirty and forty of the passages cited under S were taken from Professor Kluge's notes, and the number would have been larger had not, as already stated, Professor Kluge's criticism called attention to omissions in the earlier part of the work. To the late Dr. Grein my obligations are very great. He has done so much to remove the difficulties of one of the most difficult parts of the vocabulary—the poetical—that he has earned the gratitude of every one who attempts to work in the same field as the author of the Sprachschatz der Angelsächsischen Dichter.

In conclusion, it may not be out of place to refer to some of the difficulties which are met with in an attempt to compile an Anglo-Saxon Dictionary. The Anglo-Saxon remains are varied in respect to the subjects of which they treat, and the technical terms peculiar to some of these subjects, e.g. law, require the knowledge of a specialist. The poetical vocabulary, again, as a part of the language almost lost in later times presents many difficulties. Even where at first sight it might seem that the solution of difficulties would be most certainly furnished—in the case of glosses to Latin words—the expectation is not always realized, and at times the gloss is the only authority for both the English and the Latin word. And throughout there is the difficulty of realizing the condition of those who used the language and thus of appreciating the significance of the language they used. It is hoped, however, that the numerous citations given under many words, by shewing the actual use of those words, may help to the appreciation of their significance, and so supplement the often necessarily imperfect explanations afforded by the Modern English words that are used as the nearest equivalents to the old forms. Further, English philology has become so extensive a study that to keep pace with its developments is a task that might occupy so much time as to leave comparatively little for other work. To compile an Anglo-Saxon Dictionary calls for so much in the compiler that some leniency towards shortcomings may perhaps be looked for by any one who attempts the labour.

EXPLANATION OF REFERENCES.

In the following list a want of uniformity may be noticed in the case of some of the contractions used. This is due partly to modifications of Dr. Bosworth's forms, which it seemed convenient to make; partly to different conditions in respect to texts cited, which have been brought about while the work was in progress: some texts, that existed in MS. only, have been printed; of others, that were already printed, new editions have appeared, which were more convenient to refer to than were the old. Cross references are given below in these cases. Double references are given to passages cited from the poetry, to English editions and to Grein's Bibliothek der Angelsächsischen Poesie; in the later the contractions used are those to be found in Grein's Lexicon, and they are given together at the end of this list.

Where a reference to any citation consists of more than one part (e. g. Bt. —; Fox —), the several parts are separated by a semi-colon: where after a citation several references are given, these are separated by a colon.

When consecutive citations are taken from the same work the full reference is given only with the first (e. g. Bt. is not repeated where consecutive citations are taken from Boethius; or if the reference be of one part, e. g. Nar. —, the Nar. is not repeated).

A. D. Altenglische Dichtungen der MS. Harl. 2253, herausgegeben von K. Böddeker, Berlin, 1878.

A. P. v. Allit. Pms.

A. R. The Ancren Riwle, edited for the Camden Society (No. lvii.) by J. Morton, 1853. Quoted by page and line.

Abus. Codex Junii 23, fol. 60, in the Bodleian Library. See Wanley's Catalogue, p. 37, and Engl. Stud. viii. 62.

Ælf. Ep. 1st = L. Ælfc. P. (q.v.).

Ælf. Test. Ælfric on the Old Testament in Sweet's Anglo-Saxon Reader (1st ed.).

Ælfc. Gen. Thw. The preface to Genesis in Thwaites' edition of the Heptateuch. v. Gen.

Ælfc. Gl. Codex Junii 71, in the Bodleian Library. See Wanley's Catalogue, p. 96. Printed by Somner (Som.) at the end of his Dictionary, and again by Wright in A Volume of Vocabularies (Wrt. Voc.). In the early part of the Dictionary the page of the MS., and the page and number of the word in Somner and in Wright are given, but later the reference is to Wright only (Wrt. Voc. i.).

Ælfc. Gl.; Zup. Ælfric's Grammatik und Glossar, herausgegeben von Julius Zupitza, Berlin, 1880. Quoted by page and line.

Ælfc. Gr. Ælfric's Grammar, referred to at first in the edition by Somner, printed with his Dictionary (Som.), later in that of Zupitza (Zup. v. preceding explanation). Quoted by section of the Grammar, and by page and line of the editions.

Ælfc. pref. Gen. = Ælfc. Gen. Thw.

Ælfc. T. *or* **Ælfc. T. Lisle.** A Saxon treatise concerning the Old and New Testament. . . . Now first published in print with English of our times by William L'Isle, London, 1623. Quoted by page and line.

Ælfc. T. Grn. The same text, in vol. i. of Bibliothek der Angelsächsischen Prosa, herausgegeben von Chr. Grein. 1872. See also Ælf. Test.

Æqu. Vern. This contraction (used, but not explained, by Lye) seems to refer to the Anglo-Saxon abridgement of Bede's *De Natura Rerum* in MS. Cotton. Tiberius, B. V. (see Wanley's Catalogue, p. 216). It is printed in Popular Treatises on Science, edited for the Historical Society of Science by Wright, London, 1841 (Wrt. popl. science); and again in the 3rd vol. of Cockayne's Leechdoms (Lchdm. III). The later quotations are taken from the latter edition. v. Equin. vern.

Al. The Life of St. Alexius, edited by F. J. Furnivall, E.E.T.S., No. 69, 1878. Quoted by line.

Alb. resp. Albini responsa ad Sigewulfi interrogationes. For a text and MSS. see Anglia, vol. vii. pp. 1 sqq.

Ald. Sancti Aldhelmi Opera, edited by J. A. Giles, Oxford, 1844. Quoted by page.

Alex. The Alliterative Romance of Alexander, edited by J. Stevenson, Roxburghe Club, 1849. Quoted by line.

Alex. (Skt.). The same, edited by W. W. Skeat, E.E.T.S., No. lxvii., 1866. Quoted by line.

Alis. King Alisaunder, in Weber's Metrical Romances, vol. i., Edinburgh, 1810. Quoted by line.

Allit. Pms. Early English Alliterative Poems, edited by R. Morris, E.E.T.S., No. 1, 1864. Quoted by page and line.

Am. and Amil. Amis and Amiloun, in Weber's Metrical Romances, vol. ii.

An. Lit. Anecdota Literaria, edited by Thomas Wright, London, 1844. Quoted by page and line.

An. (*or* **Anal.**) **Th.** *or* **Th. An.** (**Anal., Anlct.**). Analecta Anglo-Saxonica, by Benjamin Thorpe, London, 1846. Quoted by page and line.

And. = St. And. (q. v.).

Andr. Grm. See Grm[m]. A. u. E.

Andr. Kmbl. The Poetry of the Codex Vercellensis, edited by J. M. Kemble for the Ælfric Society. Part 1. The Legend of St. Andrew, London, 1844.

Andr. Recd. The same poem edited for the Record Commission by Benjamin Thorpe, but not published. See Glos. Epnl. Recd.

Andrews' Old English Manor. The Old English Manor, a study in English Economic History, by Charles McLean Andrews, Baltimore, 1892.

Anglia. Anglia, Zeitschrift für Englische Philologie. Halle, 1878–

Anlct. v. An. Th.

Ap. (Apol.) Th. *or* **Th. Ap. (Apol.).** The Anglo-Saxon Version of the Story of Apollonius of Tyre, from a MS. in the Library of C. C. C., Cambridge (v. Wanley's Catalogue, p. 146), edited by Benjamin Thorpe, London, 1834. Quoted by page and line.

App. (Lib.) Scint. v. Scint.

Apstls. Crd. An interlinear version of the Apostles' Creed on folio 199 a of the MS. referred to as Ps. Lamb. (q. v.).

Apstls. Kmbl. The Fates of the Twelve Apostles in The Poetry of the Codex Vercellensis. Part II. v. Andr. Kmbl.

Apstls. Recd. The same poem edited for the Record Commission. v. Andr. Recd.

Arth. and Merl. Arthour and Merlin, a Metrical Romance edited by W. D. Turnbull, Abbotsford Club, 1838. Quoted by line.

Ass. B. Assumpcio Beate Marie, edited by J. R. Lumby, E.E.T.S., No. 14, 1866. Quoted by line.

Ath. Crd. *or* **Athan.** An interlinear version of the Athanasian Creed, folios 200 a–202 b of the MS. referred to as Ps. Lamb. (q. v.). Quoted by paragraph.

Ayenb. Dan Michel's Ayenbite of Inwyt, in the Kentish Dialect, 1340, edited by R. Morris, E.E.T.S., No. 23, 1866.

Bailey. An Universal Etymological English Dictionary, by N. Bailey, 10th edition, London, 1742.

Basil admn.; Norm. The Anglo-Saxon Remains of St. Basil's Admonitio ad filium spiritualem, edited by the Rev. Henry W. Norman, 2nd edition, London, 1849. Quoted by chapter, and by page and line.

Bd. de nat. rm. (rerum). *See under* Æqu. Vern.

Bd.; M. The Old English Version of Bede's Ecclesiastical History of the English People, edited by Thomas Miller, E.E.T.S., Nos. 95, 96, 1890–1891. Quoted by book and chapter, and by page and line.

Bd.; S. Baedae Historia Ecclesiastica a gloriosissimo veterum Anglo-Saxonum rege Aluredo Saxonice reddita, cura et studio Johannis Smith, Cantabrigiae, 1722. Quoted as in previous work.

Bd.; Whel. (Whelc.). Bedae Venerabilis Historia Ecclesiastica Anglorum, Anglo-Saxonice ex versione Ælfredi Magni Gentis et Latine, cura Abrahami Wheloci, Cantabrigiae, 1644.

Ben. Vocabularium Anglo-Saxonicum, opera Th. Benson, Oxoniae, 1701.

Beo. Kmbl. The Anglo-Saxon poems of Beowulf, the Traveller's Song and the Battle of Finnesburh, edited by John M. Kemble, 2nd edition, London, 1835.

Beo. Th. The Anglo-Saxon Poem of Beowulf, edited by Benjamin Thorpe, Oxford, 1855.

Beves. Sir Beves of Hamtune, edited by E. Kölbing, E.E.T.S., Nos. xlvi., xlviii., 1885–1886. Quoted by line.

Blickl. Gl. (Gloss.). Glosses taken from a copy of the Roman Psalter in the library at Blickling Hall. Printed at the end of the Blickling Homilies. See next paragraph.

Blickl. Homl. *or* **Homl. Blick.** The Blickling Homilies, edited by R. Morris, E.E.T.S., Nos. 58, 63, 1874–1876. Quoted by page and line.

Boutr. (Btwk.) Scrd. Screadunga. Anglo-Saxonica maximam partem inedita publicavit C. G. Bouterwek, Elberfeld, 1858. Quoted by page and line.

Brand. Popular Antiquities of Great Britain, edited, from the materials collected by John Brand, by W. C. Hazlitt. Three vols. London, 1870.

Bridf[r]. Bridferth's Enchiridion contained in MS. No. 328 in the Ashmolean Library (see Wanley's Catalogue, p. 103). Quoted by folio. This MS. is printed in Anglia viii. 298–337, and later references are to this edition by page and line.

Bt.; Fox. King Alfred's Anglo-Saxon version of Boethius de Consolatione Philosophiae, edited by the Rev. S. Fox. Bohn's Antiquarian Library, London, 1864. Quoted by chapter and paragraph, and by page and line.

Bt. Met. Fox *and* **Bt. Tupr.** The Anglo-Saxon metrical version of the metrical portions of Boethius, with a verse translation by M. Tupper. At the end of the previous work. Quoted by number of metre and line.

Bt.; Rawl. Boethii Consolationis Philosophiae libri v Anglo-Saxonice redditi ab Ælfredo; ad Apographum Junianum expressos edidit Christophorus Rawlinson, Oxoniae, 1698. Quoted by chapter and paragraph, and by page and line.

Btwk. Cædmon's Biblische Dichtungen, herausgegeben von K. W. Bouterwek. Erster Theil, Gütersloh, 1854. The references are to the Anglo-Saxon piece 'De officiis diurnalium et nocturnalium horarum,' preface, pp. cxciv–ccxxii. Quoted by page and line.

Btwk. Scrd. v. Boutr. Scrd.

Byrht. Th. The poem on the battle of Maldon in Thorpe's Analecta Anglo-Saxonica. Quoted by page and line.

C. L. Castel off Love, edited by R. F. Weymouth, Philol. Soc., 1864. Quoted by line.

C. M. Cursor Mundi, edited by R. Morris, E.E.T.S. Quoted by line.

C. R. Ben. An Anglo-Saxon version of the Benedictine Rule contained in a MS. in the library of Corpus Christi College, Cambridge. See Wanley's Catalogue, p. 122. Quoted by chapter. In the latter part of the Dictionary references are given to the work noticed under R. Ben., in which this MS. is used.

Cambr. MS. Ps. = Ps. Spl. C. (q. v.).

Canon. Hrs. Appendix to Hickes' Letters to a Popish Priest. Quoted by page and line. The piece is printed in Select Monuments of the Doctrine and Worship of the Catholic Church in England before the Norman Conquest, by E. Thompson, London, 1875 (2nd edition).

Cant. Ab. (Abac., Habac., Abac. Lamb.). A gloss of Habakkuk, 3, 2–19, contained in the same MS. as Ps. Lamb. (q. v.) on folios 189–191. Quoted by verse.

Cant. Abac. Surt. A gloss of the same material as the preceding, printed in An Anglo-Saxon and Early English Psalter, edited by J. Stevenson, Surtees Soc., No. 19. Quoted by page and line.

Cant. (Cantic.) An. A gloss of the song of Hannah (I. Sam. 2, 1–10), contained in the same MS. as Ps. Lamb. (q. v.) on folios 185 b–186 b. Quoted by verse.

Cant. Es. A gloss of Isaiah 12, 1–6, contained in the same MS. as the preceding, on folio 184. Quoted by verse.

Cant. Ez. (Cant. Ezech. Lamb.). A gloss of Isaiah 38, 10–20, contained in the same MS. as the preceding, on folios 184 b–185 b. Quoted by verse (in some instances the folio of the MS. is also given).

Cant. M. (Moys., Moys. Lamb.). A gloss of Exodus 15, 1–19, contained in the same MS. as the preceding, on folios 186 b–189. Quoted as in the preceding.

Cant. M. ad fil. (Moys. Isrl. Lamb.). A gloss of Deuteronomy 32, 1–43, contained in the same MS. as the preceding, on folios 191–195. Quoted as in the preceding.

Cant. Mar. A gloss of Luke 1, 46–55, contained in the same

MS. as the preceding, on folios 198–198 b. Quoted by verse.

Cant. Moys. Ex. (**Cantic. Moys.**); **Thw.: Cant. Moys. Thw.** A gloss of Exodus 15, 1–19, at the end of Thwaites' Heptateuch.

Cant. Zach. A gloss of Luke 1, 68–79, contained in the same MS. as Ps. Lamb. (q. v.) on folios 197–198. Quoted by verse.

Cart. Eadgif. R. A charter of Queen Eadgifu, v. Chart. Th. 201.

Cath. Ang. (**Angl.**). Catholicon Anglicum, edited by S. J. Herrtage, E.E.T.S., No. 75, 1881. Quoted by page.

Cd.; **Th.** (*later* **Cd. Th.**). Cædmon's Metrical Paraphrase of parts of the Holy Scripture, in Anglo-Saxon, by Benjamin Thorpe, London, 1832 Quoted at first by folio, and by page and line, later by page and line.

Chart. Erl. A Handbook to the Land Charters and other Saxonic Documents, by John Earle, M.A., Oxford, 1888. Quoted by page and line.

Chart. (**Ch.**) **Th.** Diplomatarium Anglicum Aevi Saxonici, by Benjamin Thorpe, London, 1865. Quoted by page and line.

Chauc. The abbreviations used in connexion with Chaucer are not given as not requiring explanation.

Chr.; **Erl.** Two of the Saxon Chronicles parallel with supplementary extracts from the others, edited by John Earle, M.A., Oxford, 1865. Quoted by year, and by page and line.

Chr.; **Gib.** Chronicon Saxonicum, Latine et Anglo-Saxonice, cum notis Edmundi Gibson, Oxon., 1692.

Chr.; **Ing.** The Saxon Chronicle, with an English translation and notes, by the Rev. James Ingram, 1823.

Chr.; **Th.** The Anglo-Saxon Chronicle, according to the several original authorities. Edited, with a translation, by Benjamin Thorpe, Master of the Rolls Series, 1861. Quoted by year, and by page, line, and column.

Chron. Abing. Chronicon Monasterii de Abingdon. Edited by Rev. J. Stevenson, Master of the Rolls Series, 1858.

Chron. Vilodun. Chronicon Vilodunense, sive de vita et miraculis sanctae Edithae, cur. W. H. Black. Quoted by line.

Cl. and Vig. Dict. An Icelandic-English Dictionary, based on the MS. collections of the late Richard Cleasby, enlarged and completed by Gudbrand Vigfusson, Oxford, 1874.

Cod. Dip. B. Cartularium Saxonicum: a collection of Charters relating to Anglo-Saxon History, by Walter de Gray Birch, London, 1883–1893. Quoted by volume, page and line.

Cod. Dip. (**Dipl.**) **Kmbl.** Codex Diplomaticus Aevi Saxonici, opera Johannis M. Kemble. Publications of the English Historical Society, 1839–1848. Quoted by volume, page and line.

Cod. Exon. v. Exon. Th.

Coll. Monast. Th. *or* **Wrt.** Colloquium ad pueros linguae Latinae locutione exercendos ab Ælfrico compilatum. Printed in Thorpe's Analecta (v. An. Th.), or in Wright's Vocabularies (v. Wrt. Voc. i.). Quoted by page and line.

Confess. Pecc. (**Peccat.**). A gloss of a 'Confessio pro peccatis ad Deum,' contained in the same MS. as Ps. Lamb. (q. v.) on folios 182 b–183 b.

Corp. Gl. (**ed.**) **Hessels.** An eighth-century Latin-Anglo-Saxon Glossary preserved in the Library of Corpus Christi College, Cambridge, edited by J. H. Hessels, Cambridge, 1890. Quoted by page and number of word.

Cot. In the earlier part of the Dictionary several glossaries found among the Cotton MSS. are referred to by this abbreviation. These glossaries are printed in Wrt. Voc. i., ii., to which works later references are given; in a supplement to the Dictionary similar references will be found to replace the abbreviation in question.

D. Arth. Morte Arthure; or the Death of Arthur, edited by Edm. Brock, E.E.T.S., No. 8, 1871. Quoted by line.

Dep. Rich. Richard the Redeles, an Alliterative Poem on the Deposition of Richard II, edited by W. W. Skeat, E.E.T.S., No. 54, 1873. Quoted by passus and line.

Destr. Tr. The Gest Historiale of the Destruction of Troy, edited by G. A. Panton and D. Donaldson, E.E.T.S., Nos. 39, 56. Quoted by line.

Deut. The Anglo-Saxon version of Deuteronomy in Thw. Hept. (q. v.) or in Bibliothek der Angelsächsischen Prosa, herausgegeben von Chr. Wilh. Mich. Grein, erster Band, 1872. Quoted by chapter and verse.

Dial. v. Gr. Dial.

Dief. Vergleichendes Wörterbuch der Gothischen Sprache, von Dr. Lorenz Diefenbach, 1851.

Dietr. Dietrich's Commentatio de Kynewulfi poetae aetate, Marburg, 1859–1860.

Dōm. L. Be Dōmes Dæge, an Old English version of the Latin poem ascribed to Bede. Edited with other short poems from the MS. in the Library of Corpus Christi College, Cambridge, by J. R. Lumby, E.E.T.S., No. 65, 1876. Quoted by page and line.

E. D. S. (**Publ.**). The publications of the English Dialect Society.

E. E. T. S. The publications of the Early English Text Society.

E. G. English Gilds, edited by Miss L. Toulmin Smith, E.E.T.S., No. 40, 1870. Quoted by page and line.

Earle A.S. Lit. Anglo-Saxon Literature. By John Earle. London: Society for Promoting Christian Knowledge, 1884.

Ecclus. The book of Ecclesiasticus.

Elen. Grm. v. Grmm. A. u. E.

Elen. Kmbl. The Poetry of the Codex Vercellensis, edited for the Ælfric Society by J. M. Kemble. Part II. Elene and Minor Poems, London, 1856.

Engl. Stud. Englische Studien. Organ für englische Philologie. Herausgegeben von Dr. Eugen Kölbing.

Ep. Gl. (**Gloss. Ep.**). The Epinal Glossary, Latin and Old-English of the eighth century. Edited by Henry Sweet. Printed for the Philological and Early English Text Societies, 1883. Quoted by page, column and line.

Equin. vern. An Anglo-Saxon summary of Bede's De Temporibus, referred to in Wanley's Catalogue under the heading De equinoctio vernali. It is printed in Lchdm. iii. pp. 232–280, and the quotations from the work are, except in the earlier part of the Dictionary, from this printed form. v. Æqu. Vern.

Erf. Gl. A Latin-Anglo-Saxon Glossary contained in a MS. preserved in the Amplonian library at Erfurt. Printed in the oldest English Texts, edited by Henry Sweet, E.E.T.S., No. 83, 1885.

Ettm. Lexicon Anglosaxonicum, edidit Ludovicus Ettmüllerus. Quedlinburgii et Lipsiae, 1851.

Ettm. Poet. Anglosaxonum poetae atque scriptores prosaici. Edidit Ludovicus Ettmüllerus. Quedlinburgii et Lipsiae, 1850.

Ex. The Anglo-Saxon version of Exodus. v. Deut.

Exod. Thw. v. preceding.

Exon.; **Th.** (*later* **Exon. Th.**). Codex Exoniensis. A Collection of Anglo-Saxon poetry, from a MS. in the library of the Dean and Chapter of Exeter, by Benjamin Thorpe, London, 1842. Quoted at first by folio, and by page and line, later by page and line.

Fer. Sir Ferumbras, edited by S. J. Herrtage, E.E.T.S., No. xxiv., 1879. Quoted by line.

Fins. Th. The Anglo-Saxon poem of the Fight at Finnesburg, edited by Benjamin Thorpe. In the same volume with Beo. Th. (q. v.).

Fl. a. Bl. Floriz and Blauncheflur, edited by J. R. Lumby, E.E.T.S., No. 14, 1866. Quoted by line.

Frag. Kmbl. A Fragment, Moral and Religious, contained in the Poetry of the Codex Vercellensis, edited by J. M. Kemble (v. Elen. Kmbl.).

Frag. Phlps. Fragment of Ælfric's Grammar, Ælfric's Glossary, and a Poem on the Soul and the Body, in the orthography of the twelfth century, edited by Sir T. Phillipps, London, 1838.

Frag. Recd. The same poem as Frag. Kmbl., printed with Andr. Recd. (q. v.).

Fulg. S. Fulgentii Regulae Monachorum, an Anglo-Saxon gloss of the Latin work contained in MS. Cott. Tib. A. 3 (see Wanley's Catalogue, p. 91).

Gam. The Tale of Gamelin, edited by W. W. Skeat, Oxford, 1884. Quoted by line.

Gaw. Sir Gawayne and the Green Knight, edited by R. Morris, E.E.T.S., No. 4, 1864. Quoted by line.

Gen. The Anglo-Saxon version of Genesis. v. Deut.

Gen. and Ex. The Story of Genesis and Exodus, edited by R. Morris, E.E.T.S., No. 7, 1865. Quoted by line.

Gen. pref. Thw. The Anglo-Saxon preface to Genesis in Thw. Hept. Quoted by page and line.

Germ. Die Bouloneser Angelsächsischen Glossen zu Prudentius. Herausgegeben von Dr. Alfred Holder. In vol. xi. (new series) of Germania. Quoted by page and number preceding the gloss. v. Gl. Prud., Gl. Prud. H., Glos. Prudent. Recd.

Gl. Amplon. Glossae Amplonianae, ed. Oehler in Jahn's Jahrb. 13, 1847.

Gl. E. A Latin-Anglo-Saxon Glossary contained in MS. Cott. Cleopatra A III. (v. Wanley's Catalogue, p. 238). Printed in Wrt. Voc. ii. pp. 70 sqq., whence, except at the beginning, quotations are taken.

Gl. M. An Anglo-Saxon Gloss of Aldhelm's De laude virginitatis, published in Mone's Quellen und Forschungen, Leipzig, 1830. Quoted by page. See Hpt. Gl., where the same gloss is referred to.

Gl. Mett. Glossae Mettenses in Mone Anzeiger, 1839.

Gl. Prud. (1). Glosses to Prudentius in Mone Anzeiger, 1839. Quoted by number of gloss. From the same MS. as that given under Germ.

Gl. Prud. (2). The same abbreviation as the preceding has also sometimes been used for another work, which elsewhere is referred to as Glos. Prud. (q. v.) or simply Prud. The quotations, however, in this case are by paragraph.

Gl. Prud. H. This is the gloss given under Germ. (q. v.). The quotations are by folio instead of by page.

Gl. Wülck. v. Wülck.

Glos. Brux. Recd. An Anglo-Saxon Vocabulary taken from a MS. in the Royal Library at Brussels. It is printed in Wrt. Voc. i. pp. 62 sqq., and to this edition alone, except in the earlier part of the Dictionary, references are given.

Glos. Epnl. Recd. The Epinal Glossary printed (but not published) in Appendix B of An Account of the most important Public Records of Great Britain (Publications of the Record Commissioners), London, 1836.

Glos. Prud. *or* **Prud.** Englische Übersetzungen der lateinischen Erklärungen von Bildern zur Psychomachie des Prudentius entlehnt: (A) einer Hs. im Britischen Museum, Cotton. Cleop. C. viii, (B) einer Cambridger Hs., Corpus Christi College 23, published by J. Zupitza in Zeitschrift für deutsches Alterthum, vol. 8 (new series), 1876. Quoted by paragraph and MS.

Glos. Prudent. Recd. The glosses given under Germ., printed in the same work as the Glos. Epnl. Recd.

Gloss. Ep. v. Ep. Gl.

Glostr. Frag. Legends of Saint Swiđun and Sancta Maria Ægyptiaca, published by John Earle, M.A., London, 1861.

Gospel of Nicodemus. Quoted from The Apocryphal New Testament. Printed for William Hone, 1820. Tenth edition, London, 1872.

Goth. Gothic; the text referred to has been Die Gothischen Sprachdenkmäler, herausgegeben von H. F. Massmann. v. Dief.

Gow. Confessio Amantis of John Gower, edited by R. Pauli, London, 1857. Quoted by volume, page and line.

Greg. Die englische Gregorlegende, herausgegeben von F. Schulz, Königsberg, 1876. Quoted by line.

Gr. (Greg.) Dial. The Anglo-Saxon version of Gregory's Dialogues. Quoted from Lye. v. Wanley's Catalogue, p. 71.

Grff. Althochdeutscher Sprachschatz von Dr. E. G. Graff. Berlin, 1834-1842.

Grm. (Grmm. Gr.). Deutsche Grammatik von Dr. Jacob Grimm. 2. Ausgabe.

Grm[m]. A. u. E. (And. u. El.). Andreas und Elene. Herausgegeben von Jacob Grimm. Cassel, 1840.

Grm[m]. D. M. Deutsche Mythologie, von Jacob Grimm. Zweite Ausgabe, Göttingen, 1844.

Grm[m]. Gesch. D. S. (Gsch.). Geschichte der deutschen Sprache, von Jacob Grimm. 3. (2.) Ausgabe, Leipzig, 1868.

Grm. Mythol. The first edition of Grmm. D. M.

Grm[m]. R. A. Deutsche Rechtsalterthümer, von Jacob Grimm. 2. Ausgabe, Göttingen, 1854.

Guthl. (Gu.); Gdwin. The Anglo-Saxon version of the Life of St. Guthlac, Hermit of Crowland, edited by C. W. Goodwin, London, 1848. Quoted by chapter (Guthl.) and by page and line (Gdwin.).

H. (K.) de visione Isaiae. The reference is to Wanley's Catalogue, p. 27, l. 9; the passage will be found Wulfst. 44, 23.

H. M. Hali Meidenhad, edited by O. Cockayne, E.E.T.S., No. 18, 1866. Quoted by page and line.

H. R. Legends of the Holy Rood, edited by R. Morris, E.E.T.S., No. 46, 1871. Quoted by page and line.

H. S. Robert of Brunne's Handling Sinne, edited by F. J. Furnivall, Roxburghe Club, 1862. Quoted by line.

H. Z. (Hpt., Hpt. Zeit[sch].). Zeitschrift für deutsches Alterthum, herausgegeben von Moritz Haupt.

Hall. (Halliw., Halwl.) Dict. A Dictionary of Archaic and Provincial Words, by J. O. Halliwell. Seventh edition, London, 1872.

Handl. Synne. v. H. S.

Harl. Gl. 978. This glossary is printed at p. 139 of Wrt. Voc. i.

Havel. The Lay of Havelok the Dane, edited by W. W. Skeat, E.E.T.S., No. iv., 1868. Quoted by line.

Hêl. Hêliand. Herausgegeben von Moritz Heyne. Paderborn, 1866.

Heli. Schmel. Heliand. Poema Saxonicum seculi noni. Edidit J. A. Schmeller, 1830.

Hem. (Heming.). Hemingi Chartularium Eccl. Wigorniensis, edidit T. Hearne, Oxon., 1723. Tom. ii.

Herb.; Lchdm. i. An Anglo-Saxon Herbarium printed in Lchdm. i. Quoted by section and paragraph (Herb.), and by page and line. See Lchdm.

Hexam. (Hex.); Norm. The Anglo-Saxon version of the Hexameron of St. Basil, edited by H. W. Norman.

2nd edition, London, 1849. Quoted by chapter (Hexam.), and by page and line (Norm.).

Hick. Thes. Linguarum veterum septentrionalium thesaurus, auctore G. Hickesio, Oxoniae, 1705.

Hick. Diss. Ep. (Hickes' Diss.). G. Hickesii de antiquae litteraturae septentrionalis utilitate dissertatio epistolaris, Oxoniae, 1703. Contained in vol. i. of the preceding.

Hom. = O. E. Homl.

Hom. de Comp. Cord. Cited by Dr. Bosworth from Lye.

Hom. 8 Cal. Jan. This homily is printed in Homl. Th. i. 28. [v. ge-þryle, the reference to which = Homl. Th. i. 34, 34.]

Homl. As[s]. Angelsächsische Homilien und Heiligenleben, herausgegeben von Bruno Assman, Kassel, 1889. [Bibliothek der Angelsächsischen Prosa, begründet von C. W. M. Grein, 3. Band.] Quoted by page and line of section.

Homl. Blick. v. Blickl. Homl.

Homl. in nat. Innoc. This homily is printed in Homl. Th. i. 76. [v. ærst, the reference to which = Homl. Th. i. 78, 18.]

Homl. Pasc. Daye. A Sermon of the Paschall Lambe to be spoken unto the people at Easter. Imprinted (with other works of Ælfric) at London by John Daye, 1567.

Homl. Pasc. Lisl. The same homily as the preceding, published in 1623 by Lisle. The homily is printed in Homl. Th. ii. 262.

Homl. Skt. Ælfric's Metrical Lives of Saints, edited by W. W. Skeat, E.E.T.S., Nos. 76, 82, 94, 1881–85–90. Quoted by volume, homily and line.

Homl. Th. The Homilies of Ælfric, edited by B. Thorpe for the Ælfric Society, London, 1844–1846. Quoted by volume, page and line.

Horn (K[ing] Horn). King Horn, edited by J. R. Lumby, E.E.T.S., No. 14, 1866. Quoted by line.

Hpt. v. H. Z.

Hpt. Gl. Die Angelsächsischen Glossen in dem Brüsseler Codex von Aldhelms Schrift De Virginitate, published in vol. ix. of Haupt's Zeitschrift, by K. Bouterwek. Quoted by page and line.

Hpt. Zeit[sch]. v. H. Z.

Hymn. ad Mat. Hymnus ad Matutinos Dies Dominicos, contained in fols. 195–196 of Ps. Lamb. Quoted by verse.

Hymn. in Dedic. Eccles. (Hymn.). The piece referred to will be found printed in Homl. Th. ii. 576 sqq.

Hymn. L. = Hymn. ad Mat.

Hymn. Lye = Hymnarium in Cott. MS. Jul. A. 6.

Hymn. Surt. Anglo-Saxon Hymnarium, edited by Rev. J. Stevenson, Surtees Society, vol. xxiii., 1851. Quoted by page and line.

Hymn. T. P. An Anglo-Saxon gloss of Dan. 3, 57–88, contained in the same MS. as Ps. Lamb. on folios 196–197. Quoted by verse.

Icel. Icelandic; the forms are taken from Cleasby and Vigfusson's Dictionary.

Invent. Crs. Recd. The poem in the Codex Vercellensis on the finding of the Cross (v. Elen. Kmbl.), edited for the Record Commission by Benjamin Thorpe, but not published. See Andr. Recd.

Jamieson. Jamieson's Dictionary of the Scottish Language, abridged by J. Johnstone. A new edition by J. Longmuir, Edinburgh, 1877.

Japx. Gysbert Japicx, a Friesian poet, who wrote about 1650.

Jellinghaus. Die Westfälischen Ortsnamen nach ihren Grundwörtern, von H. Jellinghaus. Kiel und Leipzig, 1896.

Jn. The Gospel of St. John. v. Mt.

Job Thw. A portion of Ælfric's homily on Job (v. Homl. Th. ii. 446) printed in Thw. Hept. Quoted by page and line.

Jos. (1). The Anglo-Saxon version of the book of Joshua. v. Deut.

Jos. (2). (Jos. of Arith.). Joseph of Arimathie, edited by W. W. Skeat, E.E.T.S., No. 44, 1871.

Josc. For the passage under *sliten* cited from Joscelin by Lye, see Lk. Spt. p. 2, 11. For Joscelin's Dictionary see Wanl. Cat. p. 101.

Jud. (1). The Anglo-Saxon version of the book of Judges. v. Deut.

Jud. (2) (Jud. Thw.). Where the quotation is by page and line the reference is to the matter printed in Thw. Hept. at the end of the book of Judges.

Jud. (3). See under the contractions used in Grein's Dictionary.

Jud. Civ. Lund. Judicia Civitatis Lundoniae. L. Ath. v.; Th. i. 228.

Judth.; Thw. (*later* Judth. Thw.). The poem of Judith printed at the end of Thw. Hept. Quoted by section (Judth.), and by page and line (Thw.).

Jul. (Juliana). The Liflade of St. Juliana, edited by O. Cockayne and T. Brock, E.E.T.S., No. 51, 1872. Quoted by page and line.

K. Alis. v. Alis.

Kath. The Life of Saint Katherine; in the earlier part of the Dictionary reference is to the edition of Rev. J. Morton, later to that of Dr. E. Einenkel, E.E.T.S., No. 80, 1884. Quoted by line. The correspondence of lines in the two editions is marked in the later.

Kent. Gl. Kentische Glossen des neunten Jahrhunderts, published in Zeitschrift für deutsches Alterthum, vol. ix., new series, by J. Zupitza. These glosses, from MS. Cott. Vesp. D 6, are on the book of Proverbs, and in the earlier part of the Dictionary the abbreviation used is Prov.; in this case the quotation is by chapter, in the other by the number of the gloss.

Ker. Kero, the name assumed to be that of the author of a glossary, and of a gloss of the Benedictine Rule, in the Alemannic dialect.

Kil. Etymologicum Teutonicae linguae, sive dictionarium Teutonico-Latinum, studio et opera Corn. Kiliani Dufflaei, Antverpiae, 1599.

King Horn. v. Horn.

Kmbl. Cod. Dipl. v. Cod. Dipl. Kmbl.

Kmbl. Sal. and Sat. v. Salm. Kmbl.

L.; Th. The following contractions refer to the matter contained in Ancient Laws and Institutes of England, edited by Benjamin Thorpe, and printed under the direction of the Commissioners on the Public Records of the Kingdom, 1840. Quoted by (section and) paragraph (L. —), and by volume, page and line (Th.):—

- **L. A. G.** Alfred and Guthrum's Peace.
- **L. Ælfc. C.** Canons of Ælfric.
- **L. Ælfc. E.** Ælfric's Epistle, 'Quando dividis Chrisma.'
- **L. Ælfc. P.** Ælfric's Pastoral Epistle.
- **L. Æðelb.** = L. Ethb.
- **L. Æðelst.** = L. Ath.
- **L. Alf.** Extracts from Exodus, prefixed to Alfred's Laws.
- **L. Alf. pol.** Laws of King Alfred.
- **L. Ath. i–v.** Laws of King Athelstan.
- **L. C. E.** Ecclesiastical Laws of King Cnut.
- **L. C. F.** Constitutiones de Foresta of King Cnut.
- **L. C. S.** Secular Laws of King Cnut.
- **L. de Cf.** De Confessione (Canons enacted under King Edgar).
- **L. E. B.** Ecclesiastical Compensations (Bôt).

L. Ecg. C. Ecgberti Confessionale.
L. Ecg. E. Excerptiones Ecgberti.
L. Ecg. P. i–iv. Ecgberti Poenitentiale (libri iv.).
L. Ecg. P. addit. Additamenta to the preceding.
L. E. G. Laws of Edward and Guthrum.
L. E. I. Ecclesiastical Institutes.
L. Ed. Laws of King Edward.
L. Ed. C. Laws of King Edward the Confessor.
L. Edg. i, ii. Laws of King Edgar, (i) ecclesiastical, (ii) secular.
L. Edg. C. Canons enacted under King Edgar.
L. Edg. H. Laws of King Edgar (How the Hundred shall be held).
L. Edg. S. Supplement to King Edgar's Laws.
L. Edm. B. Laws of King Edmund (of betrothing a woman).
L. Edm. C. „ „ „ (Concilium Culintonense).
L. Edm. E. „ „ „ (Ecclesiastical).
L. Edm. S. „ „ „ (Secular).
L. Eth. i–ix. Laws of King Ethelred.
L. Ethb. Laws of King Æthelbirht of Kent.
L. Ff. Of Forfang.
L. H. Laws of King Henry I.
L. H. E. Laws of Hlothhære and Eadric.
L. I. P. Institutes of Polity.
L. In. Laws of King Ine.
L. M. I. P. Modus Imponendi Poenitentiam.
L. M. L. Mercian Law.
L. N. P. L. Law of the Northumbrian Priests.
L. O. Oaths.
L. O. D. Ordinance respecting the Dúnsǽtas.
L. P. M. Of Powerful Men.
L. Pen. Of Penitents.
L. R. Ranks.
L. R. S. Rectitudines Singularum Personarum.
L. Th. C. Theodori Capitula et Fragmenta.
L. Th. P. Theodori Liber Poenitentialis.
L. Wg. Wergilds.
L. Wih. Laws of King Wihtræd.
L. Wil. i–iv. Laws of William the Conqueror.

L. Const. W. Wilkins' (v. Wilk.) edition of the text cited as L. I. P. in Thorpe's Laws.

L. Eádg., L. Eádg. Suppl., L. Eccles., L. Ecg. P. A. = L. Edg., L. Edg. S., L. E. I., L. Ecg. P. addit.

L. Edw. Conf. Schmid. The Laws of King Edward the Confessor in Schmid's A. S. Gesetz. (q.v.).

L. H. R. = H. R.

L. Lund. = L. Ath. v.

L. M. 1, 2, 3. Three books on medicine, contained in Lchdm. ii. Quoted by book and section; in the latter part of the Dictionary the references are to Lchdm. only.

L. Med. ex Quadr. = Med. ex Quadr.

L. N. F. Altenglische Legenden, neue Folge, herausgegeben von C. Horstmann, Heilbronn, 1881. Quoted by page and line.

L. S. Lives of Saints, edited by C. Hortsmann, E.E.T.S., No. 87, 1887. Quoted by page and line of poem.

L. Th. Thorpe's edition of the Laws given under L.; Th.

Lambd. Lambard's edition of the Laws printed in 1568.

Laym. Laȝamon's Brut, edited by F. Madden, Society of Antiquaries, London, 1847. Quoted by line.

Lchdm. Leechdoms, Wortcunning, and Starcraft of early England, edited by O. Cockayne, Master of the Rolls Series, 3 vols. London, 1864–1866. Quoted by volume, page and line.

Leo A. S. Names. A treatise on the local nomenclature of the Anglo-Saxons, translated from the German of Prof. H. Leo, London, 1852.

Leo A. Sax. Gl. Angelsächsisches Glossar von H. Leo, Halle, 1877.

Lev. The Anglo-Saxon version of the book of Leviticus. v. Deut.

Lk. The Gospel of St. Luke. v. Mt.

LL. Th. = L. Th.

Lupi Serm. v. Wulfst.

Lye. Dictionarium Saxonico- et Gothico-Latinum. Auctore Eduardo Lye. Edidit Owen Manning, London, 1772.

M. H. The MS. so quoted has now been printed. v. Homl. Skt.

Man. ed. Furn. (F). Robert Manning's History of England, edited by F. J. Furnivall, Rolls Series, London, 1887. Quoted by line.

Mand. The Voiage and Travaile of Sir John Maundeville, edited by J. O. Halliwell, London, 1883.

Manip. Vocab. Levins' Manipulus Vocabulorum, a riming Dictionary, 1570, edited by H. B. Wheatley, E.E.T.S., No. 27, 1867.

Mann. Manning's edition of Lye's A. S. Dict., particularly the Supplement.

Mapes. The Latin Poems commonly attributed to Walter Map, edited by T. Wright, Camden Soc., No. xvi., 1841. Quoted by page and line.

March. A comparative grammar of the Anglo-Saxon language, by F. A. March, New York, 1873.

Marg. Seinte Margarete, edited by O. Cockayne (in the same volume as the next). Quoted by line.

Marh. Seinte Marherete, þe meiden ant martyr, edited by O. Cockayne, E.E.T.S., No. 13, 1866. Quoted by page and line.

Martyr. (Martyrol.). Martyrologium in Bibl. C. C. C. Cant. D. 5. v. Wanl. Catal. p. 106. Alterum exemplar, mutilum licet, multa tamen continens quae in superiori desiderantur, occurrit in Bibl. Cott. Jul. A. 10, v. Wanl. Catal. p. 185. The MSS. thus referred to by Lye are used by Cockayne in Shrn. pp. 44–156, and from this edition most passages are taken in the Dictionary. The quotation by month and day of Martyr. makes reference to Shrn. easy.

Med. ex Quadr. An Anglo-Saxon version of the Medicina de Quadrupedis of Sextus Placitus, printed in Lchdm. i. Quoted by section and paragraph.

Med. Pec. For the passage given under *ágotenes* with this abbreviation see L. Ecg. C. 2; Th. ii. 136, 20.

Menol. Fox. Menologium seu Calendarium Poeticum, ex Hickesiano Thesauro, edited by S. Fox, London, 1830. Quoted by line.

Met[r]. Homl. English Metrical Homilies from MSS. of the 14th century, edited by J. Small, Edinburgh, 1862. Quoted by page and line.

Mid. York. Gl. A glossary of words pertaining to the dialect of Mid-Yorkshire, by C. C. Robinson, E.D.S., 1876.

Migne. Lexicon Manuale ad Scriptores mediae et infimae Latinitatis, par M. L'Abbé Migne, Paris, 1866.

Min. The Poems of Laurence Minot, edited by J. Hall, Oxford, 1887. Quoted by number of poem (or of page) and line.

Mirc. Instructions for Parish Priests by John Myrc, edited by E. Peacock, E.E.T.S., No. 31, 1868. Quoted by line.

Misc. An Old English Miscellany, edited by R. Morris. E.E.T.S., No. 49, 1872. Quoted by page and line.

Mk. The Gospel of St. Mark. v. Mt.

Mobr. Venerabilis Baedae Historia Ecclesiae Gentis Anglorum, cura G. H. Moberly, Oxon., 1869.

Mod. Confit. Confessio et oratio ad Deum, MS. Cott. Tib. A. 3, fol. 44, v. Wanl. Cat. p. 195. See an edition of this piece, Anglia xi. 112–115.

Mod. Lang. Notes. Modern Language Notes, Baltimore.

Mone. Mone's Quellen und Forschungen zur Geschichte der teutschen Literatur und Sprache, Leipzig, 1830.

Mone A. A copy of the same glossary as Glos. Brux. Recd. printed in Mone.

Mone B. A copy of the same glossary as Hpt. Gl. printed in Mone.

Morris Spec. i. Specimens of Early English, edited by R. Morris, Part I. Oxford, 1882. Quoted by page and line of section.

Mort A. Morte Arthure, edited by E. Brock, E.E.T.S., No. 8, 1865. Quoted by line.

Morte Arthure (Halliwell). From a MS. quoted in Halliwell's Dictionary.

Mt. The Gospel of St. Matthew. Several editions of various versions of the Gospels are referred to, for a detailed notice of which see Prof. Skeat's preface to his edition of St. Mark's Gospel in the series noted below under Kmbl.

Bos. The Gothic and Anglo-Saxon Gospels with the versions of Wycliffe and Tyndale, edited by J. Bosworth, London, 1865.

Foxe. The Gospels of the fower Euangelistes, translated in the olde Saxon tyme out of Latin into the Vulgare toung of the Saxons, London, printed by John Daye, 1571. This work was published by Fox, the Martyrologist.

Hat. The Hatton MS. in the Bodleian Library, at Oxford, marked 38. See Wanl. Cat. p. 76.

Jun. Quatuor D. N. Jesu Christi Euangeliorum versiones perantiquae duae, Gothica scil. et Anglo-Saxonica; illam ex Codice Argenteo depromsit Franciscus Junius, hanc curavit Thomas Mareschallus, Dordrechti, 1665.

Kmbl. The Gospel according to Saint Matthew in Anglo-Saxon and Northumbrian Versions. Cambridge, 1858. The work was begun by J. M. Kemble and completed by Mr. Hardwick. The other Gospels were edited by Prof. Skeat, who in 1887 edited this Gospel also.

Lind. MS. Cott. Nero D. 4. The Latin Text was written in the island of Lindisfarne. See Wanl. Cat. p. 250.

Rl. MS. Bibl. Reg. I. A. xiv. See Wanl. Cat. p. 181.

Rush. MS. Auct. D. ii. 19, in the Bodleian Library at Oxford. The MS. was at one time in the possession of John Rushworth, deputy-clerk to the House of Commons during the Long Parliament, and was by him presented to the Bodleian Library. See Wanl. Cat. p. 31.

Skt. v. Kmbl.

Stv. An edition of the Lindisfarne and Rushworth Gospels was published by the Surtees Society (Nos. 28, 39, 43, 48, 1854–1865), the first volume being edited by Rev. J. Stevenson, the last three by G. Waring.

Th. The Anglo-Saxon version of the Holy Gospels, edited by B. Thorpe, London and Oxford, 1842.

War. v. Stv.

N. Dictionarium Saxonico-Anglicum Laurentii Noelli, in the Bodleian Library. See Wanl. Cat. p. 102.

N. P. Nugae Poeticae. Select pieces of Old English popular poetry, edited by J. O. Halliwell, London, 1844. Quoted by page.

Nar. Narratiunculae Anglice conscriptae, edited by O. Cockayne, London, 1861. Quoted by page and line.

Nat. S. Greg. Els. An English-Saxon Homily on the Birthday of St. Gregory, translated into Modern English by Elizabeth Elstob, London, 1709 (cf. Homl. Th. ii. 116). Quoted by page and line.

Nath. (Nathan). Nathanis Judaei legatio ad Tiberium Caesarem. It is contained in a MS. preserved in the University Library at Cambridge, described in Wanl. Cat. p. 152, and has been edited in Publications of the Cambridge Antiquarian Society by C. W. Goodwin, Cambridge, 1851. v. St. And., under which abbreviation references by page and line are given except in the earlier part of the Dictionary.

Nicod. (Nic.); Thw. (Nicod. Thw.). An Anglo-Saxon version of the Gospel of Nicodemus, printed in Thw. Hept.

Num. The Anglo-Saxon version of the book of Numbers. v. Deut.

O. and N. An Old English poem of the Owl and the Nightingale, edited by F. H. Stratmann, Krefeld, 1868. Quoted by line.

O. E[ngl.] Homl. Old English Homilies, edited by R. Morris, E.E.T.S., first series, Nos. 29, 32; second series, No. 53, 1867–1868, 1873. Quoted by series, page and line.

O. E. Misc. = Misc.

O. Frs. Old Frisian; the forms are taken from Altfriesisches Wörterbuch von Karl von Richthofen, Göttingen, 1840.

O. H. Ger. Old High German. v. Grff.

O. L. Ger. Old Low German; the references are mostly to Kleinere altniederdeutsche Denkmäler, herausgegeben von M. Heyne, Paderborn, 1877.

O. Nrs. v. Icel.

O. Sax. v. Hêl.

Obs. Lun. De obseruatione lune, printed from MS. Cott. Tib. A. iii. fol. 30 b in Lchdm. iii. 184.

Octo Vit. cap[it]. A homily De octo vitiis et de xii. abusivis, in a MS. of the Bodleian, Cod. Jun. 24, p. 329 (Wanl. Cat. p. 42). It is printed in O. E. Homl. i. 296–304. Cf. also Homl. Skt. i. 16, 246–384.

Octov. Octovian Imperator in Weber's Metrical Romances, vol. iii., 1810. Quoted by line.

Off. episc[op.]. The reference seems to be to the matter printed in Thorpe's Laws from Cod. Jun. 121, and referred to as L. I. P. (e. g. *â-wildian* will be found, Th. ii. 322, 15).

Off. reg[um]. The same MS. as the preceding seems sometimes to be referred to, e. g. *efen-wel* occurs Th. ii. 324, 2: but *bæc-slitol* I have noted only Wulfst. 72, 16, where the MS. is Cod. Jun. 99 (Wanl. Cat. p. 27).

Orm. The Ormulum, edited by R. M. White, Oxford, 1852. Quoted by line.

Ors.; Bos. King Alfred's Anglo-Saxon version of the compendious history of the world by Orosius, edited by J. Bosworth, London, 1859. Quoted by book and chapter (Ors.), and by page and line (Bos.).

Ors. Hav. The edition of Orosius by Havercamp, Leyden, 1738.

Ors.; Swt. King Alfred's Orosius, edited by H. Sweet, E.E.T.S., No. 79, 1883. Quoted by book and chapter (Ors.), and by page and line (Swt.).

Ottf. Otfrid's Krist, edited by E. G. Graff, Königsberg, 1831.

P. B. Beiträge zur Geschichte der deutschen Sprache und Literatur, herausgegeben von H. Paul und W. Braune.

P. L. S. Early English Poems and Lives of Saints, edited by F. J. Furnivall, Philol. Soc., 1862. Quoted by number of piece and line (or stanza).

P. R. L. P. Political, Religious, and Love Poems, edited by F. J. Furnivall, E.E.T.S., No. 15, 1866. Quoted by page and line.

P. S. The Political Songs of England, from the reign of John to that of Edward II, edited by T. Wright, Camden Soc., No. vi., 1839. Quoted by page and line.

Palgrv. Eng. Com. Palgrave's Rise and Progress of the English Commonwealth, London, 1834.

Pall. Palladius on Husbondrie, edited by B. Lodge and S. T. Herrtage, E.E.T.S., Nos. 52 and 72, 1872 and 1879. Quoted by page and line of book.

Parten. The Romans of Partenay, edited by W. W. Skeat, E.E.T.S., No. 22, 1866. Quoted by line.

Past.; Hat. An Anglo-Saxon version of Gregory's Pastoral Care, contained in a MS. (Hatton 20) preserved in the Bodleian Library. Quoted by chapter and paragraph of an edition of the Cura Pastoralis by J. Stephen, London, 1629 (Past.), and by folio and line of MS. (Hat.).

Past.; Swt. The Anglo-Saxon version of Gregory's Pastoral Care from the Hatton MS. and the Cotton MSS., edited by H. Sweet, E.E.T.S., Nos. 45 and 50, 1871–1872. Quoted by chapter (Past.), and by page and line (Swt.).

Peccat[orum] Medic[ina] = L. Pen. (e. g. *āspīwan* may be found L. Pen. 5; Th. ii. 278, 22).

Pegge's Kenticisms. An Alphabet of Kenticisms by Samuel Pegge, 1735. E. D. S., 1876.

Piers [P.]. The Vision of William concerning Piers the Plowman (Text B), E. E. T. S., No. 38, 1869. [Texts A and C are Nos. 28 and 54.] Quoted by passus and line.

Piers P. Crede. Pierce the Ploughman's Crede, edited by W. W. Skeat, E.E.T.S., No. 30, 1867. Quoted by line.

Pl. Cr. = Piers P. Crede.

Pol. Songs Wrt. = P. S.

Pr. C. The Pricke of Conscience, by R. Rolle de Hampole, edited by R. Morris, Philol. Soc., 1863. Quoted by line.

Pref. [Ælfc.]. Thw. Ælfric's preface to Genesis in Thw. Hept. Quoted by page and line.

Pref. (Procem.) R. Conc[ord]. Prohemium regularis concordie Anglicae nationis monachorum (MS. Cott. Tib. A. 3, v. Wanl. Cat., p. 193). This is edited in Anglia, vol. xiii. p. 365, and in the later part of the Dictionary this edition is referred to.

Prehn's Rätsel des Exeterbuches. Komposition und Quellen der Rätsel des Exeterbuches, von Dr. August Prehn, Paderborn, 1883.

Proclam. H. III. The only English Proclamation of Henry III, edited by Alex. J. Ellis, Philol. Soc., 1868.

Prompt. [Parv.]. Promptorium Parvulorum, sive Clericorum, dictionarius Anglo-Latinus princeps, auctore fratre Galfrido, recensuit Albertus Way, Camden Soc., Nos. xxv., liv., lxxxix., 1843–1865. Quoted by page.

Prov. Glosses on the book of Proverbs, which are printed as noticed under Kent. Gl. Quoted by chapter (and verse).

Prov. Kmbl. Anglo-Saxon Apothegms in Salm. Kmbl. (q. v.) Part III. pp. 258–268. Quoted by number.

Prud. v. Gl. Prud. (2).

Ps. An Early English Psalter, edited by J. Stevenson, Surtees Soc., Nos. 16, 19, 1843–1847. Quoted by psalm and verse.

Ps. Grn. The edition of the metrical version of Psalms 51–150 in Grein's Bibliothek der Angelsächsischen Poesie. 2. Band. Göttingen, 1858.

Ps. Lamb. An interlinear version of the Psalms in a MS. preserved in the library of Lambeth Palace. It is thus described by Wanley: Psalterium D. Hieronymi Gallicum, Astericis et obolis, punctisque Musicis subjectis notatum, una cum interlineata Versione Saxonica, Catalogue, p. 268.

Ps. Spl. Psalterium Davidis Latino-Saxonicum vetus. A Johanne Spelmanno D. Hen. fil. editum. E vetustissimo exemplari MS. in Bibliotheca ipsius Henrici, et cum tribus aliis non multo minus vetustis collatum, Londini, 1640. The MS. used by Spelman subsequently was in the library at Stowe, and has been described by Dr. O'Conor in his account of that library. Afterwards it passed into the possession of Lord Ashburnham. Of the three collated MSS., which Spelman refers to under the letters C, T, M, the first is in the University Library at Cambridge, see Wanl. Cat. p. 152; the second is in the library of Trin. Coll. Camb., and has been edited by F. Harsley, E.E.T.S., No. 92, 1889 (Eadwine's Canterbury Psalter); the third is Arundel MS. No. 60 in the British Museum. The printed edition, as regards C and T, was collated with those MSS. for Dr. Bosworth by Dr. Aldis Wright, and many corrections were made.

Ps. Stev. *or* **Surt.** An Anglo-Saxon Psalter (printed from MS. Cott. Vesp. A. 1), edited by J. Stevenson, Surtees Soc., Nos. 16, 19, 1843–1847.

Ps. Th. Libri Psalmorum versio antiqua Latina; cum paraphrasi Anglo-Saxonica, partim soluta oratione, partim metrice composita. E Cod. MS. in Bibl. Regia Parisiensi adservato descripsit et edidit B. Thorpe, Oxonii, 1835.

Ps. Trin. Camb. = Ps. Spl. T.

Ps. Vos[sii]. An interlinear version of the Psalms in a MS. given by Isaac Vossius to Francis Junius (MS. Bodl. Junius 27). See Wanl. Cat. p. 76.

R., Lye. Ælfric's Vocabulary, transcribed by or for Junius from a MS. in the possession of Reubens the painter, v. Wanl. Cat. p. 96. It was printed by Somner at the end of his Dictionary, and will be found in Wrt. Voc. i. 15.

R. Ben. Die Angelsächsische Prosabearbeitung der Benedictinerregel, herausgegeben von A. Schröer, Kassel, 1885. Quoted (at first by chapter, later) by page and line.

R. Ben. Interl. The Rule of S. Benet. Latin and Anglo-Saxon interlinear version. Edited by H. Logeman, E.E.T.S., No. 90, 1888. Quoted (at first by chapter, later) by page and line.

R. Brun[ne]. Peter Langtoft's Chronicle (as illustrated and improved by Robert of Brunne), published by Thomas Hearne, Oxford, 1725. Quoted by page and line.

R[eg.] Conc[ord]. v. Pref. R. Conc.

R. Glouc. Robert of Gloucester's Chronicle, published by Thomas Hearne, Oxford, 1724. Quoted by page and line.

R. R. The Romaunt of the Rose, formerly attributed to Chaucer. Quoted by line.

R. S. Religious Songs, edited by Thomas Wright, Percy Soc., vol. xi., 1843. Quoted by number of piece and line.

Rask Hald. Björn Halldórsson's Icelandic-Latin Dictionary, edited by Rask, 1814.

Recd.; Wrt. Voc. v. Glos. Brux. Recd.

Rel[iq.] Ant[iq.]. Reliquiae Antiquae. Scraps from Ancient Manuscripts, edited by T. Wright and J. O. Halliwell. 2 vols., London, 1845. Quoted by volume, page and line.

Rich. Richard Coer de Lion, in Weber's Metrical Romances, vol. ii. 3–278. Quoted by line.

Rol. H. Richard Rolle of Hampole and his followers, edited by C. Horstmann. 2 vols., London, 1895. Quoted by volume, page and line.

Rood Kmbl. The Holy Rood, a poem in the Vercelli MS., published with Elen. Kmbl. (q. v.).

Rood Recd. The same poem as the preceding, printed as Andr. Recd. (q. v.).

Rtl. Rituale Ecclesiae Dunelmensis (Latin and interlinear Anglo-Saxon versions), Surtees Soc., No. 10, 1839. Quoted by page and line.

Runic Inscrip. Kmbl. On Anglo-Saxon Runes. By J. M. Kemble. Archaeologia, published by the Society of Antiquaries, vol. xxviii., London, 1840. Quoted by page and line.

Runic pm. Kmbl. A poem printed in the above paper. Quoted by page and line.

S. de Fide Cathol. This homily is printed Homl. Th. i. 274.

Salm. Kmbl. Anglo-Saxon Dialogues of Salomon and Saturn, by J. M. Kemble. Printed for the Ælfric Society, London, 1845–1848. The poetical part is quoted by line, the prose by page and line.

Sax. Engl. The Saxons in England. A History of the English Commonwealth till the period of the Norman Conquest, by J. M. Kemble. 2 vols., London, 1876.

Schmid [A. S. Gesetz.]. Die Gesetze der Angelsachsen. Herausgegeben von Dr. R. Schmid, Leipzig, 1858.

Scint. Defensoris Liber Scintillarum, with an interlinear Anglo-Saxon version, edited by E. W. Rhodes, E.E.T.S., No. 93, 1889. Quoted (at first by chapter, later) by page and line of the interlinear version. App. [Lib.] Scint. refers to the matter in pp. 223–236 of this edition.

Scint. de Praedest. = Scint., pp. 226–228.

Scóp. Th. The Scóp or Gleeman's Tale printed in Beo. Th.

Scot. Scottish. v. Jamieson.

Seebohm Vill. Comm. The English Village Community examined in its relations to the Manorial and Tribal Systems, by F. Seebohm, London, 1890.

Serm. Creat. = Homl. Th. i. 8–28. (v. ge-dæman, *where read* ge-clǣman.)

Shor[eham]. The Religious Poems of William de Shoreham, edited by T. Wright, Percy Soc. vol. xxviii., 1849. Quoted by page.

Shrn. The Shrine. A Collection of occasional papers on dry subjects, by O. Cockayne, London, 1864–1870. Quoted by page and line.

Skt. Dict. An Etymological Dictionary of the English Language, by W. W. Skeat, Oxford, 1879–1882.

Solil. Soliloquia Augustini Selecta et Saxonice reddita ab Ælfredo Rege, MS. Cott. Vitell. A. 15, fol. 1. (Printed in Shrn. pp. 163–204.) v. Wanl. Cat. p. 218.

Som. Dictionarium Saxonico-Latino-Anglicum, by E. Somner, Oxon., 1659.

Somn. De somniorum diuersitate (MS. Cott. Tib. A. iii. fol. 25 b) *and* De somniorum eventu (v. Wanl. Cat. p. 40). The two pieces are printed Lchdm. iii. pp. 198–214, 168–176. Quoted by number of paragraph in the two combined. (In the later part of the Dictionary the references are to Lchdm. iii.)

Soul Kmbl. The departed soul's address to the body, a poem in the Vercelli MS. published with Elen. Kmbl. (q. v.).

Soul Recd. The same poem as the preceding, printed with Andr. Recd. (q. v.).

Spec. Specimens of Lyric Poetry composed in England in the reign of Edward I, edited by T. Wright, Percy Soc., vol. iv., 1842. Quoted by page and line.

St. And. Anglo-Saxon Legends of St. Andrew and St. Veronica, Cambridge Antiquarian Society, Cambridge, 1851.

Swt. A. S. Prim. An Anglo-Saxon Primer by H. Sweet, Oxford, 1882.

Swt. [A. S.] Rdr. An Anglo-Saxon Reader, in prose and verse, by H. Sweet, Oxford, 1876.

Techm. Internationale Zeitschrift für allgemeine Sprachwissenschaft, begründet und herausgegeben von F. Techmer, Leipzig. Quoted by volume, page and line.

Te Dm. Lamb. (Te Deum; Lamb.). An interlinear version of the Te Deum in the same MS. as Ps. Lamb. It is also cited as Hymn ad Mat.

Te Dm. Lye. v. Wanl. Cat. p. 222.

Te Dm. Thomson. A version of the same in Thomson's Select Monuments of the Doctrine and Worship of the Catholic Church in England before the Norman Conquest, 1849.

Text. Rof. Textus de Ecclesia Roffensi. v. Wanl. Cat. p. 273.

Th. An[al.] (Anlct.). v. An. Th.

Th. Ap[ol.]. v. Ap. Th.

Th. Ch[art.] (Diplm.). v. Chart. Th.

Th. Lapbg. A History of England under the Anglo-Saxon Kings, translated from the German of Dr. J. M. Lappenberg by B. Thorpe, London, 1845.

Th. Ll. v. L.; Th.

Thw. Hept. Heptateuchus, Liber Job, et Evangelium Nicodemi; Anglo-Saxonice. Historiae Judith Fragmentum; Dano-Saxonice. Edidit Edwardus Thwaites, Oxoniae, 1698. v. Wanl. Cat. pp. 67–68, 152.

Torrent of Portugal. An English Metrical Romance, edited by J. O. Halliwell, London, 1842.

Tr. and Cr. Chaucer's Troilus and Creseyde. Quoted by book and line.

Tract. de Spir. Septif. A homily De Septiformi Spiritu. See Wulfst. 50–56.

Trev. Polychronicon Ranulphi Higden, with the English translation of John Trevisa. Rolls Series, 1865–1886. Quoted by volume, page and line.

Trist. Die Nordische und die Englische Version der Tristan-Saga, herausgegeben von E. Kölbing, Heilbronn, 1882–1883. Quoted by line.

Txts. The Oldest English Texts, edited by H. Sweet, E.E.T.S., No. 83, 1885. Quoted by page and number of gloss (or by line).

Tynd. Tyndal's version of the New Testament.

V. Ps. = Ps. Vos.

Vit. Swith. See either Glostr. Frag. or Homl. Skt. i. 21.

W. Cat. = Wanl. Cat.

W. F. (Wells Frag.). MS. of the A.S. version of the Benedictine Rule in the possession of the Chapter at Wells, printed in R. Ben.

W. S. West-Saxon.

Wald. Two leaves of King Waldere's Lay, published by George Stevens, Copenhagen. Quoted by line.

Wanl. Cat[al.]. Wanley's Catalogue of Anglo-Saxon MSS., forming the third volume of Hickes' Thesaurus, Oxoniae, 1705.

Wht. Dict. White and Riddle's Latin-English Dictionary.

Wick. v. Wyc.

Wicklif Select Wrks. Select English Works of John Wyclif, edited by T. Arnold, Oxford, 1869–1871. Quoted by volume and page.

Wilk. Leges Anglo-Saxonicae Ecclesiasticae et Civiles, edited by D. Wilkins, London, 1721. Quoted by page and line.

Will. The Romance of William of Palerne, edited by W. W. Skeat, E.E.T.S., No. i., 1867. Quoted by line.

Wrt. Biog. Brit. A. Sax. Biographia Britannica Literaria; or Biography of Literary Characters of Great Britain and Ireland. Anglo-Saxon Period. By Thomas Wright, London, 1842.

Wrt. Popl. Science. Popular Treatises on Science written during the Middle Ages, edited by Thomas Wright, London, 1841. Quoted by page and line.

Wrt. Provncl. Dictionary of Obsolete and Provincial English, compiled by Thomas Wright, London, 1837.

Wrt. Spec. v. Spec.

Wrt. Voc. [i.]. A volume of Vocabularies, edited by Thomas Wright. Privately printed, 1857. Quoted by page and number of gloss.

Wrt. Voc. ii. A second volume of Vocabularies, edited by Thomas Wright. Privately printed, 1873. Quoted by page and line.

Wülck. [**Gl.**]. Anglo-Saxon and Old English Vocabularies, by Thomas Wright. Second edition, edited by R. P. Wülcker, London, 1884. Quoted by column and line.

Wulfst. Wulfstan. Sammlung der ihm zugeschriebenen Homilien, herausgegeben von A. Napier, Berlin, 1883. Quoted by page and line.

Wyc. The Holy Bible in the earliest English versions made from the Latin Vulgate by John Wycliffe, edited by Forshall and Madden, Oxford, 1850.

York. Gl. A Glossary of words pertaining to the Dialect of Mid-Yorkshire. E. D. S. Pub., 1876.

Zacher. Das Gothische Alphabet Ulfilas und das Runen-alphabet. Eine sprachwissenschaftliche Untersuchung von Julius Zacher, Leipzig, 1855.

EXPLANATION OF THE PRINCIPAL CONTRACTIONS.

[Contractions used in Grein's Lexicon Poeticum are given separately on the next page.]

Ælfc. Gl; Som; Wrt. Voc. Ælfric's Glossary given at the end of Somner's Dictionary, and in A Volume of Vocabularies, edited by Thomas Wright (First Series, 1857).
Ælfc. Gr; Som. Ælfric's Grammar, at the end of Somner's Dictionary.
Ælfc. T. Grn. Ælfric de veteri et de novo testamento, in Grein's edition of the Heptateuch.
Alis. King Alisaunder, in Weber's Metrical Romances.
Andr. Kmbl. The Legend of St. Andrew, edited by Kemble for the Ælfric Society.
An. Lit. Anecdota Literaria, by T. Wright.
Apstls. Kmbl. The Fates of the Twelve Apostles; a fragment, in Part II. of The Poetry of the Codex Vercellensis, edited by Kemble for the Ælfric Society.
A. R. The Ancren Riwle, edited for the Camden Society by J. Morton.
Ayenb. Dan Michel's Ayenbite of Inwyt, edited for the Early English Text Society by R. Morris.
Basil admn. The Anglo-Saxon remains of St. Basil's Admonitio ad filium spiritualem, edited by H. W. Norman.
Bd; S. The Anglo-Saxon version of Bede's Ecclesiastical History, edited by Smith.
Beo. Th. The Anglo-Saxon poem of Beowulf, edited by Thorpe.
Blickl. Gl. Blickling Glosses, at the end of the Blickling Homilies.
Blickl. Homl. The Blickling Homilies, edited for the Early English Text Society by R. Morris.
Boutr. Scrd. Screadunga, edited by C. G. Bouterwek.
Bt; Fox. King Alfred's Anglo-Saxon version of Boethius De Consolatione Philosophiæ, edited by Fox (in Bohn's Antiquarian Library).
Bt. Met. Fox. The Anglo-Saxon version of the Metres of Boethius, at the end of the previous work.
Byrht. Th. The Battle of Maldon, in Thorpe's Analecta Anglo-Saxonica.
Cant. Abac. Canticum Abacuc Prophetæ, in Ps. Lamb., q. v.
Cant. Moys. Canticum Moysis, at the end of Thwaites' Heptateuch.
Cd; Th. Cædmon's Metrical Paraphrases of parts of the Holy Scriptures, edited by Thorpe.
Chart. Th. Diplomatarium Anglicum Ævi Saxonici, edited by Thorpe.
Chauc. Chaucer.
Chr; Erl. Two of the Saxon Chronicles, edited by Earle.
Cod. Dipl. Kmbl. Codex Diplomaticus Ævi Saxonici, edited by Kemble.
Coll. Monast. Th. Ælfric's Colloquy, in Thorpe's Analecta Anglo-Saxonica.
Confess. Peccat. Confessio Peccatorum, in Ps. Lamb., q. v.
Cot. Lye. A MS. of the Cotton Library quoted by Lye in his Dictionary.
Deut. Deuteronomy, in Thwaites' Heptateuch.
E. D. S. English Dialect Society.
Elen. Kmbl. Elene, or the Recovery of the Cross, edited by Kemble for the Ælfric Society.
Ex. Exodus, in Thwaites' Heptateuch.
Exon. Th. Codex Exoniensis, edited by Thorpe.
Fins. Th. The Fight at Finnesburg, at the end of Thorpe's Beowulf.
Frag. Kmbl. A Fragment, Moral and Religious, in Part II. of The Poetry of the Codex Vercellensis, edited by Kemble.
Gen. Genesis, in Thwaites' Heptateuch.
Grff. Althochdeutscher Sprachschatz von Graff.
Grmm. A. u. E. Andreas und Elene, herausgegeben von Jacob Grimm.
Grmm. D. M. Deutsche Mythologie von Jacob Grimm. Zweite ausgabe.
Grmm. Gesch. D. S. Geschichte der Deutschen Sprache von Jacob Grimm. Dritte auflage.
Grn. R. A. Deutsche Rechtsalterthümer von Jacob Grimm. Zweite ausgabe.
Guthl; Gdwin. The Anglo-Saxon version of the Life of St. Guthlac, edited by C. W. Goodwin.
Halliw. Dict. Halliwell's Dictionary of archaic and provincial words.
Herb. Herbarium in Vol. I. of Saxon Leechdoms.
Hexam. Norm. The Anglo-Saxon version of the Hexameron of St. Basil, edited by H. W. Norman.
Homl. Skt. Ælfric's Lives of Saints, edited for the Early English Text Society by W. W. Skeat.
Homl. Th. The Homilies of Ælfric, edited for the Ælfric Society by B. Thorpe.
Hpt. Gl. Angelsächsische Glossen, von Bouterwek mitgetheilt in Haupts Zeitschrift ix. (quoted from Leo's Angelsächsische Glossar).
H. R. Legends of the Holy Rood, edited for the Early English Text Society by R. Morris.
Hymn. Surt. The Latin Hymns of the Anglo-Saxon Church, edited for the Surtees Society by J. Stevenson.
Icel. Icelandic; the references being to Cleasby and Vigfusson's Icelandic Dictionary.
Jn. Skt. The Gospel of St. John, edited by Skeat. v. Mk. Skt.
Jos. Joshua, in Thwaites' Heptateuch.
Jud. Judges, in Thwaites' Heptateuch.
Judth; Thw. The poem of Judith, at the end of Thwaites' Heptateuch.
Jul. The Liflade of St. Juliana, edited for the Early English Text Society by Cockayne.
L. Alf; Th. The Laws of King Alfred, in Thorpe's Ancient Laws and Institutes. The other contractions, being the same as those used by Thorpe, are not given here.
Laym. The Brut of Laȝamon, edited by Sir F. Madden.
Lchdm. i. ii. iii. Leechdoms, Wortcunning and Starcraft of Early England, edited by Cockayne (Master of the Rolls' series, 3 vols.).
Lev. Leviticus, in Thwaites' Heptateuch.
Lk. Skt. The Gospel of St. Luke, edited by Skeat. v. Mk. Skt.
L. M; Lchdm. v. Lchdm. (L. M. = Liber Medicinalis.)
L. Med. ex Quadr; Lchdm. v. Lchdm.
Menol. Fox. Menologium or Poetical Calendar of the Anglo-Saxons, edited by Fox.
Met. Homl. English Metrical Homilies from MSS. of 14th century, edited by J. Small.
Mk. Skt. Lind. *or* Rush. The Gospel of St. Mark in Anglo-Saxon and Northumbrian versions, edited for the Syndics of the University Press by W. W. Skeat. (Lind. = Lindisfarne MS. Rush. = Rushworth MS.)
Mt. Kmbl. Lind. *or* Rush. The Gospel of St. Matthew, in Anglo-Saxon and Northumbrian versions, edited by Kemble. v. preceding.
Nar. Narratiunculæ Anglice Conscriptæ, edited by Cockayne.
Nicod; Thw. The Anglo-Saxon version of the Gospel of Nicodemus, at the end of Thwaites' Heptateuch.
Num. Numbers, in Thwaites' Heptateuch.
O. and N. An Old English poem of the Owl and the Nightingale, edited by Stratmann.
O. E. Homl. Old English Homilies, edited for the Early English Text Society by R. Morris.
O. Frs. refers to Altfriesisches Wörterbuch von Dr. Karl Freiherrn von Richthofen.
O. H. Ger. v. Grff.
Orm. The Ormulum, edited by Dr. White.
Ors; Swt. *or* Bos. The Anglo-Saxon version of Orosius, edited by Sweet *or* by Bosworth.
O. Sax. The Old Saxon poem of the Heliand.
Past; Swt. King Alfred's version of Gregory's Pastoral Care, edited for the Early English Text Society by Sweet.
Piers P. The Vision concerning Piers the Plowman, B-text, edited for the Early English Text Society by W. W. Skeat.
P. L. S. Early English Poems and Lives of Saints, edited by F. J. Furnivall.
Prompt. Parv. Promptorium parvulorum sive clericorum, lexicon Anglo-latinum princeps, edited for the Camden Society by Way.

Prov. Kmbl. Anglo-Saxon Apothegms given by Kemble in Anglo-Saxon Dialogues of Salomon and Saturn, Part III. (Ælfric Society's publications).

Ps. Lamb. Lambeth Psalter. The references are taken from the copy made under Dr. Bosworth's direction.

Ps. Spl. Psalterium Davidis Latino-Saxonicum vetus, a Johanne Spelmanno editum. (Dr. Bosworth's copy has been collated with the original MSS. and has thus been corrected in many places.)

Ps. Surt. Anglo-Saxon and Early English Psalter, edited for the Surtees Society by Stevenson.

Ps. Th. Libri Psalmorum versio antiqua Latina; cum paraphrasi Anglo-Saxonica, edidit Benjamin Thorpe.

R. Ben. Anglo-Saxon version of the Benedictine Rule (quoted from Lye).

R. Brun. Peter Langtoft's Chronicle translated and continued by Robert Manning of Brunne, edited by Hearne.

Rel. Ant. Reliquiæ Antiquæ, edited by Wright and Halliwell.

R. Glouc. Robert of Gloucester's Chronicle, edited by Hearne.

Rood Kmbl. The Holy Rood; a Dream, in Part II. of The Poetry of the Codex Vercellensis, edited for the Ælfric Society by Kemble.

Rtl. Rituale Ecclesiæ Dunelmensis, edited for the Surtees Society by Stevenson. (Compare Skeat's collation in the Philological Society's Transactions.)

Runic pm. Kmbl. Runic poem printed by Kemble in Archæologia, vol. 28.

Salm. Kmbl. Anglo-Saxon Dialogues of Salomon and Saturn, edited for the Ælfric Society by Kemble.

Schmid. A. S. Ges. Die gesetze der Angelsachsen, herausgegeben von Reinh. Schmid.

Scot. Scottish; the references being to Jamieson's Dictionary.

Shrn. The Shrine; a collection of occasional papers on dry subjects, by Cockayne.

Soul Kmbl. The Departed Soul's Address to the Body, in Part II. of The Poetry of the Codex Vercellensis, edited for the Ælfric Society by Kemble.

St. And. Anglo-Saxon Legends of St. Andrew and St. Veronica (Publications of the Cambridge Antiquarian Society).

Swt. A. S. Rdr. An Anglo-Saxon Reader in prose and verse, by Henry Sweet.

Th. An. Analecta Anglo-Saxonica, by Benjamin Thorpe.

Th. Ap. The Anglo-Saxon version of the story of Apollonius of Tyre, edited by Thorpe.

Trev. Polychronicon Ranulphi Higden, with the English translation of John Trevisa (Master of the Rolls' series).

Will. The romance of William of Palerne, edited by W. W. Skeat (Early English Text Society).

Wrt. popl. Science. Popular Treatises on Science written during the Middle Ages, edited by Wright.

Wrt. Voc. A Volume of Vocabularies, edited by Wright. (First Series, Liverpool, 1857.)

CONTRACTIONS USED BY GREIN.

Ælf. Tod. Poem on the death of Alfred, son of Ethelred, given in the Chronicle under the year 1036.

Æðelst. Poem on the victory of Athelstan, taken from the Chronicle.

Alm. Almosen, from the Codex Exoniensis, p. 467.

An. The legend of St. Andrew.

Ap. The fates of the Apostles, from the Codex Vercellensis.

Az. Azarias, from the Codex Exoniensis, p. 185.

B. Beowulf.

Bo. Botschaft des Gemahls, from the Codex Exoniensis, p. 472.

By. The death of Byrhtnoth.

Crä. Manna cræftas, from the Codex Exoniensis, p. 292.

Cri. Cynewulfs Crist, from the Codex Exoniensis, p. 1.

Dan. Daniel, in Thorpe's Cædmon, p. 216.

Deór. Deors Klage, from Codex Exoniensis, p. 377.

Dōm. Dōmes dæg, from Codex Exoniensis, p. 445.

Edg. Eádgār; poems from the Chronicle, under the years 973, 975.

Edm. Eádmund, from the Chronicle, under the year 942.

Edw. Eádweard, from the Chronicle, under the year 1065.

El. Elene, from the Codex Vercellensis.

Exod. Exodus, in Thorpe's Cædmon, p. 177.

Fä. Fæder lārcwidas, in Codex Exoniensis, p. 300.

Fin. The fight at Finnsburg.

Gen. Genesis, in Thorpes' Cædmon, p. 1.

Gn. C. Versus gnomici (Cotton MS.).

Gn. Ex. Versus gnomici, from Codex Exoniensis, p. 333.

Gú. Legend of St. Guthlac, from Codex Exoniensis, p. 104.

Hö. Höllenfahrt Christi, from Codex Exoniensis, p. 459.

Hy. Hymnen und Gebete.

Jud. The poem of Judith.

Jul. The legend of St. Juliana, in Codex Exoniensis, p. 242.

Kl. Klage der Frau, in Codex Exoniensis, p. 442.

Kr. Das heilige Kreuz, from the Codex Vercellensis.

Leás. Bī manna leáse, from the Codex Vercellensis.

Men. Menologium.

Met. The metres of Alfred.

Mōd. Manna mōd, in the Codex Exoniensis, p. 313.

Pa. Panther, in the Codex Exoniensis, p. 355.

Ph. Phönix, in the Codex Exoniensis, p. 197.

Phar. Pharao, in the Codex Exoniensis, p. 468.

Ps. Psalms, from Thorpe's edition.

Ps. C. The 50th psalm, from one of the Cotton MSS.

Rä. Riddles from the Codex Exoniensis.

Reb. Rebhuhn, from the Codex Exoniensis, p. 365.

Reim. Reimlied, from the Codex Exoniensis, p. 352.

Ruin. Ruine, from the Codex Exoniensis, p. 476.

Rūn. Runenlied, in Archæologia, vol. 28.

Sal. Salomo und Saturn; see above Salm. Kmbl.

Sat. Crist und Satan, in Thorpe's Cædmon, p. 265.

Seef. Seefahrer, in the Codex Exoniensis, p. 306.

Seel. Reden der Seelen, in the Codex Exoniensis, p. 367; see also above, Soul Kmbl.

Sch. Wunder der Schöpfung, in the Codex Exoniensis, p. 346.

Vid. Vīdsīð, in Codex Exoniensis, p. 318.

Vy. Manna wyrde, in Codex Exoniensis, p. 327.

Wal. Walfisch, in Codex Exoniensis, p. 360.

Wand. Wanderer, in Codex Exoniensis, p. 286.

A.

A. It is not necessary to speak of the form of what are often called Anglo-Saxon letters, as all Teutonic, Celtic, and Latin manuscripts of the same age are written in letters of the same form. There is one exception: the Anglo-Saxons had, with great propriety, two different letters for the two distinct sounds of our *th:* the hard þ in *th*in and soo*th*, and the soft ð in *th*ine and soo*th*e, vide **Þ, þ**. **2.** The indigenous Pagan alphabet of our Anglo-Saxon forefathers, called Runes, it must be particularly observed, not only represents our letters, but the names of the letters are significant. The Runes are chiefly formed by straight lines to be easily carved on wood or stone. For instance, the Rune ᚪ âc is not only found in inscriptions on wood and stone, but in Anglo-Saxon MSS. and printed books. In manuscripts and in books, it sometimes denotes the letter **a**; and, at other times, *the oak*, from its Anglo-Saxon name, âc *the oak*. v. **ÂC**, and **RÛN**.

B. The *short* or unaccented Anglo-Saxon **a** is contained in the following words, which are represented by modern English terms of the same import, having the sound of *a* in *man;* as Can, man, span, hand, land, sand, camp, dranc, *etc.* **2.** The short **a** is often found in the final syllables of inflections, -a, -an, -as, -aþ, *etc.* It generally appears in the radix before a doubled consonant, as swamm *a fungus*, wann *wan;* or two different consonants, as mp, mb, nt, nc, ng, *etc.*—Camp, lamb, plante, dranc, lang, *etc.* **3.** The radical short **a** can only stand before a single consonant and *st, sc*, when this single consonant and these double letters are again followed, in the inflections or formative syllables, by *a, o, u* in nouns; and by *a, o, u, e* in adjectives; and *a, o, u*, and *ia* in verbs; as Dagas, daga from dæg, hwalas from hwæl, fatu from fæt, gastas from gæst, ascas from æsc; *adj.* Smales, smale, smalost, smalu, from smæl *small;* Lates, latu, latost, from læt *late:* Stapan, faran, starian, wafian. Grimm's Deut. Gram. vol. i. p. 223, 2nd edit. 1822. In other cases, the short or unaccented **æ** is used instead of **a**. See **Æ** in its alphabetical order. **4.** The remarks in **3.** are of great importance in declining words, for monosyllables, ending in a single consonant, in *st* or *sc*, change the **æ** into **a**, whenever the consonant or consonants are followed by *a, o, u* in nouns, and *a, o, u, e* in adjectives, vide **Æ**. **5.** It must be remembered then, that a short **a** cannot stand in a word (1) when it ends in a single consonant, that is, when no inflections of *a, o, u* in nouns follow; as in Stæf, fræt: (2) when in nouns a single consonant is followed by *e;* as Stæfes, stæfe, wæter: (3) when the word has any other double consonants besides *st, sc*, though followed by *a, o, u;* as Cræft, cræfta, ægru *n. pl. of* æg: (4) in contracted words, when **æ** is not in the last syllable; as Æcer, *pl.* æceras, æcerum, contracted æcras, æcrum; wæpen, *pl.* wæpenu; mægen, *pl.* mægenu, contracted wæpnu, and mægnu. **6.** Though I have given in **C. 3.** the reasons, which Grimm assigns for making the prefixed a-, long, I believe it is generally short in *A. Sax.* as in *Eng.* a-bide = *A. Sax.* a-bîdan = bîdan, so a-cende = cende:—Ic todæg cende [cende Surt; acende Spl. T; Th.] ðê *ego hodie genui te*, Ps. Spl. 2, 7. A-beran = beran *to bear:*—Hefige byrðyna man aberan ne mæg *a man is not able to bear heavy burdens*, Mt. Bos. 23, 4. Ne bere ge sacc *nolite portare sacculum*, Lk. Bos. 10, 4. A-biddan = biddan *to ask, pray:*—Abiddaþ [biddaþ Cott.] hine *pray to him*, Bt. 42; Fox 258, 21. Ic bidde ðê, Drihten *I pray to thee, Lord*, Gen. 19, 18. It is evident by these examples that words have the same meaning with and without the prefixed a-: this a- was not prominent or long, and therefore this prefix is left unaccented in this Dictionary. **7.** a- prefixed, sometimes denotes *Negation, deterioration*, or *opposition*, as *From, out, away;* thus awendan *to turn from, subvert*, from wendan *to turn;* amôd *out of* or *without mind, mad;* adôn *to do away, banish*, composed of a *from*, dôn *to do*, vide **Æ**. The prefixed a- does not always appear to alter the signification: in this case it is generally omitted in modern English words derived immediately from Saxon,—thus, Aberan *to bear;* abrecan *to break;* abîtan *to bite.* The prefixed a-, in such cases, seems to add some little force or intensity to the original signification of the word to which it is joined,—thus, fǽran *to make afraid;* terrere: a-fǽran *to terrify, dismay, astound;* exterrere, perterrere, consternare, stupefacere.

C. The *long* Anglo-Saxon **â** is accented, and words containing this long or accented **â** are now represented by English terms, with the vowel sounded like o in *no* and *bone.* The following words have either the same or an analogous meaning, both in English and Anglo-Saxon: Hâm *home*, ân *one*, bân *bone*, hân *hone*, stân *stone*, sâr *sore*, râp *rope*, lâr *lore*, gâst *ghost*, wrât *wrote.* Sometimes the accented or long **â** is represented in English by *oa;* as Âc *an oak*, gâd *a goad*, lâd *load*, râd *road*, brâd *broad*, fâm *foam*, lâm *loam*, sâpe *soap*, âr *oar*, bâr *boar*, hâr *hoar*, bât *boat*, gât *goat*, âta *oat*, âþ *oath*, lâþ *loath.* Occasionally **â** becomes *oe* in English; as Dâ *a doe*, fâ *a foe*, tâ *toe*, wâ *woe;* but the *oe*, in these words, has the sound of *o* in *no*. The same may be said of *oa* in *oak, goad.* Hence it appears that the Anglo-Saxon **â** is represented by the modern English *o, oa*, and *oe*, which have the sound of *o* in *no* and *bone;* as Râd *rode* (*p. of ride*), râd *a road*, and dâ, *a doe.* Deut. Gram. von Jacob Grimm, vol. i. pp. 358, 397, 398, 3rd edit. 1840. **2.** The long **â** is often changed into **ǽ**; as Lâr *lore*, lǽran *to teach*, ân *one*, ǽnig *any.* **3.** The following is a precise summary from Grimm of the prefixed â-, long or accented. The prefixed â- is long because it is a contraction and represents the preposition æf *of, off, from, away, out of*, or the preposition on *on, in, upon, into*, or as the *Lat.* in and *Eng.* un; as â-dûne for æf-dûne, â-wendian for æf-wendian, â-drædan for on-drædan, â-gean for on-gean, â-týnan *to unshut, open*, Ps. Spl. 38, 13, for on-týnan, un-týnan *to open.* Â, as an inseparable particle, is long because it represents the inseparable prefixed particles ar, ur, ir, in *O. H. Ger.* and *O. Sax.* commonly expressing the meaning of the Latin prepositions *ab, ex, ad*, etc: *A. Sax.* â-hebban, *O. H. Ger.* ur-hefan *elevare; A. Sax.* â-fyllan, *O. H. Ger.* ar-fullan *implere; A. Sax.* â-beran, *O. H. Ger.* ar-peran *ferre, efferre; A. Sax.* â-scînan, *O. H. Ger.* ir-scînan *clarescere.* The peculiar force which this particle imparts to different verbs may correspond (1) to the Latin ex *out*, as â-gangan *to go out;* exire: (2) to the English *up*, as â-hleápan *to leap up;* exsilire: â-fyllan *to fill up;* implere: (3) it expresses the idea of an origin, *becoming, growing*, â-blacian *to blacken, to become black;* â-heardian *to grow hard:* (4) it corresponds to the Latin *re*, as â-geban *reddere*, â-lôsian *redimere*, â-sêcan *requirere:* (5) it is often used merely to render a verb transitive, or to impart a greater force to the transitive meaning of the simple verb,—â-beódan *offerre*, â-ceapian *emere*, â-lecgan *ponere*, â-sleán *occidere:* (6) it is used with intransitive verbs, where it has hardly any meaning, unless it suggests *the commencement* or *beginning* of the action, as â-hleahan *ridere*, â-sweltan *mori:* (7) it expresses *the end, aim*, or *purpose* of an action, as â-dômian *condemnare*, â-biddan *deprecari*, â-wirþan *perire.* But, after all, it must be borne in mind, that the various shades of its meaning are innumerable, and that, even in one and the same compound, it often assumes different meanings. For further illustration we must therefore refer to the compounds in which it occurs, Grm. ii. 818–832. I have, in justice to Grimm, given his motives for marking the prefixed â- long: I believe, however, it is short. See **B. 6.**

-a, affixed to words, denotes *A person, an agent*, or *actor*, hence, *All nouns ending in* a *are masculine, and make the gen. in* an; as from Cum *come* [*thou*], cuma *a person who comes*, or *a guest:* Swîc *deceive* [*thou*], swîca *a traitor:* Worht *wrought*, wyrhta *a workman, wright:* Fôregeng *foregoing*, fôregenga *a foregoer:* Beád or gebêd *a supplication, praying*, beáda *a person who supplicates* or *prays:* Bytl *a beetle* or *hammer*, bytla *a hammerer, builder.* Some *abstract nouns*, and words denoting *inanimate things*, end in -a; and these words, having the same declension as those which signify *Persons* or *actors*, are masculine; as Hlîsa, an; *m. fame:* Tîma, an; *m. time:* Lîchama, an; *m. a body:* Steorra, an; *m. a star:* Gewuna, an; *m. a custom, habit.*

a; *prep. acc. To, for;* in:—A worlda world *to* or *in an age of ages;* in seculorum seculum, Ps. Th. 18, 8, = on worlda world, Ps. Lamb. 20, 5, = on worulda world, Ps. Th. 103, 6.

Â, aa, aaa; *adv. Always, ever, for ever;* hence the *O. Eng.* AYE, *ever;* semper, unquam, usque:—Ac â sceal ðæt wiðerwearde gemetgian *but ever must the contrary moderate*, Bt. 21; Fox 74, 19. Ân God â on ēcnysse *one God to all eternity* [lit. *one God ever, in eternity*], Homl. Th. ii. 22, 32. Â on ēcnisse *usque in æternum*, Jos. 4, 7. Ic â ne geseah '*I not ever saw*' = *I never saw*, Cd. 19; Th. 24, 10; Gen. 375. Â = ǽfre: Nū, sceal beón â on Iī abbod *now, there shall always* [*ever*] *be an abbot in Iona*, Chr. 565; Th. 33, 2, col. 2. Nū, sceal beón ǽfre on Iī abbod *now, there shall ever* [*always*] *be an abbot in Iona*, Chr. 565; Th. 32, 11; 33, 4, col. 1. He biþ aa [ââ MS.] ymbe ðæt ân *he is for ever about that one* [*thing*], L. Th. ii. 310, 25. Aa on worulda woruld *semper in seculorum seculum*, Ps. Th. 105, 37. Nū and aaa [âââ MS.], to worulde būton ǽghwilcum ende *now and ever, to a world without any end*, Bt. 42; Fox 260, 15. Â world *for ever*, Ex. 21, 6. Â forþ *ever forth, from thence*, Bt. Tupr. 303, 31. [The original signification seems to be a flowing, referring to time, which every moment flows on, hence *ever, always*, also to ǽ, eá *flowing water, a river*. In Johnston's Index Geog. there are nineteen rivers in Europe with the name of Aa = Â.]

â, *indecl; f. A law;* lex:—Dryhtnes â *the Lord's law*, Andr. Recd. 2387; An. 1196. vide **ǼE**.

aac, e; *f. An oak:*—Aac-tūn *Acton Beauchamp, Worcestershire*, Cod. Dipl. 75; A. D. 727; Kmbl. i. 90, 19. v. Âc-tūn.

aad *a pile:*—He mycelne aad gesomnode *he gathered a great pile*, Bd. 3, 16; S. 542, 22. v. âd.

âǽdan *to lay waste;* vastare, Gen. 1280: â ǽdan, Cd. 64; Th. 77, 24. v. ǽdan.

aam, es; *m. A reed of a weaver's loom*, Exon. 109 a; Th. 417, 22; Rä. 36, 8; Cod. Lugd. Grn. v. âm.

aar *honour:*—In aar naman *in honore nominis*, Bd. 2, 6; S. 508, note 43: 5, 11; S. 626, note 36. v. **ÂR**; *f.*

aaþ *an oath:*—He done aaþ gesæh *he saw the oath*, Th. Dipl. A. D. 825; p. 71, 12. v. **Âþ**.

a-bacan, ic -bace, ðū -bæcest, -bæcst, he -bæceþ, -bæcþ, *pl.* -bacaþ; *p.* -bōc, *pl.* -bōcon; *pp.* -bacen *To bake;* pinsere, coquere:—Se hlāf þurh fȳres hǽtan abacen *the bread baked by the heat of fire*, Homl. Pasc. Daye, A. D. 1567, p. 30, 8; Lisl. 4to, 1623, p. 4, 16; Homl. Th. ii. p. 268, 9.

a-bād *expected, waited:*—And abād swâ ðeáh seofon dagas *expectavitque nihilominus septem alios dies*, Gen. 8, 12. v. abīdan.

a-bæd, abǽdon *asked; p. of* abiddan.

a-bǽdan; *p.* -bǽdde; *pp.* -bǽded *To restrain, repel, compel;* avertere, repellere, cogere, exigere:—Is fira ǽnig, ðe deáþ abǽde *is there any man, who can restrain death?* Salm. Kmbl. 957; Sal. 478. Ðæt oft wǽpen abǽd his mondryhtne *which often repels the weapon for its lord*, Exon. 114 a; Th. 437, 24; Rä. 56, 12. v. bǽdan.

a-bæligan; *p.* ode; *pp.* od *To offend, to make angry;* irritare, offendere:—Sceal gehycgan hæleða ǽghwylc ðæt he ne abælige bearn waldendes *every man must be mindful that he offend not the son of the powerful*, Cd. 217; Th. 276, 27; Sat. 195. v. a-belgan, a-bylgan.

a-bær *bore* or *took away;* sustulit, Ps. Spl. 77, 76; *p. of* a-beran.

ABAL, afol, es; *n. Power of body, strength;* vigor, vires, robur corporis:—Ðīn abal and cræft *thy strength and power*, Cd. 25; Th. 32, 9; Gen. 500. [*Orm.* afell: *O. H. Ger.* aval, *n*: *O. Nrs.* afl, *n. robur, vis: Goth.* abrs *strong*: *Grk.* ὄβρῐμος.]

a-bannan; *p.* -beónn, *pl.* -beónnon; *pp.* -bannen. **I.** *to command, order, summon;* mandare, jubere:—Abannan to beadwe *to summon to battle*, Elen. Grm. 34. **II.** *to publish, proclaim; with* ūt *to order out, call forth, call together, congregate, assemble;* edicere, avocare, citare:—Aban ðū ða beornas ūt of ofne *command thou the men out of the oven*, Cd. 193; Th. 242, 32; Dan. 428. Ðâ hēt se cyng abannan ūt ealne þeódscipe *then the king commanded to order out* [*to assemble*] *all the population*, Chr. 1006; Erl. 140, 8. v. bannan.

a-barian; *p.* ede; *pp.* ed [a, barian *to make bare;* bær, se bara; *adj. bare*] *To make bare, to manifest, discover, disclose;* denudare, prodere, in medium proferre:—Gif ðū abarast ūre sprǽce *si sermonem nostrum profers in medium*, Jos. 2, 20: R. Ben. Interl. 46: Cot. 80.

a-bāt *bit, ate:*—He abāt *he ate*, MS. Cott. Jul. E. vii. 237; Salm. Kmbl. 121, 15; *p. of* a-bītan.

abbad, abbod, abbud, abbot, es; *m:* abboda, an; *m.* **I.** *an abbot;* abbās,—the title of the male superior of certain religious establishments, thence called abbeys. The word *abbot* appears to have been, at first, applied to any member of the clerical order, just as the French Père and English Father. In the earliest age of monastic institutions the monks were not even priests: they were merely religious persons, who retired from the world to live in common, and the abbot was one of their number, whom they elected to preside over the association. In regard to general ecclesiastical discipline, all these communities were at this early time subject to the bishop of the diocese, and even to the pastor of the parochial district within the bounds of which they were established. At length it began to be usual for the abbot to be in orders; and since the sixth century monks generally have been priests. In point of dignity an abbot is generally next to a bishop. A minute account of the different descriptions of abbots may be found in Du Cange's Glossary, and in Carpentier's supplement to that work:—Se ârwurða abbad Albīnus *the reverend abbot Albinus*, Bd. pref. Riht is ðæt abbodas fæste on mynstrum wunian *it is right that abbots dwell closely in their minsters*, L. I. P. 13; Th. ii. 320, 30. Hēr Forþrēd abbud forþfērde *in this year abbot Forthred died*, Chr. 803; Erl. 60, 13. Se abbot Saxulf *the abbot Saxulf*, Chr. 675; Ing. 50, 15. Swâ gebireþ abbodan *as becometh abbots*, L. Const. W. p. 150, 27; L. I. P. 13; Th. ii. 320, 35. **II.** *bishops were sometimes subject to an abbot, as they were to the abbots of Iona:*—Nū, sceal beón ǽfre on Iī abbod, and nâ biscop; and ðan sculon beón underþeódde ealle Scotta biscopas, forðan ðe Columba [MS. Columban] was abbod, nâ biscop *now, in Iī* [*Iona*], *there must ever be an abbot, not a bishop; and to him must all bishops of the Scots be subject, because Columba was an abbot, not a bishop*, Chr. 565; Th. 32, 10–16, col. 1. [*Laym.* abbed: *O. Frs.* abbete: *N. Ger.* abt: *O. H. Ger.* abbat: *Lat.* abbās; *gen.* abbātis *an abbot: Goth.* abba: *Syr.* אַבָּא abba *father*, from *Heb.* אָב ab *father, pl.* אָבוֹת abot *fathers*.] DER. abbad-dōm, -hād, -isse, -rīce: abboda.

abbad-dōm *an abbacy*. v. abbud-dōm.

abbad-hād *the state* or *dignity of an abbot*. v. abbud-hād.

abbadisse, abbodisse, abbatisse, abbudisse, abedisse, an; *f.* [abbad *an abbot*, isse *a female* termination, *q. v.*] *An abbess;* abbatissa:—Riht is ðæt abbadissan fæste on mynstrum wunian *it is right that abbesses dwell closely in their nunneries*, L. I. P. 13; Th. ii. 320, 30: L. Const. W. 150, 21: Bd. 3, 8; S. 531, 14: Guthl. 2; Gdwin. 16, 22: Bd. 3, 11; S. 536, 38.

abbad-rīce *an abbacy*. v. abbod-rīce.

Abban dūn, e; *f. Abingdon, in Berkshire*, Chr. 985; Ing. 167, 5. v. Æbban dūn.

abbod *an abbot*, L. I. P. 13; Th. ii. 320, 30. v. abbad.

abboda, an; *m. An abbot;* abbas:—Swâ gebireþ abbodan *as becometh abbots*, L. I. P. 13; Th. ii. 320, 35. v. abbad.

abbod-rīce, abbot-rīce, es; *n. The rule of an abbot, an abbacy;* abbatia:—On his tīme wæx ðæt abbodrīce swīðe rīce *in his time the abbacy waxed very rich*, Chr. 656; Ing. 41, 1. On ðis abbotrīce *in this abbacy*, Chr. 675; Ing. 51, 12.

abbodysse *an abbess*, Guthl. 2; Gdwin. 16, 22. v. abbadisse.

abbot *an abbot*, Chr. 675; Ing. 50, 15. v. abbad.

abbud *an abbot*, Chr. 803; Erl. 60, 13: Bd. 5, 23; S. 645, 14. v. abbad.

abbud-dōm, es; *m.* [= abbod-rīce, *q. v.*] *An abbacy, the rule* or *authority of an abbot;* abbātia, abbātis jus *vel* auctoritas:—Abbuddōmes, *gen.* Bd. 5, 1; S. 613, 18. Abbuddōme, *dat.* 5, 21; S. 642, 37.

abbud-hād, es; *m. The state* or *dignity of an abbot;* abbatis dignitas:—Munuchād and abbudhād ne syndon getealde to ðysum getele *monkhood and abbothood are not reckoned in this number*, L. Ælf. C. 18; Th. ii. 348, 31.

abbudisse, an; *m. An abbess:*—Ðâ sealde seó abbudisse him sumne dǽl ðære moldan *tunc dedit ei abbatissa portiunculam de pulvere illo*, Bd. 3, 11; S. 536, 38. v. abbadisse.

a-beág *bowed down*, Beo. Th. 1555; B. 775; *p. of* a-būgan.

a-bealh *angered*, Cd. 222; Th. 290, 4; Sat. 410. v. a-belgan.

a-beátan; *p.* -beót; *pp.* -beáten *To beat, strike;* tundere, percellere:—Stormum abeátne *beaten by storms*, Exon. 21 b; Th. 58, 26; Cri. 941. v. beátan.

a-beden *asked*, Nicod. 12; Thw. 6, 15: Bd. 4, 10; S. 578, 31; *pp. of* a-biddan.

abedisse, an; *f. An abbess;* abbatissa:—Ðære abedissan betæhton *committed to the abbess*, Chr. 1048; Erl. 181, 28. v. abbadisse.

a-bēgan; *p.* de; *pp.* ed; *v. trans. To bend, bend down, bow, reduce, subdue;* incurvare, redigere, subigere:—Weorþe heora bæc swylce abēged eác *dorsum illorum semper incurva*, Ps. Th. 68, 24: Chr. 1073; Erl. 212, 1: 1087; Th. 356, 10. v. bēgan.

a-bēgendlīc; *adj. Bending;* flexibilis, Som. v. a-bēgan.

a-behōfian; *p.* ode *To behove, concern;* decere:—Mid māran unrǽde ðone him abehōfode *with more animosity than it behoved him*, Chr. 1093; Th. 360, 4. v. be-hōfian.

a-belgan, ic -belge, ðū -bilgst, -bilhst, he -bylgþ, -bilhþ, *pl.* -belgaþ; *p.* -bealg, -bealh, *pl.* -bulgon; *pp.* -bolgen, *v. trans.* [a, belgan *to irritate*] *To cause any one to swell with anger, to anger, irritate, vex, incense;* ira aliquem tumefacere, irritare, exasperare, incendere:—Ne sceal ic ðē abelgan *I would not anger thee*, Salm. Kmbl. 657; Sal. 328. Oft ic wīfe abelge *oft I irritate a woman*, Exon. 105 b; Th. 402, 20; Rä. 21, 32. He abilhþ Gode *he will incense God*, Th. Dipl. 856; 117, 20. Ic ðē abealh *I angered thee*, Cd. 222; Th. 290, 4; Sat. 410: Beo. Th. 4550; B. 2280. God abulgan *Deum exacerbaverunt*, Ps. Th. 77, 41: Ex. 32, 29. Nū hig me abolgen habbaþ *irascatur furor meus contra eos*, Ex. 32, 10. He him abolgen wurþeþ *he will be incensed against them*, Cd. 22; Th. 28, 4; Gen. 430. Wæs swȳðe abolgen *erat graviter offensus*, Bd. 3, 7; S. 530, 8.

a-beódan; *p.* -beád; *pp.* -boden; *v. a.* [a, beódan *to order*] *To announce, relate, declare, offer, command;* referre, nuntiare, annuntiare, edicere, offerre, jubere:—Ðæt he wolde ðæt ǽrende abeódan *that he would declare the errand*, Ors. 4, 6; Bos. 86, 20: Cd. 91; Th. 115, 14; Gen. 1919: 200; Th. 248, 9; Dan. 510.

a-beofian *To be moved* or *shaken, to tremble;* moveri, contremere:—Ealle abeofedan eorþan staðelas *movebuntur omnia fundamenta terræ*, Ps. Th. 81, 5. v. beofian.

a-beornan; *p.* -bearn, -barn, *pl.* -burnon; *pp.* -bornen, *v. intrans. To burn;* exardere:—Fȳr abarn *exarsit ignis*, Ps. Th. 105, 16. v. beornan.

a-beran; *p.* -bær; *pp.* -boren. I. *to bear, carry, suffer;* portare, ferre:—Ðe man aberan ne mæg *which they are not able to bear*, Mt. Bos. 23, 4. Hī ne māgon nān earfoða aberan *they cannot bear any troubles*, Bt. 39, 10; Fox 228, 3: Andr. Kmbl. 1912; An. 958: Ps. Th. 54, 11. II. *to take* or *carry away;* tollere, auferre:—Abær hine of eowdum sceápa *sustulit eum de gregibus ovium*, Ps. Spl. 77, 76: Ps. Grn. 50, 12. v. beran.

a-berd, -bered; *adj. Sagacious, crafty, cunning;* callidus, Wrt. Voc. 47, 36: Lchdm. iii. 192, 10: 188, 26: 186, 17.

a-berend-līc; *adj.* [berende *bearing*] *Bearable, tolerable, that may be borne;* tolerabilis:—Aberendlīc broc *bearable affliction*, Bt. 39, 10; Fox 228, 4, note 5.

a-berstan; *p.* -bearst, *pl.* -burston; *pp.* -borsten [a, berstan] *To burst, break, to be broken;* perfringi. v. for-berstan.

a-bet; *adv. Better;* melius:—Hwæðer ðē se ende abet līcian wille *whether the end will better please thee*, Bt. 35, 5; Fox 166, 23. v. bet.

a-beþecian; *subj.* ðū abeþecige; *p.* ode; *pp.* od [be, þeccan *to cover*] *To uncover, detect, find hidden, to discover, disclose;* detegere:—Būton ðū hit forstele oððe abeþecige *unless thou steal it, or find (it) hid*, Bt. 32, 1; Fox 114, 9.

a-bicgan; *p.* -bohte; *pp.* boht; *v. a.* [a, bycgan *to buy*] *To buy, pay for, recompense;* emere, redimere:—Gif frīman wið frīes mannes wīf geligeþ, his wērgelde abicge *if a freeman lie with a freeman's wife, let him buy her with his wergeld*, i. e. *price*, L. Ethb. 31; Th. i. 10, 7. v. a-bycgan.

a-bīdan, ic -bīde, ðū -bīdest, -bītst, -bīst, he -bīdeþ, -bīt, *pl.* -bīdaþ; *p.* -bād, *pl.* -bidon; *pp.* -biden; *v. intrans. To* ABIDE, *remain, wait, wait for, await;* manere, sustinere, expectare:—Hȳ abīdan sceolon in sin-nihte *they must abide in everlasting night*, Exon. 31 b; Th. 99, 28; Cri. 1631. Hēr sculon abīdan bān *here the bones shall remain*, 99 a; Th. 370, 18; Seel. 61. Abād swā ðeáh seofon dagas *expectavit nihilominus septem alios dies*, Gen. 8, 12. We ōðres sceolon abīdan *alium expectamus?* Mt. Bos. 11, 3. Ic abād [anbīdode Spl.] hǣlu ðīne *expectabam salutare tuum*, Ps. Surt. 118, 166. Sāwla ūre abīdyþ Driht *anima nostra sustinet Dominum*, Ps. Spl. C. 32, 20. Windes abidon *ventum expectabant*, Bd. 5, 9; S. 623, 19. Ðǣr abīdan sceal maga miclan dōmes *there the being [Grendel] shall await the great doom*, Beo. Th. 1959; B. 977: Exon. 115 b; Th. 444, 27; Kl. 53. [*Laym.* abiden; *p.* abad, abed, abeod, abod, abaod, abide, *pl.* abiden.] v. bīdan.

a-biddan, ic -bidde, ðū -bidest, -bitst, he -bit, -byt, -bitt, *pl.* -biddaþ; *p.* -bæd, *pl.* -bǣdon; *pp.* -beden *To ask, pray, pray to, pray for, obtain by asking* or *praying;* petere, precari, postulare, exorare, impetrare:—Wilt tū wit unc abiddan drincan *vis petamus bibere?* Bd. 5, 3; S. 616, 30. Abiddaþ [Cott. biddaþ] hine eáþmōdlīce *pray to him humbly*, Bt. 42; Fox 258, 21. Se ðe hwæt to lǣne abit *qui quidquam mutuo postulaverit*, Ex. 22, 14. Ne mihte ic lȳfnesse abiddan *nequaquam impetrare potui*, Bd. 5, 6; S. 619, 8. Ðā sendon hȳ tuā heora ǣrendracan to Rōmānum æfter friðe; and hit abiddan ne mihtan *then they sent their ambassadors twice to Rome for peace; and could not obtain it*, Ors. 4, 7; Bos. 87, 39. He abiddan mæg ðæt ic ðē lǣte duguða brūcan *he may obtain by prayer that I will let thee enjoy prosperity*, Cd. 126; Th. 161, 5; Gen. 2660. v. biddan.

a-bifian, -bifigan; *p.* ode, ede; *pp.* od, ed *To be moved* or *shaken, to tremble;* moveri, contremere:—For ansȳne ēcan Dryhtnes ðeós eorþe sceal eall abifigan *a facie Domini mota est terra*, Ps. Th. 113, 7. v. bifian.

a-bilgþ, a-bilhþ *anger, an offence.* v. a-bylgþ.

a-biran *to bear, carry;* portare, Bd. 1, 27; S. 491, 31. v. a-beran.

a-bīsegien *should prepossess*, Bt. 35, 1; Fox 154, 32. v. abȳsgian.

a-bit *prays*, Ex. 22, 14; *pres. of* a-biddan.

a-bītan, ic -bīte, ðū -bītest, -bītst, he -bīteþ, -bīt, *pl.* -bītaþ; *p.* -bāt, *pl.* -biton; *pp.* -biten; *v. a. To bite, eat, consume, devour;* mordere, arrodere, mordendo necare, comedere, devorare:—Gif hit wildeór abītaþ, bere forþ ðæt abitene and ne agife *si comestum a bestia, deferat ad eum quod occisum est, et non restituet*, Ex. 22, 13. He abāt his suna *he ate his children*, Salm. Kmbl. p. 121, 15. Ðæt se wōd-freca were-wulf tō fela ne abīte of godcundre heorde *that the ferocious man-wolf devour not too many of the spiritual flock*, L. I. P. 6; Th. ii. 310, 31. Mīne scēp sind abitene *my sheep are devoured*, Homl. Th. i. 242, 10. Ðū his ne abītst *non comedas ex eo*, Deut. 28, 31. v. bītan.

a-biterian, -bitrian; *p.* ode; *pp.* od *To make sour* or *bitter;* exacerbare. v. biterian, biter *bitter*.

a-bi-tweónum; *prep. dat. Between;* inter:—Ic wiht geseah horna abitweónum [hornum bitweónum, Grn; Th.] hūðe lǣdan *I saw a creature bringing spoil between its horns*, Exon. 107 b; Th. 411, 19; Rä. 30, 2. [*Sansk.* abhi: *Zend* aibi.] v. bi-tweónum.

a-blācian, -blācigan; *p.* ode; *pp.* od *To be* or *look pale, grow pale;* pallere, obrigescere:—Ablācodon *obriguerunt*, Ex. 22, 16? Lye. Ic blācige *palleo*, Ælfc. Gr. 26, 2; Som. 28, 42. Blācian from blīcan, *p.* blāc *to shine:* blǣcan *to bleach, whiten, fade.* Observe the difference between blāc, blǣc *pallid, bleak, pale*, and blæc, blaces, se blaca *black, swarthy.* DER. blācian *pallere.*

a-blǣcan; *p.* -blǣhte; *pp.* -blǣht [a, blǣcan *to bleach*] *To bleach, whiten;* dealbare, Ps. Vos. 50, 8: 67, 15.

a-blǣcnes, -ness, e; *f. A paleness, gloom;* pallor, Herb. 164; Lchdm. i. 294, 3, note 6. v. æ-blǣcnys.

a-blændan *to blind, deaden, benumb.* v. ablendan.

a-blann *rested; p. of* a-blinnan *to leave off.*

a-blāwan; *p.* -bleów; *pp.* -blāwen *To blow, breathe;* flare, efflare:—On ableów *inspiravit*, Gen. 2, 7. Ūt ablāwan *to breathe forth*, Hexam. 4; Norm. 8, 20. Nǣfre mon ðæs hlūde bȳman ablāweþ *never does a man blow the trumpet so loudly*, Exon. 117 b; Th. 451, 27; Dōm. 110. God ðā geworhte mannan and ableów on his ansȳne līflīcne blǣd *God then made man and blew into his face the breath of life*, Hexam. 11; Norm. 18, 25.

a-blāwung, e; *f. A blowing.* v. blāwung.

a-blend, se a-blenda; *adj. Blinded;* cæcatus:—Wēnaþ ða ablendan mōd *the blinded minds think*, Bt. 38, 5; Fox 206, 6. v. *pp. of* a-blendan.

a-blendan; *p.* -blende, *pl.* -blendon; *pp.* -blended, -blend; *v. a. To blind, make blind, darken, stupify;* cæcare:—Ða gyldenan stānas ablendaþ ðæs mōdes eágan *the golden stones blind the mind's eyes*, Bt. 34, 8; Fox 144, 34. Swā bióþ ablend so *are blinded*, 38, 5; Fox 206, 1. Ic sȳne ablende bealo-þoncum *I blinded their sight by baleful thoughts*, Exon. 72 b; Th. 270, 22; Jul. 469. He ablende hyra eágan *excæcavit oculos eorum*, Jn. Bos. 12, 40. Ablended in burgum *blinded as I am in these dwellings*, Andr. Kmbl. 155; An. 78. Wæs ablend *was blinded*, Mk. Bos. 6, 52: Num. 14, 44. v. blendan.

a-bleóton *sacrificed; p. pl. of* a-blōtan.

a-bleów *blew; p. of* a-blāwan.

a-blīcan; *p.* -blāc, *pl.* -blicon; *pp.* -blicen; *v. n. To shine, shine forth, to appear, glitter, to be white, to astonish, amaze;* dealbari, micare:—Sōþlīce on rihtwīsnysse ic ablīce *ego autem in justitia apparebo [micabo]*, Ps. Spl. T. 16, 17. Ofer snāw ic beó ablicen *super nivem dealbabor*, Ps. Spl. 50, 8.

a-blīcgan; *p.* ede; *pp.* ed *To shine, to be white, to astonish;* consternare:—Ic eom ablīcged *consternor*, Ælfc. Gr. 37; Som. 39, 42.

a-blignys, -nyss, e; *f. An offence.* v. a-bylgnes.

a-blindan *to blind*, Abus. 1, Lye. v. a-blendan.

a-blinnan; *p.* -blann, *pl.* -blunnon; *pp.* -blunnen *To cease, desist;* cessare, desistere, Ps. Spl. 36, 8: Bd. 4, 1; S. 563, 16.

a-blīsian; *p.* ode; *pp.* od *To blush;* erubescere:—Ōþ eówre lyþre mōd ablīsige *donec erubescat incircumcisa mens eorum*, Lev. 26, 41.

a-blōtan; *p.* -bleót, *pl.* -bleóton; *pp.* -blōten *To sacrifice;* immolare. v. blōtan.

a-blȳsgung, -blȳsung, e; *f. The redness of confusion, shame;* pudor, R. Ben. 73.

a-boden *told; pp. of* a-beódan *to bid, tell.*

a-bogen *bowed; pp. of* a-būgan, -beógan *to bow, bend.*

a-boht *bought; pp. of* a-bicgan *to buy.*

a-bolgen *angered*, Ex. 32, 10; *pp. of* a-belgan *to offend, anger.*

a-boren *carried; pp. of* a-beran *to bear.*

a-borgian; *p.* ode; *pp.* od *To be surety, to undertake for, to assign, appoint;* fidejubere:—Gif he nite hwā hine aborgie, hæfton hine *if he know not who will be his borh, let them imprison* [lit. *have, detain*] *him*, L. Ath. i. 20; Th. i 210, 8.

a-bracian; *p.* ode; *pp.* od *To engrave, emboss;* cælare:—Abracod *cælatum*, Cot. 33.

a-bradwian *To overthrow, slay, kill;* prosternare, occidere, Beo. Th. 5232; B. 2619. v. a-bredwian.

a-bræc *broke; p. of* a-brecan *to break.*

a-bræd, -brægd *drew*, Mt. Bos. 26, 51; *p. of* a-bredan, a-bregdan *to move, drag, draw.*

a-breátan; *p.* -breót, *pl.* -breóton *To break, kill;* frangere, concidere, necare:—Abreót brim-wīsan, brȳd aheorde *slew the sea-leader, set free his bride*, Beo. Th. 5852; B. 2930. v. a-breótan.

a-brecan, ic -brece, ðū -bricst, he -bricþ; *p.* -bræc, *pl.* -brǣcon; *pp.* -brocen *To break, vanquish, to take by storm, to assault, destroy;* frangere, effringere, expugnare:—Abrecan ne meahton reced *they might not break the house*, Cd. 115; Th. 150, 14; Gen. 2491. He Babilone abrecan wolde *he would destroy Babylon*, Cd. 209; Th. 259, 10; Dan. 689. Hū ǣnig man mihte swylce burh abrecan *how any man could take such a town*, Ors. 2, 4; Bos. 44, 16. DER. brecan.

a-bredan, he -brit = -brideþ, -bret = -bredeþ; *p.* -bræd, *pl.* -brudon; *pp.* -broden; *v. a. To move quickly, remove, draw, withdraw;* vibrare, destringere, eximere, retrahere:—Abræd hys swurd, *exemit gladium suum*, Mt. Bos. 26, 51. Gif God abrit *if God remove*, Bt. 39, 3; Fox

216, 5. Of mōde abrit ðæt micle dysig *he removes from his mind that great ignorance*, Bt. Met. Fox 28, 155; Met. 28, 78. Hond up abræd *he raised his hand*, Beo. Th. 5144; B. 2575. Lār Godes is abroden of breóstum *the knowledge of God is withdrawn from your breasts*, Cd. 156; Th. 194, 31; Exod. 269. v. bredan.

a-bredwian; *p.* ade; *pp.* ad *To overthrow, slay? kill?* prosternare? occidere?—Ðeáh ðe he his brōðor bearn abredwade [abradwade Th.] *although he had overthrown [exiled? killed?] his brother's child*, B. 2619.

a-brēgan; *p.* de; *pp.* ed *To alarm, frighten*; terrere:—Mec mæg grīma abrēgan *a phantom may frighten me*, Exon. 110 b; Th. 423, 7; Rä. 41, 17. Abrēgde, *p.* Bd. 3, 16; S. 543, 12: Ps. Spl. T. 79, 14.

a-bregdan; *p.* -brægd, *pl.* -brugdon; *pp.* -brogden *To move quickly, vibrate, remove, draw from, withdraw*; vibrare, destringere, eximere, retrahere:—Ðē abregdan sceal deáþ sāwle ðīne *death shall draw from thee thy soul*, Cd. 125; Th. 159, 22; Gen. 2638. Hwonne of heortan hunger oððe wulf sāwle and sorge abregde *when from my heart hunger or wolf shall have torn both soul and sorrow*, 104; Th. 137, 22; Gen. 2277. Hine of gromra clommum abrugdon *they drew him from the clutches of the furious*, 114; Th. 150, 4; Gen. 2486. v. bregdan.

ā-brēmende *ever-celebrating*, Exon. 13 a; Th. 24, 20; Cri. 387. v. brēman.

a-breótan; *p.* -breát, *pl.* -bruton; *pp.* -broten *To bruise, break, destroy, kill*; frangere, confringere, concidere, necare:—Billum abreótan *to destroy with bills*, Cd. 153; Th. 190, 14; Exod. 199. Yldo beám abreóteþ *age breaks the tree*, Salm. Kmbl. 591; Sal. 295. Hine seó brimwylf abroten hæfde *the sea-wolf had destroyed him*, Beo. Th. 3203; B. 1599. Stānum abreótan *lapidare*, Elen. Kmbl. 1017; El. 510.

a-breóðan; *p.* -breáþ, *pl.* -bruðon; *pp.* -broðen *To unsettle, ruin, frustrate, degenerate, deteriorate*; perdere, degenerare:—Hæleþ oft hyre hleór abreóðeþ *a man often unsettles her cheek*, Exon. 90 a; Th. 337, note 18; Gn. Ex. 66. Abreóðe his angin *he frustrated his enterprise*, Byrht. Th. 138, 59; By. 242. Hī abruðon ðā ðe he toþohte *they frustrated that which he had thought of*, Chr. 1004; Ing. 178, 1. Eálā ðū abroðene folc *degener O populus*, Ælfc. Gr. 8; Som. 8, 10. *Hic et hæc et hoc nugas* ðæt is abroðen on Englisc, Ælfc. Gr. 9, 25; Som. 11, 2.

abret, abrit *takes away*, Bt. 39, 3; Fox 216, 5. v. abredan.

a-brocen *broken*. v. a-brecan.

a-broden, a-brogden *opened, freed, taken away*. v. abredan, abregdan.

abrotanum = ἀβρότονον *southernwood*, Herb. 135; Lchdm. i. 250, 16. v. sūðerne-wudu.

a-broten? *crafty, silly, sluggish*; vafer, fatuus, socors:—Abroten *vel* dwǣs *vafer*, Ælfc. Gl. 9; Som. 56, 114. Abroten? *for* abroðen.

a-broðen *degeneratus*; *pp. of* a-breóðan.

a-broðennes, -ness, e; *f. Dulness, cowardice, a defect, backsliding*; ignavia, pusillanimitas. DER. a-broðen.

a-brugdon *withdrew*, Cd. 114; Th. 150, 4; Gen. 2486; *p. pl. of* a-bregdan.

a-bruðon *frustrated*, Chr. 1004; Ing. 178, 1; *p. pl. of* a-breóðan.

a-bryrdan; *p.* -bryrde; *pp.* -bryrded, -bryrd, *v. trans. To prick, sting, to prick in the heart, grieve*; pungere, compungere:—Nā ic ne beó abryrd, God mīn *non compungar, Deus meus*, Ps. Spl. 29, 14. v. bryrdan.

a-bryrdnes, -ness, e; *f. Compunction, contrition*; compunctio, contritio. v. bryrdnys, a-bryrdan.

a-brytan; *p.* -brytte; *pp.* -brytt *To destroy*; exterminare, Ps. Spl. C. 36, 9. v. brytan.

a-būfan; *adv.* [a + be + ufan] ABOVE; supra:—Swā wæ ǣr abūfan sǣdan *as we have before above said*, Chr. 1090; Th. 358, 15. DER. būfan.

a-būgan; *p.* -beág, -beáh, *pl.* -bugon; *pp.* -bogen *To bow, bend, incline, withdraw, retire*; se vertere, declinare, inclinare, averti:—Abūgaþ eádmōdlīce *inclinate suppliciter*, Coll. Monast. Th. 36, 3. Ac ðē firina gehwylc feor abūgeþ *but from thee each sin shall far retire*, Exon. 8 b; Th. 4, 22; Cri. 56. Ðǣr fram sylle abeág medu-benc monig *there many a mead-bench inclined from its sill*, Beo. Th. 1555; B. 775. v. būgan.

a-bulgan = abulgon *angered*, Ps. Th. 77, 41; *p. of* a-belgan.

a-būnden *ready*; expeditus, Cot. 72; *pp. of* a-bīndan. v. bīndan.

a-būtan, -būton; *prep. acc.* [a + be + ūtan] ABOUT, *around, round about*; circa:—Ðū tæcst Israhela folce abūtan ðone mūnt *thou shalt take the people of Israel around the mountain*, Ex. 19, 12. Abūton hī *circa eos*, Mk. Bos. 9, 14. Abūton stān *about a stone*, L. N. P. L. 54; Th. ii. 298, 16.

a-būtan, -būton; *adv.* ABOUT; circa:—Besæt ðone castel abūtan *beset the castle about*, Chr. 1088; Th. i. 357, 29. Besǣton ðone castel abūton *they beset the castle about*, Chr. 1090; Th. i. 358, 25.

a-bycgan, -bicgan; *p.* -bohte, *pl.* -bohton; *pp.* -boht [a, bycgan *to buy, procure*]. I. *to buy, pay for*; emere, redimere, L. Ethb. 31; Th. i. 10, 7. II. *to perform, execute*; præstare:—Āþ abycgan *jusjurandum præstare*, L. Wih. 19; Th. i. 40, 18.

a-byffan; *p.* ode; *pp.* od *To mutter*; mutire, Cot. 134. v. byffan.

a-bȳgan, *v. trans. To bow, bend*; incurvare, Grm. ii. 826. v. a-bēgan.

a-bȳgendlīc; *adj. Bending, flexible*; flexibilis. DER. un-abȳgendlīc.

a-bylgan, -byligan, -bylgean; *p.* de; *pp.* ed *To offend, anger, vex*; offendere, irritare, exacerbare:—Hī hine oft abylgdon [MS. -dan] *ipsi sæpe exacerbaverunt eum*, Ps. Th. 105, 32. Ða mōd abylgean ūra ðara nȳhstena *animos proximorum offendere*, Bd. 3, 19; S. 548, 17: Hy. 6, 22. v. a-belgan.

a-bylg-nes, æ-bylig-nes, æ-bylig-nys, -ness, e; *f.* [abylgan *to offend*] *An offence, scandal, anger, wrath, indignation*; offensa, ira, indignatio:—He him abylgnesse oft gefremede *he had oft perpetrated offence against him*, Exon. 84 a; Th. 317, 25; Mōd. 71.

a-bylgþ, -bilgþ, -bilhþ, e; *f. An offence, wrong, anger*; offensa, injuria, ira:—He sceal Cristes abilgþe wrecan *he ought to avenge offence to Christ*, L. Eth. 9, 2; Th. i. 340, 13: L. Pen. 16; Th. ii. 284, 6. v. æ-bylgþ.

a-byligd, e; *f. Anger*; indignatio, Ps. Th. 77, 49. v. a-bylgþ.

a-byrgan, -byrgean, -byrian *To taste*; gustare:—We cȳðaþ eów ðæt God ælmihtig cwæþ his āgenum mūðe, ðæt nān man he mōt abyrgean nānes cynes blōdes. Ǣlc ðæra ðe abyrgþ blōdes ofer Godes bebod sceal forwurþan on ēcenysse *we tell you that God Almighty said by his own mouth, that no man may taste any kind of blood. Every one who tastes blood against God's command shall perish for ever*, Homl. intitul. Hēr is hālwendlīc lār, Bibl. Bodl. MSS. Junii 99, fol. 68. Se wulf for Gode ne dorste ðæs hæfdes abyrian *the wolf durst not, for God, taste the head*, Homl. Brit. Mus. MSS. Cot. Julius, E. 7, fol. 203, Bibl. Bodl. MSS. Bodley 343. v. byrgan.

a-bȳsgian, -bȳsgan, -bȳsean, -bīsegian; *p.* ode, ade; *pp.* od, ad [a, bȳsgian *to busy*] *To occupy, preoccupy, prepossess*; occupare:—Ðeáh unþeáwas oft abīsegien ðæt mōd *though imperfections oft prepossess the mind*, Bt. 35, 1; Fox 154, 32. Biþ hyra seó swīþre symble abȳsgod ðæt hī unrihtes tiligeaþ *dextera eorum dextera iniquitatis*, Ps. Th. 143, 9. Biþ hyra seó swīþre symble abȳsgad *dextera iniquitatis*, 143, 13.

a-bȳsgung, -bīsgung, e; *f. Necessary business, employment*; occupatio, Past. 18, 1; Hat. MS. 25 a, 27, 29, 30.

a-bȳwan; *p.* de; *pp.* ed; *v. trans. To adorn, purify, clarify*; exornare, purgare:—Beóþ monna gǣstas beorhte abȳwde þurh bryne fȳres *the souls of men are brightly adorned [clarified] through the fire's heat*, Exon. 63 b; Th. 234, 24; Ph. 545. v. bȳwan.

AC, ach, ah, oc; *conj.* I. *but*; sed:—Ne com ic nā towurpan, ac gefyllan *non veni solvere, sed adimplere*, Mt. Bos. 5, 17. Brytwalas fultumes bǣdon wið Peohtas, ac hī næfdon nǣnne *the Brito-Welsh begged assistance against the Picts, but they had none*, Chr. 443; Erl. 11, 34. II. *for, because*; nam, enim, quia:—Ne se aglǣca yldan þōhte, ac he gefēng hraðe slǣpendne rinc *nor did the wretch mean to delay, for he quickly seized a sleeping warrior*, Beo. Th. 1484; B. 740. Ðū ne þearft onsittan wīge, ac nē-fuglas [wig, eácne MS.] blōdig sittaþ þicce gefylled *thou needest not oppress with war, because carrion birds sit bloody quite satiated* (lit. *thickly filled*), Cd. 98; Th. 130, 12; Gen. 2158. III. *but also, but yet*; sed etiam, sed et, sed tamen:—Nā læs weoruld men, ac eác swylce ðæt Drihtnes eowde *not only men of the world, but also* [sed etiam Bd.] *the Lord's flock*, Bd. 1, 14; S. 482, 25. Ða cwican nō genihtsumedon ðæt hī ða deádan bebyrigdon, ac hwæðere ða ðe lifigende wǣron nōht dōn woldon *the living were not sufficient to bury the dead, but yet those who were living would do nothing*, Bd. 1, 14; S. 482, 32: 2, 7; S. 509, 13. Ac swylce tunge mīn ǣlce dæge smeáþ rightwīsnysse ðīne *sed et lingua mea tota die meditabitur justitiam tuam*, Ps. Spl. 70, 26. [*R. Glouc. Orm.* ac: *Laym.* ac, æc, ah: *Scot.* ac: *O. Sax.* ak: *O. H. Ger.* oh: *Goth.* ak.]

ac; *adv. interrogative, Why, whether*; nonne, numquid:—Ðā ðū gehogodest sæcce sēcean, ac ðū gebettest mǣrum þeódne *when thou resolvedst to seek warfare, hadst thou compensated the great prince?* Beo. Kmbl. 3976; B. 1990. Ac [ah MS.] ætfileþ ðē seld unrihtwīsnesse *numquid adhæret tibi sedes iniquitatis?* Ps. Surt. 93, 20. Ac hwā dēmeþ *who shall judge?* Salm. Kmbl. 669; Sal. 334. Ac forhwon fealleþ se snāw *why falleth the snow?* 603; Sal. 301.

ac-, v. ag-, ag-lǣca, ah-, ah-lǣca.

ĀC, ǣc; *g.* e; *f.* I. *an* OAK; quercus, robur:—Ðeós āc *hæc quercus*, Ælfc. Gr. 8; Som. 7, 46. Sume āc astāh *got up into an oak*, Homl. Th. ii. 150, 31. *acc.* Āc *an oaken ship*, Runic pm. 25; Kmbl. 344, 21. Geongre āce *of a young oak*, L. M. 1, 38; Lchdm. ii. 98, 9. Of ðære āc [*for* āce], Kmbl. Cod. Dipl. iii. 121, 22. II. āc; *g.* āces; *m. The Anglo-Saxon Rune* ᚪ = a, the name of which letter, in Anglo-Saxon, is āc *an oak*, hence, this Rune not only stands for the letter a, but, for āc *an oak*, as ᚪ byþ on eorþan elda bearnum flǣsces fōdor *the oak is on earth food of the flesh to the sons of men*, Hick. Thes. vol. i. p. 135; Runic pm. 25; Kmbl. 344, 15. Ācas twegen *two A's*, Exon. 112 a; Th. 429, 26; Rä. 43, 10. [*R. Glouc.* ōk: *Chauc.* ōk, āke, oak: *O. Frs.* ēk: *Dut.* eek, eik: *North Frs.* ik: *L. Ger.* eke: *N. Ger.* eiche: *M. Ger.* eich: *O. Ger.* eih: *Dan.* eg: *Swed.* ek: *O. Nrs.* eik. *Grn.* starting from *Goth.* ayuk in áiw-dup, i. e. áiw-k-dup εἰς τὸν αἰῶνα, supposes a form ayuks, contracted to áiks, the equivalent of which would be āc, which would, therefore, indicate a tree of long durability.]

a-cægan *to name*. v. a-cīgan.

a-cænned = a-cenned *brought forth*; *pp. of* acennan.

a-cænnednys, -cænnys *nativity*. v. a-cennednes.

a-cærran *to avert;* acærred *averted.* v. a-cerran.

a-calan; *p.* -cōl, *pl.* -cōlon *To become cold;* algere, frigescere:—Nō acōl for ðȳ egesan *he never became cold for the terror,* Andr. Grm. 1267. v. calan.

ACAN; ic ace, ðū æcest, æcst, he æceþ, æcþ, *pl.* acaþ; *p.* ōc, *pl.* ōcon; *subj.* ic, ðū, he ace; *pp.* acen; *v. n. To* AKE, *pain;* dolere:—Gif mannes midrif [MS. midrife] ace *if a man's midriff ake,* Herb. 3, 6; Lchdm. i. 88, 11: Herb. Cont. 3, 6; Lchdm. i. 6; 3, 6. Acaþ mīne eágan *my eyes ake,* Ælfc. Gr. 36, MS. D; [mistiaþ = acaþ, Som. 38, 48]; dolent mei oculi, Mann. [*Laym. p.* oc: *R. Glouc. p.* ok: *Chauc.* ake: *N. L. Ger.* aken, æken.]

Âcan-tūn, es; *m.* [âcan = âcum, *pl. d. of* âc *an oak,* tūn *a town*] *Acton, Suffolk:*—Ðæt hit cymþ to Âcantūne; fram Âcantūne [MS. Âcyntūne] ðæt hit cymþ to Rigindūne *till it comes to Acton; from Acton till it comes to Rigdon,* Th. Diplm. A. D. 972; 525, 22–24. v. Âc-tūn, *and* ðæt *adv.*

acas, e; *f:* acase, axe, an; *f. An axe;* securis:—Acas, Mt. Lind. Stv. 3, 10. Acase, Lk. Rush. War. 3, 9 [id. Lind. Acasa, *a Northumbrian form*]. Axe, Mt. Rush. Stv. 3, 10. v. æx.

âc-beám, es; *m. An oak-tree;* quercus, Ettm. p. 51.

âc-cærn, âc-corn *an acorn.* v. ǽcern.

accutian? *to prove;* probare:—Accuta me *proba me,* Ps. Spl. M. 138, 22.

âc-cyn, -cynn, es; *n.* [âc *oak,* cyn *kind*] *A species of oak;* ilex, Mann.

âc-drenc, -drinc, es; *m. Oak-drink, a kind of drink made of acorns;* potus ex quercus glandibus factus. v. âc, drenc.

ace *ake, pain.* DER. acan *to ake.* v. ece.

a-cealdian; *p.* ode; *v. intrans. To be* or *become cold;* algere, frigescere, Past. 58, 9. v. a-cōlian, calan.

a-ceápian; *p.* ode; *pp.* od *To buy.* v. ceápian.

a-cearfan *to cut off:*—Acearf *abscindet,* Ps. Spl. C. 76, 8. v. a-ceorfan.

a-cēlan; *p.* de; *v. intrans. To be* or *become cold;* algere, frigescere:—Ðæs þearfan ne biþ þurst acēled *the thirst of this desire is not become cold,* Bt. Met. Fox 7, 34; Met. 7, 17. v. cēlan, calan.

Acemannes burh, burg; *g.* burge; *d.* byrig, beri; *f:* ceaster, cester; *g.* ceastre; *f.* [æce *ake,* mannes *man's,* ceaster *or* burh *city or fortress*] *Bath, Somersetshire:*—Hēr Eádgār to rīce fēng at Acemannes byrig, ðæt is at Baðan *here,* A. D. 972, *Edgar took the kingdom at Akeman's burgh, that is at Bath,* Chr. 972; Th. 225, 18, col. 3. On ðære ealdan byrig, Acemannes ceastre; ac beornas Baðan nemnaþ *in the old burgh, Akeman's Chester; but men call it Bath,* Chr. 973; Ing. 158, 26. At Acemannes beri *at Akeman's bury,* Ing. 158, note g. v. Baðan.

acen *pained.* v. acan.

âcen *oaken.* v. ǽcen.

a-cennan, ðū -censt, he -cenþ; *p.* -cende; *pp.* -cenned; *v. a. To bring forth, produce, beget, renew;* parere, gignere, renovare, renasci:—Swā wīf acenþ bearn *as a woman brings forth a child,* Bt. 31, 1; Fox 112, 2. On sārnysse ðū acenst cild *in dolore paries filios,* Gen. 3, 16. Ðā se Hǽlend acenned wæs *cum natus esset Jesus,* Mt. Bos. 2, 1. Crist wæs acenned [MS. acennyd] on midne winter *Christ was born in mid-winter,* Menol. Fox 1; Men. 1. Gregorius wæs of æðelborenre mægþe acenned *Gregory was born of a noble family,* Homl. Th. ii. 118, 7. Eal edniwe, eft acenned, synnum asundrad *all renewed, born again, sundered from sins,* Exon. 59 b; Th. 214, 19; Ph. 241. Ðonne se mōna biþ acenned [geniwod, v. geniwian] *when the moon is changed* [*born anew*], Lchdm. iii. 180, 19, 22, 28. v. cennan.

a-cenned-līc; *adj. Native;* nativus, Cot. 138.

a-cennednes, -cennes, -cennys, -cænnednys, -cænnys, -ness, e; *f. Nativity, birth, generation;* nativitas, ortus:—Manega on his acennednysse gefagniaþ *multi in nativitate ejus gaudebunt,* Lk. Bos. 1, 14: Ps. Spl. 106, 37.

a-ceócian? *p.* ode; *pp.* od *To choke;* suffocare. v. a-þrysman.

a-ceócung, e; *f. A consideration;* ruminatio, Wrt. Voc. 54, 62. v. a-ceósung.

a-ceorfan; *p.* -cearf, *pl.* -curfon; *pp.* -corfen *To cut off;* abscidere, succidere, concidere:—Of his ansȳne ealle ic aceorfe, ða ðe him feóndas syndon *concidam inimicos ejus a facie ipsius,* Ps. Th. 88, 20.

a-ceósan; *p.* -ceás, *pl.* -curon; *pp.* -coren *To choose, select;* eligere. DER. ceósan.

a-ceósung [MS. aceócung], e; *f. A consideration;* ruminatio, Wrt. Voc. 54, 62.

acer *a field,* Rtl. 145, 18. v. æcer.

a-cerran; *p.* -cerde; *pp.* -cerred *To turn, return;* vertere, reverti:—Ūton acerran ðider ðǽr he sylfa sit, sigora waldend *let us turn thither where he himself sitteth, the triumphant ruler,* Cd. 218; Th. 278, 6; Sat. 217.

a-cerrednes, -ness, e; *f. An aversion.* v. a-cerran.

ach *but;* sed:—Ach ðæs weorodes eác *but of the host also,* Andr. Recd. 3182; An. 1594. v. ac; *conj.*

âc-hāl; *adj. Oak-whole* or *sound, entire;* roboreus, integer, Andr. Grm. 1700.

a-cīgan; *p.* de; *pp.* ed *To call;* vocare, evocare:—Acīgde of corþre cyninges þegnas *he called the thanes of the king from the band,* Beo. Th. 6233; B. 3121. Sundor acīgde *called him alone, in private,* Elen. Kmbl. 1203; El. 603. Hine acīgde ūt *evocavit eum,* Bd. 2, 12; S. 513, 19.

ac-lǽc-cræft, es; *m.* [ac-lǽc = ag-lǽc *miseria,* cræft *ars*] *An evil art;* ars mala vel perniciosa:—Ðū ðē, Andreas, aclǽccræftum lange feredes *thou, Andrew, hast long betaken thyself to evil arts,* Andr. Kmbl. 2724; An. 1364.

a-clǽnsian; *p.* ode; *pp.* od *To cleanse, purify;* mundare:—Hyra nân næs aclǽnsod, būton Naaman se Sirisca *nemo eorum mundatus est, nisi Naaman Syrus,* Lk. Bos. 4, 27.

Âc-leá = Âc-leáh; *g.* -leáge; *f.* [âc *an oak,* leáh *a lea, ley, meadow; acc.* leá = leáh, *q. v.*] *The name of a place, as Oakley:*—Sinoþ wæs gegaderod æt Âcleá *a synod was assembled at Acley* or *Oakley,* Chr. 789; Ing. 79, 14. Âcleá, Chr. 782; Erl. 57, 6: 851; Erl. 67, 26; 68, 3.

âc-leáf, es; *n. An oak-leaf;* quercus folium:—Âcleáf, Lchdm. iii. 311: L. M. 3, 8; Lchdm. ii. 312, 19.

a-cleopian; *p.* ode; *pp.* od *To call, call out;* clamare, exclamare. DER. cleopian, clypian.

aclian; *p.* ode; *pp.* od [acol, acl *excited by fear*] *To frighten, excite;* terrere, terrore percellere. DER. ge-aclian.

âc-melu, *g.* -meluwes; *n. Acorn-meal;* querna farina, L. M. 1, 54; Lchdm. ii. 126, 7.

âc-mistel, e; *f. Oak mistletoe;* quercus viscum:—Genīm âcmistel *take mistletoe of the oak,* L. M. 1, 36; Lchdm. ii. 88, 4.

a-cnyssan; *p.* ede; *pp.* ed *To expel, drive out;* expellere. v. cnyssan.

a-cofrian; *p.* ode; *pp.* od *To recover;* e morbo consurgere, convalescere:—Acofraþ *will recover,* Lchdm. iii. 184, 15.

acol, acul, acl; *adj. Excited, excited by fear, frightened, terrified, trembling;* agitatus, perterritus, pavidus:—Wearþ he on ðam egesan acol worden *he had through that horror become chilled, trembling,* Cd. 178; Th. 223, 24; Dan. 124. Forht on mōde, acul for ðam egesan *fearful in mood, trembling with dread,* 210; Th. 261, 14; Dan. 726. Acol for ðam egsan *trembling with terror,* Exon. 42 b; Th. 143, 20; Gū. 664. Forht and acol *afraid and trembling,* Cd. 92; Th. 117, 18; Gen. 1955. Wurdon hie ðā acle *they then became terrified,* Andr. Kmbl. 2678; An. 1341. Fyrd-leóþ galan aclum stefnum *they sung a martial song with loud excited voices,* Cd. 171; Th. 215, 4; Exod. 578.

a-cōlian; *p.* ade, ode; *pp.* ad, od *To become cool, cold, chilled;* frigescere:—Ræst wæs acōlad *his resting-place was chilled,* Exon. 119 b; Th. 459, 28; Hö. 6. Ðonne biþ ðæt werge līc acōlad *then shall be the accursed carcase cooled,* Exon. 100 a; Th. 374, 12; Seel. 125. v. cōlian.

acolitus = ἀκόλουθος *A light-bearer;* lucifer:—Acolitus is se ðe leóht berþ æt Godes þēnungum *acolite is he who bears the light at God's services,* L. Ælf. P. 34; Th. ii. 378, 7: L. Ælf. C. 14; Th. ii. 348, 4. v. hād **II.** *state, condition;* ordo, gradus, *etc.*

acol-mōd; *adj. Of a fearful mind, timid;* pavidus animo:—Eorl acolmōd *a chief in trembling mood, fearful mind,* Exon. 55 b; Th. 195, 36; Az. 166. Þegnas wurdon acolmōde *the thanes were chilled with terror,* Andr. Kmbl. 753; An. 377.

acordan; *p.* ede; *pp.* ed *To* ACCORD, *agree, reconcile;* reconciliare, Chr. 1119; Ing. 339, 30.

a-coren *chosen; pp. of* a-ceósan. v. ceósan, gecoren.

a-corenlīc; *adj. Likely to be chosen;* eligibilis:—Biþ swīðe acorenlīc *is very estimable,* Past. 52, 8; Swt. 409, 36.

a-corfen *carved; pp. of* a-ceorfan.

a-costnod *tried; pp. of* a-costnian. v. costnian.

a-cræftan; *p.* de; *pp.* ed *To devise, plan, contrive as a craftsman;* excogitare:—Ūton ðeáh hwæðere acræftan hū we heora, an ðyssa nihta, māgan mǽst beswīcan *let us however plan how we can, in this night, most weaken them,* Ors. 2, 5; Bos. 47, 19.

a-crammian; *p.* ode; *pp.* od *To cram, fill;* farcire. v. crammian.

a-creópian; *p.* ede; *pp.* ed *To creep;* serpere, scatere:—Ðā lǽfdon hīg hit [Manhu] sume, ōþ hit morgen wæs, and hit wearþ wyrmum acreóped *dimiserunt quidam ex eis usque mane, et scatere cœpit vermibus,* Ex. 16, 20.

a-crimman; *p.* -cramm, *pl.* -crummon; *pp.* -crummen *To crumble;* friare:—Acrummen *in micas fractus,* Cot. 88: 179: 193.

âc-rind, e; *f. Oak-rind* or *bark;* querna cortex:—Nīm âcrinde *take oak-bark,* Lchdm. iii. 14, 1.

acs *an axe.* v. æx, acas.

Acsa, Axa, an; *m? The river Axe.* v. Acsan mynster.

Acsan mynster, Ascan mynster, Axan minster, es; *n.* [Acsa, an; *m? the river Axe;* mynster *a monastery: Flor.* Axanminster: *Hunt.* Acseminster] AXMINSTER *in Devonshire;* hodie *Axminster,* in agro Devoniensi; ita dictum quod situm est ad ripam fluminis *Axi:*—Se Cynewulf rīcsode xxxi wintra, and his līc līþ æt Wintan ceastre, and ðæs æðelinges æt Ascan [Acsan, Gib. 59, 3; Ing. 71, 28] mynster *Cynewulf reigned thirty-one years, and his body lies at Winchester, and the prince's at Axminster,* Chr. 755; Erl. 50, 32: Th. 86, 13, col. 1.

acse *ashes,* Cot. 40. v. asce.

acsian, acsigan; *p.* ode; *pp.* od *To ask, ask for, demand;* rogare, expostulare, exigere:—Môt ic acsian, Bd. 4, 3; S. 568, 26. Cômon corþrum miclum cuman acsian *they came in great multitudes to demand the strangers,* Cd. 112; Th. 148, 8; Gen. 2453: Lk. Bos. 20, 40. Hig hine acsodon ðæt bigspell *they asked him the parable,* Mk. Th. 4, 10. Hû mæg ǽnig man acsigan *how can any man inquire?* Bt. 35, 1; Fox 156, 6. v. ascian.

acsung, e; *f. An asking, a question, an inquiry, inquisition, interrogation, that which is inquired about, information;* interrogatio:—Uneáþe ic mæg forstandan ðîne acsunga *I can scarcely understand thy questions,* Bt. 5, 3; Fox 12, 16. v. ascung.

âc-treó, -treów, es; *n. An oak-tree;* quercus:—Under âctreó *under the oak-tree,* Exon. 115 a; Th. 443, 10; Kl. 28.

Âc-tûn, es; *m.* [âc *oak,* tûn *a town*] ACTON, *Staffordshire?*—Æt Âctûne *at Acton,* Th. Diplm. A. D. 1002; 546, 27. v. aac.

a-cucian *to revive* [cuc = cwic, Cd. 65; Th. 78, 23 = Ors. 2, 1; Bos. 38, 8]. v. a-cwician.

acul *frightened,* Cd. 210; Th. 261, 14; Dan. 726. v. acol.

â-cuma OAKUM; putamen:—Âcuman *putamina,* Mone p. 398; B. 3231. v. âcumba.

a-cuman; *p.* -cám, -com, *pl.* -câmon, -cômon; *pp.* -cumen, -cymen *To come, bear;* venire, ferre, sustinere:—Wæs of fere acumen *he had come from the vessel,* Cd. 75; Th. 93, 12; Gen. 1544. Ðæt land hig ne mihte acuman *non sustinebat eos terra,* Gen. 36, 7. Ge hyt ne mâgon nû acuman *non potestis portare modo,* Jn. Bos. 16, 12.

â-cumba, an; *m:* ǽ-cumbe, an; *n?* [cemban *to comb*]. I. *oakum, that which is combed, the coarse part of hemp,—Hards, flax, tow;* stuppa = στύππη, στύπη [v. heordas *stuppæ,* R. 68]:—Afyl ða wûnde, and mid âcumban besweðe *fill the wound, and swathe up with tow,* L. M. 1, 1; Lchdm. ii. 22, 21. Ǽcumbe *stuppa,* Ælfc. Gl. 64; Som. 69, 2; Wrt. Voc. 40, 36. II. the thing pruned or trimmed, properly of trees, and figuratively of other things, hence,—*Prunings, clippings, trimmings;* putamen, hinc,—putamina non solum arborum sunt, verum omnium rerum purgamenta. Nam quicquid ex quacumque re projicitur, putamen appellatur:—Âcumba *putamen,* Mone B. 3702. Âcumban *putamina,* 3703, p. 407. III. reduced to ashes, it was used as a substitute for σπόδιον = σποδός, *Wood ashes;* spodium Græcorum nihil aliud est, quam radix Alcannæ combusta, officinæ ustum ebur ejus loco substituunt:—To sealfe, nîm. âcumban, cneówholen *for a salve, take the ashes of oakum, butcher's broom,* L. M. 1, 33; Lchdm. ii. 80, 11. Âcumba *ashes of oakum,* 1, 47; Lchdm. ii. 120, 14.

a-cumend-lîc; *adj. Tolerable, bearable;* tolerabilis:—Acumendlîcre byþ Sodoma lande and Gomorra on dômes dæg, ðonne ðære ceastre *tolerabilius erit terræ Sodomorum et Gomorrhæorum in die judicii quam illi civitati,* Mt. Bos. 10, 15.

a-cumendlîcness, e; *f. The possibility to bring anything to pass;* possibilitas. v. cumende; *part. of* cuman.

a-cunnian; *p.* ode; *pp.* od *To prove;* probare:—Ðû acunnodest [MS. acunnudyst] us God *probasti nos Deus,* Ps. Spl. C. 65, 9. v. cunnian.

a-curon *chose; p. pl. of* a-ceósan.

a-cwǽdon *said,* Ps. Th. 72, 6; *p. of* a-cweðan.

a-cwǽlon *died,* Chr. 918; Erl. 104, 13; *p. pl. of* a-cwelan.

a-cwæþ *spoke,* Cd. 30; Th. 40, 14; Gen. 639; *p. of* a-cweðan.

a-cwalde *killed,* Ps. Vos. 104, 27: 134, 11, = a-cwealde; *p. of* a-cwellan.

a-cwân *melted, decayed,* Bd. 2, 7; S. 509, 29; *p. of* a-cwînan.

a-cwanc *quenched,* Chr. 1110; Ing. 331, 30; *p. of* a-cwincan.

a-cwealde *killed,* Cd. 69; Th. 84, 25; Gen. 1403; *p. of* a-cwellan.

a-cweccan; *p.* -cwehte; *pp.* -cweht *To move quickly, to shake, vibrate;* movere, quatere, vibrare:—Æsc acwehte *he shook the ash,* i. e. *the lance,* Byrht. Th. 140, 59; By. 310.

a-cwelan, he -cwilþ, *pl.* -cwelaþ; *p.* -cwæl, *pl.* -cwǽlon; *pp.* -cwolen, -cwelen, *v. n. To die, perish;* mori:—Ða fixas acwelaþ *pisces morientur,* Ex. 7, 18. Ofercumen biþ he ǽr he acwele *he will be overcome ere he dies,* Exon. 90 b; Th. 340, 10; Gn. Ex. 114. Monige men hungre acwǽlon *many men died of hunger,* Chr. 918; Erl. 104, 13.

a-cwellan; *p.* -cwealde; *pp.* -cweald *To kill, destroy;* interficere, necare:—Freá wolde on ðære to-weardan tîde acwellan *the Lord would destroy them in the coming time,* Cd. 64; Th. 77, 31; Gen. 1283. Ic wille mid flôde folc acwellan *I will destroy the folk with a flood,* 64; Th. 78, 21; Gen. 1296. Acwelleþ ða wyrmas *killeth the worms,* Herb. 137; Lchdm. i. 254, 22. Ðâ ðe êgor-here eorþan tuddor eall acwealde *when the water-host destroyed all the progeny of earth,* Cd. 69; Th. 84, 25; Gen. 1403. Wîges heard wyrm acwealde *the bold one in battle slew the worm, the dragon,* Beo. Th. 1777; B. 886. Steóp-cilda feala stundum acwealdon *pupillos occiderunt,* Ps. Th. 93, 6.

a-cwelledness, e; *f. A quelling, killing;* occisio. DER. cwellan.

a-cwencan; *p.* de, te, *pl.* don, ton; *pp.* ed, d, t *To quench, extinguish, put out;* extinguere:—Bæd ðæt hî ðæt leóht acwencton *prayed that they would put out the light,* Bd. 4, 8; S. 575, 40, note, MS. B. Ûre leóhtfatu synt acwencte *lampades nostræ extinguuntur,* Mt. Bos. 25, 8. Fyr ne byþ acwenced *ignis non extinguitur* Mk. Bos. 9, 44.

a-cweorran; *p.* -cwear, *pl.* -cwurron; *pp.* -cworren *To eat* or *drink immoderately, to glut, guzzle;* ingurgitare:—Swâ swâ mihti acworren fram wîne *tanquam potens crapulatus a vino,* Ps. Spl. T. 77, 71.

âc-wern, es; *n. The name of an animal, a squirrel;* scirra, sciurus, Ælfc. Gl. 19; Som. 59, 9.

a-cwerren, -cworren *drunk; pp. of* a-cweorran.

a-cweðan, he -cwyþ; *p.* -cwæþ, *pl.* -cwǽdon; *pp.* -cweden *To say, tell, answer;* dicere, eloqui, respondere:—Ðæt word acwyþ *that word says,* Beo. Th. 4099; B. 2046. Word acwæþ, wuldres aldor *he spake the word, the chief of glory,* Cd. 30; Th. 40, 14; Gen. 639. Ðæt me acweden syndon *quæ dicta sunt mihi,* Ps. Th. 121, 1. v. cweðan.

a-cwician; *p.* ode; *pp.* od *To quicken, revive, to come to life;* vivificare, reviviscere:—On ðînre mild-heortnesse me scealt acwician *in misericordia tua vivifica me,* Ps. Th. 118, 159. Ðâ acwicode ic hwon *then I revived a little,* Bd. 5, 6; S. 619, 29.

a-cwilþ *perishes:*—Ne a-cwilþ *perishes not,* Bt. 13; Fox 38, 29. v. a-cwelan.

a-cwînan; *p.* -cwân, *pl.* -cwinon; *pp.* -cwinen *To waste* or *dwindle away, decline, become extinct;* tabescere:—Ðæt fŷr acwân and adwæsced wæs *the fire declined and was extinguished,* Bd. 2, 7; S. 509, 29.

a-cwincan; *p.* -cwanc, *pl.* -cwuncon; *pp.* -cwuncen *To vanish, become extinguished, quenched;* extingui, evanescere:—Se môna acwanc *the moon was extinguished,* i. e. *eclipsed,* Chr. 1110; Ing. 331, 30.

a-cwinen *quenched.* v. a-cwînan.

a-cwolen *died,* Chr. 918; Gib. 105, 37, note a. v. a-cwelan.

a-cworren *drunk,* Ps. Spl. T. 77, 71; *pp. of* a-cweorran.

a-cwucian *to quicken.* v. a-cwician.

a-cwylan *to die,* L. H. E. 6; Th. i. 30, 3. v. a-cwelan.

acxan *ashes,* Ors. 1, 3; Bos. 27, 32. v. axe, asce.

a-cŷd *said, confirmed,* R. Ben. 27. v. a-cŷðan.

a-cyrran; *p.* -cyrde; *pp.* -cyrred, -cyrd *To avert;* avertere:—Ne ðû nǽfre gedêst, ðæt ðû mec acyrre from Cristes lofe *thou shalt never do so, that thou avert me from the love of Christ,* Exon. 67 b; Th. 251, 2; Jul. 139. Acyrred from Cristes ǽ *turned from Christ's law,* 71 b; Th. 267, 6; Jul. 411.

a-cyrredness, -cerrednes, -ness, e; *f. A turning, aversion, a turning from, apostacy, revolting;* aversio. DER. a-cyrred. v. a-cyrran.

a-cŷðan; *p.* -cŷðde; *pp.* -cŷðed, -cŷd *To show, announce, confirm;* manifestare, annuntiare, confirmare:—Yrre acŷðan *iram manifestare, irasci,* Ps. Th. 88, 39. Ǽr he hine acŷðan môte *ere he can show himself,* Exon. 89 b; Th. 336, 15; Gn. Ex. 49. Torn acŷðan *to make known* or *show one's affliction,* Exon. 78 a; Th. 293, 8; Wand. 113. Ðǽr me wæs yrre ðîn on acŷðed *in me confirmata est ira tua,* Ps. Th. 87, 7.

ÂD, aad, es; *m. A funeral pile, pile, heap;* rogus, congeries:—Ðâ onbærnde he ðone âd *then kindled he the pile,* Bd. 3, 16; S. 542, 25. Âd stôd onæled *the pile was* [*stood*] *kindled,* Cd. 141; Th. 176, 35; Gen. 2922. Hêt âd onælan *he commanded to kindle the funeral pile,* Exon. 74 a; Th. 277, 13; Jul. 580. Mycelne aad [âd MS. B. T.] gesomnode on beámum *advexit plurimam congeriem trabium,* Bd. 3, 16; S. 542, 22. [*Kath.* ad: *O. Ger.* eit *ignis, rogus.* v. *Lat.* æs-tus: *Grk.* αἶθος: *Sansk.* edh-as *wood for fuel,* from the *Sansk.* root indh *to light, kindle.*] DER. âd-fær, -fŷr, -lêg, -loma.

a-dǽlan; *p.* ede; *pp.* ed, *To part, divide, separate;* partiri, dividere, separare:—He sceal wesan of eorþan feor adǽled *he shall be far parted from the earth,* Cd. 106; Th. 140, 4; Gen. 2322. Ða wǽron adǽlede ealle of ânum *these were parted all from one,* 12; Th. 14, 13; Gen. 218: Ps. Th. 54, 20. v. dǽlan.

a-deádan, -deádian; *p.* ode; *pp.* od *To fail, decay, die, mortify, lay waste, destroy;* fatiscere, Herb. 35, Lye: Cot. 90.

a-deáf; *adj. Deaf;* surdus, Ben. v. deáf.

a-deáfian; *p.* ode, ede; *pp.* od, ed *To become* or *wax deaf;* surdescere, obsurdescere:—Adeáfede *obsurduit,* Ælfc. Gl. 100; Som. 77, 13; Wrt. Voc. 55, 17.

a-deáfung eárena *A deafening of the ears;* surditas. v. a-deáf.

âdel *a disease,* Exon. 48 b; Th. 167, 23; Gû. 1064. v. âdl.

adela, an; *m. Filth;* cœnum:—Ðæt hêr yfle adelan stinceþ *that here ill smells of filth,* Exon. 110 b; Th. 424, 1; Rä. 41, 32. [addle-pool *a pool near a dunghill: Scot.* adill, addle *foul and putrid water: N. Ger.* adel, *m. cœnum: Holst.* addeln *lotium pecudum.*] DER. adelihţ, adel-seáþ.

a-delfan; *p.* -dealf, -dylf, *pl.* -dulfon; *pp.* -dolfen *To dig, delve;* fodere, effodere:—Cleopatra hêt adelfan hyre byrigenne *Cleopatra ordered her burying place to be dug,* Ors. 5, 13; Bos. 113, 22. Seáþ adealf *lacum effodit,* Ps. Spl. 7, 16: Bd. 3, 2; S. 524, 16. Ôþ ðæt biþ seáþ adolfen *donec fodiatur fovea,* Ps. Th. 93, 12: Bd. 3, 9; S. 533, 23.

adeliht; *adj. Dirty, filthy;* cœnosus, Cot. 48.

adel-seáþ, es; *m. A sewer, gutter, sink;* cloaca. v. adul-seáþ.

adelyng *a prince,* Joh. Brompt. ad ann. 907. v. æðeling.

a-dêman; *p.* de; *pp.* ed *To judge, adjudge, doom, deem, try, abjudicate, deprive;* examinare, abjudicare, judicio facto relegare:—Lîcode Gode hire ða hâlgan sâule eác swylce mid longre hire lîchoman untrymnesse adêmde and asodene beón *it pleased God that her holy soul should also be tried and seethed with long sickness of her body,* Bd. 4, 23;

S. 595, 15. Ðū adēmest me fram duguđe *thou deprivest me of good,* Cd. 49; Th. 63, 14; Gen. 1032. v. dēman.

a-deorcian; *p.* ode, ade; *pp.* od, ad *To obscure, dim, darken, hide;* obscurare:—Adeorcad *obscuratus,* Som. v. deorcian.

adesa, eadesa, an; *m. An addice* or *adze, a cooper's instrument;* ascia, Bd. 4, 3; S. 567, 26: Wrt. Voc. p. 84, 62.

ād-fær, *nom. acc; g.* -færes; *pl. nom.* -faru; *n. The pile-way, the way to the funeral pile;* iter rogi:—Ðæt we hine gebringen on ādfære *that we may bring him on the way to the pile,* Beo. Th. 6012; B. 3010.

ād-fȳr, es; *n. A pile-fire;* ignis rogi:—Abraham ādfȳr onbran *Abraham kindled a pile-fire,* Cd. 162; Th. 203, 4; Exod. 398.

a-dihtan; *p.* -dihte, -dihtode; *pp.* -dihtod, -diht *To compose, edit, write;* facere, componere. v. dihtan.

a-dilegian, -dilgian, -dylegian; *p.* ode; *pp.* od; *v. a.* [a, dilgian *to destroy*] *To abolish, blot out, destroy, do away;* abolere, delere:—His sāwul biþ adilegod of his folce *delebitur anima illa de populo suo,* Gen. 17, 14. Ic adilgige hī *delebo eos,* Ps. Lamb. 17, 43. Adilga me of đīnre bēc *dele me de libro tuo,* Ex. 32, 32: Ps. Th. 68, 29: 108, 13, 14. Adilgode, Ps. Th. 17, 40.

a-dimmian; *p.* ode; *pp.* od, ad *To dim, darken, obscure, make dull;* obscurare:—Đeáh heora mōd sie adimmad *though their mind be obscured,* Bt. 24, 4; Fox 84, 28: Ps. Th. 68, 24.

ĀDL, ādel; *g.* ādle, *f:* ādle, an; *f. A disease, pain, a languishing sickness, consumption;* morbus, languor:—Wæs seó ādl þearl, hāt and heorogrim *the disease was sharp, hot and very fierce,* Exon. 47 a; Th. 160, 30; Gū. 951. Seó mycle ādl *the great disease, leprosy;* elephantiasis, Som. Ne hine drēfeþ ādl *disease does not afflict him,* Beo. Th. 3476; B. 1736. Đē to heortan hearde grīpeþ ādl unlīđe *fell disease gripes thee hard at heart,* Cd. 43; Th. 57, 32; Gen. 937. Đē untrymnes ādle gongum bȳsgade *infirmity has afflicted thee through attacks of disease,* Exon. 47 b; Th. 163, 8; Gū. 990. He đīne ādle ealle gehǣlde *sanavit omnes languores tuos,* Ps. Th. 102, 3. Ðæt ādla hī gehǣldon *ut languores curarent,* Lk. Bos. 9, 1. Hū manega ādla *how many diseases?* Bt. 31, 1; Fox 110, 29: Bd. 3, 12; S. 537, 6. Laman legeres ādl *the palsy.* v. leger. [*Orm.* adl *disease.* Probably akin to the *Sansk.* root indh *to burn.*] DER. feorh-ādl, fōt-, horn-, in-, lungen-, mōnaþ-: ādl-ian, -īc, -ig, -þracu, -wērig.

ādle, an; *f. A disease;* morbus:—Ne yldo ne ādle *neither age nor disease,* Exon. 112 a; Th. 430, 7; Rä. 44, 4. v. ādl.

ād-lēg, es; *m. The flame of the funeral pile;* flamma rogi:—Ādlēg æleþ flǣsc and bān *the flame of the pile burns flesh and bones,* Exon. 59 a; Th. 213, 9; Ph. 222.

ādlian, -igan; *p.* ode; *pp.* od *To ail, to be sick, to languish;* ægrotare, languere:—Ðæt se ylca biscop ān ādliende mæden gebiddende gehǣlde *ut idem episcopus puellam languentem orando sanaverit,* Bd. 5, 3; S. 615, 35. Ic ādlige *langueo,* Ælfc. Gr. 26, 2; Som. 28, 46.

ādlīc, ādlig; *adj.* [ādl *disease,* līc *like*] *Sick, ill, diseased, corrupted, putrid;* morbidus, ægrotus, tabidus, vitiatus, putidus. Hence ADDLE *egg;* putidum ovum:—Ādlige men *languentes homines,* Bd. 3, 2; S. 524, 32. Ādlig *æger* vel *ægrotus,* Wrt. Voc. 45, 59.

ād-loma, -lama? an; *m. One crippled by the flame?* cui flamma claudicationem attulit?—Earme ādloman *poor wretches, i. e.* diaboli, Exon. 46 a; Th. 156, 33; Gū. 884.

ādl-þracu; *g.* -þræce; *f. The force* or *virulence of disease;* morbi impetus:—Seó ādlþracu *the force of disease,* Exon. 46 b; Th. 159, 31; Gū. 935. v. þræc.

ādl-wērig; *adj. Weary with sickness;* morbo fatigatus:—Fonde his mon-dryhten ādlwērigne *he found his master weary with sickness,* Exon. 47 b; Th. 162, 25; Gū. 981.

a-dolfen *dug,* Ps. Th. 93, 12; *pp. of* a-delfan.

a-dōn; *p.* -dyde; *impert.* -dō; *v. a. To take away, remove, banish;* tollere, ejicere:—Ne māgon đē nū heonan adōn hyrste đa reádan *the red ornaments may not now take thee hence,* Exon. 99 a; Th. 370, 14; Seel. 57. Ðæt hȳ God đanon adō to heora āgnum lande *that God will bring them thence to their own land,* Ors. 3, 5; Bos. 56, 37. Adō đa buteran *remove the butter,* L. M. 1, 36; Lchdm. ii. 86, 22. Adō of đa buteran *take off the butter,* 86, 19. Flōd adyde mancinn *a flood destroyed mankind,* Ælfc. T. 5, 25: Gen. 7, 23: 9, 11. Adō đas wylne *ejice ancillam hanc,* Gen. 21, 10: Bt. 16, 1; Fox 50, 10: Ps. Th. 68, 14.

a-drǣdan; *p.* -drēd; *pp.* -drǣden *To fear;* timere:—He adrēd đæt folc *timuit populum,* Mt. Bos. 14, 5.

a-drǣfan, -drēfan; *p.* de; *pp.* ed *To drive away;* expellere:—Đā wearþ adrǣfed deórmōd hæleþ *then was driven away the beloved hero,* Chr. 975; Th. i. 228, 22; Edg. 44. He adrǣfed wæs *ejectus est,* Gen. 3, 24. Osrǣd wæs of rīce adrēfed *Osred was banished from his kingdom,* Chr. 790; Th. 99, 20, col. 2.

a-dreág, -dreáh *bore,* Exon. 25 b; Th. 74, 6; Cri. 1202; *p. of* a-dreógan.

a-drēd *feared,* Mt. Bos. 14, 5; *p. of* a-drǣdan.

a-drēfed *driven,* Chr. 790; Th. 99, 20, col. 2, = a-drǣfed; *pp. of* a-drǣfan.

adreminte, an; *f. The herb feverfew;* parthenium = παρθένιον, Prior 78.

a-drencan; *p.* -drencte; *pp.* -drenced; *v. a. To plunge under, to immerse, drown;* immergere:—Wolde hine adrencan on đære eá *would drown him in the river,* Bt. 16, 2; Fox 52, 36. Caines ofspring eall wearþ adrenced on đam deópan flōd, đe adyde mancinn *Cain's offspring were all drowned in the deep flood, which destroyed mankind,* Ælfc. T. 5, 24. Heora feóndas flōd adrencte, Ps. Th. 105, 10: Ex. 14, 28.

a-dreógan, -driógan; ic -dreóge, đū -dreógest, -drȳhst, he -dreógeþ, -drȳhþ; *p.* -dreág, -dreáh, *pl.* -drugon; *pp.* -drogen. I. *to act, perform, practise;* agere, perficere:—He adreág unrihte þing *gessit iniqua,* Hymn. Bibl. Cott. Jul. A. 6. Đe his iufan adreógeþ *who practises his love,* Exon. 33 b; Th. 107, 24; Gū. 63. Līf adreógan *agere vitam,* Hexam. 3; Norm. 4, 29. II. *to bear, suffer, endure;* pati, sustinere:—Hī adreógan māgan *they may bear,* Bt. 40, 3; Fox 238, 27. Ic ne mæg adreógan đīne seófunga *I cannot tolerate thy lamentations,* Bt. 11, 1; Fox 30, 20. Ðæt hie đe eáþ mihton drohtaþ adreógan *that they might the easier endure their way of life,* Andr. Kmbl. 737; An. 369. Earfeđu đe he adreág *the pains that he endured,* Exon. 25 b; Th. 74, 6; Cri. 1202. Earfeđo đe he adreáh *the pains that he endured,* Andr. Kmbl. 2971; An. 1488. v. dreógan.

a-dreógendlīc; *adj. Bearable;* tolerabilis; *part. of* a-dreógan, -līc.

a-dreópan; ic -dreópe, đū -drȳpst, he -drȳpþ; *p.* -dreáp, *pl.* -drupon; *pp.* -dropen *To shed drop by drop;* guttatim effundere:—Nū is mīn swāt adropen *now is my blood sprinkled,* An. 1427, note. v. a-þrāwan.

a-dreósan; ic -dreóse, đū -drȳst, he -dreóseþ, -drȳst; *p.* -dreás, *pl.* -druron; *pp.* -droren *To fall, decline;* labi, deficere:—Ne biþ se hlīsa adroren *fame will not decline,* non erit fama tædio affecta, Exon. 95 a; Th. 355, 19; Reim. 79.

a-drīfan, æ-drīfan; ic -drīfe, đū -drīfest, -drīfst, he -drīfeþ, -drīfþ, -drīft, *pl.* -drīfaþ; *p.* -drāf, *pl.* -drifon; *pp.* -drifen *To drive, stake, expel, pursue, follow up;* agere, pellere, expellere, repellere, sequi, prosequi:—Đa Walas adrifon sumre eá ford ealne mid scearpum pīlum greátum innan đam wætere *the Welsh staked all the ford of a certain river with great sharp piles within the water,* Chr. Introd; Th. 5, 35. Rihtwīsnyssa his ic ne adrāf fram me *justitias ejus non repuli a me,* Ps. Spl. 17, 24. Adrīfe đæt spor ūt of his scīre *let him pursue the track out of his shire,* L. Ath. v. § 8, 4; Th. i. 236, 23. Adrifene fatu *graven* or *embossed vessels,* Ælfc. Gl. 67; Som. 69, 99. v. drīfan.

a-drigan, -drygan, -drygean, -drugian, -druwian; *p.* de, ode; *pp.* ed, od *To dry, dry up, rub dry, wither;* abstergere, siccare, exsiccare:—Hlūde streámas on Æthane ealle đū adrigdest *tu exsiccasti fluvios Ethan,* Ps. Th. 73, 15.

a-drincan; *p.* -dranc, *pl.* -druncon; *pp.* -druncen *To be immersed, extinguished, quenched by water, to be drowned;* immergi, exstingui, aquis suffocari:—Līgfȳr adranc *the fire-flame was quenched,* Cd. 146; Th. 182, 18; Exod. 77. Mycele mā moncynnes adranc on đam wætere *many more of mankind were drowned in the water,* Bd. 3, 24; S. 556, 36.

a-driógan, -drióhan *to bear,* Bt. 40, 3; Fox 238, 22; MS. Cott. The Bodl. MS. has a-drióhan. v. a-dreógan.

a-drogen *done, finished;* transactus, peractus; *pp. of* a-dreógan.

a-dronc, -droncen, *for* a-dranc, -druncen; *p. and pp. of* a-drincan.

a-drugian; *p.* ode; *pp.* od *To dry;* siccari:—Đā sōna adrugode se streám *alveus siccatus est,* Bd. 1, 7; S. 478, 13. v. a-drigan.

a-druncen *drowned; pp. of* a-drincan.

a-druwian; *p.* ode; *pp.* od *To dry up;* siccari:—Ðæt đa wætera wǣron adruwode ofer eorþan *quod aquæ cessassent super terram,* Gen. 8, 11. Eorþan brādnis wæs adruwod *exsiccata erat superficies terræ,* 8, 13. v. a-drigan.

a-drygan, -dryggean *to dry,* Past. 13, 1; Hat. MS. 16 b, 6. v. adrigan.

adul-seáþ *a sewer, sink;* cloaca, Wrt. Voc. 36, 42. v. adelseáþ.

a-dumbian; *p.* ode, ede; *pp.* od, ed; *v. n. To hold one's peace, to keep silence, to become mute* or *dumb;* obmutescere:—Adumba and gā of đisum men *obmutesce et exi de homine,* Mk. Bos. 1, 25. Adumbiaþ đa fācnfullan weoloras *muta efficiantur labia dolosa,* Ps. Th. 30, 20. Ic adumbede *obmutui,* Ps. Spl. 38, 3. Ic adumbode, Ps. Lamb. 38, 10.

a-dūn, -dūne; *adv. Down, adown, downward;* deorsum:—Adūn of đam wealle *down from the wall,* Bd. 1, 12; S. 481, 21. Đa ōđre đa dura brǣcon adūne *the others broke the doors down,* Chr. 1083; Th. 352, 19. Adūne asetton *(they) put down, deposed,* Bd. 4, 6; S. 573, 35. He adūne astāh *descendit,* Ps. Spl. 71, 6: 87, 4.

a-dūn-weard; *adv. Downward;* deorsum:—Scotedon adūnweard mid arewan *they shot their arrows downward,* Chr. 1083; Th. i. 352, 14.

a-dwæscan; *p.* ede, te; *pp.* ed, t; *v. a.* [a, dwæscan *to quench*] *To quench, put out, staunch, appease;* extinguere:—Smeócende flex he ne adwæscþ *linum fumigans non extinguet,* Mt. Bos. 12, 20. Ðæt fȳr adwæsced wæs *flammæ extinctæ sunt,* Bd. 2, 7; S. 509, 29. Adwæscton *extinguerent,* 4, 8; S. 575, 41. Adwæsctum đīnum feóndum *extinctis tuis hostibus,* 2, 12; S. 514, 7. Efne swā he mid wætre đone weallendan lēg adwæsce *even as he with water the raging flame quenches,* Exon. 122 a; Th. 467, 23; Alm. 6. Eall mīn unriht adwæsc *omnes iniquitates meas dele,* Ps. Ben. 50, 10.

a-dwelian; *p.* -dwelede, -dwealde; *pp.* -dweled, -dweald [a, dwelian *to err*] *To seduce, lead into error;* seducere:—Woldon adwelian mancyn fram heora Drihtene *they would seduce mankind from their Lord*, L. Ælf. P. 29; Th. ii. 374, 31.

a-dwínan; ic -dwíne, -dwínest, -dwínst, he -dwíneþ, -dwínþ, *pl.* -dwínaþ; *p.* -dwán, *pl.* -dwinon; *pp.* -dwinen *To dwindle* or *vanish away*; vanescere. v. dwínan.

a-dýdan, -dýddan; *p.* -dýdde; *pp.* -dýded, -dýd; *v. a.* [a, dýdan *to die*] *To put to death, to destroy, kill, mortify*; perdere, occidere:—Wolde híg adýddan *would destroy them*, Ælfc. T. 22, 19. Ðæt ic náteshwon nelle heonon forþ eall flǽsc adýdan mid flódes wæterum *that I will not, by any means, henceforth destroy all flesh with the waters of a flood*, Gen. 9, 11. Ǽlc þing ðe líf hæfde wearþ adýd *everything which had life was destroyed*, Gen. 7, 23.

a-dydest, *hast banished*; expulisti, Ps. Lamb. 59, 12; *p. of* a-dón.

a-dylegian; *pres.* ic -dylegige; *p.* ode; *pp.* od *To destroy*; delere:—Ic adylegige *deleo*; ic adylegode [adeligode Som.] *delevi*; adylegod *deletum*, of ðam is gecweden letum [=lethum *death*; *Grk.* λήθη *oblivio*] deáþ, ðe adylegaþ líf *I destroy; I destroyed; destroyed*, deletum, *from which is derived* [*called*] letum *death, which destroyeth life*, Ælfc. Gr. 26; Som. 28, 32, 33. v. a-dilegian, dilgian.

a-dylf *effodit*, Ps. Th. 7, 15,=a-dealf; *p. of* a-delfan, *q. v.*

Æ. The short or unaccented Anglo-Saxon æ has a sound like *ai* in *main* and *fairy*, as appears from these cognate words:—Wæl *wail*, brædan *to braid*, nægel *a nail*, dæg, spær, læt, snæce, mæst, æsp, bær, *etc.* **2.** The short or unaccented æ stands only (1) before a single consonant; as Stæf, hwæl, dæg: (2) a single consonant followed by *e* in nouns; Stæfes, stæfe, hwæles, dæges, wæter, fæder, æcer: (3) or before *st, sc, fn, ft*; Gæst, æsc, hræfn, cræft: (4) before *pp, bb, tt, cc, ss*; Æppel, cræbba, hæbben, fætte, fættes, wræcca, næsse: (5) before double consonants, arising from the inflection of monosyllabic adjectives:—Lætne, lætre, lætra, from læt *late*; hwætne, hwætre, hwætra from hwæt *quick*. **3.** In the declension of monosyllabic nouns and adjectives, **e** is rejected from the short or unaccented **æ**, and becomes **a**, when a single consonant, or *st, sc*, is followed by *a, o, u* in nouns, and by *a, o, u, e* in adjectives; as Stæf, *pl.* stafas, *g.* stafa, *d.* stafum; hwæl, *pl.* hwalas; dæg, *pl.* dagas. *adj.* Læt *late*; *g. m. n.* lates; *d.* latum; se lata *the late*; latost, latemest, *latest*: Smæl *small*; *g. m. n.* smales; *d.* smalum; se smala *the small*, etc. See short *a* in **B. 3**, p. 1, col. 1. **4.** æ-, prefixed to words, like **a-**, often denotes *A negative, deteriorating* or *opposite signification*, as *From, away, out, without*, etc. Like **a**, **ge**, etc. æ is sometimes prefixed to *perfect tenses and perfect participles* and other words without any perceptible alteration in the sense; as Céled, æ-céled *cooled*. **5.** The Anglo-Saxon Rune for æ is ᚫ, which is also put for æsc *an ash-tree*, the name of the letter. v. æsc.

B. The long or accented ǽ has the sound of *ea* in *meat, sea*. The ǽ is found in the following words, which are represented by English terms of the same signification, having *ea* sounded as in *deal, fear*; Dǽl, fǽr, drǽd, lǽdan, brǽdo, hǽto, hwǽte, hǽþ, hǽðen, clǽne, lǽne, sǽ, ǽr, hǽlan, lǽran, tǽcan, tǽsan, tǽsel, wǽpen, *etc.* **2.** The ǽ is known to be long, and therefore accented, when in monosyllables, assuming another syllable in declining, ǽ is found before a single consonant or *st, sc*, and followed in nouns by *a, o, u*, and in adjectives by *a, o, u*, or *e*; as Blǽda *fruits*; blǽdum: Dwǽs *dull*; *g. m.* dwǽses. The ǽ is often changed into á; as Stǽnen *stony*, stán *a stone*; lǽr, lár *lore*.

Ǽ; *indecl. f. Law, statute, custom, rite, marriage*; lex, statutum, ceremoniæ, ritus, matrimonium:—God him sette ǽ ðæt ys open lagu *God gave them a statute that is a plain law*, Ælfc. T. 10, 20. Ǽ Drihtnes *the law of the Lord*, Ps. Spl. 18, 8: Mt. Bos. 26, 28. God is wísdóm and ǽ woruldbúendra *God is the wisdom and law of the inhabitants of the world*, Bt. Met. Fox 29, 165; Met. 29, 83. Cristes ǽ *the Gospel*. Bútan ǽ oððe útlaga *an outlaw*, Ælfc. Gr. 47; Som. 48, 44. Seó æftere ǽ *Deuteronomy*, Bd. 1, 27. Húslfatu hálegu ða ǽr Israela in ǽ hæfdon *the holy vessels which the Israelites formerly used in their rites*, Cd. 212; Th. 262, 29; Dan. 751. Wircaþ his bebodu and his ǽ and his dómas *observa præcepta ejus et ceremonias atque judicia*, Deut. 11, 1. Stýrde unryhtre ǽ *he reproved the unlawful marriage*, Exon. 70 a; Th. 260, 14; Jul. 297. [*O. Sax.* ēo, *m: O. Frs.* ā, ē, ēwe, ēwa, *f: Ger.* ehe, *f.* *matrimonium: M. H. Ger.* ēwe, ē, *f: O. H. Ger.* ēwa, ēha, ēa, *f: Sansk.* eva, *m. course, manner.*]

ǽ; *indecl. f. Life*; vita:—Ðæt hí ne meahtan acwellan cnyhta ǽ *that they might not destroy the young men's lives*, Exon. 55 a; Th. 195, 32; Az. 164.

ǽ; *indecl. f. A river, stream*; rivus, torrens:—On ðære ǽ ðú hý drencst *thou shalt give them to drink of the stream*; torrente potabis eos, Ps. Th. 35, 8. v. eá.

ǽ *alas!* Ǽ, Hy. 1, 1,=eá, Lamb, MS. fol. 183 b, line 11. v. ǽlá, æálá, eálá.

æálá; *interj. O! alas!* O, eheu:—Æálá ðú Scippend *O! thou Creator*, Bt. Met. Fox 4, 1; Met. 4, 1. v. eálá, ǽlá.

a-eargian; *p.* ode, ade; *pp.* od [a, eargian *torpescere*] *To become slothful*; segnis fieri:—Hý ondrédan, gif hí hwílum ne wunnon, ðæt hý tó raðe a-eargadon *they dreaded, if they did not sometimes wage war, that they should too soon become slothful*, Ors. 4, 13; Bos. 100, 20.

ǽ-bær *notorious*, L. Eth. vi. 36; Th. i. 324, 11. v. ǽ-ber.

Æbban dún, Abban dún, e; *f.* [Æbba, an; *m*: or Æbbe, an; *f*: dún *a down* or *hill*; *Æbba's* or *Æbbe's down* or *hill*] ABINGDON; Abindoniæ oppidum in agro Berceriensi:—His líc líþ on ðam mynstre æt Abban dúne *his body lies in the monastery at Abingdon*, Chr. 981; Th. 234, 34, col. 1.

a-ebbian; *p.* a-ebbode; *pp.* a-ebbad, ge-ebbod; *v. intrans. To ebb away, recede*; recedere:—Ðæt wæter wæs a-ebbad [a-ebbod MS. C. T; ge-ebbod Cant.] feala furlanga from ðám scipum *the water had ebbed many furlongs from the ships*, Chr. 897; Ing. 123, 19. v. ebbian.

æbbung, e; *f. An* EBBING; recessus aquarum:—Sǽ-æbbung *a bay*; sinus, Wrt. Voc. 41, 63. v. ebba.

ǽ-bebod, es; *n. Law, injunction of the law, command*; lex, legis mandatum:—Ðú me ǽbebod ǽrest settest *tu legem posuisti mihi*, Ps. Th. 118, 102.

ǽ-béc *law books, books of the law*; juris codices, Cot. 126.

ǽ-ber, ǽ-bær; *adj. Clear and evident by proof, manifest, apparent, notorious*; apricus, manifestus:—Se ǽbera þeóf *the notorious thief*, L. Edg. ii. 7; Th. i. 268, 22. Ǽbære manslagan *notorious homicides*, L. Eth. vi. 36; Th. i. 324, 11.

æbesen, æbesn *pasturage*; pasnagium, L. In. 49; Th. i. 132, 18, note 46. v. æfesen.

æ-bilgan, æ-bilian *to make angry*; exasperare, Ps. Spl. 67, 7. v. a-belgan.

æ-bilignes, -ness, e; *f. Indignation, anger*; indignatio, Apol. Th. v. æ-bylignes.

æ-blǽcnys, -nes, -ness, e; *f. A paleness*; pallor:—Wið æblǽcnysse ðæs líchaman *for paleness of the body*, Herb. 164, 2; Lchdm. ii. 294, 3.

æ-bléc; *adj. Pale, wan, whitish, bleak*; pallidus. v. blǽc, blác.

æ-blécing, æ-blécnys *paleness*. v. æ-blǽcnys, blácung.

ǽ-bod, es; *m. A business*; negotium:—Ǽbodas *pragmatica negotia*, Ælfc. Gl. 12; Som. 57, 94.

ǽ-boda, an; *m. A messenger of the law*; legis nuntius:—Ðá wæs frófre gǽst onsended eádgum ǽbodan *then the spirit of comfort was sent to the blessed messenger of the law*, i. e. *the preacher of the gospel*, Exon. 46 b; Th. 158, 15; Gú. 909.

ǽ-brec [eá *water*, bræc] *A catarrh, rheum*; rheuma. v. brecan.

æbs, e; *f? A fir-tree*; abies, Ælfc. Gr. 5; Som. 4, 45: 9, 26; Som. 11, 18.

æ-bylg, es; *n. Anger*; ira, indignatio, Exon. 50 b; Th. 176, 17; Gú. 1211. v. æ-bylgþ.

æ-bylgan, -byligan *To make angry*; exasperare, Ps. Spl. 65, 6. v. a-belgan.

æ-bylgþ, -bylþ, -bylygþ, e; *f*: es; *n?* [bylgþ, v. belgan] *An offence, a fault, scandal, wrong, anger, wrath, indignation*; offensa, injuria, ira, indignatio:—To æbylgþe *for offence*, Ors. 4, 1; Bos. 76, 27. He sende on hí graman æbylygþe hys *misit in eos iram indignationis suæ*, Ps. Spl. 77, 54. Cristenum cyningce gebyraþ swýðe rihte ðæt he Godes æbylþe wrece *Christiano regi jure pertinet ut injurias Deo factas vindicet*, L. C. S. 40; Th. i. 400, 10. v. a-bylgþ, a-byligd.

æ-bylignes, -ness; -nys, -nyss, e; *f. Indignation, wrath*; indignatio:—Æbylignes yrres ðínes *indignatio iræ tuæ*, Ps. Th. 68, 25. He sende on hí graman æbylignysse hys *misit in eos iram indignationis suæ*, Ps. Spl. 77, 54. v. a-bylgnes.

ǽc *also*, Th. Dipl. A. D. 804–829; 460, 9: 461, 18, 33. v. eác.

ǽc, e; *f. An oak*; quercus:—Of ðære ǽce [MS. ǽc] andlang heges to ðæm wege *from the oak and along the hedge to the road*, Kmbl. Cod. Dipl. iii. p. 78, 7. v. ác.

ǽcan *to eke*, Solil. 11. v. écan.

æced, es; *n. Vinegar*; acetum, Jn. Lind. War. 19, 30. v. eced.

æce, acc, es; *m. An ake, pain*; dolor:—Eal ðæt sár and se æce onwæg alǽded wæs *all the sore and ake were* (*led*) *taken away*, Bd. 5, 3; S. 616, 35: 5, 4; S. 617, 22. DER. acan *to ake*. v. ece.

ǽce; *adj. Eternal*; æternus:—Ðæt we ge-earnian ǽce dreámas *that we may obtain eternal delights*, Ps. C. 156. v. éce.

æced, es; *n. Vinegar*:—Onféng ðe Hǽlend ðæt æced *the Saviour received the vinegar*, Jn. Rush. War. 19, 30. v. eced.

æced-fæt, es; *n. An acid-vat, a vinegar-vessel*; acetabulum, Wrt. Voc. 25, 21. v. eced-fæt.

æced-wín, es; *n.* ACID-WINE; murratum vinum, Mk. Lind. War. 15, 23.

æ-céled *cooled*; *pp. of* æ-célan = a-célan. DER. célan.

æcelma, an; *m. A chilblain*; mula, L. M. 1, 30; Lchdm. ii. 70, 16.

ǽcen = ácen; *adj. Oaken, made of oak*; quernus, Cot. 165.

ǽcen, eácen; *pp. of* eácan *to increase*. v. eácan.

ÆCER, æcyr, es; *m.* I. *a field, land, what is sown, sown land*; ager, seges:—For ðam is se æcer geháten Acheldemah *propter hoc vocatus est ager ille Haceldama*, Mt. Bos. 27, 8. Hér ys seó bót, hú ðú meaht ðíne æceras betan *here is the remedy, how thou mayest improve thy fields*, Lchdm. i. 398, 1. Of ðæm æcere *from the field*, Bt. Met. Fox 12, 3; Met. 12, 2. Æcera þúsend *a thousand fields*, 14, 10; Met. 14, 5. II. a definite quantity of land which, in *A. Sax.* times, a yoke of oxen could plough in a day, *an* ACRE, *that is* 4840 *square yards*; jugeri spatium, jugerum, a jugo quod tantum fere spatii uno jugo boum arari posset: *also* ager – *Ger.* acker *an acre*:—Ǽlce dæg ic sceal erian fulne æcer oððe máre *omni die debeo arare integrum jugerum* [MS. *agrum*] *aut plus*, Coll. Monast. Th. 19, 21. Ðæt is se teóða æcer, eal swâ seó sulh hit gegâ *that is the tenth acre, all as the plough goes over it*, L. C. E. 8; Th. i. 366, 6. Æceras *jugera*, Cot. 109. [*O. Sax.* akkar: *O. Frs.* ekker: *O. Ger.* ahhar: *N. Ger.* acker *a field, an acre*: *Goth.* akrs: *O. Nrs.* akr: *Lat.* ager: *Grk.* ἀγρός: *Sansk.* ajra *a plain.*]

æcer-ceorl, es; *m. A field-churl, a farmer, ploughman;* agricola. DER. æcer *a field*, ceorl *a free husbandman.*

æcer-man, æcer-mon; *g.* æcer-mannes; *m. A field-man, farmer;* agricola, Ælfc. Gl. 5.

æ̂cern, æ̂cirn, es; *n.* [æ̂c = âc *oak*, corn *corn*] *The corn* or *fruit of an oak, an* ACORN, *a nut;* glans:—Æ̂cern *glans*, Ælfc. Gl. 46; Som. 65, 7. Æ̂cirnu, *pl. nom.* Gen. 43, 11. [*Spenser, Grafton*, acornes, *pl*: *N. Dut.* aker *in* aker-boom: *N. L. Ger.* ecker, *m. n*: *N. Ger.* ecker, *pl.* eckern, *m. n. glans quernea* or *fagea*: *Goth.* akran, *n. fructus*: *Dan.* agern, *n*: *Norw.* aakorn: *O. Nrs.* akarn, *n. glans silvestris.*]

æcer-spranca, æcer-spranga, an; *m.* [æcer, spranca, an; *m. a shoot, sprout*] *Young shoots springing up from acorns, saplings, the holm oak, scarlet oak;* ilex:—Æcer-spranca *ilex*, Ælfc. Gr. 9, 61; Som. 13, 48.

æcest = æcst *akest, 2nd pers. sing. pres. of* acan.

æceþ = æcþ *aketh, 3rd pers. sing. pres. of* acan.

æchir *an ear of corn*, Mt. Rush. Stv. 12, 1. v. ear.

æ-ciorfan *to cut to pieces*, Ps. Spl. 128, 4. v. a-ceorfan.

æ̂cirnu *nuts*, Gen. 43, 11. v. æ̂cern.

æc-læ̂ca, an; *m.* [æc = ag, *q. v.*] *A wretch, miscreant, monster;* miser, perditus, monstrum, Elen. Grm. 901; El. 902. v. ag-læ̂ca.

æ̂-cræft, es; *m. Law-craft and its result;* legis peritia et vires inde oriundæ:—Æ̂cræft eorla *law-craft of men*, Elen. Kmbl. 869; El. 435: Cd. 173; Th. 217, 7; Dan. 19.

æ̂-cræftig; *adj. Law-crafty, one skilled in law, a lawyer, scribe;* legis peritus:—Him æ̂cræftig andswarode *to them the skilled in law answered*, Cd. 212; Th. 262, 10; Dan. 742.

æcse *an axe*, Bd. 4, 3; S. 567, 26. v. æx.

æcst *akest, 2nd pers. sing. pres. of* acan.

æcþ *aketh, 3rd pers. sing. pres. of* acan.

æ̂cumbe *oakum;* stuppa, Wrt. Voc. 40, 36. v. âcumba.

æcyr *a field*:—Blôdes æcyr *sanguinis ager*, Mt. Foxe 27, 8. v. æcer.

æcyrf, e; *f. That which is cut off, a fragment, piece;* recisura, fragmentum:—Ðara treówa æcyrf and lâfe forbærnde wǽron *the offcuttings and leavings of the wood were burnt*, Bd. 3, 22; S. 552, 13. v. cyrf, ceorfan.

æd-, prefixed to words, denotes *Anew, again*, as the Latin re-:—Ædsceaft *re-generation.* v. ed-.

æ̂ddran *kidneys;* renes, Ps. Spl. C. 7, 10. v. æ̂dre.

æ̂der-seax, æ̂dre-seax, es; *n. A vein-knife, a lancet;* lancetta, Cot. 92.

æd-fæst [eád *substance*, fæst *fast, fixed*] *Goods, property;* bona:—Ædfæst tǽht to healdenne *property taken to hold, a pledge*, Ælfc. Gl. 14; Som. 58, 8.

æd-leán *a reward*, Th. Diplm. A. D. 804–829; 459, 11. v. ed-leán.

æ̂dr *vein, artery*, Ps. Th. 72, 17. v. æ̂dre, êdre.

ædre; *adv. Quickly, promptly, at once, forthwith;* illico, confestim, statim, protinus:—Him ðâ ædre God andswarede *God answered him forthwith*, Cd. 42; Th. 54, 4; Gen. 872. Wille ðê ða andsware ædre gecŷðan *I will quickly let you know the answer*, Beo. Th. 714; B. 354. Nû ðû ædre const sîþ-fæt mînne *now thou comprehendest at once my journey*, Exon. 52 b; Th. 184, 29; Gû. 1351. [*O. H. Ger.* atar: *O. Sax.* adro: *O. Frs.* edre *velociter.*] v. edre.

æ̂dre, æ̂ddre, êdre, an; *f*: æ̂dr, e; *f.* I. a channel for liquids, *An artery, a vein, fountain, river;* arteria, vena, fons, rivus; v. wæter-æ̂dre:—Feorh alêton þurh æ̂dra wylm *they let life forth through the fountain of their veins*, Exon. 72 b; Th. 271, 6; Jul. 478. Blêdaþ æ̂dran *the veins shall bleed*, Salm. Kmbl. 290; Sal. 144. Swât æ̂drum sprong *blood sprang from the veins*, Beo. Th. 5925; B. 2966. II. *a nerve, sinew, kidney;* nervus, ren:—Wǽron mîne æ̂dra ealle tolŷsde *renes mei resoluti sunt*, Ps. Th. 72, 17. Ðû canst mîne æ̂dre ealle *tu possedisti omnes renes meos*, 138, 11. Ðâ for ðam cŷle him gescuncan ealle æ̂dra *then all his sinews shrank because of the cold*, Ors. 3, 9; Bos. 64, 39. [*Plat.* ader: *O. Frs.* eddere, eddre: *O. Dut.* adere: *Ger.* ader: *M. H. Ger.* âder: *O. H. Ger.* âdara: *Dan.* aare: *Swed.* åder: *Norw.* aader: *O. Nrs.* æd, *f.*] DER. wæter-æ̂dre.

æ̂dre-seax *a vein-knife, lancet.* v. æ̂der-seax.

æ̂dre-weg, es; *m. A drain way, a vein, an artery;* arteria, vena. v. æ̂dre, weg *a way.*

æ-drîfan *to expel*, Ps. Spl. T. 42, 2: 43, 26. v. a-drîfan.

æd-sceaft, e; *f. A regeneration, new creation;* regeneratio:—Hî æ̂lce geáre weorþaþ to ædsceafte *they become every year a new creation*, Bt. 34, 10; Fox 150, 16. v. edsceaft.

Ædwines clif, EDWIN'S CLIFF, Chr. 761; Ing. 73, 15.

æd-wist *substance;* substantia, essentia. v. æt-wist.

æd-wît, es; *n. A reproach;* opprobrium:—Æd-wît manna *opprobrium hominum*, Ps. Spl. C. T. 21, 5. v. ed-wît.

æd-wîtan *To reproach;* exprobare:—Æd-wioton him *improperabant ei*, Mt. Lind. Stv. 27, 44. v. ed-wîtan.

æf, af, of: *prep. Of, from:* ab, de. v. compound æf-lâst and in of-.

æf-ǽst, es; *n. Envy;* invidia:—Bûtan æfǽste *sine invidia*, Bd. 5, 22; S. 644, 13. v. æf-êst.

æ̂-fæst, -fest; *adj.* [æ̂ *law*, fæst *fast, fixed*] *Firm in observing the law, religious, pious;* tenax observandi legem, religiosus, pius, justus:—Æ̂fæst hæleþ *a pious man*, Cd. 59; Th. 72, 6; Gen. 1182. Æ̂fæste men *pious men*, 86; Th. 108, 7; Gen. 1802. We æ̂fæstra dǽde dêman *we consider the deeds of the pious*, Exon. 40 a; Th. 133, 30; Gû. 497. Wæs he æ̂fæst and ârfæst *was he devout and good?* Bd. 3, 14; S. 539, 33. v. æ̂w-fæst.

æ̂-fæsten, es; *n. A legal fast;* legitimum jejunium:—III æ̂fæstenu fæste he *tribus legitimis jejuniis jejunet*, L. Ecg. C. 4; Th. ii. 138, 1.

æ̂-fæstnes, -festnes, -nys, -ness, e; *f. Firmness in the law, religion;* religio:—He wæs mycelre æ̂fæstnesse wer *he was a man of much religion*, Bd. 4, 31; S. 610, 7: 2, 9; S. 510, 30, 32.

æf-dæl; *g.* -dæles; *pl. nom.* -dalu; *n.* [æf, dæl *a vale*] *A descent;* descensus:—To æfdæle *ad descensum*, Lk. Lind. War. 19, 37. v. of-dæl.

æfdon *performed, executed*, Exon. 27 b; Th. 83, 16; Cri. 1357, = æfndon, *p. pl. of* æfnan.

æ-felle, a-felle; *adj.* [æ, fell *a skin*] *Barked, peeled, skinned;* decorticatum, Ælfc. Gl. 115; Som. 80, 34; Wrt. Voc. 61, 14.

æfen *even;* æqualis, æquus. v. efen.

ÆFEN, æ̂fyn, êfen, es; *m. The* EVEN, *evening, eventide;* vesper, vespera:—Syððan æ̂fen cwom *after evening came*, Beo. Th. 2475; B. 1235. Æ̂fen æ̂rest *vesperum primum*, Cd. 8; Th. 9, 7; Gen. 138. Æ̂fena gehwâm *in each of evenings*, 148; Th. 184, 16; Exod. 108. Æt æ̂fenne, on æ̂fenne, or to æ̂fenne, *at even, in the evening*, Ps. Spl. 29, 6. [*Laym.* aefen: *Orm.* efen: *Gow. Chauc.* even: *N. Dut.* avond: *M. Dut.* avont, *m*: *Plat.* abend, *m*: *O. Sax.* âband, *m*: *O. Frs.* âvend, *m*: *Ger.* abend, *m*: *M. H. Ger.* âbent, *m*: *O. H. Ger.* âpand, âbant, âbunt, *m*: *Dan.* aften, *m*: *Swed.* afton, *m*: *Icel.* aptan, aftan, *m*: *confr. Grk.* ὀψέ.]

æ̂fen-dreám, es; *m. Even-song;* vespertinus cantus. v. æ̂fen.

æfen-fela *as many;* totidem, Deut. 9, 11. v. efen-feola.

æ̂fen-gebêd, es; *n. An evening prayer, evening service*:—Æ̂fen-gebêd *vespertinum officium*, Ælfc. Gl. 34; Som. 62, 50.

æ̂fen-gereord, e; *f. An evening meal, a supper;* cœna, Ælfc. Gl. 58; Som. 67, 87; Wrt. Voc. 38, 13.

æ̂fen-gereordian; *p.* ode; *pp.* od *To sup* or *take supper;* cœnare. v. gereordian *to take food.*

æ̂fen-gifl, -giefl, es; *n. Evening food, supper;* cœna:—Hî sêcaþ ðæt hie fyrmest hlynigen æt æ̂fengieflum [-giflum MS. C.] *quærunt primos in cœnis recubitus*, Past. 1, 2; MS. Hat. 6 b, 20: 44, 3; MS. Hat. 61 b, 22.

æ̂fen-glôm, es; *m. The evening gloom* or *twilight;* crepusculum:—From æ̂fenglôme ôþ ðæt eástan cwom dægrêdwôma *from evening twilight there came the rush of dawn from the east*, Exon. 51 b; Th. 179, 21; Gû. 1265.

æ̂fen-grom; *adj. Fierce in the evening;* vespere ferox:—Grendel cwom eatol, æ̂fengrom *Grendel came terrible, fierce at eve*, Beo. Th. 4154; B. 2074.

æ̂fen-hlytta, an; *m. A fellow, consort, companion* or *mate;* consors, Ælfc. Gr. 9, 44; Som. 13, 6.

æ̂fen-hrepsung, e; *f. The evening close;* vesper. v. hrepsung *closing.*

æ̂fen-lâc, es; *n. An evening sacrifice;* vespertinum sacrificium:—Swylce ahafenes handa mînra, ðonne ic æ̂fenlâc secge *elevatio manuum mearum sacrificium vespertinum*, Ps. Th. 140, 3.

æfen-læ̂can *to match;* imitari. v. efen-læ̂can.

æ̂fen-læ̂can; *p.* -læ̂hte; *pp.* -læ̂ht *To grow towards evening;* advesperascere:—Hit æ̂fenlæ̂cþ *advesperascit*, Lk. Bos. 24, 29.

æfen-læ̂cend *an imitator.* v. efen-læ̂cend.

æ̂fen-leóht, es; *n. Evening light;* vespertina lux:—Siððan æ̂fen-leóht under heofenes hâdor beholen weorþeþ *after the evening light is concealed under heaven's serenity*, Beo. Th. 831; B. 413.

æ̂fen-leóþ, es; *n. An evening song;* vespertinus cantus:—Atol æ̂fenleóþ *a dreadful evening song*, Cd. 153; Th. 190, 18; Exod. 201.

æ̂fen-lîc; *adj. Vespertine, of the evening;* vespertinus, Ps. Spl. 140, 2.

æ̂fen-mete, es; *m. Evening meat, supper;* cœna, Cot. 42.

æ̂fen-rest, e; *f. Evening rest;* vespertina requies:—Sum sâre ongeald æ̂fenreste *one paid dearly for his evening rest*, Beo. Th. 2508; B. 1252.

æ̂fen-rima, an; *m.* [æ̂fen *vesper*, rima *margo, labrum*] *Twilight;* crepusculum. v. rima *a rim, margin.*

æ̂fen-sang, es; *m.* EVEN-SONG, *vespers;* vespertinus cantus, L. Ælf. C. 19; Th. ii. 350, 7.

æ̂fen-sceóp, -scôp, es; *m. An evening bard;* vespertinus cantor:—Eald æ̂fensceóp ic bringe *I bring an old evening bard*, Exon. 103 a; Th. 390, 21; Râ. 9, 5.

æ̂fen-scîma, an; *m. Evening splendour;* vespertinus splendor, Cd. 112; Th. 147, 31; Gen. 2448.

æ̂fen-spræc, e; *f. Evening speech;* vespertina loquela:—Gemunde æ̂fenspræce *he remembered his evening speech*, Beo. Th. 1522; B. 759.

æ̂fen-steorra, an; *m. The evening star;* Hesperus; the *Grk.* Ἕσπερος [*Lat.* vesper], *the evening star*, is called by Hesiod a son of Astræus and Eos, and was regarded by the ancients the same as the morning star, whence both Homer and Hesiod call him the bringer of light, *ἑωσ-φόρος*, Il. xxii. 318 : xxiii. 226. The Romans designated him by the names Lucifer and Hesperus, to characterise him as the morning or evening star:—Se steorra đe we hâtaþ ǽfensteorra, đonne he biþ west gesewen, đonne tâcnnaþ he ǽfen. Fǽrþ he đonne æfter đære sunnan on đære eorþan sceade, óþ he ofirnþ đa sunnan hindan, and cymþ wiđ fôran đa sunnan up, đonne hâten we hine morgensteorra (*q. v.*) fordam he cymþ eástan up, bodaþ đære sunnan cyme *the star which we call the evening star, when it is seen westwardly, then it betokens the evening. It then goes after the sun into the earth's shade, till it runs off behind the sun, and comes up before the sun, then we call it the morning star, because it comes up in the east, and announces the sun's approach*, Bt. 39, 13; Fox 232, 34. Se môna, mid his blâcan leóhte, dunniaþ đone beorhtan steorran, đe we hâtaþ morgensteorra: đone ilcan we hâtaþ ôđre naman, ǽfensteorra *the moon, with his pale light, obscures the bright star, which we call the morning star: the same we call by another name, the evening star*, 4; Fox 8, 3.

ǽfen-þénung, e; *f. An evening service* or *duty, evening repast, supper;* cœna, R. Concord 8. v. þegnung.

ǽfen-þeówdôm, es; *m. An evening service* or *office;* vespertinum officium, Ælfc. Gl. 34; Som. 62, 50.

ǽfen-tîd, e; *f. The eventide, evening;* vespertina hora:—Seó ǽfen-tîd đæs dæges *the eventide of the day*, Dial. 1, 10. On ǽfen-tîd *at eventide*, Cd. 111; Th. 146, 19; Gen. 2424.

ǽfen-tîma, an; *m. Evening time, eventide;* vespertinum tempus:—Đâ ǽfentîma wæs, he fêrde to Bethanîam *cum jam vespera esset hora, exiit in Bethaniam*, Mk. Bos. 11, 11.

ǽfen-tungel, es; *m. n. The evening star;* hesperus. v. tungel.

ÆFER; *adv.* EVER, *always;* unquam, semper:—Æfer ge fliton ongên God *semper contentiose egistis contra Deum*, Deut. 31, 27. v. ǽfre.

æfesen, æfesn, æbesen, æbesn, e; *f. Pasturage, the charge for pigs going into the wood to fatten on acorns;* pasnagium, pretium propter porcos in quercetum admissos:—Gif mon nîme æfesne on swînum *if* [*a man*] *any one take pasturage on swine*, L. In. 49; Th. i. 132, 18.

æf-êst, æf-ǽst, æfst, es; *n.* [æf, of=*ab*, êst *gratia*] Without favour or good-will, hence, *Envy, spite, enmity, zeal, rivalry, emulation;* livor, invidia, odium, zelus, æmulatio:—Æfst and oferhygd *envy and pride*, Cd. 1; Th. 3, 1; Gen. 29. Eald-feóndes æfêst *the old fiend's envy*, Exon. 61 b; Th. 226, 5; Ph. 401. Æfêstes *livoris*, Mone B. 2699, p. 386. Heora æfstu ealle sceamien *they all shall be ashamed of their enmities*, Ps. Th. 69. 4. Fore æfstum *from envy*, Exon. 43 a; Th. 144, 27; Gû. 684. Æfǽstum onæled *inflamed with envy*, Exon. 84 a; Th. 316, 3; Môd. 43. [*O. Sax.* ab-unst, *f. invidia: O. Frs.* ev-est *invidia: Ger.* ab-gunst, *f. invidia: O. H. Ger.* ap-anst, ap-unst, *m. invidia, livor, zelus, rancor.*]

ǽ-fest; *adj.* [ǽ *law*, fæst *fast, fixed*] *Fast* or *firm in the law, religious, devout;* religiosus:—Wæs se mon swýđe ǽfest *erat vir multum religiosus*, Bd. 4, 24; S. 598, 20. Ongunnon ǽfeste leóþ wyrcean *religiosa poemata facere tentabant*, id; S. 596, 38. v. ǽ-fæst, ǽw-fæst.

æf-êst-ful; *adj. Full of envy;* invidia plenus, invidiosus:—He is swîđe æfêstful for dînum gôde *he is very full of envy at thy prosperity*, Th. Apol. 14, 24. v. æf-êst.

æf-êstian, -êstigan; *p.* ode; *pp.* od *To envy, be envious of* or *at;* invidere:—Đes iunga man ne æfêstigaþ on nânum þingum, đe he hêr gesihþ *this young man is envious at nothing, which he here seeth*, Th. Apol. 14, 25: Cot. 119. v. æf-êst.

æf-êstig, æfstig; *adj. Envious, emulous, jealous;* invidus, æmulus:—Sum eald and sum æfêstig ealdorman *an old and an envious nobleman*, Th. Apol. 14, 19. v. æf-êst.

ǽ-festlîce; *adv. Religiously;* religiose. v. fæstlîce.

æf-êstnes, -ness; -nys, -nyss, e; *f. Envy, spite;* invidia, malignitas. DER. æf-êst.

ǽ-festnes, -ness, e; *f. Religion, devotion;* religio:—Đa đe to ǽfestnesse belumpon *quæ ad religionem pertinebant*, Bd. 4, 24; S. 597, 1. v. ǽ-fæstnes.

Æffric; *def. m.* Æffrica; *adj. African;* Afer:—Severus Câsere se wæs Æffrica cynnes *Severus Cæsar genere Afer*, Bd. 1, 5; S. 476, 5. v. Affric.

æf-îst *envy;* invidia, Mt. Lind. Stv. 27, 18. v. æf-êst.

æf-lâst, es; *m.* [æf=af *from*, lâst *a course*] *A wandering away?* aberratio, Cd. 166; Th. 207, 27; Exod. 473.

æfnan; *p.* de; *pp.* ed *To perform, execute, labour, show;* patrare, facere, laborare, præstare:—His dômas æfnaþ *they fulfil his judgments*, Exon. 32 b; Th. 102, 29; Cri. 1680. Gif hý woldun his bebodu æfnan *if they would execute his judgments*, 54 a; Th. 152, 29; Gû. 816. Wile eorlscipe æfnan *he wishes to show his dignity*, 87 a; Th. 327, 3; Wîd. 141. Æfdon unsofte *for* æfndon? 27 b; Th. 83, 16; Cri. 1357. DER. ge-æfnan. v. efnan.

æfne; *interj. Behold;* ecce:—Æfne sôþlîce sôþfæstnysse đû lufudest *ecce enim veritatem dilexisti*, Ps. Spl. 50, 7. v. efne; *interj.*

ǽfnian; *p.* ode; *pp.* od *To grow towards evening;* vesperascere, Dial. 1, 10.

ǽfnung, e; *f. Evening;* vespera:—Heó com đâ on ǽfnunge eft to Nôe *illa venit ad eum* [*Noe*] *ad vesperam*, Gen. 8, 11: Homl. Th. ii. 266. 5, 6.

ǽfre, ǽfer; *adv. Ever, always;* unquam, semper:—Nolde ǽfre *nolebat unquam*, Cd. 72; Th. 89, 14; Gen. 1480. Ne sceal ǽfre gehêran *nor shall I ever hear*, 216; Th. 275, 14; Sat. 171. Nû ic eóm orwêna đæt. unc seó êdyl-stæf ǽfre weorþe gifede ætgædere *now I am hopeless that the staff of our family will ever be given to us two together*, 101; Th. 134, 12; Gen. 2223. Đû ǽfre wǽre *tu semper fuisti*, Exon. 9 b; Th. 8, 2; Cri. 111. Ǽfre forþ *sempiternum*, Cd. 220; Th. 282, 35; Sat. 297. Ǽfre to aldre *in æternum*, 38; Th. 51, 1; Gen. 820. ǽfre=â, *q. v.*

ǽ-fremmende; *part. Fulfilling the law, religious;* legis præcepta conficiens, religiosus:—Ic lǽran wille ǽfremmende đæt ge eówer hûs gefæstnige *I will teach that you, the laws fulfilling, should make firm your house*, Exon. 75 a; Th. 281, 18; Jul. 648.

æfst *envy*, Past. 13, 2; Hat. MS. 17 a, 12: Cd. 1; Th. 3, 1; Gen. 29. v. æf-êst.

ǽfstian; *p.* ode; *pp.* od *To hasten;* festinare, accelerare. v. êfstan.

æfstig; *adj. Envious, emulous;* æmulus:—Æfstig wiđ ôđra manna yflu *æmulus contra aliena vitia*, Past. 13, 2; MS. Hat. 17 a, 11. v. æf-êstig.

æft; *adv.* AFT, *behind*, as go *aft=go astern, Afterwards, again;* postea, iterum:—Moises cwæþ æft to Israela folce *Moses said afterwards to the people of Israel*, Deut. 28, 15. Æft uferan dôgum *afterwards in later days*, Beo. Th. 4406 note; B. 2200. Đæt hî æft to him cômen *that they would come to him again*, Bt. Met. Fox 1, 130; Met. 1, 65. v. eft.

æftan; *adv. Behind;* post, pone:—Earn æftan hwît *the eagle white behind*, Chr. 937; Th. i. 206, 29; Æđelst. 63, col. 1. DER. be-æftan.

æftan-weard; *adj. Coming after, following;* posterior:—Rinc biþ on ôfeste, se mec onþýþ æftanweardne *the man is in haste, who urges me following*, Exon. 125 a; Th. 480, 3; Rä. 63, 5. v. weard II; *adj.*

æft-beteht *re-assigned*, R. Ben. 4. v. eft-betæht.

æftemest, -myst, -most; *adj. superlative of* æfter,—*After-most, last;* postremus, novissimus:—Đeós bôc is æftemyst on đære biblioþêcan *this is the last book of the Bible*, Ælfc. T. 31, 22; Grn. Ælfc. T. 16, 3. Đonne he sylf mid đam fyrmestan dǽle wiđ đæs æftemestan flûge *when he himself with the first part should flee towards the hindermost*, Ors. 4, 6; Bos. 85, 20: Mk. Bos. 12, 22: Jn. Bos. 7, 37.

æften-tîd, e; *f.* [æftan *after*] *Evening, eventide;* vespertinum tempus, vesper:—Ǽr morgenes gancg wiđ æftentîd ealle đa dêman Drihten healdeþ *exitus matutini et vespere delectaberis*, Ps. Th. 64, 9.

æfter; *prep.* [æft, *q. v;* er, *q. v.*] *dat;* rarely *acc.* I. local and temporal *dat.*—AFTER; post:—Ne far đû æfter fremdum godum *go not thou after strange gods*, Deut. 6, 14. Æfter þrîm monþum *after three months*, Gen. 38, 24. Æfter dagum *after those days*, Lk. Bos. 1, 24. Cumaþ æfter me *venite post me*, Mt. Bos. 4, 19. Æfter þrým dagum [MS. dagon] ic arîse *post tres dies resurgam*, Mt. Bos. 27, 63. Đâ eóde đæt wîf æfter him *then the wife went after him*, Bt. 35, 6; Fox 170, 13. Hâm stađeledon, ân æfter ôđrum *they established a home, one after another*, Cd. 213; Th. 266, 22; Sat. 26. Æfter đâm wordum werod eall arâs *after those words all the host rose*, Cd. 158; Th. 196, 29; Exod. 299: Exon. 28 b; Th. 86, 24; Cri. 1413. Wunder æfter wundre *wonder after wonder*, Beo. Th. 1866; B. 931: Cd. 8; Th. 9, 19; Gen. 144: Cd. 46; Th. 59, 15; Gen. 964: Cd. 143; Th. 178, 1; Exod. 5: Cd. 148; Th. 184, 18; Exod. 109: Cd. 227; Th. 304, 14; Sat. 630: Exon. 16 a; Th. 36, 8; Cri. 573: Exon. 18 a; Th. 44, 31; Cri. 711: Exon. 117 a; Th. 449, 32; Dôm. 80: Exon. 117 a; Th. 450, 3; Dôm. 82: Exon. 124 a; Th. 476, 20; Ruin. 10: Beo. Th. 170; B. 85: Beo. Th. 238; B. 119: Apstls. Kmbl. 163; Ap. 82: Andr. Kmbl. 175; An. 88: Andr. Kmbl. 265; An. 133: Exon. 39 b; Th. 130, 22; Gû. 442: Exon. 40 b; Th. 134, 5; Gû. 503: Elen. Kmbl. 859; El. 430: Elen. Kmbl. 977; El. 490: Exon. 118 a; Th. 454, 10; Hy. 4, 30. 2. extension over space or time,—*Along, through, during; κατά*, per:—Sǽton æfter beorgum *they sat along the hills*, Cd. 154; Th. 191, 9; Exod. 212. His wundra geweorc, wîde and sîde, brême æfter burgum *his works of wonder, far and wide, famed through towns*, Exon. 45 b; Th. 155, 4; Gû. 855. Đeáh ic fela for him æfter woruldstundum wundra gefremede *though I performed many miracles for them during my time in this world*, Elen. Kmbl. 725; El. 363: Exon. 55 b; Th. 196, 18; Az. 176: Judth. 10; Thw. 21, 17; Jud. 18: Salm. Kmbl. 233; Sal. 116: Exon. 108 a; Th. 412, 25; Rä. 31, 5. 3. mode or manner,—*According to, by means of;* secundum, propter:—Æfter dôme đînum gelîffæsta me *secundum judicium tuum vivifica me*, Ps. Lamb. 118, 149. He hæfþ mon geworhtne æfter his onlîcnesse *he has created man after* [secundum] *his own image*, Cd. 21; Th. 25, 19; Gen. 396. Đæt sweord ongan æfter heađoswâte wanian *the sword began to fade away by the warsweat* [*in consequence of the hot blood*], Beo. Th. 3216; B. 1606: Exon. 19 b; Th. 50, 20; Cri. 803; Andr. Kmbl. 156; An. 78: Exon. 45 b; Th. 154, 27; Gû. 849: Bt. Met. Fox 20, 93; Met. 20, 47: Exon. 110 a; Th. 421, 8; Rä. 40, 15: Beo. Th. 5499; B. 2753: Cd. 28; Th. 37, 19; Gen. 592. 4. object,—*After, about;* propter, ob, de:—Hæleþ frægn æfter æđelum *a chief asked after the heroes*, Beo. Th. 670; B. 332. Him æfter deórum men dyrne langaþ *he longs secretly after the dear man*, Beo. Th. 3762; B. 1879. Grôf æfter golde *he dug after gold*, Bt. Met. Fox 8, 113; Met. 8, 57: Elen. Kmbl. 1346; El. 675: Beo. Th. 2648; B. 1322: Beo. Th. 2688; B. 1342: Cd. 15:

Th. 18, 33; Gen. 282: Cd. 15; Th. 19, 14; Gen. 291: Cd. 92; Th. 117, 20; Gen. 1956: Cd. 98; Th. 130, 3; Gen. 2154: Cd. 203; Th. 251, 30; Dan. 571: Elen. Kmbl. 1653; El. 828: Andr. Kmbl. 74; An. 37: Beo. Th. 4913; B. 2461: Beo. Th. 4917; B. 2463: Beo. Th. 4528; B. 2268. II. *acc*; cum accusativo, *After, above, according to;* post, super, secundum:—Æfter ðás dagas *post hos dies*, Lk. Lind. War. 1, 25. He eorþan æfter wæter ǽrest sette *qui fundavit terram super aquas*, Ps. Th. 135, 6. Stefne mîne gehēr æfter mildheortnesse ðíne, Drihten *vocem meam audi secundum misericordiam tuam, Domine*, Ps. Lamb. 118, 149. [*O. Sax.* aftar, after: *O. Frs.* efter, after: *O. Dut. N. Dut.* achter: *Ger.* after, *only in compnd: M. H. Ger.* after: *O. H. Ger.* aftar: *Goth.* aftra *backward, again: Dan.* efter: *Swed.* efter: *O. Nrs.* eptir, eftir, *prep;* aptr, aftr, *adv. back, again: Sansk.* apara.]

æfter; *adv. After, then, afterwards;* post, postea, exinde:—Æfter siððan *ever afterwards, from thenceforth*, Cd. 26; Th. 35, 6; Gen. 550. Æfter to aldre *for ever after*, Cd. 22; Th. 28, 15; Gen. 436. Ðæm eafera wæs æfter cenned *a son was afterwards born to him*, Beo. Th. 24; B. 12. Word æfter cwæþ *then he spake these words*, Beo. Th. 636; B. 315. Ǽr oððe æfter *sooner or later*, Exon. 32 b; Th. 103, 22; Cri. 1692. Ic wāt æfter nū hwā mec ferede ofer flōdas *now afterwards I know who conveyed me over the floods*, Andr. Kmbl. 1808; An. 906. Ðǽr sceal ylda cwealm æfter wyrþan *then must slaughter of men take place afterwards*, 364; An. 182. Swā ðas foldan fæðme bewíndeþ ðes eástrodor and æfter west *quantum ortus distat ab occasu*, Ps. Th. 102, 12.

æftera, æftra; *adj. compar. of* æfter,—*Hinder, next, second;* posterior, sequens, alter, secundus:—Ðȳ æfteran dæge *sequenti die*, Lk. Bos. 13, 33. Ðæs æfteran monþes *mensis secundi*, Ex. 16, 1. On ðam forman dæge ðæs æftran monþes *primo die mensis secundi*, Num. 1, 18. Seó æftre, *i. e.* eá, Ethiopia land belīgeþ ūton *the next river encompasses the country of Ethiopia*, Cd. 12; Th. 15, 4; Gen. 228. Siððan ic ongon on ðone æfteran ānseld būgan *after I had begun to live in this second hermitage*, Exon. 50 b; Th. 176, 22; Gū. 1214.

æfter-boren [=æftergenga, *q. v.*] *part. Born after the father's death;* posthumus, Ælfc. Gr. 47; Som. 48, 32.

æfter-cweðan; *p.* -cwæþ; *pp.* -cweden *To speak after, repeat, to answer, revoke, renounce, abjure;* repetere, revocare:—Bebeád he ðæt him mon lengran cwidas beforan cwæde, and he symle gedēfelīce æftercwæþ *he ordered longer sayings to be spoken before him, and he always repeated them properly*, Bd. 5, 2; S. 615, 15. His brōðer griþ eall æftercwæþ *his brother renounced all peace*, Chr. 1094; Th. 360, 23. Æftercweðendra lof *the praise of the after-speaking* [*post mortem laudantium*], Exon. 82 b; Th. 310, 10; Seef. 72.

æfter-eala, an; *m. After-ale, small beer:*—Æfter-eala *sapa*, Ælfc. Gl. 33; Som. 62, 22; Wrt. Voc. 28, 5.

æfter-fæce; *adv.* [æfter *after, and the dat. of* fæc *a space*] *Afterwards, after that;* postmodum. v. fæc.

æfter-folgere, es; *m. A follower;* successor, Ors. 3, 11; Bos. 74, 36.

æfter-folgian; *p.* ode; *pp.* od *To follow after, pursue;* subsequi, persequi:—Him æfterfolgiende wǽron *they were pursuing him*, Ors. 1, 10; Bos. 32, 25.

æfter-fylging, e; *f. A following after, a sequence;* sectatio, successio. v. fylging.

æfter-fylian, -filian; *p.* de; *pp.* ed *To follow* or *come after, to succeed;* sequi, prosequi, subsequi:—Ðæs sǽs smyltnys æfterfyligeþ *serenitas maris prosequetur*, Bd. 3, 15; S. 541, 35. Ðæs æfterfiliendan tācnes *signi sequentis*, Ex. 4, 8.

æfter-fyligend, -fylgend, es; *m. One who follows* or *succeeds, a follower;* successor:—Ac Oswald his æfterfyligend hī ge-endade swā we ǽr beforan sǽdon *sed successor ejus Oswaldus perfecit ut supra docuimus*, Bd. 2, 20; S. 521, 36: Bd. 5, 23; S. 646, 2.

æfter-fylignes, -ness, e; *f. A following after, a succession, succeeding;* successio. v. fylignes.

æfter-gān [gān *to go*] *To follow after;* subsequi, Past. 15, 2?

æfter-gencnys, -nyss, e; *f.* [gengnys *a going*] *Extremity;* extremitas, R. Ben. Interl. 7.

æfter-genga, an; *m.* [genga *goer*] *One who goes* or *follows after, a follower;* successor, posthumus:—Æftergenga *posthumus*, æfter boren, se ðe biþ geboren æfter bebyrgedum fæder *one who is born after the father has been buried*, Ælfc. Gr. 47; Som. 48, 32. Ðū me ne derige, ne mīnum æftergengum *ne noceas mihi et posteris meis*, Gen. 21, 23.

æfter-gengnys, -nyss, e; *f. Succession;* posteritas. v. æfter-gencnys.

æfter-gild, -gyld, es; *n. An after-payment, a paying again* or *in addition;* secunda *vel* iterata compensatio, L. C. S. 24; Th. i. 390, 7.

æfter-hǽtu, e; *f.* [æfter *after*, hǽtu *heat*] *After-heat;* insequens calor:—Mid ungemetlīcum hærfest-wætan and æfterhǽte *from heavy harvest-rains and after-heat*, Ors. 3, 3; Bos. 55, 23.

æfter-hȳrigean; *p.* de; *pp.* ed *To follow another's example, to imitate, resemble;* imitari:—He wilnode æfterhȳrigean *he wished to imitate*, Bd. 3, 18; S. 545, 44.

æfter-leán, es; *n. An after-loan, reward, recompense, retribution;* præmium, merces:—Þearl æfterleán *hard retribution*, Cd. 4; Th. 5, 24; Gen. 76.

æfter-līc; *adj. After, second;* secundus, Cot. 191.

æfterra *second;* secundus:—Se æfterra deáþ *the second death*, Bt. 19; Fox 70, 18. Sende he eft æfterran sīðe ǽrenddracan *he sent messengers again a second time*, Bd. 2, 12; S. 513, 10. v. æftera.

æfter-rāp, es; *m. An* AFTER-ROPE, *a crupper;* postilena, Ælfc. Gl. 20; Som. 59, 54.

æfter-rīdan; *p.* -rād, *pl.* -ridon; *pp.* -riden *To ride after;* equo insequi:—Hīg ða sōna æfterridon īdelum færelde *secuti sunt eos per viam*, Jos. 2, 7.

æfter-ryne, es; *m. An encountering, meeting, running against one;* occursus:—Æfterryne his ōþ to heáhnesse his *occursus ejus usque ad summum ejus*, Ps. Spl. 18, 7.

æfter-sang, es; *m. The after-song;* posterior cantus:—Mid ðam æftersange *with the after-song*, L. Ælf. P. 31; Th. ii. 376, 6.

æfter-singend, es; *m. An after-singer;* succentor, Wrt. Voc. 28, 21.

æfter-spræc, e; *f. After-speech* or *claim;* repostulatio, L. O. 7; Th. i. 180, 23.

æfter-sprecan; *p.* -spræc, *pl.* -sprǽcon; *pp.* -sprecen [sprecan *to speak*] *To claim;* petere, repetere:—Āgnung biþ nēr ðam ðe hæfþ, ðonne ðam ðe æftersprecþ *possession is always nearer to him who has, than to him who claims*, L. Eth. ii. 9; Th. i. 290, 21.

æfter-spyrian, -spyrgean; *p.* ede; *pp.* ed *To inquire after, examine;* examinare:—Gif ge hit willaþ æfterspyrian *if ye will examine it*, Bt. 16, 2; Fox 52, 8. v. spyrian.

æfter-weard *After,* AFTERWARD, *following;* posterior, secundus:—Gif he me æfterweard weorþeþ *if he shall be after* [*afterward*] *me*, Exon. 104 b; Th. 397, 3; Rä. 16, 14. v. æfte-weard, weard; *adj.*

æfter-weardnes, -ness, e; *f. Posterity;* posteritas, Cot. 149.

æfter-wearþ beón *To be away, absent*, Bd. 3, 15; S. 542, note 6. v. æfweard.

æfter-yldo, -yld, e; *f.* I. *after-age, old age;* ætas provecta:—Ne māgon ða æfteryld in ðam ǽrestan blǽde geberan *they may not produce* [*show*] *old age in their first strength* [*youth*], Exon. 39 b; Th. 132, 3; Gū. 467. II. *an after-age, after-time;* posterius ævum:—Swā nǽnig æfteryldo syððan gemunan mæg *so as no after-age since can remember*, Bd. 1, 14; S. 482, 22.

æfte-weard; *adj.* [=æfter] *After, back, late, latter, full;* posterior:—Æfteweard lencten *full spring*, Wrt. Voc. 53, 27. Æfteweard heáfod *the back of the head*, 42, 43. Drihten ðē gesett nā on æfteweard *the Lord will not set thee in the after-part*, Deut. 28, 13.

æfte-wearde; *adv.* [æfter, wearde, weardes] *Afterward, after, behind;* post, pone:—Ðū gesihst me æftewearde *thou shalt see me behind*, Ex. 33, 23.

æf-þanc, es; *m:* æf-þanca, -þonca, -þunca, an; *m. Offence, insult, grudge, displeasure, envy, zeal;* simultas, offensa, odium, zelus:—Swindan me dyde æfþanca mīn *tabescere me fecit zelus meus*, Ps. Spl. M. 118, 139. Æfþonca gefylled *full of grudges*, Exon. 83 b; Th. 315, 4; Mod. 26. Eald æfþoncan edniwedan *they have renewed old grudges*, 72 b; Th. 271, 20; Jul. 485. Æfþancum herian *to vex with insults*, Cd. 102; Th. 135, 3; Gen. 2237.

æftyr *after, according to;* secundum, Mt. Bos. 9, 29. v. æfter I. 3.

æf-weard, æf-ward; *adj. Absent, distant;* absens:—Līcumlīce æfward *corporaliter absens*, Bd. 3, 15; S. 542, 6.

æf-weardnes, -ness, e; *f. Absence, removal, posterity;* absentia:—For ðīnre æfweardnesse *because of thy absence*, Bt. 10; Fox 28, 28.

æf-werdelsa, an; *m. Damage, detriment, loss;* detrimentum, damnum, L. Alf. 27; Th. i. 50, 28. v. æf-werdla.

æf-werdla, æf-wyrdla, æ-wyrdla, a-wyrdla, an; *m.* [æf *of*, wyrdan *to corrupt*] *Damage, injury, loss, the amercement for it;* detrimentum, jactura, damnum:—Þolie ðone æfwerdlan [æfwyrdlan MS. H.] *let him bear the damage*, L. In. 40; Th. i. 126, 16: R. Ben. 2: Cot. 104.

ǽ-fyllende; *adj.* [ǽ=*law*, fyllende *part. of* fyllan *to fill, fulfil*] *Following the law, faithful;* legem exsequens:—Seó circe ǽfyllendra *the church of the faithful*, Exon. 18 a; Th. 44, 17; Cri. 704.

ǽfyn, es; *m. The evening:*—On ǽfyn *at evening*, Cd. 17; Th. 20, 22; Gen. 313. v. ǽfen.

æ-fyrmþa; *pl. f.* [æ, fyrmþ, e; *f. washing*] *Ablutions, the sweepings of a house, the refuse of things* or *things of no value;* ablutiones, quisquiliæ:—Æfyrmþa [MS. æfyrmþe] *quisquiliæ*, Ælfc. Gr. 13; Som. 16, 22.

ÆG, æig; *g.* æges; *pl. nom. acc.* ægru; *g.* ægra; *d.* ægrum, ægerum; *n. An* EGG; ovum:—Gif hit [cild] æges bitt *if he ask for an egg*, Homl. Th. i. 250, 9. Ðæt æg [æig MS.] getācnaþ ðone hālgan hiht *the egg betokens the holy hope*, i. 250, 11. Gif he bit æg *si petierit ovum*, Lk. Bos. 11, 12. Genīm hænne æges geolocan *take the yolk of a hen's egg*, L. M. 1, 2; Lchdm. ii. 38, 6. Sceáwa nū on ānum æge, hū ðæt hwīte ne biþ gemenged to ðam geolcan, and biþ hwæðere ān æg *look now on an egg, how the white is not mingled with the yolk, and yet it is one egg*, Homl. Th. i. 40, 27, 28. On æge biþ gioleca on middan *in an egg the yolk is in the middle*, Bt. Met. Fox 20, 338; Met. 20, 169. Of ægerum *from eggs*, Exon. 59 a; Th. 214, 2; Ph. 233. Ægru lecgan *to lay eggs*, Som.

121. Æges hwîte *white of an egg.* Æmettan ægru genîm *take emmet's eggs*, L. M. 1, 87; Lchdm. ii. 156, 6. [*Ger.* ei, *n*: *M. H. Ger.* ei, *g.* eies, eiges, *pl.* eiger, *n*: *O. H. Ger.* ei, *g.* eies, eiges, *pl.* eigir, *n*: *Dan.* äg, *n*: *Swed.* ägg, *n*: *O. Nrs.* egg, *n.*]

ǽg, e; *f. water, water land, an island.* v. ǽge, îgg.

ǽg- used in composition,—*water, sea;* aqua, mare. DER. ǽg-flota, ǽg-weard. v. îg-.

ǽg- *Ever, always;* semper: either a contraction of the prefixes â, ǽ, with a *g* added, as ǽg, or derived from aa = â, âwa, ǽw. It is used in compound pronouns and adverbs, as,—ǽg-hwâ, ǽg-hwǽr, ǽg-hwilc, *etc;* but, in its place, we also find the prefix â-, as,—â-hwǽr, â-hwilc, *etc.* Both ǽg- and â- impart to their compounds a sense of universality.

ǽgan *to own*, Ps. Spl. T. 78, 12: 138, 12. v. âgan.

æge *fear;* timor, terror, Chr. 1006, Th. 257, 41. v. ege.

ǽge *the island;* insulam:—Æt eðelinga ǽge *at the island of nobles;* apud nobilium insulam, Sim. Dunelm. an. 888. v. Æðelinga îgg.

Ægeles birg *Aylesbury*, Chr. 571; Th. 32, 29. v. Ægles burg.

Ægeles ford, Egeles ford, es; *m. Ailsford*, Chr. 1016; Th. 279, 16, col. 2: 1016; Th. 282, 10, col. 2.

Ægeles þrep *Aylesthorpe*, Chr. 455; Th. 21, 32. v. Ægles þrep.

ǽgen; *adj. Own;* proprius, Bt. 14, 2; Fox 44, 23. v. âgen.

æger-felma, an; *f. Film of an egg;* membrana vitellum complectens:—Genîm ðonne ægerfelman *then take film of egg*, L. M. 1, 11; Lchdm. ii. 54, 21.

ægerum *from eggs*, Exon. 59 a; Th. 214, 2; Ph. 233. v. æg.

ǽ-gewrîtere, es; *m.* [ǽ *law*, gewrîtere *a writer*] *A writer* or *composer of laws;* legum conditor, Prov. 8.

ǽg-flota, an; *m. A floater on the sea, sailor, ship;* nauta, navis, Andr. Kmbl. 515; An. 258. v. flota.

ǽg-hwâ; *m. f.*: *neut.* ǽg-hwæt; *gen.* ǽg-hwæs [â + ge + hwâ] *Every one, everything;* quisque, quicunque:—Ǽghwâ secge *let every one say*, Exon. 88 b; Th. 333, 5; Vy. 97: 125 a; Th. 482, 4; Rä. 66, 2. Ǽghwæt heó gefôn mæg *whatever she may seize*, Bt. 25; Fox 88, 14. God ǽghwæs wealt *God governs everything*, Bt. 35, 4; Fox 160, 14. Þearfum ǽghwæs oftugon *ye denied the poor everything*, Exon. 30 a; Th. 92, 8; Cri. 1505. Se fugol is on hiwe ǽghwæs ǽnlîc *the bird is in aspect every way unique*, 60 a; Th. 219, 24; Ph. 312. Ǽghwæs orwîgne *wholly defenceless*, 72 a; Th. 268, 18; Jul. 434.

ǽg-hwǽr, â-hwǽr; *adv.* [â + ge + hwǽr]. I. *everywhere;* ubique:—God ǽghwǽr is eall, and nâhwâr todǽled *God is everywhere all, and nowhere divided*, Homl. Th. i. 286, 27. Hî ðâ farende ǽghwǽr bodedon *illi profecti prædicaverunt ubique*, Mk. Bos. 16, 20. Ǽghwǽr sindon hiora gelîcan *they are everywhere like them*, Bt. Met. Fox 10, 116; Met. 10, 58. II. *in every respect, in every way;* omnino:—Eofore eom ǽghwǽr cênra *I am in every respect bolder than a wild boar*, Exon. 110 b; Th. 423, 9; Rä. 41, 18: Ps. Th. 102, 14.

ǽg-hwæt *whatever;* quodcunque. v. ǽg-hwâ.

ǽg-hwæðer; *pron.* [â + ge + hwæðer]. I. of two, *either, each, both;* uterque:—Ǽghwæðer ôðerne earme beþehte *they embraced each other*, Andr. Kmbl. 2029; An. 1017. Beámas twegen ðara ǽghwæðer efngedǽlde heáhþegnunga hâliges gâstes *two pillars, each of which shared alike the high services of the holy spirit*, Cd. 146; Th. 183, 21; Exod. 94. II. of many, *every one, each;* unusquisque:—Heora ǽghwæðrum *to each, to every one of them*, Beo. Th. 3277; B. 1636. Ǽghwæðer ge lengre fæc ðysses lîfes ðê forgifan ge ðê eác ðæs êcan lîfes inganges wyrþne gedôn *et hujus vitæ longiora spatia concedere et ingressu te vitæ perennis dignum reddere*, Bd. 3, 13; S. 539, 2. Ǽghwæðer ge—ge *et—et*, 2, 16; S. 519, 34.

ǽg-hwanan, -hwanon, -hwonon, -hwanone, -hwonene; *adv. Everywhere, every way, on all sides;* undique:—Ǽghwanan mid wæterum ymbseald *undique aquis circumdata*, Bd. 4, 19; S. 588, 28. Hî ǽghwanon to him cômon *conveniebant ad eum undique*, Mk. Bos. 1, 45. Ǽghwonan ymb-boren mid brondum *on every side surrounded with brands*, Exon. 74 a; Th. 277, 14; Jul. 580. Ǽghwanon, Ælfc. Gr. 45; Som. 46, 57. Hine ǽghwonan ælmihtig God [MS. Good] gehealdeþ *Almighty God keeps him everywhere*, Bt. Met. Fox 7, 89; Met. 7, 45. Ǽghwonon *everywhere*, Bd. 4, 13; S. 582, 44. Ǽghwanone, 3, 6; S. 528, 18. Ǽghwonene, 3, 15; S. 541, 42.

ǽg-hwâr, ǽg-hwêr *everywhere*, Ors. 4, 1; Bos. 76, 38. v. ǽg-hwǽr.

ǽg-hwider, -hwyder; *adv. On every side, every way;* quaquaversum:—Ǽghwider ymb swâ swâ Edwines rîce wǽre *quaquaversum imperium regis Æduini pervênerat*, Bd. 2, 16; S. 519, 38. Ǽghwider wolde wîde toscrîðan *it would everywhere widely wander*, Bt. Met. Fox 20, 184; Met. 20, 92.

ǽg-hwilc, -hwelc, -hwylc; *adj.* [â + ge + hwŷ + lîc] *Every, all, whosoever, whatsoever, every one;* quicunque, unusquisque, omnis:—Ǽghwylc dæg *every day*, Mt. Bos. 6, 34. Ǽghwylce geáre *every year*, Bd. 2, 16; S. 519, 23. Hêr is ǽghwylc eorl ôðrum getrŷwe *here is every man true to the other*, Beo. Th. 2460; B. 1228. Ǽghwylcum maððum gesealde *he gave a present to every one*, Beo. Th. 2104; B. 1050. Ǽghwylcne ellþeódigra *unumquemque alienorum*, Andr. Kmbl. 51; An. 26. Wreðiaþ fæste ǽghwilc ôðer *each supports the other firmly*, Bt. Met. Fox 11, 69; Met. 11, 35. Ǽghwelce dæg *on every day*, Bt. Met. Fox 14, 9; Met. 14, 5. Ǽghwylc wille lîfes tiligan *every one wishes to cultivate life*, Exon. 27 a; Th. 81, 4; Cri. 1318. Ðû ǽghwylces canst *thou art knowing in every matter*, Andr. Kmbl. 1016; An. 508.

ǽg-hwonene; *adv. On every side;* ubique:—Ða ŷða ǽghwonene ðæt scyp fyldon *the waves filled the ship on every side*, Bd. 3, 15; S. 541, 42. v. ǽg-hwanan.

ǽg-hwyder *every way.* v. ǽghwider.

ǽ-gift, e; *f. A legal gift, restitution;* legalis dos, restitutio, Cart. Eadgif R.

æ-gilde, æ-gylde, a-gilde, a-gylde; *adv.* [æ *without*, gild *payment*] *Without compensation;* sine compensatione:—Gif he gewyrce ðæt hine man afylle, licge ægilde *if he so do that any man fell him down, let him be without compensation*, L. Eth. vi. 38; Th. i. 324, 24: L. E. G. 6; Th. i. 170, 13: L. C. S. 49; Th. i. 404, 14: L. Eth. v. 31; Th. i. 312, 12.

Ægiptisc *Egyptian.* v. Ægypte, Egiptisc.

æg-lǽc, es; *n. Misery, trouble, torment;* miseria, tribulatio, cruciatus, Elen. Grm. 1188. v. ag-lâc.

æg-lǽca, an; *m. A miserable being, wretch, monster;* miser, perditus, monstrum:—Atol æglǽca *the fell wretch*, Beo. Th. 1188; B. 592: Cd. 216; Th. 274, 28; Sat. 161: Andr. Kmbl. 2717; An. 1361. v. ag-lǽca.

ǽ-gleáw; *adj. Skilled in the law, learned, wise;* legis peritus, sagacissimus, sapientissimus:—Ðâ andswarode him sum ǽgleáw *respondit quidam ex legis peritis*, Lk. Bos. 11, 45. Ealde ǽgleáwe *elders skilled in laws*, Menol. Fox 37; Men. 19. Ðæt sceal ǽgleáwra fîndan *that a more learned man must find out*, Andr. Kmbl. 2965; An. 1485.

æg-lêca, an; *m. A wretch, miscreant*, Cd. 214; Th. 269, 14; Sat. 73. v. ag-lǽca.

Ægles burg, Ægeles burg, [burh]; *g.* burge; *f*: Ægles byrig, e; *f.* AYLESBURY, *in Buckinghamshire:*—Cûþwulf genom Ægeles burg *Cuthwulf took Aylesbury*, Chr. 571; Erl. 18, 13. Genam Ægles burh *id.* Th. 32, 29, col. 2. Genam Ægles byrig *id.* Th. 33, 27, col. 1. Betweóx Byrnewuda and Ægles byrig *betwixt Bernwood and Aylesbury*, 921; Th. 194, 19.

Ægles ford, es; *m.* AYLESFORD *on the Medway near Maidstone, Kent*, Chr. 455; Ing. 15, 15. v. Ægeles ford.

Ægles þrep, es; *n.* [þorp *a village*] AYLESTHORPE, *a village near Aylesford, Kent*, Chr. 455; Ing. p. 15, note *h;* Th. 20, 39.

Ægles wurþ, es; *m. The village of* EYLESWORTH, *Northamptonshire*, Chr. 963; Ing. 155, 9.

æg-lîm, es; *m.* [æg *an egg*, lîm *lime, glue*] EGG-LIME, *the sticky part* or *white of an egg;* ovi viscum:—Æglîm *glara*, Ælfc. Gl. 81; Som. 72, 119.

ǽg-moran; *pl. f. Eye-roots;* nervi quibus oculus cum cerebro connectitur:—Ðe beóþ on ðan ǽgmoran sâra *which are sores in the eye-roots*, Lchdm. iii. 98, 5. v. more.

ǽgnes þonces *of his own accord;* sponte, ultro. v. âgen.

ægnian; *p.* ede; *pp.* ed? *To frighten, vex;* terrere, tribulare:—Ægnian mid yrmþum *to frighten with misery*, Cd. 156; Th. 194, 23; Exod. 265.

ægru *eggs*, L. M. 1, 87; Lchdm. ii. 156, 6. v. æg.

ægsa, an; *m. Fear;* timor, Mt. Rush. Stv. 14, 26. v. egsa.

ǽg-ðer [= ǽg-hwæðer]; *pron. Either, each, both;* uterque, ambo:—Ǽgðer byþ gehealden *ambo conservantur*, Mt. Bos. 9, 17. Ǽgðer ðara eorla *each of the men*, Andr. Kmbl. 2103; An. 1053. Heora ǽgðer *either* or *both of them, each*, Gen. 21, 31. On ǽgðre hand, on ǽgðere healfe *on either hand* or *half, on both sides*, Ors. 1, 11; Bos. 34, 40: 1, 14; Bos. 37, 33. On ǽgðre healfe weard *towards both sides*, Ælfc. Gr. Ǽgðer ge—ge, *both—and, as well—as:*—Ǽgðer ge hâdes, ge êðeles þolige *let him forfeit both degree and country*, L. C. S. 41; Th. i. 400, 14. Ǽgðer ge heonan ge ðanan *both here and there.* Hî hatedon ǽgðer ge me ge mînne fæder *they hated both me and my father*, Jn. Bos. 15, 24.

ǽg-weard, e; *f. Sea-ward, sea-guard* or *guardianship;* maris [litoris] custodia:—Ic ǽgwearde heóld *I hold guard*, Beo. Th. 488, note; B. 241. v. weard.

æg-wyrt, e; *f. Egg-wort, dandelion;* leontodon taraxacum, Lacn. 40; Lchdm. iii. 28, 26.

æ-gylde; *adv. Without compensation*, L. E. G. 6; Th. i. 170, 13. v. æ-gilde.

ǽ-gylt, -gilt, es; *m.* [ǽ, gylt *guilt, fault*] *A breach* or *violation of the law, a trespass, fault;* delictum:—Ǽgiltas iúguþ-hâdes mînes ne gemun ðû *delicta juventutis meæ ne memineris*, Ps. Spl. T. 24, 7.

æ-gype, -gipe; *adj. Trifling, worthless;* nugalis:—Forðon hî dydan Drihtnes sprǽce ǽghwæs ægype *quia exacerbaverunt eloquium Domini*, Ps. Th. 106, 10.

Ægypte *Egypt*, Bd. 4, 24; S. 598, 11. v. Egypte.

æ-hiwnes, -ness, e; *f. Paleness, gloom;* pallor, deficientia coloris:—Wið æblǽcnysse and æhiwnesse ðæs lîchoman *for paleness and discoloration of the body*, Herb. 164; Lchdm. i. 294, 3.

ǽ-hlŷp, -hlîp, es; *m.* [ǽ *law*, hlŷp *a leap*] *A transgression, breach of the law, an assault;* legis transgressio, aggressus:—Se ðe ǽ-hlîp gewyrce *whoever commits an assault*, L. Ath. v. § 1, 5; Th. i. 230, 10. Þurh ǽ-hlýp *by a violation of the law*, L. Eth. v. 31; Th. i. 312, 11. v. æt-hlýp.

æht, e; *f. Valuation, estimation, deliberation, council*; æstimatio, deliberatio, consilium:—Fira bearn æht besittaþ *the sons of men sit in council*, Andr. Kmbl. 820; An. 410. Biscopas and bóceras and ealdormen æht besǽton *bishops and scribes and princes sat in council*, Andr. Kmbl. 1216; An. 608. v. eaht *deliberation, council*.

ǽht, e; *f.* [ēhtan *to persecute*] *Persecution, hostility*; persecutio, hostilitas:—Ðā wæs ǽht boden Sweóna leódum *then was persecution announced to the people of the Swedes*, Beo. Th. 5907; B. 2957. [*Ger.* acht, *f. proscriptio*: *M.H.Ger.* āhte, æhte: *O.H.Ger.* āhta, *f. persecutio.*]

ǽht, e; *f.* [ǽhte = āhte *had*; *p. of* āgan *to own, possess*]. I. *possessions, property, lands, goods, riches, cattle*; opes, substantia, possessio, greges:—He hæfde mycele ǽhta *erat habens multas possessiones*, Mk. Bos. 10, 22. Esau nam ealle his ǽhta, and eall ðæt he ǽhte *Esau took all his goods, and all that he possessed*, Gen. 36, 6. Grūndleás gītsung gilpes and ǽhta *bottomless avarice of glory and possessions*, Bt. Met. Fox 7, 30; Met. 7, 15. Israēla ǽhta *the Israelites' possessions*, Cd. 174; Th. 218, 23; Dan. 43. Genam on eallum dǽl ǽhtum sīnum *he took a part of all his possessions*, 74; Th. 90, 23; Gen. 1499. Ealle his ǽhta *omnem substantiam ejus*, Ps. Th. 108, 11. II. *possession, power*; possessio, potestas:—His miht and his ǽht ofer middangeard gebledsod *his might and power is blessed throughout the earth*, Andr. Kmbl. 3432; An. 1720. Āgan us ðis wuldres leóht eall to ǽhte *let us get all this light of glory into our possession*, Cd. 219; Th. 280, 11; Sat. 254. On āgene ǽht syllan *in possessionem dare*, Ps. Th. 104, 10, 39: 110, 4. [*Scot.* aucht: *O.H.Ger.* ēht, *f*: *Goth.* aíhts, *f*: *O.Nrs.* ǽtt, ātt *family*.] DER. gold-, māðum-, staðol-, wan-, won-.

æhta *eight*, Chr. 1070; Th. 345, 32. v. eahta.

ǽhte *had, owned, possessed*. v. āhte; *p. of* āgan.

ǽhte land, es; *n.* [ǽht *property*] *Landed property*; terra possessionis:—Forðon ðe Peohtas heora ǽhte land ðætte Angle ǽr hæfdon eft onfēngon *nam Picti terram possessionis suæ quam tenuerunt Angli receperunt*, Bd. 4, 26; S. 602, 29.

ǽhte man, mann, es; *pl.* men; *m. A husbandman, a farmer, ploughman*; colonus:—Laboratores sind yrþlingas and ǽhte men *labourers are ploughmen and husbandmen*, Ælfc. T. 40, 20.

æhtere, es; *m. An estimator, a valuer*; æstimator, Ælfc. Gl. 114; Som. 80, 25.

ǽhte swān, es; *m.* [ǽht *property*, swān *swain* or *herdsman*: *O.H.Ger.* sweinn *a herdsman*] *A cowherd, swineherd, who belongs to the property of his lord*; bubulcus, porcarius qui in peculio domini est, L. R. S. 7; Th. i. 436, 22.

ǽht-gesteald, es; *n. Possession*; possessio:—He ða brȳdlufan sceal to ōðerre ǽhtgestealdum idese sēcan *he must seek conjugal love in the possession of another woman*, Exon. 67 b; Th. 249, 22; Jul. 115.

ǽht-gestreón, es; *n. Possessions, riches*; possessio, divitiæ:—Ðonne līg eal þigeþ eorþan ǽhtgestreón *when the flame devours all the possessions of the earth*, Exon. 63 a; Th. 232, 13; Ph. 506.

ǽht-geweald, es; *m. n. Possession, power, the power of the possessor*; potestas possessoria:—Cwæþ he his sylfes sunu syllan wolde on ǽhtgeweald *he said that he would give his own son into their power*, Andr. Kmbl. 2221; An. 1112. Ðū usic bewrǽce in ǽhtgewealda *tu nos tradidisti in potestatem*, Exon. 53 a; Th. 186, 28; Az. 26.

ǽhtian [ǽht *persecution*] *to persecute*; persequi. v. ēhtan.

ǽht-spēdig; *adj. Wealthy, rich*; locuples, opulentus:—Se is betra ðonne ðū, ǽhtspēdigra feoh-gestreóna *he is better than thou, richer in money-treasures*, Exon. 67 a; Th. 248, 26; Jul. 101.

æhtung, e; *f. Estimation, valuing*; æstimatio, Ælfc. Gl. 114; Som. 80, 26. v. eahtung.

ǽht-wela, an; *m. Wealth, riches*; opes, divitiæ:—Gelufian eorþan ǽhtwelan *to love earth's riches*, Exon. 38 a; Th. 125, 24; Gū. 359: Apstls. Kmbl. 167; Ap. 84.

ǽht-welig; *adj. Rich, wealthy*; locuples:—Sum wæs ǽhtwelig gerēfa *there was a wealthy count*, Exon. 66 a; Th. 243, 29; Jul. 18.

ǽ-hwǽr; *adv. Everywhere*; ubique, Ps. Th. 88, 31. v. ā-hwǽr.

æ-hwyrfan *To turn from, avert*; avertere, Ps. Spl. T. 53, 5. v. a-hwerfan, hwyrfan, hweorfan.

æig, es; *n. An egg*; ovum:—Ðæt æig getācnaþ hiht: ǽrest hit biþ æig, and seó mōdor siððan mid hihte bret ðæt æig to bridde *the egg betokens hope: first it is an egg, and the mother then with hope cherishes the egg to a young bird*, Homl. Th. i. 250, 22–24. v. æg.

æl-; *prefix*. I. = eal *all*; totus, omnis, as æl-beorht, æl-ceald, *etc*. II. æl- = el-, ele-, *foreign*; peregrinus, as æl-fylce, æl-wihta, *etc*.

æl, e; *f. An awl*; subula:—Hwanon sceó-wyrhtan æl *unde sutori subula*, Coll. Monast. Th. 30, 33: L. Alf. 11; Th. i. 46, 10. Æl *subula*, Ælfc. Gl. 1; Som. 55, 27; Wrt. Voc. 16, 2. v. al.

æl, es; *m. Oil*; oleum:—Ða sceolon beón æle bracene *they must be beaten up with oil*, Lev. 6, 21. v. ele.

ǼL, es; *m. An* EEL; anguilla:—Hwilce fixas gefēhst ðū? ǽlas and hacodas *what fishes catchest thou? eels and haddocks*, Coll. Monast. Th. 23, 33. Ac seó þeód ðone cræft ne cūðe ðæs fiscnōðes nymþe to ǽlum ānum *sed piscandi peritia genti nulla nisi ad anguillas tantum inerat*, Bd. 4, 13; S. 582, 43. Smæl ǽl *a small eel*, Cot. 161. [*Plat. Dut. Ger.* aal, *m*: *M.H.Ger. O.H.Ger.* āl, *m*: *Swed.* äl, *m*: *Dan.* aal, *m*: *O.Nrs.* āll, *m.*] DER. ǽl-net, ǽle-puta.

ǽ-lā *O!*—Ǽlā Drihten *O Lord*, Hy. 1, 1. v. eálā, æálā.

ǽ-lǽdend, es; *m.* [ǽ *lex*, lǽdend *lator*, from lǽdan *ferre*, to move or propose a law] *A lawgiver*; legislator, Ps. Spl. 9, 21.

ǽ-lǽrende; *part. Teaching the law*; legem docens:—Siððan him nǽnig wæs ǽlǽrendra ōðer betera *since there was none other of those teaching the law better than he*, Elen. Kmbl. 1009; El. 506.

æ-lǽten *divorced*, L. C. E. 7; Th. i. 364, 23, = a-lǽten; *pp. of* a-lǽtan.

ælan; *p.* de; *pp.* ed; *v. a. To kindle, set on fire, burn, bake*; accendere, urere, comburere, coquere:—Ne ælaþ hyra leóhtfæt *neque accendunt lucernam*, Mt. Bos. 5, 15. Ūton wircean us tigelan and ælan hīg on fȳre *faciamus lateres et coquamus eos igni*, Gen. 11, 3. Fȳr æleþ uncyste *the fire burns the vices*, Exon. 63 b; Th. 233, 17; Ph. 526. Flǽsc and bān ādlēg æleþ *the fire of the pile burns flesh and bones*, Exon. 59 a; Th. 213, 9; Ph. 222. Brond biþ ontyhte, æleþ ealdgestreón *let the brand be kindled, consume the old treasure*, 19 b; Th. 51, 8. DER. in-ælan, on-.

æl-beorht *All-bright, all-shining*:—Engel ælbeorht *an all-bright angel*, Cd. 190; Th. 237, 13; Dan. 337: Exon. 15 a; Th. 32, 1; Cri. 506: 21 b; Th. 58, 2; Cri. 929: 53 b; Th. 188, 27; Az. 52. Hwīlum cerreþ eft on up rōdor ælbeorhta lēg *the all-bright flame returns sometimes again up to the sky*, Bt. Met. Fox 29, 104; Met. 29, 51. v. eall-beorht.

ǽlc; *adj.* [ā + ge + līc] *Each, any, every, all*; quisque, quivis, unusquisque, omnis:—Ǽlc gōd treów byrþ gōde wæstmas *omnis arbor bona fructus bonos facit*, Mt. Bos. 7, 17. Ǽlc wæs on twegra sestra gemete *capientes singulæ metretas binas*, Jn. Bos. 2, 6. Ǽlc hine selfa begrindeþ gāstes dugeðum *each deprives himself of his soul's happiness*, Cd. 75; Th. 91, 32; Gen. 1521. Ǽlc flǽsc *omnis caro*, Ps. Th. 64, 2. Ǽlces monnes *of every man*, Bt. Met. Fox 26, 236; Met. 26, 118. Ǽlcum *cuique*, Andr. Kmbl. 3067; An. 1536. On ǽlcere tīde *omni tempore*, Lk. Bos. 21, 36. In ǽlce tīd *in æternum*, Exon. 13 b; Th. 25, 26; Cri. 406. Ǽlce dæg *each day*, Bt. Met. Fox 27, 15; Met. 27, 8. [*Plat. Dut.* elk *each, every one.*]

æl-ceald; *adj.* [æl = eal] *All cold, most cold*; usquequaque frigidus:—Meahtest weorþan æt ðæm ælcealdan steorran ðone Saturnus hātaþ *you might be at that all-cold star which they call Saturn*, Bt. Met. Fox 24, 37; Met. 24, 19.

ælcor; *adv. Elsewhere, besides, otherwise*; alias, præter, nisi, aliter:—Forðon ðam bisceope ne wæs alȳfed ælcor būtan on myran rīdan *non enim licuerat pontificem sacrorum præter in equa equitare*, Bd. 2, 13; S. 517, 7. Ælcor *alias*, Ælfc. Gr. 38; Som. 41, 67. v. elcor.

ælcra; *adv. Otherwise*; aliter, R. Ben. 62. v. ælcor.

æl-cræftig; *adj. All-powerful, all-mighty*; omnipotens:—Nān þing nis ðīn gelīca, ne hūru ǽnig ælcræftigre *nothing is like unto thee, nor is any one more all-powerful*, Bt. Met. Fox 20, 76; Met. 20, 38.

æld *fire*, Exon. 22 a; Th. 59, 30; Cri. 960. v. æled.

æld *age*, Exon. 45 a; Th. 152, 11; Gū. 807. v. ældu.

ældan *To delay, forbear, postpone, conceal*:—Ældyst, Ps. Spl. C. 88, 37. Ælde, Ps. Surt. 77, 21: Mt. Rush. Stv. 25, 5: Bd. 1, 27; S. 491, 31; MS. B. v. yldan.

ælde *men*:—Ælda bearnum *for the sons of men*, Exon. 21 b; Th. 58, 18; Cri. 937. Ǽnig ælda cynnes *any one of the race of men*, 19 a; Th. 49, 4; Cri. 780: 44 b; Th. 151, 16; Gū. 796. Mid ældum *with men*, 13 b; Th. 25, 25; Cri. 406. v. ylde.

ælding *delay*, Mt. Rush. Stv. 24, 48. v. ylding.

ældo, aldu *the elders*; seniores, Mt. Lind. Stv. 21, 23. v. ældu.

ældran; *pl. Parents*; parentes:—Mīne ældran, Ps. C. 65; Ps. Grn. ii. 278, 65. v. yldra.

ældru, ældro, aldro *parents*, Mk. Rush. War. 13, 12: Lk. Rush. War. 2, 27, 41, 43. v. ældran.

ældu, æld, e; *f.* I. *age, old age*; sæculum, senectus:—In ðā ǽrestan ældu *in his first age*, Exon. 34 a; Th. 108, 30; Gū. 80. On ælde *in senectute*, Ps. C. 142: Ps. Surt. 91, 15: 70, 18. II. *an age, century*; ævum, centuria:—Þurh ælda tīd *per sæcula sæculorum*, Exon. 45 a; Th. 152, 11; Gū. 807. Wið ælda *against the age*, 81 a; Th. 305, 16; Fä. 89. v. yldu.

ælecung, e; *f. An allurement, a blandishment*; blandimentum, C. R. Ben. 2.

æled, *g.* ældes; *m.* [*pp. of* ælan] *Fire, conflagration*; ignis, incendium:—Æled wæs micel *the fire was great*, Cd. 186; Th. 231, 6; Dan. 243. Hāt biþ monegum egeslīc æled *the dreadful fire shall be hot to many*, Exon. 63 a; Th. 233, 9; Ph. 522. Æled weccan *to light a fire*, Cd. 140; Th. 175, 26; Gen. 2901. Ældes fulle *full of fire*, Exon. 22 a; Th. 59, 30; Cri. 960. [*O.Sax.* eld, *m. ignis*: *O.Nrs.* eldr, *m. ignis*.]

æled-fȳr, es; *n. Flame of fire*; incendii flamma, Exon. 61 a; Th. 223, 27; Ph. 366.

æled-leóma, an; *m. A gleaming fire, fire-brand;* ignis micans, Beo. Th. 6241; B. 3125.

ælednys, -nyss, e; *f. A burning;* incendium. v. æled *a fire.*

æ-leng; *adj. Long, protracted, lengthy, troublesome;* longus, molestus:—Me þincþ ðæt ðē þincen tō ǣlenge ðās langan spell *methinks that these long discourses appear to thee too lengthy,* Bt. 39, 4; Fox 218, 6.

ǣle-puta, an; *m. An* EEL-POUT; capito:—Hwilce fixas gefēhst ðū? mynas and ǣleputan *what fishes catchest thou? minnows and eel-pouts,* Coll. Monast. Th. 23, 33. [*Plat.* aalput *or* putte: *Dut.* aalpuit *or* puit aal, *m. a young eel, eel-pout.*] v. myne.

æ-lēten, æ-lǣten, a-lǣten; *part.* [from a-lǣtan *to let go*] *One let go, divorced;* repudiata uxor:—Ne on ælǣten ǣnig cristen mann ǣfre ne gewīfige *nor with one divorced let any christian man ever marry,* L. C. E. 7; Th. i. 364, 23.

ÆLF, es; *m. An* ELF; genius, incubus:—Wið ælfe gnīd myrran on wīn *against an elf rub myrrh in wine,* L. M. 2, 65; Lchdm. ii. 296, 9. Ylfe, *pl. nom. m.* Beo. Th. 224; B. 112. v. ylfe. [*Plat.* elf: *O. Dut.* alf: *Ger.* elf, *m; elbe, f;* alp, *m. nightmare,* Grm. Wörterbch. iii. 400; i. 200, 245; Grm. Mythol. 249: *M. H. Ger.* alp, alf, *m. pl;* elbe, *f: O. H. Ger.* alp, *m: Dan.* elv: *Swed.* elf: *O. Nrs.* álfr, *m.*] DER. ælf-ādl, -cyn, -nōþ, -rēd = rǣd, -sciéne, -scīnu, -scȳne, -siden, -sogoða, -þone: ylfe: ælfen, elfen, dūn-, feld-, mūnt-, sǣ-, wudu-, wylde-.

ælf-ādl, e; *f. Elf-disease;* ephialtæ morbus:—Wið ælfādle *against elf-disease,* L. M. 3, 62; Lchdm. ii. 344, 20.

æl-fæle *All-fell, very baleful;* omnino perniciosus:—Âttor ælfæle *very baleful poison,* Andr. Kmbl. 1539; An. 771. v. eal-felo.

ælf-cynn, es; *n. The elf-kind, the race of elves, elfin race;* ephialtum genus, Som. Lye:—Wyrc sealfe wið ælfcynne *work a salve against the elfin race,* L. M. 3, 61; Lchdm. ii. 344, 7.

-ælfen, -elfen, e; *f. A fairy, nymph;* nympha. *It is found only in compound words, as* Mūnt-ælfen *a mountain nymph;* oreas = ὀρειάς, ἄδος:—Wudu-elfen *a wood nymph;* dryas, *etc,* Wrt. Voc. 60, 14-19. v. -en.

æl-fer, es; *n.* [= -fær, *n.*] *The whole army;* totus exercitus:—Ymbwīcigean mid æl-fere Æthanes byrig *to surround with the whole army the town of Etham,* Cd. 146; Th. 181, 24; Exod. 66.

Ælf-nōþ, es; *m.* [ælf, nōþ *boldness, courage*] *Ælfnoth, elf courage;* nomen viri præclari in audacia, Byrht. Th. 137, 8; By. 183.

Ælfred, Alfriþ, Aldfriþ, Ealdfriþ, es; *m.* [æl *all;* ald, eald *old:* fred = friþ *peace:* v. Ælfrēd] *Alfred the wise, king of Northumbria for twenty years,* A. D. 685–705. *He was educated in Ireland for the Church, and was the first literary king of the Anglo-Saxons; Lat.* Ælfrēdus, Alfrid, Alfrīdus, Bd. 4, 26; S. 175, 4: Aldfrīdus, Bd. 5, 2; S. 183, 6: Aldfrithus, Chr. 685; Gib. 45, 24:—Fēng Ælfred [MS. Ealdfriþ] æfter Ecgfriþe to rīce, se mon wæs se gelǣredesta on gewrītum, se wæs sæd ðæt his brōðor wǣre Oswies sunu ðæs cyninges *Ecgfrith was succeeded in the kingdom by Alfred, who was said to be his brother, and a son of king Oswy, and was a man most learned in scripture;* successit Ecgfrido in regnum Alfrid, vir in scripturis doctissimus, qui frater ejus et filius Osuiu regis esse dicebatur, Bd. 4, 26; S. 603, 6-8. A. D. 685, Hēr man ofslōh Ecgferþ, and Ælfred [MS. Aldfriþ *Aldfrithus*] his brōðor fēng æfter him to rīce *here,* A. D. 685, *they slew Ecgferth, and Alfred his brother succeeded* [*took*] *to the kingdom after him,* Chr. 685; Erl. 41, 29. On Ælfredes [MS. Aldfriþes *Aldfrithi*] tīdum ðæs cyninges *in temporibus Aldfridi regis,* Bd. 5, 1; S. 614, 20. Hēr Ælfred [MS. Aldfriþ] Norþanhymbra cining forþfērde *here,* A. D. 705, *Alfred, king of the Northumbrians, died,* Chr. 705; Erl. 43, 32.

Ælfrēd, es; *m.* [ælf *an elf;* rēd = rǣd *counsel, wise in counsel:* v. Ælfred] *Alfred;* Alfrēdus. I. Alfred the Great, born A. D. 849, grandson of Egbert, and fourth son of king Ethelwulf, reigned thirty years, A. D. 871-901:—Ðā, A. D. 871, fēng Ælfrēd, Æðelwulfing, to West Seaxna rīce ... And ðes geáres wurdon ix folcgefeoht gefohten wið ðone here on ðam cinerīce be sūþan Temese; būtan ðam ðe hī Ælfrēd, ... and ealdormen, and cíningas þegnas, oft rāda on riden, ðe man nāne rīmde *then,* A. D. 871, *Alfred, son of Ethelwulf, succeeded to the kingdom of the West Saxons ... And this year nine great battles were fought against the army in the kingdom south of the Thames; besides which, Alfred ... and aldormen, and king's thanes, often rode raids on them, which were not reckoned,* Chr. 871; Erl. 77, 3-10. A. D. 897, Ðā hēt Ælfrēd cyning timbrian lange scipu ongeán ðas æscas [MS. æsceas] ða wǣron fulneáh twā swā lange swā ða ōðre; ... ða wǣron ǣgðer ge swiftran ge untealran, ge eác heárran [MS. heárra] ðonne ða ōðru; nǣron hī nāwðær ne on Frysisc gesceapen ne on Denisc; būtan swā him sylfum þūhte ðæt hī nytwyrðe beón meahton *then,* A. D. 897, *king Alfred commanded long ships to be built against the Danish ships* [æscas] *which were full nigh twice as long as the others; ... they were both swifter and steadier, and also higher than the others; they were shapen neither as the Frisian nor as the Danish, but as it seemed to himself that they might be most useful,* 897; Th. 175, 37, col. 2—177, 5, col. 2. Ðæs ilcan geáres, hēt se cyning [Ælfrēd] faran to Wiht ... Ðā gefēngon hȳ ðara scipa twā, and ða men [MS. mæn] ofslōgon ... Ða ylcan sumere, forwearþ nā læs ðonne xx scipa mid mannum mid ealle be ðam sūþ riman *in the same year* [A. D. 897], *the king* [*Alfred*] *commanded his men to go to Wight ... They then took two of the ships, and slew the men ... In the same summer, no less than twenty ships, with men and everything* [*of the Danes*], *perished on the south coast,* Chr. 897; Th. 177, 5, col. 2—179, 3, col. 2. A. D. 901, Hēr gefōr Ælfrēd cyning vii Kl Nouembris ... and ðā fēng Eádweard, his sunu to rīce *here died king Alfred, on the twenty-sixth of October ... and then Edward* [*the Elder*], *his son, succeeded to the kingdom,* Chr. 901; Th. 179, 14-18, col. 2. II. Though the talents and energy of Alfred were chiefly occupied in subduing the Danes, and in confirming his kingdom, he availed himself of the short intervals of peace to read and write much. He selected the books best adapted for his people, and translated them from Latin into Anglo-Saxon. In translating he often added so much of his own, that the Latin text frequently afforded only the subject, on which he wrote most interesting essays, as may be seen in his first work, Boethius de Consolatione Philosophiæ. 1. *Boethius was probably finished about* A. D. 888. In his preface, he thus speaks of his book and of his other occupations:—Ælfrēd, Cyning [MS. Kuning] wæs wealhstōd ðisse bēc, and hie of bēc Lēdene on Englisc wende ... swā swā he hit ða sweotolost and andgitfullīcost gereccan mihte, for ðæm mistlīcum and manigfealdum weoruld bīsgum, ðe hine oft ǣgðer ge on mōde ge on līchoman bīsgodan. Ða bīsgu us sint swīðe earfoþ rīme, ðe on his dagum on ða rīcu becōmon, ðe he underfangen hæfde; and ðeáh, ðā he ðas bōc hæfde geleornode, and of Lǣdene to Engliscum spelle gewende, and geworhte hī eft to leóðe, swā swā heó nū gedōn is *king Alfred was translator of this book, and turned it from book Latin into English ... as he the most plainly and most clearly could explain it, for the various and manifold worldly occupations, which often busied him both in mind and in body. The occupations are to us very difficult to be numbered, which in his days came upon the kingdoms which he had undertaken; and yet, when he had learned this book, and turned it from Latin into the English language, he afterwards put it into verse, as it is now done,* Bt. prooem; Fox viii. 1-10. 2. *Alfred,* having supplied his people with a work on morality in Boethius, *next translates for them the Historia Anglorum of his learned countryman Bede, about* A. D. 890. This was the king's work, for the Church says in Ælfric's Homilies, about A. D. 990,—'Historia Anglorum' ða ðe Ælfrēd cyning of Lēdene on Englisc awende *Historia Anglorum, which king Alfred turned from Latin into English,* Homl. Th. ii. 116, 30-118, 1. 3. *The third book which Alfred translated, about* A. D. 893, was the Compendious History of the World, written in Latin by the Spanish monk Orosius in A. D. 416. There is the best evidence, that the voyages of Ohthere and Wulfstan were written by the king, for we read that,—Ohthere sæde Alfrēde cyninge, ðæt he ealra Norþmanna norþmest būde *Ohthere told king Alfred that he dwelt northmost of all Northmen,* Ors. 1, 1; Bos. 19, 25. Wulfstan also uses the language of personal narrative,—Burgenda land wæs on us bæcbord *we had* [lit. *there was to us;* erat nobis] *the land of the Burgundians on our left,* Ors. 1, 1; Bos. 21, 44. This is the longest and most important specimen of Alfred's own composition. 4. We have undoubted evidence of the date of *Alfred's Anglo-Saxon translation of Gregory's Pastoral Care,* for the king thus speaks of archbishop Plegmund,—Ic hie geliornode æt Plegmunde mīnum ærcebiscepe *I learnt it from Plegmund my archbishop,* Introduction to Gregory's Pastoral, Oxford MS. Hatton 20, fol. 2. Plegmund was raised to the archbishopric in 890: Alfred was engaged with the invasion of Hastings till he was conquered in 897; Alfred, therefore, had only leisure to translate the Pastoral *between the expulsion of Hastings in* 897, *and his own death in* 901. It was certainly translated by Alfred, for he distinctly states,—Ðā ongan ic, ongemang ōðrum mislīcum and manigfealdum bīsgum ðisses kynerīces, ða bōc wendon on Englisc, ðe is genemned on Lǣden Pastoralis, and on Englisc Hierde bōc, hwīlum word be worde, hwīlum andgit of andgite *then began I, among other different and manifold affairs of this kingdom, to turn into English the book, which is called in Latin Pastoralis, and in English Herdman's book, sometimes word for word, and sometimes meaning for meaning,* Oxford MS. Hatton 20, fol. 2.

æl-fremd, æl-fremed; *adj. Strange, foreign;* alienus, alienigena:—Bearn ælfremde, Ps. Spl. 17, 47: 18, 13: 107, 10: 82, 6: Lk. Bos. 17, 18.

Ælfrīc, es; *m.* [ælf, rīc] *Ælfric;* Ælfricus. 1. Ælfric of Canterbury, the grammarian, was of noble birth, supposed to be the son of the earl of Kent. He was a scholar of Athelwold, at Abingdon, about 960. When Athelwold was made bishop of Winchester, he took Ælfric with him and made him a priest of his cathedral. Ælfric left Winchester about 988 for Cerne in Dorsetshire, where an abbey was established by Æthelmær. Ic Ælfrīc, munuc and mæssepreóst ... wearþ asend, on Æðelrēdes dæge cyninges, fram Ælfeáge biscope, Aðelwoldes æftergengan, to sumum mynstre, ðe is Cernel gehaten, þurh Æðelmæres bene ðæs þegenes *I Ælfric, monk and mass-priest ... was sent, in king Æthelred's day, from bishop Ælfeah, Æthelwold's successor, to a minster, which is called Cerne, at the prayer of Æthelmær the thane,* Homl. Th. i. 2, 1-5. He is said to have been bishop of Wilton, and he was elected archbishop of Canterbury. A. D. 995, Hēr Siric arcebisceop forþfērde, and Ælfrīc,

Wiltunscîre bisceop wearþ gecoren on Easterdæi on Ambresbyri, fram Æðelrēde cinge, and fram eallan his witan *in this year*, A. D. 995, *archbishop Sigeric died, and Ælfric, bishop of Wiltshire, was chosen on Easter-day at Amesbury, by king Æthelred, and all his witan*, Chr. 995; Th. 243, 36, col. 2—245, 3, col. 2. *This Ælfric was a very wise man, so that there was no more sagacious man in England. Then went Ælfric to his archiepiscopal see, and when he came thither, he was received by those men in orders, who of all were most distasteful to him, that was, by clerks*, Chr. 995; Th. ii. 106, 20–24. Ælfric speaks strongly against the transubstantiation in the Eucharist, which gave his Homilies so great an importance in the eyes of the English reformers: v. hūsel. He died A. D. 1006, Hēr forþfērde Ælfrîc arcebisceop *in this year, archbishop Ælfric died*, Chr. 1006; Th. 255, 35, col. 2. The preceding is the most probable biography of Ælfric, archbishop of Canterbury. Others have been written in Pref. to Homl. Th. i. pp. v–x: Lchdm. iii. pref. pp. xiv–xxix, *etc.* A list of his numerous books is given in Wright's Biographia Britannia Literaria, A. Sax. Period, pp. 485–494, and in Homl. Th. i. pp. vii–ix. 2. Ælfric Bata was the pupil of the preceding Ælfric, the grammarian. In the title of the MS. in St. John's College, Oxford, we read,—'Hanc sententiam Latini sermonis olim Ælfricus abbas composuit, qui meus fuit magister, sed tamen ego Ælfric Bata multas postea huic addidi appendices,' Wanl. Catal. p. 105, 4–7. It appears that in the time of Lanfranc, when the newest Romish doctrines relating to transubstantiation *etc.* were imposed upon the English Church by the Norman prelates, Ælfric Bata was regarded as an opponent of that doctrine, Wrt. Biog. Brit. A. Sax. p. 497.

ælf-sciéne, -sciéno; *adj. Beautiful, like an elf* or *nymph, of elfin beauty;* formosus ut genius vel nympha:—Mæg ælfsciéno = ides ælfsciéno *O woman of elfin beauty!* Cd. 86; Th. 109, 23; Gen. 1827: Cd. 130; Th. 165, 11; Gen. 2730.

ælf-scînu; *adj. Shining like an elf* or *fairy, elfin-bright, of elfin beauty;* splendidus ut genius vel nympha:—Iudiþ ides ælf-scînu *Judith, the woman of elfin beauty*, Judth. 9; Thw. 21, 11; Jud. 14.

ælf-siden, -sidenn, e; *f. The influence of elves* or *of evil spirits, the nightmare;* impetus castalidum, diaboli incubus:—Ðis is se hālga drænc wið ælfsidene and wið eallum feóndes costungum *this is the holy drink against elfin influence and all temptations of a fiend*, Lacn. 11; Lchdm. iii. 10, 23. Wið ælfsidenne, L. M. 1, 64; Lchdm. ii. 138, 23.

ælf-sogoða, an; *m.* [sogeða *juice*] *A disease ascribed to fairy influence, chiefly by the influence of the* castalides, dūnelfen, *which were considered to possess those who were suffering under the disease, a case identical with being possessed by the devil, as will appear from the forms of prayers appointed for the cure of the disease,*—Deus omnipotens expelle a famulo tuo omnem impetum castalidum; *and further on,*—Expelle diabolum a famulo tuo, L. M. 3, 62; Lchdm. ii. 348, 11. v. ælf, sogeða, sogoða.

ælf-þone, an; *f? Enchanter's nightshade;* circæa lutetiana:—Wið ælfādle nîm ælfþonan nioðowearde *against elf disease take the lower part of enchanter's nightshade*, L. M. 3, 62; Lchdm. ii. 344, 21.

æl-fylc, es; *n.* [æl, folc]. I. *a foreign land;* aliena provincia:—Ðæt hie on ælfylce on Danubie stæðe wîcedon *till they encamped in the foreign land on the banks of the Danube*, Elen. Kmbl. 72; El. 36. II. *foreigners, a foreign army, an enemy;* peregrinus exercitus, hostes:—Ðæt he wið ælfylcum ēðelstōlas healdan cūðe *that he could keep his paternal seats against foreigners*, Beo. Th. 4731; B. 2371. [*Icel.* fylki, *n.*]

æl-grēne *all-green*, Cd. 10; Th. 13, 3; Gen. 197: Cd. 74; Th. 91, 24; Gen. 1517: Bt. Met. Fox 20, 155; Met. 20, 78. v. eal-grēne.

æl-gylden *all-golden*. v. eal-gylden.

ǣ-lîc; *adj. Belonging to law, lawful;* legalis, legitimus, Bd. 1, 27, resp. 8; S. 495, 29. Tyn ǣlîcan word *the ten commandments*, Som.

æling, e; *f. Burning, burning of the mind, ardour;* ardor, flagrantia animi:—Ðȳ læs ælinge ūtadrîfe selflîcne secg *lest burning desires should excite the self-complacent man*, Bt. Met. Fox Introd. 11; Met. Einl. 6.

æling *weariness;* tædium, Bt. pref. Cot; Rawl. viii. notes, line 10.

æll-beorht *all-bright*, Exon. 26 b; Th. 78, 20; Cri. 1277. v. eall-beorht.

æll-mihtig *all-mighty*, Cd. 17; Th. 20, 19; Gen. 311. v. eall-meahtig.

æll-reord *foreign speaking, barbarous*, Bd. 1, 13; S. 481, 44. v. el-reord.

æll-þeódignes, -nys, -ness, e; *f. A going* or *living abroad, a pilgrimage*, Bd. 1, 23; S. 485, 38. v. æl-þeódignes.

ællyfta *the eleventh;* undecimus, Bd. 1, 34; S. 499, 35. v. endlefta.

æl-mǣst *adv. Almost;* fere, Chr. 1091; Th. 359, 12. v. ealmǣst.

Æl-meahtig *Almighty:*—Habbaþ we Fæder æl-meahtigne *we have the Almighty Father*, Exon. 19 a; Th. 47, 22; Cri. 759: Ps. C. 50, 85; Ps. Grn. ii. 278, 85: 50, 97; Ps. Grn. ii. 279, 97. v. eall-mihtig.

Æl-mehtig *Almighty*, Hy. 8, 14. v. eall-mihtig.

ælmes-feoh, *g.* -feós; *n. Alms, alms' money;* pecunia eleemosynæ, L. R. S. 2; Th. i. 432, 13.

ælmes-georn; *adj. Diligent in giving alms, benevolent;* beneficus, liberalis:—Sum biþ ār-fæst and ælmesgeorn *one is honest and diligent in giving alms*, Exon. 79 a; Th. 297, 13; Crä. 67. Sum man Tobias gehāten, swîðe ælmesgeorn *a man, whose name was Tobias, very diligent in giving alms*, Ælfc. T. 21, 24.

ælmes-lond *land given in frankalmoigne*. v. almes-lond.

ÆLMESSE, ælmysse, an; *f.* ALMS, *almsgiving;* eleemosyna:—Ðæt ofer sî and to lāfe sellaþ ælmessan *quod superest date eleemosynam*, Bd. 1, 27; S. 489, 30. Hwæt is us to sprecanne hū hî heora ælmessan dǣle *de faciendis portionibus et adimplenda misericordia nobis quid erit loquendum*, 1, 27; S. 489, 25. Ðæt ðîn ælmesse sȳ on dîglum *ut sit eleemosyna tua in abscondito*, Mt. Bos. 6, 4. Sōþlîce ælmessan dō *sic facias eleemosynam*, 6, 3. Ðonne he ælmessan dǣleþ *when he deals alms*, Exon. 62 a; Th. 229, 10; Ph. 453. Syle ælmyssan *give alms*, Cd. 203; Th. 252, 31; Dan. 587. Ælmessan dǣlan *or* syllan *or* dōn *to give* or *distribute alms;* eleemosynam dare, facere, Mt. Bos. 6, 2, 3. [*Scot.* almous: *O. Sax.* alamōsna, *f:* *O. Frs.* ielmisse: *Ger.* almosen, *n:* *M. H. Ger.* almuosen, *n:* *O. H. Ger.* alamuosan, *n:* *Dan.* almisse: *Swed.* almosa: *O. Nrs.* almusa, ölmusa, *f:* *from the Grk.* ἐλεημοσύνη.]

Ælm-hām, es; *m. Elmham, Norfolk*, Kmbl. Cod. Dipl. 759; 59, 17.

Æl-miht; *adj. Almighty;* omnipotens:—Wiston Drihten ælmihtne *they knew the Almighty Lord*, Cd. 182; Th. 228, 1, note a; Dan. 195.

Æl-mihteg *Almighty;* omnipotens:—Ic hæbbe me geleáfan to ðam ælmihtegan Gode *I have confidence in the Almighty God*, Cd. 26; Th. 34, 27; Gen. 544.

Æl-mihtig, -mihti *Almighty:*—Se Ælmihtiga *the Almighty*, Beo. Th. 184; B. 92: Andr. Kmbl. 497; An. 249: Elen. Grm. 1146: Exon. 9 b; Th. 8, 22; Cri. 121: Cd. 191; Th. 239, 10; Dan. 368: Hy. 10, 1: Bt. Met. Fox 9, 97; Met. 9, 49: Menol. Fox 187; Men. 95: Salm. Kmbl. 68; Sal. 34: Ps. Th. 69, 6: Bd. 3, 15; S. 541, 19: Gen. 17, 1: 35, 11: 48, 3: Ex. 6, 3: Job Thw. 167, 27. Ælmihti, Bt. Met. Fox 13, 144; Met. 13, 72: Th. Dipl. 125, 20. Se ælmihtiga God is unasecgendlîc and unbefangenlîc, se ðe ǣghwær is eall, and nāhwar todǣled *the Almighty God is unspeakable and incomprehensible, who is everywhere all, and nowhere divided*, Homl. Th. i. 286, 26. v. eall-mihtig.

æl-myrca, an; *m. All sallow, a black man, an Ethiopian;* omnino fuscus, Æthiops:—On ælmyrcan ēðel-rîce *in the realm of the Ethiopian*, Andr. Kmbl. 863; An. 432.

ælmysse, an; *f. Alms*, Cd. 203; Th. 252, 31; Dan. 587. v. ælmesse.

ǣl-net, es; *n. An eel net;* rete anguillare:—Gesomnedon ða ǣlnet ǣghwonon ðe hî mihton *retibus anguillaribus undique collectis*, Bd. 4, 13; S. 582, 44.

ǣlpig; *adj.* [= ān-lîpig, ān-lēpig, *from* ān *one*, hleáp *a leap*] *Each, single;* unicus:—Ðæt næs ān ǣlpig hîde, ne ān gyrde landes *that there was not one single hide, nor one yard of land*, Chr. 1085; Th. i. 353, 12. [*Laym.* alpi, ælpi *single, only:* Relq. Ant. W. on alpi word *one single word*, ii. 275, 3.]

ælr *an alder-tree;* alnus. v. alr, alor.

æl-reord, æl-reordig *of foreign speech, barbarous;* exterus, barbarus. v. el-reord, el-reordig.

æl-tæw, -teaw, -teow; *comp.* re; *sup.* est; *adj. All good, excellent, entire, sound, healthful, perfect, honest;* omnino bonus, sanus:—Fîndest ðū æltæwe hǣlo *thou shalt find perfect healing*, Herb. 1, 29; Lchdm. i. 80, 7; MS. B. Næfþ nō æltæwne ende *has no good end*, Bt. 5, 2; Fox 10, 29. Full æltæwe geboren *born quite [full] sound* or *healthy*, 38, 5; Fox 206, 22. Oððe ǣnig þing ǣr wǣre oððe æltæwre *if anything were before or more excellent*, Bt. 34, 2; Fox 136, 8. Ealle ða æltæwestan ofslōgen *they slew all the best men*, Ors. 4, 4; Bos. 81, 16. v. eal-teaw.

æl-tæwlîce; *adv. Well, perfectly;* bene. v. æl-tæw, -lîce.

æl-teaw, -teow *All good, sound, perfect;* omnino bonus, sanus:—Fîndest ðū ælteowe [æltæwe MS. B.] hǣlo *thou shalt find perfect healing*, Herb. 1, 29; Lchdm. i. 80, 7: Hy. 2, 13. v. æl-tæw.

æl-þeód, -þiód, e; *f. A foreign nation, foreign people, foreigners:*—Ðonne ða rîcan beóþ oððe on ælþeóde oððe on hiora āgenre gecȳððe *when the rich are among foreigners or in their own country*, Bt. 27, 3; Fox 98, 34. v. el-þeód.

æl-þeódelîce; *adv. Among foreigners, abroad;* peregre:—Swā se man ðe ælþeódelîce fērde *sicut homo qui peregre profectus*, Mk. Jun. 13, 34.

æl-þeódig, æl-þiódig; *adj. Strange, foreign;* exterus, peregrinus, barbarus:—On ælþeódig folc *to a foreign people*, Bt. 27, 3; Fox 98, 22. Ælþeódigra manna gisthūs *foreign men's guest house, an inn*, Wrt. Voc. 58, 51. Ælþeódige men acwealdon *advenam interfecerunt*, Ps. Th. 93, 6. Ne geunret ðū ælþeódige, ge wǣron ælþeódie on Egipta lande *advenam non contristabis, advenæ enim et ipsi in terra Ægypti*, Ex. 22, 21. Ðām ælþeódegan *to the foreigners*, Bt. 27, 3; Fox 100, 2. v. el-þeódig.

æl-þeódiglîce; *adv. In foreign parts, among foreigners;* peregre, Ælfc. Gr. 38; Som. 41, 26–28.

æl-þeódignes, -ness, -nyss, e; *f. A being* or *living abroad, a pilgrimage:*—On stōwe ælþeódignysse mînra *in loco peregrinationis meæ*, Ps. Spl. 118, 54: Gen. 12, 10: Bd. 4, 23; S. 593, 11.

æl-þeódine *foreign, a proselyte*, Mt. Bos. 23, 15; *for* æl-þeódigne, *acc. s. of* æl-þeódig.

æl-þeódung, e; *f. A being or living abroad;* peregrinatio, Bd. 4, 23; S. 593, 15.

æl-þiódig *foreign*, Bt. 39, 2; Fox 212, 17. v. æl-þeódig.

æl-walda *the all-powerful*, Cd. Jun. 6, 10. v. eal-wealda.

æl-wihta; *pl.* I. *strange creatures, monsters;* alieni generis entia, monstra:—Ðæt ðǽr gumena sum ælwihta eard ufan cunnode *that a man from above explored there the dwelling of strange creatures*, Beo. Th. 3004; B. 1500. II. *all created things;* omnia creata:—Helm ælwihta, engla scippend *the protector of all created things, the creator of angels*, Andr. Kmbl. 236; An. 118. v. eall-wihta.

æ-melle; *adj. Unsavoury, without taste;* insipidus, Cot. 116.

æmelnys, æmylnys, -nyss, e; *f. Loathsomeness, weariness, disdain, falsehood, unfaithfulness, false dealing, treason;* fastidium, tædium:—Hneppade sáwle mín for þrece oððe for æmelnysse *dormitavit anima mea præ tædio*, Ps. Lamb. 118, 28.

æ-men; *adj.* [æ *without*, man *man*] *Unmanned, depopulated, desolate;* hominibus nudus, non habitatus:—Stód seó dýgle stów ídel and æmen *the secret spot stood void and desolate*, Exon. 35 a; Th. 115, 9; Gú. 187.

æmete, æmette, æmytte, an; *f. An* EMMET, *ant;* formica:—Æmete *formica*, Wrt. Voc. 23, 78. Æmettan ægru genim *take emmet's eggs*, L. M. 1, 87; Lchdm. ii. 156, 6. Æmytte *formica*, Somn. 108. Níme æmettan *take emmets*, L. M. 3, 34; Lchdm. ii. 328, 7. [æ = a *from, off, away;* mete *meat, food:* Grm. (Gr. ii. 88) thinks it is connected with *O. H. Ger.* emizíc *assiduus;* ameiza *formica: O. Nrs.* ami *labour: A. Sax.* æmettig *otiosus;* æmtegian *vacare.*]

æmet-hwíl, e; *f.* [æmetta *leisure*, hwíl *while, time*] *Leisure, spare-time, respite;* otium, Ælfc. Gr. 8; Som. 8, 1.

æmet-hyll, æmett-hyll, es; *m. An* EMMET-HILL, *ant-hill;* formicetum, Past. 28, 3; Hat. MS. 37 a, 3.

æmetig; *adj. Vacant, empty, barren;* vacuus:—Hit æmetig læg *it lay barren*, Ors. 1, 10; Bos. 34, 16. v. æmtig.

æmetta *rest*, Bt. procem; Fox viii. 13. v. æmta.

æmettig *idle*, Solil. 13. v. æmtig.

æmnitta, an; *m. A balance;* statera. v. emnettan, emnian *to make equal.*

æ-mód; *adj.* [æ *without*, mód *mind*] *Out of mind, mad, dismayed, discouraged;* amens:—Forðam Rómáne wǽron swá æmóde, ðæt hý ne wéndon ðæt hí ða burh bewérian mihton *because the Romans were so out of heart, they thought that they could not guard the city*, Ors. 3, 4; Bos. 56, 12.

æmta, emta, æmetta, an; *m. Quiet, leisure, rest;* quies:—Ic ne æmtan nabbe *I have no leisure*, Bt. 39, 4; Fox 218, 9. Be his æmettan *by his leisure*, Bt. procem; Fox viii. 13.

æmtegian *to be at leisure*, Past. 18, 4; Hat. MS. 26 b, 16. v. æmtian.

æmtian, æmtegian, æmtigean; *p.* ode; *pp.* od *To be at leisure, to be vacant;* otiosum esse:—Æmtigaþ and geseóþ forðan ðe ic eom God *vacate et videte quoniam ego sum Deus*, Ps. Spl. C. 45, 10: Ælfc. Gr. 33; Som. 37, 14.

æmtig, æmteg, emtig, æmetig, emetig, æmettig; *adj. Vacant,* EMPTY, *free, idle;* vacuus, inanis:—Seó eorþe wæs æmtig *terra erat vacua*, Gen. 1, 2. Gefylde sáwle æmtige *satiavit animam inanem*, Ps. Spl. 106, 9: Mt. Bos. 12, 44: Bd. 4, 3; S. 567, 5. Híg synd emtige *they are idle*, Ex. 5, 8. Æmtege wífemen *unmarried women*, Past. 21, 8, Lye. cf. æmete.

æmtigean *to be at leisure*, Ælfc. Gr. 33; Som. 37, 14. v. æmtian.

æ-múða [æ *without*, múða *a mouth*] *cæcum intestinum*, Wrt. Voc. 44, 64.

æmyce, æmyrce; *adj. Excellent, singular;* egregius, Cot. 74.

æmylnys, -nyss, e; *f. Weariness;* tædium, Pref. R. Conc. v. æmelnys.

æmytte *an emmet;* formica, Somn. 108. v. æmete.

ǽn *one;* unus:—Wyrc ðé nú ǽnne arc *now make thee an ark*, Gen. 6, 14: Mt. Bos. 5, 36. v. án.

ænde *and*, L. Wih. 8; Th. i. 38, 16. v. and.

ændemes, ændemest *likewise, equally;* pariter, Bt. 41, 1; Fox 244, 12. v. endemes.

ændian; *p.* ode; *pp.* od *To end;* finire, Solil. 12. v. endian.

ændlefen *eleven;* undecim:—He ætýwde ændlefene *he appeared to the eleven*, Mk. Bos. 16, 14. v. endleofan.

ændlyfta *eleventh*, Bd. 2, 14; S. 517, 23. v. endlyfta.

ǽne; *adv. Once, alone;* semel, solum:—Nú ic ǽne begann to sprecanne to mínum Drihtne *quia semel cœpi, loquar ad Dominum meum*, Gen. 18, 31. Oft, nalles ǽne *often, not once*, Beo. Th. 6030; B. 3019. Ǽne on dæge *once in the day*, Bt. Met. Fox 8, 35; Met. 8, 18. Ic ðé ǽne abealh, éce Drihten *I alone angered thee, eternal Lord*, Cd. 222; Th. 290, 4; Sat. 410. v. áne *once.*

ǽneg, ǽnegu *any*:—Ǽnegu gesceaft *any creature*, Bt. 35, 4; Fox 160, 26: Cd. 26; Th. 34, 17; Gen. 539. v. ǽnig.

ǽn-ette *solitude;* solitudo, Dial. 2, 3. v. án-ád, án-ǽd.

ǽnforléten; *part. Clothed?* amictus? Ps. Spl. T. 103, 2; *amissus?* and not *amictus.* v. ánforlǽten; *pp. of* án-forlǽtan.

ǽnga *Single, sole;* unicus:—Fram ðam ǽngan hláforde *from the sole lord*, Salm. Kmbl. 766; Sal. 382. v. ánga.

ænge; *def.* se ænga; *adj. Narrow, troubled, anxious;* angustus, anxius:—Ðes ænga stede *this narrow place*, Cd. 18; Th. 23, 9; Gen. 356. Is me ænge [MS. ænige] gást innan hreðres *anxiatus est in me spiritus meus*, Ps. Th. 142, 4. v. ange, enge.

ænge; *adv. Narrowly, sadly;* anguste, anxie, triste, Ps. Th. 136, 8.

ængel *an angel*, Ps. Spl. 8, 6: 34, 7. v. engel.

Ǽnglisc *English;* Anglicus:—Hér synd on ðam íglande fíf geþeódu, Ǽnglisc, Brytwylsc, Scottysc, Pihttisc, and Bóclǽden *here are in the island five languages, English, Brito-Welsh, Scottish, Pictish, and Book-Latin*, Chr. Th. 3, 5, col. 1. v. Englisc.

ǽngum, Beo. Th. 952; B. 474, = ǽnigum *to any; dat. of* ǽnig.

ǽnig, ǽneg, áni; *adj.* [ǽn = án *one*, -ig *adj. termination;* ánig, g = y, *Eng.* any] ANY, *any one;* ullus, quisquam, aliquis:—Ðæt ǽnig man ǽnig fæt þurh ðæt templ bǽre *that any man should bear any vessel through the temple*, Mk. Bos. 11, 16. Mæg ǽnig þing gódes beón of Nazareth *a Nazareth potest aliquid boni esse?* Jn. Bos. 1, 46. Ǽniges sceates *of any treasure*, Cd. 25; Th. 32, 15; Gen. 503. Monnes ǽnges *of any man*, Exon. 10 b; Th. 13, 9; Cri. 200. Næs ðǽr ǽnigum gewin *there was no toil for any one*, Andr. Kmbl. 1776; An. 890. Ǽngum ne mæg se cræft losian *the skill may not desert any one*, Bt. Met. Fox 10, 71; Met. 10, 36. DER. nǽnig *none.*

ǽn-íge, ǽn-ígge *one-eyed*:—Gif he hí gedó ǽnígge *if he make them one-eyed*, L. Alf. 20; Wilk. 30, 11: Cot. 179. v. án-eáge.

ǽniht [ǽn = án *one*, -iht *adj. termination*] *Anything;* quicquam:—Ǽniht *quicquam*, Jn. Lind. War. 11, 49. In mec ne hæfeþ ǽniht *in me non habet quicquam*, Jn. Rush. War. 14, 30. v. stániht, -ig, -ihtig.

ǽninga; *adv. Of necessity, by all means*, Bd. 4, 16; S. 584, 32: 5, 19; S. 640, 16: Andr. Kmbl. 439; An. 220. v. áninga.

ǽn-lépnes, ness, e; *f. Solitude, privacy;* solitudo. v. án-lépnes.

ǽn-líc; *adj.* [án *one*, líc *like*] ONLY, *singular, incomparable, excellent, beautiful, elegant;* unicus, egregius, elegans, pulcher:—He hæfde án swíðe ǽnlíc wíf *he had a very excellent wife*, Bt. 35, 6; Fox 166, 30. Ǽnlíces hiwes *of an excellent shape*, Ælfc. T. 33, 15. Ðeáh hió ǽnlícu sý *though she be beautiful*, Beo. Th. 3887; B. 1941. Eal wæs ǽnlícra ðon mæge stefn areccan *all was more excellent than voice can tell*, Exon. 52 a; Th. 181, 17; Gú. 1294. Cynn Fabiane forðan hit ealra Rómána ǽnlícost wæs *because the Fabian family was the highest in rank of all the Romans*, Ors. 2, 4; Bos. 43, 28. v. án-líc.

ǽn-líce; *adv.* ONLY, *singularly, elegantly;* eleganter, Coll. Monast. Th. 35, 37.

ǽn-lípie = ǽn-lípige *singulos*, Ps. Lamb. 7, 12. v. æn-lípig.

ǽn-lípig, -lýpig, -lépig; *adj.* [án *one*, hlíp, hlýp] *Each, every, singular, solitary, private;* singuli, solus:—Þurh ǽnlípige dagas *per singulos dies*, Ps. Spl. 41, 15. Be ǽnlípigum mannum *per singulos viros*, Jos. Grn. 7, 14: C. R. Ben. 22. v. án-lípig.

ǽnne *one;* unum:—Ðú ne miht ǽnne locc gedón hwítne *non potes unum capillum album facere*, Mt. Bos. 5, 36; *acc. of* ǽn = án, *q. v.*

æ-not; *adj.* [æ *without*, not *use*] *Useless, of no use, unprofitable;* inutilis:—Ðæt hit ænote weorþe *that it be useless*, L. Eth. vi. 34; Th. i. 324, 7.

a-eóde *happened;* evenit:—Swá hit sóþlíce aeóde *so it truly happened*, H. de visione Isaiæ; *p. of* a-gán.

æpel-sceal, -scel, e; *f. An apple-shale* or *film about the kernels* or *pips;* pomi scheda, Cot. 43.

æpel-tre *an apple-tree;* malus, Wrt. Voc. 79, 79. v. æppel-treów.

æplian; *p.* ede; *pp.* ed *To make into the form of apples*, Elen. Kmbl. 2517; El. 1260. v. æpplian.

ÆPPEL, æpl, appel, apl, eapl, es; *m: nom. acc. pl. m.* æpplas; *nom. acc. pl. n.* æppla. I. *an* APPLE, *fruit generally*, Ors. Eng. 1. 3; Bos. 63, note 1; malum, pomum:—Æples gelícnes *likeness of an apple*, Exon. 59 a; Th. 213, 26; Ph. 230. Æppel unsǽlga, deáþ-beámes ofet *the unblest apple, fruit of the tree of death*, Cd. 30; Th. 40, 10; Gen. 637. Ða reádan appla *the red apples;* mala Punica, Past. 15, 5; MS. Hat. 19 b, 28. Nǽnig móste heora hrórra hrím æpla gedígean *none of their hardy fruits could withstand the frost;* occidit moros in pruina, Ps. Th. 77, 47. Genim brembel-æppel *take a bramble-fruit*, i. e. *a blackberry*, L. M. 1, 64; Lchdm. ii. 138, 27. II. *what is round as an apple, the apple of the eye, a ball, bolus, pill;* quidvis globosum, pupilla, globus, bolus, pilula:—On ðæs siweníngean eágum beóþ ða æpplas hále, ac ða brǽwas greátigaþ *in lippi oculis pupillæ sanæ sunt, sed palpebræ grossescunt*, Past. 11, 4; MS. Hat. 15 a, 18. Hí scilde swá geornlíce swá swá man déþ ðone æpl on his eágan *he protected them as carefully as a man does the apple of his eye*, Bt. 39, 10; Fox 228, 13. Írenum aplum *with iron balls*, Salm. Kmbl. 56; Sal. 28. [*Orm.* appell: *R. Glouc.* appel: *Gow.* apple: *O. Frs.* appel, *m. malum, pomum: N. Dut. L. Ger.* appel, *m: Ger. M. H. Ger.* apfel, *m: O. H. Ger.* aphul, aphol; *m: Dan.* æble, *n: Swed.* æple, *n: O. Nrs.* epli, *n: Wel.* aval: *Ir.* abhall, ubhall: *Gael.* abhal, ubhal: *Manx* ooyl: *Corn. Arm.* aval: *Lith.* obolys: *O. Slav.* jabluko.] DER. æppel-bǽre, -bearo, -cyrnel, -fealu, -hús, -leáf, -sceal, -screáda, -þorn, -treów, -tún, -wín: brembel-æppel, eág-, eorþ-, fíc-, finger-, palm-, wudu-.

æppel-bǽre; *adj. Apple-bearing, fruit-bearing;* pomifer:—Æppelbǽre treów *lignum pomiferum*, Gen. 1, 11: Hexam. 6; Norm. 12, 5.

æppel-bearo, -bearu; *g.* -bearwes; *d.* -bearwe; *acc.* -bearo; *pl. nom. acc.* -was; *g.* -wa; *d.* -wum; *m. An orchard;* pomarium, Ps. Th. 78, 2.

æppel-cyrnel, es; *n. A pomegranate;* malogranatum, malum Punicum, Cot. 128.

æppelder, æppeldor *an apple-tree.* v. apulder.

æppel-fealu; *g. m. n.* -fealuwes; *adj. Apple-fallow, apple* or *reddish yellow;* flavus ut pomum:—Mearas æppelfealuwe *bay steeds,* lit. *apple-coloured steeds,* Beo. Th. 4336; B. 2165. DER. fealo, fealu, wes; *n.*

æppel-hús, es; *n. An apple-house, a place for fruit generally;* pomarium, Wrt. Voc. 58, 55.

æppel-leáf, es; *n. An apple-leaf.* v. appel-leáf.

æppel-sceal, e; *f. A film about the kernels of an apple.* v. æpel-sceal.

æppel-screáda *Apple-shreds, apple-parings;* pomi præsegmina, quisquiliæ, Wrt. Voc. 22, 13; *nom. pl. of* æppel-screád. v. screád.

æppel-þorn *an apple-thorn, a crab-tree.* v. appel-þorn.

æppel-treów, es; *n. An apple-tree;* malus. v. æpel-tre.

æppel-tún, es; *m. An apple-garden, orchard;* pomarium, Ælfc. Gl. 24? Somn. 299.

æppel-wín, es; *n. Apple-wine, cider;* pomaceum, Cot. 117.

æppled, æpled; *part.* APPLED, *made into the form of apples, made into balls* or *bosses;* in pomorum formam redactus:—Æpplede gold *appled gold,* Exon. 63 a; Th. 232, 14; Ph. 506: 75 b; Th. 283, 30; Jul. 688. Æplede gold, Elen. Kmbl. 2517; El. 1260. v. *pp. of* æpplian.

æpplian, æplian; *p.* ede; *pp.* ed [æppel *an apple*] *To make into the form of apples, to make into balls* or *bosses;* in pomorum formam redigere, globosum facere, Exon. 63 a; Th. 232, 14; Ph. 506: 75 b; Th. 283, 30; Jul. 688: Elen. Kmbl. 2517; El. 1260.

æppuldre, æpuldre, an; *f. An apple-tree;* malus. v. apuldre.

æppuldre-tún, es; *m. An apple-tree inclosure, apple-orchard;* pomarium. v. apulder-tún.

æppyl *an apple,* Ælfc. Gr. 6; Som. 5, 57; MS. C. v. æppel.

æps, æsp, e; *f:* æpse, æspe, an; *f. An asp* or *aspen-tree, a species of poplar;* populus tremula:—Æps *sicomorus,* vel *celsa,* Wrt. Voc. 33, 27: Cot. 165. Ním æps-rinde *take asp-rind,* L. M. 3, 39; Lchdm. ii. 332, 7. Genim æpsan *take asp-tree,* 1, 36; Lchdm. ii. 86, 6. [*Chauc.* aspe: *Prompt. parv.* aspe, espe: *O. Frs.* espe, *f: Ger.* espe, *f. populus tremula: M. H. Ger.* aspe, *f: O. H. Ger.* aspa, *f: O. Nrs.* espi, *n.*]

æpsenys, -nyss, e; *f. Disgrace, dishonour, shame;* dedecus, Scint. 56.

æps-rind, e; *f. Asp-rind;* populi tremulæ cortex, L. M. 3, 39; Lchdm. ii. 332, 7. DER. æps.

ær, es; *m.* [ær = ear, *q. v.*] *Ocean; pl. The waves of the ocean:*—Ofer æra gebland *over the mingling of the waves,* Chr. 937; Th. i. 202, 38, col. 1. v. ear, ear-gebland.

ǣr, es; *n. Brass;* æs:—Siððan folca bearn ǣres [MS. ǣrest] cúðon and ísernes *since then the sons of men have known brass and iron,* Cd. 52; Th. 66, 22; Gen. 1088: Wrt. Voc. 8, 27. v. ár.

ǣr; *comp. m.* ǣra, ǣrra; *f. n.* ǣre, ǣrre; *sup.* ǣrest; *adj. Early, former, preceding, ancient;* prior, præcedens, antiquus:—On ǣrne mergen *in early morning;* primo mane, Mt. Bos. 20, 1: Mk. Bos. 16, 9: Jn. Bos. 21, 4: Ps. Spl. 5, 3, 4. Fram ǣrne mergen óþ ǣfen *from early morning till evening,* Bd. 2, 14; S. 518, 8. Swá he wæs gyrstan dæg and ǣran dæg *sicut erat heri et nudius tertius,* Gen. 31, 5. Ðæs ǣran tácnes *prioris signi,* Ex. 4, 8. Forlýst he his ǣrran gód *he loses his former good,* Bt. 35, 6; Fox 170, 22. Of deáþe woruld awehte in ðæt ǣrre líf *awoke the world from death into the former life,* Elen. Kmbl. 609; El. 305: Exon. 113 b; Th. 436, 11; Rä. 54, 12. On ðysse ǣrran béc *præcedente libro,* Bd. 4, 1; S. 563, 18. Ǣrran dagas *dies antiqui,* Ps. Th. 142, 5: Beo. Th. 1819; B. 907. Weorpe ǣrest stán *primus lapidem mittat,* Jn. Bos. 8, 7. Se hér-búendra hearpan ǣrest hlyn awehte *who first of dwellers here awoke the sound of the harp,* Cd. 52; Th. 66, 5; Gen. 1079. Se ǣresta wæs Enos háten *the first was called Enos,* 50; Th. 64, 24; Gen. 1055. Wæs seó ǣreste costung ofercumen *the first temptation was overcome,* Exon. 39 a; Th. 128, 22; Gú. 408. In ða ǣrestan ældu *in the first age,* 34 a; Th. 108, 29; Gú. 80. Ða ǣrestan ælda cynnes *the first of the race of men,* 47 a; Th. 160, 23; Gú. 948. Ðú eall oncneówe, ða ǣrestan eác ða néhstan *tu cognovisti omnia, antiqua et novissima,* Ps. Th. 138, 3. Æt ǣrestan *at the first;* primo, L. Alf. pol. 1; Th. i. 60, 2: Exon. 19 a; Th. 49, 15; Cri. 786. DER. ǣr-ádl, -cwide, -dǣd, -dæg, -deáþ, -fæder, -gestreón, -geweorc, -gewinn, -gewyrht, -ing, -morgen, -mergen, -sceaft, -wéla, -woruld.

ǣr, eár, ér; *sup.* ǣrost, ǣrest, ǣrst; *adv.* ERE, *before, sooner, earlier, formerly, already, some time ago, lately, just now, till, until;* antea, prius, mane, mature, dudum:—Gang ǣr *vade prius,* Mt. Bos. 5, 24. He wæs ǣr ðonne ic *ille erat prius quam ego,* Jn. Bos. 1, 15, 30. Ǣr on morgen *early in the morning,* Cd. 224; Th. 297, 10; Sat. 515: Ps. Th. 18, 5: Ex. 12, 22. Nóht micle ǣr *non multo ante,* Bd. 4, 23; S. 593, 21. Hwéne ǣr *scarcely before, just before,* Bt. 23; Fox 78, 25. Swýðe ǣr *very early;* valde mane, Mk. Bos. 16, 2: 1, 35. Tó ǣr *too soon,* Exon. 45 a; Th. 152, 30; Gú. 816. Hwonne ǣr *how soon? when?* quando? Ps. Th. 40, 5. Ǣrost *first,* Gen. 19, 33. Swá hit engel gecwæþ ǣrest on Ebresc *as the angel said it first in Hebrew,* Exon. 9 b; Th. 9, 11; Cri. 133: 88 b; Th. 333, 15; Gn. Ex. 4. Him cenned wearþ Cainan ǣrest *to him was born Cainan first,* Cd. 57; Th. 70, 7; Gen. 1149. Mon wæs to Godes anlícnesse ǣrest gesceapen *man was at first shapen to God's image,* 75; Th. 92, 16; Gen. 1529. Ðá ic hér ǣrest com *when I first came here,* 129; Th. 164, 8; Gen. 2711: Beo. Th. 1236; B. 616. [*Laym.* ær, ære, ear: *Orm.* ær: *R. Glouc.* er: *Wyc. Chauc. Piers* er: *T. More* ere: *O. Sax.* ér *prius, antea: O. Frs.* ér: *Ger.* eher *prius, antea: O. H. Ger.* ér, ǣr *antea, dudum, prius, quondam: Goth.* air *diluculo, mane: O. Nrs.* ár *olim, mane.*] DER. ǣr-boren, -gedón, -genemned, -gód, -gystran-dæg, -líce, -wacol.

ǣr; *conj.* ERE, *before that;* antequam, priusquam:—Ǣr heó wordum cwæþ *ere she said in words,* Cd. 222; Th. 290, 3; Sat. 409. Ǣr hie to setle gong *ere she went to her seat,* Beo. Th. 4043; B. 2019. Ǣr ge furður féran *ere that ye further proceed,* 510; B. 252. Ǣr hie on tú hweorfon *before they departed from one another,* Andr. Kmbl. 2102; An. 1052. [*O. Sax.* ér *priusquam: M. H. Ger. O. H. Ger.* ér *priusquam.*]

ǣr; *prep. d. Before;* ante:—Ǣr his swylt-dæge *before his death-day,* Cd. 62; Th. 74, 12; Gen. 1221. Ǣr dægréde *before dawn,* 223; Th. 294, 4; Sat. 466. Ǣr sunnan his nama sóþfæst standeþ, byþ his setl ǣr swylce ðonne móna *ante solem permanebit nomen ejus, et ante lunam sedes ejus,* Ps. Th. 71, 17. Ǣr ðam flóde *ante diluvium,* Mt. Bos. 24, 38. Ǣr ðé *before thee,* Bt. 41, 3; Fox 246, 26. Ǣr ðam *before that, before;* antequam, Mt. Bos. 6, 8: Exon. 61 a; Th. 224, 22; Ph. 379. Ǣr ðam ðe *before that which, till;* priusquam, Ps. Spl. 38, 18: Mt. Bos. 12, 20. [*O. Sax.* ér *ante: M. H. Ger. O. H. Ger.* ér *ante.*]

ǣra; *adj. Earlier, former;* prior, præcedens:—Ðæs ǣran tácnes *prioris signi,* Ex. 4, 8: Gen. 31, 5. v. ǣr; *adj.*

ǣr-ádl, e; *f. Early-disease;* præmaturus morbus:—Ðá ǣrádl nímeþ *when early disease takes them,* Exon. 89 a; Th. 335, 10; Gn. Ex. 31.

æra gebland [ær = ear *sea*] *The agitation of the sea,* Chr. 937; Th. 202, 38, col. 1; ear in col. 2, and p. 203, 38, col. 1; eár in col. 2. v. ear-gebland.

ǣr-boren; *p. part. First-born;* primogenitus, Cd. 47; Th. 59, 33; Gen. 973.

ærce-biscop, ærce-bisceop, es; *m. An archbishop,* Bd. 2, 3; S. 504, 35. v. arce-bisceop.

ærce-diácon, es; *m. An archdeacon.* v. arce-diácon.

ǣr-cwide, es; *m. Prophecy;* prophetia? nuntii vel doctoris loquela?—He ǣrcwide onwreáh [MS. onwearh] *he revealed the prophecy,* Exon. 83 a; Th. 313, 23; Mód. 4.

ǣr-dǣd, e; *f. Former conduct, a past deed;* ante-actum:—Wyt witodlíce be uncer ǣr-dǣdum onfóþ *nos duo quidem juste, nam digna factis recipimus,* Lk. Bos. 23, 41: Bd. 1, 6; S. 476, 24, note.

ǣr-dæg, es; *m.* I. *early day, early morn;* matutinum, mane, prima lux:—Mid ǣrdæge *at early day,* Andr. Kmbl. 440; An. 220: 3048; An. 1527: Cd. 121; Th. 155, 19; Gen. 2575. On uhtan mid ǣrdæge *in the morning at early day,* Beo. Th. 253; B. 126. To ðam ǣrdæge *on that morn,* Cd. 153; Th. 190, 12; Exod. 198. II. *in pl. Early days, former days;* dies prisci:—On ǣrdagum *in former days,* Cd. 119; Th. 153, 23; Gen. 2543: Exon. 9 a; Th. 6, 4; Cri. 79. [*O. Sax.* an ērdagun *priscis diebus: O. Nrs.* í árdaga *primis temporibus, olim.*]

ǣr-deáþ, es; *m. Early death;* mors immatura:—Regnþeófas dǣlaþ yldo, oððe ǣr-deáþ *the great thieves find age, or early death,* Cd. 169; Th. 212, 14; Exod. 539.

ærdian, ærdyan *to inhabit* [ærd = eard *earth, dwelling*]:—Ærdydon *habitabant,* Bd. 2, 9; S. 510, 15. v. eardian.

ærdon = ærndon? *from* ærnan; *þ.* de *To run, run away;* currere:—He gehleóp and his bróðru mid him begen ærdon *he fled and both hi[s] brothers ran away with him,* Byrht. Th. 137, 25; By. 191.

ærdung, e; *f.* [eard *a dwelling*] *A tabernacle,* Ps. Spl. T. 18, 5. eardung.

æ-réfnan *to bear,* Ps. Spl. T. 24, 5. v. a-rǣfnan.

ǣren, ǣryn, ǣrn; *adj. Made of b[r]ass brazen;* æneus:—Wirc ǣrenan næddran *fac serpentum æneum,* Num. 21, 8. Ǣrnum be[mum] *with brazen trumps,* Cd. 154; Th. 191, 18; Exod. 216: Ors. 2, 8; 52, 16: Ælfc. Gr. 5; Som. 4, 60.

ǣren-byt, -bytt, e; *f.* [byt *a butt, vessel*] *A brass pan* or *vesse[l]* ticula, Wrt. Voc. 25, 17.

ǣrend, ǣrende, ǣrynd, es; *n: pl. nom. acc.* ǣrendu, ǣrendo *An [errand,] a message, an embassy, news, tidings, an answer, business, ca[re;] [nun]tium, mandatum, negotium, cura:*—Ne mæg ðæs ǣrendes yldin[g] *there may not be a delay of this errand,* Andr. Kmbl. 429; He his hláfordes ǣrende secgan sceolde *he should tell his lord'[s]* Bd. 2, 9; S. 511, 19. Hí hæfdon nyt ǣrend *they had [a] errand,* 5, 10; S. 624, 21: 3, 6; S. 528, 17: L. C. S. 76; 5. He sent on his ǣrenda *he sends on his errands,* Bt. 39, 1 25. Híg lægdon ǣrende *they imposed an errand,* Chr. 10[..] 25, col. 2. He aboden hæfde Godes ǣrendu *he had an[..] messages,* Exon. 43 a; Th. 145, 17; Gú. 696: 51 b; Th 1270. Hí lufedon Godes ǣrendo *they loved God's err[ands]* 111, 27; Gú. 133. [*Laym.* arend, erend, *as in* arend-r[..]

Orm. ernde: *R. Glouc.* ernde, erinde: *O. Sax.* ārundi, *n. message: M. H. Ger.* ārant, ērende, *m. message: O. H. Ger.* āranti, āronti, ārunti, *m. nuntius; f. verbum, mandatum: Dan.* ærinde, ærend: *Swed.* ærende: *O. Nrs.* örundi, erendi, *n. negotium: Sansk.* īr *ire, to go.*] v. ār *a messenger.*

ǽren-dæg, es; *m.* [*contracted for* on ærran dæg *on a former day*] *The day before, yesterday;* pridie, Ælfc. Gl. 96; Wrt. Voc. 53, 31. v. dæg.

ǽrend-bōc, e; *f. A letter, message;* epistola, litteræ:—Hī ne mihton arǽdan engles ǽrendbēc *they might not interpret the angels' messages,* Cd. 212; Th. 261, 32; Dan. 735. v. ǽrend-gewrit.

ǽrend-gāst, es; *m. A spiritual messenger, an angel;* nuntius spiritus, angelus:—Godes ǽrendgāst *God's spiritual messenger,* Cd. 104; Th. 138, 23; Gen. 2296.

ǽrend-gewrit, ǽrend-writ, es; *n. A message* or *report in writing, a letter, an epistle, letters mandatory, a brief writing, short notes, a summary;* epistola:—Hī sendon ǽrendgewrit *mittunt epistolam,* Bd. 1, 13; S. 481, 41. On forþgeonge ðæs ǽrendgewrites *in processu epistolæ,* 1, 13; S. 481, 43: Bt. Met. Fox 1, 125; Met. 1, 63. Ǽrend-gewrit *epistola* vel *pictacium,* Wrt. Voc. 46, 64: 61, 21. Þurh his ǽrendgewritu *by his letters,* Bd. pref; S. 472, 22.

ǽrendian; *p.* ede; *pp.* ed *To go on an errand, to carry news, tidings,* or *a message, to intercede, to treat for anything, to plead the cause;* nuntium ferre, mandatum deferre, intercedere, annuntiare:—He mæg unc ǽrendian *he may bear our messages,* Cd. 32; Th. 41, 31; Gen. 665. Ða ǽrendracan, ðe his cwale ǽrndedon [Whel. ǽrenddedon] *the messengers, who had treated for his death,* Bd. 2, 12; S. 515, 4.

ǽrend-raca, ǽrend-wreca, an; *m.* [ǽrend *an errand;* raca, wreca *from* reccan *to tell,* wrecan *to utter*] *A messenger, ambassador, an apostle, angel;* nuntius, apostolus, angelus:—Se ǽrendraca nys mǽrra ðonne se ðe hine sende *non est apostolus major eo qui misit eum,* Jn. Bos. 13, 16. Sende he ǽrendracan *misit legatarios,* Bd. 5, 21; S. 642, 34. Gabriēl Godes ǽrendraca *Gabriel God's angel,* Hy. 10, 12. Ǽrendraca, Bd. 2, 9; S. 510, 27: 2, 12; S. 513, 8; 515, 3: 1, 12; S. 480, 25. Ǽrendraca *an apostle,* Wrt. Voc. 42, 1. Ǽrendraca unnytnesse *a tale-bearer,* Cot. 139. Gesibbe ǽrendracan *messengers of peace;* caduceatores vel pacifici, Wrt. Voc. 36, 6.

ǽrendran *messengers;* nuntii:—Æðele ǽrendran andswarodon [*Grn.* ǽrendracan] *the noble messengers answered,* Cd. 111; Th. 147, 4; Gen. 2434.

ǽrend-secg, es; *m. An errand-deliverer, a messenger;* legatus, nuntius:—Ic, on his gearwan, geseó ðæt he is ǽrend-secg uncres Hearran *I, by his habit, see that he is the messenger of our Lord,* Cd. 30; Th. 41, 17; Gen. 658.

ǽrend-secgan *to deliver a message;* nuntium deferre. v. secgan.

ǽrend-spræc, e; *f. A verbal message;* nuntiatio:—Ǽrendspræce abeódan *to announce a verbal message,* Exon. 123 a; Th. 472, 13; Rä. 61, 15.

ǽrendung, e; *f. A command;* mandatum, C. R. Ben. 38.

ǽrend-wreca, an; *m. A messenger, ambassador;* nuntius, legatus:—Hī onsendon ǽrendwrecan *miserunt nuntios,* Bd. 1, 12; S. 480, 25. He sende ǽrendwrecan in Gallia rīce *he sent ambassadors into the kingdom of the Gauls,* 2, 6; S. 508, 33. v. ǽrendraca.

ǽrend-writ, es; *n. A letter;* epistola, Bd. 5, 21; S. 642, 34, note. v. ǽrend-gewrit.

ǽren-geát, *for* earn-gēt *a goat-eagle;* harpe = ἅρπη, Ælfc. Gl. 17; Wrt. Voc. 21, 62. v. earn-geát.

ǽrer; *adv. Before:*—Ǽrer hit gewyrþe *before it comes to pass,* Bt. 41, 2; Fox 244, note 8. v. ǽror.

æ-rest, es; *m:* e; *f. The resurrection:*—On līfes æreste *in resurrectionem vitæ,* Jn. Bos. 5, 29: Andr. Grm. 780: Exon. 37 b; Th. 122, 29; Gū. 313. v. æ-rist.

ǽrest; *adj. First,* ERST; primus:—Weorpe ǽrest stān *primus lapidem mittat,* Jn. Bos. 8, 7: Cd. 52; Th. 66, 5; Gen. 1079. v. ǽr; *adj.*

ǽrest; *adv. First, at first;* primum, primo:—Him cenned wearþ Caīnan ǽrest *to him was born Cainan first,* Cd. 57; Th. 70, 7; Gen. 1149: 75; Th. 92, 16; Gen. 1529. v. ǽr.

ǽr-fæder; *indecl. in sing. but sometimes gen.* -fæderes *and dat.* -fædere *are found; pl. nom. acc.* -fæderas; *gen.* a; *dat.* um; *m. A forefather, father;* propator, pater, Beo. Th. 5238; B. 2622.

ǽr-fæst; *adj. Honourable, good, gracious, merciful,* Judth. 11; Thw. 24, 15; Jud. 190. v. ār-fæst.

ǽr-fæstnys, -nyss, e; *f. Honesty, goodness, piety;* pietas:—Aidanus wæs mycelre ǽrfæstnysse and gemetfæstnysse mon *Aidan was a man of much piety and moderation,* Bd. 3, 3; S. 525, 31. v. ār-fæstnes.

ærfe *an inheritance,* Heming, pp. 104, 105. v. yrfe.

ǽr-geára; *adv. Heretofore, of old;* olim, Salm. Kmbl. 860; Sal. 429: Bt. Met. Fox 20, 104; Met. 20, 52. v. geára.

ǽr-geblond *the sea agitation.* v. ǽra gebland, ear-gebland.

ǽr-gedōn; *adj. Done before;* anteactus, prior:—Wæs seó ēhtnysse unmétre and singalre eallum ðām ǽrgedōnum *quæ persecutio omnibus fere anteactis diuturnior atque immanior fuit,* Bd. 1, 6; S. 476, 24: 1, 12; S. 481, 25.

ǽr-genemned; *pp. Before-named;* prænominatus. v. ge-nemnan.

ǽr-gescod; *pp. Brass-shod, shod with brass;* ære calceatus:—Bill ǽrgescod *a brass-shod bill,* Beo. Th. 5548; B. 2777.

ǽr-gestreón, es; *n. Ancient treasure;* thesaurus antiquitus repositus:—Ðǽr wæs fela in ðam eorþ [-scræfe] ǽrgestreóna *there were many ancient treasures in that earth-cave,* Beo. Th. 4457; B. 2232: 3518; B. 1757: Exon. 22 b; Th. 62, 5; Cri. 997: Cd. 98; Th. 129, 22; Gen. 2147.

ǽr-geweorc, es; *n. An ancient work;* antiquum opus:—Enta ǽrgeweorc *the ancient work of giants,* Beo. Th. 3362; B. 1679: Andr. Kmbl. 2471; An. 1237.

ǽr-gewinn, es; *n. An ancient struggle, former agony;* antiquum certamen, pristina agonia:—Earmra ǽrgewinn *the former agony of the wretched ones,* Rood Kmbl. 37; Kr. 19.

ǽr-gewyrht, es; *n. A former work, a deed of old;* opus pristinum, facinus olim commissum:—Ða byre siððan grimme onguldon gafulrǽdenne þurh ǽrgewyrht *the children since have bitterly paid the tax through the deed of old,* Exon. 47 a; Th. 161, 17; Gū. 960: Elen. Kmbl. 2599; El. 1301. *Nom. pl.* ærgewyrhtu, Exon. 26 a; Th. 76, 18; Cri. 1241.

ǽr-glæd; *adj. Brass-bright, gleaming with brazen arms;* armis æneis coruscans, Cd. 158; Th. 196, 17; Exod. 293.

ǽr-gōd; *adj. Good before others, of prime goodness;* præ ceteris bonus:—Æðeling ǽrgōd *a prince good before others,* Beo. Th. 260; B. 130: 2662; B. 1329. Īren ǽrgōd *iron of prime goodness,* 1982; B. 989.

ǽr-gystran-dæg *ere-yesterday, the day before yesterday;* nudius tertius. v. gysternlīc dæg, gyrstan-dæg.

ærian *to plough:*—Hwilc man aþohte ǽrust myd sul to ærienne [MS. æriende] *what man thought first of ploughing with a plough?* Anlct. 113, 27. v. erian.

ǽ-riht, es; *n.* [ǽ *law,* riht *right*] *Law-right, law;* jus legum, jus:—Ða ðe fyrngewritu sēlest cunnen, ǽriht eówer *who the old writings best know, your own law,* Elen. Kmbl. 749; El. 375: 1176; El. 590.

ǽring, e; *f. The early dawn, day-break;* diluculum:—In ǽringe, æfter leóhtes cyme *at early dawn, after light's coming,* Exon. 68 a; Th. 252, 9; Jul. 160: Mk. Lind. War. 1, 35. v. ǽr; *adv.*

ǽ-risc, e; *f.* [eá *running water,* risc *a rush*] *A water-rush, bulrush;* scirpus, Ælfc. Gl. 42; Wrt. Voc. 31, 31. v. eá-risc.

æ-rist, æ-ryst, æ-rest, es; *m:* e; *f. A rising up, the resurrection;* resurrectio:—Drihtnes ærist *the resurrection of the Lord,* Menol. Fox 116; Men. 58. Æfter æriste *after resurrection,* Exon. 64 a; Th. 235, 18; Ph. 559. Ðū mīn setl swylce oncneówe and mīnne ærist æfter gecȳþdest *tu cognovisti sessionem meam et resurrectionem meam,* Ps. Th. 138, 1: Hy. 10, 55. Ærist gefremede *accomplished his resurrection,* Exon. 48 b; Th. 168, 6; Gū. 1073. Ðonne æriste ealle gefremmaþ *when all shall accomplish their resurrection,* 63 a; Th. 231, 26; Ph. 495. [*Goth.* urrists. *f.*]

ǽrist = ǽrest; *adv. First:*—Mec se wong ǽrist cende *the field first brought me forth,* Exon. 109 a; Th. 417, 10; Rä. 36, 2: *sup. of* ǽr; *adv.*

ǽr-lēst, e; *f. Dishonour, impiety, cruelty, a disgraceful deed:*—Hwelce ǽrlēste Nerōn worhte *what disgraceful deeds Nero wrought,* Bt. Met. Fox 9, 2; Met. 9, 1. v. ār-leást.

ǽr-līce, ār-līce; *adv.* [ǽr *ere, before,* līce] EARLY *in the morning;* diluculo, mane, Jn. Lind. War. 8, 2.

ærm; *adj. Poor;* pauper:—On ðære ærman byrig *in that poor city,* Chr. 1011; Th. i. 269, 1, col. 1: 1014; Th. i. 272, note 1, 3. v. earm.

ǽr-margen, es; *m. The early morning, the day-break,* Ps. Surt. 56, 9: 107, 3: 118, 148. v. ǽr-morgen.

ǽr-morgen, -mergen, es; *m. The early morning, day-break;* primum mane, matutinum, diluculum:—On ǽrmorgen *in the early morning,* Bt. Met. Fox 28, 72; Met. 28, 36. Ǽrmorgenes gancg wið æftentīd *exitus matutini et vespere,* Ps. Th. 64, 9. On ǽrmergen *diluculo,* 107, 2: 56, 10: Bd. 1, 34; S. 499, 27. Ǽrmyrgen *mane,* Ælfc. Gl. 94; Wrt. Voc. 53, 2. [*O. Nrs.* ār-morgin.]

ærn, ern, es; *n. A place, secret place, closet, an habitation, a house, cottage;* locus, locus secretior, domus, casa:—Bireþ into his ærne *beareth into his habitation,* L. In. 57; Th. i. 138, 16. [*O. Nrs.* rann, *n.*] DER. bere-ærn [-ern] *a barley place, barn,* blāc-, blæc-, blǽc-, breáw-, carc-, cweart-, cwert-, dōm-, eást-, eorþ-, fold-, gæst-, gest-, gyst-, heal-, hēdd-, holm-, hord-, mæðel-, mēdo-, meðel-, mold-, norþ-, slǽp-, sūþ-, þryþ-, west-, wīn-.

-ærn, -ern, es; *n.* [ærn *a place*] is generally used as a termination, and denotes *a place:* thus, Eorþ-ærn, es; *n. An earth-place* or *house, the grave:*—Open wæs ðæt eorþ-ærn *the grave was open,* Exon. 120 a; Th. 460, 18; Hö. 19: 119 b; Th. 459, 22; Hö. 3; Th. 460, 4; Hö. 12. Dōm-ern *a judgment-place, judgment-hall, court of justice,* Mt. Bos. 27, 27. Hēdd-ern *a heeded-place, store-house, cellar,* Lk. Bos. 12, 24.

-ærn; *adj. termination def.* se -ærna, *m;* -ærne, *f. n.* v. -ern.

ǽrn *brazen*:—Ǽrnum bēmum *with brazen trumpets*, Cd. 154; Th. 191, 18; Exod. 216. v. ǽren.

ærnan; *p.* de; *pp.* ed; *v. intrans. To run*; currere:—Ærnan *to run*, Bd. 5, 6; S. 618, 42: S. 619, 12. Ærnaþ hȳ *they run*, Ors. 1, 1; Bos. 22, 36. DER. ge-ærnan. v. yrnan.

ǽrnddedon = ǽrendedon; *p. of* ǽrendian *To go on an errand*; nuntium ferre, Bd. 2, 12; S. 515, 4.

ǽrne *Early*:—On ǽrne mergen *primo mane*, Mt. Bos. 20, 1; *acc. sing. m. of* ǽr, *adj.*

ærne-weg, es; *m.* [ærnan *to run*, weg *a way*] *A running-way, a way fit for running on, a broad road*; via cursui apta, platea:—Æt sumes ærneweges ende *at the end of some course*, Bt. 37, 2; Fox 188, 9. Gescroepe ærneweg *via apta cursui equorum*, Bd. 5, 6; S. 618, 41.

ærnian *to earn*. v. ge-ærnian.

ærning, e; *f. A running, riding*; cursus, equitatio:—Ða ðe hiora ærninge trēwaþ *those who trust in their running*, Bt. 37, 2; Fox 188, 10: Bd. 5, 6; S. 619, 15.

ærnung, e; *f. An* EARNING, *stipend, hire, wages*; merces. v. earnung.

ǽron; *adv. Before*; antea:—Ic hyt ǽron nyste *I knew it not before*, Nicod. 12; Thw. 6, 22. v. ǽr; *adv.*

ǽror, ǽrror; *prep. dat. Before*; ante, priusquam:—Næs ǽror ðē [MS. aworþe] ǽnegu gesceaft *there was not before thee any creature*, Bt. Met. Fox 20, 81; Met. 20, 41.

ǽror, ǽrror, ǽrur, ǽrer; *adv. Before, formerly*; antea, prius:—Weras on wonge wibed setton, neáh ðam ðe Abraham ǽror rǽrde *the men placed an altar in the plain, near that which Abraham had reared before*, Cd. 90; Th. 113, 7; Gen. 1883. Se ðe fela ǽror fyrena gefremede *he who before had committed many crimes*, Beo. Th. 1623; B. 809. Nemne we ǽror mǽgen fāne gefyllan *unless we before may fell the foe*, 5302; B. 2654. Ðæt hió eft cume, ðǽr hió ǽror wæs *that it again comes where it was before*, Bt. Met. Fox 13, 152; Met. 13, 76. Ǽror, on his līfdagum *before, in the days of his life*, 26, 174; Met. 26, 87: Exon. 35 b; Th. 114, 32; Gū. 181: Ps. Th. 77, 3: 91, 8: 134, 11: 135, 21: 145, 4: Menol. Fox 330; Men. 166. v. ǽr; *adv.*

ǽrost; *adv. First*, Byrht. Th. 135, 27; By. 124: Gen. 19, 33. v. ǽr.

ǽrra, ǽrre; *adj. Former, earlier*, Exon. 113 b; Th. 436, 11; Rä. 54, 12: Menol. Fox 213; Men. 108: Elen. Kmbl. 609; El. 305. v. ǽra.

ǽrra geóla *the ere or former Yule month, December*, Menol. Fox 439; Men. 221. v. geóla.

ǽrra līða *the ere or former Litha, June*, Menol. Fox 213; Men. 108. v. līða.

ǽrror; *adv. Before, formerly*:—We iú in heofonum hæfdon ǽrror wlite and weorþmynt *we once in heaven had formerly beauty and dignity*, Cd. 216; Th. 274, 9; Sat. 151: 220; Th. 283, 4; Sat. 299. v. ǽror; *adv.*

ǽrror; *prep. dat. Before*; ante:—Cymeþ eástan up ǽrror [MS. æst ror] sunnan, and eft æfter sunnan on setl glīdeþ *comes up from the east before the sun, and again after the sun glides to his seat*, Bt. Met. Fox 29, 52; Met. 29, 26. v. ǽror.

ærs *The buttocks, the hind part*; anus, podex:—Open-ærs *a medlar*, Wrt. Voc. 32, 50; Som. 64, 116. v. ears.

ǽr-sceaft, e; *f. An old creation, an ancient work*; pristina creatio, priscum opus, Exon. 124 a; Th. 477, 1; Ruin. 16.

ærsc-hen *a quail*, Ælfc. Gl. 38; Wrt. Voc. 29, 42. v. ersc-hen.

ǽrst *first*; primo, Homl. in nat. Innoc. p. 36, = ǽrost. v. ǽr; *adv.*

ǽr-ðam, ǽr-ðon *before that*, Mt. Bos. 6, 8: Exon. 61 a; Th. 224, 22; Ph. 379. v. ǽr; *prep.*

ǽr-ðam-ðe *before that which, till*, Mt. Bos. 12, 20. v. ǽr; *prep.*

ǽrur; *adv. Before*; antea:—Swā he him ǽrur, hēr on ðyssum līfe, ge-earnaþ *as he for himself before, here in this life, earneth*, Rood Kmbl. 214; Kr. 108: Ps. Th. 115, 3. v. ǽror.

ǽr-wacol; *adj. Early awake*; diluculo vigil:—For hwī eart ðū ðus ǽrwacol *why art thou thus early awake?* Apol. Th. 19, 5.

ǽr-wēla, an; *m.* [ǽr *ere, before*, wēla *wealth*] *Ancient wealth*; divitiæ antiquitus accumulatæ, Beo. Th. 5488; B. 2747.

ǽr-woruld, e; *f. The former world*; pristinus mundus:—Ðonne weorþeþ sunne sweart gewended, on blōdes hiw, seó ðe beorhte scān ofer ǽrworuld *then the sun shall be turned swart, to hue of blood, which shone brightly over the former world*, Exon. 21 b; Th. 58, 17; Cri. 937.

ǽryn *brazen*; æreus:—Ðū gesettest swā swā bogan bræsenne [ǽrynne, Spl. C.] earmas mīne *posuisti ut arcum æreum brachia mea*, Ps. Lamb. 17, 35: Ps. Spl. C. 106, 16. v. ǽren.

ǽrynde, es; *m. An interpreter*; interpres:—Ðæra byrla ealdor forgeat Iosepes ǽrynde *prepositus pincernarum oblitus est Josephi interpretis sui*, Gen. 40, 23.

ǽrynd-writ *a letter*, Lye. v. ǽrend-gewrit.

ǽryr; *adv. Before*; prius, C. Jn. 1, 30, Lye. v. ǽror.

æ-ryst, es; *m*: e; *f. The resurrection*:—Ða secgeaþ ðæt nān æryst ne sȳ *qui dicunt non esse resurrectionem*, Mt. Bos. 22, 23: 27, 53. v. æ-rist.

ǽryst; *adv. First*; primum, primo, Ps. Th. 104, 15. v. ǽrest.

ǼS, es; *n. Food, meat, carrion, a dead carcase*; esca, cibus, pabulum, cadaver:—Earn ǽses georn *the eagle eager for food*, Byrht. Th. 134, 60; By. 107. Lǽton him behīndan ðone earn ǽses brūcan *they left behind them the eagle to eat of the carrion*, Chr. 938; Th. i. 207, 30, col. 2; Æðelst. 63. Ǽse wlanc *exulting in carrion*, Beo. Th. 2668; B. 1332: Ps. Th. 146, 10. [*Dut.* aas, *n. esca, cadaver*: *Ger.* aas, *n. esca, cadaver*: *M. H. Ger.* âs, *n*: *O. H. Ger.* âs, *n. esca*: *Dan.* aas, *n*: *Swed.* as, *n.*]

ÆSC; *g.* æsces; *pl. nom. acc.* æscas, ascas; *g.* æsca, asca; *d.* æscum, ascum; *m.* I. *an ash-tree*; fraxinus excelsior:—On ðone æsc *to the ash-tree*, Cod. Dipl. Apndx. 461; A. D. 956; Kmbl. iii. 450, 3. Æsc *fraxinus*, Ælfc. Gl. 45; Som. 64, 98. II. *the Anglo-Saxon Rune* ᚫ = æ, the name of which letter in Anglo-Saxon is æsc *an ash-tree*, hence this Rune not only stands for the letter æ, but for æsc *an ash-tree*, as,—ᚫ byþ oferheáh, eldum dȳre, stīþ staðule *the ash-tree is over-high, dear to men, firm in its place*, Hick. Thes. vol. i. p. 135; Runic pm. 26; Kmbl. 344, 23. Se torhta æsc *the remarkable Rune* æsc, Exon. 112 a; Th. 429, 24; Rä. 43, 9. III. *an ash-spear, a spear, lance*; hasta fraxinea, hasta:—Byrhtnōþ wānd wācne æsc *Byrhtnoth brandished his slender ashen spear*, Byrht. Th. 132, 68; By. 43: 140, 59; By. 310. Ðe ðē æsca tīr æt gūðe forgeaf *who to thee gave glory of spears in battle*, Cd. 97; Th. 127, 10; Gen. 2108. Asca, *g. pl.* Exon. 78 a; Th. 292, 15; Wand. 99. Æscum *with spears*, Beo. Th. 3548; B. 1772: Andr. Kmbl. 2195; An. 1099. IV. because boats were made of ash,—*a small ship, a skiff, a light vessel to sail* or *row in*; navis, navigium, dromo:—Hēt Ælfrēd cyng timbrian langscipu ongēn ða æscas *king Alfred commanded to build long ships against those ships*, Chr. 897; Th. i. 174, 41. Æsc *dromo*, Wrt. Voc. 63, 34: 56, 24. [*O. H. Ger.* asc, *m*: *O. Nrs.* askr, *m. arbor, fraxinus, vas ligneum, navis, gladius*, Egils.] DER. daroþ-æsc, ceaster-: æsc-rind.

æ-scære; *adj.* [æ = a, scær, *p. of* sceran *to shear, cut*] *Without tonsure, uncut, untrimmed, neglected*; intonsus, incultus, neglectus:—Deóplīc dǽdbōt biþ, ðæt lǽwede man swā æscære beó, ðæt īren ne cume on hǽre, ne on nægle *it is a deep penitence, that a layman be so untrimmed that scissors* [*iron*] *come not on hair, nor on nail*, L. Pen. 10; Th. ii. 280, 20. v. a-scære.

æsc-berend, es; *m.* [æsc *a spear*, berende *bearing*, *part.* from beran *to bear*] *A spear* or *lance-bearer, a soldier*; hastifer:—Eorre æscberend *the fierce spear-bearer*, Andr. Kmbl. 93; An. 47: 2153; An. 1078. Ealde æscberend *the old spear-bearer*, 3072; An. 1539.

æsc-berende; *part. Spear-bearing*; hastam gerens:—Wīgena æscberendra *of warriors bearing spears*, Cd. 94; Th. 123, 7; Gen. 2041.

æsce; *g.* æscean; *f. Ashes*:—Forðon ic anlīc ætt æscean hlāfe *quia cinerem sicut panem manducabam*, Ps. Th. 101, 7: 147, 5. v. asce.

ǽsce, an; *f. Search, inquisition, examination, inquiry, trial of* or *asking after any matter* or *thing*; interrogatio, investigatio, disquisitio:—Hæfdon ealle ða ǽscean *all should have the search*, L. Ath. 5; Th. i. 230, 18.

æsceda, an; *m. A farrago, mixture, perfume*; migma, Wrt. Voc. 38, 53.

æscen *A vessel made of ash-wood, such as a bottle, bucket, pail*, etc; lagena:—Æscen ðe is ōðre namon hrygilebuc gecleopad *an ascen, its other name is called Rigelbuc*, q. *back-bucket*, Heming, p. 393.

æscen; *adj. Ashen, ash, made of ash*; fraxineus. v. æsc, -en.

Æsces dūn, e; *f.* [æsc *ash-tree*, dūn *a hill*] ASHDOWN, *the hill of the ash-tree, on the Ridgeway in Berkshire, where Alfred and his elder brother, king Ethelred, first routed the Danes*; 'dicitur Latine mons fraxini,' Asser:—Hēr gefeaht Æðerēd cyning and Ælfrēd, his brōðor, wið ealne ðone here, on Æsces dūne A. D. 871, *here fought king Æthelred and Alfred, his brother, with all the army* [*of the Danes*], *on Ashdown*, Chr. 871; Th. 139, 5, col. 1.

æsc-here, es; *m. A spear-band, company armed with spears, a ship* or *naval-band*; exercitus hastifer, exercitus navalis, Byrht. Th. 133, 53; By. 69.

æsc-holt, es; *nom. pl.* -holt; *n. Ash-wood, an ash-wood spear*; lignum fraxineum, hasta fraxinea:—Æscholt asceóc *shook his ashen spear*, Byrht. 138, 35; By. 230: Beo. Th. 665; B. 330.

æscian *to ask*; interrogare, Jud. Civ. Lund. v. acsian.

æsc-man, -mann, es; *m. A ship-man, sailor*, and hence *a pirate*; nauta, pirata:—Ǽgþer ge æscmanna ge ōðerra *both of the ship-men and of the others*, Chr. 921; Th. 195, 15: Cot. 155.

æsc-plega, an; *m.* [plega *play*] *The play of spears, war*; hastarum ludus, prœlium:—Æt ðam æscplegan, Judth. 11; Thw. 24, 31; Jud. 217.

æsc-rind, e; *f. Ash-bark*; fraxini cortex:—Nīm æscrinde *take ash-bark*, Lchdm. iii. 14, 1. Wel æscrinde *boil ash-bark*, ii. 78, 5.

æsc-rōf; *adj. Spear-famed, distinguished in battle, illustrious, noble*; hasta clarus, in prœlio strenuus, illustris, nobilis:—Eorlas æscrōfe *illustrious nobles*, Judth. 12; Thw. 26, 20; Jud. 337: Elen. Grm. 276: 202.

æsc-stēde, es; *m. The ash-spear place, place of battle*; hastæ locus, pugnæ locus:—Hī witan fundian æscstēde *they strive to know the battle place*, Exon. 83 b; Th. 314, 20; Mōd. 17.

æsc-þræc; *g.* -þræce; *pl. nom. g. acc.* -þraca; *f. Spear-strength, brunt of spears, a battle*; hastæ vis, hastarum impetus, prœlium:—Ǽt æscþræce, Cd. 98; Th. 130, 2; Gen. 2153.

æsc-þrote, an; *f*: -þrotu, e; *f.* [æsc *ash*, þrote *a throat*] ASH-THROAT, *vervain*; verbenaca, verbena officinalis, Prior, p. 242: vocabularies give the *Lat.* ferula *the fennel-giant*, but verbenaca *vervain* seems more probable from the following quotations,—Herba uermenaca [= uerbenaca, Herb. 4, = verbenaca: *Lat.* = berbena, 67, = verbena, *Lat.*] ðæt is æscþrotu *the herb verbena, that is ash-throat* [=*vervain*], Herb. cont. 4, 1; Lchdm. i. 8, 1. Niðeweardre æscþrotan *of the netherward* [*part of*] *vervain*, L. M. 3, 72; Lchdm. ii. 358, 16. Ním æscþrotan *take vervain*, 1, 88; Lchdm. ii. 156, 22. Æscþrotan, 1, 43; Lchdm. ii. 108, 6. Æscþrote, *nom.* Herb. 4, 1; Lchdm. i. 90, 1. Æscþrotu, L. M. 1, 47; Lchdm. ii. 120, 9: 2, 53; Lchdm. ii. 274, 9. Man æscþrote nemneþ *one nameth it vervain*, Herb. 4, 1; Lchdm. i. 90, 3. Genim æscþrote *take vervain*, 101, 3; Lchdm. i. 216, 11: L. M. 3, 61; Lchdm. ii. 344, 9: Lchdm. iii. 28, 14.

æsc-tír, es; *m. Spear-glory, glory in war;* hastæ gloria, belli gloria, Cd. 95; Th. 124, 27; Gen. 2069.

æsc-wert, e; *f. Ash-wort, vervain;* verbena, Mone C. 3; p. 442, 24.

æsc-wíga, an; *m. A spear-warrior;* bellator hastifer:—Eald æscwíga *an old spear-warrior*, Beo. Th. 4090; B. 2042. Æscwígan, *nom. pl.* Elen. Grm. 260.

æsc-wlanc; *adj. Spear-proud;* hasta superbus, Leo 104.

ÆSP, e; *f*: æspe, an; *f. An* ASP or *aspen-tree;* populus tremula:—Æspan rind *the rind of the asp-tree*, L. M. 1, 47; Lchdm. ii. 116, 1. v. æps.

æspen; *adj.* ASPEN, *belonging to the asp-tree;* populeus. DER. æsp.

ǽ-spring, ǽ-springe, ǽ-sprynge, es; *n.* [*ǽ water*, spring *a spring*] *A water-spring, fountain;* aquæ fons, fons:—Se æðela fugel æt ðam ǽspringe wunaþ *the noble fowl remains at the fountain*, Exon. 57 a; Th. 204, 28; Ph. 104. Ǽspringe útawealleþ of clife *a fountain springs out of a cliff*, Bt. Met. Fox 5, 23; Met. 5, 12. Ealle ǽsprynge *all springs*, Exon. 55 a; Th. 194, 5; Az. 134: 93 b; Th. 351, 8; Sch. 77. v. eá-spring.

æ-springnes, -ness, e; *f.* [aspringan *to fail*] *A failing, fainting;* defectio, Ps. Spl. T. 118, 53. v. a-sprungennes.

ǽstel, es; *m. A tablet, a table for notes, a waxed tablet;* indicatorium, astula, pugillaris. Du Cange says astula = *tabula sectilis*, referring to pugillares, under which he gives the following quotation from Cassander in Liturgicis, p. 53,—'Inter instrumenta sacra numerantur pugillares aurei sive argentei. . . . Propriè pugillares sunt tabulæ, in quibus scribi consuevit, quæ Græcè πινακίδια dicuntur.' In St. Luke i. 63, *αἰτήσας πινακίδιον, postulans pugillarem*, is in the A. Sax. Gospels, gebedenum wex-brede *a waxed tablet being asked for.* William of Malmsbury may have alluded to one of these waxed tablets in Gesta Reg. ii. § 123,—'Cum pugillari aureo in quo est manca auri.' It is most probable then that Alfred's ǽstel consisted of two waxed tablets, joined together by a hinge, and framed or covered with gold to the value of fifty mancuses. When these waxed tablets were closed, being framed or covered with gold, they would have a splendid and costly appearance, worthy the gift of a king:—Ǽstel *indicatorium*, Ælfc. Gr. 8; Som. 7, 63: Cot. 214: Ælfc. Gl. 19? Lye. Ðá ongan ic [Ælfréd cyning] ða bóc wendan on Englisc, ðe is genemned on Lǽden *Pastoralis*, and on Englisc *Hierde-bóc*, hwílum word be worde, hwílum andgit of andgite, swá swá ic hie geliornode æt Plegmunde mínum Ærcebiscepe, and æt Assere mínum Biscepe, and æt Grimbolde mínum Mæsse-Prióste, and æt Iohanne mínum Mæsse-Preóste. Siððan ic hie ða geliornod hæfde, swá swá ic hie forstód, and swá ic hie andgitfullícost areccean meahte, ic hie on Englisc awende, and to ǽlcum Biscep-stóle on mínum Ríce wille áne onsendan, and on ǽlcre biþ án Ǽstel, se biþ on fíftegum Mancessan. Ond ic bebióde, on Godes naman, ðæt nán mon ðone Ǽstel from ðære béc ne dó, ne ða bóc from ðæm Mynstre *then I* [*Alfred king*] *began to translate into English the book, which is called in Latin* Pastoralis, *and in English* Herdsman's book, *sometimes word by word, sometimes meaning for meaning, as I learned it from Plegmund my archbishop, and from Asser my bishop, and from Grimbold my presbyter, and from John my presbyter. After I had then learned it, so that I understood it as well as my understanding would allow me, I translated it into English, and I will send one copy to each bishop's see in my kingdom; and on each one there shall be one tablet, which shall be worth fifty mancuses. And in God's name, I command that no man take the tablet from the book, nor the book from the minster*, Past. Hat. MS. Pref.

æsul, es; *m. An ass;* asinus, Mt. Rush. Kmbl. 21, 2. v. esol.

æ-swáp, es; *n. pl.* æswápa *Sweepings, dust;* peripsema, purgamentum. v. a-swáp.

ǽ-swíc, ǽ-swýc, é-swíc, es; *m.* [*ǽ law*, swíc *an offence*] *An offence, a scandal, stumbling-block, sedition, deceit;* scandalum:—Ne biþ him ǽswíc *non est illis scandalum*, Ps. Th. 118, 165: Ps. Spl. 118, 165: 48, 13: 49, 21, C. To ǽswýce *in scandalum*, Ps. Th. 105, 26.

ǽ-swíca, an; *m*: ǽ-swícend, es; *m. An offender of the law, a deceiver, hypocrite, apostate;* hypocrita, apostata. v. swíca.

ǽ-swícian; *p.* ode; *pp.* od *To offend, to depart from the law, to dissemble;* scandalizare, deficere ab aliquo:—Gyf ðín swýðre eáge ðé ǽswície *si oculus tuus dexter scandalizat te*, Mt. Bos. 5, 29. v. a-swícian?

ǽ-swícung, e; *f. An offence;* scandalum:—Ðú settest ǽswícunge *ponebas scandalum*, Ps. Spl. 49, 21. v. ǽ-swíc.

æ-swind; *adj. Idle;* iners, Cot. 108. v. a-swind.

ǽ-swutol, es; *m.* [*ǽ law*, sweotol *manifest, clear, open*] *One who makes the law clear, a lawyer;* legisperitus. v. sweotol.

ǽ-swýc, es; *m. An offence;* scandalum, Ps. Th. 105, 26. v. ǽ-swíc.

ǽ-syllend, es; *m.* [*ǽ law*, syllende *giving*] *A lawgiver;* legislator, Ps. Spl. 83, 7.

ÆT; *prep.* I. *with the dative;* cum dativo AT, *to, before, next, with, in, for, against;* apud, juxta, prope, ante, ad, in, contra:—Sittende æt tollsceamule *sitting at the seat of custom*, Mt. Bos. 9, 9. Æt fruman worulde *at the beginning of the world*, Exon. 47 a; Th. 161, 7; Gú. 955. Wæs seó treów lufu hát æt heortan *the true love was hot at heart*, 15 b; Th. 34, 8; Cri. 539. Ge ne cómon æt me *ye came not to me*, Mt. Bos. 25, 43. Æt selde *before the throne*, Cd. 228; Th. 306, 12; Sat. 663. Ic áre æt him fínde *I may find honour with them*, Exon. 67 a; Th. 247, 19; Jul. 81. Ic nú æt feáwum wordum secge *I now say in few words*, Bd. 3, 17; S. 545, 14. Is seó bót gelong eal æt ðé ánum *the expiation is all ready with thee alone*, Exon. 10 a; Th. 10, 16; Cri. 153. Ne mihton hí áwiht æt me ǽfre gewyrcean *they might not ever do anything against me*, Ps. Th. 128, 1. Ðe him æt blisse beornas habbaþ *which men have for their merriment*, Exon. 108 b; Th. 414, 4; Rä. 32, 15. 2. because you approach a person or thing when you wish to take something away, as they say in Lancashire, Nottinghamshire, *etc. Take this at me*, i. e. *from me*, hence,—*Of, from;* a, ab, de:—Anýmaþ ðæt púnd æt hym *tollite ab eo talentum*, Mt. Bos. 25, 28. Leorniaþ æt me *learn by coming near me, learn at, of*, or *from me;* discite a me, Mt. Bos. 11, 29. Æt his sylfes múþe *at* or *from his own mouth*, Bd. 3, 27; S. 558, 40. Æt ðam wífe *from the woman*, Cd. 33; Th. 44, 31; Gen. 717. Ic gebád grynna æt Grendle *I endured snares from Grendel*, Beo. Th. 1864; B. 930: Ps. Th. 21, 18. 3. *the names of places are often put in the dat. pl. governed by* æt, the preposition *is then, as in Icelandic, not translated*, and the noun is read as singular:—Ðe mon hǽt æt Hǽðum *which they call Haddeby;* quem vocant Hæthe, Ors. i. 1, § 19; Bos. Eng. 47, note 57. In monasterio, quod situm est in civitate æt Baðum [MS. Bathun], Kmbl. Cod. Dipl. cxciii; vol. i. 237, 1. II. very rarely used *with the accusative;* cum accusativo To, *unto, as far as;* ad, usque ad:—Æt sǽstreámas *ad mare*, Ps. Th. 79, 11. Æt Ác-leá *at Oakley*, Chr. 789; Ing. 79, 14. v. Ác-leá. III. sometimes *æt* is separated from its case:—Ðonne wile Dryhten sylf dǽda gehýran æt ealra monna gehwám *then will the Lord himself hear of the deeds from all sorts of men* [ab omnium hominum quocunque], Exon. 99 b; Th. 372, 15; Seel. 93. [*O. Sax.* at: *O. Frs.* et, it: *O. H. Ger.* az: *Goth.* at: *O. Nrs.* at.]

æt *ate;* comedit:—He æt *he ate*, Gen. 3, 6; *p. of* etan *to eat.*

æt-, prefixed to words, like the *prep.* æt, denotes *at, to*, and *from;* ad-, ab-. v. æt; *prep.* I. 2.

ǽt, es; *m*: ǽt, e; *f.* [æt, *p. of* etan *to eat*]. I. *food;* cibus, esca:—Ǽtes on wénan *in hope of food*, Cd. 151; Th. 188, 9; Exod. 165. He us ǽt giefeþ *he gives us food*, Exon. 16 b; Th. 38, 9; Cri. 604. Oft he him ǽte heóld *he often gave them food*, Exon. 43 a; Th. 146, 12; Gú. 708: Cd. 200; Th. 247, 32; Dan. 506. II. *eating;* esus, manducatio:—Ǽfter ǽte *after eating*, Exon. 61 b; Th. 226, 13; Ph. 405. Hí to ǽte útgewítaþ *ipsi dispergentur ad manducandum*, Ps. Th. 58, 15: Andr. Kmbl. 2148; An. 1075. [*Orm.* aet: *O. Sax.* át, *n*: *O. Frs.* ét, *n*: *O. H. Ger.* áz, *n*: *O. Nrs.* át, *n. esus.*] v. etan.

ǽta, an; *m. An eater;* edax. DER. self-ǽta, *q. v.*

æt-arn *ran away*, Gen. 39, 12; *p. of* æt-irnan.

æt-bær *bore, produced*, Cd. 202; Th. 249, 31; Dan. 538; *p. of* æt-beran.

æt-befón, ic -befó; *subj.* ic, he -befó [æt, be, fón] *To take to, attach;* deprehendere, capere, invenire:—Gif hwá befó ðæt him losod wæs, cenne se ðe he hit ætbefó hwanon hit him cóme *if any one attach that which he had lost, let him with whom he attaches it declare whence it came to him*, L. Eth. ii. 8; Th. i. 288, 15: L. C. S. 23; Th. i. 388, 22. v. be-fón, æt-fón.

æt-beón *To be at* or *present;* adesse:—Ætbeón ðé we biddaþ *adesse te deposcimus*, Hymn Surt. 14, 26.

æt-beran; *p.* -bær, *pl.* -bǽron *To bear* or *carry to, bring forward, produce, bear away* or *forth;* afferre, proferre, efferre:—Hió Beówulfe medo-ful ætbær *she to Beowulf the mead-cup bore*, Beo. Th. 1253; B. 624. He wundor manig fór men ætbær *he many a wonder produced before men*, Cd. 202; Th. 249, 31; Dan. 538. Hí hyne ætbǽron to brimes faroðe *they bore him away to the sea-shore*, Beo. Th. 55; B. 28: 4261; B. 2127: 5222; B. 2614. Ðæt [wǽpen] to beadu-láce ætberan meahte *might bear forth that* [*weapon*] *to the game of war*, 3127; B. 1561.

æt-berstan, ic -berste, he -birsteþ, -byrst; *p.* -bærst, *pl.* -burston; *pp.* -borsten *To break out* or *loose, to escape, get away;* erumpere, evadere:—Ða ætbærst him sum man *evasit homo quidam*, Gen. 14, 13. Ða fíf cyningas ætburston *fugerunt enim quinque reges*, Jos. 10, 16. Ðæt he ðanon ætberste *that he escape thence*, L. C. E. 2; Th. i. 358, 25.

æt-bredan, he ætbryt; *p.* -bræd, *pl.* -brudon; *pp.* -broden, -breden; *v. a. To take away, withdraw, set at liberty, to enlarge, release, rescue;* tollere, eripere:—Se deófol ætbryt ðæt word *diabolus tollit verbum*, Lk. Bos. 8, 12. Ge ætbrudon ðæs ingehýdes cǽge *tulistis clavem scientiæ*, 11, 52. Ðæt ðe he hæfþ him biþ ætbroden *quod habet auferetur ab eo*, Mt. Bos. 13, 12: 21, 43: Ex. 22, 10. Ðe hys wealas him ætbrudon *quem abstulerant servi ejus*, Gen. 21, 25. DER. bredan.

æt-bredendlíc; *adj.* [æt-bredende, *part. of* ætbredan *to take away*]

Taking away; ablativus:—Ætbredendlíc is *ablativus:* mid ðam casu biþ geswutelod swá hwæt swá we ætbredaþ óðrum, oððe swá hwæt swá we underfóþ æt óðrum, oððe hwanon we faraþ,—Fram ðisum menn ic underféng feóh *ab hoc homine pecuniam accepi.* Fram ðisum láreówe ic gehýrde wísdóm *ab hoc magistro audivi sapientiam.* Fram ðære byrig ic rád *ab illa civitate equitavi.* Fram cyninge [MS. kyningce] ic com *a rege veni,—ablative is* ablativus: *with this case is shewn whatsoever we take away from others, or whatsoever we receive from others, or whence we proceed:—From this man I received money. From this teacher I heard wisdom. I rode from that city. I came from the king,* Ælfc. Gr. 7; Som. 6, 27–32.

æt-broden *Taken away;* ablatus:—Him biþ ætbroden *shall be taken away from him,* Mt. Bos. 13, 12: 21, 43; *pp. of* æt-bredan.

æt-bryidan; *p.* ede; *pp.* ed *To take away;* auferre:—Ðæs óðres áþ ðe mon his orf æt-bryideþ *the oath of the other from whom the cattle is taken away,* L. O. 3; Th. i. 178, 16, = æt-bredan. DER. bryidan.

æt-byrst *he will escape;* evadet, Basil. 7; Norm. 5, 12; *fut. of* æt-berstan.

æt-clifian; *p.* ode; *pp.* od; *v. intrans. To cleave to, adhere;* adhærere, Ps. Vos. 101, 6.

æt-dón, ic æt-dó; *p.* -dide; *subj.* ic, ðú, he -dó; *pp.* -dón, -dén *To take away, deprive;* eripere:—Ðæt nán preósta óðrum ne ætdó ǽnig ðara þinga *that no priest deprive another of any of those things,* L. Edg. C. 9; Th. ii. 246, 10.

ǽte, an; *f. pl.* ǽtan; *g.* ǽtena *Oats;* avena sativa, L. M. 1, 35; Lchdm. ii. 84, 5. v. áte.

æt-écan, -ýcan; *p.* -écte; *v. trans.* [æt *to, at,* eácan *to eke*] *To add to, increase;* addere, adjicere:—He ætécte *addidit,* Bd. 3, 27; S. 559, 33: Mt. Rush. Stv. 6, 27.

æt-eglan; *p.* ede; *pp.* ed; *v. intrans. To inflict pain, torment, trouble, grieve;* molestum quid injicere:—Ne mæg him ǽnig fácen feónd æteglan *any deceitful fiend may not inflict grief upon him,* Ps. Th. 88, 19.

æt-eom, -eart, -is, -ys [æt *at,* eom *am*] *I am present;* adsum:—Ðæt ríp æt-is [æt-ys, Jun.] *adest messis,* Mk. Bos. 4, 29. v. wesan *to be.*

æ-teorian; *p.* ode; *pp.* od *To fail, be wanting;* deficere:—Æteorode se heofonlíca mete *the heavenly food [manna] failed,* Jos. 5, 12.

æt-eówedniss, e; *f. A revelation;* revelatio:—To æteówednisse cynna *ad revelationem gentium,* Lk. Rush. War. 2, 32.

æt-eówian, -eówigan; *p.* de, ede; *impert.* -eów; *pp.* ed. I. *v. trans. To shew, display, manifest, declare;* ostendere, manifestare:—Æteów ðínne andwlitan *ostende faciem tuam,* Ps. Th. 79, 4, 7; 84, 6. God æteówde me *Deus ostendit mihi,* Ps. Spl. 58, 11: Mt. Bos. 13, 26. He geseah dríge stówe æteówde *he saw the dry places displayed,* Cd. 8; Th. 10, 31; Gen. 165. II. *v. intrans. To appear;* apparere, manifestari:—Æteówige drígnis *appareat arida,* Gen. 1, 9. Æteów fór Effraim *appare coram Effrem,* Ps. Th. 79, 2. v. eáwan.

æt-eówigendlíce; *adv. Evidently, demonstratively;* demonstrative,—æt-eówigende; *part. of* æt-eówian, -eówigan.

ǽtern *Venomous, poisonous;* venenosus:—Wið ǽlcum ǽternum swile *for every venomous swelling,* L. M. 1, 45; Lchdm. ii. 112, 24. v. ǽtren.

ǽternes, -ness, e; *f. Venomousness, full of poison;* venenositas. v. ǽtern.

æt-ēwung, e; *f. A shewing, manifesting, epiphany;* manifestatio, Wrt. Voc. 16, 49.

æt-fæstan; *p.* -fæste; *pp.* -fæsted; *v. trans.* [æt, fæstan *to fasten*] *To fix, fasten, drive into, afflict with, inflict on;* impingere, infigere:—Hí míne sáwle synne ætfæsten *they inflict sin on my soul,* Ps. Th. 142, 12. He him ætfæste éce edwít *opprobrium sempiternum dedit illis,* 77, 66. Bitere ætfæsted *bitterly afflicted,* 136, 8. Ne mágon we him láþ ætfæstan *we cannot afflict him with pain,* Andr. Kmbl. 2694; An. 1349.

æt-fealh *adhæsit,* Ps. Th. 118, 25; *p. of* æt-felgan.

æt-feallan; *p.* -feól, *pl.* -feóllon; *pp.* -feallen *To fall away;* cadere:—Healf wér ðǽr æt-fealþ *one half of the wer there falls away,* L. O. D. 5; Th. i. 354, 21.

æt-fecgan; *p.* -feah; *v. trans. To seize;* apprehendere:—Me ætfeah fyrhtu helle *fear of hell seized me,* Ps. Th. 114, 3.

æt-fele *Adhesion;* adhæsio?—Mín is ætfele mihtigum Drihtne *mihi autem adhærere Deo,* Ps. Th. 72, 23. v. æt-feolan.

æt-felgan; *p.* -fealh, *pl.* -fulgon; *pp.* -folgen; *v. intrans. To cleave on, adhere, stick to;* adhærere:—Mín sáwul flóre ætfealh *adhæsit pavimento anima mea,* Ps. Th. 118, 25: 118, 31: Beo. Th. 1941; B. 968: Ps. Spl. C. 62, 8.

æt-feng, es; *m. Attaching;* comprehensio:—Be yrfes ætfenge *of attaching cattle,* L. Ath. i. 9; Th. i. 204, 9. DER. æt-fón.

æt-feohtan; *p.* -feaht, *pl.* -fuhton. I. *to fight against, contend;* oppugnare:—Ætfeohtan mid frumgárum *to fight against the patriarchs,* Cd. 97; Th. 127, 25; Gen. 2116. II. *to feel earnestly, grope;* contendere, tentare circum:—Folmum ætfeohtan *with his hands to contend* or *grope,* Exon. 87 b; Th. 328, 15; Vy. 18.

æt-feolan, -fiolan; *p.* -fæl, *pl.* -fǽlon, -félon; *pp.* -folen, -feolen *To adhere, cleave* or *hang on, insist upon, stick to, continue;* insistere, adhærere:—Ætfeole mín tunge fæste gómum *adhæreat lingua mea faucibus meis,* Ps. Th. 136, 5. Is ætfeolen eác mín bán flǽsce mínum *adhæserunt ossa mea carni meæ,* Ps. Th. 101, 4. Ætfélon [MS. ætfelun] *vel* ætclofodon [MS. -fodun] *adhæserunt,* Ps. Surt. 101, 6. Me sóþlíce ætfeolan Gode gód is *mihi autem adhærere Deo bonum est,* 72, 28. Ætfeolan wæccum and gebédum *to continue in watchings and prayers,* Bd. 4, 25; S. 601, 2. DER. felan, feolan.

æt-ferian; *p.* ede; *pp.* ed; *v. trans. To carry out, take away, bear away;* auferre:—Ic ðæt hilt feóndum ætferede *I bore the hilt away from the foes,* Beo. Th. 3342; B. 1669.

æt-fiolan *to stick to, continue;* adhærere. v. æt-feolan.

æt-fleón; *p.* -fleáh, *pl.* -flugon; *pp.* -flogen [æt, fleón *to flee*] *To flee away, escape by flight, eschew;* aufugere:—Ic ána ætfleáh *I alone escaped,* Job Thw. 165, 30. Nán þing ætfleón ne mihte *nothing might remain,* Jos. 10, 35: L. C. S. 78; Th. i. 420, 7.

æt-flówan; *p.* -fleów, *pl.* -fleówon; *pp.* -flówen; *v. intrans. To flow to* or *together, to increase;* affluere:—Gyf wélan ætflówon *si divitiæ affluant,* Ps. Spl. 61, 10.

æt-fón [æt *to,* fón *to seize*] *To claim, lay claim, attach;* deprehendere, capere:—Gif se ágend hit eft ætfó *if the owner afterwards lay claim to it,* L. H. E. 7; Th. i. 30, 8: 16; Th. i. 34, 6: L. Ed. 1; Th. i. 160, 8.

æt-foran; *prep. dat.* [æt *at,* foran *fore*] *Close before, close by, before, at;* ante, pro, coram:—Ætforan eágan ðíne *ante oculos tuos,* Ps. Spl. 5, 5: 13, 7: Byrht. Th. 132, 14; By. 16. Sæt ætforan ðam dómsetle *sedit pro tribunali,* Jn. Bos. 19, 13.

æt-foran-weall, es; *m. The outer wall, out-works, a bulwark before a castle;* antemurale. v. weall; *m.*

æt-fyligan; *p.* de; *pp.* ed *To adhere to, stick to;* adhærere:—Ne ætfyligeþ ðé áhwǽr fácn ne unriht *numquid adhæret tibi sedes iniquitatis,* Ps. Th. 93, 19.

æt-gædere; *adv.* [æt, gædrian = gadrian *to gather*] *Together;* una, simul:—Twá beóþ ætgædere gríndende, Lk. Bos. 17, 35; *tweye* [wymmen] *schulen be gryndinge to gidere,* Wyc. His mǽgþe biþ ætgædere *his kindred is together,* Bt. Met. Fox 20, 320; Met. 20, 160. Gáras stódon samod ætgædere *the javelins stood altogether,* Beo. Th. 664; B. 329. Blód and wæter bú tú ætgædre *blood and water both together,* Exon. 70 a; Th. 260, 5; Jul. 292. Bismærede ungket [= uncit] men, bá ætgædre *they [men] reviled us two, both together,* Runic Inscrip. Kmbl. 354, 30. DER. gædere.

æt-gár, es; *m.* [æt, gár *a spear*] *A short spear* or *javelin, a kind of dart* or *other weapon to cast at the enemy;* framea, Cot. 188: 86. [*O. Frs.* etgér: *M. H. Ger.* azigér: *O. H. Ger.* azkér: *O. Nrs.* atgeirr.]

æt-gebicgan; *p.* -bohte; *pp.* -boht [æt, gebycgan *to buy*] *To buy for himself;* emere:—He hí æft æt ðam ágende sínne willan æt-gebicge *let him afterwards buy her at her owner's will,* L. Ethb. 82; Th. i. 24, 4.

æt-gebrengan; *p.* -gebrohte; *pp.* -gebroht; *v. trans. To bring* or *lead to;* adducere:—He ætgebrenge, ðe him sealde *let him bring the person who sold it him,* L. H. E. 7; Th. i. 30, 8.

æt-geníman; *p.* -genam, *pl.* -genámon; *pp.* -genumen *To take away by force, to pluck out, withdraw, deliver, rescue;* eripere, Cot. 77.

ǽt-giefa, -geofa, an; *m.* [ǽt *food,* gifa *a giver*] *A food-giver, feeder;* cibi dator:—Óþ ðæt se fugel his ǽtgiefan eáþmód weorþeþ *till that the bird becomes obedient to his feeder,* Exon. 88 b; Th. 332, 26; Vy. 91: 90 b; Th. 339, 22; Gn. Ex. 98.

æt-gifan; *p.* -geaf, -gaf, *pl.* -geáfon, géfon; *pp.* -gifen [æt *to,* gifan] *To give to, render, afford;* tribuere, afferre:—Ic him líf-wraðe lytle meahte ætgifan æt gúðe *I could render to him little life-protection in the conflict,* Beo. Th. 5748; B. 2878.

æt-gongan [æt *at,* gangan *to go*] *To go to, approach;* accedere:—Hét hie of ðam líge neár ætgongan *he bade them from the flame to approach nearer,* Exon. 55 b; Th. 197, 1; Az. 183.

æt-grǽpe; *adj. Grasping at, seizing;* prehendens:—Ðǽr him aglǽca ætgrǽpe wearþ *where the miserable being seized him,* Beo. Th. 2542; B. 1269.

æt-habban; *p.* -hæfde; *pp.* -hæfed *To retain, detain, withhold;* retinere, detinere, Scint. 10. DER. habban.

ǽðan *To overflow, deluge, lay waste:*—Cwæþ ðæt he wolde eall á ǽðan ðæt on eorþan wæs *said that he would for ever lay waste all that was on the earth,* Cd. 64; Th. 77, 24; Gen. 1280. v. éðan.

æðel- *noble;* nobilis:—v. the compounds æðel-boren, -borennes, -cund, *etc. from* æðele *noble.*

ǽðel, es; *m. A native country, country, land;* patria, terra:—In ðeossum ǽðele *in this country,* Cd. 215; Th. 271, 21; Sat. 108. On ǽðelum, *d. pl.* Menol. Fox 236; Men. 119. v. éðel.

Æðelbald, es; *m.* [æðele, bald *bold, brave*] *Æthelbald;* Æthelbaldus; *the eldest son of Æthelwulf. Æthelbald, the eldest brother of Alfred, was king of Wessex for five years, from* A. D. 855–860:—A. D. 855, ðá féngon Æðelwulfes ii suna to ríce; Æðelbald to Westseaxna ríce, and Æðelbryht to Cantwara ríce *then,* A. D. 855, *Æthelwulf's two sons succeeded to the kingdom; Æthelbald to the kingdom of the West Saxons, and Ethelbert to the kingdom of Kent,* Chr. 855; Th. 129, 16–19, col. 1.

A. D. 860, hēr, Æðelbald cyning forþfērde *here*, A. D. 860, *king Æthelbald died*, Chr. 860; Erl. 71, 3.

æðel-boren; *part. Noble-born, free-born, noble;* natu nobilis, nobili genere natus, nobilis:—Sum æðelboren man *homo quidam nobilis*, Lk. Bos. 19, 12. Æðelborene cild *vel* freóbearn *liberi*, Ælfc. Gl. 91; Wrt. Voc. 51, 67: Apol. Th. 19, 21. v. beran.

æðel-borennes, -ness, e; *f. Nobleness of birth;* nobilitas:—Ic ðīne æðelborennesse geseó *I see the nobleness of thy birth*, Apol. Th. 15, 18.

Æðelbryht, -berht, -briht, es; *m.* [æðele, bryht *bright, excellent.* v. beorht]. **1.** *Ethelbert king of Kent, for fifty-six years, from* A. D. 560–616. Ethelbert was converted to Christianity by the preaching of St. Augustine: v. Augustinus:—A. D. 560 [MS. 565], hēr, fēng Æðelbryht [MS. Æðelbriht] to Cantwara rīce *here*, A. D. 560, *Ethelbert succeeded to the kingdom of Kent*, Chr. 565; Erl. 17, 18. Ðā wæs ymb syx hund wintra and syxtyne winter fram Drihtnes mennyscnesse, ðæt wæs ymb ān and twentig wintra ðæs ðe Agustinus, mid his geferum, to lǽranne on Angel þeóde sended wæs, ðæt Æðelbryht Cantwara cyning æfter ðam hwīlendlīcan rīce ðæt he six and fīftig wintra wundorlīce hæfde, and ðā to ðam heofonlīcan rīce mid gefeán astāh *anno ab incarnatione Dominica sexcentesimo decimo sexto, qui est annus vicesimus primus, ex quo Augustinus cum sociis ad prædicandum genti Anglorum missus est, Æthelbryhtus* [*Æthelberht*] *rex Cantuariorum, post regnum temporale, quod quinquaginta et sex annis gloriosissime tenuerat, æterna cælestis regni gaudia subiit*, Bd. 2, 5; S. 506, 5–9. Hēr forþfērde Æðelbryht [MS. Æðelberht] Cantware cining, se rīxade lvi wintra *here*, A. D. 616, *Ethelbert king of the Kentish people died, who reigned fifty-six years*, Chr. 616; Erl. 21, 37. **2.** *Æðelbryht*, es; *m. Ethelbert the second;* Æthelbryhtus, *the second son of Æthelwulf. This Ethelbert, after the lapse of* 239 *years from the death of Ethelbert the first in* 616, *became king of Kent, Essex, Surrey, and Sussex, for five years, from* 855 *to* 860; *he succeeded to Wessex on his brother's death, in* 860, *and reigned five years more over these five counties, from* 860 *to* 865; *he was therefore king for ten years, from* A. D. 855–865:—A. D. 855, ðā fēngon Æðelwulfes ii suna to rīce; Æðelbald to Westseaxna rīce; and Æðelbryht to Cantwara rīce, and to Eástseaxena rīce, and to Sūþrigean, and to Sūþseaxena rīce *then*, A. D. 855, *Æthelwulf's two sons succeeded to the kingdom; Æthelbald to the kingdom of the West Saxons, and Ethelbert to the kingdom of Kent, and to the kingdom of the East Saxons, and to Surrey, and to the kingdom of the South Saxons*, Chr. 855; Th. 129, 16–22, col. 1. A. D. 860, hēr, Æðelbald cyning forþfērde, and fēng Æðelbryht to eallum ðam rīce his brōðor, and se Æðelbryht [MS. Æðelbriht] rīcsode v geár *here*, A. D. 860, *king Æthelbald died, and Ethelbert succeeded to all the kingdom* [*Wessex*] *of his brother, and Ethelbert reigned five years*, Chr. 860; Erl. 71, 3–10.

æðel-cund; *adj. Of noble kind* or *origin, noble;* nobilis originis:—Æðelcunde mægþ *the noble woman*, Exon. 119 b; Th. 459, 18; Hö. 1.

æðel-cundnes, -ness, e; *f. Nobleness, nobility;* nobilitas:—Mid micelre æðelcundnesse *with great nobleness*, Bt. 19; Fox 68, 31.

æðel-cyning, es; *m. The noble king*, used for *Christ;* rex nobilis, Christus:—Cristes onsȳn, æðelcyninges wlite *Christ's countenance, the noble king's aspect*, Exon. 21 a; Th. 56, 27; Cri. 907. Æðelcyninges rōd *the cross of the noble king*, Elen. Kmbl. 437; El. 219: Andr. Kmbl. 3354; An. 1681.

æðel-duguþ, e; *f. A noble attendance;* comitatus nobilis:—Hine ymbūtan æðelduguþ, eádig engla gedryht *around him a noble attendance, a blessed train of angels*, Exon. 22 b; Th. 62, 36; Cri. 1012.

æðele, eðele; *comp.* -ra; *sup.* -ast, -est, -ust; *adj.* **I.** *noble, eminent, not only in blood or by descent, but in mind, excellent, famous, singular;* nobilis, generosus, præstabilis, egregius, excellens:—Se eorl wæs æðele *the earl was noble*, Cd. 59; Th. 72, 5; Gen. 1182. He sægde Habrahame, æðeles geþingu *he told to Abraham the promises of the noble*, Andr. Kmbl. 1512; An. 757. Æðelan cynnes *of noble race*, Cd. 154; Th. 192, 6; Exod. 227. Æðelre gebyrde *of noble birth*, Bd. 2, 15; S. 518, 37. Æðelum cempan *to the noble champion*, Andr. Kmbl. 460; An. 230. Ðære æðelan [cwēne] *to the noble lady*, Elen. Kmbl. 1085; El. 545. Wuldriaþ æðelne ordfruman *they glorify the noble origin*, Exon. 13 b; Th. 25, 17; Cri. 402. Æðelum stencum *with sweet odours*, 64 a; Th. 237, 7; Ph. 586: Cd. 75; Th. 92, 24; Gen. 1533. Ðone æðelan Albanum *Albanum egregium*, Bd. 1, 7; S. 476, 34. He wæs on his mōde æðelra ðonne on woruld gebyrdum *he was in his mind more noble than in worldly birth*, Bd. 3, 19; S. 547, 26. Of ðam æðelestan cynne *of the most noble race*, 3, 19; S. 547, 25. Æðelast tungla *the noblest of stars*, Exon. 57 a; Th. 204, 6; Ph. 93: Ps. Th. 84, 10. Æðelust bearna *the noblest of heroes*, Elen. Kmbl. 950; El. 476. **II.** *noble, vigorous, young;* nobilis, novellus:—Ðīne bearn swā elebeámas æðele weaxen *thy children grow like young olive-trees;* sicut novellæ olivarum, Ps. Th. 127, 4: 143, 14. Swā swā æðele plantunga *sicut novellæ plantationes*, Ps. Spl. 143, 14. [*O. Sax.* eðili: *O. Frs.* ethel, edel: *Dut. Ger.* edel: *M. H. Ger.* edele: *O. H. Ger.* edili: *Dan. Swed.* ädel: *O. Nrs.* aðal, *n. natura, ingenium.*] DER. emn-æðele, ge-, on-, un-.

Æðelflǽd, e; *f.* [æðele, flǽd] *Æthelfled;* Æthelfleda. The eldest and most intellectual daughter of king Alfred the Great, and sister of king Edward the Elder. She married Æthelred, a Mercian nobleman, who was made viceroy of Mercia by king Alfred. He died in A. D. 912, Chr. Erl. 100, 30, and his widow Æthelfled governed Mercia most efficiently for about ten years:—Hēr com Æðelflǽd, Myrcna hlǽfdige, on ðone hālgan ǽfen Inuentione Sanctæ Crucis, to Scergeate, and ðǽr ða burh getimbrede; and, ðæs ilcan geáres, ða æt Bricge *here*, A. D. 912, *Æthelfled, the lady of the Mercians, came to Scergeat* [*Sarrat?*] *on the holy eve of the Inventio Sanctæ Crucis* [*May third*], *and there built the burgh; and in the same year, that at Bridgenorth*, Chr. 912; Th. 187, 6–10, col. 1: Chr. 913; Th. 186, 11–37, col. 2: Chr. 917; Th. 190, 37, col. 2–192, 1, col. 2: Chr. 918; Th. 192, 7, col. 2: Th. Diplm. A. D. 886–899, 138, 5–11: 138, 29–32. Æthelfled died at Tamworth in A. D. 922. Ðā on ðæm setle Eádweard cyng ðǽr sæt [æt Steanforde], ðā gefōr Æðelflǽd his swystar æt Tameworþige, xii nihtum ǽr middum sumera. Ðā gerād he ða burg æt Tameworþige; and him cierde to eall se þeódscype on Myrcna lande, ðe Æðelflǽde ǽr underþeóded wæs *then, while king Edward was tarrying there* [*at Stamford*], *Æthelfled his sister died at Tamworth, twelve nights before midsummer. Then rode he to the borough of Tamworth; and all the population in Mercia turned to him, which before was subject to Æthelfled*, Chr. 922; Erl. 108, 22–26.

æðelian; *p.* ode; *pp.* od; *v. trans. To ennoble, improve;* nobilitare. DER. ge-æðelian, un-.

æðel-īc; *adj.* [æðele *noble*, līc *like*] *Noble, excellent;* egregius:—Æðelīc onginn *a noble beginning*, Andr. Kmbl. 1775; An. 890. Stenc æðelīcra eallum eorþan frætwum [MS. frætwa] *a nobler odour than all earth's ornaments*, Exon. 96 a; Th. 358, 19; Pa. 48.

ǽðe-līc; *adj.* [ǽðe = eáðe *easy*; *adj.* līc *like*] *Easy;* facilis:—Gif ðū ne wilt us geþafian in swā ǽðelīcum þinge *si non vis assentire nobis in tam facili causa*, Bd. 2, 5; S. 507, 26. v. eáðelīc.

æðel-īce; *adv. Nobly, elegantly;* nobiliter, insigniter, Cot. 77. v. æðel-līce.

æðeling, es; *m.* [æðele, -ing *son of, originating from*]. **I.** *the son of a king, one of royal blood, a nobleman, used also in poetry for the king, God, and Christ;* regia suboles, vir nobilis:—Se iunga æðeling *regius juvenis*, Bd. 2, 12; S. 514, 27: 3, 21; S. 550, 40: 2, 14; S. 517, 22. Æðelinges bearn *the prince's child*, Beo. Th. 1780; B. 888. Be sumum Rōmāniscum æðelinge *by a certain Roman nobleman*, Bt. 16, 2; Fox 52, 19. Crist Nergende! wuldres Æðeling! *Saviour Christ! Prince of Glory!* Exon. 10 a; Th. 10, 26; Cri. 158. Ðā se Æðeling cwom in Betlem *when the Prince came in Bethlehem*, 14 a; Th. 28, 18; Cri. 448. Æðelstān cyning and his brōðor eác, Eádmund æðeling *king Æthelstan and his brother also, Edmund the noble*, Chr. 938; Th. 200, 33; Æðelst. 3. Ēce is se æðeling *the creator* [*atheling*] *is eternal*, Exon. 60 b; Th. 220, 12; Ph. 319: 119 b; Th. 459, 21; Hö. 3. Stōd æfter mandrihtne eard and ēðel, æfter ðam æðelinge [*his*] *land and dwelling-place stood after* [*waiting for*] *the man-lord, the chieftain*, 207; Th. 256, 10; Dan. 638. **II.** *man generally, in pl. men, people, used in a good and noble sense, as a derivative of* æðele *noble;* homo, homines:—Ðæs æðelinges ellen dohte *the man's courage was good*, Cd. 64; Th. 78, 4; Gen. 1288. Ða nū æðelingas, ealle eorþ-būend, Ebrēi hātaþ *which people now, all dwellers upon earth, call Hebrews*, 79; Th. 99, 17; Gen. 1647. Hēht him ceósan æðelingas *he commanded him to choose men*, 90; Th. 112, 9; Gen. 1868: 58; Th. 70, 31; Gen. 1161. DER. sib-.

Æðelinga īgg, eíg, e; *f. The island of nobles, Athelney;* nobilium insula:—Æt Æðelinga īgge *apud nobilium insulam*, Chr. 878; Th. 146, 42, col. 2. Wið..., Th. 148, 31, col. 2: Chr. 879; Th. 148, 30, col. 3.

æðel-līc; *adj. Noble;* nobilis, Andr. Kmbl. 1775; An. 890. v. æðel-īc, æðele.

æðel-līce, æðel-īce; *adv. Nobly;* nobiliter:—Wæs se wer on hālgum gewritum æðellīce gelǽred *vir erat sacris litteris nobiliter instructus*, Bd. 5, 23; S. 646, 17: 4, 26; S. 603, 9: 2, 1; S. 501, 8.

æðel-nes, -nys, -nyss, e; *f. Nobility;* nobilitas, Bd. 2, 20; S. 522, 7: Ps. Th. 118, 142, [MS. æðeles.]

æðelo; *indecl. in sing; pl. nom. acc.* æðelu, æðelo; *gen.* æðela; *dat.* æðelum; *n. Nobility, pre-eminence, origin, family, race, nature, talents, genius;* nobilitas, principatus, origo, natales, prosapia, natura, indoles, ingenium:—Ic lǽre ðæt ðū fægenige ōðerra manna gōdes and heora æðelo *I advise that thou rejoice in other men's good and their nobility*, Bt. 30, 1; Fox 108, 31. His æðelo bióþ on ðam mōde *his nobility is in the mind*, 30, 1; Fox 110, 1. Ryht æðelo biþ on ðam mōde, næs on ðam flǽsce *true nobility is in the mind, not in the flesh*, Bt. 30, 2; Fox 110, 19. Him frumbearnes riht freóbrōðor ōþþah, eád and æðelo *his own brother had withdrawn from him his wealth and pre-eminence*, Cd. 160; Th. 199, 15; Exod. 339. Ealdaþ eorþan blǽd æðela gehwylcre *earth's produce of every nature grows old*, Exon. 33 a; Th. 104, 28; Gū. 14. Hwæt his æðelu sīen *which his origin is*, 69 b; Th. 259, 23; Jul. 286. Sindon him æðelum ōðere twegen beornas geborene brōðorsibbum *to him in his family are two other men born in brotherly relationship*, Andr. Kmbl. 1377; An. 689. Þurh ðīne wordlæðe æðelum ēcne *through thy discourse great with talents*, 1271; An. 636. He eówer æðelu can *he* *knows your nobility*, Beo. Th. 790; B. 392: 3745; B. 1870. DER. fæder-æðelo, riht-.

Æðelrǣd, Æðelrēd, Æðerēd, es; *m.* [æðele *noble*, rǣd *counsel*] *Æthelred, a Mercian nobleman, the viceroy* or *governor of the Mercians;* Æthelrēd, Æthelrēdus. He married Æthelfled, the eldest and most intellectual daughter of king Alfred the Great. He styles himself *subregulus* in subscribing his name to a charter of king Alfred, A. D. 889,—Ego Æthelrēd, subregulus et patricius Merciorum, hanc donationem signo crucis subscripsi, Th. Diplm. 136, 21. His wife simply writes,—Ego Æthelflǣd consensi, Th. Diplm. 136, 23. Rīxiendum ussum Dryhtene ðæm Hǣlendan Crist. Æfter ðon ðe agān wæs ehta hund wintra and syx and hund nigontig efter his acennednesse, and ðȳ feówerteóðan gebonngēre [v. geban II], ðā ðȳ gēre gebeón [*p. of* gebannan] Æðelrēd ealderman alle Mercna weotan tosomne to Gleaweceastre, biscopas, and aldermen, and alle his dugupe; and ðæt dyde be Ælfrēdes cyninges gewitnesse and leáfe *under the rule of our Lord Jesus Christ. When* 896 *winters were passed after his birth, and in the fourth indiction year, then in that year Æthelred alderman assembled all the witan of the Mercians together at Gloucester, bishops, and aldermen, and all his nobility; and did that with the knowledge and leave of king Alfred*, Th. Diplm. A. D. 896; 139, 4-16. Æthelred died in A. D. 912. Hēr gefōr Æðelrēd, ealdorman on Myrcum *here*, A. D. 912, *died Æthelred, alderman of the Mercians*, Chr. 912; Erl. 101, 46. *His widow, Æthelfled, governed Mercia about ten years, with great vigour and success, under her brother, king Edward the Elder*, Chr. 922; Erl. 108, 22-26. v. **Æðelflǣd.**

Æðelrēd, Æðerēd, es; *m.* [æðele, rēd = rǣd *counsel*]. **1.** *Æthelred, third son of Æthelwulf, and brother of Alfred the Great. Æthelred was king of Wessex for five years*, A. D. 866-871; Æthelred, Æthelrēdus:—Hēr fēng Æðelrēd to West Seaxna rīce *here*, A. D. 866, *Æthelred succeeded to the kingdom of the West Saxons*, Chr. 866; Erl. 73, 1. Æfter Eástron gefōr Æðelrēd [MS. Æðerēd] cining; and he rīcsode [MS. rīxade] v geár *after Easter* [A. D. 871] *king Æthelred died; and he reigned five years*, 871; Erl. 77, 1. **2. Æðelrēd** *Æthelred Atheling, the second son of Edgar. Æthelred was king of Wessex, Mercia, and Northumbria, for thirty-eight years*, A. D. 978-1016:—Hēr, Æðelrēd æðeling fēng to ðam rīce *here* [A. D. 978] *Æthelred Atheling succeeded to the kingdom*, Chr. 978; Th. 232, 3, col. 1. A. D. 1016, Ðā gelamp hit ðæt se cyning Æðelrēd forþfērde *then*, A. D. 1016, *it happened that king Æthelred died*, 1016; Erl. 155, 15. **3. Æðelrēd, Æðerēd** *Æthelred, a Mercian nobleman*, Th. Diplm. A. D. 896; 139, 11: Chr. 912; Erl. 101, 46. v. **Æðelrǣd.**

Æðelstān, es; *m.* [æðele, stān *stone*] *Athelstan, the eldest son of Edward the Elder. Athelstan, who gained a complete victory over the Anglo-Danes in the battle of Brunanburh, in* A. D. 937, *was king of Wessex fourteen years and ten weeks, from* A. D. 925-940:—A. D. 925, hēr, Eádweard cyning [MS. cing] forþfērde and Æðelstān his sunu fēng to rīce *here*, A. D. 925, *king Edward died, and Athelstan his son succeeded to the kingdom*, Chr. 925; Erl. 110, 19. A. D. 940, hēr, Æðelstān cyning forþfērde, and Eádmund Æðeling fēng to rīce, and Æðelstān cyning rīcsode xiv geár, and teon wucan *here*, A. D. 940, *king Athelstan died, and Edmund Atheling succeeded to the kingdom, and king Athelstan reigned fourteen years and ten weeks*, Chr. 940; Th. 209, 13-23, col. 1.

æðel-stenc, es; *m. A noble odour;* odor nobilis, Exon. 58 b; Th. 211, 10; Ph. 195.

æðel-tungol, es; *m. A noble star;* sidus nobile, Exon. 60 a; Th. 218, 5; Ph. 290: 52 a; Th. 181, 4; Gū. 1288.

Æðel-wulf, es; *m.* [æðele *noble*, wulf *a wolf*] *Æthelwulf;* Æthelwulfus; *eldest son of Egbert and father of Alfred the Great. Æthelwulf was king of Wessex, from* A. D. 837 (v. Ecg-bryht) -855:—A. D. 837 [MS. 836], hēr, Ecgbryht cyning forþfērde, and fēng Æðelwulf his sunu to Westseaxna rīce *here*, A. D. 837, *king Ecgbryht died, and Æthelwulf his son succeeded to the kingdom of the West Saxons*, Chr. 836; Th. 117, 34, col. 1. A. D. 855, hēr, Æðelwulf cyning gefōr *here*, A. D. 855, *king Æthelwulf died*, Chr. 855; Erl. 68, 24.

Æðerēd, es; *m. The name of a king and a Mercian nobleman*, Chr. 867; Th. 130, 22, cols. 1, 2, 3; Th. 131, 22, cols. 1, 3: Chr. 912; Erl. 100, 30. v. **Æðelrēd 1, Æðelrǣd.**

æt-hīde, æt-hȳde *Put out of the hide, skinned, bowelled;* excoriatus, Cot. 42.

æt-hindan; *adv. At the back, behind, after;* a tergo, pone, post:—Se cyning fērde him æthindan *the king went after them*, Chr. 1016; Th. i. 282, 17.

æt-hleápan; *p.* -hleóp, *pl.* -hleópon; *pp.* -hleápen; *v. intrans. To leap out, to flee, escape, get away;* aufugere, evadere:—Ðēh þrǣla hwylc hlāforde æthleápe *a domino suo servus si quis aufugerit*, Lupi Serm. 1, 13; Hick. Thes. ii. 103, 4.

æt-hlȳp, es; *m.* [æt *to*, hlȳp *a leap*] *An assault;* aggressus, assultus:—For ðan æthlȳpe *for the assault*, L. Ath. i. 6; Th. i. 202, 22. v. ǣ-hlȳp.

ǢÐM, ēðm, es; *m. A vapour, breath, a hole to breathe through, a smell;* halitus, spiritus, vapor:—Hreðer ǣðme weóil *his breast heaved with breathing*, Beo. Th. 5180; B. 2593. Hū sīd se swarta ēðm seó *how vast the black vapour may be*, Cd. 228; Th. 309, 4; Sat. 704. [*Plat.* ādem, ām, *m: O. Sax.* āðom, *m: O. Frs.* ethma, ādema, ōm, *m: Dut.* ādem, *m: Ger.* athem, odem, *m: M. H. Ger.* ātem, *m: O. H. Ger.* ātam, ātum, *m. spiritus*, ἀτμή *vapor: Sansk.* ātman *breath, soul.*] v. brǣþ.

ǣðmian; *p.* ode; *pp.* od [ǣðm *vapour*] *To raise vapour, boil, to be heated, to be greatly moved;* exæstuare, Scint. 30.

æt-hredan *to deliver;* eripere:—Ic æthrede oððe ahredde *eripio*, Ælfc. Gr. 28, 3; Som. 30, 63.

æt-hreppian, Ettm. æt-hræppian, Som; *p.* ode; *pp.* od *To rap at, to knock, dash about;* impingere. v. hrepian.

æt-hrīnan; *p.* -hrān, *pl.* -hrinon; *pp.* -hrinen *To touch, take, move;* tangere, apprehendere, movere:—Ðæt ic æt-hrīne ðīn *ut tangam te*, Gen. 27, 21. He æt-hrān hyre hand *tetigit manum ejus*, Mt. Bos. 8, 15. Se unclǣna gāst hine æt-hrīnþ *spiritus apprehendit eum*, Lk. Bos. 9, 39. Nellaþ hīg ðā mid heora fingre æt-hrīnan *digito autem suo nolunt ea movere*, Mt. Bos. 23, 4.

æ-þrȳt; *adj. Troublesome, tedious;* molestus, Equin. vern. 38.

æ-þrȳtnes, -ness, e; *f. Trouble;* molestia, Lye. v. a-þrotennes.

æt-hwā; *pron. Each;* quisque:—Se is æt-hwām freónd *which is to each a friend*, Exon. 95 b; Th. 356, 22; Pa. 15.

æt-hwæga, æt-hwega, æt-hwegu *Somewhat, about, in some measure, a little;* aliquantum, aliquantulum, aliquatenus, R. Ben. interl. 73. Scīres wīnes drince æt-hwæga *let him drink somewhat of pure wine*, L. M. 2, 59; Lchdm. ii. 284, 5. Æt-hwega yfel wǣte biþ gegoten on ðæt lim *whatever evil humour is secreted on the limb*, L. M. 2, 59; Lchdm. ii. 284, 28. v. hwæt-hwæga *in* hwæt, hwega.

æt-hweorfan; *p.* -hwearf, *pl.* -hwurfon; *pp.* -hworfen [æt, hweorfan *to turn*] *To turn, return;* accedere, reverti:—Hwīlum on beorh æt-hwearf *sometimes he turned to the mount*, Beo. Th. 4587; B. 2299.

æt-hwōn; *adv. Almost;* pæne, fere. v. hwōn.

æt-hȳde *Put out of the hide, skinned;* excoriatus. v. æt-hīde.

æt-irnan; *p.* -arn, *pl.* -urnon; *pp.* -urnen; *v. intrans. To run away;* egredi:—Ðā ætarn he ūt *et egressus est foras*, Gen. 39, 12. v. yrnan.

æt-is *is present;* adest, Mk. Bos. 4, 29; *3rd pres. of* æt-eom.

æt-īwedness, e; *f. A shewing, manifestation;* ostensio:—Wæs on wēstenum ōþ ðone dæg hys ætīwednessum on Israhel *erat in desertis usque in diem ostensionis suæ ad Israel*, Lk. Bos. 1, 80. v. æt-ȳwnys.

æt-lǣdan; *p.* de; *pp.* ed *To lead out, drive away;* abigere:—Ðæt ðū ætlǣddest me mīne dōhtra *ut clam me abigeres filias meas*, Gen. 31, 26.

æt-lætness, e; *f. Desolation, destruction;* desolatio, Somn. 323.

æt-licgan; *p.* -læg, *pl.* -lǣgon; *pp.* -legen *To lie still* or *idle;* inutilem jacere:—Ðæt Godes feoh ne ætlicge *ne Dei pecunia jaceat*, Ælfc. Gr. pref; Som. 1, 27.

æt-lūtian [lūtan *to lurk*] *To lie hid;* latere, Jud. 4, 18.

Ætne, es; *m. Etna*, Bt. 15; Fox 48, 20: 16, 1; Fox 50, 5. v. Etna.

æt-nīman; *p.* -nam, *pl.* -nāmon; *pp.* -numen *To take from, to take away;* demere, adimere:—Ne wolde him beorht fæder bearn ætnīman *the glorious father would not take the child away from him*, Cd. 162; Th. 204, 5; Exod. 414.

æt-nȳhstan; *adv. At last;* tandem, Bd. 2, 2; S. 502, 26. v. nȳhst.

ætol, ætol-man, ætul-man *A glutton;* edax. v. etol.

ǣton *ate*, Mt. Bos. 13, 4; *p. of* etan.

ǣtor *Poison;* venenum. v. ǣtor-cyn, ātor.

ǣtor-cyn, -cynn, es; *n. The poison-kind;* veneni genus:—Ǣtorcyn gewurdon onwæcned *the poison-kinds arose*, Salm. Kmbl. 437; Sal. 219. v. ātor, *etc.*

ǣtren, ǣttren, ǣtern, ǣttern; *adj. Poisonous;* venenosus:—Ǣttren wæs ellorgæst *the strange guest was poisonous*, Beo. Th. 3238; B. 1617. Me of bōsme fareþ ǣtren onga *from my bosom comes a poisonous sting*, Exon. 106 b; Th. 405, 18; Rä. 24, 4: Ps. Th. 139, 3. Him æt heortan stōd ǣtterne ord [*sc.* gāres] *the poisonous point* [*of the spear*] *stood in his heart*, Byrht. Th. 136, 4; By. 146: Frag. Kmbl. 37; Leás. 20: L. M. 1, 45; Lchdm. ii. 112, 24.

ǣtren-mōd; *adj. Venom-minded;* malitiosus:—Ǣtrenmōd mon *a venom-minded man*, Exon. 91 b; Th. 343, 26; Gn. Ex. 163.

ǣtrian, ǣttrian; *p.* ede; *pp.* ed; *v. trans.* [ǣtor = ātor *poison*] *To poison, envenom;* venenare:—For ǣtredum gescotum *from poisoned arrows*, Ors. 3, 9; Bos. 68, 38; MS. C.

æt-rihte; *adv.* [æt *at*, rihte *rightly, justly, well*] *Rightly* or *justly at, near, at hand, almost;* pæne, haud multum abest quin:—Ætrihte wæs gūþ getwǣfed, nymþe mec God scylde *the contest had almost been finished, had not God shielded me*, Beo. Th. 3319; B. 1657. Wæs him endedōgor ætryhte *his final day was near*, Exon. 49 b; Th. 171, 12; Gū. 1125: 47 a; Th. 162, 4; Gū. 970.

æt-rihtost; *adv. By and by, presently;* mox. v. æt-rihte; *adv.*

æt-ryhte *Nearly, almost;* pæne, Exon. 47 a; Th. 162, 4; Gū. 970: Exon. 49 b; Th. 171, 12; Gū. 1125. v. æt-rihte.

æt-sacan; *p.* -sōc, *pl.* -sōcon; *pp.* -sacen; *v. a. n.* [æt, sacan *to charge, accuse*] *To deny, disown, abjure;* negare, detestari, abjurare:—Ða ætsacaþ ðæs ærȳstes *qui negant esse resurrectionem*, Lk. Bos. 20, 27: L. Ath. i. 4;

Th. i. 202, 2: i. 6; Th. i. 202, 12, 13. Ðá ætsóc he *at ille negavit,* Mk. Bos. 14, 68: Lk. Bos. 22, 57. Ðá ætsóc he and swerede *tunc cœpit detestari et jurare,* Mt. Bos. 26, 74. Ðá ongan he ætsacan and swerian *ille autem cœpit anathematizare et jurare,* Mk. Bos. 14, 71. v. sacan.

æt-sæcst *shalt deny; fut. of* æt-sacan:—Þríwa ðú me ætsæcst *ter me negabis,* Mk. Bós. 14, 72: Lk. Bos. 22, 34, 61. v. sacan.

æt-samne; *adv. In a sum, together:*—Begen æt-samne *both together,* Chr. 937; Th. 206, 18, col. 1; Æðelst. 58. Ealle ætsamne *all together,* Ps. Th. 148, 12. v. æt-somne.

æt-sceófan *To shove away;* removere, Leo 239. v. scúfan.

æt-sittan; *p.* -sæt, *pl.* -sǽton; *pp.* -seten; *v. intrans. To sit by, to remain, stay, wait;* adsidere:—Ðá ætsǽton ða Centiscan ðǽr beæftan *then the Kentish men remained there behind,* Chr. 905; Th. 180, 31, col. 1.

æt-slídan; *p.* -slád, *pl.* -slidon; *pp.* -sliden [æt *from, away;* v. æt I. 2: slídan *labi*] *To slip* or *slide away;* labi, elabi:—Ic ætslíde *labor,* Ælfc. Gr. 29; Som. 33, 43: 35; Som. 38, 10. Ðæt hira fót ætslíde *ut labatur pes eorum,* Deut. 32, 35.

æt-somne, æt-samne; *adv. In a sum, at once, together;* una, simul, pariter:—Eardiaþ ætsomne *habitant simul,* Deut. 25, 5. Ic gongan gefregn gingran ætsomne *I have understood that the disciples went together,* Cd. 224; Th. 298, 2; Sat. 526. Wǽr is ætsomne Godes and monna *a covenant is together of God and men,* Exon. 16 a; Th. 36, 29; Cri. 583. Blód and wæter bú tú ætsomne út bicwóman *blood and water both together came out,* 24 a; Th. 68, 34; Cri. 1113. Tyne ætsomne *ten together,* Beo. Th. 5687; B. 2847. Ealle ætsomne *omnes pariter,* Bd. 2, 13; S. 515, 38: Ps. Th. 87, 17. v. somne.

æt-speornan, -spornan, ðú -spyrnst, he -spyrnþ; *p.* -spearn, *pl.* -spurnon; *pp.* -spornen; *v. trans. To stumble, spurn at, dash* or *trip against, mistake;* cæspitare, offendere ad aliquid, impingere:—He ætspyrnþ *he stumbleth;* offendit, Jn. Bos. 11, 9, 10. Ðe-læs ðe ðín fót æt stáne ætsporne *ne forte offendas ad lapidem pedem tuum,* Mt. Bos. 4, 6. Ðe-læs ðú ætspurne [Lamb. ætsporne] æt stáne fót ðínne *ne forte offendas ad lapidem pedem tuum,* Ps. Spl. 90, 12. Ætspornen [MS. ætspurnan] ic wæs *offensus fui,* Ps. Lamb. 95, 10.

æt-springan, -sprincan; *p.* -sprang, -spranc, *pl.* -sprungon; *pp.* -sprungen; *v. intrans. To spring out;* prosilire:—Blód ætspranc *the blood sprang out,* Beo. Th. 2247; B. 1121.

æt-springnes, -ness, e; *f. A springing out, falling off, despondency;* defectio, defectio animi, Ps. Spl. T. 118, 53.

æt-spurne *offendas,* Ps. Spl. 90, 12; *subj. p. of* æt-speornan, *q. v.*

æt-spyrning *An offence, a stumbling, stumbling-block;* offensio, scandalum. DER. speornan.

ætst *shalt eat;* comedes:—Ðu ætst *thou shalt eat,* Gen. 3, 17; *for* ytst, Gen. 3, 18. DER. etan *to eat.*

æt-standan; ic -stande, ðú -standest, -stentst, he -standeþ, -stent, -stynt, *pl.* -standaþ; *p.* -stód, *pl.* -stódon; *pp.* -standen. I. *v. intrans. To stand, stand still, stop, stand near, rest, stay, stand up;* stare, adstare, restare, requiescere:—Íren on wealle ætstód *the iron stood in the wall,* Beo. Th. 1787; B. 891. Ðá ætstód se Hǽlend *then Jesus stood still,* Mk. Bos. 10, 49. Ætstód ðæs blódes ryne *stetit fluxus sanguinis,* Lk. Bós. 8, 44. Ðá ætstód se arc *requievit arca,* Gen. 8, 4: Ps. Th. 106, 24: Lk. Bos. 7, 14. Ætstódon cyningas [Ps. Th. 2, 2, arísaþ] *kings stood up;* adstiterunt reges, Ps. Spl. 2, 2: 5, 4. Ic ætstande *resto,* Ælfc. Gr. 24; Som. 25, 62: Ælfc. T. 37, 6: L. Eth. ii. 9; Th. i. 290, 3. II. *v. trans. To stop;* obturere, claudere:—Gif se mícgða ætstanden sý *if the water be stopped,* Herb. 7, 3; Lchdm. i. 98, 5. Hí habbaþ ætstandene ǽdran *they have stopped veins,* 4, 4; Lchdm. i. 90, 11.

æt-stapan; *p.* -stóp, *pl.* -stópon; *pp.* -stapen *To step forth, approach;* accedere:—He forþ ætstóp *he stepped forth,* Beo. Th. 1495; B. 745.

æt-steal, -steall, -stæl, es; *m: pl. nom. acc.* -stalas [*at a place, a fixed place*] *Station, camp station;* sedes, statio:—Æt ðam ætstealle *at the camp station,* Wald. 37; Vald. 1, 21. Æt-stælle *at the place,* Exon. 35 a; Th. 112, 26; Gú. 150. v. stæl.

æt-stent *shall stand;* consistet:—Seó eá ætstent on hire ryne *the river shall stand in its course,* Jos. 3, 13; *fut. of* æt-standan, *q. v.*

æt-stillan; *p.* ede; *pp.* ed *To still;* componere:—Sió cwacung sóna biþ ætstilled *the quaking will soon be stilled,* L. M. 1, 26; Lchdm. ii. 68, 11.

æt-swerian; *p.* -swór; *pp.* -sworen *To forswear, deny with an oath;* abjurare, L. In. 35; Th. i. 124, 11, note.

æt-swymman; *p.* -swamm, *pl.* -swummon; *pp.* -swummen *To swim out, swim;* enatare, Chr. 918; Ing. 132, 17, note *m.* v. æt; *prep.* 2.

ǽtten *should eat,* L. In. 42; Lambd. 8, 5; Wilk. 21, 24; *for* ǽten. v. etan *to eat.*

ǽtter, ǽttor, es; *n. Poison;* venenum. v. átor.

ǽtter-berende; *part. Poison-bearing, poisonous, venomous.* v. átterberende.

ǽtter-loppe, an; *f.* [átor *poison,* loppe *a silk worm, spinner of a web*] *A spider;* aranea:—And a-ýdlian oððe aswarcan oððe acwínan oððe aswindan ðú dydest swá swá ǽtterloppan oððe ryngan sáwle his *et tabescere fecisti sicut araneam animam ejus,* Ps. Lamb. 38, 12; and thou madist his lijf to faile as an yreyne [*Lat.* aranea *a spider*], Wyc. v. átor-loppe.

æt-þringan *To take away, deprive of;* eripere:—Ða ðé feorh ætþringan *who may deprive thee of life,* Andr. Kmbl. 2742; An. 1373.

ǽttren, ǽttern; *adj. Poisonous;* venenosus, Beo. Th. 3238; B. 1617: Byrht. Th. 136, 4; By. 146: Frag. Kmbl. 37; Leás. 20. v. ǽtren.

ǽttrian; *p.* ede; *pp.* ed; *v. trans. To poison, envenom;* venenare, Pref. R. Conc. v. ǽtrian.

ǽttryn; *adj. Poisonous;* venenosus:—Ǽttrynne ord *the poisonous point,* Byrht. Th. 133, 8; By. 47. v. ǽtren.

æt-wæg *took away,* Beo. Th. 2401; B. 1198; *p. of* æt-wegan.

æt-wæsend, -wesend, -weosend [æt *at,* wesende *being; part. of* wesan *to be*] *At hand, approaching, hard by;* imminens, Cot. 107.

æt-wegan; *p.* -wæg, *pl.* -wǽgon; *pp.* -wegen *To take away;* auferre:—Hama ætwæg sigle *Hama took away the jewel,* Beo. Th. 2401; B. 1198. v. wegan.

ǽt-wéla, an; *m. Abundance of food, a feast;* copia cibi, Exon. 100 a; Th. 374, 8; Seel. 123.

æt-wenian; *p.* ede; *pp.* ed [æt *from,* wenian *to wean*] *To deliver from, wean;* dissuescere, seducere, ablactare:—Ðe híg deóflum ætweneþ *who weaneth them from devils,* L. C. S. 85; Th. i. 424, 13.

æt-wesan; *p.* ic, he -wæs, *pl.* -wǽron [æt *at,* wesan *to be*] *To be present;* adesse:—Wilferþ ætwæs, eác swylce ætwǽron úre bróðru *Wilfrid adfuit, adfuerunt et fratres nostri,* Bd. 4, 5; S. 572, 12. [*Goth.* atwisan.]

æt-windan; *p.* -wánd, *pl.* -wúndon; *pp.* -wúnden *To wind off, turn away, escape, flee away;* aufugere:—Ic ána ætwánd *effugi ego solus,* Job Thw. 165, 27; Grn. Iob 1, 16: Beo. Th. 289; B. 143. Ic lǽte híg ætwíndan to wuda *dimitto eos avolare ad silvam,* Coll. Monast. Th. 26, 3.

æt-wist, æd-wist, ed-wist, e; *f.* [æt, wist *substantia, cibus*] *Substance, existence, being, presence;* substantia, præsentia:—God heora ǽhta and ætwist on-genímeþ *God takes their wealth and substance away,* Cd. 60; Th. 73, 21; Gen. 1208. Se gǽst lufaþ onsýn and ætwist yldran hádes *the spirit loves the aspect and substance of elder state,* Exon. 40 a; Th. 132, 11; Gú. 471. Him ðæt Crist forgeaf ðæt hý mótan his ætwiste brúcan *Christ gave that to them, that they might enjoy his presence,* 13 b; Th. 24, 29; Cri. 392: Gen. 7, 4.

æt-wítan; *p.* -wát, *pl.* -witon; *pp.* -witen *To reproach, blame, upbraid;* imputare, improperare, exprobrare:—Ne sceolon me on ðære þeóde þegenas ætwítan *the thanes of this people shall not reproach me,* Byrht. Th. 138, 15; By. 220. Siððan Gúþláf and Óslaf ætwiton weána dǽl *since Guthlaf and Oslaf reproached him for a part of their woes,* Beo. Th. 2304; B. 1150: Ps. Th. 88, 44: 73, 17: Ps. Spl. 31, 2. v. edwítan.

æt-ýcan; *p.* -ýcte; *pp.* -ýced, -ýct [æt, ýcan, ecan *to eke*] *To add to, augment, increase;* adjicere:—Se gesíþ ætýcte eác swylce his bénum, ðæt he his teáras geát *the earl also added to his intreaties, that he shed tears,* Bd. 5, 5; S. 617, 40: 4, 5; S. 573, 13.

æt-ýccnys, -ýcnys, -nyss, e; *f. An increase, addition;* augmentum:—Mid ætýccnysse *cum augmento,* Bd. 1, 27; S. 490, 24: 3, 22; S. 553, 14.

æ-týnan; *p.* de; *pp.* ed; *v. a.* [æ = a = on, un *un;* týnan *to shut*] *To open;* aperire:—Dura heofones he ætýnde *januas cœli aperuit,* Ps. Spl. 77, 27. v. a-týnan.

æt-ys *is present;* adest, Mk. Jun. 4, 29. v. æt-eom.

æt-ýwan; *p.* de; *pp.* ed. I. *v. trans. To shew, reveal, manifest;* ostendere, manifestare:—Ðú me ætýwdest earfoðes feala *ostendisti mihi tribulationes multas,* Ps. Th. 70, 19: Exon. 121 b; Th. 465, 34; Hö. 114: Judth. 11; Thw. 24, 6; Jud. 174. Ðá him wearþ on slǽpe swefen ætýwed *then was a dream revealed to him in sleep,* Cd. 199; Th. 247, 13; Dan. 496: Exon. 31 a; Th. 96, 19; Cri. 1576. II. *v. intrans. To appear;* apparere, manifestari:—Ealle ætýwaþ *omnes apparuerint,* Ps. Th. 91, 6. Deóful ætýwde *the devil appeared,* Andr. Kmbl. 2338; An. 1170. Nolde ǽfre siððan ætýwan *would not ever afterwards appear,* Cd. 73; Th. 89, 16; Gen. 1481. v. æteówian.

æt-ýwnys, -nyss, æt-ýwedness, æt-eówedniss, æt-íwedness, e; *f. A shewing, manifestation, laying open, a declaration;* ostensio:—Seó ætýwnys heofonlíces wundres *miraculi cœlestis ostensio,* Bd. 3, 11; S. 535, 23. Mid monigra heofonlícra wundra ætýwnysse *miraculorum multorum ostensione,* Bd. 1, 26; S. 488, 10. Óþ ætýwednessum, Lk. Foxe 1, 80.

ǽw, ǽwe, es; *n.* [ǽ *law*]. I. *law,* what is established by law, hence *wedlock, marriage, a marriage vow;* lex, matrimonium:—Ðætte ryht ǽw gefæstnod wǽre *that just law might be settled,* L. In. pref; Th. i. 102, 9: 1; Th. i. 102, 16. Rihtum ǽwe *legitimo matrimonio,* Bd. 4, 6; S. 573, 17, note. Se man ðæt ǽwe brycþ *homo qui adulterium committit,* L. M. I. P. 15; Th. ii. 268, 28. II. a female bound by the law of marriage, *a wife;* conjux legitima, uxor justa:—Se ðe hæfþ ǽwe *he who has a wife;* qui legitimam uxorem habet, L. M. I. P. 17; Th. ii. 270, 6. Gif ceorl wið óðres riht ǽwe hǽmþ *si maritus cum alterius legitima uxore adulteraverit,* 18; Th. ii. 270, 10. Se man, ðe his riht ǽwe forlǽt, and óðer wíf nímþ, he biþ ǽwbreca *the man who forsakes his lawful wife* [suam legitimam uxorem], *and takes another woman* [aliam mulierem], *he is an adulterer*, L. Ecg. P. ii. 8; Th. ii. 184, 21. Gif hwylc man wið óðres riht ǽwe hǽmþ, oððe wíf wið óðres gemæccan, fæste vii geár *if any man commit adultery with the lawful wife* [cum legitima uxore] *of another, or a woman* [mulier] *with the husband of another, let the fast be seven years*, ii. 10; Th. ii. 186, 6. vide ǽ.

ǽw; *adj. Lawful, legitimate, related by the law of marriage, married*; legitimus, nuptus, germanus:—Mid his ǽwum wífe *with his lawful wife*, L. Alf. pol. 42; Th. i. 90, 26, 29. Ǣwe gebróðru *brothers of the same marriage, own brothers*; germani fratres, Bd. 1, 27; S. 490, 28.

ǽwan, ðú ǽwest *To despise, contemn, scorn*; spernere, aversari:—Ða ðú ǽfre ne ǽwest *ea tu nunquam spernis*, Ps. C. 129.

ǽw-breca, -brica, ǽw-bryca, an; *m.* [ǽw *marriage*, breca *a breaker*] *A breaker of the marriage vow, an adulterer*; adulter:—Se ðe his ǽwe forlǽt, and nímþ óðer wíf, he biþ ǽwbryca [Wilk. ǽwbrica] *he who leaves his wife, and taketh another woman, he is an adulterer*, L. M. I. P. 16; Th. ii. 268, 30.

ǽw-bryce, es; *m. A breaking of the marriage vow, adultery*; adulterium:—Wið ǽghwylcne ǽwbryce *against all kind of adultery*, L. C. E. 24; Th. i. 374, 10: L. C. S. 51; Th. i. 404, 20: L. Edm. S; Th. i. 246, 8.

ǽwda, an; *m. A witness, one who affirms the truth by oath*; fidejussor, consacramentalis:—Hæbbe him in áþe óðerne ǽwdan gódne *let him have with him in the oath another good witness*, L. Wih. 23; Th. i. 42, 8. Mid gódum ǽwdum *by good witnesses*, L. H. E. 2; Th. i. 28, 2.

ǽwda-man, -mann, es; *m. A witness*; fidejussor, consacramentalis:—Rím ǽwdamanna *a number of witnesses*, L. H. E. 5; Th. i. 28, 12. v. ǽwda.

ǽwe, es; *n. Law*; lex, L. M. I. P. 15; Th. ii. 268, 28. v. ǽw.

ǽ-welm, -wellm, -wylm, -wylme, -wielme, es; *m.* [eá *water*, wælm *a welling* or *boiling up*] *A welling up of water, spring, fountain, source, head of a river, beginning*; aquæ fons:—Swá sum mical ǽwelm and diópe *as some great and deep spring*, Bt. 34, 1; Fox 134, 10. Seó eá cymþ eft to ðam ǽwelme *the river comes again to the source*, Fox 134, 17. Ðe mæg geseón ðone hluttran ǽwellm *who can behold the clear fountain*, 35, 6; Fox 166, 25. Gif he gesión mǽge æðelne ǽwelm ǽlces gódes [MS. goodes] *if he may see the noble fountain of all good*, 23, 7; Met. 23, 4: 20, 517; Met. 20, 259. Andlang Lígan óþ hire ǽwylm *along the Lea unto its source*, L. A. G. 1; Th. i. 152, 9. Ðære ǽwylme [MS. L. ǽwielme] is neáh ðære eá Rínes *whose spring is near the river Rhine*, Ors. 1, 1; Bos. 18, 25. God is ǽwelm and fruma eallra gesceafta *God is the beginning and origin of all creatures*, Bt. Met. Fox 29, 161; Met. 29, 81. v. eá-wylm.

æ-wén; *adj.* [æ *without*, wén *hope*] *Doubtful, uncertain*; dubius:—And eów biþ eówre líf æwéne *and your life will be doubtful to you*, Deut. 28, 66.

ǽwen-bróðor *a brother of the same marriage, an own brother*; germanus, Cot. 97. v. ǽw; *adj.*

ǽ-werd; *adj.* [ǽ *law*, werd *from* werdan *to corrupt*] *Perverse, froward, averse*; perversus. v. wyrdan *to corrupt*.

æ-werdla, an; *m. Damage, injury*, L. In. 42; Th. i. 128, 10. v. æ-wyrdla.

ǽw-fæst; *adj. Firm in observing the law, religious, bound by the law, married*; religiosus, vinculo nuptiarum constrictus:—Ǣwfæst *religiosus*, Scint. 28. Ǣwfæst man *a married man*, L. C. S. 51; Th. i. 404, 21. v. ǽ-fæst.

ǽw-fæsten, es; *n.* [ǽw *law*, fæsten *a fast*] *A fixed* or *legal fast*; legitimum jejunium:—To ǽwfæstene *for the legal fast*, Rubc. Lk. Bos. 3, 1 a, notes, p. 578.

ǽw-fæst-man *a man bound by law, a married man*; vinculo nuptiarum constrictus, L. C. S. 51; Th. i. 404, 21.

ǽw-festnys, -nyss, e; *f. Religion, piety*; religio, pietas. v. ǽfestnes.

ǽ-wintre; *adj.* [ǽ = ǽn = án *one*] *Of one winter* or *year, continuing for a year*. v. án-wintre.

ǽ-wintre-cyning, es; *m. A king* or *ruler for one winter* or *year, a consul*; consul. v. winter; *g.* wintres.

ǽwisc, e; *f. A dishonour, disgrace, offence*; dedecus, scandalum:—Cwæþ ðæt him to micel ǽwisce wǽre *said that it would be much disgrace to them*, Ors. 4, 6; Bos. 86, 26. On ǽwisce *in scandalum*, Ps. Th. 68, 23. [*Goth.* aiwisks, *n. dedecus.*]

ǽwisc; *adj. Disgraced, ashamed, abashed*; dedecoratus. v. ǽwisc-mód.

ǽwisc-berende; *part. Bearing disgrace, unchaste, lewd, unclean, shameless, impudent*; impudicus. v. ǽwisc, berende *bearing*.

ǽwisc-mód; *adj. Disgraced in mind, ashamed, abashed*; dedecoratus animo, pudore suffusus:—Ides, ǽwiscmód, andswarode *the woman, disgraced in mind, answered*, Cd. 42; Th. 55, 18; Gen. 896. Ðæt he ǽwiscmód eft sídade, heán, hyhta leás *that he abashed returned, depressed, void of hopes*, Exon. 46 a; Th. 157, 23; Gú. 896: 80 b; Th. 302, 16; Fä. 37. Gewiton hym ða Norþmen Dyflin sécan ǽwiscmóde *then the Northmen departed, abashed in mind, to seek Dublin*, Chr. 938; Th. 207, 16, col. 1; Æðelst. 56.

ǽwisc-nys, -ness, e; *f. Disgrace, obscenity, filthiness, a blushing for shame, reverence*; dedecus, obscenitas, pudore suffusio, reverentia:—Ǣwiscnys *reverentia*, Ps. Spl. C. 34, 30. On ǽwiscnesse *openly, as not being ashamed to be seen*; in propatulo, Cot. 110, 202.

ǽ-wita, an; *m.* [ǽ *lex*, wita *gnarus homo, sapiens*] *One skilled in the law, a counsellor*; legis peritus, consiliarius:—Ealdum ǽwitan ageaf andsware *gave answer to the old counsellor*, Elen. Kmbl. 907; El. 455.

ǽw-líc; *adj. Lawful*; legitimus, Procem. R. Conc. v. ǽ-líc.

ǽwnian; *p.* ode; *pp.* od [ǽw *marriage*] *To marry, wed*; connubio jungere, Leo 104. DER. be-ǽwnian.

ǽ-wrítere, es; *m. A writer, composer* or *framer of laws*; legum conditor, Prov. 8.

æwul *A wicker-basket with a narrow neck for catching fish, a* WEEL; nassa, Ælfc. Gl. 102; Som. 77, 85; Wrt. Voc. 56, 9.

ǽwum-boren; *part. Lawfully born, born in wedlock*; legitimo matrimonio natus:—Æt his dehter ǽwum-borenre *with his lawfully-born daughter*, L. Alf. pol. 42; Th. i. 90, 28. v. ǽw.

ǽwunge; *adv. Openly, publicly*; manifeste:—On ǽwunge *openly, abroad, in the sight of all*; in propatulo. v. eáwunga, eáwunge.

ǽ-wylm, es; *m. A spring, fountain, source*:—Andlang Lígan óþ hire ǽwylm *along the Lea unto its source*, L. A. G. 1; Th. i. 152, 9. v. ǽ-welm.

æ-wyrdla, -werdla, an; *m. Damage, detriment, injury*; detrimentum:—He sóna mycle wonunge and æwyrdlan wæs wyrcende ðære mærwan cyrican weaxnesse *magno tenellis ibi adhuc ecclesiæ crementis detrimento fuit*, Bd. 2, 5; S. 506, 37: 1, 3; S. 475, 21: Herb. 141; Lchdm. i. 262, 11. v. æf-wyrdla.

æ-wyrp, es; *m.* [æ = a *from*, wyrp *a cast*, from wyrpan *or* weorpan *to cast*] *A cast-away, throwing away*; abjectus, abjectio:—Ǣwyrp folces *abjectio populi*, R. Ben. 7.

ÆX = ÆCS, æsc, acas, e; *f*: acase, axe, an; *f*. what is brought to an edge, *An* AXE, *a hatchet, pickaxe*; securis, ascia:—Eallunga ys seó æx to ðæra treówa wurtrumum asett *jam enim securis ad radicem arborum posita est*, Mt. Bos. 3, 10. Mid æxum *with axes*, Ps. Th. 73, 6. On æxe *in securi*, Ps. Spl. 73, 7. Forðon seó æx [MS. H. sió æsc; seó eax B.] biþ melda, nalles þeóf *because the axe is an informer, not a thief*; quia securis acclamatrix potius est, non fur, L. In. 43; Th. i. 128, 23. [*O. Sax.* acus, *f*: *N. Dut.* akse, *f*: *Ger.* axt, *f*: *M. H. Ger.* ackes, *f*: *O. H. Ger.* achus, *f*: *Goth.* aqizi, *f*: *Dan.* ökse: *Swed.* yxa: *O. Nrs.* öx, *f*: *Lat.* ascia, *f*: *Grk.* ἀξίνη.]

æx, e; *f. An axis*; axis, Ælfc. Gr. 9, 28; Som. 11, 45. v. eax.

æxe, an; *f. Ashes*, Ps. Spl. T. 101, 10. v. axe, asce.

æxian; *p.* ode *To ask*; rogare:—Ǣxodon *asked*; interrogaverunt, Ps. Spl. T. 136, 3. v. acsian.

af- = æf- = of- *of, from, away from*; de, ex, ab. v. æf-, of-: af-god *an idol*.

a-fǽded; *part.* [*for* a-féded; *pp. of* a-fédan *to feed, nourish*] *Fed, nourished, brought up, educated*; nutritus, Bd. 1, 27; S. 489, 37.

a-fæged, -fægd; *part. Depicted, drawn*; depictus:—Bǽron anlícnysse Drihtnes Hǽlendes on brede afægde and awritene *ferebant imaginem Domini Salvatoris in tabula depictam*, Bd. 1, 25; S. 487, 4. v. a-fægrian.

a-fægniende *rejoicing*, = fægniende; *part. of* fægnian.

a-fægrian; *p.* ode; *pp.* od *To make fair* or *beautiful, to adorn, embroider*; depingere, ornare:—Mid missendlícum blóstmum wyrta afægrod *variis herbarum floribus depictus*, Bd. 1, 7; S. 478, 22.

a-fælan, -fællan; *p.* de; *pp.* ed *To overturn, overthrow, cast out, drive out, cause to stumble, offend*; evertere, prosternere, ejicere, scandalizare, Mt. Rush. Stv. 21, 12: Mk. Rush. War. 3, 23: Mt. Rush. Stv. 18, 6. v. ge-fælan.

a-fǽman; *p.* de; *pp.* ed *To foam out, breathe out*; exspumare, exhalare:—Múþ ic ontýnde mínne wíde, ðæt me mín oroþ út afǽmde *os meum aperui, et exhalavi spiritum*, Ps. Th. 118, 131.

a-fǽran; *p.* de; *pp.* ed [a, fǽran *to terrify*] *To make greatly afraid, to affright, terrify, dismay, astound*; exterrere, perterrere, consternare, stupefacere:—Ðæt heó afǽre fleógan on nette *that she may terrify flies into her net*, Ps. Th. 89, 10. Folc wæs afǽred *the folk was affrighted*, Cd. 166; Th. 206, 3; Exod. 446: Exon. 63 b; Th. 233, 15; Ph. 525: Mk. Bos. 9, 6, 15: Lk. Bos. 24, 4. Híg wurdon ealle afǽrede *erant omnes exterriti*, Gen. 42, 35: Ex. 20, 18.

a-færþ *he shall lead out*, Ps. Spl. 51, 5. v. afaran II.

a-fæstan; *p.* -fæste; *pp.* -fæsted *To fast*; jejunare:—He afæste to ǽfenes *he fasted till evening*, Bd. 3, 23; S. 554, 32: 3, 27; S. 559, 13.

afæstla; *interj. O certainly! O assuredly!* O certe:—Afæstla, and hi lá hi, and wella well, and þyllíce óðre syndon Englisc interjectiones *O certainly, and alas, and well well, and such other are English interjections*, Ælfc. Gr. 48; Som. 49, 28.

a-fæstnian; *p.* ode; *pp.* od *To fix, fasten* or *make firm, to strengthen, fortify, confirm, betroth, espouse, inscribe*; munire, firmare, consignare libris, infigere:—Ðæt we hí móton afæstnian on ðé *that we may fix them* [our eyes] *on thee*, Bt. 33, 4; Fox 132, 31: Bt. Met. Fox 20, 525; Met. 20, 263. Hú afæstnod wæs feld-húsa mǽst *how that greatest of* *field-houses was fastened*, Cd. 146; Th. 183, 2; Exod. 85: 173; Th. 218, 17; Dan. 40. Ðe he on fíf bócum afæstnode *which he inscribed in five books*, Hexam. 1; Norm. 2, 18: Deut. 32, 23. Afæstnod ic eom *infixus sum*, Ps. Spl. 68, 2.

a-fandelíc *probable*. v. a-fandigendlíc.

a-fandian, -fandigean; *p*. ode, ude, ade; *pp*. od, ud, ad; *v. a. To prove, try, to make a trial, to discover by trying, to experience*; probare, tentare, experiri:—Ðú afandodest heorte míne *probasti cor meum*, Ps. Spl. 16, 4. Lá líceteras, cunne ge afandian heofones ansýne and eorþan, húmeta ná afandige ge ðas tíde? *hypocritæ, faciem cœli et terræ nostis probare, hoc autem tempus quomodo non probatis?* Lk. Bos. 12, 56. Ðú hit hæfst afandad be ðé selfum *thou hast experienced it of thyself*, Bt. 31, 1; Fox 112, 19. Seolfor afandod eorþan *argentum probatum terræ*, Ps. Spl. 11, 7: 80, 7. Afandud, Gen. 43, 23. Afanda hwæðer Freá wille *make a trial whether the Lord will*, Cd. 101; Th. 134, 23; Gen. 2229.

a-fandigendlíc, -fandelíc, -fandodlíc; *adj. What may be tried, proved, probable*; probabilis, Scint. de prædest.

a-fandung, e; *f. A trying*; probatio, experientia, Scint. v. fandung.

a-fangen *taken, received*: assumptus, Mk. Bos. 16, 19. v. a-fón.

afara *a son*, Chr. 937; Th. 200, 41, col. 1; Æðelst. 7. v. eafora.

a-faran, he -færþ; *p*. -fór, *pl*. afóron; *pp*. -faren. I. *v. n. To depart, march, to go out of* or *from a place*; exire, egredi:—Hie of Egyptum út afóron *they marched out from Egypt*, Cd. 173; Th. 217, 14; Dan. 6. II. *v. act. To remove, lead out*; emigrare:—Afærþ ðé *emigrabit te*, Ps. Spl. 51, 5.

a-feallan; *p*. -feól, -feóll, *pl*. -feóllon; *pp*. -feallen *To fall down*; cadere:—Ðæt hús afeóll *domus cecidit*, Lk. Bos. 6, 49: Cd. 202; Th. 251, 1; Dan. 557: Jud. 16, 30. Wearþ afeallen Æðelrædes eorl *Ethelred's earl fell* [*in the battle*], Byrht. Th. 137, 46; By. 202.

a-feccan *To receive*; accipere:—He afecþ [MSS. C. T. onféhþ] me *acceperit me*, Ps. Spl. 48, 16.

a-fédan; *p*. -fédde; *pp*. -féded, -féd *To feed, nourish, rear, bring up*; nutrire, cibare, alere, pascere:—Heó bearn afédeþ *she nourishes her child*, Salm. Kmbl. 746; Sal. 372: Ps. Th. 135, 26: 83, 3. Ðæt ðú hí afédde mid ðý Godes worde *that thou didst feed them with the word of God*, Bd. 3, 5; S. 527, 34: Ors. 1, 6; Bos. 29, 10: Ps. Th. 94, 7: 99, 3: Andr. Kmbl. 1177; An. 589. He wæs aféded *he was brought up*, 1367; An. 684. He wæs aféded and gelæred *he was reared and taught*; nutritus atque eruditus est, Bd. 5, 20; S. 642, 16. Wearþ Iafeðe geóguþ aféded *to Japhet was youth brought up*, Cd. 78; Th. 96, 34; Gen. 1604: 82; Th. 102, 29; Gen. 1707. Ic eom aféd *pascor*, Ælfc. Gr. 33; Som. 36, 44. Ðá híg afédde wǽron *quibus adultis*, Gen. 25, 27.

a-féhþ *receives*; suscipit, Ps. Spl. 47, 3. DER. a-féhan. v. féhan, fón.

a-fellan; *p*. de; *pp*. ed *To fell*; cædere, prosternere, L. In. 43; Th. i. 128, 23. v. a-fyllan.

a-felle *barked*; decorticatum, R. 115. v. æ-felle.

Afen, Afn, e; *f*: Afene, an; *f*. I. AVON, *the name of a river in Somersetshire*:—Eást óþ Afene múþan *east at the Avon's mouth*, Chr. 918; Th. 190, 4. II. also of other rivers in different parts of England:—Into Afenan múþan *into Avon's mouth*, Chr. 1067; Th. 342, 5.

aféng, aféngon *took*, Ps. Spl. 47, 8: 118, 16; *p. of* a-fón.

a-feohtan; *p*. -feaht, *pl*. -fuhton; *pp*. -fohten. I. *to fight against, attack, assail*; impugnare, expugnare:—Bryttas Ongel þeóde afuhton *the Britons fought against the English nation*, Bd. 5, 23; S. 647, 1: 4, 26; S. 602, 25. Hí afuhton me *expugnaverunt me*, Ps. Th. 108, 2: Ps. Grn. 34, 1. II. *to tear* or *pluck out*; evellere:—Ǽr hit afohten foldan losige *priusquam evellatur*, Ps. Th. 128, 4. v. feohtan.

a-feóll *fell*; cecidit, Lk. Bos. 6, 49; *p. of* afeallan.

a-feormian, -igan; *p*. ode; *pp*. od; *v. trans*. [a *intensive*, feormian *to cleanse*] *To cleanse, clean thoroughly, purge, wash away*; mundare, emundare, permundare, diluere:—Mid besmum afeormod *scopis mundatus*, Lk. Bos. 11, 25. He afeormaþ his þyrscelflóre *permundabit aream suam*, Mt. Bos. 3, 12. Hyt ðone magan ealne afeormaþ *it purges the whole stomach*, Herb. 60, 3; Lchdm. i. 162, 19. Ic afeormige *diluo*, Ælfc. Gr. 28, 3; Som. 30, 49. Hit afeormaþ of ealle ða nebcorn *it will cleanse away all the face pimples*, Herb. 22, 3; Lchdm. i. 118, 24.

a-feormung, e; *f. A cleansing, purging*; purgatio, Scint. 2.

a-feorran, -ferran, -firran, -fyrran; *p*. de, ode; *pp*. ed, od *To remove, take away, expel*; removere, elongare, amovere, auferre:—Ðæs líchoman fæger and his streón mágon beón afeorred *the fairness of the body and its strength may be taken away*, Bt. 32, 2; Fox 116, 31. Ðú afeorrodyst fram me freónd and nýhstan *elongasti a me amicum et proximum*, Ps. Spl. C. 87, 19: Cd. 219; Th. 282, 9; Sat. 284.

a-feorsian, -fersian, -firsian, -fyrsian; *p*. ode; *pp*. od. I. *v. trans. To remove, take away, expel*; removere, elongare, expellere:—Ðe afeorsiaþ hine fram ðé *qui elongant se a te*, Ps. Spl. 72, 26: L. C. E. 4; Th. i. 360, 29. II. *v. intrans. To go away, depart*; emigrare:—Ic ná afeorsie *non emigrabo*, Ps. Spl. 61, 6.

afera *a son*, Cd. 95; Th. 123, 31; Gen. 2054. v. eafora.

a-féran; *p*. de; *pp*. ed *To affright, terrify*; perterrere, Chr. 1083; Th. 352, 9. . a-fǽran.

a-ferian, -igan; *p*. ede; *pp*. ed *To take away, remove, withdraw*; auferre, amovere, subducere, cum averiis vel curru vehere, averiare:—Ðæt ðú ðe aferige of ðisse folcsceare *that thou withdraw thyself from this people*, Cd. 114; Th. 149, 19; Gen. 2477. He aferede *he bore away*, Andr. Kmbl. 2355; An. 1179: Ps. Th. 135, 25: Menol. Fox 47; Men. 23. Gif he aferaþ *if he remove*; si averiat, L. R. S. 4; Th. i. 434, 8. He sceal aferian [MS. auerian = averian = aferian] *he shall remove*; debet averiare, 432, 10. v. a-feorran.

a-ferran; *p*. de; *pp*. ed *To remove, take away*; elongare, removere:—Gást háligne fram me aferredne *the holy spirit taken from me* [*acc. absol.*], Ps. C. 97: Bt. 39, 11; Fox 230, 19. v. a-feorran.

a-ferscean [a, fersc *fresh*] *To freshen, to become fresh*; salsuginem deponere:—Swá swá of ðære sǽ cymþ ðæt wæter innon ða eorþan and ðǽr aferesceaþ *thus from the sea the water enters into the earth and then becomes fresh*, Bt. 34, 6; Fox 140, 18.

a-fersian *to take away*; removere. v. a-feorsian.

a-festnian *to fix, fasten*; munire, firmare. v. a-fæstnian.

a-fétigan *to beat with the feet, to praise, applaud*; plaudere:—Ic afétige *plaudo*, Ælfc. Gr. 28, 4; Som. 31, 28.

Affric; *def. m*. Affrica; *adj*. AFRICAN; Afer, Africanus:—Severus se Cásere Affrica *Severus Cæsar Afer*, Bd. 1, 5; S. 476, 5, note. Fóron Rómane on Affrice, *acc. pl. the Romans went against* [*upon*] *the African people*, Ors. 4, 6; Bos. 84, 24: 5, 4; Bos. 105, 2: 5, 7; Bos. 106, 22. On Africum *among the African people*, 6, 1; Bos. 115, 31.

Affrica; *indecl: but Lat*. Affrica, *gen*. æ; *acc*. am; *f. Africa*:—Asia and Affrica togædere licgaþ *Asia and Africa lie together*, Ors. 1, 1; Bos. 15, 14. Ðære Affrica norþ-west gemǽre *the north-west boundary of Africa*, id; Bos. 16, 4. Nú wille we ymbe Affrica *now will we* [*speak*] *about Africa*, id; Bos. 24, 26. Hý ða þrý dǽlas on þreó tonemdon—Asiam, and Európam, and Affricam *they named the three parts by three names—Asia, and Europe, and Africa*, id; Bos. 15, 5: 5, 11; Bos. 109, 23: 6, 30; Bos. 126, 32.

Affrican, es; *m. An African*; Africanus:—Regulus feaht wið Affricanas *Regulus fought against Africans*, Bt. 16, 2; Rawl. 33, 19. v. African.

af-god, es; *n*. [af = of = æf *a, ab*; god, *n. a heathen god*] *An idol, an image*; idolum. [*Platt. Dut*. afgod, *m*: *O. H. Ger*. apcot, *n*: *M. H. Ger*. abgot, *n. m*: *Ger*. abgott, *m*: *Goth*. afguþs *impius*: *Dan. Swed*. afgud, *m*: *O. Nrs*. afguð, *m*.] v. god; *n*.

af-godnes, -ness, e; *f. Idolatry, the worshipping of images*; idololatria. v. af, god, es; *n. a heathen god*; -nes, -ness.

a-fíndan; *p*. -fánd, *pl*. -fúndon; *pp*. -fúnden *To find, detect, feel, experience*; invenire, deprehendere, experiri, sentire:—Ðe he Godes eorre afúnde *though he felt God's anger*, Ps. C. 25. Ic afínde *experior*, Ælfc. Gr. 31; Som. 35, 55. Ðis wíf wæs afúnden on unrihton hǽmede *hæc mulier deprehensa est in adulterio*, Jn. Bos. 8, 4: Bt. 35, 5; Fox 162, 31.

a-firhtan *to affright*; exterrere:—Hí flugon afirhte to múntum *they fled affrighted to the mountains*, Gen. 14, 10. v. a-fyrhtan.

a-firran; *p*. de; *pp*. ed *To remove, take away, put away, expel*; elongare, amovere, auferre:—Ðæt he him afirre frécne geþohtas *that he put away from him wicked thoughts*, Cd. 219; Th. 282, 9; Sat. 284. Crist heó afirde *Christ expelled them*, 214; Th. 269, 3; Sat. 67: Ps. Spl. T. 87, 19. v. a-feorran.

a-firsian; *p*. ode; *pp*. od *To take away, remove*; longefacere, removere:—He afirsode fram us unrihtwísnysse *longefecit a nobis iniquitates*, Ps. Spl. M. 102, 12. v. a-feorsian.

a-fleón, he -flíhþ; *p*. -fleáh, *pl*. -flugon; *pp*. -flogen. I. *v. intrans. To flee away*; effugere:—Gǽst aflíhþ *the spirit fleeth away*, Exon. 40 a; Th. 132, 20; Gú. 475: 58 a; Th. 208, 13; Ph. 155. II. *v. trans. To drive away, put to flight*; fugare:—Hí aflogene wǽron *they were put to flight*, Jud. 6, 14. DER. fleón.

a-fleótan *To float off, scum, clarify, purify liquor by scumming*; despumare. DER. fleótan.

a-fleów *overflowed*, Ors. 5, 4; Bos. 105, 9; *p. of* aflówan.

a-flian *to put to flight*; fugare, Herb. 96, 2; Lchdm. i. 208, 20. v. a-fligan.

a-fliéman; *p*. de; *pp*. ed *To cause to flee, to banish*:—Síe he afliémed *let him be* [*as one*] *banished*, L. Alf. pol. 2; Th. i. 60, 17. v. a-flýman, ge-fléman.

a-fligan; *p*. de; *pp*. ed [a, fligan] *To drive away, put to flight*; fugare, arcere:—Sóna hit ðone fefer afligeþ *it will soon put the fever to flight*, Herb. 37, 2; Lchdm i. 138, 5. Aflian [MS. B. afligan] *to put to flight*, 96, 2; Lchdm. i. 208, 20. Ic aflige míne fýnd *arcesso inimicos meos*, Ælfc. Gr. 28, 2; Som. 30, 43. Afliged beón *to be driven away*, R. Ben. cap. 48. Afliged mon *an apostate*, Prov. 6.

a-fliung, e; *f. A fleeing*; rejectio:—Mete-afliung *a rejecting of meat*; atrophia, Ælfc. Gl. 10; Som. 57, 41; Wrt. Voc. 19, 44.

a-flogen *driven away*, Jud. 6, 14; *pp. of* a-fleón.

a-flówan; *p*, -fleów, *pl*. -fleówon; *pp*. -flówen *To flow from, flow over*; effluere:—Etna fýr afleów up *the fire of Etna flowed over*, Ors. 5, 4; Bos. 105, 9.

a-flyge, es; *m.* [a, flyge *a flight*] *A flying, flight;* volatus. [*Ger.* flug, Grm. Wörterbuch; fuga?]

a-flýman; *p.* de; *pp.* ed; *v. trans.* [a, flýman] *To cause to flee, put to flight, drive away, banish, scatter, disperse;* fugare, in fugam vertere, ejicere, pellere, dispergere:—He swá manige man aflýmde *he caused so many men to flee*, Byrht. Th. 138, 61; By. 243. Ðú me aflýmst *tu me ejicis*, Gen. 4, 14. Wurdon twegen æðelingas aflýmde of Sciððian *two noblemen were driven from Scythia*, Ors. 1, 10; Bos. 32, 34. Sý he aflýmed *let him be [as one] banished*, L. Alf. pol. 2; Th. i. 60, 17, note. And eall his weored oððe ofslægen wæs oððe aflýmed *ejusque totus vel interemptus vel dispersus est exercitus*, Bd. 2, 20; S. 521, 13.

afol, es; *n. Power;* vires, robur:—Eallum his afole *with all his power*, L. I. P. 2; Th. ii. 304, 22. v. abal.

a-fón; *p.* -féng, *pl.* -féngon; *pp.* -fangen, -fongen *To receive, take, take up, hold up, support, seize, lay hold of;* suscipere, assumere, corripere, occupare, tradere:—We aféngon mildheortnysse ðíne on midle temple *suscepimus misericordiam tuam in medio templi*, Ps. Spl. 47, 8: 118, 116. Afónde *suscipiens*, 146, 6. He wæs on heofonum afangen *assumptus est in cælum*, Mk. Bos. 16, 19. Hyre se aglǽca ageaf andsware, forht afongen *to her the wretch gave answer, seized with fear*, Exon. 70 a; Th. 261, 24; Jul. 320: 25 a; Th. 73, 3; Cri. 1184. Ðæt Johannes wæs afongen *quod Johannes traditus esset*, Mt. Rush. Stv. 4, 12.

a-fónde *taking up, raising up;* suscipiens, Ps. Spl. 146, 6; *part. of* a-fón.

afor; *adj. Vehement, dire, hateful, rough, austere;* vehemens, atrox, odiosus, asper, austerus, acerbus:—Iudiþ, egesfull and afor *Judith, dreadful and vehement*, Judth. 12; Thw. 25, 13; Jud. 257. Afrum onfengum *with their dire attempts*, Exon. 40 a; Th. 133, 15; Gú. 490. Ðæt [sǽd] byþ þreóhyrne, and hyt byþ afor and sweart *the seed is three-cornered, and it is rough and swarthy*, Herb. 181, 1; Lchdm. i. 316, 11. [*Goth.* abrs *strong: O. Nrs.* æfr *sævus, vehemens, ferox.*] v. nefre.

a-fór, -fóron *departed*, Ors. 2, 4; Bos. 45, 14: Cd. 173; Th. 216, 14; Dan. 6; *p. of* a-faran.

afora *a son*, Chr. 937; Th. 200, 41, col. 3; Æðelst. 7. v. eafora.

afor-feorsian; *p.* ode; *pp.* od *To defer, delay, prolong;* prolongare:—Eardbiggengnes [MS. eardbiggendes] mín aforfeorsode is *incolatus meus prolongatus est*, Ps. Spl. 119, 5; Lambeth has, Eardbegengnes oððe elþeódignys mín afeorrad oððe gelængd is, Ps. 119, 5; *my pilgrimaging is drawen along*, Wyc. v. feorsian.

a-forhtian; *p.* ode; *pp.* od [a *intensive*, forhtian *to fear*] *To be very much afraid, to tremble with fear, to be affrighted, amazed;* expavescere:—Ðá aforhtode Isaac micelre forhtnisse *expavit Isaac stupore vehementi*, Gen. 27, 33.

á-forþ; *adv.* [á *always*, forþ *forth*] *Always, continually, daily, still;* indies, Cot. 115.

aforud *exalted;* exaltatus. v. ofer-ge-aforud.

a-fréfran; *p.* ede; *pp.* ed *To comfort, console;* consolari:—God eáðe mæg afréfran feásceaftne *God can easily comfort the distressed*, Exon. 10 b; Th. 11, 23; Cri. 175: 13 a; Th. 23, 13; Cri. 368. He mec þurh engel oft afréfreþ *he through his angel oft comforteth me*, 37 a; Th. 121, 10; Gú. 286. We weorþaþ afréfrede *facti sumus sicut consolati*, Ps. Th. 125, 1: 118, 52: Andr. Kmbl. 1275; An. 638.

a-fréfrian; *p.* ode; *pp.* od *To comfort, console;* consolari:—Forwyrnde beón afréfrod sáwle mín *renuit consolari anima mea*, Ps. Spl. 76, 3.

a-freoðan; *p.* ede; *pp.* ed *To froth;* spumare:—Lǽt afreoðan *let it froth*, L. M. 1, 47; Lchdm. ii. 118, 27. [*O. Nrs.* froða, frauð *froth;* spuma.]

Africa = Affrica *Africa;* Africa:—Affrica onginþ *Africa begins*, Ors. 1, 1; Bos. 24, 35. v. Affrica.

African, Affrican, es; *m. An African;* Africanus:—Ðá he feaht wið Africanas, he hæfde sige ofer ða Africanas *when he fought against Africans, he gained a victory over the Africans*, Bt. 16, 2; Fox 52, 39: 54, 1.

Africanisc, Afrisc; *adj. Belonging to Africa, African;* Africanus:—Africanisc æppel [MS. -isca, -ple] *a pomegranate;* malum Punicum, Cot. 133.

Afrisc; *adj. African;* Africanus:—Afrisc meówle *an African maid*, Cd. 171; Th. 215, 7; Exod. 579.

a-froefred *comforted;* consolatus, Mt. Rush. Stv. 5, 4, = a-fréfred; *pp. of* a-fréfran.

a-fúl, es; *n. A fault;* culpa. v. fúl.

a-fúlian; *p.* ode; *pp.* od; *v. n. To become foul, to putrefy, be defiled;* putrescere, putrefieri, inquinari, Scint. 66: 17. v. fúlian.

a-fúnden *found, discovered*, Jn. Bos. 8, 4: Bt. 35, 5; Fox 162, 31; *pp. of* a-findan.

a-fúndennis, -niss, e; *f. An experiment, an invention, a discovery;* experimentum, R. Ben. interl. 59.

a-fýlan; *p.* ede; *pp.* ed; *v. a.* [a, fúl *foul, unclean*] *To foul, defile, pollute, to make filthy, to corrupt;* inquinare, contaminare, fœdare:—Yfel biþ ðæt man mid flǽsc-mete hine sylfne afýle *it is sinful that any one defile himself with flesh-meat*, L. C. S. 47; Th. i. 402, 24: Past. 54, 1. Afýled *fœdatus*, Procem. Greg. Dial. v. ge-fýlan, a-fúlian.

a-fyllan; *p.* de; *pp.* ed [a, fyllan *to fill*] *To fill up* or *full, replenish, satisfy;* replere, implere:—Afyllaþ ða eorþan *replete terram*, Gen. 9, 1. He ne mæg ða gítsunga afyllan *he cannot satisfy the desires*, Bt. 16, 3; Fox 56, 16. Fýres afylled *with fire filled*, Exon. 30 b; Th. 95, 26; Cri. 1563: Cd. 215; Th. 271, 4; Sat. 100: Beo. Th. 2040; B. 1018: Ps. Th. 128, 5.

a-fyllan = a-fellan; *p.* de; *pp.* ed; *v. a.* [a, fyllan, fellan *to fell*] *To fell, to strike* or *beat down, to overturn, subvert, lay low, abolish, slay;* cædere, occidere, prosternere, dejicere, demoliri, comprimere, abrogare:—Gif mon afelle [MS. B. afylle] on wuda wel monega treówa *if any one fell in a wood a good many trees*, L. In. 43; Th. i. 128, 19. Drihten afylþ ðíne fýnd *the Lord will strike down thine enemies*, Deut. 28, 7. Hí to eorþan afyllaþ ðé *ad terram prosternent te*, Lk. Bos. 19, 44: Salm. Kmbl. 595; Sal. 297. Afylde hine *he felled him*, Salm. Kmbl. 917; Sal. 458. Wæs Waldendes lof afylled *the supreme ruler's praise was suppressed*, Chr. 975; Th. 228, 10; Edg. 38. Hú man mæg unlage afyllan *how one may abolish unjust laws*, L. C. S. 11; Th. i. 382, 8. Gif hwá óðres ryht afylle *if any one suppress another's right*, L. Ath. i. 17; Th. i. 208, 16: L. Eth. vi. 8; Th. i. 316, 26. Ðæt hine man afylle *that any one slay him*, 38; Th. i. 324, 23: v. 31; Th. i. 312, 12. v. be-fyllan, ge-.

a-fyran; *p.* ede; *pp.* ed *To remove, take away, expel;* amovere, elongare, Exon. 43 b; Th. 147, 1; Gú. 720. v. a-fyrran.

a-fýran; *p.* de; *pp.* ed, yd [a, fýran *castrare*] *To castrate;* castrare:—Afýred olfend *a dromedary, a kind of swift camel;* dromeda MS. Twegen afýryde men *duo eunuchi*, Gen. 40, 1.

a-fýrd, es; *m. A eunuch;* spado, Cot. 189. v. a-fýrida.

a-fyrhtan; *p.* -fyrhte; *pp.* -fyrhted, -fyrht *To affright, terrify;* terrere, exterrere, perterrere, timore afficere:—He afyrhted wearþ *he was affrighted*, Exon. 52 a; Th. 181, 29; Gú. 1300: Andr. Kmbl. 3057; An. 1531. Wǽran mid egsan ealle afyrhte *with dread were all affrighted*, Cd. 222; Th. 288, 22; Sat. 385. Ða weardas wǽron afyrhte *custodes exterriti sunt*, Mt. Bos. 28, 4: Bd. 3, 16; S. 543, 12, MS. T. Afirhte, Gen. 14, 10. v. a-forhtian.

afýrida, afýryda, an; *m.* [a-fýred; *pp. of* a-fýran] *A eunuch, a castrated animal, servant, courtier;* eunuchus, servus:—Se afýrida *the servant, courtier* [*eunuch*], Gen. 39, 1. Hí sealdon Iosep Putifare ðam afýrydan Faraones *vendiderunt Joseph Putiphari eunucho Pharaonis*, 37, 36.

a-fyrran, -fyran; *p.* ede, de; *pp.* ed [a *from*, fyrr *far*] *To remove, take away, expel, deliver;* amovere, avertere, elongare, auferre, eripere:—Næddran hí afyrraþ *serpentes tollent*, Mk. Bos. 16, 18. Beóþ afyrrede *are taken away*, Ps. Spl. 57, 8. Ðú afyrdest of Jacobe ða graman hæftnéd *avertisti captivitatem Jacob*, Ps. Th. 84, 1. Ðú me afyrdest frýnd ða nýhstan *elongasti a me amicum et proximum*, 87, 18: 88, 36: Bd. 2, 20; S. 522, 23: 4, 11; S. 579, 34. Afyrrinde gefeoht oððe óþ ende eorþan *auferens bella usque ad finem terræ*, Ps. Spl. C. T. 45, 9. Afyrr me feóndum mínum *eripe me de inimicis meis*, Ps. Th. 142, 10. Afyr, 118, 22: 53, 5. Ic ðé wolde cwealm afyrran *I would remove death from thee*, Exon. 28 b; Th. 87, 17; Cri. 1426. Dreám wæs afyrred *joy was removed*, 42 a; Th. 142, 9; Gú. 641. He hæfde feóndas afyrde *he had the fiends expelled*, 43 b; Th. 147, 1; Gú. 720. v. a-feorran.

a-fyrsian; *p.* ode; *pp.* od; *v. a.* [a, fyrsian *to remove*] *To remove farthest away, drive away, dispel;* pellere, propellere, auferre:—He afyrseþ gást ealdormanna *aufert spiritum principum*, Ps. Spl. 75, 12: 45, 9. Ðe deófla afyrseþ *which drives devils away*, L. C. E. 4; Th. i. 360, 29. v. a-feorsian, a-fyrran.

a-fýryda *a eunuch;* eunuchus:—Ðam afýrydan Faraones *eunucho Pharaonis*, Gen. 37, 36. v. afýrida.

a-fýsan; *p.* de; *pp.* ed. I. *to hasten;* festinare, tendere:—Feor afýsan and forþ gangan *to hasten away and to go forward*, Byrht. Th. 131, 4; By. 3. II. *to hasten away, impel, accelerate, incite, excite, make ready;* incitare, accelerare, paratum vel promptum reddere:—Ðonne he afýsed biþ *when he hastened away*, Exon. 65 a; Th. 241, 11; Ph. 654. To heofonum biþ mód afýsed *to heaven is the spirit impelled*, 65 b; Th. 241, 17; Ph. 657: 59 b; Th. 217, 3; Ph. 274: Rood Kmbl. 247; Kr. 125: Exon. 119 a; Th. 457, 22; Hy. 4. 87. Swá ǽr wæter fleówan, flódas afýsde *as the waters flowed before, the excited floods*, 22 b; Th. 61, 17; Cri. 986.

ag, es; *n? Wickedness;* nequitia:—Hí þohton and hí sprǽcon ag *cogitaverunt et locuti sunt nequitiam*, Ps. Spl. T. 72, 8. [*Goth.* aglo, *f. trouble: O. Nrs.* agi, *m. terror:* Grm. ii. 503, 20.] DER. ag-lác, ag-lǽc, -lǽca, -lác-hád, -lǽc-cræft, -lǽc-wíf.

ága, an; *m. A possessor, an owner;* possessor. v. un-ága.

a-gæf *returned;* reddidit, Cd. 196; Th. 244, 24; Dan. 453; *p. of* a-gifan.

a-gǽlan; *p.* de; *pp.* ed. I. *v. trans. To hinder, occupy, detain, delay, neglect;* impedire, retardare, morari, negligere:—Ðæt he ne agǽle gǽstes þearfe *that he delay not his spirit's welfare*, Exon. 19 b; Th. 51, 16; Cri. 817. Me ðiós siccetung hafaþ agǽled *this sighing has hindered me*, Bt. Met. Fox 2, 9; Met. 2, 5. Ic míne tíd-sangas oft agǽlde *I have often neglected my canonical hours*, L. De Cf. 9; Th. ii. 264, 11. Astrecceaþ agǽledan honda *remissas manus erigite*, Past. 11, 1; Cot. MS. And swá eall ðæt folc wearþ mid him ánum agǽled *and all the people were so occupied with him alone*, Ors. 3, 9; Bos. 68, 24. II. *v. intrans. To hesitate, be careless;* cunctari, indiligens esse:—He wihte ne agǽlde ðæs ðe þearf wæs þeódcyninges *he* *was not careless about anything that was needful for the king*, Chr. 1066; Th. 335, 15, col. 1; Edv. 33.

a-gælende; *part. enchanting;* incantans, Ps. Vos. 57, 5. v. a-galan.

a-gælwed *astonished;* consternatus, Bt. 34, 5; Fox 140, 9; MS. Cot. v. a-gelwan.

a-gǽn *gone, past;* præteritus, Cart. Uuerfriþ in app. ad Bædam, S. 772, 1, 4. v. a-gân.

a-gǽþ *happens:*—Hit agǽþ eall swâ *it happens so as* [*also*], Deut. 13, 2. v. agân, gân, hit gǽþ.

a-galan; he -gælþ; *p.* -gôl, *pl.* -gôlon; *pp.* -galen [a, galan *to sing*] *To sing, chant;* canere, cantare:—He fûsleóþ agôl *he sang the death-song*, Exon. 52 b; Th. 183, 1; Gû. 1320. Fyrdleóþ agôl wulf on walde *a war-song sung the wolf in the wood*, Elen. Kmbl. 54; El. 27: Beo. Th. 3047; B. 1521.

a-gâlan *To loose, dissolve;* remittere, Past. 11, 1; Hat. MS. 14 b, 24. v. agǽlan.

a-gan *began;* cœpit, Mk. Bos. 6, 7; *p. of* a-ginnan.

a-gân; *p.* -eóde; *pp.* -gân [a *from, away*, gân *to go*]. I. *to come to pass, happen;* præterire, transire:—Ǽr his tîd agâ [tîde ge MS.] *before his time come to pass*, Exon. 82 a; Th. 310, 3; Seef. 69; [Grn. Gloss.] Đâ sæternes dæg wæs âgân *cum transivisset sabbatum*, Mk. Bos. 16, 1. Ǽfen-fela nihta agâne wǽron *totidem noctes transierunt*, Deut. 9, 11: Andr. Kmbl. 293; An. 147: Elen. Kmbl. 2452; El. 1227. Swâ hit sôþlîce a-eóde *so it truly happened*, K. de visione Isaiæ. II. *to come forth;* provenire:—Him upp agâ horn on heafde *a horn comes forth on his head*, Ps. Th. 68, 32. III. *to approach to any one to solicit him;* procedere ad aliquem sollicitandi causa:—Ne meahton heora bregoweardas agân *might not approach their lords*, Cd. 131; Th. 166, 14; Gen. 2747.

ÂGAN, to âganne; *pres. part.* âgende; *pres. indic.* ic, he âh, đû âhst, *pl.* âgon, âgan, âgun; *p.* ic, he âhte, đû âhtest, *pl.* âhton; *subj.* ic, đû, he âge, *pl.* âgen; *p.* ic âhte, *pl.* âhten; *pp.* âgen. I. *to* OWN, *possess, have, obtain;* possidere, habere, percipere:—Đe micel âgan willaþ *who desire* [*will*] *to possess much*, Bt. 14, 2; Fox 44, 13. Nû ic âh mǽste þearfe *now I have the utmost need*, Byrht. Th. 136, 60; By. 175. Gesyle eall đæt đû âge *vende quæcumque habes*, Mk. Bos. 10, 21. Đû đe âhst dôma geweald *thou that hast power of dignities*, Elen. Kmbl. 1448; El. 726. Âh him lîfes geweald *he hath power over life*, Andr. Kmbl. 1036; An. 518: Cd. 103; Th. 137, 8; Gen. 2270. Wuna đǽm đê âgon *dwell with those who own thee*, Cd. 104; Th. 138, 18; Gen. 2293: 221; Th. 287, 3; Sat. 361. Đæt hie heofonrîce âgan *that they shall possess heaven's kingdom*, 22; Th. 27, 33; Gen. 427. Hî âgun *they possess*, Exon. 33 b; Th. 106, 33; Gû. 50. Đæt ic êce lîf âge *ut vitam æternam percipiam*, Mk. Bos. 10, 17. He sealde eall đæt he âhte *vendidit omnia quæ habuit*, Mt. Bos. 13, 46: Ps. Th. 147, 3: Beo. Th. 5210; B. 2608. Hî gewyrhto âhton *they possessed merits*, Cd. 196; Th. 244, 7; Dan. 444. Âhton, Ps. Th. 118, 79. Đæt hî sige âhten *that they had the victory*, Bd. 3, 2; S. 524, 28. Dôm âgende *possessing power*, Andr. Kmbl. 1139; An. 570: Exon. 68 a; Th. 253, 26; Jul. 186. Đeáh he feoh-gestreón âhte *although he possessed riches*, Exon. 66 b; Th. 245, 13; Jul. 44. II. to make another to own or possess, hence,—*to give, deliver, restore;* dare in possessionem, reddere, rependere:—Êđelstôwe đê ic âgan sceal *I shall give thee a dwelling-place*, Cd. 130; Th. 164, 34; Gen. 2724. On hand âgan *to deliver in hand*, Ors. 3, 11? Âgan ût *to have* or *find out*. Lett âgan ût, hû fela *permit to find out, how many*, Chr. 1085; Th. 353, 5. [Âgan is the first of the following twelve Anglo-Saxon verbs,—âgan, cunnan, dugan, durran, magan, môtan, munan, nugan, sculan, þurfan, unnan, witan, which are called *præterito-præsentia*, because they take their *new infinitives and their present tenses* from *the perfects of strong verbs with their inflections*. These new infinitives form their *p.* tenses regularly in accordance with the weak conjugations. Thus, the new infinitive âgan has *pres.* ic, he âh = âg, *pl.* âgon; *p.* âhte = âgde, *pl.* âhton = âgdon. The *inf.* âgan and the *pres.* âh, *pl.* âgon [*for* igon], retaining preterite inflections, are taken from the *p.* of a strong verb, ascertained from âh [*Goth.* áih], which shews the â of the *p. singular* in the eighth class of Grimm's division of strong verbs [Grm. i. p. 837; Koch i. p. 253], and requires by analogy, with other verbs of the same class, the *inf.* îgan, the *p. pl.* igon, and the *pp.* igen. Thus we find the original verb îgan; *p.* âh, *pl.* igon; *pp.* igen. But in âgan the â of the singular *indef.* is kept in the *pl. inf.* and *pp.* The weak *p.* âhte = âgde, *pl.* âhton = âgdon are formed regularly from the weak *infin.* âgan. The same *præterito-præsens* may be generally observed in the following cognate words:—

	inf.	*pres.*	*pl.*	*p.*
Engl.	owe, *possidere,*			ought.
Laym.	agen,	ah,	agen,	ahte.
O. Sax.	êgan,	[êh],	êgun,	êhta.
O. Frs.	âga, hâga,	âch,	âgon,	âchte.
O. H. Ger.	eigan,		eigumês.	
Goth.	áigan,	áih,	áigum,	áihta.
O. Nrs.	eiga,	â,	eigum,	âtta.]

DER. âgen, -frigea, -nama, -nyss, -slaga: âgend, -freá, -lîce: âhni-an, âgni-an, -end, -endlîc: ge-âgnian, ge-âgnigendlîc: âgenung: ǽht, e; *f.* ǽhte-land, -man, -swân: ǽhtige.

âgan, Cd. 216; Th. 274, 1; Sat. 147; *g. d. acc. etc. of* âge, an; *f. property*.

a-gangan; *pp.* -gangen, -gongen *To go or pass by* or *over, to happen, befal;* præterire, evenire:—Đâ wæs agangen, geára hwyrftum, tû hund and þreó *there were passed, in the circuits of years, two hundred and three*, Elen. Kmbl. 1; El. 1: Chr. 974; Th. 224, 33; Edg. 10. Swâ hit agangen wearþ *how it had befallen*, Beo. Th. 2473; B. 1234. Wæs đæs mǽles mearc agongen *the limit of the time was passed*, Cd. 83; Th. 103, 17; Gen. 1719: Exon. 39 b; Th. 130, 20; Gû. 441.

âge, an; *f. Property;* possessio, proprium:—Đe he to âgan nyle *which he will not have for his property*, Cd. 216; Th. 274, 1; Sat. 147. Đe đê gedafenode âgan to habbanne *quem te conveniebat proprium habere*, Bd. 3, 14; S. 540, 26.

âge, Mk. Bos. 10, 17; *subj. s. of* âgan *to own*.

a-geaf *gave up*, Jn. Bos. 19, 30; *p. of* agifan.

a-geald *rewarded*, Beo. Th. 3335; B. 1665; *p. of* agildan.

a-geán; *prep. Towards;* adversus, Chr. 1052; Th. 314, 23. v. on-geán.

ageán-fêran; *p.* de; *pp.* ed *To go again, return;* reverti, Chr. 1070; Th. 344, 31. v. ongeán-faran.

ageán-hwyrfan *To turn again, to return;* redire, Mk. Jun. 6, 31. v. agên-hwyrfan.

a-geara, -gearwa *prepared;* paratus. v. gearwa *in* gearo; *adj.*

a-gearwian *To prepare;* parare. v. gearwian.

a-geat *understood*, Ps. Spl. 118, 95; *p. of* a-gitan.

a-geát *poured out*, Cd. 47; Th. 60, 20; Gen. 984. v. a-geótan.

a-gêfan; *3rd pl. perf. of* a-gifan, *for* a-gêfon, Menol. Fox 160.

a-geldan; *p.* -geald, *pl.* -guldon; *pp.* -golden *To pay, render;* reddere:—Scilling agelde *let him pay a shilling*, L. H. E. 11, 12; Th. i. 32, 5, 9. v. a-gildan.

a-geldan; *pp.* -geald [Grn.] *To punish;* punire:—Wurdon teónlîce tôđas idge [MS. to þas idge] ageald *the greedy teeth were harmfully punished*, Exon. 61 b; Th. 226, 19; Ph. 408.

a-gelwan; *p.* ede; *pp.* ed *To stupefy, astonish;* stupefacere, consternare:—Đâ wearþ ic agelwed *then I was astonished*, Bt. 34, 5; Fox 140, 9.

a-gên; *prep. acc. Against;* adversum, contra:—Se đe nis agên eów, se is for eów *qui non est adversum vos, pro vobis est*, Mk. Bos. 9, 40. Đîn brôđor hæfþ ǽnig þing agên đê *frater tuus habet aliquid adversum te*, Mt. Bos. 5, 23. v. on-geán; *prep.*

a-gên; *adv.* AGAIN, *anew, also;* iterum, denuo, et:—Đe đê slihþ on đîn gewenge, wend ôđer agên *qui te percutit in maxillam, præbe et alteram*, Lk. Bos. 6, 29. Đâ wende he on scype agên *then he went into the ship again*, 8, 37, 40. Wæs forworht agên *was punished anew*, Cd. 214; Th. 269, 21; Sat. 76. v. on-geán; *adv.*

âgen; *adj.* [*originally the pp. of* âgan *to own, possess*]. I. OWN, *proper, peculiar;* proprius:—Sêcþ his âgen wuldor *gloriam propriam quærit*, Jn. Bos. 7, 18. Godes âgen bearn *God's own child*, Cd. 213; Th. 265, 20; Sat. 10: 109; Th. 144, 27; Gen. 2396: Bd. 3, 14; S. 539, 19. Hire âgenes hûses *of her own house*, Bt. Met. Fox 13, 60; Met. 13, 30. Binnan heora âgenre hŷde *within their own skin*, Bt. 14, 2; Fox 44, 23. On eówerne âgenne dôm *in your own decision*, Andr. Kmbl. 677; An. 339. On his âgenum dagum *in diebus ejus*, Ps. Th. 71, 7. His âgnum willan *on his own accord*, Ors. 4, 11; Bos. 98, 6. Âgna gesceafta *thy own creatures*, Bt. Met. Fox 20, 28; Met. 20, 14: Bt. 14, 2; Fox 44, 36. Đînes âgenes þonces *of thine own choice*, Bt. 8; Fox 26, 12. II. used substantively, *The property owned*, or *one's own property;* proprium:—Agife man đam âgen-frigean his âgen *let his own be rendered to the proprietor*, L. C. S. 24; Th. i. 390, 7: L. Eth. ii. 10; Wilk. 106, 38. [*Chauc.* owen: *Laym.* agen: *Plat.* egen: *O. Sax.* êgan: *O. Frs.* ein, ain, eigen, egen: *Ger. M. H. Ger.* eigen: *O. H. Ger.* eikan, eigan: *Goth.* áigin, *n. and* áihts, *f.* οὐσία: *O. Nrs.* eigin.] v. âgan.

agên-arn *met;* occurrit, Mk. Bos. 5, 2; *p. of* agên-yrnan.

agên-bewendan; *p.* de; *pp.* ed *To turn again, return;* reverti:—And đâ he hine eft agên-bewende *and then he turned himself again*, Mk. Bos. 14, 40.

agên-cuman; *p.* -com, *pl.* -cômon; *pp.* -cumen *To come again;* redire:—Đâ se Hǽlend agên-com *cum rediisset Iesus*, Lk. Bos. 8, 40.

âgend, es; *m.* [*part. of* âgan *to own*] *An owner, a possessor, the Lord;* possessor, proprietarius, Dominus:—Þreóm hundum scillinga gylde se âgend *with three hundred shillings let the owner pay*, L. H. E. 1; Th. i. 26, 9: 3; Th. i. 28, 5. Âgendes êst *the owner's favour*, Beo. Th. 6142; B. 3075. Wuldres Âgend *the Lord of glory*, Exon. 25 b; Th. 73, 32; Cri. 1198: 14 b; Th. 29, 32; Cri. 471. Se Âgend *the Lord;* Dominus, Cd. 158; Th. 196, 21; Exod. 295.

âgend-freá, an; *m. The owning lord, possessor;* dominus, possessor:—He heofona is and đisse eorþan âgend-freá *he is the owning Lord of heaven and of this earth*, Cd. 98; Th. 129, 10; Gen. 2141: Beo. Th. 3770; B. 1883.

âgend-freán; *acc. f. A mistress;* dominam:—Heó [Agar] ongan æfþancum âgend-freán herian *she [Hagar] began to vex her mistress with insults*, Cd. 102; Th. 135, 4; Gen. 2237. v. freá.

âgend-frió, -freó; *indecl. m. An owner, possessor;* possessor:—He agife ðam âgendfrió [âgend-freó MS. B.] ðone monnan *let him give up the man to the owner*, L. In. 53; Th. i. 136, 4. v. âgend-freá.

âgend-lîce; *adv. Properly, as his own;* proprie, Bd. 1, 1; S. 474, 42.

âgen-frigea, -friga, -friá, an; -frige, es; *m. An owner, possessor;* possessor:—Se âgen-frigea *the owner*, L. In. 42; Th. i. 128, 14. Agife man ðam âgen-frigean [-frigan MS. C.] his âgen *let his own be rendered to the proprietor*, L. C. S. 24; Th. i. 390, 7. Ðam âgen-frige *to the possessor*, L. In. 53; Th. i. 136, 4, MS. H. *We also find*,—Se âgena frigea *the possessor;* ðam âgenan frián *to the possessor*, L. Eth. iii. 4; Th. i. 294, 18, 17.

agên-gecyrran *To turn again, recur;* recurrere, Fulg. 9.

agên-gehweorfan; *p.* -gehwearf, *pl.* -gehwurfon; *pp.* -gehworfen *To change again, to return;* redire:—Ðâ hîg agên-gehwurfon *cum redirent*, Lk. Bos. 2, 43.

agên-hwyrfan; *p.* de; *pp.* ed *To turn again, return;* redire:—Manega agên-hwyrfdon [Jun. ageán-hwyrfdon] *multi redibant*, Mk. Bos. 6, 31.

agên-lǽdan; *p.* de; *pp.* ed *To lead back;* reducere, Anlct. Gloss.

âgen-nama, an; *m. One's own* or *proper name;* purum nomen, Fulg. 3: proprium nomen, Ælfc. Gr. 7; Som. 6, 59.

âgen-nys, -nyss, e; *f. An owning, a possession, property;* possessio, S. de Fide Cathol.

agên-sendan; *p.* -sende *To send again, send back;* remittere:—He hine agên-sende to Herode *remisit eum ad Herodem*, Lk. Bos. 23, 7: 23, 11.

âgen-slaga, an; *m. A self-slayer, self-murderer;* qui sibimet ipsi manum infert, Octo Vit. capit.

âgen-spræc, e; *f.* [âgen *own*, spræc *speech*] *One's own tongue, an idiom, the peculiarity of a language;* idioma, Ælfc. Gl. 101; Som. 77, 41. v. gecynde-spræc.

agên-standan; *p.* -stôd, *pl.* -stôdon; *pp.* -standen *To* STAND AGAINST, *urge, insist upon;* obsistere, insistere:—Ða Farisei ongunnan hefilîce him agên-standan *Pharisæi cœperunt graviter insistere*, Lk. Bos. 11, 53.

âgenung, âgnung, âhnung, e; *f. An* OWNING, *a possessing, possession, ownership, claiming as one's own, power* or *dominion over anything;* possessio, dominium:—Gif getrŷwe gewitnes him to âgenunge rŷmþ; forðam âgnung biþ nêr ðam ðe hæfþ, ðonne ðam ðe æfter-sprecþ *if a true witness make way for him to possession; because possession is nearer to him who has, than to him who claims*, L. Eth. ii. 9; Th. i. 296, 20. Be ðære âhnunge *respecting ownership*, L. Ed. 1; Lambd. 38, 25.

agên-yrnan; *p.* -arn, *pl.* -urnon; *pp.* -urnen *To run against, meet with, meet;* occurrere:—Him agênarn ân man *occurrit homo*, Mk. Bos. 5, 2. Inc agênyrnþ sum man *occurret vobis homo*, Mk. Bos. 14, 13.

a-geofan *to restore, give back, repay*, = a-gifan, Heming, p. 104.

a-geolwian [a, geolo *yellow*] *To become yellow, to make to glitter as gold;* flavescere, Herb. 42, ? Lye. v. geolwian.

a-geómrod *lamented;* lamentatus. v. geómerian.

a-geótan, -gîtan; *p.* -geát, -gêt, *pl.* -guton; *pp.* -goten. I. *v. trans. To pour out, shed, strew, spill, deprive of;* effundere, privare:—He his swât ageát *he shed his blood*, Exon. 40 a; Th. 133, 22; Gû. 493: Cd. 47; Th. 60, 20; Gen. 984. He his blôd agêt *he had spilled his blood*, Andr. Recd. 2897; [ageát, Grm. 1449; Kmbl. 2897.] Hî aguton blôd *effuderunt sanguinem*, Ps. Spl. 78, 3: Bd. 1, 7; S. 476, 30: Gen. 9, 6. Ageót cocor *effunde frameam*, Ps. Spl. 34, 3. Agoten *effusus*, Ps. Th. 78, 11. Hie wǽron agotene gôda gehwylces *they were deprived of all goods*, Judth. 10; Thw. 21, 23; Jud. 32. II. *v. intrans. To pour forth;* profluere:—Swâ ðîn swât ageát *thus thy blood poured forth*, Andr. Kmbl. 2881; An. 1443.

a-getan; *p.* de, te; *pp.* ed *To seize, take away, destroy;* corripere, eripere, delere:—Sumne sceal gâr agetan *the spear shall take one away*, Exon. 87 a; Th. 328, 11; Vy. 16: Andr. Grm. 1144: Exon. 127 b; Th. 491, 3; Rä. 80, 8. Ðǽr læg secg mænig gârum ageted *there lay many a warrior destroyed by javelins*, Chr. 937; Th. 202, 21, col. 1; Æðelst. 18. DER. getan.

a-gêton [*they*] *destroyed; 3rd pers. pl. p. of* a-gitan.

âg-hwǽr *everywhere;* ubique, Lye. v. ǽg-hwǽr.

a-giefan; *p.* -geaf; *pp.* -giefen *To restore, render, pay, give;* reddere, solvere, dare, Exon. 73 b; Th. 274, 6; Jul. 529: 26 a; Th. 77, 22; Cri. 1260. v. a-gifan.

a-gieldan *To pay, repay:*—Ðû scyle ryht agieldan *thou shalt pay just retribution*, Exon. 99 b; Th. 372, 25; Seel. 98. v. a-gildan.

a-giémeleásian; *p.* ode; *pp.* od *To neglect, despise:*—Ne agiémeleása ðû Godes swingan *noli negligere disciplinam Domini*, Past. 36, 4; Hat. MS. 47 b, 3. v. a-gîmeleásian.

a-giéta, a-gîta, an; *m. A spendthrift, prodigal;* prodigus, profligator, Past. 20, 1; Hat. MS. 29 a, 26.

a-gifan, -gyfan, -giefan, -geofan; *p.* -gæf, -geaf, -gef, *pl.* -gêfon, -geáfon; *pp.* -gifen, -giefen, -gyfen *To restore, give back, give up, leave, return, repay, render, pay, give;* reddere, restituere, tradere, relinquere, exsolvere, dare:—He wolde hine his fæder agifan *volebat eum reddere patri suo*, Gen. 37, 22. Ûton agifan ðæm êsne his wîf *let us restore to the man his wife*, Bt. 35, 6; Fox 170, 6. Eorþe ageaf ða *the earth gave up those*, Exon. 24 b; Th. 71, 15; Cri. 1156. Ðone hie ðære cwêne agêfon *they gave him up to the queen*, Elen. Kmbl. 1171; El. 587. He agæf him his leóda lâfe *he restored to him the remnant of his people*, Cd. 196; Th. 244, 24; Dan. 453. Ne agife *non restituet*, Ex. 22, 13. Hy fæder ageaf on feónda geweald *her father delivered her up into her foes' power*, Exon. 68 a; Th. 252, 6; Jul. 159. Andreas his gâst ageaf *Andrew gave up his soul*, Menol. Fox 431; Men. 217. Ageaf his gâst *tradidit spiritum*, Jn. Bos. 19, 30. Andreas carcerne ageaf *Andrew left his prison*, Andr. Kmbl. 3155; An. 1580. Him se wer ageaf andsware *to him the man returned answer*, Exon. 49 b; Th. 171, 34; Gû. 1136. Andreas agef andsware *Andrew returned answer*, Andr. Kmbl. 378; An. 189. Ic forþ agef ða, ðe ic ne reáfude ǽr *quæ non rapui, tunc exsolvebam*, Ps. Th. 68, 5: L. In. 60; Th. i. 140, 10. Siððan ge eówre gafulrǽdenne agifen habbaþ *after ye have paid your fare*, Andr. Kmbl. 592; An. 296. He him leán ageaf *he gave him a gift*, Cd. 86; Th. 108, 19; Gen. 1808: 97; Th. 128, 3; Gen. 2121: Th. Diplm. A.D. 830; 465, 31. Hî ageáfon *dono dederunt*, Judth. 12; Thw. 26, 23; Jud. 342. DER. gifan.

a-gift, e; *f? A giving back, restoration;* restitutio. v. gift, e; *f.*

a-gildan, -geldan, -gieldan, -gyldan; *p.* -geald, *pl.* -guldon; *pp.* -golden *To pay, render, repay, restore, reward, requite, permit, allow;* reddere, solvere, rependere, retribuere, concedere:—Ðû scyle ryht agieldan [agildan MS. Verc.] *thou shalt pay just retribution*, Exon. 99 b; Th. 372, 25; Seel. 98. Gyf ic ageald gyldendum me yfelu *si reddidi retribuentibus mihi mala*, Ps. Spl. 7, 4. Ðâ me sǽl ageald *as opportunity permitted to me*, Beo. Th. 3335; B. 1665: 5374; B. 2690: Cd. 93; Th. 121, 11; Gen. 2008. Aguldon me yfelu for gôdum *retribuebant mihi mala pro bonis*, Ps. Spl. 34, 14. Ða onsægdnysse ða ðe fram eów deóflum wǽron agoldene *sacrificia hæc quæ a vobis redduntur dæmonibus*, Bd. 1, 7; S. 477, 37. DER. gildan.

a-gilde, a-gylde; *adv. Without compensation*, L. C. S. 49; Th. i. 404, 14 [MS. A]: L. Eth. v. 31; Th. i. 312, 12. v. æ-gilde.

a-gilpan; *p.* -gealp, *pl.* -gulpon; *pp.* -golpen *To glory, boast, exult;* gloriari, lætari:—Wyt mâgon ðǽr dǽdum agilpan *we may there exult in our deeds*, Cd. 100 a; Th. 377, 2; Seel. 165.

a-giltan; *p.* -gilte; *pp.* -gilt *To sin, fail, do wrong;* delinquere, peccare:—Ic agilte wið eówerne Drihten *peccavi in Dominum vestrum*, Ex. 10, 16: Hy. 7, 103; Hy. Grn. ii. 289, 103. v. a-gyltan.

a-giltst *thou repayest*, Mt. Bos. 5, 33. v. giltst *in* gildan.

a-gîmeleásian, -giémeleásian; *p.* ode; *pp.* od *To neglect, despise;* negligere:—Ne agiémeleása [MS. C. agîmeleása] ðû Godes swingan *noli negligere disciplinam Domini*, Past. 36, 4; Hat. MS. 47 b, 3. v. gŷmeleásian.

a-gimmed, -gymmed; *part. Gemmed, set with gems;* gemmatus:—Agimmed and gesmiðed bend *a gemmed and worked crown, a diadem;* diadema, Ælfc. Gl. 64; Som. 69, 12; Wrt. Voc. 40, 46. Agimmed gerdel, *vel* gyrdel, *vel* angseta, *vel* hringc *a gemmed girdle* or *ring;* strophium, 64; Som. 69, 20; Wrt. Voc. 40, 51; *pp. of* a-gimmian. v. gimmian.

a-ginnan; ic aginne, ðû aginnest, aginst, he aginneþ, agineþ, aginþ, agynþ; *p.* agan, *pl.* agunnon; *pp.* agunnen; *v. a. To begin, to set upon, undertake, take in hand;* incipere:—And agynþ beátan hys efenþeówas *cœperit percutere conservos suos*, Mt. Bos. 24, 49. Hî agynnon hine tǽlan *incipiant illudere ei*, Lk. Bos. 14, 29: 23, 5. He agan hî sendan twâm and twâm *cœpit eos mittere binos*, Mk. Bos. 6, 7.

a-gîta, an; *m. A spendthrift;* prodigus, Past. 20, 2; Hat. MS. 29 b, 10.

a-gitan; *p.* -geat, *pl.* -geáton, -gêton; *pp.* -giten [a *away*, gitan *to get*] *To destroy, abolish, subvert;* destruere, exstinguere, subvertere:—He ageat gylp wera *he destroyed the vaunt of men*, Cd. 169; Th. 210, 12; Exod. 514. Hî heáfodgimme agêton *they destroyed the gem of the head*, Andr. Recd. 63; [aguton, Grm. 32; Kmbl. 63.]

a-gitan *To discover, find;* deprehendere, L. N. P. 48; Th. ii. 296, 27. v. a-gytan.

agîtan; *p.* -geát, -gêt, *pl.* -guton; *pp.* -goten *To pour out, shed;* effundere:—Swâ hwâ swâ agît mannes blôd, his blôd biþ agoten *quicumque effuderit humanum sanguinem fundetur sanguis illius*, Gen. 9, 6.

ag-lâc, æg-lǽc, es; *n.* [ag *nequitia;* lâc *ludus, donum*] *Misery, grief, trouble, vexation, sorrow, torment;* miseria, dolor, tribulatio, molestia, tristitia, cruciatus:—Of ðam aglâce *from that misery*, Exon. 101 b; Th. 383, 7; Rä. 4, 7. Aglâc dreóge *I suffer misery*, 127 b; Th. 490, 5; Rä. 79, 6. Ðǽr hie ðæt aglâc drugon *where they suffered that torment*, Cd. 185; Th. 230, 25; Dan. 238. v. ag.

ag-lâc-hâd, es; *m.* [ag *nequitia;* lâc *ludus, donum;* hâd *conditio, status*] *Misery-hood, a state of misery;* afflictionis conditio, Exon. 113 b; Th. 435, 24; Rä. 54, 5.

ag-lǽca, -lǽcea, -lêca, an; *m.* [ah-lǽca, æg-, æc-; ag-lâc, -lǽc *misery;* a *the m. of personal noun*] *A miserable being, wretch, miscreant, monster, fierce combatant;* miser, perditus, monstrum, bellator immanis:—Ne ðæt se aglǽca yldan þohte *nor did the wretch [Grendel] mean to delay that*, Beo. Th. 1482; B. 739. Earme aglǽcan *miserable wretches*, Exon. 41 a;

Th. 136, 26; Gû. 547. Satanus, earm aglǽca *Satan, miserable wretch*, Cd. 223; Th. 293, 1; Sat. 448: Exon. 69 b; Th. 258, 21; Jul. 268: 70 a; Th. 261, 22; Jul. 319: Beo. Th. 1116; B. 556: 5177; B. 2592.

ag-lǽc-cræft, es; *n. An evil art*, Andr. Kmbl. 2724; An. 1364. v. ac-lǽc-cræft.

ag-lǽcea, an; *m. A wretch, miscreant, monster;* miser, perditus, monstrum:—Wiđ đam aglǽcean *against the wretch*, Beo. Th. 5033; B. 2520: 5107; B. 2557: 5177; B. 2592. v. ag-lǽca.

ag-lǽc-wîf, es; *n. A wretch of a woman, vile crone;* monstrum mulieris, mulier perniciosa:—Grendles môdor, ides, aglǽc-wîf *Grendel's mother, the woman, vile crone*, Beo. Th. 2522; B. 1259.

ag-lêca, an; *m. A wretch, miscreant.* v. æg-lêca, ag-lǽcea.

a-glîdan; *p.* -glâd, *pl.* -glidon; *pp.* -gliden *To glide* or *slip;* labascere, Cot. 123. DER. glîdan.

âgnian = âhnian; *part.* âgnigende; *p.* ade, ode; *pp.* ad, od; *v. a. To own, possess, to appropriate to himself, to prove* or *claim as one's own;* possidere, vindicare sibi:—Hû miht đû, đonne, đe âgnian heora gôd *how canst thou, then, appropriate to thyself their good?* Bt. 14, 1; Fox 42, 26. Đone gleówstôl [MS. gleáwstôl] brôđor mîn âgnade *my brother possessed the seat of joy*, Exon. 130 a; Th. 499, 3; Rä. 88, 10. He âgnige hit *let him prove it as his own* [*keep possession of it*, Th.], L. C. S. 24; Th. i. 390, 10, 11: L. O. 13; Th. i. 184, 5. Swâ he hit âgnode [MS. B. âhnode], swâ he hit tȳmde *as he claimed it as his own, so he advocated it*, L. Ed. 1; Th. i. 160, 8. Âhnodon, Ps. Spl. 43, 4. DER. âgan.

âgniend, âhniend, es; *m. An owner, a possessor;* possessor:—Se đe ys âhniend eorþan and heofenan *qui est possessor cæli et terræ*, Gen. 14, 22.

âgniend-lîc; *adj. Possessive, pertaining to possession* or *owning;* possessivus. DER. âgniende = âgnigende; *part. of* âgnian, -lîc.

âgnung, e; *f. An owning;* possessio, L. Eth. ii. 9; Th. i. 290, 20. v. âgenung.

ag-nys, -nyss, e; *f. Sorrow, affliction;* ærumna:—On agnysse [MS. T. angnisse] mîn *in ærumna mea*, Ps. Spl. 31, 4. v. ag.

agof = agob *A word formed in the Riddles by inverting the order of the letters in the word* boga *a bow.* Agob [MS. agof] is mîn noma eft onhwyrfed *agob is my name transposed*, Exon. 106 b; Th. 405, 12; Rä. 24, 1.

a-gôl *sang;* cantavit, Beo. Th. 3047; B. 1521; *p. of* a-galan.

a-golden *repaid*, Bd. 1, 7; S. 477, 37. v. a-gildan.

âgon *they own*, Cd. 104; Th. 138, 18; Gen. 2293; *pres. pl. of* âgan.

a-gongen *passed*, Cd. 83; Th. 103, 17; Gen. 1719; *pp. of* agangan.

a-goten *poured out*, Ps. Th. 78, 11. v. a-geótan.

a-gotenes, a-gotennys, -nyss, e; *f. An effusion, a pouring* or *shedding forth, out* or *abroad;* effusio:—Agotennys teára *a shedding of tears*, Med. pec. 16.

a-græfen *engraved, carved;* cælatum, Cot. 33. v. a-grafan.

a-grafan; *p.* -grôf, *pl.* -grôfon; *pp.* -grafen *To engrave, inscribe;* sculpere, cælare, sculptare, inscribere:—He sealde Moise twâ stǽnene wexbreda mid Godes handa agrafene *dedit Moisi duas tabulas scriptas digito Dei*, Ex. 31, 18. Beó se mann awirged, đe wirce agrafene godas odđe gegotene *maledictus homo, qui facit sculptile et conflatile*, Deut. 27, 15: Lev. 26, 1. On agrafenum anlîcnyssum *in sculptilibus*, Ps. Spl. 77, 64. Se đisne beám agrôf *he inscribed this beam*, Exon. 123 a; Th. 473, 10; Bo. 12.

a-grafen-lîce, an; *n.* [a-grafen *carved*, -lîce *a body*] *That which is carved, a carved image;* sculptile:—Hî gebǽdon đæt agrafenlîce *adoraverunt sculptile*, Ps. Spl. 105, 19.

agrimonia, an; *f. Agrimony;* agrimonia eupatoria:—Genîm agrimonian *take agrimony*, L. M. 1, 2; Lchdm. ii. 36, 21: 1, 31; Lchdm. ii. 74, 15. *The native name was* garclife, *q. v.*

a-grîsan *To dread, fear greatly, shudder;* horrere:—Đæt he for helle agrîse *that he shudder for hell*, L. C. E. 25; Th. i. 374, 13.

a-grisen-lîc *horrible;* terribilis. v. angrîslîc, grîslîc.

a-grôf *inscribed*, Exon. 123 a; Th. 473, 10; Bo. 12; *p. of* a-grafan.

a-grôwan [a, grôwan *to grow*] *To grow under, to cover;* succrescere:—Seó eorþe stôd mid holtum agrôwen *the earth was* [*stood*] *covered* [*overgrown*] *with groves* [*holts*], Hexam. 6; Norm. 12, 4.

a-grȳndan; *p.* -grând, *pl.* -grûndon; *pp.* -grûnden *To ground, to descend to the earth;* ad solum descendere:—Gim astîhþ on heofonas up hȳhst on geáre and of tille agrȳnt *the gem* [i. e. *the sun*] *rises in the heavens highest in the year and descends from its station*, Menol. Fox 220; Men. 111.

agu *A pie, magpie;* pica, Ælfc. Gl. 38; Som. 63, 22; Wrt. Voc. 29, 43.

âgun *possess*, Exon. 33 b; Th. 106, 33; Gû. 50; *3rd pl. pres. of* âgan. v. âgon.

Agustin, es; *m:* Agustînus, Augustînus, i; *m: Lat. St. Augustine, the missionary sent by Pope Gregory to England*, A. D. 597; Augustînus:—A.D. 597, Hêr com Augustînus and his geferan to Engla lande *now*, A.D. 597, *Augustine and his companions came to England*, Chr. 597; Th. 35, 41, col. 2. Gregorius sende Agustîne pallium *Gregorius misit Augustino pallium*, Bd. 1, 29; S. 498, 12. Æfter Agustîne *after Augustine*, 2, 4; S. 505, 9. Đæt he sende Godes þeów Agustînum bodian Godes word Angel-þeóde *ut mitteret servum Dei Augustinum prædicare verbum Dei genti Anglorum*, Bd. 1, 23; S. 485, 27. Agustînus com on Breotone *Augustinus pervenit Brittaniam*, 1, 25; S. 486, 13. Đæt Gregorius sende Agustîno pallium *ut Gregorius Augustino pallium miserit*, 1, 29, titl; S. 498, 2. Æfter đyssum forþfêrde đâ Gode se leófa fæder Agustînus, and his lîchoma wæs ûte bebyriged nêh cyricean đara eádigra Apla' Petrus and Paulus, for đon heó đa gyta ne wæs fullîce geworht ne gehâlgod. Sôna đæs đe heó gehâlgod wæs đâ dyde mon his lîchoman in, and on đære cyricean norþ portice gedefelîce wæs bebyriged. . . . Is awriten in Sce' Agustînus byrigenne đysses gemetes gewrit:—'Hêr resteþ Domne Agustînus se ǽresta ærceb' Cantwarena burge, se geára hider fram đam eádigan Gregorie đære Rômâniscan burge B' sended wæs, and fram Gode mid wundra wyrcnesse awređed wæs, Æđelbyrht cyning and his þeóde fram deófulgylda bigonge he to Cristes geleáfan gelǽdde, and on sibbe gefyldum dagum his þênunge forþfêred wæs đa đȳ dæge septima Kł Junias on đæs ylcan cyninges rîce' *defunctus est autem Deo dilectus pater Augustinus, et positum corpus ejus foras, juxta ecclesiam beatorum apostolorum Petri et Pauli, quia ea necdum fuerat perfecta, nec dedicata. Mox vero ut dedicata est, intro inlatum, et in porticu illius aquilonali decenter sepultum est* [Sep. 13, 613]. . . . *Scriptum vero est in tumba ejusdem Augustini epitaphium hujusmodi:—'Hic requiescit domnus Augustinus Doruvernensis* [*Canterbury*] *archiepiscopus primus, qui olim huc a beato Gregorio Romanæ urbis pontifice directus, et a Deo operatione miraculorum suffultus, Ædilberctum* [*Ethelbert*] *regem, ac gentem illius ab idolorum cultu ad Christi fidem perduxit, et completis in pace diebus officii sui, defunctus est septimo kalendas Junias* [May 26, A.D. 604] *eodem rege regnante,'* Bd. 2, 3; S. 504, 30–505, 4; Mobr. 95, 10–15–96, 1–8. v. Augustînus.

Agustus; *nom. acc. gen.* Agustuses; *dat.*-Agustuse; *m.* [generally spelled incorrectly in *Anglo-Saxon MSS:* Agustus, as well as Agustinus, for *Augustus and Augustinus*, from augustus *majestic, august*, from augeo *to increase, exalt, honour, praise*]. I. *Augustus, the first Roman emperor, reigned from* A.C. 30 *to* A.D. 14:—Wearþ Agustus sârig *Augustus was grieved*, Ors. 5, 15; Bos. 114, 38. Agustuses lâtteówas *the generals of Augustus*, 5, 15; Bos. 114, 34. Bûton Agustuse sylfum *without Augustus himself*, 5, 15; Bos. 114, 35. II. *the month of August;* mensis Augustus, Menol. Fox 275; Men. 139. v. Augustus.

agute *poured out*, Gen. 4, 11; *subj. p. of* a-geótan.

a-gyfan; *p.* -geaf, *pl.* -geáfon, -gêfon; *pp.* -gyfen *To restore, give up, repay, pay, give;* reddere, tradere, solvere, dare, Mt. Bos. 27, 58: Cd. 79; Th. 98, 7; Gen. 1626: Mt. Bos. 18, 28: 21, 41: 20, 8: Exon. 127 a; Th. 489, 19; Rä. 78, 10. A-gyfen, 44 a; Th. 148, 30; Gû. 752. v. a-gifan.

a-gyldan; đu -gyltst, he -gylt; *p.* -geald, *pl.* -guldon; *pp.* -golden *To pay, render, repay, requite:*—Ic agylde *reddo*, Ælfc. Gr. 28, 8; Som. 33, 5. Đæt ic mîn gehât agylde *ut reddam vota mea*, Ps. Th. 60, 6. Đû agyldest ânra gehwylcum wyđ weorc heora *tu reddes unicuique juxta opera sua*, Ps. Spl. 61, 11. Drihtne đû agyltst đîne âþas *reddes Domino juramenta tua*, Mt. Bos. 5, 33. Nâ agylt *non solvet*, Ps. Spl. 36, 22. XII scillingas agylde đam cyninge *let him pay twelve shillings to the king*, L. H. E. 9; Th. i. 30, 15. v. a-gildan, gildan.

a-gylde; *adv. Without compensation*, L. Eth. v. 31; Th. i. 312, 12. v. æ-gilde.

a-gyltan, -giltan; *p.* -gylte, -gilte; *pp.* -gylt, -gilt [a, gyltan *to be guilty*] *To fail in duty, to commit, become guilty, offend, sin against;* delinquere, committere, admittere, peccare:—Ic agylte *ego deliqui*, Ps. Th. 118, 67. Agyltan, 74, 4: Ex. 10, 16: Hy. 7, 114: Ælfc. Gr. 28, 4; Som. 31, 39, 41. Đæt he agylte on him sylfum *ut delinquat in semet ipso*, Ps. Spl. 35, 1. Agyltan wiđ *to offend* or *sin against.* Twegen afȳryde men agylton wiđ heora hlâford *peccaverunt duo eunuchi domino suo*, Gen. 40, 1.

a-gȳmeleásian; *p.* ode; *pp.* od *To neglect, despise;* negligere. v. a-gîmeleásian, gȳmeleásian.

a-gymmed *set with gems:*—Agymmed hringc *ungulus*, Ælfc. Gl. 65; Som. 69, 30; Wrt. Voc. 40, 59. v. a-gimmed.

a-gynþ *beginneth*, Mt. Bos. 24, 49. v. a-ginnan.

a-gytan, -gitan; *p.* -geat, *pl.* -geáton; *pp.* -gyten, -giten [a *from*, gitan *to get*] *To discover, know, understand, consider;* cognoscere, intelligere, deprehendere:—Đæt hit man geornor agytan mǽge *that it may be better understood*, Ors. 2, 1; Bos. 38, 30. Gecȳđnyssa đîne ic ageat *testimonia tua intellexi*, Ps. Spl. 118, 95, 99: 48, 12. Gif đonne ǽni-man agiten wurþe *if then any one be found*, L. N. P. 48; Th. ii. 296, 27.

ah *But, but also, whether;* sed, sed et, numquid:—Ne mîþ đû, ah đînne môdsefan stađola *shrink not thou, but strengthen thy mind*, Andr. Kmbl. 2420; An. 1211: 3337; An. 1672: 3403; An. 1705: 463; An. 232: Cd. 219; Th. 281, 7; Sat. 268: 228; Th. 308, 21; Sat. 696. 'Ah and tunge mîn biþ smêgende rehtwîsnisse đîne *sed et lingua mea meditabitur justitiam tuam*, Ps. Surt. 70, 24. Ah ætfileþ đe seld unrihtwîsnesse *numquid adhæret tibi sedes iniquitatis?* Ps. Surt. 93, 20. Ah ne *nonne?* Mk. Lind. Rush. War. 6, 3. v. ac; *conj.*

ah- [= ag-, *q. v.*] DER. ah-lǽca, an; *m. a wretch*, etc.

âh *has, owns;* habet, Byrht. Th. 136, 60; By. 175; *3rd pres. of* âgan.

a-habban; *p.* -hæfde; *subj. pres. s.* -hæbbe [a *from*, habban *to have*] *To abstain, restrain*; abstinere:—Ðū ne woldest ðē ahabban fram ðam hūse ðæs forlorenan mannes *noluisti te continere a domo perditi*, Bd. 3, 22; S. 553, 36. Ðæt Herebald eallinga hine fram ðam gefīte ahæbbe *ut Herebald ab illo se certamine funditus abstineat*, 5, 6; S. 619, 4.

a-hæbban; *p.* -hōf, *pl.* -hōfon; *pp.* -hæfen *To heave up, raise, exalt*:—Hió biþ up ahæfen ofer hī selfe *she is exalted above herself*, Bt. Met. Fox 20, 437; Met. 20, 219: 25, 37; Met. 25, 19: Elen. Kmbl. 19; El. 10. v. a-hebban.

a-hafen *lifted up, raised, exalted*, Cd. 69; Th. 84, 21; Gen. 1401: Ps. Spl. 106, 25; *pp. of* a-hebban.

a-hafennes, -hafenes, -hafennys, -ness, -nyss, e; *f. A lifting up, an elevation, elation, pride*; elevatio, elatio:—Ahafenes handa mīnra *elevatio manuum mearum*, Ps. Th. 140, 3. Ahafennys *elevatio*, Ps. Spl. 140, 2. Wundorlīce ahafennyssa sǣ *mirabiles elationes maris*, 92, 6.

a-hangen *hung*, Mt. Bos. 26, 2; *pp. of* a-hōn.

a-heardian; *p.* ode; *pp.* od; *v. intrans. To harden, grow hard, become inured to anything, to last, hold out, endure*; durare, perdurare, indurescere:—On swā mycelre geþræstnesse and forhæfednesse mōdes and līchoman aheardode and awunode *he hardened and continued in so great contrition and restraint of mind and body*; in tanta mentis et corporis contritione duravit, Bd. 5, 12; S. 627, 28. Aheardaþ his gebod *perdurat ejus imperium*, R. Ben. 68. v. a-hyrdian; *v. trans.*

a-heardung, e; *f. A hardening*; induratio. v. heard, heardian, heardnes.

a-heáwan; *p.* -heów; *pp.* -heáwen *To hew* or *cut out* or *off, hew down, prepare by cutting, make smooth, plane*; excidere, resecare, succidere, levigare:—On hys niwan byrgene, ða he aheów on stāne *in monumento suo novo, quod exciderat in petra*, Mt. Bos. 27, 60. On aheáwene byrgene *in monumento exciso*, Lk. Bos. 23, 53: Bd. 3, 6; S. 528, 26. Ic wæs aheáwen holtes on ende, astyred of stefne mīnum *I was hewn down at the end of a wood, removed from my trunk*, Rood Recd. 57; Kr. 29. Aheáwen treów *cut wood, timber*; lignum, Ælfc. Gr. 8; Som. 8, 1. Of aheáwenum bordum *of hewn* or *planed boards*; de lignis levigatis, Gen. 6, 14.

a-hebban, -hæbban; ðū -hefst, he -hefeþ, *pl.* -hebbaþ; *p.* -hōf, *pl.* -hōfon; *imp.* -hefe; *pp.* -hafen *To heave up, lift up, raise, elevate, exalt, ferment*; levare, tollere, elevare, erigere, exaltare, extollere, fermentare:—Nolde his eágan ahebban up to ðam heofone *nolebat oculos ad cœlum levare*, Lk. Bos. 18, 13. To ahebbanne *levare*, Gen. 48, 17. Ðū ahōfe me on ēcne dreám *thou raisedst me to everlasting joy*, Exon. 100 a; Th. 376, 12; Seel. 153. Se ðe rōdor ahōf *who hove up the firmament*, Andr. Kmbl. 1042; An. 521. Nymþe heó wæs ahafen on ða heán lyft *unless it was raised in the high air*, Cd. 69; Th. 84, 21; Gen. 1401. Ic ahebbe ðē, Drihten *exaltabo te, Domine*, Ps. Spl. 29, 1: 117, 27. Ðū ðe ahefst me *qui exaltas me*, 9, 14: Ps. Th. 63, 6: 91, 9: 148, 13. Ne ahebbaþ ge to heá eówre hygeþancas *nolite extollere in altum cornu vestrum*, 74, 5. Ōþ he wæs eall ahafen *donec fermentatum est totum*, Mt. Bos. 13, 33.

a-hefan; *p.* -hefde; *pp.* -hefed *To heave up, lift up, raise*; levare, elevare, extendere:—Ahefdon upp ðone arc *elevaverunt arcam*, Gen. 7, 17. He ahefde upp his hand *extendit manum*, Ex. 8, 17. He ahefde up *he lifted up*, 14, 27. v. a-hebban.

a-hefednes, -ness, e; *f. An elevation, elation, pride*, = a-hafennes, Lye. v. up-a-hefednes.

a-hefen = a-hafen *raised up, exalted*, Lk. Lind. War. 13, 13: Bd. 3, 16; S. 543, 3, col. 2; *pp. of* a-hebban.

a-hefeþ *raises up, exalts*, Cd. 220; Th. 283, 27; Sat. 311: Ps. Th. 74, 7: 144, 15. v. a-hebban.

a-hefigian, -hefgian; *p.* ode; *pp.* od, ad *To make heavy* or *sad, to weigh down, burden*; gravare, contristare, deprimere:—Swā biþ ðam mōde, ðonne hit biþ ahefigad mid ðǣm ymbhogum ðisse worulde *so is it with the mind, when it is weighed down by the anxieties of this world*, Bt. 24, 4; Fox 84, 32. Ahefgade *gravati*, Mt. Lind. Stv. 26, 43. v. hefigian.

a-hefst *raisest up, exaltest*, Ps. Spl. 9, 14. v. a-hebban.

a-hēhst, -hēhþ *shalt* or *shall hang up, crucify*; appendet, suspendet, Deut. 21, 22. v. a-hōn.

a-helpan; *p.* -healp, *pl.* -hulpon; *pp.* -holpen *To help, assist*; auxiliari, adjuvare, subvenire:—Ahelpe mīn se hālga Dryhten *may the holy Lord help me*, Exon. 117 b; Th. 452, 13; Hy. 4, 1. v. helpan; *gen. dat.*

a-hēnan; *p.* de; *pp.* ed *To humble, abase, tread down* or *under foot*; humiliare, calcare:—Biþ ahēned *calcabitur*, Lk. Lind. War. 21, 24. v. hēnan, hӯnan.

a-hēneg *hung*, Ælfc. Gr. 26, 6; Som. 29, 13; *p. of* a-hōn.

a-hēng *hung*, Exon. 70 a; Th. 260, 29; Jul. 305; *p. of* a-hōn.

a-heólorian; *p.* ede, ode; *pp.* ed, od *To weigh, balance*; librare, trutinare. v. heólorian.

a-heordan? *p.* de; *pp.* ed [heorde = hyrde *a guardian, keeper*] *To set free from a guardian*; e custodia liberare:—Abreót brimwīsan, brӯd aheorde *slew the sea-leader, set free his bride*, Beo. Th. 5853; B. 2930.

a-hērian; *p.* ode; *pp.* od *To hire*; conducere, Cot. 43, 204. v. a-hӯrian.

a-hērian; *p.* ede; *pp.* ed *To praise fully, celebrate enough*; plene laudare, satis celebrare:—Ne mæg ðē ahērian hæleða ǣnig *not any men can fully praise thee*, Hy. 3, 10; Hy. Grn. ii. 281, 10; prec. 3 ad calcem Cœdm. l. 5.

a-hicgan; *p.* -hogde, -hogode; *pp.* -hugod *To devise, search, invent*, Cd. 94; Th. 122, 24; Gen. 2031. v. a-hycgan.

a-hiéðan *to destroy, lay waste, despoil*, Salm. Kmbl. 147, MS. A; Sal. 73. v. a-hӯðan.

a-hildan; *p.* -hilde; *pp.* -hilded, -hild *To incline, decline*; inclinare, declinare:—Ne ahilde ge nāðer ne on ða wynstran healfe ne on ða swīðran *non declinabitis neque ad dexteram neque ad sinistram*, Deut. 5, 32. v. a-hyldan.

a-hiscean *to hiss at, to mock*; irridere. v. hiscan.

a-hīðan *to rob, destroy*; vastare, subvertere, Exon. 87 a; Th. 328, 9; Vy. 15. v. a-hӯðan.

a-hīðend, es; *m. A robber, an extortioner*; grassator, Cot. 95.

a-hlādan; *p.* -hlōd, *pl.* -hlōdon; *pp.* -hlāden [a *from*, hlādan *to lade*] *To draw out, draw forth*; exhaurire, educere:—Ic hlāde *haurio*: ic of ahlāde [MS. C. ofhlāde] *exhaurio*, Ælfc. Gr. 30, 2; Som. 34, 41. He of hæfte ahlōd folces unrīm *he drew forth from captivity numberless people*, Exon. 16 a; Th. 35, 34; Cri. 568.

ah-lǣca, an; *m.* [ah- = ag- = æg- = æc- *nequitia*; lǣc *ludus, donum*; -a *the personal termination, q. v.*] *A miserable being, miscreant, monster*; miser, perditus, monstrum:—He wiste ðæm ahlǣcan hilde geþinged *he knew conflict was destined for the miscreant*, Beo. Th. 1297; B. 646: 1983; B. 989. v. ag-lǣca.

a-hlǣnan; *p.* de; *pp.* ed [a, hlǣnan *to lean*] *To set himself up*; exsurgere:—Se ðe hine selfne þurh oferhygda up ahlǣneþ *he who through presumption sets himself up*, Exon. 84 a; Th. 316, 24; Mōd. 53. [*M. H. Ger.* sich ūf leinan: *Ger.* sich auflehnen.]

a-hlǣnsian; *p.* ude; *pp.* ud [lǣnian *to be* or *make lean*, hlǣne *lean*] *To soak, steep, make lean*; macerare, Scint. 10.

a-hleápan; *p.* -hleóp, *pl.* -hleópon; *pp.* -hleápen [a *from*, hleápan *to leap*] *To leap, leap up*; exsilire, insilire, prosilire, desilire:—Alexander ahleóp and ofslōh hine *Alexander leaped up and slew him*, Ors. 3, 9; Bos. 67, 7. Ahleópon ðā ealle *then all jumped up*, 5, 12; Bos. 112, 24. Ahleóp ðā fōr hæleðum hilde-calla *the herald of war leaped then before the warriors*, Cd. 156; Th. 193, 25; Exod. 252: Andr. Kmbl. 1472; An. 737: 2405; An. 1204: Beo. Th. 2798; B. 1397.

a-hlehhan, -hlyhhan; *p.* -hlōh, -hlōg, *pl.* -hlōgon; *pp.* -hlahhen. I. *to laugh at*; ridere, deridere:—Ðā ðæt wīf ahlōh wereda Drihtnes *the woman then laughed at the Lord of hosts*, Cd. 109; Th. 143, 16; Gen. 2380. II. *to exult, laugh*; exultare, lætari:—Heorte mīn ahlyhheþ *lætetur cor meum*, Ps. Th. 85, 11. His mōd ahlōg *his mind laughed*, Beo. Th. 1465; B. 730: Salm. Kmbl. 358; Sal. 178. v. hlehhan.

a-hlinian; *p.* ode; *pp.* od *To loose*; solvere. v. hlinian.

a-hlōg, -hlōh *laughed at, laughed*, Cd. 109; Th. 143, 16; Gen. 2380; *p. of* a-hlehhan.

a-hlōwan *To low* or *bellow again*; reboare. v. hlōwan *to low*.

a-hlutred *purified*; purificatus, Cot. 68; *pp. of* a-hluttrian.

a-hluttrian; *p.* ede; *pp.* ed *To purify, scum, refine, cleanse*; purificare:—Ðū me ahluttra *purify me*, Ps. C. 50, 73; Ps. Grn. ii. 278, 73. Ahlutred wīn *vinum defæcatum*, Cot. 68. v. hluttran.

a-hlyhheþ *laughs at*, Ps. Th. 85, 11. v. a-hlehhan, -hlyhhan.

a-hneápan; *p.* -hneóp, *pl.* -hneópon; *pp.* -hneápen *To pluck off*; decarpere:—Heó of beáme a-hneóp wæstm biweredne *she plucked from the tree the prohibited fruit*, Exon. 45 a; Th. 153, 2; Gū. 819. [*Goth.* dishniupan, dishnaupnan *discerpere*: *O. Nrs.* hnupla *surripere*.] v. hneápan.

a-hnescian; *p.* ode; *pp.* od *To become weak*; emollire:—Ahnescodon *became weak*, Ors. 5, 3; Bos. 103, 42. v. hnescian.

āhniend, es; *m. An owner*, Gen. 14, 22. v. āgniend.

āhnodon *owned*; possederunt, Ps. Spl. 43, 4. v. āgnian.

āhnung *an owning*, L. Ed. 1; Lambd. 38, 25. v. āgenung.

a-hnyscan; *p.* -hnyscte; *pp.* -hnysct *To mock*; subsannare:—Fӯnd ūre ahnyscton us *inimici nostri subsannaverunt nos*, Ps. Spl. 79, 7. v. a-hiscean.

a-hō *hang*; suspendo, Ælfc. Gr. 26, 6; Som. 29, 12; *pres. of* a-hōn.

a-hōf *raised*, Andr. Kmbl. 1042; An. 521; *p. of* a-hebban.

a-hofyn = a-hafen *elated*, Ps. Spl. C. 130, 1; *pp. of* ahebban.

a-hōh *crucify*:—Ahōh hine *crucifige eum*, Mk. Bos. 15, 14; *impert. of* a-hōn.

a-holan; *p.* ede. *To dig*; fodere, Mt. Kmbl. Rl. 5, 29. v. a-holede.

a-hold *faithful*; fidelis, fidus. v. hold.

a-holede, an; *n. An engraved* or *embossed work*; opus lacunatum, Cot. 7; *pp. of* a-holan *to dig*.

a-holian; *p.* ode; *pp.* od [a, holian *to hollow*] *To dig*; eruere, fodere:—Gyf ðīn eáge ðē swīcaþ, ahola hyt ūt *si oculus tuus scandalizat te, erue eum*, Mt. Bos. 18, 9: 5, 29.

a-hōn, to a-hōnne; ic -hō, ðū -hēhst, he -hēhþ; *impert.* -hōh; *p.* -hēng,

-hēncg, *pl.* -hēngon; *pp.* -hongen, -hangen *To hang, crucify;* suspendere, crucifigere:—He Andreas hēt ahōn on heáhne beám *he commanded to hang Andrew on a high tree,* Exon. 70 a; Th. 261, 3; Jul. 309: Gen. 40, 19. Ic ahō *suspendo;* ic ahēncg *suspendi,* Ælfc. Gr. 26, 6; Som. 29, 12. Sealde heom to ahōnne *tradidit eis ut crucifigeretur,* Mt. Bos. 27, 26. Ahōh hine *crucifige eum,* Mk. Bos. 15, 14. On gealgan ahēhþ *he shall hang on a gallows,* Deut. 21, 22. Ðæt hī hine ahēngon *ut crucifigerent eum,* Mk. Bos. 15, 20: Mt. Bos. 27, 35: Mk. Bos. 15, 25. Ðæt he ahangen wǣre *that he should be crucified,* 15, 15: Mt. Bos. 27, 38, 44. Sȳ he ahangen *crucifigatur,* 27, 23. Pilatus on rōde ahēng rōdera Waldend *Pilate had crucified on the cross the Ruler of the skies,* Exon. 70 a; Th. 260, 29; Jul. 305: Elen. Kmbl. 419; El. 210. He ahangen wæs *he was hanged,* Elen. Kmbl. 887; El. 445: 903; El. 453.

a-hongen *hung,* Exon. 24 a; Th. 67, 26; Cri. 1094; *pp. of* ahōn.

a-hreddan; *p.* -hredde; *pp.* -hreded, -hred [a *from,* hreddan *to rid*] *To rid, liberate, set free, deliver, rescue;* liberare, eripere, eruere:—Ðæt he sceolde his folc ahreddan *that he should deliver his people,* Jud. 6, 14. Ðæt ðū us ahredde *that thou deliver us,* Exon. 13 a; Th. 23, 25; Cri. 374. Ðe ðū ahreddest *whom thou hast rescued,* Cd. 97; Th. 128, 15; Gen. 2127. He hī æt hungre ahredde *he rid them of the famine,* Ors. 1, 5; Bos. 28, 40. Loth wæs ahreded *Lot was rescued,* Cd. 96; Th. 125, 27; Gen. 2085. Ahred, 94; Th. 122, 26: Gen. 2032. Ahrede me hefiges nīdes feónda mīnra *eripe me de inimicis meis,* Ps. Th. 58, 1. Ahrede me hearmcwidum heánra manna *redime me a calumniis hominum,* 118, 134. Ic ahredde *eruo,* Ælfc. Gr. 28, 3; Som. 30, 55, 63.

a-hreded *commotus,* Ps. Th. 59, 2; Ps. Grn. ii. 158, 59, 2. v. a-hrēran.

a-hreófod; *adj. Leprous;* leprosus, Martyr. 21, Sep.

a-hreósan; *p.* -hreás, *pl.* -hruron; *pp.* -hroren [a, hreósan *to rush*] *To rush, fall, fall down;* irruere, ruere, corruere, decidere:—Bleówun windas and ahruron on ðæt hūs *flaverunt venti et irruerunt in domum illam,* Mt. Bos. 7, 25. On Godes naman ahreóse ðis tempel *in God's name let this temple fall down,* Homl. Th. i. 72, 2, 5. He ahreás *he fell,* Homl. Th. i. 192, 20.

a-hrepian; *p.* ode; *pp.* od *To touch;* tangere. v. hrepian.

a-hrēran; *p.* de; *pp.* ed [a, hrēran *to move, agitate*] *To shake, make to tremble;* commovere:—Heó ahrēred [MS. ahreded] is *commota est,* Ps. Th. 59, 2.

a-hrīnan, -hrȳnan; *p.* -hrān, *pl.* -hrinon; *pp.* -hrinen *To touch;* tangere:—Ge ne ahrīnaþ ða seámas mid eówrum ānum fingre *uno digito vestro non tangitis sarcinas,* Lk. Bos. 11, 46. Ahrȳn mūntas *tange montes,* Ps. Spl. 143, 6.

a-hruron *rushed,* Mt. Bos. 7, 25; *p. pl. of* a-hreósan.

a-hrydred *robbed;* expilatus, Cot. 73. v. aþryd.

a-hrȳnan *To touch;* tangere, Ps. Spl. 143, 6. v. a-hrīnan.

a-hrysian; *p.* ode; *pp.* od *To shake violently;* excutere:—Drihten ahrysode ða wēstan eorþan *the Lord shook violently the desert earth,* Ps. Th. 28, 6. Ahrysod ic eom *excussus sum,* Ps. Spl. 108, 22. Ahryse ða moldan of *shake the mould off,* Herb. 1, 1; Lchdm. i. 70, 8. v. hrysian.

ahse, an; *f. Ashes:*—Forðon ahsan swā swā hlāf ic æt *quia cinerem tanquam panem manducabam,* Ps. Spl. 101, 10: 147, 5. v. asce.

ahsian; *p.* ode; *pp.* od. I. *to ask, demand, call, summon before one;* interrogare, postulare, exigere:—He ongan hine ahsian *he began to call him,* Cd. 40; Th. 53, 18; Gen. 863: Deut. 4, 32: Ps. Th. 14, 2. II. *to obtain, experience;* nancisci, experiri:—He weán ahsode *he obtained woe,* Beo. Th. 2417; B. 1206: 851; B. 423. v. acsian.

āhst *hast, ownest,* Elen. Kmbl. 1448; El. 726; *2nd pers. sing. pres. indic. of* āgan.

āht, es; *n.* AUGHT, *anything, something;* aliquid, quidquam:—Nō he ðǣr āht cwices lǣfan wolde *he would leave not anything living there,* Beo. Th. 4618; B. 2314: Ps. Th. 143, 4. Ðe āhtes wǣron *who were of aught, of any account* or *value,* Chr. 992; Th. 238, 35. Ðæt ān man, ðe himsylf āht wǣre, mihte faran *that a man, who himself was aught, might go,* 1087; Th. 355, 17. v. ā-wiht.

ahta *eight,* Menol. Fox 188; Men. 95. v. eahta.

āhte, āhtest *had, owned:*—He sealde eall ðæt he āhte *he sold all that he had;* vendidit omnia quæ habuit, Mt. Bos. 13, 46; *p. of* āgan.

āht-līce; *adv. Courageously, manfully, triumphantly;* viriliter, Chr. 1071; Gib. p. 181, 16; Th. 347, 18; Ing. 277, 10; Erl. 203, 2: 210, 22.

āhton *had, owned, possessed:*—Ðe Caldeas cyningdōm āhton *the Chaldeans possessed the kingdom,* Cd. 209; Th. 258, 24; Dan. 680; *p. pl. of* āgan.

a-hūðan; *p.* -heáþ, *pl.* -hudon; *pp.* -hoden [a *from,* hūð *prey*] *To spoil, rob, plunder;* diripere, expilare, spoliare:—Fȳnd ahūðan [MS. ahudan] mid herge hordburh wera *the foes plundered with their band the treasure-city of the men,* Cd. 93; Th. 121, 8; Gen. 2007.

ā-hwā; *g.* -hwæs; *d.* -hwām; *acc.* -hwone; *pron.* [ā, hwā *who*] *Any one;* aliquis:—Gif he āhwām geweólde *if he have done violence to any one,* L. Pen. 16; Th. ii. 284, 6.

a-hwǣnan; *p.* ede; *pp.* ed *To vex, trouble;* contristare, vexare, molestare:—Gyf hwylc cyld ahwǣned sȳ *if any child be vexed,* Herb. 20, 7; Lchdm. i. 116, 8.

ā-hwænne; *adv. When, sometime;* quando:—Drihten āhwænne behealtst ðū *Domine quando respicies,* Ps. Spl. 34, 20: 7, 2. v. hwænne.

ā-hwǣr, -hwār, -hwēr, -wēr; *adv.* [ā *always, ever, every;* hwǣr *where*]. I. *everywhere, somewhere, anywhere;* uspiam, alicubi, usquequaque:—Ne mæg ic hine āhwǣr [*uspiam*] befleón, Ps. Th. 61, 6. Ne forlǣt ðū me āhwǣr eorþan, oððe ǣghwanan *non me derelinquas usquequaque,* Ps. Lamb. 118, 8: Ps. Th. 54, 24: 68, 7: 108, 12: 62, 9: 71, 12: 113, 10: 118, 39: Ps. Spl. 118, 8. II. *in any wise;* quoquo modo:—Habbe ic ðē āwēr benumen ðīnra gifena *have I in any wise deprived thee of thy gifts?* Bt. 7, 3; Fox 20, 14.

ā-hwǣrgen *everywhere;* uspiam, Bt. Met. Fox 30, 19; Met. 30, 10.

a-hwæt = -hwet = -hwetted *whetted,* Ors. 6, 30; Bos. 126, 17; *pp. of* a-hwettan.

ā-hwæðer; *adj. pron. Some one, any one, anything;* quis, aliquis, aliquid:—Nis me ege mannes for āhwæðer *non timebo quid faciat mihi homo* [*non est mihi hominis timor pro aliquo*], Ps. Th. 55, 4: 117, 6. v. āwðer, nā-hwæðer.

ā-hwār; *adv.* I. *somewhere, anywhere;* alicubi:—Ðe he āhwār gefremode *that he anywhere occasioned,* L. Pen. 16; Th. ii. 284, 6. Āhwār on lande *anywhere within the land,* L. E. G. 11; Th. i. 172, 21. II. *in any wise;* quoquo modo:—And se man, ðe wiðcwiþ ðīnum bebodum [Grn. wordum] āhwār, beó he deáþes scildig *and the man, who shall in any wise contradict* [*speak against*] *thy commands* [Grn. *words*], *he shall be guilty of death,* Jos. 1, 18. v. ā-hwǣr.

a-hwelfan [a, hwelfan] *to cast down, cover over,* Ps. Lamb. 58, 12. v. a-hwylfan.

a-hweorfan; *p.* -hwearf, *pl.* -hwurfon; *pp.* -hworfen. I. *v. trans. To turn away, convert;* avertere, convertere:—Ne lǣt ðē ahweorfan hǣðenra þrym *let not the power of the heathen turn thee away,* Andr. Kmbl. 1913; An. 959. Ðæt he of Sione ahweorfe hæft-nēd *that he would turn away captivity from Sion,* Ps. Th. 125, 1. Ðū eart of ðīnre stilnesse ahworfen *thou art moved from thy tranquillity,* Bt. 7, 1; Fox 16, 24. II. *v. intrans. To turn away, turn, move;* averti, converti:—Sigor eft ahwearf of norþ-monna nīþ-geteóne *victory turned away again from the northmen's hostile malice,* Cd. 95; Th. 124, 24; Gen. 2067. Hie of sib-lufan Godes ahwurfon *they turned away from the love of God,* Cd. 1; Th. 2, 26; Gen. 25. Ðā his gāst ahwearf in Godes gemynd *then his spirit turned to thought of God,* Cd. 206; Th. 255, 26; Dan. 630.

ā-hwēr; *adv. Everywhere;* alicubi, Ors. 3, 7; Bos. 60, 7. v. ā-hwǣr.

a-hwerfan; *p.* de; *pp.* ed *To turn away;* avertere:—Ahwerf fram synnum ðīne ansióne *averte faciem tuam a peccatis,* Ps. C. 50, 83; Ps. Grn. ii. p. 278, 83. Ahwerfed, Bt. 37, 4; Fox 192, 12. v. a-hwyrfan.

a-hwettan; *p.* -hwette; *pp.* -hwetted. I. *to whet, excite;* excitare, accendere:—Ðæt ic ðē mǣge lust ahwettan *that I may excite thy desire,* Andr. Kmbl. 606; An. 303. II. *to provide;* adhibere, subministrare:—Ic eów gōda gehwæs ēst ahwette *I will provide you the favour* [*liberal supply*] *of every good,* Andr. Kmbl. 678; An. 339. III. *to cast away, drive away;* abigere, repudiare:—God ahwet hie from his hyldo *God will cast them away from his favour,* Cd. 21; Th. 26, 13.

ā-hwider *on every side;* quoquoversum. v. ǣg-hwider.

ahwilc? [ah = ag *nequitia,* hwilc] *adj. Terrible;* terribilis, Ælfc. Gl. 116; Som. 80, 65; Wrt. Voc. 61, 43.

a-hwonan, -hwonon; *adv.* [a *from,* hwonan *whence*] *From what place, whence, somewhere, anywhere;* alicubi, Bd. 5, 12; S. 629, 16. Ahwonan ūtane *from without, outwardly, extrinsically,* Bt. 34, 3; Fox 136, 23.

a-hworfen *moved,* Bt. 7, 1; Fox 16, 24; *pp. of* a-hweorfan.

ā-hwylc *whatsoever;* qualiscunque, C. R. Ben. 46. v. ǣg-hwilc.

a-hwylfan, -hwelfan; *p.* de; *pp.* ed [a, hwylfan *to cover* or *vault*] *To cover over, overwhelm;* operire, obruere, deponere:—Seó sǣ ahwylfde Pharaones cratu *aquæ operuerunt currus Pharaonis,* Ex. 14, 27. Alege oððe ahwelf hīg *cast down* [or *cover over*] *them,* Ps. Lamb. 58, 12.

a-hwyrfan, -hwerfan; *p.* de; *pp.* ed *To turn away;* avertere:—Ðæt ic ðē meahte ahwyrfan from hālor *that I might turn thee from salvation,* Exon. 71 a; Th. 264, 6; Jul. 360. Ne ahwyrf *ne avertas,* Ps. Th. 89, 3. Ahwyrfde, *subj. perf. would cast,* Exon. 39 a; Th. 129, 33; Gū. 430.

a-hycgan, -hicgan; *p.* -hogde, -hogode; *pp.* [ge]-hugod *To devise, search, invent;* excogitare, perscrutari, invenire:—Leóhtor ðonne hit men mǣgen mōdum ahycgan *more clearly than men may in mind devise it,* Exon. 21 a; Th. 56, 20; Cri. 903. Bæd him ðæs rǣd ahicgan *besought them to devise counsel for this,* Cd. 94; Th. 122, 24; Gen. 2031: 178; Th. 224, 3; Dan. 130. Hie ahogodan heoro *they invented the sword,* Exon. 92 a; Th. 346, 9; Gn. Ex. 202. v. hycgan.

a-hȳdan; *p.* de; *pp.* ed *To hide;* abscondere, occultare:—Tungol beóþ ahȳded *the star is hidden,* Exon. 57 a; Th. 204, 12; Ph. 96: Cd. 148; Th. 184, 30; Exod. 115. Rōmāne gesomnodon al ða goldhord and sume on eorþan ahȳddon *the Romans collected all the treasures and hid some in the earth,* Chr. 418; Th. 18, 6, col. 1. v. hȳdan.

a-hyldan, -hildan; *p.* -hylde; *pp.* -hylded, -hyld. I. *to incline, recline;* inclinare, reclinare:—Ahylde ic mīne heortan *inclinavi cor meum,* Ps. Th. 118, 112. Ahyld me ðīn eáre *inclina aurem tuam ad me,* 85, 1. Ahylded, 103, 6. Hwār he his heáfod ahylde *ubi caput reclinet,* Lk. Bos. 9,

58. II. *to decline, turn away, avert from;* declinare, inclinare:—Ahyld fram yfele *declina a malo,* Ps. Spl. 36, 28. Beóþ ðé ahylded fram wíta unrím *from thee shall be averted the numberless torments,* Exon. 68 a; Th. 252, 31; Jul. 171. Se dæg wæs ahyld *dies inclinata est,* Lk. Bos. 24, 29: Ps. Th. 108, 23. Ne ahilde ge *non declinabitis,* Deut. 5, 32.

a-hyldendlíce *inclining1y;* enclitice, inclinative; *part. of* a-hyldan, -líce.

a-hyltan [a *from, away;* hylt *holds, 3rd pres. of* healdan] *should take support away, supplant;* supplantaret:—Ða þohton ðæt hí ahyltan [= ahylten] me *who thought that they should supplant me,* Ps. Th. 139, 5. v. healdan **IV**.

a-hyrdan; *p.* -hyrde, -hyrte; *pp.* -hyrded, -hyrd; *v. trans. To harden, make hard;* durare, indurare:—Ic ahyrde Pharaones heortan *ego indurabo cor Pharaonis,* Ex. 4, 21. Ahyrde hyra heortan *induravit cor eorum,* Jn. Bos. 12, 40: Ex. 8, 15. Ahyrdon heoro slíðendne *they hardened the wounding sword,* Exon. 92 a; Th. 346, 9; Gn. Ex. 202. Ecg wæs íren ahyrded heaðo-swáte *its edge was iron hardened with battle-blood,* Beo. Th. 2924; B. 1460: Ex. 8, 19: Mt. Bos. 13, 15: Ps. Th. 119, 4.

a-hyrdineg, e; *f. A hardening;* induratio, App. Scint. v. a-heardung.

a-hýrian; *p.* ode; *pp.* od *To hire;* conducere:—He úteóde ahýrian wyrhtan *exiit conducere operarios,* Mt. Bos. 20, 1: Jn. Bos. 10, 13.

a-hyrstan; *p.* -hyrste; *pp.* -hyrst *To roast, fry;* frigere. v. hyrstan.

a-hyrte *hardened,* Ex. 8, 15, = a-hyrde; *p. of* a-hyrdan.

a-hýðan, -híðan, -hiéðan *To destroy, lay waste, despoil;* vastare, abolere, subvertere:—Hí woldon Rómwara ríce geþringan, hergum ahýðan *they would conquer the empire of the Romans, lay it waste with their armies,* Elen. Kmbl. 81; El. 41. Hungor he ahýðeþ [MS. A. ahiéðeþ] *hunger despoileth it,* Salm. Kmbl. 147; Sal. 73. Ahíðan, Exon. 87 a; Th. 328, 9; Vy. 15. DER. hýðan *prædari.*

a-ídlan; *p.* ede; *pp.* ed. I. *v. intrans. To become idle, free from;* vacare:—Ðá gegyrelan from hǽlo gife ne a-ídledon *indumenta a gratia curandi non vacarunt,* Bd. 4, 31; S. 611, 6. II. *v. trans. To profane;* profanare:—Monige ðone geleáfan mid unrihte weorce a-ídledon *multi fidem iniquis profanabant operibus,* Bd. 4, 27; S. 604, 5.

a-ídlian, -igan; *p.* ode, ude; *pp.* od, ad, ud *To make useless, vain, to empty, annul, profane;* irritum facere, frustrari, exinanire, cassare, profanare:—Ic a-ídlige *frustror,* Ælfc. Gr. 25; Som. 26, 63. A-ídlian *cassare,* Cot. 43: 204: 179. He a-ídlode mín wedd *pactum meum irritum fecit,* Gen. 17, 14. Þræst his nys a-ídlude *fæx ejus non est exinanita,* Ps. Spl. 74, 8. Seó untrumnys byþ a-ídlud *the infirmity will be annulled,* Herb. 121, 2; Lchdm. i. 234, 8. Ðæt Cristes geleáfan a-ídlad wǽre *fidem profanatam esse,* Bd. 3, 30; S. 562, 7.

ain, aina *one,* Gen. 43, 6. v. ÁN II.

al, æl, eal, awul, awel, e; *f. An* AWL, *a fork, flesh-hook;* subula, fuscinula, harpago:—Þirlige his eáre mid ale *bore his ear through with an awl,* Lev. 25, 10: L. Alf. 11; Th. i. 46, 10, MS. G. [*Chauc.* oule: *Wyc.* al: *O. H. Ger.* ala, *f: M. H. Ger.* al, *f: Ger.* ahle, *f: O. Nrs.* alr, *m.*]

al *all,* Cd. 213; Th. 265, 16; Sat. 8: 214; Th. 268, 24; Sat. 60. v. eal.

a-ládian [a *from,* ládian *to clear*] *To excuse, to make excuse for;* excusare:—Hú mágon hí hí a-ládigen [MS. Cot. aládian] *how can they excuse themselves?* Bt. 41, 3; Fox 248, 21.

a-lǽdan; *p.* de; *pp.* ed [a *from,* lǽdan *to lead*]. I. *to lead, lead out, withdraw, take away;* ducere, producere, educere:—Ic alǽdde ðé of lande *eduxi te de terra,* Ps. Spl. 80, 9: Ps. Th. 80, 10: 142, 12: 103, 14: Cd. 73; Th. 90, 15; Gen. 1495. Ic eom alǽded fram leóhte *I am led out from the light,* Cd. 217; Th. 275, 27; Sat. 178: Ps. Spl. 108, 22. II. *to be produced, brought forth, to grow;* produci:—Ðú of foldan fódder neátum lǽtest alǽdan *thou permittest fodder to be produced from the earth for cattle,* Ps. Th. 103, 13. Swylce he of ægerum út alǽde *as it from an egg had been brought forth,* Exon. 59 a; Th. 214, 3; Ph. 233: 59 b; Th. 215, 11; Ph. 251.

a-lǽnan; *p.* ede; *pp.* ed *To lend;* accommodare:—Alǽned feoh *pignus,* Ælfc. Gl. 14; Som. 58, 10.

a-lǽran; *p.* ede; *pp.* ed *To teach;* docere, edocere:—Me ðíne dómas alǽr *judicia tua doce me,* Ps. Th. 118, 108.

a-lǽtan, a-létan; *p.* -lét, *pl.* -léton; *pp.* -lǽten; *v. a.* [a *from,* lǽtan *to let*] *To let go, lay down, leave, give up, lose, renounce, resign, remit, pardon, deliver;* sinere, abjicere, deponere, relinquere, remittere, condonare, relaxare, liberare:—Ðæt ðú ne alǽte dóm gedreósan *that thou wouldest not let thy greatness sink,* Beo. Th. 5323; B. 2665: Cd. 205; Th. 253, 3; Dan. 590. Ic hæbbe ánweald míne sáwle to alǽtanne *I have power to lay down my life* [*soul*], Jn. Bos. 10, 18. Ic ðæt alétan ne sceal *I will not let that go,* Solil. 8. Ðú hine alǽtst *thou lettest it go,* Bt. 25; Fox 88, 24. Swá sceal ǽghwylc mon lǽn-dagas alǽtan *so must every man leave these loan-* [*lent* or *transitory*] *days,* Beo. Th. 5175; B. 2591. Ðæt ic mǽge mín líf alǽtan *that I may resign my life,* 5494; B. 2750: Exon. 72 b; Th. 271, 16; Jul. 483. Úre leáhtras alǽt *pardon our crimes,* Hy. 6, 20; Hy. Grn. ii. 286, 20: Cd. 29; Th. 39, 9; Gen. 622. Hí wurdon alǽten líges ganga [MS. gange] *they were delivered from the flame's course,* 187; Th. 232, 20; Dan. 263. Hý heora líf aléton *they lost their lives,* Ors. 3, 8; Bos. 63, 10. Ðá ðæt fýr hie alét *when the fire left them,* 4, 7; Bos. 87, 19.

a-lǽtnes, ness, e; *f. A loss, losing;* amissio, Somn. 326.

a-lamp *happened, occurred,* Beo. Th. 1249; B. 622; *p. of* a-limpan.

alan; ic ale, ðú alest, alst, he aleþ, alþ, *pl.* alaþ; *p.* ól, *pl.* ólon; *pp.* alen. I. *to nourish, grow, produce;* alere, procreare:—Swylce eorþe ól *as the earth nourished,* Exon. 94 a; Th. 353, 35; Reim. 23. II. *to appear;* apparere:—Ða ne alaþ *which appear not;* quæ non apparent, Lk. Lind. War. 11, 44. [*Goth.* alan; *pp.* alans *crescere: O. Nrs.* ala *gignere, parere, procreare: Lat.* alere.]

a-langian; *p.* ode; *pp.* od; *v. impers.* [a, langian] *To last too long, to long for;* diutius durare, exoptare:—Me alangaþ [MS. a langaþ] *it lasts me too long,* Exon. 100 a; Th. 376, 13; Seel. 154.

alaþ *ale,* Th. Diplm. A. D. 883; 130, 3. v. ealaþ.

ald, se alda *old:*—Alde méce *with an ancient sword,* Cd. 167; Th. 209, 5; Exod. 494: Elen. Grm. 252: Bd. 3, 7; S. 530, 11. Se alda út of helle *the old one out of hell,* Cd. 213; Th. 267, 6; Sat. 34. DER. ald-er, -erdóm, -friþ, -hád, -helm, -or, -Seaxe. v. eald.

alder *an elder, author,* Bd. 2, 5; S. 507, 40. v. aldor.

alder-dóm, es; *m. Authority,* Bd. 1, 27; S. 492, 12, MS. B. v. ealdor-dóm.

Aldfriþ, es; *m.* [ald = eald *old;* friþ *peace*] *Alfred the wise, king of Northumbria:*—A.D. 685, Hér Aldfriþ féng to ríce *here,* A.D. 685, *Alfred succeeded* [*took*] *to the kingdom,* Chr. 685; Erl. 41, 29. On Aldfriþes tídum *in temporibus Aldfridi,* Bd. 5, 1; S. 614, 20. A. D. 705, Hér Aldfriþ Norþanhymbra cining forþférde *here,* A. D. 705, *Alfred, king of the Northumbrians, died,* Chr. 705; Erl. 43, 32. v. Ælfred *king of Northumbria.*

ald-hád, es; *m.* [ald = eald *old;* hád *hood*] *Old age;* senectus, = eald-hád.

Aldhelm, Ealdhelm, es; *m.* [ald = eald *old;* helm *an helmet*] ALDHELM *bishop of Sherborne;* Aldhelmus apud Scireburnam episcopus:—Hér Aldhelm be westan Selewuda bisceop forþférde *here* [A.D. 709] *Aldhelm bishop west of Selwood* [*Sherborne*] *died,* Chr. 709; Th. 68, 17, col. 2. Ealdhelm, Chr. 731; Th. 74, 31, col. 2.

aldor, es; *m.* [aldor = ealdor *an elder*]. I. *an elder, parent, author;* parens, auctor, Cd. 76; Th. 95, 14; Gen. 1578: L. H. E. pref; Th. i. 26, 6. II. *a chief, prince;* præpositus, princeps, Cd. 30; Th. 40, 15; Gen. 639: 82; Th. 103, 1; Gen. 1711: 89; Th. 111, 30; Gen. 1863: 209; Th. 259, 7; Dan. 688: Beo. Th. 744; B. 369: 1340; B. 668: Andr. Kmbl. 110; An. 55: Elen. Grm. 157: Bt. Met. Fox 26, 14; Met. 26, 7. DER. aldor-apostol, -burh, -déma, -dóm, -duguþ, -freá, -leás, -líc, -líce, -man, -mon, -nes, -ness, -þægn, -wísa. v. ealdor.

aldor, es; *n.* [aldor = ealdor *life*]. I. *life, the vital parts of the body;* vita:—Ðonne ðú of líce aldor asendest *when thou sendest life from thy body,* Cd. 134; Th. 168, 29; Gen. 2790: 126; Th. 160, 27; Gen. 2656: Elen. Grm. 132: Andr. Kmbl. 2702; An. 1353: Beo. Th. 1364; B. 680. Wit on gársecg út aldrum néþdon *we two ventured out on the sea with* [*peril to*] *our lives,* Beo. Th. 1080; B. 538: 1024; B. 510. Ðæt se wǽre his aldre scyldig *that he with his life should pay* [*be liable*], Cd. 196; Th. 244, 19; Dan. 450. Ðæt him on aldre stód here-strǽl hearda *so that the hard war-shaft stood in his vital parts,* Beo. Th. 2873; B. 1434. II. *age, in the expressions*—On aldre *ever,* to aldre *always.* On aldre, Elen. Grm. 570: Beo. Th. 3563; B. 1779: Cd. 21; Th. 26, 6; Gen. 402. To aldre, Beo. Th. 4014; B. 2005: 4990; B. 2498: Cd. 22; Th. 27, 33; Gen. 427: 22; Th. 28, 15; Gen. 436: Elen. Grm. 350: 1218. DER. aldor-bana, -bealu, -cearu, -dæg, -gedál, -leás, -leg, -ner. v. ealdor.

aldor-apostol, es; *m. The chief of the apostles;* apostolorum princeps, Bd. 3, 17; S. 543, 41, col. 2. v. ealdor-apostol.

aldor-bana, an; *m.* [aldor = ealdor *life;* bana *a destroyer*] *A life destroyer;* vitæ destructor, Cd. 49; Th. 63, 17; Gen. 1033.

aldor-bealu *vital evil,* Beo. Th. 3356; B. 1676. v. ealdor-bealu.

aldor-burh *metropolis,* Bd. 1, 26; S. 488, 20. v. ealdor-burh.

aldor-cearu, e; *f. Life-care, care for life, life-long care;* cura propter vitam, ærumna longinqua:—He wearþ eallum æðelingum to aldorceare *he became a life-care to all nobles,* Beo. Th. 1817; B. 906.

aldor-dæg; *g.* -dæges; *pl. nom. acc.* -dagas; *m. Life-day, day of life;* dies vitæ, Beo. Th. 1440; B. 718. v. ealdor-dæg.

aldor-déma, an; *m. A supreme judge, a prince;* supremus judex, princeps, Cd. 57; Th. 70, 21; Gen. 1156: 114; Th. 149, 28; Gen. 2481.

aldor-dóm *a principality,* Cd. 208; Th. 256, 16; Dan. 641: 209; Th. 258, 27; Dan. 682: Elen. Grm. 767: Lk. Lind. Rush. War. 20, 20. v. ealdor-dóm.

aldor-duguþ *a chief nobility,* Cd. 95; Th. 125, 19; Gen. 2081. v. ealdor-duguþ.

aldor-freá, an; *m. A chief lord;* princeps dominus, Cd. 174; Th. 218, 29; Dan. 46.

aldor-gedál, es; *n. A divorce* or *separation from life,* Cd. 52; Th. 65, 25; Gen. 1071: Beo. Th. 1615; B. 805. v. ealdor-gedál.

aldor-leás *lifeless,* Beo. Th. 3178; B. 1587. v. ealdor-leás.

aldor-leás *deprived of parents;* orphanus, Jn. Lind. War. 14, 18. Aldorleás [MS. aldoras], Beo. Th. 30; B. 15.

aldor-leg = -læg, es; *n. Life-law, fate:*—Ðæt ge cũðon mîne aldorlege *that ye know my life's destiny,* Cd. 179; Th. 224, 20; Dan. 139. v. ealdor-leg = -læg.

aldor-lîc *principal;* principalis. v. ealdor-lîc.

aldor-lîce; *adv.* [aldor = ealdor, -lîce] *Principally, excellently;* principaliter, magnificenter, Ps. C. 50, 103; Ps. Grn. ii. 279, 103.

aldor-mon, -monn, es; *m.* [aldor = ealdor *an elder;* mon] *An elderman, alderman, nobleman, chief;* major natu, princeps, Th. Diplm. A. D. 804–829; 459, 3: Chr. 851; Th. 120, 19, col. 1: Lk. Jun. 19, 2. v. ealdor-man.

aldor-ner, es; *n. A life's safety, refuge;* vitæ servatio, asylum:—Ne mæg ic aldor-nere mîne gesẽcan *I cannot seek my life's safety,* Cd. 117; Th. 151, 22; Gen. 2512. Ðæt we aldor-nere sẽcan mõten *that we may seek an asylum,* Cd. 117; Th. 152, 13; Gen. 2519. v. ealdor-ner.

aldornes, ness, e; *f. Authority;* auctoritas:—Se bisceop mid biscoplîcre aldornesse [ealdorlîcnysse, S. 553, 35] wæs cỹðende *episcopus pontificali auctoritate protestatus,* Bd. 3, 22; Whel. 224, 22.

aldor-þegn, aldor-þegn, es; *m. A principal thane, chief,* Cd. 214; Th. 268, 36; Sat. 66: Beo. Th. 2620; B. 1308. v. ealdor-þegn.

aldor-wîsa, an; *m. A chief ruler, chief;* principalis dux, princeps:—Æðelinga aldor-wîsa *the chief ruler of men,* Cd. 63; Th. 75, 9; Gen. 1237. v. eald-wîta.

Ald-Seaxe *the Old-Saxons,* Chr. 780; Th. 92, 29, col. 1: 885; Th. 154, 20, col. 1. v. Eald-Seaxe.

a-leáh, -leág *falsified,* Ors. 3, 6; Bos. 58, 7; *p. of* a-leógan.

a-leát *bent down:*—Aleát wið ðæs engles *bent down before the angel,* Num. 22, 31; *p. of* a-lũtan.

a-lecgan, -lecgean; he -legeþ, -legþ, -lehþ, *pl.* -lecgaþ; *p.* -legde, -lẽde, *pl.* -legdon, -lẽdon; *pp.* -legd, -lẽd; *v. trans.* [a *from,* lecgan *to lay*]. I. *to place, lay down, throw down, suppress, lay aside, cease from;* ponere, collocare, prosternere, deponere, abjicere, relinquere, omittere:—Alecgan hine *to lay him down,* Lk. Bos. 5, 19: Ors. 6, 30; Bos. 126, 25. He mec on þeóstre alegde *he laid me in darkness,* Exon. 28 b; Th. 87, 11; Cri. 1423: Beo. Th. 4395; B. 2194: 67; B. 34: 6273; B. 3141. He hond alegde *he laid down the hand,* 1673; B. 834. Hie alẽdon hine *they laid him down,* Rood Kmbl. 125; Kr. 63: Ors. 5, 13; Bos. 113, 31. Hîg gemetton ðæt cild on binne alẽd *invenerunt infantem positum in præsepio,* Lk. Bos. 2, 16: 19, 20. Hỹ hleahtor alegdon *they laid laughter aside,* Exon. 35 a; Th. 116, 1; Gũ. 200: Beo. Th. 6033; B. 3020: 1707; B. 851. Hîg alẽdon ða to hys fõtum *projecerunt eos ad pedes ejus,* Mt. Bos. 15, 30. Hîg alẽdon heora fỹnd *they threw down their enemies,* Jos. 10, 13. Unriht alecgan *to suppress injustice,* L. C. S. 7; Th. i. 380, 8. Alecgende word ðæt is *deponens verbum,* for ðan ðe he legþ him fram ða âne getâcnunge, and hylt ða õðre. Ða alecgendlîcan word getâcniaþ dǽde *deponentia verba significant actum,* swâ swâ *activa;* ac hî ge-endiaþ on *or,* swâ swâ *passiva,*—ic wraxlige *luctor,* ic sprece *loquor,* hẽr is dǽd *a deponent verb is so called in Latin, because while it keeps its passive inflections it has deposed or laid aside its passive signification, and has only an active meaning; as the Latin* luctor = ic wraxlige *I wrestle;* loquor = ic sprece *I speak, here is action,* Ælfc. Gr. 19; Som. 22, 54–57. II. *to impose, inflict upon;* imponere, immittere:—Ðũ woldest on me wrohte alecgean *thou wouldest inflict calamity upon me,* Cd. 127; Th. 162, 21; Gen. 2684. III. *to diminish, take away, refuse;* imminuere, deprimere, reprimere:—Godes lof alecgan *to diminish God's glory,* Ælfc. T. 22, 20. He nǽfre ða leán alegeþ *he never refuseth the reward,* Exon. 33 b; Th. 107, 23; Gũ. 63.

alecgende word, alecgendlîc word *a deponent verb;* deponens verbum; *part. of* a-lecgan I, *q. v.*

a-lẽd *put, laid,* Lk. Bos. 2, 16; *pp. of* a-lecgan.

a-lẽdon *laid;* posuerunt, Rood Kmbl. 125; Kr. 63; *p. of* a-lecgan.

a-lefan; *pp.* ed [a, lef *weak, feeble*] *To become weak, feeble;* languescere:—Ðæt we fæston mid gerâde, swâ ðæt ũre lîchama alefed ne wurþe *ut cum ratione jejunemus, ita ut corpus nostrum languidius ne fiat,* Bd. 3, 23; Whel. 228, 45.

a-lẽfan; *p.* de; *pp.* ed *To permit, grant;* permittere, concedere:—Ðæt he us ǽfre wille eard alẽfan *that he will ever grant us a dwelling,* Cd. 215; Th. 272, 8; Sat. 116: 219; Th. 281, 27; Sat. 278. Alẽfed *permitted,* Bt. 38, 5; Fox 206, 7. v. a-lỹfan.

a-legde *should lay,* Ors. 5, 13; Bos. 113, 31; *p. of* a-lecgan.

a-lege *lay down;* depone:—Alege oððe ahwelf hîg, eálâ ðũ Drihten *cast down* [or *cover over*] *them, O Lord!* depone eos, Domine! Ps. Lamb. 58, 12; *impert. of* a-lecgan.

a-legen *confined,* Bt. 18, 3; Fox 64, 31; *pp. of* a-licgan.

a-lẽh *belied,* Beo. Th. 160; B. 80; *p. of* a-leógan.

a-lǽnian [a, lǽnian *to be lean*] *To make lean, to soak;* macerare, Ælf. pref. Hom. p. 4.

a-leódan; *p.* -leád, *pl.* -ludon; *pp.* -loden [a, leódan *to spring*] *To grow;* germinare, crescere:—Ðe under lyfte a-loden wurde *what was grown up under heaven,* Exon. 128 a; Th. 493, 5; Rä. 81, 25: Ps. Th. 106, 36.

a-leógan; *p.* -leág, -leáh, -lẽh, *pl.* -lugon; *pp.* -logen [a, leógan *to lie, lig*] *To lie, tell lies, belie, deceive;* mentiri, confutare, non præstare:—He aleág *he belied,* Bt. Met. Fox 1, 78; Met. 1, 39. Heó hyre gehât aleáh *she belied her vow,* Ors. 3, 6; Bos. 58, 7. He beót ne alẽh *he belied not his promise,* Beo. Th. 160; B. 80. Hî aleógaþ him *they tell lies to him,* Bt. 26, 1; Fox 90, 18: L. In. 13; Th. i. 110, 12.

a-leoðian; *p.* ode; *pp.* od [lið *a limb,* to-liðian *to dissolve,* Grn.] *To dismember;* avellere, abstrahere, sejungere:—He ðæt andweorc of Adames lîce aleoðode *he dismembered the substance from Adam's body,* Cd. 9; Th. 11, 18; Gen. 177.

aler, es; *m. The alder;* alnus:—Aleres rinde seóþ *boil bark of alder,* L. M. 2, 39; Lchdm. ii. 248, 17. v. alor.

aler-holt, es; *m.* [aler *the alder;* holt *a grove, wood*] *An alder wood;* alnetum. v. alor.

a-lesan; *p.* -læs, *pl.* -lǽson; *pp.* -lesen [a, lesan *to choose*] *To choose;* eligere, seligere:—Þeóden holde hæfde him alesen *the prince had faithful ones chosen to him,* Cd. 151; Th. 189, 11; Exod. 183: 154; Th. 192, 7; Exod. 228: Elen. Kmbl. 571; El. 286: 759; El. 380.

a-lẽsan; *p.* de; *pp.* ed *To redeem;* solvere, liberare, Hy. 8, 33; Hy. Grn. ii. p. 290, 33. v. a-lỹsan.

a-lẽsend, es; *m. A redeemer;* redemptor, Bt. 42; Fox 260, 14. v. a-lỹsend.

a-lẽsenis *redemption,* Mt. Lind. Stv. 20, 28. v. a-lỹsnes.

alet, es; *m.* [alet = æled, *pp. of* ælan *to kindle*] *Fire;* ignis, Cd. 186; Th. 232, 3; Dan. 254.

a-lẽt, -lẽton *left, gave up,* Ors. 3, 8; Bos. 63, 10; *p. of* a-lǽtan.

a-lẽtan *to leave, let go;* dimittere:—Ic ðæt alẽtan ne sceal *I will not let that go,* Solil. 8: Ors. 4, 7; Bos. 87, 19. v. a-lǽtan.

a-leðran; *p.* ede; *pp.* ed *To lather;* saponem illinere:—Smire mid on niht and on morgen aleðre *smear therewith at night and in the morning lather it,* L. M. 1, 54; Lchdm. ii. 126, 11.

alẽt-lîc; *adj. Pardonable;* remissibilis. v. alẽt *gave up;* lîc *like.*

alewe, aluwe, alwe, an; *f. The aloe, bitter spice,* in the plural *aloes;* aloe:—He brohte wyrt-gemang and alewan *tulit herbarum commixtionem et aloes,* Jn. Bos. 19, 39. Murre and alwe *myrrh and aloe,* L. M. 2, 65; Lchdm. ii. 296, 20. Alwan wið untrymnessum *aloes for infirmities,* L. M. cont. 2, 64; Lchdm. ii. 174, 6. Gedõ alwan gõdne dǽl ðǽr on *put a good deal of aloes therein,* L. M. 2, 14; Lchdm. ii. 192, 5: 194, 25. Aluwan gegnîd *rub up aloes,* Lchdm. iii. 2, 15. Nim alewan [MS. alewen] *take aloes,* 104, 26: 134, 9. [אֲהָלִים ăhālīm, *pl. m.;* אֲהָלוֹת ăhāloth, *pl. f. the aloe-trees, the perfumes: Grk.* ἀλόη, ης; *f. the aloe: Lat.* alŏē, ēs; *f. the aloe, a small tree in the east, which has juicy leaves, from which the bitter gum called* aloes *is extracted.*]

Alfriþ, es; *m.* [al = all = eal, eall *all;* friþ *peace*] *Alfred the wise, king of Northumbria:*—A.D. 705, Hẽr Alfriþ, Norþhymbra cing, forþfẽrde *here,* A.D. 705, *Alfred, king of the Northumbrians, died,* Chr. 705; Th. 69, 7, col. 3. v. Ælfred *king of Northumbria.*

al-geweorc, es; *n. Tinder, touchwood, a fire-steel;* igniarium, Recd. 40, 34; Wrt. Voc. 66, 42: Cot. 107: 164.

algian; *p.* ode; *pp.* od *To defend;* defendere. DER. ge-algian. v. ealgian.

alh, alhn, es; *m. A sheltering-place, temple, fane;* asylum, templum:—Tempel Gode, alhn hâligne *a temple for God, a holy fane,* Cd. 162; Th. 202, 22; Exod. 392. [*O. Sax. O. H. Ger.* alah: *Goth.* alhs.] v. healh, hearh.

alh-stede, es; *m. A sheltering-place, city;* arx, urbs, Cd. 209; Th. 259, 1; Dan. 690. v. ealh-stede.

a-libban, -lybban; *p.* -lifde, -lyfde; *pp.* -lifd, -lyfd *To live, live after, survive;* vivere, superesse:—Ðæt heó wolde hyre lîf on fæmnanhâde alibban *that she would live out her life in maidenhood,* Ors. 3, 6; Bos. 58, 5. Hwâ unclǽnnisse lîf alifde *who lived a life of uncleanness,* Exon. 116 b; Th. 448, 32; Dõm. 63: Hy. 4, 115. Hỹ on bilwitnesse hyra lîf alyfdon *they lived a harmless life,* Ors. 1, 2; Bos. 27, 5: Ex. 21, 22.

alibbend, es; *m. A survivor, one who lives after;* superstes; *part. of* a-libban.

a-licgan, -licgean; *p.* -læg, *pl.* -lǽgon; *pp.* -legen *To lie, fail, confine, perish;* jacere, conquiescere, deficere, aboleri:—Nũ sceal eall ẽðelwyn alicgean *now all joy of country shall fail,* Beo. Th. 5764; B. 2886. His dõm alæg *its power failed,* Beo. Th. 3061; B. 1528.

a-liéfan, a-lîfan *to permit;* permittere:—Alîfe me *permitte mihi,* Deut. 3, 25. Aliéfþ, Past. 50, 4. v. a-lỹfan.

aliésan *to redeem; part.* aliésend. v. a-lỹsan.

a-lifian; *p.* ode; *pp.* od *To live;* vivere:—He geþohte ðæt he wolde on fellenum gegyrelan ealle his dagas his lîfes alifian *he resolved that he would live all the days of his life in clothing of skins,* Guthl. 4; Gdwin. 26, 13. v. a-libban.

alîhtan; *p.* -lîhte, *pl.* -lîhton; *pp.* -lîhted; *v. a.* [a, lîhtan *to light*] *To enlighten;* illuminare:—Hîg alîhton ða eorþan *illuminent terram,* Gen. 1, 15. v. lỹhtan.

a-lîhtan; *p.* -lîhte *To* ALIGHT; desilire:—Ic of alîhte *desilio,* Ælfc. Gr. 30, 3; Som. 34, 44. v. lîhtan.

a-lîhting, e; *f. Enlightening;* illuminatio:—On alîhtinge [MS. alîhtincge] andwlitan ðines *in illuminationem vultus tui*, Ps. Th. 89, 8. v. lîhting.

a-limpan; *p.* -lamp, *pl.* -lumpon; *pp.* -lumpen *To happen, befall*; evenire, accidere, contingere:—Óþ-ðæt sǽl alamp *until occasion offered*, Beo. Th. 1249; B. 622. Ðá him alumpen wæs wén *then hope had occurred to him*, Beo. Th. 1471; B. 733.

a-linnan *to cease, stop*; cessare. v. a-lynnan.

a-lîs *loose*:—Alîs me *libera me*, Ps. Spl. 7, 1; *impert. of* a-lȳsan.

a-lîsendnes *redemption*. v. a-lȳsednys.

alisian = ahsian; *p.* ode; *pp.* od *To ask*; interrogare:—Driht ahsiaþ [Spl. alisiaþ] rihtwîsne *Deus interrogat justum*, Ps. Spl. 10, 6, 5; ahsaþ, Ps. Th. 10, 5, 6.

all *all*, Th. Diplm. A.D. 804–829; 460, 36: Jn. Lind. War. 11, 50: Elen. Grm. 815. v. eal, eall.

al-lîc; *adj.* [eall *all*, lîc *like*] *Universal, general, catholic*; universus:—We ealle ða ðe asettan ðone allîcan geleáfan *nos omnes qui fidem catholicam exposuimus*, Bd. 4, 17; S. 586, 16.

all-swá *likewise, also*, Mt. Kmbl. Hat. 21, 30. v. al-swá.

allunga *altogether*; omnino:—Ðe allunga underþeóded biþ unþeáwum *who is altogether subject to vices*, Bt. 30, 2; Fox 110, 20. v. eall-unga.

All-walda, an; *m.* [eal, eall *all*, -wealda *ruler*] *All-ruler, the Almighty*, Cd. 15; Th. 19, 15; Gen. 292. v. eal-wealda.

all-wihta *all beings*:—Helm allwihta *Protector of all creatures*, Cd. 64; Th. 78, 9; Gen. 1290. Meotud allwihta *Lord of all creatures*, Exon. 53 a; Th. 185, 9; Az. 5. v. eall-wihta, wiht I, *for nom. pl.* wihta.

al-mægen, es; *n.* [eal *all*, mægen] *All power, strength, might*; omnis vis:—Gém, al-mægene, heofones tunglu *observe, with all thy power, the stars of heaven*, Bt. Met. Fox 29, 6; Met. 29, 3. v. eal-mægen.

almes-lond, es; *m. Land given* or *granted in frankalmoigne*; fundus in eleemosynam datus. v. ælmes-lond.

almes-man, -mann, es; *m. An almsman*; eleemosynarius:—Ðonne nime man uncûþ sǽd æt almesmannum *then let one take strange seed of almsmen*, Lchdm. i. 400, 17.

a-loccian; *p.* ode; *pp.* od *To entice*; allicere:—Ðæt hî aloccodan út ða, ðe ðǽr binnan wǽran *that they might entice those out, who were there within*, Ors. 4, 11; Bos. 97, 39.

a-locen *withdrawn*, Lk. Bos. 22, 41; *pp. of* a-lúcan.

a-logen *false, feigned*; mentitus, falsus; *pp. of* a-leógan.

alo-malt, es; *n. Malt used in making ale*; brasium ad cerevisiam conficiendam:—Genim alomalt *take malt for ale*, Lchdm. iii. 28, 8.

alor, aler, alr, es; *m. An* ALDER-*tree*, called ELLER and ALLER; alnus; alnus glutinosa, Lin. The alder, or rather aler, is 'an inhabitant of swamps and meadows in all Europe, the north of Africa and Asia, and North America. Its favourite station is by the side of rivulets, or in the elevated parts of marshy land where the soil is drained. Its juice contains a great abundance of tannin, which renders the bark valuable for tanning, and the young shoots for dyeing. Its foliage being large, and of a deep handsome green, the alder is rather an ornamental tree. The *alder* alnus glutinosa must not be confused with the *elder* sambucus nigra *the elder-tree*, v. ellen:—Bútan alore *except alder*, L. M. 1, 36; Lchdm. ii. 86, 9. On ðone [MS. ðane] alr *to the alder*, Cod. Dipl. Apndx. 376; A.D. 939; Kmbl. iii. 413, 5. Aleres rinde seóþ on wætre *seethe in water rind of alder*, L. M. 2, 39; Lchdm. ii. 248, 17. Alr *alnus*, Ælfc. Gl. 46; Som. 65, 5; Wrt. Voc. 33, 4. [*Plat.* eller, *f*: *Dut.* else, *f*: *O. H. Ger.* elira, erila, *f*: *Ger.* eller, erle, *f*: *O. Nrs.* elrir, ölr, *m*; elri, *n.*] DER. alor-drenc, -holt, -rind.

alor-drenc, es; *m. An alder-drink*; potus alni, L. M. 1, 40; Lchdm. ii. 106, 5.

alor-holt, es; *m. An alder-holt*. v. aler-holt.

alor-rind, es; *m. Alder-rind*; cortex alni, L. M. 1, 2; Lchdm. ii. 32, 26.

a-loten *prone, submissive, bent down*; supplex, Ælfc. Gr. 10; Som. 14, 42. v. a-lútan.

aloþ *ale*:—Wulfréd scolde gifan twá tunnan fulle hlutres aloþ, and ten mittan Wælsces aloþ *Wulfred should give two tuns full of clear ale, and ten mittan or measures of Welsh ale*, Chr. 852; Ing. 93, 16: Th. Diplm. A.D. 791–796; 40, 4, 5, 6: A.D. 804–829; p. 460, 25. v. ealaþ.

alr, es; *m. An alder-tree*; alnus, Ælfc. Gl. 46; Som. 65, 5; Wrt. Voc. 33, 4. v. alor.

Alrîca, Eallrîca, Eallerîca, an; *m*: Alarîcus, i; *m. Lat.* [al = eall *all*, rîca *a ruler*; v. rîc] *Alaric*; Alarîcus, king of the Visigoths, = the west Goths, elected A.D. 382, took Rome 410, and died the same year:—Alrîca wearþ Cristen *Alaric became a Christian* [*about* A.D. 396], Ors. 6, 37; Bos. 132, 32. Alrîca, se Cristenesta cyning, and se mildesta, mid swá lytlum nîþe abræc Róme burh, ðæt he bebeád ðæt man nánne man ne slóge,—and eác ðæt man nánuht ne wanode, ne ne yfelode ðæs ðe on ðám cyricum wǽre. And sóna ðæs, on ðam þriddan dæge, hî geféran út of ðære byrig ágenum willan; swá ðǽr ne wearþ nán hûs heora wyllan forbærned *Alaric, the most Christian and the mildest king, sacked Rome with so little violence, that he ordered no one should be slain,—and that nothing should be taken away, or injured, that was in the churches. Soon after that, on the third day, they went out of the city of their own accord; so there was not a single house burnt by their order*, Ors. 6, 38; Bos. 133, 7. Hettulf, Alrîcan mæg, Honoriuses sweóstor him to wîfe genam *Ataulf, Alaric's kinsman, took the sister of Honorius for his wife*, Ors. 6, 38; Bos. 133, 14. Seó hergung wæs, þurh Alarîcum [*acc. Lat.*] Gotena cyning, geworden *hæc inruptio, per Alarîcum regem Gothorum, facta est*, Bd. 1, 11; S. 480, 11. Ðæt Eallrîca, Gotona cyning, hyre anwaldes hî beniman woldan *that Alaric, king of the Goths, would deprive her of her power*, Ors. 2, 1; Bos. 39, 37. Eallerîca, Bt. 1; Fox 22.

al-swá *also*, L. Ethb. 70; Wilk. 6, 41. v. eal-swá.

altar, es; *m. An altar*; altare:—Beforan ðam altare *ante altare*. Mt. Bos. 5, 24.

alþes *of ale*; cervisiæ [MS. cervise], *gen. s.* Rtl. 116, 42. v. alaþ, ealaþ.

a-lúcan; *p.* -leác, *pl.* -lucon; *pp.* -locen [a, lúcan *to lock*] *To separate, take* or *pluck away, withdraw*; avellere:—He wæs fram him alocen *avulsus est ab eis*, Lk. Bos. 22, 41. Alúc ðú hine fram mínum weofode *pluck thou him away from mine altar*, L. Alf. 13; Th. i. 48, 1.

a-lútan, anlútan; *p.* -leát, *pl.* -luton; *pp.* -loten [a, lútan *to bend*] *To bend, incline, bend* or *bow down*; procumbere:—Alútende he geseah *procumbens vidit*, Lk. Bos. 24, 12. He aleát to eorþan *he bowed to the earth*, Ælfc. T. 37, 8.

aluwe, an; *f. Aloe*, Lchdm. iii. 2, 15. v. alewe.

al-waldend; *adj.* [eal *all*, waldende *ruling*] *All-ruling, almighty*; omnipotens:—Alwaldend God *Almighty God*, Exon. 123 b; Th. 474, 18; Bo. 31.

alwe *aloe*, L. M. 2, 14; Lchdm. ii. 192, 5: 2, 16; Lchdm. ii. 194, 25. v. alewe.

Al-wealda, -walda, an; *m. All-ruler, God, the Almighty*; omnium rector, Deus, omnipotens:—Noldon alwealdan word weorþian *they would not revere the all-ruler's* [*the Almighty's*] *word*, Cd. 18; Th. 21, 23; Gen. 328: Beo. Th. 1861; B. 928. Gif ðé alwalda scirian wille *if the Almighty will give* [*grant*] *thee*, Cd. 136; Th. 171, 10; Gen. 2826. v. eal-wealda.

al-wealda, -walda; *def. adj. All-powerful, almighty*; omnipotens:—Alwalda God *all-powerful God*, Exon. 25 a; Th. 73, 17; Cri. 1191: 27 b; Th. 83, 33; Cri. 1365. v. eal-wealda.

al-wihta *all-beings*, Cd. 227; Th. 303, 20; Sat. 616: Exon. 18 a; Th. 43, 11: Cri. 687: Ps. C. 50, 100; Ps. Grn. ii. 279, 100. v. eall-wihta.

a-lybban; *p.* -lyfde, *pl.* -lyfdon; *pp.* -lyfed [a, lybban *to live*] *To live, live after, survive*; vivere, superesse:—Ðæt ic alybban ne mæg *that I may not survive*, Nicod. 26; Thw. 13, 37. Heó alyfaþ *she shall live*, Ex. 21, 22. Alyfdon, Ors. 1, 2; Bos. 27, 5. v. a-libban.

alȳfan, hit -lȳfþ; *p.* -lȳfde, *pl.* -lȳfdon; *impert.* -lȳf; *pp.* -lȳfed; *v. a. To give leave, permit, grant*; permittere, concedere, tradere:—Se eorl ongan alȳfan landes *the earl began to grant the land*, Byrht. Th. 134, 26; By. 90. Alȳfe me to farenne *permitte me ire*, Mt. Bos. 8, 21. Alȳf me *permitte mihi*, Lk. Bos. 9, 59: Hy. 7, 28; Hy. Grn. ii. p. 287, 28: Ps. Th. 139, 8. Hit him Rómáne alȳfdon *the Romans granted it to him*, Ors. 4, 11; Bos. 96, 30: Beo. Th. 1315; B. 655. Wearþ Cartainum friþ alȳfed *peace was granted to the Carthaginians*, Ors. 4, 10; Bos. 96, 12: Exon. 31 a; Th. 96, 12; Cri. 1573. Hyt ys alȳfed *it is permitted*, Mt. Bos. 12, 12. Alȳfþ *licet?* Mk. Bos. 3, 4: 10, 2.

a-lyfaþ *shall live*, Ex. 21, 22; *fut. of* a-lybban.

alȳfed-lîc; *adj.* [a-lȳfed *allowed, pp. of* a-lȳfan; lîc *like*] *Allowable*; expeditus:—Alȳfedlîc þing *an allowable thing*; fas, Ælfc. Gr. 9, 25; Som. 10, 67.

alȳfed-lîce; *adv. Lawfully, allowably*; licite: = a-lȳfed *allowed*, lîce; *adv.*

alȳfednes, -ness, e; *f. Permission, leave, grant*; permissio: = a-lȳfed, -nes.

a-lȳfþ *is it allowable?* licet? Mk. Bos. 3, 4. v. a-lȳfan.

a-lȳhtan *to enlighten*; illuminare. v. a-lîhtan.

alȳhtnys, -nyss, e; *f. An enlightening, illumination, a lightness*; illuminatio:—Ðú settest unrihtwîsnysse úre on alȳhtnysse andwlitan ðînne *posuisti iniquitates nostras in illuminationem vultus tui*, Ps. Spl. 89, 8. v. a-lîhting.

a-lynian; *p.* ode; *pp.* od *To liberate, deliver, free from*; liberare:—Alynian of róde Cristes lîchaman *to deliver Christ's body from the cross*, De offic. diurn. et noct. v. a-lynnan.

a-lynnan, -linnan; *p.* -lann, *pl.* -lunnon; *pp.* -lunnen *To deliver, free from, release*; liberare, evellere:—He wolde hine alynnan of láþscipe *he would release him from calamity*, Cd. 95; Th. 123, 19; Gen. 2048.

a-lȳsan, to alȳsanne; *p.* de; *impert.* -lȳs, -lîs; *pp.* ed; *v. a. To let loose, free, deliver, liberate, to pay for loosing, to pay, redeem, ransom*; liberare, redimere:—Helias wylle hine alȳsan *Elias vult liberare eum*, Mt. Bos. 27, 49. Fæsten alȳsan *jejunium solvere*, Bd. 5, 4; S. 617, 13. Ðú to alȳsanne mannan *tu ad liberandum hominem*, Te Dm. Lamb. 195 b, 16. God alȳseþ sáwle míne of handa helle *Deus redimet animam meam de manu inferi*, Ps. Spl. 48, 16. Alȳs us of yfele *deliver us from evil*, Hy. 7, 113; Hy. Grn. ii. p. 289, 113. Alîs me *libera me*, Ps. Spl. 7, 1: Ps. Th. 53, 1: 58, 1. Alȳsaþ þearfan *liberate egenum*, 81, 4. He alȳsde leóda bearn of locan deófla *he released the sons of men from the prison of devils*, Elen. Kmbl. 361; El. 181. Ða ðe ic nā reáfode ðā ic alȳsde *quæ non rapui tunc exsolvebam*, Ps. Spl. C. 68, 6: 48, 7. Ðū beó fram him alȳsed *liberatus sis ab illo*, Lk. Bos. 12, 58. Ðā wæs of ðæm hrōran helm and byrne alȳsed *then was helm and byrnie loosed from the active chief*, Beo. Th. 3264; B. 1630. We synt alȳsde *liberati sumus*, Ps. Th. 123, 7: 107, 5. Ðæt hī wǣron alȳsede *ut liberentur*, 59, 4.

a-lȳsednys, -nyss, e; *f. Redemption, a ransom;* redemptio:—Weorþ alȳsednysse sāwle his *pretium redemptionis animæ suæ*, Ps. Spl. 48, 8. Ūre alȳsednyss *nostra redemptio*, Hymn. Surt. 83, 31.

a-lȳsend, alēsend, es; *m.* [alȳsende, *part. of* alȳsan *to deliver*] *A liberator, deliverer, redeemer;* liberator, redemptor:—Ic lufige ðē, Driht, alȳsend mīn *diligam te, Domine, liberator meus*, Ps. Spl. 17, 1, 49: 18, 16. Ic wāt ðæt mīn Alȳsend leofaþ *I know that my Redeemer liveth*, Job Thw. 167, 40: Ps. Th. 69, 7: 77, 34: 143, 2.

a-lȳsendlīc; *adj. Loosing;* solutorius:—He hine acsade, hwæðer he ða alȳsendlīcan rūne cūðe *he asked him, whether he knew the loosing runes* [literas solutorias], Bd. 4, 22; S. 591, 25.

a-lȳsing, e; *f. Redemption;* redemptio, Ps. Th. 110, 6.

a-lȳsnes, -ness, e; *f. Redemption;* redemptio, Exon. 29 b; Th. 90, 14; Cri. 1474.

a-lystan; *p.* -lyste; *pp.* -lysted, -lyst [a, lystan *to wish*] *To list, wish, desire;* desiderare:—Hwī eów alyste [ā lyste, Grn.] *why do ye desire?* Bt. Met. Fox 10, 36; Met. 10, 18.

am *am;* sum:—Ic am *ego sum*, Mt. Lind. Stv. 26, 22: 11, 29: Jn. Lind. War. 7, 34. Ic am witnesse *I am witness*, Chr. 1121; Erl. 39, 23. [vide p. 28, note 3, for the date, A. D. 1121.] v. eom.

am-, as a prefix denotes *even, equal.* v. em-, am-byr.

ām, aam, es; *m. The reed* or *slay of a weaver's loom;* pecten textorius:—Ne mec ōhwonan sceal āmas [Th. uma, Dietr. āma] cnyssan *nor shall the weaver's reeds beat me anywhere*, Exon. 109 a; Th. 417, 22; Rä. 36, 8.

a-mællad; *part. Emptied out, brought to naught;* exinanitus, Ps. Surt. 74, 9. v. a-meallud.

a-mǣn-sumian; *p.* ode; *pp.* od [a *ex*, mǣn = gemǣne *communis;* sumian = samnian *congregare*] *To excommunicate;* excommunicare:—Sīe amǣnsumod *let him be excommunicated*, L. Alf. pol. 1; Th. i. 60, 18. v. a-mān-sumian.

a-mæst *fat, fattened;* altilis:—Amæste fuglas *altilia*, Cot. 16.

a-mæstan; *p.* -mæstede; *pp.* -mæsted, -mæstd, -mæst [a, mæstan *to fatten*] *To fatten;* saginare, impinguare:—Māra ic eom and fættra ðonne amæsted swīn, bearg bellende on bōc-wuda *I am larger and fatter than a fattened swine, a barrow-pig grunting in the beech-woods*, Exon. 111 b; Th. 428, 9; Rä. 41, 105. Sāwl ðe wel spricþ, hió biþ amæst *a soul that speaketh well, she shall be fattened*, Past. 49, 2.

a-mæt *measured*, a-mǣte *measuredst*, Elen. Kmbl. 2493; El. 1248: 1456; El. 730. v. a-metan.

a-mang; *prep. c. dat.* [a-, ge-mang; *prep. inter*] AMONG, *while;* inter:—Amang ðām ðe hī ridon *while they were riding*, inter equitandum, Chr. 1046; Th. 307, 29. v. on-mang, ge-mang, on-gemang.

a-manian, -manigan; *p.* ode, ade; *pp.* od, ad [a *from*, manian *to admonish, challenge, lay claim to*] *To demand, exact;* exigere:—Gif hit se gerēfa ne amanige mid rihte *if the reeve do not lawfully exact it*, L. Ed. 5; Th. i. 162, 12. Se biscop amanige ða oferhȳrnesse æt ðam gerēfan *let the bishop exact the penalty for contempt from the reeve*, L. Ath. i. 26; Th. i. 214, 2. Amanige ðære scīre bisceop ða bōte to ðæs cynges handa *let the bishop of the shire exact the compensation into the hands of the king*, L. Edg. ii. 3; Th. i. 266, 19.

a-mānsod; *part. Excommunicated:*—Gif hwā amānsodne [MS. B. amānsumodne] oððe ūtlahne hæbbe and healde *if any one have and hold an excommunicated person, or an outlaw*, L. C. S. 67; Th. i. 410, 17.

a-mān-somod *excommunicated* = a-mān-sumod, L. Edm. E. 2; Th. i. 244, 18, MS. B. v. a-mān-sumian.

a-manst *art mindful of;* memor es, Ps. Th. 8, 5. v. a-munan.

a-mān-sumian; *p.* ode, ede, ade; *pp.* od, ed, ad [a *ex*, mān = mǣn = gemǣne *communis*, sumian = samnian *congregare*] *To excommunicate, anathematize;* excommunicare, anathematizare:—Amānsumede he hine *excommunicavit eum*, Bd. 3, 22; S. 553, 26. We amānsumiaþ mid heortan and mid mūþe ða ðe hī amānsumedan *anathematizamus corde et ore quos anathematizarunt*, 4, 17; S. 586, 10, 11. Hȳ amānsumodon ðone mæsse-preost Arrīum *they excommunicated the mass-priest Arius*, L. Ælf. C. 3; Th. ii. 344, 2. Amānsumed *excommunicated*, Chr. 675; Th. 59, 12: 963; Th. 221, 23: 1070; Th. 347, 4: L. Eth. v. 29; Th. i. 312, 1.

a-mān-sumung, -sumnung, e; *f.* [a *ex*, mān = mǣn = gemǣne *communis*, sumnung = samnung *a congregation*] *Excommunication, a curse;* excommunicatio, anathema:—Besmiten mid ðære amānsumunge *pollutus anathemate*, Jos. 7, 12: R. Ben. 51: Procem. R. Conc. v. mān-sumung.

a-māwan; *p.* -meów; *pp.* -māwen [a, māwan *to mow*] *To mow, cut off;* demetere, desecare, Ps. Th. 101, 4.

ambeht, es; *m. A servant, attendant, messenger, officer;* minister, servus, nuntius, legatus. [*O. Sax.* ambahteo, *m: O. H. Ger.* ampaht, *m: Goth.* andbahts, *m: O. Nrs.* ambâtt, *f. ancilla: Lat.* ambactus, *m. a vassal, a dependant upon a lord.*] v. ombeht, ombiht, onbeht.

ambeht, ambiht, ambieht, ambyht [an-, em-, on-], *gen.* es; *nom. acc. pl.* o; *n. An office, ministry, service, command, message;* officium, ministerium, jussum, mandatum:—Ðæm ōleccaþ ealle gesceafte, ðe ðæs ambehtes āwuht cunnon *all creatures obey him, that know aught of this service*, Bt. Met. Fox 11, 17; Met. 11, 9. Lǣste ðū georne his ambyhto *perform thou zealously his commands*, Cd. 25; Th. 33, 10; Gen. 518. [*O. Sax.* ambaht, *n. servitium, ministerium: O. Frs.* ambucht, ombecht, *n: Ger.* amt, *n: M. H. Ger.* ambahte, ambehte: *O. H. Ger.* ampahti, ampaht, ambaht, *n: Goth.* andbahti, *n: Dan.* embede, *n: Swed.* ämbete, *n: Icel.* embætti, *n: Lat.* ambĭtus, *m. pp. of* ambio.]

ambeht-hēra, an; *m. An obedient minister.* v. ombieht-hēra.

ambeht-hūs, es; *n. A workshop;* officina. v. ambiht-hūs.

ambeht-mæcg, es; *m. A servant-man.* v. ambyht-mæcg, ombiht-mæcg.

ambeht-man, -mann, es; *m. A servant-man.* v. ambiht-man.

ambeht-scealc, es; *m. An official-servant;* minister. v. anbyht-scealc, ombiht-scealc, onbyht-scealc.

ambeht-secg, es; *m. An official man, a messenger.* v. ambyht-secg.

ambeht-smiþ, es; *m. An official smith* or *carpenter.* v. ambiht-smiþ.

ambeht-þegen, es; *m. An attendant-thane, an attendant, servant.* v. ombeht-þegen, ombiht-þegen.

ām-ber, ōm-ber, ōm-bor, es; *m. n?* I. *a dry measure of four bushels;* mensura continens quatuor modios sive bussellos. v. Registri Honoris de Richm. App. p. 44, where, in an extent of the manors of Crowhurst and Fylesham, in Sussex, 8 Edw. I, we read, 'xxiii ambræ salis, quæ faciunt xii quarteria, secundum mensuram Londoniæ.' Id. p. 258, it is added: 'quarterium Londinense octo modios sive bussellos continet, AMBRA *igitur quatuor modios.*' v. Introduc. to Domesday I. p. 133:—Tyn āmbra feðra *ten ambers of feathers*, Ors. 1, 1; Bos. 20, 37. Agyfe mon hine ēlce mōnaþ āne āmbra meles *let there be given him every month one amber of meal*, L. Ath. i. procem; Th. i. 198, 6. Þritig ōmbra rues cornes, feówer āmbru meolwes *thirty ambers of rye-corn, four ambers of meal*, Th. Diplm. A.D. 791–796; 40, 9, 10. Ðæt he agefe l āmbra maltes and vi āmbra grūta *that he give fifty ambers of malt and six ambers of groats*, 835; 471, 12, 13: 832–870; 474, 23. II. *a liquid measure;* batus, cadus:—Āmber *batus*, Ælfc. Gl. 25; Wrt. Voc. 24, 58. Āmbras *cadi, lagenæ*, Cot. 31, 125: Lk. Lind. War. 16, 6. XII āmbra Wilisces ealaþ, āmber fulne buteran *twelve ambers of Welsh ale, an amber full of butter*, L. In. 70; Th. i. 146, 17, 19. XXX ōmbra gōdes Uuelesces aloþ, ðæt limpaþ to xv mittum *thirty ambers of good Welsh ale, which are equal to fifteen mittas*, Th. Diplm. A.D. 804–829; 460, 24. III. *a vessel with one handle, a tankard, pitcher, pail;* lagena, urceus, amphora, situla, hydria:—Ōmbor *lagena*, Mk. Lind. Rush. War. 14, 13. Ōmbora *urceorum*, 7, 8. Ōmbor *amphora*, Lk. Lind. War. 22, 10. [ān *one*, beran *to bear, carry: O. Sax.* ēmbar, ēmber, *m. amphora: Ger.* eimer, *m: O. H. Ger.* einpar, eimberi, *m. situla, hydria.*]

ambiht, ambieht *an office, ministry, service;* officium. v. ambeht.

ambiht-hūs, es; *n.* [ambeht *an office*, hūs *house*] *A workshop;* officina, R. Concord. 11.

ambiht-man, embeht-man, embiht-man, -mann, -monn, es; *m.* [ambeht *an office*, man *a man*] *A servant-man, servant-woman, attendant, servant, minister;* servus, pedisequus, pedisequa, minister, ministra:—Hīg habbaþ ōðre ambihtmen *they have other attendants*, L. E. I. 12; Th. ii. 410, 11: Mk. Lind. War. 9, 35.

ambiht-smiþ, es; *m.* [ambeht *an office*, smiþ *a smith*] *An official smith* or *carpenter;* præfectus fabrorum:—Cyninges ambihtsmiþ *the king's official carpenter*, L. Ethb. 7; Th. i. 4, 8.

ambyht, es; *n. An office, service;* mandatum, nuntium, Cd. 25; Th. 33, 10; Gen. 518. v. ambeht; *n.*

ambyht-mæcg, es; *m.* [ambeht *an office, service;* mæcg *a man*] *A servant-man, servant, minister;* servus:—Ðīne scealcas, ambyhtmæcgas *servi tui*, Ps. Th. 101, 12. v. ombiht-mæcg.

ambyht-secg, es; *m.* [ambeht *an office, command, message;* secg *a man, messenger*] *An official man, a messenger, ambassador;* minister, nuncius, legatus:—Ðæt ic seó gramum ambyhtsecg, nales Godes engel *that I am a minister to the malignant one, not God's angel*, Cd. 27; Th. 36, 35; Gen. 582.

am-byr: *gen. m. n.* -byres; *f.* -byrre, -byre: *dat. m. n.* -byrum; *f.* -byrre, -byre: *acc. m.* -byrne; *f.* -byre; *n.* -byr; *adj.* [am *even, equal*, byr *let it happen*, from byrian *to happen, pertain*]. What is happening even or equal,—*Favourable, fair;* æquus, secundus:—Gyf man hæfde ambyrne wind *if a man had a favourable wind*, Ors. 1, 1; Bos. 21, 20.

a-meallud, -mællad; *part. Emptied out, brought to naught;* exinanitus, Ps. Spl. 74, 8, MSS. C, M.

a-mearcian; *p.* ode; *pp.* od [a, mearcian *to mark*] *To mark out, delineate, describe, determine;* annotare, denotare, designare, describere, definire:—Hēr amearcod is hāligra hiw, þurh handmægen awriten on wealle *here is described the form of the holy ones, through might of hand carved on the wall*, Andr. Kmbl. 1448; An. 724. Ðone, ðe grūnd and sund, heofon and eorþan, amearcode mundum sīnum *him, who land and* *sea, heaven and earth, marked out with his own hands,* 1499; An. 751: R. Concord. 2.

amel, es; *m. A vessel for holy water;* amula, vas lustrale, Cot. 2.

a-meldian; *p.* ode; *pp.* od *To betray, make known;* prodere, indicare:—Ic ameldige *prodo*, Ælfc. Gr. 28, 8; Som. 33, 4. He hine ameldode *prodidit eum*, Bd. 3, 14; S. 539, 46. Ðâ wǽron hî ðǽr ameldode *proditi sunt*, 4, 16; S. 584, 26: Jos. 9, 17. v. meldian.

ameos = ἄμμεως *of ammi* or *bishop-wort; gen. of* ammi.

a-merian, -myrian; *p.* ode, ede; *pp.* od, ed *To examine, purify [generally said of melted metal]*; examinare, purgare, merum reddere:—Óðer dǽl sceal beón amered on ðam fýre, swâ hêr biþ sylfor *the other part shall be proved in the fire, as silver here is*, Bt. 38, 4; Fox 204, 1. Ðæt seolfor ðe biþ seofon síðum amered *argentum examinatum septuplum*, Ps. Th. 11, 7: Exon. 63 b; Th. 234, 22; Ph. 544: 65 a; Th. 240, 3; Ph. 633: Elen. Kmbl. 2621; El. 1312: Ps. Spl. 11, 7: 16, 4. Genim ânne cuculere fulne ameredes huniges *take a spoon-full of purified honey*, Herb. 106; Lchdm. i. 220, 12. Fýre ðú us amyrdest swâ swâ amyred biþ seolfor *igne nos examinasti sicut examinatur argentum*, Ps. Spl. 65, 9. Amerodest *examinasti*, Ps. Lamb. 65, 9.

a-merran *to hinder, trouble, disturb*, Bt. Met. Fox 8, 87; Met. 8, 44. v. a-myrran.

a-metan; *p.* -mæt, *pl.* -mǽton; *pp.* -meten; *v. trans.* [a, metan *to measure*]. I. *to mete, measure, measure out;* metiri, emetiri:—His micelnesse ne mæg nân monn ametan *his greatness no man can measure*, Bt. 42; Fox 258, 13. Mid hondum amet *measure with [thy] hands*, Cd. 228; Th. 308, 30; Sat. 700. Ðæt súsl amǽte *that he should measure his torment*, 229; Th. 310, 13; Sat. 725. Ðæt ðú hús ameten hæbbe *that thou hast measured the house*, 228; Th. 309, 16; Sat. 710: Bd. 4, 23; S. 596, 26. II. *to measure out to any one, to allot, assign, bestow;* aliquid alicui emetiri, ex mensura dare, largiri:—Ametan wolde wrece be gewyrhtum wóh-fremmendum *would mete out punishment according to their deeds to the doers of wickedness*, Bt. Met. Fox 9, 70; Met. 9, 35. Ǽr me gife unscynde mægen-cyning amæt *before the powerful king measured out to me a blameless grace*, Elen. Kmbl. 2493; El. 1248. III. *to measure out, plan, form, make;* emetiri, formare, confingere:—Ðú amǽte mundum ðínum ealne ymbhwyrft and uprâdor *thou measuredst with thine hands the whole circumference and the firmament above*, Elen. Kmbl. 1456; El. 730.

a-metan; *p.* -mette; *pp.* -mett; *v. trans.* [a, metan *to paint*] *To paint, depict, adorn;* pingere, depingere, ornare:—Swelce he hit amete and atiefre on his heortan *quasi in corde depingitur*, Past. 21, 3; Hat. MS. 30 b, 26. Firmamentum [fæstnes] mid manegum steorrum amett *the firmament adorned with many stars*, Bd. de nat. rm; Wrt. popl. scienc. 10, 12; Lchdm. iii. 254, 9.

amet-hwîl, e; *f. Leisure;* otium, Ælfc. Gr. 8; Som. 8, 1, MS. D. v. æmet-hwîl.

a-middan; *adv.* [a = on *in, into;* mid *middle*] *In the middle, into the midst;* in medium:—Arís, and stand hêr amiddan *surge, et sta in medium*, Lk. Bos. 6, 8.

ammi, ami; *g.* ameos; *n. Ammi, an African umbelliferous plant, millet, bishopwort;* ammi Copticum [ἄμμι; *g.* ἄμμεως]:—Ðeós wyrt ðe man ami, and óðrum naman milium, nemneþ *this wort which is named ammi, and by another name millet*, Herb. 164, 1; Lchdm. i. 292, 20. Óðer swilc ameos *as much more of ammi*, L. M. 2, 14; Lchdm. ii. 192, 7.

a-molsnian; *p.* ode, ade; *pp.* od, ad *To corrupt, putrefy;* putrefacere, Som. v. molsnian.

amore, an; *f. A kind of bird;* avis quædam, scorellus, Cot. 160.

Amorreas; *pl: g.* a *The Amorites;* Amorrhæi:—Seon cyning Amorrea *Sehon regem Amorrhæorum*, Ps. Th. 135, 20.

ampella, ampolla, ampulla, an; *m. A vial, bottle, flask, flagon;* ampulla, lecythus, lenticula:—Ampella *vel* ele-fæt *an oil-flask*, lecythus = λήκυθος [MS. legithum], Cot. 119. Ampella *vel* crog *lenticula*, 124. [*Ger.* ampel, *f: O. H. Ger.* ampulla, ampla, *f: O. Nrs.* ampli, hömpull, *m.*]

ampre, an; *f. Sorrel* or *dock;* rumex, Lchdm. iii. 12, 25. v. ompre.

a-munan; ic, he -man, ðú -manst, *pl.* -munon; *p.* -munde, *pl.* -mundon; *pp.* -munen *To think of, mind, consider, be mindful of, have a care for;* cogitare, reputare, memor esse, providere:—Hwæt is se mann, ðe ðú swâ miclum amanst? *quid est homo, quod memor es ejus?* Ps. Th. 8, 5. Cwǽdon hî, ðæt hie ðæs ne amundon ðe mâ ðe eówre geferan *they said, that they no more minded it than did your companions*, Chr. 755; Th. 84, 36, col. 3. v. munan.

a-mundian; *p.* ode; *pp.* od *To protect, defend;* tueri, tutari, Æthelfl. Test; Th. Diplm. A.D. 972; 522, 28. v. mundian.

a-mundon *thought of, minded*, Chr. 755; Th. 84, 36, col. 3; *p. of* a-munan.

a-myrdrian; *p.* ede; *pp.* ed *To murder, kill;* occidere, interficere, trucidare:—Ðæt man sý amyrdred *that a man be murdered*, L. C. S. 57; Th. i. 406, 25. v. myrðrian.

a-myrgan; *p.* de; *pp.* ed; *v. trans.* [a, myrgan *to be merry*] *To make merry, to gladden, cheer;* exhilarare, lætificare:—Bêc syndon breme: hî amyrgaþ módsefan manna gehwylces of þreánýdlan ðisses lífes *books are famous: they cheer the mind of every one from the necessary affliction of this life*, Salm. Kmbl. 479; Sal. 240.

a-myrian; *p.* ede, ode; *pp.* ed, od *To examine;* examinare, Ps. Spl. 65, 9. v. a-merian.

a-myrran, -merran; *p.* de; *pp.* ed [a, myrran *impedire*]. I. *to hinder, impede, obstruct, check, disturb;* impedire, turbare, obstruere:—Ðæs wêla amerþ and lǽt ða men *this wealth obstructs and hinders those men*, Bt. 32, 1; Fox 114, 3. He ofslôh fætta heora, and gecorene Israhêla he amyrde *occidit pingues eorum, et electos Israhel impedivit*, Ps. Spl. C. 77, 35. Me habbaþ hringa gespong síðes amyrred *the binding of these rings hath impeded me in my course*, Cd. 19; Th. 24, 18; Gen. 378. He ðæs eorles earm amyrde *he checked the earl's arm*, Byrht. Th. 136, 43; By. 165. II. *to dissipate, spend, distract, defile, mar, corrupt, spoil, destroy;* dissipare, perdere, consummare, corrumpere, devorare, distrahere:—Ðâ he hæfde ealle amyrrede *postquam omnia consummasset*, Lk. Bos. 15, 14, 30. Ne amyrþ he hys mêde *non perdet mercedem suam*, Mt. Bos. 10, 42. Ðeós gitsung hafaþ gumena gehwelces môd amerred *this covetousness has corrupted the mind of every man*, Bt. Met. Fox 8, 87; Met. 8, 44: 22, 8; Met. 22, 4. Eorþe wæs amyrred *corrupta est terra*, Ex. 8, 24: Ors. 3, 10; Bos. 69, 39. Ic amyrre *distraho*, Ælfc. Gr. 28, 5; Som. 32, 10.

an; *prep. In, among, into, to;* in, ad; followed by *dat.* or *acc*:—An ferþe *in the spirit*, Ps. C. 50, 110; Ps. Grn. ii. 279, 110: 50, 157; Ps. Grn. ii. 280, 157. Hió biþ eallunga an hire selfre *she is altogether in herself*, Bt. Met. Fox 20, 440; Met. 20, 220. An folcum *among the people*, Ps. C. 50, 5; Ps. Grn. ii. 276, 5. Dó glêda an glêdfæt *put embers into a chafing dish*, L. M. 3, 62; Lchdm. ii. 346, 3. Ðæt ic an forþgesceaft fêran môte *that I may come to a future state*, Ps. C. 50, 52; Ps. Grn. ii. 278, 52. v. on.

an *I give*, Alfd. Will 14, 4; *he gives*, Cd. 141; Th. 176, 22; Gen. 2915. v. unnan.

an- is used in composition. I. for A.Sax. and *against, in return;* contra, re-; as an-sacan *to strive against, to contradict;* repugnare, contradicere: an-swarian *to answer;* respondere. II. for un-, denoting *privation;* as an-bindan *to unbind;* absolvere. III. for on, in *in, to;* as an-wadan *to invade;* invadere: an-fôn *to take to one's self;* accipere. Sometimes an- appears scarcely to alter the meaning of the word before which it is placed.

-an, -anne, v. -anne, in alphabetical order, and TO; *prep.* IV. The termination of most Anglo-Saxon verbs is in -an; but -ân is found, which seems to be contracted from aa, agan, ahan, as,—gân *to go*, from gaan: smeán *to consider*, from smeagan: sleán *to slay*, from sleahan, *etc.* The termination of verbs in -ôn, appears to be a contraction from ahan, ohan, as,—fôn *to take*, from fahan: gefeón *to rejoice*, from gefeohan: teón *to draw*, from teohan, *etc.* Mrch. § 247*.

ÂN, I. *m. f. n.* ONE; unus, una, unum: *gen. m. n.* ânes; *f.* ânre *of one;* unius: *dat. m. n.* ânum; *f.* ânre *to one;* uni: *acc. m.* ânne, ǽnne; *f.* âne, *n.* ân *one;* unum, unam, unum: *instr. m. n.* âne; *f.* ânre *with one;* uno, unâ, uno: *pl. nom. acc. m. f. n.* âne *each, every one, all;* unusquisque, una-quæque, unum-quodque; singuli, æ, a: *gen. m. f. n.* ânra *of every one, all;* singulorum, arum, orum: *dat. m. f. n.* ânum *to every one, all;* singulis: *instr.* ânum *with all: def.* se âna; seó, ðæt âne *the one: gen.* ðæs, ðære, ðæs ânan *of the one: dat.* ðam, ðære, ðam ânan *to the one: acc.* ðone, ða ânan, ðæt ân *the one: instr. m. n.* ðý ânan; *f.* ðære ânan *with the one; adj*:—Ân of ðâm *unus ex illis*, Mt. Bos. 10, 29. Ân wæs on Ispania *one was in Spain*, Ors. 4, 9; Bos. 92, 19. God geworhte ǽnne mannan, Adam, of lâme *God created one man, Adam, of earth*, Homl. Th. i. 12, 28. He is ân God *Deus unus est*, Mk. Bos. 12, 29. Ðis is ân ðara gerǽdnessa *this is one of the ordinances*, L. Eth. ix. 1; Th. i. 340, 2. II. *alone, only, sole, another;* solus, alius: with these meanings it is used *definitely*, and *generally written* âna, *m. and sometimes* aina, ânna, ânga, *q. v*:—Ân God ys gôd *God alone is good;* solus [unus] est bonus, Deus, Mt. Bos. 19, 17. Ðæt ge forlǽton me ânne, and ic ne eom âna *ut me solum relinquatis, et non sum solus*, Jn. Bos. 16, 32. God âna wât hú his gecynde biþ, wífhâdes ðe weres *God alone knows how its sex is, [the sex of] female or male*, Exon. 61 a; Th. 223, 6; Ph. 355. Ðæt ge aina [ge â mâ, Grn.] gebróðra hæfdon *quod alium haberetis vos fratrem*, Gen. 43, 6. 2. *sole, alone of its kind, singular, unique, without an equal;* unicus, eximius:—Ân sunu, mǽre meotudes bearn *the only Son, illustrious child of the Creator*, Exon. 128 a; Th. 492, 7; Rä. 81, 10: Hy. 8, 14; Hy. Grn. ii. 290, 14: Bt. Met. Fox 21, 19, 25, 32; Met. 21, 10, 13, 16. Ðæt wæs ân foran eald-gestreóna *that was before a singular old treasure*, Beo. Th. 2920; B. 1458. Ðæt wæs ân cyning, ǽghwæs orleáhtre *that was a singular king, faultless in everything*, 3775; B. 1885. III. *a certain one, some one;* quidam; v. sum:—Ân man hæfde twegen suna *homo quidam habebat duos filios*, Mt. Bos. 21, 28. *In this sense it is used as* sum *in the parallel passage.*—Sum man hæfde twegen suna *homo quidam habuit duos filios*, Lk. Bos. 15, 11. 2. *sometimes, though rarely,* ân *may be used as the English article a, an.* It does not, however, appear to be generally used as an indefinite article, but more like the *Moes.* ain, or the *Lat.* unus.—When a noun was used indefinitely by the Saxons, it was without an article prefixed; as,—Þeódríc wæs Cristen *Theoderic was a Christian*, Bt. 1; Fox 2, 7. **3.** *in the following examples it seems to be used for the indefinite article a, an*:—Ân engel bodade ðâm hyrdum ðæs heofonlícan cyninges acennednysse *an angel announced to the shepherds the birth of the heavenly king*, Homl. Th. i. 38, 3. Ðâr beó ân mann stande *there shall be a man standing*, Chr. 1031; Ing. 206, 5; Erl. 162, 7. Ðâ stôd ðâr ân Iudeisc wer, ðæs nama wæs Nichodêmus *then stood there a Jewish man, whose name was Nicodemus*, Nicod. 11; Thw. 5, 38. On ânum reste-dæge *on a rest-day* or *sabbath*, Lk. Bos. 24, 1: Jn. Bos. 20, 1. Sceollon ǽnne tîman gebîdan *must wait [abide] a time*, L. C. E. 18; Th. i. 370, 18: Ors. 3, 7; Bos. 61, 36. Wirc ðê nû ǽnne arc *now make for thee an ark*, Gen. 6, 14. Âne lytle hwîle *a little while*, Bt. 7, 1; Fox 16, 4. Cynríc ofslôgon ǽnne Bryttiscne cyning *Cynric slew a British king*, Chr. 508; Ing. 21, 6. **IV.** *each, every one, all*; unus-quisque, una-quæque, unumquodque; singuli, -æ, -a. It is in this sense that it admits of a plural form: *nom. acc. pl. m. f. n.* âne; *gen. m. f. n.* ânra; *dat. m. f. n.* ânum:—Ânra gehwâ, ânra gehwylc *every one*, or, literally, *every one of all*. Swelte ânra gehwilc for his âgenum gilte *unusquisque pro peccato suo morietur*, Deut. 24, 16. Ânes hwæt, Bt. 18, 3; Fox 64, 30, denotes *anything*, literally '*anything of all*,' and is used adverbially for *at all, in any degree.* ¶ *One, other*,—Ân æfter ânum *one after another*, Jn. Bos. 8, 9: Salm. Kmbl. 771; Sal. 385. To ânum to ânum *from one to the other, only*; duntaxat. Ðæt ân, or for ân *this one thing, for one thing, only*; tantummodo, Mk. Bos. 5, 36. Hý forbærndon ânne finger, and ânne *they burnt off one finger, and then another*, Ors. 2, 3; Bos. 42, 15. Ete ǽnne and ǽnne *let him eat one and another, one after another*, Herb. 1, 20; Lchdm. i. 76, 24. On ân *in one, continually, ever*, Gen. 7, 12: Cd. 140; Th. 175, 9; Gen. 2892. DER. nân [=ne+ân *n*+*one*] *none, no one*; nullus [ne-ullus].

ân; *adv. Only*; tantum:—Cweþ ðín ân word *speak thy word only*; tantum dic verbo, Mt. Bos. 8, 8. v. ÂN II.

âna; *m. One, sole, single, solitary*; unus, unicus, solus, solitarius: *nom. f. n.* âne *one, etc*; una, unum: *gen. m. f. n.* ânan *of one*; unius=unici, unicæ, unici: *dat.* ânan *to one*; uni=unico, unicæ, unico: *acc. m. f.* ânan *one*; unum, unam; *def. numeral adj.* Ðæt [treów, *n.*] se âna is ealra beáma beorhtast geblôwen *that is the one of all the trees most brightly flourishing*, Exon. 58 b; Th. 209, 27; Ph. 177. God âna on êcnysse rîxaþ *one God ruleth to eternity*, Homl. Th. i. 28, 23. v. ÂN II.

ân-âd, ân-ǽd, es; *n.* [ân *unus*, âd=eád, eáþ *desertus, vastus*, Ett: *Goth.* áuþs ἔρημος *desertus*: v. DER. eáðe; *adj.*] *Solitude, a desert*; solitudo, desertum:—On ðam ânâde *in the desert*, Exon. 37 a; Th. 122, 12; Gû. 304: 37 b; Th. 123, 24; Gû. 327. On ânǽde *in a desert*, 122 b; Th. 471, 22; Rä. 61, 5. [*O. Sax.* ênôdi, einôdi, *f. n. solitudo*: *Ger.* einöde, *f. desertum, solitudo*: *M. H. Ger.* einoede, *f*; einoete, einôte, *n*: *O. H. Ger.* einôdi, *f*; einoti, *n. solitudo, desertum.*]

an-ælan; *p.* -ælde; *pp.* -æled, -æld [an, ælan *to light*] *To kindle, inflame, enlighten*; accendere, incendere, inflammare, illuminare:—Mid andan ðære rihtwîsnesse anæld *kindled with a zeal of righteousness*, Chr. 694; Th. 66, note 2: R. Concord. 5. v. on-ælan, in-ælan.

an-æðelian; *p.* ode, ade; *pp.* od, ad; *v. trans.* [an=un *not*, æðelian *to ennoble*] *To dishonour, degrade*; ignobilem reddere:—And ðonan wyrþ anæðelad ôþ-ðæt he wyrþ unæðele *and thence becomes degraded till he is unnoble*, Bt. 30, 2; Fox 110, 22: Bt. Met. Fox 17, 53; Met. 17, 27. v. un-æðelian.

ânan, ânum *by this alone, only*; *dat. of* ân *one*.

anan-beám, es; *m. The spindle-tree, prick-wood, prick-timber*; euonymus Europæus, L. M. 1, 32; Lchdm. ii. 78, 13.

ana-wyrm, es; *m.* [ana=an, in *in*, as in *Goth.* anahneiwan *inclinare*; wyrm *a worm*] *An intestinal worm*; lumbricus:—Gif anawyrm on men weaxe *if an intestinal worm grow in a man*, L. M. 1, 46; Lchdm. ii. 114, 13, 18, 23.

an-bærnys, on-bærnys, -nyss, e; *f.* [v. on-bærning, in-bærnis] *Incense, frankincense*; incensum, thus:—Sý gereht gebêd mîn swâ swâ anbærnys *dirigatur oratio mea sicut incensum*, Ps. Spl. 140, 2.

an-be-lǽdan; *p.* -lǽdde; *pp.* -lǽded, -lǽd *To lead* or *bring in*; inducere. DER. belǽdan, lǽdan.

an-bestingan; *p.* -bestang, *pl.* -bestungon; *pp.* -bestungen *To thrust in*; immittere, intromittere:—Ða anbestungne [Cot. MS. anbestungnan] saglas *intromissi* [scil. *circulis*] *vectes*, Past. 22, 1; Hat. MS. 33 a, 22.

an-bîd, es; *n. Awaiting, expectation*; expectatio, mora:—Ðǽr wǽron ǽrendracan on anbîde *there ambassadors were in waiting*, Ors. 3, 9; Bos. 68, 44. Næs ic on nâuht [ne, âht, âuht] îdlum anbîde, ðeáh hit me lang anbîd þûhte, ðâ ðâ ic anbîdode Godes fultumes *expectans, expectavi Dominum*, Ps. Th. 39, 1. Earmra anbîd *the expectation of the miserable*, Cd. 169; Th. 212, 2; Exod. 533: Elen. Kmbl. 1767; El. 885. v. on-bîd.

an-bîdian; *p.* ode, ude; *pp.* od *To abide, wait, wait for, expect*; morari, commorari, expectare:—Wolde ðǽr on ælþeódignisse anbîdian *ut peregrinaretur ibi*, Gen. 12, 10. Me anbîdiaþ rihtwîse ôþ-ðæt ðû afyldest me *me expectant justi donec retribuas mihi*, Ps. Spl. 141, 10. Ic anbîdude hine *expectabam eum*, 54, 8.

an-bîdung, es; *m. An abiding, tarrying, awaiting, expectation*; commoratio, expectatio:—Wîcode þreó niht on anbîdunge *moratus est tres dies*, Jos. 3, 1. Hwylc is anbîdung mîn *quæ est expectatio mea?* Ps. Spl. 38, 11.

an-bindan; ic -binde, ðû bindst, he -bint, *pl.* -bindaþ; *p.* -band, ðû -bunde, *pl.* -bundon; *pp.* -bunden; *v. a.* [an=un *un-*, bindan *to bind*] *To* UNBIND, *untie*; solvere, absolvere, religare:—Seó wiðerwearde wyrd anbint and gefreóþ ǽlc ðara ðe hió togeþiéþ *adverse fortune unbinds and frees every one of those whom she adheres to*, Bt. 20; Fox 72, 2. v. on-bindan, in-bindan.

an-biscopod; *part. Unbishoped, unconfirmed*; non confirmatus ab episcopo, L. Edg. C. 15; Wilk. 83, 40. v. un-biscopod.

ân-boren; *part. Only-born, only-begotten*; unigenitus:—Ðæt in Bethlême cyning ânboren cenned wǽre *that in Bethlehem the only-begotten king was born*, Elen. Kmbl. 783; El. 392: Exon. 16 b; Th. 39, 6.

an-brôce, an; *f. Material, wood, timber*; materies, tignum:—Æðele anbrôce *noble material*, Elen. Grm. 1029, note, p. 161.

an-bryrdan; *p.* -bryrde; *pp.* -bryrded, -bryrd; *v. a. To prick, goad, vex*; compungere, stimulare:—He hêhtende wæs menn wanspendinne, and anbryrdne heortan *persecutus est hominem inopem, et compunctum corde*, Ps. Spl. 108, 15. v. on-bryrdan, in-bryrdan.

an-bryrdnes, -ness, e; *f. Compunction, remorse*; compunctio, C. R. Ben. 70. v. on-bryrdnes.

ân-bûende; *part. Dwelling alone*; anachoreticam vitam agens:—Eáhteþ ânbûendra *persecutes those dwelling alone*, Exon. 33 b; Th. 107, 15; Gû. 59.

an-bûgan, *p.* -beáh, -beág, *pl.* -bugon; *pp.* -bogen; *v. intrans. To bend* or *bow one's self in, submit to any one*; se inflectere, se submittere alicui:—To ðon ðæt hî him anbugon *that they might submit to him*, Ors. 1, 12; Bos. 36, 25. v. on-bûgan.

anbyht-scealc, ombiht-scealc, onbyht-scealc, es; *m.* [ambeht *an office*, scealc *a servant*] *An official servant, a servant*; minister, servus:—Hraðe fremedon anbyhtscealcas swâ him heora ealdor bebeád *the official servants quickly did as their lord bade them*, Judth. 10; Thw. 21, 27; Jud. 38. v. ombiht-scealc, onbyht-scealc.

an-byrdnys, nyss, e; *f.* [an *contra*, byrdnys *status*] *Resistance*; repugnantia:—Gif ǽnig man anbyrdnysse beginþ *if any man begin resistance*, L. Edg. S. 14; Th. i. 276, 31. v. geán-byrdan.

an-byrignys, -nyss, e; *f. A tasting, taste*; gustus, Ælfc. Gl. 70; Som. 70, 51; Wrt. Voc. 42, 59. v. byrignes.

ân-cænned; *def.* se ân-cænneda; *part. Only-begotten*; unigenitus:—To ârwurþianne [MS. tarwurþienne, v. weorþianne=wurþianne *in* weorþian I] ðînne, ðone sôðan and ðone âncænnedan, Sunu *to honour thy, the true and only-begotten, Son*, Te Dm. Thomson 35, 12. v. ân-cenned.

ân-cenda=ân-cenneda *only-begotten*, Exon. 99 a; Th. 370, 2; Seel. 51. v. ân-cenned.

ân-cenned; *def.* se ân-cenneda; *part.* [ân *unus*, cennan *gignere*] *Only-begotten*; uni-genitus:—Âncenned Sunu *only-begotten Son*, Exon. 14 b; Th. 29, 18; Cri. 464. Se âncenneda Sunu *the only-begotten Son*, Jn. Bos. 1, 18: 3, 16.

ancer; *g.* ancres; *m. An anchor*; ancora, Wrt. Voc. 73, 84. v. ancor.

âncer, es; *m. An anchoret, hermit*; anachoreta:—Mid ðý he leornode be ðâm âncerum *when he learnt concerning the anchorets*, Guthl. 2; Gdwin. 18, 22. v. âncor.

âncer-lîc; *adj. Anchoretic, like a hermit*; anachoreticus, Som. v. âncor-lîc.

âncer-lîf, es; *n. An anchoret's* or *hermit's life*; anachoretica vita, Bd. 4, 28; S. 605, 6. v. âncor-lîf.

ancer-man, -mann, es; *m. An anchor-man, the man in charge of the anchor*; proreta, Ælfc. Gl. 104; Som. 77, 126. v. ancor-man.

âncer-setl, -settl, es; *n. An anchoret's cell, hermitage*; anachoretæ sedes:—Twegen hâlige menn, on âncersettle wuniende, wǽron forbearnde *two holy men, dwelling in a hermitage, were burned*, Chr. 1087; Th. 354, 23: Guthl. 4; Gdwin. 26, 10.

ancer-streng, es; *m. An anchor-string, a cable*; ancorarius funis, Solil. 4.

ancleow, es; *m. The* ANCLE; talus:—Ancleow *talus*, Ælfc. Gl. 75; Wrt. Voc. 44, 74. Lytel ancleow *taxillus*, 75; Wrt. Voc. 45, 1. [*Dut.* anklauuw, enklauuw, enkel: *Ger. M. H. Ger.* enkel, *m*: *O. H. Ger.* anchal, *m*; anchala, *f*: *Dan. Swed.* ankel: *O. Nrs.* ökul, ökli, *m.*]

an-cnâwan *To recognise*; agnoscere, Ælfc. Gr. 28, 1; Som. 30, 31. v. on-cnâwan.

ancor, ancer, oncer; *g.* ancres; *m.* [ancŏra=ἄγκυρα: uncus=ὄγκος *a hook*, v. DER.] *An anchor*; ancora:—Ðîn ancor is git on eorþan fæst *thine anchor is yet fast in the earth*, Bt. 10; Fox 30, 5. On ancre fæst *fast at anchor*, Beo. Th. 611; B. 303. On ancre râd *rode at anchor*, 3771; B. 1883. Ða ancras *the anchors*, Bt. 10; Fox 30, 10, 13: Bd. 3, 15; S. 541, 40. Ýþmearas ancrum fæste *ships* [*wave-horses*] *fast with anchors*, Exon. 20 b; Th. 54, 6; Cri. 864. [*Chauc.* ancre: *Plat. Dut. Ger. M. H. Ger.* anker, *m*: *O. H. Ger.* anchar, *m*: *Dan.* anker, *m*: *Swed.*

ankare, *m: O. Nrs.* akkéri, *m: Lat.* ancora: *Grk.* ἄγκυρα: *Lith.* inkoras; *from the Sansk.* anka *a hook.*]

ãncor, ãncer; *g.* ãncres; *m. An anchoret, hermit;* anachoreta:—Slēfleás ãncra scrūd *hermits' sleeveless garment,* Ælfc. Gl. 63; Som. 68, 111. [*O. Sax.* ēnkoro, *m: O. H. Ger.* einchoranar, *m: Grk.* ἀναχωρητής.]

ancor-bend, es; *m. An anchor-band* or *cord* or *rope.* v. oncer-bend.

ãncor-līc; *adj. Anchoretic, like a hermit;* anachoreticus. DER. v. ãncor *a hermit,* līc *like.*

ãncor-līf, ãncer-līf, es; *n. An anchoret's* or *hermit's life, a solitary life;* anachoretica vita, Bd. 4, 28; S. 605, 11.

ancor-man, ancer-man, -mann, es; *m. An anchor-man, the man in charge of the anchor;* ancorarius, proreta, Ælfc. Gl. 83; Som. 73, 66: 104; Som. 77, 126.

ancor-rãp, es; *m. An anchor-rope, a cable.* v. oncyr-rãp.

ancor-setl, es; *n. An anchor-seat, the fore-castle of a ship, the prow;* prora, Ælfc. Gl. 104; Som. 78, 11.

ãncor-stōw, e; *f. An anchoret's* or *hermit's cell, a solitary place;* anachoretæ mansio, solus locus, Bd. 5, 12; S. 627, 26.

ancra, an; *m. An anchor, ballast;* ancora *vel* saburra, Ælfc. Gl. 83; Wrt. Voc. 48, 21. v. ancor.

ãncra, an; *m. An anchoret, hermit;* anachoreta, solitarius, Ælfc. Gl. 69; Som. 70, 20.

ancre, an; *f.* [antre?] *Radish;* raphănus = ῥάφἄνος:—Ancre, ðæt is rædic *raphanus,* Mone A. 493. v. ontre.

anc-sum, anc-sum-līc *troublesome.* v. ang-sum, ang-sum-līc.

an-cuman; *p.* -com, *pl.* -cōmon; *pp.* -cumen, -cymen *To come, arrive;* advenire:—Ðã he west ancom [westan com, MS.] *when he came to the west,* Cd. 90; Th. 113, 9; Gen. 1884. DER. cuman.

ãn-cummum; *adv.* [ãn *one,* cummum *the dat. of* cuma *a comer*] *One by one, singly;* singulatim, Jn. Lind. War. 21, 25.

ãn-cyn; *g. m. n.* -cynnes; *f.* -cynre; *adj.* [ãn *one, only;* cyn *proprius*] *Only;* unicus:—Ðē seó [MS. se] hālige andett geladung,—ðinne sōðan and ãncynne sunu *te sancta confitetur ecclesia,—tuum verum et unicum* [= *proprium*] *filium,* Te Dm. Lye. v. ãn-līc.

and; *prep. dat. acc.* I. *with the dative;* cum dativo *With;* cum:—Emb eahta niht and feówerum *after eight nights with four* [*twelve nights*], Menol. Fox 419; Men. 211. Ymb twentig and fīf nihtum *after twenty with five nights,* i. e. *after twenty-five nights,* 373; Men. 188. II. *with the accusative;* cum accusativo *Against, before, on, into;* contra, apud, in; κατά:—Hæfdon dreám and heora ordfruman *had joy before their creator* [apud creatorem], Cd. 1; Th. 2, 2; Gen. 13. Ðæt is cræft eágorstreámes, wætres and eorþan, and on wolcnum eác *that is the power of the sea, of water on earth, and also in the clouds,* Bt. Met. Fox 20, 245; Met. 20, 123. Ȳþ up færeþ, ōfstum wyrceþ wæter and wealfæsten *the wave goes up* [*and*] *rapidly makes* [*worketh*] *the water into a wall* [*wall-fastness*], Cd. 157; Th. 195, 27; Exod. 283. [*O. Sax.* ant *usque ad: O. Frs.* anda, and *in, on: Goth.* and *against: O. H. Ger.* ant: *O. Nrs.* and *contra: Lat.* ante: *Grk.* ἀντί, ἄντα: *Lith.* ant *on, upon: Sansk.* anti *opposite, against, before.* Thus *and* seems to be connected with *Goth.* andi *end, A. Sax.* ende *frontier, boundary,* and *Sansk.* anta *end, boundary, limit, border,* which is probably derived from the *Sansk.* root ant, and *to bind;* hence *near* or *with,* and that which is *with* or *near,* may be *against.*]

and; *conj.* AND; et, atque, ac:—Gesceóp God heofenan and eorþan *creavit Deus cœlum et terram,* Gen. 1, 1. Cum and geseóh *veni et vide,* Jn. Bos. 1, 46. And swã forþ *and so forth;* et cætera, Ælfc. Gr. 25; Som. 26, 59.

and- [*Goth.* anda-: *Icel.* and-, önd-: *Grk.* ἀντι-] in composition denotes opposition,—*Against, without;* contra:—And-bita, and-beorma *without barm, what was unleavened;* azymos = ἄ-ζῡμος, Cot. 17. And-saca *an adversary, apostate,* Cd. 23; Th. 28, 27; Gen. 442. And-swaru *an answer,* Beo. Th. 5713; B. 2860.

anda, onda, an; *m.* emotion of mind,—*Malice, envy, hatred, anger, zeal, annoyance, vexation;* animi emotio,—rancor, invidia, indignatio, ira, zelus, molestia:—Anda *rancor,* Ælfc. Gl. 89; Som. 74, 93. Næfst ðū nãnne andan to nãnum þinge *thou hast not any envy to anything,* Bt. 33, 4; Fox 128, 18. Hyne for andan sealdon *per invidiam tradidissent eum,* Mt. Bos. 27, 18. Nyste nǣnne andan *know not any hatred,* Bt. 35, 6; Fox 168, 10. For hwilcum līþrum andan *ex prava aliqua invidia,* L. M. I. P. 12; Th. ii. 268, 11: Bt. Met. Fox 20, 72; Met. 20, 36. Habbaþ andan betweóh him *have enmity between them,* 28, 104; Met. 28, 52. On andan *in hatred,* Beo. Th. 1421; B. 708: Cd. 191; Th. 237, 28; Dan. 344. Manigum on andan *for vexation to many,* Elen. Grm. 969. For ðæm andan his rihtwīsnes [-nesse MS. Cot.] *per zelum justitiæ,* Past. 17, 1; Hat. MS. 21 b, 28. [*O. Sax.* ando, *m. indignatio, ira, zelus: O. H. Ger.* anado, anto, *m. zelus: O. Nrs.* andi, *m. halitus oris, spiritus, animus.*] DER. andian: andig.

ãn-dæge; *adj.* [ãn *one,* dæg *a day*] *For one day, lasting a day:* diurnus, unius diei:—Næs ðæt ãndæge nīþ *that was no one-day evil,* Exon. 92 a; Th. 345, 25; Gu. Ex. 195. Sǣ-weall astãh, uplang gestōd ãndægne fyrst *the sea-wall arose,* [*and*] *stood erect one day's space,* Cd. 158; Th. 197, 9; Exod. 304. Ðe hire ãndæges eágum starede *who daily gazed on her with his eyes,* Beo. Th. 3874; B. 1935.

andættan *to confess,* Th. Anlct. v. andettan.

ãn-daga, an; *m.* [dæg *a day* = daga, *q. v.*] *A fixed day, a time appointed, a day* or *term appointed for hearing a cause;* dies dictus, dies constitutus:—Gesette me ãnne ãndagan *constitue mihi tempus,* Ex. 8, 9: 9, 5: Gen. 18, 14. Ðæt gehwilc spræc hæbbe ãndagan hwænne heó gelǣst sȳ *that every suit have a term when it shall be brought forward,* L. Ed. prœm; Th. i. 158, 6: 11; Th. i. 164, 21: L. Edg. H. 7; Th. i. 260, 13: L. C. S. 19; Th. i. 386, 14. [*O. Sax.* ēn-dago, *m. dies statutus, fatalis,—terminus vitæ: O. Nrs.* ein-dagi *dies oculatus, tempus præscriptum, a verbo* eindaga *certum tempus definire.*]

ãn-dagian; *p.* ode; *pp.* od; *v. a. To appoint a day* or *term, to cite;* diem dicere, L. Edg. H. 7; Th. i. 260, 12. DER. ge-ãn-dagian. v. ãndaga.

and-beorma, an; *m. That which is without barm, unleavened, unleavened bread, the feast of unleavened bread;* azyma:—Andbita *vel* [and-]beorma *azyma,* Cot. 17. v. beorma, and-bita.

and-bīdian; *p.* ode; *pp.* od *To expect;* expectare:—Ðe andbīdiaþ ðē *qui expectant te,* Ps. Spl. 68, 8. Andbīdiaþ wildeór on þurste heora *expectabunt onagri in siti sua,* 103, 12. v. an-bīdian.

and-bīdung, es; *m. Expectation;* expectatio:—Nã ðū gescend me fram andbīdunge mīne *non confundas me ab expectatione mea,* Ps. Spl. 118, 116. v. an-bīdung.

and-bita, an; *m. That which is unleavened, unleavened bread, the feast of unleavened bread;* azyma:—Andbita *vel* and-beorma *azyma,* Cot. 17. [*Goth.* unbeistei, *f.* ἄζυμον.]

and-cwis, -cwiss, e; *f. An answer;* responsum:—Andcwis ageaf *gave answer,* Exon. 47 b; Th. 163, 26; Gū. 999.

anddetan *To confess;* confiteri:—Hyra synna anddetende *confitentes peccata sua,* Mk. Bos. 1, 5. v. andetan.

and-eáw; *adj.* [and *against,* eáw = ǣw *lawful, legitimate*] *Arrogant, presumptuous, proud;* arrogans, Scint. 46.

Andefera, an; *m.* ANDOVER, *a market town in the north west of Hampshire built on the east bank of the river Ande or Anton;* oppidum in agro Hamtunensi:—Hī ðã lǣddon Ãnlãf to Andeferan *they then led Anlaf to Andover,* Chr. 994; Th. 242, 27, col. 1; Th. 243, 26, col. 1, 12, col. 2. To Andefron, Th. 242, 26, col. 2. [*Dun.* Andeafara: *Kni.* Andever.] About the year 1164 *Simeon Durham* writes it Andeafara = Ande-eá-fara *a farer over the river Ande, on the bank of which Andover is built,* v. fara *a traveller,* faran *to go, travel, sail.* From the *A. Sax.* of the MS. Cott. Tiber. B. IV. to Andefron, of Knighton Andever, about 1395, and from the present name Andover = Ande + ōfer, another derivation may be supposed,—Ande *the river Ande,* and ōfer; *g.* ōfres; *d.* ōfre; *m. a margin, bank,* that is *a town on the bank of the river Ande.*

and-efn, es; *n.* [and, efen *even*] *An equality, a proportion, measure, an amount;* proportio:—Be hire andefne *by its proportion,* Bt. 32, 2; Fox 116, 14.

andet, andett, e; *f. Confession, praise, honour, glory;* confessio. v. *comp.* wlite-andet, andetnes.

andetan *To confess, acknowledge, give thanks* or *praise;* confiteri:—Ic ðē on folcum andete *confitebor tibi in populis,* Ps. Th. 56, 11: 98, 3: 104, 1: 135, 27. v. andettan.

andetla, an; *m. A confession;* confessio, L. Alf. pol. 22; Th. i. 76, 4.

andetnes, -ness; andetnys, -nyss, e; *f. A confession, acknowledgment, profession, giving of thanks* or *praise, praise, honour, glory;* confessio:—In andetnesse *in confessione,* Bd. 4, 25; S. 599, 42. Seó andetnes ðe we Gode andettaþ *the confession that we confess to God,* L. E. I. 30; Th. ii. 426, 33. Ðe his naman neóde sealdon him andetnes ǣghwǣr habban *ad confitendum nomini tuo,* Ps. Th. 121, 4. Is upp-ahafen his andetness, heáh ofer myclum heofone and eorþan *confessio ejus super cœlum et terram,* 148, 13: 95, 6. Andetnysse and wlite ðū scrȳddest *confessionem et decorem induisti,* Ps. Spl. 103, 2.

andetta, an; *m. One who confesses, a confessor, an acknowledger;* confessor:—Se ðæs sleges andetta sīe *who is a confessor of the slaying,* L. Alf. pol. 29; Th. i. 80, 7.

andettan, andetan, ondettan, ondetan; *p.* and-ette [and = *Lat.* re, contra; *Grk.* ἀντί; hãtan *to command, promise*] *To confess, acknowledge, give thanks* or *praise;* fateri, confiteri:—Gif he wille and cunne his dǣda andettan *if he will and can confess his deeds,* L. De. Cf. 2; Th. ii. 260, 18, 16. Ic andette Ælmihtigum Gode *I confess to Almighty God,* 6; Th. ii. 262, 20. Seó andetnes ðe we Gode ãnum andettaþ, dēþ hió us ðæt to gōde *the confession that we confess to God alone, it doth this for our good,* L. E. I. 30; Th. ii. 426, 33. Drihtne andette *confitebatur Domino,* Lk. Bos. 2, 38. Folc ðē andetten *confiteantur, tibi populi,* Ps. Th. 66, 5. Ealra godena Gode andettaþ *confitemini Domino omnium dominorum,* 135, 28. [*O. Sax.* and-hētan, ant-hētan *præcipere, vovere: O. H. Ger.* ant-heizan *proponere, spondere, polliceri, vovere.*] DER. and-detan: ge-andettan, -ondettan: andet, -an, -la, -nes, -ta, -tere, -ting.

andettean *to confess;* confiteri, Bd. 1, 1; S. 474, 3. v. andettan.

andettere, es; *m. A confessor;* confessor:—Ðæt Albanus hæfde ðone

Cristes andettere mid him *confessorem Christi penes Albanum latere*, Bd. 1, 7; S. 477, 7.

andetting, es; *m. A confession, profession;* confessio, professio. v. andettan.

and-feng, an-, on-, es; *m. A taking to one's self, taking up, a receiving, defence, defender;* assumptio, susceptio, susceptor, Lk. Bos. 9, 51: Ps. Spl. 90, 2: Cd. 218; Th. 279, 28; Sat. 245: Ps. Spl. 88, 18. v. an-feng, on-feng.

and-fenga, -fengea, -fencgea, [ond-], an; *m. A receiver, undertaker, defender;* susceptor:—Is andfenga Drihten sāwle mīnre *Dominus susceptor est animæ meæ*, Ps. Th. 53, 4: 118, 114. Ðū me, God, eart andfengea *tu, Deus, susceptor meus es*, 58, 18: 143, 2. Andfencgea, 58, 9.

and-fenge, -fencge; *adj. That which can be received, acceptable, approved, fit;* acceptabilis, acceptus, aptus:—Asette his hand ofer ðære offrunge heáfod, ðonne biþ heó andfenge *ponet manum super caput hostiæ, et acceptabilis erit*, Lev. 1, 4. Bodian Drihtnes andfenge gēr *prædicare annum Domini acceptum*, Lk. Bos. 4, 19: 4, 24. Nys andfenge Godes rīce *non est aptus regno Dei*, 9, 62. Andfencge *acceptus:* andfengra *acceptior*, Ælfc. Gr. 43; Som. 44, 47.

and-fengend, es; *m. A receiver, undertaker, defender;* susceptor:—Ūre andfengend is Iacobes God *susceptor noster Deus Jacob*, Ps. Th. 45, 6.

and-fengnes, -ness, on-, e; *f. A receiving, reception, a place for receiving, a receptacle;* receptaculum, Bd. 2, 9; S. 510, 12: Cot. 190. v. on-fangennes.

and-findende; *part. Finding, getting;* nanciscens, Cot. 138.

and-gelōman, and-lōman; *pl. m. Implements, tools, utensils;* instrumenta, Cot. 104. v. ge-lōma.

and-get, es; *n. The understanding, intellect;* intellectus, Bt. 39, 4; Fox 216, 28. v. and-git.

andgete; *adj. Manifest;* manifestus, Exon. 26 a; Th. 76, 22; Cri. 1243; [*perhaps we should read* or-gete: v. l. 1238.]

andget-full, andgit-full; *adj. Sensible, discerning, knowing;* intelligentiæ plenus, intelligens, intelligibilis:—Ðæt ǣnig mon sīe swā andgetfull [andgitfull, MS. Cot.] *that any man is so discerning*, Bt. 39, 9; Fox 226, 1: R. Ben. 7: 63.

and-giet, es; *n. understanding, intellect, knowledge;* intellectus:—Ic ðec, mon, ǣrest geworhte, and ðē andgiet sealde *I first wrought thee, O man, and gave thee understanding*, Exon. 28 a; Th. 84, 30; Cri. 1381: 117 a; Th. 449, 16; Dōm. 72. v. and-git.

andgiet-tācen, es; *n. A sensible token;* intelligibile signum:—Ge on wolcnum ðæs andgiettācen māgon sceáwigan *ye may behold a sensible token of this in the clouds*, Cd. 75; Th. 93, 3; Gen. 1539.

and-git, -giet, -gyt, -get, [ond-, on-], es; *n.* [and, git = get, *p. of* gitan *to get*]. I. *the understanding, the intellect;* intellectus:—Þurh ðæt andgit, man understent ealle ða þing, ðe he gehȳrþ oððe gesihþ *by the understanding, man comprehends* [*understands*] *all the things, which he hears or sees*, Homl. Th. i. 288, 21. Þurh ðæt andgit, seó sāwul understent *through the understanding, the soul comprehends* [*understands*], 288, 28. Ðǣr ðæt gemynd biþ, ðǣr biþ ðæt andgit and se willa *where the memory is, there is the understanding and the will*, 288, 26. Ðæs andgites mǣþ *the measure of the understanding*, Bt. 41, 4; Fox 250, 23. Andgit *intellectus*, Ælfc. Gl. 69; Som. 70, 28: Exon. 28 a; Th. 84, 30; Cri. 1381: Ps. Th. 31, 10. II. *understanding, knowledge, cognizance;* intellectus, cognitio, agnitio:—Ic ðē sylle andgit *intellectum dabo tibi*, Ps. Th. 31, 9: 91, 5. Forðan biþ andgit ǣghwǣr sēlest *therefore is understanding everywhere best*, Beo. Th. 2122; B. 1059. Nolde ic hiora andgit ǣnig habban *non agnoscebam eos*, Ps. Th. 100, 4. III. *sense, meaning, one of the senses;* sensus:—Hwīlum [he sette] andgit of andgite *sometimes* [*he put*] *meaning for meaning*, Bt. proœm; Fox viii. 3. Ða fīf andgitu ūre līchaman, ðæt is, gesihþ and hlyst, swæcc and stenc and hrepung *the five senses of our body, that is, sight and hearing, taste and smell and touch*, Homl. Th. ii. 550, 10.

andgitan; *p.* -geat; *pp.* -giten *To perceive, understand:* animadvertere, Cot. 3. v. on-gitan.

and-gite, -giete, an; *f. The intellect, understanding, knowledge;* intellectus, cognitio. v. ond-giete.

andgit-fullīc; *adj. Fully* or *clearly understood, intelligible;* omnino intellectus, intelligibilis:—Ǣlc stemn is oððe andgitfullīc oððe gemenged. Andgitfullīc stemn is ðe mid andgite biþ geclypod, swā swā is, Ic hērige ða wǣpnu, and ðone wer *arma virumque cano,—every voice is either intelligible or confused. Intelligible voice is what is spoken with understanding, as, Arms and the man I sing*, Ælfc. Gr. 1; Som. 2, 32–34.

andgit-fullīce; *comp.* or; *sup.* ost; *adv. Sensibly, clearly, plainly, distinctly, intelligibly;* intelligenter:—Swā swā he hit andgitfullīcost gereccan mihte *as he most clearly might explain it*, Bt. proœm; Fox viii. 4.

andgit-leás; *adj. Foolish, senseless, doltish;* stolidus, insipiens:—Geonge men and andgitleáse man sceal swingan *young men and foolish must be beaten* [*one shall beat*], L. M. I. P. 14; Th. ii. 268, 26.

andgit-līc; *adj. Sensible, intelligible;* intelligibilis, Solil. 11.

andgit-līce; *adv. Clearly;* liquido, Cot. 123. v. andgit-fullīce.

andgitol; *adj. understanding;* intelligibilis. v. andgyttol.

andgit-tācen, es; *n. a sensible token.* v. andgiet-tācen.

and-gyt, es; *n. the intellect, understanding, knowledge;* intellectus, cognitio:—Ðām nis andgyt *quibus non est intellectus*, Ps. Spl. 31, 11: 118, 73. Ne māgon andgyt habban? *nonne cognoscent?* Ps. Th. 52, 5: 66, 2. v. and-git.

andgyttol, andgytol; *adj. understanding, intelligent, sensible;* intelligens, intelligibilis, R. Ben. 7: 63. v. andget-full.

and-hētan; *p.* -hētte *to confess;* confiteri:—He his gyltas Gode andhētte *he confessed his offences to God*, Ps. C. 50, 29; Ps. Grn. ii. 277, 29. v. andettan.

andian, -igan; *part.* -igende; ic andie, andige, ðū andast, he andaþ, andgaþ, *pl.* andiaþ; *p.* ode; *pp.* od [anda *envy*] *To envy;* invidere:—Ic andige on ðē *invideo tibi*, Ælfc. Gr. 41; Som. 43, 58: 26; Som. 29, 3. Andgaþ *invidet*, Prov. 28.

andig; *adj. Envious;* invidus, Scint. 15.

andigende; *part. envying*, R. Ben. interl. 55. v. andian.

and-lang, -long, [ond-]; *adj. All-along, throughout, continuous, extended;* per totum, continuus, in longum porrectus:—Wæs andlangne dæg swungen *was beaten all day long*, Andr. Kmbl. 2550; An. 1276: Chr. 937; Th. 202, 27, col. 2; Æðelst. 21: Beo. Th. 4237; B. 2115.

and-lang, ond-long, on-long; *prep. only gen. On length,* ALONG, *by the side of;* in longum, per:—Lǣte yrnan ðæt blōd nyðer andlang ðæs weofudes *decurrere faciet sanguinem super crepidinem altaris;* he will let the blood run down along the altar, Lev. 1, 15. Andlang ðæs [MS. ðas] wēstenes *along the desert*, Jos. 8, 16. Andlang ðara nægla *along the nails*, Bd. 3, 17; S. 544, 30. Ðæt wæter wyrþ to eá, ðonne andlang eá to sǣ *the water runs to the river, then along the river to the sea*, Bt. 34, 6; Fox 140, 20. Andlang Mæse *along the Mase*, Chr. 882; Th. 150, 22, col. 2, 3. Andlang dīces *along the dike*, Cod. Dipl. Apndx. 442; A. D. 956; Kmbl. iii. 438, 18.

and-leán, ond-leán, es; *n. Retribution, retaliation;* retributio, talio:—Hī sculon onfōn wrāþlīc andleán *they shall receive dire retribution*, Exon. 20 a; Th. 52, 12; Cri. 832. DER. leán.

and-leofen, -lifen, -lyfen, es; *n.* I. *living, food, sustenance, nourishment, pottage;* victus, alimenta, pulmentum:—Mon to andleofne eorþan wæstmas hām gelǣdeþ *man for sustenance brings home earth's fruits*, Exon. 59 a; Th. 214, 22; Ph. 243. Ðū winnan scealt and dīne andlifne selfa gerǣcan *thou shalt labour and thyself get thy sustenance*, Cd. 43; Th. 57, 25; Gen. 933. Sealde him andlyfene *dedit eis alimenta*, Gen. 47, 17: Bd. 1, 27, resp. 8; S. 494, 16. Sealde ealle hyre andlyfene *misit totum victum suum*, Mk. Bos. 12, 44. II. that by which food is procured, *money, wages, alms;* stipendium, stips:—Ðæt he mihte dæghwāmlīce andleofene onfōn *ut quotidianam ab eis stipem acciperet*, Bd. 5, 2; S. 615, 3. Beóþ ēþhylde on eówrum andlyfenum *estote contenti stipendiis vestris*, Lk. Bos. 3, 14.

and-līcnis, -niss, e; *f. A likeness, similitude;* imago:—God gesceóp man to his andlīcnisse *creavit Deus hominem ad imaginem suam*, Gen. 1, 27. v. an-līcnes.

and-lōman, and-lūman; *pl. m. Utensils, vessels;* utensilia, vasa, Ælfc. Gl. 22: R. Ben. interl. 31. v. and-gelōman.

and-long; *adj. All-along, throughout;* per totum:—Andlonge niht *all night long*, Exon. 51 b; Th. 179, 14; Gū. 1261: Beo. Th. 5383; B. 2695. v. and-lang.

and-mitta, an; *m.* [and, mitta *a measure*] *A weight, a standard weight;* exagium. v. an-mitta.

an-drǣdan; *part.* an-drǣdende *To fear*, Cd. 156; Th. 194, 25; Exod. 266. v. on-drǣdan.

Andreas; *m. indecl. but* Andreæ *and* Andrea *are found in dat. as in Lat. and Grk. Andrew;* Andreas. [*Lat.* Andreas; *g. dat.* Andreæ; *m.* = Ἀνδρέας; *g.* ου; *dat.* ᾳ; *m.* from ἀνδρεία; *g. as manliness, manly strength* or *courage*, from ἀνήρ; *g.* ἀνδρός *a man*]:—Andreas, Simōnes brōðer Petres *Andreas, frater Simonis Petri*, Ἀνδρέας, ὁ ἀδελφὸς Σίμωνος Πέτρου, Jn. Bos. 1, 40. Hī cōmon on Andreas hūs *venerunt in domum Andreæ*, ἦλθον εἰς τὴν οἰκίαν Ἀνδρέου, Mk. Bos. 1, 29. Fram Bethsaida, Andreas ceastre and Petres *a Bethsaida, civitate Andreæ et Petri*, Jn. Bos. 1, 44. Philippus sǣde hit Andreæ *Philippus dicit Andreæ*, Φίλιππος λέγει τῷ Ἀνδρέᾳ, 12, 22. Ðā ðæt Andrea earmlīce þūhte *then that seemed pitiful to Andrew*, Andr. Kmbl. 2271; An. 1137. Ðǣr Andrea ongete wearþ wīgendra þrym *there the glory of the warriors became known to Andrew*, 3136; An. 1571. Ðis Gōdspel sceal on Andreas mæsse-dæg *this Gospel must be on St. Andrew's day*, Rubc. Mt. Bos. 4, 18–22, Notes, p. 574.

and-reccan; *p.* -reahte; *pp.* -reaht *To relate;* referre:—Ic mæg andreccan spræce *I can relate a tale*, Bt. Met. Fox 26, 3; Met. 26, 2. v. reccan.

an-drece-fæt, es; *n.* [drecan *vexare*, fæt *vas*] *A pressing-vat, a wine* or *oil vat;* emistis? *vel* trapetum, *scil.* torcular ad uvas *vel* olivas premendas, Mann; Ælfc. Gl. 26; Wrt. Voc. 25, 22.

Andred, es; *m. The name of a large wood in Kent, also the city of* ANDRED or *Andrida:* Andredes ceaster, e; *f. the Roman station* or *city of Andred, Pevensey* or *Pemsey Castle*, Sussex: Andredes leág, e; *f.*

ANDREDSLEY: Andredes weald, es; *m.* ANDRED'S WEALD, *a large wood in Kent, extending into Sussex* [v. Sandys Gavel. Ind. p. 340]:—Hine đā Cynewulf on Andred adrǣfde *then Cynewulf drove him into Andred*, Chr. 755; Th. 82, 9, col. 2. Hēr Ælle and Cissa ymbsǣton Andredes ceaster *in this year Ælle and Cissa besieged Andredescester*, 491; Th. 24, 19, col. 2. On đone wudu đe is genemned Andredes leáge *into the wood which is called Andredsley*, 477; Th. 22, 40, col. 1. Se mūþa [Limene] is on eásteweardre Cent, on đæs ilcan wuda eást ende đe we Andred hātaþ. Se wudu is westlang and eástlang cxx mīla lang odđe lengra, and xxx mīla brād. Seó eā, đe we ǣr embe sprǣcon, līđ ūt of đam wealde *the mouth* [*of the Limen*] *is in the east of Kent, at the east end of the same wood which we call Andred. The wood is, along the east and along the west*, 120 *miles long, or longer, and thirty miles broad. The river, of which we before spoke, flows out from the weald*, Chr. 893; Th. 162, 29, col. 3.

Andredes ceaster, leág, weald. v. Andred, es; *m.*

an-drysen-lic, -drysn-līc, [on-]; *adj. Terrible;* terribilis:—Swȳđe heáh God and swȳđe andrysnlīc ofer ealle godas *Dominus summus, terribilis super omnes deos*, Ps. Th. 46, 2: Past. 15, 2; Hat. MS. 19 a, 26. v. dryslīc.

an-drysne, on-drysne; *adj.* I. *terrible, fearful, dreadful;* terribilis, horrendus:—Wearþ đæt andwyrde swīđe andrysne *that answer was very fearful*, Ors. 5, 3; Bos. 104, 3. II. as causing fear, *venerable, venerated, respectable;* verendus, reverendus:—Ne biþ he nāuđer ne weorþ, ne andrysne *he is neither honourable, nor respectable*, Bt. 27, 1; Fox 94, 22: Ors. 5, 12; Bos. 112, 13.

an-drysno; *dat. pl.* an-drysnum; *f. Fear, awe, reverence;* timor, metus, reverentia:—For andrysnum *from reverence*, Beo. Th. 3596; B. 1796. v. on-drysno.

and-saca, ond-, an; *m. A denier, renouncer, an apostate, opposer, enemy;* negator, renunciator, adversarius:—Ofer eorþan andsaca ne wæs *there was not an opposer on the earth*, Cd. 208; Th. 258, 2; Dan. 669. Godes andsaca *an opposer or a forsaker of God*, 23; Th. 28, 27; Gen. 442: Beo. Th. 3369; B. 1682. Godes andsacan *God's enemies*, Cd. 219; Th. 281, 10; Sat. 269: Exon. 31 a; Th. 97, 22; Cri. 1594. Mid đām andsacum *with the apostates*, Cd. 17; Th. 21, 6; Gen. 320. v. saca.

and-sacian, -sacigan, -sacigian; *p.* ode; *pp.* od *To strive against, to deny, refuse, gainsay, forsake, abjure;* impugnare, negare, recusare, abjurare:—Ne mæg ic andsacigan *I cannot deny*, Bt. 10; Fox 26, 24. v. sacian.

and-sæc, es; *m?* [and-; sacu, sæc *strife, contention*] *Contention, resistance, denial, refusal;* contentio, repugnantia, contradictio, negatio:—Borges andsæc *inficiatio* vel *abjuratio*, Ælfc. Gl. 14; Som. 58, 16. Be borges andsæce *concerning a refusing of a pledge*, L. In. 41; Th. i. 128, 1, note 1. Đe đæs upstīges andsæc fremedon *who made denial of the Ascension*, Exon. 17 b; Th. 41, 14; Cri. 655: Elen. Grm. 472.

and-sǣte; *adj.* [and *against*, sǣtan *to lie in wait*] *Odious, hateful, abominable;* exosus, perosus, Ælfc. Gr. 33; Som. 36, 60: Ælfc. Gl. 84; Som. 73, 101; Wrt. Voc. 49, 9.

and-speornan *to stumble*, Mt. Kmbl. Rush. 4, 6. v. on-speornan.

and-spyrnes, -ness, e; *f. An offence;* scandalum, Mt. Rush. Stv. 16, 23.

and-standan [and, standan *to stand*] *To sustain, abide, stand by, bear;* sustinere:—Andstandende ongeán *contending against*, R. Ben. 1.

and-swarian, an-, ond-, on-; *p.* ede, ode, ude; *pp.* ed, od; *v. a. n. To give an answer, to* ANSWER, *respond;* respondere:—Đā ne mihton hīg him nān word andswarian *non poterant ei respondere verbum*, Mt. Bos. 22, 46. Andswarode ic *I answered*, Bt. 26, 2; Fox 92, 18. Him se yldesta andswarode *the chiefest answered him*, Beo. Th. 522; B. 258: Andr. Kmbl. 519; An. 260: Cd. 38; Th. 51, 16; Gen. 827. Him englas andswaredon *the angels answered him*, 117; Th. 152, 25; Gen. 2525. Andswarodon, 111; Th. 147, 5; Gen. 2434. DER. swarian, ond-, geand-: swerian.

and-swaru, ond-, e; *f.* [and, swaru *a speaking*] *An* ANSWER; responsum:—Andswaru līđe *a soft answer*, Scint. 77. Grim andswaru *a fierce answer*, Beo. Th. 5713; B. 2860. Hī afēngon andsware *illi acceperunt responsum*, Mt. Bos. 2, 12. Andsware bīdan wolde *would await an answer*, Beo. Th. 2991; B. 1493: Exon. 10 b; Th. 12, 11; Cri. 184: Bt. Met. Fox 22, 86; Met. 22, 43. Nū sceal he sylf faran to incre andsware *now he must come himself for your answer*, Cd. 27; Th. 35, 19; Gen. 557.

and-swerian; *p.* ade, ede, ode; *pp.* ed, od *to answer*:—Đā him andsweradan gāstas *then the ghosts answered him*, Cd. 214; Th. 268, 6; Sat. 51. Andsweredon, Elen. Grm. 397. v. and-swarian.

and-sȳn, e; *f. A face;* facies:—Woldon hī đæt hī mihton geholene beón fram andsȳne đæs cyninges *they wished that they might be hidden from the face of the king*, Bd. 4, 16; S. 584, 25. v. an-sȳn.

and-þwǣre; *adj. Perverse, froward, athwart, cross;* perversus. v. and *against*, þwǣre *quiet.*

and-timber, an-, on-, es; *n. Matter, materials, substance, a theme;* materies, materia, thema:—Lengran feóndscipes andtimber *longioris inimicitiæ materies*, Bd. 4, 21; S. 590, 19. Antymber [MSS. C. and D. antimber] *materies, materia*, Ælfc. Gr. 12; Som. 15, 54. Antimber *thema*, 9, 1; Som. 8, 21. v. timber.

and-warde; *adj. Present;* præsens:—Đis andwarde līf manna on eorþan *vita hominum præsens in terris*, Bd. 2, 13; S. 516, 14. v. and-weard.

and-wardnys, -nyss, e; *f. Presence;* præsentia:—Būtan ōđra bisceopa andwardnysse *sine aliorum episcoporum præsentia*, Bd. 1, 27; S. 491, 40. v. and-weardnes.

and-wealcan *to roll;* volvere, Th. Anlct. v. on-wealcan.

and-weald, es; *m. Power, right* or *title to anything*:—Đæt he wolde habban andweald ongeán God *that he would have power against God*, Homl. Th. i. 10, 25: Ps. Spl. 19, 7: 113, 2: Ælfc. Gl. 13; Som. 57, 121. v. ān-weald, onweald.

and-weard, -werd, -warde; *adj. Present;* præsens:—Đǣr is Dryhten andweard *where the Lord is present*, Exon. 48 b; Th. 167, 7; Gū. 1056. Andweard Gode *present with God*, 30 b; Th. 95, 29; Cri. 1564. Fōr đē andweardne *before thee present*, Cd. 40; Th. 54, 2; Gen. 871: Andr. Kmbl. 2449; An. 1226. Ōþ đisne andweardan dæg *usque in hunc præsentem diem*, Mt. Bos. 28, 15. On đis andweardan līfe *in this present life*, Bt. 10; Fox 26, 30. Đa scearpþanclan wītan đone twydǣledan wīsdōm hlutorlīce tocnāwaþ, đæt is, andweardra þinga and gāstlīcra wīsdōm *the sharp-minded wise men knew clearly the twofold wisdom, that is, the wisdom of things temporal* [*present*] *and spiritual*, MS. Cot. Faust, A. x. 150 b; Lchdm. iii. 440, 30. [*O. Sax.* and-ward *præsens*: *O. H. Ger.* ant-wart: *Goth.* and-wairþs.] DER. and-warde, and-wardnys, and-weardlīce, and-weardnes.

and-weard-līce; *adv. Presentially, in the presence of, present;* præsentialiter:—Đe hine andweardlīce gesāwon *who saw him present*, Bd. 4, 17; S. 585, 30: Elen. Grm. 1141.

and-weardnes, -ness, and-weardnys, and-wardnys, -nyss, e; *f. Presentness, presence, present time;* præsentia, præsens tempus, præsens:—Wæs ic swȳđe for his andweardnesse afyrhted *ejus præsentia eram exterritus*, Bd. 4, 25; S. 600, 42. On andweardnysse *in præsenti*, 1, 1; S. 474, 1.

and-wendan; *p.* -wende; *pp.* -wended *to change;* mutare. DER. wendan. v. on-wendan.

and-wendednys, a-wændednys, -nyss, e; *f.* [and, wended, *pp. of* wendan *to turn*, nes] *A changing, change;* mutatio, Ps. Spl. 76, 10. v. on-wendednes.

and-weorc, ond-weorc, an-weorc, es; *n. Matter, substance, material, metal, a cause of anything;* materia, cæmentum, metallum, causa:—He đæt andweorc of Adames līce aleođode *he dismembered the substance from Adam's body*, Cd. 9; Th. 11, 16; Gen. 176. Đæt leád is hefigre đonne ǣnig ōđer andweorc *plumbum cæteris metallis est gravius*, Past. 37, 3; Hat. MS. 50 a, 16. Būton andweorce *without cause*, Bt. 10; Fox 30, 2: Bt. Met. Fox 17, 32; Met. 17, 16.

and-werd; *adj. Present;* præsens:—On đisum andwerdan dæge *on this present day*, Homl. Th. ii. 284, 5. v. and-weard.

and-werdan, and-wirdan, and-wyrdan, ond-wyrdan; *p.* de; *pp.* od [and, word *a word*: *Goth.* and-waúrdyan *to answer*, waúrd *a word*: *Ger.* antwort *an answer*] *To answer;* respondere:—Abram hire andwerde *Abram ei respondit*, Gen. 16, 6.

and-wirdan; *p.* de; *pp.* od *to answer;* respondere:—Đæt wīf andwirde *the woman answered*, Gen. 3, 2. v. and-werdan.

and-wīs; *adj. Expert, skilful;* gnarus, expertus:—Yfeles andwīs *expert in evil*, Exon. 69 a; Th. 257, 8; Jul. 244. DER. wīs.

and-wīsnes, -ness, e; *f. Experience, skilfulness;* experientia. DER. and, wīsnes. v. wīs *wise.*

and-wlata, an; *m. The face, forehead*, Herb. 75, 6; Lchdm. i. 178, 16: 101, 2; Lchdm. i. 216, 9. v. and-wlita.

and-wlita, an-wlita, an; *m*: and-wlite, es; *n. The face, countenance, personal appearance, forehead, form, surface;* facies, vultus, aspectus, frons, forma, superficies:—Hleór bolster onfēng, eorles andwlitan *the bolster received his cheek, the hero's face*, Beo. Th. 1382; B. 689: Exon. 24 a; Th. 69, 20; Cri. 1123: Bt. Met. Fox 31, 33; Met. 31, 17. Leóht andwlitan đīnes *lumen vultus tui*, Ps. Spl. 4, 7: Ps. Th. 89, 8. Ealle gesceafta onfōþ æt Gode andwlitan *all creatures receive form from God*, Bt. 39, 5; Fox 218, 15. On andwlitan wīdre eorþan *on the face of the wide earth*, Cd. 67; Th. 81, 21; Gen. 1348. He hæfde blācne andwlitan *he had a pale countenance*, Bd. 2, 16; S. 519, 34. [*Plat.* antlaat, *n*: *N. H. Ger.* antlitz, *n*: *M. H. Ger.* antlütze, antlitze: *O. H. Ger.* antluzi: *O. Nrs.* andlit, *n.*]

and-wlītan; *p.* -wlāt, *pl.* -wliton; *pp.* -wliten *To look upon;* intueri:—Nō đæt hī mōsten in đone Ēcan andwlītan *that they might not look on the Eternal*, Cd. 221; Th. 288, 10; Sat. 378. DER. wlītan.

and-wlite, es; *n. The countenance, face;* vultus, facies:—Efennysse geseah andwlite his *æquitatem vidit vultus ejus*, Ps. Spl. T. 10, 8. v. and-wlita.

and-wrāþ; *adj. Hostile;* infensus:—Đam dracan he andwrāþ leofaþ *he lives hostile to the serpent*, Exon. 95 b; Th. 356, 26; Pa. 17. DER. wrāþ.

and-wyrdan, ond-wyrdan *to answer*, Ps. Th. 101, 21: 118, 42: Ors. 1, 10; Bos. 32, 20. v. and-werdan.

and-wyrde, es; *n. An answer;* responsum:—Hētan him ðæt andwyrde secgan *they commanded them to deliver this answer*, Ors. 1, 10; Bos. 32, 23: Cd. 27; Th. 36, 17; Gen. 573: Elen. Grm. 544: 618. v. and-swaru.

and-wyrding, e; *f. A consent, an agreement, a conspiring, conspiracy;* conspiratio, Cot. 46.

and-yttan *To confess, praise, thank;* confiteri:—Ic andytte ðē *ego confiteor tibi*, Mt. Bos. 11, 25. v. andettan.

āne, ǣne; *adv.* [ān *one, with the adverbial* -e] *Once, once for all, only, alone;* semel, solum, tantum:—Is ðys āne mā *this is once more*, Andr. Kmbl. 984; An. 492. Ic bydde ðē, ðæt ðū lǣte me sprecan āne feáwa worda *I pray thee, that thou let me speak only* [*once for all*] *few words*, Nicod. 11; Thw. 5, 40. Ic ðē ǣne abealh, ēce Drihten *I alone angered thee, eternal Lord*, Cd. 222; Th. 290, 4; Sat. 410.

ān-eáge, ān-ēge, ān-īge, ān-īgge; *adj.* [ān *one*, eage *an eye*] *One-eyed, blind of one eye;* monoculus, luscus:—Gif he hī gedō āneáge *if he make them one-eyed*, L. Alf. 20; Th. i. 48, 25, note. Gif hīg ānēge gedō *si luscos eos fecerit*, Ex. 21, 26.

ān-ecge; *adj. One-edged, having one edge;* unam habens aciem:—Ān-ecge sweord *a one-edged sword;* machæra, Ælfc. Gl. 52; Som. 66, 48; Wrt. Voc. 35, 36.

ān-ēge; *adj. One-eyed:*—Gif hīg ānēge gedō *si luscos eos fecerit*, Ex. 21, 26. v. ān-eáge.

ān-ēged; *part. One-eyed, blinded of one eye;* monoculus, monophthalmus, luscus:—Gif he hī gedō ānēgede *if he make them one-eyed*, L. Alf. 20; Th. i. 48, 25, note: Ælfc. Gl. 71; Som. 70, 76; Wrt. Voc. 43, 9.

a-neglod; *part. Nailed, fastened with nails, crucified;* clavis fixus, crucifixus, Som. v. næg-lian.

a-nēhst *at last, in the last place;* ad ultimum, ultimo. v. a-nīhst.

a-nemnan; *p.* de; *pp.* ed *To declare;* pronuntiare:—Godes spel-bodan eal anemdon *God's messengers declared all*, Exon. 33 a; Th. 104, 25; Gū. 13. v. nemnan.

ānes, āness, e; *f. A oneness, an agreement;* unitas:—Gewearþ him and ðam folce on Lindesige ānes *there was an agreement between him and the people in Lindsey*, Chr. 1014; Th. 274, 13. v. ān-nes.

ānes *of one, g. m. n. of* ān:—Ānes bleós *of one colour;* unicolor. Ānes geáres *of one year.* Ānes hiwes *of the same hue* or *shape.* Ānes wana *wanting of one, as* ānes wana twentig *twenty wanting one, nineteen.*

a-nescian, -hnescian; *p.* ode; *pp.* od *To make nesh, to weaken;* emollire:—He sceolde ða ānrǣdnesse anescian *poterat constantiam ejus emollire*, Bd. 1, 7; S. 477, 44. v. hnescian.

an-færeld *a journey;* iter, Nathan. 2. v. on-færeld.

ān-fāh; *adj. Of one colour;* unicolor. v. fāg.

an-fangen *received; pp. of* an-fōn.

an-fangennes, -ness, e; *f. A receiving, receptacle;* acceptio, susceptio, receptaculum, R. Ben. 2. v. on-fangenes.

ān-feald; *adj.* [ān *one*, feald *fold*] ONE FOLD, *simple, single, one alone, singular, peculiar, matchless;* simplex:—Swā mid þrȳfealdre swā mid ānfealdre lāde *either with a threefold or with a simple exculpation*, L. C. E. 5; Th. i. 364, 2: 5; Th. i. 362, 10. Ānfeald āþ *a simple oath*, L. C. S. 22; Th. i. 388, 11. Ānfeald getel *the singular number*, Ælfc. Gr. 13; Som. 16, 25. Ān-feald gewin *single combat*, R. Ben. interl. 1. Ða ānfealdan stræcan *those who are uniformly strict*, Past. 42, 1; Hat. MS. 57 b, 25.

ānfeald āþ *a simple oath*, L.C.S. 22; Th. i. 388, 11, note b. v. āþ, III.

ānfeald-līce; *adv. Singly, simply, without intermission;* simpliciter, R. Ben. 52.

ānfeald-nes, -ness, e; *f. Oneness, unity, simplicity, singleness;* simplicitas:—Ymbe ða ānfealdnesse ðare godcundnesse *concerning the oneness of the divine nature*, Bt. 35, 5; Fox 164, 18: 39, 5; Fox 218, 19. Ðā hwīle ðe hī heora ānrǣdnesse geheóldan him betwēnan and ānfealdnysse *while they had agreement and simplicity amongst themselves*, Ors. 5, 3; Bos. 104, 1.

an-feng, es; *m. A taking to one's self, a receiving, defence, defender;* assumptio, susceptio, susceptor:—Drihtnes anfeng ūre *Domini assumptio nostra*, Ps. Spl. 88, 18. He anfeng mīn *ipse susceptor meus*, 61, 2: Runic pm. 3; Hick. Thes. i. 135; Kmbl. 340, 1. v. and-feng.

an-fenga, an; *m. A receiver, an undertaker;* susceptor. v. and-fenga.

an-fenge; *adj. Acceptable, fit.* v. and-fenge.

an-fēnge *shouldest have taken*, Cd. 42; Th. 54, 10; *p. subj. of* an-fōn.

an-fengednes, -ness, e; *f. A receiving;* acceptio. v. on-fangenes.

ān-fēte; *adj. One-footed, with one foot;* monopodius, Exon. 114 b; Th. 439, 9; Rä. 59, 1.

an-fēðe *in walking*, Bt. 36, 5; Fox 180, 20. v. fēðe.

an-filt, on-filt *An* ANVIL; incus, Ælfc. Gr. 28, 6; Som. 32, 34: Ælfc. Gl. 50; Som. 65, 128; Wrt. Voc. 34, 56. [*Plat.* ambolt, ambult, *m: Dut.* aanbeeld, aenbeld, *n: O. H. Ger.* anafalz.]

an-findan *to discover, find;* deprehendere, Cot. 61. v. on-findan.

ān-floga, an; *m. Lonely flying;* solitarie volans, solivagus, Exon. 82 a; Th. 309, 25; Seef. 62.

an-fōn; *p.* -fēng; *pp.* -fangen *To take, take to one's self, receive, perceive, comprehend;* accipere, suscipere, sumere, percipere, recipere:—Ðū sceonde æt me anfēnge *thou shouldest have taken to thyself shame from me*, Cd. 42; Th. 54, 10; Gen. 875; Exon. 112 a; Th. 429, 12; Rä. 43, 3; Ps. C. 50, 135; Ps. Grn. ii. 280, 135. To anfōnne *to receive*, Bd. 3, 6; S. 528, 4. v. on-fōn.

an-forht; *adj. Fearful, timid;* timidus:—Ne þearf ðonne ǣnig anforht [MS. unforht] wesan *no one then need be fearful*, Rood Kmbl. 232; Kr. 117. DER. forht.

ān-for-lǣtan; ic -lǣte, ðū -lǣtest, -lǣtst, he -lǣteþ, -lēteþ, *pl.* -lǣtaþ; *p.* -lēt, -leórt, -leót, *pl.* -lēton; *pp.* -lǣten *To leave alone, lose, relinquish, forsake;* amittere:—Ðū nū ān-forlēte *thou hast now lost*, Bt. 7, 3; Fox 20, 12: Bd. 1, 27, resp. 3; S. 490, 25: 4, 10; S. 578, 34. v. ān; *adv. and* forlǣtan.

an-funden *found, taken; pp. of* an-findan.

ang-, *a prefix*, as in ang-breóst, ang-mōd, ang-mōdnes, ang-sum, *etc.* from ange *narrow, vexed.*

ānga, ǣnga, ēnga, *m;* ānge, *f. n; def. adj.* I. *one and no more, only, sole, single, singular;* unicus, ullus, quisquam:—Se ānga hyht *the sole hope*, Exon. 62 a; Th. 227, 14; Ph. 423: 96 b; Th. 360, 1; Pa. 73. Ðū eart dōhtor mīn ānge for eorþan *thou art my only daughter on earth*, 67 a; Th. 248, 13; Jul. 95. Abraham wolde gesyllan his swǣsne sunu, āngan ofer eorþan yrfelāfe *Abraham would give his dear son, his sole hereditary remnant on earth*, Cd. 162; Th. 203, 13; Exod. 403. Cain gewearþ to ecgbanan āngan brēðer *Cain was the murderer of his only brother*, Beo. Th. 2529; B. 1262. II. *any, every one, all;* quisque. In this sense it admits of a plural:—Secge me nū, hwæðer ðū ǣfre gehȳrdest, ðæt wīsdōm āngum ðara eallunga þurhwunode *tell me now, whether thou hast ever heard, that wisdom always remained to any of them*, Bt. 29, 1; Fox 102, 9. v. ān, II, IV.

an-gan *began*, Cd. 23; Th. 28, 26; Gen. 442. v. an-ginnan.

ang-breóst, es; *n.* [ange *narrow, contracted, troubled;* breóst *a breast*] *An asthma, a difficulty of breathing, breast-anguish;* asthma:—Wið angbreóste *against breast-anguish*, L. M. 1, 15; Lchdm. ii. 58, 15.

ange, ænge, enge, onge; *adj. Narrow, straitened, vexed, troubled, sorrowful;* angustus, anxius, vexatus, tristis:—Ðes ænga stede *this narrow place*, Cd. 18; Th. 23, 9; Gen. 356. Ufan hit is enge *it is narrow above*, Exon. 116 a; Th. 446, 14; Dōm. 22. Ðā wæs ðam cynge swīðe ange on his mōde *then the king was greatly troubled in his mind*, Ors. 2, 5; Bos. 48, 14. [*N. Ger. M. H. Ger.* enge *angustus: O. H. Ger.* angi: *Goth.* aggwus: *O. Nrs.* öngr: *Lat.* angustus: *Grk.* ἐγγύς: *Sansk.* anhu *narrow.*]

angeán; *prep. Against;* contra:—Hȳ him brohtan angeán ehta hund M fēðena *they brought against him eight hundred thousand foot*, Ors. 3, 9; Bos. 68, 9. v. on-geán; *prep.*

angel; *g.* angles; *m. A hook, a fishing-hook;* hamus:—Wurp ðīnne angel ūt *mitte hamum*, Mt. Bos. 17, 27. Swā swā mid angle fisc gefangen biþ *as a fish is caught by a hook*, Bt. 20; Fox 72, 11. [*Plat. Dut. Ger. M. H. Ger.* angel, *m: O. H. Ger.* angul, *m: O. Nrs.* öngull, *m.*]

Angel; *gen. dat. acc.* Angle; *f. Anglen in Denmark, the country between Flensburg and the Schley from which the Angles came into Britain;* Angulus, nomen terræ quam Angli ante transitum in Britanniam coluerunt:—Of Angle cōmon Eást-Engle *from Anglen came the East-Angles*, Chr. 449; Ing. 15, 1. Ðæt land, ðe man Angle hǣt *the land, which is called Anglen*, Ors. 1, 1; Bos. 18, 37. Hī ðā sendon to Angle *they then sent to Anglen*, Chr. 449; Th. 20, 12. v. Engel.

angel *an angel;* angelus, Ps. Spl. 33, 7. v. engel.

Angel-, *English;* Anglicanus,—*as in the following compounds:*—Angel-cyning, -cynn, -þeód.

Angel-cyning, es; *m. An Angle* or *English king*, Bd. 3, 8; S. 531, 8: 3, 9; S. 533, 8. v. Engle.

Angel-cynn, es; *n. The Angle* or *English race;* Anglorum gens, Bd. pref; S. 471, 23: 4, 16; S. 584, 13. v. Engle.

ān-geld, es; *n. A single payment* or *compensation*, L. In. 56; Th. i. 138, 9: L. Edg. ii. 7; Th. i. 268, 19, MS. G. v. ān-gild.

an-gelīc; *adj. Like, similar;* similis:—Ðonne ne finst ðū ðǣr nāuht angelīces *then thou wilt not find there anything of like*, Bt. 18, 3; Fox 66, 11. v. ge-līc.

Angel-þeód, e; *f. The English people;* Anglorum gens, Bd. 5, 24; S. 646, 34, 37. v. Engle.

angel-twicce, an; *f. A red worm used for a bait in angling* or *fishing;* lumbricus:—Rēn-wyrm *vel* angel-twicce *lumbricus*, Ælfc. Gl. 24; Som. 60, 30; Wrt. Voc. 24, 31. [twachel *the dew-worm*, Halwl. Dict.]

ān-genga, -gengea, an; *m.* [ān *unus, solus;* gengan *ire*] *A lone-goer, a solitary;* solivagus, solitarius:—Blōdig wæl eteþ āngenga *the lone-goer will eat my bloody corpse*, Beo. Th. 902; B. 449. Fela fyrena atol āngengea oft gefremede *many crimes the foul solitary oft perpetrated*, 332; B. 165.

ān-ge-trum, es; *n.* [ān *unicus, eximius;* ge-trum *cohors, caterva*] *A singular company;* unica cohors, eximia caterva:—Micel āngetrum *a great* [*and*] *singular company*, Cd. 160; Th. 199, 6; Exod. 334.

ân-geweald, es; *m. Power, empire, dominion;* potestas, imperium, dominatio:—Hyne ðære helle sealde on ângeweald *gave him into the power of hell*, Nicod. 29; Thw. 17, 1. v. ân-weald, ge-weald.

angil *a hook*, Coll. Monast. Th. 23, 11. v. angel.

ân-gild, -geld, -gyld, es; *n.* [ân *one*, gild *a payment, compensation*]. I. *a single payment* or *compensation, the single value of property claimed* or *in dispute,—a rate fixed by law, at which certain injuries, either to person* or *property, were to be paid for;* simplex compensatio:—Forgylde ðæt ângylde *let him pay for it with a single compensation*, L. Alf. pol. 6; Th. i. 66, 3: 22; Th. i. 76, 7: L. In. 22; Th. i. 116, 12. Forgylde ðæt yrfe ângylde *let him pay for the property with a single recompense*, L. Ath. v. § 8, 4; Th. i. 236, 24: L. Edg. H. 6; Th. i. 260, 7: L. Edg. ii. 7; Th. i. 268, 19: L. Eth. iii. 4; Th. i. 294, 17: L. O. D. 4; Th. i. 354, 15: Th. Diplm. A. D. 883; 130, 18–131, 5. II. *the fixed price* or *rate at which cattle and other goods were received as currency;* æstimatio, pretium:—Gif we ðæt ceáp-gild arǽraþ be fullan ângylde *if we raise the market-price* [*of cattle*] *to the full fixed price*, L. Ath. v. § 6, 4; Th. i. 234, 17.

an-gildan; *p.* -geald, *pl.* -guldon; *pp.* -golden *To pay for, repay, atone for;* rependere, pœnas dare:—Sum sâre angeald ǽfen-reste *one sorely paid for his evening rest*, Beo. Th. 2507; B. 1251: Ors. 6, 23; Bos. 124, 13. v. on-gildan.

an-gin, -ginn, -gyn, on-gin, es; *n. A beginning, attempt, resolve, purpose, design, undertaking, opportunity;* initium, principium, conatus, inceptum, cœptum, occasio:—Ælc angin *every beginning*, Bt. 5, 3; Fox 12, 18. Ðis synd sâra angin *initium dolorum hæc*, Mk. Bos. 13, 8. Se âna Scyppend næfþ nân anginn, ac he sylf is anginn ealra þinga *the Creator alone hath not any beginning, but he is himself the beginning of all things*, Hexam. 13; Norm. 22, 3. On anginne *in principio*, 1; Norm. 2, 26. Bûtan anginne *without beginning*, Exon. 9 b; Th. 8, 1; Cri. 111. Synt ðæra sâra anginnu *sunt dolorum initia*, Mt. Bos. 24, 8. Gif ðû ðæt angin fremest *if thou perfect that attempt*, Cd. 27; Th. 36, 27; Gen. 578. Ðâ geseah Iohannes sumne cniht swíðe glæd on môde and on anginne câf *there John saw a certain youth cheerful in mind and quick in design*, Ælfc. T. 33, 17. Abreóðe his angin *may his design perish*, Byrht. Th. 138, 59; By. 242: Cd. 178; Th. 223, 26; Dan. 125: R. Ben. 69. [*O. Sax.* angin *initium.*]

an-ginnan; *p.* -gan, *pl.* -gunnon; *pp.* -gunnen *To begin, undertake;* incipere:—Angan hine gyrwan *began to prepare himself*, Cd. 23; Th. 28, 26; Gen. 442: Bt. Met. Fox 1, 118; Met. 1, 59. v. on-ginnan.

an-gitan; *p.* -geat; *pp.* -giten *To get, lay hold of, seize;* assequi, corripere, invadere:—Hine se brôga angeat *terror seized him*, Beo. Th. 2587; B. 1291. v. on-gitan.

Angle; *g.* a; *dat.* um; *pl. m. The* ANGLES, who came from Anglen [v. Angel = Engel *Anglen*] in Denmark, and occupied the greater part of England, from Suffolk to the Frith of Forth, including Mercia. Bede says,—Ðæt mynster, Æbbercurnig, ðæt is geseted on Engla lande *the minster, Abercorn, that is seated in the land of the Angles*, or Engla land = England, Bd. 4, 26; S. 602, 35. Abercorn is on the south coast of the Frith of Forth, and at the mouth of the river Carron, where the Roman wall of Severus began, and extended to the Frith of Clyde. Bede wrote his history about A. D. 731, at which time Abercorn was within the bounds of Engla land = England:—Ðæt land, ðætte Angle ǽr hæfdon *the land, that the Angles formerly had*, Bd. 4, 26; S. 602, 30. To Anglum *to the Angles*, Chr. 443; Th. 18, 33, col. 1; 19, 30, col. 1. Ðâ cômon ða menn of þrym mægþum Germanie,—of Eald-Seaxum, of Anglum, of Iotum *then came the men from three tribes of Germany,—from Old-Saxons, from Angles, from Jutes*, Chr. 449; Th. 20, 18–21, col. 1.

Angle; *g. d. acc. of* Angel *Anglen*:—Ðæt land, ðe man Angle hǽt *the land, which they call Anglen*, Ors. 1, 1; Bos. 18, 37. v. Engel, Óngel.

Angles ég, e; *f.* [íg *an island*] ANGLESEY, so called after it was conquered by the English: it was anciently called Mona:—Hugo eorl wearþ ofslagen innan Angles êge *earl Hugo was slain in Anglesey*, Chr. 1098; Ing. 317, 31.

ang-môd, ancg-môd; *adj.* [ange *vexed*, môd *mind*] *Vexed in mind, anxious, sad, sorrowful;* anxius, sollicitus, tristis, R. Ben. 64.

ang-môdnes, -ness, e; *f. Sadness, sorrowfulness;* tristitia. v. ange *vexed*, môdnes, môdignes *pride*.

ang-nægl, es; *m. An* AGNAIL or ANGNAIL, *a whitlow, a sore under the nail;* paronychia = παρωνυχία, dolor ad ungulam. [*Frs.* ongneil: *O. H. Ger.* ungnagal.] v. ange *vexed*, nægel *a nail*.

angnes, -ness, angnis, -niss, angnys, -nyss, e; *f.* [ange *angustus, anxius;* -nes] *Narrowness, anxiety, distress, sorrow, trouble, anguish;* angustiæ, anxietas, tristitia, ærumna:—Angnes môdes *anxietas animi*, Somn. 354. On angnisse mîn *in ærumna mea*, Ps. Spl. T. 31, 4. Geswinc and angnys gemêtton me *tribulatio et angustiæ invenerunt me*, Ps. Spl. 118, 143. v. angsumnes.

an-golden *repaid, requited; pp. of* an-gildan. v. gildan.

Angol-þeód, e; *f. The English nation;* gens Anglorum, Bd. 5, 21; S. 642, 31. v. Angel-þeód.

angol-twæcce; *g.* -twæccean; *f. An earth-worm*:—Genim angoltwæccean *take an earth-worm*, L. M. 1, 39; Lchdm. ii. 100, 8. v. angeltwicce.

an-grîslîc, -grýslîc, on-grîslîc; *adj. Grisly, horrible, dreadful, horrid;* horridus, terribilis, horrendus:—Micel and angrîslîc *magnus et terribilis*, Ps. Spl. 88, 8: Ps. Th. 104, 33. DER. grîslîc.

an-grysen-lîce; *adv. Terribly;* terribiliter, Nicód. 26; Thw. 14, 22. v. an-grîslîc.

ang-set, es; *m?* ang-seta, an; *m? A disease with eruptions, a carbuncle, pimple, pustule, an eruption, St. Anthony's fire;* carbunculus:—Angset *vel* spring *carbunculus*, Ælfc. Gl. 9; Som. 57, 9; Wrt. Voc. 19, 19. Angseta *furunculus* vel *anthrax*, Ælfc. Gl. 12; Som. 57, 69; Wrt. Voc. 20, 12: Ælfc. Gl. 64; Som. 69, 19; Wrt. Voc. 40, 51.

ang-sum, anc-sum; *adj. Narrow, strait, troublesome, hard, difficult;* angustus, difficilis:—Eálâ hû neara and hû angsum is ðæt geat, and se weg ðe to lîfe gelǽdt; and swýðe feáwa synt ðe ðone weg findon *quam angusta porta, et arcta via est, quæ ducit ad vitam; et pauci sunt qui inveniunt eam*, Mt. Bos. 7, 14.

ang-sumian; *p.* ode; *pp.* od *To vex, afflict, to be solicitous;* vexare, angere, sollicitus esse. DER. angsum.

ang-sum-lîc *troublesome, anxious;* tristis, sollicitus. v. ang-sum.

ang-sum-lîce; *adv. sorrowfully;* triste. v. angsumlîc.

ang-sumnes, -ness, ang-sumnis, -niss, -nys, -nyss, e; *f. Troublesomeness, sorrow, anxiety, anguish;* angustiæ, ærumna:—Geswinc and angsumnes gemêtton me *tribulatio et angustiæ invenerunt me*, Ps. Spl. M. 118, 143. We gesâwon hys angsumnisse *nos vidimus angustiam animæ illius*, Gen. 42, 21: Jos. 7, 7. v. angnes.

ângum *to any*, Bt. 29, 1; Fox 102, 9. v. ânga.

ân-gyld, es; *n. A single payment* or *compensation*, L. Alf. pol. 6; Th. i. 66, 3: 22; Th. i. 76, 7: L. In. 22; Th. i. 116, 12. v. ân-gild.

an-gyn *a beginning*, Mk. Bos. 1, 1. v. an-gin.

an-gytan [an, gytan *to get*] *To find, discover, understand, know;* invenire, intelligere, R. Ben. 2. v. on-gitan.

an-hafen *lifted up, exalted*, Bd. 3, 6; S. 528, 9. v. an-hebban.

ân-haga, -hoga, an; *m. One dwelling alone, a recluse;* solitarius, solitarie habitans *vel* degens:—Ðǽr se ânhaga eard bihealdeþ *ibi solitarius natalem locum tenet*, Exon. 57 a; Th. 203, 20; Ph. 87. Ic eom ânhaga *I am a recluse*, 102 b; Th. 388, 1; Rä. 6, 1: Beo. Th. 4725; B. 2368. To ðam ânhagan *against the solitary*, Andr. Kmbl. 2701; An. 1353.

an-hagian; *p.* ode; *pp.* od *To be at leisure*, R. Ben. 58. v. on-hagian.

an-healdan; *p.* -heóld, *pl.* -heóldon; *pp.* -healden *To hold, keep;* tenere, servare, præstare:—Gesceaft fæste sibbe anhealdaþ *creatures keep firm peace*, Bt. Met. Fox 11, 84; Met. 11, 42.

an-hebban, -hæbban; *p.* -hôf, *pl.* -hôfon; *pp.* -hafen *To heave up, lift up, exalt, raise up, take away, remove;* elevare, erigere, exaltare, sublimare, attollere, auferre:—Ðæt ðû ðê ne anhebbe on ofermetto *that thou lift not up thyself with arrogance*, Bt. 6; Fox 14, 34. Mid ða heánnesse ðæs eorþlîcan rîces anhafen *regni culmine sublimatus*, Bd. 3, 6; S. 528, 9. v. on-hebban.

an-hefednes, -ness, e; *f. Exaltation;* exaltatio, C. R. Ben. 7.

ân-hende; *adj. One-handed, lame, imperfect, weak;* unimanus, Ælfc. Gl. 77; Som. 72, 25; Wrt. Voc. 45, 58.

ân-hoga, an; *m.* [ân-wuniende] *A lone dweller, recluse*:—Geworden ic eom swâ swâ spearwa ânhoga oððe ânwuniende on efese oððe on þecene *factus sum sicut passer solitarius in tecto*, Ps. Lamb. 101, 8. Se ânhoga *the recluse*, Exon. 60 b; Th. 222, 10; Ph. 346: 47 a; Th. 162, 3; Gû. 970. v. ân-haga.

an-hôn *to hang;* suspendere. v. on-hôn.

ân-horn, es; *m:* ân-horna, an; *m. A unicorn;* unicornis, monoceros = μονόκερως:—Ânhornes *unicornis*, Ps. Surt. 91, 11. Ðonne ânhorna *sicut unicornis*, Ps. Th. 91, 9: [MS. ônhornan], 77, 68.

ân-hrǽdlîce *unanimously*, Ps. Spl. 82, 5. v. ân-rǽdlîce.

an-hreósan *to rush upon;* irruere. v. on-hreósan.

ân-hydig; *adj. One or single minded, steadfast, firm, constant, stubborn, self-willed;* firmus, constans, pervicax:—Elnes ânhydig *steadfast in courage*, Exon. 45 b; Th. 156, 3; Gû. 869: Elen. Grm. 828. Ânhydig eorl *the stubborn chieftain*, Exon. 55 b; Th. 196, 28; Az. 181: 100 a; Th. 377, 11; Deór. 2. Wearþ ðâ ânhydig *then he became self-willed*, Cd. 205; Th. 254, 1; Dan. 605.

an-hyldan *to incline;* inclinare, R. Ben. in procem. v. on-hyldan.

an-hyrian *To emulate;* æmulari:—Ne anhyre ðû *noli æmulari*, Ps. Spl. T. 36, 8. v. onhyrian.

ân-hyrne; *adj. One-horned, having one horn;* unicornis:—Ânhyrne deór *unicornis*, vel *monoceros*, vel *rhinoceros*, Ælfc. Gl. 18; Som. 58, 129; Wrt. Voc. 22, 43.

ân-hyrned; *p. part. One-horned, having one horn;* unicornis:—Biþ upahafen swâ swâ ânhyrnedes deóres mîn horn *exaltabitur sicut unicornis cornu meum*, Ps. Lamb. 91, 10: 77, 69.

ân-hyrnende; *pres. part. Having one horn;* unicornis:—Fram hornum ânhyrnendra *a cornibus unicornium*, Ps. Spl. 21, 20: 77, 75: 91, 10: Ps. Lamb. 21, 22.

âni *any*, Bt. 38, 3; Fox 200, 27 [MS. Bod.] v. ǽnig.

a-nídan; *p.* -nídde; *pp.* -níded, *pl.* -nídde = nídede *To force*, Chr. 823; Th. 110, 33, col. 1. v. a-nýdan.

ân-íge, -ígge; *adj. One-eyed*:—Ânige *luscus*, Cot. 122. Gif he hí gedô ânígge *if he make them one-eyed*, L. Alf. 20; Th. i. 48, 25. v. ân-eáge.

a-níhst; *adv.* [a = on *in, ad*; níhst *ultimus*] *At last, in the last place*; ad ultimum, ultimo:—Ne wǽron ðæt gesíða ða sǽmestan, ðeáh ðe ic hý aníhst nemnan sceolde *they were not the worst of comrades, though I should name them last*, Exon. 86 b; Th. 326, 9; Wíd. 126.

a-niman, -nyman; *p.* -nam, *pl.* -námon; *pp.* -numen [a *from*, niman *to take*] *To take away, remove*; tollere, capere:—Animaþ ðæt pûnd æt hym *take the talent from him*, Mt. Foxe 25, 28. Animan wolde *would take*, Fins. Th. 43; Fin. 21.

âninga, ǽninga, ânunga; *adv.* [ân *one*, inga] *One by one, singly, at once, clearly, plainly, entirely, altogether, necessarily, by all means, at all events*; per singula, singulatim, plane, prorsus, omnino, necessario, ad omnem eventum:—Woldon âninga ellenrôfes môd gemiltan *they would entirely subdue the bold man's mind*, Andr. Kmbl. 2785; An. 1394. Gif ða cnihtas âninga ofslagene beón sceoldan *si necesse esset pueros interfici*, Bd. 4, 16; S. 584, 32: Beo. Th. 1272; B. 634: Judth. 12; Thw. 25, 9; Jud. 250: Jn. Lind. War. 21, 25: Bt. Met. Fox 18, 11; Met. 18, 6.

a-niðerian; *p.* ode; *pp.* od [a *intensive*, niðerian *to thrust down*] *To put down, condemn, damn*; deorsum trudere:—Ðá wurþe he aniðrod mid Iudas *then let him be cast down with Judas*, Chr. 675; Ing. 52, 12.

an-læc *A respect, regard, consideration*; respectus, Ælfc. Gr. 28, 5; Som. 31, 67.

an-lǽdan; *p.* de *To lead on* or *to*; adducere:—Ðǽr eorp-werod anlǽddon *there led on the swarthy host*, Cd. 151; Th. 190, 5; Exod. 194. v. on-lǽdan.

ân-lǽtan [ân *alone*, lǽtan *to let*] *To let alone, forbear, relinquish*; relinquere, Cd. 30; Th. 40, 24; Gen. 644.

Ân-lâf, es; *m. Olaf, king of Dublin, defeated at Brunanburh*, Chr. 937; Th. 201, 29, col. 3: 202, 37; Æðelst. 26.

ân-laga; *adj. Alone, solitary, without company*; solitarius, Cot. 198.

anlang cempa, an; *m. A regular soldier*; miles ordinarius, gregarius, Cot. 136.

ân-lâpe; *adj. Going alone, one by one*; singuli:—Ânlâpum oððe syndrigum hond gesette *singulis manus imposuit*, Lk. Lind. War. 4, 40. Ða síe awritten ânlâpum *quæ scribantur per singula*, Jn. Lind. War. 21, 25. v. ân-lêpe.

ân-lâpum; *adv. One by one*; per singula, singulatim, Jn. Lind. War. 21, 25. v. ân-lâpe, ân-lêpe.

an-lec *a respect*, Ælfc. Gr. 28, 5; Som. 31, 67, MS. D. v. anlæc.

ân-leger; *adj.* [ân *one*, leger *jacens*] *Lying with one person*; unicubus:—Ânlegere wífman *a woman with one husband*; unicuba, R. 8.

an-leofa, an; *m.* I. *food, nourishment*; victus, cibus:—Beón beraþ ǽrlícne anleofan *bees carry delicious food*, Frag. Kmbl. 36; Leás. 20. II. *a gift, alms, wages*; stips, Ælfc. Gl. 4; Som. 55, 105.

ân-lêpe, -lêpig, -lípig, -lýpig, [ǽn-]; *adj.* [ân *one*; hleáp, hlýp *a running, leap*] *Going alone, solitary, private, alone, singular, one, each one*; solivagus, solitarius, privatus, solus, singularis, unus, singulus:—Nis nân ðe eallunga wel dô, nô forðon ânlêpe *non est qui faciat bonum, non est usque ad unum*, Ps. Th. 13, 2. Ânlêpra ǽlc *each one*, Bt. Met. Fox 25, 111; Met. 25, 56. [*Ger.* einläufig, einläuftig *solivagus, singularis.*]

ân-lêpig; *adj. Solitary, private, alone.* v. ân-lípig.

ân-lêpnes, -ness, e; *f. Solitude, loneliness*; solitudo:—Ne tala ðû me, ðæt ic ne cunne ða ânlêpnesse ðínes ûtsetles *think not thou, that I know not the loneliness of thy outsitting*, Bd. 2, 12; S. 513, 41.

an-líc, on-líc; *adj. Like, similar, equal*; similis, æqualis:—Forðam ys heofena ríce anlíc ðam cyninge *ideo assimilatum est regnum cœlorum homini regi*, Mt. Bos. 18, 23. Ðæt he bióþ swíðe anlíc *that he is very like*, Bt. 37, 1; Fox 186, 11. Nis under wolcnum Drihtne ǽnig anlíc? *quis in nubibus æquabitur Domino?* Ps. Th. 88, 5: 57, 4: 72, 18: 112, 5. [*Ger.* æhnlich *similis*: *M. H. Ger.* anelích: *O. H. Ger.* anagalíh: *Goth.* analeiks: *O. Nrs.* álíkr.]

ân-líc, ǽn-líc; *adj.* [ân *one*, líc *like*] ONLY, *singular, incomparable, excellent, elegant, beautiful*; unicus, eximius, egregius, elegans, pulcher:—He is mín ânlíca-sunu *unicus est mihi filius*, Lk. Bos. 9, 38. Andett seó gelaðung ðínne sôðan and ânlícan sunu *confitetur ecclesia tuum verum et unicum filium*, Ps. Lamb. fol. 195 a, 12: Te Dm. Thomson 37, 12. Ic spearuwan swâ some gelíce gewearþ, ânlícum fugele *factus sum sicut passer unicus*, Ps. Th. 101, 5: Exon. 56 a; Th. 198, 12; Ph. 9: Beo. Th. 507; B. 251. Gesete fram deóflum oððe fram leónum ânlícan oððe ânnysse míne *restitue a leonibus unicam meam*, Ps. Lamb. 34, 17; restore thou myn oon lijf aloone [darling] fro liouns, Wyc.

an-lícast *most like*, Ps. Th. 78, 2: 89, 4, 10: 91, 11; *sup. of* an-líc.

an-líce, on-líce; *adv. In like manner, similarly*; similiter:—Anlíce swâ swâ *sicut*, Ps. Th. 123, 6. Ðæm anlícost, ðe ... *in a manner most like to his, that ...*, Bt. Met. Fox 20, 337; Met. 20, 169.

ân-líce ONLY. v. ǽn-líce.

an-lícnes, on-lícnes, and-lícnis, -lícness, -lícnyss, e; *f.* I. *a likeness, image, similitude, resemblance*; imago, similitudo:—Mon wæs to Godes anlícnesse ǽrest gesceapen *man was to God's image first shapen*, Cd. 75; Th. 92, 15; Gen. 1529. Hwæs anlícnys ys ðis? *cujus est imago hæc?* Mt. Bos. 22, 20. God gesceóp man to his andlícnisse *creavit Deus hominem ad imaginem suam*, Gen. 1, 27. On ðæs mannes sâwle is Godes anlícnyss *in the soul of the man is God's image*, Hexam. 11; Norm. 18, 21. Uton gewyrcan mannan to ûre anlícnysse and to ûre gelícnysse *faciamus hominem ad imaginem nostram et similitudinem nostram*, 11; Norm. 18, 14, 20, 21, 25. God worhte Adam to his anlícnysse. On hwilcum dǽle hæfþ se man Godes anlícnysse on him? On ðære sâwle, nâ on ðam líchaman. Ðæs mannes sâwl hæfþ on hire gecynde ðære Hâlgan Þrýnnysse anlícnysse; forðan ðe heó hæfþ on hire þreó þing, ðæt is gemynd, and andgit and willa *God made Adam in his own likeness. In which part has man the likeness of God in him? In the soul, not in the body. The soul of man has in its nature a likeness to the Holy Trinity; for it has in it three things, these are memory, and understanding, and will*, Homl. Th. i. 288, 14–19. II. *a parable*; parabola:—Ic on anlícnessum ontýne mínes sylfes mûþ *aperiam in parabolis os meum*, Ps. Th. 77, 2. v. big-spell, gelícnes, II. III. *an image, statue, idol, stature, height*; statua, simulacrum, statura:—He wundoragræfene anlícnesse geseh *he beheld a wondrously-carved image*, Andr. Kmbl. 1425; An. 713. Tobrec hira anlícnyssa *confringes statuas eorum*, Ex. 23, 24: Cd. 119; Th. 154, 33; Gen. 2565. Anlícnes *agalma*, vel *iconisma*, vel *idea*, Ælfc. Gl. 81; Som. 72, 123. Hwylc mæg ícan âne elne to his anlícnesse? *quis potest adjicere ad staturam suam cubitum unum?* Lk. Bos. 12, 25.

ân-lípie = ân-lípige *solitary, private*, Bd. 1, 15; S. 483, 45. v. ân-lípig.

ân-lípig, -lýpig; *adj.* [ân *one*; hlíp, hlýp] *Going alone, solitary, private, singular, alone*; solitarius, privatus, singularis, solus, tantus:—Se ðâ ânlýpig [MS. ânlýpi] awunode on syndrige stôwe fram ðære cyricean *qui tum in remotiore ab ecclesia loco solitarius manebat*, Bd. 4, 30; S. 609, 1. Cynelíco getimbro and ânlípige [MS. ânlípie] *publica ædificia et privata*, 1, 15; S. 483, 45. He nânwiht on hand nyman wolde bûtan his âgene gyrde ânlípige *nonnisi virgam tantum habere in manu voluit*, 3, 18; S. 546, 32. v. ân-lêpe.

an-lûtan; *p.* -leát, *pl.* -luton; *pp.* -loten *To bend down, to incline*; se inclinare, R. Ben. 53. v. on-lûtan.

ân-lýpig, -lýpi; *adj. Solitary, private*, Bd. 4, 30; S. 609, 1. v. ân-lípig.

an-medla, on-medla, on-mædla, an; *m. Pride, pomp, arrogance, presumption*; superbia, fastidium, arrogantia, præsumptio:—For ðam anmedlan ðe hie ǽr drugon *for the arrogance which they before had practised*, Cd. 214; Th. 269, 16; Sat. 74. Ðû for anmedlan in ǽht bǽre [MS. bêre] hûsl-fatu hâlegu on hand werum *thou, in thy presumption, barest for a possession the holy sacrificial vessels into the hands of men*, Cd. 212; Th. 262, 22; Dan. 748.

an-mitta, an; *m. A measure, bushel*; mensura, modius:—Habbaþ rihtne anmittan *habete justam mensuram*, Lev. 19, 35. Hæbbe ǽlc man rihtne anmittan, and rihte wǽgan, and rihte gemetu on ǽlcum þingum *pondus habebis justum et verum, et modius æqualis et verus erit tibi*, Deut. 25, 15. v. mitta.

an-môd, on-môd; *adj.* [*Ger.* anmüt *gratus*, Grimm] *Steadfast, eager, bold, courageous, daring, fierce*; constans, alacer, animosus:—Folc wæs anmôd, rôfe rincas *the folk were steadfast, renowned men*, Cd. 80; Th. 99, 23; Gen. 1650: 80; Th. 100, 10; Gen. 1662. Feónd wæs anmôd *the foe was courageous*, 153; Th. 190, 23; Exod. 203. Ðâ wearþ yrre an-môd cyning *then the daring king was wroth*, 184; Th. 229, 29; Dan. 224. Ûr byþ anmôd *a bull is fierce*, Runic pm. 2; Hick. Thes. i. 135; Kmbl. 339, 7.

ân-môd; *adj.* [ân *one*, môd *mood, mind*] *Of one mind, unanimous*; unanimis:—Ðû sôþlíce man ânmôd *tu vero homo unanimis*, Ps. Spl. 54, 14: 67, 6. Ealle ânmôde *all with one mind*, Andr. Kmbl. 3128; An. 1567. Hie ðâ ânmôde ealle cwǽdon *then they all with one mind said*, 3200; An. 1603: 3274; An. 1640: Elen. Grm. 397: 1118. [*Ger.* einmütig *unanimis*: *M. H. Ger.* einmuot: *O. H. Ger.* einmuoti *unanimis, constans.*]

ân-môdlíce; *adv. Unanimously, with one accord*; unanimiter:—Hí ânmôdlíce cômon *they came with one accord*, Jos. 11, 4: Exon. 12 b; Th. 21, 25; Cri. 340. Gesamnodon hí ealle ânmôdlíce [MS. ânmôdlíc] *congregati sunt pariter*, Jos. 9, 2.

ân-môdnes, -môdness, e; *f. Unity, unanimity*; unitas, unanimitas, Som.

ann *he gives*:—Ðê he ann *he gives thee*, Ps. Th. 74, 7 = an; *pres. of* unnan.

-anne, -enne, -ende *the termination of the declinable infinitive in the dat. governed by* to, as,—Ondrêd to faranne *timuit ire*, Mt. Jun. and Th. 2, 22, but the B. MS. of A. D. 995 has farende, also Foxe, Bos. and the Rl. MS. about A. D. 1145. The Lind., about A. D. 957, has farenne [MS. færenne]. Alýfe me to farenne *permitte me ire*, Mt. Bos. 8, 21, and B. MS. about A. D. 995. Sometimes -ende is found, because -enne = ende, as in the preceding example farende about A. D. 995. The most usual form is -anne, from the infin. -an; *g.* -annes; *dat.* -anne. v. TO; *prep.* **IV. 2**: also -enne and -ende, and Grm. iv. 111.

ân-ne *alone;* solum:—Ðæt ge forlǽton me ânne *that ȝe leeue me aloone,* Wyc; ut me solum relinquatis, Jn. Bos. 16, 32. v. ân, **II.**

ân-nes, ân-nys, ânes, -ness, e; *f.* **I.** ONENESS, *unity;* unitas:—Geleáfa sôþlîce se geleáffulla đes is; đæt ânne God on þrýnnesse and þrýnnesse on Ânnesse we ârwurþian *fides autem catholica hæc est; ut unum Deum in Trinitate et Trinitatem in Unitate veneremur,* Ps. Lamb. fol. 200 a, 13. On đa ânnysse đære hâlgan cyrican *in unitate sanctæ ecclesiæ,* Bd. 2, 4; S. 505, 7: 4, 5; S. 572, 1. We andettaþ þrýnnesse in Ânnesse efenspêdiglîce, and Ânnesse on đære þrýnnesse *confitemur Trinitatem in Unitate consubstantialem, et Unitatem in Trinitate,* 4, 17; S. 585, 37: Exon. 76 a; Th. 286, 5; Jul. 727: Hy. 8, 41; Hy. Grn. ii. 291, 41. Gesete fram deóflum ođđe fram leónum ânlîcan ođđe ânnysse mîne *restitue a leonibus unicam meam,* Ps. Lamb. 34, 17; restore thou myn oon lijf aloone [darling] fro liouns, Wyc. **II.** *a covenant, an agreement;* conventio:—Gewearþ him and đam folce on Lindesige ânes *there was an agreement between him and the people in Lindsey,* Chr. 1014; Th. 274, 13, col. 1. **III.** *loneliness, solitude;* solitudo:—Ânnys đæs wîdgillan wêstenes *the solitude of the wide desert,* Guthl. 3; Gdwin. 20, 20.

ân-nyss, e; *f. Oneness, unity, agreement, solitude;* unitas, conventio, solitudo, Bd. 2, 4; S. 505, 7. v. ân-nes.

anođa? *fear, amazement;* formido. v. onođa.

ân-pæþ, es; *nom. pl.* -pađas; *m. A single path, a pass, lonely way;* solitaria via:—Enge ânpađas, uncûþ gelâd *narrow passes, an unknown way,* Beo. Th. 2824; B. 1410: Cd. 145; Th. 181, 8; Exod. 58.

ânra *of every one; g. pl. of* ân *one,* q. v.

ân-rǽd; *adj.* [ân *one,* rǽd *counsel*] *One-minded, unanimous, agreed, persevering, resolute, prompt, vehement;* unanimus, firmus consilii, confidens, audax, vehemens:—And đonne beón hîg ânrǽde *and when they be unanimous,* L. Ath. iv. 7; Th. i. 226, 19. Đis swefen ys ânrǽde *somnium unum est,* Gen. 41, 25. Ealle ânrǽde to gemǽnra þearfe *all unanimous for the common need,* L. Edg. C. 1; Th. ii. 244, 4. Wæs seó mǽg ânrǽd and unforht *the maid was resolute and fearless,* Exon. 74 b; Th. 278, 21; Jul. 601. Eft wæs ânrǽd mǽg Hygelâces *Hygelac's kinsman was resolute again,* Beo. Th. 3062; B. 1529: Byrht. Th. 133, 2; By. 44.

ân-rǽdlîce, -rêdlîce; *adv.* [ân, rǽd *opinion, advice,* lîce] *Unanimously, resolutely, constantly;* unanimiter, constanter:—Hî þohton ânrǽdlîce [MS. ânhrǽdlîce] *cogitaverunt unanimiter,* Ps. Spl. 82, 5. Đe ânrǽdlîce wile his sinna geswîcan *who resolutely desires to abstain from his sins,* L. Pen. 17; Th. ii. 284, 17. Ânrǽdlîce wrêgende *constanter accusantes,* Lk. Bos. 23, 10.

ân-rǽdnes, -rêdnes, -nys, -ness, -nyss, e; *f.* [ân *one,* rǽdnes *opinion*] *Unanimity, concord, agreement, constancy, steadfastness, diligence, earnestness;* concordia, constantia:—Hî heora ânrǽdnesse geheóldan him betwênan *they had agreement among themselves,* Ors. 5, 3; Bos. 103, 44. Brôđerlîc ânrǽdnys *brotherly unanimity,* Scint. 11. Ânrǽdnys gôdes weorces *constancy of good works,* Oct. vit. cap. Scint. 7: Job Thw. 167, 33. *Opposed to* twýrǽdnes, un-gerǽdnes *dissention, q. v.*

ânra-gehwâ, ânra-gehwilc *every one;* unusquisque, Deut. 24, 16. v. ân, **IV.**

ân-reces; *adv. Continually, forthwith,* Chr. 1010; Th. 262, 34. v. ân-streces.

ân-rêdlîce *unanimously,* Jud. Thw. 161, 27. v. ân-rǽdlîce.

ân-rêdnes *unanimity, constancy,* Bd. 1, 7; S. 477, 43. v. ân-rǽdnes.

an-rine, es; *m.* [an *in,* ryne *a course*] *An inroad, incursion, assault;* incursio:—Fram anrine *ab incursu,* Ps. Spl. 90, 6.

an-sacan; *p.* -sôc, *pl.* -sôcon; *pp.* -sacen *To strive against, resist, deny;* impugnare, repugnare, negare:—Se đe lýhþ, ođđe đæs sôđes ansaceþ *he that lieth, or the truth resisteth,* Salm. Kmbl. 365; Sal. 182: L. In. 46; Th. i. 130, 14, 15. v. on-sacan.

an-sæc, es; *m? Contention, resistance;* contentio, repugnantia:—Bûtan ansæce *without resistance,* Chr. 796; Ing. 83, 5. v. and-sæc.

an-sægdnes, an-segdnes, -ness, e; *f.* [ansægd *affirmed; pp. of* ansecgan] *A thing which is vowed, or devoted, an oblation, a sacrifice;* sacrificium, Bd. 1, 7; S. 477, 39. v. onsægdnes.

an-sǽte *odious, hateful;* exosus, perosus, Ælfc. Gl. 84; Som. 73, 101; Wrt. Voc. 49, 9. v. and-sǽte.

an-sceát, -sceót, es; *m? The bowels;* exentera = ἔντερα, *pl. n,* Cot. 73.

an-scôd *unshod;* discalceatus. v. un-sceód.

an-scûnian *to shun;* evitare, Bt. 18, 1; Fox 60, 20. v. onscûnian.

an-scûniend-lîc, an-scûnigend-lîc *abominable;* abominabilis. v. onscûniendlîc.

an-secgan; *p.* -sægde, -sǽde; *pp.* -sægd, -sǽd *To charge against, affirm,* L. Edg. ii. 4; Wilk. 78, 12. v. on-secgan.

ân-seld, es; *m.* [ân *only,* seld *dwelling*] *A solitary dwelling, an hermitage;* habitatio solitaria:—Ic ongon on đone ânseld bûgan *I began to dwell in this hermitage,* Exon. 50 b; Th. 176, 23; Gû. 1214.

an-sendan; *p.* -sende *To send forth, send;* emittere, mittere:—Ne mǽgen hî leóhtne leóman ansendan *they cannot send forth a clear light,* Bt. Met. Fox 5, 10; Met. 5, 5: Ps. C. 50, 16; Ps. Grn. ii. 277, 16. v. on-sendan.

an-settan *to impose,* Bt. 39, 10; Fox 228, 4. v. on-settan.

an-sién, e; *f. aspect, figure:*—Idesa ansién *the aspect of the females,* Cd. 64; Th. 76, 22; Gen. 1261. Ansién đyses middan-geardes *the figure of this world,* Past. 51, 2. v. an-sýn, **II.**

an-sîn, e; *f. a view, sight, figure:*—Đîn môd wæs abîsgod mid đære ansîne đissa leásena gesǽlþa *thy mind was occupied with the view of these false goods,* Bt. 22, 2; Fox 78, 10: Bd. 5, 13; S. 633, 5. Gûþlâc wæs on ansîne mycel *Guthlac was tall in figure,* Guthl. 2; Gdwin. 18, 1. v. an-sýn, **II.**

an-sión, e; *f. a sight:*—Ne aweorp đû me fram ansióne ealra đînra miltsa *cast me not away from the sight of all thy mercies,* Ps. C. 50, 95; Ps. Grn. ii. 279, 95. v. an-sýn, **III.**

an-speca, on-spæca, an; *m.* [spæc *a speech*] *A speaker against, an accuser, a persecutor;* persecutor. v. an = and *against,* spæca *a speaker.*

an-spel, -spell, es; *n.* [an, spel *a speech*] *A conjecture;* conjectura, Cot. 56.

an-spilde; *adj.* [an = and *against,* spild *destruction*] *Anti-destructive, salutary;* salutaris:—Đæt biþ anspilde lyb wiđ eágena dimnesse *that is a salutary medicine for dimness of eyes,* L. M. 1, 2; Lchdm. ii. 30, 14.

ân-spræce; *adj. One speaking, speaking as one,* Ps. Th. 40, 7. v. -spræce.

an-standan; *p.* an-stôd, *pl.* an-stôdon; *pp.* an-standen. **I.** *to stand against, resist, withstand, to be firm* or *steadfast;* adversari. **II.** *to stand upon, inhabit, dwell;* insistere, habitare. v. on-standan.

ân-standende; *part. One standing alone:*—Ânstandende, ân-stonde, ođđe munuc *one standing alone, or a monk,* Ælfc. Gl. 3?

ân-stapa, an; *m. A lone wanderer;* solivagus, Exon. 95 b; Th. 356, 21; Pa. 15.

ân-steallet *one-stalked:*—Nim bête, đe biþ ânsteallet *take beet, which is one-stalked,* Lchdm. iii. 70, 2. v. ân-steled.

ân-steled, ân-steallet *One-stalked, having one handle* or *stalk;* unicaulis, L. M. 1, 1; Lchdm. ii. 20, 15: Lchdm. iii. 70, 2.

an-stellan; *p.* -stealde, -stalde; *pp.* -steald *To cause, establish, appoint;* instituere, constituere:—Ic đæs orleges ôr anstelle *I cause the beginning of that strife,* Exon. 102 a; Th. 386, 10; Rä. 4, 59. v. on-stellan.

ân-stonde *one standing alone, a monk.* v. ân-standende.

ân-stræc; *adj.* [ân *one;* strec *stretch,* from streccan *to stretch?*] *Of one stretch, constant, resolute, determined;* pertinax:—Đa ânstræcan sint to monianne *admonendi sunt pertinaces,* Past. 42, 2; Hat. MS. 58 a, 24.

ân-streces; *adv.* [ân *one;* streces, *gen. of* strec *a stretch*] *At one stretch, with one effort, continually;* sine intermissione:—And fôron on ânstreces dæges and nihtes *and went at one stretch day and night,* Chr. 894; Th. 170, 25.

ân-sûnd, on-sûnd; *adj.* [ân *sole, entire, wholly;* sûnd *sound*] *Sound, entire, unhurt;* sanus, integer, incolumis:—Hrôf âna genæs ealles ânsûnd *the roof alone was saved wholly sound,* Beo. Th. 2004; B. 1000. Gehwâ ânsûndan and ungewemmedne [geleáfan] healde *quisque integram inviolatamque [fidem] servaverit,* Ps. Lamb. fol. 200 a, 7. Beóþ đâ gebrosnodan bân mid đam flǽsce ealle ânsûnde eft geworden *then the corrupted bones together with the flesh will all again be made sound,* Hy. 7, 89; Hy. Grn. ii. 289, 89. Seó heofon is sinewealt and ânsûnd *heaven is circular and entire,* Bd. de nat. rm; Wrt. popl. scienc. 1, 17. v. on-sûnd.

ân-sûndnes, -ness, e; *f.* [ân, sûnd, nes] *Wholeness, soundness, integrity;* integritas:—Ânsûndnesse lufigend *a lover of integrity,* Wanl. Catal. 292, 34.

an-swarian; *p.* ode; *pp.* od *To answer;* respondere:—Ic answarige *ego respondebo,* Ps. Spl. 118, 42. v. and-swarian.

ân-swêge; *adj.* [ân *one,* swêg *a sound*] *Of the same sound, agreeing in sound, consonant;* consonus:—Ânswêge sang *symphonia,* Ælfc. Gl. 34; Wrt. Voc. 28, 40.

an-sýn, -sîn, -sién, -sión; on-, e; *f.* [an, sýn *sight, vision*]. **I.** *a face, countenance;* facies, vultus:—His ansýn sceán swâ swâ sunne *facies ejus resplenduit sicut sol,* Mt. Bos. 17, 2. Beforan đîne ansýne *ante faciem tuam,* Lk. Bos. 7, 27. Gûþlâc wæs wlitig on ansýne *Guthlac was handsome in countenance,* Guthl. 2; Gdwin. 18, 3. God ableów on his ansýne lîflîcne blǽd *God blew into his face the breath of life,* Hexam. 11; Norm. 18, 25. Fleóþ his ansýne *fugiant a facie ejus,* Ps. Th. 67, 1. Gedô đæt hiora ansýn âwa sceamige *imple facies eorum ignominia,* 82, 12. Ansýn đîn *vultus tuus,* 88, 14. Ic bidde đînre ansýne *deprecatus sum faciem tuam,* 118, 58. Ansýn ýwde *shewed his countenance,* Beo. Th. 5660; B. 2834. **II.** *a view, aspect, sight, form, figure;* aspectus, conspectus, visus, visio, species, forma, figura:—Fæger ansýne *fair in aspect,* Runic pm. 11; Hick. Thes. i. 135; Kmbl. 341, 19. Đîn môd wæs abîsgod mid đære ansîne đissa leásena gesǽlþa *thy mind was occupied with the view of these false goods,* Bt. 22, 2; Fox 78, 10. For đînre ansýne *in conspectu tuo,* Ps. Th. 68, 20: 108, 14. Se Hâlega Gâst astâh lîchamlîcre ansýne, swâ ân culfre *descendit Spiritus Sanctus corporali specie, sicut columba,* Lk. Bos. 3, 22: Cot. 74. Ansién đyses middan-geardes *figura hujus mundi,* Past. 51, 2. **III.**

a thing to be looked upon, *a sight;* spectaculum:—Ðisse ansýne Alwealdan þanc gelimpe *for this sight may thanks to the Almighty take place*, Beo. Th. 1860; B. 928. Seó ansîn wearþ mycel wundor Rômânum *the sight was a great wonder to the Romans*, Ors. 6, 7; Bos. 120, 3. IV. a view or sight producing desire or longing, and hence,—*a desire of anything, want* or *lack of anything;* desiderium, defectus:—Swâ eorþan biþ ansýn wæteres *sicut terra sine aquâ*, Ps. Th. 142, 6. [*O. Sax.* ansiun, *f. aspectus: Plat.* anseen, *n: Dut.* aanzien, *n: Ger.* ansehen, *n. aspectus, forma: M. H. Ger.* ansiune, *n: O. H. Ger.* anasiuni, *n.*]

an-tâllîc, an-tâlîc; *adj.* [an=un *not*, tâllîc *blamable*] *Unblamable, undefiled;* irreprehensibilis, immaculatus:—Æ Drihtnes antâlîc *lex Domini immaculata*, Ps. Spl. 18, 8.

Antecrist, es; *m. Antichrist;* Antichristus:—Ðonne cymþ se Antecrist, se biþ mennisc mann and sôþ deófol *then Antichrist shall come, who is human being* [*man*] *and true devil*, Homl. Th. i. 4, 14. Ðes deófol, ðe is gehâten Antecrist, ðæt is gereht þwyrlîc Crist, is ord ǽlcere leásunge and yfelnysse *this devil, who is called Antichrist, which is interpreted opposed Christ, is the origin of all leasing and evil*, Homl. Th. i. 4, 21. Togeánes Antecriste *against Antichrist*, Ælfc. T. 6, 22: Job Thw. 166, 8.

antefn=antefen, e; *f?* es; *n?* [ἀντί *opposite*, φωνή *a voice*] *An antiphon, anthem, a hymn sung in alternate parts;* antiphona, cantus Ecclesiasticus alternus:—Is ðæt sǽd, ðæt hî ðysne letanîan and antefn geleóþre stæfne sungan *fertur, quia hanc litaniam consona voce modularentur*, Bd. 1, 25; S. 487, 24.

ant-fenge; *adj. Acceptable;* acceptabilis, R. Ben. 5. v. and-fenge.

an-þracian *to fear, to be afraid, to dread;* revereri, horrere:—Ic onginne to anþracigenne *I begin to dread;* horresco, Ælfc. Gr. 35; Som. 38, 4: Ps. Spl. 69, 2. v. on-þracian.

an-þræclîc? *adj. Horrible, terrible, fearful;* horridus, horribilis, terribilis, Hymn?

ân-tîd, e; *f. The first hour;* hora prima:—Ymb ân-tîd ôðres dôgores *about the first hour of the second day*, Beo. Th. 443; B. 219.

an-timber; *g.* -timbres; *n. Matter, materials, substance, a theme;* materies, materia:—Ungehiwod antimber *rudis atque informis materia*, Alb. resp. 15, 22. v. and-timber.

antre, an; *f. Radish?* raphanus, raphanis sativa:—Dô ðonne betonican and antran *add then betony and ontre* [*radish?*], L. M. 2, 51; Lchdm. ii. 266, 3. Ancre [antre?], ðæt is rædic *raphanus*, Mone A. 493. v. ontre.

an-trumnys *infirmity;* infirmitas. v. un-trumnes.

an-tymber *matter*, Ælfc. Gr. 12; Som. 15, 54. v. an-timber.

an-týnan; *p.* de; *pp.* ed [an=un *un-*, týnan *to inclose*] *To unclose, open;* recludere, aperire:—Ic antýne on bigspellum mûþ mînne *aperiam in parabolis os meum*, Ps. Spl. 77, 2. v. un-týnan, on-týnan.

a-numen *taken away; pp. of* a-niman.

anunga *zeal, an earnest desire, jealousy;* zelus, Jn. Rush. War. 2, 17.

ânunga; *adv. Entirely, necessarily, by all means;* plane, prorsus, omnino, Beo. Th. 1272; B. 634. v. âninga.

an-wadan; *p.* -wôd *To invade, enter into;* invadere:—Hie wlenco anwôd *pride invaded them*, Cd. 173; Th. 217, 3; Dan. 17. v. on-wadan.

ân-wald, es; *m. Sole power, jurisdiction, rule:*—Ðæt se Câsere eft ânwald ofer hî âgan môste *that the Cæsar might again obtain power over them*, Bt. Met. Fox 1, 123; Met. 1, 62. Se ânwald Godes Ælmihtiges *the power of Almighty God*, 9, 95; Met. 9, 48: Exon. 63 a; Th. 232, 23; Ph. 511: Lk. Bos. 23, 7: Bd. 4, 32; S. 611, 15: Ors. 2, 1; Bos. 38, 11. v. ân-weald.

ân-walda, an; *m. A sole ruler, the sole ruler of the universe:*—Him to Ânwaldan âre gelýfde *in him as sole ruler reverently trusted*, Beo. Th. 2548; B. 1272. Ealra Ânwalda, eorþan and heofones *ruler of all, of earth and heaven*, Exon. 110 a; Th. 422, 10; Rä. 41, 4: Cd. 227; Th. 305, 5; Sat. 642. v. ân-wealda.

ân-waldan *to have sole power over, to exercise absolute rule;* solam potestatem habere, dominari:—He ðone ânwaldeþ *he rules it*, Bt. Met. Fox 29, 154. v. wealdan.

ân-waldeg? *adj. Having sole power, powerful;* solus potens:—Ðæt se sîe ânwaldegost *that he is most powerful*, Bt. 36, 5; Fox 180, 16.

an-walg, -wealg; *adj. Entire, whole, sound;* integer, Past. 52, 2. v. on-walg.

an-wann *fought against; p. of* an-winnan.

ân-weald, ân-wald, es; *m. Single, sole, monarchical*, or *royal power, empire, dominion, jurisdiction, rule, government, bidding;* solius dominatus, unius imperium, monarchia, potestas, imperium, ditio, dominatio, jus, arbitrium, nutus:—Me is geseald ǽlc ânweald *data est mihi omnis potestas*, Mt. Bos. 28, 18. Ânweald Godes is *potestas Dei est*, Ps. Spl. 61, 11. Ðîn ânweald *dominatio tua*, Ps. Th. 144, 13: 135, 20: 118, 91: Ors. 2, 1; Bos. 38, 15: Bd. 1, 3; S. 475, 12. Cyning biþ ânwealdes georn *a king is desirous of power*, Exon. 89 b; Th. 337, 4; Gn. Ex. 59. Mid ðînum âgenum ânwealde *by thine own power*, Bt. 33, 4; Fox 128, 13. Hî synd heora sylfes ânwealdes *illi sunt sui juris*, Bd. 5, 23; S. 647, 4. On his ânwealde *ad ejus nutum*, Gen. 42, 6. [*O. Nrs.* einwald, *n. singularis potestas, monarchia.*] DER. wealdan.

ân-wealda, ân-walda, an; *m.* [ân *one, sole;* wealda, walda *a ruler*] *The one* or *sole ruler of a province* or *of the universe, a sovereign, governor, magistrate, a power;* qui solus dominatur, monarcha, dominus, gubernator, magistratus, potestas:—Se Ânwealda hæfþ ealle his gesceafta befangene and getogene *the governor has caught hold of, and restrained all his creatures*, Bt. 21; Fox 74, 5. Ânwealda Ælmihtig *Almighty Ruler*, Rood Kmbl. 303; Kr. 153. Ðonne hîg lǽdaþ eów to ânwealdum *cum inducent vos ad potestates*, Lk. Bos. 12, 11. [*O. Nrs.* einwaldi, *m. solus dominus.*]

an-wealg *whole.* v. an-walg.

an-wealglîce; *adv. Wholly, soundly;* integre, Past. 33, 5; Hat. MS. 42 a, 33.

an-wealgnes, -ness, e; *f. Wholeness, soundness, entireness;* integritas. v. on-walhnes.

an-weg *away;* inde, exinde. v. on-weg.

an-weorc, es; *n. Material, cause;* materia, causa:—Bûton anweorce *without cause*, Bt. 30, 2; Fox 110, 16. v. and-weorc.

ân-wîg, es; *n? m?* [ân *one*, wîg *a contest*] *A single combat, a duel;* certamen singulare:—Ðǽr gefeaht Mallius ânwîg wið ânne Galliscne mann *there Mallius fought a single combat with a man of Gaul*, Ors. 3, 4; Bos. 56, 15: 3, 6; Bos. 57, 42. Hî gefuhton ânwîg *they fought a duel*, Ors. 3, 9; Bos. 67, 32.

ân-wîg-gearo, -gearu; *g. m. n.* -wes, -owes; *f.* -re, -rwe; *adj.* [gearo *prepared*] *Prepared for single combat;* ad singulare certamen paratus:—Wæs þeáw hyra, ðæt hie oft wǽron ânwîggearwe *it was their custom, that they oft were for single combat prepared*, Beo. Th. 2499; B. 1247. v. gearo; *adj.*

ân-wîglîce; *adv. In single combat;* singularis certaminis modo:—Ân-wîglîce feohtende *fighting in single combat*, Cot. 186.

ân-wille, *def.* se ân-willa; *adj.* [ân *one*, willa *a will*] *Having one will, following one's own will, self-willed, obstinate, stubborn;* pertinax, obstinatus, contumax:—Ânwilla *obstinatus, pertinax*, Ælfc. Gl. 90; Wrt. Voc. 51, 29. Sint to manianne ða ânwillan *admonendi pertinaces*, Past. 42. 1; Hat. MS. 57 b, 23.

ân-willîce; *adv. Obstinately, stubbornly, pertinaciously;* pertinaciter:—Ic tô ânwillîce winne wið ða wyrd *I too pertinaciously attack fortune*, Bt. 20; Fox 70, 20: Past. 7, 2; Hat. MS. 12 a, 15.

ân-wilnes, -ness, e; *f. Obstinacy, self-will, contumacy;* pertinacia, protervia, Past. 32, 1; Hat. MS. 40 a, 16, 25.

an-winnan; *p.* -wann *To fight against, to attack;* impugnare:—Him onwann [MS. L. anwann] *fought against them*, Ors. 3, 7; Bos. 61, 7.

ân-wintre, ǽ-wintre; *adj.* [ân *one*, winter *a winter*] *Of one year, one year old, continuing for a year;* hornus=horinus=ὥρινος from ὥρα, hornotînus, anniculus:—Ðæt lamb sceal beón ânwintre *erit agnus anniculus*, Ex. 12, 5.

ân-wîte, es; *n. A simple* or *single fine, a mulct* or *amercement;* simplex mulcta:—Ealle forgielden ânwîte *let them all pay a single fine*, L. Alf. pol. 31; Th. i. 80, 17.

an-wlǽta, -wlâta, an; *m. A livid bruise;* sugillatio, livor:—Wið wundspringum and anwlâtan *ad livores et sugillationes*, Med. ex quadr. 7; Lchdm. i. 356, 20. v. wlǽtan.

an-wlita, an; *m. The countenance, face;* vultus, facies, Ælfc. Gl. 70; Som. 70, 44. v. and-wlita.

an-wlite, es; *m.* [an=un *un-*, wlite *decus*] *Disgrace;* dedecus:—Sconde oððe anwlite *dedecus*, Cot. 66, Lye.

an-wlitegian; *p.* ode; *pp.* od [an=un *un-*, wlitigian *to form*] *To unform, change the form of anything;* deformare:—Ða he þwaraþ and gewlitegaþ; hwîlum eft unwlitegaþ [MS. Cot. anwlitegaþ] *these it tempers and forms; sometimes again it unforms*, Bt. 39, 8; Fox 224, 9.

an-wlô, an-wlôh; *adj.* [an=un *without*, wlôh *a fringe, ornament*] *Untrimmed, neglected, without a good grace, deformed, ill-favoured;* inornatus, deformis:—Ðîn rîce restende biþ an-wlôh *thy kingdom shall remain neglected*, Cd. 203; Th. 252, 27; Dan. 585.

an-wôd *invaded*, Cd. 173; Th. 217, 3; Dan. 17; *p. of* an-wadan.

an-wreón; *p.* -wreáh, *pl.* -wrugon; *pp.* -wrogen [an=un *un-*, wreón *to cover*] *To uncover, reveal;* revelare, R. Ben. 3. v. un-wreón, on-wreón.

an-wrigenys, -nyss, e; *f.* [an=un, wrigen, nys] *A revealing, disclosing, an opening, a sermon, homily;* explicátio, expositio. v. wrigen; *pp. of* wrîhan *to cover.*

ân-wunian; *part.* -wuniende; *p.* ode; *pp.* od *To dwell* or *be alone;* esse solitarius, Ps. Lamb. 101, 8.

ân-wuniende; *part. Dwelling alone, being alone;* solitarius:—Geworden ic eom swâ swâ spearwa ânhoga oððe ânwuniende on efese oððe on þecene *factus sum sicut passer solitarius in tecto*, Ps. Lamb. 101, 8.

an-wunigende; *part. Dwelling in, inhabiting;* inhabitans, Bt. Met. Fox 7, 93; Met. 7, 47; *part. pres. of* an-wunigan=on-wunian, *q. v.*

anxsumnes, -ness, e; *f. Anxiety*, Somn. 87: 133. v. angsumnes.

a-nýdan; *p.* -nýdde; *pp.* -nýded, *pl.* -nýdede=-nýdde [a *from*, nýdan *to compel*]. I. *to repel, thrust* or *beat back, keep from, restrain, constrain, force;* repellere, extorquere:—Hî fram his mâgum ǽr mid unrihte anýdde wǽron *they had formerly been unjustly forced from his kinsmen*, Chr. 823; Th. 111, 34. II. *with* ût *to expel, to drive* *out;* expellere, depellere, exigere:—Ic anýde hîg ût on fremde folc *I will drive them out among a strange people,* Deut. 32, 21.

a-nyman; *impert.* a-nymaþ ge *To take away;* tollere:—Anymaþ ðæt pûnd æt hym *take away that pound from him,* Mt. Bos. 25, 28: Hick. Thes. i. 192, 16, col. 2. v. a-niman.

an-ŷwan; *p.* de; *pp.* ed *To shew, demonstrate;* ostendere, demonstrare, R. Ben. 7, 11. v. eáwan.

apa, an; *m. An* APE; simia:—Wið apan bîte *against bite of an ape,* Med. ex quadr. 11, 7; Lchdm. i. 366, 24: Ælfc. Gl. 19; Som. 59, 18; Wrt. Voc. 22, 59.

a-pǽcan; *p.* -pǽhte; *pp.* -pǽht *To seduce, mislead;* seducere:—Gif hwâ ôðres mannes folgere fram him apǽce *si quis alius hominis pedisequam ab eo seducat,* L. M. I. P. 23; Th. ii. 270, 31.

a-pǽran *to pervert, turn from;* evertere, pervertere. v. for-pǽran.

a-parian; *p.* ode; *pp.* od *To apprehend, take;* deprehendere:—Seó wæs aparod on unriht-hǽmede *deprehensa est in adulterio,* Jn. Bos. 8, 3.

apelder-tûn, es; *m. An apple-tree garden.* v. apulder, apulder-tûn.

ap-flôd, es; *m. The low tide;* ledo, æstus maris, Martyr. 20, Mar. v. nêp-flôd.

a-pinsian; *p.* ode; *pp.* od, ud *To ponder, weigh, estimate;* ponderare, pensare:—Ðâ ðâ he ðæra Judea misdǽda ealle apinsode *when he estimated all the misdeeds of the Jews;* cum Judeæ singula delicta pensarentur, Past. 53, 3. DER. pinsian.

apl, es; *m; nom. acc. pl.* aplas, *m; nom. acc. pl.* apla, *n. An apple, a ball:*—Ða reádan appla [MS. C. apla] *mala Punica,* Past. 15, 5; Hat. MS. 19 b, 28: Salm. Kmbl. 55; Sal. 28. v. appel.

a-plantian; *p.* ode; *pp.* od *To plant, transplant;* plantare, transplantare:—God ðâ aplantode wynsumnisse orcerd *plantaverat autem Dominus Deus paradisum voluptatis,* Gen. 2, 8. Ge sǽdon ðissum treówe, Sý ðû awyrtwalod, and aplantod on sǽ *dicetis huic arbori, Eradicare, et transplantare in mare,* Lk. Bos. 17, 6.

Apollinus; *gen.* Apollines; *m. Apollo;* Apollo, inis; *m.* [= Ἀπόλλων, ωνος; *m.*]:—Wæs se Apollinus æðeles cynnes, Iôbes eafora *this Apollo was of noble race, the son of Jove,* Bt. Met. Fox 26, 67; Met. 26, 34. Apollines dôhtor *Apollo's daughter,* 26, 64; Met. 26, 32: Bt. 38, 1; Fox 194, 12, 19.

apostata, an; *m. An apostate;* apostata:—Hêr syndon apostatan *here are apostates,* Lupi Serm. i. 19; Hick. Thes. ii. 105, 1.

apostol, es; *m: also like the Lat.* Apostolus; *g.* -i; *m. One sent, an apostle;* apostolus [= ἀπόστολος, ἀπό *from,* στέλλω *to send*]:—Se eádiga apostol Simon *the blessed apostle Simon,* Homl. Th. ii. 492, 7. He apostolas geceás, ðæt sind ǽrendracan *he chose apostles, that are messengers,* Ælfc. T. 26, 17. Ðâ gesâwon ða apostolas Drihten *then the apostles saw the Lord,* Homl. Th. ii. 494, 28. Ða apostoli becômon to ðære byrig *the apostles came to the city,* 494, 14: 482, 18, 25, 27. Æt ðæra apostola fôtum *at the apostles' feet,* 488, 4. Ðâ fleáh ðæt folc eal to ðâm apostolum *the folk then all fled to the apostles,* 492, 12. Se ealdorman ðâ ða apostolas mid him to ðam cyninge Xerxes gelǽdde *the general then led the apostles with him to the king Xerxes,* 486, 3. Ðæra twelf apostola naman *duodecim apostolorum nomina,* Mt. Bos. 10, 2: Cd. 226; Th. 300, 27; Sat. 571: Menol. Fox 242; Men. 122. DER. ealdor-apostol.

apostol-hâd, es; *m. The apostolic office;* apostolatus:—Se apostolhâd *the apostolic office,* Apstls. Kmbl. 28; Ap. 14. Gesette bisceop ðâm leódum and gehâlgode þurh apostolhâd *set a bishop over the people and hallowed him through the apostolic office,* Andr. Kmbl. 3300; An. 1653.

apostolic; *def. m.* -a, *f. n.* -e; *adj. Apostolic;* apostolicus:—Ðâ ongunnon hî ðæt apostolîce lîf ðære frymþelîcan cyricean onhýrigean *cœperunt apostolicam primitivæ ecclesiæ vitam imitari,* Bd. 1, 26; S. 487, 31. Se papa ðe on ðam tîman ðæt apostolîce setl gesæt *the pope who at that time occupied the apostolic seat,* Homl. Th. ii. 120, 10.

appel, es; *m; nom. acc. pl.* applas, *m; nom. acc. pl.* appla; *n. An apple:*—Ða reádan appla *the red apples;* mala Punica, Past. 15, 5; Hat. MS. 19 b, 28. v. æppel.

appel-leáf, es; *n.* [lit. *apple-leaf*] *A violet;* viola, viola odorata, Harl. Gl. 978. v. æppel-leáf.

appel-screáda APPLE-SHREDS, *apple-parings.* v. æppel-screáda.

appel-þorn, es; *m. An* APPLE-THORN, *a crab-tree;* pirus malus, Cod. Dipl. Apndx. 460; A. D. 956; Kmbl. iii. 448, 20.

appel-treów *an apple-tree.* v. apple-treów.

appel-tûn *an apple-garden, orchard.* v. apple-tûn.

apple-treów, es; *n. An apple-tree;* pomus, malus, Ælfc. Gr. 5? v. æppel-treów.

apple-tûn, es; *m. An orchard;* pomarium, Cot. 146. v. æppel-tûn.

Aprêlis; *m. April;* Aprîlis mensis:—Aprêlis mônaþ *the month April,* Menol. Fox 112; Men. 56.

aprotane, an; *m. The herb southernwood, wormwood;* abrotonum = ἀβρότονον [artemisia, Lin.]:—Genim aprotanan *take wormwood,* L. M. 1, 16; Lchdm. ii. 60, 1.

apulder, apuldor; es, *n? An apple-tree;* malus, Wrt. Voc. 32, 47: L. M. 1, 23; Lchdm. ii. 66, 1: 1, 36; Lchdm. ii. 86, 6. Sûr-melsc [MS. -melst] apulder *malus matiana* [MS. *matranus*],—*pyrus malus,* Lin. *a sour-sweet apple-tree, a souring apple-tree,* Wrt. Voc. 32, 48. Swête [MS. swîte] apulder *a sweet apple-tree;* malomellus, 32, 49.

Apulder, es; *m.* [*in paludibus*] APPLEDORE, *a village in Kent, near Tenterden:*—Æt Apuldre *at Appledore,* Chr. 893; Th. 164, 10: 894; Th. 166, 41, col. 1. Æt Apoldre *at Appledore,* Th. Diplm. A. D. 1032; 328, 23. [*O. Dut.* polder, *m. palus marina pratum litorale; ager, qui est fluvio aut mari eductus, aggeribus obsepitur,* Kil.]

Apulder-comb, es; *m.* [*in paludibus vallis*] APPLEDORE COMBE, *Isle of Wight;* nomen loci in insula *Vecti,* Mann.

apulder-tûn, es; *m. An apple-tree inclosure, an apple-orchard;* malorum hortus, arborum pomiferarum hortus, Cot. 146.

apuldor-rind, apuldre-rind, e; *f. Apple-tree rind;* mali cortex:—Nim apuldorrinde *take apple-tree rind,* L. M. 1, 38; Lchdm. ii. 98, 7: 3, 47; Lchdm. ii. 338, 12: Med. ex quadr. 8; Lchdm. i. 358, 14.

apuldre, an; *f. An apple-tree;* malus:—Ðeós apuldre *hæc malus,* Ælfc. Gr. 6, 9; Som. 5, 57. v. apulder.

apuldur *an apple-tree.* v. apulder.

a-pullian; *p.* ode; *pp.* od *To pull;* vellere. v. pullian.

Aquilegia; *indecl.* [Aquileia = Ἀκυληΐα] *Aquileia in Gallia Transpadana, north of the Adriatic:*—Maximus abâd æt Aquilegia ðære byrig *Maximus encamped at the town Aquileia,* Ors. 6, 36; Bos. 131, 21.

ÂR, ǽr, es; *n.* ORE, *brass, copper;* æs; *g.* æris; *n.* v. bræs:—Bræs oððe âr *æs,* Ælfc. Gr. 5; Som. 4, 59. Israhêla folc is geworden nû me to âre on mînum ofne *versa est mihi domus Israel in æs in medio fornacis,* Past. 37, 3; Hat. MS. 50 a, 6. Grêne âr *green copper, brass;* orichalcum, Cot. 14. [*O. Sax.* êrin, *adj. æneus: Ger.* erz, *n. metallum, æs: M. H. Ger. O. H. Ger.* êr, *n. æs: Goth.* aiz, *n. æs: Dan.* erts: *Swed.* ör *a copper coin: O. Nrs.* eir, *n. æs: Sansk.* ayas *ferrum.*] DER. âr-fæt, -geótere, -gescôd, -gesweorf, -geweorc, -glæd, -sâpe, -smiþ: ǽren: ôra.

ÂR, e; *f.* I. *honour, glory, rank, dignity, magnificence, respect, reverence;* honor, dignitas, gloria, magnificentia, honestas, reverentia:—Sý him âr and onwald *be to him honour and power,* Exon. 65 b; Th. 241, 28; Ph. 663. Ne wolde he ǽnige âre wîtan *nor would he ascribe any honour,* Bd. 2, 20; S. 521, 29. He sundor lîf wæs fôreberende eallum ðâm ârum *he was preferring a private life to all honours,* Bd. 4, 11; S. 579, 8. Nyton nâne âre on nânum men *they know no respect for any man,* Bt. 35, 6; Fox 168, 25. Be ðære cirican âre *according to the rank of the church,* L. Alf. pol. 42; Th. i. 90, 10. He on his âgenum fæder âre ne wolde gesceáwian *he would not look with reverence on his own father,* Cd. 76; Th. 95, 18; Gen. 1580. II. *kindness, favour, mercy, pity, benefit, use, help;* gratia, favor, misericordia, beneficium, auxilium:—He gemunde ðâ ða âre ðe he him ǽr forgeaf, wîc-stede wêligne *he remembered then the favour which he before had conferred upon him, the wealthy dwelling-place,* Beo. Th. 5205; B. 2606. Ne mihte earmsceapen âre findan *nor might the poor wretch find pity,* Andr. Kmbl. 2260; An. 1131. Him wæs âra þearf *to him was need of favours,* Cd. 97; Th. 128, 12; Gen. 2125. To gôdre âre *to good use,* Herb. 2, 9; Lchdm. i. 82, 21: Bd. 3, 5; S. 527, 14. Eallum to âre ylda bearnum *for the benefit of all the sons of men,* Jul. A. 2. (Vid. Price's Walton, ci. note 34.) Leáf and gærs grôweþ eldum to âre *leaves and grass grow for the benefit of men,* Bt. Met. Fox 20, 199; Met. 20, 100. Ðǽr is âr gelang fira gehwylcum *there is help ready to every man,* Andr. Kmbl. 1958; An. 981. III. *property, possessions, an estate, land, ecclesiastical living, benefice;* bona, possessiones, fundus, beneficium:—He plihte to him sylfum and ealre his âre *he acts at peril of himself and all his property,* L. Eth. ix. 42; Th. i. 350, 3: Ors. 1, 1; Bos. 20, 32. Hwîlum be âre, hwîlum be ǽhte *sometimes in estate, sometimes in goods,* L. Eth. vi. 51; Th. i. 328, 11: L. C. S. 50; Th. i. 404, 18. Se ðe sitte on his âre on lîfe *he who lives on his property during life,* L. Eth. iii. 14; Th. i. 298, 9: L. Eth. vi. 4; Th. i. 316, 1, 3. Ðæt hî him andlyfne and âre forgeáfen for heora gewinne *that they should give them food and possessions for their labour,* Bd. 1, 15; S. 483, 19. [*Laym.* ære, are: *Orm.* are: *O. Sax.* êra: *O. Frs.* êre: *Dut.* eer: *Ger.* ehre, *f: M. H. Ger.* êre: *O. H. Ger.* êra: *Dan.* äre: *Swed.* ära: *O. Nrs.* æra.]

ÂR, es; *m. A messenger, legate, herald, apostle, angel, minister, servant, man, soldier;* nuntius, legatus, præco, apostolus, angelus, minister, vir:—Ðes âr sægeþ *this messenger sayeth,* Cd. 32; Th. 42, 34; Gen. 682: Beo. Th. 5559; B. 2783. Stîðlîce clypode Wicinga âr *the herald of the Vicings firmly proclaimed,* Byrht. Th. 132, 34; By. 26. Æðelcyninges âr *the noble King's messenger* [*Christ's apostle*], Andr. Kmbl. 3354; An. 1681. Hie hêton lǽdan ût hâlige âras *they commanded him to lead out the holy messengers* [*angels*], Cd. 112; Th. 148, 14; Gen. 2456: Exon. 15 a; Th. 31, 29; Cri. 503. Fæder ælmeahtig his âras hider onsendeþ *the almighty Father will send his angels hither,* Exon. 19 a; Th. 47, 23; Cri. 759. Ðâ afyrhted wearþ âr [Gûþlâces] *then* [*Guthlac's*] *servant was affrighted,* 52 a; Th. 181, 30; Gû. 1301. Lǽt gebîdan beornas ðîne, âras *let thy warriors, thy men, await,* Andr. Kmbl. 799; An. 400. [*O. Sax.* êru, *m: Goth.* áirus, *m: O. Nrs.* ârr, *m.* from the *Sansk.* root îr *to go.*] v. ǽrend.

ÂR, e; *f. An* OAR; remus:—Drugaþ his âr on borde *his oar becomes* *dry on board*, Exon. 92 a; Th. 345, 15; Gn. Ex. 188. Sume hæfdon lx āra *some had sixty oars*, Chr. 897; Th. 174, 43, col. 1. Sǽrōfe ārum bregdaþ ȳþbord [MS. yþborde] neáh *brave seamen draw the vessel near with oars*, Exon. 79 a; Th. 296, 26; Crä. 57. [*Havl.* ār: *Chauc.* oore: *Dan.* aare: *Swed.* are: *O. Nrs.* ār, *f.*] DER. ār-blæd, -gebland, -wēla, -widde, -ȳþ.

ār *before*:—Ǽrist odde ār *primo*, Mt. Kmbl. Lind. 20, 1. v. ǽr.

āra = geára? *adv. Formerly*; quondam:—Ðū me āra, God, ǽrest lǽrdest of geóguþhāde *Deus, docuisti me a juventute mea*, Ps. Th. 70, 16.

a-rād *rode*:—He ūt arād *he rode out*, Ors. 3, 7; Bos. 62, 22; *p. of* a-rīdan.

a-rǽcan; *p.* -rǽhte, -rǽcte; *pp.* -rǽht. I. *to reach, get at*; prehendere, attingere:—Ðæt man arǽcan mihte *that one could reach*, Chr. 1014; Ing. 193, 19. II. *to hold forth, reach out, hand*; porrigere:—Arǽce me ða bōc *porrige mihi librum*, Ælfc. Gr. 28, 5; Som. 31, 47. v. rǽcan.

a-rǽd, -rēd, es; *m.* [a *intensive*, rǽd *counsel*] *Counsel, welfare, safety*; consilium, commodum, salus:—Smeágende ymbe heora sāwla arǽd [arēd, MS. B; rǽd, MS. D] *considering about their souls' welfare*, L. Edm. E. pref; Th. i. 244, 6.

a-rǽd; *def.* se a-rǽda; *adj. Counselling, consulting, wise, prudent*; sagax, prudens:—Hwǽr is nū se fōremǽra and se arǽda Rōmwara heretoga *where is now the illustrious and prudent consul of the Romans?* Bt. 19; Fox 70, 6.

a-rǽd *uttered*, Bt. 23; Fox 78, 20, note 8, = a-rǽded, *pp. of* a-rǽdan.

a-rǽdan, -rēdan; *p.* -rǽdde, -rēdde, -rēde; *pp.* -rǽded, -rǽd, -rēd [rǽd *counsel*]. I. *to take counsel, care for, appoint, determine*; consilium capere, consulere alicui, decernere, definire:—Sende gewrit, on ðām he gesette and arǽdde *misit literas, in quibus decrevit*, Bd. 2, 18; S. 520, 33. Gif hit eallinga ðus arǽded sī *si omnimodis ita definitum est*, 4, 9; S. 577, 29. Ða dōmas ða ðe fram fæderum arǽdde and gesette wǽron *quæque definierunt canones patrum*, 4, 5; S. 572, 18. Hwæðere ðis betwyh heom arǽddon *his tamen conditionibus interpositis*, 4, 1; S. 564, 15. He symble þearfum arēde *semper pauperibus consulebat*, 3, 9; S. 533, 25. II. *to conjecture, guess, prophesy, interpret, utter*; conjectare, divinare, prophetizare, interpretari, eloqui:—Ne mihton arǽdan men engles ǽrend-bēc *men might not interpret the angel's messages*, Cd. 212; Th. 261, 30; Dan. 734. And him to cwǽdon, Arǽd *et dixerunt ei, Prophetiza*, Mk. Bos. 14, 65. Ðā se wīsdōm ðis spell arǽd hæfde *when wisdom had uttered this speech*, Bt. 23; Fox 78, 20, note 8: Exon. 76 b; Th. 286, 24; Wand. 5. v. rǽdan, *p.* rǽdde.

a-rǽdnis *a condition*, Bd. 4, 4; S. 571, 11. v. a-rēdnes.

a-rǽfnan, -rēfnan; *p.* ede, de; *pp.* ed *To endure, bear, suffer*; sustinere, tolerare, perferre:—Ðæt he ðæt sār mihte geþyldelīce mid smylte mōde aberan and arǽfnan *ut patienter dolorem ac placida mente sustineret*, Bd. 4, 31; S. 610, 27. Ðonne hī ðæt mægen ðære unmǽtan hǽto arǽfnan ne mihton *cum vim fervoris immensi tolerare non possent*, 5, 12; S. 627, 41. Ic þrōwade and arǽfnde *pertuli*, 2, 6; S. 508, 21: Andr. Kmbl. 1632; An. 817. Sāwl mīn symble arǽfnede *sustinuit anima mea*, Ps. Th. 129, 5: 68, 21: 64, 7. v. rǽfnan.

a-rǽfnian; *p.* ade; *pp.* ad. I. *to endure, bear, suffer, support*; sustinere, pati, supportare:—Ic arǽfnige *sustineo*, Ps. Th. 129, 4. Forðon ic edwīt for ðē oft arǽfnade *quoniam propter te supportavi improperium*, 68, 8. II. *to ponder in mind* or *heart*; animo versare, ponderare:—Maria sōþlīce heóld ealle ðās word, arǽfniende on hire heortan *but Mary kept all these words, pondering them in her heart*, Homl. Th. i. 30, 35. v. a-rǽfnan.

a-rǽfniende, -rǽfnigende; *part. Bearing in mind, considering, pondering*, Homl. Th. i. 42, 17, 30. v. a-rǽfnian.

a-rǽfniendlīc; *adj. Possible, tolerable*; possibilis, tolerabilis. DER. *part.* arǽfniende, līc.

a-rǽman; *p.* de; *pp.* ed. I. *v. trans. To raise, lift up, elevate*; excitare, erigere, elevare:—Ða ge mihton rǽdan, and eów arǽman on ðām *which ye may read, and elevate yourselves in them*, Ælfc. T. 31, 15. II. *v. intrans. To raise* or *lift up one's self, to arise*; se erigere, se elevare, surgere:—Dæges þriddan ord arǽmde *the beginning of the third day arose*, Cd. 139; Th. 174, 10; Gen. 2876: 162; Th. 203, 29; Exod. 411. [*O. H. Ger.* rāma *sustentaculum, columen.*] DER. up-arǽman, rǽman.

a-rǽran; *p.* de; *pp.* ed; *v. trans.* [a, rǽran *to rear, raise*] *To rear up, raise up, lift up, exalt, set up, build up, create, establish*; erigere, excitare, resuscitare, extollere, ædificare, creare:—Ðone stān arǽrde to mearce *lapidem erexit in titulum*, Gen. 28, 18, 22. Arǽrende þearfan *lifting up the poor*; erigens pauperem, Ps. Spl. 112, 6. Gyld of golde arǽrde *reared up an idol of gold*, Cd. 180; Th. 226, 23; Dan. 175. Arǽrde Cristes rōde *reared up Christ's rood*, Exon. 35 a; Th. 112, 27; Gū. 150. Ic arǽre ðis tempel binnan þrīm dagum *excitabo hoc templum in tribus diebus*, Jn. Bos. 2, 19, 20. Ic hine arǽre on ðam ȳtemestan dæge *ego resuscitabo eum in novissimo die*, 6, 44, 54. Weá wæs arǽred *woe was raised up*, Cd. 47; Th. 60, 26; Gen. 987. Se ðe fōre duguðe wile dōm arǽran *who desires before his nobles to exalt his dignity*, Exon. 87 a; Th. 327, 2; Wid. 140: Beo. Th. 3411; B. 1703. Ðā wæs ǽ Godes riht arǽred *then was God's right law set up*, Andr. Kmbl. 3288; An. 1647. Weofod arǽrde *ædificavit altare*, Gen. 22, 9. Eardas rūme Meotud arǽrde for mon-cynne *the Creator established spacious lands for mankind*, Exon. 89 a; Th. 334, 14; Gn. Ex. 16.

a-rǽrnes, -ness, e; *f. A raising, an exaltation*; exaltatio:—Heora hrȳre wearþ Athēnum to arǽrnesse *their fall was the raising of the Athenians*, Ors. 3, 1; Bos. 53, 42.

a-rǽsan *to rush*; irruere, Anlct.

a-rāfian *To unrove, unravel, unwind*; dissolvere:—Arāfaþ ðæt cliwen ðære twīfaldan heortan *unwinds the clew of the double heart*; dissolvit corda duplicitatibus involuta, Past. 35, 5; Hat. MS. 46 b, 1.

a-rās *arose*; surrexit, Gen. 19, 1. v. a-rīsan.

āras *messengers*, Exon. 15 a; Th. 31, 10; Cri. 493. v. ār.

a-rāsade = rēsade *suspicabatur*, Bd. 4, 1; S. 564, 48, note.

a-rāsian; *p.* ode, ade; *pp.* od, ad; *v. trans.* [a, rāsian *to raise, uncover*] *To lay open, discover, explore, detect, reprove, correct, seize*; detegere, invenire, explorare, corripere, reprehendere, intercipere:—God hæfþ arāsod ūre unrihtwīsnissa *Deus invenit nostras iniquitates*, Gen. 44, 16. Arāsian *explorare*, Gr. Dial. 2, 14. Ðǽr hȳ arāsade, reótaþ and beofiaþ, fōre freán forhte *there they detected, shall wail and tremble, afraid before the Lord*, Exon. 25 b; Th. 75, 31; Cri. 1230. Hæleþ wurdon acle arāsad for ðȳ rǽse *the men were seized with fear on account of its force*, 74 a; Th. 277, 27; Jul. 587. Se ðe wilnaþ hiera unþeáwas arāsian *qui eorum culpas corripere studet*, Past. 35, 3; Hat. MS. 45 b, 6: 35, 5; Hat. MS. 46 a, 20. Beón arāsod *reprehendi*, Fulg. 5. Arāsad wæs *interceptus est*, Cot. 109. Arāsod beón on hefygtīmum gyltum *gravioris culpa noxæ teneri*, R. Ben. 25: 34.

ār-blæd, es; *n. The oar-blade*; palmula remi, Ælfc. Gl. 103; Wrt. Voc. 56, 38.

arc, es; *m*: earc, erc, e; *f*: earce, an; *f. A vessel to swim on water, the* ARK, *a coffer, small chest* or *box*; arca, cista, cistella, cibotium = κιβώτιον:—Ðā ætstōd se arc *tunc requievit arca*, Gen. 8, 4. Wirc ðē nū ǽnne arc *fac tibi arcam*, 6, 14. Þreó hund fæðma biþ se arc on lenge, and fīftig fæðma on brǽde, and þrittig on heáhnisse *trecentorum cubitorum erit longitudo arcæ, quinquaginta cubitorum latitudo, et triginta cubitorum altitudo illius*, 6, 15. Se arc wæs geferud ofer ða wæteru *arca ferebatur super aquas*, 7, 18. [*Laym.* archen, arche, *dat*: *Dut.* ark, *f*: *Ger. M. H. Ger.* arche, *f*: *O. H. Ger.* archa: *Goth.* arka: *Dan.* ark: *O. Nrs.* örk, *f.*] v. earc.

arce- *chief* = ἀρχι = ἀρχός, a prefix; v. arce-bisceop:—Hēr Ǽlfrīc arcebisceop fērde to Rōme æfter his arce[-pallium] *this year archbishop Ælfric went to Rome after his arch-pallium*, Chr. 997; Th. 247, 2, col. 2. = Wið ðan ðe he scolde gifan heom ðone arce [MS. erce] *on condition that he should give them the arch-pallium*, 996; Th. 244, 42, note. = Forðī ðæt he scolde heom ðone pallium gifan *on condition that he should give them the pallium*, 996; Th. 245, 11, note.

arce-bisceop, arce-bysceop, arce-biscop, ærce-bisceop, erce-biscop, es; *m. The chief bishop*, ARCHBISHOP; archiepiscopus [= ἀρχι-επίσκοπος from ἀρχι = ἀρχός *a leader, chief*; ἐπίσκοπος. v. bisceop]:—Honorius se arcebysceop gehālgode Thoman his diācon, to bisceope *archbishop Honorius consecrated Thomas his deacon, as bishop*, Bd. 3, 20; S. 550, 21: 4, 1; S. 563, 6, 8, 12, 29.

arce-bisceop-rīce, arce-biscop-rīce, es; *n. An* ARCHBISHOPRIC; archiepiscopatus:—To ðam arcebisceoprīce *to the archbishopric*, Chr. 994; Th. 242, 38. Ðæt arcebiscoprīce on Cantwara byrig *the archbishopric of Canterbury*, 1114; Th. 370, 15.

arce-diācon, archi-diācon, ærce-diācon, es; *m. An* ARCHDEACON, *a bishop's vicegerent*; archidiāconus [= ἀρχι-διάκονος, from ἀρχός *a chief, leader*, and διάκονος *a deacon*]:—Becom Benedictus to freóndscipe ðæs hālgan weres and ðæs gelǽredestan, Bonefacii archidiācones *Benedictus pervenit ad amicitiam viri doctissimi ac sanctissimi, Bonifacii videlicet archidiaconi*, Bd. 5, 19; S. 638, 14. Arcediācon *archidiaconus*, Ælfc. Gl. 69; Wrt. Voc. 42, 27.

arce-stōl, es; *m.* [arce *chief*, stōl *a stool*] *An archiepiscopal see* or *seat*; sedes archiepiscopalis:—Æt his arcestōle on Cantwara byrig *at his archiepiscopal see in Canterbury*, Chr. 1115; Th. 371, 5: 1119; Th. 372, 32.

ār-cræftig; *adj.* [ār *respect*, cræftig *crafty*] *Skilful* or *quick in shewing respect, respectful, polite*; morigerus, obsequens:—Ārcræftig ār *a respectful messenger, a prophet*, Cd. 202; Th. 250, 23; Dan. 551.

arctos; *acc.* arcton; *f.* [ἄρκτος, ου, *m. f. a bear*; ἄρκτος, *f. the constellation Ursa Major*, called also ἅμαξα, carles wǽn *the churl's wain*: the bright star in Boötes is denominated by ancient astronomers and poets Ἀρκτοῦρος, *the bear-ward*]. *The constellation Ursa Major*; arct-os, -us, i; *f.* = ἄρκτος, *f*:—Arcton hātte ān tungol on norþ dǽle, se hæfþ seofon steorran, and is for ðī ōðrum naman gehāten, *septemtrio*, ðone hātaþ lǽwede menn carles wǽn. Se ne gǽþ nǽfre adūne under ðyssere eorþan, swā swā ōðre tunglan dōþ, ac he went abūtan, hwīlon adūne and hwīlon up, ofer dæg and ofer niht *one constellation is called arctos in the north part, which has seven stars, and for that is called by another name*, septemtrio, *which untaught men call the churl's wain. It never goes down under this earth, as the other constellations do, but one* *while it turns down and another while up, over day and over night,* Bd. de nat. rerum; Wrt. popl. science 16, 3-7; Lchdm. iii. 270, 9-15.

ârde; *dat.* [=arce MS?] *A mark of honour, badge of office, the pallium,* Chr. 997; Ing. 172, 7. v. ârod.

ardlîce; *adv.* [arod *quick,* lîce] *Quickly, immediately;* prompte, cito:—Êfstaþ nû ardlîce *persequimini cito,* Jos. 2, 5: Gen. 14, 14: 22, 11.

are, es; *m. A court-yard;* area, Alb. resp. 48.

âre, an; *f. Honour, honesty, favour, benefit, pity, mercy;* honor, honestas, gratia, beneficium, misericordia:—Âre [MS. aare] cyninges dôm ǽghwǽr lufade *honor regis judicium diligit,* Ps. Th. 98, 3. Mid âran *with honours,* Cd. 155; Th. 193, 12; Exod. 245. Ârna ne gŷmden *they had no regard of honour,* 113; Th. 148, 20; Gen. 2459. Us is dînra ârna þearf *to us is need of thy mercies,* Exon. 11 b; Th. 16, 19; Cri. 255. Ârna gemyndig *mindful of benefits,* Cd. 98; Th. 130, 22; Gen. 2163: Beo. Th. 2379; B. 1187. We đec ârena biddaþ *we pray thee for thy mercies,* Exon. 53 a; Th. 186, 6; Az. 15. v. âr *honour.*

a-reáfian; *p.* ode; *pp.* od [a *from,* reáfian *to tear*] *To tear from, tear asunder, separate;* diripere:—Brim [MS. bring] is areáfod *the sea is separated,* Cd. 158; Th. 196, 12; Exod. 290.

a-reaht, -reht *put forth, spoken, explained,* Exon. 24 a; Th. 69, 23; Cri. 1125: Bt. 36, 2; Fox 174, 3; *pp. of* a-reccan.

a-recan *to recount:*—Hit nis nânum men aléfed, đæt he mǽge arecan đæt đæt God geworht hæfþ *it is not permitted to any man, that he may recount that which God has wrought,* Bt. 39, 12; Fox 232, 10. v. a-reccan.

a-reccan, -recan, -reccean; ic -recce, đû -reccest, -recest, he -receþ, -recþ; *p.* -reahte, -rehte; *impert.* -rece; *pp.* -reaht, -reht; *v. trans.* I. *to put forth, stretch out, strain, raise up;* extendere, expandere, erigere:—Hondum slôgun, folmum areahtum and fŷstum eác *they struck with their hands, with outstretched palms and fists also,* Exon. 24 a; Th. 69, 23; Cri. 1125. Areahtum eágum *attonitis oculis,* Prov. 16, Lye. He mæg of woruf-torde đone þearfendan areccan *de stercore erigens pauperem,* Ps. Th. 112, 6: 144, 15. II. *to put forth, relate, recount, speak out, express, explain, interpret, translate;* proponere, exponere, enarrare, eloqui, exprimere, disserere, interpretari, reddere:—Đara sume we areccan wyllaþ *some of which we will relate,* Bd. 5, 12; S. 627, 7: Menol. Fox 138; Men. 69. Đâ se Wîsdôm đâ đis spell areht [MS. Cot. areaht] hæfde *when Wisdom then had spoken this speech,* Bt. 36, 2; Fox 174, 3: 39, 3; Fox 214, 14: Bt. Met. Fox 8, 3; Met. 8, 2. Wordum gereccan [MS. Cot. areccan] *to express in words,* Bt. 20; Fox 70, 28. Arece us đæt bigspell *edissere nobis parabolam,* Mt. Bos. 13, 36: 15, 15. Arece us đæt gerŷne *explain to us the mystery,* Exon. 9 a; Th. 5, 24; Cri. 74: 49 a; Th. 169, 16; Gû. 1095: Cd. 202; Th. 250, 5; Dan. 542. Ân ǽrendgewrit of Lǽdene on Englisc areccean *to translate an epistle from Latin into English,* Past. pref. Hat. MS. III. *to set in order, adorn, deck?* expedire, expolire, comere?—Areaht sîe *expoliatur,* Cot. 77, Lye: Exon. 94 a; Th. 353, 9; Reim. 10.

a-reccean; *p.* -reahte. -rehte; *pp.* -reaht, -reht; *v. trans. To tell out, relate, recount, express, translate;* enarrare, eloqui, exprimere, reddere:—Hwâ is đæt đe eall đa yfel, đe hî dônde wǽron, mǽge areccean *who is there that can relate all the evils which they did?* Ors. 1, 8; Bos. 31, 24: Hy. 3, 17; Hy. Grn. ii. 281, 17. Ân ǽrendgewrit of Lǽdene on Englisc areccean *to translate an epistle from Latin into English,* Past. pref. v. a-reccan.

a-reccende; *part. Explaining;* exponens, Bd. 1, 27, resp. 8; S. 494, 35. v. a-reccan.

a-receþ, -recþ *raises up;* erigit, Ps. Th. 144, 15: Ps. Spl. 145, 7. v. a-reccan.

a-rêd *counsel,* L. Edm. E. pref; Th. i. 244, 6, MS. B. v. a-rǽd.

a-rêdad *discovered,* R. Ben. 61; *pp. of* a-rêdian.

a-reddan *to liberate.* v. a-hreddan.

a-rêde *cared for,* Bd. 3, 9; S. 533, 25, = a-rêdde = a-rǽdde; *p. of* a-rǽdan, *q. v.*

a-rêdian; *p.* ode; *pp.* od, ad *To make ready, provide, furnish, execute, find, to find the way to any place, reach;* parare, præparare, exsequi, invenire, pervenire aliquo:—Us is þearf đæt we arêdian đæt ûre hlâford wille *it behoves us that we provide that which our lord wants,* L. Ath. v. § 8, 9; Th. i. 238, 25. Smeáge man hû man mǽge rǽd arêdian þeóde to þearfe *let it be considered how advantage may be provided for the behoof of the nation,* L. Eth. vi. 40; Th. i. 324, 28: L. C. S. 11; Th. i. 382, 6. Arêdod *furnished,* Som. Woruld-gerihta mon arêdian mǽge Gode to gecwêmnysse *secular rights may be executed to the pleasure of God,* L. Edg. S. 2; Th. i. 272, 24. Hî arêdian ne mâgon, đæt hî aslêpen *they cannot find out that they may slip,* Bt. Met. Fox 13, 16; Met. 13, 8. Arêdad beón *inveniri,* R. Ben. 61. Đæt đû ne mǽge đîne wegas arêdian *ut non dirigas vias tuas,* Deut. 28, 29. Đû ne mihtest gyt fulrihtne weg arêdian *thou hast not yet been able to find the most direct way,* Bt. 22, 2; Fox 78, 8: 40, 5; Fox 240, 22: Bt. Met. Fox 23, 19; Met. 23, 10. Oferdruncen man ne mæg to his hûse arêdian *a drunken man is not able to find the way to his house,* Bt. 24, 4; Fox 84, 31. Ic ne mæg ût arêdian *I cannot find the way out,* 35, 5; Fox 164, 14. Đû eart cumen innon đa ceastre, đe đû ǽr ne mihtest arêdian *thou art come into the city, which thou couldest not reach before,* 35, 3; Fox 158, 11.

a-rêdnes, -rǽdnis, -ness, e; *f. A degree, condition, covenant;* consultum, conditio:—Đâ geþafedon hî đære arêdnesse *ea conditione consenserunt,* Bd. 1, 1; S. 474, 20. Đæt wîf he onfêng đære arêdnesse *uxorem ea conditione acceperat,* 1, 25; S. 486, 33.

a-rêdod *furnished,* Som. v. a-rêdian.

a-rêfnan *to endure:*—Ic arêfnde *sustinui,* Ps. Spl. C. 68, 25. v. a-rǽfnan.

a-reht *spoken,* Bt. 36, 2; Fox 174, 3; *pp. of* a-reccan.

ârena *of mercies,* Exon. 53 a; Th. 186, 6; Az. 15, = ârna; *gen. pl. of* âre, *q. v.*

a-reódian; *p.* ode; *pp.* od [a, reódian *to redden*] *To become red, to redden, blush;* erubescere:—His andwlita eal areódode *all his countenance became red,* Apol. Th. 21, 26.

a-reósan; *p.* -reás, *pl.* -ruron; *pp.* -roren *To fall down, perish;* decidere, corruere:—Ic areóse [MS. areófe] be gewyrhtum fram feóndum mînum on îdel *decidam merito ab inimicis meis inanis,* Ps. Spl. 7, 4. v. a-hreósan.

a-rêtan; ic -rête, he -rêteþ, -rêt; *p.* -rêtte; *pp.* -rêted, -rêt; *v. trans.* [a, rêtan *to comfort*] *To exhilarate, comfort, delight, restore, refresh, set right;* exhilarare, lætificare, reficere:—Ic monigra môd arête *I exhilarate the mind of many,* Exon. 102 b; Th. 389, 12; Rä. 7, 6. Seó hwætnes đæs lîchoman geblissaþ đone mon and arêt *the vigour of the body rejoices and delights the man,* Bt. 24, 3; Fox 84, 8. Đæt ge brôđor mîne wel arêtten *that ye should well cherish my brethren,* Exon. 30 a; Th. 91, 33; Cri. 1501. Ǽghwylcum wearþ môd arêted *every one's mind was delighted,* Judth. 11; Thw. 24, 2; Jud. 167. Hî hæfdon đæt môd arêt *they had restored* or *refreshed the mind,* Bt. titl. xxii; Fox xiv, 5. Đû me hæfst arêtne on đam tweóne *thou hast set me right in the doubt,* Bt. 41, 2; Fox 246, 12: 22, 1; Fox 76, 12, MS. Cot.

arewe, an; *f. An arrow;* sagitta:—Sume scotedon adûnweard mid arewan *some shot downward with arrows,* Chr. 1083; Erl. 217, 19.

Arewe, Arwe, an; *f.* [arewe *arrow*] ARROW, the name of a river in several counties, called so either from its *swiftness* or *straightness,* also *the Orwell;* fluvii nomen:—Se here gewende đâ fram Lundene, mid hyra scypum, into Arewan [MS. Laud. Arwan] *the army* [*of the Danes*] *went then from London, with their ships, into the river Orwell* [*in Suffolk*], Chr. 1016; Erl. 157, 14. *Gibson says of Orwell,*—Hunc suspicor antiquitus fuisse pronunciatum *Arwel,* tum quod Saxonicum *A* sequentibus sæculis transiit in *O,* tum etiam quod oppidum est ad ejus ripam situm, *Arwerton* dictum; accedit quod *Harewich* ad oram hujus fluminis, olim *Arwic,* non ut conjectat Camd. *Herewic,* dici posset, Gib. Chr. Explicatio 13, col. 1.

âre-weorþ *honourable, venerable;* honore dignus, honorabilis, venerabilis, Lye. v. âr-weorþ.

âr-fæst, ǽr-fæst; *adj.* [âr *honour,* fæst *fast*] *Honourable, honest, upright, virtuous, good, pious, dutiful, gracious, kind, merciful;* honestus, probus, bonus, pius, propitius, clemens, misericors:—Ârfæste rincas *honourable chieftains,* Cd. 90; Th. 113, 29; Gen. 1894: 136; Th. 171, 9; Gen. 2825. Wæs he se mon ǽfæst and ârfæst *he was the religious and pious man;* vir pietatis et religionis, Bd. 3, 14; S. 539, 33. Wes đû đînum yldrum ârfæst simle *be thou always dutiful to thy parents,* Exon. 80 a; Th. 300, 25; Fä. 11. Ongan đâ rôdera wealdend ârfæst wiđ Abraham sprecan *then began the gracious Ruler of the skies to speak with Abraham,* 109; Th. 145, 13; Gen. 2405. Drihten biþ ârfæst his folces lande *Dominus propitius erit terræ populi sui,* Deut. 32, 43: Exon. 11 b; Th. 15, 32; Cri. 245. Đæt Drihten him ârfæst and milde wǽre *that the Lord might be to him merciful and mild,* Bd. 4, 31; S. 610, 31.

âr-fæstlîce; *adv. Honestly, piously;* honeste, pie. DER. ârfæst, lîce.

âr-fæstnes, âr-fæstnys, ǽr-fæstnys, -ness, e; *f. Honourableness, honesty, goodness, piety, clemency, mercifulness;* honestas, probitas, pietas, clementia, misericordia:—Đæt he wæs mycelre ârfæstnesse and ǽfæstnesse wer *quod vir esset multæ pietatis ac religionis,* Bd. 4, 31; S. 610, 7. Seó godcunde ârfæstnys *pietas divina,* 2, 12; S. 512, 24: 3, 13; S. 539, 1. Mid đa upplîcan ârfæstnesse *apud supernam clementiam,* 5, 23; S. 649, 8: Jos. 6, 17. For đînre ârfestnesse *of thy clemency,* Hy. 8, 24; Hy. Grn. ii. 290, 24.

âr-fæt, es; *n. A brazen vessel;* æramentum, labrum:—Fyrmþa ârfata *baptismata æramentorum,* Mk. Bos. 7, 4. Hâlgode đæt ârfæt *labrum sanctificavit,* Lev. 8, 11.

ar-faran *To go away, depart;* abire:—Ar-faraþ, Bt. Met. Fox 20, 25: Met. 20, 13 *suggests* an-faraþ, *taking* an *as an adv. away,* without referring to any authority.

âr-fest *merciful,* Ps. Spl. 102, 3. v. âr-fæst.

âr-ful, âr-full; *adj. Venerable, respectful, favourable, merciful, mild;* honorabilis, venerabilis, propitius, reverens:—Ic Ǽđelbald wæs beden from đæm ârfullan bisceope Milrede *I Æthelbald have been solicited by the venerable bishop Milred,* Th. Diplm. A. D. 743-745; 28, 22. Se đe ârfull biþ eallum unrihtwîsum đînum *qui propitiatur omnibus iniquitatibus tuis,* Ps. Spl. M. 102, 3. Cristenra manna gehwilc beó ârful fæder and mēder *Christianorum quivis reverenter habeat patrem et matrem,* Wulfst. paræn. 7.

ârful-lîce; *adv. Mildly, gently;* clementer:—Iosep hîg oncneów ârfullîce *Joseph clementer resalutavit eos,* Gen. 43, 27.

arg; *adj. Wicked, depraved, bad;* malus, pravus. ☞ An impure word only found in the Lindisfarne Gospels or the Durham Book:—Cneórisse yflo and arg *an evil and wicked generation;* generatio mala et adultera, *i. e.* prava, pigra, etc. Mt. Kmbl. Lind. 12, 39. Arg *peccatrix,* Mk. Skt. Lind. 8, 38. [*Plat. Dut. Ger. Franc. Dan. Swed.* arg: *Grk.* ἀργός *idle: Icel.* argr *effeminatus, pavidus, ignavus, malus, detestabilis.*] v. earg.

âr-gebland, es; *m. The mingling of the oars, the sea disturbed by the oars, the oar-disturbed sea;* remorum commixtio, mare remis turbatum, Andr. Kmbl. 765; An. 383. v. âr.

âr-geótere, es; *m.* [âr *brass,* geótere *a pourer*] *A caster* or *pourer of brass, melter of brass, brass-founder;* ærarius:—Ðâ wæs sum ârgeótere, se mihte dôn anlîcnessa *there was a certain brass-founder, who could make images,* Ors. 1, 12; Bos. 36, 26.

âr-gesweorf, es; *m. Brass filings;* limatura æris, L. M. 1, 34; Lchdm. ii. 80, 22. v. gesweorf, sweorfan.

âr-geweorc, es; *n. Brass-work;* æramentum, Cot. 79.

âr-gifa, an; *m. A benefit-giver;* beneficiorum dator, Exon. 78 b; Th. 294, 6; Crä. 11.

âr-glæd *bright with brass.* v. ǽr-glæd.

arhlîce *disgracefully, basely:*—Eádwine eorl wearþ ofslagen arhlîce fram his âgenum mannum *earl Eadwine was basely slain by his own men,* Chr. 1071; Erl. 210, 14; Th. 347, 12. v. earhlîce from earg, earh II. *evil, vile.*

âr-hwæt; *g. m. n.* -hwates; *f.* -hwætre; *adj.* [âr *honour,* hwæt *eager, brisk*] *Eager* or *desirous of honour, bold, valiant;* honoris cupidus, fortis:—Wealas ofercômon eorlas ârhwate *the men eager for glory overcame the Welsh,* Chr. 937; Erl. 115, 22; Th. 208, 9, col. 2; Æðelst. 73.

ârian; to ârianne; *part.* ende, gende; *p.* ede, ode; *pp.* ed, od; *v. a.* [âr *honour*]. I. *to give honour, to honour, reverence, have in admiration;* honorare, honorificare, venerari:—Is to ârianne *is to be honoured,* Bt. 32, 2; Fox 116, 14. Onsægednys lôfes âreþ me *sacrificium laudis honorificabit me,* Ps. Spl. T. 49, 24. He âraþ ða gôdan *he honoureth the good,* Bt. 41, 2; Fox 246, 19. Ic ârode ðē ofer ealle gesceafta *I honoured thee over all creatures,* Exon. 28 a; Th. 84, 33; Cri. 1383. Se rîca Rôména wita and se âroda *the rich and honoured senator of the Romans,* Bt. Met. Fox 10, 89; Met. 10, 45. II. *to regard, care for, spare, have mercy, pity, pardon, forgive;* consulere, propitium esse, misereri, parcere:—He þearfum ârede *he cared for the poor,* Bd. 3, 9; S. 533, 25. Ac ârodon heora lîfe *but they spared their lives,* Jos. 9, 21: Beo. Th. 1201; B. 598. Bûton him se cyning ârian wille *unless the king will pardon him,* L. In. 36; Wilk. 20, 39; Th. i. 124, 19. Âra ambehtum [MS. onbehtum] *pity thy servants,* Exon. 13 a; Th. 23, 17; Cri. 370. DER. ge-ârian.

Arianisc, Arrianisc; *adj.* ARIAN, *belonging to Arius, an Alexandrian, who lived in the fourth century:*—Se Arrianisca gedweolda arâs *the Arian heresy arose,* Bd. 1, 8; S. 479, 27, 18, 33. On ðam Arianiscan gedwolan *in the Arian heresy,* Ors. 6, 31; Bos. 127, 43.

a-rîdan; *p.* -râd, *pl.* -ridon; *pp.* -riden *To ride;* equitare:—He ût of ðam mann-werode arâd *he rode out from the crowd,* Ors. 3, 7; Bos. 62, 22. v. rîdan.

a-riddan, ðû -riddest [a-, riddan] *To rid, deliver;* liberare, repellere:—For hwy me ðû ædrîfe oððe ariddest *quare me reppulisti?* Ps. Spl. T. 42, 2. v. a-hreddan.

âriende, ârigende *sparing;* parcens. v. ârian.

a-riht; *adv.* ARIGHT, *right, well, correctly;* probe, recte:—Gif man hit ariht asmeáþ *if one considereth it right,* L. Edg. C. 13; Th. ii. 246, 21. v. riht.

a-rîman; *p.* de; *pp.* ed *To number, count, enumerate;* numerare, enumerare, dinumerare, recensere:—He arîman mæg regnas scûran dropena gehwelcne *he can count every drop of the rain-shower,* Cd. 213; Th. 265, 21; Sat. 11: Ps. Th. 89, 13: 146, 5. Hî arîmdon ealle bân mîne *dinumeraverunt omnia ossa mea,* Ps. Spl. C. 21, 16: Past. 16, 1; Hat. MS. 20 b, 4.

âr-ing, ârung, e; *f. Honour, respect;* honoratio:—Bûton âringe *without honour,* Ors. 5, 10; Bos. 108, 41.

a-rinnan; *p.* -ran, *pl.* -runnon; *pp.* -runnen *To run out, pass by, to disappear;* effluere, præterire:—Ðæt sý [MS. sie] cwide arunnen *that the word be run out,* Salm. Kmbl. 960; Sal. 479. v. rinnan, yrnan, a-yrnan.

a-rîsan; *part.* arîsende; *p.* arâs, *pl.* arison; *pp.* arisen; *v. n. To* ARISE, *rise, rise up, rise again, to come forth, originate;* surgere, exsurgere, resurgere, provenire, oriri:—Ic arîse *surgo,* Ælfc. Gr. 28, 5; Som. 31, 49. Micel arîseþ dryht-folc to dôme *a great multitude shall arise to judgment,* Exon. 23 a; Th. 64, 22; Cri. 1041. Ðý þryddan dæge arîsan *tertia die resurgere,* Mt. Bos. 16, 21: Exon. 23 a; Th. 64, 2; Cri. 1031. Ýdel is eów ǽr leóhte arîsan *vanum est vobis ante lucem surgere,* Ps. Spl. 126, 3. He arâs sôna *surrexit,* Gen. 19, 1. Ðâ arison ða þrî weras *surrexerunt tres viri,* Gen. 18, 16. Weorod eall arâs *the band all arose,* Beo. Th. 6053; B. 3030. Storm upp arâs *the storm rose up,* Andr. Kmbl. 2474; An. 1238. Sindon costinga monge arisene *many temptations are arisen,* Exon. 33 a; Th. 104, 20; Gû. 10. Arisen wæs sunne *exortus est sol,* Mk. Lind. War. 4, 6.

a-rîseþ *it behoveth;* oportet:—Ðætte arîseþ sunu monnes *for it bihoueth mannis sone,* Wyc. Lk. Lind. Rush. War. 9, 22; quia oportet filium hominis, Vulg. v. gerîsan.

Arîus [='Αρειος], Arrius; *g.* ii; *acc.* um; *m. A presbyter of Alexandria, founder of the Arians, born in Cyrenaica, Africa, and died in* A. D. 336:—Ðâ cwæþ Arrius ðæt Crist, Godes Sunu, ne mihte nâ beón his Fæder gelîc, ne swâ mihtig swâ he; and cwæþ, ðæt se Fæder wǽre ǽr se Sunu, and nam býsne be mannum, hû ǽlc sunu biþ gingra ðonne se fæder on ðisum lîfe.... He wolde dôn Crist læssan ðonne he is, and his Godcundnysse wurþmynt wanian *then Arius said that Christ, the Son of God, could not be equal to his Father, nor so mighty as he; and said, that the Father was before the Son, and took example from men, how every son is younger than his father in this life.... He would make Christ less than he is, and diminish the dignity of his Godhead,* Homl. Th. i. 290, 3–8, 22, 23. Hý amânsumodon ðǽr [on ðære ceastre Nicea A. D. 325] ðone mæsse-preóst Arrium, forðan ðe he nolde gelýfan ðæt ðæs lîfigendan Godes Sunu wǽre ealswâ mihtig swâ se mǽra Fæder is *they there [in the city of Nice A. D. 325] excommunicated the mass-priest Arius, because he would not believe that the Son of the living God was as mighty as the great Father is,* L. Ælf. C. 3; Th. ii. 344, 2–4.

ariwe *an arrow;* sagitta. v. arewe.

âr-leás; *def.* se âr-leása; *adj.* [âr, leás]. I. *void of honour, honourless, disgraceful, infamous, wicked, impious;* inhonestus, impius, infamis:—Him ârleáse cyn andswarode *the honourless race answered him,* Cd. 114; Th. 149, 15; Gen. 2475: 91; Th. 116, 10; Gen. 1934. Hleór geþolade ârleásra spâtl *my face endured the spittle of the impious,* Exon. 29 a; Th. 88, 7; Cri. 1436: Elen. Kmbl. 1668; El. 836. Ða ârleásan *the impious men,* Andr. Kmbl. 1117; An. 559. Wið ðam ârleásestan eretice *against the most wicked heretic,* Bd. 4, 17; S. 585, 43. Forweorþaþ se ârleása *the wicked perisheth,* Ps. Spl. 9, 5: Ps. Lamb. 1, 4, 5. Ðû scealt hweorfan ârleás of earde ðînum *thou shalt depart infamous from thy dwelling,* Cd. 48; Th. 62, 24; Gen. 1019: Exon. 28 b; Th. 87, 25; Cri. 1430. II. *pitiless, merciless, cruel;* crudelis:—Maximianus, ârleás cyning, cwealde cristne men *Maximian, the cruel king, slew Christian men,* Exon. 65 b; Th. 243, 1; Jul. 4.

ârleáslîce; *adv.* [ârleás, lîce] *Wickedly, impiously;* impie:—Ic ne dyde ârleáslîce *nec impie gessi,* Ps. Th. 17, 21: Ps. Spl. 17, 23: Exon. 40 b; Th. 136, 7; Gû. 537.

ârleás-nes, -ness, e; *f.* [ârleás *honourless, wicked,* -nes, -ness] *Wickedness, acts of wickedness, impiety;* iniquitas:—Æfter mænigo ârleásnyssa heora *secundum multitudinem impietatum eorum,* Ps. Spl. 5, 12: 64, 3. Seó wîldeórlîce ârleásnes Bretta cyninges *feralis impietas regis Brittonum,* Bd. 3, 9; S. 533, 7: 3, 19; S. 548, 18.

âr-leást, ǽr-lêst, e; *f.* [âr *honor, honestas, gratia,* -leást] *Dishonour, impiety, cruelty, a disgraceful deed;* inhonestas, impietas, crudelitas, flagitium:—Ârleásta fela *many disgraceful deeds,* Bt. Met. Fox 9, 12; Met. 9, 6.

âr-lîc; *adj.* [âr *honour,* lîc *like*]. I. *honest, honourable, noble, becoming, proper;* honestus, decorus, honorabilis, nobilis:—Ârlîc bisceopsetl *an honourable bishop-seat,* Bd. 3, 7; S. 530, 1: Ors. 2, 8; Bos. 51, 11. Is nû ârlîc ðæt we ǽfestra dǽde dēmen *it is now becoming that we consider the deeds of the pious,* Exon. 40 a; Th. 133, 29; Gû. 497. II. applied to food of a high quality,—*Delicious;* delicatus, suavis:—Ða beón beraþ ârlîcne anleofan,—hafaþ hunig on mûþe, wynsume wist *the bees produce delicious food,—have honey in the mouth, a pleasant food,* Frag. Kmbl. 36; Leás. 20: Ps. Th. 95, 8. DER. un-ârlîc.

ârlîce; *adv. Honourably, honestly, properly, mercifully;* honorifice, honeste, decenter, misericordi vel propitio animo:—He hine ârlîce bebyride *honorifice eum sepelivit,* Bd. 4, 22; S. 591, 20: Bt. 16, 2; Fox 52, 31: Cd. 127; Th. 162, 23; Gen. 2685. Waldend usser gemunde Abraham ârlîce *our Lord remembered Abraham mercifully,* 121; Th. 156, 9; Gen. 2586.

âr-lîce; *adv.* [=ǽr *early*] *Early;* diluculo, mane, Mk. Lind. War. 16, 2: Lk. Lind. War. 24, 1: Jn. Rush. War. 8, 2. v. ǽr-lîce.

arm; *adj. Miserable;* miser:—Arm leód *miserable people,* Chr. 1104; Th. 367, 15. v. earm.

armêlu *Field* or *wild rue, which is called* Mōly [=μῶλυ] *in Cappadocia and Galatia, and by some* Harmāla; *hence the botanical name* =pēgănum harmāla, Lin. vol. ii. p. 327, =πήγἄνον ἄγριον *wild rue:*—Armêlu wyl on buteran to sealfe *boil wild rue in butter to a salve,* L. M. 1, 64; Lchdm. ii. 140, 4.

âr-morgen *early dawn,* Jn. Lind. War. 18, 28: 20, 1. v. ǽr-morgen.

arn *ran,* Mk. Bos. 5, 6; *p. of* yrnan.

ârna *of honours, of mercies,* Exon. 11 b; Th. 16, 19; Cri. 255; *gen. pl. of* âre, *q. v.*

arod, es; *n? A species of herb, probably* arum=ἄρον; herbæ genus, arum:—Nim lybcornes leáf, oðđe arod *take a leaf of saffron, or arod,* L.M. 3, 42; Lchdm. ii. 336, 10. Gehwæde arodes wôses *a little of the ooze of arum,* Lchdm. iii. 2, 23.

arod; *adj. Quick, swift, ready, prepared;* celer, velox, promptus, paratus:—Đá wearþ sum to đam arod, đæt he in đæt bûrgeteld nēþde *then one became ready for this, that he ventured into the bower-tent,* Judth. 12; Thw. 25, 24; Jud. 275. [*O. Nrs.* ördugr, ördigr *arduus, difficilis, acer, vehemens.*] v. earu.

ârod *honoured,* Bt. Met. Fox 10, 89; Met. 10, 45; *pp. of* ârian, *q. v.*

ârod, es; *m?* [ârian *to honour*] *A mark of honour, badge of office, the pallium given by the pope to a bishop* or *archbishop;* honoris vel muneris signum:—Hēr Ælfrîc arcebisceop fērde to Rôme æfter his ârde [? arce, MS. *q. v.*] *this year archbishop Ælfric went to Rome after his pallium,* Chr. 997; Ing. 172, 7. v. arce-.

arodlîce, arudlîce, ardlîce; *adv. Quickly, immediately;* cito, sine mora:—Hî hebbaþ swîđe arodlîce đa earce up *arcam sine mora elevant,* Past. 22, 2; Hat. MS. 33 b, 9.

arodscipe, es; *m. Quickness, swiftness, readiness, dexterity;* velocitas, dexteritas, promptitudo:—Oft mon biþ swîđe rempende and rǽsþ swîđe dollîce on ǽlc weorc and hrædlîce, and đeáh wēnaþ men đæt hit sîe for arodscipe and for hwætscipe *sæpe præcipitata actio velocitatis efficacia putatur,* Past. 20, 1; Hat. MS. 29 b, 5. DER. un-arodscipe.

aron *estis,* Mt. Kmbl. Lind. 5, 11, = earon.

ârra *of favours, mercies, grace,* Cd. 131; Th. 166, 20; Gen. 2750; *gen. pl. of* âr.

Arrian, es; *m. Arius;* Arrianus:—Arrianes gedwola *the heresy of Arius,* Bt. Met. Fox 1, 80; Met. 1, 40. v. Arîus.

Arrianisc *Arian,* Bd. 1, 8; S. 479, 18, 27, 33. v. Arianisc.

Arrius, ii; *m. Arius,* L. Ælf. C. 3; Th. ii. 344, 3. v. Arîus.

âr-sâpe, an; *f.* [âr *ore, brass;* sâpe = sâp, *p. of* sîpan *stillare*] *Verdigris;* ærugo:—Nim ârsâpan *take verdigris,* Lchdm. iii. 14, 31.

âr-sceamu, e; *f. Verecundia:*—Ârscame, *acc.* Ps. Th. 68, 19.

Âr-scyldingas, a; *pl. m. The honoured Skyldings, Danes,* Beo. Th. 933; B. 464: 3425; B. 1710.

ars-gang, es; *m.* [ears *anus,* gang *a passage*] *Ani foramen, anus.* v. ears-gang.

âr-smiþ, es; *m.* [âr *brass,* smiþ *a smith*] *A copper-smith, a brazier, a worker in brass;* faber ærarius, Coll. Monast. Th. 30, 1.

âr-stæf, *gen.* -stæfes; *pl. nom. acc.* -stafas; *m. Favour, kindness, benefit, help;* gratia, beneficium, auxilii latio:—Fæder alwalda mid ârstafum eówic gehealde sîđa gesunde *may the all-ruling Father hold you with kindness safe on your ways,* Beo. Th. 639; B. 317. For ârstafum đû usic sôhtest *thou hast sought us for help,* 920; B. 458: Exon. 107 a; Th. 409, 5; Rä. 27, 24. v. âr, stæf.

art *art:*—Art *vel* arþ *es,* Jn. Lind. War. 1, 19. v. eom.

arþ *art,* Mk. Lind. Rush. War. 14, 70: Jn. Lind. Rush. War. 1, 19. v. eom.

âr-þegn, âr-þeng, es; *m.* [âr *honour,* þegen *a servant*] *A servant* or *minister by his place* or *employment;* servus, minister honorabilis:—Cumena ârþegn *the servant of guests,* Bd. 4, 31; Whel. 361, 14.

arudlîce *quickly.* v. arodlîce, ardlîce.

ârung, e; *f.* I. *an honouring, a reverence;* honoratio. II. *a regarding, sparing, pardoning;* remissio. v. âr *honour,* ârian.

Arwan:—Into Arwan *into the river Orwell,* Chr. 1016; Laud. MS; Erl. 157, 1. v. Arewe.

arwe *an arrow.* v. arewe.

âr-wêla, an; *m.* [âr *an oar,* wêla] *The wealth of oars, the sea;* divitiæ remorum, mare, Andr. Kmbl. 1705; An. 855.

âr-weorþ; *adj.* [âr *honour,* weorþ *worth, worthy*] *Honour-worth, honourable, venerable;* honorabilis, venerabilis, venerandus. v. âr-wurþ, âr-wyrþ.

âr-weorþe; *adv. Honourably;* honorifice, Bd. 2, 20; S. 522, 1, MS. B. v. âr-wurþlîce.

âr-weorþian, -wurþian, -wyrþian; *p.* -ode; *pp.* -od [âr *honour,* weorþian *to hold worthy*] *To hold worthy of honour, to give honour to, to honour, reverence, worship;* honorare, honorificare, honorem referre, venerari:—He ongan ârweorþian đa þrôwunge hâligra martyra *incepit honorem referre cædi sanctorum,* Bd. 1, 7; S. 479, 1. Đæt mynster seó cwēn swýđe lufode and ârwyrþode *regina monasterium multum diligebat et venerabatur,* 3, 11; S. 535, 15: Jn. Bos. 5, 23: Deut. 5, 16.

âr-weorþig; *adj. Venerable, reverend;* reverendus. v. ârwurþig.

âr-weorþlîc; *adj. Venerable;* venerabilis. v. âr-wurþlîc.

âr-weorþlîce; *adv. Honourably, reverently, solemnly, kindly;* honorifice, reverenter, solemniter, clementer, R. Ben. 58, Lye: Bd. 3, 19; S. 547, 8: 1, 27, resp. 8; S. 495, 17: Gen. 45, 4. v. âr-weorþe, -wurþlîce, -wyrþlîce.

âr-weorþnes, âr-wyrþnes, -ness, e; *f.* [âr *honour,* weorþnes *worthiness*] *Honour-worthiness, honour, dignity;* honor, dignitas, reverentia:—Æfter ârwyrþnesse swâ micles biscopes *juxta venerationem tanto pontifice dignam,* Bd. 3, 17; S. 544, 3, col. 2. Gif đû nû gemunan wilt eallra đara ârwyrþnessa *if thou now wilt be mindful of all the honours,* Bt. 8; Fox 24, 20. Mid ârweorþnesse *with honour, honourably,* R. Ben. 6, 61.

âr-weorþung, e; *f. Honour, reverence;* honor, reverentia:—On ârweorþunge *in honore,* Ps. Lamb. 48, 21. v. âr-wurþung.

âr-widđe, an; *f?* [âr *an oar,* widđe *withe*] *An oar-withe, a willow band to tie oars with;* struppus:—Ârwidđe *vel* strop *struppus,* Ælfc. Gl. 103; Som. 77, 117; Wrt. Voc. 56, 37.

arwunga, arwunge; *adv. Gratuitously;* gratis:—Arwunga ge onfēngun, arwunge ge sellaþ *gratis accepistis, gratis date,* Mt. Kmbl. Rush. 10, 8. v. earwunga.

âr-wurþ, -wyrþ; *def.* se ârwurþa; seó, đæt ârwurþe; *adj.* [âr *honour,* weorþ *worth*] *Honour-worth, honourable, venerable, reverend;* honorabilis, honorandus, venerabilis, venerandus:—Se ârwurþa wer *vir venerabilis,* Bd. 4, 18; S. 586, 22: 5, 1; S. 613, 11. Se gôda biþ simle ârwyrþe *the good is always honourable,* Bt. 39, 2; Fox 212, 23. Ârwurþe wudewe [MS. wurdewe] *or* nunne *nonna,* Ælfc. Gl. 69; Som. 70, 21; Wrt. Voc. 42, 30. Se ârwurþesta Godes andettere *reverentissimus Dei confessor,* Bd. 1, 7; S. 478, 20. Đa ârwurþan bân *honoranda ossa,* 3, 11; S. 535, 16. Đæt ârwurþe bæþ *lavacrum venerabile,* 3, 11; S. 535, 34.

âr-wurþian, -wurþigean; *p.* ode; *pp.* od; *v. a. To give honour to, to honour, reverence, worship;* honorare, honorificare, venerari:—Onsægednys lôfes ârwurþaþ me *sacrificium laudis honorificabit me,* Ps. Spl. 49, 24. Đæt ealle ârwurþion [ârwurþigeon, Jun.] đone Sunu, swâ swâ hîg ârwurþiaþ [ârwurþigeaþ, Jun.] đone Fæder; se đe ne ârwurþaþ đone Sunu, ne ârwurþaþ he đone Fæder *ut omnes honorificent Filium, sicut honorificant Patrem; qui non honorificat Filium, non honorificat Patrem,* Jn. Bos. 5, 23: Bd. 5, 19; S. 637, 6. To ârwurþianne [MS. tarwurþienne, v. weorþianne = wurþianne, in weorþian I] đînne, đone sôđan and đone âncænnedan, Sunu *to honour thy, the true and only begotten, Son,* Te Dm. Thomson 35, 12. Geleáfa sôþlîce se geleáffulla đes is; đæt ânne God on þrýnnesse and þrýnnesse on Ânnesse we ârwurþian *fides autem catholica hæc est; ut unum Deum in Trinitate et Trinitatem in Unitate veneremur,* Ps. Lamb. fol. 200 a, 15. Ârwurþa đînne fæder and đîne môdur *honora patrem tuum et matrem,* Deut. 5, 16. v. âr-weorþian.

âr-wurþig *reverend.* v. âr-weorþig, âr-weorþ.

âr-wurþigean *to honour, reverence;* honorificare, Jn. Jun. 5, 23. v. âr-wurþian.

âr-wurþlîc; *adj. Venerable;* venerabilis:—Ârwurþlîc on to seónne *venerabilis aspectu,* Bd. 2, 16; S. 519, 35. v. âr-weorþ, -wurþ.

âr-wurþlîce; *adv. Honourably, reverently, kindly, solemnly, mildly;* honorifice, solemniter, reverenter, clementer:—Hî swîđe ârwurþlîce onfangene wǽron *they were very honourably received,* Bd. 2, 20; S. 522, 1: 3, 19; S. 547, 8: 5, 19; S. 637, 33. Fram cyricean ingonge ârwurþlîce ahabban *ab ingressu ecclesiæ reverenter abstinere,* Bd. 1, 27, resp. 8; S. 495, 17. Đa grēte hîg ârwurþlîce *quos ille clementer allocutus est,* Gen. 45, 4. v. âr-weorþe, -weorþlîce.

âr-wurþung, e; *f. Honour, reverence;* honor, reverentia:—Bryngaþ Drihtne ârwurþunge *afferte Domino honorem,* Ps. Spl. T. 28, 2: Ps. Spl. 48, 12. v. âr-weorþung.

âr-wyrþ; *adj. Honourable, venerable;* honorabilis, venerandus, Bt. 39, 2; Fox 212, 23: Elen. Kmbl. 2256; El. 1129. v. âr-weorþ.

âr-wyrþian; *p.* ode; *pp.* od *To honour, reverence,* Bd. 3, 11; S. 535, 15. v. âr-weorþian.

âr-wyrþlîce; *adv. Honourably, reverently, solemnly, kindly,* R. Ben. 58. v. âr-wurþlîce.

âr-wyrþnes, -ness, e; *f. Dignity,* Bd. 3, 17; S. 544, 3, col. 2. v. âr-weorþnes.

a-rýpan; *p.* de, te; *pp.* ed, d, t *To tear off, to rip;* evellere, abscindere:—He me of hýd arýpeþ *he tears off my hide from me,* Exon. 127 a; Th. 488, 15; Rä. 76, 7. v. be-rýpan.

âr-ýþ, e; *f. An oar-wave;* unda remis pulsata:—Hærn eft onwand, ârýđa geblond *the tide turned back, the commotion of the oar-waves,* Andr. Kmbl. 1063; An. 532.

a-sæcgan; *p.* -sægde, -sǽde; *pp.* -sægd, -sǽd *To speak out, relate, tell, say, express, explain, announce, proclaim;* edicere, effari, exprimere, referre, enarrare, annunciare:—Ne mǽge we nǽfre asæcgan, hû đû æđele eart, ēce Drihten *we may never express, how excellent thou art, everlasting Lord,* Hy. 3, 13; Hy. Grn. ii. 281, 13. v. a-secgan.

a-sǽd *said out, related, told,* Bd. 4, 22; S. 590, 32; *pp. of* a-secgan, *q. v.*

a-sǽdon *said out, related, told,* Ors. 4, 6; Bos. 86, 33; *p. of* a-secgan.

a-sǽlan; *p.* -sǽlde; *pp.* -sǽled [a, sǽlan *to bind*] *To bind fast, bind;* astringere, ligare:—Synnum asǽled *bound fast by sins,* Elen. Kmbl. 2485; El. 1244: Cd. 100; Th. 132, 18; Gen. 2195: 166; Th. 207, 21; Exod. 470.

a-sændan; *p.* -sænde; *pp.* -sænd *To send forth, to send,* Apol. Th. 6, 16: 13, 5. v. a-sendan.

a-sâh *set, sank,* Chr. 1012; Th. 268, 30, col. 1; 269, 28, col. 1; 26, col. 2; *p. of* a-sîgan.

asal, asald *an ass,* Mt. Lind. Stv. 18, 6: 21, 2. v. esol.

a-sânian; *p.* ode; *pp.* od *To languish, grow weak, diminish;* languescere, laxari:—Nǽfre ic lufan sibbe forlǽte asánian *never will I permit the love of my kin to languish*, Exon. 50 a; Th. 172, 23; Gú. 1148.

asaru *Asarabacca, folefoot, hazelwort;* asărum Europæum = ἄσαρον, L. M. 2, 14; Lchdm. ii. 192, 7.

a-sáwan; *p.* -seów, -siów, *pl.* -seówon; *pp.* -sáwen *To sow;* seminare, obserere, Bt. Met. Fox 20, 499; Met. 20, 250. v. sáwan.

asca *dust;* pulvis, Mk. Lind. Rush. War. 6, 11. v. asce.

asca, ascas, ascum:—Asca *of ash spears*, Exon. 78 a; Th. 292, 15; Wand. 99. v. æsc.

a-scacan *to shake off, to shake, brandish;* excutere, Ps. Th. 67, 10. v. asceacan.

a-scádan *to separate*, L. Wih. 3; Th. i. 36, 19. v. asceádan.

a-scæcan *to shake*, Exon. 58 a; Th. 207, 20; Ph. 144: Ps. Spl. 7, 13. v. a-sceacan.

a-scære; *adj.* [a, scær; *p. of* sceran *to cut, shear*] *Without tonsure, untrimmed;* intonsus, incultus, Peccatorum Medicina 8. v. æ-scære.

a-scafan; *p.* -scóf, *pl.* -scófon; *pp.* -scafen, -scæfen *To shave;* abradere, obradere:—Ascæfen *obrasus*, Cot. 148. v. scafan.

a-scamian; *p.* ode; *pp.* od *To be ashamed, to make ashamed* or *abashed;* erubescere, pudore confundere:—Ná ascamien on me *non erubescant in me*, Ps. Spl. 68, 8. Hí ascamode swíciaþ on swíman *they wander abashed in giddiness*, Exon. 26 b; Th. 79, 31; Cri. 1299. v. scamian.

Ascan mynster *Axminster*, Chr. 755; Th. 86, 13, col. 1. v. Acsan mynster, Axan mynster.

ASCE, æsce [*g.* æscean], acse, ahse, axe, axse, æxe, an; *f.* ASH, *ashes;* cinis:—On ðære ascan *in the ashes*, Exon. 59 a; Th. 213, 27; Ph. 231: 60 a; Th. 217, 24; Ph. 285. Gebreadad weorþeþ eft of ascan *it becomes formed again from* [*its*] *ashes*, 61 a; Th. 224, 9; Ph. 373. Ascan and ýslan *ashes and embers*, 64 a; Th. 236, 18; Ph. 576: 65 a; Th. 240, 33; Ph. 648. [*O.H.Ger.* asca, *f. cinis: Goth.* azgo, *f: O.Nrs.* aska, *f.*]

a-sceacan, -scacan, -scæcan; he -sceaceþ, -sceacþ, -scæceþ, -scaceþ; *p.* -sceóc, -scóc, *pl.* -sceócon, -scócon; *pp.* -sceacen, -scacen. I. *to shake off, remove;* excutere:—Asceacaþ ðæt dust of eówrum fótum *excutite pulverem de pedibus vestris*, Mk. Bos. 6, 11. II. *to be removed, forsake, desert, flee;* excuti, fugere, aufugere, deserere:—Asceacen [Lamb. ofascacen] ic eom *excussus sum*, Ps. Spl. C. 108, 22. Ðæt Iacob wæs asceacen *quod fugeret Jacob*, Gen. 31, 22. He asceacen wæs fram Æðelréde *he had deserted from Æthelred*, Chr. 1001; Ing. 174, 15. III. *to shake, brandish, to be shaken;* vibrare, quatere, concuti, labefieri, infirmari:—His swurd he acwecþ oððe asceacþ *gladium suum vibrabit*, Ps. Lamb. 7, 13. He ascæceþ feðre *it shakes its plumage*, Exon. 58 a; Th. 207, 20; Ph. 144: Ps. Spl. 7, 13. Offa æscholt asceóc *Offa shook his ashen spear*, Byrht. Th. 138, 35; By. 230. Wilsumne regn wolcen brincgeþ, and ðonne ascaceþ God sundoryrfe *pluviam voluntariam segregabis, Deus, hereditati tuæ, etenim infirmata est*, Ps. Th. 67. 10.

a-sceádan, -scádan; *p.* -scéd, *pl.* -scédon; *pp.* -sceáden, -scáden; *v. a.* [a *from*, sceádan *to divide*] *To separate, disjoin, exclude, distinguish;* separare, segregare:—Ic mec ascéd ðara scylda *I separated myself from the guilt*, Elen. Kmbl. 937; El. 470: 2623; El. 1313. And he hine from nýtenum ascéd *and he distinguished him from beasts*, L. E. I. 23; Th. ii. 420, 8. Hí of círicean gemánan ascádene síen *they from the church communion shall be excluded*, L. Wih. 3; Th. i. 36, 19. Ðæt eálond is feor asceáden fram Hibernia *insula ab Hibernia procul secreta est*, Bd. 4, 4; S. 570, 40.

a-sceáf *expelled*, Cd. 55; Th. 68, 11; Gen. 1115; *p. of* a-scúfan.

a-scealian; *p.* ode; *pp.* od [a *from*, scealu *a scale*] *To pull off the scales* or *bark, to scale, bark;* decorticare, Cot. 79.

a-sceamian *to be ashamed*. v. a-scamian.

a-scearpan *to sharpen*, Ps. Surt. 63, 4. v. a-scirpan.

a-scéd *separated*, Elen. Kmbl. 937; El. 470; *p. of* a-sceádan.

a-sceofen *expelled*, = a-scofen, Bd. 4, 12; S. 581, 17; *pp. of* a-scúfan.

a-sceónung, e; *f. Detestation, abomination;* abominatio, Mk. Bos. 13, 14. v. a-scúnung.

a-sceóp *gave*, Cd. 161; Th. 201, 32; Exod. 381. v. a-sceppan.

a-sceortian, -scortian; *p.* ode; *pp.* od *To be short, to grow short, shorten, elapse, diminish, fail;* breviare, effluere:—Ðæt wæter asceortode *the water failed*, Gen. 21, 15. Ten þúsend geára ascortaþ *ten thousand years will elapse*, Bt. 18, 3; Fox 66, 12.

a-sceótan; he -scýt, -scýtt; *p.* -sceát, *pl.* -scuton; *pp.* -scoten [a, sceótan *to shoot*] *To shoot forth, shoot, shoot out, fall;* jaculari, cum impetu erumpere:—Hie ne mehton from him nǽnne flán asceótan *they could not shoot an arrow from them*, Ors. 6, 36; Bos. 132, 8. Ne ascýtt Sennacherib flán into ðære byrig Hierusalem *Sennacherib shall not shoot arrows into the city of Jerusalem*, Homl. Th. i. 568, 31. Ða eágan of his heáfde ascuton, and on eorþan feóllan *the eyes shot out of his head, and fell on the earth*, Bd. 1, 7; S. 478, 38.

a-sceppan; *p.* -sceóp, -scóp, *pl.* -sceópon, -scópon; *pp.* -sceapen, -scapen *To create, appoint, give;* creare, designare:—Him God naman niwan asceóp *God gave him a new name*, Cd. 161; Th. 201, 32; Exod. 381.

a-scerian *to cut from, separate*. v. a-scirian.

a-scerpan *to sharpen*. v. a-scirpan.

ASCIAN, acsian, ahsian, axian; *p.* ode; *pp.* od. I. *to* ASK, *to ask for, to demand, inquire, to call, summon before one;* interrogare, postulare, exigere:—Ðe ðú me æfter ascast *which thou askest about*, Bt. 39, 4; Fox 216, 26, 29. Ne ascige ic nú ówiht bi ðam bitran deáþe mínum *I demand now nothing for my bitter death*, Exon. 29 b; Th. 90, 16; Cri. 1475. He ongan hine ahsian *he began to call him*, Cd. 40; Th. 53, 18; Gen. 863. II. *to obtain, experience;* nancisci, experiri:—He weán ahsode *he obtained woe*, Beo. Th. 2417; B. 1206: 851; B. 423. [*Orm.* asskenn: *Laym.* axien: *O.Sax.* éscón: *O.Frs.* askia, aschia: *Dut.* eischen: *Ger.* heischen: *M.H.Ger.* eischen: *O.H.Ger.* eiscón: *Dan.* äske: *Swed.* äska: *O.Nrs.* æskja *optare: Sansk.* ish *to wish, desire.*]

a-scilian; *p.* ede; *pp.* ed [a *from*, scel *a shell*] *To take off the shell, to shell;* enucleare, Cot. 171.

a-scínan; *p.* -scán, *pl.* -scinon; *pp.* -scinen *To shine forth, to be clear, evident;* clarescere, elucere:—Hwylc wǽre his líf cúþlícor ascíneþ *vita qualis fuerit certius clarescat*, Bd. 5, 1; S. 613, 14. Ðá ðǽr ascán beáma beorhtast *then there shone the brightest of beams*, Exon, 52 a; Th. 180, 20; Gú. 1282.

a-scirian, -scyrian; *p.* ede; *pp.* ed, ud; *v. a.* [a, scirian *to share*] *To cut from, separate, divide, part, sever;* separare, sejungere, excommunicare, destinare:—He ascirede Adames bearn *he separated Adam's sons*, Deut. 32, 8. Ascyrud beón fram mannum *moveri ab hominibus*, Somn. 280. Ascyred and asceáden scylda gehwylcre *sundered and set apart from every sin*, Elen. Kmbl. 2623; El. 1313: Exon. 31 b; Th. 98, 16; Cri. 1608. Ðæt he scyle from his Scippende ascyred weorþan to deáþe niðer *that he shall be separated from his Creator by death beneath*, Exon. 31 b; Th. 99, 2; Cri. 1618.

a-scirigendlíc *disjoining, disjunctive*. v. a-scyrigendlíc.

a-scirpan, a-scyrpan, a-scerpan, a-scearpan; *p.* te, tun; *pp.* ed *To sharpen;* exacuere:—Swíðor ablendaþ ðæs módes eágan ðonne hí hí ascirpan *they rather blind the eyes of the mind than sharpen them*, Bt. 34, 8; Fox 144, 34. v. scerpan.

ascirred = ascired *separated from, saved*, Bt. 20; Fox 72, 6; *pp. of* a-scirian.

a-scofen *banished*, R. Ben. 63. v. a-scúfan.

a-scóp *gave*, Ors. 1, 8; Bos. 31, 16. v. a-sceppan.

a-scortian *to shorten*, Bt. 18, 3; Fox 66, 12. v. a-sceortian.

a-scræp *he scraped;* radebat, Job 2, 8; Thw. 166, 33; *p. of* a-screopan.

a-screádian; *p.* ode; *pp.* od *To prune, lop;* præsecare, Anlct. Gl. DER. screádian.

a-screncan; *p.* -screncte; *pp.* -screnct [a, screncan *to supplant*] *To supplant:*—Ne eft sió þræsþing ðæs líchoman ðæt mód ne ascrence mid upahæfenesse *ne aut istos afflicta caro ex elatione supplantet*, Past. 43, 9; Hat. MS. 60 b, 3.

a-screopan; *p.* -scræp, *pl.* -scrǽpon; *pp.* -screpen *To scrape off, scrape;* radere:—Ascræp ðone wyrms of his líce *testa saniem radebat*, Job 2, 8; Thw. 166, 33. v. screopan.

a-screpan, -scrypan; *pp.* en *To bear, cast* or *vomit out;* egerere, Cot. 71. v. a-screopan.

a-scrincan; *p.* -scranc, *pl.* -scruncon; *pp.* -scruncen *To shrink;* arescere. v. scrincan.

a-scrypan *to cast out*. v. a-screpan.

asc-þrotu *fennel-giant*. v. æsc-þrote, an; *f.*

a-scúfan, -sceófan; *p.* -sceáf, *pl.* -scufon; *pp.* -scofen, -sceofen [a *from*, scúfan *to shove*] *To drive away, expel, banish, repel, shove away;* expellere, pellere, abigere, extrudere, emittere:—Forþ ascúfan *to drive forward*, Exon. 129 b; Th. 498, 1; Rä. 87, 6. Me cearsorge of móde asceáf þeóden usser *our Lord has driven anxious sorrow from my mind*, Cd. 55; Th. 68, 11; Gen. 1115. He wæs asceofen and adrifen of his biscop-setle *pulsus est a sede sui episcopatus*, Bd. 4, 12; S. 581, 17.

ascung, e; *f. An asking, a question, an interrogation, inquiry, inquisition;* interrogatio, inquisitio:—Ðæs sǽdes corn biþ simle aweaht mid ascunga *the grain of this seed is always excited by inquiry*, Bt. Met. Fox 22, 81; Met. 22, 41: Bt. 5, 3; Fox 12, 16. v. acsung.

a-scúnian; *p.* ode; *pp.* od; *v. a.* [a *away*, scúnian *to shun*]. I. *to avoid, shun, fly from;* evitare, reprobare:—He mót þyllíc ascúnian *he must shun the like*, L. C. S. 7; Th. i. 380, 9: L. Ed. 4; Th. i. 162, 6. II. *to hate, detest;* odisse, detestari:—Esau ascúnode Iacob *oderat Esau Jacob*, Gen. 27, 41. Ðá ascúnodon híg hine *oderant eum*, Gen. 37, 4. III. *to accuse, reprove, convict;* arguere:—Hwylc eówer ascúnaþ me for synne *quis ex vobis arguet me de peccato?* Jn. Bos. 8, 46.

a-scúniendlíc; *adj. Detestable, abominable;* detestabilis:—Beforan Gode ys ascúniendlíc *abominatio est ante Deum*, Lk. Bos. 16, 15.

a-scúnung, a-sceónung, e; *f. An execration, abomination, a detesta-*

tion; execratio, abominatio: — Ge geseóþ ðære toworpennysse asceónunge [ascũnunge, Jun.] *videritis abominationem desolationis,* Mk. Bos. 13, 14: Ps. Spl. 58, 14.

a-scuton *shot out,* Bd. 1, 7; S. 478, 38; *p. pl. of* a-sceótan.

a-scyled *taken out of the shell, shelled;* enucleatus, Cot. 75; *pp. of* a-scilian.

a-scyndan [a *from,* scyndan *to hasten*] *To separate, remove, take away;* tollere, elongare:—Ðũ ascyndest fram me freónd *elongasti a me amicum,* Ps. Spl. M. 87, 19.

a-scyrian *to separate,* Elen. Kmbl. 2623; El. 1313. v. a-scirian.

a-scyrigendlíc; *adj.* [ascirigende *disjoining,* from ascirian] *Disjoining, disjunctive;* disjunctivus, Ælfc. Gr. 44; Som. 45, 43.

a-scyrigendlíce; *adv. Disjunctively, severally;* disjunctive, Ælfc. Gr. 44? Lye.

a-scyrpan *to sharpen,* Ps. Th. 126, 5: Ps. Spl. C. 63, 3. v. a-scirpan.

a-sealcan; *pp.* asolcen *To languish, to be* or *become weak, idle, slothful, remiss;* languescere, remittere, desidiosum fieri:—Ne lǽt ðũ ðe ðín mõd asealcan wǽrfæst willan mínes *let not thou thy mind languish* [*to be*] *observant of my will,* Cd. 99; Th. 130, 30; Gen. 2167. Asolcen fram gõdre drohtnunge *slothful for good living,* Homl. Th. i. 306, 11: 340, 35. Asolcen *accidiosus?* vel *tediosus,* Ælfc. Gl. 114; Som. 80, 18; Wrt. Voc. 60, 52. Asolcen *dissolutus, desidiosus,* R. Ben. 48. Asolcen *deses,* Ælfc. Gr. 9, 26; Som. 11, 10. Asolcen *iners,* Cot. 108. Asolcen *remissus, ignavus,* Scint. 16.

a-seárian; *p.* ode; *pp.* od *To become dry, to sear, dry up;* arescere, Lchdm. iii. 355, 24.

a-seáþ *seethed; p. of* a-seóðan.

a-sécan, -sécean; *p.* -sõhte; *pp.* -sõht [a, sécan *to seek*]. I. *to search* or *seek out, to seek for, to require, demand;* eligere, requirere, petere aliquid ab aliquo:—Asécean ða sélestan *to seek out the best,* Elen. Kmbl. 2035; El. 1019: 813; El. 407. Mid swã mycle fõreseónysse wæs ðæs líchoman clǽnnesse asõht *tanta provisione est munditia corporis requisita,* Bd. 1, 27, resp. 8; S. 496, 8. Wyllaþ me lífes asécean *they will demand my life,* Ps. Th. 118, 95. II. *to seek, go to, explore;* adire, explorare:—Ðæt fýr georne aséceþ innan and ũtan eorþan sceátas *the fire shall eagerly seek the tracts of earth within and without,* Exon. 22 b; Th. 62, 20; Cri. 1004.

a-secgan, -sæcgan; *p.* -sægde, -sǽde; *pp.* -sægd, -sǽd [a *out,* secgan *to say*] *To speak out, declare, express, tell, say, relate, explain, announce, proclaim;* edicere, effari, exprimere, referre, enarrare, annunciare:—Ic him mín ǽrende asecgan wille *I will relate to him my errand,* Beo. Th. 693; B. 344. Heofonas asecgaþ wuldor Godes *cœli enarrant gloriam Dei,* Ps. Spl. C. 18, 1. Wundor asecgan *miraculum enarrare,* Bd. 3, 2; S. 524, 39. Gif seó gemyndelíc wíse asǽd biþ *if that memorable thing be told,* 4, 22; S. 590, 32: Bt. 34, 8; Fox 144, 22: 35, 1; Fox 154, 18. Him engel Godes eall asægde *God's angel told him all,* Cd. 179; Th. 225, 19; Dan. 156. Ðã asǽdon his geféran *then said his companions,* Ors. 4, 6; Bos. 86, 33. Õþ ðæt ic asecge *donec annunciem,* Ps. Th. 70, 17.

a-secgendlíc; *adj. That which may be spoken, expressible;* effabilis, Som.

a-sellan; *p.* -sealde; *pp.* -seald *To expel, banish, deliver;* expellere, relegare, tradere, Cd. 215; Th. 270, 14; Sat. 90. v. sellan.

a-sendan, ic -sende, ðũ -sendest, -sendst, -senst, he -sent, -sendeþ, *pl.* -sendaþ; *p.* -sende; *pp.* -sended, -send *To send forth, send out, send;* emittere, mittere:—Asend gãst ðínne and biþ gescapen *emitte spiritum tuum et creabuntur,* Ps. Spl. 103, 31. Ðonne ðũ of líce aldor asendest *when thou sendest forth life from thy body,* Cd. 134; Th. 168, 29; Gen. 2790. Drihten asent hungor on eów and þurst and næcede *the Lord shall send forth on you hunger and thirst and nakedness,* Deut. 28, 48. Ðæt he wolde asendan his ãncennedan Sunu *that he would send his only-begotten Son,* Homl. Th. ii. 22, 3: Ps. Spl. 105, 15. Ic eom asend *ego missus sum,* Lk. Bos. 1, 19. DER. sendan.

a-séngan *for* a-sénian [a, sénian *to see*] *To shew, discover, manifest;* manifestare, perspicuum facere:—Ðe ic aséngan ne mæg *which I may not discover,* Exon. 70 a; Th. 261, 11; Jul. 313.

a-seón, ic -seó, ðũ -síhest, -síhst, he -síheþ, -síhþ, *pl.* -seóþ; *p.* -sãh, *pl.* -sigon, -sihon; *impert.* -seóh; *pp.* -sigen, -sihen [a *from, out;* seón, síhan *to strain*] *To strain out;* percolare:—Aseóh ðone drenc, and dõ ðonne mele fulne buteran *strain out the drink, and then add* [*do*] *a basin full of butter,* L. M. 1, 36; Lchdm. ii. 86, 16.

a-seóðan; *p.* -seáþ, *pl.* -sudon; *pp.* -soden *To boil, seethe, scorch, to purify by seething;* coquere:—Swã man seolfor aseóðeþ mid fýre *as one seethes silver by fire,* Ps. Th. 65, 9. Ðé ic geceás on ðam ofne ðe ðũ on wǽre asoden, ðæt wæs on ðínum iermþum *elegi te in camino paupertatis,* Past. 26, 1; Hat. MS. 35 a, 6. Ðæt heó mid longre hire líchoman untrumnesse asodene beón *that she should be purified by the long suffering of her body,* Bd. 4, 23; S. 595, 15. Ealle we lǽtaþ to viii healf-marcum asodenes goldes *we estimate all at eight half-marks of pure gold,* L. A. G. 2; Th. i. 154, 2.

a-seów, -siów *sowed,* Bt. 33, 4; Fox 132, 26; *p. of* a-sãwan.

a-setan *to appoint, design;* destinare, R. Conc. pref.

a-seted, -sett *set, placed, stored, built,* Beo. Th. 1338; B. 667: Mt. Bos. 3, 10; *pp. of* a-settan.

a-séðan; *p.* -séðde; *pp.* -séðed *To affirm, confirm;* affirmare, confirmare:—Sume [adverbia] syndon ad vel confirmativa, mid ðám we aséðaþ ũre spræce *some adverbs are affirmative or confirmative, with which we affirm our speech,* Ælfc. Gr. 38; Som. 40, 16.

a-séðan *to boil.* v. seóðan.

a-setnys, -nyss, e; *f. What is set* or *fixed, a statute, law;* constitutio, statum: — Eádmundes cyninges asetnysse *king Edmund's institutes,* L. Edm. E. 1; Th. i. 244, 1.

a-settan; *p.* -sette; *pp.* -seted, -sett. I. *to set, put, place, appoint, lay, set up, erect, build, to set* or *take, to plant;* ponere, statuere, constituere, instituere, collocare, deponere, desumere, plantare:—He asette his swíðran hand under Abrahames þeóh *posuit manum sub femore Abraham,* Gen. 24, 9. He hæfde Grendle togeánes seleweard aseted *he had set a hall-ward against Grendel,* Beo. Th. 1338; B. 667. Eallunga ys seó æx to ðære treówa wurtrumum asett *jam enim securis ad radicem arborum posita est,* Mt. Bos. 3, 10. Hét ðã asettan líc on eorþan *he then commanded to place the body upon the earth,* Elen. Kmbl. 1750; El. 877. Ac heó hire ðǽr wíc asette *ibique sibi mansionem instituit,* Bd. 4, 23; S. 593, 26: Exon. 108 a; Th. 411, 27; Rä. 30, 6. Hét ǽnne weall asettan *he ordered a wall to be built,* Ors. 6, 15; Bos. 122, 34. Hét hí eft asettan *he bade her again be taken,* Exon. 69 a; Th. 256, 14; Jul. 231. Ic on neorxna wonge niwe asette treów mid telgum *I planted in paradise a new tree with branches,* Cd. 223; Th. 295, 5; Sat. 481. II. síþ asettan *to make a journey;* iter facere:—He in helle ceafl síþ asette *he made his journey into the jaws of hell,* Andr. Kmbl. 3404; An. 1706: Exon. 103 a; Th. 391, 26; Rä. 10, 11.

a-sette *set, placed, built,* Bd. 4, 23; S. 593, 26; *p. of* a-settan.

asicyd; *part.* [a *from,* sũcan *to suck*] *Taken from suck, weaned;* ablactatus:—Swã swã asicyd ofer mõdor *sicut ablactatus super matre,* Ps. Spl. M. C. 130, 4.

a-siftan; *p.* -sifte; *pp.* -sift *To sift;* cribrare:—Asift þurh clãþ *sift through a cloth,* L. M. 1, 2, 21; Lchdm. ii. 36, 7. v. siftan.

a-sígan; *p.* -sãh, *pl.* -sigon; *pp.* -sigen *To decline, go down, fall down;* delabi, occidere:—Ðæt, mid ðam dynte, he nyðer asãh *that, with the blow, he fell down,* Chr. 1012; Th. 268, 30, col. 1; 269, 28, col. 1; 269, 26, col. 2. Lǽt ðínne sefan healdan freán dõmas, ða ðe hér men forlǽtaþ asígan *let thy mind observe the Lord's decrees, which here men permit to decline,* Exon. 81 a; Th. 304, 24; Fä. 75.

a-sigen *fallen; pp. of* a-sígan.

a-sindrian; *p.* ode; *pp.* od *To sunder, separate.* v. a-syndran.

a-singan; *p.* -sang, *pl.* -sungon; *pp.* -sungen [a, singan] *To sing;* canere:—Ðæt man asinge *that a man sing,* Ps. Th. 91, 1: Beo. Th. 2323; B. 1159: Bd. 3, 27; S. 559, 12.

Asirige *The Assyrians;* Assyrii:—Ðæt synd Asirige and Rõmãne *these are the Assyrians and the Romans,* Ors. 2, 5; Bos. 49, 14. v. Assyrias.

a-sittan; *p.* -sæt, *pl.* -sǽton; *pp.* -seten *To dwell together;* considere:—Secgas, mid sigecwén, aseten hæfdon, on Créca land *the men had a dwelling together with the victorious queen, in the land of the Greeks,* Elen. Kmbl. 1993; El. 998. v. sittan II.

a-slacian, -slæcian; *p.* ode, ade, ude; *pp.* od, ad, ud *To slacken, loosen, untie, remit, dissolve, enervate;* laxare, remittere, solvere, dissolvere, dimittere, hebetare, enervare, Cot. 103: 169: Prov. 19: 10. v. slacian.

a-slacigendlíc; *adj. Remissive;* remissivus:—Sume [adverbia] syndon remissiva, ðæt synd aslacigendlíce [lytlum *paulatim,* softe *suaviter, etc.*] *some* [*adverbs*] *are* remissiva, *that is remissives, etc.* Ælfc. Gr. 38; Som. 40, 29.

a-slacigendlíce; *adv. Slackly, remissly;* remisse, Ælfc. Gr. 38? Lye.

aslãd *slipped away.* v. aslídan.

a-slæccan; *p.* -slæcte; *pp.* -slæced, -slæct *To slacken, loosen, remit;* laxare, remittere. v. slæccan, slacian.

a-slæcian; *p.* ude; *pp.* ud *To dissolve;* dimittere, Cot. 62. v. a-slacian.

a-slægen *struck,* Lye. v. a-sleán.

a-slãpan; *p.* -slép, *pl.* -slépon; *pp.* -slãpen [a, slãpan = slǽpan *to sleep*] *To be sleepy, begin to sleep, fall asleep;* dormitare:—Mín sãwl aslép *dormitavit anima mea,* Ps. Th. 118, 28.

a-slãwian; *p.* ode; *pp.* od *To be heavy, dull, sluggish;* torpescere, Ors. 4, 13; Bos. 100, 20.

a-sleán; *p.* -slõh, *pl.* -slõgon; *pp.* -slegen, -slagen, -slægen *To strike, beat, hammer, to fix, erect;* ferire, icere, cædere, figere, ponere:—On býman aslegenum [Lamb. onaslagenum], Ps. Spl. 97, 6; *in tubis ductilibus,* Vulg; in trumpis beten out, Wyc. Hí aslõgan ãn geteld *tetenderunt tentorium,* Bd. 3, 17; S. 543, 33, col. 1; 5, 6; S. 619, 26. Ðe of his líchoman aslegen wæs *that was struck off his body,* Bd. 3, 12; S. 537, 34. v. sleán. DER. on-asleán; *pp.* on-aslagen.

a-slépen = a-sleópen *slip away,* Bt. Met. Fox 13, 18; Met. 13, 9. v. a-slũpan.

a-slídan; ic -slíde, ðũ -slídest, -slíst, he -slídeþ, -slít, *pl.* -slídaþ; *p.* -slãd, *pl.* -slidon; *pp.* -sliden *To slide* or *slip away;* labare:—Ne aslīt his fōt *non supplantabuntur gressus ejus,* Ps. Th. 36, 31. Ðæt mīn fōt asliden wǽre *motus est pes meus,* 93, 17. Asliden beón *labi,* Scint. 13, 24, 78.

a-slītan, -slȳtan; *p.* -slāt, *pl.* -sliton; *pp.* -slyten, -sliten; *v. a.* [a *from,* slītan *to slit*] *To cleave, rive, destroy, cut off;* discindere, diruere, abscindere:—Aslāt ða tūnas ealle *destroyed all the villages,* Bd. 3, 16; S. 542, 20. Mildheortnysse his aslȳteþ of cneórysse on cynrine *misericordiam suam abscindet a generatione in generationem,* Ps. Spl. 76, 8.

a-slōh, -slōgon *struck, fixed,* Bd. 3, 17; S. 543, 33, col. 1; *p. of* a-sleán.

a-slūpan; *p.* -sleáp, *pl.* -slupon; *pp.* -slopen *To slip away;* elabi:—Lǽt ðē aslūpan sorge of breóstum *let sorrow slip away from thy breast,* Cd. 134; Th. 169, 7; Gen. 2796. Ðæt hī ǽfre him of aslēpen [= a-sleópen] *that they may ever slip from them,* Bt. Met. Fox 13, 18; Met. 13, 9.

a-slȳtan; *p.* -slāt; *pp.* -slyten; *v. trans. To cut off:*—Aslȳteþ *abscindet,* Ps. Spl. 76, 8. v. a-slītan.

a-smeágan, -smeán; *p.* -smeáde; *pp.* -smeád *To look closely into, examine, trace out, elicit, meditate upon, consider, contemplate, ponder, judge, deem, be of opinion, think;* perscrutari, investigare, indagare, elicere, contemplari, pensare, censere:—Nū ne māge we asmeágan hū God of ðam lāme flǽsc worhte and blōd, bān and fell, fex and næglas *now we cannot trace out how of the loam God made flesh and blood, bones and skin, hair and nails,* Homl. Th. i. 236, 15. Stīge mīne ðū asmeádest *semitam meam investigasti,* Ps. Spl. 138, 2: R. Ben. 55. Asmeágende *indagantes,* Cot. 104. Asmeáde *elicuit,* Cot. 77. Gif man hit ariht asmeáþ *if one rightly considers it,* L. Edg. C. 13; Th. ii. 246, 21. Ic dēme oððe ic asmeáge *censeo,* Ælfc. Gr. 26, 2; Som. 28, 51.

a-smeágung, e; *f. Investigation, meditation;* scrutinium, investigatio, meditatio:—Þurh asmeágunge bōclīce snotornesse *through investigation of book-like wisdom,* Apol. Th. 3, 16.

a-smiðian; *p.* ode; *pp.* od; *v. trans. To forge, make, work as a smith;* fabricare:—Asmiðod *fabricatus,* Cot. 82.

a-smorian; *p.* ede, ode; *pp.* ed, od; *v. trans. To smother, choke, strangle, suffocate;* suffocare:—Asmoraþ ðæt word *suffocat verbum,* Mt. Rush. Stv. 13, 22. Hī hine on his bedde asmoredan and aþrysemodan *they smothered and stifled him on his bed,* Ors. 5, 4; Bos. 105, 5. Ðæt ge ne blōd ne þicgen, ne asmored [MS. H. asmorod] *that ye taste not blood, nor* [*what is*] *strangled,* L. Alf. 49; Th. i. 56, 26.

a-snǽsan, -snāsan; *p.* de; *pp.* ed; *v. trans.* I. *to hit* or *strike against, to stake oneself upon anything;* impingere:—Gif beforan eágum asnāse [MS. H. asnǽse] *if he stake himself before his eyes,* L. Alf. pol. 36; Th. i. 84, 14. II. *to wrest anything from another?* extorquere, L. Noel, Lye. DER. on-snǽsan, ona-.

a-snīðan; *p.* -snāþ, *pl.* -snidon; *pp.* -sniden; *v. trans. To cut off;* amputare. v. snīðan *to cut.*

a-soden *sodden, boiled, tried by seething,* Bd. 4, 23; S. 595, 15; *pp. of* a-seóðan.

a-sogen *sucked,* Cot. 193; *pp. of* a-sūgan.

a-sōht *sought out, searched,* Bd. 1, 27, resp. 8; S. 496, 8; *pp. of* a-sēcan.

a-solcen, a-swolcen; *part. Idle, lazy, dissolute, slow, slothful;* remissus, desidiosus, Homl. Th. i. 306, 11. v. a-sealcan.

a-solcennys, -nyss, e; *f. Idleness, sloth, slothfulness, sluggishness, laziness;* ignavia, desidia, pigritia:—Heora līðnys is asolcennys and nȳtennys *their mildness is sloth and ignorance,* Homl. Th. ii. 46, 11: 220, 21. Se sixta heáfodleáhter is asolcennyss *the sixth chief sin is slothfulness,* 218, 22. Þurh ūre asolcennysse *through our sluggishness,* Th. Diplm. A. D. 970; 240, 12: Homl. Th. i. 602, 8.

a-spanan; *p.* -spōn, -speón, *pl.* -spōnon, -speónon; *pp.* -spanen, -sponen; *v. trans. To allure from, entice, induce, urge, persuade, introduce secretly;* allicere, illicere, impellere, persuadere, attrahere, subintroducere:—Gif he ða cwēne gespannan [MS. B. aspanan] and gelǽran mihte, ðæt heó brūcan wolde his gesynscipes *si reginæ posset persuadere ejus uti connubio,* Bd. 4, 19; Whel. 304, 42, note. Hēr aspōn Æðelwald ðone here to unfriþe *in this year Æthelwald allured the army to a violation of the peace,* Chr. 905; Th. 180, 18, col. 1. Hine Hannibal aspōn, ðæt he ðæt gewinn leng ongan *Hannibal induced him to carry on the war longer,* Ors. 4, 11; Bos. 97, 15. He aspeón him fram ealle *he enticed all from him,* 1, 12; Bos. 35, 19: 2, 2; Bos. 41, 8: 5, 2; Bos. 102, 21. Aspeón ōðerne bisceop *subintroduxit alium episcopum,* Bd. 3, 7; S. 530, 4.

a-spāw *vomited out; p. of* a-spīwan.

a-spēdan; *p.* -spēdde; *pp.* -spēded, -spēdd *To speed, prosper;* prosperare:—Wītum aspēdde *made prosperous by their sufferings,* Andr. Kmbl. 3261; An. 1633.

a-spelian; *part.* a-speliende; *p.* ode, ade; *pp.* od, ad *To supply another's room, to be deputy* or *proxy for another, represent another;* vicario munere fungi, vicem *vel* locum alicujus supplere:—He mōste his hlāford aspelian *he might represent his lord,* L. R. 3; Th. i. 192, 3: R. Ben. 58. Aspelad beón *to have one's place supplied by another;* excusari, R. Ben. 35.

a-spendan; *p.* de; *pp.* ed [a, spendan *to spend*] *To spend entirely, consume, squander, to spend, expend, lay out, bestow, distribute;* consumere, dissipare, expendere, sumptum facere, erogare, impertiri:—Ðonne hys gestreón beóþ ðus eall aspended *when his property is thus all entirely spent,* Ors. 1, 1; Bos. 22, 43. Ic aspende yfele *distraho,* Ælfc. Gr. 47; Som. 48, 52. Ic aspende [asende MS.] oððe gife *impertior,* 37; Som. 39, 13. Aspendan þearfum *to spend on the poor;* erogare pauperibus, R. Ben. interl. 58: Scint. 1.

a-speón *enticed, secretly introduced,* Ors. 1, 12; Bos. 35, 19: Bd. 3, 7; S. 530, 4. v. a-spanan.

a-sperian *to track, trace, investigate;* investigare, Prov. 20. v. a-spyrian.

aspide, es; *m. An asp, viper, serpent;* aspis, ĭdis; *f.* = ἀσπίς, ἴδος; *f. a sort of serpent remarkable for rolling itself up in a spiral form: α negative, and* σπίζω *to extend,* Scapulæ Lexicon:—Aspidas *aspides,* Ps. Th. 139, 3. Anlīc nædran, ða aspide ylde nemnaþ *like a serpent, which men call an asp,* Ps. Th. 57, 4. Spl. Lamb. in Ps. 57, 4 *have* nædran *instead of* aspide. Ðū ofer aspide miht gangan *thou mayest go over an asp* [super aspidem], Ps. Th. 90, 13; Lamb. *has* ofer nædran, 90, 13.

a-spirian, -spirigan; *p.* ede; *pp.* ed *To search, trace:*—Aspirige hit ūt *let him trace it out,* L. Ath. iv. 2; Th. i. 222, 14. v. a-spyrian.

a-spīwan; *p.* -spāw, *pl.* -spiwon; *pp.* -spiwen *To spew out, vomit forth;* evomere, vomere:—Aspau = aspāw *evomuit,* Cot. 78: Peccat. Medic. 5.

a-spōn *allured, induced,* Chr. 905; Th. 180, 18, col. 1: Ors. 4, 11; Bos. 97, 15. v. a-spanan.

a-spreádan; *p.* de; *pp.* ed [= a-sprǽdan] *To spread forth, extend;* prætendere:—Aspreád mildheortnysse ðīne *prætende misericordiam tuam,* Ps. Spl. T. 35, 11. v. sprǽdan.

a-sprecan; *p.* -spræc, *pl.* -sprǽcon; *pp.* -sprecen [a, sprecan] *To speak out, speak;* eloqui, loqui:—Hwylc mæg ǽfre mihta Drihtnes asprecan and aspyrian *quis loquetur potentias Domini?* Ps. Th. 105, 2. Ðū asprǽce *locutus es,* 59, 5: 58, 12: 73, 21.

a-spreótan; *p.* -spreát, *pl.* -spruton; *pp.* -sproten; *v. intrans.* [a, spreótan] *To sprout forth, break forth;* progerminare, erumpi, eructare:—Swā unefne is eorþe þicce, syndon ðas mōras myclum asprotene *sicut crassitudo terræ erupta est super terram,* Ps. Th. 140, 9.

a-sprettan *to sprout out;* germinare, pullulare, Solil. 9. v. a-sprȳtan.

a-sprian; *v. a. To lay before, shew?* prætendere, Bd. 4, 19.

a-sprincan; *p.* -spranc, *pl.* -spruncon; *pp.* -spruncen *To spring up, arise;* oriri, exoriri:—Aspruncen is on þȳstrum leóht *exortum est in tenebris lumen,* Ps. Spl. 111, 4: C. R. Ben. 7. v. a-springan.

a-sprindlad; *part.* [= a-springlad? from springan *to spread,* or sprengan *to burst open*] *Torn asunder, ripped up;* diruptus, L. M. 2, 24; Lchdm. ii. 216, 7.

ā-spring *a water-spring, fountain;* scaturigo, Hom. de Comp. Cordis, Lye. v. ǣ-spring.

a-springan, -spryngan, -sprincan; *p.* -sprang, *pl.* -sprungon; *pp.* -sprungen; *v. intrans.* I. *to spring up, arise, originate, break forth;* surgere, assurgere, oriri, exoriri, rumpi, prorumpi:—Aspryngþ rihtwīsnys *orietur justitia,* Ps. Spl. 71, 7: R. Ben. 69. Asprang *ortum traxit,* Lupi Serm. 3, 7. Ðā asprungon ealle wyllspringas ðære micelan niwelnisse *rupti sunt omnes fontes abyssi magnæ,* Gen. 7, 11. II. *to spring out, lack, fail, cease, fall away;* deficere, desinere:—Asprang gāst mīn *defecit spiritus meus,* Ps. Spl. C. 76, 3. Asprong hālig *defecit sanctus,* 11, 1: 72, 19. Ne ðām fore yrmþum ðe ðǽr inwuniaþ līf aspringeþ *nor, through sorrows, shall life fail to them that dwell therein,* Exon. 32 b; Th. 103, 8; Cri. 1685: 30 b; Th. 94, 11; Cri. 1538. Wrōht wæs asprungen *strife had ceased,* Cd. 5; Th. 6, 4; Gen. 83: Ps. Th. 54, 10. Ðæt hī ne asprungan fram heora geleáfan *ne a fide deficerent,* Bd. 2, 9; S. 511, 6.

a-sprīt *shall sprout out,* Gen. 3, 18. v. a-sprȳtan.

a-spruncen *arisen.* v. a-sprincan.

a-sprungennes, -sprungennys, -ness, e; *f.* [asprungen *failed, ceased; pp. of* a-springan] *An eclipse, deficiency, failing, fainting, exhaustion;* eclipsis, defectio:—Wæs geworden sunnan asprungennys *facta erat eclipsis solis,* Bd. 3, 27; S. 558, 10. Asprungynnes nam me *defectio tenuit me,* Ps. Spl. C. 118, 53.

a-spryngan *to spring up, arise,* Ps. Spl. 71, 7. v. a-springan.

a-sprȳtan, -sprītan; *p.* -sprȳtte, -sprītte; *pp.* -sprȳted *To sprout out, cause to sprout out;* germinare:—Þornas and bremelas heó asprīt ðē *spinas et tribulos germinabit tibi,* Gen. 3, 18. v. sprȳtan, spryttan.

a-spȳlian, -spȳligan; *p.* ode; *pp.* od *To cleanse, wash, purify;* abluere:—Swīn nyllaþ aspȳligan [aspȳlian MS. Cot.] on hluttrum wæterum *swine will not wash in pure waters,* Bt. 37, 4; Fox 192, 27. [*Plat.* afspölen: *Dut.* afspoelen: *Ger.* abspülen.]

a-spyrgan *to search, explore, investigate,* Exon. 92 b; Th. 348, 16; Sch. 29. v. a-spyrian.

a-spyrgeng, e; *f. An inventing, invention;* adinventio, Cot. 186.

a-spyrian, -spyrigan, -spyrigean; *p.* ede; *pp.* ed *To search, explore, trace, discover, explain;* investigare, indagare, explorare, enucleare:—Ϸe ðe nele, be his andgites mǽðe, ða bōclīcan gewritu aspyrian, hū hī to

Criste belimpaþ *he who will not, according to the measure of his understanding, search the book-writings, how they refer to Christ,* Homl. Th. ii. 284, 30. Aspyrige hit ût *let him trace it out,* L. Ath. iv. 2; Th. i. 222, 14, note 33. Ðæt mihte ðæra twegra tweón aspyrian *that might discover the difference of the two,* Salm. Kmbl. 870; Sal. 434: Elen. Kmbl. 932; El. 467. Ic aspyrige *enucleo,* Ælfc. Gr. 26, 6; Som. 29, 18; Ps. Th. 105, 2.

assa, an; *m:* asse, es; *m. A male ass;* asinus:—Se assa geseah ðone engel *asinus cernebat angelum,* Num. 22, 23, 25. Beót ðone assan *verberabat asinum,* 22, 23, 25. Gif ðû gemête ðînes feóndes assan, lǽd hine to him *si occurreris inimici tui asino erranti, reduc ad eum,* Ex. 23, 4: 23, 5. Wîlde assan *wild asses;* onagri, Ps. Spl. C. 103, 12. Ðâ feóll se asse adûne *tum concidit asinus,* Num. 22, 27. He hæfde on olfendum and on assum micele ǽhta *he had great possessions in camels and in asses,* Gen. 12, 16: 22, 5. [*O. Nrs.* asni, *m. asinus.*] v. asse, esol.

Assan dûn, e; *f.* [assan, dûn *a hill: 'Assendun* S. Hovd. *i. e.* vertente Florent. *mons asini,'* Gib.] *Assingdon* or *Ashingdon, in Essex:*—Se cyning offêrde hî innon Eást-Seaxan, æt ðære dûne ðe man hǽt Assandûn *the king overtook them in Essex, at the hill which is called Assingdon,* Chr. 1016; Th. 282, 19, col. 2: 1020; Th. 286, 16, 19, col. 1.

asse, an; *f:* assen, e; *f. A she-ass;* asina:—Uppan assan folan sittende *sedens super pullum asinæ,* Jn. Bos. 12, 15. Finde gyt âne assene *ye [two] shall find a she-ass,* Mt. Bos. 21, 2. Rît uppan tamre assene *rides on a tame she-ass,* 21, 5. Lǽddon ða assene to him *adduxerunt asinam,* 21, 7.

Asse-dun; *adj.* [asse *asina; or* asce *ash,* cinis; dun *dun* or *grey,* fuscus] ASS-DUN or ASH-DUN, *of a dun* or *dark colour;* dosinus, cinereus:—Assedun *dosinus* vel *cinereus,* Ælfc. Gl. 79; Wrt. Voc. 46, 39. 'Glossæ Isidori: *Dosius* vel *dosinus, equus asinini pili,'* Du Cange.

ass-myre, an; *f. A mare ass, she-ass;* asina:—And xx assmyrena *and twenty of mare asses,* Gen. 32, 15.

Assyria, æ; *f. Assyria,* Cd. 12; Th. 15, 13; Gen. 232.

Assyrias; *gen.* Assyria, Assiria; *dat.* Assyrium; *pl. m. The Assyrians;* Assyrii:—Assyria ealdorduguþ *the people of the Assyrians,* Judth. 12; Thw. 26, 4; Jud. 310.

Assyrige; *gen.* a; *dat.* um; *pl. m. The Assyrians;* Assyrii:—Ðæt synd Assyrige and Rômâne *these are the Assyrians and the Romans,* Ors. 2, 5; Bar. 77, 31. v. Assyrias.

ast *a kiln;* siccatorium:—Cyln oððe ast *siccatorium,* Ælfc. Gl. 109; Som. 78, 132. v. cyln.

a-stælan [a, stælan *to steal*] *To steal out, to seduce;* obrepere:—Ðæt me nǽfre deófol on astælan ne mǽge *that the devil may never secretly creep on me* [*seduce me*], L. De. Cf. 9; Wilk. 88, 49. v. stelan.

a-stǽnan; *p.* de; *pp.* ed *To adorn with stones* or *gems;* lapidibus *vel* gemmis ornare:—Gimmum astǽned *adorned with gems,* Salm. Kmbl. 128; Sal. 63. Mid deórwyrþum gimmum astǽned *de lapide pretioso ornata,* Ps. Th. 20, 3. Astǽned gyrdel *a girdle set with stones,* Cot. 201.

a-stâh *ascended,* Chr. 1012; Th. 268, 29, col. 2; *p. of* a-stîgan.

a-standan; *p.* -stôd, *pl.* -stôdon; *pp.* -standen. I. *to stand up, get up, rise up, rise;* exsurgere, resurgere, surgere:—Ðâ astôd he semninga *exsurrexit repente,* Bd. 2, 9; S. 511, 20. He up astandeþ of slǽpe *he rises up from sleep,* Exon. 96 a; Th. 358, 4; Pa. 40. Eft lîfgende up astôdon *they stood up living again,* 24 b; Th. 71, 18; Cri. 1157. II. *to insist, persist, continue;* persistere, instare:—Ðæt hî on ðam geleáfan sôþfæstnysse symle fæstlîce astôdon and awunedon *ut in fide veritatis persisterent semper ac proficerent,* Bd. 2, 17; S. 520, 21, note: 4, 25; S. 599, 31. Hîg astôdon *illi instabant,* Lk. Bos. 23, 23.

a-steápan, -steópan, -stêpan; *p.* -steápde, -steápte; *pp.* -steáped, -steapt *To deprive, bereave, as children of their parents;* orbare, orphanum reddere:—Sîen bearn his asteápte *fiant filii ejus orphani,* Ps. Surt. 108, 9. [*O. H. Ger.* stiufan *orbare,* arstiufan *viduare: Swed.* stufwa, stubba *to cut off: O. Nrs.* stýfa *abrumpere, abscindere.*]

a-stellan; *p.* -stealde, -stalde; *pp.* -steald; *v. a. To set forth, to set, place, afford, supply, appoint, establish, ordain, undertake, undergo, begin;* statuere, collocare, instituere, præbere, stabilire, fundare, suscipere, inire:—Bîsene astellan *exemplum præbere,* Past. 3, 1; Hat. MS. 8 b, 5. Asteald to býsne *set for an example,* Ors. 2, 4; Bos. 44, 33. Crist hit astealde and tǽhte *Christ established and taught it,* Homl. Th. ii. 582, 29. Heofonas, and môna, and steorran, ða ðû astealdest *cœlos, lunam et stellas, quæ tu fundasti,* Ps. Th. 8, 4. Astealde ðæt gewin *undertook the war,* Ors. 2, 5; Bos. 46, 26. Stephanus ðone martyrdôm astealde *Stephen suffered* [*underwent*] *martyrdom,* Homl. Th. i. 50, 2. Ðone fleám ǽrest astealde Þurcytel *Thurkytel first began the flight,* Chr. 1010; Th. 262, 43. DER. up-a-stellan. v. stellan.

a-stemnian; *p.* nede; *pp.* ned [a *from,* stemnian *to build*] *To proceed from a foundation, to found, build, erect;* condere:—Ðe hî sylf astemnedon *which they themselves built,* Bd. Pref; S. 472, 17.

a-steópan *to bereave.* v. a-steápan.

a-steorfan; *p.* -stearf, *pl.* -sturfon; *pp.* -storfen *To die;* mori:—Fǽrunge astorfen *sideratus* vel *ictuatus,* Ælfc. Gl. 114; Som. 80, 29; Wrt. Voc. 61, 9: Wanl. Catal. 43, 17.

a-stêpan; *p.* -stêpte; *pp.* -stêped, -stêpt *to bereave, as children of their parents,* Gr. Dial. 1, 2: Ps. Vos. 108, 8. v. a-steápan.

a-stêpnes, -ness, e; *f. A privation;* orbatio, Cot. 187.

a-stêpte *bereaved, orphans,* Ps. Vos. 108, 8. v. a-stêpan, a-steápan.

astered *disturbed, stirred, moved; pp. of* a-sterian.

a-sterfan; *p.* de; *pp.* ed *To cause death, kill, destroy;* necare, eradicare, Mt. Rush. Stv. 15, 13. v. a-styrfan.

a-sterian; *p.* ede; *pp.* ed *To agitate, stir, move;* commovere, movere:—He astereþ ðone rôdor and ða tungla *it moves the sky and the stars,* Bt. 39, 8; Fox 224, 6, note. v. a-styrian.

asterion, es; *n.* [=ἀστέριον] *The herb pellitory, so called from its star-like form;* astericum, Herb. 61; Lchdm. i. 164, 1, 10.

a-stîfian; *p.* ede, ode; *pp.* ed *To stiffen, grow* or *wax stiff;* obrigere, Cot. 146. His sine astîfode *his sinew stiffened,* Gen. 32, 32.

a-stîfician, -stîficigan; *p.* ode; *pp.* od; *v. a. To eradicate, extirpate, destroy, exterminate;* eradicare:—Ðæt he astîficige unþeáwas *that he exterminate vices,* Bt. 27, 1; Fox 94, 23.

a-stîgan, ic -stîge, ðû -stîgest, -stîhst, he -stîgeþ, -stîhþ, *pl.* -stîgaþ; *p.* -stâg, -stâh, *pl.* -stigon; *impert.* -stîh; *pp.* -stigen [a, stîgan *to go*]. I. *to go, come, step, proceed, climb;* ire, venire, gradi, procedere, scandere:—Hwider sceal ðæs monnes môd astîgan *thither shall the mind of man go,* Exon. 32 b; Th. 103, 21; Cri. 1691. Egsa astîgeþ *dread shall come,* 102 a; Th. 385, 24; Rä. 4, 49. Word-hleóðor astâg *the sound of words came,* Andr. Kmbl. 1416; An. 708: Bd. 4, 3; S. 568, 2. Se Hâlega Gâst astâh lîchamlîcre ansýne *the Holy Spirit came in bodily form,* Lk. Bos. 3, 22. Se môt wuldres dreám astîgan *he may climb the delight of glory,* Exon. 84 b; Th. 317, 30; Môd. 73: Ps. Th. 79, 10. Ic astîge *scando,* Ælfc. Gr. 28, 6; Som. 32, 30. II. *to go in any direction:* 1. *generally indicated by a preposition* or *adverb, hence to rise, ascend, descend, etc;* surgere, ascendere, descendere:—Ðe þurh oferhyd up astîgeþ *who comes up through pride,* Cd. 198; Th. 247, 11; Dan. 495. He from helle astâg *he came from hell,* Exon. 48 b; Th. 168, 14; Gû. 1077. Ðæt he mid ðam dynte nyðær astâh *that he came down with the blow,* Chr. 1012; Th. 268, 29, col. 2. Astîgaþ [Spl. C. upastîgaþ] mûntas, and niðer astîgaþ feldas on stôwe *the mountains ascend, and the fields go down into their place;* ascendunt montes et descendunt campi in locum, Ps. Lamb. 103, 8. Moises âna astîhþ to Drihtne *Moses alone goes to the Lord;* solus Moyses ascendit ad Dominum, Ex. 24, 2. Astîh on Fasgan mûntes cnæpp *go to the top of mount Pisgah;* ascende cacumen Phasgæ montis, Deut. 3, 27. He astâh on scyp *he went into a ship;* ascendit in naviculam, Mt. Bos. 8, 23: 9, 1. He nyðer astîhþ swâ swâ rên on flýs, and swâ swâ niðer astîhþ droppetung, droppende ofer eorþan *he shall come down as rain on a fleece, and as falling* [*rain*] *comes down, dropping over the earth;* descendet sicut pluvia in vellus, et sicut stillicidium stillantium [MS. stillicidia stillantia] super terram, Ps. Lamb. 71, 6. 2. *but sometimes the direction is indicated in the sentence without a preposition:*—Hire môd astâh *her mind rose,* Cd. 101; Th. 134, 35; Gen. 2235: 205; Th. 253, 18; Dan. 597. He astîgeþ swâ se rên fealleþ on flýs *he shall come as the rain falleth on a fleece;* descendet sicut pluvia in vellus, Ps. Th. 71, 6.

a-stîgend, es; *m. A rider;* ascensor:—Hors and astîgend [MS. astîgende] aweorpeþ on sîe *equum et ascensorem dejecit in mare,* Cant. Moys. Ex. 15, 1; Thw. 29, 6. v. stîgan.

a-stîgnes, -ness, e; *f. An ascent, ascending;* ascensus, Ps. Spl. T. 103, 4.

a-stîh *go, ascend,* Deut. 3, 27; *impert. of* a-stîgan.

a-stîhst, a-stîhþ *ascendest, ascends,* Jn. Bos. 3, 13; *2nd and 3rd pres. of* a-stîgan.

a-stihtan; *p.* -stihte; *pp.* -stiht [a, stihtan *to dispose*] *To determine on;* decernere:—Fleám wearþ astiht *flight was determined on,* Chr. 998; Th. 246, 22. v. stihtan.

a-stintan; *p.* -stant, *pl.* -stunton; *pp.* -stunten = -stinted, Som. Lye, = -stint = -stynt *To make dull, to blunt, stint, assuage;* hĕbĕtare, obtundere, Scint. 12: Cot. 101. v. a-stynt, stintan.

a-stirian *to move, remove, agitate, stir up, raise,* Lk. Bos. 6, 48. v. a-styrian.

astîðian; *p.* ode, ude; *pp.* od, ud [a *intensive,* stîðian *to become hard*] *To become hard, dry, dry up, wither;* indurare, arescere:—Astîðude swâ swâ tigle miht mîn *my strength dried up as a tile,* Ps. Spl. 21, 14. Hit astîðaþ and drugaþ *induret et arescat,* 89, 6.

a-stôd *stood up, insisted,* Bd. 2, 9; S. 511, 20: Lk. Bos. 23, 23; *p. of* a-standan.

a-stondnes, -ness, e; *f. An existence, a subsistence;* subsistentia:—Âna God on þrým astondnessum *one God in three subsistences;* unum Deum in tribus subsistentiis, Bd. 4, 17; S. 585, 38.

a-storfen; *part. Starved, like a dead body;* cadaverosus, Wanl Catal. 43, 17. v. a-steorfan.

a-streahte, -streaht *stretched out; p. and pp. of* a-streccan.

a-streccan; ic -strecce, ðū -strecest, he -strecþ; *p.* -streahte, -strehte; *impert.* -strece; *pp.* -streaht, -streht; *v. a. To stretch out, to extend, prostrate,* or *lay low, to prostrate oneself, bow down*; extendere, expandere, prosternere, se prosternere, adorare:—Ðe leas he astrecce his hand *ne forte mittat manum suam,* Gen. 3, 22: 22, 12. He neowol astreaht feól on ða flōre *he fell stretched prostrate on the floor,* Bt. Met. Fox 1, 159; Met. 1, 80. Ðā feóll Abram astreht to eorþan *cecidit Abram pronus in faciem,* Gen. 17, 3. Astrehte hine to eorþan *adoravit in terram,* Gen. 18, 2: Mt. Bos. 18, 26, 29: Mk. Bos. 3, 11.

a-stregdan; *p.* -stregde; *pp.* -stregd [a, stregdan *to sprinkle*] *To sprinkle, scatter, strew*; aspergere:—Ðū astregdest me mid hysopon *asperges me hyssopo,* Ps. Spl. T. 50, 8.

astreht, astrehte *prostrated*; *pp. and p. of* a-streccan.

astrengd *Malleable*; ductilis, Ælfc. Gl. 115; Som. 80, 46; Wrt. Voc. 61, 24.

a-strīcan; *p.* -strāc, *pl.* -stricon; *pp.* -stricen *To strike*; percutere. v. strīcan.

a-striénan, -strȳnan; *p.* -strȳnde; *v. a. To engender, procreate, beget*; gignere:—Hie ðā ongunnon bearn astriénan *they began then to beget children,* Cd. 46; Th. 59, 19; Gen. 966. He bearn astrȳnde *he begat children,* 57; Th. 70, 5; Gen. 1148. v. streónan, strȳnan.

astrihilthet [astre *a house,* hold *a master,* þeowet *a fine?* Mann.] *A fine levied on a householder*; compensatio facta a domino mansionis, L. Ed. C. 26; Th. i. 454, 2, MS. L.

a-stundian *To* ASTOUND, *grieve, suffer grief, to bear*; dolere, R. Ben. 36, Mann.

a-stȳfecigan *to exterminate,* Bt. 27, 1; Fox 94, 23, note 9. v. a-stīfician.

a-styltan *to astonish*; stupescere. v. styltan.

a-stynt *made dull*; hĕbĕtātus, Cot. 101. v. a-stintan.

a-styrfan; *p.* de; *pp.* ed *To cause death, kill, slay*; necare:—Stānum astyrfed *slain with stones,* Exon. 10 b; Th. 12, 27; Cri. 192. v. a-sterfan.

a-styrian, -stirian; *p.* ode, ede; *pp.* od, ed *To remove, move, agitate, stir violently, stir up, raise*; amovere, removere, movere, commovere:—Astyre fram me wītu ðīne *amove a me plagas tuas,* Ps. Spl. 38, 13: 118, 29: Rood Recd. 59; Kr. 30. Drihten astyrede ða wēstan stōwe *commovit Dominus desertum,* Ps. Th. 28, 6: 17, 7. Simle ðonne ðǣr ān tweó ofadōn biþ, ðonne biþ ðǣr unrīm astyred *always when there is one doubt removed, then is there an innumerable multitude raised,* Bt. 39, 4; Fox 216, 19.

a-styrred *starred*; stellatus, Scint. 58.

a-styrung, e; *f. A motion*; motus, Lye. v. stirung.

a-suand = a-swand *weakened.* v. a-swindan.

a-sūcan, -sūgan; *p.* -seác, -seág, *pl.* -sucon, -sugon; *pp.* -socen, -sogen *To suck*; sugere:—Asogen wǣre *sugeretur,* Cot. 193. Sina beóþ asocene [Exon. asogene] *the sinews shall be sucked,* Soul Kmbl. 217; Exon. 99 b; Th. 373, 19; Seel. 111. v. sūcan.

a-sudon *seethed*; *p. pl. of* a-seóðan.

a-sūgan *to suck,* Exon. 99 b; Th. 373, 19; Seel. 111. v. a-sūcan.

asundran, asundron; *adv.* ASUNDER, *apart, alone, privately*; seorsum:—Eall he hys leorning-cnihtum asundron rehte *seorsum discipulis suis disserebat omnia,* Mk. Bos. 4, 34. v. sunder.

a-sundrian, -syndrian; *p.* ode, ade; *pp.* od, ad [a *from,* sundrian *to sunder*] *To put asunder, to sunder, separate, disjoin, sever*; separare:—Se deáþ asundraþ līc and sāwle *death separates body and soul,* Exon. 98 a; Th. 367, 7; Seel. 4: 50 a; Th. 172, 27; Gū. 1150. Asundrod fram synnum *separated from sins,* Elen. Kmbl. 2615; El. 1309. Asundrad, Exon. 59 a; Th. 214, 20; Ph. 242.

a-sungen *sung,* Beo. Th. 2323; B. 1159; *pp. of* a-singan.

a-suond = a-swand *languished,* Cot. 101; *p. of* a-swindan.

a-sūrian; *p.* ode; *pp.* od *To be* or *become sour, tart, bitter*; acescere, Cot. 10: 177. v. sūrian.

a-swǣman *to wander about*; vagari, Exon. 52 b; Th. 183, 12; Gū. 1326. [vide H. Z. x. 315.]

a-swǣpþ *sweeps away,* Past. 36, 8; Hat. MS. 48 b, 16; *pres. of* a-swāpan.

a-swǣrnung, -swārnung, e; *f. Bashfulness, confusion*; verecundia:—Aswǣrnung [aswǣrnunga MS. aswārnung Ps. Lamb.] mīn ongeán me is *verecundia mea contra me est,* Ps. Spl. 43, 17. v. sceamu.

a-swāf *wandered away*; exorbitavi, exorbitavit; *p. of* a-swīfan.

a-swāmian; *p.* ode; *pp.* od *To languish, fail, cease*; tabescere, deficere [H. Z. x. 315], Cd. 19; Th. 24, 12; Gen. 376.

a-swand *languished away,* Ps. Lamb. 106, 26; *p. of* a-swindan.

a-swāp, es; *n*; *pl.* a-swāpa *Sweepings, dust*; peripsema, = περίψημα, purgamentum. v. a-swāpan.

a-swāpan; he -swāpþ, -swǣpþ; *p.* -sweóp, *pl.* -sweópon; *pp.* -swōpen *To sweep off, clean*; verrere, mundare:—Hit aswǣpþ aweg ðæt yfel *abstergat mala,* Past. 36, 8; Hat. MS. 48 b, 16: Exon. 106 b; Th. 405, 21; Rä. 24, 5. Aswōpen clǣne *mundatus,* Mt. Rush. Stv. 12, 44. v. swāpan.

a-swarcan *To languish, consume*; tabescere:—A-ȳdlian oððe aswarcan oððe acwīnan oððe aswindan ðū dydest swā swā ǣtterloppan oððe ryngan sāwle his *tabescere fecisti sicut araneam animam ejus,* Ps. Lamb. 38, 12.

a-swarcian; *p.* ode; *pp.* od *To confound, dismay, abash, fear*; confundere, revereri:—Ðon gescynde and aswarcode [MS. aswarcod] beóþ *cum confusi et reveriti fuerint,* Ps. Spl. 70, 26.

a-swārnian; *p.* ode; *pp.* od *To be confounded*; confundi:—Ðæt hī aswārnian *that they be confounded,* Ps. Spl. 85, 16. v. a-swarcian.

a-swārnung, e; *f. Bashfulness,* Ps. Lamb. 43, 16. v. a-swǣrnung.

a-swearc *languished, failed,* Jos. 2, 11; *p. of* a-sweorcan.

a-sweartian; *p.* ode; *pp.* od *To blacken, darken, to be made* SWARTHY or *black, obscured, darkened*; denigrari:—Ðæt gold biþ asweartod *aurum obscuratur,* Past. 18, 4; Hat. MS. 26 b, 8.

a-swebban; *p.* -swefede, *pl.* -swefedon; *pp.* -swefed; *v. a.* [a *intensive,* swebban *to put to sleep*] *To sooth, appease, set at rest, put to death, destroy*; sopire, sedare, necare, dolere:—He ðone storm aswefede and gestilde *tempestatem sopivit,* Bd. 3, 15; S. 542, 5: Exon. 58 b; Th. 210, 15; Ph. 186. Sweordum aswebban *to put to death with swords,* Andr. Kmbl. 143; An. 72. He his ealdordōm synnum aswefede *his eldership he had destroyed by sins,* Cd. 160; Th. 199, 9; Exod. 336.

a-swefecian; *p.* ade; *pp.* ad *To eradicate*; eradicare:—Aswefecad *eradicatus,* Cot. 75: 199.

a-swefed, -swefede, -swefedon; *pp. and p. of* a-swebban.

a-swellan; *p.* -sweall, *pl.* -swullon; *pp.* -swollen *To swell*; tumere:—Se earm wæs swīðe aswollen *the arm was much swollen,* Bd. 5, 3; S. 616, 7. v. swellan.

a-sweltan; *p.* -swealt, *pl.* -swulton; *pp.* -swolten *To die*; mori, Cot. 147: 62. v. sweltan.

a-swengan; *p.* -swengde; *pp.* -swenged *To shake out* or *off, to cast forth*; excutere:—He aswengde Pharaon in ðæm reádan sǣ *excussit Pharaonem in Mari Rubro,* Ps. Surt. 135, 15.

a-sweorcan; *p.* -swearc, *pl.* -swurcon; *pp.* -sworcen [a, sweorcan *to dim, darken*] *To languish, fail*; caligare, elanguere:—Aswearc ūre mōd *elanguit cor nostrum,* Jos. 2, 11.

a-sweorfan; *p.* -swearf, *pl.* -swurfon; *pp.* -sworfen *To rub off, to file off, polish*; expolire:—To asworfenum ōran, to gesworfenum ōran *sub expolita,* Glos. Prudent. Recd. 142, 19. v. sweorfan.

a-sweotole; *adv. Clearly*; manifeste, Bt. 34, 4; Fox 138, 16. v. sweotol.

a-swerian; *p.* -swōr, *pl.* -swōron; *pp.* -sworen; *v. a. To swear*; jurare:—Ðæs deópne āþ Drihten aswōr *juravit Dominus veritatem,* Ps. Th. 131, 11. Ðæt he hine for hōle ǣr ne aswōre *non frustrabitur eam,* 131, 11. DER. swerian.

a-swīcan; *p.* -swāc, *pl.* -swicon; *pp.* -swicen; *v. a.* [a *from,* swīcan *to go*] *To go away from any one, to desert any one, to deceive, betray, offend*; desciscere, deficere ab aliquo, prodere, scandalizare:—Ne aswīc sundorwīne *do not desert a particular friend,* Exon. 80 b; Th. 301, 34; Fä. 29. Eádrīc aswāc his cynehlāforde *Eadric betrayed his royal lord,* Chr. 1016; Erl. 158, 5. Gif ðīn swīðre hand ðē aswīce *si dextra manus tua scandalizat te,* Mt. Bos. 5, 30.

a-swīcian; *p.* ode; *pp.* od *To offend*; scandalizare:—Gyf ðīn swīðre eáge ðē aswīcie [aswikie, Hat. MS.] *si oculus tuus dexter scandalizat te.* Mt. Kmbl. Rl. 5, 29.

a-swīfan; *p.* -swāf, *pl.* -swifon; *pp.* -swifen *To wander out of the way, to wander about*; exorbitare, Cot. 76: 188. v. swīfan.

a-swind, æ-swind; *adj. Slothful, sluggish, idle*; iners, Cot. 108.

a-swindan; *p.* -swand, *pl.* -swundon; *pp.* -swunden [a *away,* swindan *to languish*] *To languish away, to enervate, pine, consume away, to decay, perish, dissolve*; tabescere, torpescere, consumi:—Hwȳ ge swā aswundene sión *why are ye so enervated?* Bt. 40, 4; Fox 238, 31. Ðȳlæs ealle gesceafta aswindaþ *lest all creatures perish,* Bt. 33, 4; Fox 130, 34. Aswindan me dyde anda mīn *tabescere me fecit zelus meus,* Ps. Spl. C. 118, 139: 111, 9: 106, 26. Aswunden *reses,* Ælfc. Gr. 9, 26; Som. 11, 11. A-ȳdlian oððe aswarcan oððe acwīnan oððe aswindan ðū dydest swā swā ǣtterloppan oððe ryngan sāwle his *tabescere fecisti sicut araneam animam ejus,* Ps. Lamb. 38, 12.

a-swindung, e; *f. Idleness, sloth*; desidia. DER. aswind.

a-swōgan; *p.* -swēg, *pl.* -swēgon; *pp.* -swōgen [a, swōgan *to rush*] *To rush into, invade, overrun, choke*; irruere, invadere, occupare, suffocare:—We wīton ðæt we lufiaþ ðone æcer ðe ǣr wæs mid þornum aswōgen, and æfter ðæm ðe ða þornas beóþ aheáwene and se æcer biþ onered, bringþ gōdne wæstm *we know that we love the land which before was overrun with thorns, and after that the thorns are dug out and the land is ploughed up, brings good fruit,* Past. 52, 9; Hat. MS. 81 b, 23.

a-swolcen *idle*; iners, Cot. 108. v. a-solcen.

a-swollen *swollen,* Bd. 5, 3; S. 616, 7. v. a-swellan.

a-swond = a-swand *he weakened, enervated*; enervavit, Cot. 71; *p. of* a-swindan.

a-swondennes, -ness, e; *f. Slothfulness*; inertia. v. a-swundennes.

a-swōpen *swept, cleaned*:—Aswōpen clǣne *mundatus,* Mt. Rush. Stv. 12, 44. v. a-swāpan.

a-sworetan; *p.* te; *pp.* ed *To sigh, draw a deep breath*; suspirare:—He hefiglîce asworette *graviter suspiravit*, Bd. 3, 11; S. 536, 33. v. sworetan.

a-sworfen *polished*, Glos. Prudent. Recd. 142, 19; *pp. of* a-sweorfan.

a-swunan; *p.* -swan, *pl.* -swônon; *pp.* -swunen *To swoon*; deficere animo. v. a-swâmian.

a-swunden *weakened, slothful*, Ælfc. Gr. 9, 26; Som. 11, 11; *pp. of* a-swindan.

a-swunden-lîce; *adv. Slothfully*; segniter. v. a-swunden.

a-swundennes, -ness, -nys, -nyss, e; *f. Slothfulness, idleness*; inertia:—His lîf toscǽgde fram ussa tîde aswundennysse *vita illius a nostri temporis segnitia distabat*, Bd. 3, 5; S. 526, 35. v. a-swindan.

a-swýðerian, -swýðrian; *p.* ade; *pp.* ad *To make heavy* or *grievous, aggravate, increase, make stronger*; gravare, aggravare, ingravare, augere. v. swíðrian.

a-syndran, -syndrian; ic asyndrige; *p.* ede, ode; *pp.* ed, od [a *from*, syndrian *to sunder, part*] *To put* ASUNDER, *to separate, disjoin, sever*; separare:—Ic com mann asyndrian ongên his fæder *veni separare hominem adversus patrem suum*, Mt. Bos. 10, 35: Ps. Spl. 67, 10. Se deáþ asyndreþ lîc and sâwle *death sunders body and soul*, Soul Kmbl. 7; Seel. 4. v. a-sundrian.

a-syndrung, e; *f. A division, separation, divorce*; divortium, Cot. 68.

at- *at*; apud, ad; *used in composition for* æt-, as in at-ýwan, *p.* -ýwde; at-âwian, *p.* -âwode *ostendere*, Ps. Spl. T. 77, 14. v. at-âwian.

a-tæfran, -tiefran, -tifran; *p.* ede; *pp.* ed *To depict, paint*; depingere:—Ic hæbbe atæfred *I have depicted*, Past. 65; Hat. MS.

at-âwian; *p.* ode; *pp.* od *To shew*; ostendere:—He atâwode him *ostendit eis*, Ps. Spl. T. 77, 14. v. æt-eówian, æt-ýwan.

at-berstan; *p.* -bærst, *pl.* -burston; *pp.* -borsten *To break out, escape*; erumpere, Chr. 607; Ing. 30, 9. v. æt-berstan.

ÂTE, ǽte; *gen.* âtan; *pl.* âtan; *gen.* âtena; *f.* OATS, *tares, darnel, cockle*; avena fatua, Lin. lolium:—Nim âtena grâtan *take groats of oats*, Lchdm. iii. 292, 24. Genim mela ǽtena *take meal of oats*, L. M. 1, 35; Lchdm. ii. 84, 5: Chr. 1124; Th. 376, 6. Âte *lolium*, Cot. 126. Âtan *or* lasor *tares*; zizania, Cot. 204. [*Frs.* ôat: *O. Nrs.* ât *food.*]

a-teáh *drew out* or *away, went, came*, Exon. 29 b; Th. 91, 19; Cri. 1494: Beo. Th. 1537; B. 766; *p. of* a-teón.

a-tefred *painted*, Solil. 4. v. a-tæfran.

ate-gâr, es; *m. A javelin*; framea. v. æt-gâr.

atel *dire, terrible*:—Se atela gǽst *the dire spirit*, Exon. 34 a; Th. 109, 9; Gû. 87. v. atol, *adj.*

a-telan *to reckon*, Bt. 8; Fox 24, 21; *for* a-tellan.

atelîc; *adj.* [=atol, lîc] *Dire, terrible, horrid, foul, loathsome*; dirus, terribilis, horridus, deformis, fœdus:—Norþ-Denum stôd atelîc egesa *over the North-Danes stood dire terror*, Beo. Th. 1572; B. 784. Unwlitig swile and atelîc *tumor deformis*, Bd. 4, 32; S. 611, 17. v. atol.

a-tellan; *p.* -tealde, *pl.* -tealdon; *pp.* -teald; *v. trans.* [a, tellan] *To tell out, enumerate, reckon, explain, interpret*; dinumerare, numerare, interpretari:—Hwylc wât ânweald yrres ðînes, and for ege ðînum graman ðinum atellan *quis novit potestatem iræ tuæ, et pro timore tuo iram tuam dinumerare?* Ps. Spl. C. 89, 13. Gif ðû nû atellan wilt ealle ða blîþnessa wið ðâm unrôtnessum *if thou wilt now reckon all the enjoyments against the sorrows*, Bt. 8; Fox 24, 21, note 6. Wit gesâwon swefen, ac wyt nyton hwâ hyt unc atelle *nos duo somnium vidimus, et non est qui interpretetur nobis duobus*, Gen. 40, 8.

atelucost, R. Ben. 1; *for* atelîcost; *sup. of* atelîc *foul.*

a-temian; *p.* ede; *pp.* ed [a *intensive*, temian *to tame*] *To tame thoroughly, make very tame* or *gentle, to subdue, tame*; edomare:—Atemiaþ hira lîchoman *edomant carnem*, Past. 46, 2; Hat. MS. 66 a, 10. Sum sceal wildne fugel atemian *one shall tame the wild bird*, Exon. 88 b; Th. 332, 15; Vy. 85: 89 b; Th. 336, 11; Gn. Ex. 46: Bt. Met. Fox 13, 38; Met. 13, 19: 13, 71; Met. 13, 36. DER. un-atemed.

a-tendan; *p.* de; *pp.* ed; *v. trans.* [a *intensive*, tendan *to tind, set on fire*] *To set on fire, kindle, inflame*; accendere, incendere, inflammare;—Hî atendon hiora herebeácen *they kindled their war-beacons*, Chr. 1006; Th. 256, 24, col. 1. Hî mid fýre atendan woldan *they wished to set it on fire*, Chr. 994; Th. 241, 32, col. 2.

a-tendend, es; *m. An incendiary, inflamer, inciter*; incensor, inflammator, Scint. 78.

a-tendincg=atending, e; *f. A fire-brand, an incentive, a provoking*; incentivum, Scint. 81.

a-teón; ic -teó, ðû -týhst, he -týhþ, -tîhþ, -tíþ, *pl.* -teóþ; *p.* -teáh, *pl.* -tugon; *pp.* -togen [a *from, out*; teón *to tow, draw*]. I. *v. trans.* generally with a preposition: *to draw out* or *away, pull out, lead out, pluck, draw*; abstrahere, extrahere, ejicere, educere, trahere, ducere:—For ðam ðe he wolde ateón ðê fram Drihtne *quia voluit te abstrahere a Domino*, Deut. 13, 10. Ðonne he atîþ hine, Ps. Surt. 9, 30. Ðonne he fram atîhþ [atýgþ MS. C.] hine *dum abstrahet eum*, Ps. Spl. second 9, 11. Seó mæg ateón ǽlces cynnes âttor ût of men *which can draw poison of every kind out of man*, Ors. 5, 13; Bos. 113, 33. Mid atogenum swurde *evaginato gladio*, Num. 22, 22. He ateáh rib of sîdan *he extracted a rib from his side*, Cd. 9; Th. 11, 19; Gen. 177. Lǽt, ðæt ic ateó ða egle of ðînum eágan *sine ejiciam festucam de oculo tuo*, Lk. Bos. 6, 42. Gif ðû up atýhst and awyrtwalast of gewitlocan leása gesǽlþa *if thou pluckest up and rootest out of thy mind false felicities*, Bt. Met. Fox 12, 49; Met. 12, 25. Ðâ ic ðec from helle ateáh *when I drew thee from hell*, Exon. 29 b; Th. 91, 19; Cri. 1494: 124 b; Th. 479, 4; Rä. 62, 2. Mûþ mîn ic ontýnde, and ic ateáh to [to geteáh MS. C.] gâst *os meum aperui, et attraxi spiritum*, Ps. Spl. 118, 131. Hîg ne mihton hit ateón *non valebant illud trahere*, Jn. Bos. 21, 6. II. *to treat, use, dispose of, employ*; tractare, uti, adhibere:—Ðû ðîn âgen môst mennen ateón swâ ðîn môd freóþ *thou mayest treat thine own maidservant as thy mind inclines* (*liketh*), Cd. 103; Th. 136, 14; Gen. 2258. Ðâ his fýnd hine ne meahton ateón swâ hý woldon *when his enemies might not treat him as they would*, Ps. Th. arg. 9. Ateóh hyne swylce brôðer *tracta eum sicut fratrem*, Scint. 60: Nicod. 14; Thw. 7, 7. Hû hîg sceoldon ðæs Hǽlendes wurþ ateón *how they should dispose of the Saviour's price*, Mt. Bos. 27, 7. III. *intrans.* or with a cognate noun: *to draw to any place, betake oneself anywhere, go, come, make a journey* or *expedition*; se recipere, meare, proficisci, ire, venire, iter facere:—Siððæt se hearmscaða to Heorute ateáh *after the injurious scather came to Heorot*, Beo. Th. 1537; B. 766. Wîg-sîþ ateáh *went on a warlike expedition*, Cd. 96; Th. 126, 13; Gen. 2094: 167; Th. 208, 28; Exod. 490: 208; Th. 256, 34; Dan. 650: Exon. 37 a; Th. 120, 15; Gû. 272.

a-teorian, -teorigan; *p.* ede, ode; *pp.* ed, od; *v. intrans. To fail, become weary, cease, leave off*; deficere, fatiscere, cessare, desistere:—Geteorigende ateoraþ *deficientes deficient*, Ps. Spl. 36, 21. Ateorode hâlig *defecit sanctus*, Ps. Spl. 11, 1. Ateorode on sâre lîf mîn *defecit in dolore vita mea*, 30, 12. Hîg ateoredon smeágende mid smeáunge *defecerunt scrutantes scrutinio*, Ps. Lamb. 63, 7. Ateorodun *defecerunt*, 9, 7: Cot. 69: Greg. Dial. 1, 1: R. Ben. interl. 53.

a-teorigendlîc; *adj.* [a-teorigende *part. of* a-teorigan *to fail*, lîc] *Failing, fleeting, perishable*; caducus, fugax:—Seó yld is geteald to ǽfnunge ðises ateorigendlîcan middaneardes *that age is considered as the evening of this fleeting world*, Homl. Th. ii. 266, 6.

a-teorung, e; *f. A failing, fainting, weariness*; defectio, fatigatio. v. ge-teorung.

at-eówad, -eówed; *part. Shewn, made known*; ostensus. v. æt-eówian.

âter *poison*; venenum. v. âtor.

âter-drinca, an; *m. A poisonous potion* or *drink, poison*; potio venenata, venenum, Cot. 24. v. âtor, *etc.*

a-terian; *p.* ede; *pp.* ed *To fail, become weary*; deficere, fatigare:—Atered *fatigatus*, Ælfc. Gl. 87; Wrt. Voc. 50, 20: R. Ben. interl. 53. v. a-teorian.

âter-lâðe, an; *f. The plant cock's leg*; panicum crus galli. Betonica? Cot. 24. v. âtter-lâðe.

âter-lîc; *adj. Poison-like*; veneno similis:—Âterlîc *vel* biter *gorgoneus*, Cot. 98, = âtor-lîc.

âter-tân, es; *m. A poisonous rod, twig*; vimen venenosum:—Ecg wæs îren, âtertânum fâh *the edge was iron, tainted with poisonous twigs*, Beo. Th. 2923; B. 1459.

ÂÞ, es; *m.* I. *an* OATH, *a swearing*; juramentum:—Ðû agyltst ðîne âþas *reddes juramenta tua*, Mt. Bos. 5, 33. Ðâ behêt he mid âþe *pollicitus est cum juramento*, 14, 7, 9. He âþ swereþ þurh his selfes lîf *he sweareth an oath by his own life*, Cd. 163; Th. 205, 5; Exod. 431: Ps. Th. 131, 11. Hî sealdon unwillum hâlige âþas *they gave unwillingly holy oaths*, Bt. Met. Fox 1, 49; Met. 1, 25. Gif ðæt geswutelod wǽre, oððe him âþ burste, oððe ofercýðed wǽre *if that were made evident, or an oath failed to them, or were out-proven*, L. Ed. 3; Th. i. 160, 20. Nû on worulde hêr monnum ne deriaþ mâne âþas *now here in the world wicked* [*false*] *oaths do not inflict injury on men*, Bt. Met. Fox 4, 96; Met. 4, 48. Mid unforedan âþe *with an unbroken oath*; pleno juramento, L. Wil. ii. 3; Th. i. 489, 25. Ðæt he ðonne âþ funde gif he mæhte ungecorenne *that he bring forward the oath of persons unchosen if he could*, L. Ed. 1; Th. i. 158, 18. II. *every accusation must be verified by oath*: *the accused and his witness then replied also upon oath*; *thus*, 1. Ðæs âþ ðe his ǽhte bryideþ, ðæt he ne dǽþ ne for hete ne for hôle:—'On ðone Drihten, ne teó ic N. ne for hete ne for hôle ne for unrihtre feohgyrnesse; ne ic nân sôþre nât; bûte swâ mîn secga me sǽde, and ic sylf to sôþe talige, ðæt he mînes orfes þeóf wǽre' *The oath of him, who takes his* [*own*] *property, that he does it neither for hatred nor for envy*:—'*By the Lord, I accuse not N. neither for hatred nor for envy, nor for unlawful lust of gain; nor know I anything soother; but as my informant to me said, and I myself in sooth think, that he was the thief of my property.*' 2. Ðæs ôðres âþ ðe he is unscyldig:—'On ðone Drihten, ic eom unscyldig, ǽgþer ge dǽde ge dihtes æt ðære tîhtlan ðe N. me tîhþ' *The other's oath that he is guiltless*:—'*By the Lord, I am guiltless, both in deed and purpose, of the accusation of which N. accuses me.*' 3. His gefêran âþ ðe him mid standaþ:—'On ðone Drihten, se âþ is clǽne and unmǽne ðe N. swôr' *His companion's oath who stands with him*:—'*By the Lord, the oath is clean and unperjured which N. has sworn,*'

L. O. 4-6; Th. i. 180, 8-19. III. Ânfeald âþ [lâd] *a simple oath [exculpation]*; simplex juramentum [purgatio] hoc est, accipiat duos, et sit ipse tertius, et sic jurando conquirat simplicem purgationem. Þrŷfeald âþ *a threefold oath*; triplex juramentum, hoc est, accipiat quinque, et ipse sit sextus, L. C. S. 22; Th. i. 388, 11, 12, and note b. [*Plat.* êd: *O. Sax.* êd: *O. Frs.* eth, ed: *Dut.* eed: *Ger.* eid: *M. H. Ger.* eit; *gen.* eides: *O. H. Ger.* eid: *Goth.* aiþs: *Dan.* eed: *Swed.* ed: *O. Nrs.* eiðr, *m.*] v. ânfeald âþ.

âþ-brice, es; *m. A breaking of an oath, perjury*; perjurium, Wulf. 8.

â ðe, â ðŷ *Ever the*; unquam eo:—Â ðe, â ðŷ deórwyrþran *ever the more precious*, Bt. 14, 2; Fox 44, 2. Â ðŷ mâ *ever the more*, Bt. 40, 2; Fox 236, 30. Â ðŷ betera *ever the better*, Bt. 13; Fox 38, 9. v. ðŷ.

a-þecgan; *p.* -þegde; *pp.* -þeged, -þegd *To receive*; recipere, excipere, Exon. 100 b; Th. 380, 3, 12; Rä. 1, 2, 7.

âþe-gehât *an oath*, Ælfc. Gl. 13; Som. 57, 119; Wrt. Voc. 20, 56. v. âþ-gehât.

a-þegen; *part.* [a, þegen; *pp. of* þecgan *sumere*] *Full, stuffed out*; distentus, Cot. 63.

a-þencan, -þencean; *p.* -þohte; *pp.* -þoht. I. *to think out, devise, invent*; excogitare:—Gif we hit mægen wihte aþencan *if we may devise it in any way*, Cd. 21; Th. 26, 2; Gen. 400: 179; Th. 224, 35; Dan. 146: Ors. 1, 10; Bos. 33, 28. II. *to think, intend*; cogitare, intendere, velle:—He ðis ellenweorc âna aþohte to gefremmanne *he thought this bold work to perform alone*, Beo. Th. 5280; B. 2643.

a-þenian; *p.* ede, ode; *pp.* ed, od; *v. a.* [a *out*, þenian *to stretch*]. I. *to stretch out, extend, distend, expand, stretch*; tendere, extendere, expandere:—Aþene ðîne hand, and he hî aþenede *extende manum tuam, et extendit*, Mt. Bos. 12, 13: Ps. Th. 59, 7: 103, 3. Gif se maga aþened sîe *if the stomach be distended*, L. M. cont. 2, 2; Lchdm. ii. 158, 4. Bogan his he aþenede *arcum suum tetendit*, Ps. Spl. 7, 13. II. *to prostrate*; prosternere:—Hî aþenedon hî *they prostrated themselves*, Mt. Bos. 2, 11. III. *to stretch, apply*; intendere:—He ða geornlîce his môd aþenode on ða þing, ðe he gehŷrde *ille sollicitus in ea, quæ audiebat, animum intendit*, Bd. 4, 3; S. 567, 45.

a-þenung, e; *f. An extending, extension*; extensio. v. a-þenian.

a-þeódan; *p.* -þeódde; *pp.* -þeóded [a *from*, þeódan *to join*] *To disjoin, separate*; disjungere:—Aþeódde from Gode *disjuncti a Deo*, Gr. Dial. 2, 16.

a-þeóstrian; *p.* ode, ade, ede; *pp.* od *To overcloud, to be eclipsed*; obumbrare, obscurare:—Aþeóstrade *obscuravit*, Ps. Surt. 104, 28: Chr. 538; Th. 28, 6, col. 2, Cott. Tiber. A. vi; col. 3, Cott. Tiber. B. 1. v. a-þŷstrian.

a-þeótan; he-þŷteþ; *p.* -þeát, *pl.* -þuton; *pp.* -þoten *To wind, sound, blow*; inflare, canere:—Næfre mon ðæs hlûde horn aþŷteþ, ne bŷman ablâweþ *never so loudly one sounds a horn, nor blows a trumpet*, Exon. 117 b; Th. 451, 26; Dôm. 109. v. þeótan.

âðer *either*; alter, Ors. 3, 9; Bos. 68, 11. v. âðor.

a-þêstrian; *p.* ode; *pp.* od *To be eclipsed*; obscurari:—Seó sunne aþêstrode *the sun was eclipsed*, Chr. 538; Th. 29, 4, col. 1; Bodl. Laud. 636. v. a-þŷstrian.

âðexe, an; *f. A lizard, newt*; lacerta, Som. [*O. Sax.* egithassa: *Dut.* hagedisse: *Ger.* eidechse: *M. H. Ger.* egedehse: *O. H. Ger.* egidehsa.] v. efete.

âþ-fultum, es; *m.* [âþ *an oath*, fultum *a help, support*] *The support to an oath*, i. e. *the supporters of an oath, those who support one's oath, who will swear for another as witnesses*; sacramentales:—Freónd-leás weofod-þên, ðe âþfultum næbbe *a friendless servant of the altar, who has no support to his oath*, L. C. E. 5; Th. i. 362, 19: L. Eth. ix. 22; Th. i. 344, 23.

âþ-gehât, âþe-gehât, es; *n.* [âþ *an oath*, gehât *a promise*] *A promise on oath, sacred pledge, an oath*; sacramentum:—Âþ-wed *vel* âþe-gehât *sacramentum*, Ælfc. Gl. 13; Som. 57, 119; Wrt. Voc. 20, 56. v. âþ-wed.

a-þierran; *p.* de; *pp.* ed *To wash off* or *away, rinse, make clean, purge, clear*; diluere:—Hit is þearf, ðæt sió hond sîe ǽr geclǽnsad, ðe wille ðæt fenn of ôðerre aþierran *necesse est ut esse munda studeat manus, quæ diluere sordes curat*, Past. 13, 1; Hat. MS. 16 b, 8.

a-þiéstrian; *p.* ode; *pp.* od *To overcloud, to be eclipsed*; obscurari:—Seó sunne aþiéstrode *the sun was eclipsed*, Chr. 538; Th. 28, 6, 11, col. 1. v. a-þŷstrian.

a-þindan; *p.* -þand, *pl.* -þundon; *pp.* -þunden *To puff up, swell, inflate*; intumescere:—He ðâ ðone aþundenan sǽ gesmylte *tumida æquora placavit*, Bd. 5, 1; S. 614, 8. Gif he aþunden sŷ *if he be swollen*, Herb. 1, 21; Lchdm. i. 76, 27. Aþindaþ *occurs in* Ps. Th. 106, 25 *as a translation of* tabescebat; *the translator confounded* tabescere *with* tumescere. v. þindan.

a-þindung, e; *f. A swelling* or *puffing up*; tumor, Som. v. a-þindan.

a-þîstrian; *p.* ode; *pp.* od *To overcloud, to be eclipsed*; obscurari:—Seó sunne aþîstrode *the sun was eclipsed*, Chr. 540; Ing. 22, 22: Bt. Met. Fox 6, 8; Met. 6, 4. v. a-þŷstrian.

Athlans; *m.* ['Ατλας, αντος, *m.*] *Mount Atlas, in West Africa*; Atlas mons:—Hyre west-ende is æt ðæm beorge, ðe man Athlans nemneþ *its west end is at the mountain, which is called Atlas*, Ors. 1, 1; Bos. 16, 6.

âþ-loga, an; *m. A perjurer*; perjurus, Exon. 31 b; Th. 98, 10; Cri. 1605.

a-þoht, es; *m.* [a *out*, þoht *a thought*] *A thinking out, an excogitation, a device, an invention*; commentum, Cot. 35.

a-þohte, -þoht *thought out, thought*, Beo. Th. 5280; B. 2643; *p. and pp. of* a-þencan.

a-þolian; *p.* ode, ude; *pp.* od *To sustain, endure, suffer*; sustinere, perdurare, pati:—Hwylc aþolaþ *quis sustinebit?* Ps. Spl. 129, 3; Exon. 27 a; Th. 81, 8; Cri. 1320: Solil. 4. Ðæt him frêcne on feorh aþolude *that their soul in them suffered violently*; anima eorum in ipsis defecit, Ps. Th. 106, 4.

aðol-ware; *gen.* -wara; *dat.* -warum; *pl. m. Citizens*; cives, Exon. 92 a; Th. 346, 6; Gn. Ex. 201.

âðor; *pron. Either the one or the other, both*; alter, alteruter, uterque:—And se ðe âðor fulbrece *and he who violates either*, L. C. E. 2; Th. i. 358, 20: L. Ed. 2; Th. i. 160, 11: Hy. 10, 42; Hy. Grn. ii. 293, 42. On âðrum *on both*, Cot. 214. On âðre hand *on either hand*, Ors. 1, 14; Bos. 37, 32. v. âwðer.

a-þracian; *p.* ode; *pp.* od *To fear*; conturbari, horrescere, Ps. Spl. 6, 10: 34, 4. v. þracian.

a-þrǽstan; *p.* -þrǽste; *pp.* -þrǽst *To wrest out*; extorquere, Cot. 73. v. þrǽstan.

a-þrǽt *irksomeness*; tædium. v. a-þreát.

a-þrâwan; *p.* -þreów, *pl.* -þreówon; *pp.* -þrâwen [a, þrâwan *to throw*]. I. *to throw forth, to spill*; effundere:—Is mîn swât aþrâwen [MS. aþrowen] *my blood is spilt*, Andr. Kmbl. 2850; An. 1427. II. *to twist, wreath, twine*; contorquere:—Aþrâwenan gold-þrǽddas *twisted gold-threads*. Aþrâwenum þrǽdum *with twisted threads*, Cot. 50.

a-þreát, -þrǽt, es; *m. Irksomeness, disgust*; tædium:—Eów wæs lungre aþreát *you had soon disgust [at this]*, Elen. Kmbl. 736; El. 368. v. a-þreótan.

a-þreótan; *indef.* hit aþrŷt; *p.* -þreát, *pl.* -þruton; *pp.* -þroten. I. *impers. To weary, irk, displease, be loathsome, irksome to any one*; tædere, pigere:—Me aþrŷt *it wearies me, I am weary*, Ælfc. Gr. 33; Som. 37, 19. Hwî ne lǽte ge eów ðonne aþreótan *why then let ye [it] not to be loathsome to you?* Bt. 32, 2; Fox 116, 8. Ne sceal ðæs aþreótan þegn môdigne, ðæt he wîslîce woruld fulgonge *it must not irk therefore an energetic man, that he wisely passes his life*, Exon. 92 b; Th. 347, 31; Sch. 21. Hŷ tô ǽr aþreát, ðæt hŷ waldendes willan lǽsten *it too soon displeased them, that they should execute their sovereign's will*, 45 a; Th. 152, 30; Gû. 816: Bt. Met. Fox 29, 82; Met. 29, 40. II. *pers. To loathe, dislike, be weary of anything*; pertæsum esse:—Se cyning wæs aþroten his ællreordre gespræce *rex pertæsus erat barbaræ loquelæ*, Bd. 3, 7; S. 530, 4.

a-þrescan; *p.* -þræsc, *pl.* -þruscon; *pp.* -þroscen, -þroxen [a, þerscan *to thresh, beat*] *To rob, spoil*; spoliare, expilare:—Aþroxen *spoliatus*.

a-þriéttan; *p.* -þriétte; *pp.* -þriétted, -þriét *To weary, loathe any one*; tædio afficere aliquem:—Ic ðê hæbbe aþriét mid ðis langan spelle *I have wearied thee with this long discourse*, Bt. 39, 12; Fox 232, 19.

a-þringan; *p.* -þrang, -þrong, *pl.* -þrungon; *pp.* -þrungen [a *out*, þringan *to throng*]. I. *to throng* or *press out* or *forth, to urge out, to urge, to throng* or *press away* or *out of sight, to conceal*; extrudere, celare:—Ne mihte ic of ðære heortan heardne aþringan stŷlenne stân *I could not press out from his heart the hard and steely stone*, Salm. Kmbl. 1008; Sal. 505. Aþrungen, ût-aþrungen *celatum*, Cot. 33. II. *to rush forth, to rush*; prorumpere:—Ic of enge up aþringe *I rush up from the narrow place*, Exon. 101 b; Th. 383, 18; Rä. 4, 12.

a-þrintan; *p.* -þrant, *pl.* -þrunton; *pp.* -þrunten [a *out*, þrintan *to swell*] *To swell up*; tumere:—Ic ða wiht geseah, womb wæs aþrunten *I saw the creature, its belly was swollen up*, Exon. 109 b; Th. 419, 7; Rä. 38, 2.

a-þroten *loathed*, Bd. 3, 7; S. 530, 4; *pp. of* a-þreótan.

a-þrotennes, -þrotenes, -ness, e; *f. Tediousness, loathsomeness, wearisomeness*; tædium, Cot. 91.

a-þrotsum; *adj.* [a-þroten *pp. of* a-þreótan *to trouble*, -sum] *Troublesome, irksome, wearisome*; tædiosus, pertæsus:—Aþrotsum is *pertæsum est*, Cot. 188.

a-þrowen = a-þrâwen *thrown forth, spilt*, Andr. Kmbl. 2850; An. 1427; *pp. of* a-þrâwan.

a-þrôwian; *p.* ode; *pp.* od *To suffer*; pati. v. þrôwian.

a-þroxen *spoiled, robbed*; spoliatus; *pp. of* a-þrescan.

a-þrungen; *part. Concealed*; celatum, Cot. 33; *pp. of* a-þringan.

aþrunten *swollen up*, Exon. 109 b; Th. 419, 7; Rä. 38, 2; *pp. of* a-þrintan.

aþryd; *part. Robbed, pilled*; expressus, expilatus, Cot. 73; *pp. of* a-þryþian.

a-þrysman, -þrysemian; *p.* ede, ode; *pp.* ed, od *To suffocate with smoke* or *vapour, to suffocate, stifle*; fumo suffocare:—Hî hine on his bedde asmoredan and aþrysemodon *they smothered and stifled him in his bed*, Ors. 5, 4; Bos. 105, 6. Sunne wearþ adwæsced, þreám aþrysmed *the sun was darkened, stifled by sufferings*, Exon. 24 b; Th. 70, 5; Cri. 1134. v. þrysman.

a-þrýt *wearies*, Ælfc. Gr. 33; Som. 37, 19. v. a-þreótan.

a-þryþian; *p.* -þryþede; *pp.* -þryþed, -þryd [a *away*, þryþian from þryþ *force*] *To force from, rob, pillage;* exprimere, expilare:—Aþryd *expressus, expilatus,* Cot. 73: 74.

áþ-stæf, es; *m.* [áþ *oath*, stæf] *An oath;* juramentum, Ps. Spl. C. 104, 8.

áþ-swaring, -swerung, e; *f. An oath-swearing;* juramentum:—Gemindig wæs áþswaringe his *memor fuit juramenti sui,* Ps. Spl. 104, 8. Mid áþswerunge *with oath-swearing,* Chr. 1070; Th. 344, 27.

áþ-swaru, e; *f. An oath-swearing, a solemn oath, an oath;* juramentum:—For heora áþsware *because of their oath,* Jos. 9, 18. Ðæt he lange gehét mid áþsware *what he long had promised on oath,* Cd. 170; Th. 213, 26; Exod. 558: Ps. Th. 88, 3. Áþsware pytt *the well of the oath, Beersheba,* Gen. 46, 1.

áþ-sweord, es; *n.* [áþ *an oath*, sweord *sword*] *A sword-oath, a warrior's oath, an oath;* jusjurandum:—Ðonne bióþ brocene áþsweord eorla *then will be broken the oaths of the warriors,* Beo. Th. 4134; B. 2064.

áþ-swerung *an oath,* Chr. 1070; Th. 344, 27. v. áþ-swaring.

áþ-swyrd, es; *n. An oath;* juramentum:—Gemyndig wæs áþswyrdes [MS. áþswyrde] his *memor fuit juramenti sui,* Ps. Surt. 104, 9. v. áþ-sweord.

ÁÐUM, es; *m. A son-in-law, a daughter's husband, a brother-in-law, a sister's husband;* gener; sororis, ut et patris, sororis maritus:—Áðum *gener,* Ælfc. Gr. 8; Som. 7, 18. Hæfst ðú suna oððe dóhtra oððe áðum *habes filios aut filias aut generum,* Gen. 19, 12. Cwæþ to his twám áðumum *locutus est ad generos suos,* 19, 14: Exon. 66 b; Th. 246, 22; Jul. 65. Fór to ðam cynge his áðume *went to the king his sister's husband,* Chr. 1091; Th. 359, 6. [*Ger.* eidam *a daughter's husband: M. H. Ger.* eidem, *id: O. H. Ger.* eidum, eidam, eidem, *id.*]

a-þunden *swollen,* Bd. 5, 1; S. 614, 8; *pp. of* a-þindan.

a-þundenes, -ness, e; *f. A tumour, swelling, puffing up;* tumor:—Wið lifre swyle and aþundenesse *for swelling and puffing up of the liver,* L. M. cont. 2, 18; Lchdm. ii. 160, 18. Wið aþundenesse magan windigre *for windy swelling of the stomach,* 2, 11; Lchdm. ii. 158, 23. DER. aþindan, þindan; *pp.* þunden *swollen.*

a-þwægen *washed,* Bd. 4, 19; S. 588, 9; *pp. of* a-þweán.

a-þwǽnan; *p.* de; *pp.* ed [a *away*, þwǽnan *to soften, diminish*] *To soften, diminish, lessen, abate, take away;* diminuere, demere:—Seó sealf wile ðone swile aþwǽnan *the salve will diminish the swelling,* L. M. 3, 39; Lchdm. ii. 332, 25.

a-þwát *disappointed,* Ps. Spl. 131, 11. v. a-þwítan.

a-þweán; ic -þweá, -þweah, ðú -þweahst, -þwyhst, -þwehst, he -þwýhþ, -þwehþ, *pl.* -þweáþ; *p.* -þwóh, *pl.* -þwógon; *pp.* -þwegen [a *from, out;* þweán = þweahan *to wash*] *To wash out, to wash, cleanse, baptize, anoint;* abluere, luere, lavare, baptizare, unguere:—Gif ðú aþweán wylt *if thou wilt wash out,* Guthl. 5; Gdwin. 32, 8. Aþweah me *lava me,* Ps. Spl. 50, 3. Ðú aþweahst me *lavabis me,* 50, 8. He þegnas mid ða hálgan wyllan fulluht-bæðes aþwóh *milites sacrosancto fonte abluebat,* Bd. 4, 13; S. 582, 13: 3, 7; S. 529, 14: 1, 7; S. 478, 41. Wætere aþwegen and bebaðod *lotus aqua,* 1, 27; S. 496, 17: 4, 19; S. 588, 9. Ðæt híg aþwegene wǽren *ut baptizarentur,* Lk. Bos. 3, 12. Aþwóg *unxit,* Jn. Lind. War. 12, 3.

áþ-wed, -wedd, es; *n.* [áþ *an oath*, wed *a pledge*] *A pledge on oath, a solemn pledge;* sacramentum:—Áþ-wed *vel* áþe-gehát *sacramentum,* Ælfc. Gl. 13; Som. 57, 119; Wrt. Voc. 20, 56. v. áþ-gehát.

a-þwegen *washed,* Bd. 1, 7; S. 478, 41; *pp. of* a-þweán.

a-þweran; *p.* -þwær, *pl.* -þwǽron; *pp.* -þworen *To shake* or *stir together with a churn-staff* [*A. Sax.* þwiril], *to churn;* bacillo agitare:—Aþweran buteran *butyrum agitare,* Som. Aþwer buteran *churn butter,* L. M. 1, 45; Lchdm. ii. 112, 25. v. þweran.

a-þwítan; *p.* -þwát, *pl.* -þwiton; *pp.* -þwiten [a, þwítan *to cut off*] *To disappoint;* frustrari:—Ná aþwát [bewægde C.] him *non frustrabitur eum,* Ps. Spl. 131, 11.

a-þwóh, -þwógon *washed,* Bd. 4, 13; S. 582, 13; *p. of* a-þweán.

áþ-wyrþe; *adj. Worthy of an oath, worthy of credit;* dignus qui juret:—Gif he áþwyrþe biþ *if he be oath-worthy,* L. In. 46; Th. i. 130, 14: L. Ed. 3; Th. i. 160, 21.

á ðý *ever the;* unquam eo, Bt. 13; Fox 38, 9. v. ðý.

a-þýan; *p.* de; *pp.* ed *To press;* premere:—Wel on aþýdum sceapes smeruwe *boil in pressed sheep's grease,* L. M. 1, 8; Lchdm. ii. 54, 1. v. þýan.

aþýdum *pressed,* L. M. 1, 8; Lchdm. ii. 54, 1; *dat. of* aþýed = aþýd. v. aþýan.

a-þylgian; *p.* ode; *pp.* od *To sustain, bear, be patient, wait patiently;* sustinere:—For ǽ ðínre ic aþylgode ðé *propter legem tuam sustinui te,* Ps. Spl. 129, 4. Aþylgode sáwle mín on worde his *sustinuit anima mea in verbum ejus,* 129, 5. v. þyldigean.

a-þynnian, -þinnian; *p.* ade; *pp.* ad *To thin;* tenuare. DER. þynnian. þyn.

a-þýstrian, -þístrian, -þeóstrian, -þiéstrian, -þéstrian; *p.* ode, ade; *pp.* od *To overcloud, to be obscured* or *eclipsed;* obnubilare, obscurari:—Sýn aþýstrode eágan heora *obscurentur oculi eorum,* Ps. Spl. 68, 28. Seó sunne aþýstrade *the sun was eclipsed,* Ors. 6, 2; Bos. 117, 14. Aþýstrade *obnubilavit,* Bd. 5, 13; S. 633, 34. Ðonne aþeóstriaþ ealle steorran *then all the stars are darkened,* Bt. 9; Fox 26, 15. Byþ sunne aþeóstrod, Mk. Bos. 13, 24. Hér sunne aþýstrode *here the sun was eclipsed,* Chr. 538; Ing. 22, 18: 540; Ing. 22, 22. DER. þýstrian.

a-þýteþ *sounds,* Exon. 117 b; Th. 451, 26; Dóm. 109. v. a-þeótan.

a-þýwan; *p.* de; *pp.* ed [a *from*, þýwan *to drive*] *To lead* or *drive from, to discard;* ejicere:—He hý raðe aweg aþýwde *he soon drove them away,* Ors. 6, 36; Bos. 131, 28.

a-tiarian *to fail;* deficere, Prov. 3. v. a-teorian.

a-tiefran, -tifran; *p.* ede; *pp.* ed *To paint, describe by painting;* depingere:—Ealle ða hearga Israhéla folces wǽron atiefrede [MS. C. atifred: MS. Oth. atiefred] on ðæm wage *universa idola domus Israel depicta erant in pariete,* Past. 21, 3; Hat. MS. 30 a, 23. He atiefreþ [MS. C. atifreþ] ðæs þinges onlícnesse on his móde ðe he ðonne ymbsmeáþ *in corde depingitur quidquid fictis imaginibus deliberando cogitatur,* Past. 21, 3; Hat. MS. 30 b, 27: 30 b, 26.

a-tihtan; *p.* -tihte; *pp.* -tihted, -tiht *To attract, incite,* Bt. 32, 1; Fox 114, 3. v. a-tyhtan.

a-tíhþ, a-tíþ *draws away, draws to;* abstrahit, attrahit, Ps. Spl. second 9, 11: Ps. Surt. 9, 30. v. a-teón.

a-tihting *intention, an aim;* intentio, Scint. 6, 7. v. a-tyhtan.

a-tillan; *p.* de; *pp.* ed *To touch;* tangere, R. Ben. interl. 7. v. tillan.

a-timbrian, -timbran; *p.* ode, ede; *pp.* od, ed *To erect, build;* ædificare:—Hét ða burh atimbrian *ordered to build the city,* Ors. 3, 9; Bos. 65, 21; 66, 40; 67, 39: 6, 30; Bos. 127, 34. Búr atimbran *to build a bower,* Exon. 108 a; Th. 411, 26; Rä. 30, 5.

a-tión; *p.* -teáh, *pl.* -tugon; *pp.* -togen *To draw out, pull out;* abstrahere, extrahere:—Atió of ðæm æcere fearn and þornas *let him pull out from the field fern and thorns,* Bt. Met. Fox 12, 3; Met. 12, 2: 22, 53; Met. 22, 27.

at-íwan; *p.* ede; *pp.* ed *To appear;* apparere:—Atíwede cométa *a comet appeared,* Chr. 1066; Th. 330, 38. v. æt-ýwan.

a-togen *drawn out,* Num. 22, 22; *pp. of* a-teón.

atol, es; *n. Terribleness, terror, horror, wretchedness;* diritas, terror, horror, miseria:—Sceal atol þrówian *must suffer terror,* Cd. 222; Th. 289, 10; Sat. 395. Is ðes windiga sele atole gefylled *this windy hall is filled with horror,* 216; Th. 273, 16; Sat. 137: Exon. 26 a; Th. 77, 33; Cri. 1266.

ATOL, atul, atel, eatol; *adj. Dire, terrific, terrible, horrid, foul, loathsome;* dirus, atrox, terribilis, horridus, fœdus, teter:—Atol æglǽca *the dire miscreant,* Beo. Th. 1188; B. 592: Andr. Kmbl. 2625; An. 1314. Atol is ðín onseón *horrid is thine aspect,* Cd. 214; Th. 268, 26; Sat. 61. Atol mid égum *terrific with his eyes,* 229; Th. 310, 18; Sat. 728. Atol ýða gewealc *the terrible rolling of the waves,* 166; Th. 206, 21; Exod. 455: Beo. Th. 1700; B. 848: Exon. 81 b; Th. 306, 11; Seef. 6. Se atola *the horrid one* [*the devil*], Cd. 222; Th. 290, 10; Sat. 413. In ðeossum atolan ǽðele *in this horrid country,* 215; Th. 271, 20; Sat. 108. Atole gástas *horrid ghosts,* 214; Th. 268, 7; Sat. 51. Gúþrinc geféng atolan clommum *the warrior seized in her horrid clutches,* Beo. Th. 3008; B. 1502. [*Orm.* atell *foul, corrupt: O. Nrs.* atall, ötul *fierce;* atrox.] DER. atelíc.

atolíc; adj. [atol, líc] *Dire, horrid, loathsome;* dirus, horridus, deformis, Bd. 4, 32; S. 611, note 17. v. atelíc.

átor, áttor, áter, átter, ǽtor, ǽtter, ǽttor; *gen.* átres, áttres; *n. Poison, venom;* venenum:—Átres drync *the drink of poison,* Andr. Kmbl. 105; An. 53. Átre gelícost *most like to poison,* Cd. 216, Th. 274, 32; Sat. 162. Flór átre weól *the floor boiled with venom,* 220; Th. 284, 8; Sat. 318. Átru *venena,* Scint. 28. Wið áttrum *against poisons,* Ps. Th. 57, 4: Bd. 1, 1; S. 474, 39: Bd. 4, 23; S. 595, 1. Wið fleógendum átre *for flying venom,* L. M. 1, 45; Lchdm. ii. 112, 24. [*Orm.* atterr; *Laym.* atter: *Piers* attre: *Plat.* etter, eiter, *m. n: O. Sax.* ētar, ettar, *m: O. Dut. Dut.* etter, *m: Ger.* eiter, *n. m: M. H. Ger.* eiter, *n: O. H. Ger.* eitar, *n: Dan.* edder, *n: Swed.* etter, *n: Norw. O. Nrs.* eitr, *n.* Cf. *M. H. Ger.* eiten *to burn: Sansk.* i-n-dh and the *A. Sax.* ád *a funeral pile: O. H. Ger.* eit *ignis,* áttor then would seem to mean *a cause of burning, a pricking pain.*]

átor-berende; *part. Venom-bearing;* venenifer, L. M. 2, 1; Lchdm. ii. 176, 5. v. átter-berende.

átor-coppe, an; *f. A spider;* aranea. v. áttor-coppe.

átor-cræft, es; *m. Poison-craft, the art of poisoning, sorcery;* veneficium, Lye.

átor-cyn, es; *n. The poison-kind;* veneni genus, Salm. Kmbl. 437; Sal. 219. v. ǽtor-cyn.

átor-drinc, es; *m. Poisonous drink, poison;* potio venenata, venenum. v. áttor-drinca.

átor-drinca *poisonous drink, poison.* v. áttor-drinca.

a-torfian; *p.* ode; *pp.* od *To throw forth, to throw;* jactare, Mt. Hat. 12, 24, Lye. v. torfian.

átor-láðe, an; *f. The cock's spur grass;* panicum crus galli, v. áttor-láðe, L. M. 45; Lchdm. ii. 110, 8; 114, 11.

átor-líc *poison-like;* veneno similis. v. áter-líc.

ātor-loppe, an; *f.* [ātor, loppe *a silkworm, spinner of a web*] *A spider, spider's web*; aranea. v. ǽtter-loppe.

ātor-sceaða *a venomous destroyer.* v. āttor-sceaða.

ātor-spere, es; *n. A poisoned spear*; telum venenatum. v. āttor-spere, Exon. 105 a; Th. 399, 10; Rä. 18, 9.

ātor-tān, es; *m. A poisonous rod;* ramus venenosus. v. āter-tān, Beo. Th. 2923; B. 1459.

a-tredan; *p.* -træd, *pl.* -trǽdon; *pp.* -treden *To tread, twist from* or *out, extort;* extorquere:—Atred him ða giltas ūt *extort his sins from him*, L. De Cf. 3; Th. ii. 260, 21.

a-treddan; *p.* de; *pp.* ed *To investigate, search, examine* or *explore carefully;* scrutari, investigare:—Ðæt ic ðīn bebod beorht atredde *scrutabor mandata tua*, Ps. Th. 118, 69: 138, 2. v. treddan.

a-trendlian; *p.* ode; *pp.* od *To trundle, roll;* volutare, provolvere, Bt. Met. Fox 5, 33; Met. 5, 17.

ātren-mōd *venom-minded;* malitiosus. v. ǽtren-mōd.

ātrian *to poison, envenom;* venenare. v. ǽtrian.

ātter; *gen.* āttres; *n. Poison, venom;* venenum:—Ðæt ātter wæs sōna ofernumen *the poison was soon detected*, Bd. 1, 1; S. 474, 39. v. ātor.

ātter-berende; *part. Venom-bearing;* venenifer:—Wǽtan ātterberendum *by venom-bearing humours*, L. M. 2, 1; Lchdm. ii. 176, 5. v. ātor, *etc.*

ātter-coppe, an; *f.* [ātor *poison*, copp *a head*] *A spider;* aranea:—Swindan ðū dydest swā swā āttercoppan sāwle his *tabescere fecisti sicut araneam animam ejus*, Ps. Spl. T. 38, 15. v. āttor-coppe.

ātter-lāðe, an; *f. The cock's spur grass;* panicum crus galli:—Ātterlāðe *venenifuga* [*venom-loather*], Wrt. Voc. 30, 38. v. ātor, *etc.*

āttor; *gen.* āttres; *n. Poison, venom;* venenum, Beo. Th. 5423; B. 2715: Ps. Spl. 13, 5. v. ātor.

āttor-coppe, an; *f. A spider;* aranea:—Loppe, fleónde næddre, *vel* āttorcoppe *a spider*, Wrt. Voc. 24, 1. Āttorcoppe—wið āttorcoppan bīte *a spider—for spider's bite*, Herb. 4, 9; Lchdm. i. 92, 5, 6: Med. ex Quadr. 4, 10; Lchdm. i. 344, 15. v. ātor, *etc.*

āttor-drinca, an; *m. A poisonous drink, poison;* potio venenata, venenum, Martyrol. ad 11 Junii.

āttor-, ātter-lāðe, an; *f. The cock's spur grass, atterlothe* [*venom-loather*]; panicum crus galli:—Wið āttre, betonican and ða smalan āttorlāðan dō on hālig wæter *against poison, put betony and the small atterlothe into holy water*, L. M. 1, 45; Lchdm. ii. 110, 8; 114, 11: Herb. 45, 1; Lchdm. i. 148, 4: L. M. 1, 1; Lchdm. ii. 22, 15. Ātterlāðe *venenifuga*, Ælfc. Gl. 40; Som. 63, 88; Wrt. Voc. 30, 38. v. ātor, *etc.*

āttor-sceaða, an; *m. A poisonous destroyer, a venomous dragon, serpent;* hostis venenosus, draco venenosus, serpens:—Būtan ðam āttorsceaðan *save to the venomous destroyer*, Exon. 96 a; Th. 357, 24; Pa. 33: Beo. Th. 5670; B. 2839. v. ātor, *etc.*

āttor-spere, es; *n. A poisoned spear;* telum venenatum:—Eglum āttorsperum *with dire poisoned spears*, Exon. 105 a; Th. 399, 10; Rä. 18, 9. v. ātor, *etc.*

a-tuge *might draw away;* abstraheret, Bd. 4, 24; S. 598, 19; *p. subj. of* a-teón.

atul; *adj. Dire, terrible, horrid:*—In ðæt atule hūs *into that dire house*, Exon. 40 b; Th. 136, 1; Gū. 534: Andr. Kmbl. 106; An. 53: Ps. Th. 118, 123. v. atol.

a-tydran; *p.* ede; *pp.* ed *To procreate, create;* procreare, gignere, Elen. Kmbl. 2555; El. 1279. v. tydran.

a-tȳhst *drawest out*, Bt. Met. Fox 12, 49; Met. 12, 25. v. a-teón.

a-tyhtan, -tihtan; *p.* -tyhte, -tihte; *pp.* -tyhted, -tyht, -tiht. I. *to persuade, solicit, incite, attract, allure;* persuadere, allicere, incitare:—Ðā wæs ofer Mūntgiop monig atyhted Gota, gylpes full *then was allured over the Alps many a Goth, full of arrogance*, Bt. Met. Fox 1, 16; Met. 1, 8. Ðe beóþ atihte to ðām sōðum gesǽlþum *who are intent upon* [*attracted to*] *the true felicities*, Bt. 32, 1; Fox 114, 3. II. *to produce, procreate;* procreare, gignere:—Wīga is of dumbum twām atyhted *a warrior is produced from two dumb ones*, Exon. 113 a; Th. 433, 27; Rä. 51, 3. v. tyhtan.

a-tȳhþ *draws away;* abstrahit, *3rd sing. pres. of* a-teón.

a-tymbrian, -tymbran; *p.* ode, ede; *pp.* od, ed *To erect, build;* ædificare:—Se Cēnwalh hēt atymbran [atymbrian MS. Laud.] ða ealdan cyrican on Wintanceastre *Cenwalh ordered to build the old church at Winchester*, Chr. 643; Ing. 38, 1: 919; Ing. 133, 17. v. a-timbrian.

a-tȳnan; *p.* -tȳnde; *pp.* -tȳned, -tȳnd; *v. a.* I. [a *away, out;* tȳnan *to inclose, shut*] *to shut out, exclude;* excludere:—Ne beóþ ūt fram ðē atȳnde *ut non excludantur*, Ps. Th. 67, 27. II. [a = on, un *un*, tȳnan] *to un-shut, open;* aperire:—Nā ic atȳnde mūþ mīnne *non aperui os meum*, Ps. Spl. 38, 13. Atȳn us *aperi nobis*, Lk. Bos. 13, 25. v. on-tȳnan, un-tȳnan.

a-tyrian *to fail;* deficere. v. a-teorian.

at-ȳwan; *p.* de; *pp.* ed *To shew;* ostendere:—He atȳwde him *ostendit eis*, Ps. Spl. C. 77, 14. v. æt-ȳwan, ȳwan.

Augustīnus, i; *m; Lat.* [Augustīnus is correct in the quotations from the titles of the two following chapters of Bede, but in the A. Sax. text it is Agustīnus] *St. Augustine, the missionary sent by Pope Gregory to England*, A. D. 597, *and died May* 26, 605; Augustīnus:—Ðæt se hālga Papa Gregorius Augustīnum sende Angel-þeóde to bodiganne Godes word *ut sanctus Papa Gregorius Augustinum ad prædicandum genti Anglorum verbum Dei miserit*, Bd. 1, 23, titl; S. 485, 14. Augustīnus cumende on Breotone *Augustinus veniens Brittaniam*, 1, 25, titl; S. 486, 10. Hēr com Augustīnus and his gefēran to Engla lande *here*, A. D. 597, *Augustine and his companions came to England*, Chr. 597; Th. 35, 41, col. 2: 596; Th. 34, 37, col. 1; 35, 36, cols. 1, 2.

Augustus, i; *m; Lat.* I. *the first Roman Emperor.* v. Agustus. II. *the month of August;* mensis Augustus:—On ðam monþe ðe man Augustum nemneþ *in the month which is named August*, Herb. 7, 1; Lchdm. i. 96, 23. v. Agustus.

ā-uht, es; *n. Aught, anything;* aliquid:—Eálā, ðæt on eorþan āuht fæstlīces weorces ne wunaþ ǽfre *alas, that on earth aught of permanent work does not ever remain*, Bt. Met. Fox 6, 32; Met. 6, 16. Ðe āuht oððe nāuht āuðer worhte *which could either make aught or naught*, 20, 83; Met. 20, 42. Hwȳ biþ his ānwald āuhte ðȳ māra *why will his power be by aught the greater?* 16, 40; Met. 16, 20: Bt. 35, 5; Fox 164, 6, 10.

ā-uht; *adv. At all, by any means;* omnino, ullo modo:—Āuht ne gebētaþ hiora scearpnesse *nor by any means improve their sharpness*, Bt. Met. Fox 21, 46; Met. 21, 23: 6, 12; Met. 6, 6. v. ā-wuht, ā-wiht.

a-urnen *run out, passed*, Cd. 79; Th. 98, 6; Gen. 1626. v. a-yrnan.

āuðer *either, each*, Bt. Met. Fox 29, 19; Met. 29, 10. v. āwðer.

ĀWA, āwo; *adv. Always, ever, for ever;* semper, unquam, usque:—Āwa *always*, Ps. Th. 143, 13. Āwa *usque*, 70, 16: 138, 15: Elen. Kmbl. 1899; El. 951. Ne wile heó āwa ðæs sīþes geswīcan *nor will it ever desist from its course*, Salm. Kmbl. 646; Sal. 322. Āwa to feore *in seculum*, Ps. Th. 51, 8: 65, 6. On ēcnesse, āwa *in æternum*, 118, 89. Āwa to worlde *in seculum seculi*, 71, 19: 144, 1. Āwa to worulde *usque in seculum*, 130, 5: 132, 4. Āwa to ealdre *for evermore*, Exon. 93 a; Th. 348, 22; Sch. 32: Beo. Th. 1914; B. 955. [*O. Sax.* ēo *unquam, semper: O. H. Ger.* ēo, io *unquam, semper: Goth.* aiw *semper: Lat.* ævum *an age: Grk.* αἰεί, ἀεί *always;* αἰών *an age.*] vide ā.

a-wacan; *p.* -wōc, *pl.* -wōcon; *pp.* -wacen; *v. intrans.* I. *to* AWAKE; expergisci, expergefieri, evigilare:—Awōc of ðam slǽpe *awoke from sleep*, Gen. 9, 24. Awōc Pharao *expergefactus est Pharao*, 41, 4, 7. II. *to wake into being, to arise, be born;* oriri, provenire, nasci:—Twā þeóda awōcon *two nations arose*, Cd. 124; Th. 158, 11; Gen. 2615. v. wacan.

a-wacian; *p.* ode; *pp.* od *To awake;* expergisci, expergefieri, evigilare:—Of hefegum slǽpe awacode *e gravi somno expergefactus est*, Gen. 45, 26. v. wacian.

a-wācian, -wācigan; *p.* ode; *pp.* od; *v. intrans. To grow weak* or *effeminate, to languish, decline, fail, fall away, relax, to be indolent;* infirmari, deficere, recedere:—Awācode mid langre ealdunge *weakened with old age*, Gr. Dial. 2, 15. Awāciaþ on ðære costnunge tīman *in tempore tentationis recedunt*, Lk. Bos. 8, 13. Ðæt ne awācodon wereda Drihtne *that they might not fall away from the Lord of hosts*, Cd. 183; Th. 229, 20; Dan. 220. Gif he nā ne awācaþ *if he never relax*, L. Pen. 12; Th. ii. 280, 29. v. ge-wācian, on-.

a-wacnian, -wæcnian; *p.* cnede, cenede; *pp.* cned, cened; *v. intrans.* I. *to* AWAKEN, *come to life again, revive;* evigilare, expergefieri, reviviscere:—On dagunge he eft acwicode [awacenede MSS. Ca. O.] *diluculo revixit*, Bd. 5, 12; S. 627. 13. II. *to arise, spring, have one's origin;* suscitari, oriri, nasci:—Of ðām frumgārum folc awæcniaþ *from these patriarchs shall spring a people*, Cd. 104; Th. 138, 14; Gen. 2291. Eall heora gewinn awacnedon ǽrest fram Alexandres epistole *all their wars first arose from Alexander's letter*, Ors. 3, 11; Bos. 72, 19. v. wæcnan, on-wæcnan, on-wæcnian.

a-wǽcan; *p.* -wǽcte, -wǽhte; *pp.* -wǽced, -wǽct, -wǽht *To weaken, fatigue;* debilitare, fatigare:—Awǽht *defessus*, Hymn. Awǽht *porrectus*, Cot. 157.

a-wæccan *To awake;* suscitare, Mt. Rush. Stv. 3, 9. v. a-weccan.

a-wæcnan; *p.* ede; *pp.* ed; *v. intrans. To awake, rise up, be born;* evigilare, suscitari, nasci:—Nū is ðæt bearn cymen, awæcned *now is that child come, risen up*, Exon. 8 b; Th. 5, 9; Cri. 67.

a-wæcnian; *p.* ode; *pp.* od *To awaken, arise, spring;* evigilare, oriri:—Awæcniaþ, Cd. 104; Th. 138, 14; Gen. 2291. v. a-wacnian.

a-wǽgan; *p.* de; *pp.* ed; *v. trans. To deceive, delude, frustrate, disappoint, cause to fail;* eludere, frustrari, irritum facere:—Ðæt is sōþ ðæt ðū ǽr awǽgdest *that is true which thou before didst frustrate*, Homl. Th. ii. 418, 18. Ǽr awǽged sīe worda ǽnig *ere any word be made to fail*, Andr. Kmbl. 2876; An. 1441. Awǽged ne dō ðū wedd *irritum ne facias fœdus*, Hymn, Lye. v. wǽgan, ge-wǽgan.

a-wæh *weighed out, weighed to;* appendit, Gen. 23, 16. v. a-wegan.

a-wǽht *weakened, wearied; pp. of* a-wǽcan.

a-wæhte *aroused;* suscitavit, Bd. 4, 23; S. 596, 14. v. a-weccan.

a-wǽlan; *p.* ede, de, te; *pp.* ed. I. *v. trans. To roll away, roll back, roll to;* revolvere, advolvere:—Awǽlede ðone stān *revolvit lapidem*, Mt. Rush. Stv. 28, 2. Awǽlte ðone stān *advolvit lapidem*,

Mk. Rush. War. 15, 46. II. *to move violently, vex, afflict;* vexare:—Awǽled *vexatus*, Mk. Rush. War. 5, 18.

a-wændan; *p.* de; *pp.* ed *To turn from* or *away, to translate;* avertere, transferre:—Ðonne awænt Driht hæftnunge folces his *cum averterit Dominus captivitatem plebis suæ*, Ps. Spl. 13, 11. v. a-wendan, wændan.

a-wændednys, -nyss, e; *f. A change;* mutatio, Ps. Lamb. 76, 11. v. awendednys.

a-wænian; *p.* ede; *pp.* ed *To wean from;* ablactare:—Swá swá awæned cild *sicut ablactatus*, Ps. Lamb. 130, 2.

a-wærged, -wærgd; *pp; def. m.* -wærgda *Accursed;* maledictus:—Wit ðæs awærgdan wordum gelýfdon *we two believed the words of the accursed one*, Cd. 222; Th. 290, 16; Sat. 416. v. a-wyrged.

a-wæscen *washed;* lotus; *pp.* v. wascan. DER. un-a-wæscen.

a-wǽstan; *p.* -wǽste; *pp.* -wǽsted; *v. trans. To waste, lay waste, eat up;* vastare, carpere:—Swá swá oxa gewunaþ to awǽstenne gærs *quo modo solet bos herbas carpere*, Num. 22, 4. v. a-wéstan.

a-wanian; *p.* ode; *pp.* od *To diminish;* diminuere. v. wanian.

a-wannian; *p.* ode; *pp.* od *To wax wan* or *pale;* pallescere:—Awannod *pallidus factus*, Greg. Dial. 1, 2.

á-wár; *adv.* [=á-wǽr=á-hwǽr] *Anywhere;* alicubi:—Swilce he áwár wǽre, ǽrðan ðe he geboren wǽre *as if he were anywhere, before he was born*, Homl. Th. ii. 244, 19.

a-wariged; *part. Accursed;* maledictus. v. a-werged; *pp. of* a-wergian: awyrged; *pp. of* a-wyrgian.

a-wárnian; *p.* ode; *pp.* od *To be confounded;* confundi, Ps. Spl. M. 85, 16. v. a-swárnian.

a-warpen; *pp. cast out;* ejectus, Ps. Spl. 108, 9. v. a-worpen; *pp. of* a-weorpan.

a-weaht, a-weahte *awaked, excited, raised up*, Ps. Th. 77, 65: Bd. 3, 5; S. 526, 34; *pp. and p. of* a-weccan.

a-weallan; ic -wealle, ðú -weallest. -wylst, he -wealleþ, -wealþ, -wylþ, *pl.* -weallaþ; *p.* -weól, -weóll, *pl.* -weóllon; *pp.* -weallen; *v. intrans. To boil* or *bubble up, break forth, stream* or *gush forth, well out, flow forth, issue;* ebullire, erumpere, emanare:—Swá ǽspringe út awealleþ of clife hárum *so a water-spring wells out of a hoary cliff*, Bt. Met. Fox 5, 24; Met. 5, 12: Ps. Th. 103, 10: Ex. 8, 3: Andr. Kmbl. 3045; An. 1525. Ða fruman aweallaþ Deorwentan streámes *Deruentionis fluvii primordia erumpunt*, Bd. 4, 29; S. 607, 11. Is ðæt eác sǽd, ðæt wylle aweólle *fertur autem, quia fons ebullierit*, Bd. 5, 10; S. 625, 23: Exon. 17 a; Th. 39, 20; Cri. 625. DER. weallan.

a-weardian; *p.* ode, ede; *pp.* od, ed; *v. trans. To ward off, defend, protect;* defendere, protegere:—Hí hí sylf aweardedon *they defended themselves*, Ors. 5, 3; Bar. 182, 19. DER. weardian.

a-wearpan=a-weorpan *to cast away;* projicere:—Dust ðæt awearpþ wind *pulvis quem projicit ventus*, Ps. Spl. 1, 5.

a-weaxan; *p.* -weóx, -wóx; *pp.* -weaxen; *v. intrans. To wax, grow, arise, come forth;* crescere, oriri, provenire:—Him aweaxeþ wynsum gefeá *to them shall grow winsome delight*, Exon. 26 a; Th. 77, 7; Cri. 1253: Ps. Th. 128, 4: Exon. 103 a; Th. 391, 24; Rä. 10, 10: 103 b; Th. 392, 6; Rä. 11, 3: Elen. Kmbl. 2450; El. 1226.

a-web, es; *n. The cross threads in weaving, called the woof* or *weft;* subtegmen, Cot. 161.

a-weccan, -weccean; ic -wecce, ðú -wecest, -wecst, he -wecceþ, -weceþ, -wecþ, *pl.* -weccaþ, -wecceaþ; *p.* -weahte, -wehte, *pl.* -weahton, -wehton; *impert.* -wec, -wece, *pl.* -wecceaþ; *pp.* -weaht, -weht; *v. trans.* I. *to awake, arouse from sleep, awake from death;* e somno excitare, suscitare, resuscitare:—Hí awehton hine *excitaverunt eum*, Mk. Bos. 4, 38. Ðá wearþ aweaht Drihten swá he slǽpende *excitatus est tamquam dormiens Dominus*, Ps. Th. 77, 65. Ic hine awecce *resuscitabo eum*, Jn. Bos. 6, 40. Se Fæder awecþ ða deádan *Pater suscitat mortuos*, 5, 21. He manige men of deáþe awehte *he awoke many men from death*, Andr. Kmbl. 1167; An. 584. Awecceaþ deáde *suscitate mortuos*, Mt. Bos. 10, 8. II. *to excite, rouse, stir up, call forth, raise up, raise up children;* excitare, concitare, suscitare, resuscitare:—To ælmessan and to gódra dǽda fylignessum he hí aweahte ge mid wordum ge mid dǽdum *ad eleemosynas operumque bonorum executionem et verbis excitabat et factis*, Bd. 3, 5; S. 526, 34. Awehte wǽlníþ Babilónes brego *deadly hatred excited the prince of Babylon*, Cd. 174; Th. 218, 28; Dan. 46. Ðæs sǽdes corn biþ simle aweaht mid ascunga, eác siððan mid gódre láre, gif hit grówan sceal *the grain of this seed is always excited by inquiry, and moreover by good instruction, if it shall grow*, Bt. Met. Fox 22, 80; Met. 22, 40. Awehte ða windas of heofenum *excitavit ventos de cœlo*, Ps. Th. 77, 26. Awece ðíne mihte *excita potentiam tuam*, 79, 3. Hí his yrre aweahtan *in ira concitaverunt eum*, 77, 58, 40: Cd. 52; Th. 66, 7; Gen. 1080. Awecceþ wópdropan *calls forth tears*, Salm. Kmbl. 567; Sal. 283. He aweahte gewitnesse on Iacobe *suscitavit testimonium in Jacob*, Ps. Th. 77, 6. Ic awecce wið ðé óðerne cyning *I will raise up against thee another king*, Elen. Kmbl. 1851; El. 927. Aweccende fram eorþan wædlan *suscitans a terra inopem*, Ps. Spl. 112, 6. Awece me *resuscita me*, 40, 11. He mæg bearn aweccan [aweccean Mt. Bos. 3, 9] *potens est suscitare filios*, Lk. Bos. 3, 8. Hys bróðor sǽd awecce *suscitet semen fratri suo*, 20, 28.

a-wece *arouse, raise up*, Ps. Spl. C. T. 40, 11; *impert. of* a-weccan.

a-wecgan, -wegan; *p.* -wegde, -wegede; *pp.* -weged; *v. trans. To move, remove, shake;* movere, amovere, commovere, agitare:—Ne mihton awecgan Iob of his módes ánrǽdnysse *might not move Job from his constancy of mind*, Job Thw. 167, 33; Andr. Kmbl. 1005; An. 503. Hí ne mihton hine awecgan *they could not move it*, Homl. Th. ii. 164, 31. Mód biþ aweged of his stede *the mind is removed from its place*, Bt. 12; Fox 36, 18: Bt. Met. Fox 7, 48; Met. 7, 24. Winde aweged [MS. awegyd] hreód *arundinem vento agitatam*, Mt. Bos. 11, 7. v. wecgan.

a-wecþ *awakes, raises up*, Jn. Bos. 5, 21; *3rd pers. pres. of* a-weccan.

a-wédan; *p.* -wédde; *pp.* -wéd; *v. n. To be mad, to rage, to be angry, to go* or *wax mad, revolt, apostatize;* in furorem agi:—Awéddon ða nýtena *the cattle became mad*, Ors. 5, 10; Bos. 108, 31. Se ðe for sleápe awéd *phreneticus*=φρενιτικός, Ælfc. Gl. 78; Som. 72, 40; Wrt. Voc. 45, 72. v. wédan.

a-wefan; *p.* -wæf, *pl.* -wǽfon; *pp.* -wefen *To weave;* texere:—Wyrmas ne awǽfon *worms did not weave*, Exon. 109 a; Th. 417, 23; Rä. 36, 9: Jn. Bos. 19, 23.

a-weg; *adv.* AWAY, *out;* (this is its meaning both in and out of composition); auferendi vim habet:—Ðá eóde he aweg *autem abiit*, Mt. Bos. 19, 22. Ge drehnigeaþ ðone gnæt aweg *ye strain the gnat out;* excolantes [ex *out*, colare *to filter, strain*] culicem, Mt. Bos. 23, 24. He hí raðe aweg aþýwde *he quickly drove them away*, Ors. 6, 36; Bos. 131, 28: Ps. Th. 77, 57. v. on-weg.

aweg-adrífan *to drive* or *chase away;* expellere, Ps. Spl. C. 35, 13. v. a-drífan.

aweg-aferian *to carry away, to cart away;* evehere, Cot. 205.

aweg-alúcan [aweg *away*, alúcan *to lock out, separate*] *To shut* or *lock out, to separate;* discludere, Cot. 67.

a-wegan; *p.* -wæg, -wæh, *pl.* -wǽgon; *pp.* -wegen; *v. trans.* I. *to lift up, take* or *carry away;* levare, auferre:—Hí á sibbe gelǽraþ, ða ǽr wonsǽlge awegen habbaþ *they shall ever advise peace, which the unblest have before taken away*, Exon. 89 a; Th. 334, 25; Gn. Ex. 21: Homl. Th. i. 308, 17. II. *to weigh out, weigh to any one;* appendere:—Abraham ðá awæh feówer hund scillinga seolfres *Abraham appendit quadringentos siclos argenti*, Gen. 23, 16. Eálá gif míne synna and mín yrmþ wǽron awegene on ánre wǽgan *utinam appenderentur peccata mea et calamitas in statera*, Job 6, 2; Thw. 167, 18.

a-wegan; *p.* -wegede, -wegde; *pp.* -weged *To move, shake:*—Aweged, Bt. 12; Fox 36, 18: Bt. Met. Fox 7, 48; Met. 7, 24: Mt. Bos. 11, 7. v. a-wecgan.

aweg-animan *to take away;* sufferre, Jn. Bos. 20, 1. v. a-niman.

aweg-awyltan *to roll away;* revolvere, Mk. Bos. 16, 4. v. a-wyltan.

aweg-beran *to bear, carry* or *convey away;* asportare, Ælfc. Gr. 47; Som. 48, 37. v. beran.

aweg-cuman *to go away, to leave, escape;* dimittere:—Sume awegcómon *some escaped*, Ors. 3, 3; Bos. 55, 26. v. cuman.

a-weged *moved*, Bt. 12; Fox 36, 18; *pp. of* a-wegan *to move.*

a-wegen *taken away, weighed as in a balance*, Job 6, 2; Thw. 167, 18. v. a-wegan *to weigh.*

aweg-gán *to go away;* abire:—Ongan aweg-gán *began to go away*, Bd. 4, 22; S. 591, 1. v. gán.

aweg-geniman *to take away;* auferre. v. geniman.

aweg-gewítan; *p.* -gewát, *pl.* -gewiton; *pp.* -gewiten *To go away, depart;* discedere:—Ic eom aweg-gewiten *I am gone away*, Ors. 2, 4; Bos. 44, 36. v. ge-wítan.

aweg-gewitenes, -ness, e; *f. A going away, departure;* abscessio:—Æfter þrím geárum Willfreþes aweg-gewitenesse *post tres abscessionis Vilfridi annos*, Bd. 4, 12; S. 581, 30. v. gewítan.

aweg-lǽtan *to let* [*go*] *away, let escape;* abire permittere, L. C. S. 29; Th. i. 392, 14. v. lǽtan.

aweg-onwendan *to turn* or *move away;* amovere, Ps. Spl. C. 65, 19. v. on-wendan.

aweg-weorpan *to cast* or *throw away;* abjicere. v. aweg, weorpan.

a-wegyd *shaken*, Mt. Bos. 11, 7. v. a-wecgan.

a-weht *awaked, aroused; pp. of* a-weccan.

a-wehte *awaked, excited*, Andr. Kmbl. 1167; An. 584: Ps. Th. 77, 26; *p. of* a-weccan.

a-wehtnes, -ness, e; *f. An awaking, a stirring up, excitation, quickening, encouraging;* excitatio:—To awehtnesse lífiendra monna of sáule deáþe *ad excitationem viventium de morte animæ*, Bd. 5, 12; S. 627, 5.

awel *an awl;* subula, fuscinula, harpago=ἁρπάγη, Cot. 84: 13. v. al.

a-wellan; *p.* de; *pp.* ed *To cause to bubble, to well;* facere ut aliquid ferveat vel ebulliat:—Hreðor innan wæs wynnum awelled *the breast within was welled with joy*, Andr. Kmbl. 2037; An. 1021. v. a-weallan.

a-wend *turned, translated; pp. of* a-wendan:—Seó bóc is on Englisc awend *the book is turned* [*translated*] *into English*, Homl. Th. ii. 358, 30.

a-wendan; ic -wende, ðú -wendest, -wenst, he -wendeþ, -went, *pl.* -wendaþ; *p.* -wende; *pp.* -wended, -wend, -went. I. *v. trans. To turn away* or *off, avert, remove, to turn upside down, turn, change, translate, pervert;* avertere, vertere, mutare, transferre, subvertere:—

Ansýne ðýn awendst ðū *faciem tuam avertis*, Ps. Spl. 43, 27: Ps. Th. 73, 11: 103, 27: 101, 2: 77, 38. Heó awent hyre hūs and sēcþ geornlīce óþ heó hine fint *sche turneth vpsodoun the hous and sekith diligently til sche fynde it*, Wyc; Lk. Bos. 15, 8. He wæter awende to wīnlīcum drence *he turned water into winelike drink*, Ælfc. T. 27, 7: Ps. Spl. 101, 28: Gen. 19, 26: Cd. 14; Th. 17, 13; Gen. 259: Jn. Bos. 10, 35. 'Historia Anglorum' ða ðe Ælfrēd cyning of Lēdene on Englisc awende [*Bede's*] *Historia Anglorum, which king Alfred translated from Latin into English*, Homl. Th. ii. 116, 30–118, 1. Ðeáh ðe seó bōc on Englisc awend sý *though the book be translated into English*, 118, 5. Ne nim ðū lāc, ða awendaþ rihtwīsra word *nec accipies munera, quæ subvertunt verba justorum*, Ex. 23, 8. II. *v. intrans. To turn* or *direct oneself, to turn from, go, depart*; se vertere, ire:—Ðæt hý, mid sume searawrence, from Xerse awenden [awende MS.] *that they would by some stratagem turn from Xerxes*, Ors. 2, 5; Bos. 47, 41. Hī awendon aweg *they turned away*, Ps. Th. 77, 57. v. wendan.

a-wended-līc, -wende-līc, -wendend-līc; *adj.* [awended *changed, pp. of* awendan, līc] *Movable, changeable, alterable, mutable*; mobilis, Alb. resp. 42.

a-wendednys, a-wændednys, -nyss, e; *f. A change, alteration*; commutatio:—Nā sōþ is him awendednys *non enim est illis commutatio*, Ps. Spl. 54, 22: 88, 50.

a-wendelīc-nes, -ness, e; *f. Mutableness, mutability, changeableness, inconstancy*; mutabilitas, Som. [a-wendedlīc *changeable*, -ness].

a-wendinog, e; *f. An overthrowing, a change, ruin*; subversio, Scint. 61.

a-wenian; *p.* ede; *pp.* ed *To wean*; ablactare:—Ǣr ðone, ðæt acennede bearn, awened sī *quoadusque, qui gignitur, ablactatur*, Bd. 1, 27, resp. 8; S. 493, 33. v. wenian.

a-went, -wenþ, -wendeþ *turns*, Lk. Bos. 15, 8. v. a-wendan.

a-weódian, -weódigan; *v. a. To weed, root* or *rake up, to destroy*; sarculare:—Ðæt man aweódige unriht *that one should root up injustice*, L. C. S. 1; Th. i. 376, 7.

a-weōl *flowed forth*, Cot. 72. v. a-weallan.

a-weorpan, -wurpan, -wyrpan; ðū -wyrpst, he -wyrpþ; *p.* ic, he -wearp, ðū -wurpe, *pl.* -wurpon; *impert.* -weorp, -wurp, -wyrp ðū; *pp.* -worpen; *v. a.* [a *from*, weorpan *to throw*] *To throw* or *cast from* or *down, to cast away* or *off, cast out, to degrade, reject, divorce*; abjicere, dejicere, projicere, ejicere, propellere, repellere, reprobare, repudiare:—Ðæt he ðec aweorpe of woruldrīce *that he shall cast thee from thy worldly kingdom*, Cd. 203; Th. 253, 1; Dan. 589. Ðū awurpe hī, ðā hī wǣron upahafen *dejecisti eos, dum allevarentur*, Ps. Spl. 72, 18: 79, 9: Ps. Th. 72, 14. Is wærgðu [wærgða MS.] aworpen *the curse is cast off*, Exon. 9 a; Th. 7, 8; Cri. 98: Bt. Met. Fox 23, 12; Met. 23, 6: Bd. 3, 24; S. 557, 44: Mt. Bos. 12, 28. Ðā woldon senatus hine aweorpan *then would the senate degrade him*, Ors. 3, 10; Bos. 70, 36: Bt. 37, 4; Fox 192, 10. Ne aweorp ðū me *ne projicias me*, Ps. Spl. 70, 10. Mannes sunu gebyreþ beón aworpen *oportet filium hominis reprobari*, Mk. Bos. 8, 31. Aworpen wīf *a divorced wife*, L. Ælf. C. 7; Th. ii. 346, 6. Aworpen man biþ ā unnyt *homo apostata, vir inutilis*, Past. 47, 1; Hat. MS. 68 a, 23. Used also with the prepositions on *into*, as awurpan on *to cast into*, Mt. Foxe 13, 50. Fram *from*, Mt. Bos. 5, 29, 30. Ūt *out*, Mt. Bos. 13, 48. Under *below*, Bt. 37, 4; Fox 192, 10.

a-weorpnis, -niss, e; *f. A casting off, putting away, divorce*; repudium, Mt. Rush. Stv. 19, 7. v. a-worpenes. DER. weorpan.

a-weorþan, a-wurþan, ic -weorþe, -wurþe, ðū -wyrst, he -weorþeþ, -wyrþeþ, -wurþeþ, -wyrþ, *pl.* -weorþaþ, -wurþaþ; *p.* -wearþ, *pl.* -wurdon; *pp.* -worden; *v. intrans.* [a *from, away*, weorþan *to become*] *To cease to be, become insipid* or *worthless*; evanescere:—Gyf ðæt sealt awyrþ *if the salt become insipid*, Mt. Bos. 5, 13: Lk. Bos. 14, 34. Ðū awordena *raca*, Mt. Bos. 5, 22.

a-weosung, e; *f. The being, essence,* or *subsistence of a thing*; subsistentia, essentia, Cot. 170. v. wesan.

a-weóx *waxed, increased*, Ors. 1, 3; Bos. 27, 25. v. a-weaxan.

ā-wēr *anywhere, in any wise*, Bt. Met. Fox 8, 28; Met. 8, 14: Bt. 7, 3; Fox 20, 14. v. ā-hwǣr.

a-werd, es; *m. A spoiled* or *worthless fellow*; vappa, Ælfc. Gl. 9; Som. 56, 113; Wrt. Voc. 18, 61, = a-wered = a-werded; *pp. of* a-werdan.

a-werdan; *p.* de; *pp.* ed; *v. trans. To injure, corrupt, violate, destroy*; lædere, corrumpere, vitiare, violare. v. a-wyrdan.

a-wered *protected, worn*; *pp. of* a-werian I and III.

a-wergian, -wirgean, -wyrgian; *p.* de; *pp.* ed [a, wergian *to curse*] *To accurse, curse, condemn, malign*; maledicere, condemnare, malignari:—Helle dióful, awerged in wītum *hell's devil, accursed to torments*, Andr. Kmbl. 2599; An. 1301: Gen. 8, 21: Ps. Spl. 73, 4.

a-werian, -wergan, -wergean; *p.* ede; *pp.* ed; *v. trans.* I. *to ward off, defend, restrain, protect, cover*; defendere, prohibere, protegere:—Ðæt be hine eáþ awerian mæge *that he may easily defend him*, L. C. S. 20; Th. i. 388, 2. He hine awerede *he defended himself*, Ors. 3, 9; Bos. 68, 23, 29: 5, 3; Bos. 103, 25: Ps. Th. 105, 24. Ðū mīn heáfod scealt on gefeohtdæge feóndum awergean *obumbrasti caput meum in die belli*, 139, 7. Ðū me oft aweredest wyrigra gemōtes *protexisti me a conventu malignantium*, 63, 2: 55, 11. Ðeáh hit mon awerge wīrum ūtan *though it be covered with wires without*, Exon. 111 a; Th. 424, 30; Rä. 41, 47. II. *to ward off from oneself, spurn from oneself*; aspernari:—Aweredon ða ōðre *aspernabantur ceteros*, Lk. Rush. War. 18, 9. III. *to wear, wear out*; terere, deterere:—Awered *tritus*, R. Ben. 55. v. werian.

a-werpan *to cast away*; projicere:—Awerp from ðē *projice abs te*, Mt. Rush. Stv. 5, 29. v. a-weorpan.

a-wersian *to make worse*; deterius facere, Cart. Edwardi R. v. wyrsian.

āwesc-nis, -niss, e; *f. Disgrace, blushing for shame, reverence*, Ps. Surt. 34, 26. v. ǣwisc-nys.

a-wēst; *part. Wasted, laid waste, waste, desert*; vastatus, desertus:—Awēst wearþ *was laid waste*, Ors. 3, 9; Bos. 66, 17, 19, 21: Ps. Spl. T. 68, 30. v. a-wēstan.

a-wēstan; *p.* -wēste; *pp.* -wēsted [-wēstd], -wēst [a *intensive*, wēstan *to waste*] *To waste, lay waste, depopulate, ravage, destroy*; vastare, devastare, desertum facere, desolare:—Hī awēste *eam vastavit*, Jos. 10, 39. Hī ealle Ægypta awēston *they laid waste all Egypt*, Ors. 1, 10; Bos. 32, 26. Troia awēsted wæs *Troy was laid waste*, 2, 2; Bos. 40, 28. Eall seó þeód awēst wearþ *all the nation was laid waste*, 3, 9; Bos. 66, 17, 19, 21. Sý wunung heora awēst *fiat habitatio eorum deserta*, Ps. Spl. T. 68, 30. Widūtan awēst hīg sweord *swerd with outforth schal waaste* [*destroy*] *hem*, Wyc; foris vastabit eos gladius, Cant. Moys. Isrl. Lamb. 193 a, 25. His stede odðe stōwe hīg awēston *locum ejus desolaverunt*, Ps. Lamb. 78, 7.

a-wēstendnes, -ness, e; *f. A wasting, a laying waste*; vastatio, Som. v. a-wēstan, a-wēstende, *part*; ness.

a-wēstnis, -niss, e; *f.* [a-wēst *wasted*, ness] *Desolation*; desolatio, Lk. Rush. War. 21, 20.

āwian; *p.* ode; *pp.* od [= eówan, ýwan] *To shew*; ostendere. v. at-āwian, Ps. Spl. T. 77, 14.

a-wierdan *to corrupt*; corrumpere:—He awiert ðæt mōd *corrumpit animum*, Past. 53, 5. v. a-wyrdan.

a-wierged; *def. m.* -wiergeda, -wiergda; *pp. Accursed, wicked*; maledictus, malignus, Past. 65, 4? v. a-wyrged.

ā-wiht, ā-wyht, ā-wuht, ā-uht, āht, es; *n.* [ā *semper*, wiht *creatura, animal, aliquid*] AUGHT, *anything*; aliquid:—Unc gemǣne ne sceal elles āwiht *to us two shall not be aught else common*, Cd. 91; Th. 114, 16; Gen. 1905: Ps. Th. 55, 9. Handa hī habbaþ, ne hió hwæðere māgon gegrāpian gōdes āwiht *they have hands, and yet they may not touch anything of good*, Ps. Th. 113, 15: 58, 3: 65, 16: Bt. Met. Fox 9, 124; Met. 9, 62. Nafast ðū for āwiht ealle þeóda *pro nihil habebis omnes gentes*, Ps. Th. 58, 8. Ðæt hī geseón ne māgon āwiht *ne illi videant aliquid*, 68, 24. v. nā-wiht, nāht.

ā-wiht, ā-wyht, ā-wuht, ā-uht, āht; *adv. At all, by any means*; omnino, ullo modo:—Ne lata ðū āwiht *do not thou tarry at all*, Ps. Th. 69, 7: 77, 10, 12: 134, 19. Me ðæt riht ne þinceþ, ðæt ic ōleccan āwiht þurfe Gode æfter gōde ǣnegum *to me it seems not right, that I at all need cringe to God for any good*, Cd. 15; Th. 19, 13; Gen. 290.

a-wildian; *p.* ode; *pp.* od; *v. intrans. To become wild* or *fierce*; silvescere, efferari, Off. Episcop. 7.

a-willan; *p.* de; *pp.* ed *To cause to bubble, to boil*; facere ut aliquid ferveat vel ebulliat, coquere, decoquere:—Awilled meolc *boiled milk, pottage*; juta [jura?], Cot. 168. Awilled wīn *vel* cyren *new wine, just pressed from the grape*, or *new wine boiled till half evaporated*; dulcisapa, Cot. 62, 168. v. a-wyllan, cyren.

a-windan; ic -winde, ðū -wintst, -winst, he -wint, *pl.* -windaþ; *p.* -wand, *pl.* -wundon; *pp.* -wunden [a, windan *to wind*]. I. *v. trans. To wind, bend*; plectere, torquere:—Hī him onsetton þyrnenne helm awundenne *imponunt ei plectentes spineam coronam*, Mk. Bos. 15, 17. II. *v. trans. To strip off*; detrahere:—Gif him mon ðonne awint of ða clāþas *if any man should strip off the clothes from him*, Bt. 37, 1; Fox 186, 10: Bt. Met. Fox 25, 44; Met. 25, 22. III. *v. intrans. To whirl* or *slip off*; labi:—Gif sió æcs ðonne awient [awint, Cot.] of ðæm hielfe *if the axe then slip from the handle*, Past. 21, 7; Hat. MS. 32 b, 6.

a-windwian, -wyndwian *to winnow, blow away*; ventilare, Ps. Spl. 43, 7. v. windwian.

a-winnan; *p.* -wan, *pl.* -wunnon; *pp.* -wunnen *To labour, contend, gain, overcome*; laborare, contendere, acquirere, nancisci, superare:—Ǣlc wīs mon scyle awinnan ǣgðer ge wið ða rēðan wyrde ge wið ða wīnsuman *every wise man ought to contend both against the severe fortune and against the pleasant*, Bt. 40, 3; Fox 238, 16. Ealles ðū ðæs wīte awunne *for all this thou hast gained suffering*, Exon. 39 b; Th. 130, 18; Gū. 440. Sūsl wæs awunnen *the pain was overcome*, Cd. 208; Th. 257, 8; Dan. 654. DER. winnan.

a-wint *strips off, slips off*. v. a-windan.

a-wirdan *to destroy*, Leo 254. v. a-wyrdan.

a-wirgan; *p.* de; *pp.* ed *To strangle*; strangulare:—Gelīcost ðam ðe he hine sylfne hæfde unwitende awirged *as if he had voluntarily strangled himself*, Ors. 6, 36; Bos. 131, 38. v. a-wyrgan.

a-wirgean; *p.* de; *pp.* ed *To accurse, curse;* maledicere:—Nelle ic awirgean ꝺa eorþan *nolo maledicere terræ*, Gen. 8, 21. Awirgede woruldsorga *ye execrable worldly cares*, Bt. 3, 1; Fox 4, 25. v. a-wergian, a-wyrgian.

a-wirgnis, -niss, e; *f. A curse, cursing;* maledictio:—Sette ge awirgnisse uppan Hebal dúne *ponite maledictionem super montem Hebal*, Deut. 11, 29. v. a-wyrgednes.

áwisc-ferinend, es; *m.* [áwisc = ǽwisc *disgrace*, ferinian = firenian *to sin*] *One who sins disgracefully, a publican;* qui turpiter péccat, publicanus, Cot. 204.

a-wisnian; *p.* ade; *pp.* ad *To be dry, to become dry, wizen;* arescere:—Awisnade *vel* oferdrugade *aruit*, Lk. Lind. War. 8, 6. v. wisnian.

a-wlǽtan; *p.* -wlǽtte; *pp.* -wlǽted *To defile;* fœdare, Hymn: Mod. Confit. 1.

a-wlancian; *p.* ode; *pp.* od *To come in youthful strength, to exult, to be proud;* exultare, Leo 262. v. wlancian.

áwo; *adv. Always, ever;* semper, unquam:—Áwo *ever*, Exon. 26 b; Th. 78, 9; Cri. 1271: 32 a; Th. 101, 25; Cri. 1664. Siððan áwo *ever after*, 48 a; Th. 164, 24; Gú. 1016. Áwo to ealdre *for evermore*, 14 b; Th. 30, 13, note; Cri. 479. v. áwa.

a-wóc *awoke, arose*, Gen. 9, 24; *p. of* a-wacan.

a-wódian *to root up*. v. aweódian.

a-woffian; *p.* ode; *pp.* od *To rave, be delirious, frantic;* delirare:—Awoffod *phreneticus*, Leo 266. v. woffian.

awóh; *adv.* [a, wóh *crooked*] AWRY, *unjustly, wrongfully, badly; the same as* mid wóge *with injustice*, or *unjustly;* tortè, obliquè, malè:—Gif mon ðæt trod awóh drífe *if one wrongfully pursue the foot-step* [*tread*], L. O. D. 1; Th. i. 352, 10. Ðæt man ǽr awóh tosomne gedydon *which they before unjustly joined together*, L. Edm. B. 9; Th. i. 256, 11.

a-worden; *pp. of* a-weorþan; *def. m.* awordena *become worthless*:—Ðú awordena *raca*, Mt. Bos. 5, 22.

a-worpen *cast off, away*, Exon. 9 a; Th. 7, 8; Cri. 98; *pp. of* a-weorpan.

a-worpenes, -worpennys, -worpnes, -ness, -nyss, e; *f. A rejection, casting away, reprobation, reproving;* abjectio:—Ic eom aworpennys folces *ego sum abjectio plebis*, Ps. Spl. 21, 5. v. a-weorpnis; forwyrpnes.

a-worpen-líc; *adj. Damnable;* damnabilis, Past. 52, 8.

a-wóx *waxed, grew, rose*, Exon. 103 b; Th. 392, 6; Rä. 11, 3; *p. of* a-weaxan.

a-wræc, -wrǽcon *related*, Exon. 17 a; Th. 40, 3; Cri. 633; *p. of* a-wrecan.

a-wrǽstan, -wréstan; *p.* -wrǽste; *pp.* -wrǽst *To wrest from, to extort;* extorquere, Cot. 78. v. wrǽstan.

a-wrát *wrote*, Bd. 5, 23; S. 648, 27; *p. of* a-wrítan.

a-wráþ *bound up*, Bd. 4, 22; S. 590, 36; *p. of* a-wríðan.

a-wreáh *discovered*, Ps. Spl. 97, 3; *p. of* a-wreóhan. v. a-wreón.

a-wrecan; *p.* -wræc, *pl.* -wrǽcon; *pp.* -wrecen. I. *to drive away;* pellere, expellere:—Ðara ðe he of lífe hét awrecan *of those whom he bade to drive from life*, Exon. 130 a; Th. 498, 11; Rä. 87, 11. II. *to hit, strike;* icere, percutere:—Awrecen wælpílum *hit with darts of death*, Exon. 49 b; Th. 171, 15; Gú. 1127: 51 b; Th. 179, 11; Gú. 1260. III. *to relate, recite, sing;* narrare, enarrare, canere:—Bi ðon Iob giedd awræc *of whom Job related his lay*, Exon. 17 a; Th. 40, 3; Cri. 633: 84 a; Th. 316, 20; Mód. 51: Beo. Th. 3452; B. 1724: 4223; B. 2108. IV. *to avenge, revenge;* ulcisci:—Gif hine hwá awrecan wille *if any one will avenge him*, L. Ath. i. 20; Th. i. 210, 10, note 20. v. wrecan.

a-wreccan; *p.* -wrehte; *pp.* -wreht; *v. a. To arouse, awake, revive;* excitare, suscitare:—Ic wylle gán and awreccan hyne of slǽpe *vado ut a somno excitem eum*, Jn. Bos. 11, 11. Ðe se Hǽlend awrehte *quem suscitavit Jesus*, 12, 1. v. wreccan.

a-wrecen *banished, driven away;* extorris, Cot. 212: 5; *pp. of* a-wrecan.

a-wregennes *a discovery*. v. a-wrigenes.

a-wrehte, a-wreht *aroused, awoke;* suscitavit, suscitatus, Jn. Bos. 12, 1; *p. and pp. of* a-wreccan.

a-wreón, -wreóhan, -wrióhan, -wrión; *p.* -wreáh, *pl.* -wrugon; *pp.* -wrogen; *v. a.* [a *not*, wreón *to cover*] *To uncover, discover, disclose, open, reveal;* revelare:—Se Sunu hit awreón wyle *the Son will reveal it*, Lk. Bos. 10, 22. Ðú ðás þing lytlingum awruge *revelasti ea parvulis*, 10, 21. Drihten awreáh rihtwísnysse hys *Dominus revelavit justitiam suam*, Ps. Spl. 97, 3. Awreóh Drihtne weg ðínne *revela Domino viam tuam*, Ps. Lamb. 36, 5. DER. wreóhan, wreón.

a-wréstan *to wrest from, extort;* extorquere. v. a-wrǽstan.

a-wreðian; *p.* ede; *pp.* ed; *v. a.* [a, wreðian *to support*] *To support, underprop, sustain;* sustentare:—Agustínus fram Gode awreðed wæs *Augustin was sustained by God*, Bd. 2, 3; S. 505, 1. He, mid his crycce hine awreðiende, hám becom *he, with his crutch supporting himself, came home*, Bd. 4, 31; S. 610, 18: Past. 17, 11; Hat. MS. 25 a, 20: Exon. 37 a; Th. 121, 27; Gú. 295.

a-wrigen *revealed*, Lk. Bos. 2, 35; *pp. of* a-wríhan.

a-wrigenes, -wregennes, -ness, e; *f. A discovery, revelation;* revelatio:—To þeóda awrigenesse *ad revelationem gentium*, Lk. Bos. 2, 32.

a-wríhan; *p.* -wráh, *pl.* -wrigon; *pp.* -wrigen [a *not, un-;* wríhan *to cover*] *To uncover, reveal;* revelare:—Stefn Drihtnes awríhþ þiccetu *vox Domini revelabit condensa*, Ps. Spl. 28, 8. Awrigene synd grúndweallas [grundfeallas MS.] ymbhwyrftes eorþan *revelata sunt fundamenta orbis terrarum*, 17, 17: Lk. Bos. 2, 35.

a-wringan; *p.* -wrang, *pl.* -wrungon; *pp.* -wrungen *To wring out, to squeeze out, express;* exprimere, Cot. 196. v. wringan.

a-wrióhan, -wrión *to uncover, reveal;* revelare:—Awrióh Drihtne weg ðínne *revela Domino viam tuam*, Ps. Spl. T. 36, 5. v. a-wreón, wreón.

a-wrítan; *p.* -wrát, *pl.* -writon; *pp.* -writen; *v. a.* [a, wrítan *to engrave, write*]. I. *to write out* or *down, to transcribe, describe, compose;* transcribere, describere, conscribere, contexere:—Ðæs hálgan fæder and biscopes Sancti Cuþberhtes líf ǽrest eroico metro and æfter fæce gerǽde worde ic awrát *I wrote out the life of the holy father and bishop, St. Cuthbert, first in heroic metre, and after a space in prose*, Bd. 5, 23; S. 648, 27. Eall þurh endebyrdnesse ic awrát *cuncta per ordinem transcriberé curavi*, 5, 23; S. 648, 11. Nú hæbbe we awriten ðære súþ *now have we described the south*, Ors. 1, 1; Bos. 17, 42. Leviticus ys genemned *Ministerialis* on Lýden, ðæt ys þénungbóc, for ðam ðara sacerda þénunga sind ðár áwritene *Leviticus is called in Latin* Ministerialis, *that is service-book, because the services of the priests are described therein*, Lev. pref. Ðám ðæt hálige gewrit awriten is *quibus scriptura sancta contexta est*, Bd. 5, 23; S. 648, 43. Wéndest ðú ðæt awriten nǽre *thoughtest thou that it was not written*, Cd. 228; Th. 307, 8; Sat. 676: Ps. Th. 138, 14. Sum biþ list-hendig to awrítanne word-gerýnu *one is cunning to write down word-mysteries*, Exon. 79 b; Th. 299, 2; Crä. 96. Ðara abbuda stǽr and spell ðysses mynstres on twám bócum ic awrát *I wrote a history and narrative of the abbots of this monastery in two books*, Bd. 5, 23; S. 648, 30: 5, 23; S. 649, 11. II. *to inscribe;* inscribere, inscriptione ornare:—Wæs se beám bócstafum awriten *the beam was inscribed with letters*, Elen. Kmbl. 182; El. 91. III. *to carve, delineate, draw;* sculpere, delineare:—Sindon awritene [MS. awriten] on wealle wuldres þegnas *upon the wall are carved the thanes of glory*, Andr. Kmbl. 1451; An. 726. Hí bǽron anlícnysse Hǽlendes on brede afægde and awritene *they bore the Saviour's likeness figured and drawn on a board;* ferebant imaginem Domini Salvatoris in tabula depictam, Bd. 1, 25; S. 487, 4.

a-wríðan; *p.* -wráþ, *pl.* -wriðon; *pp.* -wriðen [a, wríðan *to wreathe, bind*]. I. *to bind up, bind, wreathe;* alligare, torquere:—Hí me gyrene awriðon [MS. awriðan] *posuerunt mihi laqueos*, Ps. Th. 118, 110. Sylfa his wúnda awráþ *he bound up his wounds;* sua vulnera ipse alligavit, Bd. 4, 22; S. 590, 36. II. *to unbind, loosen;* solvere:—Ðæt he awríðe bearn fordóndra *ut solveret filios interemptorum*, Ps. Spl. 101, 21.

a-wruge *revealedst*, Lk. Bos. 10, 21; *p. of* a-wreóhan. v. a-wreón.

a-wrungen *wrung;* *pp. of* a-wringan.

a-wrygen = a-wrigen *discovered;* *pp. of* a-wríhan.

a-wrygenes = a-wrigenes *a discovery, revealing*. v. a-wrigenes.

áwðer = á-hwæðer; *adj. pron. Either, each, one or other;* alter, alteruter:—Ne uncer áwðer *not either of us;* neuter [*ne-uter*] nostrum, Exon. 129 b; Th. 496, 29; Rä. 85, 22. Ða tungl áwðer [MS. auðer] óðres rene á ne gehríneþ, ǽr ðam ðæt óðer of gewíteþ *the stars never touch each other's course, before the other goes away*, Bt. Met. Fox 29, 19; Met. 29, 10: 20, 84; Met. 20, 42: Bt. 6; Fox 16, 3.

á-wuht [= á-wiht] *Aught, anything; at all, by any means;* aliquid; omnino, ullo modo:—Ne meahte on ðære eorþan áwuht libban *nor might aught live on the earth*, Bt. Met. Fox 20, 214; Met. 20, 107: 11, 18; Met. 11, 9: 18, 14; Met. 18, 7: Cd. 25; Th. 32, 1; Gen. 496. v. á-wiht, ná-wuht.

awul *an awl;* fuscinula *vel* tridens, Ælfc. Gl. 31; Som. 61, 78; Wrt. Voc. 27, 8. v. al.

a-wunden *bent*, Mk. Bos. 15, 17; *pp. of* a-windan.

a-wundrian; *p.* ade; *pp.* ad *To make a wonder of;* vertere quasi miraculi ad modum:—Eów sceal ðæt leás awundrad weorþan *the falsehood shall be made a wonder of for you*, Invent. Crs. Recd. 1161.

a-wunian; *p.* ode, ade; *pp.* od, ad [a, wunian *to dwell*] *To abide, remain, continue, insist;* manere, permanere, insistere:—Ðeós sibb awunade on Cristes cyrican *hæc pax mansit in ecclesia Christi*, Bd. 1, 8; S. 479, 26. He lét hit on his bósme awunian *he let it remain in his bosom*, 3, 2; S. 525, 14. He on hálgum gebédum astód and awunode *he insisted and continued in holy prayers*, 4, 25; S. 599, 31. Hreówe awunian *pœnitentiæ insistere*, 4, 25; S. 600, 11.

a-wunnen *overcome*, Cd. 208; Th. 257, 8; Dan. 654; *pp. of* a-winnan.

a-wurpan *to cast away;* projicere:—Awurp hí fram ðé *projice eam abs te*, Mt. Bos. 5, 30. v. a-weorpan.

a-wurpon *cast off*, Bd. 3, 24; S. 557, 44; *p. pl. of* a-weorpan.

a-wurþan, ic -wurþe, he -wurþeþ, *pl.* -wurþaþ; *p.* -wearþ, *pl.* -wurdon; *pp.* -worden *To cease to be, become insipid* or *worthless;* evanescere:—Ðæt ge awurþaþ [wurþaþ MS.] *that ye perish* [*cease to be*], Deut. 4, 26. v. a-weorþan.

a-wurtwarian; *p.* ude; *pp.* ud *To root up;* exterminare:—Awurtwarude hine *exterminavit eam*, Ps. Spl. M. 79, 14. v. a-wyrt-walian.

a-wygedne, Exon. 74 b; Th. 279, 21, note; Jul. 617; *for* awyrgedne *accursed; pp. of* a-wyrgian.

â-wyht [= â-wiht] *Aught, anything; at all:*—Ne hî for âwyht eorþan cyste ða sêlestan geseón woldan *pro nihilo habuerunt terram desiderabilem*, Ps. Th. 105, 20: 103, 9: 113, 14.

a-wyllan, -willan, -wellan; *p.* de; *pp.* ed; *v. trans. To cause to bubble, to boil;* facere ut aliquid ferveat vel ebulliat, coquere, decoquere:—Genim awylled hunig *take boiled honey*, Herb. 1, 20; Lchdm. i. 76, 23. Awylled wîn *defrutum*, Lye. v. wyllan.

a-wyltan; *p.* -wyltede, -wylte; *pp.* -wylted = -wyltd = -wylt; *v. a. To roll, roll away, revolve;* devolvere, volutare:—Ðæt hîg awylton ðone stân *ut devolverent lapidem*, Gen. 29, 3. Awylt *rolled away*, Lk. Bos. 24, 2.

a-wylþ *shall bubble up;* ebulliet, Ex. 8, 3. v. a-weallan.

a-wyltne *rolled away*, Lk. Bos. 24, 2; *acc. s. m. of* a-wylt; *pp. of* a-wyltan.

a-wyndwian *to blow away;* ventilare:—We awyndwiaþ [windwiaþ, Lamb.] fŷnd ûre *ventilabimus inimicos nostros*, Ps. Spl. 43, 7. v. a-windwian.

a-wyrcan; *p.* -wyrhte; *pp.* -wyrht *To do, effect;* facere, agere:—Riht awyrce *let him do right*, L. H. E. 8; Th. i. 30, 13. Ðæt ðû me gewissige bet ðonne ic awyrhte to ðê *that thou wouldest direct me better than I have done towards thee*, Bt. 42; Fox 260, 6. DER. wyrcan.

a-wyrdan, -werdan; *p.* -wyrde; *pp.* -wyrded, -wyrd; *v. trans. To injure, corrupt, destroy;* lædere, corrumpere, vitiare, violare:—Ðe he sylf awyrde *whom he himself had injured*, Homl. Th. i. 4, 24. Æðeling manig wundum awyrded *many a noble injured with wounds*, Beo. Th. 2230; B. 1113. Gif spræc awyrd weorþ *if speech be injured*, L. Ethb. 52; Th. i. 16, 5. Ðŷlæs hî [*scil.* wæstmas] rênes scûr awyrde *lest the shower of rain should destroy them* [i. e. *the fruits*], Exon. 59 b; Th. 215, 2; Ph. 247. [*O. H. Ger.* ar-wartian *violare, vitiare, fœdare, adulterare, corrumpere, depravare.*] DER. wyrdan.

a-wyrdla, an; *m. Damage;* detrimentum. v. æ-wyrdla, æf-werdla.

a-wyrdnys, -nyss, e; *f. Hurt, injury, damage, ruin, destruction;* læsio, labes, damnum:—Crist mihte, bûtan awyrdnysse his lima, nyðerasceótan *Christ could, without injury of his limbs, cast himself down*, Homl. Th. i. 170, 22. Awyrdnyss *labes*, Ælfc. Gr. 9, 27; Som. 11, 25: 13; Som. 16, 5.

a-wyrgan, -wirgan; *p.* de; *pp.* ed *To strangle, suffocate, corrupt, injure, violate;* strangulare, suffocare, corrumpere, lædere, violare:—He hine sylfne hæfde awirged *he had strangled himself*, Ors. 6, 36; Bos. 131, 38. Wommum awyrged *corrupted with sins*, Cd. 169; Th. 211, 26; Exod. 532: Exon. 30 b; Th. 95, 24; Cri. 1562: 105 b; Th. 401, 25; Rä. 21, 17. [*Ger.* erwürgen *strangulare: O. H. Ger.* arwurgian *id.*]

a-wyrgda, an; *m.* [*the def. pp. of* a-wyrgian *to curse*] *The cursed, the devil;* diabolus, Cd. 220; Th. 284, 3; Sat. 316.

a-wyrged *cursed;* malignus, maledictus, Mt. Bos. 25, 41. v. a-wyrgian.

a-wyrgedlîc; *adj. Wicked, evil;* malignus:—Awyrgedlîc geþanc *a wicked thought*, Nicod. 20: Thw. 10, 11.

a-wyrgednes, a-wyrgednys, a-wirgnis, -niss, e; *f. A cursedness, wickedness, a curse, reviling;* malignitas, maledictio:—Ðæs mid awyrgednesse [of awyrgednysse, Ps. Spl. C.] mûþ full is *cujus maledictione os plenum est*, Ps. Lamb. second 9, 7: 13, 3: Deut. 11, 29: Th. Diplm. A. D. 970; 243, 16. DER. wyrgednes.

a-wyrgendlîc; *adj. Detestable, abominable;* detestabilis, Nathan. 7.

a-wyrgian; *p.* -wyrgede; *pp.* -wyrged, -wyrgd *To curse, execrate, malign;* execrari, maledicere, malignari:—Ðû awyrgedest his cynegyrdum *maledixisti sceptris ejus*, Cant. Abac. Lamb. 3, 14: Ps. Spl. 73, 4. Nelle ic awirgean ða eorþan *nolo maledicere terræ*, Gen. 8, 21. The perfect participle signifies *execrable, wicked, detestable;* execrabilis, maledictus, malignus, malignans:—Gewîtaþ nû, awirgede woruldsorga *depart now, execrable worldly cares*, Bt. 3; Fox 4, 25. Gewîtaþ ge awyrgede fram me on ðæt êce fŷr *discedite a me maledicti in ignem æternum*, Mt. Bos. 25, 41: Exon. 30 a; Th. 93, 2; Cri. 1520. Of ðam awyrgedan wrâðan sweorde *de gladio maligno*, Ps. Th. 143, 11. Seó gegaderung ðara awyrgdra *consilium malignantium*, 21, 14. *The devil is called* Se awyrgda *the accursed*, Cd. 220; Th. 284, 3; Sat. 316. Se awyrgeda gâst *the accursed spirit*, Guthl. 7; Gdwin. 44, 12. Se awyrgda wulf *the accursed wolf*, Exon. 11 b; Th. 16, 20; Cri. 256. v. a-wergian.

âwyrn; *adv. Before?* antea, olim? Fox; Manning *says,—perhaps for* âhwǽr, *anywhere, in any place;* alicubi:—Ne hŷrde ic guman âwyrn [gumena fyrn, Grn.] ǽnigne ǽr ǽfre bringan sêlran lâre *I have not heard before any other man ever bring better lore*, Menol. Fox 200.

a-wyrpan; *p.* -wearp, *pl.* -wurpon; *pp.* -worpen *To cast away, cast out, reject, take away;* projicere, repellere, auferre:—To awyrpanne *ut auferant*, Ps. Th. 39, 16. Ahola hit ût, and awyrp hit fram ðê *erue eum* [*oculum*], *et projice abs te*, Mt. Jun. 5, 29: Ps. Th. 50, 12; Ps. Grn. ii. 149, 50, 12. v. a-weorpan.

a-wyrþ *loses its strength, becomes insipid*, Mt. Bos. 5, 13. v. a-weorþan.

a-wyrþian? [a *intensive*, wyrþian *to glorify*] *To give honour to, to glorify;* glorificare, Cant. Moys. Lye. v. weorþian.

a-wyrt-walian; *p.* ode; *pp.* od; *v. a.* [a *out*, wyrtwalian *to root, to fix roots*] *To root up, eradicate, extirpate, exterminate;* eradicare, supplantare:—Ælc plantung byþ awyrtwalod *omnis plantatio eradicabitur*, Mt. Jun. 15, 13. Ðelæs ge ðone hwǽte awyrtwalion *ne forte eradicetis triticum*, 13, 29: Lk. Bos. 17, 6: Bt. Met. Fox 12, 51; Met. 12, 26: Ps. Th. 36, 9. Awyrtwala hine *supplanta eum*, Ps. Spl. 16, 14.

a-wystelan, a-wystlan *to hiss, lisp, whistle;* sibilare. v. hwistlan.

Axa-mûþa, an; *m. Exmouth*, Chr. 1049; Th. 307, 37. v. Exan mûþa.

axan = oxan *oxen;* boves:—Sceáp and axan *oves et boves*, Ps. Spl. 8, 7. v. oxa.

axan *ashes*, Lev. 1, 16. v. axe.

Axan minster *Axminster, Devon*, Lye. v. Acsan mynster.

ax-baken; *part. Baked in ashes;* subcinericius, Gr. Dial. 1, 11.

axe *an axe*, Mt. Rush. Stv. 3, 10. v. acas, acase.

axe, an; *f. Ash, ashes;* cinis:—Swâ swâ dust oððe axe *as dust or ashes*, Bt. 33, 4; Fox 130, 9: Bt. Met. Fox 20, 211; Met. 20, 106. On ðære stôwe ðe man ða axan gît *in loco in quo cineres effundi solent*, Lev. 1, 16. Bearwas wurdon to axan and to ŷslan *the groves became ashes and embers*, Cd. 119; Th. 154, 9; Gen. 2553. v. asce.

axian, axigan, axigean; *p.* ode; *pp.* od *To ask;* interrogare:—He axode *he asked*, Ors. 2, 5; Bos. 46, 43. Ic axige me rǽdes *consulo*, Ælfc. Gr. 28, 3; Som. 31, 2. Ic axige *percunctor* [= *percontor*], 25; Som. 27, 6: Mt. Foxe 22, 46. v. acsian, ascian.

axiendlîc, axigendlîc; *adj. Interrogative, inquiring, inquisitive;* interrogativus:—Gif ic cweðe, hwâ dyde ðis? *quis hoc fecit?* ðon biþ se [hwâ *quis*] *interrogativum*, ðæt is axigendlîc, Ælfc. Gr. 18; Som. 21, 27.

axigean *to ask;* interrogare:—Ne nân ne dorste hyne axigean *neque ausus fuit quisquam eum interrogare*, Mt. Foxe 22, 46. v. axian.

axode *asked*, Ors. 2, 5; Bos. 46, 43; *p. of* axian.

axse, an; *f. Ashes;* cinis:—On axsan gehwyrfeþ *in cinerem convertit*, Bd. 4, 25; S. 600, 34. v. asce.

axung *inquiry*, Scint. 16. v. acsung.

a-ŷdlian; *p.* ode; *pp.* od *To make useless*, Ps. Lamb. 38, 12. v. a-îdlian.

a-ŷdlig; *adj. Void, empty, idle, vain;* vacuus, irritus, vanus. v. îdel.

a-yrnan, he -yrnþ; *p.* -arn, *pl.* -urnon; *pp.* -urnen [a *out*, yrnan *to run*] *To run over, to pass* or *go over, pass, go;* præterire, decurrere:—To nâhte hîg becumaþ swâ swâ a-yrnende wæter *ad nihilum devenient tamquam aqua decurrens*, Ps. Lamb. 57, 8. Swâ neáh wæs þûsend wintra a-urnen *so near was a thousand winters gone*, Chr. 973; Th. 226, 5, col. 1; Edg. 16: Cd. 79; Th. 98, 6; Gen. 1626. A-urnenre tîde *in* or *at a declining time, the time being far spent* or *gone*. A-urnen biþ *is run out, passed*, Som.

a-ŷtan; *p.* -ŷtte; *pp.* -ŷted [a *from*, ŷtan = ûtian *to out*] *To expel, drive out;* expellere:—He ðâ a-ŷtte ða Swegen ût *he then drove Sweyn out*, Chr. 1047; Th. 304, 4, col. 2. DER. ŷtan, ûtian.

azîma, orum; *pl. n. Lat. Unleavened;* infermentata, azŷma [= τὰ ἄζυμα, ἀ *without*, ζύμη *fermentation*]:—Freólsdæg azîmorum, se is gecweden eástre *dies festus azymorum, qui dicitur pascha;* ἡ ἑορτὴ τῶν ἀζύμων, ἡ λεγομένη πάσχα, Lk. Bos. 22, 1. Se dæg azîmorum *dies azymorum;* ἡ ἡμέρα τῶν ἀζύμων, Lk. Bos. 22, 7.

B

THE sound of **b** is produced by the lips; hence it is called a labial consonant, and has the same sound in Anglo-Saxon as in English. In all languages, and especially in the dialects of cognate languages, the letters employing the same organs of utterance are continually interchanged. In Anglo-Saxon, therefore, we find that *b* interchanges with the other labials, *f* and *p:*—Ic hæbbe *I have*, he hæfþ *he hath*. When words are transferred into modern English, *b* is sometimes represented by *f* or *v:*—Beber *or* befor *a beaver;* Ober, ofer, *over*. **2.** In comparing the Anglo-Saxon aspirated labial *f* with the corresponding letter in Old Saxon, the sister dialect, we find that the Old Saxons used a softer aspirated labial ƀ = *bh*. This softer aspirated ƀ generally occurs as a medial letter between two vowels; as,—

O. Sax.		*A. Sax.*		*Eng.*
graƀan	=	grafan	=	engrave
klioƀan	=	cleófan	=	cleave
geƀan	=	gifan	=	give

3. The Runic letter ᛒ not only stands for the letter **B, b,** but also for the name of the letter in Anglo-Saxon beorc *the birch-tree*. v. beorc.

bâ, bû *both; nom. f. n. acc. m. f. n. of* begen:—Ða idesa bâ *both the women*, Judth. 11; Thw. 23, 22; Jud. 133. Wæter and eorþe, sint on gecynde cealda bâ twâ *water and earth, both the two are by nature cold,*

Fox 20, 152; Met. 20, 76. Bysmeredon uncit [*Inscription* Bismærede ungket] men, bā ætgædre *they* [*men*] *reviled us two, both together*, Runic Inscrip. Kmbl. 354, 30.

baan, es; *n. A bone*:—Ne tobrǣcan ðа baan *they broke not the bones*, Homl. Daye 55, 17; Th. *has*, Ne tobrǣcon ða bān, Homl. ii. 280, 9. v. bān.

Babilōn, e; *f*: Babilōnie, Babilōnige, an; *f*: Babilōn, Babylōn, es; *f*. [v. wim-man, es; *f*.] *Babylon;* Babȳlōn, ōnis; *f*. This celebrated city of antiquity, in Mesopotamia, was built on both banks of the Euphrates. Its foundation by Nimrod is mentioned immediately after the Deluge, Gen. 10, 9, 10: 11, 9:—Nimrod [MS. Membrað], se ent, ongan ǣrest timbrian Babilōnia; and Ninus, se cyning æfter him, and Sameramis, his cwēn, hī ge-endade æfter him, on middeweardum hire rīce. Seó burh wæs getimbred on fildum lande, and on swīðe emnum. And heó wæs swīðe fæger on to lōcianne, and heó is swīðe rihte feówerscȳte. And ðæs wealles mycelnyss and fæstnyss, is ungelȳfedlīc to secgenne: ðæt he is l elna brād, and ii hund elna heáh, and his ymbgang is hund seofantig mīla, and seofeþan dǣl ānre mīle . . . Seó ylce burh Babylōnia, seó ðe mǣst wæs, and ǣrest ealra burga, seó is nū læst and wēstast *Nimrod, the giant, first began to build Babylon; and, after him, king Ninus, and then Semiramis, his queen, finished it in the middle of her reign. The city was built on open and very level land. It was very fair to look upon, and it is quite a true square. The greatness and firmness of the wall, when stated, is hardly to be believed. It is fifty ells broad, and two hundred ells high, and its circumference is seventy miles, and the seventh part of a mile . . . This very city of the Babylonians, which was the greatest and first of all cities, is now the least and most desolate*, Ors. 2, 4; Bos. 44, 17–31. Babilōn wæs mǣrost burga *Babylon was the greatest of cities*, Cd. 209; Th. 259, 19; Dan. 694. Babilōne weard *the guardian of Babylon*, 177; Th. 222, 14; Dan. 104: 178; Th. 223, 9; Dan. 117. Þurh Babilōnian burh *through the city of Babylon*, Ors. 2, 4; Bos. 44, 11. Babilōnes brego *the ruler of Babylon*, Cd. 174; Th. 218, 30; Dan. 47. Se wæs Babylōnes brego *he was the ruler of Babylon*, 79; Th. 98, 20; Gen. 1633. Ofer flōdas Babilōnes *super flumina Babylonis*, Ps. Surt. 136, 1: Ps. Spl. 136, 1. Dōhtor Babylōnes earm *filia Babylonis misera*, Ps. Surt. 136, 8: Ps. Spl. 136, 11. In Babilōne *in Babylon*, Cd. 82; Th. 102, 28; Gen. 1707. On ðære þeóde, ðe swā hātte bresne Babilōnige *in the country, that was so called powerful Babylon*, 180; Th. 226, 18; Dan. 173. [*Heb.* בָּבֶל bābĕl *the city of Belus*: *Grk.* Βαβυλών, ῶνος; *f*: *Lat.* Babȳlōn, ōnis; *f*.]

Babilōnia *Babylon, acc. Grk*, Ors. 2, 4; Bos. 44, 17. v. Babilōn.

Babilōnie, an; *f. Babylon*, Ors. 2, 4; Bos. 44, 11. v. Babilōn.

Babilōnige *Babylon*, Cd. 180; Th. 226, 18; Dan. 173. v. Babilōn.

Babilōnis *of Babylon, gen. Lat.* Ps. Th. 86, 2. v. Babilōn.

Babilōnisc; *def.* se Babilōnisca, seó, ðæt Babilōnisce; *adj. Babylonish;* Babylōnĭcus:—Dōhtor, seó Babilōnisce wræcce [MS. babilonisca wræcca] *filia Babilonis misera*, Ps. Lamb. 136, 8.

Babilōnisca, an; *m. Babylon;* Babȳlōn, ōnis; *f*:—Ofer flōd Babilōniscan *super flumina Babilonis*, Ps. Lamb. 136, 1. DER. Babilōnisc.

Babylōn *Babylon*, Cd. 79; Th. 98, 20; Gen. 1633. v. Babilōn.

baca *of backs; gen. pl. of* bæc.

BACAN; ic bace, ðū bacest, bæcest, bæcst, becest, becst, he baceþ, bæceþ, beceþ, *pl.* bacaþ; *p.* ic, he bōc, ðū bōce, *pl.* bōcon; *pp.* bacen; *v. a. To* BAKE; torrere, pinsere, coquere:—Fīf bacaþ on ānum ofene *quinque in uno clibano coquant*, Lev. 26, 26. Hī bōcon melu *coxerunt farinam*, Ex. 12, 39. [*Orm.* bakenn: *Chauc.* bake: *Wyc.* bake; *p.* boke; *pp.* bakun: *Scot.* baike *to bake; pp.* baiken; bakster *a baker*: *O. Sax.* bakan: *N. Frs.* backe: *Dut.* bakken: *Ger.* backen: *M. Ger.* bachen: *O. H. Ger.* pachan; *p.* puoch; *pp.* pachanēr: *Dan.* bage: *Swed. O. Nrs.* baka *to roast: Sansk.* bhak-tas *cooked*, from bhaj *to cook*.] DER. a-bacan: bæcere, bæcestre: bacen, niw-, ofen-.

bacen *baked; pp. of* bacan.

bac-slitol, es; *m. A backbiter;* detractor, Off. reg. 15. v. bæc-slitol.

bacu *backs; nom. acc. pl. of* bæc:—Hī me towendon heora bacu *they turned their backs on me*, Bt. Met. Fox 2, 29; Met. 2, 15.

bād, e; *f.* [from bǣdan *compellere*] *A pledge, stake, a thing distrained;* pignus:—Gif bād genumen sȳ, ðonne begyte ða bāde hām *if a pledge be taken, then shall he obtain the pledge home again*, or *back*, L. O. D. 3; Th. i. 354, 6, 7. DER. bādian; nēd-bād, nȳd. v. wed, wedd.

bād *expected, waited*, Cd. 132; Th. 167, 32; Gen. 2774; *p. of* bīdan.

Baddan-burh; *g.* -burge; *d.* -byrig; *f.* BADBURY, *Dorsetshire, formerly Baddanburgum;* Baddanburgus in quo castra metatus est Eadweardus Ælfredi fil, An. 901; haud longe a Winburna, in agro Dorsetensi:—He gewīcode æt Baddanbyrig wið Winburnan *he encamped at Badbury near Winburn*, Chr. 901; Th. 178, 26.

Badecan wylle, an; *f.* [*Badec's well*: *Flor.* A. D. 1114, Badecanwella] BAKEWELL, *Derbyshire*:—Fōr on Peac-lond to Badecan wyllan [MS. wiellon] *went into the Peak to Bakewell*, Chr. 924; Erl. 110, 12.

bādian; *p.* ode; *pp.* od; *v. a. To pledge, seize, take by way of a pledge;* pignerare, pignus auferre:—Of ǣgðran stæðe on ōðer man mōt bādian, būte man elles riht begytan mǣge *from one shore to the other one may take a pledge, unless he can get justice in another way*, L. O. D. 2; Th. i. 354, 3.

Bæbba-burh *Bamborough*, Chr. 1093; Th. 360, 6: 1095; Th. 362, 12. v. Bæbban burh.

Bæbban burh, Chr. 993; Th. 241, 17, col. 1. v. Bebban burh.

BÆC; *g.* bæces; *pl. nom. acc.* bacu, bæc; *g.* baca; *d.* bacum; *n. A* BACK; dorsum, tergum [dorsum *is opposed to* venter, *especially in animals, and* tergum *to* frons, v. hricg]:—Mīnra feónda bæc ðū onwendest to me *inimicorum meorum dedisti mihi dorsum*, Ps. Th. 17, 38. Fȳnd mīne ðū sealdest me on bæc *vel* hricc *inimicos meos dedisti mihi dorsum*, Ps. Spl. 17, 42; myn enemys thou ȝeue to me bac, Wyc. 17, 41. Ðā wendon hī me heora bæc to *then turned they their backs to me*, Bt. 2; Fox 4, 13. Hī me towendon heora bacu *they turned their backs on me*, Bt. Met. Fox 2, 29; Met. 2, 15. Ǣr hī bacum tobreden *before they turn their backs to each other*, Exon. 92 a; Th. 345, 20; Gn. Ex. 192. ¶ On bæc *retro*, Jn. Bos. 6, 66: *and* under bæc *retrorsum*, Ps. Spl. 43, 12: *at his back, behind, backward*, v. under-bæc. Clǣne bæc hæbban *to have a clean back, to be free from deceit*, L. A. G. 5; Th. i. 156, 6. Gang on bæc, Mt. Bos. 4, 10. Gā on bæc *go behind* or *away;* vade retro, Mk. Bos. 8, 33. [*Orm.* bac, bacch: *Chauc.* back: *O. Sax.* bak, *n*: *N. Frs.* beck, *n*: *O. Frs.* bek, *n*: *O. Ger.* pacho, bacho, *m*: *O. Nrs.* bak, *n*: *Scot.* back *a body of followers*. Is it allied to the root in bīgan *to bow*, as the *N. Ger.* buckel *dorsum* is to biegen?] DER. ofer-bæc, on-, under-.

bæc-bord, es; *m. The larboard* or *left-hand side of a ship, when looking towards the prow* or *head;* navigii sinistra pars:—Burgenda land wæs us on bæcbord *the land of the Burgundians was on our larboard* or *left*, Ors. 1, 1; Bos. 21, 44. [*Plat. Dut.* bakboord *the larboard*.]

bǣce *a beech-tree*, Som. Lye. v. bēce.

bæcere, es; *m. A* BAKER; pistor, Ælfc. Gl. 50; Som. 65, 109; Wrt. Voc. 34, 38. [*Plat. Dut.* bakker: *Ger.* bäcker: *Dan. Swed.* bagere: *O. Nrs.* bakari.] v. bacan.

bæce-ring, es; *m. A grate formed as a ring used for baking, a gridiron;* craticula, Cot. 99.

bæc-ern, es; *n.* [bæc from bacan *to bake*, ern *a place*] *A baking-place, a bakehouse;* pistrinum, Ælfc. Gl. 50; Som. 65, 110; Wrt. Voc. 34, 39.

bæcest *bakest*, = bacest, *2nd sing. pres. of* bacan.

bæcestre, bæcistre, bæcystre, an; *f? m.* [bacan *to bake*, heó bæc-eþ; estre, v. -isse] *A woman who bakes;* pistrix: but because afȳrde men performed that work which was originally done by females, this occupation is here denoted by a feminine termination; hence, *a baker;* pistor:—Ðā gelamp hit ðæt twegen afȳryde men agylton wið heora hlāford, Egypta cynges byrle and his bæcistre *ecce accidit ut peccarent duo eunuchi, pincerna regis Ægyptorum, et pistor, domino suo*, Gen. 40, 1. Ðara ōðer bewiste his byrlas, ōðer his bæcestran *illorum alter pincernis præerat, alter pistoribus*, 40, 2, Bæcistra ealdor *pistorum magister*, 40, 16, 20. Bæcestre *a baker;* pistor, Ælfc. Gr. 28, 1; Som. 30, 36.

bæceþ *baketh*, = baceþ, *3rd sing. pres. of* bacan.

bæc-hūs, es; *n. A* BAKEHOUSE; pistrinum, Ælfc. Gl. 22? v. bæc-ern.

bæcling; *adv.* Only used with on, *On the back, backwards, behind;* retrorsum:—On bæcling *retrorsum*, Ps. Th. 113, 5. On bæclincg, 43, 12, 19. Cer ðē on bæcling *turn thee behind me*, Cd. 228; Th. 308, 26; Sat. 698. v. ears-ling, hinder-ling.

bæc-slitol, es; *m.* [bæc *a back;* slitol *a biter*, from sliten, *pp. of* slītan *to slit, bite*] *A backbiter;* detractor, Off. reg. 15.

bæcst *bakest;* bæcþ *bakes*. v. bacan.

bæc-þearm, es; *m. The entrails;* anus, longanon:—Wrt. Voc. 283, 60. Bæcþearmas *the bowels;* extales, Ælfc. Gr. 13; Som. 16, 23. Bæcþearm *vel* snǣdel *extales*, Ælfc. Gl. 74; Som. 71, 66; Wrt. Voc. 44, 48. Bæcþearmes ūtgang *morbus*, fortasse, *ani procidentia*, Som. v. snǣdel.

bæcystre *a baker;* pistor:—Bæcystra ealdor *pistorum magister*, Gen. 41, 10. v. bæcestre.

bæd, *pl.* bǣdon *asked, besought*, Cd. 94; Th. 122, 12; Gen. 2025: 37; Th. 48, 24; Gen. 780; *p. of* biddan.

Bæda-ford-scīr *Bedfordshire*, Chr. 1011; Th. 267, 4, col. 2. v. Bedan ford-scīr.

bǣdan; *p.* de; *pp.* ed *To constrain, compel, require, solicit;* cogere, compellere, exigere, postulare, flagitare:—Ðæs his lufu bǣdeþ *whom his love constrains*, Exon. 90 b; Th. 339, 27; Gn. Ex. 100. Mǣru cwēn bǣdde byras geonge *the illustrious queen solicited her young sons*, Beo. Th. 4040; B. 2018. [*O. Sax.* bēdian *cogere aliquem ad aliquid*: *O. H. Ger.* ga-peitian: *Goth.* báidjan: *O. Nrs.* beiða *petere, postulare*.] DER. a-bǣdan, ge-.

bædd *a bed*, Vit. Swith. v. bed.

bǣdde, an; *f? A thing required, tribute;* exactum, Cot. 73.

bǣdde *solicited*, Beo. Th. 4040; B. 2018; *p. of* bǣdan.

bæddel, es; *m. A hermaphrodite;* hermaphroditus:—Wǣpen-wīfestre *vel* scritta *vel* bæddel *hermaphroditus*, Ælfc. Gl. 76; Som. 71, 125; Wrt. Voc. 45, 28. v. wǣpen-wīfestre, scritta.

bædd-ryda, an; *m. One bedridden;* clinicus, Vit. Swith. v. bedreda.

bǽdel *a beadle*, Som. Lye. v. býdel.

bǽdend, es; *m. A vehement* or *earnest persuader, a solicitor, stirrer;* impulsor, Cot. 115.

bǽde-wég, -wíg, es; *n. A cup;* poculum:—Heó scencte bittor bǽde-wēg *she poured out the bitter cup*, Exon. 47 a; Th. 161, 13; Gū. 958.

bædling, es; *m.* [bedd *a bed*] *A delicate fellow, tenderling, one who lies much in bed;* homo delicatus:—Bædlingas *effeminate men;* μαλακοί, Cot. 71: 1 Cor. 6, 9.

bǽdling, es; *m.* [from bǽdan *to compel, solicit*] *A carrier of letters* or *orders;* tabellarius, Som.

bæd-þearm, es; *m. Mentera, entera?* = ἔντερα, *pl. n. exentera?* Bæd-þearm *seems to be an error of the copyist for* bæcþearm, Ælfc. Gl. 76; Som. 71, 122; Wrt. Voc. 45, 27.

bædzere, bæzere, es; *m:* bezera, an; *m. A baptist, baptizer;* baptista:—Hie cwǽdun, sume Iohannes se bædzere *illi dixerunt, alii Ioannem Baptistam*, Mt. Rush. Stv. 16, 14: 3, 1. v. fulluhtere.

bæfta, an; *m. The after part, the back;* tergum:—Ic geseah đone bæftan *I saw the back*, Gen. 16, 13.

bæfta; *adv. Behind;* post, Gen. 32, 24. v. bæftan; *adv.*

bæftan, beftan; *prep. dat.* [be-æftan, *q. v.*] I. *after, behind;* post, pone:—Gang bæftan me *vade post me*, Mt. Bos. 16, 23. II. *behind, without;* sine:—Bæftan đam hlāforde *without the master*, Ex. 22, 14.

bæftan, bæfta; *adv.* [be-æftan, *q. v.*] *After, behind, hereafter, afterwards;* postea:—Git synd fíf hungor gēr bæftan *adhuc quinque anni residui sunt famis*, Gen. 45, 11. He āna belāf đǽr bæfta *he alone was left there behind*, Gen. 32, 24. Mycel đæs heres đe mid hyre bæftan wæs *much of the army that was behind with her*, Ors. 1, 10; Bos. 33, 23.

bæftan-sittende; *part. Idle;* reses, Ælfc. Gr. 9, 26; Som. 11, 11.

bǽg *a collar:*—Wearm lim gebundenne bǽg hwīlum berstеþ *the warm limb sometimes escapes from the bound collar*, Exon. 102 b; Th. 387, 20; Rä. 5, 8. v. beáh.

bæga *of both*, Th. Diplm. A. D. 804–829; 462, 17. v. begen.

Bægere, Bægware; *gen.* a; *dat.* um; *pl. m. The Bavarians;* Bavarii, the Boiari, *or* Bajuvarii, whose country was called Boiaria, its German name is Baiern, now called the kingdom of Bavaria:—Mid Bægerum *with the Bavarians*, Chr. 891; Th. 160, 24. Hī Maroaro habbaþ, be westan him, Þyringas, and Behemas, and Bægware healfe *they, the Moravians, have, on their west, the Thuringians, Bohemians, and part of the Bavarians*, Ors. 1, 1; Bos. 18, 42.

bǽh *a crown*, Ælflædæ Test. v. beáh.

BǼL, es; *n.* I. *fire, flame;* ignis, flamma:—Hæfde landwara līge befangen, bǽle and bronde *he had enveloped the inhabitants of the land with flame, with fire and brand*, Beo. Th. 4633; B. 2322: 4606; B. 2308. Bǽles cwealm in helle *the torment of the fire in hell*, Andr. Kmbl. 2374; An. 1188. II. *the fire of a funeral pile, in which dead bodies were burned, a funeral pile;* rogus, pyra:—Ǽr he bǽl cure *ere he chose the pile* [*the fire of the pile*], Beo. Th. 5629; B. 2818. Bǽl biþ onæled *the pile is kindled*, Exon. 59 a; Th. 212, 26; Ph. 216. [*Piers.* bal: *O. Nrs.* bāl, *n. a fire, funeral pile.*]

bǽl-blǽse, an; *f. Blaze of a flame;* flammæ candor *vel* ardor, Exon. 42 b; Th. 142, 22; Gū. 648.

bǽl-blys, e; *f. Blaze of a fire;* flammæ ardor, Cd. 184; Th. 230, 12; Dan. 232: 162; Th. 203, 9; Exod. 401.

bælc, es; *m.* I. *a* BELCH; eructatio, Mann. II. *the stomach, pride, arrogance;* stomachus, superbia, arrogantia:—He him bælc forbīgde *he bent their pride*, Cd. 4; Th. 4, 15; Gen. 54: Judth. 12; Thw. 25, 18; Jud. 267.

BÆLC, es; *m. A covering;* tegmen, peristroma, tabulatum:—He bælce oferbrǽdde byrnendne heofon *he overspread with a covering the burning heaven*, Cd. 146; Th. 182, 9; Exod. 73. [*N. Ger.* gebälk, es; *n. the beams* or *timber of a house: Icel.* bálkr.]

bælcan *to cry out;* vociferari:—He bælceþ *he cries out*, Exon. 83 b; Th. 315, 8; Mōd. 28. [*Plat.* bölken: *N. Frs.* balckien: *N. Dut.* balken: *Ger.* bolken.]

bældan *to animate, encourage;* animare, instigare:—Đū þeóde bældest to beadowe *thou encouragest the people to strife*, Andr. Kmbl. 2373; An. 1188. v. byldan.

bældu, e; *f. Confidence;* fiducia, Mt. Rush. Stv. 14, 27.

bǽl-egsa, an; *m. Terror of flame?* flammæ terror?—Bǽlegsan [bell egsan MS.] hweóp *he threatened with terror of flame*, Cd. 148; Th. 185, 12; Exod. 121.

bǽl-fýr, es; *n. A funeral fire;* rogi ignis:—Bǽlfýra mǽst *greatest of funeral fires*, Beo. Th. 6278; B. 3143: Exon. 74 a; Th. 277, 12; Jul. 579.

bælg, bælig, es; *m. A bulge, bag;* bulga, Cot. 27. v. belg.

bælig-nis, -niss, e; *f.* [from belgan *to be angry, to make angry*] *An injury;* injuria, Mt. Lind. Stv. 20, 13.

bǽl-stede, es; *m. A funeral pile place;* rogi locus, Beo. Th. 6185; B. 3097.

bǽl-þræc; *g.* -þræce; *pl. nom. g. acc.* -þraca; *f. Force of fire;* flammæ impetus:—Æfter bǽlþræce *after the fire's force*, Exon. 59 b; Th. 216, 19; Ph. 270.

bǽl-wudu, es; *m. Wood of the funeral pile;* rogi lignum, Beo. Th. 6216; B. 3112.

bǽl-wylm, es; *m. Fire's heat;* flammæ æstuatio, Exon. 70 b; Th. 262, 22; Jul. 336.

bǽm *for* bām; *dat. of* begen *both*, Bt. 38, 5, MS. Cott; Fox 206, 15: Th. Diplm. A. D. 804–829; 463, 3. v. begen.

bænc *a bench*, Som. Lye. v. benc.

bænd, es; *m. A band;* vitta:—Healfne bænd gyldenne [*dederunt*] *dimidiam vittam auream*, Text. Rof. 111, 3; Th. Diplm. A. D. 950; 501, 35: Text. Rof. 110, 23; Th. Diplm. A. D. 950; 501, 20. v. bend.

Bænesing-tūn *Bensington*, Chr. 571; Th. 32, 29, col. 1. v. Bensingtūn.

BÆR; *g. m. n.* bares; *f.* bærre: *d.* barum: *acc.* bærne: *pl. nom.* baru; *acc.* bare; *dat.* barum; *def.* se bara; seó, đæt bare; *adj.* BARE, *naked, open;* nudus:—On bær līc *on the bare body*, Exon. 125 a; Th. 482, 7; Rä. 66, 4. On barum sondum *on bare sands*, Bt. 34, 10; Fox 148, 24. Wit hēr baru standaþ unwered wǽdo *we stand here naked, unprotected by garments*, Cd. 38; Th. 50, 20; Gen. 811. [*Plat. Dut. Ger.* baar *nudus, promptus, merus, manifestus: M. H. Ger.* bar *nudus: O. H. Ger.* par, bar: the *Goth.* form is not found, but would be basis or basus: *Dan. Swed.* bar: *O. Nrs.* berr: *Slav.* bos: *Lith.* bosus; then the radical consonants would be b–s, not b–r; therefore the word is not connected with beran *ferre*. v. Grm. Wrtbch. i. 1055.] v. berie.

bær, *pl.* bǽron *bore*, Cd. 24; Th. 31, 2; Gen. 479: 178; Th. 223, 18; Dan. 121; *p. of* beran.

bǽr, e; *f.* I. *a* BIER; feretrum:—Sīe seó bǽr gearo *let the bier be ready*, Beo. Th. 6202; B. 3105. Gefærenne man brohton on bǽre *they brought a dead man on a bier*, Elen. Kmbl. 1742; El. 873. II. *a couch, pallet, litter;* grabatus:—On his þegna handum on bǽre boren wæs *manibus ministrorum portabatur in grabato*, Bd. 5, 19; S. 640, 22. [*Chauc. Wyc.* bere: *Plat.* baar, *f: O. Sax.* bāra, *f: O. Frs.* bēre, *f: Dut.* baar, *f: Ger.* bahre, *f: M. H. Ger.* bāre, *f: O. H. Ger.* bāra, *f: Dan.* baar, *f.*] v. bēr, beer, Lind. Rush. DER. beran.

bǽran; *p.* de; *pp.* ed *To bear, bear oneself;* ferre, transferre:—He ne geþafode, đæt ǽnig man ǽnig fæt þurh đæt templ bǽre, Mk. Bos. 11, 16; *he suffride not, that ony man schulde bere a vessel thurȝ the temple*, Wyc. DER. ge-bǽran.

bær-beáh; *g.* -beáges; *m. A bearing-ring, ring;* anulus, Exon. 108 b; Th. 414, 18; Rä. 32, 22.

bǽr-disc, es; *m.* [bǽr, disc *a dish*] *A dish bier* or *tray, a frame on which several dishes were brought to table at once, a course, service;* ferculum, Wrt. Voc. 26, 64.

bǽre *a bier;* feretrum, Wrt. Voc. 49, 26. v. bǽr.

-bǽre *an adjective termination* signifying *Producing, bearing*, from beran *to bear, produce;* as, wæstm-bǽre *fruit-bearing, fruitful;* frugifer: æppel-bǽre *apple-bearing;* pomifer: horn-bǽre *horn-bearing;* corniger: leóht-bǽre *light-bearing*. [*Plat. Dut.* -baar: *Ger.* -bar: *M. H. Ger.* -bǽre: *O. H. Ger.* -pāri.] v. bora.

bære-flōr, es; *m. A barley-floor, barn-floor, threshing-floor;* hordei area, area:—Þurh-clǽnsaþ his bæreflōr *permundabit aream suam*, Mt. Kmbl. Rush. 3, 12. v. bere.

bǽrende *bearing; part. of* bǽran. v. berende.

bær-fōt; *adj.* BAREFOOT or *that goeth barefooted;* nudipes, Peccat. Med. 8. [*Ger.* barfusz.]

bærlīc, es; *m? Barley;* hordeum:—Man sælde đæt æcer-sǽd bærlīc to six scillingas *one sold the acre-seed of barley for six shillings*, Chr. 1124; Th. 376, 5. v. bere.

bær-līce; *adv. Openly, nakedly*, BARELY; palam, Jn. Lind. War. 6, 29.

bærm *a bosom, lap;* sinus, Som. Lye. v. bearm.

bǽr-man, -mann, es; *nom. pl.* bǽrmenn; *d.* bǽrmannum; *m. A man who bears, a bearer, carrier, porter;* bajulus:—Đa bǽrmenn gesetton heora fōtlǽst *the porters set their footstep*, Jos. 3, 15.

bærn *a barn*, Wrt. Voc. 84, 55. v. bern.

bærnan; *p.* bærnde; *pp.* bærned; *v. a. To kindle, light, set on fire, to* BURN, *burn up;* accendere, urere, comburere, exurere:—Bærnaþ nū eówer blācern *light now your lamp*, Bd. 4, 8; S. 576, 5. Hī bærndon gecorene *they burned the chosen*, Exon. 66 a; Th. 243, 26; Jul. 16. [*Plat.* brennen; *p.* brende *ardere, urere: Dut.* branden; *p.* brande *id: O. Dut.* bernen; *p.* bernde; branden; *p.* brande *id: Ger.* brennen; *p.* brannte; *but* brinnan; *p.* brann *ardere: M. H. Ger.* brennen; *p.* brante *urere: O. H. Ger.* brennan; *p.* branta; prennan; *p.* pranta *id: O. Sax.* brinnan, brennan: *Goth.* brannjan; *p.* brannida: *Dan.* brände *ardere, urere: Swed.* bränna *urere: O. Nrs.* brenna; *p.* brendi *id.*] DER. forbærnan, ge-, on-. v. byrnan, beornan.

bærnes, bærnis, -ness, e; *f. A burning;* incendium, Bd. 1, 6; S. 476, 25. DER. an-bærnis, -bærnys, in-, on-.

bærnet, bærnyt, bernet, es; *n.* I. *a combustion, burning up;* combustio:—He wudu gelogode to his sunu bærnytte *he laid in order the wood for the burning of his son*, Gen. 22, 9. II. *arson;* incendium:—Hūsbryce and bærnet ... is bōtleás *bootless is ... house-breaking and arson*, L. C. S. 65; Th. i. 410, 5. DER. wudu-bærnet.

bærning, berning, e; *f. A* BURNING; adustio:—Sylle bærninge wið bærninge *reddat adustionem pro adustione*, Ex. 21, 25.

bærnyt *a combustion, burning*, Gen. 22, 9. v. bærnet.

-bǽro, -bǽru *a bearing*. v. forþ-, ge-, on-.

bærs, bears, es; *m. A perch;* perca, lupus:—Bærs *lupus* vel *scardo*, Ælfc. Gl. 101; Som. 77, 58; Wrt. Voc. 55, 63. [*Dut.* baars, *m: Ger.* bars, barsch, *m.*]

bærst *burst*, Byrht. Th. 140, 6; By. 284; *p. of* berstan.

bærstlian; *p.* ode; *pp.* od *To break, burst;* crepare:—Bærstlaþ *crepuerit*, Cot. 39. v. brastlian.

bær-synnig, -sinnig, -suinnih, -sunig; *adj.* [bær *bare, open;* synnig *sinful, wicked*] *Openly-wicked;* used substantively, *an open* or *public sinner, a publican;* apertus *vel* publicus peccator, publicanus:—Síe đe swǽ bærsynnig *sit tibi sicut publicanus*, Mt. Lind. Stv. 18, 17: 21, 32: Mk. Lind. War. 2, 16: Lk. Lind. War. 15, 1: Mt. Lind. Stv. 9, 10. [*O. Nrs.* ber-syndugr.]

bærwe *a grove*, Som; *dat. of* bearo.

BÆST, es; *m? n? The inner bark of a tree, of which ropes were made;* tilia:—Bæst *vel* lind *tilia*, Lye. [*Plat. Dut.* bast, *m. bark: O. Dut.* bast, *m. signifies the bark of a tree and also a rope; because the inner part of the linden* or *lime-tree was mostly used for making ropes: Ger. M.H.Ger.* bast, *m. bark: O.H.Ger.* past, *m: Dan.* bast, *m: Swed.* bast, *n: O.Nrs.* bast, *n.* The word is probably to be derived from bindan *to bind*, v. Grm. Wrtbch. i. 1148.]

bæsten; *adj. Made of bast*, BAST; tiliaceus:—Híg đá hine gebundon mid twám bæstenum rápum *then they bound him with two bast ropes*, Jud. Grn. 15, 13.

bæstere *a baptizer;* baptista:—Bæstere *baptista*, Mt. Lind. Stv. 3, 1. v. bædzere.

bæswi [=basu *purple*] *A scarlet robe;* coccinum, Cot. 208.

bǽtan; *p.* bǽtte; *pp.* bǽted; *v. a. To bridle, rein in, restrain, curb, bit;* frenum equo *vel* asino injicere, frenare, cohibere:—Esolas bǽtan *to bridle asses*, Cd. 138; Th. 173, 25; Gen. 2866. Gif he ǽr þweores windes bǽtte *if he first restrained the perverse wind*, Bt. 41, 3; Fox 250, 16. [*O.H.Ger.* beizian *mordere facere, infrenare: O.Nrs.* beita.] DER. ge-bǽtan, ymbe-.

bǽte, es; *n. A* BIT *of a bridle, a bridle, trappings, harness;* lupatum, frenum. v. gebǽte, gebǽtel.

BÆÞ, es; *pl. nom. acc.* bađu; *g.* bađa; *d.* bađum, bađan, bađon; *n.* I. *a* BATH; balneum, balneatio:—Bæþ háte weól *the bath boiled* [*welled*] *with heat*, Exon. 74 a; Th. 277, 16; Jul. 581. On hátum bađum *in hot baths*, Bd. 4, 19; S. 588, 6. II. *a font;* fons lustralis:—Hú hí hine bǽdan fullwihtes bæđes *how they had asked him for a font of baptism*, Ors. 6, 34; Bos. 130, 30. [*Plat.* bad, *n: O. Sax.* bath, *n: Dut. Ger.* bad, *n: M.H.Ger.* bat; *gen.* bades, *n: O.H.Ger.* bad, *n: Dan. Swed.* bad: *O.Nrs.* bađ, *n.*] DER. fýr-bæþ, seolh-: Bađan *Bath.*

bæđere, es; *m. A baptist;* baptista, Grm. i. 253, 38. v. bædzere.

bæþ-hús, es; *n. A* BATH-HOUSE; thermarum domus:—Bæþhús *balnearium* vel *thermarium*, Ælfc. Gl. 109; Som. 79, 13; Wrt. Voc. 58, 54. Bæþhús *vel* bæþstów *thermæ*, Ælfc. Gl. 107; Som. 78, 75; Wrt. Voc. 57, 53. v. bæþ-stów.

bæđian; *p.* ode; *pp.* od *To bathe*, Som. Lye. v. bađian.

bæþ-stede, es; *m. A place of baths;* thermarum locus:—Bæþstede *thermæ* vel *gymnasium*, Ælfc. Gl. 55; Som. 67, 7; Wrt. Voc. 37, 5.

bæþ-stów, e; *f. A bathing-place;* thermarum locus:—Bæþhús *vel* bæþstów *thermæ*, Ælfc. Gl. 107; Som. 78, 75; Wrt. Voc. 57, 53. v. bæþ-hús.

bæþ-weg, es; *m. A bath-way, the sea;* via balnei, mare:—Brecan ofer bæþweg *to break over the bath-way*, Andr. Kmbl. 445; An. 223. Bæþweges blǽst *a blast* or *wind of the sea, a sea breeze, the south wind.* Súþwind *is so called*, Cd. 158; Th. 196, 11; Exod. 290.

bǽting, béting, e; *f. A cable, a rope, anything that holds* or *restrains;* funis, retinaculum:—Lǽtan đa bétinge [Cot. bǽtinge] *to slip the cable*, Bt. 41, 3; Fox 250, 15.

bǽtte *restrained*, Bt. 41, 3; Fox 250, 16; *p. of* bǽtan.

bæzera, bæzere *a baptizer*, Mt. Rush. Stv. 11, 11, 12. v. bædzere.

bala-níþ, es; *m. Baleful malice, evil*, Ps. C. 50, 151; Ps. Grn. ii. 280, 151. v. bealo-níþ.

balca, an; *m. A* BALK, *beam, bank, a ridge;* trabs, porca, terra inter duos sulcos congesta:—On balcan lecgan *to lay in ridges*, Bt. 16, 2; Fox 54, 2. [*Piers P. Chauc.* balke *trabs: Plat.* balk, *m. id: O.Sax.* balko, *m: Dut.* balk, *m: Ger. M.H.Ger.* balke, *m: O.H.Ger.* baicho, balko, *m: Dan.* bjälke: *Swed.* bjelke: *O.Nrs.* bálkr, *m; but cf. also Gaelic* balc *a ridge of earth between two furrows*, Grm. Wrtbch. i. 1089.]

balcettan *to belch*, Som. Lye. v. bealcettan.

bald; *adj.* BOLD, *audacious, adventurous, confident;* audax, confidens:—Bald breóst-toga *a bold chief*, Salm. Kmbl. 369; Sal. 184. Hilde calla bald bord upahóf *the bold war-herald raised his shield*, Cd. 156; Th. 193, 27; Exod. 253. Wǽron hí đe baldran gewordene *confidentiores facti*, Bd. 1, 12; S. 481, 17. v. beald.

-bald, -bold; as the incipient or terminating syllable of proper names denotes *Bold, courageous, honourable;* audax, virtuosus:—Baldwin *from* bald, *and* win *a contest, battle.* Cúþbold, Cúþbald *from* cúþ *known*, bald *bold.* Eádbald *happily bold*, from ead *or* eádig *and* bald.

balde; *adv. Boldly, freely, confidently, instantly;* audacter, libere, fidenter, instanter, prone, statim, sine mora:—Hie balde gecwǽdon *they said boldly*, Cd. 182; Th. 228, 11; Dan. 200. v. bealde.

bald-líce *boldly;* fortiter:—He baldlíce beornas lǽrde *he boldly exhorted the warriors*, Byrht. Th. 140, 60; By. 311. v. beald-líce.

bald-lícost; *sup. Most bravely;* fortissime:—Đe baldlícost on đa bricge stóp *who stept on the bridge most bravely*, Byrht. Th. 134, 2; By. 78. v. beald-líce.

baldor, es; *m.* [*the comp. of* bald *is* baldor *more bold, courageous, honourable, hence*] *A prince, ruler;* princeps, dominus:—*thus*, Gumena baldor *a ruler of men*, Cd. 128; Th. 163, 4; Gen. 2693: Judth. 9; Thw. 21, 8; Jud. 9. Rinca baldor, 12; Thw. 26, 21; Jud. 339. Wígena baldor *a prince of warriors*, 10; Thw. 22, 5; Jud. 49. v. bealdor.

baldra *bolder*, Bd. 1, 12; S. 481, 17. v. bald, beald.

baldsamum, i; *n. Balsam, balm;* balsamum:—Swá swá mon héddern ontýnde đa baldsami *quasi opobalsami cellaria esse viderentur aperta*, Bd. 3, 8; S. 532, 19. v. balsam.

balewa, an; *m. The baleful* or *wicked one, Satan;* Satanas, Diabolus:—Swá inc se balewa hét *as the baleful one desired you*, Cd. 224; Th. 295, 11; Sat. 484.

balewe *wicked:*—Se inc forgeaf balewe geþohtas *he inspired you with wicked thoughts*, Cd. 224; Th. 295, 19; Sat. 488. v. bealo.

ballíce *boldly:*—Ballíce *audacter*, Mk. Lind. War. 15, 43. v. baldlíce, beald-líce.

balo *bale, evil*, Lye. DER. balo-cræft. v. bealo.

balo-cræft, es; *m. A pernicious, wicked*, or *magic art;* ars perniciosa *vel* magica, Bt. Met. Fox 26, 150; Met. 26, 75. v. bealo-cræft.

balsam, es; *n.* [balsamum, baldsamum, i; *n.*] *Balsam, balm;* balsamum:—Balsames blǽd *the balsam's fruit;* carpo balsami, Ælfc. Gl. 48; Som. 65, 54; Wrt. Voc. 33, 50. Balsames teár *the tear* or *juice of the balsam-tree;* opobalsamum, Ælfc. Gl. 48; Som. 65, 55; Wrt. Voc. 33, 51. Héddern đa balsamum on wǽre *a store-house in which was balm*, Bd. 3, 8; S. 532, 19, note.

bals-minte, an; *f.* BALSAM-MINT, *spear-mint, water-mint;* sisymbrium: *q.* mentha aquatica, Lin. Ælfc. Gl. 43; Som. 64, 52; Wrt. Voc. 31, 62.

balw; *g. m. n.* es; *f.* re *Miserable, wicked;* malus, Beo. Th. 1958; B. 977. v. bealo.

balzam *balsam:*—Se sceal on balzame beón *it shall be of balsam*, L. M. 2, 64; Lchdm. ii. 288, 23. v. balsam.

bám *with both*, Hexam. 2; Norm. 4, 22: Cd. 6; Th. 8, 23; Gen. 128; *dat. of* begen.

ban, bann, es; *n. A command, edict, interdict;* mandatum, edictum, interdictum, Grm. 3rd edit. i. 359, 8. v. ge-ban.

BÁN, baan, es; *pl.* bán; *n. A* BONE; os:—Đis ys nú bán of mínum bánum *hoc nunc os ex ossibus meis*, Gen. 2, 23. Moises nam Iosepes bán mid him *tulit Moyses ossa Ioseph secum*, Ex. 13, 19: Cd. 9; Th. 12, 9; Gen. 182. Híg synt innan fulle deádra bána *intus plena sunt ossibus mortuorum*, Mt. Bos. 23, 27. Bán míne *my bones*, Ps. Spl. 6, 2: Exon. 110 a; Th. 421, 14; Rä. 40, 18: 125 b; Rä. 68, 3: Beo. Th. 5149; B. 2578. [*Plat.* been, *n. os, crus: O.Sax. O.Frs.* bén, *n: Dut.* been, *n: Ger. M.H.Ger.* bein, *n: O.H.Ger.* pein, *n: Dan.* been: *Swed.* ben: *O.Nrs.* bein, *n.* In *Goth.* the word is preserved only in baina-bagms *a bone-tree, cornel-tree*, for *συκάμινος.* Thus, all the *Teut.* languages have the same word, the chief and oldest signification of which is os *a bone.* This is the only meaning it has in *A.Sax.* where scanca is used for *crus;* also in *O.Nrs.* the meaning *crus* is very rare, the more common word being leggr *a leg.* The *Sansk. Lat. Grk.* and the *Slav.* languages use a totally different root,—*Sansk.* asthi os: *Lat.* os: *Grk.* *ὀστέον*: the *Slav.* branch kost, *Boh.* kost, *Pol.* kosc, all with an initial *k.* Grimm, Wrtbch. i. 1381, suggests, if *crus* could be proved to be the original meaning of bán, it might be related to *βαίνειν*, in the same way as *Sansk.* asthi to *στῆναι.*] DER. breóst-bán, cin-, elpen-, hrycg-, wído-, ylpen-.

BANA, bona, an; *m. A killer, murderer, manslayer*, also applied to *the devil;* interfector, occisor, homicida, diabolus:—Đam wearþ Weohstán bana *to whom Weohstan became a murderer*, Beo. Th. 5220; B. 2613: Cd. 144; Th. 180, 3; Exod. 39. Banena byre *the son of the murderers*, Beo. Th. 4112; B. 2053. Hie nǽfre his banan folgian noldon *they never would follow his murderer*, Chr. 755; Th. 84, 33, col. 1: L. Ethb. 23; Th. i. 8, 7: L. H. E. 2, 3, 4; Th. i. 28, 1, 5, 7. On banan fæđme *in the embrace of the murderer*, i. e. *the devil*, Andr. Kmbl. 1232; An. 616. [*O.Sax.* bano: *O.Frs.* bona: *O.H.Ger.* bano: *O.Nrs.* bani.] DER. aldor-bana [-bona], bróđor-, dǽd-, ecg-, feorh-, ferhþ-, fugel-, gást-, hand-, múþ-, ord-, rǽd-, súsl-.

bán-beorgas; *pl. m. Bone defences, greaves;* ossium præsidia, ocreæ, Cot. 17: 145.

bán-brice, -bryce, es; *m. A* BONE-BREAKING or *fracture of a bone;*

ossis fractura :—Wið bānbryce genim ðysse ylcan wyrte wyrttruman *for fracture of a bone take roots of this same plant*, Herb. 15, 3; Lchdm. i. 108, 9.

BANC, e; *f. A bench*, BANK, *hillock*; tumulus, Som. v. benc.

bān-cōfa, an; *m. A bone-dwelling, the body*; ossium cubile, corpus :—Wæs se bāncōfa ādle onǣled *the body was inflamed with disease*, Exon. 46 b; Th. 159, 16; Gū. 927.

Bancorena burh, Bancorna burh; *g.* burge; *d.* byrig; *Bangor, in Wales*; civitas Bangor :—Swȳðest of Bancorena [Bancorna, B.] byrig *most chiefly from the city of Bangor*, Bd. 2, 2; S. 502, 39, note.

ban-cōða, an; *m*: -cōþ, -cōðu, e; *f*: -cōðe, an; *f*. [ban. bana *a killer*, cōða *a disease*] *A baneful disease, a fatal* or *deadly malady, erysipelas*; lethalis morbus, ignis sacer :—Wæs him inbogen bittor bancōða *a bitter malady was fixed in him*, Exon. 47 b; Th. 163, 23; Gū. 998. Wið bancōðe, ðæt is ōman, nim eolonan *for the baneful disease, that is erysipelas, take elecampane*, L. M. 1, 39; Lchdm. ii. 102, 16.

band *bound*, Cd. 143; Th. 178, 22; Exod. 15; *p. of* bindan.

banda, an; *m. A householder, husband*, Som. Lye. v. bonda.

bān-fæt; *g.* -fætes; *pl. nom. acc.* -fatu; *n. The bone vessel, the body*; ossium vas, corpus, Exon. 59 a; Th. 213, 23; Ph. 229.

ban-fāh, -fāg; *adj.* [ban, bana *a killer*, fāg *stained*] *Death* or *murder stained*; homicidio pollutus, lethifer, Beo. Th. 1564; B. 780.

bān-gebrec, es; *n. A bone-breaking*; ossium fractio, Andr. Kmbl. 2882; An. 1444.

bān-helm, es; *m. A bone-helm, shield*; ossium galea, clipeus, Fins. Th. 60; Fin. 30.

bān-hring, es; *m. A bone-ring, a neck-bone*; ossium artus, vertebra :—Ðæt hire wið halse heard grāpode, bānhringas bræc *against her neck it griped her hard, broke the bone-rings*, Beo. Th. 3138; B. 1567.

bān-hūs, es; *n. The bone-house, the chest, body*; ossea domus, pectus, corpus :—He ðæt bānhūs gebrocen hæfde *he had broken the bone-house, the breast*, or *body*, Beo. Th. 6285; B. 3147. *Hence* bānhūses weard *the body's guard, the mind*, Cd. 169; Th. 211, 9; Exod. 523.

Baningas; *pl. m. The Banings, people mentioned in the Gleeman's tale* :—Becca weóld Baningum *Becca ruled the Banings*, Scōp Th. 39; Wíd. 19.

bān-leás; *adj. Bone-less, without bones*; ossibus carens, Exon. 112 b; Th. 431, 19; Rä. 46, 3.

bān-loca, an; *m. A bone inclosure, the skin, body*; ossium clausura, caro :—Ðȳ-læs se ord ingebuge under bānlocan *lest the point enter in under the skin*, Exon. 19 a; Th. 48, 10; Cri. 769.

BANNAN, bonnan; ic banne, ðū bannest, banst, benst, he banneþ, banþ, benþ, *pl.* bannaþ; *p.* bēn, bēnn, beón, beónn, *pl.* beónnon; *pp.* bannen *To summon*; jubere, citare, convocare :—Leóde tosomne bannan *to summon the people together*, Andr. Kmbl. 2189; An. 1096: Elen. Grm. 45. [*O. Frs.* banna, bonna: *Ger. M. H. Ger.* bannen *edicere, interdicere, prohibere, expellere*: *O. H. Ger.* pannan: *Goth.* bandwjan *significare, innuere*: *O. Nrs.* banna *prohibere, interdicere.*] DER. a-bannan, ge-: ge-ban.

bannuc-camb, es; *m.* [camb *a comb*] *A wool-comb*; pecten textorium :—Bannuccamb *pecten*, Ælfc. Gl. 111; Som. 79, 77. DER. cimban.

bān-rift, bān-ryft; *pl. n. Bone coverings, greaves*; tibialia, ossium velamen, ocreæ, Cot. 174. v. bān-beorgas.

ban-segn, es; *m. A banner, an ensign*; vexillum, Cot. 23. v. treuteru.

bān-sele, es; *m. A bone-house* or *dwelling, the body*; ossium aula, corpus :—Gǣst and bānsele *soul and body*, Exon. 117 b; Th. 451, 12; Dōm. 102.

banst, he banþ *summonest, summoneth*; *2nd and 3rd pers. pres. of* bannan.

bān-wærc, es; *n. Grief, pain*, or *ache in the bones*; ossium dolor. v. bān *a bone*, wærc *pain*.

bān-wyrt, e; *f. Bone-wort, a violet, perhaps the small knapweed*; viola, centaurea minor :—Bānwyrt hæbbe croppan *bone-wort hath bunches of flowers*, L. M. 2, 51; Lchdm. ii. 266, 5. Bānwyrt *centaurea minor*, Ælfc. Gl. 44; Som. 64, 85; Wrt. Voc. 32, 21. Sió greáte bānwyrt *the great bone-wort*, L. M. 3, 8; Lchdm. ii. 312, 19: 1, 1; Lchdm. ii. 22, 15: 1, 25; Lchdm. ii. 66, 17, 20: 1, 31; Lchdm. ii. 74, 24: 1, 36; Lchdm. ii. 86, 21: 1, 59; Lchdm. 130, 11: 1, 63; Lchdm. ii. 138, 15: Herb. 165, 1; Lchdm. i. 294, 7: 152, 1; Lchdm. i. 276, 24: Lchdm. iii. 16, 6.

baorm *bosom* :—On baorm *in sinu*, Jn. Rush. War. 13, 23. v. bearm.

bar, es; *m. A bear*; ursus. v. bera.

BĀR, es; *m. A* BOAR; aper :—Cyng Willelm forbeád sleán ða heortas swylce eác ða bāras *king William forbade men to kill the stags, and also the boars*, Chr. 1087; Ing. 296, 12. Ic gefeó heortas, and bāras, and rann, and rægan, and hwīlon haran *capio cervos, et apros, et damas, et capreas, et aliquando lepores*, Coll. Monast. Th. 21, 31: Ælfc. Gr. 8; Som. 7, 14: Ps. Lamb. 79, 14. [*Dut.* beer: *M. H. Ger.* bēr: *O. H. Ger.* pēr.]

barda, an; *m. A beaked ship, a ship pointed with iron*; rostrata navis, Mone A. 131.

bare *bare, naked*, Cd. 37; Th. 48, 30; Gen. 783; *acc. pl. of* bær, *adj.*

barenian; *p.* ode; *pp.* od *To make bare*; denudare :—Sand barenodon *made bare the sand*, Cd. 166; Th. 207, 22; Exod. 470, note.

barian; *p.* ede; *pp.* ed *To make bare, discover, disclose*; denudare, prodere, in medium proferre. DER. a-barian.

barm *a bosom* :—On barme *in sinu*, Jn. Rush. War. 1, 18. v. bearm.

barn *a child*, Th. Diplm. A. D. 830; 465, 30. v. bearn.

barn *burned*, Ex. 3, 2; *p. of* beornan.

Baroc-scīr, e; *f. The bare oak shire* or BERKSHIRE, so called from a polled oak in Windsor forest, where public meetings were held, Brompt. p. 801. It was most commonly written by the Anglo-Saxons—Barruc, Bearruc, and Bearwucscīre, Chr. 860; Th. 130, 3.

bār-spere, es; *n. A* BOAR SPEAR; venabulum :—Bārspere *vel* huntigspere *venabulum*, Ælfc. Gl. 51; Som. 66, 22.

bār-spreót, es; *m. A boar spear*; venabulum. v. bār-spere.

barþ, es; *m. A kind of ship, a light vessel to sail* or *row in*; dromo :—Æsc *vel* barþ *dromo*, Ælfc. Gl. 103; Som. 77, 102; Wrt. Voc. 56, 24. v. æsc.

Barton *Barton, a corn village*; frumentaria villa. v. bere-tūn.

basilisca, an; *m. A basilisk*; basiliscus :—Ðū ofer aspide miht eáðe gangan and bealde nū basiliscan tredan *super aspidem et basiliscum ambulabis*, Ps. Th. 90, 13.

Basilius; *g.* Basilies; *m. Basil, bishop of Cæsarēa* = Καισάρεια :—Basilius se eádiga wæs swīðe hālig bisceop, on Cessarean byrig, on Grēciscre þeóde, manegra munuca fæder, munuchādes him sylf. He wæs swȳðe gelǣred and swȳðe mihtig lareów, and he munuc regol gesette mid swȳðlīcre drohtnunge. He wæs ǣr Benedictus, ðe us bōc awrāt on Lēdenre spræce leóhtre be dǣle ðonne Basilius, ac he tymde swāðeáh to Basilies tǣcinge for his trumnysse. Basilius awrāt āne wundorlīce bōc, be eallum Godes weorcum, ðe he geworhte on six dagum, 'Exameron' gehāten, swīðe deópum andgite. And he awrāt ða lāre ðe we nū willaþ on Englisceum gereorde secgean *Basil the blessed* [*born* A. D. 328, *died* 379] *was a very holy bishop in the city of Cæsarēa, a province belonging to Greece, the father of many monks, himself of the monkhood. He was a very learned and a very mighty teacher, and he appointed monastic canons with strict conduct. He was before Benedict* [*born* A. D. 480, *died* 540], *who wrote us a book in the Latin language more clear in part than Basil, but yet he appealed to the teaching of Basil for his confirmation. Basil wrote a certain wonderful book concerning all the works of God which he wrought in six days, called the 'Hexameron,' with a very deep understanding. And he wrote the advice which we now wish to tell in the English language*, Basil prm; Norm. 32, 1-14. Sancti Basilii Exameron [= ἑξάμερον], ðæt is, be Godes six daga weorcum *the Hexameron of holy Basil, that is, concerning the six days' works of God*, Hexam. 1; Norm. 1, 1-3.

basing, es; *m. A short cloak, a cloak*; chlamys = χλαμύς, pallium :—Ic geseah wurm-reádne basing *I saw a purple* [*worm* or *shell-fish reddened*] *cloak*; vidi pallium coccineum, Jos. 7, 21.

Basing, es; *m.* The name of a place, *Basing, old Basing, near Basingstoke, Hampshire*; nomen oppidi ita hodie vocatum in agro Hantoniensi :—Wið ðone here æt Basingum *with the army at Basing*, Chr. 871; Th. 138, 28, col. 2; 139, 27, col. 1, 2.

bāsnian, bāsnan; *p.* ode; *pp.* od *To expect, await*; exspectare :—Gestōd ðæt folc bāsnende *stabat populus exspectans*, Lk. Lind. War. 23, 35. Bāsnode hwæt him gifeðe wurde *he awaited what should befall him*, Andr. Kmbl. 2131; An. 1067. DER. ge-bāsnian.

bāsnung, e; *f. Expectation*; exspectatio, Lk. Lind. War. 21, 26.

baso, basu, e; *f. Purple*; purpura, Cot. 85. DER. brūn-baso, wealh-. v. basu.

baso, basu *a berry*; bacca, Grm. i. 244, 36.

baso-popig, es; *n?* [*astula regia*, Glos. Brux. Recd. 40, 57; Mone A. 354; Wrt. Voc. 66, 65] *Corn* or *red poppy*; papaver rhœas, L. Prior, p. 279.

Basterne *The people of Sarmatia in Europe* or *upper Hungary*; Bastarnæ. Lye.

basu: *g. m. n.* -wes; *f.* -re: *pl. nom. m. f. n.* -we: *def. m.* se baswa; *adj. Purple, crimson*; purpureus, phœniceus, coccineus :—Sum brūn, sum basu *part brown, part purple*, Exon. 60 a; Th. 218, 17; Ph. 296. Baswe bōcstafas *crimson characters*, Cd. 210; Th. 261, 10; Dan. 724. Basu hǣwen *of purple colour* or *hue, of scarlet* or *crimson colour*, Cot. 117. [Grimm, Wrtbch. i. 1243, connects the word with *Goth.* basi *a berry*: *Ger.* beere: *A. Sax.* berie.]

basu, e; *f. A scarlet robe*; coccinum, Grm. i. 254, 2. v. baso.

basuian; *p.* ode; *pp.* od *To be clad in purple*; purpura vestiri. v. basu.

baswa stān, es; *m.* [basu *purple*, stān *stone*] *A topaz, a precious stone varying from a yellow to a violet colour*; topazium :—Ofer gold and ðone baswon stān [= baswan stān] *super aurum et topazion*, Ps. Spl. 118, 127.

baswe *crimson* :—Baswe bōcstafas *crimson letters*, Cd. 210; Th. 261, 10; Dan. 724; *pl. of* basu, *adj.*

bat, e; *f.* I. *contention, strife*; contentio, R. Ben. 21. II.

a bat, club, staff, stick; fustis, Som. [*O. Nrs.* beit, *f;* lamina explanata *a thin board, plank.*]

BĀT, e; *f:* es; *m. A* BOAT, *ship, vessel;* linter, scapha, navicula:—Ðeós bāt glīdeþ on geofene *this boat glideth over ocean,* Andr. Kmbl. 992; An. 496. He bāt gestāg *he ascended a boat,* Exon. 52 a; Th. 181, 33; Gū. 1302. [*Plat.* boot, *n: Dut.* boot, *f: Ger.* boot, *n: Dan.* baad, *c: Swed.* bāt, *m: Icel.* bátr, *m. cymba, navicula.*] DER. mere-bāt, sǣ-, wudu-.

bāt *bit;* momordit, Beo. Th. 1488; B. 742; *p. of* bītan.

bāt, e; *f.* What can be bitten,—*Food;* esca, Ettm. 305. [*Icel.* beit, *f. pascuum;* beita, *f. esca:* bāt; *p. of* bītan *to bite.*]

bađa *of baths,* Exon. 57 b; Th. 205, 10; Ph. 110; *gen. pl. of* bæþ.

Bađan [*dat. pl. of* bæþ *a bath, q. v.*], Bađan-ceaster; *g.* -ceastre; *acc.* -ceastre, -ceaster; *f. The city of Bath, Somersetshire,* so called from its baths; Bathoniæ urbs a balneis dicta, in agro Somersetensi:—Bađan, Bađon, Bađun, *for* Bađum, æt Bađum, Cod. Dipl. 170; A. D. 796; Kmbl. i. 207, 5, *at the Baths,* or, as we now say, *at Bath* or *Bath* [v. æt, *prep.* I. 3, before names of places]; apud balneas, *vel* apud Bathoniam, *vel* apud urbem Bathoniæ. Æt Bađan, Chr. 1106; Erl. 241, 1. On Bađan, Th. Diplm. A. D. 1060; 379, 14: 436, 8. Æt Bađun, Cod. Dipl. 354; A. D. 931; Kmbl. ii. 177, 7. In monasterio, quod situm est in civitate æt Bađun, Cod. Dipl. 193; A. D. 808; Kmbl. i. 237, 1. In illa famosa urbe, quæ nominatur calidum balneum, đæt is æt đæm hātum bađum, Cod. Dipl. 290; A. D. 864; Kmbl. ii. 80, 8. Eádgār wæs to cyninge gehālgod on đære ealdan byrig, Acemannes ceastre; eác, ōđre worde, beornas Bađan nemnaþ *Edgar was consecrated king in the old town, Akemansceaster; also, by another word, men name Bath,* Chr. 973; Th. 224, 22, col. 1; Edg. 5. Genāmon þreó ceastra,—Gleawan-ceaster and Ciren-ceaster and Bađan-ceaster *they took three cities,—Gloucester, Cirencester, and Bath,* Chr. 577; Erl. 18, 20. v. Ace-mannes burh.

bađian, beđian, beđigean, ic -ige, -yge; *p.* ode, ede; *pp.* od. I. *v. trans. To wash, foment, cherish;* lavare, fovere:—Hī bađedon đone līchoman *they washed the body,* Bd. 4, 19; S. 589, 38. Wit unc in đære burnan bađodan *we two washed ourselves in that brook,* Exon. 121 b; Th. 467, 2; Hö. 132. II. *v. intrans. To* BATHE; lavari, balneare, aquis se immergere:—Seldon heó bađian wolde *she would seldom bathe,* Bd. 4, 19; S. 588, 6. Gesihþ bađian brimfuglas *he sees sea-fowls bathing,* Exon. 77 a; Th. 289, 12; Wand. 47. Bađiendra manna hūs đǣr hī hī unscrēdaþ inne *apodyterium, domus, qua vestimenta balneantium ponuntur,* Ælfc. Gl. 55; Som. 67, 9. DER. bi-bađian.

bađo *baths,* Bd. 1, 1; S. 473, 22; *acc. pl. of* bæþ.

bātian; *p.* ode; *pp.* od *To* BAIT or *lay a bait for a fish, to bait a hook;* inescare, Som.

bāt-swān, es; *m. A* BOATSWAIN; scaphiarius, proreta. v. bāt *a boat;* swān *a swain, servant.*

bātwā, būtā, būtū, būtwū; *adj.* [bā *both,* twā *two*] BOTH THE TWO, *both:*—Bātwā Adam and Eue *both Adam and Eve,* Cd. 37; Th. 47, 24; Gen. 765: Gen. 26, 35. v. begen.

bāt-weard, es; *m.* [bāt *boat,* weard *keeper*] *Keeper* or *commander of a ship;* navis custos:—He đæm bātwearde swurd gesealde *he gave a sword to the keeper of the ship,* Beo. Th. 3804; B. 1900.

BE [*abbreviated from* big = bī, *q. v.*]; *prep. dat. and instr.* 1. BY, *near to, to, at, in, on, upon, about, with;* juxta, prope, ad, secus, in, cum:—Be wege *by the way,* Mk. Bos. 8, 3. Wunode be Iordane *he dwelt by Jordan,* Cd. 91; Th. 116, 6; Gen. 1932. Be grūnde wōd *went on the ground,* Exon. 106 a; Th. 404, 29; Rä. 23, 15. Be ȳþlāfe *along the leaving of the waves,* Beo. Th. 1136; B. 566. Ic be grūnde græfe *I dig along the ground,* Exon. 106 a; Th. 403, 3; Rä. 22, 2. Be fullan *in full;* abundanter, Ps. Th. 30, 27. Be eallum *with all, altogether,* L. Ath. v. § 8, 2; Th. i. 236, 12. Ne mæg he be đȳ wedre wesan *he may not be in the open air,* Exon. 90 b; Th. 340, 18; Gn. Ex. 113. Be đam strande *upon the strand* or *shore,* Mt. Bos. 13, 48. Ne leofaþ se man be hlāfe ānum, ac be ǣlcon worde, đe of Godes mūþe gǣþ *non in solo pane vivit homo, sed in omni verbo, quod procedit de ore Dei,* Mt. Bos. 4, 4. Byrgan be deádum *to bury with the dead,* Exon. 82 b; Th. 311, 27; Seef. 98. 2. *of, from, about, touching, concerning;* de, quoad:—Be đam cilde *of* or *concerning the child,* Mt. Bos. 2, 8. Be hlīsan *of* or *about fame,* Bt. titl. xviii. xix; Fox xiv. 1. Gramlīce be Gode sprǣcan *male locuti sunt de Deo,* Ps. Th. 77, 20. Be his horse Bucefal *about his horse Bucephal,* Ors. 3, 9; Bos. 67, 39. Ahsiaþ be ealdum dagum *interrogate de diebus antiquis,* Deut. 4, 32. Mæg ic be me sylfum sōþ gied wrecan *of myself I can relate a true tale,* Exon. 81 b; Th. 306, 1; Seef. 1. Ic đis gid be đē awræc *I recited this strain of thee,* Beo. Th. 3451; B. 1723. Nysse ic be đǣre [rōde] riht *I did not know the right about the cross,* Elen. Kmbl. 2479; El. 1241. 3. *for, because of, after, by, through, according to;* pro, propter, per, secundum:—He sette word be worde *he set word for word,* Bt. procem; Fox viii. 3. Be hyra weorcum *for their works,* Exon. 26 b; Th. 79, 13; Cri. 1290. Đū scealt sunu āgan, bearn be brȳde đīnre *thou shalt have a son, a child, by thy bride,* Cd. 106; Th. 140, 11; Gen. 2326. Forlǣdd be đam lygenum *misled by the lies,* 28; Th. 37, 31; Gen. 598. Đæt ic meahte ongitan be đam gealdre Godes bearn *that I might comprehend, through that lore, God's child,* Exon. 83 a; Th. 313, 26; Mōd. 6. Hie, be wæstmum, wīg curon *they, according to his strength, choose each warrior,* Cd. 155; Th. 193, 8; Exod. 243. Nā đū be gewyrhtum ūrum woldest us dōn *thou wouldst not do to us according to our sins* [secundum peccata nostra], Ps. Th. 102, 10. 4. *beside, out of;* e, ex:—Ic đē lǣde be đam [bi đæm MS. Cott.] wege *I should lead thee out of the way,* Bt. 40, 5; Fox 240, 23. Genam hine æt eowde ūte be sceápum *tulit eum de gregibus ovium,* Ps. Th. 77, 69. 5. *sometimes* be *is separated from its case:*—Be dæges leóhte *at the light of day* or *at daylight,* Exon. 107 b; Th. 410, 17; Rä. 28, 17. Be fæder lāre *through the father's counsel,* Beo. Th. 3905; B. 1950. Ūre bān syndon toworpene be helwarena hæfte neódum *dissipata sunt ossa nostra secus infernum,* Ps. Th. 140, 9. Mīn bibod đū brǣce be đīnes bonan worde *thou didst break my command through the word of thy destroyer* [*the devil*], Exon. 28 a; Th. 85, 21; Cri. 1394. ¶ Be ānfealdum *single.* Be twīfealdum *twofold,* Ex. 22, 4. Be đam mǣstan *at the most.* Be đam đe *as,* Gen. 3, 6. [*Orm. Laym. R. Glouc. Piers P.* bi: *Chauc. Wyc.* by: *Plat.* bī: *O. Sax.* bi, be: *O. Frs.* bī, be: *Dut.* by: *Ger.* bei: *M. H. Ger.* bī: *O. H. G.* bī, pī: *Goth.* bi: *Sansk.* abhi?]

be-, bi-, big-, and **bī-** are often used as prefixes. I. when prefixed to verbs, be- and bi- either give an intensive signification to a transitive verb, or change an intransitive into a transitive verb, as,—Sprengan *to sprinkle,* be-sprengan *to be-sprinkle;* lecgan *ponere,* be-lecgan *im-ponere;* settan *to set, put,* be-settan *to be-set, surround;* fōn *to seize,* be-fōn *to surround;* gangan *to go,* be-gangan *to exercise;* reótan *plorare,* be-reótan *de-plorare.* 2. they have a privative sense, as,—Be-niman *to deprive,* be-reáfian *to bereave,* be heáfdian *to behead.* 3. sometimes they do not indicate any perceptible variation in the sense, as,—Be-cuman *to come,* be-sencan *to sink.* 4. be-, bi-, big- have the same effect when prefixed to *substantives, adjectives, and adverbs.* II. the accented bī- and big-, as prefixes, generally have the original sense of the preposition *by,* as,—Bī-cwide, big-cwide *a by-saying, proverb;* bī-spell, big-spell *a by-story, parable;* bī-wǣrlan *to pass-by;* big-standan *to stand-by.* vide I. 2.

BEÁCEN, bēcn, bēcun; *g.* beácnes; *n. A* BEACON, *sign, token, standard;* signum, significatio, typus, vexillum, portentum, miraculum; in specie de sancta cruce et de sole:—Leóht eástan com beorht beácen *light came from the east a bright beacon,* Beo. Th. 1144; B. 570. He beácen onget *he perceived the sign,* Cd. 198; Th. 246, 33; Dan. 488. Wæs beácen boden *the token was announced,* Andr. Kmbl. 2403; An. 1203. Beácnes cyme *the beacon's* [*the sun's*] *coming,* Exon. 57 b; Th. 205, 4; Ph. 107. Segn genom beácna beorhtost *he took an ensign brightest of standards,* Beo. Th. 5547; B. 2777. [*O. Sax.* bōkan: *O. Frs.* bāken: *O. H. Ger.* pouchan.] DER. fore-beácen, freođo-, heofon-, here-, sige-, sigor-, wundor-: beácn, -ian, -ung: bēcn-an, -ian: bīcn-ian: bȳcn-an, -endlīc, -iend, -iendlīc.

beácen-stān, es; *m. A stone whereon the beacon fire was made, a stone* or *tower whereon to set the beacon fire;* specula, pharus, Cot. 88.

beácne *to a sign,* Cd. 80; Th. 100, 19; Gen. 1666; *dat. of* beácen.

beácneng *a beckoning* or *nodding, a speaking by tropes* or *figures;* nutus, Cot. 139: tropologia, Cot. 201. v. beácnung.

beácnian, bȳcnian, bīcnian; *p.* ode; *pp.* od. I. *to* BECKON, *nod;* innuere:—He wæs bīcniende him *erat innuens illis,* Lk. Bos. 1, 22, 62: 5, 7. II. *to shew, indicate;* indicare, typice significare:—Swā fenix beácnaþ *as the phœnix shews,* Exon. 65 a; Th. 240, 30; Ph. 646. Đisses fugles gecynd beácnaþ hū hī beorhtne gefeán healdaþ *this bird's nature indicates how they possess bright joy,* Exon. 61 b; Th. 225, 14; Ph. 389. DER. ge-beácnian, -bēcnan.

beácniend-līc, bȳcniend-līc, bȳcnend-līc; *adj. Allegorical;* allegoricus:—Ic sette āne bōc beácniendlīcre race be Cristes cyricean *unum librum explanationis allegoricæ de Christo et ecclesia composui,* Bd. 5, 23; S. 648, 5.

beácnung, bȳcnung, beácneng, e; *f.* I. *a* BECKONING or *nodding;* nutus, Cot. 139. II. *a speaking by tropes* or *figures;* tropologia, Cot. 201.

beád *a prayer;* oratio. v. gebēd, beáda.

beád, es; *m. A table;* mensa:—Of beád *de mensa,* Lk. Lind. War. 16, 21. Beádas, Mt. Kmbl. Lind. 21, 12. v. beód.

beád *commanded,* Cd. 111; Th. 147, 1; Gen. 2432; *p. of* beódan.

beáda, an; *m. A counsellor, persuader, an exhorter* or *intreater;* suasor. v. beád.

Beada-ford-scīr, e; *f. Bedfordshire:*—Cnut wende him ūt þurh Buccingahāmscīre into Beadafordscīre *Canute went out through Buckinghamshire into Bedfordshire,* Chr. 1016; Th. 279, 16, col. 1. v. Bedan ford-scīr.

BEADO, beadu; *g. d.* beadowe, beadwe, beaduwe; *f. Battle, war, slaughter, cruelty;* pugna, strages:—Gūþ-Geáta leód, beadwe heard *the War-Goths' prince, brave in battle,* Beo. Th. 3082; B. 1539. Wit đære beadwe begen ne onþungan *we both prospered not in the war,* Exon. 129 b; Th. 497, 2; Rä. 85, 23. Beorn beaduwe heard *a man brave in battle,* Andr. Kmbl. 1963; An. 984. Đū þeóde bealdest to beadowe *thou encouragest the people to slaughter*, Andr. Kmbl. 2373; An. 1188. [*O. H. Ger.* badu-, pato-: *O. Nrs.* böð, *f. a battle: Sansk.* badh *to kill.*]

beado-cræftig; *adj. War-crafty, skilful in war, warlike*; bellicosus:—Beadocræftig beorn *a chief skilful in war*, Exon. 78 b; Th. 295, 28; Crä. 40. v. beadu-cræftig.

beado-grīma, -grīmma, an; *m. A war-mask, helmet*; bellica larva, cassis:—Ða ðe beadogrīmman bȳwan sceoldon *those who should prepare the war-helmet*, Beo. Th. 4506; B. 2257. v. beadu-grīma.

beado-hrægl, es; *n. A war-garment, coat of mail*; bellica vestis, lorica:—Beadohrægl on breóstum læg *the coat of mail lay on my breast*, Beo. Th. 1108; B. 552. v. beadu-hrægl.

beado-leóma, an; *m. A war-gleam, sword*; stragis flamma, ensis:—Ðæt se beadoleóma bītan nolde *that the war-gleam would not bite*, Beo. Th. 3050; B. 1523. v. beadu-leóma.

beado-mēce, es; *m. A battle-sword, sword of slaughter*; pugnæ ensis:—Ðæt hine-nō beadomēcas bītan ne meahton *that no battle-sword might bite it*, Beo. Th. 2912; B. 1454. v. beadu-mēce.

beado-rinc, es; *m. A soldier*; bellicosus vir:—Betst beadorinca *the best of soldiers*, Beo. Th. 2222; B. 1109: Judth. 12; Thw. 25, 24; Jud. 276. v. beadu-rinc.

beado-rōf; *adj. War-renowned, bold in war*; in pugna strenuus:—Beornas beadorōfe *war-renowned warriors*, Apstls. Kmbl. 155; Ap. 78. v. beadu-rōf.

beado-searo; *gen.* -searewes, -searwes; *n. A war-train, an engine* or *weapon of war*; bellicus apparatus:—Þurh ða heora beadosearo wǣgon *through which their war-train had moved*, Cd. 170; Th. 214, 21; Exod. 572. v. beadu-searo.

beado-wǣpen; *gen.* -wǣpnes; *dat.* -wǣpne; *n. A war-weapon*; bellica arma:—Ic beadowǣpen bere *I bear a war-weapon*, Exon. 104 b; Th. 396, 11; Rä. 16, 3. Ic swelgan onginne beadowǣpnum *I begin to swell with war-weapons*, 105 a; Th. 399, 8; Rä. 18, 8. v. beadu-wǣpen.

beado-wēg, -wēge, es; *n. A war-cup, contest, discussion*; poculum certaminis, certamen:—Him betwih beadowēg [MS. beadowīg] scencton ðæs heofonlīcan līfes *dum sese alterutrum cœlestis vitæ poculis ebriarent* [MS. *debriarent*], Bd. 4, 29; S. 607, 17. v. beadu-wēg, bǣde-wēg.

beado-weorc, es; *n. A war-work, warlike operation*; bellicum opus:—Ic eom beadoweorca sæd *I am tired of war-works*, Exon. 102 b; Th. 388, 4; Rä. 6, 2: Chr. 937; Th. 205, 40, col. 1, 2; Æðelst. 47. v. beadu-weorc.

Beado-wulf, es; *m. Beowulf*, Th. Anlct. v. Beówulf.

beadu; *gen.* beaduwe; *f. Battle, war, etc.* Andr. Kmbl. 1963; An. 984. v. beado and the following compounds.

beadu-cāf; *adj. Battle-prompt, ready for battle*; ad pugnam expeditus, Exon. 100 b; Th. 380, 20; Rä. 1, 11.

beadu-cræft, es; *m. War-craft, strength in war*; bellica vis:—Ðē gūþgewinn þurh hǣðenra hilde wōman, beorna beaducræft, geboden wyrþeþ *a war-contest will be offered to thee through the heathens' battle rush, the war-craft of heroes*, Andr. Kmbl. 437; An. 219.

beadu-cræftig, beado-cræftig; *adj. War-crafty, warlike*; bellicosus:—Fugel beaducræftig *the warlike bird*, Exon. 60 a; Th. 217, 26; Ph. 286. Beaducræftig beorn Bartholameus *a warlike chief, Bartholomeus*, Apstls. Kmbl. 87; Ap. 44.

beadu-cwealm, es; *m. A war-death, violent death*; nex:—Ðǣr he sāwulgedāl beaducwealm gebād *there he awaited the separation of the soul, a war-death*, Andr. Kmbl. 3400; An. 1704.

beadu-folm, e; *f. A war* or *bloody hand*; bellica manus:—Nān īren blōdge beadufolme onberan wolde *no iron would impair his bloody war-hand*, Beo. Th. 1984; B. 990.

beadu-grim; *adj. War-grim, war-furious*; in pugna atrox, Leo 114.

beadu-grīma, an; *m. A war-mask, helmet.* v. beado-grīma.

beadu-hrægl, es; *n. A war-garment*; bellica vestis, lorica. v. beado-hrægl.

beadu-lāc, es; *n. Play of battle, battle, war*; stragis actio, pugna:—Ǣnig mon to beadulāce ætberan meahte *any man might bear forth to the play of battle*, Beo. Th. 3126; B. 1561. To ðam beadulāce *to the battle-play*, Andr. Kmbl. 2238; An. 1120.

beadu-leóma, an; *m. A war-gleam, sword*; stragis flamma, ensis. v. beado-leóma.

beadu-mægen; *gen.* -mægnes; *n. Battle-strength, military power*; militaris vis, exercitus stragem faciens:—Beadumægnes rǣs, grīm-helma gegrind *the rush of battle-strength, the crash of grim helmets*, Cd. 160; Th. 198, 28; Exod. 329.

beadu-mēce, es; *m. A battle-sword, sword of slaughter*; pugnæ ensis. v. beado-mēce.

beadu-rǣs, es; *m. A battle-rush, onset*; pugnæ impetus:—Biter wæs se beadurǣs *the onset was bitter*, Byrht. Th. 134, 68; By. 111.

beadu-rinc, es; *m. A soldier*; bellicosus vir, miles:—Beadurincum wæs Rōm gerȳmed *Rome was laid open by the soldiers*, Bt. Met. Fox 1, 36; Met. 1, 18. v. beado-rinc.

beadu-rōf; *adj. War-renowned, bold in war*; in pugna strenuus:—Beadurōfes beácn *a beacon of the war-renowned*, Beo. Th. 6301; B. 3161. He hǣlo and frōfre beadurōfum abeád *he offered safety and comfort to the bold in war*, Andr. Kmbl. 191; An. 96. v. beado-rōf.

beadu-rūn, e; *f. A war-secret, quarrel*; jurgiosum arcanum, rixa:—Hūnferþ onband beadurūne *Hunferth unbound the war-secret*, Beo. Th. 1006; B. 501.

beadu-scearp; *adj. Battle-sharp, sharp in fight, applied to a sword*; ad pugnam acutus:—Cyning wælseaxe gebræd biter and beaduscearp *the king drew his deadly knife bitter and battle-sharp*, Beo. Th. 5401; B. 2704.

beadu-scrūd, es; *n.* [scrūd *clothes*] *Warlike apparel, warlike garmen a coat of mail*; bellicum vestimentum, lorica:—Beaduscrūda betst mīne breóst wereþ *the best of warlike garments defends my breast*, Beo. Th. 910; B. 453.

beadu-searo; *gen.* -searewes, -searwes; *n. A war-train, an engine* or *weapon of war*; bellicus apparatus. v. beado-searo.

beadu-serce, an; *f. A war-shirt, coat of mail*; bellica tunica, lorica:—Ic gefrægn sunu Wihstānes beran beadusercean *I heard that Wihstan's son bore the coat of mail*, Beo. Th. 5503; B. 2755.

beadu-þreát, es; *m. A war-host, an army*; exercitus, Elen. Kmbl. 62; El. 31.

beadu-wǣpen; *gen.* -wǣpnes; *dat.* -wǣpne; *n. A war-weapon*; bellica arma. v. beado-wǣpen.

beadu-wang, es; *m. A battle-plain*; pugnæ campus:—On beaduwange *on the battle-plain*, Andr. Kmbl. 825; An. 413.

beadu-wēg *a war-cup, contest, discussion.* v. beado-wēg.

beadu-weorc, es; *n. A war-work, warlike operation*; bellicum opus. v. beado-weorc.

beadu-weorca, an; *m. A war-worker, soldier*; miles, Grm. ii. 449, 34.

Beadu-wulf *Beowulf.* v. Beado-wulf.

be-æftan; *prep.* I. *after, behind*; post, pone:—Be-æftan *contracted to* bæftan, *q. v.* II. *without*; sine:—Beæftan ðære menego *sine turba*, Lk. Bos. 22, 6.

be-æftan; *adv. Behind, after, hereafter*; post, pone, postea:—Ðǣr beæftan forlēt eall *left there all behind*, Ors. 2, 4; Bos, 45, 14. Ðæt ic wille hēr beæftan sweotolor gereccan *that I will hereafter more clearly shew*, Bt. 11, 1; Fox 30, 29.

beærn *a son*, Ps. Spl. T. 28, 1. v. bearn.

be-ǣwnian; *p.* ode; *pp.* od *To join in marriage, marry, wed*; legitime despondere:—Bewedded and beǣwnod *wedded and married*, Chr. 1052; Th. 314, 38. v. ǣwnian.

beaf *a gad-fly*; œstrus = οἶστρος, Leo 118.

beaftan, beaftian; *p.* beaftode, beafte, *pl.* beaftodon, beafton; *pp.* beaftod *To lament*; lamentare:—We mid hondum beafton *lamentavimus*, Mt. Lind. Stv. 11, 17. v. beofian.

beág *a ring, crown*; anulus, corona, Exon. 91 a; Th. 341, 24; Gn. Ex. 131. v. beáh.

beág *gave way*, Exon. 124 a; Th. 477, 2; Ruin. 17; *p. of* būgan.

beágian, biágian; *p.* ode; *pp.* od *To crown, to set a garland on*; coronare:—Of wuldre and weorþmynt ðū beágodest hine *gloria et honore coronasti eum*, Ps. Spl. 8, 6.

beáh, beág, bǣh, bēg, bēh; *gen.* beáges; *dat.* beáge; *pl.* beágas; *m.* [beáh, beág; *p. of* būgan *to bend*] Metal made into circular ornaments, as *A ring, bracelet, collar, garland, crown*; anulus, armilla, diadema, corona. Bracelets were worn about the arms and wrists; rings on the fingers, round the ankles, the neck, and about the head. See Guide to Northern Archæology, by the Earl of Ellesmere, 8vo. 1848, p. 54; also Weinhold, Altnordisches Leben, 8vo. Berlin, 1856, p. 185. These being valuable were probably used in early times as means of exchange or as money; hence the origin of ring-money. v. Sir Wm. Betham's Essay in the Trans. of Rl. Ir. Acd. and Gent's. Mag. April 1837, pp. 372, 373, and May, p. 499:—Ic nyme ðīnne hring and ðīnne beáh and ðīnne stæf, ðe ðū on handa hæfst *capiam anulum tuum et armillam et baculum, quem manu tenes*, Gen. 38, 18, 25. Gehwearf in Francna fæðm cyninges se beáh *the collar of the king went into the grasp of the Franks*, Beo. Th. 2427; B. 1211. Sceal bryde beág *a ring shall be for a bride*, Exon. 91 a; Th. 341, 24; Gn. Ex. 131. He beágas dǣlde *he distributed bracelets*, Beo. Th. 161; B. 80. Ic frinan wille beága bryttan *I will ask the distributor of bracelets*, Beo. Th. 709; B. 352. Brūc ðisses beáges *make use of this collar*, Beo. Th. 2436; B. 1216. Se beorhta beág hlifaþ ofer heáfde *the bright garland rises over the head*, Exon. 64 b; Th. 238, 10; Ph. 602. Under gyldnum beáge *under a golden crown*, Beo. Th. 2330; B. 1163. To ðam beáge *to the crown*, Bt. 37, 2; Fox 188, 11. Se beáh gōdes [Cot. MS. beág goodes] *the crown of good*, 37, 2; Fox 188, 21. [*O. Sax.* bōg, *m: M. H. Ger.* bouc, *m: O. H. Ger.* pouc, *m: O. Nrs.* baugr, *m.*] DER. earm-beáh, -beág, heals-, rand-, scanc-, wuldor-.

beáh *submitted*, Chr. 1015; Th. 276, 22; *p. of* būgan.

beáh-gifa, beág-gifa, -gyfa, an; *m. A ring-giver, a giver of ring* or *bracelet money*; anulorum *vel* armillarum largitor:—Se geonga gewāt Eádgār of līfe, beorna beáhgifa *the young Edgar, ring-giver of men,* *departed from life*, Chr. 975; Th. 226, 36, col. 2: Byrht. Th. 140, 19; By. 290: Elen. Grm. 100: 1199: Beo. Th. 2208; B. 1102.

beáh-gifu, e; *pl. nom. acc.* a; *gen.* a, ena; *f. A ring-gift, distribution of rings* or *bracelets;* armillarum largitio:—Geongne æðeling sceolan gōde gesīðas byldan to beáhgife *good companions should exhort a young prince to a distribution of bracelets*, Menol. Fox 490; Gn. C. 15.

beáh-hord, es; *n. A ring-hoard*, Beo. Th. 1792; B. 894.

beáh-hroden [hroden; *pp. of* hreóðan] *Crown-adorned, adorned with bracelets;* armillis *vel* diademate ornatus:—Beáh-hroden [MS. beág-hroden] cwēn *a queen adorned with bracelets*, Beo. Th. 1251; B. 623.

beáh-sel, es; *n. Hall of bracelets;* domus *vel* aula in qua armillas dominus largitur, Andr. Kmbl. 3312; An. 1659.

beáh-sele, es; *m. Idem*, Beo. Th. 2358; B. 1177.

beáh-þegu, e; *f. A ring-receiving;* armillarum acceptio:—Æfter beáhþege *after the receiving of rings*, Beo. Th. 4358; B. 2176.

beáh-wriða, an; *m. A ringed wreath, armlet, bracelet;* armilla = armilla, quæ brachialis vocatur, *Cic*:—Oft hió beáhwriðan secge sealde *oft she gave a ringed wreath to the warrior*, Beo. Th. 4041; B. 2018.

beal *bellowed, roared; p. of* bellan.

beala-nīþ, es; *m. Baleful malice, evil, wickedness*, Ps. C. 50, 111; Ps. Grn. ii. 279, 111. v. bealo-nīþ.

bealcan *to emit, utter, pour out;* eructare:—Dæg ðam dæge bealceþ word *dies diei eructat verbum*, Ps. Spl. 18, 2. v. bealcettan.

bealcettan, belcettan, bealcan; *p.* te; *pp.* ted *To belch, utter, send forth, emit;* eructare, dicere, emittere:—Swēte to bealcetenne *pleasant to belch*, Bt. 22, 1; Fox 76, 32. Bealcetteþ heorte mīn word gōd *eructat cor meum verbum bonum*, Ps. Spl. 44, 1. Bealcettaþ weleras mīne lofsang *eructabunt labia mea hymnum*, Ps. Spl. 118, 171.

BEALD, bald; *adj.* BOLD, *brave, confident, of good courage;* validus, strenuus, fortis, constans, audax, fidens, bono animo, liber:—He beald in gebēde bīdsteal gifeþ *he confident in prayer maketh a stand*, Exon. 71 a; Th. 265, 28; Jul. 388. Beald reordade, eádig on elne *brave he spake, happy in courage*, Exon. 47 b; Th. 163, 24; Gū. 998. He healdeþ Meotudes ǣ beald in breóstum *bold in his breast he holds the law of the Creator*, Exon. 62 b; Th. 229, 20; Ph. 458. Hī beóþ bealde, ða ðe beorhtne wlite Meotude bringaþ *they will be of good courage, who bring a bright aspect to the Creator*, Exon. 23 b; Th. 66, 25; Cri. 1077. [*Goth.* balþs: *O. Sax.* bald: *O. Frs.* balde, *adv. quickly: O. H. Ger.* bald: *O. Nrs.* ballr.] DER. cyning-beald, cyre-, un-.

bealde, balde; *adv. Boldly, freely, instantly;* audacter, libere, fiducialiter, fidenter, instanter, prone, statim, sine mora:—Of Basan cwæþ bealde Drihten *dixit Dominus ex Basan*, Ps. Th. 67, 22. Bletsige mīne sāwle bealde Dryhten *benedic anima mea Dominum*, Ps. Th. 102, 2: 65, 18: 66, 4: 67, 24: 72, 16: 118, 130. Balde, Cd. 182; Th. 228, 11; Dan. 200: Ps. Th. 113, 25: 133, 3: 149, 8.

bealdian; *p.* ode; *pp.* od *To be brave, bear oneself bravely;* strenue *vel* fortiter se gerere:—Swā bealdode bearn Ecgþeówes *thus the son of Ecgtheow bore himself bravely*, Beo. Th. 4360; B. 2177.

beald-līce, bald-līce, bal-līce; *adv.* BOLDLY, *instantly, earnestly, saucily;* audenter, statim:—Ic bealdlīce mīnum hondum slōg *I boldly slew with my hands*, Exon. 73 a; Th. 272, 1; Jul. 492. Aoth bleów bealdlīce his horn *Aod statim insonuit buccina*, Jud. 3, 27: 3, 21.

bealdor, baldor, es; *m. A hero, prince;* princeps:—Wedera bealdor *prince of the Weders*, Beo. Th. 5127; B. 2567. Is hlāford mīn beorna bealdor *my lord is the prince of men*, Exon. 52 b; Th. 183, 24; Gū. 1332. v. baldor.

bealg *was angry*, Exon. 68 a; Th. 253, 25; Jul. 185; *p. of* belgan.

bealh *was angry, irritated; p. of* belgan.

beallucas *testiculi*, Wrt. Voc. 283, 57.

BEALO, bealu, balu; *gen.* bealowes, bealwes, bealuwes, baluwes; *dat.* bealuwe, bealwe, baluwe, bealo; *acc.* bealu, balu, bealo; *instr.* bealwe, bealuwe; *pl. gen.* bealwa, bealuwa, baluwa; *dat. instr.* balawum; balawun; *n.* I. BALE, *woe, harm, evil, mischief;* malum, calamitas, pernicies, damnum, noxa, tribulatio:—Hæfdon bealo *they had woe*, Cd. 214; Th. 269, 10; Sat. 71. Bealowes gāst *spirit of evil* [diabolus], Cd. 228; Th. 307, 19; Sat. 682. Oft heó to bealwe bearn afēdeþ *often she nourisheth her child to woe*, Salm. Kmbl. 745; Sal. 372. Him to bealwe *to their own harm*, Exon. 24 a; Th. 68, 19; Cri. 1106. Bealwe gebǣded *by calamity compelled*, Beo. Th. 5644; B. 2826. Ne ondrǣde ic ðīnra wīta bealo *I dread not the evil of thy torments*, Exon. 68 b; Th. 255, 9; Jul. 211. II. *wickedness, depravity;* malities, nequitia:—Me wið blōdhreówes weres bealuwe gehǣle *preserve me against the wickedness of the blood-thirsty man*, Ps. Th. 58, 2. [*O. Sax.* balu: *O. Frs.* balu: *O. H. Ger.* balo: *Goth.* balweins *punishment, pain: O. Nrs.* böl: *Slav.* bōl *pain.*] DER. aldor-bealo [-bealu], ealdor-, feorh-, firen-, folc-, helle-, hreðer-, leód-, mān-, morþ-, morþor-, niht-, sweord-, þeód-, un-, wīg-.

bealo-ben, -benn, e; *f. A baleful wound.* v. bealu-ben.

bealo-blonden; *pp. Mixed with bale, pernicious;* pernicie mixtus, perniciosus:—Bealoblonden nīþ *pernicious hate*, Exon. 92 a; Th. 345, 30; Gn. Ex. 198.

bealo-clom, -clomm, es; *m*: e; *f. A dire chain.* v. bealu-clom.

bealo-cræft, balo-cræft, es; *m. A wicked, pernicious,* or *magic art;* perniciosa *vel* magica ars, Bt. Met. Fox 26, 150; Met. 26, 75.

bealo-cwealm, es; *m. A pernicious* or *violent death;* perniciosa *vel* violenta mors, Beo. Th. 4523; B. 2265.

bealo-dǣd, bealu-dǣd, e; *f. A wicked, evil,* or *sinful deed;* peccatum:—Ðæt hȳ bealodǣde gescomeden *that they felt shame for a sinful deed*, Exon. 27 a; Th. 80, 4; Cri. 1302.

bealo-ful, -full; *def.* se bealo-fulla; *adj.* BALEFUL, *dire, cursed, wicked;* pestiferus, facinorosus, scelestus, malitiosus:—Bealofull *baleful*, Judth. 10; Thw. 22, 15; Jud. 63. Se bealofulla hȳneþ heardlīce *the baleful one hardly oppresseth*, Exon. 11 b; Th. 16, 27; Cri. 259. Heó ðone bealofullan alēde mannan *she laid down the odious man*, Judth. 10; Thw. 23, 2; Jud. 100. Biter bealofullum *bitter to the baleful*, Exon. 21 a; Th. 56, 31; Cri. 909.

bealo-fūs; *adj. Inclined to sin;* peccandi pronus, Exon. 94 b; Th. 354, 23; Reim. 50.

bealo-hycgende; *part. Intending evil;* perniciem moliens:—Ǣghwæðrum wæs bealo-hycgendra brōga fram ōðrum *to either of them, intending evil, was a fear of the other*, Beo. Th. 5123; B. 2565.

bealo-hydig; *adj. Intending evil, baleful-minded;* perniciem moliens, Beo. Th. 1450; B. 723.

bealo-inwit, es; *n. Guile, deceit.* v. bealu-inwit.

bealo-leás; *adj. Void of evil, innocent;* innocens, Exon. 89 b; Th. 335, 27; Gn. Ex. 39.

bealo-nīþ, beala-nīþ, bala-nīþ, es; *m. Baleful malice, evil, wickedness;* pravum *vel* perniciosum studium, pernicies, calamitas:—Him on breóstum bealonīþ weóll *baleful malice boiled in his breast*, Beo. Th. 5422; B. 2714. Bebeorh ðē ðone bealonīþ *keep from thee that baleful evil*, Beo. Th. 3520; B. 1758.

bealo-rāp, es; *m. A pernicious cord;* dirus laqueus, Exon. 13 a; Th. 23, 7; Cri. 365.

bealo-searu; *g.* -searwes; *n. A wicked machination* or *snare;* malitiosa machinatio, Exon. 72 b; Th. 270, 30; Jul. 473.

bealo-sīþ, bealu-sīþ, es; *m.* I. *an evil fortune, misfortune, calamity;* calamitas, adversa fortuna:—Bealosīþa hwōn *few* [*of*] *misfortunes*, Exon. 81 b; Th. 307, 24; Seef. 28. II. *a destructive* or *deadly path, death;* fatale iter, mors, Cd. 143; Th. 178, 1; Exod. 5.

bealo-sorg, e; *f. Baleful sorrow;* dirus ægritudo *vel* mæror, Exon. 61 b; Th. 226, 21; Ph. 409.

bealo-spell, es; *n. A baleful message* or *tale;* perniciei nuntius, Cd. 169; Th. 210, 5; Exod. 510.

bealo-þanc, -þonc, es; *m. A baleful* or *wicked thought;* prava *vel* malitiosa cogitatio, Exon. 72 b; Th. 270, 22; Jul. 469.

bealo-ware; *gen.* -wara, *pl. m. Baleful inhabitants, criminals;* scelesti. v. bealu-ware.

bealu, balu; *adj. Baleful, pernicious, wicked, malicious;* dirus, perniciosus, pravus, malus, malitiosus:—Awrītaþ hie on his wǣpne bealwe bōcstafas *they cut baleful letters upon his weapon*, Salm. Kmbl. 325; Sal. 162. v. bealo.

bealu-ben, -benn, e; *f. A baleful wound;* lethale vulnus, Cd. 154; Th. 192, 27; Exod. 238.

bealu-clom, -clomm, es; *m*: e; *f. A dire chain;* dirum vinculum:—Under bealuclommum *under dire chains*, Exon. 120 b; Th. 463, 5; Hö. 65.

bealu-dǣd, e; *f. An evil deed*, Elen. Kmbl. 1027; El. 515. v. bealo-dǣd.

bealu-inwit, es; *n. Guile, deceit;* dolus, Ps. Th. 54, 24.

bealu-sīþ, es; *m. A destructive* or *deadly path, death;* fatale iter, mors, Cd. 143; Th. 178, 1; Exod. 5. v. bealo-sīþ.

bealu-ware; *gen.* -wara; *pl. m. Baleful inhabitants, criminals;* scelesti:—Ðæt ic bealuwara weorc gebiden hæbbe *that I have endured the work of criminals*, Rood Kmbl. 155; Kr. 79.

BEÁM, es; *m.* I. *a tree;* arbor:—Se beám bude wyrda geþingu *the tree boded the councils of the fates*, Cd. 202; Th. 250, 11; Dan. 545: 23; Th. 30, 18; Gen. 468: 24; Th. 31, 1; Gen. 478. On ðæs beámes blēdum *on the branches of the tree*, 200; Th. 248, 4; Dan. 508: Exon. 114 a; Th. 437, 14; Rä. 56, 7. On ðam beáme *on the tree*, Cd. 24; Th. 31, 11; Gen. 483: Exon. 57 b; Th. 206, 6; Ph. 122. Forlǣtaþ ðone ǣnne beám *abstain from the one tree*, Cd. 13; Th. 15, 19; Gen. 235: 25; Th. 31, 28; Gen. 492. Twegen beámas stōdon ofætes gehlǣdene *two trees stood laden with fruit*, 23; Th. 30, 2; Gen. 460: Exon. 56 a; Th. 200, 4; Ph. 35. Ic beámas fylle *I fell the trees*, 101 a; Th. 381, 11; Rä. 2, 9. II. *the tree, cross;* patibulum, crux:—Wæs se beám bōcstafum awriten *the cross was inscribed with letters*, Elen. Kmbl. 181; El. 91: Exon. 24 a; Th. 67, 17; Cri. 1090. Se ðe deáþes wolde biteres onbyrigan on ðam beáme *who would taste of bitter death on the cross*, Rood Kmbl. 226; Kr. 114: Cd. 224; Th. 296, 30; Sat. 510. He on ðone hālgan beám ahongen wæs *he was hung on the holy cross*, Exon. 24 a; Th. 67, 25; Cri. 1094: 29 a; Th. 88, 29; Cri. 1447. III. *a column, pillar;* columna:—Hæfde wuldres beám werud gelǽded *the pillar of glory had led the host*, Cd. 170; Th. 214, 10; Exod. 566: 148; Th. 184, 22; Exod. 111. God hēt him fýrenne beám befōran wīsian *God commanded a pillar of fire to point out the way before them*, Ps. Th. 104, 34. Him befōran fōron beámas twegen *two pillars went before him*, Cd. 146; Th. 183, 20; Exod. 94. **IV.** *wood, a ship;* lignum, navis:—Ic of fæđmum cwom brimes and beámes *I came from the clutches of sea and ship*, Exon. 103 b; Th. 392, 13; Rä. 11, 7. **V.** *a* BEAM, *splint, post, a stock of a tree;* trabs, stipes:—Se beám biþ on đīnum āgenum eágan *trabs est in oculo tuo*, Mt. Bos. 7, 4. Bunden under beáme *bound under a beam*, Exon. 126 a; Th. 485, 9; Rä. 71, 11. Đū ne gesyhst đone beám on đīnum āgenum eágan *trabem in oculo tuo non vides*, Mt. Bos. 7, 3, 5. Heora ǽrenan beámas ne mihton fram Galliscum fýre forbærnede weorþan *their brazen beams could not be destroyed by the fire of the Gauls*, Ors. 2, 8; Bos. 52, 16. Of beáme *de stipite*, Cot. 63. **VI.** *in composition*, anything proceeding in a right line, hence,—*A ray of light, a sun*-BEAM; radius:—Comēta, se steorra, scān swilce sunne-beám *a comet, the star, shone like a sun-beam*, Chr. 678; Erl. 41, 5. **VII.** in the Northumbrian Gospels beám is put for býme *a trumpet;* tuba:—Mid beám *cum tuba*, Mt. Kmbl. Lind. 24, 31. [*Tynd.* beame: *Chauc. Wyc.* beme: *R. Glouc.* beam, bem: *Laym.* beam, bem: *O. Sax.* bôm, *m*: *N. Frs.* baem, beamme, bjemme: *O. Frs.* bām, *m*: *Dut.* boom, *m*: *Ger.* baum, *m*: *M. H. Ger.* boum, *m*: *O. H. Ger.* poum, *m*: *Goth.* bagms, *m*: *Icel.* bađmr, *m.*] DER. beg-beám, ceder-, deáþ-, ele-, fīc-, firgen-, gār-, gleó-, sige-, wer-, wudu-, wyn-.

Beám-dūn, Beán-dūn, e; *f.* BAMPTON, *Devonshire;* oppidum situm esse arbitror in agro Devoniensi, qua Somersætensibus adjacet, et vocari hodie *Bampton*, Gibson Chr. Explicatio, p. 14, col. 1:—Hēr Cynegils and Cwichelm gefuhton on Beámdūne *in this year Cynegils and Cwichelm fought at Bampton*, Chr. 614; Th. 38, 38, cols. 2, 3. [beám *a tree;* dūn *a hill, down;* collis stipitibus seu trabibus refertus, Gibson.]

Beám-fleót, es; *m.* The name of places now called *Beamfleet* [*Beamfled*, Hunt.] *Bamfleet, Benfleet, Essex;* æstuarii nomen in agro Essexiensi, hodie *Benfleet*:—Hie fōron eást to Beámfleóte *they marched east to Benfleet*, Chr. 894; Erl. 91, 15.

beámian; *p.* ede; *pp.* ed *To shine, to cast forth rays* or *beams like the sun;* radiare, Som.

beám-sceadu, e; *f. A tree-shade, the shade of a tree;* arborum umbra:—Gewitan him đā gangan under beámsceade *then they retired under the tree-shade*, Cd. 40; Th. 53, 10; Gen. 859. Hī slēpon under beámsceade *they slept under the tree-shade*, Bt. Met. Fox 8, 55; Met. 8, 28.

beám-telg, es; *m. Dye of a tree* [*ink*]; tinctura arborea [atramentum scriptorium]:—Fugles wyn beámtelge swealg *the bird's joy* [i. e. *the pen*] *swallowed dye of a tree*, Exon. 107 a; Th. 408, 9; Rä. 27, 9.

BEÁN, bién, e; *f. A* BEAN, *all sorts of pulse;* faba, legumen:—Beán pisan *a vetch*, Cot. 34: 122. [*Plat. Dut.* boon, *f*: *Ger.* bohne, *f*: *M. H. Ger.* bône, *f*: *O. H. Ger.* pōna, *f*: *Dan.* bönne: *Swed.* böna: *O. Nrs.* baun, *f*: *Lat.* faba, *f.*]

beán-belgas, beán-coddas; *pl. m.* [beán *a bean*, belg or codd *a bag*] *Bean-pods, husks, cods* or *shells;* fabarum sacculi, siliquæ:—Of đām beáncoddum *de siliquis*, Lk. Bos. 15, 16: Cot. 200.

beand, es; *m. A band, bond;* vinculum:—On beandon *in bonds* or *captivity;* in vinculis, Chr. 1069; Erl. 207, 15. v. bend.

Beán-dūn, e; *f. Bampton, Devonshire*, Chr. 614; Th. 38, 38, col. 1; 39, 37, col. 1; Erl. 20, 36; 21, 35. v. Beám-dūn.

beánen; *adj. Beany, belonging to beans;* fabarius:—Beánene melewe BEAN-MEAL, Herb. 155, 3; Lchdm. i. 282, 9.

beán-scealas BEAN-SHELLS; siliquæ, quisquiliæ, Cot. 200.

Bearan burh; *gen.* burge; *dat.* byrig; *f. Banbury, Oxfordshire.* v. Beran burh.

BEARD, es; *m.* **I.** *a* BEARD; barba:—Ne beard ne sciron *nec radetis barbam*, Lev. 19, 27; nether ge schulen schave the beerd, *Wyc.* Smyringc niđerfeól on bearde, bearde Aarones *unguentum descendit in barbam, barbam Aaronis*, Ps. Lamb. 132, 2. **II.** *the Anglo-Saxons were proud of their beards, and to shave a layman by force was a legal offence*:—Gif mon đone beard ofascire, mid XX scillinga gebēte. Gif he hine gebinde, and đonne to preoste bescire, mid LX scillinga gebēte *if a man shave off the beard, let him make amends* [*boot*] *with* XX *shillings. If he bind him, and then shave him like a priest, let him make amends* [*boot*] *with* lx *shillings*, L. Alf. pol. 35; Th. i. 84, 8. [*Laym.* baerd: *Plat. Dut.* baard, *m*: *Frs.* berd, bird, *m*: *Ger.* bart, *m*: *Icel.* bart, *n.*]

beard-leás; *adj.* BEARDLESS; imberbis. Used as a noun, it denotes those *without a beard*, as *a youth, stripling*, also *a hawk* or *buzzard;* ephebus, buteo:—Beardleás *ephebus*, vel *buteo*, Ælfc. Gl. 87; Som. 74, 51; Wrt. Voc. 50, 33.

BEARG, bearh, es; *m. A castrated boar, a barrow pig;* majālis:—Amæsted swīn, bearg bellende on bōc-wuda *a fattened swine, a barrow pig* [*castrated boar*] *grunting in beech woods*, Exon. 111 b; Th. 428, 10; Rä. 41, 106. Bearh *majalis*, Ælfc. Gl. 20; Som. 59, 31; Wrt. Voc. 22, 72. [*Plat.* borg, *m. a castrated boar pig*: *Dut.* barg, *m*: *Frs.* baerg, *m*: *Ger.* borg-schwein: *O. H. Ger.* barc, barg, *m. porcus castratus.*]

bearg, bearh *saved, secured*, Exon. 55 a; Th. 195, 21; Az. 159; *p. of* beorgan.

bearh *saved*, Cd. 124; Th. 158, 29; Gen. 2624; *p. of* beorgan.

bearht *bright*, Ps. Spl. 22, 7. v. beorht.

bearhtm, es; *m. A noise, tumult, clamour, sound, cry;* fragor, strepitus, tumultus, clamor:—Ic on đisse byrig bearhtm gehýre *I hear a tumult in this city*, Cd. 109; Th. 145, 16; Gen. 2406. v. breahtm, brecan *to break.*

bearhtm, es; *m. Brightness, glittering, scintillation, twinkling, glance;* claritas, splendor, nitor, scintillatio, acies:—Eágena bearhtm forsiteþ and forsworceþ *the brightness of the eyes vanishes and darkens*, Beo. Th. 3537; B. 1766. Đæt biþ an eágan bearhtm [MS. bryhtm] *that is in the twinkling of the eye, in a moment*, Bd. 2, 13; S. 516, 20. DER. bearht, beorht *bright.*

bearhtm-hwīl, byrhtm-hwīl, e; *f. A twinkling while, a moment;* oculi nictus tempus, momentum:—On ānre byrhtmhwīle *in momento temporis*, Lk. Bos. 4, 5.

bearhtnes *brightness.* v. beorhtnes.

bearm, es; *m. The bosom, lap;* sinus, gremium:—On eówerne bearm *in sinum vestrum*, Lk. Bos. 6, 38. Iosep hī nam of đæs fæder bearme *Ioseph eos tulit de gremio patris*, Gen. 48, 12: Cd. 216; Th. 274, 12; Sat. 153. Đā wæs fæger foldan bearm *then was earth's bosom fair*, Beo. Th. 2278; B. 1137. Alēdon leófne þeóden on bearm scipes *they laid the beloved chief in the ship's bosom*, Beo. Th. 70; B. 35: Exon. 101 b; Th. 382, 28; Rä. 4, 3. [*Chauc.* barme *the bosom*: *O. Sax.* barm, *m. sinus, gremium*: *O. Frs.* barm-bracco *a lap-dog*: *O. H. Ger.* barm, *m*: *Goth.* barms, *m*: *Icel.* barmr, *m.* I. *the brim of anything;* ora, margo; II. *the bosom;* gremium: from beran, beoran *to bear, to carry in folded arms*, or *on the bosom.*]

bearm-clāþ, es; *n. A* BARME-CLOTH [*Chauc. The Milleres Tale*, 3237], *a bosom-cloth, an apron;* sinui imposita mappula:—Bearmclāþ *mappula*, Wrt. Voc. 26, 68.

bearm-rægl, es; *m. A bosom-garment;* sinui imposita vestis *vel* mappula, Wrt. Voc. 26, 28.

bearn, es; *n. A* BEARN, *child, son, issue, offspring, progeny;* natus, infans, puer, filius, soboles, proles:—Bearn Godes *Son of God*, Elen. Kmbl. 1624; El. 814. Nū is đæt bearn cymen *now is that child come*, Exon. 8 b; Th. 5, 8; Cri. 66. Hīg næfdon nān bearn *non erat illis filius*, Lk. Bos. 1, 7. Þurh bearnes gebyrd *through the birth of a child*, Exon. 8 b; Th. 3, 18; Cri. 38. Beón mid bearne *gravidam esse*, Somn. 370. Bearn *soboles* vel *proles*, Ælfc. Gl. 91; Som. 75, 19. Geáta bearn *the sons of the Goths*, Beo. Th. 4374; B. 2184. He Noe gebletsade and his bearn *he blessed Noah and his sons*, Cd. 74; Th. 91, 1; Gen. 1505. Đys synd Israēla bearna naman *hæc sunt nomina filiorum Israel*, Ex. 1, 1. Geseah his bearna bearn *vidit filios filiorum suorum*, Job Thw. 168, 35. Ge Godes bearn, bringaþ Gode ramma bearn *filii Dei, afferte Domino filios arietum*, Ps. Th. 28, 1. [*Piers* barn *a child*: *Scot. and Northumb.* bairn: *O. Sax.* barn, *n*: *O. Frs.* bern, *n*: *O. H. Ger.* barn, *n*: *Goth.* barn, *n*: *Dan. Swed. Icel.* barn, *n. a child*: *what is borne, from* beran *to bear.*] DER. cyne-bearn, dryht-, folc-, freó-, frum-, god-, hǽlu-, hūsel-, sige-, þryþ-, woruld-. v. beran.

bearn, es; *n. A barley-place, a* BARN; horreum:—He gadereþ hys hwǽte on his bearn *congregabit triticum suum in horreum*, Mt. Kmbl. Hat. 3, 12. v. bere-ærn.

be-arn *occurred*, Wanl. Catal. 154, 5; *p. of* be-yrnan.

bearn *burned, consumed;* *p. of* beornan.

bearn-cennung, e; *f. Child-birth;* puerperium. v. cenning, *from* cennan *parere.*

bearn-eácen [bearn *a child*, eacen *increased*] *Increased, pregnant;* auctus, gravidus:—Bearneácen wīf þrōwaþ micel earfođu *a pregnant woman suffers much trouble*, Bt. 31, 1; Fox 112, 2, note 2, Cott: L. Alf. pol. 9; Th. i. 66, 23. DER. eácan.

bearn-eácnung, e; *f. Generation, conception, pregnancy;* genitura, conceptio, prægnatio. v. eácnung.

bearnende *burning;* ardens, Jn. Lind. War. 5, 35. v. bernende; *part. of* byrnan.

bearn-gebyrdo; *indecl. f. Child-bearing;* partus:—Hyre eald Metod ēste wǽre bearngebyrdo *to her the ancient Creator was gracious in her child-bearing*, Beo. Th. 1896; B. 946.

bearn-gestreón, es; *n. Child-procreation;* liberorum procreatio:—Đæt ic þolian sceal bearngestreóna: ic wiđ brýde ne mōt hǽmed habban *that I shall lack child-procreation: with a bride I may not have intercourse*, Exon. 105 b; Th. 402, 9; Rä. 21, 27.

bearn-leás; *adj. Childless;* absque liberis:—Bearnleásne ge habbaþ me gedōnne *absque liberis me esse fecistis*, Gen. 42, 36: Ex. 21, 22.

bearn-lēst, e; *f. Childlessness, want of children;* liberorum defectus *vel* orbitas, eorum conditio qui liberis carent:—For bearnlēste *for want of children*, Bt. 11, 1; Fox 32, 6.

bearn-lufe, an; *f. Child-love, love of one's own* or *of an adopted child;* liberorum amor, filii sui *vel* adoptivi amor:—Hine on bearnlufan habban wolde *eum loco adoptivi haberet*, Bd. 5, 19; S. 638, 4.

bearn-myrþra, an; *m. A child-murderer, an infanticide;* liberorum interfector, Lupi Serm. i. 19; Hick. Thes. ii. 105, 5.

bearn-teám, es; *m. A succession of children, issue, posterity;* liberorum ordo *vel* successio, soboles:—Ðæt hí to raðe woldon fultumleáse beón æt hiora bearnteámum *that they should very soon be without help from posterity,* Ors. 1, 14; Bos. 37, 19. [*Scot.* barn-teme, bairn-time *a brood of children, all the children of one mother.*]

BEARO, bearu; *gen.* bearwes; *dat.* bearwe, bearowe, bearuwe; *acc.* bearo; *pl. nom. acc.* bearwas; *gen.* -wa; *dat.* -wum; *m. A grove, wood;* nemus *vel* lucus, silva, virgultum:—Se hálga bearo sette *the holy man planted a grove,* Cd. 137; Th. 172, 7; Gen. 2840. Wæter wynsumu bearo ealne geondfaraþ *pleasant waters pervade all the grove,* Exon. 56 b; Th. 202, 10; Ph. 67. Bearu *nemus* vel *lucus,* Wrt. Voc. 32, 38. Se fugel of ðæs bearwes beáme gewíteþ *the fowl departs from the tree of the grove,* Exon. 57 b; Th. 206, 5; Ph. 122: 58 a; Th. 207, 27; Ph. 148. Wíc mid bearuwe ymbsealde *mansions surrounded with a grove,* Bd. 5, 2; S. 614, 31. In bearwe, on bearwe *or* on bearowe *in a wood,* Cot. 109. Heó begeát grēne bearwas *she gained the green groves,* Cd. 72; Th. 89, 13; Gen. 1480. [Heyne says *a bearing* or *a fruit-bearing tree, hence trees in general, a wood: O. Nrs.* börr, *m. arbor.*] DER. æppel-bearo, sun-, wudu-.

Bearocscýre, Bearucscýre, Bearwucscíre *Berkshire.* v. Barocscír.

bearo-næs, -næss, es; *m. A woody shore* or *promontory;* litus nemorosum:—Trædaþ bearonæssas *they tread the woody promontories,* Exon. 114 b; Th. 439, 5; Rä. 58, 5.

bearowe *in a wood,* Menol. Fox 496; Gn. C. 18. v. bearo.

bears *a perch;* lupus. v. bærs.

bear-swinig; *adj. openly wicked, a publican,* Lk. Rush. War. 3, 12: 15, 1. v. bær-synnig.

bearu *a grove,* Wrt. Voc. 32, 38. v. bearo.

bearug *a barrow-pig.* v. bearg.

bearuwe *with a grove,* Bd. 5, 2; S. 614, 31. v. bearo.

bearwas, bearwe, bearwes, Exon. 57 b; Th. 206, 5; Ph. 122. v. bearo.

BEÁTAN; *part.* beátende; ic beáte, ðú beátest, býtst, he beáteþ, být, *pl.* beátaþ; *p.* beót, *pl.* beóton; *pp.* beáten. I. *to* BEAT, *strike, lash, dash, hurt;* percutere, tundere, verberare, cædere, pulsare, quatere, lædere:—Agynþ beátan hys efenþeówas *cœperit percutere conservos,* Mt. Bos. 24, 49. Hwí beátst ðú me *quid me cædis?* Jn. Bos. 18, 23. Ðá Balaam beót ðone assan *cum Balaam verberaret asinam,* Num. 22, 23. Streámas staðu beátaþ *streams beat the shores,* Exon. 101 a; Th. 382, 4; Rä. 3, 6. Sǽ on staðu beáteþ *the sea lashes against the shore,* Bt. Met. Fox 6, 30; Met. 6, 15. Beóton brimstreámas *the sea-streams dashed,* Andr. Kmbl. 477; An. 239: 3084; An. 1545. Ne se bryne beót mæcgum *nor did the burning hurt the youths,* Cd. 187; Th. 232, 24; Dan. 265. II. to beat with the feet,—*to tread, trample, tramp;* calcare, proculcare:—Se mearh burhstede beáteþ *the steed tramps the castle-place,* Beo. Th. 4522; B. 2265. [*Ger.* boszen *to beat: M. H. Ger.* bōzen *id: O. H. Ger.* pōzan *id: O. Nrs.* bauta *id.*] DER. a-beátan, ge-, of-, ofa-, to-.

beátere, es; *m. A* BEATER, *fighter, champion;* pugil, Ælfc. Gr. 9, 8.

beáw-hyrnet = beó-hyrnet, -hyrnett, e; *f. A bee-hornet, gad-fly, horse-fly;* œstrus = οἶστρος:—Beáw-hyrnet *œstrus* [MS. beáw-hyrnette *œstrum, acc?*], Ælfc. Gl. 22; Som. 59, 108; Wrt. Voc. 23, 64. v. beó, hyrnet.

be-baðian, bi-baðian; *p.* ode; *pp.* od *To bathe, wash;* luere, abluere, lavare:—Wætere aþwegen and bebaðod *lotus aqua,* Bd. 1, 27; S. 496, 17.

Bebba-burh *Bamborough,* Chr. 1095; Th. 361, 39, 40: 362, 1. v. Bebban burh.

Bebban burh, Chr. 547; Th. 28, 25; 29, 24: 641; Th. 49, 3: 993; Th. 240, 17; 241, 16, col. 2: Bæbba-burh, Chr. 1093; Th. 360, 6: Bebba-burh, Chr. 1095; Th. 361, 39, 40: *gen.* -burge; *dat.* -byrig; *acc.* -burg, -burh; *f.* BAMBOROUGH, *in Northumberland:* Babbæ oppidum in provincia Northanhymbrorum:—Hēr Ida fēng to ríce, ðonon Norþanhymbra cyne-cyn onwōc, and ríxode twelf geár. He timbrode Bebban burh, seó wæs ǽrost mid hegge betýned, and ðǽr æfter mid wealle *here* [A. D. 547] *Ida began to reign, from whom arose the royal race of the Northumbrians, and reigned twelve years. He built Bamborough, which was at first inclosed by a hedge, and afterwards by a wall,* Chr. 547; Erl. 16, 7-10. From Bebban byrig *from Bamborough,* Chr. 926; Th. 199, 31. Ðá becom Penda, Myrcna cyning, to ðære cynelícan byrig, seó is nemned Bebban burh *then came Penda, king of the Mercians, to the royal city, which is named Bamborough,* Bd. 3, 16; S. 542, 18: 3, 6; S. 528, 28. Hēr wæs Bæbban burg tobrocon, and mycel herehúðe ðǽr genumen *here* [A. D. 993] *Bamborough was destroyed, and much spoil was there taken,* Chr. 993; Erl. 133, 1. [Bebba, æ; *f. Lat:* Bebbe, an; *f. Bebba, the name of a queen:* burh *a borough, corporate town;* hence Bebban burh *Bebba's burgh* or *city;* Bebbæ urbs. Bede calls it,—'Urbs regia, quæ a Regina quondam vocabulo Bebba cognominatur,' Bd. 3, 6; S. 109, 22. We thus see that the town had its name from queen Bebba. It is probable that king Ida, who built the town, did not give it this name; but his grandson, Ædilfrid, as Nennius says,—'Eadfered [= Ædilfrid] dedit uxori suæ [urbem], quæ vocatur Bebbab, et de nomine suæ uxoris suscepit nomen, id est Bebbanburch,' Nenn. 63, ed. Stevens; Bd. Gidl. 187, note 1. Bebban burh was written in succeeding ages,—Bebbanburc, Flor. A. D. 1117: Bebanburgh, Bebamburgh, Babanburch, Hunt. A. D. 1148: Babbanburch, Bebbanburc, Dun. A. D. 1164: Babanburch, Ric. A. D. 1184: Bebbamburg, Hovd. A. D. 1204: Bamburgh, Kni. A. D. 1395: now, in 1873, Bamborough.]

bebeád *commanded,* Elen. Kmbl. 1417; El. 710; *p. of* be-beódan.

be-beódan, bi-beódan; *part.* be-beódende, he be-být; *p.* be-beád, *pl.* be-budon; *impert.* be-beód; *pp.* be-boden. I. *to give a by-command* or *a gentle command,* but generally *to command, order;* jubere, præcipere, mandare:—He hys englum bebýt *angelis suis mandavit,* Lk. Bos. 4, 10. Bebeód Iosue *præcipe Iosue,* Deut. 3, 28: Ps. Th. 67, 26: Ex. 16, 16. Swā him God bebeád *as God commanded him,* Frag. Kmbl. 75; Leás. 39. Hí bebudon him *præceperunt illi,* Bd. 4, 24; S. 597, 35. Ðǽm laudbūendum is beboden, ðæt ealles ðæs ðe him on heora ceápe geweaxe, híg Gode ðone teóðan dǽl agyfen *to farmers it is commanded, that of all which increases to them of their cattle, they give the tenth part to God,* L. E. I. 35; Th. ii. 432, 27. II. *to offer, give up, commend;* offerre, commendare, mandare:—Ðū scealt leófes líc forbærnan and me lāc bebeódan *thou shalt burn the beloved's body and offer it me as a sacrifice,* Cd. 138; Th. 173, 9; Gen. 2858. On handa ðíne ic bebeóde gāst mínne *in manus tuas commendo spiritum meum,* Ps. Spl. 30, 6; Hy. 4, 5; Hy. Grn. ii. 283, 5: Ps. Th. 132, 4. III. *to announce;* nuntiare, pronuntiare:—He bebeád wyrd gewordene *he announced the event that had passed,* Cd. 197; Th. 245, 29; Dan. 470. v. beódan.

be-beódend, es; *m. One who commands, a master;* præceptor, Lk. Bos. 5, 5: 9, 33.

be-beódendlíc gemet, beódendlíc gemet, es; *n. The imperative mood;* modus imperativus:—Ðæt ōðer modus is imperativus, ðæt is bebeódendlíc; mid ðam gemete we hātaþ ōðre menn dōn sum þingc, oððe sum þingc þrōwian,—Rǽd ðū *lege,* rǽde he *legat,* beswing ðis cild *flagella istum puerum,* sí he beswungen *flagelletur.* Ðis gemet sprecþ forþwerd, and næfþ nǽnne *præteritum,* forðanðe nān mann ne hǽt dōn ðæt ðe gedōn biþ *the other mood is the imperative, that is the commanding; with this mood we order other people to do something,* or *to suffer something,—Read thou, let him read, beat this child, let him be beaten. This mood speaketh directly* [*forthward* or *to those present*], *and has no preterite, because no man commands to do what is done,* Ælfc. Gr. 21; Som. 23, 20-24.

be-beorgan; *p.* -bearg, *pl.* -burgon; *pp.* -borgen *To defend oneself, to take care;* cavere ab aliqua re:—He him bebeorgan ne con wōm *he cannot defend himself against the evil,* Beo. Th. 3497; B. 1746: 3520; B. 1758.

beber *a beaver,* Som. Lye. v. befor.

be-beran; he -byreþ; *p.* -bær *To bear* or *carry to, provide, supply;* afferre, instruere:—Gif man mannan wǽpnum bebyreþ *if one supply a man with weapons,* L. Ethb. 18; Th. i. 6, 19. v. beran.

be-biddan *to command.* v. biddan.

be-bindan; *p.* -band, -bond, *pl.* -bundon; *pp.* -bunden [be, bindan, *q. v.*] *To bind in* or *about;* inligare, Bd. 3, 11; S. 536, note 9.

be-birgan, -birigan; *p.* de; *pp.* ed *To bury;* sepelire:—Mín fæder me byd ðæt ic hine bebirgde *pater meus adjuravit me, ut eum sepelirem,* Gen. 50, 5: 50, 6. He hine bebirigde *he buried him,* Ælfc. T. Grn. 6, 2. Hine bebirgdon *sepelierunt eum,* Gen. 50, 13. Bebirged *sepultus,* 50, 14. Ðǽr wæs Isaac bebirged, and ðǽr líþ eác Lia bebirged *ibi sepultus est Isaac, ibi et Lia condita jacet,* 49, 31. v. be-byrgan.

be-birigan; *p.* de; *pp.* ed *To bury,* Gen. 49, 29. v. be-byrigan.

be-blonden; *pp. infected, dyed;* infectus, tinctus. v. blandan.

be-bod, bi-bod, es; *pl. nom. acc.* u, o; *gen.* a; *dat.* um; *n. A command, mandate, decree, order;* mandatum, jussum:—Hwilc ðære geógoþe gleáwost wǽre bōca bebodes *which of the youth was most skilful in the precepts of books,* Cd. 176; Th. 221, 2; Dan. 82. Eall ðín bebodu *omnia mandata tua,* Ps. Th. 118, 172. Ealra beboda mǽst *primum omnium mandatum,* Mk. Bos. 12, 28. Hí brǽcon bebodo *they broke the commandments,* Cd. 188; Th. 234, 28; Dan. 299.

be-bodan *to command,* Ps. Spl. 67, 31. v. be-beódan.

be-boden *commanded, commended; pp. of* be-beódan.

be-bohte *sold,* Cd. 226; Th. 301, 5; Sat. 577; *p. of* be-bycgean.

be-bond *bound,* Bd. 3, 11; S. 536, note 9; *p. of* be-bindan.

be-boren-inniht *born within a country, free of a country, native;* municipalis, Cot. 136. v. beran.

be-brecan, he, heó -briceþ, -bricþ; *p.* -bræc, *pl.* -brǽcon; *pp.* -brocen *To break off, deprive by breaking, to break to pieces, consume;* carpendo spoliare, confringere, consumere:—Beám heó abreóteþ and bebriceþ telgum *it crusheth the tree and deprives it of its twigs,* Salm. Kmbl. 592; Sal. 295. Bebrocene wǽron ealle hyra hlāfas *consumpti erant omnes eorum panes,* Gr. Dial. 2, 21.

be-bregdan; *p.* -brægd, *pl.* -brugdon; *pp.* -brogden *To pretend;* simulare, Lk. Lind. War. 20, 20. v. bregdan.

be-briceþ, -bricþ *breaks off, deprives by breaking,* Salm. Kmbl. 592; Sal. 295. v. be-brecan.

be-brocen *broken, consumed*, Gr. Dial. 2, 21; *pp. of* be-brecan.

be-brugdon *they pretended*, Lk. Lind. War. 20, 20; *p. of* be-bregdan.

be-bûgan, bi-bûgan; *p.* -beág, *pl.* -bugon; *pp.* -bogen. I. *to avoid;* avertere, evitare:—Ne meahte he ða gehðu bebûgan *he could not avoid the sorrow*, Elen. Kmbl. 1215; El. 609: Ps. Th. 138, 17. II. *to surround, encircle, encompass;* circumire, circumcingere:—Swâ wæter bibûgeþ ðisne beorhtan bôsm *so far as the water encircles this bright expanse*, Exon. 95 b; Th. 356, 4; Pa. 6: Cd. 190; Th. 236, 16; Dan. 322. III. *to reach, extend;* pertinere:—Swâ bebûgeþ gebod geond Brytenrîcu Sexna cyninges [MS. kyninges] *so far as the command of the king of the Saxons extendeth through Britain*, Menol. Fox 457; Men. 230: Beo. Th. 2451; B. 1223.

be-bycgean, -bycgan; *part.* -bycgende; *p.* -bohte; *pp.* -boht *To sell, to set* or *put to sale;* vendere:—On gold bebycgean *to sell for gold*, Bd. 2, 12; S. 514, 39. Iudas bebohte bearn wealdendes on seolfres sinc *Judas sold the child of the Almighty for a heap of silver*, Cd. 226; Th. 301, 5; Sat. 577: Ps. Th. 43, 14: 104, 15: Beo. Th. 5591; B. 2799.

be-byrd *garnished with nails, set with spikes;* clavatus, Cot. 49, Som. Lye.

be-byreþ *supplies*, L. Ethb. 18; Th. i. 6, 19; *pres. of* be-beran.

be-byrgan, be-birgan; *p.* de; *pp.* ed *To bury;* sepelire:—Bebyrgeþ bân and ýslan *buries bones and embers*, Exon. 60 a; Th. 217, 26; Ph. 286: Gen. 23, 19. To bebyrgenne *sepelire*, Mt. Bos. 27, 7: Jn. Bos. 19, 40. v. byrgan.

be-byrian; *p.* ede, ide; *pp.* ed *To bury;* sepelire:—Ðæt hî môston ða deádan bebyrian *that they might bury the dead*, Ors. 3, 1; Bos. 54, 29. Hine ârlîce bebyride *eum honorifice sepelivit*, Bd. 4, 22; S. 591, 20. v. byrian.

be-byrigan, be-birigan; *p.* ede; *pp.* ed *To cover with a mound, to bury;* tumulare, sepelire:—Bebirigaþ me *sepelite me*, Gen. 49, 29. Ða bân ðe ðǽr bebyrigede wǽron *ossa quæ ibidem fuerant tumulata*, Bd. 4, 10; S. 578, 10: 2, 1; S. 500, 15. v. byrigan.

be-byrigean *to bury*, Mt. Bos. 8, 21, 22: Bd. 4, 11; S. 580, 3. v. byrgan, byrigan.

be-byrigednes, -ness, e; *f. A burying;* sepultura:—Æfter monigum geárum his bebyrigednesse *post multos ejus sepulturæ annos*, Bd. 4, 32; S. 611, 27. v. be-byrignys.

be-byrignys, -nyss; be-byrigednes, -ness, e; *f. A burying;* sepultura:—Ne wæs ǽnig se ðe bebyrignysse sealde ðám ðe acwealde wǽron *nec erat qui interemptos sepulturæ traderet*, Bd. 1, 15; S. 484, 3.

be-bŷt *commands*, Lk. Bos. 4, 10; *3rd pres. of* be-beódan.

bec, becc, es; *m. A brook*, BECK or *small rapid stream;* rivulus:—Of ðan bece [MS. bæce] *from the beck*, Kmbl. Cod. Dipl. iii. 121, 16.

Bec *an abbey in Normandy:*—Teodbald, ðe was abbot in ðe Bec *Theobald, who was abbot of Bec*, Chr. 1140; Th. 383, 40.

bêc *books*, Hy. 7, 20; Hy. Grn. ii. 287, 20. v. bôc.

be-cæfian, be-cefian; *p.* ede; *pp.* ed *To embroider, ornament, decorate;* phalerare:—Becæfed *phaleratus*, Cot. 84. v. cæfian.

be-carcan *to take care of;* accurare, Som. Lye. v. carc *care.*

becc *a beck, brook.* v. bec.

-becc, -bec, -beck, used for the name of places, or as a termination to the names of places, denotes the situation to be near *a brook* or *river.*

becca, an; *m. A* BECK, *pick-axe, mattock;* ligo, marra, Ælfc. Gl. 2; Som. 55, 42.

bêce, bǽce, beóce, an; *f. A beech-tree, a tree bearing mast;* fagus, æsculus:—Bêce *fagus*, Wrt. Voc. 285, 21. v. bôcce, bôc.

be-ceápian; *p.* ode; *pp.* od *To sell;* vendere:—He sceolde ealle his wêlan beceápian *he should sell all his wealth*, Homl. Th. i. 62, 3. Se ðe sôþfæstnysse beceápaþ wið feó *he who sells truth for money*, ii. 244, 24. Hî beceápodon heora ǽhta *they sold their possessions*, i. 316, 4, 11, 31. Beceápa ealle ðîne ǽhta *sell all thy possessions*, ii. 400, 12. v. be-cýpan, ceápian.

be-ceásan; *p.* -ceós, *pl.* -ceóson; *pp.* -ceásen *To attack, fight, combat;* oppugnare, contendere, Leo 131. v. ceásan, ceás *strife.*

be-cefian; *p.* ede; *pp.* ed *To ornament, embroider*, Lye. v. be-cæfian.

bêcen *a beacon*, Mk. Skt. Lind. 13, 22. v. beácen.

bêcen; *adj.* BEECHEN, *made of beech;* fagineus:—Bêcen *fagineus*, Ælfc. Gl. 45; Som. 64, 101; Wrt. Voc. 32, 36.

be-ceorfan; *p.* -cearf, *pl.* -curfon; *pp.* -corfen *To* BECARVE, *cut off, to cut* or *pare away;* amputare, præcidere:—Ðâ hêt he hine heáfde beceorfan *then he ordered to cut off his head*, Bd. 1, 7; S. 478, 3.

be-ceorian; *p.* ode; *pp.* od *To complain;* obmurmurare, R. Ben. 5. v. ceorian.

be-ceówan, bi-ceówan; *p.* -ceáw, *pl.* -cuwon; *pp.* -cowen *To chew, gnaw;* corrodere:—Biþ swyra becowen [bicowen, Exon.] *the neck is gnawed*, Soul Kmbl. 218; Seel. 111.

be-cerran, -cyrran; *p.* de; *pp.* ed *To turn, turn round;* vertere, convertere, Bt. Met. Fox 13, 156; Met. 13, 78. v. be-cyrran, cyrran.

becest *bakest* = bacest; *2nd pers. pres. of* bacan.

beceþ *baketh* = baceþ; *3rd pers. pres. of* bacan.

be-clæmed; *part. p.* BECLAMMED, *glued to* or *together, emplastered, plastered over;* glutinatus, Som. v. be-clemman.

be-clǽnsian; *p.* ode; *pp.* od *To cleanse;* purgare, Lye. v. clǽnsian.

be-clemman; *p.* de; *pp.* ed *To fetter, bind, tie, inclose, glue together*, BECLAM; vincire, includere, glutinare:—Ðeáh he hie mid fîftigum clûsum beclemme *though he inclose it with fifty bonds*, Salm. Kmbl. 143; Sal. 71. Beclæmed *glutinatus*, Lye.

be-clingan; *p.* -clang, *pl.* -clungon; *pp.* -clungen [clingan, I. *to wither*, II. *to adhere*] *To* BECLING, *surround, inclose;* circumcludere, includere:—Clommum beclungen *inclosed in bands*, Elen. Kmbl. 1388; El. 696.

be-clîsan; *p.* de; *pp.* ed *To inclose;* includere, Leo 126. v. be-clýsan.

be-clîsing, e; *f. An inclosed place, a cell;* cella, Leo 126. v. be-clýsing, be-clýsan.

be-clypian, be-cleopian, be-clepian; *p.* ede, ode, ade; *pp.* ed, od, ad *To accuse, summon, sue at law;* accusare, in judicium vocare, judicio compellere:—Ǽr he clǽne sý ǽlcere spæce, ðe he ǽr beclyped wæs *before he be clear of every suit, in which he had been previously accused*, L. C. S. 28; Th. i. 392, 12: 31; Th. i. 394, 29: 73; Th. i. 414, 23.

be-clyppan, bi-clyppan; *p.* -clypte; *pp.* -clypt *To clip, embrace;* amplecti, Ps. Th. 118, 61: Mk. Bos. 9, 36. v. clyppan.

be-clýsan; *p.* de; *pp.* ed *To close in, to shut in, to inclose, to shut;* includere, concludere, claudere:—He beclýsde Iohannem *inclusit Johannem in carcere*, Lk. Bos. 3, 20: Ps. Spl. 30, 10: Jos. 10, 18. Hig hyra eágan beclýsdon *oculos suos clauserunt*, Mt. Bos. 13, 15: Exon. 12 b; Th. 20, 26; Cri. 323.

be-clýsing, e; *f. A cell.* v. be-clîsing.

bêcn, es; *n. A sign, beacon;* signum:—Mîn gebêd nû gyt bêcnum standeþ ðæt him on wîsum is wel lýcendlîce *adhuc est oratio mea in beneplacitis eorum*, Ps. Th. 140, 8: Beo. Kmbl. 6314; B. 3161. v. beácen.

bêcnan; *p.* ede; *pp.* ed *To indicate, denote, signify;* indicare, significare:—Ðe we mid ðæm bridle bêcnan tiliaþ *which we will denote by the bridle*, Bt. Met. Fox 11, 158; Met. 11, 79: Exon. 110 a; Th. 421, 31; Rä. 40, 26: 106 b; Th. 407, 5; Rä. 25, 10. v. beácnian.

be-cnâwan; *p.* -cneów, *pl.* -cneówon; *pp.* -cnâwen *To know;* cognoscere, C. R. Ben. 25. v. on-cnâwan.

bêcniendlîce; *adv. Allegorically* or *by parable;* allegorice, Som. v. bêcnan.

bêcnuncg, e; *f. A sign, token;* significatio:—Ðû bêcnuncge sealdest ðâm ðe ege ðînne elne healdaþ *dedisti metuentibus te significationem*, Ps. Th. 59, 4.

bêcnydlîc; *adj. Allegorical;* allegoricus:—Bêcnydlîcre gerecednesse *explanationis allegoricæ*, Bd. 5, 23; S. 648, 5, note. v. bêcnan.

be-cnyttan; *v. a. To knit, bind* or *tie, inclose;* ligare:—Ðe seó molde on becnit wæs *in which the mould was inclosed*, Bd. 3, 10; S. 534, 29, note. v. cnyttan, cnittan.

be-com *came, was come*, Beo. Th. 231; B. 115; *p. of* be-cuman.

be-corfen; *part. p. Cut off, beheaded;* truncatus:—Becorfen wæs heáfde *capite truncatus est*, Bd. 1, 27; S. 491, 19. v. be-ceorfan.

be-crafian; *p.* ode, ede; *pp.* od, ed *To crave.* v. crafian.

be-creópan; *p.* -creáp, *pl.* -crupon; *pp.* -cropen *To bring secretly, to creep;* irrepere:—Ðæt he sîe becropen on carcern *that he should be secretly led to prison*, Bt. Met. Fox 25, 71; Met. 25, 36.

becst *bakest* = bacest; *2nd pers. pres. of* bacan.

be-cuman; he -cymþ; *p.* -com, -cwom, *pl.* -cômon, -cwômon; *pp.* -cumen; *v. intrans.* I. *to* BECOME, *happen, befall, meet with, fall in with;* contingere, evenire, supervenire, incidere:—Syððan niht becom *after it had become night*, or *night had come*, Beo. Th. 231; B. 115. Oft becymþ se ânweald ðisse worulde to swîðe gôdum monnum *often cometh the power of this world to very good men*, Bt. 39, 11; Fox 228, 18. Ðǽm gôdum becymþ ânfeald ýfel *to the good happens unmixed evil*, Bt. 39, 9; Fox 224, 29. Him ðæs grim leán becom *this grim retribution happened to them*, Cd. 2; Th. 3, 36; Gen. 46. Him becômon fela yrmþa *much misery befell them*, Ælfc. T. 41, 21. Becom *evenit*, Ælfc. Gr. 33; Som. 37, 18. He becom on ða sceaðan *he fell among thieves*, Lk. Bos. 10, 30: R. Ben. 65. II. *to come, enter, come* or *attain to, come together;* venire, ingredi, pervenire, attingere, concurrere:—In ða ceastre becuman meahte *thou mightest come into the city*, Andr. Kmbl. 1858; An. 931. Hannibal to ðam lande becom *Hannibal came to that land*, Ors. 4, 8; Bos. 90, 14. Gehlýde mîn to ðê becume *clamor meus ad te perveniat*, Ps. Th. 101, 1. Ic eft up becom êce dreámas *I again on high attained to eternal joys*, Cd. 224; Th. 297, 4; Sat. 512. Becumen sî *concurratur*, R. Ben. 43. Becumendum to Segor *venientibus in Segor*, Gen. 13, 10.

bêcun *a beacon*, Mk. Skt. Rush. 13, 22. v. beácen.

be-cunnian; *p.* ode; *pp.* od *To assay, prove, try;* experiri. v. cunnian.

be-cweðan; ðû -cwîst, he -cwiþ; *p.* -cwæþ, *pl.* -cwǽdon; *pp.* -cweden, -cweðen. I. *to say, assert;* dicere:—Swâ ðû worde becwîst *as thou sayest by word*, Andr. Kmbl. 386; An. 193: 419; An. 210. II. *to reproach;* exprobrare:—Hî becweðaþ *exprobraverunt*, Ps. Th. 88, 44. III. *to* BEQUEATH, *to give by will;* legare:—Ealle ða mynstra and ða cyrican wǽron givene and becweðene Gode *all the minsters and churches were given and bequeathed to God*, Chr. 694; Th. 66, 6, note 2: Th. Diplm. A. D. 830; 465, 16.

be-cwom, *pl.* -cwômon *came, fell*, Cd. 160; Th. 199, 26; Exod. 344; *p. of* be-cuman.

be-cwyddod; *part. p.* [be, cwiddian *to speak*] *Bespoken, deposited;* depositum, Ælfc. Gl. 14; Som. 58, 9.

be-cyme, es; *m. A* BY-COMING, *an event* or *coming suddenly;* eventus:—Ðæs gehâtes and ðæs wîtedômes sôþ se æfterfyligenda becyme ðara wîsena gesēðþe and getrymde *cujus promissi et prophetiæ veritatem sequens rerum astruxit eventus*, Bd. 4, 29; S. 607, 35.

be-cymþ *happens*, Bt. 39, 9; Fox 224, 29. v. be-cuman.

be-cȳpan; ic -cȳpe, ðû -cȳpest, -cȳpst, he -cȳpeþ, -cȳpþ, *pl.* -cȳpaþ; *p.* ic, he -cȳpte, ðû -cȳptest, *pl.* -cȳpton; *pp.* -cȳped, -cȳpt *To sell;* vendere:—Ðû becȳptest folc ðîn *vendidisti populum tuum*, Ps. Spl. 43, 14. Gif hwâ becȳpþ his dôhtor *si quis vendiderit filiam suam*, Ex. 21, 7. Iosep becȳped wæs *venundatus est Ioseph*, Ps. Spl. 104, 16: Mt. Bos. 10, 29. v. cȳpan.

be-cyrran; *p.* -cyrde; *pp.* -cyrred, -cyred, -cyrd; *v. trans. To turn to, to give up, deliver, betray;* vertere, transferre ad:—Ælfmær hî becyrde *Ælfmær betrayed it*, Chr. 1011; Th. 266, 23. v. be-cerran.

BED, bedd, es; *n.* I. *a* BED, *couch, pallet;* stratum, lectus:—Hî ðâ inasendon ðæt bed, ðe se lama on læg, Mk. Bos. 2, 4; *thei senten doun the bedd, in whiche the sike man lay*, Wyc. To ðînum bedde *to thy bed*, Gen. 16, 2. II. *a bed in a garden;* pulvillus *vel* areola in hortis: *used in compounds, as* Wyrt-bedd *a wort bed*, Herb. 7, 1; Lchdm. i. 96, 22: Hreód-bedd *a reed bed*, 8, 1; Lchdm. i. 98, 13. [*Plat. O.Sax. Dut.* bed, *n: Ger.* bett, bette, *n: M.H.Ger.* bette, *n: O.H.Ger.* petti, *n: Goth.* badi, *n: Dan.* bed: *Swed.* bädd, *n: O.Nrs.* beðr, *m.* According to Grm. Wrtbch. i. 1722 connected with *A.Sax.* biddan: *Goth.* bidjan? for which he suggests the original meaning *to lie on the ground;* humi jacere.] DER. bed, bedd, -bolster, -clȳfa, -côfa, -felt, -ian, -ing, -ling, -reáf, -reda [-rida], -rest, -stede, -þên, -tîd: gebed, -clȳfa, -scipe.

bed *asked:*—Ic bed *petii*, Ps. Spl. 26, 7, = bæd; *p. of* biddan.

BÊD, es; *nom. acc. pl.* bêdu, bêdo; *n. A prayer, supplication, religious worship;* oratio, supplicatio, Dei cultus:—Ðæt he sceolde ða bêdu [MS. B. byldo *constancy*] anescian *that he should diminish* [*weaken*] *the prayers*, Bd. 1, 7; S. 477, 43. Bêd is chiefly found in composition, as in,—Bêd-hûs *a place for prayer*, bêd-dagas *prayer-days, Rogation-days.* The original word bêd *a prayer* was superseded by ge-bêd *a prayer, q.v.* [*Orm.* bede *a prayer; acc. pl.* bedess: *Laym. acc. s.* bede, bode *a prayer; dat. s.* ibede; *nom. pl.* beden: *R. Glouc. acc. pl.* bedes *prayers: Piers acc. pl.* bedes *prayers*,—'if I bidde any bedes:' *Piers and Chauc. also* bedes,—'a peire of bedes,'—*a set of beads* or *small balls of glass etc. on a string, for counting prayers: O.Sax.* beda; *gen. s.* bede; *dat. s.* bedu: *O.Frs.* bede: *M.H.Ger.* bete: *O.H.Ger.* beta.] DER. bêd-dagas, -hûs, -rîp: gebêd, -dagas, -hûs, -man, -ræden, -stôw. v. biddan.

Beda, an; *m. Venerable Bede, born at Monkton by Jarrow, near the mouth of the Tyne, in* A.D. 674. He wrote his *Historia Ecclesiastica gentis Anglorum about* A.D. 731, *and died May 26, at the age of* 61, *in* 735.—*He gives the following account of himself, according to king Alfred's Anglo-Saxon version, made about* 890:—Ic Beda, Cristes þeów, and Mæsse-Preóst ðæs Mynstres ðara eádigra Apostola Petrus and Paulus, ðæt is æt Wira-mûþan [*Wearmouth*] and on Gyrwum [*Jarrow*], wæs acenned on sundor-lande ðæs ylcan Mynstres.—Mid ðȳ ic wæs seofon wintre, ðâ wæs ic mid gȳmenne mînra maga seald to fêdanne and to lǣranne ðam ârwurþan Abbude Benedicte, and Ceolfriþe æfter ðon and syððan ealle tîd mînes lîfes on ðæs ylcan Mynstres eardunge, ic wæs dônde, and ealle geornnesse ic sealde to leornianne and to smeágianne hâlige gewrîto and betwyh gehald regollîces þeódscipes and ða dæghwâmlîcan gȳmenne to singanne on cyricean me symble swête and wynsum wæs ðæt ic oððe [leornode oððe] lǣrde oððe wrîte.—And ðâ ðȳ nigonteoðan geáre mînes lîfes ðæt ic Deâconhâde onfêng; and ðȳ þrittigoðan geáre Mæsse-Preóst-hâde. And ǣghwæðerne þurh þênunge ðæs ârwurþan biscopes Johannes þurh hǣse and bebod Ceolferþes ðæs Abbudes.—Of ðære tîde ðæs ðe ic Mæssepreósthâde onfêng ôþ nigon and fîftig wintra mînre yldo, ic ðâs bêc for mînre nȳdþearfe and mînra freónda of geweorcum ârwurþra Fæders wrât and sette ge eác swylce to mǣgwlite andgytes and gâstlîcra gerecenessa ic to ætȳcte [*Ego*] *Bæda, famulus Christi, et Presbyter Monasterii beatorum Apostolorum Petri et Pauli, quod est ad Viuræmuda et Ingyruum, natus sum in territorio ejusdem Monasterii.—Cum essem annorum septem* [A.D. 674 + 7 = 681] *cura propinquorum datus sum educandus reverentissimo Abbati Benedicto, ac deinde Ceolfrido cunctumque ex eo tempus vitæ in ejusdem Monasterii habitatione peragens, omnem meditandis Scripturis operam dedi atque inter observantiam disciplinæ regularis et quotidianam cantandi in ecclesia curam semper aut discere aut docere aut scribere dulce habui.—Nonodecimo autem vitæ meæ anno* [A.D. 674 + 19 = 693] *Diaconatum, tricesimo gradum Presbyteratus* [A.D. 674 + 30 = 704]. *Utrumque per ministerium reverentissimi Episcopi Johannis jubente Ceolfrido Abbate suscepi.—Ex quo tempore accepti Presbyteratus usque ad annum ætatis meæ quinquagesimum nonum* [A.D. 674 + 59 = 733], *hæc in Scripturam sanctam meæ meorumque necessitati ex opusculis venerabilium Patrum breviter adnotare sive etiam ad formam sensus et interpretationis eorum superadjicere curavi*, Bd. 5, 23; S. 647, 18–35. Hêr forþfêrde Beda *here*, A.D. 735 [MS. 734], *Bede died*, Chr. 734; Th. 77, 20, col. 1, 2, 3. *Anno* 735, *Bæda Presbyter obiit*, Bd. S. 224, 5. Sanctes Bedan bân restaþ on Gyrwa-wîc *saint Bede's bones rest in Jarrow*, L. Ælf. C. 6; Th. ii. 344, note 4, 3.

be-dǣlan, -dêlan, bi-dǣlan; *p.* -dǣlde, -dêlde; *pp.* -dǣled, -dêled *To deprive, bereave of anything, to deliver, release, free from anything;* privare, orbare, sejungere, liberare, expertem reddere:—Wuldres bedǣled *deprived of honour*, Salm. Kmbl. 760; Sal. 379. Nele hî God ǣfre gôde bedǣlan *Dominus non privabit eos bonis*, Ps. Th. 83, 13. Be ðære lyfte bedǣled *aere privatus*, Bd. de nat. rerum; Wrt. popl. scienc. 17, 11. Hî bióþ ǣlces cræftes bedǣlde *they are destitute of all ability*, Bt. 36, 6; Fox 180, 28. Hwî sceal ic beón bedǣled ǣgþer mînra sunena *cur utroque orbabor filio?* Gen. 27, 45. Gesǣlige sâwle sorgum bedǣlde *happy souls released from cares*, Cd. 220; Th. 282, 34; Sat. 296.

Beda-ford *Bedford*, Chr. 915; Th. 191, 26, col. 1. v. Bedan ford.

bêdan *to offer*, Chr. 1011; Th. 267, 12, col. 1. v. beódan III.

Bedan ford, Beda-ford, Bedcan ford, Bede-ford, Bedican ford, Biedcan ford, es; *m: dat.* -forde, -forda [*Hunt.* A.D. 1148 Bedeford: *West.* 1377 Bedford: *Kni.* 1395 Bedforde, Bedeforde: bedan = bedum *lectis*, ford *vadum:* lectos et diversoria ad vadum sonans, *Camd.*] BEDFORD; oppidi nomen:—Ða yldestan men to Bedan forda hyrdon *the first men belonged to Bedford*, Chr. 918; Ing. 133, 2. Eádweard cyning fôr to Bedan forda *king Edward went to Bedford*, 919; Ing. 133, 13. Hie gedydon æt Bedan forda *pervenirent ad Bedanfordam*, Chr. 921; Gib. 107, 40.

Bedan ford-scîr, Bæda-ford-scîr, Beada-ford-scîr, Bede-ford-scîr, e; *f.* BEDFORDSHIRE; comitatus nomen:—Hî hæfdon oferga̅n Bedan fordscîre *they had subjugated Bedfordshire*, Chr. 1011; Th. 266, 5, col. 2. Wende him ût into Bedan fordscîre *egressus est in Bedanfordsciram*, 1016; Th. 278, 16, col. 1.

Bedan heáfod, es; *m. Beda's head, Bedwin? in Wiltshire*, Chr. 675; Erl. 37, 6. v. Biedan heáfod.

bed-bolster; *gen.* -bolstres; *m. A pillow, bolster;* plumacium:—Bedbolster *plumacium*, Ælfc. Gl. 27; Som. 60, 103; Wrt. Voc. 25, 43.

Bedcan ford *Bedford*, Chr. 571; Th. 32, 27, col. 1. v. Bedan ford.

bed-clȳfa, bedd-clȳfa, bed-cleófa, bed-côfa, an; *m. A bed-chamber, closet;* cubile hominis, cubiculum:—Gang into ðînum bedclȳfan *intra in cubiculum tuum*, Mt. Bos. 6, 6.

bed-côfa, an; *m. A bed-place;* cubiculum:—Bed-côfa *vel* bûr *cubiculum*, Ælfc. Gl. 27; Som. 60, 99: Lk. Bos. 12, 3. v. bed-clȳfa.

bedd *a bed;* stratum, lectus, Cd. 101; Th. 134, 33; Gen. 2234. v. bed.

bedd *bid, command*, Lev. 6, 20, = bid, bidd; *impert. of* biddan.

bêd-dagas; *pl. nom. m. Prayer-days, Rogation-days;* orandi dies, Rogationis dies, Wanl. Catal. 20, 12.

bedd-clȳfa *a bed-chamber;* cubiculum, Gen. 43, 30. v. bed-clȳfa.

beddian, beddigan; *p.* ode; *pp.* od *To prepare* or *make a bed;* sternere:—Ic strewige oððe beddige *I make or prepare a bed*, Ælfc. Gr. 28, 1; Som. 30, 34. Fêde þearfan, and beddige him *feed the needy, and make a bed for them*, L. Pen. 14; Th. ii. 282, 16.

bedding, beding, e; *f.* I. BEDDING, *covering of a bed;* stramentum, stratum, Ælfc. Gl. 111; Som. 79, 60:—Mid mînum teárum mîne beddinge ic beþweá *lacrimis meis stratum meum rigabo*, Ps. Lamb. 6, 7. II. *a bed;* lectus:—Gyf ic astîge on bedinge strǣte mînre *si ascendero in lectum strati mei*, Ps. Spl. 131, 3.

bedd-reáf *bed-clothes.* v. bed-reáf.

bedd-redda, bedd-rida, an; *m. One bed-ridden;* clinicus, Ælfc. Gl. 77; Som. 72, 28. v. bed-reda.

bedd-rest, bed-rest, e; *f. A bed-rest, a bed;* lectus:—Me Sarran beddreste gestâh *Sarah ascended my bed*, Cd. 129; Th. 164, 16; Gen. 2715: 102; Th. 135, 25; Gen. 2248.

-bêde *exorable.* DER. eáþ-bêde, *q.v.*

be-deáglian, bi-deáglian; *p.* ode; *pp.* od *To hide, cover, conceal, keep close* or *secret;* occultare, abscondere:—Me ne meahte monna ǣnig bideáglian hwæt he hogde *nobody could conceal from me what he meditated*, Exon. 51 a; Th. 177, 12; Gû. 1226. v. be-dîglian.

be-deaht = be-þeaht *covered*, Judth. 11; Thw. 24, 29; Jud. 213; *pp. of* be-þeccan.

Bede-ford *Bedford*, Chr. 1010; Th. 264, 12, col. 1. v. Bedan ford.

Bede-ford-scîr *Bedfordshire*, Chr. 1011; Th. 266, 5, col. 1. v. Bedan ford-scîr.

be-dêglad, bi-dêglad *hidden, obscured*, Exon. 57 a; Th. 204, 15; Ph. 98; *pp. of* be-dîglian.

be-dêlan; *p.* -dêlde; *pp.* -dêled *To deprive;* privare:—Duguðum bedêled *deprived of dignity*, Cd. 215; Th. 272, 19; Sat. 122. v. be-dǣlan.

be-delfan; *p.* -dealf, *pl.* -dulfon; *pp.* -dolfen *To dig in* or *around, to bury, inter;* circumfodere, sepelire:—Ôþ ic hine bedelfe *usque dum fodiam circa illam*, Lk. Bos. 13, 8. Bedealf hyt on eorþan *he buried it in the earth*, Mt. Bos. 25, 18. Bedolfen, Elen. Kmbl. 2159; El. 1081.

be-delfing, e; *f. A digging about;* ablaqueatio:—Niðerwart treówes bedelfing *a digging about the lower part of a tree*, Ælfc. Gl. 60; Som. 68, 16; Wrt. Voc. 39, 2.

beden *prayed*, Bd. 3, 5; S. 527, 28: Th. Diplm. A.D. 743–745; 28, 22; *pp. of* biddan.

Bederices weorþ, es; *m.* [Bederices *Bederic's*, weorþ *worth, town*, or *residence*] *Bederic's worth* or *town, so called because the manor formerly belonged to Bederic, who bequeathed it to Edmund the king and martyr, hence it was subsequently called* Eádmundes burh, *St. Edmund's bury*:—On Bedericeswyrþe *at Bedericsworth*, Will 23; Th. Diplm. A. D. 970; 517, 26. *At an earlier date, in* A. D. 958, *Ælfgar records*,—Ic an ðat lond into Beodricheswrþe to Seynt Eádmundes stówe *I give the land at Bedericsworth to St. Edmund's place*, Th. Diplm. 506, 12. v. Eádmundes burh.

Bedewinda, an; *m.* BEDWIN, *Wilts*:—Ic, Ælfrêd, West-Seaxena cining [MS. cingc], an Eádweade, mînum yldran suna, ðæs landes æt Bedewindan *I, Alfred, king of the West-Saxons, give the land at Bedwin to Edward, my elder son* [lit. *made a grant of the land at Bedwin*], Alfd. Will 14, 10.

bed-felt, es; *m?* *A bed-covering*; lecti pannus, lodix, R. Ben. 55.

bêd-hûs, es; *n.* [bêd *a prayer*, hûs *a house*] *A chapel, an oratory, a place for prayer*; oratorium, Fulg. 43.

Bedican ford, es; *m. Bedford*, Chr. 571; Ing. 26, 12. v. Bedan ford.

be-dîcian; *p.* ode; *pp.* od; *v. a.* *To* BEDIKE, *to mound, to fortify with a mound*; aggere munire:—Bedîcodon ða buruh ûtan *they embanked the city without*, Chr. 1016; Th. 280, 8, col. 1.

be-didrian; *p.* ode; *pp.* od *To deceive*; decipere:—Wêndon ge, ðæt ge mihton bedidrian mînne gelîcan *think ye, that ye could deceive one like me?* Gen. 44, 15. DER. be-dyderian, dyderian.

be-dielf *dug*, Mt. Foxe 25, 18, *for* be-dealf; *p. of* be-delfan.

be-dîglian, -dîhlian, -deáglian; ic -dîglige; *p.* -dîglode; *pp.* -dîglod, -dîhlod; *v. a.* *To hide, cover, conceal, keep close* or *secret*; occultare, abscondere:—Ne hîre ðû him ðæt ðû hine bedîglige *non audias eum ut occultes eum*, Deut. 13, 8. On grîne ða ðe hî bedîglodon *in laqueo quem absconderunt*, Ps. Spl. 9, 16. Bedîglod *occultus*, Ælfc. Gr. 28, 3; Som. 31, 5.

be-dîhlian; *p.* -dîhlode; *pp.* -dîhlod *To hide.* v. be-dîglian.

beding, e; *f.* *Bedding, covering of a bed, a bed*, Ps. Spl. 131, 3. v. bedding.

be-dipped, bedypt *dipped, dyed*; tinctus. v. be-dyppan.

bedling *a delicate person.* v. bædling.

be-dofen *drowned*; submersus, Homl. Th. ii. 472, 5; *pp. of* be-dûfan.

be-dolfen *buried*, Elen. Kmbl. 2159; El. 1081; *pp. of* be-delfan.

be-dôn [be, dôn *to do*] *To shut*; claudere:—Ðæt ðû ðîne doru mihtest bedôn fæste *that thou mightest shut fast thy doors*, Ps. Th. 147, 2.

bêd-rǽden, -rǽdenn, e; *f.* *An assignment, ordinance* or *appointment*; assignatio, Som. v. ge-bêd-rǽden.

be-drǽf *drove*, Exon. 108 a; Th. 412, 5; Rä. 30, 9, = be-drâf; *p. of* be-drîfan.

be-drâf *drove*, Ors. 3, 11; Bos. 72, 38; *p. of* be-drîfan.

be-dragan; *p.* -drôg, -drôh, *pl.* -drôgon; *pp.* -dragen *To draw aside, seduce*; seducere:—Ðe hie dearnenga bedrôg *who seduced her secretly*, Cd. 29; Th. 38, 5; Gen. 602.

bed-reáf, es; *m.* *Bed-clothes, bedding*; lodix, fulcrum, lectisternia, Ælfc. Gl. 27; Som. 60, 109: 111; Som. 79, 62, 64: R. Ben. 55.

bed-reda, -rida, an; *m.* [bed *a bed*, reda = rida *from* riden *ridden, pp. of* rîdan *to ride*, hence the *def. adj.* bedreda *bedridden, and the noun* bedreda, bedrida *one bedridden*] *One* BEDRIDDEN; clinicus:—Ðǽr læg be ðam wege ân bedreda *there lay by the way one bedridden*, Homl. Th. ii. 422, 4. Arâs se bedreda, and arn blissigende *the bedridden arose, and ran rejoicing*, ii. 422, 9. Ðâ ðâ se sunderhâlga Iosias ðæt tâcn geseah on ðam bedredan [*def. adj.*] men, ðâ feól he to ðæs apostoles fôtum *when the pharisee Josias saw that miracle in the bedridden man, then fell he at the apostle's feet*, ii. 422, 11. Drihten cwæþ to sumum bedridan *the Lord said to one bedridden*, i. 472, 23.

bed-rest *a bed*; lectica, Ælfc. Gl. 66; Som. 69, 75: Judth. 10; Thw. 21, 26; Jud. 36. v. bedd-rest.

bed-rida *one bedridden*, Homl. Th. i. 472, 23. v. bed-reda.

be-drîfan; *p.* -drâf, -drǽf, *pl.* -drifon; *pp.* -drifen; *v. a.* I. *to drive, thrust on* or *upon, to compel, constrain* or *enforce one to do a thing, to pursue, follow*; cogere, compellere, agere, adigere:—Perðica hine bedrâf into ânum fæstene *Perdiccas drove him into a fastness*, Ors. 3, 11; Bos. 72, 38. Hî him hâm bedrifon [MS. bedrifan] and sige âhton *they drove them home and had a victory*, Bd. 1, 14; S. 482, 20. Wiht ða hûðe hâm bedrǽf *a creature drove the spoil home*, Exon. 108 a; Th. 412, 5; Rä. 30, 9. Ðû bedrifen [MS. bidrifen] wurde on ðas þeóstran worulde *thou wast driven into this dark world*, Exon. 28 b; Th. 86, 17; Cri. 1409. II. *to drive* or *beat against, to surround*; obruere, obducere, circumflare:—He geseah stapulas standan storme bedrifene *he saw columns standing driven by the storm*, Andr. Kmbl. 2987; An. 1496: Rood Kmbl. 123; Kr. 62. DER. drîfan.

be-drincan; *p.* -dranc, *pl.* -druncon; *pp.* -druncen *To drink in* or *up, absorb*; imbibere:—Ðonne ðæt bedruncen sý, eft hit geniwa *when that is drunk up, renew it again*, Med. ex Quadr. 2, 10; Lchdm. i. 336, 4, MS. B.

bêd-rîp, e; *f.* *The cutting* or *reaping of corn on request*; ad preces messio, L. R. S. 5; Th. i. 436, 4, note. v. bên-rîp.

be-drôg *seduced*, Cd. 29; Th. 38, 5; Gen. 602; *p. of* be-dragan.

be-droren; *pp.* *Deceived, deluded, bereaved, deprived*; deceptus, orbatus, Cd. 26; Th. 33, 31; Gen. 528: 93; Th. 120, 22; Gen. 1998; *pp. of* be-dreósan. v. dreósan, bi-droren.

be-druncen *drunk in, absorbed*, Med. ex Quadr. 2, 10; Lchdm. i. 336, 4, MS. B; *pp. of* be-drincan.

bed-ryda, an; *m.* *A bedridden man*; clinicus:—Se bedryda wearþ gehǽled sôna; and eóde him ðâ hâm, hâl on his fôtum, se ðe ǽr wæs geboren on bǽre to cyrcan *the bedridden man was soon healed; and he then went home, whole on his feet, who before was borne on a bier to church*, Glostr. Frag. 10, 4, 15-18. v. bed-reda, drî, drîan.

bed-stede, es; *m.* [bed *a bed*; stede *a place, station*; locus, situs] *A* BEDSTEAD; sponda. v. stede.

bed-þên, es; *m.* [bed *a bed*, þên *for* þegn *a servant*] *A chamberlain, a servant who has the care of a chamber*; lecti minister, camerarius, Ælfc. Gl. 27; Som. 60, 101.

bed-tîd, e; *f.* BEDTIDE, *bed time*; lecti adeundi tempus, serum, Ælfc. Gl. 95; Som. 76, 2.

bêdu *prayers*; orationes, Bd. 1, 7; S. 477, 43. v. bêd; *n.*

be-dûfan; *p.* -deáf, *pl.* -dufon; *pp.* -dofen *To bedive, put under*; submergere, Homl. Th. ii. 392, 13. v. be-dofen. DER. dûfan.

bêdul; *adj.* *Prayerful, suppliant*; petitiosus, Ælfc. Gl. 101; Som. 77, 46.

be-dulfon *buried*, Ors. 3, 6; Bos. 58, 7; *p. pl. of* be-delfan.

bed-wahrift, es; *n.* *A curtain*; cortina, Cod. Dipl. A. D. 995; Kmbl. vi. 133, 9.

be-dyderian; *p.* ode; *pp.* od *To deceive*; decipere. v. be-didrian. DER. dyderian *to deceive.*

be-dydrung, e; *f.* *A deceit, deceiving*; deceptio. DER. dydrung.

be-dyppan; *p.* -dypte, *pl.* -dypton; *pp.* -dypped; *v. trans.* *To dip, immerse*; mergere, intingere, tingere:—Se ðe bedypþ on disce mid me his hand *qui intingit mecum manum in paropside*, Mt. Bos. 26, 23. Se ðe ic rǽce bedyppedne hlâf *is cui ego intinctum panem porrexero*, Jn. Bos. 13, 26. Hîg bedypton his tunecan on ðam blôde *tinxerunt tunicam ejus in sanguine*, Gen. 37, 31. Ic bedyppe *mergo*, Ælfc. Gr. 28, 4; Som. 31, 36.

be-dyrnan, bi-dyrnan; *p.* de; *pp.* ed *To hide, conceal*; occultare:—Ne mihte him bedyrned wyrþan *it might not be hidden from him*, Cd. 14; Th. 17, 18; Gen. 261: Elen. Kmbl. 1201; El. 602: 1164; El. 584. v. dyrnan.

be-ebbian; *p.* ode, ade; *pp.* od, ad *To leave aground by ebbing*; aqua privare:—Scipu wǽron be-ebbode [be-ebbade] *the ships were left aground by the ebb*, Chr. 897; Th. 176, 30. v. ebbian.

beél, es; *n.* *A pile*; rogus, Gl. E. 6, Lye. v. bǽl.

be-eódon *dwelt, inhabited*, Bd. 1, 26; S. 488, 1; *p. of* be-gân.

beer *a bier, bed*, Cot. 23: Jn. Lind. War. 5, 8. v. bǽr.

be-fæstan, bi-fæstan; *p.* -fæste; *pp.* -fæsted. I. *to fasten, make fast, fix*; infigere:—Biþ se þridda dǽl lîge befæsted, in glêda grîpe *the third part shall be fastened in fire, into the gripe of flames*, Elen. Kmbl. 2598; El. 1300. II. *to establish*; fundare, firmare:—Wæs se bisceophâd fægere befæsted *the bishopric was fairly established*, Elen. Kmbl. 2423; El. 1213. III. *to commend, recommend, commit, deliver, put in trust, entrust*; commendare, tradere, committere:—He his geféran his freóndum wæs befæstende *socios amicis suis commendavit*, Bd. 4, 26; S. 602, 38. Ic him befæsted wæs *I was entrusted to him*, 5, 6; S. 618, 37: Ps. Th. 30, 5. Hyt gebyrede ðæt ðû befæstest feoh myneterum *oportuit te committere pecuniam numulariis*, Mt. Bos. 25, 27: L. C. S. 28; Th. i. 392, 10.

be-fæsting, e; *f.* *An entrusting.* DER. fæsting.

be-fæðman; *p.* ede; *pp.* ed *To embrace with the arms*; ulnis amplecti:—Befæðman, Cd. 163; Th. 204, 32; Exod. 428. v. fæðman.

be-fættian; *p.* ode; *pp.* od [be, fættian *to fatten*] *To make fat, anoint*; impinguare. v. ge-fættian.

be-falden *covered.* v. swegl-befalden.

be-fangen *taken*, Jos. 7, 15; *pp. of* be-fôn.

be-faran; *p.* -fôr, *pl.* -fôron; *pp.* -faren; *v. trans.* [be, faran *to go*] *To go round, to travel through, go all over, to traverse, to go, march, encompass, to surround*; peragrare, circumvenire:—Ne befaraþ ge Israhêla burga ǽrðan ðe mannes sunu cume *ye shall not go over the cities of the Israelites before the son of man come*, Mt. Bos. 10, 23. Rômâne on ungewis on ân nyrewett beféran, ôþ hý Somnite ûtan beféran *the Romans marched unwittingly into a narrow pass, till the Samnites surrounded them on the outside*, Ors. 3, 8; Bos. 63, 8: Cd. 167; Th. 209, 10; Exod. 497.

be-fealdan, bi-fealdan; *p.* -feóld, *pl.* -feóldon; *pp.* -fealden, -falden *To fold, infold, clasp, involve, surround, inwrap, cover, overwhelm*; implicare, involvere, amplecti, circumdare:—Ðû miht on ânre hand eáðe befealdan ealne middaneard *thou canst easily infold in one hand all the midearth*, Hy. 7, 119; Hy. Grn. ii. 289, 119. Ðâ he ða bôc befeóld *cum plicuisset librum*, Lk. Bos. 4, 20. He befeóld his handa mid ðæra tyccena fellum *pelliculas hædorum circumdedit manibus*, Gen. 27, 16. Meç hý-gedryht befeóld *a body of domestics surrounded me*, Exon. 94 b; Th. 353, 32; Reim. 21. DER. swegl-befalden.

be-feallan, ic -fealle, ðú -feallest, -fylst, he -fealleþ, -fylþ, *pl.* -feallaþ; *p.* -feól, -feóll, *pl.* -feóllon; *pp.* -feallen. I. *to fall; cadere*, incidere:—Ân of ðám ne befylþ on eorþan *unus ex illis non cadet super terram*, Mt. Bos. 10, 29. Hie oft befeallaþ on micel yfel *they often fall into great evil*, Past. 40, 3; Hat. MS. 53 b, 8: Cd. 18; Th. 21, 26; Gen. 330: Lk. Bos. 10, 36: Gen. 15, 12. II. *to fall off; cadere* ab aliquo; *pp.* befeallen *deprived, bereft;* orbatus, privatus:—Freóndum befeallen *bereft of friends*, Beo. Th. 2256; B. 1126: 4504; B. 2256. DER. feallan.

be-feastnian; *p.* ade; *pp.* ad *To betrothe;* desponsare:—Befeastnad *betrothed;* desponsatus, Mt. Lind. Stv. 1, 18. v. be-fæstan.

be-fêhþ *includes*, Bt. 24, 1; Fox 80, 14; *3rd pers. pres. of* be-fôn.

be-felan, -feolan; *p.* -fæl, *pl.* -fǽlon; *pp.* -feolen, -folen *To commit, commend, deliver, assign, allot;* committere, commendare, tradere, Leo 140. v. be-feolan.

be-felgan, bi-felgan; *p.* -fealg, -fealh, -felh, *pl.* -fulgon; *pp.* -folgen. I. *v. intrans. To stick* or *cling to, betake oneself;* inhærere, insistere:—Þilcum wordum heó him befelh ǽlce dæge *hujuscemodi verbis per singulos dies mulier molesta erat ei*, Gen. 39, 10. Æfter ðon ðe he ðǽr sum fæc hâlgum leornungum befealh *after he had there for a while betaken himself to holy learning*, Bd. 4, 23; S. 594, 19. Ðæt he ðám hâlwendan ongynnessum georne gefeole [befulge MS. B.] *ut cœptis salutaribus insisteret*, Bd. 5, 19; S. 637, 11, note. II. *v. trans. To deliver, transmit, consign;* tradere, committere:—He hine rôde befealg *he delivered him to the cross*, Andr. Kmbl. 2654; An. 1328.

be-fellan; *p.* de; *pp.* ed *To fell;* cædere. v. be-fyllan.

be-fêng *concubuerit*, Gen. 19, 33. v. be-fôn.

be-feohtan; *p.* -feaht, *pl.* -fuhton; *pp.* -fohten *To deprive by fighting;* pugnando privare. v. bi-feohtan.

be-feól, -feóll *fell*, Lk. Bos. 10, 36; *p. of* be-feallan.

be-feolan, bi-feolan; *p.* -fæl, *pl.* -fǽlon; *pp.* -folen, -feolen *To commit, commend, deliver, grant;* committere, commendare, tradere:—Morðor under eorþan befeolan *to commit murder under the earth*, Exon. 90 b; Th. 340, 23; Gn. Ex. 115: Cd. 202; Th. 251, 7; Dan. 560. Ðú him for inwite yfel befǽle *propter dolos disposuisti eis mala*, Ps. Th. 72, 14. Him wæs hâlig gâst befolen fæste *the holy spirit was fully granted to him*, Elen. Kmbl. 1870; El. 937: 391; El. 196. v. be-felan.

be-feóld *folded*, Lk. Bos. 4, 20; *p. of* be-fealdan.

BEFER, beofer, beofor, byfor, es; *m.* A BEAVER; castor, fiber:—Befer *fiber, castor, ponticus?* Ælfc. Gl. 19; Som. 59, 3; Wrt. Voc. 22, 47. Beofor, byfor *fiber*, Ælfc. Gr. 8; Som. 7, 13. [*Plat. Dut.* bever: *Ger. M.H.Ger.* biber: *O.H.Ger.* pipar, pipur: *Dan.* bäver: *Swed.* bäfver: *O.Nrs.* bifra, *f*: *Slav.* bobr. Grm. Wrtbch. i. 1806 connects the word with *Ger.* bauen *to build.*]

be-fêran; *p.* de; *pp.* ed *To go about, to go round, surround;* circumire, circumdare:—He lǽrende ða castel befêrde *circumibat castella in circuitu docens*, Mk. Bos. 6, 6. He befêrde ðæt Israhêlisce folc *he surrounded the people of Israel*, Ex. 14, 9. DER. fêran.

be-fician *to deceive, to go round;* decipere, Off. Episc. 8.

be-fîlan; *p.* de; *pp.* ed *To befoul, defile*:—Nâ mid meoxe befîled *not defiled with dung*, L. Ælf. P. 45; Th. ii. 384, 11. v. be-fýlan.

be-filgan; *p.* -filgde; *pp.* -filged *To follow after, pursue;* insequi:—Wolde me befilgende beón mid sâre *voluit me insequi cum dolore*, Bd. 4, 19; S. 589, 28, note. v. be-felgan.

be-flagen flǽsc, es; *n.* [MS. flæc] *The bowels;* viscera:—Beflagen flæc [=flǽsc] *vel* innoþes innewearde *viscera*, Ælfc. Gl. 75; Som. 71, 99; Wrt. Voc. 45, 7. v. be-fleán.

be-fleán; *p.* -flôg, *pl.* -flôgon; *pp.* -flagen *To flay, to skin*, or *take off the skin* or *bark;* decorticare, Cot. 62. v. beflagen flǽsc.

be-fleógan; *p.* -fleáh, *pl.* -flugon; *pp.* -flogen *To fly around* or *about;* circumvolare:—Ða spearcan beflugon on ðæs hûses hrôf *the sparks flew about on the roof of the house*, Bd. 3, 10; S. 534, 31, note.

be-fleón, to be-fleónne; *p.* -fleáh, *pl.* -flugon; *pp.* -flogen *To flee, flee away, escape;* fugere, effugere, evitare:—Hû he mihte befleón fram ðam toweardan yrre *quomodo posset fugere a ventura ira*, Bd. 4, 25; S. 599, 39. Hwider mæg ic ðînne andwlitan befleón *a facie tua quo fugiam?* Ps. Th. 138, 5: 61, 6. Nô ðæt ýðe byþ to befleónne *it is not easy to flee from that*, Beo. Th. 2010; B. 1003.

be-flôwan; *p.* -fleów, *pl.* -fleówon; *pp.* -flôwen *To overflow;* diffluere, redundare:—Wætre beflôwen *overflowed with water*, Exon. 115 b; Th. 444, 19; Kl. 49.

be-fôh *contain;* complectere, Solil. 3; *impert. of* be-fôn.

be-folen *granted*, Elen. Kmbl. 1870; El. 937; *pp. of* be-felan, be-feolan.

be-fôn, bi-fôn, ic -fô, ðú -fêhst, he -fêhþ, *pl.* -fôþ; *p.* -fêng, *pl.* -fêngon; *impert.* -fôh; *pp.* -fangen, -fongen; *v. trans.* I. *to comprehend, grasp, seize, take hold of, catch;* comprehendere, apprehendere, capere:—Swâ he ealle befêhþ ânes cræfte, heofon and eorþan *even as he comprehendeth all by his sole power, heaven and earth*, Andr. Kmbl. 653; An. 327. Habbaþ me helle clommas fæste befangen *the clasps of hell have firmly grasped me*, Cd. 19; Th. 24, 7; Gen. 374. Heó ânne hæfde befangen *she had seized one*, Beo. Th. 2594; B. 1295. Befangen on ðam fracodan gilte *deprehensus in hoc facinore*, Jos. 7, 15. Ne mihton hîg his word befôn *non potuerunt verbum ejus reprehendere*, Lk. Bos. 20, 26. Gif mon forstolenne ceáp befêhþ *if a man seize stolen cattle*, L. In. 47; Th. i. 132, 4: L. Ath. i. 9; Th. i. 204, 10. Ðæt hîg woldon ðone Hǽlend on his spræce befôn *ut caperent eum in sermone*, Mt. Bos. 22, 15. II. *to surround, encompass, encircle, envelop, contain, clothe, case, receive, conceive;* circumdare, amplecti, complecti, capere, cingere, tegere, operire, accipere, concipere:—He hafaþ ðam brîdle bû tû befangen *he has encompassed both with the bridle*, Bt. Met. Fox 11, 58; Met. 11, 29. Befongen freáwrâsnum *encircled with noble chains*, Beo. Th. 2906; B. 1451. Fýre befangen *enveloped in fire*, Beo. Th. 4540; B. 2274. Ne mihte ðes middaneard ealle ða bêc befôn *non potest capere mundus omnes eos libros*, Jn. Bos. 21, 25: Bt. 24, 1; Fox 80, 14. Befôh hit mid feáum wordum *complectere hoc paucis verbis*, Solil. 3: Ps. Th. 74, 2. Ne hêt he nâ etan ðone lîchaman ðe he mid befangen wæs *he bade them not eat that body with which he was surrounded*, Homl. Pasc. Lisl. 9, 19: Soul Kmbl. 67; Seel. 34: Job 19, 26; Thw. 168, 2. Saglas, golde befongne *poles, cased in gold*, Past. 22, 2; Hat. MS. 33 a, 25. Ic hêr hǽlu calic hæbbe befangen *calicem salutaris accipiam*, Ps. Th. 115, 4: Exon. 9 a; Th. 6, 7; Cri. 80.

be-fongen *encircled*, Beo. Th. 2906; B. 1451; *pp. of* be-fôn.

be-fôran, bi-fôran; *prep.* I. *dat.* II. *acc.* [be *by, proximity*, fôran *fore*, as æt fôran] BEFORE; ante, coram, præ:—I. *dat.* He swîðe oft befôran fremede folces rǽswum wundor æfter wundre *he very often performed before the princes of the people miracle after miracle*, Andr. Kmbl. 1237; An. 619. Ealdormen hêredon hîg befôran him *principes laudaverunt eam apud illum*, Gen. 12, 15. Hwâ ne wâfaþ ðæs, ðæt ða steorran scînaþ befôran ðam mônan, and ne befôran ðære sunnan *who wonders not at this, that the stars shine before the moon, and not before the sun?* Bt. 39, 3; Fox 214, 30. II. *acc.* He oft befôran hine com *ante illum venire consueverat*, Bd. 5, 2; S. 614, 42, note. Sweord manige gesâwon befôran beorn beran *many saw a sword borne before the hero*, Beo. Th. 2052; B. 1024. III. befôran *frequently comes after the case*:—Him befôran fêreþ leóht *light goeth before him*, Cd. 222; Th. 288, 29; Sat. 389. Him bifôran *before them*, Exon. 47 a; Th. 160, 22; Gû. 947.

be-fôran; *adv. Before, at hand, openly;* ante, antea, præ, in conspectu, in conspectum:—He sceal befôran fêran *he shall advance before*, Bt. Met. Fox 4, 35; Met. 4, 18. Wundor on eorþan he befôran cýþde *he revealed miracles on earth openly*, Andr. Kmbl. 1212; An. 606. Wæs se atola befôran *the wicked one was at hand*, Cd. 224; Th. 295, 17; Sat. 487. He befôran gengde *he went before*, Beo. Th. 2829; B. 1412.

befôran-cweðan; *p.* -cwæþ, *pl.* -cwǽdon, -cwêdon; *pp.* -cweden *To foretell;* prædicere, Bd. 4, 19; S. 588, 15, note; 5, 2; S. 615, 13, note.

befôran-gestihtian; *p.* ode; *pp.* od *To fore-ordain;* præordinare. DER. ge-stihtian.

Befor-leág *Beverley, in Yorkshire.* v. Beofer-lic.

be-fôtian, -fôtigan; *p.* ode; *pp.* od [be, fôtian, fôt *a foot*] *To befoot, to cut off the feet;* pedes abscindere, Som. v. be-heáfdian *to behead.*

be-freón; *p.* -freóde; *pp.* -freód *To free;* liberare, Ps. C. 50, 110; Ps. Grn. ii. 279, 110.

be-frinan, -frynan; *p.* -fran, *pl.* -frunon; *pp.* -frunen [be, frinan *to ask*] *To ask, inquire, learn;* interrogare, sciscitari, discere:—Ic befrine *sciscitor*, Ælfc. Gr. 25; Som. 27, 4. Herodes befran hî *Herodes didicit ab eis*, Mt. Bos. 2, 7.

beftan *after, behind, without;* post, sine, Som. Lye. v. bæftan.

be-fýlan, -fîlan; *p.* -fýlede; *pp.* -fýled, -fîled, -fýld; *v. trans.* [be, fûl *foul*] *To* BEFOUL, *pollute, defile, make filthy;* inquinare, fœdare, contaminare:—Befîled, L. Ælf. P. 45; Th. ii. 384, 11: Basil. admn. 7; Norm. 48, 23: Lchdm. iii. 208, 7: Cot. 104.

be-fyllan; *p.* -fylde; *pp.* -fylled [be, fyllan *to fill*] *To fill, fill up;* adimplere:—Befyllan, Bd. 1, 27; S. 489, 26.

be-fyllan; *p.* -fylde, -fealde; *pp.* -fylled; *v. trans.* [be, fyllan, fellan *to fell*]. I. *to fell, strike down;* cædere, prosternere, projicere:—Hwæt befealdest ðû wærfæstne rinc *why didst thou fell the upright man?* Cd. 48; Th. 62, 6; Gen. 1010. He us hæfþ befylled *he has struck us down*, 19; Th. 23, 17; Gen. 361. II. *to deprive by felling, bereave;* cædendo orbare:—Secgum befylled *bereft of his warriors*, Cd. 97; Th. 128, 10; Gen. 2124.

befylþ *falls*, Mt. Bos. 10, 29; *3rd pers. pres. of* be-feallan.

bêg, es; *m. A bracelet, ring, crown;* armilla, corona:—Hie feredon brýd and bêgas *they conveyed bride and bracelets*, Cd. 90; Th. 112, 25; Gen. 1876. Hî on beorg dydon bêgas [MS. beg] and siglu *they placed in the mound rings and jewels*, Beo. Th. 6308, note; B. 3164. v. beáh.

be-galan; *p.* -gôl, *pl.* -gôlon; *pp.* -galen [be, galan *to sing, enchant*] *To enchant;* incantare:—Gyf hwylc yfel-dǽde man ôðerne begaleþ *if any ill-doing man enchants another*, Herb. 87, 4; Lchdm. i. 190, 10.

be-gan *began*, Gen. 9, 20. v. be-ginnan.

be-gân, bi-gân, ic -gâ, ðú -gǽst, he -gǽþ, *pl.* -gâþ; *p.* -eóde, *pl.* -eódon; *pp.* -gân [be, gân *to go*]. I. *to go over, to surround, occupy, dwell, cultivate, till;* perambulare, circumdare, incolere, habitare, colere:—Ic fêrde geónd ðas eorþan and hî be-eóde *I walked through* [*over*] *the earth, and perambulated it,* Job 1, 7; Thw. 164, 16. Se ðe æcer begǽþ *he who goes over the land, a farmer,* Ælfc. Gr. 7; Som. 6, 44. Mid ðý Rômâne ðâ gyt Breotone be-eódan *dum adhuc Romani Brittaniam incolerent,* Bd. 1, 26; S. 488, 1. Hî ðone bûr ûtan be-eódon *they surrounded the dwelling without,* Chr. 755; Th. 83, 26, col. 1. II. *to go to. visit, attend, to cherish, honour, worship;* obire, colere, excolere:—Plegan begân *to go to* or *attend plays,* Ors. 6, 2; Bos. 117, 9. Ðæt mynster seó ylce cwên swýðe lufode and ârwyrþode and be-eóde *eadem regina hoc monasterium multum diligebat, venerabatur, excolebat,* Bd. 3, 11; S. 535, 15: 2, 13; S. 517, 1. III. *to commit, exercise, practise, observe;* committere, perficere, observare:—Synne, ða ic selfa be-eóde *sins, which I committed myself,* Ps. C. 50, 66; Ps. Grn. ii. 278, 66. He begǽþ unmǽtas [MS. unætas] *he commits gluttonies,* Deut. 21, 20. Begâ ðê sylfne to ârfæstnysse *exercise thyself in* or *devote thyself to piety,* 1 Tim. 4, 7: Bt. Met. Fox 8, 33; Met. 8, 17: Ps. Th. 105, 12. Ða ðe be-eódon îdelnesse *observantes vanitatem,* 30, 6: 118, 23: 119, 5: 98, 4: Bd. 2, 13; S. 517, 4.

be-gân *tilled, cultivated:*—On begânum landum *in cultivated lands,* Herb. 5, 1; Lchdm. i. 94, 6; *pp. of* be-gân.

bêgan; he bêgþ; *p.* de; *pp.* ed. I. *to bow, bend, turn;* flectere, inflectere, deprimere:—Ðeáh ðû teó hwelcne bôh of dûne to ðære eorþan, swelce ðû bêgan mǽge *though thou pull any bough down to the earth, such as thou mayest bend,* Bt. 25; Fox 88, 23. Se Ælmihtiga bêgþ ðider he wile mid his ânwealde *the Almighty bends them whither he will by his power,* Bt. Met. Fox 13, 6; Met. 13, 3: Cd. 221; Th. 288, 15; Sat. 381: Bd. 4, 11; S. 580, 10. II. *to bow to, to settle;* inflectere, insistere:—Ðara bearn swylce bêgaþ æðelum settum beámum, samed anlîce, standan on staðule stîðe wið geóguþe *quorum filii sicut novellæ plantationes stabilitæ a juventute sua,* Ps. Th. 143, 14. DER. a-bêgan, for-, ge-, ofge-. v. bygan.

be-gang, be-gong, bi-gang, bi-gong, bi-gencg, es; *m.* [be, gang *a step, proceeding*]. I. *a course, way, passage, circuit, district;* cursus, via, tenor, circuitus:—Ofer geofenes begang *over the course of ocean,* Beo. Th. 729; B. 362. Holma begang *the passage of the deeps,* Andr. Kmbl. 390; An. 195. Gârsecges begang *the circuit of ocean,* 1059; An. 530. II. *an undertaking, a business, exercise, service, religious worship;* negotium, exercitatio, cultus:—Ða willnode he hyne sylfne fram eallum begangum ðisse woruldе fremde gedôn *cupivit se ab omnibus sæculi hujus negotiis alienare,* Bd. 3, 19; S. 549, 38. On bigange ðæs âncorlîfes *in exercenda vita solitaria,* 5, 1; S. 613, 9. Ðæt heó môste healdan ðone geleáfan and bigong hire ǽfestnysse *ut fidem cultumque suæ religionis servaret,* 2, 9; S. 510, 29: 1, 7; S. 477, 21: Jos. 23, 7. Bigencg *observatio, studium,* Scint. 7.

be-ganga, bi-gonga, bi-genga, bi-gengea, an; *m. An inhabitant, a dweller, cultivator, observer, benefactor, worshipper;* incola, cultor:—Be ǽrran bigengum [begangum MS. B.] *of the first inhabitants,* Bd. 1, 1; S. 473, 7. Þearfena bigenga *a benefactor of the poor;* cultor pauperum, Bd. 3, 14; S. 540, 23: 2, 15; S. 519, 8. DER. land-begenga.

be-gangan, -gongan, bi-gangan, -gongan; *pp.* -gangen [be, gangan *to go*]. I. *to go round, surround;* circumdare:—Cartaina wæs mid sǽ ûtan befangen [begangen Cot.] *Carthage was outwardly surrounded by sea,* Ors. 4, 13; Bos. 99, 39. II. *to go to* or *after, to attend, commit, practise, exercise, perform, observe, worship;* exercere, incumbere, procurare, colere:—Begangan his gebêdu *to attend his prayers,* Bd. 3, 16; S. 542, 34, col. 1. Begangan wæccan *to attend wakes,* Bd. 3, 17; S. 545, 11. Forligru ne begange *should not commit adultery,* L. C. E. 7; Th. i. 364, 24. Ðæt ðû his bebod georne begange *that thou shouldst gladly perform his command,* Elen. Kmbl. 2339; El. 1171: Ps. Th. 118, 48. Swýðe ic begangen wæs *exercitatus sum,* Ps. Th. 76, 4: 54, 2. Gif ðû fremdu godu bigongest *if thou wilt worship strange gods,* Exon. 67 b; Th. 250, 3; Jul. 121.

begannes, -ness, e; *f.* [beginnan *to begin*] *The calends, the first day of the month;* calendæ, Cot. 202.

bêgaþ *shall settle,* Ps. Th. 143, 14; *pres. and fut. pl. of* bêgan **II.**

beg-beám, beig-beám, es; *m.* [begir *a berry,* beám *a tree*] *The mulberry-tree, the blackberry-bush, a tree bearing berries, a bramble;* morus, rubus:—Moyses æt-ýwde wið ǽnne beigbeám *Moyses ostendit secus rubum,* Μωσῆς ἐμήνυσεν ἐπὶ τῆς βάτου, Lk. Bos. 20, 37.

begea *of both,* Judth. 11; Thw. 23, 19; Jud. 128; *gen. of* begen.

bêgean *to bow, bend:*—Cneó bêgean scolden *genua flectere deberent,* Bd. 3, 17; S. 544, 39, col. 2. v. bêgan.

be-geat, be-geáton *obtained,* Ors. 3, 11; Bos. 72, 6; *p. of* be-gytan.

be-gellan *to celebrate by song, to sing.* v. bi-gellan.

be-gêmed *taken care of, governed; pp. of* be-gýman.

BEGEN; *nom. m. only, Both;* ambo; *adj. pron. pl:*—Hîg feallaþ begen on ǽnne pytt *ambo in foveam cadunt,* Mt. Bos. 15, 14. Wit wǽron begen ðâ git on geógoþfeore *we* [*Beowulf and Breca*] *were both yet in youthful life,* Beo. Th. 1077; B. 536.—*Nom. m. f. n.* bâ, bû, bô *both;* ambo, ambæ, ambo:—Ða idesa, *f.* bâ *both the women,* Judth. 11; Thw. 23, 22; Jud. 133. Þrym, *m.* sceal mid wlenco, þriste, *m.* mid cênum; sceolon bû recene beadwe fremman *pomp shall be with pride, the confident with the bold; both shall quickly promote war,* Exon. 89 b; Th. 337, 9; Gn. Ex. 62: Elen. Kmbl. 1225; El. 614. Blôd, *n.* and wæter, *n.* bû tû ætgædre eorþan sôhton *blood and water, both the two sought the earth together,* Exon. 70 a; Th. 260, 5; Jul. 292: Cd. 35; Th. 46, 29; Gen. 751.—*Nom. m. and f.* or *f. and n.* bâ, bû *both;* ambo et ambæ *vel* ambæ et ambo, *n*:—Sorgedon bâ twâ, Adam and Eue *both the two sorrowed, Adam and Eve,* Cd. 37; Th. 47, 24; Gen. 765: 39; Th. 52, 8; Gen. 840. Hî bû þêgon [MS. þegun] æppel *they both* [*Adam and Eve*] *ate the apple,* Exon. 61 b; Th. 226, 8; Ph. 402: Cd. 10; Th. 12, 18; Gen. 187. Wǽron bû tû rihtwîse befôran Gode *both the two* [*Zacharias and Elizabeth*] *were righteous before God,* Lk. Bos. 1, 6, 7: Cd. 27; Th. 36, 20; Gen. 574. Wæter, *n.* and eorþe, *f.* sint on gecynde cealda bâ twâ *water and earth, both the two are by nature cold,* Bt. Met. Fox 20, 152; Met. 20, 76. Bû samod, lîc, *n.* and sâwl, *f. both together, body and soul,* Elen. Kmbl. 1775; El. 889: Exon. 27 a; Th. 81, 20; Cri. 1326. Niwe wîn, *n.* sceal beón gedôn on niwe bytta [*acc. pl. of* bytt, *f.*], ðonne beóþ bû tû gehealden *new wine shall be put into new bottles, then both the two shall be preserved,* Mk. Bos. 2, 22.—*Gen. m. f. n.* begra, begea, bega *of both;* amborum, ambarum, amborum:—Se Hâlga Gâst, ðe gǽþ of ðam Fæder and of ðam Suna, is heora begra lufu *the Holy Ghost, who proceedeth from the Father and the Son, is the love of them both,* Hexam. 2; Norm. 4, 22: Ælfc. T. 3, 4. Heora begra eágan wurdon ge-openode *the eyes of them both were opened,* Gen. 3, 7: Cd. 90; Th. 113, 27; Gen. 1893. Hyra begea nest *earum ambarum cibum,* Judth. 11; Thw. 23, 19; Jud. 128: Ps. Th. 86, 2. Engla and deófla, weorþeþ bega cyme *of angels and of devils, of both shall be a coming,* Exon. 21 a; Th. 56, 8; Cri. 897. Heora bega fæder *earum ambarum pater,* Cd. 123; Th. 157, 4; Gen. 2600.—*Dat. m. f. n.* bâm, bǽm *to both;* ambobus, ambabus, ambobus:—Se Hâlga Gâst, ðe gǽþ of ðam Fæder and of ðam Suna, is him bâm gemǽne *the Holy Ghost, who proceedeth from the Father and the Son, is common to them both,* Hexam. 2; Norm. 4, 22: Lk. Bos. 7, 42. He sceóp bâm naman *he gave names to both,* Cd. 6; Th. 8, 23; Gen. 128: Exon. 45 b; Th. 154, 14; Gû. 842.—*Acc. m. f. n.* bâ, bû *both;* ambos, ambas, ambo:—Bysmeredon uncit [*Inscription* Bismærede ungket] men, bâ ætgædre *they* [*men*] *reviled us two, both together,* Runic Inscrip. Kmbl. 354, 30. Ða beón beraþ, bû tû ætsomne, ârlîcne anleofan and ǽtterne tægel *the bees bear excellent food and a poisonous tail, both the two together,* Frag. Kmbl. 35; Leás. 19. On bâ healfa *on both sides,* Beo. Th. 2614; B. 1305: Ps. Th. 59, 5. Sceolde bû witan ylda ǽghwilc yfles and gôdes *each of men must know both of evil and good,* Cd. 24; Th. 31, 3; Gen. 479.—*Acc. m. and f.* or *f. and n.* bâ, bû *both;* ambos et ambas *vel* ambas et ambo:—Ðæt ðæt fýr ne mæg foldan, *f.* and mereстreám, *m.* forbærnan, ðeáh hit wið bâ twâ sîe gefeged *that the fire may not burn up earth and sea, though it be joined with both the two,* Bt. Met. Fox 20, 230; Met. 20, 115. Bringaþ Drihtne, bû ætsomne, wlite, *m.* and âre, *f. bring to the Lord, both together, glory and honour,* Ps. Th. 95, 7. Hât bû tû aweg Agar fêran and Ismael *command both the two to go away, Hagar and Ishmael,* Cd. 134; Th. 169, 12; Gen. 2798. Gehwylc hafaþ ætgædre bû lîc, *n.* and sâwle, *f. each shall have together both body and soul,* Exon. 23 a; Th. 64, 13; Cri. 1036.—*Instr. m. f. n.* bâm, bǽm *with* or *by both;* ambobus, ambabus, ambobus:—Mid bǽm handum *with both hands,* Elen. Kmbl. 1607; El. 805. [*R. Brun.* beie, *gen*: *R. Glouc.* beye, bey: *Laym.* beie, beine, beigene: *Orm.* beȝenn, *gen*: *O. Scot.* baith: *O. Sax.* bêðie, bêdea: *Frs.* bêthe: *Dut.* beide: *M. Dut.* bede: *Ger. M. Ger.* beide: *N. L. Ger.* beede: *O. Ger.* pêdê, pêdô, pêdiu: *Goth.* bai *and* bayoþs; *n.* ba: *Dan.* baade: *Swed.* både: *O. Nrs.* bâðir, bâðar, bæði: *Lat.* ambo: *Grk.* ἄμφω: *Lith.* abbu; *f.* abbi: *O. Slav.* oba: *Sansk.* ubha; *dual* ubhau; *pl.* ubhe.]

be-geondan, be-iundan; *prep. acc.* [be *by,* geond, geondan *over*] BEYOND; per, trans:—Him fyligdon mycele menigu fram Iudea and fram begeondan Iordanen *secutæ sunt eum turbæ multæ de Judæa et de trans Jordanem,* Mt. Bos. 4, 25. Alîfe me to farenne and to geseónne ðæt sêloste land begeondan Iordane *transibo et videbo terram hanc optimam trans Jordanem,* Deut. 3, 25. Begeondan sǽ *in transmarinis partibus,* Bd. 5, 19; S. 639, 10. Gewendon begeondan sǽ *went beyond sea,* Chr. 1048; Erl. 180, 16. Beiundan Iordane *trans Jordanem,* Deut. 1, 5.

be-geondan; *adv. Beyond;* ultra:—Feor begeondan *far beyond,* Ælfc. Gr. 38; Som. 41, 3. v. geond; *adv.*

be-geótan, bi-geótan; he -gýt; *p.* -geát, *pl.* -guton; *pp.* -goten, -geten [be, geótan *to pour*]. I. *to pour out, to cast upon, to sprinkle, cover;* aspergere:—Ic wæs mid blôde bestêmed, begoten of ðæs guman sîdan *I was wet with blood, poured from the man's side,* Rood Kmbl. 97; Kr. 49. Mid blôde begoten *sprinkled with blood,* Chr. 734; Th. 76, 18: Herb. 96, 4; Lchdm. i. 210, 3: Rood Kmbl. 13; Kr. 7. II. *to pour into;* infundere:—He me lâre on gemynd begeát *he poured knowledge into my mind,* Elen. Kmbl. 2494; El. 1248.

be-geten, L. H. E. 2; Th. i. 28, 2; *for* be-gitan *to seize, obtain.*

be-getende *seeking out,* = be-gitende, Ps. Spl. T. 110, 2. v. be-gitan.

be-gêton *begot,* Cd. 223; Th. 294, 20; Sat. 474; *p. of* be-gitan.

beggen *both,* L. Ælf. P. 35; Th. ii. 378, 13, 15, 16; *nom. m.* = begen.

bégian; *p.* ode; *pp.* od [bēg *a crown*] *To crown;* coronare:—Ðū bēgodest us *coronasti nos*, Ps. Spl. C. 5, 15. v. beágian.

be-gietan *to get, obtain*, Exon. 65 b; Th. 242, 6; Ph. 669. v. be-gitan.

be-gîman *to guard;* custodire, Gen. 2, 15. v. be-gȳman.

be-gîmen *observation, care;* observatio, Wanl. Catal. 78, 24. v. be-gȳmen.

be-gîming, e; *f. An invention, a device;* adinventio, Ps. Spl. 105, 36.

be-gînan; *p.* -gān, *pl.* -ginon; *pp.* -ginen *To open the mouth wide, gape, yawn?* oscitare in aliquem?—Ic begīne *I yawn*, Exon. 129 b; Th. 497, 19; Rä. 87, 3.

be-ginnan, ic -ginne, ðū -ginnest, -ginst, he -ginneþ, -gineþ, -ginþ, *pl.* -ginnaþ, -ginaþ; *p.* -gan, *pl.* -gunnon; *pp.* -gunnen; *v. a.* [be, ginnan, *q. v.*] *To* BEGIN; incipere:—Nōe ðā began to wircenne ðæt land *Noe tunc cœpit exercere terram*, Gen. 9, 20: 18, 27: Hy. 10, 36; Hy. Grn. ii. 293, 36. v. on-ginnan.

be-giondan *beyond*, Past. Pref. MS. Hat. v. be-geondan.

be-girdan; *p.* -girde; *pp.* -girded *To begird*, Apol. Th. 12, 17. v. be-gyrdan.

be-gitan, -gietan, -gytan; *part.* -gitende; ic -gite, ðū -gytst, he -gyteþ, *pl.* -gytaþ; *p.* -geat, *pl.* -geáton; *pp.* -geten; *v. a.* [be, gitan *to get*] *To get, obtain, take, acquire, to seek out, receive, gain, seize, lay hold of, catch;* sumere, obtinere, assequi, acquirere, nancisci, capere, comprehendere, arripere:—Ælc mōd wilnaþ sōþes gōdes to begitanne *every mind wishes to get the true good*, Bt. 24, 2; Fox 82, 1. Hī ða burh mihton eáðe begitan *they might easily have taken the city*, Ors. 3, 4; Bos. 56, 10. He begeat ealle ða eást land *he obtained all the east country*, Ors. 3, 11; Bos. 72, 6. Hwæt begytst ðū of ðīnum cræfte *quid acquiris de tua arte?* Coll. Monast. Th. 23, 3: Ps. Th. 83, 3: 68, 37. Ðe hȳ under Alexandre begeáton *which* [*riches*] *they had gained under Alexander*, Ors. 3, 11; Bos. 73, 27: Beo. Th. 4490; B. 2249. Fin sweord-bealo begeat *misery from the sword seized Fin*, Beo. Th. 2297; B. 1146.

be-gleddian, ic -gleddige; *p.* ode; *pp.* od *To dye, stain;* inficere:—Ic begleddige *inficio*, Ælfc. Gr. 28, 6; Som. 32, 37. And begleddod is eorþe on blōdum *et infecta est terra in sanguinibus*, Ps. Spl. 105, 36.

be-glîdan; *p.* -glād, *pl.* -glidon; *pp.* -gliden *To glide* or *disappear from any one, to desert any one;* evanescere ab aliquo, derelinquere:—Unriht me eall beglīde *iniquitas a me omnis transeat*, Ps. Th. 56, 1.

be-gnagan; *p.* -gnōg, *pl.* -gnōgon; *pp.* -gnagen *To* BEGNAW, *gnaw;* corrodere, Martyrol. 9, Jul.

begne, an; *f. An ulcer, a carbuncle;* carbunculus:—Seó blace begne *the black ulcer;* carbunculus, Ælfc. Gl. 64; Som. 69, 21; Wrt. Voc. 40, 52.

be-gnornian; *p.* ode; *pp.* od *To deplore;* lugere:—Begnornodon *deplored*, Beo. Th. 6338; B. 3179.

be-gong, es; *m. A course:*—Under swegles begong *under the course of heaven*, Beo. Th. 1724; B. 860. v. be-gang.

be-gongan *to exercise*, Exon. 32 b; Th. 103, 24; Cri. 1693 [MS. bi-gongan]. v. be-gangan.

be-goten *covered*, Rood Kmbl. 13; Kr. 7; *pp. of* be-geótan.

begra *of both:*—He is heora begra lufu *he is the love of them both*, Hexam. 2; Norm. 4, 22. v. begen.

be-grafan, bi-grafan; *p.* -grōf, *pl.* -grōfon; *pp.* -grafen [be, grafan *to dig*] *To bury;* defodere, sepelire:—Rōda greóte begrafene [MS. be-grauene] *crosses buried in the sand*, Elen. Kmbl. 1666; El. 835.

be-grauen *buried*, = begrafen; *pp. of* be-grafan.

be-greósan; *p.* -greás, *pl.* -gruron; *pp.* -groren *To overwhelm fearfully;* horrore afficere, formidolose obruere?—Atole gāstas sūsle begrorene [MS. begrorenne] *the horrid spirits fearfully overwhelmed with torment*, Cd. 214; Th. 268, 9.

be-grêtan, -grǣtan; *p.* -grēt, *pl.* -grēton; *pp.* -grēten, -grǣten *To lament, bewail;* lamentare, deplorare:—Fæmnan ne wǣran geonge begrētte *virgines eorum non sunt lamentatæ*, Ps. Th. 77, 63. v. grētan.

be-grindan; *p.* -grand, *pl.* -grundon; *pp.* -grunden. I. *to grind, polish;* perfricare, polire, exacuere:—Sindrum begrunden *ground with cinders*, Exon. 107 a; Th. 408, 3; Rä. 27, 6. II. *to deprive;* privare:—Ælc hine selfa begrindeþ gāstes dugeþum *each deprives himself of his soul's happiness*, Cd. 75; Th. 91, 33; Gen. 1521. DER. grindan.

be-grîpan; *p.* -grāp, *pl.* -gripon; *pp.* -gripen; *v. trans.* [be, grīpan *to gripe*] *To* BEGRIPE, *chasten, chide;* increpare, Ps. Spl. T. 15, 7.

begrorene [MS. begrorenne] *fearfully overwhelmed*, Cd. 214; Th. 268, 9; *pp. of* be-greósan.

be-grornian *to lament, to grieve for;* mœrere, Cd. 13; Th. 16, 14; Gen. 243. v. gnornian.

be-grynian; *p.* ode; *pp.* od *To ensnare, entrap;* illaqueare, irretire:—Ðæt hīg swā beón begrynode *ut sic irretientur*, Coll. Monast. Th. 21, 17. v. grinian.

be-gunnon, be-gunnen *began, begun*, C. R. Ben. 22. v. be-ginnan.

be-gyldan; *p.* -gylde; *pp.* -gylded *To gild;* inaurare, deaurare:—Begylded fatu *vasa deaurata*, Lye. v. gyldan, gildan.

be-gȳman, be-gīman; *p.* de; *pp.* ed; *v. trans. To take care of, to keep, govern, regard, serve, attend;* custodire, curare, servare, observare, attendere:—Godes þeówum ðe ðære cyrcan begȳmaþ *to God's servants who serve the church*, L. Ælf. C. 24; Th. ii. 352, 11: Ps. Spl. 77, 63: Lk. Bos. 10, 35: Mt. Bos. 6, 1: Ps. Spl. 5, 2.

be-gȳmen, be-gīmen, e; *f. Care, regard, observation, shew, pomp;* observatio:—Mid begȳmene = μετὰ παρατηρήσεως, *with shew* or *that it can be observed*, Lk. Bos. 17, 20.

be-gyrdan, -girdan; *p.* de; *pp.* ed, or be-gyrd; *v. trans.* [be, gyrdan *to gird*]. I. *to* BEGIRD, *surround;* cingere, præcingere, accingere:—Begyrdaþ eówer lendenu *renes vestros accingetis*, Ex. 12, 11. He ðæt eálond begyrde and gefæstnade mid dīce *he begirt and secured the island with a dike*, Bd. 1, 5; S. 476, 10. God se begyrde me of mihte *Deus qui præcinxit me virtute*, Ps. Spl. 17, 34: Ps. Th. 17, 37. He wæs begyrded mid wǣpnum ðæs gāstlīcan camphādes *accinctus erat armis militiæ spiritalis*, Bd. 1, 7; S. 477, 24. II. *to clothe;* amicire:—Begyrded oððe bewǣfed leóhte swā swā mid hrægle *amictus lumine sicut vestimento*, Ps. Lamb. 103, 2.

be-gytan *to obtain*, Mt. Bos. 5, 7. v. be-gitan.

be-gytst *obtainest*, Coll. Monast. Th. 23, 3. v. be-gitan.

bêh *a crown:*—On ðone bēh *in coronam*, Bd. 5, 21; S. 643, 28. v. bēg.

be-habban, he -hæfeþ; *p.* -hæfde; *pp.* -hæfed, -hæft; *v. a.* [be *by, near*, habban *to have*]. I. *to compass, encompass, surround;* cingere, circumdare:—Ðīne fȳnd behabbaþ ðē *inimici tui circumdabunt te*, Lk. Bos. 19, 43: Jos. 6, 20. Behæfde heápa wyn Hǣlendes burg *the joy of bands surrounded the Saviour's tomb*, Exon. 120 a; Th. 460, 16; Hö. 18: Cd. 112; Th. 148, 9; Gen. 2454. II. *to comprehend;* comprehendere, continere:—Behabban hreðre *or* on hreðre *to comprehend in the mind*, Andr. Kmbl. 1633; An. 818: Exon. 92 b; Th. 347, 9; Sch. 10: Ps. Spl. 76, 9. III. *to restrain, detain, stay;* detinere:—Hī behæfdon hine *detinebant illum*, Lk. Bos. 4, 42.

be-hæfednes, -ness, e; *f. A detention, care;* conservatio:—Behæfednes fæsten *sparingness, parsimony*, Cot. 191. v. fæst-hafolnes.

be-hæftan; *p.* -hæfte; *pp.* -hæfted, *contr.* -hæftd, -hæft *To betake, take, bind;* captare, vincire:—Be-hæft *held;* captus = gehæft, *q. v.* Gen. 22, 13. v. *pp. of* hæftan. v. ge-hæftan.

be-hǽs, e; *f.* [be *by, near*, hǣs *command*] *A self-command, vow, promise.* Hence our *behest;* votum:—He fela behǣsa behēt *he promised many vows*, Chr. 1093; Th. 359, 33. v. hǣs, behāt.

be-hǽtst *vowest*, Gen. 38, 17. v. be-hātan.

be-hangen *hung round; pp. of* be-hōn.

behât, es; *n. A promise, vow;* promissum, votum:—Ic sende on eów mīnes fæder behāt *ego mitto promissum Patris mei in vos*, Lk. Bos. 24, 49. Ðonne ðū behāt behǣtst Drihtene *cum votum voveris Domino*, Deut. 23, 21. DER. be-hātan, ge-hāt.

be-hâtan, ic -hāte, ðū -hātest, -hǣtst, he -hāteþ, *pl.* -hātaþ; *p.* -hēt, *pl.* -hēton; *pp.* -hāten [be, hātan *to call, promise*, vide II] *To promise, vow, threaten;* spondere, pollicere, vovere, comminari:—Ðæt ðū me behǣtst *quod polliceris*, Gen. 38, 17. Behēt he mid āþe *cum juramento pollicitus est*, Mt. Bos. 14, 7. Ðonne ðū behāt behǣtst Drihtene *cum votum voveris Domino*, Deut. 23, 21. Drihten God behēt us wedd *Dominus Deus pepigit nobiscum fœdus*, 5, 2. Ælc yfel man him behēt *they threatened him every evil*, Chr. 1036; Ing. 209, 12; Ælf. Tod. 11.

be-hâwian; *p.* ode, ade; *pp.* od, ad *To see, see clearly;* videre:—Behāwa ðonne ðæt ðū ūtadō ðæt mot *see then clearly* [τότε διαβλέψεις] *that thou take out the mote*, Mt. Bos. 7, 5.

be-heáfdian; *p.* ode; *pp.* od; *v. trans.* [be, heáfod *head*] *To* BEHEAD; decollare:—He beheáfdode Iohannem *decollavit Iohannem*, Mt. Bos. 14, 10: Judth. 12; Thw. 25, 32; Jud. 290.

be-heáfdung, e; *f. A* BEHEADING; decollatio, L. Ath. i. prm; Th. i. 194, 21.

be-healdan, bi-healdan, ic -healde, ðū -healdest, -hylst, he -healdeþ, -hylt, -hilt, *pl.* -healdaþ; *p.* ic, he -heóld, ðū -heólde, *pl.* -heóldon; *pp.* -healden; *v. trans.* [be *near*, healdan *to hold, observe*]. I. *to hold by* or *near, possess, observe, consider, beware, regard, mind, take heed, behave, to mean, signify;* tenere, inhabitare, servare, curare, gerere:—Heora ǣ to behealdenne *to observe their laws*, Ors. 3, 5; Bos. 57, 21. Adam sceal mīnne stronglīcan stōl behealdan *Adam shall possess my strong seat*, Cd. 19; Th. 23, 28; Gen. 366. He gemetfæstlīce and ymbsceáwiendlīce hine sylfne on eallum þingum beheóld *se modeste et circumspecte in omnibus gereret*, Bd. 5, 19; S. 637, 5. Hwæt ðæt swefen beheóld *what the dream signified*, Gen. 41, 8. II. *to* BEHOLD, *see, look on;* observare, aspicere, videre:—Beheald ða tunglu *behold the stars*, Bt. 39, 13; Fox 232, 25. Loth ðā beheóld geond eall, and geseah *elevatis itaque Lot oculis, vidit*, Gen. 13, 10.

be-heáwan, bi-heáwan; *p.* -heów; *pp.* -heáwen *To beat, bruise, hew* or *cut off, to separate from, deprive of;* tundere, cædendo privare, amputare:—Beheáwene mid swingellan *tunsi per flagella*, Past. 36, 5; Hat. MS. 47 b, 15. Heáfde beheáwan *to behead*, Bt. Met. Fox 1, 85; Met.

1, 43. Hwonne me wrāþra sum aldre beheówe *when some enemy might deprive me of life*, Cd. 128; Th. 163, 21; Gen. 2701.

be-hēdan; *p.* -hēdde; *pp.* -hēded *To watch, heed, guard;* cavere, curare, Leo 178. v. hēdan.

be-hēfe, es; *m:* be-hēfnes, -ness, e; *f.* [be-hōfen] *Gain, advantage, benefit*, BEHOOF; lucrum. v. be-hōfian *to have need of.*

be-hēfe; *adj. Necessary, behoveful;* necessarius:—Ðe behēfe synd *qui necessarii sunt*, Lk. Bos. 14, 28. Behēfe þing *necessary things, necessaries*, C. R. Ben. 46. DER. efn-behēfe.

be-hegian; *p.* ede; *pp.* ed *To* BEHEDGE, *hedge around;* circumsepire. v. hegian.

be-helan, bi-helan; *p.* -hæl, *pl.* -hǣlon; *pp.* -holen *To conceal, hill* or *cover over, hide;* occultare, Beo. Th. 833; B. 414: Bd. 4, 16; S. 584, 25, note. v. helan, be-helian.

be-held *availed*, Chr. 1123; Th. 374, 23. v. be-healdan.

be-heldan [= be-healdan?] *To attend, intend;* attendere, intendere:—Wesan ðíne eáran gehȳrende and beheldende *fiant aures tuæ intendentes*, Ps. Th. 129, 2.

be-helian, bi-helian; *p.* ode, ede; *pp.* od, ed; *v. trans.* [be, helian *to cover*] *To cover, cover over, conceal, obscure, hide;* condere, sepelire:—Wurdon behelede ealle ða dūna *operti sunt omnes montes*, Gen. 7, 19. Se heofen mōt ðæt leóht behelian *the heaven may obscure the light*, Bt. 7, 3; Fox 20, 21: Elen. Kmbl. 858; El. 429.

be-helman; *p.* ede; *pp.* ed *To cover over, to cover;* cooperire:—Heolstre behelmed *covered with darkness*, Salm. Kmbl. 209; Sal. 104. v. bi-helmian.

Behēmas, *pl. m:* Bēme, *nom. acc; gen.* a; *dat.* um; *pl. m. The Bohemians;* Bohemi:—Hī Maroaro habbaþ, be westan him Þyringas, and Behēmas, and Bægware healfe *they, the Moravians, have, on their west, the Thuringians, Bohemians, and part of the Bavarians*, Ors. 1, 1; Bos. 18, 42.

be-hēng, *pl.* -hēngon *hung round; p. of* be-hōn.

be-heófian; *p.* ode; *pp.* od *To bewail, lament;* lugere, lamentari:—Heora mǣdena ne synt beheófode *virgines eorum non sunt lamentatæ*, Ps. Lamb. 77, 63. v. heófian.

be-heóld *beheld*, Gen. 13, 10; *p. of* be-healdan.

be-heonan, -heonon; *adv.* [be *by*, heonan *hence*] *On this side, close by;* cis, citra:—Get beheonon *yet nearer;* citerius, Ælfc. Gr. 38; Som. 41, 4: Cot. 33.

be-heopian; *p.* ode; *pp.* od *To hew* or *cut off;* amputare, Cd. 125; Th. 160, 2, note a; Gen. 2644, = be-heáwan? *q. v.*

be-heówe *might deprive*, Cd. 128; Th. 163, 21; Gen. 2701. v. be-heáwan.

be-hēt *promised*, Deut. 5, 2; *p. of* be-hātan.

be-hicgan *to confide, trust, rely, depend upon;* acquiescere, niti, inniti:—Ðe on Gode behicgaþ *qui in Deo acquiescunt*, R. Ben. 31. DER. hicgan.

be-hīdan; *p.* -hīdde *To hide;* abscondere:—Forðamðe ic eom nacod, ic behīdde me *quod nudus essem, abscondi me*, Gen. 3, 10, 8. v. be-hȳdan.

be-hidiglīce *carefully*, Bd. 3, 19; S. 547, 29. v. be-hydelīce.

be-hilt *beholds;* respicit, R. Ben. 8; *pres. of* be-healdan.

be-hindan; *prep. dat. Behind;* post, pone:—He lēt him behindan ciólas *he left ships behind him*, Bt. Met. Fox 26, 45; Met. 26, 23. Ligeþ him behindan hefig hrusan dǣl *behind it lies the heavy mass of earth*, 29, 106; Met. 29, 52. Ne ðē behindan nū lǣt mænige ðus micle *now leave not behind thee such a multitude of people*, Exon. 10 a; Th. 10, 19; Cri. 155.

be-hindan; *adv. Behind, back;* a tergo, pone, post:—Ac behindan beleác mid wǣge *but inclosed them behind with the wave*, Cd. 166; Th. 206, 24; Exod. 456. Ðū ðone hēhstan heofon behindan lǣtst *thou shalt leave the highest heaven behind*, Bt. Met. Fox 24, 58; Met. 24, 29.

be-hionan *on this side*, Past. pref. v. be-heonan.

be-hīring *a hiring*, Ælfc. Gl. 13; Som. 57, 123. v. be-hȳring.

be-hlād *covered*, Ors. 3, 3; Bos. 56, 6; *p. of* be-hlīdan.

be-hlǣman *to overwhelm with noise;* strepitu obruere. v. bi-hlǣman.

be-hlǣnan *to beset by leaning anything against another;* acclinando circumdare. v. bi-hlǣnan.

be-hlæstan *to load a ship;* navem onerare. v. be, hlæstan.

be-hleápan; *p.* -hleóp, *pl.* -hleópon; *pp.* -hleápen *To leap upon* or *in, to fix;* insilire:—Ðæs monnes mōd and his lufu biþ behleápen on ða lǣnan sibbe *the man's mind and his love are fixed on the fragile peace*, Past. 46, 5; Hat. MS. 67 a, 9.

be-hlehhan, bi-hlyhhan; *p.* -hlōh, *pl.* -hlōgon; *pp.* -hlahen, -hleahen *To laugh at, deride;* ridere aliquid, exultare de aliqua re:—Ic ne þearf behlehhan *I need not deride*, Exon. 52 b; Th. 183, 22; Gū. 1331. DER. hlehhan.

be-hlemman *to dash together;* collidere cum strepitu. v. bi-hlemman.

be-hlīdan; *p.* -hlād, *pl.* -hlidon; *pp.* -hliden [hlīdan *to cover*] *To cover over, to cover, close;* tegere, claudere:—Hīg awylton ðone stān, and ðone pytt eft behlidon *thei schulden turne awei the stoon, and thei schulden put it eft on the pit*, Wyc; Gen. 29, 3. Seó eorþe siððan togædere behlād *the earth then closed together*, Ors. 3, 3; Bos. 56, 6.

be-hlidenan = be-lidenan *the left* or *departed, the dead;* mortuos, Andr. Kmbl. 2179; An. 1091; *acc. pl. pp. from* be-līðan, *q. v.*

be-hlīgan, he -hlīþ *To dishonour, defame;* infamare:—Oft hī mon wōmmum behlīþ *man often defames her with vices*, Exon. 90 b; Th. 339, 29; Gn. Ex. 101.

be-hlȳðan; *p.* de; *pp.* ed *To deprive;* privare, spoliare:—Ic sceal heáfodleás behlȳðed licgan *I must lie deprived of head*, Exon. 104 a; Th. 395, 20; Rä. 15, 10.

be-hōfen *supplied, provided;* ornatus:—Ðæt ealle Godes cyricean sȳn wel behōfene *that all God's churches be well supplied* or *well provided* [*with all they have need of*], L. Edm. E. 5; Lambd. 58, 7; Wilk. 73, 13. v. be-hweorfan.

be-hōfian, bi-hōfian; *p.* ode; *pp.* od; *v. a. To have need of, to need, require;* egere, indigere. *Impersonally, it* BEHOVETH, *it concerns, it is needful* or *necessary;* oportet, interest:—Mycel wund behōfaþ mycles lǣcedōmes *a great wound has need of a great remedy*, Bd. 4, 25; S. 599, 40. He mægenes behōfaþ gōdra gūþrinca *he requires strength of good warriors*, Beo. Th. 5288; B. 2647: Exon. 98 a; Th. 367, 1; Seel. 1. Ðeáh ða scearpþanclan witan ðisse Engliscan geþeódnesse ne behōfien *though the sharp-minded wise men may not have need of this English translation*, MS. Cot. Faust A. x. 150 b; Lchdm. iii. 440, 32. Behōfaþ *oportet*, Jn. Lind. War. 3, 7. DER. a-behōfian.

be-hōf-līc; *adj. Behoveful, needful;* necessarius:—Ðæt his līf him behōflīc wǣre *quia necessaria sibi esset vita ipsius*, Bd. 5, 5; S. 618, note 3. Behōflīc is *is necessary*, Mk. Skt. Lind. 11, 3.

be-hogadnes, -ness, e; *f. Use, custom, practice;* exercitatio, Cot. 114.

be-hogian *to be anxious, solicitous, wise, very careful;* solicitum esse, C. R. Ben. 58. v. hogian, hycgan.

be-hōn; *p.* -hēng, *pl.* -hēngon; *pp.* -hangen, -hongen [be, hōn *to hang*] *To* BEHANG, *to hang round;* circumpendere, circumdare, ambire:—Behongen beón mid bellum *to be behung* or *hung round with bells*, Past. 15, 4; Hat. MS. 19 b, 7.

be-hongen *hung round*, Past. 15, 4; Hat. MS. 19 b, 7; *pp. of* be-hōn.

be-horsian; *p.* ode, ade, ude; *pp.* od, ad, ud *To deprive of a horse;* equo privare:—Ðā eóde se here to hyra scipum ... and hī wurdon ðǣr behorsode *then the army went to their ships ... and they were there deprived of their horses*, Chr. 886; Th. 152, 28, col. 3. DER. horsian.

be-hreósan, *pl.* -hreósaþ; *p.* -hreás, *pl.* -hruron; *pp.* -hroren *To rush down, fall;* ruere, corruere, incidere:—Behreósaþ on helle *incidunt in gehennam*, Lupi Serm. 5, 8.

be-hreówsian; *part.* -hreówsigende; ic -hreówsige, ðū -hreówsast, he -hreówsaþ, *pl.* -hreówsiaþ; *p.* ode; *pp.* od *To repent, feel remorse, make amends* or *reparation;* pœnitere, compungi, satisfacere:—Behreówsian *pœnitere*, Ælfc. Gr. 33; Som. 37, 22. Behreówsiaþ *compungimini*, Ps. Lamb. 4, 5. Ic behreówsige *satisfacio*, Ælfc. Gr. 37; Som. 39, 40. Behreówsigende *pœnitens*, Scint. 9. DER. hreówan, hreów.

be-hreówsung, e; *f. A lamenting, repentance, penitence;* pœnitentia:—Behreówsung oððe dǣdbōt *pœnitentia*, Ælfc. Gr. 33; Som. 37, 22.

be-hrīman; *p.* de; *pp.* ed [hrīm *rime, hoar-frost*] *To cover with rime* or *hoar-frost;* pruinis circumfundere, Exon. 115 b; Th. 444, 17; Kl. 48.

be-hringed, be-hrincged; *part.* [be, hring *a ring*] *Inclosed in a ring, encircled, surrounded;* circumdatus:—Behringed beón *to be surrounded*, Past. 21, 5; Hat. MS. 32 a, 8.

be-hrōpan; *p.* -hreóp, *pl.* -hreópon; *pp.* -hrōpen [hrōpan *to call* or *cry out*] *To scoff at, rail, trouble;* sugillare:—Ðe-læs heó cume me behrōpende *ne veniens sugillet me*, Lk. Bos. 18, 5.

be-hroren; *p. part. Fallen off, deprived of;* a quo aliquid decidit, orbatus:—Fatu hyrstum behrorene *vessels deprived of their ornaments*, Beo. Th. 5517; B. 2762; *pp. of* be-hreósan, *q. v.*

be-hrūmig; *adj. Swarthy, sooty;* fuliginosus, Martyr. 3, April. v. hrūmig.

be-hrumod; *p. part. Bedaubed, dirtied;* cacabatum, Cot. 31: 189. v. besciten.

bēhþ, e; *f. A token, sign, proof;* signum, testimonium:—Heó hēt hyre þinenne ðæs herewǣðan heáfod to bēhþe blōdig ætȳwan ðām burhleódum *she ordered her servant to shew the bloody head of the leader of the army to the citizens as a token*, Judth. 11; Thw. 24, 6; Jud. 174.

be-hwearf, es; *m. A change, an exchange;* commutatio:—On behwearfum heora *in commutationibus eorum*, Ps. Spl. 43, 14.

be-hweorfan; *p.* -hwearf, *pl.* -hwurfon; *pp.* -hworfen, -hweorfen. I. *to turn, spread about;* vertere, convertere:—Hleahtre behworfen *turned to laughter*, Andr. Recd. 3402; An. 1705. Hīg behwurfon hīg būton ðære wīcstōwe *they spread them about outside of the camp*, Num. 11, 32. II. *to turn* or *put in order, arrange;* disponere, parare:—Ðæt ealle Godes cyrcan sȳn wel behworfene [behweorfene, H.] *that all God's churches be well put in order*, L. Edm. E. 5; Th. i. 246, 12. Ðæt ǣlc preost hæbbe eal mæsse-reáf wurþlīce behworfen *that every priest have all his mass-vestments worthily arranged*, L. Edg. C. 33; Th. ii. 250, 28. DER. hweorfan.

be-hwerfan; *p.* de; *pp.* ed [be, hwerfan *to turn*] *To turn, prepare, instruct;* vertere, instruere:—Ðonne hió ǣrest sīe ūtan behwerfed *when* *it is first turned round about*, Bt. Met. Fox 13, 154; Met. 13, 77. Ic wolde mid sumre bîsne ðé behwerfan ûtan *I would instruct thee further* [ûtan *from without*] *by some example*, Bt. 34, 4; Fox 138, 27.

be-hwon *whence;* unde, Bd. 2, 2; S. 503, 2. v. hwonan.

be-hwurfon *spread about*, Num. 11, 32; *p. pl. of* be-hweorfan.

be-hwylfan; *p.* -hwylfde; *pp.* -hwylfed *To cover* or *vault over;* operire, obruere:—Ne behwylfan mæg heofon and eorþe his wuldres word *the word of his glory may not cover over heaven and earth*, Cd. 163; Th. 204, 28; Exod. 426. v. hwylfan.

be-hwyrfan *to treat, direct, exercise, practice;* tractare, exercere:—Behwyrf ðé sylfne *exerce temet ipsum*, Coll. Monast. Th. 31, 37: R. Ben. 32. v. be-hweorfan.

be-hycgan, -hicgan *to think, consider, bear in mind, trust;* meditari, considerare, sollicitum esse de re, confidere, niti:—He sceal deópe behycgan þroht þeóden-gedál *he must deeply bear in mind the dire decease of his lord*, Exon. 52 b; Th. 183, 7; Gû. 1323. Ðe on Gode behicgaþ *qui in Deo acquiescunt*, R. Ben. 31. v. hycgan.

be-hýdan, bi-hýdan; *p.* -hýdde; *pp.* -hýded, -hýdd, -hýd *To hide, conceal, cover;* abscondere, occultare, operire:—Se ðe hine behýdde fram hǽton his *qui se abscondit a calore ejus*, Ps. Spl. 18, 7: Salm. Kmbl. 604; Sal. 301. Ðæt wæs lange behýded *which was long concealed*, Elen. Kmbl. 1582; El. 793. Heolstre behýded *covered with darkness*, Elen. Kmbl. 2161; El. 1082. Behýdd *absconditum*, Mk. Bos. 4, 22.

be-hydelíce, -hidiglíce, big-hydilíce, big-hidiglíce; *adv. Carefully;* sollicite, sollerter, Bd. 1, 27; S. 489, 39: 3, 19; S. 547, 29: 4, 23; S. 595, 4.

be-hydig, bí-hidig; *adj. Careful, vigilant, wary, watchful, solicitous, anxious;* sollers:—He wæs se behydegesta [MS. behydegæsta] *erat sollertissimus*, Bd. 5, 20; S. 642, 13: 4, 7; S. 574, 33. v. hydig.

be-hýdignys, -nyss, e; *f.* [be, hýdan *to hide*] *A desert, a wilderness;* desertum:—Stefn Drihtnes tosceacende behýdignys *vox Domini concutientis desertum*, Ps. Spl. C. 28, 7.

be-hyldan *to put off, to flay, skin;* excoriare:—He hét hý behyldan *he ordered to flay it*, Ors. 4, 6; Bos. 84, 45.

be-hýpan; *p.* -hýpte; *pp.* -hýped [hýpe *a heap*] *To heap* or *cover over, surround, encompass;* contegere, circumsepire, circumdare:—He wæs mid wǽpnum and mid feóndum eall ûtan behýped *cum armis et hostibus circumseptus erat*, Bd. 3, 12; S. 537, 28.

be-hýring, -híring, e; *f. A hiring, letting out to hire;* locatio:—Behíring *vel* gehýred feoh *locatio*, Ælfc. Gl. 13; Som. 57, 123; Wrt. Voc. 20, 60. v. ge-hýran.

be-hyðelíce; *adv. More sumptuously;* sumptuosius, Cot. 186.

be-hyðlíc *sumptuous.* v. hyðelíc.

beig-beám, es; *m. A bramble;* rubus:—Moyses ætýwde wið ǽnne beigbeám *Moyses ostendit secus rubum*, Lk. Bos. 20, 37. v. begbeám.

be-innan; *prep. dat. In, within;* in, intra:—Boëtius ðá nânre frôfre beinnan ðam carcerne ne gemunde *then Boethius thought of no comfort within the prison*, Bt. 1; Fox 4, 2.

be-irnan; *impert.* be-irn; *p.* -arn, *pl.* -urnon; *pp.* -urnen *To come* or *run into;* incurrere:—Ne be-irn ðû on ða inwitgecyndo *do not run into their guilty nature*, Salm. Kmbl. 660; Sal. 329. v. be-yrnan.

be-iundan *beyond;* trans, ultra:—Beiundan Iordane *trans Iordanem*, Deut. 1, 5: 11, 30. v. be-geondan.

be-lâcan; *p.* -léc, -leólc, *pl.* -lécon; *pp.* -lâcen *To flow around, inclose;* circumfluere:—Ýþ mec lagufæðme beleólc *the wave inclosed me in its watery bosom*, Exon. 122 b; Th. 471, 26; Rä. 61, 7.

be-lâdian, ic -lâdige; *p.* ode; *pp.* od *To clear, excuse;* excusare:—Ðæt he wolde belâdian his môdor *that he might clear his mother*, Ors. 3, 9; Bos. 65, 24: Ælfc. Gr. 28, 6; Som. 32, 35. v. lâdian.

be-lâdigend, es; *m. One who makes excuses, a defender;* excusator, Ælfc. Gl. 23; Wrt. Voc. 83, 64.

be-lâdung, e; *f. An excuse;* apologeticus, excusatio:—Belâdung *apologeticus*, Ælfc. Gl. 106; Som. 78, 65; Wrt. Voc. 57, 44. v. lâdung.

be-lǽdan; *p.* -lǽdde; *pp.* -lǽd, -léd; *v. a. To bring, lead by, mislead, lead;* seducere, inferre, inducere, impellere:—Ðû belǽddest us on grin *thou hast mislead us into a snare;* induxisti nos in laqueum, R. Ben. 7. Belǽd beón mid unþeáwum *impelli vitiis*, R. Ben. 64. v. lǽdan.

be-lǽfan; *p.* de; *pp.* ed *To remain, to be left;* remanere, superesse:—Ân of him ne belǽfde *unus ex eis non remansit*, Ps. Spl. C. 105, 11. v. lǽfan.

be-læg *surrounded*, Ps. Th. 118, 153; *p. of* be-licgan.

be-lændan *to deprive of land*, Chr. 1112; Th. 369, 39. v. be-landian.

be-lǽðed; *part.* [lâþ *evil*] *Loathed, detested;* exosus. v. lâðian.

be-lǽwa, an; *m. A destroyer;* proditor, traditor. v. lǽwa.

be-lǽwan; *p.* -lǽwde; *pp.* -lǽwed; *v. a. To beway, betray;* tradere, prodere:—Ðæt he hyne wolde belǽwan *ut traderet eum*, Mt. Bos. 26, 15, 16. Heó hine belǽwde *she betrayed him*, Jud. 16, 21. Ðæt Iohannes belǽwed wæs *quod Ioannes traditus esset*, Mt. Bos. 4, 12.

be-lǽwing, e; *f. A betraying, treason;* proditio, Homl. Th. ii. 244, 22. v. be-lǽwan, lǽwa *a betrayer.*

be-lâf *remained*, Jos. 5, 1; *p. of* belífan.

be-lagen beón *to be oppressed;* opprimi, Past. 58, 1; Hat. MS.

be-lamp *happened, befell*, Beo. Th. 4928; B. 2468; *p. of* belimpan.

be-landian; *p.* ode, ede; *pp.* od, ed; *v. a. To deprive of land, to confiscate, disinherit;* terris privare:—Wearþ Eádgâr belandod *Edgar was deprived of land*, Chr. 1091; Th. 359, 5. Hí hí ǽr belandedon *they had deprived them previously of their lands*, 1094; Th. 361, 12. v. be-lendian. Opposed to gelandian *to inherit.*

belced-sweora; *adj. Possessed of an inflated neck;* inflata cervice præditus:—Ic eom belced-sweora *I am neck-inflated*, Exon. 127 b; Th. 489, 24; Rä. 79, 1.

belcentan *to utter, give forth, belch, eructate;* eructare:—Se lǽcecræft biþ swíðe swéte belcentan *the medicine is very sweet to eructate*, Bt. 22, 1, Bodl; Fox 76, note 17. v. belcettan.

belcettan; *p.* te; *pp.* ted *To utter, give forth;* eructare:—Nû míne weleras ðé wordum belcettaþ ymnas elne *eructabunt labia mea hymnum*, Ps. Th. 118, 171. v. bealcettan.

beld, beldo *boldness, rashness;* audacia. v. byld, byldo.

be-leác *shut in*, Ors. 4, 5; Bos. 81, 40; *p. of* belûcan.

be-leán; *p.* -lôh, *pl.* -lôgon; *pp.* -leahen *To hinder by blame, reprehend, reprove, forbid;* prohibere, reprobare, reprehendere:—We lǽraþ ðæt preostas oferdruncen beleán ôðrum mannum *we enjoin that priests reprehend drunkenness in other men*, L. Edg. C. 57; Th. ii. 256, 14. He him ðæt swýðe belôh *hoc multum illi prohibuit*, Bd. 5, 19; S. 638, 28, note: Beo. Th. 1027; B. 511. v. leán.

be-lecgan, bi-lecgan; *p.* -legde, -léde, *pl.* -legdon; *pp.* -legd, -léd; *v. a. To lay* or *impose upon, cover, invest, load, afflict, charge, accuse;* imponere, afficere, onerare, accusare:—Heó ðone hleóðor-cwyde husce belegde *she covered the revelation with scorn*, Cd. 109; Th. 143, 21; Gen. 2382. Papirius wæs mid Rômânum swylces dômes beléd *Papirius was invested with such authority by the Romans*, Ors. 3, 8; Bos. 63, 40. We hine clommum belegdon *we loaded him with chains*, Andr. Kmbl. 3119; An. 1562. Hí ðé wítum belecgaþ *they afflict thee with torments*, 2424; An. 1213. Gyf man sacerd belecge mid tyhtlan and mid uncræftum *if one charges a priest with an accusation and with evil practices*, L. C. E. 5; Th. i. 362, 8, 19, 21. Se ðe hine belecge *he who accuses him*, L. O. D. 6; Th. i. 354, 30: 4; Th. i. 354, 15.

be-léd *impelled*, R. Ben. 64; *pp. of* belǽdan.

be-léd = be-legd *charged, accused*, L. O. D. 4; Th. i. 354, 15; *pp. of* be-lecgan.

be-légan, bi-légan; *p.* -légde; *pp.* -légd *To surround with flame;* circumflagrare flamma:—Líge belégde *surrounded with flame* [*Ger.* umlodert mit lohe], Cd. 188; Th. 234, 22; Dan. 296. v. légan.

be-legde *covered*, Cd. 109; Th. 143, 21; Gen. 2382; *p. of* be-lecgan.

be-lendan, be-lændan; *p.* de; *pp.* ed *To deprive of land;* terris privare:—Se cyng belænde ðone eorl *the king deprived the earl of his land*, Chr. 1112; Th. 369, 39, 41: 1104; Th. 367, 11. Wearþ Eoda eorl and manege ôðre belende *earl Eudes and many others were deprived of their lands*, 1096; Th. 362, 36. v. be-landian.

belene, beolone, belone, an; *f. Henbell, henbane;* hyoscyamus niger:—Belenan meng wið rysele *mix henbane with lard*, L. M. 1, 31; Lchdm. ii. 72, 1. Dô belenan seáw *apply the juice of henbane*, 3, 3; Lchdm. ii. 310, 7. Genim beolonan sǽd *take the seed of henbane*, 1, 2; Lchdm. ii. 38, 1. v. beolone, henne-belle. [Henbane is so called from the baneful effects of its seed upon poultry, of which Matthioli says that 'birds, especially gallinaceous birds, that have eaten the seeds perish soon after, as do fishes also.' The *A. Sax.* belene and beolone, *Ger.* bilse, *O. Ger.* belisa, *Pol.* bielún, *Hung.* belénd, *Rus.* belená are words derived (according to Zeuss, p. 34) from an ancient Celtic god Belenus, corresponding to the Apollo of the Latins: 'Dem Belenus war das Bilsenkraut heilig, das von ihm Belisa und Apollinaris hiess,' Prior 109.]

be-leógan; *p.* -leág, *pl.* -lugon; *pp.* -logen *To belie, deceive by lies;* fallere:—Belogen beón *falli*, Gr. Dial. 1, 14. DER. leógan.

be-leólc *flowed around, inclosed*, Exon. 122 b; Th. 471, 26; Rä. 61, 7; *the reduplicated p. of* be-lâcan, v. lâcan, *and Goth. cognates at the end of* lâcan.

be-leóran *to pass over.* v. bi-leóran.

be-leósan, bi-leósan; *p.* -leás, *pl.* -luron; *pp.* -loren [be, leósan *to loose*] *To let go, to deprive of, to be deprived of, lose;* privare, orbare, privari, amittere:—Leóhte belorene *deprived of light*, Cd. 5; Th. 6, 9; Gen. 86: Beo. Th. 2150; B. 1073: Andr. Kmbl. 2159; An. 1081. Ðǽr ic swíðe beleás hérum, ðám ðe ic hæfde *there I was much deprived of the hairs, which I had*, Exon. 107 a; Th. 407, 35; Rä. 27, 4. v. for-leósan.

be-léwa, an; *m. A betrayer;* proditor. v. be-léweda, lǽwa.

be-léweda, an; *m. A betrayer;* proditor:—Mid Iudan ûres Drihtenes beléwedan *with Judas the betrayer of our Lord*, Wanl. Catal. 137, 38, col. 1. v. beléwa, belǽwa.

bele-wite *simple;* simplex:—Se wer wæs swíðe belewite and rihtwís *erat vir ille simplex et rectus*, Job 1, 1; Thw. 164, 2. v. bile-wit.

bel-flýs, es; *n.* [bell *a bell*, flýs *a fleece*] *The* BELL-WETHER'S FLEECE, *the fleece of a sheep that carries the bell;* tympani vellus, *i. e.* ducis gregis tintinnabulum gestantis vellus:—Bel-flȳs *id est, tympani vellus*, L. R. S. 14; Th. i. 438, 23.

BELG, belig, bylg, bylig, bilig, bælg, bælig, es; *m. A* BULGE, *budget, bag, purse, bellows, pod, husk*, BELLY; bulga, follis, siliqua, uter:—Bylg *bulga*, Cot. 27. Bylig *follis*, Ælfc. Gl. 27; Wrt. Voc. 86, 15. Bilig *uter*, Ps. Spl. M. 118, 83. [*Dut.* balg, *m*: *Ger.* balg, *m*: *M. H. Ger.* balc, *m*: *O. H. Ger.* balg, *m. follis, uter*: *Goth.* balgs, *m*: *Dan.* bælg, *m*: *O. Nrs.* belgr, *m.*] DER. beán-belg, -bælg, blāst-, mete-, wīn-. v. ge-belg.

BELGAN, ic belge, ðu bilgst, bilhst, he bilgþ, bilhþ, bylgþ, *pl.* belgaþ; *p.* ic, he bealg, bealh, ðū bulge, *pl.* bulgon; *pp.* bolgen. I. *v. reflex. acc. To cause oneself to swell with anger, to make oneself angry, irritate oneself, enrage oneself*; ira se tumefacere, se irritare, se exasperare:—Nelle ðū on ēcnesse ðē āwa belgan *non in æternum indignaberis*, Ps. Th. 102, 9. Ic bidde ðæt ðū ðē ne belge wið me *ne, quæso, indigneris*, Gen. 18, 30. Bealg hine swīðe folc-āgende *the people's lord irritated himself greatly*, Exon. 68 a; Th. 253, 25; Jul. 185. II. *intrans. To swell with anger, to be angry, to be enraged*; ira tumere, indignari, irasci:—Gē belgaþ wið me *mihi indignamini*, Jn. Bos. 7, 23. [*O. Sax.* belgan, *v. reflex*; *p.* balg; *pp.* bolgan *irasci, indignari*: *N. H. Ger.* balgen *pugnis certare*: *O. H. Ger.* belgan *tumere, irasci.*] DER. a-belgan, ge-, bolgen-mōd.

bel-hringes beácn, es; *n. A sign by bell-ringing*; signum sonitu campanæ datum, R. Ben. 43.

bel-hūs, bell-hūs, es; *n. A* BELL-HOUSE, *a room* or *tower in the castle of a Thane, generally built between the kitchen and porter's lodge, where was a bell* or *bells to summon the inhabitants to prayers*, and for other purposes; campanile *vel* campanarium, turris in qua pendent tintinnabulum *vel* tintinnabula, Du Cange, fol. 1681, col. 712; CAMPANA, col. 708:—Gif ceorl hæfde fīf hīda āgenes landes cirican and cycenan, bell-hūs ... ðonne wæs he þegen-rihtes weorþe *if a freeman had five hides of his own land, a church and kitchen, a bell-house ... then was he worthy of thane-right*, L. R. 2; Th. i. 190, 15.

be-libban; *p.* -lifde, *pl.* -lifdon; *pp.* -lifed, -lifd *To deprive of life*; vita privare:—Līc cōlode belifd under lyfte *the corpse was lifeless cold in the air*, Exon. 51 b; Th. 180, 19; Gū. 1282. v. libban.

be-licgan, he -ligeþ, -līþ, *pl.* -licgaþ; *p.* -læg, *pl.* -lǣgon, -lāgon; *pp.* -legen; *v. a.* [be *by*, licgan *to lie*] *To lie* or *extend by* or *about, to surround, encompass*; circumdare, cingere:—Hī belicgaþ us mid fyrde *circumdabunt nos exercitu*, Jos. 7, 9. Sió eá Etheopia land beligeþ ūton *the river encompasseth the Ethiopian land*, Cd. 12; Th. 15, 7; Gen. 229. Me nēd belæg *want surrounded me*, Ps. Th. 118, 153.

be-lidenes *of the left* or *departed*, Elen. Kmbl. 1752; El. 878; *gen. pp. from* be-līðan, *q. v.*

be-līfan, ic -līfe, ðū -līfest, -līfst, he -līfeþ, -līfþ; *p.* -lāf, *pl.* -lifon; *pp.* -lifen *To remain, abide, to be left*; superesse, manere, remanere:—Ne se rysel ne belīfþ ōþ morgen *nec remanebit adeps usque mane*, Ex. 23, 18. He āna belāf ðǣr bæfta *mansit solus*, Gen. 32, 24: Ps. Spl. 105, 11. Hī nāmon ðæt of ðām brytsenum belāf, seofon wilian fulle *sustulerunt quod superaverat de fragmentis, septem sportas*, Mk. Bos. 8, 8. [*Plat.* bliven; *p.* blēf: *Dut.* blijven; *p.* bleef: *Ger.* bleiben; *p.* blieb: *M. H. Ger.* belīben; *p.* be-leip: *O. H. Ger.* pi-līpan; *p.* pi-leip: *Dan.* blive; *p.* blev: *Swed.* blifva, bli; *p.* blef, ble: in *O. Nrs.* the word is wanting, as well as in *Goth.*] v. līfan.

be-lifd = -lifed *deprived of life, lifeless, inanimate*; defunctus, Exon. 51 b; Th. 180, 19; Gū. 1282; *pp. of* be-libban.

belig *a bag.* v. belg.

be-ligeþ *encompasseth*, Cd. 12; Th. 15, 7; Gen. 229. v. be-licgan.

be-limp *an event*; eventus, Lchdm. iii. 202, 28. v. gelimp.

be-limpan; *p.* -lamp, *pl.* -lumpon; *sub.* -lumpe; *pp.* -lumpen [be, limpan *to appertain*] *To concern, regard, belong, pertain, appertain*; curare, pertinere:—Ne belimpþ to ðē *non ad te pertinet*, Mk. Bos. 4, 38. Hwæt ðæs to him belumpe *what of that concerned him?* Bd. 2, 12; S. 513, 39. Hwæt belimpþ his to ðē *what of it belongs to thee?* Bt. 14, 2; Fox 42, 35. Hit belimpþ to ðære spræce *it appertains to the discourse*, Bt. 38, 2; Fox 198, 19. II. *to happen, occur, befall*; evenire, accidere, contingere:—Ðā him sió sār belamp *when that pain befell him*, Beo. Th. 4928; B. 2468.

be-lisnian, -listnian; *p.* ode; *pp.* od; *v. trans.* [be *from*, lystan *to desire*] *To evirate, emasculate, castrate*; castrare. *Part. p.* belisnod, belistnod *emasculated*:—Belisnod *spadatus, eunuchizatus*, Ælfc. Gl. 2; Som. 55, 53; Wrt. Voc. 16, 26. Used as a noun,—*A eunuch*:—Belisnod *spado, eunuchus*, Ælfc. Gr. 9, 3; Som. 8, 32. Sōþlīce synd belistnode, ðe of hyra mōdor innoðum cumaþ, and eft synt belistnode ða men ðe man belistnaþ, and eft synd belistnode ðe hīg sylfe belistnodon for heofona rīce *sunt enim eunuchi, qui de matris utero sic nati sunt, et sunt eunuchi, qui facti sunt ab hominibus, et sunt eunuchi, qui se ipsos castraverunt propter regnum cœlorum*, Mt. Bos. 19, 12. v. a-fȳran.

be-lisnod, -listnod *a eunuch*, Ælfc. Gr. 9, 3; Som. 8, 32: Ælfc. Gl. 2; Som. 55, 53. v. be-lisnian.

be-līþ *surrounds*, Cd. 12; Th. 15, 13; Gen. 232. v. be-licgan.

be-līðan; *p.* -lāþ, *pl.* -liðon = -lidon; *pp.* -liðen = -liden [be *from*, līðan *to go, sail*] *To go from, to leave*; effugere, relinquere:—Līfe belidenes līc *the body of the left by life*, i. e. *the body of the lifeless*, Elen. Kmbl. 1752; El. 878: Exon. 52 a; Th. 182, 18, note; Gū. 1312: Judth. 12; Thw. 25, 26; Jud. 280. Ða belidenan [MS. behlidenan] *the dead*; mortuos, Andr. Kmbl. 2179; An. 1091.

BELL, e; *f*: belle, an; *f. A* BELL; campana, tintinnabulum, cymbalum:—Cyrice bell *the church-bell.* Hleóðor heora bellan *a sound of their bell*, Bd. 4, 23; S. 595, note 40. Belle *tintinnabulum*, Ælfc. Gr. 5; Som. 4, 39. Hēriaþ hine on bellum *laudate eum in cymbalis*, Ps. Lamb. 150, 5. Seó lytle belle *the little bell.* Seó mycele belle *the large bell*; campana, Lye. [*Plat. Dut.* belle, bel.] v. bellan.

bell *a bellowing, roar, cry?* Cd. 148; Th. 185, 12; Exod. 121. v. bǣl-egesa.

BELLAN; *part.* bellende; ic belle, ðū bilst, he bilþ, *pl.* bellaþ; *p.* ic, he beal, ðū bulle, *pl.* bullon; *pp.* bollen *To* BELLOW, *to make a hollow noise, to roar, bark, grunt*; boare, latrare, grunnire:—Bearg bellende *a roaring* [*grunting*] *boar*, Exon. 111 b; Th. 428, 10; Rä. 41, 106. [*Ger.* bellen: *Swed.* böla: *O. Nrs.* belja.]

belle, an; *f. A bell*; tintinnabulum:—Hleóðor heora bellan *a sound of their bell*, Bd. 4, 23; S. 595, note 40: Ælfc. Gr. 5; Som. 4, 39. v. bell.

bell-hūs *a bell-house*, L. R. 2; Th. i. 190, 15. v. belhūs.

be-locen *shut up, inclosed*, Cd. 209; Th. 259, 24; Dan. 696; *pp. of* be-lūcan.

be-logen *deceived*, Gr. Dial. 1, 14. v. be-leógan.

be-lōh *forbade*, Bd. 5, 19; S. 638, 28, note. v. be-leán.

belone, an; *f. Henbane*:—Henne-belone, ōðrum naman belone *henbane, by another name bane*, Herb. 5, 1; Lchdm. i. 94, 5, note 9. v. hennebelle, belene.

be-loren *deprived*, Cd. 5; Th. 6, 9; Gen. 86; *pp. of* be-leósan.

BELT, es; *m. A* BELT, *girdle*; balteus, Cot. 25. [*O. H. Ger.* palz, balz, *m? a girdle*: *Ger.* Belt, *m. name of the narrow straits between the Danish isles*: *Dan.* belte *a belt*: *Swed.* bälte, *id*: *O. Nrs.* belti, *n. id*: *Lat.* balteus.] v. gyrdel.

be-lūcan, he -lȳcþ; *p.* -leác, *pl.* -lucon; *pp.* -locen; *v. trans.* [be, lūcan *to lock*] *To lock up, inclose, surround, shut, shut up*; concludere, recludere, includere, circumcludere, amplecti, obserare, claudere:—Drihten hī beleác *Dominus conclusit eos*, Deut. 32, 30. Gif he ðone oxan belūcan nolde *si non recluserit bovem*, Ex. 21, 29. Ðā hēt he hine gebringan on carcerne and ðǣr inne belūcan *he gave an order to take him to prison and therein lock him up*, Bt. 1; Fox 2, 26: Ors. 4, 5; Bos. 81, 40: Gen. 41, 49: Ps. Spl. C. T. 16, 11. Belocen leoðu-bendum *locked up in limb-bonds*, Andr. Kmbl. 327; An. 164. Wealle belocen *inclosed with a wall*, Cd. 209; Th. 259, 24; Dan. 696. Ðæt man belūce ǣlc deofulgyld-hūs *that one should close every idol-temple*, Ors. 6, 30; Bos. 127, 36.

be-lumpe *concerned*; pertineret, Bd. 2, 12; S. 513, 39. v. be-limpan.

belune *henbane*, Som. Lye. v. belene.

be-lȳcþ *locks*, Hexam. 5; Norm. 8, 27; *pres. of* belūcan.

be-lytegan; *p.* ade; *pp.* ad; *v. a.* [lyteg *crafty*] *To allure, inveigle, seduce*; procare:—He belytegade Crēce *he allured Greece*, Ors. 3, 7; Bos. 59, 39.

be-mǣnan, bi-mǣnan; *p.* de; *pp.* ed [be, mǣnan *to moan*, III. *q. v.*] *To* BEMOAN, *bewail, lament, mourn*; lugere, dolere, congemere:—Ða heófungdagas wǣron ðā gefyllede, ðe hīg Moisen bemǣndon *completi sunt dies planctus lugentium Moysen*, Deut. 34, 8.

be-mǣtan = be-mǣton *measured, compared*, Ors. 3, 7; Bos. 60, 43; *p. pl. of* be-metan.

Bēme; *nom. acc*; *gen.* a; *dat.* um; *pl. m. The Bohemians*; Bohēmi:—Riht be eástan syndon Bēme *right to the east are the Bohemians*, Ors. 1, 1; Bos. 18, 33. v. Behēmas.

bēme, an; *f. A trumpet*; tuba, salpinx:—Bēman blāwan *to blow the trumpet*, Cd. 227; Th. 302, 19; Sat. 602. Bēme *barbita*, Cot. 27. v. bȳme.

be-mearn *mourned*, Cd. 106; Th. 139, 14; Gen. 2309. v. be-meornan.

be-meornan; *p.* -mearn, *pl.* -murnon; *pp.* -mornen [be, meornan *to mourn*] *To mourn*, BEMOURN, *bewail, deplore*; lugere:—Ðīn ferhþ bemearn *thy soul mourned*, Cd. 106; Th. 139, 14; Gen. 2309. Nō ic ða stunde bemearn *I bemourned not the time*, Exon. 130 a; Th. 499, 12; Rä. 88, 14.

bēmere *a trumpeter*, Lye. v. bȳmere.

be-metan; *p.* -mæt, *pl.* -mǣton; *pp.* -meten; *v. trans.* [be, metan *to measure*] *To measure by, compare, estimate, consider*; metiri, commetiri, comparare, æstimare:—Ðæt hȳ ðā æt nihstan hȳ sylfe to nōhte bemǣtan *that they at last compared themselves to nought*, Ors. 3, 7; Bos. 60, 43. Ðæt hȳ nā siððan nānes anwealdes hȳ ne bemǣtan, ne nānes freódōmes *that afterwards they did not consider themselves* [*possessed*] *of any power, nor of any freedom*, 3, 7; Bos. 62, 11. Ðæt hȳ heora miclan anwealdes and longsuman hȳ sylfe siððan wið Alexander to nāhte [ne] bemǣtan *that, in respect of their great and lasting power, they estimated themselves at nothing against Alexander*, 3, 9; Bos. 65, 39: 4, 6; Bos. 86, 17.

be-mīðan, bi-mīðan; *p.* -māþ, *pl.* -miðon; *pp.* -miðen [be, mīðan *to hide*] *To hide, conceal*; abscondere, occultare:—He ne mihte hit bemīðan *non potuit latere*, Mk. Bos. 7, 24. Hī ne māgon heortan geþohtas fōre Waldende bemīđan *they cannot conceal their heart's thoughts before the Supreme*, Exon. 23 a; Th. 65, 4; Cri. 1049. He his mǣgwlite bemiđen hæfde *he had concealed his shape*, Andr. Kmbl. 1712; An. 858.

be-murcnian; *p.* ode; *pp.* od [be, murcnian *to murmur*] *To murmur, murmur greatly;* obmurmurare:—Hū ungemetlīce, ge Rōmware, bemurcniaþ *how immoderately, O Romans, do ye murmur*, Ors. 1, 10; Bos. 34, 9.

be-murnan, bi-murnan; *p.* -murnde; *pp.* -murned [be, murnan *to mourn*] *To bemoan, bewail, mourn, to care for;* lugere, curare, sollicitum esse de re:—Hwæt bemurnest đū *why bemoanest thou?* Exon. 10 b; Th. 11, 26; Cri. 176. Sīþ ne bemurneþ *he bewails not his lot*, 117 a; Th. 449, 31; Dōm. 79. Feorh ne bemurndon grǣdige gūþrincas *the greedy warriors cared not for the soul*, Andr. Kmbl. 308; An. 154.

be-mūtian *to exchange for;* commutare. v. bi-mūtian.

be-myldan [molde *mould*] *To cover with mould* or *earth, to bury, inter, hide* or *put under ground;* inhumare, humare, Cot. 101.

BEN, benn, e; *f.* [*connected with* bana *a slayer, murderer*] *A wound;* vulnus:—Ne đǣr ǣnig com blōd of benne *nor came there any blood from the wound*, Cd. 9; Th. 12, 6; Gen. 181. Heortan benne *the wounds of heart*, i. e. *sadness, grief*, Exon. 77 a; Th. 289, 17; Wand. 49. Blātast benna *the palest of wounds*, Exon. 19 a; Th. 48, 13; Cri. 771. Hī feóllon bennum seóce *they fell sick with wounds*, Cd. 92; Th. 118, 29; Gen. 1972. With this word the MSS. often confound the *pl.* of bend, as in Cd. 195; Th. 243, 12; Dan. 435, where *benne* stands for *bende:* and in Andr. Recd. 2077; An. 1040: Exon. 73 a; Th. 273, 21, note; Jul. 519, where *bennum* stands for *bendum.* v. bend. [*O. H. Ger.* bana, *f: Goth.* banya, *f: Icel.* ben, *f.*] DER. bennian, ge-.

BĒN; *gen. dat.* bēne; *acc.* bēn; *pl. nom.* bēna, bēne; *f. A praying, prayer, petition, an entreaty, a deprecation, supplication, demand.* Hence in *Chaucer* bone *and our* BOON; precatio, deprecatio, oratio, preces, postulatio:—Đeáh đe đæs cyninges bēne mid hine swīđode and genge wǣren [wæren, MS. T: wære, MSS. Ca. O.] *though the king's prayers were powerful and effectual with him*, Bd. 3, 12; S. 537, 18: 1, 4; S. 475, 32: 5, 1; S. 614, 15: 5, 21; S. 643, 6. Be ryhtes bēne *of praying for justice*, L. In. 8; Th. i. 106, 19. Đīn bēn ys gehȳred *exaudita est deprecatio tua*, Lk. Bos. 1, 13. Ic underfēng đīne bēne *suscepi preces tuas*, Gen. 19, 21. Hī heom đæra bēna forwyrdnon *they gave to them a denial of their requests*, Ors. 2, 2; Bos. 40, 34. Micelra bēna dæg *litania major*, Martyr. 25, April. [*O. Nrs.* bón, *f. a petitioner.*]

bēn, bēnn *summoned; p. of* bannan.

bēna, an; *m. A petitioner, demander;* rogator, supplex:—Gehȳr me helpys bēnan *exaudi me auxilii supplicem*, Ps. Th. 101, 2. Hȳ bēna wǣron *they were demanders*, or *they demanded*, Ors. 3, 11; Bos. 73, 36. *Hence* bēna wesan *to demand, request*, Beo. Th. 6272; B. 3140: Cd. 107; Th. 142, 6; Gen. 2357.

be-nacian; *p.* ode; *pp.* od, ed [be, nacian *nudare*] *To make naked;* denudare:—Đū benacodest grundweall ōþ hneccan *denudasti fundamentum usque ad collum*, Cant. Abac. Lamb. fol. 190 a; 13.

be-nǣman, be-nēman; *p.* -nǣmde, -nēmde; *pp.* -nǣmed, -nēmed [be, niman *to take*] *To deprive, take away;* auferre, privare:—He ne meahte hī đæs landes benǣman *he could not deprive them of their land*, Ors. 1, 10; Bos. 33, 35: Cd. 98; Th. 129, 32; Gen. 2152. Ealdre benǣman *to deprive of life*, Judth. 10; Thw. 22, 24; Jud. 76. Wuldre benēmed *deprived of glory*, Cd. 215; Th. 272, 18; Sat. 121.

BENC, e; *f. A* BENCH; scamnum, abacus:—Bugon to bence *they turned to a bench*, Beo. Th. 659; B. 327. On bence wæs helm *a helm was on the bench*, Beo. Th. 2491; B. 1243. [*Plat. O. Sax. Dut. Ger.* bank, *f: M. H. Ger.* banc, *m. f: O. H. Ger.* panch, *f: Dan. Swed.* bänk: *O. Nrs.* bekkr, *m.*] DER. ealu-benc, meodu-.

benc-sittende; *part. Sitting on a bench;* in scamno sedens, Judth. 10; Thw. 21, 20; Jud. 27: Exon. 88 a; Th. 332, 1; Vy. 78.

benc-swēg, es; *m. A bench-noise, noise from the benches, convivial noise;* clamor in scamnis ad convivium sedentium, Beo. Th. 2326; B. 1161.

benc-þel, es; *pl.* -þelu; *n. A bench-floor, a floor on which benches are put;* scamnorum tabulatum, Beo. Th. 976; B. 486: 2482; B. 1239.

bend, bænd, e; *f:* es; *m.* What ties, binds, or bends,—*A band, bond, ribbon, a chaplet, crown, ornament;* vinculum, ligamen, diadema:—Đæt benda onlȳseþ *that looseneth bonds*, Exon. 8 b; Th. 5, 12; Cri. 68. On lāþne bend *in a loathsome bond*, Cd. 225; Th. 298, 27; Sat. 539. Heora bendas towearp *vincula eorum disrupit*, Ps. Th. 106, 13: 115, 7: 149, 8. Đa benda sumes gehæftes *vincula cujusdam captivi*, Bd. 4, 22; S. 590, 28. Đā Iohannes on bendum gehȳrde Cristes weoruc *Joannes cum audisset in vinculis opera Christi*, Mt. Bos. 11, 2. Bend agimmed and gesmīđed *diadema*, Ælfc. Gl. 64; Som. 69, 12; Wrt. Voc. 40, 46. Mid golde gesiwud bend *nimbus*, 64; Som. 69, 13. DER. ancor-bend, fȳr-, hell-, hyge-, īren-, searo-, wæl-, wīte-.

bendan; *p.* bende; *pp.* bended; *v. trans.* [bend *a band*]. I. *to* BEND; flectere, tendere, intendere:—He his bogan bendeþ *intendit arcum suum*, Ps. Th. 57, 6. He bende his bogan *arcum suum tetendit*, 7, 13. II. *to bind, fetter;* vincire:—Sume hī man bende *some they bound*, Chr. 1036; Th. 294, 6, col. 2; Ing. 208, 28; Ælf. Tod. 4. DER. ge-bendan.

bend-feorm, e; *f. A feast for the reaping* [*binding*] *of corn, a harvest-feast;* firma ad congregandas segetes, firma messis:—On sumere þeóde gebyreþ bend-feorm [bēn-feorm] for rīpe *in some one province a harvest-feast is due for reaping the corn*, L. R. S. 21; Th. i. 440, 26.

bēne; *gen. dat.* s; *nom. acc. pl. of* bēn *a prayer, q. v.*

be-neah *he requires*, Elen. Kmbl. 1233; El. 618. v. be-nugan.

be-neced *naked:*—Of hæftnede benecedes *de captivitate nudati*, Cant. Moys. Isrl. Lamb. 194 b, 42; *pp. of* be-nacian.

be-nēman; *p.* -nēmde; *pp.* -nēmed *To deprive;* privare:—Wuldre benēmed *deprived of glory*, Cd. 215; Th. 272, 18; Sat. 121. v. be-nǣman.

be-nemnan; *p.* -nemde; *pp.* -nemed [be, nemnan *to name*] *To affirm, declare, stipulate;* asserere, stipulari:—Āþe benemnan *to declare by oath*, Exon. 123 b; Th. 475, 18; Bo. 49. Fin Hengeste āþum benemde *Fin declared to Hengest with oaths*, Beo. Th. 2199; B. 1097: 6131; B. 3069: Ps. Th. 88, 3: 94, 11: 88, 42.

be-neótan, bi-neótan; *p.* -neát, *pl.* -nuton; *pp.* -noten [be, neótan *to enjoy, use*] *To deprive of the enjoyment* or *use of anything;* privare:—Aldre beneótan *to deprive of life*, Beo. Th. 1364; B. 680. Heáfde beneótan *to deprive of the head, to behead*, Apstls. Recd. 92; Ap. 46: Cd. 50; Th. 63, 32; Gen. 1041: 89; Th. 110, 1; Gen. 1831.

be-neođan, be-nyđan; *prep. dat.* [be, neođan *under*] BENEATH, *below, under;* infra:—Hió biþ swīđe fior hire selfre beneođan *she is very far beneath herself*, Bt. Met. Fox 20, 444; Met. 20, 222. Gif se sconca biþ þyrel beneođan cneówe *if the shank be pierced beneath the knee*, L. Alf. pol. 63; Th. i. 96, 16, 17: 66; Th. i. 96, 31. Nis nān wuht benyđan [him] *no creature is beneath him* [*beneath God's notice*], Bt. 36, 5; Fox 180, 18.

Benesing-tūn *Bensington*, Chr. 571; Th. 33, 28, col. 1. v. Bensingtūn.

bēn-feorm, e; *f. Food required from a tenant;* firma precum, L. R. S. 21; Th. i. 440, 26, for MS. bend-feorm, *q. v.*

ben-geat, es; *pl. nom. acc.* -geato; *n. A wound-gate, the opening of a wound;* vulneris porta:—Bengeato burston *the wound-gates burst open*, Beo. Th. 2246; B. 1121.

be-niman, bi-niman; *p.* -nam, *pl.* -nāmon; *pp.* -numen [be, niman *to take*] *To deprive, bereave;* privare:—Sceolde hine yldo beniman ellendǣda *age should deprive him of bold deeds*, Cd. 24; Th. 31, 12; Gen. 484. He hine his rīces benam *eum regno privavit*, Bd. 3, 7; S. 529, 31. He us hæfþ heofonrīce benumen *he has bereft us of heaven's kingdom*, Cd. 19; Th. 23, 20; Gen. 362.

be-niđan; *adv.* [be, neođan *under*] *Beneath, below, under;* infra, subter:—Đū bist ǣfre bufan and nā beniđan *eris semper supra et non subter:* thou shalt be above only, and thou shalt not be beneath, Deut. 28, 13.

benn, e; *f. A wound;* vulnus, Cd. 9; Th. 12, 6; Gen. 181. v. ben.

bennian, bennegean; *p.* ode, ade; *pp.* od, ad [ben *a wound*] *To wound;* vulnerare:—Mec īsern bennade *iron wounded me*, Exon. 130 a; Th. 499, 7; Rä. 88, 12. Ic geseah winnende wiht wīdo bennegean [benne gean, Th.] *I saw a block* [*wood*] *wound* [lit. *to wound = wounding*] *a striving creature*, 114 a; Th. 438, 4; Rä. 57, 2. DER. ge-bennian.

be-nohte, *pl.* -nohton *enjoyed*, Andr. Kmbl. 3407; An. 1707; *p. of* be-nugan, *q. v.*

be-norþan; *adv. In the north;* partibus borealibus:—Ofer eall benorþan *everywhere in the north*, Chr. 1088; Th. 357, 10.

be-notian; *p.* ode; *pp.* od [be, notian *to use*] *To use, consume;* uti:—Hie hæfdan heora mete benotodne *they had consumed their provisions*, Chr. 894; Th. 166, 15, col. 2.

bēn-rīp, e; *f. The reaping of corn by request;* ad preces messio. Originally the tenant came to reap corn etc. at his lord's request: in time, it grew into a custom or duty, but its old designation bēn-rīp was still used:—Eác he sceal hwīltīdum geára beón on manegum weorcum to hlāfordes willan, to-eácan bēnyrþe and bēnrīpe and mǣdmǣwecte *etiam debet esse paratus ad multas operationes voluntaris domini sui, et ad* bēnyrþe, *id est, araturam precum, et* bēnrīpe, *id est, ad preces metere, et pratum falcare*, L. R. S. 5; Th. i. 436, 3-5.

bēnsian; *part.* ende; *p.* ode; *pp.* od [bēn *a prayer*, sian *or* sīgan *to fall down*] *To fall down in prayer, to pray, entreat in prayer;* supplicare, deprecari, orare:—Đrihten bēnsian *Dominum deprecari*, Bd. 4, 25; S. 601, 4. He wæs bēnsiende đa uplīcan ārfæstnesse mīnra gesynta *supplicans erat supernæ pietati pro sospitate mea*, 5, 6; S. 619, 35: 3, 12; S. 537, note 20.

Bensing-tūn, Benesing-tūn, Bænesing-tūn, es; *m.* BENSINGTON *or Benson in Oxfordshire;* Bensington in agro Oxoniensi:—Hēr Cuđulf feówer tūnas genam, Liggeanburh, and Æglesburh, and Bensingtūn, and Egoneshām *here, in* 571, *Cuthwulf took four towns,* LENBURY, *and* AYLESBURY, *and* BENSON, *and* ENSHAM, Chr. 571; Th. 32, 29, col. 2; 33, 28, col. 1; 32, 29, col. 1: 777; Th. 92, 12, col. 2.

benst, he benþ *summonest, summons; 2nd and 3rd pers. pres. of* bannan.

bên-tîd, e; *f.* [bên *a prayer,* tîd *time*] *Prayer-time, rogation-days, time for supplication;* rogationum dies:—Ðæt is heálîc dæg, bên-tîd brêmu *that is a high day, a celebrated time for supplication,* Menol. Fox 148; Men. 75.

bên-tîde, bên-tigđe, bên-tiđige; *adj.* [bên *a prayer;* tîđa, tîđe *possessing, having obtained;* compos]. I. *having obtained a prayer, benefitted, favoured, successful;* precum *vel* supplicationis compos, fortunatus:—Hie đǽr, Godes þances, swíđe bêntíđe [bêntiđige, col. 2; bêntigđe, p. 153, 10, cols. 1, 2] wurdon æfter đam gehâte *there, God be thanked, they were very successful after that vow,* Chr. 883; Th. 152, 9, col. 3. II. *accepting a prayer, exorable, gracious;* deprecabilis:—Beó đû bêntýđe *vel* gehlystfull ofer đîne þeówan *deprecabilis esto super servos tuos,* Ps. Lamb. 89, 13.

be-nugan, he be-neah, *pl.* be-nugon; *p.* be-nohte; *subj. pres.* benuge [*Goth.* binauhan, binah; *pp.* binauht, δεῖ, *oportet*] *To need, want, require, enjoy;* indigere, frui:—Ðonne he bega beneah *when he requires both,* Elen. Kmbl. 1233; El. 618: Exon. 123 b; Th. 475, 12; Bo. 46. Gif hî đæs wuda benugon *if they enjoy* [*have enjoyment of*] *the wood,* Bt. 25; Fox 88, 19. Wiđ đan đe mîn wîf đǽr benuge inganges *dummodo uxor mea fruatur ingressu,* Hick. Thes. ii. 55, 32. And siđ nô frôfre benohte *and never since he enjoyed comfort,* Andr. Kmbl. 3407; An. 1707: 2320; An. 1161. v. nugan.

be-numen *deprived,* Cd. 19; Th. 23, 20; Gen. 362; *pp. of* be-niman.

bên-yrþ, e; *f. Ploughed land;* precum aratura:—Eác he sceal hwîltîdum geára beón on manegum weorcum to hlâfordes willan, to-eácan bênyrþe and bênrîpe and mǽdmǽwecte *etiam debet esse paratus ad multas operationes voluntatis domini sui, et ad* bênyrþe, *id est, araturam precum, et* bênrîpe, *id est, ad preces metere, et pratum falcare,* L. R. S. 5; Th. i. 436, 3-5.

be-nyđan *beneath, under;* infra, Bt. 36, 5; Fox 180, 18. v. be-niđan.

BEÓ; *indecl. in s; pl. nom. acc.* beón; *gen.* beóna; *dat.* beóum, beóm; *f. A* BEE; apis. The keeping of bees was an object of much care in the economy of the Anglo-Saxons. The great variety of expressions, taken from the flavour of honey, sufficiently account for the value they placed upon it. While the bee-masters [beó-ceorlas, *v.* beó-ceorl] enjoyed their own privileges, they had to pay an especial tax for the keeping of bees:—Swâ swâ seó beó sceal losian *as the bee shall perish,* Bt. 31, 2; Fox 112, 26. Sió wîlde beó sceal forweorþan, gif hió yrringa awuht stingeþ *the wild bee shall perish, if she angrily sting anything,* Bt. Met. Fox 18, 9; Met. 18, 5. Ða beón beraþ ârlîcne anleofan and ǽterne tægel *the bees carry a delicious food and a poisonous tail,* Frag. Kmbl. 34; Leás. 19. Be đâm đe beón bewitaþ *concerning those who keep bees,* L. R. S. 5; Th. i. 434, 35. Ymbtrymedon me swâ swâ beón *circumdederunt me sicut apes,* Ps. Spl. 117, 12: Ps. Th. 117, 12. [*Dut.* bij, bije, *f: Ger.* biene, beie, *f: M. H. Ger.* bîe, *f: O. H. Ger.* pîa, *f: Dan. Swed.* bi, *n: O. Nrs.* bý, *n; generally* bý-fluga, *f. a bee-fly.*] DER. beó-breád, -ceorl, -gang, -þeóf, -wyrt.

beó *I am* or *shall be;* sum, ero: *be thou;* sis:—Gefultuma me fæste, đonne beó ic fægere hâl *adjuva me, et salvus ero,* Ps. Th. 118, 117. Ic beó *ero,* Ælfc. Gr. 32; Som. 36, 29. Beó đû *sis:* Beó he *sit,* 32; Som. 36, 30: Beo. Th. 777; B. 386. v. beón.

beó-breád, bió-breád, bî-breád, es; *n.* I. BEE-BREAD, *the pollen of flowers collected by bees and mixed with honey for the food of the larvæ;* apum panis. ☞ Quite distinct from weax *beeswax;* cera = κηρός: and hunig-camb *honey-comb;* favus:—Ic eom swêtra đonne đû beóbreád blênde mid hunige *I am sweeter than if thou blendedst bee-bread with honey,* Exon. 111 a; Th. 425, 20; Rä. 41, 59. Hî synt swêtran đonne hunig ođđe beóbreád *they are sweeter than honey or bee-bread,* Ps. Th. 18, 9. Þynceþ bîbreád swêtre, gif he ǽr bitres onbyrgeþ *bee-bread seems sweeter, if he before has had a taste of bitter,* Bt. Met. Fox 12, 17; Met. 12, 9. Hit is hunige micle and beóbreáde betere and swêtre *it is better and sweeter than much honey and bee-bread,* Ps. Th. 118, 103. II. sometimes, from a deficient knowledge of natural history, beó-breád is used for hunig-camb *honey-comb;* favus:—Swêtran [MS. swetra] ofer hunig and beóbreáde *dulciora super mel et favum,* Ps. Lamb. 18, 11. Híg brohton him dǽl gebrǽddes fisces, and beóbreád *illi obtulerunt ei partem piscis assi,* et favum mellis; οἱ ἐπέδωκαν αὐτῷ ἰχθύος ὀπτοῦ μέρος, καὶ ἀπὸ μελισσίου κηρίου *and from a honey-comb,* Lk. Bos. 24, 42.

beóce *a beech-tree.* v. bêce, bôcce, bôc.

beó-ceorl, beó-cere, es; *m. A* BEE-CEORL, *bee-farmer* or *keeper;* bocherus, apum custos:—Be đâm đe beón bewitaþ. Beóceorle gebyreþ, gif he gafolheorde healt, đæt he sylle đonne lande gerǽd beó. Mid us is gerǽd đæt he sylle v sustras huniges to gafole *concerning those who keep bees. It behoves a keeper of bees, if he hold a taxable hive* [*stock of bees*], *that he then shall pay to the country what shall be agreed. With us it is agreed that he shall pay five* sustras *of honey for a tax;* 'bochero, id est, apum custodi, pertinet, si gavelheorde, id est, gregem ad censum teneat, ut inde reddat sicut ibi mos [MS. moris] erit. In quibusdam locis est institutum, reddi v [MS. vi] mellis ad censum,' L. R. S. 5; Th. i. 434, 35-436, 2. Swâ ic ǽr be beócere cwæþ *sicut de custode apum dixi,* L. R. S. 6; Th. i. 436, 17. [beócere = *Barbarous Lat.* bocherus = beó *a bee,* cherus = herus *a master.*] DER. þeów-beócere.

BEÓD, es; *m. A table;* mensa:—Ðâ đa gebrôđru æt beóde sǽton *sedentibus ad mensam fratribus,* Bd. 3, 2; S. 525, 9. Ðû gearcodest beforan mînre gesihþe beód *vel* beódwyste *vel* mýsan *parasti in conspectu meo mensam,* Ps. Lamb. 22, 5. Beódas *lances,* Cot. 123. [*O. Sax.* biod: *O. H. Ger.* piot: *Goth.* biuds: *O. Nrs.* bjóđr.]

BEÓDAN, bíodan; ic beóde, bióde, đû beódest, býtst, býst, he beódeþ, být, *pl.* beódaþ; *p.* ic, he beád, đû bude, *pl.* budon; *pp.* boden; *v. trans.* I. *to command,* BID, *order;* jubere, mandare:—Ðâs þing ic eów beóde *hæc mando vobis,* Jn. Bos. 15, 17. He beád Iosepe đæt he bude his brôđrum *dixit ad Joseph ut imperaret fratribus suis,* Gen. 45, 17: Ors. 6, 7; Bos. 119, 38: Andr. Kmbl. 692; An. 346. II. *to announce, proclaim, inspire, bode, threaten;* nuntiare, annuntiare, nuntium *vel* mandatum deferre, prædicare, significare, inspirare, minari alicui aliquid:—He him friþ beódeþ *he announces peace to them,* Exon. 27 b; Th. 82, 20; Cri. 1341. Geácas geár budon *cuckoos announced the year,* 43 b; Th. 146, 27; Gû. 716. Him wæs hild boden *to him was war proclaimed,* Elen. Kmbl. 36; El. 18. Hwæt seó rûn bude *what that mystery boded,* Cd. 202; Th. 250, 6; Dan. 542. Geác monaþ geómran reorde, sorge beódeþ bitter in breósthord *the cuckoo exhorts with mournful voice, inspires bitter sorrow to the heart,* Exon. 82 a; Th. 309, 9; Seef. 54. Ðeáh him feónda hlôþ feorhcwealm bude *though the band of fiends threatened death to him,* 46 a; Th. 157, 6; Gû. 887: Mk. Bos. 10, 48. III. *to offer, give, grant;* offerre, præbere:—Beód him ǽrest sibbe *offerres ei primum pacem,* Deut. 20, 10. Hafa ârna þanc đara, đe đû unc bude *have thanks for the kindnesses, which thou hast offered us,* Cd. 111; Th. 147, 7; Gen. 2435. [*Plat.* bêden *to command, offer: O. Sax.* biodan *to offer: O. Frs.* biada *id: Dut.* bieden *id: Ger.* bieten *id: M. H. Ger.* biuten *id: O. H. Ger.* biotan *id: Goth.* biudan *id: Dan.* byde *to bid, offer: Swed.* bjuda *id: O. Nrs.* bjóđa *id.*] DER. a-beódan, be-, bi-, for-, ge-, on-.

beódas; *pl. m. Dishes, plates, scales;* lances, Cot. 123. v. beód.

beód-bolla, an; *m. A table-bowl, a cup, bowl;* cupa, Som.

beód-clâþ, es; *m. A table-cloth, carpet, hanging;* gausape = γαυσάπης, Ælfc. Gr. 9, 2; Som. 8, 28.

beódende *commanding,* R. Ben. 5; *part. of* beódan.

beódendlîc gemet *the imperative mood.* v. be-beódendlîc gemet.

beód-ern, es; *n.* [beód *a table,* ern *a place*] *A refectory, a dining-room;* refectorium, Ælfc. Gl. 107; Som. 78, 94; Wrt. Voc. 58, 9.

beód-fers, es; *m.* [beód *a table,* fers *a verse*] *A song* or *hymn sung during meal-time;* ad mensam carmen, hymnus, Dial. 1, 19.

beód-gæst, es; *m. A guest at table;* mensæ consors, convictor, Andr. Kmbl. 2177; An. 1090.

beód-geneát, es; *m. A table-companion;* mensæ socius, convictor, Beo. Th. 691; B. 343: 3431; B. 1713.

beód-gereordu; *pl. n.* [beód *a table,* gereord *a feast*] *A table-meal, a feast;* convivium, Cd. 74; Th. 91, 27; Gen. 1518.

beód-hrægl, beód-rægl [beód *a table,* hrægl *clothing*] *A table-cloth;* gausape = γαυσάπης, Ælfc. Gl. 30; Som. 61, 61; Wrt. Voc. 26, 60.

beód-sceát, es; *m:* beód-scýte, es; *m. A table-cloth, table-napkin, hand-towel;* mantile, mappa, Cot. 136.

beód-wist, beód-wyst, e; *f.* [beód *a table,* wist *food*] *Food placed on a table, board, a table;* mensa:—Ðû gearcodest beforan mînre gesihþe beód *vel* beód-wyste *vel* mýsan *parasti in conspectu meo mensam,* Ps. Lamb. 22, 5.

beofer, beofor, es; *m. A beaver;* castor, Ælfc. Gr. 8; Som. 7, 13. v. befer.

Beofer-lic, Beofor-lic, es; *m.* [beofer, lic? = lie, leá, leáh, *q. v. Ric.* A. D. 1184, Beverli: *Brom.* 1330, Beverlith] BEVERLEY, *Yorkshire;* Beverlea in agro Eboracensi:—Hêr forþfêrde se hâlga biscop Iohannes, and his lîc resteþ [MS. restad] in Beoferlic *here,* A. D. 721, *the holy bishop John died, and his body resteth at Beverley,* Chr. 721; Erl. 45, 25; Th. 73, 15, col. 2; Beoforlic, col. 1.

beofian; *p.* ode; *pp.* od *To tremble, quake, be moved;* tremere, contremere, commoveri:—Beofaþ eal beorhte gesceaft *all the bright creation shall tremble,* Exon. 116 b; Th. 448, 22; Dôm. 58. Seó eorþe beofode *the earth trembled,* 24 b; Th. 70, 27; Cri. 1145. Beofaþ middangeard *the mid-earth shall quake,* 20 b; Th. 55, 12; Cri. 882. For his ansýne sceal eorþe beofian *commoveatur a facie ejus universa terra,* Ps. Th. 95, 9: 103, 30. v. bifian.

beofung, e; *f. A trembling, quaking;* tremor. DER. eorþ-beofung *an earthquake.* v. bifung.

beó-gang, es; *m. A swarm of bees;* examen, Cot. 15, 164.

beógol, beógul; *adj. Agreeing, consenting, bending wholly to;* consentiens. v. ge-býgel.

beo-hâta? Cd. 156; Th. 193, 27. v. beót-hâta.

beolone, an; *f. Henbane;* hyoscyamus niger:—Genim beolonan sǽd *take seed of henbane,* L. M. 1, 6; Lchdm. ii. 50, 17: 1, 2; Lchdm. ii. 38, 1: 1, 3; Lchdm. ii. 42, 15: 1, 63; Lchdm. ii. 136, 26: 3, 37; Lchdm. ii. 328, 23. v. belene.

beóm *am,* Exon. 30 a; Th. 91, 13; Cri. 1491. v. beón.

beóm *a beam,* Chr. 1137; Erl. 262, 13. v. beám.

beó-móder; *f. A* BEE-MOTHER, *queen-bee;* chosdrus? *vel* castros? Ælfc. Gl. 22; Som. 59, 104; Wrt. Voc. 23, 61.

BEÓN [bión], to beónne; *part.* beónde; ic beó [beóm], ðú bist, byst, he biþ, byþ, *pl.* beóþ; *impert.* beó, *pl.* beóþ; *subj.* beó, *pl.* beón *To* BE, *exist, become;* esse, fieri:—Hí ne tweódon fērende beón to ðam ēcan līfe *non dubitabant esse transituros ad vitam perpetuam,* Bd. 4, 16; S. 584, 38, 18. Ðe ðǽr beón noldon *who would not be there,* Byrht. Th. 137, 13; By. 185: Exon. 100 a; Th. 376, 29; Seel. 162: Cd. 24; Th. 31, 15; Gen. 485: Mt. Bos. 19, 21: Bt. 5, 3; Fox 12, 12: Ælfc. Gr. 25; Som. 26, 48. Ic ðæs folces beó hyrde *I am the people's pastor,* Cd. 106; Th. 139, 24; Gen. 2314. Ic beó gearo sōna *I shall be soon ready,* Beo. Th. 3655; B. 1825: Exon. 71 a; Th. 264, 17; Jul. 365: Andr. Kmbl. 144; An. 72. Ic beó hāl *I shall be safe,* Mt. Bos. 9, 21: Mk. Bos. 5, 28: Ex. 3, 12. Ðonne ic stille beóm *when I am still,* Exon. 102 b; Th. 387, 5; Rä. 4, 74: 72 a; Th. 268, 26; Jul. 438: Mt. Lind. Rush. Stv. 9, 21. Ðú āna bist eallra dēma *thou alone art judge of all,* Hy. 8, 38; Hy. Grn. ii. 291, 38: Bt. Met. Fox 24, 53; Met. 24, 27: Exon. 8 b; Th. 4, 24; Cri. 57: Cd. 26; Th. 34, 16; Gen. 538: Bd. 5, 19; S. 640, 43: Mk. Lind. War. 14, 70: Lk. Lind. Rush. War. 1, 76. Ðú yrre byst *tu terribilis es,* Ps. Th. 75, 5: 101, 24: Lk. Bos. 1, 76: Deut. 23, 22. Hiora birhtu ne biþ to gesettane *their brightness is not to be compared,* Bt. Met. Fox 6, 11; Met. 6, 6. Biþ ealles leás *he will be void of all,* Cd. 217; Th. 276, 1; Sat. 182: 109; Th. 144, 19; Gen. 2392: Beo. Th. 604; B. 299: Ps. Th. 118, 142: Andr. Kmbl. 3383; An. 1695: Mt. Bos. 5, 19, 22, 37: Ors. 1, 1; Bos. 20, 18: Bt. 37, 3; Fox 190, 15. Fela biþ *many there are,* Exon. 78 a; Th. 293, 14; Crä. 1: 26 a; Th. 76, 5; Cri. 1235. Ne byþ lang *it shall not be long,* Elen. Grm. 433: Beo. Th. 3529; B. 1762. Sēlre biþ ǽghwām *it is better for every one,* Andr. Kmbl. 640; An. 320: Ps. Th. 111, 9: Beo. Th. 2009; B. 1002: Mt. Bos. 5, 14, 19, 21, 22. Yldo beóþ on eorþan ǽghwæs cræftig *age is on earth powerful of everything,* Salm. Kmbl. 583; Sal. 291: Exon. 36 b; Th. 118, 27; Gū. 246. Ðǽr wit tū beóþ *where we two are,* Exon. 125 a; Th. 480, 21; Rä. 64, 5: Beo. Th. 3681; B. 1838: Cd. 133; Th. 168, 20; Gen. 2785: Hy. 7, 88; Hy. Grn. ii. 289, 88: Ors. 1, 1; Bos. 20, 21: Bd. 4, 16; S. 585, 2: Bt. 10; Fox 30, 14: Nicod. 17; Thw. 8, 23: Mt. Rush. Stv. 26, 31. Beó ðú sunum mīnum gedēfe *be thou gentle to my sons,* Beo. Th. 2457; B. 1226: Andr. Kmbl. 428; An. 214: Exon. 81 a; Th. 305, 18; Fä. 90: Cd. 229; Th. 310, 25; Sat. 733: Jn. Bos. 3, 2. Ne beóþ ge tō forhte *be not ye too terrified,* Andr. Kmbl. 3216; An. 1611: Ps. Th. 104, 4. Ne beó ic gescynded *non confundar,* Ps. Th. 118, 6. Beón ða oferhydegan ealle gescende *confundantur superbi,* Ps. Th. 118, 78: 148, 12. [*Orm.* beon; *pres.* beo, best, beoþ, beþ; *subj.* beo, be, ben: *Laym.* beon; *pres.* beo, beost, bist, beoþ, beþ, biþ, biðe; *subj.* beo: *O. Sax.* bium, bist: *O. Frs.* bem, bim, ben, bin: *Dut.* ben: *O. Dut.* bem: *Ger. M. H. Ger.* bin: *O. H. Ger.* pim: *Slav.* byti: *Zend* bū: *Sansk.* bhū, bhavāmi.] v. eom *I am,* wesan *to be.*

beón *bees,* Ps. Spl. 117, 12: L. R. S. 5; Th. i. 434, 35. v. beó.

beón, beónn *commanded, assembled; p. of* bannan.

beón-breád *bee-bread,* Ps. Spl. 18, 11. v. beó-breád.

beón-broþ, es; *n.* Perhaps *mead, a drink of water and honey mingled and boiled together;* melicratum, L. M. 2, 24; Lchdm. ii. 216, 12.

beónde *being,* Cot. 77; *part. of* beón.

be ongewyrhtum *freely;* gratis, Ps. Spl. C. 34, 8.

BEÓR, es; *m.* I. BEER, *nourishing* or *strong drink;* cerevisia, sicera. Beer, made from malted barley, was the favourite drink of the Anglo-Saxons. In their drinking parties, they pledged each other in large cups, round at the bottom, which must be emptied before they could be laid down, hence perhaps the name of a tumbler. We are speaking of the earliest times, for beer is mentioned in Beowulf:—Gebeótedon beóre druncne oret-mecgas, ðæt hie in beór-sele bīdan woldon Grendles gūðe *the sons of conflict, drunk with beer, promised that they would await in the beer-hall the attack of Grendel,* Beo. Th. 965; B. 480. Æt beóre *at the beer,* 4088; B. 2041. ☞ Beer was the common drink of the Anglo-Saxons, hence *a convivial party* was called Gebeórscipe, *q. v: a place of entertainment,* beórsele *a beer-hall,* or beórtūn *a beer-enclosure.* Hence also the other compounds, as beór-scealc *a beer-server,* beór-setl *a beer-bench* or SETTLE, and beór-þegu *a beer-serving.* The following remark seems to be as applicable to the Anglo-Saxons as to the Icelanders,—Öl heitir með mönnum, en með Ásum bjór *ale is called, by men and by gods,* BEER, Alvismál.—Beóre druncen *drunk with beer,* Beo. Th. 1066; B. 531: Exon. 72 b; Th. 271, 22; Jul. 486. He ne drincþ wīn ne beór *vinum et siceram non bibet,* Lk. Bos. 1, 15: Deut. 14, 26. Ðæt mon geselle twelf seoxtres beóras *that they give twelve sesters of beer,* Th. Diplm. A. D. 901–909; 158, 22. II. *a beverage made of honey and water, mead;* metheglin, hydromeli, ytis, *n.* = ὑδρόμελι, ydromellum, mulsum:—Beór *ydromellum,* Ælfc. Gl. 32; Som. 61, 114; Wrt. Voc. 27, 43. Beór *mulsum,* Ælfc. Gl. 32; Som. 61, 118; Wrt. Voc. 27, 46. [*Plat.* beer, *n: Frs.* biar, *n: Dut. Ger.* bier, *n: Icel.* bjór, bjórr, *m: O. H. Ger.* pier, *n: Sansk.* pā *to drink.*] DER. beór-hyrde, -scealc, -scipe, -sele, -setl, -þegu, -tūn: gebeór, -scīpe.

beora, an; *m. A grove;* lucus *vel* nemus, Ælfc. Gl. 110; Som. 79, 39; Wrt. Voc. 59, 11. v. bearo.

beoran *to bear:*—Ic sceal beoran *I shall bear,* Cd. 216; Th. 274, 22; Sat. 158: 217; Th. 277, 17; Sat. 206. v. beran.

beorc, e; *f.* I. *a birch-tree;* betula. v. birce, byrc. II. *the Anglo-Saxon Rune* ᛒ = b, the name of which letter in Anglo-Saxon is beorc *a birch-tree,* hence this Rune not only stands for the letter *b,* but for beorc *a birch-tree,* as,—ᛒ byþ blǽda leás *a birch-tree is void of fruit,* Hick. Thes. i. 135; Runic pm. 18; Kmbl. 342, 27.

BEORCAN, ic beorce, he byrcþ; *p.* bearc, *pl.* burcon; *pp.* borcen [*Icel.* barki, *m. guttur*]. I. *to make a sharp explosive sound;* latratum *vel* sonum edere. v. gebeorc. II. *to* BARK; latrare:—Ða dumban hūndas ne māgon beorcan. We sceolon beorcan and bodigan ðām lǽwedum *dumb dogs cannot bark. We ought to bark and preach to the laymen,* L. Ælfc. C. 23; Th. ii. 350, 34. Ic hwīlum beorce swā hūnd *I sometimes bark as a dog,* Exon. 106 b; Th. 406, 16; Rä. 25, 2. Hūnd byrcþ *canis latrat,* Ælfc. Gr. 22; Som. 24, 8. Ne mæg he fram hūndum beón borcen *he may not be barked at by dogs,* Herb. 67, 2; Lchdm. i. 170, 17. [*O. Nrs.* berkja.] DER. gebeorc, borcian.

beorcen *birchen;* tiliaceus [*Kil.* bercken]. v. bircen.

Beordan īg, e; *f.* [īg *an island,* beordan = bridan = bridum *with the young of birds*] BARDNEY *in Lincolnshire;* cœnobii locus in agro Lincolniensi, Som.

beorende *bringing forth; part. of* beoran.

beorg, beorh, biorg, biorh; *gen.* beorges; *dat.* beorge; *pl. nom. acc.* beorgas; *gen.* beorga; *dat.* beorgum; *m.* I. *a hill, mountain;* collis, mons:—On Sȳne beorg *on Sion's hill,* Exon. 20 b; Th. 54, 29; Cri. 876. Ōþ ða beorgas ðe man hǽt Alpis *to the mountains which they call the Alps,* Ors. 1, 1; Bos. 18, 44; 16, 17. Ǽlc mūnt and beorh byþ genyðerod *omnis mons et collis humiliabitur,* Lk. Bos. 3, 5. Æt ðæm beorge ðe man Athlans nemneþ *at the mountain which they call Atlas,* Ors. 1, 1; Bos. 16, 6. II. *a heap,* BURROW or *barrow, a heap of stones, place of burial;* tumulus:—Worhton mid stānum ānne steápne beorh him ofer *congregaverunt super eum acervum magnum lapidum,* Jos. 7, 26. Bæd ðæt ge geworhton in bǽlstede beorh ðone heán *he commanded* [*bade*] *that you should work the lofty barrow on the place of the funeral pile,* Beo. Th. 6186; B. 3097: 5606; B. 2807: Exon. 50 a; Th. 173, 26; Gū. 1166: 119 b; Th. 459, 31; Hö. 8. [*Laym.* berȝe: *Piers* bergh; *still used in the dialect of Yorkshire: Plat.* barg: *O. Sax.* berg: *O. Frs.* berch, birg: *Ger.* berg: *M. H. Ger.* berc: *O. H. Ger.* perac: *Goth.* bairga-hei *a mountainous district: Dan.* bjærg, *n: Swed.* berg, *n: O. Nrs.* berg, *n:* derived from beorgan.] DER. ge-beorg, -beorh, heáh-, mund-, sǽ-, sand-, stān-.

beorg, berg *a protection, refuge;* præsidium, refugium. DER. heáfod-beorg, ge-beorg, scūr-beorg: cin-berg.

BEORGAN; ic beorge, ðú byrgst, byrhst, he byrgeþ, byrgþ, byrhþ, *pl.* beorgaþ; *p.* ic, he bearg, bearh, ðú burge, *pl.* burgon; *impert.* beorg, beorh, *pl.* beorgaþ, beorge ge; *pp.* borgen; *v. a.* I. *cum dat. To save, protect, shelter, defend, fortify, spare, preserve;* servare, salvare, custodire, tueri, parcere:—Beorh ðīnum feore *salva animam tuam,* Gen. 19, 17. Woldon feore beorgan *they would save their lives,* Andr. Kmbl. 3075; An. 1540. Beorh me, Drihten, swā swā man byrhþ ðām æplum on his eágum mid his brǽwum *custodi me, Domine, ut pupillam oculi,* Ps. Th. 16, 8. Ðæt se bittra bryne beorgan sceolde ǽfæstum þrīm *that the bitter burning should spare the pious three,* Exon. 53 b; Th. 189, 10; Az. 57. II. *dat. of the pers. acc. of the thing* or *following* wið,—*To defend, secure, guard against, avoid;* defendere, arcere, cavere, vitare:—Hȳ him hryre burgon *they secured him from fall,* Exon. 43 a; Th. 145, 30; Gū. 702: 55 a; Th. 195, 21; Az. 159. Hȳ beorgaþ him bealonīþ *they guard themselves against baleful malice,* 44 b; Th. 150, 19; Gū. 781. Druncen beorg ðē *from drunkenness guard thyself,* 80 b; Th. 302, 10; Fä. 34. Ðæt preóstas beorgan wið ofer-druncen *that priests avoid* [*over-drinking*] *drunkenness,* L. Edg. C. 57; Th. ii. 256, 13. [*Orm.* berrȝhenn: *Plat.* bargen: *O. Sax.* gi-bergan: *M. H. Ger.* bergen: *O. H. Ger.* perkan, bergan: *Goth.* bairgan: *Dan.* bjerge: *Swed.* berga: *O. Nrs.* biarga: *Grm. Wrtbch.* i. 1507 refers to *Grk.* φράγνυμι, φάργνυμι *to hedge round, to secure.*] DER. be-beorgan, ge-, ymb-.

beorgan *to taste;* gustare:—Fēnix of ðām wyll-gespryngum brimcald beorgeþ æt baða gehwylcum *the Phœnix tastes ocean-cold* [*water*] *from the well-springs at every bath,* Exon. 57 b; Th. 205, 9; Ph. 110. v. byrgan.

Beorg-ford, Beorh-ford, es; *m.* [beorg *a hill,* ford *a ford;* collis ad vadum] BURFORD *in Oxfordshire:*—Hēr Cūþrēd, Wæst-Seaxna cining, gefeaht ðȳ xxii geára his rīces, æt Beorgforda [MS. Beorhforda], wið Æðelbald, Myrcena cing, and hine geflȳmde *here, in 752, Cuthred, king of the West-Saxons, fought in the twenty-second year of his reign, at Burford, with Æthelbald, king of the Mercians, and conquered him,* Chr. 752; Erl. 49, 13.

beorg-hleoþ, es; *n. A mountain-brow;* montis fastigium:—Ofer beorghleoða *over the mountain-brows,* Exon. 114 a; Th. 438, 27; Rä. 58, 2. v. beorh-hliþ.

beorg-seðel, es; *n. A mountain-dwelling;* habitaculum in monte:—He ongan beorgseðel būgan *he began to inhabit a mountain-dwelling*, Exon. 34 a; Th. 108, 15; Gū. 73.

beorh; *gen.* beorges; *m. A hill, mountain;* collis, mons:—Ǽlc mūnt and beorh byþ genyðerod *omnis mons et collis humiliabitur*, Lk. Bos. 3, 5. v. beorg.

beorh *save*, Ps. Th. 16, 8; *impert. of* beorgan.

beorh-hliþ, -hleoþ, es; *n. A mountain-height, mountain-brow;* montis clivus *vel* fastigium:—Under beorhhliðe *under the mountain-height*, Elen. Kmbl. 1572; El. 788: 2015; El. 1009. Wǽron beorhhliðu blōde bestēmed *the mountain-brows were besteamed with blood*, Cd. 166; Th. 206, 7; Exod. 448. Under beorhhleoðum *among the mountain-heights*, 98; Th. 130, 13; Gen. 2159.

beorh-stal, -stōl, es; *m.* [beorh *a hill*, stal *a place, seat, dwelling*] *A hill-seat, dwelling on a hill;* sedes super collem *vel* clivum. v. burg-stal.

beorh-stede, es; *m. A mountain-place, place on a mountain, a mountain, mound;* locus in monte, mons, collis:—On beorhstede *on the mound*, Exon. 60 a; Th. 217, 22; Ph. 284.

beorht, es; *n. Brightness, a glistening, light, sight, glance, twinkling;* splendor, lumen, lux:—Ðis leóhte beorht cymeþ morgna gehwām *this pure brightness cometh each morn*, Exon. 93 a; Th. 350, 6; Sch. 59. Onfēng ðam beorhte hire eágena *received the sight* [*full sight, sparkling*] *of her eyes*, Bd. 4, 10; S. 578, 2. Ðæt biþ an eágan beorht *that is in the twinkling of an eye*, Bd. 2, 13; S. 516, note 20. v. bearhtm.

BEORHT, berht, byrht, bryht; *adj.* BRIGHT, *light, clear, lucid, splendid, excellent;* splendidus, lucidus, coruscus, clarus, formosus:—Eall ðīn līchama biþ beorht *totum corpus tuum lucidum erit*, Mt. Bos. 6, 22. Beorht ēðles wlite *the land's bright beauty*, Exon. 27 b; Th. 82, 32; Cri. 1347. Beorht sumor *bright summer*, 54 b; Th. 191, 29; Az. 95. To ðære beorhtan byrg *to the bright city*, 15 a; Th. 33, 1; Cri. 519. Beorhte burhweallas beorhte scīnaþ *the lucid city-walls shine brightly*, Cd. 220; Th. 282, 31; Sat. 295. Ðā cwom sunnan beorhtra līg *then came a fire, brighter than the sun*, Elen. Kmbl. 2218; El. 1110. Hī mōdes eágan beorhtran gedōn *they make the mind's eye clearer*, Bt. Met. Fox 21, 54; Met. 21, 27. Sum hafaþ beorhte stefne *one has a clear voice*, Exon. 79 b; Th. 298, 32; Crä. 94. II. *bright, brilliant, magnificent, noble, glorious, sublime, divine, holy;* clarus, præclarus, eximius, augustus, divus, sanctus:—In ða eástor-tīd, on ðone beorhtan dæg *in the Easter-time, on that bright day*, Exon. 48 b; Th. 168, 17; Gū. 1079. Meotud ælmihtig, beorht cyning *Almighty God, noble king*, Andr. Kmbl. 1804; An. 905. Ne wolde him beorht fæder bearn ætniman *the glorious father* [*God*] *would not take the child from him*, Cd. 162; Th. 204, 4; Exod. 414. Se ān dēma is gestæððig and beorht *the only judge is steadfast and sublime*, Bt. 36, 2; Fox 174, 20: Exon. 14 b; Th. 30, 22; Cri. 483. Mid ðȳ beorhtan gebēde *with the holy prayer* [*the Lord's prayer*], Salm. Kmbl. 87; Sal. 43. [*Wyc.* bright: *Plat.* Brecht *a proper name, f: O. Sax.* berht, beraht: *Ger. preserved in proper names as* Bertha, Albrecht: *M. H. Ger.* berht: *O. H. Ger.* peraht: *Goth.* bairhts: *O. Nrs.* biartr: *Lat.* fulgeo, flagrare: *Grk.* φλέγειν *to burn*, from the *Sansk.* root bhrāj *to shine;* bhargas *splendour, brightness.*] DER. æl-beorht, eall-, efen-, gold-, heáfod-, heofon-, hīw-, rōdor-, sadol-, sigel-, sigor-, sun-, swegl-, þurh-, wlite-.

beorhtan, berhtan, byrhtan; *p.* te; *pp.* ed *To shine;* lucere, Ps. Th. 143, 7.

beorhte; *adv. Distinctly, clearly, lucidly, brightly;* clare:—He geseah Egypta heábyrig beorhte blīcan *he saw the Egyptians' cities brightly glitter*, Cd. 86; Th. 109, 13; Gen. 1822. Ðonne seó sunne beorhtost scīneþ *when the sun shines brightest*, Bt. 9; Fox 26, 15: Beo. Th. 3039; B. 1517.

beorht-hwīl, e; *f. A glance;* ictus oculi, Lye. v. bearhtm-hwīl.

beorhtian, beorhtigan; *p.* ode; *pp.* od. I. *to shine, brighten;* clarere:—Ðǽr his geearnunge oft miclum mægenum scīnaþ and beorhtigaþ *there his earnings often shine and brighten with great virtues*, Bd. 3, 19; S. 550, 17. II. *to sound clearly* or *loudly;* clare sonare:—Beorhtode bencswēg *the bench-noise sounded loudly*, Beo. Th. 2326; B. 1161.

beorht-līc; *adj. Bright, light, clear, lucid, splendid;* lucidus, clarus, splendidus, Runic pm. 6; Hick. Thes. i. 135; Kmbl. 340, 19: Ps. Th. 67, 3.

beorht-līce; *adv. Clearly, distinctly, splendidly;* clare, splendide:—Ðæt he beorhtlīce eall geseah *ut clare videret omnia*, Mk. Bos. 8, 25: Ps. Th. 118, 98: 147, 7.

beorhtm, es; *m. Tumult;* tumultus:—Hwǽr ahangen wæs heriges beorhtme rōdera waldend *where the Lord of glory was hung up by the tumult of the host*, Elen. Kmbl. 410; El. 205. v. breahtm *a noise*, brecan *to break.*

beorht-nes, byrht-nes, -ness, -nys, -nyss, e; *f.* [beorht *bright*] BRIGHTNESS, *clearness, splendour;* splendor, claritas, nitor:—Godes beorhtnes him ymbesceán *claritas Dei circumfulsit illos*, Lk. Bos. 2, 9: Ǽlfc. Gr. 36; Som. 38, 54: Ps. Th. 118, 130. Eágena beorhtnes *brightness of the eyes*, Herb. 31, 2; Lchdm. i. 128, 13: Hy. 7, 31; Hy. Grn. ii. 287, 31.

beorht-rōdor, es; *m. The bright firmament, heaven;* æther, Cd. 146; Th. 183, 19; Exod. 94.

beorhtu, beorhto, birhtu, byrhtu, e; *f. Brightness, splendour;* claritas, splendor:—Gif hæleþa hwilc mæg ǽfre ofsión heofones leóhtes hlūtre beorhto *if any man may ever behold the clear brightness of heaven's light*, Bt. Met. Fox 21, 78; Met. 21, 39.

beór-hyrde, es; *m. A beer-keeper, butler;* cerevisiæ custos, pincerna:—Sum biþ gewittig æt wīnþege, beórhyrde gōd *one is witty at wine-bibbing, a good beer-keeper*, Exon. 79 b; Th. 297, 28; Crä. 75.

BEORMA, an; *m:* bearm, es; *m. Barm, leaven, yeast, froth;* fermentum:—Se beorma awent ða gesceafta of heora gecynde *barm changes creatures from their nature*, Homl. Th. ii. 278, 21. Wistfullian on yfelnysse beorman *to feast on the barm of evil*, ii. 278, 25. Heofena rīce is gelīc ðam beorman *cœlorum regnum simile est fermento*, Mt. Bos. 13, 33: Lk. Bos. 13, 21. Nim ele and hunig and beorman *take oil and honey and barm*, Lchdm. i. 398, 6: Exon. 71 b; Th. 266, 11; Jul. 396. [*Plat. Dut.* barm, *m. fæx: Ger.* barme, bärme, *f: Dan. Swed.* bærme *dregs, lees, barm.*] v. and-, andbita.

Beormas; *gen.* a; *pl. m. The Biarmians.*—The Biarmians inhabited the country on the shores of the White Sea, north-west of the river Dwina. Alfred calls them Beormas. They were called Biarmians by Icelandic historians, and Permiaki by the Russians, and now Permians. In the Middle Ages, the Scandinavian pirates gave the name of Permia to the whole country between the White Sea and the Ural, Malte-Brun's Univer. Geog. vol. vi. p. 419. In an Icelandic MS. on geography, written in the 14th century, Beormia and two Cwenlands are located together. Kvenlönd II, ok ero þau norþr frá Bjarmalandi. Duæ Quenlandiæ, quæ ulterius quam Bjarmia boream versus extenduntur, Antiquitates Americanæ, p. 290.—Haldorson's Lexicon Islandico-Latino-Danicum, edited by Rask, has—'Biarmaland, Biarmia, quæ ob perpetuas nives albicatur, Bjarmeland, Permien. Biarmia ortum versus ad mare album vel gandvikam sita est:'—Fela spella him sǽdon ða Beormas, ǽgþer ge of hyra āgenum lande, ge of ðǽm landum, ðe ymb hȳ ūtan wǽran; ac he nyste hwæt ðæs sōðes wæs, forðæm he hit sylf ne geseah. Ða Finnas, him þuhte, and ða Beormas sprǽcon neáh ān geþeóde *the Biarmians told him many stories, both about their own country and about the countries which were around them; but he knew not what was true, because he did not see it himself. The Finns and the Biarmians, as it seemed to him, spoke nearly the same language*, Ors. 1, 1; Bos. 20, 11—15. Ða Beormas hæfdon swīðe well gebūn hyra land *the Biarmians had very well inhabited their land*, 1, 1; Bos. 20, 7.

beorn *children*, Th. Diplm. A. D. 830; 466, 5. v. bearn.

beorn *for* bearn *burned*, Beo. Th. 3764, note; B. 1880; *p. of* beornan.

BEORN, biorn, es; *m.* [this word is only used by poets]. I. *a man;* vir:—Se beorn on waruþe scip gemētte *the man found a ship on the strand*, Andr. Kmbl. 478; An. 239: 1203; An. 602. Boētius wæs beorn bōca *Boethius was a man skilled in books*, Bt. Met. Fox 1, 103; Met. 1, 52: Exon. 83 a; Th. 313, 22; Mōd. 4. Beornes blōde *with man's blood*, Bt. Met. Fox 8, 67; Met. 8, 34. Beornas Baðan nemnaþ *men name Bath*, Chr. 973; Erl. 124, 12; Edg. 5. Beornas geonge *young men*, Cd. 184; Th. 230, 13; Dan. 232. Beorna sēlost *the best of men*, 162; Th. 203, 10; Exod. 401: Bt. Met. Fox 21, 82; Met. 21, 41. II. *a prince, nobleman, chief, general, warrior, soldier;* princeps, vir nobilis, dux, miles:—Se beorn ageaf teóðan sceát *the prince gave a tenth portion*, Cd. 97; Th. 128, 1; Gen. 2120: 176; Th. 222, 3; Dan. 99. Þurh ðæs beornes cyme *through the chief's coming*, Exon. 15 b; Th. 33, 24; Cri. 530. He ðam beorne oncwæþ *he answered the warrior*, Byrht. Th. 138, 65; By. 245. Me on beáme beornas sticedon *soldiers pierced me on the cross*, Cd. 224; Th. 297, 1; Sat. 510. Beorna beáhgyfa *bracelet-giver of warriors* or *a rewarder of heroes*, Chr. 937; Erl. 112, 2; Edg. 30. III. *rich;* dives:—Beornum and þearfum *to rich and poor*, Runic pm. 12; Hick. Thes. i. 135; Kmbl. 341, 25. [*Dan. Swed. Icel.* björn, *m. a bear;* ursus.] DER. folc-beorn, gūþ-, sige-.

BEORNAN, byrnan; ic beorne, byrne, ðū beornest, beornst, byrnest, byrnst, he beorneþ, beornþ, byrneþ, byrnþ, *pl.* beornaþ; *p.* ic, he bearn, barn, born, ðū burne, *pl.* burnon; *pp.* bornen. I. *v. n. To* BURN, *be on fire;* ardere, exardere, comburi:—Ðonne beorneþ [byrneþ, Spl.] eorre his *cum exarserit ira ejus*, Ps. Surt. 2, 13. Se ðe ǽfre nū beorneþ on bendum *he who now ever burns in bonds*, Cd. 222; Th. 290, 12; Sat. 414. Bearn [MS. beorn] breóstsefa [*their*] *spirit burned*, Exon. 15 b; Th. 34, 10; Cri. 540. Heofoncandel barn *the heavenly candle burnt*, Cd. 148; Th. 184, 31; Exod. 115. Hreðer innan born *his spirit burned within*, Exon. 46 b; Th. 158, 18; Gū. 910. Him sorga burnon on breóstum *sorrows burned in their breasts*, Cd. 37; Th. 48, 17; Gen. 777. II. *v. trans. To* BURN; urere, comburere:—Swā fȳr wudu byrneþ *sicut ignis comburit silvas*, Ps. Th. 82, 10. [*O. Sax. M. H. Ger. O. H. Ger.* brinnan: *Ger.* brennen: *Swed. O. Nrs.* brenna.] DER. a-beornan, for-, ge-. v. bærnan, byrnan, on-brinnan.

beorn-cyning, es; *m. A king of men;* virorum rex:—Māðmas ic ðe, beorncyning, bringan wylle *I will bring thee treasures, king of men*, Beo. Th. 4302; B. 2148.

beorne, an; *f. A coat of mail;* lorica, Cod. Dipl. 716; A.D. 996–1006; Kmbl. iii. 351, 26. v. byrne.

Beornica ríce, es; *n:* mægþ, e; *f. The kingdom* or *province of the Bernicians, that part of Northumbria which lies between the river Tees and the Scottish sea* or *frith;* regnum *vel* provincia Berniciorum, a Tesi ad fretum Scoticum olim pertingens:—Oswio ðone óðerne dǽl Norþanhymbra ríces hæfde, ðæt is Beornica *Oswi possessed the other part of the Northumbrian kingdom, that is Bernicia,* Bd. 3, 14; S. 539, 35: 5, 14; S. 635, 6.

Beornice; *gen.* a; *dat.* um; *pl. m. The Bernicians;* Bernicii:—Man gehálgode twegen biscopas on his stal, Bosan to Derum and Eátan to Beornicum *two bishops were hallowed in his stead, Bosa over the Deirians and Eata over the Bernicians,* Chr. 678; Th. 61, 17, col. 1: Bd. 3, 24; S. 556, 45.

beorn-þreát, es; *m. A band of men* or *warriors;* virorum turma:—Monig beornþreát *many a band of warriors,* Exon. 96 a; Th. 358, 24.

beorn-wíga, an; *m.* [wíga *a warrior*] *A soldier, hero;* loricatus bellator, Menol. Fox 447; Men. 225.

beór-scealc, es; *m. A beer-server, a butler;* cerevisiæ minister:—Beórscealca sum *some one of the beer-servers,* Beo. Th. 2485; B. 1240.

beór-scipe *a feast.* v. gebeór-scipe.

beór-sele, biór-sele, es; *m. A beer-hall, feasting-hall, hall, mansion, palace;* cerevisiæ aula, convivis recipiendis locus, aula, mansio, palatium:—In [on] beórsele *in the beer-hall,* Beo. Th. 968; B. 482: 988; B. 492: Runic pm. 14; Hick. Thes. i. 135; Kmbl. 342, 5. Gesittaþ beórselas beorna *they shall inhabit the beer-halls of chieftains,* Cd. 170; Th. 214, 2; Exod. 563.

beór-setl, es; *n. A* BEER-SETTLE or *bench;* scamnum cerevisiam bibentium:—Ofer beórsetle [MS. -sele] *on the beer-bench,* Exon. 75 b; Th. 283, 28; Jul. 687.

beor-swinig; *adj.* [=bær-synnig] *Openly-wicked, a publican,* Lk. Rush. War. 19, 2. v. bær-synnig.

beorþ, berþ, byrþ, e; *f:* es; *n?* [beorþ *bears, from* beoran, *as* byrþ birþ *from* beran] *A* BIRTH, *the act of coming into life, the thing born;* nativitas, partus, fetus, Cot. 87. Found in the compounds berþ-estre, berþ-ling: v. also beorþor, beorþor-cwelm, -þínen; hyse-beorþor. [*O. Sax.* gi-burd, *f: O. Frs.* berthe, *f: O. H. Ger.* burt, *f: Goth.* ga-baurþs, *f: O. Nrs.* burðr, *m.*] v. ge-byrd.

beór-þegu, e; *f. A beer-receiving, beer-serving, beer-drinking;* cerevisiæ acceptio *vel* ministratio, cerevisiæ potatio:—Ðæt wæs biter beórþegu *that was a bitter beer-serving,* Andr. Grm. 1533; An. 1535. Æfter beórþege *after the beer-drinking,* Beo. Th. 234; B. 117: 1239; B. 617.

beorþor, byrþor, berþor, borþor, es; *n? Child-birth, that which is born, a fetus;* partus, fetus:—Æfter beorþre *after child-birth,* Med. ex Quadr. 4, 6; Lchdm. i. 344, 1: L. M. 3, 37; Lchdm. ii. 330, 1. Ðe him hyra beorþor losie *quibus fetus pereat,* Med. ex Quadr. 4, 4; Lchdm. i. 342, 21. Mid beorþre *fetu,* Cot. 87. DER. ge-beorþor, hyse-.

beorþor-cwelm, es; *m. A dead birth, an abortion, a miscarriage;* fetus mortuus *vel* abortivus, abortus, Cot. 11.

beorþor-þínen, e; *f. A midwife;* obstetrix [beorþor *child-birth,* þínen *a maid-servant*]. v. bróðor-þínen.

beór-tún, es; *m. A beer-hall;* convivis recipiendis locus *vel* aula, Mann. v. beór-sele.

Beorwic [wíc *a village* or *residence,* Beornica *of the Bernicians;* Berniciorum vicus] BERWICK *on Tweed,* Som.

beosmriende *deceiving,* Bd. 5, 12; S. 628, 31, note, = bysmriende. v. bysmerian.

BEÓST, býst, býsting, es; *m?* BIESTINGS, *the first milk of a cow after calving;* colostrum:—Beóst *biestings;* obesta, Ælfc. Gl. 31; Som. 61, 102. Býst *colostrum,* Ælfc. Gl. 31; Som. 61, 102. Býsting, þicce meolc *biest, biestings, thick milk,* Ælfc. Gl. 33; Som. 62, 20. [*Plat.* beest, beest-melk: *Dut. Ger.* biest: *O. H. Ger.* biost: *Goth.* beist.]

BEÓT, es; *n.* I. *a threatening, threat, command, menace;* comminatio, minæ:—He ne wæs ondredende ða beótunge [beót, MSS. B. C.] ðæs ealdormannes *minas principis non metuit,* Bd. 1, 7; S. 477, 23: Exon. 68 a; Th. 253, 7; Jul. 176. II. *peril;* periculum:—Ðenden [ðen, MS.] in ðam beóte wǽron *while they were in that peril,* Cd. 187; Th. 232, 25; Dan. 265. III. *a boasting, boasting promise, promise;* jactantia, promissio gloriosa, promissum:—Wæs him gylp forod, beót forborsten *their vaunt was broken, their boasting shattered,* Cd. 4; Th. 5, 11; Gen. 70. He beót eal wið ðé sóðe gelǽste *he truly fulfilled all his promise to thee,* Beo. Th. 1051; B. 523: 160; B. 80. [*Ger. M. H. Ger.* butze, *m. larva, terriculamenta.*] DER. ge-beót, word-.

beót *beat, hurt,* Cd. 187; Th. 232, 24; Dan. 265; *p. of* beátan.

beóþ *is, are, shall be,* Exon. 44 a; Th. 149, 28; Gú. 768: 96 b; Th. 361, 20; Wal. 22: Ælfc. Gr. 25; Som. 26, 14: Th. Diplm. A.D. 743–745; 28, 27. v. beón.

beóðan *are,* Mt. Rush. Stv. 5, 11, = beóþ. v. beón.

beót-háta, an; *m.* [MS. beo = beót, gebeót *a command, decree,* háta *a caller, commander*] *A commander, leader;* imperator, dux:—Ahleóp ðá fór hæleðum hilde calla, bald beót-háta bord upahóf *then the herald of war leaped before the warriors, the bold commander* [*Moses*] *upraised his shield,* Cd. 156; Th. 193, 27; Exod. 253.

beó-þeóf, es; *m. A thief* or *stealer of bees;* apum fur, L. Alf. pol. 9; Th. i. 68, 6.

beótian, beótigan; *p.* ode, ede; *pp.* od, ed [beót I. *a threatening*]. I. *to threaten;* minari, minitari:—Agustinus is sǽd, ðæt he beótigende fórecwǽde *Augustinus fertur minitans prædixisse,* Bd. 2, 2; S. 503, 29: Exon. 67 b; Th. 250, 35; Jul. 137. II. *to boast, vow, promise;* magna loqui, polliceri, spondere:—Swá he beótode ǽr wið his beáhgifan *as he boasted before towards his ring-giver,* Byrht. Th. 140, 18; By. 290. Ful oft wit beótedan, ðæt unc ne gedǽlde nemne deáþ ána *full oft we two vowed, that naught should part us save death alone,* Exon. 115 a; Th. 442, 32; Kl. 21.

beótian; *p.* ode; *pp.* od [*from* bót *a restoring, cure*] *To become* or *grow better;* melius fieri, convalescere:—Ðá sóna gefélde ic me beótiende and wyrpende *then I felt myself soon getting better and turning;* confestim me melius habere sentirem, Bd. 5, 6; S. 620, 12.

beót-líce; *adv. In a threatening manner, threateningly;* minaciter, Jos. 8, 10: Num. 14, 44.

beótung, e; *f. A threatening, raging;* comminatio, minæ:—Beótunge dǽdum gefyldon [*they*] *followed the threatening with deeds,* Bd. 1, 15; S. 483, 39. Ðá wæs his mód mid ðám beótungum gebreged *then was his mind frightened by the threatenings,* 2, 12; S. 513, 14: 1, 7; S. 477, 23. DER. ge-beótung.

beót-word, es; *n.* I. [beót I. *a threat*] *a word of threatening, threats;* minæ:—Beótwordum spræc folcágende *the people's lord spake in words of threatening,* Exon. 68 a; Th. 253, 24; Jul. 185. II. [beót III. *a boasting*] *a word of boasting;* jactationis verbum:—Beówulf beótwordum spræc *Beowulf spake in words of boasting,* Beo. Th. 5014; B. 2510.

Beó-wulf, es; *m.* [=Beado-wulf *a war-wolf,* = *Icel.* Böðúlfr *a war-wulf*] BEOWULF, a celebrated warrior of the Scyldings' race, a record of whose heroic deeds is given in the Anglo-Saxon poem bearing his name. It appears most probable that Beowulf was originally an Old Norse heathen Saga, written in the language common at the earliest age in Denmark, Sweden, and Norway, but now only spoken in Iceland. This Saga it is hoped may yet be found in some Swedish library. The story informs us that Hrothgar built a splendid palace at Heorot in the north of Jutland. This palace was soon made a scene of slaughter, in consequence of the nightly attacks of a monster called Grendel, who carried off at one time no less than thirty thanes, for the purpose of devouring them in his retreat. These dreadful visitations are continued during a period of twelve years. Intelligence of this calamity having reached the heroic Beowulf, a relation of Hrothgar, Beowulf resolves to rid the Danish land of this monster; and, in pursuance of this design, sails from home with a company of fifteen warriors. In terrific conflicts he kills Grendel and his mother.—It was the first heroic poem by any Germanic nation, and must have been translated into Anglo-Saxon by a Christian, as is evident by Grendel's mother being spoken of as a descendant of Cain, and numerous Christian allusions, when the Danish sovereignty in England was at its height, perhaps in the reign of Canute, about A.D. 1020. If it were originally written in the Old Norse or Icelandic the Saga would be called Böðúlfr, and the translator into Anglo-Saxon would naturally write it Beado-wulf contracted to Beó-wulf:—

Beówulf wæs bréme,	*Beowulf was renowned,*
blǽd wíde sprang	*the glory of Scyld's offspring*
Scyldes eaferan	*widely spread*
Scede-landum in,	*in the Swedish lands.*
Beo. Th. 35-38; B. 18, 19.	
Heorot [Hróþgár] eardode	[*Hrothgar*] *occupied Heorot,*
sincfáge seld [MS. sel],	*the richly variegated seat.*
Beo. Th. 335; B. 166.	
[Grendel] atol æglǽca;	[*Grendel*] *the fell wretch;*
him on eaxla wearþ	*a deadly wound was manifest*
syndolh sweotol,	*in his shoulder,*
seonowa onsprungon,	*the sinews sprang asunder,*
burston bánlocan:	*the bone-inclosures burst:*
Beówulfe wearþ	*to Beowulf*
gúþhréþ gyfeðe;	*warlike fierceness was given;*
scolde Grendel ðonan	*Grendel, death-sick,*
feorhseóc fleón,	*must thence flee.*
Beo. Th. 1636-1644; B. 816-820.	
Geféng ðá be eaxla	*The War-Goths' lord*
Gúþ-Geáta leód	*seized then by the shoulder*
Grendles módor.	*Grendel's mother.*
Brægd ðá beadwe heard,	*Then the fierce warrior dragged*
feorhgeníðlan,	*the mortal foe,*
ðæt heó on flet gebeáh:	*so that she bowed on the place:*
Beo. Th. 3078-3085; B. 1537-1540.	
-- bil eal þurhwód,	-- *the falchion passed through all*
fǽgne flǽschoman,	*her fated carcase,*
heó on flet gecrong.	*she sank on the ground.*
Beo. Th. 3139-3141; B. 1567, 1568.	

beó-wyrt, e; *f.* [beó *a bee*, wyrt *a plant*] BEE-WORT, *balm-mint, sweet flag;* apiastrum, acorus = ἄκορος, acorus calamus, Lin:—Beówyrt *apiastrum*, Cot. 12: Ælfc. Gl. 39; Som. 63, 55; Wrt. Voc. 30, 9. Ðeós wyrt, ðe man on Lēden *veneriam*, and on ūre geþeóde beówyrt, nemneþ, heó biþ cenned on begānum stōwum, and on wyrtbeddum, and on mǣdum *this plant, which in Latin is called* veneria, *and in our language bee-wort, is produced in cultivated places, and in wort-beds, and in meads*, Herb. 7, 1; Lchdm. i. 96, 21: L. M. 1, 26; Lchdm. ii. 68, 4.

be-pǣcan; *part.* be-pǣcende; *p.* be-pǣhte; *pp.* be-pǣht; *v. a.* [be *by*, pǣcan *to deceive*] *To deceive, entice, seduce, draw away;* decipere, pellicere, illudere, seducere:—Seó næddre bepǣhte me *serpens decepit me*, Gen. 3, 13: Mt. Bos. 2, 16: Ælfc. Gr. 28, 5; Som. 32, 1. Ic bepǣce oððe forlǣde *seduco*, 47; Som. 48, 53: Jud. 16, 5.

be-pǣcestre, an; *f. She who deceives, flatters,* or *entices, a harlot;* pellex, Ælfc. Gr. 28, 5; Som. 32, 1.

be-pǣcung, e; *f. Lewd practice;* lenocinium, Som. v. be-pǣcan.

be-pǣht *deceived*, Mt. Bos. 2, 16; *pp. of* be-pǣcan.

be-prenan, be-preðan *To wink;* nictare:—Tele nū ða lenge ðære hwīle, ðe ðū ðīn eáge on beprenan [bepreðan, Cott.] mǣge *compare now the length of the time, wherein thou mayest wink thine eye*, Bt. 18, 3; Fox 66, 7.

bēr, beer, e; *acc.* bēr, bēre; *f. A bed;* lectus, grabatus:—Nim bēr ðīn *tolle grabatum tuum*, Jn. Lind. War. 5, 12. Nim bēre ðīne, Jn. Rush. War. 5, 12. v. bǣr.

BERA, an; *m. A* BEAR; ursus:—Dauid gewylde ðone wīldan beran *David subdued the wild bear*, Ælfc. T. 13, 26. Eofor oððe beran onginnan *to attack a boar or bear*, Exon. 92 a; Th. 344, 21; Gn. Ex. 177. Sceall gyldan ān beran fel *shall pay one bear's skin*, Ors. 1, 1; Bos. 20, 37. Bera *ursus*, Ælfc. Gl. 21; Som. 59, 69: L. Ecg. P. iv. 28; Th. ii. 212, 22. [*Laym.* beore: *Plat.* baar, *m*: *Dut.* beer, *m*: *Ger.* bär, *m*: *M. H. Ger.* ber: *O. H. Ger.* pero: *Dan.* biörn, *c*: *Swed.* biörn, *m*: *O. Nrs.* björn, *m.*]

be-rǣcan *to cause to smoke*, Herb. 14, 2; Lchdm. i. 106, note 24. v. be-rēcan.

be-rǣdan; *p.* -rǣdde; *pp.* -rǣd [be- *dis-*, rǣdan *to possess*] *To dispossess, deprive of;* privare:—He hine rīces berǣdde *he deprived him of his realm*, Andr. Kmbl. 2653; An. 1328: 266; An. 133. Hie unscyldigne feore berǣddon *they deprived the guiltless of his life*, Elen. Kmbl. 993; El. 498. Earnulf hine berǣdde æt ðam rīce *Arnulf deprived him of the kingdom*, Chr. 887; Th. 156, 32, col. 1; 33, col. 2, 3: Bt. titl. 1; Fox x. 3.

be-rǣsan; *p.* de; *pp.* ed [be, rǣsan *to rush*] *To rush into;* irruere:—Ðā ðonne hie berǣsaþ on swelce weámōdnesse *when they then rush into such anger*, Past. 40, 5; Hat. MS. 55 a, 25: Gen. 14, 15.

be-rafan; *p.* -rōf, *pl.* -rōfon; *pp.* -rafen *To bereave;* spoliare:—Ða ðe Sodoma golde berōfon [MS. berofan] *those that had bereaved Sodom of gold*, Cd. 95; Th. 125, 13; Gen. 2078. v. be-reáfian, be-reófan.

BERAN, beoran, ic bere, beore, ðū birest, birst, byrst, he bireþ, byreþ, birþ, byrþ, *pl.* beraþ; *p.* ic, he bær, ðū bǣre, *pl.* bǣron; *pp.* boren; *v. a.* I. *to* BEAR, *carry, bring, bear* or *carry a sacrifice, offer, bear off, carry out, extend, wear, support, endure, suffer;* ferre, portare, afferre, offerre, deferre, proferre, extendere, gerere, tolerare:—Ðū eall þing birest *thou bearest all things*, Bt. Met. Fox 20, 551; Met. 20, 276. Heó gār bireþ *she beareth the javelin*, Salm. Kmbl. 876; Sal. 437. Eft byreþ ofer lagustreámas leófne mannan *shall bear back over the water-streams the beloved man*, Beo. Th. 598; B. 296: 4117; B. 2055. Se ðæt wicg byrþ *he whom the horse carries*, Elen. Kmbl. 2390; El. 1196. On handum hī beraþ ðē *in manibus portabunt te*, Ps. Spl. 90, 12. Secgas bǣron beorhte frætwa *the warriors bare bright arms*, Beo. Th. 432; B. 213. Ðe bǣron byrðena on ðises dæges hǣtan *qui portavimus pondus diei et æstus*, Mt. Bos. 20, 12: Lk. Bos. 11, 27. Ne bere ge sacc *nolite portare sacculum*, Lk. Bos. 10, 4: Ex. 22, 13. Him wæs ful boren *to him the cup was borne*, Beo. Th. 2388; B. 1192: Cd. 6; Th. 8, 7; Gen. 120. Deóflum onsægdnesse bær *dæmonibus hostias offerebat*, Bd. 1, 7; S. 477, 13. Byreþ blōdig wæl *will bear off my bloody corpse*, Beo. Th. 900; B. 448. Ða wiccungdōm wīdost bǣron *who carried the magic art furthest*, Cd. 178; Th. 223, 18; Dan. 121. Ðæt ða hætt beran mōston *that they might wear* [*bear*] *a hat*, Ors. 4, 10; Bos. 96, 20, 18. Ic nelle beran eówre gȳmeleáste *I will not endure your negligence*, L. Ælf. C. 1; Th. ii. 342, 10. II. *to* BEAR, *produce, bring forth;* facere, ferre, edere, parere:—Ǣlc gōd treów byrþ gōde wæstmas *every good tree produces* [facit] *good fruits*, Mt. Bos. 7, 17: 7, 18. Ðæt wæs deáþes beám se bær bitres fela *that was the tree of death which bare much of bitter*, Cd. 24; Th. 31, 2; Gen. 479: 30; Th. 40, 26; Gen. 645. Gif he to ðæm rīce wæs on rihte boren *if he to that kingdom was rightly born*, Bt. Met. Fox 26, 92; Met. 26, 46. [*O. Sax.* beran *ferre, portare*: *O. Frs.* bera: *O. H. Ger.* beran *ferre, parere, gignere, generare*: *Goth.* bairan; *p.* bar, *pl.* berum; *pp.* bairans *to bear, carry, bring, bear children*: *O. Nrs.* bera *ferre, portare, sustinere, tolerare*: *Grk.* φέρειν: *Sansk.* bhṛi *to bear, hence Goth.* barn *a child*: *A. Sax.* bearn *a child.*] DER. a-beran, æt-, be-, for-, fōr-, forþ-, ge-, in-, on-, ōþ-, to-, under-, up-, upa-, upge-, ymb-: berende, deáþ-, feorh-, gār-, helm-, leóht-, reord-, sǣd-, sweord-, un-, wæstm-: berend, gār-, gāst-, helm-, reord-, sāwl-, segn-, tācn-: berendnis, un-: bere, -ærn, -corn, -flōr, -gafol, -græs, -hlāf, -sǣd, -tūn, -wīc: berie, berige, berge, blæc-, byrig-, hind-, streów-, wīn-: brid: bearn, cyne-, dryht-, folc-, freó-, frum-, god-, hǣlu-, hūsul-, steóp-, sweostor-, world-, þryþ-: -cennung, -eácen, -eácnung, -gebyrdo, -gestreón, -lēst, -lufe, -myrþra, -teám: bearm, -clāþ, -rægl: beorma, bearm, gebyrman: byre: ge-byrd, -dæg, -tīd, -wiglǣre, -witega: byrde, ge-, in-: frum-byrdling, in-byrdling: beorþ, berþ, berþ-estre, berþ-ling; hyse-: beorþor, -cwelm, -þīnen, hyse-: bǣr, bǣran, bǣr-disc: bǣre, æppel-, corn-, cwealm-, cwyld-, hlīs-, horn-, leóht-, lust-, wæstm-, unwæstm-: bǣrnes, lust-, wæstm-, unwæstm-: byrðen, mægen-, sorg-, syn-: bora, cǣg-, horn-, mund-, rǣd-, rǣs-, segen-, sōþ-, sweord-, tācn-, wǣg-, wǣpen-, wīg-, wōþ-, wrōht-: boren, æðel-.

Beran burh; *gen.* burge; *dat.* byrig; *f.* [*Hunt.* Beranbiri: *Kni.* Banbyry] BANBURY, *Oxfordshire*:—Hēr Cynrīc and Ceawlin fuhton wið Brettas æt Beran byrig *here*, A. D. 556, *Cynric and Ceawlin fought with Britons at Banbury*, Chr. 556; Th. 30, 9, col. 1, 2, 3.

berbēna, æ; *f. Latin:* berbēne, an; *f. Vervain;* verbēna:—Berbēna [berbēne MS. H.] Ðeós wyrt, ðe man περιστερεών, and ōðrum naman berbēnam, nemneþ, heó ys culfron swīðe hīwcūþ. *Vervain. This plant, which they call vervain, and by another name verbena, in colour is very like to doves*, Herb. 67, 1; Lchdm. i. 170, 11-14. *Verbēna officinalis* is intended by the drawing in MS. V. and by περιστερεών in Dioskorides. v. æsc-þrote.

berc *a birch-tree;* betula:—Nim birc rinde *take birch-tree rind*, L. M. 3, 39; Lchdm. ii. 332, 9. v. birce.

bere, an; *f. A female bear;* ursa. v. bera *ursus*.

BERE, es; *m. Barley;* hordeum:—Ðā hēt he him bere sǣd bringan *inde hordeum jussit afferri*, Bd. 4, 28; S. 605, 36: Ælfc. Gr. 8; Som. 7, 63. Hira flex and hira beras [MS. bernas] wǣron fordōne *eorum linum et hordea læsa sunt*, Ex. 9, 31. [*Scot. and North E.* bear, bere *barley*: *Goth.* barizeins, *adj. made of barley;* hordeaceus: *Swed. Norw. Icel.* barr, *n.* I. *spina abietis vel pinus*, II. *granum, semen, hordeum.*]

bēre *a bed; acc. sing. of* bēr.

bere-ærn, ber-ern, beren, bern, bearn, es; *n. A barley-place, a corn-place, a barn;* horreum:—He gegaderaþ his hwǣte on his bern *congregabit triticum suum in horreum*, Mt. Bos. 3, 12: 13, 30. He feormaþ hys berenes flōre *purgabit aream suam*, Lk. Jun. 3, 17. Ic towurpe mīne berenu *destruam horrea mea*, 12, 18: 12, 24: Mt. Kmbl. Lind. 3, 12: Leo 103: 110.

be-reáfian, bi-reáfian, -reáfigean, ic -reáfige; *p.* -reáfode; *pp.* -reáfod; *v. a. To* BEREAVE, *seize, spoil, take away;* eripere, spoliare, privare:—Heó hit ne mæg his gewittes bereáfian *she cannot bereave it of its faculty*, Bt. 5, 3; Fox 12, 25. Hū mæg man hys fata hyne bereáfian *quomodo potest quisquam vasa ejus diripere?* Mt. Bos. 12, 29: Mk. Bos. 3, 27. Ic ondrēd, ðæt ðū me bereáfodest ðīnra dōhtra *timui, ne violenter auferres filias tuas*, Gen. 31, 31: 43, 18: 43, 14: Ors. 3, 7; Bos. 61, 16: Cd. 40; Th. 53, 11; Gen. 859.

be-rēcan, -rǣcan [rēcan *to smoke*] *To cause to smoke;* facere ut fumet aliquid:—Berēc hit on hātum ahsum *make it smoke on hot ashes*, Herb. 14, 2; Lchdm. i. 106, 17.

be-reccan, -reccean; *p.* -reahte, -rehte; *pp.* -reaht, -reht. I. *to relate, recount, explain;* narrare, exponere:—Nū wille we sum þing scortlīce eów be him bereccan *now will we relate to you shortly something concerning him*, Nat. S. Greg. Els. 3, 2. II. *to explain one's conduct, justify one's self;* se excusare, se purgare, accusatorum criminibus respondere:—Hī simle sēceaþ endleáse lādunga, hū hie bereccan [MS. C. bereccean] mǣgen *they always seek endless excuses, how they may justify themselves*, Past. 35, 2; Hat. MS. 45 a, 19. Him wæs lȳfnesse seald ðæt he him mōste scyldan and besecgan [MS. B. bereccan] *accepit locum se defendendi*, Bd. 5, 19; S. 640, 11, note. v. reccan.

bere-corn, es; *n.* [bere *barley*, corn *a grain*] BARLEY-CORN, *a grain of barley;* hordei granum:—IX bere-corna *nine barley-corns*, L. Ath. iv. 5; Th. i. 224, 11.

bere-flōr, es; *m. A* BARLEY-FLOOR, *barn-floor;* hordei area, Lk. Lind. Rush. War. 3, 17.

bere-gafol, es; *n. Barley-rent, a tribute of barley;* hordei tributum. One of the rents paid in kind, which, by the following enactment, is fixed at the rate of six pounds weight for every labourer employed in the barley harvest:—Mon sceal simle to bere-gafole agifan æt ānum wyrhtan six pūnd-wǣga *a man shall always give for barley-rent for every labourer six pounds weight*, L. In. 59; Th. i. 140, 5.

bere-græs, es; *n.* BARLEY-GRASS, *a farrago;* hordei gramen:—Grēne beregræs *green fodder for cattle* [farrago], Ælfc. Gl. 59; Som. 67, 124.

bere-hlāf, es; *m. A* BARLEY-LOAF, *barley-bread;* hordeaceus panis. v. bere *barley*, hlāf *a loaf*.

beren, es; *n.* [bere-ærn, *q. v.*] *A barley-place, a barn;* horreum, Lk. Jun. 3, 17: 12, 18, 24.

beren; *adj. Barley, made of barley;* hordeaceus:—Genim smæl beren mela *take fine barley-meal*, L. M. 1, 36; Lchdm. ii. 86, 24. Hæfþ fīf berene hlâfas *habet quinque panes hordeaceos*, Jn. Bos. 6, 9: 6, 13. v. bere.

beren, byren; *adj.* [bera *a bear*] *Belonging to a bear, ursine;* ursinus:—Se byrdesta sceall gyldan berenne cyrtel [kyrtel MS.] oððe yterenne *the richest must pay a bear- or otter-skin vest*, Ors. 1, 1; Bos. 20, 37.

berende; *part. Bearing, fruitful;* ferens, gerens, abundans, ferax:—Wîneard berende *vitis abundans*, Ps. Spl. 127, 3: Cot. 85. Berende bôh *germen*, Ælfc. Gl. 60; Som. 68, 32. v. beran.

berendlîc; *adj. Bearable, tolerable.* v. a-berendlîc.

berendnis, -niss, e; *f. Fertility, fruitfulness;* fertilitas, Leo 110. v. un-berendnis.

be-rênian; *p.* ode; *pp.* od [regnian, rênian *to arrange*] *To cause;* moliri:—Heó wroht berênodon [berenedon MS.] *they caused strife*, Cd. 149; Th. 187, 6; Exod. 147.

be-reófan, bi-reófan; *p.* -reáf, *pl.* -rufon; *pp.* -rofen [be, reófan *to reave, rob*] *To bereave, deprive;* spoliare, privare:—Since berofene *deprived of treasure*, Cd. 144; Th. 179, 30; Exod. 36: Beo. Th. 5855; B. 2931.

be-reótan; *p.* -reát, *pl.* -ruton; *pp.* -roten *To deplore;* deplorare:—Æðelinges deáþ bereótan *to deplore the death of the noble*, Exon. 119 b; Th. 459, 27; Hö. 6.

ber-ern *a barley-place, a barn;* horreum, Mt. Kmbl. Lind. 3, 12. v. bere-ærn.

bere-sæd, es; *n. Barley-seed, barley;* hordeum, Bd. 4, 28; S. 605, 36. v. bere.

bereþ *bears, brings forth, produces, 3rd pres. of* beran, Mt. Rush. Stv. 1, 21: Hick. Thes. i. 135; Runic pm. 18; Kmbl. 342, 28.

bere-tûn, es; *m.* [bere *barley, corn;* tûn *an inclosure, a place shut in*] *A barley-inclosure, court-yard, threshing-floor, corn-farm, grange, corn-village*, BARTON; hordei area, villa frumentaria. 'BARTON, *Prædium dominicum*, vel *terræ* quas vocant *Dominicales*, hoc est, quas in distributione manerii dominus non elocavit hæreditarie, sed alendæ familiæ suæ causâ propriis manibus reservavit: *Dominicum*, Gallice *Domaine*. Vox in Devonia, inquit Spelmannus, et plaga Angliæ Occidentali bene nota,' Du Cange Glos:—Þerh-clǣnsade beretûn his *permundavit aream suam*, Mt. Kmbl. Lind. 3, 12.

bere-wîc, es; *n. A barley-village, a corn-village;* hordeaceus *vel* frumentarius vicus, Th. Diplm. A. D. 1060; 382, 12: A. D. 1093; 443, 31. v. bere-tûn.

berg *a hill, mountain*, Som. DER. berg-ælfen. v. beorg.

berg-ælfen *mountain-elves;* oreades. v. ælf, -ælfen.

bergan *to taste;* gustare:—Ða ðe ne bergaþ deáþ *qui non gustabûnt mortem*, Mt. Kmbl. Rush. 16, 28. v. byrgan.

berge, an; *f. A berry, grape*, Deut. 23, 24. v. berie II.

bergels-leóþ, es; *n. A burial ode;* sepulcrale carmen, Leo 116. v. byrgen-leóþ.

bergel-song, es; *m. A burial song;* sepulcralis cantus, Leo 116. v. byrgen-song.

bergena *of berries*, Deut. 23, 24; *g. pl. of* berie.

Berghâm-styde, es; *m.* BERHAM, *near Canterbury:*—In ðære stôwe, ðý hâtte Berghâmstyde *in the place which is called Berham*, L. Wih. pref; Th. i. 36, 6.

bergyls, es; *m. A burial-place, a sepulchre;* sepulcrum, Coll. Monast. Th. 32, 33. v. byrgels.

berh *for* bearh *shunned;* vitavit, Bd. 2, 12; S. 513, 28; *p. of* beorgan.

berht; *adj. Bright;* splendidus, clarus, Bt. Met. Fox 22, 43; Met. 22, 22. v. beorht.

berhtan *to shine;* lucere. DER. ge-berhtan. v. beorhtan.

Berhte, an; *f. Bertha;* Bercta, *the daughter of Cariberht, king of Paris*, and granddaughter of Clotaire, king of the Franks and Burgundians. *In the year* 570, *she married Æðelbryht, king of Kent.* By the queen's Christian conduct, the heathen predilections of the king were removed, and the way made clear for the preaching of Augustine in 597. v. Æðelbryht:—Ǣr ðam, becom hlîsa to him ðære cristenan ǣfestnysse, for ðon he cristen wîf hæfde, seó wæs him forgifen of Francena cyningcynne, Berhte wæs hâten. Ðæt wîf he onfêng fram hire yldrum ðære arêdnesse, ðæt heó his leáfnysse hæfde ðæt heó ðone þeáw ðæs cristenan geleáfan, and hire ǣfestnysse, ungewemmedne healdan môste, mid ðý biscop, ðone ðe hî hire to fultume ðæs geleáfan sealdon, ðæs nama wæs Leodheard *before that, a report of the Christian religion had come to him* [*Æðelbryht*] *for he had a Christian wife, who was given to him from the royal kin of the Franks, her name was Bertha. He received his wife from her parents on condition, that she should have his leave that she might hold the manner of the Christian belief, and of her religion, unspotted, with the bishop, whose name was Liudhard, whom they gave her for the help of that faith*, Bd. 1, 25; S. 486, 30–36.

berhtm-hwæt; *adj. Swift as an eye-blink;* celer ut oculi nictus:—Ðec lîgetu blâce, berhtmhwate ða ðec bletsige *the pale lightnings, swift as an eye-blink, these shall bless thee*, Cd. 192; Th. 240, 3; Dan. 381. v. bearhtm.

berhtra, *acc.* berhtre *brighter*, Bt. Met. Fox 22, 43; Met. 22, 22; *comp. of* berht, beorht, *q. v.*

berian *berries*, Ælfc. Gl. 47; Som. 65, 30; *pl. of* berie.

berian; *p.* ode, ede; *pp.* od [bær *bare*] *To bare, make naked, expose, exhibit, make a shew of;* nudare, denudare, in medium proferre, ostentare:—Benc-þelu beredon *they made bare the bench-floor*, Beo. Th. 2482; B. 1239. Ða ðe me fôr werode wisdôm bereþ *who to me make a shew of wisdom before the people*, Cd. 179; Th. 224, 27; Dan. 142. v. barenian, a-barian.

berian *to taste.* v. bergan, byrgan, on-berian.

berian = byrian *to happen.* DER. ge-berian.

be-rîdan, he -rît; *p.* -râd, *pl.* -ridon; *pp.* -riden; *v. a.* I. *to ride round, to surround, besiege;* perequitare, præcingere:—Ðæt he his gefân berîde *that he besiege his enemy*, L. Alf. pol. 42; Th. i. 90, 4. II. *to ride after, pursue;* persequi:—Ðâ berâd mon ðæt wîf *then they pursued the wife*, Chr. 901; Ing. 125, 14. He hine berâd *he rode after him*, 755; Ing. 70, 1.

BERIE, berge, berige, berigie, an; *f.* I. *a* BERRY; bacca:—Berian *berries*, Cot. 36. Bergan *berries;* baccæ, Cot. 23. Nym wînberian, ðe beóþ acende æfter ôðre berigian *take grapes, which are formed after other berries*, Lchdm. iii. 114, 5. II. *a grape;* uva. *Though* wîn-berie, *q. v. a wine-berry, is generally used in Anglo-Saxon for* a grape, *yet* berge, berige *are sometimes found, as*,—Gif ðû gange binnan ðînes freóndes wîneard, et ðæra bergena swâ fela, swâ ðû wylle, and ne ber ðû nâ mâ ût mid ðê *if thou shalt go within thy friend's vineyard, eat as many of the grapes as thou wilt, and carry not out with thee any more*, Deut. 23, 24. Beóþ ðînes wîfes wêlan gelîce swâ on wîngearde weaxen berigean, and on ðînes hûses hwommum genihtsum *the riches of thy wife shall be like as grapes may grow in a vineyard, and abundant on the corners of thy house*, Ps. Th. 127, 3. [*O. Sax.* beri, *n: Dut.* bes, *f: O. H. Ger.* beri, *n: Goth.* basi, *n: O. Nrs.* ber, *n.* The *Goth. Plat.* and *Dut.*, says Grimm [i. 1243], do not allow us to derive these words from the root of *Goth.* bairan, *A. Sax.* beran *to bear, but it is probably connected with* bær *bare, naked, signifying the bare fruit, which can be eaten immediately.* Bopp derives the *Teutonic* words and the *Lat.* bacca from *Sansk.* bhaksh *edere;* so the *Goth.* basi = bhakshya *cibus, eatable fruit.*] DER. blæc-berie, byrig-, hind-, streów-, streáw-, wîn- [-berie, -berge, -berige, -berigie].

berig *to a city*, Wrt. Voc. 84, 45, = byrig; *dat. of* burh.

berig-drenc, es; *m.* [berige *a berry*, drenc *a drink*] *Drink made of mulberries;* diamoron, Wrt. Voc. 20, 23.

berige, an; *f. A berry, grape*, Ps. Th. 127, 3. v. berie II.

berigea, an; *m. A surety*, L. H. E. 6; Th. i. 30, 5. v. byriga.

berigean *berries, grapes*, Ps. Th. 127, 3; *nom. pl. of* berige. v. berie.

berigie *a berry*, Lchdm. iii. 114, 5. v. berie I.

be-rindan; *p.* de; *pp.* ed [be *off*, rind *the bark*] *To bark, peel* or *strip off the bark;* decorticare:—Berinde *decorticavit*, Cot. 62.

be-riówsian *to repent*, Ælfc. Gr. 33, MS. D; Som. 37, 22. v. behreówsian.

bern, es; *n. A barn;* horreum:—Nabbaþ ða hrefnas hêddern ne bern *the ravens have not store-house nor barn* [cellarium neque horreum], Lk. Bos. 12, 24: 12, 18: 3, 17: Mt. Bos. 3, 12: 13, 30. Bern *horreum*, Ælfc. Gl. 109; Som. 78, 131. v. bere-ærn.

bernan *to burn;* ardere, Ælfc. Gr. 35; Som. 38, 5. v. beornan.

berne-lâc, es; *n. A burnt offering;* holocaustum:—Ic ðê bernelâc brengan môste *I must bring thee a burnt offering*, Ps. C. 50, 123; Ps. Grn. ii. 279, 123.

bernes *a burning*, Bd. 4, 21; S. 590, 21. v. bærnes.

bernet, bernett, es; *n. A burning;* incendium, R. Ben. interl. 28. v. bærnet.

berning, e; *f. A burning;* combustio, ustio, Som. Lye. v. bærning.

be-rofen *bereaved*, Beo. Th. 5855; B. 2931. v. be-reófan.

bêron *might bear, carry, bring, for* bǣren, *perf. subj. of* beran, Byrht. Th. 133, 49; By. 67.

be-rôwan; *p.* -reów, *pl.* -reówon; *pp.* -rôwen *To row round;* remigando circumnavigare, Chr. 897; Th. 176, 41.

berst *loss;* damnum, malum, ruina, Lupi Serm. i. 2: Wulfstani Archiepiscopi Ebor. Admonitio sive Paraenesis, 8. *etc.* DER. berstan. v. byrst.

BERSTAN; *part.* berstende; ic berste, ðû birst, he birsteþ, biersteþ, birst, byrst, bierst, *pl.* berstaþ; *p.* ic, he bærst, ðû burste, *pl.* burston; *pp.* borsten. I. *to* BURST, *break, fail, fall;* cum fragore dissilire, corruere, rumpi, frangi:—Heofonas berstaþ *the heavens burst*, Exon. 21 b; Th. 58, 10; Cri. 933. Burston bân-locan *the bone-inclosures burst*, Beo. Th. 1640; B. 818. Wǣgas burston *the waves broke*, Cd. 167; Th. 208, 15; Exod. 483. Ðâ burston ða weallas *muri illico corruerunt*, Jos. 6, 20: Ors. 1, 7; Bos. 29, 38. Gif him âþ burste *if an oath failed them*, L. Ed. 3; Th. i. 160, 20. II. *to make the noise of a bursting* or *breaking, to crash, dash, crack;* fragorem edere, sonare, crepare:—Brim berstende blôd-egesan hweóp *the dashing sea threatened bloody horrors*, Cd. 166; Th. 208, 2; Exod. 477. Fingras burston *his fingers cracked*, Beo. Th. 1525; B. 760. [*Laym.* bersten: *Wyc.* berste, breste: *Plat.*

barsten: *O. Sax.* brestan: *O. Frs.* bersta: *Dut. Ger.* bersten: *M. H. Ger.* bresten: *O. H. Ger.* brestan: *Dan.* bröste: *Swed.* brista: *O. Nrs.* bresta.] DER. a-berstan, æt-, for-, óþ-, to-, út-.

bersting, e; *f. A* BURSTING, *rent;* ruptura. DER. múþ-bersting, *q.v.*

berþ *a birth.* v. berþ-estre, berþ-ling, beorþ.

Berþa *Bertha;* Bercta, *Lat. f. the queen of Æðelbryht, king of Kent.* v. Berhte.

berðen, e; *f. A burthen, load;* sarcina:—Seám *vel* berðen *sarcina,* Wrt. Voc. 16, 27. v. byrðen.

berþ-estre, an; *f. A bearer of children;* genetrix, Leo 110. v. -estre.

berþ-ling, es; *m. Child-birth.* v. hyse-berþling.

berþor *child-birth.* v. beorþor, hyse-beorþor.

bert-hwíl *a moment;* momentum, R. Ben. 5. v. beorht-hwíl.

berwe; *dat. of* bearo *a grove, q. v.*

be-rýfan [= be-reófan] *to bereave;* spoliare, privare:—Ðá hí þohton þeóden-stóles rícne berýfan *then they thought to bereave the powerful of his throne,* Exon. 84 a; Th. 317, 9; Mód. 63. DER. reófan *to reave, rob, bereave.*

be-rýpan; *p.* -rýpde, -rýpte, *pl.* -rýpton; *pp.* -rýped, -rýpt *To spoil;* spoliare:—Berýpton, Bt. Met. Fox 2, 23; Met. 2, 12. v. rýpan *to rip, tear.*

be-sacan; *p.* -sóc, *pl.* -sócon; *pp.* -sacen *To dispute about anything;* in controversiam vocare. DER. un-besacen. v. sacan.

be-sæncan; *p.* -sæncte; *pp.* -sænct *to sink;* mergere, L. Ælf. P. 13; Th. ii. 368, 27. v. sencan.

be-sænct *sunk;* mersus; *pp. of* be-sæncan.

be-sæt, be-sǽton *besieged,* Ors. 1, 14; Bos. 37, 15; *p. of* be-sittan.

be-sanc *sank;* submersit, Ors. 3, 11; Bos. 75, 32; *p. of* be-sincan.

be-sárgian; *p.* ode; *pp.* od *To lament, bewail, to mourn* or *be sorry for, to condole;* lamentari, condolere, compati, deflere:—Ic besárgige *compatior,* Ælfc. Gr. 29; Som. 33, 52: Ælfc. T. 42, 1: Scint. 45, 50.

be-sárgung, e; *f. A sorrowing,* Hymn. Surt. 126, 24. v. sárgung.

be-sárigende *condoling.* v. be-sárgian, sárgian.

be-sáwan *to sow;* conserere. v. sáwan.

be-sáwe, *pl.* -sáwen *looked,* Bt. 35, 6; Fox 170, 9; *p. subj. of* be-seón.

be-scær, -scear, *pl.* -scǽron, -sceáron *sheared, shaved; p. of* be-sceran.

be-sceadan; *p.* ede; *pp.* ed *To shadow;* obumbrare:—For hwám besceadeþ heó múntas and móras *why shadoweth it mountains and moors?* Salm. Kmbl. 680; Sal. 339. v. sceadian, ofer-.

be-sceáden *separated,* L. E. I. 32; Th. ii. 430, 9; *pp. of* be-sceádan.

be-sceáf *cast,* Andr. Kmbl. 2384; An. 1193; *p. of* be-scúfan.

be-sceát *shot into, precipitated one's self,* Ors. 3, 3; Bos. 56, 5; *p. of* be-sceótan.

be-sceáwian; *p.* ode; *pp.* od *To look round upon, look on, consider, regard, watch;* circumspicere, intueri, considerare, respicere, perscrutari, providere:—Hí besceáwigende *circumspiciens eos,* Mk. Bos. 3, 5. Ic onlócige, oððe ic besceáwige *intueor,* Ælfc. Gr. 27; Som. 29, 60. Besceáwiaþ æcyres lílian *considerate lilia agri,* Mt. Bos. 6, 28. Ðú ne besceáwast nánes mannes hád *non respicis personam hominum,* Mt. Bos. 22, 16. Ðæt he Alexandres [wisan] besceáwode *that he might watch Alexander's conduct,* Ors. 4, 5; Bos. 82, 22: R. Ben. 55. DER. sceáwian.

be-sceáwigere, be-sceáwere *a beholder;* spectator, Som.

be-sceáwodnes, -ness, e; *f. A seeing, vision, sight;* visio, Ps. Spl. T. 9, 11.

be-scencan *to give to drink.* v. bi-scencan.

be-sceoren *shorn,* Bd. 5, 7; S. 621, 15, = be-scoren; *pp. of* be-sceran.

be-sceótan; he -sceóteþ, -scýt; *p.* -sceát, *pl.* -scuton; *pp.* -scoten *To shoot into, inject, precipitate one's self, to be sent, go;* injicere, se præcipitare, mitti, ire:—Ne bescýt se deófol nǽfre swá yfel geþóht in to ðám men *nunquam diabolus tam pravas cogitationes in hominem injicit,* Alb. resp. 40. Curtius besceát *Curtius se præcipitavit,* Ors. 3, 3; Bos. 56, 5. Ðæt hí on grúnd ne bescuton *ut in abyssum ne irent,* Lk. Bos. 8, 31.

be-sceran, bi-sceran, -sciran, -scyran; *p.* -scær, -scear, *pl.* -scǽron, -sceáron; *pp.* -scoren *To shear off, to shave, cut off;* attondere, amputare, præcidere:—Hý eall heora heáfod besceáron *they all shaved their heads,* Ors. 4, 11; Bos. 96, 37; capitibus rasis, Ors. Hav. 4, 20; p. 270, 5. Ðæt he to preóste bescoren beón mihte *that he might be shorn as a priest,* Bd. 4, 1; S. 564, 24. Iulianus ðeáh to preóste bescoren wǽre *though Julian had been shorn for a priest,* Homl. Th. i. 448, 29. Ic næs nǽfre ge-efsod ne nǽfre bescoren, and gif ic beó bescoren, ðonne beó ic unmihtig óðrum mannum gelíc *ferrum nunquam ascendit super caput meum, si rasum fuerit caput meum, recedet a me fortitudo mea et deficiam eroque sicut ceteri homines,* Jud. 16, 17. Man ne mót hine besciran *a man must not shear him,* Jud. 13, 5. Gif he hine to preóste bescire [bescyre MSS. B. H.], mid xxx scillinga gebéte *if he shave him like a priest, let him make amends with thirty shillings,* L. Alf. pol. 35; Th. i. 84, 7, 9. Biscær, Reim. 26. v. sceran.

be-scerian, -scirian, -scyrian, -scyrigan; *p.* ede; *pp.* ed *To deprive, separate, defraud;* privare, separare, fraudare:—Hér, A. D. 821, wærþ Ceolwulf his ríces bescered *here Ceolwulf was deprived of his kingdom,* Chr. 821; Erl. 63, 10. Ðonne ic bescired beó fram túnscíre *when I am deprived of my stewardship,* Lk. Bos. 16, 4. Ðone we sceoldan bescyrian ðære onfangenan ealdorlícnysse *quem nos privare auctoritate percepta debemus,* Bd. 1, 27; S. 492, 14. Ne syndon hí to bescyriane gemǽnsumnysse Cristes líchoman and blódes *non corporis ac sanguinis Domini communione privandi sunt,* 1, 27; S. 491, 27. He bescyraþ hine sylfne fram ðære écan méde *he separates himself from the everlasting reward,* Homl. Th. ii. 534, 34. Ná bescyreþ of gódum hí ða gangendan on unscyldignysse *non privabit bonis eos qui ambulant in innocentia,* Ps. Spl. 83, 13. Mec bescyrede Scyppend eallum *the Creator deprived me of all,* Exon. 111 b; Th. 427, 34; Rä. 41, 101. He wæs eallra his lima þénunge bescyred *he was deprived of the use of all his limbs,* Bd. 5, 5; S. 617, 38. He hæfþ us ðæs leóhtes bescyred *he hath deprived us of the light,* Cd. 21; Th. 25, 12; Gen. 392: 21; Th. 25, 16; Gen. 394. Ðæt ic meahte ongitan Godes ágen bearn, scyldum bescyredne *that I might comprehend God's own child, separated from protections [shields],* Exon. 83 b; Th. 314, 2; Mód. 8. Wuldre bescyrede *from glory separated,* Andr. Kmbl. 3235; An. 1620: Cd. 221; Th. 285, 26; Sat. 343: Exon. 8 a; Th. 3, 7; Cri. 32: 45 b; Th. 155, 29; Gú. 867: Ps. Th. 77, 29. Syndon hí to bescyriganne Cristes líchoman and blódes *corporis et sanguinis Domini privandi sunt,* Bd. 1, 27; S. 491, 34. Híg ne synt bepǽhte oððe bescyrede fram heora gewilnunge *non sunt fraudati a desiderio suo,* Ps. Lamb. 77, 30; thei weren not defraudid of her desier, Wyc. v. bi-scerian.

be-scerwan *to deprive;* privare:—Ne ðínra árna me bescerwe *do not deprive me of thy mercy,* Ps. C. 50, 98; Ps. Grn. ii. 279, 98.

be-sciered *deprived,* Chr. 821; Erl. 62, 11, = be-scired; *pp. of* be-scirian.

be-scínan; *p.* -scán; *pp.* -scinen *To shine upon, illuminate;* collustrare, illuminare:—Mec heaðosigel bescíneþ *the glorious sun shines upon me,* Exon. 126 b; Th. 486, 18; Rä. 72, 17.

be-sciran *to shear, shave,* Jud. 13, 5: L. Alf. pol. 35; Th. i. 84, 7, 9. v. be-sceran.

be-scirian *to deprive,* Lk. Bos. 16, 4. v. be-scerian.

be-scítan; *p.* -scát; *pp.* -sciten *To bedaub;* cacare:—Besciten *caccabatum,* Cot. 189. v. scítan.

be-scofen *thrust off, precipitated,* Mk. Bos. 5, 13; *pp. of* be-scúfan.

be-scoren *shorn, shaved,* Jud. 16, 17; *pp. of* be-sceran.

be-screádian *to cut off;* descindere. DER. screádian.

be-screopan; *p.* -scræp, *pl.* -scrǽpon; *pp.* -screpen *To scrape,* BESCRAPE, *make level;* radere. v. screopan.

be-scrifen; *part. Confessed, that hath undergone confession;* confessus. v. scrífan.

be-scúfan; *p.* -sceáf, *pl.* -scufon; *pp.* -scofen; *v. a. To shove, thrust, cast, hurl* or *throw, to precipitate;* intrudere, immittere, detrudere, præcipitare:—Hét hine ðá niman, and ðǽr on bescúfan *then ordered to take him, and to shove him in there,* Ors. 1, 12; Bos. 36, 38. Wá biþ ðǽm, ðe sceal sáwle bescúfan in fýres fæðm *woe shall be to him, who shall thrust a soul into the fire's embrace,* Beo. Th. 371; B. 184. Se mihtiga cyning niðer bescúfeþ in súsla grúnd *the mighty king casteth thee down into the abyss of sulphur,* Elen. Kmbl. 1883; El. 943. Ðé se Ælmihtiga heolstor besceáf *the Almighty cast thee into darkness,* Andr. Kmbl. 2384; An. 1193. Seó heord wearþ on sǽ bescofen *grex precipitatus est in mare,* Mk. Bos. 5, 13. v. scúfan, sceófan.

be-scuton *went,* Lk. Bos. 8, 31; *p. pl. of* be-sceótan.

be-scyldigian; *p.* ode; *pp.* od *To accuse;* accusare, criminari. v. scyldigian, ge-.

be-scylian; *p.* ede; *pp.* ed *To look upon, to regard;* intueri:—Ðú bescylst mid óðre eágan on ða heofenlícan þing, mid óðre ðú lócast on ðás eorþlícan *thou lookest with one eye on the heavenly things, and with the other thou lookest on these earthly [things],* Bt. 38, 5; Fox 206, 18.

be-scyran *to shave,* L. Alf. pol. 35; Th. i. 84, 7, 9, MSS. B. H. v. be-sceran.

be-scyre *should shave;* attonderet, L. Alf. pol. 35; Th. i. 84, 7, 9; *3rd pers. pres. subj. of* be-scyran.

be-scyred *deprived,* Bd. 5, 5; S. 617, 38; *pp. of* be-scyrian.

be-scyrednes, -ness, e; *f. An abdication, a casting off, depriving;* abdicatio, Cot. 14.

be-scyrian *to deprive, separate, defraud,* Bd. 1, 27; S. 492, 14: 1, 27; S. 491, 27: Homl. Th. ii. 534, 34: Ps. Spl. 83, 13: Exon. 111 b; Th. 427, 34; Rä. 41, 101: Bd. 5, 5; S. 617, 38: Cd. 21; Th. 25, 12; Gen. 392: 21; Th. 25, 16; Gen. 394: Exon. 83 b; Th. 314, 2; Mód. 8: Andr. Kmbl. 3235; An. 1620: Cd. 221; Th. 285, 26; Sat. 343: Exon. 8 a; Th. 3, 7; Cri. 32: 45 b; Th. 155, 29; Gú. 867: Ps. Th. 77, 29: Ps. Lamb. 77, 30. v. be-scerian.

be-scyrigan *to deprive,* Bd. 1, 27; S. 491, 34. v. be-scerian.

be-scyrþ *shaves; 3rd pers. pres. of* be-sceran.

be-scyrung, e; *f.* [be *from,* scerung *from* sceran *to tonsure* or *consecrate*] *A deposing, degrading, putting from holy orders;* exauctoratio, desecratio, exordinatio. DER. be-scyrian?

be-scýt *injects,* Alb. resp. 40; *3rd pers. pres. of* be-sceótan.

be-seah *looked about*, Gen. 24, 63; *p. of* be-seón.

be-seald *surrounded*, Cd. 2; Th. 3, 27; Gen. 42; *pp. of* be-sellan.

be-secgan; *p.* -sægde, -sǽde, *pl.* -sægdon, -sǽdon; *pp.* -sægd, -sǽd [be, secgan *to answer*] *To defend;* defendere:—Him wæs lýfnesse seald, ðæt he him mōste scyldan and besecgan on andweardnesse his gesacena *leave was given him, that he might shield and defend himself in the presence of his accusers*, Bd. 5, 19; S. 640, 11. v. be-reccan.

be-sellan; *p.* -sealde, -salde, *pl.* -sealdon, -saldon; *pp.* -seald [be *by, about*, sellan *to give*] *To surround, bring on;* circumdare, obducere:—Sinnihte beseald *surrounded with perpetual night*, Cd. 2; Th. 3, 27; Gen. 42.

besema, an; *m. A besom;* scopæ:—He gemēt hyt [hūs] geclǽnsod mid besemum *invenit eam* [*domum*] *scopis mundatam*, Mt. Foxe 12, 44. v. besma.

be-sencan, bi-sencan; *p.* -sencte; *pp.* -senced *To sink, immerge;* mergere, demergere:—Ic besence *mergo*, Ælfc. Gr. 28, 4; Som. 31, 36. Hreóhnys besencte me *tempestas demersit me*, Ps. Spl. 68, 3: Ps. Th. 68, 2: Menol. Fox 421; Men. 212. Ðe-læs me besencen *ne me demergant*, Ps. Th. 68, 14. Sī besenced on sǽs grūnd *demergatur in profundum maris*, Mt. Bos. 18, 6: Lk. Bos. 10, 15. Ðæt he gesāwe Satanan besencedne on ðām grūndum helle *that he saw Satan sunk in the depths of hell*, Bd. 5, 14; S. 634, 25. DER. sencan.

be-sengan; *p.* -sengde; *pp.* -senged, -sengd *To singe, scorch, burn;* ustulare, urere, æstuare:—Beren ear beseng *singe a barley ear*, L. M. 1, 51; Lchdm. ii. 124, 18. Ōðra wēron forberned oððe besenged [MS. besenced] *alia æstuaverunt*, Mt. Kmbl. Lind. 13, 6. Hī besāwon on ða besengdan burh and on ða wēstan *they looked on the burnt and wasted city*, Ors. 2, 8; Bos. 51, 42.

be-seón, -sión, bi-seón; ic -seó, ðū -sihst, he -sihþ, -syhþ, *pl.* -seóþ; *p.* ic, he -seah, ðū -sāwe, *pl.* -sāwon; *impert.* -sih; *pp.* -sewen [be *by, near, about;* seón *to see*]. I. *to look about* or *around;* circumspicere:—Sōna ðā hī besāwon hī, nānne hī mid him ne gesāwon *suddenly when they looked about them, they saw no one with him*, Mk. Bos. 9, 8. Ðā he beseah, ðā geseah he olfendas *when he looked about, then he saw the camels*, Gen. 24, 63. II. *to see, look, behold;* videre, aspicere:—Abraham beseah upp and geseah þrī weras *Abraham looked up and saw three men*, Gen. 18, 2. Eágan his on þearfena beseóþ *oculi ejus in pauperem respiciunt*, Ps. Spl. 10, 5. Besih on me *aspice in me*, Ps. Lamb. 118, 132. III. *to go to see, visit;* visere, visitare:—Beseoh wīngeard ðisne *visita vineam istam*, Ps. Th. 79, 14.

be-serian; *p.* ode; *pp.* od *To rob, plunder, deprive, deceive;* spoliare, fraudare:—He hine feore [MS. fere] beserode *he deprived him of life*, Ps. C. 50, 22; Ps. Grn. ii. 277, 22. v. be-syrwan.

be-seten *beset;* circumdatus, Ps. Th. arg. 19; *pp. of* be-sittan.

be-settan; *p.* -sette, *pl.* -setton; *pp.* -seted, -sett; *v. a.* [be *by*, settan *to set*] *To* BESET, *set near, appoint, to place, own, possess;* circumdare, collocare, ponere:—Seó cwēn ða rōde hēht mid eorcnanstānum besettan [MS. besetton] *the queen commanded them to beset the cross with jewels*, Elen. Kmbl. 2049; El. 1026. Ic ðē mægene besette *I beset thee with strength*, Andr. Kmbl. 2866; An. 1435. Wǽpna smiþ besette swīnlīcum hine *the armour-smith beset it with figures of swine*, Beo. Th. 2910; B. 1453. Se hālga wæs searoþancum beseted *the saint was beset with various thoughts*, Andr. Kmbl. 2511; An. 1257: Exon. 60 a; Th. 218, 19; Ph. 297. Domicianus ða rēðan ēhtnyssa besette on ðām cristenum *Domitian appointed the cruel persecutions of the Christians*, Ælfc. T. 32, 10. Sǽd þeówna his besetton ða *semen servorum ejus possidebit eam*, Ps. Spl. 68, 42.

be-sih *see, look, behold;* aspice, Ps. Lamb. 118, 132; *impert. of* be-seón.

be-sincan; *p.* -sanc, *pl.* -suncon; *pp.* -suncen *To sink;* submergere, demergere:—Seó burh besanc on eorþan *the city sank into the earth*, Ors. 3, 11; Bos. 75, 32. Twā byrig on eorþan besuncon *two cities sunk into the earth*, Ors. 3, 2; Bos. 54, 43. Wæs ic swīðe besuncen *I was deeply sunk*, Exon. 103 b; Th. 392, 5; Rä. 11, 3. v. sincan.

be-singan; *p.* -sang, -song, *pl.* -sungon; *pp.* -sungen *To utter enchantments, to enchant, charm, bewail;* excantare incantationibus, deplorare:—Ne sceal nān man mid galdre wyrte besingan *no man shall enchant a herb with magic*, Homl. Th. i. 476, 9. Besing *enchant*, Herb. 93, 2; Lchdm. i. 202, 13. Ge sceolon weán wōpe besingan *ye shall bewail torment with weeping*, Exon. 41 b; Th. 139, 3; Gū. 587.

besining, e; *f. A bending;* sinuatio:—Besining *sinuatio*, Ælfc. Gl. 100; Som. 77, 8; Wrt. Voc. 55, 11.

be-sión *to look about:*—Ðæt he hine ne besió *that he look not about him*, Bt. 35, 6; Fox 170, 17. v. be-seón I.

be-sittan, to be-sittanne; *p.* -sæt, -sætt, *pl.* -sǽton; *pp.* -seten [be *by, near*, sittan *to sit*]. I. *to sit round, surround, beset, besiege;* circumdare, cingere, obsidere:—Ða Læcedemonian besǽton ða burh Mæsiane tyn winter *the Lacedæmonians surrounded the city of Messene for ten years*, Ors. 1, 14; Bos. 37, 15. Se cyng lēt [hī] besittan ðone castel *the king permitted* [*them*] *to beset the castle*, Chr. 1087; Erl. 226, 9. He besæt ða sinherge sweorda lāfe *circumdedit magno exercitu ensium reliquias* [*superstites*], Beo. Th. 5864; B. 2936. He fōr to Hrofe ceastre, and besætt ðone castel *he went to Rochester, and beset the castle*, Chr. 1087; Erl. 226, 5. Hie hine besǽton on ǽlce healfe on ānum fæstenne *they beset it* [*the army*] *on every side in a fastness*, Chr. 894; Erl. 92, 23: 918; Erl. 102, 35. He wæs beseten mid his feóndum on ðære byrig *he was beset by his enemies in the city*, Ps. Th. arg. 19: Chr. 894; Erl. 92, 7. Ic eom beseten *obsideor*, Ælfc. Gr. 37; Som. 39, 8. Cassander hȳ hēt ðǽr besittan *Cassander commanded to besiege them there*, Ors. 3, 11; Bos. 74, 16. Hī þohton [MS. þohtan] hine inne to besittanne *they thought to besiege him therein*, Chr. 1094; Erl. 230, 22. Antigones hine bedrāf into ānum fæstenne and hine ðǽr besæt *Antigonus drove him into a fastness and besieged him there*, Ors. 3, 11; Bos. 73, 18: Chr. 1106; Erl. 241, 8. Gif he ðæs mægenes ne hæbbe ðæt he hine inne besitte *if he have not sufficient power that he may besiege him within*, L. Alf. pol. 42; Th. i. 90, 11. II. *to be in session, to hold sessions, to be able to sit as master of, be in possession, to possess;* considere, considere ad aliquid, possidere:—Fira bearn æht besittaþ *filii hominum ad deliberationem considunt*, Andr. Kmbl. 820; An. 410. Ealdormen æht besǽton *princes sat in council*, Andr. Kmbl. 1216; An. 608: 1254; An. 627: Elen. Kmbl. 944; El. 473. Wālā wā! ðæt is sārlīc, ðæt swā leóhtes andwlitan men sceolan āgan and besittan þȳstra ealdor *alas! it is a woful thing, that the prince of darkness should own and possess* [*have influence over by sitting* or *being near, hold, be in possession of*] *men of so bright a countenance;* heu, proh dolor! quod tam lucidi vultus homines tenebrarum auctor possidet, Bd. 2, 1; S. 501, 16.

be-siwian; *p.* ede; *pp.* ed *To sew together, to join;* jungere:—Besiwed feðergeweorc *opus plumarium*, Cot. 145. v. siwian.

be-slægen *slain, cut off*, Chr. 937; Th. 205, 28, col. 2, = be-slagen; *pp. of* be-sleán.

be-slǽpan; *p.* -slēp; *pp.* -slǽpen [be, slǽpan *to sleep*] *To sleep;* dormire:—He oft beslēp *he often slept*, L. Pen. 16; Th. ii. 284, 3.

be-slagen *slain, taken away*, Chr. 937; Th. 204, 28, col. 1; *pp. of* be-sleán.

be-sleán; *p.* -slōh, *pl.* -slōgon; *pp.* -slagen, -slægen, -slegen; *instr. To beat, strike* or *cut off, take away, bereave;* decollare, cædendo orbare, privare:—Ðǽr wæs heáfde beslagen se strengesta martyr sanct Albanus *decollatus itaque martyr fortissimus sanctus Albanus*, there the bravest martyr, St. Alban, was beheaded, Bd. 1, 7; S. 478, 33. He beslōh synsceaðan gewealde *he bereft the impious of power*, Cd. 4; Th. 4, 17; Gen. 55. Wuduwan freóndum beslægene *widows bereft of friends*, 94; Th. 121, 15; Gen. 2010.

be-slegen *slain*, Chr. 937; Th. 205, 28, col. 1, = be-slagen; *pp. of* be-sleán.

be-slēp *slept*, L. Pen. 16; Th. ii. 284, 3; *p. of* be-slǽpan.

be-slēpan; *p.* -slēpte; *subj. pl.* -slēpen; *pp.* -slēped, -slēpt *To slip, lay, place, put*, and with the preposition on, *on, upon,—to slip, put* or *lay on, to impose, clothe;* ponere, imponere, induere:—Hū hefig geoc he beslēpte on ealle *how heavy a yoke he laid on all!* Bt. 16, 4; Fox 58, 16. Beslēpen hī on hȳ bysmor *induantur confusione!* Ps. Th. 34, 24. Beslēpte mid gyldnum fnasum *in fimbriis aureis circumamicta*, 44, 15. v. slēpan.

be-slītan; *p.* -slāt, *pl.* -sliton; *pp.* -sliten *To slit, tear;* findere, lacerare:—Ðec sculon moldwyrmas monige seonowum beslītan *many mould-worms shall tear thee from thy sinews*, Exon. 99 a; Th. 371, 9; Seel. 73. Hēr sculon abīdan bān besliten seonwum *here shall abide the bones torn from the sinews*, Exon. 99 a; Th. 370, 20; Seel. 62. v. slītan.

be-slōgon, be-slōh *bereft*, Cd. 4; Th. 4, 17; Gen. 55; *p. of* be-sleán.

BESMA, besema, an; *m. A* BESOM, *broom, an instrument of punishment made of twigs, a rod;* scopæ, virga:—Geclǽnsod mid besmum *scopis mundatam*, Mt. Bos. 12, 44; clensid with bismes, Wyc. He hit [hūs] gemēt mid besmum afeormod *invenit eam* [*domum*] *scopis mundatam*, Lk. Bos. 11, 25; he fyndith it [hous] clensid with beesmes, Wyc. He [Brutus] hȳ [his fīf suna] hēt gebindan, and mid besman swingan *he* [*Brutus*] *gave orders to bind them* [*his five sons*], *and scourge them with rods* [*virgis cecidit*, Hav.], Ors. 2, 3; Bos. 42, 3. [*Frs.* besma, *m: Dut.* bézem, *m: O. Dut.* besem, bessem, *m: Ger.* besen, *m: O. H. Ger.* besamo: *Bret.* bezo, *m. a birch.*]

be-smītan; *p.* -smāt, *pl.* -smiton; *pp.* -smiten [be, smitta *smut*] *To* BESMUT, *defile, dirty, pollute, contaminate;* polluere, inquinare, coinquinare, contaminare:—Ðæt hine besmītan mǽge *quod possit eum coinquinare*, Mk. Bos. 7, 15: Cd. 127; Th. 162, 14; Gen. 2681: Judth. 10; Thw. 22, 12; Jud. 59: Exon. 81 a; Th. 305, 8; Fä. 85. Ic besmīte *polluo*, Ælfc. Gr. 28, 3; Som. 30, 49: Ps. Spl. C. 88, 34. Ðis synt ða þing ðe ðone mann besmītaþ; ne besmīt ðone mann, ðeáh he unþwogenum handum ete *hæc sunt quæ coinquinant hominem; non lotis autem manibus manducare, non coinquinat hominem*, Mt. Bos. 15, 20: 15, 18: Ps. Th. 54, 20. Besmiten mid synne *defiled with sin*, Cd. 74; Th. 91, 30; Gen. 1520: Jos. 7, 12: Bt. Met. Fox 8, 65; Met. 8, 33. Ðæt hȳg nǽron besmitene *ut non contaminarentur*, Jn. Bos. 18, 28: Ps. Th. 52, 1: 106, 16: Mk. Bos. 7, 2, 5.

be-smitenes, -ness, -nyss, e; *f. Dirtiness,* SMUTTINESS, *filthiness,* *pollution, abomination, infection;* sordes, inquinamentum, pollutio, coinquinatio :—Tilode se Drihtnes wer ða stôwe fram unsyfernyssum geclǽnsian ðara ǽrrena mâna and besmitenessa *the man of God toiled to cleanse the place from the impurities of former misdeeds and abominations,* Bd. 3, 23; S. 554, 28. Ðæt of wyrtruman besmitenysse acenned biþ *quod ex pollutionis radice generatur,* Bd. 1, 27; S. 494, 38, 41. Bûtan ǽlcere besmitennysse *without any pollution,* Homl. Th. i. 538, 28.

be-smiðian; *p.* ode; *pp.* od; *v. trans. To forge, to make* or *work as a smith does;* excudere, fabricare, fabrefacere :—Innan and ûtan îrenbendum searoþoncum besmiðod *within and without, cunningly forged with iron bands,* Beo. Th. 1554; B. 775. DER. smiðian.

be-smyred; *pp. Besmeared;* interlitum, Cot. 108. DER. smyrian.

be-snǽdan; *p.* de; *pp.* ed *To cut, lop;* amputare :—Engel hêt besnǽdan *an angel commanded to cut it,* Cd. 200; Th. 248, 16; Dan. 514. Ðæt ðæt treów sceolde, telgum besnǽded, âfeallan *that the tree, lopped of its branches, should fall,* Cd. 202; Th. 250, 34; Dan. 556.

be-snîwod; *pp.* BESNOWED, *covered with snow, snowy;* nive tectus, ninguidus :—Besnîwod *ninguidus,* Ælfc. Gl. 93; Som. 75, 94; Wrt. Voc. 52, 44. DER. snîwan.

be-snyðian; *p.* ede; *pp.* ed *To deprive;* privare :—Ongênþeów ealdre besnyðede Hǽþcyn *Ongentheow had deprived Hæthcyn of life,* Beo. Th. 5841; B. 2924: Andr. Kmbl. 2650; An. 1326: Exon. 107 a; Th. 407, 29; Rä. 27, 1.

be-solcen; *pp. Slow, inactive, dull, stupefied;* deses, torpidus :—Ðýlæs he weorþe besolcen *lest he becomes stupefied,* Past. 35, 1; Hat. MS. 45 a, 15. v. solcen.

be-sône; *adv. Soon, immediately;* mox, statim :—Cweðe se preóst besône *let the priest immediately say,* L. Ælf. C. 36; Th. ii. 358, 24. v. sôna.

beso-reádian; *p.* ode; *pp.* od [baso *red, purple,* reádian *to redden*] *To make a reddish purple;* rubefacere :—Besoreáda ða rinda ealle ûtan *make all the rinds on the outside a reddish purple [by soaking in chalybiate water?],* L. M. 1, 47; Lchdm. ii. 116, 3.

be-sorg, -sorh; *adj. Anxious, careful, dear, beloved;* sollicitus, carus :—Ðǽr wǽron ofslægene hyre þægna feówer ðe hyre besorge wǽron *there were slain four of her thanes which were dear to her,* Chr. 917; Erl. 105, 25. Papinianus wæs ealra his deorlinga besorgost *Papinianus was the most beloved of all his favourites,* Bt. 29, 2; Fox 104, 25. Besorh *carus,* R. Ben. 72.

be-sorgian, bi-sorgian; *p.* ode; *pp.* od *To be sorry for, to care for, be anxious about, fear;* curare :—Gif ðû me lufodest, ðû hit besorgodest *if thou lovedst me, thou wouldst be sorry for it,* Apol. Th. 20, 27. He deáþ ne bisorgaþ *he cares not for death,* Exon. 61 a; Th. 223, 32; Ph. 368. Ðû hæfst gesûnd gehealden eall ðæt deórwyrðoste, ðætte ðû ðe besorgod hæfdest *thou hast kept entire everything most precious, which thou wast anxious about,* Bt. 10; Fox 28, 10. Ne bisorgaþ he synne to fremman *he feareth not to perpetrate sin,* Exon. 30 b; Th. 95, 12; Cri. 1556.

be-sorh *anxious, dear, beloved,* R. Ben. 72. v. be-sorg.

be-spanan, bi-spanan; *p.* -spôn, -speón; *pp.* -spanen, -sponen; *v. trans. To allure, entice, incite, urge, induce, bring on any one;* allicere, illicere, incitare, provocare, inducere :—He deriende leóda bespeón to ðysan earde *he allured pernicious people to this land,* Chr. 959; Th. 219, 18. Gif he ǽnigne man on synne bespeóne *if he have enticed any man to sin,* L. Pen. 16; Th. ii. 284, 13. Ðæt gewin ðe hió hine on bespôn mid manigfealdon firen-lustum *the war which she brought upon him by her manifold wicked desires,* Ors. 1, 2; Bos. 26, 40.

be-sparrad *shut,* Cot. 145. v. sparran.

be-speón, be-spôn *allured, enticed,* Chr. 959; Th. 219, 18; *p. of* be-spanan.

be-spirian, -spirigan, -spyrigan; *p.* ode; *pp.* od *To inquire, trace;* inquirere, investigare :—Be ðon ðe yrfe bespirige *of him who traces cattle,* L. Ath. iv. 2; Th. i. 222, 13. Se ðe bespyrige [bespirige, Wilk.] yrfe innan ôðres land, aspirige hit ût, se ðe ðæt land âge, gif he mǽge *he who traces cattle into another's land, let him trace it out, who owns that land, if he can,* iv. 2; Th. i. 222, 14.

be-spræc, *pl.* -sprǽcon *spoke to, charged; p. of* be-sprecan.

be-spræcen *spoken to, charged,* L. Eth. ii. 9; Wilk. 105, 47, = be-sprecen; *pp. of* be-sprecan.

be-sprængan; *p.* de; *pp.* ed *To besprinkle;* aspergere, Herb. 86, 4; Lchdm. i. 190, 11, note. v. be-sprengan.

be-sprecan; *part.* -sprecende, ic -sprece, ðû -sprecest, -sprycst, he -spreceþ, -sprycþ, *pl.* -sprecaþ; *p.* -spræc, *pl.* -sprǽcon; *pp.* -sprecen, -spræcen [be *by,* sprecan *to speak*] *To speak to, to tell, pretend, plead, speak against, to complain, charge, accuse, impeach;* obloqui :—Fram stefne besprecendre oððe ofersprecendes *a voce obloquentis,* Ps. Lamb. 43, 17. Cristene Rôma besprycþ *Christian Rome complains,* Ors. 2, 4; Bos. 44, 45. Hû ge besprecaþ *how ye complain!* Ors. 1, 10; Bos. 34, 9. Hit besprecen biþ *it is charged,* L. Eth. ii. 8; Th. i. 288, 16: Ors. 1, 12; Bos. 36, 39.

be-sprengan; *p.* de; *pp.* ed *To besprinkle;* aspergere :—Bespreng me mid ysopon, ðæt ic beó geclǽnsod *asperges me hyssopo, et mundabor,* Ps. Th. 50, 8. Besprengc hyne mid ðam wætere *besprinkle him with the water,* Herb. 86, 4; Lchdm. i. 190, 11.

be-sprycþ *tells, complains,* Ors. 2, 4; Bos. 44, 45; *3rd pers. pres. of* be-sprecan.

be-spyrigan *to inquire, trace,* L. Ath. iv. 2; Th. i. 222, 14. v. be-spirian.

best; *adv. sup.* BEST, *most;* optime :—Ðe helpes best behôfaþ *who most wants help,* L. C. S. 69; Th. i. 412, 3; MS. A. [*Plat. Dut. Ger.* best, beste.] The usual form is wel *well,* bet *better,* betst *best = most.* In the text the preceding passage has betst behôfaþ *most wants.*

besta; *m:* seó, ðæt beste *the* BEST; optimus :—Scipio, se þesta Rômâna witena *Scipio, the best of the Roman senators,* Ors. 5, 4; Bos. 104, 38; Cot. MS. Tib. B. I. fol. 85 b. v. betst; *adj.*

be-stæl, *pl.* -stǽlon *stole upon,* Ors. 1, 10; Bos. 33, 33: Chr. 876; Erl. 79, 13; *p. of* be-stelan.

be-stæpþ *steps, steps upon, treads,* Jos. 1, 3; *pres. of* be-stapan.

be-standan; *p.* -stôd, *pl.* -stôdon; *pp.* -standen *To stand by* or *near, to stand around, surround, to stand on* or *upon, occupy, detain;* adstare, circumstare, circumdare, detinere :—Him bestande man *adstet quis ei,* L. Alf. P. 48; Th. ii. 384, 35. Abraham hîg bestôd on ða ealdan wîsan *Abraham stood by her after the old custom,* Gen. 23, 2. Fæderas and môddru bestandaþ heora bearna lîc *fathers and mothers stand around the corpses of their children,* Homl. Th. ii. 124, 17. Ðâ bestôdon ða Iudeas hyne ûtan *circumdederunt ergo eum Judæi,* Jn. Bos. 10, 24: Byrht. Th. 133, 51; By. 68. Ahrede me æt ðâm ðe me habbaþ ûtan bestanden *redime me a circumdantibus me,* Ps. Th. 31, 8. Ðæs wîf wæs hû hugu xl daga mid grimre âdle bestanden *cujus conjux quadraginta ferme diebus erat acerbissimo languore detenta,* Bd. 5, 4; S. 617, note 6.

be-stapan; he -stæpþ; *p.* -stôp, *pl.* -stôpon; *pp.* -stapen *To step, step upon, tread with the foot, go, enter;* gradi, calcare, ire, inire :—Eall ðæt rýmet, ðe eówer fôtswaðu on bestæpþ *omnem locum, quem calcaverit vestigium pedis vestri,* Jos. 1, 3. Se deófol into Iudan bestôp *the devil went [entered] into Judas,* Homl. Th. ii. 242, 14.

be-stelan, bi-stelan; *p.* -stæl, *pl.* -stǽlon; *subj. p.* -stǽle, *pl.* -stǽlen; *pp.* -stolen *To steal away* or *upon;* fugere, obrepere :—Gif hwâ on ôðre scîre hine bestele *if any one steal himself away into another shire,* L. In. 39; Th. i. 126, 10. Bestelan on Theodosius hindan *to steal upon Theodosius behind,* Ors. 6, 36; Bos. 131, 25. Hannibal bestæl on Marcellus *Hannibal stole upon Marcellus,* Ors. 4, 10; Bos. 94, 19: Past. 28, 6; Hat. MS. 38 a, 6. Ðâ he nihtes on ungearwe hî on bestæl, and hî swîðe forslôh and fordyde *then he stole upon them unawares by night, and grievously slew and destroyed them,* Ors. 1, 10; Bos. 33, 33. Hî nihtes bestǽlon ðære fyrde *they stole upon the army by night,* Chr. 876; Erl. 79, 13. Ðý-læs he on niht onweg fluge and bestǽle *lest he should have fled and stole away by night,* Bd. 4, 22; S. 591, 11.

be-stêman, -stýman; *p.* de; *pp.* ed *To* BESTEAM, *bedew, make damp, make wet;* humectare, madefacere, circumfundere :—Wǽron beorhhliðu blôde bestêmed *the mountain-brows were besteamed with blood,* Cd. 166; Th. 206, 8; Exod. 448. Wæs ðæs hâlgan lîc swâte bestêmed *the body of the saint was besteamed with blood,* Andr. Kmbl. 2480; An. 1241. Usses Dryhtnes rôd blôde bestêmed *our Lord's rood bedewed with blood,* Exon. 23 b; Th. 67, 10; Cri. 1086. Hwîlum hit [beácen] wæs mid wǽtan bestêmed *at times it [the beacon] was damped with wet,* Rood Kmbl. 44; Kr. 22. Ic wæs mid blôde bestêmed begoten of ðæs guman sîdan *I was wet with blood poured from the man's side,* 96; Kr. 48. Hû ðû wǽgflotan wǽre bestêmdan sund wisige *how thou directest the sailing of the wave-floater [ship] wetted with the sea,* Andr. Kmbl. 974; An. 487. Dreóre bestêmed *wet with blood,* 2949; An. 1477. DER. stêman.

be-stingan; *p.* -stang, *pl.* -stungon; *pp.* -stungen *To besting, thrust, push;* trudere, immittere, Med. ex Quadr. 5, 1; Lchdm. i. 348, 4.

be-stôd, *pl.* -stôdon *stood by* or *near, stood around, surrounded,* Gen. 23, 2: Byrht. Th. 133, 51; By. 68; *p. of* be-standan.

be-stolen *stolen,* Exon. 103 b; Th. 393, 7; Rä. 12, 6; *pp. of* be-stelan.

be-stôp *stepped, stepped into, entered,* Homl. Th. ii. 242, 14; *p. of* be-stapan.

be-streddon *heaped up;* aggeraverunt, Bd. 3, 2; S. 524, note 20. v. be-styrian.

be-streówian; *p.* ode; *pp.* od *To* BESTREW; superspargere :—Hî mid duste heora heáfod bestreówodon *sparserunt pulverem super caput suum,* Iob Grn. 2, 12.

be-streðan, -stryðan; *p.* ede, de; *pp.* ed *To heap up, erect;* aggerare, obducere :—Stânum bestreðed *heaped up with stones,* Exon. 128 b; Th. 493, 28; Rä. 81, 38. Bestryðed fæste *firmly erected,* Exon. 93 b; Th. 351, 29; Sch. 87: Bd. 3, 2; S. 524, note 20.

be-strîdan, he -strît, *pl.* -strîdaþ; *p.* -strâd, *pl.* -stridon; *pp.* -striden *To* BESTRIDE; ascendere :—Bestrîdan hors *to bestride a horse;* equum ascendere, Lye. v. be, strîdan *to stride.*

be-stroden *bespoiled, confiscated, robbed,* Cot. 108; *pp. of* be-strûdan.

be-strūdan; *p.* -streád, *pl.* -strudon; *pp.* -stroden *To bespoil, spoil, confiscate, rob;* spoliare, privare, confiscare:—Ða ðe Sodoma and Gomorra golde berōfan bestrudon stigwitum *qui Sodoma et Gomorra auro spoliarunt, incolis privarunt*, Cd. 95; Th. 125, 14; Gen. 2079. Bestroden *confiscatus*, Cot. 108.

be-strȳpan; *p.* -strȳpte; *pp.* -strȳped *To strip, rob, spoil, bereave;* exuere, spoliare:—Bestrȳpan widuwan *viduas spoliare* vel *exuere*, Off. Episc. 8. Ealle ða bestrȳpte he æt lande *he bereaved all those of land*, Chr. 1065; Erl. 196, 11.

be-stryðan; *p.* ede, de; *pp.* ed *To heap up, erect;* aggerare, obducere:—Bestryðed fæste *firmly erected*, Exon. 93 b; Th. 351, 29; Sch. 87: Bd. 3, 2; S. 524, note 20. v. be-streðan.

be-stungen *pushed*:—On næsþyrl bestungen *pushed into the nostril*, Med. ex Quadr. 5, 1; Lchdm. i. 348, 4; *pp. of* be-stingan.

be-stȳman; *p.* de; *pp.* ed *To besteam, bedew, make damp, make wet;* humectare, madefacere, circumfundere:—Drihtsele blōde bestȳmed *the princely hall besteamed with blood*, Beo. Th. 977; B. 486. v. bestēman.

be-styrian; *p.* ede; *pp.* ed [be, styrian *to move*] *To heap up, pile up;* aggerare:—His þegnas mid moldan hit bestyredon and gefæstnedon *his thanes heaped up with mould and fastened it*, Bd. 3, 2; S. 524, 20.

be-styrman; *p.* de; *pp.* ed *To* BESTORM, *storm, agitate;* flatibus agere, agitare:—Ðonne hit bestyrmaþ ðisse worulde ungeþwǣrnessa *quando ipsam agitant hujus mundi inquietudines*, Bt. 3, 2; Fox 6, 8. DER. styrman.

be-suncen *sunk*, Exon. 103 b; Th. 392, 5; Rä. 11, 3; *pp. of* besincan.

be-swāc *deceived, enticed, seduced*, Andr. Kmbl. 1226; An. 613; *p. of* be-swīcan.

be-swælan; *p.* de; *pp.* ed *To burn, sweal, scorch, singe;* adurere, ustulare:—Næs hyra feax fȳre beswæled *nor was a hair of them burned by the fire*, Cd. 195; Th. 243, 18; Dan. 438. Glēdum beswæled *scorched by gleeds*, Beo. Th. 6075; B. 3041. DER. swelan.

be-swāpan; *p.* -sweóp, *pl.* -sweópon; *pp.* -swāpen [be, swāpan *to sweep*] *To clear up, persuade, cover over, clothe, protect;* suadere, cooperire, amicire, munire:—Gif hwylc Rǣdwolde on mōd beswāpe *si qui Redualdo suadeat*, Bd. 2, 12; S. 514, 3. Hī hī mid scȳtan besweóp *she covered herself over with a sheet*, 3, 9; S. 534, 13. Beswāpen [beswapyn MS.] leóhte swā swā of rægle *amictus lumine sicut vestimento*, Ps. Spl. C. 103, 2. Ðæt he bió wið ǣlce orsorgnesse beswāpen *that he shall be protected against every pleasure*, Past. 14, 3; Hat. MS. 17 b, 21.

be-swemman; *p.* -swemde; *pp.* -swemmed, -swemd *To make to swim;* natare facere:—Ðeáh hī beswemde weorþon *though they be made to swim*, Bt. 37, 4; Fox 192, 28.

be-sweóp *covered over, clothed*, Bd. 3, 9; S. 534, 13; *p. of* be-swāpan.

be-sweðian, bi-sweðian; *p.* ede; *pp.* ed *To bind up, swathe;* ligare:—Mid ācumban besweðe *bind up with tow*, L. M. 1, 1; Lchdm. ii. 22, 21. v. sweðian, ge-sweðian.

be-swīc, big-swīc, bī-swīc, es; *m.* [be, big, bī *intensive*; swīc *deceit*, swīcan *to deceive*] *Deceit, a deceiving, treachery, snare;* fraus, deceptio, dolus = δόλος, decipula:—Būtan bræde and beswīce [bigswīce, bīswīce, Th. i. 160, 7, note 6] *absque figmento et fraude*, L. Ed. 1; Wilk. 48, 38. Bīswīcum *deceptionibus*, Mone B. 1174. Philippus ealle ða cyningas mid bīswīce ofslōh *Philip slew all the kings by treachery*, Ors. 3, 7; Bos. 60, 13. To bīswīce his nȳhstan *in dolo proximo suo*, Ps. Th. 23, 4. Beswīc *decipula*, Cot. 61. Ða woruldwēlan synt gesceapene to bīswīce monnum *worldly riches are created for a snare to men*, Bt. 14, 1; Fox 42, 3.

be-swīcan, bi-swīcan; ic -swīce, ðū -swīcest, -swīcst, he -swīceþ, -swīcþ, *pl.* -swīcaþ; *p.* -swāc, *pl.* -swicon; *pp.* -swicen; *v. a.* [be *by*, swīcan *to deceive*] *To deceive, entice, seduce, delude, betray, offend, supplant, weaken, evade;* decipere, illicere, seducere, illudere, prodere, scandalizare, supplantare, deficere, evadere:—He ongan sirwan hū he hine beswīcan mihte *he began to plot how he might deceive him*, Ors. 1, 12; Bos. 35, 19: Cd. 23; Th. 29, 17; Gen. 451. Hȳ beswīcaþ weardas *the guardians deceive them*, Exon. 116 a; Th. 446, 2; Dōm. 16: Ps. Th. 61, 9. Ne beswīc ðū ðīnne nēxtan *deceive not thy neighbour*, Lev. 19, 11. Me nædre beswāc *the serpent deceived me*, Cd. 42; Th. 55, 20; Gen. 897: Exon. 61 b; Th. 226, 30; Ph. 413: Andr. Kmbl. 1226; An. 613. We beswicon [MS. beswican] us sylfe *we have deceived ourselves*, Exon. 121 a; Th. 464, 31; Hö. 96. Hycgaþ hū ge hī beswīcen *think how ye may deceive them*, Cd. 22; Th. 28, 9; Gen. 433. Mid gedwolan beswicen *errore deceptus*, Deut. 30, 17: Exon. 97 a; Th. 363, 20; Wal. 56. Ge sind beswicene *ye are deceived*, Andr. Kmbl. 1489; An. 746. Ic beswīce *illicio*, Ælfc. Gr. 28, 5; Som. 31, 67. Gif hwā fǣmnan beswīce unbeweddode *if any one entice an unbetrothed woman*, L. Alf. 29; Th. i. 52, 5. Feóndas sōþfæstra sāwle willaþ beswīcan *fiends will seduce the souls of the righteous*, Exon. 41 a; Th. 136, 12; Gū. 540. Wæs he beswicen fram his wīfe *ab uxore sua seductus est*, Bd. 2, 15; S. 518, 29: Cd. 26; Th. 33, 32; Gen. 529. Hiora ealdormen wǣron beswicene *principes eorum seducti sunt*, Ps. Th. 106, 39. Forðamðe ðū me beswice *quia illusisti mihi*, Num. 22, 29. Sindon ge beswicene *ye are deluded*, Exon. 41 b; Th. 139, 22; Gū. 597. Us Godrīc hæfþ beswicene *Godric has betrayed us*, Byrht. Th. 138, 51; By. 238. Ðæt eów beswīcþ *hoc vos scandalizat?* Jn. Bos. 6, 61: Mt. Bos. 18, 6. Ða ðe þohton beswīcan fǣrelde mīne *qui cogitaverunt supplantare gressus meos*, Ps. Spl. 139, 5. Ūton acræftan hū we heora māgon [MS. magan] beswīcan *let us plan how we can weaken them*, Ors. 2, 5; Bos. 47, 20. Ne mæg hit wildeór beswīcan *a wild beast cannot evade it*, Salm. Kmbl. 572; Sal. 285. Ðū hafast ðīnra feónda handa beswicene *hostium manus evasisti*, Bd. 2, 12; S. 515, 23.

be-swīcende, an; *f. A deceiver, harlot;* pellex, Cot. 170.

be-swīcian; *p.* ode, ede, ade; *pp.* od, ed, ad [be, swīcian *to wander*] *To go from, evade, escape, be without, be free from;* evadere, carere:—Ða ðe ðone deáþ beswīcian myhton [myhtan MS.] *qui mortem evadere poterant*, Bd. 1, 12; S. 481, 1. Ðæt he ðone ēcan deáþ beswīcode *ut ipse mortem evaderet æternam*, Bd. 3, 23; S. 555, 36: 2, 12; S. 512, 36. Ðæt heó ðære langan untrumnesse beswīcede *se infirmitate longa carere*, Bd. 5, 4; S. 617, 24. Torhtgyþ ðære tungan onstyrenesse beswīcade *Torctgyd linguæ motu caruit*, 4, 9; S. 577, 17.

be-swincan; *p.* -swanc, *pl.* -swuncon; *pp.* -swuncen *To toil, labour, make with toil;* laborare:—Ic sende eów to rīpanne, ðæt ðæt ge ne beswuncon; ōðre swuncon, and ge eódon on hyra geswinc *ego misi vos metere quod vos non laborastis; alii laboraverunt, et vos in labores eorum introistis*, Jn. Bos. 4, 38. Ðæt hrægl is beswuncen *laboratur vestis*, Ælfc. Gr. 19; Som. 22, 48.

be-swingan; *p.* -swang, *pl.* -swungon; *pp.* -swungen *To scourge, beat;* flagellare, verberare:—Ic wæs beswungen ealne dæg *fui flagellatus tota die*, Ps. Lamb. 72, 14: Bt. Met. Fox 25, 91; Met. 25, 46. Hīg ne beóþ beswungene *non flagellabuntur*, Ps. Lamb. 72, 5: Ex. 5, 16. Ic eom beswungen *verberor*, Ælfc. Gr. 5; Som. 3, 32. Ic eom beswungen *I am beaten;* vapulo, 19; Som. 23, 3.

be-swuncen *made with toil*, Ælfc. Gr. 19; Som. 22, 48; *pp. of* beswincan.

be-swungen *beaten*, Bt. 37, 1; Fox 186, 20; *pp. of* be-swingan.

be-swylian; *p.* ede; *pp.* ed *To soil, stain;* polluere, inficere:—Hit wæs beswyled mid swātes gange *it was soiled with running of blood*, Rood Kmbl. 45; Kr. 23.

be-sylfred; *pp.* [seolfer *silver*] *Silvered*, BESILVERED; deargentatus, Ps. 67, 14, Lye. v. ofer-sylfrian.

be-sylian; *p.* ede; *pp.* ed *To soil, stain;* maculare, inquinare:—Besyled *stained;* maculatus, Bt. 16, 4; Fox 58, 18: Elen. Kmbl. 1390; El. 697. v. selian.

be-syrewian; *p.* ede; *pp.* ed *To ensnare, deceive;* circumvenire, decipere, machinare:—Hī woldon hine besyrewian *they would deceive him*, Chr. 1002; Erl. 137, 34. v. be-syrwan.

be-syrian; *p.* ode, ede; *pp.* od, ed *To rob, plunder, deprive, deceive;* spoliare, fraudare, dejicere:—Ðæt hī mǣgon besyrian ðone earman *ut dejiciant inopem*, Ps. Th. 36, 13. Cirus hȳ besyrode *Cyrus ensnared them*, Ors. 2, 4; Bos. 45, 20. Hine Rodbeard besyrede *Robert deceived him*, Chr. 1093; Erl. 229, 5. Ða Scottas heora cyng Dunecan besyredon *the Scots ensnared their king Duncan*, 1094; Erl. 230, 40. v. be-syrwan.

be-syrwan, -syrewian, -syrian, -serian; *p.* -syrwde; *pp.* -syrwed *To ensnare, deceive;* circumvenire, decipere, machinari:—Ðæt hīg woldon ðone Hǣlend mid fācne besyrwan *ut Iesum dolo tenerent*, Mt. Bos. 26, 4. Mynte se mānscaða manna cynnes sumne besyrwan *the wicked spoiler expected to ensnare one of the race of men*, Beo. Th. 1430; B. 713: 1888; B. 942: Cd. 127; Th. 162, 13; Gen. 2680. v. syrwan.

BET, bett; *adv.* [?*from* bet *well*; *comp.* betor *better? contracted to* bet; *sup.* betost *contracted to* betst, *q. v.*] BETTER; melius:—Ðā acsode he, to hwylcum tīman him bet wǣre *interrogabat ergo horam ab eis in qua melius habuerit*, Jn. Bos. 4, 52. Ðæt se hwǣte mǣge ðȳ bet weaxan *that the wheat may grow the better*, Bt. 23; Fox 78, 24. Hwonne his horse bett wurde *till his horse should be better*, Bd. 3, 9; S. 533, 34. [*Chauc. Piers* bet: *Scot.* bet: *O. Sax.* bet: *Frs. O. Frs.* bet: *M. Dut. N. Dut.* bet: *Ger.* basz: *M. H. Ger.* baz: *O. H. Ger.* baz: *O. Nrs.* betr.] DER. abet. v. wel *well*.

be-tǣcan; *p.* -tǣhte, *pl.* -tǣhton; *pp.* -tǣht; *v. a.* [be *by*, tǣcan *to teach, shew*]. I. *to shew;* ostendere:—He eów betǣcþ mycele healle *ipse ostendet vobis cænaculum magnum*, Lk. Bos. 22, 12. II. *to* BETAKE, *impart, deliver, commit, put in trust;* impertire, adsignare, tradere, commendare:—Ic betǣce hīg ðam yrþlincge *adsigno eos aratori*, Coll. Monast. Th. 20, 31. Sum man clypode hys þeówas, and betǣhte hym hys ǣhta *homo vocavit servos suos, et tradidit illis bona sua*, Mt. Bos. 25, 14; a man clepide his seruauntis, and bitoke to hem his goodis, Wyc: Gen. 9, 2: Ps. Th. 104, 17: Ors. 2, 5; Bos. 48, 6. Swā us betǣhton, ða ðe hit of frymþe gesāwon *sicut tradiderunt nobis, qui ab initio ipsi viderunt*, Lk. Bos. 1, 2: Elen. Kmbl. 1167; El. 585. Man hȳ ðære abedissan betǣhton *they committed her to the abbess*, Chr. 1052; Erl. 181, 28. Ðæt we mōton ðē betǣcan sāwle ūre *that we may commit our souls to thee*, Hy. 7, 82; Hy. Grn. ii. 289, 82: Runic pm. 20;

Kmbl. 343, 18; Hick. Thes. i. 135. III. *to send, follow, pursue;* mittere, insequi, amandare:—Betǽcan [MS. betæcen] cildru on scóle *to send children to school;* mittere pueros in scholam, Obs. Lun. § 4; Lchdm. iii. 184, 28. Mid swiftum húndum ic betǽce wildeór *with swift hounds I pursue wild beasts;* cum velocibus canibus insequor feras, Coll. Monast. Th. 21, 27. Ic betǽce fram me *amando*, Ælfc. Gr. 47; Som. 48, 35.

be-tǽcung, e; *f. A betaking;* traditio. v. be, tǽcung, be-tǽcan.

be-tǽhte, *pl.* -tǽhton *delivered, committed*, Gen. 9, 2: Chr. 1052; Erl. 181, 28; *p. of* be-tǽcan II.

be-táht *betrothed*, Mt. Lind. Stv. 1, 18, = be-tǽht; *pp. of* be-tǽcan II.

be-táhten, Chr. 654; Erl. 29, 11, = betǽhton *committed; p. of* be-tǽcan II.

bétan, ic béte; *p.* bétte; *pp.* béted; *v. trans.* [*Goth.* ô = *A. Sax.* ó, é, *thus Goth.* bôtyan = bôtan = *A. Sax.* bétan]. I. *to make better, to improve, amend, repair, restore;* emendare, reparare, reficere, mederi, expiare:—Ðæt he bétte *that he should improve*, Bd. 5, 13; S. 632, 11: Ex. 21, 22. Hú ðú meaht ðíne æceras bétan *how thou mayest improve thy fields*, Lchdm. i. 398, 1. II. joined with fýr *to mend* or *repair a fire, to light* or *make a fire, to kindle;* focum reparare. [In this sense böten is used in Low German at the present day:—Böt füer *make the fire.* So in *Frs.* fiūr boetsje *struere focum.*] Ðá hét he bétan micel fýr *then he ordered a great fire to be lighted*, Ors. 6, 32; Bos. 129, 10. III. *to remedy, compensate, make amends;* compensare:—Ic hit béte *I will remedy it*, Deut. 1, 17. [*Chauc.* bete: *Piers* bete: *R. Glouc.* bete: *Laym.* beten, bæten: *Orm.* betenn: *O. Sax.* bôtean: *Plat.* betern *to repair;* böten *to mend the fire: Dut.* baten *to profit;* beteren *to amend: O. Frs.* beta, beteria *to repair: Ger.* bessern *to repair: Goth.* bôtyan: *Dan.* böde: *Swed.* böta: *Icel.* bæta; bet *better.*] DER. gebétan, gebétung, unbéted.

betast *best;* optimus:—Betast hereféðan blícaþ *best martial bands shine*, Exon. 22 b; Th. 62, 36; Cri. 1012. v. betst; *adj.*

BÉTE, an; *f:* béte, an; *n?* BEET, *a root from which sugar is often extracted;* béta = σεῦτλον, *n:*—Sindon eáþ begeátra béte and mealwe *beet and mallow are more easily procured*, L. M. 2, 30; Lchdm. ii. 226, 25: iii. 12, 26. Wyrc drænc of ðære bétan [MS. beton] *work a drink of the beet*, Lchdm. iii. 22, 6. Beðe mid bétan leáfum *foment with leaves of beet*, L. M. 1, 39; Lchdm. ii. 100, 12: iii. 2, 8: 44, 8: 114, 13. Nim ða bétan, ðe gehwǽr weaxaþ *take the beet, which groweth anywhere*, L. M. 2, 33; Lchdm. ii. 238, 3: iii. 22, 12. Nim béte [*acc. n.*] ðe biþ ánsteallet *take beet, which is one-stalked*, iii. 70, 2. [*Dut.* beet, biet, *f: Ger.* beete, *f: O. H. Ger.* bieza, *f: Fr.* bette, *f: Ital.* bieta, *f: Lat.* beta, *f.*]

be-teáh *accused;* accusavit, Chr. 1096; Th. 362, 32; *p. of* be-teón.

be-teldan, bi-teldan; *p.* -teald, *pl.* -tuldon; *pp.* -tolden [be, teldan *to cover*, teld *a tent*]. *To cover, cover over, surround, overwhelm;* tegere, supertegere, circumdare, obruere:—He ðæt wælreáf wyrtum biteldeþ *he covers the dead spoil with herbs*, Exon. 59 b; Th. 217, 1; Ph. 273. Láme bitolden *covered with clay* [*buried*], 64 a; Th. 235, 11; Ph. 555: 64 b; Th. 238, 25; Ph. 609. Hæfde sigora weard betolden leófne leódfruman mid lofe sínum *the lord of triumphs had surrounded the dear chieftain with his praise*, Andr. Kmbl. 1976; An. 990. Fuglas hringe beteldaþ Fénix *the birds surround the Phœnix in a ring*, Exon. 60 b; Th. 221, 24; Ph. 339. Wæs wópes hring torne bitolden *the weeping circle was overwhelmed with grief*, 15 b; Th. 34, 6; Cri. 538.

be-tellan; *p.* -tealde, -telede, *pl.* -tealdon, -teledon; *pp.* -teald, -teled, -tæled; *v. a.* [be, tellan *to tell*] *To speak about, to answer, excuse, justify, clear;* excusare:—Ðæt he móste hine betellan *that he might answer him*, Chr. 1048; Erl. 180, 12. Godwine betealde hine *Godwin cleared himself*, 1052; Ing. 238, 22.

bétende; *part.* [from bétan *to make better, atone*] *Amending, atoning;* reparans, expians:—Bétende [MS. betend] crungon hergas to hrusan *the atoning bands sank to earth*, Exon. 124 a; Th. 477, 24; Ruin. 29.

be-teón; *p.* -teáh, *pl.* -tugon; *pp.* -togen. I. *to draw over* or *round, cover, surround, inclose, protect;* obducere, superinducere, circumducere, concludere, munire:—Heora scyldas wǽron betogene mid hýdum *their shields were covered with hides*, Ors. 5, 7; Bos. 107, 8. Betogen [betogan MS.] cræt *a covered carriage;* capsus, Ælfc. Gl. 49; Wrt. Voc. 34, 23. Híg betugon mycele menigeo fixa *concluserunt copiosam multitudinem piscium*, Lk. Bos. 5, 6. Se reáda æppel biþ betogen mid ánfealdre rinde, and monig corn on-innan him hæfþ *in malo punico uno exterius cortice multa interius grana muniuntur*, Past. 15, 5; Hat. MS. 19 b, 22. v. teón I. II. *to leave by law, bequeath;* legare, Th. Diplm. A. D. 1037; 567, 9. III. *to bring a charge against any one, accuse;* criminari, accusare:—Beteáh Gosfrei Bainard Willelm of Ou *Geoffrey Bainard accused William of Eu*, Chr. 1096; Th. 362, 32. Se ðe biþ betogen *he who is accused*, L. In. 54; Th. i. 136, 10: 71; Th. i. 148, 2. v. teón II.

betera, betra; *m:* betere, betre; *f. n. adj.* [*from* bet *good*, v. bet-líc *good-like, comp.* betera, betra *better; sup.* betest, betst *best*, v. besta, gód] BETTER; melior:—Ðæt hý wǽron beteran þegnas *that they were better thanes*, Ors. 4, 9; Bos. 92, 23. Ða betran tída *the better times*, 4, 9; Bos. 92, 18. To beteran tíde *to a better time*, Bd. 3, 14; S. 539, 39. Wítodlíce micle má mann ys sceápe betera? Mt. Bos. 12, 12; *hou moche more is a man betre than a sheep?* Wyc. Hit is betre *it is a better* [*thing*], Bt. 38, 7; Fox 210, 5: 29, 1; Fox 102, 6.

beterian; *p.* ode; *pp.* od [betera *better*] *To make better, ameliorate;* meliorari, emendare. v. ge-beterian.

betesta *best:*—Se betesta *the best*, Cot. 153. v. betst; *adj.*

beþ *is*, Chr. 675; Erl. 38, 8, = biþ; *3rd pers. pres. of* beón.

be-þæht *covered*, Bd. 3, 10; S. 534, 32, = be-þeaht; *pp. of* be-þeccan.

be-þærfeþ *expedit*, Mt. Rush. Stv. 19, 10, = be-þearfeþ. v. be-þearfan.

be-þeaht, -þéht *covered*, Exon. 117 a; Th. 451, 4; Dóm. 98: Elen. Kmbl. 2593; El. 1298; *pp. of* be-þeccan.

be-þearf, ic, he, ðú be-þearft *I have, thou hast, he has need*, Elen. Kmbl. 1082; El. 543: Ps. Spl. 15, 1; *pres. of* be-þurfan.

be-þearfaþ *he needs, wants;* opus habet:—Hwæt helpeþ *vel* beþearfeþ [MS. beþearfaþ] menn *what does it help to a man* or *what needs a man* [*of what use is it to a man*]? quid prodest homini? Mt. Rush. Stv. 16, 26. v. þearfan, þurfan, be-þurfan.

be-þeccan, bi-þeccan; *p.* -þeahte, -þehte, *pl.* -þeahton, -þehton; *pp.* -þeaht, -þeht *To cover, cover over, conceal;* tegere, contegere, operire:—Ða róde earme beþeahte *he covered the cross with his arm*, Elen. Kmbl. 2470; El. 1236: Cd. 185; Th. 230, 26; Dan. 239. Ǽghwæðer óðerne earme beþehte *each covered the other with his arm*, [*each embraced the other*], Andr. Kmbl. 2030; An. 1017. Mec mon biþeahte mid wǽdum *one covered me with weeds*, Exon. 28 b; Th. 87, 10; Cri. 1423: 51 b; Th. 179, 1; Gú. 1255. Hie heora líchoman leáfum beþeahton *they covered their bodies with leaves*, Cd. 40; Th. 52, 18; Gen. 845: Elen. Kmbl. 1669; El. 836. Se wæs beþeaht mid þæce *quod erat fœno tectum*, Bd. 3, 10; S. 534, note 32: Exon. 117 a; Th. 451, 4; Dóm. 98. Biþeaht *covered*, Exon. 47 b; Th. 163, 36; Gú. 1004. Heó helltregum wunodon þýstrum beþeahte *they dwelt in hell-torments covered with darkness*, Cd. 4; Th. 5, 23; Gen. 76. Synfulle beóþ þrosme beþehte *the sinful shall be covered with foulness*, Elen. Kmbl. 2593; El. 1298. Me beþeahton [Spl. C. beþehton] þeóstru *contexerunt me tenebræ*, Ps. Th. 54, 5.

beðen, e; *f? A fomentation, embrocation;* fomentum:—Mid beðenum *with fomentations*, Bd. 4, 32; S. 611, 20. v. beðing.

be-þencan, bi-þencan; *p.* -þohte, *pl.* -þohton; *pp.* -þoht *To consider, bear in mind*, BETHINK, *remember, trust, confide, entrust;* considerare, recordari, in se reverti, meminisse, fidere, confidere:—Scyle gumena gehwylc georne biþencan, ðæt us bicwom meahta Waldend *each man should well consider, that the Lord of might came to us*, Exon. 19 b; Th. 51, 27; Cri. 822. Ðæt we gǽstes wlite biþencen *that we bear in mind the spirit's beauty*, Exon. 20 a; Th. 53, 14; Cri. 850: 51 b; Th. 179, 32; Gú. 1270. Ðá beþohte he hine *then he bethought himself;* in se autem reversus, Lk. Bos. 15, 17: Ælfc. T. 35, 21. Híg beþohton ðæt híg hym seofon weras gecuron *they bethought that they would choose them seven men*, Nicod. 20; Thw. 10, 4. He beþohte swíðost to Arpelles *he trusted most in Harpalus*, Ors. 1, 12; Bos. 35, 34. Gif ðú to sǽmran gode biþencest *if thou confidest in a worse god*, Exon. 66 b; Th. 245, 30; Jul. 52. Beþohton [MS. beþohtan] hý ealle heora wígcræftas to Exantipuse *they entrusted all their military forces to Xantippus*, Ors. 4, 6; Bos. 85, 16. Cassander hæfde hys wisan beþoht to Seleucuse *Cassander had entrusted his affairs to Seleucus*, 3, 11; Bos. 74, 45.

be-þénede *served: substituted by Thorpe*, Beo. Th. 4077, for bewenede. v. be-wenian.

be-þennan; *p.* ede; *pp.* ed *To cover;* obducere:—He mec beþenede *he covered me*, Exon. 107 a; Th. 408, 15; Rä. 27, 12.

beðian, beðigean *to bathe, foment;* fovere:—Beða ða eágan *foment the eyes*, Herb. 1, 3; Lchdm. i. 72, 3: Med. ex Quadr. 4, 18; Lchdm. i. 346, 20. v. baðian.

beðigean *to wash, foment;* fovere:—Ða eágan to beðigeanne *to foment the eyes*, Med. ex Quadr. 4, 18; Lchdm. i. 346, 20; MS. H. Ic beðige *foveo*, Ælfc. Gr. 26, 5; Som. 28, 66. v. baðian.

beðing, e; *f. A fomentation, an assuaging* or *nourishing medicine;* fomentum, Bd. 4, 32; S. 611, 20; MS. B. v. beðen.

be-þoht, -þohte, -þohton *bethought, trusted, entrusted*, Ælfc. T. 35, 21: Ors. 3, 11; Bos. 74, 45; *p. and pp. of* be-þencan.

be-þorfte, -þorfton *did need*, Bt. 33, 4; Fox 128, 14; *p. of* be-þurfan.

be-þridian, -þrydian; *p.* ede; *pp.* ed [þrydian *from* þryþ *power, force*] *To force, overpower;* cogere, vi superare:—Ðæt hine man wolde beþridian mid ðam ilcan wrence *that they would overpower him by the same stratagem*, Ors. 6, 36; Bos. 132, 4. Ðæt hý án cyning swá ýðelíce on his geweald beþrydian sceolde *that one king should so easily force them under his power*, Ors. 3, 7; Bos. 59, 42: 2, 5; Bos. 47, 11.

be-þringan, bi-þringan; *p.* -þrang, *pl.* -þrungon; *pp.* -þrungen *To throng* or *press around, encompass, surround;* undique urgere, circumvenire, circumdare:—Ic wæs bísgum beþrungen *I was encompassed with misery*, Elen. Kmbl. 2488; El. 1245: 1896; El. 950. Se sceal wesan wyrmum beþrungen *he shall be surrounded with worms*, Exon. 54 a;

Th. 316, 30; Môd. 56. Fênix biþ on middum þreátum biþrungen *the phœnix is in the midst surrounded by multitudes*, 60 b; Th. 221, 27; Ph. 341.

be-þrungen *encompassed*, Elen. Kmbl. 2488; El. 1245; *pp. of* be-þringan.

be-þryccan *to press on, impress.* v. bi-þryccan.

be-þuncan *To consider, look out;* consulere, prospicere, Exon. 113 a; Th. 432, 29; Rä. 49, 7.

be-þurfan, bi-þurfan, ic, he -þearf, ðú -þearft, *pl.* -þurfon; *p.* -þorfte, *pl.* -þorfton; *subj.* -þurfe, *pl.* -þurfen; *p.* -þorfte, *pl.* -þorften; *gen.* or *acc.* or *v. n. To need, have need, want, to be in want, to require;* opus habere, egere, indigere:—Wîsdômes beþearf *he requires wisdom*, Elen. Kmbl. 1082; El. 543. Ic ârna biþearf *I need mercy*, Exon. 76 a; Th. 285, 17; Jul. 715: Ælfc. Gr. 26, 2; Som. 28, 48. Gôda mînra ðú ne beþearft *bonorum meorum non eges*, Ps. Spl. 15, 1. Ge beþurfon *indigetis*, Mt. Bos. 6, 32. We bicgaþ ða þing ðe we beþurfon *ememus necessaria*, Gen. 43, 4, 8. Mâre ðonne he beþurfe *more than he has need of*, Bt. 14, 2; Fox 44, 21.

be-þweán, ic -þweá; *p.* -þwôh, *pl.* -þwôgon; *pp.* -þwegen *To wet, bedew, wash;* rigare:—Mid mînum teárum strecednysse mîne oððe mîne beddinge ic beþweá oððe ic gelecce *lacrimis meis stratum meum rigabo*, Ps. Lamb. 6, 7.

be-þwyr; *adj.* [be, þwir *wicked*] *Perverse, depraved;* depravatus, Cot. 63.

be-þýan; *p.* -þýde, -þýdde, *pl.* -þýddon; *pp.* -þýed, -þýd *To thrust;* trudere:—Hî beþýddon *they thrust*, Ors. 4, 1; Bos. 78, 8.

be-þýddon *thrust*, Ors. 4, 1; Bos. 78, 8; *p. pl. of* be-þýan.

be-tiénan *to shut, shut up;* concludere, Ps. Spl. T. 34, 3: Cot. 58. v. be-týnan.

betigean *to be* or *make better;* meliorare:—Sôna hý betigeaþ [MS. batigeaþ] *they will be better soon*, Lchdm. iii. 54, 33. v. beterian, betrian.

be-tîhan; *p.* -tâh, *pl.* -tigon; *pp.* -tigen, -tygen [be, tîhan, II. *to bring a charge against any one*] *To accuse, impeach;* criminari, accusare:—Gif he oft betygen wǽre *if he has often been accused*, L. In. 18; Th. i. 114, 6: 37; Th. i. 124, 21: 52; Th. i. 134, 12. v. be-teón, III.

be-tîhtlian, -týhtlian; *p.* ode, ede, ade; *pp.* od, ed, ad *To accuse, charge;* accusare, criminari:—Gif he betîhtlod weorþe *if he be accused*, L. C. S. 31; Th. i. 396, 1. Ðe oft betîhtlede wǽron *who have often been accused*, L. Ath. i. 7; Th. i. 202, 25. Ælc mynetere ðe betîhtlad sî *every moneyer who is accused*, L. Eth. iii. 8; Th. i. 296, 15. Gif he betýhtlad wurðe *if he should be accused*, L. Eth. i. 1; Th. i. 280, 8, 16.

be-tilldon, be-teldon, Bd. 4, 26; S. 602, 19, *for* betǽldon *deceived.* v. tǽlan.

be-timbran; *p.* ede; *pp.* ed *To build, construct with timber;* ædificare, construere:—Hî betimbredon bêcn *they constructed a beacon*, Beo. Kmbl. 6312; B. 3160.

bêting *a cable*, Bt. 41, 3; Fox 250, 15. v. bǽting.

bêtl, es; *m.* A BEETLE; blatta:—Ða blacan bêtlas *blattæ nigro colore*, Cot. 141. v. bîtel.

bet-lîc; *adj. sup.* bet-lîcast *Good-like, excellent;* eximius:—Bold wæs betlîc *the mansion was excellent*, Beo. Th. 3854; B. 1925. Betlîcast, Exon. 8 b; Th. 5, 7; Cri. 66.

bet-nes, -ness, e; *f.* [bet *better*] *Satisfaction, amends, amendment, recompence;* satisfactio, compensatio:—Ðæt ic bûton betnesse beó mînra synna *that I am without amendment of my sins*, L. De Cf. 10; Th. ii. 264, 16.

betoce *the herb betony*, L. M. 1, 39; Lchdm. ii. 104, 4. v. betonice.

be-togen. I. *drawn over, covered, inclosed*, Ors. 5, 7; Bos. 107, 8. II. *accused*, L. In. 54; Th. i. 136, 10; *pp. of* be-teón.

betogenes, -ness, -niss, e; *f. An accusation;* accusatio:—Be cierlisces monnes betogenesse [MS. H. betogenisse] *of a churlish man's accusation*, L. In. 37, titl; Th. i. 124, note 50.

be-tolden *surrounded*, Andr. Kmbl. 1976; An. 990; *pp. of* be-teldan.

betonice, an; *f: also Lat.* betonĭca, æ; *f. The herb* BETONY; betonĭca officinālis. This species is the *common wood-betony*, the *betonĭca officinālis* of Linnæus. It is a species of the genus *Stachys*, but it was formerly a species of the genus *Betonica.* It is very plentiful in Great Britain, and formerly much used in medicine. The leaves have a rough bitter taste, and are slightly aromatic. The roots are nauseous and very bitter, and when taken act as purgatives and emetics:—Genim betonican gôdne dǽl *take a good deal of betony*, Lchdm. iii. 22, 16. Nim betonican sǽd *take seed of betony*, iii. 72, 6. Wyl on ealaþ betonican *boil betony in ale*, L. M. 1, 16; Lchdm. ii. 58, 24. Wyrc betonican and pipores seofon and xx corna tosomne getrifulad *work betony and twenty-seven corns of pepper triturated together*, 1, 21; Lchdm. ii. 64, 6: 1, 22; Lchdm. ii. 64, 16. *Latin*, Betonĭca, æ; *f*:—Ðis is seó grêne sealf,—betonĭca, rude, etc. *this is the green salve,—betony, rue, etc.* Lchdm. iii. 6, 8. Genim ðás ylcan wyrte and betonĭcam *take this same wort and betony*, Herb. 135, 3; Lchdm. i. 252, 4. [Betonĭca, quæ et Vettonĭca dicitur, quod eam Vettones = Οὐέττονες, in Hispania invenerunt, Plin. 25, 8: Prior 20.]

betost; *adj. Best;* optimus:—Nû is ôfost betost, ðæt we þeódcyning ðǽr sceáwian *now is speed best, that we may see there the great king*, Beo. Th. 6007; B. 3007. v. betst.

be-træppan, -treppan [be, treppan *to trap*] *To* BETRAP, *to entrap;* circumvallare:—Meahton hî ðone here betræppan [betreppan, col. 1] *they might entrap the army*, Chr. 992; Th. 238, 40, col. 2.

betre *better*:—Hit is betre *it is better*, Bt. 38, 7; Fox 210, 5. v. betera.

be-tredan; *p.* -træd, *pl.* -trǽdon; *pp.* -treden *To tread upon, cover;* conculcare:—Þýstru betredaþ me *tenebræ conculcabunt me*, Ps. Spl. C. 138, 10.

be-treppan *to entrap*, Chr. 992; Th. 238, 40, col. 1. v. be-træppan.

betrian, betrigan; *p.* ode; *pp.* od [bet *well*, betra *better*] *To be better, to excel, to make better, to grow better;* meliorari, emendare:—Ic betrige *melioror*, Ælfc. Gr. 25; Som. 27, 13. v. beterian, gebeterian.

betrung, bettrung, e; *f.* [betrian *to be better*] *A* BETTERING, *amending;* emendatio:—Ðæt hit wǽre heora betrung *that it was their amendment*, Bt. 38, 7; Fox 210, 13.

be-trymian; *p.* ede; *pp.* ed [be, trymian *to fortify*] *To besiege, environ;* circumdare vallo:—Ðîne fýnd ðê betrymiaþ *circumdabunt te inimici tui vallo*, Lk. Bos. 19, 43. Ge geseóþ Hierusalem mid here betrymede *ye shall see Jerusalem besieged with an army*, 21, 20.

betst, betest; *adj. sup. def.* se betsta, betesta; seó, ðæt beteste; *pos.* gôd [bet *good;* v. bet-lîc *good-like*] *Best, the best, first;* optimus, primus:—Ða þing ðe ge betstan gelîfaþ [MS. betst ongelifaþ] *ea quæ vos optima credebatis*, Bd. 1, 25; S. 487, note 12. Scipio, se besta [Laud MS. betsta] Rômana witena *Scipio, the best of the Roman senators*, Ors. 5, 4; Bos. 104, 38; Cot. MS. Tib. B. I. fol. 85 b. Se betesta *the best*, Cot. 153. He sealde ðæt betste hors *he gave the best horse*, Bd. 3, 14; S. 540, 16. Ðara betstena sumes *of some one of the best*, Bt. 30, 1; Fox 110, 5. [*Goth.* bats? *good; comp.* batiza *better; sup.* batists *best: O. Nrs. comp.* betri *better; sup.* beztr *best.*]

betst; *adv. sup. of* wel [? bet *well, q. v.*] *Best, most;* optime:—Ðæt betst lîcaþ *that pleases best*, Bt. 18, 2; Fox 64, 23. Ic him betst truwode *I most trusted them*, Bt. 2; Fox 4, 12. Albînus wæs betst gelǽred *Albinus was most learned*, Bd. pref; S. 471, 23.

betst-boren; *pp. Best-born, eldest;* major natu:—Moises clipode ða betstborenan *Moyses vocavit majores natu*, Lev. 9, 1: Gen. 50, 7: Deut. 5, 23.

bett *better*, Bd. 3, 9; S. 533, 34. v. bet.

bête *corrected*, Bd. 4, 25; S. 599, 25; *p. of* bêtan.

bettonice, an; *f. The herb betony;* betonĭca officinālis:—Genim bettonican and pipor *take betony and pepper*, Lchdm. i. 380, 24. v. betonice.

bettrung, e; *f. A bettering, ameliorating;* emendatio:—To his bettrunge [Cot. betrunge] *to his amelioration*, Past. 31, 1; Hat. MS. 39 b, 8. v. betrung.

be-tugon *shut in, inclosed;* concluserunt, Lk. Bos. 5, 6; *p. pl. of* be-teón.

be-tuh; *prep. dat. acc. Between;* inter:—He bewîcode betuh ðâm twâm hergum *he encamped between the two armies*, Chr. 894; Ing. 115, 4; Th. 164, 23, col. 2; 165, 22, col. 1; 23, col. 2. Betuh Arabia and Palestîna *between Arabia and Palestine*, Ors. 1, 3; Bos. 27, 20: Cd. 37; Th. 47, 26; Gen. 766. v. be-tweoh.

be-tux *between.* v. betux-sittan, be-tweoh.

betux-sittan *to insert, interpose, to set, put* or *bring in;* interserere. v. betux, sittan.

be-tweoh, be-tweohs, be-tweox, be-twih, be-twyh, be-twyx, be-twyxt, be-twuh, be-twuht, be-twux, be-twuxt, be-tuh, be-tux; *prep. dat. acc.* [be *by, with;* twi, twihs, tweox, twux *duo*] *Between,* BETWIXT, *among, amid, in the midst;* inter, in medio. I. *dat*:—Men and nêtenu habbaþ andan betweoh him *men and beasts have enmity between them*, Bt. Met. Fox 28, 104; Met. 28, 52. Betweohs him *among them;* in cujus medio, Ex. 34, 10. Betwyh him *among them*, Bt. 39, 12; Fox 230, 27. Betwuh ðâm wæs seó Magdalenisce Maria, and Maria Iacobes môder *inter quas erat Maria Magdalene, et Maria Iacobi mater*, Mt. Bos. 27, 56. Betwuht him *between them*, Bt. 39, 13; Fox 234, 5. Betwux wîfa bearnum *inter natos mulierum*, Lk. Bos. 7, 28. Betwuxt ðâm warum *among their wares* [*merchandise*], Nat. S. Greg. Els. 11, 14. Hǽðe stent betuh Winedum and Seaxum and Angle *Haddeby stands in the midst of the Winedi, Saxons and Angles*, Ors. 1, 19; Bos. 21, 30. II. *acc*:—Swâ lamb betweox wulfas *sicut agnos inter lupos*, Lk. Bos. 10, 3. Betwih ða mægen *inter virtutes*, Bd. 4, 9; S. 576, 28. Ne byþ swâ betweox eów *non ita erit inter vos*, Mt. Bos. 20, 26. III. *the case sometimes precedes the prep.* or *is separated from it*:—Hî him healdaþ betwuh sibbe *they keep peace between themselves*, Bt. Met. Fox 29, 8; Met. 29, 4. Him betuh *between them*, Cd. 37; Th. 47, 26; Gen. 766.

be-tweohs *among*:—Betweohs him *among them*, Ex. 34, 10. v. be-tweoh.

be-tweonan; *prep. dat. acc. Between;* inter:—Unc betweonan *between us two*, Cd. 91; Th. 114, 10; Gen. 1902. v. be-tweonum.

be-tweonum, be-tweonan, be-twinum, be-twinan, be-twynan, bi-tweon, bi-tweonum; *prep.* **I.** *dat.* **II.** *acc.* [be, bi *by, with*, tweo *two; dat.* tweonum, twinum, tweon, twin, twyn] BETWEEN, *betwixt, among, amid, in the midst;* inter, in medio. **I.** *dat.* Betweonan đām *between them*, Ps. Th. 102, 12. Betweonum đissum þingum *amid these things*, Bd. 1, 27; S. 488, note 26. Đā Iudeas cwǣdon betweonan him sylfum *then the Jews said among themselves*, Jn. Bos. 7, 35. **II.** *acc.* Đū hī betweonum wætera weallas lǣddest *thou ledest them between water-walls*, Ps. Th. 105, 9. Đā seó cwēn ongan lǣran đæt hie sybbe swā same sylfra betweonum freóndrǣdenne gelǣston *then the queen began to teach that they should hold peace also amid their friendly band*, Elen. Kmbl. 2412; El. 1207. **III.** *sometimes* betweonum *follows its case, or is separated from it:*—Đā gewearþ hī him betweonum *they then agreed between themselves*, Ors. 6, 30; Bos. 126, 24. Lēton him đa betweonum tān wisian *they let the lot decide between them*, Andr. Kmbl. 2199; An. 1101. Ne sceolon unc betweonan teónan weaxan *injury shall not wax between us two*, Cd. 91; Th. 114, 10; Gen. 1902. Hluton hell-cræftum, hǣđengildum teledon betwinum *they cast lots, counted, with hellish arts, amid heathen gods*, Andr. Kmbl. 2207; An. 1105. Gif ge habbaþ lufe eów betwynan *si dilectionem habueritis ad invicem*, Jn. Bos. 13, 35. Friþ freóndum bitweon *peace between friends*, Exon. 32 a; Th. 101, 15; Cri. 1659. **IV.** *sometimes the case is placed between* be *and* tweonum, *as,*—Be sǣm tweonum *between the seas*, Cd. 163; Th. 205, 28; Exod. 442: 170; Th. 214, 1; Exod. 562. v. bi-tweonum.

be-tweonum; *adv. Between;* inter, in medio:—Ne sī lang fæc be-tweonum *ne sit longum spatium in medio*, Bd. 4, 9; S. 577, 27.

be-tweox *between;* inter:—Nū ic eów sende swā swā lamb betweox wulfas *ecce ego mitto vos sicut agnos inter lupos*, Lk. Bos. 10, 3: 11, 51: Ps. Th. 87, 4: 88, 5: Bt. Met. Fox 11, 90; Met. 11, 45: 11, 168; Met. 11, 84: 24, 25; Met. 24, 13. v. be-tweoh.

be-twih *between.* v. betwih-licgan, be-tweoh.

betwih-licgan, he -ligeþ *To lie between;* interjacere:—Gif mycel feornys sīþfætes betwihligeþ *si longinquitas itineris magna interjacet*, Bd. 1, 27; S. 491, 39. v. be-tweoh.

be-twinan; *prep. dat. Within, among;* intra, inter:—Cwǣdon sume bōceras him betwinan *some scribes said among themselves*, Mt. Bos. 9, 3. v. be-tweonum **III.**

be-twinum *between, amid;* inter, in medio, Andr. Kmbl. 2207; An. 1105. v. be-tweonum.

be-twion; *adj.* [be *by, with;* twām, twǣm, *dat. of* twā *two*] *Double, folding, twofold;* duplex:—Mid betwion mentle *with a folding mantle;* diploide, Ps. Spl. T. 108, 28.

be-twuh; *prep. dat. acc. Between, among;* inter:—He gewīcode be-twuh đǣm twām hergum *he encamped between the two armies*, Chr. 894; Th. 164, 23, col. 1. He betwuh him wunaþ *he dwells among them*, Bt. 39, 13; Fox 234, 10: Bt. Met. Fox 29, 8; Met. 29, 4. v. be-tweoh.

be-twuht; *prep. dat. Between;* inter:—Betwuht him *between them*, Bt. 39, 13; Fox 234, 5. v. be-tweoh.

be-twux *between, among;* inter:—Nis betwux wīfa bearnum, nān mǣrra wītega, đonne Iohannes se Fulluhtere *major inter natos mulierum propheta nemo est Ioanne Baptista*, Lk. Bos. 7, 28: Gen. 3, 14. v. be-tweoh.

betwux-alegednes, -nyss, e; *f.* [betwux *between;* aleged, alegd *laid*] What is laid or placed between, *an interposition, interjection;* inter-jectio:—*Interjectio* mæg beón gecweden betwuxalegednyss on Englisc, forđanđe he līþ betwux wordum *an interjection may be called a laying between in English, because it lies between words*, Ælfc. Gr. 48; Som. 48, 61. v. betwyx-aworpennyss.

betwux-aworpennys *an interjection;* interjectio. v. betwyx-awor-pennyss.

be-twuxt *among;* inter:—Đā geseah Grēgōrius betwuxt đām warum, cȳpecnihtas gesette *then Gregory saw among their wares, youths set for sale*, Nat. S. Greg. Els. 11, 14. v. be-tweoh.

be-twyh *between, among;* inter, in medio:—Betwyh đās þing *between these things, in the mean while, whilst;* interea, Bd. 1, 27; S. 488, 26. Betwyh him *among them*, Bt. 39, 12; Fox 230, 27. v. be-tweoh.

betwyh-geset *interposed;* interpositus, Bd. 4, 9; S. 576, 42.

be-twynan; *prep. dat. Between, among;* inter:—Him betwynan *among them*, Mt. Jun. 9, 3: Jn. Bos. 16, 17. Ge habbaþ lufe eów be-twynan *dilectionem habueritis ad invicem*, Jn. Bos. 13, 35. v. be-tweonum.

be-twyx *betwixt, between:*—Betwyx wīfa bearnum *inter natos muli-erum*, Mt. Bos. 11, 11: Chr. 1126; Th. 377, 10. v. betwyx-sendan, betweoh.

betwyx-aworpennyss, e; *f. An interjection;* interjectio:—*Inter-jectio* is betwyxaworpennyss. Se dǣl līþ betwux ōđrum wordum, and geswutelaþ đæs mōdes styrunge. *Heu* geswutelaþ mōdes sārnesse *an interjection is a throwing between. This part of speech lieth between other words, and denotes a stirring of the mind.* Heu *denotes a soreness of mind*, Ælfc. Gr. 5; Som. 3, 55. v. betwux-alegednes.

betwyx-sendan *to send between;* intermittere, R. Conc. Procem.

be-twyxt *betwixt, between;* inter, Hemm. p. 403. v. be-tweoh.

be-tygen *accused*, L. In. 14; Th. i. 110, 16; *pp. of* be-tīhan.

be-tȳhþ *accuses*, L. In. 46; Th. i. 130, 12; *pres. of* be-teón.

be-tȳhtlian *to accuse*, L. Eth. i. 1; Th. i. 280, 8, 16. v. be-tīhtlian.

be-tȳnan, -tiénan, bi-tȳnan; *p.* -tȳnde, *pl.* -tȳndon; *impert.* -tȳn, -tiéne; *pp.* -tȳned, -tiéned, -tȳnd; *v. a.* [be, tȳnan *to hedge in*]. **I.** *to inclose* or *surround with a hedge, inclose, close, shut, shut up;* sepem circumdare, sepire, intercludere, claudere, occludere, concludere:—Sum hīrēdes ealdor wæs, se plantode wīngerd, and betȳnde hyne *homo erat paterfamilias, qui plantavit vineam, et sepem circumdedit ei*, Mt. Bos. 21, 33: Mk. Bos. 12, 1. Ceorles weorþig sceal beón betȳned *a churl's close ought to be surrounded with a hedge*, L. In. 40; Th. i. 126, 13. Hī hine betȳndon in ān nearo fæsten *they inclosed him in a narrow fastness*, Bd. 4, 26; S. 602, note 19. Hāteþ heáhcyning helle betȳnan *the mighty king shall command to close hell*, Salm. Kmbl. 348; Sal. 173. Đæs heán biscopes leoma on đysse byrigenne syndon betȳnde [MS. be-tyned] *pontificis summi hoc clauduntur membra sepulchro*, Bd. 2, 1; S. 500, 22: Exon. 110 b; Th. 422, 25; Rä. 41, 11. Wearþ se hālga wong bitȳned *the holy plain was closed*, 61 b; Th. 227, 7; Ph. 419. He hine inne betȳnan nolde *he would not shut it in*, L. Alf. 21; Th. i. 48, 31. He đæt folc ūte betȳnde *he shut the people out*, Ors. 4, 5; Bos. 81, 40. Hȳ betȳndon Ianes duru *they shut the doors of Janus*, 6, 7; Bos. 120, 5: 5, 14; Bos. 113, 42. Gif hwā wæterpyt betȳnedne ontȳne, and hine eft ne betȳne, gelde swelc neát swelc đǣron befealle *if any one open a water-pit [that is] shut up, and close it not again, let him pay for whatever cattle may fall therein*, L. Alf. 22; Th. i. 50, 6, 7. Betiéne togeánes hīg *conclude adversus eos*, Ps. Spl. T. 34, 3. **II.** *to end, finish, conclude;* finire:—Heó đus đæt word betȳnde *thus she ended the speech;* ita sermonem conclusit, Bd. 4, 9; S. 577, 28.

be-tyran [be, tyrwa *tar*] *To* BETAR, *to smear over, to stain a dark colour;* pice liquida inficere, *q. d.* pullo *vel* bætico colore imbuere, Æqu. vern. 2.

be-ufan; *adv.* [be, ufan] *Above;* supra:—Swā we hēr be-ufan cwǣdon *as we here have said above*, L. Ath. iv. 4; Th. i. 224, 4. v. būfan.

be-ūtan; *prep. dat.* [be, ūtan *out*] *Without;* extra:—Wundorlīc is geworden đīn wīsdōm eall, se is be-ūtan me *mirabilis facta est scientia tua ex me*, Ps. Th. 138, 4. Gif ic mīne fiđeru gefō, fleóge ǣr leóhte, ōþ đæt ic be-ūtan wese eallum sǣwum *si sumpsero pennas meas ante lucem, et habitavero in postremo maris*, 138, 7. Đa be-ūtan beóþ earce bordum *who shall be without the boards of the ark*, Cd. 67; Th. 81, 32; Gen. 1354. v. būtan.

be-waden; *part. p. A quo aliquid abiit?*—Of wombe bewaden, Exon. 130 b; Th. 499, 32; Rä. 88, 24. DER. be, wadan.

be-wǣfan; *p.* de; *pp.* ed [wǣfan *to cover*] *To befold, wrap round, cover, clothe;* obvolvere, amicire, operire, induere:—Mid ānre seȳtan bewǣfed *amictus sindone*, Mk. Bos. 14, 51: Homl. Th. ii. 242, 24. Heó nam hyre wǣfels and bewǣfde hīg *illa sustulit pallium et operuit se*, Gen. 24, 65. Martinus me bewǣfde mid đyssere wǣde *Martin clothed me with this garment*, Homl. Th. ii. 500, 34. His cempan mid wolcnreádum wǣfelse hine bewǣfdon *his soldiers clothed him in a scarlet robe*, ii. 252, 25. Ic eom reáde bewǣfed *I am clothed with red*, Exon. 126 a; Th. 484, 2; Rä. 70, 1: Past. 14, 3; Hat. MS. 17 b, 19. [*Goth.* bi-wáibyan *to wind, put round.*]

be-wæg *surrounded*, Bt. 39, 4; Fox 216, 25; *p. of* be-wegan.

be-wǣgan; *p.* de; *pp.* ed *To deceive, disappoint;* frustrari:—Ne bewǣgde him *non frustratus est eum*, Ps. Spl. C. 131, 11. v. bi-wǣgan.

be-wægnan; *p.* ede; *pp.* ed *To offer;* offerre:—Him wæs freónd-lađu bewægned *a friendly invitation was offered to him*, Beo. Th. 2390; B. 1193.

be-wǣlan; *p.* de; *pp.* ed *To afflict;* undique vexare, affligere, cru-ciare:—Wītum bewǣled *afflicted with torments*, Andr. Kmbl. 2721; An. 1363.

be-wǣpnian, -wēpnian; *p.* ede; *pp.* ed [be, wǣpen *a weapon*] *To take away arms, disarm;* armis spoliare:—Be đam đe ōđerne bewēpnaþ *de eo qui alium armis spoliaret*, L. C. S. 61, titl; Th. i. 408, 16. Gif man æt unlagum man bewǣpnige [bewepnie MS. B.] *if any one unlawfully disarm a man*, 61; Th. i. 408, 18.

be-wand *wrapped, enwrapped*, Bd. 3, 11; S. 536, 9: Lk. Bos. 2, 7; *p. of* be-windan.

be-warenian, -warnian; *p.* ode; *pp.* od *To guard, beware;* custodire, cavere:—He wel ne bewarenaþ wiđ đa unþeáwas *he does not well guard against the vices*, Bt. Met. Fox 16, 45; Met. 16, 23. Đa đe hie wiđ đa læssan scylda bewareniaþ *those who guard themselves against the lesser sins*, Past. 57, 1; Hat. MS.

be-warian, -warigan; *p.* ode; *pp.* od *To keep, guard, preserve;* custo-dire, arcere:—Bisceopas godcunde heorda bewarian and bewerian sceolon *bishops ought to guard and defend their spiritual flocks*, L. C. E. 26;

Wilk. 133, 22; Th. i. 374, 24. Ðæt ðú meaht wíte bewarigan *that thou mayest ward off punishment*, Cd. 27; Th. 35, 31; Gen. 563. v. warian.

be-warnian *to beware*, R. Ben. 7. v. be-warenian.

be-weallan; *p.* -weóll, *pl.* -weóllon; *pp.* -weallen *To boil away*; decoquere:—Óþ-ðæt þrydda dǽl sý beweallen *till the third part be boiled away*, Med. ex Quadr. 1, 3; Lchdm. i. 328, 17: 8, 10; Lchdm. i. 360, 1.

be-wealwian; *p.* ode; *pp.* od *To wallow*; volutare:—Swín on ða solu bewealwiaþ *swine wallow in the mire*, Bt. 37, 4; Fox 192, 29.

be-weardian, -weardigan; *part.* -weardigende; *p.* ode; *pp.* od *To ward, protect, keep*; custodire, protegere, observare:—Ðú, Drihten, beweardast us *tu, Domine, custodies nos*, Ps. Spl. 11, 8. Hálige englas ða dǽda beweardiaþ *holy angels protect the deeds*, L. C. E. 4; Th. i. 360, 31. Beweardigende *observantes*, Ps. Spl. 30, 7.

be-wearp *cast*, Bt. 7, 2; Fox 16, 25; *p. of* be-weorpan.

be-weaxan, bi-weaxan; *p.* -weóx, *pl.* -weóxon; *pp.* -weaxen *To overgrow, cover over*; obducere, obserere:—Sindon burgtúnas brérum beweaxene [MS. beweaxne] *the city-dwellings are overgrown with briers*, Exon. 115 b; Th. 443, 17; Kl. 31. Scyllum biweaxen *overgrown with scales*, 60 a; Th. 219, 21; Ph. 310.

be-weddian, -weddigan; *p.* ede, ode; *pp.* ed, od *To espouse, wed*; spondere, despondere:—Ic beháte oððe ic beweddige [MS. bewedige] *spondeo*, Ælfc. Gr. 26, 6; Som. 29, 10. Gif he híg his suna beweddaþ *si filio suo desponderit eam*, Ex. 21, 9. v. weddian.

be-weddung, e; *f. A betrothal, wedding*; oppigneratio, connubium:—Be wífmannes beweddunge *of a woman's betrothal*, L. Edm. B. titl; Th. i. 254, 1.

be-wefan; *p.* -wæf, *pl.* -wǽfon; *pp.* -wefen *To cover over, envelope*; obtexere, obducere:—Biþ ðæt brægen mid reáman bewefen *the brain is covered over with a membrane*, Lchdm. iii. 146, 4.

be-wegan; *p.* -wæg, *pl.* -wǽgon; *pp.* -wegen *To cover, cover over, surround*; obducere, circumdare:—Bewegen wælmiste *covered with the mist of death*, Exon. 87 b; Th. 329, 30; Vy. 42. He hí bewæg mid wuda útan *he surrounded them with wood*, Bt. 39, 4; Fox 216, 25.

be-wendan; *p.* -wende; *pp.* -wended, -wend *To turn, turn round* or *about, convert*; vertere, convertere:—Bewend to ðære menigu *conversus ad turbam*, Mk. Bos. 5, 30. Se Hǽlend bewende hyne *the Saviour turned himself about*, Mt. Bos. 9, 22: Mk. Bos. 8, 33. Æt sumum cyrre bewend *aliquando conversus*, Lk. Foxe 22, 32. v. wendan.

be-wenian; *p.* ede; *pp.* ed [be, wenian *to accustom, draw to one's self, honour*] *To entertain, take care of*; hospitio accipere:—We wǽron hér tela bewenede *we were here kindly entertained*, Beo. Th. 3646, note; B. 1821. Dryht-bearn Dena duguþa bewenede [MS. *and* Thorpe's note, 4077; bí werede, B. 2035] *a noble offspring of the Danes entertained the knights*, 4077, note.

be-weópon *wept over, bewailed*, Num. 20, 30; *p. pl. of* be-wépan.

be-weorcean *to adorn*, Elen. Kmbl. 2045; El. 1024. v. be-wyrcan.

be-weorpan, -wyrpan; ic -weorpe, ðú -wyrpst, he -weorpeþ, -wyrpþ, *pl.* -weorpaþ; *p.* -wearp, *pl.* -wurpon; *pp.* -worpen. I. *to cast, cast down, throw*; projicere, dejicere:—Seó cwén hét [híg] ðam cyninge heáfod ofaceorfan, and bewyrpan on ánne cylle *the queen commanded [them] to cut off the king's head, and to cast it into a vessel*, Ors. 2, 4; Bos. 45, 33. Hwæt bewearp ðé on ðás gnornunga *what has cast thee into these lamentations?* Bt. 7, 2; Fox 16, 25. He hæfþ us beworpen on ealra wíta mǽste *he hath cast us down into the greatest of all torments*, Cd. 21; Th. 25, 13; Gen. 393. Ic wæs hér unscildig on pytt beworpen *I was thrown here innocent into a dungeon*, Gen. 40, 15. II. *to cast about* or *over, cover over, surround*; conjicere, supertegere, cingere:—Hláford, lǽt hine [fíctreów] gyt ðis geár, óþ ic hine bedelfe, and ic hine beweorpe mid meoxe *Lord, suffer it [the fig-tree] yet this year, till I dig about it, and cast it about [surround it] with dung*, Lk. Bos. 13, 8. Oft beweorpeþ ánre þecene wundrum gewlitegad *often casts over with a covering wondrously adorned*, Exon. 128 b; Th. 493, 20; Rä. 81, 34. Hafaþ fægerne eard wætre beworpen *it hath a fair dwelling surrounded with water*, Runic pm. 28; Kmbl. 345, 8; Hick. Thes. i. 135. DER. weorpan.

be-weotian; *p.* ode; *pp.* od *To observe, watch over*; observare, curæ habere:—Draca hord beweotode *a dragon watched over the hoard*, Beo. Th. 4431; B. 2212. v. be-witian.

be-wépan; *p.* -weóp, *pl.* -weópon; *pp.* -wópen *To weep, weep over, bewail*; flere, deflere, plorare:—Ic bewépe *defleo*, Ælfc. Gr. 26, 1; Som. 28, 28. Hí beweópon Aarones forþsíþ *they bewailed Aaron's death*, Num. 20, 30. Wyduwan heora nǽron bewópene *viduæ eorum non plorabantur*, Ps. Lamb. 77, 64: Ors. 2, 8; Bos. 51, 41.

be-wépnian *to unweapon, disarm*, L. C. S. 61, titl; Th. i. 408, 16. v. be-wǽpnian.

be-werenes, -ness, e; *f.* [be-wered *forbidden*] *A forbidding*; prohibitio:—Óþ bewerenesse to onfónne ðam hálgan geryne *usque ad prohibitionem percipiendi sancti mysterii*, Bd. 1, 27; S. 496, 43.

be-werian, bi-werian, -wergan; *p.* ede, ode; *pp.* ed, od *To defend restrain*; defendere, prohibere, tueri:—Bisceopas godcunde heorda bewarian and bewerian sceolon *bishops ought to guard and defend* [tueri debent] *their spiritual flocks*, L. C. E. 26; Wilk. 133, 22; Th. i. 374, 25. Bewerede *coercuit*, Cot. 56. Bewered *prohibitus*, Bd. 1, 27; S. 493, 10. Bewerode *defendit*, Ex. 2, 17. Bewerod *prohibitus*, Ælfc. Gl. 63; Som. 68, 104. DER. werian.

be-werigend, es; *m. A defender*; protector, Ps. Spl. 27, 11.

be-werung, e; *f. A defence, fortification*; tutamen:—Bewerung strang *a strong defence*, Scint. 64.

be-wícian; *p.* ode; *pp.* od *To encamp*; castra metari:—Ælfréd cyning bewícode betuh ðám twám hergum *king Alfred encamped between the two armies*, Chr. 894; Gib. 92, 21.

be-wimman; *g.* -wimmannes; *f.* [be-wimmen, Wrt. Voc. 72, 36] *A niece*; neptis, Som. Lye. v. wimman.

be-windan, bi-windan; *p.* -wand, -wond, *pl.* -wundon; *pp.* -wunden; *v. a. To wind* or *bind around* or *about, entwine, wrap, enwrap, encircle, surround, wind, turn*; amplecti, involvere, cingere, circumdare, volvere:—Hí ísene næglas mid flexe bewundon *they wound iron nails round with flax*, Ors. 4, 1; Bos. 78, 8. Wæs bewunden *was wound round*, Andr. Kmbl. 38; An. 19. Wírum þewunden *bound round with wires*, Beo. Th. 2066; B. 1031. Iosep bewand hyne mid clǽnre scýtan *Ioseph involvit illud in sindone munda*, Mt. Bos. 27, 59: Lk. Bos. 2, 7: Bd. 3, 11; S. 536, 9. Geseah heó monnes líchoman mid scýtan bewundenne *vidit corpus hominis sindone involutum*, Bd. 4, 9; S. 576, 32. Wæs Cristes lof on fyrhþlocan bewunden *Christ's praise was entwined within his breast*, Andr. Kmbl. 116; An. 58: Beo. Th. 6283; B. 3146. Biwunden *entwined*, Exon. 69 a; Th. 256, 20; Jul. 234. Sum gǽstes þearfe móde bewindeþ *one wraps his spirit's need in his mind*, 79 b; Th. 298, 18: Crä. 87: Ps. Th. 102, 12. Wæs feorh æðelinges flǽsce bewunden *the prince's soul was wrapped in flesh*, Beo. Th. 4840; B. 2424. Mec mon folmum biwond, and mec ðá on þeóstre alegde biwundenne mid wonnum clâðum *one with hands enwrapped me, and then laid me in darkness enwrapped in dusky clothes*, Exon. 28 b; Th. 87, 9-12; Cri. 1422-1424. He wæs clâðum biwunden *he was enwrapped with clothes*, 18 b; Th. 45, 27; Cri. 725. Ðǽr is geat gylden wynnum bewunden *there is the golden gate encircled with joys*, Cd. 227; Th. 305, 21; Sat. 650: Beo. Th. 6097; B. 3052. He is wuldre biwunden *he is encircled with glory*, Exon. 65 b; Th. 241, 34; Ph. 666. Ða þreó wæter steápe stánbyrig streámum bewindaþ *the three waters surround lofty cities of stone with their streams*, Cd. 100; Th. 133, 18; Gen. 2212. Hwonne us líffreá tíre bewinde *when the Lord of life may surround us with honour*, Exon. 8 a; Th. 3, 1; Cri. 29. Ic eom bewunden mid wuldre *I am surrounded with glory*, 108 a; Th. 412, 18; Rä. 31, 2. He geseah Sennera feld sídne bewindan *he saw Shinar's field wide winding*, Cd. 205; Th. 253, 28; Dan. 602. Abraham bewand ða hleóðorcwydas on hige sínum *Abraham turned the revelations in his mind*, 107; Th. 140, 34; Gen. 2337.

be-wiste *governed, presided*, Gen. 24, 2; *p. of* be-witan.

be-witan; ic. he -wát, ðú -wást, *pl.* -witon; *p.* -wiste, *pl.* -wiston; *pp.* -witen; *v. trans.* [be *near*, witan *to know, see, take care of*] *To overlook, watch over, superintend, preside, govern, administer*; præesse, administrare:—Ðe ealle his þing bewiste *qui præerat omnibus quæ habebat*, Gen. 24, 2. Ne miht ðú leng tún-scíre bewitan *jam non poteris villicare*, Lk. Bos. 16, 2: Ex. 3, 7: 5, 14: Ors. 2, 2; Bos. 41, 33: 2, 4; Bos. 43, 21: 6, 37; Bos. 132, 21. Fæder ealle gesceafte bewát *the father watches over all creatures*, Exon. 128 a; Th. 492, 5; Rä. 81, 9. To bewitanne, Gen. 39, 4.

be-witian, -witigan, -weotian; *p.* ode; *pp.* od *To observe, take care of, administer, perform*; observare, curæ habere, exsequi, peragere:—Ne mâgon hí tunglu bewitian *they may not observe the heavenly bodies*, Exon. 89 b; Th. 335, 31; Gn. Ex. 40. Hí oft bewitigaþ sorgfulne síþ *they often perform a sorrowful journey*, Beo. Th. 2861; B. 1428: Exon. 12 b; Th. 22, 18; Cri. 353.

be-wlát *looked, beheld*, Cd. 142; Th. 177, 6; Gen. 2925; *p. of* be-wlítan.

be-wlátian; *p.* ode; *pp.* od *To see, look, behold*; videre, conspicere:—Eágan ðíne geseón oððe bewlátion [MS. bewlatiun] efnysse oððe rihtwísnesse *oculi tui videant æquitates*, Ps. Lamb. 16, 2. To gescyldnysse mínre beseoh oððe bewláta *ad defensionem meam conspice*, 21, 20.

be-wlátung, e; *f. Show, sight, pageant*; spectaculum. DER. bewlátian.

be-wlítan; *p.* -wlát, *pl.* -wliton; *pp.* -wliten *To look, behold*; spectare, respicere:—Se eádega bewlát rinc ofer exle *the happy man looked over his shoulder*, Cd. 142; Th. 177, 6; Gen. 2925.

be-wópen *bewailed*, Ors. 2, 8; Bos. 51, 41; *pp. of* be-wépan.

be-worht *made, built, covered*, Jos. 2, 1; *pp. of* be-wyrcan.

be-worpen *cast, cast down, thrown, cast about, surrounded*, Cd. 21; Th. 25, 13; Gen. 393: Gen. 40, 15: Runic pm. 28; Kmbl. 345, 8; Hick. Thes. i. 135; *pp. of* be-weorpan.

be-wrǽcon *exiled, sent forth*, Cd. 189; Th. 235, 12; Dan. 305; *p. pl. of* be-wrecan.

be-wreáh *covered, covered over, protected,* Ps. Th. 104, 34; *p. of* be-wreón.

be-wrecan, bi-wrecan; *p.* -wræc, *pl.* -wrǣcon; *pp.* -wrecen. I. *to exile, send forth;* pellere, propellere:—Ðū ūsic bewrǣce in ǣht-gewealda *thou hast exiled us into bondage,* Exon. 53 a; Th. 186, 25; Az. 25. Ða us bewrǣcon *they have sent us forth,* Cd. 189; Th. 235, 12; Dan. 305. II. *to strike* or *beat around, afflict;* circum pulsare:—We land gesōhton wære bewrecene *we sought the land beaten round [afflicted] with the sea,* Andr. Kmbl. 537; An. 269. III. *to drive* or *bring to;* appellere:—Ceólas lēton sande bewrecene *they let the keels [ships] be driven to the sand [shore],* Elen. Kmbl. 502; El. 251. DER. wrecan.

be-wrencan; *p.* -wrencte; *pp.* -wrenced [be *about,* wrenc *deceit*] *To deceive;* occultis machinationibus circumvenire, Prov. Kmbl. 34.

be-wreón; *p.* -wreáh, *pl.* -wrugon; *pp.* -wrogen *To cover, cover over, protect, clothe;* tegere, contegere, operire, protegere, velare:—Bewrugon [bewreogon MS.] me þȳstru *contexerunt me tenebræ,* Ps. Spl. 54, 5. Mid mīnum bysmre ic eom bewrogen *confusio vultus mei operuit me,* Ps. Th. 43, 17. Ðū bewruge me fram gemētinge awyrgedra *protexisti me a conventu malignantium,* Ps. Spl. 63, 2. He hī wolcne bewreáh *he protected them with a cloud,* Ps. Th. 104, 34. Ic wæs nacod, and ge me noldon bewreón *I was naked, and ye would not clothe me,* Past. 44, 7; Hat. MS. 62 b, 21.

be-wrigen, -wrigon *covered, concealed,* Bt. Met. Fox 4, 93; Met. 4, 47; *pp. and p. pl. of* be-wrīhan.

be-wrigennes, -ness, e; *f. A hiding, keeping close* or *concealing;* occultatio. DER. be-wrīhan.

be-wrīhan, bi-wrīhan; *p.* -wrāh, *pl.* -wrigon; *pp.* -wrigen *To cover over, conceal, wrap up;* velare, operire:—Se snāw bewrīhþ wyrta cīþ *the snow covers over the germ of herbs,* Salm. Kmbl. 605; Sal. 302. Ic goldwine mīnne hrusan heolstre biwrāh *I covered my bounteous patron in a cave of the earth,* Exon. 76 b; Th. 287, 32; Wand. 23. Bewrigen mid wrencum *concealed by frauds,* Bt. Met. Fox 4, 93; Met. 4, 47: Cd. 8; Th. 10, 14; Gen. 156. Bewrigenum *wrapped up, instr.* Cd. 77; Th. 95, 28; Gen. 1585. DER. be-wrigennes, wrīhan.

be-wrīhþ *covers over,* Salm. Kmbl. 605; Sal. 302; *3rd pers. pres. of* be-wrīhan.

be-wrītan, bi-wrītan; *p.* -wrāt, *pl.* -writon; *pp.* -writen *To write down, inscribe;* inscribere, Exon. 92 b; Th. 347, 27; Sch. 19.

be-wrīđan, he -wrīþ; *p.* -wrāþ, *pl.* -wriđon; *pp.* -wriđen *To bind, bind round, begird;* ligare, redimire:—Meotud bewrīþ mid his wuldre eall eorþbūend *the Creator shall wreathe with his glory all earth's inhabitants,* Exon. 18 a; Th. 45, 12; Cri. 718. Duru wundurclommum bewriđen *the door bound with wondrous bands,* 12 a; Th. 19, 33; Cri. 310. DER. wrīđan.

be-wrogen *covered, covered over;* opertus, Ps. Th. 43, 17; *pp. of* be-wreón.

be-wruge *hast protected;* protexisti, Ps. Spl. 63, 2; *2nd pers. sing. p. of* be-wreón.

be-wunden *wrapped, enwrapped,* Beo. Th. 4840; B. 2424: -wundon *wound* or *bound round,* Ors. 4, 1; Bos. 78, 8; *pp. and p. pl. of* be-windan.

be-wyddod *betrothed;* desponsatus, L. Ethb. 83; Th. i. 24, 5, = be-weddod; *pp. of* be-weddian.

be-wyrcan, -weorcean, bi-wyrcan; *p.* -worhte, *pl.* -worhton; *pp.* -worht *To work, work in, insert, make, build, cover, adorn;* elaborare, immittere, facere, ædificare, inducere, exornare:—Bewyrc us on heortan Hālige Gāst *work the Holy Ghost into our hearts,* Hy. 7, 79; Hy. Grn. ii. 288, 79. Ne wāt ic mec beworhtne wulle flȳsum *I know not that I was made with fleeces of wool,* Exon. 109 a; Th. 417, 11; Rä. 36, 3. He lǣmen fæt biwyrcan hēt *he commanded to make an earthen vessel,* 74 a; Th. 277, 3; Jul. 575. Babylōnia is mid stǣnenum wīghūsum beworht *Babylon is built with stone towers,* Ors. 2, 4; Bos. 44, 30: Jos. 2, 1. Se mid weaxe beworhte *he covered it with wax,* Ors. 2, 5; Bos. 46, 30. Ða tēþ on golde bewyrc *cover the teeth with gold,* Med. ex Quadr. 1, 1; Lchdm. i. 326, 16. Seó cwēn đa rōde hēht golde beweorcean *the queen commanded to adorn the cross with gold,* Elen. Kmbl. 2045; El. 1024.

be-wyrpan *to cast, throw,* Ors. 2, 4; Bos. 45, 33. v. be-weorpan.

be-yrnan, -irnan; he -yrnþ; *p.* -arn, *pl.* -urnon; *pp.* -urnen [be *by,* yrnan *to run*] *To run by, to come in, occur, incur;* percurrere:—Be-arn me on mōde *it occurred to my mind,* Homl. Th. i. 2, 6. Ān wundor me nū on mōd be-arn *one wonder now [runs by me into the mind] occurs to me,* Dial. 1, 10. He ne be-arn on leásunga synne *he incurred not the sin of [leasing] lying,* Dial. 1, 2: Bd. de nat. rerum; Wrt. popl. science 7, 1; Lchdm. iii. 244, 20.

bezera, an; *m:* bezere, es; *m. The baptist:*—Se bezera, Mt. Rush. Stv. 3, 1. v. bædzere.

bi *by, near, concerning.* v. be, bī.

bī *a bee;* apis: *found in the compound* bī-breád.

bī; *prep. dat.* [Bī is more frequently shortened into be. In compounds it is generally written be- or bi-; but bī- is long where it is used for big, or is a contraction, thus,—bī-spell for big-spell, and as bī-breád for beó-breád. v. be.] **1.** *dat. By, near to, at, in, upon;* juxta, prope, apud, in:—Arās bī ronde oretta *the champion arose by his shield,* Beo. Th. 5069; B. 2538. He bī sesse geóng *he went by the seat,* 5506; B. 2756. Bī stađe fæste *fast by the shore,* Exon. 96 b; Th. 361, 11; Wal. 18. Hwearf bī bence *turned by the bench,* Beo. Th. 2380; B. 1188. **2.** *dat. Of, about;* de, quoad:—Ðæt bī đē sōþfæst sægde Esaias *what Isaiah said truly of thee,* Exon. 12 a; Th. 19, 16; Cri. 301. Hȳrde ic secgan gēn bī sumum fugle *I have yet heard tell of a certain bird,* 97 b; Th. 365, 17; Reb. 1. Bī đon se wītga song *of whom the prophet sang,* 17 a; Th. 41, 4; Cri. 650. **3.** *dat. By, through, because of, after, according to, in comparison with;* per, secundum, pro, ex:—Bī hwon scealt đū lifgan *by what art thou to live?* Exon. 36 b; Th. 118, 23; Gū. 244. Bī noman gehātne *called by name,* 23 b; Th. 66, 16; Cri. 1072. Bī heofonwōman *through the crash of heaven,* 20 a; Th. 52, 18; Cri. 835. Leán cumaþ werum bī gewyrhtum *retribution shall come to men according to their works,* 27 b; Th. 84, 3; Cri. 1368: 76 a; Th. 286, 8; Jul. 728. Ðisses fugles gecynd fela gelīces bī đām gecornum Cristes þegnum *the nature of this bird is much like to the chosen servants of Christ,* 61 b; Th. 225, 12; Ph. 388. **4.** *sometimes* bī *is separated from its case:*—Bī wædes ōfre *by the shore of the sea,* Exon. 96 b; Th. 360, 22; Wal. 9.

biágian; *p.* ode; *pp.* od [beág *a crown*] *To crown;* coronare:—Ðū biágodyst hine *coronasti eum,* Ps. Spl. C. 8, 6. v. beágian.

biaþ *are; for* bióþ, Mt. Lind. Stv. 26, 31; *pl. pres. of* bión = beón.

bi-bađian; *p.* ode; *pp.* od *To bathe, wash;* lavare:—Se æđela fugel hine bibađaþ in đam burnan *the noble fowl bathes itself in the brook,* Exon. 57 b; Th. 205, 3; Ph. 107. v. be-bađian.

bi-beódan; *p.* -beád, *pl.* -budon; *pp.* -boden *To order, command, bid;* jubere, mandare, Exon. 56 a; Th. 200, 6; Ph. 36: 93 a; Th. 349, 13; Sch. 45. v. be-beódan.

biblio-þēce, an; *f.* [$\beta\iota\beta\lambda\iota o\theta\acute{\eta}\kappa\eta = \beta\iota\beta\lambda\acute{\iota}o\nu$ *a book,* $\theta\acute{\eta}\kappa\eta$ *repository, a library*]. I. *a library;* bibliotheca, C. R. Ben. 50. II. a collection of books in one volume, hence,—*The Bible;* biblia:—Hieronimus, se wurþfulla and se wīsa bōcere, ūre Biblioþēcan gebrohte to Lēdene of Grēciscum bōcum and of Ebrēiscum *Jerome, the worthy and wise author, translated our Bible out of the Greek and Hebrew books into Latin,* Ælfc. T. Grn. 16, 6–8. Se saltere ys ān bōc on đære Biblioþēcan *the psalter is one book in the Bible,* Ælfc. T. 14, 15. Iohannes awrāt đa bōc, Apocalipsis gehāten, and đeós bōc ys æftemyst on đære Biblioþēcan *John wrote the book called Revelation, and this book is the last in the Bible,* Ælfc. T. 31, 23.

bi-bod, es; *n. A command, decree, an order;* mandatum, jussum, Exon. 25 a; Th. 71, 22; Cri. 1159: Hy. 4, 34; Hy. Grn. ii. 283, 34. v. be-bod.

bī-breád, es; *n. Bee-bread;* apium panis:—Þynceþ bībreád swētre, gif he ǣr bitres onbyrgeþ *bee-bread seemeth sweeter, if he before has a taste of bitter,* Bt. Met. Fox 12, 17; Met. 12, 9. v. beó-breád I.

bī-būgan; *p.* -beág, *pl.* -bugon; *pp.* -bogen *To avoid;* avertere, Exon. 45 a; Th. 154, 9; Gū. 840. v. be-būgan.

bi-bycgong, e; *f.* [be, bycg *from* bycgan *to buy*] *A selling away;* venditio. v. bebycgean.

bi-byrgan; *p.* de; *pp.* ed *To bury,* Exon. 24 b; Th. 71, 21; Cri. 1159. v. be-byrgan.

BICCE, bice, bicge, an; *f. A* BITCH, *a female of the canine kind;* canicula:—Biccean [biccan MS. B.] meolc *bitch's milk,* Med. ex Quadr. 9, 8, 9; Lchdm. i. 362, 15, 18. [*Piers P.* bicche; *Ger.* bätze, betze, petze, *f: Icel.* bikkja, *f.*]

biccen; *adj. Belonging to a bitch;* caninus; *the adj. of* bicce.

bi-cerran *to pass by;* præterire, Mk. Lind. Rush. War. 6, 48. v. be-cerran.

bicgan *to buy, procure,* Jn. Bos. 4, 8: Beo. Th. 2615; B. 1305: Exon. 120 b; Th. 463, 11; Hö. 68: Salm. Kmbl. 403; Sal. 202: Exon. 114 a; Th. 436, 37; Rä. 55, 12. v. bycgan.

bicge *a bitch;* canicula, Ælfc. Gl. 21; Wrt. Voc. 23, 33. v. bicce.

bi-clyppan; *p.* -clypte; *pp.* -clypt *To clip, embrace, inclose, clasp;* amplecti, Exon. 59 b; Th. 217, 8; Ph. 277. v. be-clyppan.

bīcnian, bīcnigan; *part.* bīcniende; he bīcneþ; *p.* ode; *pp.* od; *v. a.* I. *to beckon, nod;* innuere:—He wæs bīcniende him *erat innuens illis,* Lk. Bos. 1, 22. Bīcnodon hī to his fæder *innuebant patri ejus,* 1, 62: 5, 7. II. *to indicate, signify, announce, shew;* indicare, significare:—He sceal mid bellan bīcnigan đa tīda *he shall with bells announce the times,* L. Ælf. C. 11; Th. ii. 346, 29. v. beácnian.

bīcnung *a sign;* signum, signatio. v. beácnung.

bi-cowen *gnawed,* Exon. 99 b; Th. 373, 20; Seel. 111; *pp. of* bi-ceówan. v. be-ceówan.

bi-cweđan; *p.* -cwæþ, *pl.* -cwǣdon; *pp.* -cweden *To say;* dicere, Exon. 37 b; Th. 123, 32; Gū. 331. v. be-cweđan.

bī-cwide *a proverb,* Prov. 22. v. big-cwide.

bi-cwom, *pl.* -cwōmon *came, entered:*—Ðā ic to hām bicwom *when I came home,* Exon. 86 a; Th. 324, 14; Wīd. 94: 20 b; Th. 53, 32;

Cri. 859: 17 a; Th. 39, 33; Cri. 631: 48 b; Th. 168, 2; Gû. 1071. Ût bicwômon [MS. bicwoman], 24 a; Th. 69, 1; Cri. 1114. v. be-com, *p. of* be-cuman.

bíd, es; *n. Delay, abiding;* mora:—Wearþ on bíd wrecen *was driven to delay* [*on delay*], Beo. Th. 5917; B. 2962. On bíd wriceþ *drives on delay,* Exon. 101 b; Th. 382, 29; Rä. 4, 3. DER. an-bíd, on-: bíd-fæst, -steal.

bi-dǽlan; *p.* -dǽlde; *pp.* -dǽled *To deprive, bereave of anything, to deliver, release, free from anything;* privare, sejungere, expertem reddere:—Duguþum bidǽled *bereft of honours,* Exon. 16 a; Th. 35, 24; Cri. 563. v. be-dǽlan.

BÍDAN, ic bíde, ðú bídest, bítst, bíst, he bídeþ, bít, *pl.* bídaþ; *p.* ic, he bád, ðú bide, *pl.* bidon; *pp.* biden; *acc. gen. To* BIDE, *abide, continue, remain, tarry, wait, await, expect, endure;* manere, remanere, morari, habitare in aliquo loco, expectare, consequi, sustinere:—Ic in wíte sceal bídan in bendum *I in torment must abide in bonds,* Cd. 214; Th. 268, 2; Sat. 49. Seó eorþe gíniende bád *the earth continued yawning,* Ors. 3, 3; Bos. 56, 4. Ðonne ðæt he ðǽr leng bide *than that he should abide there longer,* Ors. 2, 5; Bos. 48, 4. Mere stille bád *the sea remained still,* Cd. 158; Th. 197, 2; Exod. 300. Bídaþ assan on þurste *expectabunt onagri in siti sua,* Ps. Th. 103, 11. Swá mín sáwl bád *sicut expectavit anima mea,* 55, 6. He geþyldum bád *he waited patiently,* Exon. 46 a; Th. 157, 4; Gû. 886. Utan we well ðære tíde bídan *bene expectemus horam illam,* Bd. 4, 24; S. 599, 5. Bídaþ Dryhtnes dómes *they await the Lord's doom,* Exon. 23 a; Th. 63, 17; Cri. 1021. Bád sôþra gehâta *he awaited the faithful promises,* Cd. 71; Th. 86, 2; Gen. 1424. Hie ðæs bidon *for this they waited,* Exon. 10 a; Th. 10, 4; Cri. 147. In helle heó bryne welme bídan sceolden *in hell they must abide* [*endure*] *scorching heat,* Cd. 213; Th. 266, 25; Sat. 27. Ðá seó circe hér eahtnysse bád *then the church here endured persecution,* Exon. 18 a; Th. 44, 18; Cri. 704. [*Laym.* biden, ibiden; *p.* ibæd, ibad, *pl.* biden; *pp.* ibiden, ibede: *O. Sax.* bídan: *N. Frs.* bida: *O. Frs.* bidia: *N. Dut. N. L. Ger.* beiden: *N. Ger. dial.* beiten: *M. H. Ger.* bîten: *O. H. Ger.* bítan: *Goth.* beidan: *Dan.* bie: *Swed.* bida: *O. Nrs.* bíða [for bída]: *Ir. Gael.* feith.] DER. a-bídan, ge-, ofer-, on-.

BIDDAN, ic bidde, ðú biddest, bidst, bitst, he biddeþ, bit, byt, bitt, *pl.* biddaþ; *impert.* bide, *pl.* biddaþ; *p.* ic, he bæd, ðú bǽde, *pl.* bǽdon; *pp.* beden: *followed by an acc. of the person,* or *by the prep. to, and a gen. of the thing; v. trans. To ask, pray, intreat, beseech,* BID, *order, require;* petere, poscere, orare, quærere, precari, deprecari, rogare, postulare, præcipere, requirere:—Ic bidde *peto,* Ælfc. Gr. 28, 1; Som. 30, 41. Eádréd, cyning, biddeþ and hálsaþ *Eadred, king, prayeth and intreateth,* Cod. Dipl. 433; A. D. 955; Kmbl. ii. 304, 24: Ælfc. Gr. 33; Som. 37, 31. Ic bidde *precor,* 25; Som. 27, 11. Andreas ongann mere-líðendum miltsa biddan *Andrew began to ask mercy for the sea-faring men,* Andr. Kmbl. 706; An. 353. Hú hí hine bǽdon [MS. bædan] rihtes geleáfan and fullwihtes bæðes *how they had asked him the favour of a right belief and of a font of baptism,* Ors. 6, 34; Bos. 130, 30. Ongunnon ealle biddan ðæs ðe he bæd *all began to pray that which he prayed,* Bt. 35, 6; Fox 168, 30. Hý him to eów árna bǽdun *they prayed to you for compassion,* Exon. 27 b; Th. 83, 9; Cri. 1353. Bide hine *ora eum,* Ps. Spl. 36, 6. Ic bidde ðé mín Drihten *quæso Domine mi,* Gen. 19, 18. We biddaþ *quæsumus,* Ælfc. Gr. 33; Som. 37, 41. Ðone alwaldan ára biddan *to intreat the all-powerful for benefits,* Cd. 217; Th. 277, 24; Sat. 209. Gehýr, God, gebéd mín ðon ic bidde *exaudi, Deus, orationem meam cum deprecor,* Ps. Spl. 63, 1. Biddaþ *rogate,* Ps. Th. 121, 6. He bitt sibbe *rogat ea quæ pacis sunt,* Lk. Bos. 14, 32. Gif he bit æg *si petierit ovum,* 11, 12. Gif hit [cild] æges bitt *if he ask for an egg,* Homl. Th. i. 250, 9. Gif hit [cild] hine hláfes bitt *if he ask him for bread,* 250, 8. Gif he byt fisces *if he ask for a fish,* Lk. Bos. 11, 11. Bide me *postula a me,* Ps. Th. 2, 8. Hí dôþ swá ic bidde *they do as I bid,* Beo. Th. 2467; B. 1231. He bæd him hláfas wyrcan *he bade him make loaves,* Cd. 228; Th. 307, 1; Sat. 673. Ðú bitst me ðæt ic lǽde út ðis folc *præcipis ut educam populum istum,* Ex. 33, 12. Bide his me eft *de manu mea require illum,* Gen. 43, 9. [*Orm.* biddenn: *Laym.* bidde, bidden; he biddeþ, *pl.* biddeþ; *impert.* bide, bid: *O. Sax.* biddean: *Frs.* bidde: *O. Frs.* bidda: *Dut.* bidden: *N. Ger. M. H. Ger.* bitten: *O. H. Ger.* bitjan: *Goth.* bidyan: *Dan.* bede: *Swed.* bedja: *O. Nrs. poet.* biðja *petere, rogare.*] DER. a-biddan, ge-, on-: v. bedd.

biddende *praying,* Ors. 2, 5; Bos. 47, 40; *part. of* biddan.

biddere, es; *m. A petitioner;* petitor *vel* petax, Ælfc. Gl. 114; Som. 80, 19. v. biddan.

bide *pray;* ora:—Bide ðinne fæder *ora tuum patrem,* Mt. Bos. 6, 6; *sing. impert. of* biddan.

bi-deáglian *to hide, cover, conceal, keep close* or *secret,* Exon. 51 a; Th. 177, 12; Gû. 1226. v. be-deáglian.

bi-déglad *hidden, obscured:*—Bidéglad on dægréd *obscured at dawn,* Exon. 57 a; Th. 204, 15; Ph. 98; *pp. of* bi-déglian. v. be-déglad.

bídende *abiding,* Elen. Kmbl. 966; El. 484; *part. of* bídan.

bíd-fæst; *adj.* [bíd *an abiding, delay;* fæst *fast, firm*] *Stationary, firm;* stabilis:—Hyre fôta wæs bídfæst [biidfæst MS.] ôðer *one of its feet was stationary,* Exon. 114 a; Th. 438, 13; Rä. 57, 7.

bíding, e; *f. A* BIDING, *abode;* mansio, statio:—Ðǽr hý bídinge môstun tídum brúcan *where they might at times enjoy a biding,* Exon. 35 b; Th. 114, 30; Gû. 180.

bi-droren *deprived;* orbatus, Exon. 77 b; Th. 291, 8; Wand. 79; *pp. of* bi-dreósan. v. dreósan, be-droren.

bíd-steal, -steall, es; *m.* [bíd *an abiding, delay;* steal *a stall, place*] *A stand, halt;* statio, mora:—He, beald in gebéde, bídsteal gifeþ *he, bold in prayer, maketh a stand,* Exon. 71 a; Th. 265, 29; Jul. 388. Ic eofore eom céenra, ðonne he, gebolgen, bídsteal giefeþ *I am bolder than a wild boar, when he, enraged, makes a stand,* 110 b; Th. 423, 11; Rä. 41, 19.

bi-dyrnan; *p.* de; *pp.* ed *To hide, conceal;* occultare, Exon. 24 a; Th. 67, 16; Cri. 1089. v. be-dyrnan.

bie *be,* Mk. Lind. War. 10, 44, *for* bió; *subj. of* bión *to be.*

biécn *a beacon, wonder,* Ps. Spl. C. 104, 25. v. beácen.

Bieda, an; *m. Bieda the son of Port:*—Hér com Port on Brytene, and his twegan sunan, Bieda and Mægla *here,* A. D. 501, *Port came to Britain, and his two sons, Bieda and Mægla,* Chr. 501; Erl. 15, 14.

Biedan heáfod; *gen.* heáfdes; *dat.* heáfde; *m.* [Biedan *Bieda's,* heáfod *head: Flor.* Bidanheafod, A. D. 1114] BIEDA'S HEAD = *Bedwin, Wilts?*—Hér Wulfhere and Æscwine gefuhton æt Biedan heáfde *here,* A. D. 675, *Wulfhere and Æscwine fought at Bedwin,* Chr. 675; Erl. 36, 9; Th. 58, 15, col. 1, 3.

Biedcan ford *Bedford,* Chr. 571; Th. 32, 26, col. 2. v. Bedan ford.

bién-codd *beanpod,* Lk. Foxe 15, 16. v. beán-belgas.

bi-eóde *venerated,* Exon. 68 b; Th. 255, 3; Jul. 208; *p. of* bi-gán.

biereþ *bears, carries,* Exon. 58 b; Th. 211, 18; Ph. 199; *for* bireþ; *3rd pres. of* beran.

bierm *a bosom,* Ps. Spl. C. 73, 12. v. bearm.

biernende *burning, for* byrnende. v. byrnan.

biersteþ, bierst *bursts,* Exon. 102 a; Th. 386, 16; Rä. 4, 62; *3rd pres. of* berstan.

bieþ *are, for* bióþ, Mk. Lind. War. 10, 43. v. bión.

bi-férende; *part. Passing by,* Lk. Lind. War. 18, 36. v. be-féran.

bi-fæstan; *p.* -fæste; *pp.* -fæsted *To fasten, make fast, fix, commit, intrust;* infigere, committere, tradere, Exon. 97 a; Th. 362, 2; Wal. 30: 50 a; Th. 173, 26; Gû. 1166. v. be-fæstan.

bi-fangen *surrounded,* Exon. 15 b; Th. 33, 18, note; Cri. 527; *pp. of* bi-fôn. v. be-fôn.

bi-fealdan; *p.* -feóld, *pl.* -feóldon; *pp.* -fealden *To infold, involve, inwrap, cover, overwhelm;* implicare, involvere, circumdare, Exon. 9 b; Th. 8, 14; Cri. 117. v. be-fealdan.

bi-felgan; *p.* -fealh, *pl.* -fulgon; *pp.* -folgen *To deliver, transmit, consign;* tradere, committere, Exon. 72 b; Th. 271, 13; Jul. 481. v. be-felgan.

bi-féng, *pl.* -féngon *held, seized;* apprehendit, Exod. 415; Grn. i. 88, 415; *p. of* bi-fôn. v. be-fôn.

bi-feohtan; *p.* -feaht, *pl.* -fuhton; *pp.* -fohten *To deprive by fighting;* pugnando privare:—Feore bifohten *deprived of life,* Exon. 101 b; Th. 384, 23; Rä. 4, 32.

bi-feolan; *p.* -fæl, *pl.* -fǽlon; *pp.* -folen *To commit, commend, deliver;* immittere, commendare, tradere:—Bifolen in foldan *committed to earth,* Exon. 71 b; Th. 267, 18; Jul. 417: 17 b; Th. 42, 5; Cri. 668. v. be-feolan.

bifgende, bifgende *trembling, trembling with a fever:*—Bifgende *febricitantem,* Mt. Rush. Stv. 8, 14. v. bifian.

BIFIAN, bifigan, byfian, beofian; *p.* ode; *pp.* od *To tremble, shake, be moved;* tremere, contremere, commoveri:—Drihten besihþ eorþan and déþ hýg bifian *Dominus respicit terram et facit eam tremere,* Ps. Lamb. 103, 32: Rood Kmbl. 72; Kr. 36. He, bifiende, feóll to Iohannes fôtum *he, trembling, fell at John's feet,* Ælfc. T. 37, 10: Cd. 92; Th. 118, 25; Gen. 1970. Ic bifige *tremo,* Ælfc. Gr. 35; Som. 38, 8. Eorþe [eorþan MS.] bifode *terra tremuit,* Ps. Spl. 75, 8: Rood Kmbl. 83; Kr. 42. Ða wudas bifodon *the woods shook,* Bt. 35, 6; Fox 168, 8. [*O. Sax.* bibôn: *Frs.* bibbe, bibje: *O. Frs.* beva: *Dut.* beven: *Ger.* beben: *M. H. Ger.* biben: *O. H. Ger.* bibên: *Dan.* bäve: *Swed.* bäfwa: *O. Nrs.* bifast: *Lat.* pavere: *Grk.* φέβομαι: *Sansk.* bhî *to fear.*] DER. a-bifian.

bifigan *to tremble;* tremere, Ælfc. Gr. 35; Som. 38, 8. v. bifian.

bi-fleón; *part.* -fleónde *To escape, to pass by* or *under, to go away privately;* subterfugere, Cot. 192. v. be-fleón.

bi-folen *committed, commended,* Exon. 71 b; Th. 267, 18; Jul. 417; *pp. of* bi-feolan.

bi-fôn; *p.* -féng, *pl.* -féngon; *pp.* -fangen, -fongen. I. *to comprehend, grasp, seize, take hold of, attach, catch, ensnare;* comprehendere, apprehendere, reprehendere, deprehendere, capere:—Folm mec mæg bifôn *the hand may grasp me,* Exon. 111 a; Th. 425, 6; Rä. 41, 52. II. *to surround, encompass, encircle, envelop, contain, invest, clothe, case, receive, conceive;* circumdare, amplecti, capere, cingere, tegere, operire, accipere, concipere:—Flǽsce bifongen *surrounded with flesh*, Exon. 98 a; Th. 368, 33; Seel. 34. v. be-fôn.

bi-fongen *surrounded*, Exon. 98 a; Th. 368, 33; Seel. 34; *pp. of* bi-fôn. v. be-fôn.

bi-fōran; *prep. dat. Before*; ante, coram:—Wineleás guma gesihþ him bifōran fealwe wegas *the friendless mortal sees before him seared ways*, Exon. 77 a; Th. 289, 10; Wand. 46: 47 a; Th. 160, 22; Gû. 947. v. be-fōran; *prep.*

bi-fōran; *adv. Before, of old*; antea:—Swā ǽr bifōran *as ere of old*, Exon. 14 b; Th. 29, 26; Cri. 468. v. be-fōran; *adv.*

bifung, beofung, e; *f.* [bifian *to tremble*] *A trembling, shaking*; tremor:—Fyrhto oððe bifung begrāp hīg *tremor apprehendit eos*, Ps. Lamb. 47, 7: 54, 6. DER. eorþ-bifung.

bī-fylc, es; *n.* [bī *by, near to*; fylc *a tribe, country, province*] *A neighbouring people, province*, or *region*; provincia *vel* populus adjacens:—Of eallum ðyssum bīfylcum *de cunctis prope provinciis*, Bd. 3, 14; S. 540, 11.

big; *prep. dat. Of, about, concerning*; de, quoad:—Big ðam ðe ic ðē ǽr sægde *de qua tibi ante dixi*, Bd. 2, 12; S. 514, 35. v. be 2.

bi-gǽþ *commits*, Exon. 27 a; Th. 80, 18; Cri. 1308; *pres. of* bi-gân.

bi-gân, he -gǽþ; *p.* -eóde, *pl.* -eódon; *pp.* -gân. I. *to commit, exercise, observe, enjoy*; committere, exercere, observare, frui, Exon. 27 a; Th. 80, 18; Cri. 1308. II. *to honour, worship, venerate*; colere, Exon. 68 b; Th. 255, 3; Jul. 208. v. be-gân.

bīgan; *p.* de; *pp.* ed; *v. trans. To bow, bend, bend down, turn, turn back*; flectere, deflectere, incurvare, retorquere:—His cneów bīgde on eorþan *genua flexit in terram*, Bd. 5, 21; S. 643, 15: 3, 2; S. 524, 14: Mt. Bos. 27, 29: Exon. 62 b; Th. 229, 23; Ph. 459: Bd. 3, 19; S. 548, 8: Lev. 1, 15. v. bȳgan.

bi-gang, -gong, es; *m.* I. *a course, way, passage, circuit*; cursus, via, tenor, circuitus:—Tīda bigong *the course of seasons*, Exon. 11 a; Th. 15, 13; Cri. 235. II. *an undertaking, business, exercise, religious worship*; negotium, exercitatio, cultus, Bd. 5, 1; S. 613, 9. v. be-gang.

bi-gangan *to go round, go to, attend, commit, practise, exercise, worship*; exercere, incumbere, colere, Bd. 1, 7; S. 477, 33. v. bi-gongan, be-gangan.

big-cwide, bī-cwide, es; *m.* [be, big *by*; cwide *a saying*] *A by-saying, by-word, proverb, fable, tale*; proverbium, fabula:—Ge forwurðaþ þurh bigspell and bigcwidas *eris perditus in proverbium et fabulam*, Deut. 28, 37. Bīcwide *proverbium*, Prov. 22.

bige, es; *n?* [bycgan, bicgan *to buy*] *A buying, exchange, commerce, traffic*; emptio, permutatio, commercium, mercatus:—Gif gebyrige ðæt for neóde heora hwilc wið ūre bige habban wille, oððe we wið heora, mid yrfe and mid ǽhtum, ðæt is to þafianne *if it happen that from necessity any of them will have traffic with us, or we with them, with cattle and with goods, that is to be allowed*, L. A. G. 5; Th. i. 156, 2–4.

bige *buy*, Jn. Bos. 13, 29; *impert. of* bicgan.

bīge, es; *m. A bending, turning, bend, an angle, a corner*; flexus, sinus, angulus:—Se engel eóde into ānum nyrwette, ðe he ne mihte forbūgan on nāðere healfe, forðamðe ðǽr nān bīge næs *angelus ad locum angustum transivit, ubi nec ad dexteram nec ad sinistram poterat deviare*, Num. 22, 26. Bīge limes *fractura membri*, Fulg. 19. v. bȳge.

bīgean *to bow, bend*; flectere:—His cneówu bīgean *genua flectere*, Bd. 4, 31; S. 610, 23: 3, 2; S. 524, 21: Ps. Th. 94, 6. v. bȳgan.

bi-geat *obtained, seized*, Exon. 81 b; Th. 306, 12; Seef. 6; *p. of* bi-gitan. v. be-gitan.

bi-gegnes, bi-gegnys, -ness, e; *f. A going about* or *applying one's self to anything, the pursuit* or *study of anything*; studium:—Bigegnes *vel* smeágung *studium*, Ælfc. Gl. 90; Wrt. Voc. 51, 27: Gr. Dial. 1, 10. DER. eorþ-bi-gegnys.

bi-gellan; *p.* -geal, *pl.* -gullon; *pp.* -gollen *To celebrate by song, to scream*; canendo celebrare, exclamare:—Ful oft ðæt earn bigeal *the eagle screamed that often*, Exon. 81 b; Th. 307, 16; Seef. 24.

bīgels, es; *m. An arch, a vault, an arched roof*; arcus, fornix, camera, Ælfc. Gl. 93; Som. 75, 91; Wrt. Voc. 52, 41: Cot. 201. DER. for-bīgels.

bi-geng *worship, observation*, Scint. 7. v. be-gang II.

bi-geng, es; *m. Observation, worship, service*; cultus:—Bigeng *cultus*, Ælfc. Gr. 11; Som. 15, 18, MSS. C. D. He bæd hīg ðā georne, ðæt hīg būgan ne sceoldon fram Godes bigengum *he bade them then earnestly, that they should not decline from the services of God*, Jos. 23, 7. v. be-gang.

bi-genga, an; *m. An inhabitant, dweller, cultivator*; incola, cultor:—Ðæt ðæt Eálond Wiht onfēng Cristene bigengan *ut Vecta insula Christianos incolas susceperit*, Bd. 4, 16; S. 584, 2. Se ārfæsta bigenga ðæs gāstlīcan landes *pius agri spiritalis cultor*, 2, 15; S. 519, 8: Deut. Grn. 4. 3. DER. land-bigenga. v. be-ganga.

bi-geongende, bi-gongende; *part.* [*part. of* bi-gongan, v. be-gongan, be-gangan] *Passing by*; præteriens, Mk. Lind. War. 15, 21: Mk. Rush. War. 15, 21.

bi-gerdel *a purse, public purse*, Ælfc. Gl. 65; Som. 69, 35; Wrt. Voc. 40, 63. v. big-gyrdel.

biggencere, es; *m. A worker*; operator:—Ic hæbbe smiþas... and manega óðre mistlīcra cræfta biggenceras *habeo fabros... et multos alios variarum artium operatores*, Coll. Monast. Th. 30, 3.

big-geng *observation, worship*; cultus:—Biggeng [MS. biggend] *cultus*, Ælfc. Gr. 11; Som. 15, 18. v. begang.

big-gyrdel, bī-gyrdel, -gerdel; *g.* -gyrdles, -gerdles; *m.* [big, bī, gyrdel *a girdle, belt, purse*] *A belt, girdle*, and as girdles were used to carry money, hence, *a purse, public purse, treasury*; zōna = ζώνη, saccus = σάκκος, fiscus:—Næbbe ge feoh on eówrum bīgyrdlum *nolite possidere pecuniam in zonis vestris*, Mt. Bos. 10, 9. Bīgerdel *saccus*, Ælfc. Gl. 3; Som. 55, 68; Wrt. Voc. 16, 41. Cyninges [MS. kinges] gafoles bīgerdel *saccus* vel *fiscus*, 65; Som. 69, 35; Wrt. Voc. 40, 63. Biggyrdel *fiscus* vel *saccus publicus*, 17; Som. 58, 94; Wrt. Voc. 22, 11.

big-hydig, bī-hydig; *adj. Careful, watchful, solicitous, anxious*; sollicitus, sollers:—Wæs seó mōder ðære gesomnunge bīhydig [MS. B. byghydig = bighydig] *sollicita est mater congregationis*, Bd. 4, 7; Whel. 277, 27. v. be-hydig.

big-hydiglīce, -hydilīce, -hydlīce, -hidiglīce; *adv. Carefully*; sollicite, sollerter:—Ðe he bighydiglīce heóld *which he carefully held*, Bd. 4, 31; S. 611, 2. Heó hine bighydilīce [bighydlice, Whel. 324, 8] sōhte *she carefully sought him*, 4, 23; S. 595, 4. Bighidiglīce *sollicite*, 1, 27; S. 489, note 39. v. be-hydelīce.

bi-gitan, -gytan *to get, obtain, seize*; assequi, acquirere, arripere, corripere, Exon. 32 b; Th. 103, 19; Cri. 1690. v. be-gitan.

big-leofa, bī-leofa, an; *m.* [big, bī *for*, līf *life*, leofen *living, nourishment*]. I. provision by which life is maintained, *Food, victuals, nourishment*; cibus, victus, alimentum:—Ðū nimst witodlīce of eallum mettum... ðæt hīg beón ǽgðer ge ðē ge him to bigleofan *tolles igitur ex omnibus escis... et erunt tam tibi quam illis in cibum*, Gen. 6, 21. Hwæt begytst ðū of ðīnum cræfte? Bigleofan, and scrūd, and feoh *quid adquiris de tua arte? Victum, et vestitum, et pecuniam*, Coll. Monast. Th. 23, 3–6. Bigleofa *victus*, Ælfc. Gr. 28, 5; Som. 32, 6. Bīleofa *alimentum*, C. R. Ben. 49. II. that by which food is procured, *Money, wages*; stips, stipendium:—Scipe *vel* bigleofa *stipendium*, Ælfc. Gl. 12; Som. 57, 92; Wrt. Voc. 20, 33. v. an-leofa, andleofen.

big-leofan; *part.* ende; *p.* ede; *pp.* ed *To nourish, feed, support*; cibare. v. big-leofa.

bi-glīdan *to glide* or *disappear from any one, to desert any one*; evanescere ab aliquo, derelinquere, Exon. 94 a; Th. 353, 18; Reim. 14.

bīg-nes, -ness, e; *f. A bending, bowing*; flexio:—Se earm nǽnige bīgnesse on ðam elnbogan hæfde *brachium nihil prorsus in cubito flexionis habuit*, Bd. 5, 3; S. 616, 23. v. bȳgan.

bi-gong *a course*, Exon. 54 b; Th. 193, 29; Az. 129. v. be-gang.

bi-gongan *to attend, practise, observe, worship*, Exon. 44 b; Th. 150, 11; Gû. 777. v. be-gangan.

bi-grafan *to bury*; sepelire, Exon. 29 a; Th. 89, 33; Cri. 1466. v. be-grafan.

bigsen *an example*, Bd. 3, 28, MS. B; S. 560, note 35. v. bȳsen.

big-sittan; *p.* -sæt, *pl.* -sǽton; *pp.* -seten *To sit by* or *near*; adsidere:—Se bisceop ðæt geseah ðe him bigsæt *the bishop who sat by him saw it*; quo viso pontifex qui adsidebat, Bd. 3, 6; S. 528, 22.

big-spæc, e; *f. A by-speech, deceiving*; supplantatio. DER. big. spæc.

big-spell, bī-spell; *g.* -spelles; *pl. nom. acc.* -spell, -spellu; *n.* [big, bī, spell *a history*] *A by-history, a parable, fable, example, proverb, story*; parabola, fabula, exemplum, proverbium, narratio:—Gehȳre ge ðæs sāwendan bigspell *vos audite parabolam seminantis*, Mt. Bos. 13, 18. Ic ahylde on bigspelle eáre mīn *inclinabo in parabolam aurem meam*, Ps. Spl. 48, 4. Ealle ðās þing se Hǽlend spræc mid bigspellum to ðām weredum; and nān þing ne spræc he būtan bigspellum *hæc omnia locutus est Iesus in parabolis ad turbas; et sine parabolis non loquebatur eis*, Mt. Bos. 13, 34, 35: Ps. Lamb. 48, 5. Bigspellu, *acc. pl.* Lchdm. iii. 214, 15. He him rehte bīspell bī ðære sunnan *he related to him a parable of the sun*, Bt. titl. vi; Fox x. 12. Ðeáh we sculon manega and mistlīce bīsna and bīspell reccan *though we should relate many and various examples and fables*, Bt. 35, 5; Fox 166, 13, 19. Gehȳr sum bīspell *hear an example*, 37, 3; Fox 190, 21: 39, 6; Fox 220, 21. Þurh bigspell and bigcwidas *in proverbium et fabulam*, Deut. 28, 37. We sculon ðē sum bīspell reccan *we will relate a story to thee*, Bt. 35, 6; Fox 166, 27: Bt. Met. Fox 23, 17; Met. 23, 9. [*Kil.* bijspel: *Ger.* beispiel, *n*: *M. H. Ger.* bīspel, *n.*] DER. bigspell-bōc.

bigspell-bōc, e; *f.* [bigspell *parabola, proverbium*, bōc *liber*] *A book of parables, the Book of Proverbs*; proverbiorum liber:—Salomon gesette þreó bēc þurh his snoternisse: ān ys bigspellbōc *Solomon wrote three books by his wisdom: one is the Book of Proverbs*, Ælfc. T. 14, 26.

big-standan; *p.* -stōd, *pl.* -stōdon; *pp.* -standen [big = bī *by, near*, standan *to stand*] *To stand by* or *near one, to support*; stare cum aliquo, adstare, adjuvare:—Bigstandaþ me, strange geneátas *stand by me, strong associates*, Cd. 15; Th. 18, 36; Gen. 284. Ða ðe him bigstōdon *those* *who stood by him*, Byrht. Th. 137, 7; By. 182: Beo. Th. 6086; B. 3047.

big-swíc, es; *m. Deceit, guile;* fraus:—Bútan brede and bigswíce *without fraud and guile*, L. Ed. 1; Th. i. 160, 7. v. be-swíc.

big-wist, bí-wist, e; *f.* [wist *subsistence, victuals, food;* wesan *to be, exist*] *Food, nourishment, provision;* pabulum, alimentum, commeatus:—Bigwist *alimentum, pabulum*, Abus. 4. We lǽraþ, ðæt hí habban þreóra daga bíwiste *we enjoin, that they have provision for three days*, L. Edg. C. 3; Th. ii. 244, 12. He habban sceal ðám þrím geférscipum bíwiste *he must have provisions for the three classes*, Bt. 17; Fox 60, 3, 4.

bí-gyrdel *a girdle, purse*, Mt. Bos. 10, 9. v. big-gyrdel.

bi-gytan *to get, obtain, seize;* assequi, acquirere, arripere, corripere, Exon. 32 b; Th. 103, 19; Cri. 1690. v. be-gitan.

bi-healdan; *p.* -heóld, *pl.* -heóldon; *pp.* -healden. I. *to hold by* or *near, guard, observe, preserve;* tenere, inhabitare, custodire, servare, præservare:—Ðǽr se ánhaga eard bihealdeþ *there the lonely* [*bird*] *holds its dwelling*, Exon. 57 a; Th. 203, 21; Ph. 87. Mec sáwelcund hyrde bihealdeþ *a spiritual shepherd guardeth me*, Exon. 37 a; Th. 121, 15; Gú. 289. Hine weard biheóld of heofonum *a guardian from heaven guarded him*, Exon. 34 a; Th. 108, 22; Gú. 76: 54 b; Th. 193, 22; Az. 125. Se sceal ðære sunnan-síþ bihealdan *he shall observe the sun's course*, Exon. 57 a; Th. 203, 27; Ph. 90: 57 b; Th. 205, 17; Ph. 114. Háteþ mec heáh-cyning bihealdan *the high king commands* [*them*] *to preserve me*, Exon. 110 b; Th. 424, 15; Rä. 41, 39. II. *to see, look on, behold;* videre, intueri, aspicere:—Freó ðæt bihealdeþ hú me of hrife fleógaþ hylde pílas *my master beholds how the shafts of battle fly from my belly*, Exon. 105 a; Th. 399, 3; Rä. 18, 5. v. be-healdan.

bi-heáwan; *p.* -heów; *pp.* -heáwen *To hew* or *cut off, to deprive of;* cædendo privare:—Iohannes bibeád heáfde biheáwan *commanded to cut off John's head*, Exon. 70 a; Th. 260, 10; Jul. 295. v. be-heáwan.

bi-helan; *p.* -hæl, *pl.* -hǽlon; *pp.* -holen *To conceal;* occultare, Exon. 27 a; Th. 80, 23; Cri. 1311. v. be-helan.

bi-helian *to hide, conceal*, Exon. 52 b; Th. 183, 14; Gú. 1327. v. be-helian.

bi-helmian; *p.* ade; *pp.* ad *To cover over, to cover, shroud;* cooperire:—Heolstre bihelmad *shrouded with darkness*, Exon. 69 a; Th. 257, 2; Jul. 241. v. be-helman.

bi-heonan *on this side.* v. be-heonan.

bi-hlǽman *to overwhelm with noise, to fall upon;* strepitu obruere:—Ðonne foldbúende se micla dæg meahtan Dryhtnes mægne bihlǽmeþ *then the great day of the mighty Lord will fall with might upon the earth's inhabitants*, Exon. 20 b; Th. 54, 18; Cri. 870. [*O. Sax. O. H. Ger.* hlamón *crepitare.*]

bi-hlǽnan; *p.* de; *pp.* ed *To surround* or *beset by leaning anything against another;* acclinando circumdare:—Lǽmen fæt wudu-beámum, holte bihlǽnan [bilænan MS.] *an earthen vessel with forest trees, with wood beset*, Exon. 74 a; Th. 277, 7; Jul. 577.

bi-hlemman; *v. a.* [be, hlemman *to dash together*] *To dash together;* collidere cum strepitu:—He ða grimman goman bihlemmeþ fæste togædre *he dashes the grim jaws* [*gums*] *fast together*, Exon. 97 b; Th. 364, 26; Wal. 76.

bi-hlyhhan; *p.* -hlóh, *pl.* -hlógon; *pp.* -hlahen, -hleahen *To laugh at, deride;* ridere aliquid, exultare de aliqua re, Exon. 73 b; Th. 274, 1; Jul. 526. v. be-hlehhan.

bi-hófian; *p.* ode; *pp.* od *To have need of, to need, require;* egere, indigere, Exon. 37 b; Th. 123, 33; Gú. 332. v. be-hófian.

bi-hongen *behung, hung round*, Exon. 81 b; Th. 307, 1; Seef. 17; *pp. of* bi-hón. v. be-hón.

bi-hreósan; *p.* -hreás, *pl.* -hruron; *pp.* -hroren *To rush down, cover;* ruere, obruere, incidere:—Hríme bihrorene *covered with rime*, Exon. 77 b; Th. 291, 4; Wand. 77.

bi-hroren *rushed*, Exon. 77 b; Th. 291, 4; Wand. 77. v. bi-hreósan.

bi-hýdan; *p.* -hýdde; *pp.* -hýded *To hide, conceal, cover;* abscondere, occultare, operire, Exon. 61 b; Th. 227, 4; Ph. 418. v. be-hýdan.

bi-hydig *careful*, Bd. 4, 7; S. 574, 33. v. be-hydig, big-hydig.

bii; *prep. dat.* [= big = bí = be] *By, near to;* juxta, prope:—Se eádiga ærcebiscop Sanctus Laurentius bii his fóregengan Sancte Agustine bebyrged wæs *beatus archiepiscopus Laurentius juxta prædecessorem suum Augustinum sepultus est*, Bd. 2, 7; S. 509, 6. v. be I.

BIL, bill, es; *n. An old military weapon, with a hooked point, and an edge on the back, as well as within the curve, a* BILL *or a broad two-edged sword, a falchion. Whatever its shape, it must have had two edges; as, in the earliest poem, an envoy is attacked,* billes ecgum, *with the edges of a bill;* falx, marra, falcastrum, ensis curvus. Hitherto this word has only been found in poetry:—Ðá ic, on morgne, gefrægn mǽg óðerne billes ecgum on bonan stælan *then on the morrow, I have heard of the other kinsman setting on the slayer with the edges of a bill*, Beo. Th. 4963; B. 2485. Geseah ðá sige-eádig bil, eald sweord eótenisc *then he saw a victorious bill, an old giant sword*, Beo. Th. 3119; B. 1557. Abrægd mid ðý bille *he brandished with his sword*, Cd. 142; Th. 177, 17; Gen. 2931. Billa ecgum *with the edges of swords*, Cd. 210; Th. 260, 14; Dan. 709. Billum abreótan *to destroy with swords*, Cd. 153; Th. 190, 14; Exod. 199. [*Laym.* bil *a falchion: O. Sax.* bil, *n: Dut.* bijl, *f: Ger.* beil, beihel, *n: M. H. Ger.* bíle, bíl, *n: O. H. Ger.* bihal, bial, *n: Sansk.* bil *to divide;* findere.] DER. gúþ-bil, hilde-, stán-, twí-, wíg-, wudu-.

bi-lage [bí *by, near*, lagu *a law*] *A* BYE-LAW; lex privata, Chr. W. Thorn. an. 1303.

bile, es; *m? A* BILL, *beak of a bird, a proboscis, the fore part of a ship;* rostrum, proboscis = προβοσκίς:—Bile *rostrum*, Wrt. Voc. 77, 26. Ylpes bile *vel* wrót *an elephant's proboscis*, Ælfc. Gl. 18; Som. 58, 128; Wrt. Voc. 22, 42.

bíle *a bile, carbuncle, sore;* ulcus, Som. Lye. v. býl.

bi-leác *locked up, shut up*, Exon. 124 b; Th. 479, 1; Rä. 62, 1, = beleác; *p. of* be-lúcan.

bi-lecgan; *p.* -legde, -lēde; *pp.* -legd, -lēd *To lay* or *impose upon, to lay round, cover, load, afflict, charge;* imponere, afficere, onerare, accusare, Exon. 107 a; Th. 409, 6; Rä. 27, 25. v. be-lecgan.

bi-lēgan; *p.* -lēgde; *pp.* -lēgd *To surround with flame;* circumflagrare flamma:—Lēge bilēgde *surrounded with flame* [*Ger.* umlodert mit lohe], Exon. 53 a; Th. 186, 7; Az. 16. v. be-lēgan.

bile-hwít; *adj.* [bile *the beak*, hwít *white*, referring to the *beaks* of young birds, then to their nature, *Junius*] *Simple, sincere, honest, without fraud* or *deceit, meek, mild, gentle;* simplex, mitis:—Arnwi munuc wæs swíðe gód man and swíðe bilehwít *monk Arnwi was a very good man and very meek*, Chr. 1041; Erl. 169, 12. v. bilewit.

bile-hwítlíce; *adv. Honestly, simply;* honeste, simpliciter:—Andswarede Dryhthelm bilehwítlíce, forðon he wæs bylehwítre gleáwnesse and gemetfæstre gecynde man *Drycthelme respondebat simpliciter, erat namque homo simplicis ingenii ac moderatæ naturæ*, Bd. 5, 12; S. 631, 30.

bí-leofa *food*, C. R. Ben. 49. v. big-leofa.

bí-leofen, -lifen, e; *f.* [bí, leofen *living, livelihood*] *Food, provisions;* annona, pulmentum:—Bí-leofene [MS. bileouene] *annona*, C. R. Ben. 43. Bílifen *pulmentum*, Cot. 171. v. big-leofa.

bi-leóran; *p.* de, ade; *pp.* ed *To pass by* or *over;* transire, præterire:—Gif bileórade fram [MS. from] him seó [MS. ðio] tíd *si transiret ab eo hora*, Mk. Skt. Lind. 14, 35, 36. Se bileórde *qui præterivit*, Ps. Surt. 89, 4. v. leóran.

bi-leósan; *p.* -leás, *pl.* -luron; *pp.* -loren *To bereave, deprive;* orbare, privare:—Ðá afyrhted wearþ ár, elnes biloren *then the messenger was affrighted, bereft of courage*, Exon. 52 a; Th. 181, 30; Gú. 1301. v. be-leósan.

bile-wit, bele-wit, bil-wit; *adj.* [bile, wit *mind, wit*] *Merciful, mild, gentle, simple, honest;* æquanimus, mansuetus, mitis, simplex, honestus:—Bilewit Dryhten *merciful Lord*, Ps. C. 50, 99; Ps. Grn. ii. 279, 99: Bt. Met. Fox 20, 138; Met. 20, 69: 20, 510; Met. 20, 255: 20, 538; Met. 20, 269. We bletsiaþ bilewitne feder *we bless the merciful father*, Hy. 8, 8; Hy. Grn. ii. 290, 8. Gehýran ða bilewitan [MS. bylewitan] *audiant mansueti*, Ps. Spl. 33, 2. Beóþ eornustlíce gleáwe swá nædran, and bilwite [MS. bilwyte] swá culfran *estote ergo prudentes sicut serpentes, et simplices sicut columbæ*, Mt. Bos. 10, 16: 11, 29.

bile-witness, bil-witness, e; *f. Mildness, simplicity, innocence;* simplicitas:—Se God wunaþ simle on ðære heán ceastre his ánfealdnesse and bilewitnesse *God dwells always in the high city of his unity and simplicity*, Bt. 39, 5; Fox 218, 19. Hý on bilwitnesse hyra líf alyfdon *they passed their lives in simplicity*, Ors. 1, 2; Bos. 27, 5.

bil-gesleht, bill-gesliht, -geslyht, es; *n.* [bil, bill *a sword*, gesleht *a clashing, conflict, slaughter;* from sleán *to slay, kill*] *A clashing of swords, battle;* ensium concutio, pugna:—Gelpan ne þorfte beorn blandenfeax bilgeslehtes [billgeslyhtes, Cott. Tiber. A. vi; billgeslihtes, Cott. Tiber. B. i: Cott. Tiber. B. iv] *the grizzly-haired warrior needed not boast of the clashing of swords*, Chr. 937; Th. 204, 35, col. 1; Æðelst. 45.

bilgst, bilhst, he bilgþ, bilhþ *art angry, is angry; 2nd and 3rd pers. pres. of* belgan *to be angry.*

bil-hete, bill-hete, es; *m.* [bil, bill *ensis*, hete *odium*] *The hate of swords;* odium ope ensium manifestatum:—Æfter billhete *after the hate of swords*, Andr. Kmbl. 156; An. 78.

bí-libban; *p.* -lifde; *pp.* -lifed, -lifd [bí 1. *by, upon*, libban *to live*] *To live by* or *upon, to be sustained* or *supported;* vesci, sustentari:—Sciððium wearþ emleóf, ðæt hý gesáwon mannes blód agoten, swá him wæs ðara nýtena meolc, ðe hý mǽst bílibbaþ *it was as agreeable to the Scythians to see* [lit. *that they saw*] *man's blood shed, as it was* [*to see*] *the milk of their cattle, upon which they mostly live*, Ors. 1, 2; Bos. 26, 31-33. God ðás eorþan, ðe ealle cwice wihta bílibbaþ, ealle hire wæstmbǽro gelytlade *God lessened this earth, all its fruitfulness, by which all living creatures are supported*, 2, 1; Bos. 38, 8.

bi-liden *left, departed*, Exon. 52 a; Th. 182, 18, = be-liden; *pp. of* be-líðan, *q. v.*

bí-lifen *food*, Cot. 171. v. bí-leofen.

bilig *a bag, bottle, skin;* uter, Ps. Spl. M. 118, 83. v. belg.

bi-lihþ *dishonours, defames,* Exon. 90 a; Th. 337, 16; Gn. Ex. 65, = be-hlīþ; *pres. of* be-hlīgan, *q. v.*

biliþ, es; *n. An image, a representation, resemblance, likeness, pattern, example;* imago, effigies:—Biliþe wǣron eorlas Ebrēa *the men were the images [likenesses] of the Hebrews,* Cd. 187; Th. 232, 7, note a. [*O. Sax.* biliði, *n*: *Frs. O. Frs.* bilethe, byld, *n*: *Dut.* beeld, *n*: *Ger.* bild, *n*: *M. H. Ger.* bilde, *n*: *O. H. Ger.* biladi, bilidi, *n*: *Dan.* billed, billede, *n*: *Swed.* bild, *m*; belāte, *n*: *O. Nrs.* bílldr, *m. forma, aspectus;* bílæti, *n. effigies, statua,* Rask Hald.]

bill *a bill, falchion;* falcatus ensis:—Bill *falcastrum,* Ælfc. Gl. 51; Som. 66, 1; Wrt. Voc. 34, 61: Beo. Th. 5548; B. 2777. v. bil.

bill-gesliht, -geslyht *a clashing of swords,* Chr. 937; Th. 205, 35; Æðelst. 45. v. bil-gesleht.

bi-locen *locked up,* Exon. 26 a; Th. 77, 21; Cri. 1260, = be-locen; *pp. of* be-lūcan.

bilod *having a bill, nib* or *snout;* rostratus, Som. DER. bile *a bill, beak.* v. ge-bilod.

bi-loren *deprived,* Exon. 52 a; Th. 181, 30; Gū. 1301, = be-loren; *pp. of* be-leósan.

bilst, he bilþ *bellowest, bellows;* 2nd *and* 3rd *pers. pres. of* bellan.

bil-swæþ; *gen.* -swæðes, *pl. nom.* -swaðu; *n. A bill* or *sword track:*—Bilswaðu blōdige *bloody sword tracks,* Cd. 160; Th. 198, 27; Exod. 329. v. swæþ, *n.*

bi-lūcan *to lock up, inclose, surround,* Exon. 31 b; Th. 99, 14; Cri. 1624. v. be-lūcan.

bil-wetnes *innocence,* Bd. 3, 27; S. 559, 28. v. bile-witness.

bil-wit *mild,* Cd. 40; Th. 53, 4; Gen. 856. v. bile-wit.

bil-witness *simplicity,* Ors. 1, 2; Bos. 27, 5. v. bile-witness.

bi-mǣnan; *p.* de; *pp.* ed *To bemoan, bewail, lament, mourn;* lugere:—Woldan wīf wōpe bimǣnan æðelinges deáþ *the women would with weeping bewail the noble's death,* Exon. 119 b; Th. 459, 24; Hö. 4. v. be-mǣnan.

bi-mīðan; *p.* -māþ, *pl.* -miðon; *pp.* -miðen *To hide, conceal;* occultare, abscondere, Exon. 34 b; Th. 110, 33; Gū. 118: Ps. Th. 68, 6. v. be-mīðan.

bi-murnan; *p.* -murnde; *pp.* -murned *To mourn, be troubled about, care for;* lugere, curare, sollicitum esse de re, Exon. 87 a; Th. 328, 7; Vy. 14; 34 a; Th. 110, 1; Gū. 101. v. be-murnan.

bi-mūtian; *p.* ade; *pp.* ad [mūtung *mutuum,* Cot. 136] *To exchange for;* commutare:—Swā ðās woruldgestreón on ða mǣran gōd bimūtad weorþaþ *so these world-treasures shall be exchanged for the greater good,* Exon. 33 b; Th. 106, 17; Gū. 42.

BIN, binn, e; *f. A manger, crib,* BIN, *hutch;* præsepe, præsepium:—Binn *præsepe,* Ælfc. Gr. 9, 2; Som. 8, 27. Heó hine on binne ālēde *reclinavit eum in præsepio,* Lk. Bos. 2, 7, 12, 16: Exon. 18 b; Th. 45, 25; Cri. 724. On heora assena binne *in the manger of their asses,* Homl. Th. i. 30, 13, 31. [*Chauc.* binn: *Dut.* ben, *f*: *Ger.* benne, binne, *f.*]

BINDAN, to bindenne; ic binde, ðū bindest, bintst, binst, he bindeþ, bint, *pl.* bindaþ; *p.* ic, he band, bond, ðū bunde, *pl.* bundon; *pp.* bunden; *v. a. To* BIND, *tie;* ligare, alligare:—Hió bindan þenceaþ cyningas *she thinks to bind kings,* Ps. Th. 149, 8. Fæste binde swearte wealas *I bind the swart strangers fast,* Exon. 103 b; Th. 393, 21; Rä. 13, 3. Hrusan [MS. hruse] bindeþ wintres wōma *the winter's violence binds the earth,* Exon. 78 a; Th. 292, 21; Wand. 102. Hīg bindaþ hefige byrðyna *alligant onera gravia,* Mt. Bos. 23, 4. He band hine *he bound him,* Gen. 42, 24. Hrīm hrusan bond *frost bound the earth,* Exon. 81 b; Th. 307, 31; Seef. 32. Ūser Hǣlend [MS. hælendes] wæs bunden fæste *our Saviour was bound fast,* Exon. 116 b; Th. 449, 5; Dōm. 66. [*Chauc.* binde: *Laym.* binde, binden: *Orm.* bindenn: *O. Sax.* bindan: *Frs.* bynnen: *O. Frs.* binda: *Dut. Ger. M. H. Ger.* binden: *O. H. Ger.* bintan: *Goth.* bindan: *Dan.* binde: *Swed.* binda: *O. Nrs.* binda.] DER. an-bindan, be-, for-, ge-, in- [= un-], on- [= un-], un-, ymb-.

binde, an; *f.* [bindan *to bind*] *A band, wreath, head-band, fillet;* corolla, fascia:—Hió an Ceoldryþe hyre betstan [MS. betsðan] bindan *she gives to Ceoldryth her best band,* Cod. Dipl. 1290; A. D. 995; Kmbl. vi. 133, 18, 20.

bindele, byndele, byndelle, an; *f. A binding, tying, fastening with bands;* vinculis constrictio:—Be mannes bindelan *concerning [the] binding [putting in bands] of a man.* L. Alf. pol. 35; Th. i. 84, 1, note 2.

bindere, es; *m.* [bindan *to bind*] *One who binds, a* BINDER; ligator:—Ic eom bindere and swingere *I am a binder and a scourger,* Exon. 107 b; Th. 409, 25; Rä. 28, 6.

bi-neótan; *p.* -neát, *pl.* -nuton; *pp.* -noten *To deprive of the enjoyment* or *use of anything:*—On hyge hālge heáfde bineótan *to deprive the holy one in spirit of his head,* Exon. 74 b; Th. 278, 28; Jul. 604. He hine ealdre bineát *he deprived him of life,* Beo. Th. 4784; B. 2396. v. be-neótan.

bi-niman [*Goth.* bi-niman *auferre, furari;* κλέπτειν] *to deprive.* v. be-niman.

binn *a manger,* Ælfc. Gr. 9, 2; Som. 8, 27. v. bin.

binnan [be-innan]; *prep. dat. acc. Within, in, into;* intra, infra, in:—Ðe binnan ðam fæstenne wǣran *who were within the fastness,* Ors. 4, 11; Bos. 97, 39: Mt. Bos. 2, 16. Gyt ne com se Hǣlend binnan ða ceastre *nondum Iesus venerat in castellum,* Jn. Bos. 11, 30. [*Northumb.* binna, bionna: *Frs.* binnen: *O. Frs.* binna, binnia: *Dut. Kil. Ger. M. H. Ger.* binnen.] DER. innan.

bi-nom, *pl.* bi-nōmon *deprived,* Exon. 100 a; Th. 378, 15; Deór. 16: 37 b; Th. 122, 30; Gū. 313, = be-nam, -nāmon; *p. of* be-niman. v. niman.

bi-noten *deprived,* Exon. 45 b; Th. 156, 10; Gū. 872; *pp. of* bi-neótan.

bintst, binst, he bint *bindest, binds;* 2nd *and* 3rd *pers. pres. of* bindan *to bind.*

bió *I am* or *shall be,* Bt. 40, 5; Fox 240, 24; *pres. of* bión. v. beó, beón.

bió-breád *honey-comb,* Bt. 23; Fox 78, 25. v. beó-breád.

biódan *to command, announce, offer,* Beo. Th. 5777; B. 2892: Bt. 25; Fox 88, 18. v. beódan.

bióm *I am, shall be;* sum, ero:—Ic beóm hāl *vel* gehǣled ic bióm *salva ero,* Mk. Lind. Rush. War. 5, 28: Jn. Rush. War. 7, 34; 1st *pers. pres. of* bión. v. beón.

bión, ic bió, bióm, he bióþ, *pl.* bióþ, bieþ, biaþ; *subj.* bió, bie *to be;* esse, existere, fieri:—Ic bió swīðe fægn *I shall be very glad,* Bt. 40, 5; Fox 240, 24. Bióm, Jn. Rush. War. 7, 34. Hwæt iów ðȳ bet bió oððe þince *what is or appears to you the better?* Bt. Met. Fox 10, 130; Met. 10, 65: Beo. Th. 5487; B. 2747: Mk. Lind. War. 10, 44. Ne mæg hira ǣnig būtan ōðrum bión *nor can any of them exist without the others,* Bt. Met. Fox 20, 290; Met. 20, 145: 11, 102; Met. 11, 51: Bt. 33, 4; Fox 130, 26: Th. Diplm. A. D. 804; 459, 16. Ðonne bióþ brocene *then will be broken,* Beo. Th. 4132; B. 2063: Andr. Kmbl. 815; An. 408: Elen. Grm. 1289: Bt. Met. Fox 7, 46; Met. 7, 23: 24, 121; Met. 24, 61: Ps. C. 50, 80; Ps. Grn. ii. 278, 80: Mk. Lind. War. 10, 43: Mt. Lind. Stv. 26, 31. v. beón.

biór *beer,* Prov. 31. v. beór.

biorg *a hill, mountain;* collis, mons, Exon. 35 a; Th. 112, 20; Gū. 146. v. beorg.

biorhto *brightness,* Bt. 41, 1; Fox 244, 7. v. beorhtu.

biorn, es; *m. A warrior, soldier, hero;* bellator, miles, heros:—Biorn under beorge bordrand onswāf wið Geáta dryhten *the hero under the mount turned his shield's disc against the lord of the Goths,* Beo. Th. 5111, note; B. 2559. DER. folc-biorn. v. beorn II.

biór-sele, es; *m. A beer-hall, feasting-hall,* Beo. Th. 5263; B. 2635. v. beór-sele.

bióþ *is, are,* Bt. Met. Fox 7, 46; Met. 7, 23: 24, 121; Met. 24, 61; 3rd *pers. pres. of* bión. v. beón.

biótian *to threaten;* intentare, Cot. 108. v. beótian I.

biótul *a beetle, staff,* Cot. 28. v. bȳtl.

bió-wyrt *bee-wort;* apiastrum, Glos. Epnl. Recd. 153, 20. v. beó-wyrt.

BIRCE, ean; *f*: berc, beorc, byrc, e; *f. A birch-tree;* betula alba:—Genim bircean *take of the birch-tree,* L. M. 1, 36; Lchdm. ii. 86, 7: Wrt. Voc. 285, 22. [*Scot.* birk: *Plat.* barke, *f*: *Dut.* berke-boom, *m*: *Kil.* berck: *Ger.* birke, *f*: *M. H. Ger.* birke, birche, *f*: *O. H. Ger.* bircha, *f*: *Dan.* birk, *m. f*: *Swed. O. Nrs.* biörk, *f. betula vel quæcunque arbor viridis.*]

bircen, beorcen; *adj.* BIRCHEN, *belonging to birch;* betulaceus, Som. Lye. [*Kil.* bercken.]

birc-holt, es; *n. A birch holt* or *grove;* betuletum. v. byrc-holt.

bird *the young of any of the feathered tribe;* pullus:—Birdas *pullos,* Lk. Lind. Rush. War. 2, 24. v. brid.

bi-reáfian; *p.* ode; *pp.* od *To bereave;* privare, Exon. 87 b; Th. 328, 30; Vy. 25. v. be-reáfian.

bi-reófan; *p.* -reáf, *pl.* -rufon; *pp.* -rofen *To bereave, deprive;* spoliare, privare:—Rǣdum birofene *bereft of counsel,* Exon. 30 a; Th. 93, 14; Cri. 1526: 104 a; Th. 394, 22; Rä. 14, 7. v. be-reófan.

birest, he bireþ *bearest, bears,* Bt. Met. Fox 20, 551; Met. 20, 276: L. In. 57; Th. i. 138, 15; 2nd *and* 3rd *pers. pres. of* beran.

birgan; *p.* de; *pp.* ed *To cover with a mound, to bury;* sepelire:—Birge man hine ðæs ilcan dæges *sepelietur in eadem die,* Deut. 21, 23: Gen. 49, 31. DER. be-birgan. v. byrgan.

birgean *to bury:*—Iosue hēt hī birgean *Joshua ordered to bury them,* Jos. 10, 27. v. birgan.

birgels, es; *m. A burial-place, sepulchre;* sepulcrum:—Him sylfum to birgelse *in possessionem sepulcri,* Gen. 23, 9. v. byrgels.

birgen, birgenn, e; *f. A burying-place, sepulchre;* sepulcrum, Gen. 23, 4, 6: 49, 30: 50, 5: Num. 11, 34. v. byrgen.

birg-nes, -ness *a taste,* Cot. 97. v. bȳrignes.

birhtu *brightness, splendour;* claritas, splendor, Bt. Met. Fox 6, 11; Met. 6, 6: 20, 537; Met. 20, 269. v. beorhtu.

birig *to a city, for* byrig, Gen. 13, 12: Deut. 14, 27; *d. s. of* burh.

birigan *to bury.* v. be-birigan, byrigan.

birigh-man *a city officer;* ædilis, Ælfc. Gr. 9, 28; Som. 11, 29. v. byrig-man.

bī-rihte, -ryhte; *prep. dat. Near, close by;* juxta:—Geseh he on greóte gingran sîne bîryhte [Kmbl. birihte] him swefan on slǽpe *he saw his disciples near him slumbering in sleep on the sand*, Andr. Recd. 1699; An. 850.

birihto *brightness*, L. E. I. 20; Th. ii. 414, 11. v. beorhtu.

birilian, birlian, byrlian; *p.* ode, ade; *pp.* od, ad *To draw, bear;* haurire, Jn. Lind. Rush. War. 2, 8, 9.

bi-rinnan; *p.* -ran; *pp.* -runnen to run as a liquid, hence,—*To wet, bedew;* fluere, perfundere, irrigare:—Ðá wearþ beám monig blôdigum teárum birunnen, sæp wearþ to swâte *then many a tree became bedewed with bloody tears, their sap became [turned to] blood*, Exon. 25 a; Th. 72, 19–23; Cri. 1175–1177.

Birînus, i; *m.* Latin: Birîne, Byrîne, es; *m. Birinus, the first bishop of Wessex, sent by pope Honorius to Britain in* A. D. 634:—Ðære tîde ðá West-Seaxna þeód mid Cynigelse heora cyninge Cristes geleáfan onfêng, bodade him and lǽrde Godes word Birînus biscop, se mid Honorius geþeahte ðæs Papan com on Breotene .... He ðá lǽrde ðǽr godcunde lâre, and ðone cyning to Cristes geleáfan gecyrde, and hine gecristnade, and hine eft æfter fæce mid fulluhtbæðe aþwôgh mid his þeóde West-Seaxum. Hit gelamp on ða sylfan tîd ðe mon ðone cyning fullade, ðæt ðǽr wæs se hâlgesta and se sigefæstesta cyning Norþan Hymbra Oswald andweard .... Ðá sealdon hî and geáfon ðam bisceope begen ða cyningas eardungstôwe and biscopsetl on Dorceceastre, and he ðǽr, se bisceop, Gode lifde and cyricean worhte and hâlgode ... and he ðǽr his dagas ge-endode and to Drihtne fêrde, and in ðære ylcan ceastre bebyriged wæs, and eft æfter monigum geárum Hædde bisceop hêt his lîchoman up adôn and lǽdan [MS. lædon] to Winton ceastre *eo tempore* [A. D. 634] *gens Occidentalium Saxonum, (qui antiquitus Gevissæ vocabantur,) regnante Cynigilso fidem Christi suscepit, prædicante illis verbum Birino episcopo, qui cum consilio papæ Honorii venerat Brittaniam .... Itaque evangelizante illo in præfata provincia, cum rex ipse catechizatus, fonte baptismi cum sua gente ablueretur, contigit tunc temporis sanctissimum ac victoriosissimum regem Nordanhymbrorum Osualdum adfuisse .... Donaverunt autem ambo reges eidem episcopo civitatem quæ vocatur Dorcic [Dorchester], ad faciendum inibi sedem episcopalem; ubi factis dedicatisque ecclesiis ... migravit ad Dominum, sepultusque est in eadem civitate, et post annos multos Hædde episcopatum agente translatus inde in Ventam civitatem [Winchester]*, Bd. 3, 7; S. 529, 4–6; 12–16; 18–21; 22–24. Hêr forþfêrde Birînus se biscop *here*, A. D. 650, *Birinus the bishop died*, Chr. 650; Th. 51, 1, col. 2. Hêr Ægelbryht of Galwalum æfter Birîne [Byrîne, col. 2, 3] ðam Rômâniscan bisceope onfêng Wesseaxna bisceopdôme *here*, A. D. 650, *Ægelbyrht of Gaul succeeded to the bishopric of the West-Saxons after Birinus the Roman bishop*, 650; Th. 50, 1–5, col. 1.

birst, he birsteþ, birst *burstest, bursts; 2nd and 3rd pers. pres. of* berstan.

birþ *bears; 3rd pers. pres. of* beran.

bî-sæc *a bag*, Mt. Rush. Stv. 10, 10. v. sæc, codd.

bî-sǽce, es; *n? m?* I. *a visit;* visitatio:—Bâd bîsǽce betran hyrdes *waited the visit of a better keeper*, Exon. 35 b; Th. 115, 11; Gû. 188. II. *persecution, dispute, litigation;* controversia, litigatio:—Bîsǽce *in litigation*, L. Edg. C. 62; Th. ii. 258, 3. Gif ðǽr hwæt bîsǽces sŷ, seme se biscop *if there be somewhat of dispute, let the bishop settle it*, Const. vii; Th. ii. 258, note a. DER. sǽcan, sêcan *to seek, visit, persecute, dispute.*

bi-scær *sheared* or *cut off*, Reim. 26; *p. of* bi-sceran. v. be-sceran.

bi-scencan; *p.* -scencte, *pl.* -scencton; *pp.* -scenced [scencan *to give drink*, scenc *drink*] *To give to drink;* ad potionem dare:—Ge in wræcsîðe longe lifdon, lêge biscencte *ye [fallen spirits] have long lived in exile, flame being given [you] to drink*, Exon. 41 b; Th. 139, 21; Gû. 596.

bisceop, biscop, biscep, es; *m.* I. *a* BISHOP, *prelate;* episcopus:—Se bisceop is gecweden *episcopus* and is *ofersceáwigend* on Englisc, ðæt he ofersceáwige symle his underþeóddan *the bishop is called* episcopus, *that is in English*, overseer, *because he constantly oversees his subordinates*, L. Ælf. P. 37; Th. ii. 378, 28. Nis ná mâre betwyx mæsse-preóste and bisceop, bûton ðæt [Th. ii. 348, 24] se bisceop is geset to mâran bletsunge ðonne se mæsse-preóst sŷ; ðæt is, circan to hâlgigenne, and to hâdigenne preóstas, to bisceopgenne cild [Th. ii. 348, 26: MS. men to biscopienne], and to bletsigenne ele *there is no difference between a mass-priest and a bishop, but that the bishop is appointed for greater benediction [blessing] than is the mass-priest; that is, to hallow churches, and to ordain priests, to confirm children, and to bless oil*, 36; Th. ii. 378, 20; v. mæsse-preóst. Seó mǽgþ hafþ twegen bisceopas *the province has two bishops*, Bd. 4, 5; S. 573, 33. II. *a chief priest of the Jews;* pontifex:—Se forma biscop, ðe God silf gesette, wæs Aaron gehâten *the first high priest, whom God himself appointed, was called Aaron*, L. Ælf. P. 38; Th. ii. 378, 32. Scrîdde ðone bisceop mid lînenum reáfe *vestivit pontificem subucula linea*, Lev. 8, 7. Ðá astyredon ða bisceopas ða menegu *pontifices autem concitaverunt turbam*, Mk. Bos. 15, 11. Se bisceop acsode ðone Hǽlend *pontifex interrogavit Iesum*, Jn. Bos. 18, 19, 22, 24. III. *a heathen priest of the Romans and Egyptians;* the chief priest of the Romans was called *Pontifex Maximus*, which was a title assumed by the Consuls and Emperors, v. yldest-bisceop:—Sǽdon ða Ēgyptiscan bisceopas, ðæt ða Godes wundor hiora âgnum godum getealde wǽron, ðæt sint deófol-gild *the Egyptian priests said, that the godlike wonders were ascribed to their own gods, which are idols*, Ors. 1, 5; Bos. 28, 25. Bisceopas on Rôme sǽdon, ðæt heora godas bǽdon ðæt him man worhte anfiteatra *the priests in Rome said, that their gods ordered them to build an amphitheatre*, Ors. 3, 3; Bos. 55, 26. Lucinius Crassus, se consul, wæs eác Rômâna yldesta bisceop *Lucinius Crassus, the consul, was also the chief priest* [pontifex maximus] *of the Romans*, Ors. 5, 4; Bos. 104, 16. IV. *the rank of an Anglo-Saxon bishop was equal to that of the Ealdorman*, or *highest nobleman, being only inferior to the Æðeling* or *prince, for they had equal power as judges in civil courts of law,—and their* burh-brice *and* wêr-gyld *were the same:*—Bisceope gebyreþ ǽlc rihting, ge on godcundan þingan ge on woruldcundan *to a bishop belongs every direction [righting] both in divine and worldly things*, L. I. P. 7; Th. ii. 312, 9. Sculon bisceopas, mid woruld-dêman, dômas dihtan ðæt hî ne geþafian, gyf his waldan magan, ðæt ǽnig unriht up-aspringe *bishops, with temporal judges, should so direct judgments that they never permit, if it be in their power, that any injustice spring up*, 7; Th. ii. 312, 35–37. And sêce man hundred-gemôt swâ hit ǽr geset wæs; and hæbbe man þrîwa on geáre burh-gemôt; and tûwa scîr-gemôt; and ðǽr beó on ðære scîre bisceop and se ealdorman, and ðǽr ǽgðer tǽcan ge Godes riht ge woruld-riht *and let the hundred-moot be attended as it was before fixed; and thrice in the year let a city-moot be held; and twice a shire-moot; and let there be present the bishop of the shire and the ealdorman, and there each expound both God's law [right] and the world's law*, L. Edg. ii. 5; Th. i. 268, 2–5: L. C. S. 18; Th. i. 386, 4–8. Biscopes and ealdormannes burg-bryce biþ lx scillinga *a bishop's and an ealdorman's* burh-bryce *shall be sixty shillings*, L. Alf. pol. 40; Th. i. 88, 8, note 19, H. Biscopes and ealdormannes mund-brice gebête mid ii pundum *recompense a bishop's and an ealdorman's* mund-brice *with two pounds*, L. Eth. vii. 11; Th. i. 332, 1. Biscopes and ealdormannes wêr-gyld is viii þûsend þrymsa *a bishop's and an ealdorman's* wer-gild *is eight thousand thrymsas*, L. Wg. 3; Th. i. 186, 7. V. *the bishops were the best educated men of their age, and often the most energetic, their advice and assistance were, therefore, naturally sought in every case of emergency in the cabinet or in the field,—Hence Ealhstan, the bishop of Sherborne for fifty years* [Ealhstân hæfde ðæt biscoprîce l wintra æt Scyreburnan, A. D. 817–867: Chr. 867; Ing. 98, 12–14], *became a general of Egbert and of his son Æthelwulf:*—Ecgbryht, West-Seaxna cyning, sende Æðelwulf his sunu of ðære fyrde, and Ealhstân his bisceop, to Cent micele werede, and hŷ Baldrêd ðone cyning norþ ofer Temese adryfon *Egbert, king of the West-Saxons, sent his son Æthelwulf, and Ealhstan his bishop, into Kent, with a large part of the army, and drove Baldred the king northward over the Thames*, Chr. 823; Ing. 87, 6–15: 845; Ing. 92, 1. Æt Mere-tûne wearþ Heáhmund biscop ofslegen, and feala gôdra monna *at Merton bishop Heahmund was slain, and many good men*, 871; Ing. 101, 1–9. [*Orm.* bisskopp, bisscopp, bisshopp: *Laym.* biscop, bissop: *Wyc.* bischop: *O. Sax.* biskop: *Dut.* bisschop: *Ger. M. H. Ger.* bischof: *O. H. Ger.* piscof: *Goth.* aipiskaupus: *Dan.* bisp: *Swed.* biskop: *O. Nrs.* biskup: *Fr.* évêque: *Span.* obispo: *It.* vescovo: *Wel.* esgob: *Gael.* easbuig: *Ir.* easbog: *Arm.* eskop: *Slav.* biskup: *Lith.* wyskupas. *From the Lat.* episcopus [*e-piscop-us, hence O. H. Ger.* piscof: *A. Sax.* biscop: *Orm.* bisshopp: *Laym.* biscop: *Wyc.* bischop: *Eng.* bishop] = *Grk.* ἐπίσκοπος *an overseer, guardian*, from ἐπί *upon, over*,—σκοπός *one who watches*,—σκοπέω *to look, watch, consider, contemplate.*] DER. arce-bisceop, -biscop, ealdor-: bisceop-dôm, -gegyrelan, -hâd, -hyrde, -lîc, -rîce, -roc, -scîr, -seld, -seðel, -setl, -stôl, -þênung, -wîte, -wyrt: bisceopian.

bisceop-dôm, biscop-dôm, biscep-dôm, es; *m.* I. [bisceop *a bishop*, dôm *judgment*] *a bishop's doom, excommunication;* episcopi judicium, excommunicatio:—Sŷn hî begen ðæs bisceopdômes scyldige *let them both be guilty of the bishop's doom [excommunication]*, Bd. 4, 5; S. 573, note 1. II. *the province of a bishop, a bishopric;* episcopi provincia, episcopatus:—He onfêng biscopdôm Parisiace hâtte *he received the bishopric called Paris;* accepto episcopatu Parisiacæ civitatis, Bd. 3, 7; S. 530, note 10. Ps. Lamb. 108, 8. Wine heóld ðone biscepdôm iii geár *Wine held the bishopric three years*, Chr. 660; Erl. 34, 7.

bisceop-gegyrelan *episcopal robes.* v. biscop-gegyrelan.

bisceop-hâd, biscop-hâd, es; *m.* [bisceop *a bishop;* hâd *hood, condition, state*] BISHOPHOOD, *the office* or *state of a bishop, the episcopate, a bishopric;* munus episcopale, flaminium, episcopatus, episcopi provincia:—Wæs se bisceophâd befæsted *the bishopric was established*, Elen. Kmbl. 2422; El. 1212. Biscophâd *flaminium*, Cot. 86: 186. On biscophâde ge ǽr bisceophâde *in episcopatu et ante episcopatum*, Bd. 4, 6; S. 574, 2, 3: 5, 6; S. 620, 19. His bisceophâd [biscophâd, Spl.] brûcan feóndas *let his enemies enjoy his episcopate*, Ps. Th. 108, 8.

bisceop-hyrde, biscop-hyrede, es; *m. A bishop's shepherd* or *clergyman;* episcopi clericus, Cot. 44. v. hyrde.

bisceopian, biscopgan; *p.* ode; *pp.* od *To exercise the office of a bishop,* *to oversee, visit, confirm;* episcopali munere fungi, visitare, confirmare:—Se bisceop biþ gesett to hādigenne preóstas, and to bisceopgenne cild *the bishop is appointed for the ordaining of priests, and confirming of children,* L. Ælf. C. 17; Th. ii. 348, 26.

bisceop-líc, biscop-líc; *def.* se -líca, seó, ðæt -líce; *adj.* BISHOPLIKE, *episcopal, belonging to a bishop;* episcopalis, pontificalis:—He ðæt biscoplíce líf be-eóde *episcopalem vitam exercebat,* Bd. 5, 18; S. 635, 23. On bisceoplícum gerece *pontificali regimine,* 2, 15; S. 519, 13.

bisceop-ríce, biscop-ríce, es; *n.* [bisceop *a bishop,* ríce *a region*] *A* BISHOPRIC, *diocese, province of a bishop;* episcopi provincia, diœcesis = διοίκησις:—Mellitus fēng to ðam bisceopríce *Mellitus succeeded to the bishopric,* Bd. 2, 7; S. 509, note 8. Seaxulf his biscopríce onfēng *Saxulf succeeded to his bishopric,* 4, 6; S. 573, 35.

bisceop-roc, -rocc *a bishop's rochet.* v. biscop-roc.

bisceop-scír, biscop-scír, e; *f.* [bisceop *a bishop,* scír *a province*]. I. *the province of a bishop, a diocese;* episcopi provincia, diœcesis = διοίκησις, parochia = παροικία:—Bisceopscír *diœcesis* vel *parochia,* Ælfc. Gl. 68; Som. 69, 123; Wrt. Voc. 42, 4. Ðæt nǣnig bisceop ōðres bisceopscíre onswōge *ut nullus episcoporum parochiam alterius invadat,* Bd. 4, 5; S. 572, 32: 4, 13; S. 582, 1: 4, 6; S. 573, 39. He todǣlde on twā biscopscíre West-Seaxna mǣgþe *he divided the province of the West-Saxons into two dioceses,* 3, 7; S. 530, 6, 10. II. *the office of a bishop, episcopate;* episcopatus:—Seó biscopscír Wihte ðæs eálondes belimpeþ to Daniele Wintan ceastre bisceope *episcopatus Vectæ insulæ ad Danihelem pertinet episcopum Ventæ civitatis,* 5, 23; S. 646, 22. Se forlēt ða bisceopscíre *he left the episcopate;* relicto episcopatu, 3, 21; S. 551, 38.

bisceop-seld *a bishop's seat* or *residence, an episcopal see.* v. biscop-seld.

bisceop-seðel *a bishop's seat* or *residence, an episcopal see.* v. biscop-seðel.

bisceop-setl, biscop-setl, biscep-setl, es; *n.* [bisceop *a bishop,* setl *a seat*]. I. *a bishop's seat* or *residence;* sedes episcopalis:—Sæt he ðæt bisceopsetl xxxvii wintra and six mōnaþ and feówertyne dagas *he occupied the episcopal residence thirty-seven [of] years [winters] and six months and fourteen days,* Bd. 5, 23; S. 646, 9. He ðam Wine gesealde biscopsetl on Wintan ceastre *Vino in civitate Venta sedem episcopalem tribuit,* 3, 7; S. 530, 7, 14. Se eádiga Petrus se apostol gesæt biscepsetl on Rōme *the blessed Peter the apostle occupied the episcopal residence in Rome,* Chr. 45; Erl. 6, 19. II. *a bishopric;* episcopatus:—Wine wæs adrifen of his bisceopsetle *Wine was driven from his bishopric;* pulsus est Vini de episcopatu, Bd. 3, 7; S. 530, 13.

bisceop-stōl, biscop-stōl, es; *m.* [stōl *a stool, seat*] *A bishop's seat* or *residence, an episcopal see, bishopric;* sedes episcopalis, episcopatus, pontificatus:—He ne mihte ðone Rōmāniscan bisceopstōl eallunge forlǣtan *he could not altogether neglect the Roman episcopal see,* Nat. S. Greg. Els. 28, 8. Agefen to Wigorna cestre ðam bisceopstōle *given to the episcopal see at Worcester,* Th. Diplm. A. D. 883; 131, 27. Augustinus cyrde to his bisceopstōle *Augustine returned to his bishopric,* Nat. S. Greg. Els. 37, 5. Seó on setl biscopstōles wæs to ætȳced *quæ in sedem pontificatus addita est,* Bd. 5, 23; S. 646, 32.

bisceop-þēnung, e; *f.* [þēnung *duty, office*] *The duty* or *office of a bishop;* episcopi officium:—Þegnode se ārwurþa bisceop Willferþ on ðām dǣlum ða bisceopþēnunge ārwurþlíce fíf geár *the venerable bishop Wilfrith exercised the office of a bishop in those parts honourably five years,* Bd. 4, 13; S. 583, 15. Fēng Eádulf to ðære bisceopþēnunge *Eadulf succeeded to the bishop's office,* 5, 23; S. 645, 19.

bisceop-wíte *a bishop's fee for visiting.* v. biscop-wíte.

bisceop-wyrt, biscop-wyrt, biscep-wyrt, e; *f.* [wyrt *a wort, herb, plant*] BISHOP'S-WORT, *bishop's weed, betony, vervain, marsh-mallow;* ammi = ἄμμι [ammi majus, *Lin.*], betonica, verbena, hibiscum = ἰβίσκος:—Wyrc to drence æscþrotu, betonice, bisceopwyrt *make into a drink ash-throat, betony, bishop's-wort,* L. M. 1, 47; Lchdm. ii. 120, 10: 1, 23; Lchdm. ii. 66, 2, 10. Genim bisceopwyrt ða sūðernan *take the southern bishop's-wort,* L. M. 2, 54; Lchdm. ii. 274, 27. To monnes stæmne nim biscopwyrt *for a man's voice take bishop's-wort,* Lchdm. iii. 46, 26: Ælfc. Gl. 40; Som. 63, 93; Wrt. Voc. 30, 43. Genim ða brādan biscopwyrt *take the broad bishop's-wort,* Lchdm. iii. 46, 2. Betonice, ðæt is, biscopwyrt *betony, that is, bishop's-wort,* Herb. cont. 1; Lchdm. i. 2, 1. Seó læsse biscopwyrt *betonica,* Ælfc. Gl. 43; Som. 64, 49; Wrt. Voc. 31, 59. Biscopwyrt [MS. biscopwyrtil] *verbena,* 41; Som. 64, 1; Wrt. Voc. 31, 14. Biscepwyrt *hibiscum,* Wrt. Voc. 286, 15.

biscep *a bishop,* Chr. 110; Erl. 8, 11: 636; Erl. 24, 14: 690; Erl. 42, 15. v. bisceop.

biscep-dōm *the province of a bishop, a bishopric,* Chr. 660; Erl. 34, 7. v. bisceop-dōm II.

biscep-setl *an episcopal see,* Chr. 45; Erl. 6, 19. v. bisceop-setl.

biscep-wyrt *marsh-mallow,* Wrt. Voc. 286, 15. v. bisceop-wyrt.

bi-scerian, -scirian, -scyrian; *p.* ede; *pp.* ed *To deprive, separate;* privare, separare:—Wilna biscirede *from desires separated,* Exon. 48 b; Th. 166, 24; Gū. 1047. Dreámum biscyred *from joys separated,* 88 a; Th. 330, 23; Vy. 55. Faraþ nū, awyrgde, willum biscyrede engla dreámes, on ēce fír *go now, accursed, wilfully deprived of the joy of angels, into eternal fire,* 30 a; Th. 93, 3; Cri. 1520: 95 a; Th. 355, 28; Reim. 84: 42 b; Th. 142, 17; Gū. 645. v. be-scerian.

bi-scirian *to separate,* Exon. 48 b; Th. 166, 24; Gū. 1047. v. bi-scerian.

biscop *a bishop,* Chr. 910; Erl. 100, 9, 10. v. bisceop.

biscop-dōm *the province of a bishop, a bishopric,* Bd. 3, 7; S. 530, note 10. v. bisceop-dōm II.

biscopgan *to confirm,* L. Ælf. C. 18; Wilk. 155, 51. v. bisceopian.

biscop-gegyrelan; *pl. m.* [gegyrela *a garment, robe*] *Episcopal robes;* indumenta episcopalia:—He sende him biscopgegyrelan *he sent him episcopal robes,* Bd. 1, 29; S. 498, 10.

biscop-hād *the office* or *state of a bishop, the episcopate,* Cot. 86: Ps. Spl. 108, 7. v. bisceop-hād.

biscop-heáfod-lín *a bishop's head linen, an ornament which bishops wore on their heads;* infula:—Biscop-heáfod-lín *infula,* Ælfc. Gl. 64; Som. 69, 10.

biscop-líc *episcopal,* Bd. 5, 18; S. 635, 23. v. bisceop-líc.

biscop-ríce *a bishopric,* Bd. 4, 6; S. 573, 35. v. bisceop-ríce.

biscop-roc, -rocc, es; *m.* [roc, rocc *a tunic*] *A bishop's rochet;* dalmatica:—Mid biscoprocce scrȳdan *to clothe with a bishop's rochet,* Lchdm. iii. 202, 26.

biscop-scír *a diocese,* Bd. 3, 7; S. 530, 6, 10. v. bisceop-scír.

biscop-seld, es; *n.* [seld *a seat, residence*] *A bishop's seat* or *residence, an episcopal see;* sedes episcopalis:—Se cyning sealde him stōwe and biscopseld on Lindesfearona eá *rex locum sedis episcopalis in insula Lindisfarnensi tribuit,* Bd. 3, 3; S. 525, 35.

biscop-seðel; *g.* -seðles; *n.* [seðel *a seat*] *A bishop's seat* or *residence;* sedes episcopalis:—Mellitus fēng to ðam biscopseðle Contwara burge cirican *Mellitus succeeded to the episcopal residence of Canterbury church;* Mellitus sedem Doruvernensis ecclesiæ suscepit, Bd. 2, 7; S. 509, 8.

biscop-setl *a bishop's residence,* Chr. 604; Th. 38, 1. v. bisceop-setl.

biscop-stōl *an episcopal seat,* Bd. 5, 23; S. 646, 32. v. bisceop-stōl.

biscop-wíte, es; *n. A bishop's fee for visiting, procuration;* episcopo debita, Chr. 675; Erl. 38, 5.

biscop-wyrt *bishop's-wort, betony,* Lchdm. iii. 46, 26: Herb. cont. 1; Lchdm. i. 2, 1. v. bisceop-wyrt.

bi-scyrian *to deprive, separate,* Exon. 88 a; Th. 330, 23; Vy. 55: 30 a; Th. 93, 3; Cri. 1520: 95 a; Th. 355, 28; Reim. 84: 42 b; Th. 142, 17; Gū. 645. v. bi-scerian.

bi-seah *looked about,* Exon. 51 b; Th. 180, 8; Gū. 1276, = be-seah; *p. of* be-seón.

bísegu *occupation,* Bt. 33, 4; Fox 132, 28. v. bȳsgu.

bísen; *gen.* bísne, bísene; *f. An example, similitude, command, precept,* Bt. 22, 2; Fox 78, 13: 29, 1; Fox 102, 12: Exon. 40 a; Th. 133, 33; Gū. 499: Lk. Rush. War. 13, 6: Cd. 27; Th. 36, 13; Gen. 571. v. bȳsen.

bi-sencan *to sink,* Exon. 25 a; Th. 72, 8; Cri. 1169. v. be-sencan.

bi-seón; *p.* -seah *to see,* Exon. 23 b; Th. 67, 13; Cri. 1088. v. be-seón, seón.

bises; *indecl. m. A leap year;* bisextile, bisextus:—Būtan bises geboden weorþe, feorþan geáre *unless a leap year is appointed, [being] the fourth year,* Menol. Fox 64; Men. 32.

bi-settan; *p.* -sette, *pl.* -setton; *pp.* -seted, -sett *To set, beset, surround;* inserere, circumdare:—Ðonne gim in goldfate smiþa orþoncum biseted weorþeþ *when a gem has been set in a golden vessel by the artifice of smiths,* Exon. 60 a; Th. 219, 9; Ph. 304. Mid wyrtum se wilda fugel his nest biseteþ ūtan *the wild bird surrounds its nest without with herbs,* 63 b; Th. 233, 26; Ph. 530. v. be-settan.

bísgian *to occupy, busy,* Cd. 64; Th. 76, 29; Gen. 1264: Bt. proœm; Fox viii. 6. v. bȳsgian.

bísgu, e; *f. Occupation, toil, affliction, care,* Bt. proœm; Fox viii. 5, 6: Exon. 114 a; Th. 438, 14; Rä. 57, 7: 82 b; Th. 311, 6; Seef. 88: 74 b; Th. 280, 7; Jul. 625: Beo. Th. 3490; B. 1743: Bt. Met. Fox 22, 127; Met. 22, 64. v. bȳsgu.

bísgung, e; *f.* [= a-bísgung = a-bȳsgung] *Business, occupation;* negotium, occupatio:—Fint he ða ryhtwísnesse gehȳdde mid his mōdes bísgunga *he will find the wisdom concealed by the occupation of his mind,* Bt. 35, 1; Fox 156, 12. Ne forlǣte se reccere ða inneran giémenne ðæs godcundan þiówdōmes for ðære abísgunge ðara ūterra weorca *let not the ruler forsake the inner care of the divine ministration for the occupation of outer works,* Past. 18, 1; Hat. MS. 25 a, 29, 27, 30. v. bȳsgu.

bísigu *occupation, labour,* Beo. Th. 567, note; B. 281. v. bȳsgu.

bisleásung, e; *f. Fiction;* figmentum, Ps. Spl. M. 102, 13. v. leásung.

bismærian; *p.* ede; *pp.* ed *To revile;* maledicere:—Bismæredon uncit [*Inscription,* Bismærede ungket] men, bā ætgædre *they [men] reviled us two, both together,* Runic Inscrip. Kmbl. 354, 30. v. bysmerian.

bismær-word, es; *n.* [= bismer-word: bismer *opprobrium, contumelia;*

word *verbum*] *A disgraceful* or *abusive word, reproach, insult;* ignominiosum *vel* contumeliosum verbum, opprobrium, insultatio:—Mid bismærwordum *with insults*, L. H. E. 11; Th. i. 32, 5.

bismer, bismor, bysmer, bysmor; *gen.* bismeres, bysmres; *n.* [be, smeru *fat, grease*] *Filthiness, pollution, abomination, disgrace, infamy, mockery, reproach, contumely, blasphemy, calumny;* ludibrium, pollutio, abominatio, infamia, opprobrium, contumelia, blasphemia, calumnia:—Hí amyrdon heora folc on bysmore *they defiled their people with filthiness*, Ælfc. T. 15, 21. Seó stôw gewearþ swíðe mǽre for Rômâna bismere *the place became famous for the disgrace of the Romans*, Ors. 3, 8; Bos. 62, 44. His môd wæs mid ðam bismre ahwæt *his mind was whetted with that disgrace*, Ors. 6, 30; Bos. 126, 17. Hí mængdon eced and geallan togædere and hit, on his bismer, Criste gebudon *they mingled vinegar and gall together, and offered it to Christ, in mockery of him*, L. Edg. C. 39; Th. ii. 252, 17. Ðû hí, Drihten, dêst deópe to bysmre *tu, Domine, deridebis eos*, Ps. Th. 58, 8. He hâlge lâre brygdeþ on bysmer *he turneth holy lore into mockery*, Exon. 117 a; Th. 449, 14; Dôm. 71. Hí gefremedan ôðer bysmer *they made another reproach;* irritaverunt eum, Ps. Th. 105, 25: 106, 10. Dracan ðû ðysne geheowadest, hête syððan him bysmere brâde healdan *draco iste, quem formasti ad illudendum ei*, Ps. Th. 103, 25. Ðæt he dôþ to bysmore ðînum feóndum *he makes that for a reproach to thine enemies*, 8, 3. Ge gehýrdon his bysmer *audistis blasphemiam*, Mk. Bos. 14, 64. Ðæt ðû mǽge þolie bysmor on ǽlcne tîman *ut omni tempore calumniam sustineas*, Deut. 28, 29. [*O. Sax.* bismer, *n. opprobrium.*] DER. bismer-full, -leás, -leóþ, -lîc, -lîce, -nes, -spræc, -sprecan, -word: bismerian, ge-: bismerung: bismeriend.

bismer-full; *adj. Polluted, abominable, disgraceful;* pollutus, detestabilis, turpis. v. bysmor-full.

bismerian; *p.* ode, ede; *pp.* od, ed *To mock, deride, irritate, reproach, blaspheme, defame, revile;* illudere, deridere, irritare, irridere, blasphemare, calumniam facere, maledicere. DER. bismer. v. bysmerian.

bismeriend, es; *m. A deceiver;* illusor, Prov. 11, 4. DER. bismer.

bismer-leás; *adj. Without pollution, spotless, blameless;* sine pollutione, immaculatus, irreprehensus. v. bysmer-leás.

bismer-leóþ, es; *n.* [bismer *mockery, reproach;* leóþ *a song*] *A reproachful song, an incantation;* carmen invectivum, nenia, Cot. 188.

bismer-lîc, bismor-lîc; *adj.* [bismer, bismor *disgrace*, -lîc] *Disgraceful, ignominious, dirty, unpleasant;* turpis, ignominiosus, fœdus:—Mid ðam bismerlîcestan âþe *with the most disgraceful oath*, Ors. 4, 3; Bos. 79, 39: 1, 7; Bos. 29, 35. We lǽraþ, ðæt man geswîce bismorlîcra efesunga *we enjoin, that a man abstain from ignominious tonsures*, L. Edg. C. 20; Th. ii. 248, 16. On ðone bismerlîcostan eard *in the most unpleasant province*, Ors. 3, 11; Bos. 73, 34.

bismer-lîce; *adv. Disgracefully, indecently, irreverently, contemptuously, reproachfully;* probrose, indecore, inverecunde, contumeliose. v. bismor-lîce.

bismer-nes, -ness, e; *f.* [bismer *filthiness, pollution*, -nes] *A polluting, staining* or *defiling;* pollutio, Bd. 1, 27; S. 497, note 7.

bismer-spræc, -spæc, e; *f. A speaking blasphemy, blasphemy;* blasphemia. v. bysmor-spræc.

bismer-sprecan, -specan; *p.* -spræc, -spæc, *pl.* -sprǽcon, -spǽcon; *pp.* -sprecen, -specen [bismer *blasphemia*, sprecan, specan *loqui*] *To speak blasphemy, blaspheme;* blasphemiam loqui, blasphemare. v. bysmer-specan.

bismerung, e; *f. Blasphemy;* blasphemia, Mk. Skt. Hat. 3, 28. v. bysmrung.

bismer-word, es; *n. A disgraceful* or *abusive word, reproach, insult;* ignominiosum *vel* contumeliosum verbum, opprobrium, insultatio. v. bismær-word.

bismiriende *deriding;* insultans, Greg. Dial. 2, 1, = bismeriende. v. bysmerian.

bismor *a disgrace*, Chr. 992; Erl. 131, 31. v. bismer, bismor-lîc, -lîce.

bismor-lîc *disgraceful, ignominious*, L. Edg. C. 20; Th. ii. 248, 16. v. bismer-lîc.

bismor-lîce, bysmor-lîce, bysmer-lîce; *adv.* [bismer, bismor *disgrace*, -lîce] *Disgracefully, indecently, irreverently, contemptuously, reproachfully;* probrose, indecore, inverecunde, contumeliose:—Bysmerlîce *disgracefully*, Judth. 10; Thw. 23, 2; Jud. 100. Hí willaþ, binnan Godes hûse, bysmorlîce plegian *they will play irreverently within God's house*, L. Ælf. C. 35; Th. ii. 356, note 2, line 20. Worpaþ hine deófol on dômdæge bismorlîce *the devil shall cast him down contemptuously in the day of judgment*, Salm. Kmbl. 53; Sal. 27.

bismrian *to mock*, Ps. Spl. 103, 28. v. bysmerian.

bisnian *to give* or *set an example*, Bt. 33, 4; Fox 128, 20: 39, 11; Fox 230, 2. v. býsnian.

bisnung *an example;* exemplum, Ælfc. T. 5, 15. v. býsnung.

bi-sorgian *to care for, fear*, Exon. 61 a; Th. 223, 32; Ph. 368: 30 b; Th. 95, 12; Cri. 1556. v. be-sorgian.

bi-spanan; *p.* -spôn, -speón; *pp.* -spanen, -sponen; *v. trans. To allure, entice, incite, urge;* allicere, illicere, seducere, incitare, impellere:—Ic Herode in hyge bispeón, ðæt he Iohannes bibeád heáfde biheáwan *I Herod in mind incited, that he commanded John's head to be cut off*, Exon. 70 a; Th. 260, 8; Jul. 294. v. be-spanan.

bî-spell *a fable*, Bt. 35, 5; Fox 166, 19: Ors. 1, 6; Bos. 29, 11. v. big-spell.

bissexte *a leap year;* bisextus, Bd. 5, 23; S. 648, 19. v. bises.

bist *art, shalt be;* es, eris, Bd. 5, 19; S. 640, 43: Ælfc. Gr. 25; Som. 26, 28; *2nd pers. pres. and fut. of* beón.

bi-stelan; *p.* -stæl, *pl.* -stǽlon; *pp.* -stolen *To rob, deprive;* furari, privare:—Strengo bistolen *deprived of strength*, Exon. 107 b; Th. 410, 8; Rä. 28, 13. v. be-stelan.

bi-swâc *deceived, seduced*, Exon. 70 a; Th. 260, 25; Jul. 302; *p. of* bi-swîcan.

bi-sweðian; *p.* ede; *pp.* ed *To bind, wind round, inwrap;* ligare, involvere:—Hí biwundon oððe bisweðedon [biuundun ł bisueðdun MS.] hine *ligaverunt eum*, Jn. Lind. War. 19, 40. Sibbum bisweðede, sorgum biwerede *inwrapt in peace, from cares protected*, Exon. 32 a; Th. 100, 19; Cri. 1644. v. be-sweðian.

bî-swîc, es; *m. Deceit;* fraus, Ors. 3, 7; Bos. 60, 13. v. be-swîc.

bi-swîcan; *p.* -swâc, *pl.* -swicon; *pp.* -swicen *To deceive, seduce;* decipere, seducere:—Ic Nêron biswâc [MS. bisweac] *I deceived Nero*, Exon. 70 a; Th. 260, 25; Jul. 302. v. be-swîcan.

bî-swîcol; *adj.* [bî-swîc *deceit;* dolus] *Deceitful;* dolosus:—We sculon geþencean ðæt ðis lîf, ðæt we nû onlibbaþ, is bîswîcol eallum ðǽm ðe hit lufiaþ *we ought to think that this life, in which we now live, is deceitful to all those who love it*, L. E. I. prm; Th. ii. 400, 16.

bit *asks, prays*, Lk. Bos. 11, 12; *3rd pers. pres. of* biddan.

bita, an; *m.* [biten; *pp. of* bîtan *to bite*]. I. *a* BIT, *morsel, piece, fragment;* frustum, buccella:—Ne mihte hyra ǽlc ânne bitan of ðâm gelæccan *every one of them could not get a morsel*, Homl. Th. i. 182, 10. Æfter ðam bitan *post buccellam*, Jn. Bos. 13, 27. II. *anything that bites, a biter, an animal;* ferus:—Ǽnlîce [ænlige MS.] bita *singularis ferus*, Ps. Spl. 79, 14.

BÎTAN; *part.* bîtende; ic bîte, ðû bîtest, bîtst, he bîteþ, bîtt, bît, *pl.* bîtaþ; *p.* ic, he bât, ðû bite, *pl.* biton; *pp.* biten. I. *to* BITE *with the teeth;* mordere:—Ic bîte *mordeo*, Ælfc. Gr. 26, 6; Som. 29, 10. Monnan ic ne bîte nymþe he me bîte *I bite no man unless he bite me*, Exon. 125 a; Th. 482, 9, 10; Rä. 66, 5. Ǽghwâ bîteþ mec on bær lîc *every one bites me on the bare body*, 125 a; Th. 482, 7; Rä. 66, 4. Monige mec bîtaþ *many bite me*, 125 a; Th. 482, 12; Rä. 66, 6. Ðæt mǽden bât and totær ǽlcne ðe heó gerǽcan mihte *the maiden bit and tore every one whom she could reach*, Homl. Th. i. 458, 14: Beo. Th. 1488; B. 742. Biton [MS. byton] hine lýs *lice bit him*, Hexam. 17; Norm. 24, 30. Nim ðis ofæt, bît hit and byrge *take this fruit, bite it and taste*, Cd. 25; Th. 33, 12; Gen. 519. II. used metaphorically of the biting or wounding by a sword,—*to cut, wound;* cædere, vulnerare:—Se gist onfand ðæt se beadoleóma bîtan nolde *the guest found that the war-beam [the sword] would not wound*, Beo. Th. 3051; B. 1523: 2913; B. 1454. Sió ecg gewâc, bât unswîðor *the edge [of the sword] failed, cut less sharply*, 5150; B. 2578. Ðeáh mec heard bite stîðecg stýle *though the stiff-edge steel wounded me greatly*, Exon. 130 a; Th. 499, 10; Rä. 88, 13. [*Chauc. Wyc.* bite: *R. Glouc.* byten: *Laym.* biten: *Orm.* bitenn: *Northumb.* bîta *discerpere: Plat.* biten: *O. Sax.* bîtan: *O. Frs.* bita: *Dut.* bijten: *Ger.* beiszen: *M. H. Ger.* bîzen: *O. H. Ger.* bîzan: *Goth.* beitan: *Dan.* bide: *Swed.* bita: *Icel.* bíta: *Sansk.* bhid *findere, perforare.*] DER. a-bîtan, on-.

bîte, es; *m.* [bîtan *to bite*] *A* BITE, *pain, the biting* or *pain of a wound, a biting disease* or *cancer;* morsus, cancri morbus *vel* cancer:—Hyt ða wêdendan bîtas gehǽleþ *it heals the maddening bites*, Med. ex Quadr. 13, 7; Lchdm. i. 370, 14. Wið apan bîte *for the bite of an ape*, 11, 7; Lchdm. i. 366, 24: L. Ethb. 35; Th. i. 12, 5: Beo. Th. 4126; B. 2060. Þurh sweordes bîte *through the bite of the sword*, Apstls. Kmbl. 68; Ap. 34. Bîte îrena *the bite of swords*, Beo. Th. 4511; B. 2259. Gnættas cômon ofer ðæt land mid fýrsmeortendum bîtum *gnats came over the land with fire-smarting bites*, Ors. 1, 7; Bos. 29, 30. Wið canceràdle, ðæt is, bîte *against cancer-disease, that is, a biting disease*, L. M. 1, 44; Lchdm. ii. 108, 9. DER. lâþ-bîte.

bîtel, bîtela, bêtl; *m. A beetle;* blatta:—Ða blacan bêtlas *the black beetles*, Cot. 141.

bi-teldan *to cover, surround, overwhelm*, Exon. 59 b; Th. 217, 1; Ph. 273: 64 b; Th. 238, 25; Ph. 609. v. be-teldan.

bîtende *biting;* mordax, Cot. 134; *part. of* bîtan.

BITER, bitor, bitter, bittor; *g. m. n.* biteres, bitres, bittres; *f.* bitre; *sup.* biteresta, bitresta; *adj.* BITTER, *sharp, severe, dire;* amarus, acerbus, acer, dirus, atrox:—Ðæt bitereste [MS. biteroste] clyster *botri amarissimi*, Deut. 32, 32; *the clustre most bittir*, Wyc. Ðæt he bibûgan mǽge ðone bitran drync *that he may escape the bitter drink*, Exon. 45 a; Th. 154, 10; Gû. 840. Hí beheóldon bogan [MS. boga], þing [þingc MS.] biter *intenderunt arcum, rem amaram*, Ps. Spl. 63, 3: Ps. Th. 78, 5. Bitter, Exon. 82 a; Th. 309, 10; Seef. 55. Bittor, Exon. 47 a; Th. 161, 13; Gû. 958. Boda bitresta *the bitterest messenger*, Cd. 36; Th. 47, 19;

Gen. 763. Bittres; *g.* Salm. Kmbl. 658; Sal. 328. Biteres; *g.* Rood Kmbl. 225; Kr. 114. [*Orm.* bitterr: *O. Sax.* bittar: *Dut. Ger. M. H. Ger.* bitter: *O. H. Ger.* bittar: *Goth.* baitrs: *Dan. Swed.* bitter: *Icel.* bitr.] DER. þurh-biter, -bitter, winter-.

bitere *bitterly, sharply*, Ps. Th. 101, 18: 128, 2. v. bitre.

biterian, biterigan; *p.* ode; *pp.* od *To embitter, make sharp;* acerbare:—Ðætte us biterige sió hreówsung *that the repentance may be bitter to us*, Past. 54, 5. DER. a-biterian, ge-.

biter-líce, bitter-líce; *adv.* BITTERLY; amare:—He weóp biterlíce [Bos. bityrlíce] *he wept bitterly*, Mt. Jun. 26, 75. He ongan biterlíce [Smith, 600, 29, bitterlíce] wēpan *he began to weep bitterly*, Bd. 4, 25; Whelc. 337, 43.

biter-nys, -nyss, e; *f.* BITTERNESS; amaritudo:—Híg cōmon to ðære stōwe, ðe ys Mara genemned, ðæt ys on ūre lȳden biternys; ðā ne mihton híg drincan ðæt wæter, forðamðe hit wæs biter: ðā hēton híg ealle his naman Mara, ðæt ys on ūre lȳden biternys *venerunt in Mara, nec poterant bibere aquas de Mara, eo quod essent amaræ, unde et congruum loco nomen imposuit vocans illum Mara, id est amaritudinem*, Ex. 15, 23. Heortan biternys *bitterness of heart*, Homl. Th. ii. 220, 18. Ðæs mūþ full is biternysse *cujus os plenum est amaritudine*, Ps. Spl. second 9, 8. Nolde his onbyrian for ðære biternysse *he would not taste it for its bitterness*, Homl. Th. ii. 254, 18, 19.

biter-wyrde; *adj. Inclined to bitterness;* ad amaritudinem pronus:—Ne he biterwyrde næs *he was not inclined to bitterness*, Homl. Th. i. 320, 15: ii. 44, 22.

biþ *is, shall be;* est, erit, Bt. Met. Fox 6, 11; Met. 6, 6: Cd. 217; Th. 276, 1; Sat. 182; *3rd pers. pres. and fut. of* beón.

bi-þeahte, -þeaht *covered over*, Exon. 96 a; Th. 359, 11; Pa. 61: 101 a; Th. 382, 10; Rä. 3, 9; *p. and pp. of* bi-þeccan. v. be-þeccan.

bi-þearf ic *I need*, Exon. 76 a; Th. 285, 17; Jul. 715. v. bi-þurfan, be-.

bi-þeccan *to cover*, Exon. 28 b; Th. 87, 10; Cri. 1423: 51 b; Th. 179, 1; Gū. 1255. v. be-þeccan.

bi-þencan *to consider, bear in mind, confide*, Exon. 19 b; Th. 51, 27; Cri. 822: 20 a; Th. 53, 14; Cri. 850: 51 b; Th. 179, 32; Gū. 1270: 66 b; Th. 245, 30; Jul. 52. v. be-þencan.

bi-þringan *to surround*, Exon. 60 b; Th. 221, 27; Ph. 341. v. be-þringan.

bi-þryccan; *p.* -þrycte, *pl.* -þrycton; *pp.* -þrycced [þryccan *to press*] *To press on;* imprimere:—Hī hwæsne beág ymb mīn heáfod gebȳgdon, þreám biþrycton *they bent a sharp crown around my head, pressed it on with reproaches*, Exon. 29 a; Th. 88, 26; Cri. 1446.

bi-þurfan *to need, to have need*, Exon. 76 a; Th. 285, 17; Jul. 715. v. be-þurfan.

bītl *a mallet, hammer*, Past. 36, 5; Cott. MS. v. bȳtl.

bit-mǣlum; *adv.* [bit, mǣlum, *dat. pl. of* mǣl, *n.*] *Piecemeal, by bits;* mordicus, Ælfc. Gr. 38; Som. 42, 5.

bitol, es; *n. A bridle;* frænum:—On gewealde and bitole ceácan heora gebind *in camo et fræno maxillas eorum constringe*, Ps. Spl. 31, 12.

bi-tolden *covered, overwhelmed*, Exon. 64 b; Th. 238, 25; Ph. 609; *pp. of* bi-teldan. v. be-teldan.

bitre, bitere, bittre; *adv.* [biter *bitter*] *Bitterly, sharply, cruelly;* amare, acriter, atrociter:—Ic eom bitre abolgen *I am bitterly vexed*, Exon. 119 b; Th. 458, 31; Hy. 4, 109: 120 b; Th. 463, 4; Hö. 65: Beo. Th. 4651; B. 2331. Unc he bitere forgeald *he bitterly requited us*, Cd. 222; Th. 290, 21; Sat. 418. Hī geblēndon bittre tosomne unswētne drync ecedes and geallan *they mingled bitterly together an unsweet drink of vinegar and gall*, Exon. 29 a; Th. 88, 11; Cri. 1438: 119 a; Th. 457, 4; Hy. 4, 78.

bitst, he bitt *askest, he asks*, Ex. 33, 12: Homl. Th. i. 250, 8, 9; *2nd and 3rd pers. pres. of* biddan.

bītst, bīst, bīt *bidest, bides; 2nd and 3rd pers. pres. of* bīdan.

bitt *a bottle;* uter. v. byt.

bitter *bitter;* amarus, Exon. 82 a; Th. 309, 10; Seef. 55. v. biter.

bitter-líce *bitterly*, Bd. 4, 25; S. 600, 29. v. biter-líce.

bitter-nes *bitterness*, Scint. 61. v. biter-nys.

bittor *bitter*, Exon. 47 b; Th. 163, 23; Gū. 998. v. biter.

bittre *bitterly, sharply, cruelly*, Exon. 94 b; Th. 354, 24; Reim. 50. v. bitre.

bi-tweon; *prep. dat. Between;* inter, Exon. 32 a; Th. 101, 15; Cri. 1659. v. be-tweonum III.

bi-tweonum; *prep. dat. Between;* inter:—Hornum bitweonum [horna abitweonum MS. Th.] *between the horns*, Exon. 107 b; Th. 411, 19; Rä. 30, 2. v. abi-tweonum, be-tweonum.

bi-tȳnan *to close, shut up*, Exon. 61 b; Th. 227, 7; Ph. 419. v. be-tȳnan.

bityr-líce *bitterly;* amare:—Petrus weóp bityrlíce *Petrus flevit amare*, Mt. Bos. 26, 75. v. biter-líce.

bi-wǣgan; *p.* de; *pp.* ed; *v. a. To disappoint;* frustrari:—Ne biwǣgde hine *non frustratus est eum*, Ps. Surt. 131, 11. v. be-wǣgan.

bī-wærlan; *p.* de; *pp.* ed [v. bī- in be- II] *To pass by;* præterire, Lk. Lind. War. 10, 31: 11, 42: Lk. Rush. War. 11, 42. DER. wærlan.

bi-wāwan; *p.* -weów; *pp.* -wāwen *To blow against;* afflare:—Winde biwāwne [MS. biwaune] *waved* or *shaken by the wind*, Exon. 77 b; Th. 291, 2; Wand. 76. DER. wāwan.

bi-weaxan *to overgrow*. Exon. 60 a; Th. 219, 21; Ph. 310. v. be-weaxan.

bi-weddian *to espouse, betrothe, wed;* desponsare:—Wæs sió fǣmne wēlegum biweddad *the woman was betrothed to the rich one*, Exon. 66 a; Th. 244, 25; Jul. 33. v. be-weddian.

bi-werian, -wergan *to defend, restrain, forbid*, Exon. 87 b; Th. 329, 23; Vy. 38: Exon. 45 a; Th. 153, 3; Gū. 820. v. be-werian.

bi-windan *to entwine, enwrap, encircle*, Exon. 69 a; Th. 256, 20; Jul. 234: 28 b; Th. 87, 9, 12; Cri. 1422, 1424: 18 b; Th. 45, 27; Cri. 725: 65 b; Th. 241, 34; Ph. 666. v. be-windan.

bī-wist *food, provision*, Bt. 17; Fox 60, 4: L. Edg. C. 3; Th. ii. 244, 12. v. big-wist.

bī-word, -wyrd, es; *n.* [be, bī *by*, word *a word*] *A* BYEWORD, *proverb;* proverbium:—Man segþ [seið MS.] to bīworde, 'hæge sitteþ ða æceras dǣleþ' *man saith for a proverb, 'the hedge abides which fields divides,'* Chr. 1130; Erl. 259, 13. Bīword, bīwyrd *proverbium*, Cot. 157.

bi-worpen *cast about, surrounded;* cinctus:—Is ðæt ēglond fenne biworpen *the island is surrounded with a fen*, Exon. 100 b; Th. 380, 9; Rä. 1, 5, = be-worpen; *pp. of* be-weorpan.

bi-wrāh *covered*, Exon. 76 b; Th. 287, 32; Wand. 23; *p. of* bi-wrīhan. v. be-wrīhan.

bi-wrecan; *p.* -wræc, *pl.* -wrǣcon; *pp.* -wrecen *To strike* or *beat around, to surround;* circum pulsare, circumdare:—Hī sculon onfōn in fȳrbaðe wælmum biwrecene wrāþlīc andleán *they must receive dire retribution in the fire-bath surrounded with flames*, Exon. 20 a; Th. 52, 11; Cri. 832. v. be-wrecan.

bi-wrīhan; *p.* -wrāh, *pl.* -wrigon; *pp.* -wrigen *To cover*. v. be-wrīhan.

bi-wrītan; *p.* -wrāt, *pl.* -writon; *pp.* -writen [be *by*, wrītan *to write*] *To write after, by,* or *out of, to copy;* postscribere, exscribere, Past. pref; Hat. MS. v. be-wrītan.

bi-wyrcan *to make*, Exon. 74 a; Th. 277, 3; Jul. 575. v. be-wyrcan.

bixen; *adj.* [box *the box-tree*] *Belonging to box,* BOXEN, *made of box-wood;* buxeus:—Bixen box *a box made of box-wood;* pyxis, Ælfc. Gl. 26; Som. 60, 96; Wrt. Voc. 25, 36.

blāc; *adj.* I. *bright, shining;* lucidus, splendidus:—On bryne blācan fȳres *into the burning of the bright fire*, Cd. 186; Th. 231, 13; Dan. 246. Līgetta hērgen blāce dȳrne Dryhten *lightnings bright praise the beloved Lord*, Exon. 54 b; Th. 192, 16; Az. 107. Engel ða burh oferbrægd blācan lȳge, hātan heaðowealme *an angel spread over the town a bright flame, hot warlike floods*, Andr. Kmbl. 3081; An. 1543. Blācum leóhte *with bright light*, Bt. Met. Fox 4, 15; Met. 4, 8. Līgetu blāce *lightnings bright*, Cd. 192; Th. 240, 3; Dan. 381. II. BLEAK, *pale, pallid, livid, as in death;* pallidus, de moribundis et mortuis:—Biþ his līf scæcen, and he blāc *his life is departed, and he pale*, Exon. 87 b; Th. 329, 28; Vy. 41. Scylfing hreás blāc *Scylfing fell pale*, Beo. Th. 4969; B. 2488: Runic pm. 29; Kmbl. 345, 16. Blācne *pale, acc.* Judth. 12; Thw. 25, 26; Jud. 278. He hæfde blæc feax and blācne andwlitan *he had black hair and a pale countenance*, Bd. 2, 16; S. 519, 34. Se mōna mid his blācan leóhte *the moon with her pale light*, Bt. 4; Fox 6, 34. [*Prompt.* bleyke *pallidus, subalbus*, from blāc, *p. of* blīcan *to shine.*] ☞ Observe the difference between blāc *bright, shining, bleak, pale*, and blæc *black*, se blaca *the black*.

blāc *shone*, Exon. 52 a; Th. 182, 4; Gū. 1305; *p. of* blīcan.

blace berian *black berries;* mori, Ælfc. Gl. 47; Som. 65, 30. v. blæc-berie.

blāc-ern, es; *n.* [blāc *light*, ærn, ern *a place*] *A light place, a lamp, candlestick, lantern, light, candle;* lucerna:—Bæd ðæt hī ðæt blācern adwæscton *prayed that they would put out the light* [lucernam], Bd. 4, 8; S. 575, 40. Bærnaþ eówer blācern *light your candle*, Bd. 4, 8; S. 576, 6: Ps. Th. 131, 18.

blāc-hleór; *adj.* [blāc II. *pale*, hleór *a face, cheek*] *Having a pale face, pale-faced, fair;* pallidus *vel* candidus genis:—Sceolde monig blāchleór ides bifiende gān *many a pale-faced damsel must trembling go*, Cd. 92; Th. 118, 23–25; Gen. 1969, 1970; Judth. 11: Thw. 23, 18; Jud. 128.

blācian, blācigan, to blācienne, blācigenne; *p.* ode; *pp.* od [blāc *pallid, bleak, pale*] *To grow pale;* pallere, pallescere:—Ic blācige *palleo*, Ælfc. Gr. 26, 2; Som. 28, 42: 35; Som. 38, 5. Ic onginne to blācigenne [blācienne MS. C.] *pallesco*, 35; Som. 38, 6. Onsȳn blācaþ *his face grows pale*, Exon. 82 b; Th. 311, 13; Seef. 91. DER. a-blācian.

blācung, e; *f. Paleness, wanness;* pallor:—Blācung *pallor*, Ælfc. Gr. 9, 21; Som. 10, 27. On blācunge goldes *in pallore auri*, Ps. Lamb. 67, 14.

BLÆC, es; *n. Ink;* atramentum:—Ðæt hī habban blæc and bōcfel *that they have ink and parchment*, L. Edg. C. 3; Th. ii. 244, 11. Blæc *atramentum*, Wrt. Voc. 47, 3. [*Plat.* blak *ink: O.H.Ger.* blach *ink: Dan.* blæk, *n. ink: Swed.* bläck, *n. ink: Icel.* blek, *n. atramentum.*]

BLÆC; *gen. m. n.* blaces, *f.* blæcre; *def. m.* se blaca, *f. n.* blace: bleac; *adj.* BLACK, *swarthy;* niger, fuscus:—He hæfde blæc feax, and blácne andwlitan *he had black hair, and a pale* [*lean, thin*] *countenance;* nigro capillo, facie macilenta, Bd. 2, 16; S. 519, 33. Forđonđe đú ne mæht ǽnne loc hwítne gewirce ođđe blæcne *quia non potes unum capillum album facere aut nigrum,* Mt. Kmbl. Rush. 5, 36. Ofslógon đone blacan Heawald *they killed the black Heawald,* Bd. 5, 10; S. 624, 40. Đa sind blace swíđe *they are very black,* Exon. 114 b; Th. 438, 28; Rä. 58, 2. Swearte wǽron lástas, swađu swíđe blacu *swart were their footsteps, their tracks very black,* 113 b; Th. 434, 19; Rä. 52, 3. [*Icel.* blakkr *niger,* Egils. v. *A.Sax.* blæc *ink.*] ☞ Observe the difference between blæc; *gen. m. n.* blaces, se blaca *black, swarthy,* and blác *shining, pallid, bleak, pale,* from blác; *p. of* blícan *to shine;* remark also blǽc *pale, livid,* from blǽcan *to bleach, whiten.* v. blícan, blǽcan.

blǽc; *adj. Shining, pale, livid;* lucidus, pallidus, lividus:—Ís brycgade blǽce brimráde *the ice bridged the pale water road,* Grn. An. 1264. v. blǽcan *to bleach.*

blǽcan, blǽcean; *p.* de; *pp.* ed *To* BLEACH, *whiten, fade;* pallidum colorem inducere, albicare:—Blǽced *bleached,* Exon. 107 b; Th. 410, 27; Rä. 29, 5. Ne mæg ne sunne blǽcan *no sun can bleach,* Bd. 1, 1; S. 473, 20: blǽcean, note 20. DER. blícan.

blæc-berie, an; *f. A* BLACKBERRY, *mulberry;* vaccinium, morus:—Blace berian *mori,* Ælfc. Gl. 47; Som. 65, 30; Wrt. Voc. 33, 29. DER. blæc.

blæc-ern, es; *n. An inkstand;* atramentarium. DER. blæc *ink,* ærn *a place.*

blǽc-ern, es; *n.* [blǽc *light,* ærn *a place*] *Literally a lamp* or *candlestick,* also *the light itself; verbum de verbo,* candelabrum, *etiam* candela, lucerna:—Bæd đæt hí đæt blǽcern acwencton *prayed that they would put out the light* [lucernam], Bd. 4, 8; S. 575, 40, note, MS. B. Ne menn blǽcern in beornaþ *men do not light a candle* [lucernam], Mt. Kmbl. Rush. 5, 15. Blǽcern fótum mínum *lucerna pedibus meis,* Ps. Th. 118, 105. v. blác-ern.

blæc-fexed; *adj.* [blæc *black,* feax, fex *hair*] *Having black hair, black-haired;* nigris capillis:—He is blæcfexed [MS. blæcfexede] *he is black-haired,* Homl. Th. i. 456, 16.

blæc-gym; *g.* -gymmes; *m. A black fossil, called jet;* nigro-gemmeus, lapis gagates = γαγάτης, Bd. 1, 1; S. 473, 24.

blǽco, es; *n.* [blǽc *pale, livid;* blǽcan *to bleach*] *Paleness, leprosy;* pallor, lepra = λέπρα:—Blǽco *pallor,* Cot. 157. Lǽcedómas wiđ đam yflan blǽce *leechdoms against the evil leprosy,* L. M. cont. 1, 32; Lchdm. ii. 8, 1. Wiđ blǽce genim góse smero *for leprosy take goose-grease,* L. M. 1, 32; Lchdm. ii. 76, 9, 1, 4, 7, 18. v. blǽcþa.

blæc-teru; *g.* wes; *n. Black-tar, tar, naphtha, a sort of bituminous fluid;* pix fluida, naphtha, Som.

blǽcþa, an; *m:* blǽcþ-rust, es; *m. Leprosy;* vitiligo, Cot. 221. v. blǽco.

BLÆD; *gen.* blædes; *nom. pl.* blado, *n. A leaf,* BLADE; folium, palmula:—Bråd blado *broad leaves,* Cd. 48; Th. 61, 8; Gen. 994. Róđres blæd *the blade of an oar;* palmula, Ælfc. Gl. 83; Som. 73, 77; Wrt. Voc. 48, 16. [*O. Sax.* blad, *n: Frs. O. Frs.* bled, *n: Dut.* blad, *n: Ger.* blatt, *n: M. H. Ger.* blat, *n: O. H. Ger.* blat, *n: Dan. Swed.* blad, *n: Icel.* blađ, *n. folium.*] DER. ár-blæd.

blæd, e; *f. A cup, bowl, goblet, vial;* patera, phiala, Æthelfledæ Test. Lye. v. bledu.

blǽd, es; *m.* I. *a blast, blowing, breath, spirit, life, mind;* flamen, flatus, inspiratio? spiritus, vita, animus:—Gif máre blǽd windes astág [MS. astahg] *if a stronger blast of wind arose;* si flatus venti major adsurgeret, Bd. 4, 3; S. 569, 8. Þurh gǽstes blǽd *through the spirit's inspiration,* Exon. 63 b; Th. 234, 33; Ph. 549. God ableów on his ansýne liflícne blǽd *God blew into his face the breath of life,* Hexam. 11; Norm. 18, 26. His blǽd forleósan *to lose his life,* Judth. 10; Thw. 22, 16; Jud. 63. Náh seó módor geweald bearnes blǽdes *the mother hath not power over her child's life,* Salm. Kmbl. 769; Sal. 384. Beorht on blǽde *bright in life,* Elen. Kmbl. 975; El. 489. II. *enjoyment, prosperity, abundance, success, blessedness, gift, reward, benefit, glory, honour;* fruitio, prosperitas, abundantia, successus, beatitudo, donum, præmium, beneficium, gloria, dignitas:—Hyra blǽd leofaþ æt dómdæge *their enjoyment shall exist* [*live*] *at doomsday,* Exon. 31 b; Th. 100, 4; Cri. 1636. Blǽdes full *full of enjoyment,* Exon. 32 a; Th. 101, 13; Cri. 1658. Eorþan blǽdas *the enjoyments of earth,* 116 b; Th. 447, 28; Dóm. 46. He heóld blǽd mid bearnum *he possessed prosperity with his children,* Cd. 79; Th. 97, 5; Gen. 1608. Hie ne meahton blǽdes brúcan *they might not enjoy prosperity,* 90; Th. 113, 26; Gen. 1893. On his blǽde *in his prosperity,* 205; Th. 253, 26; Dan. 601. Sý him wuldres blǽd *may there be to him abundance of glory,* Exon. 65 b; Th. 241, 27; Ph. 662. Đa feóndas đæs blǽdes gebrocen hæfdon *the fiends had enjoyed their success,* Exon. 38 b; Th. 127, 28; Gú. 393. Écan lífes blǽd *the blessedness of eternal life,* Exon. 82 b; Th. 310, 24; Seef. 79. Wæs his blǽd mid God *his reward was with God,* 39 a; Th. 128, 27; Gú. 410: 20 b; Th. 55, 4; Cri. 878. Wæs heora blǽd micel *their glory was great,* Cd. 1; Th. 2, 5; Gen. 14. Hie Iudéa blǽd forbrǽcon billa ecgum *they destroyed the Jews' glory with the edges of swords,* Cd. 210; Th. 260, 13; Dan. 709. [*O. H. Ger.* blát *flatus.*] DER. fër-blǽd, wuldor-: blǽd-ágende, -dæg, -fæst, -gifa, -horn, -wéla.

blǽd, bléd, e; *f.* What is produced,—*A flower, blossom, fruit;* flos, olus, fructus:—His leáf and his blǽda ne fealwiaþ *its leaves and its flowers shall not fall;* folium ejus non decidet, Ps. Th. 1, 4. Wudu sceal blǽdum blówan *a wood shall blow with flowers,* Menol. Fox 527; Gn. C. 34. Geseh he geblówene bearwas standan, blǽdum gehrodene *he saw blowing groves stand, adorned with blossoms,* Andr. Kmbl. 2896; An. 1451. Bléda wyrta *olera herbarum,* Ps. Spl. 36, 2. He dêþ ǽlc twíg aweg on me, đe blǽda ne byrþ; and he feormaþ ǽlc đara, đe blǽda byrþ, đæt hyt bere blǽda đe swíđor *omnem palmitem in me non ferentem fructum, tollet eum; et omnem, qui fert fructum, purgabit eum, ut fructum plus afferat,* Jn. Bos. 15, 2. Beorc biþ blǽda leás *the birch-tree is fruitless* [*void of fruit*], Runic pm. 18; Kmbl. 342, 27; Hick. Thes. i. 135. Hærfest bryngþ rípa bléda *harvest brings ripe fruits,* Bt. 39, 13; Fox 234, 15: 34, 10; Fox 150, 5. Balsames blǽd *fruit of balsam,* Cot. 48.

blǽd-ágende; *part. Possessing abundance, prosperous;* abundantiam habens, prosper, Beo. Th. 2031; B. 1013.

blǽd-dæg; *g.* -dæges; *pl. nom.* -dagas; *g. pl.* -daga; *m. A prosperous* or *happy day;* prosperitatis dies, faustus dies:—Đǽr we mótun brúcan blǽddaga *where we may enjoy prosperous days,* Exon. 65 b; Th. 242, 16; Ph. 674: Cd. 60; Th. 73, 7; Gen. 1201.

blǽddre *a blister, pimple, the bladder,* Ex. 9, 9, 10: Ælfc. Gl. 75; Som. 71, 74; Wrt. Voc. 44, 56. v. blǽdre.

blǽd-fæst; *adj. Prosperous;* prosper:—Heó abreát blǽdfæstne beorn *she destroyed a prosperous hero,* Beo. Th. 2602; B. 1299. DER. ge-blǽdfæst.

blǽd-gifa, an; *m. A giver of prosperity, happiness,* or *glory;* prosperitatis, beatitudinis, *vel* gloriæ largitor:—Beorht blǽdgifa *bright giver of prosperity,* Andr. Kmbl. 167; An. 84: 1311; An. 656.

blǽd-horn, es; *m. A blast-horn, a trumpet;* classicum:—Blǽdhornas *classica,* Ælfc. Gl. 52; Som. 66, 44; Wrt. Voc. 35, 32.

blǽdre, blǽddre, an; *f.* [bláwan *to blow;* flare] That which is blown out, hence I. *an inflated swelling, blister, pimple, blain, pustule;* pustula, papula:—Be ǽghwylcum uncúþum blǽdrum đe on mannes nebbe sittaþ *of all strange blisters which exist on a man's face,* Herb. cont. 2, 19; Lchdm. i. 6, 10: Herb. 2, 19; Lchdm. i. 86, 5. Eall folc wæs on blǽdran, and đa wǽron swíđe hreówlíce berstende *all the people had blisters* [lit. *was in blister*], *and they were very painfully bursting,* Ors. 1, 7; Bos. 29, 37. On mannum and on nýtenum beóþ wunda and swellende blǽddran *there shulen ben in men and yn beestis biles and bleynes swellynge,* Wyc; Ex. 9, 9, 10. II. *the* BLADDER, *receptacle for the urine;* vesica:—Báres blǽdre *a boar's bladder,* Med. ex Quadr. 8, 12; Lchdm. i. 360, 8. Wiđ sáre đære lifre and đære blǽdran *for sore of the liver and of the bladder,* Herb. cont. 145, 2; Lchdm. i. 54, 27: Herb. 41, 2; Lchdm. i. 142, 8: 80, 1; Lchdm. i. 182, 12. Gif weaxan stánas on đære blǽdran *if stones grow in the bladder,* L. M. 3, 20; Lchdm. ii. 320, 6. Genim eoferes blǽdran *take a boar's bladder,* Med. ex Quadr. 8, 11; Lchdm. i. 360, 5. Blǽddre *vesica,* Ælfc. Gl. 75; Som. 71, 74; Wrt. Voc. 44, 56. Wiđ đære blǽddran sáre *for sore of the bladder,* Herb. 107; Lchdm. i. 220, 15: 126; Lchdm. i. 238, 10: Med. ex Quadr. 8, 11; Lchdm. i. 360, 4. [*Chauc. Wyc.* bladder: *Piers P.* bleddere: *Dut.* blaar, *f: O. Dut.* blaeder, blaere: *Ger.* blatter, *f: M.H. Ger.* bláter, *f: O.H. Ger.* blátara, *f: Dan.* blære, *m. f: Swed.* blåddra, *f: Icel.* blađra, *f.*]

blǽd-wéla, an; *m. Fruitful riches;* opes uberes:—Ic đé on đa fægran foldan gesette to neótenne neorxna wonges blǽdwélan *I set thee on the fair earth to enjoy the fruitful riches of Paradise,* Exon. 28 a; Th. 85, 16; Cri. 1392.

blǽge, an; *f. A* BLAY, *bleak, the gudgeon;* gobio = κωβιός:—Blǽge *gobio,* Ælfc. Gl. 101; Som. 77, 59; Wrt. Voc. 55, 64. [*Ger.* bleie, bleihe, *f. a blay.*]

blǽ-hǽwen, blǽ-hwen, blǽwen; *adj.* [bleó *blue,* hǽwen *hued*] *Of a blue hue, bluish, violet* or *purple colour;* cæruleus, perseus:—Moises scrídde đone bisceop [Aaron] mid línenum reáfe, and girde hine, and dyde ymbe hine blǽhwene tunecan, and léde eaxlcláþ ofer hine *Moses clothed the bishop* [*Aaron*] *with a linen garment, and girded him* [*with a girdle*], *and put around him a blue tunic, and laid a cope* [lit. *shoulder-cloth*] *upon him,* Lev. 8, 7. Blǽwen *perseus,* Ælfc. Gl. 80; Som. 72, 94; Wrt. Voc. 46, 51.

blæse, blase, an; *f.* I. *a* BLAZE, *flame;* ardor, flamma. v. bǽl-blæse. II. that which makes a blaze,—*A torch, lamp;* fax, facula, lampas = λαμπάς:—Blæse *fax,* Greg. Dial. 2, 8: Glos. Prudent. Recd. 143, 33. Iudas com đyder mid leóhtfatum, and mid blasum, and mid wǽpnum *Iudas venit illuc cum laternis, et facibus, et armis,* Jn. Bos. 18, 3. Blæsum *faculis,* Mone B. 3487. Blase *lampas,* Ælfc. Gl. 30; Som. 61, 54; Wrt. Voc. 26, 53. [*M. H. Ger.* blas, *n. fax, lampas.*]

blæsere, blasere, blysiere, es; *m.* [blæse I. *a blaze, flame*] *A burner, incendiary;* incendiarius:—Be blæserum *of incendiaries*, L. Ath. i. 6; Th. i. 202, 18. We cwǽdon be ðám blaserum *we have ordained concerning incendiaries*, L. Ath. iv. 6; Th. i. 224, 13.

blæst, es; *m.* [blæse I. *a blaze, flame*] *A burning, blaze, flame;* ardor, flamma:—Ne mæg ðǽr, rēn ne snāw, ne fȳres blæst, wihte gewyrdan *there rain nor snow, nor flame of fire can aught injure*, Exon. 56 a; Th. 198, 25; Ph. 15: Andr. Kmbl. 1674; An. 839. Ðæt he [Fēnix] onfōn mōte, þurh līges blæst, līf æfter deáþe *that it* [*the Phœnix*] *may, through the fire's flame, receive life after death*, Exon. 62 a; Th. 228, 6; Ph. 434. Lēges blæstas weallas ymbwurpon *flames of fire overwhelmed the walls*, Andr. Kmbl. 3103; An. 1554.

blǽst, es; *m.* [blāwan *to blow;* flare] *A blowing*, BLAST or *gust of wind, a breeze;* flatus:—Sǽgrundas sūþwind fornam, bæþweges blǽst *the south wind, the sea breeze, dried up the depths of the sea*, Cd. 158; Th. 196, 11; Exod. 290. [*Chauc.* blast: *Laym.* blæst: *Ger. M. H. Ger.* blast, *m*: *O. H. Ger.* blāst, *m*: *Icel.* blástr, *m.*]

blǽst-belg *bellows*, Wrt. Voc. 286, 76. v. blǣst-belg.

blǽt, ðū blǽtst *is livid, thou art livid; 3rd and 2nd pers. pres. of* blātan.

blǽt, es; *m. A bleating, a* BLEAT *like a sheep;* balatus. DER. blǽtan.

BLǼTAN; *p.* blǽtte; *pp.* blǽtted; *v.n.* [blǽt *a bleat*] *To* BLEAT; balare:—Ic blǽte swā gāt *I bleat as a goat*, Exon. 106 b; Th. 406, 17; Rä. 25, 2. Scǽp blǽt *ovis balat*, Ælfc. Gr. 22; Som. 24, 9. Hit biþ swīðe dyslīc ðæt se man beorce oððe blǽte *it is very foolish that the man bark or bleat*, 22; Som. 24, 12. [*Piers P.* blete: *Orm.* blætenn: *Dut.* bleeten, bláten: *M. Dut.* bleten: *Ger.* blaszen: *O. H. Ger.* blazan *to cry as a sheep* or *goat, to bleat.*]

blǽtesung, e; *f. A flaming, blazing, sparkling;* flagrantia, Ps. Spl. T. 76, 18.

blǽwen *light blue;* perseus, Ælfc. Gl. 80; Som. 72, 94; Wrt. Voc. 46, 51. v. blǽ-hǽwen.

blǽweþ, blǽwþ *blows*, Bt. Met. Fox 6, 15; Met. 6, 8: ðū blǽwest, blǽwst *thou blowest; 3rd and 2nd pers. pres. of* blāwan.

blan *ceased*, Bd. 1, 8; S. 479, 17; *p. of* blinnan.

BLANC; *adj.* BLANK, *white, grey;* pallidus, albus, candidus:—Gewiton mearum rīdan beornas on blancum *the warriors departed to ride on white horses*, Beo. Th. 1716; B. 856. [*Relq. Ant. W.* i, 37, 30, blonc *white*: *Dut.* blank *white, shining*: *Ger.* blank *albus*: *M. H. Ger.* blanc: *O. H. Ger.* blanch *candidus*: *Dan. Swed.* blank *bright*: *O. Nrs.* blankr *albus*, Rask Hald: hence *Span.* blanco *white*: *Fr.* blanc: *It.* bianco.]

blanca, blonca, an; *m. A white* or *grey horse;* equus albus *vel* candidus:—On blancan *on a grey horse*, Elen. Grm. 1185. [*Laym.* blank, blonk *a horse, steed*: *O. Nrs.* blakkr, *m. equus.*] DER. blanc.

bland, es; *n. A mixture, confusion;* mixtio:—Swēg swīðrode and sanges [MS. sances] bland *sound prevailed and a confusion of song*, Cd. 158; Th. 197, 19; Exod. 309. [*Icel.* bland, *n.*] DER. ge-bland, -blond, wind-.

BLANDAN, blondan, ic blande, blonde, ðū blandest, he blandeþ, blent, *pl.* blandaþ; *p.* ic, he bleónd, blēnd, ðū bleónde, blēnde, *pl.* bleóndon, blēndon; *pp.* blanden, blonden *To mix*, BLEND, *mingle;* miscere:—Ic eom on gōman gena swētra ðonne ðū beóbreád blēnde mid hunige *I am yet sweeter on the palate than if thou blendedst bee-bread with honey*, Exon. 111 a; Th. 425, 21; Rä. 41, 59. [A strong verb in all the Teutonic dialects: *Goth.* blandan; *p.* baibland; *pp.* blandans: *O. Sax.* blandan: *O. H. Ger.* blandan: *Swed. O. Nrs.* blanda.] DER. ge-blandan: ge-blondan, on-: be-blonden: ge-bland: ge-blond, ær-, ār-, ear-, earh-, sund-, ȳþ-: wind-blond.

blanden-feax, blonden-feax, -fex; *adj.* [blanden; *pp. of* blandan *to mix;* feax, fex *hair*] *Having mixed* or *grizzly hair, grey-haired, old;* comam mixtam *vel* canam habens, senex. Blanden-feax is a phrase which in Anglo-Saxon poetry is only applied to those advanced in life; and is used to denote that *mixture* of colour which the hair assumes on approaching or increasing senility, Price's Warton i. xcvi. note 20:—Gelpan ne þorfte beorn blandenfeax [MS. blandenfex, col. 2] bilgeslehtes *the grizzly-haired warrior ought not to boast of the clashing of swords*, Chr. 937; Th. 204, 34, col. 1; Ædelst. 45. Abraham ne wēnde, ðæt him Sarra, brȳd blondenfeax, bringan meahte on woruld sunu *Abram thought not that Sarah, his grey-haired wife, could bring a n into the world*, Cd. 107; Th. 141, 7; Gen. 2341: 123; Th. 157, 5; Gen. 2600: Beo. Th. 3586; B. 1791. Blondenfexa *the grizzly-haired*, 5916; B. 2962. Hruron teáras blondenfeaxum *tears fell from the grizzly-haired* [*prince*], 3750; B. 1873. Blondenfeaxe, gomele, ymb gōdne ongeador sprǽcon *the grizzly-haired, the old, spoke together about the good* [*warrior*], 3193; B. 1594.

blann *ceased, rested*, Bd. 3, 20; S. 550, 28; *p. of* blinnan.

blase *a torch, lamp*, Ælfc. Gl. 30; Som. 61, 54; Wrt. Voc. 26, 53. v. blæse II.

blasere, es; *m. An incendiary*, L. Ath. iv. 6; Th. i. 224, 13. v. blæsere.

blāst-belg, es; *m. A blast-bag, bellows;* follis, Cot. 86.

BLĀT; *comp.* blātra; *superl.* blātast; *adj. Livid, pale, ghastly;* lividus, pallidus:—Þurh ðæs beornes breóst blāt weóll waðuman streám *a livid stream bubbled in waves through the man's breast*, Andr. Kmbl. 2560; An. 1281. Hungres on wēnum, blātes beódgæstes *in expectation of hunger, of a pale table-guest*, 2177; An. 1090. Ðæt biþ frēcne wund, blātast benna *that is a dangerous wound, most ghastly of sores*, Exon. 19 a; Th. 48, 13; Cri. 771. [*O. H. Ger.* bleizza *livor.*]

blātan; *part.* blātende; ic blāte, ðū blātest, blǽtst, he blāteþ, blǽt, *pl.* blātaþ; *p.* bleót, blēt, ðū blēte, *pl.* blēton; *pp.* blāten; *intrans. To be livid, pale,* or *dark as with envy;* livere:—Hygewælmas teáh beorne on breóstum blātende nīþ *darkening* [*livid, pale*] *envy drew agitations of mind to the breast of the man*, Cd. 47; Gen. 981.

blāte; *adv. Lividly, pallidly;* livide, pallide:—Helle fȳr blāte forbærnþ biteran lēge *the fire of hell lividly burns up with a dire* [*bitter*] *flame*, Bt. Met. Fox 8, 107; Met. 8, 54. Ðæt fȳr ne mæg foldan and merestreám blāte forbærnan *the fire cannot pallidly burn up earth and sea*, 20, 229; Met. 20, 115.

blātende; *part. Darkening, making livid* or *pallid;* livens, Cd. 47; Th. 60, 14; Gen. 981. v. blātan.

BLĀWAN; *part.* blāwende; ic blāwe, ðū blāwest, blāwst, blǽwest, blǽwst, he blāweþ, blāwþ, blǽweþ, blǽwþ, *pl.* blāwaþ; *p.* bleów, blēw, *pl.* bleówon; *pp.* blāwen *To* BLOW, *breathe;* flare, sufflare. I. *v. intrans*:—Ge geseóþ sūþan blāwan *ye see the south* [*wind*] *blow*, Lk. Bos. 12, 55. Ic blāwe *flo*, Ælfc. Gr. 24; Som. 25, 41. Wind wrāðe blāweþ *the wind fiercely blows*, Bt. Met. Fox 7, 104; Met. 7, 52: Ps. Th. 147, 7. Blǽwþ gāst his and flōwaþ wæteru *flabit spiritus ejus et fluent aquæ*, Ps. Lamb. 147, 18: Bt. Met. Fox 6, 15; Met. 6, 8. Swōgaþ windas, blāwaþ brecende, bearhtma mǽste *winds shall howl, crashing blow, with the greatest of sounds*, Exon. 21 b; Th. 59, 11; Cri. 951. Se wind sūþan bleów *the wind blew from the south*, Bd. 2, 7; S. 509, 27. Bleów he on hī *he breathed on them*, Jn. Bos. 20, 22. Bleówon [MS. bleowun] windas *flaverunt venti*, Mt. Bos. 7, 25, 27. Blāwen is on smiððan *conflatur in conflatorio*, Prov. 27. II. *v. trans*:—Drihten hāteþ hēh-englas bēman blāwan *the Lord shall command the archangels to blow the trumpets*, Cd. 227; Th. 302, 19; Sat. 602. Englas blāwaþ bȳman *angels shall blow the trumpets*, Exon. 20 b; Th. 55, 10; Cri. 881. Ne blāwe man bȳman beforan ðē *let not a man blow a trumpet before thee*, Mt. Bos. 6, 2. [*Laym.* blæwen, blauwen, blawen, blowen: *Ger.* blähen: *M. H. Ger.* blæjen: *O. H. Ger.* blājan: *Lat.* flo.] DER. a-blāwan, for-, ge-, to-: blāwennys: blāwere: blāwung.

blāwen-nys, -nyss, e; *f. A blowing* or *puffing up, a windy swelling;* inflatio, sufflatio. DER. blāwan.

blāwere, es; *m.* [blāwan *to blow;* flare] *A* BLOWER; conflator:—Ídel wæs se blāwere *the blower was useless;* frustra conflavit conflator, Past. 37, 3; Hat. MS. 50 a, 24.

blāwung, e; *f.* [blāwan *to blow;* flare] *A* BLOWING; flatus:—Ðā hēt Gedeon his geferan habban heora bȳman him mid to ðære blāwunge *then Gideon commanded his companions to have their trumpets with them for the blowing*, Jud. 7, 16. DER. a-blāwung.

bleac; *def.* se bleaca; *adj. Black;* niger:—Wæs ðis gesceád ðæt for missenlīce heora feaxes hiwe, ōðer wæs cweden se bleaca Heawold, ōðer se hwīta Heawald *ea distinctione ut pro diversa capillorum specie, unus niger Hewald, alter albus Hewald diceretur*, Bd. 5, 10; S. 624, 16. v. blæc, blaca *black*.

BLEÁT; *def.* se bleáta, seó, ðæt bleáte; *adj. Wretched, miserable;* miser, miserabilis:—Ǽnig ne wæs mon on moldan ðætte meahte bibūgan ðone bleátan drync deópan deáþwēges *there was not any man on earth that could avoid the miserable drink of the deep death-cup*, Exon. 47 a; Th. 161, 24; Gū. 963. [*Scot.* blait *nudus*: *Frs.* bleat *nudus*: *O. Frs.* blat *nudus;* thi blata *pauper, miser*: *Dut.* bloot: *M. Dut.* blōt: *Ger.* blosz: *M. H. Ger.* blōz: *Icel.* blautr.]

bleáte; *adv. Wretchedly, miserably;* misere, miserabile:—He geseah ðone leófestan līfes æt ende bleáte gebǽran *he saw his dearest* [*friend*] *bearing* [*himself*] *wretchedly at life's end*, Beo. Th. 5640, note; B. 2824.

BLEÁÞ; *adj. Gentle, timid, peaceful, inactive;* timidus, imbellis, ignavus:—Ic eom to ðon bleáþ ðæt mec mæg grīma abrēgan *I am so timid that a phantom may frighten me*, Exon. 110 b; Th. 423, 4; Rä. 41, 16. Ne wæs him bleáþ hyge *his mind was not inactive*, Andr. Kmbl. 462; An. 231. [*Laym.* blæð *destitute*: *O. Sax.* blōði: *Dut.* bloode: *Ger.* blöde: *M. H. Ger.* blœde: *O. H. Ger.* blōdi: *Dan.* blöd: *Swed.* blöt: *Icel.* blauðr.] DER. here-bleáþ.

Blecinga ég, e; *f. Blekingey, the sea-coast of the Blekingians, a province on the south-west of Sweden; in A. Sax. times belonging to Denmark*, Ors. 1, 1; Bos. 22, 1.

bled, e; *f. A bowl, the dish of a balance, a scale.* v. helur-bled, bledu.

blēd, e; *f. A shoot, branch, flower, fruit;* germen, ramus, frons, flos, fructus:—Ðæt cymen [MS. cyme] grēne blēda *that green shoots come*, Cd. 200; Th. 248, 24; Dan. 518. On ðæs beámes blēdum *on the branches of the tree*, Cd. 200; Th. 248, 5; Dan. 508. Ne dreósaþ beorhte blēde *bright fruits fall not*, Exon. 56 a; Th. 200, 3; Ph. 35: 62 b; Th. 230, 2; Ph. 466. God lǽteþ hrusan syllan beorhte blēda beornum and þearfum *God lets earth give delightful fruits to rich and poor*, Hick. Thes. i. 135, 24. DER. wudu-blēd. v. blǽd.

blēdan; *p.* de; *pp.* ed [blōd *blood*] *To* BLEED, *emit blood;* sanguinem emittere:—Blēdaþ ǽdran *the veins shall bleed*, Salm. Kmbl. 290; Sal. 144. Se blēdenda fīc *the bleeding fig* or *disease*, Wanl. catal. 305, 4. Wiđ đone blēdende fīc nim murran *for the bleeding fig* or *disease take myrrh*, Lchdm. iii. 8, 1. [*Dut.* bloeden: *Ger.* bluten: *O.H.Ger.* bluotan: *Dan.* blöde: *Swed.* blöda.]

blēd-hwæt; *g.* -hwates; *adj.* [blēd *a shoot*, hwæt *quick*] *A shoot growing quickly;* germen velox:—Đonne ic hrēre bearwas blēd-hwate *then I shake the quick-growing groves*, Exon. 101 a; Th. 381, 10; Rä. 2, 9.

bledsian; *p.* ode; *pp.* od *To bless, consecrate;* benedicere, consecrare. DER. ge-bledsian. v. bletsian.

bledsung *a blessing*, Chr. 813; Erl. 60, 21. v. bletsung.

bledu, bled, blæd, e; *f. A bowl, vial, goblet, the dish of a balance, a scale;* patera, phiala, lanx, trutinæ, scala, Ælfc. Gl. 25; Wrt. Voc. 24, 44: Æthelfledæ Test. Lye. DER. helur-bled.

BLĒGEN, e; *f. A* BLAIN, *blister, bile* or *ulcer;* pustula, ulcus:—Wiđ đa blēgene, genim nigon ægra and seóþ hīg fæste *for blains, take nine eggs and boil them hard*, Lchdm. i. 380, 1. Wiđ đa blacan blēgene *against black blains*, L. M. 1, 58; Lchdm. ii. 128, 21. [*Tyndl.* blain: *Chauc.* blein: *Wyc.* bleines, *pl*: *Dut.* blein, *f*: *Dan.* blegn.]

blencan; *p.* blencte; *pp.* blenced *To deceive, cheat;* decipere, fallere:—He wrenceþ and blenceþ *he deceives and cheats*, Exon. 83 b; Th. 315, 18; Mōd. 33. [*Prov. Eng.* blench: *Icel.* blekkja *to impose upon.*]

blēnd *mixed, blended, mingled; p. of* blandan.

blendan, he blent; *p.* blende; *pp.* blended, blend; *v. trans.* [blind *cæcus*] *To* BLIND, *deprive of sight, darken;* cæcare, obscurare:—Se dæg blent and þióstraþ hiora eágan *the day blinds and darkens their eyes*, Bt. 38, 5; Fox 206, 5. Man hine blende, and hine swā blindne brohte to đām munecum *they blinded him, and brought him thus blind to the monks*, Chr. 1036; Th. 294, 17, col. 2; Ælf. Tod. 14. [*Chauc. Piers* blende: *Laym.* a-blenden: *Orm.* blendenn: *O. Frs.* blenda, blinda: *Dut.* blinden: *Ger. M.H.Ger.* blenden: *O.H.Ger.* blentjan: *Goth.* ga-blindyan: *Dan.* for-blinde: *Swed.* för-blinda: *Icel.* blinda.] DER. a-blendan, ge-.

blent *blends; 3rd pers. pres. of* blandan.

bleó *a colour, hue, complexion*, Ælfc. Gl. 79; Som. 72, 78; Wrt. Voc. 46, 35. v. bleoh.

bleó *blue* or *azure colour;* cæruleus, Som.

bleó-bord, es; *n.* [bleoh, bleó *colour*, bord *a table*] *A coloured table on which games of chess are played;* tabula colorata in qua prœlia latronum luduntur (Ettm. p. 311):—Dryhten dǽleþ sumum gūþe blǽd, sumum tæfle cræft, bleóbordes gebregd *the Lord allots to one success in war, to another skill at the table, cunning at the coloured board*, Exon. 88 a; Th. 331, 20; Vy. 71.

bleó-brygd, es; *m? n?* [bleó *colour*, bregdan *to change*] *A variegated colour;* color variegatus:—Is se fugel fæger, bleóbrygdum fāg *the bird is fair, shining with variegated colours*, Exon. 60 a; Th. 218, 9; Ph. 292.

bleó-cræft, es; *m.* BLEE-CRAFT, *the art of embroidering;* ars plumaria, ars acupingendi:—Bleócræft *ars plumaria*, Cot. 17.

bleó-fæstnes, -ness, -nyss, e; *f.* That which gives pleasure from its colour,—*Pleasure, delight;* jucunditas, deliciæ:—Niht is onleóhtnes ođđe onlīhting on bleófæstnessum [bleófæstnyssum, Spl.] ođđe ēstum mīnum *nox illuminatio est in deliciis meis*, Ps. Lamb. 138, 11.

bleó-fāg, -fāh; *adj.* [bleoh, bleó *color;* fāg, fāh *varius*] *Of various colours, party-coloured;* versicolor:—Byrne is mīn bleófāg *my byrnie is party-coloured*, Exon. 105 b; Th. 400, 18; Rä. 21, 3: Cot. 115. Oferslop bleófāh habban ǽrende fūllīc getācnaþ *to have a party-coloured overcoat betokens an unpleasant message*, Lchdm. iii. 200, 6.

BLEOH, bleó, blioh, blió; *gen.* bleós; *n. A colour, hue, complexion;* color, species:—Bleoh *color*, Ælfc. Gl. 79; Som. 72, 70; Wrt. Voc. 46, 27. Mislīc bleó *a mixed colour*, 79; Som. 72, 78; Wrt. Voc. 46, 35. Blió *color*, Prov. 23. Đæt wæs hwītes bleós swā cristalla *it was of a white colour like crystal*, Num. 11, 7. Ānes bleós *of one colour;* unicolor, concolor, Ælfc. Gl. 79; Som. 72, 76; Wrt. Voc. 46, 33: Ælfc. Gr. 9, 21; Som. 10, 35. Hwī is se rēnboga mislīces bleós *why is the rainbow of a mixed colour?* Boutr. Scrd. 21, 25. Menn māgon cēpan be đæs mōnan bleó hwylc weder toweard byþ *men may observe by the moon's colour what weather is at hand*, Bd. de nat. rerum; Wrt. popl. science 15, 9; Lchdm. iii. 268, 5. Hī brugdon on wyrmes bleó *they changed to a worm's hue*, Exon. 46 a; Th. 156, 32; Gū. 883: 71 a; Th. 264, 12; Jul. 363: Elen. Kmbl. 2210; El. 1106. Seolocenra hrægla mid mistlīcum bleowum hī ne gīmdon *they cared not for silken garments of various colours*, Bt. 15; Fox 48, 11. Mōnan bleoh habban hȳnþe getācnaþ *for the moon to have colours betokens humility*, Lchdm. iii. 206, 27. Hī habbaþ blioh and færbu ungelīce *they have different colours and forms*, Bt. Met. Fox 31, 7; Met. 31, 4. Bleóum *with colours*, Exon. 94 a; Th. 352, 31; Reim. 4: Salm. Kmbl. 301; Sal. 150. Secgaþ guman đæt Iosephes tunece wǽre bleóm bregdende *men say that Joseph's coat varied* [lit. *was varying*] *in colours*, Exon. 95 b; Th. 357, 3; Pa. 23: 87 a; Th. 327, 14; Vy. 3. Geseah ic đæt beácen wendan bleóm *I saw the beacon change in colours*, Rood Kmbl. 43; Kr. 22: Elen. Kmbl. 1515; El. 759. [*Prov. Eng.* blee: *Chauc.* blee: *O. Sax.* blī, *n*: *North Frs.* bläy: *O. Frs.* blie, bli, *n.*] DER. ge-bleoh, wundorbleó.

bleóm *in colours*, Elen. Kmbl. 1515; El. 759; *inst. pl. of* bleoh.

bleónd, *pl.* bleóndon *mixed, blended; p. of* blandan.

bleónde *hast mixed, blended; p. of* blandan.

bleó-reád, -reód; *adj.* BLUE RED, *purple, myrtle-coloured;* cæruleoruber, myrteus:—Bleóreád *myrteus*, Cot. 135. Bleóreód *myrteus*, Ælfc. Gl. 79; Som. 72, 89; Wrt. Voc. 46, 46.

bleó-stǽning, e; *f. Coloured stone-work* or *pavement, Mosaic work;* opus musivum, pavimentum segmentatum, Som. Lye: Cot. 131.

bleót *was livid, pale; p. of* blātan.

bleót, đū bleóte, *pl.* bleóton *sacrificed, sacrificedst, sacrificed; p. of* blōtan.

bleóum *in colours*, Salm. Kmbl. 301; Sal. 150; *inst. pl. of* bleoh.

bleów, bleówe, *pl.* bleówon *blew, breathed*, Jn. Bos. 20, 22; *p. of* blāwan.

bleów, đū bleówe, *pl.* bleówon *flourished, hast flourished, flourished*, Ps. Surt. 27, 7; *p. of* blōwan.

bleowum *to* or *with colours*, Bt. 18; Fox 48, 11; *dat. pl. of* bleoh.

blere, es; *m? An onyx, gem;* onyx = ὄνυξ, *m. a nail*:—Blere *onyx*, Wrt. Voc. 288, 55.

blēt, blēte, *pl.* blēton *was livid, pale; p. of* blātan.

blēt *sacrifices; 3rd pers. pres. of* blōtan.

bletsian, bletsigan; *part.* bletsiende, bletsigende; *p.* ode, ade; *pp.* od, ad; *v. a. To* BLESS, *wish happiness, consecrate;* benedicere, consecrare:—Ic Ismael ēstum wille bletsian *I will bless Ishmael with favours*, Cd. 107; Th. 142, 5; Gen. 2357: 191; Th. 238, 23; Dan. 359: Gen. 17, 16. He, bletsiende [bletsigende, Jun.], bræc đa hlāfas, and sealde his leorningcnihtum *he, blessing, brake the loaves, and gave to his disciples*, Mt. Bos. 14, 19. Ic bletsie ealle đa đe hit healden *I bless all who may observe it*, Chr. 675; Erl. 39, 25. Ic bletsige ođđe wel secge *benedico*, Ælfc. Gr. 37; Som. 39, 38. Ic bletsige đē on mīnum līfe *benedicam te in vita mea*, Ps. Lamb. 62, 5: Exon. 41 b; Th. 138, 22; Gū. 580. Đū geáres hring mid gyfe bletsast *benedices coronæ anni benignitatis tuæ*, Ps. Th. 64, 12. We đec bletsiaþ, Fæder ælmihtig *we bless thee, Father almighty*, Cd. 192; Th. 241, 6; Dan. 400: Exon. 64 b; Th. 239, 12; Ph. 620: Ps. Lamb. 128, 8. Đū bletsodest [bletsadest, Th.] Drihten eorþan đīne *benedixisti Domine terram tuam*, Ps. Spl. 84, 1. He bletsode hī *benedicebat eos*, Mk. Bos. 10, 16: Ps. Spl. 106, 38. Mid heora mūþe hīg bletsodon, and mid heora heortan hīg wergdon *ore suo benedicebant, et corde suo maledicebant*, Ps. Lamb. 61, 5. Hī hine bletsadon meáglum wordum *they blessed him in strenuous words*, Exon. 43 a; Th. 146, 6; Gū. 705. Bletsa eálā đū mīn sāwl Drihtne *benedic anima mea Domino*, Ps. Lamb. 103, 1. Bletsiaþ Drihtne ealle englas his *benedicite Domino omnes angeli ejus*, 102, 20. Neáta gehwilc naman bletsie *every* [*kind*] *of cattle bless* [*thy*] *name*, Cd. 192; Th. 240, 22; Dan. 390. Bletsien đec, Dryhten, deór and nȳten *beasts and cattle bless thee, O Lord*, Exon. 55 a; Th. 194, 26; Az. 144. [*Chauc.* blisse, blysse: *Wyc.* blisse: *Laym.* bletseiȝen: *Orm.* blettcenn, blettsenn: *Northumb.* bletsia, bloetsia, bloedsia: *Icel.* bleza, bletza, blessa: *Goth.* bleiþs *merciful, kind*, bleiþyan *to have mercy.*] DER. ge-bletsian.

bletsing-bōc, e; *f. A blessing-book;* liber benedictionum formulas continens, Wanl. catal. 80, 33.

blētst *sacrificest; 2nd pers. pres. of* blōtan.

bletsung, bledsung, e; *f. A* BLESSING; benedictio:—Sī bletsung Drihtnes ofer eów *sit benedictio Domini super vos*, Ps. Spl. 128, 7: Exon. 9 a; Th. 7, 12; Cri. 100. He onfōn sceal mīnre bletsunge *he shall receive my blessing*, Cd. 106; Th. 140, 22; Gen. 2331. Cyn his on bletsunge byþ *semen illius in benedictione erit*, Ps. Lamb. 36, 26. Mid bletsunge [bledsunge, col. 1] đæs pāpan *with the blessing of the pope*, Chr. 813; Th. 108, 22, col. 2, 3. Brohte him bletsunge, se đe him ǽ sette *benedictionem dabit, qui legem dedit*, Ps. Th. 83, 7: 113, 21. Him se beorn bletsunga leán ageaf *the prince gave him the gift of his blessings*, Cd. 97; Th. 128, 2; Gen. 2120.

blēwþ, đū blēwst *blows, thou blowest*, Ps. Spl. 102, 14; *3rd and 2nd pers. pres. of* blōwan.

BLĪCAN, ic blīce, đū blīcest, blīcst, he blīceþ, blīcþ, *pl.* blīcaþ; *p.* ic, he blāc, đū blice, *pl.* blicon; *pp.* blicen; *v. n.* I. *to shine, glitter, dazzle, sparkle, twinkle;* lucere, fulgere, coruscare, micare:—Đū đære gyldnan gesihst Hierusalem weallas blīcan *thou seest the walls of the golden Jerusalem shine*, Salm. Kmbl. 469; Sal. 235: Exon. 57 a; Th. 204, 10; Ph. 95. Mōna swā seó Godes circe beorhte blīceþ *the church of God shines brightly like the moon*, 18 a; Th. 44, 11; Cri. 701: 58 b; Th. 210, 16; Ph. 186. Blīcþ đeós beorhte sunne *this bright sun glitters*,

Cd. 38; Th. 50, 19; Gen. 811. Hý fóre leódum leóhte blícaþ *they with light shall shine before the people*, Exon. 26 a; Th. 76, 14; Cri. 1239. Heofoncandel blác ofer lagoflódas *the sun* [lit. *heaven's candle*] *shone over the water-floods*, Andr. Kmbl. 486; An. 243. Blicon bordhreóðan *bucklers glittered*, Cd. 149; Th. 187, 30; Exod. 160. Hwonne swegles tapur hǽdre blíce *when the sun* [lit. *heaven's taper*] *serenely shines*, Exon. 57 b; Th. 205, 20; Ph. 115. II. *to shine by exposure, as the bones;* denudando in conspectum dari:—Hí twigena ordum hine weallaþ óþ ðæt him bán blícaþ *they shall vex him with points of twigs until his bones appear* [*shine*], Salm. Kmbl. 289; Sal. 144. [*Laym.* blikien: *O. Sax.* blíkan: *Frs.* blike *apparere: O. Frs.* blíka: *Ger.* er-bleichen *pallescere: M. H. Ger.* blíchen *fulgere: O. H. Ger.* ar-blíchan *pallescere: O. Nrs.* blíka, blíkja: *Lat.* flag-ra-re: *Grk.* φλέγ-ω: *Lith.* blizg-ù *I shine: Sansk.* bhráj *to shine.*] DER. a-blícan.

blíce, es; *m.* [blícan II. *to shine by exposure, as the bones*] *An exposure;* denudatio:—Gif bánes blíce weorþeþ, þrím scillingum gebéte *if there be an exposure of the bone* [*by wounding*], *let amends be made with three shillings*, L. Ethb. 34; Th. i. 12, 4.

blícettan; *p.* blícette; *pp.* blícetted [blícan I. *to shine, glitter*] *To glitter, quiver;* vibrare:—Blícette *vibrabat*, Cot. 178. [*O. H. Ger.* blechazan *micare.*]

blícettung, e; *f.* [blícettan *to glitter*] *A coruscation, shining;* coruscatio:—Blícettunga *coruscationes*, Ps. Vos. 76, 18: 143, 8. [*O. H. Ger.* blechazunga, *f. fulmen.*]

blicon *shone, glittered*, Cd. 149; Th. 187, 30; Exod. 160; *p. pl. of* blícan.

blícst, he blícþ *shinest, shines*, Cd. 38; Th. 50, 19; Gen. 811; *2nd and 3rd pers. pres. of* blícan.

blids *joy, gladness*, Ps. C. 50, 99; Ps. Grn. ii. 279, 99. v. blíþs.

blin, blinn, e; *f.* [= be-lin; v. linnan *to cease*] *A ceasing, rest, intermission;* cessatio, intermissio:—Bútan blinne *without ceasing;* sine intermissione, Bd. 5, 12; S. 628, 20: Elen. Kmbl. 1648; El. 826. [*Old Eng.* blin, Ben. Jonson.] DER. un-ablinn. v. blinnan.

BLIND; *def.* se blinda, seó, ðæt blinde; *adj.* BLIND, *deprived of sight;* cæcus:—Ðá wæs him broht án deófolseóc man, se wæs blind and dumb *tunc oblatus est ei dæmonium habens, cæcus et mutus*, Mt. Bos. 12, 22: Mk. Bos. 10, 46: Cd. 115; Th. 150, 13; Gen. 2491. Ðæt ðú grápie on midne dæg, swá se blinda déþ on þístrum *ut palpes in meridie, sicut palpare solet cæcus in tenebris*, Deut. 28, 29: Mt. Bos. 23, 26. Æt-hrán he ðæs blindan hand *he took the hand of the blind* [*man*], Mk. Bos. 8, 23. Hwá geworhte mannes múþ oððe hwá geworhte dumne oððe deáfne and blindne oððe geseóndne *quis fecit os hominis aut quis fabricatus est mutum et surdum, cæcum et videntem?* Ex. 4, 11: Chr. 1036; Erl. 165, 29; Ælf. Tod. 15. Híg synt blinde, and blindra látteówas; se blinda, gyf he blindne lǽt, híg feallaþ begen on ǽnne pytt *cæci sunt, et duces cæcorum: cæcus si cæco ducatum præstet, ambo in foveam cadunt*, Mt. Bos. 15, 14: 9, 27: 20, 30: Lk. Bos. 7, 22: Andr. Kmbl. 1162; An. 581. Blinde on geþoncum *blind in thoughts*, Exon. 24 b; Th. 69, 28; Cri. 1127: Bt. Met. Fox 19, 59; Met. 19, 30. Mæg wód man blindra manna eágan ontýnan *numquid dæmonium potest cæcorum oculos aperire?* Jn. Bos. 10, 21. Manegum blindum he gesihþe forgeaf *cæcis multis donavit visum*, Lk. Bos. 7, 21: 4, 18. Ðonne ðú gebeórscype dó, clypa þearfan, and wanhále, and healte, and blinde *cum facis convivium, voca pauperes, debiles, claudos, et cæcos*, Lk. Bos. 14, 13: Ps. Th. 145, 7. Drihten onleóhteþ ða blindan [MS. blinden] *Dominus illuminat cæcos*, Ps. Lamb. 145, 8. Eálá ge dysegan and blindan *O ye foolish and blind*, Mt. Bos. 23, 17, 19, 24. ¶ Blind slite *or* slyte *a blind* or *inward wound*, i. e. *a bite, the wound of which does not appear because of the swelling of the part affected;* morsus, cujus vulnus non apparet præ tumore partis affectæ, Herb. 4, 12; Lchdm. i. 92, 25. Seó blinde netele *or* netle *the blind* or *dead nettle;* archangelica [lamium album, *Lin.*], Ælfc. Gl. 43; Som. 64, 51; Wrt. Voc. 31, 61: L. M. 1, 23; Lchdm. ii. 66, 4. Blinda mann *a parasite;* palpo, Ælfc. Gr. 36; Som. 38, 46, 47. Blinde cweartern *a blind* or *dark prison;* cæcus *vel* tenebrosus carcer:—Gebrohton hí hine binnan ðam blindan cwearterne *they brought him into the dark prison*, Homl. Th. i. 416, 28. Engel scínende ðæt blinde cweartern mid leóhte afylde *a shining angel filled the dark prison with light*, ii. 382, 6. [*O. Sax.* blind: *O. Frs. Dut. O. Dut. Ger.* blind: *M. H. Ger. O. H. Ger.* blint, *gen.* blindes: *Goth.* blinds: *Dan. Swed.* blind: *Icel.* blindr.] DER. hyge-blind, mód-.

blindan *is not found, but the Gothic* ga-blindyan *to blind, exists; so also A. Sax.* blendan *to blind*, q. v.

blind-líce; *adv. In a blind manner,* BLINDLY, *rashly;* temere:—Hú blindlíce monige sprecaþ *how blindly* [*rashly*] *many speak*, Ors. 1, 10; Bos. 34, 17.

blind-nes, -ness, -nyss, e; *f.* BLINDNESS; cæcitas:—Ðá ge blindnesse bóte forségon *when ye renounced the remedy of blindness*, Elen. Kmbl. 777; El. 389: Exon. 41 b; Th. 139, 28; Gú. 600. Ofer hyra heortan blindnesse *super cæcitate cordis eorum*, Mk. Bos. 3, 5: Elen. Kmbl. 597; El. 299. Sende ðé Drihten on ungewitt and blindnysse *percutiat te Dominus amentia et cæcitate*, Deut. 28, 28.

blinnan; *part.* blinnende; ic blinne, ðú blinnest, blinst, he blinneþ, blinniþ, blinþ, *pl.* blinnaþ; *p.* ic, he blan, blon, blann, blonn, ðú blunne, *pl.* blunnon; *pp.* blunnen; *v. intrans.* [be, linnan *to cease*] *To cease, rest, leave off;* cessare, desinere:—Seó réþnes ðæs stormes wæs blinnende *the fierceness of the storm ceased* [lit. *was ceasing*], Bd. 5, 1; S. 614, 9. Blǽd his blinniþ *his prosperity ceaseth*, Exon. 94 b; Th. 354, 29; Reim. 53. We Dryhten bletsigaþ, ne ðæs blinnaþ áwa to worulde *we bless the Lord, nor cease from this for ever*, Ps. Th. 113, 25. Seó éhtnes [MS. ehtnysse] blan *the persecution ceased*, Bd. 1, 8; S. 479, 17. Blann [blonn MS. T.] se bysceophád eall geár and ðæs óðres syx mónaþ *the bishopric was vacant* [lit. *rested*] *all one year and six months of the next*, 3, 20; S. 550, 28. Ic nóht ðon ǽr ðære ærninge blon *I naught the sooner left off from running*, 5, 6; S. 619, 15: Andr. Kmbl. 2532; An. 1267. Ðú wuldres blunne *thou forfeitedst glory*, 2760; An. 1382. Rómáne blunnon [MS. blunnun] rícsian on Breotene *Romani in Brittania regnare cessarunt*, Bd. 1, 11; S. 480, 13. Blinn from eorre and forlét hát-heortnisse *desine ab ira et derelinque furorem*, Ps. Surt. 36, 8. [*Chauc.* blinne.] DER. a-blinnan, ge-.

blinnende, an; *f.* [blinnende, *part. of* blinnan *to cease*] *A ceasing, rest, intermission;* cessatio, intermissio:—Bútan blinnendan *without ceasing;* sine intermissione, Bd. 5, 12; S. 628, note 20. v. blin.

blinnes, blinness, e; *f. Rest;* cessatio, Som. Ben. Lye. DER. blin, nes.

blinniþ *ceases*, Exon. 94 b; Th. 354, 29; Reim. 53; *3rd pers. pres. of* blinnan.

blió, blioh *a colour, hue, complexion*, Prov. 23: Bt. Met. Fox 31, 7; Met. 31, 4. v. bleoh.

bliótan *for* bleóton *sacrificed; 3rd pl. p. of* blótan *to sacrifice:*—Hú ða burhleóde on Cartaina bliótan [= bleóton] men hira godum *how the towns-people in Carthage sacrificed men to their gods*, Ors. cont. 4, 4; Bos. 11, 32.

blis, bliss, blys, blyss, e; *f.* [contracted from blíþs, *q. v.*] I. BLISS, *joy, gladness, exultation, pleasure;* lætitia, gaudium, exultatio, beatitas:—Ne seó héhste blis nis on ðám flǽsclícum lustum *the highest bliss is not in the fleshly lusts*, Bt. 33, 1; Fox 120, 5: Ps. Spl. 29, 6. On heofonum is singal blis *in heaven is eternal bliss*, Rood Kmbl. 280; Kr. 141: Exon. 18 b; Th. 47, 5; Cri. 750: 48 b; Th. 167, 5; Gú. 1055. Ðanon com ǽrest cristendóm and blis fór Gode and fór worulde *whence first came christianity and joy before God and before the world*, Chr. 1011; Erl. 146, 22. Ðú eart blis mín *tu es exultatio mea*, Ps. Spl. 31, 9. Úre bliss on ánum ðé éce standeþ *our bliss eternally remaineth in thee alone*, Ps. Th. 86, 6. Gehýrde he of hrófe ðære ylcan cyricean upp astígan ðone ylcan blisse song *audivit ascendere de tecto ejusdem oratorii idem lætitiæ canticum*, Bd. 4, 3; S. 568, 2: Bt. 24, 4; Fox 86, 32: Andr. Kmbl. 2130; An. 1066. Stefn blisse *vox exultationis*, Ps. Spl. 117, 15. Þeówiaþ Drihtne on blisse, [and] insteppaþ oððe ingáþ on gesihþe his on blisse *servite Domino in lætitia,* [*et*] *introite in conspectu ejus in exultatione*, Ps. Lamb. 99, 2. Ðis is se dæg ðæne Drihten worhte eádigum to blisse *this is the day which the Lord made for joy to the blessed*, Menol. Fox 125; Men. 62: Exon. 15 b; Th. 35, 2; Cri. 552. Ðæt bearn bringeþ blisse ðé *that infant* [*Christ*] *bringeth bliss to thee*, Exon. 8 b; Th. 5, 11; Cri. 68: Chr. 975; Erl. 126, 30; Edg. 56. Ðú eart on heofonum blissa beorhtost *thou art the brightest of joys in heaven*, Hy. 7, 10; Hy. Grn. ii. 287, 10: Exon. 26 a; Th. 77, 15; Cri. 1257. Se burgstede wæs blissum gefylled *the city-place was filled with joys*, Exon. 52 a; Th. 181, 11; Gú. 1291: 27 b; Th. 82, 31; Cri. 1347. Blissum hrémig *exulting in gladness*, Elen. Kmbl. 2273; El. 1138: Exon. 48 b; Th. 168, 18; Gú. 1079. II. *friendship, kindness, benevolence, grace;* comitas, benignitas, benevolentia, gratia:—Hí me to wendon heora bacu bitere, and heora blisse from *they turned their bitter backs on me, and* [*took*] *their friendship from* [*me*], Bt. Met. Fox 2, 30; Met. 2, 15. Þurh ðé eorþbúende ealle onfóþ blisse mínre and bletsunge *through thee all dwellers upon earth shall receive my grace and blessing*, Cd. 84; Th. 105, 30; Gen. 1761: 106; Th. 140, 21; Gen. 2331. [*Laym. Orm.* blisse.] DER. heáh-blis, -bliss, woruld-.

blisgere, es; *m. An incendiary;* incendii auctor:—Blisgeras *incendiaries*, L. Ath. i. 6; Th. i. 203, note 38. v. blæsere.

blissian, blyssian, blissigan, blissigean; *part.* blissiende, blissigende; ic blissie, blissige, ðú blissast, he blissaþ, *pl.* blissiaþ; *p.* ode, ede, ade; *pp.* od, ed, ad [blis, bliss *bliss, joy*]. I. *v. intrans. To rejoice, exult, be glad* or *merry;* lætari, gaudere, exultare, ovare:—Heora láreówas blissigende hám hwurfon *doctores eorum domum rediere lætantes*, Bd. 3, 30; S. 562, 20. Blissigende [blissiende MS. C.] *ovans*, Ælfc. Gr. 33; Som. 37, 46. Ic blissige [Spl. blissie] ofer spæce ðínre *lætabor ego super eloquia tua*, Ps. Lamb. 118, 162. Blissaþ se rihtwísa on Drihtne *lætabitur justus in Domino*, Ps. Lamb. 63, 11: 57, 11: Andr. Kmbl. 1268; An. 634. Ða ðe ondrǽdaþ ðé, geseóþ me, and hí blissiaþ *qui timent te, videbunt me, et lætabuntur*, Ps. Lamb. 118, 74: Exon. 26 b; Th. 79, 8; Cri. 1287. Hyge blissode *their spirit rejoiced*, Andr. Kmbl. 1156; An. 578. Hí on ðon swýðe blissedon *they rejoiced very much at that*, Bd. 5, 12; S. 628, 34. Blissiaþ on Drihtne *lætamini in Domino*, Ps. Lamb. 31, 11. Blyssiaþ mid me *rejoice with me*, Lk. Bos. 15, 9.

Blissie [Lamb. blissige] heorte sēcendra Drihten *lætetur cor quærentium Dominum*, Ps. Spl. 104, 3. Blissian [blissien, Th. 66, 4] and fægnian hīg þeóda *lætentur et exultent gentes*, Ps. Lamb. 66, 5. Ðæt hī blission mid Criste *that they rejoice with Christ*, Chr. 1036; Erl. 165, 17; Ælf. Tod. 9. II. *v. trans. dat.* or *acc. To make to rejoice, to gladden, delight, exhilarate*; lætificare:—Sum sceal on heápe blissian æt beóre bencsittendum *one shall in company delight the bench-sitters at beer*, Exon. 88 a; Th. 331, 34; Vy. 78. Ðā se hālga ongann hæleþ blissigean *then the saint began to gladden the man*, Andr. Kmbl. 3213; An. 1609. Ðū, God, eallum blissast *thou, O God, makest all to rejoice*, Hy. 7, 34; Hy. Grn. ii. 287, 34. Heortan manna wīndrinc blissaþ *vinum lætificet cor hominis*, Ps. Th. 103, 14. He sārig folc blissade *he gladdened the sorrowful people*, Ps. Th. 106, 32. Hyge wearþ mongum blissad *the mind of many was made to rejoice*, Exon. 24 b; Th. 71, 30; Cri. 1163. [*Laym.* blissien: *Orm.* blissen.] DER. ge-blissian: mōd-blissiende.

blissung, blisung, e; *f.* [blis, bliss *exultatio*] *A triumphing, exultation*; exultatio:—Blisunga beorgas beóþ ymbgyrde *exultatione colles accingentur*, Ps. Spl. 64, 13. DER. ge-blissung.

blīð = blīðe *sweet, pleasant*; suavis, amœnus:—Ðis ofet is swēte, blīð on breóstum *this fruit is sweet, pleasant in the stomach*, Cd. 30; Th. 41, 13; Gen. 656.

BLĪÐE; *comp.* blīðra; *superl.* blīðost; *def.* se blīða, seó, ðæt blīðe; *adj.* I. *joyful, glad, merry, cheerful, pleasant,* BLITHE; lætus, hilaris:—Beó blīðe, ðū gōda þeów *be joyful, thou good servant*, Mt. Bos. 25, 21. Wæs Iethro blīðe for eallum ðām þingum, ðe Drihten dyde Israhēla folce *Jethro was glad for all the things, which the Lord did for the people of Israel*, Ex. 18, 9. Wæs engla þreát hleahtre blīðe geworden *the host of angels became merry with laughter*, Exon. 18 b; Th. 46, 19; Cri. 739: 20 b; Th. 55, 3; Cri. 878: Cd. 178; Th. 223, 10; Dan. 117. Wæs se blīða gǣst fūs on forþweg *the blithe spirit was eager for departure*, Exon. 46 b; Th. 158, 30; Gū. 917. He bæd hine blīðne beón æt ðære beórþege *he bade him be merry at the beer-drinking*, Beo. Th. 1238; B. 617; Menol. Fox 193; Men. 98. Dō dīnes scealces sāwle blīðe *lætifica animam servi tui*, Ps. Th. 85, 3. Mid ðās blīðan gedryht [MS. gedryt] *with this joyful host*, Exon. 15 a; Th. 33, 2; Cri. 519. Ic God bletsige blīðe mōde *I will bless God with a joyful mind*, 41 b; Th. 138, 23; Gū. 580: Ps. Th. 54, 11: 65, 7: Rood Kmbl. 242; Kr. 122. Wīgan wǣron blīðe *the warriors were blithe*, Elen. Kmbl. 492; El. 246: Cd. 171; Th. 215, 12; Exod. 582: Ps. Th. 52, 8: 106, 41. Cyning wæs ðȳ blīðra *the king was the blither*, Elen. Kmbl. 192; El. 96: Bt. Met. Fox 9, 63; Met. 9, 32: Byrht. Th. 136, 5; By. 146. Hīg blīðost [blīðust MS.] wǣron *they were most merry*, Jud. 16, 25. II. *gentle, kind, friendly, clement, mild, sweet*; mansuetus, benignus, comis, clemens, mitis, suavis:—Him biþ engla Weard milde and blīðe *the Lord of angels will be mild and gentle to them*, Elen. Kmbl. 2631; El. 1317: Ps. Th. 118, 88: Beo. Th. 877; B. 436. Eallum is ūre Drihten milde and blīðe *suavis Dominus universis*, Ps. Th. 144, 9: 66, 6. Wese us beorhtnes ofer blīðan Drihtnes ūres *let the beauty* [*brightness*] *of our gentle Lord be over us*, 89, 19. Weorc ānra gehwæs beorhte blīceþ in ðam blīðan hām *the works of every one shall brightly shine in that sweet home*, Exon. 64 b; Th. 238, 5; Ph. 599. Fæder ongon, þurh blīðne geþoht, his bearn lǣran *a father began, through kind thought, to teach his son*, Exon. 80 b; Th. 302, 30; Fä. 44: Andr. Kmbl. 1941; An. 973: Ps. Th. 102, 19. Utan us biddan ðone blīðan gǣst ðæt he us gescilde wið sceáðan wǣpnum *let us pray the kind spirit* [i. e. *the Holy Ghost*] *that he shield us against the spoiler's weapons*, Exon. 19 a; Th. 48, 20; Cri. 774. Blīðe mōde *with gentle mind*, Ps. Th. 89, 18: Exon. 121 b; Th. 467, 5; Hö. 134. Hȳ wǣron blīðe wið me on heora gebǣrum, and on heora mōde hī blissedon on mīnum ungelimpe *they were friendly with me in their manner, and in their mind they rejoiced for my misfortune*, Ps. Th. 34, 15. Swylce habban sceal blīðe gebǣro *such shall have gentle demeanour*, Exon. 115 b; Th. 444, 8; Kl. 44. Hȳ se æðeling grētte blīðum wordum *the chieftain greeted her with kind words*, 68 a; Th. 252, 19; Jul. 165. III. *quiet, calm, peaceful*; tranquillus, placidus:—Lēton ðone hālgan swefan on sibbe under swegles hleó, blīðne bīdan *they left the saint sleeping in peace, calm abiding under the vault of heaven*, Andr. Kmbl. 1665; An. 835. Ðæt he smylte mōde and blīðe him eall forlēt *quod ille placida mente dimitteret*, Bd. 3, 22; S. 553, 21. Ða ȳða swȳgiaþ, blīðe weorþaþ *the waves grow silent, become calm*, Ps. Th. 106, 28. [*Chauc. R. Glouc.* blithe: *Laym.* blīðe, bliðen: *Orm.* bliþe: *O. Sax.* blīði: *North Frs.* blid: *O. Frs.* blide in blid-skip *joy*: *Dut.* blijde: *M. H. Ger.* blīde: *O. H. Ger.* blīdi: *Goth.* bleiþs: *Dan. Swed.* blid: *Icel.* blīðr.] DER. hyge-blīðe, ofer-, un-.

blīðe; *adv.* I. *joyfully, gladly*; læte:—Bletsa, mīne sāwle, blīðe, Drihten *bless the Lord joyfully, O my soul*, Ps. Th. 102, 1: Exon. 44 a; Th. 149, 9; Gū. 759. II. *kindly, mildly*; benigne, clementer:—Ðū me, milde and blīðe, þurh ysopon ahluttra *asperges me hyssopo*, Ps. C. 50, 72; Ps. Grn. ii. 278, 72: Ps. Th. 54, 17.

blīðe-heortnys, -nyss, e; *f. Merry-heartedness*; lætitia, mansuetudo. DER. blīðe, heorte, -nes.

blīðe-līce; *comp.* -līcor; *adv. Gladly, joyfully,* BLITHELY, *merrily*; læte, hilariter:—He hine blīðelīce onfēng *he received him joyfully*, Lk. Bos. 19, 6: Gen. 46, 30. Ge māgon blīðelīce hlihhan *potestis hilariter ridere*, Ors. 3, 7; Bos. 62, 28. Ðæt he ðȳ blīðelīcor þrōwode *that he the more gladly might suffer*, Bd. 5, 14; S. 634, 42.

blīðe-mōd; *adj. Blithe of mind, glad, cheerful*; lætus animo, lætus, hilaris:—Wæs ā blīðemōd bealuleás cyning [MS. kyng], ðeáh he lang ǣr, lande bereáfod, wunode wræclāstum *the innocent king was ever blithe of mind* [*cheerful*], *though he long before, bereft of land, dwelt in exile*, Chr. 1065; Erl. 196, 34; Edw. 15: Cd. 72; Th. 88, 21; Gen. 1468: 86; Th. 108, 2; Gen. 1800: 210; Th. 260, 21; Dan. 713. Hyssas wǣron blīðemōde *the youths were cheerful* [*blithe of mind*], 186; Th. 231, 26; Dan. 253.

blīð-heort; *adj.* I. BLITHE *of* HEART, *merry, joyful*; lætus corde, hilaris:—Hrefn blaca, blīðheort, bododе cuman beorhte sunnan *the black raven, blithe of heart* [*merry*], *foretold the coming of the bright sun*, Beo. Th. 3608; B. 1802: Andr. Kmbl. 2526; An. 1264. Gefēgon beornas, blīðheorte, burhweardes cyme *the men, blithe of heart, rejoiced in the coming of the prince* [lit. *the city-guardian*], Andr. Kmbl. 1319; An. 660. II. *kind of heart, merciful*; benignus corde, misericors:—Gebletsode blīðheort Cyning, Metod alwihta, wīf and wǣpned *the merciful King, Lord of all things, blessed female and male*, Cd. 10; Th. 12, 28; Gen. 192.

blīð-nes, -ness, -nyss, e; *f. Joyfulness, enjoyment, a leaping for joy, exultation, mirth*; gaudium, exultatio, hilaritas:—Gif ðū nū atelan wilt ealle ða blīðnessa wið ðām unrōtnessum *if thou wilt now reckon all the enjoyments against the sorrows*, Bt. 8; Fox 24, 22. On blīðnysse *in exultatione*, Ps. Spl. 99, 2. Blīðnysse līf *vita hilaritatis*, Lchdm. iii. 212, 1.

blīþs, blīds, e; *f. Joy, gladness*; lætitia:—Liódum to blīþse *to the gladness of the people*, Ps. C. 50, 118; Ps. Grn. ii. 279, 118. Sæle blīdse me *give me joy*, 50, 99; Ps. Grn. ii. 279, 99. [*O. Sax.* blīdsea, *f.*] DER. blīðe. v. blis.

blīþsian; *p.* ode; *pp.* od *To rejoice, be glad, blithe, merry*; lætari:—Hī tō swīðe blīþsodon *they rejoiced too much*, Past. 50, 2; Hat. MS. Blīþsa, cniht on ðīnum gióguþhāde *rejoice, young man, in thy youth*, 49, 5; Hat. MS. [*O. Sax.* blīdsean: *Ger.* blitzen *exsilire gaudio*: *O. H. Ger.* blīdēn.] DER. blīþs.

blīðust *very merry*, Jud. 16, 25, = blīðost; *superl. of* blīðe, *adj.*

BLŌD, es; *n.* BLOOD, *gore*; sanguis, cruor:—Ðæt blōd eów byþ to tācne on ðām hūsum, ðe ge on beóþ: ðonne ic ðæt blōd geseó, ðonne forbūge ic eów *erit sanguis vobis in signum in ædibus, in quibus eritis, et videbo sanguinem et transibo vos*, Ex. 12, 13: Gen. 4, 10: Jn. Bos. 6, 55: Mt. Bos. 16, 17. Wæs ðæt blōd hāt *the blood was hot*, Beo. Th. 3237; B. 1616: 3339; B. 1667: Cd. 9; Th. 12, 6; Gen. 181: Exon. 116 b; Th. 447, 15; Dōm. 40: Andr. Kmbl. 1907; An. 956. His swāt wæs swylce blōdes dropan *est sudor ejus sicut guttæ sanguinis*, Lk. Bos. 22, 44: Mt. Bos. 27, 6, 8: Gen. 4, 11: Exon. 21 b; Th. 58, 15; Cri. 936. Lā hwilc nȳtwyrþnes on mīnum blōde *quæ utilitas in sanguine meo?* Ps. Lamb. 29, 10: Lk. Bos. 22, 20: Beo. Th. 1698; B. 847. Hit biþ geworden to blōde *vertetur in sanguinem*, Ex. 4, 9: 7, 17: 29, 21. Swā hwā swā agīt mannes blōd, his blōd biþ agoten *quicumque effuderit humanum sanguinem, fundetur sanguis illius*, Gen. 9, 6: Ps. Lamb. 13, 3: 49, 13: Andr. Kmbl. 46; An. 23. Gebletsode Romulus mid his brōðor blōde ðone weall, and mid ðara sweora blōde ða cyrican, and mid his eámes blōde ðæt rīce *Romulus blessed* [*consecrated*] *the wall* [*of Rome*] *with his brother's blood, the temples with the blood of their fathers-in-law, and the kingdom with his uncle's blood*, Ors. 2, 2; Bos. 41, 5-7. Meotud ðē gebohte blōde ðȳ hālgan *the Lord bought thee with his holy blood*, Exon. 98 a; Th. 368, 26; Seel. 30: Rood Kmbl. 96; Kr. 48. Blōde fāh *stained with blood*, Beo. Th. 1873; B. 934: 3192; B. 1594: 5940; B. 2974. Begleddod is eorþe on blōdum *infecta est terra in sanguinibus*, Ps. Spl. 105, 36. Deád blōd *clotted blood, gore*; cruor, Wrt. Voc. 283, 79. [*Chauc.* blod: *Wyc.* blood: *Laym. Orm.* blod: *Scot.* bloud: *Plat.* blod, *n*: *O. Sax.* blōd, *n*: *Frs.* bloed, *n*: *North Frs.* blot, blöt, *n*: *O. Frs.* blod, *n*: *Dut. O. Dut.* bloed, *n*: *Ger.* blut, *n*: *M. H. Ger.* bluot, *n*: *O. H. Ger.* bluot, *n*: *Goth.* bloþ, *n*: *Dan. Swed.* blod, *n*: *Icel.* blóð, *n.*] DER. blōd-dolg, -egesa, -fāg, -geóte, -gīta, -gȳte, -hreów, -hreówa, -lǣtan, -lǣtere, -leás, -reád, -reów, -ryne, -seax, -seten, -siht, -spīwing, -wyrt, -yrnende: blōdig, -tōþ: blōdeg: blōdegian, ge-.

blōd-dolg, es; *n. A bloody wound*; cruentum vulnus. DER. blōd, dolg, *q. v.*

blōd-dryncas; *pl. m. Blood-sheddings, blood-shed*; sanguinis effluvium:—Seó eorþbeofung tācnade ða miclan blōddryncas *the earthquake betokened the great blood-sheddings*, Ors. 4, 2; Bos. 79, 29.

blōd-egesa, an; *m.* [egesa, egsa *fear, terror*] *Bloody horror*; cruentus terror:—Brim berstende blōdegesan hweóp *the bursting sea threatened bloody horrors*, Cd. 166; Th. 208, 3; Exod. 477.

blōdegian; *p.* ode; *pp.* od [blōdig *bloody*] *To make bloody*; cruentare. DER. ge-blōdegian.

blódes flównyss, e; *f. A bloody flux, a flowing of blood;* sanguinis fluxus:—Ðæt wíf wæs þrówiende blódes flównysse *mulier fluxum patiebatur sanguinis*, Bd. 1, 27; S. 494, 4. v. blód-yrnende, flównes.

blód-fág; *adj.* [fág *tinctus*] *Stained with blood;* sanguine tinctus:— Is me bánhús blódfág *my body* [lit. *bone-house*] *is stained with blood*, Andr. Kmbl. 2809; An. 1407: Beo. Th. 4127; B. 2060.

blód-forlǽtan; *p.* -forlét, *pl.* -forléton; *pp.* -forlǽten *To let blood, bleed;* sanguinem emittere, phlebotomare:—Ðæt heó niwan blódforlǽten wǽre on earme *that she had been lately bled in the arm;* quia phlebotomata est nuper in brachio, Bd. 5, 3; S. 616, 4.

blód-geótan *to pour out* or *shed blood;* sanguinem effundere. DER. blód, geótan.

blód-geóte, es; *m. Blood-shedding, a shedding of blood;* sanguinis effusio:—Be blódgeóte *of blood-shedding*, L. Edm. S. 4; Th. i. 248, 22, 24. v. blód-gýte.

blód-geótende; *part. Shedding blood, blood-thirsty;* sanguinem effundens, sanguinolentus:—Weras blódgeótende *viri sanguinum*, Ps. Spl. 54, 27.

blód-gíta, an; *m. A shedder of blood;* sanguinis effusor:—Ðæne wer, ðe is blódgíta, gehiscþ Drihten *the Lord hates the man who is a blood-shedder*, Ps. Lamb. 5, 8.

blód-gýte, es; *m.* [blód, gýte *a flowing, from* gýt *flows out, pres. of* geótan]. I. *a flowing* or *running of blood;* sanguinis profluvium:—Gif men blód út of nósum yrne tó swíðe, syle him drincan fífleáfan on wíne, and smyre ðæt heáfod mid ðam; ðonne óþstandeþ se blódgýte sóna *if blood run from a man out of his nostrils too much, give him to drink fiveleaf in wine, and smear the head with it; then the blood-running will soon staunch*, Herb. 3, 5; Lchdm. i. 88, 8-10. II. *a blood-shedding, bloodshed;* sanguinis effusio:—Ðǽr wæs se mǽsta blódgýte *there was the greatest bloodshed*, Ors. 4, 2; Bos. 79, 26. Wǽron ða mǽstan blódgýtas *there were the greatest blood-sheddings*, Ors. 3, 9; Bos. 67, 31. Bútan blódgýte *without bloodshed*, Bd. 1, 3; S. 475, 11.

blód-hrǽcan; *p.* te; *pp.* ed *To retch* or *spit blood;* sanguinem excreare. DER. blód, hrǽcan *to retch.*

blód-hrǽce, es; *m. A spitting of blood;* sanguinis excreatio. v. blód, hrǽce.

blód-hreów; *def.* se blód-hreówa; *adj.* [hreów *cruel*] *Blood-thirsty, cruel;* sanguinolentus, crudelis:—Me wið blódhreówes weres bealuwe gehǽle *save me from the wickedness of the blood-thirsty man*, Ps. Th. 58, 2. Blódhreówe weras ge bebúgaþ me *viri sanguinum declinate a me*, 138, 17. Se blódhreówa wer *sanguinum vir*, Ps. Grn. 54, 24; Ps. Grn. ii. 153, 24.

blódig; *def.* se blódiga, seó, ðæt blódige; *adj.* BLOODY; sanguineus, cruentus:—Ne sý him bánes bryce, ne blódig wund *let there not be to him a breaking of bone, nor a bloody wound*, Exon. 42 b; Th. 143, 33; Gú. 670: Andr. Kmbl. 2945; An. 1475. Se bræd of ðæm beorne blódigne gár *he plucked the bloody dart from the chief*, Byrht. Th. 136, 21; By. 154. Geseoh nú swá ðín swát ageát, blódige stíge *behold now where thy blood poured forth, a bloody path*, Andr. Kmbl. 2883; An. 1444. He byreþ blódig wæl *he will bear off my bloody corpse*, Beo. Th. 900; B. 448. He his mǽg ofscét blódigan gáre *he shot his kinsman with a bloody arrow*, 4872; B. 2440. Ealle him brimu blódige þuhton *all the waters seemed bloody to them*, Cd. 170; Th. 214, 20; Exod. 572. Ða hwettaþ hyra blódigan téþ *who whet their bloody teeth*, L. E. I. prm; Th. ii. 396, 6. Blódigum teárum *with bloody tears*, Exon. 25 a; Th. 72, 20; Cri. 1175. Blódig útsiht *a dysentery;* dysenteria, Ælfc. Gl. 11; Som. 57, 51; Wrt. Voc. 19, 53. [*O. Sax.* blódag: *O. Frs.* blodich: *Dut.* bloedig: *Ger.* blutig: *M. H. Ger.* bluotec: *O. H. Ger.* blótag: *Dan. Swed.* blodig: *Icel.* blóðigr.] DER. ge-blódegian.

blódig-tóþ; *adj. Bloody-toothed, cruel;* cruentus dentibus, crudelis:— Bona blódigtóþ *the bloody-toothed murderer*, Beo. Th. 4170; B. 2082.

blód-læswu, e; *f. A blood-letting;* sanguinis emissio:—Frægn se biscеop hwonne hire blódlæswu ǽrest wǽre *the bishop asked when was first her blood-letting*, Bd. 5, 3; S. 616, 12, 15. On ðære blódlæswe *in the blood-letting*, 5, 3; S. 616, 5.

blód-lǽtan; *p.* -lét, *pl.* -léton; *pp.* -lǽten *To let blood, bleed;* sanguinem emittere, phlebotomare:—Blódlǽtan móna gód ys *it is a good moon for letting blood*, Lchdm. iii. 184, 11: Bd. 5, 3; S. 616, 14.

blód-lǽtere, es; *m. A blood letter;* phlebotomarius, Ælfc. Gl. 17; Som. 58, 93; Wrt. Voc. 22, 10.

blód-leás; *adj.* BLOODLESS; exsanguis, Ælfc. Gr. 9, 28; Som. 11, 58.

blód-mónaþ '*blood-month*,' i. e. *November.* v. blót-mónaþ.

blód-reád; *adj.* BLOOD-RED; sanguineus:—Ðæt þridde cyn ys *sanguineus*, ðæt is blódreád *the third sort is* sanguineus, *that is blood-red*, Herb. 131, 1; Lchdm. i. 242, 16.

blód-reów; *adj. Sanguinary;* sanguinolentus:—Breóst-hord blódreów *a sanguinary heart* [lit. *breast-hoard* or *treasure*], Beo. Th. 3442; B. 1719.

blód-ryne, es; *m.* [ryne *a running, course*] *A running of blood, an issue;* sanguinis fluxus:—Án wíf þolode blódryne twelf geár *mulier sanguinis fluxum patiebatur duodecim annis*, Mt. Bos. 9, 20. On blódryne *in fluxu sanguinis*, Lk. Bos. 8, 43.

blód-seax, blód-sex, es; *n. A blood-knife, a lancet;* phlebotomus = φλεβοτόμον, Ælfc. Gl. 17; Som. 58, 91; Wrt. Voc. 22, 9. v. ǽder-seax.

blód-setenn, e; *f.* [blód *blood*, setenn *from* seten, *pp. of* sittan *to sit, stop*] *The stoppage of blood;* sanguinis profluentis restrictio. v. sittan.

blód-siht, e; *f. A flowing of blood;* sanguinis profluvium. DER. blód *blood*, siht *a flowing, flux.*

blód-spíwing *a spewing of blood.* v. blót-spíung.

blód-wanian; *p.* ode; *pp.* od [wanian *to diminish*] *To diminish blood;* sanguinem minuere:—Nys ná gód móna blódwanian *it is not a good moon for diminishing blood*, Lchdm. iii. 184, 16.

blód-wíte, es; *n.* [blód, wíte *mulcta*] *Blood;* sanguis:—Ná ic gegadrige gesamnunga heora of blódum oððe of blódwítum *non congregabo conventicula eorum de sanguinibus*, Ps. Lamb. 15, 4.

blód-wyrt, e; *f.* BLOODWORT or *bloody-dock from its red veins and stems;* rumex sanguineus, Lin. v. wyrt.

blód-yrnende; *part.* [blód, yrnende, *part. of* yrnan *to run, flow*] *Blood-flowing;* sanguinans, sanguine fluens:—Ðæt wíf blódyrnende þrówaþ *the blood-flowing woman suffereth* [*was suffering*], Bd. 1, 27; S. 494, note 8, B. v. blódes flównyss.

BLÓMA, an; *m.* [blów + am + a, Ettm. 314] *Metal, the metal taken from the ore*, Wrt. Voc. 34, note 1: *a mass;* metallum, massa = μᾶζα *that which adheres together like dough*, Wht. Dict:—Ísenes blóma *a mass of iron;* ferri massa, Som: Cot. 135. Blóma oððe dáh *massa*, Wrt. Voc. 85, 16; *Lye says truly, referring to this quotation*,—'Inter ea quæ pertinent ad metalla.' Blóma *is contained in one of our oldest glossaries:*— Dáh [MS. dað] *vel* blóma *massa*, Ælfc. Gl. 51; Som. 66, 9; Wrt. Voc. 34, 68. Also in a Semi-Saxon glossary of the 12th century,—Blóma *vel* dáh *massa*, Wrt. Voc. 94, 63. DER. gold-blóma.

blon, blonn *ceased;* cessavit, Bd. 5, 6; S. 619, 15: 3, 20; S. 550, note 27; *p. of* blinnan.

blonca, an; *m. A grey horse;* equus albus:—Beornas and bloncan mid *warriors and their grey horses with them*, Exon. 106 a; Th. 405, 5; Rä. 23, 18. v. blanca.

blondan *to mix, blend, mingle;* miscere. DER. ge-blondan. v. blandan.

blonden-feax; *part. Having mixed hair;* comam mixtam habens, Cd. 107; Th. 141, 7; Gen. 2341: 123; Th. 157, 5; Gen. 2600: Beo. Th. 3586; B. 1791: 5916; B. 2962: 3750; B. 1873: 3193, B. 1594. v. blanden-feax.

blóstm, es; *m:* e; *f? A blossom, flower;* flos:—Blóstm *flos*, Ælfc. Gl. 46; Som. 65, 10; Wrt. Voc. 33, 9. Blóstma hiwum *in hues of flowers*, Exon. 94 a; Th. 352, 32; Reim. 4. v. blóstma.

BLÓSTMA, blósma, an; *m.* [= blóstm *a blossom*] A BLOSSOM, *bloom, flower;* flos:—Swá swá blósma ǽceres swá he blóweþ *tamquam flos agri sic efflorebit*, Ps. Lamb. 102, 15. Ofer híne scír cymeþ mínra [minre MS.] sóþfæst blóstma *super ipsum florebit sanctificatio mea*, Ps. Th. 131, 19. Ðeáh ðe lilie sý beorht on blóstman, ic eom betre ðonne heó *though the lily be bright in its blossom, I am better than it*, Exon. 110 b; Th. 423, 26; Rä. 41, 28: Ps. Th. 102, 14. Ne feallaþ on foldan fealwe blóstman *the fallow blossoms fall not on earth*, Exon. 57 a; Th. 202, 24; Ph. 74. Ic geseah ðone fægrestan feld full grówendra blóstma *I saw the most beautiful field full of growing flowers*, Bd. 5, 12; S. 629, 20. Ellenes blósman genim *take blossoms of elder*, L. M. 2, 59; Lchdm. ii. 288, 2. Ic geseah ðǽr on weaxende blósman litlum and litlum, and æfter ðám blósmum wínberigean *I saw blossoms growing thereon by little and little, and after the blossoms grapes* [lit. *wine-berries*], Gen. 40, 10. He dysegaþ se ðe wintregum wederum wile blósman [Cot. blostman] sécan *he is foolish who will seek flowers in wintry weather*, Bt. 5, 2; Fox 10, 32. Ðænne wangas blóstmum bláwaþ *then* [i. e. *in summer*] *the fields bloom with flowers*, Menol. Fox 179; Men. 91: Exon. 82 a; Th. 308, 31; Seef. 48. [*Tynd.* blossom: *Chauc. Piers P.* blosme: *Orm.* blostme: *Dut.* bloesem, *m: O. Dut.* blosem, *Kil: Dan.* blomst, *c: Swed.* blomster, *n: Icel.* blómstr, *m.*]

blóstm-bǽrende; *part.* [blóstm, bǽran *to bear*] *Blossom-bearing;* florifer:—Seó blóstmbǽrende stów is seó stów on ðære beóþ onfangene sóþfæstra sáula *the blossom-bearing place is the place to which are taken the souls of the righteous*, Bd. 5, 12; S. 630, 14.

blóstmian; *part.* blóstmiende; *p.* ode; *pp.* od *To* BLOSSOM, *blow;* efflorere:—Seó beorhtnes ðæs blóstmiendan feldes wæs gesewen *the brightness of the blossoming field was seen*, Bd. 5, 12; S. 629, 38.

BLÓT, es; *n. A sacrifice;* sacrificium:—He ealle ða cuman to blóte gedyde *he gave all the strangers for a sacrifice*, Ors. 1, 8; Bos. 31, 4. On blóte *by sacrifice*, L. C. S. 5; Th. i. 378, 21. [*Icel.* blót, *n.*] DER. ge-blót: blótan: blót-mónaþ.

blót = blód *blood;* sanguis. v. blót-spíung.

blótan, ic blóte, ðú blótest, blétst, he blóteþ, blét, *pl.* blótaþ; *p.* ic, he bleót, ðú bleóte, *pl.* bleóton; *pp.* blóten; *v. a.* [blót *a sacrifice*] *To sacrifice, to kill for a sacrifice;* immolare, sacrificare:—Ðæt hí hiora godum ðe ýð blótan meahton *that they might the more easily sacrifice to their gods*, Ors. 2, 2; Bos. 40, 37: 4, 4; Bos. 80, 39: 5, 2; Bos. 102, 16. Ongunnon heora bearn blótan feóndum *immolaverunt filios suos dæmoniis*, Ps. Th. 105, 27: Cd. 138; Th. 173, 5; Gen. 2856.

Úre yldran on ðam mônþe bleóton â *our forefathers always sacrificed in this month*, Hick. Thes. i. 219, 57. Ða burhleóde on Cartaina bleóton [bliotan MS.] men hira godum *the inhabitants of Carthage sacrificed men to their gods*, Ors. cont. 4, 4; Bos. 11, 32. Ðæt hine mon ǽnigum godum blôte *that a man sacrifice him to any gods*, Ors. 1, 8; Bos. 31, 11. Ðæt hî ða git swîðor blôtten, ðonne hie ǽr dydon *that they should sacrifice still more than they had done before*, 4, 4; Bos. 80, 18. [*M. H. Ger.* bluoten: *O. H. Ger.* blozan, ploazzan, plozan: *Goth.* blotan: *O. Dan.* blothe: *Swed.* blota: *Icel.* blóta *sacrificare.*] DER. a-blôtan, on-.

blôt-mônaþ, es; *m.* [blôt *a sacrifice*, mônaþ *month*] *November*, the month of sacrifice, so called because at this season the heathen Saxons made a provision for winter, and offered in sacrifice many of the animals they then killed. In an account of the Saxon months, it is thus described:—Se mônaþ is nemned on Lêden *Novembris*, and on úre geþeóde blôtmônaþ, forðon úre yldran, ðâ hŷ hǽðene wǽron, on ðam mônþe hŷ bleóton â, ðæt is, ðæt hŷ betǽhton and benêmdon hyra deófolgyldum ða neát ða ðe hŷ woldon syllan *this month is called* Novembris *in Latin, and in our language the month of sacrifice, because our forefathers, when they were heathens, always sacrificed in this month, that is, that they took and devoted to their idols the cattle which they wished to offer*, Hick. Thes. i. 219, 56–58: Menol. Fox 387; Men. 195.

blôt-spiung, e; *f.* [blôt = blôd *blood*, spîwing *spewing*] *A throwing up of blood;* hæmoptois, Ælfc. Gl. 10; Som. 57, 33; Wrt. Voc. 19, 38.

blôtung, e; *f. A sacrificing, sacrifice;* sacrificium, immolatio:—Þurh heora blôtunge *per eorum sacrificium*, Ors. 3, 3; Bos. 55, 33. v. blôt.

BLÔWAN; *part.* blôwende; ic blôwe, ðú blôwest, blêwst, he blôweþ, blêwþ, *pl.* blôwaþ; *p.* ic, he bleów, ðú bleówe, *pl.* bleówon; *pp.* blôwen; *v. n.* 1. *to* BLOW, *flourish, bloom, blossom;* florere, efflorere, reflorere:—Wudu sceal blǽdum blôwan *the wood shall blow with flowers*, Menol. Fox 527; Gn. C. 34: Exon. 109 a; Th. 417, 6; Rä. 35, 9. Wæs Aarones gyrd gemêtt blôwende and berende hnyte *Aaron's rod was found blossoming and bearing nuts*, Homl. Th. ii. 8, 15. Ic eom bearu blôwende *I am a blooming grove*, Exon. 108 a; Th. 412, 22; Rä. 31, 4. Ic blôwe *floreo*, Ælfc. Gr. 26, 2; Som. 28, 44. Swâ swâ blôsma æceres swâ he blôweþ [blêwþ, Spl.] *tamquam flos agri sic efflorebit*, Ps. Lamb. 102, 15. Hió grêwþ and blêwþ and westmas bringþ *it grows and blossoms and produces fruits*, Bt. 33, 4; Fox 130, 6. Se rihtwîsa swâ palmtreów blêwþ *justus ut palma florebit*, Ps. Lamb. 91, 13. Hîg blôwaþ swâ swâ gærs eorþan *florebunt sicut fœnum terræ*, 71, 16. Aarones gyrd greów and bleów and bær hnyte *Aaron's rod grew and blossomed and bare nuts*, Homl. Th. ii. 8, 18. Bleów flǽsc mîn *refloruit caro mea*, Ps. Lamb. 27, 7. Ǽr ðon eówre treówu telgum blôwen [MS. blôwe] *ere your trees flourish with branches*, Ps. Th. 57, 8. 2. blôwan *to blossom*, is sometimes used in Anglo-Saxon instead of blâwan *to blow;* and thus, blôwan was occasionally used by the Anglo-Saxons as the present English *to blow.* We say *to blow as the wind*, and *to blow* or *blossom as a flower.* v. blâwan. [*Wyc. R. Glouc.* blowe: *Laym.* blowen: *O. Sax.* blôjan: *Frs.* bloeyen: *North Frs.* blöye: *O. Frs.* bloia: *Dut.* bloeijen: *Ger.* blühen: *M. H. Ger.* blüejen, blüen, bluon: *O. H. Ger.* bluohan, bluojan, bluon: *Lat.* florere: *Grk.* φλέω, φλοίω *to be in full vigour or bloom: Sansk.* phal *to burst, blossom.*] DER. geblôwan.

blunne, *pl.* blunnon; *pp.* blunnen *hast been deprived, ceased, rested*, Andr. Kmbl. 2760; An. 1382: Bd. 1, 11; S. 480, 13; *p. and pp. of* blinnan.

blysa, blisa, an; *m. A torch;* fax:—Ðes blisa [blysa, D.] *hæc fax*, Ælfc. Gr. 9, 59; Som. 13, 37.

blysiere, es; *m. An incendiary;* incendii auctor:—Blysieras *incendiaries*, L. Ath. i. 6; Th. i. 202, 19. v. blæsere.

blysige, an; *f. A torch;* fax:—Þæcile, blysige *fax*, Wrt. Voc. 284, 20. v. þæcele.

blyssian *to rejoice*, Lk. Bos. 15, 9. v. blissian.

bô *both;* ambo, Ps. Th. 103, 9; *nom. pl.* = bû, bâ. v. begen.

BÔC, e; *f:* bôc-treów, es; *n:* bôcce, beóce, bêce, bǽce, an; *f. A beech-tree;* fagus silvatica, fagus = φηγός, æsculus:—Bôc *fagus;* bôc *æsculus*, Ælfc. Gl. 45; Som. 64, 99, 100. [*Plat.* book, böke, *f: Dut.* beuk, beuke, *f: Kil.* boecke, buecke: *Ger.* buche, *f: Icel.* bók, *f: Lat.* fâgus, *f.* = *Grk.* φηγός, *f.*] DER. bôc-scyld, -treów, -wudu.

bôc; *g.* bôce? bêc; *d.* bêc; *acc.* bôc; *pl. nom. acc.* bêc; *g.* bôca; *d.* bôcum, bôcan; *f.* I. *a* BOOK; liber:—Seó bôc is on Englisc awend *the book is turned into English*, Homl. Th. ii. 358, 30. On fôreweard ðære bôce [MS. bôc] odðe on heáfde bǽc awriten is be me *in capite libri scriptum est de me*, Ps. Lamb. 39, 9. On fôrewardre ðyssere bêc ys awriten be me, ðæt ic sceolde ðinne willan wyrcan, Ps. Th. 39, 8; *in the hed of the boc it is write of me, that I do thi wil*, Wyc. Ic wrât bôc *I wrote a book*, Bd. 5, 23; S. 648, note 37. Adilga me of ðînre bêc *dele me de libro tuo*, Ex. 32, 32, 33. Swâ he ða bôc unfeóld so *he unfolded the book*, Lk. Bos. 4, 17, 20: Deut. 31, 26. Ða bêc befôn *to contain the books;* capere libros, Jn. Bos. 21, 25. On ðæra cininga bôcum *in the kings' books*, Ælfc. T. Lisle 21, 1: 23, 19: 40, 4. On ðære bêc *in this book*, 24, 25. Bôca bedǽled *deprived of books*, 2, 3. On fîf bêc *in five books*, Bd. 5, 23; S. 648, 31. Ðis is seó bôc Adames mǽgrace *hic est liber generationis Adam*, Gen. 5, 1: Mt. Bos. 5, 31. Feówer Cristes bêc *four books of Christ, the four gospels*, Ælfc. T. Lisle 24, 22. Bôca streón *a treasury of books, a library*, Bd. 5, 21; Whelc. 451, 30, MS. C. II. *a charter;* charta = χάρτης, *m:*—Ðis is seó bôc, ðe Æðelstân cing gebôcode Friþestâne bisceope *this is the charter, which king Æthelstan chartered to bishop Frithestane*, Th. Diplm. A. D. 938; 187, 18. Heó cŷðaþ on ðisse bêc *they declare by this charter*, Th. Diplm. A. D. 886–899; 137, 12. Ic him sealde ðæt lond on êce erfe, and ða bêc *I gave him the land in perpetual heritage, and the charters*, Th. Diplm. A. D. 872–915; 168, 10. 2. *for the books which a priest ought to possess*, v. mæsse-preóst, 2; *for his canonical hours*, v. 3. [*Chauc.* booke: *Laym.* boc, bac, *f: Orm.* boc: *Plat.* book, *n: O. Sax.* bôk, *n. f: Frs.* bok, *f;* boek, *n: O. Frs.* bok, *f. n: Dut.* boek, *n: Ger.* buch, *n: M. H. Ger.* buoch, *n: O. H. Ger.* bôh, *n: Goth.* boka, *f: Dan.* bog, *c: Swed.* bok, *f: Icel.* bók, *f: O. Slav.* bukva, *f.* All these words have evidently the same origin. *Wormius, Saxo, Junius, etc.* suppose that as bôc denotes *a beech-tree*, as well as *a book*, in the latter case it was used in reference to the material from which the Northern nations first made their books. *Wormius* infers, that pieces of wood, cut from the beech-tree, were the ancient Northern books, *Lit. Run.* p. 6. *Saxo Grammaticus* states, that Fengo's ambassadors took with them letters engraved in wood [literas ligno insculptas], because that was formerly a celebrated material to write upon, *Lib.* iii. p. 52: *Turner's Hist.* App. b. ii. ch. 4, n. 25, vol. i. p. 238. Thus the *Latin* liber, and *Greek* βίβλος *a book*, took their origin from the materials of which books were made. *Liber* originally signified *the inner bark of a tree*, and βίβλος or βύβλος, *an Egyptian plant* [Cyperus papyrus, *Lin.*], which, when divided into lamina and formed into sheets to write upon, was called πάπυρος, hence papyrus *paper. Martinius, Stiernhielmius, Wachter, Adelung, etc.* rather derive buch, bôc, etc. from bügen *to bend* or *fold in plaits*, referring to the folded leaves of the parchment. Thus distinguishing these books from their folds. The ancient *volumina* were denominated from being in rolls, or rolled in the form of cylinders. At the Council of Toledo, in the 8th century, a book was denominated *complicamentum*, that which is folded. In still earlier times, even one fold of parchment was denominated a book, and *Ker.* calls a letter puah, and *Not.* brïef puoch, lit. *a letter book.*] DER. ǽ-bêc, ǽrend-bôc, bigspell-, bletsing-; Cristes bôc; dôm-, fôr-, gôdspell-, hand-, land-, mæsse-, pistol-, rǽding-, sang-, scrift-, sîþ-, spel-, traht-, wîs-: bôc-æceras, -cest, -cræft, -cræftig, -ere, -fel, -gestreón, -hord, -hûs, -ian, -land, -lâr, -leáf, -lêden, -lîc, -rǽdere, -rǽding, -reád, -riht, -scamel, -stæf, -tǽcing, -talu, -ung.

bôc, *pl.* bôcon *baked;* coxit, coxerunt, Ex. 12, 39; *p. of* bacan.

bôc-æceras, *pl. m. Booked acres, book-land, freehold.* v. bôc-land.

bôcan = bôcum *for books*, L. Eth. vi. 51; Th. i. 328, 8; *dat. pl. of* bôc.

bôca streón *a place for books, library;* bibliotheca, Bd. 5, 21; Whelc. 451, 30, MS. C.

bôcce, beóce, bêce, bǽce, an; *f. A beech-tree;* fagus = φηγός; æsculus. v. bôc, e; *f. a beech-tree.*

bôc-cest, e; *f.* [cest, cyst *a chest*] *A book-chest, book-shop, tavern;* taberna:—Bôccest *taberna*, Ælfc. Gl. 17; Som. 58, 89; Wrt. Voc. 22, 7.

bôc-cræft, es; *m.* [bôc *a book*, cræft *art, science*] *Book-learning, learning, literature;* literatura:—Boëtius wæs in bôccræftum se rihtwîsesta *Boëthius, in book-learning, was the most wise*, Bt. 1; Fox 2, 13. Ðara bôccræfta *of the knowledge of letters, of literature*, Greg. Dial. pref. 2.

bôc-cræftig; *adj. Book-crafty* or *learned, learned in the Bible;* in libris literatus, in Bibliis doctus:—Hî breóton [MS. breotun] bôccræftige *they destroyed those learned in the Bible*, Exon. 66 a; Th. 243, 25; Jul. 16.

bôcere, es; *m. A writer, scribe, an author, a learned man, instructor;* scriptor, scriba, interpres, vir doctus *vel* literatus:—Ðâ cwæþ se bôcere, Láreów, well ðú on sôþe cwǽde *then the scribe said, Master, thou in truth hast well said*, Mk. Bos. 12, 32. Hwæt secgeaþ ða bôceras *why say the scribes?* Mt. Bos. 17, 10. Hieronimus se wurþfulla and se wîsa bôcere awrât be Iohanne *the worthy and the wise author Jerome wrote concerning John*, Ælfc. T. Lisle 32, 1. Ǽlc gelǽred bôcere forlǽt ealde þing and niwe *every learned writer brings out old things and new*, 39, 5. Swâ ðætte swâ hwæt swâ he of godcundum stafum þurh bôceras geleornode *ita ut quicquid ex divinis literis per interpretes disceret*, Bd. 4, 24; S. 596, 33. We witan ðæt, þurh Godes gyfe, þrǽl wearþ to þegene, and ceorl wearþ to eorle, sangere to sacerde, and bôcere to biscope *we know that, by the grace of God, a slave has become a thane, and a ceorl [free man] has become an earl, a singer a priest, and a scribe a bishop*, L. Eth. vii. 21; Th. i. 334, 7–9.

bôc-fel, -fell, es; *n.* [fell *skin*] *A skin prepared for books, parchment, vellum;* charta pergamena, membrana:—Bôcfel *membrana*, Ælfc. Gl. 80; Som. 72, 111; Wrt. Voc. 46, 68. Bôcfel *bargina*, 16; Som. 58, 57; Wrt. Voc. 21, 44. Ðæt hî habban blæc and bôcfel *that they have ink and vellum*, L. Edg. C. 3; Th. ii. 244, 11.

bôc-gestreón, es; *n. A book-treasury, library;* bibliotheca:—He ðider micel bôcgestreón and æđele begeat *he acquired there a great and noble library*, Bd. 5, 20; S. 642, 2.

bôc-hord, es; *n.* *A* BOOK-HOARD, *a library* or *receptacle for books, papers, etc;* bibliotheca, archivum:—Bôchord [MS. boochord] *bibliotheca* vel *armarium* vel *archivum*, Ælfc. Gl. 109; Som. 79, 4; Wrt. Voc. 58, 47.

bôc-hûs, es; *n.* *A* BOOK-HOUSE, *library;* librarium:—Bôchûs *librarium*, Ælfc. Gl. 109; Som. 79, 5; Wrt. Voc. 58, 48.

bôcian; *p.* ode; *pp.* od *To give by charter, to charter;* libro *vel* charta dare:—Oswald biscop bôcaþ Wihtelme his þegne *bishop Oswald charters to Wihthelm his thane*, Cod. Dipl. 531; A.D. 966; Kmbl. iii. 6, 9. DER. ge-bôcian.

bôc-land, -lond, es; *n.* BOOK-LAND, *land held by a charter or writing, free from all fief, fee, service or fines.* Such was formerly held chiefly by the nobility, and denominated allodialis, which we now call *freehold;* ex scripto sive charta possessa terra, terra codicillaris:—Đe on his bôclande cyricean hæbbe *who on his freehold has a church*, L. Edg. i. 2; Th. i. 262, 11: L. Ed. 2; Th. i. 160, 14. Se mon bôcland hæbbe *the man has a freehold*, L. Alf. pol. 41; Th. i. 88, 16: Bd. 2, 3; S. 504, 29: 3, 24; S. 556, 4: Cod. Dipl. 317; A.D. 871-889; Kmbl. ii. 120, 6. Hæfde Rômânum to bôclande gesealde *Romanis per testamentum tradiderat*, Ors. 5, 4; Bos. 104, 18. Bôclandes, Cot. 83. v. folc-land *and* land.

bôc-lâr, e; *f.* [lâr *lore, learning*] *Book-learning, learning;* doctrina:—Blind biþ se lâreów, gif he đa bôclâre ne cann *blind is the teacher, if he know not book-learning*, L. Ælf. C. 23; Th. ii. 352, 6.

bôc-leáf, es; *n.* *The leaf of a book, a charter;* folium codicis, charta, instrumentum donationis. v. leáf.

bôc-lêden *book-language, and as most books were written in Latin,* hence *Latin*, Chr. Erl. 3, 3. v. lêden.

bôc-lîc; *adj.* BOOK-LIKE, *biblical, bookish, relating to books;* biblicus:—Gregorius wæs fram cildhâde on bôclîcum lârum getŷd *Gregory was from childhood instructed in book-learning*, Homl. Th. ii. 118, 16. On bôclîcum gewritum *in book-writings*, 284, 24. Đæt we đa bôclîcan lâre smeágan *that we consider the book-lore*, 284, 24.

bôcod *booked, chartered.* v. bôcian, gebôcian.

bôcon *baked;* coxerunt, Ex. 12, 39; *p. pl. of* bacan.

bôc-rǽdere, es; *m.* *A reader of books, a reader;* lector, Cot. 126.

bôc-rǽding *book-reading, reading.* v. rǽding.

bôc-reád *Book-red, vermilion:* so named, because it was much used in ornamenting books; minium:—Of bôcreáde *ex minio*, Cot. 75: 176.

bôc-riht, es; *n.* BOOK-RIGHT, *the right of a will* or *charter;* testamenti rectitudo *vel* jus:—Þegenes lagu is, đæt he sŷ his bôcrihtes wyrđe *taini lex est, ut sit dignus rectitudine testamenti sui*, L. R. S. 1; Th. i. 432, 1.

bôc-scamel, es; *m.* *A reading-desk* or *seat;* pluteus, lectorium. DER. bôc, scamel *a bench.*

bôc-scyld, es; *m.* [bôc *a beech-tree*, scyld *a shield*] *A beechen shield;* fagineum scutum:—Ic ge-an [MS. geann] Siferþe mînes bôcscyldes *I give to Siferth my beechen shield*, Th. Diplm. A.D. 938; 561, 5.

bôc-stæf, es; *pl. nom. acc.* -stafas; *g.* -stafa; *d.* -stafum; *m.* *A book-staff, a letter, character;* litera, character = χαρακτήρ:—Awrîtaþ hie on his wǽpne wælnota heáp, bealwe bôcstafas *they cut upon his weapon a heap of fatal marks, baleful letters*, Salm. Kmbl. 325; Sal. 162. Engel Drihtnes wrât in wâge worda gerŷnu baswe bôcstafas *the angel of the Lord wrote on the wall mysteries of words in crimson letters*, Cd. 210; Th. 261, 10; Dan. 724. Đæt he him bôcstafas arǽdde and arehte *that he [Daniel] should read and explain the characters to them*, 212; Th. 262, 7; Dan. 740. Hwâ wrât bôcstafas ǽrest *who first wrote letters?* Salm. Kmbl. 200, 23: 192, 6. Bôcstafa *of letters*, Salm. Kmbl. 199; Sal. 99. Wæs se beám bôcstafum awriten *the beam was inscribed with letters*, Elen. Kmbl. 182; El. 91. DER. stæf.

bôc-sum; *adj.* *Obedient, flexible,* BUXOM; obediens, flexibilis. [*Frs. Halbert.* p. 540, bûchsom *flexibilis:* *Dut.* boogh-saem *flexibilis:* *Ger.* biegsam *flexibilis.*]

bôc-sumnes, -ness, e; *f.* *Obedience, pliantness,* BUXOMNESS; obedientia. [*Ger.* biegsamkeit *flexibilitas:* *Verst. Restitn.* buhsomnesse, bowsomenesse *pliableness.* *Chaucer* writes buxsomnesse, p. 211.]

bôc-tǽcing, e; *f:* bôc-talu, e; *f.* *Book-teaching, a book of decrees, writings, the scriptures, holy writ, the Bible;* Scripta Lambardo; Sacra Scriptura Bromto: rectius fortasse Sacri Canones, *vel* Liber Judicialis, Lye:—Be bôctǽcinge *ex scriptis*, L. C. S. 35; Wilk. 140, 3. Be bôctale *by scripture*, L. C. S. 38; Th. ii. 398, 21. v. dôm-bôc.

bôc-talu, e; *f.* *Book-story* or *narration, the Bible.* v. bôc-tǽcing.

bôc-treów, es; *n.* *A beech-tree;* fagus:—Bôc-treów *fagus*, Wrt. Voc. 79, 76. v. bôc *fagus.*

bôc-ung, e; *f.* *A* BOOKING, *a setting down in a book;* inscriptio. DER. bôc, ung.

bôc-wudu; *m.* BEECH-WOOD; locus fagis consitus:—On bôcwuda *in the beech-wood*, Exon. 111 b; Th. 428, 11; Rä. 41, 106.

BOD, es; *pl.* u, o, a; *n.* *A command, commandment, precept, mandate, an edict, order, message;* jussum, mandatum, edictum:—Hwæt is đæt bod micle [MS. micla] in ǽ *quod est mandatum magnum in lege?* Mt. Lind. Stv. 22, 36: Mk. Lind. Stv. 12, 28, 29, 30, 31: Lk. Lind. Stv. 2, 1. Bod on cine *diploma*, Ælfc. Gl. 80; Som. 72, 110; Wrt. Voc. 46, 67. Hwâ swâ halt đis bod [bode MS.] wurđe he ēfre wunnende mid God *whosoever observes this command, may he ever dwell with God*, Cod. Dipl. 990; A.D. 680; Kmbl. v. 29, 23. We đîne bodu brǽcon *we broke thy commandments*, Hy. 7, 109; Hy. Grn. ii. 289, 109. [*Laym.* bode, bod: *Orm.* bode: *Scot.* bode, bod: *Plat.* bod, ge-bodd, *n:* *O. Sax.* gibod, *n:* *O. Frs.* bod, *n:* *Dut.* ge-bod, *n:* *Ger.* bot, ge-bot, *n:* *M. H. Ger.* ge-bot, *n:* *O. H. Ger.* ga-bot, *n:* *Goth.* busns, *f.* in ana-busns: *Dan.* bud, *n:* *Swed.* bud, *n:* *Icel.* boð, *n.* *a commandment.*] DER. ǽ-bod, be-, bi-, for-, ge-.

boda, an; *m.* [bod *a message*, -a, *q.v.*] I. *a messenger, ambassador, herald, apostle, angel;* nuntius, legatus, præco, apostolus, angelus:—Eálâ Wîsdôm, đû eart boda and fôrrynel đæs sôđan leóhtes *O Wisdom, thou art the messenger and forerunner of true light*, Bt. 36, 1; Fox 170, 28. Me đes boda sægde wǽrum wordum *this messenger told me in cautious words*, Cd. 32; Th. 42, 30; Gen. 680: 32; Th. 43, 6; Gen. 686: 33; Th. 45, 11; Gen. 725. Heó đæs lâđan bodan lârum hŷrde *she obeyed the advice of the loathsome messenger*, 33; Th. 44, 18; Gen. 711. Đa bodan us fǽrdon *nuntii nos terruerunt*, Deut. 1, 28: Exon. 27 a; Th. 80, 9; Cri. 1305. Sende he bodan befôran his ansŷne *misit nuntios ante conspectum suum*, Lk. Bos. 9, 52: Gen. 32, 3: Exon. 24 b; Th. 71, 7; Cri. 1152. Cyninges bodan underfôn *to receive a king's ambassador*, Lchdm. iii. 210, 15. Se sôđa boda đæs hean leóhtes Agustinus wæs fram him eallum bodad *verus summæ lucis præco ab omnibus prædicatur Augustinus*, Bd. 2, 2; S. 502, 32. Brimmanna boda *præco nautarum*, Byrht. Th. 133, 12; By. 49. Gefeohtes bodan *heralds of war;* præfeciales, Ælfc. Gl. 53; Som. 66, 81; Wrt. Voc. 36, 7. Đû Drihtnes eart boda of heofnum *thou art the Lord's angel from heaven*, Cd. 26; Th. 34, 5; Gen. 533: Elen. Kmbl. 153; El. 77. Bodan hyrdum cŷđdon sôþne gefeán *angels announced to the shepherds true joy*, Exon. 14 a; Th. 28, 20; Cri. 449. II. *a foreboder, prophet;* propheta, vates:—Gleáw bodan ǽrcwide *skilled in a prophet's prediction*, Exon. 83 a; Th. 313, 23; Môd. 4. [*R. Brunne* bode: *Laym.* boden, *pl:* *O. Sax.* bodo, *m:* *Frs.* bode, boade, *c:* *O. Frs.* boda, *m:* *Dut.* bode, *m:* *Ger.* *M. H. Ger.* bote, *m:* *O. H. Ger.* boto, *m:* *Dan.* bud: *Swed.* båd, *m:* *Icel.* boði, *m.* *a messenger.*] DER. ǽ-boda, ēdel-, fôr-, heáh-, nŷd-, sîþ-, spel-, wil-.

bodad *announced, proclaimed*, Andr. Kmbl. 2241; An. 1122, = bodod; *pp. of* bodian.

boden *ordered, offered, proclaimed*, Elen. Kmbl. 36; El. 18; *pp. of* beódan.

bodere, es; *m.* *A teacher, a master;* præceptor, Lk. Rush. War. 9, 33.

bodian, bodigan, bodigean; *part.* bodiende, bodigende; *p.* ode, ede, ade, ude; *pp.* od, ed, ad, ud; *v. a.* [bod *a message*]. I. *to tell, announce, proclaim, preach;* nuntiare, annuntiare, enuntiare, narrare, prædicare, evangelizare:—Ongan se Hǽlend bodian *cœpit Iesus prædicare*, Mt. Bos. 4, 17: Mk. Bos. 1, 45: Exon. 49 a; Th. 169, 2; Gû. 1088. He ongan bodigean on Decapolim *cœpit prædicare in Decapoli*, Mk. Bos. 5, 20: Cd. 169; Th. 210, 4; Exod. 510. Ic eom asend đē đis bodian *missus sum hæc tibi evangelizare*, Lk. Bos. 1, 19: Bd. 5, 9; S. 622, 13. To bodianne godcunde lâre *ad prædicandum doctrinam divinam*, 5, 9, titl; S. 622, 4. Com se Hǽlend on Galileam Godes rîces gôdspell bodigende *venit Iesus in Galilæam prædicans evangelium regni Dei*, Mk. Bos. 1, 14: Ps. Lamb. 2, 6. Ic bodie *annuntiabo*, Ps. Th. 54, 17. Đæt ic bodige ođđe đæt ic cŷđe ealle hērunga ođđe lofunga đîne on geatum dēhter ođđe dôhtra đæs mûntes [Siones] *ut annuntiem omnes laudationes tuas in portis filiæ Sion*, Ps. Lamb. 9, 15: Exon. 103 a; Th. 391, 3; Rä. 9, 10. Me đes âr bodaþ frēcne fǽrspell *this messenger announces to me a horrible unforeseen message*, Exon. 69 b; Th. 259, 3; Jul. 276: Bt. Met. Fox 29, 45; Met. 29, 23. Heofonas bodiaþ ođđe cŷđaþ wuldor Godes *cæli enarrant gloriam Dei*, Ps. Spl. 18, 1: Salm. Kmbl. 474; Sal. 237. Đes apostol Iacobus bodode on Iudēa lande *this apostle James preached in Judea* [lit. *in the land of the Jews*], Homl. Th. ii. 412, 23. Ymb Bethleem bododon englas đæt acenned wæs Crist on eorþan *angels announced about Bethlehem that Christ was born on earth*, Hy. 10, 23; Hy. Grn. ii. 293, 23. Bodedon heofonas rihtwîsnysse his *annuntiaverunt cœli justitiam ejus*, Ps. Spl. 96, 6: Judth. 12; Thw. 25, 6; Jud. 244. Hŷ bodudon *annuntiaverunt*, Ps. Spl. 43, 1. Cŷđaþ ođđe bodiaþ betwux þeódum his gecneordnyssa ođđe his ymbhoga *annuntiate inter gentes studia ejus*, Ps. Lamb. 9, 12: Andr. Kmbl. 669; An. 335. Wæs đæt weátâcen geond đa burh bodad *the fatal token was proclaimed throughout the town*, 2241; An. 1122. II. *to foretell, predict, prophesy, promise;* prædicere, promittere:—Him đone dæg willan Drihten bodode *the Lord had foretold [promised] to him that day of desire*, Cd. 133; Th. 168, 2; Gen. 2776: Beo. Th. 3608; B. 1802. Đæt wæs oft bodod ǽr befôran fram fruman worulde *it was often foretold long before from the beginning of the world*, Elen. Kmbl. 2280; El. 1141. [*Laym.* bodien: *O. Frs.* bodia: *Icel.* boða *to announce.*] DER. fôre-bodian, ge-, to-.

BODIG, es; *n.* I. *bigness* or *height of body, stature;* statura:—Đæt se mon wǽre lang on bodige *quod esset vir longæ staturæ*,

Bd. 2, 16; S. 519, 33. Wæs Oswine se cyning on bodige heáh *king Oswine was tall in stature*, 3, 14; S. 540, 7. II. *the trunk, chest* or *parts of the chest, as the back-bone*; truncus corporis:—Bodig *truncus*, Wrt. Voc. 283, 26: *spina*, Cot. 177: 196. III. *the* BODY; corpus:—Ǽgðer ge his fēt ge his heáfod ge eác eall ðæt bodig *either his feet or his head or even all the body*, Past. 35, 3; Hat. MS. 45 b, 12. [*Wyc.* body: *R. Glouc. Laym.* bodi: *Orm.* bodiȝ: *Ger.* bottech, *m*: *Bav.* bottich, *m*: *M.H.Ger.* botech, *m*: *O.H.Ger.* botah, *m*: *Gael.* bodhag, *f.*]

bodigean *to publish, preach*, Mk. Bos. 5, 20: Cd. 169; Th. 210, 4; Exod. 510. v. bodian.

bod-lāc, es; *n. A decree, ordinance*; decretum, Chr. 1129; Ing. 359, 21; Erl. 258, 13.

bod-scipe, es; *m.* [bod *a command*, scipe] *A message, an embassy, a commandment*; nuntium, mandatum:—Swā ic him ðisne bodscipe secge *when I tell him this message*, Cd. 27; Th. 35, 10; Gen. 552. Ðā hie Godes hæfdon bodscipe abrocen *when they had broken God's commandment*, 37; Th. 48, 29; Gen. 783. DER. ge-bodscipe.

bodudon *announced*; annuntiaverunt, Ps. Spl. 43, 1, = bododon; *p. pl. of* bodian.

bodung, e; *f. A preaching, publishing, divulging*; prædicatio, pronuntiatio:—Niniuetisce men dǣdbōte dydon æt Ionam bodunge *viri Ninivitæ pœnitentiam egerunt ad prædicationem Ionæ*, Lk. Bos. 11, 32.

bodung-dæg, es; *m. An annunciation day*; annuntiationis dies:—Ðes dæg is gehāten *Annuntiatio Sanctæ Mariæ*, ðæt is Marian bodungdæg gecweden *this day is called* Annuntiatio Sanctæ Mariæ, *which is interpreted, the annunciation-day of Mary*, Homl. Th. i. 200, 25.

boēm *to both*, Th. Diplm. A. D. 830; 465, 22; *for* bām; *dat. of* begen.

Boēties, Boōtes; *m. Boötes*; Bōōtēs, æ; *m.* [= βοώτης, ου; *m. a ploughman*, from βοῦς *an ox*]. The ancient constellation, the chief star of which is the bright Arcturus, v. arctos *the bear*; Ursa Major. The modern representation of Boötes is a man with a club in his right hand, and in his left a leash, which holds two dogs:—Hwā ne wundraþ ðætte sume tunglu habbaþ scyrtran hwyrft ðonne sume habban? For ðȳ hī habbaþ swā sceortne ymbhwyrft, for ðī hī sint swā neáh ðam norþende ðære eaxe, ðe eall ðes rōdor on hwerfþ, swā nū Boēties dēþ *who wonders not that some constellations have a shorter course than others have? Therefore they have so short a course, because they are so near the north end of the axis, on which all the sky turns, as now Boötes does*, Bt. 39, 3; Fox 214, 17-24. Boōtes beorhte scīneþ *Boötes shines brightly*, Bt. Met. Fox 28, 53; Met. 28, 27.

Boētius; *nom. acc*; *g.* Boēties, Boētiuses; *d.* Boētie; *m.* [βοηθόος *warlike*] *Anicius Manlius Severinus Boëthius*, born in Rome between A. D. 470-475, was Consul in 510. He was so eminent for his integrity and talents that he attracted the attention and obtained the patronage of Theodoric the Great, king of the East or Ostrogoths. He was afterwards accused of treason, and cast into prison, where he wrote his celebrated work *De Consolatione Philosophiæ*, which king Alfred translated into *Anglo-Saxon* about A. D. 888. Being condemned to death, without a hearing, he was beheaded in prison about A. D. 524:—Ðā wæs sum consul, ðæt we heretoha hātaþ, Boētius wæs hāten. Se wæs, in bōccræftum and on worold-þeáwum, se rihtwīsesta *there was a certain consul, that we call heretoha, who was named Boëthius. He was, in book-learning and in worldly affairs, the most truly wise* [= *most righteous*], Bt. 1; Fox 2, 12-14. Se Boētius wæs ōðre naman gehāten Seuerīnus: se wæs heretoga Rōmāna *Boëthius was by another name called Severinus: he was a consul of the Romans*, Bt. 21; Fox 76, 3-4. Hū Gotan gewunnon Rōmāna rīce, and hū Boētius hī wolde berǣdan, and Þeódrīc ðā ðæt anfunde and hine hēt on carcerne gebringan *how the Goths conquered the empire of the Romans, and how Boëthius wished to deliver them, and Theodoric discovered it, and gave orders to take him to prison*, Bt. title 1; Fox x. 2-4. Hū se Wīsdōm com to Boētie ǣrest inne on ðam carcerne *how Wisdom first came to Boëthius in the prison*, Bt. title 3; Fox x. 6: 26; Fox xiv. 18. Hēr endaþ nū seó æftre frōferbōc Boētiuses [Cot. MS. æfterre frōfr-bōc Boēties] *here now endeth the second consolation-book of Boëthius*, Bt. 21; Fox 76, 2-3. Hēr endaþ nū seó þridde bōc Boēties *here now endeth the third book of Boëthius*, Bt. 35, 6; Fox 170, 23.

bog *the arm, shoulder*, Ælfc. Gl. 73; Som. 71, 16; Wrt. Voc. 44, 2. v. boh.

boga, an; *m.* [bogen; *pp. of* būgan *to bow, bend*] Anything curved,—*A* BOW, *an arch, a corner*; arcus, angulus:—Ǽteówþ mīn boga on ðām wolcnum *apparebit arcus meus in nubibus*, Gen. 9, 14. Boga sceal strǣle *a bow shall be for an arrow*, Exon. 91 b; Th. 343, 8; Gn. Ex. 154. Ðæt hīg fleón fram ansȳne bogan *ut fugiant a facie arcus*, Ps. Lamb. 59, 6. Hīg aþenodon bogan heora *intenderunt arcum suum*, 36, 14: 57, 8: 63, 4. Hī lēton gāras fleógan, bogan wǣron bysige *they let the arrows fly, bows were busy*, Byrht. Th. 134, 66; By. 110. Bogan [MS. bogen] streng *a bow-string*; anquina, Ælfc. Gl. 52; Som. 66, 37; Wrt. Voc. 35, 26. [*Wyc.* bowe, bouwe: *Laym.* boȝe, bowe: *O.Sax.* bogo, *m*: *Frs.* boage: *O.Frs.* boga, *m*: *Dut.* boog, *m*: *Ger.* boge, bogen, *m*: *M.H.Ger.* boge, *m*: *O.H.Ger.* bogo, *m*: *Dan.* bue, *c*: *Swed.* båge, *m*: *Icel.* bogi, *m. arcus.*] DER. brægd-boga, flān-, horn-, hring-, rēn-, scūr-, stān-, wīr-.

bōgan *to boast*; jactare, Scint. 46. v. bōn.

boga-net, boge-net, -nett, es; *n. A* BOW-NET, *weel, wicker-basket with a narrow neck for catching fish*; nassa:—Ǽwul *vel* boganet *nassa*, Ælfc. Gl. 102; Som. 77, 85; Wrt. Voc. 56, 9. Bogenet *vel* leáp *nassa*, 84; Som. 73, 90; Wrt. Voc. 48, 28. Bogenet *nassa*, 105; Som. 78, 41; Wrt. Voc. 57, 23.

boge-fōdder, es; *m.* [boga *a bow*, fōdder *fodder*, from fōd *food*] *A* BOW-FEEDER, *case for arrows, a quiver*; corȳtos = κωρυτός:—Boge-fōdder *corytos* [MS. *coriti*], Ælfc. Gl. 53; Som. 66, 67; Wrt. Voc. 35, 53.

bogen *bowed, bent, gave way*; *pp. of* būgan.

bogen *rosemary*, L. M. 3, 30; Lchdm. ii. 324, 25, = boðen, *q. v.*

boge-net *a bow-net, weel*, Ælfc. Gl. 105; Som. 78, 41; Wrt. Voc. 57, 23. v. boga-net.

bogen streng, es; *m.* [bogen = bogan; *gen. of* boga *a bow*; streng *a string*] *The string of a bow, a* BOW-STRING; arcus chorda, anquina, Ælfc. Gl. 52; Som. 66, 37; Wrt. Voc. 35, 26. v. boga.

bogetung, e; *f.* [bogen; *pp. of* būgan *to bend*] *A bending, crook*; anfractus, Cot. 18.

bōgian; *p.* ode; *pp.* od *To inhabit*; incolere:—Bōgodon *incoluerunt*, Ælfc. T. Lisle 21, 13. v. būgian.

bogung, e; *f.* [bogen *bent*; *pp. of* būgan *to bow, bend*] *Crookedness, perversity*; pravitas, perversitas:—Þurh heora upahefednysse and āgenre bogunge *through their arrogance and own perversity*, Homl. Th. ii. 428, 13.

boh, bog, es; *m.* [bogen *bent*; *pp. of* būgan *to bow, bend*] Anything curved or bent,—hence I. *the arm, shoulder*; armus = ἄρμός, humerus, lacertus:—Se swīðra boh *armus dexter*, Lev. 7, 32; the riȝt schuldur, Wyc. Bog *lacertus*, Ælfc. Gl. 73; Som. 71, 16; Wrt. Voc. 44, 2. Eorl sceal on eós boge rīdan *a chief shall ride on a horse's back* [lit. *shoulder*], Exon. 90 a; Th. 337, 11; Gn. Ex. 63. Ðū nymst of ðam ramme ðone swȳðran boh *tolles de ariete armum dextrum*, Ex. 29, 22. Mec se beaducāfa bogum bilegde *the battle-prompt man embraced me in his arms*, Exon. 100 b; Th. 380, 21; Rä. 1, 11. II. *the arm of a tree, a* BOUGH, *branch*; ramus, stipes, palmes:—Bōh *ramus*, Scint. 1. Boh *stipes*, Ælfc. Gr. 9, 26; Som. 11, 16. Berende boh *germen*, Ælfc. Gl. 60; Som. 68, 32; Wrt. Voc. 39, 18. Ðeáh ðū hwilcne boh ðæs treówes bȳge *though thou bendest any bough of a tree*, Bt. Met. Fox 13, 105; Met. 13, 53. Hit wearþ mycel treów, and heofenes fugelas reston on his bogum *factum est in arborem magnam, et volucres cœli requieverunt in ramis ejus*, Lk. Bos. 13, 19: Cd. 30; Th. 40, 26; Gen. 645. He astrehte his bogas ōþ ða sǣ *extendit palmites suos usque ad mare*, Ps. Lamb. 79, 12. III. *a branch of a family, offspring, progeny*; propago:—Tyddrung odðe boh *propago*, Ælfc. Gr. 36; Som. 38, 49. [*Chauc.* bow: *Piers P.* bowe: *Wyc.* boow, bouȝ, boȝ: *Orm.* boȝh: *Dut.* boeg, *m. the bow of a ship*: *Ger.* bug, *m. armus*: *M.H.Ger.* buoc, *m*: *O.H.Ger.* buoc, *m. armus*: *Dan.* bov, boug, *c. shoulder, bow of a ship*: *Swed.* bog, *m. the shoulder, haunch*: *O.Nrs.* bógr, *m. the shoulder of an animal.*] DER. wæter-boh, wīn-.

boh-scyld, es; *m. A shoulder shield*; ad humerum clypeus, Æthelst. Test. Mann. = bōc-scyld, *q. v.*

bohte, *pl.* bohton *bought*; emit, emerunt, Gen. 49, 30; *p. of* bycgan.

BOLCA, an; *m. The gangway of a ship*; forus navis:—Bolca *forus*, Cot. 86. Geseah weard beran ofer bolcan beorhte randas *the guard saw bright shields borne over the ship's gangway*, Beo. Th. 467; B. 231: Andr. Kmbl. 1203; An. 602. He on bolcan sæt *he sat on the gangway*, 610; An. 305. [*Icel.* búlki, *m. the cargo of a ship.*]

BOLD, es; *n.* I. *a building, dwelling, house*; ædificium, domicilium, domus:—Wæs ðæt bold tobrocen swīðe *the dwelling was much shattered*, Beo. Th. 1998; B. 997. Ðǣr ic wīc būge, bold mid bearnum *where I inhabit a dwelling, a house with children*, Exon. 104 b; Th. 396, 23; Rä. 16, 9. Bold wæs betlīc *the building was excellent* [*good-like*], Beo. Th. 3854; B. 1925. Nis ðæt betlīc bold [blod MS.] *that is no goodly dwelling*, Exon. 116 a; Th. 446, 16; Dōm. 23. II. *a superior house, hall, castle, palace, temple*; aula, palatium, ædes:—He him gesealde bold and bregostōl *he gave to him a habitation and a princely seat*, Beo. Th. 4398; B. 2196. Ne mōt ic brūcan burga ne bolda *I may not enjoy towns nor palaces*, Cd. 216; Th. 273, 19; Sat. 139. Ðā wæs Beówulfe gecȳðed, ðæt his sylfes hām, bolda sēlest, brynewylmum mealt *then it was made known to Beowulf, that his own home, the best of mansions, was consumed by flames of fire*, Beo. Th. 4641; B. 2326. Gewāt beorht blǣdgifa in bold ōðer *the bright giver of glory departed into another temple*, Andr. Kmbl. 1312; An. 656. [*R. Glouc.* bold: *A.Sax.* bylda *a builder*: *Eng.* to build. v. botl.] DER. feorh-bold, fold-: bold-āgende, -getæl, -getimber, -wēla.

bold-āgende; *part.* [bold *a house*, āgende *owning*] *House-owning, possessing a house*; domum possidens:—Hæleða monegum boldāgendra *to many of house-owning men*, Beo. Th. 6215; B. 3112: Exon. 90 b; Th. 339, 12; Gn. Ex. 93.

bold-getæl, es; *n.* [bold *a house,* getæl *a number, tribe, register*] *A dwelling-place, mansion, habitation, house;* domicilium, mansio, vicus, domus:—Gif mon wille of boldgetale [boldgetæle MS. B.] in óðer boldgetæl hláford sécan, dó ðæt mid ðæs ealdormonnes gewitnesse ðe he ǽr in his scíre folgode *if a man from one dwelling-place wish to seek a lord in another dwelling-place, let him do it with the knowledge of the alderman, whom he before followed in his shire,* L. Alf. pol. 37; Th. i. 86, 2; that is, *If a person who had* commended *himself, wished to take his name off the* manor-roll *of one lord, etc.* Thorpe's Laws, vol. i. p. 86, note a.

bold-getimber; *gen.* -getimbres; *pl. nom. acc.* -getimbru; *n. The timber of a house;* ædificii tignum:—Leóht [fýr] briceþ and bærneþ boldgetimbru *light [fire] breaketh and burneth the timbers of the house,* Salm. Kmbl. 826; Sal. 412.

bold-wéla, an; *m.* [bold *a house,* wéla *wealth*]. I. *a dwelling of wealth* or *happiness;* prædium, opes domesticæ:—Ne mæg ðé adón ðinne boldwélan *thou mayest not take thee thy dwelling of wealth* or *happiness,* Soul Kmbl. 118; Seel. 59. II. *paradise, heaven;* paradisus = παράδεισος, cœlum:—Ðé is neorxna wang boldwéla fægrost *paradise is to thee the fairest dwelling of happiness,* Andr. Kmbl. 206; An. 103. Adam and Æue anforléton beorhtne boldwélan *Adam and Eve forsook bright paradisal happiness,* Exon. 73 a; Th. 272, 22; Jul. 503. He gesóhte swegle dreámas, beorhtne boldwélan *he sought the joys of heaven, the bright dwelling of happiness,* Apstls. Kmbl. 65; Ap. 33. He [God] sceal rǽdan, se ðe ródor ahóf, wuldres fylde beorhtne boldwélan *he [God] shall rule, who uplifted the firmament, with glory filled the bright dwelling of wealth,* Andr. Kmbl. 1047; An. 524.

bolgen *vexed, irritated, angry; pp. of* belgan.

bolgen-mód; *adj. Enraged in mind;* iratus animo:—Him bolgenmód yrre andswarode *enraged in mind, answered them angrily,* Cd. 183; Th. 228, 26; Dan. 209: Beo. Th. 1422; B. 709: Andr. Kmbl. 255; An. 128: Exon. 40 b; Th. 135, 25; Gú. 529.

BOLLA, an; *m. Any round vessel, cup, pot,* BOWL, *a measure;* vas, cyathus = κύαθος:—Bolla *cyathus,* Glos. Epnl. Recd. 156, 16. Cærenes gódne bollan fulne meng tógædere *mingle together a good bowl full of boiled wine,* L. M. 1, 1; Lchdm. ii. 24, 19. Ðǽr wǽron bollan steápe boren æfter bencum *there were carried deep bowls behind the benches,* Judth. 10; Thw. 21, 14; Jud. 17. [*Piers P. Laym.* bolle: *O. Frs.* bolla, *m.* in kne-bolla, strot-bolla: *Dut.* bol, *m*: *Kil.* bolle *caput, globus*: *Ger.* punsch-bole, *f. a punch-bowl*: *M. H. Ger.* hirn-bolle: *O. H. Ger.* hirni-polla *the brain-pan, skull*: *Dan.* bolle, *c*: *Swed.* bål, *n*: *O. Nrs.* bolli, *m. a bowl.*] DER. beód-bolla, heáfod-, þrot-.

bollen *bellowed, roared; pp. of* bellan.

BOLSTER; *gen.* bolstres; *m. A* BOLSTER, *a pillow for the head;* cervical:—He his heáfod onhylde to ðam bolstre, and medmycel fæc onslǽpte *reclinavit caput ad cervical, modicumque obdormivit,* Bd. 4, 24; S. 599, 7. He wæs on scipe, ofer bolster slápende *erat in puppi, super cervical dormiens,* Mk. Bos. 4, 38. Hit geondbrǽded wearþ beddum and bolstrum *it was overspread with beds and bolsters,* Beo. Th. 2484; B. 1240. [*Dut.* bolster, *m. a shell*: *Kil.* bolster *culcita*: *Ger.* polster, *m. cervical*: *M. H. Ger.* bolster, *m*: *O. H. Ger.* bolstar, *n*: *Swed.* bolster, *n. a mattress*: *O. Nrs.* bólstr. *m. a bolster.*] DER. heáfod-bolster, hleór-.

BOLT, es; *pl.* boltas; *m. A* BOLT, *a warlike engine to throw bolts, arrows;* catapulta, Cot. 45. [*Chauc.* bolt: *Dut.* bout, *m*: *Kil.* bolt *sagitta*: *Ger. M. H. Ger.* bolz, *m*: *O. H. Ger.* bolz: *Dan.* bolt, *c*: *O. Nrs.* bolti, *m.*]

bón [bógan *to boast*] *To boast;* jactare:—He bóþ his sylfes swíðor micle ðonne se sélla mon *he boasts of himself much more than a better man,* Exon. 83 b; Th. 315, 9; Mód. 28.

bona, an; *m. A killer;* interfector:—Se wites bona *the destroyer of the mind [the devil],* Exon. 11 b; Th. 17, 3; Cri. 264. Fugel-bona *a bird killer,* 79 b; Th. 298, 5; Crä. 80. v. bana.

bond *bound;* ligavit, Exon. 42 b; Th. 143, 29; Gú. 668; = band; *p. of* bindan.

bonda, an; *m. A husband, an householder, a master of a family;* maritus:—Se bonda sæt *the husband dwelt,* L. C. S. 73; Th. i. 414, 21: 77; Th. i. 418, 24. v. bunda.

bonde-land, es; *n. Bond or leased land, land held under restrictions, or on conditions expressed in writing;* tributaria terra:—Án abbot, Beonne gehâten, lét Cúþbriht ealdorman x bonde-lande [x tributariorum terram, *vel* terram x manentium] æt Swinesheáfde, mid læswe and mid mǽdwe, and mid eal ðæt ðǽrto læi, and swá ðæt Cúþbriht geaf ðam abbote l punde ðǽrfore, and ilca geár ánes nihtes feorme, ouðer xxx scyllinge penega; swá eác ðæt eafter his dæi scólde ðæt land ongeán into ðam mynstre *an abbot, called Beonna, let to the alderman Cuthbriht ten 'bonde-lands' at Swineshead, with leasow and with meadow, and with all lying thereto, and so that Cuthbriht should give to the abbot fifty pounds for it, and every year one night's entertainment, or thirty shillings in pennies; and also that after his day the land should come again to the monastery,* Chr. 777; Th. 92, note 1; Cod. Dipl. 165; A. D. 786–796; Kmbl. i. 201.

bon-gár, es; *m.* [bana, ban *a killer, death?* gár *a spear*] *A death-spear;* letifera hasta, Beo. Th. 4066; B. 2031.

bonnan; *p.* beónn, *pl.* beónnon; *pp.* bonnen *To summon, call together;* citare, convocare:—Sió býman stefen and se beorhta segn bonnaþ sáwla gehwylce *the voice of the trumpet and the bright sign shall summon every soul,* Exon. 23 b; Th. 66, 6; Cri. 1067. v. bannan.

booc-hord *a library,* Ælfc. Gl. 109; Som. 79, 4; Wrt. Voc. 58, 47. v. bóc-hord.

BÓR. I. *a borer, gimlet;* terebra, Leo 121. II. *a lancet, a surgeon's* or *barber's instrument, a burin,* or *graving tool;* scalprum rasile, Cot. 63. [*Plat.* baar: *Dut.* boor, *f*: *Dan.* bor, *n*: *Swed.* borr, *m*: *O. Nrs.* bor, *m. terebra,* Rask Hald.]

bora, an; *m.* [boren; *pp. of* beran *to bear*] *One who bears* or *sustains the charge of anything, a ruler;* qui rem aliquam gerit, gestor:—Ríces boran *the rulers of the state,* Cd. 224; Th. 296, 10; Sat. 500.

-bora, an; *m.* [*from* boren; *pp. of* beran] Often used as a termination to denote *A bearer, bringer, supporter;* is qui fert, gerit; as, Cǽg-bora, horn-, mund-, rǽd-, rǽs-, segen-, sweord-, tácn-, wǽg-, wæpen-, wíg-, wóþ-, wróht-. v. -bǽre.

borcian; *p.* ade, ode *To bark;* latrare:—Hió borcade: þancode willum *it barked: thanked willingly,* Exon. 129 a; Th. 495, 11; Rä. 84, 6. v. beorcan.

BORD, es; *n.* I. *a* BOARD, *plank;* tabula sectilis, tabula:—Bord *tabula,* Wrt. Voc. 63, 80. Borda gefég *a joining of boards;* commissura, R. 62. Hwílum ic bordum sceal heáfodleás behlýðed licgan *sometimes I must lie on boards deprived of head,* Exon. 104 a; Th. 395, 18; Rä. 15, 9. Wirc ðé ǽnne arc of aheáwenum bordum *make thee an ark of planed planks,* Gen. 6, 14; fac tibi arcam de lignis levigatis, Vulg. II. what is made of a board,—*A table, shield;* mensa, clypeus:—Ic on wuda stonde, bordes on ende *I stand upon wood, at the end of the table,* Exon. 129 a; Th. 496, 15, 18; Rä. 85, 15, 16. Geweorþe bord oððe mése heora beforan him on grine *fiat mensa eorum coram ipsis in laqueum,* Ps. Spl. T. 68, 27. Scip sceal genægled, scyld gebunden, leóht bord *a ship shall be nailed, a shield bound, the light shield* [lit. *board*], Exon. 90 b; Th. 339, 16; Gn. Ex. 95: Byrht. Th. 134, 67; By. 110: Fins. Th. 58; Fin. 29. He fýsde forþ flán genehe: hwílon he on bord sceát, hwílon beorn tǽsde *he poured forth his arrows abundantly: sometimes he shot on the shield, sometimes he pierced the warrior,* Byrht. Th. 139, 46; By. 270: Beo. Th. 5041; B. 2524: Cd. 156; Th. 193, 28; Exod. 253. Ðǽr wæs borda gebrec *there was clash of shields,* Elen. Kmbl. 227; El. 114: Beo. Th. 4510; B. 2259. Beraþ bord fór breóstum *bear shields before their breasts* Judth. 11; Thw. 24, 16; Jud. 192: 12; Thw. 26, 9; Jud. 318. He mid bordum hét wyrcan ðone wíhagan *he commanded to raise with the shields the fence of war,* Byrht. Th. 134, 49; By. 101: Andr. Kmbl. 2412; An. 1207. III. *the board, covering* or *deck of a ship, the ship itself;* tabulatum, stega = στέγη, constratum, navis:—Hý twegen sceolon habban gomen on borde, in sídum ceóle *they two shall have pastime on board, in the spacious ship,* Exon. 92 a; Th. 345, 5; Gn. Ex. 183. He drugaþ his ár on borde *he draws his oar on board,* 92 a; Th. 345, 15; Gn. Ex. 188. Ofer ceóles bord *from the vessel's deck,* Exon. 20 b; Th. 54, 2; Cri. 862. Lǽd under earce bord eaforan ðíne *lead thy children under the covering of the ark,* Cd. 67; Th. 80, 23; Gen. 1333: 67; Th. 82, 4; Gen. 1357. Bord oft onféng ýða swengas *the ship often received the blows of the waves,* Elen. Kmbl. 476; El. 238. Ic wille eall acwellan ða be-útan beóþ earce bordum *I will destroy all who shall be without the boards of the ark* or *all who are not in the ark* or *ship,* Cd. 67; Th. 81, 33; Gen. 1354. IV. *with the prepositions* innan *and* útan *governing the genitive case, at home and abroad;* domi et foris:—Hie sibbe innan bordes gehióldon *they preserved peace at home* [lit. *inside the boundary*], Past. pref; Hat. MS. Man útan bordes wísdóm hieder on lond sóhte *one from abroad* [lit. *outside the boundary*] *sought wisdom in this land,* Past. pref; Hat. MS. [*Wyc.* boord: *R. Brun.* bord: *R. Glouc.* bord, borde: *Laym.* bord, beord, burd: *Orm.* bord, borde: *O. Sax.* bord, *m*: *Frs.* boerd, bord, *m*: *O. Frs.* bord, *m*: *Dut.* bord, boord, *m*: *Ger.* bord, *m. and n*: *M. H. Ger.* bort: *O. H. Ger.* bort, borti, borto, *m*: *Goth.* fotu-baurd, *n. a foot-stool*: *Dan.* bord, *n*: *Swed.* bord, *m*: *Icel.* borð, *n*: *Fr.* bord, *m*: *Span. It.* bordo, *m*: *M. Lat.* bordus: *Wel.* bwrdh, bord: *Corn.* bord, *f*: *Ir. Gael.* bord, *m*: *Armor.* bourz.] DER. bleó-bord, fámig-, gúþ-, hilde-, hleó-, nægled-, þryþ-, wǽg-, wíg-, ýþ-.

borde, an; *f. A board, table;* tabula, mensa:—Fǽmne æt hyre bordan geríseþ *it becomes a damsel to be at her board,* Exon. 90 a; Th. 337, 14; Gn. Ex. 64.

bord-gelác, es; *n.* [lácan *to play, sport, fly*] What flies against a shield, hence,—*A missile, dart;* telum:—Ðý-læs ingebúge biter bordgelác under bánlocan *lest the bitter dart enter in under the skin,* Exon. 19 a; Th. 48, 9; Cri. 769. v. bord II.

bord-hæbbende; *part.* [bord *scutum, clypeus;* habban *habere, vel* hebban, hæbban *levare, tollere*] *Shield-bearing;* scutum ferens, scutifer, Beo. Th. 5782; B. 2895.

bord-haga, an; *m.* [bord II. *a shield,* haga *a hedge*] *The cover of* *shields;* clypeorum sepimentum:—Gefeallen under bordhagan *fallen under the cover of shields*, Elen. Kmbl. 1300; El. 652.

bord-hreóða, -hrēða, an; *m.* [bord II. *a shield*, hreóðan *to cover, protect*]. I. *the cover* or *protection of the shield;* clypei tegmen *vel* tutela:—Hǣðne heápum þrungon under bordhreóðan *the heathens thronged in heaps under the cover of shields*, Andr. Kmbl. 256; An. 128: Beo. Th. 4412; B. 2203: Cd. 154; Th. 192, 23; Exod. 236. II. *a shield, buckler;* clypeus:—Blicon bordhreóðan *shields glittered*, Cd. 149; Th. 187, 30; Exod. 160. Hæfdon hie ofer bordhreóðan beácen arǣred *they had a signal reared over their bucklers*, 160; Th. 198, 9; Exod. 320. Brǣcon bordhrēðan *they broke through the bucklers*, Invent. Crs. Recd. 242; El. 122.

bord-rand, es; *m.* [bord II. *a shield*, rand *a rim, margin*] *The margin or disc of a shield;* scuti margo:—Biorn bordrand onswāf *the hero turned his shield's disc*, Beo. Th. 5112; B. 2559.

bord-stæþ, es; *pl. nom. acc.* -staðu; *n.* [stæþ *a shore, bank*] *The sea-shore;* litus:—Eágorstreámas beóton bordstaðu [bordstæðu MS.] *the ocean-streams beat the sea-shores*, Andr. Kmbl. 883; An. 442.

bord-þaca, an; *m. Board thatch, a warlike engine, a cover* or *roof of a house, a snare;* testudo, laquearium:—Bordþacan *laquearii*, Cot. 119.

bord-weall, es; *m. A board-wall, a shield;* scutorum agger, testudo, clypeus:—He bræc ðone bordweall *he broke through the board-wall*, Byrht. Th. 139, 60; By. 277: Beo. Th. 5952; B. 2980.

bord-wudu; *m. Shield-wood, a shield;* clypei lignum, clypeus, Beo. Th. 2490; B. 1243. v. bord II.

boren *borne, carried, born*, Bt. Met. Fox 26, 92; Met. 26, 46; *pp. of* beran.

boren-nes, -ness, e; *f.* [boren *born*, -nes] *Birth, nativity;* partus, nativitas. DER. æðel-borennes.

borg *a surety* or *pledge*, L. Alf. pol. 3; Th. i. 62, 8. v. borh.

borgas *sureties, debtors*, L. Eth. i. 1; Th. i. 280, 21; *pl. of* borh.

borgen *saved, protected, sheltered; pp. of* beorgan.

borges bryce *a breaking* or *breach of a suretyship* or *pledge*, L. Alf. pol. 3; Th. i. 62, 9, 10, 12. v. borh-bryce.

borg-gylda, an; *m. A usurer;* fœnerator, Ps. Spl. C. 108, 10.

borgian, he borgaþ; *p.* ode, ede; *pp.* od, ed [borh *a pledge, loan*] *To take* or *give a loan*, BORROW, *lend;* mutuari, commodare:—Ðam ðe wylle æt ðē borgian, ne wyrn ðū him *volenti mutuari a te, ne avertas*, Mt. Bos. 5, 42. Borgaþ se synfulla and nā gefillþ oððe he ne agylt *mutuabitur peccator et non solvet*, Ps. Lamb. 36, 21. Borgedon [MS. borgedan] *commodarunt*, Cot. 38. [*Chauc. R. Glouc.* borwe: *Piers P.* borwen: *Laym.* burȝen: *Plat.* borgen: *O. Frs.* borga: *Dut. Ger. M. H. Ger.* borgen: *O. H. Ger.* borgēn *cavere: Dan.* borge: *Swed.* borga: *O. Nrs.* borga *fidejubere.*] DER. a-borgian.

borgiend, es; *m.* [*part. of* borgian *to lend*] *A usurer;* fœnerator:—Smeáge borgiend [MS. borgiende] ealle spēda his *scrutetur fœnerator omnem substantiam ejus*, Ps. Spl. 108, 10.

borg-wed, -wedd, es; *n. Anything given in pledge, a promise;* vadimonium. v. wed, wedd.

BORH; *g.* borges; *d.* borge; *acc.* borh; *pl. nom. acc.* borgas; *g.* a; *d.* um; *m.* I. *a security, pledge, loan, bail;* fœnus:—Ic wille, ðæt ǣlc mann sȳ under borge ge binnan burgum ge būtan burgum *I will that every man be under security both within cities and without cities*, L. Edg. S. 3; Th. i. 274, 6. Abere se borh ðæt he aberan scolde *let the borh bear that he ought to bear*, L. Edg. ii. 6; Th. i. 268, 9. On his āgenon borge *on his own security*, L. Eth. i. 1; Th. i. 282, 10. Gif ðū feoh to borge selle *if thou give money on loan*, L. Alf. 35; Th. i. 52, 21. Be borges andsæce *concerning a denial of a bail*, L. In. 41; Th. i. 128, 1, note 1. II. *a person who gives security, a surety, bondsman, debtor;* fidejussor, debitor.—Bail was taken by the Saxons from every person guilty of *theft, homicide, witchcraft, etc:* indeed, every person was under bail for his neighbour. It is generally thought, that the borh originated with king Alfred, but the first time we find it clearly expressed, is in the Laws of Ine, v. *Turner's Hist. of A. S.* Bk. vi. Append. 3, ch. 6, vol. ii. p. 499:—Sette getreówe borgas *shall appoint true sureties*, L. Eth. i. 1; Th. i. 280, 21: 280, 6, 7, 8: L. Ed. 6; Th. i. 162, 19, 20. Ge asēcaþ eówre borgas *ye shall search out your debtors*, L. E. I. 42; Th. ii. 438, 35. [*Chauc. Wyc.* borwe: *R. Glouc.* borewes, *pl: Piers P.* borgh: *Laym.* borh: *Frs.* borch, *m: O. Frs.* borh, borch, *m: Dut.* borg, *m. and f: Ger.* borg, *m: M. H. Ger.* borc, *m.*]

borh-bryce, borg-bryce, es; *m.* [borh *a pledge*, bryce *a breaking*] *A pledge-breaking, violation of a bail;* fidejussionis violatio:—Be borhbryce *concerning a pledge-breaking*, L. Alf. pol. 3; Th. i. 62, 7, note 10. Borh-bryce, L. In. 31; Th. i. 122, note 20. Borg-bryce, L. Alf. pol. 1; Th. i. 60, 19.

borh-fæstan, geborh-fæstan; *p.* -fæste; *pp.* -fæsted [borh *a surety*, fæstan *to fasten*] *To fasten* or *bind by pledge* or *surety;* fidejussione obligare:—Man borhfæst ðam cyninge [MS. kyninge] ealle ða þægnas *they bound by pledge all the thanes to the king*, Chr. 1051; Ing. 228, 33; Erl. 181, 5.

borh-hand, borhond, e; *f. A pledge by the hand, a pledger, surety, security;* sponsor, fidejussor:—Borh-hand *sponsor, fidejussor*, Ælfc. Gl. 114; Som. 80, 15; Wrt. Voc. 60, 50: Ælfc. Gr. 9, 25; Som. 10, 66: 9, 35; Som. 12, 32.

borhigenda, an; *m.* [borh *a loan*, āgenda *a possessor*] *A usurer;* fœnerator:—Ascrudnige borhigenda ealle spēde oððe ǣhte his *scrutetur fœnerator omnem substantiam ejus*, Ps. Lamb. 108, 11.

borh-leás; *adj. Void of security;* fidejussore carens:—Gif hwā borhleás orf habbe... agife ðæt orf, and gilde xx oran *if any one have cattle borhless* [i. e. *for which no borh has been given*]... *let him give up the cattle, and pay twenty* oran [*which at* 1*s.* 4*d. each, would make* £1. 6*s.* 8*d. in our money*, v. pūnd], L. Eth. iii. 5; Th. i. 296, 1.

borh-wed, -wedd, es; *n. Anything given in pledge;* vadimonium. v. wed, wedd.

BÓRIAN; *p.* ode; *pp.* od *To* BORE, *to make a hole, perforate;* terebrare, perforare:—Wyrm ðe bōraþ treów *a worm that perforates wood;* termes *vel* teredo, Ælfc. Gl. 23; Som. 60, 4; Wrt. Voc. 24, 8. [*Tynd.* bore: *Dut.* boren: *Ger.* bohren: *M. H. Ger.* born: *O. H. Ger.* borjan, borōn: *Dan.* bore: *Swed.* borra: *Icel.* bora: *Lat.* for-are: *Zend* bar *to cut, bore.*]

born *burnt; p. of* beornan:—Forðonðe se Godes wer stronglīce innon born mid ðȳ fȳre godcundre lufan *quia vir Dei igne divinæ caritatis fortiter ardebat*, Bd. 2, 7; S. 509, 30.

bornen *burnt; pp. of* beornan.

borsten *burst; pp. of* berstan.

borþor *child-birth.* v. beorþor, hyse-beorþor.

Boruchtuari, -orum; *pl. m. Lat. A people of ancient Germany, conquered by the Old-Saxons;* Boructuari:—Ðā Swȳþbyrht hæfde bisceophāde onfongen, he gewāt to ðære þeóde Boruchtuarorum;... ac ðā æfter noht langre tīde seó ylce þeód wæs oferwunnen fram Eald-Seaxum, and ða wǣron wīde todrifene *Suidberct, accepto episcopatu, ad gentem Boructuarorum secessit;... sed expugnatis non longo post tempore Boructuaris, quolibet hi, a gente Antiquorum Saxonum, dispersi sunt*, Bd. 5, 11; S. 626, 6-11. v. Boruct-ware.

Boruct-ware; *gen.* a; *dat.* um; *pl. m:* Boructuari, -orum; *pl. m. A people of ancient Germany, occupying the country between the Rhine, the Lippe, Ems, and Weser;* Bructěri = Βρούκτεροι:—Wǣron Frysan, Rugine, Dene, Hune, Eald-Seaxan, Boructware *sunt Fresones, Rugini, Danai, Hunni, Antiqui Saxones, Boructuari*, Bd. 5, 9; S. 622, 16. Tacitus always mentions the Bructeri with the Tencteri,—Bructeri et Tencteri, Ann. xiii. 56: Hist. iv. 21, 77. Zeuss supposes they may have inhabited the country near the Lippe, which was called *Boroctra* or *Borhtergo*, Deut. Nachbarst. 353.

Bosan-hām, Bosen-hām, es; *m.* [*Flor.* A. D. 1114; *Sim. Dunelm.* 1164 Bosanham: *Hovd.* 1204 Boseham] BOSEHAM OR BOSHAM *in Sussex;* in agro Sussexiensi:—Ðā gewende Swegen to his scypum [MS. scypon] to Bosanhām *Swegen then went with his ships to Bosham*, Chr. 1049; Erl. 172, 34. Gewende ðā Swegen eorl to Bosenhām *earl Swegen then went to Bosham*, 1048; Erl. 180, 15.

BÓSG, bōsig, bōsih, es; *m? n? An ox* or *cow-stall, where the cattle stand all night in winter;* a BOOSE, as it is now called by the common people, in the Midland and Northern counties. It is now [1874] more generally used for the upper part of the stall where the fodder lies,—They say, 'you will find it in the *cow's boose*,' that is, in the place for the *cow's food;* præsepium:—Of bōsge *a præsepio*, Lk. Rush. War. 13, 15. Of bōsih *a præsepio*, Lk. Lind. War. 13, 15. [*Frs.* bos *a cottage: Ger.* banse, *m. or f: Goth.* bansts, *m. a barn: Dan.* baas, *c: Swed.* bås, *n: Icel.* bás. *m. stabulum, præsepium bovis*, Rask Hald.]

BÓSUM, bōsm, es; *m. The space included by the folding of the arms, the* BOSOM, *lap, breast, interior parts;* sinus, gremium, pectus, interna:—Ðæt ic hīg bǣre on mīnum bōsume, swā fōstormōdor dēþ cyld *ut portarem eos in sinu meo, sicut portare solet nutrix infantulum*, Num. 11, 12. Mīn gebēd on bōsme mīnum byþ gecyrred *oratio mea in sinu meo convertetur*, Ps. Lamb. 34, 13: 73, 11: 78, 12: 88, 51. Ic winde sceal swelgan of sumes bōsme *I* [i. e. *a horn*] *shall swell with wind from some one's bosom*, Exon. 104 a; Th. 395, 30; Rä. 15, 15: 109 b; Th. 419, 17; Rä. 38, 7: 127 a; Th. 489, 11; Rä. 78, 6. Gescype scylfan on scipes bōsme *make shelves in the interior* [lit. *bosom*] *of the ship*, Cd. 65; Th. 79, 5; Gen. 1306: 67; Th. 80, 21; Gen. 1332: 71; Th. 85, 6; Gen. 1410: Chr. 937; Erl. 112, 27; Æðelst. 27. Of brimes bōsme *from the sea's bosom*, Andr. Kmbl. 887; An. 444. Dō ðīne hand on ðīnne bōsum. Ðā he hīg dyde on his bōsum *mitte manum tuam in sinum tuum: cum misisset in sinum*, Ex. 4, 6, 7. Ān man mihte faran ofer his rīce, mid his bōsum full goldes, ungederad *a man might go over his kingdom, with his bosom full of gold, unhurt*, Chr. 1086; Erl. 222, 4. Ðū ðīnre mōdor bōsm sylfa gesōhtes *thou thyself soughtest thy mother's bosom*, Exon. 121 b; Th. 465, 27; Hö. 110. Ðū wuldres þrym bōsme gebǣre *thou barest the majesty of glory* [*Christ*] *in thy breast*, 9 a; Th. 6, 14; Cri. 84. [*Wyc.* bosum: *Laym.* bosm: *Orm.* bosemm: *Plat.* bussen, bossen: *O. Sax.* bōsom, *m: O. Frs.* bosm, *m: Dut.* boezem, *m: Ger.* busen, *m: M. H. Ger.* buosem, buosen, *m: O. H. Ger.* bōsam, buosam, *m. sinus.*] DER. fāmig-bōsm, swegl-.

BÔT, e; *f.* I. *help, assistance, remedy, cure;* auxilium, remedium, emendatio, sanatio:—Hēr ys seó bōt, hū ðū meaht ðīne æceras bētan *here is the remedy, how thou mayest improve thy fields,* Lchdm. i. 398, 1. Findest ðū ðǣr æt bōte and ælteowe hǣlo *thou shalt find therein a remedy and perfect healing,* Herb. 1, 29; Lchdm. i. 80, 6. Byþ hræd bōt *the cure will be quick,* Med. ex Quadr. 6, 15; Lchdm. i. 354, 11. II. *a* BOOT, *compensation due to an injured person as damages for the wrong sustained, redressing, recompense, an amends, a satisfaction, correction, reparation, restoring, renewing, repentance, an offering;* compensatio, emendatio, reparatio, oblatio:—Gif feaxfang geweorþ, L scætta to bōte *if there be a taking hold of the hair, let there be* 50 *sceats for compensation,* L. Ethb. 33; Th. i. 12, 3. For bōte his synna *for a redressing of his sins,* Bd. 4, 25; S. 599, 32: 5, 13; S. 632, 13. Bringaþ ānne buccan to bōte *bring a kid for an offering,* Lev. 4, 23, 28: L. Alf. pol. 2; Th. i. 62, 6: Bd. 1, 27; S. 489, 9. ¶ To-bōte *to-boot, with advantage, moreover, besides.* [*Piers P.* boote: *Laym. Orm.* bote: *Plat.* bote, *f: O. Sax.* bōta, *f: O. Frs.* bote, *f: Dut.* boete, *f: Ger.* busze, *f: M. H. Ger.* buoz, buoze: *O. H. Ger.* bōza, *f: Goth.* bota, *f: Dan.* bod, *c: Swed.* bot, *m: Icel.* bót, *f.*] DER. bric-bōt, bricg-, burh-, hād-, weofod-.

bōþ *boasts*:—He bōþ *he boasts,* Exon. 83 b; Th. 315, 9; Mōd. 28; *pres. of* bōn.

boðen, es; *m? n? Rosemary, darnel;* rosmarinus, rosmarinus officinalis, Lin. lolium:—Ðeós wyrt, ðe man *rosmarinum* [MS. *rosmarim*], and ōðrum naman boðen, nemneþ, byþ cenned on sandigum landum *this herb, which is called* rosmarinus, *and by another name rosemary, is produced in sandy lands,* Herb. 81, 1; Lchdm. i. 184, 5. Ceów boðenes moran *chew roots of rosemary,* L. M. 3, 4; Lchdm. ii. 310, 17. Ðeós wyrt ys boðene gelīc *this herb is like rosemary,* Herb. 149, 1; Lchdm. i. 274, 6. Boðen *lolium,* Ælfc. Gl. 101; Som. 77, 30; Wrt. Voc. 55, 35.

botl, es; *n. An abode, a dwelling, mansion, house, hall;* domus, ædes, domicilium, atrium:—Gif he him nān botl ne selþ *if he do not give him an abode,* L. In. 67; Th. i. 146, 5. Fordrīfe ðȳ botle *let him be driven from the abode,* 68; Th. i. 146, 8. Wæs Gūþlāce botles neód *Guthlac was in need of a dwelling* [lit. *there was need to Guthlac of a dwelling*], Exon. 37 a; Th. 122, 4; Gū. 300. Pharao eóde in to his botle *Pharao ingressus est domum suam,* Ex. 7, 22. Mīn se ēca dǣl in gefeán fareþ, ðǣr he fægran botles brūceþ *my eternal part* [i. e. *the soul*] *shall go into joy, where it shall enjoy a beautiful mansion,* Exon. 38 a; Th. 125, 14; Gū. 354. To ðæra sacerda ealdres botle *in atrium principis sacerdotum,* Mt. Bos. 26, 3, 58. Cynelīc botl *a kingly dwelling, a palace;* palatium, Ælfc. Gl. 81; Som. 73, 9; Wrt. Voc. 47, 16. DER. ealdor-botl, heáfod-.

bōt-leás; *adj.* [bōt *boot,* leás *less*] BOOTLESS, *unpardonable, what cannot be remedied, recompensed* or *expiated;* inexpiabilis:—Ðonne sīg ðæt bōtleás *then is that unpardonable,* L. C. E. 2; Th. i. 358, 24. Hūsbryce is bōtleás *housebreaking is unpardonable,* L. C. S. 65; Th. i. 410, 6.

botl-gestreón, es; *n.* [gestreón *riches, wealth*] *Household property, goods,* or *treasure;* domesticæ opes:—Chus wæs brytta brōðrum sīnum botlgestreóna *Cush was a dispenser of household treasures to his brothers,* Cd. 79; Th. 97, 32; Gen. 1621. Lameh onfēng æfter fæder dæge botlgestreónum *Lamech succeeded to the household goods after his father's day,* 52; Th. 65, 32; Gen. 1075; 91; Th. 116, 3; Gen. 1930.

botl-weard, -werd, es; *m.* [weard *a keeper, guardian*] *A house-steward;* ædilis:—Hōfweard *vel* byriweard *vel* botlweard *ædilis,* Ælfc. Gl. 8; Som. 56, 105; Wrt. Voc. 18, 54. Botlwerd *ædilis,* Ælfc. Gr. 9, 28; Som. 11, 29.

botl-wēla, an; *m.* [botl *a house,* wēla *weal, wealth*] *House-wealth, a collection of houses, village;* domesticæ opes, vicus:—Ðǣr is botlwēla Bethlem hāten *there is a village called Bethlem,* Cd. 86; Th. 107, 34; Gen. 1799.

BOTM, es; *m. A* BOTTOM; fundus:—Scipes botm *a ship's bottom, the keel;* carina, Ælfc. Gl. 83; Som. 73, 64; Wrt. Voc. 48, 3: 103; Som. 77, 112; Wrt. Voc. 56, 32. Satan on botme [ðære helle] stōd *Satan stood at the bottom* [*of hell*], Cd. 229; Th. 310, 5; Sat. 721: 18; Th. 21, 27; Gen. 330: 19; Th. 23, 18; Gen. 361. Heó to [ðæs fennes] botme com *she came to the bottom* [*of the fen*], Beo. Th. 3017; B. 1506. [*Chauc.* botome: *Wyc.* botme: *O. Sax.* bodom, *m: Frs.* boyem, *c: O. Frs.* boden, *m: Dut.* bódem, *m: Ger. M. H. Ger.* bodem, boden, *m: O. H. Ger.* bodam, *m: Dan.* bund, *c: Swed.* botten, *m: Icel.* botn, *m: Lat.* fundus, *m: Grk.* πυθμήν, *m: Ir.* bonn, *m: Gael.* bonn, buinn, *m: Sansk.* budhna, *m. the bottom,* from the root budh *to fathom a depth, penetrate to the bottom.*] DER. byden-botm, tunne-.

bōt-wyrþe; *adj. Pardonable, expiable, that may be atoned for;* emendabilis:—Æt bōtwyrþum þingum *among pardonable things,* L. C. E. 3; Th. i. 360, 16.

BOX, es; *m? n? The* BOX-*tree;* buxus = πύξος, buxus sempervirens, Lin:—Box *buxus,* Ælfc. Gl. 47; Som. 65, 39; Wrt. Voc. 33, 36: 79, 71. Æt ðam boxe, of ðam boxe *at the box-tree, from the box-tree,* Cod. Dipl. 1102; A. D. 931; Kmbl. v. 195, 14. [*Chauc.* box-tree: *Dut.* bos-boom: *Ger.* buchs, *m: M. H. Ger.* buhs, *m: O. H. Ger.* buhs-boum: *Dan.* bux-bom: *Swed.* bux-bom: *Lat.* buxus: *Grk.* πύξος *the box-tree* or *box-wood.*] DER. bixen.

box, es; *m? n?* [box *the box-tree*] *A wooden case made of box-wood, a* BOX; buxum, pyxis = πυξίς:—Bixen box *a box made of box-wood;* pyxis, Ælfc. Gl. 26; Som. 60, 96; Wrt. Voc. 25, 36. Forcorfen [MS. forcaruen] box *a carved box;* buxum, Ælfc. Gr. 6, 9; Som. 5, 59. Seó hæfde box mid deórwyrþre sealfe *she had a box of precious ointment,* Mt. Bos. 26, 7. Ellenes blōsman gedō on box *put blossoms of elder into a box,* L. M. 2, 59; Lchdm. ii. 288, 3. Hundteontig boxa *a hundred* [*of*] *boxes,* Jn. Bos. 19, 39. [*Chauc. R. Glouc.* box: *Dut.* bus, *f: Ger.* büchse, *f: M. H. Ger.* bühse, *f: O. H. Ger.* buhsa, *f: Lat.* buxum, *n;* pyxis, *f: Grk.* πυξίς, *f. a box.*] DER. sealf-box.

box-treów, es; *n. The* BOX-TREE; buxus = πύξος:—Ðis boxtreów *hæc buxus,* Ælfc. Gr. 6, 9; Som. 5, 59. v. box.

bracan; *p.* brōc, *pl.* brōcon; *pp.* bracen *To break, bruise* or *bray in a mortar, to beat up;* conterere, contundere:—Ðā sceolon beón ele bracene *then shall they be beaten up with oil,* Lev. 6, 21. v. brecan.

braccas; *pl. m. Breeches;* bracæ:—Braccas on swefnum geseón *to see breeches in dreams,* Lchdm. iii. 198, 28. v. brōc; *pl.* brēc, brǣc.

brac-hwīl *a glance while, a moment.* v. bearhtm-hwīl.

bracigean *to dress, mingle* or *counterfeit with brass;* ærare. v. bræsian.

BRÂD; *def.* se brāda, seó, ðæt brāde; *comp. m.* brādra, *f. n.* brādre, brǣdre; *superl.* brādost; *adj.* BROAD, *open, large, spacious, copious;* latus, expansus, amplus, spatiosus, copiosus:—Ðæt eálond on Wiht is twelf mīla brād *the isle of Wight is twelve miles broad,* Bd. 1, 3; S. 475, 19: Ors. 1, 1; Bos. 21, 4, 5, 6. Wæs his rīce brād *his kingdom was broad,* Exon. 65 b; Th. 243, 10; Jul. 8: Elen. Kmbl. 1831; El. 917: Beo. Th. 6296; B. 3158. Brād is bebod ðīn *latum est mandatum tuum,* Ps. Lamb. 118, 96. Se brāda sǣ *the broad sea,* Exon. 24 b; Th. 70, 28; Cri. 1145: Chr. 942; Erl. 116, 11; Edm. 5: Ps. Th. 79, 10. Beówulfe brāde rīce on hand gehwearf *the broad realm passed into the hand of Beowulf,* Beo. Th. 4421; B. 2207. Beorn monig seah on ðās beorhtan burg brādan rīces *many a chief looked on this bright city of a broad realm,* Exon. 124 b; Th. 478, 9; Ruin. 38. Ofer Babilōne brādum streáme we sittaþ *we sit over the broad stream of Babylon,* Ps. Th. 136, 1. On ðam brādan brime *on the broad ocean,* Exon. 55 a; Th. 194, 20; Az. 142. Se hearda þegn lēt brādne mēce brecan ofer bordweal *the fierce thane caused his broad sword to break over the shield,* Beo. Th. 5948; B. 2978. Ðū scealt ðīnum breóstum tredan brāde eorþan *thou shalt tread the broad earth on thy breast,* Cd. 43; Th. 56, 5; Gen. 907: 83; Th. 105, 12; Gen. 1752: Ps. Th. 118, 32: Exon. 22 b; Th. 61, 29; Cri. 992. He him brād syleþ lond *he will give him broad land,* Exon. 88 a; Th. 331, 29; Vy. 75. On brād wæter *on the broad water,* Ps. Th. 105, 8: Salm. Kmbl. 552; Sal. 275. Ðā he healdan mihte brād swurd *when he could hold his broad sword,* Byrht. Th. 132, 12; By. 15: 136, 38; By. 163; Beo. Th. 3096; B. 1546. Brāde synd on worulde grēne geardas *in the world there are broad green regions,* Cd. 25; Th. 32, 29; Gen. 510. Of ðām brād blado sprȳtan ongunnon *thence broad leaves began to spring,* 48; Th. 61, 8; Gen. 994. Engle and Seaxe ofer brāde brimu Brytene sōhton *the Angles and Saxons sought Britain over the broad seas,* Chr. 937; Erl. 115, 20, note; Æðelst. 71: Exon. 13 a; Th. 22, 25; Cri. 357. Sceolde he ða brādan līgas sēcan *he must seek the broad flames,* Cd. 36; Th. 47, 20; Gen. 763. Hit mæg bión syxtig mīla brād, oððe hwene brǣdre; and middeweard þrītig oððe brādre *it may be sixty* [*of*] *miles broad, or a little broader; and midway thirty or broader,* Ors. 1, 1; Bos. 21, 1, 2. Ðeáh hit ǣlce geáre sȳ brādre and brādre *though it is broader and broader every year,* 2, 6; Bos. 50, 22. Ic eom brǣdre ðonne ðes wong grēna *I am broader than this green plain,* Exon. 111 a; Th. 425, 3; Rä. 41, 50: 111 b; Th. 426, 32; Rä. 41, 82. Ðæt bȳne land is easteweard brādost *the inhabited land is broadest eastward,* Ors. 1, 1; Bos. 20, 45. Sume hyne slōgon on his ansȳne mid hyra brādum handum *some smote him on his face with their open hands,* Mt. Bos. 26, 67. Brād *amplus,* Ælfc. Gr. 37; Som. 39, 35. Seó sunne is swā brād swā eall eorþan ymbhwyrft, ac heó þincþ [MS. þingþ] us swȳðe unbrād, forðamðe heó is swīðe feorr fram ūrum gesihþum *the sun is as large as the whole compass of the earth, but he* [lit. *she*] *appears to us very small* [lit. *un-broad*], *because he is very far from our sight,* Bd. de nat. rerum; Wrt. popl. science 3, 8–11; Lchdm. iii. 236, 6–9. Ða steorran, ðe us lyttle þinceaþ [MS. þingeaþ], synd swȳðe brāde *the stars, which seem little to us, are very large,* 3, 16; Lchdm. iii. 236, 14. Se deófol brohte him brāde stānas *the devil brought large stones to him,* Cd. 228; Th. 306, 31; Sat. 672. Byþ se niwa mōna brādra [MS. braddra] gesewen *the new moon appears* [lit. *is seen*] *larger,* Bd. de nat. rerum; Wrt. popl. science 14, 14; Lchdm. iii. 264, 26. Ðǣr is brāde lond in heofonrīce *there is a spacious land in heaven's kingdom,* Cd. 218; Th. 278, 2; Sat. 215. Hī bebūgaþ brādne hwyrft *they shall inhabit the spacious orb,* 190; Th. 236, 16; Dan. 322: Exon. 53 b; Th. 187, 29; Az. 38. Ðū gearwodest beforan me brādne beód *thou preparedst a copious table before me,* Ps. Th. 22, 6. Ge onsceáwiaþ beágas and brād gold *ye will behold bracelets and ample gold,* Beo. Th. 6201; B. 3105. Ic his cynn gedō brâd and bresne *I will make his race large and powerful*, Cd. 134; Th. 169, 17; Gen. 2801. Brâd earmbeáh *a broad or large arm-bracelet;* dextrocherium, Ælfc. Gl. 114; Som. 80, 30; Wrt. Voc. 61, 10. [*Chauc. Wyc.* brod, brood: *R. Glouc.* brod: *Laym.* braed, brad, brod: *Orm.* brad: *Scot.* braid, brade: *Plat.* breed: *O. Sax.* brêd: *Frs.* bred: *O. Frs.* bred, breid: *Dut.* breed: *Ger. M. H. Ger.* breit: *O. H. Ger.* breit: *Goth.* braids: *Dan. Swed.* bred: *Icel.* breiðr: *Lat.* latus for platus: *Grk.* πλατύς: *Lith.* platùs: *Zend* frath-anh *breadth: Sansk.* pṛithu *broad, wide;* pṛith *to extend.*] DER. un-brâd, wîd-.

brâd-æx, e; *f. A broad axe, an axe;* dolatura, dolabrum:—Brâdæx *dolatura*, Cot. 68: *dolabrum*, Ælfc. Gl. 51; Som. 65, 131; Wrt. Voc. 34, 59.

Brâdan ǽ; *indecl. f.* [i. e. latus fluvius, *Hist. Eccl. Petroburg.* Bardanea, *Gib. Chr. explicatio* 15] *Broadwater;* Bradanea:—Þurh ân scýr wæter, Brâdan ǽ hâtte *through a clear water called Broadwater*, Chr. 656; Erl. 31, 17; per unam pulcram aquam, Bradanea nomine, Cod. Dipl. 984; A. D. 664; Kmbl. v. 5, 3.

Brâdan-ford, es; *dat.* -forde, -forda; *m.* [brâd *broad*, ford *a ford*] BRADFORD *in Wilts;* loci nomen vadum amplum *vel* latum significans, hodie *Bradford* in agro Wiltoniensi:—Cênwalh gefeaht æt Brâdanforda be Afne *Kenwealh fought at Bradford near the Avon*, Chr. 652; Erl. 26, 22.

Brâdan-relic, Brâdun-reolic, es; *m:* Brâdan-reíg, -eíg = îg, e; *f.* [eíg, îg *an island, broad island*] *Flat Holme, an island in the mouth of the Severn:*—Sǽton hie ûte on ðam îglande, æt Brâdanrelice *they sat outward on an island, Flat Holme*, Chr. 918; Ing. 132, 19.

brâddra *broader, larger*, Bd. de nat. rerum; Wrt. popl. science 14, 14; Lchdm. iii. 264, 26, = brâdra; *comp. def. m. of* brâd.

brâde; *adv. Broadly, widely;* late:—Fîson brâde bebûgeþ *Pison widely encompasses it*, Cd. 12; Th. 14, 23; Gen. 223: Exon. 13 a; Th. 24, 5; Cri. 380: Ps. Th. 106, 37.

Brâden, Brǽden, es; *m.* [*Flor.* Bradene: so called from its *size*, from brâd, brǽd *broad, open, spacious;* dene, es; *m. vallis, locus silvestris*, v. denu] BREDON *Forest, near Malmesbury, Wiltshire;* silvæ nomen in agro Wiltoniensi:—Hie cômon to Creccagelâde, and fôron ðǽr ofer Temese, and nâmon, ǽgðer ge on Brâdene, ge ðǽr ymbûtan, eall ðæt hie gehentan mehton *they came to Cricklade, and there they went over the Thames, and took, both in Bredon, and thereabout, all that they could carry off*, Chr. 905; Th. 180, 22, col. 1, 2.

brâd-hlâf, es; *m.* [brǽdan *to roast*, hlâf *bread*] *A biscuit, parched* or *baked bread;* paximatium = παξαμάδιον, panis torrefactus:—Brâdhlâf *paximatium*, Wrt. Voc. 288, 66.

brâdiende; *part.* [brâd *broad, spread out*] *Stretching out, extending, reaching;* amplificans, extendens, tendens;—Fram ðam heofone brâdiende niðer ôþ ða eorþan *reaching from the heavens down to the earth*, Ors. 5, 10; Bos. 108, 25. v. brǽdan.

brâd-nes, -ness, -nis, -niss, -nys, -nyss, e; *f.* [brâd *broad, large*, -nes, -nis, -nys *-ness*] BROADNESS, *extent, largeness, surface;* latitudo, amplitudo, facies, superficies:—Se rôdor belýcþ on his bôsme ealle eorþan brâdnysse *the firmament incloses in its bosom all the extent of the earth*, Hexam. 5; Norm. 8, 27. Se wǽta, gyf hit sealt byþ of ðære sǽ, byþ þurh ðære lyfte brâdnysse to ferscum wǽtan awend *the moisture, if it is salt from the sea, is turned into fresh water through the extent of the atmosphere*, Bd. de nat. rerum; Wrt. popl. science 19, 3, 27; Lchdm. iii. 278, 11; 280, 14. Gehêrde me on tobrǽdednesse oððe on brâdnesse Drihten *exaudivit me in latitudine Dominus*, Ps. Lamb. 117, 5. Salomone forgeaf God brâdnysse heortan *God gave Solomon largeness* [or *liberality*] *of heart*, Homl. Th. ii. 576, 29. Þeóstru wǽron ofer ðære niwelnisse brâdnisse *tenebræ erant super faciem abyssi*, Gen. 1, 2. Ðære eorþan brâdnis wæs adrûwod *exsiccata esset superficies terræ*, 8, 13. Byþ ðære eorþan brâdnys betweox us and ðære sunnan *the surface of the earth is between us and the sun*, Bd. de nat. rerum; Wrt. popl. science 5, 8; Lchdm. iii. 240, 14. Sumes þinges brâdnyss *the surface of something;* superficies, Ælfc. Gr. 47; Som. 48, 47. Ân wyll asprang of ðære eorþan, wætriende ealre ðære eorþan brâdnysse *fons ascendebat e terra, irrigans universam superficiem terræ*, Gen. 2, 6.

brâdost *broadest*, Ors. 1, 1; Bos. 20, 45; *superl. of* brâd.

brâdre *broader*, Ors. 2, 6; Bos. 50, 22; *comp. f. n. of* brâd.

brâd-þistel; *gen.* -þistles; *m. A thistle with long leaves, sea-holm, sea-holly;* eryngium = ἠρύγγιον, eryngium maritimum, Lin: — Brâdþistel *eryngion*, Cot. 212.

bræc, ðû brǽce, *pl.* brǽcon *broke, didst break*, Mt. Bos. 14, 19: Exon. 28 a; Th. 85, 20; Cri. 1394: Cd. 32; Th. 43, 5; Gen. 686; *p. of* brecan.

bræc, es; *n.* [bræc; *p. of* brecan *to break*] *A breaking, flowing, rheum, catarrh;* rheuma = ῥεῦμα:—Bræc *rheuma*, Ælfc. Gl. 10; Som. 57, 21; Wrt. Voc. 19, 27. DER. ge-bræc, fýr-ge-, hrǽc-ge-, neb-ge-.

brǽc *breeches;* braccæ, Som. femoralia, Wrt. Voc. 81, 63, = brêc; *pl. of* brôc, *f.*

bræc-côðu, e; *f.* [bræc *a breaking*, côðu *a disease*] *The breaking* or *falling disease, epilepsy;* epilepsia = ἐπιληψία: — Bræc-côðu, fylle-seóc *epilepsia* vel *caduca* vel *larvatio* vel *commitialis*, Ælfc. Gl. 10; Som. 57, 20; Wrt. Voc. 19, 26.

brǽce; *adj. Breaking;* violans. DER. ǽw-brǽce, un-. v. brecan.

bræc-seóc; *adj.* [bræc, seóc *sick, diseased*] *Troubled with the falling sickness, epileptic, frantic, lunatic;* epilepticus, phreneticus, lunaticus:—Sum bræcseóc man becom ðyder *phreneticus devenit ibi*, Bd. 4, 3; Whelc. 267, 45, MSS. B. C. DER. ge-bræcseóc.

bræc-seócnes, -ness, e; *f. Epilepsy;* epilepsia. DER. bræc-seóc *epileptic, frantic;* -nes *-ness.*

bræd, bred, es; *m.* [= brægd, bregd from bregdan *to braid, weave, twist*] *Fraud, deceit;* fraus, dolus:—He hit dyde bûtan brede [bræde MS. B.] and bigswîce *he did it without fraud and guile*, L. Ed. 1; Th. i. 160, 6. Ic spæce drîfe bûtan bræde and bûtan bîswîce *I prosecute my suit without fraud and without guile*, L. O. 2; Th. i. 178, 13. Bred *fucus, fraus, astus*, Cot. 10.

bræd *plucked, drew out*, Byrht. Th. 136, 20; By. 154; *p. of* bredan.

brǽd, e; *f:* brǽdo, brǽdu; *indecl. f.* [brâd *broad;* latus] BREADTH, *width, latitude;* latitudo, amplitudo:—Biþ se arc fîftig fæðma on brǽde *the ark shall be fifty fathoms in breadth;* quinquaginta cubitorum erit latitudo arcæ, Gen. 6, 15. On brǽdo his stealles *latitudine sui status*, Bd. 1, 1; S. 474, 29. Ic on brǽdu [brǽde, Spl.] gange *ambulabam in latitudine*, Ps. Th. 118, 45. Drihten me gehýrde on heáre [= heáhre, MS. hearr] brǽdu *exaudivit me in latitudine Dominus*, 117, 5. Hî habbaþ ingang swâ mycelre brǽdo swâ mon mæg mid liðeran geworpan *habet ingressum amplitudinis quasi jactus fundæ*, Bd. 4, 13; S. 583, 11. [*Chauc.* brede: *Wyc.* breede: *O. Frs.* brede, *f: Dut.* breedte, *f: Ger. M. H. Ger.* breite, *f: O. H. Ger.* breiti, *f: Goth.* braidei, *f: Dan.* brede, *c: Swed.* bredd, *f: Icel.* breidd, *f. breadth.*] DER. hand-brǽd.

brǽd *broad;* latus, Beo. Th. 4421, note. v. brâd.

brǽdan, brêdan; to brǽdanne, brêdanne; *part.* brǽdende; he brǽdeþ, brǽd; *p.* brǽdde, *pl.* brǽddon; *pp.* brǽded, brǽdd, brǽd [brâd *broad;* latus]. I. *v. trans. To make broad*, BROADEN, *extend, spread, stretch out;* dilatare, propalare, expandere:—Hî heora stôwe brǽddon *they broadened their places*, Bd. 1, 8; S. 479, 24. He gesihþ brimfuglas brǽdan feðra *he sees sea-fowls spread their wings*, Exon. 77 a; Th. 289, 13; Wand. 47. Ge wilniaþ eówerne hlîsan to brêdanne *ye wish to spread your fame*, Bt. 18, 1; Rawl. 38, 33, MS. Cot. Se wallenda lêg hine brǽdde to ðam biscope *the raging flame spread itself to the bishop*, Bd. 2, 7; S. 509, 22. Brǽddon æfter beorgum flotan feldhûsum *the sailors spread* [*themselves*] *amongst the hills with their tents*, Cd. 148; Th. 186, 1; Exod. 132. Ðæt hî his naman brǽden [MS. brǽdan] *that they spread his name*, Bt. 30, 1; Fox 108, 11. Se cyning his handa wæs uppweardes brǽdende wið ðæs heofones *the king stretched* [lit. *was stretching*] *out his hands upwards towards heaven*, Ors. 4, 5; Bos. 81, 36. II. *v. intrans. To be extended* or *developed, grow* or *rise up;* dilatari, adolescere:—Leáf and gærs brǽd geond Bretene *leaves and grass are extended* [lit. *leaf and grass is extended*] *over Britain*, Bt. Met. Fox 20, 197; Met. 20, 99. Treó sceolon brǽdan *trees shall rise up*, Exon. 91 b; Th. 343, 20; Gn. Ex. 160. [*Laym.* breden: *Scot.* brade: *Plat.* breden, bredden: *O. Sax.* brêdian, brêdôn: *Kil.* breeden: *Ger. M. H. Ger.* breiten: *O. H. Ger.* breitan: *Goth.* braidyan: *Dan.* brede: *Swed.* breda: *Icel.* breiða *to broaden.*] DER. ge-brǽdan, geond-, ofer-, to-.

BRǼDAN, brêdan, to brǽdenne; *part.* brǽdende; *p.* brǽdde; *pp.* brǽded, brǽdd; *v. a. To roast, broil, warm;* assare, fovere:—We magon brǽdan ða þing [þingc MS.] ðe to brǽdenne synd *nos possumus assare quæ assanda sunt*, Coll. Monast. Th. 29, 21. Brêdan, weormian *fovere*, Cot. 86. Brǽdende *assans*, Cot. 195. [*Laym.* breden: *Scot.* brade: *Plat.* braden, braën: *Frs.* briede: *O. Frs.* breda: *Dut.* braden: *Ger.* braten: *M. H. Ger.* brâten: *O. H. Ger.* brâtan *assare.*] DER. ge-brǽdan.

brǽde, es; *m.* [brǽdan *to roast*] *Roasted meat;* assatura:—Brǽde *assura* vel *assatura*, Ælfc. Gl. 31; Som. 61, 85; Wrt. Voc. 27, 15. [*Dut.* ge-braad, *n: Ger.* brate, *m. caro assa: M. H. Ger.* brâte, *m: O. H. Ger.* brâto, *m. assatura.*]

brǽde, an; *f. The breadth;* latum. v. lenden-brǽde.

brǽded-nes, -ness, e; *f.* [brǽded; *pp. of* brǽdan *to broaden*, -nes *-ness*] *Broadness, breadth, width, latitude;* amplitudo, latitudo. DER. to-brǽdednes. v. brâdnes.

brǽdels, es; *m?* [brǽdan *to spread* or *stretch out*] *Anything spread* or *stretched out, a carpet, covering, garment, dress;* palla, stragulum, velamentum, opertorium:—Brǽdels *stragulum*, R. 4, Lye. DER. ofer-brǽdels.

Brǽden *Bredon Forest:*—On Brǽdene ge ðǽr onbûtan *in Bredon and thereabout*, Chr. 905; Th. 180, 23, col. 1, 2. v. Brâden.

brǽding, e; *f.* [brǽdan *to spread, extend*] *A spreading;* ampliatio:—Mæg hine scamian ðære brǽdinge his hlîsan *he may be ashamed of the spreading of his fame*, Bt. 19; Fox 68, 24.

brǽding-panne, an; *f.* [brǽdan *to roast, broil*, panne *a pan*] *A frying-pan;* sartago, Cot. 173. v. brǽd-panne.

bræd-îsen, bred-îsern, es; *n.* [bræd, *p. of* bredan; îsen, îsern *iron*] *A scraping* or *graving tool, file;* scalprum, scalpellum:—Brædîsen *scal-*

þrum, scalpellum, Cot. 173. Bredísern *scalpellum,* Glos. Epnl. Recd. 162, 28.

brǽd-nys, -nyss, e; *f. Broadness; latitudo.* DER. to-brǽdnys. v. brádnes.

brǽdo *breadth, width,* Bd. 1, 1; S. 474, 29: 4, 13; S. 583, 11. v. brǽd.

brǽd-panne, an; *f.* [brǽdan *to roast,* panne *a pan*] *A frying-pan;* sartago, frixorium, Cot. 115. v. brǽding-panne.

brǽdre *broader,* Ors. 1, 1; Bos. 21, 2, = brádre; *comp. f. n. of* brád.

brǽdu *breadth, width,* Ps. Th. 117, 5: 118, 45. v. brǽd.

brægd, bregd, es; *m.* [brægd, *p. of* bregdan *to twist, braid, weave*] *Deceit, fraud;* dolus, fraus. DER. ge-brægd, -bregd, nearo-. v. bræd.

brægd *bent,* Beo. Th. 1593; B. 794; *p. of* bregdan.

brægdan *to modulate;* modulari:—Hí geherаþ hleóðrum brægdan óðre fugelas *they hear other birds modulate their songs,* Bt. Met. Fox 13, 94; Met. 13, 47.

brægd-boga, an; *m.* [brægd, *p. of* bregdan *to draw, bend,* brægd *deceit;* boga *a bow*] *A drawn* or *bent bow, a deceitful* or *fraudulent bow;* arcus incurvatus *vel* fraudulentus:—He in folc Godes forþ onsendeþ of his brægdbogan biterne strǽl *he* [*the devil*] *sendeth forth, amongst God's people, the bitter arrow from his deceitful bow,* Exon. 19 a; Th. 48, 1; Cri. 765.

brægden; *adj.* [= bregden; *pp. of* bregdan] *Deceitful, cunning, crafty;* dolosus:—Sendon [sendan MS.] hí Marium, ðone consul, ongeán Geoweorþan, á swá lytigne, and á swá brægdenne, swá he wæs *they sent Marius, the consul, against Jugurtha, as he was always so cunning, and always so crafty,* Ors. 5, 7; Bos. 106, 29.

brægd-wís; *adj.* [brægd *deceit,* wís *wise*] *Wise in deceit, crafty, fraudulent;* astutus, fraudulentus, dolosus:—Brægdwís bona *a crafty murderer,* Exon. 33 b; Th. 107, 13; Gú. 58.

BRÆGEN, brægn, bragen, es; *n. The* BRAIN; cerebrum, cerebellum:—Wið tobrocenum heáfde, and gif ðæt brægen útsíge, genim æges ðæt geoluwe *for a broken head, and if the brain appears, take the yolk of an egg,* L. M. 1, 1; Lchdm. ii. 22, 19. Brægen *cerebrum* vel *cerebellum,* Ælfc. Gl. 69; Som. 70, 38; Wrt. Voc. 42, 46. Brægn *cerebrum,* Wrt. Voc. 64, 25. Bragen *cerebrum,* 70, 25. Brægenes ádl *the disease of the brain,* L. M. 2, 27; Lchdm. ii. 222, 3. On his brægn astíge his unriht *in verticem ipsius iniquitas ejus descendet,* Ps. Th. 7, 16. [*Chauc.* brain: *R. Glouc.* brayn: *Laym.* brain, braȝen: *Plat.* brägen: *O. Frs.* brein, brin, *n: Dut.* brein, *n. cerebrum.*]

Brægent-ford *Brentford in Middlesex,* Chr. 1016; Th. 280, 26, col. 2: 1016; Th. 282, 5, col. 2. v. Brent-ford.

bræhtm *a glimpse, glittering, twinkling,* Bd. 2, 13; Whelc. 142, 23, MS. B. v. bearhtm.

brǽmbel *a bramble,* Herb. 89, 1; Lchdm. i. 192, note 6. v. brémel.

brǽmbel-brǽr, es; *m.* [brǽmbel *a bramble,* brǽr, brér *a brier*] *A bramble-brier;* tribulus, Wrt. Voc. 285, 64. v. brémel.

brǽmbel-leáf, es; *n.* [brǽmbel *a bramble,* leáf *a leaf*] *The leaf of a bramble;* rubi folium:—Nim brǽmbel-leáf *take bramble-leaves,* Lchdm. iii. 40, 26. v. brémel.

brǽmel *a bramble.* DER. brǽmel-berie. v. brémel.

brǽmel-berie, an; *f.* [brǽmel = brémel *a bramble,* berie *a berry*] *A bramble-berry;* rubi bacca:—Drince seóca of brǽmelberian gewrungene *let the sick man drink of wrung bramble-berries,* Lchdm. iii. 8, 17.

brǽr *a brier;* tribulus. DER. brǽmbel-brǽr. v. brér.

BRÆS, es; *n.* BRASS; æs:—Bræs oððe ár *æs,* Ælfc. Gr. 5; Som. 4, 59. [*O. Nrs.* bras, *n. ferumen, soldering of iron,* Rask Hald.] v. ár.

bræsen, bresen; *def.* se bræsna, seó, ðæt bræsne, bresne; *adj.* I. BRAZEN, *made of brass;* æreus, æneus:—Bræsen oððe ǽren *æneus,* Ælfc. Gr. 5; Som. 4, 59. Ðú gesettest swá swá bogan bræsenne earmas míne *posuisti ut arcum æreum brachia mea,* Ps. Lamb. 17, 35. II. *strong, powerful, bold, daring;* validus, fortis, potens, procax:—Gebeád ðá se bræsna Babilóne weard *then the bold lord of Babylon proclaimed,* Cd. 196; Th. 244, 16; Dan. 449.

bræsian, brasian, ic bræsige, ðú bræsast, he bræsaþ, *pl.* bræsiaþ; *p.* ode; *pp.* od *To cover* or *furnish with brass, to make of brass;* ærare:—Ic bræsige [MSS. C. D. brasige] *æro,* Ælfc. Gr. 36; Som. 38, 39.

bræsna *strong, bold,* Cd. 196; Th. 244, 16; Dan. 449. v. bræsen.

BRǼÞ, bréþ, es; *m. An odour, a scent, smell good* or *bad, a savour,* BREATH; odor, odoramen:—God underféng ðære wynsumnysse brǽþ *odoratus est Dominus odorem suavitatis,* Gen. 8, 21. Ongan se cealc mid ungemete stincan, ðá wearþ Iuuinianus mid ðam brǽþe ofsmorod *the plaster* [lit. *chalk*] *began to smell excessively, and Jovian was smothered with the smell,* Ors. 6, 32; Bos. 129, 12. Bréþ *odor,* Ælfc. Gl. 70; Wrt. Voc. 42, 58. [*Chauc. Piers P.* breeþ: *Ger.* bradem, *m: M. H. Ger.* bradem, *m: O. H. Ger.* bradam, *m.*] v. ǽðm.

BRǼW, breáw, breág, brég, brégh, bréhg, es; *m. An eye-lid;* palpebra:—Wið þiccum brǽwum *for thick eye-lids,* L. M. 1, 2; Lchdm. ii. 38, 9. Ðæt biþ swíðe gód sealf ðam men ðe hæfþ þicce brǽwas *that will be a very good salve for a man who has thick eye-lids,* 1, 2; Lchdm. ii. 38, 22, 12. Unwlítig swile and atelíc his eágan brégh [brég MS. C.] wyrde and wemde *an unsightly and fearful swelling harmed and corrupted his eye-lid,* Bd. 4, 32; S. 611, 18. Ðá he ðá ðam feaxe onféng ðæs hálgan heáfdes, he togesette ðam untruman bréhge *cum accepisset capillos sancti capitis, adposuit palpebræ languenti,* 4, 32; S. 611, 40. Ðá gehrán he his eágan, gemétte he hit swá hál mid ðý brǽwe *contingens oculum, sanum cum palpebra invenit,* 4, 32; S. 612, 7. Brǽwas [brégas, Surt.] his axiaþ oððe befrinaþ bearn manna *palpebræ ejus interrogant filios hominum,* Ps. Lamb. 10, 5; the eȝelidis of hym asken the sones of men, Wyc. Brǽwas *palpebræ,* Wrt. Voc. 70, 41: 282, 50. Breáwas *palpebræ,* Ælfc. Gl. 70; Som. 70, 63; Wrt. Voc. 42, 71. Gif ic selle swefnu oððe slǽp eágum mínum, and breáwum [brǽwum, Spl: brégum, Surt.] mínum hnappunga *si dedero somnum oculis meis, et palpebris meis dormitationem,* Ps. Lamb. 131, 4; I shal not ȝiue slep to myn eȝen, and to my eȝe lidis napping, Wyc. Ic eom wíde calu, ne ic breága ne brúna brúcan móste *I am very bald, nor can I make use of eye-lids nor eye-lashes,* Exon. 111 b; Th. 427, 32; Rä. 41, 100. Betwux oferbrúan and brǽwum *intercilium* [= *intercilia*], Ælfc. Gl. 70; Som. 70, 70; Wrt. Voc. 43, 4. [*O. Sax.* bráha, bráwa, *f: O. Frs.* ag-bre, *n. an eye-lid: M. H. Ger.* brá, *f: O. H. Ger.* brá, *n: Icel.* brá, *f. an eye-lid: Lat.* frons, *f. the forehead, brow: Grk.* ὀφρύς, *f. the eye-brow: Sansk.* bhrū, *f. an eye-brow, the brow.*] DER. ofer-brǽw. v. brú.

bragen *the brain,* Wrt. Voc. 70, 25. v. brægen.

BRAND, brond, es; *m.* I. *a* BRAND, *fire-brand, torch;* titio, torris:—Brand *titio* vel *torris,* Ælfc. Gl. 30; Som. 61, 76; Wrt. Voc. 27, 6. Brand *titio,* Wrt. Voc. 82, 55: Glos. Epnl. Recd. 163, 42. Bǽron brandas on bryne blácan fýres *they bare fire-brands into the burning of the bright flame,* Cd. 186; Th. 231, 12; Dan. 246. Se ád wæs ǽghwonan ymb-boren mid brondum *the funeral pile was heaped around on every side with fire-brands,* Exon. 74 a; Th. 277, 15; Jul. 581. II. *a burning, flame, fire;* incendium, flamma, ignis:—Brond þeceþ hús *the burning covers the house,* Exon. 59 a; Th. 212, 27; Ph. 216. Hæfde landwara líge befangen, bǽle and bronde *he had enveloped the land-inhabitants in flame, with fire and burning,* Beo. Th. 4633; B. 2322. Reóteþ meówle, seó hyre bearn gesihþ brondas þeccan *the woman weeps, who sees the flames covering her child,* Exon. 87 b; Th. 330, 7; Vy. 47. Ða beágas sceal brond fretan *fire shall consume the rings,* Beo. Th. 6021; B. 3014: Exon. 19 b; Th. 51, 7; Cri. 812. He his sylfes ðǽr bán gebringeþ, ða ǽr brondes wylm on beorhstede forþylmde *it* [*the Phœnix*] *brings its own bones there, which the fire's rage had before encompassed on the mound,* Exon. 60 a; Th. 217, 21; Ph. 283. Ða fýnd þoliaþ helle to-middes brand and bráde lígas *the fiends suffer fire and broad flames in the midst of hell,* Cd. 18; Th. 21, 16; Gen. 325. Hý hine ne móston bronde forbærnan *they could not consume him with fire,* Beo. Th. 4258; B. 2126. Brondas lácaþ on ðam deópan dæge *fires shall flare on that awful day,* Exon. 116 b; Th. 448, 23; Dóm. 58. Bronda *of fires,* Beo. Th. 6302; B. 3161: Exon. 116 a; Th. 445, 25; Dóm. 13. Bronda beorhtost *brightest of fires* or *lights, the sun,* 93 b; Th. 350, 17; Sch. 65. III. metaphorically from its shining, *A sword* [hence the *Eng. to* BRANDISH]; ensis:—Ic gean Eádmunde mínum [minon MS.] bréðer ánes brandes *I give to Edmund my brother one sword,* Th. Diplm. 559, 24. Ðæt hine nó brond ne beadomécas bítan ne meahton *that no sword nor battle-falchions might bite it,* Beo. Th. 2912; B. 1454. [*Chauc.* bronde *a torch: Laym.* brond, brand *a sword: Plat.* brand, *m: Frs.* brân, *c. gladius: O. Frs.* brond, brand, *m. a fire-brand: Dut.* brand, *m. a burning, fire: Ger.* brand, *m. titio, torris, ensis: M. H. Ger.* brant, *m: O. H. Ger.* brant, *m. titio, torris: Dan.* brand, *m. f: Swed.* brand, *m. a fire-brand, fire: Icel.* brandr, *m.* I. *a brand, fire-brand;* II. *the blade of a sword.*]

brand? Beo. Th. 2045, note; B. 1020, note; *an error of the copyist for* bearn *a son.*

brand-hát, brond-hát; *def.* se -háta, seó, ðæt -háte; *adj.* [brand II. *a burning,* hát *hot*] *Burning hot, very hot, ardent, passionate;* ardentissimus, vehemens, fervidus:—Brandháta níþ weóll on gewitte *ardent malice boiled in their mind,* Andr. Kmbl. 1536; An. 769. Born in breóstum brondhát lufu *ardent love burned in his breast,* Exon. 46 b; Th. 160, 2; Gú. 937.

brand-hord *ardent treasure;* ardens thesaurus. v. brond-hord.

brand-ísen, es; *n.* [brand II. *a burning,* ísen *iron*] *A* BRANDING-IRON, *a tripod;* andena, tripes:—Brandísen *andena* vel *tripes,* Ælfc. Gl. 30; Som. 61, 77; Wrt. Voc. 27, 7: 82, 54. [*Dut.* brandijzer, *n: O. Dut.* brandijser *fulcrum focarium,* Kil: *Ger.* brandeisen, *n. cauterium.*] v. Du Cange, vol. i. col. 187, Andena.

brand-rád, e; *f.* [ród I. *a rod*] *A branding-rod;* andena, Glos. Epnl. Recd. 153, 4. [*O. Frs.* brondrad: *O. Dut.* brandroede.]

brand-stæfn *the shining prowed.* v. brond-stæfn.

brang, brong, *pl.* brungon *brought; p. of* bringan.

brant, bront; *adj. High, deep, steep, difficult;* altus, arduus:—Ðæt ðú us gebrohte brante ceóle, heá hornscipe, ofer hwæles éðel, on ðære mǽgþe *that thou wouldst bring us with the steep keel, the high pinnacled ship, over the whale's home, to that tribe,* Andr. Kmbl. 545–549; An. 273–275. Ðe brontne ceól ofer lagustrǽte lǽdan cwómon *who came leading* *a high keel over the water-street*, Beo. Th. 482; B. 238. Ymb brontne ford *about the deep ford*, 1140; B. 568. Lēton ofer fīfelwǣg scrīđan brōnte brimþīsan *they let the high ships go over the ocean-wave*, Elen. Kmbl. 475; El. 238. [*Wrt. Provncl.* brant *steep*: *Dan.* brat *steep*: *Swed.* brant *precipitous*: *Icel.* brattr *steep.*]

bran-wyrt, e; *f. A bilberry shrub*; vaccinium:—Branwyrt *vaccinium*, Ælfc. Gl. 39; Som. 63, 73; Wrt. Voc. 30, 25. v. brūn-wyrt II.

brasian, brasigan, ic brasige *I cover with brass*; æro, Ælfc. Gr. 36; Som. 38, 39, Bodleian copy, C. D. v. bræsian.

brassica, an; *m. Colewort, cabbage*; brassica, æ, *f*:—Wyrta sindon betste bēte and mealwe and brassica *beet and mallow and cabbage are the best herbs*, L. M. 2, 30; Lchdm. ii. 228, 1.

BRASTL, es; *m. A noise, brustle, rustle, creak, crackle, burning?* crepitus, strepitus, fractio, arsio? Som. [*Ger.* brassel, prassel, geprassel, *n. a crackling noise.*] v. brastlung.

brastlian, brastligan, to brastlienne, brastligenne; *part.* brastliende, brastligende; he brastlaþ; *p.* ode; *pp.* od [berstan *rumpi, frangi*] *To* BRUSTLE, *rustle, crackle, make a noise, murmur*; crepare, crepitare, strepere, murmurare:—Begann to brastligenne þunor *thunder began to crackle*, Homl. Th. ii. 196, 23. Đæt treów brastliende sāh to đam hālgan were *the tree fell crackling towards the holy man*, ii. 508, 33. Brastligende mid brandum *crackling with fire-brands*, ii. 140, 16. Ge begeáton þeósterfulle wununga afyllede mid brastligendum līgum *ye have obtained dark dwellings filled with crackling flames*, i. 68, 5. Se þuner oft egeslīce brastlaþ *thunder often crackles fearfully*, Bd. de nat. rerum; Lchdm. iii. 280, 13. [*Laym.* brastlien: *Ger. M. H. Ger.* brasteln: *Swed.* prassla *to crackle.*]

brastlung, e; *f. A* BRUSTLING, *rustling, creaking, breaking, crashing*; strepitus, crepitus, fractio:—Hīg tobrǣcon đa būcas mid micelre brastlunge *they broke the pitchers with great crashing*, Jud. 7, 20. Brastlung treówa *rustling of trees*, Ælfc. Gr. 1; Som. 2, 35: Greg. Dial. 1, 2.

bratt *A cloak*; pallium:—Forlēt hrægl' ođđe bratt *remitte pallium*, Mt. Kmbl. Lind. 5, 40. [*Prov. Eng.* brat *a child's pinafore*: *Chauc.* bratt *a coarse mantle, rag*: *Wel.* brat *a rag*: *Gael.* brat *a mantle, apron, cloth.*]

breác *enjoyed*, Exon. 77 a; Th. 289, 7; Wand. 44; *p. of* brūcan.

BREÁD, breód, es; *n. A bit, fragment, morsel*, BREAD; buccella, panis:—Æfter đæt breád *post buccellam*, Jn. Lind. War. 13, 27, 30. Hī ge-ēton đæt breád *manducaverunt panem*, 6, 23. [*Chauc.* brede: *Wyc.* breed, brede: *Piers P.* breed: *R. Brun. R. Glouc.* brede: *Laym.* bred: *Orm.* bræd: *Plat.* brood, *n*: *O. Sax.* brōd, *n*: *Frs.* braed, *n*: *O. Frs.* brad, *n*: *Dut. O. Dut.* brood. *n*: *Ger.* brot, *n*: *M. H. Ger.* brōt, *n*: *O. H. Ger.* brōt, *n*: *Dan. Swed.* bröd, *n*: *Icel.* brauð, *n.* Breád is first used in a compound word in Anglo-Saxon, v. beó-breád. It was first used as a separate word in the Lindisfarne Gospels, about A. D. 946-968, and breód in the Rushworth, John 13, 27, A. D. 901-1000. Breád and breód there signify *a morsel.* In John 6, 23, Lindisfarne and Rushworth, it signifies *bread*, panis.] DER. beó-breád.

breág *an eye-lid*:—Breága *palpebrarum*, Exon. 111 b; Th. 427, 32; Rä. 41, 100. v. brǣw.

breahtm, brehtm, bearhtm, beorhtm, byrhtm, es; *m. A noise, tumult, sound, cry*; fragor, strepitus, tumultus, clamor, vociferatio:—Đā wearþ breahtm hæfen *then a noise was raised*, Exon. 36 a; Th. 118, 1; Gū. 233. Breahtem stīgeþ *a tumult rises*, 83 b; Th. 314, 25, note; Mōd. 19. Breahtmum hwurfon ymb đæt hāte hūs hǣþne leóde *the heathen people surrounded that hot house with cries*, 55 a; Th. 195, 25; Az. 161: 57 b; Th. 206, 29; Ph. 134. [*O. Sax.* brahtum, braht, *m*: *M. H. Ger. O. H. Ger.* braht, *m*: *Dan.* brag, *n*: *Swed. Icel.* brak, *n.*] DER. brecan *to break.*

breahtm *a shining, moment, glance, an atom*; scintillatio, atomus:—Breahtm *atomus*, Cot. 36: 100. v. bearhtm *brightness.*

breahtum-hwæt; *adj. Swift as the twinkling of an eye*; celer ut oculi nictus:—Đec līgetta hergen, blāce, breahtum-hwate *may the lightnings praise thee, pale, swift as the twinkling of an eye*, Exon. 54 b; Th. 192, 16; Az. 107. v. berhtm-hwæt.

breard, es; *m. A brim, margin, rim, the highest part of anything*:—To brearde heofnes *ad summum cœli*, Mk. Lind. War. 13, 27. v. brerd.

breát *destroyed*, Beo. Th. 3430; B. 1713; *p. of* breótan.

breátan, ic breáte, đū breátest, brȳtst, he breáteþ, brȳt, *pl.* breátaþ; *p.* breót, *pl.* breóton; *pp.* breáten *To break, demolish, destroy, kill*; frangere, conterere, necare:—Hī hālge cwelmdon, breóton [breotun MS.] bōccræftige [bōccræftge MS.] bærndon gecorene *they slew the holy, destroyed the book-learned, burned the chosen*, Exon. 66 a; Th. 243, 25; Jul. 16. DER. a-breátan. v. breótan.

breáw, *pl.* bruwon *brewed*; *p. of* breówan.

breáw *an eye-lid*, Ælfc. Gl. 70; Som. 70, 63; Wrt. Voc. 42, 71: Ps. Lamb. 131, 4. v. brǣw.

breáw-ern, es; *n. A brewing-place, brew-house*; coquina cerevisiæ, Grm. ii. 338, 3:—Breáwern *aporleriterium*, forte *apolyterium*, Ælfc. Gl. 55; Som. 67, 17.

brec, es; *n. A breaking, crash, noise*; fractio, fragor, strepitus. DER. ge-brec, bān-ge-, cumbol-ge-. v. brecan.

brēc *the breech, breeches*, L. M. 1, 71; Lchdm. ii. 146, 3: R. Ben. 55; *acc. s. and nom. pl. of* brōc, *f.*

breca, an; *m. A breaker*; violator. DER. ǣw-breca, wiđer-. v. brecan.

BRECAN; ic brece, đū bricest, bricst, he briceþ, bricþ, *pl.* brecaþ; *p.* ic, he bræc, đū brǣce, *pl.* brǣcon; *pp.* brocen. I. *v. trans.* 1. *to* BREAK, *burst, violate, break or burst through*; frangere, confringere, rumpere, perfringere, perrumpere:—Lēt se hearda Higelāces þegn brādne mēce brecan ofer bordweal *the fierce thane of Higelac caused his broad sword to break over the shield*, Beo. Th. 5952; B. 2980: Exon. 102 b; Th. 387, 10; Rä. 5, 3: Andr. Kmbl. 1007; An. 504: Salm. Kmbl. 202; Sal. 100. Hit þurh hrōf wadeþ, briceþ boldgetimbru *it goeth through the roof, breaketh the timbers of the house*, 825; Sal. 412: Exon. 125 a; Th. 482, 8; Rä. 66, 4. Se Hǣlend bræc đa hlāfas *Iesus fregit panes*, Mt. Bos. 14, 19: 15, 36: Beo. Th. 3027; B. 1511: 3138; B. 1567. Ne brǣcon hī nā his sceancan *non fregerunt ejus crura*, Jn. Bos. 19, 33. Swā swā fæt tigelen đū bricst hī *tanquam vas figuli confringes eos*, Ps. Spl. 2, 9. Seó wiht, gif hió gedȳgeþ, dūna briceþ *the creature, if it escape, will burst the hills*, Exon. 109 b; Th. 420, 6; Rä. 39, 6. Him egsa becom đā dēma duru in helle bræc *dread came over them when the judge burst the doors in hell*, Cd. 221; Th. 288, 15; Sat. 381. Gif hie brecaþ his gebodscipe, he him abolgen wurþeþ *if they break* [*violate*] *his commandment, he will be incensed against them*, 22; Th. 28, 3; Gen. 430. Đū mīn bibod brǣce *thou didst break my commandment*, Exon. 28 a; Th. 85, 20; Cri. 1394. Bræc se here đone friþ *the army broke* [*violated*] *the peace*, Chr. 911; Erl. 100, 16: 921; Erl. 106, 6. Heó Alwaldan bræc willan *she broke* [*violated*] *the Almighty's will*, Cd. 29; Th. 37, 34; Gen. 599. Yldran usse in oferhygdum đīn bibodu brǣcon *our forefathers in pride broke thy commandments*, Exon. 53 a; Th. 186, 13; Az. 19: Cd. 188; Th. 234, 28; Dan. 299. Gif hwā his āþ brece, bēte swā dōmbōc tǣce *if any one break his oath, let him make amends as the doom-book may teach*, L. Ed. 8; Th. i. 164, 2. Đæt ǣnig mon wǣre ne brǣce *that any man should not break the compact*, Beo. Th. 2205; B. 1100. Bióþ brocene āþsweord eorla *the oaths of the warriors will be broken*, 4132; B. 2063. He lǣteþ inwitflān brecan đone burgweal *he lets the shafts of treachery break through the town-wall*, Exon. 83 b; Th. 315, 28; Mōd. 38. Ic hwīlum ēđelfæsten brece *sometimes I break through a land-fastness*, Exon. 126 b; Th. 487, 4; Rä. 72, 23. Se storm and seó stronge lyft brecaþ brāde gesceaft *the storm and the strong blast shall break through the broad creation*, Exon. 22 b; Th. 61, 29; Cri. 992. Eádweard bræc đone bordweall *Edward broke through the wall of shields*, Byrht. Th. 139, 60; By. 277. Brǣcon bordhreóđan [*they*] *broke through the wall of shields*, Elen. Kmbl. 243; El. 122. Leóht lyftedoras bræc *the light burst through the aerial dwellings*, Cd. 155; Th. 193, 24; Exod. 251. 2. *to press, force, urge*; urgere:—Lufian hine fyrwet bræc Iulianan *desire urged him to love Juliana*, Exon. 66 a; Th. 244, 14; Jul. 27: Salm. Kmbl. 493; Sal. 247: Beo. Th. 470; B. 232: 5562; B. 2784. 3. *to rush into* a place, *take* a place *by storm*; in locum irrumpere, expugnare:—Siđđan he for wlence beorgas brǣce *since he for pride rushed into the mountains*, Exon. 35 b; Th. 114, 29; Gū. 180. Cwom [MS. cuom] feorþe healf hund scipa on Temese mūþan, and brǣcon Contwara burg and Lundenburg *three hundred and fifty ships came to the mouth of the Thames, and took Canterbury and London by storm*, Chr. 851; Erl. 66, 34. II. *v. intrans.* 1. *to break* or *burst forth, make a noise* or *crash*; erumpere, prorumpere, crepare, fremere:—Geseah streám brecan of beorge [*he*] *saw a stream burst forth from the mount*, Beo. Th. 5085; B. 2546. Wæter wynsumu of đære moldan tyrf brecaþ *pleasant waters burst forth from the turf of the earth*, Exon. 56 b; Th. 202, 9; Ph. 67. Swōgaþ windas, blāwaþ brecende, bearhtma mǣste *winds shall howl, crashing blow, with greatest of sounds*, Exon. 21 b; Th. 59, 11; Cri. 951. 2. *to sail*; navigare:—Scealtū ceól gestīgan, and brecan ofer bæþweg *thou shalt ascend a ship, and sail over the sea* [lit. *bath-way*], Andr. Kmbl. 445; An. 223: Elen. Kmbl. 487; El. 244. We brecaþ ofer bæþweg brimhengestum *we sail over the sea in ships* [lit. *sea-horses*], Andr. Kmbl. 1025; An. 513. III. *v. reflex. To retch*; screare:—Gebræd he hine seócne, and ongan hine brecan to spīwenne *he feigned himself sick, and began retching to spew*, Chr. 1003; Erl. 139, 9. [*Wyc.* breke, breek: *Piers* breken: *R. Glouc.* breke: *Laym.* breken: *Orm.* brekenn: *Plat.* broeken, breken: *O. Sax.* brekan: *Frs.* brekke: *O. Frs.* breka: *Dut.* breken: *Ger.* brechen: *M. H. Ger.* brëchen: *O. H. Ger.* brechan: *Goth.* brikan: *Dan.* bräkke: *Swed.* bråka, bräcka: *Icel.* braka *to creak.*] DER. a-brecan, be-, for-, ge-, ofer-, on-, to-, þurh-, upa-: brec, -mǣlum, -ung; ǣ-, ge-, bān-ge-, cumbol-ge-: breca, breoca, ǣw-, wiđer-: brece, hlāf-ge-: brecendlīc, una-: brecþ, edor-: bræc, -cōđu, -seóc, -seócnes; ge-, fȳr-ge-, hrǣc-ge-, neb-ge-: brǣce, ǣw-, un-: brice, bryce, ǣw-, āþ-, bān-, borh-, burh-, ciric-, cyric-, eodor-, fæsten-, freóls-, ful-, ge-, griþ-, hād-, hūs-, lah-, mund-, sām-, wed-: breahtm: broc, scip-ge-, un-.

brece, es; *n. A bit, morsel, piece*; frustum, buccella. DER. hlāf-gebrece. v. brecan.

Brecenan-mere, es; *m.* [*Bd.* Britannemere: *Flor.* Bricenanmere: *Hunt.* Brecanammere: *Hovd.* Bricenamere] *Brecknock, the capital of*

Brecknockshire in South Wales; Brechinia. Gibson says,—Ad secundum circiter milliare a Brecknock in Wallia conspicitur Brecknockmere. Arx autem quam in nostris Annalibus Æthelfleda dicitur expugnasse, fuit, opinor, apud ipsum *Brecknock*, Chr. explicatio, p. 16, col. 1:—Sende Ǽdelflǽd fyrd on Wealas, and abræc Brecenanmere *Æthelfled sent a force into Wales, and took Brecknock by storm,* Chr. 916; Th. 190, 35.

brecendlīc; *adj.* [brecende, *part. of* brecan *to break,* -līc] *Breakable;* fragilis. DER. un-abrecendlīc.

brēc-hrægel, -hrægl, es; *n.* [brēc *breeches, pl. of* brōc, *f;* hrægel *a garment*] *A sort of garment;* lumbare, diplois = διπλοΐς:—Him sī abrogden, swā of brēchrægle [mid twȳfealdum mentle, Spl.], hiora sylfra sceamu *operiantur* [*operiantur?*] *sicut diploide confusione sua,* Ps. Th. 108, 28.

brec-mǽlum; *adv.* [brece *a bit, piece;* mǽlum, *dat. pl. of* mǽl, *n.*] *By bits, piecemeal;* minutatim, Mone B. 1819.

brecþ, e; *pl. nom.* brecþa; *f.* [brecan *to break*] *A broken state, fracture,* used figuratively of mental contrition, *grief;* fractio, ærumna:—Ðæt wæs wrǽc micel wine Scyldinga, mōdes brecþa *that was great wretchedness to the friend of the Scyldings, his mind's griefs,* Beo. Th. 344; B. 171. DER. edor-brecþ.

brecung, e; *f.* [brecan *frangere*] *A* BREAKING; fractio:—On brecunge breódes *in fractione panis,* Lk. Rush. War. 24, 35.

bred, es; *pl. nom. acc.* bredu; *n. A surface, plank, board, table, tablet;* superficies, tabula, tabella:—Ðisse eorþan ymbhwyrft is, wið ðone heofon to mettanne, swilce ān lytel pricu on brādan brede *the circumference of this earth is, compared with the heaven, like a little point on a large surface,* Bt. 18, 1; Fox 62, 4. Breda þiling *vel* flōr on to þerscenne *a joining of planks* or *a floor to thrash on;* area, Ælfc. Gl. 57; Som. 67, 73; Wrt. Voc. 37, 59. Hī bǽron anlīcnysse Drihtnes on brede afægde and awritene *they bore the likeness of the Lord figured and drawn on a board;* ferebant imaginem Domini in tabula depictam, Bd. 1, 25; S. 487, 3. Lytle hūs of bredan [= bredum] *small houses with tables, eating-houses, taverns;* tabernæ *vel* gurgustia, Ælfc. Gl. 55; Som. 67, 12; Wrt. Voc. 37, 7. Ic bær ða stǽnenan bredu, on ðām wæs ðæt wedd, ðe Drihten wið eów gecwæþ *acciperem tabulas lapideas, tabulas pacti, quod pepigit vobiscum Dominus,* Deut. 9, 9. [*Dut.* berd, *n: O. Dut.* bred, *n: Ger.* bret, brett, *n: M. H. Ger.* brët, *n: O. H. Ger.* bret, *n.*] DER. wex-bred.

bred *deceit,* L. Ed. 1; Th. i. 160, 6. v. bræd.

brēd *broad,* Chr. 189; Erl. 9, 25. v. brād.

bredan; ic brede, ðū britst, brist, he brit, bret, *pl.* bredaþ; *p.* bræd, *pl.* brudon; *pp.* broden, breden. I. *to weave,* BRAID, *knit, join together, draw, pluck;* plectere, nectere, vibrare, gladium stringere:—Ic brede nett *plecto,* Ælfc. Gr. 28, 5; Som. 32, 8. Ic brede me max *plecto mihi retia,* Coll. Monast. Th. 21, 13. Beadohrægl broden on breóstum læg *the armour* [lit. *war-garment*] *joined together lay on my breast,* Beo. Th. 1108; B. 552: 3100; B. 1548. Byrhtnōþ bræd bill of scēðe *Byrhtnoth drew his battle-axe from its sheath,* Byrht. Th. 136, 36; By. 162. Hīg brudon up heora ancran *they drew up their anchors,* Chr. 1052; Erl. 184, 23. Sweord ǽr gemealt, forbarn broden mǽl, wæs ðæt blōd to ðæs hāt *the sword had already melted, the drawn brand was burnt, so hot was the blood,* Beo. Th. 3236; B. 1616. Se bræd of ðæm beorne blōdigne gār *he plucked the bloody dart from the chief,* Byrht. Th. 136, 20; By. 154. II. *to change, vary, transform;* vertere, variare, transformare:—Simon bræd his hiw ætfōran ðam cāsere, swā ðæt he wearþ fǽrlīce geþuht cnapa, and eft hārwenge *Simon changed his appearance before the emperor, so that he suddenly seemed a boy, and again a hoary man,* Homl. Th. i. 376, 11. Hǽðen cild biþ gefullod, ac hit ne bret nā his hiw wiðūtan, ðeáh ðe hit beó wiðinnan awend *a heathen child is baptized, but it varies not its aspect without, although it be changed within,* Homl. Th. ii. 268, 30. DER. a-bredan, æt-, for-, ge-, ofer-, on-, ōþ-, to-, upa-, ūta-, wið-. v. bregdan.

brēdan *to roast, broil, warm,* Cot. 86. v. brǽdan.

brēdan *to make broad,* Bt. 18, 1; Rawl. 38, 33, MS. Cot. v. brǽdan.

brēd-būr *a bed-chamber,* Hymn Surt. 34, 30: 103, 17. v. brȳd-būr.

brēden; *adj. Broad;* latus:—Seuerus geworhte weall of turfum, and brēdenne [breden MS: bred weal, col. 1: bred weall, col. 2] ðār on ufon, fram sǽ to sǽ *Severus made a wall of turfs, and a broad wall thereupon, from sea to sea,* Chr. 189; Th. 15, 22, col. 3. v. brād.

bredende; *adj.* [*part. of* bredan] *Deceitful, cunning, crafty;* dolosus:—Sendon [MS. sendan] hī Marius, ðone consul, ongeán Geoweorþan, ā swā lytigne, and ā swā bredende, swā he wæs *they sent Marius, the consul, against Jugurtha, as he was always so cunning, and so crafty,* Ors. 5, 7; Bos. 106, 29; notes, p. 24.

brēd-guma *a bridegroom,* Mt. Kmbl. Hat. 9, 15. v. brȳd-guma.

brēding-panne, an; *f.* [brǽdan *to roast,* panne *a pan*] *A frying-pan;* sartago, Wrt. Voc. 288, 38. v. brǽding-panne.

brēdi-panne, brēding-panne, an; *f.* [brǽdan *to roast,* panne *a pan*] *A frying-pan;* sartago:—Brēdipanne [MS. bredipannæ] *sartago,* Glos. Epnl. Recd. 162, 30. Brēding-panne *sartago,* Wrt. Voc. 288, 38. v. brǽd-panne.

bred-īsern *a graving iron,* Glos. Epnl. Recd. 162, 28. v. bræd-īsen.

brēg *an eye-lid,* Ps. Surt. 131, 4: Bd. 4, 32; S. 611, note 18. v. brǽw.

brega; *m. A governor, ruler, prince;* imperator, princeps:—Ðā se brega mǽra gelaðade leóf weorud *when the great prince assembled the dear company,* Exon. 14 a; Th. 29, note 1; Cri. 456, note. v. brego.

brēgan, brēgean; *p.* de; *pp.* ed; *v. a.* [brōga *fear, terror*] *To give fear, frighten, make afraid, terrify, astonish;* terrere, pavefacere, stupefacere:—Hī sǽ-ȳða swȳðe brēgaþ *the sea-waves greatly frighten them,* Runic pm. 21; Kmbl. 343, 24; Hick. Thes. i. 135. Ðeáh hī me swā brēgdon, ne dorston hī me gehrīnan *though they frightened me so, they durst not touch me,* Bd. 5, 12; S. 628, 45. Ne beó ge brēgede fram ðām ðe ðone līchaman ofsleáþ *be ye not afraid of those who slay the body,* Lk. Bos. 12, 4: 21, 9. Hȳ hine brēgdon *they terrified him,* Exon. 40 b; Th. 136, 4; Gū. 536. Ne biþ he brēged mid ǽnigum ōgan *he will not be terrified with any dread,* Herb. 73, 2; Lchdm. i. 176, 4. We hī scylen manian and brēgean *we should admonish and frighten them,* Past. 53, 8; Hat. MS. Sume wīf us brēgdon *some women astonished us,* Lk. Bos. 24, 22. DER. a-brēgan, ge-.

brēgd, brēgda *fear, terror, dread.* v. brōga, brēgnes.

BREGDAN, bredan, ic bregde, ðū bregdest, he bregdeþ, *pl.* bregdaþ; *p.* brægd, *pl.* brugdon; *pp.* brogden, bregden. I. *v. a. To move to and fro, vibrate, cast, draw, drag, change, bend, weave;* vibrare, vibrare gladium, jactare, stringere, trahere, nectere, plectere:—Git mundum brugdon *ye vibrated with your hands,* Beo. Th. 1033; B. 514. Ðæt hie ne mōste se synscaða bregdan *that the sinful spoiler might not draw them,* 1419; B. 707: Exon. 42 b; Th. 142, 23; Gū. 648. Ic underbæc bregde nebbe *I draw my face backwards,* Exon. 130 a; Th. 498, 6; Rä. 87, 8. Bōcstafa brego bregdeþ feónd be ðam feaxe *the prince of letters shall draw the fiend by his hair,* Salm. Kmbl. 200; Sal. 99. Saga, hwā mec bregde of brimes fæðmum *say, who drew me from the bosom of the ocean,* Exon. 101 a; Th. 382, 18; Rä. 3, 13. Sǽ-rōfe ārum bregdaþ ȳþbord [MS. yþborde] neáh *brave seamen draw the vessel near with oars,* 79 a; Th. 296, 26; Crä. 57. Brægd beadwe heard feorh-genīðlan *the fierce warrior dragged the mortal foe,* Beo. Th. 3082; B. 1539: 1593; B. 794. Brugdon hæleþ of scǽðum sweord *the warriors drew their swords from their sheaths,* Cd. 93; Th. 120, 8; Gen. 1991: Judth. 11; Thw. 24, 38; Jud. 229. Nǽfre hie ðæs sellīce bleóum bregdaþ *let them never so strangely change with colours,* Salm. Kmbl. 301; Sal. 150. Bleóm bregdende *changing in colours,* Exon. 95 b; Th. 357, 3; Pa. 23. Sceal mǽg nealles inwitnet ōðrum bregdan *a kinsman should not weave a net of treachery for another,* Beo. Th. 4341; B. 2167. Ic gefrægn sunu Wihstānes beran brogdne beadu-sercean *I heard that Wihstan's son bore his weaved war-sark,* 5503; B. 2755. Ðǽr wæs on eorle brogden byrne *there was on the man the woven mail-shirt,* Elen. Kmbl. 513; El. 257: Exon. 64 b; Th. 238, 11; Ph. 602. Bregden feðrum *woven with feathers,* 60 a; Th. 219, 13; Ph. 306: Ps. Th. 138, 9. II. *v. n. to turn into;* se vertere in aliquid:—Hī brugdon on wyrmes bleó *they turned into the hue of a worm,* Exon. 46 a; Th. 156, 30; Gū. 882. [*Wyc. R. Glouc.* breide: *Scot.* brade: *O. Sax.* bregdan: *O. Frs.* brida: *L. Ger.* breiden: *O. H. Ger.* brettan: *Icel.* bregða.] DER. a-bregdan, be-, for-, ge-, ofer-, on-, to-, upa-, ūta-.

Bregent-ford *Brentford in Middlesex,* Chr. 1016; Th. 280, 28, col. 1. v. Brent-ford.

brēgh *an eye-lid,* Bd. 4, 32; S. 611, 18. v. brǽw.

brēg-nes, -ness, e; *f.* [brēgan *to give fear*] *Fear, terror, dread;* terror:—Brēgnessa [MS. bregnes] ðīne hȳ gedrēfdon me *terrores tui conturbaverunt me,* Ps. Spl. T. 87, 17.

BREGO, bregu, brega, breogo; *indecl. m.* A word chiefly used by poets, denoting *A leader, governor, ruler, prince, king, Lord;* imperator, princeps, rex, Dominus:—Se beorna brego *a leader of men,* Judth. 12; Thw. 25, 11; Jud. 254. Norþmanna þregu *the leader of North men,* Chr. 937; Erl. 112, 33; Æðelst. 33. Brego engla *the ruler of angels,* Cd. 9; Th. 12, 7; Gen. 181. Brego moncynnes *ruler of mankind,* Bt. Met. Fox 20, 86; Met. 20, 43. Babilōne brego *the king of Babylon,* Cd. 187; Th. 232, 6; Dan. 256. Se brega mǽra *the great prince,* Exon. 14 a; Th. 29, note 1; Cri. 456, note. Beorna breogo *the king of men,* Andr. Kmbl. 609; An. 305. [*Icel.* bragr, *m. vir primarius, princeps.*]

brego-rīce, es; *n.* [brego *a governor, ruler, king;* rīce *a region, kingdom*] *A kingdom;* regnum:—Se wæs Babylōnes bregorīces fruma *he was the founder of the kingdom of Babylon,* Cd. 79; Th. 98, 21; Gen. 1633.

brego-stōl, breogo-stōl, es; *m.* [brego *a ruler, prince, king;* stōl *a stool, seat, throne*] *A prince's stool* or *chair, a throne, a prince's dominion, kingdom;* principis sella, thronus, regnum:—He him gesealde bold and bregostōl *he gave him a habitation and a princely seat,* Beo. Th. 4398; B. 2196: 4729; B. 2370. He hāmes niósan lēt ðone bregostōl *he left the kingdom to visit his home,* 4767; B. 2389. Breogostōl, Andr. Kmbl. 417; An. 209.

brego-weard, es; *m.* [brego *a ruler, prince;* weard *a guard, keeper*] *A royal guard, prince, lord;* princeps, dominus, Cd. 131; Th. 166, 13; Gen. 2747: 106; Th. 140, 26; Gen. 2333.

bregu *a leader, ruler, prince*, Chr. 937; Erl. 112, 33; Ædelst. 33. v. brego.

brēgyd *made afraid, frightened*, Lk. Foxe 12, 4,=brēged; *pp. of* brēgan.

brēhg *an eye-lid*, Bd. 4, 32; S. 611, 40. v. brǽw.

brehtm, es; *m. A noise, tumult, sound, cry;* fragor, strepitus, tumultus, clamor:—Ða com hæleþa þreát..... weorodes brehtme *then came the troop of heroes..... with the tumult of a host*, Andr. Kmbl. 2544; An. 1273. v. breahtm *a noise.*

brehtnian *To make a noise* or *crackling;* crepare, Cot. 202.

brehtnung, e; *f. A noise, clattering, cracking;* crepitus, Cot. 49.

brēman; *part.* brēmende; *p.* de; *pp.* ed; *v. a.* [brēme *celebrated*] *To celebrate, solemnise, make famous, have in honour;* celebrare, honorare:—Ðæt hie ðæt hālige gerȳne brēman mǽgen *that they may celebrate the holy mystery* [i. e. *the sacrament*], L. E. I. 4; Th. ii. 404, 27. Â brēmende *ever celebrating*, Exon. 13 a; Th. 24, 20; Cri. 387. We ðec, hālig Drihten, gebēdum brēmaþ *we celebrate thee, holy Lord, in our prayers*, Cd. 192; Th. 241, 17; Dan. 406: Menol. Fox 186; Men. 94. Bodiaþ and brēmaþ beorhtne geleáfan *preach and make famous bright belief*, Exon. 14 b; Th. 30, 21; Cri. 483. DER. ge-brēman.

brēmbel *a bramble*, L. M. 2, 65; Lchdm. ii. 296, 23. v. brēmel.

brēmbel-æppel, es; *m. Bramble-fruit, blackberry;* rubi pomum, L. M. 1, 64; Lchdm. ii. 138, 26: 3, 41; Lchdm. ii. 334, 12.

brēmbel-rind, e; *f.* [brēmbel *a bramble*, rind *rind, bark*] *Bramble-rind;* rubi cortex:—Genim brēmbel-rinde *take bramble-rind*, L. M. 3, 47; Lchdm. ii. 338, 11. v. brēmel.

brēmber *a bramble*, Cd. 142; Th. 177, 12; Gen. 2928. v. brēmel.

brēmblas *brambles*, Homl. Th. i. 18, 17; *pl. of* brēmbel. v. brēmel.

BRÉME, brȳme; *def.* se brēma, seó, ðæt brēme; *comp.* brēmra; *sup.* brēmest, brȳmust; *adj. Celebrated, renowned, illustrious, famous, notable,* BRIM, *glorious, esteemed;* celeber, clarus, illustris, famosus, notus, cognitus:—Og wæs brēme cyning on Basane *Og was a celebrated king in Basan*, Ps. Th. 135, 21: Menol. Fox 80; Men. 40. Ðæt is heálīc dæg, bentīd brēmu *that is a high day, a celebrated time for supplication*, 148; Men. 75. Ðis is anlīcnes ðæs brēmestan mid ðām burgwarum in ðære ceastre *this is the image of the most celebrated amongst the inhabitants in the city*, Andr. Kmbl. 1435; An. 718. Beówulf wæs brēme *Beowulf was renowned*, Beo. Th. 35; B. 18: Cd. 177; Th. 222, 13; Dan. 104. Ðā wearþ se brēma on mōde blīðe *then was the illustrious one blithe in mind*, Judth. 10; Thw. 22, 10; Jud. 57. Ne hȳrde ic bisceop brēmran *I have not heard a more illustrious bishop*, Menol. Fox 205; Men. 104. Bēc syndon brēme *books are famous*, Salm. Kmbl. 473; Sal. 237. Salomon wæs brēmra, ðeáh ðe Saturnus sumra hæfde bōca cǽga *Salomon was the more famous, though Saturn had the keys of some books*, 366; Sal. 182. Fram gebyrdtīde brēmes Cyninges *from the birth-time of the glorious King* [*Christ*], Chr. 973; Erl. 124, 20; Edg. 12. Hī Rōmāna brȳmuste wǽron *they were the most esteemed of the Romans*, Ors. 2, 2; Bos. 41, 30. [*Northumb.* brōeme *clarus.*]

brēme; *adv. Famously, notably, gloriously;* famose, solemniter, gloriose:—Is his miht ofer middangeard brēme gebledsod *his might is gloriously blessed throughout the earth*, Andr. Kmbl. 3434; An. 1721.

BRÉMEL, brēmbel, brǽmbel, brēmber, es; *m. A* BRAMBLE, *brier, blackberry bush;* tribulus, vepres, rubus fruticosus, Lin:—*Herba rubus* [*erusti* MS.=*rubus fruticosus*], ðæt is brēmel [brēmbel MS. H.] *the herb* rubus, *that is bramble*, Herb. cont. 89; Lchdm. i. 34, 21. Genim ðās wyrte ðe man brēmel [brǽmbel MS. H.] nemneþ *take this herb which a man calls bramble*, Herb. 89, 1; Lchdm. i. 192, 9. Brēmelas *vepres*, Wrt. Voc. 80, 23: Brēmlas *vepres*, Ælfc. Gr. 13; Som. 16, 15: Gl. 48; Som. 65, 52; Wrt. Voc. 33, 48. Abraham geseah ānne ramm betwux ðām brēmelum be ðām hornum gehæft *Abraham vidit arietem inter vepres hærentem cornibus*, Gen. 22, 13. Þornas and brēmelas heó asprīt ðē *spinas et tribulos germinabit tibi*, 3, 18: Homl. Th. i. 432, 34. Wið ūtwærce, brēmbel ðe sīen begen endas on eorþan *for dysentery, a bramble of which both ends are in the earth*, L. M. 2, 65; Lchdm. ii. 290, 30. Seó eorþe sylþ ðē þornas and brēmblas *the earth shall give thee thorns and brambles*, Homl. Th. i. 18, 17. He rom geseah brēmbrum fæstne *he saw a ram fast in the brambles*, Cd. 142; Th. 177, 12; Gen. 2928. [*Chauc.* brember: *Wyc.* brembil, brimbil: *Plat.* brummelbeere, *f*: *Dut.* braam, *m. a bramble;* braam-bézie, *f. a blackberry*: *Kil.* braeme, breme *rubus*: *Ger.* brom-beere, *f. a blackberry*: *O. H. Ger.* brāma, *f.*; brāmo, *m*; brāmal, *n*: *Dan.* brambær, *n*: *Swed.* brombär, *m.*] DER. heop-brēmel.

brēmel-æppel *bramble-fruit, blackberry.* v. brēmbel-æppel.

brēmel-berie *a bramble-berry.* v. brǽmel-berie.

brēmel-brǽr *a bramble-brier.* v. brǽmbel-brǽr.

brēmel-leáf *the leaf of a bramble.* v. brǽmbel-leáf.

brēmel-rind *bramble-rind.* v. brēmbel-rind.

brēmel-þyrne, an; *f.* [brēmel *a bramble*, þyrne *a thorn*] *A bramble-thorn, bramble-bush;* rubus:—On middan ānre brēmelþyrnan *de medio rubi*, Ex. 3, 2, 4.

brēmen; *adj. Illustrious, glorious;* illustris, gloriosus:—Brēmen Dryhten *the glorious Lord*, Exon. 54 b; Th. 193, 4; Az. 116: 55 a; Th. 194, 21; Az. 142. v. brēme.

Bremes burh; *gen.* burge; *dat.* byrig; *f.* BRAMSBURY or *Bramsby, Lincolnshire;* urbis *vel* arcis nomen in agro Lincolniensi:—Hēr, A. D. 909, Æðelflǽd getimbrode Bremes burh *in this year*, A. D. 909, *Æthelfled built Bramsbury*, Chr. 909; Th. 183, 30, col. 2. Hēr, A. D. 910, Æðelflǽd getimbrede ða burh æt Bremes byrig *in this year*, A. D. 910, *Æthelfled built the fortress at Bramsbury*, 910; Th. 184, 11, col. 2.

brēmlas *brambles*, Ælfc. Gr. 13; Som. 16, 15; *pl. nom. of* brēmel.

bremman; *part.* bremmende; *p.* de; *pp.* ed *To rage, roar;* rudere, fremere:—Bremman *rudere*, Cot. 192. Bremmende *rudens*, 192. Bremmde *fremuit*, Jn. Lind. War. 11, 33, 38. [*Frs.* brimje, brimme: *Dut.* brommen: *Kil.* bremmen: *Ger.* brummen: *M. H. Ger.* brimmen: *O. H. Ger.* breman: *Lat.* fremere: *Grk.* βρέμειν.]

brēmra *more illustrious*, Salm. Kmbl. 366; Sal. 182; *comp. of* brēme.

brencþ *brings*, Bt. Met. Fox 13, 120; *3rd pers. pres. of* brengan.

breneþ *burns*, Runic pm. 15; Kmbl. 342, 11; Hick. Thes. i. 135,= berneþ; *3rd sing. pres. of* bernan.

brengan; ic brenge, ðū brengest, brengst, he brengeþ, brengþ, brencþ, *pl.* brengaþ; *p.* ic, he brohte, ðū brohtest, *pl.* brohton; *pp.* broht; *v. a. To bring, adduce, lead, produce, bear, carry;* ferre, afferre, offerre, proferre:—Ðæt geár mōt brengan blōsman *the year may bring blossoms*, Bt. 7, 3; Fox 20, 22. He brengeþ æfter swegeltorht sunne *he brings after him the heavenly-bright sun*, Bt. Met. Fox 29, 46; Met. 29, 23. Eorþe sió cealde brengþ wæstma fela *the cold earth bringeth many fruits*, 20, 201; Met. 20, 101. Brencþ *brings*, 13, 120; Met. 13, 60. Wæter and eorþe wæstmas brengaþ *water and earth produce fruits*, 20, 150; Met. 20, 75. Nū scīneþ ðe leóht, ðæt ic from Gode brohte *now the light shineth, which I brought from God*, Cd. 29; Th. 38, 32; Gen. 615. Ðū brohtest *thou broughtest*, Exon. 121 a; Th. 463, 34; Hö. 80: 121 a; Th. 464, 12; Hö. 86. Gabriēl brohte *Gabriel brought*, Exon. 12 b; Th. 21, 18; Cri. 336: Cd. 156; Th. 194, 12; Exod. 259. Āras brohton *the messengers brought*, Elen. Kmbl. 1989; El. 996. Ða he hæfde ǽr him to wīfe broht *whom he had formerly married* [lit. *he had formerly taken to himself for a wife*], Bd. 3, 7; S. 529, 30. DER. ætgebrengan: forþ-brengan, ge-, ofer-, onge-, ongeán-.

brengnes, -ness, e; *f. An offering;* oblatio:—Onsægednissa and brengnesse ðū nolde *sacrificia et oblationem noluisti*, Ps. Spl. T. 39, 9.

brenning *a burning;* crematio, Som. Lye. v. bærning.

Brent-ford, Bregent-ford, Brægent-ford; *gen.* -fordes; *dat.* -forde, -forda; *m.* [Brent *the river Brent*, ford *a ford*: Brenford, *Sim. Dun*: Brendeford, *Hunt.*] BRENTFORD *in Middlesex, situate where the river Brent flows into the Thames;* oppidum in agro Middlesexiæ, in sinu quodam ubi se in Tamesin effundit Brent fluvius:—Eádmund cyng fērde ofer Temese æt Brentforda *king Edmund went over the Thames at Brentford*, Chr. 1016; Th. 282, 4, col. 1: 281, 26, col. 1.

brenting, es; *m. A ship;* navis:—Hī brentingas ofer flōda genīpu feorran drīfaþ *they drive ships from afar over the mists of floods*, Beo. Th. 5607; B. 2807.

breód *a bit, morsel, bread*, Jn. Rush. War. 13, 27. v. breád.

breodian; *p.* ode; *pp.* od *To cry out;* vociferari:—He breodaþ *he cries out*, Exon. 83 b; Th. 315, 8; Mōd. 28.

breodwian; ic breodwige, ðū breodwast, he breodwaþ, *pl.* breodwiaþ; *p.* ode; *pp.* od *To prostrate;* prosternere?—Beóþ ða gebolgne, ða ðec breodwiaþ, tredaþ ðec and tergaþ *they are enraged, they will prostrate thee, will tread and tear thee*, Exon. 36 b; Gū. 258. DER. a-bredwian.

breogo *a ruler, prince, king*, Andr. Kmbl. 609; An. 305. v. brego.

breogo-stōl *a throne, kingdom*, Andr. Kmbl. 417; An. 209. v. brego-stōl.

BREÓST, es; *n.* I. *the breast of man* or *beast;* pectus:—Ðæt mīne breóst wereþ *that defends my breast*, Beo. Th. 911; B. 453. On breóstum læg *lay on my breast*, 1109; B. 552. He beót his breóst *percutiebat pectus suum*, Lk. Bos. 18, 13. Blīð on breóstum *mild in the breast* [*stomach*], Cd. 30; Th. 41, 13; Gen. 656. Ðū gǽst on ðīnum breóste *super pectus tuum gradieris*, Gen. 3, 14. II. *the breasts;* ubera:—Ða breóst ðe ðū suce *ubera quæ suxisti*, Lk. Bos. 11, 27. Ða breóst ðe ne sīcton *ubera quæ non lactaverunt*, 23, 29. Ðǽr wearþ Alexander þurhscoten mid ānre flān underneoðan ōðer breóst *there Alexander was shot through with an arrow underneath one breast*, Ors. 3, 9; Bos. 68, 27. III. the breast as the seat of the vital powers, of the feelings, and of the affections, *The heart, mind, thought;* pectus, cor, mens:—Drihtnes wæs bām on breóstum byrnende lufu *in both their breasts there was the burning love of the Lord*, Cd. 10; Th. 12, 25; Gen. 191. Hwæðre he in breóstum ða git hērede—in heortan—heofonrīces weard *nevertheless he still in his breast—in his heart—honoured the guardian of heaven's kingdom*, Andr. Kmbl. 102; An. 51. Mæg ðīn mōd wesan blīðe on breóstum *thy mind may be blithe in thy breast*, Cd. 35; Th. 46, 28; Gen. 751. Beoran on breóstum blīðe geþohtas *to bear in our breasts blithe thoughts*, 217; Th. 277, 17; Sat. 206. Adame innan breóstum his hyge hwyrfde *Adam within his breast changed* *his mind*, 33; Th. 44, 27; Gen. 715. Ðū ūra breósta āna aspyrigend eart *tu nostrorum pectorum solus investigator es*, Hymn. Surt. 33, 21. Dēma ðū ætbist smēgan dǣda breóstes *judex aderis rimari facta pectoris*, 36, 20. Gefyll mid heofonlīcre gyfe ðe ðū gesceópe breóst *imple superna gratia quæ tu creasti pectora*, 92, 9. [*Chauc. Wyc.* brest: *R. Glouc.* breste: *Laym.* breoste: *Orm.* brest: *Plat.* borst, bost, *f*: *O. Sax.* briost, breost, *n*: *Frs.* boarst, *m. f*: *O. Frs.* brust: *Dut. Kil.* borst, *f*: *Ger. M. H. Ger. O. H. Ger.* brust, *f*: *Goth.* brusts, *f*: *Dan.* bryst, *n*: *Swed.* bröst, *n*: *Icel.* brjóst, *n.*] DER. byled-breóst, fōre-.

breóst-bān, es; *n.* [breóst *the breast*, bān *a bone*] *The* BREAST-BONE; pectoris os, pectusculum, Ælfc. Gl. 73; Som. 71, 25; Wrt. Voc. 44, 11.

breóst-bedern, es; *n. The breast-chamber, the inmost thoughts, the mind, the breast, chest;* pectoris conclave *vel* cubile, *i. e.* pectus intimum, thorax = θώραξ:—Fōran-bodig *vel* breóstbedern [MS. beden] *thorax* [MS. *torax*], Ælfc. Gl. 73; Som. 71, 26; Wrt. Voc. 44, 12.

breóst-beorh, -beorg, es; *m. A breast-defence, breast-plate;* pectoris tutamen. DER. breóst, beorg.

breóst-cearu, e; *f.* [breóst II. *the heart, mind*, cearu *care*] *The care of the heart, anxiety, grief, sorrow;* ægritudo, mæror:—Ic bitre breóst-ceare gebiden hæbbe *I have suffered bitter grief*, Exon. 81 b; Th. 306, 7; Seef. 4: 115 b; Th. 444, 9; Kl. 44.

breóst-cōfa, an; *m.* [breóst *the breast, the heart, mind*, cōfa *a cave, chamber*] *The breast-chamber, breast, heart, mind;* pectoris cubile, pectus, uber, cor, animus:—Under breóstcōfan *sub pectore*, Wanl. Catal. 48, 43. Ðū eart hiht mīn fram breóstcōfan mōdor mīnre *tu es spes mea ab uberibus matris meæ*, Ps. Lamb. 21, 10. He wæs ðe blīðra on breóst-cōfan *he was the blither in his heart*, Bt. Met. Fox 9, 64; Met. 9, 32: Cd. 27; Th. 36, 19; Gen. 574: Exon. 76 b; Th. 287, 22; Wand. 18.

breóst-gebeorh, -geborh; *gen.* -gebeorges; *m.* [breóst, gebeorh *a defence*] *A defence for the breast*, hence *a defence generally, bulwark, tower;* propugnaculum, Cot. 152.

breóst-gehygd, e; *f*: es; *n.* [breóst II. *the heart, mind*, gehygd *thought, meditation*] *The thought of the heart* or *mind, a thought;* cordis *vel* animi cogitatio, cogitatio:—Ðæt wæs gingeste word breóstgehygdum *that was the last word from his mind's thoughts*, Beo. Th. 5628; B. 2818: Andr. Kmbl. 1994; An. 999.

breóst-geþanc, -geþonc, es; *m.* [breóst II. *the heart, mind*, geþanc *thought*] *The thought of the heart* or *mind, a thought;* cordis *vel* animi cogitatio, cogitatio:—Annanias ðec, and Adzarias and Misaēl, Metod, dōmige, breóstgeþancum *Hananiah and Azariah and Mishael glorify thee, O God, in their minds' thoughts*, Cd. 192; Th. 241, 5; Dan. 400. Breóstgeþoncum, Exon. 80 b; Th. 302, 8; Fä. 33.

breóst-gewǣdu; *pl. n.* [breóst I. *the breast*, gewǣde *a garment, clothing*] *A covering for the breast, corselet;* pectoris vestimentum, lorica:—Gehwearf in Francna fæðm feorh cyninges, breóstgewǣdu, and se beáh somod *the king's life fell into the power of the Franks, his corselet, and his collar also*, Beo. Th. 2426; B. 1211: Beo. Th. 4330; B. 2162.

breóst-hord, es; *n. m.* [breóst II. *the heart, mind*, hord *a hoard, treasure*] *The breast's treasure, the thought, mind, heart;* pectoris thesaurus, cogitatio, mens, cor:—Ōþ-ðæt wordes ord breóst-hord þurhbræc *until the point* [or *issue*] *of the word broke through his mind*, Beo. Th. 5577; B. 2792. Him on ferhþe greów breóst-hord blōdreów *in his mind there grew a bloodthirsty thought*, Beo. Th. 3442; B. 1719: Exon. 82 a; Th. 309, 10; Seef. 55.

breóst-hyge, es; *m.* [breóst, hyge, hige *the mind*] *The breast-thought;* pectoris cogitatio, Andr. Elen. Grm. xxxix. v. hyge, hige.

breóst-līn, es; *n.* [breóst, līn *linen*] *A breast-linen* or *bandage, breast-cloth;* pectoralis fascia, Cot. 89.

breóst-loca, an; *m.* [breóst, loca *an inclosure*] *The breast-inclosure, the mind;* pectoris clausura, mens:—Swefen he onfōn ne meahte in his breóstlocan *he could not contain the dream in his mind*, Cd. 180; Th. 226, 7; Dan. 167: Elen. Kmbl. 2498; El. 1250.

breóst-net, -nett, es; *n.* [breóst, net *a net*] *A breast-net, covering for the breast, breast-plate;* pectorale reticulatum, thorax:—Him on eaxle læg breóstnet broden *on his shoulder lay the braided breastplate*. Beo. Th. 3100; B. 1548: Cd. 154; Th. 192, 24; Exod. 236.

breóst-rocc, es; *m.* [breóst, rocc *clothing*] *Breast-cloth;* thorax:—Breóstrocc *thorax*, Cot. 163. Stīðe and ruge breóstroccas [MS. breóst-rocces] *stiff and rough breast-clothes;* renones, Ælfc. Gl. 63; Som. 68, 114; Wrt. Voc. 40, 24.

breóst-sefa, an; *m.* [breóst *the breast*, sefa *the mind*] *The mind* or *heart in the breast, the mind, heart;* mens *vel* cor in pectore, mens, cor:—Arǣred wearþ beornes breóstsefa *the mind of the man was exalted*, Elen. Kmbl. 1606; El. 805: Exon. 15 b; Th. 34, 10; Cri. 540. Ic onsende in breóstsefan bitre geþoncas *I send into his mind bitter thoughts*, 71 b; Th. 266, 28; Jul. 405.

breóst-toga, an; *m. A breast-leader;* pectoris dux:—Sumra hæfde bald breóst-toga bōca cǣga *the bold chief had the keys of some books*, Salm. Kmbl. 369; Sal. 184.

breóst-wærc, es; *n? A breast-pain, the asthma, short windedness;* pectoris dolor *vel* morbus, forsan asthma, Lye, = ἄσθμα *short breath, a panting*. v. wærc.

breóst-weall, es; *m.* [breóst, weall *a wall*] *A wall as high as the breast, a rampart, defence;* structura in muris ad pectus alta, munimentum, propugnaculum, Cot. 199.

breóst-weorþung, e; *f.* [breóst, weorþung *a honouring*] *A breast-decoration, an ornament;* pectoris decoratio, ornamentum:—Nalles he Fres-cyninge breóstweorþunge bringan mōste *he could not bring the ornament to the Frisian king*, Beo. Th. 5001; B. 2504.

breóst-wylm, es; *m. The fountain of the breast, a breast, teat, emotion of the breast, grief;* pectoris fons, uber, pectoris æstuatio, ærumna:—Ðū eart hiht mīn fram breóstwylmum mōdor mīnre *tu es spes mea ab uberibus matris meæ*, Ps. Spl. 21, 8. He ðone breóstwylm forberan ne mihte *he could not restrain the emotion of his breast*, Beo. Th. 3758; B. 1877.

BREÓTAN; ic breóte, ðū breótest, breótst, brȳtest, brȳtst, he breóteþ, breót, brȳteþ, brȳt, *pl.* breótaþ; *p.* ic, he breát, ðū brute, *pl.* bruton; *pp.* broten; *v. a. To bruise, break, demolish, destroy;* conterere:—Hergas breótaþ *break idols*, Exon. 14 b; Th. 30, 26; Cri. 485. Heremōd breát bolgen-mōd eaxlgesteallan *Heremod in angry mood destroyed his bosom friends*, Beo. Th. 3430; B. 1713. [*O. H. Ger.* bretōn *cædere*: *Dan.* bryde: *Swed.* bryta: *Icel.* brjóta.] DER. a-breótan. v. breátan.

Breoten, e; *f. Britain;* Britannia, Bd. 1, 17; S. 484, 26. v. Bryten.

breóðan; ic breóðe, ðū breóðest, brȳst, he breóðeþ, brȳþ, *pl.* breóðaþ; *p.* breáþ, *pl.* bruðon; *pp.* broðen *To ruin, destroy;* perdere. DER. a-breóðan. v. breótan.

Breoton *Britain*, Bd. 1, 1; S. 473, 8. v. Bryten.

breótun *destroyed*, Exon. 66 a; Th. 243, 25; Jul. 16, = breóton; *p. pl. of* breátan.

BREÓWAN; ic breówe, ðū breówest, brȳwst, he breóweþ, brȳwþ, *pl.* breówaþ; *p.* breáw, *pl.* bruwon; *pp.* browen, ge-browen *To* BREW; cerevisiam coquere:—Ne biþ ðǣr nǣnig ealo gebrowen mid Estum *there is no ale brewed by the Esthonians*, Ors. 1, 1; Bos. 22, 17. Ne dranc he nānes gemencgedes wǣtan, ne gebrowenes *he drank not of any mixed or brewed fluid*, Homl. Th. i. 352, 7. [*Dut.* brouwen: *Ger.* brauen: *M. H. Ger.* briuwen: *O. H. Ger.* briuwan: *Dan.* brygge: *Swed.* brygga: *Icel.* brugga.] DER. twy-browen.

BRĒR, es; *m. A* BRIER, *the bramble;* tribulus, rubus fruticosus:—Genim brēr ðe hiopan on weaxaþ *take a brier on which hips grow*, L. M. 1, 38; Lchdm. ii. 96, 15. Sindon burgtūnas brērum beweaxene [MS. beweaxne] *the city-dwellings are overgrown with briers*, Exon. 115 b; Th. 443, 17; Kl. 31. [*Chauc. Wyc.* brere: *Orm.* breress, *pl*: *Northumb.* breer, *m*: *Fr.* bruyère *heather*: *O. Fr.* bruière: *M. Lat.* bruarium *a heath, barren land rough with brambles and bushes*, Du Cange.] DER. brǣmbel-brǣr, hind-brēr.

BRERD, breord, breard, briord, es; *m. A brim, margin, rim, top of a pot* or *vessel, a shore, bank, brink;* labrum, ora, margo, summitas, summum:—Hīg gefyldon ða ōþ ðone brerd *impleverunt eas usque ad summum*, Jn. Bos. 2, 7. Ofer brūnne brerd *over the dark brim*, Exon. 107 a; Th. 408, 8; Rä. 27, 9. Brerd vel ōfer *crepido*, Ælfc. Gl. 98; Som. 76, 81; Wrt. Voc. 54, 25. Stæþ *vel* brerd *labrum, margo*, vel *crepido*, 106; Som. 78, 44; Wrt. Voc. 57, 25. To brearde heofnes *ad summum cœli*, Mk. Lind. War. 13, 27. [*Wyc.* brerde: *Laym.* breorde: *Orm.* brerd: *O. H. Ger.* brart, brort, *m. prora, ora, labrum, margo, limbus*: *Icel.* broddr, *m. a spike*: *Sansk.* bhrishṭi, *f. a spike.*]

bresne; *adj. Strong, powerful, bold;* potens:—Ic his cynn gedō brād and bresne *I will make his race wide-spread and powerful*, Cd. 134; Th. 169, 17; Gen. 2801: 180; Th. 226, 18; Dan. 173. v. bræsen II.

bret *varies, changes; 3rd pres. of* bredan:—Hǣðen cild biþ gefullod, ac hit ne bret nā his hiw widūtan, ðeáh ðe hit beó widinnan awend *a heathen child is baptized, but it varies not its aspect without, although it be changed within*, Homl. Th. ii. 268, 30. v. bredan II.

Bret-, Bryt- *a Welshman.* v. Bret-walas, Bret-walda, Bryt-land.

Breten *Britain*, Bt. Met. Fox 20, 197; Met. 20, 99. v. Bryten.

Bretenan-mere, es; *m. The British mere* or *lake, Welshpool, Montgomeryshire;* loci nomen apud Cambrenses, Som. v. Brecenan-mere.

brēþ *breath*, Wrt. Voc. 42, 58. v. brǣþ.

brēðer *to a brother;* fratri, Lk. Bos. 12, 13; *dat. of* brōðor.

Bret-land, es; *n. Britain:*—On Bretlande *in Britain*, Ors. 6, 30; Bos. 126, 2. v. Bret-, Bryt-land.

bretta, an; *m. A steward, lord, the Lord;* dispensator, dominus, Deus:—Līfes Bretta *Lord of life*, Ps. C. 50, 122; Ps. Grn. ii. 279, 122. v. brytta.

Brettas *Britons*, Chr. Th. 4, 4, col. 1; also *Bretons*, Chr. 890; Th. 160, 10, col. 1. v. Bryttas.

brettnere *a steward;* dispensator. v. brytnere.

Bret-walas; *pl. m. The Britons of Wales;* Walli:—Cynrīc ða Bret-walas gefliémde *Cynric routed the Welsh*, Chr. 552; Th. 28, 39, col. 1.

Bret-walda, an; *m. A ruler of the Saxons in Britain, the chief Saxon king in England;* Saxonum in Britannia rex supremus. Turner and Lappenberg suppose that the Bretwalda was elected by the other Saxon kings and by the collected nobility and other electors in Britain, because

Hunt. lib. ii, about A.D. 1148, says, 'Omnia jura regni Anglorum, reges scilicet et proceres et tribunos in ditione sua tenebat:'—Ecgbryht wæs se eahteđa cyning, se đe Bretwalda wæs *Egbert was the eighth king, who was the Bretwalda*, Chr. 827; Th. 112, 21, col. 1.—There does not appear to be any historical evidence that the Bretwalda denoted any special title or office. The word is given in this alphabetical order because it occurs once in the Chronicle, and is thus written by historians; however, its more correct form appears to be brȳten-walda, *q.v.*

bric- *a bridge* [=bricg], *found in the compound* bric-bōt, *q.v.*

brica, an; *m. A breaker;* ruptor. DER. ǣw-breca, L. M. I. P. 16; Th. ii. 268, 30.

bric-bōt, e; *f. A repairing* or *restoring of a bridge;* pontis restitutio *vel* instauratio:—Bricbōta aginne man georne *let a man diligently begin the repairings of bridges*, L. Eth. vi. 32; Th. i. 322, 31: v. 26; Th. i. 310, 24.

brice, bryce, es; *m.* [*from* briceþ, brycþ, *pres. of* brecan *to break*] *A breaking, rupture, fracture, fragment, violation, breach;* fractio, ruptura, fractura, fragmentum, violatio:—Hīg hine oncneówon on hlāfes brice *cognoverunt eum in fractione panis*, Lk. Bos. 24, 35. We witon ful georne, đæt to miclan bryce sceal micel bōt nȳde *id compertum est nobis, immanis ubi facta est ruptura, ibi opus esse, ut large resarciatur*, Lupi Serm. i. 3; Hick. Thes. ii. 99, 30. Ne sȳ bānes bryce *let there not be a fracture of a bone*, Exon. 42 b; Th. 143, 32; Gū. 670. Gefēg đās bricas to ānsūndnysse *join these fragments to soundness*, Homl. Th. i. 62, 7, 9. Hī gegaderodon đa bricas *they gathered the fragments*, i. 182, 22. Wǣron seofan spyrtan afyllede mid đām bricum *seven baskets were filled with the fragments*, ii. 396, 9: i. 190, 4, 11. Đæs borges bryce *a violation* or *infraction of the pledge* or *security*, L. Alf. pol. 3; Th. i. 62, 9, 10, 12. [*Plat.* bräk, *m: Frs.* brek, *m. f: O. Frs.* breke, *m. f: Dut.* breuk, *f: Dan.* bræk, brök: *Swed.* brak, *n: Icel.* brek, *n. a fraudulent purchase of land:* like *Ger.* ge-brechen, *n. vitium;* bruch, *m. a breaking, breach,* from *Ger.* brechen, *A.Sax.* brecan *to break.*] DER. ǣw-brice, -bryce, āþ-, bān-, borh-, burh-, ciric-, cyric-, eodor-, fæsten-, freóls-, ful-, ge-, griþ-, hād-, hūs-, lah-, mund-, sām-, wed-.

brīce *use, service:*—God hīg gesceóp eallum mannum to brīce *God created them for the use of all men*, Deut. 4, 19. v. brȳce.

brīce; *adj. Useful;* utilis:—Dæg byþ eallum brīce *day is useful to all*, Runic pm. 24; Kmbl. 344, 14; Hick. Thes. i. 135. v. brȳce.

bricest, he briceþ *breakest, he breaks*, Exon. 63 a; Th. 232, 10; Ph. 504; *2nd and 3rd pers. pres. of* brecan.

bricg, e; *f. A bridge;* pons:—He hēt đa ofermetan bricge mid stāne gewyrcan *he ordered a very large bridge to be built with stone*, Ors. 2, 5; Bos. 48, 11. v. brycg.

Bricg, Brycg, e; *f.* [*Sim. Dun.* Brige: *Hovd.* Briges: *Matt. West.* Brigges]. I. *Bridgenorth in Shropshire;* oppidum in agro Salopiensi:—Æđelflǣd đa burh getimbrede æt Bricge *Æthelfled built the fortress at Bridgenorth*, Chr. 912; Th. 186, 10, col. 2; 187, 10, col. 1. II. *Bruges in Belgium;* Brugæ, Flandriæ emporium:—Heó com to Bricge begeondon sǣ *she came to Bruges beyond the sea*, Chr. 1037; Erl. 166, 7. Fērde Swegen ūt to Baldewines lande to Brycge *Sweyn went out to Baldwin's land to Bruges*, 1045; Erl. 170, 11: 1046; Erl. 175, 6: 1052; Erl. 181, 20: 1052; Erl. 182, 4.

bricg-bōt, e; *f. A repairing of a bridge;* pontis instauratio:—Bricgbōta aginne *let the repairings of bridges be begun*, L. C. S. 10; Th. i. 380, 27. v. brycg-bōt.

bricg-geweorc, es; *n.* BRIDGE-WORK, *the construction* or *reparation of a bridge;* pontis opus, pontis exstructio *vel* instauratio:—Brycggeweorc, Heming. 104, Lye. *Turner's Hist. of A.S.* App. No. 4, c. 3, vol. ii. p. 539. 8vo. 1823. v. brycg-geweorc.

Bricg-stōw, e; *f.* [Bricstowa, *Flor:* Brigestou, Bristou, *Hunt:* Brycstoue, *Sim. Dun:* Brikestow, Bristohw, *Hovd:* Bristow, *Kni:* brycg *a bridge*, stōw *a place*] BRISTOL *in Gloucestershire and Somersetshire;* Bristova in finibus agrorum Glocestriensis et Somersetensis:—Hīg fērdon to Bricgstōwe *they went to Bristol*, Chr. 1087; Erl. 224, 18.

bricg-weard, es; *m.* [bricg *a bridge*, weard *a keeper, guardian*] *A keeper* or *defender of a bridge;* pontis custos *vel* defensor:—Hī đǣr bricgweardas bitere fundon *they found there the stern defenders of the bridge*, Byrht. Th. 134, 16; By. 85.

brīcsian; *p.* ade *To profit;* prodesse, Bd. 5, 13; S. 632, 6. v. brȳcian.

bricst, he bricþ *thou shalt break, he shall break;* confringes, confringet, Ps. Spl. 2, 9; *2nd and 3rd pers. pres. and fut. of* brecan.

brīcst *shalt eat;* edes, Gen. 3, 19; *pres. and fut. of* brūcan.

brid, bridd, es; *m. The young of any of the feathered tribe;* pullus:—Earnes brid *an eagle's young*, Exon. 59 a; Th. 214, 7; Ph. 235. Þurh briddes hād *through the state of a young bird*, 61 a; Th. 224, 7; Ph. 372. Đæt hīg offrunge sealdon twegen culfran briddas *ut darent hostiam duos columbæ pullos*, Lk. Bos. 2, 24: Lev. 1, 14: Ps. Spl. 83, 3. On swealwan bridda magan *in the maw of the young ones of a swallow*, L. M. 3, 1; Lchdm. ii. 306, 7. Hit sculon beón micle briddas *it should be big young ones*, L. M. 3, 1; Lchdm. ii. 306, 14. Hrefnes briddum *corvi pullis*, Ps. Th. 146, 10. [*Chauc.* brid, bryd: *Wyc. Piers P.* brid: *Orm.* bridd: *O. Nrs.* burdr, *m. Rask*, burðr, *m. Vigf. partus.*]

brīd *a bride;* sponsa. v. brȳd.

brīd-bletsung, e; *f. A marriage-blessing;* nuptialis benedictio:—Man ne mōt sillan him brīdbletsunge *they* [*priests*] *may not give them the marriage-blessing*, L. Ælf. P. 43; Th. ii. 382, 33.

brīd-būr *a bedchamber.* v. brȳd-būr.

briddas *the young of any of the feathered tribe;* pulli. v. brid.

BRIDEL; *gen.* bridles; *m. A* BRIDLE; frenum:—Bridel *bagula?* Ælfc. Gl. 15; Som. 58, 46; Wrt. Voc. 21, 35. Bridles midl *a bridle's middle, a bit;* camus, 21; Som. 59, 61; Wrt. Voc. 23, 22: Runic pm. 21; Kmbl. 343, 26; Hick. Thes. i. 135. On hælftre and bridle ceácan heora gewrīþ *in camo et freno maxillas eorum constringe*, Ps. Lamb. 31, 9. He đæne bridel of ateáh *he took the bridle off* [*his horse*], Bd. 3, 9; S. 533, note 34. Se gemetgaþ đone bridel *he regulates the bridle*, Bt. 36, 2; Fox 174, 18. Mid his bridle *with his bridle*, Bt. 21; Fox 74, 6: Bt. Met. Fox 11, 45, 57, 157; Met. 11, 23, 29, 79; 24, 73; Met. 24, 37. He đæt gewealdleđer forlǣt đara bridla *he shall let go the rein* [*lit. governing leather*] *of the bridles*, Bt. 21; Fox 74, 31: Bt. Met. Fox 11, 151; Met. 11, 76. Drihten welt eallra gesceafta mid đām bridlum his anwealdes *the Lord governs all creatures with the bridles of his power*, Bt. 25; Fox 88, 3: Bt. Met. Fox 13, 5; Met. 13, 3. [*Chauc.* bridel, bridle: *Wyc.* brydil, bridel: *Dut.* breidel, *m: Kil.* breydel: *O. H. Ger.* brittil, *m. a bridle.*]

bridels, es; *m. A bridle;* frenum:—On bridels dōn *to put on a bridle*, Elen. Kmbl. 2348; El. 1175: 2367; El. 1185: 2396; El. 1199 v. bridel.

bridels-hring, es; *m. A bridle-ring;* in freno annulus:—Đæs cyninges sceal mearh midlum geweorþod, bridelshringum *the king's horse shall be adorned with bits, with bridle-rings*, Elen. Kmbl. 2385; El. 1194.

bridel-þwangas; *pl. m. Bridle-thongs* or *reins;* freni:—Ic wyrce bridelþwangas [MS. bridel-þwancgas] *facio frenos*, Coll. Monast. Wrt. 9, 9.

brīd-gifu, e; *f.* [brīd=brȳd *a bride*, gifu *a gift*] *A marriage-portion, dowry;* dos:—Đeós brīdgifu *hæc dos*, Ælfc. Gr. 9, 31; Som. 12, 1.

bridles *of a bridle*, Ælfc. Gl. 21; Som. 59, 61; Wrt. Voc. 23, 22; *gen. of* bridel.

bridlian; *p.* ode; *pp.* od [bridel *a bridle*] *To* BRIDLE, *curb, rule;* frenare. DER. ge-bridlian.

brig *a bridge*, Chr. 1125; Erl. 254, 19. v. bricg, brycg.

brigd, es; *n.* [bregdan *to change*] *A change, variety;* varietas:—Đæs deóres hiw brigda gehwæs wundrum lixeþ *the animal's hue of every variety wondrously shines*, Exon. 95 b; Th. 357, 9; Pa. 26. [*Icel.* brigði, *n. a change.*]

briht *bright*, Lk. Hat. 11, 34, Lye. v. bryht, beorht.

brihtan; *p.* brihte; *pp.* brihted [briht=beorht *bright*] *To brighten;* illuminare. DER. ge-brihtan. v. beorhtian.

briht-līce; *adv. Clearly, brightly;* clare, splendide:—Đæt he brihtlīce eall geseah *ut videret clare omnia*, Mk. Skt. Hat. 8, 25. v. beorht-līce.

BRIM, brym, es; *n. m. Surf, the sea, ocean, surface of the sea;* æstus aquæ, mare, pelagus=πέλαγος, æquor:—Brim sceal sealt weallan *the salt sea shall foam*, Menol. Fox 552; Gn. C. 45: Andr. Kmbl. 884; An. 442: 3147; An. 1576: Cd. 166; Th. 208, 2; Exod. 477: Exon. 95 b; Th. 356, 6; Pa. 7. Beáteþ [MS. beataþ] brim stađo [MS. stæđo] *the sea beats the shores*, Andr. Kmbl. 991; An. 496. Wæs brim blōde fāh *the sea's surface was stained with blood*, Beo. Th. 3192; B. 1594: 1699; B. 847. Ic of fæđmum cwom brimes *I came from the bosom of the sea*, Exon. 103 b; Th. 392, 13; Rä. 11, 7: Andr. Kmbl. 884; An. 442: Beo. Th. 5599; B. 2803. On đam brādan brime *on the broad ocean*, Exon. 55 a; Th. 194, 20; Az. 142: Elen. Kmbl. 505; El. 253: Menol. Fox 423; Men. 213. Brimo fæđmaþ [MS. fæđmeđ] in ceastra gehwǣre *the seas surround* [*them*] *in every city*, Elen. Kmbl. 1941; El. 972. Ealle him brimu blōdige þuhton *all the waters seemed bloody to them*, Cd. 170; Th. 214, 20; Exod. 572: Ps. Th. 106, 28: Beo. Th. 1145; B. 570. Cealde [MS. ceald] brymmas *cold seas*, Chr. 1065; Erl. 196, 31; Edw. 12. Engle and Sexe becōmon ofer brāde brimu *Angles and Saxons came over the broad seas*, Chr. 937; Th. 208, 5; Æđelst. 71: Andr. Kmbl. 1037; An. 519. [*Icel.* brim, *n. surf, the sea: Sansk.* bhram *to agitate, fluctuate.*]

brim-ceald, -cald; *adj.* [brim, ceald *cold*] *Cold as the water of the sea, ice-cold;* frigidus ut aqua maris, frigidissimus, gelidus:—Fēnix brimcald beorgeþ *the Phœnix tastes the ocean-cold* [*water*], Exon. 57 b; Th. 205, 9; Ph. 110. Wæter wynsumu of đære moldan tyrf brimcald brecaþ *pleasant waters, sea-cold, break forth from the turf of the earth*, 56 b; Th. 202, 9; Ph. 67.

brim-clif, es; *n.* [brim, clif *a cliff, rock*] *A sea-cliff;* marinus scopulus:—Đa līđende land gesāwon, brimclifu blīcan, beorgas steápe *the voyagers saw land, the sea-cliffs shine, steep mountains*, Beo. Th. 449; B. 222.

brim-faroþ? es; *n.* [brim, faroþ *the shore*] *The sea-shore;* maris litus:—Bebūgaþ brādne hwyrft ōþ đæt brimfaroþ [MS. brimfaro] *they* *shall inhabit the spacious orb unto the sea-shore*, Cd. 190; Th. 236, 17; Dan. 322.

brim-flód, brym-flód, es; *m.* [brim, flód *a flowing, flood*] *The sea's flowing, the ocean-flood, sea;* maris fluctus, cataclysmus = κατακλυσμός, mare:—Heofonsteorran búgaþ brádne hwearft óþ brimflódas *the stars of heaven encircle the spacious orb unto the ocean floods*, Exon. 53 b; Th. 187, 30; Az. 38. Brymflód *cataclysmus*, Ælfc. Gl. 115; Som. 80, 45; Wrt. Voc. 61, 23: Cot. 50.

brim-fugel; *gen.* -fugles; *m.* [brim, fugel *a bird, fowl*] *A sea-fowl, sea-gull;* marina avis:—He gesihþ baðian brimfuglas *he sees sea-fowls bathe*, Exon. 77 a; Th. 289, 12; Wand. 47.

brim-gæst, -giest, es; *m.* [brim, gæst *a guest*] *A sea-guest, sailor;* marinus hospes, nauta:—Biþ hlúd brimgiesta breahtm *the sailors' noise is loud*, Exon. 101 b; Th. 384, 9; Rä. 4, 25.

brim-hengest, es; *m.* [brim, hengest *a horse*] *A sea-horse, ship;* marinus equus, navis:—Hí brimhengest bringeþ to lande *the ship brings them to land*, Runic pm. 16; Kmbl. 342, 19; Hick. Thes. i. 135. We brecaþ ofer bæþweg brimhengestum *we sail over the sea in ships*, Andr. Kmbl. 1026; An. 513.

brim-hlæst, e; *f.* [brim, hlæst *a burden*] *The sea's burden, fishes;* maris onus, pisces:—Brúcaþ brimhlæste and heofonfugla *enjoy fishes and fowls of heaven*, Cd. 10; Th. 13, 10; Gen. 200.

brim-lád, e; *f.* [brim, lád *a way, path*] *The path of the sea, sea-way;* maris via:—Ic in brimláde bídan sceolde *I must remain on the sea's path*, Exon. 81 b; Th. 307, 27; Seef. 30. Ðe brimláde teáh *who came the sea-way*, Beo. Th. 2107; B. 1051.

brim-líðende; *part.* [brim, líðende; *part. of* líðan *to go, sail*] *Sea-faring;* per æquora navigans:—Se beót abeád brimlíðendra *he declared the threats of the sea-faring [men]*, Byrht. Th. 132, 37; By. 27. Hie ymb brontne ford brimlíðende ne letton *they have not hindered sea-faring [men] about the deep ford*, Beo. Th. 1141; B. 568.

brim-man, -mann, es; *m. A seaman, sailor;* nauta:—Brimmen wódon *the seamen proceeded*, Byrht. Th. 140, 29; By. 295. Brimmanna, *gen. pl.* 133, 12; By. 49.

brim-nesen, e; *f.* [brim, nesan *to be saved from*] *A safe sea-passage;* per æquora iter salvum:—Gif hie brimnesen settan móston *if they should make a safe sea-passage*, Elen. Kmbl. 2006; El. 1004.

brim-rád, e; *f. The sea-road, the sea;* maris cursus, mare:—Geofon swaðrode, brimrád gebád *the ocean subsided, the sea-road stopped*, Andr. Kmbl. 3172; An. 1589: 2525; An. 1264.

brim-streám, brym-streám, es; *m.* [brim, streám *a stream, river*]. I. *the sea's current, ocean-stream, the sea, ocean;* maris fluctus, mare, oceanus:—Ic on brimstreáme spræc worda worn *I spake many words on the ocean-stream*, Andr. Kmbl. 1806; An. 905. Beóton brimstreámas *the sea-streams dashed*, 477; An. 239. Ic eów ferian wille ofer brimstreámas *I will convey you over the seas*, 695; An. 348: Beo. Th. 3825; B. 1910. II. *a rapid stream, river;* fluvius rapidus, amnis:—Humbran eá, bráda brimstreám *Humber's river, broad rapid stream*, Chr. 942; Th. 208, 38, col. 1, 2, 3.

brim-þisa, an; *m:* -þise, an; *f.* [brim, -þisa, -þise *a noise*] *A ship;* navis:—He brimþisan æt sǽs faroþe sécan wolde *he would seek a ship on the sea-shore*, Andr. Kmbl. 3313; An. 1659. Léton ofer fífelwǽg scríðan bronte brimþisan *they let the high ships go over the ocean*, Elen. Kmbl. 475; El. 238.

brim-wísa, an; *m.* [brim, wísa *a leader, guide*] *A sea-leader, leader of sailors;* per maris æstum dux, nautarum dux:—Abreót brimwísan, brýd aheorde *he slew the sea-leader, set free his bride*, Beo. Th. 5852; B. 2930.

brim-wudu; *m.* [brim, wudu *wood*] *Sea-wood, a ship;* maris lignum, navis:—Brimwudu scynde leóht to hýðe *the light ship hastened to the port*, Exon. 52 a; Th. 182, 5; Gú. 1305. Meahte gesíón brecan ofer bæþweg brimwudu *he could see the ship sail over the sea*, Elen. Kmbl. 488; El. 244.

brim-wylf, e; *f.* [brim, wylf *a she-wolf*] *A sea-wolf;* marina lupa. An epithet applied to Grendel's mother:—Hine seó brimwylf abróten hæfde *the sea-wolf had destroyed him*, Beo. Th. 3202; B. 1599.

brim-wylm, es; *m.* [brim, wylm *æstus*] *The sea's surge;* maris æstus:—Brimwylm onféng hilde rince *the sea's surge received the man of war*, Beo. Th. 2993; B. 1494.

bring, es; *m.* [bringan *to bring*] *That which is brought, an offering, a sacrifice;* sacrificium, holocaustum:—Ðú onféhst bringas *acceptabis holocausta*, Ps. Trin. Camb. 50, 20. DER. on-bring.

BRINGAN; *part.* bringende; ic bringe, brincge, ðú bringst, he bringeþ, brincgeþ, bringþ, *pl.* bringaþ; *p.* ic, he brang, brong, ðú brunge, *pl.* brungon; *pp.* brungen; *v. a. To* BRING, *adduce, lead, produce, bear, carry:* ferre, adducere, ducere, producere, offerre, proferre:—Hwǽr is ðæt tiber, ðæt ðú bringan þencest *where is the gift which thou thinkest to bring?* Cd. 140; Th. 175, 7; Gen. 2891: Exon. 23 b; Th. 65, 23; Cri. 1059. Ic ðé þúsenda þegna bringe *I will bring thee thousands of warriors*, Beo. Th. 3663; B. 1829: Exon. 103 a; Th. 390, 22; Rä. 9, 5. Winter bringeþ weder ungemetcald *winter brings weather excessively cold*, Bt. Met. Fox 11, 117; Met. 11, 59: 11, 125; Met. 11, 63. Regn wolcen brincgeþ *a cloud brings rain*, Ps. Th. 67, 10. Seó eorþe westmas bringþ *the earth produces fruits*, Bt. 33, 4; Fox 130, 7. His bodan bringaþ *his angels bring*, Cd. 25; Th. 32, 28; Gen. 510: 231; Th. 286, 24; Sat. 357. Bring us hǽlo líf *bring us a life of health*, Exon. 10 a; Th. 10, 11; Cri. 150. He ða býsene from Gode brungen hæfde *he had brought the mandates from God*, Cd. 30; Th. 41, 4; Gen. 651: 176; Th. 221, 3; Dan. 82. [*Chauc. R. Brun. R. Glouc.* bringe: *O. Sax.* brengian, bringan: *Frs.* bringe: *O. Frs.* branga, bringa: *Dut.* brengen: *Kil.* brenghen: *Ger. M. H. Ger.* bringen: *O. H. Ger.* bringan: *Goth.* briggan.] DER. ge-bringan, onge-, to-, þurh-.

brinnan; *p.* bran, *pl.* brunnon; *pp.* brunnen *To burn;* ardere. DER. on-brinnan. v. beornan.

briord, es; *m. A brim, margin, rim, the highest part of anything;* labrum, ora, margo, summitas, summum:—Gefyldon ða to briorde *impleverunt eas ad summum*, Jn. Lind. War. 2, 7. v. brerd.

briosa, an; *m. A* BREESE, *gad-fly;* asilus, tabānus, Cot. 160; Wrt. Voc. 281, 32.

brist *supportest;* vehis; *for* birst, *2nd pres. s. of* beran *to bear, support:*—Ðú birst [MS. brist] ealle þing búton geswince *thou supportest all things without labour*, Bt. 33, 4; Fox 132, 36.

bristl *a bristle;* seta. v. byrst.

brit *knits;* plectit. v. bredan.

Briten, Britten, e; *f. Britain;* Britannia:—Britene ígland ys eahta hund míla lang *the island of Britain is eight hundred miles long*, Chr. Th. 3, 1, col. 3. Brittene ígland *the island of Britain*, Chr. Th. 3, 1, col. 2. v. Bryten.

Brittas; *pl. m. The Britons;* Britones, Chr. Th. 3, 31, col. 2. v. Brytas, Bryttas.

brittian *to dispense:*—Gold brittade *dispensed gold*, Cd. 59; Th. 72, 4; Gen. 1181. v. bryttian.

Brittisc *British*, Chr. Erl. 3, 3; Th. 3, 5, col. 2. v. Bryttisc.

brittnere *a steward;* dispensator, Past. 63, Lye. v. brytnere.

BRÍW, es; *m. A thick pottage made of meal, pulse, etc,* BREWIS; puls; *gen.* pultis = πόλτος *porridge:*—Ðes bríw *this pottage;* hæc puls, Ælfc. Gr. 9, 46; Som. 13, 9: Wrt. Voc. 290, 38. Swá þicce swá bríw *as thick as pottage*, L. M. 1, 36; Lchdm. ii. 88, 18: 2, 51; Lchdm. ii. 266, 25. Ete ðone bríw *let him eat the pottage*, 1, 36; Lchdm. ii. 88, 2: 2, 51; Lchdm. ii. 264, 19. Bríwas niman *pultes accipere*, Lchdm. iii. 210, 4. [*Plat.* brij, *m: Frs.* bry: *Dut.* brij, *m: Ger.* brei, *m: M. H. Ger.* brî, brîe, *m: O. H. Ger.* brî, brîo, *m.*] DER. calwer-bríw.

bríwan; *p.* de; *pp.* ed *To cook, dress food;* coquere:—Bríw his mete wið ele *dress his meat with oil*, L. M. 2, 51; Lchdm. ii. 264, 22; 266, 29. v. breówan.

BROC, es; *m? A* BROCK, *badger;* taxo = tassus [= tasso *It:* taisson *Fr.*], meles:—Broc *taxo* vel *melus*, Wrt. Voc. 78, 4: Ælfc. Gl. 19; Som. 59, 10; Wrt. Voc. 22, 53. Sum fyðerféte nýten is, ðæt we nemnaþ taxonem, ðæt ys broc on Englisc *there is a four-footed animal, which we name taxonem, that is brock in English*, Med. ex Quadr. 1, 2; Lchdm. i. 326, 12. [*Wyc.* brok: *Laym.* brockes, *pl: Dan.* brok: *Icel.* brokkr, *m: Wel. Corn.* broch: *Ir.* broc, *m: Gael.* broc, bruic, *m: Manx* broc, *m: Armor.* broc'h, *m.*]

BRÓC; *gen.* bróce; *dat.* bréc; *acc.* bróc, bréc; *pl. nom. acc.* bréc, brǽc; *gen.* bróca; *dat.* brócum; *f.* I. *the* BREECH; nates:—Under ða bréc *under the breech*, L. M. 1, 71; Lchdm. ii. 146, 3. II. *a covering for the breech, in pl.* BREECHES, *trousers, pantaloons;* braca, bracæ, femoralia:—Bréc *femoralia*, R. Ben. 55. Brǽc *femoralia*, Wrt. Voc. 81, 63. [*Chauc.* brech, *pl: Wyc.* brechis, *pl: Piers P.* brech, *pl: R. Brun.* breke, *pl: R. Glouc.* brych, *pl: Laym.* brechen, *dat. s;* breches, *pl: Scot.* breek, breik; *pl.* breeks, breiks: *Plat.* brook, broke, *f: Frs.* broek, *f. pudendorum tegumentum: O. Frs.* brok, *pl.* brek, *f: Dut.* broek, *f: Kil.* broecke *bracha: Ger.* bruch, *f. n. femorale: M. H. Ger.* bruoch, *f: O. H. Ger.* bruoh, bruoch, brôch, *n;* bruocha, *f: Dan.* brog, *c: Swed.* bracka, *f: Icel.* brók; *pl.* brækr, *f: Fr.* braie, *f: Span. Port.* braga: *Lat.* brācæ, *pl. f: Grk.* βράκαι, *pl. f: Ir.* broages: *Armor.* bragez, *m.*] DER. bréc-hrægel: wǽd-bréc.

bróc, es; *m.* [bróc, *perf. of* bracan *to break, purl, ripple*] *A* BROOK; latex, torrens:—Se bróc *the brook*, Bt. 6; Fox 14, 27. Burna oððe bróc *latex*, Wrt. Voc. 80, 69. Bróc *torrens*, Ælfc. Gl. 98; Som. 76, 78; Wrt. Voc. 54, 22. Bróc biþ onwended *the brook is turned aside*, Bt. Met. Fox 5, 38; Met. 5, 19. [*Laym.* broc: *Plat.* brook: *Dut.* broek, *f: Ger.* bruch, *m. n. palus: M. H. Ger.* bruoch, *n: O. H. Ger.* bruoh, *n.*]

bróc, es; *pl.* brócu; *n:* bróc, gebróc, metaphorically, that which violently breaks from the body or mind; hence, *Affliction, misery, tribulation, trouble, labour, adversity, a disease, malady, sickness;* afflictio, miseria, tribulatio, labor, adversitas, morbus, ægritudo:—God nyle nán unaberendlíce bróc him ansettan *God wishes not to put on them any unbearable affliction*, Bt. 39, 10; Fox 228, 4. Mid heardum bróce *with severe [hard] affliction*, Bt. 39, 11; Fox 228, 25. He on ðæm bróce nyle alǽtan ðás eorþlícan wilnunga *in affliction he will not give up these earthly desires*, Past. 37, 3; Hat. MS. 50 a, 18, 21, 22: 36, 4; Hat. MS. 47 b, 7. On đám brócum *in these afflictions*, Th. Diplm. A. D. 880–885; 485, 24. Ðæt hit sý gefreód ǽghwylcere uneáþnesse ealles woroldlíces bróces *that it be freed from every annoyance of all worldly trouble*, 1061; 389, 30: 864; 125, 13: Past. 37, 3; Hat. MS. 50 a, 7. Ðæt biþ swíđe hefig bróc *it is a very severe labour;* gravis labor est, 61, 1; Hat. MS. Eucharius wæs þearle geswenct mid langsumum bróce *Eucharius was much afflicted with a protracted disease*, Homl. Th. ii. 24, 16: 176, 32. Brócu *miseriæ*, Lye. DER. ge-bróc.

bróc, es; *m?* [bróc, *p. of* bracan] *An inferior horse, a shaking horse, jade;* caballus, equus vilior:—Ðæt hie sécen him bróc on onráde, and on wǽne, ođđe on đon đe hie á þrówian mǽgen *that they look for themselves to ride on a horse, and in a wain, or in that which they can ever endure*, L. M. 2, 6; Lchdm. ii. 184, 13. [*Chauc.* brok: *Icel.* brokkr, *m.*]

broccen *vel* gǽten roc, es; *m.* [broc *a badger*, gǽten *goaten, caprine*, roc *a garment*] *A garment made of badger* or *goat-skins, extending from the shoulders to the loins;* melotes, Ælfc. Gl. 63; Som. 68, 117; Wrt. Voc. 40, 27.

bróce *use*, Bd. 3, 22; Whelc. 221, 39, note B. C. v. brýce.

brocen *enjoyed*,=gebrocen, Exon. 38 b; Th. 127, 29; Gú. 393; *pp. of* brúcan, gebrúcan.

brocen *broken*, Beo. Th. 4132; B. 2063; *pp. of* brecan.

brócian; *part.* brócigende; ic brócie, đú brócast, he brócaþ, *pl.* bróciaþ; *p.* ode; *pp.* ge-brócod; *v. a.* [bróc *affliction*] *To oppress, vex, afflict, break up, injure, blame;* opprimere, vexare, affligere, confringere, nocere, accusare:—Ic beóde đæt hý nán man ne brócie *I command that no man oppress them*, Th. Diplm. A.D. 880–885; 492, 10. Ða manigfealdan yrmþa đa wérigan burh brócigende wǽron *manifold miseries afflicted* [lit. *were afflicting*] *the weary city*, Ors. 2, 4; Bos. 42, 36. Ða gebétan đe hí bróciaþ *to amend those whom they afflict*, Bt. 39, 11; Fox 230, 8. Se synfulla biþ gebrócod for his unrihtwísnysse *the sinful is afflicted for his unrighteousness*, Homl. Th. i. 472, 3: 474, 19. Ðæt gebrócode flǽsc gelǽrþ đæt upahæfene mód *the afflicted flesh teaches the proud mind*, Past. 36, 7; Hat. MS. 48 a, 22. We for úrum synnum gebrócode beóþ *we are afflicted for our sins*, Homl. Th. i. 476, 19. Næfde se here Angelcyn gebrócod *the army had not broken up the English race*, Chr. 897; Erl. 94, 30. Hí gefeóllon of ánre upflóran and sume swíđe gebrócode wǽron *they fell from an upper floor and some were much injured*, 978; Erl. 127, 12. Gif đé mon brócie for rihtre scylde, geþola hit wel *if a man blame thee for a just cause, bear it well*, Prov. Kmbl. 45. DER. wiđer-brócian.

bróc-líc; *adj. Sick, grieved, miserable;* æger. DER. bróc.

bróc-líce; *adv. Sickly, grievously;* ægre. DER. bróc.

bróc-minte, an; *f:* bróc-mint, e; *f.* BROOKMINT, *horsemint;* mentha sylvestris, Lin. Σισύμβριον *sisymbrium officinale:*—Brócminte. Genim đysse wyrte wós, đe man sisymbrium, and óđrum naman brócminte nemneþ *Brookmint. Take the juice of this plant, which men call σισύμβριον, and by another name, brookmint*, Herb. 107; Lchdm. i. 220, 17.

brócu *troubles; pl. of* bróc, es; *n.*

brócung, e; *f.* [bróc *affliction, sickness*] *Sickness;* ægritudo:—Þurh his brócunge *through his sickness*, Homl. Th. i. 472, 7.

bród, e; *f.* I. *a growing together, congealing, waxing hard;* concretio, Cot. 55. II. *a* BROOD; proles. v. bródig. [*R. Glouc.* brod: *Scot.* brod: *Dut.* ge-broed, *n: Ger.* brut, *f. a brood: M.H.Ger.* bruot, *f.*]

bród; *adv. Freely, of free cost;* gratis:—Bród *gratis*, Wrt. Voc. 284, 71.

broddetan, brodettan *To tremble, quake, to pant for fear;* tremere, trepidare, palpitare, Greg. Dial. 2, 25: Cot. 154, Som. Lye.

broden *woven, braided*, Beo. Th. 1108; B. 552; *pp. of* bredan.

bróđer *a brother:*—Bróđer sune *a brother's son*, Ælfc. Gl. 91; Som. 75, 27; Wrt. Voc. 51, 71. v. bróđor.

brodetung, e; *f. A work, workmanship, fashion, forged tale, a lie;* figmentum:—He oncneów brodetunge [MS. brogdetunge] úre *ipse cognovit figmentum nostrum*, Ps. Spl. C. 102, 13.

bródig; *adj.* BROODY, *brooding;* incubans:—Bródige henne *a broody hen*, Bridf.

broel, brogel, es; *n.* [corrupted from the *Mid. Lat.* brolium *or* briolium] *A park, warren stored with deer;* hence the BROYL, *a wood in Sussex, belonging to the Archbishop of Canterbury;* vivarium, hortus cervorum, Som. [*O. H. Ger.* brogil, broil.]

BRÓGA, an; *m. A prodigy, monster, trembling, fear, terror, horror, dread;* monstrum, tremor, terror, horror:—Ǽnig óđer bróga *any other prodigy*, Bt. 36, 1; Fox 172, 17. Iówer ege and bróga sie ofer ealle eorþan nítenu *terror vester ac tremor sit super cuncta animalia terræ*, Past. 17, 2; Hat. MS. 22 a, 14. Brógan đíne gedréfdon me *terrores tui conturbaverunt me*, Ps. Spl. 87, 17. Bútan brógan *without dread*, Lev. 26, 6. Hine se bróga angeat *terror laid hold of him*, Beo. Th. 2587; B. 1291. Ne con he đæs brógan dǽl *he knoweth not a portion of the terror*, Exon. 117 a; Th. 449, 15; Dóm. 71. Ðǽr is brógna [=brógena] hýhst *there is the greatest of terrors*, 116 a; Th. 446, 17; Dóm. 23. [*O. H. Ger.* brógo, *m.*] DER. bryne-bróga, gryre-, here-, spere-, wæter-, wíte-.

brogden *woven, cast*, Elen. Kmbl. 513; El. 257; *pp. of* bregdan.

brogden-mǽl, es; *n.* [brogden, *pp. of* bregdan, mǽl *a spot, mark*] *Turned* or *marked with a spot* or *sign;* tortum *vel* curvatum signum:—Beofaþ brogden-mǽl *what is marked by signs* [*the sword*] *trembles* or *glitters*, Elen. Kmbl. 1514; El. 759.

brohte, đú brohtest, *pl.* brohton; *pp.* broht *Brought, broughtest, brought*, Cd. 29; Th. 38, 32; Gen. 615: Exon. 121 a; Th. 463, 34; Hö. 80: Elen. Kmbl. 1989; El. 996: Bd. 3, 7; S. 529, 30; *p. and pp. of* brengan.

bróh-þreá; *m. f. n. indecl. but in dat. and inst. pl.* [bróh=bróg *terror*, þreá *calamitas*] *Terrific calamity;* calamitas terroris plena:—Ðæt bróhþreá Cananéa wearþ cynne getenge *the terrific calamity was grievous to the Canaanites' race*, Cd. 86; Th. 108, 29; Gen. 1813. v. þreá.

BRÓM, es; *m. The well-known shrub from which besoms are made*, hence BROOM; genista:—Bróm *genista*, Ælfc. Gl. 46; Som. 64, 130; Wrt. Voc. 32, 64: L. M. 1, 55; Lchdm. ii. 126, 12: 1, 32; Lchdm. ii. 78, 19: Wrt. Voc. 80, 16: 285, 69. Genim brómes ahsan *take ashes of broom*, L. M. 1, 2; Lchdm. ii. 32, 12. [*Chauc. Wyc.* bromes, *pl: Dut.* brem, *f: Kil.* brem *genista.*]

Bróm-dún, e; *f.* [bróm *broom*, dún *a hill*] BRUMDON, *Dorset;* hodie opinor Brumdon in agro Dorsetensi:—Ðæt gemót wæs on Brómdúne *the meeting was at Brumdon*, L. Eth. iii. 4; Th. i. 294, 14: Cod. Dipl. 1322; A. D. 1035; Kmbl. vi. 186, 13, 14.

bróm-fæsten, es; *n.* [bróm *broom*, fæsten *an inclosed place*] *A broom-field, a field, close* or *wood of broom;* myricæ campus, myricetum, genesteium, Cot. 97.

brond *a fire-brand, fire, sword*, Exon. 74 a; Th. 277, 15; Jul. 581: Beo. Th. 6021; B. 3014: 2912; B. 1454. v. brand.

brond-hát *ardent*, Exon. 46 b; Th. 160, 2; Gú. 937. v. brand-hát.

brond-hord, es; *n.* [brand II. *a burning*, hord *a hoard, treasure*] *A burning* or *ardent treasure, a treasure exciting ardent desires;* ardens thesaurus:—Se ǽr in dæge wæs dýre, scríđeþ nú deóp feor, brondhord geblówen, breóstum in forgrówen *copper was dear in* [*that*] *day, now it circulates wide and far, an ardent treasure flourishing, grown up in the hearts*, Exon. 94 b; Th. 354, 15; Reim. 46.

Brondingas; *nom. acc; gen.* a; *dat.* um; *pl. m. The Brondings, supposed to be the inhabitants of the island Brännö, lying off the coast of West Gothland in the Cattegat;* populi nomen:—Breca gesóhte swǽsne éđel, lond Brondinga *Breca sought his own country, the land of the Brondings*, Beo. Th. 1047; B. 521. Breoca weóld Brondingum *Breca ruled the Brondings*, Scóp Th. 51; Wíd. 25.

brond-stæfn; *adj. The shining prowed;* proram spuma fulgentem habens:—Storm ne mæg brecan brondstæfne *a storm cannot break the shining* [*foaming*] *prowed* [*ship*], Andr. Kmbl. 1007; An. 504.

brong *brought; p. of* bringan.

bront *high, deep, steep, difficult*, Beo. Th. 482; B. 238: 1140; B. 568: Elen. Kmbl. 475; El. 238. v. brant.

BRORD, es; *m? A prick* or *point, a lance, javelin, the first blade* or *spire of grass* or *corn, etc;* punctus, cuspis, frumenti spica, herba:—Brord *punctus*, Cot. 157. Ne furđan brordas *not even blades;* ne herbæ quidem, Bd. 4, 28; S. 605, 35. Brord *herba*, Mt. Lind. Rush. Stv. 13, 26. Ðæt brord *natum*, Lk. Lind. War. 8, 6. [*Orm.* brodd: *Dan.* bred, brodde, *m. f: Swed.* brodd, *m: O. Nrs.* broddr, *m. aculeus, telum, frons aciei* vel *agminis.*]

brosnian; *part.* brosniende; ic brosnige, đú brosnast, he brosnaþ, *pl.* brosniaþ; *p.* ode, ade; *pp.* od *To corrupt, decay, rot, perish;* corrumpi, deficere, dissolvi, perire:—Ðære fǽmnan líchoma brosnian ne mihte *the body of the maiden could not corrupt;* feminæ caro corrumpi non potuit, Bd. 4, 19; S. 587, 36. Him hyge brosnaþ *his mind corrupts*, Exon. 81 a; Th. 304, 11; Fä. 68. Brosnaþ enta geweorc, hrófas sind gehrorene *the work of giants is decaying, the roofs are fallen*, Exon. 124 a; Th. 476, 4; Ruin. 2: Beo. Th. 4512; B. 2260. Ða beámas á gréne stondaþ, nǽfre brosniaþ *the trees always stand green, never decay*, Exon. 56 a; Th. 200, 10; Ph. 38. Cristene Róma besprycþ, đæt hyre weallas for ealdunge brosnian *Christian Rome complains, that her walls decay with age*, Ors. 2, 4; Bos. 44, 45. Ðes brosnienda wéla *this perishing wealth*, Bt. 16, 1; Fox 50, 33. Brosnade burgsteal *the city-place has perished*, Exon. 124 a; Th. 477, 23; Ruin. 29. DER. gebrosnod, unge-: brosniendlíc, brosnigendlíc, un-: brosnung, ge-, un-.

brosniend-líc, brosnigend-líc; *adj. Corruptible, perishable;* corruptibilis:—Ðæt wæter is brosniendlíc wǽta *water is a corruptible fluid*, Homl. Th. ii. 270, 5, 8, 13, 33. Geneálǽhþ đam brosniendlícum wætere *he approaches the corruptible water*, ii. 270, 1. DER. un-brosnigendlíc.

brosnung, e; *f. Corruption, decay;* corruptio, defectio:—Ic niđerastíge on brosnunge *descendo in corruptionem*, Ps. Lamb. 29, 10: Homl. Th. ii. 206, 2: 268, 35: 536, 20. Wæs ne wélan brosnung *there was no decay of wealth*, Exon. 44 b; Th. 151, 25; Gú. 800. DER. ge-brosnung, un-.

brot, es; *n.* [broten; *pp. of* breótan *to break*] *A fragment;* fragmentum. [*Icel.* brot, *n.*] DER. ge-brot.

Broten *Britain*, Bd. 3, 29; S. 561, 15. v. Bryten.

broten *bruised, broken; pp. of* breótan.

BROþ, es; *n.* BROTH; jus:—Broþ *jus*, Wrt. Voc. 82, 60. Fætt broþ ge mâgon habban *pingue jus potestis habere*, Coll. Monast. Th. 29, 13. [*M.H. Ger. Bav.* brod, *n: O.H. Ger.* brôd, brôt, *n.*]

brôđar *a brother*, Th. Diplm. A.D. 830; 466, 3. v. brôđor.

brôđer *a brother*:—Ne ic hȳrde wæs brôđer mînes *nor was I keeper of my brother*, Cd. 48; Th. 62, 2; Gen. 1008: Mt. Bos. 5, 24. v. brôđor.

BRÔĐOR, brôđer, brôder, brôđur; *d.* brêđer; *but often indecl. in sing; pl. nom. acc.* brôđor, brôđer, brôđur, brôđru, brôđro, ge-brôđor, er, ru, ro, ra; *g.* brôđra, ge-brôđra; *d.* brôđrum, ge-brôđrum; *m. A* BROTHER; frater:—Ûre brôđor *noster frater, nom. s; g.* ûres brôđor *nostri fratris; dat.* ûrum brêđer *nostro fratri; acc.* ûrne brôđor *nostrum fratrem; voc.* eálâ đû ûre brôđor *O noster frater! abl.* fram ûrum brêđer *a nostro fratre: pl. nom.* ûre gebrôđra *nostri fratres; g.* ûra gebrôđra *nostrorum fratrum; dat.* ûrum gebrôđrum *nostris fratribus; acc.* ûre gebrôđra *nostros fratres; abl.* fram ûrum gebrôđrum *a nostris fratribus*, Ælfc. Gr. 15; Som. 19, 18-23. Hwǣr is đîn brôđor *ubi est frater tuus?* Gen. 4, 9: Mt. Bos. 5, 23. Brôđor Arones *Aaron's brother*, Cd. 124; Th. 158, 21; Gen. 2620: 47; Th. 60, 19; Gen. 984. Geboren brôđer *germanus frater*, Greg. Dial. 2, 13. Đînes brôđor blôd clypaþ *fratris tui sanguis clamat*, Gen. 4, 10. His brôđor bearn *his brother's child*, Beo. Th. 5231; B. 2619. Sege mînum brêđer *dic fratri meo*, Lk. Bos. 12, 13. Cain gewearþ to ecg-banan ângan brêđer *Cain became a murderer to his only brother*, Beo. Th. 2529; B. 1262: Ps. Th. 34, 14: Mk. Bos. 12, 19. Brôđor þrȳ *the three brothers*, Cd. 94; Th. 122, 28; Gen. 2033. His brôđru fôron *fratres ejus ascenderunt*, Jn. Bos. 7, 10. His brôđro cwǣdon *fratres ejus dixerunt*, 7, 3. For mîne brôđru *propter fratres meos*, Ps. Th. 121, 8. Đe ne onfô brôđru and swustra *qui non accipiat fratres et sorores*, Mk. Bos. 10, 30. Hyre brôđra deáþ *the death of her brothers*, Exon. 100 a; Th. 377, 24; Deór. 8. Gemang brôđrum *inter fratres*, Jn. Bos. 21, 23. [*Plat.* broder, *m: O. Sax.* brôthar, *m: O. Frs.* brôther, broder, *m: Dut.* broeder, *m: Ger.* bruder, *m: M.H. Ger.* bruoder, *m: O.H. Ger.* bruodar, brôdar, *m: Goth.* broþar, *m: Dan. Swed.* broder, *m: O. Nrs.* brôđir, brôdir, *m: Lat.* frater, *m: Grk.* φράτηρ: *Ir.* brathair, *m: Wel.* brawd; *pl.* brodyr, *m: Sansk.* bhrâtṛi, *from root* bhṛi [*A. Sax.* beran] *to bear, support, a brother being the natural supporter of sisters who have lost their father.*] DER. fæderen-brôđor, freó-, ge-, sige-. v. ge-brôđor.

brôđor-bana, an; *m. A brother-slayer, fratricide*; fratricida:—Ic monnes feorh sede to brôđorbanan *I will avenge man's life on the fratricide*, Cd. 75; Th. 92, 9; Gen. 1526.

brôđor-cwealm, es; *m. Brother-murder, fratricide*; fratricidium:—Se me gemonige brôđorcwealmes *who shall remind me of my fratricide*, Cd. 49; Th. 63, 10; Gen. 1030.

brôđor-gefædred *a brother by the same father*; frater ex eodem patre ortus, Ors. 3, 7; Bos. 60, 19. v. ge-fædrian.

brôđor-gemêdred *a brother by the same mother*; frater ex eadem matre ortus, Gen. Grn. 43, 29. v. ge-mêdrian.

brôđor-gyld, es; *n. Brother-retribution, vengeance for brothers*; fratrum cædis retributio:—On hyra brôđorgyld [brôđra gyld, *Thorpe*] *in vengeance for their brothers*, Cd. 153; Th. 190, 15; Exod. 199.

brôđor-leás; *adj.* BROTHERLESS; fratrem non habens, Exon. 129 a; Th. 496, 17; Rä. 85, 16.

brôđor-lîc, brôđer-lîc; *adj.* BROTHERLY; fraternus:—Þurh đa brôđorlîcan þingunge *per fraternam intercessionem*, Bd. 4, 22; S. 592, 21: Ælfc. Gr. 5; Som. 4, 57.

brôđor-lîcnes, -nys, -nyss, e; *f.* BROTHERLINESS; fraternitas:—Đîn brôđorlîcnys is on Mynstres reogolum getȳd and gelǣred *tua fraternitas Monasterii regulis erudita est*, Bd. 1, 27; S. 489, 10.

brôđor-rǣden, brôđer-rǣdenn, e; *f. Brotherhood*; fraternitas, Ælfc. Gr. 5; Som. 5, 21.

brôđor-sib, -sibb, -syb, -sybb, e; *f.* I. *brotherhood, the relationship between brothers*; cognatio fraternalis, germanitas:—Syndon him on æđelum ôđere twegen beornas, geborene brôđorsybbum [Kmbl. 1380, -sibbum] *to him in his family are other twain men, born in brotherly-relationship*, An. 690: Cot. 100. II. *brotherly love*; fraternus amor:—Hî brôđorsibbe georne bigongaþ *they earnestly cultivate brotherly love*, Exon. 44 b; Th. 150, 10; Gû. 776.

brôđor-slaga, an; *m. A* BROTHER-SLAYER; fratricida, Wrt. Voc. 85, 47. v. brôđor *a brother*, slaga *a slayer*.

brôđor-þinen, -þinenu, e; *f. A midwife at the birth of twin-brothers*; fratres geminos parturienti obstetrix, Gen. 38, 28.

brôđor-wyrt, e; *f.* BROTHER-WORT, *the herb pennyroyal*; mentha pulegium, Wrt. Voc. 68, 61.

brôđur; *m. A brother*; frater:—His âgen brôđur *his own brother*, Ps. Th. 107, 7: 132, 1. He geseh Iacobum Zebedei and Ioannem his brôđur *vidit Iacobum Zebedæi et Ioannem fratrem ejus*, Mt. Bos. 4, 21. v. brôđor.

browen *brewed, cooked; pp. of* breówan. v. ge-browen, twy-.

BRÛ; *gen. dat. acc.* brûwe; *pl. nom. acc.* brûa, brûwa; *gen.* brûwena, brûena, brûna; *dat.* brûwum; *f. A* BROW, *an eye-brow, eye-lash*; cilium, supercilium, tauto:—Brûa *cilia*, Ælfc. Gl. 70; Som. 70, 62; Wrt. Voc. 42, 70. Brûwa *cilium* [= *cilia*], Wrt. Voc. 64, 35: 282, 49. Brûwa *tautones*, Wrt. Voc. 64, 28. Ic eom wîde calu, ne ic breága ne brûna [= brûena] brûcan môste *I am very bald, nor can I make use of eye-lids nor eye-lashes*, Exon. 111 b; Th. 427, 32; Rä. 41, 100. Betweoh brûwum *intercilium* [= *intercilia*], Wrt. Voc. 64, 34: 282, 48. [*Wyc.* browe, brewe: *Laym.* breowe, bruwe, brouwe: *Prompt.* browe *supercilium: Scot.* bre, bree: *Plat.* brane: *Dut.* wenk-braaw, *f. the brow, eye-brow: O. Dut. Kil.* brauwe, brouwe, *f. cilium, supercilium: Ger.* braue, braune, *f. supercilium: M.H. Ger.* brâwe, *f: O.H. Ger.* brâwa, *f: Dan. Swed.* bryn, *f. n. a border, brink, eye-brow: Icel.* brún, *f. the eye-brow: Lat.* frons, *f. the forehead, brow: Grk.* ὀφρύς, *f. the eye-brow: Sansk.* bhrû, *f. an eye-brow, the brow.*] DER. ofer-brû. v. brǣw.

BRÛCAN, to brûcanne; ic brûce, đû brûcest, brȳcst, brîcst, he brûceþ, brȳcþ, *pl.* brûcaþ; *p.* ic, he breác, đû bruce, *pl.* brucon; *pp.* brocen; *v. a. gen. To use, make use of, to pass, spend, enjoy, have enjoyment of, to eat, bear, discharge*; uti, frui, possidere, habere, gaudere aliqua re, edere:—Đæt he beáh-hordes brûcan môste *that he might have enjoyment of the ring-hoard*, Beo. Th. 1793; B. 894. Ne benohton beornas to brûcanne *needed not men to enjoy*, Andr. Kmbl. 2321; An. 1162. Sâwla môton lîfes brûcan *souls may enjoy* [*have enjoyment of*] *life*, Andr. Kmbl. 458; An. 229. Brûceþ fôdres *enjoys* [*has an enjoyment of*] *food*, Runic pm. 28; Kmbl. 345, 5; Hick. Thes. i. 135. Brûc đisses beáges *make use of this collar*, Beo. Th. 2436; B. 1216. He giefstôlas breác *he enjoyed gifts*, Exon. 77 a; Th. 289, 7; Wand. 44. Đe hyra lîfes þurh lust brucon [MS. brucan] *who have spent their life in pleasure*, Exon. 38 b; Th. 127, 19; Gû. 388. Ne brîcst *usest not*, Deut. 28, 30. Đû brîcst đînes hlâfes *thou shalt eat of thy bread*, Gen. 3, 19. Brûcaþ, Jn. Bos. 4, 9. [*Piers P.* brouke: *Laym.* bruken: *Orm.* brukenn: *Plat.* bruken: *O. Sax.* brûkan: *Frs.* bruke: *O. Frs.* bruka: *Dut.* gebruiken: *Ger.* brauchen: *M.H. Ger.* brûchen: *O.H. Ger.* brûchan: *Goth.* brukyan: *Dan.* bruge: *Swed. Icel.* brúka.] DER. þurh-brûcan: ge-brûcan.

brûcing, e; *f. A function, an occupation, enjoyment*; functio, fruitio, occupatio, usus, Som. Lye. DER. brûcan.

brudon *spread*; dilatarunt, Cd. 154; Th. 191, 29; Exod. 222; *p. pl. of* bredan.

brugdon *laid hold of, drew*; strinxerunt, Cd. 93; Th. 120, 8; Gen. 1991; *p. pl. of* bregdan.

BRÛN; *adj.* BROWN, *dark, dusky*; fuscus, subniger, rufus, furvus:—Sum brûn *part brown*, Exon. 60 a; Th. 218, 17; Ph. 296. Brûne leóde *brown people*; Æthiopes, Cd. 146; Th. 182, 4; Exod. 70. Sió brûne ȳþ *the dusky wave*, Bt. Met. Fox 26, 58; Met. 26, 29. [*Chauc.* browne: *R. Glouc.* broune: *Frs.* brun: *O. Frs.* brun: *Dut.* bruin: *Ger.* braun: *M.H. Ger. O.H. Ger.* brûn: *Dan.* bruun: *Swed.* brun: *Icel.* brúnn.] DER. sealo-brûn.

brûna *of eye-brows*, Exon. 111 b; Th. 427, 32; Rä. 41, 100, = brûena; *gen. pl. of* brû.

Brunan burh; *gen.* Brunan burge; *dat.* Brunan byrig; *f. Brunanburh, about five miles south-west of Durham, or on the plain between the river Tyne and the Browney, Dr. Guest properly writes 'round Brunanburh;'* v. example 1; Brunæ castellum. [Brunan burh is a pure Anglo-Saxon word, and signifies *the castle of Bruna*, though in a charter of Athelstan, dated 978, the year after the battle, it is called Bruninga feld, *the plain of the Brunings, or the descendants of Bruna*, as -ing denotes, v. -ing,—'Acta est hæc præfata donatio anno ab incarnatione Domini nostri Jesu Christi DCCCCXXXVIII, in quo anno bellum factum est in loco qui *Bruninga feld* dicitur, ubi Anglis victoria data est de cælo,' Th. Diplm. 186, 34-37; Cod. Dipl. 374; A.D. 938; Kmbl. ii. 210, 33-37. *Brunanburh* was written by *Ingulf*, in A.D. 1109, Brunford: *Hunt.* in 1148, Brumesburh, Brunesburih, Brunesburh, Bruneburh: *Hovd.* in 1204, Brunnanbyrg, Brumenburh: *Brom.* in 1330, Brunneburyh.] As the exact place cannot be determined by the name of any large town now existing, it is necessary to enter into the history of the battle, and thus ascertain its most probable locality.—Sihtric, king of Northumbria, which then extended from the Humber to the Frith of Forth [v. Angle], was son of Ingwar, and grandson of Ragnar Lodbrog. Sihtric was baptized and married Athelstan's sister in A.D. 925. He soon put away his wife, and renounced Christianity. Athelstan prepared to attack him for rejecting his sister, but Sihtric died, when Anlaf his son fled to Ireland, and Athelstan added Northumbria to his dominions. All the leaders of the Anglo-Danes and the Welsh were jealous of the increasing power of Athelstan, and combined against him. Anlaf, king of Dublin, commenced the fray by sailing from Ireland with 615 ships, containing about 100 men each, making more than 61,000 men: with this force he entered the Humber. He was joined by the Anglo-Danes, by the Welsh, and by Constantine, his father-in-law, the king of the Scots. Athelstan completely routed the immense army brought against him about Brunanburh, and became the first king of England. Alfred the Great was king over all the Anglo-Saxons, but by this complete victory Athelstan became the undisputed king over all England [Engla land, *q. v.*]—The locality of Brunanburh has not yet been determined. It appears to me, it must be north of Beverley, as Athelstan is reported by Ingulf to have visited the tomb of St. John at Beverley, and to have placed his dagger on the altar, making a vow that if victory was granted to him, he would redeem it at a worthy price. The credibility of this story has been questioned; but, whatever doubt may remain, it proves that in the time of Ingulf, A. D. 1109, there was a general impression that Athelstan marched north of Beverley to oppose his invaders, and that, after the victory in the north, on returning to the south, he redeemed his pledge at Beverley by granting many privileges. Anlaf, collecting the remnant of his conquered army, could have no difficulty in returning to his ships in the Humber, as he had to pass through the country of the Anglo-Danes, his friends, and subjects of his late father.—Now all this history indicates that Anlaf marched north to unite his army with that of his father-in-law, Constantine, king of the Scots. Athelstan followed him, and their forces met about Brunanburh. I think it was on the west of Durham. I am led to this conclusion by these facts relating to the battle, and by the *Feodarium Prioratus Dunelmensis, published by the Surtees Society*, vol. lviii, in 1872. There is a plain between the rivers Wear and Browney [Brunan eá], and west of Durham, well adapted for a great battle. We find, in the present day, east and west Brandon [Brunan dūn] and Brandon castle, the property of Viscount Boyne. There is still the river Browney [Brunan eá]. In the *Feod. Dunelmen.* compiled about A. D. 1430, we find the name of a river, of persons, and of places mentioned on the west of Durham. We have 'Ultra aquam de Wer usque ad aquam de Brun,' pref. p. lv: p. 192, note. 'De Brune,' 192, 193, note: 194, note. 'Petro de Brandone,' p. 180, note. 'Petrus de Brandone,' 200, note. On looking at the map of the learned Bishop Gibson, in his Anglo-Saxon Chronicle, 4to. 1692, I find he is of my opinion, that *Brunanburh* was north of Beverley. I cannot, however, discover why he places it to the north of Northumbria. For the reasons I have stated, I believe it was to the south-west of Durham.—Dr. Guest, Master of Caius College, Cambridge, in his excellent work, *A History of English Rhythms*, 8vo. 1838, gives the following account of this battle,—'In the year 937, was fought the battle of *Brunanburh*—a battle, that involved more important interests than any, that has ever yet been fought within this Island. It was indeed a battle between races.... Round the banner of Athelstan were ranged one hundred thousand Englishmen, and before them was the whole power of Scotland, of Wales, of Cumberland, and of Ireland under Anlaf, king of Dublin, led on by sixty thousand Northmen. The song, which celebrated the victory, is worthy of the effort that gained it. This song is found in all the copies of the Chronicle, but with considerable variations. Price collated three of them: *The Dunstan* MS. Tib. A. VI; the Abingdon, Tib. B. I; and the Worcester, Tib. B. IV. I have taken copies from all these MSS, and also from the Plegmund MS. in Ben'et Library. The Dunstan MS. appears to be by far the most correct transcript of the four. Price formed a text, so as best to suit the convenience of translation. The result might have been foreseen, and is such as little encourages imitation. I shall rather give the text, as it is found in *one* of these copies—*the Dunstan MS.* v. Chr. 937; Th. 200, col. 2. Not a word need be altered, to form either good sense or good poetry,' vol. ii. pp. 60, 61. In Mr. Earle's Chronicle, 8vo. 1865, p. 113, note x, are some excellent remarks on this song.—Dr. Guest has arranged the lines according to his system of Rhythm. I have arranged them according to the Anglo-Saxon punctuation, as in the article Beówulf. Dr. Guest's text is given within brackets, when the general orthography, or the word, seemed to require alteration:—

Hēr, DCCCCXXXVII,	*Now*, A. D. 937,
Æðelstān cing,	*Athelstan king,*
eorla drihten,	*of earls the lord,*
beorna beág-gifa,	*of barons the bracelet-*[*beigh-*] *giver,*
and his brōðor eác,	*and his brother also* [*eke*],
Eádmund æðeling,	*Edmund the prince* [*etheling*],
ealdor langne tīr	*elders a long train* [*tire*]
geslōgan æt sæcce [sake],	*slew in battle,*
sweorda eccgum,	*with sword-edges,*
embe Brunan burh.	*round Brunanburh.*
Gst. Rthm. ii. 60, 26-62, 3.	
Ðǣr læg secg manig,	*There lay many a soldier,*
gārum forgrunden,—	*by the darts brought low,—*
guman norþerne,	*northern men,*
ofer scyld sceoten,	*over shield shot,*
swylce Scyttisc eác	*so also* [*eke*] *the Scotchman's*
wērig wīgges sǣd.	*wretched war-spawn.*
Gst. Rthm. ii. 64, 1-4.	
Fīfe lāgon	*Five lay*
on ðæm campstede—	*on that battle-field* [*war-stead*]—
ciningas geonge	*youthful kings*
sweordum aswefede;	*sword-silenced;*
swilce seofone eác	*so also seven*
eorlas Ānlāfes,	*earls of Anlaf,*
unrīm herges—	*a host of the robber-band—*
flotan and Scotta.	*shipmen and Scots.*
Gst. Rthm. ii. 64, 14-18.	
Gewitan him ðā Norþmen	*Went* [*gan*] *then the Northmen*
nægled-cnearrum—	*in their nailed barks—*
[dreórig daroða lāf	[*the darts' sad leavings*
on dynges mere]	*on the noisy sea*]
ofer deóp wæter,	*over deep water,*
Dyflen sēcean	*Dublin* [*Dyflen*]
eft Iraland.	*Ireland* [*the land of the Ire*] *to seek once more.*
Gst. Rthm. ii. 66, 19-22.	
Ne wearþ wæl māre	*Was no greater carnage*
on ðisum [ðys] ēglande	*ever yet,*
ǣfre gyta, . . .	*within this island, . . .*
syððan eástan, hider	*since from the east, hither*
Engle and Sexan	*up came*
upp becōman.	*Angles and Saxons* [*Engle and Sexe*].
Gst. Rthm. ii. 68, 10-15.	

Hēr, A. D. 937, Æðelstān cyning lǣdde fyrde to Brunan byrig *in this year*, A. D. 937, *king Athelstan led an army to Brunanburh*, Chr. 937; Th. 201, 25-27, col. 2. Hēr, A. D. 937, Æðelstān [Æðestan MS.] cing and Eádmund his brōðer lǣdde fyrde to Brunan byrig [MS. Brunan byri]; and ðār gefeht wið Ānlāfe [MS. Anelaf]; and, Criste fultumegende, sige hæfde *in this year*, A. D. 937, *king Athelstan and Edmund his brother led an army to Brunanburh; and there fought against Anlaf; and, Christ aiding, they had victory*, Chr. 937; Erl. 113, 2-4.

brūn-basu, -baso; *adj.* [brūn *brown*, basu *purple*] *Dark-purple, purple, purple-red, scarlet;* purpureus, ostriger, coccineus, puniceus:—Brūnbasere reádnysse *purpureo ostro*, Mone B. 6102. Brūnbasewum [MS. -bæsewum], reádum *purpureis*, 2087. Brūnbasum *purpureis*, 189. Brūnbaso *ostriger*, Cot. 145. Brūnbasne *coccineum*, Mone B. 6153. Ðȳ brūnan oððe ðȳ brūnbasewan *puniceo*, Cot. 183.

brūn-ecg; *adj.* [brūn *brown*, ecg *an edge*] *Brown-edged;* nigra acie præditus:—Byrhtnōþ bræd bill of sceðe, brād and brūnecg *Byrhtnoth drew his battle-axe from its sheath, broad and brown of edge*, Byrht. Th. 136, 38; By. 163: Beo. Th. 3096; B. 1546.

brūnēða, an; *m. A disease called* brunella *or* pruna; morbus quidam, *idem forte*, qui Belgis *bruyne*, id est, Erysipelas [= ἐρυσίπελας] cerebri. Oris vitium, cum linguæ tumore, exasperatione, siccitate, et nigredine, *vulgo*, inquit *Kilianus*, brunella, *Som*:—Ðæt biþ strang sealf and gōd wið swelcre ablāwunge and brūnēðan, and wið ðara ceácna geswelle, oððe asmorunge *that is a strong salve and good for such inflation and brunella, and for swelling of the jaws, or smothering*, L. M. 1, 4; Lchdm. ii. 48, 10-12.

brūn-fāg; *adj.* [brūn *brown*, fāg *coloured, dyed*] *Of a brown colour, brown-hued;* fulvi coloris:—Ætbær brūnfāgne helm *he bore away the brown-hued helmet*, Beo. Th. 5223; B. 2615.

brunge, *pl.* brungon; *pp.* brungen *broughtest, brought*, Cd. 30; Th. 41, 4; Gen. 651; *p. and pp. of* bringan.

brūn-wann; *adj.* [brūn *fuscus*, wan, wann *ater*] *Dark-brown, dusky;* fusco-ater:—Niht helmade brūnwann beorgas steápe *dusky night covered over the steep mountains*, Andr. Kmbl. 2613; An. 1308.

brūn-wyrt, brūne-wyrt, e; *f.* I. BROWNWORT or *water-betony;* scrofularia aquatica:—Genim bānwyrt and brūnwyrt *take bonewort and brownwort*, L. M. 1, 25; Lchdm. ii. 66, 18. Brūne wyrt, 1, 61; Lchdm. ii. 132, 7. Genim brūne wyrt *take brownwort*, 2, 51; Lchdm. ii. 268, 9, 13: 1, 39; Lchdm. ii. 100, 5: 1, 48; Lchdm. ii. 122, 16. II. *wood-betony* or *brownwort;* scrofularia nodosa:—[Genim] ða brūnan wyrt brādleáfan, sió weaxeþ on wuda *take the broad-leafed brownwort, which grows in woods*, L. M. 1, 38; Lchdm. ii. 92, 23.

brute; *pl.* bruton *bruisedst, broke*; *p. of* breótan.

brūwa *brows, eye-brows*, Wrt. Voc. 64, 35, = brūa; *pl. nom. of* brū.

bryc *a bridge;* pons:—Ðæt he dō bryc-geweorc *that he do bridge-work*, L. R. S. 1; Th. i. 432, 2. v. brycg.

bryce *a violation, infraction*, L. Alf. pol. 3; Th. i. 62, 9. v. brice.

bryce; *adj.* [brycþ, *pres. of* brecan *to break*] *Breakable, worthless, frail, fleeting;* fragilis, futilis, caducus:—Mīn bigengea gewāt bryce on feorweg *incolatus meus prolongatus est*, Ps. Th. 119, 5. DER. un-bryce.

BRȲCE, brice, es; *m.* [brȳcst, brīcst, *pres. of* brūcan *to use, enjoy*] *Use, service, the occupation* or *exercise of a thing, profit, advantage, fruit;* usus, ministerium, commodum:—Gif ðæt ōwiht brȳce wæs *if that was any use;* si hoc aliquid prodesset, Bd. 5, 14; S. 634, 8, note. Lāfe on hwylc hugu fatu gehiwade wǣron mennisces brȳces *recisuræ in vasa quælibet humani usus formarentur*, 3, 22; S. 552, 14. Brīce oððe gewuna *usus*, Ælfc. Gr. 11; Som. 15, 16. Ealle werþeóde lifgaþ bī ðām lissum, ðe ēce Dryhten gesette sīnum bearnum to brīce *all tribes of men live by the blessings, which the eternal Lord bestowed on his children for their use*, Exon. 54 b; Th. 193, 3; Az. 116. We sceoldon ða hwīlendlīcan þing to ūrum brīcum habban *we should have transitory things for* *our use*, Homl. Th. ii. 460, 28. God hîg gesceóp eallum mannum to brîce *quæ creavit Deus in ministerium cunctis gentibus*, Deut. 4, 19. Brýce *commodum*, Cot. 59. Lǽnes landes brýce *fructus*, Cot. 92. [*Plat.* bruuk: *Dut.* ge-bruik, *n*: *Kil.* bruyk: *Ger.* brauch, *m*: *O.H.Ger.* brûh, *m*: *Dan.* brug, *c*: *Swed.* bruk, *n*: *O.Nrs.* brûk, *n.* *usus, mos*, Rask Hald.]

brýce, brîce; *adj.* [brýcst, brîcst, *pres. of* brûcan *to use*] *Useful, profitable;* utilis:—He monegum on Godes cyricum brýce wæs *multis in ecclesia utilis fuit*, Bd. 3, 23; S. 555, 33. He monegum brýce lifde *vitam multis utilem duxit*, 4, 26; S. 602, 41: Ps. Th. 118, 35. DER. un-brýce.

BRYCG, bricg, e; *f.* *A* BRIDGE; pons:—Ðeós brycg *hic pons*, Ælfc. Gr. 9, 39; Som. 12, 59. Ðæt he ne myhte to ðære brycge cuman *that he could not come to the bridge*, Ors. 2, 5; Bos. 48, 14. Eádweard cyning hêt gewyrcan ða brycge ofer Treontan *king Edward commanded the bridge over the Trent to be built*, Chr. 924; Erl. 110, 10: 887; Erl. 84, 30: 1071; Erl. 210, 17: Ors. 2, 5; Bos. 46, 7. [*Chauc.* brigge: *Piers P.* brugg: *R. Brun.* brigge: *R. Glouc.* brugg: *Plat.* brugge, brügge, *f*: *Frs.* bregge: *O.Frs.* bregge, brigge, *f*: *Dut.* brug, *f*: *Ger.* brücke, *f*: *M.H.Ger.* brucke, brücke, brügge, *f*: *O.H.Ger.* brucca, *f*: *Dan.* brygge, bro, *m.f*: *Swed.* brygga, bro, *f*: *Icel.* bryggja, brú, *f.*] DER. stân-bricg.

Brycg *Bruges in Belgium*, Chr. 1052; Erl. 182, 4. v. Bricg.

brycg-bôt, bricg-bôt, e; *f.* [brycg *a bridge*, bôt *a repairing*] *A repairing* or *restoring of a bridge;* pontis restitutio *vel* instauratio:—Brycgbôta aginne man georne *let a man diligently begin the repairing of bridges*, L. C. S. 10; Th. i. 380, 27, note 65: 66; Th. i. 410, 8, note 11.

brycg-geweorc, es; *n.* BRIDGE-WORK; pontis opus:—Brycg-geweorc, Heming 104. v. bricg-geweorc.

brycgian; *p.* ade; *pp.* ad [brycg *a bridge*] *To bridge, bridge over, make a bridge;* pontem trajicere *vel* construere:—Sceal îs brycgian *ice shall bridge over* [*water*], Exon. 90 a; Th. 338, 4; Gn. Ex. 73. Ofer eástreámas îs brycgade *the ice bridged over the water-streams*, Andr. Kmbl. 2524; An. 1263. DER. ofer-brycgian.

Brycg-stôw *Bristol*, Chr. 1052; Th. 314, 27. v. Bricg-stôw.

brycg-weard *a keeper* or *defender of a bridge.* v. bricg-weard.

brýcian, brîcsian; *p.* ode, ade; *pp.* od, ad [brýce, brîce *use*] *To be of use, profit, benefit, do good;* prodesse, proficuum esse:—He his geférum brýcian gýmde *he took care to do good to his companions*, Bd. 5, 9; S. 623, 33. Hî brýcaþ monigra hǽlo *multorum saluti proficuum erit*, Bd. 4, 22; S. 590, 32. Him sylfum brîcsade *benefited himself*, Bd. 5, 13; S. 632, 6.

brýcþ, ðû brýcst *uses, thou usest; 3rd and 2nd pres. of* brûcan.

bryd, es; *n.* *A drawing, drawing out;* extractio:—Mid wǽpnes bryde *by the drawing of a weapon*, L. Alf. pol. 38; Th. i. 86, 16.

BRÝD, brîd, e; *f.* One owned or purchased,—*A* BRIDE, *woman about to be married* or *newly married, a wife, spouse, woman;* sponsa, nupta, uxor, mulier:—Seó gelaðung is gecweden Cristes brýd and clǽne mǽden *the church is called Christ's bride and a pure maiden*, Boutr. Scrd. 19, 39. Brýd *sponsa*, Ælfc. Gl. 87; Som. 74, 57; Wrt. Voc. 50, 39. Brýde lâste *with the step of a bride*, Cd. 129; Th. 164, 15; Gen. 2715. Tyn fǽmnan fêrdon ongên ðone brýdguman and ða brýde *decem virgines exierunt obviam sponso et sponsæ*, Mt. Bos. 25, 1. Se ðe brýde hæfþ, se ys brýdguma *qui habet sponsam, sponsus est*, Jn. Bos. 3, 29. Ðâ wæs Adames brýd gâste gegearwod *then Adam's bride was endued with soul*, Cd. 10; Th. 12, 16; Gen. 186. Him brýd sunu brohte *his wife brought to him a son*, Cd. 58; Th. 71, 16; Gen. 1171. Lothes brýd underbæc beseah *Lot's wife looked backwards*, 119; Th. 154, 27; Gen. 2562: Beo. Th. 4067; B. 2031. Adam ongan ôðres striénan bearnes be brýde, Cd. 55; Th. 68, 18; Gen. 1119: 86; Th. 108, 28; Gen. 1813. Loth gelǽdde brýd mid bearnum in Sǽgor *Lot led his wife with their children into Zoar*, 118; Th. 153, 11; Gen. 2537: 129; Th. 164, 22; Gen. 2718. Nerôn his brýde ofslôg self mid sweorde *Nero himself slew his wife with a sword*, Bt. Met. Fox 9, 60; Met. 9, 30: Beo. Th. 5904; B. 2956: Cd. 125; Th. 159, 21; Gen. 2638. Him brýda twâ eaforan fêddon *two wives brought forth offspring to him*, 52; Th. 65, 33; Gen. 1075. Feóllon wergend brýda, bennum seóce *the defenders of the wives fell, sick with wounds*, 92; Th. 118, 28; Gen. 1972. God me ðâs brýd forgeaf *God gave me this woman*, 26; Th. 33, 27; Gen. 526. [*Piers P.* burde: *Laym.* brude: *Orm.* brid: *O.Sax.* brûd: *Frs. O.Frs.* breid: *Dut.* bruid: *Ger.* braut: *M.H.Ger. O.H.Ger.* brût: *Goth.* bruþs νύμφη *nurus*: *Dan. Swed.* brud: *Icel.* brúðr.] v. wîf.

brýd-bed, es; *n.* *A bride-bed;* genialis torus, Ælfc. Gl. 66; Som. 69, 72; Wrt. Voc. 41, 26.

brýd-bletsung, e; *f.* *A bride's blessing;* nuptialis benedictio. v. brîd-bletsung.

brýd-bûr, es; *n.* *A bedchamber;* thalamus:—Of brýdbûre his *de thalamo suo*, Ps. Spl. 18, 5: Beo. Th. 1846; B. 921.

brýd-ealo, -eala; *gen.* -ealowes; *n.* [ealu *ale*] *A bride-ale, bride* or *marriage feast;* nuptiale convivium:—Ðǽr wæs ðæt brýdealo [Laud. MS. -eala], ðæt wæs manegra manna bealo *there was the bride-ale, which was many men's bale*, Chr. 1076; Erl. 213, 26.

brýd-ealoþ; *indecl. n.* [ealaþ *ale*] *A bride-ale, bride* or *marriage feast;* nuptiale convivium:—Hî wǽron æt ðam brýdealoþ *they were at the marriage feast*, Chr. 1075; Erl. 214, 15.

brydel; *gen.* brydles; *m.* *A bridle;* frenum, lupatum:—Brydel *bagula, salivare*, Ælfc. Gl. 21; Wrt. Voc. 23, 23. v. bridel.

brýde lâste *with conjugal footstep*, Cd. 129; Th. 164, 16; Gen. 2715. v. brýd, lâst.

brýdelîc gewrit, es; *n.* *A bride-like writing, a play;* drama, Cot. 66.

brydel-þwang, -twancg, es; *m.* *A bridle rein;* frenum. v. bridel-þwang, -twancg, Coll. Monast. Th. 27, 35.

brýden wah *a broad wall*, Bd. Whelc. 1, 8; p. 48, 27. v. brêden, wah *a wall.*

brýd-gifa *espousals;* sponsalia, Ælfc. Gl. 87; Som. 74, 53. v. brîd-gifu.

brýd-guma, brýdi-guma, an; *m.* [brýd, guma *a man*] *A bride-man, bridegroom;* sponsus:—Swâ swâ brýdguma of his brýdbûre *tamquam sponsus procedens de thalamo suo*, Ps. Th. 18, 5. Cweðe ge sceolun ðæs brýdguman cnihtas wêpan, ða hwîle ðe se brýdguma mid him byþ *numquid possunt filii sponsi lugere quamdiu cum illis est sponsus?* Mt. Bos. 9, 15: 25, 1. Se ðe brýde hæfþ, se ys brýdguma *qui habet sponsam, sponsus est*, Jn. Bos. 3, 29: Ælfc. Gl. 87; Som. 74, 55.

brýdi-guma *a bridegroom*, Ælfc. Gl. 87; Som. 74, 55. v. brýd-guma.

brýd-lâc, es; *n.* *A marriage gift* or *feast, the celebration of a marriage;* nuptiale offertorium, nuptiarum celebritates:—Ne nân preóst môt beón æt ðam brýdlâcum âhwǽr ðǽr man eft wîfaþ, oððe wîf eft ceorlaþ *nor may any priest be at the celebration of a marriage anywhere where a man marries a second wife, or a woman marries again*, L. Ælfc. C. 9; Th. ii. 346, 18.

brýd-leóþ, es; *n.* *A marriage song;* epithalamium = ἐπιθαλάμιον, Mone B. 3121: 3123.

brýd-lîc; *adj.* *Bridal;* nuptialis:—Reáf brýdlîc *vestem nuptialem*, Mt. Lind. Stv. 22, 12.

brýd-loca, an; *m.* [loca *a place shut in*] *A bride-chamber;* sponsæ cubile:—On ðæm brýdlocan *in the bride-chamber*, Homl. Blick. 9, 10.

brýd-lufe, an; *f.* [lufe *love, favour*] *A bride's love;* sponsæ amor:—He ða brýdlufan sceal sêcan *he must seek a bride's love*, Exon. 67 b; Th. 249, 20; Jul. 114.

brýd-ræst *a bride-bed;* genialis lectus, Cot. 99. v. brýd-bed.

brýd-reáf, es; *n.* *A nuptial garment;* nuptialis vestis:—Mid brýdreáf *veste nuptiali*, Mt. Lind. Stv. 22, 11.

brýd-sang, es; *m.* *A marriage song;* hymenæus = ὑμεναῖος, epithalamium = ἐπιθαλάμιον, Ælfc. Gl. 33; Som. 62, 40; Wrt. Voc. 28, 22.

brýd-þing, es; *n.* *A bride-thing, what relates to marriage, in pl. nuptials;* nuptiæ:—Gabriel wæs ðissa brýdþinga ǽrendwreca *Gabriel was the messenger of these nuptials*, Homl. Blick. 3, 13.

brydyls *a bridle*, Ps. Spl. C. 31, 12. v. bridels.

brygc *a bridge*, Wrt. Voc. 80, 50. v. brycg.

brygdan, he brygdeþ *To turn;* vertere:—He hâlge lâre brygdeþ on bysmer *he turneth holy lore to mockery*, Exon. 117 a; Th. 449, 14; Dôm. 71. DER. on-brygdan. v. bregdan.

bryht *bright*, Ps. Spl. T. 15, 6. v. beorht.

bryhtm *a glance*:—Eágan bryhtm *an eye's glance, a moment*, Bd. 2, 13; S. 516, 20. v. bearhtm.

bryidan; *p.* ede; *pp.* ed *To take;* tollere, sumere:—Ðæs âþ ðe his ǽhte bryideþ *the oath of him who takes* [Th. *discovers*] *his property*, L. O. 4; Th. i. 180, 8. v. bregdan. DER. æt-bryidan, ge-.

brym *the sea*, Cd. 100; Th. 132, 12; Gen. 2192: Chr. 1065; Erl. 196, 31; Edw. 12. v. brim.

bryme *famous*, Ors. 2, 2; Bos. 41, 30. v. brême.

brym-flôd *a deluge*, Ælfc. Gl. 115; Som. 80, 45; Wrt. Voc. 61, 23. v. brim-flôd.

brymme, es; *m.* *A* BRIM, *brink, an edge, a border, lip of a pot, and such like;* ora, margo:—Brymmas sǽs *the borders* or *shores of the sea, a strait*, Hymn. Lye. [*Chauc.* brimme: *Laym.* brimme, *dat*: *Kil.* breme: *Ger.* bram, *n*; bräme, *f.* *margo, fimbria.*]

brym-streám *the sea, a river*, Mt. Rush. Stv. 8, 18: Chr. 942; Th. 209, 38, col. 1; Edm. 5. v. brim-streám.

brýmuste *most famous*, Ors. 2, 2; Bos. 41, 30. v. brême.

bryne, byrne, es; *m.* [byrnan *to burn*] *A burning, fire, flame, heat;* ustio, ardor, incendium, ignis, flamma, fervor:—Ne se bryne beót mæcgum *the burning did not hurt the youths*, Cd. 187; Th. 232, 24; Dan. 265: Exon. 59 a; Th. 213, 24; Ph. 229: 53 b; Th. 189, 9; Az. 57. Mid ðý me of sweoran forþlifaþ seó reádnes and bryne ðæs swyles *dum mihi de collo rubor tumoris ardorque promineat*, Bd. 4, 19; S. 589, 31: Exon. 32 a; Th. 101, 22; Cri. 1662. On bryne ge gremedon Drihten *in incendio provocastis Dominum*, Deut. 9, 22: Cd. 186; Th. 231, 12; Dan. 246. Þurh fýres bryne *through the fire's burning*, 197; Th. 245, 11; Dan. 461: Exon. 64 a; Th. 236, 16; Ph. 575. Hie sceolon þrôwian biterne bryne *they shall suffer bitter burning*, Andr. Kmbl. 1231; An. 616. Ǽr ðam ðe ðæt mynster mid byrne fornumen wǽre *priusquam* *monasterium esset incendio consumptum*, Bd. 4, 25; S. 599, 18. Se biscop ða brynas ðara hûsa gebiddende adwæscte *episcopus incendia domorum orando restinxerit*, 1, 19; S. 484, 36. Brego Caldêa gewât to ðam bryne *the prince of the Chaldeans went to the fire*, Exon. 55 b; Th. 196, 27; Az. 180. Hie ðone bryne fandedon *they proved the fire*, Cd. 196; Th. 244, 29; Dan. 455: Exon. 72 b; Th. 270, 31; Jul. 473. Bryne stîgeþ heáh to heofonum *the flame rises high to heaven*, Exon. 63 a; Th. 233, 6; Ph. 520: 55 b; Th. 196, 23; Az. 178. Beóþ amerede monna gæ̂stas þurh bryne fŷres *the souls of men will be proved through the fire's heat*, 63 b; Th. 234, 25; Ph. 545: Salm. Kmbl. 124; Sal. 61. [*Laym.* brune: *O.Sax.* brunni, *m*: *Goth.* brunsts, *f*: *Icel.* bruni, *m.*] DER. fæ̂r-bryne, helle-, lêg-, lîg-, mân-, sun-.

bryne BRINE, *salt liquor*; salsugo, muria, Ælfc. Gl. 33; Som. 62, 14; Wrt. Voc. 27, 67. [*Kil.* brijn *muria.*] DER. fisc-bryne.

bryne-âdl, e; *f.* [âdl *a disease*] *A burning disease, a fever*; æstuans morbus, febris, Cot. 92.

bryne-brôga, an; *m.* [brôga *fear, dread*] *Fear* or *dread of fire*; incendii terror:—Wið brynebrôgan *against the fire's dread*, Exon. 55 a; Th. 195, 24; Az. 161.

bryne-gield, es; *n. A burnt-offering, burnt-sacrifice*; holocaustum, Cd. 140; Th. 175, 6; Gen. 2891: 142; Th. 177, 18; Gen. 2931.

bryne-hât; *adj. Burning hot*; ardentissimus:—Æ̂r se wlonca dæg bodige brynehâtne lêg *ere the awful day proclaim the burning hot flame*, Exon. 116 b; Th. 448, 9; Dôm. 51.

bryne-leóma, an; *m.* [leóma *a ray of light, beam*] *A fire-beam, flame*; flamma:—Bryneleóma stôd *the flame stood*, Beo. Th. 4616; B. 2313.

bryne-teár, es; *m.* [teár *a tear*] *A burning tear*; fervida lacrima:—Bitrum bryneteárum *with bitter burning tears*, Exon. 10 a; Th. 10, 14; Cri. 152.

bryne-welm, -wylm, es; *m. A burning flame, flame of fire, burning heat*; incendii fervor *vel* æstus:—Brynewylmum mealt gifstôl Geáta *the gift chair of the Goths was consumed by flames of fire*, Beo. Th. 4642; B. 2326: Exon. 42 a; Th. 142, 14; Gû. 644. In helle heó brynewelme bîdan sceolden sâran sorge *in hell they must endure great sorrow from the burning heat*, Cd. 213; Th. 266, 24; Sat. 27.

bryngaþ *bring*; afferte, Ps. Spl. 28, 1, = bringaþ; *impert. pl. of* bringan.

bryrdan; he bryrdeþ, bryrdþ, bryrþ; *p.* bryrde; *pp.* bryrded, bryrd [brord *stimulus, cuspis*] *To prick, goad, incite, urge, constrain*; compungere, stimulare, instigare, urgere, compellere:—Se Ælmihtiga ealle gesceafta bryrþ mid his bridlum *the Almighty constrains all creatures with his bridles*, Bt. Met. Fox 13, 5; Met. 13, 3. DER. a-bryrdan, an-, in-, on-.

bryrd-dæg, es; *m. Passion-day*; passionis dies, Som.

bryrding, e; *f. Compunction, instigation*; compunctio, impulsio. v. on-bryrding.

bryrdnys, -nyss, e; *f. A pricking, goading, stimulation, instigation*; compunctio, stimulatio, instigatio:—Mid bryrdnysse ðæs upplîcan êðles *by stimulation from the country above*, Bd. Whelc. 173, 16. DER. a-bryrdnes, an-, in-, on-.

bryrþ *urges, constrains*, Bt. Met. Fox 13, 5; Met. 13, 3; *3rd pres. of* bryrdan.

brŷsan; he brŷsþ; *p.* brŷsde; *pp.* brŷsed, ge-brŷsed *To* BRUISE; conterere. [*Wyc.* brisse: *Tynd. pp.* brosed: *Plat.* brusen *to make a rushing noise*: *Dut.* bruisen *to foam* or *roar as the sea*: *Ger.* brausen *to ferment*: *Dan.* bruse *to roar*: *Swed.* brusa *to roar*: *O.Nrs.* brúsa *æstuare.*] DER. to-brŷsan: ge-brŷsed.

Bryt- *A Welshman*; Wallus: used in compounds. v. Bryt-land.

brŷt, e; *f. A nymph, bride*; nympha [= νύμφη *a bride*], Ælfc. Gl. 88; Som. 74, 64; Wrt. Voc. 50, 45. v. brŷd.

brŷt *breaks*; *3rd pers. pres. of* breótan.

bryta, an; *m. A lord*:—Swegles brytan *lords of heaven*, Cd. 213; Th. 266, 17; Sat. 23. v. brytta.

brytan *to break*, Herb. 1, 3; Lchdm. i. 72, note 8, B: 13, 1; Lchdm. i. 104, 20: 32, 1; Lchdm. i. 130, note 12. v. bryttian.

Brytas, Bryttas, Brittas; *pl. m. The Britons*; Britones:—Hit hafdon Brytas *the Britons had it*, Chr. Th. 3, 29, col. 3. Bryttas, 3, 8, col. 1, 3: 4, 4, col. 2, 3.

brytednys, -nyss, e; *f. A breaking, bruising*; contritio. DER. to-brytednys.

Bryten, Bryton, Briten, Breoten, Breoton, Broten, Brittan, Britten, Brytten; *gen. dat. acc.* e; *f. acc. also as nom.* BRITAIN; Britannia, Cambria:—Brytene îgland is ehta hund mîla lang *the island of Britain is eight hundred miles long*, Chr. Th. 3, 1, col. 1: 3, 10, col. 1, 3. Syxtigum wintrum æ̂r ðam ðe Crist wæ̂re acenned, Gaius Iulius, Rômâna câsere [MS. kasere], mid hund-eahtatigum scipum, gesôhte Brytene *sixty years before Christ was born, Caius Julius, emperor of the Romans, with eighty vessels, sought Britain*, Chr. Th. 5, 17-21, col. 3, 1, 2. Breoton [Brytene C] is eálond ðæt wæs iû geára Albion hâten *Britain is an island that was formerly called Albion*, Bd. 1, 1; S. 473, 8: 2, 1; S. 501, 10. On Breotone *into Britain*, Bd. 1, 15; S. 483, 2. Bryten, *acc.* Exon. 45 b; Th. 155, 5; Gû. 855.

brŷten-cyning, es; *m. A powerful king*; rex præpotens, Exon. 88 a; Th. 331, 28; Vy. 75.

brŷten-grûnd, es; *m. The spacious earth*; terra spatiosa, Exon. 13 a; Th. 22, 25; Cri. 357.

Bryten-lond, es; *n. The land of Britain*; Britanniæ terra:—Maximus, se câsere, wæs on Bryten-londe geboren *Maximus, the emperor, was born in the land of Britain*, Chr. 381; Ing. 11, 9.

brŷten-rîce, es; *n. A spacious kingdom*; regnum spatiosum, Exon. 54 b; Th. 192, 17; Az. 107.

brŷten-walda, brŷten-wealda, brêten-ânwealda, an; *m*: brŷten-weald, es; *m. A powerful ruler* or *king*; præpotens rex. It is affirmed [*Kmbl. Sax. Eng.* ii. 21, *and note* 1] that the true meaning of brŷten-walda, compounded of walda *a ruler*, and the *adj.* brŷten, is totally unconnected with Brettas or Bretwalas, the name of *the British aborigines*; for brŷten is derived from breótan *to bruise, break, to break into small portions, to disperse*; and, when coupled with walda, wealda *a ruler, king*, means no more than *an extensive* or *powerful king, a king whose power is widely extended.* Many similar compounds are found, thus in Exon. 88 a; Th. 331, 28; Vy. 75 we have brŷten-cyning *a powerful king* exactly equivalent to brŷten-walda. Brŷten-grûnd *the wide expanse of earth*, 13 a; Th. 22, 25; Cri. 357. Brŷten-rîce *a spacious realm*, 54 b; Th. 192, 17; Az. 107. Brŷten-wong *the spacious world*, 13 a; Th. 24, 6; Cri. 380. The uncompounded *adj.* is used in the same sense. Breóton bold *a spacious dwelling*, Cd. 228; Th. 308, 3; Sat. 687. Turner thinks that the Bret-walda [*Hist. of A. Sax.* bk. iii. ch. 5, vol. i. pp. 318 and 378] was *a war-king*, elected by the other Anglo-Saxon kings and their nobility, as their leader in the time of war. Lappenberg [*Th. Lapbg.* i. 125-129] takes the same view; while Kemble [*Sax. Eng.* ii. 8-21] opposes both Turner and Lappenberg, asserting that there was not any general ruler or superior *war-king* elected by the Anglo-Saxons, and that even Bret-walda [*q. v.*] does not refer to the Britons, that it is so written in only one MS. of the Chr. while each of the five others has the word brŷten-, and therefore the word ought to be written as above, brŷten-walda. Of these Brŷten-waldan the Chronicle names the following eight,—Ðŷ geáre ge-eóde Ecgbriht cing Myrcna rîce, and eal ðæt be sûþan Humbre wæs, and he wæs eahtoða cing, ðe brŷtenwalda wæs. Æ̂rest wæs Ælle, [Sûþ-Seaxna] cing, se ðus mycel rîce hæfde. Se æftera wæs Ceawlin, West-Sexna cing. Se þridda wæs Æðelbriht, Cantwara cing. Se feórþa wæs Ræ̂dwald, Eást-Engla cing: fifta wæs Eádwine, Norþhymbra cing: syxta wæs Ôswald, ðe æfter him rîxode: seofoða wæs Ôsweo, Ôswaldes brôðor: eahtoða Ecgbriht, West-Seaxna cing *in this year* [A. D. 827] *king Ecgbriht subdued the kingdom of the Mercians, and all that was south of the Humber, and he was the eighth king, who was Brŷtenwalda. The first was Ælle* [A. D. 477-514], *king of the South-Saxons, who had thus much sway. The second was Ceawlin* [A. D. 560-593], *king of the West-Saxons. The third was Æthelbriht* [A. D. 593-616], *king of the men of Kent. The fourth was Rædwald* [A. D. 617?-625], *king of the East-Angles: the fifth was Eadwine* [A. D. 625-635], *king of the Northumbrians: the sixth was Oswald* [A. D. 635-642], *who reigned after him: the seventh was Oswiu* [A. D. 642-670], *Oswald's brother: the eighth was Ecgbriht* [A. D. 800-836], *king of the West-Saxons*, Chr. 827; Th. 112, 16-34, col. 2, 3: Brŷten-, Th. 113, 21: Palgrv. Eng. Com. pp. ccxxxiv-v.

brŷten-wong, es; *m.* [brŷten, wang, wong *a plain, field*] *A spacious plain* or *field, in pl. the world*; spatiosus campus, mundus:—Geond brŷtenwongas *throughout the spacious world*, Exon. 13 a; Th. 24, 6; Cri. 380.

brŷtest, brŷtst, he brŷteþ, brŷt *breakest, breaks*; *2nd and 3rd pers. pres. of* breótan.

Bryt-ford, es; *m.* [Bryt *a Briton*, ford *a ford*] BRITFORD, *near Sarum, Wiltshire*:—Tostig wæs ðâ æt Brytforda [MS. Brytfordan] mid ðam cinge [MS. kinge] *Tostig was then at Britford with the king*, Chr. 1065; Erl. 194, 38.

bryðen, es; *n? A drink, brewing*; potus:—Bryðen wæs ongunnen, ðætte Adame Eue gebyrmde æt fruman worulde *the drink was prepared, which Eve fermented for Adam at the beginning of the world*, Exon. 47 a; Th. 161, 4; Gû. 953: L. M. 1, 67; Lchdm. ii. 142, 15. Ân bryðen mealtes *one brewing of malt*, Wulfgeat's Will.

brytian *to dispense, distribute*, Past. 44, 1; Hat. MS. 61 a, 13. v. bryttian.

brŷtian *to profit*, Bd. 5, 9; S. 623, note 32, 33, T. v. brŷcian.

Bryt-land, Bryt-lond, es; *n. The land of Britain, Wales*; Britannia, Cambria:—Ðâ fôr Harold mid scipum of Brycgstôwe abûtan Brytland *then Harold went with his ships from Bristol about Wales*, Chr. 1063; Ing. 251, 21. Into Brytlande *in Walliam*, Chr. 1063; Gib. 170, 41, note 1. v. Bryten.

brytnere, es; *m. A distributor, steward*; dispensator:—Hwâ sî [MS. sie] wîs brytnere *who can be a wise steward?* Past. 63. v. brytta.

brytnian; *p.* ode, ede, ade; *pp.* od, ed, ad *To dispense, distribute*;

administer; dispensare, administrare:—He sinc brytnade *he dispensed treasure*, Beo. Th. 4756; B. 2383. Hī weolan brytnodon *they dispensed wealth*, Chr. 1065; Erl. 197, 40; Edw. 21. Æðelingas wēlan brytnedon *the nobles distributed riches*, Cd. 209; Th. 259, 14; Dan. 691. v. bryttian.

brȳtofta *espousals*; sponsalia, Ælfc. Gl. 87; Som. 74, 53; Wrt. Voc. 50, 35. v. brȳd-gifa, brīd-gifu.

Bryton *Britain*, Bd. 1, 7; S. 476, 34. v. Bryten.

Bryton-land; es; *n. British land, Britain*, Chr. 979; Th. 233, 7, col. 1.

brytsen; *gen. dat. acc.* brytsene; *pl. nom. gen. acc.* brytsena; *dat.* brytsenum; *f.* [brytan *to break*] *A broken part, fragment*; fragmentum:—Hī nāmon ða lāfa, twelf wilian fulle ðæra brytsena *tulerunt reliquias, duodecim cophinos fragmentorum plenos*, Mt. Jun. 14, 20: Jn. Bos. 6, 13. Of ðām brytsenum *de fragmentis*, Mk. Bos. 8, 8. Gaderiaþ ða brytsena *colligite fragmenta*, Jn. Bos. 6, 12.

brytta, bryta, bretta, an; *m. A bestower, dispenser, distributor, prince, lord, God?* largitor, dispensator, administrator, princeps, dominus, Deus?—Sinces brytta *a dispenser of treasure*, Cd. 89; Th. 111, 18; Gen. 1857: Judth. 10; Thw. 21, 22; Jud. 30: Beo. Th. 1219; B. 607: 3849; B. 1922: Exon. 76 b; Th. 288, 3; Wand. 25. Goldes brytta *a distributor of gold*, Cd. 138; Th. 173, 26; Gen. 2867: 93; Th. 120, 20; Gen. 1997. Beága brytta *a distributor of rings* or *bracelets*, Beo. Th. 69; B. 35: 709; B. 352: 2978; B. 1487. Synna brytta *the prince of sins, the devil*, Elen. Kmbl. 1913; El. 958. Morðres brytta *the prince of murder, the devil*, Andr. Kmbl. 2342; An. 1172. Boldes brytta *the lord of a house*, Elen. Kmbl. 323; El. 162. Lifes brytta *the Lord of life* = *God*, Cd. 6; Th. 8, 10, 24; Gen. 122, 129: Exon. 12 b; Th. 21, 14; Cri. 334: Andr. Kmbl. 1644; An. 823. Swægles brytta *the Lord of heaven* = *God*, Cd. 215; Th. 272, 24; Sat. 124: Exon. 12 a; Th. 18, 10; Cri. 281. Tīres brytta *the Lord of power* = *God*, 14 b; Th. 29, 14; Cri. 462. [*Icel.* bryti, *m. a steward, bailiff.*]

Brytta *of the Britons*, Bd. 1, 34; S. 499, 20; *gen. pl. of* Bryttas.

Bryttas, Brittas, Breotas, Brytas, Britas; *pl. m.* I. *Britons*; Britones:—Ǣrest wǣron būend ðyses landes Bryttas *the first inhabitants of this land* [*England*] *were the Britons*, Chr. Th. 3, 8, col. 1, 3. Mōd and mægen Bryttas onfēngon *the Britons took heart and power*, Bd. 1, 16; S. 484, 19: 1, 15; S. 483, 17. Ðætte Angel-þeód wæs gelaðod fram Bryttum on Breotone *that the Angle-nation was invited by the Britons into Britain*, 1, 15; S. 483, 2. II. *Bretons*; Armoricani:—Ðȳ ilcan geáre fōr se here of Sigene to Sant Laudan, ðæt is betweoh Brettum [Bryttum, col. 2, 3] and Francum *in the same year the army went from the Seine to St. Lō, which is between the Bretons and the Franks*, Chr. 890; Th. 160, 10, col. 1. Hī speónan ða Bryttas heom to *they enticed the Bretons to them*, 1075; Th. 349, 26.

Brytten, e; *f. Britain*, Chr. Th. 3, 11, col. 2. v. Bryten.

bryttian, brittian, bryttigan, brytian; *pl.* bryttigaþ; *p.* bryttade; *v. a. To divide into fragments, dispense, rule, use*; dispensare frustatim, gubernare:—Hī hit him bryttian sceoldon *they should dispense it to them*, Past. 44, 1; Hat. MS. 61 a, 13. Land bryttade *ruled the land*, Cd. 62; Th. 75, 6; Gen. 1236. Mihton mægyn bryttigan *might use force*, Cd. 4; Th. 4, 12; Gen. 52. [*Icel.* brytja *to chop, cut in pieces.*]

brȳttian; *p.* ode, ade; *pp.* od *To possess, enjoy*; possidere, frui:—Sculon wēlan bryttian *shall enjoy wealth*, Cd. 99; Th. 131, 19; Gen. 2178. Woruld bryttade *enjoyed the world*, Cd. 62; Th. 74, 22; Gen. 1226. v. brȳtian.

Bryttisc, Brittisc; *adj. British*; Britannicus:—He wæs Bryttisc *he was British*, Chr. 1075; Erl. 213, 3.

Brytt-wealas, Bryt-walas; *pl. m. The Brito-Welsh, Britons*; Britanni:—Cynrīc ða Bryttwealas geflȳmde *Cynric routed the Britons*, Chr. 552; Gib. 20, 2. Brytwalas, 167; Erl. 9, 20: 443; Erl. 11, 33: 571; Erl. 19, 15.

bū, bȳ, es; *n?* [ic būe, he bȳþ, *pres. of* būan *to dwell*] *A dwelling, habitation*; habitatio, habitaculum:—Bearn hēr bū nāmon, and ðǣr eardedon *here children obtained a dwelling, and there settled*, Ps. Th. 101, 25. Stanford and Deóra bȳ wǣron under Norþmannum *Stamford and Derby* [Deóra bȳ *habitation of deer* or *animals*] *were under the Northmen*, Chr. 942; Th. 210, 4; Edm. 8. Se ðe hūs oððe bȳ hæfde *qui domicilium habebat*, Mk. Skt. Lind. 5, 3. [*Plat.* buw, *m*: *O. Sax.* bū, *n*: *Dut.* bouw, *m*: *Ger.* bau, *m*: *M. H. Ger.* bū, bou, *m*: *O. H. Ger.* pū, *m*: *Dan.* bo, *m. f*: *Swed.* bo, *m*: *Icel.* bú, *n. domus*: *Sansk.* bhū, *f. the earth, site, place.*]

bū *both, nom. m. f.* or *n*: *acc. m. f. n. of* begen; ambæ, ambo:—Hī bū þēgon [MS. þegun] æppel *they both* [*Adam and Eve*] *ate the apple*, Exon. 61 b; Th. 226, 8; Ph. 402: Cd. 10; Th. 12, 18; Gen. 187: 82; Th. 102, 13; Gen. 1699. v. bā.

BŪAN, būgan; ic būe, ðū būst, he bȳþ; *p.* būde, *pl.* būdon; *pp.* gebūn; *v. anom.* I. *intrans. To dwell, live*; habitare, versari aliquo loco:—He būde on Eást-Englum *he dwelt among the East-Angles*, Chr. 890; Erl. 86. 29; Ors. 1, 1; Bos. 19, 26. Gif he weard onfunde būan [MS. buon] on beorge *if he found the keeper dwelling in the mount*, Beo. Th. 5676; B. 2842. II. *v. a. acc. To inhabit, occupy*; inhabitare, colere, incolere:—He lēt heó ðæt land būan *he let them inhabit the land*, Cd. 13; Th. 16, 6; Gen. 239. Ðæt ðū būst eorþan *ut inhabites terram*, Ps. Th. 36, 33. Ðæt hēr men būn ðone heán heofon *that here men inhabit the high heaven*, Cd. 35; Th. 45, 32; Gen. 735. Ne mæg mon meduseld būan *a man may not occupy the mead-bench*, Beo. Th. 6123; B. 3065. [*Plat.* buwen, bouen, buen, bujen: *O. Sax.* būan: *Frs.* bouwje: *O. Frs.* buwa, bowa: *Dut.* bouwen: *Ger.* bauen: *M. H. Ger.* buwen, biuwen, bouwen: *O. H. Ger.* būan, būwan: *Goth.* bauan: *Dan.* boe: *Swed.* bo: *Icel.* búa: *Lith.* bu-ti *to be*: *Slav.* by-ti *to be*: *Zend* bū *to be, become*: *Sansk.* bhū *to become, spring up, be, exist, live.*] DER. ge-būan: ān-būende: bū, bȳ: būgan, būgend: būgian, būian, būwian.

BUC, es; *m. A* BUCK, *a male deer*; cervus, Ælfc. Gl. 19; Som. 59, 22: Wrt. Voc. 22, 63. v. dā *a doe*.

BŪC, es; *m.* I. *the belly, stomach*; venter, alvus:—Hit is betwux tōðum tocowen and into ðam būce asend *it is chewed between the teeth and sent into the stomach*, Homl. Th. ii. 270, 34. II. *a vessel that bulges out, as a bottle, jug, pitcher*; lagena, hydria:—Būc *lagena*, Wrt. Voc. 83, 24. Þurch heora blāwunge and ðæra būca swēg *through the sound of their blowing and of the pitchers*, Jud. 7, 21. Hī tobrǣcon ða būcas mid micelre brastlunge *they broke the pitchers* [*hydrias confregerunt*] *with great crashing*, 7, 20. [*Chauc.* bouke *bulk, body*: *Plat.* buuk, *m. venter*: *O. Sax.* būk, *m. uter*: *Frs.* buk, *m. f. venter*: *O. Frs.* buk, buch, *m. venter*: *Dut.* buik, *m. belly*: *Kil.* buyck *corporis truncus*: *Ger.* bauch, *m. venter, alveus*: *M. H. Ger.* būch, *m. venter*: *O. H. Ger.* būh, *m. venter*: *Dan.* bug, *m. f. the stomach, belly* or *middle of a vessel*: *Swed.* buk, *m. belly*: *Icel.* búkr, *m. the trunk, body.*] DER. wæter-būc. v. æscen, hrygile-būc.

bucc *a cheek, part of a helmet*; buccula, Cot. 25.

BUCCA, an; *m.* [buc *a buck*] *A he-goat*, BUCK; caper, hircus:—Bucca *caper* vel *hircus*, Wrt. Voc. 78, 32. Bucca *hircus*, Ælfc. Gr. 8; Som. 7, 30. Bucca *caper* vel *hircus* vel *tragos* [= τράγος], Ælfc. Gl. 20; Som. 59, 36; Wrt. Voc. 22, 77. Gif se ealdor syngaþ, bringeþ ānne buccan to bōte *si peccaverit princeps, offerat hircum immaculatum*, Lev. 4, 23: 9, 3. He asyndrode twāhund gāta and twentig buccena *separavit capras ducentas et hircos viginti*, Gen. 32, 14: Ps. Lamb. 49, 13. Ic ne underfō of eowedum ðīnum buccan *non accipiam de gregibus tuis hircos*, 49, 9: Deut. 32, 14. Buccan horn *a buck's horn, one of the twelve signs of the zodiac, Capricorn*, Bd. de nat. rerum; Wrt. popl. science 7, 8; Lchdm. iii. 246, 3. Buccan beard *a goat's beard*, Wrt. Voc. 289, 10. [*Chauc.* buck: *Orm.* bucc: *Plat.* buk, *m*: *O. Sax.* buc, *m*: *Frs.* bok, *m. f*: *Dut.* bok, *m*: *Ger.* bock, *m*: *M. H. Ger.* boc, *m*: *O. H. Ger.* boch, *m*: *Dan.* buk, *m. f*: *Swed.* bock, *m*: *Icel.* bokki, *m.*] DER. firgen-bucca, stān-, wudu-.

Bucc-inga ham; *gen.* hammes; *m.* [*Hunt.* Bukingeham: *Brom.* Bukyngham: Bucc, -inga ham, *q. v.*] BUCKINGHAM; oppidum primarium agri Buccinghamensis:—Fōr Eádweard cyning to Buccinga hamme *king Edward went to Buckingham*, Chr. 918; Erl. 104, 18.

Buccinga ham-scīr, e; *f.* BUCKINGHAMSHIRE; ager Buccinghamensis:—Hī wendon ðanon on Buccinga hamscīre *they turned thence to Buckinghamshire*, Chr. 1010; Th. 264, 11: 1011; Erl. 144, 35: 1016; Erl. 154, 6, 24.

būc-ful, -full, e; *f. A pitcherful*:—Him wearþ ðā geboren to būcful wæteres *a pitcherful of water was then borne to him*, Homl. Th. ii. 422, 29.

bude *hast offered*, Cd. 111; Th. 147, 7; Gen. 2435: budon *offered*, Beo. Th. 2175; B. 1085; *p. s. and pl. of* beódan.

būde *dwelt*; habitavit, Ors. 1, 1; Bos. 19, 26; *p. of* būan.

būend, es; *m. A dweller*. v. būende.

būende; *part.* būend, es; *m. Inhabiting* or *dwelling*; inhabitans:—Būendra leás *void of those inhabiting* [Cd. 5; Th. 6, 16; Gen. 89] or *inhabitants, thus used as a noun*, though sometimes in composition declined as a *m.* noun, būend, es; *m*: it is *often declined* as a *m. part.* that is an *adj.* ending in e. It would then be declined *nom. s.* -būende; *gen.* -būendes; *d.* -būendum; *acc.* -buendne; but most frequently as an *adj. pl*; *nom. acc.* -būende; *gen.* -būendra [*as a noun*, būenda]; *d.* -būendum:—Mid būendum *cum habitantibus*, Ps. Lamb. 82, 8. DER. ān-būende, ceaster-būend, ēg-, eorþ-, feor-, fold-, grūnd-, hēr-, īg-, land-, neáh-, sund-, þeód-, woruld-.

būfan, būfon; *prep. dat.* [be-ufan] *Above*; super; used in opposition to *under*:—God totwǣmde ða wæteru, ðe wǣron *under* ðære fæstnisse fram ðām ðe wǣron *būfan* ðære fæstnisse *Deus divisit aquas, quæ erant* sub *firmamento ab his quæ erant* super *firmamentum*, Gen. 1, 7. Būfan ðam māran wealle *above the greater wall*, Ors. 2, 4; Bos. 44, 28. Twentig mīla būfan Lundenbyrig *twenty miles above London*, Chr. 896; Th. 172, 25. DER. ufan; *prep.*

būfan, būfon [be-ufan]; *adv. Above, before*; supra:—Be ðære būfan sǣd wæs *de qua supra dictum est*, Bd. 4, 22; S. 592, 13: Mt. Rush. Stv. 2, 9. [*Plat.* baven: *Dut.* bóven: *Ger.* boben *supra.*] DER. ufan; *adv.*

būgan; *p.* ede; *v. a. acc. To inhabit*; inhabitare, incolere:—Þenden git mōston ān lond būgan *while ye might inhabit one land*, Exon. 123 a; Th. 473, 20; Bo. 17. Ðǣr ic wīc būge *there I inhabit a dwelling*, 104 b;

Th. 396, 22; Rä. 16, 8: 103 a; Th. 389, 23; Rä. 8, 2. Ðǽr nô men bûgaþ eard *where men inhabit not a home*, 58 a; Th. 208, 18; Ph. 157. Bûgede *habitavit*, Aldh. Gl. Grn. v. bûan, bûgian.

BÛGAN; *part.* bûgende; ic bûge, ðu bûgest, býhst, býgst, he bûgeþ, býhþ, býgþ; *p.* ic, he beág, beáh, ðû buge, *pl.* bugon; *imp.* bûg, bûh; *pp.* bogen; *v. intrans. To* BOW or *bow down oneself, bend, swerve, give way, submit, yield, turn, turn away, flee*; se flectere *vel* inclinare, curvare, declinare, desistere, cedere, vertere, divertere, fugere:—Hí noldon bûgan to nânum deófolgilde *they would not bow down to any idol*, Homl. Th. ii. 18, 29: Rood Kmbl. 71; Kr. 36: Num. 25, 2. Ne eom ic wyrðe ðæt ic his sceóna þwanga bûgende uncnytte, Mk. Bos. 1, 7; *I knelinge am not worthi for to vndo the thwong of his schoon*, Wyc. Seó eá, norþ bûgende, ût on ðone Wendel-sǽ *the river, bending northward, [flows] out into the Mediterranean sea*, Ors. 1, 1; Bos. 17, 33: Exon. 103 a; Th. 390, 24; Rä. 9, 6. Seó eorþe nǽfre ne býhþ ne ufor ne nyðor ðonne se ælmihtiga Scyppend hí gestaðelode *the earth never swerves neither higher nor lower than the almighty Creator established it*, Bd. de nat. rerum; Wrt. popl. science 10, 19; Lchdm. iii. 254, 18. Hí bugon and flugon *they gave way and fled*, Chr. 999; Erl. 135, 25. Ic sceolde on bonan willan bûgan *I must submit to a murderer's will*, Exon. 126 b; Th. 486, 4; Rä. 72, 7: Beo. Th. 5829; B. 2918. Him beág gôd dǽl ðæs folces *a good part of the people submitted to him*, Chr. 913; Erl. 102, 7: 921; Erl. 108, 1. He to fulluhte beáh *he submitted to baptism*, Homl. Th. i. 386, 32: Ex. 32, 26. Hí bugon to ðam *they submitted to that*, Jos. 9, 27: Chr. 975; Erl. 125, 24. Ǽlc burhwaru wæs bûgende to him *every city was yielding to him*, Jos. 11, 19. Bûge ic to eówerum hǽðenscipe *I will turn to your heathendom*, Homl. Th. i. 70, 28. Híg bugon of ðam wege *they have turned out of the way*, Ex. 32, 8. Ðæt ge ne bugon eft to woruldþingum *that ye turn not again to worldly things*, Boutr. Scrd. 22, 46. Se Hǽlend beáh fram ðære gegaderunge *the Saviour turned away from the company*, Jn. Bos. 5, 13: Beo. Th. 5905; B. 2956. Bûh fram yfele and dô oððe wyrc gôd *diverte a malo et fac bonum*, R. Ben. in procem. He sceal bûgan *fugere debeat*, Ex. 21, 13: Gen. 19, 21: Byrht. Th. 139, 58; By. 276. Hí bugon fram beaduwe *they fled from the fight*, 137, 12; By. 185: Beo. Th. 5190; B. 2598. [*Laym.* buȝen, buwen: *Orm.* buȝhenn: *Plat.* bögen: *Dut.* buigen: *Kil.* buyghen: *Ger. M. H. Ger.* biegen: *O. H. Ger. Goth.* biugan: *Icel.* boginn *bent*: *Sansk.* bhuj *to bend.*] DER. a-bûgan, an-, be-, bi-, for-, ge-, in-, on-, under-, ymb-.

bûgend, es; *m.* [bûgende, *part. of* bûgan, bûan *to dwell*] *A dweller, an inhabitant*; habitator:—Ǽrost wǽron bûgendas [MS. bûgend] ðyses landes Bryttas *at first the inhabitants of this land [England] were Britons*, Chr. Th. 3, 7, col. 3.

bûgende *bowing, kneeling*, Mk. Bos. 1, 7. v. bûgan *to bow down.*

bûgian, bûian, bûwian, to bûgianne; *p.* ode; *pp.* od. I. *intrans. To dwell*; habitare:—Ge ðǽr bûgiaþ *ye dwell there*, Bt. 18, 1; Fox 62, 22. II. *v. a. acc. To inhabit, occupy*; inhabitare, incolere:—Ðis is land to bûgianne *this is to inhabit land*, Bt. 17; Fox 60, 4. v. bûan.

bûh *turn*:—Bûh fram yfle *diverte a malo*, R. Ben. in procem. *impert. of* bûgan *to bow, turn.*

bûh-somnes, -ness; *f.* BOWSOMENESS, *pliableness*; obedientia, Verst. Restitn. p. 211. v. bôcsumnes.

bûian *to dwell, inhabit*; habitare, incolere:—Ðæt we môston bûian *that we should dwell*, Ps. Th. 28, 8. Ðe on eorþan bûiaþ *who dwell on earth*, Ps. Th. 32, 7. Bûiaþ *inhabit*, Ps. Th. 32, 12. v. bûgian.

bule *a stud, boss, brooch*; bulla, Cot. 26. [*Ger.* bulle; *f.*]

bulentse, an; *f. The name of a plant, which, from not knowing its Latin* or *English name, I call* bulentse:—Nime bulentsan ða smalan *take the small bulentse*, L. M. 1, 47; Lchdm. ii. 118, 1.

bulge *wast angry*; *p. of* belgan.

bulgon *made angry, were angry*; *p. pl. of* belgan.

bulle *bellowedst, roaredst*; bullon *bellowed, roared*; *p. of* bellan.

bulluca, an; *m. A male calf, a* BULLOCK; vitulus, Scint. 54.

bulot, bulut *Ragged robin* or *cuckoo-flower*; lychnis, flos cuculi, Lin:—Bulot-niðeweard *the nether part of cuckoo-flower*, L. M. 1, 58; Lchdm. ii. 128, 15. Nim bulut *take cuckoo-flower*, 3, 48; Lchdm. ii. 340, 1.

bunda, bonda, an; *m.* I. *a wedded* or *married man, a husband*; maritus, sponsus:—Ne mæg nân wíf hire bondan [bundan MS. B, note 57] forbeódan, ðæt he ne môte into his cotan gelogian ðæt ðæt he wille *no wife may forbid her husband, that he may not put into his cot what he will*, L. Cnut. pol. 74; Wilk. 145, 41; Th. i. 418, 23-25; Schmd. 312, 76, § 1. Sê hit bonda, sê hit wíf *sive maritus sit, sive uxor*, Hick. Diss. Ep. 18, 40. II. *the father* or *head of a family, a householder*; paterfamilias, œconomus:—Swâ ymbe friðes bôte swâ ðam bondan [bundan MS. A. L. C. S. 8] sí sêlost and ðam þeófan sí lâðost *so concerning* frithes-bôt *as may be best for the householder* [patrifamilias] *and worst for the thief*, L. Ǽnh. Wilk. 122, 40; Eth. vi. 32; Th. i. 322, 27; Schmd. 232, § 32: L. Cnut. pol. 8; Wilk. 134, 40; Th. i. 380, 14; Schmd. 274, 8. And ðǽr se bonda [MS. B, bunda] sæt uncwyd and unbecrafod sitte ðæt wíf and ða cild on ðam ylcan unbesacen. And gif se bonda [MS. B, bunda] beclypod wǽre, etc. *and where the householder dwelt without claim* or *contest, let the wife and the children dwell in the same, without litigation. And if the householder had been cited, etc.* L. Cnut. pol. 70; Wilk. 144, 39; Th. i. 414, 21; Schmd. 310, 72. *The early Latin version is*, Et ubi bonda [bunda, L. Th. i. 526, 3], i. e. paterfamilias manserit, sine compellatione et calumpnia, sint uxor et pueri in eodem, sine querela. Et si [bunda, i. e. paterfamilias] compellatus fuerat, etc. L. Cnut. 73; Th. ii. 542, 13-15. 2. every word has its history by which its introduction and use are best ascertained. Bede tells us [Bk. i. 25, 2] that Ethelbert, king of Kent, married a Christian wife Bertha, a Frankish princess. The queen prepared the way for the friendly reception of Augustine and his missionary followers by Ethelbert in A. D. 597, who was the first to found a school in Kent, and wrote Laws which are said to be asette on Augustines dæge *established in the time of Augustine*, between A. D. 597 and 604. The cultivation and writing of Anglo-Saxon [Englisc] began with the conversion of Ethelbert. Marriage, and the household arrangements depending upon it, were regulated by the law of the church, and indigenous compound words were formed to express that law,—thus ǽ *law, divine law*; Cristes ǽ *Christi lex*. Rihte ǽ *legitimum matrimonium*, Bd. 4, 5; S. 573, 17. Ǽw *wedlock, marriage*, ǽw-boren *lawfully born, born in wedlock*: ǽw-breca, -brica, *m. wedlock breaker, an adulterer*: ǽw-fæst-man *marriage-fast-man, a wedded man, a husband*: ǽw-nian *to wed, take a wife.* 3. Hûs-bunda, -bonda *a wedded man, husband, householder*. This compound is one of the oldest in the language. It is found in the interpolated passage of Matt. xx. between vers. 28 and 29. The passage is in all the Anglo-Saxon MSS. of the Gospels, except the interlineary glosses. The Anglo-Saxon is a literal version of the Augustinian MS. in the Bodleian Library, Oxford [*Codex August.* 857 D. 2. 14], the Old Italic version, from which the text of the Latin vulgate of the Gospels was formed by St. Jerome about A. D. 384. Though we do not know the exact dates when the Gospels were translated from Latin into Anglo-Saxon, Cuthbert assures us that Bede finished the last Gospel, St. John, on May 27, 735, [see Pref. to Goth. and A. Sax. Gos. Bos. pp. ix-xii.] As the three preceding Gospels were most likely translated before St. John, then the following sentence was written before 735. Se hûs-bonda [hûs-bunda in MS. Camb. Ii, 2, 11] hâte ðê arísan and rýman ðam ôðrum *the householder bid thee rise and make room for the other*, Notes to Bosworth's Goth. and A. Sax. Gos. Mt. xx. 28, p. 576. Hûs-bonda is also used by Ǽlfric in his version of the Scriptures about 970, Ex. 3, 22. 4. Bunda, bonda *one wedded* or *bound, a husband*, from bindan; *p.* band, bundon; *pp.* bunden *to bind* must have been of earlier origin than the compound hûs-bunda. It is a well-known rule that in Anglo-Saxon *a person* or *agent* is denoted by adding *a*, as býtl *a hammer*, býtla *a hammerer*; ânweald *rule, government*, ânwealda *a ruler, governor*; bunden, bund *bound*, bunda, bonda *one bound, a husband*. Bunda might be banda as well as bonda, for *a* is often used for o, as mon for man *a man*. The early use of hûs-bunda, -bonda would at once indicate that it was not likely to be of Norse or Icelandic origin. It could not be derived from the Norse bûa *to dwell*; *part.* bûandi, bôandi *dwelling*; nor even from the *A. Sax.* bûan *to dwell*, because the *û* and *ô* are long in the *Norse* bûa *to dwell*, bûandi, bôandi *dwelling*, and in the *A. Sax.* bûan *to dwell*, bûende *dwelling*, bûend *a dweller*; while the *u* and *o* are always short in bunda and bonda. So, in other compounds, from bindan *to bind*, as bonde-land *bond* or *leased land, land let on binding conditions*. Bunda then is a pure Anglo-Saxon word derived from bindan *to bind*. Bûan *to dwell*, with the *part.* bûende *dwelling*, and the noun bûend, es; *m. a dweller*, is quite a distinct word with its own numerous compounds. v. bûende, bûend, es; *m.*

bunden *bound, tied*; bundon *bound*, Beo. Th. 3805; B. 1900; *pp. and p. of* bindan.

bunden-stefna, an; *m.* [bunden *bound*, stefna *the prow of a ship*] *A bound prow*; ligata prora:—Sǽgenga fleát ofer ýðe, bundenstefna ofer brimstreámas *the ship* [lit. *sea-goer*] *floated over the wave, the bound prow over the ocean-streams*, Beo. Th. 3824; B. 1910.

bune, an; *f. A sort of cup*; carchesium = καρχήσιον, poculi genus, Judth. 10; Thw. 21, 14; Jud. 18: Beo. Th. 5544; B. 2775: Exon. 77 b; Th. 292, 4; Wand. 94: 90 a; Th. 338, 23; Gn. Ex. 83.

Bune, Bunne, an; *f? Boulogne in France*; Bononia:—Se micla here fêrde to Bunan [Bunnan, Th. 162, 20, col. 1] *the great army went to Boulogne*, Chr. 893; Th. 163, 20, col. 3.

buoptalmon, es; *n.* [βούφθαλμον = βοῦς, ὀφθαλμός] *Ox-eye, chamomile*; anthemis nobilis, Lin:—Buoptalmon . . . heó hafaþ geoluwe blôstman eal swylce eáge, ðanon heó ðone naman onfêng *Ox-eye . . . it has yellow blossoms all like an eye, whence it took the name*, Herb. 141, 1; Lchdm. i. 262, 4.

BÛR, es; *n. A* BOWER, *cottage, dwelling, an inner room, storehouse*; tabernaculum, conclave, casa:—Wiht wolde hyre on ðære byrig bûr atimbran *a creature would construct a bower for itself in the town*, Exon. 108 a; Th. 411, 26; Rä. 30, 5. On bûre, ahôf brýd Abrahames hleahtor *in the inner room, Abraham's wife raised a laugh*, Cd. 109; Th. 144, 7;

Gen. 2386. Cumena bûr *a guest-house*, Bd. 4, 31; S. 610, 11. Bed-cófa *vel* bûr *cubiculum*, Ælfc. Gl. 27; Som. 60, 99; Wrt. Voc. 25, 39. Wæs to bûre Beówulf fetod *Beowulf was fetched to his dwelling*, Beo. Th. 2624; B. 1310. On his suna bûre *in his son's dwelling*, Beo. Th. 4902; B. 2455. Æfter bûrum *along the dwellings*, Beo. Th. 282; B. 140. [*Chauc.* boure: *Piers P.* bour: *R. Glouc.* boures, *pl*: *Laym.* bur: *Orm.* bure: *Plat.* bur, buur, *m*: *Ger.* bauer, *m*: *O. H. Ger.* bûr: *Dan.* buur, *n*: *Swed.* bur, *m*: *Icel.* búr, *n.*] DER. brýd-bûr.

burcg, e; *f. A city*:—Ðære burcge *of the city*, Bt. 18, 2; Fox 64, 18. v. burh.

bûr-cote, an; *f.* [bûr *a bower*, cote *a couch*] *A bed-chamber; cubiculum*:—On hira bûrcotum, and on hiera beddum *in their bed-chambers, and in their beds*, Past. 16, 2; Hat. MS. 20 b, 15.

burg, e; *f. A city*; urbs:—Sceal seó burg bîdan *the city shall remain*, Exon. 121 b; Th. 466, 30; Hö. 129. v. burh.

burg- = beorg- *a hill, in some compounds, as in* burg-stal, *q. v.*

burga *cities, of cities*, Mt. Bos. 11, 20: Salm. Kmbl. 613. v. burh.

burg-âgende; *part. Possessing a fortress* or *palace*; arcem *vel* palatium possidens, Elen. Kmbl. 2347; El. 1175.

burga man, es; *m. A citizen*; civis:—Sî hit burga man *sive civis sit ille*, Deut. 1, 16. v. burh-man.

burgan = burgen, Ors. 2, 5; Bos. 47, 15; *p. pl. subj. of* beorgan *to save.*

burgat, es; *pl.* burgatu; *n.* [burg *a city*, gat, geat *a gate*] *A city-gate*; urbis porta:—Ðâ Samson genam ða burggatu [MS. burgatu] and gebær on his hricge *then Samson took the city-gates and bore them on his back*, Jud. 16, 3.

burg-bryce, burh-bryce, -brice, es; *m.* I. *a breaking into a castle* or *dwelling*; castelli *vel* domus violatio, L. In. 45; Th. i. 130, 7. II. *the fine to be paid for this burglary*; mulcta ob castelli *vel* domus violationem, L. Alf. pol. 40; Th. i. 88, 7.

burgen, e; *f. A burying-place, sepulchre*, Ps. Th. 29, 9. v. byrgen.

Burgenda land, es; *n. The land of the Burgundians, an island in the west of the Baltic sea*; Boringia. Burgenda land is the Icelandic Burgundarhólmr, of which the present Danish and Swedish name Bornholm is a contraction:—Burgenda land *the land of the Burgundians*, Ors. 1, 1; Bos. 21, 44.

Burgendan; *pl. m. The Burgundians*; Burgundiones:—Burgendan habbaþ ðone ylcan sǽs earm be westan him *the Burgundians have the same arm of the sea to the west of them*, Ors. 1, 1; Bos. 19, 19. v. Burgendas.

Burgendas; *gen.* a; *pl. m*: Burgendan; *pl. m. The Burgundians*; Burgundiones. These, in Alfred's time, dwelt to the north-west of the Osti. We find them at another period on the east bank of the Oder. They have given name to the island of Bornholm in the Baltic:—Osti habbaþ be norþan him Winedas and Burgendas *the Esthonians have to the north of them the Wends and the Burgundians*, Ors. 1, 1; Bos. 19, 18. Wine Burgenda *friend of the Burgundians*, Wald. 85; Vald. 2, 14. Weóld Burgendum Gifica *Gifica ruled the Burgundians*, Scôp Th. 40; Wîd. 19: 131; Wîd. 65.

Burgende; *gen.* a; *dat.* um; *m. The Burgundians, inhabitants of Burgundy, an old province in the east of France*; Burgundiones:—Profentse hæfþ be norþan hyre ða beorgas, ðe man Alpis hǽt, and be sûþan hyre is Wendel-sǽ, and be norþan hyre and eástan synd Burgende, and Wascan be westan *Provence has on the north of it the mountains, which people call the Alps, and on the south of it is the Mediterranean sea, and on the north and east of it are the Burgundians, and on the west the Gasconians*, Ors. 1, 1; Bos. 24, 2.

bûr-geteld, es; *n.* [bûr *a bower*, geteld *a tilt, cover*] *A tilt* or *covering of a tent, a tent*; tentorium:—He in ðæt bûrgeteld nêðde *he ventured into the tent*, Judth. 12; Thw. 25, 24; Jud. 276: 10; Thw. 22, 10; Jud. 57: 12; Thw. 25, 8; Jud. 248.

burg-geat *a city-gate*, Andr. Kmbl. 1679; An. 842. v. burh-geat.

burg-hleoþ, es; *n. A fortress-height*, Exon. 107 b; Th. 409, 17; Rä. 28, 2. v. burh-hleoþ.

burg-loca, an; *m. A city-inclosure, city-barrier*, Andr. Kmbl. 2075; An. 1040: 2132; An. 1067: 1879; An. 942. v. burh-loca.

burg-lond, es; *n. City-land*; urbis solum:—Eálâ sancta Hierusalem, Cristes burglond *O holy Jerusalem, city-land of Christ!* Exon. 8 b; Th. 4, 12; Cri. 51.

burgon *preserved*, Elen. Kmbl. 268; El. 134; *p. pl. of* beorgan.

burg-ræced, es; *nom. acc. pl.* -ræced; *n. A city-dwelling, house surrounded by a wall* or *rampart of earth*; urbanæ ædes, circumvallata domus:—Beorht wǽron burgræced *bright were the city-dwellings*, Exon. 124 a; Th. 477, 9; Ruin. 22.

burg-rûnan *the fates, furies, fairies.* v. burh-rûnan.

burg-sæl, es; *nom. acc. pl.* -salu, -salo; *n. A castle-hall, city-dwelling*; arcis aula, urbana domus:—Ofer burgsalu *over the city-dwellings*, Exon. 51 b; Th. 179, 7; Gû. 1258: 52 a; Th. 182, 4; Gû. 1305: 96 a; Th. 358, 23; Pa. 50.

burg-sele, es; *m. A castle-hall, city-dwelling*; arcis aula, urbana domus:—Burgsele beofode *the castle-hall trembled*, Exon. 94 b; Th. 353, 49; Reim. 30.

burg-sittend *a city-dweller, citizen*, Bt. Met. Fox 27, 34; Met. 27, 17: Elen. Kmbl. 552; El. 276. v. burh-sittend.

burg-sittende *city-dwelling, inhabiting a city*, Cd. 52; Th. 66, 24; Gen. 1089: Exon. 12 b; Th. 21, 20; Cri. 337: 53 a; Th. 186, 14; Az. 19: 106 b; Th. 407, 10; Rä. 26, 3. v. burh-sittende.

burg-stal, -stôl, es; *m.* [burg = beorg, beorh *a hill*, stal *a place, seat, dwelling*] *A hill-seat, dwelling on a hill*; sedes super collem *vel* clivum, Cot. 209. *The name of places built on a hill, as Burstall in Suffolk, Borstall in Kent and Oxfordshire, etc.*

burg-steal, es; *m.* [burg *a fortress, city*, steal *a place*] *A city-place*; arcis locus, arx:—Brosnade burgsteal *the city-place has perished*, Exon. 124 a; Th. 477, 23; Ruin. 29. [*Ger. M. H. Ger.* burgstall.]

burg-stede *a city-place, city*, Exon. 52 a; Th. 181, 10; Gû. 1291: 124 a; Th. 476, 3; Ruin. 2. v. burh-stede.

burg-tûn, es; *m. A* BOROUGH-TOWN, *city-inclosure, city-dwelling*; urbis septum, urbana domus:—Sindon burgtûnas brêrum beweaxne *the city-dwellings are overgrown with briers*, Exon. 115 b; Th. 443, 16; Kl. 31.

burg-waran, burh-waran, *gen.* -warena; *pl. m. Inhabitants of a city, citizens*; urbis incolæ, cives:—Ealle burgwaran *all the city-inhabitants*, Exon. 121 b; Th. 467, 6; Hö. 134: 120 b; Th. 462, 23; Hö. 56. Burgwarena fruma *the chief of the citizens*, Scôp Th. 182; Wîd. 90.

burg-ware *inhabitants of a city, citizens*, Andr. Kmbl. 3164; An. 1585: Chr. 919; Th. 192, 25: Exon. 18 b; Th. 46, 25; Cri. 742. v. burh-ware.

burg-waru *the inhabitants of a city as in a body*, Andr. Kmbl. 2189; An. 1096. v. burh-waru.

burg-weall, -weal *a city-wall*, Exon. 83 b; Th. 315, 28; Môd. 38: 22 a; Th. 61, 1; Cri. 978. v. burh-weall.

burg-wîgende; *part. pl. City-warring*; used substantively, *city-warriors*; ex arce belligerentes, cives belligeri:—Swylce Hûna cyning meahte abannan to beadwe burgwîgendra *whomsoever of city-warriors the king of the Huns might summon to the fight*, Elen. Kmbl. 68; El. 34.

BURH, burg; *gen.* burge; *dat.* byrig, byrg; *acc.* burh, burg; *pl. nom. acc.* burga; *gen.* burga; *dat.* burgum; *f.* [beorh, beorg = burh, burg *the impert. of* beorgan *to defend*]. I. the original signification was *arx, castellum, mons, a castle* for defence. It might consist of a castle alone; but as people lived together for defence and support, hence *a fortified place, fortress, castle, palace, walled town, dwelling surrounded by a wall* or *rampart of earth*; arx, castellum, mons, palatium, urbs munita, domus circumvallata:—Se Abbot Kenulf macode fyrst ða wealle abûtan ðone mynstre, [and] geaf hit ðâ to nama Burh [Burch MS.], ðe ǽr hêt Medeshâmstede *the Abbot Kenulf first made the wall about the minster, and gave it then the name Burh* = Burg [Petres burh *Peter's burg* = *Peterborough*], *which before was called Meadow-home-stead*, Chr. 963; Erl. 123, 27-34; Th. 221, 34-39. ☞ The style of the Anglo-Saxon indicates a late date, perhaps about 1100 or 1200. Burg *arx*, Cot. 10. Stîþlîc stân-torr and seó steápe burh on Sennar stôd *the rugged stone-tower and the high fortress stood on Shinar*, Cd. 82; Th. 102, 15; Gen. 1700. Ôþ ðæt hie on Sodoman weall-steápe burg wlîtan meahton *till they on Sodom's lofty-walled fortress might look*, 109; Th. 145, 7; Gen. 2402. Ðǽr se hâlga heáh, steáp reced, burh timbrede *there the holy man built a high, steep dwelling, a walled town*, 137; Th. 172, 6; Gen. 2840. Burge weall *the wall of a city*; murus, Ps. Th. 17, 28. Ðæt hie geseón mihten ðære wlitegan byrig weallas *that they might see the walls of the beautiful city*, Judth. 11; Thw. 23, 24; Jud. 137: Ps. Th. 44, 13: 47, 11. On leófre byrig and hâligre *in montem sanctificationis suæ*, 77, 54: 77, 67. Ðâ fêrdon hîg þurh ða burhga *egressi circuibant per castella*, Lk. Bos. 9, 6. Eádweard cyng fôr mid fierde to Bedan forda, and beget ða burg *king Edward went with an army to Bedford, and gained the walled town*, Chr. 919; Th. 192, 24, col. 1. Ge binnan burgum, ge bûton burgum *both within walled towns, and without walled towns*, L. Edg. S. 3; Th. i. 274, 7. Ðone æðeling on ðære byrig mêtton, ðǽr se cyning ofslægen læg *they found the ætheling in the inclosure of the dwelling, where the king lay slain*, Chr. 755; Th. 84, 19, col. 1: L. Edm. S. 2; Th. i. 248, 16: L. Eth. iii. 6; Th. i. 296, 5. II. a fortress or castle being necessary for the protection of those dwelling together in cities or towns,—*a city, town, burgh, borough*; urbs, civitas, oppidum:—Rôma burh *the city Rome*, Bd. 1, 11; S. 480, 10, 12. Ða ðe in burh môton gongan, in Godes rîce *they may go into the city, [may go] into God's kingdom*, Cd. 227; Th. 303, 16; Sat. 613. Ðonne hý hweorfaþ in ða hâlgan burg *when they pass into the holy city*, Exon. 44 b; Th. 150, 26; Gû. 784. Ðæt he gesâwe ða burh *ut videret civitatem*, Gen. 11, 5. Ða burh ne bærndon *they burnt not the city*, Ors. 2, 8; Bos. 52, 8. Burge weard *the guardian of the city*, Cd. 180; Th. 226, 19; Dan. 173: Ps. Th. 9, 13. Ðonne hî eów êhtaþ on ðysse byrig *cum persequentur vos in civitate ista*, Mt. Bos. 10, 23: Exon. 15 b; Th. 34, 14; Cri. 542. Binnan ðære byrig *within the city*, Ors. 2, 8; Bos. 52, 4. Beóþ byrig mid Iudêum getimbrade *ædificabuntur civitates Judæ*, Ps. Th. 68, 36. Byrig fægriaþ *towns appear fair*, Exon. 82 a; Th. 308, 32; Seef. 48. Ðá ongan he hyspan ða burga *tunc cœpit exprobrare civitatibus*, Mt. Bos. 11, 20. On burgum *in the towns*, Beo. Th. 105; B. 53. [*Piers P. Chauc.* burghe: *R. Brun.* burgh: *R. Glouc.* borȝ: *Laym.* burh: *Orm.* burrh: *Plat.* borch, *f*: *O. Sax.* burg, *f. urbs, civitas*: *Frs.* borge, *m. f*: *O. Frs.* burch, burich, *f*: *Dut.* burgt, *f*: *Kil.* borg, borght: *Ger.* burg, *f. arx, castellum*: *M. H. Ger.* burc, *f*: *O. H. Ger.* buruc, burg, *f. urbs, civitas*: *Goth.* baurgs, *f*: *Dan.* borg, *m. f*: *Swed.* borg, *m*: *O. Nrs.* borg, *f.*] DER. ealdor-burh [-burg], fóre-, freó-, freoðo-, gold-, heáfod-, heáh- [heá-], hleó-, hord-, in-, leód-, mǽg-, medo-, meodu-, rand-, rond-, sceld-, scild-, scyld-, stán-, under-, weder-, wín-, wyn-.

burh-âgende; *part. Possessing a fortress.* v. burg-âgende.

burh-bót, e; *f. The repairing of fortresses, which was one of the burdens on all landed property*; urbium *vel* castrorum instauratio, L. Eth. v. 26; Th. i. 310, 23: vi. 32; Th. i. 322, 31: L. C. S. 10; Th. i. 380, 27: L. R. S. 1; Th. i. 432, 2.

burh-brece *a breaking into a castle*, L. In. 45; Th. i. 130, 6, note 9. v. burh-bryce.

burh-bryce, -brice, es; *m. A breaking into a castle* or *dwelling,—the fine for this burglary*, L. In. 45; Th. i. 130, 6, note 9: L. Alf. pol. 40; Th. i. 88, 7, note 16. v. burg-bryce.

burh-ealdor, -ealder; *gen.* -ealdres; *m. A ruler of a city, mayor, citizen*; urbis præfectus, municeps, Ælfc. Gr. 14; Som. 16, 55: 9, 55; Som. 13, 24.

burh-fæsten, es; *n. A city-fastness, fortress, citadel*; arx munita, castellum:—Com God sceáwigan beorna burhfæsten *God came to view the chieftains' city-fastness*, Cd. 80; Th. 101, 10; Gen. 1680.

burhg, e; *f. A fortress, city, walled-town*:—Férdon híg þurh ða burhga *egressi circuibant per castella*, Lk. Bos. 9, 6: Bd. 4, 1; S. 563, 12. v. burh.

burh-gata *city-gates*, Jos. 2, 5. v. burh-geat.

burh-geat, -gat, burg-, es; *pl. nom. acc.* u, a, o; *n. A city-gate*; urbis porta:—Æt burhgeate *at the city-gate*, Cd. 111; Th. 146, 22; Gen. 2426. Mid ðam ðe ða burhgata belocene wurdon *cum portæ clauderentur*, Jos. 2, 5. Fóre burg-geatum *before the city-gates*, Andr. Kmbl. 1679; An. 842: Exon. 120 a; Th. 461, 20; Hö. 38.

burh-geat-setl, es; *n. A town-gate-seat, where a court was held for trying causes of family and tenants*; ad urbis portam sedes, L. R. 2; Th. i. 190, 15.

burh-gemót, es; *n. A* BURGMOTE, *city-moot, meeting of townsmen, corporation*; urbis comitia:—Hæbbe man þríwa on geáre burhgemót *thrice in a year let a city-moot be held*, L. Edg. ii. 5; Th. i. 268, 3: L. C. S. 18; Th. i. 386, 4.

burh-geréfa, an; *m. A* BOROUGH-REEVE, *city-reeve, the governor and chief magistrate of a city* or *town*; urbis prætor, præfectus, præpositus, quæstor, curialis, Wrt. Voc. 18, 7: 18, 42.

burh-geþingþ, -geþincgþ, e; *f. The city council* or *assembly*, L. Eth. iii. 1; Th. i. 292, 7. v. ge-þingþ.

burhge weardas; *pl. m.* [=burge weardas] *The guardians of the city*, Cd. 212; Th. 262, 6; Dan. 740.

burh-hleoþ, burg-hleoþ, es; *n. A fortress-height, the hill on which a city is built*; clivus montis, in quo arx *vel* urbs sita est:—Forbærned burhhleoðu *scorched fortress-heights*, Cd. 146; Th. 182, 3; Exod. 70. Ic eom brungen of burghleoðum *I am brought from fortress-heights*, Exon. 107 b; Th. 409, 17; Rä. 28, 2. v. beorh-hliþ.

burh-land, es; *n. City-land*; urbis solum. v. burg-lond.

burh-leóde; *nom. acc*; *gen.* -leóda; *dat.* -leódum; *pl. m. Town-people, citizens*; cives:—Him ða burhleóde wiðcwǽdon *the citizens withstood him*, Ors. 3, 7; Bos. 61, 6: Cd. 226; Th. 300, 7; Sat. 561: Judth. 11; Thw. 24, 14; Jud. 187: 11; Thw. 24, 6; Jud. 175. [*O. Sax.* burg-liudi *incolæ, cives.*]

burh-loca, burg-loca, an; *m. A city-inclosure, city-barrier* or *defence*, as—*a wall, mound* or *moat*; urbis septum, arcis claustrum *vel* clausura:—He gelǽdde brýd mid bearnum under burhlocan, in Ságor *he led his wife with the children within the city-inclosure, into Zoar*, Cd. 118; Th. 153, 12; Gen. 2537: Andr. Kmbl. 2132; An. 1067: Beo. Th. 3860; B. 1928. He nǽnige forlét under burglocan bendum fæstne *he left not one under the city-barriers fast in bonds*, Andr. Kmbl. 2075; An. 1040: 1879; An. 942.

burh-man, -mann, es; *m. A townsman, citizen*; urbanus, civis:—Burhman *vel* burhsita *urbanus*, Ælfc. Gl. 50; Som. 65, 103; Wrt. Voc. 34, 32: Nathan. 1.

burh-ræced, es; *n. A city-dwelling.* v. burg-ræced.

burh-rǽden, -rǽdenn, e; *f. Citizenship*; municipatus, Cot. 128.

burh-riht, es; *n. The civil law*; jus civile, Som. v. riht *law.*

burh-rúnan; *pl. f.* [-rúne, an; *f.*] *The fates, furies, fairies*; parcæ, furiæ, oreades:—Burhrúnan *furiæ*, Cot. 92.

burh-sæl, es; *n. A castle-hall, city-dwelling.* v. burg-sæl.

burh-sǽta, an; *m. A dweller in a city, citizen*; civis. v. burh-séta.

burh-scipe, es; *m. A township,* [BOROUGH-SHIP], *free borough, an incorporated city* or *town*; municipium, Ælfc. Gr. 10; Som. 14, 50: Ælfc. Gl. 54; Som. 66, 104. DER. ge-burh-scipe.

burh-scír, e; *f. A city-boundary, city-liberty*; urbis territorium:—Ða yfelan leóda fíf burhscíra ðæs Sodomítisces eardes *the evil people of the five city-boundaries of the Sodomitish land*, Ælfc. T. 7, 20: Jos. 13; Thw. 152, 9: Cot. 148.

burh-sele, es; *m. A castle-hall, city-dwelling.* v. burg-sele.

burh-séta, an; *m. A city-dweller, townsman, citizen*; civis, oppidanus, Wrt. Voc. 18, 36. v. burh-sǽta.

burh-síta, an; *m. A city-dweller, citizen*:—Burhsíta *urbanus*, Wrt. Voc. 34, 32. v. burh-sǽta.

burh-sittend, burg-sittend, es; *m. A city-dweller, an inhabitant of a city, citizen*; urbis incola, civis:—Ðú scealt sunu ágan, ðone sculon burhsittende Isaac hátan *thou shalt have a son, whom the city-dwellers shall call Isaac*, Cd. 106; Th. 140, 12; Gen. 2326: 136; Th. 172, 2; Gen. 2838. Ðá wurdon blíðe burhsittende *then the citizens became merry*, Judth. 11; Thw. 23, 37; Jud. 159: Cd. 188; Th. 235, 1; Dan. 299. Ðæt is wíde cúþ burhsittendum *that is widely known to the city-dwellers*, Cd. 135; Th. 170, 18; Gen. 2815: 210; Th. 261, 11, 23; Dan. 724, 730. His gebídan ne mágon burgsittende *citizens cannot wait for him*, Bt. Met. Fox 27, 34; Met. 27, 17: Elen. Kmbl. 552; El. 276. v. burh-sittende.

burh-sittende, burg-sittende; *part. City-dwelling, inhabiting a city*; urbem incolens:—He folgode ánum burhsittendum men ðæs ríces *adhæsit uni civium regionis illius*, Lk. Bos. 15, 15. Folca bearn burgsittende *the sons of men dwelling in cities*, Cd. 52; Th. 66, 24; Gen. 1089: Exon. 12 b; Th. 21, 20; Cri. 337. Burgsittendra, *gen. pl.* 106 b; Th. 407, 10; Rä. 26, 3.

burh-spræc, -spæc, e; *f. Civil* or *courtly speech, polite behaviour, urbanity*; urbanus sermo, urbanitas, Cot. 202.

burh-staðol, es; *m. A dwelling in a city, a mansion, house*; urbana sedes, mansio, habitaculum. v. burh, staðol *in* staðel.

burh-steal, es; *m. A city-place*; arcis locus, arx. v. burg-steal.

burh-stede, burg-stede, es; *m. A city-place, city*; urbis locus, urbs:—On ðam burh-stede *in that city*, Cd. 52; Th. 65, 7; Gen. 1062: 174; Th. 218, 31; Dan. 47. Hí ágon beorhtne burhstede *they shall have a bright city-place*, 221; Th. 287, 6; Sat. 363: Beo. Th. 4522; B. 2265. Æfter burhstedum *through the cities*, Andr. Kmbl. 1161; An. 581. Se burgstede wæs blissum gefylled *the city-place was filled with joys*, Exon. 52 a; Th. 181, 10; Gú. 1291: 124 a; Th. 476, 3; Ruin. 2.

burh-þelu, e; *f. A castle-floor.* v. buruh-þelu.

burh-tún, es; *m. A city-inclosure, city-dwelling*; urbis septum, urbana domus. v. burg-tún.

burh-waran; *gen.* -warena; *pl. m. Inhabitants of a city*; cives:—Wearþ eal here burhwarena blind *all the multitude of the city-inhabitants became blind*, Cd. 115; Th. 150, 13; Gen. 2491. v. burg-waran.

burh-ware, burg-ware; *gen.* a; *dat.* um; *pl. m. Inhabitants of a city, citizens*; urbis incolæ, cives:—Him cyrdon to mǽst ealle ða burhware *almost all the inhabitants of the city turned to him*, Chr. 919; Ing. 133, 15. Se gehâten wæs mid ðǽm burhwarum Brutus *he was called Brutus by the citizens*, Bt. Met. Fox 10, 93; Met. 10, 47. Ofer burhware *over the inhabitants*, Cd. 181; Th. 226, 31; Dan. 179. Wurdon burgware blíðe on móde *the citizens were blithe in mood*, Andr. Kmbl. 3164; An. 1585. Ðá wearþ burgwarum éce gefeá *then was to the citizens everlasting joy*, Exon. 18 b; Th. 46, 25; Cri. 742.

burh-waru, burg-waru; *gen. dat.* e; *acc.* e, u; *f. The inhabitants of a city considered as a community, the whole body of citizens*; civitas, civitatis populus:—Ǽlc burhwaru wæs búgende to him *non fuit civitas quæ se traderet illis*, Jos. 11, 19. Wearþ eall seó burhwaru onstyred *commota est universa civitas*, Mt. Bos. 21, 10: Chr. 1013; Th. 271, 28, col. 1. Wæs mycel menegu ðære burhware mid hyre *erat turba civitatis multa cum illa*, Lk. Bos. 7, 12. Ic gefrægn leóde tosomne burgwaru bannan *I learnt that the people, the body of citizens, were summoned together*, Andr. Kmbl. 2189; An. 1096.

burh-waru-man, -mann, es; *m. A citizen*; civis, Bd. 1, 7; S. 479, 12.

burh-wealda, an; *m. A city-ruler, citizen*; urbis rector, civis, Bd. 1, 7; S. 479, 12, note 12.

burh-weall, burg-weall, -weal, es; *m. A city-wall*; urbis vallum, mœnia:—Burhweall *mœnia*, Ælfc. Gl. 55; Som. 66, 116; Wrt. Voc. 36, 36. Léton ðone hálgan burhwealle néh *they left the saint near the city-wall*, Andr. Kmbl. 1666; An. 835. Beorhte burhweallas *bright city-walls*, Cd. 220; Th. 282, 31; Sat. 295. Brecan ðone burgweal *to break through the city-wall*, Exon. 83 b; Th. 315, 28; Mód. 38: 22 a; Th. 61, 1; Cri. 978.

burh-weard, es; *m. A city-ward* or *guardian, city-defender*; urbis custos *vel* defensor:—Hæfde abrocene burhweardas *had slain the city-guardians*, Cd. 144; Th. 180, 2; Exod. 39: Andr. Kmbl. 1320; An. 660.

burh-wéla, an; *m. City-wealth*; urbis opes:—Þenden he burh-wélan brūcan mōste *while he might have the enjoyment of city-wealth*, Beo. Th. 6191; B. 3100.

burh-wered, es; *n. A city-multitude;* urbis multitudo:—Heánra burhwered *vulgus* vel *plebs*, Wrt. Voc. 18, 37.

burh-wīgende; *part. pl. City-warring.* v. burg-wīgende.

burh-wita, an; *m. A knowing and polished man of the city, city-counsellor, citizen;* urbanus, homo civilis, urbis consiliarius, municeps:—Portgerēfa *vel* burhwita *municeps*, Wrt. Voc. 18, 41.

burig=byrig *to a city*, Ors. 6, 23, MS. C; *the dat. of* burh *a city.*

BURN, e; *f:* burne, an; *f:* burna, an; *m.* [*from* burnon, *p. pl. of* beornan *to boil, bubble;* fervere] *A bubbling* or *running water, a* BOURN, *brook, stream, river;* torrens, rivus:—Hefe upp ðīne hand ofer burna and ofer mōras *extende manum tuam super rivos et super paludes.* Ex. 8, 5. v. burne, burna. ☞ As a prefix or termination to the names of places, burn or burne denotes that they were near a stream; as, Burnham, Burnley, Bornemouth, Radburne, Swanburne, Sherborne. [*Piers P.* bourn: *Scot.* burn: *Plat.* born, *m: O.Sax.* brunno, *m. a source: O.Frs.* burna, *m: Dut.* born, bron, *f: Kil.* borne: *Ger.* brunne, born, *m: M.H.Ger.* brunne, burne, *m: O.H.Ger.* brunno: *Goth.* brunna, *m: Dan.* brönd, *m.f: Swed.* brunn, *m: Icel.* brunnr, *m.*]

burna, an; *m. A stream, bourn;* torrens, latex:—Burna oððe brōc *latex*, Wrt. Voc. 80, 69. Scīr burna biþ gedrēfed: brōc biþ onwended *the clear stream is disturbed: the brook is turned aside*, Bt. Met. Fox 5, 37; Met. 5, 19. He hine bibaðaþ in ðam burnan *he bathes himself in the stream*, Exon. 57 b; Th. 205, 3; Ph. 107. Burna *latex*, Wrt. Voc. 54, 21. v. burn, burne.

burne, an; *f. Running water, a stream, brook, river;* torrens, rivus:—Burnan flōweþ *aquæ fluent*, Ps. Th. 147, 7. He of stān-clife stearce burnan lǣdde *he drew a strong stream from the stony rock*, Ps. Th. 135, 17. Se Hǣlend eóde ofer ða burnan Cedron *Iesus egressus est trans torrentem Cedron*, Jn. Bos. 18, 1. Burnan unrihtwīsnysse gedrēfdon me *torrentes iniquitatis conturbaverunt me*, Ps. Spl. 17, 5. Aþene ðīne hand ofer ealle flōdas, ge ofer burnan, ge ofer meras, and ofer ealle wæter-pyttas *extende manum tuam super omnes fluvios, et rivos, ac paludes, et omnes lacus aquarum*, Ex. 7, 19. Wit unc in ðære burnan baðodan ætgædre *we two bathed together in the brook*, Exon. 121 b; Th. 467, 1; Hö. 132. v. burn. DER. wylle-burne.

burne *hast burnt, wast on fire; p. of* beornan.

burne *burned*, Ors. 4, 7; Bos. 88, 45; *subj. p. of* beornan.

burn-sele, es; *m.* [burn *a spring, brook;* sele *a dwelling, mansion*] *A bath-house;* balneum, Exon. 124 a; Th. 477, 10; Ruin. 22.

būr-reáf, es; *n.* [būr *a chamber,* reáf *a garment*] *Hangings for a chamber, tapestry;* tapete, Th. Diplm. 530, 36.

burste *hast burst, broken, failed;* burston *burst, broken*, Beo. Th. 1640; B. 818; *p. of* berstan.

būr-þegen, -þēn, es; *m.* [būr *a chamber,* þegen *a servant, attendant*] *A chamber-servant, chamberlain, chancellor, secretary;* cubicularius, cancellarius, scriniarius:—Būrþēn *cubicularius*, Ælfc. Gl. 27; Som. 60, 100; Wrt. Voc. 25, 40. His þeóden þanc gesǣde ðam būrþēne *his chief gave thanks to the chamberlain*, Byrht. Th. 135, 20, note; By. 121. Būrþēn *cancellarius* vel *scriniarius*, Ælfc. Gl. 114; Som. 80, 22; Wrt. Voc. 61, 3.

burþre, an; *f. A birth, issue;* natus, partus:—Þurh ða burþran we wǣron gehǣlde, and þurh ðæt gebeorþor we wurdon alȳsde *through the issue we were saved, and through the birth we were redeemed*, Homl. Blick. 105, 20.

burug *a city*, Mt. Kmbl. Lind. 5, 14. v. burh.

buruh *a castle, city*, Fins. Th. 72; Fin. 36: Ors. 5, 5; Bos. 105, 24: Mt. Foxe 10, 11. v. burh.

buruh-þelu, e; *f.* [burh *a castle,* þelu *a plank, board*] *A castle-floor;* arcis tabulatum:—Buruhþelu dynede *the castle-floor sounded*, Fins. Th. 61; Fin. 30.

buruh-waru *the people of a city in a body*, Chr. 1013; Th. 270, 28: Deut. 21, 21. v. burh-waru.

būta; *prep.* [be, ūt *out*] *Without;* extra:—Būta ðæt lond *extra regionem*, Mk. Lind. Rush. War. 5, 10. Būta ðæm wīngeard *extra vineam*, Mt. Lind. War. 21, 39. v. būtan; *prep.*

būta; *adv. Without;* foras, foris:—He eóde būta *exiit foras*, Mk. Lind. War. 14, 68. Petrus stōd to dura būta *Petrus stabat ad ostium foris*, Jn. Rush. War. 18, 16.

būta, būte; *conj. Unless;* nisi:—Ǣnig mon wāt ðone sunu būta ðe Fæder *nemo novit filium nisi Pater*, Mt. Lind. War. 11, 27. Būta ðes ūtacunda *nisi hic alienigena*, Lk. Lind. War. 17, 18. v. būtan; *conj.*

būtā *both;* ambo:—Swelton hīg būtā *they both shall die*, Deut. 22, 22: Exon. 113 b; Th. 436, 25; Rä. 55, 6. v. būtū.

būtan, būton, būtun; *prep.* [be, ūtan *out*]. I. *with the dative;* cum dativo. 1. *out of, against;* extra, contra:—Forbærn ðæt celf būtan ðære wicstōwe *ipsum vitulum comburet extra castra*, Lev. 4, 21. Būtan leódrihte *against the law of the land*, Andr. Kmbl. 1357; An. 679. 2. *without, except;* sine, absque, præter:—Būtan leahtre *sine crimine*, Mt. Bos. 12, 5. Būtan ānum cnihte *excepto uno puerulo*, Bd. 3, 23; S. 555, 26. Būtan geþeahte *without thought*, 3, 1; S. 523, 31. Būtan ende *without end*, Exon. 11 b; Th. 17, 16; Cri. 271: L. E. I. prm; Th. ii. 400, 28. II. *with the accusative;* cum accusativo. 1. *out of;* extra:—He lǣdde hine būtan ða wīc *eduxit eum extra vicum*, Mk. Bos. 8, 23. 2. *without, except;* sine, præter:—Būtan sealm *præter psalmodiam*, Bd. 3, 27; S. 559, 10. III. sometimes *būtan* is separated from its case:—Ðæt wæs geworden būtan weres frigum *that came to pass without the favours of man*, Exon. 8 b; Th. 3, 17; Cri. 37. [*Chauc.* but: *R. Brun.* bot: *R. Glouc.* bote: *Laym.* bute, bote: *Orm.* buttan, butt: *O.Sax.* būtan, bōtan: *Frs.* buten: *O.Frs.* buta: *Dut.* buiten: *Kil.* buyten: *Ger.* bauszen.]

būtan, būton, būtun; *conj.* [be, ūtan *out*]. I. with the *subj. Unless, save that;* nisi:—Būtan ðū [eorþan spēde] gedǣlde Dryhtne sylfum *unless thou hadst bestowed [the riches of the earth] for the Lord himself*, Exon. 99 a; Th. 371, 19; Seel. 78. Būton ðæt hit sȳ ūtaworpen *nisi ut mittatur foras*, Mt. Bos. 5, 13. Būtan ǣr wyrce ēce Dryhten ende worlde *save ere the eternal Lord shall work an end of the world*, Exon. 98 a; Th. 367, 24; Seel. 12. II. with the *ind. Save* or *except that;* nisi:—Ēgorhere eall acwealde būton ðæt earce bord heóld heofona freá *the water-host destroyed all save that the Lord of heaven held the ark board*, Cd. 70; Th. 84, 26; Gen. 1403. III. without a dependent verb, *Except, save, besides, but;* nisi:—Ond eallum dagum būtan sunnan dagum *diebus cunctis excepta dominica*, Bd. 3, 23; S. 554, 32. Ic ne gehȳrde būtan hlimman sǣ *I heard nought save the sea roaring*, Exon. 81 b; Th. 307, 4; Seef. 18. Sume men sǣdon ðæt ðǣr nǣran būtan twegen dǣlas *some men said that there were but two parts*, Ors. 1, 1; Bos. 15, 6.

būte *without;* foris, Jn. Lind. War. 18, 16. v. būta; *adv.*

būte; *conj. Unless, but;* nisi, sed:—Nān þing wyrþe [geweorþe Cot.] būte hit God wille *nothing comes to pass unless God wills it*, Bt. 41, 2; Fox 244, 18: Bt. Met. Fox 18, 20; Met. 18, 10. Būte ic nāt *but I know not*, Bt. 34, 10; Fox 148, 16. Būte ge to him gecyrren *nisi convertimini*, Ps. Th. 7, 12. v. būtan; *conj.*

būte *both;* ambo:—Būte ða þinc *ambæ res*, R. Ben. interl. 5. v. būtū.

butere, an; *f.* BUTTER; butyrum [=βούτυρον, βοῦς *a cow,* τυρός *cheese*]:—Butere *butyrum*, Wrt. Voc. 82, 27. Dō ðonne mele fulne buteran *add then a basin full of butter*, L. M. 1, 36; Lchdm. ii. 86, 17, 19, 22. On ðære buteran *in the butter*, 1, 36; Lchdm. ii. 88, 1. On gōdre buteran *in good butter*, 3, 32; Lchdm. ii. 326, 18: 3, 41; Lchdm. ii. 334, 14. Ahlyttre ða buteran *purify the butter*, 3, 2; Lchdm. ii. 308, 28: Coll. Monast. Th. 34, 27. [*Wyc.* botere: *Plat.* botter, *f: Frs.* buter: *O.Frs.* butera, botera: *Dut.* bóter, *f: Ger.* butter, *f: M.H.Ger.* buter: *O.H.Ger.* butere, *f: Fr.* beurre, *m: It.* butirro, burro, *m: Lat.* butyrum: *Grk.* βούτυρον.]

buter-flēge *a butterfly;* papilio. v. buttor-fleóge.

buter-geþweor, es; *n. Butter-curd, what is coagulated, butter;* butyri coagulum, butyrum:—Buter-geþweor ǣlc and cȳsgerunn losiaþ [MS. losaþ] eów *butyrum omne et caseus pereunt vobis*, Coll. Monast. Th. 28, 19.

buteric *a bottle*, Coll. Monast. Th. 27, 35. v. buteruc.

buter-stoppa, an; *m.* [butere *butter,* stoppa *a vessel*] *A butter-vessel, butter-dish;* butyri vas, Wrt. Voc. 290, 24.

buteruc, buteric, buturuc, butruc, es; *m. A leathern bottle;* flasco, uter:—Buteruc *flasco*, Ælfc. Gl. 26; Som. 60, 76; Wrt. Voc. 25, 16. Ic bicge hȳda and fell, and wyrce of him butericas *ego emo cutes et pelles, et facio ex iis utres*, Coll. Monast. Th. 27, 35. Ðæt wæter asceortode, ðe wæs on ðam buturuce *consumpta esset aqua in utre*, Gen. 21, 15. Butruc *flasco*, Wrt. Voc. 85, 83. [*O. Sax.* buteric, *m: O.H.Ger.* butrih *uter.*]

būton *without;* sine:—Būton ǣlcum eorþlīcum fæder *without any earthly father*, Homl. Th. i. 24, 30. Būton synne ānum *without any sin*, i. 24, 35. v. būtan; *prep.*

būton; *adv. Gratuitously, without a cause;* gratis:—Forðan ðe būton hī behīddon me onforwyrde *quoniam gratis absconderunt mihi interitum*, Ps. Spl. 34, 8.

butruc *a bottle*, Wrt. Voc. 85, 83. v. buteruc.

butsa-carlas [bātes carlas, *i.e.* bāt-sǣ carlas] *Seamen, sailors;* nautæ, Chr. 1066; Ing. 259, 4.

Butting-tūn, es; *m.* BODDINGTON, *Gloucestershire:*—Offōron hie ðone here hindan æt Buttingtūne on Sæferne staðe *they followed after the army to Boddington on the bank of the Severn*, Chr. 894; Erl. 92, 22. Mr. Earle has the following pertinent note on the locality:—Two places have hitherto contended for this site, viz. Boddington near Cheltenham, and Buttington in Montgomeryshire, near Welshpool. But Mr. Ormerod [Archæologia, vol. xxix; and *Strigulensia*, p. 60] has put forward a claim for Buttinton in Tidenham, on the peninsula formed by the Severn and the Wye. There are traces of works here, though less considerable than those at Buttington in Montgomeryshire. Mr. Ormerod grounds his claim mainly upon Matthew of Westminster's 'paganos tam navali quam terrestri exercitu circumcinxit.' No such thing appears in the text before us, but to the opposite effect. One is almost tempted to suspect that this 'Verwirrer der Geschichte' [as Lappenberg calls Matthew of Westminster] caught sight of 'sciphere' in the next line, and imagined the rest. But it must be allowed, Mr. Ormerod's position has its advantages. It does not, however, suit 'ðá up be Sæferne,' if this means that they went up stream, which would seem to be its meaning, though not in Florence, Chr. Erl. notes, p. 318.

buttor-fleóge, an; *f.* [butere *butter*, fleóge *a fly*] *A* BUTTERFLY; papilio, Ælfc. Gl. 22; Som. 59, 115; Wrt. Voc. 23, 70. [*Ger.* butterfliege, *f.*] DER. niht-buttorfleóge.

bútú [bú = bá *both*, tú = twá *two*] *Both;* ambo:—Ðonne beóþ bútú gehealden *then both* [*the two*] *shall be preserved*, Mk. Bos. 2, 22. Ðá bútú abulgon Isaace and Rebeccan *then both* [*the two*] *were a grief to Isaac and Rebecca*, Gen. 26, 35: Lk. Bos. 1, 6, 7. Wit him bútú sprecaþ *we both* [lit. *we two both*] *speak to him*, Cd. 27; Th. 36, 20; Gen. 574: 39; Th. 52, 4; Gen. 838: 40; Th. 52, 22; Gen. 847. Ðǽr hie sǽton bútú *where they both* [lit. *they two both*] *sat*, 133; Th. 168, 8; Gen. 2779. v. bátwá.

bútun *without*:—Bútun geongum litlingum, and heordum *absque parvulis, et gregibus*, Gen. 50, 8. v. bútan; *prep.*

bútun *unless, save;* nisi, Mt. Bos. 11, 27: 12, 4. v. bútan; *conj.*

buturuc *a bottle*, Gen. 21, 15. v. buteruc.

búwian; *p.* ode; *pp.* od *To inhabit;* inhabitare:—Búwa eorþan *inhabita terram*, Ps. Th. 36, 3. v. búgian.

bý, es; *n?* *A dwelling, habitation;* habitatio:—Se ðe hús oððe lytel [MS. lytelo] bý hæfde in þyrgenum [MS. byrgennum] *qui domicilium habebat in monumentis*, Mk. Skt. Lind. 5, 3. Hence, by and bye in the termination of the names of places. v. bú.

BYCGAN, bicgan, bycgean; ic bycge, bicge, ðú bygest, he bygeþ, *pl.* bycgaþ, bicgaþ; *p.* bohte, *pl.* bohton; *impert.* byge, bige, *pl.* bycgaþ; *pp.* boht; *v. a.* *To* BUY, *procure;* emere, redimere:—Hí woldon mete bicgan *cibos emerent*, Jn. Bos. 4, 8. Ðæt hie bicgan scoldon *which they must buy*, Beo. Th. 2615; B. 1305: Exon. 120 b; Th. 463, 11; Hö. 68. Ðá híg férdon bycgean *dum irent emere*, Mt. Bos. 25, 10. Ic bicge *I buy*, Salm. Kmbl. 403; Sal. 202. Mete bygeþ he *he buys meat*, Exon. 90 b; Th. 340, 14; Gn. Ex. 111. Hí bycgaþ *they buy*, 33 b; Th. 106, 27, note; Gú. 47. Ðæt góde men mid feó bicgaþ *which good men buy with money*, 114 a; Th. 436, 37; Rä. 55, 12. Ðæt þohte Abraham *quam emit Abraham*, Gen. 49, 30: Chr. 963; Erl. 123, 27. Menn heora land bohton [MS. bohtan] *men bought their land*, Chr. 1066; Erl. 203, 10. Bige us to ðæs cynges þeówette *eme nos in servitudinem regiam*, Gen. 47, 19. Bige ða þing *eme ea*, Jn. Bos. 13, 29. Bycgaþ eów ele *emite oleum vobis*, Mt. Bos. 25, 9. [*Wyc.* bigge, bye, biȝe: *R. Brun.* bie: *Laym.* bugge: *Orm.* biggenn: *O. Sax.* buggean: *Frs.* bikje: *Goth.* bugyan.] DER. a-bycgan, -bicgan, be-, ge-: un-boht, unbe-, unge-.

bycgean *to buy, procure;* emere:—Híg woldon bycgean *they would buy*, Mt. Bos. 25, 10. v. bycgan.

bycgen, bycgenn, e; *f.* *A buying, selling;* emptio, Som. Ben. Lye.

býcnend-líc; *adj.* *Allegorical, mystical;* allegoricus:—Býcnendlíc racu *allegorica expositio*, Bd. 5, 23; S. 647, 42. v. beácniend-líc.

býcnian, bycnan; *p.* ode; *pp.* od *To beckon, shew, signify;* indicare:—Niht nihte býcneþ *nox nocti indicat*, Ps. Spl. 18, 2. Ðe býcnaþ [gehiwode *finxit*, Lamb: býcnaþ *fixit?*] eáge *qui finxit oculum*, 93, 9. v. beácnian.

býcniend-líc gemet, es; *n.* *The indicative mood;* indicativus modus, Ælfc. Gr. 21; Som. 23, 18, MS. C.

býcnung, e; *f.* *A figure, trope;* figura:—Under býcnunge ðæs bíges *sub figura coronæ*, Bd. 5, 22; S. 644, 10. v. beácnung.

býd = beád? *commanded, bid*, Gen. 50, 5; *p. of* beódan.

býdel, es; *m.* [beódan *to bid, order, proclaim*]. I. *one who bids* or *cries out, a herald, proclaimer, minister;* præco, nuncius:—Býdel *præco*, Ælfc. Gr. 47; Som. 48, 41: Wrt. Voc. 84, 40. Se Godes býdel *a messenger of God, minister*, Homl. Th. ii. 530, 2. Se Godes Sunu sende his býdel toforan him *the Son of God sent his proclaimer before him*, ii. 36, 25, 27. Bisceopas sindon býdelas Godes lage *bishops are proclaimers of God's law*, L. C. E. 26; Th. i. 374, 15. Biscopas sind to býdelum gesette *bishops are ordained to be ministers*, Homl. Th. ii. 320, 8. Drihten sende his býdelas ætforan him *the Lord sent his messengers* [*prophets*] *before him*, ii. 530, 9. II. *one who bids* or *summons to appear in a court of law, a* BEADLE; apparitor, exactor, bedellus:—Ðé sylle se déma ðam býdele, and se býdel ðé sende on cwertern *judex tradat te exactori, et exactor mittat te in carcerem*, Lk. Bos. 12, 58. Býdele gebýraþ, ðæt he for his wycan sý weorces frigra ðonne óðer man *bedello pertinet, ut pro servitio suo libertior sit ab operatione quam alii homines*, L. R. S. 18; Th. i. 440, 6. He þurh his býdelas his gafoles myngaþ *he reminds him of his tribute by his messengers* [lit. *beadles*], L. Edg. S. 1; Th. i. 270, 19. Aaron hét býdelas beódan,—to morgen biþ simbeldæg *Aaron commanded beadles to proclaim,—to-morrow is a feast day*, Ex. 32, 5. [*Piers P.* bedele: *Dut.* beul, *m*: *Ger.* büttel, *m*: *M. H. Ger.* bütel: *O. H. Ger.* butil, *m.*]

BYDEN, bydenn, e; *f.* I. *a bushel;* modius:—Cwyst ðú cymþ ðæt leóhtfæt ðæt hit beó under bydene aset *numquid venit lucerna ut sub modio ponatur?* Mk. Bos. 4, 21: Lk. Bos. 11, 33. II. *a barrel, tun, butt;* dolium, cupa:—Hí mec baðedon in bydene *they bathed me in a tub*, Exon. 107 b; Th. 409, 24; Rä. 28, 6. Byden *cupa*, Ælfc. Gl. 49; Som. 65, 94; Wrt. Voc. 34, 24. [*O. H. Ger.* butin *cupa.*]

byden-botm, es; *m.* *The bottom of a vessel;* fundus, Ælfc. Gl. 25; Som. 60, 49; Wrt. Voc. 24, 49.

býe *to a habitation; dat. of* bý.

byffan *to mutter;* mutire, Cot. 154. DER. a-byffan.

byfian; *p.* ode; *pp.* od *To tremble;* tremere:—Eorþe ondréd oððe byfode and heó geswác oððe heó wæs stille *terra tremuit et quievit*, Ps. Lamb. 75, 9. v. bifian.

byfor, es; *m.* *A beaver*, Ælfc. Gr. 8; Som. 7, 13, MS. T. v. befer.

býgan, bígan, bígean, bégan; he býgeþ; *p.* de; *pp.* ed; *v. trans.* *To bow, bend, turn, turn back, bow down, humble, abase;* flectere, inflectere, incurvare, retorquere, deflectere, humiliare:—Býgdest ðú ðé fór hæleðum *thou bowedst thyself before men*, Exon. 100 a; Th. 376, 11; Seel. 153. Ðeáh ðú hwilcne boh býge wið eorþan *though thou bend any bough towards the earth*, Bt. Met. Fox 13, 106; Met. 13, 53. Býgaþ hine, ðæt he on hinder gǽþ *they shall turn him back, so that he shall go backward*, Salm. Kmbl. 252; Sal. 125. He herm-cweðend hýneþ and býgeþ *humiliabit calumniatorem*, Ps. Th. 71, 5. [*Dan.* böje, boie: *Swed.* böja: *O. Nrs.* beygja.] DER. for-býgan, -bígan, ge-, on-. v. búgan.

býge, bíge, es; *m.* [býgan *to bow*] *A bowing, bending, turning, a corner, an angle, a bay, bosom, the apex of a helmet;* flexus, ancon, angulus, sinus, conus:—Ðá gestóp he to ánes wealles býge *then he stepped to a bend of a wall*, Ors. 3, 9; Bos. 68, 23: Num. 22, 26. Helmes býge *conus galeæ*, Wrt. Voc. 36, 3.

býgend-líc; *adj.* *Flexible, pliable;* flexilis, flexibilis:—Býgendlíc on ðám geþeódnessum his liða *flexibilibus artuum compagibus*, Bd. 4, 30; S. 608, 37. v. býgan.

bygest, he bygeþ *buyest, he buys*, Exon. 90 b; Th. 340, 14; Gn. Ex. 111; *2nd and 3rd pers. pres. of* bycgan.

byggan *to build;* ædificare, Som. Ben. Lye. v. býtlian.

býgnes, -ness, e; *f.* *A bending, bowing;* flexio. v. bígnes.

byg-spæc, e; *f.* *A beguiling in speech;* supplantatio, Ps. Spl. 40, 10.

býgþ, býhþ, ðú býgst, býhst *bows, thou bowest; 3rd and 2nd pers. pres. of* búgan *to bow.*

byht, es; *m.* [býgan *to bend*] *A bending, corner, dwelling, an abode, bay,* BIGHT; habitatio, dominium, sinus:—Andlang norþgeardes ðæt hit cymþ in ðone byht *along the north yard till it comes to the corner*, Cod. Dipl. 538; A. D. 967; Kmbl. iii. 18, 29: Cod. Dipl. Apndx. 308; A. D. 875; Kmbl. iii. 399, 25, 32. Eall ðæt sculon ágan eaforan ðíne, þeódlanda gehwilc, folcmægþa byht *thy sons shall own all that, each country, the dwelling of nations*, Cd. 100; Th. 133, 20; Gen. 2213. Mec ahebbaþ ofer hæleða byht ðeós heá lyft *this lofty air raises me above the dwellings of men*, Exon. 103 a; Th. 389, 26; Rä. 8, 3. Ofer wætres byht to lande *over the water's abode* [*bay*] *to the land*, Exon. 106 a; Th. 404, 23; Rä. 23, 12. [*Dut.* bogt, *f*: *Ger.* bucht, *f*: *Dan.* bugt, *m. f*: *Swed.* bugt, *m*: *Icel.* bygð, *f.*]

býing, e; *f.* *A habitation;* domus, Mk. Skt. Rush. 5, 3. v. bý.

BÝL, býle, bíle, es; *m.* *A* BILE, *blotch, sore;* carbunculus, Cot. 183. [*O. Frs.* bel, beil: *Dut.* buil, *f*: *Kil.* buyll: *Ger.* beule, *f*: *M. H. Ger.* biule, *f*: *Dan.* bule, *m. f*: *Swed.* bula, *f*: *O. Nrs.* beyla, *f.*]

BYLD, e; *f*: byldo; *f. indecl. in s.* *Constancy, boldness;* constantia:—Bídeþ þurh byldo *awaiteth with constancy*, Exon. 9 b; Th. 8, 5; Cri. 113. He sceolde ða byldo anescian *poterat emollire constantiam*, Bd. 1, 7; S. 477, note 43. [*O. H. Ger.* baldí, *f*: *Goth.* balþei, *f. boldness.*] DER. ge-byld.

bylda, an; *m.* [bold *a house*] *A* BUILDER; ædificator:—Sum biþ bylda til hám to habbanne *one is a good builder to raise a house*, Exon. 79 b; Th. 297, 29; Crä. 75.

byldan; *p.* bylde; *pp.* bylded; *v. trans.* [beald *bold;* v. byld] *To make bold, to animate, instigate, exhort, encourage, confirm;* animare, instigare, hortari, confirmare:—He Fresena cyn byldan wolde *he would encourage the race of the Frisians*, Beo. Th. 2193; B. 1094. Geongne æðeling sceolon góde gesíðas byldan *good companions should encourage a young prince*, Menol. Fox 488; Gn. C. 15. Hí bylde bearn Ælfríces *the son of Ælfric encouraged them*, Byrht. Th. 137, 60; By. 209. Swá hí ealle bylde Godríc to gúþe *so Godric encouraged them all to the war*, Byrht. Th. 141, 11; By. 320. Bǽdon hí Sigebyrht ðæt he mid him to ðam gefeohte fóre and hyra fultum trymede and bylde *rogaverunt Sigberctum ad confirmandum militem secum venire in prœlium*, Bd. 3, 18; S. 546, 20, col. 1.

býle *a bile, blotch, sore.* v. býl.

byled-breóst; *adj.* [byled, breóst *a breast*] *Puff-breasted;* rostrato pectore præditus:—Ic eom byled-breóst *I am puff-breasted*, Exon. 127 b; Th. 489, 23; Rä. 79, 1. v. gebilod.

byle-wit *merciful;* æquanimus, mansuetus:—Gehýran ða bylewitan *audeant mansueti*, Ps. Spl. 33, 2. v. byly-wit, bile-wit.

bylg *a bulge, bag*, Cot. 27. v. belg.

bylgan; *p.* de; *pp.* ed *To offend, anger, vex;* offendere, irritare, vexare. DER. a-bylgan. v. belgan.

bylgean *to bellow;* mugire, Martyr. 17, Jan. v. bellan.

Bylges leg, es; *n.* [*Flor.* Bililesleaga: *Sim. Dun.* Byligesleage: *Hovd.* Biligesleage] BISLEY, *in Gloucestershire:*—Hī cōmon to Bylges lege *they came to Bisley*, Chr. 1055; Erl. 190, 15.

bylgþ *is angry; 3rd pers. pres. of* belgan.

bylig *bellows;* follis, Wrt. Voc. 86, 15. v. belg.

byllinc *a cake;* collyris, collyrida, Cot. 208.

bylwet, bylwit *simple.* v. bile-wit.

bylwet-līce; *adv. Simply;* simpliciter, Ors. 1, 2; Bos. 26, 29. v. bile-hwītlīce.

byly-wit *merciful, kind;* æquanimus, mitis:—Bylywit fæder *merciful father*, Cd. 191; Th. 238, 32; Dan. 363. v. bile-wit.

BȲME, bēme, an; *f. A trumpet;* tuba, salpinx = σάλπιγξ:—Bȳme sang *the trumpet sounded* [lit. *sang*], Cd. 148; Th. 186, 2; Exod. 132. Ðære bȳman swēg weóx *sonitus buccinæ crescebat*, Ex. 19, 19: 20, 18: Ps. Spl. 46, 5: Exon. 23 b; Th. 65, 29; Cri. 1062. Bȳmiaþ oððe hlyriaþ on niwum mōnþe mid bȳman *buccinate in neomenia tuba*, Ps. Lamb. 80, 4. Bȳman sungon *the trumpets sounded* [lit. *sung*], Elen. Kmbl. 218; El. 109. Drēmaþ Drihtne on bȳman *psallite Domino in tubis*, Ps. Lamb. 97, 6. Seofon sacerdas blāwon mid bȳmon *septem sacerdotes clangent buccinis*, Jos. 6, 4, 13. [*Laym.* bemen, beomen; *pl. trumpets.*] DER. heofon-bȳme, here-, sige-.

bȳmere, es; *m.* [bȳme *a trumpet*] *A trumpeter;* tubicen, salpista = σαλπιστής:—Bȳmere *tubicen*, Ælfc. Gr. 9, 12; Som. 9, 24; Wrt. Voc. 73, 57. Bȳmere *salpista*, Ælfc. Gl. 114; Som. 80, 11; Wrt. Voc. 60, 47.

bȳme-sangere, es; *m.* [bȳme *a trumpet*, sangere *a singer*] *A trumpeter;* salpicta = σαλπιγκτής, Ælfc. Gl. 114; Som. 80, 13; Wrt. Voc. 60, 48.

bȳmian; *p.* ode; *pp.* od [bȳme *a trumpet*] *To sound* or *play on a trumpet;* tuba canere, buccinare:—Ic bȳme *salpizo* vel *buccino*, Ælfc. Gl. 114; Som. 80, 14; Wrt. Voc. 60, 49. Bȳmiaþ oððe hlyriaþ on niwum mōnþe mid bȳman *buccinate in neomenia tuba*, Ps. Lamb. 80, 4.

bȳn; *def.* se bȳna, seó, ðæt bȳne; *adj.* [bȳþ; *pres. of* būan *to inhabit, occupy*] *Inhabited, occupied;* habitatus:—Ðæt bȳne land is eásteweard brādost *the inhabited land is broadest eastward*, Ors. 1, 1; Bos. 20, 45. Licgaþ wilde mōras on emnlange ðæm bȳnum lande *wild mountains lie along the inhabited land*, 1, 1; Bos. 20, 44.

byndele, byndelle *a binding*, L. Alf. pol. 35; Th. i. 84, 1, MS. H. v. bindele.

byóþ *are, shall be,* = bióþ; *pres. pl. of* bión.

byrc, e; *f. A birch-tree;* betula:—Byrc *betula* [MS. *betulus*], Ælfc. Gl. 47; Som. 65, 20; Wrt. Voc. 33, 20. v. birce.

byrc-holt, es; *n. A birch holt* or *grove;* betuletum, Ælfc. Gl. 47; Som. 65, 21.

byrcþ *barks*, Ælfc. Gr. 22; Som. 24, 8; *pres. of* beorcan.

byrd *birth;* nativitas. v. ge-byrd.

byrd-dæg, es; *m. A birth-day;* natalis dies. v. ge-byrd-dæg.

byrde; *sup.* byrdest, *def.* se byrdesta; *adj. Born, well-born, noble, rich;* natus, natu *vel* genere præstans, nobilis, opulentus:—Se byrdesta sceall gyldan *the richest must pay*, Ors. 1, 1; Bos. 20, 36. DER. ge-byrde, in-. v. ge-byrd.

byrden *a burden*, Som. Ben. Lye. v. byrðen.

byrdest, se byrdesta *the highest born, most noble, richest*, Ors. 1, 1; Bos. 20, 36; *sup. of* byrde.

byrdian *to bear;* sustinere. v. for-byrdian.

byrdicge *a weaver's tool;* plumaria, N. Som. Wrt. Voc. 282, 3.

byrdnys, -nyss, e; *f. Quality, state, condition;* qualitas, status, conditio. DER. an-byrdnys, in-. v. ge-byrd.

byrd-scype, es; *m.* [byrd, ge-byrd *birth*, scype *state, condition*] *Birthship, child-bearing;* gestatio, partus:—Ic tō fela hæbbe ðæs byrdscypes bealwa onfongen *I have received too many injuries from this child-bearing*, Exon. 10 b; Th. 12, 7; Cri. 182.

byrd-tīd, e; *f. Birth-tide, time of birth;* natale tempus. v. ge-byrd-tīd.

byrdu-scrūd, es; *n.* [byrdu = bord *a shield*, scrūd *a garment, clothing*] *The covering of a shield, a shield;* clypei tegmen, clypeus:—Unc sceal sweord and helm, byrne and byrduscrūd bām gemǣne *sword and helmet, armour and shield, shall be common to us both*, Beo. Th. 5313; B. 2660.

byre; *gen.* byres; *dat.* byre; *acc.* byre: *pl. nom. acc.* byras, byre; *gen.* byra; *dat.* byrum; *m. A son, child, descendant;* natus, filius, soboles, proles:—Ðonne ǣfre byre monnes hȳrde under heofonum *than ever child of man heard under heaven*, Exon. 57 b; Th. 206, 18; Ph. 128: Beo. Th. 4113; B. 2053. Ðǣr hyre byre wǣron *where her sons were*, 2381; B. 1188. Ðæs ða byre siððan gyrne onguldon, ðe hī ðæt gyfl þēgun *for which their children since with grief have paid, that they ate that fruit*, Exon. 61 b; Th. 226, 22; Ph. 409. Mǣru cwēn bǣdde byras geonge *the illustrious queen solicited her young sons*, Beo. Th. 4040; B. 2018. Lamech bearna strȳnde; him byras wōcan eafora and idesa; he ðone yldestan Noæ nemde *Lamech begat children; to him descendants were born of sons and daughters; the eldest he named Noah*, Cd. 62; Th. 75, 1; Gen. 1233. [*Goth.* baur, *m. one born, a son: O. Nrs.* burr, borr, *m.*] v. bearn.

bȳre, es; *m. An event, the time at which anything happens, a favourable time, an opportunity;* eventus, tempus quo accidit aliquid, opportunitas, occasio, = καιρός:—Wæs ðǣr mid him ōþ ðone bȳre ðæt Swegen wearþ deád *was there with him until the time that Sweyn was dead*, Chr. 1013; Th. 272, 22. Ðā he bȳre hæfde *when he had opportunity*, Byrht. Th. 135, 21; By. 121. DER. ge-bȳre. v. ge-bȳrian.

byrele *a cup-bearer, butler*, Wrt. Voc. 290, 51: Beo. Th. 2327; B. 1161. v. byrle.

byrelian *to pour out, give to drink, serve*, Exon. 45 b; Th. 154, 13; Gū. 842. v. byrlian.

byren; *adj. Belonging to a bear;* ursinus, Som. Ben. Lye. v. beren.

byrene, an; *f. A she-bear;* ursa, Ælfc. Gl. 21; Som. 59, 70; Wrt. Voc. 23, 29. v. bera.

byreþ *bears*, Beo. Th. 598; B. 296; *3rd pers. pres. of* beran.

bȳreþ *it pertains to, it is lawful;* pertinet ad, licet, Jn. Lind. War. 10, 13. v. bȳrian.

byrg *to a city*, Exon. 15 a; Th. 33, 1; Cri. 519; *dat. of* burh.

byrga *of cities* or *inclosed dwellings, for* burga; *gen. pl. of* burh, Runic pm. 8; Kmbl. 341, 3.

byrga *a pledger, creditor*, Cot. 37. v. byrgea.

BYRGAN, birgan, byrigan, birigan, birgean, byrigean, byrian; *p.* de; *pp.* ed [beorg *tumulus*]; *v. trans. To raise a mound, to* BURY; tumulare, tumulo condere, sepelire:—Hī his līchaman on cyrican neáh weofode byrgan woldon *they would bury his body in the church near the altar*, Bd. 3, 19; S. 550, 10: Exon. 82 b; Th. 311, 27; Seef. 98. Birge man hine ðæs ilcan dæges *sepelietur in eadem die*, Deut. 21, 23. Ðǣr hine man birgde *ibi sepelierunt eum*, Gen. 49, 31. Alȳf me ǣrest byrigan mīnne fæder *permitte mihi primum sepelire patrem meum*, Lk. Bos. 9, 59: 9, 60. Hine man byrigde swā him wel gebȳrede *they buried him as well became him*, Chr. 1036; Th. 294, 21: Hy. 10, 29; Hy. Grn. ii. 293, 29. [*Wyc.* birie: *Piers P.* yburied, *pp: Chauc.* buried: *R. Glouc.* ybured: *Laym.* burien: *Orm.* birrȝenn: *Dut.* bergen: *O. Dut.* berghen condere, abscondere, servare, tueri: *Ger. M. H. Ger.* bergen: *O. H. Ger.* bergan, ga-bergan *condere, recondere: Goth.* bairgan *tueri, conservare: O. Nrs.* byrgja *includere.*] DER. be-byrgan, bi-, ge-: byrgen.

BȲRGAN, bȳrian, bȳrigan, bȳrgean, bȳrigean, beorgan; *p.* de; *pp.* ed *To taste, eat;* gustare, manducare:—Ðū ðīnes gewinnes wæstme bȳrgest *labores fructuum tuorum manducabis*, Ps. Th. 127, 2. Nymþe ðū æppel ǣnne bȳrgdest *unless thou hast tasted an apple*, Cd. 42; Th. 54, 21; Gen. 880. Hī bū þēgun æppel, bȳrgdon forbodene *they both ate the apple, tasted the forbidden* [*fruit*], Exon. 61 b; Th. 226, 11; Ph. 404. Nim ðē ðis ofæt on hand, bīt hit and bȳrge *take to thee this fruit in hand, bite it and taste*, Cd. 25; Th. 33, 12; Gen. 519. [*O. Nrs.* bergja *to taste;* gustare.] DER. a-bȳrgan, ge-, on-.

byrgea, byrigea, byriga, berigea, an; *m.* [borh, borg *a pledge, security*] *A person who gives a pledge, a surety;* fidejussor:—Gif ðū hæbbe byrgean, mana ðone ðæs āngyldes *if thou have a surety, admonish him of the recompense*, L. In. 22; Th. i. 116, 11. Mid lx scillinga gebēte ðam byrgean *let amends be made to the surety with sixty shillings*, L. Alf. pol. 18; Th. i. 72, 12, 15, 16: L. In. 31; Th. i. 122, 6. Se man ðam ōðrum byrigean geselle *let the man give surety to the other*, L. H. E. 8; Th. i. 30, 12. Gif he byrigan forwærne *if he refuse surety*, 9, 10; Th. i. 30, 15, 17. Him man wilsumne berigean geselle [MS. gefelle] *let a man give him a sufficient surety*, 6; Th. i. 30, 5. DER. leód-gebyrgea.

bȳrgean *to taste;* gustare:—He byreþ blōdig wæl, bȳrgean þenceþ, eteþ unmurnlīce *he will bear off my bloody corpse, will resolve to taste it, will eat it without repugnance*, Beo. Th. 901; B. 448. DER. a-bȳrgan. v. bȳrgan.

byrged *buried.* v. byrgan.

byrgels, birgels, bergels, es; *m. A* BURIAL-*place, sepulchre, tomb;* sepulcrum, bustum:—Byrgels *bustum*, Cot. 183. To birgelse *in possessionem sepulcri*, Gen. 23, 9. v. byrgen.

byrgen, byrgenn, birgen, byrigen, burgen, e; *f.* [beorg *tumulus*] *A burying, grave, sepulchre, tomb;* sepulcrum, monumentum, tumba:—Byrgen *sepulcrum*, Ps. Th. 48, 9: Ps. Surt. 13, 3. Hāt nū healdan ða byrgene *jube ergo custodire sepulcrum*, Mt. Bos. 27, 64: 27, 66. On ðam wyrt-tūne wæs niwe byrgen *in horto erat novum monumentum*, Jn. Bos. 19, 41: 19, 42. Com to ðære byrgene *venit ad monumentum*, Jn. Bos. 20, 1: 20, 3, 4, 6, 8, 11. Ðȳ þriddan dæge of byrgenne, of deáðe, arās Dryhten *on the third day the Lord arose from the sepulchre, from death*, Elen. Kmbl. 371; El. 186: 965; El. 484: Exon. 18 b; Th. 45, 34; Cri. 729: Ps. Th. 29, 8. Byrgenum *sepulcris*, 13, 5: Salm. Kmbl. 445; Sal. 223. On his byrgenne is awriten byrgen-leóþ *scriptum est in tumba ipsius epitaphium*, Bd. 2, 1; S. 500, 17. 2. in the districts of England first occupied by the Angles, Saxons, and Jutes, numerous extensive cemeteries of the heathen period have been examined. In these cemeteries the graves are usually arranged in rows, and are dug exactly in the same manner and form as our modern church-yard graves, which are probably copied from them. After the burial, a low circular mound was raised over the grave. From their contents we learn that the body of the deceased was buried in the full dress worn when living,—the men with their arms and military equipments,—the women with their personal ornaments and jewelry. The body was generally laid on its back, on the floor of the grave; but in the wealthier classes, it was frequently inclosed in a wooden coffin, for in A. D. 679, it is said—Æđeldryþ on treówene þruh wæs bebyriged *Ætheldrith was buried in a wooden coffin*, Bd. 4, 19; S. 588, 21; or in the Latin of Bede—Ædilthryd ligneo in locello sepulta, S. 163, 15. **3.** the belief in a future life is shewn by the care with which the relatives and friends of better condition, placed in the grave of the dead objects which it was supposed would be necessary or useful in the next world: even mere personal ornaments, or articles to which the deceased had been attached, or which can only have been placed there as tokens of affectionate remembrance. Evidence is also found of the sentiments of tenderness which followed them to their last resting-place. It was believed that the dead were exposed to evil spirits, for amulets are usually found interred with them,—especially beads of amber, which were thought to be protective against such influences. The frequent occurrence, among the earth in the grave, of bones of animals, which were commonly eaten by the Anglo-Saxons, would seem to shew that there were both sacrifices and feasting at the burial. Human bones have been found in such a position as to justify a supposition, that a slave had been slain and thrown into the grave, perhaps in the belief that he would continue to serve his master in the spiritual world. **4.** in the districts which were occupied by the Angles in Britain, and Old Saxons on the continent, νεκροκαυστία, *cremation* or *the burning* of the bodies before burial, appears to have been almost universal, among rude nations, from the age of Homer to that of Alfred. The interment, therefore, consists of an urn filled with the burnt bones. It has been supposed that cremation was originally the mode of burial in use among the Angles; and that the Saxons and Jutes buried the body entire, or that they had adopted this mode of burial when they came into Britain. See Kemble in the *Archæological Journal*, No. 48. It is recorded of the Esthonians and Old Saxons, who were a very warlike and powerful people, once occupying the whole north-west corner of Germany,—And đæt is mid Éstum þeáw, đæt đǽr sceal ǽlces geþeódes man beón forbærned; and gyf đâr man ân bân findeþ unforbærned, hî hit sceolon miclum gebêtan *it is also a custom with the Esthonians, that there men of every tribe must be burned; and if any one find a single bone unburnt, they shall make a great atonement*, Ors. 1, 1; Bos. 23, 3-5. It is certain that in Beowulf, which is supposed to be an Old Norse poem, the body of the hero is described as being burnt:—Hit sǽ-lîđend syđđan hâtan Biówulfes biorh *sea-farers may afterwards call it Beowulf's mound [barrow]*, Beo. Th. 5604-5606; B. 2806, 2807. Him đâ gegiredon Geáta leóde âd unwâclîcne, helm-behongen, hilde bordum, and beorhtum byrnum *the people of the Goths then raised for him a mighty funeral pile, hung with helmets, shields, and bright breast-plates*, 6265-6271; B. 3137-3140. Ongunnon đâ bǽl-fýra mǽst wîgend weccan: wudu-rêc astâh sweart of Swió-þole *then the warriors began to kindle the greatest of bale-fires: the wood-smoke ascended black from the Swedish pine*, 6277-6281; B. 3143-3145. Hî on beorg dydon beágas and siglu, eall swylce hyrsta *on the mound they placed rings and jewels, also ornaments*, 6307-6309; B. 3164, 3165. Đâ ymbe hlǽw ridon æđelingas ... cyning mǽnan, word-gyd wrecan *then nobles rode round the mound ... their king bewail, a verbal lay recite*, 6319-6325; B. 3170-3173. Swâ begnornodon Geáta leóde *thus the people of the Goths deplored*, 6338, 6339; B. 3179. **5.** it is probable that down to a very late period the people adhered to many of their ancient burial customs. Charlemagne, so late as the year 789, ordered his Christian Saxon subjects to bury their dead in the Christian cemeteries, and not in the tumuli of the pagans, in these words,—'Jubemus ut corpora Christianorum Saxonum ad cœmeteria ecclesiæ deferantur, et non ad tumulos paganorum,' *Capit. Carl. Mag. Walter*, tom. ii. p. 107. In England, the ordinary converts appear to have been drawn reluctantly from the burial places of their forefathers by the establishment of Christian cemeteries attached to the churches, and even there they seem long to have continued many of their old rites. A few of these ceremonies are mentioned in the Anglo-Saxon ecclesiastical laws and constitutions relating to funerals. **6.** it appears from a regulation, which, though only preserved in the laws of Henry I, evidently belonged to the Anglo-Saxon period, that as soon as any person was dead, the body was laid out, with the feet to the east and the head to the west. This law enjoins any one who, either in revenging a feud or defending himself, should kill a man, not to take anything belonging to him, whether his horse, or his helmet, or his sword, or any money he may have, but to lay out his body in the manner usually observed with the dead, the head to the west and the feet to the east, upon his shield, if he have one; and to fix his lance, and place his arms round, and attach his horse by the reins; and to go to the nearest town and give information to the first person he meets: the Latin of the law is,—'Si quis in vindictam vel in se defendendo occidat aliquem, nihil sibi de mortui rebus aliquis usurpet, non equum, non galeam, vel gladium, vel pecuniam prorsus aliquam; sed ipsum corpus solito defunctorum more componat, caput ad occidens, pedes ad oriens versum, super clipeum, si habeat; et lanceam suam figat, et arma circummittat, et equum adregniet; et adeat proximam villam, et cui prius obviaverit denunciet,' L. H. 83, § 6; Th. i. 591. **7.** during the time that the dead body remained unburied, the relations and friends assembled to watch or wake over it [this watching or waking is mentioned under the word lîc *a body*, see lîc **II**], and this proceeding was evidently accompanied with feasting and drinking carried to a very great excess. So late as the end of the tenth century, archbishop Ælfric addressed the following injunction to his clergy:—Ge ne scylan fægnigan forþ-farenra manna, ne đæt lîc gesêcan, bûton eów mann lađige đǽr-to: đænne ge đǽr-to gelađode sŷn, đonne forbeóde ge đa hǽđenan sangas đæra lǽwedra manna, and heora hlûdan cheahchetunga; ne ge sylfe ne eton, ne ne drincon đǽr đæt lîc inne lîþ, đe-læs đe ge syndon efen-lǽce đæs hǽđenscypes đe hŷ đǽr begâþ *ye shall not rejoice on account of men deceased, nor attend on the corpse, unless ye be thereto invited: when ye are thereto invited, then forbid ye the heathen songs of the laymen, and their loud cachinations; nor eat ye, nor drink, where the corpse lieth therein, lest ye be imitators of the heathenism which they there commit*, L. Ælf. C. 35; Th. ii. 356, 23-358, 5. The clergy gave little attention to these injunctions, for they are warned against being 'hunters of funerals,' and Ælfric tells us how some priests 'Fægniaþ đonne men forþfaraþ, and unbedene gaderiaþ hî to đam lîce, swâ swâ grǽdige ræmmas, đǽr đǽr hî hold geseóþ; ac heom gebîraþ mid rihte to bestandenne đa men, đe hîraþ into heora mynstre; and ne sceal nân faran on ôđres folgoþ to nânum lîce bûton he gebeden sŷ *rejoice when men depart hence, and unbidden gather about the corpse, like greedy ravens, wherever they see a dead carcase; whereas it properly becomes them to bury those men, who belong to their minster; and no one ought to go in another's following to any corpse unless he be invited*,' L. Ælf. P. 49; Th. ii. 386, 2-6. **8.** we have no reason for supposing that people who were not rich were buried in coffins, but the body, having been wrapped up in its winding-sheet, appears to have been merely laid in the grave, and then covered with earth. The first coffins used by the converted Anglo-Saxons were undoubtedly of wood [vide **2**], and it was the ecclesiastics who introduced the stone sarcophagi for eminent personages of their own order. Sebbi, king of the East-Saxons, was buried in a coffin of stone:—Gearwodan hî his lîchoman to bebyrigeanne on stǽnenre þruh *cujus [Sebbi] corpori tumulando præparaverant sarcofagum lapideum*, Bd. 4, 11; S. 580, 4. **9.** at every funeral a payment, called a soul-sceát [v. sâwel-sceát], was made to the church where the interment took place, and a legacy was also expected. A mancus of gold, or even a much higher sum, was usually paid in the case of a king or bishop, or of a person of high rank. **10.** the graves were no doubt arranged in rows and covered with small mounds, as in the older pagan cemeteries, except that the mounds were elongated instead of being circular, and had head-stones. They seem, at an early period, to have been laid north and south, like many of those in the pagan cemeteries, and not east and west, as was the position of the bodies of the nuns of Hartlepool, buried towards the end of the seventh century, which were uncovered about thirty years ago. Small flat stones, the largest less than a foot square, had been laid over the graves at Hartlepool, each bearing a cross, and the name of the person it commemorated; some engraved in Anglo-Saxon runes, and some in the Roman letters of the seventh century, for to the latter end of that period they evidently belonged. v. Thrupp's Anglo-Saxon Home, 8vo. 1860, pp. 397-405. A very valuable paper by George Rolleston, Esq. M. D. F. R. S. On the modes of sepulture in early Anglo-Saxon times in this country, reprinted from the Translations of the International Congress of Prehistoric Archæology, Third Session: Douglas's Nenia Britannica: Faussett's Inventorium Sepulchrale: Akerman's Remains of Pagan Saxondom: Wylie's Fairford Graves: Braybrooke's Saxon Obsequies: and Mr. C. Roach Smith's Collectanea Antiqua.

byrgend, es; *m. A burier;* sepultor:—Nâhtan byrgendas *non erat qui sepeliret*, Ps. Th. 78, 3.

byrgen-leóþ, es; *n. A tomb-elegy, an epitaph;* sepulcrale carmen, epitaphium:—On his byrgenne is awriten byrgen-leóþ *scriptum est in tumba ipsius epitaphium*, Bd. 2, 1; S. 500, 18.

byrgen-song, es; *m. A burial song;* cantus sepulcralis, Leo 116. v. bergel-song.

byrgen-stôw, byrigen-stôw, e; *f. A burying-place, cemetery;* sepulcri locus, cœmeterium, Cot. 75: Bd. 5, 23; S. 645, 19.

byrgere, es; *m. A burier, corpse-bearer;* vespillo, Cot. 155.

byrging [byrgung, *Ettm.*], e; *f. A burying, the act of burying;* sepultura, Jn. 20, 1, 4, Lye.

bŷrging, e; *f. Taste, tasting;* gustus, Scint. 12, Lye. [*O. Nrs.* berging, *f. gustus, sacra synaxis* vel *participatio divinæ Eucharistiæ*.] v. on-bŷrging.

byrgst, byrhst, he byrgeþ, byrgþ, byrhþ *protectest, he protects*, Ps. Th. 16, 8; *2nd and 3rd pers. pres. of* beorgan.

byrht *bright, clear, lucid, loud;* clarus, splendidus, clarisonus, Beo. Th. 2402; B. 1199: Cd. 217; Th. 275, 15; Sat. 172. v. beorht.

byrhtan *to shine;* lucere, Exon. 24 a; Th. 67, 18; Cri. 1090. v. beorhtan.

byrhtm, es; *m. Noise, tumult;* fragor, tumultus, Apstls. Kmbl. 42; Ap. 21. v. breahtm.

byrhtm-hwȳl *a moment.* v. bearhtm-hwīl.

byrht-nes *brightness,* Ps. Spl. 118, 130. v. beorht-nes.

byrhtu, e; *f. Brightness, splendour,* Exon. 26 a; Th. 76, 15; Cri. 1240. v. beorhtu.

byrht-word; *adj.* [byrht = beorht *bright,* word *a word*] *Bright of word, clear in words* or *speech;* clarus voce:—Byrhtword arās engla ordfruma *the creator of angels, bright of words, arose,* Cd. 218; Th. 279, 15; Sat. 238.

byri = byrig *to a city.* v. byri-weard.

byrian; *p.* ede, ide; *pp.* ed *To bury:*—Ðǽr hī mon byride *where they buried her,* Ors. 3, 6; Bos. 58, 9. DER. be-byrian. v. byrgan.

bȳrian, *3rd s.* bȳreþ; *p.* ede; *pp.* ed [bȳre *an event, a favourable time, an opportunity*] *To happen, pertain to, belong to;* evenire, contingere, pertinere ad [v. ge-bȳrian]: *found as v. impers: it pertains to, it concerns, it belongs to, it is lawful;* pertinet ad, oportet, licet:—Ne bȳreþ to him from scipum *non pertinet ad eum de ovibus,* Jn. Lind. War. 10, 13: Mk. Lind. War. 4, 38. Ðe ne bȳrede him to etanne *quem non licebat ei edere,* Mt. Kmbl. Rush. 12, 4. DER. ge-bȳrian.

bȳrian *to taste;* gustare. v. a-bȳrian *under* a-bȳrgan.

byrig *to a city,* Ps. Th. 44, 13: 47, 11; *dat. of* burh.

byrig, e; *f: acc. s.* byrig, byrige *A city;* urbs, civitas:—Hēr Cūþa gefeaht wiđ Brytwalas æt Biedcan forda, and genam Lygeanbyrig and Ægles byrig *in this year Cutha fought against the Brito-Welsh at Bedford, and took Lenbury and Aylesbury,* Chr. 571; Th. 33, 28. Cantwara byrig forbarn đȳ geáre *Canterbury was burnt down in this year,* 754; Th. 81, 36, col. 2. v. burh.

byrig, es; *n. A mulberry-tree;* morus:—He ofslōh byrig heora on hagule *occidit moros eorum in pruina,* Ps. Spl. 77, 52: L. M. 2, 53; Lchdm. ii. 274, 17.

byriga, an; *m. A surety;* fidejussor:—He him byrigan gesealdne hæbbe *he has given him surety,* L. H. E. 10; Th. i. 30, 17. v. byrgea.

byrigan, birigan; *p.* de; *pp.* ed *To bury;* sepelire:—Alȳf me ǽrest byrigan mīnne fæder *permitte mihi primum sepelire patrem meum,* Lk. Bos. 9, 59: 9, 60: Chr. 1036; Th. 294, 21: Hy. 10, 29; Hy. Grn. ii. 293, 29: Nicod. 21; Thw. 10, 30: 21; Thw. 11, 4. DER. be-byrigan. v. byrian, byrgan.

bȳrigan; *p.* de *To taste;* gustare:—Deáþ he đǽr bȳrigde *he there tasted death,* Rood Kmbl. 199; Kr. 101. Ðæt he hire sealde đæt wæter to bȳrigenne *ut gustandam illi daret eam aquam,* Bd. 5, 4; S. 617, 21. DER. on-bȳrigan. v. bȳrian, bȳrgan.

byrig-berge, an; *f. A mulberry;* morum:—Byrigbergena seáw selle drincan *give him to drink juice of mulberries,* L. M. 2, 30; Lchdm. ii. 230, 12.

byrigea *a surety,* L. H. E. 8; Th. i. 30, 12. v. byrgea.

byrigean *to bury.* v. byrgan, be-byrigean.

bȳrigean *to taste.* v. on-bȳrigean, bȳrgan.

byrigen, byrigenn, e; *f.* [beorg *tumulus*] *A burying-place, a sepulchre, tomb, burying;* sepulcrum, monumentum, tumba, sepultura, Bd. 4, 19; S. 588, 37: 3, 8; S. 532, 15, 17: 3, 11; S. 535, 32: 1, 33; S. 499, 7. v. byrgen.

byrigen-stōw, e; *f. A burying-place:*—He sylfa byrigenstōwe worhte *sibi ipse in locum sepulcri fecerat,* Bd. 5, 23; S. 645, 19. v. byrgen-stōw.

byrig-leóþ, es; *n. An epitaph;* epitaphium, Bd. 2, 1, Lye. v. byrgen-leóþ.

byrig-man, -mann, es; *m.* [byrig *a city,* man *a man*] *A city officer;* ædilis, Ælfc. Gr. 9, 28, MS. D; Som. 11, 29. v. burh-man.

byrignes, -ness, -nyss, e; *f. A burying, burial;* sepultura, Bd. 4, 11; S. 580, 8. DER. be-byrignys.

bȳrignes, bīrgnes, -ness, e; *f. A tasting, a taste;* gustus:—Mid bȳrignesse đæs wæteres *by the tasting of the water,* Bd. 5, 18; S. 635, 29. Bīrgness *gustus,* Cot. 97. DER. an-bȳrignys. v. bȳrgan.

Byrīne, es; *m. Birinus, the first bishop of Wessex,* Chr. 649; Th. 50, 3, col. 2, 3; 51, 2, col. 1. v. Birīnus.

byris, e; *f? A graving-iron, file;* scalprum, scalpellum:—Byris *scalprum,* Glos. Epnl. Recd. 162, 36: *scalpellum,* 162, 51. [*O. H. Ger.* bursa, *f.*]

byri-weard, es; *m.* [byrig, *dat. of* burh *a city,* weard *a guard*] *A city-guardian;* urbis custos, ædilis, Wrt. Voc. 18, 54. v. burh-weard.

BYRLE, byrele, es; *m. A cup-bearer, butler;* pocillator, calicum magister, pincerna:—Byrle *pincerna,* Ælfc. Gl. 113; Som. 80, 1; Wrt. Voc. 60, 37: 74, 16. Egipta cynges byrle *pincerna regis Ægypti,* Gen. 40, 1. Byrele *pincerna,* Wrt. Voc. 290, 51. Þurh byreles hond *through the cup-bearer's hand,* Exon. 88 a; Th. 330, 15; Vy. 51. Byrlas ne gǽldon *the cup-bearers delayed not,* Andr. Kmbl. 3065; An. 1535. Geleornedon his byrelas him betweonum *his cup-bearers planned among themselves,* Ors. 3, 9; Bos. 69, 10: Beo. Th. 2327; B. 1161. Geþohte he đæra byrla ealdor *recordatus est magistri pincernarum,* Gen. 40, 20, 21, 23. Yldest byrla *a caliculis, magister calicum,* Ælfc. Gl. 113; Som. 79, 130; Wrt. Voc. 60, 34. Ðara ōđer bewiste his byrlas, ōđer his bæcestran *alter pincernis præerat, alter pistoribus,* Gen. 40, 2. [*Laym.* birle, borle: *Orm.* birrless, *pl: Icel.* byrli, byrlari, *m.*]

byrlian, byrelian; *p.* ade; *pp.* ad [byrle, byrele *a cup-bearer*] *To pour out, give to drink, serve;* propinare:—Ic him byrlade wrōht of wēge *I poured out complaint to them from the cup,* Exon. 72 b; Th. 271, 23; Jul. 486. Feónd byrlade đære idese bittor bǽdewēg *the fiend gave the woman the bitter cup to drink,* 47 a; Th. 161, 8; Gū. 955. Ðone bitran drync Eue Adame byrelade *Eve served to Adam the bitter drink,* 45 b; Th. 154, 13; Gū. 842.

byrman; *p.* de; *pp.* ed [beorma *barm*] *To ferment with barm, to leaven;* fermentare. DER. ge-byrman.

byrnan; *part.* byrnende; he byrneþ. I. *v. intrans. To burn, to be on fire;* ardere:—Sīn eówer leóhtfatu byrnende *sint vestræ lucernæ ardentes,* Lk. Bos. 12, 35: Deut. 9, 15. Ðonne byrneþ gramen his *cum exarserit ira ejus,* Ps. Spl. 2, 13: Bd. 5, 3; S. 616, 36. II. *v. trans. To burn;* urere, comburere:—Swā fȳr wudu byrneþ *sicut ignis comburit sylvas,* Ps. Th. 82, 10. v. beornan.

BYRNE, an; *f. A corslet, coat of mail;* lorica, thorax:—Mōt he gesellan monnan and byrnan and sweord *he may give a man a corslet and a sword,* L. In. 54; Th. i. 138, 1. Ðǽr wæs on eorle brogden byrne *there was on the man the twisted coat of mail,* Elen. Kmbl. 513; El. 257. Ætbær hringde byrnan *he bore away the ringed coat of mail,* Beo. Th. 5224; B. 2615. Ongan wyrcan sīde byrnan *he began to make a large coat of mail,* Salm. Kmbl. 906; Sal. 453: Judth. 12; Thw. 26, 15; Jud. 328. [*Laym.* burne, brunie: *Ger.* brünne, *f.: M. H. Ger.* brünje, brünne, *f.: O. H. Ger.* brunja, brunna, *f.: Goth.* brunyo, *f.: Dan.* brynie, *m. f.: Swed. Icel.* brynja, *f.: O. Slav.* brunija.] DER. gūþ-byrne, heađo-, heađu-, here-, īren-, īsern-.

byrne, es; *m. A burning;* incendium:—Ǽr đam đe đæt mynster mid byrne fornumen wǽre *priusquam monasterium esset incendio consumptum,* Bd. 4, 25; S. 599, 18. v. bryne.

byrne, an; *f. Running water, a stream;* torrens, rivus:—Ofer byrnan bōsm *over the stream's bosom,* Exon. 102 a; Th. 386, 15; Rä. 4, 62. v. burne.

byrnendra *more burning,* Bd. 5, 3; S. 616, 36. v. byrnan.

byrn-hom, es; *m.* [byrne *a coat of mail,* hom *a covering, garment*] *A coat of mail;* lorica:—Beraþ bord fōr breóstum and byrnhomas *bear shields before your breasts and coats of mail,* Judth. 11; Thw. 24, 17; Jud. 192.

byrn-wīga, an; *m. A soldier clothed in armour;* loricatus miles:—Se byrnwīga būgan sceolde *the mailed warrior must submit,* Beo. Th. 5828; B. 2918: Exon. 77 b; Th. 292, 5; Wand. 94. Byrnwīgena brego *the chief of mailed soldiers,* Judth. 9; Thw. 21, 28; Jud. 39.

byrn-wīgende, -wiggende; *part. Clothed in armour, mailed;* loricatus:—Swā hire weoruda helm byrnwiggendra beboden hæfde *as the prince of the mailed armies had commanded her,* Elen. Kmbl. 447; El. 224. Gehlōdon byrnwīgendum werum wǽghengestas *they loaded the ships with men covered with armour,* Elen. Kmbl. 470; El. 235.

byrn-wīggend, es; *m. A soldier clothed in armour, a mailed warrior;* loricatus miles *vel* bellator:—Bealde byrnwīggende *bold warriors,* Judth. 9; Thw. 21, 13; Jud. 17.

byrst, es; *n. A bristle;* seta:—Byrst *seta,* Wrt. Voc. 286, 57: Glos. Epnl. Recd. 162, 49. Hyre twigu beóþ swylce swīnene [MS. swinen] byrst *its twigs are like swine bristles,* Herb. 52, 2; Lchdm. i. 156, 3. [*Frs.* boarstel, *m. f.: Dut.* borstel, *m: Ger.* borste, *f: O. H. Ger.* burst, *n;* bursti, pursta, *f: Dan.* börste, *m. f: Swed.* borst, *m: Icel.* burst, *f.*]

byrst *bursts, breaks, fails; 3rd pers. pres. of* berstan.

byrst, he byrþ *bearest, he bears, produces;* facit, Mt. Bos. 7, 17; *2nd and 3rd pers. pres. of* beran.

byrst, berst, es; *m. A loss, defect;* damnum, calamitas:—Gylde đone byrst, đe đæt fȳr ontende *reddet damnum, qui ignem succenderit,* Ex. 22, 6, 12: Ps. Th. 108, 18. We habbaþ fela byrsta gebiden *multas calamitates sumus perpessi,* Lupi Serm. i. 2; Hick. Thes. ii. 99, 21.

byrþ *a birth.* v. beorþ, byrþ-ling.

BYRÐEN, berđen, byrđyn; *gen.* byrđenne; *f. A* BURTHEN, *load, weight, bundle;* onus, sarcina, fascis:—Hefig byrđen *onus grave,* Ps. Th. 37, 4. Sorh biþ swǽrost byrđen *sorrow is the heaviest burthen,* Salm. Kmbl. 623; Sal. 311. Seám ođđe byrđen *onus,* Ælfc. Gr. 9, 32; Som. 12, 14. Byrđen *fascis,* 9, 28; Som. 11, 44: Mt. Lind. Stv. 13, 30. [*O. Sax.* burđinnia, *f: O. Frs.* berthe, berde, *f: Ger. M. H. Ger.* bürde, *f: O. H. Ger.* burdi, *f: Goth.* baurþei, *f: Dan.* byrde, *f: Swed.* börda, *f: Icel.* byrðr, byrði, *f.*] DER. mægen-byrđen, sorg-, syn-.

byrđene dǽl, es; *m. A share of a burthen, a portion;* portio, Ps. Spl. 49, 19.

byrđen-mǽlum; *adv.* [byrđen, mǽlum, *dat. pl. of* mǽl, *n.*] *By burdens;* oneribus:—Se dēma hǽt his englas gadrian đone coccel byrđen-mǽlum *the judge will command his angels to gather the tares by burdens,* Homl. Th. i. 526, 22.

byrðen-meto; *indecl; f? An excessive burden;* oneris excessus, onerosa mensura, Prov. 27, Ettm.

byrðen-strang; *adj. Burthen-strong, strong to bear burdens;* oneribus portandis robustus:—Assa is stunt nȳten, and byrðenstrang *an ass is a foolish beast, and strong for burdens,* Homl. Th. i. 208, 13.

byrþere; *gen.* byrþres; *m.* [beran *to bear, carry*] *A bearer, carrier, supporter;* portarius, vespillo, fulcimen:—Crist ðone wācan assan geceás him to byrþre *Christ chose the mean ass for his bearer,* Homl. Th. i. 210, 16. Ða byrþeras hine to byrgenne fēredon *the bearers bare him to the grave,* i. 492, 27. Seó untrumnys his gecyndes behōfode sumes byrþres *the infirmity of his nature had need of some supporter,* i. 308, 12.

byrþ-ling, beorþ-ling, es; *m. A born image, birthling, child.* v. beorþ, hyse-berþling.

byrþor, es; *n? Child-birth, a fetus;* partus, fetus:—Būtan byrþres intingan *sine partus causa,* Bd. 1, 27; S. 493, 40. v. beorþor.

byrþor-cwelm, es; *m. An abortion, a miscarriage.* v. beorþor-cwelm.

byrþor-þinen, e; *f. A midwife.* v. beorþor-þinen.

byrðyn, e; *f. A burthen;* onus:—Mīn byrðyn ys leóht *meum onus est leve,* Mt. Bos, 11, 30. v. byrðen.

Byr-tūn, es; *m.* [*Hovd.* Burhtun: *Brom.* Burton super Trent: *Stub. Kni.* Burton] BURTON *on Trent, Staffordshire;* oppidum ad ripam fluminis Trentæ, in agro Staffordiensi:—Se cyng geaf him ðæt abbotrīce on Byrtūne *the king gave him the abbacy at Burton,* Chr. 1066; Erl. 203, 16.

bȳsegu *occupation,* Bt. Met. Fox 20, 509; Met. 20, 255. v. bȳsgu.

BȲSEN, bīsen, bȳsn, e; *f.* I. *a pattern, an example, model, resemblance, similitude, parable;* norma, exemplum, modellum, similitudo, parabola:—Ðū būtan bȳsne, Ælmihtig God, eall geworhtest þing þearle gōd [good, MS.] *thou, Almighty God, madest all things very good, without a pattern,* Bt. Met. Fox 20, 85; Met. 20, 43. Seó bȳsen ðæs rihtan geleáfan Angel cyricean to Rōme gelǽded wæs *exemplum catholicæ fidei Anglorum Romam perlatum est,* Bd. 4, 18; S. 587, 11: 2, 1; S. 590, 26: 4, 23; S. 595, 10. Gūþlāc mongum wearþ bȳsen on Brytene *Guthlac was an example to many in Britain,* Exon. 35 a; Th. 112, 19; Gū. 146. Ðiós ōðru bȳsen *this other similitude,* Bt. Met. Fox 12, 13; Met. 12, 7. Æfter heora bȳsne *after their example,* Ps. Th. arg. 28: Cd. 217; Th. 276, 29; Sat. 196. On bȳsene ðære frymþelīcan cyricean *in exemplum primitivæ ecclesiæ,* Bd. 4, 23; S. 593, 40. Be sumere bīsene *by some example,* Bt. 22, 2; Fox 78, 13. Ðæt hī ealle gemyndige wǽron hyre bȳsene *that they all should be mindful of her example,* Bd. 4, 23; S. 595, 20. He bȳsene gegearwode *he gave an example,* 4, 23; S. 594, 24. He us bȳsene sealde his ārfæstnysse *he gave us an example of his piety,* Homl. Th. i. 492, 23. Wolde ic eów bȳsne onstellan *I would give you an example,* Andr. Kmbl. 1942; An. 973: Bd. 4, 27; S. 604, 1. Secgen Dryhtne lof ealra ðara bīsena ðe us his wīsdōm cȳðaþ *let us speak to the Lord praise for all the examples which manifest his wisdom,* Exon. 40 a; Th. 133, 33; Gū. 499. Ealle bēc sint fulle ðara bīsna ðara monna, ðe ǽr us wǽron [MS. wæran] *all books are full of examples of the men, who were before us,* Bt. 29, 1; Fox 102, 12. Onlīcnesse oððe bīsene *a parable;* similitudinem, Lk. Rush. War. 13, 6. II. *a command, precept, admonition;* mandatum, præceptum, admonitio:—Ic gelȳfe ðæt hit from Gode cōme, broht from his bȳsene *I believe that it came from God, brought by his command,* Cd. 32; Th. 42, 29; Gen. 680. Ðæt he ða bȳsene from Gode brungen hæfde *that he had brought those commands from God,* 30; Th. 41, 3; Gen. 651. Hwylce ðū selfa hæfst bīsne on breóstum *what precepts thou thyself hast in thy breast,* 27; Th. 36, 13; Gen. 571. Ic ðīnra bȳsna ne mæg wuht oncnāwan *I cannot understand aught of thy commands,* 26; Th. 34, 6; Gen. 533. [*Laym.* bisne, bysne, *dat. a pattern, example: Orm.* bisne *example: O. Sax.* busan, *f. in* am-busan, *f. a commandment: Goth.* ana-busns, *f. a command.*] DER. fōre-bȳsen, lār-: bȳsnian, ge-, mis-: bȳsnung, ge-.

bȳsenian *to give an example,* C. R. Ben. 2. v. bȳsnian.

bȳsenung *an example,* C. R. Ben. 61. v. bȳsnung.

bȳsgian, bīsgian, bȳsigan; *p.* ode, ade; *pp.* od, ad *To occupy, busy, fatigue, trouble, afflict;* occupare, fatigare, affligere, tribulare:—Se man biþ hērigendlīc, ðe mid gōdum weorcum hine sylfne bȳsgaþ *the man is praiseworthy, who busies himself with good works,* Homl. Th. ii. 406, 16. For ðǽm manigfealdum bīsgum, ðe hine oft ǽgðer ge on mōde ge on līchoman bīsgodon [MS. bisgodan] *on account of the manifold occupations, which often busied him* [*king Alfred*] *both in mind and in body,* Bt. prooem; Fox viii. 6: Cd. 64; Th. 76, 29; Gen. 1264. Ic eom bȳsgod on sange *occupatus sum cantu,* Coll. Monast. Th. 18, 25; Wrt. Voc. 2, 11. Ðeáh ðæs līchoman leahtras and hefignes and unþeáwas oft bȳsigen monna mōdsefan *though the sins and heaviness and vices of the body may often trouble the minds of men,* Bt. Met. Fox 22, 60; Met. 22, 30. Hine hungor bȳsgaþ *hunger afflicts him,* Exon. 97 a; Th. 363, 10; Wal. 51. Ðē untrymnes on ðisse nȳhstan niht bȳsgade *infirmity afflicted thee in this last night,* 47 b; Th. 163, 10; Gū. 991. [*Frs.* bisgje, bysgje *occupare.*] DER. a-bȳsgian, ge-: bȳsgung, a-, woruld-.

BYSGU, bīsgu, bȳsigu, bīsigu, bȳsegu, bīsegu; *gen.* e; *dat.* e; *acc.* u, o: *nom. acc. pl.* u; *gen.* a; *dat.* um; *f. Occupation, business, labour, care, toil, difficulty, trouble, affliction;* occupatio, negotium, labor, cura, opus, difficultas, dolor, tribulatio:—Ða bīsgu us sint swīðe earfoþ rīme *the occupations are to us very difficult to be numbered,* Bt. prooem; Fox viii. 6. For ðǽm manigfealdum bīsgum, ðe hine oft ǽgðer ge on mōde ge on līchoman bīsgodon [bisgodan MS.] *on account of the manifold occupations, which often busied him* [*Alfred*] *both in mind and in body,* Bt. prooem; Fox viii. 5. Of ðisum bȳsegum *from these occupations,* Bt. Met. Fox 20, 509; Met. 20, 255. Of ðissum bīsegum *from these occupations,* Bt. 33, 4; Fox 132, 28. Bȳsigum gebǽded *oppressed with labours,* Beo. Th. 5153; B. 2580. Biþ se slǽp tō fæst bīsgum gebunden *the sleep is bound too fast by cares,* Beo. Th. 3490; B. 1743: Bt. Met. Fox 22, 127; Met. 22, 64. Ōðer bīsgo dreág *the other suffered toil,* Exon. 114 a; Th. 438, 14; Rä. 57, 7: 82 b; Th. 311, 6; Seef. 88. Ōþ-ðæt he ða bȳsgu oferbiden hæfde *until he had surmounted the trouble,* Exon. 40 b; Th. 135, 2; Gū. 518. Mec his bȳsgu gehreáw *his affliction grieved me,* Exon. 43 a; Th. 144, 31; Gū. 686. Bīsigu, Beo. Th. 567, note; B. 281. Ic bīsga unrīm dreág *I suffered numberless* [*of*] *afflictions,* Exon. 74 b; Th. 280, 7; Jul. 625. Mēðe for ðām miclum [miclan MS.] bȳsgum *weary on account of the great afflictions,* 49 a; Th. 168, 25; Gū. 1083. [*Dut.* bézig-heid, *f. occupation.*] DER. nȳd-bȳsgu.

bȳsgung, e; *f. Business, occupation, care;* negotium, occupatio, cura. DER. a-bȳsgung, woruld-. v. bīsgung.

bȳsig; *adj. Occupied, diligent, laborious,* BUSY, *industrious;* occupatus, sedulus, laboriosus, negotiosus, industrius:—Bȳsig æfter bōcum *occupied over books,* Salm. Kmbl. 123; Sal. 61. Bogan wǽron bȳsige *bows were busy,* Byrht. Th. 134, 66; By. 110: Ps. Th. 58, 3. [*Chauc.* besy, bisy, bysy: *Laym.* bisi, bisie.] DER. līc-bȳsig, līf-, nȳd-, þrag-.

bȳsigan *to occupy, trouble,* Bt. Met. Fox 22, 60; Met. 22, 30. v. bȳsgian.

bȳsigu *labour,* Beo. Th. 5153; B. 2580. v. bȳsgu.

bysmer *mockery, reproach, blasphemy,* Exon. 117 a; Th. 449, 14; Dōm. 71: Ps. Th. 58, 8: 103, 25: 105, 25: 106, 10: Mk. Bos. 14, 64. v. bismer.

bysmerian, bysmrian, bismrian, bismærian, bysmorian, bysmrigan, to bismrienne, bysmrigenne; *p.* ode, ede; *pp.* od, ed [bismer, bysmer *mockery, blasphemy*] *To mock, deride, irritate, reproach, blaspheme, defame, revile;* illudere, deridere, irritare, irridere, blasphemare, calumniam facere, maledicere:—Draca ðes, ðone ðū ȳwodest to bismrienne him *draco iste, quem formasti ad illudendum ei,* Ps. Spl. 103, 28. Hī sellaþ hine þeódum to bysmrigenne *tradent eum gentibus ad illudendum,* Mt. Bos. 20, 19. Ðæt he me bysmrode *ut illuderet mihi,* Gen. 39, 17. Ðæt he bysmorode us *ut illuderet nobis,* 39, 14. Ðū, Drihten, bysmrast hī *tu, Domine, deridebis eos,* Ps. Spl. 58, 9. Us fȳnd bysmriaþ *enemies deride us,* Ps. Th. 79, 6. Ealle bysmrodon me *omnes deriserunt me,* Ps. Spl. 21, 6. Hī bysmeredon hī on ðone reádan sǽ *irritaverunt eos in rubrum mare,* Ps. Th. 105, 8. Ongunnon hī on ðām wīcum Moyses bysmrian *they began to irritate Moses in the camps,* 105, 14. Hū lange bysmraþ se wiðerwearda naman ðīnne *usquequo irritat adversarius nomen tuum?* Ps. Spl. 73, 11. Se ðe eardaþ on heofonum bysmeraþ hȳ *qui habitat in cœlis irridebit eos,* Ps. Spl. 2, 4. Se ðone Hālgan Gāst bysmeraþ, se næfþ on ēcnysse forgyfenesse *qui blasphemaverit in Spiritum Sanctum, non habebit remissionem in æternum,* Mk. Bos. 3, 29. Hī bysmeriaþ *they blaspheme,* 3, 28. Ða wegfērendan hyne bysmeredon *prætereuntes blasphemabant eum,* Mt. Bos. 27, 39, 41. Ne bysmra ðū ðīnne mǽg *non facies calumniam proximo tuo,* Lev. 19, 13. Ne lǽt bysmrian banan mancynnes ða ðīn lof beraþ *let not the murderers of men revile those who bear thy praise,* Andr. Kmbl. 2587; An. 1295. Bysmeredon hie būtū ætgædere *they reviled us both together,* Rood Kmbl. 95; Kr. 48: Andr. Kmbl. 1923; An. 964. Uton gangan ðæt we bysmrigen him *let us go that we may revile him,* 2713; An. 1359. DER. gebysmerian.

bysmer-leás; *adj.* [bismer, bysmer *pollution, abomination, disgrace;* -leás *-less*] *Without pollution, spotless, blameless;* sine pollutione, immaculatus, irreprehensus:—Ðæt he mǽge ēðles mid monnum brūcan bysmerleás *that he may enjoy the world blameless with men,* Exon. 27 a; Th. 81, 19; Cri. 1326.

bysmer-līce *disgracefully,* Judth. 10; Thw. 23, 2; Jud. 100. v. bismor-līce.

bysmer-spæc, e; *f. Blasphemy;* blasphemia:—For ðīnre bysmerspæce *for thy blasphemy,* Jn. Bos. 10, 33. v. bysmor-spræc.

bysmer-specan, ic -spece, ðū -spicst, -spycst, he -speceþ, -spicþ, -spycþ, *pl.* -specaþ; *p.* -spæc, *pl.* -spǽcon; *pp.* -specen [bismer, bysmer *blasphemia,* specan *loqui*] *To speak blasphemy, to blaspheme;* blasphemiam loqui, blasphemare:—Ðū bysmerspycst *blasphemas,* Jn. Bos. 10, 36.

bysmer-spycst *blasphemest;* blasphemas, Jn. Bos. 10, 36. v. bysmer-specan.

bysmerung *blasphemy;* blasphemia, Mk. Bos. 3, 28. v. bysmrung.

bysmor *filthiness, reproach, calumny,* Ælfc. T. 15, 21: Ps. Th. 8, 3: Deut. 28, 29. v. bismer.

bysmor-full; *adj.* [bismer, bysmor *pollution, abomination, disgrace;* full *full*] *Polluted, abominable, disgraceful;* pollutus, detestabilis, turpis:—Ðæt híg búgan ne sceoldon to ðam bysmorfullum hǽðengilde *that they should not bow to the abominable heathen idol,* Jos. 23, 7.

bysmorian *to mock,* Gen. 39, 14. v. bysmerian.

bysmor-líce *disgracefully, irreverently,* L. Ælf. C. 35; Th. ii. 356, note 2, line 20. v. bismor-líce.

bysmor-spræc, bysmur-spræc, bysmer-spæc, e; *f.* [bismer, bysmer *blasphemy;* spræc, spæc *a speaking, word, speech*] *A speaking blasphemy, blasphemy;* blasphemia:—Ðes sprycþ bysmorspræce *this* [*man*] *speaketh blasphemy;* hic blasphemat, Mt. Bos. 9, 3. Ǽlc synn and bysmurspræc byþ forgyfen mannum, sóþlíce ðæs Hálgan Gástes bysmurspræc ne byþ forgyfen *omne peccatum et blasphemia remittetur hominibus, Spiritus Sancti autem blasphemia non remittetur,* 12, 31. Ðis ys bysmorspræc *this is blasphemy,* 26, 65. For ðínre bysmerspæce *on account of thy blasphemy,* Jn. Bos. 10, 33.

bysmrian; *p.* ode; *pp.* od *To deride, irritate, reproach, defame, revile,* Gen. 39, 17: Ps. Spl. 58, 9: Ps. Th. 105, 14: Lev. 19, 13: Andr. Kmbl. 1923; An. 964. v. bysmerian.

bysmrigan *to mock, revile,* Mt. Bos. 20, 19: Andr. Kmbl. 2713; An. 1359. v. bysmerian.

bysmrung, bysmerung, e; *f.* [bismer, bysmer *infamy, blasphemy*] *Deceit, infamy, blasphemy;* illusio, infamia, blasphemia:—Ðeós bysmrung nis to ondrǽdanne *hæc illusio non est timenda,* Bd. 1, 27; S. 496, 39, 41: 497, 6. Is on ðære ylcan bysmrunge swýðe nýdþearflíc gesceád *est in eadem illusione valde necessaria discretio,* 1, 27; S. 496, 34, 21. Hió hyre firenluste fulgán ne móste bútan manna bysmrunge *she could not fulfil her wicked desire without the infamy of mankind,* Ors. 1, 2; Bos. 27, 14. Ealle sinna synd manna bearnum forgyfene, and bysmerunga, ðám ðe hí bysmeriaþ *omnia dimittentur filiis hominum peccata, et blasphemiæ, quibus blasphemaverint,* Mk. Bos. 3, 28.

bysmur-spræc *blasphemy,* Mt. Bos. 12, 31. v. bysmor-spræc.

býsnian, bísnian, býsnigan, býsenian; *p.* ode; *pp.* od [býsen, býsn *an example*] *To give* or *set an example;* exemplum dare:—We lǽraþ, ðæt preóstas aa wel býsnian *we enjoin that priests always set a good example,* L. Edg. C. 52; Th. ii. 254, 28. Gif ða láreówas wel tǽcaþ, and wel býsniaþ, beóþ hí gehealdene *if the teachers teach well, and give good example, they shall be saved,* Homl. Th. ii. 50, 3. Ne bísnode ðé nán man, forðamðe nán ǽr ðé næs *no man set thee an example, for no one was before thee,* Bt. 33, 4; Fox 128, 20. Ða bísnodon hiora æftergengum *they set an example to their successors,* 39, 11; Fox 230, 2. Gif he yfel býsnige *if he give evil example,* Homl. Th. ii. 48, 35: L. Edg. C. 66; Th. ii. 258, 17. DER. ge-býsnian, mis-.

býsnigan *to give* or *set an example,* Homl. Th. ii. 48, 35: L. Edg. C. 66; Th. ii. 258, 17. v. býsnian.

býsnung, bísnung, býsenung, e; *f.* [býsen, býsn *an example*] *An example;* exemplum:—For ðære miclan bísnunge *for the great example,* Ælfc. T. 5, 15. DER. ge-býsnung.

byst *art, shalt be,* Lk. Bos. 1, 76: Ælfc. Gr. 25; Som. 26, 12. v. beón.

býst *biestings,* Ælfc. Gl. 31; Som. 61, 102. v. beóst.

býst *commandest, offerest; 2nd pers. pres. of* beódan.

býsting, es; *m.* BIESTINGS, *the first milk of a cow after calving;* colostrum:—Býsting, þicce meolc *biestings, thick milk,* Ælfc. Gl. 33; Som. 62, 20; Wrt. Voc. 28, 3. v. beóst.

BYT, bytt, e; *f: pl.* bytta *A bottle, flagon,* BUTT, *tun;* uter, dolium:—Byt *uter,* Wrt. Voc. 85, 82. Bytt *uter,* Ælfc. Gr. 9, 18; Som. 9, 58. Ne híg ne dóþ niwe wín on ealde bytta; gyf hí dóþ, ða bytta beóþ tobrocene, and ðæt wín agoten, and ða bytta forwurðaþ. Ac híg dóþ niwe wín on niwe bytta, and ǽgðer byþ gehealden *neque mittunt vinum novum in utres veteres; alioquin rumpuntur utres, et vinum effunditur, et utres pereunt. Sed vinum novum in utres novos mittunt, et ambo conservantur,* Mt. Bos. 9, 17: Jos. 9, 4: Ps. Lamb. 32, 7. [*Ger.* butte, bütte, *f: M. H. Ger.* büte, bütte, *f: Dan.* bötte, *m. f: Swed.* bytta, *f: Icel.* bytta, *f.*]

byt *asks, prays,* Lk. Bos. 11, 11: Ex. 5, 16, = bit; *3rd pers. pres. of* biddan.

být *commands, bids, offers,* Ex. 5, 10; *3rd pers. pres. of* beódan.

byþ *is, shall be,* Mt. Bos. 5, 14. v. beón.

býþ *inhabits; 3rd pers. pres. sing. of* búan.

byþne *a keel.* v. bytne.

býtl, bítl, es; *n. m?* [být, *pres. of* beátan *to beat, strike*] *A* BEETLE, *hammer;* malleus:—Seó wífman án ðæra teldsticcena geslóh mid ánum býtle búfan his þunwengan *the woman struck one of the tent-nails with a hammer above his temples,* Jud. 4, 21. Nán mon ne gehiérde bítles swég *no man heard the sound of hammer,* Past. 36, 5; Cott. MS. [*Plat.* bötel.]

býtla, an; *m.* [býtl *a hammer,* -a *q. v.*] *A hammerer, builder;* ædificator:—Se býtla ðǽr háligne hám arǽrde *the builder raised up a holy home there,* Exon. 34 b; Th. 110, 36; Gú. 119.

býtlian; *p.* ode, ede; *pp.* od, ed [býtla *a builder*] *To build;* ædificare:—Hí ongunnon býtlian heora burh *they began to build their town,* Cd. 90; Th. 112, 33; Gen. 1880: 99; Th. 131, 15; Gen. 2176. He ne býtlaþ of ðam grúndwealle *he builds not from that foundation,* Homl. Th. i. 368, 25. Býtlode *ædificavit,* R. Ben. in proœm. Hí worhton ðæt geweorc æt Tæmeseforda, and hit búdon, and býtledon *they wrought the work at Tempsford, and inhabited it, and built,* Chr. 921; Erl. 106, 18. DER. ge-býtlian.

býtlung, e; *f.* [býtl, ung] *A building, edifice;* structura, ædificium:—Seó býtlung is ofer Criste gelogod *the building is founded on Christ,* Homl. Th. i. 368, 22.

bytne *the keel* or *bottom of a ship;* carina, Cot. 32.

býtst *commandest, offerest; 2nd pers. pres. of* beódan.

býtt *ordains,* Homl. Th. i. 358, 31, = být, *q. v.*

bytta *bottles,* Mt. Bos. 9, 17; *pl. of* byt.

bytte-hlid, es; *n. A lid of a butt;* dolii opertorium, Cot. 208: Mann.

bytt-fylling, e; *f. A filling of butts;* doliorum impletio, L. Ath. v. § 8, 1; Th. i. 236, 4.

býwan; *p.* de; *pp.* ed *To prepare, adorn;* parare, ornare:—Ða ðe beadogrímman býwan sceoldon *those who should prepare the war-helmet,* Beo. Th. 4507, note; B. 2257. [*O. Nrs.* búa *parare.*] DER. a-býwan.

C

IN Gothic and Icelandic **c** is entirely wanting, being always represented by *k.* It is remarkable that the Anglo-Saxons have seldom made use of *k;* but, following the Latin, have preferred the use of *c.* **1.** the letter *c* is found as an initial, medial, and final.—As an initial letter it corresponds to the Gothic and Icelandic *k;* as,—*A. Sax.* corn *corn, Goth.* kaurn, *Icel.* korn; *A. Sax.* ceósan *to choose, Goth.* kiusan, *Icel.* kjósa. As a medial and final letter *c* corresponds to the Gothic and Icelandic *k,*—thus *A. Sax.* æcer *a field, Goth.* akrs, *Icel.* akr; *A. Sax.* eác *also, Goth.* auk, *Icel.* ok [og]. **2.** *c* and *cc* are often changed into *h* or *hh* before *s* or *þ,* and especially before *t;* as, strehton *they stretched,* for strecton *from* streccan. Ahsian *for* acsian *or* axian *to ask;* séhþ *for* sécþ *seeks, from* sécan *to seek.* In words immediately derived from Anglo-Saxon, *k* is frequently substituted for the Anglo-Saxon *c;* as, cyning *a king;* cyn *kin* or *kindred.* Sometimes *q* or *ch;* as, cwén *queen;* cild *a child;* cin *a chin.* **3.** the Runic letter ᚳ not only stands for the letter **c**, but also for the name of the letter in Anglo-Saxon cén *a torch.* v. cén and RÚN.

cac, es; *m? Dung, excrement;* stercus, foria, merda, Som. Ben. Lye. [*Plat.* kak, kakk: *Dut.* kak, *m: Kil.* kack: *Ger.* kack, *m: Dan.* kag, *m. f: Grk.* κάκκη: *Lat.* cacare: *Grk.* κακκάω.]

cac-hús, es; *n. A privy;* latrina, Som. Ben. Lye. [*Kil.* kack-huys.]

cæd, ced, es; *m. A boat;* linter, Mone B. 120, Ettm.

cæder-beám, es; *m. A cedar-tree;* cedrus:—Hériaþ Drihten, múntas and ealle beorgas, treówu wæstmbǽru, and ealle cæder-beám *laudate Dominum, montes et omnes colles, ligna fructifera, et omnes cedri,* Ps. Spl. 148, 9. v. ceder-beám.

Cædmon, es; *m.* [Cædmon, MS. C. C. C. Oxford: Cædmon, Bd. 4, 24; S. 170, 50; Cedmon, S. 597, 12: Ceadmon, MS. B, S. 597, note 12: Cadmon, Runic Monmnts. by Prof. Stephens, fol. Cheapinghaven, 1868, p. 419, 11: cæd *linter,* mon *homo*] A man employed by the monks of Whitby in the care of their cattle in the early part of the seventh century. He is the first person of whom we possess any metrical composition in our vernacular language. So striking and similar are some of his thoughts to Paradise Lost, it has been supposed that Milton had read his Poems. He became a monk of Whitby, and died in the monastery about A. D. 680. A full account is given of him in Bede's History, bk. iv. ch. 24. The origin of his Poem is thus recorded in king Alfred's Anglo-Saxon version of Bede:—Ðá stód him sum mon æt þurh swefen, and hine hálette and grétte, and hine be his naman nemde, Cædmon [Cedmon, Bd. 4, 24; S. 597, 12], sing me hwæt-hwegu. Ðá andswarede he and cwæþ, ne con ic nán þing singan ... Eft he cwæþ, se ðe mid him sprecende wæs, hwæðere ðú meaht me singan. Cwæþ he, hwæt sceal ic singan? Cwæþ he, sing me frumsceaft. Ðá he ðá ðás andsware onféng; ðá ongan he sóna singan, in hérenesse Godes scyppendes, ða fers and ða word ðe he nǽfre ne gehýrde ... Ðá arás he from ðam slǽpe and eall ðæt he slǽpende song fæste on gemynde hæfde ... Song he ǽrest be middangeardes gesceape, and be fruman moncynnes, and eall ðæt stǽr Genesis, and eft be útgonge Israhéla folces of Ægypta lande, and be ingonge ðæs gehátlondes, and be óðrum monigum spellum ðæs hálgan gewrites Canones bóc; and be Cristes menniscnesse, and be his þrówunge, and be his uppastígnesse on heofonas; and big ðæs hálgan Gástes cyme, and ðæra Apostola láre; and eft big ðam ege ðæs toweardan dómes, and be fyrhto ðæs tintreglícan wítes, and be swétnesse ðæs heofonlícan ríces: he monig leóþ geworhte *then stood some man by him in a dream, and hailed and greeted him, and named him by his name,* 'Cædmon, canta mihi aliquid,' = *Cædmon, sing me something. Then he answered and said, I cannot sing anything . . . Again, he who was speaking with him said, Yet thou must sing to me. Said he, What shall I sing? Said he, Sing me the origin of things. When he received this answer, then he began forthwith to sing, in praise of God the Creator, the verses and the words which he had never heard . . . Then he arose from sleep, and had fast in mind all that he sleeping had sung . . . He first sang of earth's creation, and of the origin of mankind, and all the history of Genesis, and then of the departure of the people of Israel from the Egyptians' land, and of the entrance of the land of promise, and of many other histories of the canonical books of Holy Writ; and of Christ's incarnation, and of his passion, and of his ascension into heaven; and of the coming of the Holy Ghost, and the doctrine of the Apostles; and also of the terror of the doom to come, and the fear of hell-torment, and the sweetness of the heavenly kingdom: he made many poems,* Bd. 4, 24; S. 597, 11–18, 25, 26—598, 9–17. **2.** Cædmon was first published by Junius, from the Bodleian MS. the only one in existence. Junius published the Anglo-Saxon text only at Amsterdam in 1655, without a translation, in very small 4to, pp. 116. It was again published by B. Thorpe, F.S.A. in large 8vo. 1832, with an English translation, notes, and a verbal index, pp. 341. **3.** Bouterwek, with German translation and notes, an excellent vocabulary, Lateinischangelsächsisches Wörter-verzeichniss, in 2 vols. 8vo. 1854. Gütersloh bei C. Bertelsmann. **4.** Grein in 2 vols. 8vo. 1857, Text, vol. i. pp. 148.

cæfester, es; *m?* *A halter, head-stall;* capistrum, Cot. 31: 33. DER. ge-cafstrian.

cæfian, cefian; *p.* ede; *pp.* ed *To embroider;* acu pingere. DER. be-cæfian, ymb-.

CǢG; *gen.* cǣge; *pl. nom. acc.* cǣga, cǣgia; *f:* cǣge, an; *f. A* KEY; clavis:—Stæfcræft is seó cǣg ðe ðæra bōca andgytt unlȳcþ *grammar is the key that unlocketh the sense of books,* Ælfc. Gr. pref; Som. 1, 23: 9, 28; Som. 11, 54: Past. 15, 2; Hat. MS. 19 a, 17. Ge ætbrudon ðæs ingehȳdes cǣge *tulisti clavem scientiæ,* Lk. Bos. 11, 52. Saturnus sumra hæfde bōca cǣga *Saturn had the keys of some books,* Salm. Kmbl. 370; Sal. 184. Ðē ic sylle heofona rīces cǣgia *tibi dabo claves regni cælorum,* Mt. Bos. 16, 19. Gāstes cǣgum [MS. cǣgon] *with the keys of the spirit,* Cd. 169; Th. 211, 11; Exod. 524. Cǣgan, Exon. 112 a; Th. 429, 29; Rä. 43, 12. [*Chauc.* key: *Wyc.* keie, keye: *R. Glouc.* keyen, *pl: Frs.* cay, cayce *a small key: O. Frs.* kei, kai, *m: Wel.* can *to shut, inclose.*] DER. lioðu-cǣge, searo-cǣg.

cǣg-bora, an; *m. A key-bearer;* claviger, Ælfc. Gr. 8; Som. 7, 19.

cǣge, an; *f. A key;* clavis:—Cǣgan, Exon. 112 a; Th. 429, 29; Rä. 43, 12. v. cǣg.

cǣggian; *p.* ode; *pp.* od *To lock, shut fast;* obserare. DER. cǣg.

cǣg-hyrde, es; *m.* [hyrde *a keeper, guardian*] *A keeper of keys, gaoler;* clavicularius. DER. cǣg.

cǣg-loca, an; *m. The action of locking up, a key-locking, any repository locked up;* clavis et loculamentum:—Būton hit under ðæs wīfes cǣglocan [cǣglocum MS. A.] gebroht wǣre, sȳ heó clǣne, ac ðæra cǣgean heó sceal weardian; ðæt is, hire hordern, and hire cyste, and hire tege *unless it has been brought under his wife's 'lock and key,' let her be clear; for it is her duty to keep the keys of them; namely, her 'hord-ern,' and her chest, and her cupboard,* L. C. S. 77; Th. i. 418, 19–22. The Latin version reads: 'Sed suum hordern quod dicere possumus dispensam, et cistam suam, et teage, id est scrinium suum, debet ipsa custodire.' A similar provision is found in the old Scottish law: 'Tamen uxor in certis casibus respondere tenebitur; videlicet, si furtum inveniatur sub clavibus suis quas ipsa habet sub custodia et cura sua, utpote spensæ, arcæ suæ vel scrinii sui. Et si aliquod furtum sub clavibus suis inveniatur, uxor cum viro suo tamquam ei consentaneus erit culpabilis et punietur,' *Quon. Attachi.* xii. c. 7. There is a republication of the same law in the Stat. Willielmi Regis, with this variation: 'Spensa et arca robarum et jocalium suorum et de scrinio seu coffero,' xix. c. 3. We may therefore, perhaps, render the terms in the quotation above, '*locked up in her store-room, her chest, and her cupboard,*' L. Th. i. 418, note b.

cǣlan; *p.* de; *pp.* ed *To make cold* or *cool, to cool;* infrigidare, Cot. 113. DER. ge-cǣlan. v. calan.

cælc, es; *m. A cup, chalice, goblet;* calix:—Cælc oððe scenc *calicem,* Mt. Lind. Rush. Stv. 10, 42. v. calic.

cæle *A* KEEL or *bottom of a ship;* carina, Som. Ben. Lye.

cælic, es; *m. A cup, chalice, goblet;* calix:—Cælic hǣle ic onfō *calicem salutaris accipiam,* Ps. Spl. 115, 4. v. calic.

cælþ *is cold,* Hexam. 20; Norm. 28, 22; *3rd pres. of* calan.

cæmban *to comb;* pectere, Ælfc. Gr. 28, 3; Som. 30, 61, MS. D. v. cemban.

cæmpa, an; *m. A soldier;* pugnator:—Wer cæmpa *vir pugnator,* Cant. Moys. Lamb. 186 b, 3. v. cempa.

cænnan *to clear, prove;* manifestare:—Mynstres aldor hine cænne in preóstes canne *let the chief of a monastery clear himself with a priest's clearance,* L. Wih. 17; Th. i. 40, 13: 22; Th. i. 42, 3: L. Edg. S. 11; Th. i. 276, 12. v. cennan *to declare,* II.

cænnan; *p.* cænde; *pp.* cænned *To bring forth, produce;* parere:—Ðeós wyrt biþ cænned abūton dīcum *this herb is produced about ditches,* Herb. 13, 1; Lchdm. i. 104, 18, MSS. H. B. v. cennan *to beget,* I.

cænnestre, an; *f. One who has borne, a mother, dam;* genitrix. v. cynnestre.

cæn-ryn, es; *n. A generation,* Ps. Spl. 47, 12. v. cyn-ren.

cǣpe-hūs, es; *n.* [cēpa *a merchant,* hūs *a house*] *A storehouse;* armarium:—Ǣlces cynnes cǣpe-hūs *armarium,* Ælfc. Gl. 109; Som. 79, 19; Wrt. Voc. 58, 59.

CÆPPE, an; *f. A* CAP, *cape, cope, hood;* cappa, pileus, cucullus, planeta:—Cæppe *cappa,* Wrt. Voc. 81, 67. Cæppe *planeta,* Ælfc. Gl. 27; Som. 60, 114; Wrt. Voc. 25, 54: 81, 45. Gerēnod cæppe *an adorned hood;* penula, Ælfc. Gl. 27; Som. 60, 115; Wrt. Voc. 25, 55. [*Piers P.* cope: *Chauc.* cappe, cope: *Laym.* cape, cope: *Plat.* kappe: *Frs.* kæpe: *O. Frs.* kappe: *Dut.* kap, *f: Kil.* kappe: *Ger. M. H. Ger.* kappe, *f: O. H. Ger.* kappa, *f: Dan.* kaabe, kappe, *m. f: Swed.* kappa, kåpa, *f: Icel.* kápa, *f:* from *M. Lat.* cappa, 'quia capitis ornamentum est,' Isidorus.]

cærc-ærn *a prison;* carcer, Som. Ben. Lye. v. carc-ærn.

cærcian *to chirk, chirp,* Ælfc. Gr. 26, 5; Som. 29, 7, MS. C. v. cearcian.

cæren *a sort of wine, boiled wine;* defrutum, carenum, Cot. 66: L. M. 1, 1; Lchdm. ii. 24, 19. v. ceren.

cærfille, an; *f. Chervil;* cerefolium:—Cærfille *cerefolium,* Ælfc. Gl. 43; Som. 64, 45; Wrt. Voc. 31, 55. v. cerfille.

CÆRSE, cerse, an; *f.* CRESS, *watercress;* nasturtium, cardămum = κάρδαμον:—Man nasturcium, and ōðrum naman cærse [cerse B.] nemneþ *one nameth* nasturtium, *and by another name, cress,* Herb. 21, 1; Lchdm. i. 116, 17. Ðeós wyrt, cærse, ne biþ sāwen, ac heó of hyre sylfne cenned biþ on wyllon and on brōcen *this herb, cress, is not sown, but it is propagated of itself in wells and in brooks,* i. 116, 15. [*Piers P.* kerse: *Dut.* kers, *f: Ger. M. H. Ger.* kresse, *m. f: O. H. Ger.* kresso, *m.* cressa, *f.*] DER. eá-cærse, -cerse, fen-, tūn-, wylle-.

cǣs *chose,* Chr. 963; Erl. 123, 35, = ceás; *p. of* ceósan.

cæster, e; *f. A city;* civitas, Mt. Rush. Stv. 5, 14: 8, 34. v. ceaster.

CĀF; *comp.* ra, re; *sup.* est, ost; *adj. Quick, sharp, prompt, nimble, swift;* acer, celer, præceps:—Ðā geseah Iohannes sumne cniht swīðe glæd on mōde and on anginne cāf *there John saw a certain youth very cheerful in mind and quick in design,* Ælfc. T. 33, 17: R. Ben. 7: Fulg. 9. Cāf *præceps,* Glos. Prudent. Recd. 143, 32. Hēt ðā hæleða hleó healdan ða bricge wīgan wīgheardne cāfne *then the defence [the chief] of the soldiers commanded a warrior, hardy in battle and nimble, to defend the bridge,* Byrht. Th. 133, 66; By. 76. Ðæt hī sceoldon beón cāfe [MS. caue] to Godes willan *that they might be prompt for God's will,* Homl. Th. ii. 44, 31. Sume earniaþ ðæt hie sīen ðȳ cāfran *some merit that they may be the more nimble,* Bt. 34, 7; Fox 144, 8. [*R. Brun.* kof *boisterous: Relq. Ant. W.* i. 212, 8, cof: *Orm.* kafe *bold: O. Nrs.* á-kafr *promptus, velox.*] DER. beadu-cāf. v. cīfan.

cāfe; *adv. Quickly, promptly;* celeriter, prompte:—Mægen samnode cāfe to ceáse *he promptly collected his strength for the fight,* Elen. Kmbl. 111; El. 56. DER. cīfan.

cāfer-tūn, es; *m. A hall, inclosure, court, vestibule;* atrium, vestibulum:—Mycel and rūm heall *vel* cāfertūn *atrium,* Ælfc. Gl. 109; Som. 79, 21; Wrt. Voc. 58, 61: Lk. Bos. 11, 21: Jn. Bos. 18, 15: Bt. 18, 1; Rawl. 38, 30. Seó fǣmne geneálǣhte ðam cāfertūne ðyses hūses *the maiden came nigh the court of this house,* Bd. 3, 11; S. 536, 36: 5, 2; S. 615, 2: Ps. Lamb. 95, 9. For ðī ðe is betere ān dæg on ðīnum cāfertūnum ofer þūsenda hēr *quia melior est dies una in atriis tuis super milia,* Ps. Lamb. 83, 11: 95, 8: 115, 8: 121, 2: 134, 2: Ps. Th. 121, 2: 133, 2: 134, 2. Infaraþ on cāfertūnas his on ymnum *introite atria [courts] ejus in hymnis,* Ps. Spl. 99, 4: Ps. Lamb. 99, 4. DER. cīfan.

cāf-līce; *adv. Quickly, hastily, stoutly, manfully, valiantly;* velociter, viriliter:—Ðām gemettum wæs beboden ðæt hī sceoldon cāflīce etan *the partakers were commanded to eat quickly,* Homl. Th. ii. 282, 3: i. 494, 11: Glos. Prudent. Recd. 146, 38: Byrht. Th. 136, 19; By. 153: Num. 31, 6. DER. cīfan.

cāf-scype, es; *m. A quickness;* velocitas, R. Ben. 5. DER. cīfan.

cāl, es; *m. A herb, wild cole-wort;* arboracia, lapsana?—Cāl *arboracia* vel *lapsana?* Ælfc. Gl. 44; Som. 64, 73; Wrt. Voc. 32, 9. v. cawel.

CALAN, ic cale, ðū calest, cælst, he caleþ, cælþ, *pl.* calaþ; *p.* cōl, *pl.* cōlon; *pp.* calen; *v. intrans. To be* or *become cool* or *cold;* algere, frigescere:—Ðonne him cælþ, he cēpþ him hlywþe *when he is cold, he betakes himself to shelter,* Hexam. 20; Norm. 28, 22. Hwæðer ða wēlgan ne ne cale *do the rich never become cold?* Bt. 26, 2; Fox 92, 34. [*Wyc.* kele, koole: *Orm.* kelenn: *Plat.* kölen: *O. Sax.* kōlōn: *O. Frs.* kela: *Dut.* koelen: *Ger.* kühlen: *M. H. Ger.* kuolen *to become cold: O. H. Ger.* kuoljan: *Dan.* koele: *Swed.* koela: *Icel.* kala; *p.* kōl; *pp.* kalit *algere: Lat.* gelare.] DER. a-calan, of-: calian: cēlan, a-, ge-:

cēle, cȳle, fǽr-; -gicel, -wyrt: cēlnes, ge-: cēling; cēlung, ge-: cōl, -nes: cōlian, a-: ceald, cald, æl-, brim-, eal-, hrīm-, īs-, morgen-, ofer-, sin-, snāw-, wæl-, winter-: caldu, sin-: cald-heort: cealdian, a-: cīlian: cǽlan, ge-.

calc, es; *m. A shoe, little shoe, sandal;* calceus, sandalium:—Gesceóde mid calcum *calceatos sandaliis*, Mk. Bos. 6, 9: Cot. 209.

calc-rond; *adj. Round of hoof;* calceis *vel* soleis ferreis marginatus:—Calcrondes, Exon. 91 a; Th. 342, 15; Gn. Ex. 143.

cald *cold;* gelidus, frigidus:—Ðonne cymþ forst fyrnum cald *then cometh bitter cold frost*, Cd. 17; Th. 20, 28; Gen. 316: 227; Th. 304, 29; Sat. 637: Andr. Kmbl. 619; An. 310. Caldra *colder*, Exon. 111 a; Th. 425, 10; Rä. 41, 54. Caldast *coldest*, 81 b; Th. 308, 1; Seef. 33. v. ceald, calan.

cald, es; *n. Cold, coldness*, Exon. 81 b; Th. 306, 16; Seef. 8. v. ceald *frigus*.

cald-heort; *adj. Cold-hearted, unfeeling, cruel;* frigidus cordis, inhumanus, crudelis:—Cirmdon caldheorte *the cold-hearted cried out*, Andr. Kmbl. 275; An. 138. v. calan.

caldu, e; *f. Cold, coldness;* gelu, frigus. DER. sin-caldu. v. calan.

calend, es; *m.* I. *a month;* mensis:—Calend [kalend MS.] Martius rēðe *the fierce month of March*, Menol. Fox 62; Men. 31. II. *the appointed time* or *day of life;* dies, terminus vitæ:—Ǽr se dæg cyme, ðæt sȳ his calend arunnen *ere the day come, when his appointed time be run out*, Salm. Kmbl. 959; Sal. 479.

calf *a calf*, Ps. Spl. 49, 10. v. cealf.

calferu; *acc. pl. Calves;* vitulos, Ps. Surt. 49, 9. v. cealf.

calfian *to* CALVE; vitulum edere, Som. Ben. Lye. v. cealfian.

calfru *calves*, Ps. Th. 21, 10. v. cealf.

calfur *calves;* vituli:—Ymb-saldon me calfur *circumdederunt me vituli*, Ps. Surt. 21, 13: 50, 21. v. cealf.

calian; *p.* ode; *pp.* od; *v. intrans. To be* or *become cold;* algere, frigescere. v. calan.

CALIC, cælic, cælc, calc, es; *m. A cup*, CHALICE, *goblet;* calix:—Se calic mīnre blisse *the cup of my joy*, Ps. Th. 15, 5: Ps. Spl. 22, 7. Dǽl calices mīnes *pars calicis mei*, Ps. Spl. 15, 5. He genam ðone calic *accepit calicem*, Mt. Bos. 26, 27, 28: Ps. Th. 115, 4: Ps. Surt. 115, 13. [*Plat.* kelk: *O. Sax.* kelik, *m*: *O. Frs.* tzielk, tzilik, *m*: *Dut.* kelk, *m*: *Ger.* kelch, *m*: *M. H. Ger.* kelich, kelch, *m*: *O. H. Ger.* kelih, *m*: *Dan.* kalk, *m. f*: *Swed. Norw.* kalk, *m*: *Icel.* kalkr, *m;* from *Lat.* calix: *Grk.* κύλιξ.]

calla, an; *m.* [ceallian *to call*] *A herald*, found in the phrase,—hilde calla [*q. v.*] *war's herald* or *a herald of war*, Cd. 156; Th. 193, 26; Exod. 252.

CALU, caluw; *adj.* CALLOW, *bald, without hair;* calvus, glaber:—Calu oððe hnot *glaber* [MS. *glabrio*], Ælfc. Gr. 9, 3; Som. 8, 36: Exon. 111 b; Th. 427, 31; Rä. 41, 99. Monig man weorþ fǽrlīce caluw *many a man becomes bald suddenly*, Prov. Kmbl. 42. [*Wyc.* calu: *Plat.* kaal: *Frs.* keal: *Dut.* kaal: *Kil.* kael: *Ger.* kahl: *M. H. Ger.* kal: *O. H. Ger.* chalo, chalaw: *Lat.* calvus: *Ir. Gael.* calbh: *O. Slav.* golu.]

caluw *bald*, Prov. Kmbl. 42. v. calu.

calwa, an; *m. A disease which causes baldness, the mange;* alopecia = ἀλωπεκία, Cot. 12.

calwer, es; *m. Pressed curds;* calmaria? gabalacrum?—Calwer [MS. caluuær] *calmaria?* Glos. Epnl. Recd. 157, 21: *gabalacrum?* 157, 26. Calwer *gabalacrum?* Cot. 96. v. cealre.

calwer-brīw, cealer-brīw, es; *m. A thick pottage made of curds;* calviale, Wrt. Voc. 290, 37. v. brīw.

calwere, es; *m? n?* [calu *bald*] *A bald place on the top of the head, a skull, place of skulls, place for burial;* calva, calvaria, Som. Ben. Lye.

camal *a camel*, Lk. Lind. War. 18, 25. v. camel.

camb, es; *m.* [camb *joined; p. of* cimban]. I. *a comb for cleaning hair, wool, flax, etc;* pecten, Wrt. Voc. 86, 11. v. bannuc-camb, fleðe-camb, wulfes camb. II. *the crest of a cock, the crest* or *top of a helmet, etc;* crista:—Helmes camb *the helmet's crest;* crista, Ælfc. Gl. 53; Som. 66, 75; Wrt. Voc. 36, 2. Camb on hætte, *vel* on helme *a crest on the hat* or *helmet;* crista, Cot. 46. [*Orm.* camb: *Scot.* kaim: *O. Sax.* camb, *m*: *Frs.* kaem: *Dut. Kil.* kam, *m*: *Ger.* kamm, *m*: *M. H. Ger.* kamp, *m;* kambe, *f*: *O. H. Ger.* kamp, kampo, *m*: *Dan.* kam, *m. f*: *Swed.* kam, *m*: *Icel.* kambr, *m*: *Sansk.* jambha, *m. tooth.*]

camb, e; *f. A comb, an assemblage of cells in which bees store their honey;* favus:—Hī ymbþrungon me swā swā beón camba *they surrounded me as bees* [*surround*] *the combs*, Ps. Lamb. 117, 12.

cambiht [camb, iht]; *adj. Combed, having a crest;* cristatus. v. camb II.

camel, camell, camal, es; *m. A camel;* cămēlus = κάμηλος = גָּמָל:—Wæs Iohannes gegerelad mið hērum cameles [camelles, Lind.] *erat Iohannes vestitus pilis cameli*, Mk. Skt. Rush. 1, 6. Iohannes hæfde gewēde of hērum ðæra camella *Iohannes habebat vestimentum de pilis camelorum*, Mt. Kmbl. Lind. 3, 4. Se camal, Lk. Lind. War. 18, 25.

cammoc, cammuc, commuc, es; *n. m? The cammoc, kex, an umbelliferous plant, brimstone wort, hog's fennel, cow weed, cow parsley.* Kambuck *is still a name of the kexes in Suffolk*, Prior 36, 126; peucedănum officinale, = πευκέδᾰνον, *n;* πευκέδᾰνος, *f. sulphur wort, hog's fennel:*—Ðās wyrte man peucedanum, and ōðrum naman cammoc [cammuc MS. H.] nemneþ *this wort is called peucedanum, and by another name cammoc*, Herb. 96, 1; Lchdm. i. 208, 17. Wyrc gōdne drenc, elenan iii snǽda, commuces viii *make a good drink, three portions of elf dock, eight of cammoc*, L. M. 3, 30; Lchdm. ii. 324, 20.

camp, es; *m. A bond, fetter, chain;* compes:—Hió bindan þenceaþ cyningas on campum *ad alligandos reges eorum in compedibus*, Ps. Th. 149, 8. v. cops.

CAMP, comp, es; *m. A contest, war, battle;* certamen, pugna, bellum:—Ic ne gȳme ðæs compes *I care not for the contest*, Exon. 105 b; Th. 402, 26; Rä. 21, 35. Drihten tǽcþ handa mīne to gefeohte, and fingras mīne to slehte oððe to campe *Dominus docet manus meas ad prælium, et digitos meos ad bellum*, Ps. Lamb. 143, 1: Bd. 3, 24; S. 556, 21: Judth. 11; Thw. 24, 21; Jud. 200: Beo. Th. 5003; B. 2505: Chr. 937; Th. 202, 2, col. 1, 2; Æðelst. 8: Andr. Kmbl. 2651; An. 1327. Mec gesette Crist to compe *Christ has placed me in battle*, Exon. 102 b; Th. 389, 3; Rä. 7, 2: Andr. Kmbl. 468; An. 234. He ofercom campe feónda folcriht *he overcame the liberty of enemies in battle*, Cd. 143; Th. 178, 33; Exod. 21. [*Laym.* comp *a conflict*: *Plat.* kamp: *O. Frs.* kamp, komp, *m*: *Dut.* kamp, *m. a battle*: *Ger. M. H. Ger.* kampf, *m. a fight*: *O. H. Ger.* champh, *m*: *Dan.* kamp, *m. f*: *Swed.* kamp, *m*: *Norw. Icel.* kapp, *n*: *Wel.* camp, *f.*] DER. camp-dōm, -hād, -rǽden, -stede, -wǽpen, -wered, -weorud, -wīg, -wudu: comp-wǽpen, -weorod, -wīg.

camp-dōm, es; *m. Warfare;* militia, Scint. 29, 1. DER. camp.

camp-hād, es; *m. Warfare;* militia:—Hī synd bigongende woruldlīcne camphād *they are exercising worldly warfare*, Bd. 5, 24; S. 647, 9. DER. camp.

campian, compian; *p.* ode; *pp.* od [camp *war*] *To fight, contend against;* militare, pugnare:—Sceal oretta ā Gode campian *a champion shall ever fight for God*, Exon. 37 b; Th. 123, 1; Gū. 316: Bd. 1, 15; S. 483, 12. Se deófle campaþ [compaþ, Ps. Lamb. fol. 183 b, 18] *he fights for the devil*, Hy. 2, 5; Hy. Grn. ii. 281, 5. Ic longe Gode campode *I have long fought for God*, Exon. 42 a; Th. 140, 25; Gū. 615. He for his ēðle mid his leódum compode *he fought for his country with his men*, Bd. 3, 9; S. 533, 17. [*Scot.* kemp: *Dut.* kampen: *Ger.* kämpfen: *M. H. Ger.* kempfen: *O. H. Ger.* chamfan, chemfan: *Dan.* kämpe: *Swed.* kämpa: *Icel.* keppa.] DER. wið-compian.

camp-rǽden, -rǽdenn, e; *f. State* or *condition of contest, contest, war;* certandi modus, certamen, pugna:—Nō hyra þrym alæg camprǽdenne *their vigour did not fail in the contest*, Andr. Kmbl. 7; An. 4. DER. camp.

camp-stede, es; *m. The place of battle, battle-field;* locus pugnæ:—On ðam campstede *on the battle-field*, Chr. 937; Th. 204, 2, col. 1; Æðelst. 29: 937; Th. 206, 1, col. 1; Æthelst. 49. Fōr campstede [MS. campsted] sēcan *he went forth to seek the place of battle*, Bt. Met. Fox 26, 28; Met. 26, 14. DER. camp.

camp-wǽpen *a battle-weapon, military weapon.* v. comp-wǽpen.

camp-weorud, es; *n. Fighting-men, soldiers;* militia, exercitus, Bd. 3, 24; S. 556, 33. v. camp-wered.

camp-wered, -weorud, comp-weorod, es; *n.* [werod, es; *n. an army*] *Warriors, soldiers, fighting-men, army;* militia, exercitus:—Hī sceōldan for heora campwered gebiddan and to Gode þingian *they should pray and make intercession to God for their warriors*, Bd. 2, 2; S. 503, 39. Æðelhere mon slōh mid ealle his campweorude ðe he mid him brohte *Ethelhere was slain with all the fighting-men whom he had brought with him*, 3, 24; S. 556, 33. Ða ārleásan cyningas ofslegene wǽron mid heora compweorode *the wicked kings were slain with their army*, 2, 5; S. 507, 40. DER. camp.

camp-wīg *a battle.* v. comp-wīg.

camp-wudu; *gen.* -wuda; *m. War-wood, a shield;* lignum pugnæ, clipeus:—Ðonne rand dynede, campwudu clynede *then rang the shield, the war-wood sounded*, Elen. Kmbl. 101; El. 51. DER. camp.

can, cann, e; *f. A knowledge, clearance.* v. cann.

can, ic he *I know, he knows*:—Ic oððe he can, Elen. Kmbl. 1363; El. 683: Ps. Th. 88, 13. He can *he can*, Bt. 39, 2; Fox 214, 10. v. cunnan.

Cananēisc; *adj. Canaanitish;* Chananæus:—Cham ys fæder ðære Cananēiscre þeóde *Ham is the father of the Canaanitish people*, Gen. 9, 18.

canceler, es; *m. A chancellor;* cancellarius:—Se cyng Willelm betǽhte Rodbeard his cancelere ðæt biscoprīce on Lincolne *the king William transferred the bishopric of Lincoln to Robert his chancellor*, Chr. 1093; Ing. 306, 7.

cancer; *gen.* cancres; *m?* I. *a cancer, an eating* or *spreading disease;* cancer, morbus:—Gif ðū wille cancer ablendan, genim ðonne fīfleáfan ða wyrte: seóþ on wīne *if thou desire to stop a cancer, then take the herb fiveleaf: boil it in wine*, Herb. 3, 9; Lchdm. i. 88, 20. Ealne ðone bīte ðæs cancres heó afeormaþ *it clears away all the pain* [*bite*] *of the cancer*, 167, 3; Lchdm. i. 296, 22. Wið cancre, nim gāte geallan and hunig *against cancer, take goat's gall and honey*, L. M. 3, 36; Lchdm. ii. 328, 13: Herb. 32, 3; Lchdm. i. 130, 12, MS. O, note 24. Wiđ cancre *for cancer*, Med. ex Quadr. 6, 21; Lchdm. i. 354, 25. II. *a crab;* cancer, animal. v. cancer-hæbern.

cancer-âdl, e; *f. A cancer-disease, a canker;* cancer, carcinoma = καρκίνωμα:—Wiđ cancerâdle, đæt is, bîte *against cancer-disease, that is, a biting disease*, L. M. 1, 44; Lchdm. ii. 108, 9.

cancer-hæbern, es; *n.* [cancer *a crab*, hæbern = hæb-ærn *a place, dwelling-place*] *A crab-hole;* caverna, cavernula D.

cancettan; *part.* cancettende; *p.* cancette; *pp.* cancetted *To laugh aloud* or *in a cackling manner;* cachinnare:—Mæssepreóst ne sceal lufigean micelne and ungemetlîcne cancettende hleahtor *nor shall a mass-priest love great and immoderate cackling laughter*, L. E. I. 21; Th. ii. 416, 36. v. ceahhetan.

cancetung, e; *f. A laughing in a cackling manner;* cachinnus, Cot. 58. v. ceahhetung.

CANDEL, candell, condel, condell, e; *f:* candel, es; *n. A* CANDLE; candela, lampas = λαμπάς:—Hâdre scîneþ rôdores candel *the sun* [*the candle of the firmament*] *serenely shines*, Beo. Th. 3148; B. 1572. Candeles leóma *the light of a candle;* lampas, Ælfc. Gl. 67; Som. 69, 88; Wrt. Voc. 41, 41. Glâd ofer grûndas Godes condel beorht *God's bright candle glided over the grounds*, Chr. 937; Th. 202, 16, col. 1; Æđelst. 15: Exon. 51 b; Th. 179, 20; Gû. 1264: 72 a; Th. 269, 23; Jul. 454. Se sceal đære sunnan sîþ bihealdan, Godes condelle *he shall observe the sun's course, God's candle*, 57 a; Th. 204, 2; Ph. 91. [*Chauc. Laym.* candel: *Pers.* قندیل kandeel *a candle: Fr.* chandelle: *Span. It.* candela, from the *Lat.* candela, from candēre *to shine.*] DER. dæg-candel, friþ-, heofon-, mēre-, swegel-, weder-, woruld-, wyn-: candel-bora, -leóht, -mæsse, -snytels, -stæf, -sticca, -treów, -twist, -weoc, -wyrt.

candel-bora, an; *m. A* CANDLE-BEARER, *a subdeacon, a clerk;* acolythus = ἀκόλουθος, Cot. 203.

candell, e; *f. A candle;* candela, lampas. v. candel.

candel leóht, es; *n. Candle-light;* lucernæ lumen, C. R. Ben. 53. DER. candel.

Candel-mæsse, an; *f.* CANDLEMAS, the mass at the feast of purification which, in the Romish church, *is celebrated with many lighted candles;* festum purificationis beatæ Mariæ:—Æt Candelmæssan *at Candlemas*, L. Eth. ix. 12; Th. i. 342, 32. Hēr, A. D. 1014, Swegen ge-endode his dagas to Candelmæssan *here*, A. D. 1014, *Sweyn ended his days at Candlemas*, Chr. 1014; Th. 272, 25, col. 1. DER. candel.

candel-snytels, es; *m? Candle-snuffers;* emunctorium:—Candel-snytels *emunctorium*, Ælfc. Gl. 30; Som. 61, 56. DER. candel.

candel-stæf, es; *m. A candle-staff* or *stick;* candelabrum:—Ne hî ne ælaþ hyra leóhtfæt, and hit under cyfe settaþ, ac ofer candelstæf *neque accendunt lucernam, et ponunt eam sub modio, sed super candelabrum*, Mt. Bos. 5, 15.

candel-sticca, an; *m. A* CANDLESTICK; candelabrum, Chr. 1102; Th. 366, 20. DER. candel.

candel-treów, es; *n. A candlestick with branches, a candlestick;* candelabrum:—Ne menn blǣcern in beornaþ and settaþ hine under mytte, ah on candeltreów *neque accendunt lucernam et ponunt eam sub modio, sed super candelabrum*, Mt. Kmbl. Rush. 5, 15. DER. candel.

candel-twist, es; *m. A pair of snuffers;* emunctoria:—Candel-twist *emunctoria*, Ælfc. Gl. 82; Som. 73, 50; Wrt. Voc. 47, 54. DER. candel.

candel-weoc, e; *f. A wick of a candle, a torch;* funale, funis:—Candelweoca *funalia* vel *funes*, Ælfc. Gl. 67; Som. 69, 87; Wrt. Voc. 41, 40. DER. candel.

candel-wyrt, e; *f.* [candel *a candle*, wyrt *a herb, plant*] CANDLE-WORT, *hedge-taper, mullein;* lucernaria, phlomos = φλόμος, verbascum; thapsus, Lin. A plant useful for wicks of lamps:—Candelwyrt *phlomos* [MS. *fromos*] vel *lucernaria* [MS. *lucernaris*], Ælfc. Gl. 44; Som. 64, 90; Wrt. Voc. 32, 25.

cann *know, knows;* scio, scit, Ps. Th. 91, 5: 93, 11. v. cunnan.

cann, e; *f. A knowledge, cognizance, averment* or *positive assertion, clearance;* notitia, cognitio, assertio:—Mynstres aldor hine cænne in preóstes canne *let the chief of a monastery clear himself with a priest's cognizance*, L. Wih. 17; Th. i. 40, 13. Mid rihtre canne *by lawful averment*, L. H. E. 16; Th. i. 34, 12. Đanne is cirican canne riht *then is the church clearance right*, L. Wih. 21; Th. i. 42, 1. [*Kil.* konne, kunne: *Ger.* kunde, *f.*]

CANNE, an; *f. A* CAN, *cup;* crater:—Canne *crater* vel *canna*, Ælfc. Gl. 24; Som. 60, 38; Wrt. Voc. 24, 38. [*Wyc.* cannes, *pl: Plat.* kanne: *Dut.* kan, *f: Ger. M. H. Ger.* kanne, *f: O. H. Ger.* channa, *f: Dan.* kande, *m. f: Swed. Icel.* kanna, *f.*]

CANON, es; *m. A* CANON, *rule;* regula, canon = κανών:—Se canon cwæþ *the canon said*, L. Ælf. P. 31; Th. ii. 376, 26. Se canon awriten is *the canon is written*, Bd. 5, 23; S. 648, 43. Đa canonas openlîce beódaþ *the canons openly command*, L. Ælf. P. 31; Th. ii. 376, 20. Canones bôc *the book of the canon*, Bd. 4, 24; S. 598, 13.

canon-dôm, es; *m. A canonship, office of a canon;* canonicatus. v. canon, -dôm *office, state, condition.*

canonec-lîc; *adj. Canonical;* canonicus:—Æfter canoneclîcan gewunan *according to canonical custom*, Canon. Hrs. 359, 8.

canonic, es; *m. A canon, prebendary;* canonicus:—Đæt Godes þeówas, biscopas and abbodas, munecas and mynecena, canonicas and nunnan, to rihte gecyrran *that God's servants, bishops and abbots, monks and mynchens, canons and nuns, turn to right*, L. Eth. vi. 2; Th. i. 314, 17: vi. 4; Th. i. 316, 1: v. 7; Th. i. 306, 13.

canst *knowest, canst*, Andr. Kmbl. 135; An. 68: March 176; *2nd pers. sing. pres. of* cunnan.

cantel-cap, es; *m.* CANTEL-COPE, *a sort of priest's garment;* caracalla, Chr. 1070; Ing. 274, 1.

cantere, es; *m. A singer;* cantor, Som. Ben. Lye.

cantic, es; *m. A canticle, song;* canticum:—Hafaþ se cantic ofer ealle Cristes bêc wîdmǣrost word *the canticle hath the greatest repute over all Christ's books*, Salm. Kmbl. 99; Sal. 49. Đæt ic sî gebrydded þurh đæs cantices cwide *that I may be touched through the word of the canticle*, 33; Sal. 17. Moises wrât đone cantic and lǣrde Israēla folc *scripsit Moyses canticum et docuit filios Israel*, Deut. 31, 22: 31, 19: Salm. Kmbl. 47; Sal. 24: Ps. Th. 143, 10.

Cantwara burg, Cantware-burg, Cantwar-burg, -burh; *gen.* burge; *f:* Cantwara byrig, e; *f.* [Cant-wara, *gen. pl. of* Cant-ware *Kentish men*, burh *a city*] *A city* or *fortress of the men of Kent;* Cantuariorum urbs *vel* castellum. I. CANTERBURY; Durovernensis civitas:—Cantwara burg forbærn đŷ geáre *Canterbury was burnt in that year*, Chr. 754; Th. 80, 35, col. 1. Brǣcon Cantwara burh *they took Canterbury by storm*, 853; Th. 120, 28, col. 3. Đâ sealde Æđelbyrht him wununesse and stôwe on Cantwara byrig, seó wæs ealles his rîces ealdorburh *dedit ergo Ædilberctus eis mansionem in civitate Durovernensi* [*Canterbury*], *quæ imperii sui totius erat metropolis*, Bd. 1, 25; S. 487, 18: 4, 5; S. 572, 9. To Cautwarebyrig *to Canterbury*, Chr. 1009; Th. 260, 37. He wæs bebyrged innan Cantwarbyrig *he was buried within Canterbury*, 690; Th. 65, 23, col. 1: 754; Th. 81, 36. II. *Rochester;* Roffensis civitas, Roffa:—Putta Cantwara burhge bisceop, seó is cweden æt Hrofesceastre *Putta Episcopus castelli Cantuariorum, quod dicitur Rofecester*, Bd. 4, 5; Whelc. 272, 35.

Cantwara mægþ, e; *f. The county of Kent, men of Kent;* Cantianorum provincia:—On Cantwara mægþe *in the county of Kent*, Bd. pref; S. 471, 26.

Cant-ware; *gen.* a; *dat.* um; *acc.* e; *pl. m. Kentish men, inhabitants of Kent;* Cantuarii:—Of Geáta fruman syndon Cantware and Wihtsǣtan *de Jutarum origine sunt Cantuarii et Victuarii*, Bd. 1, 15; S. 483, 22. Cantwara cyningas *kings of Kentish men*, L. H. E; Th. i. 26, 4, 5: 34, 3: 36, 2. Agustinus nû on Brytene rest, on Cantwarum *Augustine now rests in Britain, among the inhabitants of Kent*, Menol. Fox 207; Men. 105.

capelein, capellan *A chaplain;* capellanus, Chr. 1099; Ing. 318, 14.

capian; he capaþ; *p.* ode; *pp.* od *To turn, incline oneself;* vertere, se inclinare:—Capaþ he up *he turns upwards*, Bd. de nat. rerum; Wrt. popl. science 15, 3; Lchdm. iii. 266, 23.

capitol, capitul, es; *m:* capitula, an; *m. A chapter;* capitulum:—Hēr onginþ se forma capitul *here begins the first chapter*, L. Ecg. P. cont. i. 1; Th. ii. 170, 3: iii. 1; Th. ii. 194, 23. On đam ende đises capitulan *in the end of this chapter*, Bt. 32, 2; Fox 116, 33.

capitol-mæsse, an; *f. Early* or *morning mass, first mass;* prima *vel* matutinalis missa:—We sungon capitol-mæssan *cantavimus primam missam*, Coll. Monast. Th. 33, 29.

cappa *a cap, cope, priest's garment;* capitulum:—Heáfod-clâþ *vel* cappa *capitulum* vel *capitularium*, Ælfc. Gl. 64; Som. 69, 15. v. cæppe.

CAPŪN, es; *m. A* CAPON; gallinaceus, capo = κάπων:—Capûn *gallinaceus*, Wrt. Voc. 63, 9: Ælfc. Gl. 39; Som. 63, 48: Wrt. Voc. 30, 3. Capûn *capo*, 39; Som. 63, 46; Wrt. Voc. 30, 1. [*Plat.* kappuun: *Dut.* kapoen, *m: Kil.* kappuyn, kaphoen: *Ger.* kapaun, *m: M. H. Ger.* kapûn, *m: Dan. Swed.* kapun, *m: O. Nrs.* kapún, *m.* Rask Hald: from the *Lat.* capo: *Grk.* κάπων.]

cara *care*, Ælfc. Gl. 89; Som. 74, 96; Wrt. Voc. 51, 9. v. cearu.

carc CARK, *care;* cura, Som. Ben. Lye. v. carc-ern.

carc-ern, carc-ærn, es; *n.* [carc *care*, or *Lat.* carcer *a prison;* ærn, ern *a place*] *A prison, a house of correction;* carcer, latomiæ:—Alǣd of carcernes clûse mîne sâwle *educ de carcere animam meam*, Ps. Th. 141, 8. Đonne þincþ him đæt he sîe on carcerne gebroht *then it seems to him that he is brought into prison*, Bt. 37, 1; Fox 186, 15. Ic wæs on carcerne [MS. Cot. carcærne] *eram in carcere*, Past. 44, 7: Hat. MS. 62 b, 22. To đam carcerne *to the prison*, Andr. Kmbl. 179; An. 90: Exon. 8 a; Th. 2, 27; Cri. 25: Cd. 227; Th. 304, 28; Sat. 637: Cot. 124: 191.

car-clife, an; *f. Agrimony;* agrimonia, Wrt. Voc. 79, 62. v. gar-clife.

care *care*, Ps. Th. 143, 18; *acc. of* caru. v. cearu.

care-lîce; *adv. Sorrowfully, miserably, wretchedly;* misere:—Me deorc earfoðe carelīce cnyssedan *dark troubles wretchedly weakened me,* Ps. Th. 85, 6.

Carendre, an; *f. A province of Germany,* now the duchy of *Carinthia* or *Kärnthen,* a crown land of the Austrian empire:—On ōðre healfe Donua ðære eá is ðæt land Carendre, sūþ ōþ ða beorgas ðe man hǣt Alpis *on the other side of the river Danube is the country Carinthia, [lying] south to the mountains which are called the Alps,* Ors. 1, 1; Bos. 18, 43. Be eástan Carendran is Pulgara land *to the east of Carinthia is the country of the Bulgarians,* 1, 1; Bos. 19, 1.

car-ful; *adj.* CAREFUL, *anxious, curious;* sollicitus, curiosus:—Drihten carful oððe ymhydig is mīnes *Dominus sollicitus est mei,* Ps. Lamb. 39, 18. Carful *curiosus,* Ælfc. Gl. 89; Som. 74, 112; Wrt. Voc. 51, 25. v. cear-ful.

carful-līce; *adv.* CAREFULLY, *diligently;* sollicite, diligenter:—Se sacerd sceal dōn carfullīce Godes þēnunga *the priest shall carefully do God's services,* L. Ælf. C. 36; Th. ii. 360, 25. Twā þing sind ðe we sceolon carfullīce scrutnian *there are two things that we should diligently attend to,* Homl. Th. ii. 82, 25.

carful-nys, -nyss, e; *f.* CAREFULNESS, *curiosity;* sollicitudo, curiositas:—Godes cwydas sind to smeágenne mid micelre carfulnysse *the words of God are to be considered with great carefulness,* Homl. Th. ii. 280, 18: Lchdm. iii. 210, 5.

carian; *p.* ode; *pp.* od *To take care, regard, heed, to be anxious;* curare, sollicitum esse:—Ðæt abbodas nǣfre idele wlænca carian *that abbots should never regard vain pomps,* L. I. P. 13; Wilk. 150, 25. Se morgenlīca dæg caraþ ymb hyne sylfne *crastinus dies sollicitus erit sibi ipsi,* Mt. Bos. 6, 34: Homl. Th. i. 66, 9. Carian *to take heed, care,* L. I. P. 14; Th. ii. 322, 5. Ða cariaþ mid wacelum mōde *they care with watchful mind,* Homl. Th. ii. 78, 2. v. cearian.

carited *charity;* caritas:—Heóld mycel carited in ðe hūs *held much charity in the house,* Chr. 1137; Erl. 263, 6.

carl, es; *m.* [=ceorl *a churl*] *A churl, rustic;* rusticus, colonus:—Carles wǣn *the churl's wain* or *waggon,* Æqu. Vern. 30, 5; Wrt. popl. science 16, 5; Lchdm. iii. 270, 11, 12; Boutr. Scrd. 29, 31. v. carles wǣn.

carl; *adj. Male, masculine;* masculus. Used in compounds, as carl-cat, -fugel, -man.

carl-cat, es; *m. A male* or *he cat;* masculus cattus, Som. Ben. Lye.

car-leás; *adj.* [caru *care,* leás *less*] CARELESS, *reckless, void of care, free;* improvidus, securus:—Wulfas sungon, carleásan deór *wolves howled, reckless beasts,* Cd. 151; Th. 188, 10; Exod. 166. He on ðam dōme freoh and carleás biþ *in judicio liber erit,* R. Ben. 2.

carleás-nes, -ness, e; *f. Freedom from care, security,* CARELESSNESS; securitas, Ælfc. Gl. 89; Som. 74, 113; Wrt. Voc. 51, 26. v. car-leás.

car-leást, e; *f. Freedom from care, security, carelessness;* securitas:—Ring on swefnum underfōn carleáste getācnaþ *to receive a ring in dreams betokens freedom from care,* Lchdm. iii. 198, 21, 29: 210, 5.

carles wǣn [*gen. of* carl] *the churl's wain, the constellation of the Great Bear;* Ursa Major:—Carles wǣn ne gǣþ nǣfre adūne under ðyssere eorþan, swā swā ōðre tunglan dōþ *the churl's wain never goes down under this earth, as other constellations do,* Bd. de nat. rerum; Wrt. popl. science 16, 5; Lchdm. iii. 270, 11, 12. v. arctos.

carl-fugel, es; *m. A male* or *cock bird;* mas avis, Som. Ben. Lye.

carl-man, -mann, es; *m. A male, man;* masculus, homo:—Ðā nāmen hī carlmen and wimmen *then took they men and women,* Chr. 1137; Ing. 366, 7.

CARR, es; *m.* I. *a stone, rock,* SCAR; petrus = πέτρος, petra = πέτρα:—Ðæt is getrahtad carr *quod interpretatur petrus,* Jn. Lind. War. 1, 42. Ðæt wæs geheáwen of carre oððe stāne *quod erat excisum de petra,* Mk. Skt. Lind. 15, 46. Se ðe gesette ða grūndas ofer carr oððe stān *qui posuit fundamenta supra petram,* Lk. Lind. War. 6, 48: Mt. Kmbl. Lind. 7, 24. II. *Charmouth, in Dorsetshire, at the mouth of the river* Carr, = the Norman Charr, or *Charmouth;* 'in agri Dorsætensis parte maritima, post *c* literam addito *h,* ad morem Normannorum, *Gib*:—Æðelwulf cyning gefeaht æt Carrum wið xxxv sciphlæsta *king Æthelwulf fought at Charmouth against the crews of thirty-five ships,* Chr. 840; Th. 120, 3, col. 1, 2, 3; 121, 3, col. 1, 2, 3: 833; Th. 116, 4, col. 1, 2, 3; 117, 4, col. 1, 2, 3. [*North Eng.* carrock: *Scot.* cairn: *Wel.* carn: *Corn.* carn, *m*: *Ir.* carn: *Gael.* carr, *m*: *Manx* carn, *m.*]

Carrum *the place of a naval engagement, near Charmouth, Dorsetshire,* Chr. 840; Erl. 67, 12. v. Carr II.

Cartaina; *indecl:* Cartaine, an; *f. Carthage;* Carthago:—Cartaina toworpen wæs *Carthage was overthrown,* Ors. 5, 2; Bos. 101, 18. Scipia hæfde gefaren to ðære niwan byrig Cartaina *Scipio had gone to the new city Carthage,* 4, 10; Bos. 93, 41: 4, 13; Bos. 99, 27. Ðæt mon ealle Cartaina towurpe *that one would overthrow all Carthage,* 4, 13; Bos. 99, 25. He þohte Cartainan toweorpan *he wished to overthrow Carthage,* 4, 13; Bos. 100, 3.

Cartaine; *nom. acc; gen.* a; *dat.* um; *pl. m. The Carthaginians;* Carthaginienses:—Wilnedon Cartaine friðes to Rōmānum *the Carthaginians sued for peace to the Romans,* Ors. 4, 6; Bos. 87, 12. Terrentius, se mǣra Cartaina sceóp, bær hætt on his heáfde *Terence, the great poet of the Carthaginians, wore a hat on his head,* 4, 10; Bos. 96, 18: 4, 11; Bos. 97, 11: 4, 13; Bos. 99, 24. Wearþ Cartainum friþ alȳfed fram Scipiau *peace was granted to the Carthaginians by Scipio,* 4, 10; Bos. 96, 11: 4, 6; Bos. 86, 32. Rōmāne wunnon on Cartaine *the Romans fought against the Carthaginians,* 4, 7; Bos. 87, 37: 4, 6; Bos. 86, 37.

carte, an; *f.* [*Lat.* charta] *Paper, a piece of paper, a deed;* charta = χάρτης:—Hig hym tosendon āne cartan, seó wæs ðus awriten [MS. awryten] *they sent a paper to him, which was thus inscribed,* Nicod. 20; Thw. 10, 5. Alecge ða sealfe on hātne clāþ oððe cartan *lay the salve on a hot cloth or on paper,* L. M. 2, 19; Lchdm. ii. 202, 10. Cartan wrītan [MS. wirtan] oððe rǣdan *to write or read a paper,* Lchdm. iii. 200, 35.

caru *care, sorrow, grief,* Lk. Bos. 10, 40: Ps. Th. 60, 1: 78, 11. v. cearu.

cāser-dōm, es; *m. An emperor's rule;* imperium:—Ðā wæs syxte geár Constantīnes cāserdōmes *then was the sixth year of Constantine's imperial rule,* Elen. Kmbl. 16; El. 8.

Cāsere, es; *m.* [= *Lat.* Cæsar; *gen.* Cæsăris] *Cæsar, an emperor;* imperator:—Wearþ Gaius Gallica cāsere *Caius Caligula was emperor,* Ors. 6, 3; Bos. 117, 18: Elen. Kmbl. 84; El. 42: 1995; El. 999. For þingum ðæs ǣrran cāseres *for the deeds of the former emperor,* Ors. 6, 4; Bos. 118, 15: Exon. 65 a; Th. 240, 6; Ph. 634: Elen. Kmbl. 524; El. 262: 1098; El. 551: 1335; El. 669. Ðæs [MS. ðes] cāseres cwēn *the woman* or *wife of the emperor;* imperatrix *vel* augusta, Wrt. Voc. 72, 58. Cāseres wīf *the emperor's wife;* imperatrix *vel* augusta, Ælfc. Gl. 68; Som. 70, 1; Wrt. Voc. 42, 10. Aulixes under hæfde ðæm cāsere cynerīcu twā *Ulysses had two kingdoms under the emperor,* Bt. Met. Fox 26, 11; Met. 26, 6. Ðā gesettan Rōmāne twegen cāseras *then the Romans appointed two emperors,* Ors. 6, 24; Bos. 124, 18. Hī hæfdon *Cæsares* ofer hīg, ðæt we cweðaþ cāseras, ða beóþ cyninga yldest *they had* Cæsares *over them, that we call emperors, who are the greatest of kings,* Jud. Thw. 161, 29. DER. heáh-cāsere.

cāsering, e; *f. A cæsaring, a coin with an emperor's image, a coin;* drachma = δραχμή, didrachma:—Gif wīf losaþ cāsering *si mulier perdiderit drachmam,* Lk. Lind. Rush. War. 15, 8. Ne unband cāsering *non solvit didrachma,* Mt. Lind. Stv. 17, 23.

cāser-līc; *adj. Cæsar-like, imperial;* imperialis, Cot. 115.

Cāsern, e; *f.* [Cāsere + en, *f. termin.* Cāseren, Cāsern] *An empress;* augusta:—Æfter ðam ðe Rōme burh getimbred wæs DCCC wintra and LXVII, fēng Adriānus to Rōmāna ānwealde. He [Cāsere] wearþ Rōmānum swā leóf, and swā weorþ, ðæt hī hine nānuht ne hēton būton fæder; and, him to weorþscype, hī hēton his wīf, cāsern [cāsere + en, *the f. termin.*] *eight hundred and sixty-seven years after the building of Rome, Hadrian succeeded to the government of the Romans. He became so dear to the Romans, and so honoured, that they never called him anything but father; and, in honour of him, they called his wife, empress,* Ors. 6, 11; Bos. 121, 5-15.

cassoc *hassock, hassock-grass,* Lchdm. iii. 24, 3. v. cassuc.

cassuc, cassoc, e; *f. Hassock, hassock-grass, rushes, sedge* or *coarse grass;* aira cæspitosa, carex paniculata, Lin:—Dō him ðis to lǣcedōme: eoforþrote, cassuc, etc. *give him for this a leechdom: everthroat, hassock, etc.* L. M. 3, 63; Lchdm. ii. 350, 23: 1, 63; Lchdm. ii. 136, 30: 3, 67; Lchdm. ii. 354, 24. To hāligre sealfe sceal cassoc *hassock shall be for a holy salve,* Lchdm. iii. 24, 3. Dō in glēde finol and cassuc and rēcels: bærn eal tosomne *put fennel and hassock and incense upon a fire: burn all together,* iii. 56, 5: L. M. 1, 62; Lchdm. ii. 134, 30: 3, 62; Lchdm. ii. 350, 6: 3, 64; Lchdm. ii. 352, 13. Weorc Cristes [MS. Criste] mǣl of cassuce fīfo *make five crosses of hassock-grass,* Lchdm. iii. 56, 8.

cassuc-leáf; *pl. n. Hassock-leaves*:—Wið eárum [earon MS.] genim ða brādan biscopwyrt and cassucleáf *for the ears take the broad bishop-wort and hassock-leaves,* Lchdm iii. 46, 2.

CASTEL, castell, es; *n. m. A town, village,* CASTLE; villa, oppidum, castellum:—Faraþ on ðæt castel [to ðam castelle, *Hat.* in ðas cæstre, *Rush.*], ðæt fōran ongeán eów ys *ite in castellum, quod contra vos est,* Mt. Bos. 21, 2. He ðā lǣrende ða castel beferde *et circuibat castella in circuitu docens,* Mk. Bos. 6, 6. His wīf wæs innan ðam castele *uxor sua fuit in castello,* Chr. 1075; Gib. 183, 3: 1053; Erl. 187, 9. Ða castelas gewunnan *castella expugnarunt,* 1069; Gib. 174, 28. [*Lat.* castellum, *dim. of* castrum *a camp, fortified place; akin to* casa *a hut, and* caveo *to guard, protect.*] DER. castel-men, -weorc.

castel-men; *gen.* -manna; *pl. m. Castle-men;* castellani:—Ða castelmen ðe wǣron on Engla lande him togeánes cōmon [MS. comen] *the castle-men who were in England came against him,* Chr. 1075; Erl. 213, 18.

castel-weorc, es; *n. Castle-work;* castellorum opus:—Hī suencten ðe men of ðe land mid castelweorces [*for* castelweorcum] *they oppressed the men of the land with castle-works* [castellis ædificandis], Chr. 1137; Th. 382, 20.

casul, e; *f?* *A cassock, short cloak;* birrhus, casŭla, lacerna, sacrum pallium [*Ger.* kasel; *f.*], Som. Ben. Lye.

cāsus; *gen.* cāsūs; *m.* [*Lat.* cāsus, from cădo *to fall; as the Grk.* πτῶσις *a fall, case, from* πίπτω *to fall*] *A case, falling* or *change to denote the relation of nouns, adjectives, and pronouns to other words in a sentence*:—Mid ðam casu *with the case*, Ælfc. Gr. 7; Som. 6, 16, 17, 20, 22, 25, 28. Ðās six cāsus *these six cases*, Som. 6, 32. Cāsus, ðæt is fyll oððe gebīgedniss *a case, that is, a declining or inflection*, Ælfc. Gr. 14; Som. 17, 23. Ða pronomina, ðe habbaþ vocativum, ðā habbaþ six casus *the pronouns which have a vocative, then have six cases*, Ælfc. Gr. 18; Som. 20, 54. v. ge-bīgednys.

CAT, catt, es; *m.* A CAT; cătus, murĭceps:—Cat *cattus* vel *murilĕgus* aut *murĭceps*, Wrt. Voc. 78, 20. Catt *murĭceps* vel *musio, murilĕgus*, Ælfc. Gl. 21; Som. 59, 71; Wrt. Voc. 23, 30. [*Piers P. Chauc.* cat: *Plat.* katte, *f*: *O. Frs.* katte, *f*: *Dut.* kat, *f*: *Kil.* katte: *Ger. M. H. Ger.* kater, *m*; katze, *f*: *O. H. Ger.* kazza, *f*: *Dan.* kat, *m. f*: *Swed.* katt, *m*: *Icel.* köttr, *m*: *Fr.* chat, *m*: *Span.* gato, *m*: *Ital.* gatto, *m*: *Lat.* cătus, *m*: *Grk.* κάττα, *f*: *Wel.* cāth: *Corn.* cath, *f*: *Ir.* cat: *Gael.* cat, cait, *m*: *Manx* cayt: *Armor.* kaz, *m.*]

cattes mint, e; *f. Cat's mint, cat-mint;* felina mentha, nepeta cataria, Lin. Som. Ben. Lye.

caul *a basket*, Cot. 45: 196. v. cawl.

CAWEL, cawl, caul, es; *m.* COLE, *colewort, cabbage;* caulis, magudăris = μαγύδᾰρις, brassica, Lin:—Caul *caula* [= *caulis*] vel *magudaris*, Wrt. Voc. 79, 44. Befeald on caules [cawles MS. H.] leáf *fold it in the leaf of a cabbage*, Herb. 14, 2; Lchdm. i. 106, 17: L. M. 1, 46; Lchdm. ii. 114, 22: 2, 24; Lchdm. ii. 214, 23. Sele him etan gesodenne cawel on gōdum broþe *give him colewort to eat sodden in good broth*, L. M. 3, 12; Lchdm. ii. 314, 15: 3, 44; Lchdm. ii. 336, 18. Wild cawel *wild cole;* brassica silvatica, Herb. 130, 1; Lchdm. i. 240, 17. Se brāda cawel *the broad colewort, cabbage*, L. M. 1, 33; Lchdm. ii. 80, 9. [*Scot.* kail, kale: *Frs.* koal, kool: *Dut.* kool, *f*: *Ger.* kohl, *m*: *M. H. Ger.* köle, kol, *m*: *O. H. Ger.* kōl: *Dan.* kaal, *m. f*: *Swed.* kal, *m*: *Icel.* kál, *n*: *Fr.* chou, *m*: *Span.* col, *m*: *Ital.* cavolo, *m*: *Lat.* caulis, *m*: *Grk.* καυλός, *m*: *Wel.* cawl: *Corn.* caul, *m*: *Ir.* cāl: *Gael.* cāl, *m*: *Manx* kail, *f*: *Armor.* kaol, *m.*]

cawel-leáf, es; *n. A cabbage-leaf;* brassicæ folium:—Nim cawel-leáf *take cabbage-leaves*, Lchdm. iii. 40, 24.

cawel-sǽd, es; *n. Cabbage-seed;* brassicæ semen:—Nim cawel-sǽd *take cabbage-seed*, Lchdm. iii. 72, 5.

cawel-stela, an; *m.* [stela *a stalk*] *A cabbage-stem;* brassicæ caudex:—Nim cawelstelan *take a cabbage-stem*, Lchdm. iii. 102, 7.

cawel-wyrm, -wurm, es; *m. A cabbage-worm, caterpillar;* curculio, eruca:—Cawelwurm *gurgulu* [= *curculio*], Ælfc. Gl. 23; Som. 59, 127; Wrt. Voc. 24, 2.

cawl, caul, ceawl, ceaul, es; *m. A basket;* sporta, corbis, cophĭnus = κόφῐνος:—Cawl *sporta*, Ælfc. Gl. 50; Som. 65, 118; Wrt. Voc. 34, 47. Hȳ heora cawlas afylled hæfdon *they had filled their baskets*, Ors. 4, 8; Bos. 90, 34. Caul *corbis*, Cot. 45: 196. Ceawlas *cophinos*, Mt. Kmbl. Lind. 14, 20. Ceaulas *cophinos*, Mk. Skt. Lind. 6, 43.

ceác, es; *m. A pitcher, jug, basin, laver;* urceus, caucus = καῦκος, luter = λουτήρ:—Ceác *urceus*, Wrt. Voc. 85, 67: Ælfc. Gl. 26; Som. 60, 80; Wrt. Voc. 25, 20. Calica fyrmþa and ceáca *baptismata calicum et urceorum*, Mk. Bos. 7, 4, 8. Ðæt he hēt ðǽr ǽrene ceácas onhōn *ut ibi æreos caucos suspendi juberet*, Bd. 2, 16; S. 520, 6. Befōran ðæm temple stōd ǽren ceác, onuppan twelf ǽrenum oxum... Se ceác wæs swā micel ðæt he oferhelede ða oxan ealle, būton ða heáfudu totodon ūt *a brazen laver stood before the temple, upon twelve brazen oxen... The laver was so large that it covered the oxen entirely, save that the heads projected out*, Past. 16, 5; Hat. MS. 21 b, 3, 4. On ðæm ceáce *in the laver*, 16, 5; Cot. MS.

ceác-bān, es; *n. The cheek-bone, jaw;* mandibula:—Ceác-bān *vel* ceácan *vel* cin-ban *mandibula*, Ælfc. Gl. 71; Som. 70, 81; Wrt. Voc. 43, 14. v. ceáce.

ceác-bora, an; *m. A jug* or *pitcher-bearer;* anhilus? Cot. 13; anthevilus? Wrt. Voc. 285, 14.

ceace *a trial, proof;* exploratio, tentamentum, experientia, N. Som. Ben. Lye.

CEÁCE, an; *f. The jaw*, CHEEK; maxilla, mala, mandibula, gena:—Ðæt tācen ðære bærnesse he on his ceácan bær *signum incendii in maxilla portavit*, Bd. 3, 19; S. 549, 16. He gehrān his ceácan *contigit maxillam ejus*, 3, 19; S. 549, 1. Ceácan *malæ, maxillæ*, Wrt. Voc. 282, 58, 59. On hælftre and bridle ceácan heora gewrīþ *in camo et freno maxillas eorum constringe*, Ps. Lamb. 31, 9. Ceácan *mandibulæ*, Wrt. Voc. 64, 46. Ceác-bān *vel* ceácan *vel* cin-bān *mandibula*, Ælfc. Gl. 71; Som. 70, 81; Wrt. Voc. 43, 14. Ðæt biþ gōd sealf wið ðara ceácna [= ceácena] geswelle *that is a good salve for swelling of the cheeks*, L. M. 1, 5; Lchdm. ii. 48, 11. [*Wyc.* cheek-boon *the jaw*: *Piers P. R. Brun.* cheke: *Chauc.* cheeke, cheke: *Plat.* käkel: *O. Frs.* keke, tziake, *f*: *Dut.* kaak, *f*: *Kil.* kaecke: *Swed.* kek, *m*: *Icel.* kjálki, *m.*]

ceác ful; *adj. A pitcher full, jug full*:—Brohte Romanus ceác fulne wæteres *Romanus brought a jug full of water*, Homl. Th. i. 428, 1. Gedō on ceác fulne wīnes *put* [*it*] *into a jug full of wine*, L. M. 1, 2; Lchdm. ii. 30, 23.

CEAF, cef, es; *pl. nom. acc.* ceafu; *n.* CHAFF; palea:—Ceaf *palea*, Ælfc. Gl. 59; Som. 68, 1; Wrt. Voc. 38, 52. Ðæt ceaf he forbærnþ on unacwencedlīcum fȳre *paleas comburet igni inextinguibili*, Lk. Bos. 3, 17. Ða ceafu he forbærnþ on unadwæscendlīcum fȳre *paleas comburet igni inextinguibili*, Mt. Bos. 3, 12. Ðæt folc wæs todrifen ofer eall Egipta land ćef to gadrienne *dispersus est populus per omnem terram Ægypti ad colligendas paleas*, Ex. 5, 7, 10, 12, 16, 18. [*R. Brun. Chauc. Laym.* chaf: *Orm.* chaff: *Plat.* kaff: *Dut.* kaf, *n*: *Ger.* kaff, *n*: *M. H. Ger.* kaf, *n.*]

CEAFER, ceafor, es; *m. A beetle*, CHAFER; brūchus = βροῦχος:—Ceafor *bruchus*, Ælfc. Gl. 23; Som. 59, 118; Wrt. Voc. 23, 72: 77, 50: 281, 45. He cwæþ and com gærshoppa, and ceaferas ðæs næs gerīm oððe getel *dixit et venit locusta. et bruchus cujus non erat numerus*, Ps. Lamb. 104, 34. [*O. Sax. Dut.* kever, *m*: *Ger.* käfer, *m*: *M. H. Ger.* këvere, *m*: *O. H. Ger.* këvar, këvaro, *m.*]

ceafer-tūn *a hall;* atrium. v. cāfer-tūn.

ceafes *a harlot;* pellex, concubina, L. C. S. 55; Th. i. 406, 16, note 26 A. v. cyfes.

CEAFL, es; *m. A bill, beak, snout, jaw, cheek;* rostrum, rictus, fauces, maxilla:—Se wīda ceafl gefylled biþ *the wide jaw is filled*, Exon. 97 b; Th. 363, 26; Wal. 59: Andr. Kmbl. 3403; An. 1705. Blōdigum ceaflum *with bloody jaws*, 318; An. 159: Exon. 26 a; Th. 77, 5; Cri. 1252. Dauid gewylde ðone wildan beran, and his ceaflas totær *David subdued the wild bear, and tore apart his jaws*, Ælfc. T. 13, 26: 14, 2. [*Wyc.* chaul: *Laym.* cheuel, chæfl, choul: *O. Sax.* kaflōs, *pl. m*: *Dut.* kevels, *pl. f*: *Ger.* kiefel, kifel, kiffel, *m.*] DER. helle ceafl.

ceahhetan; *p.* te; *pp.* ed *To laugh loud* or *in a cackling manner;* cachinnare:—Ceahhetton *they laughed in a cackling manner*, Bd. 5, 12; S. 628, 34 [= ceachetan: *Dut.* kakelen: *Kil.* gachelen: *Ger. M. H. Ger.* kachen: *O. H. Ger.* kachazzen, chahhazen: *Lat.* cachinnare: *Grk.* καχάζω: *Sansk.* kakh *to laugh*]. v. cancettan.

ceahhetung, e; *f. A loud* or *cackling laughter;* cachinnus, cachinnatio:—Ðā gehȳrde ic mycel gehlȳd and ceahhetung, swā swā ungelǽredes folces *then heard I a great noise and a cackling laughter, as of rude folk*, Bd. 5, 12; S. 628, 30. Ceahhetung *vel* cincung *cachinnatio*, Ælfc. Gl. 88; Som. 74, 86.

CEALC, es; *m. Plaster, cement*, CHALK; calx arenata, calx:—Iuuinianus wæs sume niht on ānum niwcilctan hūse: ðā hēt he bētan ðǽr-inne mycel fȳr, forðon hit wæs ceald weder. Ðā ongan se cealc mid ungemete stincan, ðā wearþ Iuuinianus mid ðam brǽþe ofsmorod *Jovian was one night in a newly-plastered house: then he ordered a great fire to be lighted therein, because it was cold weather. Then the plaster began to fume excessively, and Jovian was smothered with the vapour*, Ors. 6, 32; Bos. 129, 9-12. [*Dut.* kalk, *f*: *Kil.* kalck: *Ger.* kalk, kalch, *m*: *M. H. Ger.* kalc, *m*: *O. H. Ger.* calc, chalch: *Dan.* kalk, *m. f*: *Swed. Norw.* kalk, *m*: *Icel.* kalk, *n*: *Lat.* calx, *m. and f*: *Grk.* χάλιξ, *m. and f*: *Wel. Corn.* calch, *m*: *Ir.* calc: *Gael.* cailc, *f*: *Manx* kelk, *m.*] DER. niw-cilct.

Cealca ceaster; *gen.* ceastre; *f. The chalk city. Camden* thinks it is Tadcaster, in Yorkshire; idem, ut opinatur clarus Camdenus, quod hodie Tadcaster in agro Eboracensi, sic olim vocatum a calce ibidem copiose effossa, Som. Ben. Lye.

Cealc-hȳþ, e; *f. The name of a place, Challock, Chalk, in Kent*:—Hēr wæs geflītfullīc sinoþ æt Cealc-hȳþe *here* [*in* A. D. 785] *there was a contentious synod at Chalk*, Chr. 785; Erl. 57, 13.

cealc-stān, es; *m. Chalk-stone, chalk;* calculus, Ælfc. Gl. 25; Wrt. Voc. 85, 25. v. mealm-stān 2.

CEALD, cald; *comp.* ra; *sup.* ost; *adj.* [ceald = cald, *q. v.*] *Cool*, COLD; frigidus, gelidus:—Hū ðone cealdan magan ungelīclīce mettas lyste *how various meats please the cool stomach*, L. M. cont. 2, 16; Lchdm. ii. 160, 7. Forst se biþ fyrnum ceald *frost which is intensely cold*, Cd. 38; Th. 50, 16; Gen. 809. Ðū ðæm wætere wǽtum and cealdum foldan fæste gesettest *thou firmly settest the earth to the water wet and cold*, Bt. Met. Fox 20, 180; Met. 20, 90: 20, 152; Met. 20, 76. Wedera cealdost *the coldest of tempests*, Beo. Th. 1097; B. 546. [*Laym.* cald: *Plat.* koold, kold, kolt: *O. Sax. O. Frs.* kald: *Dut.* koud: *Kil.* koud, kaud: *Ger. M. H. Ger.* kalt: *O. H. Ger.* chalt, kalt: *Goth.* kalds, *m*; kald, *n*: *Dan.* kold: *Swed.* kall: *Icel.* kaldr: *Lat.* gelidus: *Lith.* száltas: *Lett.* salts: *Sansk.* jala.] DER. æl-ceald, brim-, eal-, hrīm-, īs-, morgen-, ofer-, sin-, snāw-, wæl-, winter-. v. calan.

ceald, cald, es; *n. Cold, coldness;* frigus:—Somod hāt and ceald *heat also and cold*, Cd. 192; Th. 239, 29; Dan. 377: Cd. 216; Th. 273, 5; Sat. 132. Hātes and cealdes *of heat and of cold*, Exon. 117 b; Th. 451, 20; Dōm. 106. Hȳ beóþ cealde geclungene *they are shrivelled with cold*, Salm. Kmbl. 609; Sal. 304. Calde geþrungen wǽron mīne fēt *my feet were pierced with cold*, Exon. 81 b; Th. 306, 16; Seef. 8. v. calan.

cealdian; *p.* ode; *pp.* od; *v. intrans. To become cold;* frigescere:—Eorþmægen ealdaþ, ellen cealdaþ [MS. cōlaþ] *earthly power grows old,* *courage becomes cold*, Exon. 95 a; Th. 354, 62; Reim. 69, Grn. Gl. DER. a-cealdian. v. calan.

cealer-brîw, es; *m. A thick pottage made of curds;* calviale, Gl. Lchdm. ii. 375, 18. v. calwer-brîw.

CEALF, celf, calf, es; *pl.* cealfru, calfru; *n.m. A* CALF; vitulus, vitula:—He genam ân fætt cealf *tulit vitulum tenerrimum*, Gen. 18, 7. He ofslôh ân fæt celf *occidit vitulum saginatum*, Lk. Foxe 15, 27. Ne onfô ic nâ of eówrum hûse cealfas *non accipiam de domo tua vitulos*, Ps. Th. 49, 10. Ðæt hâlige cealf *the holy calf*, Ps. C. 50, 137; Ps. Grn. ii. 280, 137. Me ymbhringdon mænige calfru *circumdederunt me vituli multi*, Ps. Th. 21, 10. Ic ne on-foo of hûse ðînum calferu *non accipiam de domo tua vitulos*, Ps. Surt. 49, 9. On-settaþ ofer wi-bed ðîn calfur *acc. pl. imponent super altare tuum vitulos*, 50, 21. [*Orm.* callf: *Plat.* kalf, kalv, *n*: *O. Sax.* calf, *n*: *Dut.* kalf, *n*: *Ger.* kalb, *n*: *M. H. Ger.* kalp, *n*: *O. H. Ger.* kalb, *n*: *Goth.* kalbo, *f. a young cow, heifer*: *Dan.* kalv, *m.f*: *Swed.* kalf, *m*: *Icel.* kálfr, *m.*]

cealf-âdl, e; *f.* [âdl *a disease, pain*] *A calf-disease, a sort of disease;* morbi genus, L. M. 35, Lye.

cealfa hûs, es; *n. A house for* [*of*] *calves;* vitularius, Ælfc. Gl. 1; Som. 55, 24; Wrt. Voc. 15, 24.

cealfian; *p.* ode; *pp.* od *To calve;* vitulum parere. v. cealf.

ceallian; *p.* ode; *pp.* od [calla *a caller, herald*] *To* CALL, *cry out, shout;* clamare:—Ongan [MS. ongean] ceallian ofer cald wæter Byrhthelmes bearn *the son of Byrhthelm began to shout across the cold river*, Byrht. Th. 134, 28; By. 91. [*Chauc. R. Brun.* calle: *Piers P.* callede, *p*: *O. Frs.* kaltia, kella: *Dut. Kil. Ger. M. H. Ger.* kallen: *O. H. Ger.* challôn: *Dan.* kalde: *Swed. Norw. Icel.* kalla: *Lat.* calare: *Grk.* καλεῖν.] DER. hilde calla.

cealre, calwer, es; *m. Pressed curds, a jelly made of curds* or *sour milk;* calmaria, gabalacrum?—Cealre [MS. cealfre] *calmaria*, Wrt. Voc. 290, 33. Nim sûr molcen, wyrc to cealre, and beþ mid ðý cealre *take sour curds, work them to a jelly, and foment with the jelly*, L. M. 1, 39; Lchdm. ii. 98, 25, 26. Sûr meolc wyrce cealre, and beðe mid cealre *work sour milk into jelly, and foment with the jelly*, Lchdm. iii. 42, 26. Gewirc niwne cealre *make new jelly*, L. M. 1, 44; Lchdm. ii. 108, 13. Nim ða wyrta and wyrce togadere swâ micel swâ cealras [MS. celras] *take the herbs and work them together as thick as curds*, Lchdm. iii. 118, 14. Calwer *gabalacrum*, Cot. 96. DER. cealer-brîw.

ceaol *a basket;* cophinus, Lk. Lind. War. 9, 17. v. cawl.

CEÁP, es; *m.* I. *cattle;* pecus:—Ðǽm landbûendum is beboden ðæt ealles ðæs ðe him on heora ceápe geweaxe, hîg Gode ðone teóðan dǽl agyfen *to farmers it is commanded, that of all which increases to them of their cattle, they give the tenth part to God*, L. E. I. 35; Th. ii. 432, 29. Ceápas *cattle*, Cd. 83; Th. 105, 2; Gen. 1747. His neáhgebûres ceáp *his neighbour's cattle*, L. In. 40; Th. i. 126, 15. Ceápes cwild *murrain of cattle*, Chr. 897; Erl. 94, 31. II. as cattle were the chief objects of sale, hence,—*Saleable commodities, price, sale, bargain, business, market;* pretium, negotium, pactio, venditio, forum:—Ceápas *saleable commodities, goods*, Cd. 85; Th. 106, 16; Gen. 1772: 90; Th. 112, 28; Gen. 1877. Deópum ceápe gebohte *redeemed us at a great* [*deep*] *price*, L. C. E. 18; Th. i. 370, 28. Sume wǽron to ceápe gesealde *some were sold at a price*, Nathan. 8: Gen. 41, 56. Awyrigende ceáp [MS. cep] *malignum negotium*, Lchdm. iii. 206, 32. Ic gange to ceápe *I go to market;* veneo, Ælfc. Gr. 32; Som. 36, 23. [*Laym.* cheap, chep *value, purchase*: *Plat.* koop, *m*: *O. Sax.* kop, *m. purchase, money*: *O. Frs.* kâp, *m. purchase, sale*: *Dut.* koop, *m. bargain*: *Ger.* kauf, *m*: *M. H. Ger.* kouf, *m. purchase*: *O. H. Ger.* chouf, kouf, *m. negotium*: *Dan.* kjöb, *n*: *Swed.* köp, *n. purchase*: *Icel.* kaup, *n. bargain.*] DER. land-ceáp, orleg-, searo-.

ceáp-cniht, es; *m. A hired servant, a slave;* emptitius, Cot. 72.

ceáp-dæg; *gen.* -dæges; *pl. nom. acc.* -dagas; *m. A bargaining* or *market-day*:—Ceáp-dagas *the Nones* or *stated times when the common people came to market;* nonæ, Ælfc. Gl. 96; Som. 76, 27; Wrt. Voc. 53, 36: Cot. 142.

ceáp-eádig; *adj. Rich in goods, rich in cattle*:—Nefne him hafaþ ceápeádig mon *unless a man rich in cattle retains him*, Exon. 90 b; Th. 340, 8; Gn. Ex. 108.

ceáp-ealeðel, -ealoþ, es; *n. The ale-selling place, an ale-house;* taberna, popina, cervisiarium:—Ne sceolon mæsse-preóstas æt ceáp-ealeðelum ne etan ne drincan *mass-priests should not eat nor drink at ale-houses*, L. E. I. 13; Th. ii. 410, 18.

ceáp-gyld, es; *n.* I. *bargain money;* justum rei venditæ pretium:—Þolige ðæs ceápgyld *perdat pretium emptionis*, L. Ath. i. 24; Wilk. 61, 25; Th. i. 212, 16, note 33. II. *price* or *market-price of what is stolen;* rei furto ablatæ pretium:—Gilde man ðam teónde his ceápgyld *let a man pay to the accuser the market-price* [pretium], L. C. S. 2[illegible]; Th. i. 390, 23.

ceápian; *p.* ode; *pp.* od [ceáp II] *To bargain, chaffer, trade, to contract for the purchase* or *sale of a thing, to buy, to bribe;* negotiari, emere, comparāre:—Ceápiaþ ôþ-ðæt ic cume *negotiamini dum venio*, Lk. Bos. 19, 13. He adrâf ût ealle ða ðe ceápodon iunan ðam temple *ejiciebat omnes ementes et vendentes in templo*, Mt. Bos. 21, 12. Gyfum ceápian *to bribe with gifts*, Cd. 212; Th. 262, 5; Dan. 739. Mid ðam hî ûtwǽpnedmonna freóndscipes him ceápiaþ *quibus externorum sibi virorum amicitiam comparent*, Bd. 4, 25; S. 601, 18. Mihte ýþ geceápian, gif ǽnig man ceápode *might easily buy, if any one bargained*, Ors. 5, 7; Bos. 106, 17. DER. a-ceápian, be-, ge-, ofa-.

ceáping, e; *f. A buying, marketing;* emptio:—Ðæt nân ceáping ne sý Sunnan dagum *that no marketing be on Sundays*, L. Ath. i. 24; Th. i. 212, 15, note 31. v. ceápung.

ceáp-man, cýp-man, cýpe-man; *gen.* -mannes; *dat.* -men; *pl. nom. acc.* -men; *gen.* -manna; *dat.* -mannum; *m. A* CHAPMAN, *merchant, market-man;* mercator, negotiator, nundinator:—Gif ceápman uppe on folce ceápie, dô ðæt beforan gewitnessum *if a chapman traffic up among the people, let him do it before witnesses*, L. In. 25; Th. i. 118, 12, note 32: Obs. Lun. § 14; Lchdm. iii. 190, 23. Ða cýpmen binnon ðam temple getâcnodon unrihtwîse lâreówas on Godes gelaðunge *the chapmen within the temple betokened unrighteous teachers in God's church*, Homl. Th. i. 410, 35: ii. 120, 15. Cýpemen monig cêpeþing to ceápstôwe brohte *chapmen brought many saleable things to market*, Bd. 2, 1; S. 501; 4.

ceáp-sceamul, -sceamel, es; *m.* [scamel *a bench, seat*] *A toll-booth, custom-house, treasury;* mercatorium scabellum, telonium = τελώνιον, gazophylacium = γαζοφυλάκιον:—He geseah Leui, æt ceápsceamule sittende *vidit Levi, sedentem ad telonium*, Lk. Bos. 5, 27. Ðâs word he spæc æt ceápsceamele *hæc verba locutus est in gazophylacio*, Jn. Bos. 8, 20.

ceáp-scip, es; *n. A merchant ship, trading ship;* navis mercatoria:—Hî wîcingas wurdon, and æt ânum cyrre ân c and eahtatig ceápscipa gefêngon *they became pirates, and took, at one time, one hundred and eighty trading ships*, Ors. 3, 7; Bos. 61, 2.

ceáp-setl, cêp-setl, es; *n.* [setl *a seat*] *A toll-booth, custom-house;* telonium = τελώνιον:—He geseah Leuin sittende æt hys cêpsetle *vidit Levi sedentem ad telonium*, Mk. Bos. 2, 14.

ceáp-stôw, e; *f. A market-place, a market;* forum, emporium:—Lundenceaster is monigra folce ceápstôw of lande and of sǽ-cumendra *Lundonia civitas est multorum emporium populorum terra marique venientium*, Bd. 2, 3; S. 504, 19. Cýpemen monig cêpeþing to ceápstôwe brohte *chapmen brought many saleable things to market*, 2, 1; S. 501, 5: Cot. 138.

ceáp-strǽt, e; *f.* [ceáp II. *saleable commodities*, strǽt *a street, public place, market*] *A street* or *place for merchandise, a market;* vicus mercatorius, forum, mercatus, Som. Ben. Lye.

ceápung, e; *f. Business, trade, traffic, commerce;* negotium, negotiatio:—Be ceápunge *concerning traffic* or *commerce*, L. Ed. 1; Th. i. 158, 8. Fram ceápunge þurhgangende on þýstrum *a negotio perambulante in tenebris*, Ps. Spl. C. 90, 6. Ic ne ongeat grame ceápunga *non cognovi negotiationes*, Ps. Th. 70, 15.

ceápung-gemôt, es; *n. A meeting for trade, a market;* mercatus, Cot. 133.

ceápung-þing, es; *n. A buying, setting a price;* mercatus, Som. Ben. Lye.

cear; *adj. Sorrowful, anxious, sollicitous;* angore plenus, anxius, sollicitus:—On cearum cwidum *with anxious words*, Cd. 214; Th. 269, 2; Sat. 67: 134; Th. 169, 3; Gen. 2794.

cearc, es; *m. n? Care, anxiety;* cura, sollicitudo:—Iudas ne meahte oncyrran cearces [MS. rex, = crex, = cerx, = cearx, = cearces] geniðlan *Judas could not avert the pressure of anxiety*, El. 610. v. carc.

cearc-ern, es; *n. A prison;* carcer:—Ic wæs on cearcerne *eram in carcere*, Past. 44, 7; Hat. MS. 62 b, 22. v. carc-ern.

cearcetung, e; *f. A gnashing, grinding, crashing noise, as of the teeth;* stridor, Som. Ben. Lye.

cearcian, cearcigan; *part.* cearciende; *p.* ode; *pp.* od *To chatter, creak, crash, gnash;* strīdēre, strĭdĕre, crepitare:—Cearciende têþ *gnashing the teeth; stridentes dentes*, Som. Ic cearcige oððe gristbîtige *strideo* vel *strido*, Ælfc. Gr. 26, 5; Som. 29, 7.

ceareg *sorrowful*, Andr. Kmbl. 2218; An. 1110. v. cearig.

ceare-lîce *sorrowfully, miserably, wretchedly.* v. care-lîce.

cearena *of cares* or *sorrows*, Exon. 22 a; Th. 59, 33; Cri. 962; *gen. pl. of* cearu.

cearf *carved*, Solil. in præf; *p. of* ceorfan.

cear-ful, car-ful; *adj. Careful, full of care, sad;* sollicitus:—Cleopaþ swâ cearful se gǽst to ðam duste *the spirit so sad shall call to the dust*, Exon. 98 a; Th. 368, 1; Seel. 15. Cwǽdon cearfulle, Criste lâðe, to Gûþlâce *the foes of Christ, full of care, said to Guthlac*, 41 a; Th. 136, 30; Gû. 549: 8 a; Th. 2, 26; Cri. 25.

cearful-lîce *carefully, diligently.* v. carful-lîce.

cearful-nes, -ness, e; *f. Carefulness, curiosity.* v. carful-nys.

cear-gǽst, -gêst, es; *m. A spirit of anxiety, fearful ghost;* terribilis spiritus:—In lyft astâg ceargǽsta [MS. ceargesta] cirm *in the air arose a cry of fearful ghosts* or *spirits*, Exon. 38 a; Th. 125, 34; Gû. 364.

cear-gealdor; *gen.* -gealdres; *n.* [galdor *an incantation, charm*] *A dire* or *horrible enchantment;* cantio *vel* loquela mæsta:—Helle gǽst cleopade fór corþre ceargealdra full *the spirit of hell cried before the multitude, full of dire enchantments*, Exon. 74 b; Th. 279, 24; Jul. 618.

ceari *anxious*, Exon. 100 a; Th. 376, 29; Seel. 162. v. cearig.

cearian, cearigan, carian; ic cearige, ðú cearast, he cearaþ, *pl.* cearíaþ; *p.* ode; *pp.* od [cearu *care*] *To take care, heed, to be anxious* or *sorry*; curare, sollicitum esse:—Hwæt bemurnest ðú cearigende *why mournest thou sorrowing?* Exon. 10 b; Th. 11, 27; Cri. 177. He æt gúþe ná ymb his líf cearaþ *he cares not about his life in battle*, Beo. Th. 3077; B. 1536. Ne ceara ðú fleáme dǽlan somwist incre *care not thou to part your fellowship by flight*, Cd. 104; Th. 137, 25; Gen. 2279: 130; Th. 165, 16; Gen. 2732.

cearig, ceareg, ceari; *adj.* [cearu *care, sorrow*] *Careful, sorrowful, pensive, wary*, CHARY, *anxious, grieving, dire*; sollicitus, cautus, querens, mente turbatus, dirus:—Hie bidon hwonne bearn Godes cwóme to cearigum *they waited till the child of God should come to the sorrowful*, Exon, 10 a; Th. 10, 6; Cri. 148. Ceargan reorde *in a sorrowful voice*, Andr. Kmbl. 2218; An. 1110. Wæs Meotud on beám bunden fæste cearian clomme *the Creator was bound fast on the tree with dire bond*, Exon. 116 b; Th. 449, 6; Dóm. 67. Ne þurfon wyt beón cearie æt cyme Dryhtnes *we need not be anxious at the Lord's coming*, Exon. 100 a; Th. 376, 29; Seel. 162. DER. earm-cearig, ferhþ-, gnorn-, hreów-, mód-, sorg-, winter-.

cear-leás *void of care, careless, reckless, free*. v. car-leás.

cearleás-nes *freedom from care, security, carelessness*. v. carleás-nes.

cear-leást *freedom from care, security, carelessness*. v. car-leást.

cearo *care, sorrow, grief*, Exon. 32 a; Th. 101, 23; Cri. 1663. v. cearu.

cear-seld, es; *n. A place of sorrow*; habitaculum mæroris, Exon. 81 b; Th. 306, 10; Seef. 5.

cear-síþ, es; *m.* [síþ *fortune, fate*] *A sorrowful fate, sad fortune*; curæ sors, fortuna tristis:—Cealdum cearsíþum *with cold sad fortunes*, Beo. Th. 4783; B. 2396.

cear-sorg, e; *f. Sorrowful care, anxious sorrow*; cura sollicita:—Me cearsorge of móde asceáf þeóden usser *our Lord removed anxious care from my mind*, Cd. 55; Th. 68, 9; Gen. 1114.

CEARU, caru, cearo, e; *f.* CARE, *sorrow, grief*; cura, dolor, mæror:—Cearu wæs geniwod geworden in wícum *care was become renewed in the dwellings*, Beo. Th. 2611; B. 1303: Exon. 22 b; Th. 62, 7; Cri. 998: 119 b; Th. 459, 10; Hy. 4, 114. Nis ðé nán caru *non est tibi curæ*, Lk. Bos. 10, 40: Ps. Th. 60, 1. Đonne biþ þearfendum cwíðende cearo *then shall be wailing care to the miserable*, Exon. 26 b; Th. 79, 5; Cri. 1286: 77 a; Th. 289, 29; Wand. 55. Gehýr me, ðonne ic to ðé bidde ceare full *hear me, when I, full of care, pray to thee*, Ps. Th. 140, 1. Ic sceolde ána míne ceare cwíðan *I must bewail my care alone*, Exon. 76 b; Th. 287, 4; Wand. 9: Ps. Th. 118, 145, 147. Ne cleopigaþ hí care *they speak not their care*, 113, 16: 143, 18. Đa ceare seófedun ymb heortan *sorrows sighed round my heart*, Exon. 81 b; Th. 306, 20; Seef. 10. Cearena full *full of sorrows*, Exon. 22 a; Th. 59, 33; Cri. 962. Hý in cearum cwíðaþ *they mourn in sorrows*, 35 b; Th. 115, 23; Gú. 194. Đe-læs eówer heortan gehefegode sýn on ðises lífes carum *ne forte graventur corda vestra in curis hujus vitæ*, Lk. Bos. 21, 34: 8, 14. Mid cearum hí cwíðdun *sorrowfully* [lit. *with sorrows*] *they mourned*, Exon. 24 b; Th. 69, 35; Cri. 1131: 21 a; Th. 55, 31; Cri. 892. [*Piers P.* kare: *Chauc.* care: *Laym. Orm.* care, kare: *O. Sax.* kara, *f*: *M. H. Ger.* kar, *f*: *O. H. Ger.* chara, *f*: *Goth.* kara, *f*.] DER. aldor-ceatu, breóst-, gúþ-, líf-, mǽl-, mód-, sorg-, úht-, woruld-.

cearung, e; *f.* [cearu *care*] *Pensiveness, anguish of mind, a complaint*; sollicitudo, Som. Ben. Lye.

cear-wylm, -welm, -wælm, es; *m.* [wylm *heat of mind, emotion*] *Sorrowful* or *anxious emotion, agitation*; sollicita perturbatio, agitatio:—Đa cearwylmas cólran wurþaþ *the anxious emotions become cooler*, Beo. Th. 569; B. 282. Á wæs sæc cnyssed cearwelmum *the contest was ever tossed with waves of sorrow*, Elen. Kmbl. 2513; El. 1258. Æfter cearwælmum *after anxious emotions*, Beo. Th. 4138; B. 2066.

CEÁS, e; *f*: es; *n. A quarrel, strife*; lis:—Gif man mannan wǽpnum bebyreþ ðǽr ceás weorþ *if a man supply another with weapons where there is strife*, L. Ethb. 18; Th. i. 6, 19. On ceáse *in strife*, L. Alf. 18; Th. i. 48, 17. Mearh mægen samnode to ceáse *the horse collected his strength for the strife*, Elen. Kmbl. 111; El. 56. [*O. Frs.* kase, *f. quarrel*: *O. H. Ger.* kósa, *f. eloquium, fabula*.] DER. un-ceás.

ceás *chose*, Chr. 975; Th. 226, 21; Edg. 22; *p. of* ceósan.

ceásan? *p.* ceós, *pl.* ceóson; *pp.* ceásen [ceás *strife*] *To strive, fight*; contendere. v. be-ceásan.

ceásega, an; *m. A chooser*; elector. DER. wæl-ceásega, *q. v.*

ceásnes, -ness, e; *f. Election, choice*; electio, Som. Ben. Lye.

ceást, e; *f?* es; *n? Strife, contention, murmuring, sedition, scandal*; lis, rixa, seditio:—On ceáste *in strife*, L. Alf. 18; Th. i. 48, note 34. Gif he þurh unnytte ceáste man ofsleá fæste x geár *si in inutili rixa hominem occiderit, x annos jejunet*, L. Ecg. P. iv. 68, § 22; Th. ii. 230, 29. Ne he ceáste ne astirige *he shall not stir up strife*, L. Ælf. P. 50; Th. ii. 386, 12. Folcslíte *vel* ǽswícung, sacu, ceást *seditio*, Ælfc. Gl. 15; Som. 58, 39; Wrt. Voc. 21, 30. [*Piers P.* cheeste, cheste.] v. ceás *strife*.

ceaster, cæster, cester; *gen. dat.* ceastre; *acc.* ceastre, ceaster, *pl.* ceastra; *f.* The names of places ending in -caster and -chester were probably sites of a castrum *a fortress*, built by the Romans; the Saxon word is burh, Gen. 11, 4, 5. I. generally *f.* but sometimes *n.* vide II. *A city, fort, castle, town*; urbs, civitas, castellum:—Ne mæg seó ceaster beon behýd *non potest civitas abscondi*, Mt. Bos. 5, 14. On ðære heán ceastre *in the high city*, Bt. 39, 5; Fox. 218, 18. Đá cómon ða weardas on ða ceastre *then the keepers came into the city*, Mt. Bos. 28, 11. Đú in ða ceastre gong *go thou into the city*, Andr. Kmbl. 1878; An. 941. Ælla and Cissa ymbsǽton ceaster *Ella and Cissa besieged the city*, Chr. 491; Erl. 15, 6. Se Hǽlend ymbfór ealle burga and ceastra *circuibat Iesus omnes civitates et castella*, Mt. Bos. 9, 35. II. ceaster; *gen.* ceastres; *n. A city, etc*: it is thus declined in the termination of Exan-cester, -ceaster:—Ymsǽton Exancester *besieged Exeter*, Chr. 894; Erl. 91, 9; Th. 166, 30, col. 1. Ymbsǽton Exanceaster, Th. 167, 26, col. 1, 2. Đá wende he hine west wið Exanceastres *then he turned west towards Exeter* [versus Exanceaster], Chr. 894; Erl. 91, 10; Th. 166, 31, col. 1; 29, col. 2; 167, 28, col. 1, col. 2. Se cyning hine west wende mid ðære fierde wið Exancestres *the king turned west with the army towards Exeter*, 168, 26, col. 1; 24, col. 2; 169, 21, col. 1; 18, col. 2. III. *the name of a particular place, as* CHESTER, CAISTOR, CASTOR, *the city*; hæc civitas:—He him sende scipon æfter, and Hugo eorl of Ceastre *he sent ships after him, and Hugh earl of Chester*, Chr. 1094; Erl. 230, 28: 1120; Erl. 248, 8.

ceaster-æsc, es; *m. Black hellebore*; helleborus niger:—Wyrc gódne drenc ceasteræsces *make a good drink of black hellebore*, L. M. 3, 30; Lchdm. ii. 324, 20. Nim ceasteræsc *take black hellebore*, Lchdm. iii. 28, 20: 30, 14: 56, 15.

ceaster-búend, es; *m. City-dweller*; urbem habitans:—He áteáh ceasterbúendum *he came to the city-dwellers*, Beo. Th. 1540; B. 768.

ceaster-hlid, es; *n.* [hlid *a cover*; tegmen] *Cover of a city, gate*; urbis tegmen, porta:—Đæt ǽnig meahte ðæs ceasterhlides clustor unlúcan *that any one might unlock the inclosure of the city-gate*, Exon. 12 a; Th. 20, 7; Cri. 314.

ceaster-hof, es; *n.* [hof *a house, dwelling*] *A city-dwelling*; urbis ædes:—Storm upp arás æfter ceasterhofum *a storm arose along the city-dwellings*, Andr. Kmbl. 2475; An. 1239.

Ceaster-scír, e; *f.* [ceaster III. *Chester*, scír *a shire*] *Cheshire*; ager Cestrensis:—Rodbeard wæs gecoren to bisceope to Ceasterscíre *Robert was chosen bishop of Cheshire*, Chr. 1085; Erl. 218, 21.

ceaster-ware; *gen.* -wara; *dat.* -warum; *pl. m. City-inhabitants, citizens*; cives:—Wearþ Húna cyme cúþ ceasterwarum *the coming of the Huns was known to the citizens*, Elen. Kmbl. 83; El. 42: Andr. Kmbl. 3290; An. 1648.

ceaster-waru, e; *f. Townsmen as a body, the citizens* or *city*; cives, civitas:—Đá eóde eall seó ceaster-warú *then the whole city* [*citizens as a body*] *came out*, Mt. Bos. 8, 34.

ceaster-wyrhta, an; *m. An embroiderer, damask-weaver*; polymitarius, Cot. 156.

ceaster-wyrt, e; *f. Black hellebore*; helleborus niger, Lchdm. ii. 375, 24.

ceást-full; *adj. Full of contention, tumultuous*; tumultuosus, contentiosus, Scint. 28: Fulg. 23.

ceastra *cities*, Mt. Bos. 9, 35; *pl. of* ceaster.

ceat *a thing*; res, Cot. 100:—Ceatta *cheats*; circumventiones, Som. Ben. Lye.

ceáw, *pl.* cuwon *chewed*; *p. of* ceówan.

Ceawan hlǽw, es; *m. Cheawan low*, CHALLOW:—To Ceawan hlǽwe [MS. læwe] *to Challow*, Chron. Abing. i. 138, 5: Cod. Dipl. v. 310, 33.

ceawl, ceaul *a basket*; cophinus, Mt. Lind. Stv. 14, 20: Mk. Skt. Lind. 6, 43. v. cawl.

ced *a boat*; linter, Mone B. 120. v. cæd.

cedelc, e; *f. The herb mercury*; mercurialis perennis, Lin:—Cedelc *mercurialis*, Glos. Brux. Recd. 41, 44. Herba mercurialis, ðæt is, cedelc *the herb mercurialis, that is, mercury*, Herb. cont. 84; Lchdm. i. 34, 3. Wið ðæs innoþes heardnysse genim ðás wyrte, ðe man *mercurialis*, and óðrum naman cedelc nemneþ *for hardness of the inwards take this herb, which is called* mercurialis, *and by another name mercury*, Herb. 84, 1; Lchdm. i. 186, 23.

ceder; *gen.* cedre; *f. The cedar*; cedrus = κέδρος:—God brycþ ða heán ceder on Libano *confringet Dominus cedros Libani*, Ps. Th. 28, 5. On eallum cedrum *to all cedars*, 148, 9.

ceder-beám, cæder-beám, es; *m. A cedar-tree*; cedrus = κέδρος:—Cederbeám *cedrus*, Ælfc. Gl. 47; Som. 65, 41; Wrt. Voc. 33, 38: 80, 17. Libanes cederbeámas ða ðú gesettest *cedri Libani quas plantasti*, Ps. Th. 103, 16. Ic geseah árleásne geuferodne swá swá cedertrýw ðæs wuda oððe cederbeámas ðæs holtes *vidi impium elevatum sicut cedros Libani*, Ps. Lamb. 36, 35.

ceder-treów, -trýw, es; *n. A cedar-tree*; cedrus = κέδρος:—Ic geseah árleásne geuferodne swá swá cedertrýw ðæs wuda oððe cederbeámas ðæs holtes *vidi impium elevatum sicut cedros Libani*, Ps. Lamb. 36, 35.

cef *chaff*, Ex. 5, 7, 10, 12, 16, 18. v. ceaf.

cefes, e; *f. A concubine*, L. C. S. 55; Th. i. 406, 16, note 26 B. v. cyfes.

cêgan, cêgean *to call, call upon, invoke*. Ps. Spl. 137, 4: Ps. Lamb. 74, 2: Chr. 974; Th. 224, 27, col. 2, 3; Edg. 7. v. cîgan.

cehhettung, e; *f. A laughing in a cackling manner, a laugh of scorn, scorn;* cachinnus, contemptus:—Hwelce cehhettunge ge woldon ðæs habban, and mid hwelcum hleahtre ge woldon beón astyred *what scorn ye would have at this, and with what laughter ye would be moved*, Bt. 16, 2; Fox 52, 4. v. ceahhetung.

cel, *pl.* celas *a basket*, Mt. Lind. Stv. 15, 37. v. cawl.

cêlan; *p.* de; *pp.* ed; *v. intrans. To be* or *become cold;* algere, refrigerari:—Cêlan is of untrumnysse ðæs gecynnes *algere ex infirmitate naturæ est*, Bd. 1, 27; S. 494, 15. DER. a-cêlan. v. calan.

cêle, es; *m. A cold, coldness;* frigus:—Fôr andwlîtan cêles *ante faciem frigoris*, Ps. Th. 147, 6: Bt. Met. Fox 20, 219; Met. 20, 110: 20, 225; Met. 20, 113: 20, 315; Met. 20, 158. v. cŷle.

celender, cellender, es; *n. The herb coriander;* coriandrum, L. M. 1, 4; Lchdm. ii. 44, 17: 1, 35; Lchdm. ii. 82, 6. v. celendre.

celendre, cellendre, an; *f:* celender, cellender, es; *n. The herb coriander;* coriandrum = κορίαννον, coriandrum sativum, Lin:—Celendre *coriandrum*, Ælfc. Gl. 43; Som. 64, 44; Wrt. Voc. 31, 54: 286, 16. Genim ðâs wyrte, ðe man *coliandrum*, and, ôðrum naman ðam gelîce, cellendre nemneþ *take this herb, which is called* coriandrum, *and, by another name like that, coriander*, Herb. 104, 1; Lchdm. i. 218, 16. Genim celendran seáw grênre *take juice of green coriander*, L. M. 1, 3; Lchdm. ii. 42, 4: 1, 31; Lchdm. ii. 72, 12: 3, 3; Lchdm. ii. 310, 5. Nim cellendran *take coriander*, 3, 47; Lchdm. ii. 338, 6, 7: 2, 39; Lchdm. ii. 248, 3. Genim celender and beána togædere gesodene *take coriander and beans sodden together*, 1, 4; Lchdm. ii. 44, 17. Celendres sǽd gegnîd *rub seed of coriander*, 2, 48; Lchdm. ii. 262, 21. Cellendres sǽd gedô on scearp wîn *put seed of coriander into sour wine*, 2, 33; Lchdm. ii. 236, 30. Mid cellendre *with coriander*, 1, 35; Lchdm. ii. 82, 6.

celeþonie, an; *f. The herb celandine* or *swallow-wort;* chelidonium = χελιδόνιον, chelidonium majus, Lin:—Celeþonie *celandine*, L. M. 1, 45; Lchdm. ii. 110, 21. Nim celeþonian moran *take roots of celandine*, 3, 41; Lchdm. ii. 334, 26: 3, 42; Lchdm. ii. 336, 9: 3, 60; Lchdm. ii. 344, 2. Genim celeþonian *take celandine*, 1, 2; Lchdm. ii. 38, 14: 1, 32; Lchdm. ii. 78, 27: 1, 39; Lchdm. ii. 102, 1: 1, 48; Lchdm. ii. 122, 16: 3, 2; Lchdm. ii. 306, 23.

celf *a calf*, Lk. Foxe 15, 27. v. cealf.

cêling, cêlung, e; *f. A cooling, refreshing;* refrigerium, refrigeratio, Som. Ben. Lye.

cellendre *coriander*, Herb. 104, 1; Lchdm. i. 218, 16. v. celendre.

celmert-mon, -monn, es; *m. A hired servant, hireling;* mercenarius:—He celmertmon is *mercenarius est*, Jn. Rush. War. 10, 12, 13. Celmertmonn *mercenarius*, Jn. Lind. War. 10, 12. Ða celmertmenn *mercenarii*, Lk. Lind. War. 15, 17. From celmertmonnum ðînum *de mercenariis tuis*, 15, 19: Mk. Skt. Lind. 1, 20.

cêl-nes, côl-nes, -ness, e; *f. Coolness, cool air, a breeze;* refrigerium, aura:—Ðû lǽddest us on cêlnesse *eduxisti nos in refrigerium*, Ps. Spl. C. T. 65, 11. To sêcanne wið hǽto cêlnes *quærere contra æstum auras* [*breezes*], Bd. 1, 27; S. 494, 17. DER. ge-cêlnes. v. calan.

cêlod, cêllod; *part.* [ceól *the keel of a ship*] *Formed like a keel* or *boat;* scaphiformis:—Cêlod bord *a shield shaped as a boat*, Fins. Kmbl. 57; Fin. 29. Cêllod bord, Byrht. Th. 140, 4; By. 283.

celras *curds*, Lchdm. iii. 118, 14. v. cealre.

cemban, cæmban; *p.* de; *pp.* ed [camb *a comb*, I. *q. v.*] *To* COMB; pectere:—Ic cembe *pecto*, Ælfc. Gr. 28, 3; Som. 30, 61.

cemes, e; *f. A linen night-gown, chemise;* camisia, Cot. 31.

cempa, an; *m.* [camp *war, battle*, -a, *q. v.*] *A soldier, warrior*, CHAMPION; miles, bellator, athleta = ἀθλητής:—Cempa *miles* vel *athleta*, Wrt. Voc. 72, 68. Se cempa oferwon frêcnessa fela *the champion overcame many perils*, Exon. 35 a; Th. 113, 2; Gû. 151: Andr. Kmbl. 922; An. 461: Byrht. Th. 135, 17; By. 119: Beo. Th. 2629; B. 1312. Ðâ ða cempan hine ahêngon, hî nâmon his reáf, and worhton feówer dǽlas, ǽlcum cempan ânne dǽl *milites cum crucifixissent eum, acceperunt vestimenta ejus, et fecerunt quatuor partes, unicuique militi partem*, Jn. Bos. 19, 23. Scyld sceal cempan *a shield shall be for a soldier*, Exon. 91 a; Th. 341, 22; Gn. Ex. 130: Beo. Th. 3901; B. 1948: Andr. Kmbl. 460; An. 230. Woldun hŷ geteón in orwênnysse Meotudes cempan *they would draw God's soldier into despair*, Exon. 41 a; Th. 136, 28; Gû. 548: Salm. Kmbl. 279; Sal. 139. Hûslfatu hâlegu cempan genâmon *the warriors took the holy vessels of sacrifice*, Cd. 210; Th. 260, 9; Dan. 707: Fins. Th. 29; Fin. 14. We his þegnas sind, gecoren to cempum *we are his thanes, chosen to* [*be his*] *warriors*, Andr. Kmbl. 647; An. 324. Alǽten cempa *a soldier who has served his time, a veteran;* emeritus, Ælfc. Gl. 7; Som. 56, 62; Wrt. Voc. 18, 15. Gecorene cempan *chosen soldiers, adjutants;* optiones, 7; Som. 56, 64; Wrt. Voc. 18, 17. Cempena **yldest** *a chief of soldiers, a commander;* militum tribunus, Ors. 4, 9; Bos. 91, 18. Twâ hund cempna [= cempena] *two hundred* [*of*] *soldiers:* manipulus, Ælfc. Gl. 7; Som. 56, 75; Wrt. Voc. 18, 27. Fîf hund cempena ealdor *a commander of five hundred soldiers;* cohors, 7; Som. 56, 61; Wrt. Voc. 18, 14. DER. fêðe-cempa, sige-.

CÉN, es; *m.* I. *the Anglo-Saxon Rune* ᚳ = the letter *c*, the name of which letter in Anglo-Saxon is cên *a torch;* pinus, tæda; hence this Rune not only stands for the letter *c*, but for cên *a torch*, as,—ᚳ byþ cwicera gehwâm cûþ on fŷre *torch on fire is well known to all living*, Hick. Thes. vol. i. p. 135; Runic pm. 6; Kmbl. 340, 17: Exon. 76 a; Th. 284, 28; Jul. 704. II. this Rune appears sometimes to stand for the *adj.* cêne *bold*, II. *q. v.* [*Plat.* keen: *Ger. M. H. Ger.* kien, *m. n. a fir* or *pine saturated with the gum of turpentine: O. H. Ger.* kien. kên *pinus, fax, tæda.*]

CÉNE, cŷne; *adj.* I. KEEN, *fierce, bold, brave, warlike;* acer, audax, animosus, bellicosus:—Se wæs ûþwita cêne and cræftig *who was a philosopher keen and profound*, Bt. Met. Fox 10, 101; Met. 10, 51. Stôp ût cêne collenferþ *he stept out bold* [*and*] *firm of mind*, Andr. Kmbl. 3154; An. 1580. Eofore eom ǽghwǽr cênra *than a wild boar I am everywhere bolder*, Exon. 110 b; Th. 423, 9; Rä. 41, 18. Cende cneow-sibbe cênra manna *he begat a race of brave men*, Cd. 161; Th. 200, 14; Exod. 356. Þriste mid cênum *the confident with the brave*, Exon. 89 b; Th. 337, 8; Gn. Ex. 61: Beo. Th. 1541; B. 768. II. this word is sometimes expressed by the Rune ᚳ:—Ðonne ᚳ cwacaþ *then the bold shall quake*, Exon. 19 b; Th. 50, 8; Cri. 797: Elen. Grm. 1258. [*Piers P. R. Brun. Chauc. R. Glouc. Laym.* kene: *Dut.* koen: *Ger.* kühn: *M. H. Ger.* küene, kuon: *O. H. Ger.* kôn, kôni, kuon, kuoni.] DER. dǽd-cêne, gâr-.

cênlîce; *adv. Keenly, boldly, courageously, notably;* animose, audacter, insigniter, Ælfc. T. 15, 17.

CENNAN, cænnan, cynnan; *part.* -nende; *p.* de; *pp.* ed; *v. trans.* I. *to beget, conceive, create, bring forth;* gignere, creare, facere, parere:—Ic to-dæg cende ðê *ego hodie genui te*, Ps. Spl. 2, 7. Sceal, ic nû eald wîf, cennan *shall I, now an old woman, conceive?* Gen. 18, 13. Iob sunu Waldendes freónoman cende *Job gave* [*created, made*] *a noble name to the Lord's son*, Exon. 17 a; Th. 40, 9; Cri. 636. Ðam wæs Judas nama cenned *to him was given* [*created, made*] *the name Judas*, Elen. Kmbl. 1170; El. 587: Ps. Th. 73, 7. Heó cende hyre frumcennedan sunu *peperit filium suum primogenitum*, Mt. Bos. 1, 25. II. to bring forth from the mind, *to declare, choose, ascribe, clear, prove;* advocare, confiteri, adscribere, purgare, manifestare:—Gif he cynne ðæt he hit bohte *if he declare that he bought it*, L. Edg. S. 11; Th. i. 276, 12, MS. F. Ic me to cyninge cenne Iudas *I chose Judah to me for a king*, Ps. Th. 107, 8. We deórwyrþne dǽl Dryhtne cennaþ *we ascribe the precious lot to the Lord*, Exon. 35 a; Th. 113, 8; Gû. 154. Cenne he hwanon hit him côme *let him declare whence it came to him*, L. Eth. ii. 8; Th. i. 288, 14, 21, 22, 23, 25. Gif he cenþ ðæt he hit bohte *if he declare that he bought it*, L. Edg. S. 10; Th. i. 276, 6. Mynstres aldor hine cænne in preóstes canne *let the chief of a monastery clear himself with a priest's clearance*, L. Wih. 17; Th. i. 40, 13: 22; Th. i. 42, 3: L. Edg. S. 11; Th. i. 276, 12. [*Piers P.* kennen, kenne *to teach: Chauc.* kennen *to know: R. Brun.* ken *to know: Laym.* kenne, kennen *to know, make known, acknowledge: Orm.* kennedd *begotten: O. Sax.* kennian *gignere, cognoscere: Frs.* kinnen: *O. Frs.* kanna, kenna *to know: Dut. Ger. M. H. Ger.* kennen *to know: O. H. Ger.* kannjan: *Goth.* kannyan *to make known: Dan.* kjende: *Swed.* känna: *Icel.* kenna *to know, teach.*] DER. a-cennan, ge-, on-.

cennend-lîc; *adj. Begetting, genital;* gignens, genitalis:—Ða cennendlîcan *genitalia*, Wrt. Voc. 283, 53. v. cennan.

cennestre *one who has borne, a mother*. v. cynnestre.

cenning, e; *f. Birth, a producing;* partus:—Ðære cenninge tîma *tempus pariendi*, Gen. 25, 24. DER. ed-cenning.

cenning-tîd, e; *f. The time of bringing forth, birth-time;* pariendi tempus, puerperii hora:—Ðâ wæs gefylled Elizabethe cenningtîd, and heó sunu cende *Elisabeth autem impletum est tempus pariendi, et peperit filium*, Lk. Bos. 1, 57. On ðære cenningtîde *instante partu*, Gen. 38, 27.

cennynde *producing*, Bd. 1, 27; S. 493, 23, = cennende; *part. of* cennan.

cênost *keenest, bravest, boldest*, Cd. 160; Th. 198, 14; Exod. 322; *sup. of* cêne.

Cênrêd, es; *m.* [cêne, rêd *counsel*] *Cenred, son of Ceolwald, and father of Ine, king of Wessex:*—Cênrêd wæs Ceolwalding *Cenred was the son of Ceolwald*, Chr. Th. 2, 2. Ingeld wæs Înes brôðor, and hî, begen brôðra, wǽron [MS. wareon] Cênrêdes suna: Cênrêd wæs Ceoldwalding *Ingeld was Ine's brother, and they, both brothers, were Cenred's sons: Cenred was son of Ceolwald*, Text. Rof. 61, 12-18. v. Îne.

Cent; *indecl. n. The county of* KENT; Cantium = Κάντιον:—Wæs he sended to Cent *he was sent into Kent*, Bd. 3, 15; S. 541, 24: Chr. 823; Erl. 62, 19. Se cyning wæs on Cent *the king was in Kent*, Chr. 911; Erl. 101, 37: 1009; Erl. 143, 14. Se mûþa Limene is on eastewearde Cent *the mouth of the Limen is in the east of Kent*, 893; Erl. 88, 26.

centaurie, an; *f. The herb centaury;* centaureum = κενταύριον, erythræa centaureum, Lin:—Nim centaurian *take centaury*, L. M. 2, 8; Lchdm. ii. 186, 26; 2, 39; Lchdm. ii. 248, 13.

cênþu, e; *f. Boldness;* audacia:—Cræft and cênþu *strength and boldness*, Beo. Th. 5385; B. 2696.

Centingas; *pl. m. Men of Kent, Kentish men;* Cantiani:—Hî forneáh ealle west Centingas fordydon *they ruined nearly all the west Kentish men*, Chr. 999; Th. 248, 12, col. 2: 1011; Th. 267, 7, col. 1.

Centisc; *adj.* KENTISH, *belonging to Kent;* Cantianus:—Seó Centisce fyrd com ongeán hî *the Kentish force came against them*, Chr. 999; Th. 249, 6, col. 2. Ætsǽton ða Centiscan ðǽr *the Kentish [men] remained there*, 905; Erl. 98, 23.

Cent-land, -lond, es; *n. Kentish land, Kent;* Cantium:—Eást-Seaxe syndon Temese streáme tosceádene fram Centlande *the East-Saxons are divided from Kent by the river Thames*, Bd. 2, 3; S. 504, 17: 3, 15; S. 541, note 24. Æðelrêd oferhergode Centland [Centlond, col. 1] *Æthelred ravaged Kent*, Chr. 676; Th. 60, 8, col. 2, 3. Ða Brettas forlêton Centlond *the Britons forsook Kent*, 457; Erl. 12, 19.

Cent-rîce, es; *n. The kingdom of Kent;* Cantii regnum:—Hêr Eádberht fêng to Centrîce *here*, A.D. 725, *Eadberht succeeded to the kingdom of Kent*, Chr. 725; Erl. 44, 31.

CEÓ, ció; *indecl. f. A* CHOUGH, *a bird of the genus corvus, a jay, crow, jackdaw;* cornix, graculus, monedula:—Ðeós ceó *hæc cornix*, Ælfc. Gr. 9, 64; Som. 13, 58. Ceó *gracculus* vel *monedula*, Ælfc. Gl. 37; Som. 63, 13; Wrt. Voc. 29, 36. [*Scot.* keaw: *Dut.* kauw, *f*: *M. H. Ger.* kouch, *m. a horned owl*: *O. H. Ger.* kaha, *f*: *Dan.* kaa, kaje, *m. f*: *Swed.* kaja, *f*: *Icel.* kjói, *m. a sea-bird.*]

ceóce *a cheek-bone, cheek*, Wrt. Voc. 64, 44, = ceáce, *q. v.*

ceofl *a basket;* cŏphĭnus = κόφῖνος, Lk. Rush. War. 9, 17. v. cawl.

ceol *a basket;* sporta, Mt. Kmbl. Lind. 15, 37: Mk. Skt. Lind. 8, 20. v. cawl.

CEÓL, ciól, es; *m. The* KEEL *of a ship, a ship;* carina, celox, navis:—Ðe brontne ceól ofer lagustrǽte lǽdan cwômon *who came leading a high keel over the water-street*, Beo. Th. 482; B. 238. Ðæt ðû us gebrohte brante ceóle, heá hornscipe, ofer hwæles êðel, on ðære mǽgþe *that thou wouldst bring us with the steep keel, the high pinnacled ship, over the whale's home, to that tribe*, Andr. Kmbl. 545–549; An. 273–275. Ceól *celox*, Glos. Epnl. Recd. 156, 12: Wrt. Voc. 288, 30. Ceól on lande stôd *the ship stood on land*, Beo. Th. 3829; B. 1912: Exon. 90 b; Th. 339, 20; Gn. Ex. 97. Ofer ceóles bord *from the vessel's deck*, 20 b; Th. 54, 2; Cri. 862: Andr. Kmbl. 620; An. 310. In ðam ceóle wæs cyninga wuldor *the glory of kings was in the ship*, 1707; An. 856: Exon. 81 b; Th. 306, 9; Seef. 5. He ceól gesôhte *he sought the ship*, Andr. Kmbl. 759; An. 380. Hî cômon on þrîm ceólum to Brytene *they came in three ships to Britain*, Chr. 449; Erl. 13, 3: Bt. Met. Fox 21, 22; Met. 21, 11. Ceólas lêton on brime bîdan *they let the ships abide in the sea*, Elen. Kmbl. 500; El. 250. Hwanon cômon ge ceólum lîðan *whence came ye sailing in ships?* Andr. Kmbl. 512; An. 256: Exon. 20 a; Th. 53, 18; Cri. 852. [*Plat.* keel: *Dut.* kiel, *f*: *Ger. M. H. Ger.* kiel, *m*: *O. H. Ger.* chiol, cheol, chiel, *m*: *Dan.* kiöl, *m. f*: *Swed.* köl, *m*: *Icel.* kjóll, *m.*] DER. þriéreþre-ceól.

ceola *a little cottage, a cabin;* stega, Som. Ben. Lye.

ceolas; *pl. m. Cold winds, cold;* auræ frigidæ, frigus:—Ðec ceolas weorþian Fæder, forst and snâw *thee, O Father, cold winds adore, frost and snow*, Exon. 54 b; Th. 192, 9; Az. 103.

CEOLE, ciole, an; *f. The throat,* JOWL; guttur, fauces:—Ðŷ-læs sió ceole sîe aswollen *lest the throat be swollen*, L. M. 1, 4; Lchdm. ii. 48, 26. Wið ceolan swile *for swelling of throat*, 1, 12; Lchdm. ii. 54, 23; 56, 2. Wið sweorcôðe, riges seofoþa seóþ on geswêttum wætere, swille ða ceolan mid ðŷ gif se sweora sâr sîe *for quinsy, seethe the siftings of rye in sweetened water, swill the throat with it if the neck be sore*, 1, 4; Lchdm. ii. 48, 21. Hû swête ceolum mînum spræce ðîne, ofer hunig mûþe mîne *quam dulcia faucibus meis eloquia tua, super mel ori meo*, Ps. Spl. 118, 103. Ne cleopigaþ hî, ðeáh ðe hî ceolan habban *they* [i. e. *idols*] *cry not, though they have throats*, Ps. Th. 113, 16. [*Plat.* kele: *Dut.* keel, *f*: *Kil.* keele, kele: *Ger.* kehle, *f*: *M. H. Ger.* kël, *f*: *O. H. Ger.* këla, *f*: *Lat.* gula, *f*: *Sansk.* gala, *m.*]

ceoler; *gen.* ceolre; *f. The* COLLAR *or throat;* guttur:—Sind gefægnunga Godes on ceolre oððe þrote heora *sunt exaltationes Dei in gutture eorum*, Ps. Lamb. 149, 6. v. ceole.

Ceóles îg, e; *f.* [ceól *a ship*, îg *an island*] CHELSEA, '*on the bank of the Thames, Middlesex; Somner* says, 'Insularis olim et navibus accommodata, ut nomen significat.'

Ceóles îg, e; *f.* CHOLSEY, *Berks, near Wallingford*, Chr. 1006; Th. 256, 27.

ceól-þelu, e; *f. The deck of a ship, a ship;* navis tabulatum, navis:—Ic eom hêr cumen on ceólþele *I am come here in a ship*, Exon. 123 a; Th. 473, 1; Bo. 8.

Ceolwald, es; *m.* [ceol, -wald, es; *m. power*] *Ceolwald, son of Cuthwulf, an ancestor of the West-Saxon kings:*—Ceolwald wæs Cûþwulfing *Ceolwald was the son of Cuthwulf*, Chr. Th. 2, 3. v. Cênrêd, Îne.

ceorf-æx, e; *f. A cutting axe, executioner's axe;* securis:—Wǽran ða heáfda mid ceorfæxum ofacorfena *their heads were cut off with axes*, Ors. 4, 1; Bos. 79, 7.

CEORFAN; *part.* ceorfende; ic ceorfe, ðû ceorfest, cyrfst, he ceorfeþ, cyrfþ, *pl.* ceorfaþ; *p.* ic, he cearf, ðû curfe, *pl.* curfon; *pp.* corfen; *v. a. To cut, cut down, hew, rend, tear,* CARVE, *engrave;* secare, concidere, succidere, excidere, conscindere, incidere, infindere:—He wæs hine sylfne mid stânum ceorfende *erat concidens se lapidibus*, Mk. Bos. 5, 5. He cearf of heora handa and heora nosa *he cut off their hands and their noses*, Chr. 1014; Erl. 151, 10. Hîg curfon ðone ram eall to sticceon *they cut the ram all to pieces*, Lev. 8, 20. Corfen *cut*, Exon. 107 b; Th. 410, 24; Rä. 29, 4. Treówa ceorfan *to hew trees*, Obs. Lun. § 11; Lchdm. iii. 188, 24: Cd. 200; Th. 248, 11; Dan. 511. On wuda treówa mid æxum hî curfon dura *in silva lignorum securibus exciderunt januas*, Ps. Spl. 73, 7. Curfon hie ðæt moldern of beorhtan stâne *they hewed the sepulchre out of bright stone*, Rood Kmbl. 132; Kr. 66. Ðû toslite oððe curfe hǽran mîne *thou hast rent my sackcloth;* conscidisti saccum meum, Ps. Spl. 29, 13. Îsene ceorfan *to carve* or *engrave with iron*, Past. 37, 3; Hat. MS. 50 b, 5. Ceorfende *infindens*, Cot. 111. [*R. Glouc.* carf *cut*: *Chauc.* corven, *pp*: *Scot.* kerf: *Plat.* karven: *Frs.* kerven: *O. Frs.* kerva: *Dut.* kerven: *Ger. M. H. Ger.* kerben: *Dan.* karve: *Swed.* karfva.] DER. a-ceorfan, be-, for-, of-, ofa-, to-, ymb-.

ceorfincg-îsen, es; *n. A marking* or *searing-iron;* cauterium = καυτήριον, Scint. 9.

CEORIAN, ceorigan, ciorian, cerian; *part.* ceorigende; *p.* ode; *pp.* od; *v. intrans. To murmur, complain;* murmurare, queri:—Ne underfêhþ nân ceorigende sâwul Godes rîce, ne nân ceorian ne mæg, se ðe to ðam becymþ *no murmuring soul receives God's kingdom, nor may any one murmur who comes to it*, Homl. Th. ii. 80, 11. We ne ceoriaþ *we murmur not*, ii. 80, 16. Hîg ceorodon ongeán God and Moysen *they murmured against God and Moses*, Num. 21, 5: Homl. Th. i. 338, 11: ii. 472, 1. Ic ceorige oððe cîde *queror*, Ælfc. Gr. 29; Som. 33, 52. [*Dut.* korren *to coo, as pigeons*: *Kil.* karien, koeren, koerien *gemere, instar turturis*: *Ger.* kerren *stridere*: *M. H. Ger.* kërren, kirren: *O. H. Ger.* kerren *garrire;* queran *gemere*: *Lat.* garrio: *Grk.* γηρύω: *Zend* gar *to sing*: *Sansk.* grî *sonare.*] DER. be-ceorian.

CEORL, es; *m.* I. *a freeman of the lowest class,* CHURL, *countryman, husbandman;* homo liber, rusticus, colonus:—Ceorles weorþig sceal beón betŷned *a churl's close must be fenced*, L. In. 40; Th. i. 126, 13. Se ceorl, 60; Th. i. 140, 8. Swâ we eác settaþ be eallum hâdum, ge ceorle ge eorle *so also we ordain for all degrees, whether to churl or earl* [*gentle or simple*], L. Alf. pol. 4; Th. i. 64, 3. Twelfhyndes mannes âþ forstent vi ceorla âþ *a twelve hundred man's oath stands for six churls' oaths*, L. O. 13; Th. i. 182, 19. Be ceorles gærstûne *of a husbandman's meadow*, L. In. 42; Th. i. 128, 4, 5. Landes [MS. londes] ceorl *a land's man*, Bt. Met. Fox 12, 54; Met. 12, 27. II. *a man, husband;* vir, maritus:—Ceorla cyngc *king of the commons*, Chr. 1020; Erl. 160, 23. Ealdan ceorlas wilniaþ *old men wish*, Bt. 36, 5; Fox 180, 7. Clypa ðînne ceorl *voca virum* [*husband*] *tuum*, Jn. Bos. 4, 16, 17. Ðû hæfdest fîf ceorlas *thou hast had five husbands*, 4, 18. III. *a free man*, as opposed to þeów, and to þrǽl *a slave;* or as opposed to þegen *a thane* or *nobleman*, as we say, 'gentle or simple:'—We witan ðæt, þurh Godes gyfe, þrǽl wearþ to þegene, and ceorl wearþ to eorle, sangere to sacerde, and bôcere to biscope *we know that, by the grace of God, a slave has risen to a thane, and a ceorl* [*free man*] *has risen to an earl, a singer to a priest, and a scribe to be a bishop*, L. Eth. vii. 21; Th. i. 334, 7–9. Gif ceorl geþeáh, ðæt he hæfde fullîce fîf hîda âgenes landes, cirican and cycenan [MS. kycenan], bell-hûs and burh-geat-setl, and sunder-note on cynges healle, ðonne wæs he ðonon-forþ þegen-rihtes weorþe *if a free man thrived, so that he had fully five hides of his own land, church and kitchen, bell-house and a city-gate-seat, and special duty in the king's hall, then was he thenceforth worthy of thane-right*, L. R. 2; Th. i. 190, 14–17. [*Chauc.* cherl: *Wyc.* cherl, churl: *Laym.* cheorl: *Orm.* cherl *a young man*: *Plat.* keerl: *Frs.* tzierl: *O. Frs.* tzerle, tzirle: *Dut.* karel, *m*: *Ger. M. H. Ger.* kerl, *m*: *O. H. Ger.* charal, charl, *m*: *Icel.* karl, *m.*] DER. ceorl-boren, -folc, -ian, -isc, -iscnes, -lîc, -lîce, -strang: æcer-ceorl, hûs-.

ceorl-boren; *part. Country* or *free-born, common, low-born*, opposed to þegen-boren *noble-born*:—Ne þearf he hine gyldan mâ, sŷ he þegenboren, sŷ he ceorl-boren *he need not pay more for him, be he born a thane, be he born a churl*, L. O. D. 5; Th. i. 354, 20.

ceorl-folc, es; *n. Common people, the public;* vulgus:—Ðis ceorlfolc [ceorle folc MS.] *hoc vulgus*, Ælfc. Gr. 8; Som. 7, 35. Ceorlfolc *vulgus*, 13; Som. 16, 7: Wrt. Voc. 72, 73.

ceorlian; *p.* ode; *pp.* od [ceorl *a husband*] *To take a husband, to marry;* nubere. Spoken of a woman, and opposed to wîfian *to take a wife*:—Ne wîfiaþ hîg, ne hîg ne ceorliaþ *they take not a wife, nor do they take a husband*, Mt. Bos. 22, 30. Ne nân preóst ne môt beón æt ðam brŷdlâcum âhwǽr, ðǽr man eft wîfaþ, oððe wîf eft ceorlaþ *no priest may be at a marriage anywhere, where a man marries a second wife, or a woman a second husband*, L. Ælf. C. 9; Th. ii. 346, 19.

ceorlisc, ciorlisc, cierlisc, cirlisc, cyrlisc; *adj.* [ceorl, -isc, *q. v.*] CHURLISH, *rustic, common;* rusticus, vulgaris:—Ceorlisc *rusticus*, Cot. 188. Ceorlisc hlāf *common bread;* cibarius [panis], Ælfc. Gl. 66; Som. 69, 61; Wrt. Voc. 41, 17. Ceorlisc folc *common people;* vulgus *vel* plebs, 87; Som. 74, 45; Wrt. Voc. 50, 27. Gif cierlisc [ciorlisc MS. H; cyrlisc B.] mon betygen wǽre *if a common man has been accused*, L. In. 18; Th. i. 114, 6. Se cierlisca [ceorlisce MS. B; ciorlisca H.] mon *the common man*, 37; Th. i. 124, 21. Be cierlisces [cyrlisces MSS. B. G.] monnes ontȳnesse *of the accusing of a common man*, 37; Th. i. 124, 20. Be cirliscum [ceorliscum MS. B; cyrliscum G; cierliscum H.] þeófe *of a common thief*, 18; Th. i. 114, 5. Sǽton feáwa cirlisce [cyrlisce, col. 2, 3; 165, col. 1, 2] men *a few countrymen remained*, Chr. 893; Th. 164, 4, col. 1.

ceorlisc-nes, -ness, e; *f.* CHURLISHNESS, *rudeness, vulgarity;* rusticitas, sordes. v. cyrliscnys.

ceorl-līc, ceorlīc; *adj.* CHURL-LIKE, *rustic, common;* rusticus, vulgaris:—Ceorlīc ǽhta *common property;* peculium, Ælfc. Gl. 13; Som. 57, 122; Wrt. Voc. 20, 59. v. ceorlisc.

ceorl-līce, ceorlīce; *adv. Commonly;* vulgariter, Bridf.

ceorl-strang; *adj. Strong as a man, manlike;* fortis, virilis:—Ceorlstrang fǽmne *a manlike woman;* virago, Ælfc. Gl. 5; Som. 56, 10; Wrt. Voc. 17, 18.

Ceortes īg, Certes īg, e; *f.* [*Hovd. Matt. West.* Certesie] *Cerot's island*, CHERTSEY, *in Surrey, on the bank of the Thames;* Ceroti insula, Certesia, in agro Surriensi, ad ripam Tamesis fluminis:—Ercenwold getimbrede mynster on Sūþrigena lande, be Temese streáme, on ðære stōwe ðe is nemned Ceortes īge *Earconvaldus monasterium construxerat in regione Sudergeona, juxta fluvium Tamensem, in loco qui vocatur Cerotæsei, id est, Ceroti insula*, Bd. 4, 6; S. 574, 15. Hēr drǽfde Eádgār cyng ða preóstas of Ceortes īge [Certes ige, 223, col. 3] *in this year*, A. D. 964, *king Edgar drove the priests from Chertsey*, Chr. 964; Th. 222, 5, 10.

ceorung, e; *f.* [ceorian *to murmur*] *A murmuring, complaint, grudging;* murmuratio, querimonia, querela:—Sum ceorung mihte beón gif he his behāt ne gelǽste *there might be some murmuring if he performed not his promise*, Homl. Th. ii. 80, 26, 12. Æfter ceorunge *after murmuring*, ii. 80, 9. Mōdignys acenþ ceorunge *pride begets murmuring*, ii. 222, 8. Ic gesylle fram me Israhēla ceorunge *cohibebo a me querimonias filiorum Israel*, Num. 17, 5. Beóþ cumlīðe eów betwȳnan būton ceorungum *be hospitable among yourselves without grudging*, Homl. Th. ii. 286, 14.

CEÓSAN, ciósan, ic ceóse, ðū ceósest, cȳst, he ceóseþ, cȳst, cīst, *pl.* ceósaþ; *p.* ic, he ceás, cēs, ðū cure, *pl.* curon; *impert.* ceós, *pl.* ceósaþ; *pp.* coren; *v. a.* I. *to* CHOOSE, *select, elect;* legere, seligere, eligere:—Ðæt hī woldon ōðerra wera ceósan *that they would make a choice of other husbands*, Ors. 1, 10; Bos. 32, 32. He hēht him wine ceósan *he commanded him to choose friends*, Cd. 90; Th. 112, 8; Gen. 1867: Runic pm. 29; Kmbl. 345, 15; Hick. Thes. i. 135. Drihten ðē cīst *the Lord will choose thee*, Deut. 28, 9. Hī leófne ceósaþ ofer woruldwēlan *they choose the beloved above worldly wealth*, Exon. 62 b; Th. 230, 29; Ph. 479. Bebodu ðīne ic ceás *mandata tua elegi*, Ps. Spl. 118, 173. Hēr Eádgār, Engla cyning, ceás him ōðer leóht, and ðis wāce forlēt līf *here*, A. D. 975, *Edgar, king of the Angles, chose him another light, and left this frail life*, Chr. 975; Erl. 124, 30; Edg. 22: 1041; Erl. 169, 10. Ǽfæste men him ðā wīc curon *the pious men chose them a dwelling there*, Cd. 86; Th. 108, 9; Gen. 1803: Andr. Kmbl. 808; An. 404. Ceós ðē gefēran and feoht ongēn Amalech *elige viros et pugna contra Amalec*, Ex. 17, 9: Deut. 17, 15. Ðæt ic neóbed ceóse *that I may choose a death-bed*, Exon. 63 b; Th. 235, 7; Ph. 553. Ðæt se cyning him ceóse sumne wīsne man *ut provideat rex virum sapientem*, Gen. 41, 33: Ps. Th. 105, 5. Ceósan us eard in wuldre *may we choose us a dwelling in glory*, Cd. 217; Th. 277, 14; Sat. 204. Ðæt he ōðer līf cure *that he chose another life*, Bd. 5, 19; S. 638, 6. Ǽr he bǽl cure *ere he chose the funeral pile*, Beo. Th. 5629; B. 2818: Exon. 100 a; Th. 376, 20; Seel. 157. Ðæt hī him cyning curan *ut regem sibi eligerent*, Bd. 1, 1; S. 474, 22. Ðēh ðe fell curen synnigra cynn *though the race of sinners chose death*, Andr. Kmbl. 3217; An. 1611. II. *to accept by choice* or *what is offered, to accept;* oblatum accipere, accipere:—Ðæt he ðone cynedōm ciósan wolde *that he would accept the kingdom*, Beo. Th. 4742; B. 2376. Hie curon æðelinges ēst *they accepted the chieftain's bounty*, Cd. 112; Th. 147, 20; Gen. 2442. [*Wyc. Piers P. Chauc. R. Glouc.* chese: *Laym.* cheosen: *Orm.* chesenn: *Plat.* kösen, kören: *O. Sax.* kiosan, keosan: *Frs.* kiezjen, tziezjen: *O. Frs.* kiasa, tziesa: *Dut.* kiezen: *Ger.* kiesen: *M. H. Ger.* kiusen, kiesen: *O. H. Ger.* kiusan, kiosan: *Goth.* kiusan: *Dan.* keise: *Icel.* kjósa: *Lat.* gustare: *Grk.* γεύω: *Sansk.* jush *to like, be fond of, choose.*] DER. a-ceósan, forþ-, ge-, on-, wið-, wiðer-.

CEOSEL, ceosol, cisil, cysel, es; *m? Gravel, sand;* glarea, sabulum. Hence the sand-hill in Dorsetshire is called CHESSIL:—Cisil *glarea*, Glos. Epnl. Recd. 157, 12. [*Kil.* kijsel, kesel: *Ger.* kiesel, *m*: *M. H. Ger.* kisel, *m*: *O. H. Ger.* kisil, *m.*] DER. sǽ-ceosel, sand-.

ceosel-stān, cysel-stān, es; *m. Sand-stone, gravel;* glarea, calculus:—Ceoselstān *glarea*, Wrt. Voc. 63, 70. Cyselstān *calculus*, Ælfc. Gl. 11; Som. 57, 46; Wrt. Voc. 19, 48.

ceosol, cesol, es; *m? n? A hut, cottage;* gurgustium:—Cesol *gurgustium*, Glos. Epnl. Recd. 157, 8.

ceósung, e; *f. A choosing;* electio, Som. Ben. Lye. DER. a-ceósung. v. ceósan.

ceoul *a basket;* cophĭnus, Jn. Lind. War. 6, 13. v. cawl.

CEÓWAN, to ceówenne, ic ceówe, ðū ceówest, cȳwst, he ceóweþ, cȳwþ, *pl.* ceówaþ; *p.* ceáw, *pl.* cuwon; *pp.* cowen *To* CHEW, *gnaw, eat, consume;* ruminare, manducare:—He hēt hine ceówan mid tōþum his fingras *he commanded him to gnaw his fingers with his teeth*, Homl. Th. ii. 510, 34. Ongunnon ða næddran to ceówenne heora flǽsc and heora blōd sūcan *the serpents began to chew their flesh and suck their blood*, ii. 488, 34, 27. Ðæt hīg eton ða nȳtenu ðe hira clawe todǽlede beóþ and ceówaþ *omne quod habet divisam ungulam, et ruminat in pecoribus, comedetis*, Lev. 11, 3, 4. Hī cuwon heora girdlas, and gærs ǽton *they chewed their own girdles, and ate grass*, Ælfc. T. 42, 9: Homl. Th. i. 404, 5. Ðec sculon mold-wyrmas monige ceówan *many mould-worms shall consume* [*chew, eat*] *thee*, Exon. 99 a; Th. 371, 8; Seel. 72. [*Chauc.* chewe: *Orm.* chewwenn: *Scot.* chaw, chow: *Plat.* kaujen, kauwen, kawwen: *Dut.* kaauwen: *Kil.* kauwen, kouwen, kuwen: *Ger.* käuen, kauen: *M. H. Ger.* kiuwen: *O. H. Ger.* kiuwan: *Dan.* tygge: *Swed.* tugga: *Icel.* tyggja, tyggva.] DER. be-ceówan, for-, to-.

ceowl *a basket;* sporta, Mk. Skt. Rush. 8, 8. v. cawl.

ceówung, e; *f. A chewing;* ruminatio, Som. Ben. Lye. v. cȳwung.

cēp, es; *m. A sale, bargain, business;* negotium:—Awyrigende cēp *malignum negotium*, Somn. 159; Lchdm. iii. 206, 32. Sellan to cēpe *to give for sale, sell*, Deut. 28, 68. v. ceáp II.

cēpa, an; *m. A chapman, merchant;* mercator:—Nǽnig cēpa ne seah ellendne wearod *no merchant saw a foreign shore*, Bt. Met. Fox 8, 58; Met. 8, 29. Ne geseah nān cēpa ealand *no merchant visited an island*, Bt. 15; Fox 48, 13. Cēpena þinga gewrixle *the interchange of merchants' goods, commerce;* commercium, Ælfc. Gl. 16; Som. 58, 53; Wrt. Voc. 21, 41. v. cȳpa.

CĒPAN, to cēpanne; *p.* cēpte, *pl.* cēpton; *pp.* cēped, cēpt; *v. a. gen. acc. To observe, keep, regard, await, desire, take, betake oneself to, meditate, bear;* observare, tenere, manere, appetere, captare, se conferre, meditari, portare:—Menn māgon cēpan be his bleó hwylc weder toweard byþ *men may observe by his hue what weather is coming*, Bd. de nat. rerum; Wrt. popl. science 15, 9; Lchdm. iii. 268, 5. Hīg mīnne hō oððe hōhfōt cēpaþ oððe begēmaþ *ipsi calcaneum meum observabunt*, Ps. Lamb. 55, 7: Homl. Th. ii. 324, 16: Ælfc. T. 28, 3. Ðe willaþ ðysre deópnysse cēpan *who will keep this precept*, Homl. Th. ii. 94, 7. Ðæt folc his cēpte *the people regarded him*, Homl. Th. ii. 506, 7. Hī brycge ne cēpton *they regarded not the bridge*, Chr. 1013; Erl. 148, 11. Ða sceoldon cēpan Godwines eorles *they were to lay in wait for earl Godwine*, 1052; Erl. 183, 34. Ða munecas ðæs āndagan cēpton *the monks awaited the day appointed*, Homl. Th. ii. 172, 13. He dysigra manna hērunga cēpþ *he desires the praises of foolish men*, i. 412, 7. Ðæt hī cēpaþ ðæs ydelan hlȳsan *that they desire vain renown*, ii. 566, 2. Swā hwilcne swā ic cysse, cēpaþ his sōna *whomsoever I kiss, take him forthwith*, ii. 246, 11. He nolde him nānes fleámes cēpan *he did not wish to betake himself to flight*, Ælfc. T. 36, 18. Ðonne him cælþ, he cēpþ him hlywþe *when he is cold, he betakes himself to shelter*, Hexam. 20; Norm. 28, 22. Ic gylpes cēpte *I have persevered in boasting;* jactantiæ insistebam, Mod. confitendi 1. Nele he him hearmes cēpan *he will not meditate harm against him*, Homl. Th. ii. 522, 20. He me hearmes cēpþ *he meditates harm against me*, i. 56, 3. Ðe cēpton heora deáþes *who meditated their death*, L. Ælf. C. 2; Th. ii. 342, 20. Ðæt ðū cēpe [MS. kepe] him hearmes *that thou meditate harm against him*, Basil admn. 5; Norm. 46, 4. Ne cēp [MS. kep] ðū ðīnum nēxtan fācnes *devise not deceit against thy neighbour*, 5; Norm. 46, 10. Geþyldelīce synd to cēpanne *patienter portandi sunt*, R. Ben. interl. 36. [*Chauc. R. Glouc. Laym.* kepe: *Kil.* kepen.]

cēpe-cniht, es; *m. A bought servant, slave;* venalis puer, servus:—Gregorius geseah cēpecnihtas ðǽr gesette *Gregory saw slaves placed there*, Bd. 2, 1; S. 501, 7. v. ceáp-cniht.

cēpe-man, es; *m. A chapman, merchant;* mercator:—Gif man feormaþ cēpeman *if a man entertain a chapman*, L. H. E. 15; Th. i. 32, 17. Hit cēpemen ne gefaraþ *merchants do not visit it*, Bt. 18, 2; Fox 64, 1. v. ceáp-man.

cēpe-stōw *a market-place, market;* forum, emporium, Som. Ben. Lye. v. ceáp-stōw.

cēpe-þing; *pl. n. Saleable things, goods, ware, merchandise;* venalia, merces:—Secgeaþ hī ðæt cȳpemen monig cēpeþing to ceápstowe brohte *dicunt quia mercatoribus multa venalia in forum fuissent conlata*, Bd. 2, 1; S. 501, 4. Cēpeþing [MS. cepeþingc] *merces*, Ælfc. Gl. 16; Som. 58, 52; Wrt. Voc. 21, 40.

cēping, e; *f. Traffic, merchandise;* negotiatio:—Hūs cēpinge *domum negotiationis*, Jn. Rush. War. 2, 16. To cēpinge his *ad negotiationem* *suam*, Rtl. 107, 25 Betre is tosocnung his cēpinge seolferes and goldes *melior est acquisitio ejus negotiatione argenti et auri*, 81, 14.

cēp-man, -mann, es; *m. A chapman, merchant;* mercator:—Hīg fōron mid ōđrum cēpmannum *they went with other merchants*, Gen. 42, 5. v. ceáp-man.

cēp-sceamol, es; *m. A toll-booth, seat of custom, treasury;* telonium = τελώνιον, gazophylacium = γαζοφυλάκιον:—Đās word he spræc æt cēpsceamole *hæc verba locutus est in gazophylacio*, Jn. Foxe 8, 20. v. ceáp-sceamul.

cēp-setl, es; *n. A toll-booth, seat of custom;* telonium = τελώνιον:—He geseah Leuin sittende æt hys cēpsetle *vidit Levi sedentem ad telonium*, Mk. Bos. 2, 14. v. ceáp-setl.

cer *a turn*. v. cerr, cyrr.

Cerdic, es; *m. Cerdic, the founder of the West-Saxon kingdom;* Cerdĭcus:—Đȳ geáre đe wæs agān fram Cristes acennesse cccc wintra and xcv [MS. xciiii] wintra, đā Cerdic and Cynrīc his sunu cwom up æt Cerdices ōran mid v scipum. Ond đæs ymb vi geár, đæs đe hie up cwōmon, ge-eódon West-Seaxna rīce; and đæt wǣron đa ǣrestan cyningas đe West-Seaxna lond on Wealum ge-eódon; and he hæfde đæt rīce xvi geár; and đā he gefōr, đā fēng his sunu Cynrīc to đam rīce, and heóld xxvii [MS. xvii] winter. Đā he gefōr, đā fēng Ceol to đam rīce and heóld vii geár. Đā he gefōr, đā fēng Ceolwulf to his brōđur, and he rīcsode xvii geár; and hiera cyn gǣþ to Cerdice. Đā fēng Cynegils, Ceolwulfes brōđur sunu, to rīce and rīcsode xxxi wintra; and he onfēng ǣrest fulwihte Wesseaxna cyninga; and đā fēng Cēnwalh to and heóld xxxi wintra; and se Cēnwalh wæs Cynegilses sunu *in the year that was past from the birth of Christ* 495, *then Cerdic and Cynric his son landed at Cerdic's shore from five ships. And six years after they landed, they subdued the West-Saxons' kingdom; and they were the first kings, who conquered the West-Saxons' land from the Welsh; and he had the kingdom sixteen years; and when he died, then his son Cynric succeeded to the kingdom, and held it twenty-seven winters. When he died, then Ceol succeeded to the kingdom, and held it seven years. When he died, then Ceolwulf his brother succeeded, and he reigned seventeen years; and their kin reaches to Cerdic. Then Cynegils, Ceolwulf's brother's son, succeeded to the kingdom, and reigned thirty-one winters; and of the West-Saxons' kings, he first received baptism; and then Cenwalh succeeded, and held it thirty-one winters; and Cenwalh was the son of Cynegils*, Chr. Erl. 2, 1–20. Hēr, A. D. dxxxiv, Cerdic forþfērde, and Cynrīc his sunu rīxode xxvii wintra and hie gesealdon heora twām nefum, Stufe and Wihtgāre, Wihte eáland *here*, A. D. 534, *Cerdic died, and Cynric his son reigned twenty-seven years, and they gave their two nephews, Stuf and Wihtgar, the isle of Wight*, Chr. 534; Th. 26, 40. v. Cerdices ford, Cerdices leáh, Cerdices ōra, Birīnus, Cynegils.

Cerdices ford, es; *m. Cerdic's ford, the ford of a little river in the south of Dorsetshire on* Cerdices ōra, *q. v;* Cerdĭci vadum:—Hēr Cerdic and Cynrīc West-Sexena rīce onfēngun; and đȳ ilcan geáre hie fuhton wiđ Brettas, đær mon nū nemneþ Cerdices ford *in this year Cerdic and Cynric took the kingdom of the West-Saxons; and in the same year they fought against the Britons, where it is now named Cerdic's ford*, Chr. 519; Th. 26, 21–26, col. 1.

Cerdices leáh; *gen.* leáge; *f. Cerdic's ley, in the south of Dorsetshire;* Cerdĭci campus:—Hēr Cerdic and Cynrīc [MS. Cinric] fuhtan wiđ Bryttas on đære stōwe đe is gecweden Cerdices leág [MS. Laud ford] *in this year Cerdic and Cynric fought against the Britons at the place which is called Cerdic's ley*, Chr. 527; Th. 26, 30–33, col. 3.

Cerdices ōra, Certices ōra, an; *m. Cerdic's shore, on the south of Dorsetshire*, v. Cerdices ford; Cerdĭci lītus:—Đā Cerdic and Cynrīc his sunu cwom up æt Cerdices ōran mid v scipum *then*, A. D. 495, *Cerdic and Cynric his son came up to Cerdic's shore with five ships*, Chr. Erl. 2, 3. Hēr cwōmon Cerdic and Cynrīc his sunu on Breteue, mid v scipum, in đone stede đe is gecweden Cerdices [Certices, 25, 29, col. 1, 2] ōra *here*, A. D. 495, *Cerdic and Cynric his son came to Britain, with five ships, at the place which is called Cerdic's shore*, Chr. 495; Th. 24, 31, col. 1, 2, 3: 514; Th. 26, 16, col. 1.

ceren, cæren, cyren, es; *n? New wine boiled down one third* or *one half, sweet wine;* carenum = κάροινον:—Hī, đa sylfe betweónum, indrencton mid đām cerenum đære gōdspellīcan swētnysse *between themselves, they pledged with the wines of gospel sweetness*, Guthl. 17; Gdwin. 72, 7. Cærenes gōdne bollan fulne meng togædere *mingle together a good bowl full of boiled wine*, L. M. 1, 1; Lchdm. ii. 24, 19. Cyren *vel* awilled wīn *dulcisapa*, Cot. 62.

CEREN, cyrin, e; *f. A* CHURN; vas in quo lac agitatur et butyrum cogitur, fidelia, sinum:—Cyrin *sinum*, Wrt. Voc. 290, 31. [*Prompt.* chyrne: *Scot.* kirn: *Plat.* karne: *Ger. dial.* kerne, *f: Dan.* kjerne, *m. f: Swed.* kärna, *f: Icel.* kirna, *f.*]

cerfe *shall separate;* secabit:—Ne cerfe *non secabit*, Lev. 1, 17. v. ceorfan.

CERFILLE, cærfille, cyrfille, an; *f.* CHERVIL; cærefolium = χαιρέφυλλον, chærophyllum sylvestre, Lin:—Genim đysse wyrte đe man *cerefolium*, and ōđrum naman đam gelīce cerfille nemneþ þrȳ croppas *take three heads of this herb, which is named* cerefolium, *and by the other like name chervil*, Herb. 106; Lchdm. i. 220, 9: Lchdm. ii. 72, 6. To monnes stemne nim cerfillan *for a man's voice take chervil*, 1, 83; Lchdm. ii. 152, 15: 2, 52; Lchdm. ii. 272, 10. [*Plat.* karwel: *Dut.* kervel, *f: Ger.* kerbel, *m: M. H. Ger.* kërvele, *f: O. H. Ger.* kerfola, *f: Dan.* kiörvel, *m. f: Swed.* kyrfvel, *m: Icel.* kerfill, *m.* Rask Hald: *Lat.* cærefolium; from. *Grk.* χαιρέφυλλον.] DER. wudu-cerfille.

cerg; *adj.* [= cearig, *q. v.*] *Sad, dire, wicked;* tristis, sollicitus, dirus, malus:—Cerge reótaþ fōre onsȳne ēces dēman *the wicked shall wail before the face of the eternal judge*, Exon. 20 a; Th. 52, 20; Cri. 836.

cerian *to murmur*, Wanl. Catal. 4, 6. v. ceorian.

cerlic, es; *m? n? The herb* CARLOCK or CHARLOCK; rapum sylvestre:—Nim cerlices sǣd *take seed of charlock*, L. M. 1, 39; Lchdm. ii. 102, 2: 2, 34; Lchdm. ii. 238, 30.

cernan; *p.* de; *pp.* ed [ceren *a churn*] *To churn;* agitare butyrum, Som. Ben. Lye.

cerr, es; *m. A turn, time;* versio, temporis spatium:—Æt ōđrum cerre *alio tempore*, Bt. 35, 2; Fox 156, 17. v. cyrr.

cerran; *p.* de; *pp.* ed *To turn, return;* verti, reverti:—On wōh cerde *turned to wrong, deviated;* deviavit, Cot. 61. Cer đē on bæcling *turn thee behind*, Cd. 228; Th. 308, 26; Sat. 698. Hió cerrende Criste hērdon *they returning obeyed Christ*, Ps. C. 50, 56; Ps. Grn. ii. 278, 56. Cerreþ on uprōdor leóht *light returns to the sky*, Bt. Met. Fox 29, 102; Met. 29, 50. v. cyrran.

cerrednes, -ness, e; *f.* [cerred, *pp. of* cerran; -nes] *A turning;* versio, Ben. Lye. DER. a-cerrednes. v. cyrrednes.

cerse, an; *f. Cress;* nasturtium, Herb. 21; Lchdm. i. 116, 17, MS. B: L. M. 1, 26; Lchdm. ii. 68, 4: 1, 31; Lchdm. ii. 74, 10: 128, 13: ii. 182, 15: 188, 8: ii. 340, 24. v. cærse.

Certes īg, e; *f.* CHERTSEY; Certesia:—Hēr [MS. hier] wurþan đa canonicas gedrifen ūt of ealdan mynstre fram Eádgāre cynge, and eác of niwan [MS. niwen] mynstre and of Certes īge, and of Mideltūne, and he sette đārto munecas and abbodas: to niwan [MS. niwen] mynstre Ægelgārum, to Certes īge Ordberhtum, to Mideltūne Cyneward *here the canons were driven out of the old monastery* [*at Winchester*] *by king Edgar, and also from the new monastery, and from Chertsey, and from Milton, and he placed thereto monks and abbots: Æthelgar to the new monastery, Ordberht to Chertsey,* [*and*] *Cyneward to Milton*, Chr. 964; Th. 223, 1–11. v. Ceortes īg.

Certices ōra, an; *m. Cerdic's shore;* Cerdĭci lītus:—On đone stede đe is gehāten Certices ōra *at the place which is called Cerdic's shore*, Chr. 495; Th. 25, 29, col. 1, 2: 514; Th. 27, 15, col. 1, 2. v. Cerdices ōra.

ceruille *chervil*, Lchdm. iii. 106, 19. v. cerfille.

cēs *chose, elected; p. of* ceósan.

cēse *a cheese*, L. In. 70; Th. i. 146, 19. v. cȳse.

cēse-lib *rennet* or *runnet;* coagulum, Som. Ben. Lye. v. cȳs-lib.

cesol *a cottage*, Glos. Epnl. Recd. 157, 8. v. ceosol.

cest, e; *f. A chest;* cibotium = κιβώτιον, cistella, loculus, Ælfc. Gl. 3; Som. 55, 64: Jn. Rush. War. 13, 29. v. cyst.

cester *a city*, Chr. 491; Erl. 14, 6. v. ceaster.

cete, an; *f. A cabin, cellar;* cella, Ælfc. Gl. 108; Som. 78, 99; Wrt. Voc. 58, 14. v. cote, cyte.

cetel, cetil, es; *m. A* KETTLE; căcăbus = κάκκăβος:—Cetil *cacabum*, Glos. Epnl. Recd. 155, 26. v. cytel.

cetel-hrūm, es; *m. Kettle-soot;* cacabi fuligo:—Genim cetelhrūm *take kettle-soot*, L. M. 1, 61; Lchdm. ii. 134, 2.

Cetrehta, an; *m. Catterick, near Richmond, Yorkshire;* Cataracta, oppidi nomen in agro Richmondensi:—Tūn, đe he oftust oneardode wel neáh Cetrehtan, gyt to-dæg mon his naman cneódeþ *cujus nomine vicus in quo maxime solebat habitare, juxta Cataractam, usque hodie, cognominatur*, Bd. 2, 20; S. 522, 24.

cewl *a basket*, Mt. Kmbl. Lind. 16, 9: Mk. Skt. Lind. 8, 8. v. cawl.

chor, es; *m? A dance, chorus, choir;* chŏrus = χορός:—Chor *chorus*, Wrt. Voc. 81, 21.

chor-gleów, es; *n.* [gleó, gleów *glee, joy, music*] *A musical dance, dance;* chorus = χορός:—Hērian hīg naman his on chorgleówe *laudent nomen ejus in choro*, Ps. Lamb. 149, 3: 150, 4.

cicel; *gen.* cicles; *m. A morsel, little mouthful, cake;* buccella, placenta:—Cicel *buccella*, Cot. 26: 126. Se cicel *the cake*, Lchdm. iii. 30, 21. Gemenged wiđ meolowe and to cicle abacen *mingled with meal and baked to a cake*, Med. ex Quadr. 9, 17; Lchdm. i. 364, 14. Bac hym ānne cicel *bake him a cake*, Lchdm. iii. 134, 20: L. M. 1, 46; Lchdm. ii. 114, 25: Lchdm. iii. 30, 19, 26: 96, 17.

CICEN, es; *pl. nom. acc.* cicenu; *gen.* a; *dat.* um; *n. A* CHICKEN; pullus:—Cicen *pullus*, Ælfc. Gl. 39; Som. 63, 49; Wrt. Voc. 30, 4: 281, 24. Cicen ođđe brid ođđe fola *pullus*, Wrt. Voc. 77, 37. Henne mid cicenum gesihþ ceápas eácan getācnaþ *a dream of a hen with chickens betokens trade to be increasing*, Lchdm. iii. 204, 31. Seó henn hyre cicenu under hyre fyđeru gegaderaþ *gallina congregat pullos suos sub alas*, Mt. Bos. 23, 37. Cicena mete *chickens' meat, chick-weed;* modera, alsȳne = ἁλσίνη, Ælfc. Gl. 44; Som. 64, 66; Wrt. Voc. 32, 3: 69, 27: 79, 39: L. M. 3, 8; Lchdm. ii. 312, 16: Lchdm. iii. 6, 14: 118, 29: 134, 1. [*Wyc.* chykenys, *pl: Piers P.* chicknes, *pl: Chauc.* chike: *Prompt.* chekyn: *Plat.* kiken, küken: *Dut.* kieken, kuiken, *n: Kil.* kiecken: *Ger.* küch-lein, *n: Dan.* kylling, *m.f: Swed.* kyckling, *m: Icel.* kjúk-lingr, *m: O. Nrs.* kyk-lingr, *m.* Rask Hald.]

cicene, an; *f. A* KITCHEN; coquina, culina:—Cicene [MS. cicen] *coquina* vel *culina*, Ælfc. Gl. 107; Som. 78, 77; Wrt. Voc. 57, 55. v. cycene.

cicle *to a cake*, Med. ex Quadr. 9, 17; Lchdm. i. 364, 14; *dat. of* cicel.

cīd, cȳd, es; *m? Strife, chiding, contention;* contentio, jurgium, rixa, Somn. 305. DER. ge-cīd.

CĪDAN, to cīdenne; *p.* cīdde, *pl.* cīddon, cīdon; *pp.* cīded, cīdd [cīd *strife, chiding*] *To* CHIDE, *rebuke, blame, contend, strive, quarrel, complain;* increpare, rixari, altercari, queri:—Cīdan on swefnum ceápes eácan getācnaþ *to chide in dreams betokens increase of trade*, Lchdm. iii. 208, 3: 204, 32. Rihtwīs cīdeþ me *justus increpabit me*, Ps. Spl. 140, 6. Cīdde him se Hǣlend *increpavit illum Jesus*, Lk. Bos. 4, 35: Mk. Bos. 1, 25: 8, 33: Homl. Th. i. 300, 24: ii. 44, 21. His leorningcnihtas cīddon him *discipuli ejus increpabant illos*, Lk. Bos. 18, 15. Cīde he wið God *let him blame God*, Homl. Th. i. 96, 1. Gif men cīdaþ *si rixati fuerint viri*, Ex. 21, 18. Begunnon hī to cīdenne *they begun to quarrel*, Homl. Th. ii. 158, 13. Ic cīde *altercor*, Ælfc. Gr. 25; Som. 27, 12. Ic cīde oððe ceorige *queror*, 29; Som. 33, 53. [*Wyc.* chide, chiden: *Piers P.* chiden: *Chauc.* chide: *Laym.* chiden: *Ger.* kiden, kyden *to sound.*] DER. ge-cīdan.

cīdde *told*, Gen. 9, 22, = cȳðde; *p. of* cȳðan.

CIDER, es; *m?* CIDER; vinum pomarium, Lye. [*Wyc.* sydur, sidir: *Dut.* cider, *f: Ger.* cider, *m: Fr.* cidre: *Span.* cidra: *It.* cidro, sidro.]

cīding, cȳdung, e; *f. A* CHIDING, *reproving, rebuke;* increpatio:—For his cīdinge *for his chiding*, Ors. 4, 12; Bos. 99, 8. Of cȳdunge ðīnre hī fleóþ *ab increpatione tua fugient*, Ps. Spl. T. 103, 8.

ciefes, e; *f. A concubine;* concubina, Ors. 6, 30; Bos. 126, 41. v. cyfes.

ciégan *to call, call upon, invoke*, Ps. Th. 52, 5: 74, 1. v. cīgan.

cīele, es; *m. Cold;* frigus:—For cīele nele se slāwa erian *propter frigus piger arare nonvult*, Past. 39, 2; Hat. MS. 53 a, 14, 16, 18. v. cīle.

cielf *a calf*, Ps. Spl. C. 105, 20. v. cealf.

ciellan; *pl. m. Vessels for drink, wooden tankards, leather bottles;* obbæ, Dial. 1, 5. v. cyll.

ciepe *an onion;* cæpe:—Genim ciepan *take an onion*, L. M. 1, 3; Lchdm. ii. 40, 6. v. cipe.

ciépe-mon *a merchant*, Som. Ben. Lye. v. ceáp-man.

cier, cierr, es; *m. A turn, time, business, affair;* versio, temporis spatium, negotium:—Æt ānum cierre *uno eodemque tempore*, Past. 61, 2. Mid ōðrum cierrum *with other affairs*, Past. 4, 1; Hat. MS. 9 b, 7. v. cyrr.

cierlisc *churlish, rustic*, L. In. 37; Th. i. 124, 20, 21. v. ceorlisc.

ciern, es; *n? Must* or *new wine boiled thick;* sapa, Cot. 170: 184. v. ceren.

CĪFAN? *p.* cāf, *pl.* cifon; *pp.* cifen *To quarrel;* litigare. [*Dut.* kijven *to quarrel: Ger.* keifen *to scold: Icel.* kīfa *to strive, quarrel.*] DER. cāf, cāf-līce, -scype; un-cāf-scipe: cāfer-tūn.

cifes *a harlot;* pellex, Alb. resp. 64: Cot. 150: 190. v. cyfes.

cifes-gemāna, an; *m. Fornication;* concubinātus:—We lǣraþ, ðæt man geswīce cifesgemānan [MS. cifesgemanna] *docemus, ut cessent concubinatus*, L. Edg. C. 21; Wilk. 84, 1.

CĪGAN, cīgean, cȳgan, cȳgean, ciégan, cēgan, cēgean; *part.* cīgende; *p.* de; *pp.* ed. I. *v. trans. To call, name, call upon, invoke, call together, summon;* vocare, nominare, invocare, convocare:—Drihten mæg steorran be naman cīgean ealle *the Lord can call all the stars by name*, Ps. Th. 146, 4. Ealle gewunedon hī mōder cȳgean *all were accustomed to call her mother*, Bd. 4, 23; S. 594, 39. Swā hine cīgþ Engle and Seaxe *as the Angles and Saxons call it*, Menol. Fox 366; Men. 184. Ðone [MS. þonne] niða bearn nemnaþ and cīgaþ Pentecostenes dæg *which children of men name and call the day of Pentecost*, Chr. 973; Erl. 124, 15; Edg. 7. He cīgde hungor ofer eorþan *vocavit famem super terram*, Ps. Spl. 104, 15. Ufan engla sum Abraham cȳgde *an angel from above called Abraham*, Cd. 141; Th. 176, 9; Gen. 2909. Ðū eart līðe eallum cīgendum ðē *tu es mitis omnibus invocantibus te*, Ps. Lamb. 85, 5: Ps. Spl. 146, 10. Swā hwylce daga ic ðē cīge, gehȳr me *in quacumque die invocavero te, exaudi me*, Ps. Th. 137, 4. Ðīnne naman we cīgaþ *nomen tuum invocabimus*, Ps. Lamb. 79, 19. Ðe cīgaþ naman his *qui invocant nomen ejus*, Ps. Spl. 98, 6. Abraham wordum God torhtum cīgde *Abraham called upon God with fervent words*, Cd. 86; Th. 108, 16; Gen. 1807: Ps. Th. 90, 15. God hīg ne cīgdon *Deum non invocaverunt*, Ps. Lamb. 52, 6: 78, 6: Ps. Spl. 98, 7. Us gehȳr swilce we ðē daga, Drihten, cīgen *hear us, O Lord, on whatever day we may call upon thee*, Ps. Ben. 19, 9: Ps. Grn. ii. 148, 19, 9. Moyses bebeád eorlas cīgean sweot sande neár *Moses bade his men summon the multitude near to the sand*, Cd. 154; Th. 191, 24; Exod. 219. II. *v. intrans. To cry, call;* clamare, vocare:—Abeles blōd to me cīgeþ *Abel's blood crieth to me*, Cd. 48; Th. 62, 12; Gen. 1013. Ic cīgde to Dryhtne *I called to the Lord*, Ps. Th. 117, 5. DER. a-cīgan, ge-.

cīgnis, niss, e; *f. A name, naming;* nomen, Som. Ben. Lye.

cilct; *part.* [cealc *chalk*] *Chalked;* calce illitus. DER. niw-cilct.

CILD; *gen.* cildes, *pl.* cild, *sometimes* cildru, cildra; *n. A* CHILD, *infant;* infans, puer:—Arīs and nim ðæt cild *surge et accipe puerum*, Mt. Bos. 2, 13, 14. Ðæt cild wixþ and gewurþ eft cnapa and eft syððan cniht *the child grows, and then becomes a boy, and afterwards a young man*, Hom. Sax. Þurh cildes hād *in the state of childhood*, Exon. 65 a; Th. 240, 15; Ph. 639. Eálā cild, hū eów līcaþ ðeós spæc *O pueri, quomodo vobis placet ista locutio?* Col. Monast. Th. 32, 7. Eálā ge cildra *O pueri*, 35, 33. Mid cilde beón, weorþan, or wesan *to be with child*, Bd. Whelc. 487, 22. [*Chauc. Laym. Orm.* child: *O. Sax. O. Frs.* kind, *n: Ger.* kind, *n: M. H. Ger.* kint, *n: O. H. Ger.* kind, kint, *n. proles: Goth.* kilþei, *f. fœtus: Icel.* kind, *f.*] DER. mōdor-cild, steóp-.

cilda hyrde, oððe lāreów, es; *m. A herder or teacher of children, schoolmaster;* pædagogus = παιδαγωγός, Ælfc. Gl. 80; Som. 72, 103; Wrt. Voc. 46, 60.

cilda mæsse-dæg, es; *m. Childermas [Innocents']-day;* festum innocentium:—Ðys Gōdspel sceal on cilda [MS. cylda] mæsse-dæg *this Gospel must be on Childermas [Innocents']-day, Dec. 28th*, Rubc. Mt. Bos. 2, 13–18; Notes, p. 574.

cilda trog, es; *m.* [cild, trog *a trough, cradle*] *A child's cot, cradle;* cunæ, arum, *pl. f.* Som. Ben. Lye.

cild-clāþ, es; *n. A child-cloth, a swaddling-cloth;* infantilis pannus:—Hine mid cildclāðum bewand *pannis eum involvit*, Lk. Bos. 2, 7.

cild-cradol, es; *m. A child's cradle;* cunabula, *pl.* Ælfc. Gr. 13; Som. 16, 23. On cildcradole *in a child's cradle*, Homl. Th. i. 82, 29.

cild-faru, e; *f. A carrying of children.* v. cyld-faru.

cild-fostre, -festre, an; *f. A child-fosterer, nurse;* nutrix:—Mōt he habban mid him his cildfostran [-festran, Roff.] *debet habere secum nutricem infantis sui*, L. In. 64; Wilk. 25, 4.

cild-geong; *adj. Young as a child;* infans, Andr. Kmbl. 1369; An. 685.

cild-hād, es; *m.* CHILDHOOD, *infancy;* infantia:—Of cildhāde *ab infantia*, Mk. Bos. 9, 21: Elen. Kmbl. 1826; El. 915.

cild-hama, an; *m. The womb;* matrix, uterus, Ælfc. Gl. 74; Som. 71, 57; Wrt. Voc. 44, 39.

cild-isc; *adj.* CHILDISH, *puerile;* puerilis:—Cildisc wesan *to be childish*, Cd. 106; Th. 139, 32; Gen. 2318. v. cild-līc.

cildiung-wīf, es; *n. A child-bearing woman;* puerpera, Wrt. Voc. 17, 17.

cild-līc, cildisc; *adj. Childish;* infantilis, puerilis:—Cildlīc *puerilis*, Ælfc. Gr. 5; Som. 5, 23: 9, 28; Som. 11, 38. For ðære cildlīcan yldo *propter infantilem ætatem*, Bd. 4, 8; S. 575, 28.

cildru *children*, Homl. Th. i. 80, 20; *acc. pl. of* cild.

cild-sung, e; *f. Childishness;* puerilitas, Som. Ben. Lye.

cīle, es; *m. A cold;* frigus:—Cīle wið hǣto *cold with heat*, Bt. Met. Fox 29, 101; Met. 29, 50: Gen. 8, 22. v. cȳle.

cilfer-lamb, cilfor-lamb, es; *n. A female lamb;* agna femina:—Bringe ān cilforlamb *offerat agnam*, Lev. 5, 6.

cīlian, ic cīlige; *p.* ode; *v. intrans. To be cold;* algere:—Ic cīlige *algeo*, Ælfc. Gr. 26, 3; Som. 28, 55. v. calan.

cilic, es; *m. Hair-cloth;* cilicium, Mt. Kmbl. Lind. 11, 21.

cille *a leather bag;* ascopera = ἀσκοπήρα, Wrt. Voc. 288, 37. v. cyll.

Cilt-ern, es; *n.* [ceald *cold*, ærn *place*] *The* CHILTERN, *high hills in Buckinghamshire and Oxfordshire;* montes quidam excelsi in agris Bucingamiensi et Oxoniensi:—Nāmon hī [Þurkilles here] ǣnne upgang ūt þuruh Ciltern, and swā to Oxena forda, and ða buruh forbærndon *they [Thorkell's army] took an upward course out through Chiltern, and so to Oxford, and burned that town*, Chr. 1009; Th. 262, 21, col. 1.

cim, cim-stanas; *pl. m. The bases of a pillar;* bases, Som. Ben. Lye.

cimbal, es; *m:* cimbala, an; *m. A cymbal;* cymbalum:—Cimbal *cymbalum*, Ælfc. Gl. 20; Wrt. Voc. 82, 17. Cimbalan oððe psalteras æt-hrīnan [MS. ætrīnan] saca hit getācnaþ *to touch cymbals or psalteries betokens a lawsuit*, Somn. 74; Lchdm. iii. 202, 14: Greg. Dial. 1, 9.

cimban? *p.* camb, *pl.* cumbon; *pp.* cumben *To join;* jungere. DER. camb; bannuc-camb, ñeðe-, wulfes-.

cimbing, e; *f. A joint, conjunction;* commissura, Som. Ben. Lye.

cime, es; *m. A coming*, Cd. 29; Th. 39, 1; Gen. 618. v. cyme.

cimþ *comes*, Ps. Th. 15, 11; *3rd pres. of* cuman.

CIN, cyn, e; *f. The* CHIN; mentum:—Cin *mentum*, Wrt. Voc. 71, 1. [*Chauc.* chinne: *Piers P.* chyn: *Laym.* chin: *O. Sax.* kinni, *n: O. Frs.* kin, ken: *Dut.* kin, *f: Ger. M. H. Ger.* kinn, *n: O. H. Ger.* kinni, *n: Goth.* kinnus, *f. the cheek: Dan.* kind, *m. f: Swed.* kind, *f: Icel.* kinn, *f: Lat.* gena: *Grk.* γένυς: *Sansk.* hanu, *m. f. the jaw.*] DER. cin-bān.

cin *a kind;* genus. v. cinn, cyn, cynn.

cīnan *a chink*, Bt. 35, 3; Fox 158, 28, note; *acc. of* cīne.

cīnan; *p.* cān, *pl.* cinon; *pp.* cinen *To gape, to break into chinks;* hiare, dehiscere, Som. Ben. Lye. DER. to-cīnan.

cin-bān, es; *n. The* CHIN-BONE; mandibula, mentum:—Cin-bān *man-*

dibula, Ælfc. Gl. 71; Som. 70, 81; Wrt. Voc. 43, 14. Cin-bān *mentum*, Text. Rof. 40, 1. Se ðe cin-bān forslæhþ, mid xx scillingum forgelde *let him who breaks the chin-bone pay for it with twenty shillings*, L. Ethb. 50; Th. i. 16, 1.

cin-berg, e; *f. That part of the helmet which protects the chin;* menti protectio:—Grīmhelm gespeón cining, cinberge *the king clasped his grim helmet, the protection of his chin*, Cd. 151; Th. 188, 28; Exod. 175.

cincg *a king*, Th. Diplm. A. D. 743–745; 28, 21. v. cyning.

cincung, e; *f. A loud* or *cackling laughter;* cachinnatio:—Ceahhetung, *vel* cincung *cachinnatio*, Ælfc. Gl. 88; Som. 74, 86.

cind *a kind, nature*. v. cynd.

cine, es; *m.* I. *a commander of four men*, or *a fourth part of an army;* quaternio:—Cine oððe feówer manna ealdor *quaternio*, Ælfc. Gr. 9, 3; Som. 8, 34. II. *a sheet of parchment folded into four parts, a quarto sheet;* quaternio:—Cine *quaternio*, Ælfc. Gl. 80; Som. 72, 108; Wrt. Voc. 46, 65: 75, 10. Bod on cine *a command in folded parchment;* diploma = δίπλωμα, Ælfc. Gl. 80; Som. 72, 110; Wrt. Voc. 46, 67.

CĪNE, cȳne, an; *f. A chink, fissure, vault;* rima, caverna:—Ic geseah āne lytle cȳnan [Cott. cīnan] *I saw a little chink*, Bt. 35, 3; Fox 158, 28. Cīnan *rimas*, Glos. Prudent. Recd. 149, 5. Cīnum *cavernis*, 148, 81. [*Wyc.* chyne: *Dut.* keen, *f.*]

cine-līc; *adj.* [cyn *fit, suitable*] *Of a like kind, agreeable, suitable, adequate;* congruus, competens:—Ðæt we wilnian to heom fultum be swā manegum mannum swā us cinelīc þince æt swā micelere spræce *that we desire aid from them of so many men as may seem to us adequate for so great a suit*, L. Ath. v. § 8, 3; Th. i. 236, 16.

cinen, cīnende *gaping; pp.* and *pres. part. of* cīnan.

cing *a king*, Deut. 11, 3: Chr. 894; Erl. 92, 17. v. cyning.

Cinges tūn, es; *m.* [cinges tūn *the king's town*] KINGSTON; regia villa:—Æðelstān wæs to cinge æt Cinges tūne gehālgod *Athelstan was consecrated king at Kingston*, Chr. 925; Th. 198, 7, col. 3; 8, col. 2: 979; Th. 234, 9, col. 1; 235, 6, col. 2. v. Cynges tūn.

cining *a king*, Cd. 151; Th. 188, 28. v. cyning.

cīn-līc *gaping*. v. cīne.

cinn, es; *n. A kind;* genus:—Fleógende cinn *flying kind;* volatile, Gen. 1, 20. Creópende cinn *creeping kind;* reptilia, 1, 24. Æfter his cinne *after its kind*, 1, 11. v. cyn, cynn.

cinnan, ic cinne, ðū cinnest, he cinneþ, cinniþ, *pl.* cinnaþ; *p.* ic, he can, ðū cunne, *pl.* cunnon; *pp.* cunnen *To generate, procreate;* generare, procreare:—Sorgum cinniþ *brings forth with sorrows*, Exon. 94 b; Th. 354, 28; Reim. 52. From this verb, the *p.* ic, he can are taken as a present tense. Hence it is called one of the twelve præterito-præsentia, enumerated under āgan. For cūðe the weak *p.* of cunnan, v. the *inf.* cunnan. DER. for-cinnan.

cin-tōþ, es; *m. A front tooth, grinder;* molaris, Prov. 30, Lye.

cīnu, e; *f. A chink, fissure;* rima, fissura:—Cīnu *rima* vel *fissura*, Wrt. Voc. 85, 18. Gemētte he ðæt fæt swā gehāl ðæt ðǣr nān cīnu on næs gesewen *he found the vessel so whole that there was no chink seen in it*, Homl. Th. ii. 154, 22. v. cīne, an; *f.*

ció *a chough, sort of crow;* cornicula, Wrt. Voc. 281, 2. v. ceó.

ciól, es; *m. A ship;* navis:—He lēt him behindan ciólas nigon and hundnigontig *he left behind him ninety-nine ships*, Bt. Met. Fox 26, 46; Met. 26, 23. v. ceól.

ciole, an; *f. The throat;* guttur:—Sting finger on ciolan *thrust a finger into the throat*, L. M. 1, 59; Lchdm. ii. 130, 5.

ciorian *to complain*, Ælfc. Gr. 29, MS. D; Som. 33, 52. v. ceorian.

ciorl *a rustic*, L. In. 40; Th. i. 126, 12, note 28. v. ceorl.

ciorlisc *churlish, rustic, common*, L. In. 18; Th. i. 114, 6, note 8. v. ceorlisc.

ciósan *to choose, accept*, Beo. Th. 4742; B. 2376. v. ceósan.

cīpan; *p.* cīpte, *pl.* cīpton, cīptun; *pp.* cīpt *To sell;* vendere:—Hīg cīptun *vendiderunt*, Gen. 47, 20. v. cȳpan.

cipe, ciepe, an; *f. An onion;* cæpa, allium cæpe, Lin:—Cipe *an onion*, L. M. 1, 39; Lchdm. ii. 102, 24. Genim garleac and cipan *take garlic and onion*, 1, 3; Lchdm. ii. 40, 15. Twā cipan oððe þreó gebrǣd on ahsan *roast two or three onions in ashes*, 1, 69; Lchdm. ii. 144, 14.

cipe-leac, es; *n. A leek;* cipus, Cot. 55.

cipp, es; *n? A coulter, ploughshare;* dentale:—Cipp *dentale*, Ælfc. Gl. 1; Som. 55, 7; Wrt. Voc. 15, 7.

Cippan-ham, -hamm, es; *m.* [*Hunt.* Cipenham: *Brom.* Chipenham] CHIPPENHAM, *Wilts;* villæ nomen in agro Wiltoniensi:—Hēr hine bestæl se here on midne winter ofer twelftan niht to Cippanhamme *in this year* [A. D. 878], *at mid-winter, after twelfth night, the army stole itself away to Chippenham*, Chr. 878; Erl. 79, 29. Hēr fōr se here to Cirenceastre of Cippanhamme, and sæt ðǣr ān geár *in this year* [A. D. 879] *the army went from Chippenham to Cirencester, and remained there one year*, Chr. 879; Erl. 80, 26; 81, 23.

cipresse, an; *f. The cypress-tree;* cupressus, Som. Ben. Lye. v. cypresse.

cīptun *bought*, Gen. 47, 20; *p. pl. of* cīpan. v. cȳpan.

cir *a turn, time:*—Æt ðam fiftan cire *at the fifth turn* or *time*, Lchdm. i. 214, 6, MS. B. note 8. v. cirr, cyrr.

circe, an; *f. A church;* ecclesia = ἐκκλησία:—Circe *ecclesia*, Ælfc. Gl. 107; Som. 78, 82; Wrt. Voc. 57, 58. We lǣraþ, ðæt man innan circan ǣnigne man ne birige *we enjoin that they do not bury any man within a church*, L. Edg. C. 29; Th. ii. 250, 15: Bd. 2, 7; S. 509, 5. v. cyrice.

Circe, Kirke, an; *f. Circe the sorceress;* Circe, es; *f.* = Κίρκη, ης; *f:*—Cyninges dōhtor sió Circe wæs *Circe was the king's daughter*, Bt. Met. Fox 26, 112; Met. 26, 56.

circe-weard, es; *m. A churchwarden;* ecclesiæ custos, Chr. 1131; Erl. 260, 12. v. cyric-weard.

circe-wīca, an; *m. A church-dwelling, sacristy;* sacrarium:—To ðe circewīcan *to the sacristy*, Chr. 1137; Erl. 263, 13.

circ-līc; *adj.* [circe *a church*] *Like a church, ecclesiastical;* ecclesiasticus:—Mid circlīcum þēnungum *with ecclesiastical services*, Wanl. Catal. 118, 4, col. 2. v. cyric-līc.

circ-nyt, -nytt, e; *f.* [nyt *duty, service*] *Church-duty* or *service;* ecclesiæ ministerium *vel* officium:—Sum cræft hafaþ circnytta fela *one has skill in many church-services*, Exon. 79 b; Th. 298, 27; Crä. 91.

circol-wyrde, es; *m. A calculator, reckoner;* computator:—Feówer sīðon syx byþ feówer and twentig: ða syx tīda sind genemned þurh ðæra circolwyrda gleáwnysse quadrantes *four times six are four-and-twenty: the six hours are called by the wisdom of calculators quadrants*, Bridf. 63.

circul, es; *m. A circle, the zodiac;* circulus, zodiacus = ζωδιακός:—Ðǣr ðæs emnihtes circul is geteald *where the circle of the equinox is reckoned*, Bd. de nat. rerum; Wrt. popl. science 4, 18; Lchdm. iii. 238, 23. Ætȳwdan feówer circulas onbūtan ðære sunnan *four circles appeared round the sun*, Chr. 1104; Erl. 239, 17. For ðam brādan circule ðe is *zodiacus* gehāten, under ðam circule yrnþ seó sunne *on account of the broad circle which is called* zodiacus, *under which circle the sun runs*, Bd. de nat. rerum; Wrt. popl. science 5, 20, 21; Lchdm. iii. 242, 2. Ðæt heó be-yrne ðone miclan circul zodiacum *that she runs through the great circle the zodiac*, Bd. de nat. rerum; Wrt. popl. science 7, 1; Lchdm. iii. 244, 21.

circul-ādl, e; *f. Circle-disease, the shingles;* zona, circīnus:—Lǣcedōmas wið ðære ādle ðe mon hǣt circulādl *leechdoms for the disease, which man calls the circle-disease* or *shingles*, L. M. Cont. 1, 36; Lchdm. ii. 8, 18: L. M. 1, 36; Lchdm. ii. 86, 5.

circul-cræft, es; *m. Circle-craft, the zodiac;* sphæræ cognitio:—Sceal on circule cræfte findan hālige dagas *shall by circle-craft* [or *the zodiac*] *find out holy days*, Menol. Fox 134; Men. 67.

cire-bald; *adj. Bold in decision;* arbitrii strenuus:—Ðā him cirebaldum Meotud mancynnes mōdhord onleác *then the Lord of mankind unlocked the treasure of words to him bold in decision*, Andr. Kmbl. 341; An. 171.

Ciren-ceaster, Cyren-ceaster, Cyrn-ceaster; *gen.* ceastre; *f.* [*Asser.* Cirrenceastre: *Hunt.* Cirecestre: *Brom.* Circestre] CIRENCESTER, *Cicester, Gloucestershire;* Cirencestria in agro Glocestriensi:—Hie genāmon iii ceastra, Gleawanceaster, and Cirenceaster [Cyrenceaster, col. 2, 3], and Baðanceaster *they took three cities, Gloucester, and Cirencester, and Bath*, Chr. 577; Th. 32, 41, col. 1. Æt Cirenceastre [Cyrenceastre, col, 2, 3] *at Cirencester*, 628; Th. 44, 13, col. 1. Hēr fōr se here to Cirenceastre [Cyrenceastre, col. 2, 3] of Cippanhamme, and sæt ðǣr ān geár *in this year* [A. D. 879] *the army went from Chippenham to Cirencester, and remained there one year*, 879; Th. 148, 38, col. 1: 880; Th. 150, 8, col. 1. Hēr, on Eastron, wæs micel gemōt æt Cyrenceastre *in this year* [A. D. 1020], *at Easter, there was a great council at Cirencester*, 1020; Th. 286, 12, col. 2. Him eóde on hand se cyning and ða burhware ðe wǣron on Cyrnceastre *the king came into his hands and the townspeople who were in Cirencester*, Ors. 5, 12; Bos. 110, 22.

ciric-belle, an; *f.* [cirice *a church*] *A church-bell;* ecclesiæ campana:—Of ciricbellan *from a church-bell*, L. M. 1, 63; Lchdm. ii. 136, 29.

ciric-bryce, cyric-bryce, es; *m.* [cirice *a church*, brice, bryce *a breaking, violation, breach*] *Church-breach, a breaking into a church;* in ecclesiam irruptio:—Be ciricbryce *of church-breach*, L. Ath. i. 5; Th. i. 202, 5, 6.

ciric-dōr, es; *n. A church-door;* ecclesiæ porta:—Se ðe man ofslehþ binnan ciricdōrum [MS. -derum] sylle ðære cirican cxx scillinga *let him who slays a man within church-doors give to the church* 120 *shillings*, L. Eth. vii. 13; Th. i. 332, 9.

cirice, an; *f. A church;* ecclesia = ἐκκλησία:—We lǣraþ, ðæt preóstas cirican healdan to godcundre þēnunge *we enjoin that priests keep their churches for divine service*, L. Edg. C. 26; Th. ii. 250, 3: 30; Th. ii. 250, 19. v. cyrice, circe.

ciric-friþ *church-peace*, L. Alf. pol. 2; Th. i. 62, 5. v. cyric-friþ.

ciric-fultum, es; *m.* [fultum *help, aid*] *Church-help, ecclesiastical support;* ecclesiæ auxilium:—We lǣraþ, ðæt preóstas geóguþe geornlīce lǣran ðæt hī ciricfultum habban *we enjoin that priests diligently teach youth that they may have ecclesiastical support*, L. Edg. C. 51; Th. ii. 254, 26.

ciric-griþ, cyric-griþ; es; *n. Church-peace, right of sanctuary;* ecclesiæ pax:—Stande ǽlc ciricgriþ [cyric- MS. A.] swá swá hit betst stód *let every church-peace stand as it has best stood*, L. Edg. i. 5; Th. i. 264, 25: L. E. G. 1; Th. i. 166, 20. Gif ǽnig man Godes ciricgriþ swá abrece, ðæt he binnon ciricwagum mannslaga weorþe, ðonne síg ðæt bótleás *if any man so break God's church-peace, that he be a homicide within church-walls, then let that be bootless*, L. C. E. 2; Th. i. 358, 22: 2; Th. i. 360, 4: L. Eth. vi. 14; Th. i. 318, 24: ix. 1; Th. i. 340, 1, 5.

ciriclec *ecclesiastical*, Chr. 716; Erl. 44, 19. v. cyriclíc.

ciric-mangung, e; *f. Church-mongering, the sale or purchase of ecclesiastical offices, simony;* sacrorum nundinatio:—Ǽnig man ciricmangunge ne macie *let no man commit simony*, L. Eth. v. 10; Th. i. 306, 28: vi. 15; Th. i. 318, 27.

ciric-mitta, an; *m.* [mitta *a measure, bushel*] *A church measure;* ecclesiastica mensura:—VI ciricmittan ealaþ *six church measures of ale*, Th. Diplm. A. D. 900; 144, 33.

ciric-ragu, e; *f. Church-lichen* or *moss;* ecclesiæ muscus, L. M. 1, 63; Lchdm. ii. 138, 1.

ciric-sceat, es; *m. Church-scot, church-money, tax* or *rate;* ecclesiæ census. v. cyric-sceat.

ciric-sócn, cyric-sócn, e; *f. Church-privilege;* ecclesiæ immunitas:—Be ciricsócnum *of church-privileges*, L. In. 5; Th. i. 104, 12.

ciric-þén, es; *m.* [þén *a servant, minister*] *A church-minister, clergyman;* ecclesiæ minister, clericus:—Ǽnig man ciricþén ne útige búton biscopes geþehte *let no man turn out a church-minister without the bishop's counsel*, L. Eth. v. 10; Th. i. 306, 29: vi. 15; Th. i. 318, 27.

ciric-þénung, e; *f.* [þénung *duty, service*] *Church-duty* or *service;* ecclesiæ ministerium:—We lǽraþ ðæt preóstas on ciricþénungum ealle án dreógan, and beón efenweorþe on geáres fæce on eallum ciricþénungum *we enjoin that priests in church-duties all perform service at the same time, and, in the space of a year, be like worthy in all church-duties*, L. Edg. C. 50; Th. ii. 254, 22–24.

ciric-tún, es; *m.* [tún *an inclosure*] *A church-inclosure, church-yard, cemetery;* ecclesiæ sepimentum, cœmetērium = κοιμητήριον:—Ne binnan cirictúne ǽnig hund ne cume *let not any dog come within the church-yard*, L. Edg. C. 26; Th. ii. 250, 7.

ciric-wæcce, an; *f. A church-watch* or *wake;* vigilia:—We lǽraþ ðæt man, æt ciricwæccan, swíðe gedreóh sí *we teach that a man, at the church-wakes, be very sober*, L. Edg. C. 28; Th. ii. 250, 12.

ciric-wag, es; *m. A church-wall;* ecclesiæ murus:—Se ðe ofslehþ man binnan ciricwagum biþ feorhscyldig *he who slays a man within church-walls is life-guilty*, L. Eth. viii. 13; Th. i. 332, 8: ix. 1; Th. i. 340, 5: L. C. E. 2; Th. i. 358, 23.

ciris-beám, es; *m. A* CHERRY-*tree;* cĕrăsus = κεράσος:—Cirisbeám *cerasus*, Wrt. Voc. 285, 44. Cirisbeám [MS. cisirbeam] *cerasus*, Glos. Epnl. Recd. 156, 19.

cirlisc *rustic*, Chr. 893; Erl. 88, 33. v. ceorlisc.

CIRM, cyrm, es; *m. A noise, shout, clamour, uproar;* strepitus, clamor, fragor, clangor:—Hlynn wearþ on ceastrum, cirm árleásra cwealmes on óre *din was in the cities, the clamour of the shameless at the point of death*, Cd. 119; Th. 153, 31; Gen. 2547. In the following references it is written cirm, Exon. 20 a; Th. 52, 19; Cri. 836: 22 b; Th. 62, 7; Cri. 998: 36 a; Th. 118, 5; Gú. 235: 38 a; Th. 125, 34; Gú. 364: 83 b; Th. 314, 26; Mód. 20: Andr. Kmbl. 82; An. 41: 2476; An. 1239. Cyrm, dyne *fragor*, Mone B. 4413. Cyrm *clangor*, Ælfc. Gr. 5; Som. 4, 40. Wæs on eorþan cyrm *a noise was on the earth*, Byrht. Th. 134, 61; By. 107: Andr. Kmbl. 2252; An. 1127. Hlúd herges cyrm *loud was the shout of the host*, Cd. 148; Th. 184, 14; Exod. 107. Ic gehýre synnigra cyrm swíðe hlúdne *I hear the uproar of sinners very loud*, 109; Th. 145, 17; Gen. 2407. Cyrmum *clangoribus*, Mone B. 6276. DER. here-cirm, wíg².

cirman, cyrman; *p.* de; *pp.* ed; *v. intrans.* [cirm *a noise, shout*] *To make a noise*, CHIRM, *cry out, shout;* strepere, clamare, exclamare:—Hí ongunnon cirman hlúde *they began to cry out aloud*, Judth. 12; Thw. 25, 20; Jud. 270. Ic hlúde cirme *I cry out aloud*, Exon. 103 a; Th. 390, 18; Rä. 9, 3. Ða hlúde cirmaþ *they loudly cry out*, 114 b; Th. 439, 4; Rä. 58, 4. He hlúde stefne ne cirmde *he did not cry out with a loud voice*, 113 a; Th. 432, 20; Rä. 49, 3. Swá wilde deór cirmdon *they cried out as wild beasts*, 46 a; Th. 156, 25; Gú. 880. Herewópa mǽst láðe cyrmdon *the enemies shouted the loudest of army-cries*, Cd. 166; Th. 207, 3; Exod. 461. [*Scot.* chirm: *Dut. Kil.* kermen: *Ger. M. H. Ger.* karmen *to wail.*]

Cirn-ceaster *Cirencester*, Chr. 628; Erl. 25, 14. v. Ciren-ceaster.

cirnel *a kernel*, Som. Ben. Lye. v. cyrnel.

cirpsian; *p.* ede; *pp.* ed *To crisp, curl;* crispare, Som. Ben. Lye. v. cyrpsian.

cirps-loccas *crisped* or *curled locks*, Som. Ben. Lye. v. crisp, cyrps.

cirr *a turn, business, affair;* versio, negotium:—Mid óðrum cirrum *with other affairs*, Past. 4, 1; Swt. 36, 23. v. cir, cyrr.

cirran; *p.* de; *pp.* ed *To turn;* vertere:—Him cirde to Þurferþ eorl *earl Thurferth turned to him*, Chr. 921; Erl. 107, 27: Invent. Crs. Recd. 1833; El. 915. v. cyrran.

cís; *adj. Choice, nice in eating;* fastidiosus in edendo:—Gyf hwá sý cís *if any one be choice*, Herb. 8, 2; Lchdm. i. 98, 15.

cisil *sand, gravel;* glarea, Glos. Epnl. Recd. 157, 12. v. ceosel.

cisil-stán *sand-stone*. v. ceósel-stán.

císnes, -ness, e; *f. Choiceness, niceness;* fastidium, curiositas, R. Ben. 39: L. M. 2, 1; Lchdm. ii. 174, 21. v. ceásnes.

Cisse-ceaster; *gen.* -ceastre; *f.* [*Flor.* Cissaceaster: *Sim. Dun.* Cissacestre] *Cissa's city*, CHICHESTER, *Sussex;* Cissæ castellum, Cicestria in agro Sussexiensi:—Hergodon hie upon Súþ-Seaxum neáh Cisseceastre *they harried on the South-Saxons near Chichester*, Chr. 895; Erl. 93, 27. To Cisseceastre *at Chichester*, L. Ath. i. 14; Th. i. 208, 3.

cist, e; *f. A band, company;* cohors:—On folcgetæl fíftig cista: hæfde cista gehwilc x hund tíreádigra *in the number of the people were fifty bands: each band had ten hundred illustrious warriors*, Cd. 154; Th. 192, 9–16; Exod. 229–232. DER. eóred-cist, here-.

cist *goodness, bounty*, Ælfc. T. 9, 1. v. cyst.

cist, e; *f. A chest;* cista, Wrt. Voc. 288, 31. v. cyst.

císt *chooses*, Deut. 28, 9; *3rd sing. pres. of* ceósan.

cisten-beám, es; *m. A chesnut-tree;* castanea = κάστανον:—Cistenbeám [MS. cistenbean] *castanea*, Wrt. Voc. 285, 46. v. cyst-beám.

cist-mǽlum *earnestly;* certatim, Som. Ben. Lye.

citel *a kettle*, Wrt. Voc. 288, 35. v. cytel.

CITELIAN; *p.* ode; *pp.* od *To tickle;* titillare, Ettm. [*Scot.* kittle; *Plat.* kiddeln, keddeln, kitteln, ketteln: *Dut.* kittelen, ketelen: *Ger.* kitzeln: *O. H. Ger.* kizilôn, kuzilôn: *Dan.* kildre: *Swed.* kittla: *Icel.* kitla.]

citelung, e; *f. A tickling;* titillatio:—Citelung [MS. kitelung] *titillatio*, Wrt. Voc. 289, 21.

CÍÞ, cýþ, es; *m.* I. *a young shoot of a herb* or *tree, a* CHIT, *sprout, germ, sprig, mote;* germen, festuca:—Swá dropan ofer gærsa cíþas *quasi stillæ super graminum germina*, Deut. 32, 2. Forhwí ǽlc sǽd to cíþum and wyrtrumum weorþe *why should every seed turn to germs and roots?* Bt. 34, 10; Fox 148, 32. On eallum cedrum cíþ alǽded [MS. cuþ, ciiþ = cíþ alæded] *the germ formed on all cedar trees*, Ps. Th. 148, 9. Eall eorþan cíþ *every shoot of the earth*, 103, 12. Se snáw bewríhþ wyrta cíþ *the snow covers the germ of herbs*, Salm. Kmbl. 605; Sal. 302. Seó eorþe cýþ mid hire cíþum, ðæt se tíma is geáres anginn *the earth makes known by her plants, that the time is the beginning of the year*, Homl. Th. i. 100, 16. Forst sceal lúcan eorþan cíþas *frost shall lock up the germs of the earth*, Exon. 90 a; Th. 338, 7; Gn. Ex. 75. Genim wegbrǽdan þrý cýþas *take three sprouts of plantain*, Herb. 2, 14; Lchdm. i. 84, 14. Ðú meaht gesión lytelne cíþ on ðínes bróður eágan *thou canst see a little mote in thy brother's eye*, Past. 33, 6; Cot. MS. 42 b, 32. Se smala cíþ *the small mote*, 33, 6; Hat. MS. 43 a, 2, 3. Cunna hwæðer ðú mǽge adón ðone cíþ of ðínes bróður eágan *try if thou canst remove the mote from thy brother's eye*, 33, 6; Hat. MS. 43 a, 6. II. *seed;* crementum:—Cýþ *crementum*, Glos. Brux. Recd. 38, 7; Wrt. Voc. 64, 16. Cíþ, *vel* weres sǽd *crementum*, vel *hominis semen* vel *crementum*, Ælfc. Gl. 74; Som. 71, 73; Wrt. Voc. 44, 55. [*O. Sax.* kíð, *m: O. H. Ger.* kídi, *n.*] DER. gærs-cíþ.

cíþ-fæst; *adj. Rooted, growing;* radicatus, crescens:—Se man ðe plantaþ treówa oððe wyrta he hí wæteraþ óþ-ðæt hí beóþ cíþfæste *the man who plants trees or herbs waters them until they are rooted*, Homl. Th. i. 304, 26.

citil *a kettle*, Som. Ben. Lye. v. cytel.

CLÁ, cleó, clawu; *gen. dat. acc.* clawe; *pl. nom. acc.* cleó, clawa, clawu, clawe; *gen.* clawena; *dat.* clám, clawum; *f. A nail*, CLAW, *hoof;* unguis, ungula:—Fénix fýres láfe clám biclyppeþ *the Phœnix seizes the relics of the fire with its claws*, Exon. 59 b; Th. 217, 8; Ph. 277. Nægl oððe clawu *unguis*, Ælfc. Gr. 9, 28; Som. 11, 46. Wurdon forþaborene ísene clawa *iron claws were brought forth*, Homl. Th. i. 424, 19. Sume wǽron mid ísenum clawum totorene *some were torn with iron claws*, Homl. Th. i. 542, 30. Hóf oððe clawu *ungula*, Wrt. Voc. 71, 66. Ðe clawe ne todǽlaþ *qui ungulam non dividunt*, Lev. 11, 4. Hearde cleó *hard hoofs*, Ps. Th. 68, 32. Hira clawe todǽlede beóþ *their hoofs are divided*, Lev. 11, 3. Gelícaþ Gode ofer cealf iungne forþbringende clawu [clawa, Spl.] *placebit Deo super vitulum novellum producentem ungulas*, Ps. Lamb. 68, 32. [*Wyc.* cle, clee *a hoof: Wrt. Gl. 12th cent.* p. 87, 26 clau *ungula: O. Sax.* clâuua, *f. a claw, hoof: Frs.* klauwe: *O. Frs.* klewe *a claw: Dut.* klaauw, *m: Ger.* klaue, *f. unguis, ungula: M. H. Ger.* klâ, *f: O. H. Ger.* klawa, kloa, *f. unguis, ungula: Dan.* klo, *m. f: Swed.* klo, *m: Icel.* kló, *f.*] DER. clawan, clawung, cleweða.

clæc-leás, clac-leás; *adj. Free;* immunis:—Clæcleás *immunis*, Cot. 104. Clacleás [clacles MS.] *free*, Hick. Thes. i. 149, 51, 57.

clæfer-wyrt, e; *f. Clover-wort, clover;* trifolium minus:—Nim ða smalan clæfer-wyrt nioðowearde *take the netherward part of the small clover-wort*, L. M. 1, 39; Lchdm. ii. 102, 26.

CLÆFRE, an; *n. f.* CLOVER; trifolium pratense:—Ðysse wyrte man crision and óðrum naman clæfre nemneþ *a man names this herb κίρσιον*, *and by another name clover*, Herb. 70; Lchdm. i. 172, 16. Clæfre *nom.* 172, 14. Hwīte clæfran wyrc clame *work white clover to a paste*, L. M. 1, 21; Lchdm. ii. 64, 4. Clæfre *calta* vel *trifillon*, Ælfc. Gl. 41; Som. 64, 3; Wrt. Voc. 31, 15. Nim reád clæfre *take red clover*, L. M. 3, 8; Lchdm. ii. 312, 20. Clæfran seáwes *of juice of clover*, 2, 24; Lchdm. ii. 214, 11. Nim clæfran wyrttruman *take roots of clover*, 2, 40; Lchdm. ii. 250, 12. [*Plat.* klever, klewer: *Dut.* klaver, *f*: *Ger.* klee, *m*: *M. H. Ger.* klē; *gen.* klēwes, *m*: *O. H. Ger.* klē, chlēo; *gen.* chlēwes: *Dan.* klöver, *n*: *Swed.* klöfver, *m.*]

CLǼG, es; *m?* CLAY; Samia terra, Ælfc. Gl. 56; Som. 67, 36; Wrt. Voc. 37, 26. [*Wyc.* cley: *Chauc.* clei: *Plat.* klei: *Frs.* klaey: *O. Frs.* klai: *Dut.* klei, *f*: *Kil.* kleye: *Ger.* klei, klai, *m*: *Dan.* kläg, kleg, *m. f. n*: *O. Nrs.* kleggi, *m. massa compacta*, Rask Hald. The fundamental idea is *slimy, tenacious.*]

clǽig; *def.* se clǽiga, clǽia; *adj.* CLAYEY; argillaceus:—On ðа clǽian lane, of ðære clǽian lane *to the clayey lane, from the clayey lane*, Cod. Dipl. 741; A. D. 1024; Kmbl. iv. 31, 8, 9.

Clǽig-hangra, an; *m.* [clǽig = clǽg *clay*] *Clay-hanger* or *Claybury, Essex*:—Eádmund cyning gegaderede fyrde and fērde to Lundene, eal be norþan Temese, and swā ūt þuruh Clǽighangran *king Edmund gathered a force and went to London, all north of the Thames, and so out through Clayhanger*, Chr. 1016; Erl. 156, 24.

CLǼMAN; *p.* de; *pp.* ed *To* CLAM, *smear, anoint*; linere:—Ic clæme *lino*, Ælfc. Gr. 28, 1; Som. 30, 35. Ðū wircst wununge binnan ðam arce and clæmst wiðinnan and wiðūtan mid tyrwan *mansiunculas in arca facies et bitumine linies intrinsecus et extrinsecus*, Gen. 6, 14. Clæm on ðone cancer *smear it on the cancer*, L. M. 1, 44; Lchdm. ii. 110, 4: 3, 45; Lchdm. ii. 336, 22. Clæme on ðæt geswel *smear it on the swelling*, Lchdm. iii. 38, 23. [*Wyc.* clemede *smeared*: *Kil.* kleemen: *O. H. Ger.* kleimjan, chleimen: *Icel.* kleima.] DER. ge-clǽman.

clæmende *hardening*; obfirmans, Cot. 145.

clæmming, e; *f. A blotting, daubing, smearing, hardening*; litura, oblimatio, Ælfc. Gr. 47, Som. Ben. Lye.

CLǼNE, clēne; *def.* se clǽna, seó, ðæt clǽne; *comp. m.* clǽnra, *f. n.* clǽnre; *sup.* clǽnest; *adj.* I. CLEAN, *pure, clear*; mundus, purus, merus, serenus:—Ðonne ān unclǽne gāst biþ adrifen of ðæm men, ðonne biþ ðæt hūs clǽne *when an unclean spirit is driven out of a man, then the house is clean*, Past. 39, 1; Hat. MS. 53 a, 8. Swā swā clǽne nȳten eodorcende in ðæt swēteste leóþ gehwyrfde *quasi mundum animal ruminando in carmen dulcissimum convertebat*, Bd. 4, 24; S. 598, 6: Homl. Th. i. 138, 20. Clǽne oflete, and clǽne wīn, and clǽne wæter *a pure oblation, and pure wine, and pure water*, L. Edg. C. 39; Th. ii. 252, 13. Wæs seó lyft swīðe clēne *the air was very clear*, Chr. 1110; Erl. 243, 1. Se clǽna ōþscūfeþ scearplīce *the pure* [*bird*] *flies quickly away*, Exon. 58 a; Th. 209, 8; Ph. 167. Ðæt land ic selle Cynulfe for syxtigum mancesa clǽnes goldes *I sell the land to Cynulf for sixty mancuses of pure gold*, Cod. Dipl. 313; A. D. 883; Kmbl. ii. 111, 21. Calic on handa Drihtnes wīnes [MS. win] clǽnes [MS. clænis] full is *calix in manu Domini vini meri plenus*, Ps. Spl. 74, 7. Forbærne hit man on clǽnum fīre *let a man burn it in a pure fire*, L. Edg. C. 38; Th. ii. 252, 8: Exon. 55 a; Th. 194, 11; Az. 137: Bt. Met. Fox 12, 9; Met. 12, 5. Clǽnre heortan *mundo corde*, Ps. Spl. 23, 4. Gebærnedne hlāf clǽnne seóþ on ealdum wīne *seethe the pure toasted bread in old wine*, L. M. 2, 2; Lchdm. ii. 180, 26. Cyning [MS. kynincg] sceal on Drihtne clǽne blisse habban *a king shall have pure bliss in the Lord*, Ps. Th. 62, 9. Ne acyr ðū fram ðīnum cnihte ðīn clǽne gesihþ *ne avertas faciem tuam a puero tuo*, 68, 17. Gewāt him se hālga sēcan ðone clǽnan hām *the holy one departed to seek the pure home*, Andr. Kmbl. 1956; An. 980. Hūslfatu Caldēas clǽne genāmon *the Chaldeans took the clean vessels of sacrifice*, Cd. 210; Th. 260, 10; Dan. 707. Clǽnum stefnum *with pure voices*, Elen. Kmbl. 1496; El. 750. God ðone ǽrestan ælda cynnes of ðære clǽnestan foldan geworhte *God made the first of the race of men from the purest earth*, Exon. 44 b; Th. 151, 12; Gū. 794. II. *chaste, innocent*; castus, innoxius:—Clǽne *castus*, Ælfc. Gl. 90; Som. 74, 121; Wrt. Voc. 51, 34. Clǽne [MS. cleane] oððe heofonlīc [MS. -lice] *cælebs*, Ælfc. Gr. 9, 49; Som. 13, 13. Ðū byst clǽne *absque peccato eris*, Deut. 23, 22: Chr. 1066; Erl. 198, 4; Edw. 23. Gif heó clǽne sȳ *if she be innocent*, L. Ath. v. § 1, 1; Th. i. 228, 17: L. Eth. iii. 7; Th. i. 296, 9. On hāligra clǽnre cyricean *in ecclesia sanctorum*, Ps. Th. 149, 1. Ic onfēng fǽmnan clǽne *I received a chaste damsel*, Exon. 10 b; Th. 12, 18; Cri. 187. Ðone clǽnan sacerd *the pure priest*, 9 b; Th. 9, 18; Cri. 136. Beón ða ōðre clǽne *let the others be innocent*, Gen. 44, 10. Sint spræcu Drihtnes spræcu clǽne *sunt eloquia Domini eloquia casta*, Ps. Lamb. 11, 7. Seó clǽneste cwēn *the most chaste woman*, Exon. 11 b; Th. 17, 26; Cri. 276. [*Piers P.* clene: *Laym.* clæne, clene, clane: *Orm.* clene: *Plat.* kleen *parvus*: *Frs.* klien *parvus*: *O. Frs.* klen *parvus*: *Dut.* kleen *little*: *Kil.* kleyn *exilis, minutus*: *Ger.* klein *parvus*: *M. H. Ger.* kleine *subtilis, parvus*: *O. H. Ger.* kleini *subtilis*: *Dan.* klein: *Swed.* klen *thin, slight*: *Icel.* klénn *snug, tiny.*] DER. hyge-clǽne, un-.

clǽne, clāne, clēne; *adv.* CLEAN, *entirely*; penitus, omnino:—Ne rīpe ge ðæt land tō clǽne *reap not the land too clean*, Lev. 23, 22: Ors. 4, 1; Bos. 76, 30: Bd. 3, 10; S. 534, 35. Clǽne biþ beorhtast nesta bǽle forgrunden *the brightest of nests is entirely destroyed by the fire*, Exon. 59 a; Th. 213, 18; Ph. 226: Ps. Th. 88, 37. Ðæt mīn cynn clǽne [MS. clane] gewīte *that my race be clean gone*, Cod. Dipl. 235; A. D. 835; Kmbl. i. 311, 16. Clēne *entirely*, Cd. 213; Th. 265, 14; Sat. 7.

clǽn-georn; *adj. Yearning after purity*; puritatis amans:—Clǽngeorn and cystig *yearning after purity and bountiful*, Exon. 128 a; Th. 492, 25; Rä. 81, 21. Ne māgon nā swilce men macian wununge ðam clǽngeornan Gode on clǽnre heortan *no such men can make a dwelling in a pure heart for a God desirous of purity*, Basil. admn. 7; Norm. 48, 19.

clǽn-heort; *def.* se clǽn-heorta; *adj. Clean-hearted, pure in heart*; mundo corde:—Eádige synd ða clǽnheortan, forðamðe hī God geseóþ *beati mundo corde, quoniam ipsi Deum videbunt*, Mt. Bos. 5, 8: Homl. Th. ii. 580, 33.

clǽn-līc; *adj. Pure,* CLEANLY; purus, mundus:—Mid clǽnlīcre lufe *with pure love*, Bt. 21; Fox 74, 38: Bt. Met. Fox 11, 183; Met. 11, 92.

clǽn-līce; *adv. Purely, cleanly*; purè, L. Ælf. C. 36; Th. ii. 360, 25.

clǽnnes, -ness, -niss, -nyss, e; *f.* CLEANNESS, *chastity, purity, modesty*; puritas, castimonia:—Clǽnnesse riht *castimoniæ jura*, Bd. 2, 5; S. 507, 1. Heó on clǽnnesse Gode þeówode *she served God in chastity*, 4, 9; S. 576, 21: L. Eth. v. 9; Th. i. 306, 20. Mid clǽnnesse *with purity*, L. Eth. v. 7; Th. i. 306, 15: vi. 4; Th. i. 316, 2: Ps. Th. 88, 37. Ðæt he healdan wille his clǽnnisse *that he will keep his chastity*, L. Eth. v. 6; Th. i. 306, 8. Þurh ða heálīcan clǽnnysse *through exalted purity*, Homl. Th. i. 346, 1: L. Edg. S. 1; Th. i. 272, 16: Ps. Spl. 17, 22, 26. DER. un-clǽnnes.

clǽnsend, es; *m.* [*part. of* clǽnsan = clǽnsian] *A cleanser*; purgator. DER. eár-clǽnsend.

clǽnsere, es; *m. A cleanser, purifier, priest*; purgator, Som. Ben. Lye.

clǽnsian, clēnsian, to clǽnsianne; *part.* clǽnsiende; *p.* ode, ade; *pp.* od, ad [clǽne *clean, pure*] *To* CLEANSE, *purify, chasten, clear oneself*; mundare, purgare, castigare, se liberare:—Gif man eard wille clǽnsian *if a man wishes to cleanse the land*, L. Eth. ix. 40; Th. i. 348, 25: L. C. S. 7; Th. i. 380, 7. Sió wamb biþ to clǽnsianne *the stomach is to be cleansed*, L. M. 2, 46; Lchdm. ii. 260, 12. Clǽnsie man ða þeóde *let a man cleanse the people*, L. E. G. 11; Th. i. 174, 2. Hī tiliaþ hī selfe to clǽnsianne mid ðȳ wōpe *they strive to purify themselves with mourning*, Past. 54; Hat. MS. Ðis wæter cristnaþ and clǽnsaþ cwicra menigo *this water cristeneth and purifieth a multitude of men*, Salm. Kmbl. 791; Sal. 395. Heó ða iungran lǽrde and clǽnsade ge mid hire lāre ge mid līfes bȳsne *she taught and purified the younger ones both by her doctrine and by the example of her life*, Bd. 4, 9; S. 576, 23. Clǽnsa me *munda me*, Ps. Spl. 18, 13. Clǽnsiende clǽnsode me Drihten *castigans castigavit me Dominus*, Ps. Spl. 117, 18. Gif he mid ða ādle clǽnsad beón sceolde *if he must be chastened by disease*, Bd. 4, 31; S. 610, 26. Gif hwā þeóf clǽnsian wylle *if any one will clear a thief*, L. Eth. iii. 7; Th. i. 296, 7. Preóst hine clǽnsie sylfes sōþe *let a priest clear himself by his own truth*, L. Wih. 18; Th. i. 40, 14, 16: 19; Th. i. 40, 17: 20; Th. i. 40, 19: L. Eth. ii. 8; Th. i. 288, 19: ii. 9; Th. i. 290, 10. Hine gerēfa clēnsie *let the reeve clear him*, L. Wih. 22; Th. i. 42, 4. [*Wyc. Piers P.* clense: *Orm.* clennsenn.] DER. a-clǽnsian, be-, ge-, un-: un-geclǽnsod.

clǽnsnian, clǽnsnigan; *p.* ode; *pp.* od *To cleanse, clear oneself*; se purgare:—Clǽnsnaþ [MS. clænsnoþ] he ðone *he clears him*, L. Eth. ii. 8; Th. i. 288, 20. Clǽnsnige hine sylfne *let him clear himself*, ii. 9; Th. i. 290, 11. Būton he frīnd hæbbe ðe hine clǽnsnian *unless he have friends who may clear him*, ii. 9; Th. i. 290, 13. v. clǽnsian.

clǽnsung, e; *f. A* CLEANSING, *purifying, chastening, expiation, chastity*; emundatio, purificatio, castigatio, expiatio, castitas:—Ðū towurpe hine fram clǽnsunge *destruxisti eum ab emundatione*, Ps. Lamb. 88, 45: Mk. Bos. 1, 44. Wæs Rōmāna gewuna ðæt hī clǽnsunge þweáles and bæþes sōhton *Romanorum usus fuit lavacri purificationem quærere*, Bd. 1, 27; S. 495, 15. Wæs he mid clǽnsunge forhæfednesse weorþ and mǽre *erat abstinentiæ castigatione insignis*, 4, 28; S. 606, 39. Biþ heó fremiende to his clǽnsunge *erit in expiationem ejus proficiens*, Lev. 1, 4. Ðe belumpon to ðære mynsterlīcan clǽnsunge *quæ monasticæ castitatis erant*, Bd. 5, 19; S. 637, 14. DER. ge-clǽnsung, mynster-, un-.

clæppettan; *p.* tte; *pp.* ted *To palpitate, have a palpitation*; palpitare:—Gif sino clæppette *if a sinew have palpitation*, L. M. 1, 26; Lchdm. ii. 68, 8. v. clappan.

clæppetung, e; *f. The pulse*; pulsus, Ælfc. Gl. 76; Som. 71, 109; Wrt. Voc. 45, 15. Ǽdra clæppetung *the pulse of the veins*, L. M. 2, 46; Lchdm. ii. 258, 16.

clǽsnian; *p.* ode; *pp.* od *To cleanse*; mundare, purgare:—Sceal mon clǽsnian ða yflan wǽtan *one must cleanse the evil humours*, L. M. 2, 30; Lchdm. ii. 228, 14, note 4: 2, 32; Lchdm. ii. 234, 25, note 2: 2, 35; Lchdm. ii. 240, 23, note 4: 2, 48; Lchdm. ii. 262, 17, note 2. v. clǽnsian.

clǽþ *a cloth*:—Dō on clǽþ *put on a cloth*, L. M. 2, 47; Lchdm. ii. 260, 28. v. clāþ.

clæweda *a clawing, scratching*, Past. 11, 6; MS. Oth. v. cleweda.

clâf, *pl.* clifon *clave, adhered; p. of* clîfan.

clam; *gen.* clammes; *m. n?* I. *what is clammy, mud, clay;* malagma, lutum:—Wyrc swâ to clame *so work to clam* [*a clammy substance*], Herb. 2, 11; Lchdm. i. 84, 3. Mid heardum weorcum clames *operibus duris luti*, Ex. 1, 14. II. *a bandage, what holds* or *retains, as a chain, net, fold, prison;* vinculum:—He đê clamme belegde *he loaded thee with a chain*, Andr. Kmbl. 2386; An. 1194. Of đǽm clammum *with those chains*, Bt. Met. Fox 1, 165; Met. 1, 83: Exon. 112 a; Th. 429, 30; Rä. 43, 12. Gebindan ǽrenum clammum *to bind with brazen bands*, Cd. 200; Th. 248, 28; Dan. 520: Beo. Th. 2675; B. 1335: 1931; B. 963. v. clom; *gen.* clommes.

clâm *with claws*, Exon. 59 b; Th. 217, 8; Ph. 277; *dat. of* clâ.

clamb, clomm, *pl.* clumbon *climbed; p. of* climan, climban.

clâne *clean, clear*, L. M. 2, 65; Lchdm. ii. 296, 6. v. clǽne.

clang *shrunk*, Andr. Kmbl. 2522; An. 1262; *p. of* clingan.

clappan *to* CLAP, *move, palpitate;* palpitare, Som. Ben. Lye.

CLÂTE, an; *f. The herb* CLOT-*bur, a bur that sticks to clothes, burdock, goose-grass, clivers;* philanthropos = φιλάνθρωπος, lappa, arctium lappa, galium aparine, Lin:—Đâs wyrte man *philanthropos* nemneþ, đæt ys on ûre geþeóde menlufigende, forđý heó wyle hrædlîce to đam men geclyfian: đa man eác ôđrum naman clâte nemneþ *this herb is called* philanthropos, *that is in our language men-loving, because it will readily cleave to a man: it is also named by another name clivers*, Herb. 174, 1; Lchdm. i. 306, 2-5: Ælfc. Gl. 40; Som. 63, 105; Wrt. Voc. 30, 53: 41; Som. 63, 108; Wrt. Voc. 30, 56: 66, 67. Clâte *lappa*, Wrt. Voc. 67, 75: 79, 41: Ælfc. Gl. 40; Som. 63, 91; Wrt. Voc. 30, 41. Wiđ ceolan swile clâtan wyl on ealaþ *for swelling of throat boil burdock in ale*, L. M. 1, 12; Lchdm. ii. 56, 3: 1, 45; Lchdm. ii. 110, 13: 2, 53; Lchdm. ii. 274, 3. Nim đa smalan clâtan *take the small burdock*, 1, 39; Lchdm. ii. 100, 23. Genim doccan ođđe clâtan, đa đe swimman wolde *take dock or clote, such as would swim*, 1, 50; Lchdm. ii. 122, 22. [*Wyc.* clote, cloote: *Chauc.* clote-lefe *a leaf of the clot-bur: Ger. M. H. Ger.* klette, *f: O. H. Ger.* kletta, kledda, *f.*]

CLÂÞ; *gen.* clâđes; *m.* CLOTH; pannus: in the plural, *clothes;* vestimenta:—Ne dêþ nân man niwes clâđes scyp on eald reáf *nemo immittit commissuram panni rudis in vestimentum vetus*, Mt. Bos. 9, 16. Heó đa moldan on clâđe bewand *she wound the mould in a cloth*, Bd. 3, 11; S. 536, 8. Dô on clâþ *put on a cloth*, L. M. 2, 2; Lchdm. ii. 180, 5, 10, 28: 2, 47; Lchdm. ii. 262, 2. Awring þurh clâþ *wring through a cloth*, 2, 53; Lchdm. ii. 274, 7. Hîg bewundon hine mid lînenum clâđe *ligaverunt illud linteis*, Jn. Bos. 19, 40. Đæt is heora bîwist; wǽpnu, and mete, and ealo, and clâđas *this is their provision; weapons, and meat, and ale and clothes*, Bt. 17; Fox 60, 5. Him wyrþ oftohen đara clâđa *he is deprived of the clothes*, 37, 1; Fox 186, 14: Bt. Met. Fox 25, 46; Met. 25, 23. Of đînum clâđum *a vestimentis tuis*, Ps. Th. 44, 10: Exon. 18 b; Th. 45, 27; Cri. 725: 28 b; Th. 87, 12; Cri. 1424. Ruben tær his clâđas *Reuben tore his clothes*, Gen. 37, 29: Bt. 37, 1; Fox 186, 10. [*R. Glouc.* cloth: *Laym.* clađe, clođ, claed: *Orm.* claþ: *Scot.* claith, clayth: *Plat.* kleed: *Frs.* klaed: *O. Frs.* klath, klad, kleth, *n: Dut. Kil.* kleed, *n: Ger.* kleid, *n: M. H. Ger.* kleit, *n: Dan. Swed.* kläde, *n: Icel.* klæđi, *n.*] DER. bearm-clâþ, cild-, feax-, heáfod-, sâr-, swât-.

clâþ-scear *a pair of shears.* v. scear IV.

clatrung, e; *f. Anything that makes a clattering, a drum, rattle;* crepitaculum, Cot. 51.

clauster; *gen.* claustres; *n. An inclosed place, a cloister;* claustrum:—Eálâ ge cildra, gâþ ût, bûtan hygeleáste, to claustre, ođđe to leorninge *O vos pueri, egredimini, sine scurrilitate, in claustrum, vel in gymnasium*, Coll. Monast. Th. 36, 9. Fæsten *vel* clauster *claustrum*, Ælfc. Gl. 109; Som. 79, 15; Wrt. Voc. 58, 56. v. clûstor.

clawan, ic clawe; *p.* ede; *pp.* ed [clâ *a nail, claw*] *To* CLAW; scalpere:—Ic clawe *scalpo*, Ælfc. Gr. 28, 4; Som. 31, 20. [*Dut.* klaauwen: *Ger.* klauen: *O. H. Ger.* klawjan: *Dan.* klöe: *Swed.* klå: *Icel.* klá *to scratch*, klóask *to fight with claws.*]

clawu *a nail, claw, hoof*, Ælfc. Gr. 9, 28; Som. 11, 46; Wrt. Voc. 71, 66. v. clâ.

clawung, e; *f.* [clâ *a claw*] *A pain, the gripes;* tormina:—Lǽcedômas wiđ clawunga *leechdoms for the gripes*, L. M. cont. 2, 32; Lchdm. ii. 164, 16: 2, 32; Lchdm. ii. 236, 1.

cleacian; *p.* ode; *pp.* od *To go nimbly, hurry;* festinare, trepidare:—He cleacode swîđe earhlîce to porte *he hurried very timidly to town;* in via totus trepidabat, M. H. 115 a.

cleadur *a clatter, drum, rattle;* crepitaculum, Som. Ben. Lye.

cleáf, *pl.* clufon *clove, separated; p. of* cleófan.

cleáfa, an; *m. A cellar;* cellarium:—Hwâ gefylþ cleáfan his *quis replet cellaria sua?* Coll. Monast. Th. 28, 17. v. cleófa.

Clede-mûþa, an; *m.* [*the mouth of the river Cleddy*] GLADMOUTH, CLEDMOUTH, *South Wales:*—Hêr Eádweard cyning getimbrede đa burh æt Cledemûþan *in A. D. 921, king Edward built the burgh at Cledmouth*, Chr. 921; Th. 194, 1-3, col. 3; Th. 195, 1-3, col. 1.

clemman; *p.* de; *pp.* ed [clam II. *a chain*] *To fetter, bind, inclose;* vincire, includere. DER. be-clemman.

clencan; *p.* te; *pp.* ed *To* CLINCH, *hold fast;* prehendere, prensare. v. be-clencan, *Supl.*

clêne *clean, pure, clear*, Ps. C. 50, 88; Ps. Grn. ii. 278, 88: Chr. 1110; Erl. 243, 1. v. clǽne; *adj.*

clêne *cleanly, entirely;* penitus:—Deópne ymblyt clêne ymbhaldeþ meotod *the Lord entirely upholdeth the deep expanse*, Cd. 213; Th. 265, 14. v. clǽne; *adv.*

clengan; *p.* de; *pp.* ed *To exhilarate;* exhilarare:—Dreám clengeþ *joy exhilarates*, Exon. 107 b; Th. 411, 6; Rä. 29, 8.

clênsian *to cleanse, clear oneself*, L. Wih. 22; Th. i. 42, 4. v. clǽnsian.

cleó *a claw, hoof*, Ps. Th. 68, 32. v. clâ.

cleof *a cliff, rock*, Exon. 101 b; Th. 384, 15; Rä. 4, 28. v. clif.

cleófa, cleáfa, cliófa, an; *m. That which is cloven, a cleft, chasm, den, cell, chamber;* cubîle, cellarium, cubiculum:—On heora cleófum ođđe holum hîg beóþ gelogode *in cubilibus suis collocabuntur*, Ps. Lamb. 103, 22. Unriht he byþ smeágende on his cliófan *iniquitatem meditatus est in cubîli suo*, Ps. Th. 35, 3. Sinewealt cleófa *vel* portic *absida*, Ælfc. Gl. 108; Som. 78, 122; Wrt. Voc. 58, 34. Đeós sweoster wæs ûtgangende of hire cleófan *hæc soror egressa est de cubiculo*, Bd. 4, 9; S. 576, 31. DER. clûstor-cleófa, ferhþ-, hord-, in-, nýd-. v. clýfa.

CLEÓFAN, ic cleófe, đû clýfst, he clýfþ, *pl.* cleófaþ; *p.* cleáf, *pl.* clufon; *pp.* clofen *To* CLEAVE, *separate, split;* findere, dissecare:—Cleófan *secare*, Glos. Prudent. Recd. 149, 54: *scindere*, 150, 9. Bordweall clufon aforan Eádweardes *Edward's sons clove the board-wall*, Chr. 937; Th. 200, 38, col. 3; Æđelst. 5. Clufon, Byrht. Th. 140, 4; By. 283. [*Piers P.* cleven: *Chauc.* cloven, *pp: Orm.* clofenn, *pp: Plat.* klöwen, klöven: *O. Sax.* kliođan: *Dut.* klieven, klooven: *Ger.* klieben: *M. H. Ger.* kliuben, klieben: *O. H. Ger.* kliuban: *Dan.* klöve: *Swed.* klyfva: *Icel.* kljúfa.] DER. to-cleófan: cleófa, cleáfa, clýfa, clîfa, bed-, clûstor-, ferhþ-, gebed-, hord-, in-, nýd-.

Cleofes hoo *Cliff, near Rochester*, Chr. 822; Th. 110, 14, col. 3. v. Clofes hoo.

cleofian, he cleofaþ, *pl.* cleofiaþ; *p.* ode; *pp.* od *To cleave, adhere, stick;* adhærere:—Đa đe him on cleófiaþ *those who cleave to him*, Exon. 97 b; Th. 364, 20; Wal. 73. v. clifian.

cleopian; *p.* ode; *pp.* od *To cry, call;* clamare:—Ic nû wille geornlîce to Gode cleopian *I will now earnestly call upon God*, Bt. 3, 4; Fox 6, 28: Andr. Kmbl. 2796; An. 1400. Ic cleopode to đê *clamavi ad te*, Ps. Th. 118, 146, 147. v. clypian.

cleopigend, cleopend, es; *m. A vowel;* vocalis, Som. Ben. Lye.

cleopung, e; *f. A cry;* clamor, Mt. Rush. Stv. 25, 6. v. clypung.

cleót *a clout*, Som. Ben. Lye. v. clût.

cleóđa, an; *m. A plaster, salve, poultice;* malagma:—Đone hâlwendan cleóđan *malagma*, Mone B. 2976. v. clîđa.

cleowen *a clew, ball of thread* or *yarn, ball*, Ælfc. Gl. 111; Som. 79, 68; Wrt. Voc. 59, 37: Exon. 59 a; Th. 213, 17; Ph. 226. v. cliwen.

clepian; *p.* ode; *pp.* od *To cry, call;* clamare, vocare:—Ic clepode forđanđe đû gehýrdest me eálâ đû God *ego clamavi quoniam exaudisti me Deus*, Ps. Lamb. 16, 6. v. clypian.

clepung, e; *f. A calling;* vocatio, clamor:—Se nân clepunge đǽrto nâ hafde mâre *he had not any more calling thereto*, Chr. 1129; Erl. 258, 9. Clepung mîn on ansýne ođđe on gesihþe his ineóde to his eárum *clamor meus in conspectu ejus introivit in aures ejus*, Ps. Lamb. 17, 7. v. clypung.

clerc, cleric, clerec, es; *m.* [*Lat.* clericus = κληρικός *belonging to the clergy, clerical*] *A* CLERK, *clergyman, generally a deacon* or *priest;* clericus:—Gregorius wæs clerc *Gregory was a priest*, Chr. 1129; Erl. 258, 25: 1123; Erl. 250, 20. He drâf ût đa clerca of đe biscoprîce *he drove the clergy out of the bishopric*, 963; Erl. 121, 13. Preóst ođđe cleric *clericus*, Wrt. Voc. 71, 77. We lǽraþ đæt preósta gehwilc to sinoþe hæbbe his cleric *we enjoin that every priest at a synod have his deacon*, L. Edg. C. 4; Th. ii. 244, 14. Hî wǽron ealle đæs cynges clerecas *they were all the king's clergy*, Chr. 1085; Erl. 218, 22.

clerc-hâd, cleric-hâd, cleroc-hâd, es; *m. The clerical office, priesthood;* sacerdotium, clericatus:—Clerchâdes man *a man of the clerical order*, Chr. 1123; Erl. 250, 11. Clerichâd *clericatus*, C. R. Ben. 60. Clerochâd *clericatus*, Cot. 45.

cleweda, clæweda, an; *m. A clawing, scratching;* scalpturigo, scalpurigo:—Se giecþa [gicþa MS. Cot.] biþ swîđe unsâr, and se cleweda [MS. Oth. clæweda] biþ swîđe rôw, and đeáh-hwæđere gif him mon tô longe fylgþ, he wundaþ, and wund sâraþ *the itch is very free from pain, and the scratching is very comfortable, and yet if it be kept up too long, it produces a wound, and the wound is painful*, Past. 11, 6; Hat. MS. 15 b, 23. DER. clawu, clâ *a nail, claw.*

CLIBBOR; *adj.* [clifian *to cleave, adhere*] *Sticky, adhesive;* tenax:—Weá biþ wundrum clibbor *grief is wonderfully adhesive*, Menol. Fox 485; Gn. C. 13. [*M. H. Ger.* klëber: *O. H. Ger.* klebar *adhesive.*]

cliewe *a clew*, Som. Ben. Lye. v. clywe.

CLIF, clyf, cleof, es; *n. A* CLIFF, *rock, steep descent, promontory;*

clivus, rupes, promontorium:—Ða Iudēi lǣddon Crist to ānum clife, and woldon hine niðerascūfan *the Jews led Christ to a cliff, and would cast him down*, Homl. Th. ii. 236, 33. Æt Eádwines clife *at Edwin's cliff*, Chr. 761; Th. 89, 24, col. 1. Ðæt hī ne hlipen on ðæt scorene clif *that they leap not down the abrupt cliff*, Past. 33, 1; Hat. MS. 41 a, 9. Be clifum *on the cliffs*, Exon. 81 b; Th. 306, 15; Seef. 8. Ðæt hie Geáta clifu ongitan meahton *that they might perceive the cliffs of the Gauts*, Beo. Th. 3826; B. 1911. Ofer cald cleofu *over the cold cliffs*, Andr. Kmbl. 619; An. 310: Exon. 101 b; Th. 384, 15; Rä. 4, 28. Ðū hluttor lǣtest wæter of clife clǣnum *thou lettest forth clear waters from the pure rock*, Exon. 55 a; Th. 194, 11; Az. 137: Bt. Met. Fox 5, 25; Met. 5, 13. Se ðe gecyrde clyf on wyllan wætera *qui convertit rupem in fontes aquarum*, Ps. Spl. M. C. 113, 8. God clifu cyrreþ on wæteres wellan *God turneth rocks into wells of water*, Ps. Th. 113, 8. Clif *promontorium*, Ælfc. Gl. 67; Som. 69, 117; Wrt. Voc. 41, 67. Nīlus seó eá, hyre ǣwylme, is neáh ðæm clife ðære Reádan Sǣs *the spring of the river Nile is near the promontory of the Red Sea*, Ors. 1, 1; Bos. 17, 19, 29. [*O. Sax.* klif, *n. a rock*: *Dut.* klip, *f. a rock, cliff*: *Kil.* kleppe, klippe *rupes, petra*: *Ger.* klippe, *f. rupes*: *O. H. Ger.* clep *promontorium*: *Dan.* klippe, *m. f. a rock, cliff*: *Swed.* klippa, *f*: *Icel.* klif, *n. a cliff*] DER. brim-clif, ēg-, heáh-, holm-, stān-, weal-.

clīfa, an; *m. A den, cave*; cubile, spelunca, Bd. 3, 23; S. 554, 22. v. clȳfa.

CLĪFAN, ic clīfe, ðū clīfest, clīfst, he clīfeþ, clīfþ, *pl.* clīfaþ; *p.* clāf, *pl.* clifon; *pp.* clifen *To* CLEAVE, *adhere*; adhærere. [*Piers P.* clyven: *Plat.* kleeven: *O. Sax.* bi-klīƀan: *Frs.* be-klieuwen: *O. Frs.* bi-kliva: *M. H. Ger.* klīben: *O. H. Ger.* klīban: *Dan.* kläbe: *Swed.* klibba.] DER. ōþ-clīfan; clifian, cleofian, cliofian.

clife, an; *f.* I. *the greater burdock*; arctium lappa:—Dō clifan *use burdock*, L. M. 1, 67; Lchdm. ii. 142, 16. II. *the small burdock*:—Seó smæle clife *the small burdock*, CLIVERS; galium aparine, L. M. 1, 50; Lchdm. ii. 124, 2. DER. gar-clife.

clifer; *gen.* clifres; *m. A claw, talon*; ungula:—Clifras [MS. cifras] *ungulas*, Glos. Prudent. Recd. 150, 37. Clifra *ungularum*, 149, 7. DER. clifrian.

clif-hlēp, clif-hlȳp *right down, under foot*; pessum, Cot. 155, Som. Ben. Lye.

clifian, cleofian, cliofian, clyfian; *p.* ode; *pp.* od *To cleave, adhere*; adhærere:—Hī willaþ clifian on ðǣm monnum *they will cleave to the men*, Bt. 16, 3; Fox 54, 19. Woldon hī on ðam clifian *they would cleave to him*, 16, 3; Fox 56, 10: L. M. 1, 2; Lchdm. ii. 38, 20. His flǣsces lima clifaþ ǣlc on ōðrum *each of the limbs of his flesh cleaves to another*, Past. 47; Hat. MS. Ðīn tunge clifaþ to ðīnum goman *thy tongue cleaveth to thy gums*, Homl. Th. ii. 530, 28. To ðære lifre clifiaþ *adhærent jecori*, Lev. 1, 8. Ðæt dust, ðæt of eówre ceastre on ūrum fōtum clifode, we drīgeaþ on eów *pulverem, qui adhæsit nobis de civitate vestra, extergimus in vos*, Lk. Bos. 10, 11. [*Wyc.* cleuyde *cleaved*: *Laym.* cleouieþ *cleaveth*: *O. Sax.* kliƀōn: *Dut.* kleeven: *Ger.* kleben, kleiben: *O. H. Ger.* klebēn, klebjan.] DER. æt-clifian, ge-, on-, to-, to-ge-.

clifig, clifiht; *adj.* CLIFFY, *steep*; clivosus, Ælfc. Gl. 9; Som. 56, 120; Wrt. Voc. 19, 4: Cot. 34: 209.

clifon *cleaved, adhered*; adhæserunt; *p. pl. of* clīfan.

clifrian, ic clifrige; *p.* ode; *pp.* od [clifer *a claw*] *To claw, scratch*; scabere:—Ic clifrige *scabo*, Ælfc. Gr. 28, 6; Som. 32, 25. DER. to-clifrian.

clif-stān, es; *m. A rough stone, rock*; cautes:—Clifstānas *cautes*, Cot. 44.

clif-wyrt, e; *f. Maiden-hair, water-wort, fox-glove*; agrimonia:—Clifwyrt, sume men hataþ foxes clife, sume eá-wyrt *cliff-wort, some men call fox-glove, some water-wort*, L. M. 1, 15; Lchdm. ii. 58, 3.

climan, ðū climst, he climþ; *p.* clomm *to climb*. v. climban and ofer-clomm.

CLIMBAN, ic climbe, ðū climst, he climþ, *pl.* climbaþ; *p.* clamb, *pl.* clumbon; *pp.* clumben; *v. a. To* CLIMB; scandere, ascendere:—Clumbon [MS. Clumben] upp to ðe stēpel *climbed up to the steeple*, Chr. 1070; Erl. 209, 9. Clumbon [MS. Clumben] upp to ðe hālge rōde *climbed up to the holy cross*, Erl. 209, 6. [*Laym.* climben *to climb*, he climbeth; *p.* cluombe, *pl.* clumben; *pp.* iclumben: *Orm.* climbenn *to climb*: *Dut.* klimmen *scandere*: *O. H. Ger.* klimban: *M. H. Ger.* klimmen, klam, klummen, geklummen; *Sansk.* kram *incedere, ascendere.*] DER. ofer-climan, ofer-climban; climan, clymmian.

climmian *to climb*. v. clymmian, climan, climban.

climst, he climþ *climbest, climbs*; *2nd and 3rd pers. pres. of* climan, climban.

CLINGAN, ic clinge, ðū clingst, he clingþ, *pl.* clingaþ; *p.* clang, *pl.* clungon; *pp.* clungen, geclungen. I. *to wither, pine, to* CLING [*in this sense, rarely used in English*] or *shrink up*; se contrahere, marcescere:—Clang wæteres þrym ofer eāstreámas: is brycgade blǣce brimrāde *the glory of water shrank over river streams: ice bridged a pale water-road*, Andr. Kmbl. 2522; An. 1262. Ic clinge *marcesco*, Ælfc. Gr. 35; Som. 38, 7. [*Piers P.* clyngen *to shrink, wither, pine.*] v. for-clingan, ge-clungen. II. *to* CLING, *stick close*; circumcludere, includere. v. be-clingan.

cliof *a cliff, rock, pointed rock, crag*; cautes, Cot. 30. v. clif.

cliófa *a den, chamber*, Ps. Th. 35, 3. v. cleófa.

cliofian, he cliofaþ, *pl.* cliofiaþ; *p.* ode; *pp.* od *To cleave*; adhærere:—Hī willaþ cliofian on ðǣm monnum *they will cleave to the men*, Bt. 16, 3; Fox 54, 19, note 9. v. clifian.

cliofung, e; *f. A* CLEAVING; sectio:—Cliofung *sectio*, Ælfc. Gl. 62; Som. 68, 83; Wrt. Voc. 39, 66.

cliopian; *part.* cliopende; *p.* ode; *pp.* od *To cry, call*; clamare:—Se Hǣland ongann cliopian [MS. cliopia] *the Saviour began to cry*, Mk. Skt. Lind. 10, 47. Cliopende, 9, 36: 15, 39: Mt. Kmbl. Lind. 14, 26. v. clypian, clipian.

cliowen *a clew, ball*, Mone B. 1662. v. cliwen.

clipian, clipigan, *pl.* clipiaþ; *p.* ode; *pp.* od *To make a vocal sound, call, address, invoke*; vocare, alloqui:—We clipiaþ to ǣlcum þinge *we address everything*, Ælfc. Gr. 7; Som. 6, 25. v. clypian, clipigendlīc.

clipigendlīc; *adj.* I. *calling, vocative*; vocativus:—Vocativus is clipigendlīc oððe gecīgendlīc: mid ðam casu we clipiaþ to ǣlcum þinge, Eálā ðū man cum hider *O! homo veni huc*: Eálā ðū man sprec to me *O! homo loquere ad me*: Eálā ðū lāreów tǣce me sum þing *O! magister doce me aliquid*: *vocative is calling or invoking*: *with this case we address everything, as—O! thou man come hither*: *O! thou man speak to me*: *O! thou master teach me something*, Ælfc. Gr. 7; Som. 6, 24–27. II. *making a vocal sound*; vocalis. v. clypiendlīc, clypigendlīc.

clipur, es; *m. A* CLAPPER *of a bell*; tintinnabuli *vel* campanæ malleus:—Se bend ðe se clipur ys mid gewriðen, ys swylce hyt sȳ sum gemetegung ðæt ðære tungan clipur mǣge styrian, and ða lippan æt-hwega beátan. Sōþlīce mid ðæs rāpes æt-hrīne se bend styraþ ðone [MS. ðæne] clipur *the band with which the clapper is tied, is as it were a method for moving the clapper of the tongue, and beating more or less the lips. So with the touch of the rope the band moves the clapper*, Wanl. Catal. 109, col. 2, 16–20. [*Dut.* klepel, *f*: *M. H. Ger.* klepfel, *m. tubillus*; klepfer, *m. clapper.*]

cliroc, es; *m. A clerk, priest*; clericus:—Cliroc hine clǣnsie *let a clerk clear himself*, L. Wih. 19; Th. i. 40, 17. v. clerc.

Clistūn, es; *m.* CLIST or CLYST, *near Exeter, Devon*, Chr. 1001; Gib. 132, 16; Ing. 175, 7. v. Glistūn.

clite, an; *f. The herb colt's foot*; tussilago:—Genim ða langan clitan [MS. lancge cliton] *take the long colt's foot*, Lchdm. iii. 22, 16.

clīða, clȳða, an; *m. A plaster, salve, poultice*; emplastrum, malagma = μάλαγμα:—Se wītega Isaias worhte ðam cyninge Ezechie clīðan to his dolge *the prophet Isaiah made for king Hezekiah a plaster for his sore*, Homl. Th. i. 476, 1. Clīða *malagma*, Wrt. Voc. 74, 9: Ælfc. Gr. 9, 1; Som. 8, 22. Man sceal him wyrcean clīðan toforan his heáfde *one must make him a poultice for his forehead*, Lchdm. iii. 8, 13, 16. Swylce ðǣr clȳða togelǣd wǣre *as if a poultice were laid there*, Herb. 51, 2; Lchdm. i. 154, 18. Ðyssa wyrta genim ða lǣssan, wyrc to clȳðan *take the lesser of these herbs, make it into a poultice*, 143, 5; Lchdm. i. 266, 15: 173, 4; Lchdm. i. 304, 15. Genim ðyssa wyrta wyrtruman, gecnucude mid ele, and mid hwǣtenan meluwe, and mid sāpan, ðam gemete ðe ðū clȳðan wyrce *take roots of these herbs, pounded with oil, and with wheaten meal, and with soap, in the manner in which thou wouldst make a poultice*, 184, 4; Lchdm. i. 322, 14: 130, 1; Lchdm. i. 240, 21: 125; Lchdm. i. 236, 21.

cliwen, clywen, cleowen, cliowen, es; *n.* [cliwe = clywe] *A clew, anything that is globular, a ball of thread, ball*; glomus, globus:—Cliwen *glomus*, Wrt. Voc. 66, 18: 82, 8: 282, 1. Clywen *glomus*, Ælfc. Gl. 28; Som. 61, 5; Wrt. Voc. 26, 4. Cleowen *glomer, globellum*, Ælfc. Gl. 111; Som. 79, 68; Wrt. Voc. 59, 37. Ān cliwen gōdes nettgernes *one ball of good net-yarn*, Cod. Dipl. Apndx. 461; A. D. 956; Kmbl. iii. 451, 7. Cliwenes *globi*, Mone B. 560. Mintan wel getrifulade meng wið hunig, wyrc to lytlum cliwene *mingle mint, well triturated, with honey, make it into a little ball*, L. M. 1, 48; Lchdm. ii. 122, 11. Ða ȳslan onginnaþ lūcan togædere geclungne to cleowenne *the ashes begin to combine together shrunk up into a ball*, Exon. 59 a; Th. 213, 17; Ph. 226. Arāfaþ ðæt cliwen ðære twīfaldan heortan *unravels the clew of the double heart*, Past. 35, 5; Hat. MS. 46 b, 2. Men gesāwon scīnan æt his hnolle swilce fȳren clywen *men saw shining on his crown as it were a fiery circlet*, Homl. Th. ii. 514, 2. Cliwene *glomere*, Mone B. 3713. Cleóne [= cleowene] *glomere*, 526. Cliowena *globos*, 1662.

CLOCCIAN; *p.* ode; *pp.* od *To* CLUCK, *sigh*; glocire, glocitare, singultire, bombum *sive* sonitum edere:—Ðeáh seó brōdige henn sārlīce cloccige *though the brooding hen sorely cluck*, Bridf. 76. [*Scot.* clock: *Plat.* klukken: *Dut.* klokken: *Kil.* klocken: *Ger. M. H. Ger.* klucken, glucken: *Dan.* klukke: *Swed.* klokka, klukka: *Icel.* klökkva: *Lat.* glocīre: *Grk.* κλώσσω.]

clod-hamer, es; *m? A field-fare?* turdus pilāris?—Clodhamer *vel* feldefare *a field-fare*; scorellus? [turdus pilāris? Lin.], Wrt. Voc. 63, 27.

Clod-hangra, an; *m.* [clod, hangra *a meadow*] *Clodhanger*:—Þurh ũt Clodhangran; of đan hangran andlang rõde ũt on Mules dene *out through Clodhanger; from the meadow along the road out to Mule's dean*, Cod. Dipl. 1198; A.D. 956; Kmbl. v. 374, 28.

clofen *cloven, separated; pp. of* cleófan.

Clofes hoo = Clofes hõ; *gen.* hõs; *pl. nom. acc.* hõas; *gen.* hõa; *dat.* hõum; *m. Cliff, near Rochester*:—Hēr sinoþ wæs æt Clofes hoo [æt Clofes hõ, col. 2] *in this year* [A.D. 822] *there was a synod at Cliff*, Chr. 822; Th. 111, 14, col. 1; 110, 14, col. 1, 2. Æt Clofes hõum *at Cliff*, Th. Diplm. A.D. 803; 52, 32: A.D. 825; 73, 12. Đã wæs sionoþlīc gemõt on đære mǣran stõwe đe mon hâteþ Clofes hõas *then there was a synodal meeting in the famous place which is called Cliff*, Th. Diplm. A.D. 825; 70, 11.

clof-þung, -þunc, e; *f. The herb crow-foot*, Herb. 9, 1; Lchdm. i. 98, 23, 25, MS. B: Lchdm. iii. 54, 21. v. cluf-þung.

clof-wurt *the herb buttercup*, Herb. 10; Lchdm. i. 100, 14, MS. B. v. cluf-wyrt.

CLOM; *gen.* clommes; *m*: clam; *gen.* clammes; *m. A band, bond, clasp, bandage, chain, prison*; vinculum, carcer:—Habbaþ me swã helle clommas fæste befangen *the clasps of hell have so firmly grasped me*, Cd. 19; Th. 24, 6; Gen. 373. Đes wītes clom *this bond of torture*, 215; Th. 271, 10; Sat. 103. Đysne wītes clom *this bond of torment*, 216; Th. 274, 21; Sat. 157: 223; Th. 293, 11; Sat. 453. On đissum fæstum clomme *in this fast bondage*, 21; Th. 26, 17; Gen. 408. Clommum fæste *fast in bonds*, Andr. Kmbl. 260; An. 130. Cealdan clommum *with cold bands*, 2425; An. 1214. DER. bealu-clom, fȳr-, hæfte-, helle-, wæl-, wīte-, wundor-. v. clam; *gen.* clammes; *m.*

clomm *climbed; scandit; p. of* climan.

clough *a cleft of a rock*, or *down the side of a hill*, Som. Ben. Lye.

CLŨD, es; *m. A stone, rock, hill*; saxum, rupes, collis:—Clūdas feóllan of muntum *stones fell from the mountains*, Ors. 6, 2; Bos. 117, 12. Clūd *rupes*, Ælfc. Gr. 9, 27; Som. 11, 24. Mid clūdum ymbweaxen *surrounded with rocks*, Ors. 3, 9; Bos. 67, 22. Sumra wyrta eard biþ on clūdum *the soil of some herbs is on rocks*, Bt. 34, 10; Fox 148, 24. Beorh ođđe clūd *collis*, Ælfc. Gr. 9, 28; Som. 11, 46. [*Laym.* clude, chlud *a cliff, rock*: *Orm.* cludess *hills*: *Plat.* kluut, klute, kloot: *Dut.* kluit, *f*; kloot, *m*: *Kil.* klot: *Ger.* klosz, *m. gleba*: *M.H.Ger.* klõz, *m. a lump*: *O.H.Ger.* kloz, *m. massa*: *Dan.* klode, *m. f. a ball*: *Swed.* klot, *n*: *Icel.* klót, *n. knob on a sword's hilt*: hence the *Eng.* CLOD.] DER. stān-clūd.

clūdig; *adj. Stony, rocky*; saxeus:—Đæt Norþ-manna land is on sumum stõwum swȳđe clūdig *the country of the Northmen is in some places very rocky*, Ors. 1, 1; Bos. 20, 42.

clufe *an ear of corn, a clove of garlic*; spica, Som. Ben. Lye. Clufe? *f. pl.* in e, *A clove*, the bulb or tuber of a plant, Glos. of Lchdm. ii. Twã clufe *two cloves*, L. M. 3, 41; Lchdm. ii. 336, 3. Garleaces iii clufe *three cloves of garlic*, 3, 62; Lchdm. ii. 350, 8.

clufeht, clufiht; *adj. Bulbed*; bulbosus:—Nim clufehte wenwyrt *take the bulbed wenwort*, L. M. i. 58; Lchdm. ii. 128, 17. Gegnīd on twã clufe đære clufehtan wenwyrte *rub them upon two bulbs of the bulbed wenwort*, 3, 41; Lchdm. ii. 336, 3.

clufon *clove, separated*, Chr. 937; Th. 200, 38, col. 3; Æđelst. 5; *p. pl. of* cleófan.

cluf-þung, e; *f*: cluf-þunge, an; *f*. [clufe, þung *monkshood, hellebore*; aconītum = ἀκόνιτον] *The herb crow-foot*; ranunculus sceleratus, Lin:—Clufþung *crow-foot*, L. M. 1, 1; Lchdm. ii. 20, 4: 1, 24; Lchdm. ii. 66, 14: 1, 28; Lchdm. ii. 70, 2: 1, 47; Lchdm. ii. 120, 1: 3, 8; Lchdm. ii. 312, 20: iii. 12, 27. Đeós wyrt đe man *sceleratam*, and õđrum naman clufþunge nemneþ, biþ cenned on fuhtum and on wæteregum stõwum *this herb which is called* scelerata, *and by another name crow-foot, is produced in damp and watery places*, Herb. 9, 1; Lchdm. i. 98, 24-26. Genim clufþungan wõs *take juice of crow-foot*, 110, 3; Lchdm. i. 224, 7.

cluf-wyrt, e; *f. The herb buttercup*; batrachion = βατράχιον, ranunculus acris, Lin:—Đeós wyrt đe man *batrachion*, and õđrum naman clufwyrt nemneþ, biþ cenned on sandigum landum and on feldum: heó biþ feáwum leáfum and þynnum *this herb which is called* batrachion, *and by another name buttercup, is produced on sandy lands and in fields: it is of few and thin leaves*, Herb. 10, 1; Lchdm. i. 100, 15-17: L. M. 3, 8; Lchdm. ii. 312, 13.

CLUGGE, an; *f. A bell, small bell*; campana:—Hleóđor heora cluggan, đære hī gewunedon to gebēdum gecīgde and awehte beón, đonne heora hwylc of weorulde gefēred wæs *the sound of their bell, by which they were wont to be called and awaked to prayers, when any of them had gone out of the world*, Bd. 4, 23; S. 595, 40. [*Plat.* klokke *a bell, clock*: *O.Frs.* klokke: *Dut.* klok, *f. a clock, bell*: *Ger.* glocke, *f*: *M.H.Ger.* glogge, *f*: *O.H.Ger.* glokka, *f*: *Dan.* klokke, *m. f. a bell, clock*: *Swed.* klocka, *f. a bell, clock*: *Icel.* klukka, klocka, *f.*]

clumbon; *pp.* clumben *climbed*, Chr. 1070; Erl. 209, 9; *p. pl. and pp. of* climban.

clumian; *p.* ode; *pp.* od *To murmur, mutter*; mussitare:—Hī clumiaþ mid ceaflum đǣr hī scoldon clypian *they mutter with their jaws where they ought to speak aloud*, Wanl. Catal. 30, 14.

clungon; *pp.* clungen *withered, pined*; *p. pl. and pp. of* clingan.

CLŨS, e; *f*: clūse, an; *f. An inclosure, a narrow passage, close, bond, prison*; claustrum, carcer:—Đeáh he hie mid fīftigum clūsum beclemme *though he surround it with fifty bonds*, Salm. Kmbl. 143; Sal. 71. Alǣd of carcernes clūse mīne sãwle *educ de carcere animam meam*, Ps. Th. 141, 8. He fram đære clūsan afaren wæs wiđ đara scipa *he was gone from the pass towards the ships*, Ors. 6, 36; Bos. 131, 26, 22. Đã hæfdon hȳ heora clūsan belocene *when they had closed their passes*, 3, 7; Bos. 60, 4. Annas and Caiphas wǣron forþgangende to đære clūsan *Annas and Caiaphas were going forth to the prison*, Nicod. 14; Thw. 7, 10: 16; Thw. 8, 6, 9. [*Plat.* kluse: *Dut.* kluis, *f*: *Kil.* kluyse: *Ger.* klause, *f*: *M.H.Ger.* klõse, klūs, klūse, *f*: *O.H.Ger.* klūsa, *f*: *M. Lat.* clusa, clausa: *Lat.* clausus, *pp. of* claudĕre *to shut, inclose.*]

clūse, an; *m. An inclosure*; claustrum, Ors. 6, 36; Bos. 131, 26. v. clūs.

cluster, es; *n. A* CLUSTER, *bunch*; botrus = βότρυς, *f*:—Cluster đæt bitereste *botrus amarissima*, Cant. Moys. Isrl. Lamb. 193 b, 32. v. clyster.

CLŨSTOR, clūster, clauster; *gen.* clūstres; *pl. nom. acc.* clūstor, clūstro; *n. A lock, bar, barrier, cell*; claustrum, clausura:—Meahte đæs ceasterhlides clūstor onlūcan *might unlock the lock of the city-gate*, Exon. 12 a; Th. 20, 8; Cri. 314. Wæs mid clūstre carcernes duru behliden *the door of the prison was shut with a lock*, Exon. 69 a; Th. 256, 23; Jul. 236. Đa locu feóllon [feollan MS.], clūstor of đãm ceastrum *the locks fell, the barriers from that city*, 120 a; Th. 461, 23; Hö. 40. Đæt he mihte cuman þurh đãs clūstro *that he might pass through these barriers*, Cd. 22; Th. 27, 11; Gen. 416. He hine hēht on carcernes [MS. carcerne] clūster belūcan *he commanded him to be locked in a prison's cell*, Bt. Met. Fox 1, 146; Met. 1, 73. [*O. Sax.* klūstar, *n*: *Frs.* klooster, kleaster: *O.Frs.* klaster, *n*: *Dut.* klooster, *n*: *Kil.* klooster: *Ger.* kloster, *n*: *M.H.Ger. O.H.Ger.* klõster, *n*: *Dan. Swed.* kloster, *n*: *Icel.* klaustr, *n*: *Lat.* claustra, *pl. n. a lock, bar, bolt.*]

clūstor-cleófa, an; *m. A prison-chamber, cell*; carceris cubiculum:—On clūstorcleófan *in the prison-chamber*, Andr. Kmbl. 2041; An. 1023.

clūstor-loc, clūster-loc, es; *pl. nom.* -loca; *n. A prison-lock, lock, bar*; claustellum, claustrum:—Clūstor-loca [MS. -locæ] *claustella*, Glos. Epnl. Recd. 156, 2. Clūster-loc *claustellum*, Cot. 34: *claustrum*, 181.

CLŨT, es; *m. A small piece of cloth*, CLOUT, *patch, piece of metal, plate*; pittacium, commissura, lamina:—Clūt *pittacium*, Glos. Epnl. Recd. 161, 19: *commissura*, Ælfc. Gl. 28; Som. 61, 4; Wrt. Voc. 26, 3: 82, 2. Wurdon forþaborene īsene clūtas *iron plates were brought forth*, Homl. Th. i. 424, 19. Legcaþ đa īsenan clūtas hâte glõwende to his sīdan *lay the iron plates glowing hot to his side*, Homl. Th. i. 424, 35. [*Wyc. Piers P.* clout: *Chauc.* cloutes *rags*: *Orm.* clutess, *pl*: *Dan.* klud, *m. f*: *Swed.* klut, *m*: *Icel.* klútr, *m*: *Wel.* clwt, *m*: *Gael.* clùd, clùid, *m. a clout, rag, patch.*] DER. ge-clūtod. v. clūd.

clyf *a cliff, rock*, Ps. Spl. M. C. 113, 8. v. clif.

clȳfa, clīfa, an; *m.* [cleófa, cleófan *to cleave, divide, separate*]. I. a separate place for man,—*A chamber*; cubiculum, cubile:—Ne mãge we hreppan ǣnne wyrm binnon đīnum clȳfan *we may not touch a worm in thy chamber*, Homl. Th. ii. 416, 23. On dīglum ođđe on incõfan, ođđe on clȳfum *in cubīlibus*, Ps. Lamb. 4, 5. On his incõfan ođđe on his clȳfan *in cubīli suo*, 35, 5. II. a separate place for wild beasts,—*A cave, den*; antrum, caverna, cubile:—On đãm clīfum đe dracan oneardedon *in the dens which dragons dwelt in*; in cubīlibus, in quĭbus dracōnes habitābant, Bd. 3, 23; S. 554, 22. DER. bed-clȳfa, gebed-, hord-, in-. v. cleófa.

clyfer-fēte; *adj.* [clifer *a claw, talon*] *Claw-footed, talon-footed, cloven-footed*; fissipes:—Đa fugelas đe be flǣsce lybbaþ syndon clyferfēte *the birds which live by flesh are cloven-footed*, Hexam. 8; Norm. 14, 19.

clyfian, clyfigan; *p.* ode; *pp.* od *To cleave, adhere*; adhærere:—Đæt feax đe on đam cambe clyfige somnige *let her collect the hair that cleaveth to the comb*, Med. ex Quadr. 1, 7; Lchdm. i. 332, 21, MS. B.

clyfigende ādl *a joint-disease, the gout*, Som. Ben. Lye.

clȳfst, he clȳfþ *cleavest, cleaves*; *2nd and 3rd pers. pres. sing. of* cleófan.

clyf-wyrt *clivers, fox-glove*, Ælfc. Gl. 40; Som. 63, 91; Wrt. Voc. 30, 41: 79, 41. v. clif-wyrt.

clymmian, he clymmaþ, *pl.* clymmiaþ; *p.* ode; *pp.* od [climan *to climb*] *To climb*; scandere:—Leóht clymmaþ *light ascends* [*climbeth*], Salm. Kmbl. 829; Sal. 414.

CLYMPRE, an; *n? A lump* or CLUMP *of metal, metal*; massa metalli, metallum:—Hefigere ic eom đonne unlytel leádes clympre *I am heavier than a huge clump of lead*, Exon. 111 b; Th. 426, 18; Rä. 41, 75. Wyrc greáte clympran [MS. clymppan] feówur *make four great lumps*, Lchdm. iii. 134, 31. Clympre *metallum*, Wrt. Voc. 286, 73. [*Plat.* klump: *Dut.* klomp, *m*: *Kil.* klompe: *Ger.* klump, klumpen, *m*:

Dan. klump, *m. f: Swed.* klump, *m: O. Nrs.* klumbr, klumpr, *m.* Rask Hald.]

clynan; *p.* ede; *pp.* ed [clyne *metal*] *To ring, sound;* clangere:—Rand dynede, campwudu clynede *the shield rang, the war-wood sounded,* Elen. Kmbl. 101; El. 51.

clyne, es; *m? n?* clyna, clyne, clyno; *indecl. f. A mass, lump, ball, metal;* massa, sphæra = σφαῖρα, metallum:—Clynes, trendles *sphæræ,* Mone B. 3491. Ælces cynnes wecg, *vel* ōra oðđe clyna *metallum,* Ælfc. Gl. 51; Som. 66, 8; Wrt. Voc. 34, 67. Clyne, clyno *massa, metallum,* Cot. 132: 182. Sile hym āne clyne *give him one lump,* Lchdm. iii. 134, 33. Trendel, clyne *sphæra,* Mone B. 3465. Clyne, clottum *massa,* 3478.

clypenes, -ness *an embrace,* Bd. 3, 24; S. 557, 6, note. v. clypnys.

CLYPIAN, clypigan, clipian, cleopian, clepian; *part.* clypiende, clypigende; ic clypie, clypige, đū clypast, he clypaþ, *pl.* clypiaþ; *p.* ode, ade; *impert.* clypa, *pl.* clypiaþ; *pp.* od, ad *To make a vocal sound, speak, speak aloud, to cry out, call, say;* loqui, clamare, vocare, dicere:—He ongan clypian *cœpit clamare,* Mk. Bos. 10, 47. Ne com ic rihtwīse clypian *I came not to call the righteous,* Lk. Bos. 5, 32: 19, 15. Hlūddre stæfne clypigan *to cry with a loud voice,* Bd. 4, 19; S. 589, 12, note. Clypiende *dicens,* R. Ben. 44. Mid micelre stemne clypigende *crying with a loud voice,* Homl. Th. i. 48, 5. Ic clypie to Gode *clamabo ad Deum,* Ps. Lamb. 56, 3. Drihten gehȳrþ me đonne ic clypige to him *Dominus exaudiet me cum clamavero ad eum,* Ps. Lamb. 4, 4. Đū clypast *thou callest,* Hy. 7, 45; Hy. Grn. ii. p. 288, 45. Hwī clypaþ Dauid hyne Drihten *quomodo David vocat eum Dominum?* Mt. Bos. 22, 43, 45. Ge clypiaþ me lāreów *vos vocatis me magister,* Jn. Bos. 13, 13. To đē ic clypode *ad te clamavi,* Ps. Lamb. 60, 3: 65, 17. Ic to đē, Drihten, clypade *ego ad te, Domine, clamavi,* Ps. Th. 87, 13. He clypode mid micelre stemne *he cried with a loud voice,* Homl. Th. i. 596, 5: Bd. 3, 2; S. 524, 21: Byrht. Th. 132, 33; By. 25: 139, 19; By. 256. Israēla folces prafostas clypodon to Pharaone *præpositi filiorum Israel vociferati sunt ad Pharaonem,* Ex. 5, 15: Homl. Th. i. 72, 28. Clypa đa wyrhtan *voca operarios,* Mt. Bos. 20, 8: Lk. Bos. 14, 12, 13: Jn. Bos. 4, 16. Clypiaþ hyne *vocate eum,* Ex. 2, 20. [*Wyc. Piers P. Chauc.* clepe: *Laym.* clepie, clepien, cleopie, cleopien: *Orm.* clepenn: *Scot.* clep, clepe *to call, name.*] DER. be-clypiān, forþ-, of-, on-, to-, toge-: healf-clypiende.

clypiendlīc, clypigendlīc, clipigendlīc; *adj. Making a vocal sound;* vocalis [*from* vox, vocis *the voice*]:—Syndon fīf vocales, đæt synd clypigendlīce, a, e, i, o, u. Đās fīf stafas æteówiaþ heora naman þurh hī silfe, and būton đām stafum ne mæg nān word beón awriten, and fordī hīg sind *quinque vocales* gehātene *there are five* vocales, a, e, i, o, u, *which are vocal* [*sounds*]. *These five letters indicate their names by themselves, and without these letters no word can be written, and therefore they are called the five vocal sounds,* Ælfc. Gr. 2; Som. 2, 44–46. Consonantes, đæt is samod-swēgende, fordande hī swīgaþ mid đām fīf clypigendlīcum *consonants, that is, sounding together, because they are made articulate by the five vocal sounds,* Som. 2, 50. v. sylf-swēgend.

clypnys, clypenes, -nyss, -ness, e; *f. An embrace;* complexus:—To clypnysse đæs heofonlīcan brȳdguman eádig fǣmne ineóde *ad complexum sponsi cælestis virgo beata intraret,* Bd. 3, 24; S. 557, 6.

clypol; *adj. Vocal;* vocalis, Bridf. 101.

clypola, an; *m. A vowel;* vocalis, Bridf. 101.

CLYPPAN; *p.* clypte; *pp.* clypt *To embrace, clasp,* CLIP, *cherish;* complecti, amplexari:—Đæt he his mondryhten clyppe and cysse *that he embrace and kiss his lord,* Exon. 77 a; Th. 289, 2; Wand. 42. Nāwuht đes woruldgielp is đe hie clyppaþ and lufiaþ *this worldly glory is worthless which they embrace and love,* Past. 41, 1; Hat. MS. 56 a, 3. Đā Laban gehīrde đæt Iacob wæs cumen his swustor sunu, đā arās he togeánes and clypte hine *cum audisset Laban venisse Iacob filium sororis suæ, cucurrit obviam ei complexusque eum,* Gen. 29, 13. Iosep clypte hira ǣlcne and cyste hīg and weóp *amplexatus et osculatus est Ioseph et ploravit super singulos,* 45, 15. Ongan seó abbudisse clyppan and lufian đa Godes gife *abbatissa amplexata gratiam Dei,* Bd. 4, 24; S. 598, 1. Hine sybbe and lufu swylce clyppeþ *justitia et pax complexæ sunt se,* Ps. Th. 84, 9. Clyppende *amplexans,* Prœm. R. Conc. Hȳ hī lufan fæste clyppaþ *they firmly clasp them with love,* Exon. 107 a; Th. 409, 8; Rä. 27, 26. Heáfodswīma heortan clypte *insensibility seized his heart,* Cd. 76; Th. 94, 30; Gen. 1569. Ǣghwæđer ōđerne earme beþehte, cyston hie and clypton *each embraced the other with his arm, they kissed and clasped each other,* Andr. Kmbl. 2031; An. 1018. [*Wyc. Piers P. Chauc.* clippe: *Laym.* cluppe: *Orm.* clippenn: *O. Frs.* kleppa: *Dan.* klippe: *Swed. Icel.* klippa.] DER. be-clyppan, bi-, ymb-.

clypung, clepung, e; *f. Articulation, speaking out, the forming of words, a cry;* eloquium, clamor:—Se mūþ drȳfþ ūt đa clypunge, and seó lyft biþ geslagen mid đære clypunge *the mouth produces* [*driveth out*] *the articulation, and the air is struck in the articulation,* Ælfc. Gr. 1; Som. 2, 31. Clypung mīn infærþ [ineóde, *Lamb.*] on eárum his *clamor meus introivit in aures ejus,* Ps. Spl. 17, 8. Clypunga *the kalends;* kalendæ, Ælfc. Gr. 13; Som. 16, 19.

clȳsan; *p.* de; *pp.* ed *To close, shut;* claudere. DER. be-clysan: clȳsing.

clȳsing, clȳsung, e; *f. A* CLOSING, *inclosure, conclusion of a sentence, period;* claustrum, periodus = περίοδος:—Seó fæstnung đære hellīcan clȳsinge ne geþafaþ đæt đa wiđercoran ǣfre ūtabrecon *the fastening of the hellish inclosure never allows the wicked to break out,* Homl. Th. i. 332, 20. Hī on hellīcere clȳsunge andbīdodon *they waited in the hellish inclosure,* Homl. Th. ii. 80, 6. Clȳsunga *claustra,* R. Ben. Interl. 67. Periodos is clȳsing oðđe ge-endung đæs ferses *a period is the conclusion or ending of a sentence* [lit. *verse*], Ælfc. Gr. 50, 14; Som. 51, 18. DER. be-clȳsing.

CLYSTER; *gen.* clystres; *pl. nom. acc.* clystru; *gen.* clystra; *dat.* clystrum; *n. A* CLUSTER, *bunch, branch;* botrus = βότρυς, *f.* racemus, propago:—Clyster *botrus,* Ælfc. Gl. 47; Som. 65, 32; Wrt. Voc. 33, 31. Hira wīnberie ys gealla and đæt biteroste clyster *uva eorum uva fellis et botri amarissimæ,* Deut. 32, 32. Clystru *botros,* Mone B. 2548. Clystrum *racemis,* 3835. Ic geseah wīneard, on đam wǣron þreó clystru *videbam vitem in qua erant tres propagines,* Gen. 40, 10, 12. [*Prompt.* clustyr: *Plat.* kluster: *Kil.* klister.]

clȳsung *an inclosure,* Homl. Th. ii. 80, 6. v. clȳsing.

clȳđa *a poultice;* emplastrum, malagma, Herb. 51, 2; Lchdm. i. 154, 18. v. clīđa.

CLYWE, an; *f. n? A* CLEW, *ball of thread* or *yarn, ball;* globus, glomus:—Clywe *globus,* Ælfc. Gl. 111; Som. 79, 66; Wrt. Voc. 59, 35. [*Plat.* kluwe, klouwen: *Dut.* kluwen, klouwen, *n: Kil.* klouwe, kluwe: *Ger.* kläuel, kleuel, knäuel, *n. m: M. H. Ger.* kliuwel, *n: O. H. Ger.* kliuwa, *f.* cliuwi, *n.*] v. cliwen.

clywen *a clew, ball of thread* or *yarn, ball, circlet,* Ælfc. Gl. 28; Som. 61, 5; Wrt. Voc. 26, 4: Homl. Th. ii. 514, 2. v. cliwen.

cnæd, đū cnǣde, *pl.* cnǣdon *kneaded, hast kneaded, fermented; p. of* cnedan.

CNÆP, cnæpp, cnep, es; *m. A top, cop,* KNOP; vertex, jugum, supercilium:—Uppan đæs muntes cnæp *in montis vertice,* Ex. 19, 20. Hīg astigon to đæs muntes cnæppe *ascenderunt in verticem montis,* Num. 14, 44. Ofer cneppas *trans juga,* Glos. Prudent. Recd. 149, 55. Hīg lǣddon hine ofer đæs muntes cnæpp *duxerunt illum ad supercilium montis,* Lk. Bos. 4, 29. [*Piers P.* knappe: *Chauc.* knoppes, *pl: Plat.* knoop: *O. Frs.* knop, knap, *m: Dut.* knop, *m: Kil.* knoppe: *Ger. M. H. Ger.* knopf, *m. nodus, globulus: O. H. Ger.* knoph, *m: Dan.* knap, *m. f: Swed.* knapp, *m: Icel.* knappr, *m: Wel. Ir.* cnap: *Gael.* cnap, cnaip, *m.*]

cnæpling, es; *m. A stripling, youth, boy;* adolescens, puer:—Eom ic cnæpling *I am a boy,* Homl. Th. ii. 576, 14: Mone B. 2514.

cnǣwe, cnāwe; *adj. Knowing, conscious, aware;* cognoscens, conscius. DER. ge-cnǣwe, or-.

cnǣwst, he cnǣwþ *knowest, knows; 2nd and 3rd pers. pres. of* cnāwan.

CNAPA, cnafa, an; *m.* I. *a boy, young man,* KNAVE; puer, juvenis, adolescens:—He betǣhte hys cnapan and se cnapa hit ofslōh *he gave it* [*a calf*] *to his young man and the young man slew it,* Gen. 18, 7. Heó sealde đam cnapan drincan *dedit puero bibere,* 21, 19: 22, 19: 42, 22: 48, 16: Homl. Th. i. 186, 14. Ic hæbbe sumne cnapan *habeo quemdam puerum,* Coll. Monast. Th. 19, 27. Abraham fērde mid twām cnapum to fyrlenum lande *Abraham ducens secum duos juvenes abiit in locum,* Gen. 22, 3, 5. Syle cnapan [cnafan C.] đīnum *da puero tuo,* Ps. Spl. 85, 15. Đæt wīf wearþ wrāþ đam cnapan *mulier molesta erat adolescenti,* Gen. 39, 10. II. *a servant;* servus:—He hēt his cnapan behealdan to đære sǣ *he ordered his servant to look towards the sea,* Bd. de nat. rerum; Wrt. popl. science 18, 23; Lchdm. iii. 276, 24. [*Wyc.* knaue-child *a male child: Piers P. Chauc.* knave: *Laym.* cnaue: *Orm.* cnapess, *gen: Plat.* knape, knawe: *O. Sax.* knapo, *m: Frs.* knape: *O. Frs.* knapa, knappa, *m: Dut.* knaap, *m: Kil.* knape: *Ger. M. H. Ger.* knabe, *m: O. H. Ger.* knabo, knappo: *Swed.* knape, *m: Icel.* knapi, *m.*] DER. þeów-cnapa.

CNĀWAN; ic cnāwe, đū cnāwest, cnǣwst, he cnāweþ, cnǣwþ, *pl.* cnāwaþ; *p.* cneów, *pl.* cneówon; *pp.* cnāwen *To* KNOW; noscere:—Đa byþ cnāwene *noscuntur,* Mone B. 169. [*Wyc. Piers P. Chauc.* knowen, knowe: *Laym.* i-cnawen: *Orm.* cnawenn: *O. H. Ger.* knājan: *Icel.* kná: *Lat.* novi, old form gnovi *I came to know: Grk.* γι-γνώ-σκω: *Sansk.* jñā.] DER. an-cnāwan, be-, ge-, on-, to-.

cnāwing, e; *f. Knowledge, a knowing;* cognitio, Som. Ben. Lye. DER. on-cnāwing.

CNEAR, cnearr, es; *m. A small ship, galley used for ships of the Northmen;* navis, septentrionalium naves:—Cnear on flot *the ship on float,* Chr. 937; Erl. 114, 1, notes, p. 326; Æđelst. 35. [*Icel.* knarri, *m. navis, id. qu.* knörr, *m. navis, in specie mercatoria; Ólafs Saga hins helga,* 27, 1, *ubi promiscue ponuntur* knörru *et* kaupskipum, *Egils. sub* knörr.] DER. nægled-cnear.

cneátian; *p.* ode; *pp.* od *To argue, dispute, contend;* disceptare, contendere:—Cneátian *disceptare,* Mone B. 967. Cneátiaþ *contendunt,* 1867.

cneátung, e; *f. A debate, an inquiry, a search;* disputatio, scrutinium, Scint. 14.

CNEDAN; ic cnede, ðú cnidest, cnist, he cnit, *pl.* cnedaþ; *p.* ic, he cnæd, ðú cnǽde, *pl.* cnǽdon; *pp.* cneden *To* KNEAD, *ferment;* subigere, fermentare:—Cnede to ðam [MS. ðan] hláfe *to knead bread*, Lchdm. iii. 134, 21. Óþ-ðæt sie cneden *donec fermentaretur*, Lk. Skt. Rush. 13, 21. [*Chauc.* knede: *Orm.* knedenn: *Dut. Kil.* knéden: *Ger.* kneten: *M. H. Ger.* knëten: *O. H. Ger.* knetan: *Dan.* knede: *Swed.* knåda: *Icel.* knoða.] DER. ge-cnedan.

CNEÓ, cneów, es; *n.* I. *a* KNEE; genu:—Ðæt he on cneó lecge honda and heáfod *that he lays his hands and head on his knee*, Exon. 77 a; Th. 289, 3; Wand. 42. Me synt cneówu unhále *genua mea infirmata sunt*, Ps. Th. 108, 24. Cneówa *genua*, Wrt. Voc. 283, 68. Hie on cneówum sǽton *they sat on their knees*, Cd. 181; Th. 227, 2; Dan. 180: Chr. 979; Erl. 129, 22: Ors. 3, 9; Bos. 68, 35: Exon. 48 a; Th. 164, 19; Gú. 1014. Cneó bígeþ *bends the knees*, Exon. 62 b; Th. 229, 23; Ph. 459. Cneó bégean scolden *genua flectere deberent*, Bd. 3, 17; S. 544, 39, col. 2: Elen. Kmbl. 1693; El. 848: Exon. 63 a; Th. 232, 29; Ph. 514: 112 b; Th. 431, 9; Rä. 45, 5. II. *a generation, relationship;* generatio, propinquitatis gradus:—On ánum cneówe *in generatione una*, Ps. Th. 108, 13. Óþ hund cneówa [MS. cnea] *to a hundred generations*, Exon. 124 a; Th. 476, 16; Ruin. 8. Binnan cneówe *within relationship*, L. E. G. 12; Th. i. 174, 25. In ðam þriddan cneówe mid Crécum mót man wíf niman, in fiftan mid Rómánum *in tertio propinquitatis gradu apud Græcos viro licet uxorem ducere, in quinto apud Romanos*, L. Ecg. C. 28; Th. ii. 152, note h. Binnan ðam feórþan cneówe *within the fourth degree of relationship*, L. Eth. vi. 12; Th. i. 318, 15. [*Piers P.* knowes *knees: Laym.* cneo: *Orm.* cnewwe: *Plat.* knee *knee, generation: O. Sax.* knio, kneo, *n. knee: O. Frs.* kni, kne, *n. knee, degree of relationship: Dut. Kil.* knie, *f. knee: Ger. M. H. Ger.* knie, *n: O. H. Ger.* kniu, kneo, *n: Goth.* kniu, *n: Dan.* knæ, *n: Swed.* knä, *n: Icel.* kné, *n: Lat.* genu, *n: Grk.* γόνυ, *n: Sansk.* jānu, *m. n.*]

cneódan; he cneódeþ; *p.* cneád, *pl.* cnudon; *pp.* cnoden *To give;* tribuĕre, cognominare:—He naman cneódeþ *he gives a name*, Bd. 2, 20; S. 522, 24. v. cnódan.

cneóeht; *adj.* [cneó *a knee*, -eht = -iht, *adj. termination*, q. v.] *Knotty;* geniculatus:—Sió cneóehte wenwyrt *the knotty wenwort*, L. M. 1, 64; Lchdm. ii. 140, 8.

Cneoferis burh, burg, e; *f. Burghcastle, Suffolk;* villæ nomen in agro Suffolciensi:—Ðá wæs fæger mynster getimbred on wuda neáh sǽ on sumre ceastre, seó is nemned on Englisc Cneoferis burh *erat monasterium silvanum, et maris vicinitate amœnum, constructum in castro quodam, quod lingua Anglorum Cnobheres burg, id est, urbs Cnobheri vocatur*, Bd. 3, 19; S. 547, 22. v. Cnobheres burh.

cneó-holen, es; *m. The shrub knee-holm, butcher's broom;* ruscum, Wrt. Voc. 285, 48. v. cneów-holen.

cneoht *a boy*, Bd. 2, 6; S. 508, 18: 3, 18; S. 545, 45, col. 2. v. cniht.

cneó-mǽgas, cneów-mǽgas, -mágas; *pl. m.* [cneó II. *generation*, mǽg *relation*] *Relations of the same sex or the same generation;* consanguinei:—Cneówmǽgas *relations*, Cd. 83; Th. 104, 11; Gen. 1733. From cneómǽgum *from their relations*, Chr. 937; Erl. 112, 8; Æðelst. 8. Énos ongon, mid ðám cneómágum, ceastre timbran *Enoch began, with his kinsmen, to build a city*, Cd. 50; Th. 64, 28; Gen. 1057: Andr. Kmbl. 1370; An. 685: Elen. Kmbl. 1170; El. 587.

cneord; *adj. Diligent, intent;* sollers, intentus. DER. ge-cneord.

cneord-lǽcan; *p.* -lǽhte; *pp.* -lǽht *To be diligent, study;* studere, M. H. 14 a. DER. ge-cneordlǽcan.

cneordnys, -nyss, e; *f. Diligence, study, learning;* studium, disciplina:—Cneordnysse *studio*, Mone B. 2464: *disciplina*, 1034. DER. ge-cneordnys.

cneóres, cneórys, cneóris, cneórnis, -ress, e; *f. A generation, posterity, race, tribe, family;* generatio, posteritas, gens, tribus, familia:—Cneóres *generatio*, Ælfc. Gl. 91; Som. 75, 18; Wrt. Voc. 51, 63: Mt. Bos. 1, 18. Ðeós cneórys is mánfull cneórys *generatio hæc generatio nequam est*, Lk. Bos. 11, 29. Hwí sécþ ðeós cneóris tácen *quid generatio ista signum quærit?* Mk. Bos. 8, 12: Ps. Lamb. 23, 6: Bd. 1, 27; S. 491, 9. Cneóresse *generationis*, Mone B. 896. Mid ðisse cneórysse mannum *cum viris generationis hujus*, Lk. Bos. 11, 31. Cneórisse bóc *liber generationis*, Mt. Bos. 1, 1: Ps. Th. 94, 9. Ne gesihþ nán man of ðisse wirrestan cneóresse ðæt góde land *non videbit quispiam de hominibus generationis hujus pessimæ terram bonam*, Deut. 1, 35: Ps. Th. 44, 18. On ðære þriddan cneórisse *in the third generation*, Bd. 1, 27; S. 491, 8: Mk. Bos. 8, 12: Lk. Bos. 11, 30. Fram cynrene on cneórisse *a generatione in generationem*, Ps. Lamb. 89, 1: 101, 19. Mid ðisse cneórysse *cum generatione hac*, Lk. Bos. 11, 32: 17, 25. Ealle cneóressa *omnes generationes*, Mt. Bos. 1, 17. Ðás sind ðære heofenan and ðære eorþan cneórnisse *istæ sunt generationes cæli et terræ*, Gen. 2, 4. Ðás sind Noes cneórnissa *hæ sunt generationes Noe*, Gen. 6, 9. Ða on cneóressum cýðed syndan *they are known to generations*, Ps. Th. 101, 16. Sie gefeá gehwám ðe in cneórissum cende weorþen *let there be joy to each one who in their generations shall be born*, Exon. 11 a; Th. 15, 6; Cri. 232: Cd. 190; Th. 236, 10; Dan. 319: Ps. Th. 144, 13. Cneóresse *posteritatem*, Mone B. 648. Ðære cneórisse wæs Cainan weard *Cainan was guardian of that race*, Cd. 57; Th. 70, 18; Gen. 1155: 106; Th. 139, 31; Gen. 2318. Hine weorþiaþ wera cneóressa *races of men worship him*, Ps. Th. 71, 15. Ealle wera cneórissa ðé weorþiaþ *omnes gentes adorabunt te*, 85, 8: 74, 6. Com God wera cneórissa weorc sceáwigan *God came to behold the work of the races of men*, Cd. 80; Th. 101, 8; Gen. 1679. Secgaþ on cneórissum *dicite in gentibus*, Ps. Th. 95, 9: Cd. 64; Th. 77, 12; Gen. 1274. Cneóres *tribus*, Ælfc. Gl. 49; Som. 65, 73; Wrt. Voc. 34, 8. Cneórisse cende wǽron *ascenderunt tribus*, Ps. Th. 121, 4. Se biþ wiðerbreca wera cneórissum *he shall be an adversary to the tribes of men*, Cd. 104; Th. 138, 8; Gen. 2288: Exon. 44 b; Th. 151, 7; Gú. 791. Mon awóc on ðære cneórisse cynebearna rím *one raised up in that family a number of princely children*, Cd. 82; Th. 102, 22; Gen. 1704. Of Cames cneórisse wóc wermǽgþa fela *from Ham's family arose many tribes of men*, 79; Th. 98, 29; Gen. 1637.

cneó-rím, cneów-rím, es; *n. The number of kin, progeny, family;* cognatorum numerus, progenies, familia:—Of ðam wíd folc, cneórím micel, cenned wǽron *from whom a wide-spread people, a great progeny, were born*, Cd. 79; Th. 98, 32; Gen. 1639. Cneórím [MS. cneorisn] Caines *the family of Cain*, 63; Th. 76, 12; Gen. 1256. He his cynnes cneórím ícte *he increased the progeny of his race*, 59; Th. 72, 22; Gen. 1190. Ða ðæs cynnes cneówrím ícton *they increased the progeny of the race*, 52; Th. 65, 13; Gen. 1065.

cneóris *a generation, race, tribe, family*, Mk. Bos. 8, 12: Ps. Th. 74, 6: 121, 4: Cd. 79; Th. 98, 29; Gen. 1637. v. cneóres.

cneórnis, -niss, e; *f. A generation*, Gen. 2, 4: 6, 9. v. cneóres.

cneórys *a generation*, Lk. Bos. 11, 29, 31, 32: 17, 25. v. cneóres.

cneó-sib *a race, generation*. v. cneów-sib.

cneów, es; *n.* I. *a knee;* genu:—Cneów *genu*, Ælfc. Gl. 75; Som. 71, 87; Wrt. Voc. 44, 69: 71, 52. Heó on cneów sette *she knelt down*, Elen. Kmbl. 2270; El. 1136: Ps. Th. 94, 6. Hí bígdon heora cneów beforan him *they bowed their knees before him*, Mt. Bos. 27, 29. II. *a generation;* generatio:—In ðære þeóde awóc his ðæt þridde cneów *in that nation rose the third generation from him*, Cd. 209; Th. 258, 16; Dan. 676. v. cneó.

cneów, *pl.* cneówon *knew;* p. *of* cnáwan.

cneó-wærc, cneów-wærc, es; *n? A pain in the knees;* genuum dolor:—Wið cneówærce *for a pain in the knees*, Lchdm. iii. 16, 16. Wið cneówwærce, L. M. 1, 24; Lchdm. ii. 66, 11.

cneów-holen, cneó-holen, es; *m. n?* KNEEHOLM, *knee-hulver, knee-holly, butcher's broom;* ruscum, victoriola, ruscus aculeatus, Lin:—Genim twegen scenceas fulle wóses ðysse wyrte, ðe man *victoriola*, and óðrum naman cneówholen, nemneþ *take two cups full of the juice of this herb, which is called* victoriola, *and by another name knee-holly*, Herb. 59; Lchdm. i. 162, 6. Genim cneówholen *take knee-holly*, L. M. 1, 36; Lchdm. ii. 86, 10: 1, 39; Lchdm. ii. 102, 9: 2, 51; Lchdm. ii. 266, 15: iii. 4, 29: 30, 14. Wyrc to drence twá cneówholen *make into a drink the two knee-hollies*, L. M. 1, 47; Lchdm. ii. 120, 8.

cneówian, cneówigan; *part.* cneówigende; *p.* ode; *pp.* od [cneó, cneów *a knee*] *To bow the knee, to kneel;* genuflectere:—Benedictus on his gebédum cneówode *Benedict knelt down in prayer*, Homl. Th. ii. 154, 20: 178, 33. Cneówigende *genuflectens*, Procem. R. Conc. DER. ge-cneówian.

cneówlian; *p.* ode; *pp.* od *To* KNEEL; genuflectere, MS. Tib. A. iii. fol. 94. v. cneówian.

cneów-mǽgas, -mágas *relations*, Cd. 83; Th. 104, 11; Gen. 1733: Elen. Kmbl. 1372; El. 688. v. cneó-mǽgas.

cneów-rím *progeny*, Cd. 52; Th. 65, 13; Gen. 1065. v. cneó-rím.

cneów-sib; *gen.* -sibbe; *f. A race, generation;* generatio:—Cende cneówsibbe céna manna *he begat a race of brave men*, Cd. 161; Th. 200, 13; Exod. 356.

cneówung, cnéwung, e; *f. A kneeling;* genuflectio, Bd. 3, 17; S. 544, 39, note.

cneów-wærc *a pain in the knees*, L. M. 1, 24; Lchdm. ii. 66, 11. v. cneó-wærc.

cneów-wyrste; *pl. f.* [wrist, wyrst *the wrist*] *Knee-joints;* genicula, Ælfc. Gl. 75; Som. 71, 88; Wrt. Voc. 44, 70.

cnep *a top, summit*, Glos. Prudent. Recd. 147, 55. v. cnæp.

cnídan; *p.* cnád, *pl.* cnidon; *pp.* cniden *To beat;* cædere:—Ða sume cnidon [MS. cnidun] *they beat some;* alium ceciderunt, Mt. Kmbl. Rush. 21, 35. DER. for-cnídan.

cnidest, cnist, he cnit *kneadest, kneads; 2nd and 3rd pers. pres. of* cnedan.

CNÍF, es; *m. A* KNIFE; culter, cultellus, artavus, *Low Latin* = cultellus:—Cníf *artavus*, Wrt. Voc. 82, 40. [*Chauc.* knyfes, *pl: Laym. Orm.* cnif: *Plat.* knief, kniiv: *Frs.* knyf: *Kil.* knijf: *Ger.* kneif, *m: Dan.* kniv, *m. f: Swed.* knif, *m: Icel.* knífr, *m. a knife* or *dirk.*] v. seax.

CNIHT, cneoht, cnyht, es; *m. A boy, youth, attendant, servant,* KNIGHT: hence the modern knights of a shire are so called because they serve the shire; puer, juvenis, adolescens, servus:—Sum lytel sweltende cniht *a little dying boy*, Bd. 4, 8; S. 575, 23; Ors. 3, 7; Bos. 58, 43. Tyn wintra cniht *a boy of ten years*, L. In. 7; Th. i. 106, 18: Lk. Bos. 7, 7: Bd. 5, 19; S. 637, 4: Byrht. Th. 136, 18; By. 153. Fram dīnum cnihte *a puero tuo*, Ps. Th. 68, 17. Heó cwæþ to đam cnihte *ait ad puerum*, Gen. 24, 65. Cwicne abregd cniht of āde *take the boy alive from the pile*, Cd. 141; Th. 176, 20; Gen. 2914: 162; Th. 203, 20; Exod. 406. Đū đone cnyht to us brohtest in Bethlem *thou broughtest the boy to us in Bethlehem*, Exon. 121 a; Th. 463, 33; Hö. 79. He scōle gesette in đære cneohtas and geonge menn lǣrde wǣron *he set up a school in which boys and young men were taught*, Bd. 3, 18; S. 545, 45, col. 2. Đyssum cnyhtum wes līđe *be gentle to these boys*, Beo. Th. 2443; B. 1219. Đæt hie đæs cnihtes cwealm gesōhton *that they should seek the young man's death*, Andr. Kmbl. 2243; An. 1123: 1824; An. 914. Đa cnihtas cræft leornedon *the youths learned science*, Cd. 176; Th. 221, 4; Dan. 83: 182; Th. 228, 2; Dan. 196. To cwale cnihta *for the destruction of the youths*, Cd. 184; Th. 229, 32; Dan. 226. Cnyhta *of the youths*, Exon. 55 a; Th. 195, 32; Az. 165. Wundor Godes on đām cnihtum gecȳđed wæs *the miracle of God was manifest on the youths*, Cd. 197; Th. 245, 32; Dan. 472. Moises sende cnihtas *Moyses misit juvenes*, Ex. 24, 5: Cd. 176; Th. 221, 16; Dan. 89: Cd. 195; Th. 243, 5; Dan. 431. Cnihtas wurdon ealde ge giunge ealle forhwerfde to sumum dióre *the attendants* [*of Ulysses*], *old and young, were all transformed to some beast*, Bt. Met. Fox 26, 170; Met. 26, 85. Agynþ beátan đa cnihtas and đa þīnena *cœperit percutere servos et ancillas*, Lk. Bos. 12, 45. Ic, Oswold bisceop, landes sumne dǣl sumum cnihte đæm is Osulf nama, for uncre sybbe, forgeaf *I, bishop Oswald, have given a portion of land to a knight named Osulf, for our kinship*, Cod. Dipl. 557; A. D. 969; Kmbl. iii. 49, 32: 612; A. D. 977; Kmbl. iii. 159, 25. [*Wyc.* kniȝt, knyȝt: *R. Brun.* knyght: *Chauc.* knight, knyght: *R. Glouc.* knygt: *Laym.* cniht: *Orm.* cnihtess, *pl*: *Scot.* knecht, knycht: *Plat.* knecht, knekt: *Frs.* knecht: *O. Frs.* kniucht, knecht, *m*: *Dut. Kil. Ger.* knecht, *m*: *M. H. Ger.* knëht, *m*: *O. H. Ger.* kneht, *m*: *Dan.* knegt, *m. f*: *Swed.* knekt, *m.*] DER. in-cniht, leorning-.

cniht-cild, es; *n. A male child, boy*; puer:—Wæs on đam ylcan mynstre cnihtcild sum, ne wæs yldre đonne þrȳ-wintre *there was in the same monastery a boy, he was not older than three years*, Bd. 4, 8; S. 575, 27.

cniht-gebeorþor; *gen.* -gebeorþres; *n. A boy-bearing, child-bearing*; pueri partus:—On đæm cnihtgebeorþre heó ā clǣne þurhwunode *in child-bearing she continued ever immaculate*, Homl. Blick. 3, 12.

cniht-geong; *adj. Young as a child*; puerilis, Elen. Kmbl. 1276; El. 640.

cniht-hād, es; *m. The period between childhood and manhood, youth, boyhood*, KNIGHTHOOD; pubes:—Cnihthād *pubes*, Ælfc. Gr. 9, 28; Som. 11, 50. Ōþ cnihthāde *to youth*; pube tenus, 47; Som. 48, 8.

cniht-iugoþ, e; *f. Youth, boyhood*; juventus:—Cnihtiugoþ and sumor beóþ gelīce *youth and summer are alike*, Bridf. 11: 12.

cniht-leás; *adj.* KNIGHTLESS, *without an attendant*; sine servo, M. H. 113 b.

cniht-līc; *adj. Boyish, childish*; puerilis:—Ne he cnihtlīce gālnysse næs begangende *nor was he* [*Guthlac*] *addicted to boyish levity*, Guthl. 2; Gdwin. 12, 16. Swā oft swā cnihtlīcu yldo begǣþ *as childish age is often wont*, 2; Gdwin. 12, 19.

cniht-wesende; *part. Being a boy* or *youth, while a youth*; dum puer est:—On đam mynstre on đam cnihtwesendum *in monasterio tunc puero*, Bd. 3, 12; S. 537, 17: 2, 15; S. 518, 36. Cnihtwesende *being a youth*, Exon. 85 a; Th. 320, 34; Wīd. 39: Beo. Th. 750; B. 372: 1075; B. 535.

cniht-wīse, an; *f. Youthwise, boy's manner*; pueri mos:—Sprecan æfter cnihtwīsan *to speak after the manner of a boy*, Guthl. 2; Gdwin. 12, 13.

cnittan *to knit*, Ælfc. Gr. 36; Som. 38, 22, MS. C. v. cnyttan.

Cnobheres burh; *gen.* burge; *f.* [MS. Cneoferis burh] *Burghcastle, Suffolk*; Cnobheri urbs, in agro Suffolciensi ad ostia Garionis fluvii:—Ceaster, seó is nemned on Englisc Cneoferis burh. *In his original Latin, Bede says,—Castrum*, '*quod lingua Anglorum Cnobheres burg, id est*, urbs Cnobheri *vocatur*,' Bd. 3, 19; S. 547, 22.

cnocian *to knock*. DER. ge-cnocian. v. cnucian.

cnōdan, cneódan; ic cnōde, đū cnōdest, he cnōdeþ, cneódeþ, *pl.* cnōdaþ; *p.* cneád, *pl.* cnudon; *pp.* cnoden, gecnoden *To give, assign, call, carry out, exalt*; tribuĕre, attribuĕre, efferre:—Gyt mon his naman cneódeþ *yet man calls by his name*, Bd. 2, 20; S. 522, 24. Gif hwæt welgedōnes biþ, đonne cnōdaþ him ealle mid hērenesse *if anything be well done, then all exalt him with praise*; si qua bene gesta sunt, omnes laudibus efferunt, Past. 17, 3; Hat. MS. 22 b, 3.

CNOLL, es; *m. A* KNOLL, *hill-top, cop, summit*; cacumen, vertex:—On đam teóđan mōnþe æteówodon đæra munta cnollas *decimo mense apparuerunt cacumina montium*, Gen. 8, 5. Garganus hine gemētte standan uppon đam cnolle đære heálīcan dūne *Garganus found him standing on the knoll of the high hill*, Homl. Th. i. 502, 13. Heá dūne, hyllas and cnollas *high downs, hills and knolls*, Exon. 18 a; Th. 45, 11; Cri. 717. On cnolle *in vertice*, Mone B. 927. To ufeweardum đam cnolle *ad verticem montis*, Jud. 16, 3. He hit ne sette upon đone hēhstan cnoll *he should not set it upon the highest hill-top*, Bt. titl. xii; Fox xii. 15. On đam lytlan cnolle đe Ermon hātte *Hermonis a monte modico*, Ps. Th. 41, 7. [*Prompt.* knolle: *Plat.* knülle: *Dut.* knol, *m*: *Kil.* knolle: *Ger.* knolle, knollen, *m*: *M. H. Ger.* knolle: *Dan.* knold, *m. f*: *Swed.* knöl, *m.*]

CNŌSL, es; *n. A race, progeny, offspring, kin, family*; proles, genus, generatio:—Gewīt đū nū fēran, and đīne fare lǣdan, ceápas to cnōsle *begin thou now to depart, and lead thy family, thy cattle for progeny*, Cd. 83; Th. 105, 2; Gen. 1747. Mīnes cnōsles *of my progeny*, Exon. 105 a; Th. 399, 22; Rä. 19, 4: 112 a; Th. 430, 15; Rä. 44, 9. Gōdes and yfles đǣr ic cunnade, cnōsle bidǣled *there I tried good and evil, separated from my offspring*, 85 b; Th. 321, 27; Wīd. 52. Bearn *vel* cnōsl *soboles* vel *proles*, Ælfc. Gl. 91; Som. 75, 19; Wrt. Voc. 51, 64. Cnōsle *genere*, Mone B. 1608. Hēht from hweorfan mānscyldigne cnōsle sīnum *he bade the crime-guilty depart from his kindred*, Cd. 50; Th. 64, 12; Gen. 1049. On cnōsle ođđe on cynne *in generatione*, Ps. Lamb. 32, 11. Gewāt him mid cnōsle *he departed with his family*, Cd. 83; Th. 104, 4; Gen. 1730. [*O. Sax.* knōsal, *n*: *Ger.* knösel, *m. a little man*: *O. H. Ger.* knuosli, knōsli, *n.*] DER. fæderen-cnōsl, geóguþ-.

cnossian, he cnossaþ; *p.* ode; *pp.* od *To beat, strike, dash*; tundi, quassari, illidi:—Ȳđa gewealc mec oft bigeat, æt nacan stefnan, đonne he be clifum cnossaþ *the rolling of the waves has often caught me, at the vessel's prow, when it strikes on rocks*, Exon. 81 b; Th. 306, 15; Seef. 8.

CNOTTA, an; *m. A* KNOT, *fastening, knitting*; nexus:—Cnotta *nexus*, Ælfc. Gr. 11; Som. 15, 10. Gyt hēr is ōđer cnotta ealswā earfođe *there is yet another knot equally difficult*, Homl. Th. ii. 386, 22. To onlȳsanne [MS. onlȳsenne] đa fæstan cnottan [MS. cnotten] *to loosen the fast knots*, Th. Diplm. A. D. 1035; 334, 9: Wanl. Catal. 42, 23. Mid cnottum *nexibus*, Mone B. 3128: Homl. Th. ii. 28, 26. [*Prompt.* *Chauc.* knotte: *Plat.* knutte: *Frs.* knotte: *Dut.* knot, *f*: *Kil.* knutte: *Ger.* knoten, knote, *m*: *M. H. Ger.* knode, knote, *m*: *O. H. Ger.* knodo, *m*: *Dan.* knude, *m. f*: *Swed.* knut, *m*: *Icel.* knútr, *m.*]

CNUCEL; *gen.* cnucles; *m. A* KNUCKLE, *joint*; articulus, Som. Ben. Lye. [*Prompt.* knokylle: *Relq. Ant. W.* i. 190, 30, knokelys, *pl*: *Plat.* knukkel, knüchel: *Frs.* kneukel: *O. Frs.* knokele, knokle: *Dut.* kneukel, *m*: *Kil.* knokel: *Ger.* knöchel, *m*: *Dan.* knogle, *m. f*: *Swed.* knoge, *m*: *Icel.* knúi, *m.*]

CNUCIAN, cnucigan; *p.* ode; *pp.* od *To* KNOCK, *beat, pound*; pulsare, tundere, pertundere:—Cnuciaþ and eów biþ ontȳned *pulsate et aperietur vobis*, Mt. Bos. 7, 7: Lk. Bos. 11, 9. Đām cnuciendum biþ ontȳned *pulsanti aperietur*, Mt. Bos. 7, 8: Lk. Bos. 11, 10. He cnucode æt đære dura *he knocked at the door*, Homl. Th. ii. 382, 17, 22. Ic cnucige *tundo, pertundo*, Ælfc. Gr. 28, 7; Som. 32, 56, 65. Đa leáf cnuca on ānum mortere *pound the leaves in a mortar*, Herb. 41, 4; Lchdm. i. 142, 18: 57, 1; Lchdm. i. 158, 20: 63, 7; Lchdm. i. 166, 29: 64; Lchdm. i. 168, 5: 65; Lchdm. i. 168, 11. Cnucige ealle. đa wyrta *pound all the herbs*, Lchdm. i. 382, 15. [*Prompt.* knokkyn': *Wyc. Piers P.* knocken: *Chauc.* knocke: *Plat.* knukken *to utter a deep sound*: *Icel.* knoka: *Wel.* cnociaw: *Corn.* cnoucye.] DER. ge-cnucian.

cnuian; *p.* ode; *pp.* od *To pound*, Lchdm. ii. 340, 15. v. cnuwian.

Cnut, es; *m. Cnut was the Danish king of England for twenty-one years, from* A. D. 1014–1035:—Hēr, on đissum geáre, Swegen ge-endode his dagas to Candelmæssan iii n Feb'. And se flota đā eal gecurón Cnut to cyninge *here, in this year*, A. D. 1014, *Sweyn ended his days at Candlemas, on the 3rd of the Nones of February* [*Feb. 3rd*]. *And then all the fleet chose Cnut for king*, Chr. 1014; Erl. 150, 20–22. Hēr forþfērde Cnut cing, on ii Id' Novemb' æt Sceftes byrig, and hine man ferode đānon to Winceastre, and hine đǣr bebyrigde *here departed king Cnut, on the 2nd of the Ides of November* [= *Nov.* 12] *at Shaftesbury, and they bore him thence to Winchester, and buried him there*, 1035; Erl. 164, 17–19. Hēr man drǣfde ūt Ælfgife, Cnutes cynges lāfe, seó wæs Hardacnutes cynges mōdor *here*, A. D. 1037, *they drove out Ælfgifu, widow of king Cnut, who was mother of king Hardacnut*, 1037; Erl. 167, 1. [Knúta, os, *ossis*. Leggja mōt wiđ marga prúđa knútu *cum multis splendidis* [*nitidis*] *artubus congredi*, *Hh.* 83, 1, i. e. *cum multis militibus, prædæ destinatis. Raskius, F.* vi. 403, *pro nom. propr. accipit*, a Knútr, *aut de principibus viris aut bellatoribus*, Egils.]

cnuwian, cnuian; *p.* ode; *pp.* od *To knock, pound*; pinsere:—Genim læfre neođowearde, cnuwa and wring *take the netherward part of a bulrush, pound it and wring*, Lchdm. i. 382, 18. Cnua beolenan *pound henbane*, L. M. 3, 50; Lchdm. ii. 340, 15. DER. ge-cnuwian. v. cnucian.

cnyht *a boy, youth*, Exon. 121 a; Th. 463, 33; Hö. 79: 55 a; Th. 195, 32; Az. 165: Beo. Th. 2443; B. 1219. v. cniht.

CNYLL, es; *m. A* KNELL, *sound of a bell*; signum campanæ:—Hwīlon ic gehȳre cnyll and ic arīse *aliquando audio signum et surgo*, Coll. Monast. Th. 35, 29. [*Prompt.* knyll-ynge *tintillacio*: *Relq. Ant. W.* ii. 31, cnul *sound of a bell*: *Ger.* knall, *m. fragor, crepitus*: *Dan.* knald, *n.*

sound: Swed. knall, *m. a loud noise: Wel.* cnul, cnull, *m. a passing bell.*]

CNYLLAN, cnyllsan; *p.* de; *pp.* ed *To* KNELL, *sound a bell;* pulsare, campanâ signum dare:—Ðæm cnyllende ontýned biþ *pulsanti aperietur,* Lk. Skt. Rush. 11, 10. Cnyllaþ [cnyllsaþ, Lind.] and ontýned biþ iów *pulsate et aperietur vobis,* 11, 9: 12, 36: R. Ben. 48. Cnylled *pulsatus,* R. Conc. 1. [*Ger.* knallen, knellen *crepare, fragorem edere: M. H. Ger.* knillen, knüllen *to beat: Dan.* knalde *fragorem edere: Swed.* knalla *to make a noise: Icel.* knylla *to beat with a blunt weapon.*]

cnyllsan *to knell, sound a bell,* Lk. Skt. Lind. 11, 9: 12, 36. v. cnyllan.

CNYSSAN, cnysan; *part.* cnyssende; *p.* cnyssede, cnysede, cnysde, cnyste; *pp.* cnyssed *To press, trouble, toss, strike, dash, beat, overcome;* premere, tribulare, pulsare, contundere, vincere:—Ic wæs hearde cnyssed *I was hard pressed,* Ps. Th. 117, 13. Ne lǽt úsic costunga cnyssan tó swíðe *let not temptations trouble us too much,* Exon. 122 a; Th. 469, 7; Hy. 5, 9. Me costunge [MS. costunce] cnyssaþ *trials trouble me,* Ps. Th. 63, 1: Exon. 81 b; Th. 308, 2; Seef. 33. Me costunge cnyssedan *trials troubled me,* Ps. Th. 65, 13: 85, 6: 114, 4. Cnysedon, 58, 17. Cnysdon, 119, 1. Cnysdan, 118, 143: 137, 7. Se storm biþ cnyssende ðæt scip *the storm is tossing the ship,* Past. 9, 2; Hat. MS. 13 b, 10. Ne mec sceal âmas cnyssan *the weaver's reeds shall not strike me,* Exon. 109 a; Th. 417, 22; Rä. 36, 8. Cnysseþ ðæt sâr on ða rib *the sore striketh upon the ribs,* L. M. 2, 46; Lchdm. ii. 258, 3. Ne se hearda forst cnyseþ ǽnigne *the hard frost strikes not any,* Exon. 56 b; Th. 201, 21; Ph. 59. He cnyste Petres sídan *he struck Peter's side,* Homl. Th. ii. 382, 7. Ðás stánhleoðu stormas cnyssaþ *storms dash these stony rocks,* Exon. 78 a; Th. 292, 19; Wand. 101. Gaius Iulius se Cásere Brettas mid gefeohte cnysede *Caius Julius Cæsar beat the Britons in battle,* Chr. Erl. 4, 24. Ahteniense hí mid gefeohte cnysedon *the Athenians beat them in battle,* Ors. 3, 1; Bos. 53, 5. Ðæt hine ne cnysse sió wilnung *lest desire overcome him,* Past. 19, 1; Hat. MS. 28 a, 6. [*Scot.* knuse *to press down with the knees: Plat.* knusen *to squeeze: Frs. Japx.* kniesen *to bruise: Dut.* kneuzen *to bruise: Kil.* knisschen *terere, quassare: Ger.* knüssen *to push, beat: M. H. Ger.* knüsen, knüssen *to press, push, beat: O. H. Ger.* knusjan, knussan *concutere: Goth.* knussyan *to press down: Dan.* knuse *to bruise: Swed.* knusa *to bruise: Icel.* knosa *to bruise, beat.*] DER. a-cnyssan, ge-, on-, to-, úta-

cnyssung, e; *f. A striking, stroke;* ictus:—Of ðære lyfte cnyssunge *from the striking of the air,* Ælfc. Gr. 1; Som. 2, 30. Sweng oððe cnyssung *ictus,* 43; Som. 44, 55.

CNYTTAN, cnittan; *p.* cnytte; *pp.* cnytted, cnytt, cnyt *To tie, bind,* KNIT; nectere, nexere, ligare:—Ic cnytte *necto,* Ælfc. Gr. 36; Som. 38, 22. Ic cnytte [MS. C. cnitte] *nexo,* 36; Som. 38, 23: 28, 3; Som. 30, 61. Genim ðysse ylcan coliandran sǽd, endlufon corn oððe þreóttyne, cnyte mid ánum þrǽde *take seed of this same coriander, eleven or thirteen grains, knit them with a thread,* Herb. 104, 2; Lchdm. i. 218, 20. [*Prompt.* knyttyñ' *nodo, confedero: Wyc.* knyt, knyttide, *pp: Piers P.* knytte: *R. Brun.* knytte: *Chauc.* knitte: *Laym.* icnutten, *p. pl. knotted: Plat.* knutten *nodare: Dut.* knotten *to tie: Kil.* knodden *nodare: Ger.* knoten, knöten *nodare: Dan.* knytte *to knit: Swed.* knyta *to knit, tie: Icel.* knytja *to knit together: Lat.* nodare *to tie: Sansk.* nah *to bind, tie.*] DER. be-cnyttan, ge-, un-.

cnyttels, es; *m? A knitting thread, string, thong;* nervus:—Strenga, cnyttelsa *nervorum,* Mone B. 2858.

COC, cocc, es; *m. A* COCK, *a male fowl* or *bird;* gallus, pullus:—Coc *gallus,* Ælfc. Gl. 39; Som. 63, 47; Wrt. Voc. 30, 2: 63, 8: 77, 34. Creów se cocc *gallus cantavit,* Mt. Bos. 26, 74, 34: Jn. Bos. 13, 38. Cocca *pullorum,* Mone B. 4913. Ðonne coccas cráwan *when cocks crow,* Lchdm. iii. 6, 5. [*Prompt.* cok: *Chauc.* cok, cock: *Kil.* kocke: *Dan.* kok, *m: Icel.* kokkr, *m: Fr.* coq, *m: O. Fr.* coc.] DER. sǽ-coc, wudu-.

CÓC, es; *m. A* COOK; coquus:—Cóc *coquus,* Ælfc. Gr. 28, 5; Som. 32, 7: Wrt. Voc. 82, 50. Hwæt secgaþ we be cóce *quid dicimus de coquo?* Coll. Monast. Th. 29, 5. Hí cócas gehyrstan *cooks roasted them,* Ps. Th. 101, 3. [*Prompt.* cooke: *Piers P.* coke: *Chauc.* coke: *Laym.* coc: *Plat.* kokk: *O. Sax.* kok, *m: Dut.* kok, *m: Kil.* kock: *Ger. M. H. Ger. O. H. Ger.* koch, *m: Dan.* kok, *m. f: Swed.* kock, *m; Icel.* kokkr, *m: Ital.* cuóco, *m: Lat.* cocus, coquus, *m: Wel.* cǒg: *Corn.* cog, *m: Ir. Gael.* coca: *Armor.* cok: *O. Slav.* kuchari.]

COCCEL, es; *m.* COCKLE, *darnel, tares;* zizania:—Æteówde se coccel hine *apparuerunt zizania,* Mt. Bos. 13, 26. He oferseów hit mid coccele on middan ðam hwǽte *superseminavit zizania in medio tritici,* 13, 25: Homl. Th. i. 526, 20. Se sóða Déma hǽt his englas gadrian ðone coccel *the true Judge shall bid his angels gather the cockle,* 526, 21: Mt. Bos. 13, 27, 29, 30. Coccela *zizaniorum,* Mone B. 2332. [*Prompt.* cokylle: *Wyc.* cockil, cokil: *Chauc.* cockle.]

COCER, cocor, cocur, es; *m.* I. *a quiver for arrows, a case;* pharetra = φαρέτρα:—Cocer *pharetra,* Wrt. Voc. 84, 31. Hý gyrdon flána heora on cocere *paraverunt sagittas suas in pharetra,* Ps. Spl. 10, 2. Nim ðín gesceót, ðínne cocur and ðínne bogan, and gang út *sume arma tua, pharetram et arcum, et egredere foras,* Gen. 27, 3. II. *a sword, spear;* framea:—Ageót cocor *effunde frameam,* Ps. Spl. 34, 3. Genera fram cocore míne sáwle *erue a framea animam meam,* 21, 19. [*Prompt.* cocur *cothurnus: Piers P.* cokeres *stockings: Laym.* koker, *m: Plat.* köker, käker: *O. Sax.* cocâre, *m: Frs. O. Frs.* koker: *Dut. Kil.* kóker: *Ger.* köcher, *m: M. H. Ger.* kochære, kocher, *m: O. H. Ger.* kochar: *Dan.* kogger, *n: Swed.* koger, *n.*]

cócer-panne, cócor-panne, an; *f.* [cóc *a cook,* panne *a pan*] *A cooking-pan, frying-pan;* sartago, frixorium:—On cócerpannan *in frixorio,* Ps. Th. 101, 3. Cócorpanne *sartago,* Mone B. 4694.

cócnunga, *pl. f.* [cóc *a cook*] *Things cooked, pies:*—Metegearwa and cócnunga sint to forbeódanne *meat-preparations and things cooked must be forbidden,* L. M. 2, 23; Lchdm. ii. 210, 26: 2, 32; Lchdm. ii. 236, 10.

cocor, es; *m. A sword;* framea, Ps. Spl. 21, 19. v. cocer II.

cócor-mete, es; *m.* [cóc *a cook,* mete *meat, food*] *Meat divided into four parts?* quadripartitum, Wrt. Voc. 290, 41.

cocur *a quiver,* Gen. 27, 3. v. cocer I.

cod-æppel, es; *m. A quince-pear, quince;* malum cydoneum *vel* cotoneum, Cot. 93.

CODD, es; *m. A bag, sack,* COD, *husk;* pera = πήρα, folliculus, siliqua:—Codd *folliculus,* Ælfc. Gl. 59; Som. 67, 128; Wrt. Voc. 38, 50. Ne nime ge nán þing on wege, ne gyrde, ne codd *nihil tuleritis in via, neque virgam, neque peram,* Lk. Bos. 9, 3: 22, 36: Mt. Bos. 10, 10: Mk. Bos. 6, 8. Nim wínberian coddas [MS. coddes] *take husks of the grape,* Lchdm. iii. 112, 13. [*Prompt.* codde: *Wyc.* coddes, coddis *pods: Chauc.* cod: *Scot.* cod *a pillow: Kil.* kodde *a bag, sack: Swed.* kudde, *m. a cushion: Icel.* koddi, *m. a pillow.*] DER. bién-codd, sceát-.

coelnes *coolness,* Wanl. Catal. 304, 49. v. cólnes.

coerin *boiled wine,* Cot. 61. v. ceren.

CÓFA, an; *m. A* COVE, *cave, repository, inner room, chamber, ark;* cubile, cubiculum, arca:—On cófan *in a chamber,* Exon. 125 a; Th. 480, 18; Rä. 64, 4. Wæs culufre eft of cófan sended *the dove was sent again from the ark,* Cd. 72; Th. 88, 13; Gen. 1464. On cyninga cófum *in cubilibus regum,* Ps. Th. 104, 26. DER. bán-cófa, bed-, breóst-, ferhþ-, gást-, heolstor-, hord-, hreðer-, in-, mearh-, morþor-, nýd-, rún-, þeóster-: cóf-godas.

Cofan-treó, Cofen-treó, Couen-tré, es; *n.* [a monachorum conventu sic dictum putant quidam] COVENTRY, *Warwickshire;* Coventria in agro Warwicensi:—Leófwine abbod on Cofantreó féng to ðam bisceopríce *Leofwine, abbot at Coventry, succeeded to the bishopric,* Chr. 1053; Erl. 188, 7. Leofríc líþ æt Cofentreó *Leofric lieth at Coventry,* 1057; Erl. 192, 30. Of Couentré *at Coventry,* 1066; Erl. 203, 16: 1130; Erl. 258, 37.

Cofer-flód, Cofor-flód, es; *n. m. The sea of Galilee;* Galilæum mare:—Ic fare on wæteres hricg ofer Coferflód, Caldéas sécan *I depart upon the water's back over the sea of Galilee, to seek the Chaldeans,* Salm. Kmbl. 39; Sal. 20. Ðú gewítest on Wendelsǽ, ofer Coforflód, cýððe sécean *thou goest on the Mediterranean sea, over the sea of Galilee, to seek thy country,* 407; Sal. 204.

cóf-godas; *pl. m. Household-gods;* penates, Ælfc. Gl. 113; Som. 79, 113; Wrt. Voc. 60, 20: Glos. Prudent. Recd. 152, 28.

cófincel, es; *n. A hand-mill;* pistrilla, Cot. 155.

cóf-líce *quickly,* Som. Ben. Lye. v. cáf-líce.

cóf-scipe *quickness,* Som. Ben. Lye. v. cáf-scype.

cohhetan; *p.* te; *pp.* ed *To bluster;* tumultuári:—Hí ongunnon cohhetan *they began to bluster,* Judth. 12; Thw. 25, 20; Jud. 270.

CÓL; *gen.* cóles; *pl. nom. acc.* cóla, cólu; *gen.* cóla; *dat.* cólum; *n.* COAL; carbo:—Cól *carbo,* Wrt. Voc. 86, 20: 286, 79. Swá sweart swá cól *as black as coal,* L. M. 3, 39; Lchdm. ii. 332, 19. Cól [MS. coll] *carbo,* Ælfc. Gl. 30; Som. 61, 75; Wrt. Voc. 27, 4. On hát cól *upon a hot coal,* L. M. 1, 50; Lchdm. ii. 124, 6. Cóla onælde synd fram him *carbones succensi sunt ab eo,* Ps. Spl. 17, 10, 15. Feallaþ ofer hí cólu *cadent super eos carbones,* Ps. Spl. C. 139, 11. Þurh ða cólu ðæs alteres *by the coals of the altar,* Past. 7, 1; Hat. MS. 12 a, 10. Ða twegen drýmen wurdon awende to cóla gelícnyssum *the two wizards were turned to the likeness of coals,* Homl. Th. ii. 496, 28. [*Prompt.* cole *carbo: Wyc.* colis, *pl: Chauc.* cole: *Laym.* col: *Scot.* coill, coyll: *Plat.* köle: *Frs.* koal: *O. Frs.* kole: *Dut.* kool, *m. f: Kil.* kole: *Ger.* kohle, *f: M. H. Ger.* kol, *m: O. H. Ger.* kolo, *m;* kol, *n: Dan.* kul, *n: Swed.* kol, *n: Icel.* kol, *n.*] DER. heofon-cól.

CÓL; *comp.* ra; *sup.* ost; *adj.* COOL, *cold;* frigidus:—Oft ǽspringe útwealleþ of clife hárum cól and hlutor *a fountain often springs out of a hoar rock cool and clear,* Bt. Met. Fox 5, 26; Met. 5, 13. Hrér mid sticcan óþ-ðæt hit cól síe *stir it about with a spoon till it be cool,* L. M. 3, 26; Lchdm. ii. 324, 1: 2, 51; Lchdm. ii. 270, 2: 3, 30; Lchdm. ii. 326, 6: 3, 31; Lchdm. ii. 326, 15. Wyrc him leage of ellenahsan, þweah his heáfod mid cólre *make him a ley of elder ashes, wash his head with this cold,* 3, 47; Lchdm. ii. 338, 26. Ða cearwylmas cólran wurþaþ *the anxious emotions become cooler,* Beo. Th. 570; B. 282: 4139; B. 2066. [*Prompt.* cole *algidus: R. Glouc.* cole: *Plat.* kölig, köl:

Dut. koel; *Kil.* koel: *Ger.* kühl, kühle: *M. H. Ger.* küele: *O. H. Ger.* kuol: *Dan.* kölig, köl: *Swed.* kylig.]

côledon *cooled, became cold,* Andr. Kmbl. 2514; An. 1258; *p. pl. of* côlian.

côlian; *p.* ode, ede; *v. intrans. To* COOL, *to be or become cold;* algere, refrigerari:—Lêt ðonne hyt côlian *then let it cool,* Herb. 94, 4; Lchdm. i. 204, 23. Flǽsc onginneþ côlian *the flesh begins to cool,* Runic pm. 29; Kmbl. 345, 14. Côlaþ Cristes lufu *the love of Christ cooleth,* Exon. 33 a; Th. 104, 17; Gû. 9. Sumur-hât côlaþ *summer-heat becomes cold,* Exon. 95 a; Th. 354, 58; Reim. 67. Líc côlode *the corpse became cold,* Exon. 51 b; Th. 180, 18; Gû. 1281. Weder côledon *the storms were cold,* Andr. Kmbl. 2514; An. 1258. Leomu côlodon *the limbs became cold,* Elen. Grm. 882. DER. a-côlian, ge-. v. calan.

coliandre, an; *f. The herb coriander;* coriandrum = κορίαννον:—Cnuca coliandran sǽdes nigon corn *pound nine grains of coriander seed,* Herb. 52, 2; Lchdm. i. 156, 3: 104, 2; Lchdm. i. 218, 19. v. celendre.

colla, an; *m. Rage, strife;* ardor, furor. DER. morgen-colla.

collen-ferhtan; *p.* -ferhte; *pp.* -ferhted *To make empty or void, render desolate;* exinanire:—Ða ðe cweðaþ, ge collenferhtaþ oððe aîdliaþ ôþ grundweal oððe to staðolfæstnunga on hire *qui dicunt, exinanite, exinanite usque ad fundamentum in ea,* Ps. Lamb. 136, 7.

collen-ferhþ, -ferþ, -fyrhþ; *adj.* [collen, *pp. of* cellan *to swell? p.* ceall, *pl.* cullon; *pp.* collen, Ettm: ferhþ *mind*] *Fierce-minded, bold of spirit, bold;* animi ferox, audax:—Cleopode collenferhþ cearegan reórde *the fierce-minded cried out in a sorrowful voice,* Andr. Kmbl. 2217; An. 1110. Wîgan wǽron blîðe, collenferhþe *the warriors were blithe, bold of spirit,* Elen. Kmbl. 493; El. 247: Judth. 11; Thw. 23, 22; Jud. 134. Ðonne he beót spriceþ collenferþ *when he bold of spirit utters a promise,* Exon. 77 b; Th. 290, 26; Wand. 71: Apstls. Kmbl. 107; Ap. 54. In ceól stigon collenfyrhþe *the bold of spirit stept into the ship,* Andr. Kmbl. 698; An. 349. Collenferþ *bold of spirit,* Exon. 96 b; Th. 361, 9; Wal. 17. Eódon mid collenferhþe *the bold went together,* Elen. Kmbl. 755; El. 378: 1694; El. 849. Hwæðer collenferþ cwicne gemêtte *whether he should find the bold* [*warrior*] *living,* Beo. Th. 5563; B. 2785. Cuma collenferhþ *the bold guest,* 3616; B. 1806. Hleóþrade cempa collenferhþ *the bold warrior spake,* Andr. Kmbl. 1075; An. 538. Stôp ût hræðe, collenferþ *he quickly stept out, firm of mind,* 3154; An. 1580.

collon-crôh, -crôg, es; *m. A water-lily;* nymphæa = νυμφαία:—Collоncrôh *nymphæa,* Wrt. Voc. 68, 20: Mone A. 461. Colloncrôg *nymphæa,* Cot. 140.

côl-mâse, an; *f.* [côl *coal,* mâse *a titmouse*] *A coal-titmouse, coal-tit;* parus ater:—Côlmâse *parra,* Wrt. Voc. 62, 39: *parula,* 281, 11: *bardioriolus,* Ælfc. Gl. 39; Som. 63, 52; Wrt. Voc. 30, 7. [*Dut.* koolmees, *f. a titmouse.*]

Coln, e; *f? The river* COLNE, *Essex;* Colnius, in agro Essexiensi:—Hie flugon ofer Temese, ðâ up be Colne on ânne îggaþ *they fled over the Thames, then up by the Colne to an island,* Chr. 894; Erl. 90, 28.

coln *a pebble stone;* calculus, Som. Ben. Lye.

côlne *pertaining to coals;* carbonarius, Som. Ben. Lye.

Colne-ceaster; *gen.* -ceastre; *f.* COLCHESTER, *Essex, so called from the river Colne;* Colcestria, in agro Essexiæ, ad ripam Colnii fluvii:—Hî fôron to Colneceastre *they went to Colchester,* Chr. 921; Erl. 107, 9; 108, 5.

côl-nes, -ness, e; *f.* COOLNESS, *cool air, a breeze;* refrigerium, aura:—On côlnesse *in refrigerium,* Ps. Th. 65, 11. v. cêl-nes, calan.

côlode *cooled,* Exon. 51 b; Th. 180, 18; Gû. 1281; *p. of* côlian.

côl-pyt, -pet; *gen.* -pyttes, -pettes; *m. A* COAL-PIT; carbonis fossa:—Fram Hlypegete to ðam côlpytte: fram côlpette *from Lipgate to the coal-pit: from the coal-pit,* Cod. Dipl. 1322; A.D. 1035; Kmbl. vi. 186, 9.

COLT, es; *m. A* COLT; pullus:—He asyndrode þrîtig gefolra olfendmyrena mid heora coltum, and twentig assmyrena mid heora coltum [MS. coltun] *separavit camelos fœtas cum pullis suis triginta, et asinas viginti et pullos earum,* Gen. 32, 15. [*Prompt.* colte: *Wyc. Chauc.* colt.]

colt-græig, e; *f?* [græg, grig *grey?*] *The herb colt's foot;* tussilago farfara, Lin. v. Prior 51:—Coltgræig *caballopodia* vel *ungula caballi,* Ælfc. Gl. 44; Som. 64, 63; Wrt. Voc. 31, 73.

côl-þrǽd, -þrêd, es; *m. A coal* or *blackened thread, plumb-line;* perpendiculum:—Côlþrêd *perpendiculum,* Glos. Epnl. Recd. 160, 73.

coltræppe, an; *f? Ram, whin* or *Christ's thorn;* rhamnus = ῥάμνος, Cot. 156.

Coludes burh, burhg; *gen.* burge; *dat.* byrig; *f. Colud's city, Coldingham, Berwickshire, Scotland;* Coludi *vel* Coludana urbs, Colania, in agro Barovici:—Eóde Æðeldryþ on Æbban mynstre ðære Abbudissan, seó wæs Ecfriþes faðu ðæs cyninges, ðæt is geseted on ðære stôwe ðe mon nemneþ Coludes burh *Ædilthryda intravit monasterium Æbbæ abbatissæ, quæ erat amita regis Ecgfridi, positum in loco quem Coludi urbem nominant,* Bd. 4, 19; S. 587, 42. Ǽrðamðe ðæt mynster æt Coludes byrig mid byrne fornumen wǽre *priusquam monasterium Coludanæ urbis esset incendio consumptum,* 4, 25; S. 599, 18. Hêr Coludes burh forbarn mid godcundum fŷre *in this year* [A. D. 679] *Coldingham was burnt with divine fire,* Chr. 679; Erl. 41, 12. Ðæt nunmynster ðæt mon nemneþ Coludes burhg þurh ungŷmenne synne fŷres lîge wæs fornumen *monasterium virginum quod Coludi urbem cognominant per culpam incuriæ flammis absumptum est,* Bd. 4, 25; S. 599, 19.

Columba, an; *m. An Irish priest, the Apostle of the Highlands,* born about A. D. 520, and arrived in Scotland in 565. He preached to the Picts, whose king gave him the Western Isle, Iona, in which he founded his abbey and college. Columba was abbot 32 years, and died there, at the age of 77, on the 9th of June, 597 [Bd. 3, 4; S. 106, 107: *it is not in king Alfred's A. Sax. version*]. Columba is thus spoken of in the *Chr.* A. D. 565:—Columba, messapreóst, com to Pyhtum, and hî gecyrde to Cristes geleáfan; ðæt sind ðonne [ðone MS.] wærteras [MS. wærteres] be norþum môrum; and heora cyning him gesealde ðæt êgland ðe man nemnaþ Iî, ðǽr sindon v hîda, ðæs ðe men cweðaþ. Ðǽr se Columba getymbrade mynster; and he ðǽr wæs abbot xxxii wintra; and ðǽr forþfêrde, ðâ ðâ he wæs lxxvii wintra. Ða stôwe habbaþ nû git his erfewærdas [MS. erfewærdes].... Nû, sceal beón ǽfre on Iî abbod, næs bisceop; and ðam sculon beón underþǽdde ealle Scotta biscopas, forðam ðe Columba wæs abbod, nes bisceop *Columba, mass-priest, came to the Picts, and converted them to the faith of Christ; who are now dwellers by the northern mountains; and their king gave him the island which men name Iona, where there are five hides, from what men say. There Columba built a monastery; and he was abbot there thirty-two years, and there died when he was seventy-seven years. His inheritors yet have the place.... Now, in Iona, there must ever be an abbot, not a bishop; and to him must all the bishops of the Scots be subject, because Columba was an abbot, not a bishop,* Chr. 565; Th. 31, 29, col. 1-33, 7, col. 1.

com, *pl.* cômon *came,* Beo. Th. 865; B. 430: Cd. 160; Th. 199, 20; Exod. 341; *p. of* cuman.

comb, es; *m. A low place inclosed with hills, a valley;* vallis, Som. Ben. Lye. v. cumb.

combol, es; *n. An ensign, military standard.* DER. here-combol.

comêta, an; *m. A comet;* comêta, comêtes, æ; *m.* = κομήτης, ου; *m. long-haired:*—Higegleáwe hâtaþ comêta be naman *the wise-minded call a comet by name,* Chr. 975; Th. 228, 38, col. 1, 2, 3; Edg. 52.

commuc, es; *n. m? The cammoc, kex, brimstone wort;* peucedănum officinale, Lin, L. M. 3, 30; Lchdm. ii. 324, 20. v. cammoc.

comp, es; *m. A battle, contest;* certamen, pugna, Exon. 105 b; Th. 402, 26; Rä. 21, 35: 102 b; Th. 389, 3; Rä. 7, 2: Andr. Kmbl. 468; An. 234. v. camp.

comp-dôm *warfare,* Rtl. 8, 15. v. camp-dôm.

comp-gim; *gen.* -gimmes; *m. A precious gem;* pretiosa gemma:—Mid ðâm neorxna wonges compgimmum astǽned *stoned with the gems of paradise,* Salm. Kmbl. 150, 10.

comp-hâd *warfare,* Som. Ben. Lye. v. camp-hâd.

compian *to fight, contend against;* militare, pugnare, Exon. 37 b; Th. 123, 1; Gû. 316: Bd. 1, 15; S. 483, 12: 3, 9; S. 533, 17: Ps. Lamb. fol. 183 b, 18. v. campian.

compung, e; *f. A combating, fighting, contest;* pugna, concertatio, Cot. 49.

comp-wǽpen, es; *n. A battle-weapon, military weapon;* arma:—Oft ic gǽstberend cwelle compwǽpnum *I often kill the living with battle-weapons,* Exon. 105 b; Th. 401, 9; Rä. 21, 9. v. camp-wǽpen.

comp-weorod, es; *n. An army;* exercitus, Bd. 2, 5; S. 507, 40. v. camp-wered.

comp-wîg, es; *m. n. A battle;* pugna:—Compwîge *in battle,* Judth. 12; Thw. 26, 18; Jud. 333.

con *I know, he knows; I, he can,* Cd. 227; Th. 304, 13; Sat. 629: Bd. 3, 24; S. 556, 16. v. cunnan.

côn, coon *bold,* Som. Ben. Lye. v. coon, cêne.

condel, condell, e; *f. A candle;* candela, lampas, Chr. 937; Th. 202, 16, col. 1; Æðelst. 15: Exon. 51 b; Th. 179, 20; Gû. 1264: 72 a; Th. 269, 23; Jul. 454. v. candel.

Cone-ceaster; *gen.* -ceastre; *f. Caster, a town seven miles from Newcastle;* oppidum septimo a Novo-castro milliario, N. Som. Ben. Lye.

conned *proved;* probatus, Lye. v. cunnian.

consolde, an; *f. The herb comfrey;* consolida:—Dô him ðis to lǽcedôme, streáwbergean leáf, consolde, etc. *give him this for a remedy, strawberry leaves, comfrey, etc.* L. M. 3, 63; Lchdm. ii. 350, 27.

const *knowest, canst,* Beo. Th 2759; B. 1377; *2nd pers. pres. of* cunnan.

Constantînus, *as Lat. gen.* i; *dat.* o; *acc.* um; *m: also gen.* es; *dat.* e; *m. Constantine the Great, Roman Emperor,* A. D. 306-337. He is said to have been converted to Christianity, about 312, by the vision of a luminous cross in the sky, on which was the inscription ἐν τούτῳ, νίκα *by this, conquer.* In 330 he removed the seat of empire to Byzantium, which he called after his own name Κωνσταντίνου πόλις, *the city of Constantine,* CONSTANTINOPLE:—Fêrde Constantius forþ on Breotone, and Constantînus his sunu, ðam gôdan Câsere, his rîce forlêt.

Wrîteþ Eutropius ðæt Constantînus, se Câsere, wǽre on Breotene acenned *Constantius died in Britain* [A. D. 306], *and left his kingdom to his son Constantine, the good emperor. Eutropius writes that the emperor Constantine was born in Britain*, Bd. 1, 8; S. 479, 30-32. Constantius, se mildesta man, fôr on Bryttanie, and ðǽr gefôr; and gesealde his suna ðæt rîce, Constantînuse, ðone he hæfde be Elenan his wîfe *Constantius, the most merciful man, went into Britain, and died there; and gave the empire to Constantine, his son, whom he had by Helena his wife*, Ors. 6, 30; Bos. 126, 39-41. Notes and various readings, p. 28, col. 2, § 4, 41 h, MS. C. wîfe; L. ciefese. Ðâ wæs syxte geár Constantînes câserdômes *then was the sixth year of Constantine's imperial power*, Elen. Kmbl. 15; El. 8. Ðâ sige forgeaf Constantîno cyning ælmihtig þurh his rôde *then the king Almighty gave victory to Constantine through his cross*, 289; El. 145. Mid Constantîne *with Constantine*, Ors. 6, 31; Bos. 127, 42. *Also dat.* Constantînuse, 6, 30; Bos. 127, 7, 17, 23. v. Elene.

consul, es; *m. A consul; one of the two chief magistrates of the Romans chosen annually after the expulsion of their kings;* geár-cyning, *q. v;* consul:—Him ða Rômâne æfter ðǽm [cyningum] lâtteówas gesetton, ðe hî consulas hêton, ðæt hiora rîce heólde ân geár ân man *after them* [*the kings*] *the Romans appointed over themselves leaders, whom they called consuls, that one man of them should hold power one year*, Ors. 2, 2; Bos. 41, 36. Brutus wæs se forma consul *Brutus was the first consul*, Ors. 2, 3; Bos. 41, 40, 41: 2, 4; Bos. 42, 27. Ân consul forsôc ðone [MS. þæne] triumphan *one consul* [*Fabius*] *declined the triumph*, 2, 4; Bos. 42, 43. Senâtas cômon ongeán hyra consulas *the senators came to meet their consuls*, 2, 4; Bos. 43, 5, 20, 26. Under ðâm twâm consulum *under the two consuls*, 2, 4; Bos. 42, 33, 39: 2, 4; Bos. 43, 10, 16. Hæfdon him consulas, ðæt we cweðaþ rǽdboran *they had consuls, that we call counsellors*, Jud. Thw. 161, 22. [Consul, consul-ere *to consult, take counsel*, hence *counsellor*.]

consula bêc, cyninga bêc, *pl. f. Books of consuls*, or *kings' annals, calendars;* fastorum libri, fasti, Cot. 92.

Contwara burg *Canterbury*, Chr. 851; Erl. 66, 34. v. Cantwara burg.

Cont-ware *inhabitants of Kent*, Chr. 616; Erl. 20, 38. v. Cantware.

coon *bold*, Som. Ben. Lye. v. côn, cêne.

coorta, an; *m. A band of soldiers, cohort;* cohors:—He hæfde eahta ond hund-eahtatig coortena [MS. coortana], ðæt we nû truman hâtaþ, ðæt wæs, on ðâm dagum, fîf hund manna, and ân þûsend *he had eighty-eight cohorts, which we now call bands, each of which was, in those days, one thousand five hundred men*, Ors. 5, 12; Bos. 111, 14, 17.

cop; *gen.* coppes; *m. A top*, COP, *summit;* vertex, summitas:—Coppe *summitate*, Mone B. 1576.

côp, es; *m? A cope, an outer garment worn by priests;* ependytes = ἐπενδύτης:—Côp *vel* hoppada *vel* ufrescrûd *ependeton* [= *ependytes*], Ælfc. Gl. 112; Som. 79, 83; Wrt. Voc. 59, 52.

cope-man *a merchant*, Som. Ben. Lye. v. ceáp-man.

copenere, es; *m. A lover;* amator:—Ðû eart forlegen wið manigne copenere *tu fornicata es cum amatori multo*, Past. 52, 3; Hat. MS.

copest *chiefest, most precious;* pretiosissimus, Som. Ben. Lye. v. cop *a summit.*

copian; *p.* ode, ade; *pp.* od, ad *To plunder, pillage, steal;* compilare:—Copade and stæl *compilabat*, Cot. 53.

cop-lîc *fit;* coplîce *fitly, well;* apte, Gr. Dial. 1, 1, Lye.

copor, es; *n? Copper;* cuprum:—Nim hwetstân brâdne and gnîd ða buteran on ðæm hwetstâne mid copore *take a large whetstone and rub butter on the whetstone with copper*, Lchdm. iii. 16, 22.

copp, es; *m. A cup, vessel;* calix, vas:—Calic oððe copp wætres *calicem aquæ*, Mk. Skt. Lind. 9, 41. Copp *vas*, Cot. 175. v. cuppe.

copped; *part.* [cop *a top*] *Having the top cut off, topped, polled;* capite recisus, decacuminatus:—To ðan coppedan þorne *to the topped thorn*, Cod. Dipl. 1121; A. D. 939; Kmbl. v. 240, 28, 29. Andlang weges on ða coppedan âc *along the way to the polled oak*, Th. Diplm. A. D. 900; 145, 29.

COPS, cosp, es; *m. A rope, cord, fetter;* funis, anquina, compes:—Cops *anquina* [*anguina*, MS.], Ælfc. Gl. 104; Som. 78, 10; Wrt. Voc. 56, 56. Hî sǽdon ðæt hió sceolde sleán on ða raccentan and on cospas *they said that she should throw them into chains and fetters*, Bt. 38, 1; Fox 194, 32. [*O. Sax.* cosp, *m: Lat.* compes *a fetter.*] DER. fôt-cops, hand-, swur-.

corcîþ, es; *m. An increase;* incrementum:—Loc hine geseon corcîþ getâcnaþ *capillum se videre incrementum significat*, Lchdm. iii. 212, 9. v. cîþ.

coren *chosen, elected*, Chr. 675; Th. 58, 34; *pp. of* ceósan.

corenes, -ness, e; *f.* [coren, *pp. of* ceósan *to choose*] *An election, a choice;* electio, C. R. Ben. 62. DER. ge-corenes, wið-, wiðer-.

corfen *cut, carved*, Exon. 107 b; Th. 410, 24; Rä. 29, 4; *pp. of* ceorfan.

Corfes geat, Corf-geat, es; *n.* [*Sim. Dun.* Coruesgeate: *Hovd.* Coruesgate] *Corfgate, Purbeck, Dorsetshire*:—Hêr wæs Eádweard cyning ofslægen æt Corfes geate [Corfgeate, Th. 233, 2, col. 2] *in this year* [A. D. 979] *king Edward was slain at Corfgate*, Chr. 979; Th. 232, 3, col. 2.

corflian; *p.* ode; *pp.* od [ceorfan *to cut*] *To cut up small, mince;* concidere:—Ðâs wyrta sŷ swŷðe smæl corflode *let these herbs be minced very small*, Lchdm. iii. 292, 5.

corîon, es; *n?* [= κόρῑον for κορίαννον = κορίανον, Anac. 138] *The herb coriander;* coriandrum [ὑπέρῑκον hyperîcon, Diosc. 3, 171], Som. Ben. Lye. v. celendre.

CORN, es; *n.* I. CORN, *a grain, seed, berry;* frumentum, granum, bacca:—Corn *frumentum*, Ælfc. Gl. 59; Som. 67, 122; Wrt. Voc. 38, 44. Wæs corn swâ dŷre, swâ nân man ǽr ne gemunde *corn was so dear, as no man before remembered it*, Chr. 1044; Erl. 168, 21: Homl. Th. ii. 68, 17. Hie wǽron benumene ǽgðer ge ðæs ceápes ge ðæs cornes *they were deprived both of the cattle and of the corn*, Chr. 895; Erl. 93, 18: Bd. de nat. rerum; Wrt. popl. science 10, 8; Lchdm. iii. 254, 4. Se Dêma gegaderaþ ðæt clǽne corn into his berne *the Judge will gather the pure corn into his barn*, Homl. Th. ii. 68, 18: Chr. 894; Erl. 93, 11. Hŷ heora corn ripon *they reaped their corn*, Ors. 4, 8; Bos. 90, 33: Chr. 896; Erl. 94, 6: Past. 52; Hat. MS. Corn *granum*, Wrt. Voc. 83, 16. Ðæt hwǽtene corn wunaþ âna *granum frumenti solum manet*, Jn. Bos. 12, 24: Bt. 35, 1; Fox 156, 2, 4. Senepes corn *granum sinapis*, Lk. Bos. 17, 6. Heofena rîce is geworden gelîc senepes corne, ðæt seów se man on hys æcre *simile est regnum cœlorum grano sinapis, quod homo seminavit in agro suo*, Mt. Bos. 13, 31: Lk. Bos. 13, 19. Hægl byþ hwîtust corna *hail is the whitest of grains*, Runic pm. 9; Kmbl. 341, 4; Hick. Thes. i. 135. Se æppel monig corn oninnan him hæfþ *the apple has many seeds inside it*, Past. 15, 5; Hat. MS. 19 b, 23. Ifig byrþ corn golde gelîce *ivy bears berries like gold*, Herb. 121, 1; Lchdm. i. 234, 4. Genim ðysse wyrte twentig corna *take twenty grains of this herb* [*ivy*], 121, 2; Lchdm. i. 234, 6. II. *a hard* or *cornlike pimple, a corn, kernel on the feet;* pustula, clavus:—Ðis mæg horse wið ðon ðe him biþ corn on ða fêt *this may be for a horse which has corns on his feet*, Lchdm. iii. 62, 22. [*Prompt.* corne: *Wyc. Chauc. R. Glouc.* corn: *Laym.* corn, *n: Orm.* corn: *Plat.* koren, koorn: *O. Sax.* korn, korni, kurni, *n: O. Frs.* korn: *Dut.* kóren, *n: Ger. M. H. Ger. O. H. Ger.* korn, *n: Goth.* kaurno, *n. a grain of corn: Dan. Swed. Icel.* korn, *n. a grain of corn.*] DER. giþ-corn, mete-, sand-, sund-.

corn-æsceda *Corn-sweepings, chaff;* quisquiliæ:—Æppelscreáda *vel* cornæsceda *quisquiliæ*, Ælfc. Gl. 17; Som. 58, 97; Wrt. Voc. 22, 13.

corn-appla, *pl. n. Pomegranates;* mala Punica, Mone B. 3822.

corn-bǽre; *adj. Corn-bearing;* graniger:—Corn-bǽre *graniger*, Ælfc. Gr. 8; Som. 7, 20: Homl. Th. i. 450, 11. Cornbǽrum *granigera*, Mone B. 1435.

corn-gesǽlig; *adj.* [gesǽlig *fortunate, rich*] *Wealthy in corn;* frumento opulentus:—Cild corngesǽlig biþ *a child will be wealthy in corn*, Obs. Lun. § 9; Lchdm. iii. 188, 11.

corn-gesceót, es; *n? A payment* or *contribution of corn;* frumenti solutio *vel* munus:—Se wudu beó gelǽst binnan þrým dagum æfter ðam corngesceóte *let the wood be supplied within three days after the contribution of corn*, Cod. Dipl. 942; Kmbl. iv. 278, 10.

corn-hrycce, an; *f. A* CORN-RICK; frumenti acervus:—Wearþ gemêt ðæt feoh uppon ânre cornhryccan *the money was found upon a corn-rick*, Homl. Th. ii. 178, 8.

corn-hûs, es; *n. A corn-house, granary;* granarium, Ælfc. Gl. 109; Som. 78, 130; Wrt. Voc. 58, 42.

corn-hwæcca, an; *m. A corn-chest, bin;* arca frumentaria. v. hwæcca, Som. Ben. Lye.

cornoch, es; *m. A crane;* grus, Som. Ben. Lye.

corn-treów, es; *n. A cornel-tree;* cornus:—Corntreów *cornus*, Ælfc. Gl. 46; Som. 64, 124; Wrt. Voc. 32, 58: Cot. 49.

corn-troh, -trog, es; *m.* [troh *a trough*] *A corn-trough, bin, a vessel for cleansing grains of corn;* cista frumentaria, capisterium:—Corntroh *capisterium*, Ælfc. Gl. 3; Som. 55, 62; Wrt. Voc. 16, 35.

Corn-weal, es; *m.* CORNWALL; Cornubia, Som. Ben. Lye.

Corn-wealas; *gen.* -weala; *dat.* -wealum; *pl. m. Cornishmen, the inhabitants of Cornwall in a body, Cornwall;* Cornubienses, Cornubia:—Cômon hî to lande on Cornwealum *they came to land in Cornwall*, Chr. 892; Th. 160, 39, col. 3: 997; Erl. 134, 8. v. Wealh.

corn-wurma, an; *m. A corn-worm, weevil;* vermiculus, Ælfc. Gl. 17; Som. 58, 84; Wrt. Voc. 22, 2.

cors, es; *m. A curse;* execratio, Ben. Lye. v. curs.

corsian *to curse*, Ben. Lye. v. cursian.

cor-snǽd, e; *f.* [cor, cer, cyrr *a choice;* snǽd *a bit, piece*] *A choice* or *trial piece;* panis conjurâtus, offa consecrâta. A sort of ordeal in which the person accused had placed in his mouth an ounce of bread or cheese. If he ate it freely and without hurt, he was considered innocent; but guilty, if he could not swallow it, or had a difficulty in doing so. The Host was used for this purpose in Christian times:—Gif man freóndleásne weofod-þên mid tihtlan belecge, gâ to corsnǽde *if a friendless servant of the altar be charged with an accusation, let him go to the* corsnǽd, L. Eth. ix. 22; Th. i. 344, 23: L. C. E. 5; Th. i. 362, 19. To corsnǽde *to the* corsnǽd, Th. i. 362, 25: Th. i. 344, 29.

corþer; *gen.* corþres; *n:* corþer; *gen.* corþre; *f. A band, multitude, company, troop, body, train, pomp;* multitudo, cohors, copia, pompa:—Cirmdon caldheorte, corþer ǒðrum getang *the cold-hearted cried out, troop thronged on troop,* Andr. Kmbl. 276; An. 138. Cyning corþres georn *a king desirous of pomp,* Cd. 176; Th. 221, 28; Dan. 95. Wǽron ealle ætgædere cyningas on corþre *the kings were altogether in a body,* 151; Th. 189, 27; Exod. 191: 166; Th. 207, 11; Exod. 465: Exon. 15 a; Th. 31, 11; Cri. 494: 46 a; Th. 156, 25; Gū. 880. Stīgeþ cirm on corþre *clamour arises in the company,* 83 b; Th. 314, 26; Mōd. 20. Cyning on corþre *a king amid his train,* Beo. Th. 2310; B. 1153: Ps. Th. 54, 16. On wera corþre *in the company of men,* Elen. Kmbl. 608; El. 304: 1081; El. 543: 140; El. 70. Heó cleopade fōr corþre *she cried before the assemblage,* Exon. 74 b; Th. 279, 23; Jul. 618: Bt. Met. Fox 26, 169; Met. 26, 85: Andr. Kmbl. 3428; An. 1718. Se sunu Wihstānes acīgde of corþre cyninges þegnas *the son of Wihstan called the king's thanes from the band,* Beo. Th. 6233; B. 3121. Mid corþre *with a troop,* Andr. Kmbl. 2151; An. 1077: 2244; An. 1123: 2410; An. 1206: Elen. Kmbl. 1379; El. 691. Corþre ne lytle *with no little train,* Exon. 16 a; Th. 36, 19; Cri. 578. Hēr Eádgār wæs Engla waldend corþre micelre *in this year* [A. D. 973] *Edgar became ruler of the Angles with much pomp,* Chr. 973; Erl. 124, 10; Edg. 2. Hī cwōmon in ða ceastre corþra mǽste *they came to the city with the greatest of companies,* Elen. Kmbl. 548; El. 274: Exon. 58 a; Th. 209, 7; Ph. 167. Corþrum miclum *in large bands,* Cd. 80; Th. 99, 27; Gen. 1652: 112; Th. 148, 7; Gen. 2453. [*O. H. Ger.* kortar, *n. grex: Lat.* cohors, *gen.* cohortis = cors, *gen.* cortis *a company.*] DER. hilde-corþer, mægen-.

cor-wurma, an; *m. A purple colour;* mūrex:—Corwurmum *mūrĭcĭbus,* Mone B. 6170.

COS, coss, es; *m. A* KISS; osculum:—Cos *osculum,* Wrt. Voc. 72, 44. Ic hine to mīnum cosse arǽrde *I raised him to my kiss,* Homl. Th. ii. 32, 11. Coss ðū me ne sealdest *osculum mihi non dedisti,* Lk. Bos. 7, 45. Mannes sunu ðū mid cosse sylst *osculo filium hominis tradis,* 22, 48. Betwux ðām cossum *between the kisses,* Homl. Th. i. 566, 19. Cossas syllan hearm getācnaþ *to give kisses betokens harm,* Lchdm. iii. 208, 27. [*Wyc.* cos, coss, cosse: *Laym.* coss: *Plat.* kuss: *O. Sax.* kus, *m: O. Frs.* kos, *m: Dut. Kil.* kus, *m: Ger.* kuss, *m: M. H. Ger.* kus, *m: O. H. Ger.* kus, *m: Dan.* kys, *n: Swed.* kyss, *m: Icel.* koss, *m: Wel.* cusan, *m: Corn.* cussin, *m: Sansk.* kus *to embrace.*]

Coshām, es; *m.* COSHAM *or* CORSHAM, *Wilts;* loci nomen in agro Wiltoniensi:—Læg se cyng seóc æt Coshām *the king lay sick at Corsham,* Chr. 1015; Erl. 152, 13.

cosp, es; *m. A fetter;* compes:—On cospas *into fetters,* Bt. 38, 1; Fox 194, 32. v. cops.

cossas *kisses,* Lchdm. iii. 208, 27; *acc. pl. of* cos.

cossian; *p.* ode; *pp.* od [cos *a kiss*] *To kiss;* osculari:—Heó hit cossode *she kissed it,* Homl. Th. i. 566, 19. v. cyssan.

cost, es; *m? The herb costmary;* costus = κόστος, balsamita vulgaris, Lin:—Cost *costus,* Ælfc. Gl. 39; Som. 63, 71: Wrt. Voc. 30, 23: 79, 21. Costes gōdne dǽl gebeát smæle and gegnīd to duste *beat small a good deal of costmary and rub to dust,* L. M. 2, 55; Lchdm. ii. 276, 6: 2, 24; Lchdm. ii. 212, 26. Genim pipor and cymen and cost *take pepper and cummin and costmary,* 1, 17; Lchdm. ii. 60, 15: 1, 23; Lchdm. ii. 66, 9: 1, 47; Lchdm. ii. 120, 9. Ænglisc [MS. Æncglisc] cost *English costmary, tansy;* [tanacetum vulgare, Lin.], Lchdm. iii. 24, 8.

cost; *adj.* [costian *to tempt, try, prove*] *Tried, proved;* probatus:—Cempan coste cyning weorþodon *the tried champions glorified the king,* Andr. Kmbl. 2111; An. 1057. DER. ge-cost.

costere, costnere, es; *m. A tempter;* tentator:—Manna cynnes [MS. manna kynnes] costere hafaþ acenned on ðē ða unablinnu ðæs yfelan geþohtes *the tempter of mankind* [lit. *of the race of men*] *hath begotten in thee the unrest of this evil thought,* Guthl. 7; Gdwin. 46, 9. Se costere cwæþ to him *tentator dixit ei,* Mt. Kmbl. Rush. Lind. 4, 3.

costere, es; *m? A digging tool, spade;* fossorium:—Costere *vel* delfīsen *vel* spadu *vel* pal *fossorium,* Ælfc. Gl. 2; Som. 55, 40; Wrt. Voc. 16, 14.

COSTIAN, costigan, costnian; *p.* ode, ade, ede; *pp.* od, ad, ed *To tempt, try, prove;* probare, tentare. I. *v. trans. gen. acc.* 1. *with the genitive;* cum genitivo:—Ðæs rinces se rīca ongan cyning costigan *the powerful king began to tempt the chief,* Cd. 137; Th. 172, 18; Gen. 2846. Ðū mīn costadest, Drihten *Domine, probasti me,* Ps. Th. 138, 1. He mīn costode *he tried me,* Beo. Th. 4175; B. 2084. Ūre costade, God *probasti nos, Deus,* Ps. Th. 65, 9. Costodon mīn *tentaverunt me,* Ps. Spl. C. M. 94, 8. Hī Godes costodon [MS. costodan] *tentaverunt Deum,* Ps. Th. 77, 41. Hī on wēstenne heora Godes costedon [MS. costedan] *tentaverunt Deum in inaquoso,* 105, 12, 31. Costa mīn, God *proba me, Deus,* 138, 20. 2. *with the accusative;* cum accusativo:—He ðæt folc costian lēt *he let* [*them*] *try the people,* Ors. 6, 3; Bos. 118, 6. He costode cyning alwihta *he tempted the king of all creatures,* Cd. 228; Th. 306, 28; Sat. 671: Homl. Blīck. 29, 24, 34. Hī costodon God *tentaverunt Deum,* Ps. Spl. 105, 14: Mt. Bos. 16, 1. Ne costa ðū ðīnne Drihten God *tempt not the Lord thy God,* Homl. Blick. 29, 33: Ps. Spl. C. T. 25, 2. II. *v. intrans:*—Ðonne bryne costaþ hū gehealdne sind sāwle wið synnum *when the burning proveth how abstinent are souls from sins,* Exon. 23 b; Th. 65, 24; Cri. 1059. Feówertig daga he wæs fram deófle costod *diebus quadraginta tentabatur a diabolo,* Lk. Bos. 4, 2: Homl. Blick. 29, 14. [*Laym.* i-costned, *pp. proved, tried: O. Sax.* kostōn *to try, tempt: Ger.* kosten *to taste, try by tasting;* tentare, gustare: *O. H. Ger.* kostōn *tentare: Goth.* kausyan *to taste: Icel.* kosta *to try, tempt.*] DER. fore-costian, ge-.

costigan *to tempt,* Cd. 137; Th. 172, 18; Gen. 2846. v. costian.

costigend, costnigend, es; *m. A tempter;* tentator:—Se costigend eóde to him *the tempter went to him,* Homl. Blick. 27, 4. Se costnigend *tentator,* Mt. Bos. 4, 3.

costing *a temptation,* Exon. 33 a; Th. 104, 18; Gū. 9. v. costnung.

costnere, es; *m. A tempter;* tentator:—Swā swā se geleáfa strengra biþ, swā biþ ðæs costneres miht læsse *as the faith is stronger, so is the might of the tempter less,* Homl. Th. ii. 392, 20, v. costere.

costnes, -ness, e; *f. A temptation;* tentatio, Som. Ben. Lye. DER. ge-costnes.

costnian; *part.* costnigende; *p.* ode; *pp.* od; *v. trans. gen. acc. To tempt;* tentare:—Hyne costnigende *tentantes eum,* Mt. Bos. 19, 3. Ic hys costnode *I tempted him,* Nicod. 26; Thw. 14, 15. Costnodon me *tentaverunt me,* Num. 14, 22: Ps. Lamb. 94, 9. Afanda me Drihten, and costna me *proba me Domine, et tenta me,* Ps. Spl. 25, 2. Ne costna ðū Drihten ðīnne God *non tentabis Dominum Deum tuum,* Mt. Bos. 4, 7: Lk. Bos. 4, 12. v. costian.

costnigend, es; *m. A tempter;* tentator, Mt. Bos. 4, 3. v. costigend.

costnung, costung, costing, e; *f.* [costnian, costian *to tempt, try*] *A temptation, trying, trial, tribulation;* tentatio, probatio, tribulatio:—Ðeós costnung is of ðam nīþfullan deófle *this temptation is from the malicious devil,* Boutr. Scrd. 23, 10, 8. Wæs seó ǽreste costung ofercumen *the first temptation was overcome,* Exon. 39 a; Th. 128, 24; Gū. 409: Homl. Th. ii. 156, 26: Ex. 17, 7. On ðære costnunge tīman *in tempore tentationis,* Lk. Bos. 8, 13. Æfter dæge costunge *secundum diem tentationis,* Ps. Spl. 94, 8. Ne gelǽd ðū us on costnunge *ne nos inducas in tentationem,* Mt. Bos. 6, 13: 26, 41: Mk. Bos. 14, 38: Lk. Bos. 11, 4: 22, 40, 46: Homl. Th. ii. 596, 9: 600, 16. On costunge *in tentatione,* Deut. 9, 22. Sindan costinga monge arisene *many temptations are arisen,* Exon. 33 a; Th. 104, 18; Gū. 9. Ðæt he us gescylde wið ða þūsendlīcan cræftas deófles costunga *that he shield us from the thousand crafts of the devil's temptations,* Homl. Blick. 19, 17. Micle costnunge ge gesāwon *tentationes magnas viderunt oculi tui,* Deut. 29, 3. Drecþ se deófol mancynn mid mislīcum costnungum *the devil vexes mankind with various temptations,* Boutr. Scrd. 19, 44. Seó costnung ðære ēhtnesse gestilled wæs *the trial of the persecution was stilled,* Bd. 1, 8; S. 479, 19. Me costung and sār cnyssedan *tribulation and sorrow troubled me,* Ps. Th. 114, 4. Hī on costunge cleopedan to Drihtne *clamaverunt ad Dominum cum tribularentur,* 106, 12, 18, 27: 117, 5: 142, 12. Ðonne me costunge cnysedon *in die tribulationis meæ,* Ps. Th. 58, 17: 65, 13. Me costunga cnysdan *tribulatio et angustia invenerunt me,* Ps. Th. 118, 143: 119, 1: 137, 7. DER. nȳd-costing.

costung, e; *f. A temptation, trying;* tentatio, tribulatio, Ex. 17, 7: Ps. Spl. 94, 8: Deut. 9, 22: Ps. Th. 114, 4. v. costnung.

COT, cott, es; *pl. nom. acc.* cotu; *gen.* cota; *dat.* cotum, cottum; *n. A* COT, *cottage, house, bed-chamber, den;* casa, domus, cubiculum, cubile, spelunca:—Onbūtan ða cotu *about the cots,* Cod. Dipl. 551; A. D. 969; Kmbl. iii. 35, 6. Ongeán ða cotu *towards the cots,* 559; A. D. 969; Kmbl. iii. 52, 16. We witan ðæt hȳ ne durran hȳ selfe æt hām æt heora cotum werian *we know that they dare not defend themselves at home in their own houses,* Ors. 3, 9; Bos. 69, 26. Ingā in cotte ðīnum *intra in cubiculum tuum,* Mt. Kmbl. Lind. 6, 6. In cotum [Lind. cottum] *in cubiculis,* Lk. Skt. Rush. 12, 3: 11, 7. Ge worhton ðæt to þeófa cote *fecistis illam speluncam latronum,* Mt. Bos. 21, 13. [*Prompt.* coote: *Wyc. Piers P.* cotes, *pl: Chauc.* cote: *Plat.* kate, katen: *Dut.* kot, *n: Ger.* kot, *n: Dan.* koje, *m. f: Swed.* kette, *m;* koja, *f: Icel.* kot, *n: Wel.* cwt: *Gael.* cot, *m.*]

cote, an; *f. A cot, cottage, house;* casa, domus:—Gif hwilc man forstolen þingc hām to his cotan bringe *if any man bring a stolen thing home to his house,* L. C. S. 77; Th. i. 418, 18. v. cyte.

cōða *diseases; nom. gen. acc. pl. of* cōðu.

cōð-līce; *adv.* [cōða, cōðu *a disease*] *Badly, miserably;* male, misere:—Cōðlīce racentan gerǽped *miserably bound in chains.* Bt. Met. Fox 25, 72; Met. 25, 36.

cōðu, e; *f:* cōðe, an; *f:* cōða, an; *m. A disease, sickness, pestilence;* morbus:—Mycel orfes wæs ðæs geáres forfaren þurh mistlīce cōða *much cattle was destroyed this year through various diseases,* Chr. 1041; Erl. 169, 9. Swylc cōðe com on mannum ... ðæt mænige swulton *such a disease came on men ... that many died,* Chr. 1087; Th. 353, 37. Seó miccle cōðu *the great disease, leprosy;* elephantinus morbus, Homl. Th. ii. 480, 10.

Seó cóđu đe lǽcas hâtaþ paralisin *the disease which physicians call palsy,* ii. 546, 29. He fram đære cóđe hine gehǽlde *he healed him from the disease,* i. 400, 10. Wiđ wambe cóđum *for diseases of the stomach,* L. M. 2, 32; Lchdm. ii. 234, 1. DER. ban-cóđa, -cóđu, bræc-, eár-, fǽr-, fôt-, heort-, in-, mûþ-, sweor-, un-.

cot-lîf, es; *pl. nom. acc.* -lîf; *gen.* -lîfa; *n.* [cot *a cot, cottage;* lîf, II. *a place to live in*] *A village;* villa:—Đæt cotlîf *the village,* Cod. Dipl. 828; A. D. 1066; Kmbl. iv. 191, 13: 845; Kmbl. iv. 204, 31: 855; Kmbl. iv. 211, 25: 859; Kmbl. iv. 214, 6: 864; Kmbl. iv. 217, 7. He bohte feola cotlîf *he bought many villages,* Chr. 963; Erl. 121, 24. Hý forbærndon ôđra cotlîfa fela *they burned many other villages,* 1001; Erl. 136, 32.

cot-sǽta, an; *m. An inhabitant of a cottage, a cottager;* casæ habitator, Som. Ben. Lye.

cot-setla, cote-setla, an; *m.* [MS. kot-setla, kote-setla] *A cottager;* casārius:—Cotsetlan [MS. kotsetlan] riht *a cottager's right,* L. R. S. 3; Th. i. 432, 15. Cotesetlan [MS. kotesetlan] riht, be đam đe on lande stent. On sumon he sceal ǽlce Môndæge ofer geáres fyrst his lâforde wyrcan, ôđđ iii dagas ǽlcre wucan on hærfest: ne þearf he landgafol syllan. Him gebýriaþ v æceras to habbanne, mâre gyf hit on lande þeáw sý, and tô lytel hit biþ beó hit â læsse, forđan his weorc sceal beón oft rǽde. Sylle his heorþ-pænig on hâlgan Þunres dæg, eal swâ ǽlcan frigean men gebýreþ, and werige his hlâfordes inland, gif him man beóde æt sǽ-wearde and æt cyniges deór-hege, and æt swilcan þingan swilc his mǽþ sý, and sylle his ciric-sceát to Martinus mæssan *cotsetle rectum est juxta quod in terra constitutum est. Apud quosdam debet omni die Lunæ, per anni spatium, operari domino suo, et tribus diebus unaquaque septimana in Augusto.* [*Apud quosdam, operatur per totum Augustum, omni die, et unam acram avene metit pro diurnale opere. Et habeat garbam suam quam præpositus vel minister domini dabit ei.*] *Non dabit landgablum. Debet habere quinque acras ad perhabendum, plus si consuetudo sit ibi, et parum nimis est si minus sit quod deservit, quia sæpius est operi illius. Det super heorþpenig in sancto die Jovis, sicut omnis liber facere debet, et adquietet inland domini sui, si submonitio fiat de sewarde, id est, de custodia maris, vel de regis deorhege, et ceteris rebus quæ suæ mensuræ sunt: et det suum cyricsceatum in festo sancti Martini,* L. R. S. 3; Th. i. 432, 16–434, 2.

cot-stôw, e; *f.* [stôw *a place*] *A place of cottages;* casarum situs:—On đa ealdan cotstôwa *to the old cot-places,* Cod. Dipl. 578; A. D. 973; Kmbl. iii. 97, 30.

cott *a bed-chamber,* Mt. Kmbl. Lind. 6, 6: Lk. Skt. Lind. 11, 7: 12, 3. v. cot.

cottuc, es; *m. Mallow;* malva:—Cottuc wyl on wætere *boil mallow in water,* L. M. 1, 32; Lchdm. ii. 78, 19: 1, 60; Lchdm. ii. 130, 23. Nim niđeweardne cottuc *take the netherward part of mallow,* 1, 68; Lchdm. ii. 144, 5.

cowen *chewed, eaten; pp. of* ceówan.

coxre *a quiver,* Som. Ben. Lye. v. cocer.

CRABBA, an; *m.* I. *A* CRAB, *crayfish;* cancer:—Crabba *cancer,* Ælfc. Gl. 102; Som. 77, 74; Wrt. Voc. 55, 78: 77, 68. Hwæt fêhst đû on sæ? Crabban and lopystran *quid capis in mari? Cancros et polypodes,* Coll. Monast. Th. 24, 11. II. *a sign of the zodiac, cancer;* signum zodiaci, cancer:—Feórþa đæra tâcna ys gehâten *cancer,* đæt is crabba *the fourth of the signs is called* cancer, *that is, a crab,* Bd. de nat. rerum; Wrt. popl. science 7, 5; Lchdm. iii. 244, 25. [*Dut.* krab, *f: Kil.* krabbe: *Ger.* krabbe, *f;* krebs, *m: M. H. Ger.* krebez, *m: O. H. Ger.* chrëpazo, *m: Dan.* krabbe, *m. f: Swed.* krabba, *f: Icel.* krabbi, *m: Lat.* karabus, *m: Grk.* κάραβος, *m. a crab: Sansk.* śarabha, *m. a grasshopper, crab.*]

cracettan *to* CROAK; crocitare, Gr. Dial. 2, 8, Som. Ben. Lye.

Crac-gelâd *Cricklade,* Chr. 905; Th. 180, 21, col. 2. v. Crecca-gelâd.

CRACIAN; *part.* craciende; *p.* ode; *pp.* od *To* CRACK, *quake;* crepare:—Craciendum *crepante,* Mone B. 123. Sió eorþe eall cracode *the whole earth quaked,* Ps. Th. 45, 3. [*Piers P.* craked *broke: Chauc.* crakke: *Laym.* crakeden, chrakeden, *p. pl: Plat. Dut.* kraken: *Ger. M. H. Ger.* krachen: *O. H. Ger.* krachjan, krachôn: *Gael.* crac *crepare.*]

CRADEL, cradol, es; *m. A* CRADLE; cunabula:—Cradel *cunabula, pl.* [MS. *cunabulum*], Ælfc. Gl. 27; Som. 60, 112; Wrt. Voc. 25, 52. On cradele [MS. B. cradole] *in a cradle,* L. C. S. 77; Th. i. 420, 1. [*Prompt.* credel, cradel: *R. Brun.* credille: *Chauc. R. Glouc.* cradel: *Gael.* creathail, *f. a cradle.*] DER. cild-cradol.

cradol *a cradle,* L. C. S. 77; Th. i. 420, 1, MS. B. v. cradel.

cradol-cild, es; *n. A cradle-child, infant;* e cunabulis infans:—Syndon cradolcild geþeówode *infantes e cunabulis sunt mancipati,* Lupi Serm. 1, 5; Hick. Thes. ii. 100, 30.

cræcetung, e; *f. A croaking;* crocitatio:—Cræcetung hræfena *the croaking of ravens,* Guthl. 8; Gdwin. 48, 4.

Cræcilâd *Cricklade,* Chr. 1016; Erl. 153, 5. v. Crecca-gelâd.

cræfian *to crave,* Cod. Exon. 5 b, Lye. v. crafian.

CRÆFT, es; *m.* I. *power, might, strength as of body or externals;* vis, robur, potentia:—On đam gefeohte Mǽđa cræft gefeól *in that battle the power of the Medes fell,* Ors. 1, 12; Bos. 35, 43. He cwæþ đæt đîn abal and cræft mâra wurde *he said that thy strength and power would become greater,* Cd. 25; Th. 32, 9; Gen. 500: 155; Th. 193, 13; Exod. 245: 212; Th. 262, 3; Dan. 738: Beo. Th. 2571; B. 1283. His âgnes cræftes *of his own strength,* Bt. 16, 2; Fox 54, 5. Þurh his cræftes miht *by the might of his power,* Andr. Kmbl. 1170; An. 585: Elen. Kmbl. 1112; El. 558: Exon. 24 b; Th. 70, 29; Cri. 1146. He cræft mâran hæfde *he had greater power,* Cd. 14; Th. 18, 6; Gen. 269: 22; Th. 27, 12; Gen. 416: 23; Th. 29, 21; Gen. 453: Exon. 33 b; Th. 107, 14; Gû. 58: Beo. Th. 1402; B. 699. Nýdaþ cræfte tîd *the tide forces it with power,* Salm. Kmbl. 790; Sal. 394: Cd. 23; Th. 29, 13; Gen. 449: Exon. 71 b; Th. 266, 3; Jul. 392: Beo. Th. 1969; B. 982. Mid eallum hiora cræftum *with all their forces,* Ors. 1, 13; Bos. 37, 4: Exon. 109 a; Th. 417, 24; Rä. 36, 9. He his dryhtne hýrde þurh dýrne cræftas *he obeyed his lord through secret powers,* Salm. Kmbl. 904; Sal. 451: Cd. 184; Th. 230, 1; Dan. 226: Exon. 88 b; Th. 332, 33; Vy. 94: 92 b; Th. 346, 27; Sch. 5. II. *an art, skill,* CRAFT, *trade, work;* ars, peritia, artificium, occupatio, opus:—Se cræft đæs lareówdômes biþ cræft ealra cræfta *the art of teaching is the art of all arts,* Past. 1, 1; Hat. MS. 6 b, 8. Cræft *ars,* Wrt. Voc. 73, 35. Wolde ic ânes to đê cræftes neósan *I would inquire of one art from thee,* Andr. Kmbl. 968; An. 484. He byþ forlǽten fram đam cræfte *ipse dimittetur ab arte,* Coll. Monast. Th. 31, 35. Ic gearcie híg mid cræfte mînum [MS. minon] *præparo eas arte mea,* 27, 31: Bt. 39, 4; Fox 216, 24. Seó þeód đone cræft ne cûđe đæs fiscnôþes *the people knew not the art of fishing,* Bd. 4, 13; S. 582, 43. Betweoh đâs cræftas *inter istas artes,* Coll. Monast. Th. 30, 17. On his mycclum cræfte *by his great skill,* Hexam. 1; Norm. 4, 3. Nân mon ne mæg nǽnne cræft cýđan bûtan tôlum *no man can shew any skill without tools,* Bt. 17; Fox 58, 29: Boutr. Scrd. 17, 8. Wundorlîce cræfte đû hit hæfst gesceapen *with wonderful skill thou hast made it,* Bt. 33, 4; Fox 130, 11: Ors. 1, 12; Bos. 35, 35. Cræft biþ betere đonne ǽhta *a craft* [=*trade*] *is better than wealth,* Prov. Kmbl. 20: Coll. Monast. Th. 27, 27: 28, 5, 7, 9: 30, 11. Ælces cræftes andweorc *the materials of any trade,* Bt. 17; Fox 58, 30. Hwæt begytst đû of đînum cræfte *what gettest thou by thy trade?* Coll. Monast. Th. 23, 3: 28, 3, 31. Đeáh đê đîne sǽlþa forlǽton, ne forlǽt đû đînne cræft *though thy wealth desert thee, desert not thou thy trade,* Prov. Kmbl. 57: Coll. Monast. Th. 21, 1, 11: 22, 35, 37: Bt. 17; Fox 58, 31: 17; Fox 60, 2. Mistlîcra cræfta biggenceras *workers of various trades,* Coll. Monast. Th. 30, 1. To cræftum [MS. cræftan] teón *to educate in trades,* L. Edg. C. 51; Th. ii. 254, 26. Gif đû bearn hæbbe, lǽr đa cræftas, đæt hî mǽgen be đâm libban *if thou have children, teach them trades, that they may live by them,* Prov. Kmbl. 20: 57. Seó cwên bebeád cræftum getýde girwan Godes tempel *the queen commanded men skilled in crafts* [=*trades*] *to make a temple of God,* Elen. Kmbl. 2034; El. 1018. Wæs ǽfre unbegunnen Scyppend, se đe gemacode swylcne cræft *the Creator, who made such a work, was ever without beginning,* Hexam. 1; Norm. 4, 5. III. *craft of mind, cunning, knowledge, science, talent, ability, faculty, excellence, virtue;* astutia, machinatio, scientia, facultas, præstantia, virtus:—Þurh deófles cræft *through the devil's craft,* Cd. 25; Th. 31, 29; Gen. 492. Đeáh Eue on deófles cræft bedroren wurde *though Eve had been deceived by the devil's craft,* 38; Th. 51, 7; Gen. 823: Exon. 17 b; Th. 43, 7; Cri. 685: Andr. Kmbl. 2590; An. 1296: Frag. Kmbl. 56; Leás. 30. Feóndes cræfte *by a fiend's craft,* Andr. Kmbl. 2394; An. 1198: Exon. 71 a; Th. 264, 5; Jul. 359. Mînum cræftum *by my devices,* 72 b; Th. 271, 11; Jul. 480. Beald biþ se đe onbýrigeþ bôca cræftes *he is bold who tasteth of book-knowledge,* Salm. Kmbl. 484; Sal. 242. On bôclîcum cræfte *in book-knowledge,* Boutr. Scrd. 17, 7. Đa cnihtas cræft leornedon *the youths learned science,* Cd. 176; Th. 221, 5; Dan. 83. Ic wilnode đæt mîne cræftas ne wurden forgitene *I was desirous that my talents should not be forgotten,* Bt. 17; Fox 60, 9. Đa yfelan nǽfre habbaþ nǽnne cræft *the wicked never have any ability,* 36, 3; Fox 174, 35. Seó gesceádwîsnes is synderlîc cræft đære sâwle *reason is a peculiar faculty of the soul,* 33, 4; Fox 132, 10: 32, 1; Fox 116, 3. Đa cræftas đe we ǽr ymbe sprǽcon ne sint to wiđmetanne wiđ đære sâwle cræfta ǽnne *the faculties which we have before spoken about are not to be compared with any one of the faculties of the soul,* 32, 1; Fox 116, 1, 2, 4. Omêrus on his leóþum swîđe hêrede đære sunnan cræftas *Homer in his poems greatly praised the sun's excellences,* 41, 1; Fox 244, 7. Sint đa cræftas betran đonne đa unþeáwas *the virtues are better than the vices,* 36, 5; Fox 180, 15. Simmachus is wîsdômes and cræfta full *Symmachus is full of wisdom and virtues,* 10; Fox 28, 17. Se eorþlîca ânweald nǽfre ne sǽwþ đa cræftas *earthly power never sows the virtues,* 27, 1; Fox 94, 25: 30, 1; Fox 110, 5. Nân man for his rîce ne cymþ to cræftum, ac for his cræftum he cymþ to rîce *no man by his authority comes to virtues, but by his virtues he comes to authority,* 16, 1; Fox 50, 21, 23, 24. IV. *a* CRAFT, *any kind of ship;* navis qualiscunque:—Gif massere geþeah đæt he fêrde þrîge ofer wîd-sǽ be his âgenum cræfte, se wæs đonne syđđan þegenrihtes weorþe *if a merchant thrived, so that* *he fared thrice over the wide sea in his own craft, then was he thenceforth worthy of thane-right*, L. R. 6; Th. i. 192, 10. Ic ǽfre ne geseah on sǽ leódan syllícran cræft *I never saw a more wonderful craft sailing on the sea*, Andr. Recd. 1004; An. 500. [*Wyc. Piers P. Chauc.* craft: *Laym.* cræft, craft: *Orm.* crafft: *Plat.* kraft, kracht: *O. Sax.* kraft, *m. and f*: *Frs. O. Frs.* kreft: *Dut.* kracht, *f*: *Kil.* kracht: *Ger. M. H. Ger. O. H. Ger.* kraft, *f*: *Dan.* kraft, *m. f*: *Swed.* kraft, *m*: *Icel.* kraptr, kraftr, *m.*] DER. aclǽc-cræft, ǽ-, átor-, beadu-, bealo-, bóc-, deófol-, dreám-, drý-, dwol-, ellen-, firen-, flíter-, galdor-, gleó-, gúþ-, hell-, hyge-, lǽce-, lár-, leornung-, leóþ-, leoðo-, leóðu-, mód-, morþor-, nearo-, ofer-, rím-, sang-, sceóp-, scín-, scip-, scóp-, searo-, snytro-, stæf-, sundor-, swinsung-, tungel-, tungol-, un-, wæl-, wic-, wicce-, wíg-, word-, woruld-, wóþ-, wundor-.

cræfta, an; *m.* [cræft *art*] *An artist, a craftsman, workman*; artifex:—Cræfta *artifex*, Ælfc. Gr. 10; Som. 14, 43. v. cræftiga.

cræftan; *p.* te; *pp.* ed [cræft *art*] *To exercise a craft, to build*; architectari:—Ic cræfte *architector*, Ælfc. Gr. 36; Som. 38, 35. DER. a-cræftan, ge-.

cræftca *a workman*; artifex, opifex, Wrt. Voc. 73, 36, 38. v. cræftiga.

cræftega *a workman*, Past. 37, 3; Hat. MS. 50 b, 6. v. cræftiga, cræfta.

cræftga *an artificer*, Bt. Met. Fox 11, 184; Met. 11, 92. v. cræftiga.

cræftgast *most skilful*, Bt. Met. Fox 30, 4; Met. 30, 2; *sup. of* cræftig.

cræftgian *to strengthen, make powerful*. DER. ge-cræftgian.

cræft-gleáw; *adj. Sage-minded, science-learned*; animi prudens:—Cræft-gleáwe men *sage-minded men*, Chr. 975; Erl. 126, 26; Edg. 52.

cræftica *a workman*, Ælfc. Gl. 81; Som. 73, 2; Wrt. Voc. 47, 9. v. cræftiga.

cræftig; *adj. Ingenious, skilful*, CRAFTY, *cunning, virtuous, powerful*; ingeniosus, peritus, astutus, probus, potens:—Sum biþ fugelbona hafeces cræftig *one is a fowler skilful with the hawk*, Exon. 79 b; Th. 298, 6; Crä. 81: 97 a; Th. 361, 24; Wal. 24: Ps. C. 50, 11; Ps. Grn. ii. 277, 11. Án reordode, ðam wæs Iudas nama, wordes cræftig *one spake, whose name was Judas, crafty in word*, Elen. Kmbl. 837; El. 419: Exon. 97 b; Th. 364, 18; Wal. 72: Beo. Th. 2936; B. 1466. He sende cræftige wyrhtan *misit architectos*, Bd. 5, 21; S. 643, 7. Móde ðæs cræftig *with a mind so cunning*, Exon. 79 b; Th. 299, 6; Crä. 98. Céne and cræftig *brave and virtuous*, Bt. Met. Fox 10, 101; Met. 10, 51: Bt. 36, 6; Fox 182, 10, 11. Sume men bióþ cræftige *some men are virtuous*, 39, 10; Fox 228, 7. Yldo beóþ on eórþan ǽghwæs cræftig *age is powerful over everything on earth*, Salm. Kmbl. 584; Sal. 291: Beo. Th. 3929; B. 1962: Chr. 1066; Th. 334, 1; Edw. 5. Weras wísfæste, wordes cræftige *wise men, powerful of speech*, Elen. Kmbl. 628, 630; El. 314, 315. Nán cræftigra is ðonne ðú *no one is more skilful than thou*, Bt. 33, 4; Fox 128, 18. Omērus wæs leóþa cræftgast *Homer was most skilful in poems*, Bt. Met. Fox 30, 4; Met. 30, 2. Elþeódge wíf hæfdon gegán ðone cræftgestan dǽl *strange women had overcome the most powerful part*, Ors. 1, 10; Bos. 33, 41. DER. ǽ-cræftig, æl-, ár-, beadu-, bóc-, eácen-, hyge-, lagu-, leóþ-, leoðu-, má-, mód-, rím-, rún-, searo-, sundor-, un-, wíg-.

cræftiga, cræftega, cræftica, cræftca, cræftga, an; *m. A craftsman, workman, artificer, architect*; artifex, opifex, architectus:—Se micla cræftiga *the great craftsman*, Past. 8, 1; Hat. MS. 12 b, 15: Andr. Recd. 3264; An. 1635. Cræftica [MS. D. cræftca] *artifex*, Ælfc. Gr. 10; Som. 14, 43, MS. C: Ælfc. Gl. 81; Som. 73, 2; Wrt. Voc. 47, 9. Cræftca *artifex*, Wrt. Voc. 73, 36. Ðyssera cræftcena *horum artificum*, Ælfc. Gr. 10; Som. 14, 44. Se cræftega wyrcean mæg to ðæm ðe he wile *the workman can make what he likes of it*, Past. 37, 3; Hat. MS. 50 b, 6. Cræftiga *opifex*, Ælfc. Gl. 9; Som. 56, 128; Wrt. Voc. 19, 11. Cræftca *opifex*, Wrt. Voc. 73, 38. Swá swá ǽlc cræftega þencþ his weorc *as every artificer considers his work*, Bt. 39, 6; Fox 220, 4. Se cræftga geférscipas fæste gesamnaþ *the artificer firmly unites societies*, Bt. Met. Fox 11, 184; Met. 11, 92: Exon. 8 a; Th. 1, 22; Cri. 12. Cræftiga [MS. C. cræftica] *architectus*, Ælfc. Gr. 36; Som. 38, 35, MS. D.

cræftig-líce; *adv. Workmanlike*, CRAFTILY; fabre, artificiose:—Cræftiglíce *fabre*, Cot. 84. Seó heáfodstów cræftiglíce geworht ætýwde *locus capitis fabrefactus apparuit*, Bd. 4, 19; S. 590, 1.

cræftigra *more skilful*, Bt. 33, 4; Fox 128, 18; *comp. of* cræftig.

cræft-leás; *adj. Artless, unskilful, innocent, simple, inexpert*; iners, indoctus, innocens:—Cræftleás *iners*, Wrt. Voc. 73, 50. Dǽl-leás *vel* cræftleás *expers, indoctus*, Ælfc. Gl. 18; Som. 58, 123; Wrt. Voc. 22, 36.

cræft-líc; *adj. Artificial*; artificialis, Bridfr. Som. Ben. Lye.

cræft-líce; *adv. Cunningly, craftily*; affabre:—Cræftlíce *vel* smícere *affabre*, Ælfc. Gl. 99; Som. 76, 113; Wrt. Voc. 54, 55: Ælfc. Gr. 38; Som. 41, 32. v. cræftig-líce.

cræft-searo; *gen.* -searowes; *n. An instrument of war, a device, stratagem*; machina, Som. Ben. Lye.

cræft-wyrc, es; *n. Workmanship*; artificium, Scint. 29.

cræn *a crane*, Som. Ben. Lye. v. cran.

cræsta, an; *m. A* CREST, *tuft, plume*; crista, Som. Ben. Lye.

CRÆT, crat, es; *pl. nom. acc.* cratu, crætu; *gen.* cræta; *dat.* cratum, crætum; *n. A chariot*, CART; currus, pilentum:—Cræt *currus*, Ælfc. Gl. 49; Som. 65, 91; Wrt. Voc. 34, 22: 85, 71. Betogen [MS. betogan] cræt *capsus*, 49; Som. 65, 93; Wrt. Voc. 34, 23. Wǽrun Godes cræta gegearwedra tyn þúsendo *currus Dei decem millibus*, Ps. Th. 67, 17. On horsum and on cratum *equis ac curribus*, Deut. 11, 4. Mid gebeótlícum crætum and gilplícum riddum *with threatening chariots and proud horsemen*, Homl. Th. ii. 194, 23: Ps. Spl. C. 19, 8. He hæfde cratu and rídende men *habuit currus et equites*, Gen. 50, 9: Ex. 14, 27. Heó oferarn Pharao, and ealle his crætu and riddan *it* [*the sea*] *overwhelmed Pharaoh, and all his chariots and horsemen*, Homl. Th. ii. 194, 27. Crat *pilentum* vel *petorritum*, Ælfc. Gl. 49; Som. 65, 95; Wrt. Voc. 34, 25. [*Prompt.* cart *biga, rheda, quadriga*: *Wyc.* cart, carte: *Piers P.* cartwey: *Chauc.* carte: *R. Glouc.* carte-staf: *Laym.* carte, *dat*: *Dut.* krat, *n*: *Ger.* krätze, kretze, *m. f*: *M. H. Ger.* kretze, *m. f*: *O. H. Ger.* cratto, *m*: *Icel.* kartr, *m*: *Wel.* cart: *Ir.* cairt: *Gael.* cairt, cartach, *f.*]

cræte-hors, es; *n.* [cræt *a cart*, hors *a horse*] *A cart-horse*; veredus, Ælfc. Gl. 5; Som. 56, 17; Wrt. Voc. 17, 21.

cræt-wǽn, es; *m.* [wǽn *a waggon*] *A chariot, wain*; currus:—Crætwǽn mid seolfre gegyred *a chariot mounted with silver*, Ors. 2, 4; Bos. 43, 14. Mid crætwǽne *with a chariot*, 2, 4; Bos. 43, 6. Sceoldon senátas rídan on crætwǽnum *the senators must ride in chariots*, 2, 4; Bos. 43, 9.

crǽwst, he crǽwþ *crowest, crows*, Lk. Bos. 22, 34; *2nd and 3rd pers. pres. of* cráwan.

CRAFIAN, crafigan; *p.* ode, ede; *pp.* od, ed *To ask*, CRAVE, *implore, demand, summon*; petere, postulare, in jus vocare:—Gif hwá wíte crafige *if any one crave a fine*, L. C. S. 70; Th. i. 412, 24. Se man crafode hine on hundrede *the man summoned him before the hundred court* Lchdm. iii. 288, 4. He mid rihte crafede ðás ða he crafede *he with right craved those things which he craved*, Chr. 1070; Erl. 208, 18, 23. [*Piers P.* craven: *Dan.* kræve: *Swed.* kräfva: *Icel.* krefja.] DER. be-crafian: un-crafod, unbe-.

crammian, ic crammige; *p.* ode; *pp.* od *To* CRAM, *stuff*; farcire:—Ic crammige odde fylle *farcio*, Ælfc. Gr. 30, 2; Som. 34, 36. [*Wyc.* crammyd, *pp*: *Piers P.* ycrammed, *pp.*] DER. under-crammian.

CRAN, es; *m*: e; *f. A* CRANE; grus:—Cran *grus*, Ælfc. Gr. 9, 33; Som. 12, 20: Ælfc. Gl. 38; Som. 63, 34; Wrt. Voc. 29, 53: 62, 20: 77, 16: 280, 25. [*Prompt.* crane *grus*: *Laym.* cron, crane: *Plat.* kraan: *O. Sax.* kranc, *m*: *Dut.* kraan, *f*: *Kil.* kraene: *Ger.* kranich, *m*: *M. H. Ger.* kranech, *m*: *O. H. Ger.* kranuh, *m*: *Dan.* trane, *m. f*: *Swed.* trana, *f*: *Icel.* trani, *m*; trana, *f*: *Lat.* grus, *f*: *Grk.* γέραν-os, *m. and f*: *Wel. Corn.* garan, *f*: *Ir. Gael.* garan, *m*: *Armor.* garan, *f.*]

cranc, *pl.* cruncon *yielded*; *p. of* crincan.

cranc-stæf, es; *m. A weaver's instrument*; instrumenti genus ad textores pertinentis, Som. Ben. Lye.

crang, *pl.* crungon *fell, perished, died*; *p. of* cringan.

crang *dead, killed*; mortuus, occisus, Mann.

crano-hawc [cran *a crane*; hafoc, es; *m. a hawk*] *A crane-hawk*; accipiter, qui gruem mordet, Spelm. Gl. Ben. Lye.

crápe *should creep*, Chr. 1131; Erl. 260, 3, = creápe; *p. subj. of* creópan.

crat *a waggon*, Ælfc. Gl. 49; Som. 65, 95; Wrt. Voc, 34, 25. v. cræt.

CRÁWAN, ic cráwe, ðú cráwest, crǽwst, he cráweþ, crǽwþ; *p.* creów, *pl.* creówon; *pp.* cráwen *To* CROW *as a cock*; cantare instar galli:—Ne crǽwþ se hana to-dæg *non cantabit hodie gallus*, Lk. Bos. 22, 34. Ne crǽwþ se cocc, ǽr ðú wiðsæcst me þríwa, Jn. Bos. 13, 38; *the koc schal not crowe, til thou schalt denye me thries*, Wyc. Ǽrðamðe cocc cráwe, þríwa ðú wiðsæcst mín *antequam gallus cantet, ter me negabis*, Mt. Bos. 26, 34. Ǽrðamðe se cocc cráwe, þríwa ðú me wiðsæcst, 26, 75; *bifore the cok crowe, thries thou shalt denye me*, Wyc. Ǽr hana cráwe *priusquam gallus vocem dederit*, Mk. Bos. 14, 30. Ǽr se hana cráwe, 14, 72; *bifore the cok synge*, Wyc: Lk. Bos. 22, 61. Sóna se cocc creów *statim gallus cantavit*, Jn. Bos. 18, 27. Hrædlíce ðá creów se cocc, Mt. Bos. 26, 74; *anon the cok crew*, Wyc. Se hana creów *gallus cantavit*, Mk. Bos. 14, 68: Lk. Bos. 22, 60. Ðá eftsóna creów se hana, Mk. Bos. 14, 72; *anon eftsoones the cok song*, Wyc. [*Wyc.* crowe: *Plat.* kreien, kreijen: *Dut.* kraaijen: *Kil.* kraeyen: *Ger.* krähen: *M. H. Ger.* kræjen: *O. H. Ger.* krâjan, krâhan.]

CRÁWE, an; *f.* I. *a* CROW; cornix:—Cráwe *cornix*, Ælfc. Gl. 37; Som. 63, 8; Wrt. Voc. 29, 31: 62, 29: 280, 34. II. *a raven*; corvus:—Se selþ nýtenum mete heora, and briddum cráwan cígendum hine *qui dat jumentis escam ipsorum, et pullis corvi invocantibus eum*, Ps. Spl. T. 146, 10. [*Chauc.* crow: *Plat.* kreie, kraie: *O. Sax.* krâia, *f*: *Frs. Japx.* krie: *Dut.* kraai, *f*: *Kil.* kraeye: *Ger.* krähe, *f*: *M. H. Ger.* krâ, *f*: *O. H. Ger.* krâa, *f*: *Lat.* corvus, cornix: *Grk.* κόραξ, κορώνη: *Sansk.* kārava, *m. a crow.*]

cráw-leác, es; *n.* [cráwe *a crow*, leác *a leek*] *Crow-garlic*; allium vineale, Lin:—Nim hermodactylos = ἑρμο-δάκτυλος [MS. datulus] ða wyrt . . . ðæt is on úre geþeóda ðæt greáte [MS. greáta] cráwleác

[MS. crauleac] *take the wort allium vineale . . . that is in our language the great crow-garlic*, Lchdm. i. 376, 3. Crāwan leác *hermodactylus*, Ælfc. Gl. 44; Som. 64, 84; Wrt. Voc. 32, 20.

Creacan ford *Crayford*, Chr. 456; Th. 22, 5, col. 2, 3. v. Crecgan ford.

Creácas; *gen.* Creáca; *pl. m. The Greeks;* Græci:—Mid eallan Creáca cræftum *with all the arts of the Greeks*, Ors. 1, 10; Bos. 33, 29, 31: Bos. 34, 6. v. Grēcas.

Creacc-gelād *Cricklade*, Chr. 905; Th. 181, 21, col. 1. v. Crecca-gelād.

Creácisc; *adj. Greek, Grecian;* Græcus, Ors. 1, 10; Bos. 33, 12. v. Grēcisc.

creád *pressed*, Chr. 937; Th. 204, 14, col. 1; Æðelst. 35; *p. of* creódan.

creáp, *pl.* crupon *crept, crawled*, Glostr. Frag. 6, 7: Ors. 1, 7; Bos. 29, 33; *p. of* creópan.

Creca-lād *Cricklade*, Chr. 1016; Erl. 153, 38. v. Crecca-gelād.

Crēcas; *gen.* Crēca; *pl. m. The Greeks;* Græci:—Fōr on Crēcas *he went against the Greeks*, Ors. 2, 5; Bos. 46, 15, 31. Ymbe Crēca land *about the land of the Greeks*, Ors. 1, 1; Bos. 23, 11: 23, 12, 13, 17, 22: 1, 6; Bos. 29, 6. Perseus of Crēca lande in Asiam fōr *Perseus went from the land of the Greeks into Asia*, 1, 8; Bos. 31, 14. v. Grēcas.

crecca, an; *m. A* CREEK, *bay, wharf;* crepido, Som. Ben. Lye.

Crecca-gelād, Cre-gelād, e; *f.* [gelād *a road, way: Flor.* Criccelade: *Hunt.* Crikelade: *Sim. Dun.* Criccelad: *Brom.* Criklade] CRICKLADE, *Wiltshire;* oppidi nomen in agro Wiltoniensi:—Hie hergodon ofer Mercna land ōþ hie cōmon to Creccagelāde, and fōron ðǽr ofer Temese *they harried over the Mercians' land until they came to Cricklade, and there they went over the Thames*, Chr. 905; Erl. 98, 15. On ðissum geáre com Cnut mid his here ofer Temese into Myrcum æt Cregelāde *in this year* [A. D. 1016] *Cnut came with his army over the Thames into Mercia at Cricklade*, 1016; Erl. 153, 23.

Creccan ford *Crayford*, Chr. 456; Th. 23, 4, col. 2. v. Crecgan ford.

Crēce; *gen.* a; *dat.* um; *pl. m. The Greeks;* Græci:—He belytegade ealle Crēce on his geweald *he allured all the Greeks into his power*, Ors. 3, 7; Bos. 59, 39, 40. Philippus alȳfde eallum Crēcum *Philip gave leave to all the Greeks*, 3, 7; Bos. 61, 42. v. Crēcas, Grēcas.

Crecgan ford, Creccan ford, es; *m.* [*Hunt.* Creganford: *the ford of the river Cray*] CRAYFORD, *Kent;* loci nomen in agro Cantiano:—Hēr Hengest and Æsc fuhton wið Brettas in ðære stōwe ðe is gecweden Crecgan ford *in this year* [A. D. 457] *Hengest and Æsc fought against the Britons at the place which is called Crayford*, Chr. 457; Erl. 12, 18.

Crēcisc *Grecian*, Bt. Met. Fox 26, 55; Met. 26, 28. v. Grēcisc.

crēda, an; *m.* [*Lat.* crēdo *I believe*] *The creed, belief;* symbolum fidei:—Se læssa crēda *the less* or *Apostles' creed*, Homl. Th. ii. 596, 11. We andettaþ on ūrum crēdan ðæt Drihten sitt æt his Fæder swīðran *we confess in our creed that the Lord sits at the right hand of his Father*, i. 48, 28: 274, 23. Ǽlc cristen man sceal æfter rihte cunnan his crēdan . . . mid ðam crēdan he sceal his geleáfan getrymman *every christian man by right ought to know his creed . . . with the creed he ought to confirm his faith*, 274, 20, 21. DER. mæsse-crēda.

Cre-gelād *Cricklade*, Chr. 1016; Erl. 153, 23. v. Crecca-gelād.

crencestre, crencistre, an; *f. A female weaver, a spinster;* textrix, Cod. Dipl. 1290; A. D. 995; Kmbl. vi. 131, 32.

Creocc-gelād *Cricklade*, Chr. 905; Erl. 99, 20. v. Crecca-gelād.

CREÓDAN, ic creóde, ðū creódest, crȳtst, crȳst, he creódeþ, crȳdeþ, crȳt, *pl.* creódaþ; *p.* ic, he creád, ðū crude, *pl.* crudon; *pp.* croden *To* CROWD, *press, drive;* premere, premi, pellere, pelli:—Ðonne heáh geþring on cleofu crȳdeþ *when the towering mass on the cliffs presses*, Exon. 101 b; Th. 384, 15; Rä. 4, 28. Creád cnear on flot *the bark drove afloat*, Chr. 937; Th. 204, 14; col. 1; Æðelst. 35. [*Prompt.* crowdyn' *impello: Chauc.* croude, crowde *push: Kil.* kruyen, kruyden *trudere, propellere.*]

CREÓPAN; *part.* creópende; ic creópe, ðū crȳpest, crypst, creópest, creópst, he crȳpeþ, crȳpþ, creópeþ, creópþ, *pl.* creópaþ; *p.* creáp, *pl.* crupon; *pp.* cropen *To* CREEP, *crawl;* repere, serpere:—He næfþ his fōta geweald and onginþ creópan *he has not the use of his feet and begins to creep*, Bt. 36, 4; Fox 178, 14, Cott. MS. Him cōmon to creópende fela næddran *many serpents came creeping to them*, Homl. Th. ii. 488, 21. Mægen creópendra wyrma biþ on heora fōtum *the power of reptiles* [lit. *creeping worms*] *is in their feet*, Ors. 4, 6; Bos. 84, 44: Gen. 7, 21. Nān wilde deór, ne on fyðerfōtum ne on creópendum, nis to wiðmetenne yfelum wīfe *no wild beast, neither among the four-footed nor the creeping, is to be compared with an evil woman*, Homl. Th. i. 486, 29. Lǽde seó eorþe forþ creópende cinn æfter heora hiwum *producat terra reptilia secundum species suas*, Gen. 1, 24, 25, 26. Ic creópe *repo*, Ælfc. Gr. 28, 4; Som. 31, 23. Se biþ mihtigra se ðe gǽþ ðonne se ðe crȳpþ *he is more powerful who goes than he who creeps*, Bt. 36, 4; Fox 178, 16. Hī creópaþ and snīcaþ *they creep and crawl*, Bt. Met. Fox 31, 12; Met. 31, 6. Heó creáp betwux ðām mannum *she crept among the men*, Homl. Th. ii. 394, 11: Glostr. Frag. 6, 7. Ða munecas crupon under ðam weofode *the monks crept under the altar*, Chr. 1083; Erl. 217, 22: Ors. 1, 7; Bos. 29, 33. [*Piers P.* crepen: *Chauc. R. Glouc.* crepe: *Laym.* crepen: *Plat.* krupen: *O. Sax.* criepan: *Frs.* krippen: *O. Frs.* kriapa: *Dut.* kruipen: *Kil.* kruypen: *Ger.* kriechen: *M. H. Ger.* kriuchen: *O. H. Ger.* kriuchan: *Dan.* krybe: *Swed.* krypa: *Icel.* krjúpa.] DER. be-creópan, þurh-, under-.

creópere, es; *m. A* CREEPER, *cripple;* serpens, clinicus:—Seó ealde cyrce wæs eall behangen mid criccum and mid creópera sceamelum *the old church was all hung around with crutches and with cripples' stools*, Glostr. Frag. 12, 17.

creópung, e; *f. A* CREEPING, *stealing;* obreptio, Cot. 144.

creów, *pl.* creówon *crew*, Jn. Bos. 18, 27; *p. of* crāwan.

crēpel, es; *m. A burrow;* cuniculum, Mone B. 2774.

cresse *cress*, Glos. Epnl. Recd. 162, 61. v. cærse.

CRICC, crycc, e; *f. A* CRUTCH, *staff;* baculus:—Gird ðīn and cricc ðīn me frēfredon *virga tua et baculus tuus me consolata sunt*, Ps. Spl. C. 22, 5. He, mid his cricce wreðiende, on cyricean eóde *baculo sustentans intravit ecclesiam*, Bd. 4, 31; S. 610, 28. He, mid his crycce hine awreðiende, hām becom *baculo innitens domum pervenit*, 4, 31; S. 610, 17. He mid criccum his fēðunge underwreðode *he supported his gait with crutches*, Homl. Th. ii. 134, 24. [*Laym.* crucche, *dat: Plat.* krukke, krükke: *Dut.* kruk, *f: Kil.* krucke: *Ger.* krücke, *f: M. H. Ger.* krücke, krucke, *f: O. H. Ger.* krucka, *f: Dan.* krykke, *m. f: Swed.* krycka, *f.*]

Cric-gelād *Cricklade*, Chr. 1016; Th. 276, 29, col. 2. v. Crecca-gelād.

Cridian tūn, es; *m.* [tūn *a town: Flor.* Cridiatun] CREDITON, *Devonshire, formerly the seat of the bishops of Devonshire, so called because it is situated on the banks of the river Creedy;* oppidi nomen in agro Devoniensi:—Hēr æt Kyrtlingtūne forþfērde Sideman bisceop, on hrædlīcan deáþe: se wæs Defnascīre bisceop, and he wilnode ðæt his līcræst sceolde beón æt Cridian tūne, æt his bisceopstōle *in this year* [A. D. 977] *bishop Sideman died at Kirtlington, by sudden death: he was bishop of Devonshire, and he desired that his body's resting-place might be at Crediton, at his episcopal see*, Chr. 977; Erl. 127, 35-38: Cod. Dipl. 1334; A. D. 1046; Kmbl. vi. 196, 15.

crimman; *p.* cramm, cram, *pl.* crummon; *pp.* crummen *To crumb, crumble, mingle;* friare, inserere:—Hornes sceafoðan crim on ðæt dolh *crumble shavings of horn on the wound*, L. M. 1, 61; Lchdm. ii. 132, 12. Cram *inseruit*, Glos. Prudent. Recd. 151, 33. DER. a-crimman.

crincan, ic crince, ðū crincst, he crincþ, *pl.* crincaþ; *p.* cranc, *pl.* cruncon; *pp.* cruncen *To yield;* occumbere:—Wīgend cruncon, wundum wērige *the fighters yielded, oppressed with wounds*, Byrht. Th. 140, 43; By. 302. DER. ge-crincan.

crincgan *to fall*, Byrht. Th. 140, 23; By. 292. v. cringan.

cringan, crincgan; ic cringe, crincge, ðū cringest, cringst, he cringeþ, cringþ, *pl.* cringaþ, crincgaþ; *p.* crang, crong, *pl.* crungon; *pp.* crungen *To yield,* CRINGE, *fall, perish, die;* occumbere, mori:—Sume on wæl crungon *some had fallen in the slaughter*, Beo. Th. 2231; B. 1113. Hī sceoldon begen cringan on wælstōwe *they should both fall on the battle-field*, Byrht. Th. 140, 23; By. 292: Andr. Kmbl. 2062; An. 1033: Chr. 937; Th. 202, 6; col. 2; Æðelst. 10. Crungon *they perished*, Exon. 124 a; Th. 477, 17; Ruin. 26: 124 a; Th. 477, 24; Ruin. 29. Fǽge crungon *the fated died*, Cd. 167; Th. 208, 11; Exod. 481: Beo. Th. 1275; B. 635. DER. ge-cringan. v. gringan.

crisma, an; *m.* [chrisma, ătis, *n.* = χρῖσμα, ἄτος; *n. an unction*, from χρίω [*fut.* χρίσω] *I touch the surface of a body, I rub* or *anoint*]. I. *the chrism, unction* or *holy oil, used for anointing by the Roman Catholic church after baptism;* oleum chrismătis:—Eálā ge mæsse-preóstas, mīne gebrōðra, we secgaþ eów nū ðæt we ǽr ne sǽdon, forðonðe we to-dæg sceolan dǽlan ūrne ele, on þreó wīsan gehālgodne, swā swā us gewissaþ seó bōc; *i. e. oleum sanctum, et oleum chrismatis, et oleum infirmorum*, ðæt is on Englisc, hālig ele, ōðer is crisma, and seóccra manna ele: and ge sceolan habban þreó ampullan gearuwe to ðām þrȳm elum; forðanðe we ne durran dōn hī togædere on ānum elefate, forðanðe hyra ǽlc biþ gehālgod on sundron to synderlīcre þēnunge. Mid ðam hāligan ele, ge scylan ða hǽðenan cild mearcian on ðam breóste, and betwux ða gesculdru, on middeweardan, mid rōde tācne, ǽrðanðe ge hit fullian on ðam fantwætere; and ðonne hit of ðæm wætere cymþ, ge scylan wyrcan rōde tācen uppon ðæm heáfde mid ðam hāligan crisman. On ðam hāligan fante, ǽrðanðe ge hȳ fullian, ge scylon dōn crisman on Cristes rōde tācne; and man ne mōt besprengan men mid ðæm fantwætere, syððan se crisma biþ ðǽron gedōn *O ye mass-priests, my brethren, we will now say to you what we have not before said, because to-day we are to divide our oil, hallowed in three ways, as the book points out to us;* i. e. oleum sanctum, et oleum chrismatis, et oleum infirmorum, *that is, in English, holy oil, the second is chrism, and sick men's oil: and ye ought to have three flasks ready for the three oils; for we dare not put them together in one oil vessel, because each of them is hallowed apart for a particular service. With holy oil, ye shall mark heathen children on* *the breast, and between the shoulders, in the middle, with the sign of the cross, before ye baptize it in the font water; and when it comes from the water, ye shall make the sign of the cross on the head with the holy chrism. In the holy font, before ye baptize them, ye shall pour chrism in the figure of the cross of Christ; and no one may be sprinkled with the font water, after the chrism is poured in*, L. Ælf. E. Th. ii. 390, 1-17. Mid crysman smyreþ his breóst *chrismate pectus eorum unguet*, L. Ecg. C. 36; Th. ii. 162, 1. Ðonne he crisman fecce *when he fetches chrism*, L. Edg. C. 67; Th. ii. 258, 20: L. N. P. L. 9; Th. ii. 292, 3. II. *the white vesture, called chrisom, which the minister puts upon the child immediately after dipping it in water, or pouring water upon it in baptism;* chrismale, id est, vestis candida, quæ super corpus baptizati ponitur. *In the Liturgy of Edward VI*, 1549, *it is said*, 'Then the minister shall put upon the child the white vesture, commonly called the *Chrisom;* and say, Take this white vesture for a token of the innocency, which, by God's grace, in this holy sacrament of baptism, is given unto thee,' p. 112. This white vesture was worn for a month after the child's birth, and if it died before the expiration of that time, it had the chrisom for its shroud. A child, thus dying, was called a Chrisom-child:—Wǽron eác gefullade æfter-fyligendre tíde óðre his [Eádwines] bearn of Æðelburhge ðære cwēne acende, Æðelhūn, and Æðeldriþ his dōhter, and ōðer his suna Wuscfreá hātte, ac ða ǽrran twegen under crisman forþgefērdon, and on cyrican in Eoferwīcceastre bebyrigde wǽron *baptizati sunt tempore sequente et alii liberi ejus* [*Æduini*] *de Ædilberga regina progeniti, Ædilhun, et Ædilthryd filia, et alter filius Vuscfrea quorum* primi albati *adhuc rapti sunt de hac vita* [*lit.* the former two died under chrism], *et Eburaci in Ecclesia sepulti*, Bd. 2, 14; S. 518, 1: 5, 7; S. 620, 40. Under crysmum *baptizatus in albis*, Mone B. 2096.

crism-hâlgung, e; *f. The consecration of the oil of chrism;* chrismatis consecratio, Wanl. Catal. 121, col. 2, 57.

crism-lȳsing, -līsing, e; *f. A leaving off the baptismal vest;* chrismatis solutio:—His crismlȳsing [crismlising MS. A.] wæs æt Wedmor *the leaving off his baptismal vest was at Wedmore*, Chr. 878; Erl. 81, 20. v. crisma.

crisp; *adj.* CRISP, *curly;* crispus:—He hæfde crispe loccas *he had curly locks*, Bd. 5, 2; S. 615, 30. v. cyrps.

Crist, Krist, es; *m.* CHRIST; Christus = Χριστός *the anointed one, as a translation of the Heb.* מָשִׁיחַ *Messiah:*—Se Hǽlend, ðe is genemned Crist *Iesus, qui vocatur Christus;* Ἰησοῦς, ὁ λεγόμενος Χριστός, Mt. Bos. 1, 16. Crist wæs acenned, Hǽlend gehāten *Christ was born, called Jesus* [*Saviour*], Menol. Fox 1-7. Hēr is on cneórisse bōc Hǽlendes Cristes *liber generationis Iesu Christi*, Mt. Bos. 1, 1. Hēr ys gōdspelles angyn Hǽlendes Cristes, Godes suna *initium evangelii Iesu Christi, filii Dei*, Mk. Bos. 1, 1. Beseoh onsȳne cristes ðīnes *behold the face of thine anointed*, Ps. Th. 83, 9: 88, 32, 44. Feówer Cristes bēc *the four Gospels*, Ælfc. T. Grn. 12, 27: Bd. 5, 19; S. 638, 16. Seó Cristes bōc *the Gospel*, Ælfc. T. 30, 1. Feoh būtan gewitte ne can Crist gehērian *cattle without understanding cannot praise Christ*, Salm. Kmbl. 48; Sal. 24. Ofer ealle Cristes bēc *over all Christ's books* [*Gospels*], 100; Sal. 49. On Cristes onlīcnisse *in Christ's likeness*, Salm. Kmbl. 146, 15.

cristalla, an; *m:* cristallus, i; *m. Lat.* I. *crystal;* crystallus = κρύσταλλος:—Ðæt wæs hwītes bleós swā cristalla *it was of a white colour like crystal*, Num. 11, 7. Cristallan *crystallum*, Glos. Prudent. Recd. 140, 49. He his cristallum sendeþ *mittit crystallum suum*, Ps. Th. 147, 6. II. *the herb crystallium, flea-bane, flea-wort;* crystallion = κρυστάλλιον, psyllion = ψύλλιον:—Nim cristallan and disman *take crystallium and tansy*, Lchdm. iii. 10, 29.

cristen; *def.* se cristena; *sup.* se cristenesta; *adj.* [Crist *Christ*] *Christian;* christianus:—Ǽlc cristen man hæfde sibbe *every christian man had peace*, Ors. 6, 13; Bos. 122, 7: 6, 30; Bos. 127, 22. Cristnu gesamnung *the christian church*, Ps. Th. 44, 11. Gif hwā cristenes mannes blōd ageóte *if any one shed a christian man's blood*, L. Edm. E. 3; Th. i. 246, 2: Ps. Th. 106, 31. He forbeád ðæt man nānum cristenum men ne abulge *he forbade men to annoy any christian man*, Ors. 6, 11; Bos. 121, 10: L. Edm. E. 2; Th. i. 244, 16: Elen. Kmbl. 1974; El. 989. Hī bebudon ðæt man ǽlcne cristenne man ofslōge *they commanded men to slay every christian man*, Ors. 6, 13; Bos. 121, 32. Him sealde Iustinus āne cristene bōc *Justin gave him a christian book*, 6, 12; Bos. 121, 24. Godes þeówas for eall cristen folc þingian *let the servants of God intercede for all christian people*, L. Eth. v. 4; Th. i. 304, 25: vi. 2; Th. i. 314, 18: L. C. E. 6; Th. i. 364, 7. Cristene men secgaþ *christian men say*, Bt. 39, 8; Fox 224, 14: Ors. 6, 11; Bos. 121, 8. Nero wæs ǽrest ēhtend cristenra manna *Nero was the first persecutor of christian men*, 6, 5; Bos. 119, 22: 6, 9; Bos. 120, 18: Elen. Kmbl. 1956; El. 980. Fram ōðrum cristenum mannum *from other christian men*, Ors. 6, 9; Bos. 120, 22: 6, 12; Bos. 121, 25. Hī cristene men pinedon *they tormented christian men*, 6, 11; Bos. 121, 17: 6, 19; Bos. 123, 16. Oswig se cristena cyning to his rīce fēng *Oswy the christian king succeeded to his kingdom*, Bd. 3, 21; S. 551, 30. Se cristena dōm *christianity*, Bt. 1; Fox 2, 15. Bǽdon [MS. bædan] hī ða cristenan men *they asked the christian men*, Ors. 6, 13; Bos. 121, 41: 6, 30; Bos. 127, 14. Se mon wæs se cristenesta and se gelǽredesta *the man was most christian and most learned*, Bd. 2, 15; S. 518, 43: 3, 1; S. 523, 7: 3, 9; S. 533, 6.

cristen, es; *m:* cristena, an; *m. A christian;* christianus:—He wæs cristen *he was a christian*, Bt. 1; Fox 2, 7: Chr. 167; Erl. 8, 16: Bd. 3, 21; S. 551, 4. He hēt ealle ða cristenan *he ordered all the christians*, Ors. 6, 30; Bos. 127, 10.

Cristen-dôm, es; *m. Christianity*, CHRISTENDOM, *the christian world;* christianitas:—Se cristendōm weóx on heora tīman *christianity increased in their time*, Jud. Grn. Epilog. 264, 7: Jud. Thw. 161, 21. Ǽghwylc cristen man gȳme his cristendōmes georne *let every christian man strictly keep his christianity*, L. Eth. v. 22; Th. i. 310, 5: vi. 27; Th. i. 322, 5: L. C. E. 19; Th. i. 370, 32: Ælfc. T. 28, 3. Gif hwā cristendōm wyrde *if any one violate christianity*, L. E. G. 2; Th. i. 168, 1: L. Eth. v. 1; Th. i. 304, 4, 7: L. C. S. 11; Th. i. 382, 7. On cristendōm *in christendom*, Chr. 1129; Erl. 258, 29.

cristenest, se, cristenesta *the most christian, pious, holy*, Bd. 3, 9 S. 533, 6: 2, 15; S. 518, 43; *sup. of* cristen.

Cristes bôc, e; *f.* CHRIST'S BOOK, *the Gospel;* Christi liber, evangelium, Ælfc. T. 30, 1: Salm. Kmbl. 100; Sal. 49. v. Crist.

cristlîc; *adj. Christlike, christian;* christianus:—We lǽraþ, ðæt ǽghwilc cristen man cristlīce lage rihtlīce healde *we direct, that every christian man rightly observe the christian law*, L. Eth. vi. 11; Th. i. 318, 11, note 4.

cristnian; *p.* ode; *pp.* od *To christianize, catechize;* catechizare:—Ðæt Paulinus ðǽr ðæt folc cristnode and fullode [MS. cristnade ⁊ fullade] *that Paulinus might there christen and baptize the people*, or as the original Latin of Bede has it, with greater precision,—*ut Paulinus cum eis catechizandi et baptizandi officio deditus moraretur*, Bd. 2, 14; S. 518, 7, 8; Latin 95, 34.

croc, crocc, crog, crogg, crohh, es; *m. A crock, pitcher, waterpot, flagon, a little jug* or *lentil-shaped vessel;* urceus, lagena, lenticula, legythum:—Croccas, Cot. 209: Grm. iii. 458, 15. DER. croc-wyrhta.

CROCCA, an; *m. A* CROCK, *pitcher, earthenware pot* or *pan;* vas fictile, testa, olla:—Mīn mægen ys forseárod, swā swā lǽmen crocca *exaruit velut testa virtus mea*, Ps. Th. 21, 13. Crocca *olla*, Ps. Lamb. 59, 10: Ælfc. Gr. 7; Som. 6, 53: Wrt. Voc. 82, 56. Wyl wæter on croccan *boil water in a crock*, L. M. 1, 40; Lchdm. ii. 104, 19. On ǽnne croccan ðone ðe sie gepicod ūtan *in a crock that is pitched on the outside*, 1, 2; Lchdm. ii. 26, 23. Ic gedō ðæt ðū hī miht swā eáðe abrecan, swā se croccwyrhta mæg ǽnne croccan *tamquam vas figuli confringes eos*, Ps. Th. 2, 9: Herb. 126, 2; Lchdm. i. 238, 6. [*Piers P.* krokke: *Plat.* kruke: *O. Sax.* crūka, *f:* *Frs.* kruwch: *O. Frs.* krocha, *m:* *Dut.* kruik, *f:* *Kil.* kruycke: *Ger.* krug, *m:* *M. H. Ger.* kruoc, *m:* *O. H. Ger.* krōg, *m:* *Dan.* krukke, *m. f:* *Swed.* kruka, *f:* *Icel.* krukka, *f.*]

croc-hwær, es; *m.* [hwer *an ewer*] *A kettle;* cacabus, Som. Ben. Lye.

croc-sceard, es; *n.* [sceard *a shred, fragment*] *A shred* or *fragment of a crock* or *pot, a pot*SHERD; testa, testu:—Adruwode oððe forseárode swā swā blȳwnys oððe crocsceard mægen mīn *aruit tamquam testa virtus mea*, Ps. Lamb. 21, 16. Mid ānum crocscearde *with a potsherd*, Job Thw. 166, 34: Homl. Th. ii. 452, 29. Crocsceard *testu*, Ælfc. Gr. 11; Som. 15, 29.

croc-wyrhta, crocc-wyrhta, -wirhta, an; *m. A crockworker, potter;* figulus, luti figulus:—Crocwyrhta *figulus* vel *luti figulus*, Ælfc. Gr. 28, 5; Som. 31, 62. Ic gedō ðæt ðū hī miht swā eáðe abrecan, swā se croccwyrhta mæg ǽnne croccan *tamquam vas figuli confringes eos*, Ps. Th. 2, 9. Fæt crocwirhtan *vel* tygelwirhtan *vas figuli*, Ps. Lamb. 2, 9.

croda, an; *m.* [croden, *pp. of* creódan *to crowd, press, drive*] *A crowd, press;* collisus. DER. lind-croda.

croden *crowded, pressed; pp. of* creódan.

croft, es; *m. A* CROFT, *a small inclosed field;* prædiolum, agellulus septus:—Æt ðæs croftes heáfod *at the top of the croft*, Cod. Dipl. 553; A. D. 969; Kmbl. iii. 37, 23. In ðone croft, of ðæm crofte *to the croft, from the croft*, 681; A. D. 972; Kmbl. iii. 261, 11: 679; A. D. 972-992; Kmbl. iii. 258, 27, 28.

crog, crogg, crohh, es; *m. A small vessel, chrismatory, bottle;* legythum, lenticula, lagena:—Crog oððe ampella *lenticula*, Cot. 124. v. croc.

croh, es; *m? Saffron;* crocus = κρόκος, crocus sativus, Lin:—Meng mid [MS. wid] croh *mingle it with saffron*, L. M. 2, 37; Lchdm. ii. 244, 23: Herb. 118, 2; Lchdm. i. 232, 7: Med. ex Quadr. 5, 4; Lchdm. i. 348, 14.

crohh *a pitcher;* legythum, lagena *vel* ampulla, Cot. 119. v. crog.

croma *a crumb*, Mt. Kmbl. Rush. 15, 27. v. cruma.

crompeht; *adj. Full of crumples, wrinkled;* folialis, Cot. 91.

crong *killed, perished; p. of* cringan.

CROP, cropp, es; *m.* I. *a sprout* or *top of a herb, flower, berry, an ear of corn, a bunch of berries* or *blooms, cluster;* cyma = κῦμα, thyrsus = θύρσος, spica, corymbus = κόρυμβος, racemus, uva:—Crop *cyma*, Ælfc. Gl. 60; Som. 68, 18; Wrt. Voc. 39, 4. Crop *tursus, cimia* [= *thyrsus, cyma*], 42; Som. 64, 28; Wrt. Voc. 31, 38. Dō him merscmealwan crop *give him a sprout of marsh mallow*, L. M. 3, 63; Lchdm. ii. 350, 25. Genim ðysse wyrte þrý croppas *take three sprouts of this herb*, Herb. 106; Lchdm. i. 220, 10. Genim ðysse wyrte croppas *take the tops of this herb*, 110, 4; Lchdm. i. 224, 9: 130, 1; Lchdm. i. 240, 18. Genim ðysse wyrte croppas *take berries of this herb* [*ivy*], 100, 3; Lchdm. i. 214, 3. Þegnas his ða croppas eton *discipuli ejus spicas manducabant*, Lk. Skt. Lind. 6, 1. Wið ðon biþ gôd lustmocan crop *a bunch of 'lustmock' is good for that*, L. M. 1, 38; Lchdm. ii. 92, 9. Genim lustmocan crop *take a bunch of 'lustmock,'* 1, 38; Lchdm. ii. 98, 16. Croppas *racemos*, Mone B. 2572. Croppum *uvis*, 3836. II. *the* CROP *or craw of a bird*; vesicula gutturis:—Wurp ðone cropp and ða feðera wiðæftan ðæt weofod *vesiculam gutturis et plumas projiciet prope altare*, Lev. 1, 16. III. *a kidney*; rien:—Crop *rien*, Ælfc. Gl. 76; Som. 71, 107; Wrt. Voc. 45, 13. [*Prompt.* croppe *cyma*: *Piers P.* crop: *Chauc.* crop, croppe: *Plat.* kropp: *Dut.* krop, *m*: *Kil.* krop, kroppe: *Ger. M.H.Ger.* kropf, *m*: *O.H.Ger.* kroph, *m*: *Dan.* krop, *m. f*: *Swed.* kropp, *m*: *Icel.* kroppr, *m.*] DER. ifig-crop.

cropen *crept, crawled*; *pp. of* creópan.

crop-leác, es; *n. Garlic*; allium satīvum, Lin:—Genim cropleác *take garlic*, L. M. 1, 3; Lchdm. ii. 42, 14: 3, 68; Lchdm. ii. 356, 5.

croppa, an; *m. The top* or *flower of a herb*; corymbus, pluma:—Bânwyrt hæbbe croppan *bonewort hath clusters of flowers*, L. M. 2, 51; Lchdm. ii. 266, 6. v. crop I.

croppiht; *adj.* [crop I. *a bunch, cluster*; -iht, *adj. termination*, q. v.] *Croppy, full of clusters*; racemosus, L. M. 1, 39; Lchdm. ii. 102, 12.

cruce, an; *f. A cruse, pitcher, waterpot*; urceus, urceolus:—Cruce *viciolum* [= *urceolus*], Wrt. Voc. 290, 67.

crucet-hús, es; *n. A torment house*; afflictionis domus:—Sume hí diden in crucet-hús, ðæt is in ân ceste ðæt was scort, and nareu, and undêp, and dide scærpe stânes ðerinne, and þrengde ðe man ðærinne, ðæt him bræcon alle ðe limes *some they put into a crucet-house, that is into a chest that was short, and narrow, and undeep, and put sharp stones therein, and pressed the man therein, so that they brake all his limbs*, Chr. 1137; Th. 382, 28.

crudon *crowded, pressed*; *p. pl. of* creódan.

cruft, es; *m?* crufte, an; *f. A vault, crypt, hollow place under the ground*; crypta:—Cruftan, cruftes *cryptæ*, Mone B. 2017. Crufte *crypta*, 4931. Cruftan *crypta*, 3298. [*Ger.* gruft, *f. a crypt.*]

Crúland, Crúwland, es; *n.* [Interprete Ingulpho *crúda et cœnosa terra*, Gib. Chr. explicatio, p. 22, col. 1] CROWLAND or CROYLAND, *Lincolnshire*; loci nomen in agro Lincolniensi. St. Guthlac, hermit of Crowland, passed a great part of his life and died here in A. D. 714. After his death, king Æthelbáld of Mercia founded a monastery at Crowland in A. D. 716:—Ðæt abbotríce of Crúlande *the abbacy of Crowland*, Chr. 1066; Erl. 203, 17: 963; Erl. 123, 5. Hér wæs Walþeóf eorl beheáfdod on Wincestre, and his líc wearþ gelæd to Crúlande, and he ðær is bebyrged *in this year* [A. D. 1077] *earl Waltheof was beheaded at Winchester, and his body was taken to Crowland, and he is there buried*, 1077; Th. 350, 10. Hí cômon to ðære stôwe ðe man hâteþ Crúwland *they came to the place which is called Crowland*, Guthl. 3; Gdwin. 22, 1: 12; Gdwin. 58, 12. Ðá wæs se eahtoða dæg ðæs kalendes Septembres, ðá se eádiga wer, Gúþlâc, com to ðære fóresprecenan stôwe, Crúwlande... hæfde he ðá on ylde six and twentig wintra *it was the eighth day before the kalends of September* [Aug. 24th, A. D. 699], *when the blessed man, Guthlac, came to the aforesaid place, Crowland... he was then twenty-six years of age*, Guthl. 3; Gdwin. 22, 25-24, 3: 22; Gdwin. 96, 21. v. Gúþ-lâc.

CRUMA, an; *m. A* CRUMB, *fragment*; mica:—Cruma *mica*, Wrt. Voc. 83, 1. We hêdaþ ðæra crumena ðæs hlâfes *we take care of the crumbs of the bread*, Homl. Th. ii. 114, 33. Ða hwelpas etaþ of ðâm crumum *catelli edunt de micis*, Mt. Bos. 15, 27: Lk. Bos. 16, 21. Lege on ðone magan hlâfes cruman *lay crumbs of bread on the stomach*, L. M. 2, 12; Lchdm. ii. 190, 15: Homl. Th. ii. 114, 29. [*Prompt.* crumme *mica*: *Wyc.* crummes, *pl*: *Chauc. Piers P.* cromes, *pl*: *Orm.* crummess, *pl*: *Scot.* crum: *Plat.* kröme, kroom: *Dut.* kruim, *f*: *Kil.* kruyme: *Ger.* krume, *f*: *Dan.* krumme, *m. f*: *Swed.* krumma, *f.*]

CRUMB, crump; *adj. Bent down, stooping*; cernuus, obuncus:—Crump *obuncus*, Cot. 144. Ða crumban *obunca*, 185. [*Prompt.* crombe, crome *bucus*: *Orm.* crumb: *Scot.* crummet: *O.Sax. O.Frs.* crumb: *Dut.* krom: *Ger.* krumm: *M.H.Ger.* krump: *O.H.Ger.* krumb: *Dan. Swed.* krum: *Wel.* crwm *bent*: *Corn.* crom *crooked*: *Ir. Gael.* crom *bent.*]

cruncon; *pp.* cruncen *yielded*, Byrht. Th. 140, 43; By. 302; *p. pl. and pp. of* crincan.

crundel, crundol, crundul; *gen.* crundeles, crundles; *dat.* crundle, crundelle; *m.* I. *a barrow, mound raised over graves to protect them*; tumulus:—On ðone durnan [MS. durnen] crundel; of ðam durnan crundelle on ðone þorn *to the retired barrow*; *from the retired barrow to the thorn*, Cod. Dipl. 1053; A. D. 854; Kmbl. v. 105, 26. Ðonan on morþcrundle; of morþcrundle on ðone brâdan herpæþ [MS. herpaþ] *thence to the death-barrow* [*to the tumulus of the dead*]; *from the tumulus of the dead to the broad military road*, Cod. Dipl. 543; A. D. 968; Kmbl. iii. 23, 34, 35. Ðêr þwyres ofer þrý crundelas *there across over three barrows*, Cod. Dipl. 985; Kmbl. v. 13, 32. II. in later times crundel is *n*:—On ðæt crundel *to the barrow*, Cod. Dipl. 1283; Kmbl. vi. 120, 8. [Kemble, in his Glossary Cod. Dipl. iii. pref. p. xxi, says,—'*It seems to denote a sort of water-course, a meadow through which a stream flows.*' Yet the following example in this same vol. proves that a crundel could not be *a meadow through which a stream flows*, as it was on a hill:—Crâwan crundul on Wereðan hylle *Crow's crundle on Weretha's hill*, Cod. Dipl. 698; A. D. 997; Kmbl. iii. 301, 35. Professor Leo says,—'A crundel or crundwel is *a spring* or *well, with its cistern, trough*, or *reservoir*,' and cites,—Ðonon eft on crundwylle *then again to crund-spring*, Cod. Dipl. 1188; Kmbl. v. 354, 20, 28. The crundle *on Weretha's hill* militates against Dr. Leo's view, as well as Kemble's; Mr. Thorpe therefore concludes,—'My belief is, that the word is not Anglo-Saxon, nor Germanic, but British, and signifies *a tumulus* or *barrow*, and is akin to the Welsh carneddaw *a cairn* or *heap of stones*,' Th. Diplm. Glossary, p. 654.] DER. morþ-crundel, stân-.

crungon; *pp.* crungen *yielded, perished*, Exon. 124 a; Th. 477, 17; Ruin. 26; *p. pl. and pp. of* cringan.

crupon *crept, crawled*, Ors. 1, 7; Bos. 29, 33: Chr. 1083; Erl. 217, 22; *p. pl. of* creópan.

crusene, crusne, an; *f. A robe made of skins*; mastruga:—Crusene oððe deórfellen roc *crusen or a beastfelt* or *skin garment*, Wrt. Voc. 82, 4. Crusne *mastruga*, Ælfc. Gl. 65; Som. 69, 39; Wrt. Voc. 40, 66.

cruþ *a crowd*; multitudo, turba confertissima, Som. Ben. Lye. v. creódan.

Crúwland *Crowland, Lincolnshire*, Guthl. 12; Gdwin. 58, 12. v. Crúland.

CRYB; *gen.* crybbe; *f. A* CRIB, *bed, stall*; stratum, præsepe:—Ic læg cildgeong on crybbe *I lay as a young child in a crib*, Exon. 28 b; Th. 87, 16; Cri. 1426. [*Prompt.* crybbe *præsepe*: *Orm.* cribbe: *Scot.* crufe, cruife, crofe: *Plat.* kribbe, krubbe: *O.Sax.* cribbia, *f*: *Frs. O.Frs.* kribbe, *f*: *Dut.* krib, kribbe, *f*: *Kil.* krippe: *Ger. M.H.Ger.* krippe, *f*: *O.H.Ger.* krippa, kripha, *f*: *Dan.* krybbe, *m. f*: *Swed. Icel.* krubba, *f*: *Fr.* crèche, *f*: *Prov.* crepcha: *It.* gréppia, *f*: *Slav.* kripa, *f. a basket.*]

crycc *a crutch, staff*, Bd. 4, 31; S. 610, 17. v. cricc.

crýdeþ *presses*, Exon. 101 b; Th. 384, 15; Rä. 4, 28; *3rd pers. pres. of* creódan.

crýfele *a den, passage under ground*; spelunca, meatus subterraneus, Som. Ben. Lye. v. crýpele.

crymbig *crooked*, Som. Ben. Lye. v. crumb.

crymbing, e; *f. A bending*; curvatura, Cot. 56.

crýpan; *p.* crýpte; *pp.* crýped *To creep*; repere:—He næfþ his fôta geweald and onginþ crýpan *he has not the use of his feet and begins to creep*, Bt. 36, 4; Fox 178, 14. v. creópan.

crýpele, es; *m? A den, burrow*; cuniculum, Mone B. 2774.

crýpest, crýpst, he crýpeþ, crýpþ *creepest, creeps*; *2nd and 3rd pers. pres. of* creópan.

crysma *chrism*, L. Ecg. C. 36; Th. ii. 162, 1. v. crisma.

crysum-lýsing *a leaving off the baptismal vest*, Chr. 879; Th. 148, 32, col. 3. v. crism-lýsing.

crýt = crýdeþ *crowdeth*: ðú crýtst, crýst *thou crowdest*; *3rd and 2nd pers. pres. of* creódan.

CÚ; *nom. acc*; *gen.* cúe, cú, cuus, cús; *dat.* cý; *pl. nom. acc.* cý; *gen.* cúa, cúna; *dat.* cuum, cúm; *f. A* cow; vacca, bucula:—Cú *vacca*, Wrt. Voc. 287, 56. Cú *vacca* vel *bucula*, Ælfc. Gl. 21; Som. 59, 82; Wrt. Voc. 23, 40: 78, 42. Iung cú *a young cow*; juvenca, Ælfc. Gl. 22; Som. 59, 89; Wrt. Voc. 23, 46. Ân cú wearþ gebroht to ðam temple *a cow was brought to the temple*, Homl. Th. ii. 300, 33: Chr. 1085; Erl. 218, 36. Gesomna cúe mesa *collect the dung of a cow*, L. M. 1, 38; Lchdm. ii. 98, 5. On ðære cú hricge *on the cow's back*, M. H. 194 a. Be cuus horne *of a cow's horn*, L. In. 59; Th. i. 140, 1, 3. Cús eáge *a cow's eye*, 59; Th. i. 140, 4. Of ðære cý *from the cow*, M. H. 194 a. Gif mon cú forstele *if a man steal a cow*, L. Alf. pol. 16; Th. i. 70, 24: L. In. 38; Th. i. 126, 5: L. Ath. v. § 6, 2; Th. i. 234, 1: L. O. D. 7; Th. i. 356, 5. Cúa *of cows*, Cod. Dipl. 201; A. D. 814; Kmbl. i. 253, 28. Feówertig cúna *vaccas quadraginta*, Gen. 32, 15: Cod. Dipl. 732; A. D. 1016-1020; Kmbl. iv. 10, 23: 949; A. D. 1049-1052; Kmbl. iv. 284, 8. On cuum *in vaccis*, Ps. Lamb. 67, 31. Ðú wâst, ðæt ic hæbbe hnesce litlingas and ge-eáne eówa and gecelfe cý mid me *nosti quod parvulos habeam teneros et oves et boves fætas mecum*, Gen. 33, 13: Cod. Dipl. 235; A. D. 835; Kmbl. i. 310, 18, 25, 27: 675; A. D. 990; Kmbl. iii. 255, 13. [*Prompt.* cowe *vacca*: *Piers P.* kow, cow: *R. Brun.* kie, *pl*: *Plat.* ko, *pl.* koie: *O.Sax.* kô, *f*: *Frs.* kw, *pl.* ky, *f*: *O.Frs.* ku, *f*: *Dut.* koe, *f*: *Kil.* koe, koeye: *Ger.* kuh, *f*: *M.H.Ger.* kuo, *f*: *O.H.Ger.* kua, kô, *f*: *Dan.* ko, koe: *Swed.* ko, *f*: *Icel.* kýr, *f. dat. and acc.* kú: *Lat.* cēva *a heifer*: *Sansk.* go, gaus *bos, vacca.*] DER. folc-cú, mete-.

cualme-stôw, e; *f. A place of burial;* calvariæ locus, Som. Ben. Lye. v. cwealm-stôw.

cû-butere, an; *f. Cow's butter, butter made of cow's milk;* vaccæ butyrum:—Reáde netlan awylle on hunige and on cûbuteran *boil red nettles in honey and in cow's butter*, L. M. 2, 51; Lchdm. ii. 268, 18: iii. 16, 20.

cuc *quick, alive;* vivus:—He lêt cucne *he left alive*, Ors. 6, 2; Bos. 116, 41: Gen. 1, 20: Ælfc. Gl. 35; Som. 62, 90. v. cwic.

cû-cealf, es; *n. A cow's calf;* vaccæ vitulus:—Gif man of myran folan adrîfþ oððe cûcealf *if a man drives off a mare's foal or a cow's calf*, L. Alf. pol. 16; Th. i. 70, 23.

cuceler, cuculer, cucler, es; *m. A spoon, half a drachm;* cochlear:—Fîf cuceleras fulle *five spoonsful*, Herb. 26, 3; Lchdm. i. 122, 23. Þrý cuculeras *three spoons*, 26, 3; Lchdm. i. 122, 24. [*Lat.* cochlear, âris; *n.*]

cucen *alive;* vivus, Wanl. Catal. 3, 12. v. cucon.

cucian; *p.* ode; *pp.* od *To quicken, make alive;* vivificare, Som. Ben. Lye. v. cwician.

cucler, es; *m. A spoon;* cochlear:—Ðæt seáw sele on cuclere *give the juice in a spoon*, L. M. 1, 48; Lchdm. ii. 120, 19. Genim celeþonian [MS. cileþonian] seáwes cucler fulne *take a spoon full of juice of celandine*, L. M. 1, 2; Lchdm. ii. 28, 3. *The following are examples of* cucler:—2, 1; Lchdm. ii. 178, 6: 2, 4; Lchdm. ii. 182, 23: 2, 7; Lchdm. ii. 186, 5: 2, 24; Lchdm. ii. 214, 5, 25. v. cuceler.

cucler-mǽl, es; *n.* [mǽl *a measure*] *A spoon measure;* cochlearis mensura:—Ân cuclermǽl *one spoon measure*, L. M. 2, 7; Lchdm. ii. 186, 10. Tû cuclermǽl *two spoon measures*, 1, 2; Lchdm. ii. 28, 3.

cucon, cucun *alive, quick;* vivus:—Ðæt he Wulfnôþ cuconne oððe deádne begytan sceolde *that he should take Wulfnoth alive or dead*, Chr. 1009; Erl. 142, 3. v. cuc, cwic.

cuculer, es; *m. A spoon;* cochlear:—Þrý cuculeras *three spoons*, Herb. 26, 3; Lchdm. i. 122, 24. v. cuceler.

cucumis; *gen.* eris; *m. Lat. A cucumber;* cucumis:—Cucumeres, ðæt synd eorþæppla *cucumbers, which are earth-apples*, Num. 11, 5.

cud, cudu, es; *n? A* CUD, *what is chewed;* rumen:—Ðe heora cudu ne ceówaþ: ða clǽnan nýtenu ðe heora cudu ceówaþ *which chew not the cud: the clean beasts which chew their cud*, M. H. 138 b. v. cwudu.

cudele *a cuttlefish;* sepia = σηπία:—Cudele *vel* wasescite *sepia*, Ælfc. Gl. 102; Som. 77, 82; Wrt. Voc. 56, 6.

cû-eáge, an; *f. A cow's eye;* vaccæ oculus:—Cûeáge biþ scillinges weorþ *a cow's eye is worth a shilling*, L. In. 59; Th. i. 140, 4, note 11.

cuellan *to kill*, Som. Ben. Lye. v. cwellan.

cûe mesa, an; *m. Cow's dung;* lætâmen:—Gesomna cûe mesa *collect cow's dung*, L. M. 1, 38; Lchdm. ii. 98, 5.

cuên *a queen*, Chr. 672; Erl. 34, 35: 737; Erl. 46, 22: 836; Erl. 64, 33: 855; Erl. 68, 30: 885; Erl. 84, 5: 888; Erl. 86, 18. v. cwên.

cuffie, an; *f. A cap, coif, hood, head dress;* pileus, cucullus, capitis tegmen:—Hió an Æðelflǽde hyre cuffian *she gives to Æthelfled her hood*, Cod. Dipl. 1290; A. D. 995; Kmbl. vi. 133, 20.

cugele, cugle, cuhle, an; *f. A* COWL, *monk's hood;* cucculla:—Twâ cugelan *two cowls*, R. Ben. 55. Cugle *cuculla*, Wrt. Voc. 81, 71. Seó cuhle *the cowl*, R. Ben. 55. [*Ger.* kogel, gugel, *f: M. H. Ger.* gugele, *f: O. H. Ger.* cucula, *f: M. Lat.* cuculla: *Span.* cogúlla, *f.*]

cû-horn, cuu-horn, es; *m. A cow's horn;* vaccæ cornu:—Cuuhorn [cû- MSS. B. H.] biþ twegea pæninga wurþ *a cow's horn shall be worth two pence*, L. In. 59; Th. i. 140, 2.

cû-hyrde, es; *m.* [hyrde *a keeper, guardian*] *A cowherd, person who has the charge of cows;* vaccarius, bubulcus:—Cûhyrde gebýreþ ðæt he hæbbe ealdre cû meolc vii niht, syððan heó nige cealfod hæfþ, and frymetlinge býstinge xiv niht; and gâ his metecû mid hlâfordes cû *vaccarii rectum est, ut habeat lac vaccæ veteris vii noctibus, postquam enixa erit, et primitivarum bistinguium xiv noctibus; et eat ejus vacca cum vaccis domini*, L. R. S. 13; Th. i. 438, 18–20. Cûhyrdas *bubulcos*, Mone B. 2408.

cuic *living*, Jn. Lind. War. 4, 10. v. cwic.

cuic-beám, es; *m. A juniper-tree;* juniperus. v. cwic-beám.

cuide *a saying*, Past. 35, 5; Hat. 46 b, 4. v. cwide.

cûle *a cowl*, Wanl. Catal. 131, 74, col. 1. v. cugele.

CULFRE, culufre, culefre, an; *f:* culfer, e; *f. A dove*, CULVER, *pigeon;* columba:—Se hâlega Gâst astâh swâ ân culfre *descendit Spiritus sanctus sicut columba*, Lk. Bos. 3, 22: Wrt. Voc. 77, 20: 280, 31. Wæs culufre of côfan sended *a dove was sent from the ark*, Cd. 72; Th. 88, 12; Gen. 1464. Culfer *columba*, Ælfc. Gl. 37; Som. 63, 2; Wrt. Voc. 29, 25. Ðæt hig offrunge sealdon, twegen culfran briddas *ut darent hostiam, duos columbæ pullos*, Lk. Bos. 2, 24: Ps. Th. 67, 13. On culfran hiwe *in likeness of a dove*, Homl. Th. i. 104, 21. Fyðeras culefran oferseolfrade *pennæ columbæ deargentatæ*, Ps. Lamb. 67, 14. He asende ût âne culfran *emisit columbam*, Gen. 8, 8, 10, 12. He forlêt hâswe culufran *he let out a livid dove*, Cd. 72; Th. 87, 20; Gen. 1451: 72; Th. 89, 8; Gen. 1477. Ða hâlgan apostolas wǽron swilce culfran *the holy apostles were as doves*, Homl. Th. i. 586, 1: Homl. Blick. 23, 27. Bilwyte swâ culfran *simplices sicut columbæ*, Mt. Bos. 10, 16: Ps. Th. 54, 6. [*Wyc.* culver, culvere: *Chauc.* culver: *Piers P.* colvere: *R. Glouc.* colfren, *pl: Orm.* cullfre: *Laym.* culveren, *pl: Lat.* columba.] DER. wudu-culfre.

culmille, an; *f. The lesser centaury;* erythræa centaurium, Lin:—Genim ða lytlan culmillan *take the small centaury*, L. M. 1, 16; Lchdm. ii. 58, 20. v. curmealle.

culpa, an; *m. A fault;* culpa:—Ne ic culpan in ðê ǽfre onfunde *I have never found any fault in thee*, Exon. 10 b; Th. 11, 28; Cri. 177.

culpian; *p.* ode; *pp.* od *To humiliate, cringe;* humiliare:—Hû ne is ðæt ðonne sum dǽl ermþa, ðæt mon scyle culpian to ðam ðe him gifan scyle *is not this then somewhat of misery, that a man must cringe to him who can give to him?* Bt. 32, 1; Fox 114, 15.

CULTER, cultur; *gen.* cultres; *m? A* COULTER *or* CULTER, *dagger;* culter, sica:—Hwanon ðam yrþlinge culter, bûton of cræfte mînon *unde aratori culter, nisi ex arte mea?* Coll. Monast. Th. 30, 31: Wrt. Voc. 74, 73. Cultur *sica*, 287, 5. Gefæstnodon sceare and cultre mid ðære syl *confirmato vomere et cultro aratro*, Coll. Monast. Th. 19, 21. [*Prompt.* culter: *Wyc.* culter, cultre: *Piers P.* cultour, kultour: *Fr.* coutre: *It.* coltro: *Lat.* culter: *Sansk.* kṛit *to cut.*]

culufre *a dove*, Cd. 72; Th. 88, 12; Gen. 1464. v. culfre.

cum *come:*—Nû ðû cum *now come thou*, Exon. 10 a; Th. 10, 9; Cri. 149; *imp. of* cuman.

cuma, an; *m.* [cum, *imp. of* cuman *to come;* -a, *termination*, q. v.] *A comer, guest, stranger;* advena, hospes:—Ic wæs cuma *eram hospes*, Mt. Bos. 25, 35, 38, 43: Wrt. Voc. 86, 43. Mon cýðe cynewordum, hû se cuma hâtte *let a man make known in fitting words, how the guest is called*, Exon. 112 b; Th. 430, 30; Rä. 44, 16: Beo. Th. 3616; B. 1806. Gûþlâc swýðe blîðe wæs ðæs heofonlîcan cuman *Guthlac was right glad of the heavenly guest*, Guthl. 4; Gdwin. 30, 2. Fram eallum ðâm cumum *a cunctis hospitibus*, Bd. 4, 31; S. 610, 6. Metodes þeów grêtan eóde cuman *the Lord's servant went to meet the guests*, Cd. 111; Th. 146, 32; Gen. 2431. Ðæt he wolde ǽlcne cuman swíðe ârlîce underfôn *that he would very honourably receive every stranger*, Bt. 16, 2; Fox 52, 31. Cuman ârfæste *righteous strangers*, Cd. 114; Th. 150, 3; Gen. 2486. Cômon Sodomware cuman acsian *the inhabitants of Sodom came to demand the strangers*, 112; Th. 148, 8; Gen. 2453: Ors. 1, 8; Bos. 31, 4. Cumena ârþegn *an attendant of guests*, Bd. 4, 31; S. 610, 4. Cumena bûr *a guest-chamber*, 4, 31; S. 610, 11. Cumena hûs *a guest-house, an inn*, Lk. Bos. 2, 7: 22, 11. Cumena inn *a guest-house, an inn*, Greg. Dial. 2, 22. Cumena wîcung *a guest-dwelling, an inn*, Ælfc. Gl. 58; Som. 67, 85; Wrt. Voc. 38, 11. DER. cwealm-cuma, wil-.

CUMAN; *part.* cumende; ic cume, ðû cymst, cymest, he cumeþ, cymþ, cymeþ, cimþ, *pl.* cumaþ; *p.* ic, he com, cwom, ðû côme, *pl.* cômon, cwômon; *imp. s.* cum, cym, *pl.* cumaþ; *subj. indef.* ic cume, cyme, *pl.* cumon, cumen, cymen; *p.* côme, *pl.* cômen; *pp.* cumen, cymen. I. *to* COME, *go, happen;* venire, ire, accidere, evenire:—Sceal se gâst cuman *the spirit shall come*, Soul Kmbl. 17; Seel. 9. Cuman ongunnan *they attempted to come*, Beo. Th. 494; B. 244. Cum to ðam lande, ðe ic ðê geswutelige *come to the land, which I will shew thee*, Gen. 12, 1. Ne cumon eów ðâs worde of gemynde *let not these words depart out of your mind*, Deut. 4, 9. Ðonne wîg cume *when war happens*, Beo. Th. 46; B. 23. Ðonne his fyll côme *when his fall has happened*, Cd. 200; Th. 248, 15; Dan. 513. Cumaþ ðonne mid cumendum *venientes autem venient*, Ps. Th. 125, 6. II. cuman is used with the infinitive expressing *manner* or *purpose;* as, Com fêran *came walking* or *happened to walk*, Cd. 40; Th. 52, 31; Gen. 852. Com lǽdan *came leading* or *came to lead*, 85; Th. 106, 19; Gen. 1773. Sunnan leóma cymeþ scýnan *a sunbeam shall come shining* or *begin to shine*, Exon. 21 a; Th. 56, 17; Cri. 902. Secgan cymeþ *shall come to say*, Cd. 22; Th. 28, 20; Gen. 438. Com grêtan *came to greet*, 97; Th. 126, 31; Gen. 2103. Com weorc sceáwigan *came to view the work*, 80; Th. 101, 7; Gen. 1678. [*Prompt.* cum, come: *Wyc. Chauc. Piers P.* come: *Laym.* come, cumen, cummen, kumen: *Orm.* cumenn: *Plat.* kamen: *O. Sax.* kuman: *Frs.* kommen: *O. Frs.* kuma, coma: *Dut.* komen: *Ger.* kommen: *M. H. Ger.* komen: *O. H. Ger.* queman: *Goth.* qiman: *Dan.* komme: *Swed.* komma: *Icel.* koma: *Lat.* venire: *Grk.* βαίνειν: *Sansk.* gam.] DER. a-cuman, an-, aweg-, be-, fôr-, fôre-, forþ-, ge-, in-, of-, ofer-, oferbe-, onbe-, ongeán-, þurh-, to-, tobe-, up-.

CUMB, es; *m.* I. *a hollow among hills, narrow valley*, COMB; caverna inter colles, vallis angusta:—Andlang cumbes *along the valley*, Cod. Dipl. Apndx. 354; A. D. 931; Kmbl. iii. 406, 10: 489; A. D. 962; Kmbl. iii. 457, 29. In cumb, of ðam cumbe *to a valley, from the valley*, Cod. Dipl. Apndx. 118; A. D. 770; Kmbl. iii. 380, 5. II. *a liquid measure;* mensura quædam liquidorum: hence, perhaps, our dry measure COMB *or* COOMB = four bushels:—Cumb fulne lîðes aloþ, and cumb fulne Welisces aloþ *a comb full of mild ale and a comb full of Welsh ale*, Th. Diplm. A. D. 791–796; 40, 5: Lchdm. iii. 28, 9. [*Dut.* kom, *f. a basin: Ger.* kumpf, kump, *m.* I. *a dry measure for corn and fruit;* II. *a cup, basin: M. H. Ger.* kumpf *a vessel, dry measure: O. H. Ger.* chumph *cimpus? O. Fr.* combe *a deep valley: Grk.* κύμβος *the hollow of a vessel, cup, bowl; κύμβη a basin: Wel.* cwm, *m. a hollow, deep valley: Sansk.* kumbha, *m. a pot, jug.*] DER. fild-cumb.

cumbel-gehnâd, es; *n.* [cumbel = cumbol, gehnâd *a conflict*] *A conflict of ensigns* or *banners, a battle;* signorum conflictus, prœlium, Chr. 937; Erl. 114, 15; Æđelst. 49, note.

Cumber-land, Cumbra-land, Cumer-land, es; *n.* [*Sim. Dun.* Cumbreland: *Hunt. Hovd. Brom.* Cumberland] CUMBERLAND; Cumbria:—Hēr Eádmund cyning oferhergode eal Cumbraland *in this year* [A. D. 945] *king Edmund overran all Cumberland,* Chr. 945; Th. 212, 10; 213, 10, col. 1, 2: Cumberland, 213, 10, col. 3. On đisum geáre se cyning fērde into Cumerlande [Cumberlande, col. 2] *in this year the king went into Cumberland,* 1000; Th. 248, 29, col. 1; 249, 29.

CUMBOL, cumbl, cuml, es; *n.* I. *a sign, image, military standard, ensign, banner;* signum, imago, signum militare, vexillum:—In campe gecrong cumbles hyrde *the standard's guardian fell in battle,* Beo. Th. 5004; B. 2505. Hie fōr đam cumble on cneówum sǽton *they sat on their knees before the image,* Cd. 181; Th. 227, 1; Dan. 180. Cumbol lixton wīges on wēnum *ensigns glittered in hopes of battle,* 151; Th. 188, 29; Exod. 175: Andr. Kmbl. 8; An. 4. To weallgeatum wīgend þrungon, cēne under cumblum *the warriors thronged to the wall-gates, bold beneath their ensigns,* Andr. Kmbl. 2409; An. 1206: Judth. 12; Thw. 26, 18; Jud. 333. II. *a sign* or *evidence of disease, a wound;* morbi signum, vulnus:—Se lǽce, đonne he cymþ đone untruman to snīđanne, ǽrest [MS. æresđ] he sceáwaþ đæt cumbl [cuml MS. Oth.] *the surgeon, when he comes to cut the patient, first examines the wound;* ad ægrum medicus venerat, secandum vulnus videbat, Past. 26; Hat. MS. 36 a, 7. [*O. Sax.* kumbal, *n. a heavenly sign: O. H. Ger.* cumpal *cohortes: Swed.* kummel, *n. tessera, signum: Icel.* kuml, kumbl, kubl, *n. a sign, badge, mark, war-badge.*]

cumbol-gebrec *a crash* or *clashing of banners.* v. cumbul-gebrec.

cumbol-gehnâd *a conflict of ensigns* or *banners, a battle.* v. cumbel-gehnâd.

cumbol-gehnâst, es; *n.* [cumbol I. *an ensign, banner;* gehnâst *a conflict*] *A conflict of ensigns* or *banners, a battle;* signorum conflictio, bellum:—Đæt hie beadoweorca beteran wurdon on campstede, cumbolgehnâstes *that they were better in works of war on the battle-field, at the conflict of banners,* Chr. 937; Th. 206, 2, col. 2; 207, 2.

cumbol-haga, an; *m.* [haga *a hedge*] *A compact rank, phalanx;* phalanx:—Ic sceal sēcan ōđerne under cumbolhagan cempan *I must seek another soldier in the rank,* Exon. 71 b; Th. 266, 8; Jul. 395.

cumbol-hete, es; *m.* [hete *hate*] *Warlike hate;* bellicum ódium:—Þurh cumbolhete *through warlike hate,* Exon. 75 a; Th. 280, 30; Jul. 637.

cumbol-wīga, an; *m.* [wīga *a warrior*] *A warrior, soldier;* bellator, miles, Judth. 12; Thw. 25, 5; Jud. 243: 12; Thw. 25, 14; Jud. 259.

cumbor; *gen.* cumbres; *n.* [= cumbol, *q. v.*] *A banner, standard, ensign;* signum militare:—Hroden hilte cumbor *a banner adorned on the hilt,* Beo. Th. 2048.

Cumbra-land *Cumberland,* Chr. 945; Erl. 116, 29. v. Cumber-land.

cumbul-gebrec, es; *n.* [cumbul = cumbol I, gebrec *a noise, crashing*] *A crashing of banners* or *ensigns;* signorum fragor, Ps. C. 50, 11; Ps. Grn. ii. 277, 11.

cumen *come,* Gen. 48, 2; *pp. of* cuman.

cumende *coming,* Ps. Lamb. 125, 6; *part. of* cuman.

cū-meoluc, e; *f.* [meolc *milk*] *Cow's milk;* vaccæ lac:—Gâte geallan meng wiđ cūmeoluc *mingle goat's gall with cow's milk,* L. M. 1, 3; Lchdm. ii. 40, 19.

Cumer-land *Cumberland,* Chr. 1000; Erl. 137, 1. v. Cumber-land.

cum-feorm, e; *f.* [cuma *a stranger,* feorm *food, support, hospitality*] *Entertainment of strangers;* hospitium, Th. Diplm. A. D. 848; 102, 30.

cū-migoþa, an; *m.* [migþa, migoþa *urine*] *Cow's urine;* vaccæ urina:—Gesomna cūmigoþan [MS. -migoþa] *collect cow's urine,* L. M. 1, 38; Lchdm. ii. 98, 5.

cumin *the herb cummin,* Som. Ben. Lye. v. cymen.

cuml *a wound, swelling,* Past. 26; MS. Oth. v. cumbol II.

cum-līđe; *adj.* [cuma *a comer,* līđe *mild, gentle*] *Kind to comers* or *strangers, hospitable;* hospitalis:—Cumlīđe *hospitalis,* Ælfc. Gr. 9, 28; Som. 11, 37. Cild cumlīđe *a child will be hospitable,* Obs. Lun. § 15; Lchdm. iii. 192, 1: 16; Lchdm. iii. 192, 8. Beóþ cumlīđe eów betwȳnan būton ceorungum *be hospitable among yourselves without grudging,* Homl. Th. ii. 286, 14.

cum-līđian [cuma *a guest,* līđian *to nourish*] *To lodge, to receive as a guest;* hospitari, R. Ben. Interl. 1.

cum-līđnys, -nyss, e; *f. Hospitableness, hospitality;* hospitalitas:—Cumlīđnys is swīđe hlīsful þing *hospitality is a very excellent thing,* Homl. Th. ii. 286, 16. Þurh đa cumlīđnysse *by hospitality,* 286, 2, 7, 8, 11, 13, 17, 27.

cummâse *a coal-titmouse, coal-tit,* Wrt. Voc. 281, 10. v. cōl-māse.

cum-pæder, es; *m. A godfather;* compater:—Đe Æđerēd his cumpæder healdan sceolde *which Æthelred his godfather had to defend,* Chr. 894; Erl. 92, 2.

cumul, es; *pl. nom. acc.* cumulu; *n. A glandular swelling;* tumor glandulōsus:—Wiđ cyrnlu and wiđ ealle yfele cumulu *for kernels and for all evil lumps,* Herb. 158, 5; Lchdm. i. 286, 17. v. cumbol II.

cūna *of cows,* Gen. 32, 15; *gen. pl. of* cū.

-cund, an adjective termination, denoting KIND, *sort,* or *origin, likeness;* as, æđel-cund, deóful-, engel-, eorþ-, feor-, feorran-, gǽst-, god-, heofon-, hīw-, in-, sāwel-, ufan-, up-, woruld-. [*O. Sax.* -kund *oriundus,* in godkund *divine: O. H. Ger.* -kund: *Goth.* -kunds: *Grk.* -γενής: *Lat.* -gena.]

cune-glæsse, an; *f. The herb hound's* or *dog's tongue;* cynoglossos = κυνόγλωσσον, cynoglossum officinale, Lin:—Wiđ canceradle, cuneglæsse niođoweard *for cancer, the netherward part of hound's tongue,* L. M. 1, 44; Lchdm. ii. 110, 1.

cunelle, an; *f. Thyme;* thymus [= θύμος] vulgaris:—Wyl cunellan [MS. cunille] *boil thyme,* L. M. 1, 31; Lchdm. ii. 74, 22. DER. wudu-cunelle.

cuning *a king,* Greg. Dial. MS. Hat. Bodl. fol. 9 a, 7. v. cyning.

CUNNAN, ic can, con, đū canst, const, he can, con, *pl.* cunnon; *p.* ic, he cūđe, đū cūđest, *pl.* cūđon; *subj.* cunne, *pl.* cunnen; *p.* cūđe, *pl.* cūđen; *pp.* [on]-cunnen, cūþ; *v. a.* I. *to be* or *become acquainted with, to know;* noscĕre, scire:—Ic đa stōwe ne can *I know not the place,* Elen. Kmbl. 1363; El. 683: 1267; El. 635. Ic eów ne con *I know you not,* Cd. 227; Th. 304, 13; Sat. 629. Đū canst *thou knowest,* Andr. Kmbl. 135; An. 68. Const, Beo. Th. 2759; B. 1377. Cann, Ps. Th. 91, 5: 93, 11. Conn, Exon. 43 a; Th. 145, 12; Gū. 693. Ge ne cunnon *ye know not,* Cd. 179; Th. 224, 25; Dan. 141. Đæt đū cunne *that thou knowest,* 228; Th. 308, 34; Sat. 702: Elen. Kmbl. 748; El. 374. Ic cūđe *I knew,* Cd. 216; Th. 273, 26; Sat. 142: 19; Th. 24, 30; Gen. 385: Ors. 1, 2; Bos. 26, 34. Hwanon cūđest đū me *unde me nosti?* Jn. Bos. 1, 48. Cūđon, Cd. 18; Th. 23, 10; Gen. 357: Andr. Kmbl. 1504; An. 753: Gen. 29, 5. Heó weán cūđon *they became acquainted with woe,* Cd. 4; Th. 5, 20; Gen. 74. Men ne cunnon *men know not,* Beo. Th. 327; B. 162. Ic ne conn þurh gemæcscipe monnes ōwēr *I know not anywhere of a man through cohabitation,* Exon. 10 b; Th. 13, 6; Cri. 198. II. *with inf. To know how to do, to have power, to be able,* CAN; scire, posse:—Ic can eów lǽran *I can teach you,* Cd. 219; Th. 280, 3; Sat. 250. Đe can naman đīnne neóde hērigean *qui scit jubilationem,* Ps. Th. 88, 13. Hērian ne cūđon wuldres waldend' *they knew not how to praise the ruler of glory,* Beo. Th. 367; B. 182. Dydon swā hie cūđon *they did as they could,* Cd. 187; Th. 232, 11; Dan. 258. [Cunnan is the second of the twelve Anglo-Saxon verbs, called *præterito-præsentia,* given under āgan, *q. v.* The *inf.* cunnan and the *pres.* can, *pl.* cunnon, retaining preterite inflections, are taken from the *p.* of the strong verb cinnan, ascertained from can, *pl.* cunnon, which shews the ablaut or internal change of the vowel in the *p.* tense of the twelfth class of Grimm's division of strong verbs [Grm. i. edn. 2, p. 898; Koch, i. p. 252], and requires, by analogy with other verbs of the same class, the *inf.* cinnan, *q. v.* and the *pp.* cunnen. Thus we find the original verb cinnan, *p.* can, *pl.* cunnon; *pp.* cunnen. The weak *p.* cūđe, *pl.* cūđon, *for* cunde, cundon, is formed regularly from the *inf.* cunnan. The *pp.* generally takes the weak form, in Anglo-Saxon as well as in the cognate words; but strong and weak forms are both found, in *A. Sax.* the strong on-cunnen, and the weak cūþ, and in *M. H. Ger.* the strong ver-kunnen, and the weak kunt. The same *præterito-præsens* may be generally observed in the following cognate words:—

	inf.	*pres.*	*pl.*	*p.*	*pp.*
Eng.		can,		could,	
Laym.	cunne,	can,	cunnen,	cuđe, couđe,	cuþ.
Wyc.	kunne,	can, kan,	cunnen, kunnen,	koude, kouthe,	cunde, koud.
Plat.	könen,	kann,	könen,	kunden, kunnen,	kunt.
O. Sax.	kunnan,	kan,	kunnun,	consta,	kuþ.
O. Frs.	kunna,	kan,	kunnon,	kunda,	kuth, kud.
Ger.	können,	kann,	können,	konnte,	gekonnt.
M.H.Ger.	kunnen,	kan,	kunnen,	kunde,	-kunnen, kunt.
O.H.Ger.	kunnan,	kan,	kunnumēs,	kunda, kunsta, konda, konsta,	kund.
Goth.	kunnan,	kann,	kunnum,	kunþa,	kunþs.
O. Nrs.	kunna,	kann,	kunnum,	kunna,	kunnat.]

DER. for-cunnan, on-.

cunne, *pl.* cunnen *know, can,* Cd. 228; Th. 308, 34; Sat. 702: Elen. Kmbl. 748; El. 374; *subj. pres. of* cunnan.

cunnere, es; *m. A tempter;* tentator, Mt. Lind. Stv. 4, 3.

cunnian; *p.* ode, ade, ede; *pp.* od, ad, ed; *v. a.* I. *to prove, try, inquire, search into, seek for, explore, examine, investigate, tempt, venture;* probare, tentare, explorare, requirere, experiri, periclitari:—Woldon cunnian, hwæđer . . . *they would prove, whether . . .,* Andr. Kmbl. 257; An. 129. Mōt ic nū cunnian *may I now inquire?* Bt. 5, 3; Fox 10, 34. Uncūþne eard cunnian *to seek for an unknown home,* Exon. 28 b; Th. 87, 1; Cri. 1418: Beo. Th. 2893; B. 1444. Se cunnaþ Dryhtnes meahta *he tempteth the Lord's might,* Salm. Kmbl. 454; Sal. 227. He đīn cunnode *he has proved thee,* Cd. 163; Th. 204, 16; Exod. 420: Bd. 3, 2; S. 525, 15. II. *with gen. To have experience of,* *to make trial of;* periclitari, experiri:—Gódes and yfles đǽr ic cunnade *there I had experience of good and evil,* Exon. 85 b; Th. 321, 26; Wíd. 52. Git wada cunnedon *ye made a trial of the fords,* Beo. Th. 1021; B. 508. [*Orm.* cunnenn *to try, attempt: O.H.Ger.* kunnēn *experiri, tentare.*] DER. a-cunnian, be-, ge-.

cunning, e; *f. Experience,* CUNNING; experientia, Som. Ben. Lye. v. on-cunning.

cunnung, e; *f. Probation;* probatio, tentatio, Exon. 118 a; Th. 453, 33; Hy. 4, 24.

cuopel; *gen.* cuople; *f? A coble, small ship;* navicula:—Ofstīgende hine ođđe he ofstāg in lytlum scipe ođđe in cuople *ascendente eo in naviculam,* Mt. Kmbl. Lind. 8, 23.

CUPPE, an; *f. A small drinking vessel,* CUP; poculum, obba:—Cuppe *obba,* Ælfc. Gl. 24; Som. 60, 43; Wrt. Voc. 24, 43. Nime âne cuppan *let him take a cup,* L. M. 2, 64; Lchdm. ii. 290, 2: Lchdm. iii. 72, 17: Cod. Dipl. 492; Kmbl. ii. 380, 35. Ic ge-an mînum hlâforde iv cuppan *I give four cups to my lord,* Th. Diplm. A. D. 972; 519, 24. [*Prompt. Wyc.* cuppe: *Piers P.* coppe, coupe: *Chauc.* cuppe: *R. Glouc.* coupe: *Orm.* cuppess, *pl: Laym.* cuppe: *Plat.* kop-jen, kop-ken *a little basin: Frs. O.Frs. Dut.* kop, *m: Dan.* kop, *m. f: Swed.* kopp, *m: Icel.* koppr, *m: Fr.* coupe, *f: It.* cóppa, *f: Span.* cópa, *f: Lat.* cupa, *f. a tub, cask: Grk.* κύπ-ελλον *a cup, goblet: Wel.* cwpan, *f;* cwb, *m: Ir.* cupa: *Sansk.* kūpa, kumbha, *m. a vessel for water.*] DER. scencing-cuppe, sop-.

curfon *carved,* Lev. 8, 20; *p. pl. of* ceorfan.

curmealle, curmelle, curmille, an; *f. Centaury;* centaurēum = κενταύρειον:—Wiđ ûtsihtâdle; curmealle, etc. *for diarrhœa; centaury, etc.* L. M. 3, 22; Lchdm. ii. 320, 11: 1, 32; Lchdm. ii. 76, 20. Curmille *centaury,* 1, 32; Lchdm. ii. 78, 21. Wring curmeallan seáw *wring juice of centaury,* 3, 3; Lchdm. ii. 310, 9: Lchdm. iii. 38, 26: 58, 10. Genim grêne curmeallan *take green centaury,* 10, 19: 18, 23: 28, 28: L. M. 3, 26; Lchdm. ii. 322, 21: 3, 30; Lchdm. ii. 324, 21. Wyl on ealaþ twâ curmeallan *boil in ale the two centauries,* L. M. 3, 38; Lchdm. ii. 330, 14. The centaury may be spoken of as, I. *the greater centaury;* chlora perfoliata, Lin:—Genim đâs wyrte đe Grêcas *centauria major* and Angle curmelle seó mâre nemnaþ *take this herb which the Greeks name* centaurea major *and the English the greater centaury,* Herb. 35, 1; Lchdm. i. 134, 3. Curmelle *centaurea major,* Ælfc. Gl. 42; Som. 64, 29; Wrt. Voc. 31, 39. II. *the lesser centaury;* erythræa centaurium, Lin:—Đeós wyrt đe man *centauriam minorem* and ôđrum naman curmelle seó læsse nemneþ, biþ cenned on fæstum landum *this herb which is named* centaurea minor *and by another name the lesser centaury, is produced on stiff lands,* Herb. 36, 1; Lchdm. i. 134, 17. v. eorþ-gealla.

curn-stân *a mill-stone,* Glos. Prudent. Recd. 149, 79. v. cweorn-stân.

curon *chose,* Cd. 86; Th. 108, 9; Gen. 1803; *p. pl. of* ceósan.

CURS, es; *m. A* CURSE; maledictio:—On ǽnigne man curse asettan *to set a curse on any man,* Offic. Episc. 3. Gif hîg ǽnig man ûtabrede, hæbbe he Godes curs *if any man take them away let him have God's curse,* Wanl. Catal. 81, 5: Cod. Dipl. 310; A. D. 871–878; Kmbl. ii. 107, 5: 1057; Kmbl. v. 114, 25; Chr. 656; Erl. 33, 12: 675; Erl. 39, 20, 21, 27, 28: 963; Erl. 123, 14. [*Prompt.* curce: *Wyc.* curs: *Chauc.* cursing: *R. Brun.* cursyng.]

cursian; *p.* ode, ede; *pp.* od, ed *To* CURSE; maledicere:—Cursiende [MS. cursiynde] *maledicentes,* Ps. Spl. C. 36, 23. Đe biscopes and lêred men heó cursede *the bishops and clergy cursed them,* Chr. 1137; Erl. 262, 37.

cursung, e; *f. A* CURSING, *curse, torment, hell;* maledictio, damnatio, gehenna = γέεννα:—He lufode cursunge, and heó cume him *dilexit maledictionem, et veniet ei,* Ps. Spl. C. 108, 16: Mt. Kmbl. Lind. 5, 29: 10, 28: Lk. Skt. Lind. Rush. 20, 47.

cûs *of a cow:*—Cûs eáge biþ scillinges weorþ *a cow's eye shall be worth a shilling,* L. In. 59; Th. i. 140, 4; *gen. of* cû.

CÛSC; *adj. Chaste, modest, pure, clean;* castus, purus:—Þurh cûscne siodo *through modest conduct,* Cd. 29; Th. 39, 2; Gen. 618. [*Plat.* küsk: *Dut.* kuisch: *Kil.* kuysch: *O.Sax.* kûsko, *adv: Frs.* kuwsch: *O.Frs.* kusk: *Ger.* keusch: *M.H.Ger.* kiusche, kiusch: *O.H.Ger.* kiuski, kûski *sobrius, pudicus: Dan.* kydsk: *Swed.* kysk.]

cusceote, cuscote, cuscute, an; *f.* [*Lancashire,* cowshot] *A ringdove, wood-pigeon;* palumbes, palumbă:—Cusceote *palumba,* Wrt. Voc. 280, 32. Cuscote, wuduculfre *palumbes,* 62, 27. Cuscutan *palumbes,* Glos. Epnl. Recd. 161, 58.

cûslyppe, cûsloppe, an; *f. A* COWSLIP; primula veris, Lin:—Nim wudubindes leáf and cûslyppan *take leaves of woodbine and cowslip,* L. M. 3, 30; Lchdm. ii. 326, 4: 3, 31; Lchdm. ii. 326, 10: iii. 30, 8: 46, 22. Cûsloppe *britannica,* Ælfc. Gl. 42; Som. 64, 30; Wrt. Voc. 31, 40.

cûsnis *choiceness;* fastidium, Glos. Epnl. Recd. 156, 40. v. cîsnes.

cû-tægel, -tægl, es; *m. A cow's tail;* vaccæ cauda:—Cûtægl biþ fîf penega weorþ *a cow's tail shall be worth five pence,* L. In. 59; Th. i. 140, 3, MS. B.

cuter *resin;* mastix, resina:—Cuter *mastix* vel *resina,* Ælfc. Gl. 48; Som. 65, 53; Wrt. Voc. 33, 49.

cûþ; *comp.* -ra; *sup.* -ost, -est; *adj.* [cûþ *known, pp. of* cunnan]. I. *known, clear, plain, evident, manifest;* notus, cognĭtus, manifestus:—Đæt wæs monegum cûþ *that was known to many,* Exon. 100 b; Th. 378, 21; Deór. 19: Lk. Bos. 8, 17. Cûþ is wîde *it is widely known,* Exon. 40 b; Th. 134, 14; Gû. 507. Cûþ is, đæt *it is manifest, that,* Cd. 198; Th. 246, 20; Dan. 482. Cûþ standeþ, đæt he gescylded wæs *quem esse servatum constat,* Bd. 3, 23; S. 555, 27: 1, 27; S. 492, 38. Đæt wæs đara fæstna folcum cûþost *that was of those fastnesses most known to nations,* Cd. 209; Th. 259, 16; Dan. 692. II. *known, well known, sure, safe, noted, known as excellent, famed, celebrated;* notus, certus, præstans, egregius:—Cûþe ǽrenddracan *nuntii certi,* Bd. 4, 1; S. 564, 40. Cûþran gewitnesse *certiori notitia,* Bd. 4, 19; S. 588, 40. Se cûþesta gewita *certissimus testis,* 4, 19; S. 587, 27. Cûþes werodes *of the famed host,* Cd. 154; Th. 192, 12; Exod. 230: Beo. Th. 1738; B. 867: 4362; B. 2178: Cd. 226; Th. 302, 9; Sat. 596. III. *familiar, intimate, related, friendly;* notus, familiāris, amīcus, benevŏlus:—Swâ swâ he cûþre stæfne wæs to me sprecende *quasi familiari me voce alloquens,* Bd. 4, 25; S. 600, 43. Ne sint me winas cûþe eorlas elþeódige *the strange men are no affable friends to me,* Andr. Kmbl. 396; An. 198. Feor đû me dydest freóndas cûþe *longe fecisti notos meos a me,* Ps. Th. 87, 8. Mîne cûþe *notos meos,* 87, 18: 54, 13: 131, 18. [*Wyc.* koud, kowd *known, pp. of* kunne: *Chauc.* couth, kouth, *pp. of* conne: *Orm.* cuþ, *pp. of* cunnenn: *Laym.* cuđ, cođ, icuđ *known, renowned, pp. of* cuđe *to make known: O.Sax.* kûđ *known: O.Frs.* kuth, kund, kud: *Dut.* kond: *Ger.* kund: *M.H.Ger.* kunt: *O.H.Ger.* kund: *Goth.* kunþs *known, pp. of* kunnan: *Icel.* kunnr, kuðr *known.*] DER. folc-cûþ, for-, hiw-, hîw-, in-, un-, unfor-, wîd-: cýþig, on-, un-.

cûđa, an; *m.* [cûþ *known, pp. of* cunnan; -a, *termination,* q. v.] *One known, an acquaintance, a familiar friend, a relation;* notus, cognātus:—Đû cûđa mîn *tu notus meus,* Ps. Spl. 54, 14: Lk. Bos. 2, 44. Ne clypa đû đîne frýnd ne đîne cûđan *noli vocare amīcos tuos neque cognātos,* 14, 12: 1, 58. v. cûþ.

cûđe; *adv. Clearly;* manifeste:—Ic cûđe gesette *I have clearly set,* Ps. Th. 88, 3.

cûđe, *pl.* cûđon *knew, could,* Ors. 1, 2; Bos. 26, 34; *p. of* cunnan.

cûþe-lîc, cûþ-lîc; *adj. Known, certain;* notus, Som. Ben. Lye. DER. un-cûþlîc.

cûþe-lîce; *adv. Certainly:*—Ac we đæt cûþelîce oncneówan *but that we certainly have known,* Bd. 1, 27; S. 491, 4. v. cûþlîce.

cûđe-men; *pl. m. Relations;* cognati:—Đa cûđemen *cognati,* Lk. Skt. Rush. 1, 58.

cûđen *knew, could,* Exon. 25 a; Th. 73, 6; Cri. 1185; *subj. p. of* cunnan.

cûđest *knewest, couldst; 2nd pers. p. of* cunnan.

cûþice; *adv.* = cûþlîce *Clearly;* manifeste:—Forđon ic cûþlîce [MS. cuþice] on đǽm, hêr nû cwicu lifige *quia in ipsis vivificasti me,* Ps. Th. 118, 93.

cûþ-lǽtan [cûþ = cýþ *relationship,* lǽtan *to admit*] *To enter into friendship;* societatem facere, Som. Ben. Lye.

cûþ-lîce, cûþe-lîce; *comp.* or; *adv.* I. *certainly, manifestly;* certo, aperte:—Ic cûþlîce wât *scio certissime,* Bd. 2, 12; S. 513, 42: 4, 19; S. 589, 25. Đæt his lîf đe cûþlîcor ascîneþ *cujus ut vita clarescat certius,* 5, 1; S. 613, 14, note. Acyrred cûþlîce from Cristes ǽ *turned manifestly from Christ's law,* Exon. 71 b; Th. 267, 6; Jul. 411: Ps. Th. 103, 16: 106, 6: 121, 1: 146, 4: 149, 8. II. *for, indeed, therefore;* nempe, igitur:—Cweđaþ cûþlîce *for indeed they said,* Ps. Th. 70, 10: 82, 4: Hy. 10, 20; Hy. Grn. ii. 293, 20. III. *familiarly, courteously, kindly;* familiariter, civiliter, comiter:—Đæt he đe cûþlîcor from đâm hâlgum ge-earnode in heofonum onfongen beón *quo familiarius a sanctis recipi mereretur in cœlis,* Bd. 5, 7; S. 621, 12: Cd. 111; Th. 146, 32; Gen. 2431. Đæt he eaþmêdum ellorfûsne oncnâwe cûþlîce *that he should with affability kindly treat the ready to depart,* Andr. Kmbl. 643; An. 322: Ps. Th. 118, 146, 154: 54, 16: 90, 15. DER. for-cûþlîce, in-, un-.

cûþ-nes, -ness, e; *f. Knowledge, acquaintance;* scientia, Scint. 38, Som. Ben. Lye. DER. cûđe *knew; p. of* cunnan *to know.*

cûþ-noma, an; *m. A surname;* cognomen, Mt. Kmbl. Præf. p. 8, 13.

cûđo-menn; *pl. m. Relations;* cognati:—Cûđomen *cognatos, acc. m.* Lk. Skt. Lind. 14, 12. v. cûđe-men.

cûđon *knew, could,* Cd. 18; Th. 23, 10; Gen. 357; *p. pl. of* cunnan.

cûþra *more sure,* Bd. 4, 19; S. 588, 40; *comp. of* cûþ.

cûđudyst = cýddest *innotuisti,* Ps. Spl. C. 143, 4; *2nd pers. p. of* cýđan.

Cûþ-wulf, es; *m. Cuthwulf:*—Cûþwulf wæs Cûþwining *Cuthwulf was the son of Cuthwin,* Chr. Th. 2, 3. Hêr DLXXI Cûþwulf feaht wiđ Bretwalas æt Bedcan forda *in this year,* A. D. 571, *Cuthwulf fought with the Brito-Welsh at Bedford,* Chr. 571; Th. 32, 25, col. 1.

cuu; *gen.* cuus; *f. A cow;* vacca:—Be cuus horne *of a cow's horn,* L. In. 59; Th. i. 140, 1, 3: Ps. Lamb. 67, 31. v. cû.

cuwon *chewed*, Ælfc. T. 42, 9; *p. pl. of* ceówan.

CWACIAN, cwacigan; *part.* cwaciende, cwacigende; *p.* ode; *pp.* od *To* QUAKE, *shake, tremble;* tremere, contremere:—Seó eorþe wæs cwaciende *the earth was quaking*, Ors. 2, 6; Bos. 49, 41. Seó cwacigende swustor *the quaking sister*, Homl. Th. ii. 32, 26, 31. Heó gemētte ealle hire bearn cwacigende eallum limum *she found all her children quaking in every limb*, 30, 20. Heard ecg cwacaþ *the hard edge shaketh*, Elen. Kmbl. 1513; El. 758. Cēne cwacaþ *the bold shall quake*, Exon. 19 b; Th. 50, 8; Cri. 797. Ða tēþ cwaciaþ on swīðlīcum cȳle *their teeth shall quake in the intense cold*, Homl. Th. i. 132, 27: 530, 35. Ic cwacode eal on fefore *I quaked all in a fever*, ii. 312, 19. Cwacode eorþe *contremuit terra*, Ps. Spl. C. 17, 9. Cwacode he sōna *he instantly quaked*, Homl. Th. ii. 312, 15: 32, 3, 19. [*Prompt.* quakyn̄ *tremere: Wyc. Piers P.* quaken: *R. Brun. Chauc. R. Glouc.* quake: *Laym.* quakien, cwakie.]

cwacung, e; *f. A* QUAKING, *trembling;* tremor:—Sōna biþ ætstilled sió cwacung *the quaking will soon be stilled*, L. M. 1, 26; Lchdm. ii. 68, 11. Cwacung gegrāp hīg *tremor apprehendit eos*, Ps. Spl. C. 47, 5. On cwacunge *in tremore*, Ps. Spl. C. 2, 11. Wæs se mūnt Garganus bifigende mid ormǣtre cwacunge *the mount Garganus was trembling with immense quaking*, Homl. Th. i. 504, 28. Būton cwacunge *without quaking*, ii. 32, 18.

cwǣde, *pl.* cwǣdon *said*, Ps. Th. 89, 3: Cd. 191; Th. 238, 28; Dan. 361; *2nd sing. p. and p. pl. of* cweđan.

cwæl, *pl.* cwǣlon *died; p. of* cwelan.

cwælm *death*, Som. Ben. Lye. v. cwealm.

cwælu *a violent death*, Som. Ben. Lye. v. cwalu.

cwǣman *to please*, Som. Ben. Lye. v. cwēman.

cwǣn *a queen*:—Æđelfriþ cwǣn, seó wæs Ælfrēdes swuster, forþfērde, and hire līc līþ æt Pauian *queen Æthelfrith, who was Alfred's sister, died, and her body lies at Pavia*, Chr. 888; Erl. 87, 16–18. v. cwēn.

cwært-ern *a prison*, Mt. Kmbl. Rl. 25, 43, 44. v. cweart-ern.

cwæstednys *a trembling*, Som. Ben. Lye. DER. to-cwæstednys.

cwæþ QUOTH, *said, spoke*, Deut. 32, 26: Bd. 3, 5; S. 527, 30, 31; *p. of* cweđan.

cwæđst *sayest*, Ælfc. Gr. 2; Som. 3, 7, = cweđst; *2nd pres. sing. of* cweđan.

CWALU, e; *f. A quelling with weapons, torment, a violent death, slaughter, destruction;* nex, cædes, exitium:—Se cyning Eádwine mid ārleásre cwale ofslegen wæs *rex Æduini impia nece occisus*, Bd. 2, 14; S. 517, 32: 2, 12; S. 513, 9, 12, 16. Þurh ānes engles cwale, on Cristes cwale *through an angel's death, by Christ's death*, Boutr. Scrd. 17, 38. Hū nyt is đe mīn slæge, ođđe mīn cwalu *slaughter*, ođđe mīn rotung on byrgenne? Ps. Th. 29, 8. To cwale cnihta *for the destruction of the youths*, Cd. 184; Th. 229, 32; Dan. 226. To cwale syllan *to give to death*, Exon. 70 a; Th. 259, 29; Jul. 289. To cwale lǣdan *to lead to death*, 74 b; Th. 279, 14; Jul. 613. [*Laym.* quale *murrain;* quale-huse, cwal-huse *a torture-house*: *O. Sax.* quala, *f*: *Dut.* kwaal *malum, morbus*: *Kil.* quaele *languor, ægritudo*: *Ger.* qual, *f*: *M. H. Ger.* quël, *f. torment*: *O. H. Ger.* quāla *nex, pernicies*: *Dan.* qwal, *m. f*: *Swed.* qual, *n. anguish, agony*: *Icel.* kwal- in compounds, *pain, torment.*] DER. deáþ-cwalu, feorh-, gāst-, hearm-, hell-, līg-, nīþ-, swylt-, sylf-.

cwanc, *pl.* cwuncon *disappeared; p. of* cwincan.

CWĀNIAN; *part.* cwāniende; *p.* ode, ede; *pp.* od, ed *To bewail, deplore, lament, mourn;* plorare, deplorare, queri, lugere. I. *v. trans*:—Sum sceal, leómena leás, sār cwānian *one, void of light, shall bewail his pain*, Exon. 87 b; Th. 328, 18; Vy. 19: 73 b; Th. 274, 23; Jul. 537. II. *v. intrans*:—Cwāniendra cirm *the cry of mourning men*, Exon. 20 a; Th. 52, 19, note; Cri. 836. Weras cwānedon *the men lamented*, Andr. Kmbl. 3071; An. 1538. [*Plat.* kwinen *to languish*: *Dut.* kwijnen *to linger, pine*: *Kil.* quenen, quynen *tabescere*: *M. H. Ger.* quinen *to languish*: *Goth.* qainon *lamentari, lugere*: *Icel.* kweina *to wail, lament.*]

cwānig; *adj.* [cwānian *to bewail, lament, mourn*] *Complaining, bewailing, sad;* querulus, tristis. DER. mōd-cwānig.

Cwanta-wīc, es; *n.* [wīc *a dwelling*] *St. Josse-sur-Mer* or *Estaples, the ancient name of which was Quantovic* or *Quentawich*:—Hēr wæs micel wælsliht on Lundenne and on Cwanta-wīc and on Hrōfes ceastre *in this year* [A. D. 839] *there was a great slaughter at London and at Estaples and at Rochester*, Chr. 839; Erl. 66, 17.

cwart-ern *a prison*:—Ic wæs on cwarterne *eram in carcere*, Mt. Kmbl. Hat. 25, 36, 39. v. cweart-ern.

Cwat-brycg, -bricg, e; *f.* [*Ethelw.* Cantbricge: *Flor.* Quatbrig: *Hunt.* Quadruge: *Matt. West.* Quantebridge] *Bridgenorth in Shropshire;* oppidi nomen in agro Salopiensi:—Hī gedydon æt Cwatbricge be Sæfern *they arrived at Bridgenorth on the Severn*, Chr. 896; Th. 173, 43, col. 1: col. 2 has Brygce. Æt Cwatbrycge, Th. 174, 1, col. 1, 2. Sǣton hie đone winter æt Cwatbrycge [Bricge, Th. 174, 10, col. 2; 175, 9, col. 1: Brygcge, 175, 10, col. 2] *they remained that winter at Bridgenorth*, Chr. 896; Th. 174, 11, col. 1. v. Bricg.

CWEAD, es; *n. Dung, filth, ordure;* stercus:—Sume nimaþ wearm cwead *some take warm dung*, L. M. 1, 50; Lchdm. ii. 124, 8: 2, 48; Lchdm. ii. 262, 18. Of cweade *de stercore*, Ps. Spl. 112, 6. [*Wyc.* quad, quade, *adj. bad*: *Piers P.* queed *the evil one, devil*: *Plat.* quaad, *adj. bad, evil*: *O. Frs.* quad, qwad, *adj. bad, evil*: *Dut.* kwaad, *n. evil, mischief*: *Kil.* quaed, quaet, quat, kat *stercus, oletum*: *Ger.* koth, *m. merda, lutum*: *M. H. Ger.* kāt, kōt, quat, *m. n. stercus*: *O. H. Ger.* chot *stercus*: *Zend* gūtha, *m. dirt*: *Sansk.* gūtha, *m. n. excrement.*]

cweahte, *pl.* cweahton *quaked, vibrated; p. of* cweccan.

cwealde, *pl.* cwealdon *slew*, Exon. 65 b; Th. 243, 3; Jul. 5: Ors. 4, 4; Bos. 80, 41; *p. of* cwellan.

cwealm, cwēlm, es; *m. n.* [cwelan *to die*] *Death, destruction, a violent death, slaughter, murder, torment, plague, pestilence, contagion,* QUALM; mors, pernicies, nex, cædes, homicidium, cruciatus, lues, pestis, pestilentia, contagium:—Hine se cwealm ne þeáh *death profited him not*, Exon. 74 b; Th. 278, 30; Jul. 605: Cd. 79; Th. 98, 1; Gen. 1623: Elen. Kmbl. 1349; El. 676. Him cwelm gesceód *death destroyed him*, Cd. 208; Th. 257, 36; Dan. 668. Ylda cwealm *a slaughter of men*, Andr. Kmbl. 363; An. 182. Cwealmes wyrhta *a worker of murder, a murderer*, Cd. 48; Th. 61, 29; Gen. 1004. Đider sōþfæstra sāwla mōtun cuman æfter cwealme *thither the souls of the just may come after death*, Exon. 32 b; Th. 103, 14; Cri. 1688: Cd. 166; Th. 207, 18; Exod. 468. To wera cwealme *for the destruction of men*, Andr. Kmbl. 3013; An. 1509. Ic honda gewemde on Caines cwealme mīne *I have polluted my hands in Cain's murder*, Cd. 52; Th. 67, 4; Gen. 1095. In Caines cynne đone cwealm gewræc Drihten *the Lord avenged the death* [*of Abel*] *on Cain's race*, Beo. Th. 215; B. 107: Exon. 28 b; Th. 87, 17; Cri. 1426: Andr. Kmbl. 2243; An. 1123. Đū wāst cwealm hātne in helle *thou knowest hot torment in hell*, 2374; An. 1188: 562; An. 281. Þurh deáþes cwealm *through pain of death*, Exon. 35 b; Th. 115, 26; Gū. 195: Cd. 224; Th. 296, 9; Sat. 499. Mid morþes cwealme *with pain of death*, 35; Th. 47, 9; Gen. 758. Cwealma mǣst *the greatest of torments, hell*, Exon. 31 b; Th. 99, 20; Cri. 1627. Micel cwealm wearþ đæs folces *the mortality of the people was great*, Homl. Th. ii. 122, 18. Cwealm *pestilentia* vel *contagium* vel *lues*, Ælfc. Gl. 9; Som. 57, 8; Wrt. Voc. 19, 18. Đæt us cwealm on ne become *ne forte occidat nos pestis*, Ex. 5, 3. To đam swīđe awēdde se cwealm đæt hundeahtatig manna of līfe gewiton *the plague raged to that degree that eighty men departed from life*, Homl. Th. ii. 126, 18: Exon. 89 a; Th. 335, 7; Gn. Ex. 30. On đissum geáre com micel māncwealm on Brytene īgland, and on đam cwealme forþfērde Tuda biscop *in this year* [A. D. 664] *there was a great plague in the island of Britain, and bishop Tuda died of the plague*, Chr. 664; Erl. 35, 19: Homl. Th. ii. 124, 2. Godes miltsung đone rēđan cwealm gestilde *God's mercy stilled the cruel pestilence*, ii. 126, 22. Beóþ mycele eorþan styrunga geond stōwa, and cwealmas *terræmotus magni erunt per loca, et pestilentiæ*, Lk. Bos. 21, 11. *In the following example* cwealm *is neuter*:—Sume ic þurh mislīc cwealm mīnum hondum slōg *some I slew by my hands through various deaths*, Exon. 73 a; Th. 272, 2; Jul. 493. [*Chauc.* qualm *sickness*: *Laym.* qualm *mortality, plague*: *Plat.* qualm *vapour, smoke*: *O. Sax.* qualm, *m. violent death, murder*: *Dut.* kwalm, *m. reek, moist*: *Ger.* qualm, *m. vapour, smoke*: *M. H. Ger.* qualm, *m. anguish*: *O. H. Ger.* qualm, *m. nex*: *Dan.* qwalm, *m. f. vapour, smoke*: *Swed.* qwalm, *n. sultriness.*] DER. beadu-cwealm, bealo-, brōđor-, deáþ-, feorh-, gār-, mān-, morþor-, nīþ-, orf-, ūt-, wæl-, yrf-.

cwealm-bǣre, cwylm-bǣre; *adj.* [-bǣre, an *adj.* termination; *producing, bearing*] *Death-bearing, deadly;* mortiferus:—Đeáh đe he cwealmbǣre wǣre *though he was death-bearing*, Wanl. Catal. 164, 48, col. 1. Drenc mid đam cwealmbǣrum āttre gemenged *a drink mingled with deadly poison*, Homl. Th. ii. 158, 17: 260, 11. Cwealmbǣrne *mortiferum*, Mone B. 4905. Cōmon đa cempan mid cwylmbǣrum tōlum *the soldiers came with deadly tools*, Homl. Th. ii. 260, 7.

cwealm-bǣrnes, -ness, e; *f. Destruction, ruin, deadliness, mortality;* pernicies, mortalitas. v. cwelm-bǣrnys.

cwealm-bealu; *gen.* -bealuwes; *n.* [bealo, bealu *bale, evil*] *Deadly evil;* cædis malum:—Đæt hit mōste cwealmbealu cȳđan *that it must make known the deadly evil*, Beo. Th. 3884; B. 1940.

cwealm-cuma, an; *m.* [cuma, *q. v. a comer, guest*] *A deadly guest;* advena cædem parans:—Nolde eorla hleó đone cwealmcuman cwicne forlǣtan *the refuge of the earls would not leave the deadly guest living*, Beo. Th. 1588; B. 792.

cwealm-dreór, es; *m.* [dreór *blood*] *Slaughter-gore;* sanguis cæde profusus, Cd. 47; Th. 60, 22; Gen. 985.

cwealmnes, cwylmnes, -ness, -nyss, e; *f. Torment, pain, anguish;* cruciatus:—Đa wǣron missenlīcum cwealmnyssum þrēste *qui diversis cruciatibus torti*, Bd. 1, 7; S. 479, 13. Fram swā myclum cwylmnessum *a tamque diutinis cruciatibus*, 4, 9; S. 577, 10.

cwealm-stede, es; *m.* [stede *a place*] *A death-place;* mortis locus:—To cwealmstede *ad palæstram*, Glos. Prudent. Recd. 148, 46.

cwealm-stōw, e; *f.* [stōw *a place*] *A place of execution;* patibuli *vel* supplicii locus:—He to đære cwealmstōwe lǣded wæs *he was led to the place of execution*, Bd. 1, 7; S. 478, note 38.

cwealm-þreá; *indecl; m. f. n.* [cwealm, þreá *a vexing, terror*] *Deadly terror;* letalis terror:—Mid cwealmþreá *with deadly terror*, Cd. 116; Th. 151, 12; Gen. 2507.

cwearn *a mill-stone*, Mk. Skt. Rush. 9, 42. v. cwyrn, cweorn-stān.

cweart-ern, cwert-ern, es; *n. A guard-house, prison;* custodia, carcer:—Ðæs cwearternes hirde hīg betǽhte Iosepe *custos carceris tradidit eos Ioseph*, Gen. 40, 4. Ic wæs on cwearterne *eram in carcere*, Mt. Bos. 25, 36, 39: Lk. Bos. 3, 20: Jn. Bos. 3, 24: Ælfc. Gr. 9, 18; Som. 9, 59. [*Prompt.* qwert, whert *incolumis, sanus, sospes.*]

cweartern-līc; *adj. Of* or *belonging to a prison;* carceralis:—Þurh cwearternlīce cyp *per carceralem stipitem*, Glos. Prudent. Recd. 150, 38.

CWECCAN; *part.* cweccende; ic cwecce, đū cwecest, cwecst, he cweceþ, cwecþ, *pl.* cweccaþ; *p.* cwehte, cweahte, *pl.* cwehton, cweahton; *pp.* cweaht *To vibrate, move;* torquēre, quatĕre, vibrāre, movēre:—Cweccende *torquens*, Glos. Prudent. Recd. 147, 49. Hē cwecþ his sweord *gladium suum vibrabit*, Ps. Th. 7, 12. Þegn Hrōþgāres, þrymmum cwehte *Hrothgar's thane, violently quaked*, Beo. Th. 476; B. 235. Iohannes cwehte his heáfod *John shook his head*, Ælfc. T. 36, 9. Hī cwehton [MS. cwehtun] heora heáfod *moverunt caput*, Ps. Lamb. 21, 8. Đa wegfērendan cwehton heora heáfod *the passers-by shook their heads*, Mt. Bos. 27, 39: Mk. Bos. 15, 29. [*Laym.* quecchen *to shake, move: Icel.* kwika *to move, stir.*] DER. a-cweccan.

cweccung, e; *f. A moving, wagging;* commotio:—Đū gesettest us on cweccunge heáfdes on folcum *posuisti nos in commotionem capitis in populis*, Ps. Lamb. 43, 15.

cwede *a saying*, Som. Ben. Lye. v. cwide.

cweden *spoken, said, called*, Exon. 15 b; Th. 34, 24; Cri. 547: Chr. 455; Erl. 13, 23: Bd. 5, 19; S. 636, 45; *pp. of* cweđan.

cwehte, *pl.* cwehton *shook, moved, quaked*, Beo. Th. 476; B. 235: Ælfc. T. 36, 9: Ps. Lamb. 21, 8: Mt. Bos. 27, 39: Mk. Bos. 15, 29; *p. of* cweccan.

CWELAN, ic cwele, đū cwilst, he cwelþ, cwilþ, cwylþ, *pl.* cwelaþ; *p.* cwæl, *pl.* cwǣlon; *pp.* cwolen *To die;* mori:—Cwele ic *I die*, Exon. 125 a; Th. 482, 2; Rä. 66, 1. Swā swā fixas cwelaþ gyf hī of wætere beóþ, swā eác cwelþ [cwylþ MSS. R. L.] ǽlc eorþlīc līchama gyf he byþ đære lyfte bedǽled *as fishes die if they are out of water, so also every earthly body dies if it be deprived of the air*, Bd. de nat. rerum; Wrt. popl. science 17, 9-11; Lchdm. iii. 272, 25 and note 36. [*Laym.* quelen *to die: O. Sax.* quelan *to die from a violent death* or *as a martyr: Dut.* quelen *languore tabescere: O. H. Ger.* quelan *cruciari, pati, mori.*] DER. a-cwelan, ōþ-: cwild, -bǽre, -bǽrlīce, -tīd: cwalu: cwellan, a-: cwellere: a-cwelledness: cwealm, -bǽre, -bǽrness, -bealu, -cuma, -dreór, -ness, -stede, -stōw, -þreá: cwelman, cwylman, ge-: cwylming.

cweldeht; *adj.* [cweld = cwyld *destruction*, -eht = -iht *adj. termination*, q. v.] *Mortified;* corruptionis plenus:—Wiđ wyrmǽtum līce and cweldehtum *for a worm-eaten and mortified body*, L. M. 1, 54; Lchdm. ii. 126, 4.

CWELLAN, ic cwelle, đū cwelest, cwelst, he cweleþ, cwelþ, *pl.* cwellaþ; *p.* cwealde, *pl.* cwealdon; *pp.* cwelled, cweled, cweald; *v. a. To kill, slay* = QUELL? necare, trucidare, occidere, mactare:—Đa cwelleras ne woldan hine cwellan *the executioners would not kill him*, Bd. 5, 19; S. 638, 30: Cd. 140; Th. 176, 2; Gen. 2905: Hy. 7, 105; Hy. Grn. ii. p. 289, 105. Oft ic cwelle compwæpnum *often I kill with battle-weapons*, Exon. 105 b; Th. 401, 9; Rä. 21, 9. Đū ramm cwelst *thou shalt kill the ram*, Ex. 29, 16. We cwellaþ *we kill*, Ex. 8, 26. Cwealde *had killed*, Andr. Kmbl. 3247; An. 1626. Hī stearcferþe cwellan þohtun *the stern of mind resolved to slay her*, Exon. 75 a; Th. 280. 31; Jul. 637. Đū Grendel cwealdest *thou didst slay Grendel*, Beo. Th. 2673; B. 1334. Ārleás cyning cwealde cristne men *the impious king slew christian men*, Exon. 65 b; Th. 243, 3; Jul. 5. [*Prompt.* qwellyn *suffocare: Wyc.* quellere *a killer: Piers P.* quellan *to kill: Chauc. R. Glouc.* quelle: *Laym.* quelle-n: *Orm.* cwellenn: *O. Sax.* quellian: *Dut.* kwellen *to vex: Kil.* quellen *molestare: Ger.* quälen *to vex: M. H. Ger.* queln, quellen, kellen *to press, vex: O. H. Ger.* queljan *necare: Dan.* qwäle *to quell, torture: Swed.* qwälja *to torment: Icel.* kwelja *to torment.*] DER. a-cwellan.

cwellend, es; *m.* [cwellende, *part. of* cwellan *to kill*] *A killer, slayer;* interfector:—Cwellend *sector*, Glos. Prudent. Recd. 150, 27.

cwellere, es; *m. A killer, man-slayer, executioner,* QUELLER, *tormentor;* lanio, interfector, spiculator? carnifex:—Se cwellere *the executioner*, Bd. 1, 7; S. 478, 15, 35. Đa cwelleras *the executioners;* carnifices, 5, 19; S. 638, 29. Herodes sende ǽnne cwellere, and bebeád đæt man his heáfod on ānum disce brohte *Herod sent an executioner, and commanded that they should bring his* [*John Baptist's*] *head on a dish*, Mk. Bos. 6, 27. Hyldere, ođđe cwellere, ođđe flǽsctawere [MS. flǽctawere] *lanio, vel lanista, vel carnifex, vel macellarius*, Ælfc. Gl. 113; Som. 79, 122; Wrt. Voc. 60, 27.

cwelm *destruction, death*, Cd. 208; Th. 257, 36; Dan. 668. v. cwealm.

cwelman, cwylman, cwilman; *part.* -ende; *p.* de; *pp.* ed [cwealm, cwelm *death, destruction, torment*] *To torture, torment, destroy, kill;* trucidare, cruciare:—Cwelmende fȳr *destroying fires*, Exon. 22 a; Th. 59, 28; Cri. 959. He wæs đæt folc cwilmende *he tortured the people*, Ors. 1, 12; Bos. 36, 25. He eorþ-cyningas yrmde and cwelmde *he oppressed and slew the kings of the earth*, Bt. Met. Fox 9, 94; Met. 9, 47. Mæssepreóstas wǣron cwylmde *sacerdotes trucidabantur*, Bd. 1, 15; S. 484, 1: 4, 13; S. 582, note 29. Hī hālge cwelmdon *they slew the holy*, Exon. 66 a; Th. 243, 24; Jul. 15. Đæt hī cwylmen rihte heortan *ut trucident rectos corde*, Ps. Spl. 36, 15. Đū hungre scealt cwylmed weorþan *thou shalt be put to death with hunger*, Elen. Kmbl. 1373; El. 688. [*O. Sax.* quelmian *to kill.*] DER. ge-cwelman, -cwylman.

cwelm-bǽrnys, -nyss, e; *f.* [cwealm, cwelm *death, destruction*] *Destruction, ruin, deadliness, mortality;* pernicies, mortalitas:—Cwelmbǽrnyss *pernicies*, Ælfc. Gr. 12; Som. 15, 52. Þurh myrran is gehīwod cwelmbǽrnys ūres flǽsces *by myrrh is typified the mortality of our flesh*, Homl. Th. i. 118, 3.

cwelþ *dies*, Bd. de nat. rerum; Wrt. popl. science 17, 10; *3rd pres. sing. of* cwelan.

cwēman; *part.* cwēmende; *p.* de; *pp.* ed; *v. a. dat. To give pleasure, please, delight, propitiate, satisfy;* placere, satisfacere:—Sum sceal on heápe hæleđum cwēman *one shall in company give pleasure to men*, Exon. 88 a; Th. 331, 33; Vy. 77. Ic mīnum Criste cwēman þence leófran lāce *I purpose to please my Saviour with a dearer gift*, 37 a; Th. 120, 26; Gū. 277: Ors. 1, 12; Bos. 36, 27: Cd. 220; Th. 283, 16; Sat. 305. Se đe ne þenceþ Meotode cwēman *he who thinketh not to propitiate the Creator*, 217; Th. 276, 5; Sat. 184: Exon. 69 a; Th. 257, 25; Jul. 252: Ps. Th. 91, 3: 94, 1. God tostencþ bān heora đa đe mannum cwēmendra *Deus dissipavit ossa eorum qui hominibus placent*, Ps. Spl. 52, 7. Ic cwēme Drihtne on rīce lȳfigendra *placebo Domino in regione vivorum*, 114, 9: Ps. Th. 53, 6. Esne his hlāforde cwēmeþ *a servant gives pleasure to his master*, 122. 2. Martiras Meotode cwēmaþ *martyrs give delight to the Creator*, Cd. 228; Th. 305, 31; Sat. 655: Exon. 39 a; Th. 130, 5; Gū. 433: Ps. Th. 71, 10. Nǽnig man scile orþances ūtabredan wǽpnes ecgge, đeáh đe him se wlite cwēme *no man should draw forth the weapon's edge without a cause, although its beauty please him*, Salm. Kmbl. 332; Sal. 165. Đæt we cwēman Criste *that we please Christ*, Cd. 226; Th. 302, 8; Sat. 596. Đam ic georne cwēmde *whom I have earnestly propitiated*, Exon. 48 b; Th. 167, 11; Gū. 1058. Him lofsangum cwēmdon [MS. cwemdan] *cantaverunt laudes ejus*, Ps. Th. 105, 11. [*Laym.* queme, cweme, iquemen, icweme *to please: Orm.* cwemenn: *Ger.* bequemen *to accommodate.*] DER. ge-cwēman.

cwēme; *adj.* [cwēman *to please*] *Pleasant, pleasing, grateful, acceptable, fit;* gratus, acceptus, congruus. DER. ge-cwēme.

cwēming, e; *f. A pleasing, satisfying;* placentia, satisfactio, Greg. Dial. 4, 28.

cwēmnys, -nyss, e; *f. A satisfaction, an appeasing, a mitigation;* satisfactio:—Cwēmnys uncysta *satisfactio vitiorum*, Bd. 1, 27; S. 495, 32.

CWÉN; *gen. dat.* cwēne; *acc.* cwēn, cwēnn, cwēne; *pl. nom. acc.* cwēne, cwēna; *gen.* cwēna; *dat.* cwēnum; *f:* cwēne, cwȳne; *gen. dat. acc.* cwēnan, cwȳnan; *pl. nom. acc.* cwēnan; *gen.* cwēnena; *dat.* cwēnum; *f.* I. *a woman;* femina:—Seó clǽneste cwēn ofer eorþan *the purest woman upon earth*, Exon. 12 a; Th. 17, 27; Cri. 276. Þurh đa æđelan cwēnn *through the noble woman*, 25 b; Th. 73, 34; Cri. 1199. Cwēna sēlost *the best of women*, Menol. Fox 334; Men. 168. Ealdra cwēna spell *old women's talk;* anilis fabula, Ælfc. Gl. 100; Som. 77, 20; Wrt. Voc. 55, 24. Ic wæs feaxhār cwēne *I was a hoary-headed woman*, Exon. 126 b; Th. 487, 13; Rä. 73, 1. On cwēnena brōce, of cwēnena brōce *to the women's brook, from the women's brook*, Cod. Dipl. Apndx. 426; A. D. 949; Kmbl. iii. 429, 34. II. *a wife;* uxor:—Abrahames cwēn *Abraham's wife*, Cd. 103; Th. 136, 17; Gen. 2259. Hæleđa cwēnum *to the wives of the warriors*, 169; Th. 210, 7; Exod. 511. Gif preóst cwēnan forlǽte, and ōđre nime, anaþema sit *if a priest forsake his wife, and take another, let him be excommunicated*, L. N. P. L. 35; Th. ii. 296, 1. Gif man mid esnes cwȳnan geligeþ, be cwicum ceorle, ii gebēte *if a man lie with an 'esne's' wife, her husband still living, let him make twofold amends*, L. Ethb. 85; Th. i. 24, 9. III. *a king's* or *emperor's wife, a* QUEEN, *empress;* regina, imperatrix, augusta:—Cwēn *regina*, Ælfc. Gl. 68; Som. 69, 128; Wrt. Voc. 42, 8: 72, 56: Mt. Bos. 12, 42: Lk. Bos. 11, 31: Ors. 1, 10; Bos. 33, 23: 3, 11; Bos. 73, 37: Chr. 672; Erl. 35, 37: 722; Erl. 45, 26: Beo. Th. 1851; B. 923: Elen. Kmbl. 494; El. 247. Đæs [MS. đes] cāseres cwēn *imperatrix* vel *augusta*, Wrt. Voc. 72, 58. Oft on ānre tīde acenþ seó cwēn and seó wyln *the queen and the slave often bring forth at one time*, Homl. Th. i. 110, 27: Elen. Kmbl. 832; El. 416: 1113; El. 558: Beo. Th. 2311; B. 1153. Seo ylce cwēn Samēramis *the same queen Sameramis*, Ors. 1, 2; Bos. 27, 6. Đǽr wearþ Marsepia, sió cwēn, ofslagen *Marpesia, the queen, was slain there*, 1, 10; Bos. 33, 22, 24: Elen. Kmbl. 756; El. 378: Bt. Met. Fox 26, 178; Met. 26, 89. Đeós cwēn *this queen*, Elen. Kmbl. 1064; El. 533: 1099; El. 551. He wæs on đære cwēne gewealdum *he was in the queen's power*, 1217; El. 610: 2269; El. 1136. Đone hie đære cwēne agēfon *they gave him up to the queen*, 1171; El. 587: 2257; El. 1130. Aðelwulf cyng Carles dōhtor hæfde to cwēne *king Æthelwulf had the daughter of Charles for his queen*, Chr. 885; Erl. 85, 3: 1017; Erl. 161, 10: 1048; Erl. 180, 21. Mid ða æðelan cwēn *with the noble queen*, Elen. Kmbl. 550; El. 275: Beo. Th. 1334; B. 665: Exon. 86 a; Th. 324, 29; Wīd. 102. Ofslōh ge ðone cyning, ge ða cwēne *slew both the king and the queen*, Ors. 3, 11; Bos. 74, 4: Homl. Th. i. 438, 21: Exon. 90 a; Th. 338, 22; Gn. Ex. 82. Cyningas and cwēne *kings and queens*, 113 a; Th. 433, 15; Rä. 50, 8. Hiora twā wǣron heora cwēna, Marsepia and Lampida wǣron hātene *two of them, called Marpesia and Lampeto, were their queens*, Ors. 1, 10; Bos. 33, 14, 35. Se wæs Melcolmes sunu cynges and Margarite ðære cwēnan *he was the son of king Malcolm and queen Margaret*, Chr. 1097; Erl. 234, 37. [*Prompt.* quene *regina;* quen, womann of lytylle price: *Wyc.* queene: *Piers P.* queyne, queene: *R. Brun. R. Glouc.* quene: *Laym.* quen-e, *f*: *Orm.* cwen: *Scot.* queyn, quean *a young woman*: *Plat.* quene: *O. Sax.* cwān, cwēna, *f. uxor*: *Dut.* kween, *f. a married woman*: *Kil.* quene *uxor, mulier*: *Ger.* königin, *f*: *M. H. Ger.* kone, kon, *f. uxor*: *O. H. Ger.* quena, chena, chone, *f. mulier, conjux, uxor*: *Goth.* qens, *f. mulier, uxor*: *Dan.* qwinde, kone *mulier, uxor*: *Swed.* qwinna, *f. mulier, uxor;* kåna, *f. a low woman*: *Icel.* kona, kuna, kwán, kwǽn *a woman, wife, queen*: *Grk.* γυνή *femina, genitrix*: *Slav.* shena: *Sansk.* gnā, jani, *f. a woman, wife, mother.*] DER. dryht-cwēn, folc-, gūþ-, sige-, þeód-.

Cwēna land *the land* or *country of the Quaines*, Ors. 1, 1; Bos. 21, 10. v. Cwēnas, Cwēn-land.

Cwēnas; *gen.* a; *pl. m. The Quaines;* Cayani. *The inhabitants of* Cwēn-land, *q. v*:—Is to-emnes ðæm lande sūþeweardum, on ōðre healfe ðæs mōres, Sweōland, ōþ ðæt land norþeweard; and to-emnes ðæm lande norþeweardum, Cwēna land. Ða Cwēnas hergiaþ hwīlum on ða Norþmen ofer ðone mōr; hwīlum ða Norþmen on hȳ; and ðǣr sint swīðe micle meras fersce geond ða mōras; and beraþ ða Cwēnas hyra scypu ofer land on ða meras, and ðanon hergiaþ on ða Norþmen. Hȳ habbaþ swȳðe lytle scypa, and swȳðe leóhte *over against the land* [*Finland*] *southward, on the other side of the waste, is Sweden, northward up to the land; and over against the land northward is the land of the Quaines. The Quaines sometimes make war on the Northmen over the waste; sometimes the Northmen on them; and there are very large fresh lakes beyond the wastes; and the Quaines carry their boats over land into the lakes, and thence make war on the Northmen. They have very little boats, and very light*, Ors. 1, 1; Bos. 21, 8–15.

cwencan; *p.* cwencte; *pp.* cwenced, cwenct *To extinguish*, QUENCH; extinguere. DER. acwencan.

cwēne, cwȳne, an; *f. A woman, wife, queen, common woman, harlot;* femina, uxor, regina, meretrix:—Ic wæs feaxhār cwēne *I was a hoary-headed woman*, Exon. 126 b; Th. 487, 13; Rä. 73, 1. Cwēnan forlǣtan *to forsake a wife*, L. N. P. L. 35; Th. ii. 296, 1. Mid esnes cwȳnan *with an 'esne's' wife*, L. Ethb. 85; Th. i. 24, 9. Margarite ðære cwēnan *of queen Margaret*, Chr. 1097; Erl. 234, 37. Wið āne cwēnan fylþe adreógaþ *cum una meretrice spurcitiem exercent*, Lupi Serm. 1, 11; Hick. Thes. ii. 102, 26. v. cwēn.

cwēn-fugol, es; *m. A female* or *hen bird;* avis feminea, Som. Ben. Lye.

Cwēn-land, es; *n. Cwēn-land* lies between the White Sea [Cwēn Sǣ] and Norway, north of the Gulf of Bothnia. The country east and west of the Gulf of Bothnia, from Norway to the Cwēn or White Sea, including Finmark on the north. Malte-Brun says that the inhabitants of Cwēn-land were a Finnish race. They were called Quaines, and by Latin writers Cayani. Gerchau maintains, in his history of Finland, 1810, that the Laplanders only were called Finns, and that they were driven from the country by the Quaines. 'They settled in Lapland, and on the shores of the White Sea, which derived from them the name of Quen Sea or Quen-vik.'... Adamus Bremensis happened to be present at a conversation, in which king Swenon spoke of Quen-land or Quena-land, the country of the Quaines, but as the stranger's knowledge of Danish was very imperfect, he supposed the king had said Quinna-land, the country of women or Amazons; hence the absurd origin of his Terra Feminarum, mistaking the name of the country, for quinna *a woman.* Malte-Brun's Universal Geog. Edin. 1827, vol. vi. p. 495.—Dr. Latham's Germania of Tacitus, 174, 179:—Sweón habbaþ be sūþan him ðone sǣs earm Osti; and be eástan him Sermende; and be norþan him ofer ða wēstennu is Cwēn-land *the Swedes have, to the south of them, the Esthonian arm of the sea; and to the east of them the Sermende; and to the north of them, over the wastes, is Cwēn-land*, Ors. 1, 1; Bos. 19, 21–23: 21, 10.

cwēn-līc; *adj.* QUEENLY, *feminine;* muliebris:—Ne biþ swylc cwēnlīc þeáw *such is not a feminine custom*, Beo. Th. 3885; B. 1940.

cwēnn *a woman*, Exon. 25 b; Th. 73, 34; Cri. 1199; *acc. s. of* cwēn.

Cwēn-sǣ; *gen.* -sǣs; *m. The White Sea;* hyperboreus oceanus:—Fram ðære eá Danais, west ōþ Rīn ða eá... and eft sūþ ōþ Donua ða eá... and norþ ōþ ðone gārsecg, ðe man Cwēnsǣ hǣt: binnan ðǣm syndon manega þeóda; ac hit man hǣt eall, Germania *from the river Don, westward to the river Rhine... and again south to the river Danube... and north to the ocean, which is called the White Sea: within these are many nations; but they call it all, Germania*, Ors. 1, 1; Bos. 18, 21–28. v. Cwēnas, Cwēn-land.

cweoc *quick, alive*, Symb. Athan. Lye. v. cwic.

cweodo *a cud, quid*, L. M. 2, 14; Lchdm. ii. 192, 6. v. cwudu.

cweorn, e; *f*: cweorne, an; *f. A mill, hand-mill, quern*, Mt. Kmbl. Hat. 24, 41: Ex. 11, 5. v. cwyrn.

cweorn-bill, es; *n.* [bil *a bill, falchion*] *A stone chisel for dressing querns;* lapidaria, Cot. 125.

cweorn-stān *a mill-stone*, Mk. Bos. 9, 42: Lk. Bos. 17, 2. v. cwyrn-stān.

cweorn-tēþ; *pl. m. Molar teeth, grinders;* molares, Wrt. Voc. 282, 75.

cwert-ern, es; *n. A prison*:—Ðe-læs ðū sȳ on cwertern send *ne forte in carcerem mittaris*, Mt. Bos. 5, 25: Lk. Bos. 12, 58. v. cweart-ern.

cweþ *says*, Ælfc. Gr. 15; Som. 18, 45, = cweðeþ; *3rd pres. sing. of* cweðan.

cweþ ðū *say thou*, cweðe he *let him say*, cweðaþ, cweðe ge *say ye*, Ælfc. Gr. 33; Som. 37, 33, 39: Mt. Bos. 3, 9: Gen. 50, 19; *impert. of* cweðan.

CWEÐAN, to cweðanne; *part.* cweðende; ic cweðe, ðū cweðest, cweðst, cwæðst, cwiðst, cwyðst, cwīst, cwȳst, he cweðeþ, cweþ, cwiþ, cwyþ, *pl.* cweðaþ; *p.* ic, he cwæþ, ðū cwǣde, *pl.* cwǣdon; *impert.* cweþ, cweðe, *pl.* cweðaþ, cweðe; *subj.* cweðe, *pl.* cweðen; *p.* cwǣde, *pl.* cwǣden; *pp.* cweden *To say, speak, call, proclaim;* dicere, loqui, vocare, indicere. I. *v. trans*:—Ic ðē wolde lofsàng cweðan *laudem dixi tibi*, Ps. Th. 118, 164: Rood Kmbl. 230; Kr. 116. For ðam worde ðe se Wealdend cwyþ *for the word which the Lord shall speak*, Rood Kmbl. 220; Kr. 111. Gehȳraþ hwæt se unrihtwīsa dēma cwyþ *audite quid judex iniquitatis dicit*, Lk. Bos. 18, 6. Him ða word hī cweðaþ *they say the words to him*, Exon. 13 b; Th. 25, 15; Cri. 401. Ne cwæþ ic wiht *I spake not aught*, 125 a; Th. 482, 1; Rä. 66, 1: Bt. Met. Fox 10, 69; Met. 10, 35. Drihten cwæþ word to Noe *the Lord spake words to Noah*, Cd. 74; Th. 91, 11; Gen. 1510: Beo. Th. 5318; B. 2662: Andr. Kmbl. 658; An. 329. Arrīus se gedwola cwæþ gemōt ongeán ðone bisceop *Arius the heretic proclaimed a synod against the bishop*, Homl. Th. i. 290, 12. Alȳs mīne sāwle of ðām welerum ðe wom cweðen *deliver my soul from the lips which may speak evil*, Ps. Th. 119, 2. Hī geornlīce smeádon hwæt he cwǣde *they earnestly considered what he said*, Bd. 3, 5; S. 527, 37. On ðære stōwe ðe is cweden Ægeles þrep *at the place which is called Aylesthorpe*, Chr. 455; Erl. 13, 23: Exon. 11 a; Th. 13, 32; Cri. 211. II. *v. intrans*:—Hwæt māgon we cweðan ongēn ūrne hlāford *what can we say to our lord?* Gen. 44, 16: Cd. 229; Th. 310, 24; Sat. 732. Hū hie cweðan woldon *how they would speak*, 201; Th. 249, 17; Dan. 531: Exon. 28 a; Th. 84, 22; Cri. 1377. Ðæt is wundor to cweðanne *quod mirum dictu est*, Bd. 3, 6; S. 528, 10. Ðus cweðende, he forþfērde *hæc dicens, expiravit*, Lk. Bos. 23, 46: Homl. Th. i. 380, 2, 21: Ps. Th. 104, 10. Ic cweðe to ðysum, and ic cweðe to ōðrum *dico huic et alii*, Mt. Bos. 8, 9: Ælfc. Gr. pref; Som. 1, 39: 5; Som. 3, 27: 15; Som. 17, 36: 18; Som. 21, 26, 27, 29, 59, 61, 63. Ic cweðe *aio, inquio*, 33; Som. 37, 31, 37. Ðū cweðst *ais*, 33; Som. 37, 31: Ps. Lamb. 87, 11. Gif ðū cwæðst *if thou sayest*, Ælfc. Gr. 2; Som. 3, 7. Ðū cwiðst *inquis*, 33; Som. 37, 38. Ðū cwyðst *thou sayest*, 2; Som. 3, 8: 5; Som. 3, 27, 32, 33, 36: 15; Som. 17, 36: 18; Som. 21, 62. Ðū cwīst ðæt ic ðē andwyrdan scyle *thou sayest that I must answer thee*, Bt. 5, 3; Fox 12, 16: Num. 11, 22, 23: 23, 12: Ps. Th. 87, 12. Ðū cwȳst ðæt ic me gebiddan sceole to dumbum stānum *thou sayest that I must pray to dumb stones*, Homl. Th. i. 424, 9: Ælfc. Gr. 5; Som. 3, 29: Ps. Th. 88, 16. Man cweðeþ *dicet homo*, Ps. Th. 57, 10. He cweþ *he says*, Ælfc. Gr. 5; Som. 3, 50: 15; Som. 18, 45. He cweþ *ait*, 33; Som. 37, 31. Ðonne cwiþ se engel *then the angel shall speak*, Exon. 32 b; Th. 102, 7; Cri. 1669: Beo. Th. 4088; B. 2041. Swā hwylc swā cwyþ to ðisum munte *quicumque dixerit huic monti*, Mk. Bos. 11, 23: Mt. Bos. 7, 21: Jn. Bos. 4, 10: 16, 18. He cwyþ *inquit*, Ælfc. Gr. 33; Som. 37, 38. We cweðaþ *we say*, Ælfc. Gr. 18; Som. 21, 67. Ge cweðaþ *ye say*, Deut. 28, 67. Sume men cweðaþ on Englisc ðæt hit sié feaxede steorra *some men say in English that it* [*a comet*] *is a long-haired star*, Chr. 891; Erl. 88, 18. Hīg cweðaþ *they say*, Deut. 31, 17: Exon. 12 a; Th. 18, 14; Cri. 283: Cd. 63; Th. 75, 13; Gen. 1239. Hī cweðaþ *aiunt, inquiunt*, Ælfc. Gr. 33; Som. 37, 32, 38. Ic cwæþ *dixi*, Deut. 32, 26: Ps. Lamb. 29, 7: 39, 8: Jn. Bos. 11, 42. Ðū cwǣde, ðæt ðū me woldest wel dōn *tu locutus es, quod benefaceres mihi*, Gen. 32, 12: Andr. Kmbl. 2822; An. 1413: Ps. Th. 89, 3. Ðū cwǣde *inquisti*, Ælfc. Gr. 33; Som. 37, 39. He cwæþ sylf to me *ipse dixit mihi*, Gen. 20, 5: Ex. 1, 15: Lev. 6, 19, 24: Num. 10, 36: Deut. 1, 34: Jos. 3, 6: Jud. 4, 18: Mt. Bos. 8, 4: Mk. Bos. 2, 5: Lk. Bos. 2, 48: Jn. Bos. 5, 8: Fins. Th. 48; Fin. 24. Hīg cwǣdon him betwȳnan *mutuo loquebantur*, Gen. 37, 19: Num. 16, 3: Cd. 191; Th. 238, 28; Dan. 361: Beo. Th. 6342; B. 3181: Elen. Kmbl. 1138; El. 571. Hī cwǣdon *aiebant*, Ælfc. Gr. 33; Som. 37, 33. Ðus cweþ *thus say*, Ex. 19, 3. Cweþ ðū *ai, inque*, Ælfc. Gr. 33; Som. 37, 33, 39. Cweðe he *inquiat*, 33; Som. 37, 39. Ne cweðaþ betwux eów *say not among yourselves*, Mt. Bos. 3, 9. Cweðe ge *say ye*, Gen. 50, 19. Ðý-læs ðú cweðe *lest thou shouldest say*, Cd. 98; Th. 129, 18; Gen. 2145: Ælfc. Gr. 7; Som. 6, 16: 21; Som. 23, 28, 38. Gif se þeówa cweðe ðæt he nelle fram ðē faran *if the servant should say that he will not go from thee*, Deut. 15, 16. Ðý-læs cweðen [MS. cweðan] óðre þeóda *lest other nations should say*, Ps. Th. 78, 10. Gif ic cwǣde *if I said*, 72, 12. Hú wunda cwǣden to hæleðum *how the wounds spake to men*, Exon. 114 b; Th. 441, 13; Rä. 60, 17. Ðæt is wel cweden *that is well spoken*, 15 b; Th. 34, 24; Cri. 547. [*Piers P.* quod *quoth: Chauc.* quethe: *Orm.* cwaþþ *said: Laym.* queð, i-queð, quaeð, quað *quoth*; iqueðen, *pp. said: O. Sax.* queðan, quethan: *O. Frs.* quetha, queda, quan: *M. H. Ger.* quiden, kiden: *O. H. Ger.* quedan: *Goth.* qiþan: *Dan.* qwaede: *Swed.* kwaeda: *Icel.* kveða: *Lat.* in-quit *quoth: Sansk. root* kath *to converse with any one.*] DER. a-cweðan *to say, tell*, æfter-, be-, bi-, for-, fōre-, ge-, hearm-, on-, onbe-, onge-, to-, wið-.

cweðs ðú lá = cwýst ðú lá *O! sayest thou?* numquid? Ps. Lamb. 7, 12. v. cwýst ðú, cweðan.

cweðst *sayest, speakest*, Ps. Lamb. 87, 11; *2nd pres. sing. of* cweðan.

CWIC, cwyc, cwuc, cuc; *def.* se cwica, seó, ðæt cwice; *adj. Alive*, QUICK; vivus, vivax:—Enoch cwic gewāt mid cyning engla *Enoch departed alive with the king of angels*, Cd. 60; Th. 73, 25; Gen. 1210: Exon. 16 b; Th. 37, 8; Cri. 590: Ps. Th. 118, 57. Cwyc *alive*, 104, 8. Ne biþ se cwuca nyttra ðe se deáda, gif him his yfel ne hreówþ *the quick* [*living*] *is not better than the dead, if he repent not of his evil*, Bt. 36, 6; Fox 182, 20. Se iunga wæs cwices mōdes *the youth was of a quick mind*; erat adolescens animi vivacis, Bd. 5, 19; S. 637, 37. He nō ðǣr āht cwices lǣfan wolde *he would leave naught alive there*, Beo. Th. 4618; B. 2314. Ǣlc wuht cwices [cwuces Cot.] biþ innanweard hnescost *everything alive is inwardly softest*, Bt. 34, 10; Fox 150, 5. Ne ofsleá ic ǣlc þing cuces *non percutiam omnem animam viventem*, Gen. 8, 21: Wrt. Voc. 85, 51. On cwicum ceápe *in live stock*, L. Ath. i. prm; Th. i. 194, 6: Homl. Blick. 39, 18. Æt cwicum [cwicon MS.] menn *for a living man*, L. Eth. iii. 1, 2; Th. i. 292, 10, 13. Be cwicum ceorle *the husband being alive*, L. Ethb. 85; Th. i. 24, 9. On cucum [MS. cucan] ceápe *in live stock*, Cod. Dipl. 1201; A. D. 956; Kmbl. v. 378, 20. Seó sealf ðone wyrm ðǣron deádne gedēþ, oððe cwicne ofdrīfþ *the salve will make the worm therein dead, or drive it away alive*, L. M. 3, 39; Lchdm. ii. 332, 26. Hie ǣnigne cwicne ne mētton *they found not any alive*, Andr. Kmbl. 2166; An. 1084: Elen. Kmbl. 1378; El. 691. Abraham leófa, ne sleah ðīn āgen bearn, ac ðú cwicne abregd cniht of āde, eaforan ðīnne *beloved Abraham, slay not thine own child, but take thou the boy, thy son, alive from the pile*, Cd. 141; Th. 176, 19; Gen. 2914: Beo. Th. 1589; B. 792: Exon. 90 b; Th. 340, 21; Gn. Ex. 114: Ps. Th. 118, 154. Ic hyne eft cwycne ageaf *I gave him back again alive*, Nicod. 26; Thw. 14, 28, 38. Tiberius forneáh nǣnne ðæra senātussa ne lēt cucne *Tiberius left hardly any of the senators alive*, Ors. 6, 2; Bos. 116, 41: L. C. S. 25; Th. i. 390, 21. Cwice, *acc. f. alive*, Glos. Prudent. Recd. 148, 51. Gif hió cwic bearn gebyreþ *if she bare a live child*, L. Ethb. 78; Th. i. 22, 4. Snīþ ðæt cwice līc *cut the body alive*, L. M. 1, 35; Lchdm. ii. 84, 29. Cwicre stæfne *with the living voice*; viva voce, Bd. 4, 18; S. 586, 39. Cwice *quick, alive, pl. nom. m.* Ps. Th. 105, 5: Andr. Kmbl. 258; An. 129. Hīg in to helle cuce sīðodon *descenderunt vivi in infernum*, Num. 16, 33: Chr. 794; Erl. 59, 23. Ðe ealle cwice wihta bīlibbaþ *by which all creatures alive are supported*, Ors. 2, 1; Bos. 38, 8. Se Ælmihtiga līf gesceóp cynna gehwylcum ðara ðe cwice hwyrfaþ *the Almighty created life for each of the kinds that go to and fro alive*, Beo. Th. 197; B. 98. Cwyce secgeaþ his wundorweorc *his wondrous works alive shall speak*, Ps. Th. 104, 1. Ða cwican nō genihtsumedon ðæt hī ða deádan bebyrigdan *those alive were not enough to bury the dead*, Bd. 1, 14; S. 482, 31. Cwicera manna *of men alive*, Judth. 11; Thw. 24, 41; Jud. 235: Runic pm. 6; Kmbl. 340, 17; Hick. Thes. i. 135. Ðǣr biþ cwicra gewin *there shall be strife of the quick*, Exon. 22 b; Th. 62, 8; Cri. 998: 51 a; Th. 177, 7; Gū. 1223: Salm. Kmbl. 792; Sal. 395. Ðú bist dēma cwucra ge deádra *thou art the judge of quick and dead*, Hy. 8, 39; Hy. Grn. ii. 291, 39. He is God cwucera gehwelces *he is the God of each of those alive*, Bt. Met. Fox 29, 160; Met. 29, 80. Blis astīhþ cwicera cynna cyninge *the joy of quick kinds ascends to the king*, Menol. Fox 183; Men. 93: Andr. Kmbl. 1823; An. 914: Judth. 12; Thw. 26, 12; Jud. 324. Cwicra wihta *of beings alive*, Exon. 107 b; Th. 411, 5; Rä. 29, 8. His is mycel sǣ, ðǣr is unrim cwycra *his is the great sea, where is a countless number of things alive*, Ps. Th. 103, 24. Ic wille mid flōde acwellan cynna gehwilc cucra wuhta *with a flood I will destroy every kind of creatures alive*, Cd. 65; Th. 78, 23; Gen. 1297. Be cwicum mannum *the men being alive*, L. Eth. ix. 4; Th. i. 340, 18: L. C. E. 3; Th. i. 360, 9. Cwycum and deádum *to quick and dead*, Hy. 7, 117; Hy. Grn. ii. 289, 117. Wylle on glēdum cwicum *boil on live coals*, L. M. 2, 28; Lchdm. ii. 224, 20. On cwicum wǣdum *in living garments*, Salm. Kmbl. 280; Sal. 139. To dēmenne ǣgðer ge ðām cucum ge ðām deádum *to judge both the quick and the dead*, Homl. Th. ii. 596, 20: 598, 6: Num. 16, 48. Seó wiht bindeþ cwice *the creature will bind the quick*, Exon. 109 b; Th. 420, 8; Rä. 39, 7. Ðe ðǣr cwice mēteþ fȳr *who shall find there fires alive*, 22 a; Th. 59, 27; Cri. 959. Dēman ða cucan and deádan *judicare vivos et mortuos*, Ps. Lamb. fol. 199 a, 25: 202 a, 27. [*Wyc.* quyk: *Piers P. R. Brun.* quik: *Chauc.* quik, quick: *R. Glouc.* quyc: *Laym.* cwic, cwik, quic, quike: *Orm.* cwicc, cwike: *Plat.* quik, qwikk: *O. Sax.* quik, quic: *Frs.* quick: *O. Frs.* quik: *Dut.* kwik: *Kil.* quick: *Ger.* keck *gay, brisk*; quecksilber *mercury: M. H. Ger.* quëc, këc: *O. H. Ger.* quek, quik, chuech: *Goth.* qius, *gen.* qiwis *vivus: Dan.* quik: *Swed.* kwick: *Icel.* kwikr, kykr: *Lat.* vivus *alive*; victum, *supine of* vivere *to live: Grk.* βίος *life: Sansk.* jīva *vivus.*] DER. healf-cwic, sām-.

cwic-ǣht, cwyc-ǣht, e; *f.* [ǣht *cattle*] *Live stock, cattle*; pecus:—Gebēte on cwicǣhtum [cwyc- MS. B.] *let amends be made in live stock*, L. Alf. pol. 18; Th. i. 72, 12.

cwic-beám, es; *m. The* QUICKBEAM, *a sort of poplar? forte* populus tremula? cariscus, juniperus:—Genim cwicbeám *take quickbeam*, L. M. 1, 23; Lchdm. ii. 66, 1. Cwicbeám *cariscus*, Ælfc. Gl. 46; Som. 64, 119; Wrt. Voc. 32, 53.

cwicbeám-rind, e; *f. Bark of quickbeam*:—Wyl on wætere cwicbeámrinde *boil bark of quickbeam in water*, L. M. 1, 32; Lchdm. ii. 78, 12: 1, 36; Lchdm. ii. 86, 5.

cwice, an; *f. Quick-growing grass, couch-grass, quitch-grass*; gramen:—Cwice *gramen*, Ælfc. Gl. 42; Som. 64, 24; Wrt. Voc. 31, 34. Genym ðysse wyrte leáf, ðe man *gramen*, and óðrum naman cwice nemneþ *take leaves of this herb, which is named* gramen, *and by another name quitch*, Herb. 79; Lchdm. i. 182, 8: Lchdm. iii. 12, 28: 16, 8. Genim cwican *take quitch*, L. M. 2, 51; Lchdm. ii. 268, 10. [*Plat.* qwäk, queek, quek, quik *viticum repens: Dut.* kweek-gras, *n. dog's grass: Ger.* quecke, *f. any grass with creeping roots: Dan.* qwik-græs *couch-grass: Swed.* qwick-hwete, *n. dog's grass growing among wheat.*]

cwicen, cwucen, cucen, cucon, cucun; *adj.* [cwic *alive*, -en *adj. termination*] *Alive, quick*; vivus:—Hwā cwicenne me on ðysum ealdre frēfrade *who comforted me quick* [*living*] *in this life*, Ps. Th. 118, 82. We ne māgon hātan deádne mon for cwucene *we cannot call a dead man quick* [*living*], Bt. 36, 6; Fox 182, 20. Ðone cyning hī brohton cucenne to Iosue *regem viventem obtulerunt Iosue*, Jos. 8, 23: Homl. Th. i. 294, 15. Gewylde man hine swā cucenne [cucunne MS. D: cwicne G.] swā deádne *let them seize him whether alive or dead*, L. Edg. ii. 7; Th. i. 268, 18. Ðæt he Wulfnóþ cuconne oððe deádne begytan sceolde *that he should take Wulfnoth alive or dead*, Chr. 1009; Erl. 142, 3. Genim cucune hrefn *take a live crab*, L. M. 3, 2; Lchdm. ii. 306, 20, 21.

cwic-feoh; *gen.* -feós; *n. Living property, cattle*; vivum munus, pecus, Som. Ben. Lye.

cwic-fȳr, es; *n. Living fire, fire of brimstone, sulphur*; ignis vivus, sulphur:—Gifeóll ðæt fȳr and cwicfȳr of heofne *pluit ignem et sulphur de cœlo*, Lk. Skt. Rush. 17, 29.

Cwichelmes hlǣw, Cwicchelmes hlǣw, Cwicelmes hlǣw, es; *m.* [hlǣw *a heap, barrow, small hill: Flor.* Cuiccelmeslawe: *Hunt.* Chichelmeslaue: *Hovd.* Cwichelmelow: *Cwichelm's hill*; Cwichelmi agger] CUCKHAMSLEY *hill* or *Cuchinslow, Berkshire, a large barrow on a wide plain overlooking White Horse Vale*; Cwichelmi agger in agro Berchensi:—Wendon to Wealingæforda, and ðæt eall forswǣldon; and wǣron him ðā āne niht æt Ceóles ēge, and wendon him ðā andlang Æsces dūne to Cwichelmes [Cwicelmes, Th. 256, 28, col. 1: Cwicchelmes, 257, 27, col. 1] hlǣwe, and ðǣr onbīdedon beótra gylpa, forðan oft man cwæþ, gif hī Cwichelmes [Cwicelmes, col. 1] hlǣwe gesōhton, ðæt hī nǣfre to sǣ gangan [gangen MS.] ne sceoldan *they went to Wallingford, and burned it all down; and were then one night at Cholsey, and then went along Ashdown to Cuckhamsley hill, and there tarried out of threatening vaunt, because it had often been said, if they came to Cuckhamsley hill, that they would never go to the sea* Chr. 1006; Th. 256, 25–32, col. 2. Æt Cwicelmes hlǣwe *at Cuckhamsley hill*, Th. Diplm. A. D. 995; 288, 24. On Cwicelmes hlǣw *to Cuckhamsley hill*, 291, 28.

cwic-hrērende; *part.* [hrēran *to move*] *Quick-moving?*—Wilt ðú biddan ðē gesecge sīdra gesceafta cræftas cwichrērende *wilt thou desire that he tell thee the quick-moving powers of wide-spread creatures?* Exon. 92 b; Th. 346, 28; Sch. 5.

cwician, cwycian, cucian; *p.* ode, ade; *pp.* od, ad [cwic *alive, quick*]. I. *v. intrans. To come to life*, QUICKEN; vīvĕre et spīrāre:—Wǣron ða leoma cwiciende *the limbs were quickening*, Greg. Dial. 4, 36. Smire mid ða sāran limu, hie cwiciaþ sōna *smear the sore limbs therewith, they will soon quicken*, L. M. 3, 47; Lchdm. ii. 338, 25. Se synfulla mid godcundre onbryrdnysse cucaþ *the sinful quickens with divine stimulation*, Homl. Th. i. 494, 15. II. *v. trans. To make alive*, QUICKEN; vivificare:—Me ðīn spræc cwycade *eloquium tuum vivificavit me*, Ps. Th. 118, 50. Ðú us cwica *quicken thou us*, 79, 17. [*Prompt.* qwycchyn *movēre: Wyc.* quikene, quykne, quycken *to revive: Piers P.* quykne *to bring to life: Chauc.* quiken *to become* or *make alive: Plat.* queken, *v. n. and a. to grow, cultivate: O. Sax.* -quikōn, -quiccōn: *Dut.* kweeken *to foster, manure, cultivate: Kil.* quicken, quecken *nutrire, alere, educare: Ger.* er-quicken *to refresh: M. H. Ger.* quicken, kücken *to make alive*: *O. H. Ger.* quikjan *vivificare*: *Dan.* qwæge: *Swed.* qwicka: *Icel.* kweykja, kweykwa.] DER. a-cwician, ed-, ge-, ge-ed-.

cwic-lifian, -lifigan; *p.* -lifode; *pp.* -lifod *To live*; vivere:—Cwiclifigende *living*, Salm. Kmbl. 840; Sal. 419. Ðǣr sceal fæsl wesan cwiclifigendra cynna gehwilces *there shall be food for each of living kinds*, Cd. 65; Th. 79, 14; Gen. 1311.

cwic-seolfor; *gen.* -seolfres; *dat.* -seolfre; *n.* QUICKSILVER; vivum argentum:—Wið magan wærce; rudan sǣd and cwicseolfor *for pain of stomach; seed of rue and quicksilver*, L. M. 3, 69; Lchdm. ii. 356, 19. Cwicseolfor *argentum vivum*, Cot. 16.

cwic-sūsl, cwyc-sūsl, es; *n*: e; *f.* [sūsl *sulphur, brimstone, torment, punishment*] *Living punishment, hell-torment*; sempervivum tormentum, infernum, barathrum = βάραθρον:—Cwicsūsl *vel* helelīc deópnes *barathrum, vorago profunda*, Ælfc. Gl. 54; Som. 66, 96; Wrt. Voc. 36, 20. Satanas ðæs cwicsūsles ealdor ðære helle *Satan the chief of the living torment of hell*, Nicod. 26; Thw. 14, 12. On ðam cwicsūsle *in hell-torment*, 25; Thw. 13, 30: Exon. 16 a; Th. 35, 21; Cri. 561: 97 a; Th. 362, 18; Wal. 38. Of ðysse cwycsūsle *from this hell-torment*, Nicod. 30; Thw. 17, 28. Faraþ ða unrihtwīsan into ēcere cwicsūsle, mid deófle and his awyrigedum englum *the unrighteous will go into everlasting torment, with the devil and his accursed angels*, Homl. Th. ii. 108, 31.

cwic-treów, es; *n. The asp* or *aspen-tree*; populus tremula, Lin:—Cwictreów *cresis? tremulus*, Ælfc. Gl. 47; Som. 65, 26. v. cwic-beám.

cwicu, cwico, cucu = cuc; *nom. acc. m. f. n*: *pl. nom. acc. m. f. n.* cwicu, cwico, cucu; *adj. Alive, quick*; vivus:—Cwicu *alive, nom. m.* Ps. Th. 118, 93. Cwico wæs ic *I was living*, Exon. 125 a; Th. 482, 1; Rä. 66, 1: Beo. Th. 6178; B. 3093. Cucu *vivus*, Wrt. Voc. 85, 56. Samson miccle mā on his deáþe acwealde, ðonne he ǣr cucu dyde *Samson multo plures interfecit moriens, quam ante vivus occiderat*, Jud. 16, 30: Boutr. Scrd. 18, 11: Homl. Th. i. 52, 20: ii. 212, 33: Cod. Dipl. 897; Kmbl. iv. 233, 5, 13. Ne sēcþ seó cucu [turtle] nǣfre hire ōðerne gemacan *the quick [living turtle-dove] never seeks to itself another mate*, Homl. Th. i. 142, 14. Heó sōna cucu arās *she instantly arose alive*, ii. 26, 32. Gif hit cucu [cwicu MS. G.] feoh wǣre *if it were live cattle*, L. Alf. 28; Th. i. 52, 1. Ælc þing ðe cucu byþ *everything which is alive*; animal, Wrt. Voc. 78, 50. Ic hæfde ferþ cwicu *I had a soul alive*, Exon. 126 b; Th. 487, 21; Rä. 73, 5. Ic hæfde feorh cwico *I had a soul alive*, 103 b; Th. 392, 11; Rä. 11, 6: 104 a; Th. 394, 14; Rä. 14, 3. Teón ða wæteru forþ swimmende cynn cucu on līfe *producant aquæ reptile animæ viventis*, Gen. 1, 20: Ex. 22, 4. Hī cwico nǣron *they were not alive*, Exon. 24 b; Th. 69, 36; Cri. 1131. Cwicu *quick [living]*, *pl. nom. n.* Ps. Th. 108, 24. Cwicu *quick [living]*, *pl. acc. m.* 87, 18. He clifu cyrreþ on cwicu wæteres wellan *he turneth the rocks to quick [living] springs of water*, 113, 8. v. cwic.

cwicu-līce; *adv. In a living manner, vigorously*; vivide:—Me on weg ðīnne lǣde cwiculīce *in via tua vivifica me*, Ps. Th. 118, 37.

cwid-bōc, e; *f. The Book of Proverbs*; proverbiorum liber:—Be ðæm is awriten on Salomonnes cwidbōcum *about which it is written in the Proverbs of Solomon*, Past. 36, 8; Cot. MS.

cwiddung, cwyddung, e; *f. A saying, tale, report, speech*; dictum, sermunculus:—Manegra manna cwyddung is *it is a saying of many men*, Bd. de nat. rerum; Wrt. popl. science 10, 28; Lchdm. iii. 256, 4. Æt fræmdra monna cwiddunge *from the report of strangers*, Bt. 18, 4; Fox 66, 25. Nā swilce he nyste manna cwyddunga be him *not as though he knew not the sayings of men concerning him*, Homl. Th. i. 366, 7.

cwide, cwyde, cwyðe, es; *m.* I. *the expression of a thought, a sentence, period*; sententia:—We todǣlaþ ða bōc to cwydum, and siððan ða cwydas to dǣlum, eft ða dǣlas to stæfgefēgum, and siððan ða stæfgefēgu to stafum; ðon beóþ ða stafas untodǣledlīce, forðonðe nān stæf ne biþ nāht, gif he gǣþ on twā. Ælc stæf hæfþ þreó þing, *nomen, figura, potestas*, ðæt is nama, and hiw, and miht *we divide the book into sentences, and then the sentences into words [parts], again the words into syllables, and then the syllables into letters; now the letters are indivisible, because a letter is nothing if divided into two [if it go in two]. Every letter has three properties*, nomen, figura, potestas, *that is a name, and a form, and a sound [power]*, Ælfc. Gr. 2; Som. 2, 37-41. II. *a saying, proverb, speech, discourse, sermon, will*; dictum, dictio, sermo, homilia, testamentum:—Eówer cwide stande *may your saying stand*, Jos. 2, 21. Singende ðone ealdan cwide *singing the old adage*, Bt. 14, 3; Fox 46, 29. Þurh ryhtlīcne cwide [MS. cuide] and dōm *through a righteous sentence and judgment*, Past. 35, 5; Hat. MS. 46 b, 4. On ǣgðer ðæra bōca sind feówertig cwyda, būton ðære fōresprǣce *in each of these books there are forty discourses, without the preface*, Homl. Th. ii. 2, 14: i. 28, 20. Ætfōran ǣlcum cwyde we setton ða swutelunge on Lēden *before each discourse we have set the argument in Latin*, ii. 2, 17. Ðes [MS. ðis] is Byrhtrīces nīhsta cwide *this is Byrhtric's last will*, Th. Diplm. A. D. 950; 500, 24: A. D. 958; 509, 3: A. D. 998; 541, 25: A. D. 1002; 543, 33. Ðæt se cwyde standan mōste *that the will might stand*, A. D. 950; 501, 11: A. D. 972; 519, 17: A. D. 997; 539, 22: A. D. 996-1006; 549, 11. Cwydas dōn *to make wills*, Lchdm. iii. 210, 30. III. *a legal enactment, decree*; edictum, decretum:—Swa hit ǣr Eádmundes cwide wæs *as it was formerly the enactment of Edmund*, L. Edg. H. 2; Th. i. 258, 9. Swā ūre ealra cwide is *as is the decree of us all*, L. Eth. i. 4; Th. i. 284, 5: L. C. S. 33; Th. i. 396, 19. [*Laym.* cwide, quide-n *a testament*; *pl.* quides, cwides *speeches, words*: *O. Sax.* quidi, *m. speech, saying*: *O. H. Ger.* quidī, *f. n. dictum, verbum*: *Goth.* qiss, *f. speech*: *Icel.* qwiðr, *m. a saying, word, speech.*] DER. ǣr-cwide, big-, ed-, ge-, gegn- [geagn-, gēn-], galdor-, gilp-, heard-, hearm-, hleóðor-, hosp-, lār-, leahtor-, mæðel-, meðel-, sār-, sib-, sōþ-, teón-, torn-, wiðer-, wom-, word-: cwidian.

cwide-gied, -giedd, es; *n.* [gid, gied *a song, lay*] *A song, ballad*; carmen:—Fela cūþra cwidegiedda *many [of] known songs*, Exon. 77 a; Th. 289, 28; Wand. 55.

cwide-leás *speechless, intestate*. v. cwyde-leás.

cwidian, cwiddigan, cwydian, cwyddian; *p.* ode; *pp.* od [cwide, cwyde *a saying*] *To speak, say*; dicere:—Ongan hine hyspan and hearm cwiddigan [cwidian, Cot.] *he began to revile and speak ill of him*, Bt. 18, 4; Fox 66, 33.

cwid-rǣden *an agreement*; pactum. v. gecwid-rǣden.

cwidu *what is chewed, a cud*, QUID, L. M. 2, 3; Lchdm. ii. 182, 3: 2, 4; Lchdm. ii. 182, 17. v. cwudu.

cwiert-ern *a prison*, Mt. Kmbl. B. 25, 36, 39. v. cweart-ern.

cwiferlīce; *adv. Anxiously*; sollicitè, C. R. Ben. 64.

cwild *a plague, pestilence, murrain, destruction*, Wrt. Voc. 75, 54: Ælfc. Gr. 9, 27; Som. 11, 25: Chr. 897; Erl. 94, 31: Ps. Spl. C. 28, 9: 31, 8. v. cwyld.

cwild-bǣre; *adj. Pestilence-bearing, deadly*; pestiferus, Scint. 53: 63.

cwild-bǣrlīce; *adv. Pestilentially, destructively*; pestifere, Scint. 8.

cwilde flōd, es; *n. m. The destruction's flood, deluge*; diluvium, Ps. Spl. C. 28, 9. v. cwyld.

cwild-tīd *a dead time*. v. cwyld, cwyl-tīd.

cwilman *to torture, kill*, Ors. 1, 12; Bos. 36, 25. v. cwelman.

cwilst, he cwilþ *diest, dies*; *2nd and 3rd pers. pres. of* cwelan.

cwiman *to come*; venire, *the supposed infin. of* cwom, *q. v.*

cwīnan; *p.* cwān, *pl.* cwinon; *pp.* cwinen *To waste* or *dwindle away*; tabescere. DER. a-cwīnan.

cwincan, ic cwince, ðū cwincst, he cwincþ, *pl.* cwincaþ; *p.* cwanc, *pl.* cwuncon; *pp.* cwuncen *To disappear, vanish, decrease*; evanescere, diminuere, deficere, Leo A. Sax. Gl. 209. DER. a-cwincan.

cwīnod *wasted*, Bt. 10; Fox 28, 29. v. cwānian.

cwis, cwiss, e; *f.* [cweðan *to say, speak*] *A saying, speaking*; locutio. DER. and-cwis, ge-: un-cwis.

cwist *sayest, speakest*, Bt. 5, 3; Fox 12, 13: Ps. Th. 87, 12, = cweðst; *2nd pres. sing. of* cweðan.

CWIÞ, es; *m*: cwiða, an; *m. The womb*; matrix, uterus:—Beðe mid ðone cwiþ *bathe the womb therewith*, L. M. 3, 37; Lchdm. ii. 330, 2: 3, 38; Lchdm. ii. 330, 19. Cwiþ *matrix*, Ælfc. Gl. 76; Som. 71, 118. Wið ðæs cwiðan sāre *for soreness of the womb*, Herb. 165, 2; Lchdm. i. 294, 11. [*O. H. Ger.* quiti: *Goth.* qiþus, *m*: *Swed.* qwed: *Icel.* kwiðr.]

cwiþ *saith, speaks*, Exon. 14 a; Th. 28, 28; Cri. 453: 30 a; Th. 92, 35; Cri. 1519, = cweðeþ; *3rd pres. sing. of* cweðan.

cwīðan, cwȳðan; he cwīðeþ; *p.* de; *pp.* ed *To speak* or *moan in grief, mourn, lament*; lamentāre, plangĕre:—Wōpe cwīðan *with weeping to lament*, Cd. 48; Th. 61, 13; Gen. 996. Ic sceolde āna mīne ceare cwīðan *I must alone mourn my care*, Exon. 76 b; Th. 287, 4; Wand. 9. We cwīðdon [MS. cwiðdun] *lamentavimus*, Mt. Bos. 11, 17. Fǣmnan ne synd cwȳðede [cwyðde MS.] *virgines non sunt lamentatæ*, Ps. Spl. C. 77, 69. Adames cyn cwīðeþ *Adam's race lamenteth*, Exon. 22 a; Th. 59, 34; Cri. 962. Hȳ in cearum cwīðaþ *they mourn in sorrows*, Exon. 35 b; Th. 115, 23; Gū. 194. Ðonne biþ þearfendum cwīðende cearo *then shall be wailing care to the miserable*, 26 b; Th. 79, 5; Cri. 1286. [*O. Sax.* quīðean: *Swed.* quida: *Icel.* kwíða *to feel anxiety about.*]

cwiðend-līc; *adj. Proper, peculiar, natural*; genuīnus, Cot. 96, Som. Ben. Lye.

cwið-nes, -ness, e; *f. A wailing, lamentation*; lamentum, Greg. Dial. 3, 15, 37.

cwiðst *sayest, speakest*, Ælfc. Gr. 33; Som. 37, 38, = cweðst; *2nd pres. sing. of* cweðan.

cwoellan *to kill*; necare, interficere:—Sōhton hine Iudēas to cwoellanne *quærebant eum Judæi interficere*, Jn. Lind. War. 5, 18. v. cwellan.

cwolen *died*; *pp. of* cwelan.

cwolstan *to swallow*. DER. for-cwolstan, *q. v.*

cwom, *pl.* cwōmon *came*; venit, venerunt; have the same meanings as the *contracted forms* com, *pl.* cōmon, *p. of* cuman, *q. v.* The *p. indic.* cwom, *pl.* cwōmon, -an, -un; *p. subj.* cwōme:—Ðā hleóðor cwom *when the sound came*, Cd. 181; Th. 226, 29; Dan. 178. Ðā ðū ǣrest cwōme *when thou first camest*, Exon. 39 a; Th. 129, 25; Gū. 426. Hwonne bearn Godes cwōme *when the child of God should have come*, 10 a; Th. 10, 6; Cri. 148. To Hierusalem cwōmon *they came to Jerusalem*, Elen. Kmbl. 547; El. 274. Cwōman englas *angels came*, Exon. 15 b; Th. 34, 21; Cri. 545. Wuldres āras cwōmun *messengers of glory came*,

15 a; Th. 31, 11; Cri. 494. Cwom, *pl.* cwōmon, *seem to be from* cwiman, *which I have not found in A. Sax. It is in Goth.* qiman [*pronounced* kwiman = cwiman]; *p.* qam, *pl.* qemum; *pp.* qumans *to come;* venire. *Goth.* Ni mag qiman [kwiman = cwiman]. *A. Sax.* Ic ne mæg cuman *I cannot come,* Lk. Bos. 14, 20. v. cwiman, cuman.

cwuc; *def.* se cwuca *alive, quick,* Bt. 36, 6; Fox 182, 20. v. cwic.

cwucen *alive, quick,* Bt. 36, 6; Fox 182, 20. v. cwicen.

cwuda *a cud, quid,* L. M. 2, 2; Lchdm. ii. 178, 26: 2, 52; Lchdm. ii. 270, 28. v. cwudu.

CWUDU, cwuda, cweodo, cwidu, cudu; *gen.* ues, wes; *n. What is chewed, a cud, quid;* manducatum, rumen:—Ðe heora cudu ne ceówaþ: ða clǽnan nýtenu ðe heora cudu ceówaþ *which chew not their cud: the clean beasts which chew their cud,* M. H. 138 b. ¶ Hwít cwudu *white cud, mastich;* an odoriferous gum from the mastich-tree, which was called by Lin. *pistacia lentiscus.* This gum was used for chewing in the East; *mastiche* = μαστίχη:—Hwít cwudu *mastich,* L. M. 1, 23; Lchdm. ii. 66, 3. Gedó gódne dǽl ðǽron hwítes cweodowes *put a good deal of mastich therein,* 2, 14; Lchdm. ii. 192, 6. Ofersceade mid hwítes cwidues duste *sprinkle over with dust of mastich,* 2, 3; Lchdm. ii. 182, 3. Of hwítum cwidue and wíne *with mastich and wine,* 2, 4; Lchdm. ii. 182, 17. Hwít cwudu gecnuwa swíðe smale *pound mastich very small,* 1, 13; Lchdm. ii. 56, 5: 1, 8; Lchdm. ii. 54, 3: 1, 47; Lchdm. ii. 118, 29: 3, 2; Lchdm. ii. 308, 24. Genim ele and gedó hwít cwuda on ðone ele *take oil and put mastich into the oil,* 2, 2; Lchdm. ii. 178, 26: 2, 52; Lchdm. ii. 270, 28. Nim hwít cudu *take mastich,* Lchdm. iii. 72, 15: 124, 25: 134, 10. [*Prompt.* cudde: *Wyc.* code, quede, quide, kude: *Orm.* cude.]

cwuncon; *pp.* cwuncen *disappeared, vanished; p. pl. and pp. of* cwincan.

cwyc *alive, quick:*—Cwyc *alive,* Ps. Th. 104, 8: Nicod. 26; Thw. 14, 28, 38. v. cwic.

cwyc-ǽht *live stock:*—On cwycǽhtum *in live stock,* L. Alf. pol. 18; Th. 1, 72, 12, note 28. v. cwic-ǽht.

cwycian *to make alive, quicken,* Ps. Th. 118, 50. v. cwician **II.**

cwyc-súsl *hell-torment,* Nicod. 30; Thw. 17, 28. v. cwic-súsl.

cwyddian; *p.* ode; *pp.* od *To speak, say;* dicere:—Ðæt me oferhydige ǽfre ne mótan hearm cwyddian *that the proud may never speak evil of me,* Ps. Th. 118, 122. Crist hí befran hú men cwyddodon be him *Christ asked them how men spake concerning him,* Homl. Th. ii. 388, 31. v. cwidian.

cwyddung *a saying,* Homl. Th. i. 366, 7. v. cwiddung.

cwyde. I. *a sentence;* sententia, Ælfc. Gr. 2; Som. 2, 38. **II.** *a discourse, sermon:*—Smeágaþ ðysne cwyde *consider this sermon,* Homl. Th. i. 28, 20: ii. 2, 14: 2, 17. v. cwide.

cwydele, an; *f. An inflamed swelling;* pustula, varix:—Cwydele *pustula,* Ælfc. Gl. 9; Som. 57, 10; Wrt. Voc. 19, 19. Cwydele *vel* hwylca *varix,* 76; Som. 71, 129; Wrt. Voc. 45, 32.

cwyde-leás; *adj. Speechless, intestate;* mutus, intestatus:—He læg cwydeleás, bútan andgite *he lay speechless, without sense,* Homl. Th. i. 86, 26. Gif hwá cwydeleás of ðyssum lífe gewíte *if any one depart this life intestate,* L. C. S. 71; Th. i. 412, 27.

cwydian; *p.* ode; *pp.* od *To speak, say;* dicere:—Menn cwydodon *men said,* Chr. 1085; Erl. 217, 38. v. cwidian.

cwydol; *adj.* [cweðan *to say, speak*] *Speaking, saying;* dicens, loquens. DER. wyrig-cwydol, *q. v.*

cwyd-rǽden *an agreement;* pactum. v. gecwid-rǽden.

cwyld, cwild, es; *m. n:* cwyld, cwild, e; *f.* [cweald, *pp. of* cwellan *to kill*] *A plague, pestilence, murrain, destruction;* pestis, pestilentia, clades:—Boreas ealne ðone cwyld *m.* afligþ *Boreas* [*the north wind*] *drives every plague away,* Bd. de nat. rerum; Wrt. popl. science 18, 9; Lchdm. iii. 276, 7. Cwilde *f.* flód *the flood of destruction, deluge;* diluvium, Ps. Spl. C. 28, 9: 31, 8. Auster mistlíce cwyld *n.* blǽwþ geond ðas eorþan *auster* [*the south wind*] *blows various plagues through this earth,* Bd. de nat. rerum; Wrt. popl. science 17, 26; Lchdm. iii. 274, 17. Cwild [cwyld MSS. C. D.], *m. f.* or *n. clades,* Ælfc. Gr. 9, 27; Som. 11, 25. Cwild, *m. f.* or *n. pestis,* Wrt. Voc. 75, 54. Mid ceápes cwylde *m. f.* or *n. with a murrain of cattle,* Chr. 897; Th. 174. 22, col. 2; 175, 20. Se ðe on þrymsetle cwyldes *m.* or *n.* ná sæt *qui in cathedra pestilentiæ non sedit,* Ps. Spl. C. 1, 1: Mone B. 2711. Cwyld-tíd *or* cwyl-tíd *evening time;* conticinium:—Cwyl-tíd *vel* gebed-giht *conticinium,* Ælfc. Gl. 16; Som. 58, 63; Wrt. Voc. 21, 50. v. cwyld-seten. DER. mon-cwyld.

cwyld-bǽre; *adj. Pestilence-bearing, deadly.* v. cwild-bǽre.

cwyld-bǽrlíce; *adv. Pestilentially.* v. cwild-bǽrlíce.

cwyld-full; *adj. Destructive, pernicious;* perniciosus:—Cwyldfulle wæfersēne *perniciosum spectaculum,* Mone B. 1259.

cwyld-róf; *adj. Devoted to slaughter;* necandi strenuus:—Deór cwyldróf = wulfas *the beasts devoted to slaughter = wolves,* Cd. 151; Th. 188, 10, 11 = 7; Exod. 166 = 164.

cwyld-seten, cwyl-seten, e; *f.* [cwyld, cwyl = cweald, *pp. of* cwellan *to kill: Icel.* kweld, *n. evening:* as if the night *quelled* or *killed* daylight] *A setting in of the evening, the first part of the night;* conticinium:—Cwylseten *conticinium,* Mone B. 3747. Cwylsetene *conticinio,* 3748. Cwyldsetene *galli cantu,* 4677.

cwylla, an; *m. A well, spring;* fons:—Riht súþ be eástan ðam cwyllan óþ ða wýde strǽte *right south by east of the spring as far as the wide road,* Cod. Dipl. 409; A. D. 946; Kmbl. ii. 265, 32. [*Ger.* quelle, *f. a spring, source, fountain.*]

cwylm *destruction, slaughter,* Glos. Prudent. Recd. 152, 12. v. cwealm.

cwylman; *p.* ede; *pp.* ed *To kill, torment,* Ps. Spl. 36, 15: Elen. Kmbl. 1373; El. 688. v. cwelman.

cwylm-bǽre; *adj. Death-bearing, pernicious;* mortiférus:—Cómon ða cempan mid cwylmbǽrum tólum *the soldiers came with deadly tools,* Homl. Th. ii. 260, 7. v. cwealm-bǽre.

cwylmd = cwylmed *killed,* Bd. 1, 15; S. 484, 1; *pp. of* cwylman.

cwylmende, cwilmende; *part. Tormenting;* crucians, Ors. 1, 12; Bos. 36, 25. v. cwelman.

cwylmian; *part.* cwylmigende; *p.* ode; *pp.* od [cwealm *pain, torment*] *To suffer, suffer torment* or *pain;* cruciāri:—Heó sceal ēcelíce cwylmian *it* [*the soul*] *shall suffer eternally,* Homl. Th. ii. 232, 29. Ða mánfullan beóþ ǽfre cwylmigende on helle súsle *the sinful shall ever be suffering pain in hell torment,* 608, 11. We cwylmiaþ *we suffer torment,* 416, 5. Gehwylce mánfulle geféran on ðám ēcum tintregum cwylmiaþ *all wicked associates shall suffer in everlasting torments,* i. 526, 27.

cwylming, e; *f.* [cwylmian *to suffer*] *Torture, trouble, suffering, a cross;* cruciātus, crux:—Cwylminge [MS. cwylmingce] *cruciātu,* Mone B. 3178. Se ðe ne nimþ hys cwylminge, and fyligþ me, nys he me wyrðe *qui non accipit crucem suam, et sequĭtur me, non est me dignus,* Mt. Bos. 10, 38: Lk. Bos. 9, 23.

cwylmnes *torment,* Bd. 4, 9; S. 577, 10. v. cwealmnes.

cwylþ *dies,* Bd. de nat. rerum; Lchdm. iii. 272, note 36; *3rd pres. sing. of* cwelan.

cwyl-tíd *dead time,* Ælfc. Gl. 16; Som. 58, 63; Wrt. Voc. 21, 50. v. cwyld.

cwýne *a wife,* L. Ethb. 85; Th. i. 24, 9. v. cwēn, cwēne.

CWYRN, cweorn, e; *f:* cweorne, an; *f. A mill, hand-mill,* QUERN; mola:—Twá beóþ æt cwyrne grindende: án byþ genumen, and óðer byþ lǽfed *duæ molentes in mola: una assumētur, et una relinquētur,* Mt. Bos. 24, 41. Ðæt híg grundon on cwyrne *popŭlus illud frangēbat mola,* Num. 11, 8. Æt ðære cweornan *ad molam,* Ex. 11, 5. [*Prompt.* querne *mola manualis: Wyc. Chauc.* querne: *Plat.* queern, qwern *a handmill: O. Sax.* querna, *f: O. Frs.* quern: *Dut. Kil.* querne: *M. H. Ger.* kürne, kürn, kurn, *f: O. H. Ger.* quirn, *f: Goth.* qairnus, *m.* or *f: Dan.* qwærn, *m. f: Swed.* qwarn, *f: Icel.* kwern, kwörn, *f.*] DER. esul-cwyrn, hand-.

cwyrn-bill *a stone chisel for dressing querns.* v. cweorn-bill.

cwyrn-burne, an; *f. A mill-stream;* molāris torrens, Som. Ben. Lye.

cwyrn-stán, cweorn-stán, es; *m. A mill-stone;* molaris lapis, mola:—Cwyrnstán *mola,* Wrt. Voc. 83, 8. Ðæt him wǽre getiged án ormǽte cwyrnstán to his swuran, and he swá wurde on deóppre sǽ besenced *that an immense mill-stone was tied to his neck, and he was so sunk in the deep sea,* Homl. Th. i. 514, 17: Mt. Bos. 18, 6. Án cweornstán *lapis molaris,* Lk. Bos. 17, 2: Mk. Bos. 9, 42.

CWYSAN; *p.* de; *pp.* ed *To crush,* QUASH, *shake, bruise, dash against;* quassare, terere, allidere:—Se ðe forgníðeþ oððe cwysþ lytlungas ðíne to stáne *qui allidet parvulos tuos ad petram,* Ps. Lamb. 136, 9. Ðú genyðeredest oððe ðú cwysdest me *allisisti me,* 101, 11. [*Prompt.* quaschyñ *quassāre: R. Brun.* quassed, *p. quashed: Plat.* quesen, quetsen *to crush: O. Sax.* quetsan *to push, squeeze: Frs.* quetsen *vulnerare: O. Frs.* quetsene *a bruise: Dut.* kwetsen *to bruise, wound, injure: Kil.* quetsen *quassare, lædere: Ger.* quetschen *to squeeze: M. H. Ger.* quetzen *to squeeze: Goth.* qistyan *to destroy: Dan.* qwæste *to squeeze: Swed.* qwäsa *to squash, bruise, wound: Icel.* kwista *to destroy, cut down: Fr.* casser *to break: Lat.* quassare, quatere *to batter, break in pieces.*] DER. for-cwysan, to-.

cwýst *sayest, speakest,* Homl. Th. i. 424, 9, = cweðst; *2nd pres. sing. of* cweðan.

cwýst ðú, cwýst ðú lá, cwýst tú lá *sayest thou?* used in questions, as *interrog. adv.* numquid?—Cwýst ðú eom ic hyt? Mt. Bos. 26, 22 *whether it am I?* Wyc. note rr; numquid ego sum? Vulg: Ps. Spl. 29, 12: 7, 12. v. cweðan.

cwyð, e; *f.* [= cwide, cwyde] *A word, saying;* verbum, dictum:—Him ða cwyðe frecne scódon *these words overwhelmed him with woe,* Cd. 78; Th. 96, 18; Gen. 1596. v. cwide.

cwyþ *saith, speaks,* Jn. Bos. 16, 18: Rood Kmbl. 220; Kr. 111, = cweðeþ; *3rd pres. sing. of* cweðan.

cwýðan *to lament,* Ps. Spl. C. 77, 69. v. cwíðan.

cwyðe *a saying,* S. Greg. Hom. 23, 104, Lye. v. cwide.

cwyðele *an inflamed swelling.* v. cwydele.

cwyðst *sayest, speakest,* Ælfc. Gr. 18; Som. 21, 62, = cweðst; *2nd pres. sing. of* cweðan.

cȳ *cows*, Gen. 33, 13; *acc. pl. of* cū.

CYCENE, cicene, an; *f. A kitchen;* coquīna, culīna:—Cycene *coquīna*, Wrt. Voc. 82, 49: *culīna*, Mone B. 3731. Ðæt seó cycene [MS. kycene] eal forburne *that the kitchen was all burning*, Homl. Th. ii. 166, 5, 11. Wurpon hī ða anlīcnysse inn to heora cycenan [MS. kycenan] *they cast the image into their kitchen*, ii. 166, 3. Gif ceorl hæfde cirican and cycenan [MS. kycenan] *if a free man had a church and a kitchen*, L. R. 2; Th. i. 190, 15. [*Piers P.* kytchen: *Chauc.* kichen: *Plat.* köke, käke: *Dut.* keuken, *f*: *Kil.* kokene, keuckene: *Ger.* küche, *f*: *M. H. Ger.* küche, küchen, kuche, kuchen, *f*: *O. H. Ger.* kuchina, *f*: *Dan.* kjökken, *n*: *Swed.* kök, *n*: *Icel.* kock-hús: *Fr.* cuisine, *f*: *Prov.* cozina: *Span.* cocina, *f*: *It.* cucina, *f*: *Lat.* coquīna, *f*: *Wel.* cegin, *f*: *Corn.* cegin, keghin, *f*: *Ir.* cucann: *Armor.* kegin: *Lith.* kukne: *Russ.* kuchnja.]

cȳdde *said, told*, Chr. 1066; Th. 336, 21, = cȳdde; *p. of* cȳðan.

cȳdung *a chiding*, Ps. Spl. T. 103, 8. v. cīding.

CȲF, e; *f*: cȳfe, an; *f. A vessel, vat, cask, bushel;* dolium, modius:—Cȳf *dolium*, Ælfc. Gl. 25; Som. 60, 48; Wrt. Voc. 24, 48. Stōd ðǣr ān æmtig cȳf *an empty cask stood there*, Homl. Th. ii. 178, 34. Cȳfe *dolium*, Wrt. Voc. 83, 25. Se hēt afyllan āne cȳfe mid ele *he commanded a vat to be filled with oil*, Homl. Th. i. 58, 25. Under cȳfe *sub modio*, Mt. Bos. 5, 15. [*Prompt.* kowpe *crater*: *Plat.* kope *dolium*: *O. Sax.* côpa, *f. dolium*: *Dut.* kuip, *f. a tub*: *Kil.* keuwe, kuype *cupa, dolium*: *Ger.* kufe, *f. a vessel*: *M. H. Ger.* kuofe, *f. cupa*: *O. H. Ger.* kuofa, *f. dolium, tunna*: *Dan.* kippe, kyper, *m. f. a dyer's tub*: *Swed.* kyp, *m. a dyer's tub*; kupa, *f. a case, box*: *Icel.* kúpa, *f. a bowl, basin, box*: *Fr.* cuve, *f*: *Span.* cuba, *f. cask for wine* or *oil*: *M. Lat.* cuppa, *f*: *Lat.* cupa, *f. a tun*: *Grk.* κύπ-ελλον *a tub, cask*: *Sansk.* kūpa *a cistern;* kumbha *vessel for water.*]

CYFES, cyfys, cifes, ciefes, e; *f*: cyfese, an; *f. A concubine, handmaid;* concubina, pellex, ancilla:—Cyfes *pellex*, Wrt. Voc. 86, 73. Of cifise *ex pellīce*, Mone B. 4553. Se ðe hæbbe riht wīf, and eác cifese [MS. A. ceafese; B. cefese] ne dō him nān preóst nān ðara gerihta, ðe man cristenum men dōn sceal *he who has a right wife, and also a concubine, let no priest do for him any of those rites, which ought to be done for a christian man*, L. C. S. 55; Th. i. 406, 16, and note 26. Cyfys [= cyfes] oððe bepǣcystre [MSS. C. D. bepæcestre] *pellex*, Ælfc. Gr. 28, 5; Som. 32, 1. Constantius gesealde his suna ðæt rīce, Constantinuse, ðone he hæfde be Elenan his ciefese *Constantius gave the empire to Constantine, his son, whom he had by Helena his concubine* [*wife*, v. notes to Ors. Bos. p. 28, col. 2], Ors. 6, 30; Bos. 126, 41. Gif he cyfesan hæbbe, and nāne riht ǣwe, he āh ðæs to dōnne swā him geþincþ; wīte he ðeáh ðæt he beó on ānre gehealden, beó hit cyfes, beó hit ǣwe *si concubinam habeat, et nullam legitimam uxorem, erit ei proinde quod ipsi videbitur faciendum; sciat tamen ut cum una ei manendum sit, sit concubina, sit uxor*, L. Ecg. P. ii. 9; Th. ii. 186, 2-5: L. M. I. P. 17; Th. ii. 270, 6, 9: Boutr. Scrd. 22, 22. Be ðīnre cyfese *super ancilla tua*, Gen. 21, 12. [*Laym.* chevese, chivese *a concubine*: *Plat.* keves: *Dut.* kevis, *f. a concubine*: *Kil.* kevisse, kiese *pellaca, concubina*: *Ger.* kebse, *f. concubina, pellex*: *M. H. Ger.* kebes, kebese, kebse, *f. concubina*: *O. H. Ger.* kebis, kebisa, *f. pellex, concubina*: *Icel. Vigf.* kefsir, *m. concubitor, concubinus*: *O. Nrs. Rask Hald.* képsi, kéffir *servus molestus, oblocutor.*]

cyfes-boren; *def.* se cyfes-borena; *part. Born in concubinage, base-born;* e concubīna genĭtus:—His cyfesborena brōðor siððan rīxode, se ðe wende to Scottum *his base-born brother afterwards reigned, who had gone to the Scots*, Homl. Th. ii. 148, 17.

cyfes-hād, es; *m. Whoredom, adultery, concubinage;* pellicātus, Cot. 186.

cyfys *pellex*, Ælfc. Gr. 28, 5; Som. 32, 1. v. cyfes.

cȳgan, cȳgean *to call, call upon, invoke*, Bd. 4, 23; S. 594, 39: Cd. 141; Th. 176, 9; Gen. 2909: Ps. Spl. 78, 6. v. cīgan.

cȳging, e; *f. A calling, naming;* appellatio, Som. Ben. Lye. v. cȳgan.

cȳgling, es; *m. A relation;* cognātus:—Cȳgling his *cognātus ejus*, Jn. Rush. War. 18, 26. v. cȳðling.

cyld, es; *n. Cold, coldness;* frigus:—For cylde *præ frigŏre*, Coll. Monast. Th. 19, 29. v. ceald *frigus*.

cyld, es; *n. A child*, Bt. 36, 5; Fox 180, 6: Mt. Jun. 2, 13, in the title. v. cild.

cyld-faru, e; *f. A carrying of children;* parvulōrum subvectio:—Ðæt hīg nymon wǣnas to hira cyldfare *ut tollant plaustra ad subvectiōnem parvulōrum*, Gen. 45, 19.

CȲLE, cīle, cēle, es; *m. A cold, coldness,* CHILL; frīgus:—Ne mæg fȳres feng ne forstes cȳle somod eardian *the grasp of fire and chill of frost cannot dwell together*, Salm. Kmbl. 708; Sal. 353. Befōran ansīne cȳles *ante faciem frigŏris*, Ps. Spl. 147, 6. Nabbaþ we to hyhte nymþe cȳle and fȳr *we have nought in hope, save chill and fire*, Cd. 220; Th. 285, 10; Sat. 335. Hȳ wyrcaþ ðone cȳle hine on *they bring the cold upon him*, Ors. 1, 1; Bos. 23, 6, 8. [*Prompt.* cole *algor*: *Piers P. Laym. Orm.* chele *chill, cold*: *Plat.* köle, *f. pain*: *Ger.* kühle, *f*: *M. H. Ger.* küele, *f*: *O. H. Ger.* kuolī, *f*: *Dan.* köle, *m. f. coolness of the air*: *Swed.* kyla, *f. a chill*: *Icel.* kylr, *m. a gust of cold air*: *Lat.* gelu.] DER. fǣr-cȳle.

cȳle-gicel, es; *m. An icicle;* frigŏris stiria:—Land wǣron freórig cealdum cȳlegicelum *the lands were frozen with cold icicles*, Andr. Kmbl. 2521; An. 1262: Exon. 56 b; Th. 201, 20; Ph. 59. v. gicel.

CYLEN, cyln, e; *f. A* KILN, *an oven;* fornacŭla, siccatōrium:—Cylene *fornacŭlæ*, Cot. 86. Cyln *vel* ast *siccatōrium*, Ælfc. Gl. 109; Som. 78, 132; Wrt. Voc. 58, 44. [*Prompt.* kylne: *Icel.* kylna, *f*: *Wel.* kylyn, *m.*]

cylenisc; *adj. Like a kiln;* fornāceus, Som. Ben. Lye.

cyleþenie, an; *f. The herb celandine;* chelidonium majus:—Cyleþenie, Herb. 75; Lchdm. i. 176, 15, 18. v. celeþonie.

cylew, cylu; *adj. Spotted, speckled;* guttātus:—Cylew *guttātus*, Cot. 99. Cylu *guttātus*, Ælfc. Gl. 80; Som. 72, 92; Wrt. Voc. 46, 49.

cȳle-wyrt, e; *f. Sour-sorrel;* oxylapăthum, Cot. 216.

cylin, cyline heorþ *a kiln;* fornacŭla. v. cylen.

CYLL, e; *f*: cylle, cille, an; *f*: cylle, es; *m. A leather bottle, flagon, vessel;* uter, ascopēra = ἀσκοπήρα:—Gesomnigende swā swā on cylle wætera sǣs *congregans sicut in utrem aquas maris*, Ps. Spl. C. 32, 7. Ðas cylle *istum utrem*, Greg. Dial. 3, 37. Swā ðū on hrīme setest hlance cylle *sicut uter in pruina*, Ps. Th. 118, 83. Flaxe oððe cylle *asscopa* [= *ascopēra*], Ælfc. Gl. 5; Som. 56, 27; Wrt. Voc. 17, 32. Æmtige cillan *vacuum utrem*: ða cillan *istum utrem*, Greg. Dial. 3, 37. Gefylde he ðære cyrcan cyllan *implevit lampades ecclesiæ*, 1, 5. He gegaderode eall sǣwætru tosomne, swylce hī wǣron on ānum cylle *congregans sicut in utrem aquas maris*, Ps. Th. 32, 6. Seó cwēn [Tomyris] hēt ðæt heáfod bewyrpan on ānne cylle se wæs afylled mannes blōdes *the queen* [*Tomyris*] *ordered the head to be thrown into a vessel which was filled with man's blood*, Ors. 2, 4; Bos. 45, 34. Se ðe fæstne hider cylle [MS. kylle] brohte . . . gif hwelc þyrelne cylle [kylle MS.] brohte to ðys burnan *who has brought hither a water-tight bottle . . . if any has brought to this spring a leaky bottle*, Past. 65; Hat. MS. [*Icel.* kyllir, *m. a bag* or *pouch.*] DER. stōr-cylle, -cille.

cyln *a kiln*:—Cyln *vel* ast *siccatorium*, Ælfc. Gl. 109; Som. 78, 132; Wrt. Voc. 58, 44. v. cylen, ast.

cylu *spotted*, Ælfc. Gl. 80; Som. 72, 92; Wrt. Voc. 46, 49. v. cylew.

cym *come*, Exon. 13 a; Th. 23, 22; Cri. 372; *impert. of* cuman.

cymast *most beautiful*, Ps. Th. 86, 2; *superl. of* cyme, *adj.*

cyme, cime, es; *m.* [cuman *to come*] *A coming, an approach, advent;* adventus:—Me is ðīn cyme on myclum þonce *gratus mihi est multum adventus tuus*, Bd. 4, 9; S. 577, 21: Exon. 21 a; Th. 56, 8; Cri. 897: 21 a; Th. 57, 10; Cri. 916: 44 b; Th. 152, 2; Gū. 802: 56 b; Th. 201, 9; Ph. 53: 69 b; Th. 258, 3; Jul. 259. Wearþ Hūna cyme cūþ ceasterwarum *the approach of the Huns was known to the citizens*, Elen. Kmbl. 82; El. 41. He ongeat ðone intingan heora cymes *he understood the cause of their coming*, Bd. 2, 2; S. 504, 1. He wītgode hū his ealdormenn sceoldon fægnian his cymes of his wræcsīðe *he prophesied how his chief men should rejoice at his coming from his banishment*, Ps. Th. arg. 23. Syxtygum wintra ǣr Cristes cyme *sixty* [*of*] *years* [*winters*] *before the coming of Christ*, Bd. 1, 2; S. 475, 4: Exon. 23 a; Th. 64, 1; Cri. 1031: 100 a; Th. 376, 30; Seel. 162: 57 b; Th. 205, 4; Ph. 107: 59 b; Th. 214, 27; Ph. 245: 68 a; Th. 252, 11; Jul. 161: Elen. Kmbl. 2454; El. 1228. Morgensteorra bodaþ ðære sunnan cyme *the morning star announces the sun's approach*, Bt. 39, 13; Fox 234, 4. Hyht wæs geniwad þurh ðæs beornes cyme *hope was renewed through the chief's coming*, Exon. 15 b; Th. 33, 24; Cri. 530: 47 a; Th. 160, 17; Gū. 945: 56 b; Th. 200, 28; Ph. 47: 63 a; Th. 231, 16; Ph. 490: Cd. 151; Th. 189, 4; Exod. 179: Elen. Kmbl. 2170; El. 1086. Þurh mīnne cime *through my coming*, Cd. 29; Th. 39, 1; Gen. 618. Gefēgon beornas burhweardes cyme *the men rejoiced at the coming of the prince*, Andr. Kmbl. 1320; An. 660: Menol. Fox 62; Men. 31. Ic ne wāt hwonan his cymas [MS. cyme] sindon *I know not whence his comings are*, Exon. 50 b; Th. 175, 18; Gū. 1196: Beo. Th. 520; B. 257. DER. be-cyme, eft-, forþ-, from-, geán-, hēr-, hider-, hleóðor-, ofer-, ongeán-, seld-, þrym-, to-, up-, ymb-, ym-.

cyme; *adj. Becoming, convenient, suitable, lovely, beautiful, splendid;* commŏdus, conveniens, aptus, splendĭdus:—Cumaþ nū and geseóþ, hū cyme weorc Drihten worhte *come now and see what lovely works the Lord has wrought*, Ps. Th. 65, 4. Ðe on Chananēa cymu worhte wundur *qui fecit mirabilia in terra Chanaan*, 105, 18. Gif ic mīne gewǣda on wītehrægl cyme cyrde *if I turned my beautiful garments into sackcloth*, Ps. Th. 68, 11. Ðæt ðū sī cymast ceastra Drihtnes *that thou may be the most beautiful of the cities of the Lord*, Ps. Th. 86, 2. DER. un-cyme.

cymed, es; *n. The plant wall-germander; forte* chamædrys = χαμαίδρυς, teucrium chamædrys, Lin:—Genim cymed *take germander*, L. M. 1, 16; Lchdm. ii. 58, 20: 1, 15; Lchdm. ii. 58, 16. Nim cymed *take germander*, 1, 39; Lchdm. ii. 102, 20.

cymen, es; *m. n. The herb cummin;* cŭmīnum = κύμῑνον, cŭmīnum, cyminum, Lin:—Ge tiógoðiaþ eówre mintan and eówerne dile and eówerne cymen [MS. kymen] *ye tithe your mint and your dill and your cummin*, Past. 57; Hat. MS. Dō ðæt cymen on.eced *put the cummin into* *vinegar*, L. M. 2, 44; Lchdm. ii. 256, 6. Cymen *cyminum*, Ælfc. Gl. 44; Som. 64, 64; Wrt. Voc. 32, 1: Herb. 155, 1; Lchdm. i. 280, 23: L. M. 2, 39; Lchdm. ii. 246, 23: iii. 6, 16: 24, 9. Cymenes *of cummin*, Herb. 152, 1; Lchdm. i. 276, 21: L. M. 2, 2; Lchdm. ii. 180, 20: 2, 15; Lchdm. ii. 192, 15: 2, 30; Lchdm. ii. 228, 26: 2, 44; Lchdm. ii. 256, 6. Wyrc sealfe of cymene *make a salve with cummin*, 2, 22; Lchdm. ii. 206, 20. Genim cymen *take cummin*, Herb. 94, 2; Lchdm. i. 204, 16: 376, 5: L. M. 1, 2; Lchdm. ii. 36, 11: 1, 17; Lchdm. ii. 60, 15: 1, 48; Lchdm. ii. 120, 24: 2, 6; Lchdm. ii. 184, 15: 2, 24; Lchdm. ii. 214, 17: iii. 28, 11: 72, 14. Cymenes sǽd *seed of cummin*, L. M. 3, 12; Lchdm. ii. 314, 21. Cymenes dust *dust of cummin*, 3, 23; Lchdm. ii. 322, 3.

cymen *come*, Exon. 8 b; Th. 5, 8; Cri. 66; *pp. of* cuman.

Cymên, es; *m. Cymen, son of Ælle, who was the first Bretwalda* [v. Bret-walda, brȳten-walda]; Cymēnus:—For example, v. Cymēnes ōra.

Cymēnes ōra, an; *m. Cymen's shore, near Wittering, Sussex;* Cymēni lītus, qui ibi naves ad terram appulit. Nunc nomen amisit, sed fuisse prope *Wittering*, in agro Sussexiensi, Charta Donatiōnis quam Cedwalla Rex Ecclesiæ Selsiensi fecit, planissĭme convincit, Camd. Camden and, after him, Gibson say, in the preceding Latin, this place was near Wittering on the coast of Sussex. They rely on a Charter which Kemble [Cod. Dipl. 992] has marked as spurious, but which was no doubt constructed with a regard for probability. In this Charter [Cod. Dipl. 992; A. D. 683; Kmbl. v. 33, 22] the name occurs as Cumeneshora, a form which countenances Ingram's guess that Shoreham is the place; quasi *Cymenes*horeham, v. Chr. Erl. 281, A. D. 477:—Hēr, A. D. 477, com [MS. cuom] Ælle on Bretonlond, and his iii suna, Cymen, and Wlencing, and Cissa, mid iii scipum, on đa stōwe đe is nemned Cymēnes ōra, and đǽr ofslōgon monige Wealas, and sume on fleáme bedrifon on đone wudu đe is genemned Andredes leáge *in this year*, A. D. 477, *Ælle came to Britain, and his three sons, Cymen, and Wlencing, and Cissa, with three ships, at the place which is named Cymen's shore, and there slew many Welsh, and drove some in flight into the wood which is named Andredsley*, Chr. 477; Erl. 12, 28–32.

cym-līc; *adj. Comely, convenient, lovely, beautiful, splendid;* aptus, commodus, splendidus:—Hierusalem, đū wǽre swā swā cymlīc ceaster getimbred *Jerusalem, thou wert built as a beautiful city*, Ps. Th. 121, 3: Exon. 108 b; Th. 415, 24; Rä. 34, 2.

cym-līce; *comp.* -līcor; *adv. Conveniently, fitly, beautifully, splendidly;* commode, apte, splendide:—Andetaþ Drihtne, and his ēcne naman cēgaþ cymlīce *confitemini Domino et invocate nomen ejus*, Ps. Th. 104, 1: 98, 7. Cymlīcor ceól gehlādenne *a more fitly laden ship*, Andr. Kmbl. 721; An. 361: Beo. Th. 75; B. 38.

cym-līcor *more aptly* or *fitly*, Andr. Kmbl. 721; An. 361: Beo. Th. 75; B. 38; *comp. of* cym-līce.

cymst, cymest *comest*, Cd. 203; Th. 252, 28; Dan. 585: Beo. Th. 2769; B. 1382; *2nd pres. sing. of* cuman.

cymþ, cymeþ *comes*, Cd. 17; Th. 20, 26; Gen. 315: Beo. Th. 4123; B. 2058; *3rd sing. pres. of* cuman.

cyn *the chin;* mentum. v. cin.

CYN, cynn, es; *n.* I. *every being of one kind, a kindred, kind, race, nation, people, tribe, family, lineage, generation, progeny*, KIN; genus, gens, natio, populus, stirps, tribus, familia, natales, origo, generatio, proles, progenies:—Đæt hie ne mōton ǽgnian mid yrmþum Israhēla cyn *that they may not hold in misery the race of Israel*, Cd. 156; Th. 194, 24; Exod. 265: 170; Th. 213, 21; Exod. 555. Monna cynn *hominum genus*, Exon. 20 b; Th. 55, 23; Cri. 888: 98 b; Th. 370, 1; Seel. 50: Cd. 212; Th. 261, 33; Dan. 735. Eorþan cynn *terræ tribus*, Ps. Th. 71, 18. Eal engla cynn *all the race of angels*, Exon. 75 a; Th. 281, 10; Jul. 644. Eall gimma cynn *all kinds of gems*, Andr. Kmbl. 3037; An. 1521. Fōr cynn æfter cynne *tribe went after tribe*, Cd. 161; Th. 200, 3; Exod. 351. Đis cynn ne byþ ūtadryfen *hoc genus non ejicitur*, Mt. Bos. 17, 21. Đæt wīf wæs hǽđen, Sirofenisces cynnes *erat mulier gentīlis, Syrophœnissa genere*, Mk. Bos. 7, 26. Lā næddrena cyn *progenies viperarum*, Mt. Bos. 3, 7. Of cynne on cynn *from generation to generation;* a progenie in progeniem, Ps. Th. 84, 5: 88, 1. Adames cyn *the race of Adam*, Cd. 222; Th. 289, 35; Sat. 408: Exon. 22 a; Th. 59, 33; Cri. 961. Ymb fisca cynn *de piscium genere*, Exon. 96 b; Th. 360, 6; Wal. 1. DER. cyn-recen, cynn-recceniss, -ren, -ryn: ælf-cyn, -cynn, ātor-, cyne-, deór-, earfoþ-, engel-, eormen-, eorþ-, fæderen-, feorh-, fīfel-, fisc-, fleóh-, from-, frum-, fugel-, fugol-, gim-, gum-, hǽđen-, helle-, heoloþ- [=hæleþ-], hwǽte-, lǽce-, man-, mēdren-, ōm-, orf-, sigor-, treó-, wǽpned-, wer-, wyrm-, wyrt-. II. in grammar,—*Gender;* genus:—Syndon twā cynn,—*masculinum*, đæt is werlīc, and *femininum*, wīflīc. Werlīc cynn biþ đes wer *hic vir: there are two genders*,—masculine, *that is manlike*, and feminine, *womanlike. Masculine gender is* đes wer *this man*, Ælfc. Gr. 6; Som. 5, 27, 28. Ælc nȳten biþ ođđe he, ođđe heó *every animal is either he, or she*, 6; Som. 5, 34. Neutrum is nāđor cynd, ne **werlīces**, ne wīflīces *neuter is neither kind, neither of male nor of female*, 6; Som. 5, 32. Đis gebȳraþ oftost to nāđrum **cynne**, swā swā is đis word *hoc verbum: this oftest belongeth to the neuter gender, as is* đis word *this word*, 6; Som. 5, 35. Twīlīces cynnes đæt is *dubii generis*, 6; Som. 5, 46. Sume naman sȳnd ōđres cynnes on ānfealdum getele, and ōđres cynnes on mænigfealdum getele *some nouns are of one gender in the singular number, and of another gender in the plural number*, 13; Som. 16, 25. The *m. f. n.* occur in the following sentence, indicated by the articles se, seó, đæt:—Seó sāwel ys mā đonne se līchama, and se līchama mā đonne đæt reáf *anima plus est quam esca, et corpus plus quam vestimentum*, Lk. Bos. 12, 23. III. *a sex;* sexus:—Hwæđeres cynnes bearn heó cennan sceal *of which sex she shall bear a child*, Lchdm. iii. 144, 6. [*Wyc.* kyn *family, generation: Chauc.* kin: *Piers P.* kynne: *R. Glouc. R. Brun.* kyn: *Laym.* cun, kun *race, progeny, kind: Orm.* kin: *O. Sax.* kunni, cunni, *n. race: Dut.* kunne, *f. gender: Kil.* konne, kunne *genus, species, sexus: O. Frs.* ken, kin, kon, *n. genus: M. H. Ger.* künne, *n. family: O. H. Ger.* kunni, *n. genus, gens: Dan.* kjön, *n. genus: Swed.* kön, *n. sex;* kynne, *n. disposition: Icel.* kyn, *n. a kind, kin: Lat.* genus, gens: *Grk.* γένος: *Sansk.* janus *gens.*]

cyn, cynn; *adj. Akin, suitable, fit, proper;* congruus, condignus:—Đæt is cyn *that is proper* or *reasonable*, Bt. 33, 1; Fox 122, 4. Swā hit cynn [cyn Cot.] was *as was suitable* or *fit*, 35, 4; Fox 162, 24. Swylce hit kyn [cyn MS. B; cynn H.] sié *as it may be right*, L. In. 42; Th. i. 128, 11. Hit ys cyn *it is proper*, Ps. Th. 29, 11: 9, 34: 138, 20.

cyncg *a king*, L. E. G. pref; Th. i. 166, 3. v. cyning.

CYND, es; *n.* I. *nature*, KIND; natura:—Gif hió hire cynd healdan wile *if she desire to retain her nature*, Bt. 35, 4; Fox 160, note 21, MS. Cot. II. *a sort, gender;* natura, genus:—Neutrum is nāđor cynd, ne werlīces, ne wīflīces *neuter is neither sort* [*gender*], *neither of male nor of female*, Ælfc. Gr. 6, 3; Som. 5, 32. [*Prompt.* keende, kyynde *genus: Wyc.* kynde *nature: Piers P.* kynde *nature, race, kind: Laym.* i-cunde *nature, kind, race: Orm.* kinde *nature, kind, race: O. Sax.* kind, *n. a child: Dut.* kind, *n. a child: Ger.* kind, *n. a child: M. H. Ger.* kint, *gen.* kindes, *n. a child: O. H. Ger.* kind, kint, *n. proles: Icel.* kind, *f. species, race, kind: Lat.* gent-em, *acc. of* gens.] DER. ge-cynd.

cynde; *adj. Natural, innate, inborn;* naturalis, innatus, ingenitus:—Cniht weóx and þāg swā him cynde wǽron *the boy waxed and thrived as to him was natural*, Cd. 132: Th. 167, 26; Gen. 2771. DER. ge-cynde, un-, unge-.

cynde-līc; *adj. Natural*, KINDLY; naturalis, ingenitus:—Sīdra gesceafta cræftas cyndelīce *the kindly powers of wide-spread creatures*, Exon. 92 b; Th. 346, 27; Sch. 5. DER. ge-cyndelīc, unge-.

cyne-, used in compounds, signifying *kingly, royal, special;* regius, præ-. v. cyne-bænd, -bearn, -boren, -bōt, -botl, -cyn, -dōm, etc.

cȳne; *adj. Bold, brave;* audax:—Cyninga cȳnost *bravest of kings*, Ps. C. 50, 3; Ps. Grn. ii. p. 276, 3. DER. searo-cȳne. v. cēne.

cȳne, an; *f. A chink, fissure;* rima:—Đæs leóhtes scīma þurh đa cȳnan đære dura ineóde *the glare of the light came through the chinks of the door*, Bd. 4, 7; S. 575, 19.

cyne-bænd, es; *m.* [bend, bænd *a band, chaplet, crown*] *A royal crown, a diadem;* regia corona, diadema = διάδημα, Som. Ben. Lye.

cyne-bearn, es; *n. A kingly child, royal offspring;* regius puer, regia proles:—Ne mihton oncnāwan đæt cynebearn *they might not acknowledge the royal child*, Andr. Kmbl. 1131; An. 566. Wuldres cynebearn *the royal child of glory*, Menol. Fox 316; Men. 159: Cd. 82; Th. 102, 23; Gen. 1704.

cyne-boren; *part. Of royal birth;* regia stirpe natus, M. H. 12 a.

cyne-bōt, e; *f.* [bōt *boot, compensation*] *A king's compensation* or *recompense;* regis compensatio:—Gebīraþ seó cynebōt đām leódum *the king's compensation belongs to the people*, L. Wg. 1; Th. i. 186, 4: L. M. L; Th. i. 190, 8.

cyne-botl, es; *n.* [botl *a dwelling*] *A kingly dwelling, a palace;* palatium, Wrt. Voc. 86, 27.

cyne-cyn, -cynn, es; *n.* [cyne *regius, regalis;* cyn, cynn, *gens, stirps, familia*] *A royal race, royal lineage, royal offspring* or *family;* gens regia, proles regia, stirps *vel* familia regia:—Of Francena cynecynne *de gente Francorum regia*, Bd. 1, 25; S. 486, note 32: 2, 14; S. 518, 3. He wæs hiora cynecynnes *he was of their royal race*, Bt. Met. Fox 26, 83; Met. 26, 42. He wæs cynecynnes *he was of royal lineage*, Bt. 38, 1; Fox 194, 14: Bd. 3, 18; S. 546, 39, col. 1: L. Wg. 1; Th. i. 186, 18.

cyne-dōm, es; *m.* [dōm *power, dominion*] *A royal dominion* or *power, kingdom, realm;* imperium, regnum, sceptrum, potestas:—Cynedōm *sceptrum*, Ælfc. Gl. 69; Som. 69, 127; Wrt. Voc. 42, 7. We willaþ đæt ān cynedōm fæste stande ǽfre on þeóde *we will that one kingship stand fast for ever in the nation*, L. N. P. L. 67; Th. ii. 302, 8. Hanna wæs mid ungemete đæs cynedōmes gyrnende *Hanno had an immoderate longing for the kingdom*, Ors. 4, 5; Bos. 81, 43: L. Wg. 1; Th. i. 186, 4: Ps. C. 50, 149; Ps. Grn. ii. 280, 149. Rūmes cynedōmes *augustæ potestatis*, Mone B. 3931. For đam cynedōme *for the kingdom*, L. M. L; Th. i. 190, 6. Claudius Orcadas eáland to Rōmwara cynedōme geþeódde *Claudius Orcadas insulas Romano adjecit imperio*, Bd. 1, 3; S. 475, 7: Chr. 47; Erl. 6, 26. He đone cynedōm ciósan wolde *he would choose* *the kingdom*, Beo. Th. 4741; B. 2376: L. Eth. ix. 42; Th. i. 350, 3. Ðætte ryhte cynedômas þurh ûre folc gefæstnode wǽron *that just royal governments might be settled throughout our people*, L. In. pref; Th. i. 102, 9.

cyneg *a king*, Jos. 10, 5: Homl. Th. ii. 540, 17. v. cyning.

cyne-geard *a royal wand, sceptre*, Ælfc. Gl. 68; Som. 69, 127; Wrt. Voc. 42, 7. v. cyne-gyrd.

cyne-gerd *a sceptre*, Ælfc. Gl. 6; Som. 56, 47; Wrt. Voc. 18, 2. v. cyne-gyrd.

cyne-gerela, an; *m.* [gerela *a robe*] *A kingly robe*; regius vestitus:—Gif mon wolde him awindan of ðǽs cynegerelan [MS. -gerelum] *if any one would strip off from him these kingly robes*, Bt. Met. Fox 25, 45; Met. 25, 23.

cyne-gewǽdu; *pl. n.* [gewǽde *a garment, robe*] *Royal robes*; regiæ vestes:—He onfêng cynegewǽdum *he took the royal robes*, Bd. 1, 6; S. 476, 19.

cyne-gild, -gyld, es; *n.* [gild *compensation*] *A king's compensation*; regis compensatio:—To bôte on cynegilde [-gylde MS. H.] *as offering for the king's compensation*, L. M. L. Th. i. 190, 7.

Cynegils, es; *m. Cynegils, sixth king of the West Saxons*; Cynegilsus:—Cynegilses, *gen.* Chr. Erl. 2, 20: Chr. 688; Erl. 42, 10. Hêr, A. D. 611, Cynegils fêng to rîce on Wesseaxum, and heóld xxxi wintra *here, Cynegils succeeded to the kingdom of the West Saxons, and held it thirty-one years*, 611; Erl. 20, 33. Hêr, A. D. 635, Cynegils [MS. Kynegils] wæs gefullod fram Byrîne ðam biscope on Dorcaceastre, and Oswold Norþhymbra cining his onfêng *here, Cynegils was baptized by Birinus the bishop of Dorchester, and Oswold, king of Northumbria, was his sponsor*, 635; Erl. 25, 33. Cynegils onfêng ǽrest fulwihte Wesseaxna cyninga *Cynegils was the first of the West Saxon kings who received baptism*, Erl. 2, 16.

cyne-gôd; *adj. Excellent, noble*; præstans, nobilis:—Him cynegôdum *to him excellent*, Cd. 78; Th. 96, 5; Gen. 1590. Him ðâ cynegôde on Carran æðelinga bearn eard genâmon *then the noble children of men took them a dwelling in Harran*, 83; Th. 104, 16; Gen. 1736: 182; Th. 228, 2; Dan. 196: 195; Th. 243, 8; Dan. 433: Exon. 85 b; Th. 321, 34; Wîd. 56.

cyne-gold, es; *n. Royal gold, a crown*; diadema = διάδημα, corona:—Þeódnes cynegold sôþfæstra gehwone glengeþ *the Lord's crown shall adorn each of the just*, Exon. 64 b; Th. 238, 17; Ph. 605.

cyne-gyrd, -geard, -gerd, e; *f.* [gyrd *a rod, wand*] *A royal wand, sceptre*; sceptrum:—Cynegyrd *sceptrum*, Wrt. Voc. 72, 55. Cynegeard *sceptrum*, Ælfc. Gl. 68; Som. 69, 127; Wrt. Voc. 42, 7. Cynegerd *sceptrum*, 6; Som. 56, 47; Wrt. Voc. 18, 2. Hî to ðæs caseres cynegyrde gebugon *they submitted to the emperor's sceptre*, Homl. Th. ii. 502, 16.

cyne-hâd, es; *m.* [hâd *form, condition*] *A royal personage* or *condition, dignity, kinghood*; regia persona *vel* dignitas:—Ðæt se cynehâd [MS. cynehade] ðæs hâlgan weres êce gemynd hæfde *ut regia viri sancti persona memoriam haberet æternam*, Bd. 3, 11; S. 535, 30, note. Ic Ælfrêd, gifendum Criste, mid cynehâdes mǽrnesse, geweorþaþ hæbbe cûþlîce ongiten *I Alfred, adorned, by the grace of Christ, with the dignity of a king have well perceived*, Greg. Dial. MS. Hat. fol. 1, 1.

cyne-hâm, es; *m.* [hâm *a house, dwelling, home*] *A royal residence*; regia villa:—On ðam cynehâme ðe is gecýged Bearwe *at the royal residence which is called Barrow*, Cod. Dipl. 90; A. D. 716–743; Kmbl. i. 109, 15. On his âgenum cynehâmum *in his own royal residences*, 598; A. D. 978; Kmbl. iii. 138, 7.

cyne-helm, -healm, es; *m.* [helm *a crown*] *A crown, diadem*; corona, diadema:—Cynehelm *corona, diadema*, Ælfc. Gl. 51; Som. 66, 14; Wrt. Voc. 35, 5: Mone B. 2166. Cynehealm *diadema*, Wrt. Voc. 74, 56. Wundon cynehelm of þornum, and asetton ofer hys heáfod *plectentes coronam de spinis posuerunt super caput ejus*, Mt. Bos. 27, 29: Jn. Bos. 19, 2, 5. Cynehelme *corona*, Mone B. 3019. For cynehelme *for a royal diadem*, Homl. Blick. 23, 34.

cyne-hlâford, es; *m.* [hlâford *a lord*] *A royal lord, sovereign lord, king*; regius *vel* supremus dominus, rex:—Be his cynehlâfordes geþafunge *with the permission of his royal lord*, Cod. Dipl. 593; A. D. 965–975; Kmbl. iii. 127, 8. Æt his leófan cynehlâforde Eádgâre cyninge *from his dear sovereign lord king Edgar*, 583; A. D. 963–975; Kmbl. iii. 111, 26: 598; A. D. 978; Kmbl. iii. 138, 22: Chr. 1016; Erl. 158, 5, 17, 29. Ðæt we ealle ânum cynehlâforde holdlîce hýran *that we all faithfully obey one sovereign lord*, L. Eth. vi. 1; Th. i. 314, 10. Utan ǽnne cynehlâford holdlîce healdan *let us faithfully support one sovereign lord*, v. 35; Th. i. 312, 21: ix. 44; Th. i. 350, 12.

cynelec; *adj. Royal*; regalis:—In ðæm cynelecan tûne *in the royal town*, Bd. 3, 17; S. 543, 21, col. 2. v. cyne-lîc.

cyne-lîc, cynellîc, cynelec; *adj. Kingly, royal, regal, belonging to the state, public*; regius, regalis, publicus:—Eádward cyng man bebyrigde bûtan ǽlcum cynelîcum wurþscipe *king Edward was buried without any kingly honour*, Chr. 979; Erl. 129, 3. Ðæt is cynelîc þing *that is a royal thing*, Exon. 124 b; Th. 478, 26; Ruin. 48. Wæs ðæs ylcan mynstres abbudisse on ða tîd seó cynellîce fǽmne Ælflǽd *præerat quidem tunc eidem monasterio regia virgo Ælbflæd*, Bd. 4, 26; S. 603, 3. Ðæt se cynelîca hâd ðæs hâlgan weres êce gemynd hæfde *ut regia viri sancti persona memoriam haberet æternam*, 3, 11; S. 535, 30. In ðæm cynelecan tûne *in the royal town*, Bd. 3, 17; S. 543, 21, col. 2. Cynelîcre *publica*, Glos. Prudent. Recd. 145, 30. Cynelîco getimbro and ânlîpie *publica ædificia et privata*, Bd. 1, 15; S. 483, 45. Chaldêas cynelîcan getimbro mid fýre fornâmon [MS. fornaman] *the Chaldeans destroyed the royal buildings with fire*, 1, 15; S. 483, 42. He onfêng cynelîcum gewǽdum and com on Breotone *he took the royal robes and came into Britain*, 1, 6; S. 476, 19, note. Wið ða cynelîcan âdle ðe man *aurriginem* nemneþ *ad morbum regium, hoc est*, auriginem [= auruginem], Herb. 87, 1; Lchdm. i. 190, 14. Cynelîc reáf *trabea*, Ælfc. Gl. 63; Som. 68, 122; Wrt. Voc. 40, 30. Cynelîc [MS. kyne-] botl *palatium*, 81; Som. 73, 9; Wrt. Voc. 47, 16.

cyne-lîce; *adv. Royally*; regie:—Ðû miltse on us gecýþ cynelîce *shew mercy royally on us*, Exon. 10 a; Th. 10, 24; Cri. 157.

cynelîc-nys, -nyss, e; *f. Royalty, as shewn in the deportment, a kingly likeness*; regia dignitas:—For his cynelîcnysse ge môdes ge onsýnes *for his kingliness both of his mind and appearance*, Bd. 3, 14; S. 540, 9.

cynellîc *kingly, royal*, Bd. 4, 26; S. 603, 3. v. cyne-lîc.

Cyne-mǽres ford, es; *m.* [*Flor.* Kimeresford: cyne *royal*; mǽre *a mere*; ford *a ford*] KEMPSFORD, *Gloucestershire*:—Râd Æðelmund alderman ofer æt Cynemǽresforda *alderman Æthelmund rode over at Kempsford*, Chr. 800; Erl. 60, 6.

cyne-rîce, -rýce, es; *n. A royal region* or *possession, a kingdom, realm*; regnum:—Secg monig wyscte ðæt ðæs cynerîces ofercumen wǽre *many a warrior wished that there was an end of that kingdom*, Exon. 100 b; Th. 378, 34; Deór. 26. Fêng his bearn to cynerîce *his child succeeded to the kingdom*, Chr. 975; Erl. 126, 5; Edg. 31: 1066; Erl. 201, 1: 1076; Erl. 215, 2. On ðý cynerîce be sûþan Temese *in the kingdom south of the Thames*, 871; Erl. 76, 9. On cynerýce *in the realm*, Exon. 53 b; Th. 187, 23; Az. 35. He ge-eóde ealle ða cynerîcu ðe on Crêcum wǽron *he over-ran all the kingdoms which were in Greece*, Ors. 3, 7; Bos. 58, 39. Cynerîca mǽst *greatest of kingdoms*, Exon. 85 a; Th. 321, 1; Wîd. 39. Ðæt he ealdordôm âgan sceolde ofer cynerîcu *that he should possess eldership over the kingdoms*, Cd. 158; Th. 198, 5; Exod. 318: Bt. Met. Fox 26, 12; Met. 26, 6.

cyne-rôf; *adj.* [rôf *famous*] *Royally famous, noble*; nobilis:—Wolde ic ânes to ðê, cynerôf hæleþ, cræftes neósan *I would inquire of thee of one art, noble hero*, Andr. Kmbl. 967; An. 484: 1169; An. 585. Cirdon cynerôfe *the noble ones turned*, Judth. 12; Thw. 26, 6; Jud. 312: 11; Thw. 24, 21; Jud. 200.

cyne-scipe, es; *m. Kingship, royalty, honour*; regia dignitas:—Hæbbe ic mînes cynescipes gerihta *I may have my rights of royalty*, L. Edg. S. 2; Th. i. 272, 27. Me to fullum cynescipe *to my perfect royalty*, 2; Th. i. 272, 25. Him sylfum to cynescipe *in honour of himself*, L. Edg. i. prm; Th. i. 262, 4: L. C. E. prm; Th. i. 358, 6.

cyne-setl, es; *n.* [setl *a seat*] *A royal seat, throne*; imperii sedes, solium:—Constantinopolis is nû ðæt heáhste cynesetl ealles eástrîces *Constantinople is now the chief royal seat of all the eastern empire*, Ors. 3, 7; Bos. 61, 11. Ðe sit on his cynesetle *qui sedet in solio ejus*, Ex. 11, 5.

cyne-stôl, es; *m.* [cyne *royal*, stôl *a seat, stool*] *A royal throne* or *dwelling, chief city, capital*; thronus, urbs regia, arx, metropolis:—On his cynestôle *on his kingly throne*, Exon. 25 b; Th. 75, 6; Cri. 1217: Elen. Kmbl. 659; El. 330. Of cynestôlum *from royal seats*, Exon. 96 a; Th. 358, 22; Pa. 49. Constantinopolis is Crêca cynestôl *Constantinople is the royal dwelling-place of the Greeks*, Bt. 1; Fox 2, 22: Ors. 3, 9; Bos. 65, 45. Cynestôle Creácas wióldon *the Greeks possessed the metropolis*, Bt. Met. Fox 1, 95; Met. 1, 48: Menol. Fox 208; Men. 105. We becômon to ðam cynestôle, ðǽr getimbred wæs tempel Dryhtnes *we came to the royal city, where the temple of the Lord was built*, Andr. Kmbl. 1332; An. 666. Ðǽr heó ǽfre forþ wunian môten cestre and cynestôl *where they may evermore possess cities and a kingly throne*, Cd. 220; Th. 283, 1; Sat. 298: Chr. 975; Erl. 125, 31. Sancta Hierusalem, cynestôla cyst *holy Jerusalem, choicest of royal cities*, Exon. 8 b; Th. 4, 11; Cri. 51.

cyne-strǽt, e; *f. A royal street* or *road*; regia via, publicum, Cot. 153.

Cynete, an; *f.* I. *the river* KENNET *which rises in Wiltshire*; fluvii nomen qui originem suam habet in agro Wiltoniensi:—Ǽrest on Cynetan, ðæt up andlang strêmes ... ðæt eft innan Cynetan strêm *first to the Kennet, then up along the stream ... then again to the river Kennet*, Cod. Dipl. 792; A. D. 1050; Kmbl. iv. 122, 21, 26: Cod. Dipl. Apndx. 378; A. D. 939; Kmbl. iii. 413, 22, 30: Cod. Dipl. 1120; A. D. 939; Kmbl. v. 238, 17, 25, 35: 1152; A. D. 944; Kmbl. v. 300, 16, 18: 1199; A. D. 956; Kmbl. v. 376, 6, 16: 1282; A. D. 984; Kmbl. vi. 118, 1, 6. II. KENNET, *a village on the river Kennet in Wiltshire*; villæ nomen in agro Wiltoniensi:—Wæs fyrd gesomnod æt Cynetan *a force was assembled at Kennet*, Chr. 1006; Erl. 140, 23.

cyne-þrym; *gen.* -þrymmes; *m.* [þrym *a multitude, majesty, glory*] *A kingly host, royal majesty* or *glory;* regia multitudo, regis majestas:—Mid cyneþrymme *with a kingly host,* Cd. 209; Th. 260, 8; Dan. 706: Exon. 120 b; Th. 462, 12; Hö. 51. He cwom on cyneþrymme *he came in royal majesty,* Ps. Th. 95, 12. Ryhtfremmende cyneþrym cýðaþ *the righteous doers shall proclaim the royal majesty,* Exon. 65 a; Th. 240, 5; Ph. 634: Andr. Kmbl. 2645; An. 1324. Ðú me gecýðdest cyneþrymma wyn *thou declaredst to me joy of kingly glories,* Exon. 120 b; Th. 463, 23; Hö. 74.

cyne-wíse, an; *f.* [wíse *an affair*] *The state, republic, commonwealth;* respublica:—Se náht freomlíces ongan on ðære cynewísan *he began nothing profitable in the state,* Bd. 1, 3; S. 475, 21. Rehte ða cynewísan *rempublicam rexit,* 1, 5; S. 476, 8.

cyne-wiððe, an; *f. A royal wreath, diadem;* redimiculum:—Cynewiððan *redimicula,* Mone B. 6270: Cot. 185.

cyne-word, es; *n.* [word *a speech*] *A proper speech* or *word;* proprium verbum:—Mon cýðe cynewordum, hú se cuma hátte *let a man make known in fitting words, how the guest is called,* Exon. 112 b; Th. 430, 29; Rä. 44, 16.

Cynewulf, es; *m. An Anglo-Saxon poet, who has preserved his name in Runes, in his poem on Elene's Recovery of the Cross.* Mr. Kemble will best describe his own discovery.—In the Vercelli MS. is contained a long poem on the finding of the Cross by the Empress Helena [= Elene]. After the close of the poem, and apparently intended as a tail-piece to the whole book, comes a poetical passage, in which the author principally refers to himself, and after a reference to his own increasing age and the change from the strength and joyousness of youth, he breaks out, in the 15th Canto, into a moralizing strain, in which he concludes his work. The following thirty lines, containing Runes, form a portion of this Canto:—

Á wæs sæc óþ-ðæt,	*Ever was contest till then,*
cnyssed cearwelmum	*with waves of sorrow tossed*
ᚳ [cén] drúsende,	**C** [*the torch*] *sinking,*
ðeáh he, in medohealle	*though he, in meadhall*
máþmas, þege	*treasures, handled*
æplede gold,	*appled gold,*
ᚣ [yr] gnornode,	**Y** [*sorrow*] *he mourned,*
ᚾ [nýd] geféra,	**N** [*need*] *his consort,*
nearu sorge dreáh,	*narrow sorrow he suffered,*
enge rúne,	*a close rune,*
ðǽr him ᛖ [éh] fóre	*where* **E** [*the horse*] *before him*
mílpaðas mæt,	*measured the mile-paths,*
módig þrægde	*proudly hastened*
wírum gewlenced.	*with wires adorned.*
ᚹ [wén] is geswíþrad,	**W** [*hope*] *is overpowered,*
gomen æfter gearum,	*my joy in my old age,*
geógoþ is gecyrred	*youth is turned back*
ald onmedla.	*my old pride.*
ᚢ [úr] wæs geára	**U** *I was of old*
geógoþhádes glǽm,	*a gleam of youth,*
nú synt geárdagas	*now are the days of my life*
æfter fyrstmearce	*after the appointed space*
forþgewitene,	*departed,*
lífwynne geliden,	*the joy of life flowed away,*
swá ᛚ [lagu] toglídeþ,	*as* **L** [*lake or water*] *glideth,*
flódas gefýsde.	*the floods that hasten.*
ᚠ [feoh] ǽghwam biþ	**F** [*wealth*] *will be for every man*
lǽne under lyfte,	*failing under the heaven,*
landes frætwe	*the ornament of the land*
gewítaþ under wolcnum.	*will depart under the welkin.*

Elen. Kmbl. 2512-2541; El. 1257-1272.

The extreme rudeness and abruptness of these lines, and the apparent uselessness of the Runes, led me to suspect that there was more in them than merely met the eye. This I found to be the case; for, on taking the Runes out of the context, using them as single letters and uniting them in one word, they supplied me with the name **CYNEWULF**, undoubtedly no other than the author of the poems. I cannot here bestow space upon a long argument to shew who this *Cynewulf* was. I believe him to have been the Abbot of Peterborough of that name, who flourished in the beginning of the eleventh century, who was accounted in his own day a celebrated poet, both in Latin and Anglo-Saxon, whose works have long been lost, but whose childish ingenuity has now enabled us with some probability to assign to him the authorship of the Vercelli and Exeter Codices, Archæologia, vol. xxviii. 1840, by Kemble, pp. 327-372. The Reverend Jn. Earle, M. A. etc. Rector of Swanswick, with some pertinent remarks, supposes Cynewulf to be the same person as Cyneweard. v. Chr. Erl. Introduction, pp. xx-xxii.

cyng *a king,* Chr. 664; Erl. 34, 20: 894; Erl. 91, 32: L. Ath. iv. pref; Th. i. 220, 1. v. cyning.

cyngc *a king,* L. Edg. S. 1; Th. i. 270, 7. v. cyning.

Cynges tún, es; *m.* [cynges tún *king's town*] KINGSTON; regia villa:—Aðelstán wæs to cynge æt Cynges túne gehálgod *Athelstan was consecrated king at Kingston,* Chr. 924; Th. 199, 8, col. 1: 979; Th. 234, 10, col. 2. Æt Cyninges tún *at Kingston,* Chr. 979; Th. 235, 9, col. 1. v. Cinges tún, Cyninges tún.

cyning, cyng, es; *m.* [cyn *people,* -ing *originating from, son of*]. I. *a king, ruler, emperor;* rex, imperator. He is the representation of the people, and springs from them, as a son does from his parents. The Anglo-Saxon king was elected from the people; he was, therefore, the king of the people. He was the chosen representative of the people, their embodiment, the child, not the father of the people. He was not the lord of the soil, but the leader of his people. He completed the order of freemen, and was the summit of his class. As the freeman [ceorl] was to the noble [æðele], so was the noble to the king. The Anglo-Saxon king was the king of a tribe or of a people, but never of the land. We read of kings of the West Saxons or of the Mercians, but not of Wessex or of Mercia. The king was, in truth, essentially one with the people, by them and their power he reigned; but his land was like theirs, private property. It was not the feudal system, and was never admitted that the king was owner of all the land in a country:—Se cyning mildelíce onféng *the king received* [*him*] *gladly,* Ors. 1, 8; Bos. 30, 44. Se Iudéa cyning *the king of the Jews;* ὁ βασιλεὺς τῶν Ἰουδαίων, Mt. Bos. 2, 2. Saul wæs gecoren ǽrest to cyninge on Israhéla þeóde *Saul was first chosen king of the people of Israel,* Ælfc. T. 13, 3. Eart ðú wítodlíce cyning *ergo rex es tu?* οὐκοῦν βασιλεὺς εἶ σύ; Jn. Bos. 18, 37. Cyninges botl *a king's dwelling, palace,* Bd. 2, 14; S. 518, 18. Cyninga [MS. cininga] bóc *the book of kings,* Ælfc. T. Grn. 6, 38: 8, 3. Cyninga [MS. kyninga] byrgen *a burying-place of kings;* mausoleum, bustum, Ælfc. Gl. 85; Som. 74, 3; Wrt. Voc. 49, 27. Maximian, árleás cyning *Maximian, the wicked emperor,* Exon. 65 b; Th. 243, 1; Jul. 4. 2. *a spiritual King, God, Christ;* Deus, Christus:—Heofona Cyning *the King of heaven,* Andr. Kmbl. 3008; An. 1507: 3017; An. 1511: Cd. 137; Th. 172, 18; Gen. 2846. Crist is ealra cyninga Cyning *Christ is King of all kings,* Homl. Th. ii. 588, 9: Exon. 9 b; Th. 9, 17; Cri. 136: 11 a; Th. 14, 6; Cri. 215: Andr. Kmbl. 1955; An. 980. 3. *the devil;* diabolus, satánas:—Hellwarena cyning *the king of hell's inhabitants,* Exon. 70 a; Th. 261, 28; Jul. 322. Se ofermóda cyning, Satan *the haughty king, Satan,* Cd. 18; Th. 22. 9; Gen. 338. II. *Anglo-Saxon kings were at first elected from a family* or *class, by* Witena gemót *the assembly of the wise.* 2. *fidelity was sworn to them by the people,* in the following words:—Ðus man sceal swerigean hyld-áþas. 'On ðone Drihten, ðe ðes háligdóm is fóre hálig, ic wille beón N. hold and getríwe, and eal lufian ðæt he lufaþ, and eal ascúnian ðæt he ascúnaþ, æfter Godes rihte and æfter woroldgerysnum, and nǽfre, willes ne gewealdes, wordes ne weorces, ówiht dón ðæs him láþre biþ; wið ðam ðe he me healde swá ic earnian wille, and eall ðæt læste ðæt uncer fórmǽl wæs, ðá ic to him gebeáh and his willan geceás *thus shall a man swear oaths of fidelity* [or *homage*]. *By the Lord, before whom this relic is holy, I will be to N. faithful and true, and love all that he loves, and shun all that he shuns, according to God's law, and according to the world's principles, and never, by will nor by force, by word nor by deed, do aught of what is loathful to him; on condition that he keep me as I am willing to deserve, and all that fulfil that our agreement was, when I submitted to him and chose his will,*' L. O. 1; Th. i. 178, 2-9. If this was taken in A. D. 924, it was not long before the power of the king was limited, for we have the following oath administered to Æðelréd, when he was consecrated king at Kingston in A. D. 978, as is stated in the Chronicle,—On ðys geáre wæs Æðelréd to cininge gehálgod æt Cinges túne *in this year Æthelred was consecrated king at Kingston,* Chr. 978 [MS. 979]; Th. 234, 9, col. 1. 3. *the king took a corresponding oath to his people.* The words of the king's oath are,—Ðis gewrit is gewriten, stæf be stæfe, be ðam gewrite ðe Dúnstán arcebisceop sealde úrum hláforde æt Cinges túne á on dæg ðá hine man hálgode to cinge, and forbeád him ǽlc wedd to syllanne bútan ðysan wedde, ðe he up on Cristes weofod léde, swá se bisceop him dihte. 'On ðære hálgan Þrýnnesse naman, Ic þreó þing beháte cristenum folce, and me underþeóddum:—*Án ǽrest,* ðæt ic Godes cyrice and eall cristen folc mínra gewealda sóðe sibbe healde. *Oðer* is, ðæt ic reáflác and ealle unrihte þing eallum hádum forbeóde. *Þridde,* ðæt ic beháte and bebeóde on eallum dómum riht and mildheortnisse, ðæt us eallum ǽrfæst and mildheort God þurh ðæt his écean miltse forgife, se lifaþ and ríxaþ' *this writing is copied, letter for letter, from the writing which archbishop Dunstan delivered to our lord at Kingston on the very day when he was consecrated king, and he forbade him to give any other pledge but this pledge which he laid upon Christ's altar, as the bishop instructed him.* '*In the name of the Holy Trinity, three things do I promise to this christian people, my subjects.* First, *that I will hold God's church and all the christian people of my realm in true peace.* Second, *that I will forbid rapine and all injustice to men of all conditions.* Third, *that I promise and enjoin justice and mercy in all judgments, whereby the just and merciful God may give us all his eternal favour who liveth* *and reigneth,*' Relq. Ant. W. ii. 194. 4. from the freedom with which the educated spoke of the Doom's Day Survey of William the Conqueror, indicating their love of freedom, *we have no reason to suppose this oath was the first oath taken by kings in our limited monarchy.* The spirit of the monks may be seen in the following extract from the Chronicle:—Willelm, Engla landes cyng, ðe ðâ wæs sittende on Normandige, forðig he âhte ǽgðer ge Engla land ge Normandige... sende ðâ ofer eall Engla land into ǽlcere scîre his men... Swâ swýðe nearwelîce he hit lett ût aspyrian, ðæt næs ân ǽlpig hîde, ne ân gyrde landes, ne, furðon, hit is sceame to tellanne, ac hit ne þuhte him nân sceame to dônne, ân oxa [MS. oxe], ne ân cû, ne ân swîn næs belyfon, ðæt næs gesæt on his gewrite, and ealle ða gewrita wǽron gebroht to him syððan *William, king of England, who was then resident in Normandy, for he owned both England and Normandy... then sent his men over all England into each shire... So very narrowly did he commission them to trace it out, that there was not one single hide, nor a rood of land, nay, moreover, it is shameful to tell, though he thought it no shame to do it, not an ox, nor a cow, nor a swine was left, that was not set down in his writ, and all the recorded particulars were afterwards brought to him,* Chr. 1085; Erl. 218, 2-4... 24, 25... 33-38. 5. the Anglo-Saxon king *had royal power to pardon transgressors:*—Gif hwâ in cyninges healle gefeohte, oððe his wǽpn gebrede, and hine mon gefô; sié ðæt on cyninges dôme, swâ deáþ, swâ lîf, swâ he him forgifan wille *if any one fight in the king's hall, or draw his weapon, and he be taken; be it in the king's power, either death or life, or pardon,* L. Alf. pol. 7; Th. i. 66, 8, 9. Sié on cyninges dôme hwæðer he lîf âge ðe nâge *be it in the king's power whether he shall or shall not have life,* L. In. 6; Th. i. 106, 3, 4. Bûton him cyning [MS. kyning] ârian wille *unless the king will be merciful to him,* 36; Th. i. 124, 19. Ðæt he wǽre his feores scyldig, bûton he cyng gesôhte, and he him his feorh forgifan wolde; eall swâ hit ǽr æt Greátan leá and æt Exan ceastre and æt Þunres felda gecweden wæs *that he should be liable in his life, unless he should flee to the king, and he should give him his life; all as it was before ordained at Greatley and at Exeter and at Thundersfield,* L. Ath. v. § 1, 4; Th. i. 230, 6-9: L. Edm. S. 6; Th. i. 250, 11: L. Edg. ii. 7; Th. i. 268, 24, 25: L. Eth. iii. 16; Th. i. 298, 14: vii. 9; Th. i. 330, 24. 6. *of all forfeits the king had one half*—to healfum:—Fô se cyng to healfum,—to healfum ða men ðe on ðære râde beón *let the king take possession of half, of* [*the other*] *half the men, who may be in the riding* [*shall take possession*], L. Ath. i. 20; Th. i. 210, 6, 7. 7. *treasure-trove, or treasure or money found, of which the owner was unknown, belonged to the king.* It is designated in Anglo-Saxon charters by the words—ealle hordas bûfan eorþan, and binnan eorþan *all hoards above the earth, and within the earth.* As we learn from Beowulf, in early and heathen times, much treasure was buried in the mound raised over the ashes of the dead, besides what was burned with the body:—Hî on beorg dydon bêgas [MS. beg] and siglu, forlêton eorla gestreón eorþan healdan, gold on greóte, ðǽr hit nû gên lîfaþ ylдum swâ unnyt swâ hit ǽr wæs *they placed rings and jewels in the mound, they left the treasure of earls to the earth to hold, gold in the dust, where it now yet remains as useless to men as it was before,* Beo. Th. 6307-6318; B. 3164-3169. The legend of Guthlac [about A.D. 700, v. Crûland] supplies a very early instance of the search for gold and silver in the mounds:—Wæs ðǽr on ðam eálande sum hlâw mycel ofer eorþan geworht, ðone ylcan men iú geára for feós wilnunga gedulfon and brǽcon: ðâ wæs ðǽr on ôðre sîdan ðæs hlâwes gedolfen swylce mycel wæterseáþ wǽre *there was on the island a great mound raised upon the earth, which some men of yore had dug and broken up in hopes of treasure: then there was dug up on the other side of the mound as it were a great water-pit,* Guthl. 4; Gdwin. 26, 4-8. 8. *Pastus* or *Convivium* = Cyninges feorm. The king visited different districts personally or by deputy to see that justice was done to all his subjects. In these periodical journeys the king received support and entertainment wherever he went. Hence perhaps the privileges of our judges. In A.D. 814 Cênwulf released the bishop of Worcester from a *pastus* of twelve men, whom he was bound to find. This was so great an expense that the exemption was worth an estate of thirteen hides, v. Cod. Dipl. 203; A.D. 814; Kmbl. i. 256. 9. *Vigilia* = heáfodweard *head ward,* or *a proper watch set over the king, which he claimed when he came into any district.* The sǽweard or *coast guard* was also a regal right, performed by the tenants of those land owners whose estates lay contiguous to the sea. 10. *the mint or coinage of money.* The king exercised a superintendence over the circulating medium. Æðelrǽd not only enacted that there should be no moneyers besides the king's, but that their number should be diminished:—Nân man ne âge nænne mynetere bûton cyng *let no man have a moneyer except the king,* L. Eth. iii. 8; Th. i. 296, 15. Ut monetarii pauciores sint quam antea fuerint, iv. 9; Th. i. 303, 2. 11. *the grant of a market, with power to levy tolls, was also a royalty,* Cod. Dipl. 1075; A.D. 873-899; Kmbl. v. 142: 1084; A.D. 904; Kmbl. v. 157. v. The Rights of Anglo-Saxon Kings, explained more fully in *Kemble's Saxons in England,* 2 vols. 8vo. 1849. Bk. ii. chap. 2; vol. ii. pp. 29-103. [*Prompt.* kynge: *Wyc.* kyng: *Piers P. Chauc.* king: *R. Glouc.* kyng: *Laym. Orm.* king: *Plat.* kŏnig: *O. Sax.* kuning, cunig, *m*: *Frs.* kening: *O. Frs.* kining, kinig, kening, keneng, koning: *Dut.* koning, *m*: *Kil.* koningh, *m*: *Ger.* könig, *m*: *M. H. Ger.* künic, künec, künc, *m*: *O. H. Ger.* kuning, *m*: *Dan.* konning, konge, *m*: *Swed.* konung, kong, kung, *m*: *Icel.* konungr, kóngr, *m*: *Lett.* kungs *dominus.*] DER. æðel-cyning, Angel-, beorn-, brýten-, eorþ-, êðel-, folc-, gâst-, geár-, gûþ-, hǽðen-, heáh-, heofon-, leód-, mægen-, rôdor-, sǽ-, segn-, self-, sige-, sôþ-, swegl-, þeód-, þrym-, þryþ-, woruld-, wuldor-.

cyning-bald; *adj. Kingly* or *nobly bold;* nobiliter audax:—Fērdon forþ cyningbalde men *the nobly bold men went forth,* Beo. Th. 3273; B. 1634.

cyning-cynn, es; *n.* [cynn *a sort, race,* v. cynn] *A royal race;* regium genus:—Of ðæs strýnde monigra mǽgþa cyningcynn fruman lǽdde *the royal race of many tribes drew its beginning from his stock,* Bd. 1, 15; S. 483, 30. Eanfriþ wæs ðære mǽgþe cyningcynnes *Eanfrith was of the royal race of that province,* 3, 1; S. 523, 14. Penda wæs se fromesta esne of Mercna cyningcynne *Penda was the boldest man of the royal race of the Mercians,* 2, 20; S. 521, 9. v. cyne-cyn.

cyning-dôm, es; *m.* [-dôm *dominion, power*] *Kingly power, a* KINGDOM; regimen, regnum:—Cyningdôm habban *to have kingly power,* Cd. 173; Th. 216, 7; Dan. 3. Metod ðec aceorfeþ of cyningdôme *the Lord will cut thee off from thy kingdom,* 202; Th. 251, 24; Dan. 568. Caldêas cyningdôm âhton *the Chaldeans held the kingdom,* 209; Th. 258, 24; Dan. 680. v. cyne-dôm.

Cyninges tûn *Kingston,* Chr. 979; Th. 235, 9, col. 1. v. Cynges tûn.

cyninges wyrt, e; *f. The herb marjoram;* sampsuchum = σάμψυχον, origanum majorana, Lin:—Cyninges wyrt *sampsuchum,* Mone A. 529.

cyning-feorm, cyninges feorm, e; *f.* [feorm *food, support*] *Royal purveyance, tribute for the royal household;* regis firma:—Ic heó gefreóge êcelîce ðæs gafoles, ðe hió nû get to cyninges handa ageofan sceolan of ðam dǽle ðe ðǽr ungefreód to lâfe wæs ðære cyningfeorme, ge on hlutrum alaþ, ge on beóre, ge on hunige, ge hryðrum, ge on swýnum, ge on sceápum *I free them for ever from the impost which they have still to pay into the king's hand, from that portion, which was there left unfreed of the royal purveyance, whether in pure ale, or in beer, or in honey, or in oxen, or in swine, or in sheep,* Cod. Dipl. 313; A.D. 883; Kmbl. ii. 111, 4-9. Ðe cyninges feorm to belimpe *to which the royal purveyance belongs,* L. Alf. pol. 2; Th. i. 60, 24.

cyning-gereord, -gereorde, es; *n.* [gereord *food, a repast, feast*] *A royal feast;* regis convivium:—Cyning-gereorde *fercula,* Cot. 93.

cyning-gierela, an; *m. A royal crown, diadem;* regalis tænia [= ταινία] diadema = διάδημα, Som. Ben. Lye.

cyning-rîce *a kingdom,* Som. Ben. Lye. v. cyne-rîce.

cyn-lîc; *adj.* [cyn *suitable, fit*] *Becoming, fitting;* dĕcōrus:—Suilce iów cynlîc þynce *as to you may seem fitting,* Th. Diplm. A.D. 804-829; 461, 36. Swâ him rihtlîc and cynlîc þince *as to them may seem just and becoming,* Th. Diplm. A.D. 905; 493, 12.

cyn-lîce; *adv. Becomingly, fitly;* congruenter:—Hî cynlîce to ðê cleopiaþ *they fitly call upon thee,* Ps. Th. 64, 14: 118, 57, 82, 145, 147: 126, 2.

cynn, es; *n. A sort, kind;* genus, Ps. Th. 144, 13. v. cyn.

cynn *suitable, fit,* Bt. 35, 4; Fox 162, 24: L. In. 42; Th. i. 128, 11, MS. H. v. cyn.

cynnan *to declare, clear, prove;* advocāre, purgāre, manifestāre:—Gif he cynne ðæt he hit bohte *if he declare that he bought it,* L. Edg. S. 11; Th. i. 276, 12, note 7. v. cennan II.

cynnestre, an; *f.* [cennan *to bring forth,* -estre *a female* termination, *q. v.*] *One who brings forth, a mother;* genitrix, mater:—Ðæt cild oncneów Marian stemne, cynnestran *the child knew the voice of Mary, the mother,* Homl. Th. i. 352, 27.

cynning-stân, es; *m.* [cennan II. *to try, prove;* stân *a stone*] *A trying-stone;* tessera:—Cynning-stân on tæfle *a little wooden tower on the side of a gaming-board, hollow and having steps inside, through which the dice were thrown upon the board;* pyrgus [= πύργος], turricula, Ælfc. Gl. 61; Som. 68, 65; Wrt. Voc. 39, 48.

cynn-recceniss, e; *f.* [reccenys *a narration, history*] *A reckoning of relationship, a genealogy;* genealogia, Mt. Kmbl. Lind. 1, title.

cyn-recen; *gen.* -recenne; *f. A pedigree, genealogy, parentage;* generatio, genealogia, parentela, Som. Ben.

cyn-ren, -ryn, es; *n.* [cyn *a kindred, race, nation, family, generation;* ren, ryn *a course*] *A family course, family, generation, kind, nation, posterity;* generatio, genus, natio, progenies, propago:—He forlêt his rîce and his cynren *he left his country and his family,* Bt. 38, 1; Fox 194, 27. Cynren *generatio,* Wrt. Voc. 72, 49. Ðis ys Thares cynryn *this is the generation of Terah,* Gen. 11, 27. On cynrynum cynrena [MS. kynrynum kynrena] *in generationes generationum,* Ps. Lamb. 71, 5. On ðam fiftan dæge ûre Drihten gesceóp ða mycelan hwalas on heora cynrynum *on the fifth day our Lord created the great whales with their kinds,* Hexam. 8; Norm. 14, 8. Fisc sceal on wætere cynren cennan [MS. cynran cennen] *a fish shall propagate his kind in the water,*

Menol. Fox 515; Gn. C. 28. Cynrenu *genera*, Scint. 53. Ic andette đē on cynrenum [cynrenon MS.], Drihten *confitebor tibi in nationibus, Domine*, Ps. Spl. 17, 51. Lā ge nædrena cynryn *progenies viperarum*, Mt. Bos. 12, 34. Cynren *propago*, Ælfc. Gl. 91; Som. 75, 17; Wrt. Voc. 51, 62.

Cynrîc, es; *m. Cynric, the second king of the West Saxons, son of Cerdic*, q. v; Cynrîcus:—Hēr, A. D. ccccxcv, cōman twegen ealdormen on Brytene, Cerdic and Cynrîc his sunu, mid v scipum on đone stede đe is gecweden Cerdices ōra, and đȳ ilcan dæge hie gefuhtan wiđ Wealum *here*, A. D. 495, *came two aldormen to Britain, Cerdic and Cynric his son, with five ships, at the place which is called Cerdic's shore* [*on the south of Dorsetshire*, v. Cerdices ōra], *and on the same day they fought against the Welsh*, Chr. 495; Th. 24, 26-33. Hēr Cerdic forþfērde, and Cynrîc his sunu rîcsode forþ xxvi wintra *in this year* [A. D. 534] *Cerdic died, and Cynric his son reigned for twenty-six years*, 534; Erl. 14, 32.

cyn-ryn, es; *n. A family course, generation;* generatio, progenies, Gen. 11, 27: Ps. Lamb. 71, 5: Hexam. 8; Norm. 14, 8: Mt. Bos. 12, 34. v. cyn-ren.

CYP; *gen.* cyppes; *m. A* CHIP, *beam, log, trunk of a tree;* festuca, trabs, stipes:—Cyppes *stipĭtis*, Glos. Prudent. Recd. 148, 80. Cyp *stipitem*, 150, 39. [*Prompt.* chyppe *assula*: *Chauc.* chippes, *pl*: *R. Brun.* chip: *Kil.* kippen *cudere*: *Icel.* kippa *to pull, snatch;* kippr, *m. a pull, shock, spasm.*]

cȳp, e; *f. A measure, bushel;* modius, dolium:—Under cȳpe *sub modio*, Mt. Kmbl. Hat. 5, 15. Cȳpe *dolium*, Mone B. 3630. v. cȳf.

cȳpa, cēpa, an; *m.* [ceáp II]. I. *a factor, merchant, trader;* negotiator, mercator:—Đā đǣr fōron Madianisce cȳpan *then there passed Midianitish merchants*, Gen. 37, 28. Cȳpa *mercator*, Glos. Prudent. Recd. 140, 38. Đās hālgan cȳpan, Petrus and Andreas, mid heora nettum and scipe him đæt ēce līf geceápodon *these holy traders, Peter and Andrew, with their nets and ship bought for themselves everlasting life*, Homl. Th. i. 580, 19. Drihten adrǣfde đillîce cȳpan of đam hālgan temple *the Lord drove such chapmen from the holy temple*, 406, 24. II. what a merchant has his goods in,—*A basket;* cofinus = κόφῐνος:—Man nam đa gebrotu đe đār belifon, twelf cȳpan fulle *sublatum est quod superfuit illis, fragmentorum cophĭni* [κόφῐνοι] *duodecim*, Lk. Bos. 9, 17. [*Scot.* couper, coper *one who buys and sells*: *O. Frs.* kapere, *m. a purchaser*: *Dut.* kooper, *m*: *Ger.* käufer, *m*: *M. H. Ger.* koufer, *m*: *O. H. Ger.* koufâri, *m*: *Dan.* kjöber: *Swed.* köpare, *m*: *Lat.* caupo *a merchant*: *Grk.* κάπηλος *one who sells provisions*: *Lith.* kupczus *mercator.*] DER. mynet-cȳpa.

cȳpan, cīpan; ic cȳpe, đū cȳpest, cȳpst, he cȳpeþ, cȳpþ, *pl.* cȳpaþ; *p.* cȳpte, đū cȳptest, *pl.* cȳpton, cīptun *To sell;* vendere:—Ic wylle cȳpan *volo vendere*, Coll. Monast. Th. 27, 19. Ic cȳpe mīne þingc *ego vendo meas res*, 26, 33. Hwǣr cȳpst đū fixas đīne *ubi vendis pisces tuos?* 23, 21. Đū sældest *vel* cȳptest folc đīn *vendidisti populum tuum*, Ps. Spl. T. 43, 14. Sǣde đām đe đa culfran cȳpton *dixit his qui columbas vendebant*, Jn. Bos. 2, 16. Gāþ to đām cȳpendum and bycgaþ eów ele *ite ad vendentes et emite vobis oleum*, Mt. Bos. 25, 9: Gen. 47, 20. [*Prompt.* chepyn' *licitari*: *Chauc.* chepe *to buy, market*: *Piers P.* chepen *to buy*: *Scot.* coup *to buy and sell*: *Plat.* kopen, köpen *to buy*: *O. Sax.* kōpōn *to bargain*: *Frs.* keapjen: *O. Frs.* kapia *to buy*: *Dut.* koopen *to buy*: *Ger.* kaufen: *M. H. Ger.* koufen: *O. H. Ger.* koufēn, koufōn *mercari*: *Goth.* kaupon *to bargain*: *Dan.* kjöbe *to buy*: *Swed.* köpa *to buy*: *Icel.* kaupa, *p.* keypti *to bargain.*] DER. be-cȳpan, ge-. v. ceápian.

cȳpe-cniht, es; *m. A bought servant, slave;* venalis puer, servus:—Đā geseah he cypecnihtas *he then saw slaves*, Homl. Th. ii. 120, 18.

cȳpe-man, -mann, es; *m. A merchant*, Bd. 2, 1; S. 501, 4. v. ceápman.

cypera, an; *m. A* KIPPER, *salmon in the state of spawning;* salmo ova gignens:—Đonne eów fōn lysteþ leax ođđe cyperan *when you desire to catch a salmon or a kipper*, Bt. Met. Fox 19, 23; Met. 19, 12.

cyperen; *adj. Coppery, belonging to copper;* æreus:—Seóþ on cyperenum citele *seethe it in a copper kettle*, L. M. 1, 15; Lchdm. ii. 56, 19. Dō on cyperen fæt *put it into a copper vessel*, 1, 2; Lchdm. ii. 36, 1. Gemultan ealle đa anlîcnessa togædere, đe đǣr binnan wǣran, ge gyldene, ge sylfrene, ge ǣrene, ge cyperene *all the statues, which were in it, of gold, and of silver, and of brass, and of copper, were melted together*, Ors. 5, 2; Bos. 101, 22. Forđonđe he forgnǣþ gatu cyperene *quia contrivit portas æreas*, Ps. Spl. 106, 16. Cyperen hwer *a copper ewer* or *vessel;* cucuma, Ælfc. Gl. 26; Som. 60, 83; Wrt. Voc. 25, 23.

cȳpe-þing; *pl. n. Saleable things, merchandise;* merces, Cot. 133. v. cēpe-þing.

cȳping, cȳpingc, cīping, e; *f.* [ceáping, ceáp *a price*, q. v. II]. I. *a bargaining, setting a price, marketing, chapping, traffic;* negotiatio, nundina:—Đæt nān cȳping ne sȳ Sunnan dagum *that no marketing be on Sundays*, L. Ath. i. 24; Th. i. 212, 15: v. 10; Th. i. 240, 9. Đa ealdorbiscopas geþafedon đæt đǣr cȳping binnan gehæfd wǣre *the high-priests allowed chapping to be held therein*, Homl. Th. i. 406, 6. Cȳpingc *negotiatio*, Ælfc. Gl. 81; Som. 73, 18; Wrt. Voc. 47, 25. Sunnan dæges cȳpinge we forbeódaþ ǣghwār *we forbid Sunday's traffic everywhere*, L. N. P. L. 55; Th. ii. 298, 21. Cȳpingce, L. C. E. 15; Th. i. 368, 15. Ne fortruwige he hiene æt đære cīpinge *let them not be too confident of their bargain*, Past. 44, 6; Hat. MS. 62 b, 9. Cȳpinga *nundinæ*, Ælfc. Gr. 13; Som. 16, 21. Đæt hī Sunnan dæges cȳpinga georne geswīcan *that they strictly abstain from Sunday marketings*, L. Eth. vi. 44; Th. i. 326, 21: vi. 22; Th. i. 320, 12: v. 13; Th. i. 308, 11: ix. 17; Th. i. 344, 7. II. *a market-place, market;* forum:—Đæs tūnes cȳping and seó innung đara portgerihta gange into đære hālgan stōwe *let the market of the town and the revenue of the port dues go to the holy place*, Cod. Dipl. 598; A. D. 978; Kmbl. iii. 138, 10. To-middes đære cȳpinge *in the midst of the market*, M. H. 117 a. Andlang strǣte ūt on đa cȳpinge, swā up anlang cȳpinge *along the road out to the market-place, so up along the market-place*, Cod. Dipl. 720; A. D. 1012; Kmbl. iii. 359, 12, 13.

cȳp-man; *gen.* -mannes; *m. A chapman, merchant;* mercator:—Đa cȳpmen binnon đam temple getācnodon unrihtwīse lāreówas on Godes gelađunge *the chapmen within the temple betokened unrighteous teachers in God's church*, Homl. Th. i. 410, 35: ii. 120, 15. Drihten adrǣfde of đam temple đa cȳpmen *the Lord drove the chapmen from the temple*, i. 406, 1. Sume synt cȳpmenn *alii sunt mercatores*, Coll. Monast. Th. 19, 7. Be cȳpmanna fōre *of the journeying of chapmen*, L. In. 25; Th. i. 118, 11, note 27, B. G. v. ceáp-man.

Cyppan-ham, -hamm *Chippenham, Wilts*:—Hēr hine bestæl se here to Cyppanhamme *here the army stole itself away to Chippenham*, Chr. 878; Th. 146, 21, col. 2, 3: 880; Th. 148, 39, col. 3. v. Cippan-ham.

cypresse, an; *f. The cypress;* cupressus [= κυπάρισσος], cupressus sempervirens, Lin:—Of cypressan *from the cypress*, Lchdm. iii. 118, 21.

cypsed; *pp. Bound, fettered;* compeditus. DER. ge-cypsed. v. cyspan.

cȳp-strǣt, e; *f.* [cȳp = ceáp II, strǣt *a street*] *A street* or *place for merchandise, cheap street;* vicus mercatorius:—Andlang cȳpstrǣte *along cheap street*, Cod. Dipl. 1291; A. D. 996; Kmbl. vi. 135, 17.

cyrc, e; *f. A church;* ecclesia:—Cristes cyrc *Christ's church*, Chr. 1066; Erl. 202, 1. In đære cyrce *in the church*, 1070; Erl. 209, 40. Đa cyrce *the church*, 1070; Erl. 209, 36. v. cyrce, cyrice.

cyrc-bræce, es; *m. Church-breach, a breaking into a church;* in ecclesiam irruptio:—Đa heáfodleahtras sind, mansliht, cyrcbræce, etc. *the chief sins are, murder, church-breach, etc.* Homl. Th. ii. 592, 4. v. ciricbryce.

cyrce; *gen.* cyrcan, cyrcean; *f. A church;* ecclesia:—Seó cyrce mid hire portice mihte fīf hund manna eáđelīce befōn on hire rȳmette *the church with her porch could easily contain in its space five hundred men*, Homl. Th. i. 508, 13: ii. 584, 3: 592, 22. Cyrcan duru *a church's door*, i. 64, 31. Crist is se grundweall đære gāstlīcan cyrcan *Christ is the foundation of the spiritual church*, ii. 588, 22. Ne sceal cyrcean timber to ænigum ōđrum weorce, būton to ōđre cyrcean *ligna ecclesiæ non debent ad aliud opus poni, nisi ad aliam ecclesiam*, L. Ecg. P. A. 16; Th. ii. 234, 16, 17. v. cyrice.

cyrce weard *a warden of the church, sacristan*, Chr. 1070; Erl. 207, 33. v. cyric-weard, cyrc-weard.

cyrc-hālgung *hallowing* or *consecrating a church*, Homl. Th. ii. 582, 27. v. cyric-hālgung.

cyrc-lîc *ecclesiastical*, Chr. 716; Th. 70, 35, col. 3: L. Ælf. C. 33; Th. ii. 356, 13: Homl. Th. i. 600, 8. v. cyric-lîc.

cyrc-þēnung *church-service*, Glos. Prudent. Recd. 145, 81. v. ciricþēnung.

cyrc-þingere, es; *m. A priest;* sacerdos:—Sacerd *vel* cyrcþingere *sacerdos*, Ælfc. Gl. 68; Som. 70, 14; Wrt. Voc. 42, 23. v. þingere II, cyric-þingere.

cyrc-weard, cyric-, -werd, es; *m. A churchwarden, sacristan;* ecclesiæ custos, sacri scriniarius:—Cyrcweardes þēnung *a churchwarden's duty*, Greg. Dial. 1, 5. Æđelstān cyric-weard [MS. -wyrd] fēng to đam abbodrîce æt Abban dūne *Æthelstan, warden of the church, succeeded to the abbacy at Abingdon*, Chr. 1044; Th. 300, 26. Cyrcweard *sacri scriniarius*, Ælfc. Gl. 114; Som. 80, 23; Wrt. Voc. 61, 4. Cyrcwerd *æditus*, R. Conc. 1. Se bisceop befran đone cyrcweard hwǣr đæs hālgan wǣpnu wǣron *the bishop asked the sacristan where the weapons of the saint were*, Homl. Th. i. 452, 2. Đā wæs ān cyrce weard Yware wæs gehāten *there was a sacristan called Yware*, Chr. 1070; Erl. 207, 33.

cyrde, *pl.* cyrdon *turned, returned*, Lk. Bos. 14, 21: Jn. Bos. 6, 66; *p. of* cyrran.

cyre, es; *m.* [ceósan *to choose*] *Choice, free choice, free will;* electio, hæresis = αἵρεσις, optio, arbitrium:—Cyre [MS. kyre] *hæresis*, Ælfc. Gl. 3; Som. 55, 84; Wrt. Voc. 16, 55. Cyre *optio*, Glos. Prudent. Recd. 146, 52. God forgeaf him āgenne cyre, forđanđe đæt is rihtwīsnys đæt gehwylcum sȳ his āgen cyre geþafod *God gave them their own free will, for it is righteousness that to every one be allowed his own free will*, Homl. Th. i. 112, 4, 5, 8, 11, 22: 12, 14: 110, 35: 292, 32: ii. 490, 16. Ic wylle đæt hȳ sȳn heora freólses wyrđe and hyra cyres *I will that they be worthy of their freedom and their free will*, Cod. Dipl. 314; A. D. 880-885; Kmbl. ii. 116, 30. Hwī wæs se man betǣht to his ágenum cyre *why was the man* [*Adam*] *committed to his own free will?* Boutr. Scrd. 17, 25. Mid cyre *arbitrio*, Mone B. 1344: 2616. [*Laym.* cure, *m. choice*: *Plat.* köre *election*: *Dut.* keur, *f. choice*: *Kil.* keur, kore *optio*, *electio*, *arbitrium*: *Ger.* kür, kur, chur, *f. election*: *M. H. Ger.* kür, küre, *f. examination*, *election*: *O. H. Ger.* churi, *f. deliberatio*, *electio*: *Dan.* kaar, *n. choice*: *Swed.* kor *electio*: *Icel.* kjörr, keyr, *n. choice, decision.*]

cyre-áþ, es; *m.* [cyre *a choice*, áþ *an oath*] *The select oath, the oath sworn by the accused, together with a certain number of consacramentals selected by him out of a fixed number of persons named to him by the judge*; juramentum electum, quod quis præstabat cum aliquot conjuratoribus ab ipso selectis e quibusdam a judice nominatis [Schmd. 566]:—Nemne him man x men and begite ðara twegen and sylle ðone áþ ... and stande ðæs cyre-áþ ofer xx peninga *let there be named ten men to him and let him get two of them and give the oath ... and let his select oath stand for over twenty pence*, L. Ath. i. 9; Th. i. 204, 15. v. un-gecoren áþ.

cyre-bald *bold in decision*; arbitrii strenuus. v. cire-bald.

cyre-líf, es; *n. A choice of life, where on decease of a lord, the cultivators choose a lord for themselves*; optio vitæ, ubi, mortuo domino, villani sibi dominum eligunt:—Ic bidde, on Godes naman, and on his háligra, ðæt mínra maga nán ne yrfewearda ne geswence nán nǽnig cyrelíf ðara ðe ic foregeald, and me West-Seaxena wítan to rihte gerehton, ðæt ic hí mót lǽtan swá freó swá þeówe, swáðer ic wille; ac ic, for Godes lufan and for mínre sáwle þearfe, wylle ðæt hý sýn heora freólses wyrðe and hyra cyres; and ic, on Godes lifiendes naman, beóde ðæt hý nán man ne brócie, ne mid feós manunge, ne mid nǽnigum þingum, ðæt hý ne mótan ceósan swylcne mann swylce hý wyllan *I pray in the name of God, and his saints, that no one of my kinsmen nor heirs molest any choice of life of those for whom I have paid, and the witan of the West Saxons have rightly confirmed to me, that I might leave them either free or servile, as I will; but I, for love of God and for my soul's need, will that they be entitled to their freedom and their choice; and I, in the name of the living God, command that no man oppress them, either by exaction of money, or in any other way, so that they may not choose whatever lord they will*, Cod. Dipl. 314; A. D. 880–885; Kmbl. ii. 116, 24–33.

cyren *must, wine boiled down*; dulcisapa:—Awilled wín *vel* cyren *dulcisapa*, Cot. 62. v. a-willan, ceren.

Cyren-ceaster, Cyrn-ceaster *Cirencester, Cicester, Gloucestershire*:—Æt Cyrenceastre *at Cirencester*, Chr. 1020; Th. 286, 12, col. 2: Ors. 5, 12; Bos. 110, 22. v. Ciren-ceaster.

cyrf, e; *f? A cutting off, an instrument to cut with*; abscissio, ferrum abscissionis:—Cyrf *abscissio*, R. Ben. 28. Be ðisum cyrfe *of this cutting*, Homl. Th. ii. 406, 33. Cyrf *ferrum abscissionis*, C. R. Ben. 40. DER. æ-cyrf, of-.

CYRFÆT, cyrfet, es; *m? A gourd*; cucurbita:—Cyrfæt *cucurbita*, Ælfc. Gl. 43; Som. 64, 38; Wrt. Voc. 31, 48. Hwerhwettan oððe cyrfet gesihþ on swefnum untrumnysse getácnaþ *to see in dreams a cucumber or a gourd betokens ailment*, Somn. 43; Lchdm. iii. 200, 16. Wylde cyrfet *wild gourd*, colocynthis = κολοκυνθίς, Ælfc. Gl. 39; Som. 63, 58; Wrt. Voc. 30, 12. Wild cyrfet *vel* hwit wíngeard *bryonia* = βρυωνία, 44; Som. 64, 81; Wrt. Voc. 32, 17. [*Plat.* körbs, körwitz, kürwes, *m*: *Dut.* kauwoerde, *f. a gourd*: *Kil.* kauwoorde, kouworde: *Ger.* kürbiss, *m*: *M. H. Ger.* kürbez, *m*: *O. H. Ger.* kurbiz, *m*: *Fr.* gourde, *f*: *O. Fr.* gougourde: *Lat.* cucurbita.]

cyrfel, es; *m.* [cyrf *a cutting off*] *A little stake, a peg*; paxillus:—Cyrfel *vel* litel stigul [= sticel?] *paxillus*, Ælfc. Gl. 29; Som. 61, 46; Wrt. Voc. 26, 45.

cyrfille, an; *f. Chervil*; cærefolium:—Nim cyrfillan *take chervil*, Lchdm. iii. 12, 13: 46, 25. v. cerfille.

cyrfst, he cyrfþ *carvest, carves*; *2nd and 3rd pers. pres. of* ceorfan.

cyric *a church*. v. *in the compounds* cyric-ǽwe, -belle, -bóc, -bót, -bryce, -burh, -dór, -friþ, -fultum, -georn, -geriht, -griþ, *etc.*

cyric-ǽwe, ciric-ǽwe, es; *n. An ecclesiastical marriage*; ecclesiasticum matrimonium:—Hí, þurh heálícne hád, ciricǽwe underféngan *they, through holy orders, have entered into an ecclesiastical marriage*, L. I. P. 23; Th. ii. 334, 14. v. cyric; ǽw, ǽwe.

cyric-belle *a church-bell*; ecclesiæ campana. v. ciric-belle.

cyric-bóc, e; *f. A church-book*; liber continens ritus et ceremonias ecclesiæ:—To ǽghwælcre neóde man hæfþ on cyricbócum mæssan gesette *masses for every necessity have been placed in church-books*, Lupi Serm. 2, 3; Hick. Thes. ii. 107, 32.

cyric-bót, ciric-bót, e; *f. Church-repair*; ecclesiæ reparatio:—To cyricbóte *for church-repair*, L. Eth. vi. 51; Th. i. 328, 6. To ciricbóte sceal eall folc fylstan mid rihte *all people must lawfully give assistance to church-repair*, L. C. S. 66; Th. i. 410, 12: L. Eth. ix. 6; Th. i. 342, 8.

cyric-bryce *church-breach, a breaking into a church*, L. Ath. i. 5; Th. i. 202, 6, MSS. B. L. v. ciric-bryce.

Cyric-burh; *gen.* -burge; *dat.* -byrig; *f.* [*Hunt.* Cereburih: *Brom.* Cyrebury: *the church city*] *Chirbury, Shropshire*; loci nomen in agro Salopiensi:—Æðelflǽd ða burh getimbrede æt Cyricbyrig *Æthelfled built the fortress at Chirbury*, Chr. 913; Th. 186, 35, col. 2; 187, 35, col. 1.

cyric-dór *a church-door*; ecclesiæ porta. v. ciric-dór.

CYRICE, cirice, cyrce, circe; *gen.* an, ean; *f*: cyric, ciric, *in the compound* cyric-ǽwe, etc. q. v. cyrc, e; *f.* circ, *in the compound* circ-líc, etc. q. v. I. *the* CHURCH *as a temporal and spiritual body*; ecclesia = ἐκκλησία:—Seó cyrice on Breotone hwæt hwugu fæc sibbe hæfde *the church in Britain for some time had peace*, Bd. 1, 8; S. 479, 17. Seó Godes circe, seó circe ǽfyllendra *the church of God, the church of the faithful*, Exon. 18 a; Th. 44, 8, 16; Cri. 699, 703. To ðære ánnesse ðære hálgan Cristes cyrican *to the unity of Christ's holy church*, Bd. 1, 26; S. 488, 13. Agustinus on Cent ðære frymþelícan cyrican líf and láre wæs onhýrigende *Augustine in Kent imitated the life and lore of the early church*, 1, 26; S. 487, 27. Gregorius féng to biscophâde ðære Rómániscan cyrican *Gregory succeeded to the bishopric of the Roman church*, 1, 23; S. 485, 23: 1, 4; S. 475, 29. Ongunnon hí ðæt apostolíce líf ðære frymþelícan cyricean onhýrigean *they began to imitate the apostolic life of the early church*, Bd. 1, 26; S. 487, 32. Fram ðam biscope ðære Rómániscan cyricean *by the bishop of the Roman church*, 1, 13; S. 481, 38. On Norþanhymbra þeóde and cyrican *in the nation and church of the Northumbrians*, 2, 20; S. 521, 19. On ðære hálgan Rómánisce cyricean *in the holy Roman church*, 1, 27; S. 489, 33, 38. Hǽlend Crist is se grundweall ðære gástlícan cyrcan *Jesus Christ is the foundation of the spiritual church*, Homl. Th. ii. 588, 22. Ealle Godes cyrcan sind getealde to ánre cyrcan, and seó is geháten gelaðung *all God's churches are accounted as one church, and that is called a congregation*, ii. 580, 22. On cirícean Crist Drihten God bletsige *in ecclesiis benedicite Dominum Deum*, Ps. Th. 67, 24. Hí hýndon and hergedon Godes cyrican *they oppressed and harried God's church*, Bd. 1, 6; S. 476, 21. Crist getimbrode ða gástlícan cyrcan, ná mid deádum stánum ac mid lybbendum sáwlum *Christ built the spiritual* [lit. *ghostly*] *church, not with dead stones but with living souls*, Homl. Th. ii. 580, 12. II. *a church, the material structure*; ecclesia:—Ðǽr wæs cyrice geworht *a church was built there*, Bd. 1, 7; S. 479, 6: 1, 26; S. 487, 42. Wæs cirice gehálgod *a church was consecrated*, Andr. Kmbl. 3291; An. 1648. Ðæt seó cyrce afealle *that the church may fall down*, Homl. Th. i. 70, 27. Godes cyrce is úre gebédhús *God's church is our prayer-house*, ii. 584, 3. Circe *ecclesia*, Ælfc. Gl. 107; Som. 78, 82; Wrt. Voc. 57, 58. Awriten mid ðám bróðrum ðære cyricean æt Lindesfarena *written by the brethren of the church at Lindesfarne*, Bd. pref; S. 472, 29. Nim úre cyrcan mádmas *take our church's treasures*, Homl. Th. i. 418, 14, 17. Nis ná alýfed ðæt ðæs mynstres hláford sylle ðære cyrcean land to óðre cyrcean *non licet monasterii domino terram ecclesiæ alii assignare ecclesiæ*, L. Ecg. P. A. 25; Th. ii. 236, 15, 16. Ceadwala cining wæs gebyrged innan Sce Petres cyrican *king Ceadwalla was buried in St. Peter's church* [*at Rome*], Chr. 688; Erl. 43, 7. Hí on cyrican in Eoferwíceastre bebyrigde wǽron *they were buried in the church at York*, Bd. 2, 14; S. 518, 2. Æðelbyrht cyning on cyricean ðara eádigra apostola Petrus and Paulus bebyriged wæs *king Æthelbert was buried in the church of the blessed apostles Peter and Paul*, 2, 5; S. 506, 22. On eorþlícere cyrcan líþ stán ofer stáne *in an earthly church stone lies over stone*, Homl. Th. ii. 582, 17: i. 452, 2: 504, 8: 506, 11, 18. Se Cénwalh hét atimbrian ða cyrican on Wintan-ceastre *Cenwalh commanded the church at Winchester to be built*, Chr. 641; Erl. 27, 13. Eádwine cyning wæs gefullod fram Pauline ðam bisceope on Eoferwíceastre, ðý hálgestan Eásterdæge, on sancti Petres cyricean ðæs apostoles, ðá he ðǽr hræde geweorce of treówe cyricean getimbrede, syððan he gecristnad wæs ... and sóna ðæs ðe he gefullad wæs, he ongan, mid ðæs bisceopes láre, máran cyrican and hýhran stǽnene timbrian, and wyrcean ymb ða cyrican útan ðe he ǽr worhte *king Edwin was baptized by bishop Paulinus on the most holy Easter day, in the church of St. Peter the apostle at York, when he had there built a church of wood, with hasty work, after he was christened ... and soon after he was baptized, he began, by the bishop's advice, to build a larger and higher church of stone, and to construct it about the church which he had formerly wrought*, Bd. 2, 14; S. 517, 22–30: Chr. 626; Erl. 23, 40; 25, 2: Bd. 2, 3; S. 504, 23, 27: 2, 14; S. 518, 18: 2, 16; S. 519, 22. Hió cirican getimbrede, tempel Drihtnes, on Caluarie *she built a church, a temple of the Lord, on Calvary*, Elen. Kmbl. 2014; El. 1008. Se hét ciricean getimbran, Godes tempel *he commanded a church to be built, a temple of God*, Andr. Kmbl. 3265; An. 1635. Hí ðǽrofer cyrcan arǽrdon and weofod *they raised a church and altar thereover*, Homl. Th. i. 506, 15, 19, 25, 35. Ne wǽron cyrican getimbrede *churches were not built*, Bd. 2, 14; S. 518, 16. Ða menigfealdan cyrcan ateoriaþ *the manifold churches will decay*, Homl. Th. ii. 582, 6. Ða cyrcean, ðe beóþ fram ðám bisceopum gehálgode, sceolon mid hálig wætere beón geondstrédde *ecclesiæ, ab episcopis illis consecratæ, aqua benedicta debent aspergi*, L. Ecg. P. A. 5; Th. ii. 232, 20. On éhtnysse Godes cyrcena *in the persecution of God's churches*, Bd. 1, 6; S. 476, 22. On ðám lácum geleáfsumra ðe hí to

Godes cyricum bringaþ *of the gifts of the faithful which they bring to God's churches*, 1, 27; S. 488, 39. On Cristes cyrican ða ðe on Brytene wǽron *in Christ's churches which were in Britain*, 1, 8; S. 479, 26. Constantínus hét ðæt man cyricean timbrede, and ðæt man belúce ǽlc deófulgyldhús *Constantine ordered churches to be built, and every heathen temple to be closed*, Ors. 6, 30; Bos. 127, 36: Bd. 1, 8; S. 479, 22, 23. Maximian, árleás cyning, cwealde cristne men, circan fylde *Maximian, the wicked emperor, slew christian men, overthrew churches*, Exon. 65 b; Th. 243, 4; Jul. 5. On ðison geáre barn Cristes cyrc *in this year* [A.D. 1066] *Christchurch* [*Canterbury*] *was burnt*, Chr. 1066; Erl. 202, 1. Cyrice weard, cyrce weard *a warden of a church*, 1043; Erl. 169, 33: 1070; Erl. 207, 33. In ðære cyrce *in the church*, 1070; Erl. 209, 40. Ða cyrce *the churches*, 1070; Erl. 209, 36. **III.** *a heathen temple;* templum paganum:—Gebletsode Romulus mid ðara sweora blóde ða cyrican *Romulus consecrated the temples with the blood of their fathers-in-law*, Ors. 2, 2; Bos. 41, 7. [*Prompt.* chyrche: *Wyc.* cherche: *Piers P.* kirk: *Chauc.* chirche: *R. Glouc.* chirches, *pl*: *Laym.* chirche, chireche, *f*: *Scot.* kirk: *Plat.* karke, kerke: *O. Sax.* kirika, *f*: *Frs.* tjercke: *O. Frs.* kerke, sthereke, sziurke, tsiurike, *f*: *Dut.* kerk, *f*: *Kil.* kercke: *Ger. M. H. Ger.* kirche, *f*: *O. H. Ger.* kiricha, *f*: *Dan.* kirke, *m. f*: *Swed.* kyrka, *f*: *Icel.* kirkja, *f*: *Grk.* κυριακή [οἰκία] *the Lord's* [*house*].] DER. cyric-ǽwe, -belle, -bóc, -bót, -bryce, -burh, -dór, -friþ, -fultum, -georn, -geriht, -griþ, -hád, -hálgung, -líc, -mangung, -mitta, -neód, -nyt, -pæþ, -ragu, -réna, -sang, -sangere, -sceat, -sócn, -stíg, -þén, -þénung, -þingere, -tíd, -tún, -wæcce, -wǽd, -wag, -waru, -weard.

cyric-friþ, ciric-friþ, es; *m. n. Church-peace, right of sanctuary;* ecclesiæ pax:—Cyricfriþ *church-peace*, L. Ethb. 1; Th. i. 2, 6. Ciricfriþes [cyric- MS. H.] to bóte *as compensation for the church-peace*, L. Alf. pol. 2; Th. i. 62, 5.

cyric-fultum *church-help, ecclesiastical support.* v. ciric-fultum.

cyric-georn; *adj. Diligent in attending church;* ad ecclesiam libenter frequens, L. Ecg. C. prm; Th. ii. 132, 15.

cyric-geriht, es; *n. A church-due;* ecclesiæ debitum:—Hí gyrnaþ heora sceatta on teoðungum, and on eallum cyricgerihtum *they desire their monies for tithes, and for all church-dues*, L. I. P. 19; Th. ii. 328, 1.

cyric-griþ, es; *n. Church-peace;* ecclesiæ pax:—Stande ǽlc cyricgriþ swá swá hit betst stód *let every church-peace stand as it has best stood*, L. Edg. i. 5; Th. i. 264, 25, MS. A. v. ciric-griþ.

cyric-hád, es; *m.* [hád **II.** *degree, order*] *A church-degree, order of the church;* ecclesiæ ordo:—For ðám seofon cyrichádum [-hádan MS.] ðe se mæssepreóst, þurh Godes gife, geþeáh ðæt he hæfde, he biþ þegenrihtes wyrðe *for the seven orders of the church, which the mass-priest, through the grace of God, has acquired, he is worthy of thane-right*, L. O. 12; Wilk. 64, 41.

cyric-hálgung, cyrc-hálgung, e; *f. Church-hallowing, consecration of a church;* encænia = ἐγκαίνια, ecclesiæ consecratio:—Ðys sceal to cyrichálgungum *this shall be for the consecration of a church*, Rubc. Jn. Bos. 10, 22; Notes, p. 580. Æt ðære ealdan cyrchálgunge *at the old church-hallowing*, Homl. Th. ii. 582, 27.

cyric-líc, circ-líc, cyrc-líc; *adj. Like a church, ecclesiastical;* ecclesiasticus:—Cyriclíc wer *vir ecclesiasticus*, Bd. 2, 20; S. 522, 21. Magister cyriclíces sanges *magister ecclesiasticæ cantionis*, 2, 20; S. 522, 27. Fram ǽlcere cyriclícre gesamnunge *a quaque ecclesiastica congregatione*, L. Ecg. P. A. 30; Th. ii. 236, 35. Hie heóldan ða cyriclícan sceare *they observed the ecclesiastical tonsure*, Chr. 716; Th. 70, 34, col. 2. Ðæt cyriclíce stǽr úres eálondes and þeóde ic wrát on fíf béc *I* [*Bede*] *wrote the ecclesiastical history of our island and nation in five books*, Bd. 5, 24; S. 648, 31. Cyriclíce preóstas *ecclesiastici presbyteri*, L. Ecg. P. A. 5; Th. ii. 232, 17. Monad mid gelomlícre smeáwunge and leornunge cyriclícra gewrita *admonitus ecclesiasticarum frequenti meditatione scripturarum*, Bd. 5, 21; S. 642, 26: 5, 23; S. 645, 15. Mid óðrum cyriclícum bócum *cum cæteris ecclesiasticis voluminibus*, 5, 20; S. 642, 1.

cyric-mangung *church-mongering, simony*, L. Eth. vi. 15; Wilk. 121, 19. v. ciric-mangung.

cyric-mitta *a church-measure.* v. ciric-mitta.

cyric-neód, e; *f. Church-need;* ecclesiæ necessitas:—Riht is ðæt man betǽce ǽnne dǽl preóstum, óðerne dǽl to cyricneóde, þriddan dǽl ðám þearfum *it is right that one part* [*of the alms*] *be delivered to the priests, a second part for the need of the church, a third part for the poor*, L. Edg. C. 55, note 4; Th. ii. 256, 30.

cyric-nyt, -nytt *church-duty* or *service.* v. circ-nyt.

cyric-pæþ, es; *m. A church-path;* ad ecclesiam semita:—Of ðære díce on ðæne cyricpæþ *from the ditch to the church-path*, Cod. Dipl. 736; A. D. 1021-1023; Kmbl. iv. 19, 9.

cyric-ragu *church-lichen* or *moss.* v. ciric-ragu.

cyric-réna, an; *m.* [rán *robbery*] *Church-robbery, sacrilege;* sacrilegium:—On cyricrénan *in sacrileges*, L. Eth. vi. 28; Th. i. 322, 20.

cyric-sang, -song, es; *m. A church-song;* ecclesiasticum carmen:—He ða cyricsangas lǽrde, ðe hí ǽr ne cúðan *quæ illi non noverant, carmina ecclesiastica doceret*, Bd. 5, 20; S. 642, 8. He wæs on cyricsonge se gelǽredesta *qui cantandi in ecclesia erat peritissimus*, 2, 20; S. 522, 25.

cyric-sangere, es; *m. A church-singer;* ecclesiæ cantator:—He sumne æðelne cyricsangere begeat, se wæs Mafa háten *he got a famous church-singer, who was named Mava*, Bd. 5, 20; S. 642, 5.

cyric-sceat, ciric-sceat, es; *m. Church-scot, church-money, tax* or *rate;* ecclesiæ census. Church-scot was at first a certain measure of corn paid to the church. In a charter of Bishop Werfrith, those to whom it was granted, agreed,—Ðæt hí agefen élce gére þreó mittan hwǽtes to ciricsceatte to Clife *that they should give yearly to Cliff three measures of wheat as church-scot*, Bd. S. 772, 8. Be cyric-sceattum. Cyric-sceattas sín agifene be Sće Martines mæssan. Gif hwá ðæt ne gelǽste, sié he scyldig lx scill. and be xii fealdum agife ðone ciric-sceat *of church-scots. Let church-scots be given at Martinmas. If any one do not perform that, let him forfeit sixty shillings, and give the church-scot twelvefold*, L. In. 4; Th. i. 104, 8-11. Ðæt neád-gafol úres Drihtnes; ðæt sýn, úre teoðunga and cyric-sceattas *the necessary tribute of our Lord; that is, our tithes and church-scots*, L. Edg. S. 1; Th. i. 270, 25. Cyric-sceat was also a general word, and included not only corn, but poultry or any other provision, that was paid in kind to the church. So in the Inquisition of the Rents of the Abbey of Glastonbury, A.D. 1201:—In churchscet lx gallinas et semen frumenti ad tres acras, *Chartul. de Glaston. MS.* f. 38: L. In. 61; Th. i. 140, 12-14: L. Ath. i. prm; Th. i. 196, 7-10: L. Edm. E. 2; Th. i. 244, 15-18: L. Edg. i. 2; Th. i. 262, 10-17: L. Eth. vi. 18; Th. i. 320, 1-2: L. Eth. ix. 11; Wilk. 114, 19-22; Th. i. 342, 27-29.

cyric-sócn *a church-privilege*, Cod. Dipl. 870; Kmbl. iv. 220, 19. v. ciric-sócn.

cyric-stíg, e; *f.* [stíg *a way, path*] *A church-path;* ad ecclesiam callis:—Of ðam hylle on cyricstíge, of cyricstíge on ða blacan þyrnan *from the hill to the church-path, from the church-path to the black-thorn*, Cod. Dipl. 1368; Kmbl. vi. 220, 19, 20.

cyric-þén *a minister of the church*, L. I. P. 25; Th. ii. 340, 13. v. ciric-þén.

cyric-þénung *church-service*, L. I. P. 23; Th. ii. 334, 30. v. ciric-þénung.

cyric-þingere *a priest.* v. cyrc-þingere.

cyric-tíd, e; *f. Church-time, time of service in a church;* in ecclesia ministerii tempus:—His cyrictída on rihtlícne tíman *his church-hours at the right time*, L. I. P. 8; Th. ii. 314, 20.

cyric-tún *a church-inclosure, church-yard.* v. ciric-tún.

cyric-wæcce *a church-watch* or *wake*, L. Edg. C. 28; Wilk. 84, 30. v. ciric-wæcce.

cyric-wǽd, e; *f. A church-garment;* ecclesiæ vestimentum:—To cyricwædum [MS. -wædan] *for church-garments*, L. Eth. vi. 51; Th. i. 328, 8.

cyric-wag *a church-wall*, L. Eth. vii. 13; Wilk. 111, 17. v. ciric-wag.

cyric-waru, e; *f. A church-congregation;* in ecclesia congregatio:—On cyricware *in a church-congregation*, L. O. 13; Th. i. 184, 12.

cyric-weard, -wyrd *a churchwarden*, Chr. 1044; Th. 300, 26, col. 1. v. cyrc-weard.

cyrin *a churn;* sinum, Wrt. Voc. 290, 31. v. ceren.

Cyring-ceaster *Cirencester*:—Æt Cyringceastre *at Cirencester*, Chr. 1020; Th. 286, 13, col. 1. v. Ciren-ceaster.

cyrlisc *rustic, rural;* rusticus, L. In. 18; Th. i. 114, 6, note 8, B. v. ceorlisc.

cyrliscnys, -nyss, e; *f.* CHURLISHNESS, *clownishness, rudeness;* rusticitas, Som. Ben. Lye.

cyrm *a noise, shout, uproar*, Andr. Kmbl. 2313; An. 1158: Scint. 55: Cot. 86. v. cirm.

cyrman *to cry out, shout*, Cd. 166; Th. 207, 3; Exod. 461. v. cirman.

cyrn *a churn;* sinum. v. ceren.

Cyrn-ceaster *Cirencester*:—On Cyrnceastre *in Cirencester*, Chr. 1020; Th. 287, 12, col. 1. v. Ciren-ceaster.

cyrnel, cyrnl; *gen.* es; *dat.* cyrnele; *pl. nom. acc.* cyrnlu; *gen.* cyrnla; *n. m?* **I.** *a* KERNEL, *grain;* nucleus, granum:—Men geseóþ oft ðæt of ánum lytlum cyrnele cymþ micel treów; ac we ne mágon geseón on ðam cyrnele náðor ne wyrtruman, ne rinde, ne bogas, ne leáf; ac God forþtíhþ of ðam cyrnele treów, and wæstmas, and leáf *men often see that of one little kernel comes a great tree; but in the kernel we can see neither root, nor rind, nor boughs, nor leaves; but from the kernel God draws forth tree, and fruits, and leaves*, Homl. Th. i. 236, 16-20. Cyrnel *granum*, Ælfc. Gl. 46; Som. 65, 8; Wrt. Voc. 33, 7. Nim ðone cyrnel ðe byþ innan ðan persogge *take the kernel which is within the peach*, Lchdm. iii. 102, 6. Genim of pínhnyte xx geclǽnsodra cyrnela *take twenty* [*of*] *cleansed kernels of the nuts of the stone pine*, L. M. 2, 2; Lchdm. ii. 180, 19. Sele ða cyrnlu ðæs eorþifiges on hátum wætre drincan *give him the grains of the ground ivy in hot water to drink*, 2, 39; Lchdm. ii. 248, 26. **II.** *a hard* *concretion in the flesh, an indurated gland* or *strumous swelling;* toles, glandulæ duriores, quæ succrescunt in isto tumore, quem strumam dicimus:—Wið cyrnlu *for kernels* [or *swelled glands*], Herb. 14, 2; Lchdm. i. 106, 13, 19: Herb. cont. 4, 3; Lchdm. i. 8; 4, 3: 14, 2; Lchdm. i. 12; 14, 2: Herb. 4, 3; Lchdm. i. 90, 8: Med. ex Quadr. 3, 7; Lchdm. i. 340, 14. Lege ofer ða cyrnlu *lay it over the kernels* or *swelled glands,* Herb. 14, 2; Lchdm. i. 106, 19. Wið cyrnla sāre *for sore of kernels* or *swelled glands,* Med. ex Quadr. 6, 3; Lchdm. i. 352, 1. Lege to ðām cyrnlum [MS. -lun] *lay to the kernels* or *swelled glands,* Herb. 75, 5; Lchdm. i. 178, 13. [*Prompt.* kyrnel: *Plat.* karn: *Dut.* kern, *f*: *Kil.* kerne: *Ger.* kern, *m*: *M. H. Ger.* kërne, kërn, *m*: *O. H. Ger.* kerno, *m*: *Dan.* kjerne, *m. f*: *Swed.* kärna, *f*: *Icel.* kjarni, *m.*] DER. æppel-cyrnel.

cyrps; *adj. Curly;* crispus, tortus:—He is blæcfexede and cyrps *he is black-haired and curly,* Homl. Th. i. 456, 17. Cyrpsum loccum *with curly locks,* Mone B. 1236.

cyrpsian; *p.* ode; *pp.* od *To crisp, curl;* crispare, asperare:—Cyrpsiendum [MS. cyrpisiendum] *crispantibus,* Mone B. 1239. Cyrpsaþ [MS. cypsaþ] *asperat,* Glos. Prudent. Recd. 144, 61.

cyrr, cerr, cirr, cierr, es; *m. A turn, space of time, an occasion, affair;* versio, vices, temporis spatium, negotium:—Æt ðam feórþan cyrre [sǣle, *q. v.*] *at the fourth turn* or *time,* Herb. 100, 3; Lchdm. i. 214, 5, 6, 7, 8: Gen. 38, 18. Æt sumum cyrre *at some turn* or *time, when;* aliquando, Lk. Bos. 22, 32. Se biþ abīsgod, on færelde mid ōðrum cierrum *who is busied, in a journey with other affairs,* Past. 4, 1; Hat. 9 b, 7. [*Laym.* chærre, cherre: *Plat.* keer, kere, *f*: *Dut.* keer, *m*: *Ger.* kehr, kehre, *f*: *M. H. Ger.* kēre, *f.* kēr, *m*: *O. H. Ger.* kēra, *f.* kēr, *m.*] DER. ed-cyrr, frum-, ofer-, on-, sǣ-.

cyrran, ic cyrre, ðū cyrrest, he cyrreþ, *pl.* cyrraþ; *p.* cyrde, *pl.* cyrdon; *pp.* cyrred. I. *to turn;* vertere:—He clifu cyrreþ on wæteres wellan *he turneth rocks into wells of water,* Ps. Th. 113, 8. Gif ic mīne gewǣda on wīte-hrægl cyme cyrde *et posui vestimentum meum cilicium,* Ps. Th. 68, 11. Cyrred, *pp. turned,* Exon. 107 b; Th. 410, 25; Rä. 29, 4. II. *to be turned, to turn himself, to go, return;* verti, se vertĕre, ire, reverti:—Ðū wille cyrran *thou wilt be turned,* Cd. 91; Th. 115, 13. Nū cyrrest *now turnest thyself,* Elen. Kmbl. 1329; El. 666. Hī cyrraþ *they return,* Ps. Th. 69, 3. Cyrdon *returned,* Cd. 195; Th. 243, 8; Dan. 433. [*Laym.* charren: *Scot.* cair, kair *to drive backwards and forwards*: *Plat.* keren: *O. Sax.* kēran: *Frs.* keeren: *O. Frs.* kera: *Dut.* keeren: *Kil.* keren, kerien *verrere*: *Ger.* kehren *verrere, vertere*: *M. H. Ger.* kēren: *O. H. Ger.* kerjan *verrere, vertere*: *Dan.* kjöre: *Swed.* köra *to drive*: *Icel.* keyra *to whip, lash, drive.*] DER. a-cyrran, -cerran, be-, for-, ge-, mis-, ofer-, on-. ongeán-, to-, under-, ymb-.

cyrrednes, -ness, e; *f. A turning, conversion;* versio, conversio. v. a-cyrrednes, ge-.

cyrse, an; *f. Cress;* nasturtium, Lacn. 89; Lchdm. iii. 58, 22. v. cærse.

cyrs-treów, es; *n. A cherry-tree;* cerăsus = κεράσος, Ælfc. Gl. 46; Som. 64, 123; Wrt. Voc. 32, 57. v. ciris-beám.

CYRTEL, kyrtel; *gen.* cyrtles; *m. A* KIRTLE, *vest, garment, frock, coat;* palla, tunica:—Cyrtel *vel* oferbrǣdels *palla,* Ælfc. Gl. 4; Som. 55, 86; Wrt. Voc. 16, 56. Ic gean sancte Æðelþryþe ānes wullenan cyrtles [kyrtles MS.] *I give to saint Æthelthryth one woollen kirtle,* Cod. Dipl. 782; A. D. 1046; Kmbl. iv. 107, 7. Bicgaþ cyrtlas *buy kirtles,* Homl. Th. i. 64, 13. Ðam ðe wylle on dōme wið ðē flītan, and niman ðīne tunecan [cyrtel oððe hrægl, Mt. Kmbl. Lind.] lǣt him tō ðīnne wǣfels *ei qui vult tecum judicio contendere et tunicam tuam tollere, dimitte ei et pallium,* Mt. Bos. 5, 40; to hym that wole stryue with thee in dome, and take awey thi coote, leeue thou to hym and thin ouer clothe, Wyc. Næbbe ge ne twā tunecan [cyrtlas, Mt. Kmbl. Lind.] *nolite possidere neque duas tunicas,* 10, 10; nyl ȝe welden nether two cootis, Wyc: Lk. Lind. War. 3, 11. Berenne cyrtel [kyrtel MS.] *a bear-skin vest,* Ors. 1, 1; Bos. 20, 38. [*Prompt.* kyrtyl *tunica*: *Piers P.* kirtel: *R. Brun.* kirtelle: *Chauc.* kirtel: *Laym.* curtel: *Orm.* kirrtell: *Plat.* kiddel: *Dut.* kiel, *m*: *Kil.* kedel, kele: *Ger.* kittel, *m*: *M. H. Ger.* kitel, kittel, *m*: *Dan.* kjortel, *m. f*: *Swed.* kjortel, *m*: *Icel.* kyrtill, *m.*]

cyrten; *adj. Beautiful, elegant;* venustus:—Hlīsful and cyrten *famous and beautiful,* Homl. Th. ii. 220, 29. Ful cyrtenu ceorles dōhtor *a churl's very beautiful daughter,* Exon. 106 b; Th. 407, 16; Rä. 26, 6.

cyrten-lǣcan; *p.* -lǣhte; *pp.* -lǣht *To make lovely, to beautify;* venustare:—Ic cyrtenlǣce *venusto,* Ælfc. Gl. 99; Som. 76, 115; Wrt. Voc. 54, 57.

cyrten-līce; *adv. Notably, solemnly, cunningly;* notabiliter, solemniter, subtiliter, Scint. 38.

CȲSE, cēse, es; *m*: cȳsa, an; *m. A* CHEESE; caseus:—Cȳse *caseus,* Wrt. Voc. 82, 26: 290, 32. Niwe gāte cȳse *new goat's cheese,* Med. ex Quadr. 6, 5, 6, 7; Lchdm. i. 352, 5, 7, 9. Ferscne cȳse on lege *lay on fresh cheese,* L. M. 1, 39; Lchdm. ii. 102, 14: 1, 53; Lchdm. ii. 126, 1: Lchdm. iii. 96, 22. Nim cȳsan *take cheese,* 96, 21. Tyn cēsas [cȳsas B. H.] *ten cheeses,* L. In. 70; Th. i. 146, 19. [*Prompt.* chese: *Plat.* kese: *O. Sax.* kēsi, *m*: *Dut.* kaas, *f*: *Kil.* kaese, kese: *Frs.* tzys: *O. Frs.* kise, tzise, *m*: *Ger.* käse, *m*: *M. H. Ger.* kæse, *m*: *O. H. Ger.* kasi, *m*: *Lat.* caseus: *Wel.* caws, *m*: *Corn.* caus, cos, ces, *m*: *Ir.* cais: *Gael.* caise: *Manx* caashey, *m*: *Armor.* caouz.]

cȳse-fæt, es; *n. A cheese-vat;* vas pro caseo asservando, calăthus = κάλăθος, Cot. 53.

cȳse-hwæg, es; *n. Cheese-whey;* siringia:—Ða rinda wyl on cȳsehwæge *boil the rinds in cheese-whey,* L. M. 3, 39; Lchdm. ii. 332, 9.

cysel *gravel, sand;* glarea. v. ceosel.

cysel-stān *gravel,* Ælfc. Gl. 11; Som. 57, 46; Wrt. Voc. 19, 48. v. ceosel-stān.

cȳs-gerunn, es; *n?* [ge-runnen *coagulatus*] *Rennet* or *runnet, a substance used to produce curd;* lactis coagulum:—Butergeþweor ǣlc and cȳsgerunn losaþ eów *butyrum omne et caseus pereunt vobis,* Coll. Monast. Th. 28, 19.

cȳs-lyb, -lybb, es; *pl. nom. acc.* -lybbu; *n.* [cȳse *cheese,* lyb, lib *a drug*] *Cheese-drug, rennet* or *runnet;* casei coagulum:—Haran cȳslybb syle drincan ðam wīfe *give the woman a hare's runnet to drink,* Med. ex Quadr. 4, 14; Lchdm. i. 346, 4. Ða meolc geren mid cȳslybbe *turn the milk with rennet,* Lchdm. iii. 18, 11. Cȳslybbu *coagula,* Glos. Prudent. Recd. 141, 25.

cyspan; *p.* ede; *pp.* ed [cosp *a fetter*] *To bind, fetter;* compedĭbus constringĕre:—Sǣdon ðæt hió sceolde cyspan mænigne *they said that she would bind many,* Bt. Met. Fox 26, 154; Met. 26, 77.

cyssan; *p.* cyste; *pp.* cyssed; *v. a.* [cos *a kiss*] *To* KISS; osculari:—Ic cysse ðē *osculor te*: ic eom fram ðē cyssed *osculor a te,* Ælfc. Gr. 19; Som. 22, 51, 52. Ic cysse, ðū cyst, he cyst *osculor, oscularis, osculatur,* 25; Som. 26, 58, 59. Swā hwæne swā ic cysse, se hyt is *quemcumque osculatus fuero, ipse est,* Mt. Bos. 26, 48. Hwīlum mec on cōfan cysseþ *sometimes he kisses me in a chamber,* Exon. 125 a; Th. 480, 19; Rä. 64, 4. Mec weras cyssaþ *men kiss me,* 108 a; Th. 412, 27; Rä. 31, 6: 104 a; Th. 395, 6; Rä. 15, 3. Ic cyste *osculatus sum,* Ælfc. Gr. 25; Som. 26, 60. He hine cyste *he kissed him,* Homl. Th. ii. 422, 34: ii. 426, 12: Bd. 3, 6; S. 528, 23. He cyste hyne *osculatus est eum,* Mt. Bos. 26, 49: Gen. 48, 10. Ǽghwæðer ōðerne cyston hie *they kissed each other,* Andr. Kmbl. 2031; An. 1018. Ðæt he his mondryhten clyppe and cysse *that he embrace and kiss his lord,* Exon. 77 a; Th. 289, 2; Wand. 42. [*Prompt.* kissin: *Wyc.* kisse: *Piers P.* kissen: *R. Brun.* kisse: *Chauc.* kisse: *R. Glouc.* cussede, *p*: *Laym.* cusseþ: *O. Sax.* kussian: *O. Frs.* kessa: *Dut.* kussen: *Ger. M. H. Ger.* küssen: *O. H. Ger.* kussjan, kussan: *Goth.* kukyan: *Dan.* kysse: *Swed.* kyssa: *Icel.* kyssa: *Grk.* κυνεῖν, *inf. aor.* κύσαι *to kiss*: *Sansk.* kus *amplecti.*] DER. ge-cyssan.

CYST, cist, cest, e; *f. A* CHEST, *coffer, coffin, sheath, casket;* capsa, capsella, cista, cistella, loculus:—Hire cyste *cistam suam,* L. C. S. 77; Th. i. 418, 21. He ða cyste æt-hrān *tetigit loculum,* Lk. Bos. 7, 14. On cyste dyde *condidit in capsella,* Bd. 3, 11; S. 536, 9. Ðæt hī woldan his bān on niwe cyste gedōn *ut ossa illius in novo recondita loculo locarent,* 4, 30; S. 608, 30: 3, 6; S. 528, 29. Cist *cista,* Wrt. Voc. 288, 31. Cest *cistella,* Ælfc. Gl. 3; Som. 55, 64; Wrt. Voc. 16, 37. [*Chauc.* cheste: *Scot.* kist, kyst: *Dut.* kist, kast: *Kil.* kiste: *O. Frs.* kiste: *Ger. M. H. Ger.* kiste, *f*: *O. H. Ger.* kista, *f*: *Dan.* kiste, *m. f*: *Swed. Icel.* kista, *f*: *Lat.* cista: *Grk.* κίστη *a chest, box*: *Manx* kishtey, *m. a chest*: *Armor.* kest, *f. a basket.*] DER. bōc-cest.

cyst, cist, e; *f.* [ceósan *to choose*]. I. *choice, election;* optio, electio:—Ic ðē cyst abeád *I have offered thee a choice,* Cd. 91; Th. 115, 14; Gen. 1919. Ðonne beóþ gesomnad, on ða swīðran hond, ða clǣnan folc, Criste sylfum gecorene bi cystum *then shall be assembled, on the right hand, the pure people, chosen by election by Christ himself,* Exon. 25 b; Th. 75, 19; Cri. 1224: Ps. Th. 64, 4. II. *with gen. pl. What is chosen;* æstimatio:—Īrena cyst *what is chosen of swords,* Beo. Th. 1350; B. 673: 1609; B. 802: 3398; B. 1697. Wǣpna cyst *what is chosen of weapons,* 3123; B. 1559. Symbla cyst *what is chosen of feasts,* 2469; B. 1232. Him gewāt Abraham eástan eágum wlītan on landa [MS. lande] cyst *Abraham departed from the east to look with his eyes on what is chosen of lands* [*Canaan*], Cd. 86; Th. 107, 26; Gen. 1795. Wedera cyst *what is chosen of weathers,* 191; Th. 238, 6; Dan. 350. Sancta Hierusalem, cynestōla cyst *holy Jerusalem, what is chosen of royal thrones,* Exon. 8 b; Th. 4, 11; Cri. 51. Folgoþa cyst *what is chosen of services,* 13 b; Th. 24, 27; Cri. 391. Godwebba cyst, ðæs temples segl *what is chosen of textures, the veil of the temple,* 24 b; Th. 70, 8; Cri. 1135. Eardrīca cyst *what is chosen of habitations* [*the garden of Eden*], 45 a; Th. 153, 14; Gū. 825. Eardwīca cyst *what is chosen of dwellings,* 98 a; Th. 366, 21; Reb. 15. Ic swefna cyst secgan wylle *I will relate what is chosen of dreams,* Rood Kmbl. 1; Kr. 1. Burga cyst, Rōm *what is chosen of cities, Rome,* Bt. Met. Fox 1, 35; Met. 1, 18. III. *excellence, virtue, munificence, goodness;* præstantia, virtus, largitas, bonitas:—Þiónde on eallum cystum and cræftum *flourishing in all excellencies and virtues,* Bt. 38, 5; Fox 206, 23: Exon. 79 b; Th. 299, 22; Crä. 106. Hī hēton heom seggan ðæs landes cysta *they bade them be told of the excellencies of the land,* Chr. 449; Erl. 12, 6. Frōd fæder freóbearn lǣrde cystum eald *a wise father,* *old in excellencies, taught his dear son,* Exon. 80 a; Th. 300, 7; Fä. 2. Wēnaþ menn ðæt he hit dō for cystum [kystum MS.] *men think that he does it for virtue,* Past. 20, 1; Hat. MS. 29 a, 27. Ðæt ðū ðīne cysta cȳðe *that thou mayest shew thy virtues,* Prov. Kmbl. 46. Cystum gōd *good in virtues,* Chr. 1065; Erl. 199, 6; Edw. 23: Beo. Th. 1738; B. 867: 1850; B. 923. Seó gitsung gedēþ gitseras lāðe, and ða cysta gedōþ ða leóftǣle *covetousness makes misers loathsome, and munificence makes them estimable,* Bt. 13; Fox 38, 16. Hū me cynegōde cystum dohten *how the noble munificently treated me,* Exon. 85 b; Th. 322, 1; Wīd. 56. Þurh Godes micclan cyste *through the great goodness of God,* Homl. Th. ii. 468, 14. For his micclan ciste *of his great goodness,* Ælfc. T. 9, 1. [*Laym.* custe *manner, quality: O. Sax.* kust, *f. choice: Frs. O. Frs.* kest, *f. choice: Ger.* kurst = kur, *f. election: M. H. Ger.* kust, *f. manner of choosing: O. H. Ger.* kust, *f. æstimatio, electio, virtus: Goth.* ga-kusts, *f. what has been tried, a trial;* kustus, *m. examination: Icel.* kostr, *m. trial, choice.*] DER. gum-cyst, hilde-, un-.

cyst; *adj. Desirable;* desiderabilis:—Ne hī for āwyht eorþan cyste ða sēlestan geseón woldan *pro nihilo habuerunt terram desiderabilem,* Ps. Th. 105, 20.

cȳst *choosest, chooses; 2nd and 3rd pers. pres. of* ceósan.

cyst-beám, es; *m.* [beám *a tree*] *A chestnut-tree;* castănea = κάστανος:—Cystel *vel* cystbeám *castănea,* Ælfc. Gl. 46; Som. 65, 6; Wrt. Voc. 33, 5.

cystel, e; *f? A chestnut-tree,* Ælfc. Gl. 46; Som. 65, 6; Wrt. Voc. 33, 5. v. cyst-beám.

cyste-līce; *adv.* [cyst *munificence*] *Munificently;* largiter:—Sȳ wuldor and lof ðam wēlegan Drihtne, se ðe his gecorenan swā cystelīce wurþaþ *be glory and praise to the bounteous Lord, who so munificently honours his chosen,* Homl. Th. ii. 154, 2. Cystelīce *largiter,* Ælfc. Gr. 38; Som. 41, 42. Ic gife cystelīce *largior,* 31; Som. 35, 54. Cystelīce dǣlan *to distribute bountifully,* Homl. Th. ii. 228, 18.

cysten = cystan *to get, procure, get the value of;* acquirere, æquiparare facere:—Se man ðe hafde ān pūnd he ne mihte cystan [MS. cysten] ǣnne peni at ānne market *the man who had a pound could not get the value of a penny at a market,* Chr. 1125; Erl. 253, 28: 1124; Erl. 252, 39.

cystig; *adj. Munificent, benevolent, bountiful, liberal, generous, good;* munificus, largus, probus, bonus:—Cystig *largus,* Ælfc. Gr. 38; Som. 41, 41; Wrt. Voc. 76. 4. Ðæt he sié cystig *that he be benevolent,* Past. 20, 2; Cot. MS. Seó mōdor clǣngeorn biþ and cystig *the mother is pure and bountiful,* Exon. 128 a; Th. 492, 25; Rä. 81, 21. Cystig *largus* vel *dapsilis,* Ælfc. Gl. 82; Som. 73, 34; Wrt. Voc. 47, 38: *larga,* Glos. Prudent. Recd. 145, 51. Bióþ ðǣm to ungemetlīce cystige *they are immoderately generous to them,* Past. 44, 6. DER. un-cystig.

cystignes, cystines, -ness, -nyss, e; *f. Bountifulness, goodness, munificence;* liberalitas, largitas, munificentia:—Cystignesse, cystignysse *liberalitatis,* Mone B. 2511. Cystines *liberalitas,* 2494. We sceolon oferwinnan woruldlīce gytsunge mid cystignysse ūres clǣnan mōdes *we must overcome worldly covetousness by the bounty of our pure mind,* Homl. Th. ii. 222, 20.

cyst-leás; *adj. Fruitless, reprobate;* reprŏbus:—Him [God] ðā se cystleása [Cain] cwealmes wyrhta andswarode *then the reprobate [man] Cain, the worker of murder, answered God,* Cd. 48; Th. 61, 28; Gen. 1004.

cystlīc; *adj. Munificent;* munifĭcus, Som. Ben. Lye.

cystlīce; *adv. Munificently;* largiter, Ælfc. Gr. 38. v. cystelīce.

cȳs-wuce, an; *f.* [cȳse *cheese,* wuce *a week*] *Cheese-week, the last week of eating cheese before Lent;* septimana dominicæ quinquagesimæ. In the Greek church quinquagesima Sunday is the last day on which cheese may be eaten till Easter. The same rule prevailed in monasteries of the Benedictine order, which only were known in England before the Conquest. 'Abstinentiam ovorum et casei incipimus feria secunda post quinquagesimam:'—Ðis sceal on Wōdnes dæg, on ðære syxteóðan wucan ofer Pentecosten; and on Frīge dæg innan ðære cȳs-wucan *this [Gospel] must be on Wednesday, in the sixteenth week after Pentecost; and on Friday within the cheese-week,* Rubc. Mt. Bos. 5, 43, Notes, p. 575.

CȲTA, an; *m. A* KITE, *bittern;* milvus, būteo, Ælfc. Gl. 37; Som. 63, 9; Wrt. Voc. 29, 32: Glos. Brux. Recd. 37, 3; Wrt. Voc. 63, 17. [*Piers P.* kytte: *Chauc.* kyte: *Wel.* cud, *m.*]

cyte, cote, an; *f. A cot, cottage, bedchamber, cell;* casa, cubiculum, cella:—Tær ðæt hors ðæt þæc of ðære cytan hrōfe *the horse tore the thatch off the roof of the cottage,* Homl. Th. ii. 136, 17. Hī hine lǣddon ūt of ðære cytan *they led him out of the cottage,* Guthl. 5; Gdwin. 36, 8. Gecyrde he to sumes hyrdes cytan *he turned into a shepherd's cottage,* Homl. Th. ii. 136, 14. In ðæm he hæfde cirican and cytan *in hac habuit ecclesiam et cubiculum,* Bd. 3, 17; S. 543, 24; col. 2. Cyte *cella,* Wrt. Voc. 85, 75. Wæs sum munuc on nēhnesse his cytan eardiende *in vicinia cellæ illius habitabat quidam monachus,* Bd. 5, 12; S. 630, 42. Leóht of heofenum gefylde ða cytan *a light from heaven filled the cell,* Homl. Th. ii. 546, 34.

CYTEL, citel, cetel, es; *m. A kettle, brazen* or *copper pot, cauldron;* căcăbus = κάκκăβος, lĕbes = λέβης:—Hwer *vel* cytel *lebes:* cytel *cacăbus,* Ælfc. Gl. 26; Som. 60, 84, 85; Wrt. Voc. 25, 24, 25. Cytel *cacăbus,* Wrt. Voc. 82, 57. On niwum cytele *in a new kettle,* L. M. 1, 3; Lchdm. ii. 44, 2. On cyperenum citele *in a copper kettle,* 1, 15; Lchdm. ii. 56, 19. On micelne citel, on læssan citel *in a large kettle, in a smaller kettle,* 1, 38; Lchdm. ii. 98, 10, 12. Ceteles hrūm *kettle-soot,* 1, 72; Lchdm. ii. 148, 10. Genim tyn-āmberne cetel *take a kettle holding ten ambers,* L. M. 1, 36; Lchdm. ii. 86, 13. [*Prompt.* ketyl, chetyle: *Wyc.* ketels, cheteles, *pl: Plat.* ketel: *O. Sax.* ketil, *m: Dut.* ketel, *m: Frs.* tjettel: *O. Frs.* ketel, szetel, tsetel, *m: Ger.* kessel, *m: M. H. Ger.* kezzel, *m: O. H. Ger.* kezil, *m: Goth.* katils, *m: Dan.* kjedel, kedel, *m. f: Swed.* kittel, *m: Icel.* ketill, *m.*]

cytel-hrūm *kettle-soot.* v. cetel-hrūm.

cytere, an; *f. A harp;* cithăra = κιθάρα:—Arīs saltēre and cytere *exsurge, psaltērium et cithăra,* Ps. Spl. C. 56, 11.

CȲÞ, cȳþþ, e; *f.* I. *knowledge;* notitia, cognitio, scientia:—Cȳþþe *notitiæ,* Mone B. 4214. Of mīnre sylfre cȳþþe *from my own knowledge,* Bd. 5, 24; S. 647, 18. Ðe nāne cȳþþe to Gode næfdon *who have had no knowledge of God,* Homl. Th. i. 396, 28. Ðære godcundan cȳþþe *divinæ cognitionis,* Bd. 5, 22; S. 644, 13, 16. II. *relation, relationship,* KITH; familiaritas, munus:—Gif he to ðam cyninge furðor cȳþþe hæbbe *if he have further relation to the king,* L. C. S. 72; Th. i. 414, 17. III. *a known land, native country, region, place;* situs naturalis, natale solum, patria regio:—Ðis is mīn āgen cȳþ *this is my own country,* Bt. Met. Fox 24, 98; Met. 24, 49. On heora āgenre cȳþþe *in their own country,* Bt. 27, 4; Fox 100, 11. Eorlas on cȳþþe *men in the country,* Andr. Kmbl. 1467; An. 735. Cniht of cȳþþe *a boy from his country,* Cd. 134; Th. 169, 15; Gen. 2800. Ðū meaht to heora cȳþþe becuman *thou mayest come to their country,* Bt. Met. Fox 12, 47; Met. 12, 24. Gif ðū gewītest cȳþþe sēcean *if thou goest to seek thy country,* Salm. Kmbl. 408; Sal. 204. Cȳþ *region,* Bt. 33, 4; Fox 130, 14. Ðǣr ūre cȳþþ wæs *there was our place,* Ps. Th. 121, 2: 119, 5. [*Piers P.* kith, kyth *relationship: Laym.* cuððe, *f. country, race, kin: Orm.* cuþe *acquaintance: Plat.* kunde, kunne *knowledge: O. Frs.* kethe, kede *news: Dut.* kunde, *f. knowledge, kindred: Kil.* konde *notitia: Ger.* kunde, *f. knowledge, news: M. H. Ger.* künde, kunde, *f. knowledge, acquaintance, home: O. H. Ger.* kundi, *f.* in un-kundi *fraus: Goth.* kunþi, *n. knowledge: Dan.* kynde, *m. f: Swed.* kund, *m. a customer: Icel.* kynni, *n. acquaintance.*] DER. eald-cȳþ, -cȳþþ, feor-, ge-, on-.

cȳþ, es; *m.* I. *a sprout, germ;* germen:—Genim wegbrǣdan þrȳ cȳþas *take three sprouts of plantain,* Herb. 2, 14; Lchdm. i. 84, 14. II. *seed;* crementum:—Cȳþ *crementum,* Glos. Brux. Recd. 38, 7; Wrt. Voc. 64, 16. v. cīþ.

CȲÐAN; *p.* ic, he cȳðde, cȳdde, ðū cȳðdest, cȳddest; *pp.* cȳðed. I. *to make known, tell, relate, proclaim, announce;* nuntiare, annuntiare, narrare, referre, effari, prædicare:—Wordum cȳðan *to make known in words,* Cd. 102; Th. 135, 14; Gen. 2242: Exon. 12 a; Th. 19, 7; Cri. 297. Ongan Dryhtnes ǣ georne cȳðan *he began the Lord's law gladly to proclaim,* Elen. Kmbl. 398; El. 199: 2510; El. 1256. Cȳþ *narra,* Lk. Bos. 8, 39: Mt. Bos. 2, 8: Gen. 37, 14: Bd. 2, 9; S. 511, 32. Cȳðdon Cristes gebyrd *they announced Christ's birth,* Exon. 8 b; Th. 5, 5; Cri. 65: Ps. Th. 77, 7: 101, 16. Cȳðe his neáhgebūrum *let him tell to his neighbours,* L. Edg. S. 7; Th. i. 274, 20. II. *to declare, reveal, manifest, shew, perform, confess, confirm, testify, prove;* notum facere, revelare, manifestare, ostendere, perhibere, confiteri, testari, probare:—Ic him cȳðde ðīnne naman *notum feci eis nomen tuum,* Jn. Bos. 17, 26. Wīsdōm sceoldon weras Ebrēa wordum cȳðan [MS. cyddon] *the Hebrew men must reveal wisdom by words,* Cd. 176; Th. 221, 33; Dan. 97. Ellen cȳðan *to manifest valour,* Beo. Th. 5384; B. 2695. Wundor cȳðan *to perform a miracle,* Elen. Kmbl. 2222; El. 1112: Andr. Kmbl. 1142; An. 571. Ðe me cȳþ beforan mannum *qui confitebitur me coram hominibus,* Mt. Bos. 10, 32: Jn. Bos. 1, 20. Cȳdde, Bd. 4, 25; S. 600, 30. Ðū cȳddest *tu innotuisti,* Ps. Spl. 143, 4. He cȳþ *testatur,* Jn. Bos. 3, 32: 1, 15. Mid āþe cȳðan *to prove on oath,* L. C. S. 15; Th. i. 384, 10. Eallra heora dōme wæs cȳðed [MS. kyþed] *omnium judicio probatum est,* Bd. 5, 19; S. 640, 13. [*Piers P.* couthen: *Chauc.* kithe, kythe: *Laym.* cuðe, cuðen: *Orm.* kiþenn: *O. Sax.* kúðian, kundan: *O. Frs.* ketha, keda: *Ger. M. H. Ger.* künden: *O. H. Ger.* kundjan, kundan: *Goth.* kunþyan: *Dan.* kynde: *Swed.* kunna: *Icel.* kynna.] DER. a-cȳðan, for-, ge-, of-, ofer-.

cȳðere, es; *m.* I. *a witness;* testis:—Onarison on me cȳðeras unrihtwīse *insurrexerunt in me testes iniqui,* Ps. Spl. 26, 18. Cȳðras *testes,* 34, 13. Hwī gewilnige we gyt cȳðera *quid adhuc desideramus testes?* Mk. Bos. 14, 63. II. *a martyr, one who bears witness by his death;* martyr = μάρτυρ *a witness:*—Stephănus is se forma cȳðere *Stephen is the early martyr,* Homl. Th. ii. 34, 13. Þurh ðæs hālgan cȳðeres þingunge *through the pleading of the holy martyr,* 28, 33. Eallum cȳðerum *to all martyrs,* 34, 23.

-cȳðig *-known?* notus? *Only used in the compounds* on-cȳðig, un-, *q. v.* In German, however, kündig *known,* is used as a simple word, and as a compound.

cýð-lǽcan; *p.* -lǽhte; *pp.* -lǽht *To become known;* innotescere:—Cýðlǽce *innotescat,* Mone B. 4286.

cýð-líc, cýðe-líc; *adj. Manifest;* manifestus. v. ge-cýðelíc.

cýþling *a relation;* cognātus, Jn. Lind. War. 18, 26. v. cúða.

cýð-nes, -nys, -ness, -nyss, e; *f. A witness, testimony, testament;* testimonium, testamentum:—Sume sǽdon leáse cýðnesse agēn hine *quidam falsum testimonium ferebant adversus eum,* Mk. Bos. 14, 57. Cýðnys, 14, 59: Jn. Bos. 3, 32, 33: Bd. 2, 7; S. 509, 17. Cýðnys *testamentum,* Ps. Spl. 24, 15. DER. ge-cýðnes.

cýþþe; *gen. dat. acc. of* cýþ, Bt. 27, 3; Fox 100, 1, Cott. note 1.

cýððu, e; *f. A native country, home;* situs natalis:—Fugel his cýððu sēceþ *the bird seeks its home,* Exon. 59 b; Th. 217, 9; Ph. 277: Exon. 119 b; Th. 459, 9; Hy. 4, 114. v. cýþ.

cyt-wēr, es; *m.* [wēr *a weir*] *A weir with a kiddle* or *a cut for a fish trap;* kidellus, machina piscatoria in fluminibus ad salmones, aliosque pisces intercipiendos:—On Sæuerne xxx cytwēras *thirty 'cyt-wērs' on the Severn,* Cod. Dipl. Apndx. 461; A. D. 956; Kmbl. iii. 450, 13, 15, 20, 21, 23.

cýwst, he cýwþ *chewest, chews; 2nd and 3rd pers. pres. of* ceówan.

cýwung, cíwung, e; *f. A chewing;* ruminatio, Ælfc. Gl. 99; Som. 76, 121; Wrt. Voc. 54, 62. v. ceówung, ceówan.

D

D is sometimes changed into **ð**, as Ic wurde, *or* Ic wurðe: snídan, sníðan *to cut.* **2.** *d* and *t* are often interchanged, as mētte *met,* for mētde. **3.** nouns ending in *d* or *t* are generally feminine, as Gebyrd, e; *f. birth:* Miht, e; *f. might, power.* **4.** a word terminating with ed, d [*Icel.* at, t: *Ger.* et, t] indicates that a person or thing is furnished or provided with that which is expressed by the root, and is usually considered as a participle, although no verb may exist to which it can be assigned; such words have, therefore, generally ge prefixed to them; as gehyrned *horned;* gesceód *shod,* Rask's Gr. by Thorpe, § 326. **5.** the perfect participle ends in ed, od, but when the letters *t, p, c, h, x,* and *s,* after another consonant, go before the infinitive an, the vowel before the terminating *d* is not only rejected, but *d* is changed into *t;* as from dyppan *to dip* would be regularly formed dypped *dipped,* contracted into dyppd, dyppt, and dypt *dipped.* **6.** the Rune ᛞ not only represents the letter *d,* but stands for dæg *a day.* v. dæg **III.** and **RÚN.**

DÁ; *gen.* dān; *f.* [*that is* dae = dā; *gen. dat. acc.* daan = dān; *pl. nom. acc.* daan = dān; *gen.* daena = dāna; *dat.* daaum = dāum] *A* DOE; dama:—Dā *damma* vel *dammula,* Ælfc. Gl. 13; Wrt. Voc. 78, 28. [*Prompt.* doo *dama: Wyc.* doo: *Chauc.* does, *pl: Dan.* daa *a doe.*] v. buc, bucca; *m. a buck.*

daag *anything that is loose, dagling, dangling;* sparsum, Wrt. Voc. 288, 67. v. dāg.

DǢD; *gen. dat.* dǽde; *acc.* dǽde, dǽd; *pl. nom. acc.* dǽda, dǽde; *f. A* DEED, *action;* actio, actus, factum:—Dǽd *actio,* Ælfc. Gr. 9, 3; Som. 8, 38: *actus,* 11; Som. 15, 12. Be ðam ðe seó dǽd sý *according as the deed may be,* L. Eth. v. 31; Th. i. 312, 10: vi. 38; Th. i. 324, 23: L. C. E. 3; Th. i. 360, 13. Seó ārfæste dǽd *the goodly deed,* Bd. 3, 6; S. 528, 22: Cd. 28; Th. 37, 24; Gen. 594: 226; Th. 301, 4; Sat. 576: Bt. Met. Fox 9, 36; Met. 9, 18: Chr. 1036; Erl. 165, 11; Ælf. Tod. 6. Gesǽton land unspēdigran ðonne se frumstōl wæs, ðe hie, æfter dǽde, ofadrifen wurdon *they inhabited a land more barren than the first settlement was, which they, after their deed, were driven from,* Cd. 46; Th. 59, 15; Gen. 964. For ðære dǽde *for that deed,* 125; Th. 159, 23; Gen. 2639: 126; Th. 161, 24; Gen. 2670. Hió speón hine on ða dimman dǽd *she urged him to that dark deed,* 32; Th. 43, 3; Gen. 685. Sceolde he dǽd ongyldan *he must expiate the deed,* 15; Th. 19, 23; Gen. 295: 17; Th. 20, 15; Gen. 309: 25; Th. 32, 23; Gen. 507: Beo. Th. 5772; B. 2890: Elen. Kmbl. 772; El. 386. Ða aleegendlīcan word getācniaþ dǽde *the deponent verbs signify action,* Ælfc. Gr. 19; Som. 22, 56. Ic wraxlige *I wrestle;* luctor, hēr is dǽd *here is action,* 19; Som. 22, 57. Mid ðisre dǽde *with this deed,* Homl. Th. i. 218, 7: Exon. 103 b; Th. 393, 8; Rä. 12, 7. Ne sindon him dǽda dyrne *deeds are not dark to him,* 23 a; Th. 65, 5; Cri. 1050: 39 b; Th. 130, 12; Gū. 437. Ðæt his gōde dǽda swýðran wearþan ðonne misdǽda *that his good deeds be more prevailing than his misdeeds,* Chr. 959; Erl. 121, 5. Opene weorþaþ monna dǽde *men's deeds shall be open,* Exon. 23 a; Th. 64, 34; Cri. 1047. Ðū scealt þrōwian ðīnra dǽda gedwild *thou shalt expiate the error of thy deeds,* Cd. 43; Th. 57, 2; Gen. 922: 188; Th. 233, 27; Dan. 282: Bd. pref; S. 471, 13: Exon. 53 a; Th. 185, 16; Az. 8. Ðeáh ðe he dǽda gehwæs dyrstig wǽre *although he were daring in every deed,* Beo. Th. 5668; B. 2838: Elen. Kmbl. 2563; El. 1283. In his dǽdum *in his deeds,* Exon. 82 a; Th. 308, 17; Seef. 41: 76 a; Th. 284, 34; Jul. 707: Cd. 29; Th. 38, 6; Gen. 602: Chr. 755; Erl. 49, 21. Wile Dryhten sylf dǽda gehýran *the Lord himself will hear of the deeds,* Exon. 99 b; Th. 372, 14; Seel. 91: Beo. Th. 393; B. 195. Dǽda his hī ongeáton *facta ejus intellexerunt,* Ps. Spl. 63, 10. Ðæt we ǽfæstra dǽde dēmen *that we consider the deeds of the pious,* Exon. 40 a; Th. 133, 31; Gū. 498: 44 a; Th. 148, 13; Gū. 744: Ps. Th. 118, 17, 43. Gōdum dǽdum *by good deeds,* Cd. 74; Th. 91, 5; Gen. 1507: 91; Th. 116, 14; Gen. 1936: Exon. 53 a; Th. 185, 5; Az. 3: Ps. Th. 104, 7: 124, 1: 135, 3. [*Prompt.* dede *factum: Wyc.* dedis, *pl: R. Brun.* dedes, *pl: Chauc. R. Glouc.* dede: *Laym. Orm.* dede, *f: O. Sax.* dād, *f: Frs.* diede, dæd: *O. Frs.* dede, *f: Dut.* daad, *f: Kil.* dæd: *Ger.* that, *f: M. H. Ger.* tat, *f: O. H. Ger.* tāt, *f: Goth.* deds, *f: Dan.* daad, *m. f: Swed.* dåd, *f: Icel.* dáð, *f.*] DER. ǽr-dǽd, bealu-, deófol-, ellen-, fācen-, firen-, gleó-, gōd-, gu-, iu-, lof-, mægen-, mis-, oncýþ-, syn-, weá-, wel-, wom-, won-, yfel-.

dǽd-bana, an; *m.* [dǽd *a deed,* bana *a killer*] *An evil-doer, a perpetrator of murder;* homicida:—Gif man gehādodne mid fǽhþe belecge, and secge ðæt he wǽre dǽdbana *if any one charge one in holy orders with enmity, and say that he was a perpetrator of homicide,* L. Eth. ix. 23; Th. i. 344, 26.

dǽd-bēta, an; *m. A deed amender, penitent;* maleficii compensator:—Se dǽdbēta *the penitent,* L. M. I. P. 3; Th. ii. 266, 16.

dǽd-bētan; *part.* -ende; *p.* -bētte; *pp.* -bēted *To make amends, give satisfaction, to be penitent, to repent;* maleficium compensare, malum bono pensāre, pœnitere:—His sāwle wūnda dǽdbētende gelācnian *to heal the wounds of his soul by making amends,* Homl. Th. i. 124, 14. Dǽdbēte *shall make amends,* L. C. S. 41; Th. i. 400, 16: L. Eth. ix. 26; Th. i. 346, 6. Ðæt he sealde sōðe gebýsnunge eallum dǽdbētendum, ðe to Drihtene gecyrraþ *that he should give a true example to all, who shall turn to the Lord by doing amend deeds,* Ælfc. T. 38, 4.

dǽd-bōt, e; *f. An amends-deed, repentance, penitence;* pœnitentia, maleficii compensatio:—Behreówsung oððe dǽdbōt *pœnitentia,* Ælfc. Gr. 33; Som. 37, 22. Deóplīc dǽdbōt biþ, ðæt lǽwede man swā æscære beó, ðæt īren ne cume on hǽre, ne on nægle *it is a deep penitence, that a layman be so untrimmed, that scissors* [*iron*] *come not on hair, nor on nail,* L. Pen. 10; Th. ii. 280, 17: 3; Th. ii. 278, 8. Eornostlīce dōþ mēdemne weastm ðære dǽdbōte *facite ergo fructum dignum pœnitentiæ,* Mt. Bos. 3, 8: Lk. Bos. 3, 3, 8. Būton hý to rihtre dǽdbōte gecyrran *unless they turn to right repentance,* L. Edm. E. 6; Th. i. 246, 16: Chr. 963; Erl. 123, 15, 21. Dōþ dǽdbōte: sōþlīce genēalǽceþ heofona rīce *pœnitentiam agite: appropinquavit enim regnum cœlorum,* Mt. Bos. 3, 2: L. M. I. P. 1; Th. ii. 266, 5. Þurh dǽdbōte *through penance,* L. Pen. 4; Th. ii. 278, 19: L. Edm. E. 3; Th. i. 246, 3. Dǽdbōta sind gedihte on mislīce wīsan *penances are devised in various ways,* L. Pen. 13; Th. ii. 282, 3.

dǽd-bōtnys, -nyss, e; *f. Penitence;* pœnitentia, Scint. 9.

dǽd-cēne; *adj. Deed-bold;* agendo fortis, audax:—Com ingān ealdor þegna, dǽdcēne mon *the prince of thanes, the deed-bold man, came entering,* Beo. Th. 3294; B. 1645.

dǽd-from; *adj. Deed-strong;* agendo strenuus:—Hī beóþ ðý dǽdfromran *they are so much the more energetic,* Ps. Th. 109, 8.

dǽd-fruma, an; *m.* [dǽd *a deed,* fruma **II.** *an author, inventor*] *A deed-doer, perpetrator, labourer;* facinoris *vel* facinorum auctor, actor:—Eádmund cyning, dýre dǽdfruma *king Edmund, the dear deed-doer,* Chr. 942; Erl. 116, 9; Edm. 3: Andr. Kmbl. 149; An. 75. Grendel, diór dǽdfruma *Grendel, the dire perpetrator,* Beo. Th. 4186; B. 2090. Cain and Abel, ða dǽdfruman, dugeþa strýndon, wēlan and wiste *Cain and Abel, the original labourers, acquired goods, wealth and food,* Cd. 46; Th. 59, 27; Gen. 970.

dǽd-hata, an; *m.* [hatian *to hate*] *A deed-hater;* facinorum osor:—Deógol dǽdhata *a secret deed-hater,* Beo. Th. 555; B. 275.

dǽd-hwæt, *pl.* -hwate, -hwatan; *adj. Deed quick* or *active, strenuous, bold;* promptus et expeditus ad agendum, acer, strenuus:—Hæleþ dǽdhwate *men prompt of deed,* Exon. 65 b; Th. 242, 26; Jul. 2. Ge wǽron dǽdhwæte *ye were bold of deeds,* Elen. Kmbl. 584; El. 292: Exon. 13 a; Th. 24, 15; Cri. 385. Ða dǽdhwatan geond ðone ofen eódon *the bold of deed went through the oven,* Cd. 191; Th. 238, 12; Dan. 353.

dǽd-leán, es; *n. A deed-loan* or *reward, a recompence;* factorum præmium:—Him eallum wile mihtig Drihten dǽdleán gyfan *the mighty Lord will give them all a recompence,* Cd. 156; Th. 194. 20; Exod. 263.

dǽd-líc; *adj. Deedlike, active;* activus:—Twegen dǽlnimende cumaþ of ðam dǽdlīcum worde *duo participia veniunt a verbo activo,* Ælfc. Gr. 24; Som. 25, 30. Dǽdlīce word *activa verba,* Ælfc. Gr. 19; Som. 22, 28. Ðās and ðylīce synd *activa,* ðæt synd dǽdlīce gehātene, forðanðe hī geswuteliaþ dǽda *these and the like are* activa, *which are called active, because they declare actions,* 19; Som. 22, 30, 37.

dǽdon, dǽdun *did, made:*—Ðæt hie to mete dǽdon *that they made for food,* Cd. 33; Th. 45, 6; Gen. 722; *p. pl. of* dōn.

dǽd-róf; *adj. Deed-famed, illustrious, valiant;* agendo celeber *vel* strenuus:—Abraham andswarode, dǽdrōf, Drihtne sīnum *Abram the deed-famed answered his Lord,* Cd. 99; Th. 131, 8; Gen. 2173: 121; Th. 156, 16; Gen. 2589.

dǽd-scûa, an; *m.* [scûa *a shade*] *One who acts in the dark;* in tenebris agens, diabolus:—Deorc dǽd-scûa *a dark deed actor* [*the devil*], Exon. 11 b; Th. 16, 22; Cri. 257. v. deáþ-scûa.

dǽd-weorc, es; *n. A work of works, great work;* facinus egregium:—Hereþreátas for ðam dǽdweorce Drihten hêredon *the army-bands praised the Lord for that great work*, Cd. 170; Th. 214, 26; Exod. 575.

dæftan; *p.* dæfte; *pp.* dæft *To make convenient* or *ready, put in order;* apparare, sternere:—Ðæt he sceolde gearcian and dæftan his weg [MS. weig] *that he might prepare and make ready his way*, Homl. Th. i. 362, 8. Menn dæftaþ heora hûs *men put their houses in order*, ii. 316, 7. Dæfte *straverat*, Glos. Prudent. Recd. 149, 73. DER. ge-dæftan.

dæft-lîce; *adv.* DEFTLY, *aptly, fitly;* commode, opportune. DER. ge-dæftlîce, unge-.

DÆG; *gen.* dæges; *pl. nom. acc.* dagas; *m:* daga, an; *m.* I. *a* DAY; dies:—Se dæg segþ ðam ôðrum dæge Godes wundru *one day to another tells of God's wonders*, Ps. Th. 18, 2. God hêt ðæt leóht, dæg *God called the light, day*, Gen. 1, 5. Se þridda dæg *the third day*, Gen. 1, 13. Emnihtes dæg *the day of equinox;* æquinoctium, Menol. Fox 347; Men. 175. Wintres dæg *the winter's day* or *beginning of winter*, Menol. Fox 401; Men. 202. II. *the time of a man's life;* tempus vitæ humanæ:—On midle mînra dagena *in the midst of my days*, Ps. Th. 101, 21. Heora dagena tîd *dies eorum*, 77, 32. On þreóra monna dæg *in three men's days* or *lives*, Bd. App. S. 771, 45. III. *the Anglo-Saxon Rune* ᛞ = the letter *d*, the name of which letter in Anglo-Saxon is dæg *a day;* hence this Rune not only stands for the letter *d*, but for dæg *a day*, as,—ᛞ byþ Drihtnes sond, deóre mannum *day is the Lord's messenger, dear to men*, Hick. Thes. vol. i. p. 135; Runic pm. 24; Kmbl. 344, 9. IV. *the daily service of the early English church is recorded, referring to the example of the Psalmist*, thus,—Dauid cwæþ seofon sîðon on dæg ic sang ðê, Drihten, to lofe,—Ðæt is Ǽrst on ǽrne morgen;—Eft on undern-tîde; and 3 on midne dæg,—and 4 on nôn,—and 5 on ǽfen,—and 6 on fôran niht,—and 7 on ûhtan tîman *David said,—seven times in a day, O Lord, I sang to thee in praise, that is,—First, in early morning* [*at break of day*];—*Next at nine o'clock;—and 3ly at midday;—and 4ly at the nones*, 3 *o'clock;—and 5ly at even, at* 6 *o'clock, the* 12*th or an even or equal part of the* 24 *hours from* 6 *a.m. to* 12 *p.m;—and 6ly at the fore night* [*at* 9 *o'clock*];—*and 7ly at midnight, that is from* 12 *o'clock at night, to* 3 *or later in the morning* ǽr dægrêde *before dawn*, Canon. Hrs. 361, 7-362, 6: Ælfc. Gl. 95; Som. 75, 126-76, 1; Wrt. Voc. 53, 7-15. v. tîd-sang. ¶ On dæg *in the day, by day.* To dæg *to-day.* Dæg ǽr *the day before.* On ǽrran dæg *on a former day.* Ôðre dæg *another day.* [*Laym.* dæi, dai: *Orm* da33: *Plat.* dag: *O. Sax* dag, *m: Frs.* dey: *O. Frs.* di, dei, dach, *m: Dut.* dag, *m: Ger.* tag: *M. H. Ger. O. H. Ger.* tac, tag, *m: Goth.* dags, *m: Swed. Dan.* dag, *m: Icel.* dagr, *m: Lat.* dies: *Sansk.* div, dyaus, *m. f. day.*] DER. ǽr-dæg, blǽd-, deáþ-, dôm-, eald-, ealdor-, earfoþ-, ende-, feorh-, freóls-, fyrn-, gang-, geár-, gebêd-, gebyrd-, gefeoht-, geheald-, geld-, gemynd-, geswinc-, gewin-, gyrstan-, lǽn-, lîf-, mǽl-, mid-, ræst-, sîþ-, swylt-, symbel-, tîd-, weder-, weorc-, wic-, wil-, win-, winter-, wyn-: heó-dæg: ân-dæge: daga, ân-daga.

dæg-candel, -condel, -candell, e; *f. Day-candle, the sun;* diei candela, sol:—Dægcondel, Exon. 130 b; Th. 499, 34; Rä. 88, 26. Dryhten forlêt dægcandelle scînan *the Lord permitted the sun* [*the day-candle*] *to shine*, Andr. Kmbl. 1670; An. 837. DER. candel.

dæges; *adv.* [*from gen. of* dæg] *Daily;* die:—Dæges and nihtes *die ac nocte*, Ps. Th. 1, 2: Bt. 35, 6; Fox 168, 7: Chr. 894; Erl. 93, 5. DER. ig-dæges, y-dæges.

dæges eáge, êge, an; *n.* [dæges, *gen. of* dæg *a day;* eáge, êge *an eye: a day's eye*] *A* DAISY; bellis perennis, Lin:—Dæges eáge *consolida*, Wrt. Voc. 79, 14. Dæges êge *consolida*, Ælfc. Gl. 42; Som. 64, 26; Wrt. Voc. 31, 36: Lchdm. iii. 292, 8.

dæg-fæsten, es; *n.* [fæsten *a fast*] *A day's fast;* diei jejunium:—Is se ǽresta lǽcedôm dægfæsten, ðæt mon mid ðý ða wambe clǽnsige, ðæt hió ðý ðe leóhtre sié *the first remedy is a day's fast, that, with that, a man may cleanse the stomach, that it may be the lighter*, L. M. 2, 25; Lchdm. ii. 216, 25.

dæg-feorm, e; *f.* [feorm *food, sustenance*] *Food for a day;* unius diei victus:—Âne dægfeorme *a day's sustenance*, Cod. Dipl. 477; A. D. 958; Kmbl. ii. 355, 5.

dæg-hluttre; *adv.* [hluttre *brightly, clearly*] *Brightly as day;* clare instar diei:—Dýre Dryhtnes þegn dæghluttre scân *the Lord's dear minister shone brightly as day*, Exon. 42 b; Th. 143, 23; Gû. 665.

dæg-hwam; *adv. Daily;* quotidie:—Nim cneówholen dæghwam *take knee holly daily*, L. M. 1, 39; Lchdm. ii. 102, 10. Lufiaþ ða ðe dæghwam Dryhtne þeówiaþ *they love those who daily serve the Lord*, Exon. 33 b; Th. 106, 34; Gû. 51: 38 a; Th. 125, 20; Gû. 357.

dæg-hwamlîc, -hwomlîc; *def.* se -lîca, seó, ðæt -lîce; *adj. Daily;* diurnus, quotidianus:—Hit ealle beorhtnysse dæghwamlîces leóhtes oferswýðde *it overshone all the brightness of the daily light*, Bd. 4, 7; S. 575, 20. Syle us to-dæg ûrne dæghwamlîcan hlâf *panem nostrum quotidianum da nobis hodie*, Lk. Bos. 11, 3: Mt. Bos. 6, 11: Homl. Th. i. 264, 31. Betwyh gehald regollîces þeódscipes and ða dæghwamlîcan gýmenne to singanne on cyricean, me symble swête and wynsum wæs ðæt ic oððe leornode, oððe lǽrde, oððe wrîte *inter observantiam disciplinæ regularis et quotidianam cantandi in ecclesia curam, semper aut dicĕre, aut docēre, aut scribĕre dulce habui*, Bd. 5, 23; S. 647, 26 28. To dæghwomlîcum bigleófan *for their daily subsistence*, Homl. Th. ii. 118, 30.

dæg-hwamlîce; *adv. Daily;* quotidie:—Ic dæghwamlîce mid eów wæs *quotidie eram apud vos*, Mk. Bos. 14, 49. Se brôðor dæghwamlîce wæs wyrse and wyrse *the brother was daily worse and worse*, Bd. 4, 32; S. 611, 24.

dæg-hwîl, e; *f.* [dæg *day*, hwîl *time*] *Day-time, time of life;* diei hora *vel* tempus:—Ðæt he dæghwîla gedrogen hæfde, eorþan wynne *that he had finished his days, his joy of earth*, Beo. Th. 5445; B. 2726.

dæg-hwomlîc *daily*, Homl. Th. ii. 118, 30. v. dæg-hwamlîc.

dægian *to dawn, become day*, Som. Ben. Lye. v. dagian.

dǽglan *secret, hidden, unknown*, Bt. 25; Fox 88, 26; *acc. pl. def. of* dǽgol = dîgol.

dæg-lang, -long; *adj. Lasting a day:*—Dæglongne fyrst *per totam diem*, Salm. Kmbl. 1000; Sal. 501.

dæg-langes; *adv. During one day, for a day;* per unam diem:—Beó ðê stille dæglanges ðînre fyrdinge *be still for a day from thy march*, Homl. Th. ii. 482, 29. v. dæg-lang.

dæg-lîc; *adj. Daily;* quotidianus:—Twâ dæglîc fæsten oððe þreó dæglîc is genôh to healdenne *biduanum vel triduanum sat est observare jejunium*, Bd. 4, 25; S. 600, 8.

dæg-mǽl, es; *n.* [mǽl *a mark*] *A day-mark, an instrument for telling the hour, a dial, clock;* horologium = ὡρολόγιον = ὥρα *an hour;* λόγιον *a telling, an announcement*, Ælfc. Gl. 30; Som. 61, 58; Wrt. Voc. 26, 57.

dæg-mǽls-pîlu [*for* dæg-mǽles pîl], e; *f. The style of a dial;* horologii gnomon, Ælfc. Gl. 30; Som. 61, 59.

dæg-mêl-sceáwere, es; *m. Who* or *what shews the time of day;* horoscopus, Ælfc. Gl. 112; Som. 79, 103: 4; Som. 56. 2.

dæg-mete, es; *m.* [dæg *a day*, mete *meat, food*] *Daily food;* quotidianus cibus:—Dæg-mete *agapis*, Cot. 15, Som. Ben. Lye.

dæg-rêd, -rǽd, es; *n. Dawn, daybreak, early morning;* dilūcŭlum, matutīnum, aurōra:—Dægrêd *dilūcŭlum*, Ælfc. Gl. 95; Som. 75, 127; Wrt. Voc. 53, 8. Syxta is *matutīnum* vel *aurōra* ðæt is dægrêd [-ræd MS. R.] *the sixth is* matutīnum *vel* aurōra *that is dawn*, Bd. de nat. rerum; Wrt. popl. science 6, 18; Lchdm. iii. 244, 5. Ðis wæs eall geworden ǽr dægrêde *this was all performed ere daybreak*, Cd. 223; Th. 294, 4; Sat. 466: Homl. Th. i. 508, 32: 592, 22. Betweox ðam dægrêde [-rǽde MS. R.] and sunnan upgange *between dawn and sunrise*, Bd. de nat. rerum; Wrt. popl. science 6, 19; Lchdm. iii. 244, 6. Cwom Maria on dægrêd *Mary came at dawn*, Exon. 119 b; Th. 459, 34; Hö. 9: 57 a; Th. 204, 15; Ph. 98: Cd. 222; Th. 289, 27; Sat. 404: Salm. Kmbl. 429; Sal. 215. Se Hǽlend com on dægrêd to ðam temple *Iesus dilūcŭlo venit in templum*, Jn. Bos. 8, 2: Lk. Bos. 24, 1: Ex. 8, 20. To ǽfenne þurhwunaþ wôp and on dægrêd blisse *ad vespĕrum demorābĭtur fletus et ad matutīnum lætĭtia*, Ps. Lamb. 29, 6: Gen. 32, 22. Ðæt leóht, ðe we hâtaþ dægrêd, cymþ of ðære sunnan *the light, which we call dawn, cometh from the sun*, Bd. de nat. rerum; Wrt. popl. science 2, 29; Lchdm. iii. 234, 29. Ic-gâ ût on dægrǽd *exeo dilūcŭlo*, Coll. Monast. Th. 19, 13: Ælfc. T. 24, 11.

dægrêd-lîc; *adj. Of* or *belonging to the morning, early;* matutinus, matutinalis:—Fram heordnesse dægrêdlîce *a custodia matutina*, Ps. Lamb. 129, 6. We sungon dægrêdlîce lofsangas *cantavimus matutinales laudes*, Coll. Monast. Th. 33, 27.

dægrêd-sang, es; *m. Morning song;* matutīna cantio, C. R. Ben. 20.

dægrêd-wôma, an; *m.* [dægrêd *daybreak, dawn*, wôma *a noise, rushing*] *Rush* or *noise of dawn;* auroræ strepitus:—Ôþ-ðæt eástan cwom ofer deóp gelâd dægrêdwôma, wedertâcen wearm *until there came from the east over the deep way the rush of dawn, a warm weather-token*, Exon. 51 b; Th. 179, 24; Gû. 1266: Andr. Kmbl. 249; An. 125.

dæg-rîm, es; *n.* [dæg *day*, rîm *a number*] *A number of days, a course of days;* dierum numerus:—Wiste ðe geornor ðæt his aldres wæs ende gegongen, dôgora dægrîm *he knew the better that his life's end was passed, his days' number*, Beo. Th. 1650; B. 823. Upon ðæt îgland ðǽr Apollines dôhtor wunode dægrîmes worn *upon the island where Apollo's daughter dwelt a number of days*, Bt. Met. Fox 26, 66; Met. 26, 33: Cd. 47; Th. 60, 1; Gen. 975: 67; Th. 80, 20; Gen. 1331. On his dægrîme *in his number of days*, Exon. 83 b; Th. 314, 10; Môd. 12. Dægrîme frôd *wise in number of days*, 130 a; Th. 498, 15; Rä. 88, 2: Cd. 99; Th. 131, 9; Gen. 2173.

dæg-rima, an; *m.* [dæg *day*, rima *a rim, edge*] *Daybreak, morning;* aurora:—Hwæt is ðeós ðe astîhþ swilce arîsende dægrima *what is this which ascends like the rising morn?* Homl. Th. i. 442, 33. Dægrima *aurora*, Ælfc. Gl. 95; Som. 75, 128; Wrt. Voc. 53, 9: Hymn. Surt. 8, 21.

Dægsan stân, Degsa-stân, Dæg-stân, es; *m.* [*Flor. Hunt.* Degsastan: *the stone of Degsa*] DAWSTON or *Dalston, Cumberland;* loci nomen in agro Cumbriæ:—Hēr Ǽgþan Scotta cyng feaht wið Dælreoda, and wið Æðelferþe, Norþhymbra cynge, æt Dægstāne [Dægsan stāne, Th. 37, 26], and man ofslōh mǣst ealne his here *in this year* [A.D. 603] *Ægthan king of the Scots fought against the Dalreods, and against Æthelfrith, king of the Northumbrians, at Dawston, and almost all his army was slain*, Chr. 603; Th. 36, 24-29, col. 1. Wæs ðis gefeoht geworden on ðære mǣran stōwe ðe cweden is Degsastān *this battle was fought in the famous place which is called Dawston*, Bd. 1, 34; S. 499, 32.

dæg-sceald, es; *m.* [dæg *day*, sceald = scild, scyld *a shield*] *A day shield* or *screen;* diei velamen:—Dægscealdes hleó wand oter wolcnum *the day shield's shade* [i.e. *the pillar of cloud*] *rolled over the clouds*, Cd. 146; Th. 182, 22; Exod. 79.

dæg-steorra, an; *m.* [dæg *a day*, steorra *a star*] *The day star;* lucifer, aurora:—Seó sunne and se mōna, and ǣfensteorra and dægsteorra, and ōðre þrȳ steorran, ne synd nā fæste on ðam firmamentum *the sun and the moon, and the evening star and the day star, and three other stars, are not fast in the firmament*, Bd. de nat. rerum; Wrt. popl. science 15, 28; Lchdm. iii. 270, 3: Ælfc. T. 24, 11. Upasprungen scīnþ dægsteorra *ortus refulget lucifer*, Hymn. Surt. 27, 23. Nū gǣþ dægsteorra up *jam ascendit aurora*, Gen. 32, 26. Ǽr dægsteorran ic cende ðē *ante luciferum genui te*, Ps. Spl. 109, 4.

dæg-ðerlīc [= dæg-hwæðer-līc]; *adj. Daily, present;* diurnus, hodiernus:—Ðis dægðerlīce gōdspel sprecþ ymbe ðæra Iudēiscra þwyrnysse *this daily gospel speaks of the perversity of the Jews*, Homl. Th. ii. 224, 29. On ðisre dægðerlīcan rǣdinge *in this daily lecture*, i. 194, 24. Se gōdspellere Lucas beleác ðis dægðerlīce gōdspel mid feáwum wordum *the evangelist Luke concluded the gospel of this day with few words*, i. 90, 8. Ðās dægðerlīcan þēnunga *these daily services*, ii. 86, 24. Hī þeónde þurhwunodon ōþ ðisum dægðerlīcum dæge *they have continued prospering to this present day*, ii. 132, 14: i. 28, 28: 32, 8.

dæg-þern, e; *f. A day's space;* diei spatium:—Lǣt simle dægþerne betweonum *leave always a day's space between*, L. M. 2, 39; Lchdm. ii. 248, 20: 2, 51; Lchdm. ii. 268, 1.

dæg-tīd, e; *f.* [dæg *day*, tīd *time*] *Day-time, time;* diei tempus:—On ðære dægtīde *at that time*, Cd. 80; Th. 100, 4; Gen. 1659. On dægtīdum *in the day-time*, Exon. 105 a; Th. 398, 26; Rä. 18, 3: 126 a; Th. 484, 23; Rä. 71, 6.

dæg-tīma, an; *m.* [tīma *time*] DAY-TIME, *day;* diurnum tempus, dies:—Þurh dægtīman oððe geond dæg sunne ne forswǣle ðē ne mōna *per diem sol non uret te, neque luna*, Ps. Lamb. 120, 6.

dæg-wæccan; *pl. f.* [wæcce *a watching*] *Day-watchings;* excubiæ, Ælfc. Gl. 7; Som. 56, 68; Wrt. Voc. 18, 20.

dæg-weard, es; *m.* [weard *a watchman*] *A day-watchman;* excubitor, vigil, Ælfc. Gl. 7; Som. 56, 69; Wrt. Voc. 18, 21.

dæg-weorc, es; *n.* [weorc *work*] *A day's work;* diei opus:—Him mihtig God ðæs dægweorces deóp leán forgeald *the mighty God recompensed to him a high reward for that day's work*, Cd. 158; Th. 197, 30; Exod. 315: 167; Th. 209, 28; Exod. 506: Byrht. Th. 136, 8; By. 148. Æt ðam dæg-weorce *at that day's work*, Elen. Kmbl. 291; El. 146. Ðætte he ðæt dægweorc dreóre gebohte *that he bought that day's work with blood*, Cd. 149; Th. 187, 14; Exod. 151: 169; Th. 210, 21; Exod. 518.

dæg-weorþung, e; *f.* [weorþung *an honouring, celebration*] *A commemoration* or *celebration of a feast-day;* diei festi celebratio:—Ðe on gemynd nime ðære deórestan dægweorþunga rōde under rōderum *who may bear in remembrance the honouring of the day of the most precious cross under the firmament* [i.e. *the feast of the Invention of the Cross*], Elen. Kmbl. 2466; El. 1234.

dæg-wine, es; *n?* *A day's pay;* diarium:—Dægwine *diarium*, Ælfc. Gl. 33; Som. 62, 32; Wrt. Voc. 28, 15. Dægwine *pensum* vel *diarium*, 64; Som. 69, 9; Wrt. Voc. 40, 43. v. wine.

dæg-wist, e; *f.* [wist *food*] *A day's food;* diei victus:—Ðæt he him dægwistes tiðode *that he would give him a day's food*, Homl. Th. ii. 134, 30.

dæg-wōma, an; *m.* [wōma *a noise*] *The rush of day, the dawn;* diei apparitio, aurora:—Dægwōma becwom, morgen mǣretorht *the dawn came, the beautiful morning*, Cd. 160; Th. 199, 26; Exod. 344. Dægwōman bitweon and ðære deorcan niht *between dawn and the dark night*, Exon. 50 b; Th. 175, 7; Gū. 1191.

DÆL; *gen.* dæles; *dat.* dæle; *pl. nom. acc.* dalu, dalo; *n. A* DALE, *den, gulf;* vallis, barathrum:—Ðæs dæles se dǣl *the part of the dale*, Ors 1, 3; Bos. 27, 29. In deóp dalu *into the deep dales*, Exon. 130 a; Th. 498, 21; Rä. 88, 5: 56 a; Th. 199, 11; Ph. 24. We synd aworpene on ðās deópan dalo *we are cast into these deep dens* [*hell*], Cd. 22; Th. 27, 21; Gen. 421. On ðæt deópe dæl deófol gefeallaþ *devils shall fall into the deep gulf*, Exon. 30 b; Th. 93, 26; Cri. 1532. [*Prompt.* dale *vallis: Piers P. Chauc. Laym. Orm.* dale: *Plat.* daal: *O. Sax.* dal, *n: Frs.* dalle, dol: *O. Frs.* del, deil: *Dut.* dal, *n: Ger.* thal, *n: M. H. Ger. O. H. Ger.* tal, *n: Goth.* dal, *n: Dan.* dal, *m. f: Swed.* dal, *m: Icel.* dalr, *m: Wel.* dôl: *Corn.* dol, *f: Ir. Gael.* dail: *Manx* dayll, *f.*] DER. of-dæl.

DǢL, es; *m.* I. *a part, portion,* DEAL; pars, portio:—Ðæs dæles se dǣl *the part of the dale*, Ors. 1, 3; Bos. 27, 29. Ðū offrast teóðan dǣl smedeman *thou shalt offer a tenth deal of flour;* offeres decimam partem similæ, Ex. 29, 36, 40. Hī heora gōd on swā manige dǣlas todǣlaþ *they divide their goods into so many parts*, Bt. 33, 2; Fox 122, 26. Micel dǣl bewylledes wæteres on huniges gōdum dǣle *a great deal of boiled water in a good deal of honey*, L. M. 2, 20; Lchdm. ii. 202, 27. Gōdne dǣl *a good deal*, L. M. 2, 55; Lchdm. ii. 276, 6. Ðæs īglandes mycelne dǣl *a great deal of the island*, Chr. 189; Ing. 9, 11. Fæder, syle me mīnne dǣl mīnre ǣhte, ðe me to gebȳreþ, Lk. Bos. 15, 12; *fadir, gyue to me the porcioun of substaunce, that byfallith to me*, Wyc. Be dǣle *in part, partly*, Chr. 1048; Erl. 178, 5. Sume dǣle *in some part, partly*, Cot. 154. II. *a part of speech in grammar;* pars orationis:—Eahta dǣlas sind *partes orationis sunt octo*, Ælfc. Gr. 5; Som. 3, 22. Interjectio is betwyxaworpennyss. Se dǣl līþ betwux ōðrum wordum, and geswutelaþ ðæs mōdes styrunge *an interjection is a throwing between. This part of speech lieth between other words, and denotes a stirring of the mind*, 5; Som. 3, 55. III. *a part of a sentence, a word;* verbum:—We todǣlaþ ða bōc to cwydum, and siððan ða cwydas to dǣlum, eft ða dǣlas to stæfgefēgum *we divide the book into sentences, and then the sentences into words* [*parts*], *again the words into syllables*, Ælfc. Gr. 2; Som. 2, 37-39. [*Prompt.* dele: *Wyc.* deel: *Piers P.* del, deel: *Chauc.* del, delle: *Laym.* dæle, dal, del: *Orm.* dæl, dale, del: *Scot.* dail: *Plat.* deel: *O. Sax.* dēl, deil, *m: Frs.* deel: *O. Frs.* del, *m: Dut.* deel, *n: Kil.* deel, deyl: *Ger.* theil, *m: M. H. Ger.* teil, *m: O. H. Ger.* teil, *m. n: Goth.* dails, *f: Dan.* deel, *m. f: Swed.* del, *m: Icel.* deill, *m: Sansk.* dal *findere.*] DER. eást-dǣl, niðer-, norþ-, sūþ-, west-: or-dǣle.

dǣlan; *p.* de; *pp.* ed; *v. a* [dǣl *a part, deal*] *To divide, separate, distribute, bestow, spend, dispense,* DEAL, DOLE; dividĕre, distribuĕre, separāre ab aliquo:—Israēlas ongunnon dǣlan ealde mādmas *the Israelites began to divide old treasures*, Cd. 171; Th. 215, 17; Exod. 584. Onfōþ and dǣlaþ betwux eów *accipĭte et divĭdĭte inter vos*, Lk. Bos. 22, 17: Ps. Spl. 21, 17: 111, 8. Mathusal māgum dǣlde gestreón *Mathuselah distributed the treasure to his brethren*, Cd. 52; Th. 65, 21; Gen. 1069. Dǣlde eall ðæt heó āhte *she had spent all that she had*, Mk. Bos. 5, 26. [*Prompt.* delyn: *Wyc.* delen: *Piers P.* delen, dele, deelen: *Chauc.* dele: *R. Brun.* daile: *R. Glouc.* dele: *Laym.* dælen, dalen, delen: *Orm.* dælenn: *Plat.* delen: *O. Sax.* dēlian, deilan: *Frs.* deelen: *O. Frs.* dela: *Dut.* deelen: *Kil.* deelen, deylen: *Ger.* theilen: *M. H. Ger.* teilen: *O. H. Ger.* teiljan: *Goth.* dailyan: *Dan.* dele: *Swed.* dela: *Icel.* deila.] DER. a-dǣlan, be-, bi-, for-, ge-, to-.

dǣledlīce *by itself, apart*, Som. Ben. Lye. DER. ge-dǣledlīce, to-.

dǣlend, es; *m.* [dǣlende, *part. of* dǣlan *to divide*] *A dealer, divider, distributor;* divīsor:—Hwā sette me dēman, oððe dǣlend, ofer inc *quis me constituit judĭcem, aut divisōrem, super vos?* Lk. Bos. 12, 14.

dǣlere, es; *m. A* DEALER, *divider, distributor, agent;* divīsor, sequester:—Dǣlere *divīsor*, Ælfc. Gl. 33; Som. 62, 28; Wrt. Voc. 28, 11: 74, 15. Ic wæs dǣlere betwix Gode and eów *ego sequester et medius fui inter Domĭnum et vos*, Deut. 5, 5. Ðam wǣdlan gedafenaþ ðæt he gebidde for ðane dǣlere *on the indigent it is incumbent that he pray for the distributor*, Homl. Th. i. 256, 33. God gesette ðone wēlegan dǣlere on his gōdum *God appointed the wealthy a distributor of his goods*, ii. 102, 28.

dælf, es; *n?* [delfan *to dig*] *Anything dug out, a* DELF, *ditch;* fossa, scrobis:—Eástweard to cynges dælf *eastward to the king's delf*, Chr. 963; Erl. 122, 17: 963; Erl. 123, 6.

dǣling, e; *f. A dividing, parting;* partitio, Som. Ben. Lye. DER. to-dǣling.

dǣl-leás; *adj.* [dǣl *a part, portion*] *Without a part, portionless, deficient;* expers:—Dǣlleás *vel* cræftleás *expers, indoctus*, Ælfc. Gl. 18; Som. 58, 123; Wrt. Voc. 22, 36: 90; Som. 75, 2; Wrt. Voc. 51, 47.

dǣl-mǣlum; *adv.* [mǣlum, *dat. pl. of* mǣl, *n.*] *By parts* or *pieces;* partim, Ælfc. Gr. 38; Som. 41, 59: *particulātim*, Mone B. 148: 3549: *paulātim*, 2635.

dǣl-neomend *a sharer, partaker*, Ps. Th. 118, 63. v. dǣl-nimend.

dǣl-niman; *p.* -nam, *pl.* -nāmon; *pp.* -numen *To take part, to participate;* participāre. v. dǣl-nimend, *etc.*

dǣl-nimend, -nymend, -neomend, es; *m.* [nimende, *part. of* niman *to take*]. I. *a taker of a part, a sharer, partaker, participator;* particeps:—Ðæt se Hǣlend dǣlnimend wǣre ūre deádlīcnysse *that the Saviour was a partaker of our mortality*, Homl. Th. i. 36, 33. Se nīþfulla is ðæra deófla dǣlnimend *the envious is a participator with devils*, i. 606, 5. Ic eom dǣlneomend ðe heom ondrǣdaþ ðē *particeps ego sum omnium timentium te*, Ps. Th. 118, 63. Tofōran eallum his dǣlnymendum on ðære menniscnysse *before all his participators in humanity*, Homl. Th. ii. 230, 26. II. in grammar,—*A participle;* participium:—Participium is dǣlnimend: he nimþ ǣnne dǣl of naman, and ōðerne of worde *a participle is a taker of parts: it takes one part from a noun, and the other from a verb*, Ælfc. Gr. 5; Som. 3, 40. Sume adverbia cumaþ of dǽlnimendum *some adverbs come from participles*, 38; Som. 41, 11.

dǽl-nimendlíc *sharing, partaking, participial*, Som. Ben. Lye.

dǽl-nimendnes, -ness, e; *f. A sharing, participation*; participatio :—Ðære dǽlnimendnes [-nimendes] his on ðæt sylfe *cujus participatio ejus in id ipsum*, Ps. Spl. 121, 3.

dǽl-nimung, e; *f. A share, portion*; portio :—Dǽlnimung oððe spēde mīn on lande lyfigendra *portio mea in terra viventium*, Ps. Lamb. 141, 6.

dǽl-numelnes, -ness, e; *f.* [numol *taking, receiving*] *A sharing, partaking, participation*; participatio :—Ðære dǽlnumelnes is hire on ðæt sylfe *cujus participatio est ejus in id ipsum*, Ps. Lamb. 121, 3.

dǽl-nymend *a sharer, participator*, Homl. Th. ii. 230, 26. v. dǽlnimend.

dǽma, an; *m. A judge*; judex, arbiter :—Bēte swā mycel swā dǽman tǽcan *subjacebit damno quantum arbitri judicaverint*, Ex. 21, 22. v. dēma.

Dæne; *pl. nom. acc*; *gen.* Dæna; *m. The Danes*; Dani :—Dæna lagu *the law of the Danes*, L. C. S. 15; Th. i. 384, 3, note 4. v. Dene.

dæne-land, es; *n.* [dænu *a valley*] *A valley*; convallis :—Dæneland getelda ic amete *convallem tabernaculorum metibor*, Ps. Lamb. 59, 8.

dænn, es; *n. A den*; cubile :—Godwine geann Leófwine ðæs dænnes æt Swīðrǽdingdænne *Godwine gives to Leofwine the den at Surrenden*, Cod. Dipl. 1315; A. D. 1020; Kmbl. vi. 178, 8, 13. v. denn.

dænnede *became slippery*, Chr. 937; Erl. 112, 12, = dennode; *p. of* dennian.

dænu, e; *f. A vale, valley*; convallis :—On ðisse sārgan dæne *in convalle lacrymarum*, Ps. Th. 83, 6. v. denu.

Dærenta-mūþa, Derta-mūþa, an; *m.* [mūþa *the mouth of a river*] *Dartmouth, Devonshire*; Tremunda, in agro Devoniæ :—Hī fērdon to Dærentamūþan [Dertamūþan, Th. 310, 5, col. 2] *they went to Dartmouth*, Chr. 1049; Th. 310, 6, col. 1.

dærst, es; *m. Leaven*; fermentum :—Ongelīc is dærste *simile est fermento*, Lk. Lind. War. 13, 21. *Rush. has dat. pl.* Gelīc is dærstum, Lk. Rush. War. 13, 21: 12, 1: 22, 1. DER. ge-dærsted.

dærstan, derstan; *pl. f? Dregs, lees*; fæx :—Nyle he ða dærstan him dōn unbrȳce *verumtamen fæx ejus non est exinanita*, Ps. Th. 74, 8. Ða derstan beóþ gōde *the dregs will be good*, L. M. 1, 2; Lchdm. ii. 38, 18, 19. Wið ecedes derstan *with lees of vinegar*, 1, 39; Lchdm. ii. 98, 24.

dæru, e; *f. Harm*; damnum :—His brōðer to dære and to lættinge *to the harm and hindrance of his brother*, Chr. 1101; Erl. 237, 18. v. daru.

dafen; *adj. Becoming, fit, suitable*; decens, congruus, conveniens. DER. ge-dafen: dafenian, ge-: dafenigendlīce, ge-: dafenlīc, ge-, unge-: dafenlīce, ge-, unge-; dafenlīcnes, ge-, unge-.

dafenian, dafnian; *p.* ode; *pp.* od *To be seemly* or *becoming*; decere :—Swā swā dafnaþ munuce *as becomes a monk*; sicut decet monacho, Coll. Monast. Th. 35, 5. DER. ge-dafenian, -dafnian.

dafenigendlīce *suitably, conformably*. DER. ge-dafenigendlīce.

dafenlīc, dafnlīc; *adj. Becoming, fit, suitable*; decens, congruus, conveniens :—Dafnlīcum *congruis*, Mone B. 1359. DER. ge-dafenlīc, unge-.

dafenlīce *becomingly, properly, fitly*. DER. ge-dafenlīce, unge-.

dafenlīcnes, -nys, -nyss, e; *f. A fit time, opportunity*; opportunitas :—Ðū forsihst on dafenlīcnyssum gedrēfednysse *despicis in opportunitatibus in tribulatione*, Ps. Spl. C. second 9, 1. DER. ge-dafenlīcnes, unge-.

dafnaþ *becomes*, Coll. Monast. Th. 35, 5; *3rd pres. sing. of* dafenian.

dāg, es; *n? What is dangling*; sparsum :—Dāges hlæfþe *sparsio*, Wrt. Voc. 288, 68. v. daag.

daga, an; *m. A day*; dies,—found in the compound word ān-daga, *q. v*; also v. dæg II.

dagas *days*, Bd. 1, 1; S. 473, 32: 474, 31; *pl. nom. acc. of* dæg.

dagena *of days*; dierum :—Him bebeád seofon dagena fæsten *enjoined them a fast of seven days*, Homl. Th. i. 434, 21: Exon. 31 a; Th. 97, 8; Cri. 1587: Menol. Fox 128; Men. 64; *gen. pl. of* daga.

dages *daily*; die, Ps. Lamb. 1, 2. v. dæges, dæg.

dagian, dagigan; *p.* ode; *pp.* od [dagas *days, pl. of* dæg *a day*] *To* DAWN, *to become day, be day*; lucescere :—Mīn leóht me tocymeþ ðonne hit dagian ongynneþ *mea lux, incipiente aurora, mihi adventura est*, Bd. 4, 8; S. 576, 7: 4, 9; S. 576, 30. Ne ðis ne dagaþ eástan *this dawns not from the east*, Fins. Th. 4; Fin. 3. Swylce hit ealle niht dagie [dagige MSS. P. S.] *as though it were day all night*, Bd. de nat. rerum; Wrt. popl. science 12, 9; Lchdm. iii. 260, 1. [*Prompt.* dagyn': *Piers P. Chauc.* dawe: *Laym.* dæȝen, daiȝen, daȝiȝen: *Plat.* dagen: *Dut.* dágen: *Kil.* daghen: *Ger. M. H. Ger.* tagen: *O. H. Ger.* tagēn: *Dan.* det daget *it dawns*: *Swed. Icel.* daga.] DER. ān-dagian, ge-ān-.

dagung, e; *f. A dawning, dawn, day-break*; aurora, tempus matutinum, diluculum :—Betwux hancrēd and dagunge *between cock-crowing and dawn*, Chr. 795; Erl. 59, 26: 802; Erl. 61, 19. Eóde he ūt on dagunge of ðam hūse *egressus est tempore matutino de cubiculo*, Bd. 3, 27; S. 559, 1. On dagunge he eft acwicode and semninga uppasæt *diluculo reviviscens ac repente residens*, 5, 12; S. 627, 13: 4, 8; S. 576, 9: 4, 23; S. 596, 17. On dagunge ðæs fiftan dæges *quinta inlucescente die*, 5, 19; S. 640, 26.

DĀH, dōh; *gen.* dāges; *m?* DOUGH; farina subacta, massa = μάζα :—Blōma oððe dāh *massa*, Wrt. Voc. 85, 16: 94, 63. Dāh [MS. dað] *vel* blōma *massa*, Ælfc. Gl. 51; Som. 66, 9; Wrt. Voc. 34, 68. Cned hyt ðæt hit sī swā þicce swā dōh *knead it that it may be as thick as dough*, Lchdm. iii. 88, 17. Wyrc clam of dāge *make a paste of dough*, L. M. 3, 59; Lchdm. ii. 342, 18. [*Prompt.* dowe *pasta*: *Wyc.* dough: *Plat.* deeg: *Dut.* deeg, *n*: *Kil.* deegh *massa*: *Ger.* teig, *m*: *M. H. Ger.* teic, *gen.* teiges: *O. H. Ger.* teig, *m*: *Goth.* daigs, *m. dough*; deigan *to make dough*: *Dan.* deig, *m. f*: *Swed.* deg, *m*: *Icel.* deig, *n*: *Sansk.* dih *to smear, plaster*.]

dāhle *hid*, Bd. 4, 27; S. 604, 24, = dīgle; *pl. nom. acc. of* dīgol.

dahum *to days*, Bt. 4; Fox 8, 5, = dagum; *dat. pl. of* dæg.

dāl, es; *n. A division, allotment, portion*, DOLE; discrimen, divisio, portio :—Ic sette dāl betwux ðīn folc and mīn folc *ponam divisionem inter populum meum et populum tuum*, Ex. 8, 23. Is ðes middangeard dālum gedǽled *this earth is divided into parts*, Exon. 33 a; Th. 105, 18; Gū. 25. Swā beóþ mōd-sefan dālum gedǽled, sindon dryht-guman ungelīce *dispositions are distributed by parts, while people are unlike*, 83 b; Th. 314, 29-32; Mōd. 21-23. DER. ge-dāl, to-.

Dalamensan; *gen.* -ena; *pl. m. The Dalamensan*; Dalamensæ: a Slavonic race, who dwelt in Misnia on both sides of the river Elbe :—Be norþan eástan Maroara syndon Dalamensan, and be eástan Dalamensan [MS. Dalamensam] sindon Horithi, and be norþan Dalamensan [MS. Dalomensam] sindon Surpe *to the north-east of the Moravians are the Dalamensan, and to the east of the Dalamensan are the Horithi, and to the north of the Dalamensan are the Surpe*, Ors. 1, 1, § 12; Bos. 19, 4-6.

dalc, dolc, es; *m. A clasp, buckle, brooch, bracelet*; fibula, spinther, regula :—Preón *vel* oferfeng *vel* dalc *fibula*, Ælfc. Gl. 64; Som. 69, 22; Wrt. Voc. 40, 53. Dalc *spinther*, Ælfc. Gr. 9, 18; Som. 9, 63. Ic geseah sumne gildenne dalc on fiftigum entsum *vidi regulam auream quinquaginta siclorum*, Jos. 7, 21. Dolc oððe preón *spinther*, Wrt. Voc. 74, 59.

dalf *dug*, Mt. Kmbl. Lind. 21, 33, = dealf; *p. of* delfan.

dap-fugel *the dip-fowl* or *diver, a gull*; mergus, mergulus, Som. Ben. Lye. v. dop-fugel.

daraþ, dareþ *a dart, spear, javelin*, Exon. 66 b; Th. 246, 27; Jul. 68: Beo. Th. 5689; B. 2848. v. daroþ.

dareþ-lācende, deareþ-lācende; *part.* [daroþ, dareþ *a dart, spear*; lācende, *part. of* lācan *to play*] *Playing with a dart, dart-brandishing*; telo ludens :—Beornþreát monig ōfestum gefȳsde, dareþlācende *many a band of nobles hurried with haste, dart-brandishing*, Exon. 96 a; Th. 358, 29; Pa. 53. Dareþlācendra *of the dart-players*, Elen. Kmbl. 1298; El. 651. Deareþlācende stæðe wīcedon *the dart-players bivouacked on the shore*, 73; El. 37.

daro *hurt, harm*, Bd. 3, 2; S. 525, 17. v. daru.

daroþ, daraþ, dareþ, es; *m.* [derian *to hurt*] *A* DART, *spear, javelin, weapon*; telum, jaculum, hasta :—Daroþ sceal on handa *the spear shall be in the hand*, Menol. Fox 502; Gn. C. 21. Forlēt daroþ of handa fleógan *let a dart fly from the hand*, Byrht. Th. 136, 11; By. 149: 139, 17; By. 255. Reórdode rīces hyrde, daraþ hæbbende *the realm's guardian spake, raising his spear*, Exon. 66 b; Th. 246, 27; Jul. 68. Daroþas wǽron weó ðære wihte *darts were an affliction to the creature*, 114 a; Th. 438, 8; Rä. 57, 4. Þurh daroþa gedrep *through the stroke of darts*, Andr. Kmbl. 2886; An. 1446. Dareþa *of darts*, Chr. 937; Th. 207, 11; Æðelst. 54. Ða ne dorston dareþum lācan *who durst not play with javelins*, Beo. Th. 5689; B. 2848. [*Prompt.* darte: *Wyc.* dartis, *pl*: *R. Brun.* darte: *Chauc.* dart: *O. H. Ger.* tart *lancea*: *Swed.* dart, *m. a dagger*: *Icel.* darraðr, *m. hasta*.]

daroþ-æsc, es; *n? An ash-dart*; jaculum fraxineum :—Daroþæsc flugon *ash-darts flew*, Elen. Kmbl. 280; El. 140.

DARU, daro, e; *f. Hurt, harm, damage*; damnum, noxa :—Hwelc is māre daru *what is a greater hurt?* Bt. 29, 2; Fox 106, 14. Gemētte he his earm and his hand swā hāle and swā gesūnde swā him nǽfre bryce ne daro gedōn wǽre *he found his arm and his hand so hale and so sound, as if breach or hurt had never been done to them*, Bd. 3, 2; S. 525, 17. Him to dare *to his harm*, Exon. 42 b; Th. 144, 2; Gū. 672. Ne astrece ðū ðīne hand būfon ðam cilde, ne him nāne dare ne gedō *stretch thou not thine hand over thy son, nor do him any harm*, Homl. Th. ii. 60, 35. Būton ǽlcere dare *without any hurt*, i. 102, 8. Ðæt mōd mid þwyrlīcum geþohtum hogaþ ōðrum dara *the mind will meditate harm to others with perverse thoughts*, i. 412, 28. [*Kil.* dere, deyre *nocumentum*: *O. H. Ger.* tara, *f.*]

Daðan, es; *m. Dathan, one of the sons of Eliab*, Num. 26, 9 :—Æfter ðam arison Chore and Hon, Daðan and Abiron ongeán Moisen *after that Korah and On, Dathan and Abiram rose up against Moses*, Num. 16, 1: 16, 27, 32: Deut. 11, 6. [דָּתָן *Dāthān*.]

Datia, Ors. 1, 1, § 12; Bos. 19, 3, = Datie; *gen.* Datia; *pl. m. The* DACIANS; Dāci; *gen.* ōrum; *m.* = Δακοί *A celebrated warlike people in Upper Hungary, in Transylvania, Moldavia, Wallachia, and in*

Bessarabia. They were originally of the same race as the Getæ. Trajan crossed the Danube and conquered the country in A D. 106, and colonised it with Romans. At a later period Dacia was invaded by the Goths; and as Aurelian considered it more prudent to make the Danube the boundary of the Empire, he resigned Dacia to the barbarians, removed the Roman inhabitants to Mœsia, and gave to the Dacians the name of the Aureliani, who inhabited that part of the province along the Danube in which they were settled:—And be eástan ðæm sind Datie [MS. Datia] ða ðe iu wǽron Gotan *and to the east of them [the Wisle] are the Dacians who were formerly Goths*, Ors. 1, 1, § 12; Bos. 19, 3.

Dauid, es; *m. David;* Dāvid, īdis; *m:*—Dauid sang ðysne syxtan sealm *David sang this sixth psalm*, Ps. Th. arg. 6. Dauides sealm *the psalm of David*, Ps. Th. arg. 4. Dauides sunu *David's son*, Homl. Blick. 15, 18, 20. Crist onwrāh, in Dauides dȳrre mǽgan, ðæt is Euan scyld eal forpynded *Christ revealed that, in David's dear kinswoman, the sin of Eve is all turned away*, Exon. 9 a; Th. 7, 4; Cri. 96. [דָּוִד, דָּוִיד *Dāvīd*, from דּוּד *dūd affection.* We have, in the same meaning, the classical name *Erasmus*, from ἐράσμιος *lovely, affectionate.*]

deācon *a levite, deacon;* levītes:—Aaron ðīn brōður, deācon, hæfþ gōde spræce *Aaron frater tuus, levītes, eloquens est*, Ex. 4, 14. v. diācon.

deācon-hād *deaconhood, deaconship;* diaconātus, Bd. 5, 23; S. 647, 29. v. diācon-hād.

DEÁD; *def.* se deáda; seó, ðæt deáde; *adj.* DEAD; mortuus:—Lazarus ys deád *Lazarus mortuus est*, Jn. Bos. 11, 14: Mt. Bos. 9, 24: Jud. 3, 25: Elen. Kmbl. 1761; El. 882: Beo. Th. 939; B. 467: Exon. 126 b; Th. 487, 19; Rä. 73, 4. Næs ðǽr nān þing deád of ðām *nec erat quidquam mortuum de his*, Ex. 9, 7: 21, 34. Me hātran sind Dryhtnes dreámas ðonne ðis deáde līf *the Lord's joys are more exciting to me than this dead life*, Exon. 82 a; Th. 309, 31; Seef. 65. Sceal yrfe gedǽled deádes monnes *the inheritance of a dead man shall be divided*, 90 a; Th. 338, 19; Gn. Ex. 81. Græf deádum men heófeþ *the grave shall groan for the dead man*, 91 b; Th. 342, 29; Gn. Ex. 149. Mec deádne ofgeáfun fæder and mōder *father and mother gave me up as dead*, 103 a; Th. 391, 7; Rä. 10, 1: Beo. Th. 2623; B. 1309. Brihtrīc þohte ðæt he Wulfnōþ cuconne oððe deádne begytan sceolde *Brihtric thought that he would get Wulfnoth alive or dead*, Chr. 1009; Erl. 142, 3. Ealle synd deáde *mortui sunt omnes*, Ex. 4, 19: Mt. Bos. 28, 4: Ps. Th. 113, 24. Deáde of duste arīsaþ þurh Drihtnes miht *the dead shall rise from the dust through power of God*, Cd 227; Th. 302, 24; Sat. 605: Exon. 25 a; Th. 72, 30; Cri. 1180. Hī ǽton deádra lāc *manducavērunt sacrifĭcia mortuōrum*, Ps. Th. 105, 22: Mt. Bos. 23, 27. Land dryrmyde deádra hrǽwum *the land mourned over the corpses of the dead*, Cd. 144; Th. 180, 6; Exod. 41: Elen. Kmbl. 1299; El. 651: 1887; El. 945. Be deádum *for the dead*, Exon. 82 b; Th. 311, 27; Seef. 98. Mid ðām deádum fellum *with the dead skins*, Boutr. Scrd. 20, 29. Ne dō hȳ to deádan *ne occidĕris eos*, Ps. Th. 58, 10: 61, 3: Ex. 21, 35, 36. Ne willaþ eów andrǽdan deáde fēðan *dread ye not dead bands*, Cd. 156; Th. 194, 26; Exod. 266: Exon. 24 b; Th. 71, 21; Cri. 1159: Andr. Kmbl. 2156; An. 1079. Lǽt deáde bebyrigean hyra deádan *let the dead bury their dead*, Mt. Bos. 8, 22. Ne hūru wundur wyrceaþ deáde *numquid mortuis facies mirabilia?* Ps. Th. 87, 10. [*Prompt.* dede: *Wyc.* ded: *Piers P.* deed: *Chauc.* dede: *R. Glouc.* ded: *Plat.* dood: *O. Sax.* dōd: *Frs.* dea: *O Frs.* dad, dath: *Dut.* dood: *Ger.* todt: *M. H. Ger. O. H. Ger.* tōt: *Goth.* dauþs: *Dan. Swed.* död: *Icel.* dauðr.] DER. woruld-deád.

deád-bǽre; *def.* se deád-bǽra, seó, ðæt deád-bǽre; *adj. Death-bearing, deadly;* mortĭfer, lethālis, lethĭfer:—Deádbǽre *lethāle*, Mone B. 1859. Se drenc deádbǽra wæs *the drink was deadly*, Homl. Th. ii. 158, 22. Ðæt ðīn heorte forhtige for ðam deádbǽrum drence *that thy heart may fear the deadly drink*, i. 72, 16. Deádbǽre sprancan *lethifĕras labruscas*, Mone B. 1993.

deád-bǽrende; *part. Death-bearing, deadly;* mortĭfer:—Se Arrianisca gedwola ðæt deádbǽrende āttor his getreówleásnysse on eallum middangeardes cyricum strēgde *the Arian heresy spread the death-bearing venom of its truthlessness in all the churches of the earth*, Bd. 1, 8; S. 479, 34. v. deáþ-berende.

deád-bǽrlīc; *adj. Deadly;* mortĭfer:—Him ne deraþ, ðeáh hī hwæt deádbǽrlīces drincon *si mortifĕrum bibĕrint, non eis nocēbit*, Mk. Bos. 16, 18.

deád-bǽrnes, -ness, e; *f. A killing, mortification;* mortificātio, Mone B. 3934.

deád blōd *dead blood, congealed blood*, Wrt. Voc. 283, 79. v. blōd.

deád-boren; *part. Dead-borne;* mortuus fœtus:—Deádboren tuddur *mortuus fœtus*, Herb. 63, 2; Lchdm. i. 166, 3.

deád-līc; *def.* se deád-līca, seó, ðæt deád-līce; *adj.* DEADLY, *mortal;* mortālis, morticīnus:—Ðæt ān deádlīc man mihte ealne middaneard oferseón *that a mortal man could see over all the world*, Homl. Th. ii. 186, 5. Rōmāne deádlīcne sige gefōran *the Romans gained a deadly victory*, Ors. 3, 8; Bos. 63, 33. Se cyning and monige of his folce lufodon ðis deádlīce līf *the king and many of his people loved this deadly life*, Bd. 3, 30; S. 561, 41: Boutr. Scrd. 20, 29. We onlybbaþ on ðisum deádlīcum līfe *we live in this deadly life*, 30, 12. Deádlīce *morticīnas*, Glos. Prudent. Recd. 145, 23. DER. un-deádlīc.

deád-līce; *adv. Mortally;* lethalĭter, Cot. 123.

deád-līcnys, -nyss, e; *f. Deadliness, mortality;* mortalĭtas:—Ðæt he dǽlnimend wǽre ūre deádlīcnysse *that he was a partaker of our mortality*, Homl. Th. i. 36, 34. He becom on ða tīde ðære myclan deádlīcnysse *tempŏre mortalitātis adveniens*, Bd. 3, 23; S. 555, 9: 3, 30; S. 561, 38. Ealle his gefēran on ðære deádlīcnysse ðæs wæles of worulde genumene wǽron *omnes sŏcii ipsōrum mortalitāte [cædis] de sæcŭlo rapti*, 3, 27; S. 558, 36. He hæfde ealle deádlīcnyssa aworpen *he had cast off all mortalities*, Homl. Th. ii. 290, 1. DER. un-deádlīcnys.

deád-rægl *clothing of the dead, a shroud;* pallium sepulchrāle, Som. Ben. Lye.

deád-spring, es; *m.* [spring *an ulcer*] *A malignant ulcer, carbuncle;* carbuncŭlus:—Wið wūnda and wið deádspringas *for wounds and ulcers*, Herb. 4, 2; Lchdm. i. 90, 5: 9, 2; Lchdm. i. 100, 1: 87, 3; Lchdm. i. 190, 24: 91, 7; Lchdm. i. 200, 17.

DEÁF; *adj.* DEAF; surdus:—Deáf *surdus* vel *surdaster*, Ælfc. Gl. 77; Som. 72, 21; Wrt. Voc. 45, 54. Ic swā swā deáf ne gehȳrde *ego tamquam surdus non audiēbam*, Ps. Lamb. 37, 14. Eart ðū dumb and deáf *thou art dumb and deaf*, Exon. 99 a; Th. 370, 26; Seel. 65. Næddran deáfre *aspĭdis surdæ*, Ps. Lamb. 57, 5. Hwā geworhte dumne oððe deáfne *quis fabricātus est mutum et surdum?* Ex. 4, 11. Hī lǽddon him ǽnne deáfne and dumbne *addūcunt ei surdum et mutum*, Mk. Bos. 7, 32: Exon. 113 a; Th. 433, 3; Rä. 50, 2. Anlīc nædran seó hī deáfe dēþ *like an adder which makes herself deaf*, Ps. Th. 57, 4. Eálā deáfa and dumba gāst *surde et mute spīrĭtus*, Mk. Bos. 9, 25. Deáfe gehȳraþ *surdi audiunt*, Mt. Bos. 11, 5: Mk. Bos. 7, 37: Lk. Bos. 7, 22: Andr. Kmbl. 1154; An. 577. Ðæt ic dumbum and deáfum deófolgieldum gaful onhāte *that I promise tribute to dumb and deaf idols*, Exon. 68 a; Th. 251, 24; Jul. 150. Ne wirige ðū deáfe *curse not the deaf*, Lev. 19, 14. Deáf corn *deaf* or *barren corn*, Past. 52, 9; Hat. MS. [*Prompt.* deffe *surdus*: *Wyc.* def: *Piers P.* deef, *pl.* deve: *Chauc.* deef: *R. Glouc.* deve: *Plat.* doov: *O. Sax.* douf: *O. Frs.* dāf: *Dut.* doof: *Ger.* taub: *M. H. Ger.* toup: *O. H. Ger.* toup, doup: *Goth.* daubs, daufs *hardened, obdurate*: *Dan.* döv: *Swed.* döf: *Icel.* daufr.] DER. a-deáf: deáfian, a-: deáfu: a-deáfung.

deáf *dived*, Exon. 126 b; Th. 487, 18; Rä. 73, 4; *p. of* dūfan *to dive*, q v.

deáfian *to become* or *wax deaf.* v. a-deáfian.

deáf-līc; *adj.* [deáf = dēfe *fitting, proper*] *Suitable, fitting, proper;* conveniens:—Deáflīc to gehīrenne on heálīcum gemōte *fitting to be heard at a public assembly*, Ælfc. T. 15, 4. v. ge-dēfe.

deáfu, e; *f.* [deáf *deaf*] *Deafness;* surditas:—Wið eárwærce and wið deáfe *for ear-ache and for deafness*, L. M. 1, 3; Lchdm. ii. 40, 8. Wið eárena deáfe *for deafness of ears*, 1, 3; Lchdm. ii. 40, 20.

deag, es; *m. A day;* dies:—Æfter feáum deagum *after a few days*, Bd. 5, 9; S. 623, 7. v. dæg.

deág *is of use, is good, avails*, Exon. 8 a; Th. 2, 19; Cri. 21: 10 b; Th. 12, 22; Cri. 189; *pres. of* dugan.

deágan; ic deáge, ðū deágest, deágst, dȳhst, he deágeþ, deágþ, dȳgþ, dȳhþ, *pl.* deágaþ; *p.* deóg, *pl.* deógon; *pp.* deágen *To dye, colour;* tingĕre:—Heoro-dreóre deáþfǽge deóg *the death-doomed dyed it with fatal gore*, Beo. Th. 1704; B. 850.

deáge *of a colour* or *dye*, Homl. Th. ii. 254, 5; *gen. of* deáh.

deággede *gouty*, Ælfc. Gl. 77; Som. 72, 12; Wrt. Voc. 45, 46. v. deág-wyrmede.

deágian, dēgian; *p.* ode; *pp.* od [deáh *a colour, dye*] *To colour,* DYE; fucāre, inficĕre, tingĕre:—Deágian *fucāre*, Mone B. 1245: *inficĕre*, 6225. Dēgian *tingĕre*, 6251. DER. ge-deágod, twī-gedeágod.

deáglenes *solitariness*, Cot. 18. v. dīgolnes.

deágol *secret*, Exon. 110 b; Th. 424, 14; Rä. 41, 39: L. M. 2, 66; Lchdm. ii. 298, 8: Bd. 3, 16; S. 542, 34, MS. T. v. dīgol.

deágollīce, deágolīce *secretly*, L. E. I. 45; Th. ii. 440, 33: L. M. 2, 66; Lchdm. ii. 298, 6. DER. un-deágollīce. v. dīgollīce.

deágolnes *hiding-place*, Bd. 4, 27; S. 604, 22. v. dīgolnes.

deágung, e; *f. A dyeing, colouring;* tinctūra:—Deágung *tinctūra*, Ælfc. Gr. 28, 5; Som. 31, 59. Ne mihte nān eorþlīc cyning swā wlītige deágunge his hræglum begytan swā swā rōse hæfþ *no earthly king could get such beautiful dyeing for his garments as the rose has*, Homl. Th. ii. 464, 10.

deág-wyrmede, deággede; *part.* [deág = deáw *dew*, wyrm *a worm*] *Dew-wormed, gouty;* podagrĭcus = ποδαγρικός:—Deágwyrmede *vel* deággede *podagrĭcus*, Ælfc. Gl. 77; Som. 72, 12; Wrt. Voc. 45, 46.

deáh *is of use, is good* or *virtuous, avails*, Herb. 2, 22; Lchdm. i. 86, 18: Bt. 27, 2; Fox 98, 15: Exon. 80 b; Th. 303, 5; Fä. 48: Beo. Th. 1151; B. 573; *pres. of* dugan.

deáh; *gen.* deáge; *f. A colour,* DYE; tinctūra, fucus, stĭbium, murex:—Deáh *tinctūra*: reád deáh *coccus*, Ælfc. Gl. 64; Som. 69, 5, 6; Wrt. Voc. 40, 39, 40. Deáge *tinctūræ*, Mone B. 6226. Mid ðære deáge hiwe *with the colour of the dye*, Homl. Th. ii. 254, 5. Deáge *fuco*, Mone B. 1080: 6224. Twí-gedeágadre deáge *bis tincto cocco*, 1094. Deáge *stĭbio*, 4649: *rubenti*, 6235: *murĭce*, 6268. Reádre deáge *rubro stĭbio*, 1242.

deáhl [= deágol]; *def.* se deáhla; seó, ðæt deáhle; *adj. Dark, secret;* obscūrus, secrētus:—Ðære deáhlan neahte *of the dark night*, Bd. 2, 6; S. 508, 13. v. dígol.

deal, deall; *adj. Proud, exulting, eminent;* superbus, clarus:—Fugel feðrum deal *a bird proud of feathers*, Exon. 59 b; Th. 216, 10; Ph. 266. Bǽr-beágum deall *proud of bearing rings*, 108 b; Th. 414, 18; Rä. 32, 22. Sum sceal wildne fugel atemian, fiðrum dealne *one shall tame the wild bird, exulting in his plumes*, 88 b; Th. 332, 21; Vy. 88. Wíggendra þreát cōmon, æscum dealle *a troop of warriors came, proud with their spears*, Andr. Kmbl. 2195; An. 1099: Exon. 106 a; Th. 404, 22; Rä. 23, 11. Ðǽr swíþferhþe sittan eódon, þryþum dealle *the strong of soul went to sit there, proud of their strength*, Beo. Th. 992; B. 494. Sprǽcon wlonce monige, dugeþum dealle *many proud ones spake, eminent with virtues*, Cd. 89; Th. 111, 1; Gen. 1849.

dealf *dug*, Mt. Bos. 25, 18; *p. of* delfan.

deapung, e; *f. A dipping;* immersio, Som. Ben. Lye. v. dyppan.

dear; ic, he *I dare, he dares*, Gen. 44, 34: Beo. Th. 1373; B. 684; *pres. of* durran.

dearf, *pl.* durfon *laboured; p. of* deorfan.

dearnunga, dearnenga, dearninga; *adv.* [dyrne *secret, obscure*] *Secretly, privately, clandestinely;* clam, occulte, clandestīno:—He wolde dearnunga mid mándǽdum menn beswícan *he would secretly deceive men with wicked deeds*, Cd. 23; Th. 29, 14; Gen. 450. Gif ðín bróðor ðé lǽre dearnunga *si tibi voluĕrit persuadēre frater tuus clam*, Deut. 13, 6: Jn. Bos. 19, 38. Oððe eáwunga oððe dearnunga *either publicly or privately*, L. Edg. ii. 8; Th. i. 270, 5: L. Ath. v. § 1, 2; Th. i. 228, 21. Be ðon ðe mon dearnenga [dearnunga MSS. G. H.] bearn gestriéne *in case a man beget a child clandestinely*, L. In. 27; Th. i. 120, 1, 2: L. Alf. 6; Th. i. 44, 17. Ðeáh heó dearnenga fordōn wurde *though she was secretly seduced*, Cd. 30; Th. 39, 21; Gen. 629: 29; Th. 38, 5; Gen. 602. Hwæt he dearninga on hyge hogde *what he secretly meditated in his mind*, Exon. 51 a; Th. 177, 13; Gū. 1226. DER. un-dearnunga.

dearr-líc; *adj. Daring, rash;* temerārius, Som. Ben. Lye.

dearr-scipe, es; *m. Rashness, presumption;* temerĭtas, Som. Ben. Lye.

dearst ðū *thou darest*, Beo. Th. 1061; B. 527; *2nd pres. sing. of* durran.

DEÁþ, es; *m.* DEATH; mors:—Ðeáh ðe him se bitera deáþ geboden wǽre *though bitter death were announced to them*, Cd. 183; Th. 229, 26; Dan. 223: Exon. 31 b; Th. 98, 6; Cri. 1603: Beo. Th. 899; B. 447: 5773; B. 2890. Se deáþ cymþ *death comes*, Bt. 8; Fox 26, 6: Chr. 1065; Erl. 198, 7; Edw. 26. Hí ofercume unþinged deáþ *vĕniat mors super illos*, Ps. Th. 54, 14. Nis me ðæs deáþes sorg *there is no fear of death to me*, Exon. 38 a; Th. 125, 7; Gū. 350: 40 a; Th. 133, 25; Gū. 495: Cd. 25; Th. 31, 28; Gen. 492: Elen. Kmbl. 1165; El. 584: Bt. 8; Fox 26, 6. Ðū ðe upahefst me of geatum deáþes *qui exaltas me de portis mortis*, Ps. Lamb. 9, 15. He is deáþes scyldig *reus est mortis*, Mt. Bos. 26, 66: Ps. Th. 54, 4: 72, 3. Gif hwā sié deáþes scyldig *if any one be guilty of death*, L. In. 5; Th. i. 104, 13: 27; Th. i. 120, 3. He men of deáþe worde awehte *he woke men from death with his word*, Andr. Kmbl. 1166; An. 583: Exon. 14 b; Th. 29, 23; Cri. 467: 41 b; Th. 139, 25; Gū. 598. Gif he man to deáþe gefylle beó he ūtlah *if he fell a man to death let him be an outlaw*, L. E. G. 6; Th. i. 170, 10: L. C. S. 2; Th. i. 376, 18: Chr. 979; Erl. 129, 10: Boutr. Scrd. 17, 25: 18, 11. Eall ðæt gemōt sōhte leáse saga ongēn ðone Hǽlend, ðæt híg hyne to deáþe sealdon *omne consĭlium quærēbat falsum testimōnium contra Iesum, ut eum morti tradĕrent*, Mt. Bos. 26, 59: 20, 18: Ps. Th. 114, 8: 117, 18. Fram deáþe to lífe *a morte in vitam*, Jn. Bos. 5, 24. Deáþ he ðǽr bȳrigde *he there tasted death*, Rood Kmbl. 199; Kr. 101: Cd. 228; Th. 306, 17; Sat. 665: Exon. 119 b; Th. 459, 25; Hö. 5. Þurh fǽrlícne deáþ *through sudden death*, L. C. S. 71; Th. i. 412, 29. Unrōt ys mín sáwl óþ deáþ *tristis est anĭma mea usque ad mortem*, Mt. Bos. 26, 38: 16, 28: Ex. 10, 17: Deut. 30, 15. He sceal deáþe sweltan *he shall perish by death*, L. Alf. 14, 15; Th. i. 48, 3, 7, 8. Ðæt ðū deáþe sweltest *that thou shalt perish by death*, Exon. 67 b; Th. 250, 11; Jul. 125. Deáþe cwylman *mortificāre*, Ps. Spl. 108, 15. Ðæt he deáþa gedāl dreógan sceolde *that he should undergo death*, Exon. 36 a; Th. 116, 12; Gū. 206. Gegang ða deáþa bearn ðe hí dēmaþ nū *possĭde filios morte punitōrum*, Ps. Th. 78, 12. Deáþas *spirits, ghosts;* manes, Cot. 134. [*Wyc.* deeth: *Chauc.* deth: *Laym.* dæd, dæð, deað, deð, *m: Orm.* dæþ: *O. Sax.* dōð, *m: Frs.* dead, dea: *O. Frs.* dad, dath, *m: Dut.* dood, *m: Ger.* tod, *m: M. H. Ger.* tōt, *m: O. H. Ger.* tōd, *m: Goth.* dauþus, *m: Dan.* död, *m. f: Swed.* död, *m: Icel.* dauði, *m.*] DER. ǽr-deáþ, ende-, gūþ-, mere-, swylt-, wæl-, wundor-.

deáþ-bǽre *death-bearing, deadly*, Som. Ben. Lye. v. deád-bǽre.

deáþ-beám, es; *m. A death-tree, tree of death;* mortis arbor, mortifĕra:—Deáþbeámes ofet *fruit of the tree of death*, Cd. 30; Th. 40, 13; Gen. 638.

deáþ-bed, -bedd, es; *n. A death-bed, grave;* mortis stratum, sepulcrum:—Nū is wilgeofa deáþbedde fæst *the kind giver is now fast in his death-bed* [= *grave*], Beo. Th. 5795; B. 2901.

deáþ-berende; *part. Death-bearing, deadly;* mortĭfer:—Eue sealde deáþberende gyfl *Eve gave the deadly fruit*, Exon. 45 a; Th. 153, 8.

deáþ-bērnis, -niss, e; *f. Death, destruction, pestilence;* pernĭcies, pestilentia:—Deáþbērnisse oððe uncūþo ādlo *pestilentiæ*, Lk. Skt. Lind. 21, 11.

deáþ-cwalu, e; *f. A deadly pain* or *plague, agony;* mortis dolor:—Sió wērge sceólu hreósan sceolde in wíta forwyrd, ðǽr hie in wylme nū dreógaþ deáþcwale *the wretched crew were compelled to fall into the ruin of punishment, where they now suffer deadly pains in flame*, Invent. Crs. Recd. 1533; El. 766. Ne geweóx he him to willan, ac to deáþcwalum Deniga leódum *he waxed not for their benefit, but for a deadly plague to the Danes' people*, Beo. Th. 3428; B. 1712.

deáþ-cwealm, es; *m.* [cwealm *a violent death, slaughter*] *Slaughter;* nex:—Ic wræc deáþcwealm Denigea *I avenged the slaughter of the Danes*, Beo. Th. 3344; B. 1670.

deáþ-cwylmende, -cwylmmende; *part.* [cwelman, cwylman *to destroy, kill*] *Put to death, destroyed, killed;* mortificātus:—Geāhna bearn adȳdra oððe deáþcwylmmendra *possĭde filios mortificatōrum*, Ps. Lamb. 78, 11.

deáþ-dæg, es; *m. Death-day, day of death;* mortis dies:—Æfter deáþdæge *after the day of death*, Beo. Th. 376; B. 187: Menol. Fox 581; Gn. C. 60. To ðínum deáþdæge *to thy death-day*, Exon. 98 a; Th. 369, 6; Seel. 37.

deáþ-denu, e; *f. The valley of death;* mortis vallis:—In ðisse deáþdene *in this valley of death*, Exon. 12 b; Th. 21, 33; Cri. 344. In ðas deáþdene *in this death-vale*, Exon. 61 b; Th. 226, 35; Ph. 416.

deáþ-drepe, es; *m. Death-stroke;* letālis ictus:—Ðȳ deáþ-drepe *in the death-stroke*, Cd. 167; Th. 209, 6; Exod. 495. v. drepe.

deáþ-fǽge; *adj.* [deáþ *death*, fǽge *fated, doomed*] *Death-doomed;* morti addictus:—Deáþfǽge deóg *the death-doomed had dyed it*, Beo. Th. 1704; B. 850.

deáþ-gedāl, es; *n.* [gedāl *a separation*] *A deathly separation, separation of body and soul in death;* letālis separātio:—Næs egle [MS. engle] on mōde deáþgedāl *the deathly separation was not oppressive to his soul*, Exon. 46 b; Th. 159, 33; Gū. 936.

deáþ-godas; *pl. m. Death-gods, spirits, ghosts;* manes, Cot. 134.

deáþ-lēg, es; *m.* [lēg *a flame*] *A death-flame;* letālis flamma:—Wihta gehwylce deáþlēg nimeþ *the death-flame shall seize each creature*, Exon. 22 a; Th. 61, 12; Cri. 983.

deáþ-líc; *adj. Deadly, mortal, good and bad angels;* mortālis:—Ðis is bísen ðara sōþena gesǽlþa, ðara wilniaþ ealle deáþlíce men to begitanne *this is an example of the true goods, which all mortal men desire to obtain*, Bt. 24, 2; Fox 80, 30. Híg gesetton hrǽwas oððe ða deáþlícan ðínra þeówana mettas fugelum heofonan *posuĕrunt mortiçīna servōrum tuōrum escas volatilĭbus cœli*, Ps. Lamb. 78, 2.

deáþ-lícnes *mortality*, Som. Ben. Lye. v. deád-lícnys.

deáþ-mægen; *gen.* -mægnes; *n. A deadly power* or *band;* letifĕra caterva, Exon. 45 b; Th. 155, 28; Gū. 867.

deáþ-ræced, es; *n.* [ræced, reced *a house*] *A death-house, sepulchre;* mortis domus, sepulcrum:—Deáþræced onhliden weorþaþ *the death-houses shall be opened*, Exon. 56 b; Th. 200, 30; Ph. 48.

deáþ-rǽs, es; *m.* [rǽs *a rush*] *Death-rush, rushing of death;* mortis impĕtus:—Ealle deáþrǽs forfēng *the death-rush clutched them all*, Andr. Kmbl. 1990; An. 997.

deáþ-reów; *adj.* [reów *cruel*] *Deadly cruel, savage;* atrox:—Com seofona sum to sele geongan deóful deáþreów *a savage devil came with seven others unto the hall*, Andr. Kmbl. 2629; An. 1316.

deáþ-scūa, an; *m.* [scūa *a shade*] *The shadow of death, death;* mortis umbra, mors, Beo. Th. 322; B. 160.

deáþ-scūfa, an; *m.* [scūfa = scūwa *a shade*] *The shadow of death, death;* mortis umbra, mors:—Forðanðe nis on deáþe oððe on deáþscūfan, ðe gemyndig sȳ ðín *quoniam non est in morte, qui memor sit tui*, Ps. Lamb. 6, 6.

deáþ-scyld, e; *f.* [deáþ *death;* scyld *sin, crime*] *A death-fault, capital crime;* capitāle crīmen:—Gif gehādod man hine forwyrce mid deáþscylde *if a man in orders ruin himself with capital crime*, L. E. G. 4; Th. i. 168, 22; L. C. S. 43; Th. i. 400, 27.

deáþ-scyldig; *adj.* [deáþ *death*, scyldig *guilty*] *Death-guilty, condemned;* damnātus:—Gif deáþscyldig man scriftsprǽce gyrne *if a man guilty of death desire confession*, L. E. G. 5; Th. i. 168, 24: L. C. S. 44; Th. i. 402, 3.

deáþ-sele, es; *m.* [deáþ *death;* sele *a dwelling, hall*] *A death-hall;* mortis aula:—In ðam deáþsele *in the death-hall*, Exon. 48 b; Th. 166, 25; Gū. 1048. On wítehūs, deáþsele deófoles *into the house of torment, the death-hall of the devil*, 30 b; Th. 94, 8; Cri. 1537: 97 a; Th. 362, 1; Wal. 30.

deáþ-slege, es; *m.* [slege *a blow, stroke*] *A death-blow;* letālis ictus:—

þurh deáþslege *through deadly stroke*, Exon. 102 b; Th. 388, 27; Rä. 6, 14.

deáþ-spere, es; *n.* [spere *a spear*] *A deadly spear;* letālis hasta:—Dol him ne ondrǽdeþ deáþsperu *the foolish will not dread the deadly spears*, Exon. 102 a; Th. 385, 32; Rä. 4, 53.

deáþ-stede, es; *m.* [deáþ *death*, stede *a place*] *A death-place;* mortis campus:—Lāgon on deáþstede drihtfolca mǽst *the greatest of people lay on their death-place*, Cd. 171; Th. 216, 1; Exod. 589.

deáþ-þēnunga; *pl. f.* [þēnung *a service*] *Funeral services, funerals;* exsĕquiæ, Cot. 74.

deáþ-wang, es; *m.* [deáþ *death*, wang *a field, plain*] *A death-plain;* mortis campus:—Hī swǽfon dreóre druncne, deáþwang rudon *they slept drunken with blood, made the death-plain red* or *bloody*, Andr. Recd. 2009; An. 1005.

deáþ-wēge, es; *n.* [deáþ *death*, wēge *a cup*] *A deadly cup;* mortis pōcŭlum:—Ǽnig ne wæs mon on moldan đætte meahte bibūgan đone bleátan drync deópan deáþwēges *there was not any man on earth that could avoid the miserable drink of the deep deadly cup*, Exon. 47 a; Th. 161, 25; Gū. 964.

deáþ-wērig; *adj. Death-weary, dead;* mortuus:—Ne mōston deáþwērigne Deniga leóde bronde forbærnan *the Danes' people could not consume the death-weary one with fire*, Beo. Th. 4256; B 2125.

deáþ-wīc, es; *n.* [deáþ *death*, wīc *a mansion*] *A mansion of death;* mortis mansio:—He gewāt deáþwīc seón *he departed to see the mansion of death*, Beo. Th. 2555; B. 1275.

deáþ-wyrda; *pl. f.* [wyrd *fate*] *Death-events, fates;* fata, Cot. 89.

DEÁW, es; *m. n.* DEW; ros:—Swā swā deáw đære dūne đætte [se, Th; se đe, Spl.] niđerastāh on munte odđe to dūne *sicut ros Hermon qui descendit in montem Sion*, Ps. Lamb. 132, 3. On morgen wæs đæt deáw abūtan đa fyrdwīc *mane ros jacŭit per circuĭtum castrōrum*, Ex. 16, 13: Num. 11, 9. Deáw and deór scūr đec dōmige *the dew and heavy rain exalt thee*, Cd. 192; Th. 239, 18; Dan. 372: Exon. 16 b; Th. 38, 19; Cri. 609: 108 a; Th. 412, 11; Rä. 30, 12: Deut. 32, 2. Þurh dropunge deáwes and rēnes *through the dropping of dew and rain*, Ps. Th. 64, 11. Syle đē God of heofenes deáwe *det tibi Deus de rore cœli*, Gen. 27, 28, 39. [*Prompt.* dewe: *Piers P. Chauc.* dewes, *pl*: *Orm.* dæw: *Plat.* dau, *m*: *Frs.* dauwe, douwe: *O. Frs.* daw, *m*: *Dut.* dauw, *m*: *Kil.* dauw, dauwe: *Ger.* thau, tau, *m*: *M. H. Ger. O. H. Ger.* tou, *n*: *Dan.* dug, dugg, *m. f*: *Swed.* dagg, *m*: *Icel.* dögg, *f.*] DER. mele-deáw, sun-.

deáw-driás, es; *m?* [dreósan *to fall*] *A fall of dew, dew-fall;* rōris cāsus:—Deáwdriás on dæge weorþeþ winde geondsāwen *the dew-fall in day is scattered by the wind*, Cd. 188; Th. 233, 17; Dan. 277.

deáwian *to* DEW, *bedew;* rorāre, Som. Ben. Lye.

deáwig; *adj.* DEWY; roscĭdus:—Gūþcyste onþrang deáwig-sceaftum *the war-tribe pressed onwards with dewy shafts*, Cd. 160; Th. 199, 25; Exod. 344. Đara breósta biþ deáwig wǽtung *there is a dewy wetting of the breasts*, L. M. 2, 46; Lchdm. ii. 258, 17.

deáwig-feđere; *def.* se -feđera, seó, đæt -feđere; *adj. Dewy-feathered;* roscĭdus pennis:—Sang se wanna fugel, deáwigfeđera *the sad fowl sang, dewy of feathers*, Cd. 93; Th. 119, 24; Gen. 1984. Hwreópon herefugolas. deáwigfeđere *the fowls of war screamed, dewy-feathered*, 150; Th. 188, 4; Exod. 163.

deáw-wyrm, es; *m. A ringworm, tetter;* impetīgo:—Wiđ deáwwyrmum genim doccan *for ringworms take dock*, L. M. 1, 50; Lchdm. ii. 122, 21: 124, 5, 7.

deccan; *impert.* dec *To cover;* tegĕre:—Dec ānne clāþ đǽr of *cover a cloth therewith*, Herb. 47, 1; Lchdm. i. 150, 19. DER. ge-deccan. v. þeccan.

Decem-ber; *gen.* -bris; *m.* [dĕcem *ten*: *Sansk.* vāra: *Pers.* bār *time, space: the tenth month* of the Romans, beginning with March, and as we begin with January, it is our twelfth month] *The month of December;* Dĕcember, bris, *m*:—Mōnaþ Decembris, ǽrra iūla [geóla] *the month of December, the former yule*, Menol. Fox 437; Men. 220; *January being after* yule *or* Christmas is called Se æftera geóla *the after yule*, Cott. Tibĕrius. B. i; Hick. Thes. i. 212, 57.

declīnigendlīc; *adj. Declinable;* declīnābĭlis:—Feówer synd *declinabĭlia*, đæt is declīnigendlīce *four are* declinabĭlia, *that is declinable*, Ælfc. Gr. 50, 3; Som. 51, 7.

declīnung, e; *f. A declension;* declīnātio:—Seó forme declīnung *the first declension*, Ælfc. Gr. 7; Som. 6, 3. On fīf declīnungum *in five declensions*, 6. 2.

dēd *dead*, Chr. 1129; Erl. 258, 22. v. deád.

dēda *of deeds*, Ps. C. 50, 147; Grn. ii. 280, 147, = dǽda; *gen. pl. of* dǽd.

defe; *adj. Becoming, fit, suitable;* dĕcens, congruus, convĕniens. DER. ge-dēfe, lǽr-ge-, un-ge-: dēfelīc, ge-: dēfelīce, ge-, un-ge-.

dēfe-līc *becoming, fit.* DER. ge-dēfelīc.

dēfe-līce *becomingly, fitly, suitably.* DER. ge-dēfelīce, un-ge-.

Defenas, Defnas; *gen.* a; *dat.* um; *pl. m. Devonians, the inhabitants of Devonshire in a body, Devonshire;* Devonienses, Devŏnia:—Hē wæs Weala gefeoht and Defena [Defna, Th. 110, 16] *in this year* [A. D. 823] *there was a fight of the Welsh and Devonians*, Chr. 823; Th. 111, 16, col. 1, 2. Ǽgđer ge on Defenum [Defnum, col. 2] ge welhwǽr be đæm sǽriman *both in Devon and elsewhere on the sea-shore*, Chr. 897; Th. 176, 8, col. 1: 981; Th. 234, 31: 997; Th. 246, 5. Forþférde Ælfgār on Defenum *Ælfgar died in Devonshire*, Chr. 962; Th. 218, 38.

Defena scīr, Defna scīr, e; *f.* [*Hunt.* Deuenesire, Dauenescyre: *Hovd.* Daveneshire: *Brom.* Deveneschire: *Kni.* Devenchire, Devenschyre] DEVONSHIRE; Devŏnia:—He wæs on Defena scīre *he was in Devonshire*, Chr. 878; Th. 146, 33, col. 1: 851; Th. 120, 20, col. 1. Hī ymbsǽton ān geweorc on Defna scīre *they besieged a fortress in Devonshire*, 894; Th. 166, 28. Sideman wæs Defna scīre bisceop *Sideman was bishop of Devonshire*, 977; Th. 230, 16.

Defenisc; *adj. Of* or *belonging to Devonshire;* Devŏniensis:—Gesomnede man ormǽte fyrde Defenisces folces *an immense force of Devonshire people was collected*, Chr. 1001; Th. 250, 5.

dēfre; *adj. Timely, seasonable*, Som. Ben. Lye; *comp. of* dēfe?

deg *a day*, Th. Diplm. A. D. 830; 465, 21: A. D. 972; 520, 7. v. dæg.

dēg *profits;* prodest, Mt. Kmbl. Lind. 16, 26, = deág, deáh; *pres. of* dugan.

dēg *a colour, dye*, Som. Ben. Lye. v. deáh.

dēgelīce [dēgel-līce] *secretly*, Bt. Met. Fox 1, 127; Met. 1, 64. v. dīgollīce.

dēgelnis *solitude*, Mt. Lind. Stv. 6, 4, 6. v. dīgolnes.

dēgian *to colour, dye*, Mone B. 6251. v. deágian.

dēgle *secret, hidden*, Lk. Lind. War. 8, 17; *nom. n. of* dēgol. v. dīgol.

dēglīce *secretly*, Mt. Lind. Stv. 20, 11. v. dīgollīce.

dēgol *obscurity, mystery*, Elen. Grm. 340: Exon. 46 b; Th. 159, 11; Gū. 925. v. dīgol.

dēgol *secret, unknown*, Exon. 8 b; Th. 3, 24; Cri. 41: 104 b; Th. 397, 17; Rä. 16, 21. v. dīgol; *adj.*

dēgol-ful; *adj. Full of secret, mysterious;* secrēti plēnus, mystĭcus:—Ic mīđan sceal dēgolfulne dōm mīnne *I must conceal my mysterious power*, Exon. 127 b; Th. 491, 14; Rä. 80, 14.

dēgollīce *secretly*, Mk. Rush. War. 9, 28. v. dīgollīce.

dēgolnis *solitude*, Mt. Lind. Stv. 6, 6. v. dīgolnes.

dēgullīce *secretly*, Mt. Rush. Stv. 1, 19. v. dīgollīce.

dēgulnes *solitude*, Mt. Rush. Stv. 6, 4, 6. v. dīgolnes.

dēhter *to a daughter*, Exon. 67 b; Th. 251, 7, Jul. 141; *dat. of* dōhtor.

dehtnung *a disposing*, Prov. 24. v. dihtnung.

Deira rīce *the kingdom of the Deirians*, Som. Ben. Lye. v. Dera rīce.

delan; *p.* dæl, *pl.* dǽlon; *pp.* dolen *To fall, sink;* lābi:—Ǽrđon engla weard for oferhygde dæl on gedwilde *ere the angels' guardian for pride sank into error*, Cd. 1; Th. 2, 22; Gen. 23.

dēlan *to divide*, Cant. Moys. Ex. 15, 10; Thw. notes, p. 29, 10. v. dǽlan.

delf, es; *n. A delving, the act of digging;* fossio, Th. Anlct. DER. ge-delf, stān-ge-. v. dælf.

DELFAN; ic delfe, đū delfest, dilfst, he delfeþ, dilfþ, *pl.* delfaþ; *p.* ic, he dealf, đū dulfe, *pl.* dulfon; *subj.* delfe, *pl.* delfen: *p.* dulfe, *pl.* dulfen; *pp.* dolfen; *v. a. To dig, dig out*, DELVE; fŏdĕre, effŏdĕre:—Ne mæg ic delfan *fŏdĕre non văleo*, Lk. Bos. 16, 3. Ongan he eorþan delfan *he began to dig the earth*, Elen. Kmbl. 1655; El. 829. Ic delfe *fŏdio*, Ælfc. Gr. 28, 6; Som. 32, 45. Đǽr þeófas hit delfaþ *ubi fures effŏdiunt*, Mt. Bos. 6, 19, 20: Exon. 111 b; Th. 427, 27; Rä. 41, 97. Ic dealf đisne pytt *ego fodi pŭteum istum*, Gen. 21, 30. Se dealf deópe *qui fodit in altum*, Lk. Bos. 6, 48. Wæterpyttas đe ge ne dulfon *wells which ye dug not*, Deut. 6, 11. Hī dulfon āne mycle dīc *they dug a great ditch*, Chr. 1016; Erl. 155, 22: Ex. 7, 24: Ps. Lamb. 21, 17: Ps. Th. 56, 8. Swelce hwā delfe eorþan *as if any one should dig the earth*, Bt. 40, 6; Fox 242, 5. Gif se delfere đa eorþan nō ne dulfe *if the digger had not dug the earth*, 40, 6; Fox 242, 7. [*Prompt.* delvyn' *fŏdĕre*: *Wyc.* delue: *Piers P.* delven: *Chauc.* delve: *Laym.* dælfen, deluen: *Orm.* dellfeþþ *burieth*: *Plat.* dölben: *O. Sax.* bi-delban *to bury*: *Frs.* dollen: *O Frs.* delva, dela: *Dut.* delven: *Ger.* delben: *M. H. Ger.* tëlben: *O. H. Ger.* bi-telban *sepelīre.*] DER. a-delfan, be-, ge-, of-, þurh-, under-, upa-, ūta-.

delfere, es; *m. A digger;* fossor:—Gif se delfere đa eorþan nō ne dulfe *if the digger had not dug the earth*, Bt. 40, 6; Fox 242, 7.

delfing, es; *m.* A DELVING, *digging, laying bare, exposing;* ablaqueātio:—Niderwart treówes delfing, bedelfing *ablaqueātio*, Ælfc. Gl. 60; Som. 68, 15; Wrt. Voc. 39, 2. DER. be-delfing.

delf-īsen, es; *n. A digging-iron, spade;* fossōrium:—Costere *vel* delfīsen *vel* spadu *vel* pal *fossōrium*, Ælfc. Gl. 2; Som. 55, 40; Wrt. Voc. 16, 14: Cot. 90.

delu, e; *f*: *pl. nom. gen. acc.* dela; *dat.* delum *A teat, nipple;* mamma:—Wǽron forbrocene đa dela hiora mǽgdenhādes ... bióþ forbrocene đa wæstmas đæra dela *fractæ sunt mammæ pubertātis eārum ... pubertātis mammæ franguntur*, Past. 52; Hat. MS. [*O. H. Ger.* tila, tili, *f. mamma.*]

dem, demm, es; *m. Damage, mischief, harm, injury, loss, misfortune;*

damnum, mălum, noxa, injūria, detrīmentum, calămĭtas:—Ðǣr wæs ān swā micel dem *there was so great a loss*, Ors. 6, 14; Bos. 122, 21. Be ðæs demmes ehte *pro damni æstimatiōne*, Ex. 22, 5. He ðone demm his giémeliéste gebētan ne mæg *he cannot remedy the mischief of his neglect*, Past. 36, 3; Hat. MS. 47 a, 22. Ne wēne ic ðæt ǣnig man atellan mǣge ealne ðone dem ðe Rōmānum gedōn wearþ *I do not think that any man can tell all the harm which was done to the Romans*, Ors. 2, 8; Bos. 51, 28. Hit oft gebȳraþ ðæt seó leáse wyrd ne mæg ðam men dōn nǣnne dem *it often happens that deceitful fortune can do no injury to a man*, Bt. 20; Fox 70, 23. He geman ðone demm oððe ðæt bismer, ðæt him ǣr gedōn wæs *he remembers the injury or the disgrace that was formerly done to him*, Past. 33, 7; Hat. MS. 43 b, 2: Ors. 2, 4; Bos. 43, 29. Ōðrum monnum þyncþ ðæt hie mǣstne demm [dem MS. Cott.] þrōwigen *it seems to other men that they suffer the greatest misfortune*, Past. 14, 5; Hat. MS. 18 a, 26.

DÉMA, an; *m.* [dēman *to deem, judge, think*]. I. *a deemer, thinker, judge, an umpire;* censor, consul, jūdex, arbĭter:—Ic eom se dēma *I am the judge*, Exon. 42 b; Th. 144, 8; Gū. 675: 69 a; Th. 257, 19; Jul. 249: Judth. 10; Thw. 22, 12; Jud. 59. Se Dēma gegaderaþ ðæt clǣne corn into his berne *the Judge shall gather the pure corn into his barn*, Homl. Th. ii. 68, 17: i. 526, 21. Gehȳraþ hwæt se unrihtwīsa dēma cwyþ *audīte quid judex iniquitātis dicit*, Lk. Bos. 18, 6, 2: Ps. Lamb. 74, 8: Ps. Th. 67, 6: Wrt. Voc. 72, 66. Dēma *judex*, vel *censor*, vel *arbĭter*, Ælfc. Gl. 68; Som. 70, 9; Wrt. Voc. 42, 18: 86; Som. 74, 21; Wrt. Voc. 50, 5: *consul*, Ælfc. Gr. 9, 10; Som. 9, 16. Sceall ǣghwylc ðǣr riht gehȳran dǣda gehwylcra, þurh ðæs dēman mūþ *there shall every one hear the right of all his deeds, through the judge's mouth*, Elen. Kmbl. 2564; El. 1283: Exon. 69 b; Th. 257, 33; Jul. 256. Him egsa becom fōr dēman *dread came over them before their judge*, Cd. 221; Th. 288, 13; Sat. 380: 175; Th. 220, 15; Dan. 71. Ic ðone dēman in dagum mīnum wille weorþian *I will worship the judge in my days*, Exon. 41 b; Th. 139, 8; Gū. 590. Besencte syndon wið stān dēman heora *absorpti sunt juxta petram judĭces eōrum*, Ps. Lamb. 140, 6. Dēman *censōres*, vel *judĭces*, vel *arbitri*, Ælfc. Gl. 8; Som. 56, 87; Wrt. Voc. 18, 39. Ealra dēmena ðam gedēfestan *to the most benevolent of all judges*, Exon. 93 a; Th. 350, 3; Sch. 58. Ǣrmorgenes gancg wið ǣfentīd ealle ða dēman Drihten healdeþ *exĭtus matutīni et vespĕre delectabĕris*, Ps. Th. 64, 9. II. *the judge, who gave a wrong judgment, was subject to a fine of one hundred and twenty shillings; and if a man could not obtain justice, the judge to whom he applied was fined thirty shillings. As the judge represented the king, he was at the king's disposal:*—Se dēma, ðe ōðrum wōh dēme, gesylle ðam cynge hundtwelftig scillinga to bōte, būtan he mid āþe gecȳðan durre, ðæt he hit nā rihtor ne cūðe, and þolige ā his þegenscipes, būtan he hine æt ðam cynge gebicge, swā swā he him geþafian wille, and amanige ðære scīre bisceop ða bōte to ðæs cynges handa *let the judge, who judges wrong to another, pay to the king one hundred and twenty shillings for a fine, unless he dare to prove on oath, that he knew it not more rightly, and let him forfeit for ever his thaneship, unless he will buy it of the king, so as he is willing to allow him, and let the bishop of the shire exact the fine* [*and pay it*] *into the king's hands*, L. Edg. ii. 3; Th. i. 266, 15-20. Gif hwā him ryhtes bidde befōran hwelcum scīrmen oððe ōðrum dēman, and abiddan ne mǣge, and him wedd. mon sellan nelle, gebēte xxx scillinga, and binnan vii nihton gedō hine ryhtes wierþne *if any one demand justice before a sheriff or other judge, and cannot obtain it, and the man will not give him a promise, let him make compensation with thirty shillings, and within seven days do him justice*, L. In. 8; Th. i. 106, 20-108, 2. [*Laym.* deme *a judge: Orm.* deme *a chief, ruler, judge: O. H. Ger.* tuomo, *m. judex, dux.*] DER. ealdor-dēma, heofon-, sige-.

dēman, to dēmanne, dēmenne; *part.* dēmende; ic dēme, ðū dēmest, dēmst, he dēmeþ, dēmþ, *pl.* dēmaþ; *p.* dēmde, *pl.* dēmdon; *impert.* dēm, dēme, *pl.* dēmaþ, dēme ge; *pp.* dēmed; *v. trans. dat. acc.* [dōm *judgment, opinion*] *To* DEEM, *judge, think, consider, estimate, reckon, determine, examine, prove, doom, condemn;* judicāre, arbitrāri, æstimāre, censēre, recensēre, decernĕre, sancīre, examināre, condemnāre:—He com dēman eorþan *venit judicāre terram*, Ps. Lamb. 95, 13: Elen. Kmbl. 621; El. 311: Exon. 63 a; Th. 231, 25; Ph. 494. Nellen ge dēman, ðæt ge ne sȳn fordēmede *nolīte judicāre, ut non judicemĭni*, Mt. Bos. 7, 1. Eorþan to dēmanne *judicāre terram*, Ps. Th. 97, 8: Bd. 4, 3; S. 569, 27. To dēmenne ǣgðer ge ðām cucum ge ðām deádum *to judge both the quick and the dead*, Homl. Th. ii. 596, 20: 598, 6. Dēmende *judging*, Past. 15, 6; Hat. MS. 20 a, 19. Ic rihtwīsnessa dēme *justĭtias judicābo*, Ps. Lamb. 74, 3. Ðæs ðe ic dēme *ut arbĭtror*, Bd. 1, 27; S. 497, 5. Ic dēme oððe asmeáge *censeo*, Ælfc. Gr. 26, 2; Som. 28, 51. Ic dēme oððe ic gefette oððe ic hālgige *sancio*, 30, 1; Som. 34, 33. Ðū dēmst [Th. dēmest] folctruman on emnysse *judĭcas popŭlos in æquitāte*, Ps. Lamb. 66, 5. Nǣfre God dēmeþ ðæt ǣnig ðæs earm geweorþe *God never deems* [= *decrees*] *that any should become so poor*, Exon. 78 b; Th. 294, 17; Crā. 16. Ðis fȳr æfter weorca ge-earnunge ānra gehwylcum dēmeþ and bærneþ *iste rogus juxta merĭta opĕrum singŭlos examĭnat*, Bd. 3, 19; S. 548, 27. He dēmþ folcum mid rihte *judicābit popŭlos cum justĭtia*, Ps. Th. 9, 9: Ps. Lamb. 95, 13. Ðam ylcan dōme ðe ge dēmaþ, eów biþ gedēmed *in quo judĭcio judicātis, judicabimĭni*, Mt. Bos. 7, 2. He monige dēmde to deáþe *he doomed many to death*, Elen. Kmbl. 997; El. 500. Moises and Aaron gegaderodon ealle ðās and dēmdon him *quos Moyses et Aaron congregavērunt recensentes eos*, Num. 1, 18. Ne dēm nān unriht ... dēme rihte ðīnum nēxtan *non injuste judicābis ... juste judĭca proxĭmo tuo*, Lev. 19, 15. Rihtlīce dēmaþ eálā ge suna manna *recte judicāte filii homĭnum*, Ps. Lamb. 57, 2: 81, 3. Hū lange dēme ge unrihtwīsnesse *usquequo judicātis iniquitātem?* 81, 2. Ne wæs sōna his hālgung [MS. halgunge] dēmed *nec statim ordinātio decrēta*, Bd. 4, 28; S. 606, 22. Beóþ his dagas swylce dēmde gelīce swā ðū on scimiendre sceade lōcige *dies ejus sicut umbra prætĕreunt*, Ps. Th. 143, 5. [*Wyc. Piers P. Chauc.* demen: *R. Glouc.* ydemd, *pp*: *Laym.* demenn: *Orm.* deme, demen: *O. Sax.* dōman, duomian: *O. Frs.* dēma: *M. H. Ger.* tüemen: *O. H. Ger.* tuomian: *Goth.* domyan: *Dan.* dömme: *Swed.* döma: *Icel.* dæma.] DER. a-dēman, for-, ge-, to-.

dēmend, es; *m. A judge, an umpire;* jūdex, arbĭter:—God sceal on heofenum dǣda demend *God shall be in the heavens judge of actions*, Menol. Fox 531; Gn. C. 36: Exon. 76 a; Th. 286, 1; Jul. 725: Andr. Kmbl. 173; An. 87: 2379; An. 1191.

dēmere, es; *m. A* DEEMER, *judge;* jūdex, L. Alf. 18; Th. i. 48, note 38.

demm *damage, mischief, harm*, Ex. 22, 5: Ors. 2, 4; Bos. 43, 29. v. dem.

demman; *p.* de; *pp.* ed *To* DAM, *stop water;* obturāre flūmen, Som. Ben. Lye. [*O. Frs.* demma, damma: *Dut.* dammen: *Ger.* dämmen: *M. H. Ger.* temmen: *O. H. Ger.* bi-temman *occupāre*: *Goth.* faurdammyan *to dam*: *Dan.* dämme: *Swed.* dämma: *Icel.* demma.] DER. fordemman.

Dena lagu, lag, lah, e; *f. The law of the Danes, Danish law;* Danōrum lex, Danisca lex. v. Dene.

Dena mearc *the land of the Danes, Denmark*, Ors. 1, 1; Bos. 21, 33. v. Dene-mearc.

den-bera; *pl. n. Lat.* [bearo *a grove, wood*] *Swine-pastures, places yielding mast for the fattening of hogs;* pascua porcōrum:—Pascua porcōrum quæ nostra lingua Saxonĭca denbera nominămus, Cod. Dipl. 288; A. D. 863; Kmbl. ii. 75, 27: 281; A. D. 858; Kmbl. ii. 65, 6. Adjectis denberis in commūni saltu, 160; A. D. 765-791; Kmbl. i. 194, 34: 179; A. D. 801; Kmbl. i. 216, 26: 198; A. D. 811; Kmbl. i. 248, 17: 239; A. D. 838; Kmbl. i. 317, 20.

dencgan *to knock, ding;* tundĕre, Som. Ben. Lye.

dene, an; *f. A valley;* vallis:—Dene *vallis*, Ælfc. Gr. 9, 28; Som. 11, 55: Wrt. Voc. 80, 44: Ælfc. Gl. 97; Som. 76, 64; Wrt. Voc. 54, 8. Ǣlc dene biþ gefylled *every valley shall be filled*, Homl. Th. i. 360, 33. Seó dene ðe ðū gesāwe *vallis illa quam aspexisti*, Bd. 5, 12; S. 630, 3. Seó dene wæs afylled mid manna sāwlum *the valley was filled with men's souls*, Homl. Th. ii. 350, 9. Seó micele byrnende dene *the great burning valley*, ii. 352, 20. v. denu.

dene, es; *m. A valley;* vallis:—Abram com and eardode wið ðone dene Mambre *Abram venit et habitāvit juxta convallem Mambre*, Gen. 13, 18. v. denu.

Dene; *nom. acc; gen.* a; *dat.* um; *pl. m. The Danes;* Dāni:—Ðā ða Engle and Dene to friþe and to freóndscipe fullīce fēngon *when the English and Danes fully took to peace and to friendship*, L. E. G; Th. i. 166, 7. Gif hlāford his þeówan freóls-dæge nȳde to weorce, gylde lahslihte inne on Dena lage, and wīte mid Englum *if a lord oblige his servant to work on a festival-day, let him pay penalty within the Danish law, and fine among the English*, L. E. G. 7; Wilk. 53, 1. Sunnan dæges cȳpinge gif hwā agynne þolie ðæs ceápes, and twelf ōrena mid Denum, and xxx scillingas mid Englum *if any one engage in Sunday marketing, let him forfeit the chattel, and twelve ores among the Danes, and thirty shillings among the English*, L. E. G. 7; Th. i. 170, 16.

Dene-mearc, -marc, e; *f*: -marce, -mearce, -merce, an; *f.* DENMARK; Dānia, Cimbrĭca Chersonēsus = Χερσόνησος, *f. a land island, peninsula; from* χέρσος, χέρρος *land, and* νῆσος, ου; *f. an island* [Dene *the Danes*,—denu *a plain, vale, valley;* and mearc *a boundary.* The Saxon Chronicle, in 1005, 1023, 1036, has Denemearc; Denmearc, in 1019, 1075; Denmarc, in 1070 and 1119. In Danish mark signifies *a country;* hence Denmark *the low country of the Danes:* so Finmark *the low country of the Finns.* Wulfstan [Alfred, A. D. 892] is the most early writer hitherto known, who mentions Denmark]:—Wulfstān sǣde ðæt he gefōre of Hǣðum. Weonoþland him wæs on steór-bord, and on bæc-bord him wæs Langa land, and Lǣland, and Falster, and Scon-ēg; and ðās land eall hȳraþ to Denemearcan *Wulfstan said that he went from Haddeby. He had Weonodland on the right, and Langland, Laaland, Falster, and Sconey on his left; and all these lands belong to Denmark*, Ors. 1, 1; Bos. 21, 39, 41-43. Ða īgland in Denemearce hȳraþ *these islands belong to Denmark*, 1, 1; Bos. 21, 38.

Denisc; *def.* se Denisca; *adj.* DANISH; Dānicus:—Gif man ofslagen weorþe, ealle we lǣtaþ efen dȳrne, Engliscne and Deniscne *if a man be slain, we estimate all equally dear, English and Danish*, L. A. G. 2;

Th. i. 154, 1. Wiđ Deniscne here *against the Danish army*, Chr. 837; Erl. 66, 7: 845; Erl. 66, 23. Nǽron hí náwđer ne on Frysisc gesceapen ne on Denisc *they were shapen neither as the Frisian nor as the Danish*, Chr. 897; Th 177, 3, col. 2. Hér, A.D. 872, Ælfréd cyning gefeaht wiđ feówer sciphlæstas Deniscra monna *here*, A.D. 872, *king Alfred fought against four ship-crews of Danish men*, 872; Th. 150, 28, col. 1. Đá com đǽm Deniscum scipum flód to *then the tide came to the Danish ships*, 897; Th. 176, 37, col. 1. Com đá se Denisca flóta to Sandwíc *then*, A.D. 1006, *the Danish fleet came to Sandwich*, 1006; Th. 257, 4, col. 1.

Deniscan; *gen.* ena; *pl. m.* [Denisca, *def. of* Denisc; *adj.*] *The Danish men, the Danes;* Dānĭci viri, Dāni:—Hér, A. D. 835, Ecgbryht, Westseaxna cing, geflýmde ge đa Wealas ge đa Deniscan *here*, A. D. 835, *Ecgbryht, king of the West Saxons, routed both the Welsh and the Danes*, Chr. 835; Th. 116, 13-23, col. 1, 2. Đa Deniscan áhton wælstówe geweald *the Danes obtained power of the battle-place*, Chr. 833; Erl. 65, 19: 837; Erl. 67, 8: 840; Erl. 67, 13: 871; Erl. 75, 15: 871; Erl. 77, 6: 999; Erl. 134, 26. On đæra Deniscena healfe wæs ofslægen Eoric cyning *king Eric was slain on the side of the Danes*, Chr. 905; Erl. 99, 32: 910; Erl. 100, 15. v. Denisc.

Denisses burna, an; *m.* DENISESBURN, *the river Denis;* Denisi rivus:—On đære stówe đe Engle nemnaþ Denisses burna *in loco qui lingua Anglōrum Denises burna, id est rivus Denisi vocātur*, Bd. 3, 1; S. 524, 10.

DENN, es; *n. A* DEN; cubīle, lustrum? [lustra MS.]:—Denn *cubile*, Ælfc. Gr. 9, 2; Som. 8, 27. Wild-deóra holl and denn *lustrum ferārum* [MS. *lustra*], Ælfc. Gl. 110; Som. 79, 38; Wrt. Voc. 59, 10. Se lég-draca gewát dennes niósian *the fire-dragon went to visit his den*, Beo. Th. 6082; B. 3045. Geseah he wundur on đæs wyrmes denn *he saw wonders in the dragon's* [lit. *worm's*] *den*, 5512; B. 2759. [*Prompt.* deñ *specus*: *Wyc.* den: *Chauc.* dennes *caves*: *Laym.* denne: *Dut.* denne, *f. deck of a ship*: *Kil.* denne *ārea, antrum*: *Ger.* tenne, *f. area*: *M. H. Ger.* tenne, *n. area*: *O. H. Ger.* tenni, *n. area.*]

dennian; *p.* ode, ade; *pp.* od, ad *To become slippery;* lubrĭcum fiĕri:—Feld dennode [dennade, col. 1] secga swáte *the plain became slippery with the blood of soldiers*, Chr. 937; Th. 203, 10, col. 2; Æđelst. 12.

den-sǽte; *m. pl. Dwellers in valleys* or *plains;* vallicŏlæ. v. sǽte.

denu, e; *f:* dene, an; *f:* dene, es; *m. A plain, vale, dale, valley;* vallis, convallis:—Seó denu đe đú gesáwe weallendum lígum *vallis illa quam aspexisti flammis ferventĭbus*, Bd. 5, 12; S. 630, 3, note, MS. B. Seó stów đǽr seó denu wæs *the place where the valley was*, 5, 12; S. 630, note 3, MS. T. Ælc denu biþ gefylled *omnis vallis implebĭtur*, Lk. Bos. 3, 5. Đá becóme wit to ánre dene, seó wæs ormǽtlíce deóp and wíd, and forneán on lenge unge-endod *we two then came to a valley, which was immensely deep and wide, and in length almost endless*, Homl. Th. ii. 350, 6: Bd. 5, 12; S. 627, 36: Ps Lamb. 83, 7: Bt. Met. Fox 7, 73; Met. 7, 37: Salm. Kmbl. 458; Sal. 229. From Ebron dene *de valle Hebron*, Gen. 37, 14. He gebirgde hine on đære dene Moab landes ongeán Phogor *sepelīvit eum in valle terræ Moab contra Phogor*, Deut. 34, 6. Dene getelda ic mete *convallem tabernaculōrum dimētiar*, Ps. Spl. 107, 7. Dena genihtsumiaþ of hwǽte *valles abundābunt frumento*, 64, 14: Exon. 115 b; Th. 443, 14; Kl. 30. Dene, *nom. pl.* Exon. 56 a; Th. 199, 11; Ph. 24. Đú đe asendst wyllas on denum *qui emittis fontes in convallĭbus*, Ps. Lamb. 103, 10: Exon. 107 b; Th. 409, 18; Rä. 28, 3. [It is often used as a termination of the names of places situate in *a plain* or *valley*, as *Tenterden, etc.*] DER. deáþ-denu.

deófel-líc; *adj. Diabolical, devilish;* diabolĭcus:—Mid deófellícum wiglungum *with devilish incantations*, Homl. Th. i. 102, 11.

deófel-seócnys, -nyss *devil-sickness*, Mt. Bos. 4, 24. v. deófol-seócnes.

deófles *of the devil*, Andr. Kmbl. 86; An. 43; *gen. of* deófol.

deóflíc, deófel-líc; *adj. Devilish, diabolical;* diabolĭcus:—Úre heofenlíca Hláford đone deóflícan deáþ nyđeratræd *our heavenly Lord trod down the diabolical death*, Nicod. 29; Thw. 16, 40. Undergeat se apostol đás deóflícan fácn *the apostle perceived these diabolical wiles*, Homl. Th. i. 62, 31. Mid deóflícum wiglungum *with diabolical incantations*, i. 102, 15.

DEÓFOL, deóful, dióful; contracted to deófl; *gen.* es; *dat.* e; *nom. pl.* deóflu, deófol; *gen.* deófla; *m. n. The* DEVIL; diabŏlus. I. *m.* Nú þencþ menig man and smeáþ hwanon deófol cóme? Đonne wite he đæt God gesceóp, to mǽran engle, đone đe nú is deófol; ac God ne gesceóp hine ná to deófle; ac đá đá he wæs mid ealle fordón and forscyldgod þurh đa miclan upahefednysse and wiđerweardnysse, đá wearþ he to deófle awend, se đe ǽr wæs mǽre engel geworht *now many a man will think and inquire whence the devil came? Then let him know that God created, as a great angel, him who is now the devil; but God did not create him as the devil; but when he was wholly done for and guilty towards God, through his great haughtiness and enmity, then became he changed to the devil, who before was created a great angel*, Homl. Th. i. 12, 18-23. Se deófol ne wunode ná on sóþfæstnysse, forđamđe seó sóþfæstnyss nis náteshwon on him *the devil abided not in the truth, because the truth is not in any wise in him*, Hexam. 10; Norm. 16, 18. Đæt he đone deófol adríſe *ut dæmŏnium ejicĕret*, Mk. Bos. 7, 26. II. *n.* Him biþ đæt deófol láþ *the devil is loathly to them*, Salm. Kmbl. 246; Sal. 122. Hyre đæt deófol oncwæþ *the devil addressed her*, Exon. 72 b; Th. 270, 5; Jul. 460. Heó đæt deófol genom *she took the devil*, 69 b; Th. 259, 27; Jul. 288. Heó đæt deófol teáh bendum fæstne *she drew the devil fast in bonds*, 73 b; Th. 274, 17; Jul. 534. On deófla ealdre he drífþ út deóflu *in princĭpe dæmoniōrum ejicit dæmŏnes*, Mt. Bos. 9, 34. Deófol, *nom. pl.* Exon. 30 b; Th. 93, 27; Cri. 1532: *acc. pl.* Exon. 118 b; Th. 455, 18; Hy. 4, 51. [*Prompt.* dewle, devylle: *Wyc.* deuel: *Piers P.* deovel: *Chauc.* deuill: *Laym.* deauel, deouel: *Orm.* deofell, defell: *Plat.* düvel, düwel, *m*: *O. Sax.* diubal, diobol, diabol, diuvil, *m*: *Frs.* deal, dijvel, *m*: *O. Frs.* diovel, divel, *m*: *Dut.* duivel, *m*: *Ger.* teufel, *m*: *M. H. Ger.* tiuvel, tievel, *m*: *O. H. Ger.* tiufal, *m*: *Goth.* diabaulus, *m*: *Dan.* diævel, dievel, *m*: *Swed.* djefvul, *m*: *Icel.* djöfull, *m*: *Lat.* diabŏlus, *m*: *Grk.* διάβολος *an accuser* or *slanderer*, *m*; from διαβάλλω *to cast* or *dart through* or *against*; figuratively, *to stab with an accusation* or *slander*; διά *through, against, and* βάλλω *to cast.* Διάβολος = ἀντίδῐκος *an opponent, adversary* = שָׂטָן *m. Satan, q. v.*] DER. helle-deófol, hilde-.

deófol-cræft, es; *m. Devil-craft, the black art, witchcraft;* dæmoniăca ars:—Þurh dígolnesse deófolcræftes *per dæmoniacæ artis arcāna*, Bd. 4, 27; S. 604, 9. Hí nalæs mid deófolcræfte ac mid godcunde mægene gewelgade cóman *illi non dæmoniaca sed divīna virtūte prædĭti veniēbant*, Bd. 1, 25; S. 487, 1.

deófol-cund *diabolical.* v. deóful-cund.

deófol-dǽd, e; *f. A devil-deed, diabolical deed;* diabŏli machinātio, diabolĭcum facĭnus:—Hie wlenco anwód deófoldǽdum *pride invaded them with diabolical deeds*, Cd. 173; Th. 217, 5; Dan. 18.

deófol-gild, deóful-gild, diófol-gild, -geld, -gield, -gyld, es; *n.* [deófol, gild *tribute, worship*] *Devil-worship, sacrifice to devils, idolatry, an idol, an image of the devil;* diabŏli *vel* dæmŏnum cultus, idololatrīa = εἰδωλολατρεία, idōlum, simulacrum:—Đæt man mihte dón heora deófolgyld *that they might do their devil-worship*, Ors. 3, 3; Bos. 55, 29, 33, 37: Andr. Kmbl. 3372; An. 1690: Exon. 66 b; Th. 245, 29; Jul. 52: Bd. 1, 7; S. 477, 4: L. Ecg. C. 38; Th. ii. 162, 22, note 6. Betwih deófolgyldum lifdon *inter idōla vivĕrent*, Bd. 3, 30; S. 562, 19: Exon. 68 a; Th. 251, 25; Jul. 150. Beóþ deófolgyld dysigra þeóda gold and seolfur *simulacra gentium argentum et aurum*, Ps. Th. 134, 15: 113, 12: Bd. 3, 30; S. 561, 43: Cd. 145; Th. 180, 18; Exod. 47: Elen. Grm. 1041: Cot. 118.

deófol-gylda, an; *m.* [gild = gyld *a worship*, with -a *a worshipper*] *A worshipper of the devil, an idolater;* idololatres = εἰδωλολάτρης:—Đa deófolgyldan gecwǽdon đæt hí woldon đone apostol to heora hǽđenscipe geneádian *the idolaters said that they would force the apostle to their heathenship*, Homl. Th. i. 70, 23.

deófolgyld-hús *a heathen temple.* v. deófulgyld-hús.

deófol-scín, es; *pl. nom. acc.* -scínnu; *n.* [scín *a vision, phantom, demon*] *A diabolical vision, phantom, demon;* dæmoniăcus vīsus, dæmon:—Deófolscín *dæmoniăcus visus*, M. H. 106 b. Deófolscínnu *dæmŏnia*, Scint. 7.

deófol-seóc; *def.* se deófol-seóca; *adj.* [seóc *sick*] *Devil-sick, possessed with a devil;* dæmŏnium hăbens, dæmoniăcus:—Đá wæs him broht án deófolseóc man *tunc oblātus est ei dæmŏnium habens*, Mt. Bos. 12, 22: 9, 32. Híg brohton him manege deófolseóce *obtulērunt ei multos dæmŏnia habentes*, 8, 16. Deófolseóc *dæmoniăcus*, Ælfc. Gl. 78; Som. 72, 34; Wrt. Voc. 45, 66. Hí đa ofsettan deófolseócan forléton *they forsook the possessed demoniacs*, Homl. Th. i. 64, 26.

deófol-seócnes, deóful-seócnes, deófel-seócnes, -ness, -nyss, e; *f. Devil sickness, possession with the devil;* dæmŏnium = δαιμόνιον:—Deófolseócnessa us synd on đínum naman underþeódde *dæmŏnia subjiciuntur nobis in nomĭne tuo*, Lk. Bos. 10, 17. Sume we gesáwon on đínum naman deófolseócnessa útadrífende *vidĭmus quemdam in nomĭne tuo ejicientem dæmŏnia*, Mk. Bos. 9, 38: 16, 17: Lk. Bos. 9, 49: 13, 32. He sealde him mihte ofer ealle deófolseócnessa *dedit illis virtūtem super omnia dæmŏnia*, Lk. Bos. 9, 1. Đe hæfdon deófolseócnesse *habentes dæmŏnia*, Mt. Bos. 8, 28. Deófolseócnysse he hæfþ *dæmŏnium habet*, Lk. Bos. 7, 33. Deófulseócnysse *dæmŏnium*, Mt. Bos. 11, 18. Đe đa deófulseócnyssa hæfdon *qui dæmŏnia habuĕrant*, 8, 33. Deófelseócnyssa *dæmŏnia*, 4, 24.

deófol-wítga, an; *m. A devil-prophet, soothsayer, wizard;* vates diabolĭcus, magus:—Him andswaredon deófolwítgan *the soothsayers answered him*, Cd. 178; Th. 223, 31; Dan. 128.

deóful *the devil*, Mt. Bos. 13, 19. v. deófol.

deóful-cund; *adj. Devil-kind* or *similar, diabolical;* diabŏlĭcus:—Gewát se deófulcunda *the diabolical departed*, Judth. 10; Thw. 22, 14; Jud. 61.

deóful-gild, -gyld *idolatry, an idol*, Andr. Kmbl. 3372; An. 1690: Ors. 6, 36; Bos. 131, 41: Bd. 3, 1; S. 523, 23: 3, 30; S. 562, 15. v. deófol-gild.

deófulgyld-hús, es; *n. A heathen temple;* paganōrum templum:—Constantinus hét ðæt man cyriceau timbrede, and ðæt man belūce ǽlc deófulgyldhūs *Constantine ordered churches to be built, and every heathen temple to be closed*, Ors. 6, 30; Bos. 127, 36.

deóful-seócnys, -nyss *devil-sickness*, Mt. Bos. 8, 33: 11, 18. v. deófol-seócnes.

deóg, *pl.* deógon *dyed, coloured*, Beo. Th. 1704; B. 850; *p. of* deágan.

deógol *secret*, Beo. Th. 555; B. 275: Elen. Grm. 1093. v. dīgol.

deógollīce *secretly*:—Deógollīce folcrǽd fremede *secretly did public benefits*. Andr. Kmbl. 1241; An. 621. v. dīgollīce.

DEÓP, dióp; *adj.* DEEP, *profound, stern, awful, solemn;* prŏfundus, grăvis, sōlemnis:—Ðes pytt is deóp *this well is deep*, Jn. Bos. 4, 11. Deóp wæter *the deep water*, Exon. 54 b; Th. 193, 19; Az. 124. Fīftena stōd deóp ofer dūnum flōd elna *the flood stood fifteen ells deep over the hills*, Cd. 69; Th. 84, 15; Gen. 1398. Noe oferlāþ ðone deópestan drencflōda *Noah sailed over the deepest of drowning floods*, 161; Th. 200, 29; Exod. 364. Hū hēh and deóp hell seó *how high and deep hell is!* 228; Th. 309, 9; Sat. 707. Deópra dolga *of deep wounds*, Exon. 114 a; Th. 438, 7; Rä. 57, 4. Wǽrun ðīne geþancas þearle deópe *nimis profundæ factæ sunt cogitatiōnes tuæ*, Ps. Th. 91, 4. Deóp leán *a deep requital*, Cd. 167; Th. 209, 29; Exod. 506. Þurh deópne gedwolan *through profound error*, Exon. 70 a; Th. 260, 22; Jul. 301. Onguldon deópra firena *they atoned for their deep crimes*, 45 a; Th. 153, 23; Gū. 830. Þurh deópne dōm *through stern doom*, 42 a; Th. 142, 8; Cū. 641. On ðam deópan dæge *on that awful day*, 116 b; Th. 448, 24; Dōm. 59. Ðū mīne sāwle ofer deópum deáþe gelǽddest *eripuisti anĭmam meam de morte*, Ps. Th. 114, 8. Deópne āþ Drihten aswōr *jurāvit Domĭnus solemne jurāmentum*, 131, 11. Moyses sægde hālige spræce, deóp ǽrende *Moses delivered a holy speech, a solemn message*, Cd. 169; Th. 210, 20; Exod. 518. [*Prompt. Wyc.* depe: *Piers P.* dupe: *Chauc. R. Glouc.* depe: *Laym.* deop, deap: *Orm.* deope, depe, deop, dep: *Plat.* deep, deip: *O. Sax O. Frs.* diop, diap: *Dut.* diep: *Kil.* duyp: *Ger. M. H. Ger.* tief: *O. H. Ger.* tiuf: *Goth.* diups: *Dan.* dyb: *Swed.* djup: *Icel.* djúpr.] DER. un-deóp.

deóp, dȳp. dióp, es; *n:* dȳpe, an; *f. Depth, the deep, abyss;* prŏfundum:—Ne me forswelge sǽ-grundes deóp *ne me absorbeat profundum*, Ps. Th. 68, 15. Adō me of deópe deorces wæteres *libĕra me de profundo aquārum*, 68, 14. Ic slōh gārsecges deóp *I struck the ocean's deep*, Cd. 147; Th. 195, 24; Exod. 281: Beo. Th. 5091; B. 2549: Exon. 93 b; Th. 351, 21; Sch. 83.

deópe, diópe; *comp.* -or; *sup.* -ost; *adv. Deeply, profoundly, thoroughly, entirely, earnestly;* prŏfunde, gravĭter, subtīlĭter, penĭtus, solemnĭter:—He wearþ deópe gedolgod *he became deeply wounded*, Exon. 113 b; Th. 435, 25; Rä. 54, 6. Gedrēfede ða deópe syndan *turbāti sunt gravĭter*, Ps. Th. 106, 26. Se ðis līf deópe geond þenceþ *who profoundly contemplates this life*, Exon. 77 b; Th. 291, 29; Wand. 89. Būton he ðe deóppor hit gebēte *unless he amend it the more earnestly*, Cod. Dipl. 773; A. D. 1044; Kmbl. iv. 87, 13. Ðæt ðū deópost cunne *what thou most thoroughly knowest*, Exon. 88 b; Th. 333, 10; Gn. Ex. 2. Nis mīn bān wið ðē deópe behȳded *non est* [*pĕnĭtus*] *occultātum os meum abs te*, Ps. Th. 138, 13. Nū ic ðē halsie deópe *now I beseech thee earnestly*, Exon. 121 a; Th. 465, 22; Hö. 108.

deóp-hycgende; *part. Deeply meditating;* contemplābundus, Exon. 49 a; Th. 168, 29; Gū. 1085; Elen. Grm. 353: 881.

deóp-hydig; *adj. Deeply meditating, thoughtful;* contemplābundus:—Cwicra gehwylc deóp-hydigra *each thoughtful being*, Exon. 117 a; Th. 450, 31; Dōm. 96: 47 a; Th. 162, 12; Gū. 974.

deóplic; *adj. Deep;* prŏfundus:—Deóplīc dǽdbōt biþ *it is a deep penitence*, L. Pen. 10; Th. ii. 280, 17: Exon. 98 a; Th. 367, 5; Seel. 3: 49 a; Th. 169, 32; Gū. 1103.

deóp-līce, dióp-līce; *comp.* -līcor; *sup.* -līcost; *adv.* DEEPLY, *profoundly, thoroughly;* profunde, subtīlĭter:—Þearle deóplīce ðū sprycst *valde profunde loquĕris*, Coll. Monast. Th. 32, 9: Exon. 49 a; Th. 169, 13; Gū. 1094: Bt. Met. Fox 22, 5; Met. 22, 3. Dióplīce spirigan æfter ryhte *to search deeply after truth*, Bt. 35, 1; Fox 154, 19. Wit sculon deóplīcor ymbe ðæt beón *we two must inquire more deeply about it*, 5, 3; Fox 12, 12. Ðe deóplīcost Dryhtnes gerȳno reccan cūðon *who most profoundly could relate the Lord's mysteries*, Elen. Kmbl. 559; El. 280.

deópnes, diópnes, -ness, -nys, -nyss, -niss, e; *f.* DEEPNESS, *depth, an abyss;* prŏfundum, altitūdo, ăbyssus = ἄβυσσος, vŏrāgo:—Onafæstnod ic eom on līme deópnesse . . . ic com on deópnysse sǽ *infixus sum in līmo profundi . . . vēni in altitudĭnem măris*, Ps. Lamb. 68, 3. Ǽnig ne wāt ða deópnesse Drihtnes mihta *no one knows the depth of the Lord's might*, Hy. 3, 33; Hy. Grn. ii. 282, 33. Is neowelnes oððe deópnes swā swā scrūd oððe hrægl gegyrlu oððe wǽfels his *est abyssus sicut vestimentum amictus ejus*, Ps. Lamb. 103, 6. Deópnys *abyssus*, Ælfc. Gl. 98; Som. 76, 91; Wrt. Voc. 54, 35. Nywelnes oððe deópnys deópnissa gecīgd *abyssus abyssum invŏcat*, Ps. Lamb. 41, 8. On ðære hellīcan deópnysse *in the hellish abyss*, Nicod. 24; Thw. 12, 20. Gesettende on goldhordum dióҏnyssa oððe nywelnyssa *ponens in thesauris abyssos*, Ps. Lamb. 32, 7. Cwicsūsl *vel* helelīc deópnes *barathrum, vorăgo profunda*, Ælfc. Gl. 54; Som. 66, 97; Wrt. Voc. 36, 20.

deóp-þancol; *adj. Deep-thinking, contemplative;* cogitābundus, contemplātīvus, Som. Ben. Lye. DER. un-deópþancol.

DEÓR, diór, es; *n. An animal, any sort of wild animal, a wild beast,* DEER; *mostly in contrast to domestic animals;* fĕra, bestia:—Is ðæt deór pandher hāten *the animal is called panther*, Exon. 95 b; Th. 356, 16; Pa. 12. Ðæt is wrætlīc deór, hiwa gehwylces *that is a curious beast, of every hue*, 95 b; Th. 356, 29; Pa. 19. God geworhte ðære eorþan deór æfter hira hiwum, and ða nītenu on heora cynne *fēcit Deus bestias terræ juxta spĕcies suas, et jumenta in genĕre suo*, Gen. 1, 25. Uton wircean man to andlīcnisse, and to ūre gelīcnisse, and he sig ofer ða deór *faciāmus homĭnem ad imagĭnem, et similitudĭnem nostram, et præsit bestiis*, 1, 26. Lǽde seó eorþe forþ cuce nītena on heora cinne, and deór æfter heora hiwum *prodūcat terra anĭmam viventem, jumenta in genĕre suo, et bestias terræ secundum spĕcies suas*, 1, 24. Ohthere hæfde, ðā he ðone cyningc sōhte, tamra deóra unbebohtra syx hund. Ða deór hī hātaþ hrānas *Ohthere had, when he came to the king, six hundred of tame* DEER *unbought* [non emptus *untrafficked* or *traded in*]. *These* DEER *they call reins*, Ors. 1, 1; Bos. 20, 25–27. Rēðe deór *a fierce beast;* bellua, Ælfc. Gl. 18; Som. 58, 126. Ānhyrne deór *a one-horned beast, unicorn, rhinoceros;* unicornis *vel* monocĕros *vel* rinocĕros, μονόκερως *vel* ῥινόκερως, 18; Som. 58, 130; Wrt. Voc. 22, 43: 78, 1. [*R. Brun. Chauc. R. Glouc.* der: *Laym. Orm.* deor, der: *Plat.* deert, *n*: *O. Sax.* dier, *n*: *O. Frs.* diar, dier, *n*: *Dut.* dier, *n*: *Ger.* thier, *n*: *M. H. Ger.* tier, *n*: *O. H. Ger.* tior, tier, *n*: *Goth.* dius, *n*: *Dan.* dyr, *n*: *Swed.* djur, *n*: *Icel.* dýr, *n*: *Grk.* θήρ *a wild beast.*] DER. heá-deór, mere-, rāh-, sǽ-, wǽg-, wild-.

deór, diór, dȳr; *adj.* [deór *an animal*]. **I.** *brave, bold,* as a wild beast; fortis, strēnuus:—Se hālga wæs to hofe lǽded, deór and dōmgeorn *the holy one was led to the house, bold and virtuous*, Andr. Kmbl. 2617; An. 1310: Exon. 108 b; Th. 414, 6; Rä. 32, 16. Nis mon in his dǽdum to ðæs deór *there is not a man so bold in his deeds*, Exon. 82 a; Th. 308, 17; Seef. 41. Ðæt wæs se deóra, Didimus wæs hāten *that was the bold one, he was called Didymus*, Cd. 225; Th. 299, 1; Sat. 543. Georne gewyrcan deóres dryhtscipes *to zealously labour for bold rulership*, Salm. Kmbl. 775; Sal. 387. Deórum dǽdum *by bold deeds*, Exon. 82 b; Th. 310, 17; Seef. 76. Wǽron mancynnes dugoþa dȳrust *they were of mankind the bravest of people*, Cd. 174; Th. 218, 10; Dan. 37. **II.** *heavy, severe, dire, vehement;* grăvis, dīrus, vehĕmens:—Deór scūr *heavy rain*, Cd. 192; Th. 239, 18; Dan. 372. Diór dǽdfruma *the dire perpetrator, Grendel*, Beo. Th. 4186; B. 2090. Ðone deóran sīþ *the severe journey*, Salm. Kmbl. 723; Sal. 361. Swenga ne wyrnaþ deórra dynta *they are not sparing of strokes, severe blows*, Salm. Kmbl. 245; Sal. 122. DER. deór-līc, -mōd: heaðo-deór, hilde-.

Deóra bȳ, Deór-bȳ, es; *n?* [*Hunt.* Dereby, Derebi: *Ethel.* Derebi: deór *an animal, deer;* bȳ *a dwelling, habitation; a habitation of deer* or *animals*] DERBY; Derbia:—Hēr Ǽðelflǽd, Myrcna hlǽfdige, begeat ða burh ðe is gehāten Deóra bȳ *in this year* [A. D. 917] *Æthelfled, lady of the Mercians, obtained the burgh which is called Derby*, Chr. 917; Erl. 105, 24: 942; Erl. 116, 14; Ǽdm. 8. Hēr wæs eorþstyrung on Deórbȳ *in this year* [A. D. 1049] *there was an earthquake at Derby*, 1049; Erl. 173, 18.

Deora mǽgþ, Deora rīce *the province* or *kingdom of the Deirians*, Som. Ben. Lye. v. Dera mǽgþ, Dera-rīce.

deóran, dȳran; *p.* ede; *pp.* ed *To hold dear, love;* cārum habēre:—Heó deóraþ mīne wīsan *they love my ways*, Exon. 103 b; Th. 393, 9; Rä. 12, 7. Dȳran sceolde he his dreámas on heofonum *he should hold dear his joys in heaven*, Cd. 14; Th. 17, 9; Gen. 257.

deór-boren, diór-boren; *comp.* -ra; *sup.* -est; *adj. Noble-born, noble;* nātu nōbilis:—Ða ilcan riht dō man be ðam deórborenran *let the same rights be done with respect to the nobler-born*, L. In. 34; Th. i. 124, 3.

Deór-bȳ *Derby*, Chr. 1049; Erl. 195, 35. v. Deóra bȳ.

Deórbȳ-scīr, Deórbī-scīr, e; *f.* [*Brom.* Derbyschire] DERBYSHIRE; ager Derbiensis:—He fōr sūþ mid ealre ðære scīre, and mid Snotinghamscīre, and Deórbȳscīre [Deorbīscīre, Erl. 194, 20] *he went south with all the shire, and with Nottinghamshire, and Derbyshire*, Chr. 1065; Erl. 195, 35.

DEORC; *def.* se deorca, seó, ðæt deorce; *adj.* DARK, *obscure, gloomy, sad;* tenebrōsus, obscūrus:—Niht-helm geswearc, deorc ofer dryhtgumum *the helm of night grew murky, dark o'er the vassals*, Beo. Th. 3584; B. 1790: Exon. 30 b; Th. 95, 22; Cri. 1561: 101 b; Th. 384, 2; Rä. 4, 21. Hī me asetton on seáþ [MS. sceaþ] hinder, ðǽr wæs deorc þeóstru, and deáþes scūa *posuĕrunt me in lacu inferiōri, et in tenĕbris, et in umbra mortis*, Ps. Th. 87, 6: Lk. Bos. 11, 34. Biþ se deorca deáþ ge-endad *the dark death shall be ended*, Exon. 63 a; Th. 231, 34; Ph. 499: Ps. Th. 101, 9. Seó deorce niht gewīteþ *the dark night departs*, Exon. 57 a; Th. 204, 16; Ph. 98. Adō me of deópe deorces wæteres *libĕra me de profundo aquārum*, Ps. Th. 68, 14. He hī of ðām þȳstrum ðanon alǽdde, and of deáþes scūan deorcum generede *eduxit eos de tenĕbris, et umbra mortis*, 106, 13. On ðære deorcan niht *in the dark night*, Andr. Kmbl. 2922; An. 1464: Exon. 50 b; Th. 175, 8; Gū. 1191. Drihten sealde him dimne and deorcne deáþes scūwan *the Lord gave him death's* *shadow dim and dark*, Cd. 223; Th. 293, 14; Sat. 455: Exon. 61 a; Th. 225, 2; Ph. 383. Ðū dæg settest, and deorce niht *tuus est dies, et tua est nox*, Ps. Th. 73, 16: 142, 4. Wæs ðæs fugles flyht dyrne and dēgol ðām ðe deorc gewit hæfdon on hreðre *the bird's flight was hidden and secret to those who had a dark understanding in their breasts*, Exon. 17 a; Th. 40, 18; Cri. 640: Cd. 5; Th. 7, 19; Gen. 108. Se ðis deorce līf deópe geondþenceþ *he profoundly contemplates this dark life*, Exon. 77 b; Th. 291, 28; Wand. 89. Feónd seondon rēðe, dimme and deorce *our foes are fierce, dim and dark*, Cd. 215; Th. 271, 13; Sat. 105: Ps. Th. 73, 19: 113, 12. Gebrecu fēraþ deorc ofer dreohtum [MS. dreontum] *the crashes go dark over multitudes*, Exon. 102 a; Th. 385, 15; Rä. 4, 45: 48 b; Th. 168, 1; Gū. 1071. Cwīst ðū oncnāwaþ hī wundru ðīne, on ðām dimmum deorcan þȳstrum *numquid cognoscentur in tenebris mirabĭlia tua?* Ps. Th. 87, 12. He wāt deorce grundas *he knows the dark places*, 134, 6: 145, 6. Ðū scealt andettan hwæt ðū þurhtogen hæbbe deorcum gedwildum *thou shalt confess what thou hast accomplished by dark errors*, Exon. 72 b; Th. 270, 4; Jul. 460: Beo. Th. 556; B. 275. Þurhdrifon hī me mid deorcan næglum *they pierced me with dark nails*, Rood Kmbl. 91; Kr. 46. [*Prompt.* derke: *Wyc.* derk-: *Chauc.* dark-: *Piers P.* derk: *R. Glouc.* derk: *O. H. Ger.* tarni *latens*, tarhnjan *occultāre*: *Icel.* dökkr: *Gael.* dorch *dark, black, dusky*.] DER. deorce: deorcian, a-: deorcung.

deorce; *adv. Darkly, sadly*; obscūre:—Ðū his dagena tīd deorce gescyrtest *minorasti dies tempŏris ejus*, Ps. Th. 88, 38. Nǣfre ge heortan geþanc deorce forhyrden *nolīte obdurāre corda vestra*, 94, 8.

deorc-full; *adj. Darksome, dark*; tenebrōsus:—Deorcfull wæg *via tenebrōsa*, Scint. 59.

deorcian; *p.* ode; *pp.* od *To darken, to grow dark*; obscurāre, obscūre facĕre. DER. a-deorcian. v. deorc.

deorc-līce; *adv. Darkly, horridly*; tetrum, Glos. Prudent. Recd. 142, 7.

deorcung, e; *f. Twilight*; crepuscŭlum:—Tweóne leóht *vel* deorcung *crepuscŭlum*, Ælfc. Gl. 94; Som. 75, 122; Wrt. Voc. 53, 3. Deorcunge, ǣfnunge *crepuscŭlo*, Mone B. 178.

deór-cynn, es; *n. Animal-kind, beast-kind*; animālium *vel* bestiārum gĕnus:—Sume wurdon to ðam deórcynne ðe mon hāt tigris *some were turned to the kind of beast which man calls tiger*, Bt. 38, 1; Fox 196, 1. On ðam syxtan dæge God gescōp eall deórcynn *on the sixth day God created all kinds of animals*, Bd. de nat. rerum; Wrt. popl. science 2, 16; Lchdm. iii. 234, 14: Hexam. 9; Norm. 14, 27. To mistlīcum deórcynnum *to various kinds of beasts*, Bt. 38, 1; Fox 196, 2.

DEÓRE, dióre; *adj.* I. DEAR, *beloved*; cārus, dilectus, familiāris:—Deóre wæs he Drihtne ūrum *he was dear to our Lord*, Cd. 14; Th. 17, 17; Gen. 261: 214; Th. 269, 32; Sat. 82: Exon. 105 a; Th. 399, 13; Rä. 18, 10. Dæg byþ deóre mannum *day is dear to men*, Runic pm. 24; Hick. Thes. i. 135; Kmbl. 344, 10. His se deóra sunu *his dear son*, Cd. 218; Th. 279, 25; Sat. 243: Exon. 76 a; Th. 286, 2; Jul. 725. Âhte ic holdra ðȳ læs, deórre duguþe *I owned the less of faithful ones, of dear attendants*, Beo. Th. 980; B. 488. He æfter deórum men dyrne langaþ *he longs secretly after the dear man*, Beo. Th. 3762; B. 1879: Ps. Th. 119, 1. Ic me on mīnne Drihten deórne getreówige *ego in te sperābo, Domĭne*, Ps. Th. 54, 24: 77, 69: 88, 17. He gedǣlde him deóre twā *he separated two dear to him*, Cd. 131; Th. 166, 8; Gen. 2744. Deórast ealra *dearest of all*, Exon. 76 a; Th. 284, 15; Jul. 697. Ðīn mildheortnes standeþ deórust *thy mercy is most dear*, Ps. Th. 102, 16. Aldorþegn ðone deórestan *the dearest chief*, Beo. Th. 2622; B. 1309. II. *dear of price, precious, of great value, desirable, excellent, glorious, magnificent, noble, illustrious*; pretiōsus, magni æstimandus, desiderabĭlis, eximius, gloriōsus, magnifĭcus, nobĭlis, illustris:—Deóre [MS. deor] hit is *pretiōsum est*, Ælfc. Gl. 35; Som. 62, 82; Wrt. Voc. 28, 60. Sege me hwæðer se ðīn wēla deóre seó ðē *tell me whether thy wealth is precious to thee*, Bt. 13; Fox 38, 6. Ðeáh gold gōd seó and deóre [dióre MS. Cot.] *though gold is good and precious*, 13; Fox 38, 11. Deórum mādme *for the precious treasure*, Beo. Th. 3060; B. 1528. On Dryhtnes naman deórum *in the Lord's precious name*, Ps. Th. 117, 10. Gesāwon dryncfæt deóre *they had seen the precious drinking vessel*, Beo Th. 4500; B. 2254. Deóran since *with precious metal*, Exon. 12 a; Th. 19, 31; Cri. 309. Deóre māþmas *precious treasures*, Beo. Th. 4464; B. 2236. Gōd hlīsa biþ betera and deórra [diórra MS. Cot.] ðonne ǣnig wēla *good fame is better and more precious than any wealth*, Bt. 13; Fox 38, 24: Exon. 128 b; Th. 493, 16; Rä. 81, 31. Ða me synd golde deórran *they are dearer to me than gold*, Ps. Th. 118, 127. Sinc biþ deórost *treasure is most precious*, Menol. Fox 480; Gn. C. 10. Hwæt ðē deórast [diórust MS. Cot.] þince: hwæðer ðe gold ðe hwæt? *what seems to thee most precious: whether gold or what?* Bt. 13; Fox 38, 10: Exon. 103 b; Th. 393, 13; Rä. 12, 9. In ðam deóran hām *in that desirable home*, Exon. 45 b; Th. 154, 15; Gū. 843: Cd. 218; Th. 278, 10; Sat. 219. On getȳnum ðe ymb Dryhtnes hūs deóre syndan *in the courts which are glorious about the Lord's house*, Ps. Th. 115, 8. Ðǣr seó deóre scōlu leófne lofiaþ *where the glorious assemblage praise the beloved*, Exon. 64 a; Th. 235, 21; Ph. 560. Ðeáh hwā æðele sié, duguþum dióre *though any be noble, magnificent in riches*, Bt. Met. Fox 10, 57; Met. 10, 29. Deóre rīce Engla landes *in the glorious kingdom of England*, Chr. 1065; Erl. 196, 38; Edw. 19. Is mīn mōdor mægþa cynnes ðæs deórestan *my mother is of the noblest race of women*, Exon. 109 a; Th. 416, 11; Rä. 34, 10. [*Prompt. Wyc. Piers P. R. Brun. Chauc. R. Glouc.* dere: *Laym.* deore, dure: *Orm.* deore, dere: *Plat.* dür: *O. Sax.* diuri: *Frs.* djoer: *O. Frs.* diore, diure: *Dut.* dier: *Ger.* theuer: *M. H. Ger.* tiure: *O. H. Ger.* tiuri: *Dan. Swed.* dyr: *Icel.* dȳrr *dear, precious*.] DER. deóran: deór-boren, -līce, -ling, -wurþe, -wyrþe, -wurþnes, -wyrþnes: un-deóre. v. dȳre.

deóre, dióre; *adv. Dearly, with great price*; cāre, magno:—Deóre he hit bohte *vel* sealde *he bought* or *sold it dearly*; care vendĭdit, Ælfc. Gl. 35; Som. 62, 84; Wrt. Voc. 28, 62. Dióre gecēpte drihten Crēca Troia burh *the lord of the Greeks dearly bought the city of Troy*, Bt. Met. Fox 26, 37; Met. 26, 19. DER. un-deóre.

deóren; *adj.* [deór *an animal, wild beast*] *Of* or *belonging to a wild beast*; bestiālis:—Mid deórenum ceaflum *bestialĭbus rictĭbus*, Mone B. 3289.

deoreþ-sceaft, es; *m.* [deoreþ = daroþ *a dart*, sceaft *a shaft, handle*] *A dart-shaft, a spear*; hasta:—Under deoreþsceaftum *amid the dart-shafts*, Cd. 93; Th. 119, 23; Gen. 1984.

deorf, es; *n. Labour, trouble, tribulation*; lăbor, tribulātio. DER. ge-deorf.

deór-fald, es; *m. A deer-fold, a park, an inclosure for deer*; cervōrum hortus, vivārium, saltus, Som. Ben. Lye.

DEORFAN, ic deorfe, ðū dyrfst, he dyrfþ, *pl.* deorfaþ; *p.* dearf, *pl.* durfon; *pp.* dorfen *To labour*; laborāre:—Ne wiðcweðe ic to deorfenne gyt, gif ic nȳdbehēfe eom gyt ðīnum folce *I refuse not to labour still, if I am yet needful to thy people*, Homl. Th. ii. 516, 26. Þearle ic deorfe *I labour very much*, Coll. Monast. 19, 13. [*O. Sax.* far-dervan *to perish*: *Ger. M. H. Ger.* ver-derben *to destroy, perish*.] DER. ge-deorfan.

deór-fellen; *adj.* [fell *a skin*] *Made of beast-skins*; ex pellĭbus ferārum:—Crusene oððe deórfellen roc *crusen or a beast-skin garment*; mastrūga, Wrt. Voc. 82, 4.

deór-friþ, es; *n. Deer-protection, game-protection*; cervōrum tūtēla:—Se cyng Willelm sætte mycel deórfriþ, and he lægde laga ðǣrwið, ðæt swā hwā swā slōge heort oððe hinde, ðæt hine man sceolde blendian *king William constituted much protection to game, and he laid down laws therewith, that whosoever should slay hart or hind should be blinded*, Chr. 1086; Erl. 222, 25-27.

Deór-hām, es; *m.* [deór *a wild beast*, hām *home, dwelling*] DERHAM, *Gloucestershire*, DEREHAM, *Norfolk*; lŏcōrum nōmen in agris Glocestriæ et Norfolciæ:—Hī iii ciningas ofslōgon in ðære stōwe ðe is gecweden Deórhām *they slew three kings at the place which is called Derham*, Chr. 577; Erl. 19, 21. On ðysum geáre Wihtburge līchama wearþ gefunden eal gehāl and unformolsnod æt [MS. a] Deórhām, æfter fīf and fīfti geáran ðæs [MS. þas] ðe heó of ðysum līfe [MS. liue] gewāt *in this year* [A. D. 798] *the body of Wihtburh was found at Dereham, all whole and uncorrupted, five and fifty years after she had departed from this life*, Chr. 798; Th. 105, 15-21, col. 3.

deór-hege, es; *m.* [hege *a hedge, fence*] *A deer-fence*; cervōrum sepīmentum:—Deórhege to cyniges hāme *the deer-fence for the royal mansion*, L. R. S. 1; Th. i. 432, 4: 2; Th. i. 432, 11: 3; Th. i. 432, 24.

Deór-hyrst, es; *m.* [hyrst *a hurst, copse, wood*] DEERHURST, *Gloucestershire*; lŏci nōmen in agro Glocestriæ:—Æt Olanīge wið Deórhyrste *at Olney near Deerhurst*, Chr. 1016; Th. 282, 40, col. 2. On Deórhyrste *at Deerhurst*, Chr. 1053; Th. 322, 13, col. 2.

deoriende *hurting*, Chr. 959; Erl. 121, 4, = deriende; *part. of* derian.

deór-līc; *adj.* [deór I. *brave, bold*] *Bold*; fortis:—Breca nǣfre git swā deórlīce dǣd gefremede *Breca never yet performed such a bold deed*, Beo. Th. 1174; B. 585.

deór-līce; *adv. Preciously, worthily*; prĕtiōse, digne:—To hwan hió ða næglas sēlost and deórlīcost gedōn meahte *to what she might best and most worthily employ the nails*, Elen. Kmbl. 2315; El. 1159.

deór-ling, diór-ling, dȳr-ling, es; *m. A dearling*, DARLING, *minion, favourite*; unĭce dīlectus, dēlĭciæ:—Gif ðē līcode his dysig, swā wel swā his dysegum deórlingum dyde *if his folly had pleased thee, as well as it did his foolish favourites*, Bt. 27, 2; Fox 96, 23: Wanl. Catal. 127, 49, col. 2. Se godcunda ānweald gefriþode his diórlingas [deórlingas MS. Cot.] *the divine power saved his darlings*, Bt. 39, 10; Fox 228, 11. He his diórlingas duguþum stēpte *he decked his favourites with honours*, Bt. Met. Fox 15, 15; Met. 15, 8. Iohannes se Godspellere, Cristes dȳrling *John the Evangelist, Christ's darling*, Homl. Th. i. 58, 1: Menol. Fox 230; Men. 116.

deór-mōd; *adj.* [deór I. *brave, bold*; mōd *mood, mind*] *Bold of mind, brave*; fortis animi:—Wearþ adrǣfed deórmōd hæleþ *the brave hero was driven away*, Chr. 975; Erl. 126, 18; Edg. 44: Exon. 46 b; Th. 159, 11; Gū. 925: 79 b; Th. 298, 22; Crā. 89: Andr. Kmbl. 1251; An. 626: Fins. Th. 46; Fin. 23. On felda ðam ðe deórmōde Diran hēton *in the plain which the brave men called Dura*, Cd. 180;

Th. 226, 14; Dan. 171. Deórmōdra sīþ *the march of the brave*, 147; Th. 183, 25; Exod. 97.

deór-net, -nett, es; *n. A beast-net, hunting-net;* rēte venātĭcum, cassis:—Deórnet *cassis*, Ælfc. Gl. 84; Som. 73, 91; Wrt. Voc. 48, 29.

deornunga *secretly*, L. In. 27; Wilk 19, 12. v. dearnunga.

deór-tūn, es; *m.* [tūn *an inclosure*] *A deer-inclosure;* cervōrum sepīmentum, Som. Ben. Lye.

Deorwente, an; *f.* [deor = *Celt.* dwr *water;* went *turned, bent;* v. wendan] *The river* DERWENT, *in Yorkshire, Derbyshire, Cumberland, and Durham;* quatuor fluviōrum nomen in agris Eboracensi Derbiensi Cumbriensi et Dunholmensi:—Be Deorwentan ðære eá *by the river Derwent* [*Yorkshire*], Bd. 2, 9; S. 511, 18: 2, 13; S. 517, 16. Of ðam ðe ða fruman awealláþ Deorwentan streámes *from which the beginnings of the river Derwent spring*, 4. 29; S. 607, 11.

deór-wyrþe, -wurþe; *adj.* [deóre *dear*, weorþe *worth*] *Precious, dear, of great worth* or *value;* prĕtiōsus:—Ðā he funde ðæt ān deórwyrþe meregrot *inventa autem una prĕtiōsa margarīta*, Mt. Bos. 13, 46. Deórwurþe *prĕtiōsus*, Wrt. Voc. 85, 61. Ealra gecorenra hālgena deáþ is deórwurþe on Godes gesihþe *the death of all the chosen saints is precious in the sight of God*, Homl. Th. i. 48, 34. Ofer gold and stāne deorwyrþum *super aurum et lapĭdem prĕtiōsum*, Ps. Lamb. 18, 11: 20, 4. We deórwyrþne dǣl Dryhtne cennaþ *we ascribe the precious lot to the Lord*, Exon. 35 a; Th. 113, 7; Gū. 154. Hī wurdon gehwyrfede to deórwurþum gymmum *they were turned to precious gems*, Homl. Th. i. 64, 5. Hī nǣfre swā deórwurþe gymstānas ne gemētton *they have never before met with such precious gems*, i. 64, 10. Ðæt is git deórwyrþre ðonne monnes līf *it is even more valuable than man's life*, Bt. 10; Fox 28, 38. Ðū hæfst gesund gehealden eall ðæt deórwyrþoste *thou hast kept entire everything most precious*, Bt. 10; Fox 28, 9. Mid ðam deórwurþustan reáfe *with the most valuable raiment*, Gen. 27, 15.

deór-wyrþnes, -wurþnes, -ness, e; *f. Preciousness, a precious thing, treasure;* res prĕtiōsa:—Mid eallum deórwyrþnessum *with all precious things*, Bt. 7, 4; Fox 22, 31. Ðe ða frēcnan deórwurþnessa funde *who found the dangerous treasures*, 15; Fox 48, 24.

dēpan; *p.* te; *pp.* ed *To dip, baptize;* baptizāre:—Dēpiþ *vel* dyppeþ *baptizābit* = βαπτίσει, Mt. Rush. Stv. 3, 11. v. dyppan.

Dēprobane; *indecl. f. An island in the Indian ocean, Ceylon;* Taprŏbăna = Ταπροβάνη:—Be sūþan eástan ðam porte is ðæt īgland Dēprobane *to the south-east of the port* [*Calymere*] *is the island Ceylon*, Ors. 1, 1; Bos. 16, 16. v. Tāprabane.

Dera mǣgþ, e; *f.* [Dere *the Deirians*, mǣgþ *a province, region, country*] *The country of the Deirians, Deira, being part of Northumbria, situate between the Tyne and Humber;* Deirōrum provincia:—In Dera mǣgþe *in provincia Deirōrum*, Bd. 2, 14; S. 518, 14. v. Dera rīce.

Dera rīce, es; *n.* [Dere *the Deirians*, rīce *a kingdom*] *The kingdom of the Deirians, Deira;* Deirōrum regnum:—Fēng to Dera rīce *suscēpit regnum Deirōrum*, Bd. 3, 1; S. 523, 9. Se hæfde Dera rīce *qui in Deirōrum partĭbus regnum habēbat*, 3, 23; S. 554, 8.

Dere; *gen.* Dera; *pl. m. The Deirians, inhabitants of Deira between the rivers Tyne and Humber;* Deīri:—Andswarede him mon and cwæþ ðæt hī Dere nemde wǣron *responsum est quod Deīri vocārentur*, Bd. 2, 1; S. 501, 21, 22: Homl. Th. ii. 120, 34, 35. Mid ðysses cyninges geornesse ða twā mǣgþa Norþan Hymbra Dere and Beornice on āne sibbe geteáh *hujus industria regis Deirōrum et Berniciōrum provinciæ in unam sunt pācem*, Bd. 3, 6; S. 528, 30. He wæs vii winter Dera cyning *he was king of the Deirians seven years*, 3, 14; S. 539, 32. Man gehālgode ii biscopas on his stal, Bosan to Derum, and Eatan to Beornicum *two bishops were consecrated in his stead, Bosa to Deira* [lit. *to the Deirians*], *and Eata to Bernicia*, Chr. 678; Erl. 41, 7. v. Dera mǣgþ.

deregaþ *injure*, Bt. 4; Fox 8, 16, = deriaþ; *pres. pl. of* derian.

DERIAN, derigan; *part.* deriende, derigende; ic derige, ðū derast, derest, he deraþ, dereþ; *pl.* deriaþ, deregaþ; *p.* ode, ede; *pp.* od, ed; *v. trans. dat. To injure, hurt, harm, damage;* nocēre, lædĕre, obesse:—Him ða stormas derian ne māhan [derigan ne mǣgon MS. Cot.] *the storms cannot hurt him*, Bt. 7, 3; Fox 22, 6: Bt. Met. Fox 12, 8; Met. 12, 4. He ne forlēt mannan derian heom *non relĭquit homĭnem nocēre eis*, Ps. Lamb. 104, 14. Derigende *nŏcens*, Ælfc. Gr. 9, 38; Som. 12, 51. Dēm Driht derigende [deriende MS. T; ða deriendan, Lamb.] me *judĭca Domĭne nocentes me*, Ps. Spl. 34, 1. Ic derige *noceo*, Ælfc. Gr. 43; Som. 44, 41: Ps. Lamb. 88, 34. Hit me ne deraþ *it shall not hurt me*, Homl. Th. i. 72, 13: Boutr. Scrd. 31, 18. Hió oft dereþ unscyldegum *she often injures the guiltless*, Bt. Met. Fox 4, 71; Met. 4, 36: 26, 221; Met. 26, 111. On woruld monnum ne deriaþ māne āþas *wicked oaths inflict no injury on men in the world*, 4, 95; Met. 4, 48: Past. 59; Hat. MS. Nāuht ne deregaþ monnum māne āþas *wicked oaths in no wise injure men*, Bt. 4; Fox 8, 16. He derode manna gesihþum *he injured men's sight*, Homl. Th. i. 454, 21: Hexam. 16; Norm. 24, 3: Chr. 1033; Erl. 164, 2: Boutr. Scrd. 18, 3. Gif ðū ðīnum cristenum brēðer deredest *if thou injuredst thy christian brother*, Homl. Th. i. 54, 22. Him ōwiht ne derede *naught harmed them*, Cd. 188; Th. 233, 11; Dan. 274: 23; Th. 30, 24; Gen. 471. Ðæt ðū me ne derige *ne nŏceas mihi*, Gen. 21, 23. Swā hwæt swā mannum derige, ðæt is eall for ūrum synnum *whatsoever is injurious to men, is all for our sins*, Homl. Th. i. 16, 25. [*Piers P.* dere: *Chauc.* dere: *Laym.* derede, *p*: *O. Sax.* derian: *Frs.* deare, derre: *O. Frs.* dera: *Dut.* deren: *O. H. Ger.* terjan, terran *nocēre.*] DER. ge-derian: un-deriende.

deriendlīc, derigendlīc; *def.* se -līca, seó, ðæt -līce; *adj. Injurious, noxious, hurtful;* nocīvus, noxius, nŏcens:—Deriendlīc *nocīvus*, Fulg. 20: *noxius*, Hymn. Surt. 5, 7. Hit ne biþ ðam men derigendlīc *it will not be injurious to a man*, Boutr. Scrd. 20, 18. Ðæt we forbūgan ǣlc þing derigendlīces *vitēmus omne noxium*, Hymn. Surt. 14, 13: 37, 16: 93, 3. Afyrsa hǣtan derigendlīce *aufer calōrem noxium*, 10, 31. Him wǣron derigendlīce dracan and næddran *serpents and adders were noxious to them*, Hexam. 17; Norm. 24, 32. Hīg swīðe gedrehton ða deriendlīcan *the hurtful greatly afflicted them*, Ælfc. T. Grn. 11, 35. Ðæt ðū derigendlīce ætbrede *ut noxia subtrăhas*, Hymn. Surt. 133, 7. Us he gehealde fram derigendlīcum *nos servet a nocentĭbus*, 9, 7.

dēr-ling *a darling*:—Dērling mīn *dīlectus meus*, Mt. Kmbl. Lind. 12, 18. v. deór-ling.

derne *secret, hidden*, Ps. C. 50, 70; Ps. Grn. ii. 278, 70. v. dyrne.

dern-geliger, e; *f*: dern-geliger-scipe, es; *m. A secret lying, adultery;* clandestīnus concubĭtus, adultĕrium:—In derngeligerscipe [MS. dernegilegerscipe] *in adultĕrio*, Jn. Rush. War. 8, 3. v. ge-liger.

dern-unga; *adv.* [derne, unga *a termination*] *Secretly;* clam:—Dernunga *clam*, Mt. Kmbl. Rush. 2, 7. v. dearnunga.

derodine? *scarlet dye*, Past. 14, 4; Hat. MS. 18 a, 3. v. dyrodine.

derstan *dregs, lees*, L. M. 1, 2; Lchdm. ii. 38, 18, 19: 1, 39; Lchdm. ii. 98, 24. v. dærstan.

derung, e; *f. An injuring, harming;* læsio, injūria, nocumentum, Greg. Dial. 3, 16.

dēst *doest, dost*, Jn. Bos. 6, 30; dēþ *does*, Basil admn. 4; Norm. 40, 29; *2nd and 3rd sing. pres. of* dōn.

diācon, deācon, es; *m. A deacon, minister of the church, levite;* diācŏnus = διάκονος *a servant, waiting man* = *Lat.* minister, levīta, levītes = λευίτης:—Diāconus is þēn, ðe þēnaþ ðam mæsse-preóste, and ða offrunga sett uppon ðæt weofod, and gōdspell eác rǣt æt Godes þēnungum. Se mōt fulligan cild, and ðæt folc hūsligan [i. e. he mōt eác hlāf sillan, gif þearf biþ *he may also give the bread, if need be*, L. Ælf. P. 34; Th. ii. 378, 12] *deacon is a minister, who ministers to the mass-priest, and sets the offerings upon the altar, and also reads the gospels at God's services. He may baptize children, and housel the people*, L. Ælf. C. 16; Th. ii. 348, 12. [Gif frigman] diācones feoh [stele], vi gylde [forgylde] *if a freeman steal the property of a deacon, he must repay sixfold*, L. Ethb. 1, 4; Th. i. 2, 5; 4, 3; about A. D. 599. Swylce diācon hine clǣnsie so *let a deacon clear himself*, L. Wih. 18; Th. i. 40, 16: L. Eth. ix. 20; Th. i. 344, 15: L. C. E. 5; Th. i. 362, 12, 17: Bd. 3, 20; S. 550, 21. We nū gehȳrdon of ðæs diācones mūþe *we have now heard from the mouth of the deacon*, Homl. Th. i. 152, 3. Ða Iudēas sendon diāconas *misērunt Iudæi levītas* [Wyc. *dekenys*], Jn. Bos. 1, 19. Diācon *levīta* [Wyc. *dekene*], Lk. Bos. 10, 32. Ða apostolas gehādodon seofon diāconas... Ðæra diācona wæs se forma Stephănus... Hī mid gebēdum and bletsungum to diāconum gehādode wurdon *the apostles ordained seven deacons... The first of the deacons was Stephen... They were ordained deacons with prayers and blessings*, Homl. Th. i. 44, 10, 13, 20: 416, 9, 11. DER. arce-diācon, erce-, under-. v. hād II.

diācon-hād, es; *m. The office of a deacon, deaconship;* diaconātus:—On diāconhāde *in deaconship*, Homl. Th. ii. 120, 13.

diācon-þēnung, e; *f.* [þēnung *duty, office*] *The duty* or *office of a deacon;* diaconātus offĭcium:—He diāconþēnunge mycelre tīde brūcende wæs *diaconātus offĭcio non pauco tempŏre fungebātur*, Bd. 4, 3; S. 570, 28.

dīc, es; *m. A* DIKE, *a bank formed by throwing the earth out of the ditch;* vallum, id est tumŭlus, qui terra effossa exstructus est:—Andlang dīces *along the dike*, Cod. Dipl. Apndx. 442; A. D. 956; Kmbl. iii. 438, 18. Ondlong ridiges on ðone dīc *along the ridge to the dike*, 620; A. D. 978; Kmbl. iii. 169, 2; iii. 168, 35. On ānne micelne dīc *to a great dike*, iii. 169, 7. Of ðæm dīce *from the dike*, iii. 169, 2. To ðæm ealdan dīc *to the old dike*, Th. Diplm. A. D. 905; 494, 17. On ðone dīc *to the dike*, 494, 37. [*O. Sax.* dīc, *m. a dike, dam*: *O. Frs.* dik, *m. a dike, dam*: *Dut.* dijk, *m. a dike*: *Ger.* deich, *m. a mound*: *Sansk.* dehī, *f. a mound, bank, rampart.*] DER. ȳlen-dīc [eáland-dīc].

dīc, e; *f.* I. *a ditch, the excavation* or *trench made by throwing out the earth, a channel for water;* fossa, excavātio *vel* scrŏbis unde terram fodĕrant:—Ðonne to ðære dīce hyrnan *then to the corner of the ditch*, Th. Diplm. A. D. 905; 495, 21. Ðonne on ðone weg, ðe scȳt ofer ða dīc *then to the way, that leads over the ditch*, Th. Diplm. A. D. 900; 145, 27. On ða dīc *to the ditch*, Cod. Dipl. Apndx. 441; A. D. 956; Kmbl. iii. 437, 11, 15, 27. Of ðam brōc on ða ealdan dīc *from the brook to the old ditch*, 556; A. D. 969; Kmbl. iii. 48, 21. On ða reádan dīc *in the reedy ditch*, Cod. Dipl. 1172; A. D. 955; Kmbl. v. 332, 13. Binnon lytlum fæce wendon to Lundene; and dulfon ðā āne mycele dīc, on ða sūþ-healfe, and drōgon heora scipa [scypo MS. Cot. Tiber. B. i; scipo MS. Cot. Tiber. B. iv] on west-healfe ðære brycge *within a little space they went to London; and they then dug a great ditch, on the south side, and dragged their ships to the west side of the bridge*, Chr. 1016; Th. 281, 4-7, col. 1. II. *sometimes* dîc, es; *m. is found to denote—a ditch* or *channel for water*:—Ymbûtan ðone weall [Babilônes] is se mǽsta dîc, on ðam is yrnende se ungefôglecesta streám; and, wiðûtan ðam dîce, is geworht twegra elna heáh weall *round the wall* [*of Babylon*] *is a very great ditch, in which runs the deepest stream; and, outside the ditch, a wall is built two ells high*, Ors. 2, 4; Bos. 44, 26, 27. [*Prompt.* dyke *fossa*: *Piers P.* dyk, dych *a ditch*: *Chauc.* dich *a ditch*: *Laym.* dic, dich, *f. a ditch*: *Plat.* diek, dîk, *m. a pond*: *Frs.* dijck, *m. vallum*: *Ger.* teich, *m. a pond*: *M. H. Ger.* tîch, *m. a pond*: *Dan.* dige, *n. a ditch*: *Swed.* dike, *n. a ditch, trench*: *Icel.* díki, dík, *n. a ditch.*]

dîcere, es; *m. A ditcher, digger;* fossor, Ælfc. Gl. 60; Som. 68, 21; Wrt. Voc. 39, 7.

dîcian; *p.* ode; *pp.* od *To* DIKE, *bank, mound;* aggĕrāre, cingĕre:—Ðǽr Severus hêt dîcian and eorþwall gewyrcan *there Severus commanded to raise a bank and to make an earth wall*, Bd. 1, 12; S. 481, 9. DER. be-dîcian, ge-.

dîcung, e; *f. A ditching, digging;* fossio, Ælfc. Gl. 60; Som. 68, 20; Wrt. Voc. 39, 6.

dide *did*, Chr. 616; Erl. 23, 5, = dyde; *p. of* dôn.

didon *did*, Hy. 7, 107; Hy. Grn. ii. 289, 107, = dydon; *p. pl. of* dôn.

diégel *hidden, obscure*, Past. 43, 2; Hat. MS. 59 a, 17. v. dîgol.

diégel-lîce *secretly*, Som. Ben. Lye. v. dîgol-lîce.

diégelnes *solitude, recess*, Bt. 13; Fox 38, 26. v. dîgolnes.

dielf *dug.* v. be-dielf.

dielgian *to destroy*, Past. 55, 2. v. dilgian.

dierne *hidden, secret*, Elen. Kmbl. 2160; El. 1081. v. dyrne I.

Difelin, Dyflen, Dyflin, es; *m?* [*Hovd.* Diveline] *Dublin;* Dublāna:—Gewiton him ða Norþmen ofer deóp wæter Difelin [Dyflen, Th. 206, 14, col. 2: Dyflin, 207, 14, col. 1] sêcan *the Northmen departed over the deep water to seek Dublin*, Chr. 937; Th. 206, 14, col. 1; Æðelst. 56.

dîgel *hidden, secret*, Greg. Dial. Hat. MS. fol. 1 a, 20; Homl. Th. ii. 314, 17. v. dîgol.

digelan *to hide*, Som. Ben. Lye. v. dîglian.

dîgel-lîce *secretly*, Ors. 6, 21; Bos. 123, 29. v. dîgollîce.

dîgelnes, dîgelnys *solitariness, recess*, Ps. Spl. second 9, 10: Ors. 2, 1; Bos. 39, 40. v. dîgolnes.

dîgle, dîgele *secret, hidden*, Mk. Bos. 4, 22: Ælfc. Gr 33; Som. 37, 24; *nom. n. of* dîgol.

dîgle; *adv. Secretly;* secrēto, clam:—Ic to ðê, Drihten, dîgle cleopode *clamāvi ad te, Domĭne, secrēto*, Ps. Th. 141, 5. Dîgle *furtim*, Glos. Prudent. Recd. 144, 30.

dîglian; *p.* ede, ode; *pp.* od *To hide;* occŭlĕre, occultāre:—Hî on wudum and on wêstenum and on scræfum hî hýddon and dîgledon *se silvis, ac desertis abdĭtisve speluncis occŭlĕrant*, Bd. 1, 8; S. 479, 22. DER. be-dîglian, ge-deigelian.

dîglîce *secretly*, Mt. Bos. 17, 19. v. dîgollîce.

dîglod *hidden*, Fulg. 16; *pp. of* dîglian.

digneras, dýneras; *pl. m. Small pieces of money;* folles, dēnārii:—Digneras *folles*, Cot. 93. Dýneras *folles*, Ælfc. Gl. 106; Som. 78, 55; Wrt. Voc. 57, 35.

DÎGOL, dýgol, dēgol, es; *n. Concealment, a secret place, secret, darkness, the grave, mystery;* secrētum, abscondĭtum, sepulcrum, mystērium:—Ðæt ðîn ælmesse sý on dîglum *ut sit eleemosўna tua in abscondĭto*, Mt. Bos. 6, 4. He wât dîglu heortan *ipse nōvit abscondĭta cordis*, Ps. Spl. 43, 24: 50, 7. Mægen he cýðde on dîgle *he revealed his power in secret*, Andr. Kmbl. 1251; An. 626. He ðý þriddan dæge of dîgle arâs *he rose the third day from the secret place* [*the grave*], Exon. 96 a; Th. 359, 13; Pa. 62.

dîgol, dýgol, diógol; *gen. m. n.* dîgles, *f.* dîgolre; *def. nom. m.* dîgla; *f. n.* dîgle; *adj. Secret, hidden, private, dark, obscure, profound, abstruse, unknown;* secrētus, occultus, obscūrus, ignōtus:—Se þeóden gewât sêcan dîgol land *the king departed to seek a secret land*, Andr. Kmbl. 1396; An. 698. He âna gesæt on dîgolre stôwe *he sat alone in a secret place*, Bd. 3, 27; S. 559, 2. Sôþlîce nis nân þing dîgle, ðæt ne sý geswutelod *non est enim occultum, quod non manifestētur*, Lk. Bos. 8, 17. He ðǽr wolde dîgol beón *he would there be hidden*, Bd. 3, 14; S. 539, 44. On dîgle, deorce stôwe *in an obscure, dark place*, Ps. Th. 142, 4. Is seó forþgesceaft dîgol and dyrne *the future condition is dark and secret*, Menol. Fox 585; Gn. C. 62. Me Daniel dýglan swefnes sôðe gesǽde *Daniel said soothly to me of the dark dream*, Cd. 198; Th. 246, 21; Dan. 482. Ðæt wit mǽgen smeálîcor sprecan and diógolran wordum *that we two may argue more closely and with profounder words*, Bt. 13; Fox 36, 32. [*Laym.* digelliche *secretly*: *O. H. Ger.* tougal *opācus, obscūrus, occultus.*]

dîgol-lîce, dîgolîce; *adv. Secretly;* secrēto, clam:—His leorning-cnihtas hine dîgollîce ahsodon *discipŭli ejus secrēto interrogābant eum*, Mk. Bos. 9, 28: Ps. Th. 9, 29. Albānus hæfde ðone Cristes andettere dîgollîce mid him *Alban had Christ's confessor secretly with him*, Bd. 1, 7; S. 477, 7. Se dîgolîce lâcnod wæs fram his wûndum *who was secretly healed of his wounds*, 4, 16; S. 584, 30. DER. un-deágollîce.

dîgolnes, dîgolnys, -ness, -nyss, e; *f. Solitariness, solitude, privacy, secrecy, mystery, hiding-place, recess;* solitūdo, abscondĭtum quid, secrētum, arcāna, latebra:—He to dîgolnesse and to stilnesse becom ðære godcundan sceáwunge *he came to the privacy and stillness of the divine contemplation*, Bd. 4, 28; S. 605, 10. Se cyning his geþohte ðære cwêne on dîgolnysse onwreáh *rex cogitatiōnem suam reginæ in secrēto rĕvelāvit*, 2, 12; S. 514, 36. Him Dryhten synderlîce his dîgolnysse onwreáh *Domĭnus ei specialĭter sua revēlābat arcāna*, 4, 3; S. 567, 20. Nǽnig ðara andweardra his heortan deágolnesse him helan dorste *nullus præsentium latebras ei sui cordis celāre præsumpsit*, 4, 27; S. 604, 22.

dîgul *secret*, Ps. Th. 106, 23. v. dîgol.

dîhglum, dîhlum = dîglum *secret, retired, shady*:—On dîhglum stôwum *in shady places*, Herb. 38; Lchdm. i. 138, 22. On dîhlum *in secret*, Mt. Bos. 6, 6; *dat. pl. of* dîgol, *q. v.*

dîhlîce *secretly*, Mt. Bos. 1, 19: 24, 3. v. dîgollîce.

dîhlum *in secret*, Mt. Bos. 6, 6. v. dîhglum.

DIHT, es; *n?* I. *a setting in order, disposing, contriving, disposition, conduct, consultation, deliberation, purpose;* disposĭtio, excogitātio, consĭlium, propŏsĭtum:—God gefylde on ðam seofoðan dæge his weorc ðe he worhte on wunderlîcum dihte, and he on ðam seofoðan dæge geswâc ðæs dihtes ðæs deóplîcan cræftes *God completed on the seventh day his works which he had wrought with wondrous contriving, and on the seventh day he ceased from the disposition of the profound art*, Hexam. 12; Norm. 20, 10, 14. Hit stent on ûrum âgenum dihte hû us biþ æt Gode gedêmed *it stands by our own conduct how we shall be judged before God*, Homl. Th. i. 52, 32. Ða mâgas ðe æt ðam dihte wǽron þolian ðone ylcan dôm *cognāti qui illi consĭlio interfuĕrint patiantur eandem sententiam*, L. M. I. P. 16; Th. ii. 270, 4. Ic eom unscyldig, ǽgðer ge dǽde ge dihtes, æt ðære tîhtlan *I am guiltless, both in deed and purpose, of the accusation*, L. O. 5; Th. i. 180, 16. II. *a dictating, direction, order, command;* dictātio, directio, jussum, mandātum:—Moyses underfêng of Godes sylfes dihte ealle ða deópnyssa ðe he on fîf bôcum syððan afæstnode *Moses received from the dictating of God himself all the mysteries which he afterwards inscribed in five books*, Hexam. 1; Norm. 2, 17. Saul wearþ Gode ungehýrsum and nolde faran be his dihte *Saul was disobedient to God and would not walk by his direction*, Homl. Th. ii. 64, 3: L. E. G. pref; Th. i. 166, 19: L. C. S. 71; Th. i. 412, 30. Ealle ða þing ðe he dyde, he dyde be his dihte *all the things which he did, he did by his* [*God's*] *command*, Gen. 39, 3. [*Dut.* dicht, *n. poetry*: *Ger.* dicht, ge-dicht, *n. a poem*: *M. H. Ger.* tihte, *f. a composing;* tihte, *n. a poem, fiction*: *O. H. Ger.* dihta, *f. dictation, fiction*: *Dan.* dight, *n. a poem, fiction*: *Swed.* dikt, *m. a fable, poem*: *Icel.* dikt, *n. a composition*: *Lat.* dictum *a saying, order.*]

dihtan, ic dihte; *p.* ic, he [dihtde =] dihte, dyhte, *pl.* dihton; *pp.* dihted; *v. a.* I. *to set in order, dispose, arrange, appoint, direct, compose;* parāre, dispōnĕre, instruĕre, constituĕre, compōnĕre:—Abram ðâ dyde, swâ swâ him dyhte Sarai *Abraham then did as Sarah arranged*, Gen. 16, 3: Jn. Bos. 18, 14. Ic eów dihte, swâ mîn Fæder me rîce dihte *ego dispōno vobis, sīcut dispŏsuit mihi pater meus regnum*, Lk. Bos. 22, 29. Ðǽr se Hǽlend heom dihte *ubi constituĕrat illis Iesus*, Mt. Bos. 28, 16: 25, 19. II. *to order, dictate, indite;* dirigĕre, dictāre:—Hî didon ðâ, swâ swâ him dihte Iosue *then they did as Joshua ordered them*, Jos. 8, 8. Drihten dihte him hwæt he dôn sceolde *Domĭnus omnia opĕra ejus dirĭgēbat*, Gen. 39, 23. [*Wyc.* diting *an inditing, writing*: *Piers P. Chauc.* dighte *to dispose*: *Laym.* dihte, dihten *to rule, dispose, indite*: *Plat.* tichten *to fix, appoint, dispose*: *Dut. Ger.* dichten *carmĭna compōnĕre*: *Kil.* dichten *dictāre*: *M. H. Ger.* tihten *fingĕre*: *O. H. Ger.* dihtôn *dictāre*: *Dan.* digte *to make poems*: *Swed.* dikta *to fable, feign*: *Icel.* dikta *to compose, feign*: *Lat.* dictāre *to dictate.*] DER. a-dihtan, ge-.

dihtaþ *dictates*, Bd. 1, 27; S. 490, 21, = dihteþ; *3rd pres. sing. of* dihtan.

dihtere, dihtnere, es; *m. An informant, expounder, disposer, manager, steward;* auctor, commentātor, expŏsĭtor, dispensātor:—Ic wrîte swâ me ða dihteras sǽdon ðe his lîf geornost cûðon *I write as the informants who knew his life most accurately told me*, Guthl. prol; Gdwin. 4, 23; 6, 8. Dihtere *commentātor, expŏsĭtor*, Ælfc. Gl. 49; Som. 65, 86; Wrt. Voc. 34, 18. Dihtnere *dispensātor*, 33; Som. 62, 29; Wrt. Voc. 28, 12. Hwâ ys getrýwe and gleáw dihtnere, ðæne se hlâford geset ofer his hîrêd *quis est fidēlis dispensātor, et prudens, quem constĭtuet Domĭnus supra famĭliam suam?* Lk. Bos. 12, 42: Homl. Th. ii. 344, 5.

dihtig; *adj. Doughty;* valĭdus, Cd. 93; Th. 120, 11; Gen. 1993. v. dyhtig.

dihtnere *an arranger, a steward;* dispensātor, Lk. Bos. 12, 42. v. dihtere.

dihtnung, e; *f. A disposing, ordering;* disposĭtio, condĭtio:—Ealle ðîure synd dihtnunge underþeódde *omnia tuæ sunt conditiōni subjecta*, Wanl. Catal. 293, 50, col. 1. DER. ge-dihtnung.

DILE, dyle, es; *m.* DILL, *anise;* anēthum = ἄνηθον, anēthum graveōlens, Lin:—Genim diles blôstman *take blossoms of dill*, L. M. 1, 1; Lchdm. ii. 20, 7. Genim diles sǽdes âne yntsan *take one ounce of seed* *of dill*, L. M. 2, 12; Lchdm. ii. 190, 9: 2, 15; Lchdm. ii. 192, 14. Selle him mon dile gesodenne on ele *let a man give him dill sodden in oil*, 2, 23; Lchdm. ii. 236, 15. Ge tiogođiaþ eówre mintan and eówerne dile and eówerne cymen *ye tithe your mint and your dill and your cummin*, Past. 57; Hat. MS: Mt. Bos. 23, 23. Genim đas wyrte, đe man *anēthum*, and ōđrum naman dyle, nemneþ *take this herb, which is named* anēthum, *and by another name dill*, Herb. 123, 1; Lchdm. i. 234, 20: Wrt. Voc. 79, 9. [*Dut.* dille, *f*: *Ger.* dill, *m*; dille, *f*: *M. H. Ger.* tille: *O. H. Ger.* tilli *anēthum*: *Dan.* dild, *m. f*: *Swed.* dill, *m.*]

DILEGIAN, dilgian, dielgian; *p.* ode; *pp.* od *To destroy, abolish, blot out, erase*; delēre, abŏlēre:—Gif se wrītere ne dilegaþ đæt he ǽr wrāt *if the scribe does not erase what he wrote before*, Past. 54, 5; Hat. MS. Swā swā fenn strǽta ic dilgie hīg *ut lutum plateārum delēbo eos*, Ps. Spl. 17, 44. To dielgianne hira synna *to blot out their sins*, Past. 55, 2; Hat. MS. [*Orm.* dillghenn: *O. Sax.* far-diligōn *delēre*: *Frs.* dylgjen: *O. Frs.* diligia: *Ger.* tilgen: *M. H. Ger.* tīligen, tilgen: *O. H. Ger.* tiligōn.] DER. a-dilegian, -dilgian, for-: un-dilegod.

dilfst, he dilfþ *diggest, digs*; *2nd and 3rd pers. pres. of* delfan.

dilgian *to destroy*; delēre, Ps. Spl. 17, 44. v. dilegian.

DIM; *def.* se dimma, seó, đæt dimme; *adj.* DIM, *dark, obscure, hidden*; obscūrus, tenebrōsus:—Đes wīda grund stōd deóp and dim *this wide abyss stood deep and dim*, Cd. 5; Th. 7, 12; Gen. 105: 24; Th. 30, 36; Gen. 478. Nǽnegum þuhte dæg on þonce, gif sió dimme niht ǽr ofer eldum egesan ne brohte *the day would seem delightful to none, if the dark night did not bring terror over men*, Bt. Met. Fox 12, 32; Met. 12, 16. Com hæleđa þreát to đære dimman ding *the troop of heroes came to the dark dungeon*, Andr. Kmbl. 2541; An. 1272: Cd. 215; Th. 271, 27; Sat. 111. On đære dimman ādle *in the hidden malady*, Exon. 49 b; Th. 171, 31; Gū. 1135. Drihten sealde him dimne and deorcne deáþes scūwan *the Lord gave them death's shadow, dim and dark*, Cd. 223; Th. 293, 14, note; Sat. 455. Nabbaþ we to hyhte nymþe đone dimman hām *we have nought in hope save this dim home*, Cd. 221; Th. 285, 14; Sat. 337. Hió speón hine on đa dimman dǽd *she urged him to that dark deed*, 32; Th. 43, 3; Gen. 685. On đis dimme hol *in this dim hole*, Bt. 2; Fox 4, 11: Andr. Kmbl. 2618; An. 1310. Sindon dena dimme *the dells are dim*, Exon. 115 b; Th. 443, 14; Kl. 30: Cd. 215; Th. 271, 13; Sat. 105: Ps. Th. 108, 8. Cwīst đū oncnāwaþ hī wundru đīne on đām dimmum deorcan þȳstrum *numquid cognoscentur in tenēbris mirabĭlia tua?* 87, 12. [*Piers P.* dymme: *Chauc.* dim: *O. Frs.* dim: *Ger. dial.* dimmer: *M. H. Ger.* timber, timmer: *O. H. Ger.* timbar: *Icel.* dimmr *dark.*]

dim-hofe, dym-hofe, an; *f. A lurking-place, hiding-place*; latĭbŭlum, lătēbra:—He gesette þȳstru dymhofan ođđe dymnes ođđe behȳdednesse his *pŏsuit tenēbras latĭbŭlum suum*, Ps. Lamb. 17, 12. Dimhofan *latĕbræ*, Ælfc. Gr. 13; Som. 16, 21. Dimhofum *latĭbŭlis*, Mone B. 85. Gregorius on dymhofum [MS. -hofon] ætlūtode *Gregory concealed himself in hiding-places*, Homl. Th. ii. 122, 33.

dimlīc, dymlīc; *adj. Dim, secret, hidden, concealed*; obscūrus, clandestīnus:—Of dimlīcum *clandestīnis*, Mone B. 872. Nā swylce he todrǽfe đa dymlīcan þeóstra *not as if he dispelled the dim darkness*, L. Ælf. C. 14; Th. ii. 348, 7.

dimmian *to dim, darken, obscure*; obscūrāre. DER. a-dimmian, for-.

dimnes, dymnys, -ness, -nyss, e; *f.* DIMNESS, *darkness, obscurity*; cālīgo, obscūrĭtas:—Dimnes *cālīgo*, Ælfc. Gl. 94; Som. 75, 120; Wrt. Voc. 53, 1. Đis biþ gōd lǽcedōm wiđ eágna dimnesse *this is a good remedy for dimness of eyes*, L. M. 1, 2; Lchdm. ii. 26, 9. Wolcnu and dimnys on his ymbhwyrfte *nubes et cālīgo in circuitu ejus*, Ps. Lamb. 96, 2: Mone B. 3240. Se dæg is þeóstra dæg and dimnysse *the day is a day of darkness and dimness*, Homl. Th. i. 618, 17. Dymnys *cālīgo*, Ælfc. Gr. 9, 3; Som. 8, 56.

dim-scūa, an; *m.* [scūwa, scūa *a shade, shadow*] *Dimness, darkness*; tenēbræ:—Oft hira mōd onwōd under dimscūan deófles lārum *their mind often went under darkness by the devil's lore*, Andr. Kmbl. 281; An. 141.

dincge, dyncge, an; *f. Ploughed land, fallow land*; novāle:—Dincge *nŏvāle*, Wrt. Voc. 66, 56. Dyncgum *novālĭbus*, Mone B. 1434: 2326.

ding, e; *f. A dungeon, prison*; carcer:—Com hæleđa þreát to đære dimman ding *the troop of heroes came to the dark dungeon*, Andr. Kmbl. 2541; An. 1272.

dingiung, e; *f. A dunging, manuring*; stercŏrātio:—Dingiung *stercŏrātio*, Ælfc. Gl. 1; Som. 55, 5; Wrt. Voc. 15, 5.

dinig, dingc, e; *f? Dung*; fimus:—Dinig *fimus*, Ælfc. Gl. 1; Som. 55, 6; Wrt. Voc. 15, 6. Dingc [MS. dingce] *thymiāma*, Mone B. 4795. v. dung.

dinne, es; *m. A storm, tempest*; procella:—On dinnes mere *on a stormy sea*, Chr. 938; Ing. 144, 24; Whel. 556, 44.

diófol-gild, es; *n. Devil-worship, an image of the devil, an idol*, Ors. 1, 5; Bos. 28, 27. v. deófol-gild.

diógol *secret, obscure, profound*, Bt. 13; Fox 36, 32. v. dīgol; *adj.*

dióhlu *secrets*, Prov. 11. v. dīgol.

dióp *deep*, Prov. 22. v. deóp; *adj.*

dióp *depth*, Ps. Spl. T. 64, 7. v. deóp.

diópe *deeply, solemnly*, Beo. Th. 6131; B. 3069. v. deópe.

dióplīce *deeply*, Bt. 35, 1; Fox 154, 19. v. deóplīce.

diópnys, -nyss *deepness, depth, an abyss*; ăbyssus = ἄβυσσος, Ps. Lamb. 32, 7. v. deópnes.

diór *heavy, severe, dire*, Beo. Th. 4186; B. 2090. v. deór; *adj.* **II.**

diór *a beast, animal*, Bt. Met. Fox 26, 183; Met. 26, 92: 27, 21; Met. 27, 11. v. deór.

diór-boren *noble-born, noble*:—Apollines dōhtor diórboren *Apollo's noble-born daughter*, Bt. Met. Fox 26, 103; Met. 26, 52. v. deór-boren.

dióre *dear, precious, glorious, magnificent*, Bt. 13; Fox 38, 10, MS. Cott: Bt. Met. Fox 10, 57; Met. 10, 29. v. deóre.

dióre *dearly, with great price*, Bt. Met. Fox 26, 37; Met. 26, 19. v. deóre.

diór-ling *a darling*, Bt. Met. Fox 15, 15; Met. 15, 8. v. deórling.

diór-wyrþe *precious, costly*, Bt. 15; Fox 48, 5. v. deór-wyrþe.

dippan; *p.* de, te; *pp.* ed, d, t *To dip*, Ps. Spl. 67, 25: Ex. 12, 22. v. dyppan.

DISC, es; *m. A plate, bowl*, DISH; discus, cătīnus, părŏpsis:—Eallswā se disc *also the dish*, L. Ælf. C. 22; Th. ii. 350, 23. Disc *discus*, Wrt. Voc. 82, 22: 290, 20. Clǽnsa ǽryst đæt wiđinnan ys calices and disces *munda prius quod intus est calĭcis et paropsĭdis* = παροψίς, ἴδος; *f.* Mt. Bos. 23, 26. Þweah đæt gewrit of đam disce *wash the writing off the dish*, L. M. 1, 62; Lchdm. ii. 136, 9. Syle me on ānum disce Iohannes heáfod đæs Fulluhteres *da mihi in disco caput Ioannis Baptistæ*, Mt. Bos. 14, 8, 11: Mk. Bos. 6, 25, 27. Se đe his hand on disce mid me dypþ *qui intingit mecum manum in cătīno*, 14, 20. On disce *in părŏpsĭde*, Mt. Bos. 26, 23. Bebeád đæt mon đone disce tobrǽce to styccum and đām þearfum gedǽlan *discum confringi, atque paupĕrĭbus minūtātim divĭdi præcēpit*, Bd. 3, 6; S. 528, 21. Discas lāgon *dishes lay* [*there*], Beo. Th. 6088; B. 3048. Ic gefrægn ānne mannan him on bearm hlādan bunan and discas *I heard that one man loaded in his bosom cups and dishes*, 5544; B. 2775. Ge clǽnsiaþ đæt wiđūtan ys, caliceas and discas *mundātis quod deforis est călĭcis et parop*[*s*]*ĭdis*, Mt. Bos. 23, 25. [*Prompt.* dysshe: *Wyc.* disch, dishe *a disc, quoit*: *Piers P.* dissh: *Chauc.* dish: *Laym.* disc: *Plat.* disch, *m. table*: *O. Sax.* disk, disc, *m. a table*: *Dut.* disch, *m. a dining-table*: *Ger. M. H. Ger.* tisch, *m. a table*: *O. H. Ger.* tisc, *m. discus, mensa, fercŭlum*: *Dan.* disk, *m. f. a table, dish*: *Swed.* disk, *m. a counter*: *Icel.* diskr, *m. a plate*: *Lat.* discus: *Grk.* δίσκος *a round plate, quoit, dish.*] DER. bǽr-disc, hlæd-, hūsel-.

disc-berend, es; *m. A dish-bearer*; discĭfer, Cot. 65.

discipul, es; *m. A disciple, scholar*; discĭpŭlus:—Se wæs iu on Brytene Bosles discipul *discipŭlus quondam in Brittania Boisili*, Bd. 5, 9; S. 622, 28. Crist cwæþ to his discipulum *Christ said to his disciples*, Boutr. Scrd. 22, 45: Homl. Th. ii. 266, 33: 320, 13.

discipul-hād, es; *m.* DISCIPLEHOOD, *pupilage*; discipŭlātus:—Đysses discipulhāde Cūþberht wæs eádmōdlīce underþeóded *hujus discipŭlātui Cudberct humĭlĭter subdĭtus*, Bd. 4, 27; S. 603, 39.

disc-þēn, es; *m.* [þegen, þēn *a minister, servant*] *A dish-servant, dish-bearer, minister of food, sewer*; discĭfer, discophŏrus, cibi minister:—Discþēn *discĭfer* vel *discophŏrus*, Ælfc. Gl. 30; Som. 61, 68; Wrt. Voc. 26, 65. Godes engel gebrohte đone discþēn đǽr he hine ǽr genam *the angel of God brought the minister of food where he had before taken him*, Homl. Th. i. 572, 9.

disg *foolish*, Deut. 32, 21. v. dysig.

disig *folly*, Hy. 7, 107; Hy. Grn. ii. 289, 107. v. dysig.

disme, an; *f? The herb tansy?* tanacētum?—Nim cristallan and disman *take crystallium and tansy*, Lchdm. iii. 10, 29.

distæf, es; *m.* [dis = *Gael.* dos *a bush, tuft*; stæf *a staff*] *A* DISTAFF; colus:—Distæf *colus*, Ælfc. Gl. 28; Som. 61, 15; Wrt. Voc. 26, 14: 82, 9.

dō *do*, Elen. Kmbl. 1078; El. 541; *impert. of* dōn.

DOCCE, an; *f.* DOCK, *sorrel*; lăpăthum = λάπαθον, rumex:—Đeós wyrt đe man *lăpăthum*, and ōđrum naman docce nemneþ, biþ cenned on sandigum stōwum, and on ealdum myxenum *this herb which is called* lăpăthum, *and by another name dock, is produced in sandy places, and on old dunghills*, Herb. 14, 1; Lchdm. i. 106, 10–12, note 14: L. M. 3, 63; Lchdm. ii. 350, 26: Wrt. Voc. 67, 54. Doccan moran dust *dust of root of dock*, L. M. 1, 54; Lchdm. ii. 126, 6. Sume seóđaþ bētan ođđe doccan on geswēttum wīne *some seethe beet or dock in sweetened wine*, L. M. 2, 25; Lchdm. ii. 218, 7: 1, 38; Lchdm. ii. 96, 11: 1, 76; Lchdm. ii. 150, 10. Seó fealwe docce *the fallow dock*; rumex marĭtĭma *vel* palustris, L. M. 1, 49; Lchdm. ii. 122, 19. Seó reáde docce *the red dock*; rumex sanguĭnea, L. M. 1, 49; Lchdm. ii. 122, 19: 1, 50; Lchdm. ii. 124, 2. Seó scearpe docce *the sharp* or *sour dock, sorrel*; oxylăpăthum = ὀξυλάπαθον, rumex acētōsa, Som. Ben. Lye. Docce seó đe swimman wille *the dock which will swim, the water-lily*; nymphæa, L. M. 3, 71; Lchdm. ii. 358, 8: 2, 65; Lchdm. ii. 292, 11: 1, 50; Lchdm. ii. 122, 21. [*Chauc.* docke *a sour herb*: *Kil.* docke, blæderen *the herb colt's foot.*] DER. eá-docce, sūr-, wudu-.

DOCGA, an; *m. A* DOG; canis:—Docgena *canum*, Glos. Prudent. Reed. 148, 23. [*Piers P. R. Glouc.* dogge: *Chauc.* dogges, *pl*: *Plat.*

dogge *a big dog*: *Dut.* dog, *m. a bull-dog*: *Ger.* dog, dogge, docke, *m.f. canis molossus Anglĭcus*: *Dan.* dogge, *m.f*: *Swed.* dogg, *m. a mastiff*.]

dóchtor *a daughter*, Ælfc. Gl. 91; Som. 75, 22; Wrt. Voc. 51, 66. v. dóhtor.

doefe *perfect*, Mt. Kmbl. Rush. 19, 21. v. défe.

doeg *a day*, Mt. Kmbl. Lind. 27, 62. v. dæg.

doema *a judge*, Mt. Kmbl. Lind. 5, 25. v. déma.

doeman *to judge*, Mt. Kmbl. Lind. 7, 1. v. déman.

dóende *doing*, Ps. Spl. 102, 6, = dónde; *part. of* dón.

dóere, es; *m. A doer, worker;* opĭfex:—Dóere, ðæt is Gást se hálga *opĭfex, id est Spīrĭtus sanctus*, Rtl. 198, 13.

doeþ-bérnis, -niss *a pestilence*, Lk. Skt. Rush. 21, 11. v. deáþ-bérnis.

dofen *dived, dipped;* mersus, immersus; *pp. of* dúfan.

Dofere, Dofre, an; *f.* [*Hunt.* Douere, Doure: *Sim. Dun. Kni.* Dovere: *Hovd.* Dowere: *Brom.* Dover: *Thorn.* Dovore: *Wel.* dwfr *water*] DOVER; Dubris, Dofris, is; *f*:—His men cóman to Doferan *his men came to Dover*, Chr. 1050; Th. 313, 20, col. 2: 1051; Th. 317, 25, col. 2. On ðam ylcan geáre com Eustatius up æt Doferan *in the same year Eustace landed at Dover*, 1052; Th. 312, 26, col. 2: 1095; Th. 361, 21. He to Dofran gewende *he went to Dover*, 1048; Th. 313, 32, 34, 35, col. 1; 315, 18, col. 1: 1052; Th. 319, 26, col. 1.

dofung, e; *f. Dotage;* deliramentum:—Dofunga *deliramenta*, Cot. 69: Mone B. 1621: 4192. Dofunga *insĭdias*, Mone B. 2721.

dóger *a day;* dies:—Dógera *of days*, Bd. 4, 3; 569, 4. v. dógor.

dógian; *p.* ode; *pp.* od *To bear, suffer;* pati?—Ic dógode *I suffered*, Exon. 100 b; Th. 380, 17; Rä. 1, 9.

DÓGOR, dóger, es; *m. n. A day;* dies:—Ymb ántíd óðres dógores *about the first hour of the second day*, Beo. Th. 444; B. 219: 1215; B. 605. He to ðam ýtemæstan dógore becom *he came to his last day*, Bd. 4, 8; S. 575, 30, 39. Ðys dógor ðú geþyld hafa weána gehwylces *do thou have patience this day for every woe*, Beo. Th. 2794; B. 1395. Ðý dógore *in that day*, 3599; B. 1797: Judth. 9; Thw. 21, 10; Jud. 12. Uferan dógore *at a later day*, Past. 38, 8; Hat. MS. 52 b, 7: Ors. 4, 5; Bos. 82, 15. Dógor beóþ mín forþscriðen *my days will be departed*, Exon. 48 a; Th. 164, 14; Gú. 1011. He dógora gehwám dreám gehýrde hlúdne in healle *he heard loud merriment each day in the hall*, Beo. Th. 176; B. 88: Bt. Met. Fox 13, 42; Met. 13, 21: 22, 122; Met. 22, 61. His dógora wæs rím aurnen *the number of his days was run out*, Cd. 79; Th. 98, 5; Gen. 1625: 119; Th. 155, 12; Gen. 2571. Emb ahta dógera rímes *after the number of eight days*, Menol. Fox 189; Men. 96. He wæs his ðara nýhstana dógera gemyndig *he was mindful of his last days*, Bd. 4, 3; S. 569, 4. His forgifnesse gumum to helpe dǽleþ dógra gehwám Dryhten weoroda *the Lord of hosts dealeth his forgiveness each day in help to men*, Exon. 14 a; Th. 27, 9; Cri. 428: 33 a; Th. 105, 23; Gú. 27: Beo. Th. 2184; B. 1090. Ic mána fela æfter dógrum dyde *I did many evils during my days*, Hy. 4, 51; Hy. Grn. ii. 284, 51. Þrió dógor *for the space of three days;* triduo, Mt. Kmbl. Lind. 15, 32. Uferan dógrum *in later days*, Beo. Th. 4407; B. 2200. [*Icel.* dægr, dœgr, *n. a day*: *Goth.* -dogs; *adj.* in ahtau-dogs *on the eighth day;* fidur-dogs *on the fourth day*.] DER. dógor-gerím, -rím: ende-dógor. v. dæg.

dógor-gerím, es; *n.* [gerím *a number*] *Number of days, allotted time of life;* diērum numĕrus, vitæ spătium:—Wæs eall sceacen dógorgerímes *all the number of his days was departed*, Beo. Th. 5449; B. 2728. Nǽfre he sóþra swá feala wundra gefremede dógorgerímum *he could never have performed so many true miracles during his life*, Elen. Kmbl. 1556; El. 780.

dógor-rím, es; *n.* [rím *a number*] *Number of days, time of life;* diērum numĕrus, vitæ spătium:—Óþ-ðæt ende cymeþ dógorrímes *till the end of the number of days cometh*, Exon. 62 b; Th. 231, 6; Ph. 485. Náne forlét deáþ dógorríme *death lets none escape after a number of days*, Bt. Met. Fox 10, 133; Met. 10, 67. Is ðes þroht to ðæs heard dógorrímum *this suffering is so hard in the days of my life*, Elen. Kmbl. 1406; El. 705.

dóh *dough*, Lchdm. iii. 88, 17. v. dáh.

dóhtar *a daughter*, Th. Diplm. A.D. 830; 466, 4. v. dóhtor.

dohte *benefited*, Chr. 1006; Erl. 140, 13: dohtest *shouldst benefit*, Deut. 15, 11; *p. of* dugan.

dóhter *a daughter*:—Lothes dóhter *Lot's daughter*, Cd. 123; Th. 157, 22; Gen. 2610. v. dóhtor.

dohtig; *def.* se dohtiga; *adj.* [dohte, *p. of* dugan *to avail*] DOUGHTY, *valiant, good;* fortis, valĭdus, probus:—Forþférde Hacun, se dohtiga eorl, on sǽ *Hakon, the doughty earl, died at sea*, Chr. 1030: Erl. 162, 40. Ðyssa þinga is gecnǽwe ǽlc dohtig man on Cent [MS. Kænt] and on Súþ-Seaxum [MS. -Sexan] *every good man in Kent and in Sussex is cognizant of these things*, Th. Diplm. A.D. 1016-1020; 313, 19. v. dyhtig.

dohton *benefited, were honest*, Bt. 18, 3; Fox 64, 37; *p. pl. of* dugan.

DÓHTOR, dóhtur, dóhter; *indecl. in sing. but the dat.* déhter *is found*: *pl. nom. acc.* dóhtor, dóhtra, dóhtru, dóhter; *gen.* dóhtra; *dat. instr.* dóhtrum; *f. A* DAUGHTER; fīlia:—Mín dóhtor is deád *fīlia mea dēfuncta est*, Mt. Bos. 9, 18. Gelýf, dóhtor *confīde, filia*, 9, 22. Ðú fram mínre dóhtor onwóce *thou from my daughter wast born*, Cd. 223; Th. 292, 11; Sat. 439. Ðá wæs ellen-wód fæder wiđ déhter *then was the father furious with his daughter*, Exon. 67 b; Th. 251, 7; Jul. 141: Gen. 29, 18: Mk. Bos. 7, 26, 29: Homl. Th. ii. 26, 33. Ðæm forgeaf Hréðel ángan dóhtor *to whom Hrethel gave his only daughter*, Beo. Th. 755; B. 375. Cynincga dóhtor *regum filiæ*, Ps. Th. 44, 10. Fægnigan dóhtra *exultent filiæ*, Ps. Spl. 47, 10: Ps. Th. 44, 14. Heora dóhtru *eorum filiæ*, 143, 15. Ðæt ðú me bereáfodest ðínra dóhtra *ne violenter auferres filias tuas*, Gen. 31, 31. Fyllaþ eorþan sunum and dóhtrum *fill the earth with sons and daughters*, Cd. 10; Th. 13, 5; Gen. 198. Ðú scealt cennan sunu and dóhtor *thou shalt bring forth sons and daughters*, 43; Th. 57, 7; Gen. 924. Suna and dóhter *filios et filias*, Ps. Th. 105, 27. [*Wyc.* douȝtir: *Piers P.* doughtres, *pl*: *Chauc.* doughter, doughtre: *R. Brun.* doughter: *R. Glouc.* dogtren, *pl*: *Laym.* dohter, douter, doȝter: *Orm.* dohhterr: *Plat.* dogter, dochter, *f*: *O. Sax.* dohtar, dohtor, dohter, *f*: *Frs.* dochter, doayter: *O. Frs.* dochter, *f*: *Dut.* dochter, *f*: *Ger.* tochter, *f*: *M. H. Ger.* tohter, *f*: *O. H. Ger.* tohtar, *f*: *Goth.* dauhtar, *f*: *Dan.* datter, *f*: *Swed.* dotter, *f*: *Icel.* dóttir, *f*: *Grk.* θυγάτηρ, *f*: *Lith.* dukte: *Zend* dughdhar: *Sansk.* duhitṛi, *f. a daughter*, properly *a milkmaid*, from duh *to milk*.] DER. steóp-dóhtor.

dóhtur *a daughter*:—Ðære Herodiadiscean dóhtur *Herodiădis fīlia*, Mt. Bos. 14, 6. v. dóhtor.

DOL; *def.* se dola, seó, ðæt dole; *adj.* DULL, *foolish, erring, heretical;* stŏlĭdus, stultus, hærĕtĭcus = αἱρετικός:—Dol biþ se ðe him his Dryhten ne ondrǽdeþ *foolish is he who dreads not his Lord*, Exon. 83 a; Th. 312, 7; Seef. 106: 89 a; Th. 335, 17; Gn. Ex. 35: Salm. Kmbl. 447; Sal. 224. Ge weorþmyndu in dolum dreáme Dryhtne gieldaþ *ye pay reverence to the Lord in foolish joy*, Exon. 39 a; Th. 130, 8; Gú. 435. Óþ hie to dole wurdon *until they became foolish*, Cd. 18; Th. 22, 14; Gen. 340. Ne ondrǽdaþ ða dolan *the foolish are not afraid*, Past. 7, 2; Hat. MS. 12 a, 25. Ða dolan rǽdas *stŏlĭda consulta*, Cot. 189. Ic dole hwette *I excite the dull*, Exon. 103 b; Th. 393, 1; Rä. 12, 3: 107 b; Th. 410, 16; Rä. 28, 17: Ps. Th. 118, 126. [*Chauc.* dul: *Orm.* dill *sluggish*: *Plat.* dul *mad*: *O. Sax.* dol *stultus*: *Frs.* dol, *mad*: *Dut.* dol *insānus*: *Ger.* toll *mad*: *M. H. Ger.* tol, dol *mad*: *O. H. Ger.* tol *stultus*: *Goth.* dwals: *Icel.* dulr *silent, close*.]

dolc *a buckle*, Wrt. Voc. 74, 59. v. dalc.

dolc-swaðu *scars*, Ps. Lamb. 37, 6, = dolh-swaðu; *pl. nom. of* dolh-swæþ.

dolfen *dug*; *pp. of* delfan. v. a-dolfen.

dolg *a wound, scar*, L. M. 1, 45; Lchdm. ii. 114, 1: Exon. 24 a; Th. 68, 24; Cri. 1108. v. dolh.

dolg-ben, -benn, e; *f.* [ben *a wound*] *A wound;* vulnus:—Dolgbennum þurhdrifen *pierced through with wounds*, Andr. Kmbl. 2793; An. 1399.

dolg-bót *compensation for a wound*, L. Alf. pol. 23; Th. i. 78, 7. v. dolh-bót.

dolgian; *p.* ode; *pp.* od [dolg = dolh *a wound*] *To wound;* vulnĕrāre:—Dolgdon, *p. pl.* Exon. 114 b; Th. 441, 2; Rä. 60, 11. DER. ge-dolgian.

dol-gilp, es; *m.* [dol *foolish*; gilp *pride, haughtiness*] *Foolish pride, vain-glory;* vana glōria:—Git wada cunnedon for dolgilpe *ye both made trial of the fords for foolish vaunt*, Beo. Th. 1022; B. 509.

dolg-rune *pellitory*, L. M. 1, 25; Lchdm. ii. 66, 16. v. dolh-rune.

dolg-sealf *a wound salve, poultice for a wound*, L. M. cont. 1, 38; Lchdm. ii. 8, 26, 29. v. dolh-sealf.

dolg-slege, es; *m.* [slege *a blow*] *A wounding blow;* vulnĕrans ictus:—Þurh dolgslege *through a wounding blow*, Andr. Kmbl. 2948; An. 1477. Deáh he sáres swá feala deópum dolgslegum dreógan sceolde *although he must suffer so much pain through deep wounding blows*, 2489; An. 1246.

DOLH, dolg, es; *n. A wound, scar of a wound, cut, gash, sore;* vulnus, cicatrix, ulcus:—Cnua gréne betonican and lege on ðæt dolh gelóme, óþ-ðæt ðæt dolh [sý] gebátod *pound green betony and lay it on the wound frequently, until the wound is bettered*, L. M. 3, 33; Lchdm. ii. 328, 2, 3: 1, 38; Lchdm. ii. 96, 9, 15, 16: 1, 72; Lchdm. ii. 148, 21. Gyf yfele dolh oððe wunda on heáfde sýn, genim ðas ylcan wyrte *if evil cuts or wounds be on the head, take this same herb*, Herb. 122, 2; Lchdm. i. 234, 15. Me ecga dolg eácen weorþaþ *to me the edges' sores become increased*, Exon. 102 b; Th. 388, 25; Rä. 6, 13. Deópra dolga *of deep gashes*, 114 a; Th. 438, 7; Rä. 57, 4. To deópum dolgum *for deep wounds*, L. M. 1, 45; Lchdm. ii. 114, 1. Wið ða sweartan dolh, genim ðas ylcan wyrte *for black scars, take this same herb*, Herb. 10, 3; Lchdm. i. 100, 23: Homl. Blick. 91, 1. Ðám biþ grorne dolg sceáwian *it shall be sad to them to behold the scars*, Exon. 25 b; Th. 74, 16; Cri. 1207: 24 a; Th. 68, 24; Cri. 1108. Blód-dolh *a blood-letting wound*, L. M. 1, 72; Lchdm. ii. 148, 12, 15. [*Frs.* dolge *vulnus*: *O. Frs.* dolch, dulg, dolech, dulich, *n. vulnus*: *O. H. Ger.* tolg, *n. vulnus*:

Goth. dulgs, m. culpa: Icel. dólg, n. direful enmity.] DER. feorh-dolh, heoru-, seono-, syn-.

dolh-ben, -benn a wound. v. dolg-ben.

dolh-bôt, dolg-bôt, e; f. [bôt compensation] A wound-fine or compensation for a wound; vulnĕris compensātio:—Bête dolgbôte [dolhbôte MS. H.] let him make compensation for the wound, L. Alf. pol. 23; Th. i. 78, 7.

dolh-drenc, es; m. [drenc a drink] A wound-drink, potion for a wound; vulnĕrāria pōtio:—Dolhdrenc: ribbe nioðeweard and ufeweard cnuwa smale a wound-drink: pound small the netherward and upward part of ribwort, L. M. I, 38; Lchdm. ii. 98, 1: I, 38; Lchdm. ii. 96, 19, 22.

dolh-rune, dolg-rune, dulh-rune, an; f. The herb pellitory, which grows upon walls; perdīcium = περδίκιον, parietāria officinālis, Lin:—Wið lungen-âdle; dolhrune, etc. for lung-disease; pellitory, etc. L. M. 2, 52; Lchdm. ii. 268, 16: Herb. 83, 1; Lchdm. i. 186, 12, 13: Lchdm. iii. 16, 9. Dulhrune pellitory, L. M. 3, 8; Lchdm. ii. 312, 16. To sealfe wið springe, nim dolhrunan for a salve against a pustule, take pellitory, I, 33; Lchdm. ii. 80, 8: I, 38; Lchdm. ii. 96, 11: 3, 65; Lchdm. ii. 354, 1: Lchdm. iii. 4, 10: 38, 26. Genim dolgrunan take pellitory, L. M. I, 25; Lchdm. ii. 66, 16: I, 47; Lchdm. ii. 120, 5.

dolh-sealf, dolg-sealf, e; f. [sealf a salve, poultice] A wound-salve, poultice for a wound; vulnĕrārium emplastrum:—Dolhsealf; genim wegbrǽdan sǽd, getrifula smale, scead on ða wunde, sôna biþ sêlre a wound-salve; take seed of waybroad, bray it small, put [shed] it on the wound, soon it will be better, L. M. I, 38; Lchdm. ii. 90, 27: I, 38; Lchdm. ii. 96, 2, 7, 10, 13. Grundeswelge ða ðe weaxaþ on worþigum biþ gôd to dolhsealfe the groundsel which grows in highways is good for a wound-salve, I, 38; Lchdm. ii. 92, 27. Hēr sindon dolhsealfa to eallum wundum here are wound-salves for all wounds, I, 38; Lchdm. ii. 90, 23. Dolgsealf wið lungen-âdle a wound-salve for lung-disease, L. M. cont. I, 38; Lchdm. ii. 8, 29. Dolgsealfa wið eallum wundum wound-salves for all wounds, L. M. cont. I, 38; Lchdm. ii. 8, 26.

dolh-slege a wounding blow. v. dolg-slege.

dolh-smeltas; pl. m. Linen bandages; tæniæ = ταινίαι:—Tæppan vel dolhsmeltas [MS. dolsmeltas] tæniæ [MS. tenia], Ælfc. Gl. 4; Som. 55, 93; Wrt. Voc. 16, 64. v. tæppan, from tæppa, m.

dolh-swæþ; gen. -swæðes; pl. nom. acc. -swaðu, -swaðo; n: dolh-swaðu, e; f: -swaðo; indecl. f. [swæþ, swaðu a trace, vestige] A trace of a wound, a scar; cicatrīcis vestīgium, cĭcātrix:—Dolhswæþ [MS. -swæð] cĭcātrix, Ælfc. Gl. 85; Som. 73, 115; Wrt. Voc. 49, 22. Forrotodon gewemmede and hîg synt dolhswaðu [dolcswaþu MS: dolhswaðo, Spl.] mîne putruērunt et corruptæ sunt cicatrices meæ, Ps. Lamb. 37, 6. Dolhswaðu cĭcātrix, Wrt. Voc. 85, 50. Ðæt seó þynneste dolhswaðo and seó læste ætýwde that the thinnest and the least scar was to be seen, Bd. 4, 19; S. 589, 19.

dolh-wund; adj. [wund wounded] Wounded; vulnĕrātus:—He on swîman læg druncen and dolhwund he lay in stupor drunk and wounded, Judth. 10; Thw. 23, 6; Jud. 107.

dol-lîc, dol-līg; adj. Foolish, rash; stultus, temĕrārius:—He manna mǽst mǽrþa gefremede, dǽda dollîcra he of men had achieved most glories, rash deeds, Beo. Th. 5285; B. 2646. Druncen beorg ðē and dollīg word guard thyself from drunkenness and foolish words, Exon. 80 b; Th. 302, 11; Fä. 34.

dollîce; adv. Foolishly, rashly; stulte, insāne:—Spræc heálīg word dollîce wið Drihten sînne he spake proud words foolishly against his Lord, Cd. 15; Th. 19, 22; Gen. 295: Homl. Th. ii. 330, 26. Ne man ne sceal drincan, oððe dollîce etan binnan Godes hûse nor may any one drink, nor foolishly eat within God's house, L. Ælf. C. 35; Th. ii. 356, note 2, line 10: Past. 20, 1; Hat. MS. 29 b, 4.

dol-sceaða, an; m. [dol foolish; sceaða a robber] A foolish or rash robber; temĕrārius spoliātor:—God eáðe mæg ðone dolsceaðan dǽda getwǽfan God may easily sever the doltish robber from his deeds, Beo. Th. 962; B. 479.

dol-scipe, es; m. [dol foolish; scipe termination, q. v.] Foolishness, folly, error; stultĭtia, error:—Giongra monna dolscipe hî ofslihþ the folly of young men kills them, Past. 50, 2; Hat. MS.

dol-spræc, e; f. [spræc a speaking, talk] Foolish or vain talk, loquacity; fātuus sermo:—Ðylæs we, for dolspræce, tô wîdgangule weorþen lest, from loquacity, we wander too far, Past. 49, 4; Hat. MS.

dol-willen, es; n. Rashness, madness; temĕrĭtas, dementia:—Ðū þurh ðîn dolwillen gedwolan fylgest thou followest error through thy rashness, Exon. 68 b; Th. 254, 24; Jul. 202.

dol-willen; adj. Rash, mad; temĕrārius, dēmens:—Ic ðec gedyrstig and ðus dolwillen gesôhte I have sought thee thus daring and rash, Exon. 72 a; Th. 269, 17; Jul. 451.

dol-wîte, es; n. [dol foolish, audacious = Ger. toll-kühn; wîte a punishment] Punishment for audacity, temerity or fool-hardiness; temerĭtātis pœna:—Nales dolwîte no punishment for audacity, Exon. 107 a; Th. 408, 25; Rä. 27, 17.

DÔM, es; m. I. DOOM, judgment, judicial sentence, decree, ordinance, law; jūdĭcium, sententia, decrētum, jus, lex:—Hit ys Godes dôm Dei jūdĭcium est, Deut. I, 17: Jn. Bos. 12, 31. Dômes dæg jūdĭcii dies, Mt. Bos. 10, 15: 11, 22, 24. Ðam ylcan dôme ðe ge dēmaþ, eów biþ gedēmed in quo jūdĭcio jūdicavĕrītis, judicabĭmĭni, Mt. Bos. 7, 2: Ex. 6, 6: 23, 6. Æfter eówrum âgnum dôme according to your own judgment, Bt. 14, 2; Fox 44, 35. Sŷn hî bisceopes dôme scyldig let them be liable to the bishop's sentence, Bd. 4, 5; S. 573, 1. Ðone ryhtan dôm the righteous sentence, Exon. 27 b; Th. 84, 6; Cri. 1369: 42 a; Th. 142, 8; Gû. 641. Hie noldon hyra þeódnes dôm þafigan they would not obey their lord's decree, Cd. 181; Th. 227, 21; Dan. 190: Exon. 65 a; Th. 240, 21; Ph. 642. On gewritum findaþ dôma gehwilcne ðara ðe him Drihten bebeád they find in the scriptures each of the ordinances which the Lord commanded him [Moses], Cd. 169; Th. 211, 2; Exod. 520. Ðis syndon ða dômas ðe Æðelbirht cyning asette on Agustinus dæge these are the laws which king Ethelbert established in Augustine's day, L. Ethb. pref; Th. i. 2, 2: L. H. E. pref; Th. i. 26, 3. Be Înes dômum of Ine's laws, L. In. pref; Th. i. 102, 1. II. a ruling, governing, command; rectio, gubernātio, impĕrium:—Dôme Drihten eorþan ymbhwyrft ealle gesette Dŏmĭnus correxit orbem terræ, Ps. Th. 95, 9: Exon. 39 a; Th. 129, 3; Gû. 415: Beo. Th. 5708; B. 2858. III. might, power, dominion, majesty, glory, magnificence, honour, praise, dignity, authority; potentia, potestas, majestas, glōria, splendor, honor, laus, dignĭtas, auctōrĭtas:—Ðǽr wearþ Lacedemonia âuweald and heora dôm alegen there was the dominion of the Lacedæmonians and their power laid low, Ors. 3, 1; Bos. 53, 30. Hî on dryhtlîcestum dôme lifdon they lived in most lordly majesty, Exon. 82 b; Th. 311, 1; Seef. 85. Sigemunde gesprong dôm unlytel no little glory sprang to Sigemund, Beo. Th. 1775; B. 885: 1913; B. 954. Hæfde Daniel dôm micelne in Babilônia Daniel had much honour in Babylon, Cd. 180; Th. 225, 33; Dan. 163. Eów Dryhten geaf dôm unscyndne the Lord gave you shameless glory, Elen. Kmbl. 730; El. 365. Se ðe wile dôm arǽran who desires to exalt his dignity, Exon. 87 a; Th. 327, 2; Wîd. 140. Dryhten â dôm âge, leóhtbǽre lof may the Lord ever have glory, bright praise, Exon. 80 a; Th. 299, 33; Crä. 111. Dôme gewurþad honoured with glory, Beo. Th. 3295; B. 1645. Dôma sēlast best of dignities, Exon. 122 a; Th. 467, 20; Alm. 4. IV. will, free will, choice, option; arbitrium, optio:—On eówerne âgenne dôm in your own will, Andr. Kmbl. 677; An. 339. Ðæt he beáh-hordes brūcan môste selfes dôme that he might enjoy the ring-hoard of his own free will, Beo. Th. 1794; B. 895: 5545; B. 2776. V. sense, meaning, interpretation; significātio, interprĕtātio:—Ge sweltaþ deáþe nymþe ic dôm wite sôþan swefnes ye shall perish by death unless I know the interpretation of my true dream, Cd. 179; Th. 224, 29; Dan. 143. [Prompt. dome: Wyc. dom, dome, doom: Piers P. doom, dome: Chauc. dome: Laym. Orm. dom: O. Sax. O. Frs. dôm, m. jūdĭcium, arbitrium, honor: Dut. doeming, f. condemnation: Kil. doeme jūdĭcium: Ger. in the termination -tum, -thum -dom: M. H. Ger. O. H. Ger. tuom, m. n. jūdĭcium: Goth. doms, m. judgment: Dan. dom, m. f: Swed. dom, m: Icel. dómr, m: Sansk. dhâman, n. a dwelling-place, state, condition, law, from dhâ to put.]

-dôm, es; m. as the termination of nouns is always masculine, and denotes Dominion, power, authority, property, right, office, quality, state, condition; as Cyne-dôm a king's power, office, etc. a kingdom; freó-dôm freedom; hālig-dôm holiness; wîs-dôm wis-dom; i. e. the state or condition of being free, holy, wise.

dôm-bôc; f. [bôc a book, q. v.] DOOM-BOOK, a book of decrees or laws; līber judiciālis:—Bête be ðam ðe seó dôm-bôc secge let him pay a fine according as the doom-book may say, L. Ath. i. 5; Th. i. 202, 7: L. Edg. i. 3; Th. i. 262, 23: i. 5; Th. i. 264, 20. Swâ hit on ðære dôm-bēc stande as it stands in the doom-book, L. Ed. prm; Th. i. 158, 4. Ne þearf he nânra dômbôca ôðerra cēpan he need not heed any other doom books, L. Alf. 49; Th. i. 56, 30. Ôþ-ðæt he com to ðâm dômbôcum, ðe se heofenlîca Wealdend his folce gesette until he came to the doom-books, which the heavenly Ruler appointed for his people, Homl. Th. ii. 198, 18.

dôm-dæg, es; m. [dômes dæg doom's day, L. E. I. 25; Th. ii. 422, 10: Salm. Kmbl. 649; Sal. 324] DOOMSDAY, judgment-day; dies jūdĭcii:—Ǽr he dômdæges dyn gehýre before he shall hear doomsday's din, Salm. Kmbl. 545; Sal. 272. Æt dômdæge, Exon. 31 b; Th. 99, 3; Cri. 1619. On dômdæge, 99 b; Th. 372, 19; Seel. 95: Cd. 227; Th. 302, 15; Sat. 600. On ðam miclan dômdæge in die jūdĭcii, L. Ælf. P. 40; Th. ii. 380, 39. Ðæt he dômdæg [dômes dæg MS. B.] ondrǽde that he dread doomsday, L. C. E. 25; Th. i. 374, 13.

dôm-eádig; adj. Blessed with power; pŏtens, nōbĭlis, beātus, glōria abundans:—Wæs ðære fǽmnan ferþ geblissad dômeádigre [-eadigra MS.] the damsel's soul, the noble one's was rejoiced, Exon. 69 b; Th. 259, 26; Jul. 288: 32 a; Th. 101, 11; Cri. 1657: 43 a; Th. 145, 23; Gû. 699: Cd. 63; Th. 75, 29; Gen. 1247.

dômere, es; m. A judge; jūdex:—Swâ him dômeras [dēmeras MS. H.] gereccen as the judges may prescribe to him, L. Alf. 18; Th. i. 48, 18. Heretogan and dômeras hæfdon mǽstne weorþscipe consuls and judges *had most honour*, Bt. 27, 4; Fox 100, 13. Settaþ ða to dōmerum *appoint them judges*, Past. 18, 2; Hat. MS. 26 a, 6.

Domer-hām, Domar-hām, es; *m.* DAMERHAM, *Wiltshire;* loci nomen in agro Wiltoniensi:—Æðelflǽd æt Domerhāme, Ælfgāres dōhter ealdormannes, was his cwēn *Æthelfled at Damerham, daughter of Ælfgar the alderman, was his [king Edmund's] queen*, Chr. 946; Erl. 117, 25. Ic gean ðæs landes æt Domarhāme into Glæstinga byrig *I give the land at Damerham to Glastonbury*, Th. Diplm. A. D. 972; 519, 30.

dōm-ern, es; *n. A judgment-place, a court-house;* forum judiciāle, tribūnal, prætōrium:—Dōmern *tribūnal*, Glos. Prudent. Recd. 143, 70. Ðā underfēngon ðæs dēman cempan ðone Hǽlend on ðam dōmerne, and gegaderodon ealne ðone þreát to heom *tunc mīlites præsĭdis suscĭpientes Iēsum in prætōrium, congregāvērunt ad eum universam cohortem*, Mt. Bos. 27, 27: Jn. Bos. 18, 28, 33: 19, 9: Homl. Th. ii. 422, 1. Wyðūtan hys dōmern *outside his judgment-hall*, Nicod. 10; Thw. 5, 9.

dōm-fæst; *adj.* [fæst *fast, firm*] *Firm in judgment, just, firm, powerful;* justus, pōtens:—Noe wæs dōmfæst and gedēfe *Noah was just and meek*, Cd. 64; Th. 78, 2; Gen. 1287: 108; Th. 143, 8; Gen. 2376: Exon. 54 b; Th. 192, 1; Az. 99. Syle us to-dæg dōmfæstne blǽd *give us to-day firm prosperity*, 122 a; Th. 469, 1; Hy. 5, 6. Twelfe wǽron dǽdum dōmfæste *the twelve were powerful in deeds*, Apstls. Kmbl. 9; Ap. 5. Ic sēce swegelcyning, dōmfæstra dreám *I seek the King of heaven, the joy of the just*, Exon. 48 b; Th. 167, 6; Gū. 1056.

dōm-fæstnes, -ness, e; *f.* [fæstnes *firmness*] *Firmness of judgment, judgment;* jūdicii integritas, jūdicium:—Mildheortnessa and dōmfæstnes ic singe *misericordiam et jūdicium cantābo*, Ps. Lamb. 100, 1.

dōm-georn; *adj.* [georn *desirous, eager*] *Eager for justice, ambitious, just, virtuous;* justitiæ appētens, justus:—Se hālga wæs to hofe lǽded, deór and dōmgeorn *the holy one was led to the house, dear and virtuous*, Andr. Kmbl. 2617: An. 1310. Hleóþrodon dugoþ dōmgeorne *the ambitious rulers spake*, 1385; An. 693: Exon. 76 b; Th. 287, 20; Wand. 17: Elen. Kmbl. 2579; El. 1291.

dōm-hūs, es; *n.* [hūs *a house*] *A judgment-house;* cūria, epicaustērium, capitōlium:—Dōm-hūs *cūria*, Ælfc. Gl. 55; Som. 67, 1; Wrt. Voc. 36, 44. Dōm-hūs *vel* mōt-hūs *epicaustērium*, 107; Som. 78, 74; Wrt. Voc. 57, 52. Dōm-hūs *capĭtōlium*, 107; Som. 78, 97; Wrt. Voc. 58, 12.

dōm-hwæt; *adj.* [hwæt *quick, strenuous*] *Strenuous in judgment;* in jūdicio strēnuus:—We hine dōmhwate, dǽdum and wordum hērgen holdlīce *we strenuous, may praise him faithfully in deeds and words*, Exon. 14 a; Th. 27, 11; Cri. 429.

dōmian; *p.* ode; *pp.* od [dōm *justice, glory*] *To praise, glorify;* celebrāre, gloriam tribuĕre:—Annanias ðec and Adzarias and Misael Metod dōmige *Hananiah and Azariah and Mishael may glorify thee, O Lord*, Cd. 192; Th. 241, 4; Dan. 399: 192; Th. 239, 19; Dan. 372.

dōm-leás; *adj. Inglorious, powerless, hapless;* inglōrius, impŏtens, infortūnātus:—Æðelingas gefricgean dōmleásan dǽd *nobles shall hear of your inglorious deed*, Beo. Th. 5772; B. 2890. Sceolon nū ǽfre dreógan dōmleáse gewinn *now we shall ever wage powerless war*, Cd. 218; Th. 279, 3; Sat. 232. Ealle swylt fornam, druron dōmleáse *death tore them all away, hapless they fell*, Andr. Kmbl. 1989; An. 997.

dōm-līc; *adj. Judicial, glorious;* judiciālis, gloriōsus:—Dōmlīc *judiciālis*, Ælfc. Gr. 9, 28; Som. 11, 36. Wǽron hwæðre monge ða ðe Meotude gehȳrdun dǽdum dōmlīcum *there were yet many who obeyed the Creator with glorious deeds*, Exon. 62 a; Th. 228, 28; Ph. 445: 62 a; Th. 229, 8; Ph. 452.

dōm-līce; *adj. Judicially, powerfully, gloriously;* judicialĭter, potenter, gloriōse:—Sȳn me ðīne handa on hǽlu nū, and ðæt dōmlīce gedōn weorþe *fiat manus tua et salvum me facias*, Ps. Th. 118, 173: Exon. 54 b; Th. 193, 19; Az. 124: Judth. 12; Thw. 26, 10; Jud. 319.

Dommoc-ceaster *Dunwich, Suffolk*, Bd. 2, 15; S. 519, 12. v. Domuc.

domne, es; *m. A lord;* dŏminus:—Hēr resteþ domne Agustinus, se ǽresta ærcebisceop Cantwarena burge *here resteth lord Augustine, the first archbishop of Canterbury*, Bd. 2, 3; S. 504, 43. Mīn domne bisceop *my lord bishop*, 3, 14; S. 540, 25: 3, 19; S. 548, 23.

dōm-setl, es; *n.* [dōm *judgment*, setl *a seat*] *A judgment-seat, tribunal;* tribūnal:—Ðis dōmsetl *hoc tribūnal*, Ælfc. Gr. 9, 5; Som. 9, 2. Se gerēfa hēt Iulianan ūt gelǽdan to his dōmsetle *the count bade Juliana be led out to his judgment-seat*, Exon. 73 b; Th. 274, 16; Jul. 534: 68 a; Th. 252, 12; Jul. 162. On his dōmsetle *pro tribūnāli*, Mt. Bos. 27, 19.

dōm-settend, es; *m. One sitting in judgment, a judge, a lawyer;* jurisconsultus, Cot. 113.

Domuc, e; *f?* Dommoc-ceaster; *gen.* -ceastre; *f. Dunwich, on the sea coast of Suffolk, the seat of the first East Anglian bishopric, which was subsequently fixed at Norwich;* loci nomen in agri Suffolciensi ora maritima:—Alfhun bisceop forþfērde on Sudberi, and he wearþ bebyrged in Domuce, and Tīdfriþ wearþ gecoren æfter him *bishop Alfhun died at Sudbury, and he was buried at Dunwich, and Tidfrith was chosen after him*, Chr. 798; Th. 105, 9–13, col. 3. Felix se bisceop, se com of Burgundana rīces dǽlum, onfēng biscopsetl on Dommocceastre, and mid ðȳ he seofontyne winter on bisceoplīcum gerece fōre wæs, ðǽr he on sibbe his līf ge-endode *Felix episcŏpus, qui de Burgundiōrum partĭbus venit, accēpit sedem episcopātus in civitāte Domnoc, et cum decem ac septem annos eidem provinciæ pontificāli regimĭne præesset, ibĭdem in pace vitam finīvit*, Bd. 2, 15; S. 519, 12.

DŌN, to dōnne; *part.* dōende, dōnde; ic dō, ðū dēst, he dēþ, *pl.* dōþ; *p.* ic, he dyde, ðū dydest, *pl.* dydon; *impert.* dō, *pl.* dōþ; *subj.* dō, *pl.* dōn, dō; *p.* dyde, *pl.* dyden; *pp.* dōn, dēn *To* DO, *make, cause;* agĕre, facĕre:—Ne mōt ic dōn ðæt ic wylle *non licet mihi quod volo facĕre?* Mt. Bos. 20, 15: Chr. 876; Erl. 79, 12: 994; Erl. 133, 17: Cd. 10; Th. 12, 23; Gen. 189: Beo. Th. 2349; B. 1172: Bt. Met. Fox 19, 78; Met. 19, 39. Alȳfþ on restedagum wel dōn, oððe yfele *licet sabbătis benefacĕre, an male?* Lk. Bos. 6, 9. He sǽde ðæt he hit nāhte to dōnne *he said that he ought not to do it*, Chr. 1070; Erl. 208, 5: 1091; Erl. 227, 13: Mt. Bos. 12, 2: Exon. 26 b; Th. 79, 11; Cri. 1289. Hyt ys alȳfed on restedagum wel to dōnne *licet sabbătis benefacĕre*, Mt. Bos. 12, 12. Dōende [dōnde, Lamb.] *faciens*, Ps. Spl. 102, 6. Eádig ys se þeów, ðe hys hlāford hyne gemēt ðus dōndne, ðonne he cymþ *beātus ille servus, quem cum venĕrit domĭnus ejus, invenĕrit sic facientem*, Mt. Bos. 24, 46: Lk. Bos. 12, 43. Ic dō *ago*, Ælfc. Gr. 28, 6; Som. 32, 12: *făcio*, 28, 6; Som. 32, 36. Ic dō oððe wyrce *făcio*, 33; Som. 37, 47. Ic dō gyt *faxo*, 33; Som. 37, 43. Ic dō ðæt gyt beóþ manna fisceras *făciam vos fĭeri piscatōres homĭnum*, Mt. Bos. 4, 19. Ðū dēst *faxis*, Ælfc. Gr. 33; Som. 37, 44. Hwī dēst ðū wið me swā *why doest thou with me so?* Gen. 12, 18: Jn. Bos. 6, 30. Se ðe hit dēþ, se biþ mycel *he who does it shall be great*, Mt. Bos. 5, 19: 13, 23: 18, 35: Boutr. Scrd. 19, 41: Ælfc. Gr. 33; Som. 37, 44: Salm. Kmbl. 364; Sal. 181: Ps. Th. 139, 12: Bt. Met. Fox 9, 123; Met. 9, 62: Beo. Th. 2121; B. 1058. Se ārleása dēþ ðæt fȳr cymþ ufan *the impious one will cause fire to come from above*, Homl. Th. i. 6, 7: Mt. Bos. 5, 32. Gyf ge ðæt dōþ *if ye do that*, Mt. Bos. 5, 47. Ne winne ge ongēn ða ðe eów yfel dōþ *strive not against those who do you wrong*, Mt. Bos. 5, 39: 12, 2. Ðæt cild weóx swā swā ōðre cild dōþ *the child grew as other children do*, Homl. Th. i. 24, 35: 18, 26: Boutr. Scrd. 18, 13: Cd. 60; Th. 73, 18; Gen. 1206: Exon. 34 a; Th. 109, 35; Gū. 100. Ne dyde ic for fācne *I did it not for fraud*, Cd. 128; Th. 162, 34; Gen. 2691. Ðū ondsæc dydest *thou madest denial*, Andr. Kmbl. 1854; An. 929. Ðæt dyde unhold mann *inĭmīcus homo hoc fecit*, Mt. Bos. 13, 28: Boutr. Scrd. 20, 2: Cd. 33; Th. 44, 12; Gen. 708: Exon. 24 a; Th. 68, 4. Iosep dyde swā Drihtnes engel him bebeád *Joseph fecit sicut præcēpit ei angĕlus Domĭni*, Mt. Bos. 1, 24: Ps. Th. 93, 7. Se wilnode ðæs westdǽles, swā se ōðer dyde ðæs eástdǽles *he wished for the west part, as the other did for the east part*, Ors. 3, 9; Bos. 66, 26: Boutr. Scrd. 18, 2: Cd. 215; Th. 272, 10; Sat. 117: Rood Kmbl. 226; Kr. 114: Beo. Th. 893; B. 444: Exon. 8 a; Th. 2, 11; Cri. 17. He ne cūðe hwæt ða cynn dydon *he knew not what the people did*, Cd. 92; Th. 116, 31; Gen. 1944: Exon. 53 a; Th. 186, 10; Az. 17. Hīg dydon swā hwæt swā hīg woldon *fecĕrunt quæcumque voluĕrunt*, Mt. Bos. 17, 12: Chr. 1001; Erl. 137, 9. Reced weardode unrīm eorla, swā hie oft ǽr dydon *countless warriors guarded the mansion, as they had often done before*, Beo. Th. 2481; B. 1238: Cd. 227; Th. 304, 6; Sat. 625: Exon. 14 a; Th. 28, 32; Cri. 455. Dō *fac*, Ælfc. Gr. 33; Som. 37, 47. Dō swā ic ðē bidde *do as I pray thee*, Cd. 101; Th. 134, 16; Gen. 2225: Elen. Kmbl. 1078; El. 541. Dōþ wel ðām ðe eów yfel dōþ *benefacĭte his qui odĕrunt vos*, Mt. Bos. 5, 44: Cd. 106; Th. 140, 6; Gen. 2323: Exon. 41 a; Th. 137, 24; Gū. 564: Beo. Th. 2467; B. 1231: Ps. Th. 30, 28. Dōþ his sīðas rihte *make his paths straight*, Mt. Bos. 3, 3: Ps. Th. 61, 8: 67, 4. Beheald ðæt ðū ðas dǽde ne dō *see that thou do not this deed*, Homl. Th. i. 38, 25. Ðæt he dō ealle hāle *ut salvos facĕret omnes*, Ps. Th. 75, 6: 118, 126. Ðæt heó dō ðæt ðæt heó ǽr dyde *that she may do that which she before did*, Bt. 25; Fox 88, 35, 36. Hwæt dō we ðæt we wyrceon Godes weorc *quid faciēmus ut operēmur opĕra Dei?* Jn. Bos. 6, 28: Exon. 99 b; Th. 372, 28; Seel. 99. Hwæt dō ge māre *quid amplius facĭtis?* Mt. Bos. 5, 47. Ðeáh hī wom dōn *though they commit sin*, Exon. 81 a; Th. 304, 15; Fä. 70: Cd. 109; Th. 145, 26; Gen. 2411: Ps. Th. 95, 7. ¶ Dōn dǽdbōte *to do penance, repent*, Mt. Bos. 3, 2: 4, 17: 11, 20, 21: 12, 41. Dōn edleán *to give a reward*, Boutr. Scrd. 22, 37. Dōn fram *to depart*, Ps. Lamb. 17, 22. Dōn in *to put in* or *into*, Bd. 2, 3; S. 504, 33: L. M. 1, 1; Lchdm. ii. 22, 13: Cd. 100; Th. 248, 31; Dan. 521. Dōn neóde *to supply want*, Basil. admn. 4; Norm. 40, 29. Dōn preóste *to give to a priest*, L. Edg. i. 2; Th. i. 262, 15. Dōn of *to take off, doff*, L. M. 1, 36; Lchdm. ii. 86, 15: Beo. Th. 5610; B. 2809. Dōn on *to put on, in*, or *into, to don*, L. M. 1, 1; Lchdm. ii. 18, 13; 24, 1: 1, 2; Lchdm. ii. 30, 5; 32, 14, 15, 17, 21: Herb. 1, 7; Lchdm. i. 72, 21: 2, 7; Lchdm. i. 82, 12: 13, 2; Lchdm. i. 104, 23: Beo. Th. 2293; B. 1144: 6307; B. 3164: Elen. Kmbl. 2348; El. 1175: Exon. 88 b; Th. 332, 19; Vy. 87: Hy. 9, 55; Hy. Grn. ii. 292, 55: Mt. Bos. 9, 16, 17. Dōn to *to put to*, Past. 49, 2; Hat. MS: L. M. 1, 2; Lchdm. ii. 28, 15. Dōn to witanne *to do to wit, to make to know* or *understand*, Past. 46, 8; Hat. MS. 68 a, 12: Prov. Kmbl. 11. Betre dōn *to prefer*, Bd. 2, 2; S. 502, 15. For nāuht dōn *to consider as naught*, Past. 38, 1; Hat. MS. 50 b, 19: Lev. 26, 15:

Deut. 31, 16. Furðor dôn *to prefer, esteem*, Past. 17, 7; Hat. MS. 23 b, 14. Gifta dôn *to keep nuptials*, Somn. 186; Lchdm. iii. 208, 21. Huntaþ dôn *to be hunting*, 239; Lchdm. iii. 212, 3. Gode dôn *to render to God*, L. Edg. C. 54; Th. ii. 256, 2. Gýmen [MS. gyman] dôn *to take care, regard*, Ors. 3, 9; Bos. 68, 25. Munuclíf dôn *to lead a monastic life*, Bd. 4, 23; S. 593, 19. On wôh dôn *to pervert*, Past. 2, 1; Cot. MS. To cyninge dôn *to make a king*, Ors. 6, 4; Bos. 118, 25: Bt. Met. Fox 15, 26; Met. 15, 13. Wrace dôn *to take revenge*, L. In. 9; Th. i. 108, 4. [*Prompt.* doon': *Wyc.* don, doon: *Piers P.* doon: *Chauc.* do *to cause*: *Laym.* don, do: *Orm.* don: *Plat.* doon: *O. Sax.* dôn, duôn, duan, dôan: *Frs.* dwaen, dien: *O. Frs.* dua: *Dut.* doen: *Ger.* thuen, thun: *M. H. Ger.* tuon: *O. H. Ger.* tuoan, tuon: *Sansk.* dhā *ponĕre.*] DER. a-dôn, be-, for-, ge-, in-ge-, of-, of-a-, ófer-, on-, on-ge-, óþ-, to-, to-ge-, un-, under-, up-a-, út-a-.

Dona-feld; *gen.* -feldes; *dat.* -felde, -felda; *m.* TANFIELD, *near Ripon, Yorkshire;* Campodŏnum in agro Eboracensi:—On Ðonafelda, ðǽr wæs ða cyninges botl, hêt Eádwine ðǽr cyricean getimbrian *in Campodōno, ubi tunc etiam villa rēgia erat, Æduini rex fecit basilĭcam*, Bd. 2, 14; S. 518, 17.

dôn-líc; *adj. Active;* practĭcus = πρακτικός, Cot. 149.

Donua; *indecl. f. The river Danube;* Danūbius = Δανούβιος:—Súþ óþ Donua ða eá, ðære ǽwylme is neáh ðære eá Rînes *south to the river Danube, whose spring is near the river Rhine*, Ors. 1, 1; Bos. 18, 24, 29. On óðre healfe ðære eá Donua *on the other side of the river Danube*, 1, 1; Bos. 18, 31, 43.

dooc *the south wind;* notus, auster, Som. Ben. Lye.

dop-enid, -ænid, e; *f.* [ened *a duck*] *A dipping-duck, a moorhen, fen-duck, coot;* fulĭca, fulix:—Dop-enid *fulĭca*, Ælfc. Gl. 38; Som. 63, 30; Wrt. Voc. 29, 50. Ganot, dop-ænid *fulix*, Glos. Epnl. Recd. 156, 53.

dop-fugel, es; *m. A dipping-fowl, a water-fowl, a moorhen;* mergus, mergŭlus:—Dop-fugel *mergus*, Wrt. Voc. 280, 12. Dop-fugel *mergŭlus*, Glos. Brux. Recd. 36, 6; Wrt. Voc. 62, 6.

doppettan; *p.* te; *pp.* ed *To dip often, dip in, immerse;* mersāre:—Geseah he swymman scealfran on flôde, and gelôme doppettan adûne to grunde, êhtende þearle ðære eá fixa *he saw gulls swimming on the water, and frequently dipping down to the bottom, eagerly pursuing the fishes of the river*, Homl. Th. ii. 516, 7. Ic doppette *merso*, Ælfc. Gr. 36; Som. 38, 21. v. dyppan.

Dor, es; *m.* DORE, *Derbyshire;* loci nomen in agro Derbiensi:—Ecgbryht Wesseaxna cyning lǽdde fierd to Dore wiđ Norþan Hymbre *Egbert king of the West Saxons led an army to Dore against the Northumbrians*, Chr. 827; Erl. 64, 7.

DÔR, es; *pl. nom. acc.* dôr, dôru, dûru; *n. A large door;* porta:—Ðæt ðû ðíne dôru mihtest bedôn fæste *that thou mightest shut fast thy doors*, Ps. Th. 147, 2. Gáþ nû on his dôru *intrāte portas ejus*, Ps. Th. 99, 3. Hôh ða wyrte on ðam [MS. ðan] dôre *hang the herbs on the door*, Lchdm. iii. 56, 29. Forðon he ǽren dôr eáðe gescéneþ [MS. gesceeneþ] *quia contrīvit portas æreas*, Ps. Th. 106, 15. Dûru *doors*, Exon. 97 b; Th. 364, 29. [*Prompt.* dore: *Wyc. Piers P. Chauc.* dore: *Laym.* dure, dore: *Plat.* döre *a door;* door *a gate:* *O. Sax.* dor, *n. a door, gate:* *Frs.* doare, doar: *O. Frs.* dore, dure *a door:* *Ger.* thüre, *f. a door;* thor, *n. a gate:* *Goth.* daúr, *n;* daúro, *f:* *Dan.* dör, *n:* *Swed.* dörr, *f:* *Icel.* dyrr, *f:* *O. Nrs.* dyrr, *n:* *Grk.* θύρα: *Sansk.* dvār, *f;* dvāra, *n.*] DER. Fífel-dôr, hel-, helle, weall-. v. dûru, *f.*

dora, an; *m. A humble-bee, dumble-*DORE; bombus terrestris, attăcus = ἄττăκος:—Dora *atticus* [= *attăcus*] vel *burdo* [= *Fr. bourdon*], Ælfc. Gl. 22; Som. 59, 112; Wrt. Voc. 23, 68. Doran hunig *dumbledore's honey*, L. M. 1, 2; Lchdm. ii. 28, 20. Celeþenian seáw gemeng wiđ dorena hunig *mingle juice of celandine with dumbledores' honey*, 1, 2; Lchdm. ii. 26, 7. Ða ahsan gemenge wiđ dorena hunig *mix the ashes with dumbledores' honey*, Lchdm. ii. 28, 26.

Dorce-ceaster, Dorces ceaster, Dorca-ceaster, Dorceaster; *gen.* -ceastre; *f.* [*Bd.* Dorcinca, Dorcic: *Hunt.* Dorecestre: *Brom.* Dorkecestre: *Matt. West.* Dorcestre] DORCHESTER, *Oxfordshire, the episcopal seat of the first bishop of the West Saxons, which was subsequently removed to Lincoln;* Durocastrum, in agri Oxoniensis parte Berceriensi finitĭma:—Hêr Cynegils [MS. Kynegils] wæs gefullod fram Byríne ðam biscope on Dorcaceastre *in this year* [A. D. 635] *Cynegils was baptized at Dorchester by bishop Birinus*, Chr. 635; Th. 47, 4, col. 1. Hêr wæs Cwichelm gefullod on Dorceceastre [Dorces ceastre, Th. 46, 10, col. 1] *in this year* [A. D. 636] *Cwichelm was baptized at Dorchester*, 636; Th. 47, 9, col. 1: 639; Th. 46, 18, col. 2; 47, 17, col. 1. Æt Dorceceastre [Dorceastre, Th. 175, 28, col. 2] *at Dorchester*, 897; Th. 174, 31, col. 1, 2; 175, 27, col. 1. Geáfon ðam biscope begen ða cyningas eardungstôwe and biscopsetl on Dorceceastre *both the kings* [*Cynegils of the West Saxons and Oswald of the Northumbrians*] *gave the bishop* [*Birinus*] *a dwelling-place and episcopal see at Dorchester*, Bd. 3, 7; S. 529, 20. Ætla wæs on Dorceceastre to bisceope gehâlgod *Ætla was consecrated bishop of Dorchester*, 4, 23; S. 594, 11. Hêr Wulstân arcebiscop onfêng eft biscopríces, on Dorceceastre *in this year* [A. D. 954] *archbishop Wulfstan again received a bishopric, at Dorchester*, Chr. 954; Th. 215, 26, col. 1.

dorfen *laboured, perished; pp. of* deorfan. v. ge-deorfan.

Dorm-ceaster; *gen.* -ceastre; *f.* [by the Britons called Cair-Dorm, by *Antonīnus* Durobrivæ, from the passage over the water; and the Anglo-Saxons, for the same reason, called it also Dornford] *Dornford* or *Dorgford, in Huntingdonshire, on the river Nen*, Som. Ben. Lye.

Dorn-sǽte, Dor-sǽte; *gen.* -sǽta; *dat.* -sǽtum, -sǽton, -sǽtan; *pl. m.* [dor = *Celt.* dwr, dur *water;* -sǽte *dwellers, inhabitants: dwellers by water*] *Inhabitants* or *men of Dorsetshire, people of Dorsetshire in a body,* DORSETSHIRE; Dorsetenses, Dorsetia:—Ðý ilcan geáre gefeaht Æðelhelm wiđ Deniscne here mid Dornsǽtum [Dorsǽtan, Th. 118, 17, col. 2; Dorsǽton, 119, 17, col. 1; Dorsǽtum, 119, 16, col. 2] *in the same year* [A. D. 837] *Æthelhelm fought against the Danish army with the Dorset-men*, Chr. 837; Th. 118, 17, col. 1. Mid Dornsǽtum [Dorsǽtum, Th. 120, 12, col. 2, 3; Dorsǽton, 121, 11, col. 1, 2, 3] *with the Dorset-men*, 845; Th. 120, 12, 36. Alfwold wæs bisceop on Dorsǽtum *Alfwold was bishop of Dorset*, 978; Th. 232, 7, col. 1: 982; Th. 234, 38: 236, 8: 1015; Th. 276, 13; 277, 13. Hí up eódon into Dorsǽton [Dorsǽtan, Th. 247, 19] *they went up into Dorsetshire*, 998; Th. 246, 19: Cod. Dipl. 1302; A. D. 1006; Kmbl. vi. 155, 6: 1334; A. D. 1046; Kmbl. vi. 195, 31. On Dorsǽtan *in Dorsetshire*, Cod. Dipl. 841; Kmbl. iv. 200, 26: 871; Kmbl. iv. 221, 5: Chr. 1078; Th. 350, 17.

Dornwara ceaster; *gen.* ceastre; *f.* [*the city of the inhabitants of Dorsetshire*] DORCHESTER, *the chief town of Dorsetshire;* Dorcestria, agri Dorsetensi caput:—Ðis wæs gedôn in ðam cynelícan setle on ðære stôwe ðe is genæmned Dornwara ceaster *this was done in the royal residence in the place which is named Dorchester*, Th. Diplm. A. D. 864; 126, 8: Cod. Dipl. 1061; A. D. 868; Kmbl. v. 119, 26.

dorste, *pl.* dorston *durst*, Ors. 1, 10; Bos. 33, 30: 4, 11; Bos. 97, 14; *p. of* durran.

Dorwit-ceaster; *gen.* -ceastre; *f. Canterbury;* Dorobernia:—Hrôfes ceaster is xxiv míla fram Dorwitceastre *Rochester is twenty-four miles from Canterbury*, Chr. 604; Erl. 21, 24.

dott, es; *m. A* DOT, *small spot, speck;* punctum:—Geopenige mon ðone dott, and binde ðone clíðan to ðan swyle *let the speck* [*at the head of a boil*] *be opened, and the poultice be bound to the swelling*, Lchdm. iii. 40, 14.

drabbe *dregs, lees,* DRAB; fæces, Som. Ben. Lye. [*Prompt.* draffe *segestārium, drascum:* *Wyc.* draf *dreg, refuse;* draffis *dregs:* *Piers P. Chauc. Laym.* draf *dregs:* *Dut.* draf, *m.*]

DRACA, an; *m.* I. *a dragon;* draco:—Draca ðes ðone ðû ýwodest *draco iste quem formasti*, Ps. Spl. 103, 28. Tredan león and dracan *conculcāre leonem et dracōnem*, Ps. Th. 90, 13. Ðû fortrydst leóna and dracena *thou shalt be a treader down of lions and dragons*, Ps. Spl. 90, 13: Ps. Th. 148, 7. II. *a serpent;* serpens:—Is ðæt deór pandher, se is æt-hwâm freónd, bûtan dracan ânum *the beast is the panther, which is to each a friend, save to the serpent only*, Exon. 95 b; Th. 356, 24; Pa. 16. III. *the serpent = the devil;* diabŏlus:—Worpaþ hine deófol, draca egeslíce *the devil, the fearful dragon, shall cast him down*, Salm. Kmbl. 52; Sal. 26: Exon. 96 a: Th. 359, 4; Pa. 57. [*R. Glouc.* dragon: *Laym.* drake, *m:* *Orm.* drake: *Plat.* drake, *m:* *Dut.* draak, *m:* *Ger.* drache, *m:* *M. H. Ger.* trache, tracke, *m:* *O. H. Ger.* tracho, *m:* *Dan.* drage, *m. f:* *Swed.* drake, *m:* *Icel.* dreki, *m:* *Fr.* dragon, *m:* *Span.* dragón, *m:* *Ital.* dragóne, *m:* *Lat.* draco: *Grk.* δράκων *a dragon*, from δέρκομαι *to flash, gleam.*] DER. eorþ-draca, fýr-, lég-, líg-, níþ-, sǽ-.

dracan blôd, es; *n. Dragon's blood, a pigment obtained from the dragon's blood-tree;* cinnabăris = κιννάβăρι, Cot. 210. v. dracentse.

dracentse, dracente, dracanse, draconze, an; *f. Dragon-wort, dragons;* dracontea = δρακόντιον, arum dracuncŭlus, Lin:—*Herba dracontea*, ðæt ys dracentse, Herb. Cont. 15, 1; Lchdm. i. 12; 15, 1. Ðeós wyrt, ðe man *dracontea* and óðrum naman dracentse nemneþ, ys sǽd ðæt heó of dracan blôde acenned beón sceolde *this herb, which is named* dracontea, *and by another name dragons, is said to be produced from dragon's blood*, Herb. 15, 1; Lchdm. i. 106, 22. Nim dracentan wyrtruman [MS. wyrtruma] *take roots of dragons*, Lchdm. iii. 114, 8. Dracanse *dragons*, iii. 24, 3. Draconzan, *acc. dragons*, L. M. 3, 62; Lchdm. ii. 350, 7.

DRǼDAN; ic drǽde, ðû drǽdest, drǽtest, drǽst, he drǽdeþ, drǽt, *pl.* drǽdaþ; *p.* drêd, dreórd, *pl.* drêdon; *pp.* drǽden *To* DREAD, *fear;* timēre, pavēre: *found in the compounds* a-drǽdan, an-, on-drǽdan, on-drǽd-endlíc, on-drǽd-ing: of-drǽd. [*Wyc.* drede, dreed: *Piers P. Chauc.* drede: *Laym.* dreden: *Orm.* drædenn, dredenn: *O. Sax.* ant-drâdan, an-drâdan: *M. H. Ger.* en-trâten: *O. H. Ger.* an-trâtan.]

drǽf, drâf, e; *f. A driving out, an expulsion;* expulsio:—Be drǽfe [drâfe MS. B.] *of expulsion*, L. In. 68; Th. i. 146, 6. DER. ût-drǽf.

drǽfan; *p.* de; *pp.* ed *To drive;* agĕre, pellĕre. DER. a-drǽfan, ge-, to-, ge-drǽfnes, to-drǽfednes, ût-drǽfere. v. drífan.

drǽfend, es; *m. A hunter;* venātor:—Sum biþ deóra drǽfend *one is a hunter of beasts*, Exon. 78 b; Th. 295, 24; Crä. 38.

dræge, es; *n? A* DRAG, *drag-net;* tragŭla, verricŭlum:—Dræg-net *vel* dræge *tragŭla*, Ælfc. Gl. 1; Som. 55, 13; Wrt. Voc. 15, 13. Dræge *tragŭla* vel *verricŭlum*, 105; Som. 78, 40; Wrt. Voc. 57, 22.

drægeþ, đū drægest *drags, thou draggest; 3rd and 2nd pers. pres. of* dragan.

dræg-net, -nett, es; *n. A drag-net;* tragum, verricŭlum:—Dræg-net *vel* dræge *tragŭla*, Ælfc. Gl. 1; Som. 55, 13; Wrt. Voc. 15, 13. Drægnet *verricŭlum*, 84; Som. 73, 89; Wrt. Voc. 48, 27.

drægþ, đū drægst *drags, thou draggest*, Past. 56, 2; Hat. MS; *3rd and 2nd pers. pres. of* dragan.

dræhþ, đū dræhst *drags, thou draggest; 3rd and 2nd pers. pres. of* dragan.

drǣn *a drone*, Wrt. Voc. 77, 48. v. drān.

drænc *a drink*, L. M. I. P. 10; Th. ii. 268, 6. v. drinc.

drǣp, đū drǣpe, *pl.* drǣpon *struck; p. of* drepan.

drǣtest, drǣst, he drǣt *dreadest, dreads; 2nd and 3rd pers. pres. of* drǣdan.

drāf, e; *f.* [drāf *drove, p. of* drīfan] *A* DROVE, *herd, band;* armenta, grex, agmen:—Đā đā seó ormǣte micelnyss his orfes on đære dūne læswede, sum mōdig fearr wearþ āngencga, and đære heorde drāfe oferhogode *when the immense multitude of his cattle was grazing on the mountain, an unruly bull wandered alone, and despised the companionship of the herd*, Homl. Th. i. 502, 10. Oft twegen sǣmen ođđe þrȳ hwīlum drīfaþ đa drāfe cristenra manna fram sǣ to sǣ *sæpe duo tresve e pirātis christianōrum agmen congregātum a mari usque ad mare compellunt*, Lupi Serm. i. 15; Hick. Thes. ii. 103, 34. Hī drifon heora drāfa into Medewæge *they drove their herds into the Medway*, Chr. 1016; Erl. 157, 4, 16.

drāf *drove*, Chr. 1099; Ing. 318, 16; *p. of* drīfan.

DRAGAN, ic drage, đū drægest, drægst, dræhst, he drægeþ, drægþ, dræhþ, *pl.* dragaþ; *p.* drōg, drōh, *pl.* drōgon; *pp.* dragen. I. *v. a. To* DRAG, *draw;* trahĕre:—Eall đæt đa beón dragen toward đa drāne dragaþ fraward *all that the bees draw towards them the drones draw from them*, Chr. 1127; Th. 378, 24, 25. Simon Petrus drōg đæt nett on eorþe *Simon Petrus traxit rete in terram*, Jn. Lind. War. 21, 11. Hī me drōgon, and ic hit nyste ... hit mon drægþ swā hit ne gefret *traxērunt me et ego non sensi ... trahĭtur et nequaquam sentit*, Past. 56, 2; Hat. MS. Hī drōgon heora scipa on west-healfe đære brycge *they dragged their ships to the west side of the bridge*, Chr. 1016; Erl. 155, 9, 23. II. *v. intrans. To draw oneself, to draw, go;* se conferre, ire:—Drōgon swā wīde swā wegas to lǣgon *they went as far as the roads lay before them*, Andr. Kmbl. 2465; An. 1234. Ongon dragan Dryhtnes cempa *the Lord's champion began to go*, Exon. 43 a; Th. 145, 23; Gū. 699. [*Wyc.* drow, droȝ, drowȝ *drew: Laym.* draȝen, drawe *to draw: Orm.* draghenn *to draw: Plat.* drāgen *to bear, endure: O. Sax.* dragan *to bear: Frs.* dreagjen, dreagen, dreyn: *O. Frs.* drega, draga *to bear: Dut.* dragen *to bear: Ger. M. H. Ger.* tragen *to bear, endure: O. H. Ger.* tragan *portăre: Goth.* dragan *to carry: Dan.* drage *to draw, carry: Swed.* draga *to wear: Icel.* draga *to drag, carry: Lat.* trahĕre *to pull.*] DER. bedragan, ūt-.

DRĀN, drǣn, e; *f. A* DRONE; fucus:—Drān *fucus*, Ælfc. Gl. 22; Som. 59, 106; Wrt. Voc. 23, 62. Drǣn *fucus*, Wrt. Voc. 77, 48. Đǣr he wunede eall riht swā drāne dōþ on hīue: eall đæt đa beón dragen toward đa drāne dragaþ fraward *he abode there just as drones do in a hive: all that the bees draw towards them the drones draw from them*, Chr. 1127; Erl. 256, 20, 21. [*Piers P.* drane: *Plat.* drone: *O. Sax.* drān, *f. fucus: Ger.* drone, thräne, *f;* dran, *m. fucus: M. H. Ger.* tren, *m. fucus: O. H. Ger.* treno, *m. attăcus, fucus: Dan.* drone, *m. f: Swed.* drönje, drön-are, *m: Grk.* ἀν-θρήν-η, *f. a hornet, bee: Sansk.* druṇa, *m. a bee;* dhraṇ *to sound.*]

dranc *drank*, Gen. 9, 21; *p. of* drincan.

dreá *a magician, wizard*, Salm. Kmbl. 89, MS. A; Sal. 44. v. drȳ.

dreág, dreáh *did, suffered*, Exon. 74 b; Th. 280, 9; Jul. 626: Cd. 145; Th. 180, 22; Exod. 49; *p. of* dreógan.

dreahnian; *p.* ode; *pp.* od *To strain out, drain;* excolāre:—Dreahna ūt þurh wyllene clāþ *drain [it] out through a woollen cloth*, Lchdm. iii. 72, 23. v. drehnigean.

dreahte, đū dreahtest, *pl.* dreahton; *pp.* dreaht *Vexed, vexedst, troubled*, Exon. 98 a; Th. 368, 6; Seel. 17; *p. and pp. of* dreccan.

DREÁM, es; *m.* I. *joy, pleasure, gladness, mirth, rejoicing, rapture, ecstasy, frenzy;* jubĭlum, lætĭtia, gaudium, delīrium:—Đǣr biþ drincendra dreám se micla *there is the great joy of drinkers*, Exon. 88 a; Th. 332, 3; Vy. 79: Beo. Th. 999; B. 497: Cd. 169; Th. 211, 25; Exod. 531. Đǣr biþ engla dreám *there [in heaven] is joy of angels*, Exon. 32 b; Th. 102, 22; Cri. 1676: Elen. Kmbl. 2461; El. 1232: Apstls. Kmbl. 96; Ap. 48. Ic eam ealles leás ēcan dreámes *I am bereft of all eternal joy*, Cd. 216; Th. 275, 8; Sat. 168: 217; Th. 276, 2; Sat. 182: Exon. 27 b; Th. 82, 24; Cri. 1343: Rood Kmbl. 285; Kr. 144. In dolum dreáme *in foolish joy*, Exon. 39 a; Th. 130, 8; Gū. 435. In đam uplīcan engla dreáme *in the exalted joy of angels*, 9 a; Th. 7, 17; Cri. 102. He dreám gehȳrde hlūdne in healle *he heard loud mirth in the hall*, Beo. Th. 177; B. 88. Sorh cymeþ in manna dreám *sorrow cometh into the joy of men*, Frag. Kmbl. 3; Leás. 2: Exon. 35 a; Th. 114, 2; Gū. 166. Heó mōton āgan dreáma dreám mid Gode *they may possess joy of joys with God*, Cd. 220; Th. 283, 32; Sat. 314: Exon. 16 a; Th. 36, 22; Cri. 580: Apstls. Kmbl. 163; Ap. 82. Eart đū dumb and deáf, ne sindan đīne dreámas wiht *thou art dumb and deaf, thy pleasures are naught*, Exon. 99 a; Th. 370, 27; Seel. 65. Dreáma leás *void of joys, joyless*, Beo. Th. 1705; B. 850: Cd. 2; Th. 3, 23; Gen. 40: 5; Th. 7, 18; Gen. 108. Ic dreáma wyn sceal āgan mid englum *I shall possess joy of joys with angels*, Exon. 42 b; Th. 142, 31; Gū. 652. Hie forþ heonon gewiton of worulde dreámum *they have departed hence from the world's joys*, Rood Kmbl. 263; Kr. 133: Exon. 43 b; Th. 146, 19; Gū. 712. Hēr ge-endode eorþan dreámas Eádgār Engla cyning *in this year [A. D. 975] Edgar, king of the Angles, ended the pleasures of earth*, Chr. 975; Erl. 124, 29; Edg. 21: Exon. 32 b; Th. 102, 5; Cri. 1668. Sēcan mid sibbe swegles dreámas *to seek in peace the joys of heaven*, Andr. Kmbl. 1618; An. 810: Cd. 14; Th. 17, 9; Gen. 257: Exon. 26 a; Th. 76, 28; Cri. 1246: Judth. 12; Thw. 26, 31; Jud. 350. On swylcum wōdum dreáme *in such insane ecstasy or frenzy*, Ors. 3, 6; Bos. 58, 14: Homl. Th. i. 524, 34: 526, 1: ii. 50, 28: 110, 18, 31. II. what causes mirth,—*An instrument of music, music, rapturous music, harmony, melody, song;* orgănum = ὄργανον, musĭca, concentus, harmŏnia = ἁρμονία, modulātio, modus, melōdia = μελῳδία, cantus:—Ne māgon đam breahtme bȳman ne hornas, ne hearpan hlyn, ne organan swēg, ne ǣnig đara dreáma đe Dryhten gescōp gumum to gliwe in đas geómran woruld *trumpets nor horns can [equal] that sound, nor sound of harp, nor organ's tone, nor any of those kinds of music which the Lord hath created for delight to men in this sad world*, Exon. 57 b; Th. 206, 29–207, 10; Ph. 134–139. On saligum we ahōfon ođđe ahēngon dreámas ūre *in salicĭbus suspendĭmus orgăna nostra*, Ps. Lamb. 136, 2. Sǣde se engel đæt se dreám wǣre of đam upplīcum werode *the angel said that the melody was from the celestial host*, Homl. Th. ii. 342, 10: Exon. 52 a; Th. 181, 9; Gū. 1290. Werhādes men ongunnon symle đone dreám, and wīfhādes men him sungon ongeán andswariende *men always begun the melody, and women answering sung in turn*, Homl. Th. ii. 548, 12: Cd. 220; Th. 284, 28; Sat. 328. Iohannes gehȳrde swylce bȳmena dreám *John heard, as it were, the sound of trumpets*, Homl. Th. ii. 86, 35. Dreáme *harmŏnia, modulatiōne*, Mone B. 2528, 2529. Dreámas *concentus*, 4940. Dreámum *modis*, Glos. Prudent. Recd. 143, 9. [*Laym,* dræm, dream, drem, *m. joy, rejoicing: Orm.* dræm *sound.*] DER. dreám-cræft, -ere, -hæbbende, -healdende, -leás, -līc, -nes, -swinsung: drēman, drȳman, freá-: drēme, drȳme, ge-, unge-: ēđel-dreám, gleó-, god-, gum-, heofon-, man-, medu-, sele-, sin-, swegl-, woruld-, wuldor-, wyn-.

dreám-cræft, es; *m. The art of music, music;* musica:—Gedēþ se dreámcræft đæt se mon biþ dreámere *the art of music causes the man to be a musician*, Bt. 16, 3; Fox 54, 31.

dreámere, es; *m. A musician;* musĭcus, Bt. 16, 3; Fox 54, 31.

dreám-hæbbende; *part.* [dreám I. *joy,* hæbbende *having, possessing*] *Possessing bliss, joyful;* lætābundus:—Þrymmas weóxon dreámhæbbendra *the glories of the possessors of bliss increased*, Cd. 4; Th. 5, 34; Gen. 81.

dreám-healdende; *part.* [healdende *holding*] *Holding joy, joyful;* lætābundus:—Beó đū sunum mīnum gedēfe, dreámhealdende *be thou gentle to my sons, holding them in joy*, Beo. Th. 2459; B. 1227.

dreám-leás; *adj. Joyless, sad;* mæstus:—Dreámleás gebād *he continued joyless*, Beo. Th. 3445; B. 1720: Cd. 202; Th. 251, 4; Dan. 558. Đis is dreámleás hūs *this is a joyless house*, Exon. 31 b; Th. 99, 22; Cri. 1628.

dreám-līc; *def.* se -līca, seó, đæt -līce; *adj. Joyous, musical;* jucundus, musĭcus:—Dreámlīc ođđe wynsum sȳ him spæc [MS. spæce] mīn *jucundum sit ei eloquium meum*, Ps. Lamb. 103, 34. Đa dreámlīcan *musĭca*, Cot. 133.

dreámnes, -ness, e; *f. A singing;* cantio:—Word dreámnessa ođđe sanga *verba cantiōnum*, Ps. Lamb. 136, 3.

dreám-swinsung *mirth-harmony, harmony*, Cot. 4. v. swinsung.

dreáp, *pl.* drupon *dropped; p. of* dreópan.

dreápian *to drop*, Ps. Surt. 67, 9. v. dreópian.

dreárung, e; *f. A falling;* destillātio, Cd. 191; Th. 238, 3; Dan. 349. v. dreórung.

dreás *rushed, fell; p. of* dreósan.

dreás *soothsayers;* hariŏli, Prov. 23, = drȳas; *pl. nom. of* drȳ.

DRECCAN, dreccean, drecan, ic drecce, drece, đū drecest, drecst, he dreceþ, drecþ, *pl.* dreccaþ, drecceaþ; *p.* [drechede = drehde =] drehte, dreahte, *pl.* drehton, dreahton; *pp.* [dreched = drehed = dreht, dreaht] dreht, dreaht *To vex, afflict, trouble, torture, torment;* vexāre, affligĕre, tribulāre, turbāre, cruciāre:—Mec sorg dreceþ *sorrow vexeth me*, Cd. 99; Th. 131, 21; Gen. 2179. Drecþ se deófol mancynn mid mislīcum costnungum *the devil vexes mankind with various temptations*, Boutr. Scrd. 19, 44. Me Agar drehte dōgora gehwam *Hagar hath vexed me each day*, Cd. 102; Th. 135, 27; Gen. 2249. Yrfweardnysse đīne hī drehton *hæreditātem tuam vexavērunt*, Ps. Spl. 93, 5: Chr. 897; Erl. 95, 7. Ic drece *vexo*, Ælfc. Gr. 24; Som. 25, 44. Đeáh hine se ymbhoga đyssa woruldsǣlþa wrāđe drecce *though the anxious care of* *these worldly goods severely afflicts him*, Bt. Met. Fox 7, 108; Met. 7, 54: Homl. Th. i. 156, 21. Ne wendaþ hine wyrda, ne hine wiht dreceþ *fates change him not, nor doth aught afflict him*, Exon. 88 b; Th. 334, 1; Gn. Ex. 9: Bt. Met. Fox 7, 50; Met. 7, 25. Đonne míne fýnd me drecceaþ *dum afflīgit me inimīcus*, Ps. Th. 42, 2. Ic ðé bebeóde ðæt ðú nánum men ne drece *I command thee that thou afflict no man*, Homl. Th. ii. 296, 5. On ðam écan lífe ðǽr ne cymþ nán deófol ne nán yfel mann, ðe us mǽge dreccan *in the eternal life there will come no devil nor evil man who may trouble us*, i. 272, 10. Hwí drecst ðú leng ðone láreów *why troublest thou the master longer?* Mk. Bos. 5, 35. Hí hine dreccaþ *they trouble him*, Ps. Th. arg. 25: Homl. Th. ii. 540, 34. To hwon dreahtest ðú me *for what* [*why*] *hast thou tortured me?* Exon. 98 a; Th. 368, 6; Seel. 17. Gif hine dreccean mót ðissa yfla hwæðer *if either of these evils can torment it*, Bt. Met. Fox 5, 80; Met. 5, 40. [*Piers P.* drecchen *to vex*: *Chauc.* drecche: *Laym.* i-dræcched, -dracched, -drecched, *pp. injured, disturbed.*] DER. ge-dreccan.

dreccednys, -nyss, e; *f. Vexation, affliction, tribulation*; vexātio, afflictio, tribulātio:—He ðære dreccednysse geswác *he ceased the affliction*, Homl. Th. i. 454, 28. DER. ge-dreccednys.

dreccing, e; *f. Tribulation*; vexātio, Som. Ben. Lye.

dréd, *pl.* drédon *dreaded, feared*; *p. of* drǽdan.

DRÉFAN; *part.* dréfende; *p.* dréfde; *pp.* dréfed *To disturb, agitate, disquiet, vex, trouble*; commovēre, turbāre, conturbāre, tribulāre, contristāre:—Uparǽr mód úre dréfende *erīge mentes nostras turbĭdas*, Hymn. Surt. 127, 6. Đonne ic wado dréfe *when I disturb the waters*, Exon. 103 a; Th. 389, 24; Rä. 8, 2. Đú dréfst hí *turbābis eos*, Ps. Spl. 82, 14. For-hwý unrót eart sáwle mín, and for-hwon dréfst me *quare tristis es anĭma mea, et quare conturbas me?* Ps. Spl. 41, 6, 15: 42, 5. Dréfaþ *conturbant*, Mone B. 2613. Ne lagu dréfde *it disturbed not the water*, Exon. 106 a; Th. 404, 31; Rä. 23, 16. Đæt ðú lagu dréfde *that thou mightest disturb the water*, Exon. 123 a; Th. 473, 26; Bo. 20. Gewát him on nacan, dréfan deóp wæter *he departed in the bark, to agitate the deep water*, Beo. Th. 3812; B. 1904. Hwý ge scylen eówer mód dréfan *why should ye trouble your mind?* Bt. Met. Fox 27, 3; Met. 27, 2. He to náhte gelǽdeþ ða dréfendan us *ipse ad nihĭlum dedūcet tribulantes nos*, Ps. Spl. 59, 13. To-hwý gemænigfylde synd ða ðe dréfaþ me *quid multiplicāti sunt qui tribŭlant me?* Ps. Spl. 3, 1. For-hwí dréfe ge eówru mód *why vex ye your minds?* Bt. 39, 1; Fox 210, 24. For-hwý dréfed ic gange, ðonne swencþ me feónd *quare contristātus incēdo, dum afflīgit me inimīcus?* Ps. Spl. 41, 13. [*Laym.* i-drefed, *pp. disturbed*; to-drefed, -dreved *oppressed*: *Orm.* dræfedd, dreofedd, drefedd *disturbed, troubled*: *Plat.* dröven: *O. Sax.* drōƀian, druovan *turbāri, conturbāre*: *Kil.* droeven *tristāri, turbāre*: *Ger.* trüben: *M. H. Ger.* trüeben: *O. H. Ger.* truobjan: *Goth.* drobyan *to trouble, confound*: *Dan.* be-dröve: *Swed.* be-dröfva.] DER. ge-dréfan, to-: un-dréfed. v. dróf.

dréfednes, -ness, -nyss, e; *f. Vexation, affliction, tribulation*; vexātio, afflictio, tribulātio:—Syððon cómon [comen MS.] ealle dréfednysse [MS. dræuednysse] and ealle ifele to ðone mynstre *after that all troubles and all evils came to the monastery*, Chr. 1066; Erl. 203, 31. DER. ge-dréfednes.

dréfing, e; *f. A disturbing*; conturbātio, Ælfc. Gl. 5; Som. 56, 24; Wrt. Voc. 17, 29.

dréfliende; *part. Troubled with rheum*; rheumatĭcus = ῥευματικός:—Saftriende *vel* dréfliende *rheumatĭcus*, Ælfc. Gl. 77; Som. 72, 14; Wrt. Voc. 45, 48.

dréfre; *adj. Agitated, disturbed*; turbulentus, C. R. Ben. 64. v. dróf.

drege *dry*, Prov. 16. v. drige.

drehnigean, drehnian, dreahnian; *p.* ode; *pp.* od *To strain out*, DRAIN; excolāre, percolāre:—Lá blindan látteówas, ge drehnigeaþ ðone gnæt aweg *duces cæci, excolantes culĭcem*, Mt. Bos. 23, 24.

drehte, *pl.* drehton; *pp.* dreht *Vexed, afflicted*, Cd. 102; Th. 135, 27; Gen. 2249: Ps. Spl. 93, 5; *p. of* dreccan.

dréman, drýman; *p.* de; *pp.* ed [dreám *joy, music*] *To rejoice, to play on an instrument*; jubilāre, psallĕre:—Drémaþ Gode Iacobes *jubĭlāte Deo Iacob*, Ps. Spl. 80, 1. Drémaþ oððe fægniaþ on gesihþe cyninges *jubĭlāte in conspectu regis*, Ps. Lamb. 97, 7. We drémaþ mægnu ðínum *psallēmus virtūtes tuas*, Ps. Spl. 20, 13. Drémaþ oððe singaþ cyninge úrum *psallĭte regi nostro*, Ps. Lamb. 46, 7: 97, 5. [*Laym.* dremen, dreomen *to revel, resound*: *O. Sax.* drōmian *jubĭlāre*.] DER. freá-dréman.

dréme, drýme; *adj.* [dreám II. *music, melody, harmony*] *Melodious, harmonious*; canōrus:—Mid dremere stefne *canōra voce*, Mone B. 2538. DER. ge-dréme, -drýme, unge-.

drenc, es; *m.* I. *a* DRENCH, *dose, draught, drink*; pōtus, pōtio:—Wið útsiht-ádle drenc *a dose for diarrhœa*, L. M. cont. 3, 22; Lchdm. ii. 300, 23. Drenc *pōtus*, Ælfc. Gr. 11; Som. 15, 16: Wrt. Voc. 82, 46: *pōtio*, 74, 7. Se drenc deádbǽra wæs *the drink was deadly*, Homl. Th. ii. 158, 22. Wín nys drenc cilda *vinum non est pōtus puerōrum*, Coll. Monast. Th. 35, 19: Homl. Th. ii. 158, 17. Wið sídan sáre ðære swíðran hwíte clæfran wyrc to drence *for sore of right side make white clover to a drink*, L. M. 1, 21; Lchdm. ii. 64, 4: 1, 23; Lchdm. ii. 64, 27: Homl. Th. ii. 158, 16. Wyrc drenc wið hwóstan *make a dose for cough*, L. M. 1, 15; Lchdm. ii. 56, 18. Sele him oft styrgendne drenc *give him often a stirring drink*, 1, 42; Lchdm. ii. 106, 25. Se yrþling sylþ us hláf and drenc *arātor dat nobis panem et potum*, Coll. Monast. Th. 31, 3. Hí ðone gástlícan drenc druncon *they drank the spiritual drink*, Homl. Th. ii. 202, 3. Drenc wyð áttre *a dose* or *antidote against poison*; theriāca = θηριακή, Ælfc. Gl. 12; Som. 57, 78; Wrt. Voc. 20, 20. Swylfende drenc *a dose to be gulped* or *swallowed down, a pill*; catapŏtium = καταπότιον, 12; Som. 57, 80; Wrt. Voc. 20, 22. II. *a drowning*; demersio, submersio:—Sume drenc fornam on lagostreáme *drowning took off some in the water-stream*, Elén. Kmbl. 272; El. 136. Gæst in deáþ-sele drence bifæsteþ scipu mid scealcum *the guest commits ships and crews to the death-hall by drowning*, Exon. 97 a; Th. 362, 2; Wal. 30. DER. berig-drenc, dolh-, dust-, ofer-, wyrt-.

DRENCAN; *part.* drencende; *p.* ic, he drencte, ðú drenctest, *pl.* drencton; *pp.* drenced; *v. a.* I. *to give to drink, to* DRENCH, *make drunk*; potum *vel* potiōnem dāre, potāre, inebriāre:—Of burnan willan ðínes ðú drenctest [Th. drencst] hí *torrente voluntātis tuæ potābis eos*, Ps. Spl. 35, 9. Đú drenctest us mid wíne *potasti nos vino*, 59, 3. On þurste mínum hí drencton me mid ecede *in siti mea potavērunt me acēto*, 68, 26. Drencende *inebrians*, 64, 11. Se inwida dryht-guman síne drencte mid wíne *the wicked one made his people drunk with wine*, Judth. 10; Thw. 21, 21; Jud. 29. II. *to drown*; submergĕre, Ps. Th. 106, 17. [*Wyc.* drenche: *Piers P.* drenchen, drenche: *Chauc.* drenche: *Plat.* drenken: *O. Sax.* drenkan: *Frs.* drinssen: *O. Frs.* drenka, drinka, drinsa *to drown*: *Dut.* drenken *to drench*: *Ger.* tränken *to give to drink*: *M. H. Ger.* trenken: *O. H. Ger.* trankjan, trenkjan *potāre*: *Goth.* dragkyan *to give to drink*: *Swed.* dränka *to drown*: *Icel.* drekkja *to drown.*] DER. a-drencan, for-, ge-, in-, ofer-, ofge-, on-. v. drincan.

drenc-cuppe, an; *f. A drinking-vessel, a cup*; pocŭlum, Wrt. Voc. 82, 42.

drenc-fæt, es; *n.* [fæt *a vessel*] *A drinking-vessel, cup*; calix = κύλιξ:—Gást ýsta oððe storma is dǽl drencfætes heora oððe heora calices *spirĭtus procellārum est pars calĭcis eorum*, Ps. Lamb. 10, 7: 15, 5: 22, 5. v. drinc-fæt.

drenc-flód, drence-flód, es; *m.* [drenc II. *a drowning*, flód *a flood*] *A drowning-flood, deluge*; dilŭvium:—Noe oferláþ ðone deópestan drencflóda [MS. dren-flóda] *Noah sailed over the deepest of deluges*, Cd. 161; Th. 200, 30; Exod. 364. Fíftena stód deóp ofer dúnum se [MS. sæ] drenceflód elna *the deluge stood fifteen ells deep over the hills*, 69; Th. 84, 16; Gen. 1398.

drenc-horn, es; *m. A drinking-horn*; potōrium cornu:—Ic geann into ðære stówe ðone drenc-horn ðe ic ǽr [MS. ér] æt ðam hírēde gebohte *I give to that place the drinking-horn which I formerly bought from the brotherhood*, Cod. Dipl. 722; Kmbl. iii. 361, 31.

drenc-hús, es; *n. A drinking-house*; potionārium:—Ǽlces cinnes drenc-hús *potionārium*, Ælfc. Gl. 110; Som. 79, 30; Wrt. Voc. 59, 4.

DRENG, es; *m. A warrior, soldier*; bellātor, miles:—Forlét drenga sum daroþ of handa fleógan *one of the warriors let fly a dart from his hand*, Byrht. Th. 136, 10; By. 149. [*Laym.* dring *a thane, warrior, servant*: *Dan.* dreng *a boy, youth*: *Swed.* dreng, dräng, *m. a man, servant, soldier*: *Icel.* drengr, *m. a youth, valiant man.*]

drenge *a drink*:—Drenge ðú sylst us *potum dabis nobis*, Ps. Spl. 79, 6. v. drenc.

dreó-cræft, es; *m. Magical art, magic*; magĭca ars:—Simon se drý þurh dreócræft worhte ǽrene næddran, and ða hie styredan *Simon the sorcerer made brazen serpents by magic, and they moved of themselves*, Homl. Blick. 173, 21. v. drý-cræft.

DREÓGAN, to dreóganne; *part.* dreógende; ic dreóge, ðú dreógest, drýhst, he dreógeþ, drýhþ, dríhþ, *pl.* dreógaþ; *p.* ic, he dreáh, dreág, ðú druge, *pl.* drugon; *pp.* drogen; *v. trans.* I. *to do, work, perform, to pass life, to fight*; ăgĕre, făcĕre, perfĭcĕre, patrāre, vitam ăgĕre, militāre:—To dreóganne wordum and dǽdum willan ðínne *to do thy will by words and deeds*, Cd. 107; Th. 141, 23; Gen. 2349. Đe he dreógan sceolde *which he had to do*, Exon. 37 b; Th. 122, 28; Gú. 312. Hwæt dreógest ðú *what dost thou?* Exon. 69 a; Th. 257, 14; Jul. 247. Þeódnes willan dreógeþ *he does the will of the Lord*, Exon. 38 a; Th. 125, 20; Gú. 357. Gif mæsse-preóst oððe munuc hǽmed-þingc dríhþ, fæste x geár *si presbȳter vel monăchus fornicatiōnem commisĕrit, x annos jejūnet*, L. M. I. P. 28; Th. ii. 272, 22. Drugon ðæt dæges and nihtes *fecērunt hoc die ac nocte*, Ps. Th. 54, 8. Gewin drugon *they fought*, Beo. Th. 1601; B. 798. Drugon wǽpna gewin *they fought the strife of arms, they waged war*, Exon. 92 b; Th. 346, 7; Gn. Ex. 201. Hú manega gefeoht he ðǽr dreógende wæs *how many battles he was there fighting*, Ors. 1, 11; Bos. 35, 9. II. *to bear, suffer*, DREE, *endure*; ferre, pati, sustinēre, tolerāre:—Mán ne cúðon dón ne dreógan *they knew not to do nor suffer crime*, Cd. 10; Th. 12, 23; Gen. 190. Đe ða earfeða oftost dreógeþ *who oftenest suffers those afflictions*, Exon. 52 b; Th. 183, 19; Gú. 1329. Earfeða dreág *suffered hardships*, Exon. 74 b; Th. 280, 9; Jul. 626. Swá ðæt fæsten dreáh *who endured that bondage*, Cd. 145; Th. 180, 22; Exod. 49. We lǽraþ ðæt man ǽnig gedrinc, and

P 2

ǽnig unnit ðár ne dreóge *we teach that man suffer not there any drinking, nor any vanity*, L. Edg. C. 28; Th. ii. 250, 14. III. *to enjoy;* frui:—He sibbe dreáh *he enjoyed peace*, Cd. 130; Th. 165, 28; Gen. 2738. Symbel-wynne dreóh *enjoy the pleasure of the feast!* Beo. Th. 3569; B. 1782. IV. *v. intrans. To be employed, be busy;* ăgĕre, negōtiōsum esse:—Nǽnig manna wāt hū mīn hyge dreógeþ, bȳsig æfter bōcum *no man knows how my mind is employed, busy over books*, Salm. Kmbl. 122, MS. B; Sal. 60. Dreógan, *inf.* Cd. 104; Th. 137, 31; Gen. 2282. Dreág, *p.* Exon. 53 a; Th. 185, 5; Az. 3. [*Chauc.* drye *to suffer, endure: Laym.* driȝen, drigen, drien *to suffer, do: Orm.* dreghenn *to suffer, endure: Scot.* dre, dree, drey *to suffer: Goth.* driugan *to do military service.*] DER. a-dreógan, ge-.

dreóh-lǽcan *magicians, sorcerers;* magi, Som. Ben. Lye. v. drȳ.

DREÓPAN; ic dreópe, ðū drȳpst, he drȳpþ, *pl.* dreópaþ; *p.* dreáp, *pl.* drupon; *pp.* dropen *To drop;* stillāre, Prov. 19. [*Chauc.* droppe: *Piers P.* droppen: *Plat.* drüppen: *Dut.* druipen: *Kil.* droppen, druppen *manāre: Frs.* drippen: *O. Frs.* driapa: *Ger.* tropfen, triefen: *M. H. Ger.* triufen: *O. H. Ger.* triufan: *Dan.* dryppe: *Swed.* drypa: *Icel.* drjúpa *to drip.*] DER. a-dreópan.

dreópian, dreápian, dropian, drupian; *p.* ode, ede; *pp.* od, ed *To drop;* stillāre, distillāre:—Swā dropa, ðe on ðas eorþan dreópaþ *as a drop, which droppeth on this earth*, Ps. Th. 71, 6. Heofonas [MS. Heofenas] dreápedun *cæli distillāvērunt*, Ps. Surt. 67, 9. Myrre and cassia dropiaþ of ðīnum clāðum *myrrh and cassia drop from thy clothes*, Ps. Th. 44, 10. Heofanas drupodon *cæli distillāvērunt*, Ps. Spl. 67, 9.

DREÓR, es; *m. Blood;* cruor:—Ic his blōd ageát, dreór on eorþan *I shed his blood, his gore on earth*, Cd. 49; Th. 63, 12; Gen. 1031. Dreóre fāhne *stained with gore*, Beo. Th. 898; B. 447. Dreóre druncne *drunk with blood*, Andr. Kmbl. 2005; An. 1005. [*O. Sax.* drōr, *m. cruor, sanguis: M. H. Ger.* trōr, *m. n. a dripping, blood: O. H. Ger.* trōr *cruor: Icel.* dreyri, dröri, *m. blood.*] DER. cwealm-dreór, heoru-, sāwel-, wæl-. v. dreósan.

dreórd, *pl.* dreórdon, dreórdun *dreaded, feared*, Mt. Kmbl. Rush. 9, 8: 19, 25, = drēd, *pl.* drēdon; *p. of* drǽdan.

dreór-fāh; *adj. Stained with gore;* cruentātus, Beo. Th. 974; B. 485.

dreórgian; *p.* ode; *pp.* od [dreór *blood*] *To be dreary, to fall, to perish;* mærēre, cadĕre, corruĕre:—Ðās hofu dreórgiaþ *these courts are dreary*, Exon. 124 a; Th. 477, 26; Ruin. 30.

dreórig, dreóreg, dreórg, driórig; *def.* se dreóriga, dreórega, seó, ðæt dreórige; *adj.* I. *bloody, gory, glorious;* cruentus, cruentātus, gloriōsus:—Wæter stōd dreórig and gedrēfed *water stood gory and troubled*, Beo. Th. 2838; B. 1417: Ps. Th. 135, 20: Exon. 72 b; Th. 271, 14; Jul. 482. Hwæt druh ðū dreórega *lo thou gory dust!* Soul Recd. 33; Seel. 17. II. *sad, sorrowful, pensive,* DREARY; mœstus:—Hīg wurdon swīðe dreórige *they became very sorrowful*, Gen. 44, 13: Mk. Bos. 14, 19. On ðas dreórgan tīd *in this sorrowful tide*, Exon. 48 b; Th. 167, 10; Gū. 1058. [*Wyc.* drerg, dreri, drury *sad: Chauc.* drery *sad: Laym.* druri, dreri *sad: Orm.* dreorig, drerig *sad: O. Sax.* drōrag *cruentus: Dut.* treurig *sad: Ger.* traurig *sad: M. H. Ger.* trūrec *sad: O. H. Ger.* trūrag *mœstus: Icel.* dreyrigr, dreyrugr *bloody.*] DER. heoru-dreórig. v. dreósan.

dreórig-ferþ; *adj. Sad in soul;* tristis animo:—Dreórig-ferþe *sad in soul*, Exon. 24 a; Th. 68, 26; Cri. 1109.

dreórig-hleór; *adj. Sad of countenance;* tristis facie:—Sumne dreórighleór in eorþ-scræfe eorl gehȳdde *a man sad of countenance has hidden one in an earth-grave*, Exon. 77 b; Th. 291, 17; Wand. 83.

dreórig-līce; *adv. Drearily, mournfully;* mœste, Anlct. v. dreór-līc.

dreórig-mōd; *adj. Sad of mind;* tristis animo:—Abraham drāf dreórig-mōd tū of earde *Abraham drove the two sad of mind from his habitation*, Cd. 134; Th. 169, 24; Gen. 2804.

dreórignys, dreórinys, -nyss, e; *f.* DREARINESS, *sadness;* mœstĭtia:—Gif he ne gehulpe hire sārlīcan dreórinysse *if he might not relieve her painful dreariness*, Greg. Dial. MS. Hat. fol. 5 a, 8.

dreór-līc, dreórilīc; *adj.* I. *bloody;* sanguinolentus:—Ne wearþ dreórlīcre [dreórilīcre, col. 2] dǽd gedōn syððan Dene cōmon *no bloodier deed was done since the Danes came*, Chr. 1036; Th. 294, 9; Ælf. Tod. 6. II. *mournful, sad;* mœstus, tristis:—Dreórilīc frēcednys *triste periculum*, Glos. Prudent. Recd. 151, 83.

dreór-sele, es; *m. A dreary, desolate-looking hall;* domus mœstĭtiæ:—On dreórsele *in the dreary hall*, Exon. 115 b; Th. 444, 20; Kl. 50.

dreórung, dreárung, e; *f. A falling;* destillātio:—Ðonne on sumeres tīd sended weorþeþ dropena dreórung *when a falling of drops is sent in summer's time*, Exon. 54 a; Th. 189, 23; Az. 64. v. dreósan.

DREÓSAN; ic dreóse, ðū drȳst, he dreóseþ, drȳst, *pl.* dreósaþ; *p.* dreás, *pl.* druron; *pp.* droren *To rush, fall, perish;* cadĕre, ruĕre:—Wæstmas ne dreósaþ *the fruits do not fall*, Exon. 56 a; Th. 200, 2; Ph. 34. Dreóseþ deáw and rēn *dew and rain fall*, 16 b; Th. 38, 19; Cri. 609. Druron dōmleáse *they fell ingloriously*, Andr. Kmbl. 1989; An. 997. Swylgþ seó gitsung ða dreósendan wēlan ðisses middangeardes *avarice swallows the perishable riches of this earth*, Bt. 12; Fox 36, 13: Bt. Met. Fox 7, 32; Met. 7, 16. [*Laym.* drese *to fall down: O. Sax.* driosan *cadĕre: Goth.* driusan *to fall.*] DER. a-dreósan, ge-.

DREPAN; ic drepe, ðū drepest, dripest, dripst, he drepeþ, dripeþ, dripþ, *pl.* drepaþ; *p.* ic, he drep, dræp, ðū drǽpe, *pl.* drǽpon; *pp.* drepen, dropen *To strike;* percŭtĕre:—Ic sweorde drep ferhþgenīþlan *I struck the deadly foe with my sword*, Beo. Th. 5753; B. 2880. Ðonne biþ on hreðre, under helm drepen biteran strǽle *then he will be stricken with the bitter shaft in the breast, beneath the helmet*, Beo. Th. 3495; B. 1745. Wæs him feorh dropen *his life was stricken*, Beo. Th. 5955, note; B. 2981. [*Plat.* drëpen *to hit: Dut. Ger.* treffen: *M. H. Ger.* triffen: *O. H. Ger.* trefan *tangĕre, percutĕre, pulsāre: Dan.* dræbe *to slay: Swed.* dræpa *to kill, slay: Icel.* drepa *to hit.*]

drepe, drype, es; *m. A slaying, stroke, violent death;* occīsio:—He drepe þrōwade *he suffered the stroke* [*death-stroke*], Beo. Th. 3183; B. 1589. DER. deáþ-drepe.

drepen, drepenn, e; *f. A stroke;* percussio. v. gemynd-drepen.

dresten = drestan; *pl. f? Dregs, lees;* fæx:—Dresten his nys aīdlude *fæx ejus non est exinanita*, Ps. Spl. T. 74, 8. v. dærstan.

drettan *to consume.* DER. ge-drettan.

drī, es; *m. A sorcerer, magician;* magus:—Be drīan = drīum *by sorcerers*, Glostr. Frag. 10, 30. v. drīan.

drīan = drīum = drȳum *with sorcerers*, Glostr. Frag. 10, 30: as fisceran and fugeleran = fiscerum and fugelerum, Ors. 1, 1; Bos. 20, 5; *the dative plural of* drī, drȳ, fiscere, and fugelere, *q. v.*

driás, es; *m?* [dreósan *to fall*] *A falling, fall;* casus. DER. deáw-driás.

drican [= drincan] *to drink*, Somn. 112, 113; Lchdm. iii. 204, 22, 23: Ps. Spl. 77, 49. v. drincan.

drī-cræfteg *skilful in magic*, Ex. 7, 11. v. drȳ-cræftig.

drie *dry*, Ex. 14, 21: Bt. 5, 2; Fox 10, 31. v. drige.

drif, e; *f.* I. *a fever;* febris:—Seó drif [sio drif MS.] *febris*, Mt. Kmbl. Rush. 8, 15. II. but drif, es; *m.* or *n.* in the following example:—Full-neáh ǽfre ǽe ōðer man wearþ on ðam wyrrestan yfele, ðæt [MS. þet] is on ðam drife *almost every other man was in the worst evil, that is with fever*, Chr. 1087; Th. 353, 38. DER. ge-drif.

DRĪFAN, drȳfan, ic drīfe, ðū drīfest, drīfst, he drīfeþ, drīfþ, drīft, *pl.* drīfaþ; *p.* ic, he drāf, ðū drife, *pl.* drifon, dreofon; *pp.* drifen. I. *v. trans. To* DRIVE, *force, pursue;* pellĕre, mināre, impellĕre, persĕqui:—Se gerēfa hie wolde drīfan to ðæs cyninges tūne *the reeve would drive them to the king's vill*, Chr. 787; Erl. 56, 13. Se Hǽlend ongan drīfan of ðam temple syllende and bicgende *Iesus cœpit ejicĕre vendentes et ementes in templo*, Mk. Bos. 11, 15. Sum mæg ofer sealtne sǽ sundwudu drīfan *one can drive a vessel over the salt sea*, Exon. 17 b; Th. 42, 24; Cri. 677. For hwan ðū us, God, woldest fram ðē drīfan *ut quid repulisti nos, Deus?* Ps. Th. 73, 1. Ic drīfe sceáp mīne to heora lease *mino oves meas ad pascua*, Coll. Monast. Th. 20, 11. Ic ða of Drihtnes drīfe ceastre *I will drive them from the Lord's city*, Ps. Th. 100, 8. Ða wēregan neát, ðe man daga gehwam drīfeþ and þirsceþ, ongitaþ hira gōddēnd *the brute animals, which man drives and beats every day, understand their benefactors*, Elen. Kmbl. 716; El. 358. Flinte ic eom heardra, ðe ðis fȳr drīfeþ of ðissum strongan stȳle *I am harder than flint, which this fire drives from this strong steel*, Exon. 111 b; Th. 426, 24; Rä. 41, 78. Hwīlum ðæt drige drīft ðone wǽtan *sometimes the dry drives away the wet*, Bt. Met. Fox 29, 98; Met. 29, 48. Us drīfaþ ða ællreordan to sǽ *the barbarians drive us to sea*, Bd. 1, 13; S. 481, 44: Beo. Th. 5609; B. 2808. Ōðerne he drāf mid sticele, ōðrum he wiðteáh mid bridle *the one he drove with a goad, the other he restrained with a bridle*, Past. 40, 3; Hat. MS. 54 b, 12. Abraham drāf dreorig-mōd tū of earde *Abraham drove the two sad of mind from his dwelling*, Cd. 134; Th. 169, 23; Gen. 2804. Ne eart ðū se sylfa God, ðe us swā drife *nonne tu, Deus, qui repŭlisti nos?* Ps. Th. 59, 9. Hī drifon scipu into Medwæge *they drove the ships into the Medway*, Chr. 1016; Erl. 157, 16. Hīg hyne drifon ūt *ejēcērunt eum foras*, Jn. Bos. 9, 35. Ðā hīg eów drifon *cum vos persequerentur*, Deut. 11, 4. Hī dreofon hine onweg *they drove him away*, Bd. 2, 5; S. 507, 27. Ge fleóþ, ðeáh eów man ne drīfe *fugiētis, nemīne persĕquente*, Lev. 26, 17. Ðæt he on wræc drife his selfes sunu *that he should drive into exile his own son*, Cd. 134; Th. 168, 32; Gen. 2791. Drīfan drȳcræft *to exercise magic*, Bt. Met. Fox 26, 107; Met. 26, 54. Ceáp drīfan *to drive* or *transact a bargain*, R. Ben. 57. Mangunge drīfan *to follow a trade*, Homl. Th. ii. 94, 34. Spæce *or* spræce drīfan *to prosecute a suit, urge a cause*, L. O. 2; Th. i. 178, 13: L. Ælf. C. 35; Th. ii. 356, note 2, 4: Th. Diplm. 376, 11. Wōh drīfan *to practise wrong*, L. I. P. 11; Th. ii. 320, 4. II. *v. intrans. To drive, rush with violence;* ruĕre:—Ic com mid ðȳ heáfde and mid handa on ðone stān drīfan *I came driving on the stone with my head and hands*, Bd. 5, 6; S. 619, 23. [*Wyc.* dryue: *Piers P.* dryven: *Chauc.* drife, drive: *Laym.* driuen, driue: *Orm.* drifenn: *Plat.* drīwen, drīben: *O. Sax.* drīban *agĕre, pellĕre: Frs.* drieuwen: *O. Frs.* driva: *Dut.* drijven: *Ger.* treiben: *M. H. Ger.* trīben: *O. H. Ger.* trīban: *Goth.* dreiban: *Dan.* drive: *Swed.* drifva: *Icel.* drífa.] DER. a-drīfan, be-, for-, ge-, in-, of-, ofa-, ofer-, þurh-, to-, ūt-, ūta-, wið-.

Driffeld; *gen.* es; *dat.* a, e; *m.* [*in* A. D. 1360 *it was written* Dyrffeld] *Great* DRIFFIELD, *in the East Riding of Yorkshire;* oppĭdi nomen in agro Eboracensi:—Hēr Aldfriþ Norþan Hymbra cining forþfērde, on xix kl' Jan. on Driffelda *in this year* [A. D. 705] *Alfred, king of the Northumbrians, died at Driffield, on the 19th of the kalends of January* [*December 14th*], Chr. 705; Erl. 43, 33.

drigan, drygan, drigean; *p.* de; *pp.* ed; *v. a.* [drige *dry*] *To* DRY, *make dry, rub dry, wipe;* siccāre, tergĕre, extergĕre:—Se hāta sumor giereþ and drigeþ sǣd and blēda *the hot summer prepares and dries seeds and fruits*, Bt. Met. Fox 29, 120; Met. 29, 60. Ðæt dust, ðæt of eówre ceastre on ūrum fōtum clifode, we drigeaþ on eów *pulvĕrem, qui adhæsit nobis de civitāte vestra, extergĭmus in vos*, Lk. Bos. 10, 11. Heó ongan mid hyre teárum his fēt þweán, and drigde mid hyre heáfdes feaxe *lacrўmis cœpit rigāre pedes ejus, et capillis capĭtis sui tergēbat*, Lk. Bos. 7, 38, 44. Seó drigde his fēt mid hyre loccum *extersit pedes ejus capillis suis*, Jn. Bos. 11, 2: 12, 3. DER. a-drigan, -drygan, ge-, ofa-, ūta-.

DRIGE, dryge, drīe; *def.* se driga, dryga, drīa; seó, ðæt drige, dryge, drīe; *adj.* DRY; siccus, arĭdus:—Se wind blǣwþ norþan and eástan, heálīc, and ceald, and swīðe drige [drīe MSS. P. L.] *the wind blows from the north-east, violent, and cold, and very dry*, Bd. de nat. rerum; Wrt. popl. science 18, 8; Lchdm. iii. 276, 6. Drige wudu *dry wood, firewood;* ligna, Wrt. Voc. 80, 31. Adrugode se streám swā ðæt he mihte dryge ofergangan *the stream dried up so that he might go over dry*, Bd. 1, 7; S. 478, 14: Exon. 111 b; Th. 426, 22; Rä. 41, 77. Tunge biþ drige *the tongue is dry*, L. M. 2, 46; Lchdm. ii. 258, 8. Seó [MS. sie] eorþ is dryge *the earth is dry*, Bt. 33, 4; Fox 128, 34: Andr. Kmbl. 3161; An. 1583. Læg ān drīe strǣt þurh ða sǣ *a dry road lay through the sea*, Ex. 14, 21. Ðæs fȳres gecynd is hāt and drīe *the nature of fire is hot and dry*, Boutr. Scrd. 18, 22, 23. Hwīlum ðæt drige drīft ðone wǣtan *sometimes the dry drives away the wet*, Bt. Met. Fox 29, 97; Met. 29, 48. Seó sǣ, ūtflōwende, gerȳmde þreóra mīla drīes færeldes *the sea, flowing out, made room for a dry passage of three miles*, Homl. Th. i. 564, 18. Ða sacerdas ætstōdon on ðam grunde on drigre moldan on middan ðære eá be drīum grunde *sacerdōtes stābant per siccam humum in medio Iordānis*, Jos. 3, 17. Gif hīg on grēnum treówe ðās þing dōþ, hwæt dōþ hīg on ðam drigum *si in virĭdi ligno hæc faciunt, in arĭdo quid fiet?* Lk. Bos. 23, 31: Ps. Th. 105, 9. Drihten gewende ða sǣ to drīum *mare Domĭnus vertit in siccum*, Ex. 14, 21. Betwux ðære drygan and ðære cealdan eorþan and ðam hātan fȳre *between the dry and the cold earth and the hot fire*, Bt. 33, 4; Fox 128, 37. Ðæt seó sǣ drigne grund ðam folce gegearcige *that the sea should prepare dry ground for the people*, Homl. Th. i. 564, 24. In drygne seáþ *into a dry pit*, Invent. Crs. Recd. 1388; El. 693. Worhte his tolme foldan drige *arĭdam fundavērunt manus ejus*, Ps. Th. 94, 5: Cd. 8; Th. 10, 29; Gen. 164. Uppan drīe eorþan *super arĭdam*, Ex. 4, 9. Se ðe gecyrde sǣ on drige land *qui convertit mare in arĭdam*, Ps. Spl. 65, 5. Dō drige pic to *add dry pitch*, L. M. 2, 38; Lchdm. ii. 246, 14. Ða drigan eorþan *the dry earth*, Bt. 33, 4; Fox 130, 2. Hwīlum flīht se wǣta ðæt dryge *sometimes the wet drives away the dry*, Bt. 39, 13; Fox 234, 11. Wǣron ða wareþas drige *the shores were dry*, Ps. Th. 105, 9. Wegas syndon dryge *the ways are dry*, Cd. 157; Th. 195, 28; Exod. 283. Drīra *arentum*, Glos. Prudent. Recd. 151, 22. Dysegaþ se ðe wile sǣd ōþfæstan ðām drīum [drygum, Cot.] furum *he does foolishly who will sow seed in the dry furrows*, Bt. 5, 2; Fox 10, 31. Hī fērdon oððe fōron on drigum flōdum *abiērunt in sicco flumĭna*, Ps. Lamb. 104, 41. He gǣþ geond drige stōwa *ambŭlat per loca arĭda*, Mt. Bos. 12, 43: Ps. Th. 65, 5. Se wyrcþ drige [drīe MSS. P. L.] wolcnu *it makes dry clouds*, Bd. de nat. rerum; Wrt. popl. science 18, 2; Lchdm. iii. 274, 24. Fram ðære burnan ðe he drigum fōtum ofereóde *from the brook which he went over with dry feet*, Bd. 1, 7; S. 478, 32. Mid drīum handum *with dry hands*, L. M. 2, 3; Lchdm. ii. 182, 8. Ðæt Israhēlisce folc gā drīum fōtum innan ða sǣ *ut gradiantur filii Israel in medio mari per siccum*, Ex. 14, 16, 29. [*Wyc.* drie: *Piers P.* drye: *Chauc.* drey: *Orm.* driȝȝe: *Plat.* dröge, drüge, dræge: *Dut.* droog: *Ger.* trocken: *M. H. Ger.* trucken: *O. H. Ger.* trukan *siccus: Dan.* dröi *solid: Swed.* dryg *heavy: Icel.* drjúgr *solid, substantial.*]

drīgian, ðū drīgast; *p.* ode; *pp.* od [dreógan *to suffer, endure*] *To suffer, endure;* tolerāre, pati:—Ðū on ðisum andweardan līfe mā earfoða drīgast *thou sufferest more troubles in this present life*, Guthl. 5; Gdwin. 32, 13.

drig-nes, dryg-nes, -ness, -nis, -niss, -nyss, e; *f.* DRYNESS; siccĭtas:—Ðære drignesse ne sceal he huniges onbītan ac eald wīn *for the dryness he must not taste of honey but old wine*, L. M. 2, 27; Lchdm. ii. 222, 19. Æteówige drignis *let dryness appear;* appāreat ărĭda, Gen. 1, 9. God gecīgde ða drignisse eorþan *vŏcāvit Deus ārĭdam terram*, 1, 10. On drignysse *in ināquōso*, Ps. Spl. 77, 20. Drygnessa his handa gescōpan *siccam mănus ejus formāvērunt*, Ps. Lamb. 94, 5.

Driht', Driht *the Lord*, used with or without the apostrophe in Spelman's Psalms for all the cases of Drihten. v. Dryht'.

driht, e; *f. A multitude, an army*, Cd. 146; Th. 182, 21; Exod. 79: Cd. 47; Th. 61, 6; Gen. 993. v. dryht.

driht-ealdor, drihte ealdor; *gen.* ealdres; *m. The lord of a feast;* architriclīnus:—Se drihtealdor cwæþ to ðam brȳdguman *the lord of the feast said to the bridegroom*, Homl. Th. ii. 70, 25, 28. Se drihte ealdor ðæs wīnes onbȳrgde *gustāvit architriclīnus vinum*, Jn. Bos. 2, 9. Beraþ ðære drihte ealdre *ferte architriclīno*, 2, 8. v. dryht-ealdor.

drihten; *gen.* drihtnes, drihtenes; *m. A ruler, lord, the Lord:*—Gumena drihten *lord of men*, Cd. 205; Th. 254, 18; Dan. 613. Eorla drihten *lord of earls*, Beo. Th. 2105; B. 1050. Drihten Crēca *lord of the Greeks*, Bt. Met. Fox 26, 38; Met. 26, 19. Drihten mīn *my lord*, Cd. 101; Th. 134, 15; Gen. 2225. Witig Drihten, rōdera Rǣdend *the wise Lord, Ruler of the skies*, Beo. Th. 3113; B. 1554. Drihten wereda *the Lord of hosts*, Beo. Th. 4378; B. 2186. Ēce Drihten wið Abrahame spræc *the Lord eternal spake with Abraham*, Cd. 106; Th. 139, 1; Gen. 2303. Ic eom Drihten ðīn God *ego sum Domĭnus Deus tuus*, Ex. 20, 2. Þurh ūrne Drihten Crist *through our Lord Christ*, L. Ælf. P. 39; Th. ii. 380, 3. On ðæm naman Drihtnes ūres Godes *in nomĭne Dŏmĭni Dei nostri*, Ps. Th. 19, 7. Se seofoða ys Drihtnes restedæg ðīnes Godes *septĭmo die sabbătum Domĭni Dei tui est*, Ex. 20, 10. Eálā Drihtenes þrym *O majesty of the Lord*, Cd. 216; Th. 274, 34; Sat. 164: Ps. Lamb. 26, 13: Ps. Th. 68, 37. v. dryhten.

Drihten-līc; *def.* se -līca, seó, ðæt -līce; *adj. Belonging to the Lord, Lordly;* Domĭnĭcus:—Drihtenlīces *Domĭnĭci*, Mone B. 429. Angelþeóde ðæs Drihtenlīcan geleáfan gife geleornode *gens Anglōrum Domĭnĭcæ fidei et dona discĕret*, Bd. 3, 3; S. 525, 29. He nǣfre mete onfēng būtan ðȳ Drihtenlīcan dæge *he never took meat except on the Lord's day*, 4, 25; S. 599, 30.

Drihten-līce; *comp.* -līcor; *adv. According to the Lord, by the Lord;* secundum Domĭnum, a Domĭno:—Ðæt he Drihtenlīcor mǣge beón hālig genemned *that he may be called holy by the Lord*, L. E. I. 21; Th. ii. 418, 9.

drihten-weard, es; *m.* [weard *a keeper, guardian*] *A guardian lord, king;* domĭnus custos, rex:—On ðam drihtenweard deópne wisse sefan sīdne geþanc *in whom the guardian lord knew* [*to exist*] *deep ample thought of mind*, Cd. 201; Th. 249, 24; Dan. 535.

driht-folc *a nation*, Cd. 144; Th. 179, 26; Exod. 34. v. dryht-folc.

driht-gesīþ, es; *m.* [gesīþ *a companion*] *An associate, attendant;* satelles:—Nān ne feól drihtgesīþa *none of the associates fell*, Fins. Th. 84; Fin. 42.

driht-guma, an; *m. A popular man, man of the people, a warrior, retainer*, Beo. Th. 2781; B. 1388: 198; B. 99. v. dryht-guma.

drīhþ *does, performs, commits*, L. M. I. P. 28; Th. ii. 272, 22; *3rd pres. sing. of* dreógan.

drihtin-beáh; *gen.* -beáges; *dat.* -beáge; *m.* [drihtin = drihten *a lord*, beáh *a ring, bracelet*] *A lord-ring* or *money paid for slaying a freeman.* In the laws of Edward the Confessor it is called Manbōte:—Manbōte in lege Anglōrum, regi et archiepiscōpo, iii marc̄ de homĭnĭbus suis; episcōpo comĭtātus, comĭti comĭtātus, et dapĭfēro regis, xx sol̄; barōnĭbus cetĕris, x solid̄, L. Ed. C. 12; Th. i. 447, 28–31. Gif man frigne mannan ofsleahþ, cyninge l scillinga to drihtin-beáge *if any one slay a freeman,* [*let him pay*] *fifty shillings to the king, as 'drihtin-beah,'* L. Ethb. 6; Th. i. 4, 6, 7.

driht-līc, driht-lec *lordly*, Menol. Fox 511; Gn. C. 26: Cd. 33; Th. 168, 12; Gen. 2781. v. dryht-līc.

driht-līce *in a lordly manner*, Cd. 98; Th. 129, 4; Gen. 2138. v. dryht-līce.

driht-nē; *pl. nom. acc.* -nēas; *m. A dead body of a host;* cadāver agmĭnis:—Ofer drihtnēum *over the bodies of the slain*, Cd. 150; Th. 188, 5; Exod. 163. v. nē.

Drihtnes *of the Lord;* Dŏmĭni, Ex. 20, 10; *gen. of* Drihten. v. dryhten.

driht-scipe *rulership*, Cd. 24; Th. 31, 14; Gen. 485. v. dryht-scipe.

driht-sele *a princely hall*, Beo. Th. 974; B. 485. v. dryht-sele.

driht-weras; *pl. m.* [wer *a man*] *Men, chieftains;* popŭlāres viri:—Ōþ-ðæt drihtweras duguþum gefōran ðǣr is botlwēla Bethlem hāten *till that the fellow men journeyed to where there is a village called Bethel*, Cd. 86; Th. 107, 32; Gen. 1798. Ðū mōst heonon hūþe lǣdan ealle, būton dǣle ðissa drihtwera *thou mayest lead all the spoil hence, save the part of these chieftains*, 98; Th. 129, 27; Gen. 2150.

drīme *joy;* jubĭlum, Cot. 109. v. dreám.

DRINC, drync, es; *m:* drinca, an; *m:* drince, an; *f.* DRINK, *a drink, draught;* potus, haustus:—Mīn blōd ys drinc *sanguis meus est potus*, Jn. Bos. 6, 55. Ic ofþyrsted wæs gǣstes drinces *I was thirsty for the soul's drink*, Exon. 98 a; Th. 369, 15; Seel. 41. Hēr gefōr Harþacnut swā ðæt he æt his drince stōd *in this year* [A. D. 1042] *Harthacnut died as he stood at his drink*, Chr. 1042; Erl. 166, 34. Ic mīnne drinc mengde mid teárum *potum meum cum fletu tempĕrābam*, Ps. Th. 101, 7. Swā hwylc swā sylþ ānne drinc cealdes wæteres ānum ðyssa lytylra manna *quicumque potum dedĕrit uni ex minĭmis istis calĭcem aquæ frigĭdæ*, Mt. Bos. 10, 42. We ðē drinc sealdon *dedĭmus tibi potum*, 25, 37: Bt. Met. Fox 8, 43; Met. 8, 22. Nǣron ðā mistlīce drincas *there were not then various drinks*, Bt. 15; Fox 48, 5: Bt. Met. Fox 8, 18; Met. 8, 9.

[*Wyc.* drynk: *Piers P.* drenke: *Chauc.* drinke: *Laym.* drænc, drench, drinc: *Orm.* drinnc, drinnch: *Plat.* drunk, drank, *m: O.Sax.* drank, *m. n: Frs.* dranck: *O.Frs.* drank in compounds: *Dut.* dranc, dronc, *m: Ger.* trank, trunk, *m: M.H.Ger.* tranc, *n. m;* trunc, *m: O.H.Ger.* trank, *n. potus;* trunk, *m. haustus: Goth.* draggk, dragk, *n. drink: Dan.* drik, *m.f: Swed.* drick, dryck, *m: Icel.* drekka, *f. beverage.*] DER. ātor-drinc, ge-, mān-, medo-, ofer-, wīn-, wīnge-.

drinca, an; *m:* drince, an; *f.* [drinc *drink*] *Drink;* potus:—Eáðe we māgon geseón hwǣr se drinca is *we can easily see where the drink is,* Ors. 5, 8; Bos. 107, 30. He wolde beran drincan his gebrōðrum *he would bear drink to his brethren,* Homl. Th. ii. 180, 5. He bæd him drincan and heó him blīðelīce sealde *he asked for drink and she gave it him gladly,* Jud. 4, 19: Basil admn. 4; Norm. 42, 24. He bæd God ðæt he him asende drincan *he prayed God to send him drink,* Jud. 15, 18. Drince mylsce drincan sió gebēt ða biternesse *let him drink a mulled drink which will amend the bitterness,* L. M. 1, 42; Lchdm. ii. 108, 2. DER. āttor-drinca, on-.

drincan, to drincenne, ic drince, ðū drincst, he drincþ, dryncþ, *pl.* drincaþ; *p.* dranc, *pl.* druncon; *pp.* druncen [drinc *drink*]. I. *to* DRINK, *imbibe;* bibĕre, potāre, imbĭbĕre:—He dranc of ðam wīne, ðā wearþ he druncen *bibens vinum inebriātus est,* Gen. 9, 21: Lev. 10, 9. We ǣton and druncon befōran ðē *manducāvĭmus coram te, et bibĭmus,* Lk. Bos. 13, 26. Ðonne hīg druncene beóþ *cum inebriāti fuĕrint,* Jn. Bos. 2, 10. II. the Anglo-Saxons often drank to excess, as is evident by the exhortation of Abbot Ælfric to his friend Sigferd, to whom he dedicated his Treatises on the Old and New Testaments:—Ðū woldest me laðian, ðā ðā ic wæs mid ðē ðæt ic swīðor drunce, swilce for blisse. Ac wite ðū, leóf man, ðæt se ðe ōðerne neádaþ ofer his mihte to drincenne ðæt se mōt aberan heora begra gild, gif him ǣnig hearm of ðam drence becymþ. Ūre Hǣlend forbeád ðone oferdrenc. Ða lāreówas alēdon ðone unþeáw þurh heora lāreówdōm and tǣhton ðæt se oferdrenc fordēþ untwīlīce ðæs mannes sāwle and his gesūndfullnysse. Unhǣl becymþ of ðam drence *when I was with thee, thou wouldest urge me to drink very much, as it were for bliss. But know thou, dear friend, that he who forces another man to drink more than he can bear, shall answer for both, if any harm come thereof. Our Saviour hath forbidden over drinking. The learned fathers have also put down that bad habit by their wise teaching, and taught that the over drinking surely destroys a man's soul and soundness. Unhealthiness cometh after* [*over*] *drinking,* Ælfc. T. 43, 6–17. [*Piers P.* drinken: *Chauc.* dronken, *pp: Laym.* drinchen, drinken: *Orm.* drinnkenn: *Plat.* drinken: *O.Sax.* drinkan: *Frs.* drincken: *O.Frs.* drinka: *Dut.* drinken: *Ger. M.H.Ger.* trinken: *O.H.Ger.* trinkan: *Goth.* drigkan: *Dan.* drikke: *Swed.* dricka: *Icel.* drekka.] DER. a-drincan, be-, for-, ge-, ofa-, ofer-, on-.

drince-fæt, es; *n. A cup;* calix:—Ic geseah Pharaones drincefæt on mīnre handa *vidēbam călĭcem Pharaōnis in manu mea,* Gen. 40, 11, 13. v. drinc-fæt.

drince-leán, es; *n. Tributary drink, scot-ale, the contribution of tenants to purchase ale for the entertainment of their lord or his steward on the fee,* Glos. to Th. Laws, vol. ii. *Or, perhaps, the ale given by the seller to the buyer on concluding a bargain;* retrĭbūtio potus *vel* præmium bibendi:—Drinceleán and hlāfordes riht gifu stande ǣfre unawend *let the tributary drink and the lord's rightful gift ever stand unchanged,* L. C. S. 82; Th. i. 422, 2: L. N. P. L. 67; Th. ii. 302, 7.

drincere, es; *m. A* DRINKER; potātor:—Drincere wīnes *potātor vini,* Mt. Kmbl. Lind. 11, 19.

drinc-fæt, drince-fæt, drync-fæt, drenc-fæt; *gen.* -fætes; *pl. nom. acc.* -fatu; *n.* [fæt *a vessel*] *A drinking-vessel, cup;* pōcŭlum, calix = κύλιξ:—Beóþ heora drincfatu gefyldu *their drinking-vessels shall be filled,* Ps. Th. 10, 7.

drinc-lagu, e; *f. Drinking-law;* assisa potus:—Statūtum, scilĭcet edictum, lex, *vel* constĭtūtio de potus vendendi mensūris, Som. Lye.

drinc-wērig; *adj. Drink weary, satisfied with drinking;* potu defessus, temūlentus, Cot. 124.

driórig *bloody;* cruentātus, gloriōsus:—Driórigne, *acc.* Beo. Th. 5572; B. 2789. v. dreórig.

dripest, dripst, he dripeþ, dripþ *strikest, strikes; 2nd and 3rd pers. pres. of* drepan.

dris-līc *fearful.* DER. on-dris-līc. v. dryslīc.

drisn, e; *f? A wig, false hair;* capillāmentum, galerĭcŭlum:—Rupe *vel* drisne *capillāmenta,* Ælfc. Gl. 35; Som. 62, 96; Wrt. Voc. 28, 73. v. rupe.

DRŌF; *adj. Draffy, dreggy, dirty, troubled;* sordĭdus, turbŭlentus, turbĭdus:—Se ðe his brōðor hataþ, he hæfþ unstilnesse, and swȳðe drōf [MS. drofi] mōd *he that hateth his brother has disquietude, and a very troubled mind,* Basil admn. 4; Norm. 44, 16. Flōd drōf *a turbid flood,* Somn. 102; Lchdm. iii. 204, 11. [*Laym.* drof *disturbed, grieved: O. Sax.* drōbi, druobi *turbĭdus, nubĭlus: Kil.* droef *turbĭdus, turbŭlentus, fecŭlentus: Ger.* trübe *troubled, obscure, dark, dull, sad: M.H.Ger.* trüebe: *O.H.Ger.* truobi *turbĭdus, turbātus.*] DER. ge-drōf.

drōf-denu, e; *f. A den* or *valley where droves of cattle feed;* armentōrum cubile. Locus nemorōsus armentōrum receptui accommŏdus, Som. Ben. Lye. v. drāf.

drōf-līc; *adj. Agitated, disturbed, troublesome, irksome, sad;* turbŭlentus, molestus:—Him biþ fȳr ongeán, drōflīc wīte *before them shall be fire, sad punishment,* Exon. 116 a; Th. 446, 8; Dōm. 19.

drōf-man, -mann, es; *m. A drove-man, cattle-keeper;* būbulcus, Som. Ben. Lye. v. drāf.

drōfnys, -nyss, e; *f. Dirtiness, sedition;* turbulentia, Som. Ben. Lye.

drōg *drew,* Jn. Lind. War. 21, 11; *p. of* dragan.

drogan = drugon *suffered;* tolerārunt, Bt. 38, 1; Card. 302, 21; *p. pl. of* dreógan.

droge, an; *f? Dung,* DRAUGH; stercus:—Nim monnes drogan *sume stercus humānum,* L. M. 3, 36; Lchdm. ii. 328, 16.

drogen *done, worked; pp. of* dreógan.

drōgon *drew,* Andr. Kmbl. 2465; An. 1234; *p. pl. of* dragan.

drōh *dragged, drew; p. of* dragan.

droht, es; *m? Manner* or *condition of life;* vitæ condĭtio:—Hū he his wīsna trūwade, drohtes, on ðære dimman ādle *how he trusted in his morals, his manner of living, in that hidden malady,* Exon. 49 b; Th. 171, 31; Gū. 1135. v. drohtaþ.

droht *drawn, draught;* tractus, haustus, Cot. 202, Som. Ben. Lye.

drohtaþ, drohtoþ, es; *m.* [dreógan *to do, suffer, pass life, live*] *Conversation, manner* or *way of life, condition, conduct, society;* condĭtio vitæ, stātio, conversātio:—Is se drohtaþ strang ðam ðe lagolāde cunnaþ *severe is the way of life for him who trieth a sea-journey,* Andr. Kmbl. 626; An. 313: 2770; An. 1387: Exon. 20 a; Th. 53, 28; Cri. 857. Duguþ and drohtaþ *virtue and converse,* Exon. 42 b; Th. 143, 4; Gū. 656. Ne wæs his drohtoþ swylce he on ealderdagum ǣr gemētte *his condition was not such as he had before found in his life-days,* Beo. Th. 1517; B. 756. Ðæt hie ðe eáþ mihton ofer ȳða geþring drohtaþ adreógan *that they might the easier endure their way of life over the clash of waves,* Andr. Kmbl. 737; An. 369: 2564; An. 1283: Exon. 103 a; Th. 389, 20; Rä. 7, 10. Hī mā lufedon dióra drohtaþ *they loved more the society of beasts,* Bt. Met. Fox 26, 183; Met. 26, 92. Drohtaþ sēcan *to seek a sojourn,* Cd. 86; Th. 109, 6; Gen. 1818: Exon. 61 b; Th. 227, 1; Ph. 416.

drohtian *to converse, live,* Bd. 1, 27; S. 488, 37: 5, 6; S. 618, 28: Salm. Kmbl. 894; Sal. 446. v. drohtnian.

drohtigen *that ye converse; pl. pres. subj. of* drohtian. v. drohtnian.

drohtnian, drohtian; *part.* drohtniende, drohtiende, drohtende; *p.* ode, ade; *pp.* od, ad *To converse, dwell* or *keep company with, pass life, live;* versāri, conversāri, dēgĕre, vitam āgĕre:—Bī bisceopum, hū hī mid heora gefērum drohtian and lifigean scylon *de episcŏpis, qualĭter cum suis clerĭcis conversentur,* Bd. 1, 27; S. 488, 37: Hy. 4, 89; Hy. Grn. ii. 285, 89. Cild ic eom under gyrde drohtniende *puer sum sub virga dēgens,* Coll. Monast. Th. 34, 23. Wæs he on his gefērscipe drohtiende *in clero illius conversātus,* Bd. 5, 6; S. 618, 28. Hī drohtende duguþe beswīcaþ *they by converse deceive the virtuous,* Exon. 97 a; Th. 362, 6; Wal. 32. Ic drohtnige *conversor,* Ælfc. Gr. 37; Som. 39, 15. Drohtnaþ on temple God *versātur in templo Deus,* Hymn. Surt. 44, 7. To hwām drohtaþ heó mid us *why dwelleth she with us?* Salm. Kmbl. 894; Sal. 446: Exon. 57 a; Th. 203, 22; Ph. 88. We drohtniaþ *degĭmus,* Hymn. Surt. 113, 17. Ða ungeleáffullan, ðe būton Godes gelaðunge dwollīce drohtniaþ *the unbelieving, who live in error without the church of God,* Homl. Th. ii. 60, 14. Se in ðam mynstre eardode and drohtnade *qui in illo monastĕrio degēbat,* Bd. 4, 25; S. 601, 32. Fela wītegan under ðære ǣ Gode gecwēmelīce drohtnodon *many prophets under the old law passed their days acceptably to God,* Homl. Th. ii. 78, 34. Ðæt mid Suna Meotudes drohtigen dæghwamlīce *that ye converse daily with the Son of God,* Andr. Kmbl. 1363; An. 682.

drohtnung, drohtung, e; *f.* [droht *vitæ condĭtio*] *Conversation, condition, conduct, life, actions;* conversātio, condĭtio, stātio, actio:—Hira drohtnung sī afandud *quorum conversātio sit probāta,* Deut. 1, 13. Manega hālige bēc cȳðaþ his [Gregoriuses] drohtnunge and his hālige līf *many holy books manifest his* [*Gregory's*] *conduct and his holy life,* Homl. Th. ii. 116, 29. Of ðære munuclīcan drohtnunge *from the monastic life,* 120, 12. Sume on mynsterlīcre drohtnunge on reogollīcum līfe getreówlīce Drihtne þeówdon *some served the Lord truly in monastic conversation in regular life,* Bd. 3, 27; S. 558, 24: Bd. de nat. rerum; Wrt. popl. science 4, 5; Lchdm. iii. 238, 4. On micelre drohtnunge *in great renown,* L. Ælf. P. 40; Th. ii. 380, 33. He his līf in Gode mid wyrþre drohtunge gefylde *vitam in Deo digna conversātiōne complēvit,* Bd. 5, 6; S. 620, 24. On ðæra Apostola drohtnunge *in the Acts of the Apostles,* R. Ben. 33. Ōþ-ðæt he full hāl sȳ on his drohtnungum *until he be full sound in his conditions,* Homl. Th. i. 126, 2.

DROPA, an; *m.* I. *a* DROP; stilla, gutta, stillicĭdium:—Dropa *gutta* vel *stilla,* Ælfc. Gl. 97; Som. 76, 70; Wrt. Voc. 54, 14. Yrnþ dropmǣlum swīðe hluttor wæter, ðæt gecīgdon ða ðe on ðære stōwe wunodon *stillam,* ðæt is dropa *very pure water runs* [*there*] *drop by drop, which those who dwelt in the place called* stilla, *that is drop,* Homl. Th. i. 510, 1. Flōwe min spræc swā dropan ofer gærsa cīþas *fluat elŏquium* *meum quasi stillæ super gramĭna*, Deut. 32, 2. Snāw cymþ of đam þynnum wǣtan, đe byþ upatogen mid đære lyfte, and byþ gefroren ǣr đan đe he to dropum geurnen sȳ *snow comes of the thin moisture, which is drawn up with the air, and is frozen before it be run into drops*, Bd. de nat. rerum; Wrt. popl. science 19, 14; Lchdm. iii. 278, 25. His swāt wæs swylce blōdes dropan on eorþan yrnende *est sudor ejus sīcut guttæ sanguĭnis decurrentis in terram*, Lk. Bos. 22, 44. Swā dropa, đe on đas eorþan dreópaþ *as a drop which droppeth on this earth*, Ps. Th. 71, 6. Heó ōđerne dropan on đæt ōđer eáge dyde *she put [did] another drop on the other eye*, Guthl. 22; Gdwin. 98, 3. Nime ānne eles dropan *take a drop of oil*, Orş. 4, 7; Bos. 88, 11: L. M. 1, 2; Lchdm. ii. 34, 26. Swā swā dropan dropende ofer eorþan *sīcut stillicĭdia stillantia super terram*, Ps. Spl. 71, 6. Dropan stīgaþ *the drops shall rise*, Salm. Kmbl. 90; Sal. 44. Dropena dreorung *a fall of drops*, Exon. 54 a; Th. 189, 23; Az. 64: Cd. 191; Th. 238, 3; Dan. 349: 213; Th. 265, 23; Sat. 12. II. *a disease, paralysis?* morbus, parălȳsis = παράλυσις:—Wiđ fōt-ādle, and wiđ đone dropan *against gout [foot disease] and against the paralysis [the drop]*, Lchdm. i. 376, 1. Wiđ đone dropan *against the paralysis [the drop]*, Herb. 59; Lchdm. i. 162, 4, 7. Heó ǣlc yfel blōd and đæne dropan gewyldeþ *it subdues all evil blood and the paralysis [the drop]*, 124, 1; Lchdm. i. 236, 13. [*Wyc.* droppes, *pl*: *Laym.* drope: *Plat.* droppen, drüppen, *m*: *O. Sax.* dropo, *m*: *O. Frs.* dropta *dropping*: *Dut.* drop, *m*: *Kil.* droppe: *Ger.* tropfen, *m*: *M. H. Ger.* tropfe, *m*: *O. H. Ger.* trofo, tropfo, *m. gutta*: *Dan.* dryp, *n*; draabe, *m. f*: *Swed.* droppe, *m*: *Icel.* dropi, *m.*] DER. hleór-dropa, rēn-, spēd-, wǣg-, wōp-, wrōht-.

dropan, droppan; *pres. part.* ende; *p.* ede; *pp.* ed *To drop*; stillāre:—Swā swā dropan dropende ofer eorþan *sīcut stillicĭdia stillantia super terram*, Ps. Spl. 71, 6. Droppende, Ps. Lamb. 71, 6. DER. dropa *a drop*.

dropen *stricken*:—Wæs feorh dropen *life was stricken*, Beo. Th. 5955, note; B. 2981; *pp. of* drepan.

dropen *dropped*; *pp. of* dreópan.

drop-fāg *stronius?* Wrt. Voc. 289, 27.

drop-fāh, -fāg; *adj.* [dropa *a drop*, fāh *coloured, stained*] *Drop-coloured, variegated in spots, spotted*; stillātus:—Stillātus, đæt is on ūre geþeóde, dropfāh *stillātus, that is in our language, spotted*, Herb. 131, 1; Lchdm. i. 242, 14. Wiđ dropfāgum andwlatan *for a spotted face*, Med. ex Quadr. 5, 6; Lchdm. i. 348, 21.

dropian *to drop*, Ps. Th. 44, 10. v. dreópian.

drop-mǣlum; *adv. By drops, drop by drop*; guttātim:—Yrnþ drop-mǣlum swīđe hluttor wæter *very clear water runs drop by drop*, Homl. Th. i. 508, 34. v. mǣl III.

droppan *to drop*:—Droppende *stillans*, Ps. Lamb. 71, 6. v. dropan.

droppetian, droppetan; *p.* ode, ede; *pp.* od, ed *To drop, fall by drops, distil*; distillāre:—Heofonas droppetodon fram ansȳne Godes *cœli distillāvērunt a facie Dei*, Ps. Lamb. 67, 9. Fōr ansȳne Drihtnes heofonas droppetaþ *the heavens drop before the face of the Lord*, Ps. Th. 67, 9.

droppetung, e; *f. A dropping, falling by drops, drop by drop*; stillicĭdium:—Swā swā niđer astīhþ droppetung droppende ofer eorþan *as falling [rain] comes down, dropping over the earth*, Ps. Lamb. 71, 6.

dropung, e; *f. A dropping*; stillicĭdium:—Þurh dropunge deáwes and rēnes *through dropping of dew and rain*, Ps. Th. 64, 11: Ps. Vos. 71, 6. v. droppetung.

droren *fallen, perished*; *pp. of* dreósan.

dros DROSS, *filth, lees*; sordes, fæx, aurĭcŭla, Cot. 14. [*Kil.* droes *fæx.*] v. drosna.

drosen-līc; *adj. Brittle, weak*; frăgĭlis, Som. Ben. Lye.

DROSNA, drosne, *nom. acc*; *gen.* drosna; *dat.* drosnum; *pl. f. Grounds, sediment, lees, dregs*; fæx, fæces:—Đās drosna *hæc fæx*, Ælfc. Gr. 9, 70; Som. 14, 14: Wrt. Voc. 83, 22. His drosna [drosne, Ps. Spl. T. 74, 8] nis aīdlad *fæx ejus non est exinānīta*, Ps. Lamb. 74, 9. Drosna *fæces*, Ælfc. Gl. 33; Som. 62, 25; Wrt. Voc. 28, 8. He gelǣdde me of fenne drosna *eduxit me de luto fæcis*, Ps. Spl. 39, 2. Of đām drosnum *from the dregs*, Ps. Th. 39, 1. Hī druncon ōþ đa drosna *usque ad fæces bibērunt*, Ælfc. Gr. 47; Som. 47, 45. Eles drosna *dregs of oil*; amurca = ἀμόργη, Ælfc. Gl. 47; Som. 65, 18; Wrt. Voc. 33, 18. [*Kil.* droessem *fæx*: *Ger.* drusen, *f. fæx*: *M. H. Ger.* truosen, *f. barm, yeast*: *O. H. Ger.* truosana, trōsana *fæx, amurca.*]

drugaþ, drugoþ, e; *f.* [drige *dry*] *A* DROUGHT, *dryness*; siccĭtas, arĭdĭtas:—Drugaþ [MS. drugaþe] *siccĭtas* vel *arĭdĭtas*, Ælfc. Gl. 96; Som. 76, 35; Wrt. Voc. 53, 43. Drugaþ ođđe hǣþ *siccĭtas*, Wrt. Voc. 76, 77. Bearn Israēla eódon þurh drugoþe *fīlii Israel ambulāvērunt per siccum*, Ps. Lamb. fol. 189 a, 21.

drugian, he drugaþ, *pl.* drugiaþ; *p.* ode; *pp.* od; *v. n.* [drige *dry*] *To become dry, wither*; arescĕre:—Drugaþ his ār on borde *his oar becomes dry on board*, Exon. 92 a; Th. 345, 15; Gn. Ex. 188. On mergen swā wyrt gewīteþ, on mergen blōweþ and fareþ, on ǣfen afylþ, astīđaþ, and drugaþ *mane sīcut herba transeat, mane flōreat et transeat, vespĕre decĭdat, indūret, et arescat*, Ps. Spl. 89, 6. Gif đæt wæter hī ne geþwǣnde, đonne drugode hió *if the water moistened it [the earth] not, then it would become dry*, Bt. 33, 4; Fox 130, 8. DER. a-drugian, for-, ge-: un-adrugod.

drugon *suffered, endured*, Beo. Th. 1601; B. 798; *p. pl. of* dreógan.

drugung, e; *f. A dryness, a dry place*; siccĭtas, inăquōsus lŏcus:—Hī costadon God in drugunge *temptāvērunt Deum in siccĭtāte*, Ps. Surt. 105, 14: 77, 17.

druh, es; *m. Dust*; pulvis:—Hwæt! druh đū dreórega *lo! thou gory dust!* Soul Recd. 33; Seel. 17.

druncaþ *drink*, Exon. 99 b; Th. 373, 23; Seel. 114, = drincaþ; *pres. pl. of* drincan.

druncen *drunken*, Gen. 9, 21; *pp. of* drincan. DER. un-druncen, wīn-druncen.

druncen, es; *n?* e; *f? Drunkenness*; ēbriĕtas:—Đæt he ne onbīte ǣniges þinges đe druncen ofcume *that he taste not anything from which drunkenness may come*, L. Pen. 11; Th. ii. 280, 23. Druncen beorg đē and dollīg word *guard thyself from drunkenness and foolish words*, Exon. 80 b; Th. 302, 10; Fä. 34. Gif hit þurh druncen gewurþe, bēte đe deóppor *si ex ebriĕtāte accidĕrit, eo grāvius emendet*, L. M. I. P. 41; Th. ii. 276, 12. Gif đū hwæt on druncen misdō, ne wīt đū hit đam ealoþe *if thou have misdone in drunkenness, blame not the drink*, Prov. Kmbl. 39. DER. ofer-druncen.

druncen-georn; *adj. Drink-desirous, drunken*; bĭbax, ebriōsus, R. Ben. 4.

druncen-hād, es; *m.* [MS. -hed] *Drunkenness*; ebriĕtas:—Þurh heora druncenhād [MS. -hed] *through their drunkenness*, Chr. 1070; Th. 345, 42.

druncen-læt; *adj. Slow*; lentus, Cot. 124.

druncennes, druncennys, druncenys, -ness, e; *f.* DRUNKENNESS; ebriĕtas:—Warniaþ eów, đe-læs eówer heortan gehefegode sȳn on druncenesse *attendĭte autem vobis ne forte graventur corda vestra in ebrietāte*, Lk. Bos. 21, 34. Đa hūs đa đe on to gebiddenne geworhte wǣron syndon nū on hūs gehwyrfed oferǣta and druncennesse *the houses which were built to pray in are now turned into houses of gluttony and drunkenness*, Bd. 4, 25; S. 601, 13. Mid druncennysse *by drunkenness*, Ors. 1, 6; Bos. 29, 17. For đære druncenysse *because of the drunkenness*, Gen. 19, 33, 35. On druncennysse and on wiste hiora wombe þeówiaþ, nas Gode *in drunkenness and feasting they minister to their belly, not to God*, L. Eccl. 45; Wilk. 195, 25; L. E. I. 45; Th. ii. 440, 38. v. drincan II.

druncen-scipe, es; *m. Drunkenness*; ebriĕtas, Som. Ben. Lye.

druncen-wille; *adj. Drunken*; ebrius:—Drincþ mid đām druncen-willum [drucen-willum MS.] monnum *bibit cum ebriis*, Past. 17, 8; Hat. MS. 24 a, 23.

drunc-mennen, es; *n. A drunken maid-servant*; ebria ancilla, Exon. 103 b; Th. 393, 32; Rä. 13, 9.

druncne *drunken*, Beo. Th. 965; B. 480; *nom. pl. of* druncen, *pp.*

druncnian; *p.* ode; *pp.* od. I. *to be* or *become drunk*; inebriāri:—Iohannes se Fulluhtere ne dranc nāđor ne wīn, ne beór, ne ealu, ne nān đære wǣtan đe menn of druncniaþ *John the Baptist drank neither wine, nor beer, nor ale, nor of the liquor from which men become drunk*, Homl. Th. ii. 38, 7. Đonne đa gebeóras druncniaþ *when the guests are drunk*, ii. 70, 27. II. *to sink, drown*; mergi:—Mid [MS. miđ] đȳ he ongann druncnian [MS. druncnia] *cum cœpisset mergi*, Mt. Kmbl. Lind. 14, 30. DER. on-druncnian.

druncning, e; *f. A drinking*; ebriĕtas:—Drencfæt ođđe calic mīn drincende ođđe on druncninge lā hū scīnende ođđe hū beorht is *calix meus inebrians [in ebriĕtāte] quam præclārus est*, Ps. Lamb. 22, 5.

druncon *drank*, Lk. Bos. 13, 26; *p. pl. of* drincan.

drupian *to drop*, Ps. Spl. 67, 9. v. dreópian.

drupon *dropped*; *p. pl. of* dreópan.

druron *fell*, Andr. Kmbl. 1989; An. 997; *p. pl. of* dreósan.

drūsan, drūsian; *part.* drūsende; *p.* ode, ade; *pp.* od, ad; *v. intrans. To sink, become low, slow, inactive, to* DROWSE; cadĕre, lentum *vel* segnem esse:—Cēn drūsende *the sinking flame*, Elen. Kmbl. 2514; El. 1258. Lagu drūsade, wǣldreóre fāg *the stream became slower, stained with deadly gore*, Beo. Th. 3265; B. 1630. He drūsende deáþ ne bisorgaþ *he cares not for death when he becomes inactive [by age]*, Exon. 61 a; Th. 223, 31; Ph. 368: 52 b; Th. 184, 33; Gū. 1353. v. dreósan.

druwian *to become dry, wither.* DER. a-druwian, for-. v. drugian.

DRȲ, drī; *gen.* drȳs; *dat. acc.* drȳ; *pl. nom. acc.* drȳas; *gen.* drīra? *dat.* drȳum, drīum; *m. A magician, sorcerer, wizard*; magus, malĕfĭcus:—Drȳ *magus*, Wrt. Voc. 74, 41. Petres wiđerwinna wæs sum drȳ, se wæs Simon gehāten: đes drȳ wæs mid đam awyrgedum gāste afylled *Peter's adversary was a certain sorcerer, who was called Simon: this sorcerer was filled with the accursed spirit*, Homl. Th. i. 370, 32: 374, 18: 376, 3: 380, 16: Homl. Blick. 173, 8, 18, 28, 32: 175, 6, 17, 31: 183, 17: 187, 32. He getengde wiđ đæs drȳs *he hastened towards the magician*, Homl. Th. i. 374, 5. Petrus cwæþ to đam drȳ *Peter said to the sorcerer*, i. 372, 6: 380, 21: Homl. Blick. 173, 2, 9, 33: 175, 25. Hī woldon forbærnan đone drȳ *they would burn the magician*, Homl. Th. i. 372, 30: 374, 22: 376, 10: 380, 23: Homl. Blick. 173, 11, 30: 175, 1: 181, 33. Đū miht mid đȳ gebēde blōd onhǽtan ðæs deófles drý *thou mayest with prayer heat the blood of the devil's wizard*, Salm. Kmbl. 89; Sal. 44. Hý drýas wǽron *they were sorcerers*, Exon. 70 a; Th. 260, 23; Jul. 301: Andr. Kmbl. 67; An. 34. Hý getrymedon hyra drýas *their magicians encouraged them*, Ors. 1, 7; Bos. 30, 21. Cwǽdon ða drýas to Pharaone *dixērunt malefĭci ad Pharaōnem*, Ex. 8, 19: 9, 11. Drîra [drîa?] *magōrum*, Mone B. 4018. Herodes biswicen wæs from drýum oððe tungulcræftgum *Herōdes insulsus erat a magis*, Mt. Kmbl. Lind. 2, 16. Ðýlæs-ðe se deófol us be drîum [MS. drian] mâge *lest the devil have power over us by sorcerers*, Glostr. Frag. 10, 30. [*Orm.* drig-menn *magicians*: *Gael.* draoi, draoidh, druidh, *m. a druid, magician.*]

drý-cræft, es; *m.* [cræft *craft, art*] *Magical art, magic, sorcery;* ars magĭca *vel* malĕfĭca:—Hí sǽdon ðæt hió sceolde mid hire drýcræft ða men forbredan *they said that she should overthrow the men by her sorcery*, Bt. 38, 1; Fox 194, 30. Gif hí hwylcne drýcræft hæfdon *si quid malĕfĭcæ artis habuissent*, Bd. 1, 25; S. 486, 40: Ex. 7, 11. Sum man wæs mid drýcræfte bepǽht *some man was deceived by magic*, Homl. Th. i. 448, 13. Warna ðé ðæt ðú ne gîme drýcræfta ne swefena ne hwatena *nec inveniātur in te, qui ariolos sciscĭtētur et observet somnia atque augŭria*, Deut. 18, 10. Drîfan drýcræftas *to exercise magical arts*, Bt. Met. Fox 26, 107; Met. 26, 54. Mid drýcræftum *by sorceries*, Ors. 1, 7; Bos. 30, 22.

drý-cræftig, drî-cræfteg; *adj.* [cræftig *crafty, skilful*] *Skilful* or *crafty in magic* or *sorcery, magical;* magĭcæ artis perītus, magĭcus:—Sió, hí sǽdon, sceolde bión swíðe drýcræftigu *she, they said, would be very skilful in sorcery*, Bt. 38, 1; Fox. 194, 20. Pharaon gegaderude ealle ða drîcræftegustan men *vocāvit Pharao sapientes et malĕfĭcos*, Ex. 7, 11.

drýfan *to drive;* pellĕre:—Sceoldon drýfan *should drive*, Ors. 2, 4; Bos. 43, 10. v. drîfan.

drýfan; *p.* de, *pl.* don; *pp.* ed *To trouble, vex;* vexāre:—Mǽst hine drýfdon his âgene men [MS. mæn] *his own men vexed him most*, Chr. 1118; Erl. 246, 34. v. drēfan.

drygan; *p.* de; *pp.* ed *To dry, make dry, rub dry, wipe;* siccāre, tergĕre, extergĕre:—Se hâta sumor drygþ and gearwaþ sǽd and blêda *the hot summer dries and prepares seeds and fruits*, Bt. 39, 13; Fox 234, 14. Cômon twegen seolas of sǽlîcum grunde, and hí mid heora flýse his fêt drygdon *two seals came from the sea-ground, and they dried his feet with their fur*, Homl. Th. ii. 138, 12. Hie beóþ oft drygde *they are often dried*, Past. 11, 4; Hat. MS. 15 a, 19. v. drigan.

dryge *dry*, Exon. 111 b; Th. 426, 22; Rä. 41, 77: Andr. Kmbl. 3161; An. 1583: Cd. 157; Th. 195, 28; Exod. 283. v. drige.

drygge *dry*, Bt. Met. Fox 7, 31; Met. 7, 16. v. drige.

dryg-nes, -ness *dryness*, Ps. Lamb. 94, 5. v. drig-nes.

dryht, driht, e; *f. A people, multitude, army, in pl. men;* pŏpŭlus, multĭtūdo, căterva, fămĭlia, hŏmĭnes:—Dryhtum to nytte *for use to people*, Exon. 113 a; Th. 433, 25; Rä. 51, 2. Ic dryhtum þeówige *I serve multitudes*, 104 a; Th. 394, 9; Rä. 13, 15: Cd. 146; Th. 182, 21; Exod. 79. Ðæt ðý deáþ-drepe drihta [MS. drihte] swǽfon *that the armies slept in the swoon of death*, Cd. 167; Th. 209, 7; Exod. 495: 217; Th. 275, 26; Sat. 177. Drihta bearnum *to the children of men*, 47; Th. 61, 6; Gen. 993: Exon. 95 b; Th. 357, 7; Pa. 25. [*Laym.* drihte *retinue*: *O. Sax.* druht, *only in composition, as* druht-folc *comĭtātus, pŏpŭlus*: *Frs.* dregte: *O. Frs.* dracht, drecht: *M. H. Ger. O. H. Ger.* truht, trut, *f. multitude*: *Icel.* drótt, *f. pŏpŭlus.* v. *Goth.* ga-drauhts, *m. a soldier*, from driugan *to do military service*: *A. Sax.* dreógan.] DER. folc-dryht, -driht, mago-; gedriht, gedryht, hí-, hý-, sib-, wil-.

Dryht', Driht', or without the apostrophe Dryht, Driht *The Lord;* Dŏmĭnus; chiefly used in the interlinear Psalms, published by Spelman and by the Surtees' Society, for all the cases of Dryhten, Drihten.

dryht-bearn, es; *n. A child of the people, a noble child;* puer pŏpŭlāris, nŏbĭlis:—Dryhtbearn Dena *the Danes' princely child*, Beo. Th. 4076; B. 2035.

dryht-cwēn, e; *f. A noble queen;* dŏmĭna et rēgĭna:—Dryhtcwēn duguþa *a noble queen of chieftains*, Exon. 86 a; Th. 324, 21; Wíd. 98.

dryht-ealdor, driht-ealdor, drihte ealdor, es; *m. The ruler of a household, meeting,* or *feast, a bridesman;* dŏmĭnus, archi-triclĭnus, parănymphus = παράνυμφος:—Brýdguma *vel* dryhtealdor *parănymphus*, Ælfc. Gl. 87; Som. 74, 60; Wrt. Voc. 50, 42.

dryhten, drihten; *gen.* dryhtnes, dryhtenes; *m.* I. *a ruler, lord, prince;* dŏmĭnus, princeps:—Geáta dryhten *the Goths' lord*, Beo. Th. 2973; B. 1484. Eorla dryhten *lord of earls*, Beo. Th. 4666; B. 2338. Dryhten Higelâc *lord Higelac*, Beo. Th. 4005; B. 2000. In gemynd his dryhtnes naman brohte *it brought his lord's name into his mind*, Exon. 114 b; Th. 440, 25; Rä. 60, 8. II. *the supreme ruler, the Lord; chiefly used for God and Christ;* Dŏmĭnus:—Him Dryhten sylf, heofona heáhcyning, hlyt getǽhte *the Lord himself, high king of heaven, assigned a lot to them*, Andr. Kmbl. 10; An. 5. Dryhtna Dryhten *the Lord of lords*, Andr. Kmbl. 1747; An. 876. Dryhten God *the Lord God*, Exon. 96 a; Th. 358, 33; Pa. 55. Dryhten Crist *the Lord Christ*, Exon. 41 a; Th. 137, 25; Gú. 564. Ðe in Dryhtnes noman cwôme *who camest in the Lord's name*, Exon. 13 b; Th. 26, 5; Cri. 413. We fór Dryhtene iu dreámas hefdon *we formerly had joys before the Lord*, Cd. 214; Th. 267, 26; Sat. 44. [*Laym.* drihten: *Orm.* drihtin: *O. Sax.* drohtin: *O. Frs.* drochten *Lord*, only used for *God* and *Christ*: *O. H. Ger.* truhtîn *dŏmĭnus*: *Icel.* dróttinn *princeps.*] DER. freá-dryhten, freó-, gum-, hleó-, man-, sige-, weoruld-, wine-.

dryhten-beáh *a lord-ring.* v. drihtin-beáh.

dryhten-bealo, -bealu; *gen.* -bealowes; *n.* [bealo *evil*] *Profound misery, extreme evil;* permagna calămĭtas:—He sceal dreógan dryhtenbealo *he shall suffer profound misery*, Exon. 88 a; Th. 330, 22; Vy. 55. Ellen biþ sēlast ðâm ðe sceal dreógan dryhtenbealu *courage is best for those who must suffer extreme evil*, 52 b; Th. 183, 6; Gú. 1323.

dryhten-dōm, es; *m.* [-dôm *termination*, q. v.] *Sovereignty, majesty;* dŏmĭnātus, majestas:—Se hâlga hērede on hēhþo heofoncyninges dryhtendôm *the saint praised the majesty of heaven's king on high*, Andr. Kmbl. 1997; An. 1001.

Dryhten-lîc *belonging to the Lord, Lordly.* v. Drihten-lîc.

Dryhten-lîce *according to the Lord, by the Lord.* v. Drihten-lîce.

dryhten-weard *a guardian-lord, king.* v. drihten-weard.

dryht-folc, driht-folc, es; *n.* [folc *a people*] *A nation, multitude;* pŏpŭlus, multĭtūdo:—Micel arîseþ dryhtfolc to dôme *a great multitude shall arise to judgment*, Exon. 23 a; Th. 64, 23; Cri. 1042. Dryhtfolca helm *a protector of nations*, 107 a; Th. 408, 24; Rä. 27, 17. Wæs deáþe gedrenced drihtfolca mǽst *the greatest of nations was drenched with death*, Cd. 144; Th. 179, 26; Exod. 34: 160; Th. 198, 13; Exod. 322: 171; Th. 216, 2; Exod. 589.

dryht-gesíþ *an associate, attendant.* v. driht-gesíþ.

dryht-gestreón, es; *n.* [gestreón *a treasure*] *A nation's* or *people's treasure;* pŏpŭli ŏpes:—Eodor gefylled dryhtgestreóna *an inclosure filled with people's treasures*, Exon. 105 a; Th. 398, 25; Rä. 18, 3.

dryht-guma, driht-guma, an; *m. A popular man, man of the people, warrior, retainer, follower,—pl. men, people;* vir pŏpŭlāris *vel* nŏbĭlis, mîles, sătelles,—hŏmĭnes:—Semninga biþ, ðæt ðec, dryhtguma, deáþ oferswýðeþ *suddenly it will be, that thee, warrior, death overpowers*, Beo. Th. 3540; B. 1768. Druncne dryhtguman dôþ swâ ic bidde *the drunken retainers do as I bid*, 2466; B. 1231. Weccaþ of deáþe dryhtgumena bearn, eall monna cynn *the sons of men, all mankind, shall wake from death*, Exon. 20 b; Th. 55, 22; Cri. 887. Beóþ môdsefan dǽlum gedǽled, sindon dryhtguman ungelîce *dispositions are by parts distributed, people are unlike*, 83 b; Th. 314, 31; Môd. 22: 79 a; Th. 297, 23; Crä. 72.

drýhþ, ðú drýhst *does, thou doest; 3rd and 2nd pers. pres. of* dreógan.

dryht-leóþ, es; *n.* [leóþ *a song*] *A lordly song;* nŏbĭle carmen:—Be ðam Dauid cyning dryhtleóþ agōl *king David sang a lordly song of him*, Elen. Kmbl. 684; El. 342.

dryht-lîc, driht-lîc, driht-lec; *comp.* -lîcra; *sup.* -lîcest; *adj. Lordly, noble, distinguished;* princĭpālis, nŏbĭlis, exĭmius:—We gehýrdon ðæt mid Sigelwarum yppe wearþ dryhtlîc dôm Godes *we have heard that the lordly doom of God was revealed among the Ethiopians*, Apstls. Kmbl. 129; Ap. 65: Exon. 94 b; Th. 354, 1; Reim. 39. Sweord sceal on bearme, drihtlîc îsern *the sword shall be in the bosom, lordly iron*, Menol. Fox 511; Gn. C. 26. Him drihtlîcu mǽg þuhte *she seemed a noble damsel to them*, Cd. 89; Th. 111, 2; Gen. 1849. Cwæþ drihtlecu mǽg, brýd to beorne *his noble mate, his wife, spake to the chief*, 133; Th. 168, 12; Gen. 2781. Drihtlîce cempan hyra sweord getugon *the noble warriors drew their swords*, Fins. Th. 29; Fin. 14: Beo. Th. 2320; B. 1158. Hí on dryhtlîcestum dôme lifdon *they lived in the most lordly power*, Exon. 82 b; Th. 310, 35; Seef. 85.

dryht-lîce, driht-lîce; *adv. In a lordly manner, divinely;* nobĭlĭter:—God leóht and þýstro gedǽlde dryhtlîce *God divinely parted light and darkness*, Exon. 11 a; Th. 14, 32; Cri. 228. Abraham fôr eorlum drihtlîce spræc *Abram spake in a lordly manner before the people*, Cd. 98; Th. 129, 4; Gen. 2138.

dryht-māþm, es; *m.* [mâþm *a treasure*] *A noble* or *lordly treasure;* nŏbĭles ŏpes:—Wearþ dryhtmâþma dǽl forgolden *his share of noble treasures was paid for*, Beo. Th. 5678; B. 2843.

dryht-nē *a dead body of a host.* v. driht-nē.

dryhtnes *of a lord*, Exon. 114 b; Th. 440, 25; Rä. 60, 8; *gen. of* dryhten.

dryht-scipe, driht-scipe, es; *m.* [-scipe *termination*] *Rulership, lordship, domination, dignity;* domĭnātus, dignĭtas:—Ðara dôm leofaþ and hira dryhtscipe *their dignity and their lordship shall live*, Elen. Kmbl. 899; El. 451. For hwam nele mon him on giógoþe georne gewyrcan deóres dryhtscipes *why will not man in youth zealously work for himself bold rulership?* Salm. Kmbl. 775; Sal. 387. Sceolde hine yldo beniman ellendǽda dreámas and drihtscipes *age must take from him the joys of bold deeds and of rulership*, Cd. 24; Th. 31, 14; Gen. 485. Nalles feallan lêt dôm and drihtscipe *he let not his power and domination sink*, Cd. 60; Th. 73, 4; Gen. 1199. Ne lǽt ðîn dryhtscipe feallan *let not thy mighty rule fall*, Wald. 12; Vald. 1, 7.

dryht-sele, driht-sele, es; *m.* [sele *a dwelling, hall*] *A princely dwelling, hall;* aula:—Draca hord eft gesceát, dryhtsele dyrnne *the* *dragon darted back to his hoard, his secret hall,* Beo. Th. 4629; B. 2320: 1538; B. 767. Wæs drihtsele dreórfāh *the princely hall was stained with blood,* 974; B. 485.

dryht-sib, -sibb, e; *f.* [sib *peace, kinship*] *Peace between two nations, lordly kinship;* pax *vel* amīcitia inter duas gentes:—Ic Headobeardna ne talige dryhtsibbe dǽl Denum unfǽcne *I esteem not part of the Heathobeards' lordly kinship to the Danes guileless,* Beo. Th. 4142; B. 2068.

dryht-weras *men, chieftains.* v. driht-weras.

dryht-wuniende; *part.* [wuniende, *part. of* wunian *to dwell*] *Dwelling among people;* in pŏpŭlo dĕgens:—Ðara ǽghwylc mōt dryhtwuniendra dǽl onfōn *each of those dwelling among people may receive a share,* Exon. 78 a; Th. 293, 26; Crä. 7.

drȳman; *part.* drȳmende; *p.* de; *pp.* ed *To rejoice, be joyful;* jubĭlāre:—Hī mōtun drȳman mid Dryhten *they may rejoice with the Lord,* Exon. 32 b; Th. 102, 27; Cri. 1679. Him gefylgan ne mæg drȳmendra gedryht *the multitude of the joyful cannot follow him,* Exon. 60 b; Th. 222, 13; Ph. 348. Eall druncon and drȳmdon *all drunk and rejoiced,* Cd. 133; Th. 168, 11; Gen. 2781. Drȳmaþ Gode eall eorþe *jubĭlāte Deo omnis terra,* Ps. Spl. 97, 5, 7: 46, 1. v. drēman.

drȳme *a song,* Som. Ben. Lye. v. dreám.

drȳ-men *magicians, sorcerers,* Homl. Th. ii. 472, 14. v. drȳ.

drȳming, e; *f. A soft* or *murmuring noise;* sŭsurrus, Som. Ben. Lye. v. dreám.

drync, es; *m. Drink, a drink, draught;* potus, haustus:—Ðǽr wæs ǽlcum genōg drync *there was enough drink for each,* Andr. Kmbl. 3069; An. 1537. Ic ofþyrsted wæs gāstes drynces *I was thirsty for the soul's drink,* Soul Kmbl. 82; Seel. 41. Drync ðū selst us *potum dabis nobis,* Ps. Lamb. 79, 6: Andr. Kmbl. 44; An. 22: Exon. 29 a; Th. 88, 12; Cri. 1439. Of mistlīcum dryncum *from various drinks,* Bt. 37, 1; Fox 186, 17. DER. heoru-drync, ofer-. v. drinc.

drync-fæt, es; *n. A drinking-vessel;* pōcŭlum:—Gesāwon dryncfæt deóre *they saw the precious drinking-vessel,* Beo. Th. 4500; B. 2254: 4601; B. 2306. v. drinc-fæt.

dryncþ *drinks,* Ps. Spl. 74, 8; *3rd pres. sing. of* drincan.

dryngc, es; *m. Drink;* potus:—Dryngc mīnne [MS. min] mid wōpe ic gemengde *potum meum cum fletu tempĕrābam,* Ps. Spl. 101, 10. v. drinc.

drynge *I drink,* Ps. Spl. 49, 14; *for* drince. v. drincan.

drypan; *p.* de, te; *pp.* ed *To drop, moisten;* stillāre, humectāre:—Nime ānne eles dropan, and drype on ān mycel fȳr *take a drop of oil, and drop it on a large fire,* Ors. 4, 7; Bos. 88, 11: L. M. 1, 3; Lchdm. ii. 40, 5: 7, 24, 28, 30. Heó drypte in ða eágan *she dropped it on the eyes,* Guthl. 22; Gdwin. 98, 2. Mīne handa drypton myrran *my hands dropped myrrh,* Homl. Th. i. 118, 4. He bæd ðæt Lazarus mōste his tungan drypan *he prayed that Lazarus might moisten his tongue,* i. 330, 29. DER. ge-drypan. v. dropa.

drype, es; *m. A stripe, blow;* ictus:—Ðēh ðū drype þolie *though thou suffer a stripe,* Andr. Kmbl. 1910; An. 957: 2436; An. 1219. v. drepe.

drȳpst, he drȳpþ *droppest, drops; 2nd and 3rd pers. pres. of* dreópan.

dryre, es; *m. Fall, decline, ceasing;* cāsus, lapsus, cessātio:—Hrīmes dryre *a fall of rime,* Exon. 56 a; Th. 198, 27; Ph. 16. Ðǽr wæs ne dreámes dryre *there was no ceasing of joy,* 44 b; Th. 152, 1; Gū. 802. DER. fǽr-dryre. v. dreósan.

dryrmian *to make sad, to be made sad, to mourn;* lugēre:—Dryrmyde, Cd. 144; Th. 180, 5; Exod. 40. v. drysmian.

drys-līc, dris-līc; *adj. Fearful, terrible;* terrĭbĭlis:—Ahwilc *vel* egeslīc *vel* dryslīc *terrĭbĭlis,* Ælfc. Gl. 116; Som. 80, 65; Wrt. Voc. 61, 43. v. on-drislīc, an-drysenlīc, an-drysne, drysne.

drysmian, dryrmian; *p.* ode; *pp.* od *To become dark, gloomy, to be made sad, to mourn;* calīgāre, obscūrāri, mœstĭtia affici, lugēre:—Ōþ-ðæt lyft drysmaþ *until the air grows gloomy,* Beo. Th. 2755, note; B. 1375.

drysnan; *p.* ede; *pp.* ed *To put out, quench, extinguish;* extinguĕre:—Ðæt fȳr ne biþ drysned *ignis non extinguĭtur,* Mk. Skt. Rush. 9, 46. DER. ge-drysnan, un-drysnende, un-adrysnendlīc.

drysne *terrible;* revĕrendus. v. on-drysne.

drȳst *rushest, rushes; 2nd and 3rd pers. pres. of* dreósan.

DUBBAN; *p.* ade; *pp.* ad *To strike,* DUB, *create;* percŭtĕre, creāre:—Se cyng dubbade his sunu Henric to rīdere *the king dubbed* [or *created*] *his son Henry a knight,* Chr. 1085; Erl. 219, 1. [*R. Brun.* dubbid, *p: Chauc.* dubbed: *Laym.* dubben: *Swed.* dubba: *Icel.* dubba, dybba: *Fr.* dauber *to strike.*]

DUCE, an; *f. A* DUCK; anas:—On ducan seáþe, of ducan seáþe *to the duck's pond, from the duck's pond,* Cod. Dipl. 538; A. D. 967; Kmbl. iii. 18, 16, 17: Apndx. 308; A. D. 875; Kmbl. iii. 399, 18. [*Piers P. Chauc.* doke: *Plat.* düker: *Kil.* duycker *mergus.*]

dūfan, ic dūfe, ðū dȳfst, he dȳfþ, *pl.* dūfaþ; *p.* ic, he deáf, ðū dufe, *pl.* dufon; *pp.* dofen *To* DIVE, *sink;* mergi:—Ic deáf under ȳðe *I dived under the wave,* Exon. 126 b; Th. 487, 18; Rä. 73, 4: 113 b; Th. 434, 23; Rä. 52, 5. Dūfe seo hand æfter ðam stāne ōþ ða wriste *let the hand dive after the stone up to the wrist,* L. Ath. iv. 7; Th. i. 226, 16. Gif ðū dȳfst *if thou sinkest,* Homl. Th. ii. 392, 35. Mid ðam ðe he deáf *when he was sinking,* ii. 392, 2: 390, 21. DER. be-dūfan, ge-, onge-, þurh-: dȳfan.

dūfe-doppa, an; *m. A pelican;* pelĭcānus = πελέκανος:—Gelīc geworden ic eom niht-hræfne oððe dūfedoppan wēstennes *simĭlis factus sum pelĭcāno sol̄ĭtūdĭnis,* Ps. Lamb. 101, 7.

dūfian; *p.* ode, ede; *pp.* od, ed *To sink, immerge;* immergĕre, Ben. Lye.

DUGAN; *part.* dugende; ic, he deah, deag; ðū duge, *pl.* dugon; *p.* dohte, *pl.* dohton *To avail, to be of use, able, fit, strong, vigorous, good, virtuous, honest, bountiful, kind, liberal;* valēre, prōdesse, frūgi esse, bŏnum esse, mŭnĭfĭcum, *vel* lībĕrālem se præbēre:—Ðonne his ellen deah *when his valour avails,* Beo. Th. 1151; B. 573: Andr. Kmbl. 920; An. 460: Bt. 29, 2; Fox 106, 1. Se ðe his heorte deah *he whose heart is good,* Cd. 219; Th. 282, 8; Sat. 283. Hūru se aldor deah [Th. þeāh, Beo. 744], se ðǽm headorincum hider wīsade *the chief is able indeed, who has led the warriors hither,* B. 369. Ðeáh ðū headorǽsa gehwǽr dohte, grimre gūþe *though thou hast everywhere been vigorous in martial onslaughts, in grim war,* Beo. Th. 1057; B. 526. Gif he ǽr ne dohte *if he were not before virtuous,* Bt. 27, 2; Fox 98, 14. Dō ā ðætte duge *do ever what is virtuous,* Exon. 80 a; Th. 300, 10; Fä. 4. Ðet him nāðor ne dohte ne innhere ne ūthere *so that neither the in-army nor the out-army was of use to them,* Chr. 1006; Th. 257, 15, col. 1. Swā swā hī sceoldon, gif hī dohton *as they ought, if they were honest,* Bt. 18, 3; Fox 64, 37. Ðæt ðū dohtest ðīnum brēðer and wædlan and þearfan *that thou be bountiful to thy brother, to the poor, and to the needy,* Deut. 15, 11. Ðū us wel dohtest *thou wast truly kind to us,* Beo. Th. 3647; B. 1821: 2693; B. 1344. Hū me cyne-gōde cystum dohten *how the good by race were munificently liberal to me,* Exon. 85 b; Th. 322, 1; Wīd. 56: 86 a; Th. 324, 4; Wīd. 89. Ða sceolon eall dugende beón swā swā hit gedafenaþ ðam hāde *they shall all be virtuous so as is befitting the order,* L. Ælf. C. 16; Th. ii. 348, 16. [Dugan is the third of the twelve Anglo-Saxon verbs called *præterito-præsentia,* and given under āgan, *q. v.* The *inf.* dugan and the *pret.* deah, *pl.* dugon, *retaining preterite inflections,* are taken from the *p.* of a strong verb deogan, *p.* deah, *pl.* dugon; *pp.* dogen, ascertained from deah; *pl.* dugon, which shews the ablaut or internal change of the vowel in the *p.* of the twelfth class of Grimm's division of strong verbs [Grm. i. p. 898; Koch, i. p. 252], and requires by analogy with other verbs of the same class the *inf.* deogan and the *pp.* dogen; thus we find the original verb deogan, *p.* deah, *pl.* dugon; *pp.* dogen. The weak *p.* dohte, *pl.* dohton [= duhte, duhton], is formed regularly from the *inf.* dugan. The same *præterito-præsens* may be generally observed in the following cognate words:—

	inf.	*pres.*	*pl.*	*p.*
Piers P. Orm.		degh, dægh,		
O. Sax.	dugan,	dōg,	dugun,	
O. Frs.	duga,	duch,		
M. H. Ger.	tugen,	touc,		tohte,
O. H. Ger.	tugan,	touc,	tugun, *3rd pers. pl.*	tohta,
Goth.	dugan,	dáug,	dugum,	daúhta.]

dugeþ, dugoþ *good, virtuous, honourable;* bonus, probus, Mann. v. duguþ; *adj.*

dugoþ-gifu, e; *f.* [dugoþ = duguþ, gifu *a gift*] *Liberality, munificence;* largĭtas, munificentia:—Ic Wulfstān Lundeniscra manna bisceop mīnes hlāfordes dugoþgife ǽfre geþwǽrige *I Wulfstan, bishop of the London men, ever consent to my lord's munificence,* Cod. Dipl. 715; A. D. 1006; Kmbl. iii. 350, 36.

duguþ, dugoþ, e; *f.* [dugan *vălēre*]. I. *manhood* and *all who have reached manhood;* ætas vĭrīlis [*O. H. Ger.* an dero tugende *in vĭrīli ætāte,* tugent daz ist die metilscaft des menniskinen alteris *vires, hoc est mĕdia vĭrīlis ætas,* Graff's Sprch. v. 372]:—Todǽlan duguþe and geógoþe *to distribute to old and young,* Andr. Kmbl. 304; An. 152. Ȳmb-eóde ðā ides Helminga duguþe and geógoþe dǽl ǽghwylcne *then the Helmings' dame went round every part* [*group*] *of old and young,* Beo. Th. 1246; B. 621: 323; B. 160: 3352; B. 1674: Andr. Kmbl. 2245; An. 1124. II. *multitude, troops, army, people, men, attendants, the nobles, nobility, the heavenly host;* cōpiæ, exercĭtus, pŏpŭlus, hŏmĭnes, comĭtātus, prŏcĕres, mīlitia cœlestis:—Duguþ samnade *the multitude collected,* Andr. Kmbl. 250; An. 125: 2542; An. 1272. Āhte ic holdra ðȳ læs, deórre duguþe *I owned the less of faithful ones, of dear attendants,* Beo. Th. 980; B. 488. Dugoþ Israhēla *the army of Israel,* Cd. 146; Th. 183, 13; Exod. 91: 167; Th. 209, 17; Exod. 500. Duguþe ðīnre *to thy people,* Hy. 7, 69; Hy. Grn. ii. 288, 69. Ðæt is duguþum cūþ *that is known to men,* Andr. Kmbl. 1364; An. 682. Ðū ðe in Dryhtnes noman dugeþum cwōme *thou who camest in the Lord's name to men,* Exon. 13 b; Th. 26, 6; Cri. 413. Be ðām hringum mon mihte witan hwæt Rōmāna duguþe gefeallen wæs *by the rings one might know how many of the nobility of the Romans had fallen,* Ors. 4, 9; Bos. 91, 11: 3, 11; Bos. 74, 30: 1, 12; Bos. 35, 43. Se cining wæs gefullod mid eallum his dugoþe *the king was baptized with all his nobility*, Chr. 626; Th. 43, 29: 1016; Th. 283, 30. He spræc mid duguþe ealdrum *lŏcūtus est cum magistrātĭbus*, Lk. Bos. 22, 4: 12, 11. Dugoþ Drihten hērigaþ *the heavenly host praises the Lord*, Cd. 170; Th. 213, 2; Exod. 546: Exon. 23 b; Th. 65, 32; Cri. 1063. *God and Christ are called* duguþa helm, dryhten, dēmend, etc. *helmet, lord, ruler, etc. of the hosts* or *heavenly hosts*, Cd. 216; Th. 274, 35; Sat. 164: Exon. 19 a; Th. 49, 7; Cri. 782: Andr. Kmbl. 173; An. 87. III. *majesty, glory, magnificence, power, virtue, excellence, ornament;* majestas, magnificentia, potentia, virtus, dĕcus:—Ealra duguþa duguþ, Drihten Hǣlend *majesty of all majesties, Lord Saviour*, Hy. 3, 24; Hy. Grn. ii. 282, 24. He sōhte Drihtnes duguþe *he sought* [*entered into*] *the Lord's glory*, Cd. 60; Th. 73, 15; Gen. 1205. Wuldre benēmed, duguþum bedēled *bereft of glory, deprived of power*, Cd. 215; Th. 272, 19; Sat. 122: 212; Th. 263, 21; Dan. 765: Exon. 16 a; Th. 35, 24; Cri. 563. Seó duguþ ðæs wlītes ðe on gimmum biþ *the excellence of the beauty, which is in gems*, Bt. 13; Fox 40, 3. On ðǣm is swiotol sió gifu and ealla ða duguþa hiora fæder *in whom is manifest the ability and all the virtues of their father*, 10; Fox 28, 32. Simmachus seó duguþ ealles moncynnes *Symmachus the ornament of all mankind*, 10; Fox 28, 12. IV. *advantage, gain, good, happiness, prosperity, riches, blessings, salvation;* commŏdum, lucrum, bŏnum, prospĕrĭtas, divĭtiæ, ŏpes, sălus:—Hwæt ðū us to duguþum gedōn wille *what thou wilt do to our advantage*, Andr. Kmbl. 683; An. 342. Adrifen from duguþum *driven from good*, Cd. 106; Th. 140, 5; Gen. 2323. Gifa ðe him to duguþe Drihten scyrede *the gifts which the Lord had bestowed on him for his happiness*, 176; Th. 221, 12; Dan. 87. He him duguþa blǣd forgeaf *he gave them abundance of prosperity*, 121; Th. 156, 2; Gen. 2582. On ðære dægtīde duguþe wǣron *there were riches at that time*, 80; Th. 100, 5; Gen. 1659. Eallum bidǣled duguþum and dreámum *deprived of all blessings and joys*, Exon. 28 b; Th. 86, 16; Cri. 1409: Cd. 43; Th. 57, 18; Gen. 930. V. *benefit, gift;* benefĭcium, mūnus, dŏnum:—Secgan Drihtne þonc duguþa gehwylcre *to say thanks to the Lord for all benefits*, Exon. 16 b; Th. 38, 4; Cri. 601: 96 a; Th. 359, 3; Pa. 57: Cd. 74; Th. 91, 10; Gen. 1510. VI. *that which is seemly, suitable, seemliness;* dĕcōrum:—He cūðe duguþe þeáw *he knew the usage of decorum* [*decorous usage*], Beo. Th. 724; B. 359; 6330; B. 3175. Æfter dugeþum *according to seemliness*, Cd. 104; Th. 137, 31; Gen. 2282. [*Laym.* duȝeðe *nobles: Plat.* dögt, *f. solidness: O. Frs.* duged, *f. power: Ger.* tugend, *f. virtus: M. H. Ger.* tugent, *f: O. H. Ger.* tugad, *f. vis, rōbur, virtus: Dan.* dyd, *f: Swed.* dygd, *f: Icel.* dygð, *f. virtue.*] DER. æðel-duguþ, ealdor-, heofon-, woruld-.

duguþ, dugoþ, dugeþ; *adj. Good, honourable;* bonus, probus, Mann. v. dugeþ; *adj.*

duguþ-gifu, e; *f. Liberality;* munificentia, Som. Ben. Lye. v. dugoþ-gifu.

duhte *did good*, Chr. 1013; Erl. 149, 5, = dohte; *p. of* dugan.

dulfon *dug*, Ps. Th. 56, 8; *p. pl. of* delfan.

dulh-rune *pellitory*, L. M. 3, 8; Lchdm. ii. 312, 16. v. dolh-rune.

dulmūnus; *gen. pl.* dulmūna; *m. The war-ship of the Greeks, which king Alfred assures us would hold a thousand men;* longa nāvis. These ships were the μακρὰ πλοῖα or νῆες μακραί, generally called in Greek ὁ δρόμων, ωνος, *m. the light war-vessel of the Greeks.* They were the longæ nāves *the long war-ships* of the Romans, which had often more than fifty rowers. The Romans called their vessel drŏmo, ōnis, defining it as *a fast rowing vessel*, evidently deriving their word from the Greek δρόμων, Cod. Just. 1, 27, 1, § 8; Cassiod. Var. 5, 17, *init.* where it is described as 'trĭrēme vehĭcŭlum rēmŏrum tantum nŭmĕrum prōdens, sed hŏmĭnum făcies dīlĭgenter abscondens.' Some suppose that Alfred derived his word dulmūnus from the *Icel.* drómundr, *m.* which Egilsson, in his Lexĭcon Poētĭcum, Hafniæ, 8vo. 1860, explains 'nāvis grandior, cūjus gĕnĕris tantum extra regiōnes septemtriōnāles, ut in māri mediterrāneo, mentio fit,' S. E. i. 582, 3, Orkn. 82, 1, 3. Vigfusson, in his Icelandic-English Dictionary, 4to. Oxford, 1869–1874, in drómundr gives only the Latin and Greek, and O. H. Ger. drahemond as cognates. What Orosius calls longas nāves, Alfred translates dulmūnus in Anglo-Saxon. As we read in the Anglo-Saxon Chronicle of A. D. 897; Th. i. 174, 41,—Hēt Ælfrēd cyng timbrian lang-scipu ongēn ða æscas *king Alfred commanded to build long-ships against those ships*, v. ÆSC IV.—Alfred, in his translation of Orosius, says:—Ǣr he [Ercol] ongan mid Creáca scypum, ðe mon dulmūnus hǣt, ðe man segþ ðæt ān scip mǣge ān þūsend manna *before he* [*Hercules*] *began with Grecian ships, which are called dulmunus, of which it is said that one ship can hold a thousand men*, Ors. 1, 10; Bos. 33, 31–33. He [Xersis] hæfde scipa ðæra mycclena dulmūna ān M and ii hund *he* [*Xerxes*] *had one thousand two hundred of the large ships, dulmunus*, Ors. 2, 5; Bos. 46, 32, 33. v. Glossārium ad scriptōres mĕdiæ et infĭmæ Latinĭtātis Dŏmĭni Du Cange, Dufresne; Francofurti ad Mœnum, 3 vols. fol. 1681, Dromōnes.

DUMB; *def.* se dumba, seó, ðæt dumbe; *adj.* DUMB, *speechless, mute;* mūtus, e-linguis:—Eart ðū dumb and deáf *thou art dumb and deaf*, Exon. 99 a; Th. 370, 26; Seel. 65: 108 b; Th. 414, 7; Rä. 32, 16. Beó ðū dumb ōþ-ðæt ðæt cild beó acenned *be thou dumb until the child shall be born*, Homl. Th. i. 202, 7: L. Alf. pol. 14; Th. i. 70, 14. Dumb *mūtus*, Wrt. Voc. 75, 36: Mt. Bos. 12, 22: Lk. Bos. 11, 14. Se dumba fæder *the dumb father*, Homl. Th. i. 354, 27: Salm. Kmbl. 457; Sal. 229. Se dumba spræc *lŏcūtus est mūtus*, Mt. Bos. 9, 33: Lk. Bos. 11, 14. Dumbes *elinguis*, Glos. Prudent. Recd. 143, 1. Hīg brohton him dumbne man *obtŭlērunt ei hŏmĭnem mūtum*, Mt. Bos. 9, 32: Mk. Bos. 9, 17: Ex. 4, 11. Gesēgun ða dumban gesceaft *they saw the dumb creation*, Exon. 24 b; Th. 69, 30; Cri. 1128: 113 a; Th. 433, 3; Rä. 50, 2. Ða ōðre nigon consonantes synd gecwedene *mūtæ*, ðæt synd dumbe *the other nine consonants are called* mūtæ, *which are dumb*, Ælfc. Gr. 2; Som. 3, 1, 2. He dyde ðæt deáfe gehȳrdon, and dumbe sprǣcon *surdos fĕcit audīre, et mūtos lŏqui*, Mk. Bos. 7, 37: Mt. Bos. 15, 31. Ic sceal dǣda fremman swā ða dumban neát *I shall do deeds such as the dumb cattle*, Andr. Kmbl. 134; An. 67. Dumbra *of the dumb*, Salm. Kmbl. 158; Sal. 78. Be dumbera manna dǣdum *of dumb men's deeds*, L. Alf. pol. 14; Th. i. 70, 13. Hī forgeáfon dumbum spræce *they gave speech to the dumb*, Homl. Th. i. 544, 33: 424, 10: Andr. Kmbl. 1153; An. 577: Exon. 68 a; Th. 251, 24; Jul. 150. [*Piers P.* dombe: *Wyc.* doumbe: *Chauc.* dombe: *Laym.* dumbe: *Orm.* dumb: *O. Sax.* dump *stultus: Frs.* domme, dom: *O. Frs.* dumbe, dume *stultus, mūtus: Dut.* dom *stupid: Ger.* dumm *stupid: M. H. Ger.* tump *stupid: O. H. Ger.* tumb *mūtus, stultus: Goth.* dumbs *mute: Dan.* dum *stupid: Swed.* dum *stupid;* dumb *mute: Icel.* dumbr *mute.*] DER. dum-nys: a-dumbian.

dumle? *the pelican;* onocrŏtălus = ὀνοκρόταλος, Cot. 23.

dumnys, -nyss, e; *f.* DUMBNESS, *speechlessness;* loquendi impotentia, Som. Ben. Lye.

DUN; *adj.* DUN, *a colour partaking of brown and black;* fuscus, aquĭlus:—Dun *fuscus*, Cot. 141, 147: *natius* [= *nātīvus*?], Ælfc. Gl. 79; Som. 72, 86; Wrt. Voc. 46, 43. Dunn *balidus* [= βαλιός?], Wrt. Voc. 289, 28. On ðone [MS. ðonne] dunnan stān *to the dun stone*, Cod. Dipl. 1120; A. D. 939; Kmbl. v. 238, 32. [*Chauc.* dunne, donne *dark-coloured: Ir.* dunn *a dun colour: Wel.* dwn *dun, swarthy, dusky: Gael.* donn *brown-coloured.*] DER. asse-dun.

DŪN, e; *pl. nom. acc.* dūna, dūne; *f. A mountain, hill*, DOWN; mons, collis:—Seó dūn, ðe se Hǣlend ofastāh, getācnode heofenan rīce *the mountain, from which Jesus descended, betokened the kingdom of heaven*, Homl. Th. i. 120, 21: 502, 2, 7: Exon. 101 b; Th. 384, 1; Rä. 4, 21. Ðeós dūn *hic mons*, Ælfc. Gr. 9, 39; Som. 12, 58: 5; Som. 4, 8: Ps. Lamb. 67, 16: Wrt. Voc. 80, 42. Hie be hliðe heáre dūne eorþscræf fundon *they found an earth-cavern by the slope of a high hill*, Cd. 122; Th. 156, 26; Gen. 2594: Homl. Th. i. 502, 13. Betwux ðære dūne Sion, and ðam munte Oliueti *between mount Sion and the mount of Olives*, i. 440, 15: 502, 2, 9: 120, 10. Genōh lange ge wunodon on ðisse dūne *suffĭcit vobis, quod in hoc monte mansistis*, Deut. 1, 6: Gen. 31, 54: Mt. Bos. 24, 3. Stōpon stīðhycgende on ða dūne up *the stout-hearted went aloft upon the hill*, Elen. Kmbl. 1430; El. 717: Bt. Met. Fox 19, 20; Met. 19, 10: Cd. 228; Th. 307, 21; Sat. 683. Ðec heá duna hērgen *high downs praise thee*, Exon. 54 b; Th. 193, 6; Az. 117. Of denum and of dūnum *from dells and from downs*, 107 b; Th. 409, 18; Rä. 28, 3: Cd. 69; Th. 84, 15; Gen. 1398: 71; Th. 85, 28; Gen. 1421. Seó wiht dūna briceþ *the creature will burst the hills*, Exon. 109 b; Th. 420, 6; Rä. 39, 6. Wurdon behelede ealle ða hēhstan dūna under ealre heofenan. And ðæt wæter wæs fīftyne fæðma deóp ofer ða hēhstan dūna *operti sunt omnes montes excelsi sub unĭverso cœlo. Quindĕcim cŭbĭtis altior fuit aqua super montes, quæ operuĕrat*, Gen. 7, 19, 20. He gehleápeþ heá dūne *he shall leap the high downs*, Exon. 18 a; Th. 45, 10; Cri. 717. Seó stōw is on Oliuetes dūne ufeweardre *the place is on the high mount of Olives*, Homl. Blick. 125, 19. [*R. Glouc.* dounes *hills: Laym.* dune, *f: Orm.* dun *a hill: Plat.* dūnen *sandhills on the seashore: Dut.* duin, *n: Kil.* duyne *agger mărinus: Ger.* düne, *f: O. H. Ger.* dūn, dūna *mons: Fr.* dune, *f: Span.* dúnas, *pl. f: Ital.* dúna, *f. an elevation of sand thrown up by the sea: Ir.* dun, *m. a fortified hill, fortress: Corn.* dun, din, *f. a hill.*] DER. a-dūn, -dūne, of-.

dūn; *adj. Mountainous, hilly;* montānus:—To dūn-landum *to hilly lands*, Deut. 1, 7. v. dūn-land.

dūn-elfen, e; *f.* [-ælfen *a fairy*] *A down* or *mountain-fairy;* castălis, ĭdis; *f. one of the muses;* castălĭdes, um, *f.* Ælfc. Gl. 113; Som. 79, 112; Wrt. Voc. 60, 19.

dūne-ward, dūne-weard *downward*, Som. Ben. Lye. v. a-dūnweard.

dun-falu, dun-fealu; *adj.* [dun *dun*, fealu *fallow-coloured*] *Dun* or *tawny colour;* color cervōrum:—Dun-fealu [MS. -falu] *cervīnus*, Ælfc. Gl. 79; Som. 72, 88; Wrt. Voc. 46, 45. v. fealo.

DUNG, e; *f.* DUNG; fimus, stercus:—Ic hine bedelfe, and ic hine beweorpe mid dunge *fŏdiam circa illam et mittam stercŏra*, Lk. Skt. Hat. 13, 8. [*Wyc.* dong, dung: *Piers P. Chauc.* donge: *Frs.* dong: *O. Frs.* dung: *Ger.* dung, *m. manure: M. H. Ger.* tunc, *f: O. H. Ger.* tunga, *f: Dan.* dynge, *m. f. a heap of dung: Swed.* dȳnga, *f: Icel.* dyngja, *f. a heap, dung.*]

Dūn-holm, es; *m.* [*Flor.* Dunhelm: *Brom.* Durem, Durham: dūn *a hill*, holm *wa'er, an island*] DURHAM; Dunelmia:—Hēr forlēt Ægelrīc bisceop his bisceoprīce æt Dūnholm *in this year* [A.D. 1056] *bishop Ægelric left his bishopric at Durham*, Ch. 1056; Erl. 191, 14. Ða menn hine befōron innan ðære burh æt Dūnholme *the men surrounded him in the burgh at Durham*, Chr. 1068; Erl. 205, 34: 1072; Erl. 211, 9, 29: 1075; Erl. 212, 35: 1080; Erl. 216, 12: 1087; Erl. 224, 6, 32: 1087; Erl. 226, 9: 1096; Erl. 232, 39.

dūn-land, es; *n. Down* or *hilly land;* terra montāna: *it is opposed to* feld-land *plain* or *level land*:—Faraþ to Amorrēa dūne and to ōðrum feld-landum and dūn-landum and to unhēheran landum *venīte ad montem Amorrhæōrum et ad cētēra campestria atque montāna et humīliōra lŏca*, Deut. 1, 7.

dūn-lendisc; *adj. Hilly, mountainous land;* montānus:—Sume sind *derivatīva*, swā dūn-lendisc *montānus*, Ælfc. Gr. 5; Som. 4, 10.

Dunnan tūn, es; *m. Dunna's town = Dunnington.*

dunnian, he dunnaþ, *pl.* dunniaþ; *p.* ode; *pp.* od *To make of a dun* or *a dark colour, to obscure, darken;* obscūrāre:—Se mōna ða beorhtan steórran dunnaþ [MS. dunniaþ] *the moon obscures the bright stars*, Bt. 4; Fox 6, 35.

dūn-sǣte; *gen.* -sǣta; *dat.* -sǣtum, -sǣtan; *pl. m.* [dūn *a mountain*, -sǣte *dwellers, inhabitants*] *Mountaineers, inhabitants of the mountains of Wales;* montĭcŏlæ Walliæ:—Ðis is seó gerǣdnes ðe Angelcynnes witan and Wealhþeóde rǣdboran betweox Dūnsǣtum [MS. Dūnsētan] gesetton *this is the ordinance which the witan of the English race and the counsellors of the Welsh nation established among the inhabitants of the mountains of Wales*, L. O. D. pref; Th. i. 352, 2. Be Wentsǣtum and Dūnsǣtum. Hwīlon Wentsǣte hȳrdon into Dūnsǣtan, ac hit gebȳreþ rihtor into West-Sexan: ðyder hȳ scylan gafol and gislas syllan. Eác Dūnsǣte beþyrfan, gif heom se cyning an, ðæt man hūru friþgislas to heom lǣte *of the Gwents* [i. e. *the people of West Wales, in Carmarthenshire, Pembrokeshire, and Cardiganshire*] *and the Dūnsǣte. Formerly the Gwents belonged to the Dūnsǣte, but more properly they belong to the West Saxons: thither they shall give tribute and hostages. The Dūnsǣte also need, if the king grant it to them, that at least peace-hostages be allowed them*, L. O. D. 9; Th. i. 356, 16-20.

dūn-scrǣf; *gen.* -scræfes; *pl. nom. acc.* -scrafu; *gen.* -scrafa; *dat.* -scrafum, -scræfum; *n.* [dūn *a mountain*, scræf *a den, cave*] *A mountain-cave;* montāna caverna:—Dūnscrafu, *nom. pl. mountain-caves*, Exon. 56 a; Th. 199, 12; Ph. 24. He sēceþ dȳgle stōwe under dūnscrafum *he seeks a secret place among the mountain-caves*, 96 a; Th. 357, 32; Pa. 37. Weras woldon to dūnscræfum drohtoþ sēcan *the men would seek a refuge in mountain-caves*, Andr. Kmbl. 3076; An. 1541.

Dūn-stān, es; *m. Dunstan;* Dunstānus:—Hēr S. Dūnstān wearþ geboren *in this year* [A.D. 925] *St. Dunstan was born*, Chr. 925; Th. 199, 4, col. 3. Hēr Eádmund cing betǣhte Glæstinga beri S. Dūnstāne, ðǣr he siððan ǣrest abbod wearþ *in this year* [A.D. 943] *king Edmund delivered Glastonbury to St. Dunstan, where he afterwards first became abbot*, 943; Th. 211, 17-21, col. 3. On ðam ylcan geáre wæs Dūnstān abbod adrǣfed ofer sǣ *in the same year* [A.D. 957] *abbot Dunstan was driven away over sea*, 957; Th. 217, 2-4, col. 1. Hēr Eádgār sende æfter S. Dūnstāne, and geaf [MS. gif] him ðæt bisceoprīce on Wigarceastre, and syððan ðæt bisceoprīce on [MS. an] Lundene *in this year* [A.D. 959] *Edgar sent after St. Dunstan, and gave him the bishopric of Worcester, and afterwards the bishopric of London*, 959; Th. 219, 25-29, col. 3. Hēr Scē Dūnstān fēng to arcebisceoprīce *in this year* [A.D. 961] *St. Dunstan succeeded to the archbishopric* [*of Canterbury*], 961; Th. 218, 34, col. 1. On ðissum geáre ealle ða yldestan Angelcynnes witan gefeóllon æt Calne of ānre upflōran, būton se hālga Dūnstān arcebisceop āna ætstōd uppan ānum beáme; and sume ðǣr swīðe gebrōcode wǣron, and sume hit ny [= ne] gedydon mid ðam līfe *in this year* [A.D. 978] *all the chief witan of the English race fell at Calne from an upper floor, but the holy archbishop Dunstan alone stayed upon a beam; and some there were very much maimed, and some did not escape with life*, Chr. 978; Th. 231, 30-39, col. 1. Hēr Dūnstān se hālga arcebisceop forlēt ðis līf, and gefērde ðæt heofonlīce *in this year* [A.D. 988] *the holy archbishop Dunstan departed this life, and passed to the heavenly* [*life*], 988; Th. 239, 9-11, col. 1.

dūn-strǣt, e; *f. A hilly road;* via montāna, Som. Ben. Lye.

dunung, e; *f. A noise;* crĕpĭtus, Som. Ben. Lye.

dūr, es; *n. A door.* v. dūru, *pl. nom. n.* v. dōr, *n.*

dūre, an; *f. A door;* ostium, jānua:—To ðære dūran *at the door*, Mk. Bos. 1, 33. v. dūru.

dūre-leás; *adj. Doorless;* sine jānua:—Dūreleás is ðæt hūs *the house is doorless*, Anlct. 153, 24, col. 2.

dūreras; *m. Folding doors;* valvæ, Cot. 183.

dūre-þinen *a female door-keeper*, Jn. Bos. 18, 16. v. dūru-þinen.

dūre-weard, -werd, es; *m. A door-ward, door-keeper*, Mk. Bos. 13, 34: Wrt. Voc. 81, 12: L. Ælf. C. 11; Th. ii. 346, 28. v. dūru-weard.

durfon *laboured, perished; p. pl. of* deorfan.

durne; *adj. Retired, secret;* reclūsus, secrētus:—On ðone durnan [MS. durnen] crundel; of ðam durnan crundelle on ðone þorn *to the retired barrow; from the retired barrow to the thorn*, Cod. Dipl. 1053; A. D. 854; Kmbl. v. 105, 26. v. dyrne.

DURRAN, ic, he dear, ðū dearst, *pl.* durron, durran; *p.* dorste, *pl.* dorston, dorstan; *pp.* dorren *To* DARE, *presume;* audēre:—Ne dear ic hām faran *I dare not go home*, Gen. 44, 34: Ex. 32, 30: Cd. 40; Th. 54, 1; Gen. 870. Gif ðū Grendles dearst neán bīdan *if thou darest abide near Grendel*, Beo. Th. 1059; B. 527: Andr. Kmbl. 2700; An. 1352. Gif he gesēcean dear *if he dares to seek*, Beo. Th. 1373; B. 684. Ne durran we ōwēr gefēran *we dare not go anywhere*, Exon. 70 b; Th. 262, 10; Jul. 330. Hī durron, Bd. 1, 27; S. 491, 33. Hwæðer ðū durre gilpan *whether thou dare boast*, Bt. 14, 1; Fox 40, 22: Bt. Met. Fox 11, 107; Met. 11, 54. Sēc gif ðū dyrre *seek it if thou durst*, Beo. Th. 2763; B. 1379. Hwæðer he winnan dorste *whether he durst fight*, Ors. 4, 11; Bos. 97, 14: Cd. 121; Th. 156, 15; Gen. 2589. Hī dorston, Beo. Th. 5688; B. 2848: dorstan, Bd. 3, 11; S. 536, 41. Gif hī dorsten *if they durst*, Bt. Met. Fox 1, 54; Met. 1, 27. [Durran is the fourth of the twelve Anglo-Saxon verbs, called *præterito-præsentia*, and given under āgan, *q. v.* The *inf.* durran and the *pres.* dear, *pl.* durron, retaining preterite inflections, are taken from the *p.* of the verb, ascertained from dear, *pl.* durron, which shews the ablaut or internal change of the vowel in the *p.* tense of the twelfth class of Grimm's division of strong verbs [Grm. i. p. 898; Koch, i. p. 252], and requires by analogy with other verbs of the same class the *inf.* deorran = deorsan [*Goth.* daursan] and the *pp.* dorren. Thus we find the original verb deorran = deorsan; *p.* dear, *pl.* durron; *pp.* dorren. The weak *p.* dorste, *pl.* dorston [= durste, durston], is formed regularly from the *inf.* durran = dursan. The same *præterito-præsens* may be generally observed in the following cognate words:—

	inf.	*pres.*	*pl.*	*p.*
Engl.	dare,	dare,	dare,	durst,
Wyc.	dore,	dar,	durn,	
Laym. Orm.		der, darr,	durren,	durste,
O. Sax.	gi-durran,	gi-dar,		gi-dorsta,
O. Frs.	thura,	thur, dur,	thuron,	thorste,
M. H. Ger.	turren,	tar,	turren,	torste,
O. H. Ger.	turran,	tar,	turrumēs,	torsta,
Goth.	daursan,	dars,	daursum,	daursta.]

durste *durst*, Chr. 1154; Erl. 266, 4, = dorste; *p. of* durran.

dūr-stodl, es; *n. A door-post;* postis:—Dūr-stodl *postes*, Wrt. Voc. 290, 15. v. dūru-stod.

dūru; *gen.* e; *dat.* e, a; *acc.* e, a, u; *pl. nom.* a; *gen.* ena; *dat.* um; *acc.* a, u; *f:* dūre, an; *f. An opening, a door, the door of a house;* ostium, jānua, fŏris:—Dūru ymbstandennesse welerum mīnum '*keep the door* [*opening* ostium] *of my lips*,' Eng. versn. Ps. Lamb. 140, 3. Seó dūru wæs belocen *clausa erat jānua*, Mt. Bos. 25, 10. Dūru sōna on arn *soon he rushed on the door*, Beo. Th. 1447; B. 721. Dūra, Andr. Kmbl. 1998; An. 1001. Ðā ða dūra wǣron belocene *cum fores essent clausæ*, Jn. Bos. 20, 19. Of ðære dūra *from the door*, Mt. Bos. 26, 71. Belocenum dūrum *janŭis clausis*, Jn. Bos. 20, 26. DER. eág-dūru, fōre-, helle-, hlīn-: dūru-leás, -stod, -þegn, *m.* -þīnen = þignen, *f.* -weard: dȳr: ge-dȳre, ofer-gedȳre. v. dōr, *n.*

dūru; *pl. n. Doors*, Exon. 97 b; Th. 364, 29; Wal. 78, = dōru. v. dōr, *n.*

dūru-leás *doorless;* sine janua. v. dūre-leás.

dūru-stod, e; *f.* [stod = studu *a post*] *A door-post;* ostii postis, Cot. 157. v. dūr-stodl.

dūru-þegn, es; *m.* [þegen *a servant*] *A door-keeper;* jānĭtor:—Dūruþegnum wearþ hildbedd stȳred *the death-bed was spread for the door-keepers*, Andr. Kmbl. 2182; An. 1092.

dūru-þīnen, dūre-þīnen, e; *f. A female door-keeper;* ancilla ostiāria:—Cwæþ seó dūruþīnen to Petrē *dīcit Petro ancilla ostiāria*, Jn. Bos. 18, 17. Se leorningcniht cwæþ to ðære dūreþīnene *discĭpŭlus dixit ostiāriæ*, 18, 16.

dūru-weard, dūre-weard, -werd, es; *m. A door-keeper;* jānĭtor, ostiārius:—Se man beóde ðam dūrewearde, ðæt he wacige *homo janĭtōri præcēpit ut vigĭlet*, Mk. Bos. 13, 34. Ostiārius is dūruweard se ðe circan cǣgan healt *ostiārius is the door-keeper who holds the keys of the church*, L. Ælf. P. 34; Th. ii. 378, 5. Dūreweard *ostiārius*, Wrt. Voc. 81, 12. Ne sceal nān dūruwerd forsecgan nānne rǣdere mid nānre wrohte *non lĭcet ostiārio ulli accūsāre lectōrem ullum ulla accusātiōne*, L. Ecg. C. 41; Th. ii. 168, 1, 3. Ostiārius [MS. Hostiārius] is ðære cyrcean dūrewerd, se sceal mid bellan bīcnigan ða tīda, and ða cyrcan unlūcan geleáffullum mannum, and ðām ungeleáffullum belūcan wiðūtan *ostiārius is the door-keeper of the church, who shall announce the hours with bells, and unlock the church to believing men, and shut the unbelieving without*, L. Ælf. C. 11; Th. ii. 346, 28-30. v. hād II.

DUST, es; *n.* DUST; pulvis:—Hwæðer ðē ðæt dust hērige *numquid confitēbĭtur tibi pulvis?* Ps. Th. 29, 9: Ps. Lamb. 77, 27. Ligeþ dust ðǣr hit wæs *the dust shall lie where it was*, Exon. 99 b; Th. 373, 8; Seel. 105: 108 a; Th. 412, 10; Rä. 30, 12. Hió wǣre fordrugod to duste *it would be dried to dust*, Bt. Met. Fox 20, 207; Met. 20, 104: Salm. Kmbl. 630; Sal. 314: Exon. 98 a; Th. 368, 4; Seel. 16: Bd. 4, 30; S. 608, 30. Hí beóþ duste gelícran, đonne hit wind tobláwþ *tamquam pulvis, quem projĭcit ventus a făcie terræ*, Ps. Th. 1, 5: 89, 6. Asceacaþ đæt dust of eówrum fótum *excŭtĭte pulvĕrem de pĕdĭbus vestris*, Mk. Bos. 6, 11: Lk. Bos. 10, 11. [*Wyc. Chauc.* dust: *R. Glouc.* douste: *R. Brun.* doste: *Laym.* dust, doust, *n*: *Orm.* dusst: *Plat.* dust, *m*: *O. Frs.* dust: *Dut.* duist: *Ger.* dust, *m. pulvis*: *Dan.* dyst, *m. f*: *Icel.* dust, *n*: *Sansk.* dhū-li, *m*; from dhū *to shake*, Willms. 457.]

dust-drenc, es; *m. A drink made of the seeds of herbs rubbed to dust*; pōtio ex herbārum quārumdam semĭnĭbus, in pulvĕrem redactis, compŏsĭta:—Wyrc gōdne dustdrenc: nim merces sǽd, and finoles sǽd, dilesǽd, etc.... gegníd ealle wel to duste: dō đæs dustes gōdne cuclerfulne on strang hluttor eala *make a good dust-drink* [*thus*]: *take seed of marche, and seed of fennel, dill-seed, etc.... rub all well to dust: put a good spoonful of the dust into strong clear ale*, L. M. 3, 12; Lchdm. ii. 314, 17-23.

dust-sceáwung, e; *f.* [sceáwung *a beholding, contemplation*] *A dust-viewing, contemplation of dust*; pulvĕris spectātio *vel* contemplātio:—He gewát from đære dustsceáwunga *he departed from the contemplation of the dust*, Homl. Blick. 113, 29.

duþhamor, dyþhomar, es; *m. Papȳrus* = πάπυρος:—Duþhamor *papȳrus*, Ælfc. Gl. 43; Som. 64, 39; Wrt. Voc. 31, 49.

DWǼS; *adj. Dull, foolish, stupid*; hĕbes, stultus, fătuus:—Dwǽs *vel* sott *hĕbes*, Ælfc. Gl. 88; Som. 74, 79; Wrt. Voc. 50, 59: 74, 35: Ælfc. Gr. 9, 26; Som. 11, 5. Abroten *vel* dwǽs *văfer* vel *fătuus* vel *sōcors*, Ælfc. Gl. 9; Som. 56, 115; Wrt. Voc. 18, 62. Dwǽs *indŏcĭlis*, Glos. Prudent. Recd. 152, 26. [*Plat.* dwas: *O. Frs.* dwes: *Dut.* dwaas.] DER. ge-dwǽs.

dwæscan; *p.* dwæscede, dwæscte; *pp.* dwæsced, dwæsct *To extinguish, put out*; extinguĕre:—Dryhten lǽnan lífes leahtras dwæsceþ *the Lord extinguishes the crimes of this frail life*, Exon. 62 b; Th. 229, 17; Ph. 456: 128 b; Th. 493, 19; Rä. 81, 33. Feóndscype dwæscaþ, sibbe sāwaþ on sefan manna *extinguish enmity, sow peace in the minds of men*, 14 b; Th. 30, 28; Cri. 486. DER. a-dwæscan, to-: un-adwæscendlíc.

dwǽs-nys, -nyss, e; *f. Dulness, foolishness, stupidity*; hĕbĕtūdo, stultĭtia, stūpĭdĭtas:—Dwǽsnys *vel* sotscipe *hĕbĕtūdo*, Ælfc. Gl. 88; Som. 74, 80; Wrt. Voc. 50, 60.

dwala *an error, doubt*:—Nānnes dwala is *non dubium est*, Mt. Kmbl. Præf. p. 2, 13. v. dwola.

dwalian; *p.* ede; *pp.* ed *To err*; errāre:—Híg dwaledon *errāvērunt*, Ps. Lamb. 57, 4. v. dwelian I.

dwān, *pl.* dwinon *pined, dwindled*; *p. of* dwīnan.

dwǽs-líht, es; *n.* [dwǽs *dull*, líht *light*] *A false light*; ignis fatuus, Som. Ben. Lye.

dwealde, *pl.* dwealdon *deceived*, Bt. 35, 5; Fox 164, 32; *p. of* dwellan.

DWELAN, ic dwele, đū dwelest, dwilst, he dweleþ, dwilþ, *pl.* dwelaþ; *p.* ic, he dwæl, đū dwǽle, *pl.* dwǽlon; *pp.* dwolen; *v. n. To be led into error, err*; in errōrem dūci, errāre. [*O. Sax.* far-dwelan *to neglect*: *O. H. Ger.* twelan *torpēre*.] DER. ge-dwelan: dwelian, a-, ge-, ofa-: dwellan, ge-.

DWELIAN, dweligan, dweoligan, dwalian, dwolian, dwoligan; *part.* dweliende, dweligende; ic dwelige, đū dwelast, he dwelaþ, *pl.* dweliaþ, dweligaþ, dweligeaþ; *p.* ode, ede; *pp.* od, ed. I. *v. n. To be led into error, err*; in errōrem dūci, errāre:—Dwelian he dyde híg on wæglǽste ođđe būtan wege, and nā on wege *errāre fecit eos in invio, et non in via*, Ps. Lamb. 106, 40. Wæs đæt dweligende sceáp ongeán fered *the wandering sheep was brought back*, Homl. Th. i. 340, 4. Dysige men, dweligende, sēcaþ đæt héhste gōd on đa sāmran gesceafta *foolish men, erring, seek the highest good in the worse creatures*, Bt. 33, 1; Fox 120, 12. Đa seofon dweligendan steorran *the seven wandering stars, the planets*, Boutr. Scrd. 18, 26, 29. Ge dweliaþ *errātis*, Mt. Bos. 22, 29. Hū ne dweligaþ ge *nonne ĭdeo errātis?* Mk. Bos. 12, 24. Swȳđe ge dweligeaþ *multum errātis*, 12, 27. Đa ongunnon clypian đæt se rihtwísa dwelode *they begun to say that the righteous man erred*, Homl. Th. ii. 300, 17. He dyde đæt ge dwelodon of đam wege *ut errāre te facĕret de via*, Deut. 13, 5. Hí dwelodon on þwyrlícum dǽdum *they erred in perverse actions*, Homl. Th. ii. 398, 7: 46, 26. Hí dweledon *errāvērunt*, Ps. Spl. 57, 3. II. *v. a. To lead into error, mislead, deceive*; in errōrem dūcĕre, decĭpĕre:—Đæt folc dweliende *misleading the people*, Homl. Th. ii. 492, 35. Ic đē ne dwelode *I have not deceived thee*, Bt. 35, 5; Fox 166, 1; 164, 32, MS. Bod. Me þincþ đæt đū me dwelige *methinks that thou misleadest me*, 35, 5; Fox 164, 12. [*O. Sax.* duelan *errāre*: *Frs.* dwæljen, dwyljen *to err*: *O. Frs.* dwela, dwila *to err*: *Dut.* dwálen *to err*.] DER. a-dwelian, ge-, ofa-.

DWELLAN, ic dwelle, đū dwelest, dwelst, he dweleþ, dwelþ, *pl.* dwellaþ; *p.* dwealde, dwelede; *pp.* dweald, dweled. I. *v. a. To lead into error, deceive, mislead*; in errōrem dūcĕre, decĭpĕre:—Ic đē ne dwelle *I do not deceive thee*, Bt. 35, 5; Fox 166, 1, MS. Cot. Đū sǽdest đæt ic đē dwealde *thou saidst that I deceived thee*, 35, 5; Fox 164, 32. Me þincþ đæt đū me dwelle *methinks that thou misleadest me*, 35, 5; Fox 164, 12, MS. Cot. II. *v. a. To prevent, hinder, delay*; impĕdīre, tardāre:—Ic dysge dwelle *I delay the foolish*, Exon. 103 b; Th. 392, 27; Rä. 12, 3. Ne hine wiht dweleþ, ādl ne yldo *nothing prevents him, disease nor age*, Beo. Th. 3475, note; B. 1735. Se ealda dweleþ miltse mid māne *the old one* [*the devil*] *prevents mercy with wickedness*, Frag. Kmbl. 62; Leás. 33. III. *v. n. To continue, remain*, DWELL; mănēre, habĭtāre:—Nero on đam holte on cȳle and on hungre dwelode, óþ-đæt hine wulfas totǽron *Nero remained in the wood, in cold and hunger, until wolves tore him to pieces*, Homl. Th. i. 384, 10. [*Piers P.* dwelle *to inhabit*: *Chauc.* dwell *to inhabit*: *Orm.* dwellenn *to dwell, delay*: *O. Sax.* bi-dwelian *to delay, prevent*: *M. H. Ger.* twelen *morāri*: *O. H. Ger.* twālōn, twaljan, tweljan *morāri, impĕdīre*: *Dan.* dwæle *to tarry, delay, dwell*: *Swed.* dwäljas *to dwell*: *Icel.* dwala *to delay*; dwelja *to dwell, wait, stay*.] DER. ge-dwellan.

dweola, dweolda *error, heresy*. DER. ge-dweola, -dweolda. v. dwola.

dweoligan; *part.* dweoligende *To err*; errāre:—Hí to đām dweoligendum lǽcedōmum deófolgylde efeston *they hastened to the erring cures of idolatry*, Bd. 4, 27; S. 604, 7. v. dwelian I.

DWEORG, dweorh, es; *m. A dwarf*; nānus:—Dweorg *pygmæus* vel *nānus* vel *pūmilio*, Ælfc. Gl. 114; Som. 80, 20; Wrt. Voc. 61, 1. Dweorh *nānus*, Wrt. Voc. 73, 53. [*Plat.* dwark, dwarf, *m*: *Frs.* dwirg: *O. Frs.* dwirg: *Dut.* dwerg, *m. f*: *Ger.* zwerg, *m*: *M. H. Ger.* twerc, *n*: *O. H. Ger.* twerg, *m*: *Dan.* dværg, dverg, *m. f*: *Swed.* dverg, *m*: *Icel.* dvergr, *m.*]

dweorge-dwosle, -dwostle, an; *f.* [dweorg *a dwarf*] *The herb pennyroyal*; mentha pulēgium, Lin:—Herba pollēgion [= pulēgium], đæt is dweorge-dwosle, Herb. cont. 94, 1; Lchdm. i. 38, 12. Đeós wyrt, đe man *pollēgium* [= *pulēgium*], and ōđrum naman dweorge-dwosle nemneþ *this herb, which is called* pulēgium, *and by another name pennyroyal* [*dwarf dwosle*], Herb. 94, 1; Lchdm. i. 204, 6, 7: 156, 2; Lchdm. i. 282, 23: iii. 6, 19. Nim dweorge-dwoslan *take pennyroyal*, Herb. 106; Lchdm. i. 220, 10: iii. 6, 12. Dweorge-dwostle *pennyroyal*, L. M. 1, 48; Lchdm. ii. 120, 23: 2, 53; Lchdm. ii. 274, 9, 13. Lege dweorge-dwostlan gecowene on *lay on chewed pennyroyal*, 2, 30; Lchdm. ii. 228, 19: 2, 32; Lchdm. ii. 236, 10: 3, 1; Lchdm. ii. 304, 29: iii. 74, 5.

dwēs *dull*, Som. Ben. Lye. v. dwǽs.

dwild, dwyld, es; *n. Error, heresy, a prodigy, spectre*; error, hærĕsis = αἵρεσις, prodĭgium, spectrum:—Wærþ mycel dwyld on Cristendōm *there was much error in Christendom*, Chr. 1129; Erl. 258, 29. On Engla land feole dwild weáren geseogen and geheórd *many prodigies were seen and heard in England*, 1122; Erl. 249, 13. DER. ge-dwild, -dwyld, mis-gedwield.

dwilman *to confuse, perplex, confound*. DER. for-dwilman.

dwimor, dwimer, dwymer, es; *n. An illusion, delusion, apparition, phantom*; error, fallācia, phantasma = φάντασμα. DER. ge-dwimor.

dwimor-líc; *adj. Visionary*; tamquam per visum, Som. Ben. Lye. DER. ge-dwymorlíc.

DWÍNAN, ic dwíne, đu dwínest, dwínst, he dwíneþ, dwínþ, *pl.* dwínaþ; *p.* dwān, *pl.* dwinon; *pp.* dwinen *To pine, fade*, DWINDLE, *waste away*; tabescĕre:—Đonne dwíneþ seó wamb sōna *then soon will the belly dwindle*, Herb. 2, 4; Lchdm. i. 82, 2. Dwinon *tabuērunt*, Cot. 190. [*Wyc.* dwyne, *p.* dwynede *to pine, waste away*: *Chauc.* dwined, *pp. wasted, shrunk*: *Plat.* dwinen *to vanish*: *Kil.* dwijnen *extenuāre, perīre*: *Dan.* tvine *to weep, vanish*: *Swed.* twina *to languish, pine away*: *Icel.* dvína, dvina *to dwindle, pine away*.] DER. a-dwínan, for-, ge-.

dwola, an; *m.* [dwolen, *pp. of* dwelan *to err*] *Error, heresy*; error, hærĕsis = αἵρεσις:—Seó mǽgþ on dwolan wæs lifigende *provincia in errōre versāta est*, Bd. 2, 15; S. 518, 42. Se [Arrianisca] dwola on đam niwan sinoþe geniđerad wæs *Arriāna hærĕsis in Nicæna synŏdo damnāta erat*, 1, 8; S. 479, 36, MS. B. DER. ge-dwola.

dwol-cræft, es; *m.* [cræft *a craft*] *Foolish craft, magic*; prāva *vel* magĭca ars:—Him geblēndon drȳas þurh dwolcræft drync unheórne *the wizards mixed for them through magic a fatal drink*, Andr. Kmbl. 67; An. 34.

dwolema *darkness, chaos*, Bt. Met. Fox 5, 86; Met. 5, 43. v. dwolma.

dwolian, dwoligan; *part.* dwoliende, dwoligende; *p.* ede; *pp.* ed *To wander out of the way, err*; errāre:—Þurh monige stōwe dwoliende *wandering through many places*, Bd. 4, 3; S. 570, 11. Dysige men, dwoliende, sēcaþ đæt héhste gōd on đa sǽmran gesceafta *foolish men, erring, seek the highest good in the worse creatures*, Bt. 33, 1; Fox 120, 12, MS. Cot. Hider and đider dwoligende *wandering hither and thither*, 36, 5; Fox 180, 12. To đām dwoligendum deófolgyldum *to the erring idolatry*, Bd. 4, 27; S. 604, 7, MS. B. Híg dwoliaþ on heortan *hi errant corde*, Ps. Lamb. 94, 10. Đa synfullan dwoledon *peccātōres errāvērunt*, Ps. Surt. 57, 4. DER. ge-dwolian. v. dwelian I.

dwol-líc; *def.* se -líca, seó, đæt -líce; *adj. Foolish, erring, heretical*; stultus, hærĕtĭcus:—Nis đis nān dwollíc sagu *this is not a foolish saying*, Jud. 15, 19. Hȳ adwæscdon đa dwollícan lāra *they extinguished the heretical doctrines*, L. Ælf. C. 33; Th. ii. 356, 11.

dwol-líce; *adv. Foolishly, heretically*; stulte, hærĕtĭce:—Ne man ne mōt drincan, ne dwollīce plegan, ne etan innan cyrican *no one may drink, nor foolishly play, nor eat in a church*, L. Ælf. E; Th. ii. 392, 16: L. Ælf. C. 33; Th. ii. 356, 12. Ðe dwollīce leofaþ *who lives in heresy*, Hexam. 20; Norm. 28, 17.

dwolma, dwolema, an; *m. Chaos, a chasm, gulph*; chaos, *n*. = χάος, τό, hiātus:—Dwolma *chaos*, Cot. 40: 204. Betweox us and eów is mycel dwolma getrymed *inter nos et vos chaos magnum firmātum est*, Lk. Bos. 16, 26. Ða twegen tregan teóþ to-somne wiđ đæt mōd fōran mistes dwoleman *the two vexations draw together before the mind a chaos of darkness*, Bt. Met. Fox 5, 86; Met. 5, 43. DER. dwilman, for-.

dwolung, e; *f. Dotage*; delirāmentum, Cot. 69.

dworge-dwostle, an; *f. Pennyroyal*; pulēgium:—Nim dworgedwostlan *take pennyroyal*, Lchdm. iii. 100, 25, 27. v. dweorge-dwoslē.

dwyld *error, heresy*, Chr. 1129; Erl. 258, 29. DER. ge-dwyld. v. dwild.

dwyrge-dwysle, an; *f. Pennyroyal*; pulēgium:—Hylwyrt ođđe dwyrge-dwysle *pollēgia* [= *pulēgium*], Wrt. Voc. 79, 54. v. dweorge-dwosle.

dyd, e; *f. A deed*; actum:—Se consul [Fauius] gedyde đa bysmerlīcestan dyde *the consul* [*Fabius*] *did the most disgraceful deed*, Ors. 5, 2. Barrington, A. D. 1773, 180, 15. v. dǽd.

dȳdan; *p*. dȳdde, *pl*. dȳddon; *pp*. dȳded, dȳdd, dȳd; *v. a*. [deád *dead*] *To put to death, kill*; morti trādere, occīdere:—Ne dȳde man ǽfre on Sunnan dæges freólse ǽnigne forwyrhtne man *let not a man ever put any condemned man to death on the festival of Sunday*, L. C. S. 45; Th. i. 402, 9. DER. a-dȳdan.

dyde *did*, Bt. 25; Fox 88, 36; *p. of* dōn.

dyde; *acc. sing. of* dyd [dyde *what was done, p. of* dōn *to do*] *a deed*; actum, Ors. 5, 2; Barrington, 180, 15, = dǽde, Ors. 5, 2; Bos. 102, 21.

dyderian, dydrian; *p*. ode; *pp*. od; *v. trans. To deceive, delude*; illūdere:—Me þincþ đæt đū me dwelige and dyderie [dwelle and dydre, Cot.], swā mon cild dēþ *methinks that thou misleadest and deludest me, as any one does a child*, Bt. 35, 5; Fox 164, 12. DER. be-dyderian, bedidrian.

dyderung, dydrung, e; *f. An illusion, delusion, pretence*; delūsio, simŭlātio:—Ðæs hālgan andwerdnyss acwencte đæs deófles dyderunge *the presence of the saint quenched the delusion of the devil*, Homl. Th. ii. 140, 19. Hit wæs đæs deófles dydrung *it was an illusion of the devil*, ii. 166, 6. He nys wīs đe mid dydrunge hyne sylfne beswīcþ *non est sapiens qui simulātiōne semet ipsum decĭpit*, Coll. Monast. Th. 33, 3. DER. be-dydrung.

dydest *didst, didst put*, Hy. 9, 55; Hy. Grn. ii. 292, 55: dydon *they did*, Lk. Bos. 10, 13; *p. of* dōn.

dydrin, es; *m? A yolk*; vitellus:—Nim æges dydrin *take the yolk of an egg*, L. M. 1, 38; Lchdm. ii. 92, 20. [*Bav.* dottern, *m*.]

dȳfan; *p*. de; *pp*. ed *To dip, immerse*; immergĕre:—Mec feónda sum dȳfde on wætre *some enemy dipped me in water*, Exon. 107 a; Th. 407, 32; Rä. 27, 3. He hine on đam streáme sencte and dȳfde *he sank and immersed himself in the stream*, Bd. 5, 12; S. 631, 22. [*Icel.* dýfa *to dip*.] v. dūfan.

dyfen, e; *f. Desert, reward*; merĭtum:—Æft heora ge-earnungum and dyfene *juxta eorum merĭta*, C. R. Ben. 2.

dȳfing, e; *f. A diving*; immersio, urīnātio, Som. Ben. Lye.

Dyflen, Dyflin *Dublin*, Chr. 937; Th. 206, 14, col. 2; 207, 14, col. 1; Æđelst. 55. v. Difelin.

dȳfst, he dȳfþ *divest, dives*; *2nd and 3rd pers. pres. of* dūfan.

dȳgan; *p*. dȳgde; *pp*. dȳged [dugan *vălēre*] *To do good, benefit*; prodesse, vălēre:—Ic secge đæt sió fōrespræc ne dȳge nāuđer ne đam scyldigan, ne đam đe him fore þingaþ *I say that the defence does no good either to the guilty or to him who pleads for him*, Bt. 38, 7; Fox 210, 6. Ðæt ys to gelȳfenne đæt hit dȳge *it is to be believed that it may benefit*, Herb. 2, 15; Lchdm. i. 84, 19. DER. ge-dȳgan, -dīgan, -dēgan.

dȳgel *secret, unknown*, Beo. Th. 2719; B. 1357: *gen. pl*. dȳgelra, Exon. 92 b; Th. 347, 26; Sch. 18. v. dīgol.

dȳgle *secret, hidden*, Exon. 35 b; Th. 115, 7; Gū. 186: Cd. 178; Th. 224, 2; Dan. 130; *def. nom. f. n. of* dȳgol. v. dīgol.

dȳgol *darkness*, Exon. 39 b; Th. 130, 13; Gū. 437. v. dīgol.

dȳgol *secret, hidden*. v. dȳgle, dīgol.

dȳhst, he dȳgþ, dȳhþ *dyest, dyes*; *2nd and 3rd pers. pres. of* deágan.

dyht *a direction*, Chr. 1097; Erl. 234, 18. v. diht.

dyhte *arranged*, Mt. Bos. 25, 19: Gen. 16, 3; *p. of* dyhtan. v. dihtan.

DYHTIG, dihtig; *adj*. [dugan *vălēre*] *Doughty, strong*; vălĭdus:—Sweord ecgum dyhtig *a sword doughty of edges*, Beo. Th. 2578; B. 1287. Dihtig, Cd. 93; Th. 120, 11; Gen. 1993. [*Piers P.* douhty, doghty: *Chauc.* douhty: *Laym.* duhti: *Orm.* duhtig: *Plat.* dugtig: *Ger.* tüchtig: *M. H. Ger.* tühtic *able, strong, fit*: *O. H. Ger.* tugad-ig *virtuous*: *Dan.* dygtig: *Swed.* dugtig: *Icel.* dygđugr.] v. dohtig.

dyle *dill*, Wrt. Voc. 79, 9. v. dile.

dylsta? *pl*. dylstan *Matter, corruption, mucus*; tabum, mucus:—Fleó đa mettas đa đe him dylsta on innan wyrcen *let him avoid the meats which may work mucus in his inside*, L. M. 2, 29; Lchdm. ii. 226, 10. Ðǽr dylstan on synd *whereon the mucus is*, 1, 31; Lchdm. ii. 72, 20.

dylstiht; *adj*. [dylsta *matter*; -iht, *adj. termination*, q. v.] *Mattery, mucous*; mucōsus:—Gif hie dylstihte sién *if they be mucous*, L. M. 1, 29; Lchdm. ii. 70, 9.

dym-hofe *a lurking-place, hiding-place*, Ps. Lamb. 17, 12: Homl. Th. ii. 122, 33. v. dim-hofe.

dymlīc *dim, obscure*:—Ða dymlīcan þeóstra *the dim darkness*, L. Ælf. C. 14; Th. ii. 348, 7. v. dimlīc.

dymnys *dimness, darkness*:—Dymnys *cālīgo*, Ælfc. Gr. 9, 3; Som. 8, 56. v. dimnes.

dyncge *ploughed land*, Mone B. 1434: 2326. v. dincge.

DYNE, dyn, es; *m. A* DIN, *noise*; sonus, fragor, strepitus:—Se dyne becom hlūd of heofonum *the din came loud from heaven*, Cd. 223; Th. 294, 5; Sat. 466. Cyrm, dyne *fragor*, Mone B. 4413: Cd. 221; Th. 288, 13; Sat. 380: 222; Th. 289, 7, 27; Sat. 394, 404. Ǽr he dōmdæges dyn gehȳre *ere he shall hear doomsday's din*, Salm. Kmbl. 546; Sal. 272: 650; Sal. 324. Dyne *fragōre*, Mone B. 4425. [*Chauc.* dinne: *Dan.* dön, *n. a loud noise*: *Swed.* dån, *n. a din, noise*: *Icel.* dynr, *m. a din, noise*.] DER. eorþ-dyne: ge-dyn, swēg-.

dȳneras *small pieces of money*, Ælfc. Gl. 106; Som. 78, 55; Wrt. Voc. 57, 35. v. digneras.

dyngan; *p*. ede; *pp*. ed [dung *dung*] *To* DUNG, *manure*; stercŏrāre. [*Piers P.* dongen: *Wyc.* dunge: *Frs.* dongjen: *O. Frs.* donga, denga: *Ger.* düngen: *M. H. Ger.* tungen: *Dan.* dynge *to heap up*.] DER. gedyngan.

dynge, dinge, dynige, es; *m? A noise, dashing, storm*; sonus, strepĭtus, procella:—On dynges mere *on the sea of noise*, Gst. Rthm. ii. 66, 20; Chr. 937; Th. 206, 12, col. 2. v. dyne.

dynian, he dyneþ; *p*. ede; *pp*. ed; *v. intrans*. [dyne *a din, noise*] *To make a noise*, DIN, *resound*; fragōrem edĕre, sŏnāre, perstrĕpĕre, clangĕre:—Gif eáran dynien *if the ears din*, L. M. 1, 3; Lchdm. ii. 40, 1: 42, 24. Dyneþ upheofon *heaven above shall resound*, Exon. 116 b; Th. 448, 25; Dōm. 59: 21 b; Th. 58, 5; Cri. 931. Hleóđor dynede *the noise resounded*, Andr. Kmbl. 1478; An. 740: Beo. Th. 1538; B. 767: Fins. Th. 61; Fin. 30: Judth. 10; Thw. 21, 18; Jud. 23: Exon. 94 b; Th. 353, 46; Reim. 28. Dynedon scildas *the shields rang*, Judth. 11; Thw. 24, 24; Jud. 204. [*O. Sax.* dunian *fragōrem edĕre*: *Swed.* dåna *to make a noise, ring*: *Icel.* dynja *to gush, shower*: *Lat.* tonāre *to make a loud noise, to thunder*: *Sansk.* dhan, dhvan *to sound, to cause a sound*.]

dynige *mountainous places*; montāna, L. M. 3, 8; Lchdm. ii. 312, 21, Som. Ben. Lye.

DYNT, es; *m*. I. *a stroke, stripe, blow*; ictus, plaga, percussio:—He, mid đam dynte, nyđer astāh *he, with the blow, fell down*, Chr. 1012; Th. 268, 29, col. 2: Jn. Lind. Rush. War. 18, 22. Ondrǽden him đone dynt *let them fear the stroke*, Past. 45, 2; Hat. MS. 64 b, 23. II. the mark or noise of a blow,—*A bruise*, DINT, *noise, crash*; contusio, impressio, sonus:—Gif dynt sie, scilling; gif he heáhre handa dyntes onfēhþ, scilling forgelde *if there be a bruise, a shilling*; *if he receive a right hand bruise, let him* [*the striker*] *pay a shilling*, L. Ethb. 58; Th. i. 18, 1. Ne wyrnaþ deórra dynta *they are not sparing of severe dints*, Salm. Kmbl. 245; Sal. 122. Wyrcþ hlūdne dynt *makes a loud crash*, Bt. 38, 2; Fox 198, 9. [*Piers P. Chauc.* dint *a blow, knock*: *R. Brun.* dynt: *R. Glouc.* dunt, *pl*. dyntes: *Orm.* dinnt *a blow, stroke*: *Icel.* dyntr, dyttr, *m*; dynta, *f. a dint*.]

dȳp, es; *n. The deep*; profundum:—Ofer dȳpe, Exon. 101 b; Th. 384, 1; Rä. 4, 21. v. deóp.

dȳpan; *p*. dȳpde = dȳpte [dȳp *deep*] *To make deep, deepen, increase, augment*; profundius reddĕre, augēre:—We cwǽdon be đām blaserum, đæt man dȳpte đone āþ be þrȳfealdum *we have ordained concerning incendiaries that the oath be augmented threefold*, L. Ath. iv. 6; Th. i. 224, 14. [*Laym.* ideoped, *pp. deepened*: *Frs.* djepjen: *O. Frs.* diupa: *Dut.* diepen: *Ger.* tiefen in ver-tiefen *to make deeper*: *M. H. Ger.* tiefen *to deepen*: *Goth.* ga-diupyan: *Dan.* for-dybe: *Swed.* för-djupa: *Icel.* dýpka *to become deeper, to deepen*.]

dȳpe, an; *f*: dȳp, es; *n. Depth, the deep, sea*; profundum, altĭtūdo, altum:—Hīg næfdon đære eorþan dȳpan *non habēbant altitūdĭnem terræ*, Mt. Bos. 13, 5. Ascūfaþ hine ūt on middan đære dȳpan *thrust him out into the middle of the deep*, Homl. Th. i. 564, 8. Teóh hit on dȳpan *duc in altum*, Lk. Bos. 5, 4. v. deóp.

DYPPAN, dippan; ic dyppe, he dypþ, dyppeþ, *pl*. dippaþ; *p*. dypte; *pp*. dypped, dypd = dypt; *v. a. To* DIP, *immerge, baptize*; immergĕre, intingĕre, tingĕre, baptīzāre:—Se đe his hand on disce mid me dypþ *qui intingit mecum manum in cātino*, Mk. Bos. 14, 20. Dyppe his finger đǽron *let him dip his finger therein*, Lev. 4, 17. Biþ dipped fōt đīn on blōde *ut intingātur pes tuus in sanguĭne*, Ps. Spl. 67, 25. Dippaþ ysopan sceaft on đam blōde *fascĭcŭlum hyssōpi tingĭte in sanguĭne*, Ex. 12, 22. Ic eówic dēpu ođđe dyppe, se eówic dēpiþ ođđe dyppeþ *ego baptizo vos, ipse baptizābit vos*, Mt. Rush. Stv. 3, 11. Dyppende *baptizantes*, 28, 19.

[*Wyc.* dippe: *Orm.* dippesst *dippest: Plat.* döpen *to baptize: O. Sax.* dôpian *baptīzāre: Dut.* doopen *to baptize, immerge: Ger.* taufen *to baptize: M. H. Ger.* toufen *to baptize: O. H. Ger.* toufēn *baptīzāre: Goth.* daupyan *to baptize.*] DER: be-dyppan, ge-, onbe-.

dýr, es; *n. A door;* ostium, jānua:—We lǽraþ, ðæt mæssepreósta oððe mynsterpreósta ǽnig ne cume binnan circan dýre būton his oferslipe *we enjoin, that no mass-priest, or minster-priest, come within the church-door without his upper vestment,* L. Edg. C. 46; Th. ii. 254, 9. v. dór.

dýr *brave, bold,* Cd. 174; Th. 218, 10; Dan. 37. v. deór I.

dýran *to hold dear, love:*—Dýran *to hold dear,* Cd. 14; Th. 17, 9; Gen. 257. v. deóran.

Dyra wudu, Dera wudu; *gen. dat.* wuda; *m.* [Dere *the Deirians,* wudu *a wood: the wood of the Deirians*] *Beverley, Yorkshire;* oppĭdi nomen in agro Eboracensi:—Se sōþfæsta Berhthun eft wæs abbud ðæs mynstres ðæt ys gecýged on Dyra wuda *veracissĭmus Bercthun nunc abbas monastĕrii quod vocātur in Derauuda, id est, in silva Derōrum,* Bd. 5, 2; S. 614, 29. He wæs bebyriged in Sce' Petres portice on his mynstre ðæt is cweden in Dera wuda *sepultus est in portĭcu sancti Petri, in monastĕrio suo, quod dicĭtur in silva Derōrum,* 5, 6; S. 620, 21. Iohannes fōr to his mynstre on Dera wuda *John went to his monastery at Beverley,* Chr. 685; Erl. 41, 35.

dýre; *adj.* I. *dear, beloved;* cārus, dilectus:—Se wæs him dýre *he was dear to him,* Lk. Bos. 7, 2: Gen. 44, 5: L. Eth. vii. 22; Th. i. 334, 12: Chr. 942; Erl. 116, 9; Edm. 3: Cd. 63; Th. 75, 28; Gen. 1247: Exon. 42 b; Th. 143, 22; Gū. 665: Runic pm. 26; Kmbl. 344, 24; Hick. Thes. i. 135, 51: Ps. Th. 87, 1: Exon. 32 a; Th. 100, 33; Cri. 1651: Ps. Th. 88, 3: Exon. 9 a; Th. 7, 5; Cri. 96: Cd. 25; Th. 32, 22; Gen. 507: Exon. 54 b; Th. 192, 18; Az. 108: Ps. Th. 131, 5: Exon. 120 b; Th. 463, 14; Hö. 70: Menol. Fox 381; Men. 192: Elen. Kmbl. 583; El. 292. II. *dear of price, precious, costly;* prĕtiōsus, magni æstimandus:—On ðisum gēre wæs corn swā dýre swā nān man ǽr ne gemunde, swā ðæt se sester hwǽtes eóde to lx penega, and eác furðor *in this year* [A. D. 1044] *corn was so dear as no man before remembered it, so that the sester of wheat went for sixty pence, and even more,* Chr. 1044; Erl. 168, 21: Exon. 94 b; Th. 354, 13; Reim. 45: Exon. 113 a; Th. 433, 12; Rä. 50, 6: Beo. Th. 4106; B. 2050: 4601; B. 2306: Beo. Th. 6089; B. 3048: 6253; B. 3131: Wanl. catal. 32, 16. v. deóre.

dyrfst, he dyrfþ *labourest, labours; 2nd and 3rd pers. pres. of* deorfan.

dýrling *a darling:*—Þeódnes dýrling Iohannes *John, the Lord's darling,* Menol. Fox 230; Men. 116. v. deórling.

dyrnan; *p.* de; *pp.* ed; *v. a.* [dyrne *hidden, secret*] *To hide, secrete, restrain;* occultāre, celāre, obscurāre, cohibēre:—Ðeáh hī hit ǽr swīðe dyrndon *though they had before quite hidden it,* Ors. 5, 10; Bos. 108, 15. Ne mihte Iosep hyne leng dyrnan *non se potĕrat ultra cohibēre Ioseph,* Gen. 45, 1. DER. be-dyrnan, bi-, ge-.

dyrne, es; *n. A secret;* secrētum:—Nelle ic ðē mīn dyrne gesecgan *I will not tell thee my secret,* Exon. 88 b; Th. 333, 11; Gn. Ex. 2.

DYRNE, dierne; *def.* se dyrna, seó, ðæt dyrne; *adj.* I. *close, hidden, secret, obscure;* occultus, secrētus, latens, obscūrus:—Ðā ðæt wīf geseah, ðæt hit [wīf] him næs dyrne *when the woman saw that she* [*the woman*] *was not hid from him,* Lk. Bos. 8, 47: Elen. Kmbl. 1443; El. 723: Menol. Fox 585; Gn. C. 62. Ne sceal dyrne sum wesan *nothing shall be secret,* Beo. Th. 548; B. 271. Ðýlæs ða smyltnesse ðæs dōmes gewemme oððe se dierna [dyrna MS. Cot.] æfst oððe tō hræd ierre *lest secret envy or too hasty anger corrupt the calmness of judgment,* Past. 13, 2; Hat. MS. 17 a, 12. Draca hord eft gesceát, dryhtsele dyrnne *the dragon darted back to his hoard, his secret hall,* Beo. Th. 4629; B. 2320. Hie hafaþ in siofan innan dyrne wūnde *they have within their mind a secret wound,* Frag. Kmbl. 57; Leás. 30. Ne sindon him dǽda dyrne *deeds are not hidden from him,* Exon. 23 a; Th. 65, 5; Cri. 1050: 39 b; Th. 130, 12; Gū. 437: 39 b; Th. 131, 32; Gū. 464. Ne dō ðū ne dyrne ðīne ða deóran bebodu *non abscondas a me mandāta tua,* Ps. Th. 118, 19: 134, 6. II. *dark, deceitful, evil;* tenebricōsus, subdŏlus:—Dyrne deófles boda wearp hine on wyrmes līc *the devil's dark messenger changed himself into a worm's body,* Cd. 24; Th. 31, 24; Gen. 490. Ðū mid ligenum fare þurh dyrne geþanc *thou mayest come with lies through evil design,* 26; Th. 34, 3; Gen. 532: Exon. 115 a; Th. 442, 13; Kl. 12. Sceal mǽg nealles inwit-net ōðrum bregdan dyrnum cræfte *a kinsman should not braid a net of treachery for another with deceitful craft,* Beo. Th. 4342; B. 2168. He to forþ gestōp dyrnan cræfte *he had stept forth with evil craft,* 4569; B. 2290. Ides sceal dyrne cræfte hire freónd gesēcan *the woman shall with deceitful art seek her friend,* Menol. Fox 547; Gn. C. 43. Dyrnra gāsta *of evil spirits,* Beo. Th. 2718; B. 1357: Exon. 71 a; Th. 264, 22; Jul. 368. [*Piers P. Chauc.* derne: *Laym.* deorne, derne *secret: Orm.* dærne *secret, hidden: O. Sax.* derni *secret: O. Frs.* dern, dren in compounds *occultus: O. H. Ger.* tarni *latens.*] DER. un-dyrne.

dyrne-geliger; *gen.* -geligre; *f.* [dyrne *secret,* geliger *a lying*] *A secret lying, adultery;* adultĕrium:—Heó hæfde dyrne-geligre *she* [*Eurydice*] *had secret adultery,* Ors. 3, 11; Bos. 73, 39: Ps. Spl. C. 72, 26. v. geliger.

dyrn-gewrit, es; *n.* [dyrne *secret,* gewrit *a writing*] *A secret writing, in the pl. books whose authors are not known, the apocryphal books;* occulta scripta, apocrypha, Cot. 10.

dyrn-licgan; *part.* -licgende, -licgynde [dyrne *secret,* licgan *to lie*] *To lie secretly, to fornicate;* fornicāri:—Dyrnlicgynde *fornicāti sunt,* Ps. Spl. C. 105, 36.

dyrodine, derodine? *Scarlet dye* or *colour;* coccus = κόκκος:—On ðæs sacerdes hrægle wæs dyrodine twegera bleó *on the priest's raiment there was twice-dyed scarlet,* Past. 14, 6; Hat. MS. 18 b, 1. Ðæt hrægl wæs beboden ðæt scolde bión geworht of purpuran and of tweóbleóm derodine *superhumerale ex purpura et bis tincto cocco fieri præcipitur,* 14, 4; Hat. MS. 18 a, 3.

dyrre *durst,* Beo. Th. 2763; B. 1379; *subj. pres. of* durran.

dýrre *dearer, more precious;* pretiōsior, carior, *comparative of* dýre II:—Forðonðe hī sint dýrran ðonne ǽnige ōðre *because they are dearer than any others,* Ors. 5, 2; Bos. 101, 25.

dýrsian *to honour, glorify.* DER. ge-dýrsian.

dyrst, e; *f. Tribulation;* tribŭlātio. DER. ge-dyrst.

dyrste-līce; *adv. Boldly;* audacter:—Dyrstelīce *audācĭter,* Ælfc. Gr. 38; Som. 41, 66. Iosep dyrstelīce in to Pilate eóde *Ioseph audacter introīvit ad Pilātum,* Mk. Jun. 15, 43. DER. ge-dyrstelīce.

dyrstig; *adj. Daring, bold, rash;* audax, ausus:—Ðeós and ðis dyrstige *audax,* Ælfc. Gr. 9, 60; Som. 13, 41. Dyrstig oððe gedyrstlǽht *ausus,* 41; Som. 43, 29. Hū wǽre ðū dyrstig ofstician bār *quomŏdo fuisti ausus jugŭlāre aprum?* Coll. Monast. Th. 22, 13: Bd. 2, 6; S. 508, 25, note: Nicod. 12; Thw. 6, 23. Ðeáh ðe he dyrstig wǽre *though he were daring,* Beo. Th. 5669; B. 2838. DER. ge-dyrstig, unge-.

dyrstigan; *p.* ede; *pp.* ed *To dare.* v. ge-dyrstigan.

dyrstig-līce; *adv. Boldly;* audacter, Mk. Bos. 15, 43. v. dyrste-līce.

dyrstignes, dyrstnes, -nyss, e; *f. Boldness, presumption, arrogance, rashness;* audācia, temĕrĭtas:—Sió gedyrstignes [MS. Cot. dyrstignes] his mōdes *præsumptio spirĭtus,* Past. 13, 2; Hat. MS. 17 a, 15. Ðæt ðīn mōd ne beó ahafen mid dyrstignysse [dyrstnysse, Nat. S. Greg. Els. p. 39, note 1] *that thy mind be not lifted up with arrogance,* Homl. Th. ii. 132, 4. DER. ge-dyrstignes.

dyrsting-panne, an; *f. A frying-pan;* sartāgo, frixōrium, Ælfc. Gl. 25; Som. 60, 59; Wrt. Voc. 25, 1. v. hyrsting-panne.

dyrst-lǽcan; *p.* -lǽhte; *pp.* -lǽht *To dare;* audēre:—Ðæt nān ne dyrstlǽce ceósan hlāfordas of lǽwedan mannan *that none dare to choose lords of laical men,* Chr. 796; Ing. 82, 26. DER. gedyrst-lǽcan, lǽcan.

dyrst-līc; *adj. Bold;* audax. v. un-dyrstlīc.

dyrstnys, -nyss *arrogance,* Nat. S. Greg. Els. p. 39, note 1. v. dyrstignes.

dýr-wurþe; *comp. m.* -wurþra; *f. n.* -wurþre; *adj. Of great worth* or *value, precious;* prĕtiōsus:—Seó ðe dýrwurþre wǽre eallum māþmum *quæ omnĭbus ornamentis prĕtiōsior est,* Bd. 2, 12; S. 514, 40. v. deór-wyrþe.

dyseg *foolish,* Bt. Met. Fox 19, 57; Met. 19, 29. v. dysig.

dysegian, dysigan, dysian; *part.* dysigende, dysiende; he dysegaþ; *p.* ede, ode; *pp.* ed, od; *v. intrans.* [dysig *foolish*]. I. *to be foolish, act foolishly, err;* ineptīre, errāre:—Ða, dysiende, wēnaþ ðætte ðæt þing sié ǽlces weorþscipes wyrþe *they, foolish, think that the thing is worthy of all estimation,* Bt. 24, 4; Fox 86, 9. He dysegaþ, se ðe wile sǽd ōþfæstan ðām drīum furum *he does foolishly, who will sow seed in the dry furrows,* 5, 2; Fox 10, 30. Ðæt ða dysegien *that they are foolish,* 24, 4; Fox 86, 9, MS. Bod. Ðæt hī on heortan hyge dysegedon *hi errant corde,* Ps. Th. 94, 10. II. *to talk foolishly, blaspheme;* blasphēmāre:—Manega ōðre þing hīg him to cwǽdon dysigende *alia multa blasphēmantes dicēbant in eum,* Lk. Bos. 22, 65. He dysegaþ *blasphēmat,* Mk. Bos. 2, 7.

dyselīc *foolish,* Bd. 4, 27; S. 604, 2. v. dys-līc.

dysg; *adj. Foolish, weak, ignorant;* stultus, ignorans:—Dysgum monnum *by ignorant men,* Bt. 33, 4; Fox 130, 28. v. dysig.

dysgung, e; *f. Silliness, foolishness;* stultĭtia:—Wið dysgunge *against foolishness,* L. M. 1, 66; Lchdm. ii. 142, 1.

dysi *folly,* Bt. 36, 1; Fox 172, 8. v. dysig.

dysi *stupid,* Bt. Met. Fox 28, 130; Met. 28, 65. v. dysig; *adj.*

dysian; *part.* dysiende *to be foolish,* Bt. 24, 4; Fox 86, 9. v. dysegian.

DYSIG, dyseg, dysg, disig, disg, dysi; *adj.* DIZZY, *foolish, unwise, stupid;* stultus, insipiens, insānus:—Dysig nā ongyt ðās ðing *stultus non intellĭgit hæc,* Ps. Spl. 91, 6. He biþ swā dysig and swā ungewiss *he is so foolish and so ignorant,* Bt. 11, 2; Fox 34, 25. Ða dysige men *foolish men,* 33, 3; Fox 126, 8. Ða dysegan sint on gedwolan wordene *the foolish are in error,* Bt. Met. Fox 19, 57; Met. 19, 29. Hīg sint dysegran *they are more foolish,* 19, 82; Met. 19, 41. Cyninga dysegast *the most foolish of kings,* 15, 22; Met. 15, 11. Dysegum neátum *jumentis insipientĭbus,* Ps. Th. 48, 11. Dysgum monnum *by unwise men,* Bt. 33, 4; Fox 130, 28: Bt. Met. Fox 28, 130; Met. 28, 65: Deut. 32, 21. [*Plat.* dusig, dösig, düsig *giddy: O. Frs.* dusig *giddy: Dut.* duizelig *giddy: Ger.* dusig, däsig *stupid;* duselig *giddy: O. H. Ger.* tusig *stultus, hĕbes.*]

dysig, disig, dysi, es; *n. An error, ignorance, folly, foolishness;* error, stultĭtia, insānia, insĭpientia:—Ðæt is hefig dysig *that is a grievous folly*, Bt. Met. Fox 19, 1; Met. 19, 1: Bt. 32, 3; Fox 118, 7. Ðē līcode his dysig and his unrihtwīsnes *his folly and his injustice pleased thee*, 27, 2; Fox 96, 22. Dysi and unrihtwīsnes nū rīcsaþ ofer ealne middaneard *folly and wickedness now reign over all the mid-earth*, 36, 1; Fox 172, 8. Fægniaþ irmingas hiera āgnes dysiges and hearmes *the wretches rejoice at their own folly and sorrow*, Past. 35, 4; Hat. MS. 46 a, 14: Bt. 36, 5; Fox 180, 6. Ulcinienses and Thrusci ða folc forneáh ealle forwurdon for heora āgnum dysige *the Volscians and the Etruscans nearly all perished through their own folly*, Ors. 4, 3; Bos. 79, 43: Bt. 18, 2; Fox 64, 4. Ne lōcaþ nǣfre to īdelnesse, ne to leásungum, ne to dysige *non respexit in vanĭtātes, et insānias falsas*, Ps. Th. 39, 4. Mīne wūnda rotedan and fūledon for mīnum dysige *computruērunt et deteriorāvērunt cicatrīces meæ, a făcie insĭpientiæ meæ*, 37, 5. Abigall forswigode ðæt dysig hiere fordruncnan hlāfordes *Abigail concealed the folly of her drunken lord*, Past. 40, 4; Hat. MS. 55 a, 12, 15: 45, 2; Hat. MS. 64 b, 25. Līfes weard of mōde abrit ðæt micle dysig *the guardian of life removes from his mind that great ignorance*, Bt. Met. Fox 28, 156; Met. 28, 78: 19, 77; Met. 19, 39: Bt. 39, 3; Fox 216, 5: Past. 30; Hat. MS. 39 a, 5. Ðeáh ic mid dysige þurhdrifen wǣre *though I was thoroughly penetrated with folly*, Elen. Kmbl. 1410; El. 707: Ps. Th. 75, 4. We sinna fela didon for ūre disige *we committed many sins through our foolishness*, Hy. 7, 107; Hy. Grn. ii. 289, 107.

dysig-dōm, es; *m. Foolishness, ignorance;* impĕrītia, Pref. R. Conc.

dysig-nes, dysi-nes, -ness, e; *f. Folly*, DIZZINESS, *blasphemy;* stultĭtia, blasphēmia:—Wǣron heó mid elreordre dysignesse onblāwne *inflāti erant barbăra stultĭtia*, Bd. 2, 5; S. 507, 13. Of manna heortan yfele geþancas cumaþ, dysinessa *de corde hŏmĭnum malæ cogĭtātiones procēdunt, blasphēmia*, Mk. Bos. 7, 22.

dys-lic, dyse-līc; *def.* se -līca, seó, ðæt -līce; *adj. Foolish, stupid;* stultus:—Hit biþ swīðe dyslīc ðæt se man beorce oððe blǣte *it is very foolish that the man bark or bleat*, Ælfc. Gr. 22; Som. 24, 11: Bd. 1, 27; S. 493, 11. Oft ge dyslīce dǣd gefremedon *often ye have done a foolish deed*, Elen. Kmbl. 771; El. 386. From ðæm līfe ðæs dyselīcan gewunon *a vita stultæ consuetūdĭnis*, Bd. 4, 27; S. 604, 2. On dyslīcum geswincum *in foolish labours*, Past. 18, 2; Hat. MS. 26 a, 11.

dys-lice; *adv. Foolishly;* stulte:—Se Godes cunnaþ ful dyslīce *he tempteth God very foolishly*, Salm. Kmbl. 455; Sal. 228. Dyslīce ðū dydest *stulte opĕrātus es*, Gen. 31, 28.

dystig; *adj.* DUSTY; pulvĕrŭlentus, Cot. 183.

dyþhomar *papyrus* = πάπυρος:—[Nim] dyþhomar [*take*] *papyrus*, L. M. 1, 41; Lchdm. ii. 106, 17. v. duþhamor.

DYTTAN; *p.* de; *pp.* ed *To* DIT, *close* or *shut up;* opprĭmĕre, occlūdĕre, obtūrāre:—Ongunnon ða Farisēi his mūþ dyttan *cœpĕrunt Pharisæi os ejus opprĭmĕre*, Lk. Bos. 11, 53. Anlīc nædran seó dytteþ hyre eáran *secundum similitūdĭnem serpentis obtūrantis aures suas*, Ps. Th. 57, 4. [*Laym.* dutte, *p. pl. stopt: Orm.* dittenn *to shut, stop: O. Nrs.* ditta *rimas occlūdĕre*, Rask Hald.] DER. for-dyttan.

dyxsas *dishes, platters*, Mt. Foxe and Jun. 23, 25, = discas; *pl. acc. of* disc.

E

A. Anglo-Saxon words, containing the short or unaccented vowel *e*, are often represented by modern English words of the same meaning, having the sound of *e* in *net, met;* as, Nett, bedd, weddian, hell, well, denn, fenn, webb, ende. **2.** the short *e* in Anglo-Saxon generally comes (1) before a double consonant; as, Nebb, weccan, tellan, weddian: (2) before any two consonants; as, Twentig, sendan, bernan: (3) before one or two consonants, when followed by a long or by a final vowel; as, Sele, henne. **3.** e is often contracted from ea; as, Ceaster and cester *a burgh, fortified town;* eahta and ehta *eight.*

B. Words containing the long or accented Anglo-Saxon *ē* are very frequently represented by English terms of the same signification, with the sound of *e* in *heel;* as, Rēc, mēd, hēl, cwēn, gēs, fēt, tēþ, hēdan, fēdan, mētan *to meet.* Some remarks on the accented *ē* in Grimm's Deutsche Grammatik, 2nd Edit. Göttingen, small 8vo. 1822, vol. i. pp. 229, 230: 3rd Edit. small 8vo. 1840, vol. i. pp. 361, 362, may be found useful, and are especially recommended to the student of Anglo-Saxon. **2.** it is, however, difficult to say when the *ē* is long in Anglo-Saxon, but it may be useful to remember, the *ē* is often long before the single consonants *l, m, n, r, c, d, f, g, s, t,* and *þ;* as, in hēl *a heel*, fēlan *to feel*, dēman *to deem, think*, fēnix *a phœnix*, hēr *here*, gēs *geese*, fēt *feet*, fēdan *to feed*, tēþ *teeth*, bēc *books*, blēgen *a blain*, drēfan *to trouble.*

C. The Runic ᛖ not only stands for the vowel *e*, but also for the name of the letter in Anglo-Saxon, eh *a war-horse.* v. eh *a war-horse*, and **RŪN.**

-e, in the termination of nouns, denotes a person; as, Hyrde, es; *m. A shepherd, from* hyrdan *to guard.* The vowel *-e* is also used to form nouns denoting inanimate objects; as, Cȳle, es; *m. Cold:* cwide, es; *m. A saying, testament:* brice, es; *m. A breach:* wlite, es; *m. Beauty.* These are mostly derived from verbs, and are masculine, but when derived from adjectives they are feminine; as, Rihtwīse, an; *f. Justice.*

-e is the termination of derivative adjectives; as, Wyrðe *worthy*, from wyrþ *worth:* forþgenge *forthcoming, increasing.*

-e is also the usual letter by which adverbs are formed from adjectives ending in a consonant; as, Rihte *rightly*, sōþlīce *truly*, yfele *badly.*

ē; *dat.* or *inst. to* or *from a river:*—Of ðære ē Indus *from the river Indus*, Ors. 1, 1; Bos. 16, 25; *dat. sing.* v. eá.

EÁ; *often indeclinable in the sing, but* eás *is sometimes found in gen; and* ē, ǣ, eǣ *in dat; pl. nom. acc.* eá, eán; *gen.* eá; *dat.* eáum, eám, eán; *f:* ǣ; *indecl. f. Running water, a stream, river, water;* flŭvius, flūmen, torrens, aqua:—Eá of dūne *water from the hill*, Menol. Fox 520; Gn. C. 30. Seó feorþe eá ys gehāten Eufrates *flŭvius quartus est Euphrātes*, Gen. 2, 14: Bd. 3, 24; S. 556, 34, 46. On twā healfe ðære eás *on the two sides of the river*, Chr. 896; Th. 172, 39, col. 1. On ōðre healfe ðære eá [MS. L. eás] *on the other side of the river*, Ors. 1, 1; Bos. 20, 3. Be ðære eá ōfrun *by the banks of the river*, Gen. 41, 3: Ors. 1, 3; Bos. 27, 28: 2, 4; Bos. 44, 13. Be ðære eá *by the river*, Chr. 896; Th. 172, 35, col. 2. Ða eá oferfaran wolde *would go over the river*, Ors. 2, 4; Bos. 44, 2. On ðæm lande syndon twā mycele eá Idaspes and Arbis *in the country are two great rivers, Hydaspes and Arabis*, Ors. 1, 1; Bos. 16, 34. Lǣt streámas weallan, eá in flēde *let streams well out, a river in flood*, Andr. Kmbl. 3006; An. 1506. Ðās synd ða feówer eán of ānum wyllspringe *these are the four streams from one well-spring*, Ælfc. T. 25, 19. He hī upforlēt on feówer hund eá and on syxtig *he divided it into four hundred and sixty streams*, Ors. 2, 4; Bos. 44, 9. Betweox ðām twām eáum *between the two rivers*, Ors. 5, 2; Bos. 102, 34. Ofer ðām eám *super flumĭna*, Ps. Th. 23, 2. Betweoh ðǣm twām eán *between the two rivers*, Ors. 1, 1; Bos. 16, 28. On feówer eán *into four streams*, Gen. 2, 10. [*Laym.* æ, *f: Orm.* æ: *O. Sax.* aha, *f: O. Frs.* a, e, *f: Ger.* aa, *f. name of rivers* or *brooks;* -ach suffix of river-names: *M. H. Ger.* ahe, *f: O. H. Ger.* aha, *f: Goth.* ahwa, *f: Dan.* aa, *m. f: Swed.* å, *f: Icel.* á, *f: Lat.* aqua.] v. ǣg-, ēg-, ēh-, īg-.

eá, eáw *oh! alas! commonly* eá-lā; *interjec.* q. v.

eác; *prep. dat. With, in addition to, besides;* cum, præter:—Gif ðū sunu āge, oððe swǣsne mǣg, oððe freónd ǣnigne eác ðissum idesum, alǣde of ðysse leód-byrig *if thou have a son, or beloved kinsman, or any friend with* [*in addition to*] *these damsels, lead* [*them*] *from this city*, Cd. 116; Th. 150, 31; Gen. 2500. Ðæt gēr wæs ðæt sixte eác feówertigum *that year was the six and fortieth*, i. e. *the sixth with the fortieth*, or *the sixth increased with forty*, Bd. 1, 3; S. 475, 16: 1, 13; S. 481, 35, 39: Bt. Met. Fox 1, 87; Met. 1, 44. DER. to-eác. v. eác; *conj.*

EÁC; *conj.* I. EKE, *also, likewise, moreover, and;* etiam, quoque, et:—Abeád eác Adame ēce Drihten *the Lord eternal announced also to Adam*, Cd. 43; Th. 57, 8; Gen. 925. Eác we ðæt gefrugnon *we also have heard that*, Exon. 12 a; Th. 19, 15; Cri. 301: Cd. 174; Th. 220, 8; Dan. 68: Beo. Th. 195; B. 97. Hondum slōgun, folmum areahtum and fystum eác *struck with their hands, with outstretched palms and with fists also*, Exon. 24 a; Th. 69, 24; Cri. 1125: 9 b; Th. 9, 18; Cri. 136: Cd. 69; Th. 82, 35; Gen. 1372. And ge sceolon eác þweán eówer ǣlc ōðres fēt *and likewise ye ought to wash one another's feet*, Jn. Bos. 13, 14, 9. Ic eów secge, eác māran ðonne wītegan *I say unto you, and more than a prophet*, Mt. Bos. 11, 9. Adam hæfde nigen hund wintra and þrītig eác *Adam had nine hundred winters, and thirty also*, Cd. 55; Th. 68, 31; Gen. 1126: 58; Th. 71, 3; Gen. 1165. Fīf and syxtig wintra hæfde and eác þreó hund *he had five and sixty winters, and also three hundred*, 62; Th. 74, 4; Gen. 1217: 74, 34; Gen. 1232. Ne his wordum eác woldan gelȳfan *et non credĭdērunt in verbis ejus*, Ps. Th. 105, 20. II. eác hwæðre, hwæðre eác *Nevertheless, however;* nihilōmĭnus:—Eác hwæðre ceald lyft is gemenged *the cold air nevertheless is mingled*, Bt. Met. Fox 20, 156; Met. 20, 78. Wæs me hwæðre eác lāþ *nevertheless it was to me unpleasant*, Exon. 100 b; Th. 380, 23; Rä. 1, 12. **2.** eác swilce, swylce eác *So also, also, moreover, very like, even so, as if;* parimŏdo, tamquam:—Ða apostoli gesetton eác swilce lārspell to ðām leódscipum ðe to geleáfan bugon *the apostles moreover gave instructions to the nations submitting to the faith*, Ælfc. T. 27, 20. Ðā wæs eác swilce se scucca him betwux *there was also the devil between them*, Th. Anlct. 37, 9: Ps. Th. 55, 4: 108, 29. Eác swylce heó sprecende sȳ to eallum mancynne *as if it spoke to all mankind*, Ors. 2, 4; Bos. 44, 34. Wīte þoliaþ swilce eác ða biteran rēcas *they suffer torments, so also the bitter reeks*, Cd. 18; Th. 21, 17; Gen. 325: Judth. 12; Thw. 26, 20, 25, 30; Jud. 338, 344, 349: Exon. 120 b; Th. 462, 5; Hö. 47: 34 b; Th. 112, 1; Gū. 137. Swylce grūndas eác *so also the abyss*, 10 a; Th. 9, 35; Cri. 145. **3.** ge eác swylce *Quin et:*—Eall ðæt he on ānweald onfēng ge eác swylce monige Brytta eáland Angelcynnes rīce underþeódde *quæ omnia sub ditiōne accēpit quin et Mevanias insŭlas impĕrio subjŭgāvit Anglōrum*, Bd. 2, 9; S. 510, 16. **4.** eác swā *So also, even so, likewise:*—Swā ðeós world eall gewīteþ, and eác swā some, đe hire on wurdon atydrede *so all this world goes away, and even so those who were born upon it*, Elen. Grm. 1278. Se is eác wealdend ealra đara đe đǽr in wuniaþ ungesewenlīcra, and eác swā same đara đe we eágum on lōciaþ *he is also the ruler of all those creatures which therein dwell invisible, and even so of those that we behold with our eyes*, Bt. Met. Fox 11, 10; Met. 11, 5: 11, 19; Met. 11, 10: 11, 171; Met. 11, 86. Sió gesceádwīsnes sceal đære wilnunge waldan and irsunge eác swā *the reason ought to govern the will and the anger likewise*, 20, 398; Met. 20, 199: 20, 384; Met. 20, 192. [*Wyc.* eke: *Chauc.* eek, eke: *R. Glouc.* ek: *Laym.* æc, ac, ec, eke, æke: *Plat.* ook: *O. Sax.* ōk *etiam, quoque*: *Frs.* ak, eak: *O. Frs.* ak, oke *also, and*: *Dut.* ook: *Ger.* auch *etiam, quoque*: *M. H. Ger.* ouch: *O. H. Ger.* ouh *etiam*: *Goth.* auk *because*: *Dan.* og *and*: *Swed.* och *and*; ock *also*: *Icel.* og *atque, et*: *O. Nrs.* auk, ōk *etiam.*] v. ēc, ǽc.

EÁCA, an; *m. An addition*, EEKING, *increase, usury, advantage;* additāmentum:—Đeáh mīn bān and blōd būtū geweorþen eorþan to eácan *though my bones and blood both become an increase to the earth*, Exon. 38 a; Th. 125, 10; Gū. 352. Þincþ đē lytel eáca đīnra gesǽlþa *does it seem to thee little addition to thy felicities?* Bt. 20; Fox 72, 12. Is witena gehwām wōpes eáca *there is increase of weeping to every man*, Salm. Kmbl. 922; Sal. 460. Ic [Ælfrīc Abbod] geset hæbbe feówertig lārspella, and sumne eácan đǽrto *I [Abbot Ælfric] have composed forty sermons, and some addition thereto*, Ælfc. T. 27, 18. Gif he hæfþ sumne eácan yfeles *if he has some addition of evil*, Bt. 38, 3; Fox 200, 19. For đæs yfles eácan *for the addition of evil*, 200, 21. Ne gehēne đū hine mid đȳ eácan *oppress him not with the usury*, L. Alf. 35; Th. i. 52, 23; *neque humĭlia illum ūsūra tua*, Wilk. 31, 45. ¶ To eácan *besides, moreover*:—Đæt wæs to eácan ōđrum unarīmedum yflum *that was besides other innumerable evils*: literally, *in* or *for, addition to, etc.* Bt. 1; Fox 2, 11. To eácan himselfum *besides himself*: literally, *in addition to*, Bt. 26, 2; Fox 92, 20. Ōđer is to eácan andgete *the second is moreover manifest*, Exon. 26 a; Th. 76, 21; Cri. 1243. DER. mægen-eáca, ofer-.

EÁCAN; *p.* eóc, *pl.* eócon; *pp.* eácen, ēcen *To be increased, augmented, enlarged, indued;* augēri, increscĕre:—Adam wearþ gāste eácen *Adam was with spirit indued*, Cd. 48; Th. 61, 23; Gen. 1001: Exon. 102 b; Th. 388, 26; Rä. 6, 13. Eácen feoh *increased cattle*, Cd. 74; Th. 91, 25; Gen. 1517. Heó wæs mago-timbre be Abrahame eácen worden *she had been increased with offspring by Abraham*, Cd. 102; Th. 135, 2; Gen. 2236: 123; Th. 157, 14; Gen. 2606: 132; Th. 167, 15; Gen. 2766. Đæt þurh bearnes gebyrd brȳd eácen wearþ *that through child-bearing the bride was increased*, Exon. 8 b; Th. 3, 19; Cri. 38. Heó ongieten hæfde đæt heó eácen wæs *she had discovered that she was pregnant*, Exon. 100 a; Th. 378, 4; Deór. 11. Ælmihtig eácenne gāst in sefan sende *the Almighty sent an enlarged spirit into his soul*, Cd. 198; Th. 246, 27; Dan. 485. Is dōhtor mīn eácen, upliden *my daughter is magnified, exalted*, Exon. 109 a; Th. 416, 13; Rä. 34, 11. [*Wyc.* echen, eche, eeche: *Chauc.* eche: *R. Glouc.* eche: *Orm.* ekenn: *Scot.* eik: *O. Sax.* ōkian, ōcōn: *O. Frs.* aka: *O. H. Ger.* auhōn: *Goth.* aukan: *Dan.* öge: *Swed.* öka: *Icel.* auka: *Lat.* aug-eo: *Grk.* αὔξ-ω: *Lith.* aug-u *to increase.*]

eácen; *adj.* [*pp. of* eácan] *Increased, great, vast, powerful;* auctus, magnus, pŏtens, grăvidus:—Eácne fuglas *the teeming fowls*, Cd. 98; Th. 130, 12; Gen. 2158. Se wæs æđele and eácen *who was noble and vigorous*, Beo. Th. 398; B. 198: Exon. 10 b; Th. 13, 20; Cri. 205. Eald sweord eácen *an old, powerful sword*, Beo. Th. 3330; B. 1663: 4286; B. 2140. Eácne eardas *the vast dwellings*, 3246; B. 1621. Insende eácne egesan *he sent in mighty terror*, Salm. Kmbl. 947; Sal. 473. Cræfte eácen *great in skill*, Exon. 128 a; Th. 492, 26; Rä. 81, 21: 14; Rä. 81, 15: 103 a; Th. 391, 21; Rä. 10, 8. Nǽron ge swā eácne mōd-geþances *ye were not so powerful in mental thought*, Cd. 179; Th. 224, 14; Dan. 136. DER. feorh-eácen, mægen-. v. ēcen.

eácen-cræftig; *adj. Exceedingly strong;* vălidus, pollens, ingens:—Wæs đæt yrfe eácencræftig *that heritage was exceedingly strong*, Beo. Th. 6095; B. 3051: 4549; B. 2280.

eá-cerse, an; *f. Water*-CRESS; nasturtium aquātĭcum:—Eácersan getrifula odđe geseóþ on buteran *bruise or seethe water-cress in butter*, L. M. 1, 38; Lchdm. ii. 94, 4.

eácnian, eácnigan, eánian; *part.* -iende, -igende; *p.* ode, ade *To increase, to be augmented, to become pregnant, to bring forth;* augēri, concipĕre, parturīre:—Ellen eácnade *the fortitude increased*, Exon. 94 b; Th. 353, 51; Reim. 31: Ps. Spl. 7, 15. Eácniende wīf *muliĕrem prægnantem*, Ex. 21, 22. DER. ge-eácnian, to-ge-. v. eánian.

eácnigende; *part. Bringing forth;* partŭriens:—Đǽr sārnessa swā swā eácnigendes wīfes *ibi dolōres ut partŭrientis*, Ps. Lamb. 47, 8; *part. of* eácnigan. v. eácnian.

eácnung, e; *f. Increase, a conception;* conceptio:—Hū đū eácnunge onfēnge bearnes þurh gebyrde *how thou didst receive increase through child-bearing*, Exon. 9 a; Th. 5, 26; Cri. 75. DER. bearn-eácnung, ge-.

EÁD, es; *n. A possession, riches, prosperity, happiness, bliss;* possessio, ŏpes, dīvĭtiæ, prospĕrĭtas, felīcĭtas, beatĭtūdo:—Se him đæt eád gefēþ *who gives the happiness to it*, Exon. 60 b: Th. 220, 13; Ph. 319. Se rinc ageaf eorþcunde eád *the prince gave up earthly happiness*, Cd. 79; Th. 98, 8; Gen. 1627. Niótan đæs eádes *to have enjoyment of the bliss*, Cd. 21; Th. 26, 5; Gen. 402. [*O. Sax.* ōd, *n. estate, wealth*: *O. H. Ger.* ōt, *n. prædium*: *Icel.* auđr, *m. riches, wealth.*]

eád; *adj. Rich, wealthy, blessed, happy;* dīves, opŭlentus, beātus:—Ic đē eád mǽg gecȳđe *I will shew thee the blessed virgin*, Exon. 70 b; Th. 263, 19; Jul. 352: Cd. 151; Th. 189, 17; Exod. 186.

eádan; *p.* eód, *pl.* eódon; *pp.* eáden *To give, concede, grant;* dăre, concēdĕre:—Swā him eáden wæs *as was granted to them*, Bt. Met. Fox 31, 18; Met. 31, 9. Is æfestum eáden *it [the soul] is given to envy*, Exon. 118 b; Th. 455, 7; Hy. 4, 46. Ac me eáden wearþ *but it was granted to me*, 10 b; Th. 13, 10; Cri. 200.

Eádbald, -bold, es; *m.* [eád *happy*, bald *bold*] *Eadbald, son of Ethelbert, king of Kent. He succeeded his father to the kingdom of Kent in* A. D. 616, *and died in* A. D. 640:—Hēr Æđelbryht Contwara cyning forþfērde, and Eádbald his sunu fēng to rīce, se forlēt his fulluht and leofode on hǽđenum þeáwe, swā đæt he hæfde his fæder lāfe to wīfe *in this year* [A. D. 616] *Ethelbert, king of the Kentish people, died, and Eadbald his son succeeded to the kingdom, who disregarded his baptism, and lived in heathen manner, so that he had his father's widow to wife*, Chr. 616; Th. 40, 2-9: Bd. 2, 5; S. 506, 36. Hēr Eádbald [Eádbold, col. 2] Cantwara cining forþfērde, se wæs cining xxiv wintra *in this year* [A. D. 640] *Eadbald, king of the Kentish people, died, who was king twenty-four years*, Chr. 640; Th. 47, 20, col. 1: Bd. 3, 8; S. 531, 6.

eádeg *happy*, Cd. 72; Th. 89, 6; Gen. 1476. v. eádig.

eadesa *an adze*, Ps. Surt. 73, 6. v. adesa.

Eádes burh; *gen.* burge; *dat.* byrig; *f.* [*Hunt.* Edesbirh: *Brom.* Edesbury] EDDESBURY, *Cheshire*; loci nomen in agro Cestriensi:—Æđelflǽd Myrcna hlǽfdige đa burh getimbrede æt Eádes byrig *Æthelfled, lady of the Mercians, built the fortress at Eddesbury*, Chr. 913; Th. 186, 30, col. 2.

eád-fruma, an; *m. Author of happiness;* beatitūdĭnis auctor:—Ēce eádfruma *the eternal author of happiness*, Exon. 15 b; Th. 33, 27; Cri. 532: Andr. Kmbl. 2585; An. 1294.

eádga, eádge *happy*, Cd. 90; Th. 113, 10; Gen. 1885: Exon. 67 a; Th. 249, 1; Jul. 105. v. eádig.

Eádgār, es; *m.* [eád *happy*, gār *spear*] *Edgar, second son of Edmund, and grandson of Alfred the Great. Edgar, in* A. D. 955, *succeeded to the kingdom of Mercia; and, at the death of his brother Eadwig, in* A. D. 959, *to the kingdoms of Wessex and Northumbria, over which he reigned sixteen years. He was, therefore, king for twenty years, from* A. D. 955-975:—Hēr, A. D. 955, Eádgār fēng to Myrcena rīce *here Edgar succeeded to the kingdom of Mercia*, Chr. 955; Erl. 119, 32. Hēr, A. D. 959, forþfērde Eádwīg cing, and Eádgār his brōđor fēng to rīce, ǽgđer ge on West-Seaxum, ge on Myrcum, ge on Norþhymbrum *here king Eadwig died, and Edgar his brother succeeded to the kingdom, as well of the West-Saxons as of the Mercians, and of the Northumbrians*, Chr. 959; Th. 216, 10-15, col. 2. Hēr, A. D. 975, Eádgār cing forþfērde *here king Edgar died*, Chr. 975; Th. 227, 19, col. 3.

eádgian; *p.* ode; *pp.* od [eád *bliss*] *To bless, enrich;* beatĭfĭcāre, Exon. 8 a; Th. 2, 16; Cri. 20.

eád-giefu, e; *f. Gift of blessedness;* beatitūdĭnis dōnum:—Đæt hī ēce eádgiefe ānforlēton *that they forsook the eternal gift of blessedness*, Exon. 73 a; Th. 272, 20; Jul. 502: 74 a; Th. 276, 8; Jul. 563. v. eád-gifu.

eád-gifa, -giefa, an; *m. Giver of prosperity* or *happiness;* prospĕrĭtātis *vel* beatitūdĭnis dātor:—Engla eádgifa *bliss-giver of angels*, Andr. Kmbl. 147; An. 74: 901; An. 451: Exon. 15 b; Th. 34, 22; Cri. 546.

eád-gifu, -giefu, e; *f. Blessed grace, gift of blessedness;* beāta grātia, beatitūdĭnis dōnum:—Đæt đū me ne lǽte of lofe hweorfan đīnre eádgife *that thou let me not turn from the praise of thy blessed grace*, Exon. 69 b; Th. 259, 2; Jul. 276.

eád-hrēđig; *adj. Happy, blessed;* beātus:—Eádhrēđig mǽg *O blessed maiden!* Exon. 69 b; Th. 257, 34; Jul. 257. Eádhrēđige mǽgþ *the blessed maidens*, Judth. 11; Thw. 23, 22; Jud. 135. v. eáþ-hrēđig.

eádi- *happy*. v. Ps. Th. 64, 14, *in* eádig-līc, eádi-līc.

eádig, eádeg; *adj.* [eád *happiness, prosperity;* ig] *Happy, blessed, prosperous, fortunate, rich, perfect;* beātus, fēlix, gaudii plēnus, faustus, abundans, opŭlentus, dīves:—Se eádega wer *the happy man*, Cd. 72; Th. 89, 6; Gen. 1476. Se eádga *the blessed [man]*, 90; Th. 113, 10; Gen. 1885. Seó eádige *the blessed [maid]*, Elen. Grm. 618. Seó eádge *the blessed [maid]*, Exon. 67 a; Th. 249, 1; Jul. 105. Forđon se biþ eádig *therefore he shall be blessed*, Cd. 220; Th. 283, 13; Sat. 304. Eádig on eorþan *rich on earth*, 98; Th. 129, 21; Gen. 2147: Exon. 22 b; Th. 63, 3; Cri. 1014. Ōđer biþ unlǽde on eorþan, ōđer biþ eádig *the one is miserable on earth, the other fortunate*, Salm. Kmbl. 732; Sal. 365. Earm ic wæs on ēđle đīnum đæt đū wurde eádig on mīnum *I was poor in thy residence that thou mightest be rich in mine*, Exon. 29 b; Th. 91, 25; Cri. 1497: 30 b; Th. 95, 8; Cri. 1554. Æđeling eádig *a prosperous noble*, Beo. Th. 2454; B. 1225. Eádig and ānmōd *blessed and steadfast*, Andr. Kmbl. 107; An. 54: Exon. 43 b; Th. 146, 29;

Gū. 717. Eádig on elne *perfect in courage*, 47 b; Th. 163, 25; Gū. 999. To ðissum eádigan hām *to this happy home*, Cd. 228; Th. 306, 7; Sat. 660. Habbaþ eádigne bearn ealle ymbfangen *all have encircled the blessed child*, 216; Th. 273, 29; Sat. 144. Eádigra gedryht *the company of the blessed*, Exon. 32 a; Th. 101, 26; Cri. 1664. Eádgest, *superl*:—Ðǣr he to ðām eádgestum ǣrest mæþleþ *where he first shall speak to those most blessed*, Exon. 27 b; Th. 82, 13; Cri. 1338. [*Laym.* ædie, eædi, eadi, edi *blessed, beautiful*: *Orm.* ædig *blessed*: *O. Sax.* ōdag *rich, happy*: *O. H. Ger.* ōtag *dīves*: *Goth.* audags *blessed*: *Icel.* auðigr, auðugr *rich, opulent.*] DER. ceáp-eádig, dōm-, efen-, eft-, hrēþ-, hwæt-, sige-, sigor-, tīr-.

eádigan *to bless, enrich*; beatificāre, App. Scint. Lye. v. eádgian.

eádig-lic, eádi-līc; *adj. Happy, prosperous*; prosper, abundans, faustus:—Biþ ðæt ǣrende eádiglīcre *that errand will be more prosperous*, Exon. 100 a; Th. 375, 1; Seel. 131. Cumaþ eádilīc wæstm on wangas *convalles abundābunt frumento*, Ps. Th. 64, 14.

eádig-līce; *adv. Happily*; felīce:—Ða drihtguman lifdon eádiglīce *the retainers lived happily*, Beo. Th. 200; B. 100.

eádignes, -ness, e; *f. Happiness*; beatĭtūdo, opŭlentia:—Ic sceal ȳcan eádignesse *I shall increase happiness*, Exon. 108 a; Th. 413, 4; Rä. 31, 9: 83 a; Th. 313, 7; Seef. 120: Bt. 40, 4; Fox 240, 8.

eádi-lic; *adj. Happy*, Ps. Th. 64, 14. v. eádiglīc.

ead-leán *a reward*, Som. Ben. Lye. v. edleán.

ead-leánnung, e; *f. Proper recompense, remuneration, retribution*; retrĭbūtio, Ps. Spl. 54, 22. v. ed-leánung.

eád-lufe, an; *f. Happiness of love*; beatĭfĭcans ămor:—Ēce eádlufan *the eternal happiness of love*, Exon. 67 a; Th. 248, 31; Jul. 104.

eád-mēd, es; *n. Humility*; humĭlĭtas, generally found in the pl:—Ic eádmēdu efnan þence *humiliātus sum*, Ps. Th. 118, 107. On mīnum eádmēdum *in humilĭtāte mea*, 118, 92. v. eáþ-mēd.

eád-mēdan; *p.* de *To humble*; humiliāre, Ps. Spl. 74, 7: 38, 3. DER. ge-eádmēdan. v. eáþmēdan.

eád-mēde; *adj. Humble*; humĭlis anĭmi:—Ic eom eádmēde *humiliātus sum*, Ps. Th. 115, 1: 118, 75. v. eáþ-mēde.

eád-mēdlic *humble, respectful*, Anlct.

eád-mōd, eáþ-mōd; *adj. Humble, meek, mild*; hŭmĭlis, Mt. Bos. 11, 29.

eád-mōdan *to humble*; humĭliāre, Ps. Spl. T. 17, 29. v. eáþ-mōdian.

eád-mōdlic *humble, respectful*, Anlct.

eád-mōdlīce; *adv. Humbly, submissively*; humĭlĭter, Ps. Spl. 130, 3: Ps. Th. 114, 2. v. eáþ-mōdlīce.

eád-mōdnes, eád-mōdnys, -ness, -nyss, e; *f. Humbleness, humility, humanity*; humĭlĭtas:—Crist eardaþ on ðære dene eádmōdnesse *Christ dwells in the vale of humility*, Bt. 12; Fox 36, 23: Ps. Spl. 9, 13. v. eáþ-mōdnis.

Eádmund, es; *m.* [eád *happy*, mund *protection*]. 1. Edmund the Martyr, king of East Anglia, was of the Old-Saxon race. He began to reign in A. D. 855. 'Anno Domĭnĭcæ incarnatiōnis DCCCLV,—Eadmundus Orientālium Anglōrum gloriosissĭmus cœpit regnāre VIII. Kalend. Januārii, id est die natālis Dōmĭni, anno ætātis suæ decĭmo quarto,' Asser, p. 7, 26-30. He reigned fifteen years, and his death is thus recorded,—Hēr, A. D. 870, fōr se here ofer Myrce innon Eást-Ængle;—and, on ðam geáre, Sc̄e Eádmund [MS. Ædmund] cining him wið gefeaht, and ða Deniscan sige nāman, and ðone cining ofslōgon, and ðæt land eall gé-eódon *here the army went over Mercia into East-Anglia;—and, in that year, St. Edmund the king fought with them, and the Danes gained the victory, and slew the king, and overran all that land*, Chr. 870; Erl. 73, 29-75, 1. 2. *Edmund Atheling, second son of Edward the Elder, and younger brother of Athelstan, whom he succeeded. Edmund was king of Wessex for six years and a half, from* A. D. 940-946:—Hēr, A. D. 940, Æðelstān cyning forþfērde, and Eádmund Æðeling fēng to rīce *here king Athelstan died, and Edmund Atheling succeeded to the kingdom*, Chr. 940; Th. 209, 13-20, col. 1. Hēr, A. D. 946, Eádmund cyning forþfērde, on Sc̄s Agustīnus mæssedæge, and he hæfde rīce seofoðe healf geár; and ðā fēng Eádrēd Æðeling, his brōðor, to rīce *here king Edmund died, on St. Augustine's mass-day* [*May 26th*], *and he held the kingdom six years and a half; and then Eadred Atheling, his brother, succeeded to the kingdom*, Chr. 946; Erl. 116, 33-36. 3. *Edmund Ironside, son of Æthelred Atheling. Edmund began to reign in* A. D. 1016, *and died the same year*:—A. D. 1016, ðā gelamp hit ðæt se cyning Æðelrēd forþfērde, and ealle ða witan ða on Lundene wǣron, and seó burhwaru gecuron Eádmund to cyninge *then it happened that king Æthelred died, and all the witan that were in London, and the townsmen chose Edmund for king*, Chr. 1016; Erl. 155, 15-19. A. D. 1016, ðā to Sc̄e Andreas mæssan, forþfērde Eádmund cyng *then, on St. Andrew's mass-day* [*Nov. 30th*], *king Edmund died*, Chr. 1016; Th. 284, 12, col. 2.

Eádmundes burh; *gen.* burge; *dat.* byrig; *f.* [Eádmundes *Edmund's*, burh *the town*] *St. Edmundsbury, Bury St. Edmunds, Suffolk*:—Hēr, A. D. 1046, forþfērde Æðelstān abbot on Abban dūne and fēng Spearhafoc munuc to of Sc̄e Eádmundes byrig *here died Æthelstan, abbot of Abingdon, and monk Spearhawk of St. Edmundsbury succeeded*, Chr. 1046; Erl. 170, 15.

eád-nes, -nys, -ness, -nyss, e; *f. Happiness, prosperity*; beatĭtūdo:—Ōs byþ eorla gehwām eádnys *mind is to every man prosperity*, Hick. Thes. vol. i. 135, 8; Runic pm. 4; Kmbl. 340, 10. Ongan he wurþigan eádnysse and hȳrsumnysse *he began to esteem happiness and obedience*, Guthl. 2; Gdwin. 18, 16. v. ēþnes.

eá-docce, an; *f. A water-dock*; rŭmex aquatĭca, Lchdm. ii. 379.

eador; *adv. Together*; una, simul:—Eall eador *all together*, Cd. 119; Th. 154, 18; Gen. 2557. Ðā wæs eall eador [geador, Kmbl.] *there was all together*, Andr. Recd. 3253; An. 1629. v. geador.

eador *a hedge, dwelling*. v. edor.

eador-geard, es; *m. The inclosure of arteries, the body*; dŏmus vēnārum, corpus; aula septa, Grm. Andr. Elen. 129, 4. Lǣtaþ spor eadorgeard [ealdorgeard, Kmbl.] sceoran, fǣges feorhhord *let the spur raze the dwelling* [*of arteries?* or *of life?*], *the soul-hoard of the mortal*, Andr. Recd. 2362; An. 1183. v. ǣdre.

Eádrēd, es; *m.* [eád *happy*, rēd = rǣd *counsel*] *Eadred Atheling, third son of Edward the Elder. Eadred was king of Wessex and Northumbria, for nine years and a half, from* A. D. 946-955:—Hēr, A. D. 946, fēng Eádrēd Æðeling to rīce *here Eadred Atheling succeeded to the kingdom*, Chr. 946; Erl. 116, 35. Hēr, A. D. 955, Eádrēd [MS. Ædrēd] cyning forþfērde, and fēng Eádwīg to rīce, Eádmundes sunu *here king Eadred died, and Eadwig, Edmund's son, succeeded to the kingdom*, Chr. 955; Erl. 119, 8.

Eadulfes næs, Ealdulfes næs, næss, es; *m. Eadulf's ness, Walton-on-the-Naze?* Ædulphi promontōrium in agro Essexiensi:—Ða ōðre fōron on Eást-Seaxon to Eadulfes næsse *the others went on to Essex, to Eadulf's ness*, Chr. 1049; Ing. 220, 24: 1051; Th. 319, 2, col. 2: 1052; Th. 321, 10.

eád-wacer, es; *m. A watchman of property*; bonōrum custos, Exon. 101 a; Th. 380, 30; Rä. 1, 16.

Eádweard, -ward, es; *m.* [eád *happy*, weard *ward, guardian*]. 1. *Edward the Elder, the eldest son of Alfred the Great. Edward was king of Wessex for twenty-four years, from* A. D. 901-925:—Hēr, A. D. 901, gefōr Ælfrēd cyning, and fēng Eádweard his sunu to rīce *here king Alfred died, and Edward his son succeeded to the kingdom*, Chr. 901; Erl. 97, 8-10. Hēr, A. D. 925, Eádweard cyning [MS. cing] forþfērde, and Æðelstān his sunu fēng to rīce *here king Edward died, and Æthelstan his son succeeded to the kingdom*, Chr. 925; Erl. 110, 19. 2. *Edward the Martyr, son of Edgar. Edward was king of Wessex, Mercia, and Northumbria, for three years, from* A. D. 975-978:—Hēr, A. D. 975, Eádweard, Eádgāres sunu, fēng to rīce *here Edward, Edgar's son, succeeded to the kingdom*, Chr. 975; Th. 227, 37, col. 1. Hēr, A. D. 978, wearþ Eádweard cyning gemartyrad *here king Edward was martyred*, Chr. 978; Th. 232, 1-3, col. 1. 3. *Edward the Confessor, son of Æthelred. Edward was king of England for twenty-four years, from* A. D. 1042-1066:—Hēr, A. D. 1042, wæs Eádward gehālgod to cinge on Wincestre *here Edward was consecrated king at Winchester*, Chr. 1042; Erl. 168, 2. Hēr, A. D. 1066, forþfērde Eádward [MS. Eáduuard] cyning [MS. king], and Harold eorl fēng to ðam rīce *here king Edward died, and earl Harold succeeded to the kingdom*, Chr. 1066; Erl. 198, 1.

eád-wēla, an; *m. Happy weal, riches, happiness, blessedness*; divĭtiæ, opŭlentia, felīcĭtas, beatĭtūdo:—Sumum eádwēlan dǣleþ *to some he dispenses riches*, Exon. 88 a; Th. 331, 12; Vy. 67: 59 b; Th. 215, 10; Ph. 251: 80 a; Th. 301, 17; Fä. 20. Sāwul fundaþ to ðam longan gefeán in eád-wēlan *the soul tendeth to that lasting joy into happiness*, 48 b: Th. 167, 22; Gū. 1064: 64 a; Th. 237, 6; Ph. 586.

Eádwīg, es; *m.* [eád *happy*, wīg *war*] *Eadwig, son of Edmund. Eadwig was king of Wessex and Northumbria for four years, from* A. D. 955-959:—Hēr, A. D. 955, fēng Eádwīg to rīce, Eádmundes sunu *here Eadwig, Edmund's son, succeeded to the kingdom*, Chr. 955; Erl. 119, 8. Hēr, A. D. 959, Eádwīg cyning forþfērde, and fēng Eádgār his brōðor to rīce *here king Eadwig died, and Edgar his brother succeeded to the kingdom*, Chr. 959; Erl. 119, 11.

eǣ; *dat.* or *abl. To* or *by a river*:—Be ðære eǣ *by the river*, Chr. 896; Th. 172, 35, col. 1. v. eá.

eæd-leǣnian *to reward*; retrĭbuĕre, Ps. Spl. T. 17, 22. DER. ge-eædleǣnian. v. edleǣnian.

eældian *to grow old*; inveterascĕre, Ps. Spl. T. 17, 47: 31, 3. v. ealdian.

eællenge; *interj. Behold*; en, ecce, Ps. Spl. T. 53, 4. v. eallenga.

eærdung, e; *f. A tabernacle*; tabernăcŭlum, Ps. Spl. T. 59, 6. v. eardung.

eærfoðian *to trouble*; tribŭlāre, Ps. Spl. T. 12, 5: 41, 14.

eærfoþnes, -ness, e; *f. Difficulty, trouble*; diffĭcultas, tribŭlātio, Ps. Spl. T. 33, 19: 65, 10: 117, 5. v. earfoþnes.

eærpung, e; *f. A harping, harp*; cĭthăra, Ps. Spl. T. 32, 2. v. earpa.

eæþ-mōd; *adj. Mild*; mītis, Ps. Spl. T. 24, 10. v. eáþ-mōd.

eafera *a son*, Beo. Th. 2374; B. 1185. v. eafora.

eá-fisc, -fix, es; *m. A river-fish;* flŭviālis piscis:—Iór byþ eáfixa [sum] *eel* [?] *is a river-fish*, Runic pm. 28; Kmbl. 345, 4. Eáfiscas sēcan *to seek river-fishes*, Bt. Met. Fox 19, 48; Met. 19, 24.

eafor, es; *m. A boar, wild boar;* aper:—Sume wǣron eaforas *some were wild boars*, Bt. Met. Fox 26, 161; Met. 26, 81. v. eofor.

eafora, eafera, eafra, eofera, afora, afera, afara, an; *m. An offspring, successor, heir, son;* prōles, successor, fīlius:—Wearþ Adamę eafora fēded *a son was born to Adam*, Cd. 55; Th. 67, 23; Gen. 1105: 82; Th. 103, 3; Gen. 1712: Bt. Met. Fox 26, 69; Met. 26, 35. Ne wearþ Heremōd swā eaforum Ecgwēlan *Heremod was not so to Ecgwela's successors*, Beo. Th. 3424; B. 1710. Ðæt we on Adame and on his eafrum andan gebētan *that we repair our wrongs on Adam and his offspring*, Cd. 21; Th. 25, 24; Gen. 399. [*O. Sax.* abaro, *m. prōles, filius.*]

eafor-heáfod-segn, es; *m. A boar-head banner;* signum ad capĭtis aprīni similitūdĭnem fabrĭcātum, *vel* signum apri præcĭpuum:—Hēt in beran eaforheáfodsegn *he bade the boar-head banner to be borne in*, Beo. Th. 4311; B. 2152.

eafoþ, es; *n. Strength, violence, might;* vis:—Wæs seó mǣg ānrǣd and unforht, eafoða gemyndig *the maid was resolved and fearless, of her strength mindful*, Exon. 74 b; Th. 278, 22; Jul. 601. Him Geáta sceal eafoþ and ellen gebeódan *a Goth shall offer him strength and valour*, Beo. Th. 1208; B. 602. Heremōdes hild sweþrode, eafoþ [MS. earfoþ] and ellen *Heremod's war had ceased, his strength and energy*, 1808; B. 902: 4687; B. 2349. Hie unlǣdra eafoðum gelȳfdon *they believed in the might of savage spirits*, Andr. Kmbl. 284; An. 142. Unlǣdra eafoþ *the violence of the wretched men*, 59; An. 30. v. eofoþ.

eág-æppel, es; *m. The apple of the eye;* pupilla, Som. Ben. Lye.

eágan beorht, es; *n. An eye's glance, a moment;* ocŭli micātio, momentum, Bd. 2, 13; S. 516, 20, MSS. C. B. v. eágan bryhtm.

eágan brēgh, e; *f. An eyebrow;* palpebra, Bd. 4, 32; S. 611, 18. v. brǣw.

eágan bryhtm, es; *m. An eye's twinkle, a moment;* ocŭli micātio, momentum, Bd. 2, 13; S. 516, 20. v. eágan beorht.

eá-gang, es; *m. A water-course;* flumĭnis cursus:—On ðære eágang *in the water-course*, Ors. 2, 4; Bos. 44, 13.

eágan weán, wenn *A ringworm, tetter;* impetīgo:—Eágan weán *vel* wearhbrǣde *impetīgo*, Ælfc. Gl. 73; Som. 71, 9; Wrt. Voc. 43, 62.

eága-swind *the eyelid, the cheek;* gĕna, Som. Ben. Lye; Grm. Gr. iii. 401 *proposes* eágan-spind.

eág-dūru, e; *f. An eye-door, a window;* fenestra, Martyr. 12, Jan. Lye.

EÁGE, ēge; *gen. dat.* -an; *acc.* -e; *pl. nom. acc.* -an, -on; *gen.* -ena, -na; *dat.* -um, -on; *n.* I. *an* EYE; ocŭlus:—Gyf ðīn swȳðre eáge ðē ǣswīcie *si ocŭlus tuus dexter scandalĭzat te*, Mt. Bos. 5, 29. Mīnra eágna leóht *light of my eyes*, Exon. 67 a; Th. 248, 14; Jul. 95. Eágena gesihþ *the sight of the eyes*, Andr. Kmbl. 60; An. 30. Eágum to wynne *to their eye's delight*, Exon. 26 a; Th. 76, 26; Cri. 1245. II. *the eye of a needle;* forāmen:—Þurh nǣdle eáge *per forāmen acus*, Mt. Bos. 19, 24: Lk. Bos. 18, 25. [*Piers P.* eighe, *pl.* eighen: *Wyc.* eiȝe, eȝe, iȝe, yȝe, *pl.* eiȝen: *Chauc. R. Glouc.* eye, *pl.* eyen: *Laym.* eȝe, *pl.* eȝene, æȝene: *Orm.* eghe, *pl.* eghne, ehhne, ehne: *Scot.* ee, e: *Plat.* ooge, *pl.* aagen: *O. Sax.* ōga, *n*; *pl.* ōgun: *O. Frs.* age, ag, ach, oge, *n*; *pl.* agon: *Dut.* oog, *n*: *Ger.* auge, *n*: *M. H. Ger.* ouge, *n*: *O. H. Ger.* ouga, auga, *n*: *Goth.* augo, *n*: *Dan.* öie, *n*: *Swed.* öga, *n*; *pl.* ögon: *Icel.* auga, *n*: *Lat.* oc-ulus, *m*: *Grk.* ὄκος, ὄκκος, *m*: *Lith.* akis, *f*: *Sansk.* aksha, *n.*]

eág-ece, es; *m. Eye-ache;* ocŭlōrum dŏlor, Som. Ben. Lye.

eáge-spring, -sprinc, es; *n.* [eáge *an eye;* spring *a spring*] *A spring* or *twinkling of the eye;* ocŭli ictus, Som.

eág-fleá *A spot in the eye;* albūgo, Ælfc. Gl. 73; Som. 71, 10.

eág-gebyrd, e; *f. The nature* or *power of the eye;* ocŭli nātūra, Exon. 60 a; Th. 219, 3; Ph. 301.

eág-hill, es; *m. An eyebrow;* supercĭlium, Mann.

eág-hringas; *pl. m. The eyebrows, eyelids;* palpebræ, genæ? Som. Ben. Lye.

eágh-þyrl *a window*, Bd. 4, 3; S. 568, 6. v. eág-þyrl.

eágor-streám, es; *m. A water-stream, ocean;* māre, Andr. Kmbl. 882; An. 441: Bt. Met. Fox 20, 244; Met. 20, 122. v. ēgor-streám.

eág-sealf, e; *f. Eye-salve;* colliria, Ælfc. Gl. 12; Som. 57, 82.

eág-seoung, -sioung, e; *f. An eye-disease;* glaucōma, Cot. 97: 170, Lye.

eág-sēung, e; *f. Eye-seeing, eye-sight;* ocŭlōrum acies, Som. Ben. Lye.

eág-sȳne; *adj. Visible to the eye;* ocŭlis conspĭcuus, Andr. Kmbl. 3099; An. 1552.

eág-þyrl, ēg-þyrl, ēh-þyrl, es; *n. An eye-hole, a window;* fenestra:—Ontȳnde se bisceop ðæt eág-þyrl ðære cyricean *apĕruit episcŏpus fenestram oratōrii*, Bd. 4, 3; S. 568, 6: 5, 12; S. 629, 15.

eág-wræc, es; *n. A pain of the eyes;* ocŭlōrum dŏlor, Med. ex Quadr. 9, 4; Lchdm. i. 362, 1.

eág-wyrt, e; *f. Eye-wort, eye-bright;* ocŭlāria, L. M. 3, 30; Lchdm. ii. 324, 19.

eáh- *eye-*, = eág-, in compounds, *q. v.*

eáh-mist, es; *m. Eye-mist* or *dimness;* ocŭlōrum calīgātio, Som. Ben. Lye.

eáh-streám *a water-stream*, Exon. 25 a; Th. 72, 6; Cri. 1168. v. eá-streám.

eaht, æht, eht, e; *f. Deliberation, council;* delibĕrātio, consĭlium, Exon. 80 a; Th. 301, 24; Fä. 24.

EAHTA, ahta, æhta, ehta *eight;* octo:—Eahta dagas *dies octo*, Lk. Bos. 9, 28. Būton ðām eahta mannum *except eight men*, Ælfc. T. 6, 26. To eahta geára fyrste *for a space of eight years*, Jud. 3, 8. Æfter eahta dagum *post dies octo*, Jn. Bos. 20, 26. He hēht eahta mearas on flet teón *he commanded eight steeds to be led into the court*, Beo. Th. 2075; B. 1035. [*Wyc.* eighte: *Laym.* æhte, æhten, eahte, ehte: *Orm.* ehhte: *O. Sax.* ahto: *O. Frs.* achta, achte, acht: *Dut. Ger.* acht: *M. H. Ger.* aht, eht: *O. H. Ger.* ahtō: *Goth.* ahtau: *Dan.* otte: *Swed.* åtta: *Icel.* átta: *Fr.* huit: *Span.* ocho: *Ital.* otto: *Lat.* octo: *Grk.* ὀκτώ: *Sansk.* ashṭan.] DER. eahta-teóða, -toða, -tyne: hund-eahtatig.

eáhtan, ēhtan, iehtan. I. *to observe, judge;* observāre, æstimāre, reputāre:—We māgon eáhtan and sōþe secgan ðæt *we may judge and soothly say that*, Exon. 30 b; Th. 94, 34; Cri. 1550. Wile fæder eáhtan hū suna bringen sāwle *the father will judge how his sons bring their minds*, 23 b; Th. 66, 20; Cri. 1074. II. *c. gen. To watch any one, pursue, persecute;* persĕqui:—Bona eáhteþ ānbūendra *the murderer persecutes lone dwellers*, Exon. 33 b; Th. 107, 15; Gū. 59: 37 b; Th. 123, 4; Gū. 317: Ps. Th. 118, 150. [*O. Sax.* ahtian *persĕqui:* *O. Frs.* achta, echta, achtia *damnāre, judicāre:* *Ger.* æchten *proscribĕre:* *M. H. Ger.* āhten, æhten: *O. H. Ger.* āhtian, āhtōn, ahtēn *persĕqui.*] v. ōht.

eahta-teóða; *m:* eahta-teóðe; *f. n. adj. The eighteenth;* duodevicēsĭmus:—On ðam eahtateóðan geáre *in the eighteenth year*, Ors. 6, 2; Bos. 117, 10. Ðysne eahtateóðan sealm Dafid sang *David sang this eighteenth psalm*, Ps. Th. arg. 18.

eahtatig *eighty*. v. hund-eahtatig.

eahta-tyne, ehta-tyne; *adj.* EIGHTEEN; octōdĕcim:—Hīg him þeówodon eahtatyne geár *they served him eighteen years*, Jud. 3, 14: 10, 8.

eahteða, eahteoða *eighth*, Exon. 47 b; Th. 164, 11; Gū. 1010: Menol. Fox 6; Men. 3. v. eahtoða.

eahtian, eahtigan, ehtian; *p.* ode, ade, ede; *pp.* od. I. *to meditate, devise, deliberate;* meditāre, reputāre, deliberāre:—Eahtade hū wynna þorfte brūcan *he meditated how he might enjoy delights*, Exon. 37 b; Th. 122, 17; Gū. 307. Sum dōmas con, ðǣr dryhtguman rǣd eahtiaþ *one understands dooms, where people devise counsel*, 79 a; Th. 297, 24; Crä. 73: 74 b; Th. 279, 6; Jul. 609: Andr. Kmbl. 2325; An. 1164: Beo. Th. 2819; B. 1407: 347; B. 172. II. *to esteem;* æstimāre:—Eahtodon eorlscipe and his ellen-weorc *they esteemed his bravery and his valiant works*, Beo. Th. 6327; B. 3174.

eáhtnes, ēhtnes, -nys, -ness, -nyss, e; *f. Persecution;* persecūtio:—Se eáhtnysse ahōf *who raised persecution*, Exon. 65 b; Th. 243, 2; Jul. 4: 18 a; Th. 44, 18; Cri. 704.

eahtoða, eahteða, ehteoða, ehtuða; *m:* -ðe; *f. n: adj. The eighth;* octāvus:—Eahtoðan sīðe *an eighth time*, Exon. 80 b; Th. 303, 26; Fä. 59.

eahtung, æhtung, e; *f. A price, an estimation;* æstimātio, Som. Ben. Lye. v. ehtung.

eáhum *with eyes;* = eágum; *pl. dat.* or *inst. of* eáge, Bt. 5, 1; Fox 8, 25, MS. Bod.

EAL, eall; *gen. m. n.* ealles; *f.* ealre, eallre; *dat. m. n.* eallum; *f.* ealre, eallre; *acc. m.* ealne, eallne, *f.* ealle, *n.* eal; *inst.* ealle; *pl. nom. acc.* ealle, ealla; *gen.* ealra, eallra; *dat.* eallum; *sometimes used indecl; adj.* I. ALL; tōtus, omnis, cunctus, unĭversus:—Eal ða earfeðu *all the pains*, Exon. 25 b; Th. 74, 5; Cri. 1202: 118 a; Th. 452, 25; Hy. 4, 7: Andr. Kmbl. 1889; An. 947. Eal here *the whole host*, Cd. 114; Th. 150, 12; Gen. 2490: Salm. Kmbl. 645; Sal. 322. Eal ic *I all*, Exon. 115 a; Th. 443, 13; Kl. 29. Ealles ðæs gafoles *of all the tribute*, Exon. 16 a; Th. 35, 16; Cri. 559. Ealre worlde *of all the world*, Hy. 7, 57: 11, 20. Ealles ðæs *of all that*, Exon. 119 a; Th. 456, 19; Hy. 4, 69. Ealne ðisne ymbhwyrft *all this orb*, 110 b; Th. 423, 1; Rä. 41, 14. Ealne ðone egesan *all the terror*, Cd. 202; Th. 250, 3; Dan. 541. Geond ealne middangeard *tōto orbe*, Bd. 2, 4; S. 505, 26. Ealne weg *always*, Bt. 38, 4; Fox 204, 10, 11. Ealle ða gesceaft *all the creation*, Bt. Met. Fox 20, 37; Met. 20, 19. Ealle ǣ *unĭversam legem*, Deut. 4, 8. Ðīne ealle gebann *omnia mandāta tua*, Ps. Th. 118, 86. Ealle gesceafte *all creatures*, Andr. Kmbl. 2997; An. 1501. Ealle ða þing *omnia*, Gen. 1, 31: Deut. 4, 3. Ealle þing *cuncta*, Bd. 1, 26; S. 487, 34: Mk. Bos. 9, 23. Ealle ða gelǣredestan men *plūres vĭri doctissĭmi*, Bd. 2, 2; S. 502, 38. Ealle his bigengan *omnes cultōres ejus*, Deut. 4, 3. Ealla gesceafta *all creatures*, Bt. Met. Fox 13, 14; Met. 13, 7: 20, 105; Met. 20, 53: Bt. 39, 13; Fox 234, 24. Ealle mægne *with all power*, Bt. Met. Fox 26, 128; Met. 26, 64. Ealle gemete *omni mŏdo*, Bd. 1, 27; S. 496, 39. Ealra ðara gifena *for all the gifts*, Exon. 41 b; Th. 138, 18; Gū. 578. Earmost ealra wihta *poorest of all creatures*, 110 a; Th. 421, 7; Rä. 40, 14. On eallum biþ ðæm līchoman *it is in* *all the body*, Bt. Met. Fox 20, 360; Met. 20, 180. Eallum heora eaforum *to all their offspring*, Cd. 26; Th. 35, 5; Gen. 550. Eal wæs ðæt mearcland *the border-land was all*, Andr. Kmbl. 37; An. 19. Ealles ðū ðæs wīte awunne *for all this thou hast obtained suffering*, Exon. 39 b; Th. 130, 18; Gū. 440. Ealra we healdaþ sancta symbel *we keep the feast of all the saints*, Menol. Fox 396; Men. 199. Ealle wyrd forsweóp mīne māgas *fate has swept away all my kinsmen*, Beo. Th. 5621; B. 2814. Ðeáh hit wið ealle sié eft gemenged weoruld-gesceafta *though it is still mixed with all worldly creatures*, Bt. Met. Fox 20, 255; Met. 20, 128. Þreó eal on ān *all three in one*, Exon. 22 a; Th. 60, 16; Cri. 970. Ðæs ealles nōwīht *nothing of all that;* nil omnīmŏdis, Bd. 4, 11; S. 579, 21. Fram him eallum *by them all*, 2, 2; S. 502, 32. On woruld ealle *through the whole world*, Cd. 32; Th. 42, 16; Gen. 674. His earfoðo ealle ætsomne *all his woes at once*, 216; Th. 272, 30; Sat. 127. We ealle *we all*, Exon. 120 b; Th. 463, 12; Hö. 69. Feówer eallum *to all four*, 113 b; Th. 434, 28; Rä. 52, 7. Me ealne, Ps. C. 50, 98. Hit eal *it all*, Beo. Th. 3220; B. 1608. Iob sæt ðā sārlīce eal on ānre wūnde *Job sat there doleful all* [*covered with*] *a wound*, Job Thw. 166, 32. Wæs ðæt bold tobrocen swīðe eal inneweard *all the dwelling was much shattered within*, Beo. Th. 2000; B. 998. He līfes gesteald in ðam ēcan hām eal sceáwode *he saw all the dwelling-place of life in the eternal home*, Exon. 12 a; Th. 19, 24; Cri. 305. Ðæs we ealles sculon secgan þonc *for all that we ought to give thanks*, 16 b; Th. 38, 24; Cri. 611. Sió his rīces wæs ealles ēðel-stōl *it was the metropolis of his whole empire*, Bt. Met. Fox 9, 21; Met. 9, 11. Hie ðā ānmōde ealle cwǣdon *they all said then unanimously*, Andr. Kmbl. 3201; An. 1603. Niðða bearna ǣrest ealra *first of all the children of men*, Cd. 56; Th. 69, 15; Gen. 1136. Us is eallum neód *to us all it is needful*, Exon. 11 b; Th. 15, 33; Cri. 245. II. *without substantive, and sometimes governing the genitive*:—Eal [*acc. n.*] ic recce *I govern all*, Exon. 110 b; Th. 424, 2; Rä. 41, 33. We oncnāwaþ eal [*acc. n.*] ðæt we geworhton *we acknowledge all that we have done*, Hy. 7, 91. Hæfde unlifgendes eal gefeormod *he had devoured all the lifeless*, Beo. Th. 1493; B. 744. Him ealles þonc ǣghwā secge *let each give thanks to him for all*, Exon. 88 b; Th. 333, 4; Vy. 97. Ðē sié ealles þonc meorda and miltsa *thanks be to thee for all, for the rewards and mercies*, 118 b; Th. 456, 14; Hy. 4, 66. Sindon ealle nyt *all are useful*, 114 a; Th. 437, 20; Rä. 56, 10. Ealle ætsomne *omnes parĭter*, Bd. 2, 13; S. 515, 38. Ofer ealle *over all*, Elen. Grm. 386. Ealra aldor *chief of all*, Cd. 228; Th. 306, 14; Sat. 664: Elen. Grm. 372. Āna wið eallum *alone against all*, Beo. Th. 292; B. 145: Cd. 218; Th. 279, 28; Sat. 245. Metod eallum weóld gumena cynnes *the Creator ruled over the whole of the race of men*, Beo. Th. 2119; B. 1057. III. ealles, ealle, ealra *are sometimes used, almost adverbially*:—Ealles gelīcost *most like of all*, Cd. 188; Th. 233, 13; Dan. 275. Ealles mǣst *maxĭme*, Bd. 2, 4; S. 505, 7: Ps. Th. 119, 3. Ealles edgiong *quite young again*, Exon. 64 a; Th. 236, 28; Ph. 581: Ps. Th. 138, 14. Ealles tō swīðe *all too readily*, L. C. S. 3; Th. i. 376, 22: Nicod. 17; Thw. 8, 18: Bt. Met. Fox 5, 59; Met. 5, 30. Ealles swā swīðe *all so readily*, 4, 70; Met. 4, 35: 12, 64; Met. 12, 32. Sille ic ðē ealle xxx pūnda *I will give thee thirty pounds in all*, Salm. Kmbl. 25; Sal. 13. Mid ealle *altogether;* pĕnĭtus, Bd. 1, 12; S. 480, 38: Ors. 2, 4; Bos. 45, 21: Chr. 893; Th. 162, 24: Exon. 22 a; Th. 60, 28; Cri. 976. Ealra swīðost *maxĭme* [*Ger.* aller-meist], Bd. 2, 4; S. 505, 22: Cd. 18; Th. 22, 8, 36; Gen. 337, 351. Ealra wǣron fīfe *in all they were five*, Exon. 112 b; Th. 432, 1; Rä. 47, 6. [*Wyc. Piers P.* al, *pl.* alle: *Chauc.* all: *Laym.* al: *Orm.* all, alle: *O. Sax.* al: *Frs. O. Frs.* al, ol: *Dut.* al, alle, alles: *Ger.* all, aller, alle, alles: *M. H. Ger.* al, *inflected* aller, alliu, alleȝ, elliu, elle, alle: *O. H. Ger.* al, all: *Goth.* alls: *Dan. Swed.* al: *Icel.* allr, öll, allt, alt: *Grk.* ὅλος.]

eal, e; *f. An awl;* subūla:—Þurhþyrlige his eáre mid eale [mid āne eale, Roff.] *perfōret aurem illīus subūla*, L. Alf. 11; Wilk. 29, 12. v. al.

eala *ale*:—Eala *cervīsia, celia*, Ælfc. Gl. 32; Som. 61, 106; Wrt. Voc. 27, 35. v. ealu.

eálā, æálā, ǣlā, hēlā; *interj. O! alas! Oh!* eheu! euge! proh:—Eálā ge næddran *O! ye serpents*, Mt. Bos. 23, 33: 23, 37. Eálā, eálā *euge, euge*, Ps. Spl. 69, 4. Eálā eálā! oððe wel wel! *ahah ahah! or well well!* euge euge! *vel* bene bene! Ps. Lamb. 34, 25. Æálā, ðū Scippend *O, thou Creator*, Bt. Met. Fox 4, 1; Met. 4, 1. Ǣlā Drihten leóf, Hy. 1, 1: 2, 1. Eálā! gif he wolde *O that he would*, Bt. Met. Fox 9, 105; Met. 9, 53. Eálā hwæt se forma wǣre *alas! that the first should have been*, 8, 109; Met. 8, 55. Eálā! ðæt hit wurde *O! that it might be*, 8, 77; Met. 8, 39. Eálā! ðǣr we māgon geseón *alas! there we may see*, Exon. 27 a; Th. 80, 27; Cri. 1313. v. eáw.

eá-lād, e; *f. A water-way;* aquōsa via:—Frēcne þuhton egle eálāda *the fearful water-ways appeared terrible*, Andr. Kmbl. 881; An. 441.

eala-hūs, eal-hūs, es; *n. An ale-house;* taberna:—On eala-hūse *in an ale-house*, L. Eth. iii. 1; Th. i. 292, 9.

eá-land, -lond, es; *n. Water-land, an island;* insūla [eás land *island*, lit. *water's land, land of water*, v. *gen.* eás in eá]:—Ne geseah nān cēpa eáland *no merchant visited the island*, Bt. 15; Fox 48, 13. Ðæs fægerne gefeán habbaþ eálanda mænig *lætentur insŭlæ multæ*, Ps. Th. 96, 1. Cumaþ hī of eálandum ūtan *they shall come forth from the islands*, 71, 10. Swylce he eác Orcadas ða eálond to Rōmwara rīce geþeódde *Orcădas ētiam insŭlas Rōmāno adjēcit impĕrio*, Bd. 1, 3; S. 475, 13: Beo. Th. 4657; B. 2334: Exon. 52 a; Th. 181, 27; Gū. 1299: 96 b; Th. 360, 27; Wal. 12: 361, 17; Wal. 21: 60 a; Th. 217, 28; Ph. 287. v. īg-land.

eala-scōp, es; *m. An ale-poet*, L. N. P. L. 41; Th. ii. 296, 12. v. ealu-scōp.

ealaþ, ealoþ, alaþ, alþ, aloþ, eoloþ; *n: indecl. in s. but gen.* alþes, Rtl. 116, 42, *Ale;* cervīsia:—Twelf ambra Wilisces ealaþ [MS. B. ealoþ] *twelve ambers of Welsh ale*, L. In. 70; Th. i. 146, 17: Ors. 5, 3; Bos. 103, 33. v. ealu.

ealaþ-wyrt, e; *f. Ale-wort;* cervīsia mustea, nova, Som. Ben. Lye.

eal-beorht *all-bright*. v. eall-beorht.

ealc *each*:—He ofslōh ða hǣðenan on ealcum gefeohte *he slew the heathen in every fight*, Ælfc. T. 13, 18. v. ǣlc.

eal-ceald *all-cold*. v. æl-ceald.

eal-cræftig *all-powerful, all-mighty*. v. æl-cræftig.

eal-cyn *of every kind, universal*. v. eall-cyn.

EALD, ald; *adj. comp.* yldra, eldra, eoldra; *sup.* yldest. I. *old, ancient;* vĕtus, ætāte provectus, priscus, antīquus:—Ic eom nū eald *I am now old*, Lk. Bos. 1, 18. Eald ǣfensceóp *an old evening-bard*, Exon. 103 a; Th. 390, 21; Rä. 9, 5: Beo. Th. 4426; B. 2210. Ealde ȳþmearas *old horses of the waves*, Exon. 20 b; Th. 54, 5; Cri. 864. Geongum and ealdum *to young and old*, Beo. Th. 144; B. 72. Hwæt niwes oððe ealdes *what of new or old*, Exon. 115 a; Th. 441, 24; Kl. 4. Se ealda *the old one* [*Satan*], Frag. Kmbl. 61; Leás. 32. Eald enta geweorc *the old work of giants*, Exon. 77 b; Th. 291, 24; Wand. 87: 60 b; Th. 220, 16; Ph. 321: 86 b; Th. 326, 1; Wīd. 122. Of ðære ealdan moldan hātaþ hȳ upp-astandan *he bids them to arise up from the old mould*, 21 a; Th. 55, 25; Cri. 889. Ða ealdan wūnde *the old wounds*, 24 a; Th. 68, 23; Cri. 1108. Mid ðȳ ealdan līge *with the ancient flame*, 30 b; Th. 94, 28; Cri. 1547. Ða ealdan race *the old story*, 28 a; Th. 85, 26; Cri. 1397. Wrecaþ ealdne nīþ *avenge your ancient grudge*, 74 b; Th. 280, 3; Jul. 623. II. *eminent, great, exalted;* eminens, præstans, excelsus: *it has the same meaning in compounds*, v. eald-wīta:—Nā ðæt ǣlc eald sȳ, ac ðæt he eald sȳ on wīsdōme *not that every one is old, but that he is old in wisdom*, L. Ælf. C. 17; Th. ii. 348, 21. [*Wyc.* eld, elde, olde: *Chauc.* elde, olde: *Laym.* æld, alde, olde: *Orm.* ald: *O. Sax.* ald: *Frs.* aod, aud, oad: *O. Frs.* ald: *Dut.* oud: *Ger. M. H. Ger. O. H. Ger.* alt: *Goth.* alþeis *old.*] DER. efen-eald, ofer-, or-.

eald-a-wered *worn, wasted with age;* vetustus, R. Ben. 51, Lye. v. eald-wērig.

eald-cwēn, e; *f. An old wife, an old crone;* vĕtŭla:—Ealdra cwēna spell *vĕtŭlārum fābŭla*, R. 100.

eald-cȳþ, eald-cȳððu, e; *f. The old country;* prisca patria:—Ðæt he his ealdcȳððu sēcan mōte *that he may seek its old country*, Exon. 62 a; Th. 228, 9; Ph. 435: 61 a; Th. 222, 19; Ph. 351: 18 b; Th. 46, 16; Cri. 738.

eald-dagas; *pl. m. Ancient days, days of old;* prisci dies:—In ealddagum, Exon. 12 a; Th. 19, 19; Cri. 303: Ors. 3, 7; Bos. 61, 44: Bd. 4, 27; S. 604, 41, MS. B.

eald-dōm, es; *m. Age;* vĕtustas:—Hyre ānweald is hreósende for ealddōme *her power is decreasing from age*, Ors. 2, 4; Bos. 45, 4.

ealde *men:* homines, Ps. Th. 93, 9. v. ylde.

eald-ealdfæder *a great-grandfather;* proăvus, Som. Ben. Lye.

ealder *an elder*, R. Ben. 4. v. ealdor.

ealdermen *aldermen*, Jud. Thw. 157, 32. v. ealdorman.

eald-fæder, ealde-fæder; *indecl. in s. but sometimes gen.* -fæderes *and dat.* -fædere *are found; pl. nom. acc.* -fæderas; *gen.* a; *dat.* um; *m. A grandfather, ancestor;* ăvus, antecessor:—Ealdefæder ăvus, Ælfc. Gl. 91; Som. 75, 6; Wrt. Voc. 51, 51. Ðū forþfærst to ðīnum ealdfæderum *tu ībis ad patres tuos*, Gen. 15, 15: Beo. Th. 751; B. 373. v. fæder 2.

eald-feónd, eald-fīnd, es; *m. An ancient foe, arch-fiend, Satan;* antīquus inĭmīcus, diăbŏlus:—Ealdfeónda cyn *the tribe of ancient foes*, Cd. 174; Th. 219, 20; Dan. 57: 196; Th. 244, 26; Dan. 454: Exon. 16 a; Th. 35, 32; Cri. 567. Ðæt he ne lēte him ealdfeónd oncyrran mōd from his Meotude *that he did not let the ancient fiend turn his mind from his Creator*, 37 b; Th. 124, 7; Gū. 336: 62 a; Th. 229, 2; Ph. 449: 121 a; Th. 464, 18; Hö. 89. v. eald-geniþla, eald-gewinna, eald-hettende.

eald-gecynd, es; *n. Old* or *original nature;* antīqua nātūra *vel* indŏles:—Wudu-fuglas on treówum ealdgecynde wuniaþ *the wood-birds live in the trees in their old nature*, Bt. Met. Fox 13, 79; Met. 13, 40: 25, 114; Met. 25, 57: Exon. 54 b; Th. 193, 26; Az. 127.

eald-geneát, es; *m. An old companion;* vĕtus cōmes:—Se wæs ealdgeneát *he was an old companion*, Byrht. Th. 140, 58; By. 310. v. eald-gesīþ.

eald-geniþla, an; *m. An ancient foe, arch-fiend, Satan;* antīquus inĭmīcus, diăbŏlus:—Ðe-læs him ealdgeniþlan scyððan cōmon *lest the old* *foes might come to injure him*, Andr. Kmbl. 2098; An. 1050: Judth. 11; Thw. 24, 37. Ealdgeníþla, helle hæftling *the old fiend, hell's captive*, Andr. Kmbl. 2682; An. 1343. v. eald-feónd.

eald-gesegen, e; *f. An old saga;* antīqua narrātio:—Se ðe eald-gesegena worn gemunde *who remembered a great number of old sagas*, Beo. Th. 1743; B. 869.

eald-gesíþ, es; *m. An old companion;* vĕtus cŏmes:—Gewiton eald-gesíþas *the old companions departed*, Beo. Th. 1711; B. 853: Andr. Kmbl. 2210; An. 1106. v. eald-geneát.

eald-gestreón, es; *n. An old treasure;* antīquus thēsaurus:—Ic ðé ða fǽhðe leánige ealdgestreónum *I will recompense thee for the strife with old treasures*, Beo. Th. 2766; B. 1381: Beo. Th. 2921; B. 1458: Exon. 31 a; Th. 96, 8; Cri. 1571.

eald-geweorc, es; *n. An ancient work, the world;* priscum ŏpus, mundus:—Freán ealdgeweorc *the ancient work of the Lord*, Bt. Met. Fox 11, 80; Met. 11, 40: 20, 232; Met. 20, 116.

eald-gewin, -gewinn, es; *n. An ancient conflict;* antīquum bellum:—Ðæt wæs eald-gewinn *that was an ancient conflict*, Elen. Kmbl. 1290; El. 647: Beo. Th. 3566; B. 1781.

eald-gewinna, an; *m. An old foe;* antīquus inĭmīcus:—Grendel wearþ, eald-gewinna, ingenga mín *Grendel, my old foe, became my invader*, Beo. Th. 3556; B. 1776. v. eald-feónd.

eald-gewyrht, es; *n. An ancient action;* prisca actio:—He þrówode for Adames ealdgewyrhtum *he suffered for Adam's ancient actions*, Rood Kmbl. 198; Kr. 100: Beo. Th. 5307; B. 2657.

eald-hád, es; *m. Old age;* senectus. v. ald-hád.

Ealdhelm *Aldhelm*, Chr. 731; Th. 74, 31, col. 2, 3; Aldhelm, 74, 31, col. 1. v. Aldhelm.

eald-hettende; *pl. m. Old foes;* antīqui inĭmīci, Judth. 12; Thw. 26, 11; Jud. 321. v. eald-feónd.

eald-hláford, es; *m.* [eald *old, ancient;* hláford *a lord*] *An old* or *ancient lord;* pristīnus domĭnus:—Ecg wæs íren eald-hláfordes *the sword of the old lord was iron*, Beo. Th. 5550; B. 2778. He hæfde heora eald-hláfordes sunu on his gewealde *he had the son of their old lord in his power*, Ors. 3, 11; Bos. 74, 25. Se Cásere wæs heora eald-hláford cynnes *the Cæsar was of the kin of their ancient lords*, Bt. 1; Fox 2, 22. He sende ǽrend-gewrit eald-hláfordum *he sent letters to the ancient lords*, Bt. Met. Fox 1, 126; Met. 1, 63.

eald-hryter-flǽsc, es; *n. A side of meat cut off;* succīdia, Ælfc. Gl. 31; Som. 61, 101; Wrt. Voc. 27, 29. *Mann. suggests* eald-hryðer-flǽsc *adulti bŏvis căro*. v. hrysel.

ealdian; *p.* ode; *pp.* od *To grow* or *wax old;* senescĕre, inveterascĕre:—Syððan ic ealdode *postquam consĕnui*, Gen. 18, 12: Jn. Bos. 21, 18: Exon. 33 a; Th. 104, 27; Gú. 14. DER. for-ealdian.

eald-líc; *adj. Old, senile, venerable;* sĕnīlis, grăvis:—Ealdlíc *sĕnīlis*, Ælfc. Gr. 9, 28; Som. 11, 38: *grăvis*, Off. Episc. 1.

eald-móder, ealde-móder; *f. A grandmother;* avia:—Ealde-móder *avia*, Ælfc. Gl. 91; Som. 75, 9; Wrt. Voc. 51, 54.

ealdnys, -nyss, e; *f.* OLDNESS, *age;* vĕtustas:—Ealdnyss *vĕtustas*, Ælfc. Gr. 5; Som. 5, 21. We awurpon ða derigendlícan ealdnysse *we have cast off pernicious age*, Homl. Th. i. 194, 25.

ealdor, ealdur, aldor; *gen.* ealdres; *dat.* ealdre; *pl. nom. acc.* ealdras; *m.* I. *an* ELDER, *parent, head of a family, author;* părens, paterfamĭlias, auctor:—Úre ealdras ða ǽrestan menn *prīmi părentes nostri*, Bd. 1, 27; S. 493, 3. Ðæt unriht ðe his ealdras ǽr gefremedon *inīquĭtas patrum ejus*, Ps. Th. 108, 14. Sum hírédes ealdor wæs *hŏmo erat paterfamĭlias*, Mt. Bos. 21, 33. Þýstra ealdor *tenebrārum auctor*, Bd. 2, 1; S. 501, 16. II. *an elder, chief, governor, prince;* sĕnior, præpŏsĭtus, princeps:—Ðæs folces ealdoran *seniōres pŏpŭli*, Lev. 4, 15. Hundredes ealdor *centŭrio*, Mt. Bos. 8, 5: Ælfc. Gl. 6; Som. 56, 58. Ðæra byrla ealdor *the chief butler*, Gen. 40, 9. Cwæþ se Hǽlend to ðæs temples ealdrum *dixit Iesus ad magistrātus templi*, Lk. Bos. 22, 52: C. R. Ben. 25. Ðæt wæs ealdor heora *that was their chief*, Cd. 221; Th. 287, 27; Sat. 373. Heofna ealdor *the prince of the heavens*, Cd. 226; Th. 300, 20; Sat. 567. Ealdor þegna *the prince of thanes*, Beo. Th. 3293; B. 1644. Egesful ealdor *a dreadful prince*, Exon. 70 b; Th. 262, 7; Jul. 329. He ofer his ealdre gestód *he stood opposite his sovereign*, 55 b; Th. 196, 1; Az. 167. Ealdras of Zabulone *princĭpes Zabulon*, Ps. Th. 67, 25: 82, 9. [*Wyc.* eldren, eldres *fathers, seniors: Laym.* ældere, aldere *a chieftain;* ældere, ælderen, alderen *ancestors, parents: Plat.* elder, *m. senior; in pl. parents: O. Sax.* aldiro, aldro, *m. ancestor; pl.* eldiron *parents: Dut.* ouder *a parent; pl.* ouders, ouderen, *m. parents: O. Frs.* alder *a parent: Ger.* eltern, ältern *parents: M. H. Ger.* altern *parents: O. H. Ger.* altiron, eltiron *parents: Dan.* ældre *elder, older;* for-ældre *parents: Swed.* äldre *elder, older;* for-äldrar *parents.*] v. yldra.

EALDOR, aldor, es; *n:* e; *f?* I. *life;* vita:—Ealdres æt ende *at life's end*, Beo. Th. 5573; B. 2790. Ðe him wolde ealdres geunnan *which would grant him life*, Andr. Kmbl. 2263; An. 1133. On ðissum ealdre *in this life*, Ps. Th. 87, 14. Deáþ geþryðeþ ealdor ánra gehwæs *death expels the life of every one*, Exon. 62 b; Th. 231, 10; Ph. 487. Nalles for ealdre mearn *he cared not for life*, Beo. Th. 2889; B. 1442. He æt wíge gecrang ealdres scyldig *he succumbed in battle, his life forfeiting*, 2680; B. 1338: 4128; B. 2061. Ne wæs me feorh ðá gén ealdor in innan *there was as yet no soul, no life within me*, Exon. 103 a; Th. 391, 10; Rä. 10, 3: Andr. Kmbl. 2276; An. 1139: Salm. Kmbl. 711; Sal. 355. Swá biþ geóguþe þeáw, ðǽr ðæs ealdres egsa ne stýreþ *so is the wont of youth, where fear of life checks not*, Exon. 38 b; Th. 127, 24; Gú. 391. On ealdre ealre *in the whole life*, Ps. Th. 126, 6. II. *age, in the expressions,* on ealdre, on aldre *ever;* unquam *and* to ealdre *always;* semper, *which are used not only with regard to the duration of life, but also in general for an unlimited period of time, independently or with the addition of* á, áwa, ǽfre, æfter, éce *as well in positive as in negative sentences:*—Ne mæg hine on ealdre ǽnig onhréran *non commovēbītur in æternum*, Ps. Th. 124, 1: 79, 15. Ne weorþe ic on ealdre ǽfre gescended *non confundar in æternum*, 70, 1: 118, 80. Ic ǽr ǽfre on ealdre ne wolde melda weorþan *I never before would be the narrator*, Exon. 50 b; Th. 175, 29; Gú. 1202. Him gewearþ yrmþu to ealdre *misery was to them for ever*, 73 a; Th. 272, 24; Jul. 504. Á to ealdre, 116 a; Th. 446, 28; Dóm. 29. Ǽfre to ealdre, 56 b; Th. 200, 13; Ph. 40. Áwa to ealdre, 14 b; Th. 30, 13; Cri. 479. Éce to ealdre, 18 a; Th. 43, 17; Cri. 690: Menol. Fox 303; Men. 153. [*O. Sax.* aldar, *n. ætas: O. Frs.* alder *age* in alderlong: *Dut.* ouder in ouder-dom *lifetime: Ger. M. H. Ger.* alter, *n. age: O. H. Ger.* altar, *n. ætas, ævum, vĕtustas, sĕnectus: Goth.* alds, *f. ævum: Dan.* alder, *m. f. age: Swed.* ålder, *m. age: Icel.* aldr, *m. age, life, period, everlasting life.*]

ealdor-apostol, aldor-apostol, es; *m. The chief apostle, the chief of the apostles;* princeps apostŏlōrum:—He mynster getimbrede on áre Sc̄e Petres ðæs ealdorapostoles *he built a monastery in honour of St. Peter, the chief apostle*, Bd. 4, 18; S. 586, 26.

ealdor-bana *a life-destroyer;* vitæ destructor. v. aldor-bana.

ealdor-bealu, aldor-bealu; *gen.* -bealuwes, -bealwes; *n. Vital evil;* malum vitæ affĭciens:—Fá þrówiaþ ealdor-bealu egeslíc *the hostile shall suffer terrific vital evil*, Exon. 31 b; Th. 98, 31; Cri. 1616.

ealdor-biscop, es; *m. An elder* or *chief bishop, an archbishop;* sĕnior episcŏpus, archiepiscŏpus; *the Pope is so called by king Alfred:*—Ðá wæs Vitalianus Papa ðæs apostolícan setles ealdorbiscop *then Pope Vitalian was the chief bishop of the apostolic seat;* sedi apostŏlĭcæ præerat, Bd. 4, 1; S. 563, 23: 2, 13; S. 516, 1: 5, 8; S. 621, 39. v. bisceop.

ealdor-botl, es; *n. A royal house* or *villa;* rēgālis villa:—Ðǽr wæs ðá cyninges ealdorbotl *ubi tunc erat villa rēgālis*, Bd. 2, 9; S. 511, 18.

ealdor-burh, -burg; *gen.* -burge; *f. A royal city, metropolis;* rēgia arx, metrŏpŏlis:—On Cantwara byrig, seó wæs ealles his ríces ealdorburh *in cīvĭtāte Doruvernensi, quæ impĕrii sui tōtius erat metrŏpŏlis*, Bd. 1, 25; S. 487, 19: 1, 13; S. 482, 6. Godes ealdorburg *God's royal city*, Exon. 114 b; Th. 441, 8; Rä. 60, 15.

ealdor-cearu *life-care, care for life, life-long care.* v. aldor-cearu.

ealdor-dæg, ealder-dæg, aldor-dæg; *gen.* -dæges; *pl. nom. acc.* -dagas; *m. Life-day, day of life;* vitæ dies:—On ealderdagum *in the days of his life*, Beo. Th. 1518; B. 757: 1440; B. 718.

ealdor-déma *a supreme judge, a prince.* v. aldor-déma.

ealdor-dóm, ealdur-dóm, aldor-dóm, alder-dóm, es; *m.* [ealdor *an elder, a chief;* dóm *dominion, power*] *Eldership, authority, magistracy, principality;* auctōrĭtas, magistrātus, princĭpātus, prīmātus, dŭcātus:—He his ealdordóm synnum aswefede *he* [*Reuben*] *had destroyed his eldership by sins*, Cd. 160; Th. 199, 8; Exod. 335. Is heora ealdordóm gestrangod *confortātus est princĭpātus eōrum*, Ps. Th. 138, 15: Cd. 60; Th. 73, 1; Gen. 1197: Exon. 58 a; Th. 208, 20; Ph. 158: 66 a; Th. 244, 10; Jul. 25. Theodor ealdordóm hæfde *Theodōrus prīmātum hăbēbat*, Bd. 4, 28; S. 606, 26, 6. Ealdordóm *dŭcātus*, Ælfc. Gl. 6; Som. 56, 48; Wrt. Voc. 18, 3. Ealdordómas *vel* ða héhstan wurþscipas *fasces*, 112; Som. 79, 85; Wrt. Voc. 59, 53: 68; Som. 70, 4; Wrt. Voc. 42, 13.

ealdor-duguþ, aldor-duguþ, e; *f. The chief nobility;* procĕres, Judth. 12; Thw. 26, 5; Jud. 310.

ealdor-freá *a chief lord.* v. aldor-freá.

ealdor-gedál, aldor-gedál, es; *n. Separation from life, death;* vitæ divortium, mors:—Óþ his ealdorgedál *until his death*, Cd. 92; Th. 118, 2; Gen. 1959.

ealdor-gesceaft, e; *f. Condition of life;* vitæ condĭtio, Exon. 110 a; Th. 421, 24; Rä. 40, 23.

ealdor-gewinna, an; *m. Vital adversary;* adversārius qui vitæ insĭdiātur, Beo. Th. 5799; B. 2903: Exon. 40 b; Th. 134, 10; Gú. 505.

ealdor-lang; *adj. Life-long;* sempĭternus:—Hí ealdorlangne tír geslógon æt sæcce *they won life-long glory in the battle*, Chr. 937; Erl. 112, 3; Æðelst. 3.

ealdor-leás, aldor-leás; *adj. Lifeless;* vita prīvātus:—Hie gefricgeaþ freán úserne ealdorleásne *they shall hear our lord* [*is*] *lifeless*, Beo. Th. 5998; B. 3003.

ealdor-leás *deprived of parents.* v. aldor-leás.

ealdor-leg, aldor-leg, -læg, es; *n.* [ealdor, læg; *p. of* licgan] *Life-law,* *fate, death;* fātum, mors:—Æfter eáldorlege *after death*, Exon. 51 a; Th. 177, 29; Gū. 1234.

ealdorlíc, aldorlíc; *adj. Principal, chief, excellent;* princĭpālis, magnĭfĭcus:—Ealdorlíc *princĭpālis*, Ælfc. Gr. 9, 28; Som. 11, 37. Ealdorlíc ānnyss *princĭpālis unĭtas*, Hymn. Surt. 1, 5. Ealdorlíce Gāste *Spīrĭtu princĭpāli*, Ps. Grn. 50, 13; ii. 149, 13.

ealdor-líce; *adv. Excellently.* v. aldor-líce.

ealdorlícnes, -ness, -nys, -nyss, e; *f. Principality, authority;* auctōrĭtas:—Ne syllaþ we đē ǣnige ealdorlícnysse *nullam tibi auctōrĭtātem trĭbuĭmus*, Bd. 1, 27; S. 492, 12, 15, 22, 26. Mid māran ealdorlícnysse *mājōre auctōrĭtāte*, 3, 22; S. 553, 3, 35.

ealdor-man, -mann, -mon, ealdur-, aldor-, eldor-, es; *m.* [eald *old, not only in age, but in knowledge*, v. eald, hence ealdor *an elder;* man *hŏmo*]. I. *an elderman*, ALDERMAN, *senator, chief, duke, a nobleman of the highest rank, and holding an office inferior only to that of the king;* mājor nātu, sĕnātor, prŏcer, princeps, prīmas, dux, præfectus, trĭbūnus, quīcunque est aliis grădu aut nātu mājor. The title of Ealdorman or Aldorman denoted civil as well as military pre-eminence. The word *ealdor* or *aldor* in Anglo-Saxon denotes princely dignity: in Beowulf it is used as a synonym for cyning, þeóden, and other words applied to royal personages. Like many other titles of rank in the various Teutonic languages, it, strictly speaking, implies age, though practically this idea does not survive in it any more than it does in the word *Senior*, the original of the feudal term *Seigneur*. Every shire had its ealdorman, who was the principal judicial officer of the shire, and also the leader of its armed force. The internal regulations of the shire, as well as its political relation to the whole kingdom, were under his immediate guidance and supervision,—the scīr-gerēfa, or sheriff, being little more than his deputy, and under his control. The dignity of the ealdorman was supported by lands within his district, which appear to have passed with the office,—hence the phrases, đæs ealdormonnes lond, mearc, gemǣro, etc. which so often occur. The ealdorman had also a share of the fines and other monies levied to the king's use; though, as he was invariably appointed from among the higher nobles, he must always have possessed lands of his own to the extent of forty hides, v. *Hist. Eliens*. ii. 40. The ealdormen of the several shires seem to have been appointed by the king, with the assent of the higher nobles, if not of the whole witena gemōt, and to have been taken from the most trustworthy, powerful, and wealthy of the nobles of the shire. The office and dignity of ealdorman was held for life,—though sometimes forfeited for treason and other grave offences; but it was not strictly hereditary:—Fram đām brōđrum and đām ealdormannum *a fratrĭbus ac majōrĭbus*, Bd. 5, 14; S. 634, 10: 5, 19; S. 637, 6. Ofslōgon Rōmāna ealdorman *slew a Roman noble*, Ors. 5, 10; Bos. 108, 30. Ealdormen, *nom. pl. princĭpes*, Ps. Th. 67, 24: Gen. 12, 15. Đæt he his ealdormen lǣrde *ut erŭdīret princĭpes suos*, Ps. Th. 104, 18. Ān ealdormann *unus de princĭpĭbus*, 81, 7. Ealdormenn Iudan *princĭpes Jŭda*, 67, 25: 82, 9: Mt. Bos. 20, 25: Mk. Bos. 6, 21. His ealdormannum and his þegnum *suis dŭcĭbus ac ministris*, Bd. 3, 3; S. 526, 1: 4, 15; S. 583, 27. Arbatus his ealdorman, đe he gesct hæfde ofer Mēđas đæt land *Arbaces, his chief officer, whom he had set over the country of the Medes*, Ors. 1, 12; Bos. 35, 17: 2, 1; Bos. 38, 35: Bd. 4, 12; S. 580, 34: 1, 13; S. 481, 40. Đæt se ylca đa dōhter đæs ealdormannes blinde onlīhte *ut idem fīliam trĭbūni cæcam inlumināvĕrit*, 1, 18; S. 484, 30: Bt. 10; Fox 28, 31. II. the new constitution introduced by Cnut, who reigned in England from A. D. 1014 to 1035, reduced the ealdorman to a subordinate position,—one eorl, *Nors*. jarl, being placed over several shires. The Danish kings ruled by their eorlas or jarls, and the ealdormen disappeared from the shires. Gradually the title ceased altogether, except in the cities, where it denoted an inferior judicature, much as it now does among ourselves:—Đis is đonne seó woruldcunde gerǣdnes, đe ic [Cnut] wille, mid mīnan witenan rǣde, đæt man healde ofer eall Engla land *this is then the secular ordinance which I* [*Cnut*], *with the counsel of my witan, will, that it be observed over all the land of the English*, L. C. S. pref; Th. i. 376, 3, 4. Đæt is đonne ǣrest đæt ic wylle; đæt man rihte laga upp-arǣre, and ǣghwilce unlaga georne afylle, and đæt man aweódige and awyrtwalige, ǣghwylc unriht, swā man geornost mǣge, of đissum earde *this is then the first that I will; that right laws be established, and all unjust laws carefully suppressed, and that every injustice be weeded out and rooted up, with all possible diligence, from this land*, L. C. S. 1; Th. i. 376, 5-8. And habbe man þrīwa on geára burh-gemōt, and twā scīr-gemōt *and thrice a year let there be a borough meeting, and twice a shire meeting*, L. C. S. 18; Th. i. 386, 4, 5. v. eorl, scīrgerēfa, and hūscarl.

ealdor-mon, -monn, es; *m. An elderman, alderman, nobleman, chief;* mājor nātu, princeps:—Ebrinus se ealdormon *Ebrinus mājor dŏmus rēgiæ*, Bd. 4, 1; S. 564, 33: 2, 13; S. 515, 32. v. ealdor-man.

ealdor-ner, aldor-ner, es; *n. A life-salvation, life's safety, refuge, asylum;* vitæ servātio, refŭgium:—Cwom him to āre and to ealdor-nere *he came to them for mercy and for their life's salvation*, Exon. 53 b; Th. 189, 4; Az. 54. v. ner.

ealdor-sacerd, es; *m. A high priest;* summus sacerdos:—Ongan eáldorsacerd hyspan *the high priest began to revile*, Andr. Kmbl. 1340; An. 670.

ealdor-scype, es; *m. Eldership, supremacy;* principātus, prīmātus:—Đa on þeódum ealdorscype habbaþ *they have eldership among the nations*, Mk. Bos. 10, 42. Ealdorscype healdan *prīmātum tĕnēre*, Coll. Monast. Th. 30, 17.

ealdor-stōl, es; *m. The lord's seat;* domĭni sēdes:—Āhte ic ealdorstōl *I possessed the lord's seat*, Exon. 94 b; Th. 353, 36; Reim. 23.

ealdor-þegn, aldor-þegn [-þægn], es; *m. The principal thane* or *servant;* princĭpālis minister:—Ealdorþegnas *principal servants*, Menol. Fox 257; Men. 130. Hie đæt đām ealdorþegnum cȳđan eódon *they went to announce it to the principal thanes*, Judth. 12; Thw. 25, 4; Jud. 242.

ealdor-wīsa *a chief ruler.* v. aldor-wīsa.

eald-riht, es; *n. An ancient right;* vĕtus jus *vel* privĭlēgium:—He him gehēt đæt hȳ ealdrihta ǣlces mōsten wyrđe gewunigen *he promised them that they should remain possessed of each of their ancient rights*, Bt. Met. Fox 1, 71; Met. 1, 36: 1, 114; Met. 1, 57. Bǣdon hine đæt he him to heora ealdrihtum gefultumede *they prayed him that he would succour them with respect to their ancient rights*, Bt. 1; Fox 2, 24.

Eald-Seaxe, Ald-Seaxe; *gen.* -Seaxa; *dat.* -Seaxum; *pl. m:* Eald-Seaxan; *pl. m. The Old-Saxons;* antīqui Saxŏnes; *the German* or *continental Saxons occupying the territory between the Eyder and the Weser:*—Hēr Eald-Seaxe [Ald-Seaxe, Th. 92, 29, col. 1] and Francan gefuhton *in this year* [A. D. 779] *the Old-Saxons and the Franks fought*, Chr. 779; Th. 93, 29, col. 1, 2. Gegadrode mycel sciphere on Eald-Seaxum [Ald-Seaxum, col. 1] *a large naval force assembled among the Old-Saxons*, 885; Th. 154, 20, col. 2, 3: 449; Th. 20, 20, 26: 924; Th. 199, 10: Bd. 5, 10; S. 624, 12, 22. Be norþan Đyringum syndon Eald-Seaxan and be norþan westan him syndon Frysan, and be westan Eald-Seaxum is Ælfe mūþa đære eá and Frysland *to the north of the Thuringians are the Old-Saxons, and to the north-west of them are the Friesians, and to the west of the Old-Saxons is the mouth of the river Elbe and Friesland*, Ors. 1, 1; Bos. 18, 34: Bos. 19, 14.

eald-spell, es; *n. An old story;* antīqua narrātio:—Ælfrēd us eald-spell reahte *Alfred told us an old story*, Bt. Met. Fox introduc. 2; Met. Einl. 1. On ealdspellum *in old tales*, Bt. 39, 4; Fox 216, 19.

eald-spræc, e; *f. An old speech, history*, Leo A. Sax. Gl. 149.

Ealdulfes næs, Chr. 1052; Th. 321, 10. v. Eádulfes næs.

ealdung, e; *f. Age;* sĕnectus:—Rōma besprycþ đæt hyre weallas for ealdunge brosnian *Rome complains that her walls decay from age*, Ors. 2, 4; Bos. 44, 45. DER. ealdian.

ealdur *a prince*, Jn. Foxe 16, 11. v. ealdor.

ealdur-dōm *authority, principality*, Ps. Th. 113, 2. v. ealdor-dōm.

ealdur-man, -mann, es; *m. An elderman, alderman, nobleman;* mājor nātu, princeps:—Nelle ge on ealdurmenn āne getreówian *nōlīte confīdere in princĭpĭbus*, Ps. Th. 145, 2: 118, 161. v. ealdor-man.

eald-wērig; *adj. Vile of old;* jampridem malignus:—Ealdwērige Egypta folc *the folk of Egypt vile of old*, Cd. 145; Th. 180, 24; Exod. 50.

eald-wīf, es; *n. An old woman;* anus, anŭla, vĕtŭla:—Sceal ic nū ealdwīf cennan *num vere parĭtūra sum anus*, Gen. 18, 13: Ælfc. Gl. 88; Som. 74, 67; Wrt. Voc. 50, 48.

eald-wita, an; *m.* [eald *old*, wita *one who knows*] *One old* or *eminent in knowledge, a priest;* presbȳter:—Presbiter is mæsse-preóst ođđe eald-wita; nā đæt ǣlc eald sȳ, ac đæt he eald sy on wīsdōme *presbyter is the mass-priest or one eminent in knowledge; not that every one is old, but that he is old in wisdom*, L. Ælf. C. 17; Th. ii. 348, 20: Bd. 2, 16; S. 519, 29.

eald-writere, es; *m. An antiquarian, one that writes of old* or *ancient matters;* antīquārius, Som. Ben. Lye.

ealeđe-tūn, es; *m. An ale-house;* taberna, Som. Ben. Lye.

eal-fela *Very much, full many;* permultum:—Se mæg ealfela singan and secgan *he can sing and say very much*, Exon. 17 b; Th. 42, 2; Cri. 666: Beo. Th. 1742; B. 869: 1770; B. 883.

eal-felo *All-fell, very baleful;* omnīno pernĭciosus:—Eal-felo āttor *very baleful venom*, Exon. 106 b; Th. 405, 28; Rā. 24, 9. v. æl-fæle, fell.

eal-fremd *foreign;* aliēnus. v. æl-fremd.

eal-geador, eall-geador; *adv. Altogether;* omnīno:—Đǣr wæs ealgeador Grendles grāpe *there was altogether Grendel's grasp*, Beo. Th. 1675; B. 835. v. geador.

eal-gearo, eall-gearo; *adj. All ready* or *prepared;* omnīno promptus *vel* părātus:—Beorh ealgearo wunode on wonge *the mountain stood all ready on the plain*, Beo. Th. 4475; B. 2241: 155; B. 77: 2465; B. 1230.

eal-geleáflīc *believed by all;* catholĭcus. v. eall-geleáflīc.

ealgian, algian; *p.* ode; *pp.* od *To defend;* defendĕre:—Nemne we mǣgen feorh ealgian þeódnes *unless we may defend the life of the prince*, Beo. Th. 5304; B. 2655: 5329; B. 2668. Hī æt campe wiđ lāþra gehwæne land ealgodon *they defended the land in conflict against every foe*, Chr. 937; Th. 202, 4; Æđelst. 9: Andr. Kmbl. 20; An. 10: Beo. Th. 2413; B. 1204: R. Ben. 64: 69. DER. ge-ealgian, -algian.

eal-grēne, eall-grēne, æl-grēne; *adj. All-green;* omnīno vĭrĭdis:—Gesēgun eorþan ealgrēne *they saw the earth all-green,* Exon. 24 b; Th. 69, 31; Cri. 1129.

eal-gylden, eall-gylden; *adj. All-golden;* omnīno aurĕus:—Swȳn eal-gylden *the all-golden swine,* Beo. Th. 2227; B. 1111.

ealh *a residence, temple.* v. alh, healh.

eal-hālig *all-holy;* omnīno sanctus. v. eall-hālig.

ealh-stede, alh-stede, eolh-stede, es; *m. A protecting* or *sheltering place, city, temple;* lŏcus qui præbet tūtēlam, arx, templum:—In ðære wīdan byrig, ealhstede eorla *in the wide city, the sheltering place of men,* Cd. 208; Th. 258, 11; Dan. 674.

eal-hūs *an ale-house,* Som. Ben. Lye. v. eala-hūs.

eal-hwīt *all-white.* v. eall-hwīt.

eá-lifer, e; *f.* [eá *water,* lifer *liver*] *Liverwort?* eupătōrium cannăbĭnum, Lin:—Eálifer hātte wyrt gnīd on ealaþ *rub in ale the herb called liverwort,* L. M. 1, 22; Lchdm. ii. 64, 21: 2, 24; Lchdm. ii. 216, 14.

eal-īren *all of iron.* v. eall-īren.

eal-īsig *all-icy;* omnīno glaciālis. v. eall-īsig.

eá-līðend, es; *m. A wave-sailor, sailor;* qui æquor navĭgat:—Wǣron eorlas onlīce eálīðendum *the men were like sailors-over-the-wave,* Andr. Kmbl. 502; An. 251.

eall; *adj. All;* tōtus:—Eall *tōtus,* Ælfc. Gr. 18; Som. 21, 10. Eall ðīn līchama *all thy body,* Mt. Bos. 6, 22. Eall ðeós woruld *all this world,* Cd. 29; Th. 38, 9; Gen. 604: Exon. 20 a; Th. 52, 34; Cri. 843: Lk. Bos. 23, 18: Jn. Bos. 11, 50: Mk. Bos. 4, 34: Andr. Kmbl. 652; An. 326: 2294; An. 1148: 2867; An. 1436: Bt. Met. Fox 26, 121; Met. 26, 61: 28, 9; Met. 28, 5: Beo. Th. 4091; B. 2042: 4181; B. 2087: Exon. 22 a; Th. 60, 5; Cri. 965: Salm. Kmbl. 2; Sal. 1: Bt. 38, 4; Fox 204, 9: Bd. 1, 12; S. 480, 35: 1, 26; S. 487, 37: Ors. 2, 4; Bos. 45, 15. v. eal.

ealla, an; *m. Gall, bile;* fel:—Hym man drincan mengde myd eallan and myd ecede *one mingled him a drink with gall and with vinegar,* Nicod. 26; Thw. 14, 18. Wið ðæs eallan [geallan MS. H.] togotennysse *for effusion of the bile,* Herb. 146, 2; Lchdm. i. 270, 4: 141, 2; Lchdm. i. 262, 12. v. gealla.

eall-beorht, æll-beorht, æl-beorht; *adj. All-bright;* pĕnĭtus splendĭdus, fulgentissĭmus:—Englas eall-beorhte *angels all-bright,* Cd. 224; Th. 297, 23; Sat. 522.

eall-cyn; *adj. Of every kind, universal;* omnĭgĕnus, unĭversus:—Eallcyn sǣd getreówfulra [Iacobes MSS. C. T.] *unĭversum semen Iacob,* Ps. Spl. 21, 22.

eallenga, eællenge; *adv. Altogether, utterly;* prorsus, omnīno:—Ðonne wæs se ōðer eallenga sweart *then was the other utterly black,* Cd. 24; Th. 30, 35; Gen. 477.

Eallerīca, an; *m. Alaric, king of the Goths:*—Rædgota and Eallerīca Rōmāne burig abrǣcon *Rhadgast and Alaric broke into the city of Rome,* Bt. 1; Fox 2, 2. v. Alrīca.

eall-geador; *adv. Altogether,* Andr. Kmbl. 2196; An. 1099. v. eal-geador.

eall-gearo; *adj. All-ready;* omnīno promptus:—Ic beóm eall-gearo *I am all-ready,* Exon. 106 b; Th. 405, 19; Rā. 24, 4. v. eal-gearo.

eall-geleáflīc; *adj.* [geleáflīc *believed*] *Believed by all, catholic;* cathŏlĭcus = καθολικός:—Ðæt monega cyricean on Hibernia, lǣrendum Athamnano, ða eallgeleáflīcan Eástran onfēngon *ut plurĭmæ Scottōrum ecclesiæ, instante Adamnano, cathŏlĭcum Pascha suscēpĕrint,* Bd. 5, 15; S. 635, 10.

eall-grēne; *adj. All-green;* omnīno vĭrĭdis:—Hwā furðum teóde eorþan eall-grēne *who first produced the earth all-green,* Andr. Recd. 1599; An. 799. v. eal-grēne.

eall-gylden; *adj. All-golden;* omnīno aurĕus:—He geseah segn eall-gylden *he saw an ensign all-golden,* Beo. Th. 5528; B. 2767: Judth. 10; Thw. 22, 3; Jud. 46. v. eal-gylden.

eall-hālig; *adj. All-holy;* omnīno sanctus:—Drihten, ðū earce eart eall-hāligra *O Lord, thou art the ark of the all-holy,* Ps. Th. 131, 8.

eall-hwīt; *adj. All-white;* omnīno albus:—On eallhwītre þryh *in an all-white coffin,* Th. Diplm. A. D. 970; 241, 11.

eal-līc *universal, general, catholic,* Som. Ben. Lye. v. al-līc.

ealling; *adv. Always;* semper:—Ealling byþ, ymb tyn niht ðæs, tiid [= tīd] geweorþad Barþolomeus *the time of Bartholomew is always honoured about ten nights from hence,* Menol. Fox 304; Men. 153: 344; Men. 173. v. ealneg.

eallinga; *adv. Altogether, wholly;* prorsus, omnīno:—He eallinga ne adiligaþ eów *he will not altogether destroy you,* Deut. 4, 31: Salm. Kmbl. 835; Sal. 417. v. eallunga.

eall-īren; *adj. All of iron;* omnīno ferrĕus:—He hēht gewyrcean eall-īrenne wīgbord wrætlīc *he commanded a wondrous battle-shield, all of iron, to be made,* Beo. Th. 4665; B. 2338.

eall-īsig; *adj. All-icy;* omnīno glaciālis:—Saturnus is se cealda eall-īsig tungel *Saturn is the cold all-icy star,* Bt. Met. Fox 24, 45; Met. 24, 23. Se is eall-īsig *it is all icy,* Bt. 36, 2; Fox 174, 13.

eall-mægen, al-mægen, es; *n. All-power, all-might;* omnis vis:—Gif hī, eall-mægene, ne þiówoden þeódne mǣrum *if they, with all might, served not the illustrious Lord,* Bt. Met. Fox 29, 193; Met. 29, 98.

eall-mihtig, -meahtig, -mehtig, -mihteg [el-, æl-, æll-]; *adj. Almighty;* omnĭpŏtens:—Drihten eallmihtig *Domĭnus Deus,* Ps. Th. 93, 22.

eall-nacod; *adj. Entirely naked;* omnīno nūdus:—Ic eom eallnacod *I am all naked,* Cd. 42; Th. 54, 3; Gen. 871.

eallneg; *adv. Always;* semper:—Ðū eallneg siófodest ðæt hī eallneg nǣron on wīte *thou always didst lament that they were not always punished,* Bt. 38, 4; Fox 204, 10, 11, MS. Cot. v. ealneg.

eall-niwe; *adj. All-new;* omnīno nŏvus:—He wearþ gebunden mid eallniwum rāpum *nŏvis funĭbus vinctus est,* Jud. 16, 11.

eallnunge; *adv. Altogether;* omnīno, C. R. Ben. 55. v. eallunga.

eall-reord *foreign speaking, barbarous,* Bd. 1, 23; S. 485, 32. v. el-reord.

Eallrīca, an; *m. Alaric, king of the Goths:*—Eallrīca Gotona cyning *Alaric, king of the Goths,* Ors. 2, 1; Bos. 39, 37. v. Alrīca.

eall-rūh; *adj. All-rough;* omnīno hirsūtus:—Se wæs reád and eall rūh *he was red and all hairy,* Gen. 25, 25.

eall-swā; *adv. Also, so, so as, likewise, even as, even so;* sīcut:—Eall-swā he sǣde *sīcut dixit,* Mk. Bos. 14, 16. v. eal-swā.

eall-tela; *adv. Quite well;* omnīno bĕne, Cd. 91; Th. 114, 17; Gen. 1905.

eallunga, allunga, eallenga, eællenge, eallinga, eallnunge; *adv. Altogether, entirely, quite, indeed, at all, assuredly, utterly;* prorsus, omnīno, profecto:—Ðæt ge eallunga ne swerion *non jurāre omnīno,* Mt. Bos. 5, 34: Exon. 21 b; Th. 57, 23; Cri. 923: Bt. Met. Fox 25, 131; Met. 25, 66: Bt. 10; Fox 30, 3. Eallunga Godes rīce on eów becymþ *profecto pervēnit in vos regnum Dei,* Lk. Bos. 11, 20.

eall-wealda; *adj. All-ruling, almighty;* omnĭpŏtens:—Eallwealdan Gode *to almighty God,* Andr. Recd. 414; An. 205. v. eal-wealda.

eall-wihta, al-wihta, æl-wihta; *pl.* [eall *all, every;* wiht *creature*] *All beings;* omnia creāta:—Cyning eall-wihta *king of all creatures,* Andr. Kmbl. 3204; An. 1605: Cd. 47; Th. 60, 7; Gen. 978: 5; Th. 7, 28; Gen. 113. v. wiht I, *for* wihta, *nom. pl.*

eall-wundor, es; *n.* [wundor *a wonder*] *A very wonderful thing;* res omnīno mirābĭlis:—Weras fyrdleóþ gōlon [MS. galan] eall-wundra fela *the men sung a martial song of many very wonderful things,* Cd. 171; Th. 215, 5; Exod. 578.

eal-mægen *all power, all might.* v. eall-mægen.

eal-mǣst, æl-mǣst; *adv.* ALMOST; totum fere, pene:—Hit is eal-mǣst mid hāligra manna naman geset *sanctōrum hŏmĭnum nōmĭnĭbus totum fere obsĭtum est,* Bd. Whelc. 448, 18; Homl. Th. ii. 466, 22.

eal-mihtig; *adj. All-mighty;* omnĭpŏtens:—On Godes ealmihtiges naman *in the name of almighty God,* Th. Diplm. A. D. 886–899; 138, 34. v. eall-mihtig.

eal-myrca *an Ethiopian.* v. æl-myrca.

eal-nacod *entirely naked.* v. eall-nacod.

ealneg, ealnig, ealllneg; *adv.* [ealne weg, Bt. 38, 4; Fox 204, 10, 11] *Always, quite;* semper, prorsus:—Ȳþ wið lande ealneg winneþ *the wave contends always against the land,* Bt. Met. Fox 28, 114; Met. 28, 57: Ors. 3, 7; Bos. 62, 36. Ðe ǣfre biþ ealnig smylte *which ever is quite calm,* Bt. Met. Fox 21, 30; Met. 21, 15.

ealning; *adv. Always;* semper:—Swā he ealning dyde æt Saltwīc *as he always did at Saltwich,* Th. Diplm. A.D. 886–899; 138, 15. v. ealling, ealneg.

eal-niwe *all-new, quite new.* v. eall-niwe.

eal-nōsu, eall-nōsu, eall seó nāsu, e; *f. All nose* or *all the nose, a swelling of the uvula;* columella, columna nasi:—Eal ufweard nōsu *tota ascendens columna nasi,* Ælfc. Gl. 71; Som. 70, 86; Wrt. Voc. 43, 18. Eall-nōsu, Mann: eal-nōsu *the swelling of the uvula;* columella. v. Som. Eall seó nāsu *columna,* Wrt. Voc. 282, 64.

ealo *ale,* Ors. 1, 1; Bos. 22, 17: Bt. 17; Fox 60, 5. v. ealu.

ealo-benc, e; *f. An ale-bench:*—In ealo-bence *on the ale-bench,* Beo. Th. 2062; B. 1029. v. ealu-benc.

ealo-fæt, es; *n. An ale-vat, vessel in which ale was left to ferment;* lăcus:—Under ðæt ealo-fæt *under the ale-vat,* L. M. 1, 67; Lchdm. ii. 142, 12.

ealo-gāl; *adj. Ale-drunk;* cervĭsia inebriātus:—Ic gehȳre ealogālra gylp *I hear the boast of the ale-drunken,* Cd. 109; Th. 145, 19; Gen. 2408.

ealo-geweorc, es; *n. Ale-work, brewing;* cervĭsiæ coctio:—On ðære byrig wæs ǣrest ealo-geweorc ongunnen *in that city ale-brewing was first begun,* Ors. 5, 3; Bos. 103, 35.

eálond, es; *n. An island;* insŭla:—Breoton is gārsecges eálond *Brittānia est oceāni insŭla,* Bd. 1, 1; S. 473, 8: 1, 3; S. 475, 13. v. eáland.

ealoþ *ale,* L. In. 70; Th. i. 146, 17, MS. B. v. ealaþ.

ealo-wǣge, es; *n. The ale-cup:*—Se ðe bær hroden ealowǣge *who bare the ornamented ale-cup,* Beo. Th. 995; B. 495. Ofer ealowǣge *over the ale-cup* [*during a drinking*], Beo. Th. 966; B. 481. v. ealu-wǣge.

ealo-wōsa, an; *m. Ale-wetter* or *drinker;* cervĭsiæ inebriātor *vel* pōtor:—

Sumum yrrum ealowōsan, were wīnsadum *from one irritated as an ale-drinker, a wine-sated man*, Exon. 87 b; Th. 330, 10; Vy. 49.

eal-riht; *adj. All-right;* pĕnĭtus rectus, R. Ben. 72, Lye.

eal-sealf, e; *f.* [eal *all*, sealf *salve*] *The herb called the oak of Jerusalem* or *the oak of Cappadocia;* ambrŏsia, Som. Ben. Lye: = ἀμβροσία *a perfumed salve, a plant;* ambrŏsia mărĭtĭma, Diosc. 3, 129, L. S. Lex. under ἀμβροσία.

eal-seolcen; *adj. All-silken;* holosērĭcus = ὁλοσηρικός, Ælfc. Gl. 62; Som. 68, 92; Wrt. Voc. 40, 3.

eal-swā, eall-swā; *adv.* ALSO, *so, so as, likewise, even as, even so;* simĭlĭter, sīcut:—Cristenum cyninge gebȳreþ đæt he sȳ ealswā hit riht is *it is the duty of a Christian king to be as it is right*, L. I. P. 2; Th. ii. 304, 8, 22. Đā cwæþ he ealswā to đām ōđrum *dixit simĭlĭter ad altĕrum*, Mt. Bos. 21, 30. Gewurþe đē, ealswā đū wylle *fiat tĭbi sīcut vis*, Mt. Bos. 15, 28. [*Piers P. Chauc.* als *also: Laym.* alse, al so, al swa, al swo *as, so, also, thus, as if: Orm.* allse, alls, allswa, all swa *also, as, so: O. Sax.* alsō *simĭlĭter, tanquam, sīcut, quăsi, quum: Frs.* als, az, alsa *sīcut, cum, ita, si: O. Frs.* alsa, olsa *ita, cum: Dut.* als *when, if;* alzoo *thus, so: Ger.* also *thus;* als *as, when: M. H. Ger.* als, alsō, alse *thus, when: O. H. Ger.* al sō *ut, sīcut, vĕlut, sic.*]

eal-tēaw; *adj.* [eal *all*, teaw = tæw *good*] *Entirely good;* omnīno bŏnus:—Gif he ealteawne ende gedreógeþ *if he enjoys a very good end*, Cd. Jun. 110, 16; Hy. 2, 13; Hy. Grn. ii. 281, 13.

EALU, ealo, es; *n: generally indecl. in sing.* ALE; cervĭsia, sīcĕra:—Ne he ealu ne drince nǣfre ođđe wīn *let him never drink ale nor wine*, Jud. 13, 4. Iohannes se Fulluhtere ne dranc nāđor ne wīn, ne beór, ne ealu *John the Baptist drank neither wine, nor beer, nor ale*, Homl. Th. ii. 38, 7: Bt. 17; Fox 60, 5, MS. Cot: L. M. 1, 47; Lchdm. ii. 120, 15: Beo. Th. 1542; B. 769. [*Chauc. Laym.* ale: *O. Sax.* alo in alo-fat, *n. an ale-cup: Dan. Swed. Icel.* öl, *n.*]

ealu-benc, ealo-benc, e; *f. An ale-bench;* scamnum cervĭsiam bibentium:—On ealu-bence *on the ale-bench*, Beo. Th. 5726; B. 2867.

ealu-clȳfe *an ale-house*, Som. Ben. Lye. v. eala-hūs.

ealu-fæt *an ale-vat*, Som. Ben. Lye. v. ealo-fæt.

ealu-gafol, es; *n.* [gafol *tax, tribute*] *Tribute* or *excise paid for ale;* cervĭsiæ trĭbūtum:—On sumen lande gebūr sceal syllan hunig-gafol, on suman mete-gafol, on suman ealu-gafol *in one place a boor shall give honey-tribute, in another meat-tribute, in another ale-tribute*, L. R. S. 4; Th. i. 434, 32.

ealu-gāl *ale-drunken.* v. ealo-gāl.

ealu-geweorc *ale-brewing.* v. ealu.

ealu-malt *malt used for making ale.* v. ealu, alo-malt.

ealu-sceop, es; *m. An ale-brewer, a brewer;* cervĭsiārius, Som. Ben. Lye.

ealu-scōp, eala-scōp, es; *m. An ale-poet:*—We lǣraþ, đæt ǣnig preóst ne beó ealu-scōp *we teach that no priest be an ale-poet*, L. Edg. C. 58; Th. ii. 256, 15.

ealu-wǣge, es; *n. An ale-cup;* pătĕra, scyphus:—Dōhtor Hrōþgāres eorlum ealuwǣge bær *Hrothgar's daughter bore the ale-cup to the earls*, Beo. Th. 4047; B. 2021.

ealu-wōsa *ale-wetter* or *drinker.* v. ealo-wōsa.

Eal-walda, an; *m. All-ruler, the Almighty;* omnium rector, Cd. 14; Th. 16, 20; Gen. 246. v. Eal-wealda.

eal-weald; *adj. All-powerful, almighty;* omnĭpŏtens:—Ǣrende ealwealdan Gode wæs sprecen *a message was spoken to the all-powerful God*, Andr. Kmbl. 3239; An. 1622.

Eal-wealda, an; *m. All-ruler, God, the Almighty;* omnium rector, Deus, omnĭpŏtens:—For đam ealwealdan [MS. alwealdan] *for the all-ruler* [*God*], Cd. 19; Th. 23, 13; Gen. 359. Noldon ealwealdan [MS. alwealdan] word weorþian *they would not revere the all-ruler's* [*the Almighty's*] *word*, 18; Th. 21, 23; Gen. 328.

eal-werlīce; *adv. All-manly, liberally, freely;* prorsus virīlĭter, benigne:—Ealwerlīce [MS. ealwerlīc] dō Driht *benigne fac Domine*, Ps. Spl. 50, 19.

eal-wihta *all beings.* v. eall-wihta.

eal-wundor *a very wonderful thing.* v. eall-wundor.

eam *am:*—Ic eam biddende Drihten *ad Deum deprĕcātus sum*, Ps. Th. 141, 1. Ic eam leás ēcan dreámes *I am bereft of eternal joy*, Cd. 216; Th. 275, 7; Sat. 168: Exon. 10 a; Th. 11, 8; Cri. 167: Exon. 36 a; Th. 116, 34; Gū. 217: Mt. Rush. Stv. 11, 29. v. eom.

EÁM, es; *m. An* EAM, *uncle chiefly on the mother's side;* avuncŭlus:—Eám *avuncŭlus*, Wrt. Voc. 72, 42: Beo. Th. 1766; B. 881: Exon. 112 b; Th. 431, 35; Rä. 47, 6: Chr. 1066; Erl. 203, 17. Nim đē wīf of Labanes dōhtrum đīnes eámes *accĭpe tibi inde uxōrem de filiābus Labāni avuncŭli tui*, Gen. 28, 2: 29, 10: Ors. 1, 12; Bos. 35, 32: 2, 2; Bos. 41, 7: Bd. 5, 19; S. 637, 33. Romŭlus slōh his eám *Romulus slew his uncle*, Ors. 2, 3; Bos. 41, 43: Chr. 1046; Erl. 175, 5, 23. Mīn eám *avuncŭlus meus:* mīnes eámes fæder *avuncŭlus meus magnus:* mīnes eámes yldre fæder *proavuncŭlus meus:* mīnes eámes þridde fæder *abavuncŭlus meus*, Ælfc. Gl. 93; Som. 75, 65–71; Wrt. Voc. 52, 21–24. [*Chauc.* eem, eme: *Laym.* æm, eam, æem, hem: *Plat.* oom, *m: Dut.* oom, *m: Frs.* yem, yeme: *O. Frs.* em, *m: Ger.* ohm, oheim, *m: M. H. Ger.* ōheim, oeheim, *m: O. H. Ger.* ōheim, *m.*] For an uncle on the father's side, v. fædera.

eám, eán *to waters:*—Ofer đām eám *sŭper flūmĭna*, Ps. Th. 23, 2. Betweoh đām twām eán *between the two waters*, Ors. 1, 1; Bos. 16, 28; *dat. pl. of* eá.

eánian, eánigan; *part.* eánigende; *p.* eánode; *pp.* eánod [eáw = eówu *a female sheep, a ewe*] *To* YEAN, *bring forth as a ewe;* enīti, parturīre:—He genam hine of eówedum sceápa, fram eánigendum he genam hine *sustŭlit eum* [*Dāvĭdem*] *de grĕgĭbus ovium, de post fetantes* [*oves*] *accēpit eum*, Ps. Lamb. 77, 70. DER. ge-eán. [*Prompt.* enyn', *brynge forthe kyndelyngys* [*A. Sax.* litlingas]. The verb *to ean* or *yean*, which is commonly applied only to the bringing forth of lambs, here appears to have had anciently the more general signification of the word from which it is derived, *A. Sax.* eánian *enīti, partŭrīre: Wyc.* ene, eene, ȝeene, ȝene, yeene *sheep with lambs*, Ps. 143, 13: Is. 40, 11: *Dut. dial.* oonen *to produce young.*]

eá-ōfer, es; *m. A river-bank;* rīpa flūmĭnis:—Be sǣwaroþe, and be eá-ōfrum *by the sea-shore, and by river-banks*, Bt. Met. Fox 19, 43.

eapl *an apple*, Cd. 222; Th. 290, 7; Sat. 411. v. æppel.

ear, ær, es; *m. Sea, ocean;* măre, oceănus:—Hyre [dūne] deorc on lāst eare geblonden ōđer fereþ *dark on its* [*the down's*] *track goes another mixed with the ocean*, Exon. 101 b; Th. 384, 3; Rä. 4, 22. v. ear-gebland, ear-grund.

EAR, es; *n. An* EAR *of corn;* spīca:—Seó eorþe wæstm beraþ, ǣrest gærs, syđđan ear, syđđan fulne hwǣte on đam eare *terra fructĭfĭcat, primum herbam, deinde spīcam, deinde plēnum frumentum in spīca*, Mk. Bos. 4, 28. Đa seofon fullan ear getācniaþ seofon wæstmbǣre geár and wēlige *septem spīcæ plēnæ septem ubertātis anni sunt*, Gen. 41, 26, 27. Pharao rehte Iosepe be đām oxum and be đām earum *Pharaoh told Joseph of the oxen and of the ears* [*of corn*], Gen. 41, 17. Hīg onguunun pluccian đa ear *cœpērunt vellĕre spīcas*, Mt. Bos. 12, 1: Mk. Bos. 2, 23: Lk. Bos. 6, 1. Him þuhte, đæt he gesāwe seofon ear weaxan on ānum healme fulle and fægre *septem spīcæ pullŭlābant in culmo uno plēnæ atque formōsæ*, Gen. 41, 5: Lev. 23, 22: Deut. 23, 25. [*Wyc.* eere, ere: *R. Glouc.* eres, *pl: Plat.* aar, aare: *Dut.* aar, *f: Ger.* ähre, *f;* äher, *n: M. H. Ger.* äher, eher, *n: O. H. Ger.* ahir, eher, *n: Goth.* ahs, *n: Dan. Swed. Icel.* ax, *n.* Grimm supposes the root of these words to be ak *sharp*, and refers to *Lat.* acus, acies, acidus: *Ger.* ecke *a corner.*]

eár *before*, Chr. 1041; Th. 299, 15, col. 1. v. ǣr.

EÁR, es; *m. The Anglo-Saxon Rune* ᛠ, which stands for the letters *eá:* v. Steph. Runic Monmnts. p. 100, 11; 117, col. 7: and p. 137: *the earth, the ground;* hŭmus:—ᛠ byþ egle eorla gehwylcum, đonne fæstlīce flǣsc onginneþ hrāw cōlian, hrusan ceósan to gebeddan *the ground is hateful to every man, when surely the flesh beginneth to cool as a corpse, to choose the earth for a consort*, Runic pm. 29; Kmbl. 345, 10: Hick. Thes. i. 135, 57. [*Icel.* aurr, *m. hŭmus.* Hylja auri *hŭmo condĕre*, Kormak's Saga.]

earan *are*, Th. Diplm. A. D. 804–829; 463, 1. v. eom.

earbe, an; *f? A tare;* ervum:—Dō earban to *add tares*, L. M. 1, 26; Lchdm. ii. 68, 4. v. earfe.

earc, e; *f:* earce, an; *f.* I. *the ark of Noah;* arca:—Noe on đa earce eóde *Noah went into the ark*, Mt. Bos. 24, 38: Lk. Bos. 17, 27. Under earce bord *under the boards of the ark*, Cd. 67; Th. 80, 23; Gen. 1333. Earce bordum *with the boards of the ark*, 67; Th. 81, 33; Gen. 1354. II. *a chest, the ark of the covenant;* cista, cistella:—Cest *vel* earc *cibōtium* = κιβώτιον, vel *cistella*, Ælfc. Gl. 3; Som. 55, 64; Wrt. Voc. 16, 37. On earce *in the chest*, Exon. 124 b; Th. 479, 3; Rä. 62, 2. Ǣt Godes earce *to the ark of God*, Cd. 212; Th. 262, 30; Dan. 752: Ps. Th. 131, 8. v. earce, *f;* arc, *m.*

earce, an; *f. The ark;* arca:—Đū earce eart eall-hāligra *tu arca sanctĭfĭcātiōnis tuæ*, Ps. Th. 131, 8. v. earc II.

eár-clǣnsend, es; *m.* [eáre, clǣnsian *to cleanse*] *An ear-cleanser, the little finger;* dĭgĭtus aurĭcŭlāris:—Eárclǣnsend [MS. earclæsnend] *aurĭcŭlāris*, Wrt. Voc. 283, 24.

earcnan-stān, es; *m. A precious stone, gem;* gemma, lăpis prĕtiōsa:—Se earcnanstān *the precious stone*, Exon. 25 a; Th. 73, 27; Cri. 1196. v. eorcnan-stān.

eár-cōđu, e; *f.* [eáre, cōđu *a disease*] *An ear-disease;* parōtis = παρωτίς:—Eár-cōđu *parōtĭdes*, Ælfc. Gl. 11; Som. 57, 57; Wrt. Voc. 20, 1.

EARD, es; *m.* I. *native soil* or *land, country, province, region, place of residence, dwelling, home;* sŏlum nātīvum, patria, rĕgio, dŏmĭcĭlium:—Sumra wyrta ođđe sumes wuda eard biþ on dūnum, sumra on merscum . . . on đære stōwe đe his eard biþ *the native soil of some herbs or of some wood is on hills, some in marshes . . . in the place which is its native soil*, Bt. 34, 10; Fox 148, 22–26. He com to his earde *vēnit in patriam suam*, Mt. Bos. 13, 54. Nys nān wītega būtan wurþscype, būton on hys earde *non est prophēta sine hŏnōre, nisi in patria sua*, 13, 57. Eard *patria*, Ælfc. Gl. 97; Som. 76, 57; Wrt. Voc. 54, 1. Đis is mīn āgen cȳþ, eard and ēđel *this is my own country, dwelling, and home*, Bt. Met. Fox 24, 99; Met. 24, 50. Đū gebunde đæt fȳr đæt hit ne mæg cuman to his āgenum earde *thou hast bound the fire, that it may not come to its own region*, Bt. 33, 4; Fox 130, 32, 24. Ne đǣr elþeódige eardes brūcaþ *strangers enjoy no dwelling there*, Andr. Kmbl. 560; An. 280. Earda leás *deprived of dwellings*, Cd. 128; Th. 163, 29; Gen. 2705. Earda sēlost *happiest of dwellings* [*heaven*], Hy. 7, 29; Hy. Grn. ii. 287, 29: Exon. 42 a; Th. 141, 16; Gū. 628: 36 b; Th. 120, 7; Gū. 268. Fīfel-cynnes eard *the dwelling of the Fifel race*, Beo. Th. 209; B. 104. Of ðan heofon-fugelas healdaþ eardas *super ea volucres cæli habĭtābunt*, Ps. Th. 103, 11. Eard gemunde *he remembered his home*, Beo. Th. 2263; B. 1129. **II.** *earth* or *land, in contrast to water, as a firm place on earth* or *on land;* terra, terra firma:—He gefæstnude foldan staðelas, eorþan eardas *he made fast foundations of the ground, the firm places of the earth*, Ps. Th. 103, 6. Eard git ne const frēcne stōwe, ðǽr ðū findan miht secg *thou dost not yet know the land, perilous place, where thou mayest find the man*, Beo. Th. 2759; B. 1377: Exon. 38 b; Th. 128, 4; Gū. 399: 129 a; Th. 495, 20; Rä. 85, 6. Lǽt nū gebīdan on earde *let us now abide on land*, Andr. Kmbl. 799; An. 400. From hrōf eardes *a summo terræ*, Mk. Lind. War. 13, 27. Gǽst and līc geador sīðedan on earde *soul and body journeyed together on earth*, Exon. 76 a; Th. 285, 16; Jul. 715. **III.** *state, station, condition;* sĭtus, condĭtio:—Fundiaþ ǽlc gesceaft ðider swīðost, ðider his eard and his hǽlo swīðost bióþ *every creature chiefly tends thither, where its station, and its health especially is*, Bt. 34, 11; Fox 150, 22. Man us tyhhaþ twegen eardas, Drihtenes āre oððe deófles þeówet *two conditions are appointed to us, the glory of God or bondage of the devil*, Hy. 7, 97; Hy. Grn. ii. 289, 97. [*Orm.* ærd *place, region: Laym.* ærde, ard *land, earth: O. Sax.* ard, *m. habĭtātio: Dut.* aard, *m. nature, temper: Kil.* ærd: *Ger.* art, *f. nātūra, indōles, mŏdus, spĕcies, gĕnus: M. H. Ger.* art, *gen.* ardes, *m;* art, *gen.* arte, *f. nātūra, indōles: O. H. Ger.* art, *f. arātio; der. of* erian *to plough?*] DER. ēðel-eard, herh-, middan-, somud-, wīc-.

eard-begenga, -begænga, -begenda, an; *m.* [beganga, begenga *a dweller*] *An inhabitant, dweller;* incŏla:—Eardbegenga wæs sāwle mīn *incŏla fuit anĭma mea*, Ps. Lamb. 119, 6. Ðā ðā hīg wǽron eardbegendan *cum essent incŏlæ*, Ps. Lamb. 104, 12. Eardbegængan *incŏlæ*, Ps. Spl. M. 104, 11.

eard-begengnes, -biggengnes, -ness, e; *f. An abode, habitation;* habĭtātio, incŏlātus:—Eardbegengnes oððe elþeódignys mīn afeorrad oððe gelængd is *incŏlātus meus prolongātus est*, Ps. Lamb. 119, 5. Eardbiggengnes [MS. eardbiggendes] mīn aforfeorsode is *incŏlātus meus prolongātus est*, Ps. Spl. 119, 5.

eard-ēðel-riht, es; *n. Land-inheritance right, patrimonial right;* patrium jus, Beo. Th. 4402; B. 2198.

eard-ēðel-wyn, -wynn, e; *f. Joy of an estate;* prædii gaudium:—He me lond forgeaf, eardēðelwyn *he gave me land, joy of property*, Beo. Th. 4979; B. 2493. v. ēðel-wyn.

eard-fæst; *adj. Earth fast, settled, established in a place, abiding;* sōlo fixus, habĭtans:—Ðe eardfæst byþ on Hierusalem *qui habĭtat in Hierusalem*, Ps. Th. 124, 1: Exon. 44 a; Th. 149, 8; Gū. 758: Cd. 136; Th. 171, 27; Gen. 2834: Bt. Met. Fox 7, 76; Met. 7, 38: Ors. 5, 4; Bos. 105, 11: 6, 33; Bos. 129, 33.

eard-geard, es; *m. A dwelling-place, the earth;* habĭtātiōnis lŏcus, terra:—In ðam eardgearde *in that dwelling-place* [*in Jerusalem*], Exon. 8 b; Th. 4, 19; Cri. 55. Ȳðde ðisne eardgeard ælda Scyppend *the Creator of men overwhelmed this world*, 77 b; Th. 291, 20; Wand. 85.

eard-gyf, es; *n. A gift from one's native land;* patrium dōnum:—Kynincgas eard-gyfu bringaþ: *Spl.* has, cyningas gyfa togelǽdaþ: *rēges dōna addūcent*, Ps. Th. 71, 10.

eard-hæbbendra [=eard, hæbbendra], Ps. Th. 86, 6; *gen. pl. of* eard-hæbbende; *part. pres. of* eard-habban = habban *to have*.

eardian, eardigan, eardigean, ærdian; *part.* eardiende, eardigende, eardende; ic eardige, ðū eardast, he eardaþ, *pl.* eardiaþ, eardigaþ; *p.* ode, ade, ede; *pp.* od, ad, ed. **I.** *v. intrans. To dwell, live, feed;* habĭtāre:—Heofenes fugelas eardian māgon under his sceade *possunt sub umbra ejus aves cæli habĭtāre*, Mk. Bos. 4, 32: Exon. 129 b; Th. 496, 24; Rä. 85, 19: Ps. Th. 67, 6: Ps. Spl. 2, 4: 5, 5. Eardigan, Bt. 33, 4; Fox 130, 10. Loth ne dorste on ðam fæstenne leng eardigean *Lot might not longer dwell in that fastness*, Cd. 121; Th. 156, 19; Gen. 2591: Ps. Spl. C. 112, 8. Ic eardige, Ps. Th. 60, 3. Ðū eardast, Hy. 5, 1; Hy. Grn. ii. 285, 1. Ðǽr his hīrēd eardaþ *where his flock feeds*, Cd. 226; Th. 302, 2; Sat. 592. Æt helle dūru dracan eardigaþ *dragons dwell at the gate of hell*, 215; Th. 270, 30; Sat. 98. On earda eorðan *dwell on earth*, Ps. Spl. 36, 3. Ðeáh hī somod eardien *though they dwell together*, Bt. Met. Fox 20, 292; Met. 20, 146. For yfelnesse ðara eardiendra ðǽr on ðære byrig *a malĭtia inhabĭtantium in eo*, Bd. 4, 25; S. 599, 22: Ps. Th. 82, 6: 135, 27: Ps. Spl. 16, 13. Eardendra, Ps. Th. 106, 33. Abram eardode on ðam lande Chanaan *Abram habĭtāvit in terra Chanaan*, Gen. 13, 12. Eardodon, Beo. Th. 6093; B. 3050. Se me be healfe eardade *who dwelled by my side*, Exon. 129 b; Th. 496, 26; Rä. 85, 20. Eardedon, 9 b; Th. 8, 30; Cri. 125. **II.** *v. trans. To inhabit;* inhabĭtāre, incŏlĕre:—Peohtas ongunnon eardigan ða norþ-dǽlas ðysses eálondes *Picti habĭtāre per septentriōnāles insŭlæ partes cœpērunt*, Bd. 1, 1; S. 474, 18. Sceolde wīc eardian elles hwergen *he should inhabit a dwelling elsewhere*, Beo. Th. 5172; B. 2589: Ps. Th. 104, 19. DER. ge-eardian, on-, on-eardiend.

eardigendlīc; *adj. Inhabitable;* habĭtābĭlis:—Seó stōw eardigendlīc wæs geworden *lŏcus habĭtābĭlis factus est*, Bd. 4, 28; S. 605, 21.

earding, e; *f. A habitation, dwelling;* habĭtăcŭlum:—Ðǽr we mōtun āgan eardinga *where we may possess dwellings*, Exon. 65 b; Th. 242, 14; Ph. 673. v. eardung.

eard-land, es; *n. Country;* patria:—Sealde heora eardland eall Israhēlum *dĕdit terram eōrum hærēdĭtātem Israel*, Ps. Th. 134, 12.

eard-rīce, es; *n. A dwelling-land;* terra habĭtātiōnis:—Eardrīca cyst *the best of habitations* [*Paradise*], Exon. 45 a; Th. 153, 14; Gū. 825.

eard-stapa, an; *m. A land-stepper, wanderer;* terras peragrans, peregrīnātor:—Swā cwæþ eard-stapa *so said a wanderer*, Exon. 76 b; Th. 286, 25; Wand. 6.

eard-stede, es; *m. A dwelling-place;* lŏcus habĭtātiōnis:—Ða swētestan somnaþ and gædraþ wyrta wynsume and wudublēda to ðam eardstede *it* [*the Phœnix*] *collects and gathers pleasant herbs and forest leaves to that dwelling-place*, Exon. 58 b; Th. 211, 9; Ph. 195.

eardung, eærdung, ærdung, e; *f. A habitation, a dwelling, tabernacle;* habĭtātio, habĭtăcŭlum:—Is geworden eardung his on Sion *facta est habĭtātio ejus in Sion*, Ps. Spl. 75, 2: 32, 14: Ps. Spl. T. 77, 32: Ps. Th. 106, 3: Hy. 6, 11; Hy. Grn. ii. 286, 11: Bd. 4, 28; S. 605, 20. v. earding.

eardung-burh; *gen.* -burge; *f. A dwelling-city, city of tabernacles;* tabernacŭlōrum urbs:—Hīg getimbrodun Pharaones eardungburga Phiton and Rameses *ædĭfĭcāvĕrunt urbes tabernacŭlōrum Pharaōni Phithon et Ramesses*, Ex. 1, 11.

eardung-hūs, es; *n. A habitation;* habĭtăcŭlum:—Gemǽne eardunghūs *commūne habĭtăcŭlum*, Bd. 4, 28; S. 605, 26.

eardung-stōw, e; *f. A dwelling-place, a tent, tabernacle;* habĭtātiōnis lŏcus, tabernăcŭlum:—On eallum eówrum eardungstōwum *in cunctis habĭtăcŭlis vestris*, Ex. 12, 20: Ps. Th. 106, 6: Jn. Bos. 14, 2: Bd. 4, 28; S. 605, 19.

eard-wīc, es; *n. A dwelling-place;* habĭtātiōnis lŏcus:—Ðonne ic sceal eardwīc uncūþ gesēcan *when I shall seek the uncouth dwelling-place*, Apstls. Kmbl. 185; Ap. 93. He getimbreþ eardwīc niwe *it builds a new dwelling-place*, Exon. 62 a; Th. 228, 1; Ph. 431.

eard-wrecca, -wreca, an; *n.* [eard I. *native country;* wrecca = wræcca *an exile*] *One banished from his native country, an exile;* exsul:—Þurh eardwrecena feormunge *by harbouring of exiles*, L. Alf. pol. 4; Th. i. 62, 16, note 24.

EÁRE, an; *n: nom. acc. sing.* eáre; *nom. acc. pl.* eáran *The* EAR *of man* or *an animal;* auris:—Ðæs eáre slōh Petrus *of cujus abscīdit Petrus aurĭcŭlam*, Jn. Bos. 18, 26: Mk. Bos. 7, 33, 35: 14, 47: Ælfc. Gl. 71; Som. 70, 92; Wrt. Voc. 43, 23: Ps. Th. 140, 8: Exon. 128 b; Th. 494, 19; Rä. 83, 3: Cd. 216; Th. 275, 13; Sat. 171. [*Wyc.* eer, eere, ere: *Piers P.* ere: *Chauc.* ere: *Orm.* ære: *Plat.* oor, *n: O. Sax.* ōra, *n: Frs.* ær, ear, eare: *O. Frs.* are, ar, *n: Dut.* oor, *n: Ger.* ohr, *n: M. H. Ger.* ōre, *n: O. H. Ger.* ōra, *n: Goth.* auso, *n: Dan.* öre, *n: Swed.* öra, *n: Icel.* eyra, *n: Lat.* auris, *f: Grk.* οὖς, *n: Lith.* ausis, *f.*]

eáre-finger, es; *m. An ear-finger, the little finger;* aurĭcŭlārius dĭgĭtus, minĭmus dĭgĭtōrum:—Eárefinger *aurĭcŭlārius*, Wrt. Voc. 71, 34.

eáre-lippric, eár-lipric, e; *f:* eór-lipric, es; *n. A flap of the ear;* aurĭcŭla:—In eárlipricum, *dat. pl.* Mk. Lind. War. 7, 33. Eárliprica, *acc. pl.* Mk. Rush. War. 7, 33: Jn. Rush. War. 18, 26. Ða eárelipprica, *acc. pl.* Mk. Lind. War. 14, 47.

earendel, earendil, es; *m? A shining light, ray;* jŭbar:—Leóma, earendil *jŭbar*, Glos. Epnl. Recd. 158, 25. Eálā earendel! engla beorhtast! ofer middangeard monnum sended *O ray! brightest of angels! sent to men over mid-earth*, Exon. 9 b; Th. 7, 20; Cri. 104. [*O. H. Ger.* Orendel, *nn. pr.*]

EARFE, earbe, an; *f? A tare;* ervum, orŏbus = ὄροβος:—Earfan wyl on wætere *boil tares in water*, L. M. 1, 8; Lchdm. ii. 52, 16. [*Dut.* erwt, *f. pea: Kil.* erwete, erte, *f: Ger.* erbse, *f. a pea: M. H. Ger.* areweiȝ, erweiȝ, *f: O. H. Ger.* araweiȝ, arawīȝ, erbiȝ *pisum: Dan.* ært, ert, *m. f. a pea: Swed.* ärt, *f. a pea: Icel.* ertr, *f. pl. peas.*]

earfednyme *an heir;* hēres, Lk. Skt. Hat. 20, 14. v. yrfenuma.

EARFEÐE, earfoþ, es; *pl. nom. acc.* u, o, a; *n. Hardship, labour, difficulty, trouble, suffering, woe;* lăbor, mŏlestia, tribŭlātio:—Ic ðæt earfeðe wonn *I suffered the hardship*, Exon. 28 b; Th. 87, 21; Cri. 1428. Earfoðes feala *tribŭlātiōnis multum*, Ps. Th. 70, 19. Earfoðu, 21, 9: 24, 15: 68, 27. Ðe ða earfeða dreógeþ *who suffers those afflictions*, Exon. 52 b; Th. 183, 18; Gū. 1329. Earfeðum, Ps. Th. 106, 5, 27. Earfoða dǽl *a deal of sufferings*, Cd. 9; Th. 12, 4; Gen. 180. [*Plat.* arbeed, *f: Hel.* arabēd, arbed, *f;* arabēdi, arbēdi, *n: O. Sax.* arbeit, *f;* arbeithi, arbeidi, arvit, *n: Frs.* aerbeyde: *O. Frs.* arbeid, arbed, *n: Dut.* arbeid, *m: Ger.* arbeit, *f: M. H. Ger.* arbeit, arebeit, *f: O. H. Ger.* arabeit, arbeit, *f: Goth.* arbaiþs, *f: Dan.* arbeid, arbeide, *n: Swed.* arbete, *n: Icel.* erfiði, erviði, *n. toil, labour, distress.*] DER. firen-earfeðe, -earfoþ, ge-, mægen-, mōd-, woruld-.

earfeðe, earfoþ; *adj. Hard, difficult, troublesome;* diffĭcĭlis, mŏlestus:—

Nis me earfeđe to geþolianne willan Dryhtnes mīnes *it is not hard for me to endure the will of my Lord*, Exon. 48 a; Th. 166, 6; Gū. 1038. Đa bīsgu us sint swīđe earfoþ *the occupations are to us very difficult*, Bt. prœm; Fox viii. 7. Earfođest *most difficult*, Bt. 39, 4; Fox 216, 15. [*Orm.* arrfeþþ *difficult.*]

earfeþ-mæcg, es; *m. An unhappy* or *unfortunate man*: infortūnātus hŏmo:—Se endestæf earfeþmæcgum weālīc weorþeþ *the end to the unfortunate is miserable*, Exon. 87 a; Th. 328, 3; Vy. 11. v. earfoþ-mæcg.

earfeþ-sīþ *a misfortune, calamity*:—Earfeþsīđas *calamities*, Andr. Kmbl. 2568; An. 1285. v. earfoþ-sīþ.

earfoþ, es; *n. Hardship, trouble*; lăbor, tribŭlātio:—Mā earfođa *more of troubles*, Guthl. 5; Gdwin. 32, 13. v. earfeđe.

earfoþ; *adj. Hard, difficult*, Bt. prœm; Fox viii. 7. v. earfeđe; *adj.*

earfoþ-cyn, -cynn, es; *n. A violent generation*; prāva gens:—Đæt wæs earfoþcynn yrre and rēđe *gĕnus prāvum et peramārum*, Ps. Th. 77, 10.

earfoþ-dæg, es; *m. A trouble-day, day of trouble*; tribulātiōnis dies:—Ic on earfoþ-dæge Drihten sōhte *in die tribulātiōnis Deum exquīsīvi*, Ps. Th. 76, 2.

earfoþ-fere; *adj. Difficult to pass*; diffĭcĭlis transĭtu, Scint. 10.

earfoþ-hāwe; *adj. Difficult to be seen*; diffĭcĭlis vīsu:—Earfoþhāwe is *it is difficult to be seen*, Bt. Met. Fox 20, 303; Met. 20, 152: Bt. 33, 4; Fox 130, 30.

earfoþ-hwīl, e; *f. A time of hardship*; mŏlestum tempus:—Ic earfoþhwīle þrōwade *I suffered a time of hardship*, Exon. 81 b; Th. 306, 5; Seef. 3.

earfoþ-hylde; *adj. Ill-inclined, ill-disposed, ill-natured*; malĕvŏlus, malignus:—Se đe earfoþhylde biþ, and gyrnþ đæra þinga đe he begitan ne mihte, būton twȳn him geneālǣhþ se hreófla Giezi *he who is ill-inclined, and yearns for the things which he could not obtain, without doubt to him approximates the leper Gehazi*, Homl. Th. i. 400, 1.

earfoþ-lǣre; *adj. Difficult to be taught, dull*; diffĭcĭlis doctu:—Earfoþlǣran brōđru *indŏcĭles fratres*, Greg. Dial. 2, 3.

earfoþ-lǣte; *adj. Difficult to be sent forth*; diffĭcĭlis emissu:—Earfoþlǣte micga *a painful discharge of urine, strangury*; strangūria = στραγγουρία, Ælfc. Gl. 11; Som. 57, 47; Wrt. Voc. 19, 49.

earfoþ-līc; *adj. Irksome*; laboriōsus:—Eall is earfoþlīc eorþan rīce *the realm of earth is all irksome*, Exon. 78 a; Th. 292, 28; Wand. 106. Gif eów ǣnig þing þince earfoþlīce *si diffĭcĭle vōbis vīsum ălĭquid fuĕrit*, Deut. 1, 17.

earfoþ-līce; *adv. With difficulty, reluctantly, sorely, hardly*; diffĭcĭle, invīte, ægre:—Earfoþlīce wæs gūþ getwǣfed *the contest had been parted with difficulty*, Beo. Th. 3318; B. 1657: 3276; B. 1636: Mk. Bos. 10, 23. Se ellen-gǣst earfoþlīce þrage geþolode *the potent ghost reluctantly endured for a time*, Beo. Th. 173; B. 86: Exon. 98 a; Th. 369, 8; Seel. 38. Đā wæs gegongen earfoþlīce *then it befel sorely*, Beo. Th. 5636; B. 2822: Andr. Kmbl. 1028; An. 514. Hī ōþ-eódon earfoþlīce *they hardly escaped*, Beo. Th. 5861; B. 2934.

earfoþlīcnes, -ness, -nyss, e; *f. Difficulty, pain*; diffĭcultas:—Heó earfoþlīcnysse [-nesse MS. B.] đæs migþan astyreþ *it stirreth a difficulty of the urine* [*strangury*], Herb. 143, 1; Lchdm. i. 266, 3. Wiđ đæs migþan earfoþlīcnyssa [-nysse MS. H: -nesse MS. B.] *for difficulties of the urine*, 156, 3; Lchdm. i. 284, 4.

earfoþ-mæcg, earfeþ-mæcg, es; *m. An unhappy man*; infortūnātus hŏmo:—Se earfoþmæcg up lōcode *the afflicted man looked up*, Cd. 206; Th. 255, 12; Dan. 623.

earfoþnes, -ness, -niss, -nyss, e; *f. Difficulty, hardship, anxiety, tribulation, misfortune*; diffĭcultas, lăbor, angustiæ, tribŭlātio, infortūnium:—God ealle þing gediht būton earfoþnysse *God regulates all things without difficulty*, Bd. de nat. rerum; Wrt. popl. science 19, 5; Lchdm. iii. 278, 13. Wiđ wīfa earfoþnyssum [-nessum MS. B.] *for the difficulties of women*, Med. ex Quadr. 2, 7; Lchdm. i. 334, 18. He geheóld his rīce mid myclum geswince and earfoþnessum [-nyssum, Th. 278, 40, col. 2; -nissum, 279, 41, col. 1] *he held his kingdom with much labour and hardships*, Chr. 1016; Th. 278, 41, col. 1. Būtan micelre earfoþnysse *without much tribulation*, Homl. Th. i. 476, 13: Boutr. Scrd. 20, 35. Būtan earfoþnyssum *without tribulations*, Homl. Th. i. 476, 11. Mihte we đȳ ēþ geþolian swā hwæt earfoþnessa swā us on becōme *we might the more easily bear whatsoever misfortunes come upon us*, Bt. 10; Fox 30, 12.

earfoþ-recce; *adj.* [reccan *to relate*] *Difficult to be told*; diffĭcĭlis narrātu, Lupi Serm. 5, 3, Lye.

earfoþ-rīme; *adj. Difficult to be numbered*; diffĭcĭlis numĕrātu:—Đa bīsgu us sint swīđe earfoþrīme *the occupations are to us very difficult to be numbered*, Bt. prœm; Fox viii. 7.

earfoþ-sǣlig; *adj. Unblessed*; infēlix:—Ne biþ ǣnig đæs earfoþsǣlig mon on moldan *there is not any man on earth so unblessed*, Exon. 78 b; Th. 294, 1; Crā. 8.

earfoþ-sīþ, earfeþ-sīþ, es; *m. A laborious journey, misfortune, calamity*; mŏlestum ĭter, infortūnium, calămitas:—Weoru geferaþ earfoþsīđa *ye travel plenty of laborious journeys*, Andr. Kmbl. 1355; An. 678: Cd. 72; Th. 89, 5; Gen. 1476. Se folc-toga findan sceolde earfoþsīđas *the nation's leader should find calamities*, 208; Th. 257, 13; Dan. 657: Exon. 88 a; Th. 330, 30; Vy. 59. Đū wāst ānra gehwylces earfeþsīđas *thou knowest every man's calamities*, Andr. Kmbl. 2568; An. 1285.

earfoþ-tǣcne; *adj. Difficult to be shewn*; diffĭcĭlis demonstrātu:—Eorþe and wæter earfoþtǣcne wuniaþ on fȳre *earth and water dwell in fire difficult to be shewn*, Bt. Met. Fox 20, 294; Met. 20, 147.

earfoþ-þrag, e; *f. Time of tribulation*; mŏlestum tempus:—Ā syđđan earfoþþrage þolaþ *ever after will suffer a time of tribulation*, Beo. Th. 572; B. 283.

EARG, earh; *comp.* eargra, earhra; *sup.* eargost; *adj.* I. *inert, weak, timid, cowardly*; iners, ignāvus, segnis, tĭmĭdus:—Se earga fēđe Brytta *ăcies segnis Brittŏnum*, Bd. 1, 12; S. 481, 19. Ful oft mon wearnum tīhþ eargne *full oft one urges the inert with threats*, Exon. 92 a; Th. 345, 14; Gn. Ex. 188. Ne biþ swylc earges sīþ *such is not the path of the cowardly*, Beo. Th. 5076; B. 2541: Ors. 6, 36; Bos. 131, 27. II. *evil, wretched, vile*; prāvus, imprŏbus:—Đa cyningas, đe æfter Romuluse rīcsedan, wǣran eargran đonne he wǣre *the kings who reigned after Romulus, were more vile than he was*, Ors. 2, 2; Bos. 41, 24. Tarcuinius hiora eallra eargost wæs *Tarquin was the most vile of them all*, 2, 2; Bos. 41, 26. Swā fela eargra worda *so many evil words*, Cd. 27; Th. 36, 32; Gen. 580: Exon. 26 b; Th. 79, 29; Cri. 1298. [*Chauc.* erke *indolent, indisposed*: *Laym.* ærȝh *timid*: *Scot.* arch, argh, ergh *averse*: *Frs.* erg *bad, wicked*: *O. Frs.* erch, erg, arg *bad*: *Dut.* erg *bad*: *Ger.* arg *bad, wicked*: *M. H. Ger.* arc *mălus, prāvus*: *O. H. Ger.* arg *avārus, prāvus*: *Dan.* arg, arrig *bad, wicked, passionate*: *Swed.* arg *angry*: *Icel.* argr *emasculate, effeminate.*] DER. un-earg.

earge; *adv. Inertly, badly*; segnĭter, măle:—Earge gē đæt lǣstun *ye performed that badly*, Exon. 30 a; Th. 92, 3; Cri. 1503.

ear-gebland, ear-geblond, earh-geblond, es; *n. Wave-mingling*; oceăni turbātio, undārum commixtio:—Ofer eargebland [æra gebland, col. 1] land gesōhtan *they sought the land over the ocean* [lit. *the wave-mingling*], Chr. 937; Th. 202, 38, col. 2: Th. 203, 38, col. 1, 2: Bt. Met. Fox 8, 59; Met. 8, 30.

eár-gespeca, eár-gespreca, an; *m. An ear-speaker, a whisperer*; aurĭcŭlārius, susurro, Cot. 14.

earg-faru, e; *f. A flight* or *shooting of an arrow*, Exon. 71 b; Th. 266, 26; Jul. 404. v. earh-faru.

eargian *to be slothful, dull, idle*; torpescĕre. DER. a-eargian.

eargra *weaker*, Bt. 26, 2; Fox 92, 27, = *comp. of* earg.

ear-grund, es; *m. The ocean's ground*; oceăni fundus, Exon. 53 b; Th. 188, 3; Az. 40.

eargscipe, earhscipe, es; *m. Idleness, sloth*; ignāvia, Lye.

earh *ocean*. DER. earh-geblond. v. ear.

earh; *adj. Swift, fleeing through fear, timorous, weak*; fŭgax, Ælfc. Gr. 9, 60; Som. 13, 43: Byrht. Th. 138, 50; By. 238. v. earg.

EARH, e; *f*: arewe, an; *f. An* ARROW; sagitta:—Earh āttre gemǣl *the arrow stained with poison*, Andr. Recd. 2661; An. 1333. [*Laym. Chauc.* arwe: *Piers P.* arwe, *pl.* arewes: *Wyc.* arewe, arwe: *Goth.* arhwazna, *f. telum*: *O. Nrs.* ör; *gen.* örvar, *f. sagitta.*]

earh-faru, e; *f.* [earh *an arrow*; faru *a going, journey, passage*] *A flight of arrows*; sagittārum vŏlātus:—Habbaþ scearp speru, atole earhfare *they have sharp spears, a terrible flight of arrows*, Salm. Kmbl. 259; Sal. 129. Mid earhfare *with a flight of arrows*, Andr. Kmbl. 2097; An. 1050. Đa us gescildaþ wiđ sceđđendra eglum [MS englum] earhfarum *they shall shield us against the enemies' noxious flights of arrows*, Exon. 19 a; Th. 47, 28; Cri. 762.

earh-geblond *wave-mingling*, Elen. Kmbl. 477; El. 239. v. ear-gebland.

earhlīce; *adv. Fearfully, timidly, disgracefully, basely*; trepĭde, remisse, ignāve, turpĭter:—Earhlīce *timidly*, Gen. 20, 4. Hī hine earhlīce ofslōgon *they basely slew him*, Chr. 1086; Erl. 223, 9. v. earh.

earhra *weaker*, Bt. 26, 2; Fox 92, 27, MS. Bod. v. earg.

eár-hring, eár-ring, es; *m. An ear-ring*; inauris:—Nymaþ gyldene eár-hringas of eówer wīfa eáron *tollĭte inaures aureas de uxōrum vestrārum auribus*, Ex. 32, 2: Ælfc. Gl. 4; Som. 55, 91. v. eár-spinl.

eá-risc, e; *f. A water-rush, bulrush*; scirpus, juncus, Cot. 219: R. 42? Lye. v. ǣ-risc.

eá-riþ, es; *m. A water-stream*; aquæ rīvus:—Đǣr synd fūle eáriþas yrnende *there are foul running water-streams*, Guthl. 3; Gdwin. 20, 5.

eá-rixe, an; *f. A water-rush*:—Nim eárixena wyrtruman *take roots of water-rushes*, Lchdm. iii. 122, 8. v. eá-risc.

eár-læppa, an; *m.* [eáre *an ear*, læppa *a lap*] *An ear-lap*; pinnŭla:—Eár-læppa *vel* ufweard [MS. ufwaard] eáre *pinnŭla*: flǣran *vel* eár-læppan *pinnŭlæ*, Ælfc. Gl. 71; Som. 70, 83, 84; Wrt. Voc. 43, 15, 16.

eár-loccas; *pl. m.* [eár = ǣr *before*] *Forelocks*; antiæ, Ælfc. Gl. 64; Som. 69, 16; Wrt. Voc. 40, 49.

EARM, es; *m.* I. *an* ARM, *the limb extending from the shoulder to the hand*; brachium:—Gif se earm biþ forad būfan elmbogan, đǣr sculon xv scillinga to bōte *if the arm be broken above the elbow, there shall be fifteen shillings for compensation*, L. Alf. pol. 54; Th. i. 94, 24: 66; Th. i. 96, 28. Earm *brachium*, Wrt. Voc. 64, 69: 71, 22: 283, 7:

Ps. Lamb. 88, 22: 97, 1. On mycelnysse earmes dînes *in magnitūdĭne brachii tui*, Cant. Moys. Lamb. 187 b, 16: Ps. Th. 70, 17: 78, 12. He worhte mægne on hys earme *fēcit potentiam in brachio suo*, Lk. Bos. 1, 51: Ex. 6, 6: Ps. Lamb. 76, 16: 135, 12: Beo. Th. 4711; B. 2361. Se đe earm þurhstinþ vi scillingum gebēte: gif earm forbrocen weorþ, vi scillingum gebēte *let him who stabs [another] through the arm make amends with six shillings: if the arm be broken, let him make amends with six shillings*, L. Ethb. 53; Th. i. 16, 7, 8: Byrht. Th. 136, 43; By. 165. Ānra gehwylc wiđ earm gesæt, hleonade wiđ handa *each one rested on his arm, leaned on his hand*, Cd. 223; Th. 291, 18; Sat. 432: Beo. Th. 1503; B. 749. Ǣghwæđer ōđerne earme beþehte *each embraced the other with his arm*, Andr. Kmbl. 2030; An. 1017: Elen. Kmbl. 2470; El. 1236. Forđanđe earmas synfulra beóþ tobrocene ođđe beóþ tobrytte *quŏniam brachia peccatōrum contĕrentur*, Ps. Lamb. 36, 17: 43, 4. Næfde sēllīcu wiht exle ne earmas *the wonderful thing had not shoulders nor arms*, Exon. 108 b; Th. 415, 4; Rä. 33, 6: 129 a; Th. 494, 24; Rä. 83, 6. Đe me mid his earmum worhte *who made me with his arms*, Cd. 26; Th. 34, 28; Gen. 544: Ps. Th. 90, 11. Muscl đæs earmes *the muscle of the arm; tōrus vel muscŭlus vel lăcertus*, Ælfc. Gl. 72; Som. 70, 123; Wrt. Voc. 43, 48. II. *anything projecting from a main body, as an inlet of the sea* or *ocean, etc*; sĭnus, rāmus:—Đæs sǣs earm *an arm of the sea*, Ors. 1, 1; Bos. 19, 10, 15, 19, 21. Earmes, 23, 20: 24, 16, 17. Gārsecges earm, Ors. 1, 1; Bos. 18, 23: 19, 9. [*Wyc.* arm: *Chauc.* arme: *Laym.* ærm, arm: *Orm.* arrmess, *pl*: *Plat. O. Sax.* arm, *m*: *Frs.* earm: *O. Frs.* erm, arm, *m*: *Dut. Ger. M. H. Ger.* arm, *m*: *O. H. Ger.* arm, aram, *m*: *Goth.* arms, *m*: *Dan.* arm, *m. f*: *Swed.* arm, *m*: *Icel.* armr, *m*: *Lat.* armus, *m*: *Grk.* ἁρμός, *m. the shoulder-joint*: *Sansk.* īrma, *m. the arm.*] DER. sǣ-earm: earm-beáh, -boga, -gegyrela, -hreád, -scanca, -slīfe, -strang, -swīþ.

EARM, ærm, arm; *comp.* earmra; *sup.* earmost; *adj.* I. *poor, miserable, helpless, pitiful, wretched*; pauper, mĭser:—Đā com ān earm wuduwe *cum vēnisset vĭdua una pauper*, Mk. Bos. 12, 42, 43: Bt. 39, 2; Fox 212, 16. Nū eart tū earm sceađa *now art thou a miserable wretch*, Cd. 214; Th. 268, 19; Sat. 57: 226; Th. 301, 9; Sat. 579: Ps. Th. 136, 8. Earm biþ se him his frȳnd geswīcaþ *miserable is he whom his friends betray*, Exon. 89 a; Th. 335, 22; Gn. Ex. 37. Se wæs ord-fruma earmre lāfe *who was the chief of the poor remnant*, Cd. 179; Th. 225, 11; Dan. 152. Gē sindon earme ofer ealle menn *you are wretched above all men*, Andr. Kmbl. 1351; An. 676. Nō ic gefrægn earmran mannan *I have not heard of a more miserable man*, Beo. Th. 1159; B. 577. Ic wolde cweđan đæt hī wǣron earmoste *I should say that they were most miserable*, Bt. 38, 2; Fox 198, 13: Exon. 110 a; Th. 421, 6; Rä. 40, 14. II. *the poor and destitute for whom the church made a provision*; paupĕres:—Be teóđunge. Se cyng and his witan habbaþ gecoren and gecweden, ealswā hit riht is,—đæt þridda [MS. þriddan] dǣl đare teóđunge, đe to circan gebȳrige, gā to ciric-bōte;—and ōđer dǣl đām Godes þeówum;—þridde Godes þearfum, and earman þeówetlingan *concerning tithe. The king and his witan have chosen and decreed, as is just,—that a third part of the tithe, which belongs to the church, go to church-repair;—and a second part to the servants of God;—a third to God's poor, and the needy in thraldom*, L. Eth. ix. 6; Th. i. 342, 6–9. v. þearfa. [*Laym.* ærm: *Plat. O. Sax.* arm: *Frs.* earm: *O. Frs.* arm, erm: *Dut. Ger. M. H. Ger.* arm: *O. H. Ger.* arm, aram: *Goth.* arms: *Dan. Swed.* arm: *Icel.* armr.]

earm-beáh; *gen.* -beáges; *dat.* -beáge; *m. An arm-ring, bracelet*; armilla:—Brād earmbeáh *a broad* or *large arm-bracelet*; dextrochĕrium, Ælfc. Gl. 114; Som. 80, 30; Wrt. Voc. 61, 10. Earmbeága fela *many bracelets*, Beo. Th. 5520; B. 2763.

earm-boga, an; *m. An arm-bow, elbow*; brachii curvātūra, Som. Ben. Lye.

earm-cearig; *adj. Miserable and sad*; mĭser et tristis:—Hū ic, earmcearig, īscealdne sǣ, winter wunade *how I passed a winter, miserable and sad, on the ice-cold sea*, Exon. 81 b; Th. 306, 27; Seef. 14: 76 b; Th. 287, 26; Wand. 20.

earme; *adv. Wretchedly, badly*; mĭsĕre, măle:—He lyt ongeat đæt him swā earme gelamp *he little knew that it would fall out to him so badly*, Cd. 76; Th. 94, 26; Gen. 1567.

earm-gegyrela, -gegirela, an; *m.* [gegyrela *clothing, apparel*] *A bracelet to be worn on the right arm*; dextrāle:—Earmgegirelan *dextrālia*, Cot. 63.

earm-heort; *adj. Tender-hearted, merciful*; misĕricors, Greg. Dial. 1, 2.

earm-hreád, e; *f. An arm-ornament*; brachii ornāmentum:—Earmhreáda [MS. earm reade] twā *two arm-ornaments*, B. 1194. v. hreódan.

earmian; *p.* ode; *pp.* od; *v. reflex. To commiserate, feel pity*; misĕrēri:—Hwam ne mæg earmian swylcere tīde *who cannot feel pity for such a time?* Chr. 1087; Th. 354, 2.

earming, erming, yrming, es; *m. A wretched* or *miserable being*; mĭser:—Earming *mĭser*, Ælfc. Gr. 8; Som. 7, 18: Ælfc. Gl. 77; Som. 72, 17; Wrt. Voc. 45, 50: 75, 33. Syle đīn eáre đīnum earminge *give thy ear to thy wretched one*, Ps. Lamb. fol. 183 b, 17. Ne ondrǣd đē, lā earming. git đū hæfst līfes hiht *dread not, O wretched man, thou hast yet hope of life*, Ælfc. T. 37, 2. Đa đe đæs wēlan gitsiaþ, hī biþ symle wædlan and earmingas on hyra mōde *they who covet wealth are always poor and miserable beings in their mind*, Prov. Kmbl. 50.

earmlīc; *sup.* earmlīcost; *adj. Miserable, wretched*; mĭser:—Đǣr sceal earmlīc ylda cwealm æfter wyrþan *then must afterwards miserable slaughter of men take place*, Andr. Kmbl. 363; An. 182. Wǣs gehȳred earmlīc ylda gedræg *the wretched tumult of men was heard*, Andr. Kmbl. 3108; An. 1557: Beo. Th. 1618; B. 807: Bd. 5, 13; S. 632, 29. Đæt is earmlīcost ealra þinga *this is the most wretched of all things*, Bt. Met. Fox 19, 55; Met. 19, 28: 27, 32; Met. 27, 16: 28, 148; Met. 28, 74.

earmlīce; *adv. Miserably, wretchedly*; mĭsĕre:—He wæs earmlīce beswicen *he was wretchedly beguiled*, Bd. 5, 13; S. 632, 26: 1, 12; S. 481, 21: Cd. 81; Th. 101, 35; Gen. 1692: Exon. 88 a; Th. 330, 20; Vy. 54. Earmlīcor *more miserably*, Bd. 5, 14; S. 635, 3.

earm-scanca, an; *m. An arm-bone* [=*shank*]; crus:—Gif đa earmscancan beóþ begen forade *if the arm-bones be both broken*, L. Alf. pol. 55; Th. i. 94, 26.

earm-sceapen; *adj. Miserable, wretched*; mĭser:—Ne mihte earmsceapen āre findan *the poor wretch might not find pity*, Andr. Kmbl. 2259; An. 1131: 2689; An. 1347: Beo. Th. 2707; B. 1351: Cd. 206; Th. 255, 30; Dan. 632.

earm-slīfe, an; *f. An arm-sleeve*; brachīle, R. Ben. Interl. 55.

earm-strang; *adj. Arm-strong, muscular*; tōrōsus, Ælfc. Gl. 72; Som. 70, 124; Wrt. Voc. 43, 49.

earm-swīþ; *adj. Arm-powerful, muscular, strong*; lacertōsus, Cot. 123: 200.

earmþu, e; *f. Misery, poverty*; mĭsĕria:—Gif đa earmþa ealle sōđe sint *if the miseries are all true*, Bt. 38, 2; Fox 198, 14, 16. v. yrmþu.

earmung, e; *f. Misery, poverty*; mĭsĕria:—Hió biþ eádgum leóf, earmunge tǣse [earmum getǣse, Grn.] *she is dear to the rich, benevolent to poverty*, Exon. 128 a; Th. 492, 28; Rä. 81, 22.

Ear-mūþa, an; *m.* [ear *the sea, the river Yare*, mūþa *the mouth*] *Great* YARMOUTH, *Norfolk*; oppĭdum in agro Norfolciensi, et in insŭla Vecti, Lye.

EARN, es; *m. An eagle*; aquĭla:—Se earn *the eagle*, Herb. 31, 2; Lchdm. i. 128, 10. Earn *aquĭla*, Ælfc. Gl. 36; Som. 62, 107; Wrt. Voc. 29, 5: 62, 1: 77, 12: 280, 1. Swā earn his briddas spænþ to flihte and ofer hīg fliceraþ, swā he tobrǣdde his feđeru *sīcut aquĭla provŏcans ad vŏlandum pullos suos et super eos vŏlĭtans expandit ālas suas*, Deut. 32, 11. Ūrigfeđera earn sang ahōf *the dewy-feathered eagle raised his song*, Elen. Kmbl. 58; El. 29: 222; El. 111: Judth. 11; Thw. 24, 27; Jud. 210: Byrht. Th. 134, 60; By. 107: Exon. 111 a; Th. 426, 1; Rä. 41, 67. Biþ ge-edniwad swylce earnes geógeþ đīn *renŏvābĭtur ut aquĭlæ juventus tua*, Ps. Lamb. 102, 5. Earnes brid *an eagle's young*, Exon. 59 a; Th. 214, 7; Ph. 235. Earnes mearh *an eagle's marrow*, Lchdm. iii. 14, 24. Se wonna hrefn fela earne secgan *the dark raven [shall] say much to the eagle*, Beo. Th. 6044; B. 3026: Exon. 59 a; Th. 214, 12; Ph. 238: Ps. Th. 102, 5. Ic onhyrge đone haswan earn *I imitate the dusky eagle*, Exon. 106 b; Th. 406, 21; Rä. 25, 4: Chr. 937; Erl. 115, 12; Ǣđelst. 63. Swā hwǣr swā hold byþ, đæder beóþ earnas gegaderode *ubicumque fuĕrit corpus, illic congrĕgābuntur et aquĭlæ*, Mt. Bos. 24, 28. Cōmon earnas on flyhte *eagles came in flight*, Andr. Kmbl. 1725; An. 865. He sende blōdige earnas *he sent bloody eagles*, Salm. Kmbl. 943; Sal. 471. [*Chauc.* erne: *R. Glouc.* ern: *Laym.* ærn, erne: *Orm.* ærn: *Scot.* ern, erne, eirne, earn: *Plat.* arend, aarn, aarnd: *Dut.* arend, *m*: *Ger.* aar, *m*: *M. H. Ger.* arn, *m*: *O. H. Ger.* arn, aro, *m*: *Goth.* ara, *m*: *Dan.* örn, *m. f*: *Swed. Icel.* örn, *m.*]

earn, es; *n. A house, cottage*; căsa:—On đære stōwe đe is gecīged æt hwītan earne *in the place which is called [at] Whitern [white house, candĭda căsa]*, Bd. 5, 24; S. 646, 31. v. ærn.

earn-cyn, -cynn, es; *n. Eagle-kind*; gĕnus aquĭlæ:—Ne ete ge nān þing earncynnes *do not eat anything of the eagle-kind*, Lev. 11, 13.

earne *active*, Exon. 101 a; Th. 380, 31; Rä. 1, 16; *acc. of* earu.

earn-geáp? [earn *an eagle*, geáp *shrewd, cunning*] *A vulture, species of falcon*; vultur, harpe = ἅρπη:—Earn-geáp? *vultur*, Ælfc. Gl. 38; Som. 63, 32; Wrt. Voc. 29, 51. Earn-geáp? *arpa* [=*harpe*], Glos. Brux. Recd. 36, 2; Wrt. Voc. 62, 2, Ben. Lye. v. earn-geát.

earn-geát, e; *f.* [gǣt, gāt *a goat*] *The goat-eagle, vulture*; harpe = ἅρπη, vultur, Glos. Epnl. Recd. 153, 40: Mone A. 2.

EARNIAN; *p.* ode, ade, ede; *pp.* od, ad; *v. trans. gen. acc. To* EARN, *merit, deserve, get, attain, labour for*; mĕrēri:—Byþ geseald đære þeóde đe hys earnaþ *it shall be given to the nation which deserves it*, Mt. Bos. 21, 43. Hū monna gehwylc earnode ēces līfes *how every man merited eternal life*, Exon. 23 a; Th. 65, 9; Cri. 1052. Đā he ne earnade elles wuhte *when he did not earn anything else*, Bt. Met. Fox 9, 39; Met. 9, 20. Gē đæs earnedon *ye merited this*, Exon. 27 b; Th. 83, 2; Cri. 1350. Uton we friþes earnian *let us merit peace*, 98 a; Th. 366, 17; Reb. 13. He hæfþ đæt đæt he earnaþ *he has that which he earns*, Bt. 37, 2; Fox 188, 6. [*Plat.* arnen, arnden *to reap*: *O. Frs.* arn, *f. messis*: *Kil.* arnen, ernen *mĕtĕre sĕgĕtem*: *Ger.* ernten, ärnten *to reap, harvest*:

M. H. Ger. arnen *to reap: O. H. Ger.* arnēn *mĕrēri;* arnōn *mĕtĕre: Goth.* asans, *f. harvest.*] DER. ge-earnian.

earning, e; *f. A merit;* mĕrĭtum:—Nō ðæs earninga ǽnige wǽron *for this were not any merits,* Exon. 118 b; Th. 456, 17; Hy. 4, 68. v. earnung.

earning-land, es; *n. Land earned* or *made freehold* = bōc-land, Cod. Dipl. 679; A.D. 972–992; Kmbl. iii. 259, 10; Sax. Engl. i. 312, note 2.

Earnulf, Arnulf, es; *m. Arnulf, emperor of Germany from* A.D. 887 to 899, *nephew of Charles le Gros* = *Ger. Karl der Dicke:*—Ðý ilcan geáre, forþfērde Carl, Francna cyning; and Earnulf, his brōður sunu, hine vi wicum ǽr he forþfērde, berǽdde æt ðam rīce *in the same year, Charles, king of the Franks, died; and six weeks before he died, Arnulf, his brother's son, bereft him of the kingdom,* Chr. 887; Th. 156, 30. Mid Earnulfes geþafunge *with the consent of Arnulf,* 887; Th. 156, 36.

earnung, earning, e; *f. An* EARNING, *desert, reward, good turn, compassion;* mĕrĭtum, misĕrātio, compassio:—For earnunge ēcan līfes *for the reward of eternal life,* Hy. 6, 26; Hy. Grn. ii. 286, 26. Hwylce earnunga uncre wǽron *such deserts have been ours,* Exon. 100 a; Th. 377, 3; Seel. 166. Se gewuldorbeágaþ ðē on earnunga *qui cŏrōnat te in miseratiōnĭbus,* Ps. Spl. 102, 4. DER. ge-earnung.

earon *are,* Ps. Th. 101, 21: Th. Diplm. A.D. 887; 133, 37; 134, 1; *3rd pres. pl. of* eom.

earp; *adj. Dark, dusky;* fuscus:—Earpan gesceafte, fūs ofer folcum, fȳre swǽtaþ *the dark creatures* [*clouds;* nubes], *hurrying over the people, sweat fire,* Exon. 102 a; Th. 385, 10; Rä. 4, 42. v. eorp.

earpa *a harp,* Ps. Spl. 107, 2. v. hearpa.

eár-plǽttan; *p.* -plætte; *pp.* -plætted [eáre *an ear,* plættan *to strike*] *To strike on the ear, to box the ear;* cŏlăphum incŭtĕre:—Se byrle ðone apostol eár-plætte *the cup-bearer struck the apostle on the ear,* Homl. Th. ii. 520, 12.

eár-preón, es; *m. An ear-pin, ear-ring;* inauris:—Eárpreón *vel* eár-ring *inauris,* Ælfc. Gl. 65; Som. 69, 50; Wrt. Voc. 41, 7. Earpreónas *vel* eár-hringas *inaures,* 4; Som. 55, 91; Wrt. Voc. 16, 61.

eár-ring *an ear-ring,* Ælfc. Gl. 65; Som. 69, 50; Wrt. Voc. 41, 7. v. eár-hring.

EARS, ærs, es; *m. The breech, the buttocks, the hind part;* ānus, pōdex. [*Piers P.* ers: *Chauc.* ers, erse: *Plat.* aars, ars, eers, *m: Frs.* earse, earz: *O. Frs.* ers: *Dut.* aars, *m: Ger.* arsch, *m: M. H. Ger. O. H. Ger.* ars, *m. cūlus, pōdex: Dan.* ars, arts, *m. f: Swed.* ars, *m: Icel.* ars, rass, *m.*] DER. open-ærs: ears-ende, -gang, -ling, -lȳre, -ode, -þerl.

eár-scrypel, es; *m. An ear-scraper, ear-finger;* dĭgĭtus auricŭlāris:—Eár-scrypel *auricŭlāris,* Glos. Brux. Recd. 38, 75; Wrt. Voc. 65, 3.

eár-sealf, e; *f. An* EAR-SALVE, L. M. 1, 3; Lchdm. ii. 40, 1.

ears-ende, es; *m. The breech, the buttocks;* nātes:—Ears-ende [MS. -endu] *nătes,* Wrt. Voc. 65, 36: [MS. -enda], 283, 61.

ears-gang, es; *m. Āni fŏrāmen, ānus.* v. ars-gang.

ears-ling; *adv.* Only used adverbially with on,—*On the back, backwards;* retrorsum:—Sȳn hī gecyrde on earsling *be thei turned awey bacward,* Wyc; avertantur retrorsum, Ps. Th. 34, 5. Gān hȳ on earsling *avertantur retrorsum,* 6, 8. v. bæcling, hinderling.

ears-lȳre, es; *m?* [lȳre = līra *muscle*] *The breech-muscle, the breech;* nātes:—Earslȳre *nătes,* Ælfc. Gl. 74; Som. 71, 71; Wrt. Voc. 44, 53.

earsode; *part. Having a breech, breeched;* tergōsus, Ælfc. Gl. 77; Som. 72, 4; Wrt. Voc. 45, 38.

eár-spinl, e; *f.* [spinl = spindel *a spindle*] *An ear-ring;* inauris, Prov. 25. v. eár-hring.

ears-þerl, es; *n.* [þerl = þyrel *a hole*] *Fŏrāmen āni, ānus:*—Ears-þerl *ānus* vel *verpus,* Ælfc. Gl. 74; Som. 71, 72; Wrt. Voc. 44, 54.

eart *art:*—Ðū eart ðē selfa ðæt hēhste good *thou thyself art the highest good,* Bt. Met. Fox 20, 90; Met. 20, 45: Bt. 10; Fox 26, 23: Ælfc. Gr. 32; Som. 36, 26: Beo. Th. 710; B. 352: 1016; B. 506: Andr. Kmbl. 2378; An. 1190: Elen. Grm. 808: Exon. 13 b; Th. 25, 19; Cri. 403: Ps. Th. 51, 8: Salm. Kmbl. 658; Sal. 328: Cd. 26; Th. 34, 4; Gen. 532: 214; Th. 268, 19; Sat. 57: Nicod. 4; Thw. 2, 34: Mk. Bos. 14, 70; *2nd pers. sing. of* eom.

earþ *art,* Cd. 205; Th. 254, 9; Dan. 609: Bt. 33, 4; Fox 128, 4. v. eom.

eárðan *before that;* antĕquam, Chr. 1041; Th. 299, 15, col. 1. v. ǽr; *adv.*

earþling *a farmer.* v. yrþling.

earu; *adj. Quick, active, ready;* cĕler, alăcer, parātus:—Gehȳrest ðū uncerne earne hwelp *hearest thou our active whelp?* Exon. 101 a; Th. 380, 31; Rä. 1, 16. [*Sansk.* ara *quick.*] v. arod.

earun *are,* Ps. Th. 104, 7; *pl. pres. of* eom.

eár-wærc, es; *n. Ear-ache, a pain in the ear;* auris dŏlor:—Wið eár-wærce *for ear-ache,* L. M. 1, 3; Lchdm. ii. 40, 7.

eár-wicga, eór-wicga, an; *m. An* EARWIG or *worm;* vermis *vel* forfĭcŭla aurĭcŭlāris:—Wið eárwicgan *against earwigs,* L. M. cont. 1, 3; Lchdm. ii. 2, 14: L. M. 1, 3; Lchdm. ii. 40, 1: 1, 3; Lchdm. ii. 44, 4. v. wicga.

earwunga [earnunga?]; *adv. Without cause;* grātis:—Afuhtan me earwunga *expugnāvērunt me grātis,* Ps. Th. 108, 2: 68, 4: 118, 161: 119, 6. v. arwunga, earnung, būtan ge-earnungum *grātis,* s. v. ge-earnung.

eás *of a river:*—On twā healfe ðære eás *on the two sides of the river,* Chr. 896; Th. 172, 39, col. 1; *gen. of* eá, *q. v.*

eá-spring, ǽ-spring, es; *n. A water-spring, fountain;* ăquæ fons, fons:—Ðæt Cūþbyrhtus ān eáspring of drigre eorþan up gelǽdde *ut Cudberct fontem de arente terra produxĕrit,* Bd. 4, 28; S. 605, 6.

EÁST, es; *m. The* EAST; ŏriens:—Óþ Indēas eáste wearde *unto the Indies towards the east,* Bt. Met. Fox 16, 36; Met. 16, 18. Sió sunne norþ eft and eást otēweþ *the sun appears again in the north and east,* i. e. *in the north-east,* 13, 118; Met. 13, 59. Ðæt eálond on Wiht is þrittiges mīla lang eást and west; and twelf mīla brād sūþ and norþ *Vecta insŭla hăbet ab ŏriente in occāsum triginta circĭter mīlia passuum; ab austro in bŏream duodĕcim,* Bd. 1, 3; S. 475, 19. [*Wyc.* est, eest: *Piers P.* eest: *Chauc.* est: *Laym.* æst, east: *Orm.* æst: *Plat.* oost: *O. Sax.* ōst-ar *towards the east: Frs.* æst, east: *O. Frs.* asta, ost: *Dut.* oost, oosten, *n: Ger.* ost, osten, *m: M. H. Ger.* ōsten, *n: O. H. Ger.* ōst, ōstan, *m: Dan.* öst, östen, öster: *Swed.* öster, *m: Icel.* austr, *m.*] DER. eástan, eástan-sūþan: Eást-Centingas, -dǽl, -ende, -Engle, -folc, -Francan, -healf, -land, -lang, -rīce, -rihte, -sǽ, -Seaxe: eáster, eáster-ǽfen, -dæg, -fæsten, -feorm, -līc, -mōnaþ, -niht, -þēnung, -tīd, -wuce.

Eást; *adj.* EAST, *easterly;* orientālis:—Eást *used mostly in composition as a noun,* Eást-Engle *East-Angles,* Bd. 5, 24; S. 646, 19. Eást-Seaxe *East-Saxons,* 5, 24; S. 646, 19. Eást-Francan *East-Franks,* Ors. 1, 1; Bos. 18, 30: Chr. 891; Erl. 88, 3. v. eást, es; *m.*

eásta, an; *m. The east;* ŏriens:—He fērde syððan to ðam mūnte, be eástan Bethel *inde transgrĕdiens ad montem, qui erat contra ŏrientem Bethel,* Gen. 12, 8. Be eástan Rīne syndon Eást-Francan *to the east of the Rhine are the East-Franks,* Ors. 1, 1; Bos. 18, 29, 31, 33, 39, 45. Be eástan *in the east,* Bt. Met. Fox 29, 65; Met. 29, 33: Chr. 878; Erl. 80, 9: 894; Erl. 92, 19. v. eást, es; *m.*

eá-stæþ *a river-bank;* flūmĭnis rīpa. v. eá, stæþ *a shore, bank.*

eástan, eásten; *adj. East;* orientālis:—Eástan sūþan wind *south-east wind;* vulturnus, Ælfc. Gl. 54; Som. 66, 86; Wrt. Voc. 36, 12. Norþan eástan wind *eurus, euroauster,* 54; Som. 66, 87; Wrt. Voc. 36, 13. Eásten wind *subsŏlānus,* 54; Som. 66, 82; Wrt. Voc. 36, 8.

eástán, eásten, ēstan; *adv. From the east, easterly;* ab ŏriente:—Gif wind cymþ westan oððe eástan *if the wind come westerly or easterly,* Cd. 38; Th. 50, 10; Gen. 806: 80; Th. 99, 20; Gen. 1649: 86; Th. 107, 24; Gen. 1794. Æðeltungla wyn eástan līxeþ *the delight of the noble stars shines easterly,* Exon. 60 a; Th. 218, 6; Ph. 290: 57 a; Th. 204, 24; Ph. 102: 20 b; Th. 55, 19; Cri. 886. Eásten hider *from the east hither,* Cd. 27; Th. 35, 16; Gen. 555. Hwonne up cyme æðelast tungla ēstan līxan *when the noblest of stars riseth up shining easterly,* Exon. 57 a; Th. 204, 8; Ph. 94.

eástan-sūþan *south-eastern,* Ælfc. Gl. 54; Som. 66, 86; Wrt. Voc. 36, 12. v. eástan; *adj.*

Eást-Centingas; *pl. m. The East Kentians, men of East Kent;* Cantii ŏrientis habitātōres:—Ealle Eást-Centingas friþ wið ðone here genāmon *all the men of East Kent made peace with the army,* Chr. 1009; Th. 260, 39.

eást-dǽl, es; *m. The eastern part, the east;* terræ pars orientālis, ortus:—Cirus, Persa cyning, hæfde mǽst eallne ðæne eást-dǽl awēst *Cyrus, king of the Persians, had laid waste almost all the east,* Ors. 2, 4; Bos. 43, 43: Exon. 55 b; Th. 197, 20; Ph. 2. Eást-dǽl *ortus,* Ps. Lamb. 102, 12.

eásten; *adj. East;* orientālis. v. eástan; *adj.*

eásten; *adv. From the east, easterly;* ab ŏriente. v. eástan; *adv.*

eást-ende, es; *m. The east-end;* pars orientālis:—Æt ðæs wuda eást-ende *at the east-end of the wood,* Chr. 893; Th. 162, 28.

Eást-Engle; *pl. m. The East-Angles;* ŏrientes Angli:—Of Engle cōman Eást-Engle and Middel-Engle *from Angeln came the Angles of the east and the middle Angles,* Bd. 1, 15; S. 483, 24.

eásten-wind, es; *m. The east wind;* subsŏlānus. v. eástan; *adj.*

eáster, eástor; *gen.* eástres; *pl. nom. acc.* eástro; *gen.* eāstrena; *dat.* eástron, eástran [= eástrum]; *n:* eástre, an; *n.* I. *Easter, the feast of Easter;* pascha = πάσχα:—On dæge symbeles eástres *in die solemni paschæ,* Lk. Lind. War. 2, 41. Wæs ðære ylcan nihte ðara hālgan Eástrena, ðæt seó cwēn cende dōhtor ðæm cyninge *it was on that same holy night of Easter, that the queen bore to the king a daughter,* Bd. 2, 9; S. 511, 28. Æfter twām dagum beóþ eástro *post bĭduum pascha fiet,* Mt. Bos. 26, 2. Freóls-dæg, se is gecweden Eástre *a feast day which is called Easter,* Lk. Bos. 22, 1. II. *the passover, paschal lamb;* pascha:—To eástron *for the Easter lamb,* Mt. Bos. 26, 17. Ðā hī eástron offrodon ... ðæt ðū eástron ete *quando pascha immŏlābant ... ut mandūces pascha,* Mk. Bos. 14, 12. [*Ger. M. H. Ger.* ostern, *f: Ker.* ōstarun, ōstrun: *Otfr.* ōstarā, ōstoron *dea, pascha: A. Sax.* Eástre, *the goddess of the rising sun, whose festivities were in April. Hence used by Teutonic christians for the rising of the sun of righteousness, the feast of the resurrection, Bd. de Temp. Rat. Works,* vol. ii. p. 81: *Grimm's Deut. Mythol.* 8vo. 1855, pp. 180–183.]

eáster, eástor; *adj. Easter;* paschālis:—Ðys sceal on eáster-ǽfen *this belongs to easter-even*, Rubc. Mt. Bos. 28, 1; Notes, p. 577, 28, 1 a. Eáster-tīd *easter-tide* or *time*, Homl. Th. ii. 266, 15, 19, 21. Eáster-mōnaþ *easter-month, April*, Menol. Fox 142; Men. 72.

eáster-ǽfen, eástor-ǽfen, es; *m. Easter-even;* dies ante festum paschæ:—Ðys sceal on eáster-ǽfen *this [gospel] must be on easter-even*, Rubc. Mt. Bos. 28, 1; notes, p. 577, 28, 1 a.

eáster-dæg, eástor-dæg, es; *m. Easter-day;* dies paschālis:—Com he to ðam cyninge ðȳ ǽrestan eáster-dæge *pervēnit ad rēgem prīmo die paschæ*, Bd. 2, 9; S. 511, 17.

eáster-fæsten, es; *n. Easter-fast;* quadrāgēsīma, jejūnium paschāle:—On fōreweard eáster-fæsten *in the beginning of the easter-fast;* incipiente quadrāgēsīma, Bd. 5, 2; S. 614, 37.

eáster-feorm, eástor-feorm, e; *f. Easter-feast* or *repast;* paschālis firma:—On sumere þeóde gebȳreþ winter-feorm [and] eáster-feorm *in quibusdam lŏcis dătur firma nātālis Dŏmĭni, et firma paschālis*, L. R. S. 21; Th. i. 440, 26.

eáster-līc, eástor-līc; *adj. Easter, paschal;* paschālis:—Hȳ fōron to Hierusalem to ðam eásterlīcan freólse *they went to Jerusalem to the paschal feast*, Lk. Bos. 2, 42: Homl. Th. ii. 32, 15: 284, 1.

eáster-mōnaþ, es; *m. Easter-month;* Aprīlis mensis:—Eáster-mōnaþ cymeþ *easter-month comes*, Menol. Fox 142; Men. 72.

eást-ern, -erne; *adj.* [ern *a place*] EASTERN, *oriental;* orientālis:—Ðonne cymþ eásterne wind *then comes the eastern wind*, Cd. 17; Th. 20, 27; Gen. 315. Se wer wæs swīðe mǽre betwux eallum eásternum *erat vir ille magnus inter omnes orientāles*, Job Thw. 164, 7.

eáster-niht, e; *f. Easter-night;* nox paschālis:—In ðære eáster-niht *in the easter-night*, Exon. 120 a; Th. 460, 10; Hö. 15.

eáster-þēnung, e; *f. The paschal feast, paschal lamb, the passover;* pascha:—Hīg gegearwodon him eáster-þēnunge *parāvērunt ei pascham*, Mt. Bos. 26, 19.

eáster-tīd, eástor-tīd, e; *f. Easter-tide;* paschæ tempus:—Se Hǽlend geheóld ða eáster-tīde *the Saviour kept the easter-tide*, Homl. Th. ii. 242, 21: 266, 15, 19, 21.

eáster-wuce, eástor-wice, an; *f. Easter-week;* paschālis septimāna:—Ðys sceal on Sæternes dæg, on ðære eáster-wucan *this [gospel] must be on Saturday in easter-week*, Rubc. Jn. Bos. 20, 1, 11; Notes, p. 580, 20, 1 a, 11 a: 21, 1; Notes, p. 580, 21, 1 a.

eá-steþ, eá-stæþ, es; *n. A river-bank;* flūmĭnis rīpa:—Hī on ðam eásteðe ealle stōdon *they all stood on the river-bank*, Byrht. Th. 133, 40; By. 63.

eásteweard *eastward*, Bt. 18, 1; Fox 60, 31. v. east; *m.*

eást-folc, es; *n. Eastern people;* pŏpŭlus orientālis, Som. Ben. Lye.

Eást-Francan; *pl. m. East-Franks;* Franci orientāles:—Wyð norþan Donua ǽwylme, and be eástan Rīne, syndon Eást-Francan *to the north from the spring of the Danube, and to the east of the Rhine, are the East-Franks*, Ors. 1, 1; Bos. 18, 30. Mid Eást-Francum *with the East-Franks*, Chr. 891; Erl. 88, 3.

eást-healf, e; *f. The east-side;* orientāle lătus, plăga orientālis:—Ðe on eást-healfe ðære eá wǽron *who were on the east side of the river*, Chr. 894; Th. 170, 9, col. 2. On eást-healfe Iericho *contra orientālem plăgam urbis Iericho*, Jos. 4, 19: Lev. 1, 16.

Eást-land, es; *n. The east country, Esthonia [Eastland], the country of the Osti* or *Estas;* orientālis terra, terra Esthonia:—Iacob com to ðam eástlande *Iacob vēnit in terram orientălem*. Gen. 29, 1. Eástland is swȳðe mycel *Esthonia is very large*, Ors. 1, 1; Bos. 22, 12.

eást-lang; *adv. Along the east;* orientem versus:—Se wudu is eástlang and westlang hund twelftiges mīla lang oððe lengra *the wood, from east to west [lit. along the east and along the west], is one hundred and twenty miles long, or longer*, Chr. 893; Th. 162, 30.

eástor-ǽfen, es; *m. Easter-even;* dies ante festum paschæ:—On eástor-ǽfen *on easter-even*, L. E. I. 41; Th. ii. 438, 24. v. eáster-ǽfen.

eástor-dæg, es; *m. Easter-day;* dies paschālis:—Ðȳ sylfan eástor-dæge *on the same easter-day*, Bd. 5, 23; S. 645, 36. v. eáster-dæg.

eástor-feorm, e; *f. Easter-feast* or *repast;* firma paschālis:—Eallum ǽhte-mannum gebȳreþ mid-wintres feorm and eástor-feorm *omnĭbus ehtemannis jūre compĕtit nātālis firma et paschālis firma*, L. R. S. 9, 1; Th. i. 436, 33. v. eáster-feorm.

eástor-līc; *adj. Easter, paschal;* paschālis:—On ðære sylfan eástor-līcan symbelnesse *on the same easter-feast*, Bd. 4, 28; S. 606, 23: 3, 24; S. 557, 40. v. eáster-līc.

eástor-tīd, e; *f. Easter-tide;* paschæ tempus:—In ða eástor-tīde *in the easter-tide*, Exon. 48 b; Th. 168, 10; Gū. 1075; Bd. 5, 23; S. 645, 36. v. eáster-tīd.

eástor-wice, an; *f. Easter-week;* septimāna paschālis:—Ealle ða dagas ðære eástor-wican *all the days of the easter-week*, L. E. I. 41; Th. ii. 438, 25. v. eáster-wuce.

eástran, eástron; *dat. pl. of* eáster; *gen.* -tres, *q. v.* Eástron *seems to be used for other cases in the pl.*

eástre, an; *n. Easter. the feast of easter;* pascha, Lk. Bos. 22, 1. v. eáster.

eá-streám, es; *m. A water-stream, a river;* rīvus:—Heóldon forþryne eástreámas heora *the river-streams held their onward course*, Cd. 12; Th. 14, 9; Gen. 216. Ofer eástreámas is brycgade blāce brimrāde *over the river-streams the ice bridged a pale water-road*, Andr. Kmbl. 2523; An. 1263. v. ēg-streám, eáh-streám.

eá-streám-ȳþ, e; *f. A river-stream-flood;* rīvi fluctus, Cd. 192; Th. 240, 11; Dan. 385.

eást-rīce, es; *n. East kingdom, eastern country, eastern part of a country;* orientāle regnum, orientālis rĕgio, Chr. 893; Th. 162, 19, col. 1, 3: Ors. 2, 1; Bos. 39, 21, 27.

eást-rihte; *adv. East right, towards* or *in the east;* contra ortum sōlis:—We witan ōðer eálond eást-rihte *nōvĭmus insŭlam aliam contra ortum sōlis*, Bd. 1, 1; S. 474, 15.

eástro *easter*, Mt. Bos. 26, 2; *nom. acc. pl. of* eáster.

eást-rōdor, es; *m. The eastern part of heaven;* pars orientālis cœli, ortus:—Ðes eást-rōdor *ortus*, Ps. Th. 102, 12.

eástron; *dat. pl. of* eáster, eástor.

eást-sǽ, es; *f. The east sea, sea on the east side of a country;* orientāle măre, Bd. 1, 12; S. 481, 8: 1, 15; S. 483, 40.

Eást-Seaxe; *gen.* -Seaxa; *dat.* -Seaxum; *pl. m:* -Seaxan; *gen.* -Seaxena, -Seaxna; *dat.* -Seaxum; *pl. m. The East-Saxons, people of Essex;* orientāles Saxŏnes:—Hēr Eást-Seaxe onfēngon geleáfan and fulwihtes bæþ *in this year [A. D. 604] the East-Saxons received the faith and bath of baptism*, Chr. 604; Th. 36, 33, col. 2, 3: 823; Th. 110, 31, col. 1: 894; Th. 170, 19, col. 1: 904; Th. 181, 16, col. 2. Of Seaxum cōman Eást-Seaxan and Sūþ-Seaxan and West-Seaxan *from the Saxons came the East-Saxons and the South-Saxons and the West-Saxons*, Bd. 1, 15; S. 483, 23. To-ætēcte ðisse gedrēfnisse storm Sæberhtes deáþ Eást-Seaxna cyninges *the death of Saberht, king of the East-Saxons, increased the storm of this disturbance*, 2, 5; S. 507, 6. Mellitum Agustinus sende Eást-Seaxum to bodigenne godcunde lāre *Augustine sent Mellitus to preach divine doctrine to the East-Saxons*, 2, 3; S. 504, 16: Chr. 604; Th. 36, 37, col. 1: 921; Th. 194, 34: 994; Th. 242, 10. Eást-Seaxena, -Seaxna land, rīce, þeód *the country, kingdom* or *nation of the East-Saxons*, Chr. 895; Th. 173, 7, col. 2: 836; Th. 118, 6, col. 1: 855; Th. 128, 15, col. 1; 129, 20: Bd. 4, 11; S. 579, 4: 2, 3; S. 504, 21.

eást-weard, eást-werd *eastward, in the east*, Ælfc. Gr. 38; Som. 40, 7. v. eást.

eást-weg, es; *m. East-way;* orientālis via:—On eást-wegas *in the east-ways*, Cd. 174; Th. 220, 11; Dan. 69: Elen. Kmbl. 509; El. 255.

eáþ; *adv. Easily;* facĭlĭter:—Dryhten mæg gehwone eáþ gescildan *the Lord may easily shield each*, Exon. 40 b; Th. 135, 23; Gū. 528: Cd. 95; Th. 124, 6; Gen. 2058. Hie ðe eáþ mihton adreógan *they the easier might endure*, Andr. Kmbl. 735; An. 368. v. ēþ, ȳþ. v. eáðe; *adj.*

eáþ-bēde; *adj. Exorable;* deprĕcābĭlis:—Wes ðīnum scealcum wel eáþbēde *deprĕcābĭlis esto super servos tuos*, Ps. Th. 89, 15.

eáþ-bēne; *adj. Exorable;* deprĕcābĭlis:—Eáþ-bēne *deprĕcābĭlis*, Som. Ben. Lye; Ps. Grn. ii. 200, 15, note.

EÁÐE, ēðe, ȳðe; *comp. m.* eáðera, eáðra; *f. n.* eáðere, eáðre; *sup.* eáðost; *adj. Easy, smooth;* făcĭlis, lēvis:—Gode þancedon ðæs ðe him ȳþ-lāda eáðe wurdon *they thanked God for that the wave-paths had been easy [= smooth] to them*, Beo. Th. 462; B. 228. Eáðere ys olfende to farenne þurh nǽdle þyrel, ðonne se rīca and se wēlega on Godes rīce gā *it is an easier [thing] for a camel to go through a needle's eye than a powerful and wealthy man to go into God's kingdom*, Mk. Bos. 10, 25. Eáðre is ðæt heofen and eorþe gewīton, ðonne ān stæf of ðære ǽ fealle *it is an easier [thing] that heaven and earth pass away than one letter of the law fail*, Lk. Bos. 16, 17. [*Chauc.* ethe, eythe *easy;* esy *light, gentle: R. Glouc.* eþ: *Laym.* æðe, eð: *Orm.* æþ: *Scot.* eith, eyth, eth: *O. Sax.* ōði: *Icel.* auð, adverbial prefix, *easy.*] DER. un-eáðe.

eáðe; *sup.* eáðost, -ust; *adv. Easily, readily, soon, perhaps;* facĭlĭter:—Ða burh mihton eáðe begitan *they might easily have taken the city*, Ors. 3, 4; Bos. 56, 10: Beo. Th. 961; B. 478. Ic eáðe forbær rūme regulas *I readily preferred the lax rules*, Exon. 39 b; Th. 131, 22; Gū. 459. We ðē eáðe gecȳðaþ sīþ ūserne *we readily proclaim our adventure to thee*, Andr. Recd. 1721; An. 861. Hwā mæg eáðost [eáðust MS. B.] ða dūru ontȳnan *who may most easily open the door?* Salm. Kmbl. 71; Sal. 36: Cd. 174; Th. 219, 6; Dan. 50: Ps. Th. 76, 10. DER. un-eáðe. v. ēðe.

eáðelīc, ǽðelīc; *comp. m.* -līcra; *f. n.* -līcre: *adj. Easy, possible;* făcĭlis:—Ealle þing synt mid Gode eáðelīce *with God all things are possible*, Mt. Bos. 19, 26. Hwæt is eáðelīcre *what is easier?* 9, 5. DER. un-eáðelīc. v. ǽðe-līc.

eáðelīce, ēðelīce, ȳðelīce; *comp.* or; *sup.* ost, ust; *adv. Easily;* făcĭle:—Eáðelīcor mæg se olfend gān þurh ānre nǽdle eáge *it is easier for a camel to go through the eye of a needle*, Lk. Bos. 18, 25. He sōhte hū he eáðelīcost hine gesealde *he sought how he might most easily betray him*, 22, 6. DER. un-eáðelīce.

eáþ-fere; *adj. Easily trod, easy;* facĭlis ĭtu:—Eáþfere weg *iter* vel *ĭtus*, Ælfc. Gl. 56; Som. 67, 48; Wrt. Voc. 37, 35.

eáþ-fynde; *adj. Easy to be found;* făcĭlis inventu:—Ðā wæs eáþfynde *then was easy to be found*, Beo. Th. 276; B. 138: Cd. 93; Th. 120, 12; Gen. 1993. v. ēþ-fynde, ȳþ-.

eáþ-gesýne *easy to be seen, visible.* v. ēþ-gesȳne = ȳþ-gesēne.

eáþ-gete; *adj. Easily got, got ready, prepared*; făcilis adeptu, parātus:—Him wæs eáþgete ele to đam baþe *oil was made ready for his bath*, Ælfc. T. 32, 14. v. ēþ-begete.

eáþ-hrēđig; *adj. Blessed*; beātus:—Seó eáþhrēđige Elene *the blessed Elene*, Elen. Kmbl. 531; El. 266; *for* eád-hrēđig, *q.v.*

eáþ-hylde *satisfied, contented.* v. ēþ-hylde.

eáþ-lǣre; *adj. Easily taught, teachable*; dŏcĭbĭlis:—Ealle eáþlǣre beóþ Godes *ĕrunt omnes dŏcĭbĭles Dei*, Jn. Bos. 6, 45.

eáþ-mēd, es; *n. Humility, affability, kindness*; humĭlĭtas, humānĭtas, generally found in the *pl*:—Ac mīne [MS. min] eáþmēdu geseah *vĭde humĭlĭtātem meam*, Ps. Th. 118, 153: 135, 24. On mīnum eáþmēdum *in humĭlĭtāte mea*, 118, 50. For eáþmēdum *in humility*, Exon. 53 a; Th. 186, 5; Az. 15: 13 a; Th. 22, 29; Cri. 359. v. eád-mēd.

eáþ-mēdan *To adore*; adōrāre:—Eáþmēdaþ feorr *adōrābĭtis prŏcul*, Ex. 24, 1. DER. ge-eáþmēdan. v. eádmēdan.

eáþ-mēde; *adj. Of an easy mind, humble*; mītis, hŭmĭlis:—He gebētte mid eáþmēde ingeþance *he expiated with humble mind*, Ps. C. 50, 152; Ps. Grn. ii. 280, 152. v. eád-mēde.

eáþ-mēdum; *adv.* [*dat. pl. of* eáþmēd] *Humbly, kindly*; humĭlĭter, benignĭter:—Eáþ-mēdum *humbly*, Exon. 46 a; Th. 157, 15; Gū. 892. Đæt he eáþmēdum oncnāwe *that he should treat* [*him*] *kindly*, Andr. Kmbl. 641; An. 321. Gewāt him se hālga eáþmēdum *the holy one departed kindly*, 1957; An. 981.

eáþ-metto; *indecl. sing*; *pl. nom. acc.* -metta; *f. Humility*; humĭlĭtas:—Geseóh mīne eáþmetto *vĭde humĭlĭtātem meam*, Ps. Th. 9, 13: 24, 16. On đam stāne eáþmetta *on the rock of humility*, Bt. 12; Fox 36, 22: Bt. Met. Fox 7, 65; Met. 7, 33.

eáþ-mōd; *adj. Humble, lowly, obedient*; hŭmĭlis, obēdiens:—Gif đū eáþmōdne eorl gemēte *if thou meet a lowly person*, Exon. 84 b; Th. 318, 5; Mōd. 78. He eáþmōde him eorlas funde *he found men obedient to him*, Menol. Fox 195; Men. 99. His ætgiefan eáþmōd weorþeþ *he becomes obedient to his feeder*, Exon. 88 b; Th. 332, 27; Vy. 91. v. eád-mōd.

eáþ-mōdian *to obey*; obēdīre. v. ge-eáþ-mōdian.

eáþ-mōdlīce; *adv. Humbly*; humĭlĭter:—Abiddaþ hine eáþmōdlīce *pray to him humbly*, Bt. 42; Fox 258, 21. v. eádmōdlīce.

eáþ-mōdnis, -nys, -niss, -nyss, e; *f. Humility*; humĭlĭtas:—Mid micelre eáþmōdnisse *with great humility*, Th. Diplm. A. D. 804–829; 459, 15. On eáþmōdnysse mīne *in humĭlĭtāte mea*, Ps. Spl. 118, 50. v. eádmōdnes.

eáþnes, -ness, e; *f. Easiness*; facĭlĭtas. v. ēþnes, eád-nes.

eatogeđa *eighth*:—Seó eatogeđe *the eighth*, Bd. 4, 5; S. 573, note 10. v. eahtođa.

eatol; *adj. Dire, terrible*; dīrus, terrĭbĭlis:—Gæst yrre cwom, eatol *the guest came angry, terrible*, Beo. Th. 4154; B. 2074: 4949, note; B. 2478. v. atol.

Eatole *Italy*; Itălia, Som. Ben. Lye.

Eatol-ware; *pl. m. Italians*; Ităli, Som. Ben. Lye.

eáu-fæstnys, -nyss, e; *f.* [eáu = ǣw, ǣ *law*; fæstnys *firmness*] *Firmness in the law, religion, devotion*; relĭgio:—Be eáufæstnysse and wundorlīcre ārfæstnysse Ōswaldes cyninges *de relĭgiōne ac piĕtāte miranda Osualdi rēgis*, Bd. 3, 6; S. 528, 2. v. ǣ-fæstnes.

eáum *to rivers*, Ors. 5, 2; Bos. 102, 34; *dat. pl. of* eá.

eáw, eáw-lā *oh! alas!* O! eheu! Bt. Met. Fox 9, 109; Met. 9, 55. v. eálā.

eáwan; *p.* de; *pp.* ed *To shew, manifest*; ostendĕre, manifestāre:—Hī þenceaþ þreá þearle þeódum eáwan *they intend to shew a severe chiding to the nations*, Ps. Th. 149, 7. He eáweþ him egsan *he shews them terror*, Exon. 33 b; Th. 107, 11; Gū. 57: Beo. Th. 557; B. 276. Ne sindon đīne ǣhta wiht, đa đū monnum eáwdest *thy possessions are nought, which thou didst shew to men*, Exon. 99 a; Th. 371, 14; Seel. 75. Nǣfre wommes tācn eáwed weorþeþ *the sign of crime shall never be manifested*, 8 b; Th. 4, 20; Cri. 55: 22 a; Th. 59, 22; Cri. 956. [*O. Frs.* auwa, awa.] DER. ge-eáwan, ōþ-. v. ȳwan.

eáwesclīce; *adv.* [eáwan *to shew, manifest*] *Openly*; pălam:—Đætte seó sāwl in deágolnisse þrōwiende wæs, đætte se līchoma eáwesclīce fōretācnode *quod anĭma in occulto passa sit, căro pălam præmonstrābat*, Bd. 3, 19; S. 549, 17.

eáw-fæst; *adj.* [eáw = ǣw, ǣ *law*; fæst *fast, fixed*] *Firm in observing the law, religious, pious*; relĭgiōsus, pius:—Gregorius wæs of æđelborenre mægþe and eáwfæstre acenned *Gregory was born of a noble and pious family*, Homl. Th. ii. 118, 7. Se eáwfæsta papa *the pious pope*, ii. 118, 8. Mid eáwfæstum þeáwum *relĭgiōsis mōrĭbus*, Bd. 3, 23; S. 555, 4. v. ǣ-fæst.

eáw-fæstnys, -nyss, e; *f.* [eáw = ǣw, ǣ *law*; fæstnys *firmness*] *Firmness in the law, religion, piety*; relĭgio, piĕtas:—Mid gelīcere eáwfæstnysse *with similar piety*, L. E. I. 41; Th. ii. 438, 26. v. ǣ-fæstnes.

eáwu, e; *f. A ewe*; ovis fēmĭna:—Agefe mon to Liming l eáwa and v cȳ *let fifty ewes and five cows be given to Lyming*, Th. Diplm. A. D. 835; 470, 29, 32. v. eówu.

eáwunga, eáwunge; *adv.* [eáwan *to shew, manifest*] *Openly, publicly*; mănĭfeste, pălam, cōram:—God eáwunga cymeþ *Deus mănĭfeste vĕniet*, Ps. Spl. 49, 3. He wearþ dīgellīce cristen, forđon he eáwunga ne dorste *he was secretly a christian, because he durst not openly*, Ors. 6, 21; Bos. 123, 29: Exon. 126 b; Th. 487, 2; Rä. 72, 22. Ođđe eáwunga ođđe dearnunga *either publicly or privately*, L. Edg. ii. 8; Th. i. 270, 5. Eáwunge *cōram*, Ælfc. Gr. 38; Som. 41, 55.

eá-wylm *a welling or boiling up of water, spring*, Lye. v. ǣwelm.

eá-wyrt, e; *f. River-wort, burdock*; arctium lappa, Lin:—Genim clifwyrt, sume men hātaþ foxes clife, sume eá-wyrt *take cliff-wort, some men call* [*it*] *fox-glove, some river-wort*, L. M. 1, 15; Lchdm. ii. 58, 4: iii. 74, 10. Nim eáwyrte niođowearde *take the netherward* [*part*] *of burdock*, L. M. 1, 87; Lchdm. ii. 154, 14.

eax *an axe*; secūris:—Seó eax *the axe*, L. In. 43; Th. i. 128, 23, note 65, MS. B. v. æx.

EAX, ex, æx, e; *f. An axis, axle-tree*; axis:—Neáh đam norþende đære eaxe *near the north end of the axis*, Bt. 39, 3; Fox 214, 20: 39, 13; Fox 232, 33: Bt. Met. Fox 28, 44; Met. 28, 22: 29, 36; Met. 29, 18. On đære ilcan eaxe hwerfeþ eall rūma rōdor *all the spacious sky turns on the same axis*, 28, 30; Met. 28, 15. Ymb đa eaxe *about the axis*, Bt. 39, 3; Fox 214, 23. On wǣnes eaxe hwearfaþ đa hweól, and sió eax stent stille *the wheels turn on the waggon's axle-tree, and the axle-tree stands still*, 39, 7; Fox 220, 27, 30, 31: 39, 8; Fox 224, 5. Sió nafu ferþ nēhst đære eaxe *the nave goes nearest to the axle-tree*, 39, 7; Fox 222, 2, 12, 20, 21, 22, 28. Twegen steorran synd gehātene *axis*, đæt is ex, forđamđe se firmamentum went on đām twām steorran, swā swā hweogel tyrnþ on eaxe, and fordī hī standaþ symle stille *two stars are called* axis, *that is axle-tree, because the firmament turns on the two stars, as a wheel turns on an axle-tree, and because they always stand still*, Bd. de nat. rerum; Wrt. popl. science 16, 12–15; Lchdm. iii. 270, 20–23. [*Wyc.* ax-tre, ex-tre *an axle-tree*: *Plat.* asse: *Dut.* as, *f*: *Ger.* achse, axe, *f*: *M. H. Ger.* ahse, *f*: *O. H. Ger.* ahsa, *f*: *Dan.* axe, *m. f*: *Swed.* axel, *m*: *Icel.* axull, öxull, *m*; öxul-tré, *n*: *Lat.* axis, *m*: *Grk.* ἄξων, *m*: *Lith.* aszis, *f*: *Sansk.* aksha *the axle of a wheel, a wheel, car.*]

Eaxan ceaster, e; *f*: es; *n.* v. ceaster *Exeter, Devon*:—Wende he hine wiđ Eaxan ceastres *he turned towards Exeter*, Chr. 894; Th. 167, 28, col. 2: 894; Th. 169, 17, col. 2: 895; Th. 173, 10, col. 2. v. Exan ceaster.

Eaxan minster; *gen.* -minstres; *n. The minster on the river Ex, Axminster, Devon*; oppĭdum in agro Devōniensi, Som. Ben. Lye. v. Acsan mynster.

Eaxan mūþa, an; *m. The mouth of the river Ex, Exmouth, Devon*:—To Eaxan mūþan *to Exmouth*, Chr. 1001; Ing. 174, note a. v. Exan mūþa.

EAXEL, eaxl, exl, e; *f*: eaxle, an; *f. The shoulder*; hŭmĕrus:—Standeþ [MS. standaþ] me hēr on eaxelum *stands here on my shoulders*, Wald. 92; Vald. 2, 18. Gefēng he be eaxle Grendles mōdor *he seized Grendel's mother by the shoulder*, Beo. Th. 3078; B. 1537. He forlēt earm and eaxle *he left arm and shoulder*, 1948; B. 972. He gewērgad sæt freán eaxlum neáh *he sat wearied near his lord's shoulders*, 5699; B. 2853: 722; B. 358. Hæfde earmas and eaxle *it had arms and shoulders*, Exon. 129 a; Th. 494, 24; Rä. 83, 6. Gif eaxle gelæmed weorþeþ *if a shoulder be lamed*, L. Ethb. 38; Th. i. 14, 2. He hit set on his exla *impōnit eam in hŭmĕros suos*, Lk. Bos. 15, 5: Andr. Kmbl. 3148; An. 1577. [*Laym.* exle, *dat*: *O. Sax.* ahsla, *f*: *O. Frs.* axle, axele, *f*: *Ger.* achsel, *f*: *M. H. Ger.* ahsel, *f*: *O. H. Ger.* ahsala, *f*: *Goth.* amsa, *m*: *Dan.* axel, *m. f*: *Swed.* axel, *m*: *Icel.* öxl, *f*: *Lat.* axilla, *f.*]

eaxl-clāþ, es; *m. A shoulder-cloth, scapular*; humĕrāle:—Lēde eaxlclāþ ofer hine *desŭper humĕrāle ei impŏsuit*, Lev. 8, 7.

eaxle, an; *f. A shoulder*; hŭmĕrus:—Gif eaxle gelæmed weorþeþ *if a shoulder be lamed*, L. Ethb. 38; Th. i. 14, 2. v. eaxel, eaxl.

eaxle-gespan; *gen.* -gespannes; *n. The shoulder-span*:—Fīfe gimmas wǣron on đam eaxlegespanne *five gems were on the shoulder-span*, Rood Kmbl. 17; Kr. 9.

eaxl-gestealla, an; *m. A shoulder companion, nearest friend, bosom friend, comrade*; cŏmes qui est a lătĕre, sŏcius intĭmus, commīlito:—Deád is Æschere, mīn eaxlgestealla *Æschere is dead, my bosom friend*, Beo. Th. 2656; B. 1326. Hæfde wīgena tō lyt, eaxlgestealna *he had too few of warriors, comrades*, Elen. Kmbl. 127; El. 64. Ic eom æđelinges eaxlgestealla *I am a noble's bosom friend*, Exon. 127 a; Th. 489, 2; Rä. 78, 1. Heremōd breát eaxlgesteallan *Heremod destroyed his bosom friends*, Beo. Th. 3432; B. 1714.

EBBA, an; *m? An* EBB *or receding of water*; rĕcessus măris:—Nēpflōd *vel* ebba ledona, Ælfc. Gl. 105; Som. 78, 29; Wrt. Voc. 57, 11. Ebba [MS. ebbe] *recessus*, 105; Som. 78, 36; Wrt. Voc. 57, 18. Ebba [MS. ebbe] *vel* gyte-streám *rheuma*, 105; Som. 78, 38; Wrt. Voc. 57, 20. Gewrixle đæs flōdes and đæs ebban *change of the flood and the ebb*,

Bt. 21; Fox 74, 30. Com flōwende flōd æfter ebban *the flowing flood came after the ebb,* Byrht. Th. 133, 45; By. 65: Bt. Met. Fox 11, 138; Met. 11, 69. [*Chauc.* ebbe: *Plat.* ebbe, *f*: *O. Frs.* ebba, *n*: *Dut.* eb, *f*: *Kil.* ebbe: *Ger. M. H. Ger.* ebbe, *f*: *O. H. Ger.* ebba, *f*: *Dan.* ebbe, *m. f*: *Swed.* ebb, *m.*]

ebbian; *p.* ode, ade; *pp.* od, ad [ebba *an ebb*] *To ebb;* recēdĕre, refluĕre:—Will-flōd ongan lytligan eft, lago ebbade sweart under swegle *the well-flood began again to lessen, the water ebbed dark under the firmament,* Cd. 71; Th. 85, 12; Gen. 1413. DER. a-ebbian, be-, ge-: æbbung, sǣ-.

ēbere-morþ, es; *n.* [ǣber *clear, manifest;* morþ *murder*] *Open murder, manslaughter;* homĭcīdium manĭfestum, L. H. 12, § 1; Th. i. 522, 27, Som. Ben. Lye.

Ebreisc; *adj. Hebrew, belonging to Jews;* Hebræus:—Nychodēmus awrāt eall mid Ebreiscum stafum *Nicodemus wrote all in Hebrew letters,* Nicod. pref; Thw. 1, 4. Of Seme com ðæt Ebreisce folc *from Shem came the Hebrew people,* Ælfc. T. 7, 25.

ebur-þring, es; *m. The celestial sign Orion,* Som. Ben. Lye. v. eofor-þring.

ebylgan *to be angry;* īrasci, Ben. Lye. v. a-belgan.

ebylgnes, -ness, e; *f. Anger, indignation;* īra:—On ebylgnesse his *in indignātiōne ejus,* Ps. Spl. T. 29, 5. v. æbylignes.

ēc; *conj.* EKE, *also;* etiam:—Ða us ēc bewrǣcon *who also have sent us forth,* Cd. 189; Th. 235, 12; Dan. 305: 151; Th. 190, 5; Exod. 194. Ēc sceoldon his þegnas ðǣr gewunian *his followers must also inhabit there,* 220; Th. 284, 23; Sat. 326: Beo. Th. 6254, note; B. 3131: Ps. Th. 131, 17. v. eác.

ēcan, ǣcan, īcan, iécan, ȳcan, ȳcean, ic ēce, ðū ēcest, he ēcþ, *pl.* ēcaþ; *p.* ēcte, *pl.* ēcton, ēhton; *pp.* ēced [eáca *an addition*] *To* EKE, *increase, prolong, add;* augēre, appōnĕre:—Ðū scealt ēcan ðīne yrmþu *thou shalt increase thy wretchedness,* Andr. Kmbl. 2767; An. 1386. Gē ēcaþ eówre ermþe *ye increase your poverty,* Bt. 26, 2; Fox 94, 9. Ðæt ēcþ his ermþa *that augments his misery,* 29, 1; Fox 102, 19. Ēcte ðæt spell mid leóþe *he prolonged the speech with verse,* 12; Fox 36, 6: Ps. Th. 104, 20. Hī hira firena furður ēhton *appŏsuērunt adhuc peccāre ei,* 77, 19. Ðæt se awyrgeda ne ēce, ðæt he hine leng myclie ofer eorþan *ut non appōnat ultra magnĭfĭcāre se hŏmo sŭper terram,* 9, 38. Hwæt biþ ðē ealles seald oððe ēced swā from ðære inwitfullan yflan tungan *quid dētur tĭbi aut quid appōnātur tĭbi a lingua dŏlōsa?* 119, 3. DER. æt-ēcan, ge-, to-, to-æt-, to-ge-: to-æt-ȳcnys.

ēcce-līc; *adj. Eternal, perpetual, everlasting;* æternālis:—Upahebbaþ gatu ēccelīce *elevāmĭni portæ æternāles,* Ps. Spl. 23, 7. v. ēce-līc.

ece, æce, ace, es; *m. An* AKE, *pain;* dŏlor:—Efne swā se bisceop ðone ece and ðæt sār mid him ūt bǣre *as if the bishop had borne the ake and the sore out with him,* Bd. 5, 3; S. 616, 37: 5, 4; S. 617, 22. DER. acan.

ĒCE, ǣce; *gen. m. n.* ēces; *gen. f.* ēcre, ēcere; *dat. m. n.* ēcum; *f.* ēcre, ēcere; *def.* se ēcá, ēcea; seó, ðæt ēce; *gen.* ēcan, ēcean; *adj. Eternal, perpetual, everlasting;* sempĭternus, æternus:—Ðis ys sōþlīce ēce līf *hæc est autem vīta æterna,* Jn. Bos. 17, 3. Onwōd ēce feónd folcdriht wera *the eternal foe pervaded the nation of men,* Cd. 64; Th. 76, 23; Gen. 1261. Ðē sīe ēce hērenis *eternal praise be to thee,* Exon. 13 b; Th. 26, 10; Cri. 415. Ðæt is ēcu rest *that is eternal rest,* Bt. Met. Fox 13, 142; Met. 13, 71. Godes ēce bearn *God's eternal child,* Exon. 18 b; Th. 46, 29; Cri. 744. Swā him se ēca bebeád *as the Eternal bade him,* Cd. 107; Th. 142, 28; Gen. 2368. Ēces word *the Eternal's word,* Exon. 61 b; Th. 225, 33; Ph. 398. Fōre onsȳne ēcan Dryhtnes *before the face of the eternal Lord,* 64 b; Th. 238, 7; Ph. 600. To ēcre gemynde *for a continual remembrance,* Homl. Blick. 127, 22. Wæs me andfencge ēcere hǣlu *tu es susceptor salūtis meæ æternæ,* Ps. Th. 88, 23. Ic þanc secge ēcum Dryhtne *I say thanks to the eternal Lord,* Beo. Th. 5584; B. 2796. Andetaþ ðam ēcean Gode *confitēmĭni Deo æterno,* Ps. Th. 135, 27. Cēgaþ his ēcne naman *invocāte nōmen ejus æternum,* 104, 1. On ðone ēcan eard ussa sāwla *to the eternal region of our souls,* Bt. Met. Fox 23, 21; Met. 23, 11. He him ēce meaht geceás *he chose to himself eternal power,* Exon. 45 b; Th. 154, 34; Gū. 852. He us sealde ēce staðelas *he gave us eternal seats,* 17 b; Th. 41, 26; Cri. 661. Se ðe ða ēcan āgan wille sōþan gesǣlþa *he who will possess the eternal true felicities,* Bt. Met. Fox 7, 57; Met. 7, 29. Ðæt he walde ēcra gestealda *that he shall rule the eternal mansions,* Elen. Kmbl. 1601; El. 802. Eorþan ðū gefyllest ecum wæstmum *thou fillest the earth with eternal fruits,* Ps. Th. 64, 9. Se mec āna mæg ēcan meahtum geþeón þrymme *who alone by his eternal powers can tame me with power,* Exon. 111 b; Th. 427, 23; Rā. 41, 90. [*Orm.* eche: *O. Sax.* ēwig: *O. Frs.* ewch, ewig, iowich, iowigh: *Dut.* eeuwig: *Ger.* ewig: *M. H. Ger.* ēwic, ēwec: *O. H. Ger.* ēwīg: *Goth.* ayuk-duþs *eternity*: *Dan. Swed.* evig.] DER. efen-ēce.

ēce; *adv. Ever, evermore, eternally, perpetually;* in æternum, semper, contĭnuo, perpĕtuo:—Hie on friþe lifdon ēce mid heora aldor *they lived ever in peace with their chief,* Cd. 1; Th. 2, 16; Gen. 20. Ðǣr he ēce sceal hāmfæst wesan *where he shall for ever sojourn,* Exon. 30 b; Th. 95, 9; Cri. 1554. Ðe wunaþ ēce *qui mănet in æternum,* Ps. Th. 54, 19. Ēce standeþ Godes hand-geweorc *God's handywork standeth evermore,* Canon. Hrs. 369, 17. Ðǣr is help gelong ēce to ealdre *there is our help for evermore at hand,* Exon. 75 a; Th. 281, 14; Jul. 646. Wunaþ symble ēce *mănet in sēcŭlum sēcŭli,* Ps. Th. 110, 2. Wunaþ ēce forþ *mănet in sēcŭlum sēcŭli,* Ps. Th. 118, 90.

ECED, æced, æcced, es; *n. m.* ACID, *vinegar;* acētum:—Ðā stōd ān fæt full ecedes *vas ergo ĕrat pŏsĭtum acēto plēnum,* Jn. Bos. 19, 29. Se Hǣlend onfēng ðæs ecedes *the Saviour received the vinegar,* Jn. Bos. 19, 30. Onfēng ðe Hǣlend ðæt æced, Jn. Rush. War. 19, 30. Drync ecedes *a drink of vinegar,* Exon. 29 a; Th. 88, 13; Cri. 1439. Mid ecede *with vinegar,* Ps. Th. 68, 22. Wyl niðewearde netelan on ecede, dō oxan geallan on ðæt eced *boil the netherward [part] of nettle in vinegar, add ox gall to the vinegar,* L. M. 3, 7; Lchdm. ii. 312, 8, 9. Lege hit in ðone eced *lay it in the vinegar,* Lchdm. iii. 18, 2. [*Plat.* etik, *m*: *O. Sax.* ekid, *n*: *Dut.* edik, eek, *m*: *Ger.* essich, essig, *m*: *M. H. Ger.* ezzich, *m*: *O. H. Ger.* ezih, *m*: *Goth.* akeit, *n*: *Dan.* eddike, *m. f*: *Swed.* ättika, *f*: *Icel.* edik, *n.*] DER. eced-fæt, æced-fæt, -wīn.

eced-fæt, æced-fæt, es; *n. An acid-vat, a vinegar-vessel;* acētābŭlum, Ælfc. Gl. 114; Som. 80, 32; Wrt. Voc. 61, 12.

eced-wīn, es; *n. Acid-wine.* v. æced-wīn.

ēce-līc, ēcce-līc; *adj. Eternal, perpetual, everlasting;* æternālis:—Upahebbaþ gatu ēcelīce *elevāmĭni portæ æternāles,* Ps. Spl. 23, 9. Ēccelīc *eternal,* 23, 7.

ēce-līce; *adv. Eternally, ever;* perpĕtuo, Ælfc. Gr. 38; Som. 42, 1. Ic ðas tīde Eástrena ēcelīce healdan wille *vŏlo hoc tempus Paschæ perpĕtuo observāre,* Bd. 5, 21; S. 643, 20.

ēcen *great, powerful;* magnus, pŏtens, Andr. Kmbl. 1271; An. 636: 1763; An. 884, = eácen; *pp. of* eácan *augēri.*

ecer *an acre,* Som. Ben. Lye. v. æcer.

ECG, e; *f. An* EDGE, *a sharpness, blade, sword;* ăcies, acūmen, glădius, ferrum:—On sweordes ecge *on the edge of the sword,* Lk. Bos. 21, 24. Hyne ecg fornam *the sword had destroyed him,* Beo. Th. 5538; B. 2772. Ecg wæs īren *the edge was iron,* 5549; B. 2778. Ecg grymetode *the blade rang,* Cd. 162; Th. 203, 24; Exod. 408. Ecga [MS. ecge] mihton helpan æt hilde *swords might help in battle,* Beo. Th. 5360; B. 2683: 5649; B. 2828. Mid gryrum ecga *with terrors of swords,* 971; B. 483. Æscum and ecgum *with spears and swords,* 3548; B. 1772. Billa ecgum *with edges of bills,* Cd. 210; Th. 260, 14; Dan. 709. [*Wyc.* egge: *Laym.* egge, agge: *Orm.* egge: *Plat.* egge, *f*: *O. Sax.* eggia, *f*: *Frs.* ig: *O. Frs.* eg, ig, *f*: *Kil.* egghe, *f*: *Ger. M. H. Ger.* ecke, *f*; eck, *n*: *O. H. Ger.* ekka, *f*: *Dan.* eg, *m. f*: *Swed.* egg, *m*: *Icel.* egg, *f*: *Lat.* ăcies, acūmen: *Grk.* ἀκή, ἀκίς, ἀκμή: *Sansk.* aśri, *f. ăcies, ensis.*] DER. brūn-ecg, heard-, stīþ-, stȳl-, twȳ-.

ecgan; *p.* de; *pp.* ed; *v. trans.* [ecg *an edge*] *To give an edge, to sharpen;* acuĕre. Ecged *edged, sharpened, only found in compositions,* as twig-ecged *two-edged;* biceps, *q. v.*

ecg-bana, -bona, an; *m. A sword-killer, murderer;* glădio cædens, occīsor:—Cain gewearþ to ecgbanan āngan brēðer *Cain became the murderer of his only brother,* Beo. Th. 2528; B. 1262. Ecg-bona, 5006; B. 2506.

Ecg-bryht, -briht, -berht, -byrht, es; *m.* [ecg *edge, sword;* bryht *bright, excellent*] *Egbert;* Ecgbryhtus; *king of Wessex for thirty-seven years and seven months, from* A. D. 800–837. Egbert chose Swithun [v. Swīþhūn] for the preceptor to his son Æðelwulf, the heir to the throne of Wessex:—Hēr, A. D. 800, Ecgbryht fēng to Wesseaxna rīce *here,* A. D. 800, *Egbert succeeded to the kingdom of the West-Saxons,* Chr. 800; Erl. 60, 4. Hēr, A. D. 837 [MS. 836], Ecgbryht cyning forþfērde, se rīcsode xxxvii wintra and vii mōnþas *here,* A. D. 837, *king Egbert died, who reigned thirty-seven years and seven months,* Chr. 836; Th. 117, 25, col. 1.

Ecg-bryhtes stān, es; *m. Brixton Deverill, Wilts?*—He gerād to Ecgbryhtes stāne be eástan Sealwyda *he rode to Egbert's stone, on the east of Selwood,* Chr. 878; Th. 148, 3, col. 1.

ecg-clif *a sea cliff* or *shore,* B. 2893, = ēg-clif, *q. v.* Beo. Th. 5778.

ecg-heard; *adj. Hard of edge;* ăcie dūrus:—Lǣtaþ spor, īren ecg-heard, ealdorgeard sceoran *let the spur, the iron hard of edge, raze the dwelling of life,* Andr. Kmbl. 2363; An. 1183.

ecg-hete, es; *m. Sword-hate, hostile hate;* ŏdium glădiis manifestātum, bellum:—Ne gesacu ōhwǣr ecghete eóweþ *nor strife shews anywhere hostile hate,* Beo. Th. 3480; B. 1738.

ecg-plega, an; *m. A play of swords, sword-fight, battle;* pugna:—Hie ðām ealdorþegnum cȳðan eódon atolne ecgplegan *they went to inform the principal thanes of the cruel sword-fight,* Judth. 12; Thw. 25, 6; Jud. 246.

ecg-þræc; *gen.* -þræce; *pl. nom. gen. acc.* -þraca; *f. Sword-strength, war* or *savage courage;* glădiōrum impĕtus:—He ne þearf atole ecg-þræce *he needs not the cruel sword-strength,* Beo. Th. 1196; B. 596.

ecg-wæl, es; *n. Sword's wail, slaughter;* strāges glădio cæsōrum:—

On ecgwæle [MS. ecgwale] *amid the slaughter of swords*, Cd. 96; Th. 126, 2; Gen. 2089.

ecilma, an; *m. A chilblain;* pernio, Som. Ben. Lye. v. æcelma.

ēcne *great; acc. of* ēcen.

ēc-nes, -nis, -nys, -ness, -niss, -nyss, e; *f. Eternity, everlasting;* æternĭtas:—Ðæt we wuldres eard in ēcnesse āgan mōsten *that we for ever might possess the abode in glory*, Exon. 25 b; Th. 74, 9; Cri. 1204: Ps. Th. 118, 152. On ēcnisse *for ever*, Cd. 23; Th. 30, 18; Gen. 469. On ēcnysse *for ever*, Mk. Bos. 3, 29: Ps. Th. 110, 6: 118, 44.

ēcra *of eternal*, Elen. Kmbl. 1601; El. 802; *gen. pl. of* ēce.

ēcre *for continual*, Homl. Blick. 127, 22; *dat. f. of* ēce.

ēc-sōþ, ēc-sōþlīce *but truly, but also;* sed autem, vēre, Som. Ben. Lye.

ēc-sōþlice *but truly.* v. ēc-sōþ.

ēd [eád *happiness*] *Safety, security, happiness;* sălus, asȳlum:—Ēd monne *safety of men, the ark*, Cd. 70; Th. 84, 30, Mann. Some think ed signifies *a renewing, restoration, regeneration;* renŏvātio: then ed monne might be translated, *regeneration of men. Grn. corrected* ed monne *into* edniowne *renewed:*—Ðā he hine [ēgor-here] upp forlēt edniowne [*acc. referring to* hine = ēgor-here] streámum stīgan *when he allowed it* [*the water-flood-'host'*] *renewed to mount up in streams*, Gen. 1405.

ed-, prefixed to words, denotes *anew, again*, as the Latin re- *meaning* rursus, dēnuo, itĕrum. Edniwian *to renew, to make new again;* renŏvāre. [*Wyc.* ed-: *Plat. O. Frs.* et- in etmal: *M. H. Ger.* ite-: *O. H. Ger.* it-, ita-: *Goth.* id-: *O. Nrs.* ið-.]

-ed used as a termination of *pp.* v. D 4, 5.

ēd- = ād *a funeral pile.* v. ēd-wylm.

ed-cenning, e; *f. Regeneration;* regenĕrātio:—On edcenninge *in regenĕrātiōne*, Mt. Bos. 19, 28.

ed-cer, -cir, -cyr, -cerr, -cirr, -cyrr, es; *m. A return;* reversio, rĕdĭtus:—Ne hī edcerres ǣfre mōton wēnan *they may never think of return*, Cd. 223; Th. 293, 7; Sat. 451. Edcir ðære ādle *a return of the disease*, Past. 33, 7; Cot. MS. Edcyr of wræcsiþe [MS. spræc-siðe] *postlīmĭnium*, Ælfc. Gl. 15; Som. 58, 28; Wrt. Voc. 21, 22. DER. cyrr.

ed-cēlness, e; *f. A recooling, pleasant coolness;* refrigĕrātio, Ps. Spl. 65, 11? Lye.

ed-cucian, -cwician; *p.* ode, ade; *pp.* od, ad *To re-quicken, revive;* reviviscĕre, Greg. Dial. 1, 12, Lye. DER. ge-edcucian, -cwician.

ed-cwide, es; *m. A relation, retelling;* relātio, Lye.

ed-cyr, -cyrr, es; *m. A return;* rĕdĭtus, Wrt. Voc. 21, 22. v. ed-cer.

ēde, es; *n. A flock;* grex:—Wæs ðǣr ēde *erat ibi grex*, Lk. Lind. War. 8, 32: 12, 32. v. eówde.

eder, es; *m. A hedge, house;* sēpes, dŏmus:—Hryðge ða ederas *the houses* [*are*] *ruinous*, Exon. 77 b; Th. 291, 5; Wand. 77. v. eodor.

eder-gong, es; *m. A home-seeking;* desīdĕrium dŏmus:—Ðǣr nǣfre cymeþ edergong *there never comes a home*, Exon. 32 b; Th. 102, 21; Cri. 1676.

edesc-hen *an edish hen, a quail;* cŏturnix, Ps. Surt. 104, 40. v. edisc-hen.

ed-geong, ed-giong; *adj. Growing young again;* rejuvĕnescens:—Of ascan edgeong weseþ *from ashes he becomes young again*, Exon. 61 a; Th. 224, 10; Ph. 373.

ed-gifan; *p.* -geaf, *pl.* -geáfon; *pp.* -gifen *To give again, restore;* reddĕre, Leo, A. Sax. Gl. 108.

ed-gift, e; *f. A re-giving, restitution;* restĭtūtio, Lye.

ed-gild, es; *n. A re-payment;* rĕ-sŏlūtio, Leo, A. Sax. Gl. 250. v. gild.

ed-giong; *adj. Growing young again;* rejuvĕnescens, Exon. 64 a; Th. 236, 28; Ph. 581. v. ed-geong.

ed-grōwung, e; *f. A re-growing;* recĭdīva, Ælfc. Gl. 60; Som. 68, 26; Wrt. Voc. 39, 12.

ed-gyldend, es; *m. A remunerator, rewarder;* remunĕrātor, Scint. 33, Som. Ben. Lye.

ed-hwyrft, es; *m. A returning, return;* rĕdĭtio, rĕdĭtus:—He ne wēneþ, ðæt him ðæs edhwyrft cyme *he will not hope that its return may come*, Exon. 89 b; Th. 336, 3; Gn. Ex. 42: Beo. Th. 2566; B. 1281.

edisc, es; *n.* [ed-, *Lat.* re- *again;* isc *a termination, generally an adj.* but also es; *n.*] I. EDISH or *aftermath, pasture;* pascua:—Wǣrun we his sceáp, ða he on his edisce afēdde *we were his sheep, which he fed in his pasture*, Ps. Th. 94, 7: 99, 3. II. *a park;* vīvārium, Cot. 207, Lye.

edisc-hen, -henn, e; *f. An* EDISH HEN, *quail;* cŏturnix:—Hī bǣdon, and com edischen *petiērunt, et vēnit cŏturnix*, Ps. Spl. 104, 38. Edeschen '*the edisse-henne*,' Ps. Surt. 104, 40. v. ersc-hen.

edisc-weard, es; *m. The keeper of edish, of a park, warren, etc;* vivarii custos, Wrt. Voc. 288, 12, Som. Ben. Lye. v. edisc.

ed-lǣcan; *p.* -lǣhte; *pp.* -lǣht *To repeat, renew;* repĕtĕre, renŏvāre, Som. Ben. Lye.

ed-lǣcung, e; *f. A repetition;* repetītio:—He sceal God biddan ðæt he hyne gehealde wið ðara ǣrgedōnra yfla edlǣcunge *he shall pray to God to preserve him against a repetition of the evils before committed*, L. E. I. 21; Th. ii. 416, 42.

ed-leǣnian, ed-leánian; *p.* ode; *pp.* od *To reward, recompense, renew, remit;* retrĭbuĕre:—He edleǣnaþ me *retrĭbuit mihi*, Ps. Spl. T. 17, 26. DER. leánian.

ed-leǣnung, e; *f. A rewarding;* retrĭbūtio:—For edleǣnunge *propter retrĭbūtiōnem*, Ps. Spl. T. 118, 112. v. ed-leánung.

ed-leán, ead-leán, æd-leán, es; *n.* [ed *or* ead; leán *a loan*] *A reward, recompense, requital, retribution;* præmium, retrĭbūtio:—Edleánes dæg *retrĭbūtiōnis dies*, Lk. Bos. 4, 19. Ðæt edleán, Bt. 3, 4; Fox 6, 19: Andr. Kmbl. 2457; An. 1230. For edleáne *propter retrĭbūtiōnem*, Ps. Spl. 118, 112.

ed-leánian *to reward;* remunĕrāre, Som. Ben. Lye. DER. leánian.

ed-leánung, e; *f. A rewarding, recompense;* retrĭbūtio:—Nylle ðū forgytan ealle edleánunga *vel* edleán his *nōli oblīvisci omnes retrĭbūtiōnes ejus*, Ps. Lamb. 102, 2. v. ed-leǣnung.

ed-lesende, ed-lesendlīc; *adj. Reciprocal, relative;* relātīvus:—Gif ic cweðe, ðū wāst hwā ðys dyde *tu scis quis hoc fēcit*, ðon biþ se [hwā] *quis rĕlātīvum*, ðæt is edlesendlīc, Ælfc. Gr. 18; Som. 21, 30: 38; Som. 40, 62.

ed-lesung, e; *f. A relation, relating;* relātio, Ælfc. Gr. 18; Som. 21, 58.

ēd-mōd; *adj. Mild, obedient;* obēdiens, mītis, Ben. Lye.

ēd-mōdian, -mōdigan; *p.* ode; *pp.* od *To be humble, to obey;* obēdīre:—Hi ēdmōdigaþ him *obēdiunt ei*, Mk. Lind. War. 1, 27.

ed-neowe; *adj. Renewed;* renŏvātus:—Eart ðū edneowe *renŏvātus es*, Ps. Th. 102, 5: Cd. 17; Th. 20, 25; Gen. 314. v. ed-niwe.

ed-niowunga; *adv. Anew;* dēnuo:—Ðe eów eágena leóht bōte gefremede edniowunga *who healed anew the light of your eyes*, Elen. Kmbl. 599; El. 300.

ed-niwan; *adv. Anew, again;* de nŏvo, dēnuo:—Eów gebȳraþ ðæt gē beón acennede edniwan *ŏportet nos nasci dēnuo*, Jn. Bos. 3, 7: 3, 3.

ed-niwe, ed-neowe; *adj. New, again new, renewed;* renŏvātus:—Eft cymeþ feorh edniwe *renewed life returns*, Exon. 59 a; Th. 213, 12; Ph. 223: 61 a; Th. 224, 4; Ph. 370: Bt. Met. Fox 11, 77; Met. 11, 39.

ed-niwe; *adv. Anew, again;* dēnuo:—Swā se fugel weorþeþ gomel æfter geárum geong edniwe *thus the bird becomes old after years and young again*, Exon. 59 b; Th. 215, 25; Ph. 258.

ed-niwian; *part.* igende; *p.* ode, ede; *pp.* od, ed *To make new, to renew;* renŏvāre:—Ðū edniwast ansīne eorþan *renŏvābis făciem terræ*, Ps. Spl. 103, 31. Hȳ fǣringa eald æfþoncan edniwedon [MS. edniwedan] *they suddenly renewed the old grudge*, Exon. 72 b; Th. 271, 21; Jul. 485. DER. ge-ed-niwian.

ed-niwinga; *adv. Anew;* dēnuo:—Se fugel līf eft onfēhþ edniwinga *the bird receives again life anew*, Exon. 63 b; Th. 234, 2; Ph. 534: Andr. Recd. 1569; An. 784.

ed-niwung, e; *f. A renewing, reparation, renovation;* repărātio:—Seó feórþe dǣl sceal beón to edniwunge Godes cyricean *the fourth part shall be to a renewing of God's church*, Bd. 1, 27; S. 489, 9.

ēdo *a flock;* grex:—Ge-eode [MS. ge-eāde] all suner *vel* ēdo in sǣ *ăbiit tōtus grex in măre*, Mt. Kmbl. Lind. 8, 32. v. eówde.

edor, eder, es; *m. A hedge, fence, place inclosed by a hedge, fold, dwelling, house;* sēpes, dŏmus, tectum:—Gif frīman edor gegangeþ *if a freeman forcibly enter a dwelling*, L. Ethb. 29: Th. i. 10, 3. Under edoras *under dwellings*, Cd. 112; Th. 147, 25; Gen. 2445: 114; Th. 150, 5; Gen. 2487. Ederas *houses*, Exon. 77 b; Th. 291, 5; Wand. 77. v. eodor.

edor-brecþ, e; *f.* [edor, brecþ *fractio*] *A fence-breaking, house-breaking;* sēpis fractio, dŏmus fractio:—Gif frīman edorbrecþe gedēþ *if a freeman commit house-breaking*, L. Ethb. 27; Th. i. 8, 15. v. eodor-brice.

edor-brice, -bryce *a fence-breaking*, L. Alf. pol. 40; Th. i. 88, 10, note 25. v. eodor-brice.

edre; *adv. Immediately, at once, forthwith;* stătim, prōtĭnus, illĭco:—Edre him ða eorlas agēfon ondsware *the earls gave answer to him immediately*, Andr. Kmbl. 801; An. 401: 1285; An. 643: 1900; An. 952: Invent. Crs. Recd. 1300; El. 649. v. ædre.

ēdre *an artery, vein;* artēria, vēna, Som. Ben. Lye. v. ǣdre.

ed-recan; *p.* te; *pp.* ed *To ruminate;* rumĭnāre, Som. Ben. Lye. v. eodorcan.

ed-recedroc, -rocc, es; *m. The belching thing;* rūmen, Cot. 169, Som. Ben. Lye.

ed-rine, es; *m. A meeting;* occursus, Ps. Spl. T. 18, 7.

edring, e; *f. A refuge, return;* refŭgium:—Dust ne mæg him edringe ǣnge gehātan *the dust may not promise any refuge to him*, Exon. 99 b; Th. 373, 11; Seel. 107. v. edor.

ed-roc, es; *m. A chewing again, chewing the cud, considering;* rūmen, rumĭnātio:—Wasend *vel* edroc *rūmen*, Ælfc. Gl. 72; Som. 70, 116; Wrt. Voc. 43, 43. Cīwung *vel* edroc, *vel* aceócung *rumĭnātio*, Ælfc. Gl. 99; Som. 76, 121, 122; Wrt. Voc. 54, 62.

ed-sceaft, æd-sceaft, e; *f. A new creation, new birth;* regĕnĕrātio:—Com swefnes wōma, hū woruld wǣre wundrum geteód ungelīc yldum ōþ edsceafte *the terror of a dream came, how the world was wondrously framed unlike to men until regeneration*, Cd. 177; Th. 222, 30; Dan. 112: Bt. 34, 10; Fox 150, 14, 16.

ed-staðelian; *p.* ode; *pp.* od [ed *again*, staðelian *to establish*, staðol *a foundation*] *To establish again, re-establish, restore*; restĭbĭlīre, Som. Ben. Lye.

ed-staðelig; *adj. Firm, strong*; firmus:—Beó se awirged, ðe ǽfre eft gedó edstaðelige ðas burh Hiericho *mălĕdictus vir qui suscitāvĕrit et ædĭfĭcāvĕrit* [*restĭbĭlĭtam fēcĕrit*] *cīvĭtātem Jĕrĭcho*, Jos. 6, 26.

ed-staðelung, e; *f. An establishing again, re-establishment, renewing*; repărātio, R. Ben. 36.

ed-þingung, e; *f. A reconciliation*; reconcĭliātio:—Edþingung *reconcĭliātio*, Ælfc. Gl. 90; Som. 74, 127; Wrt. Voc. 51, 40.

ēdulf-stæf, es; *m. A family staff* or *support, stay of the house*; prædii sustentācŭlum, Cd. 55; Th. 68, 16. v. ēðyl-stæf.

ed-wendan; *p.* -wende; *pp.* -wended; *v. intrans. To return, desist from, cease*; reverti, cessāre:—Gyf him edwendan ǽfre scolde bealuwa bīsigu *if ever the tribulation of evils should return to him*, Beo. Th. 565; B. 280.

ed-wenden, e; *f. A reverse, alteration, end*; mūtātio, āversio, cessātio:—Edwenden cwom *a reverse came*, Beo. Th. 4383, note; B. 2188. Ǽr ðon edwenden worulde geweorþe *ere that an end shall be to the world*, Exon. 56 b; Th. 200, 14; Ph. 40.

ed-wendu, e; *f. An alteration, change, end*; mūtātio, cessātio:—Ǽghwylc ðissa earfoða ēce standeþ, būtan edwende *all these sufferings are eternal, without a change*, Salm. Kmbl. 951; Sal. 475.

ed-wielle *A whirlpool, dizziness*; vortex āquæ, Cot. 86.

ed-wihte; *pron. Anything, something*; ălĭquid:—Nǽfre hleówlora [MS. hleor-lora] æt edwihtan mon weorþeþ *a man is never deprived of protection in anything*, Cd. 92; Th. 117, 15; Gen. 1954. [Ed = *A. Sax.* æt *in* æt-hwæga *somewhat*; ălĭquantum: æt-hwōn *almost*; fĕre: *Ger.* et: *M. H. Ger.* ete: *O. H. Ger.* etta, eta, ede.]

ed-winde *A winding again, a vortex*; vortex:—Edwinde *vortex*, Ælfc. Gl. 98; Som. 76, 92; Wrt. Voc. 54, 36.

ed-wist, e; *f.* [ed *re-, anew, again*; wist *support*] *Being, subsistence, existence, essence, substance*; substantia:—Ic adilegie ealle ða edwiste, ðe ic geworhte *dēlēbo omnem substantiam, quam fēci*, Gen. 7, 4. v. ætwist.

edwistfull; *adj.* [edwist *substance*, full *full*] *Existing, substantial, substantive*; substantiālis, Som. Ben. Lye. v. edwistlīc.

edwistlīc; *adj. Existing, subsisting, substantial, substantive*; substantiālis:—Ic eom, is edwistlīc word *I am is the substantive* [*existing*] *verb*, Ælfc. Gr. 32; Som. 36, 24. DER. efen-edwistlīc.

ed-wīt, æd-wīt, es; *n. A reproach, disgrace, blame, contumely, scorn*; opprobrium, probrum, ignōmĭnia, cavillātio:—Wæs him on gemynde yfel and edwīt *the evil and contumely was in his mind*, Bt. Met. Fox 1, 109; Met. 1, 55. Ealle beóþ aweaxen of edwīttes ȳða heáfdum *all shall be grown over by the heads of the waves of scorn*, Salm. Kmbl. 57; Sal. 29. Ne þearf ðē on edwīt Abraham settan *Abraham need not put thee in reproach*, i. e. *reproach to thee*, Cd. 130; Th. 165, 7; Gen. 2728. And me eác fela ðīnra edwīta on gefeóllon *et opprobria exprobrantium tibi cecĭdērunt sŭper me*, Ps. Th. 68, 9: 73, 21.

ed-wītan; *p.* -wāt, *pl.* -witon; *pp.* -witen *To reproach, blame, upbraid*; exprobrāre:—Hosp edwītendre ðē hruron ofer me *opprobria exprobrantium tibi cecĭdērunt sŭper me*, Ps. Spl. 68, 12. v. æt-wītan.

ed-wītfullīce; *adv. Disgracefully*; probrōse, Cot. 195, Lye.

edwīt-līf, es; *n. A disgraceful life*; probrōsa vīta:—Deáþ biþ sēlla eorla gehwylcum ðonne edwītlīf *death is better for every man than a disgraceful life*, Beo. Th. 5775; B. 2891.

edwīt-scype, es; *m. Cowardice*; ignāvia, ignōmĭnia:—Þurh edwītscype *ignōmĭnĭōse*, Wald. 23; Vald. 1, 14.

edwīt-spræc, e; *f. Contemptuous speech, scorn*; opprobrium, imprŏpĕrium, cavillātio:—Ðȳ-læs ic scyle þrōwian edwītspræce *lest I shall suffer contemptuous speech*, Andr. Kmbl. 161; An. 81: Ps. Th. 88, 43: 101, 6.

edwīt-spreca, an; *m. A blame-speaker, scoffer, caviller*; cavillātor:—Him edwītsprecan ermþu gehēton *the cavillers threatened him with affliction*, Exon. 39 a; Th. 129, 8; Gū. 418.

edwīt-stæf, es; *m. A disgraceful letter, reproach, scandal, disgrace, dishonour*; opprobrium:—Eom ic to edwīt-stæfe eallum geworden *factus sum opprobrium omnĭbus*, Ps. Th. 108, 24: 78, 4: 118, 42.

ēd-wylm, es; *m.* [= ād *a funeral pile*, wylm *heat, fire*] *Heat of fire, burning heat*; flammæ æstuātio:—Se fǽcna gebroht hafaþ æt ðam ēdwylme ða ðe him oncleófiaþ *the beguiler has brought into that burning heat those who cleave to him*, Exon. 97 b; Th. 364, 19; Wal. 73.

ed-wyrpan; *p.* -wyrpte; *pp.* -wyrped *To recover, become better*; mĕlĭōrāri, Ben. Lye. DER. ge-edwyrpan.

ed-wyrping, e; *f. Recovery, a growing better, recovering*; recŭpĕrātio:—Ān eáwfæst mynecenu læg swīðe geswenct, orwēne ǽlcere edwyrpinge *a pious mynchen lay greatly afflicted, hopeless of any recovery*, Homl. Th. ii. 26, 29.

Ēfe, an; *f. Eve*:—Ēfe *Eve*, Cd. 222; Th. 290, 1; Sat. 408. v. Ēua.

efel; *adj. Evil, bad*; prāvus, mălus, Som. Ben. Lye. v. yfel.

efe-lang; *adj.* [= efen *even*, lang *long*] *Even-long, equally long, oblong?* [*Wrt. Provncl.* evelong = *oblong*]; æque longus, oblongus:—Ðæt hol ðæt he efe-lang ǽr gefylde *the oblong hole which he filled before*, Exon. 112 b; Th. 431, 13; Rä. 45, 7.

efe-lāste, efen-lāste, an; *f.* [lǽstan *to last, continue, endure*] *The everlasting*; gnaphălium, Lin:—Genim efelāstan *take everlasting*, L. M. 1, 1; Lchdm. ii. 20, 3: 1, 32; Lchdm. ii. 78, 19: 1, 47; Lchdm. ii. 120, 2: 2, 65; Lchdm. ii. 292, 4. Nim efelāstan ufewearde *take the upper* [*part*] *of everlasting*, L. M. 2, 56; Lchdm. ii. 276, 20. Efelāste *herba mercŭriālis*, Som. Ben. Lye.

efeleác, es; *n. An onion, a scallion*; cæpa, Som. Ben. Lye.

EFEN, efn, æfen; *adj.* EVEN, *equal*; æquus, plānus, æquālis:—Mōdes gecynde grēteþ grorn efen winde *the disposition of his mind approached sadness equal to the wind*, Exon. 94 b; Th. 354, 22; Reim. 49. On efen, *adv. together*; simul, una:—Englas on efen blāwaþ bȳman *angels shall blow the trumpet together*, Exon. 20 b; Th. 55, 10; Cri. 881: Ps. Th. 116, 1. On efen, *prep. On even ground, on a level, by, near, aside with*; in æquāli, juxta:—Him on efn ligeþ ealdor-gewinna *by him lies his vital adversary*, Beo. Th. 5798; B. 2903. [*Wyc. Piers P. Chauc.* even: *Laym.* æfne, efne: *Orm.* efenn: *Plat.* even, ewen, effen: *O. Sax.* eban: *Frs.* even: *O. Frs.* ivin, even: *Dut.* even, effen: *Ger.* eben: *M. H. Ger.* eben, ëbene: *O. H. Ger.* eban: *Goth.* ibns: *Dan.* jävn: *Swed.* jemn: *Icel.* jafn, jamn.] DER. un-efen.

efen, efne; *adv. Evenly, equally, just so*; æque:—Wunedon ætsomne efen swā lange swā him lȳfed wæs *they dwelled together just so long as was permitted to them*, Bt. Met. Fox 20, 487; Met. 20, 244: Exon. 41 a; Th. 137, 24; Gū. 564.

ēfen, es; *n. Evening*; vesper:—Ēfna gehwām *each evening*, Exon. 50 b; Th. 176, 27; Gū. 1216. v. ǽfen.

efen-, efn-, efne-, in composition, denotes *even, equal*, represented by co-, con-, com-, *as*

efen-æðele *equally noble*. v. emn-æðele.

efen-behēfe *equally useful* or *necessary*. v. efn-behēfe.

efen-beorht; *adj. Equally bright*; æque splendĭdus:—Heofonsteorran ealle efen-beorhte ǽfre ne scīnaþ *the stars of heaven do not ever shine all equally bright*, Bt. Met. Fox 20, 465; Met. 20, 233: 20, 461; Met. 20, 231.

efen-bisceop, efn-biscop, es; *m. A co-bishop*; co-episcŏpus:—Mid Laurentio and Justo his efenbisceopum *cum Laurentio et Justo co-episcŏpis*, Bd. 2, 5; Whelc. 122, 38.

efen-blissian; *part.* -blissiende; *p.* ode; *pp.* od [blissian *to rejoice*] *To rejoice with, to rejoice equally*; congrātŭlāri:—Efenblissiende Breotone on his geleáfan, monige eálond blissiaþ *Britain equally rejoicing in his belief, many isles shall rejoice*; congrātŭlante in fide ejus Brittania, lætentur insŭlæ multæ, Bd. 5, 24; S. 647, 14.

efen-ceaster-wearan; *gen.* ena; *pl. m. Fellow-citizens*; concīves:—Efenceasterwearan ðæs heofonlīcan rīces *concīves regni cœlestis*, Bd. 1, 26; S. 488, 16.

efen-cuman; *p.* -com, *pl.* -cōmon; *pp.* -cumen; *v. intrans. To come together, convene, assemble together, agree*; convĕnīre:—Līcode us efencuman *plăcuit convĕnīre nos*, Bd. 4, 5; S. 572, 5. Efencumendum monegum bisceopum *convenientĭbus plūrĭmis episcŏpis*, Bd. 3, 28; S. 560, 11.

efen-dȳre; *adj. Equally dear*; æque cārus:—Ða syndon efen-dȳre *they are equally dear*, L. A. G. 2; Th. i. 154, 3.

efen-eádig; *adj. Equally blessed*; æque beātus:—Efeneádig bearn *equally blessed child*, Hy. 8, 21; Hy. Grn. ii. 290, 21.

efen-eald, efn-eald; *adj. Co-eval, of the same age*; co-ævus, co-ætāneus:—Ic æt efenealdum ǽfre ne mētte māran snyttro *I never met with greater prudence among those of his age*, Andr. Kmbl. 1105; An. 553: Bd. 5, 19; S. 637, 19. Nǽnig efen-eald him *no one of like age with him*, Exon. 85 a; Th. 321, 2; Wīd. 40. Plegende mid his efen-ealdum *playing with his co-evals*, Homl. Th. ii. 134, 4.

efen-eardigende *Dwelling together*; cohăbĭtans:—Ðæt ðū sunu wǽre efen-eardigende mid ðīnne ēngan Freán *that thou his son shouldst be dwelling together with thy sole Lord*, Exon. 11 a; Th. 15, 16; Cri. 237.

efen-ēce, emn-ēce; *adj. Co-eternal*; co-æternus:—Ǽr ðon up-stīge efenēce bearn āgnum fæder *ere that the co-eternal child ascended to his own father*, Exon. 14 b; Th. 29, 19; Cri. 465.

efen-edwistlīc; *adj. Consubstantial, of the same substance*; consubstantiālis:—Se Hālga Gāst is ðæs Fæder Gāst and ðæs Suna, him bām efenedwistlīc *the Holy Ghost is the Spirit of the Father and of the Son, consubstantial with them both*, Homl. Th. ii. 362, 27. Ic gelȳfe on ǽnne Crist, ðone āncennedan Godes Sunu, acennedne nā geworhtne, efenedwistlīcne ðam Fæder *I believe in one Christ, the only begotten Son of God, begotten not made, consubstantial with the Father*, ii. 596, 30.

efen-ēhþ, -nēhþ, e; *f. A plain*; plānĭties:—On ǽlcre efen-ēhþe *on every plain*, Chr. 894; Th. 170, 36.

efen-esne, es; *m. A fellow-servant*; conservus. v. efne-esne.

efen-etan *to eat as much as any one*. v. efn-etan.

efen-fela, -feola; *indecl. So many, as many*; tŏtĭdem, tot:—Eardas rūme Meotud arǽrde efen-fela bega þeóda and þeáwa *the Creator* *established spacious lands, as many of both nations and manners,* Exon. 89 a; Th. 334, 17; Gn. Ex. 17. Hilde abbudisse efen-feola wintra in munuclīfe Drihtne gehālgode *Hild abbatissa tŏtĭdem annos in Monastĭca vīta Dŏmĭno consecrāvit,* Bd. 4, 23; S. 592, 42.

efen-gedǣlan *to share alike.* v. efngedǣlan.

efen-gefeón; *p.* -gefeah, *pl.* -gefǣgon; *pp.* -gefǣgen *To rejoice together;* congaudēre:—Efengefeóndum eallum đam folce *congaudente ūnĭverso pŏpŭlo,* Bd. 3, 22; S. 553, 13.

efen-gelīc; *adj. Like, co-equal;* sĭmĭlis, consĭmĭlis, co-æquālis:—Cweđaþ to hyra efengelīcon *dīcunt co-æquālĭbus,* Mt. Bos. 11, 16.

efen-gemæcca, an; *m. A companion, husband;* consors, consortii jūre æquālis, Som. Ben. Lye. v. efn-gemæcca.

ēfen-gereord, e; *f. An evening repast, supper;* cœna, Som. Ben. Lye.

ēfen-gereordian *To sup;* cœnāre, Som. Ben. Lye.

efen-hāda-bisceop, es; *m. A co-bishop;* co-episcŏpus, Greg. Dial. 1, 5.

efen-hæfdling, es; *m. An equal, fellow, fellow-mate;* co-æquālis, co-ætāneus:—Gesomnode miccle scōle his geþoftena and hys efen-hæfdlingas *he collected a great troop of his companions and equals,* Guthl. 2; Gdwin. 14, 3.

efen-heáh; *adj. Equally high;* æque altus, Salm. Kmbl. 85, 28.

efen-heáp, es; *m. A fellow-soldier, soldier of the same band;* commănĭpŭlāris, Som. Ben. Lye.

efen-hērenis, -niss, e; *f. A praising together;* collaudātio, Ps. Spl. C. 32, 1.

efen-hērian; *v. trans. To praise together;* collaudāre, Som. Ben. Lye.

efen-hleóđor, -hleóđres; *m. A sounding together, concordance of voices* or *sounds, united voice;* concentus:—Bletsiaþ Bregu sēlestan efenhleóđre đus *they bless the most excellent Lord thus with united voice,* Exon. 64 b; Th. 239, 15; Ph. 621.

efen-hleta, -hlytta, an; *m. A consort, companion, fellow;* consors:—Hæfde Oswio efenhletan đære cynelīcan wurþnysse *hăbuit Oswiu consortem rēgiæ dignĭtātis,* Bd. 3, 14; S. 539, 29: 5, 8; S. 621, 27. Đæt we beón efenhlyttan his wuldres *that we be companions of his glory,* Homl. Th. i. 34, 1. Smyrode đē God đīn mid ele blisse toforan đīnum efenhlyttum *unxit te Deus tuus ŏleo lætĭtiæ præ consortĭbus tuis,* Ps. Lamb. 44, 8.

efen-hlytta, an; *m. A consort, companion;* consors, Ælfc. Gr. 9, 44; Som. 13, 6, MSS. C. D. v. efen-hleta.

efen-lǣcan; *p.* -lǣhte; *pp.* -lǣht *To be equal, like, to imitate;* imĭtāri, Lye. v. ge-efenlǣcan.

efen-lǣcend, es; *m. An imitator;* imĭtātor, Scint. 2, Lye.

efen-lǣcestre, an; *f. A female imitator;* imĭtatrix, Som. Ben. Lye.

efen-lǣcung, e; *f. A matching* or *making like* or *equal;* imĭtātio, æquipărātio, Som. Ben. Lye.

efen-lāste, an; *f. The everlasting;* gnaphălium:—Genim efenlāstan nyđowearde *take the netherward [part] of everlasting,* Lchdm. iii. 2, 2. v. efe-lāste.

efen-līc; *adj. Even, equal;* æquālis:—Nǣnig efenlīc đam in worlde gewearþ wīfes gearnung *a woman's desert was in the world not equal to that,* Exon. 8 b; Th. 3, 20; Cri. 39: Bd. 4, 17; S. 585, 38.

efen-līca, an; *m. An equal;* æquālis. v. efn-līca.

efen-līce; *adv.* EVENLY, *alike;* æque:—Efenlīce Godes man *æque Deo dēvōtus,* Bd. 3, 23; S. 554, 16.

efen-līcnes, -ness, e; *f. Evenness, equality;* æquālĭtas. v. efn-līcnes.

efen-ling, es; *m. A consort, an equal.* v. efn-ling.

efen-mǣre *equally great.* v. efnmǣre.

efen-metan; *v. trans. To make equal, to compare;* compărāre, Som. Ben. Lye.

ēfen-męte, es; *m. Even-meat, supper;* cœna, Som. Ben. Lye.

efen-micel; *adj. Equally great;* æque magnus:—Đū meahte spēd efen-micle Gode āgan ne mōste *thou mightest not possess abundance of power equally great with God,* Exon. 28 b; Th. 86, 4; Cri. 1403.

efen-mid; *adj. Middle;* mĕdius, plāne mĕdius:—On đisse eorþan efen-midre *in mĕdio terræ,* Ps. Th. 73, 12.

efen-neáh; *adv. Equally near;* æque vīcīne:—Strīceþ ymbūtan efenneáh gehwæđer *it holds its course around equally near everywhere,* Bt. Met. Fox 20, 282; Met. 20, 141.

efen-niht, e; *f. Even-night, equinox;* æquinoctium, Bd. Whelc. 493, 38.

efen-nys, efyn-nis, -niss, -nes, e; *f.* EVENNESS, *equality;* æquālĭtas:—Efennys gecȳđnys đīn on ēcnysse *æquĭtas testĭmōnia tua in æternum,* Ps. Spl. 118, 144: 10, 8.

efen-rīce; *adj. Equally mighty, of equal power;* æquālis potentiæ, æquipollens:—Wǣron hī eft efenrīce *they were again of equal power,* Bd. 5, 10; S. 624, 27.

efen-sārig; *adj. Even* or *equally sorry;* æque tristis, compassus:—He wearþ hyre sāre efensārig *ille ĕrat ejus dŏlōri compassus,* Greg. Dial. 2, 1, Lye.

efen-sārignyss, e; *f. Compassion;* compassio, Lye.

efen-scearp; *adj. Equally sharp;* æque acūtus:—Hī heora tungan teóþ sweorde efen-scearpe *exăcuērunt ut glădium linguas suas,* Ps. Th. 63, 3.

efen-scyldig; *adj. Equally guilty,* L. C. S. 77; Th. i. 420, 2.

efen-spēdiglīc, efne-spēdelīc; *adj.* [efen, spēdiglīc *substantiam hăbens*] *Consubstantial;* consubstantiālis:—Þrȳnnesse in ānnesse efenspēdiglīce *Trinĭtātem in unĭtāte consubstantiālem,* Bd. 4, 17; S. 585, 37.

efen-swīþ; *adj. Equally strong.* v. efn-swīþ.

ēfen-þēnung, e; *f. Even-food, supper;* vespertīna refectio, Fulg. 42, Mann.

efen-þeówa, an; *m:* efen-þeów, efn-þeów, es; *m. A fellow-servant;* conservus:—Astrehte hys efen-þeówa hyne and bæd hyne *procĭdens conservus ejus rŏgābat eum,* Mt. Bos. 18, 29. Hū ne gebȳrede đē gemiltsian đīnum efen-þeówan *nonne ergo oportuit te misĕrēri conservi tui?* Mt. Bos. 18, 33. He gemētte hys efen-þeówan *he found his fellow-servant,* 18, 28. Gesāwon hys efen-þeówas đæt *his fellow-servants saw that,* 18, 31.

efen-þrōwian; *p.* ode; *pp.* od *To suffer together, to compassionate, commiserate;* compăti, commĭsĕrāri, Past. 16, 1; Hat. MS. 20 a, 25, 26.

efen-þrōwung, e; *f. A suffering together, compassion;* compassio, Som. Ben. Lye.

efen-þwær; *adj. Agreeing;* concors, Procem. R. Conc. Lye.

efen-towistlīc; *adj. Consubstantial;* consubstantiālis, Som. Ben. Lye.

efen-wǣge, an; *f. Even-weight;* æquipondium, Som. Ben. Lye.

efen-wel *even, well, equally;* æque, sĭmĭlĭter, Off. Regum 10, Lye.

efen-weorcan; *v. trans. To co-operate;* co-opĕrāri, Som. Ben. Lye.

efen-weorþ; *adj. Even worth, equivalent;* æque dignus, æquĭvălens, L. Edg. C. 50; Th. ii. 254, 23.

efen-werod, es; *n. A soldier of the same company, a fellow-soldier;* commănĭpŭlāris, Som. Ben. Lye.

efen-wesende *co-existent;* co-existens:—Đū mid Fæder đīnne gefyrn wǣre efenwesende *thou wast co-existent with thy Father of old,* Exon. 12 b; Th. 22, 11; Cri. 350.

efen-wiht *even-weight;* æquipondium, Som. Ben. Lye.

efen-wyrcan, -weorcan; *v. trans. To co-operate;* co-opĕrāri:—Efenwyrcend *co-opĕrātor,* Bd. 5, 20; S. 641, 27.

efen-wyrcung, e; *f. A co-operating;* co-opĕrātio, Som. Ben. Lye.

efen-wyrhta, an; *m. A fellow worker;* co-opĕrātor:—Com he to Rōme mid hys efenwyrhtan and gefēran đæs ylcan weorces Ceólferþ *vēnit Rōmam cum co-opĕrātōre ac sŏcio ejusdem opĕris Ceolfrido,* Bd. 4, 18; S. 586, 28.

efen-wyrđe; *adj. Equally worthy;* condignus:—Mid efenwyrđum dǣdum *condignis actĭbus,* Bd. 3, 27; S. 559, 24: 4, 6; S. 574, 18.

efen-yrfe-weard, es; *m. A co-heir;* cŏhēres:—Sibba, his gefēra and efenyrfeward đæs ylcan rīces *Sebbe, sŏcius ejus et cŏhēres regni ejusdem,* Bd. 3, 30; S. 562, 2. Swylce gedafenaþ đæt hī engla efenyrfeweardas on heofonum sīn *tāles angĕlōrum in cœlis dĕcet esse cŏhērēdes,* 2, 1; S. 501, 19.

ēfeostlīce; *adv. Quickly, hastily;* cĕlĕrĭter:—He bebeád him đæt he ēfeostlīce sceolde to him cuman *he commanded him that he should quickly come to him,* Chr. 1114; Th. 370, 19.

efer, es; *m. A wild boar;* ăper, Anlct. v. eofor.

efer-fearn *fĭlix arbŏrātĭca,* Ælfc. Gl. 42; Som. 64, 14; Wrt. Voc. 31, 25. v. eofor-fearn.

Efer-wīc *York,* Chr. 188; Th. 15, 25, col. 3. v. Eofor-wīc.

EFES, e; *f. Eaves of a house, a brim, brink, edge, side;* margo, lātus:—Geworden ic eom swā swā spearwa ānhoga ođđe ānwuniende on efese ođđe on þecene *factus sum sīcut passer solĭtārius in tecto,* Ps. Lamb. 101, 8. To đære efese *to the edge,* Cod. Dipl. 353; A. D. 931; Kmbl. ii. 172, 22. Bī swā hwađerre efese [MS. efes] *on whichever side,* Chr. 894; Erl. 90, 13. [*Wyc.* evese *brow of a hill: Laym.* eovesen, *dat. pl. eaves: Plat.* oese, ese: *O. Frs.* ose *edges of the roof: Ger. Bav. dial.* obesen *porch of a church: M. H. Ger.* obese, *f. vestĭbŭlum: O. H. Ger.* opasa *atrium, vestĭbŭlum: Goth.* ubizwa, *f. a hall, porch: Icel.* ups, *f. eaves.*]

efes-drypa, an; *m. Eaves-drip;* stillĭcĭdium. v. yfes-drypa, -dropa.

efesian, efosian, efsian; *p.* ode; *pp.* od [efes *the eaves,* q. v.] *To cut in the form of eaves, to round, to shear;* in rŏtundum attondēre, tondēre:—Ne gē eów ne efesion ne beard ne sciron *neque in rŏtundum attondēbĭtis cŏmam nec rādētis barbam,* Lev. 19, 27. Ic efesige ođđe ic scere scēp ođđe hors *tondeo ŏves aut ĕquos,* Ælfc. Gr. 26, 6; Som. 29, 9. DER. ge-efesian, -efsian.

ēfest, e; *f. A hastening;* festīnātio. v. ōfost.

ēfestan, to ēfestanne; *p.* ēfeste, *pl.* ēfeston; *impert.* ēfest, *pl.* ēfestaþ; *pp.* ēfested *To hasten, make haste, be quick;* propĕrāre, concurrĕre, festīnāre:—Hwylcum wegum to ēfestanne sȳ to ingange his rīces *quĭbus sit viis ad ingressum regni illĭus propĕrandum,* Bd. 2, 2; S. 502, 20. He ēfeste norþweard *he hastened northward,* Chr. 1016; Erl. 154, 10. Hī to đām dweoligendum lǣcedōmum deófolgylde ēfeston and scyndon *ad errātĭca idolatriæ medicāmĭna concurrēbant,* Bd. 4, 27; S. 604, 7. To gefultumianne me ēfest *ad adjŭvandum me festīna,* Ps. Lamb. 69, 2. v. ēfstan.

efesung, e; *f. A polling, rounding, shearing, compassing;* tonsūra, Som. Ben. Lye.

efesung-sceara, an; *f. A pair of scissors* or *shears;* forfex, Som. Ben. Lye.

efete, an; *f. An* EFT, *a newt, lizard;* lăcerta:—Efete *lăcerta* vel *stĭlio*, Ælfc. Gl. 24; Som. 60, 18; Wrt. Voc. 24, 22. [*Wyc.* euete *a lizard.*] v. āđexe.

efn; *adj. Even, equal;* æquus, plānus, æquālis:—On efn, *adv. Together;* sĭmul, ūna, Ps. Th. 116, 1. On efn, *prep. On even ground, by, near, aside with;* in æquāli, juxta, Beo. Th. 5798; B. 2903. v. efen.

efnan; *p.* ede, de; *pp.* ed; *v. trans.* I. *to throw down, prostrate, level, lay low;* prosternĕre:—Ic efne to eorþan ealdne ceorl *I throw down the old churl to earth*, Exon. 107 b; Th. 409, 28; Rä. 28, 8. II. *to perform, execute, labour, achieve;* patrāre, perpetrāre, facĕre, præstāre:—Ic ǣ đīne efne and healde *custōdiam lēgem tuam*, Ps. Th. 118, 44: 118, 131, 143. Ōþ-đæt his byre mihte eorlscipe efnan *until his son might achieve a valorous deed*, Beo. 5237; B. 2622. Đe ǣr eorlscipe efnde *who before performed valorous deeds*, 6006; B. 3007. Hie efndon unrihtdōm *they executed unrighteousness*, Cd. 181; Th. 227, 7; Dan. 183. Hie đat efnedon sōna *they performed that soon*, Elen. Kmbl. 1423; El. 713. Efn elne đis *perform this boldly*, Exon. 80 a; Th. 300, 18; Fä. 8. DER. ge-efnan.

efn-behēfe; *adj.* [behēfe *necessary*] *Equally useful* or *necessary;* æque ūtĭlis *vel* necessārius:—Is điós ōđru bȳsen efnbehēfu *this other similitude is equally necessary*, Bt. Met. Fox 12, 14; Met. 12, 7.

efn-biscop, es; *m. A co-bishop;* co-episcŏpus:—Mid Laurentio and Justo his efnbiscopum *cum Laurentio et Justo co-episcŏpis*, Bd. 2, 5; S. 507, 30. v. efen-bisceop.

efne, an; *f? Alum;* alūmen, styptēria = στυπτηρία:—Efne *alūmen* vel *stiptūra* [= *styptēria*], Ælfc. Gl. 41; Som. 63, 126; Wrt. Voc. 31, 12. Efne *alūmen*, 56; Som. 67, 38; Wrt. Voc. 37, 28.

efne [= efen]; *adv. Even, exactly, precisely, just, alike, likewise, just now;* plāne, æque, omnīno, mŏdŏ, jam prīdem:—He wintra hæfde efne hund-seofontig ǣr him sunu wōce *he had just seventy winters ere a son was born to him*, Cd. 57; Th. 70, 24; Gen. 1158. We đē willaþ ferigan efne to đam lande *we will convey thee even to the land* [*to the very land;* in eandem terram], Andr. Kmbl. 587; An. 294: Bt. Met. Fox 8, 95; Met. 8, 48. On witte weallende byrnþ efne sió gitsung *even the covetousness* [i. e. *the just-mentioned covetousness*] *burns raging in his mind*, 8, 91; Met. 8, 46. Gif ic on helle gedō hwyrft ǣnigne, đū me æt-byst efne rihte *si descendĕro in infernum, părĭter ades*, Ps. Th. 138, 6. He hæfde eorþan and up-rōdor efne gedǣled *he had divided the earth and firmament alike*, Cd. 146; Th. 182, 16; Exod. 76. [v. efn-gedǣlan.] Ic ǣ đīne efnast healde *I keep thy law most exactly*, Ps. Th. 118, 77. Efne swā *even so, even as:*—And efne swā he đec gemētte meahtum gehrodene *and even so he found thee adorned with virtues*, Exon. 12 b; Th. 21, 5; Cri. 330. Deór efne swā some æfter đære stefne on đone stenc faraþ *just so goes the beast after the voice in that odour*, 96 a; Th. 358, 30; Pa. 53. Lixte se leóma efne swā of heofene scīneþ rōdores candel *the beam shone even as from heaven shines the candle of the firmament*, Beo. Th. 3146; B. 1571. He Hengestes heáp hringum þēnede efne swā swīđe swā he Fresena cyn byldan wolde *he should serve Hengest's band with rings even as abundantly as he would encourage the Frisian race*, Beo. Th. 2188; B. 1092. He efne swā swīđe hī lufode, đæt... *he loved her even so greatly, that...* [adeo ut], Bt. Met. Fox 26, 129; Met. 26, 65. v. efen; *adv.*

efne; *interj. Lo! behold! truly! indeed;* en, ecce, certe, prŏfecto:—Đā se tān gehwearf efne ofer ǣnne ealdgesīđa *then indeed went the lot over one of the old comrades*, Andr. Kmbl. 2209; An. 1106. And efne! đā ætȳwde Moyses and Helias *et ecce appăruērunt Moyses et Elias*, Mt. Bos. 17, 3. Efne swā biþ gebletsad beorna ǣghwylc *ecce sic benedīcētur hŏmo*, Ps. Th. 127, 5. Efne me God fultumeþ *ecce Deus adjŭvat me*, 53, 4: 54, 7: 86, 3: 118, 40: 138, 3.

efn-eald *co-eval:*—Efneald *æquævus* vel *coætāneus*, Ælfc. Gl. 9; Som. 56, 119; Wrt. Voc. 19, 3. v. efen-eald.

efne-cuman; *v. intrans. To convene;* convĕnīre:—Efne-cōmon to him *convenĭēbant ad eum*, Mk. Rush. War. 1, 45. v. efen-cuman.

efne-esne, es; *m. A fellow-servant;* conservus:—Efne-esne đīn ic eom [MS. am] *conservus tuus sum*, Rtl. 70, 41: Mt. Kmbl. Lind. 18, 33.

efne-nū; *interj. Behold now;* ecce:—Efnenū ge-eácnode unrihtwīsnesse *ecce partŭrit injustĭtia*, Ps. Lamb. 7, 15.

efnes, -ness, -nyss, e; *f. Evenness, equity, justice;* æquĭtas:—Efnes syndon dōmas đīne *æquĭtas sunt jūdĭcia tua*, Ps. Spl. 118, 75: Ps. Lamb. 118, 144. He dēmþ ymbhwyrft eorþan on efnesse *ipse judĭcābit orbem terræ in æquĭtāte*, Ps. Lamb. 9, 9. Đū gelīffæst me on efnesse ođđe emnesse đīnre *vivĭfĭcābis me in æquĭtāte tua*, 142, 11. Eágan đīne geseón ođđe bewlātiun efnysse ođđe rihtwīsnesse *ocŭli tui vĭdeant æquĭtātes*, 16, 2. v. efen-nys.

efne-spēdelīc; *adj. Of the same substance, consubstantial;* consubstantiālis:—On þrȳm hādum efenspēdelīcum *in trĭbus persōnis consubstantiālĭbus*, Bd. 4, 17; S. 585, 38. v. efen-spēdiglīc.

efn-etan *to eat as much as any one?* or *to become equal, to equal?* par esse ălĭcui ĕdendo? æquāre, æmŭlāri:—Ic mēsan mæg meahtelīcor and efn-etan ealdum þyrse *I can feast more heartily and eat as much as the old giant*, Exon. 111 a; Th. 425, 28; Rä. 41, 63.

efn-ēđe; *adj. Equally easy;* æque făcĭlis:—Is efnēđe up and of dūne to feallanne foldan đisse *it is equally easy for this earth to fall up and down*, Bt. Met. Fox 20, 333; Met. 20, 167.

efn-gedǣlan; *p.* de; *pp.* ed; *v. trans. To share alike;* in æquāles partes divĭdĕre:—Beámas twegen đara ǣghwæđer efngedǣlde heáhþegnunga hāliges gāstes *two pillars, each of which shared alike the high services of the holy spirit*, Cd. 146; Th. 183, 22; Exod. 95.

efn-gęmæcca, an; *m.* [gemæcca *a companion*] *A fellow-companion, associate, fellow;* consors:—Đa beóþ hira gelīcan and hira efngemæccan on hira gecynde *they are their equals and their fellows in their nature*, Past. 29; Hat. MS. 38 b, 16.

efn-līc; *adj. Equal;* æquus. v. efenlīc.

efn-līca, an; *m. An equal;* æquālis:—Nis nān efnlīca đīn *there is no one thine equal*, Bt. Met. Fox 20, 38; Met. 20, 19. v. efen-līca.

efn-līcnes, -ness, e; *f. Evenness, equality;* æquālĭtas:—Hie healdaþ mā geferrǣdenne and efnlīcnesse đonne ealdordōm *they observe companionship and equality more than authority*, Past. 17, 9; Hat. MS. 24 b, 6.

efn-ling, es; *m. A consort, an equal, a fellow;* consors, Ps. Spl. T. 44, 9.

efn-mǣre; *adj. Equally great, illustrious, renowned;* æstĭmātus, æque illustris, conspĭcuus:—He đone wēlegan wædlum efn-mǣrne gedēþ *he makes the rich equally great to the poor*, Bt. Met. Fox 10, 63; Met. 10, 32.

efn-swīþ; *adj. Equally strong;* æque vălĭdus:—Manigu ōđru gesceaft efn-swīđe him *many other creatures equally strong with them*, Bt. Met. Fox 11, 88; Met. 11, 44.

efn-þeów, es; *m. A fellow-servant;* conservus:—Đæm hlāforde is to cȳđanne, đæt he ongiete đæt he is efnþeów his *it is to be made known to the master, that he understand that he is his fellow-servant*, Past. 29; Hat. MS. 38 b, 18. v. efen-þeówa.

efor, es; *m. A wild boar;* āper:—Hiene ofslōg ān efor *a wild boar slew him*, Chr. 885; Erl. 82, 34. Sume sceoldan bión eforas *some should be wild boars*, Bt. 38, 1; Fox 194, 34. v. eofor.

efor-fearn, es; *n. A species of fern, polypody;* rădiŏlus, polȳpŏdium = πολυπόδιον:—*Herba rădiŏla* đæt is efor-fearn, Herb. cont. 85; Lchdm. i. 34, 7. Đeós wyrt, đe man *rădiŏlum*, and ōđrum naman efor-fearn, nemneþ, ys gelīc fearne, and heó byþ cenned on stānigum stōwum, and on ealdum hūs-stedum, and heó hæfþ on ǣghwylcum leáfe twā endebyrdnyssa fægerra pricena, and đa scīnaþ swā gold *this plant, which is named* rădiŏlus, *and by another name everfern, is like fern, and it is produced in stony places, and in old homesteads, and it has on each leaf two rows of beautiful spots, and they shine like gold*, Herb. 85, 1; Lchdm. i. 188, 10–14: L. M. 1, 17; Lchdm. ii. 60, 13. v. eofor-fearn.

Eforwīc-ingas *inhabitants of York*, Chr. 918; Th. 193, 9, col. 1. v. Eoforwīc-ingas.

efosian *to cut in the form of eaves, to round, shear;* tondēre:—Hine man efosode *eum totondērunt*, Gen. 41, 14. v. efesian.

ēfre *ever, always*, Chr. 675; Erl. 38, 26. v. ǣfre.

efsian, efsigean *to cut in the form of eaves, to round, shear;* tondēre:—Man ne mōt hine efsian *no one shall shear him*, Jud. 13, 5: Past. 18, 7; Hat. MS. 27 b, 11, 24. v. efesian.

ēfstan, ēfestan; *p.* ēfstte, ēfste, *pl.* ēfston, ēfstun; *impert.* ēfst, ēfste, *pl.* ēfstaþ; *pp.* ēfsted, ēfst; *v. intrans.* [ōfest, ōfost, ōfst *haste*] *To hasten, draw near, approach, make haste, be quick;* festīnāre, prŏpĕrāre, concurrĕre, appropinquāre, accelĕrāre:—Uton nū ēfstan seón wundur *let us now hasten to see the wonders*, Beo. Th. 6193; B. 3101: Rood Kmbl. 67; Kr. 34. He ēfste [ēfstte, Th. 278, 23, col. 2] norþweard *he hastened northward*, Chr. 1016; Th. 278, 22, col. 1. Abraham ēfste in to đam getelde *festīnāvit Abraham in tabernācŭlum*, Gen. 18, 6: Lk. Bos. 19, 6: Beo. Th. 2990; B. 1493: Cd. 139; Th. 174, 2; Gen. 2872. Hī ēfston ōþ to gatum deáþes *appropinquāvĕrunt usque ad portas mortis*, Ps. Spl. 106, 18: Byrht. Th. 137, 55; By. 206. Hī geneálǣhton ođđe ēfstun [ēfston, Ps. Spl. 15, 3] *accelĕrāvĕrunt*, Ps. Lamb. 15, 4. Ēfst ardlīce đyder *festīna ĭbi*, Gen. 19, 22: Lk. Bos. 19, 5. Ēfst [Th. ēfste] ođđe neálǣce đæt đū generige me *accĕlĕra ut ēruas me*, Ps. Spl. 30, 2. Ēfstaþ and lǣdaþ hine to me *festīnāte et addūcĭte eum ad me*, Gen. 45, 13: Boutr. Scrd. 22, 42: Homl. Th. ii. 88, 32. Ēfstaþ đæt ge gangon þurh đæt nearwe geat *hasten that ye go through the narrow gate*, Lk. Bos. 13, 24. Đæt we to đē mid ealre heortan ēfston *that we may hasten to thee with all our heart*, Homl. Th. ii. 600, 3. To đam đe hit ēfst wæs *ad quam festīnātum erat*, Prov. 20. DER. ge-ēfstan.

eft; *adv. Again, second time, then, afterwards;* ĭtĕrum, dēnuo, rursus, re-, deinde, ĭtem:—Eft lufigende God *ĭtĕrum āmans Deum*, Ælfc. Gr. 43; Som. 44, 58. Asende Noe ūt eft culfran *Noe rursus dīmīsit cŏlumbam*, Gen. 8, 10: Mt. Bos. 4, 7, 8: Ælfc. Gr. 38; Som. 40, 51, 52: Chr. 790; Erl, 56, 38: 828; Erl. 64, 10: 1046; Erl. 170, 17: 797; Erl. 58, 16: Chr. 838; Erl. 66, 13. Eft *ĭtem*, Bd. 4, 8; S. 575, 38: 5, 5; S. 617, 34. Eft on Cent forbærnde *afterwards burned in Kent*, Chr. 685;

Erl. 40, 20. [*Piers P.* eft *again*: *Wyc.* eft, efte *again*: *Laym.* æft, afte, eft, efte *afterwards*: *Orm.* efft *afterwards, again*: *O. Sax.* eft *again*: *O. Frs.* eft, efta *behind, afterwards, then*: *Goth.* afta *behind, back.*] v. æft.

eft-agyfan *To give back*; reddĕre, i. e. re-dāre, Bd. 2, 1; S. 500, 19.

eft-betǽht, æft-betēht *Re-assigned, re-delivered, given back*; re-consignātus, R. Ben. 4. v. be-tǽcan.

eft-cerran *To return*; redīre:—Eftcerdon *reversi sunt*, Lk. Skt. Lind. 10, 17.

eft-cuman *To come back*; revenīre:—He hēt ealle eftcuman *he commands all to come again*, Bt. 39, 13; Fox 234, 25. Eft-cymeþ *comes again*, Bd. 2, 13; S. 516, 21.

eft-cyme, es; *m. A coming again, return*; rĕdĭtus, reversio:—Ðæt eorlwerod sæt on wēnum eftcymes leófes monnes *the warrior band sat in expectation of the return of the dear man*, Beo. Th. 5785; B. 2896: Exon. 121 b; Th. 466, 33; Hö. 130. Treófugla tuddor tācnum cȳđdon eádges eftcyme *the tree-fowls' offspring by signs made known the blessed man's return*, Exon. 43 a; Th. 146, 11; Gū. 708.

eft-eádig; *adj. Rich*:—Efteádig [ēst-, Th: sēft-, Grn.] secg *the favoured mortal*, Exon. 82 a; Th. 309, 12; Seef. 56.

eft-edwītan *To reprove, upbraid again*; re-probāre, Mt. Kmbl. Lind. 21, 42.

efter *after*, Cod. Dipl. 1073; A. D. 896; Kmbl. v. 140, 7; Th. Diplm. A. D. 896; 139, 8. v. æfter.

eft-gecīgan, eft-gecīgean *To recall, call back*; re-vocāre:—Sende he đone biscop hī to sōþfæstnysse geleáfan eft-gecīgean *he sent the bishop to call them again to the belief of the truth*, Bd. 3, 30; S. 562, 10.

eft-hweorfan *To turn back, return*; rĕ-vertĕre:—Æfter tīde eft-hweorfende to heofonum *after a time returning again to the heavens*, Bd. 4, 3; S. 568, 29. Eft-hwurfon *returned again*, 5, 6; S. 619, 9.

eft-leán, es; *n.* [leán *a reward*] *A recompense*; retrĭbūtio:—He eft-leán wile ealles gēnomian *he will surely take a recompense*, Exon. 24 a; Th. 68, 8; Cri. 1100.

eft-lēsing, e; *f. Redemption*; redemptio, Mt. Kmbl. Lind. 20, 28.

eft-ongēn-bīgan *To untwist again, to unwreathe*; re-torquēre:—Eft-ongēn-bīgde *retorsit*, Cot. 189.

eft-sīþ, es; *m. A journey back, return*; rĕdĭtus:—Âr wæs on ōfoste, eftsīđes georn *the messenger was in haste, desirous of return*, Beo. Th. 5560; B. 2783. Landweard onfand eftsīþ eorla *the land-warden perceived the return of the warriors*, Beo. Th. 3786; B. 1891: 2669; B. 1332.

eft-sittan; *p.* -sæt, *pl.* -sǽton; *pp.* -seten *To sit again, reside*; resĭdēre:—Ic eftsitte ođđe ic uppsitte *resĭdeo*, Ælfc. Gr. 26, 5; Som. 29, 6.

eft-sōna; *adv.* [eft *again*, sōna *soon*] EFTSOONS, *soon after, again, a second time*; itĕrum:—He hī lǽrde eftsōna *he taught them again*, Mk. Bos. 10, 1.

eft-spellung, e; *f. A recapitulation*; re-capitŭlātio, Cot. 171.

eft-swā-micel *Even so much*; tantundem:—Eft-swā-miceles *for so much, at that price*; tantīdem, Som. Ben. Lye.

eft-wyrd, e; *f. Future fate, day of judgment*; futūrum fātum, judĭcii dies, Cd. 169; Th. 212, 15; Exod. 539.

eftyr *after*; post, Lye. v. æfter.

efyn-gelīc; *adj.* [efen *even*, gelīc *like*] *Even-like, alike, equal, co-equal*; co-æquālis, Som. Ben. Lye.

efynnis *Evenness, equity*; æquālĭtas, equĭtas, Ps. Spl. C. 110, 7. v. efennys.

efyr *a boar*, Ps. Spl. C. 79, 14. v. eofor.

ēg, e; *f. Water, sea*; aqua, māre. Used to denote,—*The sea coast*:—Blecinga ēg *Blekingley, the coast of the Blekingians*, Ors. 1, 1; Bos. 22, 1. Scon-ēg *Sconey*. v. ēg-.

ēg-. Used in composition:—*water, sea*; aqua, māre. DER. ēg-būende, -clif, -land, -streám. v. īg-.

ēgan *to fear, dread*. DER. on-ēgan, *q. v.*

ēg-būende; *pl. m. adj.* Used as a noun, *An island dweller*; ad aquam *vel* in insŭla hăbĭtans:—On đǽre ealdan byrig Acemannes ceastre; hie ēgbūendas [MS. egbuend] Bađan nemnaþ *in the old town* Akemansceaster [*the pained man's city*]; *the islanders call it Bath*, Chr. 974; Th. 224, 20, col. 2, 3; Edg. 4. Gehwæm ēgbūendra *to each of the islanders*, 975; Th. 230, 5; Edg. 57. v. īg-būende.

ēg-clif, es; *n. A water-cliff* or *shore*; scŏpŭlus [= σκόπελος *a look-out place*] măris, lītus:—Ofer ēgclif [MS. ecgclif] đæt eorl-werod sæt *the warrior band sat on the ocean's shore*, Beo. Th. 5778; B. 2893.

EGE, æge, eige, es; *m. Fear, terror, dread*, AWE; tĭmor, terror, formīdo:—Eorþcyningcgum se ege standeþ *terrĭbĭli ăpŭd rēges terræ*, Ps. Th. 75, 9. On đǽm dagum wæs mycel ege fram đǽm wīfmannan *in those days there was a great dread of these women*, Ors. 1, 10; Bos. 33, 26; Bt. Met. Fox 1, 143; Met. 1, 72. Ege Drihtnes *tĭmor Dŏmĭni*, Ps. Spl. 18, 10. Beó eówer ege and ōga ofer ealle nītenu *terror vester ac trĕmor sit sŭper cuncta anĭmālia terræ*, Gen. 9, 2. Nis me ege mannes for āhwæđer *non timēbo quid făciat mĭhi hŏmo*, Ps. Th. 55, 4: 117, 6. Wearþ hit swā mycel æge fram đam here *there was so great awe of the army*, Chr. 1006; Erl. 140, 31. Gefeallaþ [MS. gefeællæþ] ofer hī eige and fyrhto *fear and dread shall fall upon them*, Cant. Moys. Ex. 15, 19; Thw. 30, 19. Ða Bryttas mid mycclum ege flugon to Lunden-byrig *the Britons fled to London in great terror*, Chr. 456; Erl. 13, 29: 823; Erl. 63, 24. Nā đū ondrǽdst fram ege nihtlīcum *non tĭmēbis a tĭmōre nocturno*, Ps. Spl. 90, 5: Ps. Th. 118, 38: Bd. 5, 13; S. 632, 24. Ðū hæfdest eorþlīcne ege *thou hadst earthly awe*, Homl. Th. i. 596, 8: Ors. 3, 9; Bos. 64, 9. Syleþ eallum mete, đām đe his ege habbaþ *escam dĕdit timentĭbus se*, Ps. Th. 110, 3: 59, 4. Ðe him Metodes ege, on his dǽdum, Drihten forhtaþ *qui tĭmet Dŏmĭnum*, 127, 5. [*Laym.* eȝe, eiȝe, eie, æie, *m. awe, dread, anger*: *Orm.* eȝȝe: *M. H. Ger.* ege, *f*: *O. H. Ger.* egi, agi, *m. terror*: *Goth.* agei, *f*: *Dan.* ave, *m. f*: *Icel.* agi, *m. terror, discipline.*] DER. tīd-ege.

ēge; *gen. dat. acc. of* ēg *water*, Chr. 47; Th. 11, 6, col. 3. v. ēg.

ēge; *n. An eye*:—Mid ēgum *with eyes*, Cd. 229; Th. 310, 18; Sat. 728. Gif đīn ēge *if thine eye*, Mt. Rush. War. 5, 29. v. eáge; *n.*

egean *To harrow* or *break clods*; occāre, Som. Ben. Lye.

ege-full; *adj. Fearful, terrible*; terrĭbĭlis:—Mǽre God, and mihtig and egefull *Deus magnus, et pŏtens et terrĭbĭlis*, Deut. 10, 17. Hit wæs swīđe egefull *it was very terrible*, Bt. 18, 2; Fox 64, 14. v. eges ful.

ege-healdan *To hold in fear, correct*; corrĭpĕre, Ps. Spl. T. 93, 10.

ege-lāf, e; *f. What had escaped horror*; horrōris resĭduum:—Ege-lāfe [MS. ece-lāfe], *acc.* Exod. 370.

ege-leás; *adj. Fearless*; impăvĭdus, Past. 36, 1, Lye.

egeleás-līce; *adv. Fearlessly*; impăvĭde:—Hie nū egeleás-līcor and unnytlīcor brūcaþ đære mildheortlīcan Godes giefe *they now enjoy the merciful gifts of God the more fearlessly and uselessly*, Past. 36, 1; Hat. MS. 46 b, 9.

Egeles ford, es; *m. Ailsford*:—Eádrīc gewende đone cyning ongeán æt Egeles forda *Eadric went to meet the king at Ailsford*, Chr. 1016; Th. 282, 10, col. 1. v. Ægeles ford.

egen *fear*; tĭmor, Wanl. Catal. p. 14, line 7, note z. DER. ege.

egenu *a little round heap*; glŏmŭlus, Som. Ben. Lye.

egenwirht *Hire, wages, a gift*; merces, Ps. Spl. T. 126, 4.

ege-nys, eges ful-nes, -ness, e; *f. Fearfulness, fear*; tĭmor, Ps. Spl. T. 88, 39.

egesa, egsa, ægsa, an; *m.* [ege *fear*] *Fear, horror, dread*; tĭmor, horror, terror, formīdo:—Him gāsta weardes egesa on breóstum wunode *fear of the guardian of spirits dwelt in his breast*, Cd. 138; Th. 173, 24; Gen. 2866: Beo. Th. 1572; B. 784: Andr. Kmbl. 789; An. 445: Rood Kmbl. 170; Kr. 86: Judth. 12; Thw. 25, 10; Jud. 252. Būtan Godes egsan [MS. B. egesan] *without fear of God*, Bd. 4, 12; S. 581, 1: Cd. 178; Th. 223, 23; Dan. 124: Andr. Kmbl. 914; An. 457. Sió dimme niht ofer eldum egesan ne brohte *the dim night did not bring terror over men*, Bt. Met. Fox 12, 34; Met. 12, 17: Cd. 202; Th. 250, 3; Dan. 541: Ps. Th. 66, 6. Egesan geaclod *terrified with fear*, Andr. Kmbl. 1609; An. 806: Beo. Th. 5465; B. 2736. [*O. Sax.* egiso, *m*: *M. H. Ger.* egese, eise, *f. horror*: *O. H. Ger.* ekiso, *m*; egis, agis, *n. horror*: *Goth.* agis, *n. fear, terror, horror.*] DER. bǽl-egsa, blōd-egesa, flōd-, folc-, glēd-, hild-, līg-, niht-, þeód-, wæter-.

ēgesa, ēgsa, an; *m.* [ēkso; *m. possessor*: *O. Sax. Heli.* āgan *to own*] *An owner*; possessor:—Ēgesan ne gȳmeþ *heeds not the owner*, Beo. Th. 3519; B. 1757.

eges ful, ege-ful, -full; *adj.* [eges ful *full of fear* =] *Fearful, terrible, wonderful*; tĭmōre plēnus, terrĭbĭlis, admīrābĭlis:—Ðū [God] eart egesful *tu* [*Deus*] *terrĭbĭlis es*, Ps. Lamb. 75, 8: Cd. 177; Th. 222, 17; Dan. 106: Exon. 30 a; Th. 93, 20; Cri. 1529. Bera sceal on hǽþe, eald and egesfull *the bear shall be on the heath, old and terrible*, Menol. Fox 519; Gn. C. 30: Beo. Th. 5850; B. 2929. Drihten ys mǽre God and mihtig and egefull *Dŏmĭnus est Deus magnus et pŏtens et terrĭbĭlis*, Deut. 10, 17: Bt. 18, 2; Fox 64, 14. Eálā Drihten, lā hū egesful ođđe hū wundorlīc is đīn nama *Dŏmĭne, quam admīrābĭle est nōmen tuum!* Ps. Lamb. 8, 2, 10.

eges fullīc; *adj. Full of fear, fearful, awful*; terrĭbĭlis:—Hū egesfullīc he is in geþeahtingum ofer monna bearn *quam terrĭbĭlis est in consĭliis sŭper fīlios homĭnum*, Bd. 4, 25; S. 601, 36. Egesfullīcran, *nom. pl. more full of terror*, Salm. Kmbl. 93; Sal. 46.

eges ful-nes, -ness, e; *f. Fulness of fear, formidableness*; formīdŏlōsĭtas:—Eges fulnes, L. I. P. 3; Th. ii. 306, 21. v. egenys [= ege, -nys, -nes.]

eges grime, grimme, an; *f. A witch, sorceress*; vĕnēfĭca, malĕfĭca, Som. Ben. Lye.

egesian; *p.* ode; *pp.* od *To affright*; terrēre, Som. Ben. Lye. v. egsian.

egesig *terrible, horrible*. v. eiseg.

eges līc; *def.* se eges līca, seó, đæt eges līce; *adj.* [eges līc *a likeness of fear* =] *Fearful, terrible, dreadful, terrific, horrible, awful*; terrĭbĭlis, terrĭfĭcus, horrĭbĭlis, horrendus:—Eorþscræf egeslīc *a fearful cavern*, Andr. Kmbl. 3174; An. 1590. Egeslīc æled eágsȳne wearþ *the terrible fire was visible to the eye*, 3098; An. 1552: Rood Kmbl. 148; Kr. 74. Eálā hū egeslīc đeós stōw ys *quam terrĭbĭlis est lŏcus iste!* Gen. 28, 17.

He is egeslíc God, ofer ealle godu eorþbûendra *Dominus terribilis est super omnes deos*, Ps. Th. 95, 4: 88, 6: Ps. Spl. 46, 2. Wæs ðǽr swíðe egeslíc geatweard *there was a very horrible gatekeeper*, Bt. 35, 6; Fox 168, 18. Ðæs egeslícan ðæt ðú dó feóndes aídlian awyrgede syrwunga *horrendi făcias hostis văcuisse (?) malignas insĭdias*, Hymn. Surt. 47, 24. Egeslícne cwide sigora Weard ofer ðæt fǽge folc forþ forlǽteþ *the Lord of victories shall send forth a dreadful utterance over the fated folk*, Exon. 30 a; Th. 92, 30; Cri. 1516. Fá þrówiaþ ealdor-bealu egeslíc *the hostile shall suffer terrific vital evil*, 31 b; Th. 98, 31; Cri. 1616. Ðæt he monig þing ge egeslíce ge willsumlíce geseah *that he saw many things both awful and delightful*, Bd. 5, 12; S. 627, 29. Se ðe worhte egeslícu on sǽ ðære reádan *qui fēcit terribĭlia in māri rubro*, Ps. Lamb. 105, 22. Wæs heora sum ðám óðrum egeslícra *one of them was more dreadful than the others*, Bd. 5, 13; S. 633, 3. Daga egeslícast *most terrible of days*, Exon. 23 a; Th. 63, 20; Cri. 1022.

eges líce; *adv.* [eges líce *in likeness of fear* =] *Fearfully*; terrĭbĭlĭter:—Hí náht ne belimpaþ to ðam þunere ðe on ðyssere lyfte oft egeslíce brastlaþ *they do not appertain to the thunder which in this atmosphere often crackles fearfully*, Bd. de nat. rerum; Wrt. popl. science 19, 26; Lchdm. iii. 280, 13. Worpaþ hine deófol on dómdæge egeslíce *the devil shall fearfully cast him down in the day of doom*, Salm. Kmbl. 52; Sal. 26.

egesung, e; *f. A threatening, fear, dread;* commĭnātio, R. Ben. interl. 27, Som. Ben. Lye. v. egsung.

egeðe *a rake, harrow;* rastrum, Som. Ben. Lye.

egeðere, es; *m. A raker;* occātor, Som. Ben. Lye.

eggian; *p.* ode; *pp.* od *To* EGG, *excite;* excĭtāre, Ben. Lye.

égh-þyrl, es; *n. An eye hole, a window;* fenestra:—Ðæs leóhtes scíma þurh ða cýnan ðære dúra and þurh ða éghþyrla ineóde *the glare of the light entered through the chinks of the door and through the windows*, Bd. 4, 7; S. 575, 20. v. eág-þyrl.

ég-hwelc *all, every*, Jn. Rush. War. 8, 34. v. ǽg-hwilc.

Egipte, Egypte; *gen.* a; *dat.* um; *pl. m. The Egyptians, the people of Egypt in a body, Egypt;* Ægyptii:—Ðæt Egipte ne forwurþon *that the Egyptians perish not*, Gen. 41, 36. Egipta land, Egypta land *the land of the Egyptians, Egypt*, Gen. 12, 10, 11, 14, 20: 13, 10: 21, 21: 37, 25, 28, 36: 39, 1. Egipta cyng, Egypta cyng *the king of Egypt*, Gen. 40, 1: Ex. 3, 18, 19: 5, 4. Egypta ealdor *a prince of the Egyptians*, Gen. 42, 6. Egipta here *the host of the Egyptians*, Deut. 11, 4. Fóron Iosepes týn gebróðru to Egiptum *Joseph's ten brothers went to Egypt*, Gen. 42, 3: 45, 9. Hunger fornam swíðust Egipte *famine oppressed the Egyptians most*, Gen. 47, 13.

Egiptisc, Egyptisc; *def.* se Egiptisca, Egiptiscea; seó, ðæt Egiptisce; *adj. Belonging to Egypt, Egyptian;* Ægyptius:—Hér is ides Egyptisc *here is an Egyptian woman*, Cd. 101; Th. 134, 19; Gen. 2227. Fram ðære Egiptiscan eá *from the Egyptian river*, Gen. 15, 18. Hine gebohte Egiptisc man *an Egyptian man bought him*, 39, 1: Ex. 2, 11, 19. Ðisra Egiptiscra manna *of these Egyptian men*, Gen. 50, 11. Se Egiptiscea cyng *the Egyptian king*, Ex. 1, 17. Beforan ðam Egiptiscean folce *before the Egyptian people*, 3, 21, 22. Þurh Egiptisce galdru *through Egyptian enchantments*, 7, 11. Ðæt Egiptisce folc *the Egyptian people*, 11, 7. Ða Egyptiscan *the Egyptians*, Ex. 14, 18, 31. Iosep sealde hwǽte ðám Egiptiscan mannum *Joseph sold corn to the Egyptian men*, Gen. 41, 56.

egiðe *a rake*, Som. Ben. Lye. v. egeðe.

EGL, e; *f. A mote;* festūca:—Hwí gesihst ðú ða egle on ðínes bróðor eágan *quid vides festūcam in ocŭlo fratris tui?* Lk. Bos. 6, 41, 42. [*Ger.* egel, achel, *f. festūca, arista.*]

eglan *to trouble*, Judth. 11; Thw. 24, 12; Jud. 185. v. eglian.

ég-land, ég-lond, es; *n. Water-land, an island;* insŭla:—We witan óðer égland *we know another island*, Chr. Erl. 3, 10. Geond ðis égland *throughout this island*, Chr. 641; Erl. 27, 11. In ðæt églond *on the island*, Exon. 96 b; Th. 361, 7; Wal. 16. Églond monig *many an island*, 89 a; Th. 334, 12; Gn. Ex. 15: 100 b; Th. 380, 8; Rä. 1, 5: Bt. Met. Fox 1, 31; Met. 1, 16. v. íg-land.

EGLE; *adj. Troublesome, hateful, loathsome, horrid;* mŏlestus, odiōsus, infestus, turpis:—He him sylfum byþ egle *he is loathsome to himself*, Basil admn. 8; Norm. 50, 24: Cd. 209; Th. 258, 21; Dan. 679. Gif egle wǽron *if they were troublesome*, Exon. 126 a; Th. 485, 20; Rä. 71, 16. Ðý-læs sceaðan mihton egle ondsacan *lest the horrid apostates might injure [him]*, Andr. Kmbl. 2297; An. 1150: 2916; An. 1461. Eglum áttor-sperum *with horrid venomed spears*, Exon. 105 a; Th. 399, 10; Rä. 18, 9. [*Goth.* agls *shameful, disgraceful;* aglus *difficult, troublesome.*]

eglian, eglan, elan; hit egleþ, eleþ; *p.* ode, ade; *pp.* od, ad; *v. trans. chiefly used impersonally with dat. of person. To trouble, pain, grieve,* AIL; molestāre, dŏlēre:—Ðæt he us eglan móste *that he could trouble us*, Judth. 11; Thw. 24, 12; Jud. 185. Me egleþ [eleþ, MS. H.] swýðe *it grieves me much*, L. Edm. S. proœm; Th. i. 246, 22. Him nǽfre syððan seó ádl ne eglode *the illness never ailed him afterwards*, Guthl. 12; Gdwin. 60, 8: 13; Gdwin. 60, 19. Ðæt him stranglíce eglade *it afflicted him severely*, Chr. 1086; Erl. 220, 33. Gif men innan wyrmas eglen [eglien MS. B.] *if worms trouble a man within*, Herb. 2, 10; Lchdm. i. 82, 22. [*Piers P. Chauc.* eylen, eilen *to ail: Orm.* eȝȝlenn: *Plat.* echeln, öcheln *to be vexed, grieved at anything: Ger.* ekeln: *Goth.* aglyan *to molest*, in us-aglyan.] DER. æt-eglan, ge-.

Egones hám, Egnes hám, es; *m.* [*Ethelw.* Ignesham: *Flor.* Eignesham: *Hunt.* Aegnesham: *Gerv.* Egenesham] ENSHAM or EYNSHAM, *Oxfordshire;* lŏci nōmen in agro Oxoniensi:—Hér Cúþwulf feaht wið Bretwalas and genom Egones hám *in this year* [A. D. 571] *Cuthwulf fought against the Britons and took Eynsham*, Chr. 571; Erl. 18, 14. Into Egnes hám *at Eynsham*, Cod. Dipl. 714; A. D. 1005; Kmbl. iii. 344, 16.

egor *nine ounces* or *inches, a span;* dodrans, Cot. 64, Som. Ben. Lye.

égor- *water, the sea;* aqua, măre. [*Icel.* ægir, *m.*] DER. égor-here, -streám.

égor-here, es; *m. The water-host, the deluge;* undārum exercĭtus, dilŭvium:—Se égorhere eorþan tuddor eall acwealde *the water-host destroyed all the earth's progeny*, Cd. 69; Th. 84, 23; Gen. 1402: 75; Th. 92, 31; Gen. 1537.

égor-streám, eágor-streám, es; *m. A water-stream, water, the sea;* unda, flŭvius, măre:—Ðiós eorþe mæg and égorstreám cræfta náne adwæscan ðæt ðæt him on innan sticaþ *this earth and sea can by no means extinguish that which in them remains*, Bt. Met. Fox 20, 236; Met. 20, 118. Égorstreámas swógan *the water-streams sounded*, Cd. 69; Th. 83, 4; Gen. 1374.

egsa, ægsa, an; *m. Fear, horror, dread;* tĭmor, horror, terror:—Egsa com ofer me *tĭmor vēnit sŭper me*, Ps. Spl. 54, 5: Exon. 20 a; Th. 52, 26; Cri. 839: Cd. 221; Th. 288, 12; Sat. 379. Beóþ egsan of heofene *ĕrunt terrōres de cœlo*, Lk. Bos. 21, 11: Cd. 148; Th. 186, 10; Exod. 136. v. egesa.

égsa, an; *m. An owner;* possessor:—Égsan wyn *the owner's pleasure*, Exon. 90 b; Th. 340, 7; Gn. Ex. 107. v. égesa.

egsian; *p.* ode; *pp.* od [egsa *fear*] *To frighten;* terrēre:—Oft Scyld egsode eorl *Scyld often frightened man*, Beo. Th. 11; B. 6. DER. ge-egsian.

ég-streám, éh-streám, es; *m. A water-stream, a river, the sea;* aquæ fluctus, flūmen, măre:—Hæfde Metod égstreám eft gecyrred *the just Creator had averted the stream*, Cd. 71; Th. 85, 15; Gen. 1415. Here wícode égstreáme neáh *the host encamped near the river*, Elen. Kmbl. 132; El. 66: Beo. Th. 1158; B. 577. v. eá-streám.

egsung, e; *f.* [egsa *fear*] *A terrible act, frightening, threatening;* terrĭbĭle, commĭnātio:—Strencþe egsunga oððe egesfulra þinga ðínra hí cweðaþ *virtūtem terrĭbĭlium tuōrum dīcent*, Ps. Lamb. 144, 6. Mid egsunge *by threatening*, Jud. Thw. 161, 37.

egþa, an; *m. An instrument to beat out corn;* trĭbŭla, Ælfc. Gl. 2; Som. 55, 52; Wrt. Voc. 16, 25.

egþe *a rake*, Som. Ben. Lye. v. egeðe.

égðer *either*:—Égðer ge—ge *both—and*, Gen. 4, 22. v. ǽgðer.

ég-þyrl *a window*:—Þurh ðæs húses égþyrl *through the window of the house*, Jos. 2, 15. v. eág-þyrl.

égum *with eyes*, Cd. 229; Th. 310, 18; Sat. 728; *dat. pl. of* ége = eáge; *n.* q. v.

é-gylt *a fault*, Ps. Spl. T. 31, 5. v. ǽ-gylt.

Egypte; *pl. m. The Egyptians*, Ors. 1, 7; Bos. 30, 21. v. Egipte.

Egyptisc *Egyptian*, Ex. 6, 5. v. Egiptisc.

egys full *fearful*, Ps. Spl. C. 46, 2. v. eges ful.

eh, es; *n.* I. *a war-horse, charger;* equus bellātor:—Ða ða hors óþbær, eh and eorlas *which bore away the horses, the chargers, and chiefs*, Exon. 106 a; Th. 404, 21; Rä. 23, 11. II. *the Anglo-Saxon Rune* ᛖ = e, the name of which letter in Anglo-Saxon is eh *a war-horse*,—hence, this Rune not only stands for the letter e, but for eh *a war-horse, charger*, as,—ᛖ [eh] byþ for eorlum *the war-horse is for chiefs*, Hick. Thes. i. 135, 37; Runic pm. 19; Kmbl. 343, 3. v. eoh.

éh- *water*, used in composition. v. íg.

ehennys, -nyss, e; *f. Modesty;* pŭdor, Som. Ben. Lye.

eher *an ear of corn*, Mk. Lind. War. 4, 28. v. ear.

eh-heólođe, an; *f. The plant elecampane* or *horseheal;* inŭla hĕlĕnium, Lin, L. M. 1, 32; Lchdm. ii. 76, 20.

éhst *highest*, Ps. Spl. 49, 15, = heáhst, héhst; *superl. of* heáh.

éh-streám, es; *m. A water-stream, ocean*:—Heliseus éhstreám sóhte, leólc ofer lagu-flód *Heliseus sought the ocean, bounded over the water-flood*, Exon. 75 b; Th. 283, 1; Jul. 673. v. ég-streám, eá-streám.

ehsýne *a face, countenance;* făcies, Som. Ben. Lye. v. an-sýn.

eht *value, estimation*:—Be ðæs demmes ehte *pro damni æstĭmātiōne*, Ex. 22, 5. v. eaht.

ehta *eight*:—Ehta dagas gefyllede wǽron *consummāti sunt dies octo*, Lk. Bos. 2, 21. v. eahta.

éhtan; he éht, *pl.* éhtaþ; *p.* éhte, *pl.* éhton; *pp.* ehted *To follow after, chase, pursue, persecute, annoy, afflict;* persĕqui, trĭbŭlāre, afflīgĕre,—*followed by gen.* or *acc*:—Ne éht he nánre wuhte *he pursues not anything*, Bt. 42; Fox 258, 3. Húndas míne wildeór éhton *cănes mei fĕras persĕquēbantur*, Coll. Monast. Th. 21, 15. Ðonne hí eów éhtaþ on ðysse byrig *cum persĕquentur vos in cĭvĭtāte ista*, Mt. Bos. 10, 23:

5, 11: Ælfc. Gr. 29; Som. 33, 48: 25; Som. 26, 63. Đara đe mīn ēhtaþ *tribŭlantium me*, Ps. Th. 26, 14: 118, 157. Đū us ahreddest æt đām đe ūre ēhton *libĕrasti nos ex affligentĭbus nos*, Ps. Th. 43, 9. v. eáhtan, ōht.

ehta-tyne; *adj. Eighteen*; octō-dĕcim:—Wēne gē đæt đa ehtatyne wǣron scyldige *pŭtātis quia illi dĕcem et octo dēbĭtōres fuĕrint?* Lk. Bos. 13, 4, 16. v. eahta-tyne.

ēhtend, es; *m. A persecutor*; persĕcūtor:—Domicianus wearþ ēhtend cristenra manna *Domitian was a persecutor of christian men*, Ors. 6, 9; Bos. 120, 18. He dreág ēhtendra nīþ *he endured the persecutors' malice*, Exon. 40 a; Th. 133, 28; Gū. 496. Ic his ēhtendas ealle geflȳme *I will put all his persecutors to flight*, Ps. Th. 88, 20.

ehteođa, ehteđa *eighth*:—On đam ehteođan dæge *on the eighth day*, Lk. Bos. 1, 59. v. eahtođa.

ēhtere, ēhtre, es; *m. A persecutor*; persĕcūtor:—Ēhtere *persĕcūtor*, Wrt. Voc. 74, 44. Of ēhtere *ex persecūtōre*, Bd. 1, 7; S. 478, 19. Sanctus Albanus cȳđde đām ēhterum Godes geleáfan đæt he cristen wǣre *Saint Alban told the persecutors of God's truth that he was a christian*, 1, 7; S. 477, 22. Gebiddaþ for eówre ēhteras *pray for your persecutors*, Mt. Bos. 5, 44: Bd. 1, 7; S. 476, 37.

ēh-þyrl *eye-hole, a window*:—Đū wircst ēhþirl *thou makest a window*, Gen. 6, 16: Jos. 2, 18. v. eág-þyrl.

ehtian *to esteem, deem, value*; æstĭmāre:—Swā monnum riht is to ehtienne *quantum homĭnĭbus æstĭmāre fas est*, Bd. 5, 6; S. 618, 30: Beo. Th. 2449; B. 1222: Cd. 193; Th. 241, 25; Dan. 410. v. eahtian.

ēhting, e; *f. Persecution*; persĕcūtio, Ors. 6, 23; Bos. 124, 11, notes, p. 28. 1.

ēhtnes, ēhtnys, -ness, -nyss, e; *f. Persecution*; persĕcūtio:—Seó ēhtnes đara cristenra manna *the persecution of christian men*, Ors. 6, 23; Bos. 124, 11: Ps. Th. 118, 139. Fram Iudēa ēhtnesse *from the persecution of the Jews*, Ps. Th. arg. 17: Mt. Bos. 13, 21: Chr. 2; Erl. 4, 30. Eádige synd đa đe ēhtnysse þoliaþ for rihtwīsnysse *beati qui persecūtiōnem patiuntur propter justĭtiam*, Mt. Bos. 5, 10: Bd. 1, 6; S. 476, 22: 1, 8; S. 479, 19, 21. v. eáhtnes.

ehtođa, ehtuđa *eighth*, Ex. 22, 30. v. eahtođa.

ēhtre *a persecutor*, Bd. 1, 7; S. 476, 37, MS. B. v. ēhtere.

ehtung, e; *f. Deliberation, council*; delībĕrātio:—Ehtunga ealle hæfdon *cogĭtāvērunt*, Ps. Th. 82, 3. v. eahtung.

eíg, e; *f. An island*; insŭla:—Wiđ eíge *near the island*, Chr. 878; Th. 148, 29, col. 1. v. īg.

eige *fear*, Cant. Moys. Ex. 15, 19; Thw. 30, 19. v. ege.

eíg-land, es; *n.* [eá *water* = eíg, land *land*] *Water-land, an island*; insŭla:—On đis eíglande *in this island*, Chr. 937; Erl. 115, 15. v. īg, eá, īg-land = eá-land.

eiseg; *adj.* [= egseg, egeseg, from egesa *fear*] *Terrible, horrible*; terrĭbĭlis:—Cleopaþ đonne se alda ūt of helle, wriceþ word-cwedas wēregan reorde, eisegan stefne *then the chief calleth out of hell, uttereth words with accursed speech, with horrible voice*, Cd. 213; Th. 267, 6–10; Sat. 34–36.

el-, ele- *foreign, strange*; peregrīnus, externus. v. el-land, ele-land.

ēl *an eel*, Som. Ben. Lye. DER. Ēl-īg. v. ǣl.

-el, -ol, a termination denoting persons, as, Fōrrīdel *an outrider*; bȳdel *a herald*. It denotes also inanimate objects; as, Gyrdel *a girdle*; stȳpel *a steeple*.

elan *to trouble, pain, grieve*, L. Edm. S. procœm; Th. i. 246, 22, note 33. v. eglian.

ēlas *hedgehogs*, Ps. Spl. T. 103, 19. v. īl.

el-boga, ele-boga, eln-boga, an; *m. An* ELBOW; cŭbĭtum, ulna:—Elboga *cŭbĭtum*, Ælfc. Gl. 72; Som. 70, 125; Wrt. Voc. 43, 50. Fæđm betwux elbogan [MS. elboga] and hand-wyrste *a cubit, between the elbow and wrist*; cŭbĭtum, 72; Som. 70, 126; Wrt. Voc. 43, 51. [*Chauc. R. Glouc.* elbowe: *Plat.* ellbagen, *m*: *Dut.* elleboog. *m*: *Ger.* elbogen, elnbogn, ellenbogen, *m*: *M.H.Ger.* ellenboge, elenboge, *m*: *O.H.Ger.* elinbogo: *Dan.* albue, *m. f*: *Icel.* albogi, alnbogi, olbogi, ölbogi, ölnbogi, *m. elbow*.]

ēlc *each*, Mk. Skt. Rush. 16, 15. v. ǣlc.

elch, es; *m. The* ELK; alces, cervus alces, Lin. Som. Ben. Lye. [*Dut.* ellend, elland, eland, *m. tragĕlaphus, hircocervus, anĭmal sĕptentriōnālis regiōnis*: *Ger.* elk, *m*; commonly elen, elend, *n. m*; elen-thier, *n*: *M.H.Ger.* ëlch, ëlhe, *m*: *O.H.Ger.* elaho, eliho, elho, elocho, elch, *m*; *Dan.* els-dyr, *n*: *Swed.* elg, *m*: *Icel.* elgr, *m*: *Lat.* alces, *f*: *Grk.* ἄλκη, *f. an elk*.]

elcian; *part.* elcigende; *p.* ode; *pp.* od; *v.n. To put off, delay*; mŏrāri, differre, cunctāri, tempus trăhĕre:—Ic latige on sumere stōwe, ođđe ic elcige *mŏror*, Ælfc. Gr. 25; Som. 27, 14. Đæt he leng ne elcode to his geleáfan *that he no longer delayed his belief*, Homl. Th. ii. 26, 1. v. latian.

elcor, elcur, ælcor; *adv. Elsewhere, otherwise, besides, except*; alias, alĭter, præter, nisi:—Gif hit hwæt elcor biþ *sin alias*, Bd. 4, 28; S. 605, 17. [*O.Frs.* ekker, elker, elkes *alias*: *O.Sax.* elcor *alias*: *O.H.Ger.* elichor, elicor, elihor *prorsus, ultra, amplius*: *Dan.* ellers: *Swed.* eljest *else*: *Icel.* ellegar, elligar, ellar, ella *alias*.]

elcra; *comp. adj.* [elcian *to put off, delay*; elcung *lateness, delay*] *Latter*; postĕrior:—Gif hie cumaþ of ōđrum biterum and yfelum wǣtum, đa đe wyrceaþ ōman, đonne beóþ đa elcran to stillanne ōþ-đæt đe hie unstrangran weorþan *if they come from other bitter and evil humours, which cause inflammations, then are the latter to be stilled until they become less strong*, L. M. 2, 1; Lchdm. ii. 178, 12–15.

elcung, e; *f. A delay*, R. Ben. 5, 71, Lye. v. eldung.

elcur; *adv. Otherwise*; alias, Mt. Rush. Stv. 6, 1: 9, 17: Lk. Lind. War. 5, 37. v. elcor.

eld *age*:—Sió forme eld *the first age*, Bt. Met. Fox 8, 7; Met. 8, 4: Bt. 15; Fox 48, 2. v. yldu.

eldan *to tarry*, Som. Ben. Lye. v. yldan.

eldcung *delay*, Bt. 38, 3; Fox 202, 17, MS. Cot. v. eldung.

elde *men*, Elen. Kmbl. 949; El. 476: Beo. Th. 5215; B. 2611: Andr. Kmbl. 2115; An. 1059: Bt. Met. Fox 20, 199; Met. 20, 100. v. ylde.

eldendlīc; *adj. Slow, slack*; pĭger, tardus, Som. Ben. Lye.

eldo *old age*, Beo. Th. 4229; B. 2111. v. yldu.

eldor *a prince*, Som. Ben. Lye. v. ealdor.

eldor-man *an alderman*, Th. Diplm. A. D. 883; 129, 25. v. ealdorman.

eldra *elder, older*; sĕnior:—Heora eldran fæder *of their older father, of their grandfather*, Bt. 10; Fox 28, 32, MS. Cot; *comp. of* eald.

eldran *elders, parents*, Bt. Met. Fox 1, 115; Met. 1, 58: 13, 55; Met. 13, 28. v. yldra.

eldre; *comp?* *omne*:—Ne dyde he āhwǣr swā eldran cynne *non fēcit tālĭter omni nātiōni*, Ps. Th. 147, 9.

eldung, eldcung, elcung, e; *f. Delay*; mŏra:—Hit is eldung and anbīd đæs hēhstan dēman *it is the delay and waiting of the highest judge*, Bt. 38, 3; Fox 202, 17. v. ylding.

ELE, es; *m.* OIL; ŏleum:—Eles gecynd is đæt he wile oferstīgan ǣlcne wǣtan: ageót ele uppon wæter ođđe on ōđrum wǣtan, se ele flȳt bufon: ageót wæter uppon đone ele, and se ele abrecþ up and swimþ bufon *it is the nature of oil that it will rise above every fluid: pour oil upon water or on another fluid, the oil will float above: pour water upon the oil, and the oil will break through and swim above*, Homl. Th. ii. 564, 11–14. Ele *ŏleum*, Ælfc. Gl. 32; Som. 61, 109; Wrt. Voc. 27, 38: Ps. Lamb. 108, 18: 140, 5. Hund sestra eles *centum cădos ŏlei*, Lk. Bos. 16, 6: Ps. Lamb. 4, 8. Of eówrum ele *de ŏleo vestro*, Mt. Bos. 25, 8. Mid mīnum hālgan ele *ŏleo sancto meo*, Ps. Lamb. 88, 21. Đū amæstest ođđe đū gefætnodest on ele heáfod mīn *impinguasti in ŏleo căput meum*, Ps. Lamb. 22, 5: 103, 15. Genexode synt his spræcu ofer ele *mollīti sunt sermōnes ejus sŭper ŏleum*, 54, 22. Hī ne nāmon nānne ele mid hym *non sumpsĕrunt ŏleum secum*, Mt. Bos. 25, 3, 4, 9: Lk. Bos. 10, 34: Gen. 28, 18: Lev. 2, 1, 6. Đū nymst ānne holne hlāf mid ele gesprengedne *tolles tortam pānis unīus crustŭlam conspersam ŏleo*, Ex. 29, 23: Lev. 2, 4: Ps. Lamb. 44, 8: Lk. Bos. 7, 46. Eles drosna *dregs of oil*; amurca = ἀμόργη, Ælfc. Gl. 47; Som. 65, 18; Wrt. Voc. 33, 18. [*Wyc. Chauc.* oile: *Orm.* ele: *Scot.* olye: *Plat.* oelje: *O.Sax.* olig, *n*: *Frs.* oalje: *O.Frs.* olie: *Dut.* olie, *f*: *Ger.* öl, *n*: *M.H.Ger.* ol, öl, *n*: *O.H.Ger.* olei, *n*: *Goth.* alew, *n*: *Dan.* olie, *m. f*: *Swed.* olja, *f*: *Icel.* olea, olía, *f*: *Lat.* oleum, *n*: *Grk.* ἔλαιον, *n. olive oil*; ἐλαία, *f. olive-tree, olive fruit*.] DER. wyn-ele.

ēle *a lamprey*, Som. Ben. Lye. v. ǣl.

ele-bacen; *pp. Oil-baked, baked in* or *with oil*; ŏleo coctus, ŏleātus:—Manna hīg gadredon and grundon on cwyrne ođđe britton and sudon on croccan and worhton hlāfas đǣrof: đa wǣron hīg swilce hīg wǣron elebacene *pŏpŭlus collĭgens Man frangēbat mŏla sive tĕrēbat in mortārio, cŏquens in olla et făciens ex eo tortŭlas săpōris quăsi pānis ŏleāti*, Num. 11, 8.

ele-beám, es; *m.* [ele *oil*, beám *a tree*] *An olive-tree*; ŏlea, ŏlīva:—Elebeám *ŏlea* vel *ŏlīva*, Ælfc. Gl. 32; Som. 61, 111; Wrt. Voc. 27, 40: 47; Som. 65, 18; Wrt. Voc. 33, 17: 80, 25: 285, 70: Ps. Lamb. 51, 10. Heó brohte elebeámes twīg *she brought a twig of olive-tree*, Cd. 72; Th. 88, 30; Gen. 1473. Heó brohte ān twīg of ānum elebeáme *illa portāvit rāmum ŏlīvæ*, Gen. 8, 11. Ealle eówre elebeámas forwurþaþ *all your olive-trees shall perish*, Deut. 28, 40: Ps. Th. 127, 4. Syndon bearn đīne swā swā nywlīcra elebergena ođđe guógaþ elebeáma *sunt fīlii tui sīcut novellæ ŏlīvārum*, Ps. Lamb. 127, 3. Dō swā on đīnum wīnearde and on đīnum elebeámon *ĭta făcies in vīnea et in ŏlīvēto tuo*, Ex. 23, 11. He eów sylþ elebeámas đe gē ne plantudon *dĕdĕrit tibi ŏlīvēta quæ non plantasti*, Deut. 6, 11. Unwæstmbǣre elebeám *an unfruitful* or *wild olive-tree*; ŏleaster, Ælfc. Gl. 47; Som. 65, 19; Wrt. Voc. 33, 19: Ælfc. Gr. 8; Som. 7, 15.

ele-beámen; *adj. Of* or *belonging to the olive-tree*; ŏleāgĭnus, Ælfc. Gl. 32; Som. 61, 110; Wrt. Voc. 27, 39.

ele-berge, an; *f.* [ele *oil*; berge = berie *a berry*] *An olive, the fruit of an olive-tree*; ŏlīva:—Swā swā eleberge wæstmbǣra *sīcut ŏlīva fructĭfĕra*, Ps. Spl. 51, 8. Syndon bearn đīne swā swā nywlīcra elebergena ođđe guógaþ elebeáma *sunt fīlii tui sīcut nŏvellæ ŏlīvārum*, Ps. Lamb. 127, 3.

He ûteóde on ðæne mûnt Oliuarum, ðæt is Elebergena *egressus ībat in montem Ŏlīvārum*, Lk. Bos. 22, 39.

ele-boga, an; *m. An elbow;* ulna, Wrt. Voc. 71, 24. v. el-boga.

ele-byt, -bytt, e; *f.* [ele *oil*, byt *a bottle*] *An oil vessel* or *cruet, a chrismatory;* lentĭcŭla:—Elebyt ǽrenu *lentĭcŭla*, Cot. 121.

ele-fæt, es; *n. An oil-vat, cruise* or *pot;* emĭcādium:—Elefæt *emĭcūdium* [= *emĭcădium*, v. Du Cange, vol. ii. 238], Ælfc. Gl. 26; Som. 60, 79; Wrt. Voc. 25, 19. Stǽnen elefæt *ălăbastrum*, 24; Som. 60, 40; Wrt. Voc. 24, 40.

elehtre, eluhtre, an; *f. The plant lupine;* lūpīnus albus, Lin:—Elehtre *lupine*, L. M. 2, 34; Lchdm. ii. 238, 30: 2, 65; Lchdm. ii. 296, 24: 3, 22; Lchdm. ii. 320, 12. Hafa clam geworht of elehtran *have a plaster made of lupine*, L. M. 3, 39; Lchdm. ii. 332, 21. Genim elehtran *take lupine*, Herb. 46, 3; Lchdm. i. 148, 22: L. M. 1, 33; Lchdm. ii. 80, 16: 1, 62; Lchdm. ii. 134, 13: 1, 64; Lchdm. ii. 138, 27: 1, 66; Lchdm. ii. 142, 2: 3, 41; Lchdm. ii. 334, 5: iii. 56, 26.

ele-lænde; *adj. Strange, foreign;* peregrīnus:—Elelændra eorþbigennys *cŏlōnia, peregrīnōrum cultūra*, Ælfc. Gl. 54; Som. 66, 102; Wrt. Voc. 36, 25.

ele-land, es; *n. A foreign country;* externa terra:—Ðǽr ic on elelande âhte stôwe *there I owned a place in a foreign country*, Ps. Th. 118, 54.

ele-lendisc; *adj. Strange, foreign;* advĕna, aliēnus:—Elelendisc ic eom mid ðē *advĕna ĕgo sum ăpud te*, Ps. Lamb. 38, 13. Bearn elelendisce ferealdodon *fĭlii alieni invetĕrāti sunt*, Ps. Lamb. 17, 46.

elene, an; *f. The herb elecampane;* inŭla hĕlēnium, Lin:—Genim niođowearde elenan *take the netherward part of elecampane*, L. M. 3, 26; Lchdm. ii. 322, 15: 3, 47; Lchdm. ii. 338, 14. v. eolone.

Elene, an; *f. Helena;* Helĕna = Ἑλένη: *The wife of the Roman emperor Constantius, and mother of Constantine the Great:*—Constantius gesealde his suna ðæt rīce, Constantinuse, ðone he hæfde be Elenan, his wīfe *Constantius gave the empire to his son Constantine whom he had by Helena his wife*, Ors. 6, 30; Th. 496, 33. His [Constantînes] môdor wæs cristen, Elena gehâten, swîđe gelýfed mann, and þearle eáwfæst *his [Constantine's] mother was a christian, called Helena, a very faithful person, and very pious*, Homl. Th. ii. 306, 3. ☞ See Ors. Bos. Notes and Various Readings, p. 28, col. 2, in proof that *Helena was the lawful wife of Constantius*:—Ðâ him Elene forgeaf sincweorþunga *then Helĕna gave him treasures*, Elen. Kmbl. 2434; El. 1218. Fôr Elenan cneó *before the knee of Helĕna*, 1693; El. 848: 1903; El. 953. Se Câsere [Constantînus] hēht Elenan *the emperor Constantine told Helena*, Elen. Kmbl. 2003; El. 1003: 2124; El. 1063. Elene, 438; El. 219: 1204; El. 604: 1236; El. 620.

ele-sealf, e; *f. Oil-salve, sweet balm;* nardus = νάρδος, ambrŏsia = ἀμβροσία, Cot. 3: 146.

ele-seocche, an; *f?* [ele *ŏleum*, seocche = seohhe *colātōrium*] *A vessel for straining oil, an oil-strainer?*—Eleseocche *fisclum?* Ælfc. Gl. 66; Som. 69, 85; Wrt. Voc. 41, 38.

eleþ, es; *m. A man;* hŏmo:—Witon ðæt se eleþ ēce bîdeþ *they know that the man eternally abideth*, Exon. 33 b; Th. 106, 8; Gû. 38. v. hæleþ.

ele-treów, es; *n. An oil-tree, olive-tree;* ŏlīva:—Swâ swâ eletreów wæstmbǽra *sīcut ŏlīva fructĭfĕra*, Ps. Spl. C. T. 51, 8. Swâ niwe planta eletreówa *sīcut nŏvellæ ŏlīvārum*, Ps. Spl. C. 127, 4.

ele-twig, es; *n. An olive twig, a small branch of olive*, Cot. 146.

-elfen, e; *f.* [ælf *an elf*, en *a feminine termination*] *A fairy, nymph;* nympha: *used only as a termination*:—Dûn-elfen *castălĭdes;* feld-elfen *moïdes (?);* wudu-elfen *dryădes;* wylde-elfen *hamadryădes;* sǽ-elfen *naïădes*, Ælfc. Gl. 112, 113; Som. 79, 108–112; Wrt. Voc. 60, 15–19. v. -ælfen.

el-hygd, e; *f. Strange thought, distraction;* perturbātio:—Môdes elhygd *distraction of the mind*, L. M. 2, 46; Lchdm. ii. 258, 18.

Élig, e; *f.* [ēl = ǽl *an eel*, îg *an island*] *The isle of* ELY, *Cambridgeshire;* insŭla Eliensis in agro Cantabrigiensi:—Is Élig ðæt land on Eást-Engla mǽgþa, hû hugu syx hund hîda, on eálondes gelîcnesse; is eall mid fenne and mid wætere ymbseald, and fram genihtsumnesse ǽla đa đe on ðâm ylcan fennum fongene beóþ hit naman onfēng *the land Ely is in the province of the East-Angles, of about six hundred hides, in the likeness of an island; it is all encompassed with a fen and with water, and took its name from the abundance of eels which are caught in the same fen*, Bd. 4, 19; S. 590, 3–6. Hēr Sċe Æđeldryht ongon ðæt mynster æt Élîge *in this year* [A. D. 673] *St. Ætheldryth began the monastery at Ely*, Chr. 673; Th. 58, 4. Æđeldryþ wæs abbudisse geworden on ðam þeódlande đe is gecýged Élîge, ðǽr heó mynster getimbrade *Ætheldryth became abbess in the country which is called Ely, where she built a monastery*, Bd. 4, 19; S. 588, 1.

Élig-burh, Éli-burh; *gen.* -burge; *dat.* -byrig; *f. The city of Ely, Cambridgeshire;* urbs Eliensis in agro Cantabrigiensi:—Man hine lǽdde to Élîgbyrig [Élîbyrig, Th. 294, 15, col. 2] *they led him to Ely*, Chr. 1036; Th. 294, 16, col. 1.

ēliōtrōpus, ēliōtrōpos *the turnsole*, Herb. 137; Lchdm. i. 254, 10, 16. v. hēliotropus.

el-land, es; *n. A foreign country, strange land;* externa terra:—Mægþ sceal, geómormôd, elland tredan *a maiden, sad of mind, shall tread a strange land*, Beo. Th. 6031; B. 3019.

ellarn *an elder-tree*, Som. Ben. Lye. v. ellen.

ellefne; *adj. Eleven;* undĕcim:—Ellefne orettmæcgas *eleven champions*, Andr. Recd. 1331; An. 664. v. endleofan.

ELLEN; *gen.* elnes; *m. n. Strength, power, vigour, valour, courage, fortitude;* vis, rōbur, vĭgor, virtus, fortĭtūdo:—Wîsdôm hæfþ on him feówer cræftas, đara is ân wærscipe, ôđer metgung, þridde is ellen, feórþe rihtwîsnes *wisdom has in it four virtues, of which one is prudence, another temperance, the third is fortitude, the fourth justice*, Bt. 27, 2; Fox 96, 34: Beo. Th. 1151; B. 573: Cd. 64; Th. 78, 5; Gen. 1288: Exon. 52 b; Th. 183, 4; Gû. 1322: Andr. Kmbl. 920; An. 460: Menol. Fox 491; Gn. C. 16. Ðâ him wæs elnes þearf *when he had need of valour*, Beo. Th. 5745; B. 2876: Cd. 47; Th. 59, 32; Gen. 972: Exon. 45 b; Th. 156, 3; Gû. 869: Andr. Kmbl. 2002; An. 1003: Elen. Kmbl. 1446; El. 725: Salm. Kmbl. 21; Sal. 11: Ps. Th. 118, 23. Wæs Gûþlâc on elne strong *Guthlac was strong in courage*, Exon. 36 b; Th. 119, 34; Gû. 264: 62 b; Th. 231, 4; Ph. 484: Beo. Th. 5624; B. 2816. Hæfde him on innan ellen untweódne *he had within him unwavering courage*, Andr. Kmbl. 2485; An. 1244: Beo. Th. 5384; B. 2695. Ic gefremman sceal eorlîc ellen *I shall perform a manly deed of valour*, Beo. Th. 1278; B. 637. Ne lǽt ðîn ellen gedreósan *let not thy strength sink*, Wald. 10; Vald. 1, 6: Beo. Th. 1208; B. 602: Exon. 120 b; Th. 463, 7; Hö. 66: Apstls. Kmbl. 6; Ap. 3. Ellen fremman *to do a deed of valour*, Andr. Kmbl. 2418; An. 1210: Beo. Th. 6; B. 3. Moyses bebeád folc hycgan on ellen *Moses bade the people think on valour*, Cd. 154; Th. 191, 22; Exod. 218: Fins. Th. 21; Fin. 11: Ps. Th. 93, 2. Engel hine elne trymede *an angel strengthened him with courage*, Exon. 35 a; Th. 113, 21; Gû. 161: Cd. 98; Th. 129, 2; Gen. 2137: Beo. Th. 5715; B. 2861: Andr. Kmbl. 1966; An. 985: Rood Kmbl. 67; Kr. 34: Ps. Th. 128, 5. Elne *with strength, power*, or *courage, strongly, powerfully, courageously;* strēnue, fortĭter, Beo. Th. 3938; B. 1967: Exon. 80 a; Th. 300, 18; Fä. 8: Ps. Th. 52, 5: 59, 4: 118, 4, 176. [*Orm.* ellennlæs *powerless: O. Sax.* ellien, ellen, *n. strength, manhood: M. H. Ger.* ellen, *n. strength, manhood: O. H. Ger.* ellan, *m. zēlus, rōbur, virtus: Goth.* alyan, *n. zeal: Icel.* eljan, elja, *f. endurance, energy.*] DER. mægen-ellen.

ELLEN, es; *n. The elder-tree;* sambūcus nigra, a small tree whose branches are filled with a light spongy pith. The fruit is a globular, purplish-black berry, of which wine is often made, called *elder-berry wine.* It is quite distinct from alor *the alder-tree*, q. v:—Ellenes blôsman genim *take blossoms of elder*, L. M. 2, 59; Lchdm. ii. 288, 2. Genim đas wyrte, đe man sambūcus = σαμβύκη [MS. samsuchon = σάμψυχον] and ôđrum naman ellen, hâteþ *take this wort, which is named sambucus, and by another name elder*, Herb. 148, 1; Lchdm. i. 272, 14. Genim ellenes leáf *take leaves of elder*, L. M. 1, 27; Lchdm. ii. 68, 23: 2, 30; Lchdm. ii. 228, 4. [*Plat.* elloorn, *m: Ger. M. H. Ger.* holder, holunder, *m: O. H. Ger.* holder, holuntar, *m: Dan.* hyld, *m. f;* hyldetræ, *n: Swed.* hyll, *f.*]

ellen; *adj. Of elder, elder-;* sambūceus:—Genim ellenne sticcan *take an elder-stick*, L. M. 1, 39; Lchdm. ii. 104, 7.

ellen-campian; *p.* ode, ede; *pp.* od, ed *To contend vigorously;* fortĭter pugnāre:—Ellencampian *pugĭlāre*, Cot. 4. Ellencampedon *pugĭlāvērunt*, Cot. 40.

ellen-cræft, es; *m. Strength, power;* virtus, pŏtentia:—Ahebbaþ hâligne heofena Drihten, usserne God ellencræfta *exalt the holy Lord of heaven, our God of powers*, Ps. Th. 98, 5.

ellen-dǽd, e; *f.* [ellen *valour*, dǽd *a deed*] *A deed of valour, bold* or *valiant deed;* virtūtis factum:—Sceolde hine yldo beniman ellendǽda *age should deprive him of bold deeds*, Cd. 24; Th. 31, 13; Gen. 484: Judth. 12; Thw. 25, 22; Jud. 273. He secgan hýrde ellendǽdum *he heard tell of valiant deeds*, Beo. Th. 1756; B. 876: 1804; B. 900.

el-lende, ele-lænde; *adj. Strange, foreign;* extĕrus, peregrīnus:—Nǽnig cēpa ne seah ellendne wearod *no merchant saw a foreign shore*, Bt. Met. Fox 8, 60; Met. 8, 30. In ellende *in foreign land, afar*, Mt. Kmbl. Rush. 21, 33: 25, 14.

Ellen-dûn, Ellan-dûn, e; *f.* [*Flor.* Ellandun, i. e. mons Eallæ: *Will. Malm.* Hellendune: *Hunt.* Elendune] *Allington, near Amesbury, Wilts;* lŏci nōmen in agro Wiltoniensi:—Hēr gefeaht Ecgbryht cyning and Beornwulf cyning on Ellendûne [Ellandûne, Th. 111, 21, col. 2] *in this year Egbert and Beornwulf fought at Allington*, Chr. 823; Th. 110, 20.

ellen-gǽst, es; *m. A bold* or *powerful spirit;* pŏtens spīrĭtus:—Se ellengǽst *the powerful spirit* [*Grendel*], Beo. Th. 172; B. 86.

ellen-gôdnes *zeal*, Bd. 3, 3; S. 525, 32, note. v. ellen-wôdnes.

ellen-heard; *adj. Hard of courage, bold, courageous;* fortis, strēnuus:—Wæs eorl ellenheard searoþancum beseted *the courageous warrior was beset with various thoughts*, Andr. Kmbl. 2509; An. 1256: Exon. 49 b; Th. 172, 3; Gû. 1138.

ellen-lǽca, an; *m. A champion;* pŭgil, agōnista, Cot. 15.

ellen-leás; *adj. Lacking courage;* fortĭtūdĭne cārens:—Ic sceal sēcan ðderne ellenleásran cempan *I must seek another less courageous soldier,* Exon. 71 b; Th. 266, 7; Jul. 394.

ellen-líce; *adv. Boldly, daringly;* fortĭter, strēnue, pŏtenter:—Wíf beorn acwealde ellenlíce *the woman daringly slew a warrior,* Beo. Th. 4250; B. 2122.

ellen-mǽrþ, e; *f.* [mǽrþ *greatness, glory*] *Glory of valour* or *courage;* fortitūdĭnis glōria:—Grendel nihtweorce geféh, ellenmǽrþum *Grendel rejoiced in his night-work, his valour-glories,* Beo. Th. 1660; B. 828.

ellen-rind, e; *f. Elder-rind* or *bark;* sambūci cortex:—Well ellenrinde niðewearde *boil the nether part of elder-rind,* L. M. 1, 32; Lchdm. ii. 78, 5: 1, 54; Lchdm. ii. 126, 5: 1, 68; Lchdm. ii. 128, 14.

ellen-róf; *adj. Remarkably strong, powerful, daring, brave;* rōbustus, strēnuus, fortis:—Strang oððe ellenróf *rōbustus,* Ælfc. Gr. 9, 22; Som. 10, 52. Beó ðú gestrangod and ellenróf *confortāre et esto rōbustus,* Jos. 1, 7, 9: Cd. 89; Th. 110, 26; Gen. 1844: Beo. Th. 685; B. 340: Exon. 96 a; Th. 358, 3; Pa. 40: Judth. 10; Thw. 23, 7; Jud. 109: Wald. 79; Vald. 2, 11. Hí woldon ániuga ellenrófes mód gemiltan *they would entirely subdue the bold man's mind,* Andr. Kmbl. 2784; An. 1394. Gif ic ǽnigne ellenrófne geméte *if I find any brave man,* Exon. 71 a; Th. 265, 17; Jul. 382. Ellenrófe weras *the bold men,* Exon. 106 b; Th. 405, 9; Rä. 23, 20: Cd. 94; Th. 122, 33; Gen. 2036: Andr. Kmbl. 2284; An. 1143.

ellen-sióc; *adj.* [sióc = seóc *sick, diseased, infirm, languid*] *Infirm* or *languid from want of strength;* invălĭdus, dēbĭlis:—Hwæðer he cwicne geméte in ðam wongstede Wedra þeóden ellensiócne *whether he should find the languid prince of the Goths alive on the field,* Beo. Th. 5567; B. 2787.

ellen-spræc, e; *f. Powerful speech;* pŏtens sermo:—He ne meahte ellenspræce, hleóðor ahebban *he could not raise his voice, his powerful speech,* Exon. 49 b; Th. 171, 18; Gú. 1128.

ellen-þríst; *adj. Bold in courage, bold;* audax:—Ða idesa ellenþríste *the bold women,* Judth. 11; Thw. 23, 22; Jud. 133.

ellen-weorc, es; *n. A work of valour, valiant* or *powerful act;* fortitūdĭnis ŏpus, res fortĭter gesta:—He wæs ánrǽd ellenweorces *he was steadfast in his work of valour,* Andr. Kmbl. 464; An. 232. Gif ðú ðæt ellenweorc aldre gedígest *if thou escapest with life from that work of valour,* Beo. Th. 1326; B. 661: 5279; B. 2643: Exon. 42 a; Th. 140, 20; Gú. 613. Ellenweorca *of valiant acts,* Beo. Th. 4789; B. 2399. Ellenweorcum *by valiant acts,* Andr. Kmbl. 2740; An. 1372.

ellen-wód, e; *f?* [wód *mad*] *Zeal;* zēlus = ζῆλος:—Me ðínes húses heard ellenwód æt *zēlus dŏmus tuæ cŏmēdit me,* Ps. Th. 68, 9.

ellen-wód; *adj.* [wód *mad*] *Raging, furious;* fŭriōsus:—Wæs ellenwód fæder wið déhter *the father was furious with his daughter,* Exon. 67 b; Th. 251, 4; Jul. 140.

ellen-wódian; *p.* ode; *pp.* od [ellen-wód *zeal*] *To strive with zeal, emulate;* æmŭlāri:—Nylle ðú elnian oððe ellenwódian [MS. ellenwondian] on yfelwillendum *nōli æmŭlāri in malignantĭbus,* Ps. Spl. C. 36, 1.

ellen-wódnes, -ness, e; *f. Zeal, envy, emulation, ardour;* zēlus = ζῆλος, fervor:—Swindan me dyde ellenwódnes mín *tabescĕre me fēcit zēlus meus,* Ps. Spl. T. 118, 139: 78, 5. Aidanus hæfde Godes ellenwódnesse and his lufan micle *Aidan had much zeal and love for God,* Bd. 3, 3; S. 525, 32. He wæs mid wylme mycelre ellenwódnesse onbærned *zēlo magni fervōris accensus est,* 4, 24; S. 598, 22.

ellen-wyrt, e; *f. Elderwort, wallwort, danewort, dwarf-elder;* sambūcus ĕbŭlus, Lin:—Genim ðas wyrte, ðe man *ĕbŭlum,* and óðrum naman ellenwyrte nemneþ, and eác sume men wealwyrt hátaþ *take this herb, which is named* ĕbŭlum, *and by another name elderwort, and some men also call it wallwort,* Herb. 93, 1; Lchdm. i. 202, 5: Wrt. Voc. 67, 12, 64: 69, 17.

ELLES; *adv.* ELSE, *otherwise, in another manner;* ălĭter, ălĭōquin, ălĭunde, sĕcus:—Elles *ălĭter,* Ælfc. Gr. 38; Som. 41, 7, 67. Elles næbbe ge méde mid eówrum fæder *ălĭōquin mercēdem non hăbēbĭtis ăpud patrem vestrum,* Mt. Bos. 6, 1: Mk. Bos. 2, 21. Gif hit elles sý *sin autem,* Lk. Bos. 10, 6. He stýhþ elles ofer *ascendit ălĭunde,* Jn. Bos. 10, 1. Hí ne mihton elles bión *they could not else exist,* Bt. 39, 13; Fox 234, 30: Bt. Met. Fox 9, 104; Met. 9, 52: Chr. 1044; Erl. 168, 17: Beo. Th. 5034; B. 2520: Exon. 67 b; Th. 249, 18; Jul. 113. Hwá aríst elles of Syon bútan ðú *who else shall arise out of Sion but thou?* Ps. Th. 13, 11. Hwæt elles is *quid est ălĭud?* Bd. 1, 27; S. 494, 15. Nyton hwæt hý elles sprecon *they know not what else they speak,* Ps. Th. 43, 16. Áhwǽr *or* ǽghwǽr elles *anywhere else,* Ps. Th. 71, 12: 102, 15. Ná elles, ná hú elles *not otherwise, no how else;* haud sĕcus, Ælfc. Gr. 38; Som. 42, 3: Bt. 32, 1; Fox 114, 8. Nówiht elles *nothing else;* nil ălĭud, Bd. 2, 14; S. 518, 8. Elles áwiht, ówiht *or* wuht *anything else;* ălĭud quid, Cd. 32; Th. 42, 33; Gen. 682: 91; Th. 114, 16; Gen. 1905: Exon. 82 a; Th. 308, 27; Seef. 46: 115 a; Th. 443, 1; Kl. 23: Bt. Met. Fox 9, 40; Met. 9, 20. Elles hwæt *anything else,* Bd. 4, 3; S. 569, 8. Elles hwǽr, hwár, hwérgen *or* hwider *elsewhere;* ălĭorsum, L. Eth. v. 12; Th. i. 308, 5: L. C. E. 13; Th. i. 368, 6: Beo. Th. 277; B. 138: 5173; B. 2590: Ælfc. Gr. 38; Som. 40, 7. [*Wyc. Piers P.* ellis: *Chauc. R. Glouc.* elles: *Orm.* elless: *Scot.* els, ellis: *O. Frs.* elles, ellis: *M. H. Ger.* alles *ălĭter: O. H. Ger.* alles, elles, ellies *ălĭōquin: Goth.* allis *at all: Swed.* eljest: *Lat.* ălias.]

elles hwá *any;* ali-quis, March. § 136, 5 a.

ellícor; *adv. Elsewhere, otherwise,* Ælfc. Gr. 38, Lye, Ettm. v. elcor.

ellm, es; *m. An elm;* ulmus:—On ellmum *in ulmis,* L. Edg. C. 16; Wilk. 83, 47. v. elm.

ellnung, e; *f. Emulation, zeal;* æmŭlātio:—Hí hæfdon Godes ellnunge *æmŭlātiōnem Dei hăbēbant,* Bd. 5, 22; S. 644, 8. v. elnung.

ellor; *adv. Elsewhere;* ălias, ălĭorsum:—Heó ðæt leóht geseah ellor scríðan *she saw the light depart elsewhere,* Cd. 37; Th. 48, 9; Gen. 773: 133; Th. 168, 17; Gen. 2784: Judth. 10; Thw. 23, 9; Jud. 112: Beo. Th. 110; B. 55.

ellor-fús; *adj.* [fús *ready, quick*] *Desirous* or *ready to go elsewhere, ready to depart;* pĕregre eundi cŭpĭdus, ălĭorsum īre părātus:—Óþ-ðæt gást, ellorfús, gangan sceolde to Godes dóme *until his spirit, ready to depart, must go to God's judgment,* Cd. 79; Th. 97, 7; Gen. 1609. He his hláford geseah ellorfúsne *he saw his lord ready to depart* [*about to die*], Exon. 48 a; Th. 165, 11; Gú. 1027: Andr. Kmbl. 375; An. 188.

ellor-gást, -gǽst, es; *m. A spirit living* or *going elsewhere, a departing spirit;* spīrĭtus ălĭbi dēgens:—Scolde se ellorgást on feónda geweald síðian *the departing spirit must go into the power of fiends,* Beo. Th. 1619; B. 807. Ellorgǽst *a departing spirit,* 3238; B. 1617. Hie gesáwon twegen ellorgǽstas *they saw two spirits living elsewhere,* 2702; B. 1349.

ellor-síþ, es; *m. A journey elsewhere, departure, death;* ălĭbi ĭter, mors:—Symble biþ gemyndgad eaforan ellorsíþ *his offspring's death will always be remembered,* Beo. Th. 4893; B. 2451.

ell-reord; *adj. Foreign-speaking, barbarous;* barbărus:—Eallum ellreordum cynnum *cunctis barbăris nātiōnĭbus,* Bd. 4, 2; S. 565, 31. v. el-reord.

ell-reordig; *adj. Foreign-speaking, barbarous;* barbărus:—Óðer [heretoga] wæs ðam hǽðenan réþra and grimra forðon he ellreordig wæs *alter* [*dux*] *quia barbărus ĕrat, pāgāno sævior,* Bd. 2, 20; S. 521, 21, 24: 3, 6; S. 528, 10. v. el-reord.

ell-þeód, ell-þiéd, e; *f. A strange people, foreign nation;* pĕregrīna gens:—Hý fóron on ellþiéde *they went into a foreign land,* Ors. 4, 4; Bos. 81, 6. v. el-þeód.

ell-þeódig -þiódig; *adj. Strange, foreign, a stranger, a foreigner:*—Ellþeódigra *of the foreigners,* Cd. 89; Th. 110, 8; Gen. 1835: Lk. Lind. War. 17, 18: 24, 18. v. el-þeódig.

ellyn *zeal,* Ps. Spl. C. 118, 139. v. ellen.

ELM, ellm, es; *m. An* ELM, *elm-tree;* ulmus:—Genim elmes rinde *take bark of elm,* L. M. 1, 6; Lchdm. ii. 52, 9. [*Chauc.* elmes, *pl: Dut.* olm, *m: Ger.* ulme, *f: M. H. Ger.* ëlm, *f: O. H. Ger.* elm, helmboum: *Dan.* alm, älm, *m. f: Swed.* alm, *f: Icel.* almr, álmr, *m: Lat.* ulmus, *f.*] DER. elm-rind.

elm-boga, an; *m. An elbow;* cŭbĭtum:—Gif se earm biþ forad búfan elmbogan *if the arm be broken above the elbow,* L. Alf. pol. 54; Th. i. 94, 24. v. el-boga.

el-mehtig *almighty,* Ps. C. 77 [Pfr. Germ. 10, 427]. v. eal-mihtig.

elmestlíc; *adj. Charitable;* mĭsĕrĭcors:—Swé hit him bóem rehtlícast and elmestlícast wére *as might be most righteous and most charitable for both,* Th. Diplm. A. D. 830; 465, 23.

el-mihtig *almighty:*—God elmihtiga *almighty God,* Chr. 1086; Th. 353, 32. v. eal-mihtig.

elm-rind, e; *f.* ELM-RIND or *bark;* ulmi cortex:—Elmrind *bark of elm,* L. M. 1, 47; Lchdm. ii. 116, 2. Well elmrinde *boil elm-rind,* 1, 32; Lchdm. ii. 78, 5. Nim elmrinde *take elm-rind,* 1, 38; Lchdm. ii. 98, 8: 3, 29; Lchdm. ii. 324, 15. Genim elmrinde gréne *take elm-rind green,* 1, 56; Lchdm. ii. 126, 15. Mid elmrinde *with elm-rind,* 1, 25; Lchdm. ii. 66, 23.

ELN, e; *f.* I. *an* ELL, *a measure of length, the space from the point of the elbow to the end of the middle finger, eighteen inches.* This is the *Heb.* אַמָּה [amma] *a cubit:* the *Lat.* cŭbĭtus *a cubit,* ulna *an ell.* Liddell and Scott say πῆχυς = *cŭbĭtus,* and *ulna an ell* properly contain twenty-four δάκτυλοι [δάκτυλος, the breadth of a finger, about $\frac{3}{4}$ of an English inch]:—Τίς δὲ ἐξ ὑμῶν μεριμνῶν δύναται προσθεῖναι ἐπὶ τὴν ἡλικίαν αὐτοῦ π ῆ χ υ ν ἕνα; Mt. 6, 27; iþ *whas izwara maurnands mag anaaukan ana wahstu seinana aleina aina?* Mt. Bos. Goth. 6, 27; quis autem vestrum cōgĭtans pŏtest adjĭcĕre ad stătūram suam *cŭbĭtum* ūnum? Mt. Vulg. 6, 27; hwylc eówer mæg sóþlíce geþencan ðæt he ge-eácnige áne *elne* to hys anlícnesse? Mt. Bos. 6, 27; Wycl. says *cubite;* Tynd. *cubit.* It is therefore presumed that the *Grk.* πῆχυς = *Heb.* אַמָּה was eighteen inches; for twenty-four δάκτυλοι x by $\frac{3}{4}$ = [.75] = eighteen inches. In the parallel passage, Lk. Bos. 12, 25, there is not any Gothic; the *Grk. Lat.* and *A. Sax.* are the same as in the preceding verse. Lk. Bos. 12, 25 is, therefore, not quoted. Hí wǽron unfeor fram lande, swylce hit wǽre twá hund elna *non longe ĕrant a terra, sed quăsi cŭbĭtis dŭcentis* [18 in. x 200 ÷ 12 = 300 ft.], Jn. Bos. 21, 8. Fíftena stód deóp ofer dúnum se drenceflód monnes elna *the deluge stood deep over the downs, fifteen ells of man,* Cd. 69; Th. 84, 17; Gen. 1399. Eln *ulna,* Glos. Brux. Recd. 38, 62; Wrt. Voc. 64, 71. II. *the Royal*

Persian ell, or *cubit, is very nearly* 20$\frac{1}{2}$ *inches;* for Herodotus says that the *πῆχυς βασιλήϊος*, bk. i. § 178, is 3 *δάκτυλοι* longer than the common Grk. *πῆχυς* = *cubit* or *ell:* 24 *δάκτυλοι*, i.e. 24 + 3 = 27 *δάκτυλοι;* 27 × [$\frac{3}{4}$ of an inch and $\frac{1}{12}$ of an 8th, *δάκτῠλος a finger's breadth* = about $\frac{75}{100}$ of an inch, that is $\frac{3}{4}$ of an inch and $\frac{1}{12}$ of an 8th = $\frac{3}{4}+\frac{1}{96}$ = $\frac{72}{96}+\frac{1}{96}=\frac{73}{96}$ = .76] .76 = 20$\frac{52}{100}$ [= 20$\frac{1}{2}$ inches, and $\frac{2}{100}$ or $\frac{1}{50}$ of an inch]:—Se weall Babilônes is fîftig elna brâd, and twâ hund elna heáh .... and ymbûtan đone weall is se mǽsta dîc .... and wiđûtan đam dîce is geworht twegra elna heáh weall *the wall of Babylon is fifty ells broad, and two hundred ells high .... and round the wall is a very great dike .... and outside the dike a wall is built two ells high*, Ors. 2, 4; Bos. 44, 23–28. **III.** *the ell in A. Sax. was sometimes about* 24 *inches, or* 2 *feet:*—Se hwæl biþ micle læssa đonne ôđre hwalas: ne biþ he lengra đonne syfan elna lang; ac, on his âgnum lande, đa beóþ eahta and feówertiges elna lange, and đa mǽstan, fîftiges elna lange; đara, he sǽde, đæt he syxa sum ofslôge syxtig on twâm dagum *this whale is much less than other whales: it is not longer than seven ells; but, in his own country* [*Norway*], *they are eight and forty ells long, and the largest, fifty ells long; of these, he said, that he was one of six, who killed sixty in two days*, Ors. 1, 1; Bos. 20, 18–23. In giving the size of the Horse-whale or Walrus, and of the Whale, Ohthere, a Norwegian, would most probably calculate by the measure of Scandinavia, the ell of Norway, Sweden, and Denmark. Molbeck, in his Dansk Ordbog, thus defines it:—'Alen, et vist længdemaal, som deles i 24 tommer ... Tomme een 12te fod, og een 24de alen,' ... That is, *Ell, a certain measure of length, which is divided into* 24 *inches .... An inch one* 12*th of a foot, and one* 24*th of an ell.* King Alfred, in his Anglo-Saxon version of Orosius, followed the calculation of Ohthere, who says that the Horse-whale or Walrus is 7 ells long, that is 14 feet, and the Whales 48 ells, and the largest 50, that is 96 feet, and the largest 100 feet long. These calculations approach very nearly to those given by Mr. Broderip, who says the length of the Walrus is from 10 to 15 feet, and Dr. Scoresby, who gives the length of the Physalus to be about 100 feet, Ors. Eng. p. 43, note 45. **2.** ells of different lengths were used in Anglo-Saxon times; and, even in the present day, 3 sorts of ells are known in England:—*The Flemish ell* is 3 quarters of a yard or 27 inches; *the English* 5 quarters or 45 inches; and *the French* 6 quarters or 54 inches. [Early English, *Wrt. spec.* 35, ân elne long: *R. Glouc.* 429, 3, elnen, *pl: Plat.* eel, *f: Frs.* jelne: *O. Frs.* ielne, elne, *f: Dut.* el, elle, *f: Ger.* elle, *f: M. H. Ger.* elne, eln, elline, ellen, *f: O. H. Ger.* elina, elna, elle, *f: Goth.* aleina, *f: Dan.* alen, *f: Swed.* aln, *f: Icel.* alin, *f: Lat.* ulna, *f: Grk.* ὠλένη, *f.* Eln *the ell* is found in *A. Sax.* eln-boga, el-boga *the elbow: Dut.* elle-boog: *Ger.* ellen-boge.] Ell is an old Teutonic word being used in the oldest German, the Gothic translation of Ulphilas about A. D. 360: in Anglo-Saxon about 895. The date of its use in other parts of Europe may be ascertained by referring to the languages quoted above, and in the list of contractions where the names and dates of the authors are given.

eln-boga, an; *m. An elbow;* cŭbĭtum:—Se earm nǽnige bîgnesse on đam elnbogan hæfde *the arm had no bending at the elbow*, Bd. 5, 3; S. 616, 23. v. el-boga.

elnes *of strength*, Beo. Th. 3063; B. 1529; *gen. of* ellen.

elnes = ellenes *of elder:*—Elnes rinde sele *give elder-rind*, L. M. 2, 30; Lchdm. ii. 230, 14. v. ellen *an elder-tree.*

eln-gemet, es; *n. An ell-measure, the length of an ell, two feet?* cŭbĭtālis mensūra, ulnæ mensūra:—Đæt fær gewyrc fîftiges wîd, þrittiges heáh, þreó hund lang elngemeta *make the vessel fifty wide, thirty high, three hundred long, of ell measures*, Cd. 65; Th. 79, 10; Gen. 1309. v. eln **I.** and **III.**

elnian; *part.* elnende; *p.* ode, ade; *pp.* od, ad [ellen *strength*]. **I.** *to make strong, strengthen;* confortāre:—Elnode he hine and sæt upp *confortātus sēdit in lectŭlo*, Gen. 48, 2. **II.** *to strive with zeal after another, endeavour to be equal, emulate;* æmŭlāre, zēlāre:—Nyl đû elnian betwih awergde, ne elnende đû sié dônde unrehtwîsnisse *nōli æmŭlāre inter mălignantes, neque æmŭlātus fueris făcientes iniquĭtātem*, Ps. Surt. 36, 1, 7. Ic elnode [elnade, Ps. Th. 72, 2] ofer đa unrihtwîsan *zēlāvi sŭper iniquos*, Ps. Spl. C. 72, 3. Ne elna đû *ne æmŭlēris*, Ps. Surt. 36, 8. DER. ge-elnian.

elnung, ellnung, e; *f. Zeal, hot emulation, envy;* zēlus, æmŭlātio:—Elnung *zēlus*, Rtl. 192, 5. Elnung ođđe æfista hûses đînes ge-et [= geæt] mec *zēlus dŏmus tuæ cŏmēdit me*, Jn. Lind. War. 2, 17.

elone *the herb elecampane*, L. M. 1, 23; Lchdm. ii. 66, 2. v. eolone.

elp *an elephant*, Som. Ben. Lye. v. ylp.

elpen-bǽnen; *adj. Made of ivory;* ĕburnĕus:—Fram hûsum elpenbǽnenum *a dŏmĭbus ĕburnĕis*, Ps. Lamb. 44, 10.

elpen-bân, es; *n. An elephant's bone, ivory;* ĕbur:—Elpenbânum *with ivory*, Ps. Spl. 44, 10: Cot. 71. v. ylpen-bân.

elpend, es; *m. An elephant;* ĕlephas = ἔλεφας:—Hwæđer ge seón mâran on eówrum lîchoman đonne elpend *if ye were greater in your body than the elephant*, Bt. 32, 1; Fox 114, 25. Elpendes hŷd wyle drincan wǽtan gelîce and spinge dêþ *an elephant's hide will drink wet like a sponge*, Ors. 5, 7; Bos. 107, 10. He genêþde under ânne elpend *he went boldly under an elephant*, Ors. 4, 1; Bos. 77, 20: 78, 9. He hæfde xx elpenda *he had twenty elephants*, 4, 1; Bos. 77, 5: 5, 7; Bos. 107, 8. To đâm elpendum [MS. elpendan] *to the elephants*, 4, 1; Bos. 77, 26. Hêt Pirrus dôn đa elpendas on đæt gefeoht *Pyrrhus ordered the elephants to be brought into the battle*, 77, 16, 23: 78, 5, 28.

elpend-tôþ, es; *m. An elephant's tooth;* ĕlephantis dens, Cot. 78.

elra; *comp? Stranger:*—He ne mêtte on elran men mundgripe mâran *he did not find a stronger hand-gripe in a stranger man*, Beo. Th. 1509; B. 752.

el-reord, ell-reord, æl-, æll-, eall-; *adj. Foreign-speaking, barbarous;* barbărus:—Wǽron heó mid elreordre dysignesse onblâwne *inflāti ĕrant barbăra stultĭtia*, Bd. 2, 5; S. 507, 13: 1, 5; S. 476, 11: 1, 14; S. 482, 12: Ps. Surt. 113, 1.

el-reordig, ell-reordig; *adj. Foreign-speaking, barbarous;* barbărus, pĕregrīnus:—Of gramum folce đa elreordige ealle wǽron *de pŏpŭlo barbăro*, Ps. Th. 113, 1.

el-reordignes, -ness, e; *f. Barbarousness, outlandishness;* barbăries, Som. Ben. Lye.

el-riord; *adj. Barbarous;* barbărus:—Mid elriordre dysignesse *barbăra stultĭtia*, Bd. 2, 5; Whelc. 122, 3. v. el-reord.

el-þeód, æl-þeód, el-þiód [ell-]; *gen.* e; *pl. nom. acc.* a, e; *f. A foreign nation, strange people;* gens pĕregrīna, alienĭgĕnæ, pĕregrīni:—Êhton elþeóda *they pursued the strange nations*, Elen. Kmbl. 277; El. 139. Fôre elþeódum *before strange nations*, Exon. 27 b; Th. 82, 12; Cri. 1337: 23 b; Th. 67, 6; Cri. 1084. On ellþeóde *among a strange people*, Andr. Kmbl. 1943; An. 974: Exon. 123 b; Th. 474, 25; Bo. 36.

el-þeódian *foreigners;* barbăros, = el-þeódigan; *acc. pl. def. of* el-þeódig, Bd. 1, 14; S. 482, 12, note.

el-þeódig, æl-þeódig, el-þiódig [ell-]; *adj. Strange, foreign, barbarous, one who is abroad;* pĕregrīnus, barbărus, advĕna, alienĭgĕna, qui pĕregre est:—Eorlas elþeódige *strange men*, Andr. Kmbl. 397; An. 199. Þearfum and elþeódigum symble eáþmôd *paupĕrĭbus et pĕregrīnis semper hŭmĭlis*, Bd. 3, 6; S. 528, 10, note. Đæt Bryttas đa elþeódian of heora gemǽrum adrîfan *ut Brittōnes barbăros suis e fīnĭbus pĕpŭlĕrint*, 1, 14; S. 482, 12, note. Nû cwom elþeódig *now a stranger has come*, Elen. Kmbl. 1813; El. 908: Cd. 124; Th. 159, 3; Gen. 2629. Hwonne me wrâþra sum ellþeódigne aldre beheówe *when some enemy might bereave me, a stranger, of life*, 128; Th. 163, 20; Gen. 2701: Exon. 82 a; Th. 308, 11; Seef. 38: 87 b; Th. 329, 5; Vy. 29. Đa elþeódigan ealle Drihten lustum healdeþ *Dŏmĭnus custōdit advĕnam*, Ps. Th. 145, 8: 110, 4. v. el-þeód.

el-þeódiglîce, æl-þeódiglîce; *adv. In foreign parts, among foreigners;* pĕregre. v. æl-þeódiglîce.

el-þeódignes, -þeódines, æl-þeódignes, -ness, -nyss, e; *f. A being or living abroad, pilgrimage;* pĕregrīnātio:—Ferde on elþeódignysse *pĕregre prŏfectus est*, Mt. Bos. 21, 33. On elþeódinysse, 25, 14. Elþeódignys ođđe eardbegengnes mîn afeorrad ođđe gelængd is *incŏlātus meus prōlongātus est*, Ps. Lamb. 119, 5. v. eard-begengnes.

el-þeódisc; *adj. Foreign, strange;* pĕregrīnus:—To bebyrgenne elþeódisce men *in sĕpultūram pĕregrīnōrum*, Mt. Bos. 27, 7. v. el-þeódig.

el-þiód, e; *f. A foreign nation:*—In elþióde *pĕregre*, Mt. Rush. Stv. 21, 33. v. el-þeód.

el-þiódgian, -þiódigian; *p.* ode; *pp.* od [el, þeód *a people*] *To live in foreign parts, to lead a pilgrim's life;* pĕregrīnāri:—Wilnode he on neáweste đara hâligra stôwe to tîde elþiódgian on eorþan *cŭpīvit in vīcīnia sanctōrum lŏcōrum ad tempus pĕregrīnāri in terris*, Bd. 5, 7; S. 621, 12.

el-þiódig *strange, foreign*, Bt. 39, 2; Fox 212, 17, note 3: Ors. 3, 7; Bos. 62, 35: Mt. Lind. Stv. 25, 14. v. el-þeódig.

eltst *eldest;* nātu maxĭmus:—Seó mǽgþ asprang of Noes eltstan suna, se wæs gehâten Sem *that family sprang from Noah's eldest son who was called Shem*, Homl. Th. i. 24, 7, = yldest; *sup. of* eald.

eluhtre, an; *f. The plant lupine;* lūpīnus albus, Lin:—Wyl eluhtran on ealaþ *boil lupine in ale*, L. M. 1, 41; Lchdm. ii. 106, 11: 1, 63; Lchdm. ii. 136, 26. v. elehtre.

êlys *hedgehogs*, Ps. Spl. C. 103, 19. v. îl.

em-, in composition, denotes *even, equal:* v. efen *even*, emb *about.* v. em-lîcnes, em-niht, etc.

emb, embe *about, round, around:*—Emb eahta niht *about eight nights*, Menol. Fox 418; Men. 210: 76; Men. 38: 188; Men. 95: 109; Men. 54: 259; Men. 131: 449; Men. 226. Embe fîf niht *about five nights*, Menol. Fox 21; Men. 11: 30; Men. 15: 38; Men. 19: 82; Men. 41: 385; Men. 194. v. ymb.

embe-fær, es; *n.* [fær *a going, journey*] *A going round, circuit;* circuĭtus:—Embefær tûna *circuĭtus villārum*, Procem. R. Conc.

embe-gân *to go round*, Lye. v. ymb-gân.

embe-gang, es; *m. A going round, circuit;* circuĭtus:—Se embegang đara landa *the circuit of the lands*, Cod. Dipl. Apndx. 402; A. D. 944;

Kmbl. iii. 421, 6. Se mōna hæfþ læstne embegang *the moon has the least circuit*, Boutr. Scrd. 18, 38. Embegang dōn *processiōnem fācĕre*, R. Conc. 3. v. ymbe-gang.

embe-gyrdan; he -gyrt; *p.* -gyrde; *pp.* -gyrded *To surround, begird;* circumcingĕre:—Gārsecg embegyrt gumena rīce *the ocean surrounds the kingdoms of men*, Bt. Met. Fox 9, 81; Met. 9, 41. v. ymb-gyrdan.

embeht, es; *n. An office, serving;* ministĕrium:—Ymb oft embehte *circa frĕquens ministĕrium*, Lk. Skt. Lind. 10, 40. v. ambeht.

embehtian; *p.* ode, ade; *pp.* od, ad *To minister, serve;* ministrāre:—Heó embehtade odde gehērde him *ministrābat eis*, Mt. Kmbl. Lind. 8, 15. Embehtaþ *ministrābit*, Lk. Skt. Lind. 12, 37.

embeht-mon, -monn, es; *m. A servant-man, servant, minister;* servus, minister:—Allra embehtmonn *omnium minister*, Mk. Lind. War. 9, 35. v. ambiht-man.

embehtsumnes, -nis, -niss, e; *f. A compliance, kind attention;* obsĕquium:—He dēmeþ embehtsumnisse [MS. embehtsumise] odde hērnisse *arbitrētur obsĕquium*, Jn. Lind. War. 16, 2.

embe-hydignes, -ness, e; *f. Solicitude;* sollĭcĭtūdo, C. R. Ben. 43, Lye. v. ymb-hydignys.

Embene; *pl. m. The inhabitants of Amiens, Amiens, in Picardy, France;* Ambiānum:—Hēr fōr se here up on Sunnan to Embenum, and dǽr sæt ān geár *in this year* [A. D. 884] *the army went up the Somme to Amiens, and remained there one year*, Chr. 884; Erl. 82, 17.

embe-smeágung, e; *f. A considering about, experience;* empīria = ἐμπειρία:—Manega embesmeágunga *empīria*, Ælfc. Gl. 82; Som. 73, 49; Wrt. Voc. 47, 53.

embe-þencan; *part.* -þencende; *p.* -þohte; *pp.* -þoht *To think about, to be anxious for, careful;* sollĭcĭtus esse:—Ne beó ge embeþencende hū odde hwæt ge sprecon, odde andswarion *nōlīte sollĭcĭti esse quālĭter aut quid respondeātis, aut quid dīcātis*, Lk. Bos. 12, 11. v. ymbe-þencan.

embe-ūton; *adv. About;* circum:—Ān of dām de dār embe-ūton stōdon *one of those who stood there about*, Mk. Bos. 14, 47. v. ymbe-ūtan; *adv.*

emb-feran; *p.* -ferde; *pp.* -fered *To go round, surround;* circuīre:—Hig geond feówertig daga embferdon done eard *they went round the country for forty days*, Num. 13, 26.

embiht, es; *m. A servant;* minister:—Ða embihtas *ministri*, Jn. Rush. War. 7, 46. v. ambeht; *m.*

embiht, es; *n. An office;* offĭcium:—Gefylde wǽron da dagas embihtes his *implēti sunt dies offĭcii ejus*, Lk. Skt. Lind. 1, 23. v. ambeht; *n.*

embiht-mon, -monn, es; *m. A servant-man, servant, minister;* servus, minister:—Allra embihtmon *omnium minister*, Mk. Rush. War. 9, 35. v. ambiht-man.

emb-long *at length*, Som. Ben. Lye.

emb-rin, es; *n.* [= emb-īren *an encircling iron*] *A fetter;* compes:—Embrin *balus?* Cot. 203: Wrt. Voc. 288, 1.

emb-ryne, es; *m. A running round, a course, revolution, anniversary;* revŏlūtio, circuĭtus:—Tyn embrynas *quinquennia jam dĕcem*, Glos. Prudent. Recd. 139, 1. v. ymb-rene.

emb-sittan; *p.* -sæt, *pl.* -sǽton; *pp.* -seten *To sit round* or *about, surround, beset, besiege;* circumsĕdēre, obsĭdēre:—Porsenna and Tarcuinius embsǽton Rōme burh *Porsenna and Tarquin surrounded Rome*, Ors. 2, 3; Bos. 42, 11. He besirede dæt folc de hī embseten hæfdon *he deceived the people who had besieged them*, Ors. 4, 5; Bos. 83, 3. v. ymb-sittan.

emb-snīdan; *p.* -snāþ, *pl.* -snidon; *pp.* -sniden, -snyden *To cut round, circumcise;* circumcīdĕre:—Ðæt dæt cild embsnyden wǽre *ut circumcīdĕrētur puer*, Lk. Bos. 2, 21. v. ymb-snīdan.

emb-stemn; *adv. By turns;* vĭcissim:—Embstemn *vel* dǽr gemang *vĭcissim*, Glos. Prudent. Recd. 140, 2.

emb-ūtan *about, round;* circum, circa:—Guton [MS. geoton; dæs celfes blōd] embūtan dæt weofod *they poured* [*the blood of the calf*] *round the altar*, Lev. 1, 5, 11. v. ymb-ūtan; *prep.*

emb-wlātian; ic -wlātige; *p.* ode; *pp.* od *To look about, contemplate;* contemplāri:—Ic embwlātige *contemplor*, Ælfc. Gr. 25; Som. 27, 5, MS. D. v. ymb-wlātian.

emb-wlātung, e; *f. A viewing, contemplation;* contemplātio:—Hī brūcaþ dære incundan embwlātunge his godcundnysse *they enjoy the closest contemplation of his divinity*, Homl. Th. i. 348, 7. v. ymb-wlātung.

em-cristen *a fellow-christian*, L. Ed. C. 36; Th. i. 461, 1. v. emne-cristen.

eme *deceit, fraud;* fraus, Som. Ben. Lye.

emel, e; *f. A canker-worm, caterpillar, weevel;* ērūca, brūchus = βροῦχος:—He sealde emele odde treówyrme wæstm heora *dĕdit ērūcæ fructus eōrum*, Ps. Spl. C. 77, 51. He sǽde and com gærshoppe and emel dæs næs nā gerīm *dixit et vĕnit lŏcusta, et brūchus cūjus non ĕrat nŭmĕrus*, 104, 32. v. ymel.

emertung, e; *f. A tickling, an itching;* prūrīgo:—Emertung *prūrīgo*, Ælfc. Gl. 11; Som. 57, 61; Wrt. Voc. 20, 5.

emetig; *adj. Empty, vacant;* văcuus, văcans:—He gemēteþ hit [hūs] emetig *invĕnit eam* [*dŏmum*] *văcantem*, Mt. Kmbl. Rush. 12, 44. v. æmtig.

em-fela; *adj. Equally many;* tŏtĭdem:—Gān inn emfela manna of ǽgdre healfe *let equally as many men of either side go in*, L. Ath. iv. 7; Th. i. 226, 20. v. efen-fela.

em-hydig; *adj. Anxious about, solicitous;* sollĭcĭtus, C. R. Ben. 33. v. ymb-hydig.

emitte, an; *f. An emmet, ant;* formīca:—Emittan *formīcæ*, Prov. 30. v. æmete.

em-lang; *adj. Equally long;* ejusdem longitūdĭnis, L. M. 2, 36; Lchdm. ii. 242, 15.

em-leóf; *adj. Equally dear;* æque cārus:—Him wearþ emleóf, dæt hȳ gesāwon mannes blōd agoten, swā him wæs dara nȳtena meolc *it was equally dear to them to see man's blood shed, as it was* [*to see*] *the milk of their cattle*, Ors. 1, 2; Bos. 26, 32.

em-līce; *adv. Even-like, evenly, equally, patiently;* æquālĭter, æquanĭmĭter:—Hū emlīce hit gelamp *how evenly it happened!* Ors. 2, 1; Bos. 39, 25: 3, 6; Bos. 57, 41. He done eard ealne emlīce dǽlde betwux twelf mægþum *he divided all the country equally among the twelve tribes*, Homl. Th. ii. 214, 12: Boutr. Scrd. 29, 11; Lchdm. iii. 266, 22. He forbær Godes swingele swīde emlīce *he bare God's scourging very patiently*, Homl. Th. ii. 98, 12. v. efen-līce.

em-līcnes, -ness, e; *f. Evenness, equality, equity;* æquĭtas:—He dēmþ folc on emlīcnesse *judĭcābit pŏpŭlos in æquĭtāte*, Ps. Spl. T. 95, 10: 110, 7: 118, 75. v. efen-līcnes.

em-micel; *adj. Equally much;* æque multus:—Em-micel ealra *equally much of all*, L. M. 1, 2; Lchdm. ii. 30, 5. v. emn-micel, efen-micel.

emn; *adj. Even, equal, plain, level, just;* æquus, plānus, æquālis:—Ðæs wīsan monnes mōd biþ swīde emn *the wise man's mind is very even*, Past. 42, 1; Hat. MS. 58 a, 16: 17, 5; Hat. MS. 23 a, 7: Ps. Th. 10, 8. Næs ic nǽfre swā emnes mōdes *I was never of so even a mind*, Bt. 26, 1; Fox 90, 25. Seó burh wæs getimbred on swīde emnum lande *the city was built on very level land*, Ors. 2, 4; Bos. 44, 20: Past. 4, 2; Hat. MS. 10 a, 14. Habbaþ emne wǽga and emne gemetu and sestras *stătēra justa et æqua sint pondĕra, justus mŏdius æquusque sextārius*, Lev. 19, 36. On emn *on even ground, by, near;* in æquāli, juxta, Gen. 16, 12: 21, 19: Jos. 10, 5: Homl. Th. i. 30, 16: Byrht. Th. 137, 9; By. 184. To emnes *over against, opposite;* adversus, contra, Ors. 1, 1; Bos. 21, 8; 3, 9; Bos: 68, 25: Cod. Dipl. 1102; A. D. 931; Kmbl. v. 194, 32; 195, 2. v. efen.

emn-, emne-, in composition, *even, equal*, as efen:—Emne-cristen *a fellow-christian*. Emn-sceólere *a school-fellow*.

emn-ædele; *adj. Equally noble;* æque nōbĭlis:—Ealle sint emn-ædele *all are equally noble*, Bt. 30, 2; Fox 110, 17: Bt. Met. Fox 17, 27; Met. 17, 14.

emne; *comp.* emnor, emnar; *adv. Equally, even, exactly, precisely, just;* æquālĭter, æque, omnīno:—Sió sunne and se mōna habbaþ todǽled betwuht him done dæg and da niht swīde emne *the sun and the moon have divided the day and the night very equally between them*, Bt. 39, 13; Fox 234, 6: Bt. Met. Fox 29, 72; Met. 29, 35: Ps. Th. 9, 8. Crist hiene selfne ge-eáþmēdde emne ōþ done deáþ *Christ humbled himself even unto death*, Past. 41, 1; Hat. MS. 56 a, 22: 50; Hat. MS: Cd. 92; Th. 116, 28; Gen. 1943: Bt. Met. Fox 9, 76; Met. 9, 38: 13, 89; Met. 13, 45: Andr. Kmbl. 227; An. 114: 441; An. 221: 665; An. 333. Ne wēne ic dæt ǽnige twegen lātteówas emnar gefuhton *I do not think that any two leaders fought more equally*, Ors. 3, 1; Bos. 53, 32. v. efne.

emn-ēce; *adj. Co-eternal;* coæternus:—Is emnēce mægenþrymnes *est coæterna majestas*, Ps. Lamb. fol. 200, 25. Ealle þrȳ hādas emnēce him sylfum synt *totæ tres personæ coæternæ sibi sunt*, 201, 27. v. efen-ēce.

emne-cristen, em-cristen, es; *m. A fellow-christian;* co-christiānus:—His emnecristen *fratrem suum in Christo*, L. Ed. C. 36; Wilk. 209, 18.

emne-līce *evenly, equally*, Som. Ben. Lye. v. efen-līce.

emnes, -ness, -niss, -nyss, e; *f. Evenness, equity, justice;* æquĭtas:—Drihten dū geliffæst me on efnesse odde emnesse dīnre *Dŏmĭne vivĭfĭcābis me in æquĭtāte tua*, Ps. Lamb. 142, 11. Emnesse geseah anwlita his *æquĭtātem vĭdit vultus ejus*, 10, 8. He dēmþ ymbhwyrft eorþan on emnisse *ipse judĭcābit orbem terræ in æquĭtāte*, Ps. Spl. 9, 8. Eágan dīne geseón emnyssa *ŏcŭli tui vĭdeant æquĭtātes*, 16, 3: 51, 3: 110, 7. v. efen-nyss.

emnett, es; *n? Level ground, a plain;* plānĭties, campus:—He hæfde on dam emnette gefaren *he had marched on the level ground*, Ors. 4, 8; Bos. 89, 38.

emnettan, emnyttan, to emnettenne; *p.* te; *pp.* ed *To make even* or *equal, to regulate;* æquāre, coæquāre:—Synt to emnettenne be dissere emnihte *they are to be regulated by this equinox*, Bd. de nat. rerum; Wrt. popl. science 11, 15; Lchdm. iii. 256, 24. Ic emnytte *coæquo*, Ælfc. Gr. 47; Som. 48, 56. DER. ge-emnettan.

emn-gōd; *adj. Equally good;* æque bŏnus:—Nān wuht nis betere donne God ne emngōd him *no creature is better than God nor equally good with him*, Bt. 34, 3; Fox 138, 7. Nyton nāuht emngōd *they know nothing equally good*, 34, 2; Fox 136, 4.

emnian *to equal, to make alike*, Som. Ben. Lye.

em-niht, es; *n.* [em, emn *equal;* niht *night*] *Equal day and night, equinox;* æquĭnoctium :—On emnihtes dæg, ðæt is ðonne se dæg and seó niht gelīce lange beóþ *on the day of the equinox, that is when the day and night are equally long*, Bd. de nat. rerum; Wrt. popl. science 12, 19; Lchdm. iii. 260, 13. Ver is lencten tīd, seó hæfþ emnihte *spring is the lenten tide, which hath an equinox*, 8, 28; Lchdm. iii. 250, 10. Autumnus is hærfest, ðe hæfþ ōðre emnihte *Autumn is harvest, which hath the other equinox*, 9, 1; Lchdm. iii. 250, 11. On ðæs hærfestlīcan emnihtes ryne *in the course of the harvest [autumnal] equinox*, Lchdm. iii. 238, 27. To hærfestes emnihte *at the autumnal equinox*, Th. Diplm. A.D. 902; 151, 11.

emnis, -niss *evenness, equity*, Ps. Spl. 9, 8. v. emnes.

emn-land *even land, a plain*, Som. Ben. Lye.

emn-līce; *adv. Equally, evenly;* æquālĭter, æque:—Ðæt hine ealle emnlīce hērian *that all praise him equally*, Ps. Th. 32, 1: Bt. 13; Fox 38, 34, MS. Cot. v. efen-līce.

emn-micel, em-micel; *adj. Equally great;* æque magnus:—Habbaþ emnmicelne willan to cumenne *they have equally great desire to come*, Bt. 36, 4; Fox 178, 10: 42; Fox 256, 10. v. efen-micel.

emn-neáh; *prep. Equally near;* æque prŏpe:—On ǣlcere stōwe he is hire emn-neáh *it is in every place equally near it*, Bt. 33, 4; Fox 130, 23. v. efen-neáh.

emn-rēðe; *adj.* [rēðe *cruel*] *Equally cruel;* æque sævus:—Romulus and Brutus wurdon emnrēðe *Romulus and Brutus were equally cruel*, Ors. 2, 3; Bos. 41, 42.

emn-sâr, es; *n. Equal sorrow* or *contrition;* æquālis dŏlor:—Hie ne māgon ealneg ealla on āne tīd emnsâre hreówan *they cannot always repent of all at one time with equal sorrow*, Past. 53, 3; Hat. MS.

emn-sârian *to be alike sorry, to condole;* condŏlēre, Som. Ben. Lye.

emn-sârig *equally sorry*, Som. Ben. Lye. v. em-sârig, efen-sârig.

emn-sceólere, es; *m. A fellow-scholar;* condiscĭpŭlus:—He ofslōh his emnsceólere *he slew his fellow-scholar*, Ors. 3, 9; Bos. 67, 12.

emnys, -nyss *evenness, equity*, Ps. Spl. 16, 3: 51, 3: 110, 7. v. emnes.

emnyttan *to make equal*, Ælfc. Gr. 47; Som. 48, 56. v. emnettan.

empire *an empire;* impĕrium, Lye.

em-rene, es; *m. A circle;* circŭlus, C. R. Ben. 18. v. ymb-rene.

em-sârig; *adj. Equally sorry;* æque tristis:—Hī woldon ðæt ða ōðre wīf wǣran emsârige heom *they wished the other women to be equally sorry with themselves*, Ors. 1, 10; Bos. 33, 1. v. efen-sârig.

em-snīðan; *p.* -snāþ, *pl.* -snidon; *pp.* -sniden *To circumcise;* circumcīdĕre:—Ge emsnīðaþ ðæt flǣsc eówres fylmenes *circumcīdētis carnem præpūtii vestri*, Gen. 17, 11. v. ymb-snīðan.

em-swāpen *clothed;* amictus, Som. Ben. Lye. v. ymb-swāpan.

emta, an; *m. Leisure;* ōtium:—On emtan to smeágeanne *to study at leisure*, Bd. pref. S. 471, 10. Ic get emtan næbbe *I have not leisure yet*, Bt. 38, 2; Fox 196, 24. v. æmta.

emtig; *adj. Empty, idle;* vacuus, ōtiōsus:—Hīg synt emtige *they are idle*, Ex. 5, 8. v. æmtig.

em-trymming, e; *f. A fortress, fence;* mūnīmentum, Som. Ben. Lye. v. ymb-trymming.

em-twā *two even parts, halves;* dīmĭdia:—Ne dǣlaþ on emtwā heora dagas *non dīmĭdiābunt dies suos*, Ps. Lamb. 54, 24. He tobærst on emtwā *he burst asunder into halves*, Homl. Th. ii. 250, 26.

-en. I. *m.* forms only a few masculine *terminations* of nouns; as, þeóden; *gen.* þeódnes; *m. a king*, from þeód *people:* dryhten; *gen.* dryhtnes; *m. a lord*, from dryht *people, subjects.* II. *f.* -en forms many feminine nouns = the *Ger.* -in, *Dan.* -inde; as, þīnen, e; *f. a maid-servant* [*Ger.* dienerin], from þēn [*Ger.* diener]: þeówen, e; *f. a female slave*, from þeów: wylen; *gen.* wylne; *f. the same*, from weal *a slave:* mennen, e; *f. a maid-servant*, from manna: gyden, e; *f. a goddess*, from god: munecen, e; *f. a nun*, from munec: câsern [= câsere + en], e; *f. an empress*, from câsere: fyxen, e; *f. a she-fox*, from fox. Also -en forms many nouns of the *f.* gender [corresponding to the *Icel.* -n, -in]; as, Segen; *gen.* segne; *f. tradition, saying, Icel.* sögn: gȳmen, e; *f. heed, care:* byrgen, e; *f. a tomb:* sylen, e; *f. a gift:* byrðen, e; *f. a burden:* hiwrǣden; *gen.* hiwrǣdenne; *f. a family, house:* and several others in -rǣden; as, Gecwydrǣden, e; *f. an agreement, contract:* mǣg-rǣden, e; *f. relationship:* gefēr-rǣden, -rǣdenn, e; *f. a train, company, congregation.* III. some nouns in -en are neuters [corresponding to the *Icel.* -in, -en]; as, Mægen, es; *n. strength, might* = *Icel.* megin, magn: mǣden, es; *n. a maiden:* wēsten, es; *n. a waste, desert:* swefen, es; *n. a dream:* midlen, es; *n. a middle:* fæsten, es; *n. a fortress, fastness.*

-en is a termination of adjectives,—hence from fȳr *fire* is fȳren *fiery;* stǣn *a stone;* stǣnen *stony:* -en is also the termination of *pp.* in strong verbs; arisen *risen*, from arīsan *to rise;* dolfen *digged*, from delfan *to dig;* witen *known*, from witan *to know.*

ēn = ǣn = ān- *one*, as,—ǣn-līc, *q. v.* = ān-līc; ēn-wintre *one winter, q. v;* ēn-līc = ān-līc, *q. v;* ēn-līpig = ān-līpig, *q. v.*

encgel, es; *m. An angel;* angĕlus:—Hālig encgel *a holy angel*, Cd. 226; Th. 301, 24; Sat. 586, = engel *an angel.*

ēnd; *adv. Formerly, of old;* prius, ōlim:—Ic adreág fela siððan ðū ēnd to me in sīðadest *I have suffered much since thou didst come to me of old*, Exon. 120 b; Th. 463, 16; Hö. 71.

-end, es; *m.* the ending of nouns, denoting the agent:—Wegferend, es; *m. a way-faring man.*

ENDE, es; *m.* I. *an* END; fīnis, termĭnus:—Ac nys ðonne gyt se ende *sed nondum est fīnis*, Mt. Bos. 24, 6. Ā būtan ende *ever without end*, L. E. I. prm; Th. ii. 400, 28. Ðæt hī ðæs gewinnes sumne ende gedyden *that they would make an end of the war*, Ors. 2, 2; Bos. 41, 1. Ðū eart eallra þinga fruma and ende *thou art the beginning and end of all things*, Bt. Met. Fox 20, 549; Met. 20, 275: Andr. Kmbl. 1112; An. 556. II. *a corner, part, sort;* angŭlus, pars, spĕcies:—Ðæt sylfe wæter ðæt hī ða bān mid þwōgan, gutan in ǣnne ende ðære cyricean *the selfsame water that they washed the bones with, they poured into one corner of the church* [in angŭlo sacrārii], Bd. 3, 11; S. 535, 33. Harold of-slōh ðǣr mycelne ende ðæs folces *Harold slew there a great part of the people*, Chr. 1052; Gib. 166, 22; Th. 319, 14, col. 1. On feówer endum ðyses middangeardes *in the four parts of this world*, Ors. 2, 1; Bos. 38, 21. Ofer ealle eorþan endas *over all parts of the earth*, Ps. Th. 18, 4. Ne hæfde wit ōðer uncymran hors and ōðres endes *numquid non hăbuĭmus ĕquos vīliōres, vel ălias spĕcies*, Bd. 3, 14; S. 540, 27. [*Chauc. Wyc.* ende: *O. Sax.* endi, *m. n: Frs.* eyn, eyne: *O. Frs.* enda, einde, eind, ein, *m: Dut.* einde, *n: Ger.* ende, *n: M. H. Ger.* ende, *n. m: O. H. Ger.* anti, enti, *m. n: Goth.* andeis, *m: Dan.* ende, *m. f: Swed.* ände, *m: Icel.* endi, endir, *m: Sansk.* anta, *m.*] DER. eást-ende, norþ-, west-, woruld-.

-ende, the termination forming the active participle:—Wegfer-ende *way-faring:* also found for -enne. v. -anne.

ende-byrd, es; *n? An arranging, arrangement, order;* ordo:—Se Ælmihtiga ealra gesceafta endebyrd wundorlīce gemetgaþ *the Almighty wonderfully regulates the arrangement of all creatures*, Bt. Met. Fox 13, 8; Met. 13, 4.

ende-byrdan; *p.* de; *pp.* ed *To set in order, adjust, dispose;* dispōnĕre, Ps. Spl. 49, 6.

ende-byrdes; *adv. Orderly, for order;* per ordĭnem, ordĭnātim:—Ðe him rōdera Weard endebyrdes gesette *which the Guardian of the skies has orderly appointed for them*, Bt. Met. Fox 11, 41; Met. 11, 21. Ðū ðysne middangeard todǣldest swā hit getǣsost wæs endebyrdes *thou hast divided this middle earth as it was most suitable for order*, 20, 23; Met. 20, 12.

ende-byrdlīc; *adj. Belonging to order, ordinal;* ordĭnālis:—Endebyrdlīce naman *ordĭnālia nōmĭna*, Ælfc. Gr. 49; Som. 49, 53.

ende-byrdlīce; *adv. Orderly, in order, in succession;* successīve:—Ealle ðās wǣron endebyrdlīce bisceophāda brūcende on Myrcna þeóde *all these in succession enjoyed the bishopric of Mercia*, Bd. 3, 24; S. 558, 4. Endebyrdlīce *in order*, Bt. 33, 4; Fox 128, 7.

ende-byrdnes, -byrnes, -ness, e; *f. Order, disposition, method, way, manner, means;* ordo:—Ōþ endebyrdnesse *ex ordĭne*, Lk. Bos. 1, 3. On endebyrdnesse *in ordĭne*, 1, 8.

ende-dæg; *gen.* -dæges; *pl. nom. acc.* -dagas; *gen.* -daga; *dat.* -dagum; *m. The last day, the day of one's death;* dies suprēmus, dies mortis:—Ðā wæs endedæg ðæs ðe Caldēas cyningdōm āhton *then was the last day that the Chaldeans held the kingdom*, Cd. 209; Th. 258, 22; Dan. 679. Ic sceal endedæg mīnne gebīdan *I shall await my last day*, Beo. Th. 1279; B. 637. Ān endedæg *one ending day*, Apstls. Kmbl. 157; Ap. 79.

ende-deáþ, es; *m.* [ende *an end;* deáþ *death*] *Final death;* mors vītam fīniens:—Līf būtan endedeáþe *life without final death*, Exon. 32 a; Th. 101, 4; Cri. 1653.

ende-dōgor, es; *m. n. The final day, day of one's death;* fīnālis dies, mortis dies:—Wæs endedōgor neáh geþrungen *the final day was near at hand*, Exon. 46 a; Th. 158, 8; Gū. 905: 49 b; Th. 171, 11; Gū. 1125: 50 a; Th. 174, 7; Gū. 1174. Ðæt eorlwerod sæt on wēnum endedōgores *the warrior band sat in expectation of the final day [death]*, Beo. Th. 5784; B. 2896. Nis nū swīðe feor ðam ȳtemestan endedōgor *it is now not very far to the utmost final day*, Exon. 49 b; Th. 172, 8; Gū. 1140. Bād se endedōgor *he awaited [his] final day*, 51 b; Th. 179, 10; Gū. 1259.

ende-lāf, e; *f.* [ende *an end;* lāf *a remainder, remnant*] *The last remnant;* extrēmum relĭquum:—Ðū eart endelāf usses cynnes *thou art the last remnant of our race*, Beo. Th. 5618; B. 2813.

ende-leán, es; *n.* [leán *a reward*] *A final reward;* fīnālis retrĭbūtio:—Him ðæs æfter becwom yfel endeleán *for this an evil final reward came on him afterwards*, Cd. 181; Th. 227, 15; Dan. 187. Him endeleán þurh wæteres wylm Waldend sealde *the Almighty gave to them a final reward through the water's rage*, Beo. Th. 3389; B. 1692.

ende-leás; *adj.* ENDLESS, *infinite, eternal;* infīnītus, perpĕtuus, æternus:—Ðæt is endeleás wundor *that is an endless wonder*, Bt. 36, 1; Fox 172, 18: Exon. 100 b; Th. 379, 8; Deór. 30: Andr. Kmbl. 1389; An. 695. Hȳ sceolon sâr endeleás forþ þrōwian *they must thenceforth suffer endless pain*, Exon. 31 b; Th. 99, 30; Cri. 1632: 69 a; Th. 257, 22;

Jul. 251. Ða earmþa beóþ endeleáse ðe ēce bióþ *those miseries are endless which are eternal*, Bt. 38, 2; Fox 198, 16.

ende-leáslīce; *adv.* ENDLESSLY, *eternally*; infīnīte, Som. Ben. Lye.

ende-leásnys, -nyss, e; *f.* ENDLESSNESS, *eternity*; infīnītas, Ælfc. Gr. 18; Som. 21, 58.

ende-līf, es; *n. An end of life, death*; vīta fīnīta, mors:—Wurdon hie deáþes on wēnan, ādes and endelīfes *they were in expectation of death, of the funeral pile and end of life*, Elen. Kmbl. 1166; El. 585.

ende-mæst *endmost, last*; extrēmus, Som. Ben. Lye.

ende-mes, endemest, ændemes, ændemest; *adv. Equally, likewise, in like manner, together*; părĭter:—Forðon ic ne mæg eal ða monigfealdan yfel endemes areccan *because I cannot equally reckon all the manifest evils*, Ors. 2, 5; Bos. 49, 11: 3, 10; Bos. 69, 36. Ne mæg hió ealle endemest gescīnan *nor can she equally shine upon all*, Bt. 41, 1; Fox 244, 9.

endemestnes, -ness, e; *f. An extremity*; extrēmĭtas, R. Ben. interl. 6.

ende-nêhst, -nȳhst, ende-nēxta, ende-nīhsta; *adj. The nighest end, the last, uttermost*; ultĭmus:—Drihten, ðū oncneówe ealle ða nywestan odðe ða endenīhstan [MS. ændenihstan] *Dŏmĭne, tu cognōvisti omnia novissĭma*, Ps. Lamb. 138, 5. Februārius se mōnaþ is ealra scyrtst and endenȳhst *February is the shortest and last month of all*, Bd. de nat. rerum; Wrt. popl. science 13, 28; Lchdm. iii. 264, 8.

ende-rīm, es; *n. The final number, the number*; fīnālis nŭmĕrus:—Daga enderīm he gesette *he set the number of days*, Cd. 213; Th. 265, 24; Sat. 12.

ende-sǣta, an; *m. An end* or *border inhabitant, one stationed at the extremity of a territory*; līmĭtis incŏla, Beo. Th. 487; B. 241.

ende-spæc, e; *f. An end-speech, epilogue*; epĭlŏgus, Reg. Conc. in Epĭlŏgo.

ende-stæf; *pl. nom. acc.* -stafas; *m. An epilogue, conclusion, destruction*; epĭlŏgus, perorātio:—Heó endestæf gesceáwiaþ *they shall behold their end*, Cd. 225; Th. 298, 30; Sat. 541.

endian, ændian; *p.* ode; *pp.* od *To* END, *make an end*; fīnīre, dēsĭnēre:—Hī hit endian sceoldon *they should end it*, Ps. Th. 9, 6. v. ge-endian.

endleofan, endlufon, endlyfun, *inflected cases of* endleof, endluf, endlyf [end = ān *one*; unus; leof = lif, *from* līfan *to leave*; relinquĕre, Grm. ii. 947, *or* end = ān *one*; lif *ten*; dĕcem; *existing in Teutonic languages only in the words for* 11 *and* 12; *A. Sax.* end-lif *and* twē-lf = twā-lf = twâ-lif, Grm. Gsch. § 246] ELEVEN; undĕcim = ἕν-δεκα:—Ōsrēd ðæt rīce hæfde endleofan wintra *Osred held the kingdom for eleven years*, Bd. 5, 18; S. 635, 20. Mid hīra endlufon sunum *cum undĕcim fīliis*, Gen. 32, 22. Endleofan steorran *eleven stars*, Gen. 37, 9: Chr. 71; Th. 13, 3, col. 3. [*Wyc.* enleuene, enleuen, enleue: *R. Glouc.* endleve: *Laym.* elleoue, elleouen: *Plat.* elv, elwen: *O. Sax.* ellevan: *Frs.* alve, alue: *O. Frs.* andlova, elleva: *Dut.* elf: *Ger.* eilf, elf: *M. H. Ger.* einlif, einlef: *O. H. Ger.* einlif: *Goth.* ainlif: *Dan.* elleve: *Swed.* elfva: *Icel.* ellifu.] v. twelf.

endlyfta, ændlyfta, ællyfta; seó, ðæt, -e; *adj. The eleventh*; undĕcĭmus:—On ðam endlyftan mōnþe *undĕcĭmo mense*, Deut. 1, 3. Endlyfta ðæra tâcna ys gehâten āquārius *the eleventh of the signs is called ăquārius*, Bd. de nat. rerum; Wrt. popl. science 7, 9; Lchdm. iii. 246, 3.

endung, e; *f. An* ENDING, *end*; finis, consummātio:—Ðæt rīp is worulde endung *messis consummātio sæcŭli est*, Mt. Bos. 13, 39. DER. ge-endung.

end-werc, es; *n.* [werc = wærc *pain*] *A pain in the buttocks*; nătium dŏlor:—Ðes drænc is gōd wið endwerce *this drink is good for pain in the buttocks*, Lchdm. iii. 50, 11.

ENED, e; *f.* I. *a duck*; ănas, *gen.* ănătis; *f.* ănĕta:—Ōþ enede mēre *to the duck's mere*, Cod. Dipl. 204; A. D. 814; Kmbl. i. 258, 5. Ened *ănĕta*, Ælfc. Gr. 7; Som. 6, 52: Wrt. Voc. 77, 22: 280, 8. II. ened, es; *m. A drake*; ănas, ănĕtārius, mascŭlus istīus ăvis:—Ened *a drake?* ănas, *gen.* ănătis; *m.* Ælfc. Gl. 36; Som. 62, 122; Wrt. Voc. 29, 18. Ened *a drake?* larax? Wrt. Voc. 280, 9. [*Dut.* eend, end, *f. a duck*; *m. a drake*: *Ger.* ente, *f. a duck*; enterich, *m. a drake*: *M. H. Ger.* ant, *f. a duck*; *m. a drake*: *O. H. Ger.* anut, anit *ănas*: *Dan.* and, *m. f*: *Swed.* and, *f. a wild duck*: *Icel.* önd, *f. pl.* endr, andir *a duck*: *Lat.* ănas, *gen.* ănătis, *m. f*: *Grk.* νῆττα, νῆσσα, *f. a duck.*]

eneleác, es; *n. An onion*; cæpe:—We hæfdon porleác and eneleác *in mentem nōbis vĕniunt porri et cæpe*, Num. 11, 5. v. enneleác.

enetere, ēnitre; *adj. Of a year old*; annĭcŭlus:—Ðū dēst ǣlce dæg on ðæt weofod twā ēnetere lamb *făcies in altāri agnos annĭcŭlos duos per singŭlos dies*, Ex. 29, 38. v. ān-wintre.

ênga *sole*:—Mid ðīnne ēngan Freán *with thy sole Lord*, Exon. 11 a; Th. 15, 17; Cri. 237. v. ānga.

enge *from confinement*, Cd. 71; Th. 86, 23; Gen. 1435. v. engu.

enge; *def.* se enga; *adj. Narrow, anxious*; angustus, anxius:—Ufan hit is enge *it is narrow above*, Exon. 116 a; Th. 446, 14; Dōm. 22: 47 a; Th. 162, 3; Gū. 970. Of ðam engan hofe *from that narrow house*, 73 b; Th. 274, 12; Jul. 532: 8 a; Th. 3, 6; Cri. 32. Enge ānpaðas *narrow passes*, Cd. 145; Th. 181, 8; Exod. 58; Beo. Th. 2824; B. 1410. Helle wisceþ, ðæs engestan ēðel-rīces *shall wish for hell, the narrowest realm*, Salm. Kmbl. 213; Sal. 106. v. ange.

ENGEL, ængel, angel, engyl; *gen.* engles; *dat.* engle; *pl. nom. acc.* englas, engel; *gen.* engla; *dat.* englum; *m. An* ANGEL, *a messenger*; angĕlus = ἄγγελος:—Se engel him to cwæþ *dixit illis angĕlus*, Lk. Bos. 2, 10: 1, 13: Mt. Bos. 28, 5: Gen. 22, 12. Godes engel stōd on emn hī *the angel of God stood before them*, Homl. Th. i. 30, 15, 17: Mt. Bos. 1, 20, 24: Jn. Bos. 5, 4. Ðæt mæg engel ðīn eáþ geferan *that thine angel may more easily travel*, Andr. Kmbl. 387; An. 194. Þurh ðæs engles word *through the angel's word*, Exon. 20 a; Th. 51, 31; Cri. 824: 34 b; Th. 110, 11; Gū. 106: Salm. Kmbl. 901; Sal. 450: Homl. Th. i. 30, 22. He ðam engle oncwæþ *he spake to the angel*, Cd. 141; Th. 176, 12; Gen. 2910: Lk. Bos. 2, 13. God sent his engel befōran ðē *Dŏmĭnus mittet angĕlum suum cōram te*, Gen. 24, 7: 16, 7. Māran cȳðde habbaþ englas to Gode ðonne men *angels are more like God than men*, Homl. Th. i. 10, 3. Englas blāwaþ bȳman *angels shall blow the trumpet*, Exon. 20 b; Th. 55, 9; Cri. 881: 14 a; Th. 28, 17; Cri. 448. Cōmon twegen englas *vēnērunt duo angĕli*, Gen. 19, 1, 12, 15. Beheóldon ðæt [MS. ðær] engel Dryhtnes ealle *all the angels of the Lord beheld it*, Rood Kmbl. 18; Kr. 9. Hēr sindon nigon engla werod *here are nine hosts of angels*, Homl. Th. i. 10, 14: 12, 8: Elen. Kmbl. 2559; El. 1281. Engla rīce *the kingdom of angels*, 2460; El. 1231. Engla beorhtast *brightest of angels*, Exon. 9 b; Th. 7, 21; Cri. 104. Gif ðū in heofonrīce habban wille eard mid englum *if thou wilt have in heaven's realm a dwelling with angels*, Elen. Kmbl. 1240; El. 622: Andr. Kmbl. 1197; An. 599: 3440; An. 1724. Mid hys englum *cum angĕlis suis*, Mt. Bos. 16, 27. Englas God worhte, ða sind gāstas, and nabbaþ nǣnne līchaman *God created angels, which are spirits, and have no body*, Homl. Th. i. 276, 1. Mannes sunu sent his englas *mittet fīlius hŏmĭnis angĕlos suos*, Mt. Bos. 13, 41: Mk. Bos. 13, 27. [*Wyc.* aungel: *Chauc.* aungel: *Laym.* engles, *pl*: *Orm.* enngell: *O. Sax.* engil, *m*: *Frs.* ingel: *O. Frs.* angel, angl, engel, *m*: *Dut. Ger. M. H. Ger.* engel, *m*: *O. H. Ger.* engil, *m*: *Goth.* aggilus, *m*: *Dan.* engel, *m. f*: *Swed.* engel, *m*: *Icel.* engill, *m*: *Lat.* angĕlus, *m*: *Grk.* ἄγγελος, *m. f. a messenger, angel.*] DER. heáh-engel, heofon-, up-.

Engel; *gen.* Engle; *f. Anglen in Denmark, the country from which the Angles came into Britain*; Angŭlus, terra quam Angli ante transitum in Britanniam cŏluērunt:—Of Engle cōman Eást-Engle, and Middel-Engle, and Myrce, and eall Norþhembra cynn *from Anglen came the East-Angles, and Middle-Angles, and Mercians, and all the race of the Northumbrians*, Bd. 1, 15; S. 483, 24. v. Angel.

engel-cund; *adj. Angelic*; angĕlĭcus = ἀγγελικός:—God him giefe sealde engelcunde *God gave him angelic grace*, Exon. 34 a; Th. 108, 13; Gū. 72.

engel-cyn, -cynn, es; *n.* [engel *angĕlus*; cyn, cynn *gĕnus*] *The angel race* or *order*; gĕnus *vel* ordo angĕlōrum:—Wæs ðæt engelcyn [MS. encgelcyn] genemned *the angel race was named*, Cd. 221; Th. 287, 12; Sat. 366. Ðū sitest ofer ðam engelcynne *thou sittest above the angel race*, Elen. Kmbl. 1463; El. 733. Hæfde se Ealwalda engelcynna tyne getrymede *the Almighty had ten established orders of angels*, Cd. 14; Th. 16, 21; Gen. 246: Andr. Kmbl. 1434; An. 717.

engel-līc, engle-līc; *adj. Angelic*; angĕlĭcus:—He ge-earnode ðæt he wæs brūcende engellīcre gesihþe *angĕlĭca mĕruit vīsiōne perfrui*, Bd. 3, 19; S. 547, 13.

Engla feld; *gen.* feldes; *dat.* felda, felde; *m.* [*Hovd.* Englefeld: *Brom.* Englefelde: *Matt. West.* Anglefeld; *Angles' field, the field of the English*] ENGLEFIELD OR INGLEFIELD, *near Reading, Berkshire*; lŏci nōmen in agro Berkeriensi:—Hēr cwom se here to Reádingum on West-Seaxe, and ðæs ymb iii niht ridon ii eorlas up: ðā gemētte hie Æðelwulf aldorman on Engla felda, and him ðǣr wið gefeaht, and sige nam *in this year* [A. D. 871] *the army came to Reading in Wessex, and three nights after two earls rode up: then alderman Æthelwulf met them at Inglefield, and there fought against them, and gained the victory*, Chr. 871; Erl. 74, 5–8.

Engla land, es; *n. The land of the Angles* or *Engles*, ENGLAND; Anglōrum terra. It extended in the time of Bede, A. D. 731, from the present Lincolnshire to the Frith of Forth, on the south of which Æbbercurnig is located:—Ðæt mynster Æbbercurnīg, ðæt is geseted on Engla lande *the minster Abercorn, that is seated in the land of the Angles*, or Engla land = England, Bd. 4, 26; S. 602, 36.

Englan; *gen.* ena; *dat.* um; *acc.* an; *pl. m. The Angles*; Angli:—Ða Wealas flugon ða Englan [= Engle, Th. 22, 27, col. 2, 3] *the Welsh fled from the Angles*, Chr. 473; Th. 23, 26, col. 2; 23, 27, col. 1. Betweox Wealan and Englan *between the Welsh and Angles*, L. O. D. 2; Th. i. 354, 2: 3; Th. i. 354, 10. v. Engle, Angle *the Angles*.

englas *angels*, Homl. Th. i. 276, 1. v. engel.

Engle, Angle; *pl. nom. acc*; *gen.* a; *dat.* um; *pl. m*: Englan; *gen.* ena; *pl. m. The Angles*; Angli *The inhabitants of Anglen in Denmark*. Anglen was the province from which the English derived their being and name. Anglen [v. Engel] lies on the south-east part of the Duchy of Sleswick, in Denmark. The majority of settlers in Britain were from Anglen and the neighbourhood, hence this country and people derived their name *England* and *English*, England being derived from Engla land *the land* or *country of the Angles*:—On dǽm landum eardodon Engle, ǽr hȳ hider on land cōmon *the Angles* [*Engles*] *dwelt on these lands before they came hither on land* [i. e. *before they came to England*], Ors. 1, 1; Bos. 21, 36. Engla cyningas *kings of the Angles*, Bd. 2, 15; S. 518, 38. Betweox Wealum and Englum *between the Welsh and English*, L. O. D. 2; Th. i. 352, 14.

Engle *of Anglen*, Bd. 1, 15; S. 483, 24; *gen. dat. acc. of* Engel *Anglen*, q. v.

engle-līc; *adj. Angelic;* angĕlĭcus:—Englelīce ansȳne hī habbaþ *angĕlĭcam hăbent făciem*, Bd. 2, 1; S. 501, 18. v. engel-līc.

Englisc, Ænglisc; *adj.* ENGLISH; Anglĭcus:—Hēr syndon on đis īglande [Britene] fīf geþeóda [MS. þeóda], Englisc, and Brytisc, ... and Scyttisc, and Pihtisc, [and Bōc-Lǽden] *here are in this island* [*Britain*] *five languages, English, and British, ... and Scottish, and Pictish,* [*and Book-Latin*], Chr. Th. 3, 3–6, col. 3, 2. Đæt is on Englisc, mīn God *that is in English, my God*, Mt. Bos. 27, 46. On Englisc *in English*, Bd. 3, 19; S. 547, 22. On Englisc land, ne Englisc on Wilisc *in England* [*English land*], *nor English in Welsh*, L. O. D. 6; Wilk. 126, 3. Awendan of Lēdene on Englisc *to translate from Latin into English*, Ælfc. pref. Gen. 1, 4. Seó bōc is on Englisc awend *the book is turned* [*translated*] *into English*, Homl. Th. ii. 358, 30. Ic [Ælfrīc Abbod] gesett hæbbe wel feówertig lārspella on Engliscum gereorde *I* [*Abbot Ælfric*] *have composed about forty sermons in the English tongue*, Ælfc. T. 27, 17. Đeáh đa scearpþanclan witan đisse Engliscan geþeódnesse ne behōfien *though the sharp-minded wise men need not this English translation*, MS. Cot. Faust. A. x. 150 b; Lchdm. iii. 440, 31.

Englisc-man, -mon, es; *m. An Englishman;* Anglĭcānus:—Ic wille đæt gē fēdaþ ealle wæga ān earm Engliscmon *I will that ye entirely feed one poor Englishman*, L. Ath. i. prm; Th. i. 198, 5.

engu, e; *f. Narrowness, confinement, a narrow place;* angustiæ:—Of enge *from confinement*, Cd. 71; Th. 86, 23; Gen. 1435: Exon. 101 b; Th. 383, 17; Rä. 4, 12. On enge, Th. 383, 3; Rä. 4, 5. [*Ger. M. H. Ger.* enge, *f. angustiæ: O. Nrs.* öngum, *dat. pl. angustiis.*]

engyl, es; *m. An angel;* angĕlus:—His engyl ongan ofermōd wesan *his angel began to be presumptuous*, Cd. 14; Th. 17, 19; Gen. 262: 15; Th. 19, 18; Gen. 293: Mt. Bos. 11, 10. v. engel.

enid *a duck, drake, coot, water-fowl;* ănăs, ănĕta, fulĭca, Som. Ben. Lye. v. ened.

ēnig *any*, Th. Diplm. A. D. 830; 466, 1. v. ǽnig.

ēnitre; *adj. Of a year old;* annĭcŭlus:—Gif seó offrung beó of sceápon ođđe of gātum, bring ēnitre offrunge *if the offering be of sheep or of goats, bring an offering of a year old*, Lev. 1, 10. v. ēnetere.

ēn-līc *only;* ūnĭcus, Lye. v. ān-līc.

en-līhtan *to enlighten*, Som. Ben. Lye. v. on-līhtan.

ēn-līpig *each;* singŭlāris, Ælfc. Gr. 49, Lye. v. ān-līpig.

-enne *the termination of the declinable infinitive in the dat. governed by* to, as,—To farenne *to go*, Mt. Bos. 8, 21. v. -anne.

enneleác, ennelēc, eneleác, ynneleác, yneleác, es; *n.* [leác *a leek, onion*] *An onion;* cæpe, ūnio:—Enneleác *an onion*, Glos. Brux. Recd. 41, 19; Wrt. Voc. 67, 34. Ennelēc *cæpe*, Ælfc. Gl. 40; Som. 63, 106; Wrt. Voc. 30, 54.

ent, es; *m. A giant;* gĭgas = γίγας:—He geblissode swā swā se mǽsta ođđe swā swā ent to ge-yrnanne weg his *exultāvit ut gĭgas ad currendam viam ejus*, Ps. Lamb. 18, 6: Ps. Spl. 32, 16: Wrt. Voc. 73, 52. Nembroþ se ent *Nimrod the giant*, Boutr. Scrd. 21, 35: Ors. 2, 4; Bos. 44, 17. Dauid eóde to ānwīge ongeán đone ent Goliam *David went in single combat against the giant Goliath*, Ælfc. T. 14, 3: Ors. 1, 10; Bos. 33, 29. Entas wǽron ofer eorþan on đām dagum *gĭgantes ĕrant sŭper terram in diēbus illis*, Gen. 6, 4: Homl. Th. i. 318, 15. He seah on enta geweorc *he looked on the work of giants*, Beo. Th. 5428; B. 2717: Exon. 77 b; Th. 291, 24; Wand. 87: Andr. Kmbl. 2988; An. 1497: Menol. Fox 463; Gn. C. 2. v. eten, eóten.

ent-cyn, -cynn, es; *n. Giant-kind, giant-race;* gĭgantum gĕnus:—We gesāwon of đam entcynne Enachis bearna micelra wæstma *vĭdĭmus monstra quædam fīliōrum Enac prōcēræ stătūræ*, Num. 13, 34.

entisc *belonging to* or *made by a giant, giant;* gigantēus:—Lēt entiscne helm brecan *he caused the giant helmet to break*, Beo. Th. 5951; B. 2979. v. eótenisc.

entse, an; *f. A shekel, Jewish money;* siclus:—Ic geseah twāhund entsena hwītes seolfres and sumne gildenne dalc on fīftigum entsum *vīdi dŭcentos siclos argenti rēgŭlamque auream quinquāginta siclōrum*, Jos. 7, 21. v. yntse.

ēn-wintre; *adj. Of a year old;* annĭcŭlus:—Ēnwintre *vecta?* Wrt. Voc. 287, 60. v. ān-wintre.

eo. I. unaccented, *generally* stands before *two consonants* lc, ld, lf, rc, rd, rf, rg, rh, rl, rm, rn, rp, rr, rt, rþ, x; as, Geolca *a yolk*, sceolde *should*, seolfor *silver*, deorc *dark*, sweord *a sword*, ceorfan *to carve*, beorgan *to protect*, beorht *bright*, eorl *earl*, beorma *barm*, eornost *earnest*, weorpan *to throw*, steorra *a star*, heorte *the heart*, eorþe *the earth*, meox *dung*. II. eó accented, the diphthong, generally stands before the consonants c, d, f, g, h, l, m, n, p, r, s, st, t, w; as, Seóc *sick*, beódan *to bid*, þeóf *a thief*, fleógan *to fly*, hreóh *rough*, hweól *a wheel*, leóma *a ray of light*, beón *to be*, deóp *deep*, beór *beer*, ceósan *to choose*, breóst *the breast*, fleótan *to float*, leóþ *a song*, ceówan *to chew*. 2. eó is also the termination of many words, and then the ó in eó is always accented; as, Beó *a bee;* ic beó *I shall be;* freó *free;* gleó *glee;* seó *the;* seó *sim, sis, sit;* treó *a tree;* þreó *three*, etc

eó the Runic character for these letters is ᛇ. v. eóh = īw *a yew-tree.*

eóc, eócon *increased; p. of* eácan.

eóc *safety, help, succour*, Wald. 45; Vald. 1, 25. v. geóc.

eóde, es; *n. A flock;* grex:—Đæt lytle eóde *pŭsillus grex*, Lk. Skt. Rush. 12, 32. v. eówde.

eóde, đū eódest, *pl.* eódon *went, delivered*, Ps. Th. 60, 4: 67, 21: 94, 11; *p. of* gān.

EODOR, eoder, eodur, edor, eder, es; *m.* I. *a hedge, fence, enclosure, dwelling, house;* sēpes, sēpīmentum, dŏmus, tectum:—Hēht đā eahta mearas on flet teón in under eoderas *he commanded then eight steeds to be led into the court under the enclosures*, Beo. Th. 2078; B. 1037. II. *a limit, end, region, zone;* ōra, margo, extrēmĭtas, plăga, rĕgio:—Gescōp heofon and eorþan and holma bigong eodera ymbhwyrft [*he*] *created heaven and earth and the seas' expanse, the circuit of zones*, Exon. 67 b; Th. 249, 17; Jul. 113. III. *a prince, sovereign, protector;* princeps, tūtor:—Ic đē biddan wille, eodor Scyldinga, ānre bēne *I will entreat of thee, sovereign of the Scyldings, one boon*, Beo. Th. 860; B. 428: 2092; B. 1044: Exon. 90 a; Th. 339, 6; Gn. Ex. 90. [*O. Sax.* edor, *m: M. H. Ger.* ëter, *m. n: O. H. Ger.* ëtar: *Icel.* jaðarr, jöðurr, *m.*] DER. edor-brecþ, -brice, eder-gong, eodor-brice, -wīr.

eodor-brice, edor-brice, -bryce, es; *m.* [eodor, edor *a hedge, fence;* brice, bryce *a breach, breaking*] *A fence-breaking;* sēpis fractio *vel* violātio:—Ceorles eodorbryce [Th. i. 88, 10, note 25, edorbryce, edorbrice] biþ fīf scillinga *for breaking a churl's fence shall be five shillings*, L. Alf. pol. 36; Lambd. 31, 31.

eodorcan, edorcan; *part.* eodorcende; *p.* te; *pp.* ed *To chew, ruminate;* rūmĭnāre:—He eall mid hine gemynegode and swā swā clǽne nȳten eodorcende [*Whelc.* ođer cende] in đæt swēteste leóþ gehwyrfde *ipse cuncta rĕmĕmŏrando sēcum et quăsi mundum ănĭmal rūmĭnando in carmen dulcissĭmum convertēbat*, Bd. 4, 24; S. 598, 7.

eodor-wīr, es; *m. A wire-enclosure;* cingulum, sēpiens fīlum mĕtallĭcum, *Grn*:—Ic eom mundbora mīnre heorde, eodorwīrum fæst *I am the protector of my flock, fortified by wire-enclosures*, Exon. 105 a; Th. 398, 23; Rä. 18, 2.

eodur, es; *m. A prince, sovereign, protector;* princeps, tūtor:—Him Hrōþgār gewāt, eodur Scyldinga *Hrothgar departed, the Scyldings' protector*, Beo. Th. 1330; B. 663. v. eodor.

eofel *evil*, Bt. 7, 3; Fox 22, 19. v. yfel.

eofer *a boar*, Ps. Th. 79, 13: Beo. Th. 2228; B. 1112: 2660; B. 1328. v. eofor.

eofera, an; *m. A successor;* successor:—Æfter Eorpwalde Rǽdwaldes eoferan *post Earpualdum Redualdi successōrem*, Bd. 3, 18; S. 545, 35, col. 1. v. eafora.

eofer-spreót, es; *m. A boar-spear;* contus ad vēnātiōnem ūsĭtātus:—Mid eoferspreótum *with boar-spears*, Beo. Th. 2879; B. 1437. v. eofor-spreót.

Eofer-wīc *York*, Chr. 189; Th. 15, 28, col. 2. v. Eofor-wīc.

Eofes-ham, Eues-ham; *gen.* -hammes; *m.* [*Flor.* Euesham: *Hovd.* Heuesham: *Brom.* Euesham: *Kni.* Evisham, Evysham, Ewesham, Evesham] EVESHAM, *Worcestershire;* oppĭdi nomen in agro Vigorniensi:—Đæs gēres forþfērde Æfic se æđela decanus on Eofesham *in this year* [A. D. 1037] *died Æfic the noble dean at Evesham*, Chr. 1037; Th. 294, 36, col. 2. Ælfward wæs abbad on Eofeshamme ǽrest *Ælfward was first abbot of Evesham*, Chr. 1045; Th. 303, 2. Đæs ylcan geáres man hālgode đæt mynster on Eofeshamme on vi id' Octobris *in the same year* [A. D. 1054] *was consecrated the monastery at Evesham, on the 6th of the Ides of October* [*October 10th*], Chr. 1054; Th. 322, 34, col. 1; 324, 3, col. 2: 1078; Th. 350, 15.

eofet *a debt*, L. Alf. pol. 22; Wilk. 39, 35. v. eofot.

eofne; *interj. Behold!* ecce!—Eofne! đa đe fyrsiaþ hīg fram đē losiaþ *ecce! qui elongant se a te pĕrĭbunt*, Ps. Lamb. 72, 27: 82, 3. v. efne.

EOFOR, eofer, eafor, efor, efer, efyr, ofor, es; *m.* I. *a boar, a wild boar;* ăper:—Fornam hine eofor of wuda *extermĭnāvit eam ăper de silva*, Ps. Spl. 79, 14; Ps. Th. has,—Hine ūtan of wuda eoferas wrōtaþ 79, 13: Exon. 110 b; Th. 423, 8; Rä. 41, 18: 92 a; Th. 344, 20; Gn. Ex. 176. Sele đū him flǽsc eofores *give him boar's flesh*, L. M. 2, 4; Lchdm. ii. 182, 14. II. *the figure of a boar on a helmet;* signum apri sŭper gălеam:—Swȳn eal-gylden, eofer īren-heard *the swine all-golden, the boar iron-hard*, Beo. Th. 2228; B. 1112: 2660; B. 1328. [*Ger.* eber, *m: M. H. Ger.* ëber, *m: O. H. Ger.* ebur, *m: Icel.* jöfurr, *m.*] DER. eofor-cumbol, -fearn, -līc, -spreót, -swīn, -þring, -þrote, -wīc, -wīc-ceaster, -wīcingas, -wīc-scīr: eoforen, eoforen-denu.

eofora *a successor*. v. eafora.

eofor-cumbol, eofur-cumbol, -cumbul, es; *n.* [cumbol *a banner*]

A boar-banner; signum ad apri simĭlĭtūdĭnem fabrĭcātum:—Ðǽr wæs on eorle ǽnlīc eoforcumbul *there was on the man a beauteous boar-shaped ensign,* Elen. Kmbl. 517; El. 259.

eoforen; *adj. Belonging to a boar;* aprīnus, Som.

eoforen-denu, e; *f. A boar-vale;* aprīna vallis, Som. Ben. Lye.

eofor-fearn, efor-fearn, efer-fearn, es; *n.* [fearn *a fern*] *A species of fern, polypody;* polypŏdium vulgāre, Lin:—Eoforfearn *fĭlix mĭnūta, polypŏdium,* Glos. Brux. Recd. 41, 36; Wrt. Voc. 67, 51. Eoforfearn *fĭlĭcīna, fĭlix arbŏrātĭca,* 41, 66; Wrt. Voc. 68, 1. Wiđ đon sceal eoforfearn *polypody shall* [*do*] *for that,* L. M. 1, 12; Lchdm. ii. 56, 1: 1, 63; Lchdm. ii. 138, 15: 2, 51; Lchdm. ii. 266, 16. Genim eoforfearnes mǽst *take most of polypody,* L. M. 1, 15; Lchdm. ii. 56, 20: 1, 59; Lchdm. ii. 130, 9: iii. 74, 4. Eoforfearn dō on hunig *put polypody into honey,* L. M. 1, 60; Lchdm. ii. 130, 24: 1, 87; Lchdm. ii. 154, 17: iii. 56, 19.

eofor-līc, es; *n. A boar-likeness;* apri sĭmŭlacrum:—Eoforlīc scionon *boar's likenesses shone,* Beo. Th. 612; B. 303.

eofor-spreót, eofer-spreót, es; *m. A boar-spear;* vēnābŭlum, Cot. 200. v. eofer-spreót.

eofor-swīn, es; *n. A boar pig, male swine;* verres:—Eoforswīnes cwead *verris stercus,* L. M. 2, 48; Lchdm. ii. 262, 18.

eofor-þring, es; *m. Orion?* v. ebur-þring.

eofor-þrote, an; *f.* [eofor *a boar,* þrote *the throat*] *The carline thistle;* carlina acaulis, Lin:—Eoforþrote *colucus? colicus?* Glos. Brux. Recd. 41, 64; Wrt. Voc. 67, 79: 291, 7. Wiđ heáfodece sceal eoforþrote *carline thistle shall* [*serve*] *for head-ache,* Lchdm. iii. 12, 25: 24, 7: L. M. 1, 31; Lchdm. ii. 74, 18: 1, 48; Lchdm. ii. 122, 13: 1, 62; Lchdm. ii. 134, 19, 28: 3, 8; Lchdm. ii. 312, 16. Nim eoforþrotan sǽd *take seed of carline thistle,* 3, 12; Lchdm. ii. 314, 18. Eoforþrotan awyl on ealaþ *boil carline thistle in ale,* 1, 45; Lchdm. ii. 110, 12, 23: 2, 53; Lchdm. ii. 274, 2: 3, 26; Lchdm. ii. 322, 24: 3, 48; Lchdm. ii. 340, 1.

Eofor-wīc, Eofer-wīc, Efer-wīc, Euer-wīc, es; *n.* [*Hunt.* Eouerwic, Eouorwic, Euerwic: *Dun.* Eworwic: *Hovd.* Eboracum] YORK; Ebŏrācum:—Seuerus ge-endode on Eoforwīc *Severus ended* [*his days*] *at York,* Chr. 189; Th. 15, 28, col. 1.

Eofor-wīc-ceaster; *gen.* -ceastre; *f. York:*—On đære cyricean Eoforwīcceastre *in Eboracensi ecclēsia,* Bd. 5, 24; S. 646, 29: Chr. 644; Th. 48, 20.

Eofor-wīcingas, *pl. m. Yorkists, people of York;* Eboracenses:—Hæfdon Eoforwīcingas gehāten đæt hie on hire rǽdenne beón woldan *the people of York had promised that they would be at her disposal,* Chr. 918; Th. 192, 9.

Eofor-wīc-scīr, e; *f.* YORKSHIRE; comĭtātus Eboracensis:—Fōran đa þegnas ealle on Eoforwīcscīre to Eoferwīc *all the thanes in Yorkshire went to York,* Chr. 1065; Th. 332, 7.

eofot, eofut, eofet, es; *n. A debt, crime;* dēbĭtum, culpa:—Be eofotes andetlan. Gif mon on folces gemōte ge-yppe eofot *of confession of debt. If a man declare a debt at a folk-mote,* L. Alf. pol. 22; Th. i. 76, 6. Reht ođđe eofut ođđe scyld *dēbĭtum,* Mt. Kmbl. Lind. 18, 25. Godes āgen bearn, unscyldigne eofota gehwylces, hēngon on heáne beám fæderas usse *our fathers hung up God's own son on a high tree, guiltless of every crime,* Elen. Kmbl. 846; El. 423.

eofoþ, es; *n. Strength, violence, might,* Beo. Th. 5062, note; B. 2534. v. eafoþ.

eoful-sæc, es; *n?* [eoful = yfel *evil,* sacan *to accuse*] *Evil accusation, blasphemy;* blasphēmia:—Đæt đū eofulsæc ǽfre ne fremme wiđ Godes bearne *that thou never make blasphemy against God's son,* Elen. Kmbl. 1045; El. 524.

eofur-cumbol, es; *n. A boar-banner,* Elen. Kmbl. 151; El. 76. v. eofor-cumbol.

eógoþ, e; *f. Youth;* jŭventus:—Duguþe and eógoþe *with old and young,* Andr. Kmbl. 2245; An. 1124. v. geóguþ.

eoh; *nom. acc: gen.* eohes = eoes = eōs; *m. A war-horse, charger;* ĕquus bellātor:—He gehleóp đone eoh *he mounted the charger,* Byrht. Th. 137, 20; By. 189. Eorl sceal on eōs bōge *a chief shall* [*ride*] *on horse-back,* Exon. 90 a; Th. 337, 11; Gn. Ex. 63. [*O. Sax.* 'ehu-scalc *servus ĕquārius, compos: a* scalc *servus et* ehu *ĕquus, quod et nōmen cūjusdam lĭtĕræ rūnĭcæ Saxŏnĭcæ est;' Heli. Schmel: O. Nrs.* jó-r *vel* ió-r,—'*sŏnus hūjus lĭtĕræ ĭdem fuit, atque hŏdie, in lingua vĕtĕre, sed ad fĭgūram et nōmen quod attĭnet, non distinguēbātur ab i:' Egils.*—*gen.* jó-s, ió-s; *dat.* jó, ió; *acc.* jó, ió, ó; *pl. gen. acc.* jóa, ióa.] v. eh.

eóh = īw; *m. The Anglo-Saxon Rune* ᛇ = eó, the name of which letters in Anglo-Saxon is eóh = īw *a yew-tree;* taxus,—hence this Rune not only stands for the diphthong eó, but for eóh *a yew-tree,* as,—ᛇ [Eóh] biþ ūtan unsmēđe treów, heard, hrusan fæst *yew is outwardly an unsmooth tree, hard, fast in the earth,* Hick. Thes. i. 135, 25; Runic pm. 13; Kmbl. 341, 26. v. īw and RŪN.

eoldra, eolldra *older,* Bt. 16, 1; Fox 50, 7. Eolldra fæder *grandfather,* Bt. 10; Fox 28, 32; *comp. of* eald.

eolet, es; *n. The sea, ocean;* măre, ōceănus:—Đā wæs sundliden eoletes æt ende *then was the sea-voyage at the end of the ocean,* Beo. Th. 453, note; B. 224.

EOLH, eolc; *gen.* eolhes, eolces, eolcs, eolx; *m.* [eolx *vĭdētur genĭtīvus ab* eolc, eolh, Ettmül. Poet. 288, 15, note] *An* ELK; alces. The Rune ᛉ = x seems to stand for *the genitive* of this word in the Runic poem,—hence, this Rune not only stands for the letter *x,* but for eolhx = eolcx = eolcs = eolces *of an elk,* as,—ᛉ [eolhx = eolces] secg eard [seccard MS.] hæfþ oftust on fenne, wexeþ on wætere *elk's sedge hath its place* [*earth*] *oftest in fen, waxeth in water,* Hick. Thes. i. 135, 29; Runic pm. 15; Kmbl. 342, 7. Eolx secg *papilluum,* Wrt. Voc. 286, 36. [*O. H. Ger.* elaho: *M. H. Ger.* elch: *O. Nrs.* elgr: *Lat.* alces: *Grk.* ἄλκη.] v. RŪN.

eolh-sand *amber;* electrum, Cot. 75.

eolh-stede *a sheltering-place, a temple,* An. 1644. v. ealh-stede.

eolhx, eolx; *gen. sing. of* eolh, eolc *an elk.*

eolone, eolene, elone, elene, an; *f. The plant elecampane;* ĭnŭla hĕlĕnium, Lin:—Genim eolonan *take elecampane,* L. M. 1, 15; Lchdm. ii. 58, 18: 1, 32; Lchdm. ii. 76, 4: 1, 36; Lchdm. ii. 86, 11. Wyrc sealfe of eolonan *make a salve of elecampane,* L. M. 1, 28; Lchdm. ii. 70, 5. Eolene *elecampane,* L. M. 1, 23; Lchdm. ii. 66, 9.

eoloþ *ale,* L. In. 70; Th. i. 146, 17, MS. H. v. ealaþ.

eom [eam, am], đū eart [earþ, art, arþ], he is, ys; *I am, thou art, he is;* sum, es, est: *pl.* sind, sindon [synd, sint, synt, sient, sindan, sindun, syndon, syndan, syndun, siendon, seondon, seondan, siondon, siondan, syondon; earon, earun, earan, aron]: *pl. we, ye, they are;* sŭmus, estis, sunt: *subj.* sī, sȳ, [sig, sige, sīe, sȳe, seó, sió] *if I, if thou, if he be;* sim, sis, sit; *pl.* sīn, sȳn [sīe, sīen, seón] *if we, if ye, if they be;* sīmus, sītis, sint:—Ic eom, *sum,* is edwistlīc word and gebȳraþ to Gode ānum synderlīce, forđanđe God is ǽfre unbegunnen, and unge-endod on him sylfum, and þurh hine sylfne wunigende 'Sum,' *I am, is the substantive verb, and belongs exclusively to God alone, because God is ever without beginning, and without end in himself, and existing by himself,* Ælfc. Gr. 32; Som. 36, 24–26. Ic eom weg, and sōþfæstnys, and līf *ĕgo sum via, et vērĭtas, et vīta,* Jn. Bos. 14, 6. Ic sylf hit eom *ego ipse sum,* Lk. Bos. 24, 39. Ic eom *I am,* Beo. Th. 676; B. 335: Fins. Th. 49; Fin. 24: Exon. 102 b; Th. 388, 1; Rä. 6, 1: Cd. 19; Th. 24, 4; Gen. 372: Cd. 215; Th. 270, 28; Sat. 97: Ps. Th. 68, 6: Bd. 5, 19; S. 640, 40. [*Orm.* amm, arrt, iss, *pl.* arrn, sinndenn; *subj.* sī: *Laym.* eam, am, æm, em; eart, art, ært; his; *pl.* sunden, sundeþ, senden, sonden; *subj.* seo, sī; *pl.* seon, seoþ: *O. Sax.* is, ist, *pl.* sind, sint, sindon, sindun; *subj.* sī, sīn: *O. Frs.* is, send; *subj.* se, sie: *Ger.* ist, sind; *subj.* sei, seien: *M. H. Ger. O. H. Ger.* ist, sint; *subj.* sī, sīn: *Goth* im, is, ist, *pl.* sijum, sijuþ, sind; *subj.* sijau, sijais, sijai; *pl.* sijaima, sijaiþ, sijaina: *O. Nrs.* em, ert, er, erum, eruþ, eru; *subj.* sē, sēr, sē, *pl.* sēim, sēiþ, sēi: *Grk.* εἰμί, ἐστί: *Slav.* jesmi, jesti: *Sansk.* asmi, asti.] DER. neom. v. wesan.

eom = heom *to them;* illis, Gen. 20, 8.

eond *yond, beyond;* ultra, per, Nicod. 19; Thw. 9, 28. v. geond.

eonde *a species;* spĕcies, Bd. 3, 14; S. 540, 16, note. v. ende.

eond-lȳhtan; *p.* -lȳhtde = -lȳhte; *pp.* -lȳhted = -lȳhtd = -lȳht [eond = geond *through;* lȳhtan *to shine*] *To shine through, enlighten;* perlūmĭnāre, illūmĭnāre:—We ealle eondlȳhte wǽron *we were all enlightened,* Nicod. 24; Thw. 12, 21. Swylce gylden sunna wǽre ofer us ealle eondlȳhte *a golden sun as it were shone over us all,* 24; Thw. 12, 23.

eond-send *overspread,* Nicod. 27, Lye. v. geond-sendan.

eonu *moreover;* porro, Som. Ben. Lye.

eorcnan-stān, eorcan-stān, eorclan-stān, earcnan-stān, es; *m. A precious stone, pearl, topaz;* lăpis prĕtiosus, gemma, tŏpāzion = τοπάζιον, τόπαζος; *m. the yellow* or *oriental topaz,* Ps. Spl. M. C. 118, 127: Elen. Kmbl. 2048; El. 1025: Exon. 64 b; Th. 238, 12; Ph. 603. Eorcanstān, 124 b; Th. 478, 7; Ruin. 37. Eorclanstān, Beo. Th. 2420, note; B. 1208. [*O. Nrs.* iarknasteinn, *m. lăpis pellūcĭdus: Goth.* airknis; *adj. good, holy: O. H. Ger.* erchan *egrĕgius, summus.*]

eord *the earth, ground,* Som. Ben. Lye. v. eorþe, eard.

eordian; *p.* ode; *pp.* od *To dwell, inhabit;* hăbĭtāre:—Đa on līfes hūs eordiaþ *they dwell in the house of life,* Ps. Th. 134, 21. v. eardian.

eóred, eórod, es; *n. Cavalry, a band, legion, troop;* equĭtātus, lĕgio, turma:—Hie gesāwon eóred lixan *they saw the band glittering,* Cd. 149; Th. 187, 28; Exod. 157. Eórod sceal getrume rīdan *a troop shall ride in a body,* Exon. 90 a; Th. 337, 12; Gn. Ex. 63. Legio, đæt is on ūre geþeóde, eóred *legion, that is in our tongue, a troop,* Lk. Bos. 8, 30. v. weorod, weorud.

eóred-cist, eórod-cist, -cyst, -cest, -ciest, e; *f.* [eóred *a band, troop;* cist *a company*] *A company, troop;* turma, lĕgio:—Wesseaxe eórodcistum [eóredcystum, Th. 202, 28, col. 2; 203, 28] on lāst legdun lāđum þeódum *the West-Saxons in troops followed the footsteps of the hostile nations,* Chr. 937; Th. 202, 28, col. 1. Eóredcystum *in troops,* Exon. 96 a; Th. 358, 27; Pa. 52. Fōr fyrda mǽst eóredcestum *the greatest of armies marched in bands,* Elen. Kmbl. 71; El. 36. Eóredciestum faraþ *they go in bands,* Exon. 60 b; Th. 220, 25; Ph. 325.

eóred-geatwe; *pl. f. Military trappings;* armāmenta:—Se eów geaf eóred-geatwe *who gave to you military trappings,* Beo. 5724; B. 2866.

eóred-mæcg, es; *m.* [mæcg *a man*] *A horseman;* ĕques:—Hæfdon xi eóredmæcgas frīd-hengestas *the horsemen had eleven war-horses*, Exon. 106 a; Th. 404, 6; Rä. 23, 3.

eóred-man *a horseman;* ĕques, Som. Ben. Lye. v. eórod-man.

eóred-þreát, es; *m.* [þreát *a host, troop*] *A band, company;* turma, lĕgio:—Atol eóredþreát *a horrid band*, Exon. 102 a; Th. 385, 23; Rä. 4, 49.

eored-wered, es; *n.* [werod, wered *a company, multitude*] *A band, company, multitude;* exercĭtus, lĕgio:—Eóredweredu đara deófla *lĕgiōnes sive exercĭtus dæmŏnum*, Greg. Dial. 1, 10.

eorendel *the first dawn.* v. earendel.

eorfeđe *difficult;* diffĭcĭlis, Mt. Kmbl. Rush. 7, 14. v. earfeđe.

eorg *weak;* segnis:—Đam eorgan Sisaran *to the weak Sisera*, Jud. 5; Thw. 156, 8. v. earg.

eó-risc *a bulrush;* scirpus. v. eá-risc.

EORL, es; *m.* I. *an Anglo-Saxon nobleman of high rank, the yarl of the Danes, about the same as an ealdorman.* He who was in early times styled *ealdorman*, was afterwards denominated *an earl;* cŏmes, sătelles princĭpis. This title, which was introduced by the Jutes of Kent, occurs frequently in the laws of the kings of that district, the first mention of it being:—Gif on eorles tūne man mannan ofslæhþ xii scillinga gebēte *if a man slay a man in an eorl's town, let him make compensation with twelve shillings*, L. Ethb. 13; Th. i. 6, 9, 10. Its more general use among us dates from the later Scandinavian invasions, and though originally only a title of honour, it became in later times one of office, nearly supplanting the older and more Saxon one of 'ealdorman:'—Swā we eác settaþ be eallum hādum, ge ceorle ge eorle *so also we ordain for all degrees, whether to churl or earl*, L. Alf. pol. 4; Th. i. 64, 3. Se eorl nolde nā geþwǣrian *the earl would not consent*, Chr. 1051; Ing. 227, 13, 23: 228, 4, 28, 35, 36: 229, 10, 21, 25, 26. II. *a man, brave man, hero, general, leader, chief;* vir, pŭgil, vir fortis, dux:—Eorlas on cȳþþe *men in the country*, Andr. Kmbl. 1467; An. 735. Him se Ebrisca eorl wīsade *the Hebrew man* [*Lot*] *directed them*, Cd. 112; Th. 147, 24; Gen. 2444. Đa eorlas þrȳ, *nom. pl. the three men*, 95; Th. 123, 16; Gen. 2045. Eorlas wēnaþ *men think*, 86; Th. 109, 22; Gen. 1826. Fŏr eorlum *before the people*, 98; Th. 129, 1; Gen. 2137. Þegna and eorla *of thanes and earls*, Bt. Met. Fox 25, 15; Met. 25, 8. Geared gumum gold brittade, se eorl wæs æđele *Jared dispensed gold to the people, the man was noble*, Cd. 59; Th. 72, 5; Gen. 1182. [*Piers P.* eerl: *Chauc.* erl: *R. Glouc.* erles *noblemen: Laym.* eorl: *Orm.* eorless, *pl: O. Sax. Hel.* erl, *m. a man, nobleman, male offspring, boy: Icel.* jarl, earl, *m. a gentleman, nobleman, warrior, chief.*]

eorl-cund; *adj. Earl kind, noble;* nobĭlis:—Gif mannes esne eorlcundne mannan ofslæhþ þreóm hundum scillinga gylde se āgend *if a man's servant slay a man of an earl's degree, let the owner pay three hundred shillings*, L. H. E. 1; Th. i. 26, 8.

eorl-dōm, es; *m. An* EARLDOM, *the province* or *dignity of an earl*, the same as ealdor-dōm, v. *Turner's Hist.* b. viii. c. 7; cŏmĭtis mūnus:—Ælfgār eorl fēng to đam eorldōme đe Harold ǣr hæfde *earl Ælfgar succeeded to the earldom which Harold had before*, Chr. 1053; Erl. 189, 14.

eorl-gebyrd, e; *f.* [gebyrd *birth*] *Noble birth, nobility;* nōbĭlĭtas:—Eorlgebyrdum *by noble birth*, Bt. Met. Fox 9, 52; Met. 9, 26: 10, 54; Met. 10, 27.

eorl-gestreón, es; *n.* [gestreón *treasure*] *Noble treasure, riches;* dīvĭtiæ:—Nis him gād eorlgestreóna *he lacks not noble treasures*, Exon. 123 b; Th. 475, 10; Bo. 45: Beo. Th. 4481; B. 2244.

eorl-gewǣde, es; *n.* [gewǣde *clothing*] *Manly clothing, armour;* vĭrīlis vestītus:—Gyrede hine Beówulf eorlgewǣdum *Beowulf clad himself in armour*, Beo. Th. 2888; B. 1442.

eorlīc [=eorl-līc]; *adj. Manly;* vĭrīlis:—Eorlīc ellen *manly strength*, Beo. Th. 1278; B. 637. v. eorlisc, eorl-līc.

eorlīce [=eorl-līce]; *adv. Manfully, strongly, greatly;* vĭrīlĭter, vĕhĕmenter, multum:—Gebealh heó swīđe eorlīce wiđ hire suna *she was very greatly incensed against her son*, Cod. Dipl. 755; Kmbl. iv. 54, 30.

eór-lippric, es; *n. A flap of the ear*, Jn. Lind. War. 18, 26. v. eárelippric.

eorlisc, eorl-līc; *adj.* EARLISH, *earl-like, like an earl;* nōbĭlis:—Eorlisc, L. Ath. v. prm; Th. i. 228, 8. Eorllīc [MS. eorlīc], Beo. Th. 1278; B. 637.

eorl-mægen, es; *n. A host of men;* vĭrōrum turma:—Sió cwēn bebeád ofer eorlmægen āras fȳsan *the queen commanded messengers to hasten throughout the mass of the people*, Elen. Kmbl. 1958; El. 981.

eorl-riht, es; *n. An earl's right* or *privilege;* cŏmĭtis jus *vel* privĭlēgium:—Gif þegen geþeáh, đæt he wearþ to eorle, đonne wæs he syđđan eorlrihtes weorþe *if a thane thrived, that he became an earl, then he was thenceforth worthy of an earl's right*, L. R. 5; Th. i. 192, 8.

eorl-scipe, -scype, es; *m. Manliness, bravery, courage, supremacy, nobility;* vĭrīlĭtas, nōbĭlĭtas:—Hī eahtodon eorlscipe and his ellenweorc *they valued his manliness and his valiant works*, Beo. Th. 6327; B. 3174: Scōp. Th. 283; Wīd. 141: Beo. Th. 3458; B. 1727: 4272; B. 2133. Eorlscipes, Salm. Kmbl. 22; Sal. 11. He eorlscype fremede *he effected supremacy*, Exon. 85 a; Th. 320, 31; Wīd. 37.

eorl-werod, es; *n.* [werod *a company, troop*] *A band of men, warrior band;* vĭrōrum turma:—Đǣr đæt eorlwerod sæt *the warrior band sat there*, Beo. Th. 5779; B. 2893.

Eorman-rīc, Eormen-rīc, es; *m. The celebrated king of the Ostrogoths* or *East Goths, the Alexander of the Goths;* Eormanrīcus, v. Gota III, Alrīca, and þeód-rīc:—Eormanrīc āhte wīde folc Gotena rīces *Ermanric possessed the wide nations of the kingdom of the Goths*, Exon. 100 a; Th. 378, 25; Deór. 21. Weóld Eormanrīc Gotum *Ermanric ruled the Goths*, Scōp. Th. 38; Wīd. 18. Ic wæs mid Eormanrīce *I was with Ermanric*, 178; Wīd. 88. Đæt wæs inn-weorud Eormanrīces *that was the household band of Ermanric*, 224; Wīd. 111. He searo-nīđas fealh Eormenrīces *he fell into the guileful enmity of Ermanric*, Beo. Th. 2406; B. 1201. *For the anachronisms and inconsistences I would refer to W. Grimm's* Deutsche Heldensage, *where may be found the particulars of this celebrated hero.*

eormen, eorman; *adj. Universal, immense, whole, general;* universālis, immensus, permagnus, tōtus, ūniversus. *Used in composition, as in* eormen-cyn, -grund, -lāf, -rīc, -strȳnd, -þeód.

eormen-cyn, -cynn, es; *n. The human race;* hūmānum gĕnus:—God gesceapo ferede ǣghwylcum on eorþan eormencynnes *God has borne his decrees to every one of the human race on earth*, Exon. 88 b; Th. 333, 3; Vy. 96: Beo. Th. 3918; B. 1957.

eormen-grund, es; *n.* [grund *ground, earth*] *The spacious earth;* immensa terra:—Ofer eormengrund *over the spacious earth*, Beo. Th. 1722; B. 859.

eormen-lāf, e; *f. The great legacy;* immensum rĕlĭquum:—He eormenlāfe gehȳdde *he had hidden the great legacy*, Beo. Th. 4460; B. 2234.

Eormen-rīc *Ermanric*, Beo. Th. 2405; B. 1200. v. Eorman-rīc.

eormen-strȳnd, e; *f. The great generation;* permagna gĕnĕrātio:—Đū eart eorre eormenstrȳnde *thou art of an angry, great* [*heathen*] *generation*, Salm. Kmbl. 659; Sal. 329.

eormen-þeód, e; *f. A great people;* permagnus populus. v. yrmenþeód.

eormþu *poverty, calamity:*—Eormþa, Bt. 7, 4; Fox 22, 29. Eormþum, 23; Fox 78, 31. v. yrmþu.

eornan *to run;* currĕre, Ps. Surt. 57, 8. v. yrnan.

eornende *running; part. of* eornan = yrnan.

eornes, eornest *a duel, combat;* duellum, Som. Ben. Lye.

eornest *earnest, earnestness*, Exon. 24 a; Th. 68, 9; Cri. 1101. v. eornost.

eorneste *earnest, serious*, Exon. 20 a; Th. 51, 32; Cri. 825: Homl. Th. i. 386, 20. v. eornoste; *adj.*

eorneste *in earnest, earnestly*, Bt. Met. Fox 13, 56; Met. 13, 28: 16, 44; Met. 16, 22. v. eornoste; *adv.*

eornestlīce *earnestly;* stŭdiōse. v. eornostlīce.

eornfullīce; *adv. Earnestly;* stŭdiōse. v. eornostlīce.

eornfullnes, -ness, e; *f. Earnestness, anxiety;* dīlĭgentia, sollĭcĭtudo:—Eornfullness đisse worulde *sollĭcĭtūdo istius sæcŭli*, Mt. Bos. 13, 22. v. geornfulnes.

eornigende *murmuring;* murmŭrans, L. E. I. 21; Th. ii. 416, 16.

eornlīce; *adv. Diligently;* dīlĭgenter:—Genim đas wyrte eornlīce gecnucude mid ecede *take this herb diligently pounded with vinegar*, Herb. 87, 2; Lchdm. i. 190, 21. v. geornlīce.

EORNOST, eornust, eornest, e; *f.* EARNEST, *earnestness, zeal;* sērium, stŭdium:—Mid swelcum eorneste [eornoste MS. Cot.] *with such zeal*, Past. 15, 1; Hat. MS. 18 b, 27. On eornost, eornust *or* eornoste *in earnest, earnestly*, Ælfc. T. 12, 8: Homl. Th. ii. 250, 30: Mt. Bos. 5, 18: 13, 17: Gen. 14, 15. Þurh eorneste *in earnest, sternly*, Exon. 24 a; Th. 68, 9; Cri. 1101. [*Wyc.* ernes, eernes, ernest *earnest, pledge: Chauc.* erneste *zeal: Laym.* eornest *conflict: Frs.* ernste: *O. Frs.* ernst: *Dut.* ernst, *m: Ger.* ernst, *m: M. H. Ger.* ërnest, ërnst, *m: O. H. Ger.* ërnust, ërnost, ërnest, *n. f. vigor, sērium.*]

eornoste, eorneste; *adj. Earnest, serious;* sērius, stŭdiōsus:—On eornostne hige *with earnest intention*, Cod. Dipl. 942; Kmbl. iv. 278, 15. Biþ eorneste đonne eft cymeþ, rēđe and ryhtwīs *he will be earnest when he comes again, stern and just*, Exon. 20 a; Th. 51, 32; Cri. 825. Mid eornestum mōde *with earnest mind*, Homl. Th. i. 386, 20.

eornoste, eorneste; *adv. In earnest, earnestly, seriously, courageously, strongly;* sērio, strēnue, sēdŭlo, vĕhĕmenter:—He feaht eornoste *he fought earnestly*, Byrht. Th. 140, 1; By. 281: Judth. 11; Thw. 24, 39; Jud. 231. Hió onginþ eorneste racentan slītan *she will begin in earnest to sever her chains*, Bt. Met. Fox 13, 56; Met. 13, 28: 16, 44; Met. 16, 22.

eornostlīce; *adv.* EARNESTLY, *strictly, truly;* sēdŭlo:—Sunnan dæges cȳpingce we forbeódaþ eornostlīce *we strictly forbid marketing on Sunday*, L. C. E. 15; Th. i. 368, 15.

eornostlīce, eornustlīce; *conj. Therefore, but;* ergo, ĭgĭtur, ĭtăque:—Abram đā eornostlīce astirode his geteld *mōvit ĭgĭtur tabernăcŭlum suum Abram*, Gen. 13, 18. Eornostlīce ealle cneóressa fram Abraham, ōþ Dauid synd feówertyne cneóressa *omnes ĭtăque gĕnĕrātiōnes ab Abraham* *usque ad David, genĕrātiōnes quatuordĕcim*, Mt. Bos. 1, 17. Beóþ eornustlíce gleáwe *estōte ergo* [οὖν] *prūdentes*, Mt. Bos. 10, 16, 26: 2, 1: 13, 40.

eornust *earnest, earnestness*, Mt. Bos. 13, 17. v. eornost.

eornustlíce *therefore, but*, Mt. Bos. 2, 1: 10, 16, 26: 13, 40. v. eornostlíce.

eórod, es; *n. A band, legion, troop*; turma, lĕgio:—Wíse men tealdon ān eórod to six þūsendum, and twelf eórod sind twā and hundseofontig þūsend *wise men have reckoned a legion at six thousand, and twelve legions are seventy-two thousand*, Homl. Th. ii. 246, 28, 29, 25: Jud. Thw. 161, 36. v. eóred.

eórod-man, -mann, es; *m. A horseman*; ĕques:—Líhte se eórod-man *desĭluit ĕques*, Bd. 3, 9; S. 533, 33.

eorp, earp; *adj. Dark, dusky, brown, swarthy*; fuscus, badius:—Eorp werod *the swarthy host* [*the Egyptians*], Cd. 151; Th. 190, 4; Exod. 194: Exon. 113 a; Th. 433, 21; Rä. 50, 11. [*Icel.* jarpr *brown.*]

eorre, es; *n. Anger, wrath*; īra:—Warniaþ eów ðæs Drihtenes eorres and mīnes *beware of the Lord's anger and of mine*, L. Ath. i. prm; Th. i. 196, 33: Ps. Lamb. 101, 11. v. yrre.

eorre; *adj. Angry, enraged, fierce*; īrātus, īrācundus:—He us eorre gewearþ *he has become angry with us*, Cd. 219; Th. 280, 27; Sat. 261: Elen. Kmbl. 801; El. 401. Þurh eorne hyge *through angry mind*, 1367; El. 685. Nalæs late wǣron eorre æscberend to ðam orlege *the fierce spear-bearers were not slow to the onset*, Andr. Kmbl. 93; An. 47: 2153; An. 1078. v. yrre; *adj.*

eorringa; *adv. Angrily*; īrāte:—Hine eorringa gesēceþ bōcstafa brego *the prince of letters shall angrily seek him*, Salm. Kmbl. 198; Sal. 98. v. yrringa.

eorsian *to be angry*, Ps. Spl. 4, 5: Mt. Kmbl. Rush. 5, 22. v. yrsian.

eorsung *anger*, Cant. Moys. Ex. 15, 8; Thw. 29, 8. v. yrsung.

eorþ, e; *f. The earth*; terra:—Seó [MS. sie] eorþ is dryge and ceald, and ðæt wæter wǣt and ceald *the earth is dry and cold, and the water wet and cold*, Bt. 33, 4; Fox 128, 34. v. eorþe.

eorþ-æppel, es; *m*: *nom. acc. pl. n.* -æppla *An earth-apple, a cucumber*; cŭcŭmis:—Cŭcŭmĕres, ðæt synd eorþæppla *cucumbers, which are earth-apples*, Num. 11, 5. Eorþæppel *mandrăgŏra*, Ælfc. Gl. 44; Som. 64, 79; Wrt. Voc. 32, 15.

eorþ-ærn, es; *n. An earth-place, a tomb, sepulchre*; spēlunca, sĕpulcrum:—Open wæs ðæt eorþærn *the sepulchre was open*, Exon. 120 a; Th. 460, 18; Hö. 19. In ðæt eorþærn *in the sepulchre*, 119 b; Th. 460, 4; Hö. 12: Exon. 119 b; Th. 459, 22; Hö. 3.

eorþ-beofung, e; *f. An earthquake*; terræ mōtus:—Seó eorþbeofung tācnade ða miclan blōd-dryncas *the earthquake betokened the great blood-sheddings*, Ors. 4, 2; Bos. 79, 28. v. eorþ-bifung.

eorþ-bifung, -beofung, e; *f.* [bifung *a trembling, shaking*] *An earthquake*; terræ mōtus:—Ðǣr wearþ geworden micel eorþbifung *terræ mōtus factus est magnus*, Mt. Bos. 28, 2. Híg gesāwon ða eorþbifunge *vidērunt terræ mōtum*, 27, 54.

eorþ-bigegnys, -bigennys, -nyss, e; *f. Earth-cultivation, attention to agriculture*; terræ cultūra, agricultūræ stŭdium:—Elelændra eorþbigennys *cŏlōnia*, id est *peregrīnōrum cultūra*, Ælfc. Gl. 54; Som. 66, 103; Wrt. Voc. 36, 25. v. eard-begengnes, el-þeódignes.

eorþ-bigenga, an; *m.* [bigenga *an inhabitant, dweller*] *An inhabitant of the earth*; terrĭcŏla, terrigĕna:—Ðæt he eorþbigengan awecce hine to ondrǣdanne *ut terrĭgĕnas ad tĭmendum se suscĭtet*, Bd. 4, 3; S. 569, 22.

eorþ-būend, es; *m. An earth dweller, inhabitant*; terrĭcŏla:—Eorþbūend, Ps. Th. 65, 1: 101, 13: 118, 4. v. būend, būende.

eorþ-burh; *gen.* -burge; *dat.* -byrig; *f. An earth mound* or *burying place*; agger, hŭmātio:—To ðare eorþ-byrig *to the earth mound*, Cod. Dipl. Apndx. 335; A.D. 903; Kmbl. iii. 403, 31.

eorþ-byrig, e; *f. An earth mound*; agger:—Eorþ-byrig [MS. -byre], Ælfc. Gl. 56; Som. 67, 45; Wrt. Voc. 37, 33.

eorþ-cafer, es; *m. An earth-chafer, a cock-chafer*; taurus:—Eorþcaferas *tauri*, Ælfc. Gl. 24; Som. 60, 23; Wrt. Voc. 24, 26. v. ceafer.

eorþ-cend; *pp.* [cend = cenned *born*] *Earth-born*; terrigĕna:—Eorþcende *terrĭgĕnæ*, Ps. Spl. C. 48, 2.

eorþ-crypel, -cryppel; *gen.* -crypeles, -cryples, -crypples; *m. A creeper on the earth, one having the palsy, a paralytic person*; părălytĭcus = παραλυτικός:—In ðære ðe eorþcrypel [se eorþcryppel, Lind.] læg *in quo părălytĭcus jăcēbat*, Mk. Skt. Rush. 2, 4: Lk. Skt. Lind. 5, 18. Se Hǣlend cwæþ to ðæm eorþcrypele [eorþcrypple, Lind.] *Iēsus ait părălytĭco*, Mk. Skt. Rush. 2, 5. To cweðanne ðæm eorþcryple *dīcĕre părălytĭco*, Mk. Skt. Rush. Lind. 2, 9. Brengende to him ðone eorþcrypel *fĕrentes ad eum părălytĭcum*, Mk. Skt. Lind. Rush. 2, 3: Mt. Kmbl. Lind. 9, 2. Gebrohtun him eorþcryplas *obtŭlērunt ei părălytĭcos*, Mt. Kmbl. Lind. 4, 24.

eorþ-cund; *adj. Earthly, terrestrial*; terrestris:—Se rinc ageaf eorþcunde eád *the prince gave up earthly happiness*, Cd. 79; Th. 98, 8; Gen. 1627.

eorþ-cyn, -cynn, es; *n. The earth-kind, terrestrial species*; gĕnus terricŏlārum:—Eallum eorþcynne *for each terrestrial species*, Cd. 161; Th. 201, 10; Exod. 370.

eorþ-cyning, es; *m.* [cyning *a king*] *An earthly king, king of the land*; terræ rex:—Sceótend Scyldinga to scypum feredon eal ingesteald eorþcyninges *the Scyldings' warriors conveyed all the house chattels of the king of the land to their ships*, Beo. Th. 2315; B. 1155. Ðam æðelestan eorþcyninga *for the noblest of earthly kings*, Elen. Kmbl. 2346; El. 1174: Cd. 162; Th. 202, 23; Exod. 392: 189; Th. 235, 14; Dan. 306. Eorþcyningum [MS. -cynincgum] se ege standeþ *terrĭbĭli ăpud rēges terræ*, Ps. Th. 75, 9. He eorþcyningas yrmde and cwelmde *he oppressed and slew the kings of the earth*, Bt. Met. Fox 9, 93; Met. 9, 47: Ps. Th. 88, 24.

eorþ-draca, an; *m. An earth-dragon*; drăco in antro dēgens:—Sió wund ongon, ðe him se eorþdraca geworhte, swelan and swellan *the wound, which the earth-dragon had made in him, began to burn and swell*, Beo. Th. 5417; B. 2712: 5642; B. 2825.

eorþ-dyne, es; *m. Earth din, an earthquake*; terræ mōtus:—On ðisan gēre wæs micel eorþdyne *in this year* [A.D. 1060] *was a great earthquake*, Chr. 1060; Erl. 193, 31: 1122; Erl. 249, 14.

EORÞE, an; *f*: eorþ, e; *f.* I. *the* EARTH *in opposition to the sea, the ground, soil*; terra, hŭmus, sŏlum:—God gecīgde ða drignisse eorþan, and ðæra wætera gegaderunga he hēt sǣs *vŏcāvit Deus ārĭdam terram, congrĕgātiōnesque ăquārum appellāvit măria*, Gen. 1, 10. Spritte seó eorþe grōwende gærs and sǣd wircende and æppelbǣre treów wæstm wircende æfter his cinne, ðæs sǣd sig on him silfum ofer eorþan *germĭnet terra herbam vĭrentem et făcientem sēmen et lignum pōmĭfĕrum făciens fructum juxta gĕnus suum, cujus sēmen in sēmetipso sit sŭper terram*, Gen. 1, 11, 12, 24, 25, 28, 29: Cd. 57; Th. 69, 32; Gen. 1144: Exon. 62 b; Th. 231, 11; Ph. 487: Beo. Th. 3069; B. 1532: Elen. Kmbl. 1655; El. 829: Bt. Met. Fox 8, 118; Met. 8, 59. Ic ðec ofer eorþan geworhte, on ðære ðū scealt yrmþum lifgan and to ðære ilcan scealt eft geweorþan *I made thee on earth, on which thou shalt live in misery and shalt become the same again*, Exon. 16 b; Th. 39, 12-19; Cri. 621-624: 38 a; Th. 125, 10; Gū. 352. Cain wæs eorþan tilia *fuit Cain agrĭcŏla* [lit. *a tiller of the earth*], Gen. 4, 2. II. *the* EARTH, *terrestrial globe*; tellus:—On anginne gesceóp God heofenan and eorþan *in the beginning God created heaven and earth*, Gen. 1, 1, 2, 17, 20, 26: 2, 1, 4: Cd. 98; Th. 129, 9; Gen. 2141: Exon. 16 b; Th. 38, 18; Cri. 608. Se Ælmihtiga eorþan worhte *the Almighty made the earth*, Beo. Th. 185; B. 92. Drihtnes is eorþe and fulnysse oððe gefyllednes hyre *the earth is the Lord's and the fulness thereof*, Ps. Lamb. 23, 1: Ex. 9, 29: Deut. 10, 14. Ðæt gē ne swerion þurh eorþan, forðamðe heó ys Godes fōtscamul *that ye swear not by the earth, because it is God's foot-stool*, Mt. Bos. 5, 35. [*Piers P. Wyc.* erthe: *Laym.* eorðe, eorðen, earþe, erþe: *Orm.* eorþe, erþe: *Plat.* eerde, *f*: *O. Sax.* erða, *f*: *Frs.* yerd: *O. Frs.* irthe, erthe, erde, *f*: *Dut.* aarde, *f*: *Ger. M. H. Ger.* erde, *f*: *O. H. Ger.* erda, erada, *f*: *Goth.* airþa, *f*: *Dan.* jord, *m. f*: *Swed.* jord, *f*: *Icel.* jörð, *f. earth, land, estate.*]

eorþ-fæst, -fest; *adj. Earth-fast, fixed in the earth*; in terra firmus:—To ānum [MS. ane] eorþfestum treówe *to a tree firm in the earth*, Th. Anlct. 122, 10.

eorþ-fæt, es; *n. An earthen vessel, the body*; vas terrâ factum, corpus:—Se gǣst nimeþ swā wīte swā wuldor, swā him in worulde ðæt eorþfæt ǣr geworhte *the spirit receives either punishment or glory, as the body has worked for him before in the world*, Exon. 98 a; Th. 367, 15; Seel. 8.

eorþ-gealla, an; *m.* [gealla *gall*] *The herb* EARTH-GALL, *the lesser centaury*; fel terræ, erythræa centaurium, Lin:—Eorþgealla [MS. -gealle] *fel terræ* vel *centauria*, Wrt. Voc. 79, 50: Ælfc. Gl. 41; Som. 64, 5; Wrt. Voc. 31, 17. Eorþgealla *centauria*, Mone A. 373. Nim centaurian, ðæt is *fel terræ*, sume hātaþ eorþgeallan *take centaury, that is* fel terræ, *some call it earth-gall*, L. M. 2, 8; Lchdm. ii. 186, 27.

eorþ-gemet, es; *n. Earth-measure, geometry*; geometria = γεωμετρία, Cot. 95.

eorþ-gesceaft, e; *f.* [gesceaft *a creature*] *An earthly creature*; terrestris creatūra:—Men habbaþ [MS. habbæþ] geond middangeard eorþgesceafta ealle oferþungen *men have all surpassed earthly creatures throughout the middle earth*, Bt. Met. Fox 20, 387; Met. 20, 194.

eorþ-græf, es; *n. A hole dug in the earth, a ditch, well*; fossa, pŭteus:—Isernes dǣl eorþgræf pæðeþ *a part of iron passes the well*, Exon. 114 b; Th. 439, 26; Rä. 59, 9.

eorþ-grāp, e; *f. Earth's grasp, the hold of the grave*; terræ comprĕhensio:—Eorþgrāp hafaþ waldend wyrhtan *earth's grasp* [i.e. *the grave*] *holdeth its mighty workmen*, Exon. 124 a; Th. 476, 12; Ruin. 6.

eorþ-hele, es; *m. A heap*; tŭmŭlus:—Wæs ðæt deáw abūtan ða fyrdwīc, swilce hit hagoles eorþhele wǣre *the dew was about the camp, as it were a heap of hail*, Ex. 16, 14.

eorþ-hnutu, -nutu, e; *f. An earth-nut*; būnium flexuōsum:—Of ðam cumbe in eorþnutena þorn *from the combe to the earth-nut thorn*, Cod. Dipl. Apndx. 308; A.D. 875; Kmbl. iii. 399, 7.

eorþ-hūs, es; *n. An earth-house, den, cave*; hypŏgæum = ὑπόγαιον, subterrāneum :—Eorþhūs *hypŏgæum* vel *subterrāneum*, Ælfc. Gl. 110; Som. 79, 37; Wrt. Voc. 59, 9. Rōmāne him worhton eorþhūs for ðære lyfte wylme *the Romans built for themselves earth-houses because of the boiling heat of the air*, L. M. 1, 72; Lchdm. ii. 146, 16.

eorþ-ifi, es; *n. Ground ivy;* hĕdĕra nigra :—Eorþ-ifies *of ground ivy;* hĕdĕræ nigræ, L. M. 1, 2; Lchdm. ii. 30, 17. v. eorþ-ifig.

eorþ-ifig, -yfig, -ifi, -iui, es; *n. Earth* or *ground ivy;* hĕdĕra nigra, hĕdĕra terrestris, glechoma hĕdĕrācea :—Genim hederan nigran, ðe man ōðrum naman eorþifig nemneþ *take* hĕdĕra nigra, *which one calleth by another name ground ivy*, Herb. 100, 1; Lchdm. i. 212, 20.

eorþ-iui [=ivi], es; *n. Ground ivy;* hĕdĕra nigra :—Eorþ-iui [MS. eorðiuī], Herb. 100; Lchdm. i. 212, 18, note 17, MS. B. v. eorþ-ifig.

eorþ-līc; *def.* se -līca; seó, ðæt -līce; *adj.* EARTHLY, *terrestrial;* terrēnus, terrestris :—He wæs eorþlīc cing *he was an earthly king*, Chr. 979; Erl. 129, 9. Hī eorþlīces āuht ne haldeþ *nothing earthly holds them*, Bt. Met. Fox 20, 331; Met. 20, 166. Ða twelf bōcland him gefreóde eorþlīces camphādes and eorþlīcere hērenysse to bigongenne ðone heofonlīcan camphād *dōnātis duodĕcim possessiuncŭlis terrārum, in quibus ablāto stŭdio mīlĭtiæ terrestris, ad exercendam mīlĭtiam cælestem*, Bd. 3, 24; S. 556, 41. Ðū meahte ǣlc eorþlīc þing forsión *thou mayest look down upon every earthly thing*, Bt. Met. Fox 24, 13; Met. 24, 7. Hine nolden his eorþlīcan māgas wrecan *his earthly kinsmen would not avenge him*, Chr. 979; Erl. 129, 11, 15. Gif ic eów eorþlīce þing sǣde *si terrēna dixi vobis*, Jn. Bos. 3, 12. Hió ðǣs lǣnan lufaþ eorþlīcu þing *she loves these transitory earthly things*, Bt. Met. Fox 20, 447; Met. 20, 224. Ðū gegæderast ða hiofonlīcan sāwla and ða eorþlīcan līchoman *thou bringest together the heavenly souls and the earthly bodies*, Bt. 33, 4; Fox 132, 23. He forsihþ ðās eorþlīcan gōd *he despises these earthly goods*, 12; Fox 36, 25: 33, 4; Fox 132, 14, 18.

eorþ-līce; *adv. In an earthly manner;* terrŭlenter :—Eorþlīce *terrŭlenter*, Glos. Prudent. Recd. 145, 20.

eorþ-ling, es; *m. A farmer;* terræ cultor :—Eorþling *birbicaliolus?* Glos. Brux. Recd. 36, 50; Wrt. Voc. 63, 4; Mone A. 50. v. yrþ-ling.

eorþ-mægen, es; *n. Earthly power;* terræ vis :—Eorþmægen ealdaþ *earthly power grows old;* terræ vīres invĕtĕrascunt, Exon. 95 a; Th. 354, 61; Reim. 69: Ettmül. Poet. pref. xviii. 59; p. 223, 69.

eorþ-mistel, es; *m. The plant basil;* clīnŏpŏdium = κλινοπόδιον :—Genim eorþmistel *take basil*, L. M. 1, 36; Lchdm. ii. 86, 21.

eorþ-nafela, -nafola, -nafala, -nafla, an; *m. Earth-navel, asparagus;* aspărăgus officinālis :—Nim eorþnafelan *take asparagus*, Lchdm. iii. 40, 23. Genim eorþnafolan wyrtruman *take roots of asparagus*, Herb. 126, 2; Lchdm. i. 238, 5. Wyll miclan eorþnafolan *boil the great asparagus*, Lchdm. iii. 18, 7. Eorþnafala *asparagus*, iii. 6, 15. Genim eorþnaflan [MS. B. -nafelan] *take asparagus*, Herb. 97, 1; Lchdm. i. 210, 8.

eorþ-reced, es; *n.* [reced *a house*] *An earth-house, a cave;* subterrānea dŏmus, antrum :—Hū ða stānbogan ēce eorþreced healde *how the stone arches held the eternal earth-house*, Beo. Th. 5431; B. 2719.

eorþ-rest, e; *f. A resting* or *lying on the ground;* chămeunia = χαμευνία, Cot. 31.

eorþ-rīce, es; *n. A kingdom of the earth, earth's kingdom, the earth;* terræ regnum, terra :—Geond ealle eorþrīcu *per omnia regna terræ*, Deut. 28, 25: Bt. Met. Fox 4, 74; Met. 4, 37. He eorþrīcum eallum wealdeþ *regnum ipsīus omnĭbus domĭnābĭtur*, Ps. Th. 102, 18. On eorþrīce *on earth's kingdom, on earth*, Cd. 22; Th. 27, 18; Gen. 419: 23; Th. 29, 22; Gen. 454: 26; Th. 35, 1; Gen. 548.

eorþ-rima, an; *m. A kind of plant, dodder?* herbæ gĕnus, cuscuta? L. M. 3, 41; Lchdm. ii. 334, 12.

eorþ-scræf, es; *n. An earth-cavern, a grave;* căverna, antrum, sĕpulcrum :—Hie be hliðe heáre dūne eorþscræf fundon, ðǣr Loth wunode *they found by the slope of a high hill an earth-cavern, where Lot dwelt*, Cd. 122; Th. 156, 27; Gen. 2595: Exon. 115 a; Th. 443, 11; Kl. 28. Eardiaþ on eorþ-scræfum *hăbĭtant in sĕpulcris*, Ps. Th. 67, 7: Andr. Kmbl. 1605; An. 804.

eorþ-sele, es; *m.* [sele *a hall*] *An earth-hall, cave;* subterrānea aula, antrum :—Eald is ðes eorþsele *this earth-hall is old*, Exon. 115 a; Th. 443, 12; Kl. 29. Mec se mānsceaða of eorþsele ūt gesēceþ *the atrocious spoiler will seek me out from his earth-hall*, Beo. Th. 5023; B. 2515. He eorþsele āna wisse *he alone knew the earth-hall*, 4811; B. 2410.

eorþ-slihtes; *adv.* [slihtes, *old gen. of* sliht *destruction, slaughter*, like nihtes of niht] *In an earth-destroying manner;* in mŏdo vastante terram :—Swā swā oxa gewunaþ to awēstenne gærs, ōþ ða wirttruman, eorþslihtes mid tōðum *as an ox is accustomed to consume grass with his teeth, even to the roots, in an earth-destroying manner*, Num. 22, 4.

eorþ-stede, es; *m.* [stede *a place*] *An earth-place;* terræ lŏcus :—Ðā hī ðæt ðīn fægere hūs on eorþstede gewemdan [MS. gewemdaþ] *in terra pollŭērunt tabernacŭlum*, Ps. Th. 73, 7.

eorþ-styrennis, -niss, e; *f.* [styrenes *motion*] *An earthquake;* terræ mōtus :—Eorþstyrennis gewarþ micelu *terræ mōtus factus est magnus*, Mt. Kmbl. Rush. 28, 2.

eorþ-styrung, -stirung, e; *f. An earth-stirring, earthquake;* terræ mōtus :—Eorþstyrung fela burhga ofhreás . . . þreóttyne byrig þurh eorþstyrunge afeóllon *an earthquake has overthrown many cities . . . thirteen cities fell through an earthquake*, Homl. Th. i. 608, 27, 29: 244, 17. Micele eorþstyrunga beóþ gehwǣr *great earthquakes shall be everywhere*, i. 608, 18. Ðā wearþ mycel eorþstirung *there was a great earthquake*, Nicod. 15; Thw. 7, 17.

eorþ-tilia, an; *m. An earth-tiller, husbandman;* agrĭcŏla :—Mīn fæder ys eorþtilia *păter meus agrĭcŏla est*, Jn. Bos. 15, 1.

eorþ-tilþ, e; *f.* [tilþ *culture*] *Earth-tillage, agriculture;* agrĭcultūra :—Eorþtilþ *agrĭcultūra*, Coll. Monast. Th. 30, 27.

eorþ-tudor; *gen.* -tudres; *n.* [tuddor *progeny*] *Progeny of earth, men;* terrestris prōgĕnies, hŏmĭnes :—Ðis ys se dæg ðe Drihten geworhte eallum eorþtudrum eádgum to blisse *this is the day which the Lord made for bliss to all happy men*, Ps. Th. 117, 22.

eorþ-tyrewa, an; *m.* [tyrwa *tar*] *Earth-tar, asphalte;* bĭtūmen :—Se weall is geworht of tigelan and eorþtyrewan *the wall* [*of Babylon*] *is built with bricks and earth-tar*, Ors. 2, 4; Bos. 44, 25.

eorþ-wæstm, e; *f. Fruit of the earth;* terræ frux :—Mycel eorþwæstm *frūgum cōpia*, Bd. 1, 14; S. 482, 13. Eorþwæstme grōwaþ *fruits grow*, Ps. Th. 103, 12. Wæs seó stōw wædla eorþwæstma *ĕrat lŏcus frūgis inops*, Bd. 4, 28; S. 605, 18. On eorþwæstmum genōh þuhte *abundance appeared in the fruits of the earth*, Bt. Met. Fox 8, 12; Met. 8, 6.

eorþ-waru, e; *f:* -ware; *gen.* -wara; *pl. m:* -waran; *gen.* -warena; *pl. m. Inhabitants* or *population of the earth;* terrĭcŏlæ, terrĭgĕnæ :—Heofonwaru and eorþwaru *cælĭcŏlæ et terrĭcŏlæ*, Hy. 7, 95; Hy. Grn. ii. 289, 95. Crist sibb is heofonware and eorþware *Christ is the peace of the inhabitants of heaven and of the inhabitants of the earth*, Ors. 3, 5; Bos. 57, 27. Dēm eorþware *jūdĭca terram*, Ps. Th. 81, 8: 98, 1: 144, 13. Gehȳraþ ðās, eorþware *audīte hæc, terrĭgĕnæ*, Ps. Spl. 48, 2: Exon. 13 a; Th. 24, 9; Cri. 382. Ðæt cynebearn acenned wearþ eallum eorþwarum *the royal child was born for all the inhabitants of the earth*, Andr. Kmbl. 1135; An. 568: Exon. 41 b; Th. 138, 21; Gū. 579: Bt. Met. Fox 13, 120; Met. 13, 60: Menol. Fox 124; Men. 62. Hēr wynnaþ earme eorþwaran *miserable inhabitants of earth strive here*, Bt. Met. Fox 4, 113; Met. 4, 57: 17, 1; Met. 17, 1. Ofer ealle eorþwaran *over all the inhabitants of earth*, Past. 43, 9; Hat. MS. 60 b, 7.

eorþ-weall, es; *m. An earth-wall, mound;* agger :—Under eorþweall *under the earth-wall*, Beo. Th. 6171; B. 3090. Mid eorþwealle *with an earth-wall*, Bd. 1, 5; S. 476, 10: 4, 28; S. 605, 24.

eorþ-weard, es; *m. An earth-guard;* terræ custos :—Hæfde līgdraca eorþweard forgrunden *the fire-dragon had destroyed the earth-guard*, Beo. Th. 4658; B. 2334.

eorþ-weg, es; *m. An earth-way;* terrestris via :—Hió me woldan ðisses eorþweges ende gescrīfan *consummāvērunt me in terra*, Ps. Th. 118, 87. Þurh ða rōde sceal rīce gesēcan of eorþwege ǣghwylc sāwl *every soul shall seek the kingdom away from earth through the cross*, Rood Kmbl. 237; Kr. 120: Exon. 58 b; Th. 209, 29; Ph. 178: Ps. Th. 71, 11. Of eorþwegum *from the earthly ways*, Elen. Kmbl. 1468; El. 736.

eorþ-wēla, an; *m. Earth-wealth, fertility;* terrestres dīvĭtiæ, fertĭlĭtas :—Mid Egyptum wearþ syfan geár se ungemetlīca eorþwēla *for seven years there was very great fertility in Egypt*, Ors. 1, 5; Bos. 28, 3. Biþ him eorþwēla ofer ðæt ēce līf *earthly wealth to them is above the eternal life*, Exon. 33 a; Th. 105, 34; Gū. 33. Ne ic me eorþwēlan ōwiht sinne *I care naught for earth's wealth*, Exon. 37 a; Th. 121, 17; Gū. 290. Sum him Metudes ēst ofer eorþwēlan ealne geceóseþ *one chooses his Creator's favour above all earthly wealth*, 79 b; Th. 298, 20; Crā. 88.

eorþ-weorc, es; *n. Earth-work;* terræ ŏpus :—Hīg on eorþweorcum gehȳnede wǣron *in terræ ŏpĕrĭbus premēbantur*, Ex. 1, 14.

eorþ-yfig, es; *n. Ground ivy;* hĕdĕra terrestris, Herb. 100; Lchdm. i. 212, 18. v. eorþ-ifig.

eór-wicga *an earwig;* blatta, Ælfc. Gl. 24; Som. 60, 20; Wrt. Voc. 24, 24. v. eár-wicga.

eóryd *a legion*, Mt. Foxe 26, 53. v. eóred.

eós *of a war horse*, Exon. 90 a; Th. 337, 11; Gn. Ex. 63; *gen. sing. of* eoh.

eosol *an ass*, Wrt. Voc. 287, 50. v. esol.

eóster *easter*, Lk. Skt. Lind. Rush. 22, 8, 15. v. eáster.

eosul *an ass*, Mt. Kmbl. Rush. 21, 5. v. esol.

eosul-cwearn, e; *f. An ass-mill, a mill turned by asses;* ăsĭnāria mŏla, Cot. 16.

Eota land, es; *n. The land of the Jutes, Jutland;* Jūtia :—Mǣgþ seó is gecȳd Eota land *a province which is called Jutland*, Bd. 4, 16; S. 584, 24. v. Iotas.

EÓTEN, es; *m.* I. *a giant, monster, Grendel;* gĭgas, monstrum, Grendel :—Wæs se grimma gǣst Grendel, Caines cyn,—ðanon untydras ealle onwōcon, eótenas and ylfe and orcnēas, swylce gigantas *Grendel was the grim guest, the race of Cain,—whence unnatural births all sprang forth, monsters, elves, and spectres, also giants*, Beo. Th. 204–226; B. 102–113. Eóten, *nom. sing.* Beo. Th. 1526; B. 761. Eótena, *gen. pl.* Beo. Th. 846; B. 421. II. Eótenas, *gen.* a; *dat.* um; *pl. m. the Jutes, Jutlanders, the ancient inhabitants of Jutland in the north of Denmark;* Jūtæ :—Eótena treówe *the faith of the Jutes*, Beo.

Th. 2148; B. 1072: 2180; B. 1088: 2286; B. 1141: 2294; B. 1145. [*O. Nrs.* jötunn, *m.*] v. ent, eten.

eótenisc, eótonisc; *adj. Belonging to* or *made by a giant, giant;* giganteus, a gigante factus:—Geseah ðá eald sweord eótenisc *then he saw an old giant sword,* Beo. Th. 3120; B. 1558. Ætbær eald sweord eótonisc *bore away the old giant sword,* 5225; B. 2616. v. entisc.

Eotol-ware; *gen.* -wara; *dat.* -warum; *pl. m. Inhabitants of Italy, Italians, Italy;* Ităli, Itălia:—He sinoþ gesomnade Eotolwara biscopa *cōgĕret synŏdum episcŏpōrum Ităliæ,* Bd. 2, 4; S. 505, 33.

eóton *ate,* Chr. 998; Erl. 135, 20, = ǽton; *p. pl. of* etan.

eótonisc, Beo. Th. 5225; B. 2616: 5950; B. 2979. v. eótenisc.

eóton-weard, e; *f. Giant-protection;* contra gigantem protectio:—Seleweard eótonweard abeád *the hall-guard offered protection against the giant* [*Grendel*], Beo. Th. 1341, note; B. 668.

eow, es; *m? A griffin;* gryps = γρύψ, gryphus:—Eow, fiðerfōte fugel *griffin, a four-footed bird;* griffes [= gryphus], Ælfc. Gl. 18; Wrt. Voc. 22, 44. v. giw.

eow, es; *m.* I. *the yew;* taxus, L. M. 3, 63; Lchdm. ii. 350, 24. v. íw. II. *the mountain ash;* ornus? Ælfc. Gl. 47; Som. 65, 40; Wrt. Voc. 33, 37.

eów *to you,* YOU; vōbis, vos; ὑμῖν, ὑμᾶς; *pers. pron; dat. acc. pl. of* ðú, Ex. 6, 8: Mt. Bos. 6, 16: 5, 46: Lk. Bos. 12, 28. v. gē.

eów; *interj. Wo! alas!* væ! heu!—Eów me! *heu mihi!* Ps. Spl. T. 119, 5. v. wā.

eówa *ewes, female sheep; pl. nom. acc. of* eówu.

eówan; *p.* de; *pp.* ed; *v. trans. To shew, manifest, confer;* ostendĕre, manifestāre, conferre:—Ne gesacu ōhwǽr ecghete eóweþ *nor strife anywhere shews hostility,* Beo. Th. 3480; B. 1738. Ðá gēn Abrahame eówde selfa hālige spræce *then he himself shewed again to Abraham a holy speech,* Cd. 98; Th. 130, 24; Gen. 2164. Ealne ðone egesan, ðe him eówed wæs *all that terror which was shewn to him,* 202; Th. 250, 4; Dan. 541. v. eáwan, ȳwan.

eów-berge, an; *f. A yew-berry;* taxi bacca, L. M. 3, 63; Lchdm. ii. 350, 24.

eówcig; *adj. Of* or *belonging to a ewe;* ad ŏvem fēmĭnam pertĭnens:—Mid eówcigre wulle *with ewe's wool,* L. M. 1, 31; Lchdm. ii. 74, 5. v. eówocig.

eówd *a flock, herd, sheepfold,* Ælfc. Gr. 9, 2, 61; Som. 8, 27; 13, 47. v. eówde.

eówde, eówede, eówode, es; *n:* eówd, eówod, e; *f. A flock, herd;* grex:—*Neuter,* Ðæt Drihtnes eówde *the Lord's flock,* Bd. 1, 14; S. 482, 25: 2, 6; S. 508, 15. We wǽrun sceáp eówdes ðīnes *nos ŏves grĕgis tui,* Ps. Th. 78, 14. He genam hine æt eówde, ūte be sceápum *tŭlit eum de grĕgĭbus ŏvium,* 77, 69. Ne scealt ðū ðæt eówde ānforlǽtan *thou shalt not desert the flock,* Andr. Kmbl. 3334; An. 1671. Hafaþ se awyrgda wulf tostenced, Dryhten, ðīn eówde *hath the accursed wolf scattered thy flock, O Lord?* Exon. 11 b; Th. 16, 23; Cri. 257. Ofer ðīn āgen eówde sceápa *sŭper ŏves grĕgis tuæ,* Ps. Th. 73, 1: 118, 111. He gelǽdde hī swā swā eówde [eówode, Ps. Lamb. 77, 52] on wēstne *perduxit eos tanquam grĕgem in deserto,* Ps. Spl. 77, 57. Of eówdum [eówedum, Ps. Lamb. 77, 70] sceápa *de grĕgĭbus ŏvium,* Ps. Spl. 77, 76. *Feminine,* Ðeós eówd *hic grex,* Ælfc. Gr. 9, 61; Som. 13, 47. He ðæt sceáp bær on his exlum to ðære eówde *he bare the sheep on his shoulders to the flock,* Homl. Th. i. 340, 2. Ic wylle ahreddan mīne eówde wið eów *I will deliver my flock from you,* i. 242, 13. **2.** eówd, e; *f. A sheepfold, fold;* ŏvīle:—Eówd *ŏvīle,* Ælfc. Gr. 9, 2; Som. 8, 27. Sceal beón ān eówd and ān hyrde *there shall be one fold and one shepherd,* Homl. Th. i. 244, 1, 3. Ic hæbbe ōðre scēp ðe ne sind nā of ðisre eówde *I have other sheep which are not of this fold,* Homl. Th. i. 242, 35: 244, 6: ii. 114, 21.

eówe, es; *m. f. A sheep,* L. In. 55; Th. i. 138, 6, MSS. G. H. v. ēwe, es.

eówe *of a ewe,* L. In. 55; Th. i. 138, 6, note 11, MS. B. v. eówu.

eówede *a flock,* Ps. Lamb. 77, 70. v. eówde.

eówena *of ewes:*—Twāhund eówena *two hundred sheep,* Gen. 32, 14. v. eówu.

eowend *membrum vĭrīle,* L. Alf. pol. 25; Th. i. 78, 15.

eowendende; *part. Returning;* rĕdiens, Ps. Spl. 77, 44. v. awendan.

eówer *of you;* vestrûm *vel* vestri, ὑμῶν; *gen. pl. of pers. pron.* ðū:—A.. eówer *ūnus vestrûm,* Mt. Bos. 26, 21. Eówer sum *one of you,* Beo. Th. 502; B. 248. Eówer ǽnig *any of you,* Cd. 22; Th. 27, 34; Gen. 427. v. gē.

eówer YOUR; vester, vestra, vestrum, ὑμέτερ-ος, -α, -ον; *adj. pron:*—Biþ eówer blǽd micel *your prosperity shall be great,* Cd. 170; Th. 214, 3; Exod. 563. Sceal eall ēðel-wyn eówrum cynne leófum alicgean *all joy of country shall fail to your beloved kindred,* Beo. Th. 5763; B. 2885.

eówer-lendisc; *adj. Of your land* or *country;* vestras:—Eówerlendisc *vestras,* Ælfc. Gr. 15; Som. 17, 45.

eówes *a sheep's,* L. In. 55; Th. i. 138, 6, note 11, MSS. G. H. v. ēwes.

eówestras *sheepfolds,* Som. Ben. Lye. v. ēwestre.

eówian; *p.* ode; *pp.* od *To shew;* ostendĕre:—Hī eówodon me ða wunde *monstrāvērunt mihi vulnus,* Bd. 4, 19; S. 589, 17. Ðā hēt he his tungan forþdōn of his mūþe, and him eówian *linguam prōferre ex ōre, ac sĭbi ostendĕre jussit,* Bd. 5, 2; S. 615, 6. v. eáwan, ȳwan.

eówic *you; acc. pl. of pers. pron.* ðū:—Fæder alwalda mid ār-stafum eówic gehealde *may the all-ruling Father with honour hold you,* Beo. Th. 640; B. 317. Eówic grētan hēt *bade to greet you,* 6182; B. 3095. v. gē.

eówih = eówic *you; acc. pl. of pers. pron.* gē *ye.*

Eowland, es; *n. Oeland, an island on the coast of Sweden;* Oelandia:—Wǽron us ðās land, ða synd hātene Blecinga ēg, and Meore, and Eowland, and Gotland, on bæcbord *we had, on our left, those lands which are called Blekingey, and Meore, and Oeland, and Gothland,* Ors. 1, 1; Bos. 22, 1.

eówocig, eówcig; *adj. Of* or *belonging to a ewe;* ad ŏvem fēmĭnam pertĭnens:—Mid eówocigre wulle *with ewe's wool,* L. M. 1, 3; Lchdm. ii. 42, 25.

eówod, e; *f. A flock, herd;* grex, Homl. Th. ii. 514, 23. v. *n.* and *f.* in eówode.

eówode, es; *n:* eówod, e; *f. A flock, herd;* grex:—*Neuter,* He gebrohte hīg swylce eówode on wēstene *perduxit eos tamquam grĕgem in deserto,* Ps. Lamb. 77, 52. *Feminine,* He nȳtenum lǽcedōm forgeaf, ahredde fram wōdnysse, and hēt faran aweg to ðære eówode ðe hī ofadwelodon *he gave medicine to animals, saved them from madness, and bade them go away to the herd from which they had strayed,* Homl. Th. ii. 514, 21–23. v. eówde.

eówo-humele, an; *f. The female hop-plant;* humŭlus fēmĭna:—Genim eówohumelan *take the female hop-plant,* L. M. 3, 61; Lchdm. ii. 344, 8.

eówre *your,* Deut. 32, 11; *acc. of* eówer.

EÓWU; *gen.* eówe; *pl. nom. acc.* eówa; *gen.* eówena; *dat.* eówenum; *f:* ēwe, an; *f. A* EWE, *female sheep;* ŏvis fēmĭna:—*Ewes were milked by the Anglo-Saxons. The milk was used for domestic purposes: butter and cheese were made from it; for Ælfric teaches the shepherd* [sceáphyrde] *to say,* 'On fōrewerdne morgen ic drīfe sceáp mīne to heora lease, and ic agēnlǽde hīg to heora loca, and melke hīg tweówa on dæg, and cȳse and buteran ic dō *in prīmo māne mīno ŏves meas ad pascua, et rĕdūco eas ad caulas, et mulgeo eas bis in die, et cāseum et butyrum făcio,*' Coll. Monast. Th. 20, 11–19. Twāhund eówena, and twentig rammena *two hundred ewes, and twenty rams,* Gen. 32, 14. Eówu biþ, mid hire geonge sceápe, scilling weorþ *a ewe, with her young sheep, shall be worth a shilling,* L. In. 55; Th. i. 138, 7, MS. B. Be eówe weorþe *of a ewe's worth;* de ŏvis prĕtio, L. In. 55; Th. i. 138, 6, note 11, MS. B. Wyl on eówe meolce hindhioloðan *boil water agrimony in ewe's milk,* L. M. 1, 70; Lchdm. ii. 144, 22. v. ram, *the m. of* eówu. [*Plat.* ouwe, ouw *a female sheep: Frs.* eij, ei, *n. ŏvis fēmĭna: Dut.* ooi, *f. a ewe-lamb: Ger. Swiss Dial.* au, auw, ow, *f. a female sheep: M. H. Ger.* owe, *f. a female sheep: O. H. Ger.* awi, owi, au, *f. ovĭcŭla, agna: Goth. in the words* aweþi, *n. a herd of sheep;* awistr, *n. a sheepfold: Lat.* ŏvis, *f: Grk.* ὄϊς, *m. f. a sheep: Lith.* awis, *f. a sheep: Sansk.* āvi, *m. f. a sheep.*]

eówunga; *adv. Openly;* pălam, Mk. Rush. War. 8, 32. v. eáwunga.

epegitsung, e; *f. Avarice, covetousness;* avārĭtia, Ps. Spl. T. 118, 36.

epiphania = ἐπιφάνια *the Epiphany, the manifestation of Christ to the Gentiles.* v. twelfta dæg.

epistol, e; *f. A letter;* ĕpistŏla:—Eall heora gewinn awacnedon ǽrest fram Alexandres epistole *all their wars arose first from a letter of Alexander,* Ors. 3, 11; Bos. 72, 20. [*Ger.* epistel, *f: M. H. Ger.* epistole, *f: O. H. Ger.* epistula, *f: Goth.* aipistaule, *f: Lat.* ĕpistŏla, *f: Grk.* ἐπιστολή, *f.*] v. pistol.

epl, eppl *an apple,* Ps. Spl. 78, 1. v. æppel.

epse *an asp-tree,* Som. Ben. Lye. v. æps.

ēr *ere, before,* Th. Diplm. A. D. 830; 465, 30. v. ǽr.

ēran *a shrill sound, the ears;* tinnulus, aures, Som. Ben. Lye. v. eáre.

er-bleadd, es; *n.* [er = ear *an ear of corn,* bleadd = blæd *a blade, leaf*] *A stalk, stem, blade, haulm, straw, stubble;* stĭpŭla:—Ðū asendest yrre ðīn and hit æt hī swā swā erbleadd *mīsisti īram tuam, quæ devŏrābit eos sīcut stĭpŭlam,* Cant. Moys. Ex. 15, 8; Thw. 29, 8.

erc *an ark, a chest:*—Erc gehālgunge ðīnre *arca sanctĭfĭcātiōnis tuæ,* Ps. Surt. 131, 8: Lk. Rush. War. 17, 27. v. earc II.

erce-biscop *an archbishop,* Bd. 2, 20; S. 521, 42. v. arce-bisceop.

erce-diācon *an archdeacon;* archidiăconus, Wrt. Voc. 71, 80: Homl. Th. i. 416, 29: 418, 16. v. arce-diācon.

erce-hād, es; *m. Archhood, an archbishop's pall, his dignity, of which the pall was a sign;* pallium:—Ðæt his æftergengan symle ðone pallium and ðone ercehād æt ðam apostolīcan setle Rōmāniscre gelaðunge feccan sceoldon *that his successors should always fetch the pall and the archiepiscopal dignity from the apostolic seat of the Roman church,* Homl. Th. ii. 132, 10.

Ercol, es; *m:* Erculus, i; *m. Lat. Hercules;* Hercŭles:—Hȳ Ercol ðǽr gebrohte *Hercules brought them there,* Ors. 3, 9; Bos. 68, 6. Erculus wæs Iobes sunu *Hercules was the son of Jove,* Bt. 39, 4; Fox 216, 23.

-ere, -er, es; *m.* as the termination of many nouns, signifies a person or agent. v. fulwer *and* fullere *a fuller, bleacher*, Mk. Bos. 9, 3: from wer *a man;* plegere *a player;* sǣdere *a sower;* wrītere *a writer.*

erede *ploughed, eared*, Ors. 1, 1; Bos. 20, 31; *p. of* erian.

eregende *ploughing*, Lk. Bos. 17, 7, = erigende; *part. of* erian, erigan.

ēren; *adj. Brazen;* æreus, Ps. Spl. T. 17, 36: 106, 16. v. ǣren.

ērest *first;* imprīmis, C. R. Ben. 4. v. ǣrest.

eretic; *adj. Heretical;* hærĕtĭcus, Bd. 4, 13, Lye.

erfe, es; *n. An inheritance;* hērēdĭtas:—Freólsgefa āge his erfe *let the freedom-giver have his heritage*, L. Wih. 8; Th. i. 38, 16. v. yrfe.

erfe-gewrit, es; *n. A charter of donation;* dōnātiōnis charta, Heming, p. 120, Lye.

erfeđe; *adj. Difficult, troublesome;* diffĭcĭlis, mŏlestus:—For hwon erfeđo sindon gē đæm wīfe *quid mŏlesti estis mŭlieri?* Mt. Kmbl. Lind. 26, 10. v. earfeđe.

erfe-weard, es; *m. An heir;* hēres:—Đū eart erfeweard ealra þeóda *tu hērēdĭtābis in omnĭbus gentĭbus*, Ps. Th. 81, 8. Forleórt he đæs hwīlewendlīcan rīces erfeweardas his suna þrié *tres fīlios suos regni tempŏrālis hērēdes relīquit*, Bd. 2, 5; Whelc. 121, 41. v. yrfe-weard.

erfe-weardnis, -niss, e; *f. An inheritance;* hērēdĭtas:—Erfeweardnis mīn *hērēdĭtas mea*, Rtl. 3, 34. v. yrfe-weardnes.

ergende *ploughing*, Chr. 876; Th. 144, 32, col. 1, = erigende; *part. of* erian, erigan.

erhe, erhlīce *fearfully*, R. Ben. Interl. 5. v. earh-līce.

ERIAN, erigan, erigean, to erianne, eriganne, erigenne; *part.* erigende; *p.* ede; *pp.* ed; *v. a. To plough*, EAR; ărāre:—For cīele nele se slāwa erian [erigan MS. Cot.] *propter frīgus pĭger ărāre nonvult*, Past. 39, 2; Hat. MS. 53 a, 14, 15. Nylle erigean [erian MS. Cot.] *nonvult ărāre*, 39, 2; Hat. MS. 53 a, 18. Mīne æceras ic erige *mei agros āro*, Ælfc. Gr. 15; Som. 19, 44. Đū erast *thou ploughest*, Homl. Th. i. 488, 24. Đǣr yrþling ne eraþ *where husbandman ploughs not*, i. 464, 25. Đæt lytle đæt he erede, he erede mid horsan *the little that he ploughed, he ploughed with horses*, Ors. 1, 1; Bos. 20, 31. Era mid dīnum oxan *plough with thine ox*, Prov. Kmbl. 67. Hit is tīma to erigenne [eriganne MS. D.] *tempus est ărandi*, Ælfc. Gr. 24; Som. 25, 17. Me is to erigenne [erianne MS. D.] *ărandum est mĭhi*, 24; Som. 25, 19. Hæfst đū æceras to erigenne [eriganne MS. D.] *hăbes agros ad ărandum?* 24; Som. 25, 20. Erigende ic geþeó *ărando prōfĭcio*, 24; Som. 25, 18. Hwylc eówer hæfþ eregendne þeów *quis vestrum hăbet servum ărantem?* Lk. Bos. 17, 7. Ergende *ploughing*, Chr. 876; Th. 144, 32, col. 1. [*Wyc.* ere, eren, eeren *to plough: Piers P.* erien, erie, erye: *Chauc.* ere: *Laym.* ærien: *O. Frs.* era: *Dut. Kil.* erien, eren, eeren, æren: *Ger.* ären, eren: *M. H. Ger.* ern: *O. H. Ger.* aran, erran *ărāre: Goth.* aryan *to plough: Swed.* ärja: *Icel.* erja: *Lat.* ărāre: *Grk.* ἀροῦν *to plough, till.*] DER. ge-erian, on-.

ering-lond, es; *n. Arable land;* arvum, Cod. Dipl. 1339; Kmbl. vi. 200, 7.

eriung, e; *f. A ploughing, earing;* ărātio, Ælfc. Gl. 1; Som. 55, 3; Wrt. Voc. 15, 3.

erk, e; *f. The ark;* arca:—Noe on erke eóde *Noe in arcam intrāvit*, Lk. Skt. C. C. 17, 27. v. arc.

Ermanrīc, es; *m. The celebrated king of the Ostro-Goths* or *East-Goths.* v. Eormanrīc.

erming, es; *m. A miserable* or *wretched being;* mĭser:—Đæt is sió ān frōfer erminga æfter đām ermþum đisses līfes *that is the only comfort of the wretched after the calamities of this life*, Bt. 34, 8; Fox 144, 29. v. earming.

Erming-strǣt, e; *f.* [here-man-strǣt *via strāta mīlĭtāris*, Som.] *Erming-street. One of the four great Roman roads in Britain*, Som. Lye. v. Wætlinga-strǣt.

ermþu, e; *f. Misery, calamity;* mĭsĕria:—Cwom ofer eorþan ermþu *misery came upon the earth*, Ps. Th. 104, 14: Exon. 11 b; Th. 17, 17; Cri. 271: Andr. Kmbl. 2325; An. 1164: Bt. Met. Fox 16, 15; Met. 16, 8. Æfter ermþum *after calamities*, Bt. 34, 8; Fox 144, 30: Elen. Kmbl. 1533; El. 768. v. yrmþu.

ern *a place*, Som. Ben. Lye. v. ærn.

ern, es; *m. An eagle;* ăquĭla, Lye. v. earn.

-ern; *def. m.* -erna; *f. n.* -erne; an adjective termination from ærn, ern *a place*, denoting, as *-ern* in English, *Towards a place:*—Godrum se Norþerna cyning forþfērde *Godrum, the Northern king, died*, Chr. 890; Th. 160, 1. He forþbrohte Sūþerne wynd *transtŭlit austrum*, Ps. Spl. 77, 30. Fram deófle Sūþernum *a dæmŏnio mĕrĭdiāno*, Ps. Spl. 90, 6. Betwux eallum Eásternum *inter omnes orientāles*, Job Thw. 164, 7. Þurh đone smyltan Sūþan Westernan wind *through the mild South-western wind*, Bt. 4; Fox 8, 8.

ernþ, e; *f. Standing corn, the crop;* sĕges:—Hī swā swa ripe ernþ fortreddon hī ealle *they trod them all down like ripe corn*, Bd. 1, 12; S. 480, 35, note. DER. earnian.

ērra *the former*, Som. Ben. Lye. = ǣrra; *comp. of* ǣr.

ersc, es; *n. A park, preserve;* vīvārium, Ben. Lye. v. edisc.

ersc-hen, ærsc-hen, -hæn, -henn, e; *f. A quail;* cōturnix, perdix:—Erschen *cōturnix*, Wrt. Voc. 77, 36. Hī bǣdon and com erschen *pĕtiērunt et vēnit cŏturnix*, Ps. Spl. M. C. 104, 38. Erschæn *cōturnix*, Wrt. Voc. 63, 22. Drihten gesende swā micel fugolcyn on hira wīcstōwe swilce erschenna, đæt is on Lȳden cōturnix *ascendens cōturnix co-opĕruit castra*, Ex. 16, 13. v. edisc-hen.

-es is the termination of the genitive case singular, in the greater part of Anglo-Saxon nouns.—Cyninges botl *a king's palace.*—Abrahames God *Abraham's God.* In English *e* is omitted, but its place is denoted by an apostrophe.

-es is the termination of adverbs in many cases where the noun is not so formed; as nihtes *by night, nightly;* nēdes *of necessity, necessarily.*

Esau; *gen.* Esawes [Esaues]; *dat.* Esawe; *m.* [Esau עֵשָׂו *hairy*, from עָשָׂה *to be hairy*] *Esau:*—Sōþlīce Iacob sende bodan to Esawe his brēđer *mīsit autem Jacob nuntios ad Esau fratrem suum*, Gen. 32, 3. Esau, 32, 8: 33, 4, 8, 15, 16. Alīse me of Esawes handa mīnes brōđur *ērue me de mănu fratris mei Esau*, 32, 11. Đa handa synd Esaues handa *the hands are the hands of Esau*, 27, 22. Esauwe *to Esau*, 32, 18. Esau, 32, 17, *acc.* Esauw, 33, 1, *acc.*

Escan ceaster *Exeter;* Exonia, Chr. 876, 877; Erl. 78, 13, 16. v. Exan ceaster.

Esces dūn *Ashdown:*—In Esces dūne *at Ashdown*, Cod. Dipl. 998; Kmbl. v. 41, 15. v. Æsces dūn.

esl, e; *f. A shoulder;* hūmĕrus:—He on esle ahōf *he raised* [*him*] *on his shoulder*, Cd. 228; Th. 307, 18; Sat. 681. v. eaxel.

ESNE, es; *m. A man of the servile class, a servant, retainer, man, youth;* mercēnārius, servus, vir, jŭvĕnis. The esne was probably a poor freeman from whom a certain portion of labour could be demanded in consideration of his holdings, or a certain rent [gafol, *q. v.*] reserved out of the produce of the hives, flocks or herds committed to his care. He was a poor mercenary, serving for hire, or for his land, but was not of so low a rank as the þeów or wealh:—Ānan esne gebȳreþ to metsunge xii pūnd gōdes cornes, and ii scīpæteras and i gōd mete-cū, wudurǣden be landsīde *ūni æsno*, id est, *inŏpi, contingunt ad victum xii pondia bŏnæ annōnæ, et duo scæpeteras*, id est, *ŏvium corpŏra, et una bŏna convictuālis vacca, et sartĭcāre juxta sĭtum terræ*, L. R. S. 8; Th. i. 436, 26–28. Gif man mid esnes cwȳnan geligeþ, be cwicum ceorle, ii gebēte *if a man lie with an 'esne's' wife, her husband still living, let him make twofold amends*, L. Ethb. 85; Th. i. 24, 9. Gif man mannes esne gebindeþ, vi scillinga gebēte *if a man bind* [*another*] *man's esne, let him make amends with six shillings*, 88; Th. i. 24, 15. Gif esne ofer dryhtnes hǣse þeów-weorc wyrce an Sunnan ǣfen, efter hire setlgange, ōþ Mōnan ǣfenes setlgang, lxxx scillinga se dryhtne gebēte. Gif esne dēþ, his rāde, đæs dæges, vi se wiđ dryhten gebēte, ođđe sīne hȳd *if an esne do servile labour, contrary to his lord's command, from sunset on Sunday-eve till sunset on Monday-eve* [that is, *from sunset on Saturday till sunset on Sunday*], *let him make amends to his lord with eighty shillings. If an esne do* [*servile work*] *of his own accord on that day* [*Sunday*], *let him make amends to his lord with six shillings, or his hide*, L. Wih. 9, 10; Th. i. 38, 18–22. Ic eom đīn āgen esne, Dryhten *O Dŏmĭne, ĕgo sum servus tuus*, Ps. Th. 115, 6: Gen. 24, 61, 66: Exon. 112 a, 112 b; Th. 430, 9, 17, 31; Rä. 44, 5, 9, 17. On đīnes esnes gebēd *in ŏrātiōnem servi tui*, Ps. Th. 79, 5. Ic Dauide, dȳrum esne, on āþsware ǣr benemde *jūrāvi David servo meo*, Ps. Th. 88, 3. He him Dauid geceás, deórne esne *ēlēgit David servum suum*, 77, 69. Wæs se ofen onhǣted, hine esnas mænige wurpon wudu on innan *the oven was heated, many servants cast wood into it*, Cd. 186; Th. 231, 9; Dan. 244: Ps. Th. 68, 37. Twā hund-teontig and fīftig đara monna esna and mennena he gefullode *servos et ancillas dŭcentos quinquāginta baptĭzāvit*, Bd. 4, 13; S. 583, 20: Ps. Th. 78, 11. Ān esne of Leuies hīwrǣdene *vir de dŏmo Levi*, Ex. 2, 1: 11, 2. Se hwata esne *the brave man*, Bt. 40, 3; Fox 238, 10. Penda, se fromesta esne *Penda, vir strēnuissĭmus*, Bd. 2, 20; S. 521, 8. Ealle we synd ānes esnes suna *omnes fīlii ūnīus vĭri sŭmus*, Gen. 42, 11, 13. Uton agifan đæm esne his wīf *let us give to the man his wife*, Bt. 35, 6; Fox 170, 7. [*O. H. Ger.* asni, *m. mercēnārius: Goth.* asneis, *m. a hireling.*] DER. fyrd-esne.

esne-wyrhta, an; *m. A hireling, mercenary;* mercēnārius:—Esne-wyrhta *mercēnārius*, Greg. Dial. 2, 3. Eallum frióum monnum đās dagas sién forgifene būtan þeówum mannum and esnewyrhtum *to all freemen let these days be given, but not to slaves and hirelings*, L. Alf. pol. 43; Th. i. 92, 3.

esn-līce; *adv. Manfully, valiantly;* virīlĭter:—Onginnaþ esnlīce and beóþ stađulfæste *virīlĭter ăgĭte et confortāmĭni*, Deut. 31, 6. Hwæt dō gē, brōđur, dōþ esnlīce *what ye do, brother, do manfully*, Past. 47; Hat. MS. Hopa nū to Drihtne, and dō esnlīce *expecta Dŏmĭnum, et virīlĭter ăge*, Ps. Th. 26, 16: 30, 28.

ESOL, esul, es; *m. An ass;* ăsĭnus:—His ēstfulnesse wiđteáh se esol đe he onuppan sæt *the ass, upon which he* [*Balaam*] *sat, opposed his zeal*, Past. 36, 7; Cot. MS. Gif đǣr befeólle on ođđe oxa ođđe esol *if an ox or an ass fell into it*, Past. 63; Hat. MS. Ongan đā his esolas bǣtan *began then to bridle* [*bit*] *his asses*, Cd. 138; Th. 173, 25; Gen. 2866.

[*O. Sax.* esil, *m*: *Dut.* ezel, *m*: *Ger. M.H. Ger.* esel, *m*: *O. H. Ger.* esil, *m*: *Goth.* asilus, *m*: *Slav.* osilu.] v. assa, asse.

essian; *p.* ode; *pp.* od *To waste, consume*; tābescĕre:—Essian me dyde æfþanca mīn *tābescĕre me fēcit zēlus meus*, Ps. Spl. M. 118, 139.

ĒST, es; *m*: ēst, e; *f.* I. *will, consent, grace, favour, liberality, munificence, bounty*; bĕnĕplăcĭtum, consensus, grātia, bĕnĕvŏlentia, mūnĭfĭcentia:—Ofer mīne ēst *against my will*, Andr. Kmbl. 2438; An. 1217. Ofer ēst Godes *against God's consent*, Exon. 61 b; Th. 226, 10; Ph. 403. Þurh ēst Godes *through grace of God*, 44 b; Th. 151, 21; Gū. 798: Elen. Kmbl. 1968; El. 986. Hie on þanc curon æðelinges ēst *they accepted thankfully the chieftain's bounty*, Cd. 112; Th. 147, 21; Gen. 2443. He gearwor hæfde āgendes ēst ǣr gesceáwod *he had previously more fully experienced the owner's favour*, Beo. Th. 6142; B. 3075: Andr. Kmbl. 965; An. 483. II. *delicacies*; dēlĭciæ:—Ðā ðe synd on ēstum *qui sunt in dēlĭciis*, Lk. Bos. 7, 25. Ēstas *dēlĭciæ*, Ælfc. Gr. 13; Som. 16, 16. Cyninga wist *vel* ēstas *dăpes*, Ælfc. Gl. 65; Som. 69, 56; Wrt. Voc. 41, 13. [*Orm.* esstess, *pl. dainties*: *O. Sax.* anst, *f. favour, grace*: *O. Frs.* enst, est *favour*: *Ger.* gunst, *f. favour*: *M. H. Ger. O. H. Ger.* anst, *f. grātia*: *Goth.* ansts, *f. favour*: *Dan.* yndest, *m. f.*: *Swed.* ynnest, *m. favour*: *Icel.* ást, *f. love, affection.*]

-est, the termination of the superlative degree, perhaps from ēst *abundance*.

ēstan *from the east, easterly*, Exon. 57 a; Th. 204, 8; Ph. 94. v. eástan; *adv.*

ēste; *adj. Gracious, bountiful*; bĕnignus:—Ðæt he him ealra wæs āra ēste *that he was bountiful to him in all gifts*, Cd. 74; Th. 91, 8; Gen. 1509. Ðæt hyre eald Metod ēste wǣre bearngebyrdo *that the Lord of old was gracious to her in her child-bearing*, Beo. Th. 1895; B. 945.

Ēste, Ēstas; *nom. acc*: *gen.* Ēsta; *dat.* Ēstum; *pl. m. The Esthonians* or *Osterlings* are a Finnish race,—the Ēstas of Wulfstan and the Osterlings of the present day. They dwelt on the shores of the Baltic on the east of the Vistula:—Ðæt Witland belimpeþ to Ēstum *Witland belongs to the Esthonians*, Ors. 1, 1; Bos. 22, 5. Ne biþ nǣnig ealo gebrowen mid Ēstum, ac ðǣr biþ medo genōh *no ale is brewed by the Esthonians, but there is mead enough*, Bos. 22, 17, 19: 23, 3.

ēste-līce, ēst-līce; *adv. Kindly, gladly, delicately, daintily*; bĕnigne, lĭbenter, delĭcāte:—Ēstelīce *bĕnigne*, Ps. Spl. T. 50, 19: R. Ben. 71. Ēstelīce *delĭcāte*, Scint. 27: Prov. 29. We ðē ēstlīce mid us willaþ ferigan *we will gladly convey thee with us*, Andr. Kmbl. 583; An. 292.

ēster *easter*, Som. Ben. Lye. v. eáster.

ēst-ful; *adj.* [ēst *bounty*] *Full of kindness, devoted to, ready to serve*; dēvōtus, vōtīvus, offĭcĭōsus:—Ēstful *dēvōtus*, Greg. Dial. 1, 3, 11. Ēstful *vel* gehȳrsum *offĭcĭōsus*; ēstful *vōtīvus*, Ælfc. Gl. 115; Som. 80, 54, 56; Wrt. Voc. 61, 32, 34.

ēstful-līce; *adv. Kindly, devotedly*; dēvōte, Greg. Dial. 2, 16.

ēstfulnes, -ness, e; *f. Fulness of liberality, devotion, zeal*; dēvōtio:—Hī leorniaþ mid fulre ēstfulnesse ða sōðan gōd to sēcanne *they learn to seek the true good with full devotion*, Past. 58, 1; Hat. MS. His ēstfulnesse wiðteáh se esol ðe he onuppan sæt *the ass, on which he* [*Balaam*] *sat, opposed his zeal*, Past. 36, 7; Cot. MS.

ēstig; *adj. Gracious, bounteous*; bĕnignus:—Duguþa ēstig *bounteous in benefits*, Exon. 95 b; Th. 356, 23; Pa. 16.

ēstines, -ness, e; *f. Benignity, kindness, bounteousness*; bĕnignĭtas:—Drihten selþ ēstinesse *Dŏmĭnus dăbit bĕnignĭtātem*, Ps. Spl. T. 84, 13: 64, 12.

ēst-land, es; *n. East-land, east country, the east*; terra ŏrientālis, Som. Ben. Lye. v. Eást-land.

ēst-līce; *adv. Gladly*; lĭbenter, bĕnigne:—We ðē ēstlīce mid us willaþ ferigan *we will gladly convey thee with us*, Andr. Kmbl. 583; An. 292. v. ēste-līce.

Ēst-mere, es; *m.* [ēst = eást *east*, mere *a lake*] *The Frische Haff*, or *fresh water lake which is on the north of east Prussia*. Hav or Haf signifies a sea, in Danish and Swedish. It is written Haff in German, and it is now used to denote all the lakes connected with the rivers on the coast of Prussia and Pomerania. The Frische Haff is about sixty miles long, and from six to fifteen broad. It is separated by a chain of sand banks from the Baltic Sea, with which, at the present time, it communicates by one strait called the Gat. This strait is on the north-east of the Haff, near the fortress of Pillau, *Malte Brun's Univ. Geog.* vol. vii. p. 14. This Gat, as Dr. Bell informs me, 'seems to have been formed, and to be kept open by the superior force of the Pregel stream.' This gentleman has a perfect knowledge of the Frische Haff and the neighbourhood, as he received his early education in the vicinity, and matriculated at the University of Königsberg, near the west end of the Haff. I am indebted to Dr. Bell for the map of the celebrated German Historian, Professor Voigt, adapted to his 'Geschichte Preussens von den ältesten Zeiten, 9 vols. 8vo, Königsberg, 1827–1839.' In this map there are four openings from the Frische Haff to the Baltic. 'It is certain,' says Malte Brun, 'that in 1394 the mouth of one strait was situated at Lochsett, six or eight miles north of the fortress of Pillau.' Voigt's map gives the year 1311. Id. vol. vii. p. 15. The next is the Gat of Pillau, at present the only opening to the Baltic, with the date 1510. The third Gat, marked in the map with the date 1456, is about ten or twelve miles south-west of Pillau; and the fourth, without any date, is much nearer the west end of the Frische Haff:—Seó Wisle līþ ūt of Weonodlande, and līþ in Ēstmere; and se Ēstmere is hūru fīftene mīla brād. Ðonne cymeþ Ilfing eástan in Ēstmere of ðæm mere, ðe Truso standeþ in staðe *the Vistula flows out of Weonodland and runs into the Frische Haff* [*Estmere*]; *and the Frische Haff is, at least, fifteen miles broad. Then the Elbing comes from the east into the Frische Haff, out of the lake* [*Drausen*] *on the shore of which Truso stands*, Ors. 1, 1; Bos. 22, 5–8.

ēst-mete, es; *m. Delicate meat, dainties, luxuries*; delĭcātus cĭbus, daps, dēlĭciæ:—Ðeós sand oððe ēstmete *hæc daps*, Ælfc. Gr. 9, 54; Som. 13, 20. Seó wuduwe ðe lyfaþ on ēstmettum, heó ne lyfaþ nā, ac heó is deád. Ðeós Anna, ðe we embe sprecaþ, ne lufude heó nā ēstmettas, ac lufude fæstenu *the widow who liveth in luxuries, she liveth not, but she is dead. This Anna, of whom we speak, loved not luxuries, but loved fasts*, Homl. Th. i. 146, 34–148, 1.

-estre, -istre, -ystre, an; *f.* are the feminine terminations of nouns of action, same as the Latin -ix and English -ess; *as* Fiðelestre *a female fiddler*, Wrt. Voc. 73, 62: hleápestre *a female dancer*, 73, 71: lǣrestre *an instructress*: myltestre *meretrix* vel *scortum*, Wrt. Voc. 86, 72: rǣdistre *a female reader*, Wrt. Voc. 72, 7: sangestre [MS. sangystre] *a songstress*, Wrt. Voc. 72, 5: seámestre *a seamstress*, 74, 13.

ēstum; *adv.* [*dat.* or *inst. pl. of* ēst, *q. v.*] *Willingly, gladly, kindly, bounteously*; lĭbenter, bĕnigne, mūnĭfĭcenter:—He Freán hȳrde ēstum *he obeyed the Lord willingly*, Cd. 92; Th. 117, 11; Gen. 1952: Ps. Th. 140, 3. Him wæs wunden gold ēstum ge-eáwed *twisted gold was kindly offered to him*, Beo. Th. 2392; B. 1194. Ic Ismael ēstum wille bletsian *I will bless Ishmael bounteously*, Cd. 107; Th. 142, 4; Gen. 2356.

esul *an ass*, Som. Ben. Lye. v. esol.

esul-cweorn, e; *f. A mill-stone turned by an ass*; mŏla asĭnāria, Cot. 16.

ē-swīc, e; *f. Disgrace, offence*; scandălum:—Nis in him ēswīc *non est in illis scandălum*, Ps. Surt. 118, 165. In ēswīc *in scandălum*, 68, 23. v. ǣ-swīc.

ē-swīca, an; *m. A hypocrite, heathen*; hypocrĭta, ethnĭcus:—Ðū ēswīca *hypocrĭta*, Mt. Kmbl. Lind. 7, 5. Ēswīca *ethnĭcus*, 18, 17. v. ǣ-swīca.

ETAN, to etanne; *part.* etende; ic ete, ðū etest, etst, itst, ytst, ætst, he, heó, hit, yt, ytt, et, ett, eteþ, ieteþ, iteþ, yteþ, *pl.* etaþ; *p.* ic, he æt, ðū ǣte, *pl.* ǣton; *subj. indef.* ic ete, æte, *pl.* eten; *p.* ǣte, *pl.* ǣten; *pp.* eten; *v. a. To* EAT, *consume, devour*; ĕdĕre, cŏmĕdĕre, mandūcāre, vescĕre:—Ðū scealt greót etan *thou shalt eat dust* [*grit*], Cd. 43; Th. 56, 9; Gen. 909: 43; Th. 57, 28; Gen. 935. Seó leó bringþ hungregum hwelpum hwæt to etanne *the lioness brings to hungry whelps somewhat to eat*, Ors. 3, 11; Bos. 71, 38. Rȳnde him manna [mete] to etanne *pluit illis manna ad mandūcandum*, Ps. Spl. 77, 28. Ðæt treów wæs gōd to etanne *quod bŏnum esset lignum vescendum*, Gen. 3, 6. Etende *eating*, Ps. Th. 105, 17. Ic ete *ĕdo*, ðū etst [ytst MS. D.] *es*, he et [ett MS. C; ytt D.] *est*; we etaþ *ĕdĭmus*, gē etaþ *ĕdĭtis*, hī etaþ *ĕdunt*, Ælfc. Gr. 32; Som. 36, 18, 19. Ðū itst oððe drincst *thou eatest or drinkest*, Bt. 14, 1; Fox 42, 14. Ðū ytst wyrta *thou shalt eat herbs*, Gen. 3, 18. Ðū ætst *thou shalt eat*; cŏmĕdes, Gen. 3, 17. Ðe ytt hlāf *qui mandūcat pānem*, Jn. Bos. 13, 18. Se tō seldan ieteþ *he too seldom eats*, Exon. 90 b; Th. 340, 16; Gn. Ex. 112. Ne wiht iteþ *nor eats a thing* [*creature*], 114 b; Th. 439, 28; Rä. 59, 10. Gē etaþ *ye eat*, Gen. 3, 5. Ðū ǣte of ðam treówe *thou hast eaten of the tree*; cŏmēdisti de ligno, Gen. 3, 17. He æt ða offring-hlāfas *pānes prōpŏsĭtiōnis cŏmēdit*, Mt. Bos. 12, 4. He æt *he ate*, Gen. 3, 6. Fuglas ǣton ða *vŏlucres cŏmēdērunt ea*, Mt. Bos. 13, 4. Ðeáh ðe gē of ðam treówe eten [MS. eton] *though ye should eat of the tree*, Gen. 3, 4. Ðæt gē ne ǣton *ut non cŏmĕdĕrētis*, 3, 1, 3. [*Tynd.* eat: *Wyc. Chauc.* ete: *Piers P.* eten, ete: *R. Glouc.* ete: *Laym.* æten, eten: *Orm.* etenn: *Northumb.* eta: *Plat.* eten: *O. Sax.* etán: *Frs.* ytten: *O. Frs.* eta, ita: *Dut.* eten: *Ger.* essen: *M. H. Ger.* ëzzen: *O. H. Ger.* ezan, ezzan: *Goth.* itan; *p.* at, etum; *pp.* itans: *Dan.* äde: *Swed.* äta: *Icel.* eta: *Lat.* ĕd-o: *Grk.* ἔδ-ω: *Sansk.* ad *to eat.*] DER. fretan [= for-etan], ge-etan, of-, ofer-, þurh-, under-.

ete-lond, es; *n. Pasture land*; pascua terra:—Ǣgðer ge etelond ge yrþlond [MS. eyrðlond] *both pasture land and arable land*, Cod. Dipl. 299; A. D. 869; Kmbl. ii. 95, 14.

eten, es; *m. A giant*; gĭgas, Ps. Spl. T. 32, 16: 18, 6. v. ent.

eten = eton *should eat*, Gen. 3, 4; *subj. of* etan.

etere, es; *m. An* EATER, *a consumer, devourer*; vŏrax:—Etere *vŏrax*, Mt. Kmbl. Lind. 11, 19. Eteras *commessātōres*, Prov. 18.

etest *shalt eat*; cŏmēdes, Ps. Th. 127, 2; *2nd fut. of* etan.

et-felgan; *p.* -fealh, *pl.* -fulgon; *pp.* -folgen *To cleave* or *stick to, adhere*; adhærēre:—Nā etfilgþ me heorte þweor *a wicked heart cleaves not to me*, Ps. Spl. T. 100, 4. v. æt-felgan.

ēþ; *adv. More easily*:—Ðæt ic ðȳ ēþ mǣge ðæt sōþe leóht on ðē gebringan *that I may the more easily bring upon thee the true light*,

Bt. 5, 3; Fox 14, 20: 19; Fox 70, 3. Ðū meaht ēþ gecnāwan *thou mightest more easily know*, Bt. Met. Fox 12, 43; Met. 12, 22: 10, 75; Met. 10, 38. v. eáþ; *adv.*

ēþ, e; *f. A wave;* unda:—Ēþ *unda*, Ælfc. Gl. 98; Som. 76, 79; Wrt. Voc. 54, 23. v. ȳþ.

ēđan; *p.* de; *pp.* ed *To overflow, lay waste;* vastāre:—Đā eác ēđan gefrægn eald-feónda cyn win-burh wera *then also I heard that the tribe of ancient foes laid waste the people's beloved city*, Cd. 174; Th. 219, 19; Dan. 57. v. ȳđan.

Eđan-dūn, e; *f.* [*Hunt.* Edendune: *Matt. West.* Ethendune] EDDINGTON, *near Westbury, Wiltshire;* lŏci nōmen in agro Wiltonensi:—He fōr to Eđandūne *he went to Eddington*, Chr. 878; Erl. 81, 12.

ēþ-begete; *adj. Easily got, got ready, prepared;* făcĭlis adeptu, părātus:—Đā wæs grim andswaru ēþbegete *there was a fierce answer ready*, Beo. Th. 5714; B. 2861. v. eáþ-gete.

eþ-cwide, eþ-cwiđe *a rehearsal*, Som. Ben. Lye. v. ed-cwide.

ēđe; *adj.* [ēđan *to lay waste*] *Laid waste, desert, desolate;* vastātus:—Đæt he geheólde ēđne ēđel *that he might hold the desert land*, Cd. 175; Th. 220, 28; Dan. 78.

ēđe; *comp.* ēđre; *sup.* ēđost; *adj. Easy, ready, mild, soft;* făcĭlis, mītis:—Ne wæs đæt ēđe sīþ *that was no easy enterprise*, Beo. Th. 5166; B. 2586. Eall đū đīn yrre ēđre gedydest *mītĭgasti omnem īram tuam*, Ps. Th. 84, 3: Mk. Bos. 2, 9: Elen. Kmbl. 2586; El. 1294. v. eáđe; *adj.*

ēđe; *sup.* ēđest; *adv. Easily;* făcĭlĭter, Hy. 1, 6; Hy. Grn. ii. 280, 6. v. eáđe; *adv.*

ĒÐEL, æđel, ǣđel; *gen.* ēđles; *dat.* ēđle, ēđele; *m. n.* I. *one's own residence* or *property, inheritance, country, realm, land, dwelling, home;* prædium ăvītum, fundus herediтārius, patria, terra, sēdes, dŏmĭcĭlium, tabernăcŭlum:—Đis is mīn āgen cȳþ, eard and ēđel *this is my own country, dwelling and home*, Bt. Met. Fox 24, 99; Met. 24, 50. Hēr sceal mīn wesan eorþlīc ēđel *here shall be my earthly country*, Exon. 36 a; Th. 117, 30; Gū. 232. Ic ealne geondhwearf ēđel Gotena *I traversed all the country of the Goths*, 86 b; Th. 325, 10; Wīd. 109. Nān wītega nis andfenge on his ēđele *nēmo prophēta acceptus est in patria sua*, Lk. Bos. 4, 24. Se ēđel ūþgenge wearþ Adame and Ēuan *the country became alien to Adam and Eve*, Exon. 45 a; Th. 153, 11; Gū. 824: Th. 152, 29; Gū. 816. Onfōþ mīnes Fæder rīce, beorht ēþles wlite *receive my Father's realm, the land's bright beauty*, 27 b; Th. 82, 32; Cri. 1347. Ic ferde to foldan ufan from ēþle *I went to earth from the realm above*, Cd. 224; Th. 296, 2; Sat. 496. Engla ēđel *the dwelling of angels*, Andr. Kmbl. 1049; An. 525. Hæleđa ēđel *the dwelling of heroes*, 41; An. 21. Đæt he sīþ tuge eft to ēþle *that he would go his way again home*, Exon. 37 b; Th. 123, 21; Gū. 326: 36 b; Th. 119, 1; Gū. 248. Ēþles neósan *to visit their home*, Andr. Kmbl. 1660; An. 832: 32; An. 16. On heora ēđele *in tabernăcŭlis eōrum*, Ps. Th. 68, 26. 2. *the following three examples are neuter:*—Đæt earme ēđel *mĭsĕra patria*, Bd. 1, 12; S. 480, 37. He wolde eft đæt ēđel sēcan his hwīlendlīcan rīces *tempŏrālis sui regni sēdem repĕtiit*, 3, 22; S. 552, 33. His rīces ēđel đæt he hæfde *sēdem regni quam tĕnuit*, 4, 1; S. 563, 14. II. *the Anglo-Saxon Rune* ᛟ = œ́, the name of which letter in Anglo-Saxon is œ́đel, ǣđel, ēđel *one's native country*,—hence, this Rune not only stands for the letters œ́, but for œ́đel = ēđel *one's native country*, as,—ᛟ [ēđel] byþ oferleóf ǣghwylcum men *a native country is over-dear to every man*, Hick. Thes. i. 135, 45; Runic pm. 23; Kmbl. 344, 3: Beo. Th. 1045; B. 520: 1830; B. 913. [*O. Sax.* ōđil, *m. domĭcĭlium, patria, prædium avītum: O. Frs.* ēthel, *m: O. H. Ger.* uodal, *n. prædium: Icel.* ōðal, *n. fundus avitus.*] DER. fæder-ēđel.

ēđel-boda, an; *m. A native preacher, the apostle of a country;* indĭgēnus prædĭcātor, patriæ apostŏlus:—He ēđelbodan wiste *he knew the native preacher*, Exon. 47 a; Th. 162, 15; Gū. 976.

eđel-boren; *adj. Noble-born;* nōbĭlis natu, Prov. 31. v. æđel-boren.

ēđel-cyning, es; *m. A country's king, king of the land;* patriæ *vel* terræ rex:—Eall ǣr-gestreón ēđelcyninga *all ancient treasure of the kings of the land* [*earth*], Exon. 22 b; Th. 62, 6; Cri. 997.

ēđel-dreám, es; *m. Domestic pleasure, joy from one's country;* dŏmestĭcum gaudium, patriæ gaudium:—He heóld ā ēđeldreámas *he ever possessed domestic joys*, Cd. 78; Th. 97, 4; Gen. 1607.

eđele; *adj. Noble, famous, excellent;* nōbĭlis, egrĕgius:—Syle us on earfođum eđelne fultum *da nōbis auxĭlium de trĭbŭlātiōne*, Ps. Th. 107, 11. v. æđele.

ēđel-eard, es; *m. A native dwelling;* patrium domĭcĭlium:—Abraham wunode ēđeleardum *Abraham abode in the native dwellings*, Cd. 92; Th. 116, 33; Gen. 1945.

ēđel-fæsten, es; *n. Land-fastness, a country's fortress;* patriæ mūnīmentum:—Ic ēđelfæsten brece *I break through a land-fastness*, Exon. 126 b; Th. 487, 3; Rä. 72, 22.

ēđelīce; *adv. Easily;* facĭlĭter:—Đū eall þing birest ēđelīce būton geswince *thou bearest all things easily without labour*, Bt. Met. Fox 20, 552; Met. 20, 276. Đæt đū mǣge cumon ēđelīcost *that thou mayest most easily come*, Bt. 41, 5; Fox 254, 17. v. eáđelīce.

ēđelīcnes, -ness, e; *f. Easiness;* facĭlĭtas, Cot. 82. DER. un-ēđelīcnes. v. eáþnes.

eđeling *a noble, prince*, Chr. 617; Erl. 23, 17: 972; Erl. 125, 7. v. æđeling.

Eđelinga īg *the island of nobles, the island of Athelney*, Som. Ben. Lye. v. Æđelinga īgg.

ēđel-land, -lond, es; *n. A native land, a country;* patria, terra:—Đā wæs gūþ-hergum wera ēđelland geond-sended *then with hostile bands was the people's native land overspread*, Cd. 92; Th. 118, 20; Gen. 1968: 69; Th. 83, 14; Gen. 1379. On ēđelland đǣr Salem stōd *into the country where Salem stood*, 174; Th. 218, 15; Dan. 39. Sēceþ eádig ēđellond *seeks* [*its*] *happy native land*, Exon. 59 b; Th. 217, 12; Ph. 279: 42 a; Th. 141, 17; Gū. 628.

ēđel-leás; *adj. Countryless, homeless;* patria *vel* dŏmo cărens, extorris, exul:—Đæt đū ēđelleásum dēman wille *that thou art willing to adjudge to me homeless*, Andr. Kmbl. 148; An. 74. Ēđel-leáse đysne gyst-sele gihþum healdaþ [healdeþ MS.] *the homeless hold this guest-hall in memory*, Cd. 169; Th. 212, 3; Exod. 533.

ēđel-mearc, e; *f. One's country's boundary;* patriæ līmes:—Him đā Abraham gewāt of Egipta ēđelmearce *Abraham then departed from the Egyptians' country's boundary*, Cd. 85; Th. 106, 9; Gen. 1768: 90; Th. 112, 22; Gen. 1874: 100; Th. 133, 8; Gen. 2207.

ēđel-rīce, es; *n. A native-realm, native-country;* patrium regnum, patria:—Đæt đū mōste mīnes ēđelrīces neótan *that thou mightest enjoy my native realm*, Exon. 29 a; Th. 89, 24; Cri. 1462: Andr. Kmbl. 239; An. 120: 864; An. 432: Salm. Kmbl. 214; Sal. 106.

ēđel-riht, -rieht, es; *n. A land* or *country's right;* patrium jus:—Wǣron orwēnan ēđelrihtes *they were hopeless of country's right*, Cd. 154; Th. 191, 8; Exod. 211. Stōd seó dȳgle stōw īdel and æmen ēđelriehte feor *the secret spot stood void and desolate, far from patrial-right*, Exon. 35 b; Th. 115, 10; Gū. 187. DER. eard-ēđel-riht.

ēđel-seld, es; *n. A native seat, settlement;* patria sēdes, dŏmĭcĭlium:—Sceoldon đa rincas sēcan ellor ēđelseld *the chieftains must seek a settlement elsewhere*, Cd. 90; Th. 113, 32; Gen. 1896.

ēđel-setl, es; *n. A native seat, a settlement;* patria sēdes, dŏmĭcĭlium:—Him đā eard geceás and ēđelsetl *chose him then a dwelling and a settlement*, Cd. 91; Th. 115, 30; Gen. 1927. v. ēđel-seld.

ēđel-stæf, es; *m. A family staff* or *support, stay of the house;* prædii sustentăcŭlum. v. ēđyl-stæf.

ēđel-stađol, es; *m. A native settlement;* patrium habĭtăcŭlum:—Hū he ēđelstađolas eft gesette, swegel-torhtan seld *how he might replenish the native settlements, heaven-bright seats*, Cd. 5; Th. 6, 25; Gen. 94.

ēđel-stōl, es; *m.* I. *a paternal-seat, native-seat, country, habitation;* patria sēdes, patria, dŏmĭcĭlium:—Eafora æfter yldrum ēđelstōl heóld *the son after his parents ruled the paternal-seat*, Cd. 56; Th. 69, 2; Gen. 1129. He ēđelstōlas healdan cūđe *he could hold* [*his*] *paternal-seats*, Beo. Th. 4732; B. 2371. Engla ēđelstōl *native-seat of angels*, Exon. 8 b; Th. 4, 13; Cri. 52: 86 b; Th. 326, 1; Wīd. 122. Đē is ēđelstōl eft gerȳmed *to thee a habitation is again assigned*, Cd. 73; Th. 89, 23; Gen. 1485: 74; Th. 91, 19; Gen. 1514. II. *a chief city, metropolis;* urbs prīmāria, metrŏpŏlis = μητρόπολις:—He hēt forbærnan Rōmāna burig, sió his rīces wæs ealles ēđelstōl *he ordered to burn up the city of the Romans, which was the metropolis of his whole empire*, Bt. Met. Fox 9, 21; Met. 9, 11.

ēđel-stōw, e; *f. A dwelling-place;* habĭtātiōnis lŏcus:—Đē wīc geceós, ēđelstōwe *choose thee a habitation, a dwelling-place*, Cd. 130; Th. 164, 33; Gen. 2724: 50; Th. 64, 19; Gen. 1052.

ēđel-þrym, -þrymm, es; *m. One's country's dignity;* dignĭtas *vel* glōria patriæ:—He ēđelþrym onhōf *he exalted his country's dignity*, Cd. 79; Th. 98, 23; Gen. 1634.

ēđel-turf, ēđyl-turf; *gen.* -turfe; *dat.* -tyrf; *f. Native turf* or *soil, native country, country;* patrium sŏlum, patria, terrĭtōrium:—On mīnre ēđeltyrf *on my native turf*, Beo. Th. 824; B. 410. Đā com leóf Gode on đa ēđelturf *then came the friend of God into that country*, Cd. 85; Th. 106, 20; Gen. 1774: 127; Th. 162, 6; Gen. 2677: Exon. 60 b; Th. 220, 17; Ph. 321.

ēđel-weard, es; *n. A country's guardian* or *ruler, a king;* patriæ custos *vel* dŏmĭnus, rex:—Wæs đæt frōd cyning, eald ēđelweard *that was a wise king, an old country's guardian*, Beo. Th. 4426; B. 2210. Giómonna gestrión sealdon unwillum ēđelweardas *the wealth of men of old their country's guardians unwillingly gave up*, Bt. Met. Fox 1, 48; Met. 1, 24.

ēđel-wyn, -wynn, e; *f. Joy of country;* patriæ gaudium:—Nū sceal eall ēđelwyn eówrum cynne leófum alicgean *now shall all joy of country to your beloved kindred fail*, Beo. Th. 5762; B. 2885. DER. eard-ēđelwyn.

eđer *a hedge;* sēpes, Som. Ben. Lye. v. eodor.

ēþfynde; *adj. Easily found*, Cd. 171; Th. 215, 6; Exod. 579. v. eáþ-fynde, ȳþ-fynde.

ēþ-gesȳne; *adj. Easy to be seen, visible;* făcĭlis vīsu, vīsĭbĭlis:—Đǣr biþ ēþgesȳne þreó tācen *there shall be easy to be seen three signs*, Exon. 26 a; Th. 76, 6; Cri. 1235: Beo. Th. 2225; B. 1110. v. ȳþ-gesȳne.

éðgiende *breathing;* anhēlans, Cot. 1. v. éðian.

éðgung, e; *f. A breathing, inspiration;* inspīrātio:—Of éðgunge gāstes graman ðínes *ab inspīrātiōne spīrĭtus iræ tuæ,* Ps. Spl. T. 17, 18. v. éðung.

éþ-hylde; *adj. Easily inclined, satisfied, contented;* contentus:—On ānum were éþhylde heó ne biþ *she will not be contented with one man,* Obs. Lun. § 19; Lchdm. iii. 194, 1. Beóþ éþhylde on eówrum andlyfenum *contenti estōte stīpendiis vestris,* Lk. Bos. 3, 14.

éðian, éðigean; *p.* ode; *pp.* od. I. *to breathe, inspire;* hālāre, spīrāre, inspīrāre:—He leórt tācen forþ, þurh fýres bleó, up éðigean *he let a token forth breathe up, through colour of fire,* Elen. Kmbl. 2211; El. 1107. Se gāst éðaþ *the spirit breathes,* Greg. Dial. 2, 21. Hý ealle éðiaþ *they all breathe,* 4, 3. Éðode him on ðone múþe *inspīrāvit ei in os,* Martyrol. ad 28 April. II. *to smell;* ŏdōrāre:—Habbaþ opene nōse, ne māgon éðian *nares hābent et non ŏdōrābunt,* Ps. Th. 113, 14.

éðiende *abounding.* v. ýðian.

éðle *to a home,* Exon. 37 b; Th. 123, 21; Gú. 326: éðles *of a home,* Andr. Kmbl. 1660; An. 830; *dat. and gen. of* éðel *a home;* domĭcĭlium.

éðm, es; *m. Breath, steam, vapour;* hālĭtus, spīrĭtus, văpor:—Hú síd se swarta éðm seó *how wide the black vapour is,* Cd. 228; Th. 309, 4; Sat. 704. Ne lǽte on ðone éðm *let him not allow the vapour on [it],* L. M. 1, 32; Lchdm. ii. 78, 24. v. ǽðm.

éþnes, -ness, e; *f. Easiness, facility, favour;* facĭlĭtas:—He gemunde ðara éþnessa and ðara ealdrihta ðe hí under ðām Cāserum hæfdon *he remembered the favours and the ancient rights which they had under the Cæsars,* Bt. 1; Fox 2, 16. v. eáðnes.

éðode *breathed, inspired,* Martyrol. ad 28 April; *p. of* éðian.

éðre *more easy,* Mk. Bos. 2, 9; *comp. of* éðe. v. eáðe; *adj.*

et-hrínan *to touch,* Som. Ben. Lye, v. æt-hrínan.

eðða; *conj. Or;* aut:—Hú se cuma hātte, eðða se esne *how the guest is called, or the servant,* Exon. 112 b; Th. 430, 31; Rä. 44, 17: Mt. Kmbl. Rush. 5, 18. v. oððe.

éðung, éðgung, e; *f. Breath, a breathing, inspiration;* hālĭtus, spīrātio, inspīrātio:—He læg swā swā deád mon, nemne þynre éðunge ætýwde *quăsi mortuus jăcēbat, hālĭtu tantum pertĕnui quia vīvĕret demonstrans,* Bd. 5, 19; S. 640, 24. Éðung *spīrātio,* Ælfc. Gl. 79; Som. 72, 63; Wrt. Voc. 46, 21. Of éðunge gāstes graman ðínes *ab inspīrātiōne spīrĭtus iræ tuæ,* Ps. Spl. C. 17, 18.

éðyl, es; *m. A native country, country;* patria, terra:—Gesǽton eard and éðyl unspēdĭgran ðonne se frumstōl wæs *they inhabited a dwelling and a country more barren than was the first settlement,* Cd. 46; Th. 59, 11; Gen. 962: 73; Th. 90, 9; Gen. 1492. v. éðel.

éðyl-stæf, éðulf-stæf, es; *m. A family staff* or *support, stay of the house;* prædii sustentācŭlum:—Ic eom orwēna ðæt unc se [seó MS.] éðylstæf ǽfre weorþe gifeðe *I am hopeless that to us two the staff of the family will ever be by lot,* Cd. 101; Th. 134, 11; Gen. 2223. v. éðel-stæf.

éðyl-turf; *gen.* -turfe; *dat.* -tyrf; *f. Native turf* or *soil, native country, country;* patrium sōlum, patria, terrĭtōrium, Cd. 12; Th. 14, 26; Gen. 224: 129; Th. 163, 33; Gen. 2707. v. éðel-turf.

Etna; *indecl?* Etne, Ætne, es; *m. Etna, the volcano of Sicily;* Ætna, æ; *f.* = Αἴτνη, ης; *f.* 1. Etna [MS. Eðna] ðæt sweflene fýr tācnode, ðā hit upp of helle geate asprang on Sicilia ðam lande, and fela ofslōh mid bryne and mid stence [Ors. B. C. 458] *Etna betokened the brimstone fire, when it sprang up from the door of hell in the island of the Sicilians and slew many by burning and stench,* Ors. 2, 6; Bos. 50, 16–19. This is much abridged from Ors. 2, 14; Hav. 123–127. Though Alfred has given the impression of his age, respecting volcanoes, Orosius only speaks thus of Etna,—Ætna ipsa, quæ *tunc* cum excĭdio urbium atque agrōrum crebris eruptiōnibus æstuābat, *nunc* tantum innoxia spĕcie ad prætĕrĭtōrum fĭdem fūmat, Hav. 124, 2–4. On ðam geáre, asprang up Etna fýr on Sicilium, and māre ðæs landes forbærnde ðonne hit ǽfre ǽr dyde *in that year* [B. C. 135], *fire sprang up from Etna among the Sicilians, and burnt more of the land than it ever did before,* Ors. 5, 2; Bos. 103, 16. Etna fýr afleów up swā brād and swā mycel, ðæt feáwa ðara manna mihte beón eardfæste, ðe on Lipara wǽron ðam īglande, ðe ðær nīhst wæs, for ðære hǽte and for ðam stence *the fire of Etna flowed up so broad and so great, that few of the men, who were in the island Lipara, which was next to it, could abide in their dwellings, for the heat and for the stench,* 5, 4; Bos. 105, 9–12. 2. Etne, Ætne, es; *m:*—Se múnt, ðe nū monna bearn Etne hātaþ, on īglonde Sicilia swefle byrneþ, ðæt mon helle fýr hāteþ wíde, forðæm hit simle biþ sinbyrnende *the mountain, which now the children of men call Etna, burns in the island of Sicily with sulphur, that men widely call fire of hell, because it ever is perpetually burning,* Bt. Met. Fox 8, 96–104; Met. 8, 48–52. Nū manna gitsung is swā byrnende, swā ðæt fýr on ðære helle, seó is on ðam múnte ðe Ætne hātte *now the covetousness of men is as burning as the fire in the hell, which is in the mountain that is called Etna,* Bt. 15; Fox 48, 20. Se byrnenda swefl ðone múnt bærnþ, ðe we hātaþ Ætne *the burning brimstone burneth the mountain, which we call Etna,* 16, 1; Fox 50, 5.

Etne, Ætne, es; *m. Etna:*—Monna bearn Etne hātaþ *the children of men call Etna,* Bt. Met. Fox 8, 97; Met. 8, 49. Ðe Ætne hātte *which is called Etna,* Bt. 15; Fox 48, 20. v. Etna.

et-nēhstan; *adv. At nighest, at last, lastly;* postrēmo, nŏvissĭme, Som. Ben. Lye. v. æt-nýhstan.

etol; *adj. Voracious, gluttonous;* ĕdax:—Etol *ĕdax,* Ælfc. Gr. 9, 60; Som. 13, 44. v. ettul-man.

eton *should eat,* Gen. 3, 4, = eten; *subj. of* etan *to eat.*

et-somne; *adv. Together;* conjuncte, sĭmul:—Et-somne cwom lx monna *sixty men came together,* Exon. 106 a; Th. 404, 1; Rä. 23, 1. v. æt-somne.

etst, he et *eatest, eats;* es, est, Ælfc. Gr. 32; Som. 36, 18; *2nd and 3rd pers. pres. of* etan.

ettan *to pasture land;* depascĕre:—Eal ðæt land ðæt man āðer oððe ettan oððe erian mæg *all the land that they could either pasture or plough,* Ors. 1, 1; Bos. 20, 41.

ettul-man, es; *m. A gluttonous man;* vŏrax hŏmo:—Hēr ys ettulman *ecce hŏmo vŏrax,* Mt. Bos. 11, 19.

ettulnys, -nyss, e; *f. Greediness, gluttony;* edācĭtas, Som. Ben. Lye.

Éua, æ; *f. Lat:* Ēve, Ēfe, an; *f. Eve;* Hēva:—Éua, ðæt is līf; forðanðe heó is ealra libbendra mōdor *Hēva, id est vīta; eo quod māter esset cunctōrum vīventium,* Gen. 3, 20. Be Éuan his gemæccan *by Eve* [Hēvam] *his wife,* 4, 1. Éua, Homl. Th. i. 16, 27. Éuan scyld *Eve's sin,* Exon. 9 a; Th. 7, 6; Cri. 97. [*Heb.* חַוָּה from חָיָה *to live.*]

euen *even,* Som. Ben. Lye. v. efen.

Euer-wíc *York,* Chr. 189; Th. 14, 23, col. 1. v. Eofor-wíc.

Eues-ham, es; *m. Evesham,* Chr. 1077; Erl. 215, 15. v. Eofes-ham.

eufæstnys, e; *f. Sincerity, religion;* relĭgio, Ælfc. T. 28, 11. v. ǽ-fæstnes.

eúwu *a ewe,* Heming, p. 129. v. eówu.

ēw-bryce *adultery,* Som. Ben. Lye. v. ǽw-bryce.

ēwe, an; *f. A ewe;* ŏvis fēmĭna:—Ēwe biþ, mid hire giunge sceápe, scilling weorþ *a ewe, with her young sheep, shall be worth a shilling,* L. In. 55; Th. i. 138, 7. v. eówu.

ēwe, es; *common gender A sheep, generally as* ŏvis:—Be ēwes weorþe *of a sheep's worth;* de ŏvis prĕtio, L. In. 55; Th. i. 138, 6. v. eówu.

ēwede *a flock,* Ps. Spl. T. 77, 57. v. eówde.

ewerdla *damage.* v. æf-werdla.

ēwes *a sheep's,* L. In. 55; Th. i. 138, 6: *also* eówes in MSS. G, H; *gen. of* ēwe, es; *f. m.*

ēwestre, es; *m. A sheepfold;* ŏvīle, Cot. 7. v. eówestras.

ēwiscnes, -ness, e; *f. Disgracefulness, impudence, shamelessness;* impŭdentia, Som. Ben. Lye. v. ǽwiscnys.

ēwyde *a flock,* Ps. Spl. C. 77, 57. v. eówde.

ewyrdlu *damage.* v. æf-werdla.

ex, e; *f. An axe;* secūris. v. æx.

ex *an axis;* axis, Som. Ben. Lye. v. eax.

Ex, es; *m:* Exa, an; *m. The river Ex;* Isca, *in Devon.* v. Exan ceaster, Exan múþa.

exāmeron, es; *n. A work on the six days of creation;* hexæmĕron = ἑξα-ήμερον = ἕξ *six,* ἡμέριος, ον *relating to a day:*—Exāmeron, ðæt is be Godes six daga weorcum *Hexameron, that is concerning the six days' works of God,* Hexam. Norm. 1. Basilius awrāt āne wundorlīce bōc, be eallum Godes weorcum, ðe he geworhte on six dagum, Exāmeron gehāten *Basil wrote a wonderful book about all the works of God, which he wrought in six days, called Hexameron,* Basil prm; Norm. 32, 12.

Exan ceaster, Eaxan ceaster, Exe cester, es; *n.* [*Flor.* Exancestre, Excestre: *Hovd.* Excester; Ex, Exa *the river Ex:* ceaster; *gen.* ceastres; *n.* v. ceaster *a city*] EXETER, *Devon;* cīvĭtas Exoniæ in agro Devōniensi, ad rīpam Iscæ flūminis:—Se here Exan ceaster beseten hæfde *the army had beset Exeter,* Chr. 895; Th. 172, 12. He wende hine wið Exan ceastres *he turned towards Exeter,* Chr. 894; Th. 166, 31. Wið Exan cestres *towards Exeter,* Chr. 894; Th. 168, 26, col. 1. Exacester, Chr. 1003; Th. 252, 14, col. 1. Eaxeceaster, Execiester, Th. 253, 14, col. 1, 2. v. ceaster II.

Exan múþa, Eaxan múþa, Axa-múþa, an; *m:* Exan múþ, es; *m. The mouth of the river Ex,* EXMOUTH, *Devon:*—Se here com to Exan múþan *the army came to the mouth of the Ex,* Chr. 1001; Th. 249, 36. To Exan múþe *to Exmouth,* Th. 249, col. 2, 36. To Axa-múþan *to Exmouth,* Chr. 1049; Th. 307, 37.

exl, e; *f. Shoulder;* hŭmĕrus:—He hit set on his exla *impōnit in humeros suos,* Lk. Bos. 15, 5: Andr. Kmbl. 3148; An. 1577. v. eaxel.

ex-odus, i; *m.* [*Lat.* exodus = *Grk.* ἐξ *out;* ὁδός, *f. way, path, travelling*] *A going out;* exĭtus:—Exodus on Grēcisc, Exitus on Lýden, Útfæreld on Englisc *Exodus* [Ἔξοδος, *f.*] *in Greek, exitus in Latin, a going out in English,* Ex. Thw. Title. v. út-færeld.

exorcista, an; *m. A caster out of spirits,* L. Ælf. P. 34; Th. ii. 378, 6. v. hād II, hālsigend.

F

At the end of syllables, and between two vowels, the Anglo-Saxon *f* is occasionally represented by *u*, the present English *v*; it is, therefore, probable that the Anglo-Saxon *f* in this position had the sound of our present *v*, as Luu, luf=lufu *love;* fīf *five;* hæuþ, hæfþ *haveth;* Euen, efen *even*. In the beginning of Anglo-Saxon words, *f* had the sound of the English *f*, as Fīf *five*, finger *finger*, finn *fin*, fisc *fish*. The Rune ᚠ not only stands for the letter *f*, but for Feoh, which, in Anglo-Saxon, signifies *money, wealth*. v. feoh IV and RŪN.

fā *hostile;* hostīles:—Fā þrōwiaþ bealu egeslīc *the hostile shall suffer fearful evil*, Exon. 31 b; Th. 98, 30; Cri. 1615; *pl. nom. acc. of* fāh.

faag *of a varying colour*. v. fāg.

faca *of spaces*, Andr. Kmbl. 2741; An. 1373; *gen. pl. of* fæc.

facade *acquired*, Ors. 3, 11; Bos. 75, 28; *p. of* facian.

FĀCEN, fācn, es; *pl. nom. acc.* fācnu; *gen.* fācna; *n. Deceit, fraud, guile, treachery, malice, wickedness, evil, crime;* dŏlus, fraus, nēquĭtia, mālĭtia, inīquĭtas, prævārĭcātio:—Eádig wer ðam ðe nā ætwīteþ Drihten synna, and nys on gāste his fācen *beātus vir cui non impŭtābit Dŏmĭnus peccātum, nec est spīrĭtu ejus dŏlus*, Ps. Spl. 31, 2: Ps. Lamb. 35, 4. Hēr is Israhēlisc wer, on ðam nis nān fācn *ecce vēre Israelīta, in quo dŏlus non est*, Jn. Bos. 1, 47. Ðis fācn *hæc fraus*, Ælfc. Gr. 9, 36; Som. 12, 34. Ne ætfyligeþ ðē āhwǣr fācn ne unriht *numquid adhæret tĭbi sēdes inīquĭtātis*, Ps. Th. 93, 19. Fācnes cræftig *skilled in guile*, Exon. 97 a; Th. 361, 24; Wal. 24: 62 a; Th. 229, 4; Ph. 450. He ðæs fācnes fintan sceáwaþ *he sees the sequel of treachery*, 83 b; Th. 315, 16; Mōd. 32. Gif heó ðæs fācnes gewīta nǣre *if she were not privy to the crime*, L. Ath. v. 1, § 1, 2; Th. i. 228, 17, 21. Ic feóde fācnes wyrcend *făcientes prævārĭcātiōnes odīvi*, Ps. Th. 100, 3: 139, 10. Ne dyde ic for fācne *I did it not for fraud*, Cd. 128; Th. 162, 34; Gen. 2691: Exon. 73 a; Th. 272, 10; Jul. 497. Būtan ǣghwylcum fācne *without any guile*, L. O. 2; Th. i. 178, 14. He hī ðonne būtan fācne fēdeþ syððan *pāvit eos sĭne mălĭtia cordis sui*, Ps. Th. 77, 71: 93, 22. He lādige ða hand mid ðe man tȳhþ ðæt he ðæt fācen mid worhte *let him clear the hand therewith with which he is charged to have wrought the fraud*, L. Ath. i. 14; Th. i. 206, 24. Fācen ne dō ðū *ne fraudem fēcĕris*, Mk. Bos. 10, 19. Eorl ōðerne spreceþ fægere beforan, and ðæt fācen swā ðeáh hafaþ in his heortan *one man speaks another fair before his face, and nevertheless hath evil in his heart*, Frag. Kmbl. 9; Leás. 5: Menol. Fox 574; Gn. C. 56. Hī fācen and unriht acwǣdon *lŏcūti sunt nēquĭtiam*, Ps. Th. 72, 6: 94, 9. Ðæt he him nān fācn mid nyste *that he knew of no guile in him*, L. C. S. 29; Th. i. 392, 16: L. O. 9; Th. i. 182, 3. Se Hǣlend hyra fācn gehȳrde *cognĭta Iesus nēquĭtia eōrum*, Mt. Bos. 22, 18. Him yfle ne mæg fācne sceððan *evil may not injure them by guile*, Exon. 64 b; Th. 237, 25; Ph. 595: 70 b; Th. 263, 15; Jul. 350. Nōðer he ðȳ fācne mæg biwergan *nor may he defend himself from that evil*, 87 b; Th. 329, 22; Vy. 38. Innan of manna heortan yfele geþances cumaþ, fācnu *ab intus ĕnim de corde hŏmĭnum mălæ cōgĭtātiōnes prōcēdunt, dŏlus*, Mk. Bos. 7, 22. Ðū tō fela fācna gefremedes in flǣschoman *thou hast perpetrated too many guiles in the body*, Exon. 41 a; Th. 137, 12; Gū. 558: Cd. 125; Th. 160, 16; Gen. 2651. [*Orm.* fakenn: *Plat.* faxen, *pl. fun: O. Sax.* fēkn, *n. a fraud, deceit: M. H. Ger.* veichen, *n: O. H. Ger.* feihan, *n: Icel.* feikn, *f. a token, an omen.*]

fācen-dǣd, e; *f. A wicked deed, sin;* peccātum:—For fyrenfulra fācendǣdum *pro peccātōrĭbus dērĕlinquentĭbus*, Ps. Th. 118, 53.

fācen-ful, fācn-ful, -full; *def.* se -fulla, seó, ðæt -fulle; *adj. Deceitful, crafty;* fraudŭlentus, dŏlōsus:—Se fācenfulla [MS. fakenfulla] fægere word spreceþ *the deceitful man speaks fair words*, Basil admn. 5; Norm. 46, 5. Mūþ ðæs fācenfullan ofer me geopened is *os dŏlōsi sŭper me ăpertum est*, Ps. Lamb. 108, 2. Fram menn fācenfullum [MS. fakenfullum] genera me *ab hŏmĭne dŏlōso ērue me*, 42, 1. Drihten alēs sāwle mīne fram tunge fācenfulre *Dŏmĭne lībĕra ănĭmam meam a lingua dŏlōsa*, 119, 2: 108, 3. On fācnfulre tungan *lingua dŏlōsa*, 51, 6. Ðæne wer ðe is blōdgīta oððe geótende oððe wer blōda and fācenfulne gehiscþ oððe onscunaþ Drihten *vĭrum sanguĭnum et dŏlōsum abŏmĭnābĭtur Dŏmĭnus*, 5, 8. Dō ðū feorr fram ðē ða fācenfullan [MS. fakenfullan] hiwunge *make far from thee deceitful dissimulation*, Basil admn. 5; Norm. 46, 9. Weras [MS. weres] bloda and fācnfulle ne dǣlaþ [MS. dæla] on emtwā heora dagas *vĭri sanguĭnum et dŏlōsi non dimĭdiābunt dies suos*, Ps. Lamb. 54, 24.

fācen-fulnes, -ness, e; *f. Deceitfulness, deceit;* fraudŭlentia, Som. Ben. Lye.

fācen-gecwis, e; *f. A wicked consent, conspiracy;* conspīrātio, Cot. 46.

fācen-geswipere, es; *n. Deceitful counsel, deceit;* consĭlium astūtum, dŏlus:—Hī on ðīnum folce fācengeswipere syredan *in plēbem tuam astūte cōgĭtāvērunt consĭlium*, Ps. Th. 82, 3.

fācen-leás; *adj. Without deceit, simple, innocent;* simplex, Som. Ben. Lye.

fācen-līc; *adj. Deceitful;* dŏlōsus, R. Ben. in prooem: Ors. 3, 1? Lye.

fācen-līce; *adv. Deceitfully, fraudulently;* dŏlōse, fraudŭlenter:—Ðīn brōðor com fācenlīce and nam ðīne bletsunga *vēnit germānus tuus fraudŭlenter et accēpit benedictiōnem tuam*, Gen. 27, 35. Ða leásan men fācenlīce þencaþ *false men think treacherously*, Frag. Kmbl. 49; Leás. 26.

fācen-searu, fācn-searu; *gen.* -searwes; *n. A treacherous wile, treachery;* machĭnātio dŏlōsa:—Þurh fācnsearu *by treachery*, Ps. Th. 55, 1. Gefylled fācensearwum *filled with treacherous wiles*, Exon. 83 b; Th. 315, 7; Mōd. 27.

fācen-stæf, fācn-stæf, es; *pl. nom. acc.* -stafas; *m. A deceitful* or *treacherous deed;* nēquĭtia:—Nalles fācnstafas fremedon *they perpetrated no treacherous deeds*, Beo. Th. 2041; B. 1018.

fācen-tācen, es; *n. A false sign, sign of crimes;* scĕlĕrum signum:—Hafaþ fācentācen feores *they shall have the false sign of life*, Exon. 30 b; Th. 95, 32; Cri. 1566.

facg, fagc, es; *n? A flat-fish, plaice;* plătesia, Ælfc. Gl. 102; Som. 77, 64; Wrt. Voc. 55, 69.

facian; *p.* ode, ade; *pp.* od, ad *To acquire;* acquīrĕre:—Ðe he him sylfum facade Mæcedonia onweald *because he wished to get the government of the Macedonians for himself*, Ors. 3, 11; Bos. 75, 28.

fācn *deceit*, Jn. Bos. 1, 47. v. fācen.

fācne; *def.* se fācna; seó, ðæt fācne; *adj. Deceitful, fraudulent, factious;* subdŏlus, dŏlōsus, factiōsus:—Fācna *dŏlōsus*, Cot. 85: *factiōsus*, 198. Gif hit fācne is *if it be fraudulent*, L. Ethb. 77; Th. i. 22, 2. Fācnum wordum *with factious words*, Cd. 214; Th. 268, 35; Sat. 65. v. fǣcne; *adj.*

fācne; *adv. Deceitfully, fraudulently;* dŏlōse, fraudŭlenter:—Ic his feóndas fācne gegyrwe mid scame *inĭmīcos ejus induam confūsiōne*, Ps. Th. 131, 19: 138, 18. v. fǣcne; *adv.*

fācn-ful, -full *deceitful*, Ps. Lamb. 51, 6: 54, 24. v. fācen-ful.

fācon *deceit*, Jn. Lind. War. 1, 47. v. fācen.

fācyn-full *deceitful*, Prov. 14. v. fācen-ful.

fadian; *p.* ode; *pp.* od *To set in order, dispose, direct, guide;* ordĭnāre, dispōnĕre, dirĭgĕre:—Word and weorc freónda gehwylc fadige mid rihte *let every friend guide his works and words aright*, L. C. E. 19; Th. i. 372, 1. DER. ge-fadian, mis-.

fadung, e; *f. A setting in order, disposing, dispensation;* ordo, ordĭnātio, dispŏsĭtio:—Fadung *ordo, ordĭnātio*, R. Ben. 65: *dispŏsĭtio*, 18. Swā swā hit ðære godcundlīcan fadunge gelīcode *as it seemed good to the divine dispensation*, Homl. Th. i. 274, 31. DER. ge-fadung, mis-.

FÆC, es; *pl. nom. acc.* facu; *gen.* faca; *n. Space, interval, distance, portion of time;* spătium, intervallum, tempŏris intervallum:—On swā lytlum fæce *in so short a space*, Elen. Kmbl. 1917; El. 960. Ðæt wæs on fæce syxtig furlanga fram Hierusalem *quod ĕrat in spătio stădiōrum sexāginta ab Ierūsălem*, Lk. Bos. 24, 13. Hī binnon lytlan fæce gewendon to Lundene *they within a little space went to London*, Chr. 1016; Erl. 155, 22. Myccle fæce *multo intervallo*, Bd. 1, 1; S. 473, 10. Ymb lytel fæc *after a little time*, Elen. Kmbl. 543; El. 272: 765; El. 383. Þurh lytel fæc *for a little space*, Exon. 35 b; Th. 115, 6; Gū. 185. Se þeódwīga þreónihta fæc swīfeþ on swefote *the noble creature is dormant in slumber a three nights' space*, 96 a; Th. 357, 34; Pa. 38. Geseah he ānre stōwe fæc *vīdit ūnius lŏci spătium*, Bd. 3, 10; S. 534, 19. Unfyrn faca *in a little time*, Andr. Kmbl. 2741; An. 1373. Twegra dæga fæc *two days' space;* duārum diērum spătium, R. Ben. 53. Fīfwintra fæc *five years' space;* olympias, Ælfc. Gl. 16; Som. 58, 69; Wrt. Voc. 21, 56. Lytel fæc *a little time, interval;* intervallum, Ælfc. Gr. 47; Som. 48, 35: Beo. Th. 4472; B. 2240. Æfter fæce *after a while, afterwards;* postmŏdum, Bd. 3, 5; S. 527, 16: 5, 23; S. 645, 33. [*Plat.* fak: *Frs.* feck *cămĕra, spătium, intervallum: O. Frs.* fek, fak: *Dut.* vak, *n. an empty place* or *space: Ger.* fach, *n. any inclosed space: M. H. Ger.* vach, *n: O. H. Ger.* fah *mœnia: Dan.* fag, *n. a department, office: Swed.* fack, *n. a compartment.*]

fæccan *to fetch*, L. E. G. 3; Th. i. 168, 11, note 13. v. feccan.

fæcele, an; *f. A torch;* fax:—Fæcele stānes *fax scŏpŭli*, Cot. 169. v. þæcele.

fǣcne, fācne; *adj. Deceitful, fraudulent, guileful, wicked;* subdŏlus, dŏlōsus, mălignus, nēquam:—Swā oft sceaða fǣcne forfēhþ eorlas *as oft the guileful robber surprises men*, Exon. 20 b; Th. 54, 20; Cri. 871. Hæfde fǣcne hyge *he had a crafty soul*, Cd. 23; Th. 29, 1; Gen. 443. Of firenfulra fǣcnum handum *from the deceitful hands of the wicked*, Ps. Th. 81, 4: 105, 10: 136, 3. DER. fela-fǣcne, un-.

fǣcne, fācne; *adv. Maliciously, disgracefully;* mălĭgne, turpĭter:—Gif me mīn feónd fǣcne wyrgeþ *si inĭmīcus meus mălĕdixisset mĭhi*, Ps. Th. 54, 11: 55, 2: 65, 2: 111, 7, 9.

fǣdde *fed*, Chr. 994; Erl. 133, 26, = fēdde; *p. of* fēdan.

FÆDER, feder; *indecl. in sing. but gen.* fæderes *and dat.* fædere *are sometimes found; pl. nom. acc.* fæderas; *gen.* a; *dat.* um; *m. A* FATHER; păter:—Fæder and mōdor *a father and mother;* hic et hæc parens, Ælfc. Gr. 9, 38; Som. 12, 48. On Fæder geardas *in the dwellings of the Father*, Salm. Kmbl. 832; Sal. 415. Mid fæder ðīnne *with thy father*, Exon. 12 b; Th. 22, 9; Cri. 349. We bletsiaþ bilewitne Feder *we bless* *the merciful Father*, Hy. 8, 8; Hy. Grn. ii. 290, 8. Sunu his fæderes *son of his father*, Cd. 226; Th. 301, 12; Sat. 580. Ðis is se ilca God, ðone fæderas cūðon *this is the same God, whom your fathers knew*, Andr. Kmbl. 1504; An. 753: Elen. Kmbl. 796; El. 398. Ne sleá man fæderas for suna gylton, ne suna for fædera gilton *non occīdentur patres pro filiis, nec filii pro patrĭbus*, Deut. 24, 16. Bebeád fæderum ussum *mandāvit patrĭbus nostris*, Ps. Th. 77, 7. **2.** 1 Fæder *păter:* 2 ealda [MS. ealde] fæder *ăvus:* 3 þridda [MS. þridde] fæder *proăvus:* 4 feówerþa [MS. feówerþe] fæder *ăbăvus:* 5 fīfta [MS. fīfte] fæder *ătăvus:* 6 sixta fæder *sextus pater*, trĭtăvus, Ælfc. Gl. 90, 91; Som. 75, 4-14; Wrt. Voc. 51, 49-59: 72, 18-23: Nat. S. Greg. Els. p. 4, note. [*Wyc.* fader, fadir: *Piers P. Chauc.* fader: *Laym.* fæder, fader, uader: *Orm.* faderr: *Plat.* vader, *m: O. Sax.* fader, fadar, *m: Frs.* faer: *O. Frs.* feder, fader, feider, *m: Dut.* vader, *m: Ger. M. H. Ger.* vater, *m: O. H. Ger.* fatar, fater, *m: Goth.* fadar; *gen.* fadrs; *dat.* fadr, *m: Dan. Swed.* fader, *m: Icel.* faðir, *m: Lat.* păter, *m: Grk.* πατήρ, *m: Sansk.* pi-tṛi *from* pā *to guard, preserve.*] DER. ǣr-fæder, eald-, forþ-, fōster-, god-, heáfod-, heáh-, sōþ-, steóp-, wealdend-, wuldor-: fædera, ge-fædera, suhter-.

fædera, fædra, an; *m. An uncle, a father's brother;* patruus:—Mīn fædera *patruus meus*, Wrt. Voc. 52, 13. Bān hire fæderan *patrui sui ossa*, Bd. 3, 11; S. 535, 16: 3, 24; S. 556, 28: Cd. 90; Th. 114, 7; Gen. 1900. Mīnes fæderan þridda fæder *my uncle's great grandfather*, Wrt. Voc. 52, 16. [*O. Frs.* federia, *m: O. H. Ger.* fataro, *m.*] DER. suhtor-fædra, suhter-ge-fædera. v. eám *an uncle on the mother's side.*

fæder-æðelo; *indecl. n.* [æðelo *nobility, origin*] *Fatherly nobility, origin, ancestry, fatherly honours;* gĕneālōgia păterna, nōbĭlĭtas hērēdĭtāria:—Ða ðe mǣgburge mǣst gefrunon, fæderæðelo gehwǣs *those who most understand kinship, the ancestry of each*, Cd. 161; Th. 200, 24; Exod. 361. He scolde fæderæðelum onfōn *he should succeed to his father's honours*, Beo. Th. 1826; B. 911.

fæderen, fædern, fædren; *adj. Paternal, belonging to a father;* păternus, Cd. 79; Th. 98, 10; Gen. 1628.

fæderen-brōðor, es; *m. A brother from the same father;* frāter ex eōdem patre ŏriundus:—Ic fram ðē wearþ fæderenbrōðrum *exter factus sum fratrĭbus meis*, Ps. Th. 68, 8.

fæderen-cnōsl, fædren-cnōsl, es; *n.* [cnōsl *a race, kin*] *A paternal race, father's kin;* păterna prōgĕnies, părentēla:—Be ðæs fædrencnōsles wēre *according to the 'wer' of the father's kin*, L. Alf. pol. 9; Th. i. 68, 2.

fæderen-cyn, fædren-cyn, -cynn, es; *n.* [cyn *a race, kin*] *A paternal kin* or *race;* păternum gĕnus:—Hiera ryht fæderencyn [fædrencynn, Th. 87, 14, col. 1] gǣþ to Cerdice *their direct paternal kin goes to Cerdic*, Chr. 755; Th. 86, 14, col. 1. We areccan ne māgon ðæt fædrencynn *we cannot tell the paternal kin*, Exon. 11 b; Th. 16, 4; Cri. 248.

fæderen-healf, fædren-healf, e; *f. The father's side;* păterna pars:—Hira nān næs on fædrenhealfe togeboren, būton him ānum *none of them on the paternal side was born thereto, except him alone*, Chr. 887; Erl. 86, 5.

fæderen-mǣg, fædern-mǣg, fædren-mǣg, -māg, es; *m.* [mǣg *a relation*] *A relation on the father's side, paternal relative;* a patre cognātus, agnātus:—Cain gewearþ to ecgbanan fæderenmǣge *Cain became the murderer of his father's son*, Beo. Th. 2530; B. 1263. Fædrenmǣga mǣgleás *kinless of paternal relatives*, L. Alf. pol. 27; Th. i. 78, 20. Fædrenmǣgum hiora dǣl mon agife *let their share be given to the paternal kindred*, 8; Th. i. 66, 22. Fædernmāgas *agnāti*, Ælfc. Gl. 92; Som. 75, 37; Wrt. Voc. 51, 79.

fæderen-mǣgþ, e; *f. Paternal kindred;* păterna cognātio:—VIII fæderenmǣgþe *eight of the paternal kindred*, L. E. G. 12; Th. i. 174, 19.

fæder-ēðel; *gen.* -ēðles; *m.* [ēðel *a country, home*] *Father-land, paternal home;* păterna rĕgio, patria:—Scipia swōr ðæt him leófre wǣre, ðæt he hine sylfne acwealde ðonne he forlēte his fæderēðel *Scipio swore that he would rather kill himself than leave his father-land*, Ors. 4, 9; Bos. 91, 20. He bebeád, ðæt ǣlc cōme to his fæderēðle *he gave orders that every one should come to his father's home*, 5, 14; Bos. 114, 18, 22.

fæder-ēðel-stōl, es; *m. Father-land, paternal-seat;* patria, sēdes patria:—Carram ofgif, fæderēðelstōl *renounce Harran, thy father-land*, Cd. 83; Th. 105, 4; Gen. 1748: Exon. 15 a; Th. 32, 22; Cri. 516.

fæder-feoh, -fioh; *gen.* -feós; *n. A father-fee,—the marriage portion which reverted to the father, if his daughter became a widow, and returned home*, Fæder-feum, dos a patre accepta, L. Ethb. 81; Th. i. 24, 1, note a. v. *Du Cange* in voce.

fæder-geard, es; *m. A paternal habitation;* păternum dŏmĭcĭlium:—Fædergeardum feor *far from his paternal habitations*, Cd. 50; Th. 64, 20; Gen. 1053.

fæder-gestreón, es; *n. A father's property, patrimony;* patrĭmōnium, Cot. 152.

fædering-mǣg, es; *m. A paternal relation;* a patre cognātus, agnātus, L. Ethb. 81; Th. i. 24, 1. v. fæderen-mǣg.

fæderleás; *adj.* FATHERLESS; orbus patre, orphănus, Ps. Vos. 93, 6.

fæder-līc; *def.* se -līca, seó, ðæt -līce; *adj. Of* or *belonging to a father*, FATHERLY, *paternal, ancestral;* patrius, păternus, patrōnymĭcus:—Wæs he to ðære fæderlīcan healle gelǣdd *he was led to his father's hall*, Guthl. 2; Gdwin. 12, 11. Ðȳlæs toworpen sīen frōd fyrngewritu and ða fæderlīcan lāre forlēten *lest the wise old scriptures should be overturned and our ancestral lore deserted*, Elen. Kmbl. 862; El. 431. Sume syndon patronimica, ðæt synd fæderlīce naman *some are patronymics, which are fatherly nouns*, Ælfc. Gr. 5; Som. 4, 52.

fædern-mǣg, -māg *a paternal relative*, Ælfc. Gl. 92; Som. 75, 37; Wrt. Voc. 51, 79. v. fæderen-mǣg.

fæder-rīce, es; *n. A paternal kingdom;* păternum regnum:—In heora fæderrīce *in their paternal kingdom*, Cd. 220; Th. 283, 22; Sat. 308.

fæder-slaga, an; *m. A father-slayer;* parrĭcīda, Ælfc. Gl. 85; Som. 73, 113; Wrt. Voc. 49, 20.

fæderyn-cyn, -cynn, es; *n. A paternal kindred* or *race*, Cd. 170; Th. 213, 29; Exod. 559. v. fæderen-cyn.

fædra, an; *m. A paternal uncle*, Chr. 901; Th. 178, 22. v. fædera.

fædren *paternal, belonging to a father;* păternus. v. fæderen.

fædren-cnōsl *father's kin*, L. Alf. pol. 9; Th. i. 68, 2. v. fæderen-cnōsl.

fædren-cyn, -cynn *a paternal kin*, Exon. 11 b; Th. 16, 4; Cri. 248. v. fæderen-cyn.

fædren-healf *the paternal side*, Chr. 887; Erl. 86, 5. v. fæderen-healf.

fædren-mǣg *a paternal relative*, L. Alf. pol. 27; Th. i. 78, 20. v. fæderen-mǣg.

fædrunga, an; *m. A paternal relation, any parental relation;* cognātus a patre, părens:—Feóndes fædrunga *the fiend's parent* [i. e. *Grendel's mother*], Beo. Th. 4262; B. 2128. [*O. H. Ger.* fatarungo, *m.* v. Grm. ii. 363.]

fædyr *a father*, Mt. Foxe 23, 9. v. fæder.

FǢGE; *def.* se fǣga, seó, ðæt fǣge; *comp.* -ra; *sup.* -est; *adj.* **I.** *fated, doomed, destined;* prŏpĕræ morti dēvōtus, cui mors immĭnet:—Æt fōtum feóll fǣge cempa *the fated warrior fell at his feet*, Byrht. Th. 135, 17; By. 119: Exon. 89 a; Th. 335, 2; Gn. Ex. 27. Næs ic fǣge ðā gyt *I was not yet doomed*, Beo. Th. 4289; B. 2141: 5943; B. 2975. Pharaon gefeól, and his fǣge werud, on ðam Reádan Sǣ *excussit Pharaōnem, et exercĭtum ejus, in Māri Rubro*, Ps. Th. 135, 15. Lǣtaþ gāres ord ingedūfan in fǣges ferþ *let the javelin-point pierce the life of the doomed one*, Andr. Kmbl. 2665; An. 1334; Salm. Kmbl. 318; Sal. 158. Hogodon georne hwā ðǣr mid orde ǣrost mihte on fǣgean men feorh gewinnan *they were earnestly anxious who there might first take life with a spear from the doomed man*, Byrht. Th. 135, 28; By. 125. Wyrd ne meahte in fǣgum leng feorg gehealdan *fate might not longer preserve life in the destined*, Exon. 48 a; Th. 165, 19; Gū. 1031. Bil eal þurhwōd fǣgne flǣschoman *the falchion passed through all her fated carcase*, Beo. Th. 3140; B. 1568. On ðæt fǣge folc *in the fated band*, Elen. Kmbl. 233; El. 117. Wræce bīsgodon fǣge þeóda *the fated people were busied in evil*, Cd. 64; Th. 76, 30; Gen. 1265. Fǣge swulton on geofene *the destined perished in the ocean*, Andr. Kmbl. 3059; An. 1532. Scipflotan fǣge feóllan *the death-doomed shipmen fell*, Chr. 937; Erl. 112, 12; Æðelst. 12. Ādl fǣgum feorh ōþ-þringeþ *disease will expel life from the fated*, Exon. 82 b; Th. 310, 7; Seef. 71: Judth. 11; Thw. 24, 27; Jud. 209. Nō ðȳ fǣgra wæs *that was not the more fated*, Cd. 162; Th. 203, 6; Exod. 399. **II.** *dead, killed, slain;* mortuus, occīsus:—Todǣlan werum to wiste fǣges flǣschoman *to distribute the flesh of the slain to the men for food*, Andr. Kmbl. 307; An. 154. Ofer ðæt fǣge hūs *over the dead house*, Elen. Kmbl. 1759; El. 881. Hirdas lǣgon gǣsne on greóte, fǣgra flǣschaman *the keepers lay lifeless on the sand, the carcases of the slain*, Andr. Kmbl. 2171; An. 1087. Fǣgum stæfnum *with dead bodies*, Cd. 166; Th. 207, 5; Exod. 462. **III.** *accursed, condemned;* execrātus, damnātus:—Egeslīcne cwide sylf sigora Weard ofer ðæt fǣge folc forþ forlǣteþ *the Lord of victories himself shall send forth a dreadful utterance over the condemned folk*, Exon. 30 a; Th. 92, 33; Cri. 1518. On ðæt deópe dæl gefeallaþ synfulra here, fǣge gǣstas *the band of the sinful shall fall into the deep gulf, accursed spirits*, 30 b; Th. 94, 3; Cri. 1534. **IV.** *feeble, timid;* imbēcillus, tĭmĭdus:—Nis mīn breóstsefa forht ne fǣge *my mind is not afraid nor feeble*, Exon. 37 a; Th. 120, 33; Gū. 281. Ne willaþ eów andrǣdan deáde fēðan, fǣge ferhþlōcan *dread ye not dead bands, feeble carcases*, Cd. 156; Th. 194, 27; Exod. 267. [*Laym.* feie: *O. Sax.* fēgi: *Dut.* veeg: *Ger.* feig *tĭmĭdus, ignāvus: M. H. Ger.* veige: *O. H. Ger.* feigi: *Icel.* feigr.] DER. deáþ-fǣge, slege-, un-: un-fǣglīc.

FǢGEN, fægn; *comp.* fægenra; *sup.* fægnost; *adj.* FAIN, *glad, joyful, rejoicing, elate;* lætus, gaudens, hĭlăris, elātus:—Fægen fylle *joyful in slaughter*, Exon. 96 a; Th. 357, 27; Pa. 35. Wīta ne sceal tō fægen *the sagacious must not be too elate*, 77 b; Th. 290, 20; Wand. 68: Cd. 100; Th. 131, 26; Gen. 2182. Ic bió swīðe fægn [Cott. gefægen] gif ðū me lǣdest ðider ic ðē bidde *I shall be very glad if thou leadest me whither I desire thee*, Bt. 40, 5; Fox 240, 25. He, on ferþe fægn fācnes and searuwa, wælhriów wunode *he, rejoicing in his mind in stratagem and frauds, remained a tyrant*, Bt. Met. Fox 9, 73; Met. 9.

37. Ferdon forþ þonon, ferhþum fægne *they went forth thence, rejoicing in their minds*, Beo. Th. 3270; B. 1633. Wǽron ealle fægen in firnum *they were all glad in their sufferings*, Cd. 223; Th. 292, 3; Sat. 435: Andr. Kmbl. 2084; An. 1043. Lyt monna wearþ lange fægen ðæs ðe he ōðerne bewrencþ *few men rejoice long in what they have got by deceiving others*, Prov. Kmbl. 34. Fægenra *more joyful*, Bt. Met. Fox 12, 24; Met. 12, 12. Fægnost *most joyful*, Exon. 81 b; Th. 306, 26; Seef. 13. [*Piers P.* fayn: *Chauc.* fain, fawe: *R. Glouc.* fawe, fayn: *Laym.* fæin, fain: *O. Sax.* fagan: *Icel.* feginn.] DER. ge-fægen, on-, wil-.

fægenian; *p.* ode; *pp.* od *To rejoice;* gaudēre:—Ceruerus ongan fægenian mid his steorte *Cerberus began to wag* [*rejoice with*] *his tail*, Bt. 35, 6; Fox 168, 17. v. fægnian.

FÆGER, e; *f. Beauty, fairness;* pulchrĭtūdo:—Ðæs līchoman fæger *the body's beauty*, Bt. 32, 2; Fox 116, 30. [*O. H. Ger.* fagarî, *f.*]

fæger, fægr; *comp. m.* fægerra; *f. n.* fægerre; *sup.* -est, -ost, -ast, -ust; *adj.* [fæger *beauty, fairness*] FAIR, *beautiful, joyous, pleasant, pleasing, sweet;* pulcher, dĕcōrus, lætus, jucundus, dulcis:—Swā fæger swā swā Alcibiades wæs *as fair as Alcibiades was*, Bt. 32, 2; Fox 116, 18, 24, 25. Seó wæs fæger *which was fair*, Bd. 1, 7; S. 478, 22, 23. On hrusan ne feól fæger foldbold *the fair earthly dwelling fell not on the ground*, Beo. Th. 1550; B. 773: 2278; B. 1137. Biþ swā fæger fugles gebǽru *the bird's bearing is so pleasing*, Exon. 57 b; Th. 206, 11; Ph. 125. Hió dumb wunaþ, hwæðre hyre is on fōte fæger hleóðor *it continues dumb, yet there is in its foot a sweet voice*, 108 b; Th. 414, 9; Rä. 32, 17. Wæs geforþad ðīn fægere weorc *thy beautiful work was done*, Hy. 9, 24; Hy. Grn. ii. 291, 24. Mīn se ēca dǽl fægran botles brūceþ *my eternal part shall enjoy a fair mansion*, Exon. 38 a; Th. 125, 13; Gū. 353. Is mīn flǽsc swylce, for fægrum ele, frēcne onwended *căro mea immūtāta est propter ŏleum*, Ps. Th. 108, 24. Us wuldres weard þurh lāre speón to ðam fægeran gefeán *the Lord of glory drew us by his teaching to fair joy*, Andr. Kmbl. 1195; An. 598. Forht ic wæs for ðære fægran gesyhþe *I was terrified at the beautiful sight*, Rood Kmbl. 41; Kr. 21. Segnas stōdon on fægerne swēg *the banners rose at the joyous sound*, Cd. 170; Th. 214, 8; Exod. 566. Wīte ðū ðæt ðū ānforlēte Dryhtnes ðone fægran gefeán *know thou that thou didst lose the Lord's fair joy*, Elen. Kmbl. 1894; El. 949: Exon. 33 a; Th. 105, 6; Gū. 19. Gif ðū gesihst ansīne ðīne fægere blisse getācnaþ *if you see your face fair it betokens bliss*, Lchdm. iii. 212, 30, 31. Ōþ-ðæt heó reste stōwe fægere funde *until she found a joyous resting-place*, Cd. 72; Th. 88, 18; Gen. 1467. Se ǽðela geaf giestlīðnysse fægre on flette *the noble gave a fair entertainment in his abode*, 112; Th. 147, 29; Gen. 2447: Exon. 123 b; Th. 474, 27; Bo. 37. Cyning wæs ðȳ blīðra on fyrhþsefan þurh ða fægeran gesihþ *the king was blither in his mind through the joyous vision*, Elen. Kmbl. 196; El. 98. Ic ðē on ða fægran foldan gesette *I set thee on the pleasant earth*, Exon. 28 a; Th. 85, 12; Cri. 1390: 41 b; Th. 139, 30; Gū. 601. He wīc āhte fæger and freólīc *he had a dwelling fair and goodly*, Cd. 83; Th. 103, 22; Gen. 1722. Gimmas stōdon fægere æt foldan sceátum *beautiful gems stood at the extremities of the earth*, Rood Kmbl. 14; Kr. 8. Folcstede fægre wǽron *the towns were pleasant*, Cd. 91; Th. 116, 9; Gen. 1933: Exon. 26 b; Th. 79, 23; Cri. 1295. Ðeáh he fæger word ūtan ætȳwe *although it outwardly shew fair words*, Frag. Kmbl. 31; Leás. 17. Swā beóþ gelīce ða leásan men ða ðe mid tungan treówa gehātaþ fægerum wordum *such resemble false men who with the tongue promise fidelity in fair words*, 48; Leás. 26: Ps. Th. 89, 17. Wyllan onspringaþ fægrum foldwylmum *wells spring forth with pleasant bubblings from earth*, Exon. 56 b; Th. 202, 3; Ph. 64: 64 b; Th. 238, 26; Ph. 610. Heofon is betera, and heálīcra, and fægerra ðonne eall his innung, būton monnum ānum *the heaven is better, and higher, and fairer than all which it includes, except men alone*, Bt. 32, 2; Fox 116, 10: Exon. 43 b; Th. 147, 2; Gū. 720. Ne hȳrde ic sīþ ne ǽr on ēgstreáme idese lǽdan mægen fægerre *I never heard before or since that a female led on the ocean-stream a fairer power*, Elen. Kmbl. 484; El. 242. Ðǽr hī sceáwiaþ frætwe fægerran [MS. fægran] *where they behold a fairer decoration*, Exon. 60 b; Th. 221, 5; Ph. 330. Hī to ðam fægrestan heofonrīces gefeán hweorfan mōstan *they might depart to the fairest joy of heaven's realm*, Exon. 45 a; Th. 152, 14; Gū. 808. Wlitig is se wong eall mid ðām fægrestum foldan stencum *all the plain is beauteous with the sweetest odours of earth*, 56 a; Th. 198, 10; Ph. 8. Ðē is neorxna wang boldwēla fægrost *paradise is to thee the fairest dwelling of happiness*, Andr. Kmbl. 206; An. 103. Ōþ-ðæt he Adam gearone funde, and his wīf somed, freó fægroste *until he found Adam ready, and his wife also, fairest woman*, Cd. 23; Th. 29, 28; Gen. 457. Se biþ gefeána fægrast *that shall be the sweetest of joys*, Exon. 32 b; Th. 102, 1; Cri. 1666. Fægerust mægþa sōhte weroda God *the fairest of virgins sought the God of hosts*, Menol. Fox 294; Men. 148: 226; Men. 114. [*Chauc.* faire: *Laym.* fæiȝer, fæire, fære, faire, feier, ueir: *O. Sax.* fagar: *M. H. Ger.* fager: *O. H. Ger.* fagar: *Goth.* fagrs *adapted, fit*: *Dan.* fager, fauer, faver: *Swed.* fager: *Icel.* fagr.] DER. un-fæger.

fægere, fægre, fegere; *adv. Pleasantly, softly, gently, fairly, beautifully;* suāvĭter, bĕnigne, cōmĭter, dĕcenter, pulchre:—Fægere leohte ðæt land lago yrnende *the running water pleasantly washed the land*, Cd. 12; Th. 13, 30; Gen. 210: Ps. Th. 125, 1: Menol. Fox 283; Men. 143: Elen. Kmbl. 2423; El. 1213. He fægere mid wætere oferwearp wuldres cynebearn *he gently sprinkled with water the royal child of glory*, Menol. Fox 314; Men. 158. Him fægere ēce Drihten andswarode *the eternal Lord answered him fairly*, Cd. 107; Th. 141, 27; Gen. 2351: Frag. Kmbl. 8; Leás. 5. Fægere he syngþ *pulchre cantat*, Ælfc. Gr. 38; Som. 40, 32: Elen. Kmbl. 1483; El. 743: Runic pm. 18; Kmbl. 342, 32; Hick. Thes. i. 135, 36: Ps. Th. 60, 3: 62, 7: 118, 117. DER. un-fægere.

fægernes, fægernys, -ness, -nyss, e; *f.* FAIRNESS, *beauty;* pulchrĭtūdo:—On heofona wuldres fægernesse *with the beauty of heaven's glory*, Homl. Blick. 159, 16. Mid ðīnum hiwe oððe wlite and fægernysse ðīnre begēm *spĕcie tua et pulchrĭtūdĭne tua intende*, Ps. Lamb. 44, 5.

fæger-wyrde; *adj. Fair in word, fairly speaking;* suāvĭlŏquus, dĕcenter lŏquens:—Wes ðū ðīnum yldrum ārfæst symle, fægerwyrde *be thou ever dutiful to thy parents, fair in word*, Exon. 80 a; Th. 300, 26; Fä. 12.

fægir; *adj. Fair;* pulcher:—Þurh fægir word *with fair words*, Cd. 42; Th. 55, 24; Gen. 899. v. fæger.

fægn *glad, joyful*:—Ic bió fægn *I shall be glad*, Bt. 40, 5; Fox 240, 25. v. fægen.

fægnian, fægenian, fagnian, fagenian, fahnian; *p.* ode; *pp.* od [fægen, fægn *glad, joyful*] *To rejoice, be glad, exult, applaud, to be delighted with, to wish for;* gaudēre, jubĭlāre, lætāri, exultāre, plaudĕre, appĕtĕre:—Ne sceal he tō ungemetlīce fægnian ðæs folces worda *he ought not to rejoice immoderately at the people's words*, Bt. 30, 1; Fox 108, 9: 108, 7, 10, MS. Cott. Onginnaþ fægnian mid folmum *plaudent mănĭbus*, Ps. Th. 97, 8. Ic afētige oððe fægnige [MS. fegnige] *plaudo*, Ælfc. Gr. 28, 4; Som. 31, 28. Fægnaþ Israhēla *lætābĭtur Israel*, Ps. Spl. 13, 11. We fægniaþ smyltre sǽ *we rejoice at the serene sea*, Bt. 14, 1; Fox 40, 18. Fægniaþ fealdas *gaudēbunt campi*, Ps. Spl. 95, 11: Bt. Met. Fox 29, 187; Met. 29, 95. Fægnode mīn cild on mīnum innoþe *exultāvit in gaudio infans in ŭtĕro meo*, Lk. Bos. 1, 44. Fægnodon ealle *all rejoiced*, Bt. Met. Fox 1, 66; Met. 1, 33. Fægniaþ Gode ealle eorþe *jubĭlāte Deo omnis terra*, Ps. Spl. 65, 1. Fægniaþ rihtwīse *exultāte justi*, 31, 14. Hwæðer ðū fægerra blōstmena fægnige *dost thou rejoice in fair blossoms?* Bt. 14, 1; Fox 40, 25. Ðeáh he ðæs fægnige *though he rejoice at this*, 30, 1; Fox 108, 11. DER. ge-fægnian, on-.

fægnung, e; *f. A rejoicing, exultation;* jubĭlātio, exultātio:—Is eádig folc ðæt ðe can wyndreámas oððe fægnunge *est beātus pŏpŭlus qui scit jubĭlātiōnem*, Ps. Lamb. 88, 16. On fægnunga hī rīpaþ *in exultātiōne mĕtent*, Ps. Spl. 125, 6, 8. Fægnunga Godes *exultātiōnes Dei*, 149, 6. DER. ge-fægnung.

fǽg-nys, -nyss, e; *f. Difference, diversity, variety;* vărietas:—Ymbgyrd oððe ymbwǽfd mid missenlīcum oððe mid fǽgnyssum *circumamicta varietātĭbus*, Ps. Lamb. 44, 15.

fægr *fair*, Bd. 3, 14, Lye. v. fæger.

fægre; *adv. Pleasantly, slowly, fairly, beautifully;* suāvĭter, pĕdĕtentim, pulchre:—Ðæt on foldan fægre stōde wudubeám *that a forest-tree pleasantly stood on earth*, Cd. 199; Th. 247, 17; Dan. 498: Exon. 59 b; Th. 217, 2; Ph. 274. Fægre *pĕdĕtentim*, Ælfc. Gr. 38; Som. 40, 30. v. fægere.

fægrian; *p.* ode; *pp.* od [fæger *fair*] *To become fair* or *beautiful;* pulchrescĕre:—Byrig fægriaþ *towns become fair*, Exon. 82 a; Th. 308, 32; Seef. 48. DER. a-fægrian.

fǽgþ, e; *f. Hostility;* hostīlĭtas:—On ða fǽgþe *in that hostility*, Andr. Kmbl. 567; An. 284, = fǽhþ, *q. v.*

FǼHÞ, fǽgþ, e; *f*: fǽhþe, an; *f*: fǽhþo, fǽhþu; *indecl. f. Feud, vengeance, enmity, hostility, deadly feud, that enmity which the relations of the deceased waged against the kindred of the murderer;* capĭtālis inĭmīcĭtia, vindĭcātio, hostīlĭtas, factio ob hŏmĭnem interemptum:—Sió fǽhþ gewearþ gewrecen wrāþlīce *the feud was wrathfully avenged*, Beo. Th. 6115; B. 3061: 4798; B. 2403. Ne gefeáh he ðære fǽhþe *he rejoiced not in the enmity*, 218; B. 109: Exon. 29 a; Th. 88, 17; Cri. 1441. He nō mearn fore fǽhþe and fyrene *he mourned not for his enmity and crime*, Beo. Th. 274; B. 137: 3079; B. 1537. Gif man gehādodne mid fǽhþe belecge *if a man in holy orders be charged with deadly feud*, L. C. E. 5; Th. i. 362, 21: L. Eth. ix. 23; Th. i. 344, 25. Fǽhþe ic wille on weras stælan *I will place vengeance on men*, Cd. 67; Th. 81, 27; Gen. 1351: 227; Th. 305, 2; Sat. 641. Gif hwā ǽnigne man ofsleá, ðæt he wege sylf ða fǽhþe *if any one slay any man, that he himself bear the feud*, L. Edm. S. 1; Th. i. 248, 3, 9: L. In. 74; Th. i. 150, 2. He geþingade þeódbūendum wið Fæder swǽsne fǽhþa mǽste *he appeased for mankind the greatest feud with his dear Father*, Exon. 16 b; Th. 39, 5; Cri. 617. On ða fǽgþe *in that hostility*, Andr. Kmbl. 567; An. 284. Wæs seó fǽhþe open on ūhtan *the deadly feud was open at early morn*, Cd. 222; Th. 289, 30; Sat. 405. Ðæt ys sió fǽhþo *that is the feud*, Beo. Th. 5990; B. 2999: 4971; B. 2489. Sceal ic fǽhþu dreógan *I must endure enmity*, Exon. 115 a; Th. 443, 7; Kl. 26. [*Plat.* vede, fede, veide: *O. Frs.* feithe, faithe, feythe, faythe, *f*: *Dut.*

veete, *f: Ger.* fehde, *f: M.H.Ger.* vêhede, vêde, *f: Dan.* feide, *m. f. feud, war.*] DER. wæl-fǽhþ.

fǽhþ-bôt, e; *f. Feud-amends, compensation for engaging in a feud* or *quarrel*; inimīcitiārum compensātio:—Ne þearf ǽnig mynster-munuc mid rihte fǽhþbôte biddan, ne fǽhþbôte bētan *no minster-monk may lawfully demand feud-amends, nor pay feud-amends*, L. Eth. ix. 25; Th. i. 346, 2: L. C. E. 5; Th. i. 362, 27.

fǽhþe, an; *f. Deadly feud;* capĭtālis inĭmīcĭtia:—Wæs seó fǽhþe open ûhtan *the deadly feud was open at early morn*, Cd. 222; Th. 289, 30; Sat. 405. v. fǽhþ.

fǽhþo, fǽhþu; *indecl. f. Feud, enmity;* capĭtālis inĭmīcĭtia:—Ðæt is sió fǽhþo *that is the feud*, Beo. Th. 5990; B. 2999: 4971; B. 2489. Sceal ic fǽhþu dreógan *I must endure enmity*, Exon. 115 a; Th. 443, 7; Kl. 26. v. fǽhþ.

fægiger; *adj. Fair, beautiful;* pulcher:—Fægigrestan heowes *of the most beautiful colour*, Bd. 3, 14; Whelc. 199, 34, MS. Cantab. v. fæger.

fæla *many*, Nicod. 17; Thw. 8, 18. v. fela.

fǽ-lǽcan, fā-lǽcan; *p.* -lǽhte; *pp.* -lǽht *To be at deadly enmity, to be at feud;* inĭmīcĭtiam capĭtālem mŏvēre:—Gif hwā heora ǽnigne fǽlǽce [fālǽce MS. L.] *if any one be at feud with any of them*, L. Ath. i. 20; Th. i. 210, 10.

fæle; *adj. Fell.* DER. æl-fæle. v. felo.

fǽle; *adj. Faithful, true, dear, good;* fĭdēlis, constans, cārus, bŏnus:—Wes us fǽle freónd *be a faithful friend to us*, Cd. 130; Th. 165, 1; Gen. 2725: 135; Th. 170, 26; Gen. 2819: Exon. 35 a; Th. 112, 15; Gû. 144: Elen. Kmbl. 175; El. 88: Ps. Th. 66, 3: 70, 4: 77, 34: 94, 7. Se fǽla fugel *the faithful bird*, Exon. 17 a; Th. 40, 27; Cri. 645. Wese āwā friþ on Israhēla fǽlum folce *let peace ever be with the faithful people of Israel*, Ps. Th. 148, 14. Mid Ealhhilde, fǽlre freoðuwebban *with Ealhild, the faithful peace-weaver*, Exon. 84 b; Th. 319, 2; Wîd. 6: Ps. Th. 76, 3: 118, 155. Nafaþ æt gefeohte fǽlne helpend *he has not a faithful helper in battle*, Ps. Th. 88, 36: 113, 18: 120, 1. Ðone fǽlan geþanc *the true thought*, 138, 20. Ne afyr ðū me fǽle spræce *take not away from me true speech*, 118, 43. Ðīn fǽle hūs *thy dear house*, 78, 1. Onfôh me fǽle Drihten *accept me dear Lord*, 118, 116. Sprǽcon fǽle freoðoscealcas to Lothe *the faithful ministers of peace spake to Lot*, Cd. 115; Th. 150, 25; Gen. 2497. He his folc genam swā fǽle sceáp *abstŭlit sīcut ŏves pŏpŭlum suum*, Ps. Th. 77, 52: 78, 14: 99, 3. DER. un-fǽle.

fǽle; *adv. Faithfully, truly, well;* fĭdēlĭter, apte, bĕne:—Ðū mīne fēt fǽle beweredest *thou faithfully protectedst my feet*, Ps. Th. 55, 11: 84, 1: 90, 4.

fælg, e; *f:* fælge, an; *f. A felly, a part of the circumference of a wheel;* canthus, Som. Ben. Lye. v. felg.

fælging *a harrow;* occa, Som. Ben. Lye. v. fealga.

fællan; *p.* de; *pp.* ed *To offend;* scandălīzāre:—Gif ðīn ēge aswīcaþ ðē oððe fælle ðec *si ŏcŭlus tuus scandălīzat te*, Mt. Kmbl. Rush. 5, 29, 30: 18, 8.

fælniss, e; *f. An offence;* scandălum:—From fælnissum *ab scandălis*, Mt. Rush. Stv. 18, 7.

fælsian; *p.* ode; *pp.* od *To cleanse, purify;* lustrāre:—Ðæt ic mōte Heorot fælsian *that I may purify Heorot*, Beo. Th. 869; B. 432. He Hrōþgāres sele fælsode *he had purified Hrothgar's hall*, Beo. Th. 4694; B. 2352. DER. ge-fælsian.

fǽm *foam*, Som. Ben. Lye. v. fām.

fǽman; *p.* de; *pp.* ed [fām *foam*] *To* FOAM or *froth;* spūmāre:—Fǽmþ *spūmat*, Lk. Bos. 9, 39. Fǽmende *spūmans*, Mk. Bos. 9, 20. DER. a-fǽman.

fǽmig; *adj. Foamy;* spūmōsus:—Ðæt ceól scyle fǽmig rīdan ȳða hrycgum *that the foamy vessel shall ride on the waves' backs*, Exon. 101 b; Th. 384, 24; Rä. 4, 32. v. fāmig.

fǽmnan *of a virgin*, Exon. 66 b; Th. 246, 10; Jul. 59; *gen. of* fǽmne.

fǽmnan hād, fǽmn-hād, es; *m.* [fǽmne *a virgin, woman*] *Virginity, maidenhood, womanhood;* virgĭnĭtas:—Ic fǽmnan hād mīnne geheóld *I preserved my maidenhood*, Exon. 9 a; Th. 6, 31; Cri. 92. Þurh fǽmnan hād *through womanhood*, Cd. 224; Th. 296, 1; Sat. 495. On fǽmnan hāde *in virginity*, Ors. 3, 6; Bos. 58, 5. Heó lyfode mid hyre were seofen geár of hyre fǽmnhāde *vixĕrat cum vĭro suo annis septem a virgĭnĭtāte sua*, Lk. Bos. 2, 36.

FǢMNE, fēmne, an; *f.* [fēmĭna *a woman*] *A virgin, damsel, maid, woman;* virgo, puella, fēmĭna:—Wæs ðæs ylcan mynstres abbudisse on ða tīd seó cynellīce fǽmne Ælflǽd *prææerat quĭdem tunc eidem monastērio rēgia virgo Ælbflæd*, Bd. 4, 26; S. 603, 3, 6: 4, 8; S. 575, 34: Gen. 2, 23: Mt. Bos. 1, 23. Seó fæmne wæs Sarra hāten *the damsel was called Sarah*, Cd. 83; Th. 103, 23; Gen. 1722: 101; Th. 134, 17; Gen. 2226. Sceal fēmne hire freónd gesēccan *the damsel shall seek her lover*, Menol. Fox 548; Gn. C. 44. Geseah ic līchoman ðære hālgan Godes fǽmnan *vidi corpus sacræ Deo virgĭnis*, Bd. 4, 19; S. 589, 15, 43: 4, 19; S. 588, 36. Wæs ðære fǽmnan ferþ geblissad *the damsel's soul was rejoiced*, Exon. 69 b; Th. 259, 24; Jul. 287: 66 b; Th. 246, 10; Jul. 59: 67 a; Th. 247, 15; Jul. 79. Be ðære grimman untrumnysse ðære fǽmnan *de acerba puellæ infirmĭtāte*, Bd. 3, 9; S. 534, 7: 4, 8; S. 576, 11. Cirliscre fǽmnan *of a churlish woman*, L. Alf. pol. 11; Th. i. 68, 14: L. Alf. 29; Th. i. 52, 7: Apstls. Kmbl. 57; Ap. 29. Ðære fǽmnan līchoma brosnian ne mihte *fēmĭnæ căro corrumpi non pŏtuit*, Bd. 4, 19; S. 587, 36. Hæfde Nērgend fægere fôstorleán fǽmnan forgolden, ēce to ealdre *the Saviour had repaid the fair reward of fostering to the virgin, in eternal life*, Menol. Fox 302; Men. 152. Gif hwylc man hine wið fǽmnan forlicge *si hŏmo quis cum puella fornĭcātus fuĕrit*, L. Ecg. P. 4, 68; Th. ii. 228, 10. He mid fǽmnan on flet gǽþ *he walks with the woman in the court*, Beo. Th. 4074; B. 2034. Ic of ðam torhtan temple Dryhtnes onfēng freólīce fǽmnan clǽne *I joyfully received a pure damsel from the bright temple of the Lord*, Exon. 10 b; Th. 12, 18; Cri. 187: 66 a; Th. 244, 13; Jul. 27. Gemētte he ðǽr sume fǽmnan *invēnit puellam ĭbi*, Bd. 3, 9; S. 534, 4, 9: L. Ecg. P. 4, 68; Th. ii. 230, 15. Worhte God freólīcu fǽmnan *God wrought a goodly woman*, Cd. 9; Th. 12, 12; Gen. 184: L. Alf. 29; Th. i. 52, 5. Aryson ealle ða fǽmnan *surrexērunt omnes virgĭnes illæ*, Mt. Bos. 25, 7, 11: Ps. Spl. 44, 16: Ps. Th. 77, 63: Ps. Lamb. 148, 12: Bd. 4, 19; S. 589, 39. Sīðedon fǽmnan and wuduwan *the damsels and widows departed*, Cd. 94; Th. 121, 14; Gen. 2010. Heó mynster getimbrade Gode willsumra fǽmnena *constructo monastērio virgĭnum Deo devōtārum*, Bd. 4, 19; S. 588, 2. Fela fǽmnena *many damsels*, Exon. 120 b; Th. 462, 8; Hö. 49. Byþ heofena rīce gelīc ðām tȳn fǽmnum *sĭmĭle ĕrit regnum cælōrum dĕcem virgĭnĭbus*, Mt. Bos. 25, 1. Onfôþ ðǽm fǽmnum *receive the damsels*, Cd. 113; Th. 149, 7; Gen. 2471. [*O. Sax.* fēmea, fēhmia, *f: Frs.* fæm, *f: O. Frs.* famne, fomne, femne, fovne, fone, *f: Icel.* feima, *f: Lat.* fēmĭna, *f. a female, woman.*]

fǽmnenlīc; *adj. Virginlike;* virgĭnālis, Som. Ben. Lye.

fǽmn-hād *virginity;* virgĭnĭtas, Lk. Bos. 2, 36. v. fǽmnan hād.

fæn, fænn, es; *n. m. A fen, mud;* pālus, lŭtum:—Mid fænne *with a fen*, Bt. 18, 1; Fox 62, 26. Swā swā fænn strǽtena ic adilgige hī *ut lŭtum plăteārum dēlēbo eos*, Ps. Lamb. 17, 43. v. fen.

fæna *a vane, standard*, Som. Ben. Lye. v. fana.

fæng-tôþ, es; *m.* [fang, *q.v;* tôþ *a tooth*] *A fang tooth;* dens cănīnus, Text. Roff. p. 39, 26.

fæniht; *adj.* [fæn *a fen*, iht *an adj. termination*] FENNY, *marshy, dirty, muddy;* pălustris, Som. Ben. Lye.

fænn *a fen*, Ps. Lamb. 17, 43. v. fæn, fen.

fær; *nom. acc: gen.* færes; *dat.* fære; *pl. nom. acc.* faru; *gen.* fara; *dat.* farum, *n:* fær; *gen. dat. acc.* fære; *pl. nom. gen. acc.* fara; *dat.* farum; *f?* [*from* faran *to go*]. I. *a going, journey, way, journeying, expedition;* iter, expĕdītio bellĭca:—Ānes dæges fær *ĭter diei*, Lk. Bos. 2, 44. Gôdige folces fær *facilitate the people's journeying*, L. Pen. 15; Th. ii. 282, 9. Ðæt wæs fær micel *that was a great expedition*, Invent. Crs. Recd. 1295; El. 646. II. that in which a journey or voyage is made,—*a vehicle, vessel, ship;* vehĭcŭlum, nāvis:—Ðū ðær [Th. Grn. ðæt *that*] fær gewyrc *make thou that vessel*, Cd. 65; Th. 79, 6; Gen. 1307. Fær Noes *Noah's ark*, Cd. 66; Th. 80, 4; Gen. 1323. [*Piers P. Chauc.* fare: *Laym.* fære, fare, uare: *Plat.* foore, foor, *f: Dut.* voer, *n: Ger.* fuhre, *f: M. H. Ger.* var, *f: O. H. Ger.* fuora, *f;* far, *n: Dan.* fōre, *n: Swed.* fora, *f: Icel.* fōr, *f. a journey.*] DER. ād-fær, ge-, in-, ofer-, ongeán-, ūt-, þurh-.

FǢR, fēr, es; *m.* FEAR, *danger, peril;* tĭmor, terror, pĕrĭcŭlum:—Hie se fǽr begeat *the peril overwhelmed them*, Beo. Th. 2141; B. 1068. Fǽr ongēton *they felt fear*, Cd. 166; Th. 206, 16; Exod. 452. [*Wyc. R. Glouc.* fere: *Plat.* vare, *f. danger: O. Sax.* fār, *m. insĭdiæ: Dut.* gevaar, *n. danger: Kil.* vaer *mĕtus: Ger.* fahr, ge-fahr, *f. pĕrĭcŭlum: M. H. Ger.* vār, vāre, *m. snares: O. H. Ger.* fāra, *f. insĭdiæ, pĕrĭcŭlum: Dan.* fare, *m. f. danger: Swed.* fara, *f. peril: Icel.* fár, *n. harm, plague.*] v. fǽr; *adj. sudden.*

fǽr, fēr, es; *m. A fever;* febris:—Wið þriddan dæges fǽre and feórþan dæges fǽre *for a third day's fever and a fourth day's fever*, L. M. cont. 1, 62; Lchdm. ii. 12, 27. v. fefer.

fǽr; *adj. Fair, beautiful;* pulcher:—Hors ðæs fǽrestan heowes *a horse of the most beautiful colour*, Bd. 3, 14; S. 540, 16, note. v. fæger.

fǽr; *adj. Sudden, intense, terrible, horrid;* sŭbĭtus, terrĭbĭlis, horrĭdus. Used in the compounds,—Fǽr-bifongen, -bryne, -cōðu, -cwealm, -cȳle, -deáþ, -dryre, -fyll, -gripe, -gryre, -haga, -inga, -līc, -līce, -nīþ, -sceaða, -scyte, -searo, -slide, -spel, -unga, -wundor, -wyrd.

færan *to go;* īre:—Ic fære eo, Ælfc. Gr. 30, 5; Som. 34, 67. v. faran.

fǽran; *p.* de; *pp.* ed [fǽr *fear*] *To terrify, frighten;* terrēre:—Bodan us fǽrdon *nuntii nos terruērunt*, Deut. 1, 28. DER. a-fǽran.

fǽr-bēna, an; *m. A husbandman, peasant, churl;* rustĭcus:—Gif hit sī fǽrbēna, gilde xii ōr *if it be a churl, let him pay twelve ores*, L. N. P. L. 50; Th. ii. 298, 6.

fǽr-bifongen; *adj. With perils encompassed;* pĕrĭcŭlis *vel* terrōrĭbus circumventus:—Fǽrbifongen ic ðǽr furðum cwom *I had just come there encompassed with perils*, Beo. Th. 4022; B. 2009.

fǽr-bryne, es; *m. A terrible heat;* terrĭbĭle incendium:—Hālig God wið fǽrbryne folc gescylde *the holy God shielded the people against the intense heat*, Cd. 146; Th. 182, 7; Exod. 72.

FÆRBU, e; *f. Colour;* cōlor:—Habbaþ færbu ungelíce and mǽgwlitas *they have colour and species unlike*, Bt. Met. Fox 31, 7; Met. 31, 4. [*Ger.* farbe, *f.*]

færcodon *brought*, Chr. 1009; Th. 261, 30, = fercodon; *p. pl. of* fercian, *q. v.*

fǽr-cōðu, e; *f. Sudden sickness* or *death, apoplexy;* repentīna ægrĭtūdo *vel* mors, apoplexia = ἀποπληξία, Som. Ben. Lye.

fǽr-cwealm, es; *m. A sudden pestilence;* repentīna pestĭlentia:—Æt ðæm fǽrcwealme ðe his leódscipe swýðe drehte and wanode *in the pestilence which much afflicted and decreased his people*, L. Edg. S. 1; Th. i. 270, 8.

fǽr-cȳle, es; *m. A terrible cold;* terrĭbĭle frīgus:—Geondfolen fýre and fǽrcȳle *filled with fire and intense cold*, Cd. 2; Th. 3, 30; Gen. 43.

færd *an army, expedition;* exercĭtus, expĕdītio mīlĭtāris, Som. Ben. Lye. v. fyrd.

fǽr-deáþ, es; *m. Sudden death;* repentīna mors, Cot. 14.

fǽr-dryre, es; *m. A sudden* or *pernicious fall;* repentīnus *vel* pernĭciōsus lapsus:—Con he sídne ræced fæste gefégan wið fǽrdryrum *he can firmly compact the spacious dwelling against sudden falls*, Exon. 79 a; Th. 296, 9.

færeld, fareld, færelt, es; *n.* [fær *a going*, faran *to go*]. I. *a way, going, motion, journey, course, passage, progress, expedition, company, one who accompanies in the journey of life, a relation;* via, ĭter, cursus, gressus, expĕdītio, cognāta:—Hwā ne wundrige wolcna færeldes *who does not express a wonder of the way of the clouds?* Bt. Met. Fox 28, 4; Met. 28, 2. Wǽnes sió eax welt ealles ðæs færeldes *the axle-tree of a waggon regulates all its going*, Bt. 39, 7; Fox 220, 29. Â byþ on færylde *it is ever in motion*, Runic pm. 17; Kmbl. 342, 24; Hick. Thes. i. 135, 33. On ðissum geáre næs nān færeld to Rōme *in this year there was no journey to Rome*, Chr. 889; Th. 158, 33, col. 1. On færelde *in ĭtĭnĕre*, Past. 4, 1; Hat. MS. 9 b, 6. Ða habbaþ færeld *they have a course*, Bt. Met. Fox 28, 22; Met. 28, 11. Ne beó gē afyrhte þurh geswince ðæs langsuman færeldes, oððe þurh yfelra manna ymbe-spræce *be ye not afraid through the toil of the tedious journey, or through the conversation of evil men*, Homl. Th. ii. 128, 2. Se esne rehte ðā Isaace eall hys færeld *then the servant told Isaac all his journey*, Gen. 24, 66: Ps. Spl. 36, 33: 139, 5. On færelde *in the expedition*, Runic pm. 27; Kmbl. 345, 2; Hick. Thes. i. 135, 54. On ðam færelde *in the progress*, Bt. 39, 7; Fox 222, 19. On ðam færelde *in the company*, Ors. 4, 6; Bos. 84, 36. Færeld ðīn *cognāta tua*, Lk. Rush. War. 1, 36. Færeldu [MS. færeldtu] *lustra, meātus*, Cot. 125: 134. II. a particular passage,—*The passover of the Jews;* transĭtus, phase, id est transĭtus, *Vulg.* [= τὸ πάσχα, *indecl.*]:—Gāþ and nymaþ nýten þurh eówer hīwrǽdene, and offriaþ phase, ðæt ys færeld *īte tollentes ănĭmal per fămĭlias vestras, et immŏlāte phase*, Ex. 12, 21; go ȝe, and take a beeste by ȝoure meynees, and offre ȝe fase [*passover*], Wyc. Hit ys Godes færeldes offrung *victĭma transĭtus Dŏmĭni est;* it is the sacrifice of the Lord's passover, Ex. 12, 27. Biþ Drihtnes færeld *phase Dŏmĭni est*, Lev. 23, 5; is pask [*the passover*] of the Lord, Wyc. DER. an-færeld, fyrd-, in-, ofer-, on-, ūt-, ymb-.

færeld-freóls, es; *m. The passover feast;* transĭtûs *vel* paschæ festum, phase:—Hīg worhton phase, ðæt ys færeld-freóls *they kept the passover, that is the passover feast;* fēcērunt phase, id est paschæ festum, Jos. 5, 10.

færeldtu? *passages;* meātus, lustra, Cot. 125: 134. v. færeld.

færelt, es; *n. A going, progress, expedition;* ĭter, gressus, expĕdītio:—Wænes sió eax welt ealles ðæs færeltes *the axle-tree of a waggon regulates all its going*, Bt. 39, 7; Fox 220, 29, note 26. On ðæm færelte *in the progress*, 39, 7; Fox 222, 19, note 18. On færelte *in ĭtĭnĕre*, Past. 4, 1; Swt. 36, 22. He ðæt færelt swīðost þurhteáh *he most chiefly undertook that expedition*, Ors. 4, 10; Bos. 93, 31. Ðæt Scipia ðæs færeltes consul wǽre *that Scipio was the leader of the expedition*, 4, 10; Bos. 95, 2: 4, 10; Bos. 93, 34. Æt ðam ǽrran færelte *in the former expedition*, 4, 10; Ors. 92, 31: 4, 10; Bos. 93, 37. v. færeld.

færeng, e; *f. A swooning, trance;* dēlĭquium, Cot. 79.

fære-sceat, -sceatt, es; *m. Fare-scot, passage-money;* naulum, prĕtium transĭtus, Som. Ben. Lye.

færest, færeþ *goest, goeth*, Bt. Met. Fox 24, 56; Met. 24, 28: Elen. Kmbl. 2546; El. 1274; *2nd and 3rd pers. pres. and fut. of* faran.

fǽr-fyll, e; *f. A sudden* or *pernicious fall, a precipice;* repentīnus cāsus, præceps:—On fǽrfyll *in præceps*, Cot. 112.

fǽr-gripe, es; *m. A sudden* or *pernicious grasp;* sŭbĭtanea *vel* perniciōsa arreptio:—Him hrīnan ne mihte fǽrgripe flōdes *the flood's sudden grasp could not touch him*, Beo. Th. 3036; B. 1516. Under fǽrgripum *during his sudden grasps*, Beo. Th. 1480; B. 738.

fǽr-gryre, es; *m. A perilous horror;* terror perĭcŭlōsus:—Ða hyssas þrý fǽrgryre fýres oferfaren hæfdon *the three youths had passed through the fire's dire horror*, Cd. 197; Th. 245, 14; Dan. 463. Wið fǽrgryrum *against perilous horrors*, Beo. Th. 350; B. 174.

færh *a little pig;* porcellus, Glos. Epnl. Recd. 161, 40. v. fearh.

fǽr-haga, an; *m. A peril-hedge;* perīcŭlōrum sēpes:—He his mōdsefan wið ðam fǽrhagan fæste trymede *he firmly strengthened his mind against the peril*, Exon. 46 b; Th. 159, 27; Gū. 933.

fǽringa, fǽringca, fǽrunga, fǽrunge; *adv.* [fǽr *sudden*, -inga, -unga *adverbial terminations*] *Suddenly, quickly, by chance;* sŭbĭto, repente, forte:—Fǽringa hī geteorodon *sŭbĭto defēcērunt*, Ps. Spl. C. 72, 19. Ðū fǽringa gehogodest sæcce sēcean *thou suddenly resolvedst to seek conflict*, Beo. Th. 3980; B. 1988: Exon. 46 b; Th. 158, 20; Gū. 911: Bt. Met. Fox 28, 82; Met. 28, 41. Ðonne he fǽringa cymþ *cum vēnĕrit repente*, Mk. Bos. 13, 36. Fǽrincga fýr wudu byrneþ *fire quickly burneth a wood*, Ps. Th. 82, 10.

fǽrlīc, feárlīc; *def.* se fǽrlīca, seó, ðæt fǽrlīce; *adj. Sudden, unexpected, quick;* sŭbĭtus, repentīnus:—Him becom fǽrlīc yfel *a sudden plague came upon them*, Ors. 4, 5; Bos. 81, 22: Gen. 19, 19. Fǽrlīc geþoht *a sudden thought*, Hexam. 14; Norm. 22, 5. Fǽrlīc rēn *sudden rain;* imber, Ælfc. Gl. 94; Som. 75, 113; Wrt. Voc. 52, 63. Þurh fǽrlīcne [feárlīcne MS. A.] deáþ *through sudden death*, L. C. S. 71; Th. i. 412, 28. Se fǽrlīca dæg *repentīna dies*, Lk. Bos. 21, 34. Se fǽrlīca deáþ *sudden death*, Homl. Th. ii. 22, 19.

fǽrlīce, fērlīce, feárlīce; *adv. Suddenly, immediately, by chance;* sŭbĭto, repente, forte:—Cometæ synd gehātene ða steorran ðe fǽrlīce and ungewunelīce æteówiaþ *the stars are called comets which appear suddenly and unusually*, Bd. de nat. rerum; Wrt. popl. science 16, 20; Lchdm. iii. 272, 3: Gen. 14, 15: 19, 32: Job Thw. 165, 23: Bt. 38, 2; Fox 198, 8: Exon. 77 a; Th. 290, 6; Wand. 61. He fǽrlīce hrýmþ *sŭbĭto clāmat*, Lk. Bos. 9, 39: Ps. Lamb. 63, 6: Coll. Monast. Th. 22, 17.

færm *a supper, feast*, Mt. Kmbl. Lind. 22, 2, 3, 4. v. feorm.

fǽr-nīþ, es; *m. A sudden* or *pernicious hostility, mischief;* pernĭciōsa hostīlĭtas:—Sorh is me to secganne hwæt Grendel hafaþ fǽrnīða gefremed *it is sorrow for me to say what sudden mischiefs Grendel has perpetrated*, Beo. Th. 956; B. 476.

færnys, -nyss, e; *f. A passage, fare;* transĭtus:—Ðǽr monna færnys mǽst wæs *juxta publĭcos viārum transĭtus*, Bd. 2, 16; S. 520, 5.

færr, es; *n. A passing;* transĭtus:—Nis faru oððe færr *non est transĭtus*, Ps. Lamb. 143, 14. v. fær; *n.*

færs *verse;* versus, Ælfr. præf. p. 3, Lye. v. fers.

fǽr-sceaða, an; *m. A sudden* or *dangerous enemy;* sŭbĭtum damnum infĕrens hostis:—Ðæt he on ðam fǽrsceaðan feorh geræhte *that he might reach the life of the dangerous enemy*, Byrht. Th. 135, 62; By. 142.

fǽr-scyte, es; *m. A sudden* or *pernicious shot;* imprōvīsus *vel* fătālis jactus:—We fæste sculon wið ðam fǽrscyte wearde healdan *we should firmly hold ward against that sudden shot*, Exon. 19 a; Th. 48, 4; Cri. 766: 35 a; Th. 113, 13; Gū. 157.

fǽr-searo; *gen.* -searwes; *n. An insidious artifice;* insĭdiōsa machĭnātio:—Feónda fǽrsearo *the sudden artifice of foes*, Exon. 19 a; Th. 48, 11; Cri. 770.

fǽr-slide, es; *m. A sudden fall;* imprōvīsus lapsus:—Ðū geheólde fēt mīne wið fǽrslide *thou keptst my feet from sudden fall*, Ps. Th. 114, 8.

fǽr-spel, -spell, es; *n. A sudden message, sudden news, horrible message;* imprōvīsus *vel* terrĭbĭlis nuncius:—Hie him fǽrspel bodedon *they announced to them the sudden news*, Judth. 12; Thw. 25, 5; Jud. 244. On fyrd hyra fǽrspell becwom *the sudden tidings came in their tent*, Cd. 148; Th. 186, 8; Exod. 135. He ðæs fǽrspelles mōdsorge wæg hefige æt heortan *he bare mental sorrow heavy at heart at the sudden news*, Exon. 48 a; Th. 165, 4; Gū. 1023. For ðam fǽrspelle *at the sudden news*, Andr. Kmbl. 2173; An. 1088. Wæs seó fǽmne for ðam fǽrspelle egsan geaclad *the damsel was chilled with terror at the horrible message*, Exon. 69 b; Th. 258, 19; Jul. 267. Me ðes ār bodaþ frēcne fǽrspell *this messenger announces an impious horrible message to me*, 69 b; Th. 259, 4; Jul. 277.

færst, færsþ *goest*, Gen. 4, 12; færþ *goes*, Bt. Met. Fox 20, 432; Met. 20, 216; *2nd and 3rd pres. sing. of* faran.

færþ, es; *m. n. The mind;* mens:—On færþe *in the mind*, Bt. Met. Fox 27, 47; Met. 27, 24. v. ferþ.

fǽrunga, fǽrunge; *adv. Suddenly, quickly, by chance;* sŭbĭto, repente, forte:—Fǽrunga *forte*, Ælfc. Gr. 38; Som. 41, 28: Jos. 9, 7. Fǽrunge astorfen *sīdĕrātus* vel *ictuatus*, Ælfc. Gl. 114; Som. 80, 29; Wrt. Voc. 61, 9. v. fǽringa.

fǽr-wundor; *gen.* -wundres; *n. A sudden* or *stupendous wonder;* inŏpīnātum et stŭpendum mīrācŭlum:—Gē onlōciaþ fǽrwundra sum *ye behold a stupendous wonder*, Cd. 157; Th. 195, 20; Exod. 279.

fǽr-wyrd, e; *f. A terrible fate, destruction, perdition;* terrĭbĭle fātum, intĕrĭtus, perdĭtio:—He wēnþ ðæt ðone mon ǽr mǽge gebrengan on fǽrwyrde *that he thinks may bring the man earlier to a terrible fate*, Past. 62; Hat. MS.

færyld, es; *n. A motion, journey;* via, Runic pm. 17; Kmbl. 342, 24; Hick. Thes. i. 135, 33. v. færeld.

fæs, fæss, fas, es; *pl. nom. acc.* fasu; *n. A fringe;* fimbria:—On fæsum gyldenum *in fimbriis aureis*, Ps. Spl. C. 44, 15. Wíf gehrán fas [fæss, Rush.] oððe wlóh wǽdes his *mŭlier tĕtĭgit fimbriam vestīmenti ejus*, Mt. Kmbl. Lind. 9, 20: 14, 36. Micclaþ fasu hiora *magnĭficant fimbrias*, Mt. Kmbl. Rush. 23, 5.

FÆSL, es; *m? n? Offspring, progeny;* fētus, prōles, sŭbōles:—Ðǽr sceal fæsl wesan cwiclifigendra cynna gehwilces *there shall be offspring of every living kind*, Cd. 65; Th. 79, 13; Gen. 1310: 67; Th. 80, 17; Gen. 1330. To fæsle *for progeny*, 67; Th. 82, 8; Gen. 1359. [*Plat.* fasel *sŭbōles*: *Dut. Kil.* fasel, vasel *fētus in ŭtĕro*: *Ger.* fasel, *m. fētus, sŭbōles*: *M. H. Ger.* vasel, *n. fētus*: *O. H. Ger.* fasal, *f. fētus*: *Icel.* fösull, *m. a brood*.]

FÆST; *adj.* FAST, *fixed, firm, stiff, solid, constant, fortified;* fixus, firmus, sŏlĭdus, constans, mūnītus:—Ealle mǽst steorran synd fæste on ðam firmamentum *almost all stars are fixed in the firmament*, Bd. de nat. rerum; Wrt. popl. science 15, 26; Lchdm. iii. 268, 23: Andr. Kmbl. 2983; An. 1494. Fæste móde *fixa mente*, Bd. 4, 3; S. 569, 14: Exon. 8 a; Th. 1, 10; Cri. 6. Se wille fæst hús timbrian *he will build a firm house*, Bt. 12; Fox 36, 7, 10: Cd. 151; Th. 189, 1; Exod. 178. Mid fæstum geleáfan *with firm faith*, Boutr. Scrd. 20, 27: Cd. 21; Th. 26, 17; Gen. 408. Ðeós wyrt biþ cenned on fæstum stówum *this herb is produced on solid places*, Herb. 20, 1; Lchdm. i. 114, 12: 45, 1; Lchdm. i. 148, 5. On fæstum landum *on stiff lands*, 36, 1; Lchdm. i. 134, 18. On ðam weorce fæste *in ŏpĕre isto constantes*, Jos. 9, 27. Seó burh wæs fæst *the city was fortified*, Bd. 3, 16; S. 542, 19. Micle burga óþ heofun fæste *urbes magnæ ad cælum usque mūnītæ*, Deut. 1, 28. Fæst innoþ *restricta alvus*, Herb. 1, 12; Lchdm. i. 74, 11. [*Laym.* faste, feste: *Orm.* fasst: *Plat.* fast: *O. Sax.* fast: *Frs. O. Frs.* fest: *Dut.* vast: *Ger.* fest: *M. H. Ger.* vast, veste: *O. H. Ger.* fasti, festi: *Dan. Swed.* fast: *Icel.* fastr.]

-fæst, as a termination, denotes *fast, very, perfectly, effectually*, as the English *fast asleep, perfectly asleep; Ǽ-fæst fast in the law, firm, religious;* Sóþ-fæst *fast in truth, true, just;* Staðol-fæst *steadfast, steady;* Unstaðol-fæst *unsteady, unsteadfast.* DER. ǽ-fæst, ǽr-, ǽw-, ár-, bíd-, blǽd-, cíþ-, dóm-, eard-, gemet-, gif-, gin-, gryre-, hals-, hám-, heáh-, hróf-, hyge-, leoðu-, líf-, mægen-, rǽd-, rægol-, sige-, sigor-, somod-, sóþ-, stæþ-, staðol-, stede-, þeáw-, þrym-, tír-, treów-, un-, unstaðol-, wǽr-, wís-, wlitig-, wuldor-.

fæstan, -nian; *p.* fæste; *pp.* fæsted [fæst *fast, firm*]. I. *to fasten, make fast* or *firm, entrust, commit, commend;* firmāre, commendāre, Lk. Lind. War. 23, 46. II. some have taught and now teach that he who fasts properly, fastens or secures his salvation, hence, perhaps,—*To* FAST; jējūnāre:—Ne mágon hí fæstan *non possunt jējūnāre*, Mk. Bos. 2, 19. [*Wyc.* fastiden, *p. pl. fastened, made firm;* fasten = *to fast*: *Piers P.* festnen *to fasten;* fasten *to fast*: *Orm.* fesstnenn *to fix;* fasstenn *to fast*: *Plat.* vesten *to fasten;* fasten *to fast*: *O. Sax.* festian, festan *to fasten*: *Frs.* festgjen *to fasten*: *O. Frs.* festigia *to fasten;* festia *to fast*: *Dut.* vesten *to fasten;* vasten *to fast*: *Ger.* festen *commonly* be-festigen *to fasten;* fasten *to fast*: *M. H. Ger.* vesten *to fasten;* vasten *to fast*: *O. H. Ger.* fastjan, festan *firmāre;* fastēn *to fast*: *Goth.* fastan *to fasten, fast*: *Dan.* fæste *to fasten;* faste *to fast*: *Swed.* fästa *to fasten;* fasta *to fast*: *Icel.* festa *to fasten;* fasta *to fast*.] DER. æt-fæstan, a-, be-, bi-, ge-, gelíf-, gesige-, líf-, óþ-.

fæste, feste; *comp.* fæstor; *adv.* I. *fast, firmly;* fixe, firme:—Sceát he mid his spere ðæt hit sticode fæste on ðam hearge *he shot with his spear that it stuck fast in the temple*, Bd. 2, 13; S. 517, 12: Cd. 8; Th. 10, 14; Gen. 156: Jos. 6, 1. Swíðe fæste tosomne gelímed *very firmly cemented together*, Bt. 35, 2; Fox 156, 35: Exon. 22 a; Th. 61, 5; Cri. 980. He heóld hyne fæstor *he held him more firmly*, Beo. Th. 288; B. 143. II. *fastly, quickly;* cĕlĕrĭter:—Fæste geþúfe *cĕlĕrĭter frŭtĭcans, luxŭrians*, Cot. 123: 198.

fæsten, es; *n.* [fæstan II. *to fast*]. I. *a fast, fasting;* jējūnium:—Ðis feówertigfealde fæsten wæs asteald on ðære ealdan gecýðnysse *this fortyfold fast was established in the old testament*, Homl. Th. ii. 100, 1. Nis ðæs mannes fæsten náht, ðe hine sylfne on forhæfednysse dagum fordrencþ *the man's fasting is naught, who inebriates himself on days of abstinence*, 608, 23: Homl. Blick. 37, 31. Twá dæglíc fæsten oððe þreó dæglíc is genóh to healdenne *bĭduānum vel trĭduānum sat est observāre jējūnium*, Bd. 4, 25; S. 600, 8. Ðes gearlíca ymryne us gebrincþ efne nú ða clǽnan tíd lenctenlíces fæstenes *this yearly course just now brings us the pure time of the lenten fast*, Homl. Th. ii. 98, 25: Homl. Blick. 27, 23. Ðæs feówertiglícan fæstenes *quadrāgēsĭmæ*, Bd. 3, 23; S. 554, 38. Gif mæsse-preóst folc miswyssige æt fæstene *if a mass-priest misdirect the people about a fast*, L. E. G. 3; Th. i. 168, 9: L. N. P. L. 11; Th. ii. 292, 11. Búton þurh gebédu and on fæstene *nisi in ōrātiōne et jējūnio*, Mk. Bos. 9, 29: Ps. Lamb. 34, 13. Hí fæsten lufiaþ *they love fasting*, Exon. 44 b; Th. 150, 18; Gú. 780. Gif mon his heówum in fæsten flǽsc gefe *if a man during a fast give flesh-meat to his family*, L. Wih. 14; Th. i. 40, 9: L. E. G. 8; Th. i. 172, 6. Þurh gebéd and fæsten *per ōrātiōnem et jējūnium*, Mt. Bos. 17, 21: Ps. Th. 68, 10. We úrne líchoman clǽnsiaþ mid fæstenum and mid gebédum *we cleanse our bodies with fastings and prayers*, Homl. Blick. 39, 2. On fæstenum and on hálsungum *jējūniis et obsecrātiōnibus*, Lk. Bos. 2, 37: Ps. Th. 108, 24. Freólsa and fæstena healde man rihtlíce *let festivals and fasts be rightly kept*, L. Eth. vi. 22; Th. i. 320, 10. II. *a fastness, fortress, bulwark, place of strength, a castle, wall;* mūnīmentum, arx, castellum:—Ealle hire fæstenu híg fordilegodon mid fýre *all her strongholds they destroyed with fire*, Jos. 11, 12. Nearo fæsten *narrow fastness*, Bd. 4, 26; S. 602, 20. III. *an inclosed place, cloister;* claustrum:—Fæsten *vel* clauster *claustrum*, Ælfc. Gl. 109; Som. 79, 15; Wrt. Voc. 58, 56. [*O. Sax.* festi, *f. fortress, strength*: *O. Frs.* fest *junction*: *Dut.* vest, *f. a city wall, fortress*: *Ger.* feste, *f. a fortress*: *M. H. Ger.* veste, *f. firmness, solidity, fortress*: *O. H. Ger.* fastí, festí, *f. firmĭtas, rōbur, arx*: *Dan.* fæste, *n. a handle*: *Swed.* fäste, *n. firmament, castle*: *Icel.* festa, *f. a pledge;* festr, festi, *f. that by which a thing is fastened*.] DER. burh-fæsten, ǽdel-, lagu-, sǽ-, þell-, weall-, wudu-.

fæsten-behæfednes, -ness, e; *f. Parsimony, niggardliness;* parsĭmōnia, Cot. 191.

fæsten-brice, -bryce, es; *m.* [fæsten *a fast*, brice, bryce *a breaking, breach*] *A breach of a fast, fast-breaking,* BREAKFAST; jējūnii violātio, jentācŭlum:—On fæstenbricum [MS. fæstenbricon] *in breaches of fasts*, L. Eth. vi. 28; Th. i. 322, 19.

fæsten-dæg, es; *m. Fast-day;* jējūnii dies, C. R. Ben. 54.

fæsten-díc, es; *m. A castle-ditch;* arcis fossa:—Andlang riþe óþ ðone fæstendíc *along the stream to the castle-ditch*, Cod. Dipl. 204; A. D. 814; Kmbl. i. 257, 32. v. díc; *f.* II.

fæsten-geat, es; *n. A fortress* or *city gate;* arcis *vel* urbis porta:—Wið ðæs fæstengeates folc onette *the people hastened to the city gate*, Judth. 11; Thw. 23, 38; Jud. 162.

fæsten-geweorc, es; *n. Fortification work, fortification;* fortĭfĭcātio, arcium mūnīmentum, Heming, p. 104.

fæstennes, -ness, e; *f. Fastness, a walled town;* castellum, Som. Ben. Lye. v. fæstnes.

fæsten-tíd, e; *f. Fast-tide* or *time;* jējūnii tempus:—Man sceal freólstídum [MS. -tidan] and fæstentídum [MS. -tidan] geornlícost beorgan *one ought most earnestly to take care at festival-times and fast-times*, L. C. S. 38; Th. i. 398, 17. Yfel biþ ðæt man riht fæstentíde ǽr mǽle ete *it is bad that any one, at a lawful fast-time, eat before the time*, 47; Th. i. 402, 23: L. Edg. C. 25; Th. ii. 250, 2.

fǽster-módor *a foster-mother*, Bt. 3, 1; Fox 4, 30, MS. Cot. v. fóster-módor.

fæstes; *adv. By chance;* forte, Cot. 88.

fæst-gongel; *adj. Firm and sure going, faithful, constant;* sēcūrus progressus, fīdēlis:—Sum geþyld hafaþ, fæstgongel ferþ *one has patience, a faithful soul*, Exon. 79 b; Th. 298, 4; Crä. 80.

fæst-hafol, -hafel, -hafod; *adj. Fast-having, sparing, miserly;* tĕnax, parcus, sordĭdus:—Fæsthafol *tĕnax*, Ælfc. Gr. 9, 60; Som. 13, 44. Fæsthafol strængþ *tĕnax vĭgor*, Hymn. Surt. 11, 2. Fæsthafel *tĕnax*, Ælfc. Gl. 82; Som. 73, 42; Wrt. Voc. 47, 46. Sint to manianne ða fæsthafolan *the miserly are to be admonished*, Past. 45, 2; Cot. MS. Fæsthafod oððe uncystig *tĕnax*, Wrt. Voc. 76, 5.

fæst-hafolnes, -ness, e; *f. Fast-havingness, sparingness, economy;* parcĭtas:—Fæsthafolnesse *parcĭtātem*, Past. 60; Hat. MS.

fæst-hydig; *adj. Steadfast in mind;* constans anĭmo:—Ic ðé wát fæsthydigne *I know thee steadfast in mind*, Cd. 67; Th. 81, 18; Gen. 1347: Exon. 90 b; Th. 339, 30; Gn. Ex. 102.

fæsting, e; *f. An entrusting, act of confidence;* commendātio:—Gif hwá óðrum his unmagan óþfæste, and he hine on ðære fæstinge forferie *if any one commit his infant to another's keeping, and he die during such keeping*, L. Alf. pol. 17; Th. i. 72, 5. DER. be-fæsting.

fæstingan *to fasten, make firm;* firmāre:—Ic fæstinge mín wedd mid eów *firmābo pactum meum vobiscum*, Lev. 26, 9. v. fæstnian.

fæsting-men, festing-men, -menn; *pl. m.* [fæsting *an entrusting*, men, v. man *a man*] *Servants of the king entrusted to the keeping of the monasteries while going from place to place;* servi rēgii ad cūram monastēriōrum commendāti in regno obeundo:—Terram lībĕrābo ab refectiōne et hăbĭtu illōrum omnium qui dīcuntur fæstingmen, Th. Diplm. A. D. 822; 65, 17: A. D. 821; 64, 11: A. D. 841; 92, 19. Festingmenn, A. D. 823; 67, 2: A. D. 828; 79, 30.

fæstlíc; *adj.* FASTLIKE, *firm;* firmus:—Wæs se fruma fæstlíc *the man was firm*, Exon. 44 a; Th. 148, 15; Gú. 745: Cd. 220; Th. 284, 22; Sat. 325. Eálá! ðæt on eorþan áuht fæstlíces weorces ne wunaþ ǽfre *alas! that on earth aught of permanent work does not ever remain*, Bt. Met. Fox 6, 32; Met. 6, 16. Gehyge ðú fæstlícne rǽd *devise firm counsel*, Cd. 203; Th. 252, 30; Dan. 586. Fæstlíce fórescyttelsas *firm bars*, Exon. 12 a; Th. 20, 3; Cri. 312.

fæstlíce; *comp.* or; *sup.* ost; *adv. Firmly, constantly, fast, quickly;* firmĭter, constanter, cĕlĕrĭter:—Hig fæstlíce weóxon *they constantly increased*, Jud. 4, 24. Færþ micle fæstlícor *goes much more firmly*, Bt. 39, 7; Fox 220, 30. DER. un-rǽd-fæstlíce, wuldor-fæstlíce.

fæst-mód; *adj. Constant in mind;* constans anĭmo:—He wiste hú fæstmód he wæs on his geleáfon *he knew how constant in mind he was in his belief*, Ors. 6, 33; Bos. 129, 28.

fæstmód-staðol, es; *m. A state of constancy of mind, constancy;* constantis animi stātus, constantia, Off. Episc. 1.

fæstn *a fasting;* jejūnium:—Mid fæstnum *with fastings*, Nat. S. Greg. Els. 34, 28. v. fæsten I.

fæstn *a fortification;* mūnīmentum:—Ðara fæstna *of those fortifications*, Cd. 209; Th. 259, 15; Dan. 692. v. fæsten II.

fæst-nes, -niss, -ness, -nyss, e; *f. Firmament, firmness, stability, fastness, fortification;* firmāmentum, firmĭtūdo, mūnīmen, propugnācŭlum:—Firmamentum [fæstnes] is ðeós rōderlīce heofen, mid manegum steorrum amett... Seó [fæstnes] firmamentum tyrnþ symle onbūtan us under ðyssere eorþan and būfan, ac ðǣr is ungerīm fæc betweox hyre and ðære eorþan *the firmament is this ethereal heaven, adorned with many stars... The firmament always turneth about us under this earth and above it, but there is an immeasurable space between it and the earth*, Lchdm. iii. 254, 8-13. Gewurþe nū fæstnis tomiddes ðām wæterum... And God geworhte ða fæstnisse, and totwǣmde ða wæteru, ðe wǣron under ðære fæstnisse, fram ðām, ðe wǣron būfan ðære fæstnisse... And God hēt ða fæstnisse, heofenan *fiat firmāmentum in mĕdio aquārum... Et fēcit Deus firmāmentum, divisitque aquas, quæ erant sub firmāmento, ab his, quæ erant sŭper firmāmentum... Vŏcāvitque Deus firmāmentum, cœlum*, Gen. 1, 6-8. Behealdaþ nū ða wīdgilnesse, and ða fæstnesse heofenes *behold now the immensity, and the firmness of heaven*, Bt. 32, 2; Fox 116, 5. Ymbtrymming oððe fæstnyss *mūnīmen*, Ælfc. Gr. 9, 12; Som. 9, 32. DER. rǣd-fæstnes, sōþ-, staðol-. v. rōdor.

fæstnian, festnian; *p.* ode, ede; *pp.* od, ed *To* FASTEN, *secure, confirm, bind;* firmāre, vincīre:—Hie handa fæstnodon *they fastened his hands*, Andr. Kmbl. 97; An. 49: Ps. Th. 47, 11. We willaþ griþ fæstnian *we will confirm the peace*, Byrht. Th. 132, 53; By. 35. DER. a-fæstnian, ge-.

fæstnung, e; *f. A* FASTENING, *confirmation;* fixūra:—Būton ic geseó ðæra nægla fæstnunge on his honda *nisi vīdĕro in manĭbus ejus fixūram clavōrum*, Jn. Bos. 20, 25.

fæst-rǣd; *def.* se fæst-rǣda; *adj. Firm in purpose, steadfast, constant, inflexible;* firmus consĭlii, constans:—Se fæstrǣda Cato *the steadfast Cato*, Bt. 19; Fox 70, 7: Bt. Met. Fox 10, 97; Met. 10, 49. Gehȳrde fæstrǣdne geþoht *he heard a steadfast resolution*, Beo. Th. 1225; B. 610: Ps. Th. 134, 3. DER. un-fæst-rǣd.

fæst-rǣdlīce; *adv. Boldly, constantly;* constanter, Wulfst. Par. 5.

fæst-rǣdnes, -ness, e; *f. Fixed state of mind, fortitude, resolution;* fortĭtūdo:—Mōt ic nū cunnian hwōn ðīne [MS. ðinne] fæstrǣdnesse *may I now inquire a little concerning thy fortitude?* Bt. 5, 3; Fox 10, 35. DER. un-fæstrǣdnes.

fæst-steall; *adj. Fast-standing;* firmĭter stans:—Wǣron fæststealle fōtas mīne on ðīnum cāfertūnum *stantes erant pĕdes nostri in atriis tuis*, Ps. Th. 121, 2.

FÆT, es; *pl. nom. acc.* fatu, fata; *gen.* fata; *dat.* fatum; *n. A vessel, cup,* VAT; vas, cālix:—Swā swā fæt crocwirhtan oððe tygelwirhtan ðū tobrytst hīg *tamquam vas fĭgŭli confringes eos*, Ps. Lamb. 2, 9. Fætes botm *the bottom of a vessel;* vāsis fundum, Cot. 92. Mid ðam fæte *with the vessel*, Homl. Th. ii. 158, 19. He oferwrīhþ nān man mid fæte his onælede leóhtfæt *nēmo autem lucernam accendens, opĕrit eam vāse*, Lk. Bos. 8, 16. In seolfren fæt *in a silver vessel*, Elen. Kmbl. 2050; El. 1026. He mid rōde tācne ðæt fæt bletsode *he blessed the vessel with the sign of the cross*, Homl. Th. ii. 158, 19. On ðæt fæt *in călĭcem*, Gen. 40, 11. Geseah he fyrnmanna fatu *he saw vessels of men of yore*, Beo. Th. 5515; B. 2761. Gecuron hīg ða gōdan on hyra fatu *elēgĕrunt bŏnos in vāsa*, Mt. Bos. 13, 48. Adrifene fatu *graven* or *embossed vessels*, Ælfc. Gl. 67; Som. 69, 99; Wrt. Voc. 41, 49. Ne mæg man ðone strangan his ǣhta and his fatu bereáfian, and on his hūs gān *nēmo pŏtest vāsa fortis ingressus in dŏmum dirĭpĕre*, Mk. Bos. 3, 27. Hū mæg man ingān on stranges hūs, and hys fata hyne bereáfian *quōmŏdo pŏtest quisquam intrāre in dŏmum fortis, et vāsa ejus dirĭpĕre*, Mt. Bos. 12, 29. [*Prompt.* fate *cupa: Scot.* fat *a cask, barrel: O. Sax.* fat, *n: Plat.* vat, fat, *n: Dut.* vat, *n: Ger.* fass, *n: M. H. Ger.* vaȝ, *n: O. H. Ger.* faz, *n: Dan.* fad, *n: Swed. Icel.* fat, *n.*] DER. ār-fæt, bān-, drinc-, eorþ-, gold-, hord-, hūsel-, lām-, leóht-, līc-, lyft-, māðum-, sealm-, sinc-, sync, -stān-, wǣg-, wæter-.

fæt, es; *m. A journey, going, path;* meātus, passus, gressus, ĭter, *used only in compound words.* v. fæt-hengest, sīþ-fæt.

fæt; *adj. Fat;* pinguis:—Fæt *pinguis*, Wrt. Voc. 83, 45. Mid fætre lynde *with fat grease*, Ps. Th. 80, 15. v. fætt.

fæt, fætt, es; *n? A thin plate of metal, gold-leaf, ornament;* lāmĭna, bractea:—Sceal se hearda helm, hyrsted golde, fætum, befeallen *the hard helmet, adorned with gold, with ornaments, shall be fallen off*, Beo. Th. 4504, note; B. 2256. To ðæs ðe he goldsele gumena wisse, fættum fāhne *until he perceived the golden hall of men, variegated with ornaments*, 1436; B. 716.

fæted, fætt; *part. Covered with gold, gilt, golden, ornamented;* bracteātus:—Ðæt sweord fāh and fæted *the sword coloured and ornamented*, Beo. Th. 5395; B. 2701. Gesāwon fæted wǣge, dryncfæt deóre *they saw the golden cup, the precious drinking vessel*, Beo. Th. 4499; B. 2253: 4553; B. 2282: Exon. 113 b; Th. 434, 27; Rä. 52, 7: Andr. Kmbl. 601; An. 301.

fæted-hleór, es; *n. Ornamented cheek;* phălĕrāta gĕna:—He hēht ðā eahta mearas fætedhleóre on flet teón *then he commanded to lead into court eight steeds with ornamented cheek*, Beo. Th. 2076; B. 1036.

fæted-sinc, es; *n. Gilded treasure;* bracteātus thēsaurus = θησαυρός:—Ðeáh ic ðē lyt syllan mihte fætedsinces *though I might give to thee a little of gilded treasure*, Andr. Kmbl. 955; An. 478.

fætels, fetels, es; *pl. nom. acc.* fætelsas, fætels; *m. n. A vessel, vat, sack, bag, pouch;* vas, saccus, pēra = πήρα, marsūpium = μαρσύπιον:—Dō on swylc fætels swylce ðū wille *put [it] into whatever vessel thou wilt*, Lchdm. iii. 16, 26. Ðeáh man asette twegen fætels full ealaþ oððe wæteres, hȳ gedōþ ðæt ōðer biþ oferfroren *if a man set two vats full of ale or of water, they cause that either shall be frozen over*, Ors. 1, 1; Bos. 23, 8. Seó mǣgþ gebrohte heáfod blōdig on ðam fætelse *the woman brought the bloody head in the bag*, Judth. 11; Thw. 23, 18; Jud. 127. Ic bicge hȳda and fell, and wyrce of him pusan and fætelsas *ĕgo ĕmo cŭtes et pelles et făcio ex iis pēras et marsūpia*, Coll. Monast. Th. 28, 1. DER. mete-fætels.

fætelsian; *p.* ode; *pp.* od *To put into a vessel;* in vas infundĕre:—Fætelsa and heald hyt *put it into a vessel and preserve it*, Med. ex Quadr. 1, 3; Lchdm. i. 328, 17.

fætere *light, negligent;* levis, remissus, Som. Ben. Lye.

fæt-fellere, es; *m. Abatis;* aliter *abax?* Ælfc. Gl. 113; Som. 79, 118; Wrt. Voc. 60, 25.

fæt-gold, es; *n. Gold drawn out into thin plates;* in lāmĭnas dēductum aurum, B. 1921.

fæðem, es; *m. Bosom, lap;* sĭnus, grĕmium:—In fæðem *in sĭnu*, Jn. Lind. War. 1, 18. v. fæðm.

fæt-hengest, es; *m. A road horse;* itĭnĕris ĕquus:—Ne fæt-hengest *nor a road horse*, Exon. 106 a; Th. 404, 27; Rä. 23, 14.

fæðer *a feather*, Deut. 32, 11. v. feðer.

fæðer-homa *a feather-covering, the wings*, Cd. 22; Jun. 11, 1. v. feðer-hama.

FÆÐM, es; *m: also in prose* fæðm, e; *f.* I. *the embracing arms;* brachia amplexa, circumdăta:—Hī fæðmum clyppaþ *they will clasp them in their arms*, Exon. 107 a; Th. 409, 8; Rä. 27, 25. He wæs upphafen engla fæðmum *he was upraised in the arms of angels*, Exon. 17 a; Th. 41, 6; Cri. 651. Wæs Gūþlāces gǣst gelǣded engla fæðmum *the spirit of Guthlac was led in the arms of angels*, Exon. 44 a; Th. 148, 33; Gū. 754. Ðā hēt līfes brytta englas sīne fæðmum ferigean leófne *then the giver of life commanded his angels to bear the dear one in their arms*, Andr. Kmbl. 1647; An. 825. II. what embraces or contains,—*A lap, bosom, breast;* quicquid complectĭtur *vel* comprehendit alĭquid, sĭnus, grĕmium, interna, pectus:—Me on fæðme sticaþ *places me in the bosom*, Exon. 103 b; Th. 394, 1; Rä. 13, 11. On fæder fæðme *in the bosom of the father*, Menol. Fox 583; Gn. C. 61. He lǣdeþ in his ānes fæðm ealle gesceafta *he leadeth into the bosom of himself alone all creatures*, Exon. 93 a; Th. 349, 34; Sch. 56. Deáþ in eorþan fæðm sendaþ lǣne līchoman *death sends frail bodies into earth's bosom*, Exon. 62 b; Th. 231, 11; Ph. 487. Heó losaþ ne on foldan fæðm *she shall not escape into earth's bosom*, Beo. Th. 2790; B. 1393. To Fæder fæðmum *in his Father's bosom*, Beo. Th. 378; B. 188. Uppastōd of brimes bōsme on bātes fæðm egesa ofer ȳþlid *terror uprose from the bosom of the sea on the lap of the boat over our wave-ship*, Andr. Kmbl. 888; An. 444. Ðara ðe līfes gāst fæðmum þeahte *of those who covered in their breasts the spirit of life*, Cd. 64; Th. 77, 28; Gen. 1282. In fæðm fȳres *into the bosom of the fire*, Cd. 184; Th. 230, 16; Dan. 234. Astāg mægna gold-hord in fǣmnan fæðm *the treasury of might [Christ] descended into a virgin's womb*, Exon. 19 b; Th. 49, 19; Cri. 788. III. that part of the arm on which one leans, hence—*A cubit, the length from the elbow to the wrist, said to be estimated at one foot six inches or 18 inches;* cŭbĭtus. v. eln:—Fæðm betwux elbogan and handwyrste *a cubit is betwixt the elbow and wrist*, Ælfc. Gl. 72; Som. 70, 126; Wrt. Voc. 43, 51. Þreó hund fæðma biþ se arc on lenge *trĕcentōrum cŭbĭtōrum ĕrit longĭtūdo arcæ*, Gen. 6, 15. And ðū getīhst his heáhnisse togædere on ufeweardum to ānre fæðme *et in cŭbĭto consummābis summĭtātem ejus*, Gen. 6, 16. IV. *both the arms extended, now a* FATHOM = *six feet;* spătium utriusque brachii extensiōne contentum, Cot. 162? Lye. V. the arms extended for embracing or protecting,—*An embrace, protection;* amplexus, complexus, protectio:—Wæs wīf Abrahames lǣded on fremdes fæðm *the wife of Abraham was led to the embrace of a stranger*, Cd. 124; Th. 159, 7; Gen. 2631. Sceolde monig ides bifiende gān on fremdes fæðm *many a damsel trembling must go into the embrace of a stranger*, Cd. 92; Th. 118, 26; Gen. 1971. Þurh flōdes fæðm *through the embrace of the flood*, Andr. Kmbl. 3230; An. 1618. Hæfde wederwolcen wīdum fæðmum eorþan and uprōdor gedǣled *the storm-cloud had divided with wide embraces the earth and firmament above*, Cd. 146; Th. 182, 14; Exod. 75. Hwā mec bregde of brimes fæðmum *who drew me from the embrace of ocean?* Exon. 101 a; Th. 382, 19; Rä. 3, 13. VI. in the hands or power of,—*Grasp, power;* pŏtestas, ditio:—Gehwearf ðā in Francna fæðm feorh cyninges *the life of the king then departed into the power* [*grasp*] *of the Franks*, Beo. Th. 2424; B. 1210. Gē of feónda fæðme weorþen *ye escape from the power of enemies*, Cd. 158; Th. 196, 20; Exod. 294. Ðe ic alȳsde feóndum of fæðme *which I released from the power of foes*, Exon. 29 b; Th. 91, 2; Cri. 1486. VII. what is extended,—*An expanse, abyss, deep;* expansum, tractus, superficies, abyssus, profundum:—Siððan leóhtes weard ofer ealne foldan fæðm fȳr onsendeþ *after that the guardian of light shall send fire over all the expanse of earth*, Exon. 116 b; Th. 448, 14; Dōm. 54. Bodiaþ beorhtne geleáfan ofer foldan fæðm *preach the bright faith throughout the expanse of the earth*, Andr. Kmbl. 671; An. 336. Se brāda sǣ bræc on eorþan fæðm *the broad sea broke on to the tract of earth*, Exon. 24 b; Th. 70, 32; Cri. 1147. Swā hie wið eorþan fæðm þūsend wintra ðǣr eardodon *as if they had rested there on the plain of earth a thousand winters*, Beo. Th. 6091; B. 3049. Hie on flōdes fæðm ceólum lācaþ *they sail in ships on the expanse of the flood*, Andr. Kmbl. 503; An. 252. [*Chauc.* fadmen, *pl. fathoms*: *Laym.* ueðme *fathom*: *Plat.* fadem, faem *a thread, cubit*: *O. Sax.* faðmōs, *pl. m. the hands and arms*: *Dut.* vadem, vaam, *f. a fathom*: *Kil.* vadem *fīlum quod intra mānus extensas contĭnētur, mensūra mānuum expensārum, ulna, passus*: *Ger.* faden, fadem, *m. a thread, cubit*: *M. H. Ger.* vadem, vaden, *m*: *O. H. Ger.* fadam, fadum, *m. n. fīlum*: *Dan.* favn, *m. f*: *Swed.* famn, *m*: *Icel.* faðmr, *m. a fathom.*] DER. heoru-fæðm, lagu-, wæl-.

fæðmian, fæðman; *p.* ade, ede; *pp.* ad, ed *To* FATHOM, *embrace, contain, envelope, clasp, devour;* amplecti, complecti, contĭnēre, comĕdĕre:—Hie lēton flōd fæðmian frætwa hyrde *they let the flood embrace the treasures' guardian*, Beo. Th. 6257; B. 3133: Andr. Kmbl. 3176; An. 1591. Feorhcynna fela fæðmeþ ēglond *an island contains many of mortal kinds*, Exon. 89 a; Th. 334, 11; Gn. Ex. 14. Wæter fæðmedon *the waters enveloped them*, Andr. Kmbl. 3143; An. 1574. Ðæt mīnne līchaman glēd fæðmie *that fire should clasp my body*, Beo. Th. 5298; B. 2652. Heora geóguþe fȳr fæðmade *jŭvĕnes eōrum comēdit ignis*, Ps. Th. 77, 63. DER. be-fæðman, ofer-: sīd-fæðmed.

fæðm-līc; *adj. Bending, winding;* sinuōsus, Cot. 202.

fæðm-rīm, es; *n. Fathom-measure;* cŭbĭtōrum *vel* ulnārum nŭmĕrus:—Is ðæt torhte lond twelfum hērra fæðmrīmes *that glorious land is higher by twelve of fathom-measure*, Exon. 56 a; Th. 199, 21; Ph. 29.

fætian *to fetch;* addūcĕre, Lye. v. fetian.

fætnes, -ness, -nyss, e; *f.* [fæt *fat*] FATNESS; pinguēdo, adeps:—Hī habbaþ fætnesse *they have fatness*, Ps. Th. 16, 9. Of fætnysse hwǣtes *ex adĭpe frūmenti*, Ps. Lamb. 80, 17. Fætnysse heora hī beclȳsdon *thei han closide togidere her fatnesse*, Wyc; ădĭpem suum conclūsērunt, Ps. Spl. 16, 11. Mid ungle oððe mid fætnysse lamba *cum ădĭpe agnōrum*, Cant. Moys. Isrl. Lamb. 192 a, 14.

FÆTT, fett, fæt; *adj.* FAT, *fatted;* pinguis, sāgīnātus, crassus:—Seó fætte gelynd *the fat grease*, Ps. Th. 62, 5. Ðīn fæder ofslōh ān fætt cealf *occīdit păter tuus vitŭlum săgīnātum*, Lk. Bos. 15, 27, 23, 30: Gen. 18, 7. Ðonne hīg etaþ and fulle beóþ and fætte *cum comēdĕrint et sătūrāti crassique fuĕrint*, Deut. 31, 20: Gen. 41, 2: Ps. Spl. 21, 30: Ors. 4, 13; Bos. 100, 25, 26: Ps. Lamb. 21, 13. Ða fættan fearas me ofsǣton *tauri pingues obsēdērunt me*, Ps. Th. 21, 10. He ofslōh heora fættan *occīdit pingues eōrum*, Ps. Lamb. 77, 31: Gen. 41, 4. Māra ic eom and fættra ðonne amæsted swīn *I am larger and fatter than a fattened swine*, Exon. 111 b; Th. 428, 8; Rä. 41, 105. Bringon eall ðæt ðǣrinne fættest sī *offĕrent quidquid pinguēdĭnis est intrinsĕcus*, Lev. 3, 3. [*Piers P. Chauc.* fat: *Laym.* uatte, fatte, *pl*: *Frs.* fet: *O. Frs.* fat: *O. Sax.* feit: *Dut.* vet: *Ger.* fett, feist: *M. H. Ger.* veiȝ, veiȝt, veiȝet: *O. H. Ger.* feizt: *Dan.* feed, fed: *Swed.* fet: *Icel.* feitr.]

fætt; *part. Covered with gold, gilt, golden, ornamented;* bracteātus:—Sincgestreónum fættan goldes *with precious treasures of rich gold*, Beo. Th. 2190; B. 1093: 4484; B. 2246. Fættan golde *with rich gold*, 4210; B. 2102. Hwanon ferigeaþ gē fætte scyldas *whence bear ye your ornamented shields?* 672; B. 333. v. fæted.

fættian; *p.* ode; *pp.* od *To* FATTEN; pinguĕfăcĕre, pinguescĕre:—Fættiaþ wlitige wēstenes *the feire thingis of desert schulen wexe fatte*, Wyc; pinguescent spĕciōsa deserti, Ps. Spl. 64, 13. v. ge-fættian, ge-fætnian.

fæx *deceit;* fūcus, Cot. 91, Lye.

fæx *hair*, Jn. Lind. War. 11, 2. v. feax.

FĀG, fāh; *def.* se fāga, seó, ðæt fāge; *adj. Coloured, stained, dyed, tinged, shining, variegated;* tinctus, cŏlōrātus, vărius, versicŏlor, discŏlor:—Wæter wældreóre fāg *water stained with deadly gore*, Beo. Th. 3267; B. 1631. Ðæt sweord fāh and fæted *the sword blood-stained and ornate*, 5395; B. 2701: 2576; B. 1286. Bleóbrygdum fāg *shining with variegated colours*, Exon. 60 a; Th. 218, 9; Ph. 292. Gār golde fāh *a weapon shining with gold*, Menol. Fox 503; Gn. C. 22. Fȳrmǣlum fāg *variegated with marks of fire*, Andr. Kmbl. 2269; An. 1136. Fāh *vărius* vel *discŏlor*, Ælfc. Gl. 79; Som. 72, 79; Wrt. Voc. 46, 36: 77, 3. Fultum ðū him afyrdest fāgan sweordes *avertisti adjūtōrium glădii ejus*, Ps. Th. 88, 36. Ic geann Ælmǣre ānes fāgan stēdan *I give to Ælmær one pied steed*, Th. Diplm. 560, 38. Ofer næddran and fāgum wyrme ðū gǣst *sŭper aspĭdem et basiliscum ambŭlābis*, Ps. Spl. C. 90, 13. He me habban wile dreóre fāhne *he will have me stained with gore*, Beo. Th. 898; B. 447. He geseah steápne hrōf golde fāhne *he saw the steep roof shining with gold*, 1858; B. 927. On fāgne flōr feónd treddode *the fiend trod on the variegated floor*, 1454; B. 725. Slōh ðone feóndsceaðan fāgum mēce *slew the enemy with a blood-stained sword*, Judth. 10; Thw. 23, 4; Jud. 104. He geseah since fāge *he saw variegated treasures*, Beo. Th. 3234; B. 1615. Fāgum sweordum *with shining swords*, Judth. 11; Thw. 24, 18; Jud. 194. [*Laym.* fæh: *O. Sax.* fēh: *Ger.* fech: *M. H. Ger.* vēch: *O. H. Ger.* fēh: *Goth.* faihs in filu-faihs *many-coloured.*] DER. ban-fāh, bleó-fāg, blōd-, brūn-, dreór-, gold-, haso-, reád-, searo-, sinc-, stān-, swāt-, tigel-, wæl-, won-, wyrm-.

fāg *guilty, criminal, outlawed, hostile*, Beo. Th. 2531; B. 1263. v. fāh.

fagc *A plaice, flounder;* platesia, Coll. Monast. Th. 24, 12. v. facg.

fagen; *adj. Glad;* lætus:—Wǣron ða burhware fagene *the citizens were glad*, Ors. 5, 3; Bos. 103, 32. v. fægen.

fagenian; *p.* ode; *pp.* od *To rejoice, to be glad;* gaudēre:—He fagenode ðæs *he rejoiced at it*, Bt. 16, 4; Fox. 58, 9. Hīg fagenodon *gāvīsi sunt*, Lk. Bos. 22, 5. v. fægnian.

fāgettan, fāgetan, fāggetan; *p.* te; *pp.* ed *To turn colour, change, vary;* văriāre:—Se mōna fāggeteþ [fāgetteþ MS. R; fāgeteþ MS. P] oððe asweartaþ *the moon turns colour or becomes dark*, Bd. de nat. rerum; Lchdm. iii. 240, 23; Wrt. popl. science 5, 15.

fāgetung, e; *f. A changing, change;* vărietas, dīversĭtas:—Hēr is ðære lyfte fāgetung *here is a changing of the air*, Homl. Th. ii. 538, 33.

fāgian; *p.* ode; *pp.* od *To shine, glitter, vary;* văriāre:—Swā hit nū fāgaþ *so it now varies*, Bt. Met. Fox 11, 79; Met. 11, 40. Hī fāgiaþ *they vary*, Bt. 21; Fox 74, 13.

fagnian; *p.* ode; *pp.* od *To rejoice, be delighted with, wish for;* gaudēre, appĕtĕre:—Fagnian *to rejoice*, Bt. 30, 1; Fox 108, 7, 10. Herodes fagnode, ðā he ðone Hǣlend geseah *Hĕrōdes, vīso Jēsu, gāvīsus est*, Lk. Bos. 23, 8. To hwon fagnast ðū ðæs ðe ðū ǣr hæfdest *why dost thou long for what thou formerly hadst?* Bt. 14, 2; Fox 42, 32.

fāgnys, -nyss, e; *f. A scab, ulcer, eruption;* scăbies, ulcus, eruptio:—Lāþlīc biþ ðæs hreóflian līc mid mislīcum fāgnyssum *loathsome is the body of the leper with divers scabs*, Homl. Th. i. 122, 22. Ðæt Crist ūre sāwle fram synna fāgnyssum gehǣlan mǣge *that Christ may heal our soul from the ulcers of sins*, 122, 25. Seó fāgnys aweg gewāt *the eruption went away*, Homl. Th. ii. 178, 15. Unlybba awende his hiw to wunderlīcere fāgnysse *poison turned his appearance to a wonderful eruption*, 178, 12.

fāgung, e; *f. Difference, diversity, variety;* vărietas, Gr. Dial. 2, 27.

fāh *coloured;* tinctus, colōrātus:—Blōde fāh *coloured with blood*, Beo. Th. 1873; B. 934. v. fāg; *adj. coloured.*

FĀH, fāg; *pl. nom. acc.* fā; *gen.* fāra; *dat.* fāum; *adj. Guilty, criminal, proscribed, outlawed, inimical, hostile;* sons, reus, proscriptus, inĭmīcus, infensus, infestus:—Dǣdum fāh *guilty of* [*wicked*] *deeds*, Cd. 216; Th. 274, 19; Sat. 156. Mid dǣdum fāh, Ps. Th. 105, 28. Firendǣdum fāh *guilty of sinful deeds*, Exon. 22 b; Th. 62, 13; Cri. 1001: 66 b; Th. 246, 9; Jul. 59. Fyrendǣdum fāg, Beo. Th. 2006; B. 1001. Firendǣdum fā, *nom. pl.* Exon. 31 b; Th. 99, 31; Cri. 1633. Leahtrum fāh *guilty of crimes*, Exon. 97 b; Th. 364, 6; Wal. 66. Leahtrum fā, *nom. pl.* Exon. 20 a; Th. 52, 7; Cri. 830: 30 b; Th. 94, 12; Cri. 1539. Māne fāh *guilty of crime*, Beo. Th. 1960; B. 978. Māne fā, *nom. pl.* Andr. Kmbl. 3196; An. 1601. Synnum fāh *guilty of sins*, Frag. Kmbl. 28; Leás. 16: Exon. 118 b; Th. 456, 9; Hy. 4, 64. Mid synnum fāh, Cd. 217; Th. 275, 32; Sat. 180. Weorcum fāh *guilty of* [*wicked*] *works*, Elen. Kmbl. 2484; El. 1243. Ðeáh ðū from scyle freómāgum feor fāh gewītan *though thou, outlawed, shalt depart far from thy kindred*, Cd. 50; Th. 63, 29; Gen. 1039: Exon. 31 b; Th. 98, 34; Cri. 1617: Andr. Kmbl. 3406; An. 1707: Elen. Kmbl. 1535; El. 769. He fāg gewāt *he outlawed departed*, Beo. Th. 2531; B. 1263. Beó he fāh wið ðone cyng *let him be hostile to the king*, L. Ath. i. 20; Th. i. 210, 11: Cd. 215; Th. 270, 28; Sat. 97: Wald. 101; Vald. 2, 2?. Me beswāc fāh wyrm þurh fægir word *the hostile serpent deceived me with fair words*, Cd. 42; Th. 55, 24; Gen. 899: Cd. 166; Th. 207, 31; Exod. 475: Exon. 127 b; Th. 490, 22; Rä. 80, 5. Fāgum wyrme *to the hostile serpent*, Cd. 42; Th. 55, 35; Gen. 904. Nemne we mǣgen fāne gefyllan *unless we may fell the foe*, Beo. Th. 5303; B. 2655. Fā þrōwiaþ ealdorbealu egeslīc *the hostile shall suffer terrific vital evil*, Exon. 31 b; Th. 98, 30; Cri. 1615. Fāra monna *of hostile men*, Andr. Kmbl. 2045; An. 1025: Beo. Th. 1160; B. 578. Fāum folmum *with hostile hands*, Cd. 4; Th. 4, 31; Gen. 62: 114; Th. 149, 33; Gen. 2484. [*Chauc.* foo *a foe*: *R. Glouc.* fon *foes*: *Laym.* i-fa, i-fo, fo *a foe*: *M. H. Ger.* vēch, ge-vēch *hostile*: *O. H. Ger.* fēh, ga-fēh *inĭmīcus*: *Goth.* fayan *to be hostile, to reproach.*] DER. gryre-fāh, nearo-, syn-.

fāh-man, -mon, es; *m. A foeman, an enemy;* inĭmīcus:—Gif hie fāhmon [fāhman MS. H.] geierne *if a foeman flee to it*, L. Alf. pol. 5; Th. i. 64, 9.

fahnian; *p.* ode; *pp.* od *To rejoice;* gaudēre:—Hī fahnodon *gāvīsi sunt*, Mk. Bos. 14, 11. v. fægnian.

fahnys *a rejoicing;* jūbĭlātio, Som. Ben. Lye.

faht *fought,* Chr. 1122; Erl. 249, 23, = feaht; *p. of* feohtan.

fā-lǣcan *to be at deadly enmity, to be at feud,* L. Ath. i. 20; Th. i. 210, 10, MS. L. v. fǣ-lǣcan.

fald, e; *f?* *A* FOLD, *a sheepfold, an ox-stall, stable;* septum, ŏvīle, būcētum, bŏvīle, stăbŭlum:—Into sceápa falde *in ŏvīle ovium,* Jn. Bos. 10, 1: L. R. S. 4; Th. i. 434, 13. Hryđra fald *būcētum,* Ælfc. Gl. 1; Som. 55, 22; Wrt. Voc. 15, 22: Gen. 18, 7. Scēpen steal *vel* fald *bŏvīle, stăbŭlum,* Ælfc. Gl. 1; Som. 55, 23; Wrt. Voc. 15, 23. Fald ođđe hūs be wege *stăbŭlum,* Wrt. Voc. 85, 72. [*Wyc.* fold: *Orm.* faldes, *pl.*] DER. riþ-fald.

fald-gang, es; *m. Fold-going, putting sheep in fold to manure the land;* secta faldæ, servĭtium, quo tĕnēbātur vassallus ŏves ipsīus ad ŏvīle dŏmĭni perdūcĕre, fundi dŏmĭnĭcālis stercŏrandi grātia. v. Spelm. Glos. Lye.

fald-gang-penig, es; *m. Fold-going money, money paid by a vassal to be free from sending sheep to fold on his lord's land;* nummus dŏmĭno sŏlūtus a vassallo, ut a secta faldæ līběrārĕtur, Som. Ben. Lye.

fald-wurþ; *adj. Fold-worthy, liberty of folding;* falda, sive lībertāte faldagii dignus, dōnātus, Som. Ben. Lye.

falewe *fallow* or *pale yellow,* Som. Ben. Lye. v. fealo.

falewende *yellow coloured;* flavescens, Cot. 191.

fallende *falling,* Bd. 5, 6; S. 618, 24, = feallende; *part. of* feallan.

FALS, es; *n. A* FALSE*hood, fraud, counterfeit;* falsum:—Būtan ǣlcon false *without any fraud,* L. Eth. vi. 32; Th. i. 322, 29: L. C. S. 8; Th. i. 380, 16. Se đe ofer đis fals wyrce, þolige đæra handa đe he đæt fals mid worhte *he who after this shall make a counterfeit* [*coin*], *let him forfeit the hands with which he made the counterfeit,* L. C. S. 8; Th. i. 380, 16, 17, 20, 22. Hwī tīhþ ūre hlāford us swā micles falses *why doth our lord accuse us of so great a fraud?* Gen. 44, 7. [*Orm.* falls: *O. Frs.* falsk, falsch: *Ger.* falsch, *m. n*: *M. H. Ger.* valsch, *m*: *Icel.* fals, *n*: *Lat.* falsum, *n.*]

Falster *an island in the Baltic,* Ors. 1, 1; Bos. 21, 43.

FĀM, es; *n.* FOAM; spūma:—Đæt fām of đam mūþe eóde *the foam went out of the mouth,* Bd. 3, 9; S. 533, 32: 3, 11; S. 536, 14: Ælfc. Gl. 98; Som. 76, 89; Wrt. Voc. 54, 33: Exon. 101 a; Th. 382, 1; Rä. 3, 4. [*Ger.* feim, *m*: *M. H. Ger.* veim, *m*: *O. H. Ger.* feim, faim, *m*: *Sansk.* phena, *m. n. foam, froth, scum.*] v. fǣman.

fām-blāwende; *def.* se -blāwenda; *part. Foam-blowing, emitting foam;* spūmam efflans:—Se lēg fāmblāwenda seáþ and se fūla đone đū gesāwe, đæt wæs helle tintreges mūþ *pŭteus ille flammĭvŏmus ac pūtĭdus quem vīdisti, ipsum est os gehennæ,* Bd. 5, 12; S. 630, 12, note, MS. T.

fāmgian; *p.* ode; *pp.* od *To foam;* spūmāre:—Flōd fāmgode *the flood foamed,* Cd. 167; Th. 208, 10; Exod. 481.

fāmig, fǣmig; *adj.* FOAMY; spūmōsus:—Fāmig sǣ *the foamy sea,* Cd. 72; Th. 87, 22; Gen. 1452. Fāmige flōdas *foamy floods,* 100; Th. 133, 19; Gen. 2213: Exon. 101 b; Th. 383, 32; Rä. 4, 19: Salm. Kmbl. 315; Sal. 157.

fāmig-bord, es; *n. A foaming bank;* spūmōsa margo:—On streám fāmigbordum [MS. -bordon] *on a stream with foamy banks,* Bt. Met. Fox 26, 52; Met. 26, 26.

fāmig-bōsm, es; *m. A foamy bosom;* spūmōsus sĭnus, Cd. 167; Th. 209, 2; Exod. 493.

fāmig-heals; *adj. Foamy-necked;* spūmōsus in collo:—Sǣ-genga fōr, fleát fāmigheals *the sea-goer went, the foamy-necked floated,* Beo. Th. 3822; B. 1909: 441; B. 218: Andr. Kmbl. 993; An. 497.

fāmwæstas *molles,* Cot. 131.

fan *a fan.* v. fann, fon.

FANA, an; *m. A standard, flag,* VANE; vexillum:—Fana hwearfode, scīr on sceafte *the standard waved, bright on the shaft,* Bt. Met. Fox 1, 20; Met. 1, 10: Cd. 155; Th. 193, 18; Exod. 248. [*Chauc.* fane *a vane*: *Plat.* fane, *f*: *O. Sax.* fano, *m*: *O. Frs.* fona, fana, *m*: *Dut.* vaan, *f*: *Ger.* fane, fahne, *f*: *M. H. Ger.* vane, van, *m*: *O. H. Ger.* fano, *m*: *Goth.* fana, *m*: *Dan.* fane, *m. f*: *Swed.* fana, *f*: *Icel.* fāni, *m*: *Lat.* pannus, *m*: *Grk.* πῆνος, *m.*] DER. gūþ-fana.

fand *found,* Cd. 72; Th. 87, 30; Gen. 1456; *p. of* findan.

fandere, es; *m. A tempter, trier;* tentātor, Som. Ben. Lye.

fandian, fandigan; to fandienne; *p.* ede, ode; *pp.* ed, od; *v. trans. gen. dat. acc. To try, tempt, prove, examine, explore, seek, search out;* tentāre, prŏbāre, exāmĭnāre, expĕrīri, inquīrĕre, vestīgāre:—Gif đē ǣfre geweorþeþ đæt đū wilt ođđe mōst weorolde þióstro eft fandian *if it should happen that thou wilt or must again explore the world's darkness,* Bt. Met. Fox 24, 113; Met. 24, 57. Ic bohte ān getȳme oxena, nū wille ic faran and fandian hyra *jŭga boum ēmi quinque, et eo prŏbāre illa,* Lk. Bos. 14, 19. Ic wille fandigan nū hwæt đa men dōn *I will now seek to know what those men do,* Cd. 109; Th. 145, 24; Gen. 2410. Đæm weorce to fandienne *to prove the work,* Ors. 1, 12; Bos. 36, 37. He gārsecg fandaþ *he tempteth the ocean,* Runic pm. 25; Kmbl. 344, 20; Hick. Thes. i. 135, 50. Đū fandodest us God *prŏbasti nos Deus,* Ps. Spl. 65, 9. Ferdon đa Pharisēi, and his fandedon *exiērunt Pharisæi, tentantes eum,* Mk. Bos. 8, 11. Hȳ fandodon mīn *tentāvērunt me,* Ps. Th. 34, 16; 40, 6. Ne fanda đīnes Drihtnes *tempt not thy Lord,* Homl. Th. i. 166, 21. Fanda mīn, Drihten *prŏba me, Dŏmĭne,* Ps. Th. 25, 2: Deut. 6, 16. [*Piers P.* fonden: *Chauc.* fonde: *Laym.* fondien: *Orm.* fandenn: *O. Sax.* fandōn: *Frs.* fanljen: *O. Frs.* fandia, fandlia: *Dut. Kil.* vanden: *Ger.* fanden, fahnden: *M. H. Ger.* venden: *O. H. Ger.* fantōn *tentāre, explōrāre.*] DER. a-fandian, ge-.

fandlīc *hostile;* hostīlis. DER. a-fandelīc.

fandung, e; *f. A temptation, trial, proof;* tentātio, prŏbātio, inquīsītio:—Ôđer is seó fandung đe Iacob se apostol embe spræc *the other is the temptation of which the apostle James spoke,* Boutr. Scrd. 23, 8. Scearplīcu and smeálīcu fandung đæs mōdes *the sharp and searching temptation of the mind,* Past. 21, 3; Hat. MS. 30 a, 26. Đære lufe fandung is đæs weorces fremming *the proof of love is the performance of work,* Homl. Th. ii. 314, 28. On đære fandunge *in temptation,* Boutr. Scrd. 23, 8. He of earce forlēt hāswe culufran on fandunga *he let out a livid dove from the ark on trial,* Cd. 72; Th. 87, 21; Gen. 1452. DER. a-fandung.

fang, es; *m.* [fangen; *pp. of* fōn *to take,* q. v.] what is taken, *A booty;* captūra, præda:—Hī fang woldon fōn *they would take booty,* Chr. 1016; Th. 281, 30. [*Laym.* feng, ueng *booty*: *Scot.* fang *a capture*: *O. Frs.* fang, feng, *m*: *Dut.* vang, *m*: *Ger.* fang, *m*: *M. H. Ger.* vanc, *m*: *O. H. Ger.* fang, *m. captūra*: *Dan.* fang, *n*: *Swed.* fång, *n*: *Icel.* fang, *n. a catching.*] DER. feax-fang, feoh-, fore-, for-, under-.

fangen *taken;* captus:—Hēr beóþ fangene seólas and hrōnas *here are caught seals and whales,* Bd. 1, 1; S. 473, 16; *pp. of* fōn *to take.*

fangen-nes, -ness, e; *f. A taking.* DER. on-fangeness, under-.

FANN, e; *f?* *A* FAN, *implement for winnowing grain;* vannus, ventilābrum:—Fann *vannus,* Ælfc. Gl. 50; Som. 65, 114; Wrt. Voc. 34, 43. Đæs fann ys on his handa, and he afeormaþ his þyrscelflōre *cujus ventilābrum in mănu sua, et permundābit āream suam,* Mt. Bos. 3, 12: Lk. Bos. 3, 17. [*Chauc.* fan: *Dut.* wan, wanne, *f*: *Ger. M. H. Ger.* wanne, *f*: *O. H. Ger.* wanna, *f*: *Swed.* vanna, *f*: *Lat.* vannus, *f.*]

fant, font, es; *m. Fountain, spring;* fons, tis, *m;* pure water, that which holds pure or holy water, *The font for baptism;* baptistērium = βαπτιστήριον:—Ne dō man nǣnne ele to đam fante *let no one put any oil into the font,* L. Ælf. C. 36; Th. ii. 358, 35; Wilk. 159, 32. v. fant-fæt, fant-wæter, font-wæter.

fant-fæt; *gen.* fant-fætes; *pl. nom. acc.* fant-fatu; *n. A font vessel, the font for baptism;* baptistērii vas:—Hǣđen cild biþ gebroht synfull þurh Adames forgǣgednysse, to đam fant-fæte, ac hit biþ aþwogen fram eallum synnum wiđinnan, đeáh đe hit wiđūtan his hiw ne awende *a heathen child is brought to the font-vessel, sinful through Adam's transgression, but it is washed from all sins within, though without it change not its appearance,* Homl. Th. ii. 268, 29–33.

fant-wæter, font-wæter, es; *n. Font-water, baptismal water;* baptistērii aqua:—Đæt hālige fant-wæter, đe is gehāten līfes wyl-spring, is gelīc on hiwe ōđrum wæterum *the holy font-water, which is called the well-spring of life, is in appearance like other waters,* Homl. Th. ii. 268, 34.

fara, an; *m. A farer, traveller;* viātor. v. ge-fara, mere-, nȳd-, tīd-.

fāra, Andr. Kmbl. 2045; An. 1025; *gen. pl. of* fāh *hostile.*

FARAN, to farenne; ic fare, đū farest, færest, færst, færsþ, he fareþ, færeþ, færþ, *pl.* faraþ; *p.* fōr, *pl.* fōron; *pp.* faren, A word expressing every kind of going from one place to another, hence I. *to go, proceed, travel, march, sail;* īre, vādĕre, incēdĕre, transīre, migrāre, nāvĭgāre:—Faran ofer feldas *to go over fields,* Exon. 108 b; Th. 415, 8; Rä. 33, 8. Nū wylle ic faran *now I will go,* Lk. Bos. 14, 19, 31. We fōron *transīvĭmus,* Ps. Spl. 65, 11. Ic fōr fram đē *I went from thee,* Gen. 31, 31. Constantius, se mīldesta man, fōr on Bryttanie, and đǣr gefōr *Constantius, the mildest man, went into Britain, and there died,* Ors. 6, 30; Bos. 126, 39. Fōr fāmig scip *the foaming ship sailed,* Cd. 71; Th. 85, 19; Gen. 1417. II. *to* FARE, *happen, to be in any state;* versāri in ălĭqua re, se hăbēre ălĭquo mŏdo, Cd. 26; Th. 34, 2; Gen. 531. Ic fare būtan bearnum *I have no children* [lit. *I go without children*], Gen. 15, 2. Hū mæg se man wel faran *how can the man fare well?* Ælfc. T. 40, 3. [*Piers P.* faren, fare: *Wyc. Chauc.* fare: *Laym.* fære, færen, faren, uaren: *Orm.* farenn: *Plat.* faren: *O. Sax.* faran: *Frs.* ferren: *O. Frs.* fara: *Dut.* vāren: *Ger.* fahren, faren: *M. H. Ger.* varn: *O. H. Ger.* faran: *Goth.* faran: *Dan.* fare: *Swed.* fara: *Icel.* fara: *Sansk.* pṛi *to bring over.*] DER. a-faran, be-, for-, forþ-, ge-, geond-, in-, of-, ofer-, on-, ōþ-, þurh-, to-, ūt-, wiđ-, ymbe-.

faraþ-lācende; *part. Swimming;* nătans:—Fiscas faraþlācende *swimming fishes,* Exon. 97 b; Th. 364, 34; Wal. 80. v. faroþ-lācende.

fare *in a journey,* Gen. 8, 1. v. faru.

fareld *a journey:*—Þurh geswinc đæs fareldes *through fatigue of the journey,* Nat. S. Greg. Els. 29, 10; and MS. at foot of plate facing Title. v. færeld.

fareþ-lācende; *part. Sailing;* nāvĭgans:—Fareþlācendum *nāvĭgantĭbus,* Exon. 96 b; Th. 360, 14; Wal. 5. v. faroþ-lācende.

Fariseisc; *def.* se Fariseisca; *adj. Pharisean;* Phărīsæus:—Bæd hine sum Fariseisc man đæt he ǣte mid him *rŏgāvit illum quĭdam Phărīsæus ut prandĕret ăpud se,* Lk. Bos. 11, 37. Ongan se Fariseisca on him smeágan and cweđan *Phărīsæus cœpit intra se repŭtans dīcĕre,* 11, 38.

Cômon to him ða bôceras and Fariseisce *accessērunt ad eum Scrībæ et Phărīsæi*, Mt. Bos. 15, 1. Ða Fariseiscan synt gedrēfede *Phărīsæi scandălīzāti sunt*, 15, 12.

Farnea eálond, es; *n. Farn island, on the coast of Northumberland, near Lindisfarne;* Farnensis insŭla, Som. Ben. Lye.

faroþ, es; *n? The floating of the waves, a billow, the shore;* fluctuātio măris, unda, lītus:—Hī hyne ætbǽron to brimes faroþe *they bore him away to the sea's shore*, Beo. Th. 56; B. 28. Fūs on faroþe *ready on the shore*, Andr. Kmbl. 509; An. 255. DER. brim-faroþ, mere-, sǽ-, waroþ-.

faroþ-hengest *a sea-horse, ship.* v. fearoþ-hengest.

faroþ-lācende, faraþ-lācende, fareþ-lācende; *part.* [lācan *to sail*] *Sailing, swimming;* nāvĭgans, nătans:—Faroþlācende *sailing*, Andr. Kmbl. 1014; An. 507. Gewīciaþ faroþlācende on ðam eálonde *the seafaring* [*men*] *encamp on that island*, Exon. 96 b; Th. 361, 15; Wal. 20.

faroþ-rīdende; *part. Wave-riding, sailing;* nāvĭgans:—We on sǽbāte wada cunnedon, faroþrīdende *we in the sea-boat made a trial of the fords, riding over the waves*, Andr. Kmbl. 879; An. 440.

faroþ-strǽt, e; *f. The sea-street, the sea;* marĭtĭma via, măre:—Ic ongiten hæbbe ðæt ðū on faroþstrǽte feor ne wǽre *I have understood that thou wert not far from us upon the sea*, Andr. Kmbl. 1795; An. 900: 622; An. 311.

FARU, e; *f.* I. *a going, journey, passage;* ĭter, profectio, ĭtio, transĭtus:—Hit ys Godes faru *est transĭtus Dŏmĭni* [*passover*], Ex. 12, 11. II. *family, what is movable;* fămĭlia, cŏmĭtātus:—God ðā gemunde Noes fare *God then remembered Noah's family*, Gen. 8, 1. Mid ealre fare, and mid eallum ǽhtum *with all his family, and with all his possessions*, 12, 5. Abram ðā ferde of Egipta lande mid ealre his fare *Abram then went from the land of the Egyptians with all his family*, 12, 20. Gewīt ðū nū feran and ðīne fare lǽdan ceápas *begin thou now to depart and lead thy family and thy cattle*, Cd. 83; Th. 105, 1; Gen. 1746. III. *expedition, march;* expĕdītio, agmen migrantium:—He ðas fare lǽdeþ *he leadeth this expedition*, Cd. 170; Th. 213, 19; Exod. 554. v. fær; *n. and f.* [*Piers P. Chauc.* fare: *Laym.* fære, fare, uare, faren: *O. Frs.* fare, fera, fere, fer, *f*: *Ger.* far, fahr, *f. res mōbĭlis*: *M. H. Ger.* var, *f. ĭter*: *O. H. Ger.* fuora, *f. ĭtio*: *Icel.* för, *f. a journey, expedition.*] DER. earh- [earg-] faru, forþ-, fyrd-, gār-, hægl-, man-, streám-, wǽg-, wolcen-, ȳþ-.

fas *a fringe*, Som. Ben. Lye. v. fæs.

fast *fast*, Som. Ben. Lye. v. fæst *fast, firm.* v. fæstan II.

fastitocalon [=ἀσπιδοχελώνη: Dietrich ἄστυ τὸ καλόν] *A large whale;* bālæna = φάλαινα:—Ic wille cȳðan bī ðam miclan hwale, ðam is noma cenned fastitocalon *I will make known concerning the great whale, to which the name Fastitocalon is given*, Exon. 96 b; Th. 360, 18; Wal. 7.

fatan; *p.* fōt, *pl.* fōton; *pp.* faten *To go;* īre, volvi, volvĕre. v. fetan, fetian.

faðu, e; *f*: faðe, an; *f. A father's sister, paternal aunt;* ămĭta:—Faðu *ămĭta*, Ælfc. Gr. 6; Som. 5, 55: Wrt. Voc. 72, 43. Mīn faðu *ămĭta mea;* mīnra faða mōder *ămĭta mea magna;* mīnre faðan yldre mōder *proamĭta mea;* mīnre [MS. mīnra] faðan þridde mōder *abămĭta mea*, Ælfc. Gl. 92, 93; Som. 75, 60-64; Wrt. Voc. 52, 17-20. Seó wæs Ecfriþes faðu ðæs cyninges *quæ erat ămĭta rēgis Ecgfridi*, Bd. 4, 19; S. 587, 41. Būton hit sȳ his mōder, oððe sweoster, oððe faðu, oððe mōddrie *unless it be his mother, or sister, or father's sister, or mother's sister*, Homl. Th. ii. 94, 32. Ic gean mīnre faðan Leófware ðæs heáfodbotles on Purleá *I give to my aunt Leofware the chief dwelling at Purley*, Cod. Dipl. 1293; A. D. 998; Kmbl. vi. 138, 23. v. mōddrie *a maternal aunt.*

fatu, fata *vats, vessels*, Mk. Bos. 3, 27: Mt. Bos. 12, 29. v. fæt.

Faul; a word used as a charm against the bite of an adder:—Sume ān word wið nædran bīte lǽraþ to cweðenne, ðæt is, Faul *some teach us against bite of adder to speak one word, that is, Faul*, L. M. 1, 45; Lchdm. ii. 114, 2.

feá; *indecl. n.* FEE, *money, goods;* pĕcūnia:—Gif ðū ðisses mannes feá in his synnum deádes ne onfēnge *si hujus vĭri in peccātis suis mortui pĕcūniam non accēpisses*, Bd. 3, 19; S. 549, 10. v. feoh.

feá, an; *m. Joy;* gaudium:—Him he gehēt ēcne feán *he promised him everlasting joy*, Bd. 1, 25; Whelc. 76, 1. v. ge-feá.

feá; *adj. Few;* pauci:—Ðis feá āna dōþ *a few only do this*, Bd. 4, 25; S. 601, 8. Ðæt hēr wǽre mycel rīp [MS. riip] and feá wyrhtan *that a great harvest was here and few workmen*, 1, 29; S. 498, 5. Feá ðæt gedȳgaþ *few escape from that*, Exon. 102 a; Th. 386, 6; Rä. 4, 57. Feá worda cwæþ *he said few words*, Beo. Th. 5318; B. 2662. He feára sum befōran gengde *he with a few went before*, Beo. Th. 2828; B. 1412. Ealle nemne feáum ānum *all save a few only*, Beo. Th. 2167; B. 1081. Nales feám sīþum *not a few times*, Elen. Kmbl. 1633; El. 818: Andr. Kmbl. 1210; An. 605. v. feáwa.

feá; *adv. Even a little, ever so little;* părum:—Ne māgon feá gangan *they cannot walk even a little*, Ps. Th. 134, 18.

feágan, to feágenne [feá, gefeá *joy*] *To rejoice;* lætāri, plaudĕre:—To feágenne on blisse þeóde ðīnre *ad lætandum in lætĭtia gentis tuæ*, Ps. Lamb. 105, 5. Flōdas feágaþ oððe hafetiaþ mid handa *flūmĭna plaudent mănu*, 97, 8.

feaht *fought*, Byrht. Th. 139, 14; By. 254; *p. of* feohtan.

feala; *adj. Many, much;* multum, multa:—Ne spræc ic worda feala *non lŏcūtus sum verbōrum multa*, Ps. Th. 76, 4: 77, 43: 105, 27. On feala wīsan *multis mŏdis*, Coll. Monast. Th. 25, 11. v. fela.

feala-fōr, feale-fōr, e; *f? A fieldfare?* turdus pĭlāris?—Fealafōr *torax?* Cot. 174, Som. Ben. Lye. v. feolu-fōr, felde-fare.

feala-hiw, es; *n. A varied colour:*—Feala-hiwes hrægel *pŏlymĭta*, Ælfc. Gl. 63; Wrt. Voc. 40, 14. v. hiw.

feald *a field*, Ps. Spl. 77, 15: 64, 12. v. feld.

feald, es; *n. A fold, inclosure, field;* septum, ăger, Som. Ben. Lye. DER. ge-feald.

-feald, the termination of numerals, as ān-feald *one-fold, single;* twī-feald or twȳ-feald *two-fold, double;* þreó-feald or þrȳ-feald *three-fold, treble;* seofon-feald *seven-fold;* manig-feald *manifold.* [*O. Sax.* -fald: *O. Frs.* -fald: *M. H. Ger.* -valt: *O. H. Ger.* -falt: *Goth.* -falþs.]

FEALDAN, ic fealde, ðū fealdest, fylst, he fealdeþ, fylt, *pl.* fealdaþ; *p.* feóld, *pl.* feóldon; *pp.* fealden [feald *a fold*] *To* FOLD *up, wrap;* plĭcāre:—Gōd scipstȳra hǽt fealdan ðæt segl *a good pilot gives order to furl the sail*, Bt. 41, 3; Fox 250, 14. Ic fealde *plĭco;* ic feóld *plĭcui* vel *plĭcāvi*, Ælfc. Gr. 24; Som. 25, 50. He feóld his fēt uppan his bedd *collēgit pĕdes suos sŭper lectŭlum*, Gen. 49, 32. Fingras feóldon [MS. feóldan] mec *fingers folded me*, Exon. 107 a; Th. 408, 4; Rä. 27, 7. Ðæt he hine fealde swā swā bōc *that it fold itself like a book*, Ps. Th. 49, 5. [*Wyc.* folden, falt, *pp. bent, bowed: Chauc.* folden: *Dut.* vouwen: *Ger.* falten: *M. H. Ger.* valten, valden: *O. H. Ger.* faldan: *Goth.* falþan: *Dan.* folde: *Swed.* fålla: *Icel.* falda.] DER. be-fealdan, bi-, ge-, onbe-, ongeán-, tobe-, to-, un-.

feale, *pl. nom. acc.* fealewe *fallow, pale yellow, dusky*, Chr. 937; Th. 204, 16, col. 1: Andr. Kmbl. 3177; An. 1591. v. fealo.

fealewe, *yellow;* flāvus, Cot. 81. v. fealo.

fealewian *to grow yellow, ripen, wither as leaves*, Salm. Kmbl. 627; Sal. 313. v. fealwian.

fealga *harrows*, Glos. Epnl. Recd. 160, 24; *pl. nom. acc. of* fealh.

FEALH; *gen.* fealge; *f. A harrow;* occa:—Fealh *occa*, Cot. 197. Fealga *occas*, Glos. Epnl. Recd. 160, 24. [*Ger.* felge: *M. H. Ger.* vëlge, *f*: *O. H. Ger.* fëlga, *f. flexūra, rădius, canthus, occa.*]

fealh *underwent*, Beo. Th. 2405; B. 1200; *p. of* felgan.

feall, e; *f? A trap, pitfall;* decĭpŭla, Lye, Ettm.

FEALLAN, to feallanne; *part.* feallende; ic fealle, ðū feallest, fealst, felst, fylst, he fealleþ, fealþ, felþ, fylþ, *pl.* feallaþ; *p.* feól, feóll, *pl.* feóllon; *pp.* feallen; *v. intrans. To* FALL, *fall down, fail;* cădĕre, decĭdĕre, procĭdĕre, defĭcĕre:—Hī sceolon raðe feallan on grimne grund *they shall fall rapidly into the grim abyss*, Exon. 30 a; Th. 93, 15; Cri. 1526: Beo. Th. 2145; B. 1070: Ps. Th. 87, 4: Rood Kmbl. 85; Kr. 43. Enoch nalles feallan lēt dōm *Enoch let not his power fail*, Cd. 60; Th. 73, 3; Gen. 1198. To feallanne *to fall*, Bt. Met. Fox 20, 335; Met. 20, 168. Gyf ðū feallende to me ge-eádmētst *si cădens adorāvĕris me*, Mt. Bos. 4, 9: Lk. Bos. 10, 18. Heofones steorran beóþ feallende *stellæ cœli ĕrunt decĭdentes*, Mk. Bos. 13, 25. Ðis līf is lǽnlīc and feallende *this life is transitory and failing*, L. E. I. prm; Th. ii. 400, 16. Ic fealle *cădo*, Ælfc. Gr. 28, 7; Som. 32, 54. Se rēn fealleþ *the rain falls*, Ps. Th. 71, 6: Exon. 56 b; Th. 201, 25; Ph. 61: Salm. Kmbl. 603; Sal. 301. Se hagol fealþ *the hail falls*, Ex. 9, 19: Bt. 6; Fox 14, 29: Boutr. Scrd. 18, 25. Him on innan felþ muntes mægenstān *a huge mountain-stone falls into it*, Bt. Met. Fox 5, 30; Met. 5, 15. Se ðe fylþ uppan ðysne stān, he byþ tobrȳsed *qui cecĭdĕrit sŭper lăpĭdem istum, confringĕtur*, Mt. Bos. 21, 44: Bd. de nat. rerum; Wrt. popl. science 19, 15; Lchdm. iii. 278, 25. Hīg feallaþ begen on ǽnne pytt *ambo in fŏveam cădunt*, Mt. Bos. 15, 14, 27: Bd. de nat. rerum; Wrt. popl. science 15, 21, 22: Exon. 57 a; Th. 202, 23; Ph. 74: Salm. Kmbl. 628; Sal. 313: Ps. Th. 57, 7. He on hrusan ne feól *he fell not on the earth*, Beo. Th. 1549; B. 772: Fins. Th. 83; Fin. 41: Byrht. Th. 135, 31; By. 126: Bt. Met. Fox 1, 161; Met. 1, 81: Exon. 108 a; Th. 412, 11; Rä. 30, 12. Ic feóll befōran Drihtne *procĭdi ante Dŏmĭnum*, Deut. 9, 18. Feóll Abram astreht to eorþan *cĕcĭdit Abram prōnus in făciem*, Gen. 17, 3: Beo. Th. 5830; B. 2919: Byrht. Th. 135, 16; By. 119: Andr. Kmbl. 1835; An. 920: Ps. Th. 77, 27. Feónda feorh feóllon þicce *the lives of the foes fell thickly*, Cd. 95; Th. 124, 20; Gen. 2065: Beo. Th. 2089; B. 1042: Byrht. Th. 135, 1; By. 111: Elen. Kmbl. 253; El. 127. Ðæt heó feólle *that it fell*, Boutr. Scrd. 18, 25. [*Piers P.* fallen: *Wyc.* falle: *Chauc.* falle: *Laym.* falle, fallen, fællen, uallen: *Orm.* fallenn: *O. Sax. Frs.* fallan: *O. Frs.* falla: *Dut.* vallen: *Ger.* fallen: *M. H. Ger.* vallen: *O. H. Ger.* fallan: *Dan.* falde: *Swed. Icel.* falla.] DER. a-feallan, be-, ge-, of-, onbe-, on-, ōþ-, to-.

FEALO, fealu, feale; *def.* se fealwa; *adj.* FALLOW, *pale yellow* or *red coloured as withered grass or leaves, dusky, bay?* flāvus, gilvus, fuscus:—Fealo līg feormaþ and fēnix byrneþ *the yellow flame consumes and burns the Phœnix*, Exon. 59 a; Th. 213, 1; Ph. 218: 104 b; Th. 396, 8; Rä. 16, 1. Fealu *busius?* [=*fuscus?*], Ælfc. Gl. 79; Som. 72, 81;

Wrt. Voc. 46, 38. Se fealwa holen *the fallow* or *withered holly leaf*, Exon. 114 a; Th. 437, 19; Rä. 56, 10. Cing ūt gewāt on fealone [fealene, col. 1] flōd *the king departed on the dusky flood*, Chr. 937; Th. 204, 16, col. 2; Æđelst. 36: Beo. Th. 3904; B. 1950. Sum fealone wǣg stefnan steóreþ *one steers the prow* [*on*] *the dusky wave*, Exon. 79 a; Th. 296, 19; Crä. 53. Fleón fealone streám *to escape the dusky stream*, Andr. Kmbl. 3074; An. 1540. Lang is đeós sīþfæt ofer fealuwne flōd *this journey is long over the dusky flood*, 841; An. 421. Sindon fealwe fōtas *the feet are yellow*, Exon. 60 a; Th. 219, 22; Ph. 311. Ne feallaþ đǣr fealwe blōstman *fallow blossoms fall not there*, 57 a; Th. 202, 24; Ph. 74. Fealwe mearas *bay horses*, Beo. Th. 1735; B. 865. Se beorg tohlād and in forlēt fealewe wǣgas *the hill opened and let in the dusky waves*, Andr. Kmbl. 3177; An. 1591. Meahte ǣghwylc wegan fealwe linde *each could bear the yellow shields*, Cd. 94; Th. 123, 14; Gen. 2044. Wineleás guma gesihþ him bifōran fealwe wegas *the friendless mortal sees before him seared ways*, Exon. 77 a; Th. 289, 11; Wand. 46: Beo. Th. 1837; B. 916. [*Chauc.* falwe: *Laym.* falewe, *pl*: *O. Sax.* falu: *Dut.* vaal: *Kil.* vael, vaeluwe: *Ger.* fal, fahl, falb: *M. H. Ger.* val: *O. H. Ger.* falo, falw: *Icel.* fölr *pale, fallow*: *Lat.* pallĭdus *pale*: *Sansk.* palita *grey.*] DER. æppel-fealu.

fealo *many*, Beo. Th. 5508, note; B. 2757, note. v. fela.

feá-lōg; *adj. Destitute*; destĭtūtus:—Ne eam ic swā feálōg monna weorudes *I am not so destitute of a host of men*, Exon. 36 a; Th. 116, 34; Gū. 217.

fealo-hilte; *adj. Having a yellow* or *golden handle*; căpŭlo flāvo *vel* aureo instructus:—Feóll to foldan fealohilte swurd *the golden-hilted sword fell to the earth*, Byrht. Th. 136, 45; By. 166.

fealþ *falleth, falls*, Bt. 6; Fox 14, 29; *3rd pers. pres. of* feallan.

fealu *fallow, pale yellow, dusky*, Ælfc. Gl. 79; Som. 72, 81; Wrt. Voc. 46, 38: Andr. Kmbl. 841; An. 421. v. fealo.

fealu; *gen.* fealuwes, fealwes; *n. Fallow ground, ground ploughed lying fallow after a crop*; nŏvāle:—Andlang weges ōþ đone brōc, đe scȳt to fealuwes leá *along the way to the brook, which shoots to the field of fallow ground*, Cod. Dipl. 399; A. D. 944; Kmbl. ii. 251, 1. DER. fealo *a yellowish light red, like marly ground recently ploughed.*

fealuwian *to wither*, Bt. Met. Fox 11, 116; Met. 11, 58. v. fealwian.

fealvor, es; *m. A species of water-fowl, the sultana-hen*; porphyrio = πορφυρίων:—Fealvor *porphyrio*, Wrt. Voc. 280, 17. v. felofor.

fealwa *fallow*, Exon. 114 a; Th. 437, 19; Rä. 56, 10; *def. m. nom. sing. of* fealo.

fealwe *fallow, pale yellow, dusky, bay*, Exon. 57 a; Th. 202, 24; Ph. 74: 60 a; Th. 219, 22; Ph. 311: Beo. Th. 1735; B. 865: 1837; B. 916; *nom. acc. pl. of* fealo.

fealwian, fealewian, fealuwian; *p.* ode; *pp.* od *To grow yellow, ripen, to wither as leaves*; flāvescĕre:—On hærfest hit fealwaþ *in harvest it ripens*, Bt. 21; Fox 74, 23. His leáf ne fealwiaþ *its leaves shall not wither*, Ps. Th. 1, 4. Lytle hwīle leáf beóþ grēne, đonne hȳ eft fealewiaþ, feallaþ on eorþan *a little while the leaves are green, then they grow yellow again, fall to the earth*, Salm. Kmbl. 627; Sal. 313. Fealuwaþ *withers*, Bt. Met. Fox 11, 116; Met. 11, 58.

feán *joy*, Bd. 1, 25; Whelc. 76, 1; *acc. of* feá.

feánes, -ness, e; *f. Fewness*; paucĭtas:—Seó feánes nȳdde đara sacerda đæt ān bisceop beón sceolde ofer tū folc *paucĭtas sacerdōtum cōgēbat ūnum antistĭtem duōbus pŏpŭlis præfĭci*, Bd. 3, 21; S. 551, 33. v. feáwnes.

fear, es; *m. A bull, an ox*; taurus, bos:—Gif he hrīđeru offrian wille, bringe unwemme fear ođđe heáfre *si de bobus vŏluĕrit offerre, marem sive fēmĭnam immacŭlāta offĕret*, Lev. 3, 1. v. fearr.

feára *of a few*, Beo. Th. 2828; B. 1412. v. feá *few*, feáwa.

fearh, færh, ferh, es; *pl.* fearas; *m. A little pig, a* FARROW, *litter*; porcellus:—Fearh *porcellus*, Wrt. Voc. 78, 40. Fearas *suilli* vel *porcelli* vel *nefrendes*, Ælfc. Gl. 20; Som. 59, 35; Wrt. Voc. 22, 76.

fearh-hama, an; *m. A little stem*; caulĭcŭlus:—Fearh-hama *caulĭcŭlus*, Ælfc. Gl. 76; Som. 71, 117; Wrt. Voc. 45, 22.

feárlīc *sudden*, L. C. S. 71; Th. i. 412, 28, MS. A. v. fǣrlīc.

feárlīce; *adv. Suddenly, quickly*; sŭbĭto:—He ōđre fyrde hēt feárlīce abannan *he commanded another army to be quickly summoned*, Chr. 1095; Erl. 232, 6: 1120; Erl. 248, 12. v. fǣrlīce.

fearm, es; *m. A freight, cargo, load*; ŏnus nāvis:—Ofer holmes hringc hof sēleste fōr mid fearme *the most excellent house* [*the ark*] *sailed over the ocean's orb with its freight*, Cd. 69; Th. 84, 7; Gen. 1394. [*Icel.* farmr, *m. a fare, freight, cargo.*]

FEARN, FERN, es; *n. A* FERN; fĭlix:—Fearn *fĭlix*, Ælfc. Gl. 42; Som. 64, 10; Wrt. Voc. 31, 21: 67, 45: 79, 64. Genim đysse wyrte wyrttruman, đe man *fĭlĭcem* and ōđrum naman fearn nemneþ *take a root of this plant, which is named* fĭlix, *and by another name fern*, Herb. 78; Lchdm. i. 180, 25. Atió ǣrest of đa þornas, and đa fyrsas, and đæt fearn *draw out first the thorns, and the furze, and the fern*, Bt. 23; Fox 78, 22: Bt. Met. Fox 12, 5; Met. 12, 3. Đæt micle fearn *the large fern*; aspĭdium fĭlix, L. M. 1, 56; Lchdm. ii. 126, 14: Lchdm. i. 380, 19. [*Chauc.* ferne: *Dut.* váren, *n*: *Kil.* væren: *Ger.* farn, farren, *m*: *M. H. Ger.* varm, varn, *m*: *O. H. Ger.* farm, farn, *n*: *Sansk.* parṇa, *n. a leaf, plant, tree.*] DER. eofor-fearn, fen-.

fearn-bed, es; *n. A fern-bed*; fĭlĭcētum, R. 85, Lye.

Fearn-dūn, e; *f.* [*Hunt.* Ferandune: *Brom.* Farandon: fearn *fern*, dūn *a hill*] *Faringdon, Berkshire?* or *Farndon, Northamptonshire?*—Hēr Eádweard cing gefōr on Myrcum æt Fearndūne *in this year* [A. D. 924] *kind Edward died in Mercia at Farndon*, Chr. 924; Th. 198, 1, col. 2, 3.

Fearn-ham, -hamm, es; *m.* FARNHAM, *in Surrey*; lŏci nōmen in agro Surreiensi:—Sió fierd him wiđ gefeaht æt Fearnhamme *the army fought against them at Farnham*, Chr. 894; Erl. 90, 26.

fearn-leás, -lēs; *adj. Fernless, without fern*; sine fĭlĭce, Hem. p. 86.

fearoþ-hengest, es; *m.* [fearoþ = faroþ, *q. v.*] *A sea-horse, ship*; mărīnus equus, nāvis:—Fearoþhengestas gearwe stōdon *the ships stood ready*, Elen. Kmbl. 452; El. 226.

FEARR, es; *m.* I. *a bull, an ox*; taurus, bos:—Fearr *taurus*, Ælfc. Gr. 8; Som. 7, 30. He geworhte ānes fearres anlīcnesse of āre *he made an image of a bull with brass*, Ors. 1, 12; Bos. 36, 29. Fearras fætte ofsettun ođđe ymbsǣton me *tauri pingues obsēdērunt me*, Ps. Lamb. 21, 13: Mt. Bos. 22, 4. Ete ic flǣscmettas fearra *mandūcābo carnes taurōrum*, Ps. Lamb. 49, 13: 67, 31: Gen. 32, 15. II. *the Bull, one of the twelve signs of the zodiac*; taurus:—Ōđer đæra tācna ys gehāten *taurus*, đæt is fearr *the second of the signs is called* taurus, *that is a bull*, Bd. de nat. rerum; Wrt. popl. science 7, 4; Lchdm. iii. 244, 24. [*Dut.* var, varre, *m*: *Ger.* farre, farr, *m*: *M. H. Ger.* var, varre, *m*: *O. H. Ger.* farri, farro, far, *m*: *Icel.* farri, *m. a bullock.*]

feá-sceaft; *adj. Having few things, poor, naked, destitute*; mĭser, pauper, destĭtūtus:—Freónda feásceaft *destitute of friends*, Cd. 97; Th. 126, 24; Gen. 2100: 114; Th. 149, 23; Gen. 2479: Andr. Kmbl. 2257; An. 1130. Ic feásceaft eom *I am destitute*, Cd. 99; Th. 131, 13; Gen. 2175: Beo. Th. 13; B. 7. Feásceaft guma *the miserable man*, Beo. Th. 1950; B. 973: Andr. Kmbl. 3110; An. 1558: Exon. 119 b; Th. 459, 5; Hy. 4, 112. Wæs bēn getiđad feásceaftum men *the prayer was granted to the poor man*, Beo. Th. 4559; B. 2285: 4775; B. 2393. God eáđe mæg afrēfran feásceaftne *God may easily comfort the poor* [*one*], Exon. 10 b; Th. 11, 23; Cri. 175: Andr. Kmbl. 733; An. 367. Hwider fundast đū, feásceaft ides *whither art thou hastening, poor damsel?* Cd. 103; Th. 137, 6; Gen. 2269. Nō feásceafte findan meahton æt đam æđelinge *the poor could not prevail with the prince*, Beo. Th. 4735; B. 2373: Exon. 13 a; Th. 23, 13; Cri. 368.

feá-sceaftig; *adj. Poor, destitute*; pauper, destĭtūtus, mĭser:—Feásceaftig ferþ *poor soul*, Exon. 81 b; Th. 307, 19; Seef. 26.

feasten, es; *n. A fastness, fortress*; mūnīmentum:—Hī on đam feastene wǣron *they were in the fastness*, Chr. 877; Erl. 79, 23. v. fæsten II.

feastlīce; *adv. Firmly, constantly, stoutly*; firmĭter, constanter:—Hī feastlīce fēngon *they stoutly engaged*, Chr. 1004; Erl. 139, 32: 1008; Erl. 141, 17. v. fæstlīce.

FEÁWA, feá; *pl. nom. acc.* feáwe, feáwa, feá; *gen.* feáwena, feáwera, feára; *dat.* feáwum, feáum, feám; *adj.* FEW; pauci:—Feáwa đara manna mihte beón eardfæste *few of the men could abide in their dwellings* [lit. *could be earth-fast* or *settled*], Ors. 5, 4; Bos. 105, 10: Deut. 4, 27: Mt. Bos. 9, 37: Lk. Bos. 10, 2. Hit þūhte him feáwa daga *it seemed to him a few* [*of*] *days*, Gen. 29, 20. Feáwe [Spl. feáwa] gewordene hī syndon *pauci facti sunt*, Ps. Lamb. 106, 39. Wesan dagas his feáwe [feáwa, Spl. 108, 7] *fiant dies ejus pauci*, 108, 8. Đā đā hīg wǣron on gerīme [MS. gehrime] feáwa ođđe scortum, feáwoste and eardbegendan ođđe inlænde his *when they were few or short in number*, [*yea*] *very few and inhabitants of it* [*Canaan*], Ps. Lamb. 104, 12. Hira feáwa on weg cōmon *few of them came in the way*, Chr. 918; Erl. 104, 9: Deut. 28, 62. Inne on đæm fæstenne sǣton feáwa cirlisce men *a few countrymen sat within the fastness*, Chr. 893; Erl. 88, 33. Feáwa synt đe đone weg findon *pauci sunt qui invĕniunt viam*, Mt. Bos. 7, 14: Lk. Bos. 13, 23. Feáwa synt gecorene *pauci sunt electi*, Mt. Bos. 20, 16: 22, 14. Drihten, gedō đæt heora menigo sȳ læsse đonne ūre feáwena nū is, and tostencte hī geond eorþan libbende of đis lande *Dŏmĭne, a paucis de terra dīvĭde eos in vīta eōrum*, Ps. Th. 16, 13. Ic đē of Caldēa ceastre alǣdde, feáwera [MS. feowera] sumne *I led thee, one of a few, from the Chaldeans' city*, Cd. 100; Th. 132, 30; Gen. 2201. Eustatius ætbærst mid feáwum mannum *Eustace escaped with a few men*, Chr. 1048; Erl. 178, 4. Efter feáwum dagum *after a few days*, 1070; Erl. 206, 2. Be đissum feáwum forþspellum *by these few intimations*, Exon. 84 a; Th. 316, 11; Mōd. 47. Ic đē feáwe dagas mīnra mǣttra mōde secge *paucĭtātem diērum meōrum enuntia mihi*, Ps. Th. 101, 21. Feáwa fixa *paucos piscĭcŭlos*, Mt. Bos. 15, 34: Mk. Bos. 8, 7. Feáwa untrume he gehǣlde *paucos infirmos cūrāvit*, Mk. Bos. 6, 5. Đū wǣre getrȳwe ofer feáwa *sŭper pauca fuisti fĭdēlis*, Mt. Bos. 25, 23. He biþ wītnod feáwum wītum *vāpŭlābit paucis plāgis*, Lk. Bos. 12, 48. [*Wyc. Chauc. R. Glouc.* fewe: *Laym.* feue, feuȝe: *Orm.* fæwe: *Plat.* fege, vöge: *O. Sax.* fāh: *O. Frs.* fē: *O. H. Ger.* fōh: *Goth.* faus, faws:

Dan. faa: *Swed.* få: *Icel.* fár: *Lat.* paucus, paulus: *Grk.* παῦρος *few;* παύω *I make to cease.*]

feáwera *of a few,* Cd. 100; Th. 132, 30; *gen. pl. of* feáwa.

feáwnes, feánes, -ness, e; *f.* FEWNESS; paucĭtas:—Ða feáwnesse ođđe ȝehwǣdnesse dagena mīnra cȳþ me *paucĭtātem diērum meōrum nuntia mihi,* Ps. Lamb. 101, 24.

FEAX, fex, es; *n. Hair of the head, the locks;* cæsăries, cŏma, căpillus:—Nimeþ đæt feax to *the hair holdeth on,* Med. ex Quadr. 4, 11; Lchdm. i. 344, 20: L. M. 1, 87; Lchdm. ii. 156, 7. Ne feax ne fel *neither hair nor skin,* Exon. 74 a; Th. 278, 1; Jul. 591: Cd. 195; Th. 243, 18; Dan. 438. Feax *cæsăries,* Ælfc. Gr. 12; Som. 15, 53. Licgaþ æfter lande loccas todrifene, fex on foldan *throughout the land lie my driven locks, hair upon the ground,* Andr. Kmbl. 2853; An. 1429. God tofylleþ feaxes scadan, đe hēr on scyldum swǣrum eódon *Deus conquassābit vertĭcem căpilli perambulantium in delictis suis,* Ps. Th. 67, 21: 68, 4. Bōcstafa brego bregdeþ feónd be đam feaxe *the prince of letters shall draw the fiend by his hair,* Salm. Kmbl. 201; Sal. 100: Beo. Th. 3298; B. 1647. Wiđ feallendum feaxe *for falling hair,* Med. ex Quadr. 4, 11; Lchdm. i. 344, 18. Mid hyre heáfdes feaxe *căpillis căpĭtis sui,* Lk. Bos. 7, 38. Swāt ǣdrum sprong forþ under fexe *blood sprang forth from the veins under his hair,* Beo. Th. 5926; B. 2967. Æled lǣtaþ on đæs feóndes feax *they shall let fire upon the fiend's hair,* Salm. Kmbl. 261; Sal. 130: Judth. 12; Thw. 25, 27; Jud. 281. He hæfde blæc feax *he had black hair,* Bd. 2, 16; S. 519, 34. [*Laym.* uæx: *O. Sax.* fahs, *n: O. Frs.* fax: *M. H. Ger.* vahs, *m: O. H. Ger.* fahs, *n. cæsăries, cŏma: Icel.* fax, *n. a mane.*] DER. blanden-feax, blonden-, gamol-, un-, up-, won-, wunden-.

feax-clāþ, es; *m. A head-cloth, hair-band, fillet;* fascia crīnālis, Cot. 93.

feaxe; *adj. Having hair;* cŏmātus. DER. ge-feaxe.

feax-eacas, -eacon? *Hair hanging down the forehead, forelocks;* antiæ frontis, sive a fronte dependentes, Cot. 6, Som. Ben. Lye.

feaxede, fexede; *adj. Having long hair, long-haired;* cŏmātus:—Sume men cweđaþ đæt cometa sīe feaxede [fexede, Th. 162, 9, col. 2, 3; 163, 10] steorra, forđæm đǣr stent lang leóma of, hwīlum on āne healfe, hwīlum on ǣlce healfe *some men say that a comet is a long-haired star, because there stands a long ray from it, sometimes on one side, sometimes on each side,* Chr. 891; Th. 162, 9-14, col. 1. DER. ge-feaxode, -fexode, sīd-fexede.

feax-fang, es; *m. A taking hold by the hair;* cŏmæ prehensio:—Gif feax-fang geweorþ *if there be a taking hold of the hair,* L. Ethb. 33; Th. i. 12, 3; Wilk. 5, 1.

feax-feallung, e; *f. Falling off* or *loss of the hair, the mange;* crīnium amissio, alōpĕcia = ἀλωπεκία:—Feaxfeallung *alōpĕcia,* Ælfc. Gl. 11; Som. 57, 56; Wrt. Voc. 19, 58.

feax-gerǣdian; *p.* ode; *pp.* od [gerǣdian *to make ready*] *To dress* or *trim the hair;* crīnes compōnĕre, Som. Ben. Lye.

feax-hār; *adj. Hoary-haired;* cŏmam cānam hăbens:—Ic wæs feaxhār *I was hoary-haired,* Exon. 126 b; Th. 487, 13; Rä. 73, 1.

feax-nǣdel, e; *f. A hair-needle, curling-iron, crisping-pin;* călămistrum, ăcus crīnĭbus intorquendis sive crispandis adhĭbita:—Feaxnǣdel *călămistrum,* Ælfc. Gl. 4; Som. 55, 101; Wrt. Voc. 17, 4.

feax-net, -nett, es; *n. A hair-net, net-work cap for confining the hair;* rētĭcŭlum căpillis continendis, rīcŭla:—Feaxnet *rētĭcŭlum,* Ælfc. Gl. 4; Som. 55, 89; Wrt. Voc. 16, 59: *rīgŭla* [= *rīcŭla,* Car. Ains.], Som. 55, 96; Wrt. Voc. 16, 66.

feax-preón, es; *m. A hair-pin;* discrīmĭnāle:—Uplegene *vel* feax-preónas *discrīmĭnālia,* Ælfc. Gl. 4; Som. 55, 99; Wrt. Voc. 17, 2.

feax-sceacga, an; *m. A bush of hair;* cæsăries, crīnium fascĭcŭlus, Som. Ben. Lye.

feax-sceacged; *part. Having hair, hairy;* cŏmātus, Cot. 54.

feber-ādl, e; *f. A fever-disease, fever;* febris:—Forleórt đa of feber-ādlum *dīmĭsit eam febris,* Mt. Kmbl. Lind. 8, 15. v. fefer-ādl.

febrig; *adj. Feverish;* febrĭcŭlōsus:—Gif he sȳ febrig *if he be feverish,* Herb. 1, 28; Lchdm. i. 78, 26.

Februarius, i; *m. Lat. February;* nōmen mensis:—Sīgeþ Februarius *February approaches,* Menol. Fox 35; Men. 18. v. Sol-mōnaþ.

fec, es; *n. A space, portion of time;* spătium, tempŏris intervallum:—Æfter litlum fece *after a little time,* Chr. 1015; Erl. 152, 4. v. fæc.

FECCAN, feccean, fæccan; *p.* feahte, fehte; *pp.* feaht, feht *To* FETCH, *bring to, draw;* addūcĕre, tollĕre, afferre, haurīre:—Đæt he sceolde hine feccan *that he should fetch him,* Bd. 4, 1; S. 564, 43: Chr. 1017; Erl. 161, 10: Gen. 27, 42, 45: Ex. 2, 5. Com ān wīf wæter feccan *vēnit mŭlier haurīre ăquam,* Jn. Bos. 4, 7, 15. He his dōhter lēt feccean *he caused his daughter to be fetched,* Chr. 1121; Erl. 248, 35. Ic fecce wæter *affĕram pauxillum ăquæ,* Gen. 18, 4. Hig feccaþ đīne sāwle fram đē *they will fetch away thy soul from thee,* Lk. Bos. 12, 20. Đās menn đē feccaþ *these men fetch thee,* Num. 22, 20. Gif preóst crisman ne fecce [fæcce MS. B.] *if a priest fetch not the chrism,* L. E. G. 3; Th. i. 168, 11. Se đe ys uppan hys hūse, ne gā he nyđer đæt he ǣnig þing on his hūse fecce *qui in tecto, non descendat tollĕre alĭquid de dŏmo sua,* Mt. Bos. 24, 17: L. Edg. C. 67; Th. ii. 258, 20. Đæt gē đisne eówerne brōđur feccon *that ye fetch this your brother,* Gen. 42, 34. [*Laym.* fæchen: *Orm.* fecchenn: *O. Frs.* faka *to prepare, make ready.*] DER. a-feccan, ge-.

fecele *a torch,* Som. Ben. Lye. v. fæcele, þæcele.

fecgan; *p.* feah *To seize;* răpĕre. DER. æt-fecgan, ge-.

FĒDAN; *part.* fēdende; he fēdeþ, fēt, fētt; *p.* ic, he fēdde, đū fēddest, *pl.* fēddon; *pp.* fēded, fēdd. I. *to* FEED, *nourish, support, sustain, bring up, educate;* pascĕre, cĭbāre, nutrīre, enutrīre, sustentāre, edŭcāre:—Mægen mon sceal mid mete fēdan *a man must feed strength with meat,* Exon. 90 b; Th. 340. 22; Gn. Ex. 115. Wā eácniendum and fēdendum on đām dagum *væ autem prægnantĭbus, et nutrientĭbus in illis diēbus,* Mt. Bos. 24, 19: Lk. Bos. 21, 23. Đū us fēdest teára hlāfe *cĭbābis nos pāne lacrymārum,* Ps. Th. 79, 5. Se deópa seáþ dreórge fēdeþ *the deep pit feedeth the dreary,* Exon. 30 b; Th. 94, 25; Cri. 1545: 36 b; Th. 118, 26; Gū. 245. He đē fēdeþ *ipse te enutriet,* Ps. Th. 54, 22. Eówer heofonlīca fæder hīg fēt *păter vester cœlestis pascit illa,* Mt. Bos. 6, 26. Se mīlda Metod fēt eall đætte grōweþ wæstmas on weorolde *the merciful Creator nourishes all fruits which grow in the world,* Bt. Met. Fox 29, 139; Met. 29, 70. He fētt đa đe þurh dǣdbōte him to būgaþ *he feeds those who turn to him by repentance,* Homl. Th. ii. 396, 29. He me well fētt *me bĕne pascit,* Coll. Monast. Th. 22, 33: 30, 27. Mægeþ and mæcgas fēdaþ hine fægre *lasses and lads feed him kindly,* Exon. 113 a; Th. 434, 9; Rä. 51, 8. God, đū đe me fēddest fram cildhāde ōþ đisne dæg *Deus, qui pascit me ab adolescentia mea in præsentem diem,* Gen. 48, 15. Mec seó friþe mǣg fēdde *the kind woman fed me,* Exon. 103 a; Th. 391, 23; Rä. 10, 9. He fēdde hīg *sustentāvit eos,* Gen. 47, 17. He fēdde me *edŭcāvit me,* Ps. Spl. 22, 2. We đē fēddon *pāvimus te,* Mt. Bos. 25, 37. Fēd freólīce feora wōcre *feed freely the living progeny,* Cd. 67; Th. 81, 8; Gen. 1342. Gif he nāt hwā hine cwicne fēde *if he knows not who may feed him living,* Exon. 90 b; Th. 340, 21; Gn. Ex. 114. Đū bist fēded on wēlum his *pascĕris in dīvĭtiis ejus,* Ps. Spl. 36, 3: Ps. Th. 130, 4. Fēdd beón *pastus esse, pasci,* R. Conc. 10. II. *to bring forth, produce;* gignĕre, prodūcĕre:—Wæstmas fēdan *to bring forth fruits,* Cd. 46; Th. 59, 8; Gen. 960. Cucra wuhta, đara đe lyft and flōd lǣdaþ and fēdaþ *of living things, which air and flood train and bring forth,* 65; Th. 78, 25; Gen. 1298. Ides eaforan fēdde *a female brought forth offspring,* 50; Th. 64, 23; Gen. 1054. Đā wearþ eafora fēded *then was an heir brought forth,* 58; Th. 70, 27; Gen. 1159: 82; Th. 103, 3; Gen. 1712. [*Wyc. Chauc.* fede: *Piers P.* feden: *Laym.* feden, ueden: *Orm.* fedenn: *Scot.* fede: *Plat.* voden, vōden, fōden, fūden: *O. Sax.* fōdjan, fuodjan: *Frs.* fieden: *O. Frs.* foda, feda: *Dut.* voeden: *Ger.* füttern: *M. H. Ger.* vuoten, vüeten: *O. H. Ger.* fuotjan: *Goth.* fodyan: *Dan.* føde: *Swed.* föda: *Icel.* fæða: *Lat.* pascĕre: *Grk.* πατέομαι *to eat: Sansk.* pitu, *m. nourishing food.*] DER. a-fēdan, ge-.

fēdels, es; *m. A fatling;* altĭlis:—Fēdels *altĭle,* Ælfc. Gl. 22; Som. 59, 95; Wrt. Voc. 23, 51: *altĭlis,* 114; Som. 80, 7; Wrt. Voc. 60, 43.

feder *a father,* Chr. 1052; Th. 319, 17: Hy. 8, 8; Hy. Grn. ii. 290, 8: 8, 43; Hy. Grn. ii. 291, 43. v. fæder.

federa, fedra, an; *m. An uncle, a father's brother;* patruus:—Se wæs Ælfrīces sunu Ēdwines federan *he was the son of Ælfric, Edwin's uncle,* Chr. 634; Erl. 25, 25: 737; Erl. 47, 24. Ēdwines fedran suna *Edwin's uncle's son,* Chr. 643; Erl. 27, 19. v. fædera.

fēdesl, es; *m?* e; *f? A feeder, provider;* obsōnātor:—Cyninges fēdesl xx scillinga forgelde *let the king's feeder be paid for with twenty shillings,* L. Ethb. 12; Th. i. 6, 8.

fēding, e; *f. A feeding;* pastio:—Seó fēding đara sceápa *the feeding of the sheep,* Past. 5, 2; Hat. MS. 10 b, 11. v. fēdan *to feed.*

fēdnes, -ness, e; *f. Nourishment;* nutrīmentum:—On lustfullnysse đǣr biþ synne fēdnes *in delectātiōne fit peccāti nutrīmentum,* Bd. 1, 27; S. 497, 25.

FEFER, fefor, es; *m. A* FEVER; febris:—Se fefer hine forlēt *relĭquit eum febris,* Jn. Bos. 4, 52. Gif him fefer derige *if fever vex him,* Herb. 46, 2; Lchdm. i. 148, 19. Se fefor *the fever,* Mt. Bos. 8, 15. Ǣr hym đæs feferes wēne *before he expects the fever,* Herb. 2, 12; Lchdm. i. 84, 7. Wiđ fefre *for fever,* L. M. 1, 62; Lchdm. ii. 134. 14, 27. Wiđ đone cōlan fefor *against cold fever,* Herb. 138, 2; Lchdm. i. 256, 10. Đa feforas beóþ fram anȳdde *the fevers will be forced away,* 143, 4; Lchdm. i. 266, 13. On mycelum feferum *magnis febrĭbus,* Lk. Bos. 4, 38. Wiđ đa stīđustan feferas, genim đas sylfan wyrte and gedrige hȳ *for the strongest fevers, take this same herb and dry it,* Herb. 20, 3; Lchdm. i. 114, 16: 38, 2; Lchdm. i. 138, 3. Ǣlces dæges fefer *an every day* or *quotidian fever,* L. M. 1, 62; Lchdm. ii. 134, 24. Þriddan dæges fefer *a tertian fever,* 1, 62; Lchdm. ii. 134, 21. Feórþan dæges fefer *a quartan fever,* Herb. 2, 12; Lchdm. i. 84, 5. [*Piers P.* feveres, *pl: Chauc.* fevere: *Plat.* fever, *n: Ger.* fieber, *n: M. H. Ger.* vieber, *n: O. H. Ger.* fiebar, *n: Dan.* feber, *m. f: Swed.* feber, *m: Lat.* febris, *f.*]

fefer-ādl, fefor-ādl, e; *f.* [ādl *a disease*] *Fever-disease, fever;* febris:—Heó wæs swenced mid hǣto and mid bryne feferādle *she had been afflicted with the heat and burning of a fever,* Bd. 5, 4; S. 617, 28. Wiđ feferādle *for fever disease*, L. M. 1, 62; Lchdm. ii. 134, 13. Sleá đe Drihten mid feforādle and mid cīle *percŭtiat te Dŏmĭnus febri et frīgŏre*, Deut. 28, 22.

fefer-fuge, an; *f. The herb feverfew;* febrĭfŭgia:—Feferfuge *febrĭfŭgia*, Ælfc. Gl. 40; Som. 63, 89; Wrt. Voc. 30, 39: Herb. 36; Lchdm. i. 134, 15. Genim feferfugean blōstman *take blossoms of feverfew*, Lchdm. i. 374, 3.

fefer-seóc; *adj. Fever-sick, feverish;* febrĭcĭtans, Cot. 88.

fefor *a fever*, Mt. Bos. 8, 15. v. fefer.

fefor-ādl *fever-disease, fever*, Deut. 28, 22. v. fefer-ādl.

FĒGAN; *p.* de; *pp.* ed *To join, bind, unite, fix;* jungĕre, pangĕre:—Heó fēgeþ mec on fæsten *she binds me in a fastness*, Exon. 107 a; Th. 407, 22; Rä. 26, 9. Freóndscipe fēgþ *it unites friendship*, Somn. 128; Lchdm. iii. 206, 4. Hió me on nearo fēgde *she fixed me in a strait*, Exon. 124 b; Th. 479, 12; Rä. 62, 6. [*Laym.* fiede *wrote: Orm.* feȝest *joinest;* feȝȝed, *pp. composed: Plat.* fōgen: *O. Sax.* fōgian: *Frs.* fuwgjen: *O. Frs.* foga: *Dut.* voegen: *Ger.* fügen: *M. H. Ger.* vüegen: *O. H. Ger.* fuogjan, fuogan: *Dan.* föie: *Swed.* foga: *Lat.* păciscor *to make a contract: Grk.* πήγνυμι *to join, fasten: Sansk.* paś *to bind.*] DER. ge-fēgan, up-fēgean.

feger, fegr *fair;* pulcher, Solil. præf. v. fæger.

fegere *fairly, beautifully*, Hy. 8, 43; Hy. Grn. ii. 291, 43. v. fægere.

fēging, e; *f. A conjunction;* conjunctio:—Geþeódnes ođđe fēging is conjunctio *a joining is a conjunction*, Ælfc. Gr. 5; Som. 3, 47, MS. D.

fēhan, đū fēhst, he fēhþ *to take, seize;* captāre, Bt. 35, 5; Fox 164, 16: Exon. 107 b; Th. 410, 1; Rä. 28, 9. v. afēhþ, fōn.

FEL, felo, fæle; *adj.* FELL, *cruel, savage;* crūdēlis, sævus. [*Wyc.* fel, felli *crafty: Piers P.* fell *fierce: Chauc.* felle *strong, fierce: Laym.* felle, *pl. cruel: Scot.* fell *keen, hot, acute: O. Frs.* fal: *Dut. Kil.* fel *violent: O. Fr.* fel *cruel, wicked: Ital.* fello *wicked: Ir.* feal *bad, naughty, evil.*] DER. æl-fæle, eal-felo, wæl-fel.

FEL, FELL, es; *n. A* FELL, *skin, hide;* pellis, cŏrium, cŭtis:—Fel *pellis*, Wrt. Voc. 65, 11: 86, 37: 283, 33. Næs hyre feax ne fel fȳre gemǣled *neither her hair nor skin was marked by the fire*, Exon. 74 a; Th. 278, 1; Jul. 591. Fell *pellis*, Wrt. Voc. 71, 18. Felles ne rēcceþ *he cares not for my skin*, Exon. 127 a; Th. 488, 12; Rä. 76, 5. Đæt celf hīg bærndon būtan đære wīcstōwe mid felle and mid flǣsce *vĭtŭlum cum pelle et carnĭbus crĕmans extra castra*, Lev. 8, 17. Hie blōd and fel þēgon *they ate the blood and skin*, Andr. Kmbl. 46; An. 23: Ors. 1, 1; Bos. 20, 37. Đæs cealfes flǣsc and fell and gōr đū bærnst ūte būton fyrdwīcon *carnes vĭtŭli et cŏrium et fĭmum combūres fŏris extra castra*, Ex. 29, 14. Fell hongedon on seles wæge *the skins hung on the wall of the room*, Exon. 104 a; Th. 394, 15; Rä. 14, 3. Đæt gafol biþ on deóra fellum *the tribute is in skins of animals*, Ors. 1, 1; Bos. 20, 33: Boutr. Scrd. 20, 29: Gen. 27, 16. Se byrdesta sceall gyldan fīftyne mearþes fell *the richest must pay fifteen skins of the marten*, Ors. 1, 1; Bos. 20, 36. Sió wæs orþoncum gegyrwed dracan fellum *it was cunningly prepared with dragon's skins*, Beo. Th. 4183; B. 2088. [*Wyc. Piers P.* fel: *Chauc. Orm.* fell: *O. Sax.* fel, *n*: *Frs. O. Frs.* fel, *n*: *Dut.* vel, *n*: *Ger.* fell, *n*: *M. H. Ger.* vël, *n*: *O. H. Ger.* fel, *n*: *Goth.* fill, *n*: *Icel.* fell, *n*: *Lat.* pellis, *f. a skin, hide: Grk.* πέλλα, *f. a hide, leather.*]

FELA, fæla, feala, feola; *adj. indecl.* I. with *gen. Many, much;* multum, multa:—Nis nū fela folca *there is not now much people;* multum pŏpŭlōrum, Exon. 81 a; Th. 304, 8; Fä. 67. Nāh ic fela goldes *I have not much gold;* multum auri, Exon. 119 b; Th. 458, 14; Hy. 4, 100. Fela sceal gebīdan leófes and lāþes *much shall abide of loved and loathed*, Beo. Th. 2125; B. 1060. Fela meoringa *many obstacles;* multa impĕdīmentōrum, Cd. 145; Th. 181, 16; Exod. 62. Fela is đæra þinga *many a one is there of the things*, Bt. 41, 3; Fox 250, 10. Fela swylces *much of the same*, Coll. Monast. Th. 24, 13. II. *many things, much, very;* multa, multum, in prīmis, cum maxĭme:—Fela đū didest *multa fēcisti*, Ps. Spl. 39, 7: Ps. Spl. C. 31, 13. Hie fela wiston *they knew many things;* multa, Cd. 143; Th. 179, 16; Exod. 29. Fela ic hæbbe geþolod to dæg *multa passa sum hŏdie*, Mt. Bos. 27, 19. Fela fricgende *inquiring much*, Beo. Th. 4218; B. 2106. Hū fela *how many;* quam multa, Exon. 25 a; Th. 72, 27; Cri. 1179. He ongan hī fela lǣran *cœpit illos dŏcēre multa*, Mk. Bos. 6, 34. III. so *many . . . as;* tot . . . quot:—Ic ne mæg swā fela [gefōn], swā fela swā ic mæg gesyllan *non possum tot căpĕre, quot possum vendĕre*, Coll. Monast. Th. 23, 27. [*Wyc.* fele, feel: *Piers P. Chauc.* fele: *Laym.* fele, feole, vele, uæle: *Orm.* fele: *Scot.* feil, fiel: *Plat.* veel: *O. Sax.* filu, filo: *Frs.* foll, full: *O. Frs.* fel, ful: *Dut.* veel: *Ger.* viel: *M. H. Ger.* vil: *O. H. Ger.* filo, filu: *Goth.* filu: *Icel.* fjöl-, used only as a prefix, *much: Lat.* plus: *Grk.* πολύς: *Sansk.* puru, pulu *much, many.*] DER. eal-fela, efen-, em-.

fela-fǣcne; *adj. Very crafty;* multĭdŏlōsus:—Wineleás mon genimeþ him wulfas to gefēran felafǣcne deór *a friendless man takes wolves for his comrades very crafty animals*, Exon. 91 b; Th. 342, 26; Gn. Ex. 148.

fela-feald; *adj. Manifold;* multiplex:—Dōmas đīne synd neowelnys micellu ođđe felafeald *jūdĭcia tua sunt abyssus multa*, Ps. Spl. 35, 6.

fela-frēcne; *adj. Very wild* or *savage;* valde fĕrox:—Ūr biþ fela-frēcne deór *a wild bull is a very savage beast*, Runic pm. 2; Kmbl. 339, 9; Hick. Thes. i. 135, 3.

fela-geómor; *adj. Very sad;* valde tristis:—Gewāt him se gōda, felageómor *the good [king] departed, very sad*, Beo. Th. 5892; B. 2950.

fela-geong; *adj. Very young;* valde jŭvĕnīlis:—He sægde felageongum *he said to the very young [man]*, Exon. 80 b; Th. 303, 15; Fä. 53.

fela-geonge; *adj. Having travelled much;* valde peregrinātus:—Wilt đū fricgan felageongne ymb forþgesceaft *wilt thou ask one who has travelled much about the creation?* Exon. 92 b; Th. 346, 23; Sch. 3.

fela-hrōr; *adj. Very strenuous;* valde strēnuus:—Him Scyld gewāt felahrōr *Scyld departed very strenuous*, Beo. Th. 53; B. 27.

fela-leóf; *adj. Much-beloved;* valde cārus:—Sceal ic mīnes felaleófan fǣhþu dreógan *I must endure enmities for my much-loved [friend]*, Exon. 115 a; Th. 443, 6; Kl. 26.

fela-meahtig; *adj. Much mighty;* valde pŏtens:—Felameahtig God *the much mighty God*, Exon. 90 a; Th. 338, 10; Gn. Ex. 76. Bletsien đec fiscas and fuglas, felameahtigne *may fishes and birds bless thee, much mighty!* 55 a; Th. 194, 17; Az. 140: Th. 195, 14; Az. 156.

fela-mōdig; *adj. Very daring;* fortissĭmus:—Men from đæm holmclife hafelan bǣron felamōdigra *the men bore from the shore the heads of the very bold*, Beo. Th. 3278; B. 1637.

felan; *p.* fæl, *pl.* fǣlon; *pp.* folen *To stick, adhere;* hærēre:—Đæt ic in ne fele *ut non inhæream*, Ps. Surt. 68, 15. v. feolan.

FĒLAN; *p.* de; *pp.* ed; *v. a. gen. To* FEEL, *perceive, touch;* sentīre, tangĕre:—Heó fēleþ mīnes gemōtes *she perceives my meeting*, Exon. 107 a; Th. 407, 23; Rä. 26, 9. Hī đæs fēlaþ *they feel it*, Exon. 103 a; Th. 389, 16; Rä. 7, 8. [*Wyc.* felen, feele: *Chauc.* fele: *Plat.* fölen: *O. Sax.* gi-fōlian: *Frs.* fielen: *O. Frs.* fēla: *Dut.* voelen: *Ger.* fühlen: *M. H. Ger.* vüelen: *O. H. Ger.* fuoljan, fuolēn: *Dan.* föle.] DER. ge-fēlan.

fela-sinnig; *adj. Very sinful;* valde facĭnŏrōsus:—Đǣr đū findan miht felasinnigne secg *where thou mayest find the very sinful man*, Beo. Th. 2762; B. 1379.

fela-specol; *adj. Speaking much, loquacious;* magnĭloquus, lŏquax:—Mǣden felaspecol *a loquacious maiden*, Obs. Lun. § 7; Lchdm. iii. 186, 26. Tostencþ Drihten tungan đa felaspecolan *disperdat Dŏmĭnus linguam magnĭlŏquam*, Ps. Spl. 11, 3.

fela-specolnys, -nyss, e; *f. Talkativeness, loquacity;* lŏquācĭtas, Scint. 54.

fela-wlonc; *adj. Very stately;* valde magnĭfĭcus:—Mec brȳd triedeþ, felawlonc, fōtum *the bride treads me, very proud, with her feet*, Exon. 103 b; Th. 393, 28; Rä. 13, 7.

fel-cyrf, e; *f?* [fel *skin*, cyrf *a cutting off*] *The foreskin;* præpūtium, Cot. 217.

FELD, feald; *gen.* es; *dat.* a, e; *m. A* FIELD, *pasture, plain, an open country;* campus, campestria:—Se ædela feld wrīdaþ under wolcnum *the noble field flourishes under the skies*, Exon. 56 a; Th. 199, 16; Ph. 26. Feld *campus*, Wrt. Voc. 80, 48. Weaxaþ hrađe feldes blōstman *the flowers of the field quickly grow*, Bt. Met. Fox 6, 19; Met. 6, 10. On felda đam đe deórmōde Dīran hēton *in the field which the brave men call Dura*, Cd. 180; Th. 226, 13; Dan. 170: Byrht. Th. 138, 56; By. 241. He sette fōretācn his on felda Taneos *pŏsuit prōdĭgia sua in campo Taneos*, Ps. Spl. 77, 48. On đam felde *upon the plain*, Salm. Kmbl. 427; Sal. 214. Hie gesōhton Sennera feld *they sought the plains of Shinar*, Cd. 80; Th. 100, 23; Gen. 1668: 205; Th. 253, 27; Dan. 602. Hīg fundon ānne feld *invĕnērunt campum*, Gen. 11, 2. Habbaþ feldas eác fægere blisse *gaudēbunt campi*, Ps. Th. 95, 12: Ps. Lamb. 103, 8. On Moabes feldum *in campestrĭbus Moab*, Deut. 34, 8. On fealda *in campo*, Ps. Spl. 77, 15. Fealdas đīne beóþ gefylled of genihtsumnysse *campi tui replēbuntur ubertāte*, 64, 12. [*Piers P.* felde: *Wyc.* feld, felde, feeld: *Chauc. R. Glouc.* feld: *Laym.* feld, ueld, feold, uald: *Orm.* feld: *O. Sax.* feld, *m*: *Frs.* fjild: *O. Frs.* feld, field: *Dut.* veld, *n*: *Ger.* feld, *n*: *M. H. Ger.* velt, *n*: *O. H. Ger.* feld, *n*: *Dan.* fælled, *m. f*: *Swed.* fält, *n*: *Icel.* fold, *f.*] DER. here-feld, sun-, wæl-, wudu-.

feld-beó; *f. A field-bee, locust;* āpis campestris, attăcus = ἀττακός:—Feld-beó *adticus* [= *attăcus*], Wrt. Voc. 281, 38.

feld-ciric, e; *f.* -circe, an; *f. A field-church, country church;* campestris ecclēsia:—Feldcirice griþbryce is, đǣr legerstōw ne sig, mid þrittigum scillingum *the 'grith-bryce' of a field-church, where there is no burial-place, is thirty shillings*, L. C. E. 3; Th. i. 360, 21. Æt feldcircan *for a field-church*, L. Eth. ix. 5; Th. i. 342, 3.

felde *felled*, Exon. 109 b; Th. 419, 11; Rä. 38, 4; *p. of* fellan.

felde-fare, an; *f? A* FIELD-FARE? turdus pilāris?—Clodhamer *vel* feldefare *a field-fare;* scorellus? [turdus pilāris? Lin.], Wrt. Voc. 63, 27.

feld-elfen, e; *f. A wood fairy* or *nymph;* hămādryas = ἁμαδρυάς:—Feld-elfen *moides?* Ælfc. Gl. 113; Som. 79, 109; Wrt. Voc. 60, 16.

feld-gangende, -gongende; *part. Field-going, moving over a plain;* campum peragrans:—Feldgangende feoh *pĕcus campum peragrans*, Soul Kmbl. 161; Seel. 81: Salm. Kmbl. 45; Sal. 23. Feldgongende feoh *cattle traversing the field*, Exon. 99 a; Th. 371, 25; Seel. 81, note: Salm. Kmbl. 309; Sal. 154.

feld-hryðer, es; *n. A field ox* or *heifer;* campestris bos sive vĭtŭlus, Chart. ad calc. C. R. Ben.

feld-hûs, es; *n. A field-house, tent;* tentōrium, tabernăcŭlum :—Feldhûsa mǽst *greatest of tents*, Cd. 146; Th. 183, 3; Exod. 85. Brǽddon æfter beorgum flotan feldhûsum *the sailors spread* [*themselves*] *amongst the hills with their tents*, 148; Th. 186, 3; Exod. 133: Cd. 154; Th. 191, 31; Exod. 223.

feld-land, es; *n. Field-land, a plain;* plānĭties. It is opposed to dûn-land *hilly land:*—Faraþ to Amorrēa dûne and to ôðrum feld-landum and dûn-landum and to unhéheran landum *vĕnite ad montem Amorrhæōrum et ad cētĕra campestria atque montāna et hŭmĭliōra lŏca*, Deut. 1, 7: 11, 30.

feldlîc; *adj. Fieldlike, country, rural;* campester :—Feldlîc *campester*, Ælfc. Gr. 9, 18; Som. 10, 4. On feldlîcre stôwe *in lŏco campestri*, Lk. Bos. 6, 17. On feldlîcum wunungum *in campestrĭbus habĭtācŭlis*, Jos. 10, 40.

feld-mædere, an; *f.* [mædere, mæddere *madder*] *Field-madder, rosemary;* rosmărīnum :—Feldmædere *rosmărīnum*, Glos. Brux. Recd. 42, 34; Wrt. Voc. 68, 49.

feld-minte, an; *f. Field* or *wild mint;* silvestris menta, mentastrum :—Feldminte *mentarium?* [= *mentastrum*], Glos. Brux. Recd. 43, 3; Wrt. Voc. 69, 18.

feld-more, an; *f:* -moru, e; *f.* [more *a root*] *A parsnip, carrot;* pastĭnāca :—Feldmore *parsnip*, L. M. 3, 14; Lchdm. ii. 316, 21. Feldmore [MS. -mora] *pastĭnāca*, Ælfc. Gl. 42; Som. 64, 32; Wrt. Voc. 31, 42. Nim feldmoran sǽd *take seed of parsnip*, L. M. 3, 12; Lchdm. ii. 314, 19: iii. 72, 3. Wyrtdrenc of feldmoran sele drincan *give to drink a herb-drink of parsnip*, L. M. 1, 48; Lchdm. ii. 122, 15. Dô on eala feldmoran *put parsnip in ale*, 1, 66; Lchdm. ii. 142, 5: 3, 32; Lchdm. ii. 326, 17: iii. 22, 18. Herba pastināca silvātica, ðæt is feldmoru *the herb pastĭnāca silvātĭca, that is parsnip*, Herb. cont. 82, 1; Lchdm. i. 32, 25. Feldmoru biþ cenned on sandigum stôwum and on beorgum *parsnip is produced on sandy places and on hills*, Herb. 82, 1; Lchdm. i. 186, 3: L. M. 2, 53; Lchdm. ii. 274, 26. Feldmore niðeweard *the nether part of parsnip*, L. M. 1, 40; Lchdm. ii. 104, 14.

feld-oxa, an; *f. A field* or *pasture ox;* pascuālis bos :—Feldoxan *pascuāles bŏves*, Hymn. in Dedic. Eccles.

feld-rude, an; *f. Wild rue;* silvestris rūta, Ben. Lye: Lchdm. Glos. vol. iii. p. 325.

feld-swam, -swamm, es; *m. A field mushroom, toadstool;* fungus, Cot. 87.

feld-swop *bradigaco?* Cot. 25, Lye. Feld-uuop *bradigabo?* Glos. Epnl. Recd. 154, 72.

feld-wêsten, es; *n. A field waste* or *desert;* campestris solĭtūdo :—Begeondan Iordane on ðam feldwêstene wið ða reádan sǽ *trans Iordanem in solĭtūdĭne campestri contra măre rubrum*, Deut. 1, 1.

feld-wurma *the plant wild marjoram.* v. felt-wurma.

feld-wyrt, e; *f. Field-wort, gentian;* gentiāna :—Feldwyrt *gentiāna*, Wrt. Voc. 68, 7. Herba gentiāna, ðæt ys feldwyrt *the herb gentiāna, that is, field-wort*, Herb. cont. 17, 1; Lchdm. i. 12, 16. Ðeós wyrt, ðe man gentiānam, and ôðrum naman feldwyrt nemneþ, heó biþ cenned on dûnum *this herb, which is called gentian, and by another name field-wort, is produced on downs*, Herb. 17, 1; Lchdm. i. 110, 2.

fele-ferþ? [fele = fela *many?*] *A kind of worm under blocks having many feet*, Som; vermĭcŭla quædam multĭpĕda, Lye :—Feleferþ *centumpellio*, forte *centupĕda*, Ælfc. Gl. 17; Som. 58, 86; Wrt. Voc. 22, 4.

fêle-leás; *adj.* [fêlan *to feel*] *Devoid of feeling;* insensĭlis :—Biþ his lîf scæcen and he fêleleás *his life is departed and he devoid of feeling*, Exon. 87 b; Th. 329, 26; Vy. 40.

FELG, e; *f:* felge, an; *f. A* FELLY, *part of the circumference of a wheel;* canthus = κανθός, absis rŏtæ :—Ælces spācan biþ ôðer ende fæst on ðære nafe, ôðer on ðære felge *one end of every spoke is fixed in the nave, the other in the felly*, Bt. 39, 7; Fox 222, 3, 7, 10. Ða felga hangiaþ on ðâm spācan *the fellies depend on the spokes*, 222, 13, 19, 21, 27. Neár ðâm felgum *nearer to the fellies*, 222, 11. Felge [MS. felga] *canthus*, Ælfc. Gl. 2; Som. 55, 48; Wrt. Voc. 16, 21. Ðæt hweól hwerfþ ymbûton, and sió nafa, nêhst ðære eaxe, sió færþ micle fæstlîcor and orsorglîcor ðonne ða felgan dôn *the wheel turns round, and the nave, being nearest to the axle-tree, goes much more firmly and more securely than the fellies do*, Bt. 39, 7; Fox 220, 30. [*Wyc.* felijs, felys *fellies: Plat.* falge, felge, *f: Dut.* velg, *f: Ger.* felge, *f: M. H. Ger.* vëlge, *f: O. H. Ger.* felga, *f: Dan.* fælge, *m. f.*]

felgan, ic felge, ðû filgst, filhst, he filgþ, filhþ, *pl.* felgaþ; *p.* fealg, fealh, *pl.* fulgon; *pp.* folgen *To stick to, betake oneself to, go* or *come under, below* or *beneath anything, to go into, enter a place, to undergo;* inhærēre, sŭbīre, inīre, intrāre :—Ôþ he on fleáme fealh *until he betook himself to flight*, Ors. 4, 8; Bos. 89, 42. Hŷ ymb ða geatu feohtende wǽron ôþ hŷ ðǽrinne fulgon *they were fighting about the gates until they entered therein*, Chr. 755; Th. 87, 3, col. 1. Siððan inne fealh Grendles môdor *when Grendel's mother came in*, Beo. Th. 2567; B. 1281. He searonîþas fealh Eormenrîces *he underwent the guileful enmity of Ermanric*, 2405; B. 1200. [*O. Sax.* bi-felhan *trădĕre, mandāre, condĕre: Frs.* be-feljen: *O. Frs.* bifella: *Dut.* be-velen: *Ger.* be-fehlen *mandāre: M. H. Ger.* be-vëlhen *condĕre, mandāre: O. H. Ger.* fëlahan, felhan *condĕre: Goth.* filhan *to hide, bury: Icel.* fela: *Lat.* se-pĕlīre *to hide, bury.*] DER. æt-felgan, be-, bi-, ge-, wið-. v. felan, feolan.

feligean; *p.* de; *pp.* ed *To follow;* sĕqui :—Uton gân and feligean fremdum godum *eāmus et sĕquāmur deos aliēnos*, Deut. 13, 2. v. fylgean.

fell, es; *n. A fell, skin;* pellis :—Fell *pellis*, Ælfc. Gr. 9, 28; Som. 11, 56: Wrt. Voc. 71, 18. Cealfes fell *vĭtŭli cŏrium*, Ex. 29, 14. v. fel *a skin.*

fell, es; *m. Ruin, death;* lapsus, ruīna :—Ðêh ðe fell curen synnigra cynn *though the race of sinners chose death*, Andr. Kmbl. 3217; An. 1611. v. fyll.

fell; *adj. Fell, cruel, severe;* crūdēlis, Som. Ben. Lye. v. fel; *adj.*

fellan, fyllan; ic felle, ðû felest, felst, he feleþ, felþ, *pl.* fellaþ; *p.* felde, *pl.* feldon; *pp.* felled; *v. trans. To cause to fall, to fell, cut* or *throw down, strip off, destroy;* cædĕre, sternĕre, projĭcĕre, abjĭcĕre, dejĭcĕre, destruĕre :—Gefered ðǽr hit felde *borne where it was thrown down*, Exon. 109 b; Th. 419, 11; Rä. 38, 4. DER. a-fellan, be-. v. fyllan, feallan.

fellen; *adj.* [fel *skin*] *Made of skins;* pellĭceus :—Fellen gyrdel wæs ymbe his lendenu *ĕrat zōna pellĭcea circa lumbos ejus*, Mk. Bos. 1, 6. God worhte Adame and his wîfe fellene reáf and gescrîdde hî *fēcit Deus Adam et uxōri ejus tunĭcas pellĭceas et induit eos*, Gen. 3, 21. Fellen hæt *a hat made of skin, a felt hat;* gălērus *vel* pileus, Ælfc. Gl. 18; Som. 58, 111; Wrt. Voc. 22, 26.

felle-wærc, es; *n. The falling sickness, epilepsy;* epĭlepsia = ἐπιληψία :—Ðæt deáh wið fellewærce *it is good for epilepsy*, L. M. 2, 1; Lchdm. ii. 178, 8. v. fylle-wærc.

fel-nys, -nyss, e; *f. Cruelty, fierceness;* crūdēlĭtas, Som. Ben. Lye.

fêlnyss, e; *f.* [fêlan *to feel*] *Feeling;* sensus :—Gærs and treówa lybbaþ bûtan fêlnysse... nŷtenu lybbaþ and habbaþ fêlnysse bûtan gesceáde *grass and trees live without feeling... beasts live and have feeling without reason*, Homl. Th. i. 302, 15, 16. DER. ge-fêlniss.

felo; *adj. Fell, baleful;* perniciosus. DER. eal-felo. v. fæle, fel; *adj.*

felofor, fealvor, es; *m. A species of water-fowl, the sultana-hen;* porphyrio = πορφυρίων :—Felofor *porphȳrio*, Glos. Epnl. Recd. 161, 36.

felsan *to recompense;* expiāre, Som. Ben. Lye.

FELT, es; *m?* FELT; pannus *vel* lāna coactĭlis, impĭlia, Som. Ben. Lye:—Felt *centrum?* vel *filtrum?* Ælfc. Gl. 21; Som. 59, 59; Wrt. Voc. 23, 20. [*Plat.* filt, *m: Dut.* vilt, *n: Ger.* filz *m. n. carded wool, felt: M. H. Ger.* vilz, *m. felt: O. H. Ger.* filz, *m: Dan.* filt, *m. f: Swed.* filt, *m.*]

felþ *falls*, Bt. Met. Fox 5, 30; Met. 5, 15; *3rd pers. pres. of* feallan.

fel-tûn, es; *m. An enclosed place, garden, privy, dunghill;* secessus, latrīna, sterquĭlīnium :—Se wîsdôm and ôðre cræftas licgaþ forsewene swâ swâ meox under feltûne *wisdom and other virtues lie despised like dirt on a dunghill*, Bt. 36, 1; Fox 172, 11. In feltûn *in secessu*, Mt. Kmbl. Lind. 15, 17: Mk. Skt. Lind. 7, 19. In feltûne oððe mixen *in sterquĭlīnium*, Lk. Skt. Lind. Rush. 14, 35.

felt-wurma, an; *m.* [felt = feld?] *The plant wild marjoram;* orīgānum, Som. Ben. Lye: Lchdm. Glos. vol. iii. p. 349, col. 2, 32.

felt-wyrt, e; *f. The plant mullein;* verbascum thapsus, Lin :—Ðeós wyrt, ðe man verbascum, and ôðrum naman feltwyrt nemneþ, biþ cenned on sandigum stôwum and on myxenum *this plant, which is named verbascum, and by another name mullein, is produced in sandy places and on dunghills*, Herb. 73, 1; Lchdm. i. 174, 19–21. Feltwyrt *avadonia?* Wrt. Voc. 79, 5.

fêmne, an; *f. A virgin, young woman;* virgo :—Fêmne sceal hire freónd gesêcan *the virgin shall seek her friend*, Menol. Fox 548; Gn. C. 44. v. fǽmne.

FEN, fenn, fæn, fænn, es; *n. m. A* FEN, *marsh, mud, dirt;* pălus, lŭtum, līmus, sordes :—Ic fûlre eom ðonne ðis fen swearte *I am fouler than this swart fen*, Exon. 110 b; Th. 423, 33; Rä. 41, 31. Fenn *lŭtum*, Ælfc. Gr. 13; Som. 16, 6: *līmus, lŭtum*, Ælfc. Gl. 57; Som. 67, 61; Wrt. Voc. 37, 48. Þyrs sceal on fenne gewunian *the spectre shall dwell in the fen*, Menol. Fox 545; Gn. C. 42: Beo. Th. 2595; B. 1295. Se ðe môras heóld, fen and fæsten *who held the moors, the fen and fastness*, Beo. Th. 208; B. 104. Hió wyrcþ ðæt fenn ðe man hâteþ Meotedisc *it forms the fen which is called Mæotis*, Ors. 1, 1; Bos. 15, 19. He underféhþ ðæt fenn ðara þweándra *he receives the dirt of the washers*, Past. 16, 5; Hat. MS. 21 b, 20. Is Êlig ðæt land eall mid fenne and mid wæter ymbseald *est Elge pălūdĭbus circumdăta vel ăquis*, Bd. 4, 19; S. 590, 4. Is ðæt êglond fenne biworpen *the island is surrounded with a fen*, Exon. 100 b; Th. 380, 9; Rä. 1, 5. Fennas and môras *fens and moors*, Bt. 18, 1; Fox 62, 14. On ðâm fennum *in pălūdĭbus*, Bd. 4, 19; S. 590, 5. Eall ôþ ða fennas norþ *as far north as the fens*, Chr. 905; Erl. 98, 21: 1010; Erl. 143, 27. [*Piers P.* fen: *Wyc.* fen, fenne: *Laym.* fenne, uenne, *dat;* fenes, *pl: Scot.* fen: *Plat.* fenne: *Frs.* finne: *O. Frs.* fenne, fene: *Dut.* veen, *n: Kil.* ven, venne: *Ger.* fenne, *n: O. H. Ger.* fenna, fennî, *f: Goth.* fani, *n. mud, dirt: Icel.* fen, *n. a fen, quagmire.*]

fen-cerse, an; *f. Fen-cress, water-cress;* nasturtium offĭcĭnāle, Lin:—Wyl fencersan *boil water-cress,* L. M. 1, 8; Lchdm. ii. 52, 15: 1, 61; Lchdm. ii. 132, 5.

fēncg = fēng *took; p. of* fōn, *q. v.*

fen-fearn, fen-fern, es; *n. The fen* or *water-fern, flowering fern, the herb christopher, osmund-royal;* osmunda rēgālis, Lin. salvia?—Fenfearn *salvia,* Ælfc. Gl. 42; Som. 64, 8; Wrt. Voc. 31, 19. v. fearn.

fen-fixas; *pl. m. Fen-fishes;* pălustres pisces, Som. Ben. Lye. v. fisc.

fen-freoðo; *indecl. f. Fen-asylum;* ăsȳlum in pălūde:—He in fenfreoðo feorh alegde *he laid down his life in his fen-asylum,* Beo. Th. 1706; B. 851.

fen-fugelas; *pl. m. Fen-birds, fen-fowl;* pălustres ăves, Som. Ben. Lye. v. fugel.

feng, es; *m.* [fōn *to take*]. I. *a grasp, span, hug, embrace;* amplexus, captus:—Ic fāra feng feore gedīgde *from the grasp of foes I with life escaped,* Beo. Th. 1160; B. 578. Fȳres feng *the grasp of fire,* Salm. Kmbl. 707; Sal. 353. II. *what is taken, booty;* captum, præda:—Hī feng woldon fōn *they would take the booty,* Chr. 1016; Th. 280, 30, col. 2: 33, col. 1. DER. an-feng, and-, fore-, ofer-, on-, to-, under-. v. fang.

fēng, *pl.* fēngon *took,* Beo. Th. 5970; B. 2989: Salm. Kmbl. 866; Sal. 432; *p. of* fōn.

fengel, es; *m. A prince;* princeps:—Wīsa fengel geatolīc gengde *the wise prince stately went,* Beo. Th. 2805; B. 1400. Snottra fengel *the sagacious prince,* Beo. Th. 2954; B. 1475: 4318; B. 2156. Hringa fengel *prince of rings,* 4680; B. 2345.

fen-gelād, es; *n. Fen-path;* pălustris via, pălus:—Hie warigeaþ frēcne fengelād *they inhabit the dangerous fen-path,* Beo. Th. 2722; B. 1359.

feng-net, -nett, es; *n. A net for catching;* retiacŭlum:—Feallaþ firenfulle on heora fengnettum *cădent in retiacŭlo ejus peccātōres,* Ps. Th. 140, 12.

fen-hliþ, -hleoþ, es; *n.* [hliþ *a declivity, slope*] *A fen-slope, bank of a fen;* păluster clīvus, pălūdis rīpa:—Scolde Grendel fleón under fenhleoþu *Grendel must flee under the fen-slopes,* Beo. Th. 1645; B. 820.

fen-hōp, es; *n. A fen-heap* or *mound?* pălūdis agger?—He meahte fleón on fen-hōpu *he might flee to the fen-mounds,* Beo. Th. 1532; B. 764.

fēnix, es; *m.* I. *the fabulous bird phœnix* = φοῖνιξ:—Fēnix, swā hātte ān fugel on Arabiscre þeóde, se leofaþ fīf hund geára, and æfter deáþe eft arīst ge-edcucod, and se fugel getācnaþ ūrne ærīst on ðam endenēhstan dæge *phœnix, so a bird in Arabia is called, which lives five hundred years, and after death rises again re-quickened, and the bird betokens our resurrection at the last day,* Ælfc. Gr. 9, 64; Som. 13, 56-58. Se fugel se is fēnix hāten *the bird which is called phœnix,* Exon. 57 a; Th. 203, 19; Ph. 86. Fēnix byrneþ *phœnix burns,* 59 a; Th. 213, 2; Ph. 218: 60 b; Th. 221, 26; Ph. 340. II. *a genus of palms, the date tree* or *date palm;* phœnix dactylĭfĕra:—Ðǣr he heánne beám wunaþ ðone hātaþ men fēnix, of ðæs fugles noman *there it inhabits a lofty tree, which men call phœnix, from the bird's name,* Exon. 58 a; Th. 209, 21; Ph. 174.

fen-land, es; *n. Fen-land, marshy land;* pălustris terra:—Hī ealle Egypta awēston, būtan ðǣm fenlandum *they laid waste all Egypt, except the fen-lands,* Ors. 1, 10; Bos. 32, 26. He þurh ða fenland reów *he rowed through the fen-lands,* Guthl. 9; Gdwin. 50, 13.

fen-līc; *adj. Fenlike, marshy, fenny;* păluster:—Fenlīc *păluster,* Ælfc. Gr. 9, 18; Som. 10, 4. Of ðam fenlīcum adelan *from the fenlike mud,* Homl. Th. ii. 472, 7. Betwyx ða fenlīcan gewrido ðæs wīdgillan wēstenes he āna ongan eardian *he began to dwell alone among the fenny thickets of the wide wilderness,* Guthl. 3; Gdwin. 22, 9.

fen-minte, an; *f. Fen-mint, water-mint;* silvestris menta, Lin:—Fenminte *fen-mint,* L. M. 1, 3; Lchdm. ii. 40, 8.

fenn *a fen, marsh, mud, dirt,* Past. 16, 5; Hat. MS. 21 b, 20: Ps. Spl. 17, 44. v. fen.

fennig, fenneg; *adj.* FENNY, *marshy, muddy, dirty;* pălustris, ulīgĭnōsus, lŭtōsus:—Fennig æcer *ulīgĭnōsus ăger,* Ælfc. Gl. 57; Som. 67, 70; Wrt. Voc. 37, 56. Gif sió hond biþ fennegu *if the hand is dirty,* Past. 13, 1; Hat. MS. 16 b, 8.

fenol *the herb fennel;* fēnĭcŭlum, Wrt. Voc. 79, 8. v. finol.

fen-ȳce, an; *f.* [ȳce *a frog*] *A fen-frog;* pălūdis rāna:—Me is fenȳce fōre hreþre *a fen-frog is more rapid than I in its course,* Exon. 111 a; Th. 426, 9; Rä. 41, 71.

feó *for* or *with cattle* or *money,* Cd. 126; Th. 161, 2; Gen. 2659: Beo. Th. 2765; B. 1380; *dat. and instr. of* feoh.

feóde, *pl.* feódon *hated,* Ps. Th. 118, 163; *p. of* feón, feógan.

FEÓGAN, feógean, fiógan, feón, fión; *part.* feógende; ic feóge, he feógeþ, feóþ, *pl.* feógaþ, feógeaþ; *p.* feóde, *pl.* feódon, feódun, feódan *To hate, persecute;* ōdisse, ōdio hăbēre, infestāre:—Uton we firene feógan *let us hate crimes,* Exon. 98 a; Th. 366, 16; Reb. 13. He hī alȳsde of feógendra folmum *lĭbĕrāvit eos de mănu ōdientium,* Ps. Th. 105, 10. Ic unrihte wegas ealle feóge *omnem viam inīquam ŏdio hăbui,* Ps. Th. 118, 128: 138, 19. Ða wēregan neát nales feógaþ frȳnd hiera *the brute animals hate not their friends,* Elen. Kmbl. 719; El. 360. Ðe me earwunga ealle feógeaþ *qui ōdērunt me grātis,* Ps. Th. 68, 4: 73, 22. Ic feóde fācnes wyrcend *făcientes prævarĭcātiōnes ōdivi,* Ps. Th. 100, 3: 118, 113. Hī Dryhtnes ǣ feódon *they hated the Lord's law,* Exon. 66 a; Th. 243, 21; Jul. 14: Elen. Kmbl. 711; El. 356. Ðe feódun sybbe *qui ōdērunt pācem,* Ps. Spl. C. 119, 6. Hī Godes tempel feódan *they hated God's temple,* Exon. 18 a; Th. 44, 27; Cri. 709. Ða ðe hine feódan *qui ōdērunt eum,* Ps. Th. 67, 1: 82, 2: 85, 16: 104, 21. Feógeaþ [fiógaþ MS. T.] yfel *ōdīte mălum,* Ps. Spl. C. 96, 10. [*O. H. Ger.* fiēn: *Goth.* fiyan, fian: *Icel.* fjá *to hate.*]

feó-gȳtsung, e; *f. Money-desire* or *greed, avarice;* pĕcūniæ cŭpīdo, avārĭtia:—Ðæt he sceolde his treówe for feógȳtsunge and lufan forleósan *that he should lose his truth for desire and love of money,* Bd. 2, 12; S. 514, 40.

FEOH, fioh; *gen.* feós; *dat.* feó; *n.* I. *cattle, living animals;* pĕcus, jūmenta:—Gif ðē become ōðres monnes giémeleás feoh [G and H] on hand *if the stray cattle of another man come to thy hand,* L. Alf. 42; Th. i. 54, 9. Feoh būtan gewitte *the cattle without understanding,* Salm. Kmbl. 46; Sal. 23. Wiht seó ðæt feoh fēdeþ *a thing which feeds the cattle,* Exon. 109 a; Th. 416, 21; Rä. 35, 2. Ic sealde him gangende feoh *I gave him live stock* [*walking cattle*], Cd. 129; Th. 164, 23; Gen. 2719. II. cattle being used in early times as a medium of exchange, hence *Money, value, price, hire, stipend,* FEE, *reward;* pĕcūnia, merces:—Næbbe gē feoh on eówrum bīgyrdlum *nŏlīte possĭdēre pĕcūniam in zōnis,* Mt. Bos. 10, 9. Se ðe his feoh to unrihtum wæstmsceatte ne syleþ *qui pĕcūniam suam non dĕdit ad ūsūram,* Ps. Th. 14, 6. Ðæt he him sealde wið feoh ðæt scræf *ut det illi spēluncam pĕcūnia,* Gen. 23, 9. Ic ðē ða fǣhþe feó leánige *I will recompense thee for the strife with money,* Beo. Th. 2765; B. 1380. III. as property chiefly consisted of cattle, hence *Goods, property, riches, wealth;* bŏna, dīvitiæ, ŏpes:—His feoh onfōn fremde handa *dīrĭpiant aliēni omnes dīvĭtias ejus,* Ps. Th. 108, 11. Ne wilniaþ nāues ōðres feós *wish for no other riches,* Bt. 14, 2; Fox 44, 22. We ðē feoh syllaþ *we will give thee wealth,* Cd. 130; Th. 165, 2; Gen. 2725: Ors. 2, 4; Bos. 43, 22. IV. the Anglo-Saxon Rune ᚠ = f, the name of which letter in Anglo-Saxon is feoh *money, wealth,*—hence this Rune not only stands for the letter *f,* but for feoh *money,* as,—ᚠ [= feoh] byþ frōfur fira gehwylcum *money is a consolation to every man,* Runic pm. 1; Kmbl. 339, 1; Hick. Thes. i. 135, 1. ᚠ [= feoh] on foldan *wealth on earth,* Exon. 19 b; Th. 50, 28; Cri. 808: Elen. Grm. 1270. [*Piers P.* fee: *Chauc.* fee: *Laym.* feoh, feo, *n*: *Orm.* fe, fehh: *Plat.* vee, veih, *n. cattle*: *O. Sax.* fē, fio; *Hel.* fehu, *n. pĕcus, ŏpes*: *O. Frs.* fia, fya, *n*: *Dut.* vee, *n*: *Kil.* veech, vee *pĕcus*: *Ger.* vieh, *n*: *M. H. Ger.* vihe, *n*: *O. H. Ger.* fihu, *n*: *Goth.* faihu, *n. cattle, goods*: *Dan.* fæ, *n*: *Swed.* fä, *n*: *Icel.* fé, *n. cattle, goods*: *Lat.* pĕcus, *n*: *Lith.* pekus *cattle*: *Sansk.* paśu, *m. cattle.* 'The importance of cattle in a simple state of society early caused an intimate connection between the notion of cattle, and of money or wealth. Thus we have *Lat.* pĕcus *cattle;* pĕcūnia *money;* and *Goth.* faihu *cattle, possessions,* is identical with *O. H. Ger.* fihu, fehu; *Ger.* vieh *cattle;* *Icel.* fé *cattle, money;* *A. Sax.* feoh *cattle, riches, money, price, reward,*' Wgwd.] DER. cwic-feoh, hǣðen-, woruld-.

FEOHAN, feón; *part.* feónde; *p.* feah, *pl.* fǣgon; *pp.* fegen *To rejoice, be glad, exult;* gaudēre, lætāri, exultāre:—Se feónde [MS. feond] gespearn fleótende hreáw *the exulting* [*raven*] *perched on the floating corpses,* Cd. 72; Th. 87, 11; Gen. 1447. [*O. Sax.* gi-fehōn *to make to rejoice*: *O. H. Ger.* gi-fēhan, gi-vēhan *gaudēre.*] DER. ge-feohan, -feón.

feoh-bōt, fioh-bōt, e; *f. A pecuniary recompence;* nummāria compensātio:—Feohbōt arīseþ *a pecuniary recompence shall arise,* L. Eth. vi. 51; Th. i. 328, 4. Ðæt hī mōston ðære fiohbōte [ðæra feohbōta MS. H.] onfōn *that they might receive the pecuniary recompence,* L. Alf. 49; Th. i. 58, 8.

feoh-ern, es; *n. A money-place, treasury;* gazophylacium = γαζοφυλάκιον, Som. Ben. Lye,

feoh-fang, es; *m. Fee-taking, taking a bribe;* pĕcūniæ acceptio:—For feohfange *for bribery,* L. C. S. 15; Th. i. 384, 8.

feoh-gafol, es; *n. Usury, a duty, tax;* ūsūra, Som. Ben. Lye.

feoh-georn; *adj. Desirous of money, avaricious, covetous;* avārus, Som. Ben. Lye.

feoh-gesteald, es; *n. Possession of riches;* dīvĭtiārum possessio:—Ne þorfton ða þegnas feohgestealda [MS. -gestealde] wēnan *the followers needed not expect possession of riches,* Exon. 75 b; Th. 283, 25; Jul. 685.

feoh-gestreón, es; *n. Treasure, riches;* thēsaurus = θησαυρός, dīvitiæ:—Næbbe ic ne feohgestreón *I have no riches,* Andr. Kmbl. 602; An. 301: Exon. 66 a; Th. 245, 10; Jul. 42. Elþeódig hafaþ mec bereáfod feohgestreóna *a stranger has bereaved me of my treasures,* Elen. Kmbl. 1818; El. 911: Salm. Kmbl. 64; Sal. 32: Exon. 67 a; Th. 248, 27; Jul. 102.

feoh-gīfre; *adj.* [gīfre *greedy*] *Greedy of money, avaricious, covetous;* pĕcūniæ ăvĭdus, ăvārus:—Wita sceal ne tō feohgīfre *the sagacious must not be too greedy of money,* Exon. 77 b; Th. 290, 21; Wand. 68.

feoh-gift, -gyft, e; *f. A money-gift, precious gift;* pĕcūniæ dōnum *vel* largītio, prĕtiōsum dōnum:—Fromum feohgiftum *with bounteous money-gifts*, Beo. Th. 41; B. 21. Nō he ðære feohgyfte scamigan þorfte *he needed not feel shame at the precious gift*, 2055; B. 1025. Æt feohgyftum *with money-gifts*, 2182; B. 1089.

feoh-gîtsere, es; *m. A miser;* pĕcūniæ ăvārus:—Eálā! hwæt se forma feohgîtsere wǣre on worulde *alas! that the first miser should have been in the world*, Bt. Met. Fox 8, 110; Met. 8, 55. Ðæm feohgîtsere *to the miser*, Bt. 7, 4; Fox 22, 26.

feoh-gyrnes, -ness, e; *f. Money-desire, avarice;* avārĭtia, L. Ath. Lye.

feoh-gŷtsung *desire of money, avarice.* v. feó-gŷtsung.

feoh-hof, es; *n. A treasury;* ærārium, Som. Ben. Lye.

feoh-hord, es; *m. A money-hoard;* ærārium, Cot. 212.

feoh-hûs, es; *n. A treasure-house;* ærārium, Ælfc. Gl. 108; Som. 78, 104; Wrt. Voc. 58, 19.

feoh-lǣnung, e; *f. Money-lending, mortgage;* fenĕrātio:—Feohlǣnung būtan borge *hypothēca* [= ὑποθήκη], Ælfc. Gl. 14; Som. 58, 14; Wrt. Voc. 21, 9.

feoh-leás; *adj. Moneyless, priceless;* pĕcūniæ ĭnops, sine prĕtio:—Ða ðe feohleáse wǣron him scipu begēton *they who were moneyless got themselves ships*, Chr. 897; Erl. 94, 27. Ðæt wæs feohleás gefeoht *that was a priceless fight*, Beo. Th. 4873; B. 2441.

feoh-leásnes, -ness, e; *f. Poverty;* pĕcūniæ inōpia, paupertas, Som. Ben. Lye.

feoh-sceat, -sceatt, es; *n. Money-tribute, wages;* trĭbūtum, merces:—Nō ic wið feohsceattum ofer folc bere Drihtnes dōmas *I bear not the Lord's decrees among nations for wages*, Cd. 212; Th. 262, 14; Dan. 744.

feoh-spillung, -spilling, e; *f. Money-wasting, profusion;* pĕcūniārum effūsio *vel* profūsio:—Man ðǣr ne gespǣdde būtan manmyrringe and feohspillinge *man gained naught there except loss of men and waste of money*, Chr. 1096; Erl. 233, 30.

feoh-strang; *adj. Money-strong, possessing cattle* or *money;* pĕcuārius, pĕcūniōsus:—Feohstrang man *pĕcuārius*, Ælfc. Gl. 58; Som. 67, 112; Wrt. Voc. 38, 35. Feohstrang *pĕcūniōsus*, 88; Som. 74, 71; Wrt. Voc. 50, 51.

feoht, es; *n. A* FIGHT, *battle;* pugna, prœlium:—Wæs he þencende ðæt he ðæt feoht forlēte *he was thinking that he would give up the fight*, Bd. 3, 14; S. 539, 39. God tǣceþ handa mīne to feohte *Deus dŏcet mănus meas ad prœlium*, Ps. Spl. 143, 1. [*Laym.* fæht, faht: *Scot.* fecht, facht: *O. Sax.* fehta, *f*: *Frs.* fjuecht: *O. Frs.* fiucht: *Dut.* ge-vecht, *n*: *Ger.* ge-fecht, *n*: *M. H. Ger.* vëhte, *f*: *O. H. Ger.* fehta, *f*.] DER. ge-feoht, inge-, ofer-, ūtge-.

FEOHTAN; *part.* feohtende; ic feohte, ðū feohtest, he feohteþ, fiht, *pl.* feohtaþ; *p.* ic, he feaht, ðū fuhte, *pl.* fuhton; *pp.* fohten *To* FIGHT, *contend, make war, combat, struggle;* prœliāri, pugnāre, bellāre, contendĕre, decertāre, collīdĕre:—Mec mīn freá feohtan hāteþ *my lord commands me to fight*, Exon. 102 b; Th. 389, 10; Rä. 7, 5: 104 b; Th. 398, 2; Rä. 17, 1. Gyf hwylc cyning wyle faran and feohtan agēn ōðerne cyning *quis rex itūrus committĕre bellum adversus ălium rēgem*, Lk. Bos. 14, 31. Ealle on ðone cining feohtende wǣron *all were fighting against the king*, Chr. 755; Erl. 49, 35: 994; Erl. 133, 11. Ic feohte *prœlior*, Ælfc. Gr. 25; Som. 27, 7. Feohteþ se feónd *the fiend fights*, Salm. Kmbl. 995; Sal. 499: L. Eth. vii. 15; Th. i. 332, 14: L. C. S. 60; Th. i. 408, 12. Drihten fiht for eów *Dŏmĭnus pugnābit pro vōbis*, Ex. 14, 14: Wrt. Voc. 78, 1. Monige synd, ðe to me feohtaþ *multi qui bellant me*, Ps. Th. 55, 3: 58, 1. Cūþwulf feaht wið Bretwalas *Cuthwulf fought against the Brito-Welsh*, Chr. 571; Erl. 18, 12: 661; Erl. 35, 9: 871; Erl. 75, 19. Ða litlingas fuhton on hire innoþe *collīdēbantur in ŭtĕro ejus parvŭli*, Gen. 25, 22. Stuf and Wihtgār fuhton [fuhtun, Erl. 14, 22] wið Bryttas *Stuf and Wihtgar fought against the Britons*, Chr. 514; Erl. 15, 23. Wītodlīce mīne þegnas fuhton *ministri mei utique decertārent*, Jn. Bos. 18, 36. Be ðon ðe mon on cynges healle feohte *in case a man fight in the king's hall*, L. Alf. pol. 7; Th. i. 66, 7: 39; Th. i. 88, 2. Ðeáh him feohtan on firas monige *although many men fight against it*, Runic pm. 26; Kmbl. 344, 27; Hick. Thes. i. 135, 52. [*Piers P.* fighten: *Laym.* fæhten, fahten: *Orm.* fihhtenn: *Scot.* fecht: *O. Sax.* fehtan: *Frs.* fjuechten: *O. Frs.* fiuchta: *Dut.* vechten: *Ger.* fechten: *M. H. Ger.* vehten: *O. H. Ger.* fehtan: *Dan.* fegte, fægte: *Swed.* fäkta.] DER. a-feohtan, æt-, be-, bi-, ge-, ofer-, on-, wið-.

feohte, an; *f. A fight, combat;* pugna:—Wearþ him seó feohte tō grim *the fight was too severe for them*, Exon. 84 a; Th. 317, 16; Mōd. 66. Nō ic gefrægn heardran feohtan *I have not heard of a harder fight*, Beo. Th. 1157; B. 576: Exon. 102 b; Th. 388, 7; Rä. 6, 4: Andr. Kmbl. 2045; An. 1025. We ðæt ellenweorc feohtan fremedon *we have achieved that valourous deed by fighting*, Beo. Th. 1922; B. 959.

feohtere, es; *m. A fighter, warrior;* pugnātor, bellātor, Ben. Lye.

feoht-lâc, es; *n. A fighting, fight;* pugna:—Gif ciricgriþ abrocen beó, bētan man georne, sī hit þurh feohtlāc, sī hit þurh reáflāc *if church-peace be broken, be it through fighting, be it through robbery, let amends be strictly made*, L. Eth. ix. 4; Th. i. 340, 20: L. C. E. 3; Th. i. 360, 11: L. C. S. 48; Th. i. 402, 28.

feoht-wîte *a fine for fighting.* v. fyht-wīte.

feól *fell*, Beo. Th. 1549; B. 772; *p. of* feallan.

FEÓL, e; *f. A* FILE; līma:—Ic eom lāf fȳres and feóle *I am the leaving of fire and file*, Exon. 126 a; Th. 484, 7; Rä. 70, 4. Mīn heáfod is homere geþuren, sworfen feóle *my head is beaten with a hammer, rubbed with a file*, 129 b; Th. 497, 18; Rä. 87, 2. [*Prompt. Parv.* file: *Dut.* vijl, *f*: *Ger.* feile, *f*: *M. H. Ger.* vîle, *f*: *O. H. Ger.* fîhala, fîla, *f*: *Dan.* fiil, *m. f*: *Swed.* fil, *m*: *Icel.* þél, *f. a file*.]

feola *many*, Bd. 5, 19; S. 637, 15. v. fela.

feolan, fiolan, felan; *p.* fæl, *pl.* fǣlon, fēlon; *pp.* folen, feolen. I. *to cleave, stick, adhere;* adhærēre:—Ðæt ic in ne fele *ut non inhæream*, Ps. Surt. 68, 15. II. *to reach, come, pass;* procēdĕre, pervĕnīre:—Ne meahton hī ofer mere feolan *they could not pass over the sea*, Exon. 106 a; Th. 404, 10; Rä. 23, 5. DER. æt-feolan, be-, bi-, ge-, geond-.

feóld, *pl.* feóldon *folded up*, Ælfc. Gr. 24; Som. 25, 50: Exon. 107 a; Th. 408, 4; Rä. 27, 7; *p. of* fealdan.

feól-heard; *adj. File-hard, hard like a file;* instar līmæ dūrus:—Hī lēton of folman feólhearde speru *they let the file-hard spears from their hands*, Byrht. Th. 134, 63; By. 108.

feó-lif? [feó = feoh?] *Munificence, bounty;* munĭfĭcentia, D. Som. Ben. Lye.

feóll *fell*, Beo. Th. 5830; B. 2919; *p. of* feallan.

feóllon *fell*, Beo. Th. 2089; B. 1042; *p. pl. of* feallan.

feolo *many*, Cd. 222; Th. 290, 26; Sat. 421. v. fela.

feolu-fôr, e; *f*? *A field-fare;* turdus pĭlāris?—Feolufōr *torax*? Wrt. Voc. 289, 17. v. feala-fōr.

feon, feonn, es; *m. A fen;* pălus:—Geond ða feonnas *about the fens*, Chr. 1010; Erl. 143, 29: 656; Erl. 31, 10, 26. v. fen.

feón, he feóþ; *p.* feóde, *pl.* feódon *To hate;* ōdisse:—He feóþ sāwle his *ōdit ănĭmam suam*, Ps. Spl. C. 10, 6: Cd. 43; Th. 56, 13; Gen. 911: Exon. 31 a; Th. 97, 31; Cri. 1599. Ic unrihta gehwylc feóde *iniquĭtātem ŏdio hăbui*, Ps. Th. 118, 163. Hie ðē feódon *they hated thee*, Elen. Kmbl. 711; El. 356. v. feógan.

feón *to rejoice, be glad.* v. feohan, ge-feón.

feónd, fiónd, fȳnd, fiénd, es; *pl. nom. acc.* feóndas, fȳnd, feónd; *gen.* feónda; *dat.* feóndum; *m.* [feógan, feón *to hate*] *A* FIEND, *enemy, foe, the devil;* ōsor, inĭmīcus, hostis, diabŏlus = διάβολος:—Seó ydelnes is ðære sāwle feónd *idleness is the soul's enemy*, L. E. I. 3; Th. ii. 404, 9. Ēhteþ feónd sāwle mīne *persĕquātur inĭmīcus anĭmam meam*, Ps. Spl. 7, 5. Se feónd his diórlingas duguþum stēpte *the fiend decked his favourites with honours*, Bt. Met. Fox 15, 14; Met. 15, 7: Beo. Th. 1455; B. 725: 1500; B. 748. Feónd *hostis* vel *ōsor*, Wrt. Voc. 86, 45. Se feónd mid his gefērum eallum feóllon of heofnum *the devil with all his company fell from heaven*, Cd. 16; Th. 20, 10; Gen. 306: Salm. Kmbl. 140; Sal. 69: 995; Sal. 499. Nā fægnian fȳnd mīn ofer me *non gaudēbit inĭmīcus meus sŭper me*, Ps. Spl. 40, 12. Stearcheort onfand feóndes fōtlāst *the stout of heart found the foe's foot-trace*, Beo. Th. 4567; B. 2289. Gif ðū gemēte ðīnes feóndes oxan oððe assan, lǣd hine to him *si occurrĕris bŏvi inĭmīci tui aut asĭno erranti, reduc ad eum*, Ex. 23, 4: Lk. Bos. 10, 19. Se ðæm feónde ætwand *he escaped from the fiend*, Beo. Th. 289; B. 143: Bt. Met. Fox 25, 31; Met. 25, 16. Ðū feónd oferswīðdest *thou shalt overcome thy foe*, Elen. Kmbl. 186; El. 93: Cd. 144; Th. 179, 21; Exod. 32. Ðū fiónd geflǣmdest *thou didst put the enemy* [*the devil*] *to flight*, Hy. 8, 25; Hy. Grn. ii. 290, 25. Genāmon me ðǣr strange feóndas *strong enemies took me there*, Rood Kmbl. 60; Kr. 30: 65; Kr. 33. Fȳnd syndon eówere *they are your enemies*, Judth. 11; Thw. 24, 18; Jud. 195: 12; Thw. 26, 10; Jud. 320. Eówre fȳnd feallaþ befōran eów *cădent inĭmīci vestri in conspectu vestro*, Lev. 26, 8, 16: Deut. 32, 31. Ðīne feónd fǣcne forwurdan *inĭmīci tui sonāvērunt*, Ps. Th. 82, 2: 91, 8. Hȳ fæder ageaf on feónda geweald *her father delivered her up into her foes' power*, Exon. 68 a; Th. 252, 7; Jul. 159: Elen. Kmbl. 135; El. 68. Ic agilde wrace mīnum feóndum *reddam ultiōnem hostĭbus meis*, Deut. 32, 41, 43: Jos. 10, 25. Ealle ic mihte feóndas gefyllan *I might have felled all his foes*, Rood Kmbl. 75; Kr. 38. Ðū swutole mihtest tocnāwan ðīne frīnd and ðīne fȳnd [fiénd Cot.] *thou mightest clearly distinguish thy friends and thy foes*, Bt. 20; Fox 72. 21. Lufiaþ eówre fȳnd *dilĭgĭte inĭmīcos vestros*, Mt. Bos. 5, 44: Lk. Bos. 6, 27, 35. Hió ofer heora feónd fæste getrymede *confirmāvit eum sŭper inĭmīcos ejus*, Ps. Th. 104, 20: 107, 12. Ne murnþ nāuðer ne friénd ne fiénd *he regards neither friend nor foe*, Bt. 37, 1; Fox 186, 8. Wæs wera ēðelland geondsended feóndum *the people's native land was overspread with enemies*, Cd. 92; Th. 118, 22; Gen. 1969. [*Piers P.* fend: *Wyc.* fend, feend: *Chauc.* feend: *Laym.* feond, ueond, *m*: *Orm.* fend: *Plat.* fijend, fijnd, *m*: *O. Sax.* fīond, fīund, fīunt, fīand: *Frs.* fynne: *O. Frs.* fiand, fiund, *m*: *Dut.* vijand, *m*: *Ger.* feind, *m*: *M. H. Ger.* vîant, vîent, vînt, *m*: *O. H. Ger.* fîant, fîent, *m*: *Goth.* fiyands, *m*: *Dan. Swed.* fiende, *m*: *Icel.* fjándi, *m.*] DER. eald-feónd, þeód-: ge-fȳnd.

feónd-ǣt, es; *m. Eating of the sacrifice to an idol;* diabŏlĭca mandūcātio:—Hī ðæs feondǣtes Finees awerede *Phinehas restrained them from eating of the sacrifice to an idol*, Ps. Th. 105, 24, notes, p. 445.

feónd-grâp, e; *f.* *A hostile grasp;* hostīlis arreptio :—Ðæt ic ânunga eówra leóda willan geworhte, oððe on wæl crunge, feóndgrâpum fæst *that I alone would work your people's will, or bow in death, fast in hostile grasps*, Beo. Th. 1276; B. 636.

feónd-gyld, es; *n.* *Devil-worship, sacrifice to devils, idolatry, an idol;* diăbŏli cultus, diabŏlĭcum sacrifĭcium, idōlatria, idōlum :—Ðá he on ðam folce feóndgyld gebræc *when he destroyed idolatry amongst the people*, Ps. Th. 105, 24.

feóndlic; *adj.* *Fiendlike, hostile;* hostīlis, hostĭcus :—Feóndlíc *hostĭcus* vel *hostīlis*, Ælfc. Gl. 84; Som. 73, 95; Wrt. Voc. 49, 3.

feóndlíce; *adv.* *Hostilely;* hostīlĭter :—Hyre þurh yrre ageaf andsware fæder feóndlíce *her father in anger gave answer hostilely*, Exon. 67 b; Th. 249, 27; Jul. 118.

feónd-rǽden, e; *f.* [rǽden *a condition*] *Fiend-condition, enmity;* inĭmīci condĭtio, inĭmīcĭtia :—Ic sette feóndrǽdene betweox ðé and ðam wífe *inĭmīcĭtias pōnam inter te et mŭlĭĕrem*, Gen. 3, 15.

feónd-rǽs, es; *m.* *A fiendish violence;* hostīlis impĕtus :—Ic feóndrǽs gefremede, fǽhþe geworhte *I committed fiendish violence, wrought enmity*, Cd. 42; Th. 55, 26; Gen. 900.

feónd-sceaða, -scaða, an; *m.* *A fiend-enemy, dire enemy, robber;* hostis nŏcīvus, latro :—Slóh ðone feóndsceaðan fágum méce *she* [*Judith*] *slew the dire enemy* [*Holofernes*] *with a blood-stained sword*, Judth. 10; Thw. 23, 4; Jud. 104. Me to grunde teáh fáh feóndscaða *a hostile foe drew me to the ground*, Beo. Th. 1112; B. 554. Ic sceal forstolen hreddan, flýman feóndsceaðan *I shall rescue the stolen, make the robber flee*, Exon. 104 a; Th. 396, 5; Rä. 15, 19.

feónd-scipe, -scype, es; *m.* *Fiendship, enmity;* inĭmīcĭtia, hostīlĭtas :—Ðæt ys se feóndscipe *that is the enmity*, Beo. Th. 5991; B. 2999: Exon. 95 a; Th. 354, 60; Reim. 68. For feóndscipe ðæs gemynegodan cyninges *propter inĭmīcĭtias mĕmŏrāti rēgis*, Bd. 4, 13; S. 581, 42: Cd. 128; Th. 163, 1; Gen. 2691: Ps. Th. 105, 30. He Rǽdwaldes feóndscipe fleáh *he fled from the enmity of Rædwald*, Bd. 3, 18; S. 545, 40, col. 2: Cd. 29; Th. 38, 21; Gen. 610: Exon. 122 a; Th. 468, 5; Phar. 3: Elen. Kmbl. 711; El. 356. Hí feóndscype rǽrdon *they raised enmity*, Exon. 66 a; Th. 243, 22; Jul. 14: Exon. 14 b; Th. 30, 28; Cri. 486. Fleónde Rǽdwaldes feóndscypas *inĭmīcĭtias Redualdi fŭgiens*, Bd. 3, 18; S. 545, 38, col. 1.

feónd-seóc; *adj.* *Fiend-sick, demoniac;* dæmŏnĭăcus :—Ðætte seó ylce eorþe mihte to hǽle feóndseócra manna and óðra untrumnyssa *ut ipsa terra ad ăbĭgendos ex obsessis corpŏrĭbus dæmŏnes grātiæ salutāris hăbēret effectum*, Bd. 3, 11; S. 535, 35.

feónd-seócnes, -ness, e; *f.* *Fiend-sickness, demonology;* dæmŏnĭăcus morbus, Som. Ben. Lye.

feóndulf? [feónd *a fiend*, ulf = wulf *a wolf?*] *A fiend, enemy, rascal, scoundrel;* furcĭfer :—Feóndulf *furcĭfer, furca dignus*, Glos. Prudent. Recd. 146, 82.

feóng, e; *f.* *Hatred;* ŏdium, Bd. 3, 11; S. 535, note 20. v. feóung.

feor; *adj.* *Perverse, depraved;* prāvus :—Mid feorum lífe *by a perverse life*, Bd. 5, 13; S. 633, note 33. v. þweor.

FEOR, feorr, fior; *comp.* fyrr, fyr, fier; *sup.* fyrrest; *adv.* I. FAR, *at a distance;* prŏcul, longe :—Ðá wǽron ðás wundru feor and wíde gemǽrsode and gecýðed *quĭbus pătĕfactis ac diffāmātis longe lāteque mīrācŭlis*, Bd. 3, 10; S. 535, 2: 3, 16; S. 542, 16. Hyra heorte is feor [feorr, Mt. Bos. 15, 8] fram me *cor eōrum longe est a me*, Mk. Bos. 7, 6: Bt. Met. Fox 24, 4; Met. 24, 2. Ðá gyt ðá he wæs feor his fæder, he hyne geseah *when he was yet far from his father, he saw him*, Lk. Bos. 15, 20. Nóht feor úrum mynstre *non longe a monastērio nostro*, Bd. 5, 4; S. 617, 5: Cd. 50; Th. 63, 28; Gen. 1039. Feor and neáh *far and near*, Exon. 13 b; Th. 24, 25; Cri. 390: Cd. 143; Th. 177, 27; Exod. 1: Beo. Th. 2447; B. 1221: Andr. Kmbl. 1276; An. 638. We witan heonan nóht feor óðer eálond *nōvĭmus insŭlam ălĭam esse non prŏcul a nostra*, Bd. 1, 1; S. 474, 15: Beo. Th. 3615; B. 1805. Feor ðú dydest cúþan míne fram me *longe fēcisti nōtos meos a me*, Ps. Lamb. 87, 9. Hit feor on óðre wísan wæs *it was far otherwise;* longe ălĭter ĕrat, Bd. 3, 14; S. 539, 44. II. *beyond, moreover;* ultra, porro :—Ge feor hafaþ fǽhþe gestǽled *and moreover she hath set up a deadly feud*, Beo. Th. 2684; B. 1340. [*Piers P. Chauc.* fer: *R. Glouc. Wyc.* fer, ferr: *Laym.* feor, fer, ueor, feorre: *Orm.* feorr: *Plat.* feere, fere *afar*: *O. Sax.* fer: *Frs.* fier: *O. Frs.* fir, fer: *Dut.* ver, verre: *Ger.* fern: *M. H. Ger.* vërre: *O. H. Ger.* fer: *Goth.* fairra: *Dan.* fiern: *Swed.* fjerran: *Icel.* fjarri *far off*: *Lat.* porro: *Grk.* πόρρω: *Sansk.* pra *forth, away*.] DER. un-feor.

feor, feorr; *comp. m.* fyrra, firra; *f. n.* fyrre, firre; *adj.* *Far, distant, remote;* longinquus, remōtus :—Feorres folclondes *of a far country*, Exon. 115 b; Th. 444, 14; Kl. 47. Hér is gefered ofer feorne weg æðelinga sum innan ceastre *here a noble is come from a long way off into the city*, Andr. Kmbl. 2348; An. 1175: 382; An. 191: 504; An. 252.

feora *of souls* or *beings*, Exon. 38 a; Th. 126, 7; Gú. 367: Cd. 161; Th. 202, 7; Exod. 384; *gen. pl. of* feorh.

feoran; *p.* feorude *To remove afar off;* elongāre :—Ic feorude *elongāvi*, Ps. Spl. C. 54, 7. v. feorran.

feor-búend, es; *m.* *One dwelling far off;* prŏcul habĭtātor :—Nú ge feorbúend, mínne gehýraþ ânfealdne geþoht *now ye far-dwellers, hear my simple thought*, Beo. Th. 514; B. 254.

feor-cumen; *part.* *Come from afar;* perĕgrīnus, perĕger ventus :—Feorcumen [MS. feorcuman] man *a far-come man, a foreigner*, L. In. 20; Th. i. 114, 15, note 30, MS. B.

feor-cund, feorr-cund; *adj.* *Come from afar;* perĕgrīnus :—Gif feorcund mon, oððe fremde, bútan wege geond wudu gonge, and ne hriéme ne horn bláwe, for þeóf he biþ to prófianne, oððe to sleánne oððe to aliésanne *if a far-come man, or a stranger, journey through a wood out of the highway, and neither shout nor blow his horn, he is to be held for a thief, either to be slain or redeemed*, L. In. 20; Th. i. 114, 15–116, 2.

feor-cýþ, -cýþþ, e; *f.* *A far country;* remōta terra :—Feorcýþþe beóþ sélran gesóhte *far countries are better* [*when*] *sought*, Beo. Th. 3681, note; B. 1838.

feord *an army, force, expedition*, Chr. 1066; Erl. 203, 11: 1140; Erl. 265, 8. v. fyrd.

feordian; *p.* ode; *pp.* od *To be at war;* bellum gĕrĕre :—Hí feordodan wið Ætlan Húna cininge *they were at war with Ætla king of the Huns*, Chr. 443; Erl. 11, 35. v. fyrdian.

feording *military service*, Chr. 675; Erl. 38, 2, note 6. v. fyrding.

feore *to, for* or *with life*, Exon. 39 a; Th. 128, 32: Beo. Th. 1161; B. 578; *dat. and inst. of* feorh.

feores *of life*, Exon. 30 b; Th. 95, 32; Cri. 1566; *gen. of* feorh.

feorg *life, soul, spirit*, Exon. 82 b; Th. 311, 19; Seef. 94: 104 a; Th. 394, 14; Rä. 14, 3. v. feorh.

feorg-bold, es; *n.* *The dwelling of life, the body;* ănĭmæ dŏmus, corpus :—Hrǽw cólode, fæger feorgbold *the corpse grew cold, the fair dwelling of life*, Rood Kmbl. 145; Kr. 73.

feorg-bona, an; *m.* *A life-destroyer;* vītæ interfector :—He him feorgbona weorþeþ *he becomes a life-destroyer to him*, Exon. 97 a; Th. 362, 24; Wal. 41. v. feorh-bana.

feorg-gedâl, es; *n.* *Life-separation, death;* vītæ divortium, mors :—Siððan líc and leomu and ðes lífes gǽst asundrien somwíst hyra þurh feorg-gedâl *when body and limbs and this life's spirit sunder their fellowship through death*, Exon. 50 a; Th. 172, 29; Gú. 1151. v. feorh-gedâl.

FEORH, feorg, fiorh, ferh, fyorh; *gen.* feores; *dat. inst.* feore; *pl. nom. acc.* feorh; *gen.* feora; *dat. inst.* feorum; *n. m.* I. *life, soul, spirit;* vīta, ănĭma :—Nǽniges mannes feorh to lore wearþ *no man's life was lost*, Bd. 4, 21; S. 590, 23: Beo. Th. 2425; B. 1210: Ps. Th. 106, 4. Nó wæs feorh æðelinges flǽsce bewunden *the prince's soul was not surrounded with flesh*, Beo. Th. 4839; B. 2424: Exon. 103 a; Th. 391, 9; Rä. 10, 2. Ðonne him ðæt feorg losaþ *when his life perishes*, 82 b; Th. 311, 19; Seef. 94. Ne biþ him feores wén *there will be no hope of his life*, L. M. 2, 51; Lchdm. ii. 264, 19: Bd. 5, 3; S. 616, 8: Bt. 14, 3; Fox 46, 27: Exon. 115 b; Th. 445, 4; Dóm. 2: Cd. 162; Th. 203, 15; Exod. 404. Feores aþolian *to endure life*, Exon. 27 a; Th. 81, 7; Cri. 1320. Feores berǽdan *to deprive of life*, Andr. Kmbl. 266; An. 133. Feores getwǽfan *to separate from life*, Beo. Th. 2871; B. 1433. Feores geunnan *to grant life*, L. Eth. ix. 1; Th. i. 340, 8: L. C. E. 2; Th. i. 358, 26: Andr. Kmbl. 358; An. 179. Feores ongildan *to give up* or *sacrifice one's life*, Andr. Kmbl. 2204; An. 1103. Feores onsæcan *to make an attempt against one's life*, Beo. Th. 3889; B. 1942. Feores onsécan *to bereave of life*, Exon. 75 b; Th. 283, 13; Jul. 679. Feores orwéna *hopeless of life*, Exon. 87 b; Th. 329, 27; Vy. 40: Andr. Kmbl. 2216; An. 1109. Feores récan *to care for life*, Byrht. Th. 139, 27; By. 260. Feores scyldig *guilty of life, liable in one's life*, L. Alf. pol. 4; Th. i. 64, 1: L. Ath. i. 4, 6; Th. i. 202, 3, 12: v. § 1, 4; Th. i. 230, 6: L. Eth. iii. 16; Th. i. 298, 14: v. 30; Th. i. 312, 6: vi. 37; Th. i. 324, 17: L. C. S. 58; Th. i. 408, 4. Feores þolian *to forfeit life*, L. C. S. 78; Th. i. 420, 10. Feores unnan *to grant life*, Exon. 68 b; Th. 254, 3; Jul. 191. Feores unwyrðe *unworthy of life*, 30 b; Th. 95, 27; Cri. 1563. Feores wyrðe *worthy of life*, L. Ath. iv. 4; Th. i. 224, 3. Ðæt man forgá þýfþe be his feore *that a man forego theft by his life*, L. Ath. i. 20; Th. i. 210, 3: Exon. 105 b; Th. 401, 28; Rä. 21, 18: Beo. Th. 3690; B. 1843: Ps. Th. 54, 24. Beorh ðínum feore *salva ănĭmam tuam*, Gen. 19, 17: Cd. 89; Th. 110, 14; Gen. 1838: Beo. Th. 2590; B. 1293: Byrht. Th. 137, 31; By. 194: Elen. Kmbl. 268; El. 134: Andr. Kmbl. 3075; An. 1540. Â to feore *for evermore*, Exon. 32 b; Th. 102, 25; Cri. 1678. Ǽfre to feore, Ps. Th. 118, 165: Exon. 111 a; Th. 425, 33; Rä. 41, 65. Âwa to feore, Ps. Th. 51, 8. Lange to feore, Ps. Th. 132, 4. Syððan to feore *in æternum*, 54, 22: 101, 25: 106, 8. To wídan feore *for ever*, Cd. 170; Th. 213, 5; Exod. 547: Exon. 11 a; Th. 15, 3; Cri. 230: Beo. Th. 1871; B. 933: Andr. Kmbl. 211; An. 106: Elen. Kmbl. 421; El. 211: Ps. Th. 71, 17. Hæbbe his feorh *let him have his life*, L. In. 5; Th. i. 104, 14: L. Ath. v. § 1, 4; Th. i. 230, 7: L. Edg. ii. 7; Th. i. 268, 24: L. C. S. 26; Th. i. 392, 3: Ors. 2, 5; Bos. 48, 23: Chr. 937; Erl. 114, 2; Æðelst. 36. Ymb cyninges feorh sierwian *to plot against the king's life*, L. Alf. pol. 4; Th. i. 62, 15. Ðú ðín feorh hafast *thou* *hast thy life*, Beo. Th. 3703; B. 1849: Cd. 116; Th. 151, 17; Gen. 2510: Andr. Kmbl. 1908; An. 956: Exon. 47 b; Th. 164, 10; Gû. 1009. Ðǽr he eardaþ ealne wîdan feorh *where he shall dwell for evermore*, 14 a; Th. 27, 31; Cri. 439. He mîn feorg freoðaþ *he will protect my life*, 36 a; Th. 116, 28; Gû. 214: Apstls. Kmbl. 116; Ap. 58. He sylfes feore beágas bohte *he has bought rings with his own life*, Beo. Th. 6019; B. 3013: Exon. 106 b; Th. 406, 9; Rä. 24, 14. Hî bǽdan hiora feorum fôddurgeafe *pĕtĕrent escas anĭmābus suis*, Ps. Th. 77, 20: Cd. 184; Th. 229, 32; Dan. 226: Beo. Th. 147; B. 73. Freónda feorum *with the lives of friends*, Beo. Th. 2616; B. 1306. II. *a living being, person*; hŏmo, persōna:—Ða yldestan Chus and Cham hâtene wǽron, fulfreólîce feorh, frumbearn Chames *the eldest were called Cush and Canaan, most liberal beings, Ham's firstborn*, Cd. 79; Th. 97, 25; Gen. 1618. Feónda feorh feóllon þicce *the bodies of the foes fell thickly*, 95; Th. 124, 19; Gen. 2065. Feora fæsl *offspring of the living*, 67; Th. 80, 17; Gen. 1330: 67; Th. 81, 9; Gen. 1342: 161; Th. 200, 23; Exod. 361: 161; Th. 202, 7; Exod. 384. Ðæt is sârlîc ðæt swâ fæger feorh sceolan âgan þýstra ealdor *it is grievous that the prince of darkness should own such beautiful beings*, Bd. 2, 1; S. 501, 15. [*O. Sax.* ferah, ferh, *n. life, soul*: *Ger.* ferch, *n. vīta, sanguis*: *M. H. Ger.* vërch, *n. life*: *O. H. Ger.* fërah, ferh, *n. ănĭma, vita*: *Goth.* fairhwus *world*: *Icel.* fjör, *n. life*.] DER. geógoþ-feorh, geóguþ-, wîde-.

feorh-âdl, e; *f. A mortal disease, fatal sickness*; fatālis morbus:—Biþ his feorhâdl getenge *his fatal sickness is near*, L. M. 3, 22; Lchdm. ii. 320, 20. Herodes lǽfde fîf suna, þrý he hêt acwellan on his feorhâdle, ǽrðan ðe he gewîte *Herod left five sons, three he commanded to be slain in his last illness, ere he departed*, Homl. Th. i. 478, 13.

feorh-bana, -bona, feorg-bona, an; *m. A life-destroyer, murderer*; vītæ interfector, hŏmĭcīda:—Ðû Abele wurde to feorhbanan *thou hast been for a life-destroyer to Abel*, Cd. 48; Th. 62, 26; Gen. 1020. Hî gesâwon feorhbanan fuglas slîtan *they saw birds tearing the murderers*, 96; Th. 125, 32; Gen. 2088. He ne meahte on ðam feorhbonan fǽhþe gebêtan *he might not avenge the feud on the murderer*, Beo. Th. 4921; B. 2465.

feorh-bealo, -bealu; *gen.* -bealowes, -bealuwes; *n. Life-bale, mortal affliction, deadly evil*; vītæ mălum, lētāle mălum:—Gûþdeáþ fornam, feorhbealo frêcne, fyra gehwylcne leóda mînra *war-death, a cruel life-bale, has taken every man of my people*, Beo. Th. 4492; B. 2250. Ic me ðæt feorhbealo feor aswâpe *I sweep that deadly evil far from me*, Exon. 106 b; Th. 405, 20; Rä. 24, 5: Beo. Th. 314; B. 156. Ðǽr wæs hondsció, feorhbealu fǽgum *there was [his] glove, deadly evil to the fated*, 4160; B. 2077: 5067; B. 2537.

feorh-ben, -benn, e; *f.* [ben *a wound*] *A life-wound, mortal wound*; lētāle vulnus:—Feorhbennum seóc *sick with mortal wounds*, Beo. Th. 5473; B. 2740.

feorh-berende; *part. Life-bearing, living*; vītam fĕrens, vivens:—Heó wile gesêcan ǽghwylcne feorhberendra *it will seek each of those bearing life*, Exon. 110 a; Th. 420, 19; Rä. 40, 6: Cd. 92; Th. 117, 17; Gen. 1955.

feorh-bold *the dwelling of life, the body*. v. feorg-bold.

feorh-bona *a life-destroyer, murderer*, Beo. Th. 4921; B. 2465. v. feorh-bana.

feorh-cwalu, ferh-cwalu, e; *f. Life-slaughter, death*; vītæ cædes, mors:—Æfter feorhcwale *after death*, Exon. 97 b; Th. 364, 27; Wal. 77. He sôhte hû he sârlîcast, þurh ða wyrrestan wîtu, meahte feorhcwale findan *he sought how he could invent a death most painfully, through the worst torments*, 74 a; Th. 276, 28; Jul. 573.

feorh-cwealm, es; *m. A mortal pang, death, slaughter*; mors, cædes:—Ne þearft ðû ðê ondrǽdan deáþes brôgan, feorhcwealm nû giet *thou needest not dread the pain of death, the mortal pang as yet*, Cd. 50; Th. 63, 26; Gen. 1038. Ðeáh him feónda hlôþ feorhcwealm bude *though the band of fiends threatened death to him*, Exon. 46 a; Th. 157, 6; Gû. 887. Mîn sceal golden wurþan feorhcwealm *my slaughter shall be requited*, Cd. 55; Th. 67, 19; Gen. 1103.

feorh-cyn, -cynn, es; *n. Living kind*; vīventium gĕnus:—Bealocwealm hafaþ fela feorhcynna forþ onsended *pernicious death has sent forth many living kinds*, Beo. Th. 4524; B. 2266: Exon. 89 a; Th. 334, 10; Gn. Ex. 14.

feorh-dæg, es; *pl. nom. acc.* -dagas; *gen.* -daga; *dat.* -dagum; *m. A life-day*; vītæ dies:—Ðæt Ismael feorhdaga on woruldrîce worn gebîde *that Ishmael may abide many life-days in the world*, Cd. 107; Th. 142, 8; Gen. 2358.

feorh-dolh, -dolg, es; *n. A life-wound, deadly wound*; lētāle vulnus:—Geseóþ nû ða feorhdolg ðe gefremedon ǽr on mînum folmum *see now the deadly wounds which they ere inflicted on my palms*, Exon. 29 a; Th. 89, 10; Cri. 1455.

feorh-eácen; *part. Endued with life, living*; vītâ auctus, vivens:—Feorheáceno cynn inc hýraþ eall *all races endued with life shall obey you two*, Cd. 10; Th. 13, 17; Gen. 204.

feorh-gebeorh; *gen.* -gebeorges; *n. Life's security, refuge*; vītæ servātio, refŭgium:—He gelǽdde ofer lagustreámas mâþmhorda mǽst on feorhgebeorh *he led the greatest of store-houses over the water-streams for refuge*, Cd. 161; Th. 201, 8; Exod. 369.

feorh-gedâl, feorg-gedâl, es; *n. Life-separation, death*; vītæ divortium, mors:—Sceal feorhgedâl æfter wyrþan *death must afterwards take place*, Andr. Kmbl. 362; An. 181: 2854; An. 1429: Exon. 50 a; Th. 174, 5; Gû. 1173.

feorh-gener, es; *n. Life-safety, salvation of life*; vītæ servātio:—Bûton se cyningc him feorhgeneres unne *unless the king grant him salvation of life*, L. Edg. ii. 7; Th. i. 268, 25.

feorh-geníþla, an; *m. A life-enemy, deadly foe*; qui vītæ insĭdiātur, lētālis hostis:—He brægd feorhgeníþlan, ðæt heó on flet gebeáh *he dragged the deadly foe, that she bowed on the place*, Beo. Th. 3084; B. 1540: 5859; B. 2933.

feorh-gifa, -giefa, an; *m. Giver of life*; vītæ dātor:—Me onsende sigedryhten mîn, folca feorhgiefa, gǽst hâligne *my glorious Lord, Giver of life to people, sent a holy spirit to me*, Exon. 50 b; Th. 176, 20; Gû. 1213. Gesêgon on heáhsetle heofones waldend, folca feorhgiefan *they saw on his throne heaven's Ruler, Giver of life to nations*, 15 b; Th. 35, 10; Cri. 556.

feorh-gifu, -giefu, e; *f. The gift of life*; vītæ dōnum:—Secgas feorhgiefe gefêgon *men rejoiced in the gift of life*, Exon. 94 a; Th. 353, 1; Reim. 6.

feorh-gôma, an; *m.* [gôma *the gums, jaws*] *Fatal* or *deadly jaws*; fatāles fauces:—Se deópa seáþ mid wîta fela, frêcnum feorhgômum, folcum scendeþ *the deep pit [hell] afflicts people with many torments, with rugged fatal jaws*, Exon. 30 b; Th. 94, 32; Cri. 1549.

feorh-hord, es; *n. Life's treasure, the soul, spirit*; vītæ thēsaurus, ănĭma:—Lîf biþ on sîþe, fǽges feorhhord *life is on its journey, the spirit of the fated*, Exon. 59 a; Th. 213, 7; Ph. 221. Hâd wereþ feorhhord feóndum *armour defends the soul from foes*, Wald. 100; Vald. 2, 22: Exon. 49 b; Th. 170, 26; Gû. 1117: Andr. Kmbl. 2365; An. 1184.

feorh-hûs, es; *n. Life's house, spirit's house, the body*; vītæ *vel* ănĭmæ dŏmus, corpus:—Gâr oft þurhwôd fǽges feorhhûs *the dart often pierced the body of the fated*, Byrht. Th. 140, 32; By. 297.

feorh-hyrde, es; *m. Life-guardian* or *protector*; vītæ custos *vel* protector:—He hine bæd ðæt he him feorhhyrde wǽre *he prayed that he would be his life-protector*, Bd. 2, 12; S. 513, 5: Hy. 9, 8; Hy. Grn. ii. 291, 8.

feorh-lâst, es; *m. A life-step, step taken to preserve one's life, flight*; vītæ vestigium, gressus vītæ servandæ causâ lātus, fŭga:—He onweg ðanon on nicera mere, fǽge and geflýmed, feorhlâstas bær *he bore his life-steps away thence to the monsters' mere, death-doomed and put to flight*, Beo. Th. 1697; B. 846.

feorh-leán, es; *n. Life's reward* or *gift*; vītæ præmium:—Woldon hie ðæt feorhleán fâcne gyldan *they would requite life's gift with fraud*, Cd. 149; Th. 187, 12; Exod. 150.

feorh-lege, es; *m.* [lege = leg, lagu *law*] *Life-law, fate, death*; vītæ lex, fātum, mors:—Ðæt on ðone hâlgan handa sendan to feorhlege fæderas usse *that our fathers lay their hands on the holy one unto death*, Elen. Kmbl. 913; El. 458. Ic on mâþma hord mînne bebohte feorhlege *I have bought my fate for treasures' hoard*, Beo. Th. 5592; B. 2800.

feorh-lîf, es; *n. Life*; vīta:—On ðînre gesihþe ne biþ sôþfæst ǽnig, ðe on ðisse foldan feorhlîf bereþ *non justĭfĭcābĭtur in conspectu tuo omnis vīvens*, Ps. Th. 142, 2.

feorh-loca, an; *m. Life's inclosure, the breast*; ănĭmæ claustrum, pectus:—Eom ic, in mînum feorhlocan, breóstum, inbryrded to ðam betran hâm *I am, in my life's inclosure, in my breast, impelled to the better home*, Exon. 42 a; Th. 141, 11; Gû. 625.

feorh-lyre, es; *m. Loss of life*; vītæ perdĭtio:—Gif feorhlyre wurþe *if there be loss of life*, L. E. B. 3; Th. ii. 240, 14.

feorh-ner, -nere, es; *n. Life's preservation* or *salvation, a refuge, sustenance, nourishment, food*; vītæ servātio, refŭgium, ălīmentum, cibus:—Monigfealde sind gôd ðe us dǽleþ to feorhnere Fæder ælmihtig *manifold are the goods which the Father almighty distributes to us for life's preservation*, Exon. 96 b; Th. 359, 33; Pa. 72: 16 b; Th. 38, 21; Cri. 610. Ðe worhte weoroda Dryhten to feorhnere fira cynne *which the Lord of hosts wrought for salvation to the race of men*, Elen. Kmbl. 1792; El. 898: Cd. 190; Th. 237, 18; Dan. 339. Hî nô ðonan lǽtaþ on gefeán faran to feorhnere *they will not let them go thence in joy to a refuge*, Exon. 31 a; Th. 97, 28; Cri. 1597. Fuglas heora feorhnere on ðæs beámes blêdum nâme [= nâmon] *birds took their refuge on the tree's branches*, Cd. 200; Th. 248, 3; Dan. 507. Hwîlum him to honda, hungre geþreátad, fleág fugla cyn, ðǽr hý feorhnere fundon *sometimes the race of birds, forced by hunger, flew to his hands, where they found sustenance*, Exon. 46 a; Th. 157, 10; Gû. 889. Beóþ Godes streámas gôde wætere fæste gefylde, ðanan feorhnere findaþ foldbûend *flūmen Dei replētum est ăqua, părasti cĭbum illōrum*, Ps. Th. 64, 10.

feorh-rǽd, es; *m. Life-benefit, an action tending to the soul's benefit*; id quod vītæ prodest, actio ad ănĭmæ sălūtem tendens:—Ðæt hie feorhrǽd fremedon *that they should do what would benefit their souls*, Andr. Kmbl. 3306; An. 1656.

feorh-scyldig; *adj. Life-guilty, liable in one's life;* vītæ reus, morte dignus:—Gif feorhscyldig man cyning gesōhte *if a man who had forfeited his life sought the king,* L. Eth. vii. 4; Th. i. 330, 10. Se ðe ofslehþ man binnan ciricwagum, he biþ feorhscyldig *he who slays a man within church-walls, he is liable in his life,* vii. 13, 15; Th. i. 332, 8, 14.

feorh-seóc; *adj. Life-sick, mortally wounded;* letālĭter vulnĕrātus:—Scolde Grendel ðonan feorhseóc fleón *Grendel must flee thence mortally wounded,* Beo. Th. 1644; B. 820.

feorh-sweng, es; *m. A life-blow, deadly blow;* lētālis ictus:—Hond feorhsweng ne ofteah *his hand withdrew not the deadly blow,* Beo. Th. 4972; B. 2489.

feorh-þearf, e; *f. Distress of life, urgent need;* vītæ necessĭtas:—Drihten me hraðe gefultuma æt feorhþearfe *Dŏmĭne ad adjŭvandum me festīna,* Ps. Th. 69, 1.

feorh-wund, e; *f. A life-wound, mortal wound;* lētāle vulnus:—He ðǽr feorhwunde hleát *he sank there with a mortal wound,* Beo. Th. 4760; B. 2385.

feorlen; *adj. Far off, distant, remote;* longinquus:—Se gingra sunu ferde wræclīce on feorlen rīce *adolescentior fīlius pĕregre profectus est in rĕgiōnem longinquam,* Lk. Bos. 15, 13. v. fyrlen.

feor-lond, es; *n. A far country, distant land;* remōta terra:—Feorlondum on *in distant lands,* Exon. 95 b; Th. 356, 12; Pa. 10.

FEORM, fiorm, fyrm, e; *f.* I. *food, provision, goods, substance;* victus, substantia, bŏna:—Nō ðū ymb mīnes ne þearft līces feorme leng sorgian *thou needest not longer care about my body's food,* Beo. Th. 906; B. 451. Hī bærndon and awēston ðæs cynges feorme hāmas [MS. hames] *they burnt and laid waste the king's provision-homes* [or *farms*], Chr. 1087; Erl. 224, 13. Twegra daga feorme *provision for two days;* firmam duōrum diērum, Th. Diplm. A. D. 950; 501, 23; 504, 14: Chr. 777; Erl. 55, 10. Gewāt him mid cnósle, ofer Caldēa folc feran mid feorme, fæder Abrahames *the father of Abraham departed with his family, with his goods, to travel over the Chaldeans' nation,* Cd. 83; Th. 104, 6; Gen. 1731: 126; Th. 161, 2; Gen. 2659. Gewiton him eástan ǽhta lǽdan, feoh and feorme *they departed from the east leading their possessions, cattle and substance,* Cd. 80; Th. 99, 22; Gen. 1650. II. *an entertaining, entertainment, feast;* hospĭtālĭtas, convīvium, cœna:—Gif mon cierliscne monnan fliéman feorme teó *if a man accuse a churlish man of the entertaining of a fugitive,* L. In. 30; Th. i. 120, 16. Ān dǽl bisceope and his hīrēde for feorme and onfangenysse gesta and cumena *ūna portio episcŏpo et fămĭliæ propter hospĭtālĭtātem atque susceptiōnem,* Bd. 1, 27; S. 489, 7. Ðætte ælþeódige bisceopas sȳn þoncfulle heora gæstlīþnesse and feorme *ut episcŏpi peregrini contenti sint hospĭtālĭtātis mūnĕre oblāto,* 4, 5; S. 573, 3. To ðære ēcan feorme *to the eternal feast,* Homl. Th. ii. 372, 5. He gegearwode mycele feorme *magnam cœnam fēcit,* Mk. Bos. 6, 21: Lk. Bos. 14, 12, 16: Homl. Th. ii. 370, 31: 372, 1, 3. III. *a place where provisions are kept, provision-quarters of an army;* victus stătio:—Se here eódan him to heora gearwan feorme ūt þuruh Hamtūnscīre into Bearrucscīre to Reádingon *the army went to their ready provision-quarters out through Hampshire into Berkshire to Reading,* Chr. 1006; Th. 256, 20-22, col. 1. IV. *use, benefit, profit, enjoyment;* ūsus, fructus:—Ða swīðe lytle feorme [fiorme MS. Hat.] ðara bōca wiston, forðæmðe hie heora nān wuht ongietan ne meahton *they got very little benefit from the books, because they could not understand anything of them,* Past. pref; Cot. MS. [*Chauc.* farme *meal: Laym.* feorme, veorme *feast.*] DER. bēn-feorm, bend-, cyning-, eáster-, eástor-, gyt-, swīþ-, winter-: orfeorme.

feorma; *adj. First;* prīmus:—Ða feorman men *the first men,* Exon. 73 a; Th. 272, 15; Jul. 499. v. forma.

feormend-leás; *adj. Wanting a polisher;* pŏlītōre cărens:—Geseah he orcas stondan, fyrnmanna fatu, feormendleáse, ðǽr wæs helm monig eald and ōmig *he saw bowls standing, vessels of men of yore, wanting a polisher, there was many a helmet, old and rusty,* Beo. Th. 5516, note; B. 2761. v. feormynd.

feormere, es; *m. One who supplies with food, a purveyor,* FARMER; obsōnātor:—Se ðe mā manna [MS. manne] inlǽde ðonne he sceole, būton ðæs stīwerdes leáfe and ðæra feormera, gylde his ingang *he who introduces more men than he should, without leave of the steward and of the purveyors, let him forfeit his admission,* Cod. Dipl. 942; Kmbl. iv. 278, 19-21.

feorm-fultum, es; *m. Food-support, purveyance;* victus auxĭlium, commeātus, prōcūrātio:—Ðæt him nān man ne þearf to feormfultume nān þingc syllan, būtan he sylf wille *that no man need give him anything as purveyance, unless he himself be willing,* L. C. S. 70; Th. i. 412, 22.

feormian; *part.* feormende; *p.* ode, ade; *pp.* od; *v. a.* [feorm *food*]. I. *to supply with food, feed, support, sustain, entertain, receive as a guest, cherish, benefit, profit;* victum suppĕditāre, epŭlāre, suscĭpĕre, suscĭpĕre hospĭtio, fŏvēre, cūrāre, vălēre:—Ðæt ic [cyning] bebeóde eallum mīnan gerēfan ðæt hī on mīnan āgenan rihtlīce tilian, and me mid ðam feormian; and ðæt him nān man ne þearf to feormfultume nān þingc syllan, būtan he sylf wille *that I* [*the king*] *command all my reeves that they justly provide on my own, and feed* [*supply with food, maintain*] *me therewith; and that no man need give them anything as purveyance* [*food-support*], *unless he himself be willing,* L. C. S. 70; Th. i. 412, 22. Feorma, mihtig Dryhten, mīnre sāwle *mighty Lord, sustain my soul,* Exon. 118 b; Th. 454, 33; Hy. 4, 42. Āh he feormendra lyt lifgendra *he has few of entertainers living,* Exon. 87 b; Th. 329, 7; Vy. 30. Ðæt se, ðe hine feormode, and se, ðe gefeormod wæs, sȳn hī begen bisceopes dōme scyldig *that he, who entertained him, and he, who was entertained, be both guilty to the bishop's doom,* Bd. 4, 5; S. 572, 44. Feorma mec hwæðre, ðeáh ðe ic fremede mā gylta *yet cherish me, though I have committed more crimes,* Exon. 118 a; Th. 453, 36; Hy. 4, 25. Feorma ðū in ðīnum ferþe gōd *cherish thou good in thy soul,* Exon. 80 b; Th. 303, 10; Fä. 51: Ps. Th. 77, 69. Forðon hī ongeáton ðætte seó hālwende onsægedness to ēcre alȳsnesse swīþrade and feormade ge līchoman and sāwle *for they understood that the wholesome sacrifice availed and profited* [vălēret] *to the eternal redemption both of body and of soul,* Bd. 4, 22; Whel. 318, 25-27. II. *to feed on, devour, consume;* vesci, comĕdĕre, consūmĕre:—Fealo līg feormaþ and Fēnix byrneþ *the yellow flame consumes and burns up the Phœnix,* Exon. 59 a; Th. 213, 1; Ph. 218. III. *to cleanse,* FARM or *cleanse out;* mundāre, purgāre, expiāre:—He feormaþ his bernes flōre *he will cleanse the floor of his barn,* Lk. Bos. 3, 17; purgābit āream suam, Vulg. He feormaþ ǽlc ðara, ðe blǽda byrþ, ðæt hyt bere blǽda ðe swīðor *omnem, qui fert fructum, purgābit eum, ut fructum plus affĕrat,* Jn. Bos. 15, 2. Seofon dagas ðū feormast ðæt weofod, Ex. 29, 37; *seuen daies thow shalt clense the auter,* Wyc; septem diēbus expiābis altāre, Vulg. DER. a-feormian, ge-.

feorm-riht, es; *n. Right in an estate;* in prædio jus, Heming, p. 50, Mann.

feormþ, e; *f. A harbouring, an entertaining, a cleansing;* susceptio, hospĭtium. purgātio. v. fyrmþ.

feormung, e; *f.* I. *a harbouring, an entertaining;* susceptio, hospĭtium:—Þurh wreccena feormunge *by the harbouring of exiles,* L. Alf. pol. 4; Th. i. 62, 16. II. *a cleansing, polishing;* purgātio, pŏlītio:—Gif sweordhwīta ōðres monnes wǽpn to feormunge onfō *if a sword-polisher receive another man's weapon for polishing,* L. Alf. pol. 19; Th. i. 74, 9. DER. a-feormung, niht-.

feormynd [= feormend], es; *m.* [feormian III. *to cleanse*] *A cleanser, furbisher, polisher;* purgātor, pŏlītor:—Feormynd swefaþ, ða ðe beadogrīmman bȳwan sceoldon *the polishers are dead, who should prepare the war-helmet,* Beo. Th. 4505, note; B. 2256.

feornes, -nys, -ness, -nyss, e; *f.* FARNESS, *distance;* longinquĭtas:—Gif mycel feornys sīþfætes betwihligeþ *si longinquĭtas itĭnĕris magna interjăcet,* Bd. 1, 27; S. 491, 39.

feorr; *adj. Far, distant;* longinquus:—Ðeáh him mon feorr land gehēte *though a distant land was promised him,* Past. 50; Hat. MS: Andr. Recd. 850; An. 423. v. feor; *adj. far.*

feorr; *adv. Far, at a distance;* prŏcul, longe:—Hyra heorte is feorr fram me *cor eōrum longe est a me,* Mt. Bos. 15, 8. Hī feorr ætstōdon *de longe stĕtĕrunt,* Ps. Spl. 37, 12. Seó sunne gǽþ eall swā feorr adūne on nihtlīcre tīde under ðære eorþan swā heó on dæg bufan up astīhþ *the sun goes quite as far down under the earth in the night time as it rises above it in the day,* Bd. de nat. rerum; Wrt. popl. science 2, 22; Lchdm. iii. 234, 20. v. feor; *adv.*

feorran, feorrane, feorren; *adv. Afar, far off, at a distance, from far;* a longe, prŏcul, longe, e longinquo:—Ðǽr wǽron manega wīf feorran *ĕrant ĭbi mŭlĭĕres multæ a longe,* Mt. Bos. 27, 55: Mk. Bos. 5, 6. Folgiaþ feorran ðære hālgan earce *follow at a distance from the holy ark,* Jos. 3, 3. Swīðe feorran ymbūton *very far about,* Bt. 39, 5; Fox 218, 11. Ic eom hider feorran gefered *I have journeyed hither from far,* Cd. 25; Th. 32, 4; Gen. 498: Beo. Th. 728; B. 361: Andr. Kmbl. 48; An. 24: Elen. Kmbl. 1982; El. 993: Rood Kmbl. 114; Kr. 57: Salm. Kmbl. 357; Sal. 178: Exon. 103 a; Th. 389, 15; Rä. 7, 8: Boutr. Scrd. 17, 11. Feorran and neán *from far and near,* Beo. Th. 1683; B. 839: Exon. 60 b; Th. 220, 26; Ph. 326: Cd. 50; Th. 64, 8; Gen. 1047. Petrus hym fyligde feorrane *Petrus sequēbātur eum a longe,* Mt. Bos. 26, 58. Feorren, Cd. 89; Th. 110, 10; Gen. 1836.

feorran; *p.* de; *pp.* ed *To remove to a distance, withdraw;* remŏvēre, elongāre:—Ne wolde feorhbealo feorran *he would not withdraw the mortal bale,* Beo. Th. 314; B. 156. DER. a-feorran, of-.

feorran-cund; *adj. Having a distant origin, coming from afar;* e longinquo ortus:—Sōna him seleþegn, sīþes wērgum, feorrancundum forþ wīsade *forthwith the hall-thane guided him forth, weary from his journey, coming from afar,* Beo. Th. 3594, note; B. 1795. v. feor-cund.

feorren; *adv. From far;* e longinquo:—Uncer twega feorren cumenra *of us two come from far,* Cd. 89; Th. 110, 10; Gen. 1836. v. feorran; *adv.*

feorsian, fyrsian; *p.* ode; *pp.* od *To go beyond, remove;* ultĕrius procēdĕre, elongāre:—Ðū meaht feorsian *thou mayest go beyond,* Bt. Met. Fox 24, 52; Met. 24, 26. DER. a-feorsian, -fyrsian, afor-feorsian.

feor-studu, e; *f. A slanting post?* obstĭpum, Som. Ben. Lye:—Feorstuðu *obstupum?* Wrt. Voc. 290, 11.

feorþ, es; *n. The soul, spirit, life;* anĭma, vīta:—Feorþ biþ on sīþe *his soul shall be on its journey*, Exon. 87 b; Th. 328, 32; Vy. 26. v. ferþ.

feórþa, feówerþa; seó, ðæt feórþe, feówerþe; *adj. The* FOURTH; quartus:—Wæs gewórden ǽfen and mergen se feórþa dæg *the evening and morning were the fourth day*, Gen. 1, 19. Seó feórþe eá ys gehâten Eufrates *flŭvius quartus ipse est Euphrātes*, 2, 14. Hér bóc Boëties onginþ seó feórþe *here begins the fourth book of Boethius*, Bt. 35, 6; Fox 170, 24: 40, 4; Fox 240, 9. Ðæt feórþe cyn *the fourth tribe*, Cd. 158; Th. 197, 20; Exod. 310. Feórþan dǽles rîca *a ruler of a fourth part, tetrarch*; tetrarcha, Lk. Bos. 3, 1. On ðære feórþan mǽgþe *generātiōne quarta*, Gen. 15, 16. Com se Hǽlend embe ðone feórþan hancrēd to him *Iēsus quarta vĭgĭlia noctis vēnit ad eos*, Mt. Bos. 14, 25. Ða folctogan feórþan síðe æðeling lǽddon to ðam carcerne *the leaders of the people led the noble to the dungeon the fourth time*, Andr. Kmbl. 2915; An. 1460.

feórþes fôt *four-footed*; quadrŭpes:—Feórþes fôt neát *a four-footed beast*; bestia quadrŭpes, Som. Ben. Lye.

feórþling, es; *m*: feórþung, e; *f*. *in Anglo-Saxon*; but *m. in Northumb.* v. *last example. A fourth part of a thing*, FARTHING; quadrans:—Ðes feórþling oððe feórþa [MS. feórþan] dǽl þinges *hic quadrans*, Ælfc. Gr. 9, 37; Som. 12, 35. Ǽr ðû agylde ðone ŷtemestan feórþling [MS. feórþlingc] *dōnec reddas nŏvissĭmum quadrantem*, Mt. Bos. 5, 26: Lk. Bos. 12, 59. Geseah he sume earme wudewan bringan twegen feórþlingas *vīdit quandam vĭduam paupercŭlam mittentem æra mĭnūta duo*, Lk. Bos. 21, 2: Mk. Bos. 12, 42. Twegen [MS. tuoge] stycas, ðæt is feórþung penninges *duo mĭnūta, quod est quadrans*, Mk. Skt. Lind. 12, 42. Feórþungas, *acc. pl.* Lk. Skt. Lind. Rush. 21, 2.

feórþ-rîce, es; *n. Dominion over a fourth part*; tetrarchia = τετραρχία, Som. Ben. Lye.

feórþung, e; *f*: *but in Northumb. m. A fourth part, a farthing*, Mk. Skt. Lind. Rush. 12, 42. v. feórþling.

feorting, e; *f*. *Crĕpĭtus ventris*:—Feorting *pēdātio*, Ælfc. Gl. 79; Som. 72, 64; Wrt. Voc. 46, 22.

feor-weg, es; *m. A far* or *long way*; via longinqua:—Mîn bigengea ȝewât bryce on feorweg *incŏlātus meus prolongātus est*, Ps. Th. 119, 5: Exon. 36 a; Th. 117, 22; Gû. 228. Drihten asent þeóda ofer eów of feorwegum *addūcet Dŏmĭnus sŭper te gentem de longinquo*, Deut. 28, 49: Beo. Th. 73; B. 37: Ps. Th. 67, 26. On feorwegas *in distant ways*, Andr. Kmbl. 1855; An. 930: Exon. 87 b; Th. 329, 1.

feorwit-georn; *adj. Curious, inquisitive*; cūriōsus, Som. Ben. Lye. v. firwet-georn.

feorwit-geornes, -ness, e; *f. Curiosity*; cūriōsĭtas, Som. Ben. Lye. v. firwet-geornes.

feós *of cattle, money*, or *wealth*, Ors. 2, 4; Bos. 43, 15: Chr. 999; Erl. 134, 36: Bt. 14, 2; Fox 44, 22; *gen. of* feoh.

feostnode *confirmed*, Chr. 656; Erl. 32, 22: 963; Erl. 121, 32, = fæstnode; *p. of* fæstnian.

feoter, feotur; *gen.* feotre, feoture; *f. A fetter*; compes:—Mid feotrum [Rush. feoturum] *compĕdĭbus*, Mk. Skt. Lind. 5, 4. v. feter.

feóþ *shall hate*, Cd. 43; Th. 56, 13; Gen. 911. v. feón.

feoðer-scête *four-cornered, square*; quadrangŭlus, quadrātus, Som. Ben. Lye. v. feówer-scŷte.

feotod, feotud *called for, fetched*; arcessītus, Som. Ben. Lye, = fetod; *pp. of* fetian.

feóung, fióung, feóng, e; *f. Hatred, enmity*; ŏdium, inĭmīcĭtia:—His unriht and his feóung wurþ ðeáh swíðe open *invēnīret inīquĭtātem suam et ŏdium*, Ps. Th. 35, 2. Hî me settan feóunge for mînre lufan *pŏsuērunt ŏdium pro dilectiōne mea*, 108, 4. Hî ealdum feóungum [feóngum MS. B.] hine êhton *vĕtĕrānis eum ŏdiis insĕquēbantur*, Bd. 3, 11; S. 535, 20. v. feógan, feón *to hate*.

FEÓWER, feówere; *nom. acc; gen.* feówera, feówra; *dat.* feówerum: *Sometimes used indecl.* FOUR; quătuor:—Wurdon feówer cyninges þegnas ofslægene *four king's thanes were slain*, Chr. 896; Erl. 94, 4: Cd. 75; Th. 93, 16; Gen. 1546: Ælfc. T. 25, 19, 20. Feówer síðon *four times*; quăter, Ælfc. Gr. 38; Som. 40, 67. Felamôdigra feówer scoldon geferian to ðæm goldsele Grendles heáfod *four of those much daring ones must convey Grendel's head to the gold-hall*, Beo. Th. 3279; B. 1637. Hwæt beóþ ða feówere fǽges râpas *what are the four ropes of the doomed man?* Salm. Kmbl. 663; Sal. 331: 667; Sal. 333. Þrittig wæs and feówere feores onsôhte wîgena cynnes *there were thirty-four of the race of men bereft of life*, Exon. 75 b; Th. 283, 12; Jul. 679. Feówra sum *one of four*, L. Wih. 19; Th. i. 40, 17: 21; Th. i. 40, 21. Of ðisum feówer bôcum *of these four books*, Ælfc. T. 27, 17. From feówerum foldan sceátum *from the four corners of the world*, Exon. 20 b; Th. 55, 5; Cri. 879: Menol. Fox 419; Men. 211. Embe feówer wucan *after four weeks*, 30; Men. 15: 313; Men. 158. Ic sette feówer bêc *I composed four books*, Bd. 5, 24; S. 647, 37. Sylle feówer scêp for ân *restĭtuet quătuor ŏves pro ūna ŏve*, Ex. 22, 1: Jn. Bos. 19, 23. Seó hæfde feówere fêt under wombe *it had four feet under its belly*, Exon. 109 b; Th. 418, 10; Rä. 37, 3. [*Wyc.* foure: *Laym.* feour, feouwer, feowere, feor, fower, four: *Orm.* fowwerr, fowwre: *Plat.* veer: *O. Sax.* fiwar, fiuwar, fior: *Frs.* fjouver: *O. Frs.* fiuwer, fior: *Dut. Ger. M. H. Ger.* vier: *O. H. Ger.* fior: *Goth.* fidwor: *Dan.* fire: *Swed.* fyre: *Icel.* fjórir: *Lat.* quătuor: *Grk.* τέσσαρες; *Æolic* πίσυρες: *Wel.* pedwar: *Lith.* keturì: *Sansk.* ćatur, ćatvāras.]

feówera; *gen. pl. of* feówer *four*: = feáwera; *gen. pl. of* feáwa *a few*.

feówer-feald; *adj.* FOURFOLD; quadruplus:—Gif ic ǽnigne bereáfode, ic hit be feówerfealdum agyfe *si quid ălĭquem defraudāvi, reddo quadruplum*, Lk. Bos. 19, 8.

feówer-fealdan *to make fourfold*; quadruplĭcāre, Som. Ben. Lye.

feówer-fête, fiówer-fête, fiér-fête, fiðer-fête, fyðer-fête, -fôte, -fôtte; *adj. Four-footed*; quadrŭpes:—Se ælmihtiga God eallum mancinne forgeaf ða feówerfêtan deór *the almighty God gave to all mankind the four-footed beasts*, Ælfc. T. 8, 26. Ǽlces cynnes feówerfêtes feós ân *one of each kind of four-footed cattle*, Ors. 2, 4; Bos. 43, 15. Hî sceoldon [MS. sceoldan] bringan feówerfêtes twâ hwîte *of four-footed* [*cattle*] *they must bring two white*, 2, 4; Bos. 43, 8. Eádbyrht bisceop, feówerfôttra nŷtena ðone têðan dǽl, to þearfum syllan wolde *bishop Eadbert would give the tenth part of his four-footed cattle to the poor*, Bd. 4, 29; S. 608, 17. v. flox-fôte, feówer-scŷte.

feówer-gild, es; *n. A fourfold payment* or *compensation*; quadruplex compensātio:—Ǽlc tîhtbŷsig man gilde feówergilde *let every man of bad repute pay with fourfold compensation*, L. Eth. iii. 3; Th. i. 294, 10.

feówer-scŷte, fyðer-scŷte, fiðer-scŷte, -scîte, feðer-scîte, -sciȝte, -scette; *adj.* [sceát *a corner*] *Four-cornered, quadrangular, square*; quadrangŭlus, quadrātus:—Seó burh is feówerscŷte *the city is quadrangular*, Ors. 2, 4; Bos. 44, 21.

feówertene *fourteen*, Mt. Kmbl. Rush. 1, 17. v. feówertyne.

feówerteóða, *m*; seó, ðæt, feówerteóðe, *f. n*; *adj. The fourteenth*; quartus dĕcĭmus:—Se wæs feówerteóða fram Agusto ðam Câsere *who was the fourteenth from Augustus Cæsar*, Bd. 1, 4; S. 475, 27. Ðæs feówerteóðan dæges *of the fourteenth day*, Ex. 12, 18. On ðam feówerteóðan dæge *quarta dĕcĭma die*, Lev. 23, 5: Jos. 5, 10. Healdaþ ðæt ôþ ðone feówerteóðan dæg ðæs mônþes *servābĭtur usque ad quartam dĕcĭmam diem mensis hujus*, Ex. 12, 6.

feówerþa; seó, ðæt feówerþe; *adj. The fourth*; quartus:—Is feówerþe lyft *the fourth is air*, Bt. Met. Fox 20, 122; Met. 20, 61. v. feórþa.

feówerþa-fæder [MS. feówerþe-fæder]; *indecl. in sing. A great-great-grandfather*; ăbăvus, Ælfc. Gl. 91; Som. 75, 12; Wrt. Voc. 51, 57.

feówerþe-môder; *indecl. in sing*; but *dat. sing.* -mêder; *pl. nom. acc.* -môdra; *gen.* -môdra; *dat.* -môdrum; *f. A great-great-grandmother*; ăbăvia, Ælfc. Gl. 91; Som. 75, 13; Wrt. Voc. 51, 58.

feówertig; *gen.* feówertigra; *dat.* feówertigum, feówertig; *adj.* FORTY; quadrāginta:—Ne ofsleah ic hîg, gif ðǽr beóþ feówertig *non percŭtiam propter quadrāginta*, Gen. 18, 29. Æfter ðæra feówertigra daga getele *after the number of forty days*, Num. 14, 34. On feówertigum geárum *quadrāginta annis*, 14, 34: Jn. Bos. 2, 20. Hie begêton feówertig bearna *they begat forty* [*of*] *children*, Cd. 223; Th. 294, 22; Sat. 475: 228; Th. 306, 21; Sat. 667. Israhêla bearn ǽton heofonlîcne mete feówertig wintra *fīlii Israel comēdērunt Manna*; *n.* [μάννα; *n*; אֶת־הַמָּן] *quadrāginta annis*, Ex. 16, 34: Gen. 32, 15: 50, 3. Feówertig [feówertigum MS. B.] scillingum gebête *let him make amends with forty shillings*, L. Alf. pol. 10; Th. i. 68, 11.

feówertigeða, feówertigoða; *m*: -tigoðe, *f. n*; *adj. Fortieth*; quadrāgēsĭmus:—Feówertigeða *quadrāgēsĭmus*, C. R. Ben. 25. On ðam feówertigôðan [MS. feówerteóðan] geáre *in the fortieth year*; quadrāgēsĭmo anno, Deut. 1, 3.

feówertig-feald; *adj. Fortyfold*; quadrāgēnārius, Ælfc. Gr. 49; Som. 50, 19.

feówertig-lîc; *adj. Of* or *belonging to forty*; quadragēnārius:—He bebeád ðæt feówertiglîce fæsten healden beón *jejūnium quadrāginta diērum observāri præcēpit*, Bd. 3, 8; S. 531, 10. Ealle tîd ðæs feówertiglîcan fæstenes *tōtum quadrāgēsĭmæ tempus*, 3, 23; S. 554, 31.

feówertyne; *adj.* FOURTEEN; quătuordĕcim:—Feówertyne cneóressa *gĕnĕrātiōnes quătuordĕcim*, Mt. Bos. 1, 17. Cômon feówertyne Geáta gongan *fourteen Goths came marching*, Beo. Th. 3287; B. 1641: Andr. Kmbl. 3185; An. 1595. Ôþ-ðæt feówertyne niht ofer Eástron *until fourteen nights after Easter*, L. In. 55; Th. i. 138, 8, MS. B. Rachel acende feówertyne suna *Rachel bore fourteen sons*, Gen. 46, 22.

feówra *of four*, L. Wih. 19; Th. i. 40, 17, = feówera; *gen. pl. of* feówer.

feówrþa, *m*; seó, ðæt feówrþe; *adj. The fourth*; quartus:—Feowrþe is fŷr *the fourth is fire*, Bt. 33, 4; Fox 128, 30. v. feórþa.

feówrtig; *adj. Forty*; quadrāginta:—Ceorliscum men feówrtigum scillingum gebête *cŏlōni quadrāginta sŏlĭdis emendet*, L. Alf. pol. 10; Wilk. 37, 23. v. feówertig.

feowung, e; *f*. [feohan *to rejoice*] *A rejoicing, an enjoying, glorying*; gaudium, glōria, Hpt. Gl. 433; Leo A. Sax. Gl. 95, 10.

feówurtig; *adj. Forty*; quadraginta:—Ðâ ðâ he fæste feówurtig dagâ and feowurtig nihta *cum jejūnasset quadraginta diēbus et quadraginta noctĭbus*, Mt. Bos. 4, 2. v. feówertig.

fer, es; *n*. I. *a going, journey*; ĭter:—Wið fere *juxta ĭter*, Ps. Spl. M. 139, 6. II. *a vessel, ship*; nāvis:—Wæs se sunu

Lamehes of fere acumen *the son of Lamech was come from the vessel* [=*ark*], Cd. 75; Th. 93, 12; Gen. 1544. v. fær; *n.*

fēr, es; *m. A fever;* febris:—Wið ǽlces dæges fēre *for an every day's fever*, L. M. cont. 1, 62; Lchdm. ii. 12, 28. v. fǽr, fefer.

fēr, es; *m. Fear, terror;* tĭmor:—Mid fēre foldbūende se micla dæg meahtan Dryhtnes bihlǽmeþ *the great day of the mighty Lord shall strike earth's inhabitants with fear*, Exon. 20 b; Th. 54, 13; Cri. 868. v. fǽr; *m.*

fera, an; *m. A companion;* sŏcius, Som. Ben. Lye. v. ge-fera.

feran, to ferenne; *part.* ferende; *p.* ferde, *pl.* ferdon; *pp.* fered [fer *a journey*] *To go, make a journey, set out, travel, march, sail;* īre, ĭter făcĕre, proficisci, transire, migrāre, nāvĭgāre:—He hine to cyninge feran hēt *he called him to go to the king*, Bd. 3, 23; S. 554, 39: Cd. 109; Th. 144, 32; Gen. 2398: Exon. 28 b; Th. 86, 31; Cri. 1416: Beo. Th. 53; B. 27: Andr. Kmbl. 347; An. 174: Elen. Kmbl. 429; El. 215; Ps. Th. 118, 3: Bt. Met. Fox 4, 35; Met. 4, 18: Judth. 9; Thw. 21, 10; Jud. 12: Byrht. Th. 132, 64; By. 41. Ðā hī swā mycelne sīþfæt feran sceoldan *when they must go so great a journey*, Bd. 3, 15; S. 541, 30; 1, 23; S. 485, 38. He on morne feran wolde *he wished to set out in the morning*, Bd. 2, 6; S. 508, 7. Ic wegas ðīne þence to ferenne fōtum mīnum *I think to go thy ways with my feet*, Ps. Th. 118, 59. Folc ferende *travelling people*, Cd. 80; Th. 99, 28; Gen. 1653: Exon. 103 a; Th. 390, 12; Rä. 8, 9: Ps. Th. 125, 5. Ic fere geond foldan *I travel over the earth*, Exon. 101 a; Th. 381, 2; Rä. 2, 5: Ps. Th. 140, 12. Ðū mid mildse mīnre ferest *thou goest with my grace*, Andr. Kmbl. 3345; An. 1676. Mon fereþ feor *a man goes far*, Exon. 91 a; Th. 342, 20; Gn. Ex. 146; Salm. Kmbl. 614; Sal. 306: Menol. Fox 327; Men. 165. Āc fereþ gelōme ofer ganotes bæþ *a ship* [lit. *oak*] *often saileth over the sea* [lit. *sea-fowl's bath*], Runic pm. 25; Kmbl. 344, 18; Hick. Thes. i. 135, 49. Ða ðe heonon feraþ *those who go hence*, Cd. 228; Th. 305, 29; Sat. 654: Exon. 102 a; Th. 385, 14; Rä. 4, 44. Ic ferde to foldan ufan from ēþle *I went to earth from the realm above*, Cd. 224; Th. 295, 30; Sat. 495: Ps. Th. 142, 11. Mid Gode Noe ferde *Noe cum Deo ambŭlāvit*, Gen. 6, 9: Andr. Kmbl. 1323; An. 662: Exon. 42 b; Th. 143, 18; Gū. 663. Ferde his hlīsa to Galilea rīce *prōcessit rūmor ejus in omnem rĕgiōnem Gălilææ*, Mk. Bos. 1, 28: Homl. Th. ii. 358, 5. Sum sǽdere ferde to sāwenne his sǽd *a sower went to sow his seed*, ii. 88, 12: 90, 10. He ferde fram him and wæs fered on heofen *recessit ab eis et ferēbātur in cœlum*, Lk. Bos. 24, 51. He eft hām ferde *he went home again*, Bd. 2, 9; S. 512, 5: 3, 11; S. 536, 9. Hilde of deáþe ferde to līfe *Hilda de morte transīvit ad vītam*, Bd. 4, 23; S. 595, 32. He ferde ofer sǽ *he went over the sea*, Boutr. Scrd. 17, 7: 19, 2: Chr. 1140; Erl. 265, 39. God ferde forþ *ăbiit Dŏmĭnus*, Gen. 18, 33. Ferde Constantius forþ on Breotone *Constantius died* [lit. *went forth*] *in Britain*, Bd. 1, 8; S. 479, 29. Hī ferdon to Rōme *they went to Rome*, Chr. 737; Erl. 47, 22: Gen. 11, 31: Boutr. Scrd. 22, 18: Beo. Th. 3268; B. 1632. He hī lǽrde ðæt hī ferdon on ðæt geweorc ðæs Godes wordes *in ŏpus eos verbi proficisci suādet*, Bd. 1, 23; S. 485, 39. Hī ferdon ongēn ðone brȳdguman *exiērunt obviam sponso*, Mt. Bos. 25, 1. Hī ofer sǽ ferdon *they went over the sea*, Chr. 1087; Erl. 226, 7, 12. Tīd is ðæt ðū fere *it is time that thou goest*, Exon. 51 b; Th. 179, 30; Gū. 1269: Andr. Kmbl. 448; An. 224. Ǽr gē furður feran *ere ye go further*, Beo. Th. 513; B. 254. DER. be-feran, for-, forþ-, ge-, geond-, of-, ofer-, þurh-, to-. v. faran.

fer-bed, -bedd, es; *n. A bed for a journey;* ĭtĭnĕris lectus:—Ferbed *bajunula?* Ælfc. Gl. 66; Som. 69, 78; Wrt. Voc. 41, 32.

fēr-blǽd, es; *m.* [fēr- = fǽr- *sudden*, blǽd *a blast*] *A sudden* or *fearful blast;* repentīnus flātus:—Ic lǽran wille ðæt gē eówer hūs gefæstnige, ðȳ-læs hit fērblǽdum windas toweorpan *I will exhort that ye make your house firm, lest winds overthrow it with sudden blasts*, Exon. 75 a; Th. 281, 21; Jul. 649.

fercian; *p.* ode; *pp.* od *To bring, assist, help, support;* ferre, adjŭvāre, subvĕnīre, sustentāre:—Hī fercodon ða scypo eft to Lundenne *they brought the ships again to London*, Chr. 1009; Th. 260, 31, col. 2. On ðisum līfe we ateoriaþ gif we us mid bigleofan ne ferciaþ *in this life we faint if we support not ourselves with food*, Homl. Th. i. 488, 33. DER. ge-fercian.

fēr-clam; *gen.* -clammes; *m.* [fēr- = fǽr- *sudden*, clam *what holds*] *A sudden seizing;* arreptio repentīna angustiæ perīcŭlōsæ, Grn. Exod. 119. v. oferclamme, clam, clom.

fercung, e; *f. A sustaining;* sustentātio, Som. Ben. Lye.

fercuþ; *adj. Frugal, thrifty;* frūgālis, frūgi, Cot. 203.

ferd *an army*, Chr. 1140; Erl. 265, 28. v. fyrd.

ferde, *pl.* ferdon *went*, Bd. 2, 9; S. 512, 5: Chr. 737; Erl. 47, 22; *p. of* feran.

ferd-faru, e; *f. A military expedition;* mīlĭtāris expĕdītio, expĕdītio contra hostes, Heming, p. 234, Lye. v. fyrd-faru.

ferd-mon, -monn, es; *pl. nom. acc.* -men; *m. A soldier;* mīles:—Ðæt feoh mon ðām ferdmonnum sellan sceolde *the money should be given to the soldiers*, Bt. 27, 4; Fox 100, 14. Cyning sceal hæbban ferdmen *a king must have soldiers*, 17; Fox 58, 33, MS. Cot. v. fyrd-man.

ferd-rinc, es; *m. A warrior, soldier;* bellātor, mīles:—He fromne ferdrinc fere beserode *he deprived the brave warrior of life*, Ps. C. 50, 22; Ps. Grn. ii. 277, 22. v. fyrd-rinc.

ferd-wīte *a fine for neglecting to pay the contribution to the army*, L. In. 51; Th. i. 134, 10, note 23, MS. B: Th. Diplm. A. D. 1044; 359, 3. v. fyrd-wīte.

ferd-wyrt, e; *f.* [= feld-wyrt?] *Field-wort? gentian?* gentiāna?—Nim ferdwyrt *take gentian* (?), L. M. 1, 87; Lchdm. ii. 154, 15. v. feld-wyrt.

fere; *adj. Passable, able to go;* meābĭlis. DER. earfoþ-fere, eáþ-, ge-, un-, un-ge-.

fere *with life*, Ps. C. 50, 22; Ps. Grn. ii. 277, 22; *inst. of* ferh *life.*

fered *carried*, Lk. Bos. 24, 51; *pp. of* ferian.

fereld, es; *n. A way, going, step;* gressus:—Fulfrema stepas oððe paðas oððe fereldu mīne on sīþfætum ðīnum *perfĭce gressus meos in sēmĭtis tuis*, Ps. Lamb. 16, 5. v. færeld.

fēren *fiery, burning;* igneus, ignītus, Som. Ben. Lye. v. fȳren.

ferend, es; *m.* [*part. of* feran] *A traveller, messenger, sailor;* pere-grīnātor, nuncius, nauta:—He hēt gefetigan ferend snelle *he commanded swift messengers to be fetched*, Exon. 66 b; Th. 246, 12; Jul. 60. Him ða ferend on fæste wuniaþ *the sailors firmly rest on him*, 97 a; Th. 361, 25; Wal. 25.

fere-scæt, es; *m. Fare-scot, passage-money;* naulum, Cot. 138.

fere-soca, an; *m.* [ferh *a pig*, soca? = socc *a sock*] *A bag made of swine's skin;* sibæa:—Feresoca *sibba*, Wrt. Voc. 289, 1. v. Littleton, Glossārium Lătīno-þarbărum *under* sibæa.

fergan; *p.* ede; *pp.* ed. I. *to carry, convey, bear;* portāre, vehĕre, ferre:—We willaþ Hlāford fergan to ðære beorhtan byrg *we will bear the Lord to the bright city*, Exon. 15 a; Th. 32, 26; Cri. 518: 104 b; Th. 397, 1; Rä. 16, 13. Bearn fergaþ and fēdaþ fæder and mōdor *father and mother carry and lead the child*, 87 a; Th. 327, 21; Vy. 7. II. *to go;* īre:—Ic seah rǽplingas in ræced fergan *I saw captives going into a house*, Exon. 113 b; Th. 435, 2; Rä. 53, 1. v. ferian.

fer-grunden *ground to pieces, mangled*, Chr. 937; Erl. 114, 9, = for-grunden; *pp. of* for-grindan.

ferh; *gen.* feres; *dat. inst.* fere; *n. m. Life;* vīta:—Ferh ellen wræc *power drove out life*, Beo. Th. 5406; B. 2706. He fromne ferdrinc fere beserode *he deprived the brave warrior of life*, Ps. C. 50, 22; Ps. Grn. ii. 277, 22. Ealne wīdan ferh *to all eternity*, Exon. 44 b; Th. 151, 3; Gū. 789. v. feorh.

ferh, es; *m. A pig;* porcus, Wrt. Voc. 286, 47. v. fearh.

ferh-cwæle? [= -cwalu?] *A murrain of hogs;* lues porcīna, Som. Ben. Lye.

ferh-cwalu, e; *f. Life-destruction, slaughter;* internĕcio, Cot. 114. v. feorh-cwalu.

ferht *fear, fright, dread;* păvor, tĭmor, Som. Ben. Lye. v. fyrhto.

ferht, es; *m. n. The mind;* mens:—He mæg rihtwīsnesse findan on ferhte *he may find wisdom in his mind*, Bt. Met. Fox 22, 119; Met. 22, 60. v. ferhþ.

ferhþ, fyrhþ, ferþ, ferht, es; *m. n.* I. *the soul, spirit, mind;* animus, mens:—Ðīn ferhþ bemearn *thy spirit mourned*, Cd. 106; Th. 139, 14; Gen. 2309: Elen. Kmbl. 347; El. 174: Salm. Kmbl. 358; Sal. 178. Ferhþes fōreþanc *forethought of mind*, Beo. Th. 2124; B. 1060. His geleáfa wearþ fæst on ferhþe *his faith became firm in his spirit*, Elen. Kmbl. 2071; El. 1037: Exon. 100 a; Th. 375, 2; Seel. 132: Cd. 40; Th. 53, 32; Gen. 870: Beo. Th. 1512; B. 754: Ps. Th. 85, 11. Ðæt he andsware ǽnige ne cunne findan on ferhþe *that he cannot find any answer in his mind*, Bt. Met. Fox 22, 103; Met. 22, 52: Beo. Th. 2337; B. 1166: Cd. 161; Th. 200, 11; Exod. 355: Elen. Kmbl. 2325; El. 1164. He wiste ferhþ guman *he knew the man's soul*, Cd. 134; Th. 169, 2; Gen. 2793. Ne lǽt ðū ðīn ferhþ wesan sorgum asǽled *let not thy soul be bound with sorrows*, Cd. 100; Th. 132, 17; Gen. 2194. Noe læg ferhþe forstolen *Noah lay deprived of mind*, Cd. 76; Th. 95, 15; Gen. 1579: Ps. Th. 131, 2. Hī ferdon forþ ðonon, ferhþum fægne *they went forth thence, rejoicing in their minds*, Beo. Th. 3270; B. 1633: 6334; B. 3177. II. *life;* vīta:—Wīdan ferhþ, *acc. for a long life, for ever*, Elen. Kmbl. 1598; El. 801. DER. collen-ferhþ, -ferþ, -fyrhþ: dreórig-, freórig-, gāl-, gamol-, gleáw-, sār-, sārig-, stærced-, stearc-, sterced-, stīþ-, sweorcend-, swīþ-, swoncen-, swȳþ-, wērig-, wīde-. v. feorh.

ferhþ-bana, an; *m. A life-destroyer, murderer;* vītæ destructor, interfector:—Fyrst ferhþbana *the first life-destroyer*, Cd. 162; Th. 203, 5; Exod. 399.

ferhþ-cearig; *adj. Anxious in soul;* anĭmo sollĭcĭtus:—Sarra ongan, ferhþcearig, to were sīnum mæþlan *Sarah, anxious in soul, began to speak to her consort*, Cd. 101; Th. 133, 28; Gen. 2217.

ferhþ-cleófa, an; *m. The mind's cave, breast;* mentis cŭbīle, pectus:—Eádig byþ se wer, se ðe him ege Drihtnes on ferhþcleófan, fæste gestandeþ *beātus vir, qui tĭmet Dŏmĭnum*, Ps. Th. 111, 1.

ferhþ-cōfa, an; *m. The mind's cave, breast;* mentis cŭbīle, pectus:—

On ferhþcófan *in his mind's cave* or *breast*, Cd. 123; Th. 157, 8; Gen. 2603: Ps. Th. 108, 17.

ferhþ-frec; *adj. Bold in spirit;* anĭmōsus:—Ferhþfrecan Fin begeat sweordbealo *misery from the sword seized Fin the bold in spirit*, Beo. Th. 2296; B. 1146.

ferhþ-friđende *life-saving.* v. ferþ-friđende.

ferhþ-genīþla, an; *m. A life-enemy, deadly foe;* vītæ hostis, lētālis hostis:—Ic sweorde drep ferhþgenīþlan *I struck the deadly foe with my sword*, Beo. Th. 5754; B. 2881.

ferhþ-gewit *mental wit, understanding.* v. ferþ-gewit.

ferhþ-gleáw, fyrhþ-gleáw; *adj. Prudent in mind, sagacious;* anĭmo prūdens, săpiens:—Đǽr hie Iuditþe fundon ferhþgleáwe *they found Judith there prudent in mind*, Judth. 10; Thw. 21, 29; Jud. 41. Þūsenda manna ferhþgleáwra *of a thousand sagacious men*, Elen. Kmbl. 653; El. 327.

ferhþ-grim *fierce of spirit.* v. ferþ-grim.

ferhþ-līc *rational, just, equitable.* v. ferht-līc.

ferhþ-loca, ferþ-loca, fyrhþ-loca, an; *m. Soul-inclosure, bosom, body;* mentis clausūra, pectus, corpus:—Đæt đīn nama, Crist, in ūrum ferhþlocan sī feste gestađelod *that thy name, O Christ, be firmly established in our soul's inclosure*, Hy. 6, 5, 32; Hy. Grn. ii. p. 286, 5, 32. Ne willaþ eów andrǽdan fǽge ferhþlocan *dread ye not feeble bodies*, Cd. 156; Th. 194, 27; Exod. 267.

ferhþ-lufe *soul's love, mental love.* v. fyrhþ-lufe.

ferhþ-sefa, ferþ-sefa, firhþ-sefa, fyrhþ-sefa, an; *m. The mind's sense, intellect;* mens:—Cwēn gefeah on ferhþsefan *the queen rejoiced in her mind*, Elen. Kmbl. 1696; El. 850: 1787; El. 895.

ferhþ-wērig *soul-weary, sad.* v. ferþ-wērig, fyrhþ-wērig.

ferht-līc; *adj. Rational, wise, just, equitable;* rationālis, săpiens, æquus:—Drihten ferhtlīc riht folcum dēmeþ *Dŏmĭnus jūdĭcābit pŏpŭlos in æquĭtāte*, Ps. Th. 95, 10.

ferian, ferigan, ferigean, fergan; to ferianne; *p.* ode, ede; *pp.* od, ed [fer = fær *a journey*]. I. *to carry, convey, bear, lead, conduct;* ferre, portāre, vehēre, dedūcēre, afferre:—Hēht wīgend đæt hālige treó him befōran ferian *he commanded the warriors to carry the holy tree before him*, Elen. Kmbl. 215; El. 108: Cd. 67; Th. 80, 18; Gen. 1330. We đē willaþ ferigan freólīce ofer fisces bæþ *we will gladly convey thee over the fish's bath* [*the sea*], Andr. Kmbl. 585; An. 293. Hēt līfes brytta englas sīne ferigean leófne ofer lagufæsten *the giver of life commanded his angels to bear the dear one over the stronghold of the waves*, 1647; An. 825. To ferianne *ad portandum*, Gen. 46, 5. Ic ferige onbūtan *circumfĕro*, Ælfc. Gr. 47; Som. 48, 33. Mec merehengest fereþ ofer flōdas *the vessel conveys me over the floods*, Exon. 104 a; Th. 395, 13; Rä. 15, 7: 114 b; Th. 439, 16; Rä. 59, 4. Hī hine feriaþ ofer fisces bæþ *they bear it over the fish's bath* [*the sea*], Runic pm. 16; Kmbl. 342, 17; Hick. Thes. i. 135, 31. Hwanon ferigeaþ gē fætte scyldas *whence bear ye your stout shields?* Beo. Th. 671; B. 333. Folc đīn đū feredest swā sceáp *deduxisti sīcut ŏves pŏpŭlum tuum*, Ps. Th. 76, 17. He ferode đone to his mynstre mid ārwurþnysse *he bare it to his minster with honour*, Homl. Th. ii. 358, 7: Chr. 1009; Erl. 141, 23. Us ofer ārwēlan æđeling ferede *a noble one conducted us over the realm of oars* [*the sea*], Andr. Kmbl. 1706; An. 855. Hī đone sanct ferodon to đære byrig *they conveyed the saint to the city*, Homl. Th. ii. 518, 29. Đē on folmum feredan *in mănĭbus portābunt te*, Ps. Th. 90, 12: 82, 3. Feriaþ mid eów of đære eorþan wæstmum *afferte nōbis de fructĭbus terræ*, Num. 13, 21. He wæs fered on heofen *ferēbātur in cælum*, Lk. Bos. 24, 51. II. *to betake oneself to;* se gerēre, versāri:—Đū aclǽccræftum lange feredes *thou hast long betaken thyself to evil arts*, Andr. Kmbl. 2725; An. 1365. Hī on līge feredon *they betook themselves to lying*, Ps. Th. 58, 12. III. *to go, depart;* vehi, īre:—Mid friþe ferian *to depart in peace*, Byrht. Th. 136, 68; By. 179. Đonne God geond wēstena wīde feraþ *Deus, dum transgrediĕris per desertum*, Ps. Th. 67, 8. [*Laym.* uerien: *Plat.* fören: *O. Sax.* fōrian: *Frs.* fieren: *O. Frs.* fera: *Ger.* führen: *M. H. Ger.* vüeren: *O. H. Ger.* fuorjan, fōrjan: *Goth.* faryan *to convey a ship, row: Dan.* føre: *Swed.* föra: *Icel.* ferja *to transport, carry by sea.*] DER. a-ferian, æt-, ge-, of-, ōþ-, to-, wiđ-.

Feriatus, es; *m. A Spanish robber*, Ors. 5, 2; Bos. 102, 19. v. Uariatus.

feriend, ferigend, es; *m.* [*part. of* ferian *to bear, bring*] *A bringer, leader;* dux:—Flōdes ferigend [MS. B. feriend] *bringer of the flood*, Salm. Kmbl. 161; Sal. 80.

ferigan, ferigean *to carry, convey, bear*, Andr. Kmbl. 585; An. 293: 1647; An. 825: Ælfc. Gr. 47; Som. 48, 33: Beo. Th. 671; B. 333. v. ferian.

fering, e; *f. A going, travelling, journeying;* peregrīnātio, ĭter:—On đære feringe *in that journeying*, Exon. 87 a; Th. 326, 20; Wīd. 131. DER. forþ-fering.

fēringa *suddenly;* extemplo, imprōvīso, Prov. 3. v. fǽringa.

fērlīc *sudden, unlooked for, horrible;* repentīnus, horrendus, Som. Ben. Lye. v. fǽrlīc.

fērlīce *suddenly*, Ps. Spl. T. 63, 4. v. fǽrlīce.

fern, es; *n. Fern;* fĭlix:—Fern [MS. B. fearn], Herb. 78; Lchdm. i. 180, 23. v. fearn.

fernes, -ness, e; *f. A going, passing;* gressus, transĭtus:—Ne đǽr fernes is *non est transĭtus*, Ps. Th. 143, 18. DER. ofer-fernes.

ferran *to remove, take away.* DER. a-ferran. v. feorran.

fērrece? [fēr = fȳr?] *A fire-pan;* bătillum, Cot. 161, Som. Fērrece *vatilla*, Wrt. Voc. 287, 7.

ferren, ferlen; *adj. Far off, distant, remote;* longinquus:—On ferren [ferlen MS. Rl.] land *in regiōnem longinquam*, Lk. Skt. Hat. 19, 12. v. feorlen, fyrlen.

fers, færs, fyrs, es; *n. A* VERSE, *sentence, title;* versus, carmen:—Periodos is clȳsing, ođđe ge-endung đæs ferses *a period is the conclusion, or ending of the sentence*, Ælfc. Gr. 50, 14; Som. 51, 18. Ic fersige ođđe ic wyrce fers *versĭfĭcor*, 37; Som. 39, 3, MSS. C. D. Ongan he sōna singan đa fers *stătim ipse cœpit cantāre versus*, Bd. 4, 24; S. 597, 18.

FERSC; *adj.* FRESH, *pure, sweet;* dulcis:—Eufrates is mǽst eallra ferscra wætera, and is yrnende þurh middewearde Babilōnian burh *Euphrates is the greatest of all fresh waters* [*rivers*], *and runs through the middle of the city of Babylon*, Ors. 2, 4; Bos. 44, 10. Gyf se wǽta sealt byþ of đære sǽ, hit byþ þurh đære sunnan hǽtan to ferscum wæterum awend *if the moisture be salt from the sea, it is turned to fresh water through the heat of the sun*, Bd. de nat. rerum; Lchdm. iii. 278, 9–12; Wrt. popl. science 19, 3. [*Chauc.* freisshe: *Laym.* freche: *Plat.* frisk: *Frs.* fersck: *O. Frs.* fersk, fersch, farsch: *Dut.* versch: *Ger.* frisch: *M. H. Ger.* vrisch: *O. H. Ger.* frisc: *Dan.* frisk, fersk: *Swed.* frisk, färsk: *Icel.* friskr: *Wel.* ffres.]

fer-scipe, es; *m. Society, fellowship;* sŏcietas:—To healfum fō se cyng, to healfum se ferscipe *dīmĭdium căpiat rex, dīmĭdium sŏciĕtas*, L. Ath. v. 2; Wilk. 65, 19. DER. ge-ferscipe.

fer-scrifen; *part.* [= for-scrifen; *pp. of* for-scrīfan *to disregard, abandon*] *Disregarded, abandoned;* addictus:—Ferscrifen [MS. færscribæn] *addictus*, Glos. Epnl. Recd. 153, 53. Ferscrifen *addictus* [Lye *has* ferscrifer = ferscrifen? *abdictus*], Cot. 14.

fersian; *p.* ode; *pp.* od *To make verse;* versĭfĭcāre:—Ic fersige ođđe ic wyrce fyrs *versĭfĭcor*, Ælfc. Gr. 37; Som. 39, 3.

ferþ, ferþþ; *gen.* -es; *dat.* -e; *m. n.* I. *the soul, spirit, mind;* anĭmus, mens:—Wæs đære fǽmnan ferþ geblissad *the damsel's soul was rejoiced*, Exon. 69 b; Th. 259, 25; Jul. 287: 89 a; Th. 334, 21; Gn. Ex. 19. Hī gemētton ferþþes frōfre *they found comfort of soul*, 46 a; Th. 157, 21; Gū. 895. On ferþe fægn *rejoicing in mind*, Bt. Met. Fox 9, 73; Met. 9, 37: Andr. Kmbl. 2968; An. 1487. Gefeóþ gē on ferþþe *rejoice ye in spirit*, Exon. 14 b; Th. 30, 7; Cri. 476: 70 b; Th. 262, 5; Jul. 328. Đīnne ferþ, *acc. m. thy mind*, 88 b; Th. 333, 9; Gn. Ex. 1. Sum hafaþ fæstgongel ferþ *one has a constant soul*, 79 b; Th. 298, 4; Crä. 80: 81 b; Th. 307, 19; Seef. 26. Ferþum gleáw *sagacious in soul*, 128 a; Th. 493, 10; Rä. 81, 28. Ferþþum, 114 b; Th. 440, 15; Rä. 60, 3. II. *life;* vīta:—Lǽtaþ gāres ord ingedūfan in fǽges ferþ *let the javelin's point dig into the life of the doomed one*, Andr. Kmbl. 2665; An. 1334. DER. dreórig-ferþ, freórig-, sārig-, stearc-, swīþ-, wērig-, wīde-. v. ferhþ.

ferþ-friđende; *part.* [friđian *to protect*] *Life-saving;* vītam servans:—Forlēt ferþfriđende wellan on gesceap þeótan *he let his life-saving fountains be poured into a vessel*, Exon. 109 b; Th. 419, 25; Rä. 39, 3.

ferþ-gewit, -gewitt, es; *n. Mental wit, understanding;* mentis intellectus:—Đeáh hī ferþgewit ǽnig ne cūđen *though they knew not any mental wit*, Exon. 25 a; Th. 73, 4; Cri. 1184.

ferþ-grim; *adj. Fierce of spirit;* anĭmo sævus:—Frēcne and ferþgrim *rugged and fierce of spirit*, Exon. 67 b; Th. 251, 6; Jul. 141: 96 b; Th. 360, 13; Wal. 5.

ferþ-loca, an; *m. The soul's inclosure, bosom;* mentis clausūra, pectus:—Hyre wæs Cristes lof in ferþlocan *praise of Christ was in her soul's inclosure*, Exon. 69 a; Th. 256, 19; Jul. 234: 76 b; Th. 287, 12; Wand. 13. v. ferhþ-loca.

ferþ-sefa, an; *m.* [sefa *the faculty of perceiving;* sensus] *The mind;* mens:—Fæstnian ferþsefan *to fix in the mind*, Exon. 92 b; Th. 347, 29; Sch. 20. v. ferhþ-sefa.

ferþþ *the soul, mind.* v. ferþ.

ferþþes, ferþþe *of a soul, to a soul*, Exon. 46 a; Th. 157, 21; Gū. 895: 14 b; Th. 30, 7; Cri. 476; *gen. and dat. of* ferþ.

ferþ-wērig; *adj. Soul-weary, sad;* mæstus:—Freórig and ferþwērig *trembling and soul-weary*, Exon. 49 b; Th. 171, 21; Gū. 1130: 20 a; Th. 52, 9; Cri. 831. v. fyrhþ-wērig.

ferwett-full; *adj.* [ferwett = fyrwet *curiosity*] *Curious, anxious;* sollĭcĭtus:—Ferwettfulle men *sollĭcĭti*, Lk. Skt. Rush. 12, 26.

fēsian, he fēseþ; *p.* ode; *pp.* od; *v. a. To drive away, put to flight;* fŭgāre, in fŭgam ăgĕre:—Đæt oft on gefeohte ān fēseþ tyne *ut in pugna ūnus sæpe dĕcem in fŭgam ēgĕrit*, Lupi Serm. i. 14; Hick. Thes. ii. 103, 20. DER. to-fēsian. v. fȳsian.

feste; *adv. Fastly, firmly:*—Ic hæbbe genōg feste on gemynde *I have it firmly enough in my mind*, Bt. 36, 3; Fox 176, 24. v. fæste.

festen, es; *n. A fastness, fortress;* mūnīmentum:—Hī manige festena and castelas abrǽcon *they demolished many fastnesses and castles,* Chr. 1094; Erl. 230, 35. v. fæsten II.

festen-mon, -monn, es; *m. A surety;* fĭdējussor, Som. Ben. Lye. v. fēster-man.

fēster *food, nourishment, foster-*, in the compounds fēster-bearn, -fæder, -man, -mōdor. v. fōster.

fēster-bearn, es; *n. A foster-child;* ălumnus:—Fēsterbearn *ălumni*, Martyrol. ad 22 Martii. v. fōster-bearn.

fēster-fæder, es; *m. A foster-father, nourisher;* altor, nutrītor:—Fēsterfæder *altor*, Wrt. Voc. 284, 72. Ætȳwde me mīn iú magister and fēsterfæder *appārŭit măgister quondam meus et nutrītor*, Bd. 5, 9; S. 622, 34. v. fōster-fæder.

fēster-man, es; *m. A foster-man, bondsman, security;* fīdējussor:—Ælc preóst finde him xii fēstermen *let every priest find for himself twelve bondsmen*, L. N. P. L. 2; Th. ii. 290, 15.

fēster-mōdor, -mōdur; *f. A foster-mother, nurse;* altrix, nutrix:—Fēstermōdor *altrix*, Wrt. Voc. 284, 73. Wīfmonna lāreów and fēstermōdur *māter et nutrix fēmĭnārum*, Bd. 4, 6; S. 574, 17. v. fōster-mōdor.

festing-men, -menn *servants of the king entrusted to the keeping of the monasteries while going from place to place*, Th. Diplm. A. D. 823; 67, 2: A. D. 828; 79, 30. v. fæsting-men.

festlīce; *adv. Firmly, vigorously;* firmĭter:—Hī on ða burh festlīce feohtende wǽron *they were vigorously fighting against the town*, Chr. 994; Erl. 133, 11. v. fæstlīce.

festnes, -ness, e; *f. A fastness, firmament;* firmāmentum:—Weorc handa his bodaþ festnes [MS. fesnesse] *ŏpĕra mănuum ejus annuntiat firmāmentum*, Ps. Spl. T. 18, 1. v. fæstnes.

festnian *to confirm;* confirmāre:—Ic Ceólrēd abbud ðas ūre selene mid Cristes rōde tācne trymme and festnie *I Ceolred abbot ratify and confirm this our gift with the sign of Christ's cross*, Th. Diplm. A. D. 852; 106, 10-12. DER. ge-festnian. v. fæstnian.

fēstrian; *p.* ode, ude; *pp.* od, ud *To foster, nourish;* nutrīre:—Fēstrud beón *nutrīri*, Scint. 81. v. fōstrian.

fet *fetches, brings*, Prov. Kmbl. 61; *3rd sing. pres. of* fetian.

fēt *to* or *for a foot, feet*, Ex. 21, 24: Ps. Lamb. 72, 2: Mt. Bos. 18, 8; *dat. sing. and nom. acc. pl. of* fōt.

fēt *feeds*, Mt. Bos. 6, 26, = fēdeþ; *3rd sing. pres. of* fēdan.

fetan; *p.* fæt, *pl.* fǽton; *pp.* feten *To make, travail, join;* făcĕre, procreāre, jungĕre. [*Goth.* fitan; *p.* fat, *pl.* fetum; *pp.* fitans *to travail in birth;* partŭrīre.] v. fetian.

fēte; *adj. Provided with feet, footed;* pĕdĭbus instructus. v. ān-fēte, twȳ-, þrȳ-, feówer-.

FETEL; *gen.* feteles, fetles; *m. A girdle, belt;* cingŭlum, balteus:—Sweordum and fetelum *with swords and belts*, Bt. Met. Fox 25, 19; Met. 25, 10. Mid fetlum *with belts*, Bt. 37, 1; Fox 186, 5. [*Ger.* fessel, *f: M. H. Ger.* vezzel, *m: O. H. Ger.* fazzil, fezzil, fezil, *m. balteus: Icel.* fetill, *m. a strap, belt.*]

fetel-hilt, es; *n. A belted hilt;* căpŭlus baltĕo instructus:—He gefēng fetelhilt *he seized the belted hilt*, Beo. Th. 3130; B. 1563.

fetels, es; *m. A little vessel, bag;* vas, saccus:—Fōrwerede fetelsas *saccos vĕtĕres*, Jos. 9, 5. v. fætels.

FETER, fetor, e; *f. A* FETTER, *chain for the feet;* compes, pĕdĭca:—He fēdeþ swā on feterum *he feeds him thus in fetters*, Exon. 88 b; Th. 332, 20; Vy. 88; Ps. Th. 78, 11. Ān sceal inbindan forstes fetre *one shall unbind fetters of frost*, Exon. 90 a; Th. 338, 9; Gn. Ex. 76. Ic mōdsefan mīnne sceolde feterum sǽlan *I must bind my thought in fetters*, 76 b; Th. 287, 29; Wand. 21: Salm. Kmbl. 141; Sal. 70. [*O. Sax.* feterōs, *pl. m: Ger.* fesser, *f: M. H. Ger.* vëzzer, *f: O. H. Ger.* fëzzera: *Icel.* fjöturr, *m. a fetter of iron.*]

feterian *to fetter*. DER. ge-feterian.

feter-wrāsen *a chain, fetter*. v. fetor-wrāsen.

fēða, an; *m.* I. *a band on foot, infantry, a host, troop, tribe, company;* phălanx pĕdestris, pĕdĭtes, lĕgio, ăcies, trĭbus, căterva:—Eórod sceal getrume rīdan, fæste fēða stondan *a band of horse* [= *cavalry*] *shall ride in a body, a band of foot* [= *infantry*] *stand fast*, Exon. 90 a; Th. 337, 13; Gn. Ex. 64. Fēða [MS. fēðu] *lĕgio*, Ælfc. Gl. 7; Som. 56, 73; Wrt. Voc. 18, 25. Se earga fēða Brytta *ăcies segnis Brittŏnum*, Bd. 1, 12; S. 481, 19, MSS. B, C. Fēða eal gesæt *the band all sat*, Beo. Th. 2853; B. 1424. Iudisc fēða *the tribe of Judah*, Cd. 158; Th. 197, 25; Exod. 312. Se fēða com up to earde *the company came up to their home*, 223; Th. 293, 19; Sat. 457. Ðǽr wæs ungemetlīc wæl geslagen Persa, and Alexandres næs nā mā ðonne hund-twelftig on ðam rǽde-here, and nigon on ðam fēðan *there was a very great slaughter made of the Persians, and no more than a hundred and twenty in Alexander's cavalry, and nine in the infantry*, Ors. 3, 9; Bos. 64, 28. He cwiþ to ðara synfulra sāwla fēðan *he shall say to the band of sinful souls*, Exon. 30 a; Th. 93, 1; Cri. 1519. Ic him on fēðan beforan wolde *I would* [*go*] *before him in the host*, Beo. Th. 4987; B. 2497: 5830; B. 2919: Cd. 220; Th. 284, 19; Sat. 324. Ðū here fȳsest, fēðan to gefeohte *thou leadest a host, a troop to battle*. Andr. Kmbl. 2377; An. 1190. Fōr fyrda mǽst, fēðan trymedan *the greatest of armies marched, the infantry were strong*, Elen. Kmbl. 70; El. 35. Fēðan sǽton *the bands sat*, Andr. Kmbl. 1182; An. 591. Ymb ðæt hēhsetl standaþ engla fēðan *hosts of angels stand around the throne*, Cd. 218; Th. 278, 13; Sat. 221: Beo. Th. 2659; B. 1327. Ðǽr wæs Persa X M ofslagen gehorsedra, and eahtatig M fēðena *there were slain ten thousand of the Persians' cavalry and eighty thousand of the infantry*, Ors. 3, 9; Bos. 65, 2: 68, 9. Ne willaþ eów andrǽdan deáde fēðan *dread ye not dead bands*, Cd. 156; Th. 194, 26; Exod. 266. Hī bǽdon ðæt hī mōston ofer ðone ford faran, fēðan lǽdan *they gave orders to go over the ford, to lead the troops onward*, Byrht. Th. 134, 23; By. 88. Gerǽrud fēða *an arranged band;* ăcies: getrimmed fēða *cŭneus:* gangende [MS. gangend] fēða *a moving band;* agmen, Ælfc. Gl. 7; Som. 56, 74, 79, 82; Wrt. Voc. 18, 26, 31, 34. II. *a battle;* pugna:—He beald in gebēde bīdsteal gifeþ, fæste on fēðan *he bold in prayer maketh a stand, firmly in battle*, Exon. 71 a; Th. 265, 30; Jul. 389. DER. gum-fēða, here-.

fēðan; *p.* de; *pp.* ed *To lead;* dūcĕre:—Bearn fergaþ and fēðaþ fæder and mōdor *father and mother carry and lead the child*, Exon. 87 a; Th. 327, 21.

Fēðan-leag; *gen.* -leage; *f.* [*Flor.* Fethanleah: *Hunt.* Fedhalnea, Fedhanlea: *Matt. West.* Frithenleia] *Frethern, Gloucestershire?*—Hēr Ceáwlin and Cūþa fuhton wið Brettas in ðam stede ðe mon nemneþ Fēðanleag [Fēðanlea, Th. 35, 8, col. 1] *in this year* [A. D. 584] *Ceawlin and Cutha fought against the Britons at the place which is called Frethern*, Chr. 584; Th. 34, 9.

fēðe, es; *n. The power of going on foot, walking, going, motion, pace;* făcultas pĕdĭbus eundi, ambŭlātio, gressus, passus:—Ðæra hǽðenra anlīcnyssa habbaþ fēt būtan fēðe *the idols of the heathen have feet without the power of going*, Homl. Th. i. 366, 27. An fēðe mihtigost *most powerful in walking*, Bt. 36, 5; Fox 180, 21. He nāhte his fēðes geweald *he had no power of walking*, Homl. Th. i. 336, 9. Hit is nædrena gecynd ðæt heora fēðe biþ on heora ribbum *it is the nature of serpents that their power of going is in their ribs*, Ors. 4, 6; Bos. 84, 44. On fēðe lēf [MS. līf] *lame in walking*, Exon. 87 b; Th. 328, 16; Vy. 18. Sum sceal on fēðe gongan *one shall go on foot*, 87 b; Th. 328, 33; Vy. 27. Swift ic eom on fēðe *I am swift of pace*, Exon. 104 b; Th. 396, 10; Rä. 16, 2: Beo. Th. 1944; B. 970. Habbaþ hringa gespong afyrred me mīn fēðe *the clasping of rings has taken from me my power of going*, Cd. 19; Th. 24, 17; Gen. 379. He fēðe ne sparode *he spared not pace*, 117; Th. 153, 6; Gen. 2534.

fēðe-cempa, an; *m. A foot-soldier, champion;* pĕdester mīles:—Fēðecempa, *nom.* Beo. Th. 3092; B. 1544: 5698; B. 2853.

fēðe-gang, es; *m. A foot-journey;* pĕdestre iter:—Ne mæg ic aldornere mīne swā feor heonon fēðegange gesēcan *I cannot seek my life's safety so far hence by a foot-journey*, Cd. 117; Th. 152, 1; Gen. 2513.

fēðe-georn; *adj. Desirous of going;* meandi cŭpĭdus:—Sió fēðegeorn fremman onginneþ *desirous of going it resolves to proceed*, Exon. 108 a; Th. 413, 21; Rä. 32, 9.

fēðe-gest, es; *m. A pedestrian guest;* pĕdester advĕna:—Fēðegestas eódon in on ða ceastre *the pedestrian guests went into the city*, Elen. Kmbl. 1687; El. 845. Wæs gerȳmed fēðegestum flet *the hall was cleared for the pedestrian guests*, Beo. Th. 3956; B. 1976.

fēðe-here, es; *m. A foot army, infantry;* pĕdestris exercĭtus, pĕdĭtātus:—On his fēðehere wǽron XXXII M *in his infantry were* 32,000, Ors. 3, 9; Bos. 64, 17.

fēðe-hwearf, es; *m. A company on foot, pedestrian multitude;* pĕdestris căterva:—On fēðehwearfum *amongst the pedestrian multitude*, Exon. 35 a; Th. 113, 24; Gū. 162.

fēðe-lāst, es; *m. A footstep, pace;* passus, gressus:—Hie fēðelāste forþ onettan *they hastened forth with pace*, Judth. 11; Thw. 23, 25; Jud. 139. Ferdon forþ ðonon fēðelāstum *they went forth thence with their footsteps*, Beo. Th. 3269; B. 1632.

fēðe-leás; *adj. Footless;* pĕdĭbus cărens:—Ðū scealt faran fēðeleás *thou shalt go footless*, Cd. 43; Th. 56, 6; Gen. 908: Exon. 127 a; Th. 488, 7; Rä. 76, 3.

fēðe-man, -mann, es; *m. A footman* or *soldier;* pĕdestris mīles, pĕdes, Som. Ben. Lye.

fēðe-mund, e; *f. A foot-hand;* mănus gressus. Used for the fore-feet of the badger:—Ic sceal fromlīce fēðemundum þurh steápne beorg strǽte wyrcan *I* [*a badger*] *shall strenuously work a road through a steep mountain with my fore-feet*, Exon. 104 b; Th. 397, 10; Rä. 16, 17.

FEÐER; *gen. dat. acc.* feðere; *pl. nom. acc.* feðera, feðra, feðre; *f.* I. *a* FEATHER; penna, plūma:—Mid nīre [= niwre] feðere *with a new feather*, Herb. 122, 1; Lchdm. i. 234, 13: L. M. 1, 39; Lchdm. ii. 102, 8. Gedō feðere on ele *put a feather in oil*, L. M. 1, 18; Lchdm. ii. 62, 11. Swanes feðre, *nom. pl. swan's feathers*, Exon. 57 b; Th. 207, 6; Ph. 137. Wurp ða feðera wið æftan ðæt weofod *plūmas projĭciet prŏpe altāre*, Lev. 1, 16: Cd. 72; Th. 88, 26; Gen. 1471. Se fēnix ascæceþ feðre *the phœnix shakes its feathers*, Exon. 58 a;

Th. 207, 21; Ph. 145: 58b; Th. 212, 5; Ph. 205. Feðrum bifongen *clad with feathers*, 61 a; Th. 224, 23; Ph. 380: Bt. Met. Fox 24, 10; Met. 24, 5. II. in the *pl.* sometimes used for *Wings*; ālæ, pennæ:—Mec wǽgun feðre on lifte *wings bore me in air*, Exon. 107 b; Th. 409, 20; Rä. 28, 4. Ic hæbbe swíðe swifte feðera, ðæt ic mæg fliógan ofer ðone heán hrôf ðæs heofones *I have very swift wings, that I can fly over the high roof of heaven*, Bt. 36, 2; Fox 174, 4: Ps. Lamb. 54, 7: 138, 9. He gesihþ brimfuglas brǽdan feðra *he sees sea-fowls spread their wings*, Exon. 77 a; Th. 289, 13; Wand. 47. Cômon earnas on flyhte, feðerum hrêmige *eagles came in flight, exulting in their wings*, Andr. Kmbl. 1728; An. 866: Bt. Met. Fox 24, 17; Met. 24, 9. Fugel feðrum strong *a bird strong of wings*, Exon. 57 a; Th. 203, 18; Ph. 86: 57 b; Th. 206, 7; Ph. 123: 58 a; Th. 208, 29; Ph. 163: 60 b; Th 222, 11; Ph. 347. III. what is made of a feather, *A pen*; penna, călămus:—Feðer *a pen*; penna, Wrt. Voc. 75, 16. Nim ðíne feðere and wrît fîftig *take thy pen and write fifty*, Lk. Bos. 16, 6. [*Chauc.* feder: *Plat.* fedder: *O. Sax.* fethera, *f*: *Dut.* veder, veer, *f*: *Ger.* feder, *f*: *M. H. Ger.* vëdere, vëder, *f*: *O. H. Ger.* fedara, *f*: *Dan.* fjeder, *m. f*: *Swed.* fjäder, *m*: *Icel.* fjoðr, *f*: *Lat.* penna, old forms pesna, petna, *f*: *Grk.* πτερόν, *n. a feather*; πέτομαι *to fly*: *Sansk.* pat *to fly*.] DER. halsre-feðer, hleow-, wrîting-. v. fiðere.

feðer-, *four-*, used only in the compounds,—feðer-fôte, -sceátas, -scette, -scîte, -scitte. v. fiðer-, fyðer-.

feðeran, feðran *to provide with feathers* or *wings*. DER. ge-feðeran, -feðran.

feðer-bed, -bedd, es; *n. A feather-bed*; culcĭta:—Feðerbed *culcĭtes* [=*culcĭta*], Ælfc. Gl. 27; Som. 60, 102; Wrt. Voc. 25, 42.

feðer-berende; *part. Bearing feathers, feathered*; pennĭger, Cot. 150.

feðer-cræft, es; *m. The art of feather-embroidering*; plūmāria ars, Som. Ben. Lye.

feðere, feðre; *def.* se feðera, feðra; seó, ðæt feðere, feðre; *adj. Feathered*; pennis prædītus. DER. deáwig-feðere, haswig-, îsig-, salwig-, ûrig-.

feðer-fôte; *adj. Four-footed*; quadrūpes:—Eádbyrht feðerfôtra [MS. -fôta] neáta ðone tēðan dǽl to þearfum syllan wolde *Eadbyrht would give the tenth part of four-footed cattle to the poor*, Bd. 4, 29; S. 608, 17, note, MS. B. v. feówer-fête, fiðer-fête, fyðer-fête, -fôte.

feðer-gearwe; *pl. f.* [gearwe *clothing*] *Feather-gear, the feathering of an arrow*; pennis vestītus:—Sceaft feðergearwum fûs *an arrow prompt with its feather-gear*, Beo. Th. 6229; B. 3119.

feðer-geweorc, es; *n. Feather-embroidered work*; plūmārium ŏpus:—Feðergeweorc besiwed *ŏpus plūmārium intextum*, Cot. 145.

feðer-hama, -homa, an; *m. Feather-covering, feathers, plumage, wings*; plūmārum tegmen, plūma, pennæ, ālæ:—Geseó ic him his englas ymbe hweorfan mid feðerhaman *I see his angels encompass him with feathery wings*, Cd. 32; Th. 42, 6; Gen. 670. Eall biþ geniwad, feorh and feðerhoma *all is renewed, its life and plumage*, Exon. 60 a; Th. 217, 14; Ph. 280. Ðæt he mid feðerhoman fleógan meahte *that he might fly with wings*, Cd. 22; Th. 27, 13; Gen. 417.

feðer-sceátas; *pl. m. Four corners* or *quarters*; quătuor plăgæ:—Eall ðeós leóhte gesceaft feðersceátum full feohgestreóna *all this bright creation in its four quarters full of treasures*, Salm. Kmbl. 63; Sal. 32.

feðer-scette; *adj. Four-cornered*; quadrangŭlāris, in quătuor plăgas porrectus:—Eall ðeós leóhte gesceaft, feðerscette, full fyrngestreóna *all this bright creation, four-cornered, full of ancient treasures*, Salm. Kmbl. 63, MS. B; Sal. 32, note. v. feðer-scîte.

feðer-scîte, -scitte, -scette; *adj. Four-cornered, quadrangular*; quadrangŭlāris:—Feðerscîte tæfel *four-cornered tables*; tesseræ *vel* lepuscŭlæ, Ælfc. Gl. 61; Som. 68, 66; Wrt. Voc. 39, 49. Lytle feðerscitte flôr-stânas *little four-cornered floor-stones*; tessellæ, 61; Som. 68, 67; Wrt. Voc. 39, 50. v. feówer-scŷte, fiðer-scŷte, -scîte, fyðer-scŷte.

fêðe-spêdig; *adj. Speedy of foot*; lĕvĭpēs:—Sum biþ on londe snel, fêðespêdig *one is swift on land, speedy of foot*, Exon. 79 a; Th. 296, 18; Crä. 53.

fêðe-wîg, -wigg, es; *n? m? A foot-battle*; pĕdestris pugna:—Fêðe-wîges *of the foot-battle*, Beo. Th. 4717; B. 2364: Wald. 88; Vald. 2, 16.

feðm, es; *m. A bosom*; sĭnus:—On feðme heora *in sĭnu eōrum*, Ps. Spl. T. 78, 13. v. fæðm II.

feðra, feðre *feathers, wings*, Exon. 57 b; Th. 207, 6; Ph. 137: 58 b; Th. 212, 5; Ph. 205: 77 a; Th. 289, 13; Wand. 47; *nom. acc. pl. of* feðer.

feðrum *with feathers* or *wings*, Bt. Met. Fox 24, 10; Met. 24, 5: Exon. 60 b; Th. 222, 11; Ph. 347; *inst. pl. of* feðer.

fêðu *a band on foot, a host*; lĕgio, Ælfc. Gl. 7; Som. 56, 73; Wrt. Voc. 18, 25. v. fêða.

fetian, fetigean, fetigan; he fetaþ, fet; *p.* fette; *pp.* fetod *To fetch, bring to, marry*; addūcĕre, applĭcāre, uxōrem dūcĕre:—He hêht him fetigean to sprecan sîne *he bade to fetch his counsellors to him*, Cd. 126; Th. 161, 17; Gen. 2666. Fetigan, Judth. 10; Thw. 21, 26; Jud. 35. He ôðer fetaþ *ăliam duxĕrit*, Mt. Bos. 19, 9. Ǽlc ydel fet unhǽlo *all idleness brings illness*, Prov. Kmbl. 61. Se forma fette wîf, and forþferde *prīmus, uxōre ducta, defunctus est*, Mt. Bos. 22, 25: Gen. 48, 10. Wæs to bûre Beówulf fetod *Beowulf was fetched to his bower*, Beo. Th. 2625; B. 1310. DER. ge-fetian, -fætian. v. feccan.

fetlum *with belts*, Bt. 37, 1; Fox 186, 5. v. fetel.

fetor, e; *f. A fetter*; compes:—Îsern fetor *forfex*, Cot. 86. Îsen fetor *bălus*, Cot. 23. v. feter.

fetor-wrâsen, e; *f.* [wrâsen *a chain*] *A fetter, chain*; cătēna, compes:—Hraðe siððan wearþ fetorwrâsnum fæst *he was soon fast bound in fetters*, Andr. Kmbl. 2215; An. 1109.

fett; *adj. Fat*; pinguis:—He biþ anlîcost fettum swînum *he is most like to fat swine*, Bt. 37, 4; Fox 192, 26. v. fætt.

fette *fetched, brought, married*, Gen. 48, 10: Mt. Bos. 22, 25; *p. of* fetian.

fettian; *p.* ode; *pp.* od [fitt *contention, strife, fight*] *To contend, strive, dispute*; certāre, contendĕre, dispŭtāre:—Saturnus and Saloman fettodon ymbe heora wîsdôm *Saturn and Salomon contended about their wisdom*, Salm. Kmbl. p. 178, 7.

feuer-fuge, an; *f. Feverfew*; febrĭfŭgia:—Feuerfuge *feverfew*, Lchdm. iii. 12, 25. v. fefer-fuge.

fex, es; *n. Hair of the head, the locks*; cæsăries:—Fex *cæsăries*, Ælfc. Gl. 69; Som. 70, 39; Wrt. Voc. 42, 47: 70, 32. v. feax.

fexede *having long hair, long-haired*, Chr. 891; Th. 162, 9, col. 2, 3; 163, 10. v. feaxede.

fic *deceit, fraud, guile*. DER. ge-fic.

FÎC, es; *m.* I. *a* FIG, *the fruit of the fig-tree*; fīcus: found at present only in the following compounds in the sense of a tree or fruit, etc.—fîc-æppel, -beám, -leáf, -treów. II. *a disease so called, the piles, hemorrhoids*; fīcus:—Wið seóndum ômum, ðæt is fîc *for running erysipelas, that is the 'fig,'* L. M. cont. 1, 39; Lchdm. ii. 10, 7: L. M. 1, 39; Lchdm. ii. 102, 12. Lǽcedômas and drencas and sealfa wið fîce *medicines and drinks and salves for the 'fig,'* L. M. cont. 1, 57; Lchdm. ii. 12, 18. Gif se fîc [MS. uîc] weorþe on mannes setle geseten *if the 'fig' be settled on a man's fundament*, Lchdm. iii. 30, 16. Se blēdenda fîc *the bleeding 'fig,'* iii. 38, 8. Wið ðone blēdendne [MS. blēdende] fîc nim murran ða wyrt *for the bleeding 'fig' take the plant sweet-cicely*, iii. 8, 1. [*Plat.* fige, *f*: *Dut.* vijg, *f*: *Ger.* feige, *f*: *M. H. Ger.* vîge, *f*: *O. H. Ger.* fîga, *f*: *Lat.* fīcus, *f.* and *m.*]

fîc-âdl, e; *f.* [fîc II. *the piles, hemorrhoids*] *The fig-disease*; fīcus morbus:—Wið fîcâdle drenc and beðing *a drink and fomentation for the fig-disease*, L. M. cont. 3, 48; Lchdm. ii. 302, 24: L. M. 3, 48; Lchdm. ii. 340, 1.

fîc-æppel, -appel, es; *m*; *pl. nom. acc.* -æppla; *n. A fig-apple* or *fruit, a fig*; fīcus, cārica:—Fîcappel *cārica*, Ælfc. Gl. 46; Som. 64, 125; Wrt. Voc. 32, 59. Ne hîg of þornum fîcæppla ne gaderiaþ *neque de spīnis collĭgunt fīcus*, Lk. Bos. 6, 44: Mt. Bos. 7, 16.

fîc-beám, es; *m.* [beám *a tree*, v. I.] *A fig-tree*; fīcus:—Fîcbeám *fīcus*, Ælfc. Gl. 46; Som. 64, 122; Wrt. Voc. 32, 56. Behealdaþ ðone fîcbeám *vidēte fīculneam*, Lk. Bos. 21, 29. Forwurdan heora wîngeardas and fîcbeámas *percussit vīneas eōrum et fīculneas eōrum*, Ps. Th. 104, 29.

fîc-leáf, es; *n. A fig-leaf*; fīci fŏlium:—Hîg siwodon fîcleáf and worhton him wǽdbrêc *consuērunt fŏlia fīcus et fēcērunt sibi pĕrizŏmăta*, Gen. 3, 7.

ficol; *adj.* FICKLE, *crafty*; versĭpellis, inconstans, Prov. 14.

fîc-treów, es; *n. A* FIG-TREE; fīcus:—Forscranc ðæt fîctreów *fīcus ārŭit*, Mk. Bos. 11, 21: Mt. Bos. 21, 20: Wrt. Voc. 80, 11. Ðæs fîctreówes *of the fig-tree*, Mk. Bos. 11, 13. Leornigeaþ bigspel be ðam fîctreówe *ab arbŏre fīci discĭte părăbŏlam*, Mt. Bos. 24, 32: Mk. Bos. 13, 28. Hî gesâwon ðæt fîctreów forscruncen of ðam wyrtruman *vīdērunt fīcum ārĭdam factam a rādīcĭbus*, 11, 20: Mt. Bos. 21, 19. He ofslôh wîngeardas heora and fîctreów heora *percussit vīneas eōrum et fīculneas eōrum*, Ps. Spl. 104, 31.

fîc-wyrm, es; *m. A* FIG-WORM, *a worm originating from the fig-disease*; vermis ex fīco morbo ŏriens:—Feallaþ ða fîcwyrmas on ða beðinge *dēcĭdent fīci morbi vermes in balneo*, L. M. 3, 48; Lchdm. ii. 340, 8.

fîc-wyrt, e; *f. The herb* FIG-WORT; fīcāria herba, fīcus, Ælfc. Gl. 41; Som. 63, 119; Wrt. Voc. 31, 6.

fieder *a father*, Cant. Moys. Ex. 15, 2; Thw. 29, 2. v. fæder.

fiell, es; *m. A fall, ruin, destruction*; cāsus, lapsus, ruīna:—He wirþ swîðe raðe on fielle *he very quickly falls*, Past. 39, 3; Hat. MS. 53 b, 17. v. fyll.

fiénd *a fiend*:—Murnþ nâuðer ne friénd ne fiénd *regardeth neither friend nor foe*, Bt. 37, 1; Fox 186, 8. v. feónd.

fiénd-wîc, es; *n. An enemy's dwelling, a camp*; hostium vīcus, castra:—Hî feóllon on middele fiéndwîce heora *cĕcĭdērunt in mĕdio castrōrum eōrum*, Ps. Spl. T. 77, 32.

fier; *adv.* [fier, *comp. of* feor, *adv. far*] *Farther*; longius, ultĕrius:—Ðeáh ðû nû fier [fyr MS. Bod.] sîe ðonne ðû wǽre *though thou art now* *farther than thou wast*, Bt. 5, 1; Fox 8, 33. We areccan ne māgon ðæt fædrencynn fier ōwihte *we cannot reckon the paternal kin any degree farther*, Exon. 11 b; Th. 16, 5; Cri. 248. v. fyr, fyrr.

fiér *four*, in the compound fiér-fēte. v. feówer.

fierd, e; *f. An army, force, expedition*; exercĭtus, expĕdītio:—Of ðære fierde *from the army*, Chr. 823; Erl. 62, 18: 876; Erl. 78, 9: 885; Erl. 82, 23: 919; Erl. 104, 26. Ǣr sió fierd gesamnod wǣre *ere the army was assembled*, Chr. 894; Erl. 90, 21. v. fyrd.

fierdian; *p.* ede; *pp.* ed *To march*; proficisci:—Mid ðære scīre ðe mid him fierdedon *with the division which marched with him*, Chr. 894; Erl. 90, 33. v. fyrdian.

fierdleás; *adj. Without a force* or *army, unprotected*; exercĭtu cărens:—Hit ðonne fierdleás wæs *it was then without a force*, Chr. 894; Erl. 90, 13. v. fyrdleás.

fieren-full *wicked*, Bt. Met. Fox 15, 13; Met. 15, 7, note. v. firen-full.

fiér-fēte; *adj. Four-footed*; quadrŭpes:—Sume fiérfēte *some are four-footed*, Bt. Met. Fox 31, 21; Met. 31, 11. v. feówer-fēte.

FIERSN, fyrsn, e; *f. The heel*; calx:—Ðū scealt fiersna sǣtan *thou* [*the serpent*] *shalt lie in wait for her* [*Eve's*] *heels*, Cd. 43; Th. 56, 17; Gen. 913. [*Ger.* ferse, *f*: *M.H.Ger.* vërsen, *f*: *O.H.Ger.* fërsana, fërsina, fërsna, *f*: *Goth.* fairzna, *f*: *Grk.* πτέρνα, *f. the heel*: *Sansk.* pārshṇi, *m.f. the heel.*]

fierst, es; *m. The ceiling of a chamber*; lăquear:—Fierst *lăquear*, Glos. Epnl. Recd. 158, 66. v. fyrst II.

fierst, es; *m. A space of time, time*; tempŏris spătium, tempus:—Forgif ðū me fierst and ongiet *give me time and understanding*, Exon. 118 a; Th. 453, 28; Hy. 4, 21. v. fyrst.

FĪF FIVE; quinque. 1. *generally indecl*:—Hyra fīf wǣron dysige, and fīf gleáwe *quinque ex eis ĕrant fătuæ, et quinque prūdentes*, Mt. Bos. 25, 2: Lev. 26, 8. Cōmon ða fīf cynegas *ascendērunt quinque rēges*, Jos. 10, 5, 16. Ðæra fīf hlāfa *quinque pānum*, Mt. Bos. 16, 9. Of fīf hlāfum *from five loaves*, Andr. Kmbl. 1179; An. 590: Jn. Bos. 6, 13. We nabbaþ hēr būton fīf hlāfas and twegen fixas *non hăbēmus hic nĭsi quinque pānes et duos pisces*, Mt. Bos. 14, 17: Lk. Bos. 9, 13, 16: Jn. Bos. 6, 9: Gen. 14, 9; 47, 2. Wintra hæfde fīf and hundteontig *he had a hundred and five winters*, Cd. 56; Th. 69, 5; Gen. 1131: 59; Th. 71, 29; Gen. 1178: 85; Th. 106, 26; Gen. 1777. Fīf sīðon *quinquies*, Ælfc. Gr. 38; Som. 40, 67. Fīf wintra fæc *lustrum quinquennium*, Ælfc. Gl. 16; Som. 58, 70; Wrt. Voc. 21, 57. 2. *but nom. acc. pl.* fīfe; *gen.* fīfa; *dat.* fīfum *are sometimes found*:—Fīfe cininges lāgon *five kings lay* [*dead*], Chr. 937; Th. 204, 1, col. 2; 205, 1; Æðelst. 28. Burga fīfe wǣron under Norþmannum *five towns were under the Northmen*, Chr. 942; Th. 208, 39; Edm. 5. Git sceolon fīfe geár *adhuc quinque anni restant*, Gen. 45, 6. Ðǣr fīfe [gimmas] wǣron *there were five* [*gems*], Rood Kmbl. 16; Kr. 8. Him togeánes fīfe fōron folc-cyningas *five kings of nations marched against them*, Cd. 93; Th. 119, 3; Gen. 1974. Beóþ fīfe on ānum hūse todǣlede *ĕrunt quinque in dŏmo ūna divīsi*, Lk. Bos. 12, 52. Wǣron fīfe eorla and idesa *there were five men and women*, Exon. 112 b; Th. 432, 1; Rā. 47, 6. Wintra hæfde twā hundteontig and fīfe *he had two hundred and five winters*, Cd. 83; Th. 104, 28; Gen. 1742. Ān ðissa fīfa *one of these five*, Bt. 33, 3; Fox 126, 14. Būton fīfum *except five*, Chr. 897; Erl. 95, 28. [*Laym.* fif, uiuen: *Plat.* five, fiwe: *O.Sax.* fīf, vīf: *Frs.* fyf: *O.Frs.* fif: *Dut.* vijf: *Ger.* fünf: *M.H.Ger.* vunf, vünf: *O.H.Ger.* fimf, finf: *Goth.* fimf, fif: *Dan. Swed.* fem: *Icel.* fimm: *Corn.* pemp: *Lat.* quinque: *Grk.* πέντε; *Æolic* πέμπε: *Sansk.* pañćan.]

Fīf burhga *or* burga; *pl. f. The Five towns*, viz. *Leicester, Lincoln, Nottingham, Stamford, and Derby*; quinque cīvĭtātes:—On fīf burhga geþincþe *in the assembly of the Five towns*, L. Eth. iii. 1; Th. i. 292, 6. Ferde se æðeling ðanon in to fīf burgum [burhgum, Th. 276, 7, col. 2] *the noble went thence to the Five towns*, Chr. 1015; Th. 276, 7, col. 1; 277, 7: 1013; Th. 270, 17, col. 2.

fīfe *five*. v. fīf 2.

fīf-ecgede; *adj. Five-edged, five-cornered*; quinquangŭlus:—Fīfecgede *quinquangŭlus*, Ælfc. Gr. 49; Som. 50, 61.

fīfel, es; *n? m? A sea-monster, monster, giant*; monstrum mărīnum, gĭgas:—Þurh fīfela gefeald forþ onette *through the field of the monsters he hastened forth*, Wald. 76; Vald. 2, 10. [*Icel.* fífl, *m.* I. *a fool, clown, boor.* II. *a monster, giant.*]

fīfel-cyn, -cynn, es; *n. A monster-race*; monstrōrum mărīnōrum gĕnus:—Fīfelcynnes eard *the monster-race's abode*, Beo. Th. 209; B. 104.

fīfel-dōr, es; *n. Monster* or *terror-door, the river Eider*, the boundary between Holstein and Schleswig; monstrōrum mărīnōrum porta:—Bī fīfeldōre *by the monster-door*, Exon. 85 a; Th. 321, 8; Wīd. 43.

fifele? *a buckle, button*; fībŭla, Som. Ben. Lye. v. figel.

fīfel-streám, es; *m. The frightful* or *horrid stream, the ocean*; ōceănus:—Nǣnigne merehengesta mā ðonne ǣnne ferede on fīfelstreám *he led not more than one of the sea-horses on the ocean*, Bt. Met. Fox 26, 51; Met. 26, 26.

fīfel-wǣg, es; *m. The terrific wave, the ocean*; ōceănus:—Lēton ofer fīfelwǣg scrīðan bronte brimþisan *they let the high ships go over the ocean*, Elen. Kmbl. 473; El. 237.

fīf-feald; *adj. Five-fold*; quintuplex, quīnārius:—Fīffeald *quīnārius*, Ælfc. Gr. 49; Som. 50, 16.

fīf-fealde, -falde, an; *f. A butterfly*; pāpĭlio, Som. Ben. Lye:—Fīffealde *pāpĭlio*, Wrt. Voc. 281, 40. Fīfaldæ *pāpĭlio*, Glos. Epnl. Recd. 160, 78.

fīf-flēre; *adj.* [flōr *a floor*] *Five-floored, five-storied*; quinque tăbŭlātis constans:—Se arc wæs fīfflēre *the ark was five-floored*, Boutr. Scrd. 21, 6.

fīf-hund, -hundred *five hundred*; quingenti:—Fīfhund *quingenti*, Ælfc. Gr. 49; Som. 49, 48. Fīfhund sīðon *five hundred times*; quingenties, 49; Som. 50, 32. Fīfhund cempena ealdor *a chief of five hundred soldiers*; cohors, Ælfc. Gl. 7; Som. 56, 61; Wrt. Voc. 18, 14. Fundon fīfhund forþsnotterra *they found five hundred of eminently wise men*, Elen. Kmbl. 757; El. 379. Fīfhundred *quingenti*, Num. 1, 46.

fīf-leáf, es; *n*: -leáfe, an; *f. Fiveleaf, cinquefoil*; potentilla reptans, quinquefŏlium:—Fīfleáfe, Ælfc. Gl. 43; Som. 64, 54; Wrt. Voc. 31, 64: 68, 69: 79, 33: 286, 40: Herb. 3; Lchdm. i. 86, 20. Fīfleáfan seáw *juice of fiveleaf*, Herb. 3, 2; Lchdm. i. 86, 24. Genim fīfleáfan wyrtwalan *take the root of fiveleaf*, Herb. 3, 3; Lchdm. i. 86, 28. Genim fīfleáfan ða wyrt *take the herb fiveleaf*, Herb. 3, 5; Lchdm. i. 88, 3, 9, 11, 14, 17, 20.

fīfta; *m*: seó, ðæt fīfte; *adj. The* FIFTH; quintus:—Se fīfta dæg *the fifth day*, Gen. 1, 23. Fīfta wæs Eádwine, Norþan Hymbra cyning *the fifth was Edwin king of the Northumbrians*, Chr. 827; Erl. 64, 3. Hēr onginnþ seó fīfte bōc Boēties *here begins the fifth book of Boëthius*, Bt. 40, 4; Fox 240, 9. Ǣr ðam fīftan geáre *before the fifth year*, Lev. 19, 25. Ðæt gē habbon wæstmas, and syllaþ ðam cynge ðone fīftan dǣl *ut frūges hăbēre possĭtis, quintam partem rēgi dăbĭtis*, Gen. 47, 24, 26.

fīfta fæder; *m. The fifth father*; ătăvus:—Felix, se pāpa wæs his [Gregories] fīfta fæder *Felix, the pope was his* [*Gregory's*] *fifth father, that is*—reckoning Gregory's father as the first generation, his fifth father would be his great-grandfather's grandfather, Homl. Th. ii. 118, 9.

fīftegða *the fifteenth*, Bd. 4, 26; S. 602, 21. v. fīfteóða.

fīf-tene *fifteen*; quindĕcim:—Fīftena sum *one of fifteen*, Beo. Th. 420; B. 207: Cd. 69; Th. 84, 14; Gen. 1397. v. fīf-tyne.

fīfteogoða; *adj. The fiftieth*; quinquāgēsĭmus:—Se fīfteogoða *quinquāgēsĭmus*, Ælfc. Gr. 49; Som. 50, 1. v. fīftigoða.

fīfteóða, fīftēða, fīftegða, fȳfteogeða; seó, ðæt fīfteóðe; *adj. The* FIFTEENTH; quintus dĕcĭmus:—Mōna [MS. mone] se fīfteóða *the fifteenth moon*, Lchdm. iii. 190, 29. Ðam fīfteóðan geáre *anno quinto dĕcĭmo*, Lk. Bos. 3, 1. Under ðam fīftēðan dæge Kalendarum Octobris *sub die quinta decĭma Kalendas Octobres*, Bd. 4, 17; S. 585, 20. Heó leórde ðȳ fīfteóðan dæge *transīvit die quinta dĕcĭma*, 4, 23; S. 592, 39. Ðȳ fīftegðan geáre *in the fifteenth year*, 4, 26; S. 602, 21.

fīftig FIFTY; quinquāginta:—Fīftig yntsena scolfres *quinquāginta siclos argenti*, Deut. 22, 29. Fīftig wintra *fifty winters*, Beo. Th. 5459; B. 2733. Fīftig wintru, 4424; B. 2209. Se wæs fīftiges fōtgemearces lang *he was fifty feet of measure long*, 6076; B. 3042.

fīftigfeald; *adj. Fiftyfold, containing fifty*; quinquāgēnārius:—Fīftigfeald *quinquāgēnārius*, Ælfc. Gr. 49; Som. 50, 19.

fīftigoða, fīftigeða, fīfteogoða; *m*: seó, ðæt fīftigoðe; *adj. The fiftieth*; quinquāgēsĭmus:—Fīftigoða *quinquāgēsĭmus*, Gr. Dial. 2, 2. Fīftigeða, C. R. Ben. 25. Ðæt fīftigoðe [MS. fīfteóðe] gēr biþ hālig *the fiftieth year shall be holy*; sanctĭfĭcābis annum quinquāgēsimum, Lev. 25, 10.

fīf-tyne, -tene *fifteen*; quindĕcim:—Fīftyne fæðma *fifteen* [*of*] *cubits*, Gen. 7, 20. Fīftyne suna *fifteen* [*of*] *sons*, Boutr. Scrd. 21, 32. He slōh fīftyne men *he slew fifteen men*, Beo. Th. 3169; B. 1582. He on wēstenne wīceard geceás fīftyne geár *he chose a dwelling in the wilderness fifteen years*, Exon. 46 b; Th. 158, 13; Gū. 908. Fīftyno, *acc. n.* Cd. 57; Th. 70, 10; Gen. 1151.

fīf-wintre; *adj. Of* or *belonging to five years, five years old*; quinquennis:—Fīfwintre *quinquennis*, Ælfc. Gr. 49; Som. 50, 45.

fīgan *to be* or *become an enemy, be at enmity*; inĭmīcāri, inĭmīcĭtias exercēre, Som. Ben. Lye. v. feógan.

figel? fifele? *A buckle, button*; fībŭla, Cot. 85, Lye.

fihle, es; *m? n? A cloth, rag*; pannus:—Fihles reádes *panni rŭdis*, Mt. Kmbl. Lind. 9, 16.

fiht *fights*, Ex. 14, 14; *3rd sing. pres. of* feohtan.

fihtung, e; *f. A fighting*; pugnātio, dimĭcātio, Som. Ben. Lye.

fiht-wīte, es; *n. A fine for fighting*; pugnæ mulcta:—He āh fihtwīte *he has fines for fighting*, L. C. S. 15; Th. i. 384, 3, note 6, MS. B. v. fyht-wīte.

fild; *adj. Of* or *pertaining to a level field, even, flat, level*; campester:—Seó burh wæs getimbred on fildum lande *the city* [*Babylon*] *was built on level land*, Ors. 2, 4; Bos. 44, 20.

fild, es; *m? n?* e; *f? A milking, the quantity of milk drawn at one milking*; lactis quantĭtas sĕmel mulcta:—Gif fild sȳ awyrd *if a milking be spoilt*, L. M. 1, 67; Lchdm. ii. 142, 14. DER. fild-cumb.

fild-cumb, es; *m.* [cumb II. *a liquid measure*] *A milk-pail*;

mulctrāle, mulctrum:—Gif meoluc sīe awyrd, bind tosomne wegbrǣdan and giþrifan and cersan, lege on đone fildcumb, and ne sete đæt fæt niđer on eorþan seofon nihtum *if milk be spoilt, bind together waybroad and cockle and cress, lay them on the milk-pail, and set not the vessel down on the earth for seven nights*, L. M. 3, 53; Lchdm. ii. 340, 23-25.

filgst, filhst, he filgþ, filhþ *stickest to, sticks to; 2nd and 3rd pers. pres. of* felgan.

filian; *p.* filide *To follow;* sĕqui:—Fīf eówer filiaþ hira hundteontig *persĕquentur quinque de vestris centum ălĭēnos*, Lev. 26, 8. He filide me *he followed me*, Deut. 1, 36. v. fylgean.

filiende; *part. Rubbing;* fricans, Cot. 90.

fill, e; *f. Fulness, satiety, gluttony;* sătietas, inglŭvies:—He þurh fille unriht gefremode *he did wrong through gluttony*, L. Pen. 16; Wilk. 95, 58. v. fyll.

fille, an; *f. The plant thyme;* serpyllum = ἕρπυλλον:—Fille *serpyllum*, Wrt. Voc. 79, 47: Lchdm. iii. 34, 30.

filled *filled*, = fylled; *pp. of* fyllan.

film, es; *m. A* FILM, *skin, husk;* cŭtĭcŭla, Som. Ben. Lye. v. fylmen.

filma, an; *m. A cleft;* rīma, Cot. 180.

filstan *to help, aid, assist*:—Gif he nelle filstan *if he will not help*, L. N. P. L. 54; Th. ii. 298, 19. v. fylstan.

filþ *filth, impurity, rottenness*, Som. Ben. Lye. v. fylþ.

FIN, finn, es; *m. A* FIN; pinna:—Ne ete gē nānne fisc būton đa đe habbaþ finnas and scilla *ye shall not eat any fish except those that have fins and scales*, Lev. 11, 9. [*Plat.* finne, *f: Dut.* vin, *f: Ger.* finne, *f: M. H. Ger.* vinne, *f: Dan.* finne, *m. f: Swed.* fena, *f: Lat.* pinna, *f.*]

fin? *A heap, pile;* strues, Cot. 195, Lye. DER. wudu-fin.

fina, an; *m. A woodpecker;* pīcus:—Fina *pīcus*, Ælfc. Gl. 38; Som. 63, 26; Wrt. Voc. 29, 46: 77, 31: 281, 4: Glos. Brux. Recd. 36, 33; Wrt. Voc. 62, 33.

FINC, es; *m. A* FINCH; fringilla:—Finc *fringilla*, Glos. Brux. Recd. 36, 37; Wrt. Voc. 62, 37: Glos. Epnl. Recd. 156, 57. [*Plat.* fink, finke, *m: Dut.* vink, *m: Ger.* fink, finke, *m: M. H. Ger.* vinke, *m: O. H. Ger.* finco, fincho, *m: Dan.* finke, *m. f: Swed.* fink, *m: Wel.* pinc, *m.*] DER. gold-finc, rago-.

fincer, es; *m. A finger;* digĭtus:—Dō hider fincer đīnne *infer digĭtum tuum huc*, Jn. Rush. War. 20, 27. v. finger.

Finchamstede, -stæde, es; *m.* FINCHAMPSTEAD, *Berkshire;* lŏci nōmen in agro Berkeriensi:—Đises geáres to đan sumeran, innan Barrucscīre æt Finchamstæde, ān mere blōd weóll *in the summer of this year* [A. D. 1098], *at Finchampstead in Berkshire, a pool welled out blood*, Chr. 1098; Th. 364, 4.

FINDAN, to findanne; ic finde, đū findest, findst, fintst, finst, he findeþ, fint, *pl.* findaþ; *p.* fand, fond, funde, *pl.* fundon; *pp.* funden; *v. trans. To* FIND, *invent, imagine, devise, contrive, order, dispose, arrange, determine;* invĕnīre, dispōnĕre, consŭlĕre:—Hīg ne mihton nāne findan *non invĕnĕrunt*, Mt. Bos. 26, 60: Bd. 1, 15; S. 483, 39. Ne mihte earmsceapen āre findan *nor might the poor wretch find pity*, Andr. Kmbl. 2260; An. 1131: 1960; An. 982. To findanne *to find*, Ps. Th. 76, 16. Ic hine finde ferþ stađelian *I find him strengthening his spirit*, Exon. 71 a; Th. 264, 14; Jul. 364: 67 a; Th. 247, 20; Jul. 81. Đǣr đū wrađe findest *there thou shalt find help*, Elen. Kmbl. 168; El. 84: Andr. Kmbl. 2698; An. 1351. Findst đū đǣr fīf mǣgþa *thou findest there five generations*, Boutr. Scrd. 22, 19, 20. Finst đū *thou findest*, Bt. 18, 3; Fox 66, 11. Se đe forstolen flǣsc findeþ *he who finds stolen flesh*, L. In. 17; Th. i. 114, 2. Nimþ eall đæt hió fint *she will seize all she finds*, Bt. Met. Fox 13, 68; Met. 13, 34. Đǣr hī fulle dagas findaþ sōna *dies plēni invĕnientur in eis*, Ps. Th. 72, 8: 64, 10. Se cyning to nytnysse fand his leódum *rex ūtĭlĭtāti suæ gentis consŭluit*, Bd. 2, 16; S. 520, 3. Heó nō reste fand *she found no rest*, Cd. 72; Th. 87, 30; Gen. 1456: 94; Th. 123, 6; Gen. 2040. Ic grundhyrde fond *I found the ground-keeper*, Beo. Th. 4279; B. 2136: Exon. 49 b; Th. 171, 2; Gū. 1120. Ic funde *I found*, Beo. Th. 2977; B. 1486: Gen. 12, 20. Đū fundest *thou foundest*, Ps. Th. 16, 3. Swā we ǣr fundon *as we before determined*, L. Alf. pol. 18; Th. i. 72, 10. Wolde ic đæt đū funde đa *I would that thou wouldst find them*, Elen. Kmbl. 2157; El. 1080: Cd. 72; Th. 87, 6; Gen. 1444. Se cyng hæfde funden, đæt ... *the king had contrived, that* ..., Chr. 918; Erl. 104, 3. [*Piers P.* fynden: *Laym.* finde, finden, ifinde, uinde, uinden: *Orm.* findenn: *Plat.* finnen: *O. Sax.* findan: *Frs.* fynnen: *O. Frs.* finna: *Dut.* vinden: *Ger.* finden: *M. H. Ger.* vinden: *O. H. Ger.* findan: *Goth.* finþan: *Dan.* finde: *Swed.* finna: *Icel.* finna.] DER. a-findan, an-, ge-, ofer-, on-, to-.

findele, an; *f?* es; *n? An invention, a device;* adinventio, inventum, Som. Ben. Lye.

findig; *adj. Considerable, good, heavy;* pondĕrōsus:—Findig corn *heavy corn*, Lye. DER. ge-findig.

finel, es; *m. Fennel;* fēnicŭlum:—Fineles *of fennel*, Herb. 97, 1; Lchdm. i. 210, 8, MS. B. v. finol.

FINGER; *gen.* fingeres, fingres; *dat.* fingre; *pl. nom. acc.* fingras; *gen.* fingra, fingrena; *m. A* FINGER; digĭtus:—Finger *digĭtus*, Wrt. Voc. 71, 26. Send Lazarum, đæt he dyppe his fingeres liþ on wætere, and mīne tungan gecǣle *mitte Lazarum ut intingat extrēmum digĭti sui in aquam, ut refrīgĕret linguam meam*, Lk. Bos. 16, 24. Gif ic on Godes fingre deófla ūtadrīfe *si in digĭto Dei ejĭcio dæmŏnia*, 11, 20. On đæm lytlan fingre *in the little finger*, Bt. Met. Fox 20, 359; Met. 20, 180. Ne gelȳfe ic, būton ic dō mīnne finger on đæra nægla stede *nisi mittam digĭtum meum in lŏcum clāvōrum non crēdam*, Jn. Bos. 20, 25, 27: Lev. 4, 17. Wulfere mid his fingre gewrāt on Cristes mǣl *Wulfhere wrote with his finger on Christ's cross*, Chr. 656; Erl. 32, 23. Nellaþ hīg đa mid heora fingre æt-hrīnan *digĭto suo nōlunt ea mŏvēre*, Mt. Bos. 23, 4: Lk. Bos. 11, 46. Fingras *digĭti*, Wrt. Voc. 64, 78: 283, 18. Rand sceal on scylde, fæst fingra gebeorh *a boss shall be on the shield, the sure protection of fingers*, Menol. Fox 535; Gn. C. 38: Elen. Kmbl. 239; El. 120. Ic geseó heofonas đīne, weorc đīnra fingra [MS. fingrena] *vĭdēbo cœlos tuos, ŏpĕra digĭtōrum tuōrum*, Ps. Lamb. 8, 4. Sum mæg fingrum hearpan stirgan *one can awaken the harp with fingers*, Exon. 17 b; Th. 42, 6; Cri. 668: Beo. Th. 3015; B. 1505. [*Laym.* finger, fenger: *O. Sax.* fingar, *m: Frs.* finger: *O. Frs.* finger, fingr, *m: Dut.* vinger, *m: Ger. M. H. Ger.* finger, *m: O. H. Ger.* fingar, *m: Goth.* figgrs, *m: Dan.* finger, *m. f: Swed.* finger, *m. n: Icel.* fingr, *m.*] DER. eáre-finger, gold-, hring-, lǣce-, leáw-, middel-, scyte-.

finger-æppel, es; *m: nom. acc. pl.* -æppla, -appla; *n. A* FINGER-APPLE, *finger-fruit, a date;* dactȳlus:—Fingerappla *dactȳlos*, Mone B. 542. Fingerapplum *dactȳlis*, 3830.

finger-līc; *adj. Of* or *belonging to a finger* or *ring;* dĭgĭtālis, annŭlāris, Wrt. Voc. 65, 2.

fini; *adj. Decayed, mouldy;* corruptus, mūcĭdus:—Finie hlāfas *mouldy loaves*, Jos. 9, 5. v. fynig.

finiht; *adj.* [fin *a fin*] *Having fins, finny;* pinnĭger:—Scilfixas finihte *finny shell fishes*, L. M. 2, 37; Lchdm. ii. 244, 25.

Finn, es; *m. Fin, the king of the North Frisians*:—Finn [MS. Fin] Fresna cynne *Fin of the race of the Frisians*, Scōp. Th. 55; Wīd. 27. Be Finnes eaferum in Fres-wæle *of Fin's offspring in Friesland*, Beo. Th. 2140; B. 1068. v. Finns buruh.

Finnas; *gen.* a; *pl. m.* I. the Finns generally, including Scride-finnas and Ter-finnas, are the inhabitants of the north and west coast from Halgoland [v. map in Ors. Bos.] to the White Sea, as defined by Ohthere in the following example:—Ne mētte Ohthere nān gebūn land, syđđan he fram his āgnum hāme [Hālgoland, *q. v.*] fōr; ac him wæs ealne weg wēste land on đæt steór-bord, būtan fisceran, and fugeleran, and huntan, and đæt wǣron ealle Finnas *Ohthere had not met with any inhabited land, since he came from his own home* [*Halgoland*]; *but the land was uninhabited all the way on his right, save by fishermen, fowlers and hunters, and they were all Finns*, Ors. 1, 1; Bos. 20, 3-6. Đa Finnas and đa Beormas sprǣcon neáh ān geþeóde *the Finns and the Biarmians spoke nearly the same language*, 1, 1: Bos. 20, 14: 19, 29. II. *Finwood, between Gothland and Smöland, in the south of Sweden*:—Đā Beówulf sǣ ōþbær, flōd æfter faroþe, on Finna land *then the sea bore Beowulf away, the flood along the shore, on the Fins' land*, Beo. Th. 1165; B. 580. Not *Finland*, but the *Fins' land;* for how could Beowulf, in his swimming-match with Breca, be borne by the sea to Finland? Thorpe thinks the following extract may, however, afford a solution of the difficulty,—'Their [the Fins'] name is probably still to be found in the district of Finved [Finwood], between Gothland and Smöland. This inconsiderable and now despised race has, therefore, anciently been far more widely spread, and reached along the Kullen [the chain of mountains separating Norway from Sweden] down to the Sound, and eastward over the present Finland,' *Petersen, Danmarks Historie i Hedenold* i. p. 36. Ic wæs mid Finnum *I was with the Fins*, Scōp. Th. 153; Wīd. 76. DER. Scride-finnas, Ter-.

finnas *fins*, Lev. 11, 9; *pl. nom. acc. of* fin.

Finns buruh = Finnes burh; *gen.* -burge; *f. Finnsburg*:—Swylce eal Finnes buruh [MS. Finns] fȳrenu wǣre *as if all Fin's castle were on fire*, Fins. Th. 72; Fin. 36. *This Finnsburg is no doubt the same as the Finneshām mentioned by Beowulf*,—Swylce hie æt Finnes hām findan meahton *such as they might find at Finnesham*, Beo. Th. 2316; B. 1156. v. Finn.

FINOL, finul, finel, fynel, fenol, es; *m:* finule, finugle, an; *f. The plant* FENNEL; fēnĭcŭlum:—Finol *fēnĭcŭlum*, Glos. Brux. Recd. 41, 28; Wrt. Voc. 67, 43: L. M. 2, 34; Lchdm. ii. 238, 29. Genim finoles wyrttruman *take roots of fennel*, 1, 37; Lchdm. ii. 90, 6: 2, 11; Lchdm. ii. 188, 19: 2, 16; Lchdm. ii. 194, 23. Of đam finole *from the fennel*, 2, 14; Lchdm. ii. 190, 22. Seóþ on đam ecede đone finol *seethe the fennel in the vinegar*, 2, 16; Lchdm. ii. 194, 26. [*Ger.* fenchel, *m: M. H. Ger.* venchel, *m: O. H. Ger.* fenachal, fenihil: *Lat.* fēnĭcŭlum, *n.*]

finol-sǣd, es; *n. Fennel seed;* fēnĭcŭli sēmen:—Finolsǣd gnīd to duste *reduce fennel seed to dust*, Lchdm. iii. 28, 3.

finst *findest*, Bt. 18, 3; Fox 66, 11, = findest; *2nd sing. pres. of* findan.

finta, an; *m.* I. *a tail;* cauda:—Đonne is se finta fægre gedǣled *then is the tail* [*of the phœnix*] *beautifully divided*, Exon. 60 a; Th. 218, 15; Ph. 295. II. *what follows, a sequel, the consequence* *of an action;* consĕquentia:—Ðonne he ðæs fácnes fintan sceáwaþ *when he sees the consequence of treachery,* Exon. 83 b; Th. 315, 17; Mód. 32: Exon. 74 b; Th. 278, 31; Jul. 606.

fintst, he fint *findest, finds,* Bt. Met. Fox 13, 68; Met. 13, 34; *2nd and 3rd pers. pres. of* findan.

finugle, an; *f. Fennel;* fēnĭcŭlum:—Wyl on ealoþ finuglan *boil fennel in ale,* L. M. 1, 39; Lchdm. ii. 104, 1: 1, 66; Lchdm. ii. 142, 2. v. finol.

finul, es; *m:* finγle, an; *f. Fennel;* fēnĭcŭlum:—Genim ðysse wyrte wyrttruman, ðe man *fēnĭcŭlum,* and óðrum naman finul nemneþ *take roots of this herb, which is named* fēnĭcŭlum, *and by another name fennel,* Herb. 126, 1; Lchdm. i. 238, 1: 382, 1. Genim finules niðeweardes *take some of the netherward part of fennel,* L. M. 1, 60; Lchdm. ii. 130, 18. Finule *fennel,* Lchdm. iii. 34, 30. v. finol.

fióde *hated,* Bt. 39, 1; Fox 212, 5; *p. of* fiógan, fión.

fiógan, fión; *p.* fióde, *pl.* fiódon *To hate;* ōdisse:—Fiógaþ yfel *ōdīte mălum,* Ps. Spl. T. 96, 10. Ðæt is unriht ǽghwelcum men ðæt he óðerne fióge *it is wicked in every man that he should hate another,* Bt. Met. Fox 27, 47; Met. 27, 24. v. feógan.

fioh; *gen.* fiós; *dat.* fió; *n. Cattle, property, a portion;* pĕcus, ŏpes, dos:—Gif ðē becume óðres monnes giémeleás fioh on hand *if the stray cattle of another man come to thy hand,* L. Alf. 42; Th. i. 54, 9: L. Ethb. 81; Th. i. 24, 1. v. feoh.

fioh-bōt, e; *f. A pecuniary recompence;* nummāria compensātio, L. Alf. 49; Th. i. 58, 8. v. feoh-bōt.

fiolan; *p.* fæl, *pl.* fǽlon; *pp.* folen *To reach, proceed, come;* procēdĕre, pervĕnīre:—Hit fiolan ne mæg eft æt his ēþle *it cannot come again to its own region,* Bt. Met. Fox 20, 308; Met. 20, 154. v. feolan.

fión; *p.* fióde, *pl.* fiódon *To hate;* ōdisse:—Ic fióde cyrcean awyrgedra *ōdīvi ecclēsiam malignantium,* Ps. Spl. T. 25, 5. Hit nǽre nō manna ryht, ðæt hiora ǽnig óðerne fióde *it would not be right in men, that any of them should hate another,* Bt. 39, 1; Fox 212, 5. v. feógan.

fiónd *a fiend,* Hy. 8, 25; Hy. Grn. ii. 290, 25. v. feónd.

fiónd-geld, es; *n. Devil-worship,* Mt. Lind. Stv. 4, 24. v. feónd-gyld.

fior; *adv. Far, at a distance;* prŏcul, longe:—Hió biþ swíðe fior hire selfre beneoðan *she is very far beneath herself,* Bt. Met. Fox 20, 443; Met. 20, 222. v. feor.

fiorh; *gen.* fiores; *dat.* fiore; *n. Life, spirit;* vīta, ănĭma:—Būton hiora āgnum fiore *except their own life,* Bt. 39, 11; Fox 230, 1. v. feorh I.

fiorm *use, benefit, profit, enjoyment,* Past. pref; Hat. MS. v. feorm IV.

fiórþa, seó, ðæt fiórþe; *adj. The fourth;* quartus:—Seó [MS. þio] fiórþe bōc *the fourth book,* Bt. 40, 4; Fox 240, 9, note 14. v. feórþa.

fióung, e; *f. Hatred;* ōdium:—Mid unrihtre fióunge *with evil hatred,* Bt. 39, 1; Fox 210, 24. DER. unriht-fióung. v. feóung.

fiówer-fēte; *adj. Four-footed;* quadrŭpes:—Sume biþ fiówerfēte *some are four-footed,* Bt. 41, 6; Fox 254, 27. v. feówer-fēte.

fīr, es; *n. Fire;* ignis:—Þurh ðæs fīres fnæst *through the fire's blast,* Exon. 74 a; Th. 277, 29; Jul. 588. v. fȳr.

FIRAS, fyras; *gen.* a; *dat.* um; *pl. m. Living beings, the chief of living beings, men, mankind;* hŏmĭnes, vĭri, gĕnus hūmānum:—Firas monige *many men,* Runic pm. 26; Kmbl. 344, 28; Hick. Thes. i. 135, 52. Me wītan ne þearf Waldend fira *the Ruler of men need not upbraid me,* Beo. Th. 5476; B. 2741: 182; B. 91: Andr. Kmbl. 581; An. 291: 1840; An. 922: Elen. Kmbl. 2153; El. 1078: 2343, El. 1173. Biþ ānra gehwylc flǽsce bifongen fira cynnes *every one of the race of men shall be invested with flesh,* Exon. 63 b; Th. 234, 5; Ph. 535: 73 a; Th. 273, 1; Jul. 509: 92 b; Th. 347, 18; Sch. 14. Fira bearn *children of men,* Cd. 21; Th. 26, 17; Gen. 408. Firum uncūþ *unknown to men,* Bt. Met. Fox 4, 78; Met. 4, 39. Teóde firum foldan freá Ælmihtig *terram custos hūmāni gĕnĕris omnĭpŏtens creāvit,* Bd. 4, 24; S. 597, 23. [*O. Sax.* firihós, *pl. m. men, people, mankind: Icel.* firar, *pl. m. men, people.*]

fird, e; *f. A force, army, expedition;* exercĭtus, expĕdītio:—Ne mehte seó fird hie nā hindan offaran *the force could not overtake them,* Chr. 894; Erl. 93, 7: 895; Erl. 93, 22: 905; Erl. 98, 19. Fōr Eádweard cyng mid firde to Steanforda *king Edward went with an army to Stamford,* 922; Erl. 108, 17. v. fyrd.

fird-cræft, es; *m. A war design, an expedition;* expĕdītio:—Mid hiora firdcræfte *by their expedition,* Num. 22, 4.

firding, e; *f. An expedition, army;* expĕdītio, exercĭtus:—Swíðe micel folc ðū hæfst on ðīnre firdinge to ðam gefeohte *very much people thou hast in thine army for the battle,* Jud. 7, 2. v. fyrding.

fird-stemn, es; *m. An army-corps;* exercĭtus cohors:—Ðā se fird-stemn fōr hām, ðā fōr óðer ūt *when the army-corps went home, then another went out,* Chr. 921; Th. 195, 19.

FIREN, fyren, e; *pl. nom. acc.* firene, firena; *f.* I. *a wicked deed, sin, crime;* scĕlus, crīmen, peccātum:—Næs ðǽr gefremed firen æt giftum *there was no sin committed at the nuptials,* Hy. 10, 17; Hy. Grn. ii. 293, 17. Nū eft gewearþ flǽsc firena leás *flesh is again become void of sins,* Exon. 9 b; Th. 8, 25; Cri. 123: Elen. Kmbl. 2625; El. 1314: Salm. Kmbl. 897; Sal. 448. Firina gehwylc *each sin,* Exon. 8 b; Th. 4, 21; Cri. 56. Lȳsde of firenum *released from sins,* 25 b; Th. 74, 22; Cri. 1210: Elen. Kmbl. 1814; El. 909. Uton we firene feógan *let us hate crimes,* Exon. 98 a; Th. 366, 16; Reb. 13: Ps. Th. 58, 3. Firena fremman *to perpetrate crimes,* Cd. 1; Th. 2, 14; Gen. 19: Salm. Kmbl. 632; Sal. 315. II. *tribulation, torment, suffering, pain;* trĭbŭlātio, tormentum, crŭciātus:—Mid firenum *with torments,* Exon. 29 a; Th. 88, 16; Cri. 1441: 41 b; Th. 139, 26; Gū. 599. Wǽron ealle fægen in firnum *they were all glad in their sufferings,* Cd. 223; Th. 292, 3; Sat. 435. [*O. Sax.* firina, *f. a wicked deed, crime, sin: O. Frs.* firne, ferne, *f: O. H. Ger.* firina, *f. crīmen, scĕlus, făcĭnus: Goth.* fairina, *f. crimination: Icel.* firn, *n. pl. a shocking thing, abomination.*] DER. folc-firen, hell-.

firen-bealu; *gen.* -bealuwes; *n. A sinful evil;* peccātum scĕlestum:—On him Dryhten gesihþ firenbealu lāþlīc *in them the Lord shall see loathly sinful evil,* Exon. 26 b; Th. 78, 19; Cri. 1276.

firen-cræft, es; *m. A sinful craft, wickedness;* scĕlesta ars, nēquĭtia:—Hī Dryhtnes ǽ feódon þurh firencræft *they hated the Lord's law in their wickedness,* Exon. 66 a; Th. 243, 21; Jul. 14.

firen-dǽd, fyren-dǽd, -dēd, e; *f. A wicked or sinful deed, crime;* scĕlestum făcĭnus:—Ðæt hie firendǽda tō frece wurdon *that they were too audacious in wicked deeds,* Cd. 121; Th. 155, 29; Gen. 2580: Exon. 118 a; Th. 453, 35; Hy. 4, 25. Firendēda, Ps. C. 50, 44; Ps. Grn. ii. 277, 44. Firendǽdum fāh *stained with sinful deeds,* Exon. 22 b; Th. 62, 13; Cri. 1001: 31 b; Th. 99, 31; Cri. 1633.

firen-earfeðe *a sinful woe.* v. fyren-earfeðe.

firen-fremmende; *part. Committing sins;* scĕlĕra committens:—Ðæt he for ælda lufan firenfremmendra fela þrōwade *that he suffered much for love of men committing crimes,* Exon. 24 a; Th. 69, 9; Cri. 1118.

firen-full, fyren-full, -ful; *adj. Sinful;* făcĭnŏrōsus, scĕlestus:—Swā firenfulle heora aldorþægn unreordadon *thus the sinful addressed their principal chief,* Cd. 214; Th. 268, 34; Sat. 65. Gif ðū wylt ða firen-fullan fyllan mid deáþe *if thou wilt fell the wicked with death,* Ps. Th. 138, 16. Firenfulra *of the wicked,* Exon. 40 b; Th. 135, 30; Gū. 532: Ps. Th. 81, 4: 124, 3.

firen-georn; *adj. Sinful;* peccandi prōnus:—Firengeorne men *sinful men,* Exon. 31 b; Th. 98, 12; Cri. 1606.

firenian, firnian, fyrenian, fyrnian; *p.* ede; *pp.* ed. I. *to sin;* peccāre:—Firenaþ ðus ðæt flǽschord *thus will the body sin,* Exon. 99 b; Th. 373, 3; Seel. 103. Ða ðe firnedon beóþ beofigende *they who sinned shall be trembling,* Cd. 227; Th. 303, 29; Sat. 621. II. *to revile;* călumnĭāri:—Heó firenaþ mec wordum *she reviles me with words,* Exon. 105 b; Th. 402, 24; Rä. 21, 34. [*O. H. Ger.* firinōn *scĕlĕrāre: Goth.* fairinon *to criminate.*]

firenlīc; *adj. Wicked;* mălĭtiōsus, mălignus:—Hió me wrāþra wearn worda sprǽcon, fǽcne, firenlīcu *they spoke to me a multitude of wrathful words, deceitful, wicked,* Ps. Th. 108, 2.

firenlīce *vehemently, rashly.* v. fyrenlīce.

firen-ligerian *to commit fornication;* fornĭcāri. v. fyren-ligerian.

firen-lust, fyren-lust, es; *m. Sinful lust, luxury, wantonness;* lĭbīdo, luxŭria:—Mid ðȳ ðā ongon firenlust weaxan *cœpit cum quĭbus luxŭria crescĕre,* Bd. 1, 14; S. 482, 22: Past. 27; Cot. MS. Hī firenlusta frece ne wǽron *they were not desirous of luxuries,* Bt. Met. Fox 8, 29; Met. 8, 15. Þurh firenlustas *through sinful lusts,* Exon. 29 b; Th. 90, 32; Cri. 1483: 44 a; Th. 150, 8; Gū. 775.

firen-synnig; *adj. Sinful;* făcĭnŏrōsus, scĕlestus:—Firensynnig folc *sinful people,* Exon. 28 a; Th. 84, 25; Cri. 1379.

firen-þearf *great distress, dire need.* v. fyren-þearf.

firen-weorc, es; *n. A wicked work, crime;* scĕlestum ŏpus, scĕlus:—Hī firenweorc beraþ *they bear their wicked works,* Exon. 26 b; Th. 80, 1; Cri. 1301: 28 a; Th. 85, 30; Cri. 1399.

firen-wyrcende; *part. Evil-doing, committing sin;* mălum făciens, peccans:—Me of folmum afere firenwyrcendra *take me out of the hands of those committing sin,* Ps. Th. 70, 3. Ic fyrenwyrcende oft elnade *I often emulated evil-doing [men],* 72, 2.

firen-wyrhta *an evil-doer, sinner.* v. fyren-wyrhta.

firgen, fyrgen, es; *n. A mountain, mountain-woodland;* mons, saltus. [*Goth.* fairguni, *n. a mountain: Icel.* Fjörgyn, *f. Mother-earth.*] DER. firgen-beám, -bucca, -gāt, -holt, -streám.

firgen-beám *a mountain-tree.* v. fyrgen-beám.

firgen-bucca *a mountain-buck.* v. firgin-bucca.

firgend-streám *a mountain-stream,* Andr. Kmbl. 3144; An. 1575. v. firgen-streám.

firgen-gāt, firgin-gāt, e; *pl. nom. acc.* -gǽt; *f. A mountain-goat, chamois;* montāna *vel* saltuensis capra, ībex:—Firgengāt [MS. firing-gāt] *ibex,* Ælfc. Gl. 20; Som. 59, 39; Wrt. Voc. 23, 2. Firgengāt *mountain-goat,* Cot. 109: 116. Firgingǽt [MS. -gǽtt] *ibices,* Glos. Epnl. Recd. 158, 31.

firgen-holt *a mountain-wood.* v. fyrgen-holt.

firgen-streám, fyrgen-streám, firgend-streám, firigend-streám, es; *m,*

A mountain-stream, the ocean; montānum *vel* saltuense flūmen, oceănus;—Hió ðæt līc ætbær under firgenstreám *she bore the corpse away under the mountain-stream*, Beo. Th. 4263; B. 2128. Fugel on firgenstreám lōcaþ georne *the bird looks earnestly into the mountain-stream*, Exon. 57 a; Th. 204, 20; Ph. 100. Wæs ic firgenstreámum swīðe besuncen *I was deeply sunk in mountain-streams*, 103 b; Th. 392, 4; Rä. 11, 2. Ymb ealra land gehwilc flōwan firgenstreámas *mountain-streams [shall] flow over every land*, Menol. Fox 555; Gn. C. 47. Fleów firgendstreám *the mountain-stream flowed*, Andr. Kmbl. 3144; An. 1575. Ofer firigendstreám *over the ocean*, Andr. Kmbl. 779; An. 390.

firgin-bucca, an; *m. A mountain-buck, wood-buck;* montānus *vel* saltuensis căper:—Firginbucca ðæt ys wudubucca *a mountain-buck that is a wood-buck*, Med. ex Quadr. 5, 1; Lchdm. i. 348, 2. v. firgen-bucca.

firgin-gǣt *mountain-goats*, Glos. Epnl. Recd. 158, 31. v. firgen-gāt.

firhþ-sefa, an; *m. The mind;* mens:—On firhþsefan *in his mind*, Elen. Kmbl. 425; El. 213. v. ferhþ-sefa.

fīrige *let him make a fire*, L. Pen. 14; Wilk. 95, 30. v. fȳrian.

firigend-streám *a mountain-stream, the ocean*, Andr. Kmbl. 779; An. 390. v. firgen-streám.

firing-gāt *a mountain-goat*, Ælfc. Gl. 20; Som. 59, 39; Wrt. Voc. 23, 2. v. firgen-gāt.

firmetan; *p.* firmette, *pl.* firmetton; *pp.* firmeted *To request, pray;* pĕtĕre, rŏgāre:—Rōmāne hī firmetton ðæt hī ðæt gewin forlēton *the Romans requested them that they would leave off the siege*, Ors. 4, 8; Bos. 89, 21.

firna *sins, crimes*, Cd. 216; Th. 274, 27; Sat. 160; *acc. pl. of* firen.

firne *crime*, Cd. 227; Th. 305, 3; Sat. 641; *dat. of* firen.

firnian *to sin*, Cd. 227; Th. 303, 29; Sat. 621. v. firenian.

firnum, fyrnum; *adv.* [*dat.* or *inst. pl. of* firen *a sin, crime*] *Fearfully, intensely;* formīdŏlōse, immānĭter:—Nǣre firnum ðæs deóp merestreám *the sea-stream would not be so fearfully deep*, Cd. 39; Th. 51, 26; Gen. 832.

firra; *m:* firre; *f. n. adj.* [*comp. of* feor, *adj. far*] *Farther;* ultĕrior:—On ðære firran Ispānie *in the farther Spain*, Ors. 4, 11; Bos. 97, 26. v. fyrra.

firran *to remove, take away.* DER. a-firran. v. feorran.

fīr-scofl *a fire-shovel;* bătillum, Som. Ben. Lye. v. fȳr-scofl.

first, es; *m. A rafter, beam, perch;* tĭgillum, pertĭca:—First *paratica?* [=*pertica*], Wrt. Voc. 290, 3. v. fyrst.

first, es; *m. A space of time, time;* tempŏris spătium, tempus:—Ðā wæs first agān *then was the time expired*, Andr. Kmbl. 293; An. 147. Ōþ ðone first ðe hie wurdon swīðe meteleáse *until the time that they were very destitute of food*, Chr. 918; Erl. 104, 12: Bt. 38, 1; Fox 194, 27. v. fyrst.

first *first*, Chr. 675; Erl. 39, 28. v. fyrst.

first-mearc *an interval of time;* intercăpēdo, Som. Ben. Lye. v. frist-mearc.

firþriende *furthering;* promŏvens, M. A. 1, p. 223, Lye. v. fyrþran.

firwet *curiosity.* DER. firwet-georn, -geornes. v. fyrwet.

firwet-georn; *adj. Very inquisitive, curious;* cūriōsus:—Ða ðe firwetgeorne weorþaþ *they who are very inquisitive*, Bt. 39, 3; Fox 216, 4: Bt. Met. Fox 28, 151; Met. 28, 76. v. fyrwet-georn.

firwet-geornes, -ness, e; *f. Curiosity, anxiety;* sollĭcĭtūdo, Cot. 60.

FISC, es; *pl. nom. acc.* fiscas, fixas, fisceas; *gen.* fisca, fixa; *dat.* fiscum, fixum; *m. A* FISH; piscis:—Fisc *piscis*, Wrt. Voc. 65, 60: 77, 57: 281, 54. Fisc sceal on wætere cynren cennan [MS. cynran cennen] *the fish shall propagate his kind in the water*, Menol. Fox 514; Gn. C. 27: Salm. Kmbl. 841; Sal. 420. Hīg brohton him dǣl gebrǣddes fisces, and beóbreád *illi obtŭlērunt ei partem piscis assi, et făvum mellis*, Lk. Bos. 24, 42: Mt. Bos. 7, 10: Deut. 4, 18. We ðē willaþ ferigan freólīce ofer fisces bæþ *we will freely convey thee over the fish's bath*, Andr. Kmbl. 586; An. 293: Exon. 116 b; Th. 447, 14; Dōm. 39. Nim ðone ǣrestan fisc *take the first fish*, Mt. Bos. 17, 27: Jn. Bos. 21, 13. Bletsien ðec fiscas and fuglas *may fishes and birds bless thee*, Exon. 55 a; Th. 194, 16; Az. 140: 97 b; Th. 364, 33; Wal. 80. Ða fixas, ðe wǣron on ðam flōde, wurdon deáde *pisces qui ĕrant in flūmĭne, mortui sunt*, Ex. 7, 21: Ors. 5, 4; Bos. 105, 15. Earmra fisca *of poor fishes*, Salm. Kmbl. 164; Sal. 81: Bt. Met. Fox 11, 133; Met. 11, 67. Hīg betugon mycele menigeo fixa *conclūsērunt piscium multĭtūdĭnem cōpiōsam*, Lk. Bos. 5, 6: Mt. Bos. 15, 34: Mk. Bos. 6, 43: 8, 7. Hī gefēngon þreó hund fixa missenlīcra cynna *they caught three hundred fishes of diverse kinds*, Bd. 4, 13; S. 583, 1. Mid fiscum *with fishes*, Exon. 22 a; Th. 60, 10; Cri. 967: 126 b; Th. 487, 19; Rä. 73, 4. He afēdde of fixum twām and of fīf hlāfum fīf þūsendo *he fed five thousand from two fishes and from five loaves*, Andr. Kmbl. 1178; An. 589: Mk. Bos. 6, 41. We nabbaþ hēr, būton fīf hlāfas and twegen fixas *non hăbēmus hic, nisi quinque pānes, et duos pisces*, Mt. Bos. 14, 17: Lk. Bos. 9, 13: Jn. Bos. 6, 9: 21, 10: Gen. 1, 26. Heora fisceas forwurdan *occīdit pisces eōrum*, Ps. Th. 104, 25. [*Wyc.* fische: *Chauc.* fissch, fissche: *Laym.* fisc, uisc, *m: Orm.* fisskess *fishes, pl: Plat.* fisk, *m: O. Sax.* fisc, visc, *m: Frs.* fisck: *O. Frs.* fisk: *Dut.* visch, *m: Ger.* fisch, *m: M. H. Ger.* visch, *m: O. H. Ger.* fisc, *m: Goth.* fisks, *m: Dan.* fisk, *m. f: Swed.* fisk, *m: Icel.* fiskr, *m: Lat.* piscis, *m: Wel.* pysg, *m: Corn.* pesc, pysc, pisc, *m: Armor.* pesc: *Ir.* iasg, iasc, *m: Gael.* iasg, éisg, *m.*] DER. eá-fisc, horn-, hran-, hron-, mere-, sǣ-.

fiscaþ, es; *m. A fishing;* piscātus:—Ðǣr biþ swȳðe mycel fiscaþ *there is very much fishing*, Ors. 1, 1; Bos. 22, 14. v. fiscoþ.

fisc-bryne *fish-brine;* piscium salsūgo:—Fiscbryne *liguamen?* vel *gărum*, Ælfc. Gl. 32; Som. 62, 13; Wrt. Voc. 27, 66.

fisc-cynn, -cinn, es; *n. The fish kind, kind of fishes;* piscium gĕnus:—Is heofena rīce gelīc asendum nette on ða sǣ, and of ǣlcum fisccynne gadrigendum *sĭmĭle est regnum cœlōrum săgēnæ missæ in măre, et ex omni gĕnĕre piscium congrĕganti*, Mt. Bos. 13, 47. God gesceóp ðā ða micelan hwalas and eall libbende fisccinn on heora hiwum *then God created the great whales and every living kind of fishes after their kinds*, Gen. 1, 21: Ælfc. T. 8, 25.

fisceran = fiscerum *with fishers*, Ors. 1, 1; Bos. 20, 5; *dat. pl. of* fiscere. v. fugeleran, drīan.

fiscere, es; *m.* I. *A* FISHER; piscātor:—Ic eom fiscere *ĕgo sum piscātor*, Coll. Monast. Th. 23, 1: Wrt. Voc. 73, 40. Hī wǣron fisceras *ĕrant piscātōres*, Mt. Bos. 4, 18: Mk. Bos. 1, 16. Ðæra Terfinna land wæs eall wēste, būtan ðǣr huntan gewīcodon, oððe fisceras, oððe fugeleras *the land of the Terfinns was all waste, save where the hunters, fishers or fowlers encamped*, Ors. 1, 1; Bos. 20, 9. Ða fisceras eódon, and wōxon heora nett *piscātōres descendĕrant et lăvābant rētia*, Lk. Bos. 5, 2. Fiscerum [MS. fisceran] *with fishers*, Ors. 1, 1; Bos. 20, 5. II. *the bird king-fisher;* alcēdo:—Fiscere *rapariolus?* [=*rīpāriolus?*], Ælfc. Gl. 38; Som. 63, 44; Wrt. Voc. 29, 62.

fisc-hūs, es; *n. A fishing-house;* piscīnāle, Ælfc. Gl. 108; Som. 78, 105; Wrt. Voc. 58, 20.

fiscian, fixian; *p.* ode; *pp.* od *To fish;* piscāri:—Ðonne gē fiscian willaþ *when ye wish to fish*, Bt. 32, 3; Fox 118, 12.

fisc-mere, es; *m. A fish-pond;* piscīna, vīvārium, Som. Ben. Lye.

fisc-naþ, es; *m? A fishing;* piscātus:—On fiscnaþe *by fishing*, Bd. 4, 13; S. 582, 41. v. fisc-nōþ.

fisc-net, -nett, es; *n. A net of fishes, fishing net;* piscium rēte, piscātōrium rēte:—Hī tugon hyra fiscnett *trăhentes rēte piscium*, Jn. Bos. 21, 8. Hwȳ gē ne settan on sume dūne fiscnet eówru *why do ye not set your fishing nets on some hill?* Bt. Met. Fox 19, 21; Met. 19, 11.

fisc-noþ, -naþ, es; *m? A fishing;* piscātus:—Seó þeód ðone cræft ne cūðe ðæs fiscnoþes *the people knew not the art of fishing*, Bd. 4, 13; S. 582, 43.

fiscoþ, fiscaþ, fixoþ, es; *m? A fishing;* piscātus:—On fiscoþe, Ors. 1, 1; Bos. 19, 30: on fixoþ *afysshynge* (Tyndale) Jn. Bos. 21, 3.

fisc-pōl, es; *m? A fish-pool, fish-pond;* piscīna, vīvārium:—Fiscpōl *vīvārium*, Ælfc. Gl. 98; Som. 76, 94; Wrt. Voc. 54, 38: 80, 66: *piscīna*, Som. 76, 95; Wrt. Voc. 54, 39. On fiscpōle *in a fish-pool*, Lchdm. iii. 212, 15.

fisc-wēr, es; *m.* [wēr II. *a draught of fishes*] *A draught of fishes;* piscium captūra:—Lǣtaþ eówre nett on ðone fiscwēr *laxāte rētia vestra in captūram [piscium]*, Lk. Bos. 5, 4.

fisc-wylle, -welle; *adj.* [cf. weallan *to swarm*] *Full of fish, abounding in fish;* piscĭbus abundans, piscōsus:—Ðæt eálond is fiscwylle *the island is abounding in fish*, Bd. 1, 1; S. 474, 41. Fiscwyllum wæterum *flŭviis piscōsis*, 1, 1; S. 473, 15. Fiscwelle *bisarius?* [=*piscārius*], Wrt. Voc. 66, 8.

fisting, e; *f. Fesciculatio? forte* fistulātio, Som. 72, 65; Ælfc. Gl. 79; Wrt. Voc. 46, 23.

fit, fitt, es; *n? Strife, a fight, contest;* rixa, pugna, certāmen:—He slōh and fylde feónd on fitte *he struck and felled the enemy in fight*, Cd. 95; Th. 124, 33; Gen. 2072. v. fettian, fitung.

fit, fitt, e; *f. A song, poem;* cantĭlēna, carmen:—Ðā se Wīsdōm ðas fitte asungen hæfde *when Wisdom had sung this song*, Bt. 30, 1; Fox 106, 29. On fitte *in song, verse*, Bt. Met. Fox introduc. 17; Met. Einl. 9.

fiter-sticca, an; *m. A tent-nail;* clāvus tentōrii:—Fitersticca *clāvus tentōrii*, Ælfc. Gl. 110; Som. 79, 42; Wrt. Voc. 59, 14.

FIÐELE, an; *f. A fiddle;* fĭdĭcŭla, Som. Ben. Lye. [*Piers P.* fithele: *Chauc.* fithul: *Laym.* fiðele: *Plat.* fidel, *f: Dut.* vedel, veel, *f: Ger.* fiedel, fidel, *f: M. H. Ger.* videle, videl, *f: O. H. Ger.* fidula, *f: Dan.* fiddel, *m. f: Icel.* fiðla, *f: M. Lat.* fidula, vidula: *Lat.* fĭdes, *f. a string, guitar.*]

fiðelere, es; *m. A fiddler;* fĭdĭcen:—Fiðelere *fĭdĭcen*, Ælfc. Gr. 9, 12; Som. 9, 25: Wrt. Voc. 73, 61.

fiðelestre, an; *f.* [fiðele *a fiddle*, -estre *a female termination*, q. v.] *A female fiddler;* fĭdĭcĭna, Wrt. Voc. 73, 62.

fiðer- *four-* in the compounds fiðer-fēte, -scȳte. v. fyðer-, feówer.

fiðer-berende; *part. Bearing wings, winged;* ālĭger, Cot. 9: 170.

fiðere, es; *n. A wing;* āla: more often found in the *pl. nom. acc.* fiðera, fiðeru, fiðru, fyðera, fyðeru, fyðru; *gen.* fiðera, fyðera, fyðerena; *dat. inst.* fiðerum, fiðrum, fyðerum; *n:* also the forms are sometimes found *pl. nom. acc.* fiðeras, fyðeras; *m. Wings;* ālæ, pennæ:—Gif his ōðer fiðere forod biþ *if one of its wings* [lit. *one wing of it*] *is broken,*

Homl. Th. ii. 318, 29. Fiđera [Spl. fyđera : Lamb. fyđeras] beóþ culfran fægeres seolfres *pennæ cŏlumbæ sunt deargentātæ*, Ps. Th. 67, 13. Sindon đa fiđru hwīt *the wings are white*, Exon. 60 a; Th. 218, 20; Ph. 297. Bearn manna under wǣfelse odđe on gescyldnesse đīnra fiđera [Spl. fyđera] hopiaþ *fīlii hŏmĭnum in tegmĭne ālārum tuārum spērābunt*, Ps. Lamb. 35, 8: 56, 2: 60, 5. Gehȳd me under đīnra fiđera [Lamb. fyđerena] sceade *sub umbra ālārum tuārum protĕge me*, Ps. Th. 16, 8. Under fiđerum [Th. fiđrum : Lamb. fyđerum] his đū hopudest *sub pennis ejus spērābis*, Ps. Spl. 90, 4: Lk. Bos. 13, 34. Nabbaþ hī æt fiđrum fultum *they have no help from wings*, Bt. Met. Fox 31, 15; Met. 31, 8. Fleáh ofer fiđera [Th. fiđeru : Lamb. fydru] winda *vŏlāvit sŭper pennas ventōrum*, Ps. Spl. 17, 12: Homl. Th. ii. 318, 27. Abred of đa fiđeru *take off the wings*, Lev. 1, 17: Ps. Th. 54, 6: 138, 7: Salm. Kmbl. 528; Sal. 263. Se fōtum tredeþ fiđru [Spl. fyđeru: Lamb. fyđeras] winda *qui ambŭlat sŭper pennas ventōrum*, Ps. Th. 103, 4: Bt. Met. Fox 24, 1; Met. 24, 1: Exon. 65 a; Th. 241, 7; Ph. 652: 109 b; Th. 418, 18; Rä. 37, 7. Ac đǣr ic mōste đīn mōd gefiđerigan mid đām fiđerum, đæt đū mihtest mid me flióġan *but if I were allowed to furnish thy mind with wings, that thou mightest fly with me*, Bt. 36, 2; Fox 174, 6: Ps. Th. 60, 3: 62, 7: 148, 10. Hī mid hyra fiđrum weardiaþ [MS. wearþ] *they protect with their wings*, Exon. 13 b; Th. 25, 3; Cri. 395: 55 a; Th. 195, 23; Az. 160: 60 b; Th. 220, 7; Ph. 316: 88 b; Th. 332, 21; Vy. 88: Elen. Kmbl. 1482; El. 743. Him fiđeras ne fultumaþ *wings support them not*, Bt. 41, 6; Fox 254, 26. v. feđer II.

fiđer-fēte, -fōte; *adj. Four-footed;* quădrŭpes:—Ǣlcum fiđerfētum neáte *for any four-footed beast*, Med. ex Quadr. 1, 3; Lchdm. i. 328, 13. Eallum fiđerfētum nȳtenum *to all four-footed beasts*, 1, 3; Lchdm. i. 330, 4. Fiđerfōte fugel *a four-footed bird, griffin*; griffus, gryps = γρύψ, Wrt. Voc. 78, 2. v. feówer-fēte.

fiđerian, fiđerigan, fiđrian *to give wings to, provide with wings.* DER. ge-fiđerian.

fiđer-leás; *adj. Wingless;* ālis cārens:—Sum sceal of heán beáme fiđerleás feallan *one wingless shall fall from a high tree*, Exon. 87 b; Th. 328, 23; Vy. 22.

fiđer-scȳte, -scīte; *adj. Four-cornered, quadrangular, square;* quadrangŭlus, quadrātus:—Fiđerscȳte setel *siliquastrum* vel *cathedra quadrāta*, Ælfc. Gl. 116; Som. 80, 66; Wrt. Voc. 61, 44. Seó cyrce wæs eal of fiđerscītum marmstānum geworht *the church was built all of quadrangular marble stones*, Homl. Th. ii. 496, 35. v. feówer-scȳte.

fiđru *wings*, Exon. 60 a; Th. 218, 20; Ph. 297: 65 a; Th. 241, 7; Ph. 652; *pl. nom. acc. of* fiđere.

fiđrum *to* or *with wings*, Bt. Met. Fox 31, 15; Met. 31, 8: Elen. Kmbl. 1482; El. 743; *pl. dat. and inst. of* fiđere.

fittan; *p.* te; *pp.* ed *To sing;* cantāre:—Nū ic fitte gēn ymb fisca cynn *now again I sing about [the] kind of fishes*, Exon. 96 b; Th. 360, 5; Wal. 1. [*Dut.* vitten *to criticise.*]

fitung, fytung, e; *f. A fighting, quarreling;* rixa:—Ascūnige man swīđe fracodlīce fitunga *let a man earnestly shun shameful fightings*, L. Eth. vi. 28; Th. i. 322, 14.

fīwan *to hate;* ŏdio hăbēre, inĭmīcāri, Som. Ben. Lye. v. feógan, feón.

fixas *fishes*, Ex. 7, 21: Mt. Bos. 14, 17: Lk. Bos. 9, 13; *pl. nom. acc. of* fisc, *q. v.*

fixen, e; *f. A she-fox*, VIXEN; vulpes fēmĭna, Som. Ben. Lye.

fixen; *adj.* [fox *a fox*] *Of* or *belonging to a fox;* vulpīnus:—Fixen hȳd *a fox-skin*, Med. ex Quadr. 3, 15; Lchdm. i. 342, 11.

fixian; *p.* ode; *pp.* od [fisc = fix *a fish*] *To fish;* piscāri:—Ic fixige *piscor*, Ælfc. Gr. 25; Som. 27, 11. For hwī ne fixast đū on sǣ *cur non piscāris in māri?* Coll. Monast. Th. 24, 1. v. fiscian.

fixoþ, es; *m? A fishing;* piscātus:—Ic wylle gān on fixoþ *vādo piscāri*, Jn. Bos. 21, 3. v. fiscoþ.

FLĀ, flaa; *gen. dat. acc.* flān; *pl. nom. acc.* flān; *gen.* flāna; *dat.* flānum; *f.* [flae, *gen.* flaan = flān; *f.*] *An arrow, a dart, javelin;* săgitta, tēlum, jăcŭlum:—Flā *săgitta* vel *tēlum*, Wrt. Voc. 84, 27: Ælfc. Gr. 8; Som. 7, 60: Ælfc. Gl. 52; Som. 66, 35; Wrt. Voc. 35, 24. Flaa *tēlum* vel *ŏbĕliscus* = ὀβελίσκος, 53; Som. 66, 63; Wrt. Voc. 35, 49. Wīdnyt *vel* flā *jăcŭlum* vel *funda*, 18; Som. 58, 106; Wrt. Voc. 22, 21. Wearþ Alexander þurhscoten mid ānre flān underneoþan ōđer breóst *Alexander was shot through with an arrow underneath one breast*, Ors. 3, 9; Bos. 68, 27. He gedēþ his flān fȳrena *săgittas suas ardentĭbus effēcit*, Ps. Th. 7, 13: 90, 6: Deut. 32, 42. Flāna scūras *showers of arrows*, Elen. Kmbl. 234; El. 117: Judth. 11; Thw. 24, 33; Jud. 221. Sī he mid stānum oftorfod odđe mid flānum ofscotod *lăpĭdĭbus opprĭmētur aut confŏdiētur jăcŭlis*, Ex. 19, 13: Ps. Th. 10, 2. [*Chauc.* flo; *pl.* flone: *Laym.* fla, flo: *Icel.* fleinn, *m. a dart.*] v. flān.

flacea *flakes of snow;* flocci nĭvis, Som. Ben. Lye.

flacge, an; *f. A poultice;* cataplasma, Cot. 55.

flacor; *adj. Flickering;* vŏlĭtans:—Flacor flānþracu feorhhord onleác *the flickering arrow's force unlocked life's treasury*, Exon. 49 b; Th. 170, 25; Gū. 1117. Ofer scildhreādan sceótend sendaþ flacor flāngeweorc *warriors send flickering arrow-work over the shield's defence*, 17 b; Th. 42, 21; Cri. 676.

flǣc *flesh;* căro, Ælfc. Gl. 69; Som. 70, 31; Wrt. Voc. 42, 39. v. flǣsc.

flǣh *a flea;* pūlex, Som. Ben. Lye. v. fleá.

flǣm, es; *m. Flight;* fŭga:—He deófla afyrseþ and on flǣme gebringeþ *he sends away devils and puts them to flight*, L. C. E. 4; Wilk. 128, 15. v. fleám.

flǣman, flēman; *p.* de; *pp.* ed *To cause to flee, put to flight;* fŭgāre. DER. ge-flǣman, -flēman. v. flȳman.

flǣn *a lance;* frămea, Ps. Spl. 16, 14. v. flān.

flǣre, an; *f. An earlap;* pinnŭla auris:—Flǣran = eár-læppan *pinnŭlæ aurium* = *aurĭcŭlæ*, Ælfc. Gl. 71; Som. 70, 84; Wrt. Voc. 43, 16. v. eár-læppa.

FLǢSC, es; *pl. nom. acc.* flǣsc; *gen.* flǣsca, flǣscea; *dat.* flǣscum; *n:* flēsc, es; *n.* FLESH; căro:—Se gāst is hræd, and đæt flǣsc ys untrum *spīrĭtus promptus est, căro autem infirma*, Mt. Bos. 26, 41: Mk. Bos. 14, 38. Đæt Word wæs geworden flǣsc, and wunode on us *the Word became flesh, and dwelt in us*, Homl. Th. i. 40, 17: Exon. 9 b; Th. 8, 25; Cri. 123: 16 b; Th. 37, 23; Cri. 597. Sōþlīce mīn flǣsc is mete, and mīn blōd ys drinc *căro ĕnim mea vēre est cĭbus, et sanguis meus vēre est pōtus*, Jn. Bos. 6, 55: Lk. Bos. 3, 6: Gen. 2, 23: 6, 3: Ps. Spl. 15, 9: Ps. Lamb. 55, 4: 77, 39. Ge-endung ealles flǣsces com ætfōran me *fīnis ūnĭversæ carnis vēnit cōram me*, Gen. 6, 13, 19: Jn. Bos. 1, 13. In flǣsce *in the flesh*, Bt. Met. Fox 20, 475; Met. 20, 238: Apstls. Kmbl. 73; Ap. 37. Ryht æđelo biþ on đam mōde, næs on đam flǣsce *true nobility is in the mind, not in the flesh*, Bt. 30, 2; Fox 110, 19. Beóþ twegen on ānum flǣsce *ĕrunt duo in carne una*, Mt. Bos. 19, 5: Mk. Bos. 10, 8. Þurh đæt flǣsc *through the flesh*, Exon. 27 a: Th. 80, 12; Cri. 1306: 13 b; Th. 26, 17; Cri. 418. Flǣsce bifongen *invested with flesh*, 84 a; Th. 316, 13; Mōd. 48: 98 a; Th. 368, 33; Seel. 34. Genam he ān ribb of his sīdan and gefylde mid flǣsce *tŭlit ūnam de costis ejus et replēvit carnem pro ea*, Gen. 2, 21. Beóþ đa syngan flǣsc scandum þurhwaden *the sinful flesh shall be penetrated with scandals*, Exon. 26 b; Th. 78, 31; Cri. 1282. Flǣsca gehwylc *omnis căro*, Ps. Th. 144, 21. He afēdeþ flǣscea [MS. flǣcsea] ǣghwylc *qui dat escam omni carni*, 135, 26. [*Piers P.* flesshe: *Wyc.* fleisch, fleixh, flehs: *Laym.* flæsce, flas, flæs: *Orm.* flæsh: *Plat.* fleesk, fleesch, *n: O. Sax.* flēsk, fleisk, *n: Frs.* flæsck, flæsch: *O. Frs.* flask, flesk, *n: Dut.* vleesch, *n: Ger.* fleisch, *n: M. H. Ger.* vleisch, *n: O. H. Ger.* fleisc, *n: Dan.* flesk, *n. bacon, pork: Swed.* fläsk, *n. pork, bacon: Icel.* flesk, *n. pork, ham, bacon.*]

flǣsc-ǣt, es; *m.* [ǣt *food*] *Flesh food;* carneus victus, R. Ben. 36.

flǣsc-cōfa, an; *m.* [flǣsc *flesh*, cōfa *a chamber*] *The flesh chamber, the body, flesh;* căro:—Gefæstna mid ege đīnum flǣsccōfan mīne *confīge tĭmōre tuo carnes meas*, Ps. Lamb. 118, 120.

flǣsc-cwellere, es; *m. A butcher, hangman;* lănius, carnĭfex, Som. Ben. Lye.

flǣsc-cȳping, e; *f.* [cȳping II. *a market-place, market*] *A flesh-market, meat-market;* măcellum:—Flǣsccȳping [MS. flæc-cyping] *măcellum*, Ælfc. Gl. 55; Som. 67, 14; Wrt. Voc. 37, 8.

flǣsceht; *adj. Fleshy, fleshly;* carneus, Som. Ben. Lye.

flǣsc-gebyrd, e; *f. Flesh-birth, incarnation;* incarnātio:—Flǣscgebyrde *incarnātiōnis*, Mone B. 499.

flǣsc-hama, -homa, an; *m. Flesh-covering, the body, a carcase;* carnis tegmen, corpus:—Læg mīn flǣschoma in foldan bigrafen *my body lay buried in earth*, Exon. 29 a; Th. 89, 32; Cri. 1466: 47 b; Th. 163, 35; Gū. 1004. Bil eal þurhwōd fǣgne flǣschoman *the falchion passed all through her fated carcase*, Beo. Th. 3140; B. 1568: Andr. Kmbl. 307; An. 154. Lǣgon on greóte fǣgra flǣschaman *the carcases of the slain lay on the sand*, 2171; An. 1087.

flǣsc-hamian *to become incarnate;* carnem humānam induĕre. v. hama, ge-flǣschamod.

flǣsc-hord, es; *n. The flesh-hoard, the body;* carnis thesaurus, corpus:—Firenaþ đus đæt flǣschord *thus will the body sin*, Exon. 99 b; Th. 373, 3; Seel. 103; Soul Kmbl. 203.

flǣsc-hūs, es; *n. A flesh-house;* carnis offĭcīna:—Flǣschūs *carnāle*, Ælfc. Gl. 108; Som. 78, 102; Wrt. Voc. 58, 17.

flǣsc-līc; *adj. Fleshly, carnal;* carnālis:—Unrihtlīc biþ đæt se cristena mann flǣsclīce lustas gefremme *unlawful it is for the christian man to indulge in fleshly lusts*, Homl. Th. ii. 100, 18. Swā swā đa gōdan fæderas gewuniaþ heora flǣsclīce bearn þreágean *sīcut bŏni patres carnālibus fīliis sŏlent discĭplīnam tĕnēre*, Bd. 1, 27; S. 490, 16. Hwæt gōdes magan we secgan on đa flǣsclīcan unþeáwas *what good shall we say of the fleshly vices?* Bt. 31, 1; Fox 110, 25: Boutr. Scrd. 21, 43: Past. 11, 4; Hat. MS. 15 a, 17.

flǣsc-līcnes, -ness, -nys, -nyss, e; *f. Fleshliness, incarnation;* incarnātio:—Se đe wile smeágan ymbe đa gerȳnu Cristes flǣsclīcnysse *he who will inquire about the mystery of Christ's incarnation*, Homl. Th. ii. 278, 35: 280, 22.

flǣsc-mangere, es; *m. A fleshmonger, butcher;* carnis vendĭtor, măcellārius, lănius, Cot. 57: 125: Cod. Dipl. 1291; A. D. 996; Kmbl. vi. 135, 17, 18.

flǽsc-maðu, e; *f. A fleshworm, maggot;* vermis carnem infestans, Ælfc. Gl. 24; Som. 60, 19; Wrt. Voc. 24, 23.

flǽsc-mete, es; *pl. nom. acc.* -mettas; *m.* FLESH-MEAT, *flesh;* carnĕus cĭbus, căro:—Hū wæs mancynne flǽscmete alýfed æfter ðam flōde *why was fleshmeat allowed to mankind after the flood?* Boutr. Scrd. 21, 16. Mid flǽscmete *with flesh-meat,* L. C. S. 47; Th. i. 402, 24. Gē etaþ flǽscmettas eówre hreáwe *mandūcābĭtis carnes vestras crūdas,* Coll. Monast. Th. 29, 11: Ps. Lamb. 49, 13.

flǽscnes, -ness, e; *f. Incarnation;* incarnātio, Hem. 57. DER. ge-flǽscnes.

flǽsc-strǽt, e; *f. A* FLESH-STREET, *meat-market;* carnāle, carnis offĭcīna, măcellum:—Flǽscstrǽt [MS. flæc-stræt] *măcellum,* Ælfc. Gl. 55; Som. 67, 14; Wrt. Voc. 37, 8.

flǽsc-tawere, es; *m. A flesh-tawer* or *tormentor, an executioner;* lănio, carnĭfex:—Hyldere, oððe cwellere, oððe flǽsctawere [MS. flæc-tawere] *lănio, vel lănista, vel carnĭfex, vel măcellārius,* Ælfc. Gl. 113; Som. 79, 120; Wrt. Voc. 60, 27.

flǽsc-wyrm, es; *m. A* FLESH-WORM, *maggot;* tĕrēdo, vermis carnem infestans:—Wið flǽscwyrmum *against flesh-worms,* L. M. 1, 51; Lchdm. ii. 124, 19.

flæðe-camb [MS. -comb], fleðe-camb, es; *m. A weaver's comb;* pecten, pectĭca, Glos. Brux. Recd. 40, 15; Wrt. Voc. 66, 23.

flāh; *adj. Insidious, artful, deceitful, fraudulent;* subdŏlus, fraudŭlentus, infestus:—Ðonne ðæt gecnāweþ flāh feónd gemāh *when the deceitful impious fiend knows that,* Exon. 97 a; Th. 362, 19; Wal. 39.

flān, es; *m.* e; *f.* [flān; *gen.* flānes; *m* flān; *gen.* e; *f.*] *An arrow, a dart;* săgitta, tēlum:—Þurh flānes flyht *through the flight of an arrow,* Byrht. Th. 133, 56; By. 71. Fram flāne fleógendre *a săgitta vŏlante,* Ps. Spl. 90, 6: Beo. Th. 4868; B. 2438. Ðīne flāna synt afæstnode [MS. afæstnade] on me *săgittæ tuæ infixæ sunt mihi,* Ps. Th. 37, 2: 44, 7: Ps. Spl. 56, 6. Ic afæstnie mīne flāna on him *săgittas meas complēbo in eis,* Deut. Grn. 32, 23. v. flā.

flān-boga, an; *m. An arrow-bow;* arcus săgittis aptus:—Se ðe of flānbogan fyrenum sceóteþ *who wickedly shoots from his arrow-bow,* Beo. Th. 3492; B. 1744: 2870; B. 1433.

flān-geweorc, es; *n. Arrow-work;* jaculatōrius apparātus:—Flacor flāngeweorc *flickering arrow-work,* Exon. 17 b; Th. 42, 21; Cri. 676.

flān-hred; *adj. arrow-swift;* săgittārius expedītus, Grn. Reim. 72.

flāniht; *adj. Belonging to darts;* ad tēla pertĭnens, jăcŭlātōrius, jăcŭlātus, Cot. 112. v. flān.

flān-þræc, -þracu; *gen.* -þræce; *pl. nom. gen. acc.* -þraca; *f. Arrows' force;* săgittārum impĕtus:—Wið flānþræce, Exon. 71 a; Th. 265, 20: Jul. 384. Flānþracu, Exon. 49 b; Th. 170, 25; Gū. 1117.

flāt, *pl.* fliton *strove, contended; p. of* flītan.

FLAXE, an; *f. A* FLASK, *bottle;* flasca, flasco, lăgēna:—Flaxe *flasca,* Ælfc. Gl. 25; Som. 60, 65; Wrt. Voc. 25, 7. Twā treówene fatu wīnes fulle, ða syndon on folcisc flaxan gehātene *duo lignea vāsa vīno plēna, quæ sunt vulgo flascōnes vŏcāta,* Greg. Dial. 1, 9: 2, 13. Ic bicge hýda and fell, and wyrce of him flaxan *ĕgo ĕmo cŭtes et pelles, et făcio ex iis flascōnes,* Coll. Monast. Th. 27, 37. [*Plat.* flaske, *f: Dut.* flesch, *f: Ger.* flasche, *f: M. H. Ger.* vlasche, vlesche, *f: O. H. Ger.* flasca, *f: Dan.* flaske, *m. f: Swed.* flaska, *f: Icel.* flaska, *f: M. Lat.* flasca, flasco, Du Cange.] DER. wæter-flaxe.

flax-fōte, flox-fōte, flohten-fōte; *adj. Broad-footed, flat-footed, web-footed;* palmĭpes:—Ða fugelas ðe on flōdum wuniaþ syndon flaxfōte, ðæt hī swimman mǽgen [MS. magon] *the birds that dwell in waters are web-footed, that they may swim,* Hexam. 8; Norm. 14, 15.

FLEÁ, an; *m.* I. *a* FLEA; pūlex:—Fleá *pūlex,* Wrt. Voc. 78, 68. Κόνυζα fleán acwelleþ *fleabane kills fleas,* Herb. 143; Lchdm. i. 266, 2. Gorst cwelþ ða fleán *gorse killeth the fleas,* 142; Lchdm. i. 264, 15. Wið fleán *against fleas,* 142; Lchdm. i. 264, 14. v. fleó. II. *a speck, speck* or *disease in the eye;* albūgo, -ĭnis, *f.* măcŭla:—Wið fleán and wið eágena sāre *against white specks and against sore of eyes,* Herb. 24; Lchdm. i. 120, 16. [*Plat.* flo, flö *a flea: Dut.* vloo, *f. a flea: Ger.* floh, *m. a flea: M. H. Ger.* vlōch, *m. a flea: O. H. Ger.* flōh, flōch, *m. a flea: Icel.* fló, *f. a flea: Lat.* pūlex, *f. a flea.*] DER. eág-fleá. v. fleah.

fleág *flew,* Exon. 46 a; Th. 157, 9; Gū. 889; *p. of* fleógan.

fleah *a flea;* pūlex, Glos. Epnl. Recd. 161, 42. v. fleá.

fleah, fleó, flió, flié, flīg; *indecl. n:* fleá, an; *m. A white spot in the eye;* albūgo:—Þurh ðone æpl ðæs eágan mon mæg geseón, gif him ðæt fleah on ne gǽþ, gif hine ðonne ðæt fleah mid ealle ofergǽþ, ðonne ne mæg he nōht geseón *a man can see with the pupil of the eye, if the white speck does not spread over it, if the white speck spreads all over it, then he cannot see anything,* Past. 11, 4; Hat. MS. 15 b, 4. Se hæfþ eallinga fleah on his mōdes eágum *he has altogether a white speck in the eyes of his mind,* 11, 4; Hat. MS. 15 b, 1.

fleáh *flew,* Ps. Spl. 17, 12; *p. of* fleógan.

fleáh *fled,* Ps. Lamb. 113, 3; *p. of* fleón.

fleám, flǽm, es; *m.* [fleón *to flee*] *Flight;* fūga:—Ðæt eówer fleám on wintra ne geweorþe *ut non fiat fūga vestra in hieme,* Mt. Bos. 24, 20: Chr. 998; Erl. 135, 19. Wurdon feówer on fleáme folccyningas *four kings of nations were in flight,* Cd. 95; Th. 125, 4; Gen. 2074: Chr. 477; Erl. 12, 31: L. C. E. 4; Th. i. 360, 29: Jos. 7, 4. Nū sceal æðelingas gefricgean fleám eówerne *now nobles shall hear of your flight,* Beo. Th. 5771; B. 2889: Ps. Th. 141, 5: Ps. Spl. 88, 23. Fleám gewyrcan *to take to flight,* Byrht. Th. 134, 9; By. 81. Efne ic feor gewīte, fleáme dǽle *ecce elongāvi fūgiens,* Ps. Th. 54, 7: Andr. Kmbl. 3087; An. 1546. Crist nolde ða þrōwunge mid fleáme forbūgan *Christ would not by flight avoid his passion,* Homl. Th. i. 206, 6: Chr. 937; Erl. 114, 3; Æðelst. 37. [*Laym.* flæm, fleam, flem *flight.*]

fleáming *a runaway,* Grm. Gr. ii. 351, 11. v. flýming.

fleán; *p.* flōh, *pl.* flōgon; *pp.* flagen *To flay, pull off the skin;* excŏriāre, deglūbĕre, Cot. 61. [*Laym.* flan, flean *to flay: Dut. Kil.* vlaen vlaeghen: *Swed.* flå: *Icel.* flá.] DER. be-fleán.

fleard, es; *n. Trifles;* nūgæ:—Gif friþgeard sī on hwæs lande, abūton stān, oððe treów, oððe wille, oððe swilces ǽnige fleard *if there be an inclosed space on any one's land, about a stone, or a tree, or a well, or any trifles of such kind,* L. N. P. L. 54; Th. ii. 298, 17. Flearde *fraude,* Mone B. 1530. [*Orm.* flærd *mockery: Scot.* flird: *Icel.* flærð, *f. deceit.*] DER. ge-fleard.

fleardian; *p.* ode; *pp.* od *To trifle, err;* nūgāri, errāre:—Fleardian *nūgāri,* Off. Episc. 7: *errāre,* Scint. 31.

fleát *floated,* Beo. Th. 3822; B. 1909; *p. of* fleótan.

fleaðe, fleoðe, an; *f. The water-lily;* nymphæa alba, Lin:—Of fleaðan wyrte *from the plant of the water-lily,* L. M. 2, 51; Lchdm. ii. 264, 20.

fleá-wyrt, e; *f.* FLEA-WORT, *flea-bane;* pūlĭcāria, psyllium = ψύλλιον, cŏnyza = κόνυζα:—Fleáwyrt *parirus?* Wrt. Voc. 287, 23.

FLEAX, flex, es; *n.* FLAX; līnum:—Of ðære eorþan cymeþ ðæt fleax *flax comes from the earth,* Past. 14, 6; Hat. MS. 18 b, 13. Fleax *līnum,* Wrt. Voc. 82, 6. Þurh ðæt fleax *by the flax,* Past. 14, 6; Hat. MS. 18 b, 14. Swīðe hwīt fleax *very white flax;* bissum [= byssus = βύσσος], Ælfc. Gl. 62; Som. 68, 94; Wrt. Voc. 40, 5. [*Wyc.* flax, flaxe, flex, flexe: *Chauc.* flex: *Plat.* flass, *n: Frs.* flægs: *O. Frs.* flax, *n: Dut.* vlas, *n: Ger.* flachs, *m: M. H. Ger.* vlahs, *m: O. H. Ger.* flahs, *m: Lat.* flectĕre, plectĕre: *Grk.* πλέκειν *to plait, twine, twist, weave.*]

fleaxen; *adj. Flaxen;* līneus, Som. Ben. Lye.

flēc *flesh,* Chr. 1137; Gib. 239, 27. v. flǽsc.

fled *a dwelling, abode,* Lchdm. iii. 54, 17. v. flet.

flēd, es; *n.* [flōd *a flood*] *A flowing, flood;* flūmen:—Eá in flēde *the river in its flow,* Cd. 12; Th. 15, 12; Gen. 232: Andr. Kmbl. 3006; An. 1506. cf. Grein, inflēde.

flēde; *adj. Flooded, overflowed;* tŭmĭdus:—Wæs seó eá to ðan flēde *the river was so flooded,* Ors. 2, 5; Bos. 48, 13. Seó eá flēde wæs *the river was flooded,* Ors. 2, 4; Bos. 44, 7. Tiber flēdu wearþ *the Tiber was flooded,* Ors. 4, 7; Bos. 87, 20. DER. ofer-flēde.

flēding, e; *f. A flowing, an inundation;* fluxus:—Se ele geswāc ðære flēdinge *the oil ceased from the flowing,* Homl. Th. ii. 180, 2.

flēge *a fly;* cúlĭcem, Mt. Kmbl. Lind. 23, 24. v. fleóge.

flēgende *flying;* vŏlans, Bd. 1, 7, Lye, = fleógende; *part. of* fleógan.

flēma, an; *m. A fugitive;* profŭgus:—Ðū flēma scealt wīdlāst wrecan *thou shalt go a fugitive into far exile,* Cd. 48; Th. 62, 27; Gen. 1020: L. C. S. 13; Th. i. 382, 23: Obs. Lun. § 7; Lchdm. iii. 186, 23. v. flýma.

flēman; *p.* de; *pp.* ed *To cause to flee, put to flight;* fŭgāre. DER. ge-flēman. v. flǽman, flýman.

flene, an; *f. What is made soft, batter:*—Wyl ða flenan *boil the batter,* L. M. 1, 38; Lchdm. ii. 98, 11. v. flyne.

fleó *a flea;* pūlex, Ælfc. Gl. 23; Som. 60, 6; Wrt. Voc. 24, 10. v. fleá.

fleó; *indecl. n. A white speck, disease of the eye;* albūgo:—Ðæs eágan wǽron mid fleó and mid dimnesse twelf mōnþ ofergān *whose eyes had been for a twelvemonth overspread with the white speck and with dimness,* Guthl. 22; Gdwin. 96, 14. v. fleah.

FLEÓGAN, flíogan, to fleógenne; *part.* fleógende; ic fleóge, ðū fleógest, he fleógeþ, *pl.* fleógaþ; *p.* ic, he fleág, fleáh, ðū fluge, *pl.* flugon; *pp.* flogen [fleóge *a fly*]. I. *v. intrans. To* FLY *as with wings;* vŏlāre:—Ðæt he mid feðerhoman fleógan meahte *that he might fly with wings,* Cd. 22; Th. 27, 14; Gen. 417: Bt. Met. Fox 24, 3; Met. 24, 2. Ic hæbbe swīðe swifte feðera, ðæt ic mæg flíogan ofer ðone heán hrōf ðæs heofones *I have very swift wings, that I can fly over the high roof of heaven,* Bt. 36, 2; Fox 174, 5. Hwā me sealde to fleógenne fiðeru swā culfran *quis dăbit mihi pennas sĭcut cŏlumbæ, et vŏlābo?* Ps. Th. 54, 6. Geseah he ða wērian gāstas þurh ðæt fýr fleógende *he saw the accursed spirits flying through the fire,* Bd. 3, 19; S. 548, 34: Bt. Met. Fox 31, 22; Met. 31, 11. Gif ic mīne fiðeru gefō, fleóge ǽr leóhte *si sumpsĕro pennas meas ante lūcem,* Ps. Th. 138, 7. Se fugel fleógeþ *the bird flies,* Exon. 60 b; Th. 220, 18; Ph. 322: Beo. Th. 4539; B. 2273. Me of hrife fleógaþ hylde pīlas *shafts of battle fly from my belly,* Exon. 105 a; Th. 399, 4; Rä. 18, 6. Fleág fugla cyn *the race of birds flew,* Exon. 46 a; Th. 157, 9; Gū. 889: 86 b; Th. 326, 12; Wīd. 127. He fleáh ofer fyðru winda *vŏlāvit sŭper pennas ventōrum,* Ps. Lamb. 17, 11: Cd. 72; Th. 87, 29; Gen. 1456. Ða englas twegen him on twā healfa flugon *the two angels flew on both sides of him*, Bd. 3, 19; S. 548, 32: Exon. 43 a; Th. 146, 14; Gū. 709. **II.** *v. intrans. To flee, flee from;* fŭgĕre, effŭgĕre:—Ðæt he nolde fleógan *that he would not flee*, Byrht. Th. 139, 56; By. 275. Fleógende *fŭgiens*, Ps. Spl. 54, 7. Hī fleógaþ mid ðām feóndum *they flee with the fiends*, Exon. 116 a; Th. 446, 6; Dōm. 18. v. fleón I. [*Laym.* fleon: *Orm.* fleghenn: *Plat.* flegen: *Frs.* flega: *O. Frs.* fliaga: *Dut.* vliegen: *Ger.* fliegen: *M. H. Ger.* vliegen: *O. H. Ger.* fliugan, fleogan: *Dan.* flyve: *Swed.* flyga: *Icel.* fljúga.] DER. be-fleógan, forþ-, ge-, of-, ōþ-, up-, ymb-.

FLEÓGE, an; *f. A* FLY; musca:—Fleóge *musca*, Wrt. Voc. 77, 53: 281, 33. For ðē ic gebidde and ðeós fleóge færþ fram ðē *ōrābo Dŏmĭnum et recēdet musca a Pharaōne*, Ex. 8, 29. Ðæt ðǣr ne beóþ nāne fleógan *ut non sint ĭbi muscæ*, 8, 22. Ic sende on ðē eall fleógena cynn *ĕgo immittam in te omne gĕnus muscārum*, 8, 21, 24. He adrāf ða fleógan fram Pharaone *abstŭlit muscas a Pharaōne*, 8, 31: Ps. Th. 89, 10. Hundes fleóge *a dog-fly*; cynomya = κυνόμυια, Ælfc. Gl. 21; Som. 59, 79; Wrt. Voc. 23, 37: 23; Som. 59, 119; Wrt. Voc. 23, 73: Ps. Spl. 104, 29. Hundes fleóge *rĭcĭnus*, Ælfc. Gl. 21; Som. 59, 80; Wrt. Voc. 23, 38. [*Laym.* fleȝen, fleie, *pl. flies*: *Plat.* flege, *f*: *O. Sax.* fliuga, *f*: *Dut.* vlieg, *f*: *Ger.* fliege, *f*: *M. H. Ger.* vliege, *f*: *O. H. Ger.* fliuga, fleoga, fliega, *f*: *Dan.* flue, *m. f*: *Swed. Icel.* fluga, *f*.] DER. buttor-fleóge.

fleógende; *part. Flying, winged;* vŏlans, vŏlŭcer:—Fleógende *vŏlŭcer*, Ælfc. Gr. 9, 18; Som. 9, 66.

fleógendlīc; *adj. Flying, winged;* vŏlātĭlis:—Fleógendlīc *vŏlātĭlis*, Ælfc. Gr. 9, 28; Som. 11, 41.

fleóg-ryft, es; *n.* [fleóge *a fly*, ryft *a garment, veil, curtain*] *A fly-net, net for keeping off flies;* vēlāmen ad muscas prohĭbendas, cōnōpeum = κωνωπεῖον:—Fleógryft *cōnōpeum*, Cot. 46. v. fleóh-net.

fleógynda, fleógenda, an; *m.* [fleógende, *part. of* fleógan *to fly*] *A flying creature, bird, fowl;* vŏlātĭle:—Ic oncneów ealle fleógyndan heofones *cognōvi omnia vŏlātĭlia cœli*, Ps. Spl. C. 49, 12; ic oncneów all ða fleógendan [MS. flēgendan] heofenes *cognōvi omnia vŏlātĭlia cœli*, Ps. Surt. 49, 11: Ps. Spl. C. 77, 31.

fleóh-cyn, -cynn, es; *m. A kind of flies;* muscārum gĕnus:—Fleóhcynnes feala flugan on gemǣru *sciniphes in omnĭbus fīnĭbus eōrum*, Ps. Th. 104, 27.

fleóh-net, -nett, es; *n. A fly-net, net for keeping off flies;* cōnōpeum = κωνωπεῖον:—Fleóhnet *cōnōpeum*, Ælfc. Gl. 84; Som. 73, 92; Wrt. Voc. 48, 30. Fleóhnet *vel* micgnet *cōnōpeum*, 106; Som. 78, 42; Wrt. Voc. 57, 24. Ðǣr wæs eallgylden fleóhnet *there was an all-golden fly-net*, Judth. 10; Thw. 22, 3; Jud. 47. v. fleóg-ryft.

FLEÓN, flión, to fleónne, flíónne; *part.* fleónde, flíónde; ic fleó, ðū flīhst, flȳhst, he flīhþ, flȳhþ, *pl.* fleóþ, flióþ, flȳþ; *p.* ic, he fleáh, ðū fluge, *pl.* flugon; *pp.* flogen. **I.** *v. trans. To* FLEE, *escape, avoid;* fŭgĕre, effŭgĕre, vītāre:—Ic heonon nelle fleón fōtes trym *I will not flee hence a footstep*, Byrht. Th. 138, 68; By. 247: Andr. Kmbl. 3074; An. 1540. He sceal swīðe flión ðisse worulde wlite *he must quickly flee this world's splendour*, Bt. Met. Fox 7, 60; Met. 7, 30. Ðū tilast wædle to fliónne *thou toilest to avoid poverty*, Bt. 14, 2; Fox 44, 7. Fleónde *fŭgiens*, Ps. Lamb. 54, 8: Cd. 95; Th. 125, 17; Gen. 2080. Se wlite ðæs līchoman is swīðe flíónde *the beauty of the body is very fleeting*, Bt. 32, 2; Fox 116, 17. Ic fleó *fŭgio*, Ælfc. Gr. 36; Som. 38, 20: 28, 6; Som. 32, 47. He flīhþ ða wædle *he flees from poverty*, Bt. 33, 2; Fox 122, 33. He flȳhþ yfla gehwilc *he flees every evil*, Exon. 62 b; Th. 229, 25; Ph. 460: 81 a; Th. 305, 3; Fä. 82. Fleóþ his ansȳne, ða ðe hine feódan *fŭgiant a făcie ejus, qui ōdĕrunt eum*, Ps. Th. 67, 1: 103, 17. Hī flȳþ [Cott. flióþ] ðæt hī hatiaþ *they avoid what they hate*, Bt. 41, 5; Fox 252, 27. Sǣ geseah and heó fleáh *măre vīdit, et fūgit*, Ps. Lamb. 113, 3: Bt. Met. Fox 1, 40; Met. 1, 20. Hwæt is ðē sǣ ðæt ðū fluge *quid est tibi măre quod fūgisti?* Ps. Lamb. 113, 5. Ða hyrdas flugon *pastōres fūgĕrunt*, Mt. Bos. 8, 33: Ps. Lamb. 30, 12: Elen. Kmbl. 267; El. 134. Fleóþ on feorweg *flee far away*, Exon. 36 a; Th. 117, 22; Gū. 228. Ðæt ic mān fleó *that I flee evil*, Ps. Th. 93, 14. **II.** *to put to flight, rout, conquer;* fŭgāre, vincĕre:—Hundteóntig eówer fleóþ hira tyn þūsendu *your hundred shall put to flight their ten thousands*, Lev. 26, 8. **III.** *v. intrans. To fly as with wings;* vŏlāre:—Ic fleó *vŏlo*, Ælfc. Gr. 36; Som. 38, 16: Ps. Lamb. 54, 7. Culfran fleóþ him floccmǣlum *doves fly flockwise*, Homl. Th. i. 142, 9. v. fleógan I. [*Wyc.* fle: *R. Glouc.* fle: *Laym.* fleon: *Orm.* fleon, flen: *Plat.* flugten: *O. Sax.* fliohan: *Frs.* flan: *O. Frs.* flia: *Dut.* vlieden: *Ger.* fliehen: *M. H. Ger.* vliehen: *O. H. Ger.* fliuhan: *Goth.* þliuhan: *Dan.* flye: *Swed.* fly: *Icel.* flýja.] DER. a-fleón, æt-, be-, for-, in-, ofer-, ongeán-, ōþ-, þurh-, to-, up-, ūt-, ūta-, ūt-ōþ-.

fleós, es; *n. A fleece;* vellus:—Gilde ðæt fleós mid twām pæningum *let the fleece be paid for with two pence*, L. In. 69; Th. i. 146, 11, note 23, MS. B. In fleós *in vellus*, Ps. Surt. 71, 6. v. flȳs.

FLEÓT, fliét, es; *m*: fleóte, an; *f.* **I.** *a place where vessels float, a bay, gulf, an arm of the sea, estuary, the mouth of a river, a river, stream;* hence the names of places, as *Northfleet, Southfleet, Kent;* and in London, *Fleetditch;* sīnus, æstuārium, rīvus:—Se Abbod Petrus wæs besenced on sumne sǣs fleót, se wæs hāten Am-fleót *abbas Petrus demersus est in sĭnu măris, qui vŏcātur Amfleat*, Bd. 1, 33; S. 499, 6, note. Fleót *æstuārium*, Cot. 14. Ispānia land is eall mid fleóte ymbhæfd *the country of Spain is all encompassed with water*, Ors. 1, 1; Bos. 24, 3. Fleótas *æstuāria*, Glos. Epnl. Recd. 154, 46: Wrt. Voc. 63, 69. **II.** *a raft, ship, vessel;* rătis, nāvis:—Ic gebycge bāt on sǣwe, fleót on faroþe *I buy a boat on the sea, a vessel on the ocean*, Exon. 119 b; Th. 458, 13; Hy. 4, 100. [*Laym.* fleote *a fleet of ships*: *Plat.* fleet *a small river*: *O. Frs.* flet, *n. a river*: *Dut.* vliet, *m. a rivulet, brook*: *Ger.* fliesz, *m. n. fluentum*: *M. H. Ger.* vliez, *m. n. a rivulet*: *O. H. Ger.* fluz, *m. a river*: *Icel.* fljót, *n. a river*.]

fleótan; *part.* fleótende; ic fleóte, ðū flȳtst, he flȳt, *pl.* fleótaþ; *p.* fleát, *pl.* fluton; *pp.* floten [fleót *a stream*] *To* FLOAT, *swim;* fluctuāre, nătāre, nāvĭgāre:—Ðæt scip sceal fleótan mid ðȳ streáme *the ship must float with the stream*, Past. 58; Hat. MS. Nō he fram me flōdȳðum feor fleótan meahte *he could not float far from me on the waves*, Beo. Th. 1089; B. 542. Se feónde [MS. feond] gespearn fleótende hreáw *the exulting [fowl] perched on the floating corpses*, Cd. 72; Th. 87, 12; Gen. 1447. Fleótendra ferþ nō ðǣr fela bringeþ cūþra cwidegiedda *the spirit of seafarers brings there not many known songs*, Exon. 77 a; Th. 289, 26; Wand. 54. Ageót ele uppon wæter oððe on ōðrum wǣtan, se ele flȳt būfon *pour oil upon water or on another fluid, the oil will float above*, Homl. Th. ii. 564, 13. Oft scipu scrīðende scrinde fleótaþ *illic nāves pertransībunt*, Ps. Th. 103, 24. Fleát fāmigheals forþ ofer ȳðe *the foamy necked one floated forth over the wave*, Beo. Th. 3822; B. 1909. [*Piers P.* fleten: *Wyc. Chauc.* flete: *Orm.* fletenn: *Scot.* fleit, flete: *Plat.* fleten: *O. Sax.* fliotan: *O. Frs.* fliata: *Dut.* vlieten: *Ger.* fliessen: *M. H. Ger.* vliuzen: *O. H. Ger.* fliuzan, fleozan: *Dan.* flyde: *Swed.* flyta: *Icel.* fljóta: *Lat.* fluĕre *to flow*: *Grk.* πλεῖν *to navigate*: *Sansk.* plu *to float, swim*.] DER. a-fleótan.

fleóte, an; *f. A stream, river;* rīvus:—To ðære fleótan *to the stream*, Cod. Dipl. Apndx. 123; A. D. 774; Kmbl. iii. 381, 7. v. fleót I.

fleoðe, an; *f. The water-lily*:—Of fleoðan wyrte *of the plant of the water-lily*, L. M. 2, 51; Lchdm. ii. 266, 28. v. fleaðe.

fleótig; *adj. Swift, fleet, rapid;* cĕler, vēlox:—Swift wæs on fōre, fleótga [= fleótiga] on lyfte [MS. fleotgan lyfte] *it was swift in its course, rapid in the air*, Exon. 113 b; Th. 434, 22; Rä. 52, 4.

fleót-wyrt, e; *f. Floatwort, seaweed?* alga? L. M. 2, 52; Lchdm. ii. 268, 28.

fleów, *pl.* fleówon *flowed, issued*, Jn. Bos. 19, 34: Ps. Lamb. 77, 20; *p. of* flōwan.

fleówþ *flows*, Ex. 3, 17, = flēwþ; *3rd sing. pres. of* flōwan.

flēre *having a floor, floored.* DER. fīf-flēre.

flēring, e; *f. A* FLOORING; contăbŭlātio:—On ðære nyðemestan flēringe wæs heora gangpyt and heora myxen, on ðære ōðre flēringe wæs ðæra nȳtena fōda gelogod, on ðære [MS. ðone] þriddan flēringe [MS. flēringa] wæs seó forme wunung, and ðǣr wunodon ða wildeór and ða reðan wurmas, on ðære feorþan flēringe [MS. flēringa] wæs ðæra tamra nȳtena steall, on ðære fīftan flēringe wæs ðæra manna wunung mid wurþmynte gelogod *on the lowermost flooring [of the ark] was their privy and dunghill, on the second flooring the food of the cattle was placed, on the third flooring was the first dwelling, and there dwelt the wild beasts and fierce serpents, on the fourth flooring was the stall of the tame cattle, on the fifth flooring the dwelling of the men was placed with honour*, Boutr. Scrd. 21, 6-10: Homl. Th. i. 536, 11, 13: ii. 164, 5. Ðū macast þreó flēringa binnan ðam arce *tristĕga făcies in arca*, Gen. 6, 16. DER. up-flēring.

flēs, es; *n. A* FLEECE; vellus:—Be sceápes gonge mid his flēse *of a sheep's going with its fleece*, L. In. 69; Th. i. 146, 9, note 20, MS. G. v. flȳs.

flēsc, es; *n. Flesh;* căro:—We hæfdon hlāf and flēsc genōh on Egipta lande *in terra Ægypti sedēbāmus sŭper ollas carnium et comĕdēbāmus pānem in sătŭrĭtāte*, Ex. 16, 3. v. flǣsc.

fleswian; *p.* ede; *pp.* ed *To mutter, whisper;* susurrāre:—Mid ðȳ he ðā geswippre mūþe līcettende ǣrend rehte [MS. wrehte] and leáse fleswede *when he then told a feigned message with his crafty mouth, and falsely whispered;* cum sĭmŭlātam lēgātiōnem ōre astūto volvĕret, Bd. 2, 9; S. 511, 20.

FLET, flett, es; *n.* **I.** *the ground, floor of a house;* ārĕa:—Ne cume on bedde, ac licge on flette *let him not come into a bed, but lie on a floor*, L. P. M. 2; Th. ii. 286, 21. Heó on flet gecrong *she sank on the ground*, Beo. Th. 3141; B. 1568: 3085; B. 1540. **II.** *a dwelling, habitation, house, cottage, hall;* hăbĭtātio, dŏmus, căsa, aula:—Gif ðæt flet geblōdgad wyrþe *if the house be stained with blood*, L. H. E. 14; Th. i. 32, 14. Gif man mannan an ōðres flette mānswara hāteþ *if one man call another a perjurer in another's cottage*, 11; Th. i. 32, 4: L. In. 39; Th. i. 86, 21. Him se æðela geaf giestlīþnysse fægre on flette *the noble gave them a fair entertainment in his dwelling*, Cd. 112; Th. 147, 29; Gen. 2447: Beo. Th. 2054; B. 1025. Scilling agelde ðam ðe ðæt flet āge *let him pay a shilling to him who owns the dwelling*, L. H. E. 11, 12, 13; Th. i. 32, 6, 9, 12. Hī fǣrlīce flet ofgeáfon *they suddenly gave up the hall*, Exon. 77 a; Th. 290, 7; Wand. 61:

Beo. Th. 3903; B. 1949: 4039; B. 2017. [*Laym.* ulette *floor: Scot.* flet, flett *a house: Plat.* flet *a bedroom in the upper floor of a peasant's house: O. Sax.* flet, fletti, *n. the floor of a house, deal, house, hall: O. Frs.* flet *a house: Ger. dial.* fletz *aula, ārea: M. H. Ger.* vletze, *n. ārea: Icel.* flet, *n. a set of rooms, house.*]

flêt, e; *f. Cream, skimming, curds;* flos lactis, lactis crēmor exemptus, coagŭlum:—Flêt *flos lactis*, Cot. 37. Hwît sealt dô on reám oððe gôde flête *put white salt into cream or good skimmings*, L. M. 3, 10; Lchdm. ii. 314, 2. v. flête.

flête, fliéte, flŷte, an; *f:* flêt, e; *f.* [fleótan *to float*] What floats on the surface, hence,—*Cream, skimming, curds;* flos lactis, lactis crēmor exemptus, coagŭlum:—Genim cûmeoluc bûtan wætere, lǽt weorþan to flêtum, geþwer to buteran *take cow's milk without water, let it become cream, churn it to butter*, L. M. 1, 44; Lchdm. ii. 108, 22. Hafa clǽne flêtan *have clean curds*, L. M. 1, 2; Lchdm. ii. 38, 19. Menge wið flêtan, and nân ôðer molcen þicge *let him mingle it with curds, and eat no other milk-food*, L. M. 2, 51; Lchdm. ii. 264, 26.

flet-gesteald, flett-gesteald, es; *n. Dwelling-place, household goods;* hăbĭtātio, dŏmestĭcæ ŏpes:—Lamech onfêng fletgestealdum *Lamech succeeded to the dwelling-places*, Cd. 52; Th. 65, 31; Gen. 1074.

fleðe-camb, es; *m. A weaver's comb;* pecten, pectĭca, Ælfc. Gl. 110; Som. 79, 47; Wrt. Voc. 59, 18. v. flæðe-camb.

flet-mon *a sailor*, Som. Ben. Lye. v. flot-man.

flet-pæþ *a house-path, floor.* v. flett-pæþ.

flet-rest, e; *f. Domestic couch, sleeping quarters in the hall;* lectus domestĭcus:—Sum fletreste gebeág *one bowed to the domestic couch*, Beo. Th. 2487; B. 1241.

flet-sittend, es; *m. A court-resident;* in aula sĕdens:—Ðâ wæs flet-sittendum fægere gereorded *there was a feast fairly arranged to the court-residents*, Beo. Th. 3580; B. 1788. Ða ic Freáware fletsittende nemnan hŷrde *whom I heard the court-residents call Freaware*, 4049; B. 2022. Ðǽr wǽron boren æfter bencum orcas fulle fletsittendum *there were full jugs carried along the benches to the court-residents*, Judth. 10; Thw. 21, 15; Jud. 19: 21, 24; Jud. 33.

flett *the floor of a house, a dwelling, habitation;* sēdes, hăbĭtātio, Som. Ben. Lye. v. flet.

flett-gesteald, es; *n. Household goods, domestic wealth;* domestĭcæ ŏpes:—Geomor fæder flettgesteald freóndum dǽlde *Gomer distributed his father's domestic wealth to his friends*, Cd. 79; Th. 97, 11; Gen. 1611. v. flet-gesteald.

flett-pæþ, es; *pl. nom. acc.* -paðas; *m. A house-path, floor;* dŏmi sēmĭta, păvīmentum:—Ðæt ðû flettpaðas mîne trǽde *that thou hast trodden my house-paths*, Cd. 130; Th. 165, 10; Gen. 2729.

flet-werod, es; *n. Court-host, the court-retainers;* aulĭci:—Is mîn fletwerod, wîgheáp, gewanod *my court-host, the company in war, is diminished*, Beo. Th. 957; B. 476.

fleúwþ *flows*, Ps. Lamb. 57, 9,=flêwþ; *3rd sing. pres. of* flôwan.

flêwsa, an; *m.* [flôwan *to flow*] *A flowing, flux;* fluxus:—Wið innoþes flêwsan *for flux of inwards*, Herb. 53, 2; Lchdm. i. 156, 14: Med. ex Quadr. 6, 9; Lchdm. i. 352, 15. Wið wîfes flêwsan *for flux of a woman*, Herb. 89, 2; Lchdm. i. 192, 12: 128; Lchdm. i. 240, 2: 178, 6; Lchdm. i. 312, 10. Ðŷ sylfan dæge hyt ðone flêwsan belûceþ *eōdem die fluxum comprĭmet*, 178, 6; Lchdm. i. 312, 16: 175, 3; Lchdm. i. 308, 1. Heó ða flêwsan gewrîþ *it stops the flux*, 128; Lchdm. i. 240, 5.

flêwst, he flêwþ *flowest, flows*, Ex. 3, 8; *2nd and 3rd sing. pres. of* flôwan.

flex, es; *n. Flax;* līnum:—Smeócende flex he ne adwæscþ *līnum fūmĭgans non extinguet*, Mt. Bos. 12, 20. Eall hira flex and hira bernas wǽron fordône *līnum et hordeum læsum est*, Ex. 9, 31. v. fleax.

flicce, es; *n? A flitch of bacon;* succĭdia, perna:—Flicce *perna*, Wrt. Voc. 86, 13: 286, 51. [*Plat.* flikke, *m. a spot, piece: Ger.* fleck, *m. n;* flecke, *m. a rag, piece, spot, place: M. H. Ger.* vlëc, *m. a piece: O. H. Ger.* fleccho, *m. măcŭla: Dan.* flik, flikke, *m. f. a piece, rag: Swed.* flik, *m. a lap: Icel.* flik, *f. a rag;* flikki, *n. a flitch of bacon.*]

flicerian, flicorian; *p.* ode; *pp.* od [fleógan *to fly*] *To move the wings, flutter*, FLICKER; mōtāre ālas, vŏlĭtāre:—Ic flicerige *vŏlĭto*, Ælfc. Gr. 36; Som. 38, 16. Swâ earn his briddas spænþ to flihte and ofer hîg fliceraþ *sīcut ăquĭla prōvŏcans ad vŏlandum pullos suos et sŭper eos vŏlĭtans*, Deut. 32, 11. Ân blac þrostle flicorode ymbe his neb *a black thrush flickered about his face*, Homl. Th. ii. 156, 22. [*Dut.* flakkeren, flikkeren: *Ger.* flackern: *M. H. Ger.* vlackern: *O. H. Ger.* flokarôn.]

flié; *indecl. n. A white speck, disease of the eye;* albūgo:—Wið flié eágsealf *an eye-salve for the white speck*, L. M. 1, 2; Lchdm. ii. 32, 12, 17, 18, 20, 23, 26: 3, 2; Lchdm. ii. 308, 9. Ǽgðer mæg adôn flié of eágan *either can remove the white speck from the eye*, 3, 2; Lchdm. ii. 308, 26. v. fleah.

fliéman feorm, e; *f. The harbouring of a fugitive;* fūgĭtīvi susceptio, L. In. 30; Th. i. 120, 16. v. flŷman fyrmþ.

fliés, es; *n. A fleece;* vellus:—Be sceápes gonge mid his fliése. Sceáp sceal gongan mid his fliése ôþ midne sumor, oððe gilde ðæt fliés mid twâm pæningum *of a sheep's going with its fleece. A sheep shall go with its fleece until midsummer, or let the fleece be paid for with two pence*, L. In. 69; Th. i. 146, 9–11. v. flŷs.

fliét, es; *m. A raft, ship, vessel;* rătis, nāvis:—Fliét *rătis*, Cot. 200. v. fleót II.

fliéte, an; *f. Cream, curds;* flos lactis, coagŭlum:—Fliéte *verbĕrātum:* geþworen [MS. geþrofen] fliéte *churned cream;* lactudiclum? Wrt. Voc. 290, 27, 28. Dô on ðæt fæt swâ fela swâ ðara fliétna ðǽron clifian mǽge *put into the vessel as much of the curds as may cleave thereon*, L. M. 1, 2; Lchdm. ii. 38, 20. v. flête.

flîg; *indecl. n. A white speck, disease of the eye;* albūgo, Wrt. Voc. 285, 2. v. fleah.

fligan; *p.* de; *pp.* ed *To put to flight;* fŭgāre. DER. a-fligan.

flige-wîl, es; *m.* [flige=flyge *vŏlātus;* wîl *a wile, deceit*, q. v.] *A flying wile, dart of Satan;* vŏlans astūtia, diabŏli sagitta:—Gefylled feóndes fligewîlum, fâcensearwum *filled with the fiend's* [*Satan's*] *flying darts, with treacherous wiles*, Exon. 83 b; Th. 315, 6; Môd. 27.

flîhst, he flîhþ *fleest, flees*, Bt. 33, 2; Fox 122, 33; *2nd and 3rd pres. sing. of* fleón.

fliht, es; *m. A flight;* vŏlātus:—Swâ earn his briddas spænþ to flihte *sīcut ăquĭla prōvŏcans ad vŏlandum pullos suos*, Deut. 32, 11: Exon. 13 b; Th. 25, 11; Cri. 399. v. flyht.

flîma, an; *m. A runaway, fugitive;* profŭgus, Cot. 151. v. flŷma.

flind, e; *f. Genetrix*, Cot. 98, Lye.

FLINT, es; *m.* FLINT, *a rock;* sĭlex, petra:—Flint *sĭlex*, Ælfc. Gl. 58; Som. 67, 94; Wrt. Voc. 38, 19: 85, 21. Flinte ic eom heardra *I am harder than flint*, Exon. 111 b; Th. 426, 23; Rä. 41, 78. Ðæt ðû gesomnige flint unbrǽcne *that thou unite the unfragile flint*, Exon. 8 a; Th. 1, 11; Cri. 6: Salm. Kmbl. 202; Sal. 100. Flintum heardran *harder than flints*, Exon. 25 a; Th. 73, 13; Cri. 1189. Hîg cômon to ðam flinte, and Moyses ætfôran him eallum slôh mid ðære girde tûwa ðone flint, and fleów sôna of ðam flinte wæter *they came to the rock, and Moses struck the rock twice with his rod before them all, and immediately water flowed from the rock*, Num. 20, 10, 11. [*M. H. Ger.* vlins, *m. sĭlex: Dan.* flint, *m. f: Swed.* flinta, *f.*]

flint-grǽg; *adj. Flint-grey;* cānus:—Ic sceal to staðe þŷwan [MS. þyran] flintgrǽgne flôd *I shall impel the flint-grey flood to the shore*, Exon. 101 b; Th. 383, 31; Rä. 4, 19.

flió; *indecl. n. A white speck, disease of the eye;* albūgo, Glos. Epnl. Recd. 153, 12. v. fleah.

fliógan *to fly;* vŏlāre:—Ic mæg fliógan ofer ðone heán hrôf ðæs heofones *I can fly over the high roof of the heaven*, Bt. 36, 2; Fox 174, 5. v. fleógan.

flión *to flee;* fŭgĕre:—He sceal flión ðisse worulde wlite *he must flee this world's splendour*, Bt. Met. Fox 7, 60; Met. 7, 30. v. fleón.

flîs *a fleece;* vellus, Wrt. Voc. 66, 30: 282, 13. v. flŷs.

FLÎT, es; *n. Scandal, contention, strife;* scandălum, contentio:—Togeánes sunu môdor ðîne ðû settest flît *adversus fīlium matris tuæ pōnēbas scandălum*, Ps. Spl. T. 49, 21. [*Laym.* flit, *n. dispute: Scot.* flyte: *Plat.* flit, fliit, fliet, *m. diligence: O. Sax.* flît, *m. contention, contest: O. Frs.* flit *diligence: Dut.* vlijt, *f. diligence: Ger.* fleiss, *m: M. H. Ger.* vlîz, *m: O. H. Ger.* flîz, *m.*] DER. ge-flît, sund-flît.

flîta, an; *m.* [flîtan *to contend*] *A fighter, striver, foe.* DER. ge-flîta, wið-, wiðer-.

flîtan; *part.* flîtende; ic flîte, ðû flîtest, flîtst, he flîteþ, flît, *pl.* flîtaþ; *p.* flât, *pl.* fliton; *pp.* fliten *To strive, contend, dispute, rebel;* contendĕre, certāre, dispŭtāre, jurgāre:—Ic flîtan gefrægn on fyrndagum môdgleáwe men, gewêsan ymbe hyra wîsdôm *I have learnt that in days of yore men wise of mood contended, struggled about their wisdom*, Salm. Kmbl. 359; Sal. 179. Ðam ðe wylle on dôme wið ðê flîtan, and niman ðîne tunecan, lǽt him tô ðînne wǽfels *ei, qui vult tecum jūdĭcio contendĕre, et tŭnĭcam tuam tollĕre, dimitte ei et pallium*, Mt. Bos. 5, 40. Flîtende *contending*, Beo. Th. 1836; B. 916. Hwî flîtst ðû wið ðînne nêxtan *quāre percŭtis proxĭmum tuum?* Ex. 2, 13. Flîteþ *strives*, Exon. 95 a; Th. 354, 47; Reim. 62. Ne flît he *non contendet*, Mt. Bos. 12, 19. Flât he wið ânne Israhêliscne man *jurgātus est cum vĭro Israhēlīta*, Lev. 24, 10: Bd. 4, 16; S. 584, note 31. Me þincþ nû ðæt ðîn gecynd and ðîn gewuna flîte swîðe swîdlîce wið ðæm dysige *methinks now that thy nature and thy habit contend very powerfully against error*, Bt. 36, 4; Fox 178, 28. [*Scot.* flyte; *p.* flet *to scold: M. H. Ger.* vlîzen: *O. H. Ger.* flîzan.] DER. ofer-flîtan, ôþ-, wiðer-.

flît-cræft, es; *m. The art of disputing, logic;* disceptandi ars, dialectĭca:—Flîtcræft *dialectĭca*, Mone B. 3030.

flît-cræftlîc; *adj. Of* or *belonging to disputation, dialectical, logical;* dialectĭcus=διαλεκτικός:—Mid flîtcræftlîcum *dialectĭcis*, Mone B. 3147.

flîtend, es; *m.* [flîtende, *part. of* flîtan *to strive*] *A wrangler, quarrelsome person;* certans, lītigans:—Flîtend *certans*, Cot. 181. Flîtend *lītĭgans*, Mone B. 2927.

flîter-cræft, es; *m. The art of disputing, logic;* dialectĭca, Som. Ben. Lye. v. flît-cræft.

flîtere, es; *m. A brawler, wrangler, schismatic;* rŭbŭla, schismătĭcus—

σχισματικός:—Flītere răbŭla, Cot. 208: Glos. Epnl. Recd. 161, 81. Flītera schismatĭcōrum, Mone B. 2816.

flīt-ful, -full; *adj. Contentious, dialectical;* contentiōsus, dialectĭcus = διαλεκτικός:—Flītfulles *dialectĭcæ*, Mone B. 3304. Flītfulra *dialectĭcōrum*, 3164. DER. ge-flītful.

flīt-georn, -gern, es; *m. One desirous of contention, a quarreller;* lītĭgātor, vĭtĭlīgātor, rixātor:—Flītgern *lĭtĭgātor*, Prov. 25. DER. ge-flītgeorn.

flītlīce *contentiously, earnestly, eagerly;* certātim, stŭdiōse. DER. ge-flītlīce.

flīt-mǣlum; *adv.* [mǣlum, *dat. pl. of* mǣl, *n.*] *By strife, strifewise, eagerly, earnestly;* certātim:—Flītmǣlum *certātim*, Mone B. 199. DER. ge-flītmǣlum.

FLŌC, es; *n. A sole, kind of flat fish;* plătessa, passer:—Flōc *plătessa*, Glos. Brux. Recd. 39, 67; Wrt. Voc. 65, 70: 281, 49. Flōc *pansor?* [=*passer*], Ælfc. Gl. 102; Som. 77, 80; Wrt. Voc. 56, 4. Fagc and flōc *plătesias et plătessas*, Coll. Monast. Th. 24, 12, 13. [*Icel.* flóki, *m. a kind of halibut;* passer, sŏlea.]

flocan; *p.* ede; *pp.* ed or floccan *To clap, strike;* plaudĕre, complōdĕre:—Heó floceþ hyre folmum *she claps with her hands*, Exon. 105 b; Th. 402, 23; Rä. 21, 34.

FLOCC, es; *m. A* FLOCK, *band, company, division;* grex, căterva, turma:—Gif Esau cymþ to ānum flocce and đone ofslihþ, se ōđer flocc byþ gehealden *si vĕnĕrit Esau ad ūnam turmam et percussĕrit eam, ălia turma servābĭtur*, Gen. 32, 8. Mid đam mānfullum flocce *with the ungodly company*, Ælfc. T. 34, 22: 35, 8. Him mon mid ōđrum floccum sōhte *they were sought by other bands*, Chr. 894; Erl. 90, 14. Ic hīg eft ongeán oferfare mid twām floccum [MS. floccon] *cum duābus turmis regrĕdior*, Gen. 32, 10. [*Wyc.* floc: *Chauc.* flok: *Laym.* floc *a host: Orm.* flocc: *Dan.* flok, *m. f: Swed.* flock, *m. a crowd: Icel.* flokkr, *m. a troop, band.*]

flocc-mǣlum, floc-mǣlum; *adv.* [mǣlum, *dat. pl. of* mǣl, es; *n. a measure*, q. v.] *By flocks, flockwise, in companies;* grĕgātim, cātervātim:—Fleóþ him floccmǣlum *they fly by flocks*, Homl. Th. i. 142, 9: Num. 2. 34. Hī hȳ flocmǣlum slōgon *they slew them in companies*, Ors. 2, 5; Bos. 46, 6. Hī ferdon ǣghweder flocmǣlum *they went everywhere in flocks*, Chr. 1011; Erl. 145, 25.

floc-rād, e; *f. A riding company, a troop;* turma:—Đā fundon hie ōđre flocrāde, đæt rād ūt wiđ Lygtūnes *then they raised another troop, which rode out towards Leighton*, Chr. 917; Erl. 102, 15. Fōron hie æfter đæm wealda hlōþum and flocrādum *they went through the wood in bands and troops*, 894; Erl. 90, 13.

FLŌD, es; *n. m.* I. *a flowing of water, flow, flowing water, wave, tide,* FLOOD, *sea, running stream, river;* flūmen, fluctus, fluentum, æstus, accessus, flŭvius:—Đæt flōd [*n.*] eóde of stōwe đære winsumnisse to wætrienne neorxena wang; đæt flōd [*n.*] ys đanon todǣled on feówer eán *flŭvius egrĕdiēbātur de lŏco voluptātis ad irrĭgandum părădīsum; flŭvius inde dīvĭdĭtur, in quătuor căpĭta*, Gen. 2, 10. Flōd [*m.* or *n.*] *vel* yrnende eá *flūmen*, Ælfc. Gl. 97; Som. 76, 73; Wrt. Voc. 54, 17. Flōd [*m.* or *n.*] *flūmen* vel *flŭvius*, Wrt. Voc. 80, 57. Flōd [*m.* or *n.*] ođđe ȳþ *fluctus*, Ælfc. Gr. 11; Som. 15, 11. Flōd [*m.* or *n.*] *accessus*, Ælfc. Gl. 105; Som. 78, 35; Wrt. Voc. 57, 17. Hwenne đæt flōd [*n.*] byþ ealra hēhst and ealra fullost *when the tide is highest and fullest of all*, Chr. 1031; Erl. 162, 5: 897; Erl. 96, 6. Se flōd [*m.*] onsprang *the flood departed*, Andr. Kmbl. 3269; An. 1637. Com flōwende flōd [*m.* or *n.*] æfter ebban ... se flōd [*m.*] ūt gewāt *the flowing tide came after the ebb ... the tide receded*, Byrht. Th. 133, 45, 58; By. 65, 72. Cynn đa đe flōd [*m.* or *n.*] wecceþ inc hȳraþ *races which the water bringeth forth shall obey you two*, Cd. 10; Th. 13, 18; Gen. 204: Beo. Th. 1095; B. 545: Andr. Kmbl. 3091; An. 1548: Exon. 106 a; Th. 404, 12; Rä. 23, 6. Flōdes [*m.* or *n.*] ryne *flūmĭnis impĕtus*, Ps. Lamb. 45, 5. Đæs sǣes flōdes [*m.* or *n.*] weaxnes *an increasing of the sea's tide*, Bd. 5, 3; S. 616, 16. Hie on flōdes [*m.* or *n.*] fæđm ceólum lācaþ *they sail in ships on the bosom of the sea*, Andr. Kmbl. 503; An. 252: Beo. Th. 83; B. 42: Salm. Kmbl. 161; Sal. 80. On Iordanes flōde [*m.* or *n.*] *in Iordānis flūmĭne*, Mk. Bos. 1, 5. Se wuldorcyning gesette ȳþum heora onrihtne ryne, rūmum flōde [*m.* or *n.*] *the king of glory appointed to the waves, to the spacious flood, its just course*, Cd. 8; Th. 10, 36; Gen. 167: Exon. 25 a; Th. 72, 8; Cri. 1169: Beo. Th. 3780; B. 1888: Andr. Kmbl. 530; An. 265. Cyning ūt gewāt on fealene flōd [*m.*] *the king departed on the dusky flood*, Chr. 937; Erl. 114, 2; Ædelst. 36: Beo. Th. 3904; B. 1950: Andr. Kmbl. 841; An. 421: Exon. 101 b; Th. 383, 31; Rä. 4, 19. Sió eá forþ mid micle flōde [*m.* or *n.*] ūt on đa sǣ flōweþ *the river flows forth out to the sea with a great flow*, Ors. 1, 1; Bos. 15, 20: Cd. 8; Th. 10, 15; Gen. 157: Andr. Kmbl. 1907; An. 956: Exon. 103 b; Th. 392, 3; Rä. 11, 2. Đǣr cōmon flōd [*n.*] *vēnērunt flūmĭna*, Mt. Bos. 7, 27. Upahōfon flōd [*n.*] Driht, upahōfon flōdas [*m.*] stefne his, upahōfon flōd ȳþe his *elēvāvērunt flūmĭna Dŏmĭne, elēvāvērunt flūmĭna vōcem suam, elēvāvērunt flūmĭna fluctus suos*, Ps. Spl. 92, 4, 5. Flōdas [*m.*] feágaþ ođđe hafetiaþ mid handa samod *flūmĭna plaudent mănu sĭmul*, Ps. Lamb. 97, 8. Fāmige flōdas [*m.*] *foamy floods*, Cd. 100; Th. 133, 19; Gen. 2213: Ps. Th. 68, 14: Exon. 125 b; Th. 482, 19; Rä. 67, 4. Flōda [*m.* or *n.*] begong *the floods' course*, Beo. Th. 2999; B. 1497: Ps. Th. 65, 11. Đa fugelas đe on flōdum [*m.* or *n.*] wuniaþ syndon flaxfōte *the birds which dwell in waters are web-footed*, Hexam. 8; Norm. 14, 14: Exon. 22 a; Th. 61, 5; Cri. 980. Ofer flōd, *n.* [flōdas, *m.* Lamb.] he gegearwode hine *sŭper flūmĭna præpărāvit eum*, Ps. Spl. 23, 2. Đū adrygdest flōd, *n.* [flōdas, *m.* Spl.] *tu siccasti flŭvios*, Ps. Lamb. 73, 15. He gewende to blōde heora flōdas [*m.*] *convertit in sanguĭnem flūmĭna eōrum*, 77, 44: Andr. Kmbl. 1811; An. 908. II. *the Flood, deluge;* dilŭvium:—Ȳđode đæt flōd [*n.*] ofer eorþan *aquæ dilŭvii inundāvērunt sŭper terram*, Gen. 7, 10, 17: Mt. Bos. 24, 39: Lk. Bos. 17, 27: Boutr. Scrd. 21, 11, 13. Flōd [*m.* or *n.*] ofslōh giganta cyn *the flood slew the race of giants*, Beo. Th. 3383; B. 1689: Cd. 69; Th. 83, 28; Gen. 1386. Ic gebringe flōdes [*m.* or *n.*] wæteru ofer eorþan, đæt ic ofsleá eall flǣsc *ĕgo addūcam aquas dilŭvii sŭper terram, ut interfĭciam omnem carnem*, Gen. 6, 17: 7, 6, 7: 9, 11. Noe lyfode þreóhund geára and fīftig geára æfter đam flōde [*m.* or *n.*] *vixit Noe post dilŭvium trecentis quinquāginta annis*, Gen. 9, 28: Mt. Bos. 24, 38: Boutr. Scrd. 21, 12, 13, 16, 18, 29: Cd. 75; Th. 93, 13; Gen. 1544. Ic wille mid flōde [*m.* or *n.*] folc acwellan *I will destroy the people with a flood*, 64; Th. 78, 20; Gen. 1296: Boutr. Scrd. 21, 21, 22. Flōdas [*m.*] Noe oferlāþ *Noah sailed over the floods*, Cd. 161; Th. 200, 25; Exod. 362. [*Laym.* flod, ulod, *n: Orm.* flod: *Plat.* flood, *f: O. Sax.* flōd, fluod, *m. f. n;* fluot, *f: Frs.* floede: *O. Frs.* floed, flod, *n: Dut.* vloed, *m: Ger.* fluth, *f: M. H. Ger.* vluot, *f. m: O. H. Ger.* flōt, fluot, *f;* flōz *fluxus: Goth.* flōdus, *f: Dan.* flod, *m. f: Swed.* flod, *m. a flood, river: Icel.* flóð, *n. inundation, deluge.*] DER. brim-flōd, Cofer-, drenc-, geofon-, heáh-, lagu-, mere-, nēp-, sǣ-, wæter-, will-.

flōd-blāc; *adj. Flood-pale, made pale by water, that is, by drowning;* per ăquam pallĭdus:—Flōdblāc here *the flood-pale host*, Cd. 167; Th. 209, 11; Exod. 497.

flōde, an; *f. A place where anything flows, a channel, sink, gutter;* cloāca, lăcūna, Cot. 44: 193, Som. Ben. Lye.

flōd-egsa, an; *m. Flood-dread;* ăquārum terror:—Flōdegsa becwom gāstas geómre *flood-dread seized on their sad souls*, Cd. 166; Th. 206, 4; Exod. 446.

flōd-līc; *adj.* FLOODLIKE; flŭviālis:—Flōdlīc *flŭviālis*, Ælfc. Gr. 9, 28; Som. 11, 36.

flōd-weard, e; *f. A flood-guard, sea-wall;* măris custōdia, măris mūrus:—Flōdwearde slōh *he struck the sea-wall* [i. e. *the wall caused by dividing the Red Sea*], Cd. 167; Th. 209, 3; Exod. 493.

flōd-weg, es; *m. A flood-way, watery way, the sea;* mărīna via, măre:—Sǣmen fōron flōdwege *the seamen went on the sea*, Cd. 147; Th. 184, 12; Exod. 106. Fōr flōdwegas *went the watery ways*, Exon. 109 b; Th. 418, 22; Rä. 37, 9: 82 a; Th. 309, 4; Seef. 52.

flōd-wudu; *m. Flood-wood, a ship;* mărīnum lignum, nāvis:—Swā we ofer cald wæter ceólum līđan, geond sīdne sǣ flōdwudu fergen *as if we journey in vessels over the cold water, convey our ships through the wide sea*, Exon. 20 a; Th. 53, 21; Cri. 854.

flōd-wylm, es; *m. Flood-boiling, raging flood;* ăquārum fluctus:—Flōdwylm ne mæg manna ǣnigne gelettan *a raging flood may not hinder any man*, Andr. Kmbl. 1032; An. 516.

flōd-ȳþ, e; *f. A flood-wave;* măris unda:—Nō he fram me flōdȳþum feor fleótan meahte *he could not float far from me on the flood-waves*, Beo. Th. 1088; B. 542.

floga, an; *m.* [flogen, *pp. of* fleógan *to fly;* fleón *to flee*] *One who flies or flees, a fugitive;* fŭgĭtīvus. DER. ān-floga, gūþ-, lyft-, uht-, wīd-.

flogen *flown; pp. of* fleógan.

flogen *fled, escaped; pp. of* fleón.

flogettan; *p.* te; *pp.* ed *To fluctuate;* fluctuāre, Scint. 77.

flōh, e; *f. That which is flown off, a fragment, piece;* fragmen, frustum:—Flōh stānes *a piece of stone;* glēba sĭlĭcis, Cot. 99.

flohten-fōte; *adj. Web-footed;* palmĭpes:—Ne ete flohtenfōte fugelas *let him not eat web-footed birds*, L. M. 1, 36; Lchdm. ii. 88, 9. v. flax-fōte.

flooc, es; *n. A sole;* plătessa, Glos. Epnl. Recd. 161, 31. v. flōc.

FLŌR; *gen.* flōre; *dat.* flōre, flōra; *acc.* flōr, flōre; *f:* flōr, es; *m. A* FLOOR; păvīmentum, sŏlum, ārea:—Flōr on hūse *a floor in a house;* excussōrium, Ælfc. Gl. 29; Som. 61, 34; Wrt. Voc. 26, 33. Flōr *păvīmentum*, Wrt. Voc. 290, 10. Flōr *păvīmentum* vel *sŏlum*, Wrt. Voc. 81, 7. Breda þiling *vel* flōr on to þerscenne *a joining of planks* or *a floor to thresh on*, Ælfc. Gl. 57; Som. 67, 73; Wrt. Voc. 37, 59. Scipes flōr *a ship's floor, gangway;* fōri, Ælfc. Gl. 103; Som. 77, 116; Wrt. Voc. 56, 36. Īs glisnaþ glæshluttur, flōr forste geworht *ice glittereth transparent as glass, a floor caused by frost*, Runic pm. 11; Kmbl. 341, 18; Hick. Thes. i. 135, 22. Flōr āttre weól *the floor* [*of hell*] *boiled with venom*, Cd. 220; Th. 284, 8; Sat. 318: 213; Th. 267, 17; Sat. 39. Swā swā ǣlces hūses wah biþ fæst ǣgđer ge on đære flōre, ge on đæm hrōfe, swā biþ ǣlc gōd on Gode fæst, forđæm he is ǣlces gōdes ǣgđer ge hrōf ge flōr *as the wall of every house is fixed both to the floor and to the roof, so is every good fixed in God, for he is both the roof and* *the floor of every good*, Bt. 36, 7; Fox 184, 11-14. Ætfealh mīn sáwul flōre [flōra, Spl.] *adhæsit pāvimento anĭma mea*, Ps. Th. 118, 25. He gang æfter flōre *he went along the floor*, Beo. Th. 2636; B. 1316. Ðū ðæm wættere foldan to flōre gesettest *thou settest the earth for a floor to the water*, Bt. Met. Fox 20, 181; Met. 20, 91. On flōra *on the floor*, Cd. 215; Th. 271, 24; Sat. 110: Homl. Th. ii. 56, 33: 334, 35. He gefeóll on ða flōr *he fell on the floor*, Bt. 1; Fox 4, 3: 33, 4: Fox 130, 4. He feól on ða flōre, Bt. Met. Fox 1, 161; Met. 1, 81: Judth. 10; Thw. 23, 8; Jud. 111. He feormaþ his bernes flōre *purgābit āream suam*, Lk. Bos. 3, 17. On fāgne flōr feónd treddode *the fiend trod on the variegated floor*, Beo. Th. 1454; B. 725. [*Orm.* flor: *Plat.* floor: *Dut.* vloer, *m*: *Ger.* flur, *f. field*: *M.H.Ger.* vluor, *m. sĕges*: *O.H.Ger.* flūr *sĕges*: *Icel.* flór, *m. a floor, pavement*: *Wel.* llawr, *m. a floor.*] DER. bere-flōr, helle-, þirsce-, þyrscel-, up-.

flōr-stān, es; *m. A floor-stone, stone used for pavement*; tessĕra pāvīmento sternendo designāta:—Lytle feðerscitte flōrstānas *little four-cornered floor-stones*; tessellæ, Ælfc. Gl. 61; Som. 68, 67; Wrt. Voc. 39, 50.

flot, es; *n.* [floten, *pp. of* fleótan *to float*] *Water deep enough for sustaining a ship, the sea*; ăqua sătis alta ad nāvem sustĭnendam, măre:—Ongan eorla mengu to flote fȳsan *the multitude of warriors began to hasten to the sea*, Elen. Kmbl. 451; El. 226: Andr. Kmbl. 3393; An. 1700. Wǣron ða ūtlagas ealle on flote *the outlaws were all afloat* [lit. *on the sea*], Chr. 1070; Erl. 209, 24. We willaþ on flot feran *we will depart on the sea*, Byrht. Th. 132, 64; By. 41: Chr. 937; Erl. 114, 1; Æðelst. 35. [*Plat.* flot: *Dut.* vlot: *Ger.* floss: *M.H.Ger.* vlōz, *m. river, raft*: *Icel.* flot; á flot *on* or *afloat.*]

FLOTA, an; *m.* [floten, *pp. of* fleótan *to float*]. I. *a ship, vessel, fleet*; nāvis, classis:—Flota stille bād on sole *the vessel abode still in the mud*, Beo. Th. 608; B. 301: 426; B. 210. Næs se flota swā rang *no fleet was so insolent*, Chr. 975; Erl. 125, 26: 1006; Erl. 140, 6. Mid ðæm flotan *with the fleet*, 904; Erl. 98, 12. Lǣt nū geferian flotan ūserne to lande *let our ship now go to land*, Andr. Kmbl. 794; An. 397: Beo. Th. 594; B. 294. II. *a sailor, pirate*; nauta, pīrāta:—Flota mōdgade *the sailor proudly moved*, Cd. 160; Th. 198, 32; Exod. 331. Brǣddon æfter beorgum flotan feldhūsum *the sailors spread themselves amongst the hills with their tents*, 148; Th. 186, 3; Exod. 133: 154; Th. 191, 31; Exod. 223. Ða flotan, wīcinga fela *the pirates, vikings many*, Byrht. Th. 133, 25; By. 72. [*Scot.* flote *a fleet*: *Dut.* vloot, *f. a fleet*: *Ger.* flotte, *f. a. fleet*: *Dan.* flaade, *m. f*: *Swed.* flotta, *f*: *Icel.* floti, *m. a fleet.*] DER. ǣg-flota, ge-, hærn-, sǣ-, scip-, wǣg-.

floten *floated, swam*; *pp. of* fleótan.

floterian, flotorian; *p.* ode; *pp.* od *To* FLUTTER, *be disquieted* or *troubled, be carried by the waves*; fluctuāre, fluctĭbus ferri:—Ðīn heorte floteraþ on gȳtsunge *thy heart flutters* or *is disquieted with covetousness*; cor tuum fluctuat avārĭtia, Homl. Th. ii. 392, 28. Flotorode *fertur fluctĭbus*, Glos. Prudent. Recd. 150, 1. Flotorodon *prævŏlant*, 150, 10.

flot-herge, es; *m. A naval force*; nāvālis exercĭtus:—Hygelāc cwom faran flotherge *Hygelac came faring with a naval force*, Beo. Th. 5822; B. 2915. v. here, herge *an army*.

flotian; *part.* flotigende; *p.* ode; *pp.* od [floten, *pp. of* fleótan *to float*] *To float*; fluitāre:—Beó ān scip flotigende swā nēh ðan lande swā hit nȳxt mǣge *let a ship be floating as near the land as it nearest can*, Chr. 1031; Erl. 162, 6.

flot-man, -mann, -mon, -monn, es; *m. A float-man, sailor, pirate*; nauta, pīrāta:—Wīcing oððe flotman *pīrăta*, Wrt. Voc. 73, 74. Flotmen *pīrātæ*, Lupi Serm. i. 14; Hick. Thes. ii. 103, 19. Flotmanna *nautārum*, Mone B. 114. Flotmonna freá *chief of mariners* [*Noah*], Cd. 72; Th. 89, 3; Gen. 1475.

flot-scip, es; *n. A floating ship, light bark*; barca, cĕlox:—Flotscip *barca*, Ælfc. Gl. 103; Som. 77, 100; Wrt. Voc. 56, 22: Glos. Brux. Recd. 37, 18; Wrt. Voc. 63, 32. Flotscip *cēlox*, Ælfc. Gl. 103; Som. 77, 114; Wrt. Voc. 56, 34.

flot-smere, es; *n.* [smeru *fat, grease*] *Floating fat, scum of a pot*; pinguēdo ollæ sŭpernătans, Som. Ben. Lye.

flot-weg, es; *m. A sea-way, the sea*; mărīna via, măre:—He sceolde faran on flotweg *he must journey on the sea*, Exon. 123 b; Th. 475, 1; Bo. 41.

FLŌWAN; *part.* flōwende; ic flōwe, ðū flōwest, flēwst, he flōweþ, flēwþ, *pl.* flōwaþ; *p.* fleów, *pl.* fleówon; *pp.* flōwen *To* FLOW, *issue*; fluĕre, fluctuāre, inundāre:—Ðæt ealle eán eft flōwan māgon *that all waters may flow again*, Boutr. Scrd. 21, 16. Flōwan mōt ȳþ ofer eall lond *the wave may flow over all the land*, Salm. Kmbl. 644; Sal. 321: Ps. Th. 77, 21: 104, 36: Menol. Fox 555; Gn. C. 47. Com flōwende flōd *the flood came flowing*, Byrht. Th. 133, 44; By. 65. Ic flōwe *fluo*, Ælfc. Gr. 28, 5; Som. 32, 4. Lagu flōweþ ofer foldan *water shall flow over the earth*, Exon. 115 b; Th. 445, 2; Dōm. 1: Bt. Met. Fox 5, 28; Met. 5, 14: Ps. Th. 67, 2: 68, 1: 103, 10: 147, 7. On ðæt land ðe flēwþ meolece and hunie *in terram quæ fluit lacte et melle*, Ex. 3, 8: Num. 13, 28: 14, 8: 16, 14: Ps. Spl. 57, 8: Bd. de nat. rerum; Wrt. popl. science 15, 19; Lchdm. iii. 268, 16. Lybbendes wætres flōd flōwaþ of his innoþe *flūmĭna de ventre ejus fluent ăquæ vīvæ*, Jn. Bos. 7, 38: Ps. Lamb. 147, 18. Sǣstreámas flōwaþ *sea-streams flow*, Ps. Th. 92, 5. Fleów blōd ūt and wæter *exīvit sanguis et ăqua*, Jn. Bos. 19, 34. Fleów firgend-streám *the mountain-torrent flowed*, Andr. Kmbl. 3144; An. 1575. He slōh stān and fleówon wæteru, and burnan fleówon oððe ȳþgodon *percussit petram et fluxērunt ăquæ, et torrentes inundāvērunt*, Ps. Lamb. 77, 20: 104, 41. Deáh ðe wealan flōwen *dīvĭtiæ si affluant*, Ps. Th. 61, 11. [*Chauc.* flowen: *Orm.* flowenn: *Plat.* floien, flojen: *Dut.* vloeien: *M.H.Ger.* vlæjen, vlæen: *O.H.Ger.* flawjan, flewēn: *Icel.* flóa *to flood*: *Lat.* flu-ĕre: *Grk.* πλώ-ω *to swim*: *Sansk.* plu *to float, swim.*] DER. a-flōwan, æt-, be-, forþ-, geond-, of-, ofer-, to-, to-be-, under-.

flōwednys, -nyss *a flowing, flux, torrent*. DER. ofer-flōwednys, to-.

flōwnys, -nyss, e; *f. A flowing, flŭx, torrent*; fluxus, torrens:—Ðæt wīf wæs þrōwiende blōdes flōwnysse *mŭlier fluxum pătiēbātur sanguĭnis*, Bd. 1, 27; S. 494, 5. Burnan oððe flōwnyssa unrihtwīsnyssa gēdrēfdun me *torrentes iniquĭtātis conturbāvērunt me*, Ps. Lamb. 17, 5. DER. ofer-flōwnys.

flox-fōte; *adj. Web-footed*; palmĭpes, Hexam. 8; Norm. 14, 15, note x. v. flax-fōte.

fluge *fleddest*; fugisti, Ps. Lamb. 113, 5; *2nd pers. sing. p. of* fleón.

flugol; *adj.* [fleógan *to fly*; fleón *to flee*] *Apt to fly* or *flee, flying swiftly, swift*; fŭgax:—Flugol *fŭgax*, Ælfc. Gr. 9, 60; Som. 13, 43.

flugon *flew*, Bd. 3, 19; S. 548, 32; *p. pl. of* fleógan.

flugon *fled, escaped*, Cd. 166; Th. 206, 15; Exod. 452; *p. pl. of* fleón.

flustrian; *p.* ode; *pp.* od *To plait, weave*; plectĕre:—Flustriende *plectens*, Cot. 176, Som. Ben. Lye.

fluton *floated, swam*; *p. pl. of* fleótan.

flȳcþ *flees*, Chr. 473; Ing. 16, note o, = flȳhþ; *3rd pers. pres. of* fleón.

flyge, es; *m.* [fleógan *to fly*] *A flying, flight*; vŏlātus:—Se fugel flyges cunnode *the bird made trial of his flying*, Exon. 17 a; Th. 40, 28; Cri. 645. Wið flyge gāres *against an arrow's flight*, 79 a; Th. 297, 11; Crā. 66. Ic sceal on flyge earda neósan *I shall in flight visit lands*, Cd. 215; Th. 271, 28; Sat. 112. [*Ger.* flug, *m*: *M.H.Ger.* vluc, *m. O.H.Ger.* flug, *m*: *Icel.* flug, *n*; flugr, *m. vŏlātus.*] DER. a-flyge.

flyge-reów; *adj.* [reów *wild, fierce, cruel*] *Wild-flying, wild in flight*; vŏlātu fĕrus:—Flygereówe þurh nihta genipu neósan cwōmon, hwæðere . . . *the wild-flying* [*evil spirits*] *came in the darkness of night to find out, whether* . . ., Exon. 37 b; Th. 123, 10; Gū. 320.

flyge-wīl *a flying wile, cunning trick*. v. flige-wīl.

flyht, fliht, es; *m.* [fleógan *to fly*] *A flight*; vŏlātus:—Wæs ðæs fugles flyht dyrne and dēgol *the bird's flight was hidden and secret*, Exon. 17 a; Th. 40, 15; Cri. 639. On flyhte *in flight*, Elen. Kmbl. 1485; El. 744: Cd. 215; Th. 271, 29; Sat. 112. Se ðe nafaþ fugles flyht *who has not the flight of a bird*, Salm. Kmbl. 451; Sal. 226: Exon. 17 a; Th. 41, 12; Cri. 654. Earnas feredon sāwle flyhte on lyfte *eagles conveyed the soul in flight through the sky*, Andr. Kmbl. 1732; An. 868: Nicod. 26; Thw. 14, 36. [*Laym.* fliht, fluht, flut: *Orm.* flihht: *Scot.* flocht: *Plat.* flugt, *f*: *O.Sax.* fluht, *f*: *Frs.* flechte: *O.Frs.* flecht, *f*: *Dut.* vlugt, *f*: *Ger.* flucht, *f*: *M.H.Ger.* vluht, *f*: *O.H.Ger.* fluht, *f*: *Dan.* flugt, *m. f*: *Swed.* flykt, *m.*]

flyht-clāþ, es; *m. A joining, binding* or *tying together*; commissūra, conjunctūra, lĭgātūra, Som. Ben. Lye.

flȳhþ, ðū flȳhst *flees, thou fleest*, Exon. 81 a; Th. 305, 3; Fä. 82; *3rd and 2nd pers. pres. of* fleón.

flyht-hwæt; *adj. Flight-prompt*; in vŏlātu strēnuus:—Weras mundum mearciaþ on marmstāne frætwe flyhthwates *men design with hands in marble stone the plumage of the prompt in flight* [*phœnix*], Exon. 60 b; Th. 221, 15; Ph. 335. Se fēnix ascæceþ feðre, flyhthwate *the phœnix shakes its feathers, prompt for flight*, 58 a; Th. 207, 21; Ph. 145.

flȳma, flēma, an; *m. One who flees, a runaway, an exile, outlaw, a man who had fled for any offence, and whose flight was equivalent to a conviction*; profŭgus, fūgĭtīvus, exul:—Ðū bist flȳma geond ealle eorþan *profŭgus ĕris sŭper terram*, Gen. 4, 12: 4, 16. He monigra geára tīde flȳma wæs *multo annōrum tempŏre profŭgus văgābātur*, Bd. 2, 12; S. 513, 3: Ps. Th. 77, 37. Beó he syððan flȳma *let him be henceforth a fugitive*, L. Ath. i. 2; Th. i. 200, 10: i. 20; Th. i. 210, 13, 14. DER. here-flȳma.

flȳman; *p.* de; *pp.* ed *To cause to flee, put to flight, rout, banish*; fŭgāre:—Ic sceal flȳman feóndsceaðan *I shall cause the hostile-spoiler to flee*, Exon. 104 a; Th. 396, 5; Rä. 15, 19. Hī mec sōna flȳmaþ *they soon put me to flight*, 105 a; Th. 398, 12; Rä. 17, 6. Hie God flȳmde *God routed them*, Cd. 97; Th. 127, 24; Gen. 2115. DER. a-flȳman, ge-, ūt-, ūta- [-flǣman, -flēman]. v. fleón.

flȳman fyrmþ, fliéman feorm, e; *f. A fugitive's food* or *support, the offence of harbouring a fugitive, the penalty for such an offence*; fŭgĭtīvi susceptio:—Ðis syndon ða gerihta ðe se cyning āh ofer ealle men on Wes-sexan; ðæt is . . . and flȳmena fyrmþe *these are the rights which the king possesses over all men in Wessex*; *that is* . . . *and* [*the penalty*] *for harbouring a fugitive*, L. C. S. 12; Th. i. 382, 14: Th. i. 382, 21. Gif mon cierliscne monnan fliéman feorme teó *if a man accuse a churlish man of harbouring a fugitive*, L. In. 30; Th. i. 120, 16.

flȳming, es; *m. A fugitive, runaway, exile*; profŭgus, fūgĭtīvus, exul, Som. Ben. Lye. v. fleáming, flȳma.

flyne, flene, an; *f. What is made soft, batter;* fluĭdum quid:—Gewyrce to flynan micelne citel fulne *work a large kettle full into a batter,* L. M. 1, 38; Lchdm. ii. 98, 6. Geót ꝺa flynan on *pour the batter on,* 1, 38; Lchdm. ii. 98, 10.

FLȲS, flís, fliés, flēs, fleós, es; *n. A fleece, wool;* vellus, lānūgo:—Ðis flȳs *hoc vellus,* Ælfc. Gr. 9, 32; Som. 12, 12. Gilde ꝺæt flȳs mid twām pæningum *let the fleece be paid for with two pence,* L. In. 69; Th. i. 146, 11, MS. H. Mid his flȳse *with its fleece,* L. In. 69; Th. i. 146, 9, 10, MSS. B. H. He nyꝺerastīhþ swā swā rēn on flȳs *descendet sĭcut plŭvia in vellus,* Ps. Lamb. 71, 6: Ps. Th. 147, 5. Of flȳsum mīnra sceápa wǣron gehlyde þearfena sīdan *the sides of the poor were clothed with the fleeces of my sheep,* Job Thw. 165, 2. Wulle flȳsum *with fleeces of wool,* Exon. 109 a; Th. 417, 12; Rä. 36, 3. Flȳs *lānūgo,* Cot. 122. [*Piers P.* flus: *Plat.* fliis *vellus*: *Dut.* vlies, *n*: *Ger.* vlies, fliesz, *n*: *M. H. Ger.* vlies, *n.*]

flȳte, an; *f. Cream;* flos lactis:—Dō flȳtan to *add cream,* L. M. 1, 34: Lchdm. ii. 80, 23. v. flēt.

flȳte, es; *m?* [fleótan *to float*] What floats, hence,—*A boat, punt;* pontōnium:—Flȳte *pontōnium,* Ælfc. Gl. 103; Som. 77, 103; Wrt. Voc. 56, 25: 63, 35.

flyþ, es; *m. Flight;* vŏlātus:—Forgeaf ꝺām fugelum flyþ geond ꝺas lyft *he gave to the birds flight through this air,* Hexam. 8; Norm. 14, 10. v. flyht.

flȳþ *flee, flee from, avoid,* Bt. 41, 5; Fox 252, 27; *pres. pl. of* fleón.

flȳtst, he flȳt *floatest, floats,* Homl. Th. ii. 564, 13; *2nd and 3rd pers. pres. of* fleótan.

fnæd, es; *pl. nom. acc.* fnadu, fnado; *gen.* fnada; *dat.* fnadum; *n. A hem, edge, fringe;* fimbria:—Fnæd *fimbria,* Wrt. Voc. 81, 66. Ān wīf æt-hrān hys reáfes fnæd *mŭlier tĕtĭgit fimbriam vestīmenti ejus,* Mt. Bos. 9, 20: Bd. 1, 27; S. 494, 6, MS. B: Ps. Th. 132, 3. Hīg mǣrsiaþ heora reáfa fnadu *magnĭfĭcant fimbrias,* Mt. Bos. 23, 5. Fnado *vel* læppan *fimbriæ* [MS. *timbria*], Ælfc. Gl. 64; Som. 68, 128; Wrt. Voc. 40, 33. On fnadum gyldenum *in fimbriis aureis,* Ps. Lamb. 44, 14.

fnæs, es; *pl. nom. acc.* fnasu; *gen.* fnasa; *dat.* fnasum; *n. A fringe;* fimbria:—Mid gyldnum fnasum *in fimbriis aureis,* Ps. Th. 44, 15. v. fæs, fnæd.

FNÆST, es; *m. A puff, blast, breath;* flātus, anhēlĭtus:—Ūre fnæst ateoraþ *our breath faileth,* Hexam. 4; Norm. 8, 18. Þurh ꝺæs fīres fnæst *through the fire's blast,* Exon. 74 a; Th. 277, 29; Jul. 588. Hyt bringþ forþ ꝺone [MS. ꝺane] fnæst *it will bring forth the breath,* Lchdm. iii. 100, 13: 116, 24. Fnæstas [MS. fnæstiaþ] swīꝺe beóþ fortogene *the breathings are very hard drawn,* L. M. 2, 36; Lchdm. ii. 242, 7. [*O. H. Ger.* fnastōn *anhēlāre*: *Dan.* fnyse *to puff*: *Swed.* fnysa *to snort*: *Icel.* fnasa *to sneeze*: *Grk.* πνέω *I blast, puff.*]

fnæstiaþ, L. M. 2, 36; Lchdm. ii. 242, 7, = fnæstas? *pl. of* fnæst.

fneósung, e; *f. A sneezing;* sternūtātio, sternūtāmentum:—Snytingc *vel* fneósung *sternūtātio* vel *sternūtāmentum,* Ælfc. Gl. 79; Som. 72, 62. [*Wyc.* fnesynge, fnesing: *Icel.* fnasan, fnösun *a sneezing.*]

fnēsan *to sneeze.* [*Icel.* fnœsa *to sneeze.*] DER. ge-fnēsan.

fnora, an; *m. A sneezing, sneeze;* sternūtātio, Wrt. Voc. 289, 4.

fō *I take; 1st sing. pres. indic. of* fōn. Ne ne fō he *he may not take,* L. Ælf. C. 30; Th. ii. 354, 2; *3rd sing. pres. subj. of* fōn.

foca, an; *m. A cake baked on the hearth;* pānis sub cĭnĕre pistus:—Wirc focan *fac subcĭnĕrĭcios pānes,* Gen. 18, 6.

FŌDA, an; *m.* FOOD, *nourishment;* ălĭmentum:—On ꝺære ōꝺre flēringe wæs ꝺæra nȳtena fōda gelogod *on the second flooring* [*of the ark*] *the food of the cattle was placed,* Boutr. Scrd. 21, 8. Fōda fȳres, holt *food of fire, wood,* Scint. 12. Būton ꝺam gōdspellĭcan fōdan *without the evangelical food,* Homl. Th. ii. 396, 31. [*Orm.* fode: *Plat.* fōde, vōde: *Goth.* fōdeins, *f*: *Dan.* føde, *m. f*: *Swed.* föda, *f*: *Icel.* fæði, *n.*]

fōdder, fōddor, fōddur, fōder, fōdor; *gen.* fōdres; *dat.* fōdre; *n.* I. FODDER, *dry food for cattle, hay, corn, provender, food generally;* jūmenti pābŭlum, fœnum, ĕdūlium, pābŭlum, esca, victus:—Ða ungesceádwīsan neát ne wilniaþ nānes ōꝺres feós to eácan ꝺam fōdre *the irrational cattle desire no other wealth in addition to the fodder,* Bt. 14, 2; Fox 44, 23. Wolde syllan his assan fōddur *ut dăret jūmento pābŭlum,* Gen. 42, 27. Fōdder neátum *fœnum jumentis,* Ps. Th. 103, 13. We fōdder horsum ūrum habbaþ *pābŭla ĕquis nostris hăbēmus,* Coll. Monast. Th. 31, 29. Fōddur, Ps. Th. 77, 20; [mettas, Ps. Spl. 77, 21] *ut pĕtĕrent escas anĭmābus suis.* Fōddor, Exon. 96 a; Th. 357, 28; Pa. 35. Fōdor, Runic pm. 25; Kmbl. 344, 17; Hick. Thes. i. 135, 49. Brūceþ fōdres *has an enjoyment of food,* Runic pm. 28; Kmbl. 345, 6; Hick. Thes. i. 135, 55. Gif ꝺam ꝺe ꝺæs beþurfe fȳr and fōddor *let him give fire and food to him who needs it,* L. Pen. 15; Th. ii. 282, 26. II. *a case from which anything is fed, a case, cover, sheath;* thēca = θήκη:—Fōdder *thēca,* Ælfc. Gl. 53; Som. 66, 68; Wrt. Voc. 35, 54. v. boge-fōdder. [*Laym.* fodder, uodder *fodder, meat*: *Plat.* foder, voder, voer: *Dut.* voeder, voēr, *n. fodder, provender*: *Ger.* futter, *n*: *M. H. Ger.* vuoter, *n*: *O. H. Ger.* fuotar, *n*: *Goth.* fōdr, *n. a sheath*: *Dan. Swed.* foder, foer, *n*: *Icel.* fóðr, *n. pābŭlum.*] v. fōꝺer.

fōdder-brytta, an; *m. A fodder-distributor, fodderer, herdsman;* pābŭlātor:—Horshyrde *vel* fōdderbrytta *pābŭlātor,* Ælfc. Gl. 9; Som. 56, 122; Wrt. Voc. 19, 6.

fōddor-þegu, fōddur-þegu, fōdor-þegu, e; *f.* [þegu *a taking, receiving*] *A taking or receiving food, food;* cĭbi acceptio, cĭbus:—Ðæt hie tobrugdon, blōdigum ceaflum, fira flǣschoman him to fōddorþege *that they tore asunder, with bloody jaws, the bodies of men for their food,* Andr. Kmbl. 320; An. 160. Lēton him ꝺa betweonum tān wīsian hwylcne hira ǣrest ōꝺrum sceolde to fōddurþege feores ongildan *they let the lot decide between them which of them first should give up to the rest his life for food,* 2203; An. 1103. Ðǣr hī mētaþ fōdorþege gefeán [MS. gefeon] *where they find the joy of taking food,* Exon. 59 b; Th. 215, 4; Ph. 248.

fōddur-wēla, an; *m. Abundance of food;* cĭbi cōpia:—Fere fōddurwēlan folcscipe dreógeþ [*a ship*] *performs the bringing* [i. e. *a ship brings,* Grn.] *abundance of food to people,* Exon. 108 b; Th. 415, 12; Rä. 33, 10.

fōdnōþ, es; *m? Food, nourishment;* ălĭmentum, Som. Ben. Lye.

fōdrere, es; *m. A fodderer, forager;* pābŭlātor:—Þunor ofslōh xxiv heora fōdrera *thunder killed twenty-four of their foragers,* Ors. 4, 1; Bos. 78, 1.

fōg, es; *n. A joining, joint;* conjunctio, commissūra, Som. Ben. Lye. DER. ge-fōg, stān-ge-.

fōge *fitly, aptly, comprehensibly.* DER. un-ge-fōge.

fōgere, es; *m. A suiter, wooer;* prŏcus:—Fōgere [MS. foghere] *prŏco,* Mone B. 4287. v. wōgere.

fōh *take*:—Fōh to me *take from me;* accĭpe a me, Cd. 228; Th. 308, 2; Sat. 686; *impert. of* fōn.

fōh *comprehensible, measurable, moderate.* DER. un-ge-fōh.

fōhlīc *comprehensible, measurable, moderate.* DER. un-ge-fōhlīc.

fōhlīce *comprehensibly, measurably, moderately.* DER. un-ge-fōhlīce.

fohten *fought, contended; pp. of* feohtan.

FOLA, an; *m. A* FOAL, *colt;* pullus, poledrus:—Cicen oꝺꝺe brid oꝺꝺe fola *pullus,* Wrt. Voc. 77, 37. Fola *poledrus,* Ælfc. Gl. 20; Som. 59, 50; Wrt. Voc. 23, 11. Hī gemētton ꝺone folan ūte *invēnērunt pullum fŏris,* Mk. Bos. 11, 4, 5: Mt. Bos. 21, 2, 5. [*Piers P.* fole: *Plat.* falen, vale: *Frs.* fole: *O. Frs.* folla, *m*: *Dut.* volen, veulen, *n*: *Ger.* fohle, *m*; füllen, *n*: *M. H. Ger.* vole, vol, *m*; vüli, vüln, *n*: *O. H. Ger.* folo, *m. pullus, poledrus*; fuli, *n. pullus, pultrinus*: *Goth.* fula, *m*: *Dan.* fole, *m. f*; føl, *n*: *Swed.* föl, *n*: *Icel.* foli, *m*: *Lat.* pullus, *m. a young animal*: *Grk.* πῶλος, *m. f. a foal.*]

FOLC, es; *n.* [Folc being a neuter noun, and a monosyllable, has the *nom. and acc. pl.* the same as the *nom. and acc. sing*: *it is a collective noun in* English, *and has not the plural form* folks *but by a modern corruption*] *The* FOLK, *people, common people, multitude, a people, tribe, family;* pŏpŭlus, gens, nātio, vulgus, plebs, cīves, hŏmĭnes, exercĭtus, multĭtūdo:—Twā folc beóþ todǣled, and ꝺæt folc oferswīþ ꝺæt ōꝺer folc *two nations shall be divided, and the one folk shall overcome the other folk,* Gen. 25, 23. Ðæt folc wæs Zachariam geanbīdigende *ĕrat plebs expectans Zachăriam,* Lk. Bos. 1, 21. Micel folc mid hym *cum eo turba multa,* Mt. Bos. 26, 47. Hie awerede ꝺæt folc *the people defended it,* Chr. 921; Erl. 106, 10, 33. Gif folces man syngaþ *if a man of the people sin,* Lev. 4, 27. Ðæs folces hlīsa *the people's praise,* Bt. 30, 1; Fox 108, 16. He slōh folces Denigea fȳftyne men *he slew of the Danes' folk fifteen men,* Beo. Th. 3168; B. 1582. Folces hyrde *the people's shepherd,* Beo. Th. 1224; B. 610: 3668; B. 1832: 5282; B. 2644. Eallum folce to friþe *to the peace of all the people,* L. Edg. S. 15; Th. i. 278, 7. Eádmund cyning cȳþ eallum folce *Edmund king makes known to all people,* L. Edm. S; Th. i. 246, 17. Se ꝺe sȳ folce ungetrȳwe *he who may be untrue to the people,* L. C. S. 25; Th. i. 390, 17. Man swencte ꝺæt earme folc *one harassed the poor people,* Chr. 999; Erl. 135, 32. Se eorl earfoþlīce gestylde ꝺæt folc *the earl hardly stilled the people,* Chr. 1052; Erl. 187, 4, 3. Þurh ūre folc *throughout our folk,* L. In. prm; Th. i. 102, 9. Beó se þeóf ūtlah wiꝺ eall folc *let the thief be an outlaw to all people,* L. C. S. 30; Th. i. 394, 24. He gesōhte Sūþ-Dena folc *he sought the people of the South-Danes,* Beo. Th. 931; B. 463: 1049; B. 522: 1390; B. 693: 2362; B. 1179. Folce gestēpte sunu Ōhtheres *with people he supported Ohthere's son,* Beo. Th. 4776; B. 2393. Ða folc fǣhþe towehton *the people excited enmity,* 5888; B. 2948: 2849; B. 1422. Freáwine folca *friend of peoples,* 864; B. 430: 4038; B. 2017: 4849; B. 2429. Folcum gefrǣge *famed among nations,* 109; B. 55: 530; B. 262: 3715; B. 1855. Mec wolcna strengu ofer folc byreþ *the clouds' strength bears me over people,* Exon. 103 a; Th. 390, 5; Rä. 8, 6. Folgad folcum *followed by peoples,* Cd. 226; Th. 300, 4; Sat. 559. [*Laym.* folc, uolc: *Orm.* follc: *O. Sax.* folk, folc, *n*: *Frs.* folck: *O. Frs.* folk, *n*: *Dut. Ger.* volk, *n*: *M. H. Ger.* volc, *m*: *O. H. Ger.* folc, folch, folk, *n*: *Dan. Swed.* folk, *n*: *Icel.* fólk, *n.*] DER. dryht-folc, here-, mægen-, sige-, sūþ-, wīd-.

folc-āgende; *part. Folk-owning;* pŏpŭlum possĭdens:—Bealg hine swīꝺe folcāgende *the folk-owning* [*man*] *was much irritated,* Exon. 68 a; Th. 253, 26; Jul. 186: Beo. Th. 6218; B. 3113. Nis se foldan sceat mongum gefēre folcāgendra *the tract of earth is not easy of access to many folk-owning* [*men*], Exon. 56 a; Th. 198, 4; Ph. 5.

folc-bealo; *gen.* -bealowes; *n. Folk-torment, torment by many, a great torment;* ingens mălum *vel* crŭciātus:—Petrus and Paulus þrōwedon on Rôme folcbealo þreálīc *Peter and Paul suffered grievous torment by the people at Rome,* Menol. Fox 248; Men. 125.

folc-bearn, es; *n. A folk-child, a child of man;* pŏpŭli fīlius, hŏmĭnis fīlius:—Swilc biþ mǽgburh menigo đīnre, folcbearnum frome *such shall be the family of thy people, excellent in children,* Cd. 100; Th. 132, 16; Gen. 2194. Þurh đē eorþ-búende ealle onfóþ, folcbearn, freodo and freóndscipe *through thee all dwellers upon earth, the children of men, shall receive peace and friendship,* 84; Th. 105, 28; Gen. 1760.

folc-beorn *a popular man.* v. folc-biorn.

folc-biorn, es; *m. A popular man;* pŏpŭlāris vir:—Folc-biorn, Beo. Th. 4444; B. 2221.

folc-cū; *f. The folk's cow, a cow of the herd;* pŏpŭli vacca:—Under folc-cūm [MS. folcum] *inter vaccas popŭlōrum,* Ps. Th. 67, 27; among the kien of puplis, Wyc. 67, 31. v. cū.

folc-cūþ; *adj. Known to the people, folk-known, well-known, public, celebrated;* pŏpŭlis nōtus, publĭcus, cĕleber:—Wæs his freádrihtnes folccūþ nama Agamemnon *his lord's celebrated name was Agamemnon,* Bt. Met. Fox 26, 18; Met. 26, 9. Folc-cūþne rǽd *a discourse known to nations,* Bt. Met. Fox introduc. 18; Met. Einl. 9. Be folc-cūþum strǽtum *by the public roads,* Bd. 2, 16; S. 520, 4.

folc-cwēn, e; *f. Folk's queen, queen of the people;* pŏpŭli rēgīna:—Eóde freólīcu folc-cwēn to hire freán sittan *the noble queen of the people went to sit by her lord,* Beo. Th. 1286; B. 641.

folc-cyning, es; *m. Folk's king, king of nations, king of the people;* pŏpŭli rex:—Nealles folc-cyning fyrdgesteallum gylpan þorfte *the people's king needed not to boast of his comrades in arms,* Beo. Th. 5738; B. 2873: 5460; B. 2733. Folc-cyninge *for the king of nations,* Cd. 131; Th. 166, 25; Gen. 2753. Fīfe folc-cyningas *five kings of nations,* 93; Th. 119, 4; Gen. 1974: 95; Th. 125, 5; Gen. 2074. cf. *O. Sax.* folk-kuning.

folc-dryht, -driht, e; *f.* [dryht, driht *a multitude*] *A multitude of people, an assemblage;* pŏpŭli multĭtūdo, cŏmĭtātus:—Folcdryht wera bifōran *before the assemblage of men,* Exon. 23 b; Th. 66, 5; Cri. 1067. Folcdriht, Cd. 64; Th. 76, 24; Gen. 1262.

folce-firen, e; *f. A folk-crime, public crime;* pŏpŭli scĕlus:—Wǽrlogona sint folcefirena hefige *the public crimes of the faithless are heavy,* Cd. 109; Th. 145, 23; Gen. 2410.

folce-getrum, es; *n. A host of people;* exercĭtus:—Mid heora folcegetrume *with their band of people,* Cd. 95; Th. 123, 18; Gen. 2046, note. v. folc-getrum.

folc-egsa, an; *m. Folk-terror;* publĭcus terror, formīdo:—Đū towurpe fæsten his for folcegsan *pŏsuisti mūnĭtiōnes ejus in formīdĭnem,* Ps. Th. 88, 33.

folc-firen *a folk-crime.* v. folce-firen.

folc-freá, an; *m. Folk's lord, lord of a nation;* pŏpŭli dŏmĭnus:—Hie đæt cūþ dydon heora folcfreán *they made that known to their nation's lord,* Cd. 89; Th. 111, 7; Gen. 1852.

folc-frig, folc-frȳ; *adj. Folk-free;* līber ăpud plēbem:—Beó he syđđan folcfrig *be he afterwards folk-free,* L. C. S. 45; Th. i. 402, 17. Se sié folcfrȳ *let him be folk-free,* L. Wih. 8; Th. i. 38, 15. cf. *Grm. RA.* 349.

folc-gefeoht, es; *n. Folk-battle, a great battle, pitched battle;* publĭca pugna, plēnum prælium:—Đa Sciđđie noldon hine gesēcan to folcgefeohte *the Scythians would not attack him in a pitched battle,* Ors. 2, 5; Bos. 46, 5. Wurdon ix folcgefeoht gefohten *nine great battles were fought,* Chr. 871; Erl. 77, 7: 887; Erl. 87, 9. On þrīm folcgefeohtum *in three pitched battles,* Ors. 3, 9; Bos. 66, 11. cf. *Icel.* fôlk-orrusta.

folc-gemōt, -mōt, folces gemōt, es; *n. A folk-meeting;* pŏpŭli consessus. The folc-gemōt was *a general assembly of the people* of a town, city or shire, and was held annually on the first of May, but it could be convened on extraordinary occasions by ringing the moot-bell,—'Cum ălĭquid vēro inŏpīnātum, vel dŭbium, vel mălum contra, regnum, vel contra cŏrōnam dŏmĭni rēgis, forte in ballīvis suis sŭbĭto emersĕrit, dēbent, stătim pulsātis campānis quod Anglĭce vŏcant mōtbel convŏcāre omnes et ūnĭversos, quod Anglĭce dīcunt folcmōte, i. e. *vŏcātio et congrĕgātio pŏpŭlōrum, et gentium omnium,* quia ĭbi omnes convĕnīre dēbent... Stătūtum est quod dēbent pŏpŭli omnes, et gentes ūnĭversæ singŭlis annis, sĕmel in anno scīlĭcet convĕnīre, scīlĭcet in căpĭte kal. Maii,' Th. Anglo-Saxon Laws, vol. i. 613, note a. The folc-gemōt was forbidden to be held on Sundays:—On folcgemōte *at the folk-moot,* L. Alf. pol. 34; Th. i. 82, 12, 13: L. Ath. i. 2; Th. i. 200, 8: iv. 1; Th. i. 220, 23. On folcgemōte [-mōte, L.], L. Ath. i. 12; Th. i. 206, 11. On folces gemōte, L. Alf. pol. 22; Th. i. 76, 5. Gif he folcgemōt [folces gemōt, MS. H.] mid wǽpnes bryde arǽre *if he disturb the folk-moot by drawing his weapon,* L. Alf. pol. 38; Th. i. 86, 16. Sunnan dæges we forbeódaþ ǽlc folcgemōt, būton hit for mycelre neódþearfe sī *we forbid every Sunday folk-moot, unless it be for great necessity,* L. C. E. 15; Th. i. 368, 16: L. N. P. L. 55; Th. ii. 298, 22. Sunnan dæges freóls healde man georne, and folcgemōta on đam hālgan dæge geswīce man georne *let Sunday's festival be diligently kept, and folk-moots be carefully abstained from on that holy day,* L. Eth. v. 13; Th. i. 308, 11: vi. 22; Th. i. 320, 12: L. Edg. C. 19; Th. ii. 248, 14. v. folc-mōt, folc-land. v. Stubbs' Const. Hist. folk-moot.

folc-gerēfa, an; *m. A folk-reeve, a people's governor;* pŏpŭli præpŏsĭtus:—Folcgerēfa *actionātor,* Ælfc. Gl. 5; Som. 56, 25; Wrt. Voc. 17, 30. v. Du Cange, sub voce Actionator.

folc-geriht, es; *n. Folk-right;* publĭcum jus:—Feola syndon folcgerihtu *there are many folk-rights,* L. R. S. 21; Th. i. 440, 25. v. folc-riht.

folc-gesetness, e; *f. A decree* or *ordinance of the people;* plēbiscītum, Som. Ben. Lye.

folc-gesīþas; *gen.* -gesīþa; *m. The nobles of a country;* păres, nōbĭles, gentis cŏmites, pŏpŭlāres:—Syndon deáde folcgesīþas *the nobles of the country are dead,* Cd. 98; Th. 128, 29; Gen. 2134: Bt. Met. Fox 1, 140; Met. 1, 70. Wiđ đām nēhstum folcgesīþum *with the nearest rulers of the people,* Cd. 193; Th. 241, 29; Dan. 412.

folc-gestælla, an; *m. An adherent, follower;* gentis cŏmes:—Cræft folcgestælna *a force of adherents,* Cd. 15; Th. 18, 10; Gen. 271. v. folc-gestealla.

folc-gesteálla, -gestælla, an; *m. A noble companion;* gentis cŏmes, pŏpŭlāris:—Mid swilcum mæg man fōn folcgesteallan *with such, one may obtain adherents,* Cd. 15; Th. 19, 6; Gen. 287.

folc-gestreón, es; *n. A public treasure;* pŏpŭli dīvĭtiæ:—Đa leóde leng ne woldon Elamitarna aldor swīđan folcgestreónum *those nations would no longer strengthen the Elamites' prince with the public treasures,* Cd. 93; Th. 119, 17; Gen. 1981.

folc-getæl, es; *n. A number of people;* pŏpŭli nŭmĕrus:—On folcgetæl fiftig cista *in the number of people* [*were*] *fifty bands,* Cd. 154; Th. 192, 9; Exod. 229.

folc-geþrang, es; *n. Folk-throng, a crowd;* pŏpŭli căterva:—Þurh đæt folcgeþrang *through the crowd,* Ors. 3, 9; Bos. 68, 30.

folc-getrum, folce-getrum, es; *n. Folk-host;* exercĭtus:—Folcgetrume gefaren hæfdon *they had come with a host,* Cd. 93; Th. 119, 29; Gen. 1987. DER. getrum.

folc-gewinn, es; *n. Folk's war, battle;* bellum:—Wæs monig Gota gelysted folcgewinnes *many a Goth was desirous of battle,* Bt. Met. Fox 1, 19; Met. 1, 10.

folcisc; *adj. Folkish, common, vulgar, popular;* rustĭcus, plēbēius:—Gif man folciscne mæsse-preóst mid tīhtlan belecge *if a man charge a secular mass-priest with an accusation,* L. Eth. ix. 21; Th. i. 344, 19: L. C. E. 5; Th. i. 362, 16. Folcisce men *common men,* Bt. 30, 1; Fox 108, 23: 35, 6; Fox 168, 24. Đæt hī folciscra gemōta geswīcan *that they abstain from popular meetings,* L. Eth. vi. 44; Th. i. 326, 21.

folc-lǽsung, e; *f. Public lying, slander;* publĭcum mendācium:—Gif mon folclǽsunge gewyrce *si quis publĭcum mendācium confingat,* L. Alf. pol. 28; Wilk. 41, 19. v. folc-leásung.

folc-lagu, e; *f. Folk* or *public law;* publĭca lex:—Gif hwā folclage wirde *if any one corrupt the law of the people,* L. N. P. L. 46; Th. ii. 296, 22. Folclaga wyrsedon *the laws of the people were corrupted,* Lupi Serm. i. 5; Hick. Thes. ii. 100, 19.

folc-land, -lond, es; *n.* [folc *folk,* land *land*]. I. *the land of the folk* or *people.* It was the property of the community. It might be occupied in common, or possessed in severalty; and, in the latter case, it was probably parcelled out to individuals in the folc-gemōt, *q. v.* or court of the district, and the grant sanctioned by the freemen who were there present. While it continued to be folc-land, it could not be alienated in perpetuity; and, therefore, on the expiration of the term for which it had been granted, it reverted to the community, and was again distributed by the same authority. Spelman describes folc-land as 'terra pŏpŭlāris, quæ jūre commūni possĭdētur—sĭne scripto,' Gloss. Folcland. In another place he distinguishes it accurately from bōc-land: 'Prædia Saxŏnes duplĭci tĭtŭlo possĭdēbant; vel scripti auctōrĭtāte, quod bōc-land vŏcābant, vel pŏpŭli testĭmōnio, quod folc-land dixēre,' Id. Bocland:—Eác we cwǽdon hwæs se wyrđe wǽre đe ōđrum ryhtes wyrnde, āđor ođđe on bōc-lande ođđe on folc-lande, and đæt he him geāndagode of đam folc-lande, hwonne he him riht worhte befōran đam gerēfan. Gif he đonne nān riht næfde ne on bōc-lande ne on folc-lande, đæt se wǽre đe rihtes wyrnde scyldig xxx scillinga wiđ đone cyning; and æt ōđrum cyrre, eác swā: æt þriddan cyrre, cyninges oferhȳrnesse, đæt is cxx scillinga, būton he ǽr geswīce *also we have ordained of what he were worthy who denied justice to another, either in book-land or in folk-land, and that he should give him a term respecting the folk-land, when he should do him justice before the reeve. But if he had no right either to the book-land or to the folk-land, that he who denied the right should be liable in 30 shillings to the king; and for the second offence, the like: for the third offence, the king's penalty, that is, 120 shillings, unless he previously desist,* L. Ed. 2; Th. i. 160, 10-17. All lands, whether bōc-land or folc-land, were subject to the Trĭnōda Necessĭtas. Under this denomination are comprised three distinct imposts, to which all landed possessions, not excepting those of the church, were subject, viz:—[*a*] Brycg-bōt *for keeping the bridges, and highways in repair.* [*b*] Burh-bōt *for keeping the burghs, or fortresses, in* *an efficient state of defence.* [*c*] Fyrd *a contribution for maintaining the military and naval force of the kingdom*:—Gif hwā Burh-bōte, oððe Brycg-bōte, oððe Fyrd-fare forsitte; gebēte mid hund-twelftigum scillinga ðam cyningce on Engla lage, and on Dena lage, swā hit ǽr stōd *if any one neglect Burh-bôt, or Brycg-bôt, or Fyrd-fare; let him make amends with one hundred and twenty shillings to the king by English law, and by Danish law, as it formerly stood*, L. C. S. 66; Th. i. 410, 8–10. Þegenes lagu is, ðæt he sȳ his bōc-rihtes wyrðe, and ðæt he þreó þinc of his lande dō, fyrd-færeld, and burh-bōte, and brycg-geweorc [MS. bryc-] *thane's law is, that he be worthy to make his will, and that he perform three things for his land, military service, repairs of fortresses, and of bridges*, L. R. S. 1; Th. i. 432, 1–3. II. Folk-land was subject to many burthens and exactions from which book-land was exempt. The possessors of folk-land were bound to assist in the reparation of royal vills, and in other public works. They were liable to have travellers and others quartered on them for subsistence. They were required to give hospitality to kings and great men in their progress through the country, to furnish them with carriages and relays of horses, and to extend the same assistance to their messengers, followers, and servants, and even to the persons who had charge of their hawks, horses, and hounds. Such at least are the burthens from which lands are liberated when converted by charter into book-land. 2. Folk-land might be held by freemen of all ranks and conditions. It is a mistake to imagine with Lambarde, Spelman, and a host of antiquaries, that it was possessed by the common people only. Still less is Blackstone to be credited, when, trusting to Somner, he tells us it was land held in villenage by people in a state of downright servitude, belonging, both they and their children and effects, to the lord of the soil, like the rest of the cattle or stock upon the land. [Blackstone, ii. 92.]—A deed published by Lye, exposes the error of these representations. [*Anglo-Saxon Dict.*, App. ii. 2.] Alfred, a nobleman of the highest rank, possessed of great estates in book-land, beseeches King Alfred, in his will, to continue his folk-land to his son, Æthelwald; and if that favour cannot be obtained, he bequeaths, in lieu of it, to his son, who appears to have been illegitimate, ten hides of book-land at one place, or seven at another. From this document it follows, first, that folk-land was held by persons of rank; secondly, that an estate of folk-land was of such value, that seven, or even ten hides of book-land were not considered as more than equivalent to it; and, lastly, that it was a life-estate, not devisable by will, but in the opinion of the testator, at the disposal of the king, when by his own death it was vacated. 3. It appears also from this document, that the same person might hold estates both in book-land and in folk-land; that is, he might possess an estate of inheritance of which he had the complete disposal, unless in so far as it was limited by settlement; and with it he might possess an estate for life, revertible to the public after his decease. In the latter times of the Anglo-Saxon government it is probable there were few persons of condition who had not estates of both descriptions. Every one was desirous to have grants of folk-land, and to convert as much of it as possible into book-land. Money was given and favour exhausted for that purpose. 4. In many Saxon wills we find petitions similar to that of Alfred; but in none of them is the character of the land, which could not be disposed of without consent of the king, described with the same precision. In some wills, the testator bequeaths his land as he pleases, without asking leave of any one [Somner's *Gavelkind*, 88, 211; Hickes, *Pref.* xxxii; *Diss. Epist.* 29, 54, 55, 59; Madox, *Formul.* 395]; in others he earnestly beseeches the king that his will may stand, and then declares his intentions with respect to the distribution of his property [Lambarde, *Kent*, 540; Hickes, *Diss. Epist.* 54; Gale, i. 457; Lye's *Append.* ii. 1, 5; Heming, 40];—and in one instance he makes an absolute bequest of the greater part of his lands, but solicits the king's consent to the disposal of a small part of his estate [Hickes, *Diss. Epist.* 62.] There can be no doubt that book-land was devisable by will, unless where its descent had been determined by settlement; and a presumption, therefore, arises, that where the consent of the king was necessary, the land devised was not book-land, but folk-land. If this inference be admitted, the case of Alfred will not be a solitary instance, but common to many of the principal Saxon nobility. 5. That folk-lands were assignable to the thegns, or military servants of the state, as the stipend or reward for their services, is clearly indicated in the celebrated letter of Bede to Archbishop Ecgbert [Smith's *Bede*, 305–312]. In that letter, which throws so much light on the internal state of Northumberland, the venerable author complains of the improvident grants to monasteries, which had impoverished the government, and left no lands for the soldiers and retainers of the secular authorities, on whom the defence of the country must necessarily depend. He laments the mistaken prodigality, and expresses his fears that there will be soon a deficiency of military men to repel invasion, no place being left where they can obtain possessions to maintain them suitably to their condition. It is evident from these complaints, that the lands so lavishly bestowed on the church had been formerly the property of the public, and at the disposal of the government. If they had been book-lands, it could have made no difference to the state whether they belonged to the church or to individuals, since in both cases they were beyond its control, and in both cases were subject to the usual obligations of military service. But if they formed part of the, folk-land, or property of the public, it is easy to conceive how their conversion into book-land must have weakened the state, by lessening the fund out of which its military servants were to be provided. 6. A charter of the eighth century conveys to the see of Rochester certain lands on the Medway, as they had been formerly possessed by the chiefs and companions of the Kentish kings. [*Text. Roffens.* 72, edit. Hearne; Kemble, *Cod. Dipl.* No. cxi.] In this instance folk-land, which had been appropriated to the military service of the state, appears to have been converted into book-land, and given to the church, L. Th. ii. Glossary, Folc-land: Sandys' *Gavel.* 97. v. Stubbs' Const. Hist. folk-land. v. fyrd, scip-fyrd, bōc-land.

folc-lār, e; *f. Popular instruction, a sermon;* pŏpŭlāris institūtio *vel* instructio, hŏmīlia, sermo, Cot. 143, Som. Ben. Lye. v. lār.

folc-leásung, e; *f. Folk-leasing, public lying, slander;* publĭcum mendācium, cālumnia:—Be folcleásunge gewyrhtum. Gif mon folcleásunge gewyrce, mid nānum leóhtran þinge gebēte ðonne him mon aceorfe ða tungan of *of those committing slander. If a man commit slander, let him make amends with no lighter thing than that his tongue be cut out*, L. Alf. pol. 32; Th. i. 80, 19–82, 1.

folc-līc; *adj. Folklike, common;* pŏpŭlāris, commūnis:—Folclīc lār *hŏmīlia* [MS. *ŏmīlia* = ὁμιλία], Ælfc. Gl. 35; Som. 62, 75; Wrt. Voc. 28, 53. He sǽde ðæt he folclīc man wǽre *rustĭcum se fuisse respondit*, Bd. 4, 22; S. 591, 6: Nar. 18, 4.

folc-lond *folk-land;* pŏpŭli terra, Exon. 115 b; Th. 444, 14; Kl. 47. v. folc-land.

folc-mægen, es; *n. People's force;* pŏpŭli rōbur:—Ðā ðǽr folc-mægen fōr *then there marched a people's force*, Cd. 160; Th. 199, 31; Exod. 347.

folc-mǽgþ, e; *f. A nation-tribe, tribe;* nātio, trĭbus:—Folc-mǽgþa *of nation-tribes*, Cd. 64; Th. 77, 18; Gen. 1277.

folc-mǽlum *in bands*, Chr. 1011; Erl. 145, 5, = floc-mǽlum. v. flocc-mǽlum.

folc-mǽre; *nom. pl. n.* folc-mǽro; *adj. Folk-known* or *popular;* cĕlĕber, pŏpŭlōsus:—Ofer folc-mǽro land *over celebrated lands*, Cd. 86; Th. 108, 5; Gen. 1801.

folc-mōt, es; *n. A popular assembly;* pŏpŭli consessus:—On folcmōte *at the folk-moot*, L. Ath. i. 12; Th. i. 206, 11, note 25. v. folc-gemōt.

folc-nēd, e; *f. A people's need;* pŏpŭli necessĭtas:—Him wīsode wolcen unlytel daga ǽghwylce, swā hit Drihten hēt; and him ealle niht, ōðer beácen, fȳres leóma, folcnēde heóld *a large cloud directed them every day, as the Lord commanded it; and to them all night, another sign, a pillar of fire, supplied the people's need*, Ps. Th. 77, 16.

folc-rǽd, -rēd, es; *m. A public benefit, that which serves for the good of the people;* publĭcum bĕnĕfĭcium:—Dryhten gumena folcrǽd fremede *the Lord of men did public benefits*, Andr. Kmbl. 1243; An. 622. He folcrēd fremede *he accomplished public benefit*, Beo. Th. 6004, note; B. 3006.

folc-rǽden, -rǽdenn, e; *f. A nation's law;* plēbiscītum:—Sum mæg folcrǽdenne gehycgan *one may deliberate a nation's law*, Exon. 79 a; Th. 295, 32; Crä. 42.

folc-riht, -ryht, es; *n. Folkright, common law, public right, the understood compact by which every freeman enjoys his rights as a freeman;* publĭcum jus, commūne = τὸ κοινόν:—Arǽre up Godes riht; and heonanforþ lǽte manna gehwylcne, ge earmne ge eádigne, folcrihtes wyrðe, and him man rihte dōmas dēme *let God's right be exalted; and henceforth let every man, both poor and rich, be worthy of folk-right, and let a man have right dooms judged to him*, L. C. S. 1; Th. i. 376, 10: L. Ed. 11; Th. i. 164, 20: L. Edg. ii. 1; Th. i. 266, 4: L. Eth. vi. 8; Th. i. 316, 28. Hit he becwæþ mid fullan folcrihte *he bequeathed it with full folk-right*, L. O. 13; Th. i. 184, 1: 2; Th. i. 178, 13. To folcryhte *to folk-right*, L. Ath. i. 2; Th. i. 200, 7: i. 8; Th. i. 204, 7: i. 23; Th. i. 212, 1. He him forgeaf wīcstede wēligne, folcrihta gehwylc, swā his fæder āhte *he had given him the wealthy dwelling place, every public right, as his father had possessed*, Beo. Th. 5209; B. 2608. Gesealde wǽpna geweald ofercom mid ðȳ feónda folcriht *he gave him power of weapons with which he overcame the folkright* [*liberty*] *of enemies*, Cd. 143; Th. 179, 1; Exod. 22.

folc-riht, -ryht; *adj. According to folk-right, lawful;* secundum publĭcum jus, lēgālis:—Sīe he wyrðe folcryhtre [-rihtre MS. G.] bōte *let him be worthy of lawful compensation*, L. Alf. 13; Th. i. 46, 25.

folc-sæl, es; *pl. nom. acc.* -salo; *n. A folk-building;* pŏpŭlāris ædes:—Ic folcsalo bærne *I burn public structures*, Exon. 101 a; Th. 381, 3; Rä. 2, 5.

folc-scearu, -sceru, -scaru, e; *f. A division of the people, nation, multitude;* nātio, provincia:—Ðæt hie hine onsundne gebrohten of ðære folcsceare *that they should bring him uninjured from that tribe of people*, Cd. 90; Th. 112, 17; Gen. 1872: 114; Th. 149, 20; Gen. 2477. Ðū ūsic woldest on ðisse folcsceare besyrwan *thou wouldest deceive us among* *this nation*, 127; Th. 162, 12; Gen. 2680: 136; Th. 171, 16; Gen. 2829: Andr. Kmbl. 1368; An. 684: Elen. Kmbl. 1933; El. 968. Geond ða folcsceare *among the nation-host*, Cd. 85; Th. 106, 34; Gen. 1781. On ðisse folcscere *in this country*, Elen. Kmbl. 804; El. 402. Bûton folcscare *except the host of people*, Beo. Th. 146; B. 73.

folc-sceaða, an; *m. People's tyrant, villain;* pŏpŭli tyrannus:—Ðæs weorudes ða wyrrestan fâ folcsceaðan feówertyne gewiton in forwyrd sceacan *of the host the worst, hateful villains, fourteen departed into destruction*, Andr. Kmbl. 3184; An. 1595.

folc-scipe, es; *m. People;* nātio, pŏpŭlus:—Fere fôddurwêlan folcscipe dreógeþ [*a ship*] *brings* [lit. *performs the bearing of*] *abundance of food to people*, Exon. 108 b; Th. 415, 13; Rä. 33, 10. [*O. Sax.* folkskepi.]

folc-slite, es; *m. A folk-slit, sedition;* sēdĭtio:—Folcslite *vel* ǽswîcung, sacu, ceást *sēdĭtio*, Ælfc. Gl. 15; Som. 58, 38; Wrt. Voc. 21, 30.

folc-stede, -styde, es; *m. Folk* or *dwelling-place;* pŏpŭli lŏcus, habĭtācŭlum:—Folcstede gumena *the dwelling-place of men*, Andr. Kmbl. 40; An. 20. On folcstede *in the folk-place*, Chr. 937; Erl. 114, 7; Æðelst. 41: Exon. 102 b; Th. 388, 21; Rä. 6, 11. On ðam folcstede *in the folk-place*, Judth. 12; Thw. 26, 10; Jud. 320: Andr. Kmbl. 357; An. 179. Ic gehêt ðê folcstede *I promised thee a dwelling-place*, Cd. 100; Th. 132, 31; Gen. 2201. Folcstede frætwian *to decorate the dwelling-place*, Beo. Th. 152; B. 76. Se ðe gegân dorste folcstede fâra *he who durst go into the folk-place of the hostile*, Beo. Th. 2930; B. 1463. Ðǽr folcstede fægre wǽron *where the dwelling-places were fair*, Cd. 91; Th. 116, 8; Gen. 1933. Fram ðam folcstyde *from the folk-place*, Cd. 93; Th. 120, 25; Gen. 2000.

folc-stôw, e; *f. A public place, country place;* publĭcus *vel* rustĭcus lŏcus:—He ferde ge þurh mynsterstôwe ge þurh folcstôwe *discurrĕre per urbāna et rustĭca lŏca sŏlēbat*, Bd. 3, 5; S. 526, 27.

folc-sweót, es; *m.* [sweót, *m. a band*] *A multitude of people, multitude;* pŏpŭli multĭtūdo, caterva:—Folcsweóta mǽst *greatest of multitudes*, Cd. 171; Th. 215, 2; Exod. 577.

folc-talu, e; *f. Folk-reckoning, genealogy;* pŏpŭli enŭmĕrātio, genealŏgia:—On folctale *in the genealogy*, Cd. 161; Th. 201, 29; Exod. 379.

folc-toga, an; *m. A popular leader, commander* or *leader of the people;* pŏpŭli dux, princeps:—Frome folctogan *pious leaders*, Andr. Kmbl. 15; An. 8. Ferdon folctogan *the nation's chieftains came*, Beo. Th. 1682; B. 839. Fyllan folctogan *to fell the people's chieftains*, Judth. 11; Thw. 24, 17; Jud. 194. [*O. Sax.* folk-togo.]

folc-truma, an; *m.* [truma *a band, troop*] *A host of people, people;* pŏpŭli cohors, pŏpŭlus:—Cweðe eall folctruma, sý ðæt, sý ðæt oððe beó hit swâ *dīcet omnis pŏpŭlus, fiat, fiat*, Ps. Lamb. 105, 48. Folctruman andettaþ ðê *pŏpŭli confĭtēbuntur tĭbi*, 44, 18. Drihten dêmþ folctruman *Dŏmĭnus jūdĭcat pŏpŭlos*, 7, 9: 9, 9: 46, 4.

folcû [folc *people*, cû *a cow*] *A cow of the herd:*—Under folcûm *inter vaccas pŏpŭlōrum*, Ps. Th. 67, 27. Folcûm, for folc-cûm, from folcû, like wildeór, wyrtruma, for wild-deór, wyrt-truma, etc. v. folc-cû.

folc-wêlig, -wêleg; *adj. Rich in people, populous;* pŏpŭlo dīves, abundans:—Folcwêlega *populous*, Cot. 153.

folc-weras; *gen.* -wera; *pl. m. Men of the people, people;* pŏpŭlāres, pŏpŭlus:—Hâtaþ Fîson folcweras *people call it Pison*, Cd. 12; Th. 14, 21; Gen. 222: 89; Th. 110, 30; Gen. 1846. [*O. Sax.* folk-werôs.]

folc-wiga, an; *m. A warrior;* bellātor:—Folcwîgan wicge wegaþ *warriors on horseback bear me*, Exon. 104 a; Th. 395, 26; Rä. 15, 13.

folc-wita, an; *m. A senator;* publĭcus consĭliārius:—Sum biþ folcwita *one is a senator*, Exon. 79 b; Th. 297, 33; Crä. 77.

fold-ærn, es; *n.* [folde *the earth*, ærn *a place*] *An earth-place, a cave, sepulchre;* terrēnus lŏcus, sepulcrum:—Foldærne fæst *fast in the earth-house = sepulchre*, Exon. 18 b; Th. 45, 36; Cri. 730: 47 b; Th. 163, 36; Gû. 1004.

fold-bold, es; *n.* [folde *the earth*, bold *a dwelling*] *The land-dwelling, royal palace;* terrestris dŏmus, rēgia aula, arx:—Ne feól fæger foldbold *the fair earthly dwelling fell not*, Beo. Th. 1550; B. 773.

fold-bûend, -bûende; noun from pres. part. v. bûend, *pl. m. Earth-dwellers, earth's inhabitants, inhabitants of a land* or *country;* terrĭcŏlæ:—Ðanan feorhnere findaþ fold-bûend *thence earth's inhabitants find nourishment*, Ps. Th. 64, 10: Beo. Th. 4541; B. 2274. Ðone Grendel nemdon foldbûende *whom earth's inhabitants named Grendel*, Beo. Th. 2714; B. 1355: Elen. Kmbl. 2026; El. 1014: Exon. 25 a; Th. 72, 25; Cri. 1178: 121 a; Th. 465, 9; Hö. 101. Hý ongytan mihton ðæt wæs fôremǽrost foldbûendum receda *they might perceive what was the grandest of houses to earth's inhabitants*, Beo. Th. 624; B. 309: Bt. Met. Fox 8, 8; Met. 8, 4: Exon. 53 a; Th. 186, 24; Az. 24. Deáþ rîcsade ofer foldbûend *death ruled over earth's inhabitants*, Exon. 45 b; Th. 154, 17; Gû. 844. Mid fêre fold-bûende se micla dæg meahtan Dryhtnes bihlǽmeþ *the great day of the mighty Lord shall strike earth's inhabitants with fear*, Exon. 20 b; Th. 54, 14; Cri. 868. Ðæt eorþwaran ealle hæfden foldbûende fruman gelîcne *that all mortals, inhabitants of the earth, had a like beginning*, Bt. Met. Fox 17, 3; Met. 17, 2. Ðone fugel hâtaþ foldbûende Filistina fruman uasa mortis *the inhabitants of the land, the princes of the Philistines, call the bird vāsa mortis*, Salm. Kmbl. 560; Sal. 279. Ic hæbbe me on hrycge ðæt ǽr hâdas wreáh foldbûendra *I have on my back what ere covered the persons of dwellers on earth*, Exon. 101 a; Th. 381, 18; Rä. 2, 13: 32 b; Th. 106, 2; Gû. 35.

FOLDE, an; *f.* I. *the earth, dry land;* tellus, terra:—He gesêceþ fægre land ðonne ðeós folde *he shall seek a fairer land than this earth*, Cd. 218; Th. 277, 32; Sat. 213: 84; Th. 106, 3; Gen. 1765: 100; Th. 133, 2; Gen. 2204: Exon. 73 a; Th. 272, 14; Jul. 499: 120 a; Th. 460, 21; Hö. 20: Bt. Met. Fox 11, 86; Met. 11, 43: 20, 118; Met. 20, 59. Folde wæs ðâ gyt græs ungrêne *the earth was as yet not green with grass*, Cd. 6; Th. 7, 35; Gen. 116: 12; Th. 14, 7; Gen. 215: Exon. 43 b; Th. 146, 26; Gû. 715. Stôd bewrigen folde mid flôde *the dry land stood covered with water*, Cd. 8; Th. 10, 15; Gen. 157. Geblissad mid ðâm fægrestum foldan stencum *made blissful by the sweetest odours of earth*, Exon. 56 a; Th. 198, 11; Ph. 8: Cd. 161; Th. 201, 9; Exod. 369. Foldan bearm *or* fæðm *the bosom of the earth*, Beo. Th. 2278; B. 1137: 2790; B. 1393: Exon. 93 b; Th. 351, 4; Sch. 75: 125 b; Th. 482, 20; Rä. 67, 4. Foldan sceát *a region* or *tract of the earth*, Exon. 9 a; Th. 5, 21; Cri. 72: 20 b; Th. 55, 6; Cri. 879: 116 a; Th. 445, 20; Dôm. 10: Bt. Met. Fox 4, 103; Met. 4, 52: Cd. 75; Th. 92, 26; Gen. 1534: 199; Th. 247, 25; Dan. 502: 213; Th. 265, 6; Sat. 3: Beo. Th. 193; B. 96. On ðisse foldan *on this earth*, Salm. Kmbl. 953; Sal. 476: Cd. 121; Th. 155, 24; Gen. 2577: Exon. 19 b; Th. 50, 28; Cri. 808: Beo. Th. 2396; B. 1196: Menol. Fox 283; Men. 143: Rood Kmbl. 261; Kr. 132. Teóde fîrum foldan Freá ælmihtig *fīliis hŏmĭnum terram omnĭpŏtens creāvit*, Bd. 4, 24; S. 597, 24: Cd. 8; Th. 10, 9; Gen. 154: Exon. 12 b; Th. 20, 22; Cri. 321. II. *a land, country, district, region, territory;* rēgio, tractus, plăga, terrĭtōrium:—Wæs wera gûþhergum ēðelland geondsended, folde feóndum *the people's native land was overspread with hostile bands, their country with enemies*, Cd. 92; Th. 118, 22; Gen. 1969: Exon. 56 a; Th. 199, 21; Ph. 29. Unlytel dǽl sîdre foldan geondsended wæs bryne *no small part of the wide land was overspread with burning*, Cd. 119; Th. 154, 5; Gen. 2551. Nyste hine on ðære foldan fira ǽnig *none of the men in the land knew him*, Salm. Kmbl. 547; Sal. 273: Menol. Fox 29; Men. 15. Ðæt land gesêc ðe ic ðê ýwan wille, brâde foldan *seek the land which I will show thee, a spacious country*, Cd. 83; Th. 105, 12; Gen. 1752: Exon. 123 b; Th. 474, 27; Bo. 37: Salm. Kmbl. 431; Sal. 216. Ðû eart hyht ealra ðe feor on sǽ foldum wuniaþ *thou art the hope of all who dwell in lands far in the sea* [i.e. *in islands*], Ps. Th. 64, 6. III. *the ground, soil;* hŭmus, sŏlum:—He gefeóll to foldan *he fell to the ground*, Judth. 12; Thw. 25, 27; Jud. 281: Andr. Kmbl. 1474; An. 738: Exon. 29 a; Th. 88, 34; Cri. 1450: Elen. Kmbl. 1970; El. 987. Him heortan blôd foldan gesêceþ *his heart's blood seeks the ground*, Salm. Kmbl. 316; Sal. 157: Exon. 103 b; Th. 393, 17; Rä. 13, 1. Foldan begræfen *buried in the ground*, Elen. Kmbl. 1944; El. 974: Exon. 63 a; Th. 231, 17; Ph. 490: Ps. Th. 142, 4. IV. *earth, clay;* terræ lĭmus, lŭtum:—God ðone ǽrestan ælda cynnes of ðære clǽnestan foldan geworhte *God made the first of the race of men from the purest earth*, Exon. 44 b; Th. 151, 14; Gû. 795. [*Laym.* folde: *O. Sax.* folda, *f: Icel.* fold, *f. a field, earth.*]

fold-græf, es; *n. An earth-grave;* sepulcrum:—He ahôf of foldgræfe *he raised* [*it*] *from an earthly grave*, Elen. Kmbl. 1686; El. 845. Of foldgrafum *from the earth-graves*, Exon. 23 a; Th. 63, 27; Cri. 1026.

fold-grǽg; *adj.* [grǽg *grey*] *Earth-grey, earth-coloured;* instar terræ cānus:—Eá of dûne sceal foldgrǽg fêran *earth-coloured water shall proceed from a hill*, Menol. Fox 521; Gn. C. 31.

fold-hrêrende; *part. touching, moving on, the earth;* terram tangens *vel* peragrans:—Deóra foldhrêrendra *of earth-enlivening beasts*, Exon. 95 b; Th. 356, 2; Pa. 5. cf. mold-hrêrende.

fold-ræst, e; *f. Earth-rest;* sepulcrālis requies:—Weorþeþ foldræste æt ende *shall be at the end of their earth-rest*, Exon. 23 a; Th. 63, 34; Cri. 1029.

fold-wæstm, es; *m. Earth-fruit;* quidquid terra gignit:—Fægrum foldwæstmum *with fair fruits of earth*, Exon. 65 a; Th. 241, 10; Ph. 654.

fold-weg, es; *m.* I. *earth-way;* terrestris via:—On foldwege *on the earth-way*, Cd. 95; Th. 123, 24; Gen. 2050: 116; Th. 151, 17; Gen. 2510: 139; Th. 174, 4; Gen. 2873: Beo. Th. 3271; B. 1633. Foldwegas, Beo. Th. 1736; B. 866: Exon. 96 a; Th. 358, 25; Pa. 51. II. *the earth in general;* terra:—On ðissum foldwege *on this earth*, Exon. 30 a; Th. 93, 22; Cri. 1530. On foldwege *on the earth*, Andr. Kmbl. 412; An. 206. Cwicra ǽngum on foldwege *to any living on earth*, Exon. 51 a; Th. 177, 8; Gû. 1224.

fold-wêla, an; *m. Earth-wealth;* terrestres ŏpes:—Foldwêla fealleþ *earthly wealth decays*, Exon. 95 a; Th. 354, 59; Reim. 68.

fold-wong, es; *m. Earth-plain;* terræ campus:—On foldwong *on earth's plain*, Exon. 22 a; Th. 60, 25; Cri. 975.

folgaþ, es; *m.* I. *a train, retinue;* id quod sĕquĭtur, cŏmĭtātus:—Him wæs lâþ to amyrrene his âgenne folgaþ *he was loath to injure his own retinue*, Chr. 1048; Erl. 178, 12. II. *service of* *a follower;* cŏmĭtis servĭtus, ministĕrium:—Hwæt is betere ðonne ðæs cyninges folgaþ *what is better than the king's service?* Bt. 29, 1; Fox 102, 6. Heó fægerne folgaþ hæfdon uppe mid englum *they had a fair service above with angels*, Cd. 220; Th. 284, 30; Sat. 329. Ic gewát folgaþ sēcan *I departed to seek my service*, Exon. 115 a; Th. 442, 8; Kl. 9. Áhte ic fela wintra folgaþ tilne, holdne hláford *I had for many years a good service, a kind lord*, 100 b; Th. 379, 25; Deór. 38. v. folgoþ. v. Stubbs' Const. Hist. comitatus.

folgen *stuck to, went into; pp. of* felgan.

folgere, es; *m.* I. *a* FOLLOWER, *attendant, disciple;* assecla, pĕdĭsĕquus, assectātor:—Folgere *assecla*, Ælfc. Gl. 113; Som. 79, 131; Wrt. Voc. 60, 35. Hwæt wille we sprecan be ðam cyninge, and be his folgerum *what shall we say about the king, and about his followers?* Bt. 29, 1; Fox 104, 10. Ðý þriddan dæge þeóda Wealdend arās, and he feówertig daga folgeras síne rūnum arētte *on the third day the Ruler of nations arose, and for forty days he comforted his followers [=disciples] with words*, Hy. 10, 35; Hy. Grn. ii. 293, 35. II. *one of a class of freemen who has no dwelling of his own, but is the follower* or *retainer of another, for whom he performs certain agricultural services;* folgārius, ūnus ex lībĕrōrum ordĭne qui ălĭcūjus clientēlæ *vel* servĭtio sese addīcit, fămŭlus qui fŏco proprio căret, aut sub stīpendio et servĭtii ălĭcūjus præstātiōne possĭdet:—Folgere gebýreþ, ðæt he on twelf mōnþum ii æceras gearnige, ōðerne gesāwene and ōðerne unsāwene; sǽdige sylf ðæne, and his mete, and scōung, and glōfung him gebýreþ: gyf he māre geearnian mæg [MS. mæig], him biþ sylfum fremu *folgārio compĕtit, ut in duodĕcim mensĭbus duas acras hăbeat, ūnam sēmĭnātam, ălĭam non; sed ĭdem sēmĭnet eam, et victum suum, et calciamenta dēbet hăbēre, et cĭrotĕcas [=chīrothēcas]: si plus deservit, ipsi commŏdum ĕrit*, L. R. S. 10; Th. i. 438, 4-7: L. C. S. 20; Th. i. 386, 23. DER. æfter-folgere.

folgian; *p.* ode, ade, ede; *pp.* od, ad, ed; *v. trans. dat. and acc.* I. *to* FOLLOW, *go behind, run after, pursue;* sĕqui, insĕqui:—Míne sceáp gehýraþ míne stefne, and hig folgiaþ me *ŏves meæ vōcem meam audiunt, et sĕquuntur me*, Jn. Bos. 10, 27. He folgode feorhgeníþlan *he pursued his deadly foes*, Beo. Th. 5858; B. 2933. Þegn folgade *a thane went behind it*, Exon. 109 b; Th. 419, 8; Rä. 38, 2: 129 a; Th. 495, 4; Rä. 84, 2. We sōþfæstes swaðe folgodon *we followed the true one's track*, Andr. Kmbl. 1346; An. 673. Ðæt mínre spræce spēd folgie *that success follow my word*, Ps. Th. 55, 4. Gif ceorl acwyle be libbendum wífe and bearne, riht is ðæt hit ðæt bearn mēdder folgige *if a husband die, his wife and child yet living, it is right that the child follow the mother*, L. H. E. 6; Th. i. 30, 4. Ðæt ðære spræce spēd folgode *that success would follow that speech*, Cd. 109; Th. 144, 4; Gen. 2384. II. *to follow as a servant, attendant* or *disciple;* cŏmĭtāri, adhærēre alicui, servīre, subdĭtus esse:—Cwǽdon hí ðæt him nǽnig mǽg leófra nǽre ðonne hira hláford, and hí nǽfre his banan folgian noldon *they said that no kinsman was dearer to them than their lord, and they would never follow [=serve] his murderer*, Chr. 755; Erl. 50, 20. Folgian líchoman luste *to follow [=serve] the body's lust*, R. Ben. 4. Ne mæg nān þeów twām hláfordum þeówian: he ānum folgaþ and ōðerne forhogaþ *nēmo servus pŏtest duōbus dŏmĭnis servīre: ūni adhærēbit et altĕrum contemnet*, Lk. Bos. 16, 13. He forlǽteþ lāre ðíne and mānþeáwum mínum folgaþ *he shall desert thy doctrine and follow my evil customs*, Elen. Kmbl. 1857; El. 930. Him folgiaþ in ðam gladan hām gǽstas gecorene *chosen spirits follow [=serve] him [Christ] in that glad home*, Exon. 64 b; Th. 237, 16; Ph. 591. He folgode ānum burhsittendum men ðæs ríces *adhæsit ūni cīvium rēgiōnis illius*, Lk. Bos. 15, 15: Homl. Th. ii. 500, 10. Dō ðæt mid ðæs ealdormonnes gewitnesse ðe he ǽr in his scíre folgode *let him do it with the knowledge of the alderman whom he before followed in his shire*, L. Alf. pol. 37; Th. i. 86, 4, 7: L. Ath. i. 8; Th. i. 204, 5: i. 22; Th. i. 210, 21: iv. 1; Th. i. 220, 21. We lǽraþ, ðæt ǽnig preóst ne underfō ōðres scōlere, būton ðæs leáfe ðe he ǽr folgode *we enjoin, that no priest receive another's scholar, without leave of him whom he previously followed*, L. Edg. C. 10; Th. ii. 246, 15. Ðeáh hie hira beággyfan banan folgedon *though they followed [=served] their ring-giver's murderer*, Beo. Th. 2209; B. 1102. Ðæt ǽlc folgie swylcum hláforde swylcum he wille *that each follow [=serve] such lord as he will*, L. Ath. iv. 1; Th. i. 222, 1. Wæs on eorþan ēce Drihten feówertig daga folgad folcum, ǽr he to heofonríce astāh *on earth the Lord eternal was followed [=attended] by people for forty days, ere he ascended into heaven*, Cd. 226; Th. 300, 4; Sat. 559. DER. æfter-folgian, ge-. v. fylgean.

folgoþ, folgaþ, es; *m.* [folgoþ=folgaþ; *3rd sing. pres. of* folgian *to follow.*] I. that which follows,—*A train, retinue;* id quod sĕquĭtur, cŏmĭtātus:—Ā to his folgoþe and to his þénunge ða æðelestan men cōmon *the noblest men always came to his retinue and to his service*, Bd. 3, 14; S. 540, 11. On Swegenes eorles folgoþe *among the train of earl Sweyn*, Chr. 1048; Erl. 178, 16. II. service of a follower,—*A service, office, official dignity;* cŏmĭtis servĭtus, ministĕrium, offĭcium, præpŏsĭtūra:—Se biscop amanige ða oferhýrnesse æt ðam gerēfan ðe hit on his folgoþe sý *let the bishop exact the penalty for contempt from the reeve in whose service it may be*, L. Ath. i. 26; Th. i. 214, 3. He folgode Iuliane, and he on ðam folgoþe ealle fūlnysse forbeáh, lybbende swā swā munuc *he followed Julian, and in that service he avoided all foulness, living as a monk*, Homl. Th. ii. 500, 12. On ðý eahtateóðan geáre ðe Ōswold arcebisceop to folgoþe fēng *in the eighteenth year [from that] in which archbishop Oswald took office*, Cod. Dipl. 620; A. D. 978; Kmbl. iii. 168, 23. Beó se gerēfa būton his folgoþe *let the reeve be without [=deprived of] his official dignity*, L. Ath. v. § 11; Th. i. 240, 19. Ualentinianus wæs Iulianuses cempena ealdorman: he him bebeád ðæt he forlēte ðone his cristendōm oððe his folgoþ; ðā wæs him leófre ðæt he forlēte his folgoþ ðonne ðone cristendōm *Valentinian was chief of Julian's soldiers: he [Julian] commanded him to give up christianity or his office; then it was dearer to him to give up his office than christianity*, Ors. 6, 33; Bos. 129, 16-19. Habbaþ folgoþa cyst mid Cyninge *they [the angels] have the choicest of services with their King*, Exon. 13 b; Th. 24, 26; Cri. 390. III. *condition of life;* condĭtio vītæ:—Ōðer biþ unlǽde, ōðer biþ eádig... hwæðres biþ hira folgoþ betra *one is miserable, the other is fortunate... of which of them is the condition better?* Salm. Kmbl. 740; Sal. 369. DER. under-folgoþ.

FOLM; *gen. dat.* folme; *acc.* folm, folme; *pl. nom. acc.* folme, folma; *f:* folme, an; *f. The palm of the hand, the hand;* palma, mănus:—Folm mec mæg bifōn *the hand may grasp me*, Exon. 111 a; Th. 425, 6; Rä. 41, 52: Ps. Th. 79, 15. Of sceaðan folme *from the hand of the foe*, Andr. Kmbl. 2268; An. 1135. Ne hafaþ hió fōt ne folm *it has not foot nor hand*, Exon. 110 a; Th. 420, 27; Rä. 40, 10. Heó genam cūþe folme *she took the well-known hand*, Beo. Th. 2610; B. 1303: Salm. Kmbl. 339; Sal. 169: Ps. Th. 128, 5. Mægþ scearpne mēce of sceáðe abræd swíðran folme *the woman [Judith] drew the sharp sword from its sheath with her right hand*, Judth. 10; Thw. 22, 26; Jud. 80: Beo. Th. 1500; B. 748. For ðām næglum ðe ðæs Nergendes fēt þurhwōdon and his folme *for the nails which pierced the Saviour's feet and his hands*, Elen. Kmbl. 2130; El. 1066: Exon. 108 b; Th. 415, 3; Rä. 33, 5. Hæfde unlifigendes gefeormod fēt and folma *he had devoured the feet and hands of the lifeless*, Beo. Th. 1494; B. 745. Nāh geweald fōta ne folma *he shall not have the power of feet nor of hands*, Exon. 107 b; Th. 410, 12; Rä. 28, 15. Me of folmum afere firenwyrcendra *take me out of the hands of those committing sin*, Ps. Th. 70, 3: Beo. Th. 319; B. 158. Geseóþ ða feorhdolg ðe gefremedon on mínum folmum and on fōtum *see the deadly wounds which they inflicted on my palms and in my feet*, Exon. 29 a; Th. 89, 12; Cri. 1456. On ðone eádgan andwlitan helfūse men hondum slōgun, folmum areahtum, and fýstum eác *wicked men struck on the blessed visage with their hands, with outstretched palms, and fists also*, Exon. 24 a; Th. 69, 23; Cri. 1125. Ic ðē wreó and scylde folmum mínum *I will cover and shield thee with my hands*, Cd. 99; Th. 131, 4; Gen. 2171: Exon. 28 b; Th. 87, 9; Cri. 1422: Beo. Th. 1449; B. 722: Judth. 10; Thw. 23, 1; Jud. 99: Andr. Kmbl. 1044; An. 522: Elen. Kmbl. 2150; El. 1076; Ps. Th. 68, 5. [*O. Sax.* folmōs, *m. pl. the hands: O. H. Ger.* folma, *f. palma: Swed.* famla *to grope: Dan.* famle *to grope: Icel.* fálma *to grope about: Lat.* palma, *f: Grk.* παλάμη, *f. the palm of the hand.*] DER. beadu-folm, gearo-, mān-.

folme, an; *f.* [folm *the palm of the hand*] *The hand;* mănus:—Worhte his folme foldan drige *his hand made the dry land*, Ps. Th. 94, 5. Forlēt drenga sum daroþ fleógan of folman *one of the warriors let fly a dart from his hand*, Byrht. Th. 136, 12; By. 150. Ða ísenan næglas, ðe wǽron adrifene þurh Cristes folman *the iron nails, which were driven through Christ's palms*, Homl. Th. ii. 306, 16. v. folm.

fon *a fan*, Lk. Skt. Rush. 3, 17. v. fann.

FÓN, to fōnne; ic fō, ðū fēhst, he fēhþ, *pl.* fōþ; *p.* ic, he fēng, ðū fēnge, *pl.* fēngon; *impert.* fōh, *pl.* fōþ; *subj. pres.* fō, *pl.* fōn; *p.* fēnge, *pl.* fēngen; *pp.* fangen, fongen; *v. trans. To grasp, catch, seize, to seize with hostile intention, take, undertake, accept, receive;* mănu comprehendĕre, captāre, căpĕre, accĭpĕre:—Ne sceolde fōn bíspell *should not take a fable*, Bt. 35, 5; Fox 166, 20. Mæg man fōn folcgesteallan *one may take his adherents*, Cd. 15; Th. 19, 6; Gen. 287. On ōðer weorc to fōnne *to take to other work*, Bt. 39, 4; Fox 218, 4: Chr. 1009; Erl. 142, 28. Heó him to-geánes fēng *she grasped at him*, Beo. Th. 3089; B. 1542. Se ðe mec fēhþ ongeán *he who is hostile towards me*, Exon. 107 b; Th. 410, 1; Rä. 28, 9: Beo. Th. 3515; B. 1755. We fōþ nū on ða axunga ðǽr we hí ǽr forlēton *we will now take up the questions where we before left them*, Boutr. Scrd. 18, 44. Fēngon Æðelwulfes twegen suna to ríce *Æthelwulf's two sons took to the kingdom*, Chr. 855; Erl. 70, 17. Ne preóst ne fō to woruldspræcum *let not a priest take to worldly conversations*, L. Ælf. C. 30; Th. ii. 354, 2. Ðū fēhst on uncūþe *thou takest to the unknown*, Bt. 35, 5; Fox 164, 16. Hēr beóþ fangene seólas and hronas *here are caught seals and dolphins*, Bd. 1, 1; S. 473, 16. Hí feng woldon fōn *they would take the booty*, Chr. 1016; Erl. 156, 28, 12. Ðā fēng Ælfred to ðam ríce *then Ælfred took to the kingdom*, Chr. 871; Erl. 76, 3: Jud. 13, 1. Fōh to me *take from me;* accipe a me, Cd. 228; Th. 308, 2; Sat. 686. Fōþ him on *accĭpĭte eum*, Bd. 5, 13? Lye. Ǽlas fongene beóþ *anguillæ căpiuntur*, Bd. 4, 19; S. 590, 5. [*Piers P.* fangen, fongen: *Chauc.* fonge: *Laym.* fon, ifon: *Orm.* fon: *O. Sax.* fāhan, fangan: *Frs.* fean, fangen: *O. Frs.* fa: *Dut.* vangen, vaan: *Ger.* fangen, fahen: *M. H. Ger.* vāhen: *O. H. Ger.*

fāhan: *Goth.* fahan: *Dan.* faa, faae: *Swed.* få, fånga: *Icel.* fá, fanga: *Lat.* pangĕre *to fasten: Grk.* πήγνυμι *to fasten: Sansk.* paś *to bind.*] DER. a-fōn, æt-, an-, be-, bi-, for-, fōr-, fōre-, ge-, ofer-, on-, þurh-, to-, under-, ūta-, wiđ-, ymb-, ymbe-.

fond *found*, Cd. 119; Th. 154, 1; Gen. 2549; *p. of* findan.

fongen *taken:*—Ǽlas fongene beóþ *anguillæ căpiuntur*, Bd. 4, 19; S. 590, 5; *pp. of* fōn.

FONT, es; *m. A* FONT, *fountain*, Som. Ben. Lye. [*Lat.* fons; *gen.* fontis, *m.*] v. font-wæter.

font-bæþ, es; *n. A font-bath, baptism;* baptismus, Som. Ben. Lye.

font-wæter, es; *n. Font, fountain* or *spring water;* fontāna ăqua:—Wyrc drenc font-wæter *make a font-water drink*, L. M. 3, 62; Lchdm. ii. 350, 6. v. fant-wæter.

foor, es; *m. A pig, hog;* porcaster:—Foor *porcaster*, Ælfc. Gl. 19; Som. 59, 28; Wrt. Voc. 22, 69: Glos. Epnl. Recd. 161, 39. v. fōr.

FOR; *prep. dat. acc. and inst.* I. *with the dative;* cum dătīvo. 1. FOR, *on account of, because of, with, by;* pro, propter, per:—Nys đeós untrumnys nā for deáþe, ac for Godes wuldre *infirmĭtas hæc non est ad mortem, sed pro glōria Dei*, Jn. Bos. 11, 4. Đæt he đone dǽl Willferþe for Gode gesealde to brūcanne *ut hanc* [*partem*] *Vilfrido, ūtendam pro Dŏmĭno offerret*, Bd. 4, 16; S. 584, 11. Eardas rūme Meotud arǽrde for moncynne *the Creator established spacious lands for mankind*, Exon. 89 a; Th. 334, 15; Gn. Ex. 16. Aguldon me yfelu for gōdum *retrĭbuēbant mihi māla pro bŏnis*, Ps. Spl. 34, 14. He wearþ sārig for his synnum *he was sorry for his sins*, Exon. 117 a; Th. 450, 15; Dōm. 88. Ne dyde ic for fācne, ne for feóndscipe, ne for wihte *I did it not for fraud, nor for enmity, nor for aught*, Cd. 128; Th. 162, 34; Gen. 2691. Đe for đām lārum com *that came by reason of those wiles*, Cd. 29; Th. 37, 32; Gen. 598. Moyses wearþ gebȳsgad for heora yfelum *vexātus est Moyses propter eos*, Ps. Th. 105, 25. Đæt hī dydon for đǽm þingum *they did it for these reasons*, Bt. 35, 4; Fox 162, 21. Ūre gāst biþ swīđe wīde farende for his gecynde, nalles for his willan *our spirit is very widely wandering, by reason of its nature, not by reason of its will*, Bt. 34, 11; Fox 152, 4, 5. For hwilcum þingum *quas ob res*, Ælfc. Gr. 44; Som. 46, 15. Se wæs in đam fīre for Freán meahtum *he was in the fire by the Lord's power*, Exon. 54 a; Th. 189, 26; Az. 65. For dæge ođđe for twām *per ūnum aut duos dies*, Ex. 21, 29. 2. *according to;* pro, sĕcundum, juxta:—Eall sió lufu biþ for gecynde, nallas for willan *omne illud dēsīdĕrium juxta nātūram est, non juxta vŏluntātem suam*, Bt. 34, 11; Fox 152, 14, 15. Ic gelȳfe to đē, đæt đū me, for đīnum mægenspēdum, nǽfre wille ānforlǽtan *I believe in thee, that thou, according to thy great power, never wilt desert me*, Andr. Kmbl. 2572; An. 1287. For đam, for đan, for đon, for đam đe, for đan đe, for đon đe *for that, for that which, for this reason that, because, for that cause, therefore.* II. *with the accusative;* cum accūsātīvo. *For, instead of;* pro, lŏco, vĭce:—Archelāus rīxode on Iudēa þeóde for đæne Hērōdem [='Ηρώδης] *Archĕlāus* [='Αρχέλαος] *regnāvit in Jūdæa pro Hērōde*, Mt. Bos. 2, 22. Eáge for eáge, and tōþ for tōþ *ŏcŭlum pro ŏcŭlo, et dentem pro dente*, Mt. Kmbl. Hat. 5, 38. Nafast đū for āwiht ealle þeóda *pro nihil hăbēbis omnes gentes*, Ps. Th. 58, 8. Hæfdon heora Hlāford for đone hēhstan God *they held their Lord for the most high God*, Bt. Met. Fox 26, 88; Met. 26, 44. III. *with the instrumental;* cum ablātīvo. *For, on account of, because of, through;* pro, propter, per:—We sinna fela didon for ūre disige *we committed many sins through our foolishness*, Hy. 7, 107; Hy. Grn. ii. 289, 107. Hine feor forwræc Metod for đȳ māne *the Creator banished him far for that crime*, Beo. Th. 220; B. 110. Acol for đȳ egesan *trembling for the terror*, Andr. Kmbl. 2533; An. 1268. Hæleþ wurdon acle arāsad for đȳ rǽse *the men were seized with fear on account of its force*, Exon. 74 a; Th. 277, 27; Jul. 587. Ne murn đū for đī mēce *mourn not for the sword*, Wald. 43; Vald. 1, 24. For đȳ, for đī, for đȳ đe, for đī đe *for that, therefore, wherefore, because;* proptĕrea, quia. [*Piers P. Chauc.* for: *Laym.* for, uor: *Orm.* forr: *Plat.* för, vör: *O. Frs.* fori, fóre, for: *Dut.* voor: *Ger.* für: *M. H. Ger.* vür, vüre: *O. H. Ger.* fora, furi: *Goth.* faur, faura: *Dan.* for: *Swed.* för: *Icel.* fyrir: *Lat.* pro.]

for- is used in composition in Anglo-Saxon exactly as the English *for:* it often deteriorates, or gives an opposite sense, or gives strength to the words before which it is placed; in which case it may be compared with Gothic *fra-*, Dutch and German *ver-* [different from the Dutch *voor*, and German *vor*]. Forbeódan *to forbid;* fordēman *to condemn;* forcūþ *perverse, corrupt;* fordōn *to destroy, to do for.*—Sometimes fōr denotes an increase of the signification of the word before which it is placed, and is then generally to be in English *very;* valde, as fōr-eáđe *very easily*, Homl. Th. ii. 138, 35: fōr-oft *very often*, Bd. de nat. rerum; Wrt. popl. science 11, 8; Lchdm. iii. 256, 16. For- and fōr-, *or* fōre- are often confounded, though they are very different in meaning; as forseón [*Flem.* versien] *to overlook, despise;* fōr- *or* fōreseón [*Flem.* veursien] *to foresee.*—If a word, having for, fōr *or* fōre prefixed, cannot be found under for-, fōr- *or* fōre-, it must be sought under the simple term, and the sense of the preposition added; thus, fōr- *or* fōre-sendan is from sendan *to send*, and fōr-, fōre *before, to send before, etc.* [On the vowel in fōr, fōre, see remark in the preface.]

FŌR, fōre; *prep. dat. acc. Before, fore;* ante, cōram, in conspectu, præsente *vel* audiente ălĭquo, præ, priusquam. I. *dat:*—Fōr Gode and fōr [fōre Cott.] mannum *cōram Deo et hŏmĭnĭbus*, Bd. 5, 20; S. 641, 37. He fōr eaxlum gestōd Deniga freán *he stood before the shoulders of the lord of the Danes*, Beo. Th. 722; B. 358. Fōr horde *before the hoard*, Beo. Th. 5555; B. 2781. Ic hefde dreám micelne fōr Meotode *I had great joy before the Creator*, Cd. 214; Th. 269, 34; Sat. 83. We fōr Dryhtene iu dreámas hefdon *we formerly had joys before the Lord*, 214; Th. 267, 26; Sat. 44. He gehālgode fōr heremægene wīn of wætere and wendan hēt *he hallowed before the multitude wine from water and bade it change*, Andr. Kmbl. 1172; An. 586. Geónge þūhton men fōr his eágum *they seemed young men before his eyes*, Cd. 111; Th. 146, 28; Gen. 2429. Wlytig heaw fōr bearnum manna *spĕcĭōsus forma præ fīliis hŏmĭnum*, Ps. Spl. 44, 3. II. *acc:*—Ne dear forþgān fōr đē *I dare not come forth before thee*, Cd. 40; Th. 54, 2; Gen. 871. He his mōdor fōr ealle menn geweorþode *he esteemed his mother before all mankind*, Rood Kmbl. 184; Kr. 93. Fōr đæt folc *cōram pŏpŭlo*, Ps. Th. 67, 8. [*Wyc.* for-*fore-*, as for-goer *a fore-goer: Plat.* vor: *O. Sax.* for, far, fur, furi: *Dut.* voor: *Ger.* vor: *M. H. Ger.* vor, vore: *O. H. Ger.* fora, furi: *Goth.* faur, faura: *Dan.* for: *Swed.* för: *Icel.* fyrir: *Lat.* præ: *Grk.* πρό *before: Sansk.* pra- *before.*]

fōr, e; *f.* [fōr, *p. of* faran *to go*] *A going, setting out, journey, course, way, approach;* ītio, profectio, ĭter, cursus, sēmĭta, accessus:—Fōr wæs đȳ beorhtre *the course was the brighter*, Exon. 105 a; Th. 400, 11; Rä. 20, 8. Me is fenȳce fōre hreþre *a fen-frog is more rapid than I in its course*, 111 a; Th. 426, 10; Rä. 41, 71. He hine ofteáh đære fōre *subtraxit se illi profectiōni*, Bd. 5, 9; S. 623, 23: Ps. Th. 104, 33. He đyder on đære fōre wæs *he was on the journey thither*, Guthl. 16; Gdwin. 68, 1: Exon. 112 b; Th. 430, 19; Rä. 44, 11: 120 a; Th. 461, 9; Hö. 33. He sōna ongann fȳsan to fōre *he soon began to hasten for the way*, Cd. 138; Th. 173, 12; Gen. 2860. Ne can ic Abeles ōr ne fōre *I know not Abel's coming nor going*, 48; Th. 61, 33; Gen. 1006. Đū scealt đa fōre geferan *thou shalt go the journey*, Andr. Kmbl. 431; An. 216: 673; An. 337: Exon. 40 b; Th. 136, 8; Gū. 538. Đū ongeáte fōre mīne *intellexisti sēmĭtam meam*, Ps. Th. 138, 2. Hī wendon heora fōre to Cantwarbyrig *they went their way to Canterbury*, Chr. 1009; Erl. 142, 17: 1004; Erl. 139, 24. Đara lāreówa fōre headoradon *doctōrum arcēbant accessum*, Bd. 4, 27; S. 604, 29. DER. forþ-fōr, sǽ-.

fōr, foor, es; *m. A pig, hog;* porcaster:—Fōr *porcaster*, Wrt. Voc. 286, 48.

fōr *went*, Gen. 31, 31; *p. of* faran.

fōra, L. C. S. 33; Th. i. 396, 17, note 51 *has this reading for* fōr, *or* fōre *before;* ante, *q. v.* under for-, *or* fōre.

forad; *part. adj. Broken, weakened, void;* fractus, lăbĕfactus:—Gif se earm biþ forad būfan elmbogan *if the arm be broken above the elbow*, L. Alf. pol. 54; Th. i. 94, 24: 62, 63; Th. i. 96, 14, 17. Gif đa earmscancan beóþ begen forade *if the arm-bones be both broken*, 55; Th. i. 94, 26. Beó đæt ordāl forad *let the ordeal be void*, L. Ath. i. 23; Th. i. 212, 9: iv. 7; Th. i. 228, 1. v. forod.

fōra-gleáwlīce *providently, carefully, prudently;* prōvĭde, R. Ben. interl. 3. v. fōre-gleáwlīce.

for-aldod *antiquated*, Solil. 11, = for-ealdod; *pp. of* for-ealdian.

fōran; *prep. Before;* ante:—Fōran Andreas mæssan *before Andrew's mass-day*, Chr. 1010; Erl. 144, 13. ¶ Fōran ongeán *opposite;* contra:—Fōran ongeán eów *contra vos*, Mt. Bos. 21, 2. Fōran ongēn Galileam *contra Galilæam*, Lk. Bos. 8, 26. Fōran ongeán đa burh *ex adverso contra urbem*, Jos. 8, 5. Fōran-to *before*, Chr. 920; Erl. 104, 31. v. fōran-to. DER. æt-fōran, be-, bi-, on-, to-, wiđ-.

fōran; *adv. In front, before;* ante, antequam, prius:—Wonnum hyrstum fōran gefrætwed *adorned in front with dark trappings*, Exon. 113 b; Th. 436, 2; Rä. 54, 8: Chr. 894; Erl. 93, 11. Is se fugel fæger fōran *the bird is fair before*, Exon. 60 a; Th. 418, 10; Ph. 292. DER. be-fōran, bi-, on-.

fōr ān, *only;* tantum, tantummŏdo:—Gelȳf fōr ān μόνον πίστευε, *tantummŏdo crēde*, Mk. Bos. 5, 36. Fōr ān ic beó hāl, gyf ic hys reáfes æthrīne *si tĕtĭgĕro tantum vestīmentum ejus, salva ĕro*, Mt. Bos. 9, 21. Fōr ān eówre yrfe sceal beón hēr *ŏves tantum vestræ et armenta remăneant*, Ex. 10, 24.

fōran-bodig, es; *n. The forebody, chest;* pectus:—Fōran-bodig *vel* breóst-bedern [MS. breost-beden] *thōrax* = θώραξ [MS. *tōrax*], Ælfc. Gl. 73; Som. 71, 26; Wrt. Voc. 44, 12.

fōran-dæg, es; *m. Before day* or *dawn;* antelūcānum tempus, Som. Ben. Lye.

fōran-heáfod, es; *n. The forehead;* antĕrior pars căpĭtis, frons:—On fōran-heáfde *on the forehead*, Homl. Th. ii. 266, 13: Nar. 15, 13.

fōran-niht, e; *f. The fore-night, early part of the night, dusk of the evening;* antĕrior pars noctis, crĕpuscŭlum:—Lǽd hine ūt of đam hūse on fōrannihte *lead him out of the house in the dusk*, Herb. 8, 2; Lchdm. i. 98, 18: fram foran-nihte *per noctem*, Nar. 35, 9.

fōran-onsettende; *part.* [*part. of* fōran-onsettan] *Closing in;* præclūdens, Bd. 5, 1; S. 613, 31, note. v. fōre-settan.

fôran-to; *prep. Before;* ante:—Fôran-to Eástron *before Easter*, Chr. 921; Erl. 104, 37. Fôran-to middum sumera *before midsummer*, 920; Erl. 104, 31: fôran-to uhtes antelūcānum tempus, Nar. 15, 31. v. to-fôran.

fôr-arn *ran before*, Jn. Bos. 20, 4; *p. of* fôr-yrnan.

fôra-sceáwian; *p.* ode; *pp.* od *To foresee, forethink, consider;* prævĭdēre, præcōgĭtāre, consīdĕrāre:—Fôrasceáwod beón *consīdĕrāri*, R. Ben. interl. 64. v. fôre-sceáwian.

fôra-sceáwung, e; *f. Foresight, forethought, consideration:*—Fôrasceáwung *consīdĕrātio*, R. Ben. interl. 34. v. fôre-sceáwung.

fôr-âþ, es; *m. A fore-oath, an oath first taken;* præjūrāmentum, antejūrāmentum:—Ofgâ his spræce mid fôrâþe *let him begin his suit with a fore-oath*, L. O. D. 6; Th. i. 354, 31. v. fôre-âþ.

for-bæran *to forbear:*—Hwâ mæg forbæran *who can forbear?* Bt. 36, 1; Fox 172, 13. v. for-beran.

for-bærnan, -bearnan, to -bærnenne; *part.* -bærnende; *p.* -bærnde, *pl.* -bærndon; *pp.* -bærned, -bærnd; *v. trans. To burn up, consume;* ūrĕre, combūrĕre:—Nerōn hêt forbærnan ealle Rôme burh *Nero commanded to burn up all the city of Rome*, Bt. 16, 4; Fox 58, 3: Cd. 138; Th. 173, 8; Gen. 2858: Exon. 30 b; Th. 94, 21; Cri. 1543: Beo. Th. 4258; B. 2126. Isaac bær wudu to forbærnenne ða offrunge *Isaac bare wood to burn the offering*, Homl. Th. ii. 60, 26: Mt. Bos. 13, 30. Swâ swâ lêg forbærnende muntas *sicut flamma combūrens montes*, Ps. Spl. 82, 13. Ic forswæle oððe forbærne ūro, Ælfc. Gr. 28, 4; Som. 31, 11. Man hine forbærneþ *one burns him*, Ors. 1, 1; Bos. 22, 44. Ða ceafu he forbærnþ on unadwæscendlīcum fȳre *pāleas combūret igni inextinguĭbĭli*, Mt. Bos. 3, 12: Bt. 15; Fox 48, 22: 33, 4; Fox 130, 12. Hī hine forbærnaþ *they burn him*, Ors. 1, 1; Bos. 22, 26. Līg forbærnde ða ârleásan *flamma combussit peccātōres*, Ps. Lamb. 105, 18: Boutr. Scrd. 22, 40: Chr. 685; Erl. 40. 20. Hī ǽr Mul forbærndon *they had formerly burnt Mul*, Chr. 694; Erl. 43, 21: 894; Erl. 91, 25: 1001; Erl. 136, 31: 1055; Erl. 190, 4. Nim ǽnne sticcan... forbærn done ôðerne ende *take a stick... burn the one end*, Bd. de nat. rerum; Wrt. popl. science 17, 15; Lchdm. iii. 274, 4. Ðæt seó sunne mid hyre hǽtan middaneardes wæstmas forbærne *that the sun with her heat burn up the fruits of the earth*, Wrt. popl. science 9, 6; Lchdm. iii. 250, 17. Ðæt he werod forbærnde *that it [the pillar of fire] would burn up the host*, Cd. 148; Th. 185, 16; Exod. 123. Hwī ðeós þyrne ne sī forbærned *quare non combūrātur rŭbus*, Ex. 3, 3: Chr. 687; Erl. 42, 1: Cd. 146; Th. 182, 3; Exod. 70: Exon. 22 b; Th. 62, 26; Cri. 1007. Beó se forbærnd *combūrētur*, Jos. 7, 15. cf. *Ger.* verbrennen.

for-bærnednes, -ness, -nyss, e; *f. A burning up;* ustio:—Wið forbærnednysse [-nesse MS. B.] *for a burning*, Herb. cont. 168, 2; Lchdm. i. 62, 19: Herb. 168, 2; Lchdm. i. 298, 10.

for-bærst, *pl.* -burston *burst asunder*, Beo. Th. 5354; B. 2680: Bt. 18, 4; Fox 68, 6; *p. of* for-berstan.

for-barn *burnt*, Beo. Th. 3236; B. 1616; *p. of* for-beornan.

for-beád *forbade*, Cd. 30; Th. 40, 11; Gen. 637; *1st and 3rd sing. p. of* for-beódan.

for-beáh *avoided*, Byrht. Th. 141, 21; By. 325; *p. of* for-būgan.

for-bearan *to forbear*, Scint. 11. v. for-beran.

for-bearn *burnt*, Boutr. Scrd. 22, 33; *p. of* for-beornan.

for-bearnan; *p.* de; *impert. pl.* -bearnaþ; *pp.* ed *To burn up, consume by fire;* combūrĕre:—Lǽdaþ hig forþ and forbearnaþ hig *prodūcĭte eam ut combūrātur*, Gen. 38, 24. Hī forbearndon Beorn ealdorman *they consumed Beorn alderman*, Chr. 779; Erl. 55, 36: 1052; Erl. 185, 4. v. for-bærnan.

for-bêgan; *p.* de; *pp.* ed *To bow down, bend down, humble, abase, destroy;* deprĭmĕre, hūmĭliāre, immĭnuĕre:—Ðæt gê gūþfreán gylp forbêgan *that ye may humble the warrior's pride*, Andr. Kmbl. 2668; An. 1335: 3141; An. 1573: Cd. 223; Th. 294, 8; Sat. 468. v. for-bȳgan.

for-beódan, -biódan, to -beódanne; *part.* -beódende; *p.* ic, he -beád, ðū -bude, *pl.* -budon; *pp.* -boden [*Ger.* ver-bieten] *To* FORBID, *prohibit, restrain, suppress;* prohĭbēre, vĕtāre, interdīcĕre:—Nelle gê hig forbeódan cuman to me *nōlīte eos prohĭbēre ad me vĕnīre*, Mt. Bos. 19, 14: L. C. S. 77; Th. i. 418, 24. To forbeódanne *to forbid*, L. Alf. 49; Th. i. 56, 1. Ðisne we gemētton forbeódende ðæt man ðam Cāsere gafol ne sealde *hunc invĕnĭmus prohĭbentem trĭbūta dāre Cæsări*, Lk. Bos. 23, 2. Ic forbeóde *prohĭbeo:* ic forbeád *prohĭbui:* forboden *prohĭbĭtum*, Ælfc. Gr. 26, 2; Som. 28, 34, 35. Ic forbeóde *vĕto*, Ælfc. Gr. 24; Som. 25, 49. Būton ðū forgange ðæt ic ðē forbeóde *unless thou forgo that which I forbid thee*, Homl. Th. i. 14, 8: Chr. 675; Erl. 38, 22. Fram eallum wege yfelum ic forbeád fêt mīne *ab omni via măla prohĭbui pĕdes meos*, Ps. Spl. 118, 101. Ðone hire forbeád Drihten *which the Lord forbade her*, Cd. 30; Th. 40, 11, 29; Gen. 637, 646: Gen. 3, 1: Mt. Bos. 3, 14. We him forbudon *prohĭbuimus eum*, Mk. Bos. 9, 38: Lk. Bos. 9, 49. Ne forbeód him nâ ðīne tunecan *tŭnĭcam nōli prohĭbēre*, 6, 29: Num. 11, 28. Lǽtaþ ða lytlingas to me cuman, and ne forbeóde gê him *suffer the little ones to come unto me, and forbid them not*, Mk. Bos. 10, 14: Lk. Bos. 18, 16. Sunnan daga cȳpinga forbeóde man georne *let Sunday marketings be strictly forbidden*, L. Eth. ix. 17; Th. i. 344, 7. Hit forboden wæs *it was forbidden*, iii. 8; Th. i. 296, 13: Chr. 1048; Erl. 177, 21. Ðū Adame sealdest wæstme ða inc wǽron fæste forbodene *thou gavest to Adam the fruits which were strictly forbidden to you two*, Cd. 42; Th. 55, 16; Gen. 895.

for-beódendlīc; *adj. Forbidding-like, dissuasive;* prohĭbĭtōrius, dehortātōrius:—Sume synd *dehortātīva*, ðæt synd forbeódendlīce oððe mistihtendlīce *some are* dehortātīva, *which are dissuasive*, Ælfc. Gr. 38; Som. 40, 8.

for-beornan, -byrnan; *p.* -bearn, -barn, -born, *pl.* -burnon; *pp.* -bornen, -burnen; *v. n. To burn up, be destroyed by fire, be consumed;* combūri, ignĭbus consūmi:—On ðære Sodomitiscra gewītnunge forbearn seó eorþe *in the punishment of the Sodomites the earth was burnt*, Boutr. Scrd. 22, 33. Forbarn broden mǽl *the drawn brand was burnt*, Beo. Th. 3236; B. 1616: 3338; B. 1667. Hit gelamp, ðæt se ylca tūn forbarn [forborn, col. 2], and seó cyrice *evēnit, vīcum eundem, et ipsum părĭter ecclēsiam ignĭbus consūmi*, Bd. 3, 17; S. 544, 27, col. 1: Chr. 816; Erl. 62, 7. Forburnon xv tūnas *fifteen towns burned*, Ors. 6, 1; Bos. 115, 37. He geseah, ðæt seó þyrne barn and næs forburnen *vĭdēbat, quod rŭbus ardēret et non combūrērētur*, Ex. 3, 2: Bd. 3, 17; S. 544, 20, col. 1. Wǽron ða bende [MS. benne] forburnene *the bands were burnt*, Cd. 195; Th. 243, 12; Dan. 435.

for-beran; *p.* -bær, *pl.* -bǽron; *pp.* -boren [for *for;* beran *to bear*] *To* FORBEAR, *abstain, refrain, restrain, bear with, endure, suffer;* abstĭnēre, sustĭnēre, comprĭmĕre, reprĭmĕre, tŏlĕrāre, păti, ferre:—Ðæt he ðone breóstwylm forberan ne mihte *that he might not restrain the fervour of his breast*, Beo. Th. 3759; B. 1877. Hī firenlustas forberaþ in breóstum *they restrain sinful lusts in their breasts*, Exon. 44 b; Th. 150, 9; Gū. 776. Seó æftere cneóris ealle gemete is to forberanne *sĕcunda gĕnĕrātio a se omni mŏdo dēbet abstĭnēre*, Bd. 1, 27; S. 491, 9. Ic forbær ðē *sustĭnui te*, Ps. Spl. 24, 22. Yfelu forberan ne sceal *măla tŏlĕrāre non dēbet*, Past. 21, 5; Hat. MS. 31 b, 2. Hū lange forbere ic eów *quousque pătiar vos?* Mt. Bos. 17, 17. Ðonne him mon yfel dō, he hit sceal geþyldelīce forberan *when one does him evil, he shall patiently endure it*, Glostr. Frag. 112, 18: Mk. Bos. 14, 4. [cf. *Goth.* frabairan *to endure.*]

fôr-beran, fôre-beran; *p.* -bær; *pp.* -boren [fôr, fôre *before;* beran *to bear*] *To fore-bear, to bear* or *carry before, to prefer;* præferre:—Ðæt ic fôrbær rūme regulas and rēðe môd geongra monna *that I preferred the lax rules and rough minds of young men*, Exon. 39 b; Th. 131, 22; Gū. 459. Ðætte nǽnig bisceop hine ôðrum fôrbere *ut nullus episcŏpōrum se præfĕrat altĕri*, Bd. 4, 5; S. 573, 10.

for-berstan, he -birsteþ; *p.* -bærst, *pl.* -burston; *pp.* -borsten *To break, burst asunder, fail;* contĕri, dirumpi, exstingui:—Wên nǽfre forbirsteþ *hope never fails*, Exon. 64 a; Th. 236, 2; Ph. 568. Heora bogan forberstaþ *arcus eōrum contĕrātur*, Ps. Th. 36, 14. Forbærst sweord Beówulfes *Beowulf's sword burst asunder*, Beo. Th. 5354; B. 2680: Bt. 18, 4; Fox 68, 6. Ðæt him forberste se sweora *that his neck break*, L. Eth. iii. 4; Th. i. 294, 16: Prov. Kmbl. 19. Wæs him beót forborsten *their threat failed*, Cd. 4; Th. 5, 11; Gen. 70.

fôr-bêtan *to make full amends for anyone* or *anything;* compensāre pro ălĭquo, Som. Ben. Lye. v. fôre-bêtan.

for-bīgan, -bīgean; *p.* de; *pp.* ed *To bow down, bend down, humble, abase, depreciate, avoid, pass by;* hūmĭliāre, prætĕrīre:—Bælc forbīgde *he humbled their pride*, Cd. 4; Th. 4, 15; Gen. 54: 4; Th. 5, 12; Gen. 70: Exon. 85 b; Th. 321, 19; Wīd. 48: Wald. 47; Vald. 1, 26. Litlingas nellaþ forbīgean (cf. forbūgan) me *parvŭli nōlunt prætĕrīre me*, Coll. Monast. Th. 29, 3. v. for-bȳgan.

for-bīgels, es; *m. An arch, a vault, an arched roof;* arcus, fornix, cămĕra = καμάρα:—Forbīgels *arcus*, Ælfc. Gl. 29; Som. 61, 32; Wrt. Voc. 26, 31. v. bīgels.

for-bindan; ic -binde; *p.* -band, *pl.* -bundon; *subj. pres.* -binde, *pl.* -binden; *pp.* -bunden *To bind* or *tie up;* allĭgāre:—Ne forbinden gê nâ ðǽm þyrstendum oxum ðone mūþ *ye may not tie up the mouth of the thirsting oxen*, Past. 16, 5; Hat. MS. 21 b, 7.

for-biódan *to forbid:*—He wel meahte ðæt unriht him eáðe forbiódan *he might well easily forbid that injustice to him*, Bt. Met. Fox 9, 108; Met. 9, 54. v. for-beódan.

for-birsteþ *fails*, Exon. 64 a; Th. 236, 2; Ph. 568; *3rd sing. pres. of* for-berstan.

for-blâwan; *p.* -bleów, *pl.* -bleówon; *pp.* -blâwen *To blow away, inflate;* inflāre:—Com ân wind, ond forbleów hie ūt on sǽ *there came a wind, and blew them out on to the sea*, Ors. 5, 4; Bos. 105, 19. Gif mon sīe forblâwen *if a man be inflated*, L. M. 2, 34; Lchdm. ii. 240, 4.

for-blindian; *p.* ode, ade; *pp.* od, ad *To blind;* obcæcāre:—Wæs forblindad *ĕrat obcæcātum*, Mk. Skt. Rush. 6, 52. v. blendan *to blind.*

fôr-bôc, e; *f.* [fôr *a journey*, bôc *a book*] *A journey-book, itinerary;* itĭnĕrārium:—Fôrbôc [MS. fôrebôc], sīþbôc *itĭnĕrārium*, Mone B. 1994.

for-bod, es; *n. A forbidding, prohibition, countermand;* prohĭbĭtio:—Ðæt hit ðara manna forbod wǽre *that it was forbidden by those men* [lit. *that it was the forbidding of those men*], L. Alf. pol. 41; Th. i. 88, 19. On Godes forbode *with God's prohibition*, L. N. P. L. 61; Th. ii. 300, 12.

fór-boda, an; *m. A foreboder, forerunner, messenger;* prænuntius:—Gódes fórboda *God's messenger,* L. N. P. L. 2; Th. ii. 290, 6.

for-boden *forbidden,* L. Eth. iii. 8; Th. i. 296, 13; *pp. of* for-beódan.

for-bogen *avoided,* App. Lit. Scint. Lye; *pp. of* for-búgan.

for-boren *forborne, restrained, endured,* Bt. 38, 4; Fox 204, 18: L. M. 1, 45; Lchdm. ii. 114, 8; *pp. of* for-beran.

for-born *burnt,* Chr. 816; Erl. 62, 7: *p. of* for-beornan.

for-borsten *bursted, failed,* Cd. 4; Th. 5, 11; Gen. 70; *pp. of* forberstan.

for-brecan; *part.* -brecende; ðú -brecest, -bricst, -brycst, he -breceþ, -bricþ; *p.* -bræc, *pl.* -brǽcon; *pp.* -brocen *To break, break in two, bruise, crush, violate;* frangĕre, confringĕre, contĕrĕre, commĭnuĕre, vĭŏlāre:—Wolde heofona helm helle weallas forbrecan *heaven's chieftain would break down hell's walls,* Exon. 120 a; Th. 461, 13; Hö. 35. Stefn Drihtnes forbrecendes cederbeám, and forbricþ Drihten cederbeám ðæs holtes *vox Dŏmĭni confringentis cedros, et confringet Dŏmĭnus cedros Lĭbăni,* Ps. Spl. 28, 5. Ðú forbrycst ðone earm ðæs synfullan *thou shalt break the arm of the sinful,* Ps. Th. 9, 35. Ic sumra fét forbræc bealosearwum *I have broken the feet of some by wicked snares,* Exon. 72 b; Th. 270, 30; Jul. 473. He helle dúru forbræc *he brake hell's door,* Cd. 223; Th. 294, 8; Sat. 468: Ps. Spl. 106, 16. Forbrǽcon Rómáne heora áþas *the Romans broke their oaths,* Ors. 3, 8; Bos. 63, 31: Cd. 37; Th. 49, 27; Gen. 798. Forbrec oððe tobryt earm ðæs synfullan *contĕre brachium peccātōris,* Ps. Lamb. second 9, 15. Ne forbrece [MS. forbræce] gé nán bán on him *os non commĭnuētis ex eo,* Jn. Bos. 19, 36. Ðæt man forbrǽce hyra sceancan *ut frangĕrentur eōrum crūra,* 19, 31. Hie gebod Godes forbrocen hæfdon *they had broken God's command,* Cd. 33; Th. 43, 30; Gen. 698.

for-bredan; *p.* -bræd, *pl.* -brudon; *pp.* -broden *To transform;* transformāre:—Sceolde beornas forbredan *should transform men,* Bt. Met. Fox 26, 149; Met. 26, 75: Bt. 38, 1; Fox 194, 31. DER. bredan.

for-bregdan; *p.* -brægd, *pl.* -brugdon; *pp.* -brogden *To cover;* obdūcĕre:—Ic mist-helme forbrægd eágna leóman *I covered the light of their eyes with a mantle of mist,* Exon. 72 b; Th. 270, 25; Jul. 470.

for-brict *crushed,* L. E. I. 2; Th. ii. 404, 5, = for-britt; *pp. of* forbritan.

for-bricþ *breaks,* Ps. Spl. 28, 5; *3rd sing. pres. of* for-brecan.

for-brittan; *p.* -britte; *pp.* -britted, -britt *To break in pieces, smash, bruise;* confringĕre, contĕrĕre:—God forbriteþ téþ heora on múþe heora *Deus contĕret dentes eōrum in ōre ipsōrum,* Ps. Spl. 57, 6. Hú he forbritte ealle his bígengan *quōmŏdo contrīvĕrit omnes cultōres ejus,* Deut. 4, 3. Beóþ ǽlce uncysta forbritte [MS. forbricte] *all vices shall be crushed,* L. E. I. 2; Th. ii. 404, 5. v. for-bryttan.

for-brocen *broken,* Cd. 33; Th. 43, 30; Gen. 698; *pp. of* for-brecan.

for-brycst *breakest* or *shalt break,* Ps. Th. 9, 35; *2nd sing. pres. of* for-brecan.

for-brytednys, -nyss, e; *f. Bruisedness, sorrow;* contrītio:—Forbrytednys and ungesǽlignys [synd] on wegum heora *contrītio et infēlīcĭtas [sunt] in viis eōrum,* Ps. Spl. 13, 7.

for-bryttan, -brittan; he -bryteþ, -brytt; *p.* -brytte; *pp.* -bryted, -bryt *To break in pieces, smash, bruise, crush;* confringĕre, contĕrĕre, conquassāre:—Tocwysed hreód he ne forbrytt *arundĭnem quassātam non confringet,* Mt. Bos. 12, 20. Moises forbrytte ðæt celf eall to duste *Moyses vĭtŭlum contrīvit usque ad pulvĕrem,* Ex. 32, 20. Forbryt ðú earm synfulles *contĕre brachium peccātōris,* Ps. Spl. second 9, 18. Ðæt ðú sí forbryt *dōnec contĕrāris,* Deut. 28, 24. Ǽlc ðe fylþ ofer ðone stán, byþ forbryt *omnis, qui cecĭdĕrit sŭper illum lăpĭdem, conquassābĭtur,* Lk. Bos. 20, 18.

for-budon *forbade,* Mk. Bos. 9, 38; *p. pl. of* for-beódan.

for-búgan; *part.* -búgende; *p.* -beáh, *pl.* -bugon; *impert.* -búh, *pl.* -búgaþ; *pp.* -bogen; *v. trans. To bend from, pass by, decline, avoid, shun, eschew;* recēdĕre, prætĕrīre, declīnāre, evītāre, devītāre:—He mæg forbúgan ða þegnunga *he can decline the ministrations,* Past. 7, 2; Hat. MS. 12 a, 14: Wald. 25; Vald. 1, 15. Hú man sélost mæg synna forbúgan *how a man may best avoid sin,* Ælfc. T. 15, 2: Homl. Th. i. 82, 26: 206, 6: Num. 22, 26. Se wer wæs forbúgende yfel *ĕrat vir recēdens a mălo,* Job Thw. 164, 3. Næs ðæt ná se Godríc ðe ða gúþe forbeáh *this was not the Godric who had fled from the war,* Byrht. Th. 141, 21; By. 325. Ðá he ðæt geseah, he hine forbeáh *viso illo, præterivit;* Lk. Bos. 10, 31, 32: Num. 22, 23. Forbúh *devita,* Scint. 88. Forbúgaþ unrihtwýsnysse *eschew unrighteousness,* Homl. Th. i. 28, 21: 180, 13. Ǽghwylc cristen man unriht hǽmed georne forbúge *let every christian man carefully eschew unlawful concubinage,* L. Eth. v. 10; Th. i. 306, 26: vi. 11; Th. i. 318, 11. Forbogen beón *evitāri,* App. Lit. Scint. Lye. (*Orm.* forrbuȝhenn *to avoid, refuse.*)

for-búgennys, -nyss, e; *f. An avoiding, eschewing, a declining;* declīnātio, Som. Ben. Lye.

for-burnen *burnt,* Ex. 3, 2; *pp. of* for-beornan.

for-burnon *burnt,* Ors. 6, 1; Bos. 115, 37; *p. pl. of* for-beornan.

for-býgan, -bígan, -bígean, -bégan; *p.* de; *pp.* ed *To bow down, bend down, abase, humble, destroy;* deprimĕre, humiliāre, imminuĕre:—He hellwarena heáp forbýgde *he humbled the multitude of hell's inmates,* Exon. 18 b; Th. 46, 3; Cri. 731: Exon. 120 a; Th. 461, 13; Hö. 35. v. býgan.

for-byrd, e; *f. A forbearing, an abstaining from;* abstĭnentia:—Ðæt nán forbyrd nǽre æt geligere betwuh nánre sibbe *that there should be no abstaining from concubinage between any kindred,* Ors. 1, 2; Bos. 27, 15.

for-byrdian, -byrdigan; *p.* ode; *pp.* od *To forbear, wait for;* sustĭnēre:—Sáwla úre forbyrdigaþ Driht *ănĭma nostra sustĭnet Dŏmĭnum,* Ps. Spl. 32, 20.

for-byrnan *to burn up*:—Hig forbyrnaþ *they burn up,* Jn. Bos. 15, 6. v. for-beornan.

FORCA, an; *m. A* FORK; furca:—Litel forca *furcilla,* Ælfc. Gl. 66; Wrt. Voc. 41, 37. [*Laym.* forken, furken, *pl. the gallows: Plat.* furke, forke, fork, *f: Dut.* vork, *f: M. H. Ger.* furke, *f: Icel.* forkr, *m: Lat.* furca, *f: Wel.* ffwrch, *m;* fforch, *f: Armor.* forc'h, *f.*]

for-ceorfan; *part.* -ceorfende; ic -ceorfe, ðú -ceorfest, -cirfst, -cyrfst, he -ceorfeþ, -cyrfþ, *pl.* -ceorfaþ; *p.* ic, he -cearf, ðú -curfe, *pl.* -curfon; *pp.* -corfen *To cut* or *carve out, cut down, cut off* or *away, cut through, divide;* excīdĕre, concīdĕre, succīdĕre, incīdĕre, intercīdĕre:—Ðí-læs ðe se Hláford háte us mid deáþes æxe forceorfan *lest the Lord command to cut us down with the axe of death,* Homl. Th. ii. 408, 28. Forceorfende *intercīdens,* Ps. Lamb. 28, 7. Ic forceorfe *succīdo, incīdo,* Ælfc. Gr. 28, 4; Som. 31, 34. Ðú forcirfst heora horsa hóhsina *ĕquos eōrum subnervābis,* Jos. 11, 6. Ðú forcyrfst hit *thou wilt cut it down,* Homl. Th. ii. 408, 8. Drihten se rihtwísa forheáweþ oððe forcyrfþ hnollas synfulra *Dŏmĭnus justus concīdet cervīces peccātōrum,* Ps. Lamb. 128, 4. Ðæt heó healfne forcearf ðone sweoran him *so that she half cut through his neck,* Judth. 10; Thw. 23, 5; Jud. 105. Rómáne Leóne ðæm pápan his tungan forcurfon *the Romans cut out the tongue of Pope Leo,* Chr. 797; Erl. 58, 13: Ors. 4, 6; Bos. 86, 33. Forceorf hine, hwí ofþricþ he ðæt land *succīde illam, ut quid ĕtiam terram occŭpat?* Lk. Bos. 13, 7: Homl. Th. ii. 408, 4. Ǽlc treów, ðe gódne wæstm ne bringþ, byþ forcorfen *omnis arbor, quæ non făcit fructum bŏnum, excīdētur,* Mt. Bos. 3, 10: Homl. Th. ii. 406, 32. Ðæt we ne beón forcorfene *that we may not be cut down,* 408, 25.

for-ceówan; *p.* -ceáw, *pl.* -cuwon; *pp.* -cowen *To chew off, bite off;* corrōdĕre:—Forceáw he his ágene tungan *he bit off his own tongue,* Bt. 16, 2; Fox 52, 24.

for-cerran *to avoid.* v. for-cyrran.

for-cinnan, ic -cinne, ðú -cinnest, he -cinneþ, *pl.* -cinnaþ; *p.* ic, he -can, ðú -cunne, *pl.* -cunnon; *pp.* -cunnen [for, cinnan *gĕnĕrāre*] *To repudiate;* rejĭcĕre:—Hine forcinnaþ ða cyrican ge túnas *the churches as well as houses shall repudiate him,* Salm. Kmbl. 215; Sal. 107.

for-cirfst *cuttest* or *shalt cut,* Jos. 11, 6; *2nd sing. pres. of* forceorfan.

for-clingan; *p.* -clang, *pl.* -clungon; *pp.* -clungen *To shrink up;* marcescĕre:—Wǽron sume on forclungenum treówe ahangene *some were hung up on a shrunken tree,* Nath. 8. [*Orm.* forrclungenn *withered.*]

for-clýsan; he -clýseþ, -clýst; *p.* de; *pp.* ed [clýsan *to close, shut*] *To close* or *shut up;* occlūdĕre:—Ðis sceal to ðám eárum [MS. ðan earen] ðe wind oððe wæter forclýst *this shall [do] for the ears which wind or water closes up,* Lchdm. iii. 92, 24.

for-cneów, es; *n. A progeny, race;* progĕnies, Lye.

for-cnídan; *p.* ic, he -cnád, ðú -cnide, -cnyde, *pl.* -cnidon; *pp.* -cniden *To beat* or *break into pieces, dash* or *throw down;* commĭnuĕre, contĕrĕre, collīdĕre:—Ic gewanie oððe forcníde hig swá swá dust *commĭnuam eos ut pulvĕrem,* Ps. Spl. 17, 44. Ealle trumnysse hláfes he forcnád *omne firmāmentum pānis contrīvit,* 104, 15. Setl his on lande ðú forcnyde *sēdem ejus in terra collīsisti,* 88, 43. v. for-gnídan.

for-corfen *cut down,* Mt. Bos. 3, 10; *pp. of* for-ceorfan.

for-cuman; *p.* -com, -cwom, *pl.* -cómon, -cwómon; *pp.* -cumen, -cymen *To surpass, overcome, destroy, harass, wear out;* supĕrāre, vexāre:—Hæfde ðá se snotra sunu Dauides forcumen and forcýðed Caldéa eorl *then had the wise son of David overcome and surpassed in knowledge the earl of the Chaldeans,* Salm. Kmbl. 353; Sal. 176: Andr. Kmbl. 2651; An. 1327. Yrfe ðín eall forcóman *hærēdĭtātem tuam vexāvērunt,* Ps. Th. 93, 5. Bring us hǽlo líf, wérigum wíteþeówum, wópe forcymenum *bring to us weary slaves, worn out by weeping, a life of health,* Exon. 10 a; Th. 10, 13; Cri. 151. [*O. Sax.* far-kuman; *Ger.* ver-kommen *to overcome, destroy.*]

fór-cuman; *p.* -com, -cwom, *pl.* -cómon, -cwómon; *pp.* -cumen [fór *before;* cuman *to come*] *To* FORE-COME, *go before, prevent;* prævĕnīre:—Arís, Drihten, fórcum hí *exurge, Dŏmĭne, prævĕni eos,* Ps. Spl. 16, 14. Ic fórcom on rípunga *prævĕni in matūrĭtāte,* 118, 147. [*Ger.* vorkommen *to come before, occur.*]

for-curfon *cut out,* Chr. 797; Erl. 58, 13; *p. pl. of* for-ceorfan.

for-cúþ; *comp. m.* -cúþera, -cúþra; *sup. m.* -cúþesta, -cúþosta; *adj.* [cúþ *known, excellent*] *Perverse, bad, infamous, wicked;* perversus, mălus, nēquam:—Mánfull oððe forcúþ *nēquam,* Ælfc. Gr. 9, 78; Som. 14, 30. Se yfela, swá he oftor on ðære fandunge abrýþ, swá he forcúþra biþ *the oftener the evil man sinks under temptation, the more wicked he will be,* Homl. Th. i. 268, 30. Wearþ he and ealle his geferan forcúþran and wyrsan đonne ǽnig ōđer gesceaft *he and all his companions became more wicked and worse than any other creature*, i. 10, 35. Hī habbaþ đæs mennisces đone betstan dǽl forloren, and đone forcūþestan [forcūþeran MS. Bod.] gehealden *they have lost the best part of humanity, and kept the worst* [*worse*], Bt. 37, 3; Fox 192, 4. Oft đa eallra forcūþestan men cumaþ to đam ānwealde and to đam weorþscipe *the most wicked men of all often come to power and dignity*, 16, 3; Fox 54, 21. Hwæđer he wolde đām forcūþestum mannum folgian *would it follow the most wicked men?* 16, 3; Fox 54, 10, 27. Đa Sodomitiscan menn wǽron đa forcūþostan *hŏmĭnes Sŏdŏmītæ pessĭmi ĕrant*, Gen. 13, 13. [*Goth.* frakunþs *despised.*] DER. unforcūþ.

for-cūþlīce; *adv. Perversely, across;* perverse, transverse:—Đæra cynega swuran forcūþlīce trǽdon *colla rēgum pĕdĭbus calcārent*, Jos. 10, 24.

for-cweđan; *p.* -cwæþ, *pl.* -cwǽdon; *pp.* -cweden *To rebuke, censure, revile, refuse, reject;* incrĕpāre, maledīcĕre, recūsāre, rejīcĕre:—Ne sceal hine mon cildgeong ne forcweđan *one must not while a young child rebuke him*, Exon. 89 b; Th. 336, 14; Gn. Ex. 49. Đa fortrūwodan forsióþ ōđre menn and eác forcweđaþ [MS. forcueđaþ] *the presumptuous despise and also revile other men*, Past. 32, 1; Hat. MS. 39 b, 27. Se wīsa Catulus forcwæþ Nonium đone rīcan *the wise Catulus censured Nonius the rich*, Bt. 27, 1; Fox 94, 32. Drihten forcwæþ swelce ælmessan *the Lord rejected such alms*, Past. 45, 4; Hat. MS. 65 a, 26.

for-cwolstan; *p.* te; *pp.* ed *To swallow down;* haurīre:—Fīfleáfan seáwes þrȳ bollan fulle lytle sceal forcwolstan *he shall swallow down three little bowls of the juice of cinque-foil*, L. M. 1, 4; Lchdm. ii. 48, 18.

for-cwom, *pl.* -cwōmon *came upon;* sŭpervēnit, sŭpervēnērunt:—Egsa me and fyrhtu ealne forcwōmon *tĭmor et trĕmor vēnērunt sŭper me*. Ps. Th. 54, 5. v. for-com, -cōmon; *p. of* for-cuman.

for-cwysan; *p.* de; *pp.* ed *To shake violently;* conquassāre:—He forcwysde heáfda on eorþan manigra *he shook violently the heads of many in the earth*, Ps. Spl. 109, 7.

for-cymen *overcome, harassed, worn out*, Exon. 10 a; Th. 10, 13; Cri. 151; *pp. of* for-cuman.

for-cyrfst, he -cyrfþ *cuttest down, he cuts down*, Homl. Th. ii. 408, 8: Ps. Lamb. 128, 4; *2nd and 3rd sing. pres. of* for-ceorfan.

for-cyrran; *p.* de; *pp.* ed *To turn again, subvert, avoid;* pervertĕre, subvertĕre, evītāre:—Būton deáþ hī ne māgon forcyrran *except they cannot avoid death*, Bt. 41, 2; Fox 246, 8.

for-cȳđan; *p.* de; *pp.* ed *To surpass* or *excel in knowledge;* scientia excellĕre *vel* supĕrāre:—Hæfde se snotra sunu Davides forcumen and forcȳđed Caldēa eorl *the wise son of David had overcome and surpassed in knowledge the leader of the Chaldeans*, Salm. Kmbl. 353; Sal. 176: 411; Sal. 206.

FORD; *gen.* fordes; *dat.* forde, forda; *m. A* FORD; vădum:—Ford *vădum*, Ælfc. Gl. 97; Som. 76, 66; Wrt. Voc. 54, 10: 80, 51. Hie flugon ofer Temese būton ǽlcum forda *they fled over the Thames without any ford*, Chr. 894; Erl. 90, 28. Neáh đam forda, đe man hǽt Welinga ford *near the ford which is called Wallingford*, Ors. 5, 12; Bos. 110, 20. Æt đam forda [Th. forde] *at the ford*, Byrht. Th. 134, 8; By. 81. Đa Walas adrifon sumre eá ford ealne mid scearpum pīlum greátum *the Welsh staked the ford of a river all with great sharp piles*, Chr. Erl. 5, 9, 12. Ofer đone ford *trans vădum*, Ælfc. Gr. 47; Som. 47, 38: Byrht. Th. 134, 22; By. 88: Beo. Th. 1140; B. 568. He oferfōr đone ford *transīvit vădum*, Gen. 32, 22. He mihte fordas oferrīdan, đonne he to hwylcere eá cōme *he might ride over the fords, when he came to any river*, Bd. 3, 14; S. 540, 17. [*Laym.* uord, ford: *Scot.* firth, frith *a bay: O. Frs.* forda: *Dut. Kil.* voord *vădum*: *Ger.* furt, *f*: *M. H. Ger.* vurt, *m*: *O. H. Ger.* furt, *n*: *Dan.* fjord, *m. f. a bay, gulf*: *Swed.* fjärd, *m. a bay*: *Icel.* fjörðr, *m*: *Grk.* πόρος, *m. a ford, ferry.*]

for-dǽdla *a destroyer*. v. mān-fordǽdla.

for-dǽlan; *p.* de; *pp.* ed *To deal out, expend;* dispensāre, erŏgāre:—Seó fordǽlde on lǽcas eall đæt heó āhte *quæ in mĕdĭcos erogāvĕrat omnem substantiam suam*, Lk. Bos. 8, 43. [*Goth.* fradailjan *to give away*: *Dut.* ver-deelen *to divide, distribute*: *Ger.* ver-theilen *to distribute.*]

for-deáþ *destroys, does for*, Wanl. Catal. 112, 65, col. 2, = for-dēþ; *3rd sing. pres. of* for-dōn.

for-dēman, to for-dēmanne; *p.* de: *pp.* ed *To condemn, damn;* dijudĭcāre, damnāre, condemnāre:—Đæt hig hine gesealdon đām ealdron to dōme, and to đæs dēman ānwalde to fordēmanne *ut tradĕrent illum princĭpātui, et potestāti præsĭdis*, Lk. Bos. 20, 20. On middele sōþlīce godas he fordēmþ *in mĕdio autem deos dijūdĭcat*, Ps. Spl. 81, 1. Đā geseah Iudas đe hyne belǽwde, đæt he fordēmed wæs, đā ongan he hreówsian *tunc vĭdens Iudas, qui eum tradĭdit, quod damnātus esset, pænĭtentia ductus*, Mt. Bos. 27, 3. Nellen gē dēman, đæt gē ne sȳn fordēmede *judge not, that ye be not condemned*, 7, 1. Đæt man cristene men, for ealles tō lytlum, to deáþe ne fordēme *that christian men, for all too little, be not condemned to death*, L. Eth. v. 3; Th. i. 304, 17. [*O. Sax.* fardōmjan: *O. H. Ger.* firtuoman: *Dut.* verdoemen *to condemn.*]

for-dēmednes, -ness, e; *f. Condemnation, proscription;* condemnātio, proscriptio:—Þurh tyn winter full Godes cyricena bærnesse, and unsceađiendra fordēmednesse, and slege hāligra martyra unblinnendlīce dōn wæs *per dĕcem annos, incendiis ecclēsiārum, proscriptiōnĭbus innŏcentum, cædĭbus martyrum incessābĭlĭter acta est*, Bd. 1, 6; S. 476, 25.

for-demman; *part.* -demmende; *p.* de; *pp.* ed *To shut* or *dam up;* obtūrāre:—Swā swā nædran deáfe, and fordemmende eáran heora *sīcut aspĭdis surdæ, et obtūrantis aures suas*, Ps. Spl. T. 57, 4. [*Goth.* faurdammjan *to stop up*: *Ger.* verdammen *to embank, dam up.*]

for-dēn *done for, destroyed, defiled*, Exon. 25 b; Th. 74, 15; Cri. 1207; *pp. of* for-dōn.

for-dēþ *does for, destroys*, L. Edg. S. 14; Th. i. 278, 1; *3rd pres. sing. of* for-dōn.

for-dettan *to shut up;* obtūrāre, Prov. 21. v. for-dyttan.

for-dician; *p.* ode; *pp.* od *To obstruct, shut*, or *fence off with a ditch;* fossā obstruĕre, Som. Ben. Lye.

for-dilgian, -diligian; *p.* ode, ade; *pp.* od, ad *To blot out, destroy;* dēlēre, obnūbĭlāre, oblĭtĕrāre:—He wolde ealle his þeóde fram đām gingrum ōþ đa yldran fordōn and fordilgian *he would do for and blot out all his nation from the younger to the elder*, Bd. 3, 24; S. 556, 13: 5, 21; S. 643, 26. He đā ōđer werod đære [MS. đara] mānfullan þeóde fornam and fordilgade *sic cētĕras nefandæ mīlĭtiæ cōpias delēvit*, 2, 2; S. 504, 7: 5, 13; S. 633, 34. Đæt hī ōþ forwyrd ǽghwǽr fordiligade ne wǽron *ne usque ad internĕciōnem usquequaque delērentur*, Bd. 1, 16; S. 484, 17. [*Orm.* forrdillʒenn: *Dut.* ver-delgen: *Ger.* ver-tilgen *to extirpate, destroy.*]

for-dimmian; *p.* ode; *pp.* od *To make very dim, darken, obscure;* obnūbĭlāre, obfuscāre, obscūrāre, R. Conc. 1.

for-dōn, to for-dōnne; he -dēþ; *p.* ic, he -dyde, đū -dydest, *pl.* -dydon; *subj. pres.* -dō, *pl.* -dōn; *p.* -dyde, *pl.* -dyden; *pp.* -dōn, -dēn. I. *to do for, destroy, kill;* perdĕre, destruĕre, dēlēre, contĕrĕre, interfĭcĕre, occīdĕre:—Ondrǽdaþ đone, đe mæg sāwle and līchaman fordōn on helle *tĭmēte eum, qui pŏtest et ănĭmam et corpus perdĕre in gehennam*, Mt. Bos. 10, 28: Mk. Bos. 3, 6: Gen. 18, 23: Chr. 1013; Erl. 149, 2, 24: L. Ath. iv. 1; Th. i. 220, 23. He wolde ealle his þeóde fordōn and fordilgian *tōtam ejus gentem dēlēre et extermĭnāre decrēvĕrat*, Bd. 3, 24; S. 556, 13: Deut. 9, 19. He wolde Aaron fordōn *vŏluit Aaron contĕrĕre*, Deut. 9, 20. Đæt he mǽge fordōn đa unsceđđendan *ut interfĭciat innŏcentem*, Ps. Th. 9, 28. He sēcþ hine to fordōnne *quærit perdĕre eum*, Ps. Th. 36, 32. Ic fordō hig *ego disperdam eos*, Gen. 6, 13. Đe đæne scyldigan rihtlīce fordēþ *who lawfully does for the guilty*, L. Edg. S. 14; Th. i. 278, 1. Be đam wīfmen đe hire bearn fordēþ *de mŭlière quæ infantem suum occīdit*, L. Ecg. P. cont. ii. 2; Th. ii. 180, 3. Se bisceop towearp and fordyde đa wigbed *pontĭfex ipse polluit ac destruxit eas āras*, Bd. 2, 13; S. 517, 18: Chr. 986; Erl. 130, 11: 1075; Erl. 214, 15: Deut. 9, 4. Đū fordydest ǽlcne man *perdĭdisti omnem*, Ps. Lamb. 72, 27. Se here fordydon eall đæt he oferferde *the army destroyed all that it passed over*, Chr. 1016; Erl. 157, 12. Hī fordydon me *consummāvērunt me*, Ps. Lamb. 118, 87. Đæt ic hig fordō *ut contĕram eum*, Deut. 9, 14. Đæt he fordō *ut perdat*, Jn. Bos. 10, 10: Bt. Met. Fox 20, 260; Met. 20, 130. Đæt we hig fordōn *ut perdāmus illos*, Gen. 19, 13. Đȳ-læs hī fordōn ōđra gesceafta *lest they destroy other creatures*, Bt. 39, 13; Fox 234, 9. Đæt he eów ne fordyde *ne dēlēret vos*, Deut. 9, 25. Đȳ-læs hī ōđra fordyden æđela gesceafta *lest they should destroy other noble creatures*, Bt. Met. Fox 29, 91; Met. 29, 45. Hū oft ic hæbbe fordōn đa Egiptiscan *quotiens contrīvĕrim Ægyptios*, Ex. 10, 2. II. *to seduce, defile, corrupt;* sedūcĕre, scĕlĕrāre:—Đeáh heó dearnenga fordōn wurde mid ligenum *though she* [*Eve*] *was secretly seduced with lies*, Cd. 30; Th. 39, 22; Gen. 629. Deáþfirenum fordēn *defiled by deadly sins*, Exon. 25 b; Th. 74, 15; Cri. 1207. On đa firenum fordōne sorgum wlītaþ *on which the defiled by sins shall sorrowfully look*, Exon. 24 a; Th. 68, 16; Cri. 1104. Đǽr wæs cirm micel, fordēnera gedræg *there was a great noise, a tumult of the defiled*, Andr. Kmbl. 85; An. 43. Seóđeþ swearta lēg synne on fordōnum *the swart flame of sin shall seethe on the corrupted*, Exon. 22 b; Th. 62, 2; Cri. 995. [*O. Sax.* fardōn: *Dut.* ver-doen *to destroy, kill*: *Ger.* ver-thun *to waste.*] Used by Shakespeare.

for-drencan; *p.* -drencte; *pp.* -drenced, -drenct *To make drunk, inebriate, intoxicate;* madefăcĕre, inebriāre:—Uton fordrencan ūrne fæder mid wīne *let us make our father drunk with wine*, Gen. 19, 32, 33. Nis đæs mannes fæsten nāht, đe hine sylfne on forhæfednysse dagum fordrencþ *the man's fasting is naught who inebriates himself on days of abstinence*, Homl. Th. ii. 608, 24. Đās men sindon mid muste fordrencte *these men are drunken with new wine*, i. 314, 22, 23.

for-drīfan; *p.* -drāf, *pl.* -drifon; *pp.* -drifen *To drive away, force, compel, drive out, eject, banish;* pellĕre, prōpellĕre, compellĕre, cōgĕre, expellĕre:—Sumne sceal hreóh fordrīfan *the tempest shall drive one away*, Exon. 87 a; Th. 328, 10; Vy. 15. Hine se streám fordrāf *the stream drove him*, Ors. 2, 4; Bos. 44, 3: Judth. 12; Thw. 25, 25; Jud. 277: Andr. Kmbl. 538; An. 269. Norþhymbra fordrifon heora cining Alhrēd of Eoferwīc *the Northumbrians drove their king Alhred from York*, Chr. 774; Erl. 53, 33: 954; Erl. 119, 6. Fordrīf hī *expelle eos*, Ps. Th. 5, 11. Sió wunode on đam īglande đe se cyning on fordrifen wearþ *she dwelt in the island on which the king was driven*, Bt. 38, 1; Fox 194, 21. Hió geseah đone fordrifenan cyning *she saw the driven king*, 194, 23.

Lufiaþ fordrifene, forðamðe gē sylfe wǣron fordrifene and ūtancymene on Egipta lande *vos ămāte pĕrĕgrīnos, qui et ipsi fuistis advĕnæ in terra Ægypti*, Deut. 10, 19, 18. [*Laym.* men al for-dreuen: *O. Sax.* fordrīƀan: *Dut.* ver-drijven: *Ger.* ver-treiben *to drive away, banish.*]

for-drincan; *p.* -dranc, *pl.* -druncon; *pp.* -druncen *To make drunk, inebriate*; madefăcĕre, ebriāre:—Gedrēfde hī syndon and astyrede syndon swā swā fordruncen [MS. fordruncon] man *turbāti sunt et mōti sunt sīcut ebrius*, Ps. Lamb. 106, 27. Abigall forswīgode· ðæt dysig hiere fordruncnan hlāfordes *Abigail concealed the folly of her drunken lord*, Past. 40, 4; Hat. MS. 55 a, 13. [*Laym.* for-drunkene cnihtes.]

for-drugian, -druwian; *p.* ode; *pp.* od *To dry up, parch, wither;* arescĕre, siccāri:—He forheardaþ and fordrugaþ *indūret et arescat*, Ps. Lamb. 89, 6. Hió wǣre fordrugod to duste *it would be dried to dust*, Bt. Met. Fox 20, 207; Met. 20, 104. [*Dut.* ver-droogen: *Ger.* vertrocknen *to dry up.*]

for-druncen, -druncn *drunken*, Past. 40, 4; Hat. MS. 55 a, 13; *pp. of* for-drincan.

for-druwian; *p.* ode; *pp.* od *To dry up, wither;* arescĕre:—He byþ aworpen ūt swā twīg, and fordruwaþ *mittētur fŏras sīcut palmes, et arescet*, Jn. Bos. 15, 6. [*A.R.* vor-druwede, *pp. pl.*] v. for-drugian.

for-dwilman; *p.* de; *pp.* ed *To confound;* confundĕre:—Ða mistas fordwilmaþ ða sōþan gesiehþe *the mists confound the true sight*, Bt. 5, 3; Fox 14, 17.

for-dwīnan, he -dwīneþ, -dwīnþ; *p.* -dwān, *pl.* -dwinon; *pp.* -dwinen *To dwindle away, vanish;* evānescĕre:—Fordwīneþ heó sōna *it soon will dwindle away*, Herb. 2, 2; Lchdm. i. 80, 17. Mannes ege hrædlīce fordwīnþ *awe of man quickly vanishes*, Homl. Th. i. 592, 12. Se sceocca fordwān of his gesihþe *Satan vanished from his sight*, ii. 504, 4. [*Chauc.* hondes for-dwīned: *Dut.* ver-dwijnen *to vanish.*]

for-dyde, *pl.* -dydon *did for, destroyed*, Deut. 9, 1: Ps. Lamb. 118, 87: for-dyde, *pl.* -dyden *should do for, destroy*, Deut. 9, 25: Bt. Met. Fox 29, 91; Met. 29, 45; *p. indic. and p. subj. of* for-dōn.

for-dyttan; *part.* -dyttende; *p.* -dytte; *pp.* -dytted, -dytt, -dyt *To close or shut entirely up, stop up;* oppīlāre, claudĕre, obstruĕre:—Swā swā næddran deáfre, and fordyttendre hire eáran *sīcut aspĭdis surdæ, et obtūrantis aures suas*, Ps. Lamb. 57, 5. Ǣlc unrihtwīsnes fordyt mūþ hire *omnis inīquĭtas oppīlābit os suum*, 106, 42. Is fordyt mūþ sprecendra unrihte þing *obstructum est os lŏquentium inīqua*, 62, 12. Ða wilspringas ðære miclan niwelnisse wurdon fordytte *clausi sunt fontes abyssi*, Gen. 8, 2. [*Laym.* for-dut, *pres. sing. indic.*]

fore = for, *q. v; prep. dat. acc.* I. *for, on account of, for the sake of;* pro, propter, per; *with the dative;* cum dātīvo:—Ne syndon to lufianne ða wīsan fore stōwum, ac for gōdum wīsum stōwe syndon to lufianne *non pro lŏcis res, sed pro bŏnis rēbus lŏca amanda sunt*, Bd. 1, 27; S. 489, 41. Fore miltsum *for his mercies*, Exon. 46 b; Th. 159, 25; Gū. 932. He lāþ biþ ǣghwǣr fore his wonsceaftum *he is everywhere unwelcome on account of his misfortunes*, 87 b; Th. 329, 10; Vy. 32. He fore his mondryhtne mōdsorge wæg *he bare mental sorrow for his master*, Exon. 48 a; Th. 165, 5; Gū. 1024. Nō mearn fore fǣhþe and fyrene *he mourned not on account of his enmity and crime*, Beo. Th. 273; B. 136. Gē scofene wurdon fore oferhygdum in ēce fȳr *ye were thrust into eternal fire on account of pride*, Exon. 41 b; Th. 140, 6; Gū. 606. II. = for, *q. v. for, on account of, for the sake of;* pro, propter, per; *with the accusative;* cum accusātīvo:—Gehālgode fore hine Damiānum *consecrāvit pro eo Damiānum*, Bd. 3, 20; S. 550, 33. III. sometimes fore is separated from its case, v. III. *in* fōre:—Ðæt he hine fore gebǣde *that he might pray for him*, Bd. 5, 5; S. 618, 2. He ahongen wæs fore moncynnes mānforwyrhtum *he was hanged for the evil deeds of mankind*, Exon. 24 a; Th. 67, 27; Cri. 1095. Se þegn fore fæder dǣdum swefeþ *the thane sleeps for his father's deeds*, Beo. Th. 4125; B. 2059.

fōre = fōr; *prep. dat. acc.* I. *before;* cōram, ante, in conspectu, præsente *vel* audiente ălĭquo, ante; *with the dative;* cum dātīvo:—Se ār Godes ānne wīsfæstne wer gehālgode fōre ðam heremægene *the messenger of God consecrated a wise man before the host*, Andr. Kmbl. 3299; An. 1652. Fela gē fōre monnum mīðaþ *ye conceal much before men*, Exon. 39 a; Th. 130, 10; Gū. 436. Hȳ fōre leódum leóhte blīcaþ *they shall shine brightly before the people*, 26 a; Th. 76, 13; Cri. 1239. Gehealdne sind sāwle wið synnum fōre sigedēman *souls have been preserved from sins before the judge triumphant*, Exon. 23 b; Th. 65, 28; Cri. 1061. Fōre Waldende *before the Lord*, 23 b; Th. 66, 12; Cri. 1070. Fōre onsȳne ēcan Dryhtnes standaþ stīþferhþe *the stout-hearted stand before the face of the eternal Lord*, Andr. Kmbl. 1441; An. 721. Fōre eágum *before the eyes*, Exon. 27 a; Th. 81, 15; Cri. 1324. II. *before;* ante, *with the accusative;* cum accusātīvo:—Sendon hira bēne fōre bearn Godes *they sent their petition before the Son of God*, Andr. Kmbl. 2056; An. 1030. Ne sceal ic mīne onsȳn fōre eówere mengu mīðan *I shall not conceal my countenance before your multitude*, Exon. 43 a; Th. 144, 17; Gū. 679. Fōre þreó niht *before three nights*, Andr. Kmbl. 369; An. 185. III. sometimes fōre follows its case or is separated from it:—On ðone Drihten ðe ðes hāligdōm is fōre hālig *by the Lord before whom this relic is holy*, L. O. 1, 2; Th. i. 178, 3, 12. Ðes ār me fōre stondeþ *this messenger stands before me*, Exon. 69 b; Th. 259, 5; Jul. 277. Cumaþ him fōre *come before him*, Ps. Th. 94, 6. Scīneþ ðē leóht fōre *the light shines before thee*, Cd. 29; Th. 38, 30; Gen. 614. Him wēpan fōre *plōrēmus cōram eo*, Ps. Th. 94, 6.

fōre; *adv. Before, aforetime, formerly;* antea, ōlim, quondam:—He on Ægypta lande worhte fōre wundur mǣre *he aforetime did great wonders in the land of Egypt*, Ps. Th. 77, 14.

fōre; *gen. dat. acc. of* fōr *a going, journey, course, approach*, Exon. 111 a; Th. 426, 10; Rä. 41, 71: Bd. 5, 9; S. 623, 23: 4, 27; S. 604, 29. v. fōr, e; *f.*

fōre- *before*, used in composition as the English *fore-*.

fōre-ætȳwian; *p.* ede; *pp.* ed *To fore-show, to go before and show the way;* præmonstrāre, Som. Ben. Lye. v. æt-eówian, -ȳwan.

for-ealdian, -ealdigean, -ealldian; *p.* ode; *pp.* od [for-, eald *old*] *To grow* or *wax old, become old;* senescĕre, veterascĕre, inveterascĕre:—Wyrceaþ seódas, ða ðe ne forealdigeaþ *făcĭte vōbis saccŭlos, qui non veterascunt*, Lk. Bos. 12, 33. Bearn elelendisce forealdodon *fīlii aliēni inveterāti sunt*, Ps. Lamb. 17, 46. Forealldodon ða gewritu *the writings waxed old*, Bt. 18, 3; Fox 64, 37. Ne forealdige ðeós hand ǣfre *nunquam inveterascat hæc mănus*, Bd. 3, 6; S. 528, 24. Ǣlc ānweald biþ sōna forealdod *every power soon becomes old*, Bt. 17; Fox 60, 10: 39, 8; Fox 224, 11. Ðe forealdode wǣron *who were grown old*, Homl. Th. ii. 500, 4. [*Ger.* ver-alten *to grow old.*] DER. eldian, eald.

fōre-astreccan; *p.* -astreahte, -astrehte; *pp.* -astreaht, -astreht *To lay* or *stretch out before;* prōsternĕre:—Ðæt he fōreastrehte hig on wēstene *ut prōsternĕret eos in deserto*, Ps. Spl. T. 105, 25. [*Ger.* vor-strecken *to stretch forth.*]

fōre-āþ, fōr-āþ, es; *m. A fore-oath, an oath first taken;* antejūrāmentum, præjūrāmentum, præjūrātio:—So called because it was that by which every accuser or plaintiff commenced his accusation or suit against the accused or defendant. To this the defendant opposed his own fōre-āþ, thereby pleading not guilty to the charge. The oaths both of plaintiff and defendant were supported by consacramentals, respecting the number of which see L. H. 66, § 8; Th. i. 569: v. also **Āþ II, III.** If the fōre-āþ of the accuser failed, the charge was quashed and the accused set at liberty:—Ofgā ǣlc man his tīhtlan mid fōreāþe *let every man begin his charge with a fore-oath*, L. Ath. i. 23; Th. i. 212, 5. Agife ðone fōreāþ on feówer ciricum *let him make his fore-oath in four churches*, L. Alf. pol. 33; Th. i. 82, 7. Ofgā his spræce mid fōrāþe *let him begin his suit with a fore-oath*, L. O. D. 6; Th. i. 354, 31: L. Ath. iv. 2; Th. i. 222, 16. Ofgā man ānfealde lāde mid ānfealdan fōrāþe and þrȳfealde lāde mid þrȳfealdan fōrāþe *one may proceed to a simple exculpation with a simple fore-oath and to a threefold exculpation with a threefold fore-oath* L. C. S. 22; Th. i. 388, 15; cf. Schmid, Ges. der Angelsachsen, forāþ.

fōr-eáðe; *adv. Very easily;* perfăcĭle:—God mæg fōreáðe unc ǣt fōresceáwian *God can very easily provide food for us two*, Homl. Th. ii. 138, 35.

fōre-beácen, -beácn, es; *n. A fore-token, prodigy, wonder;* prodĭgium, portentum, ostentum:—Ic eom swā fōrebeácen folce manegum *tamquam prodĭgium factus sum multis*, Ps. Th. 70, 6. Fōrebeácna *prodĭgiōrum* 104, 23. He sigetācen sende manegum, fōrebeácn feala folce Ægipta *mīsit signa et prodĭgia in mĕdio Ægypti*, 134, 9: Ps. Lamb. 77, 43: Mt. Bos. 24, 24. Sōþlīce leáse cristas and leáse wītegan arīsaþ, and wyrcþ, fōrebeácnu *exsurgent ĕnim pseudochristi, et pseudoprophētæ, et dăbunt signa et portenta*, Mk. Bos. 13, 22: Deut. 13, 1. Būton gē tācna and fōrebeácna geseón, ne gelȳfe gē *except ye see signs and wonders, ye will not believe*, Jn. Bos. 4, 48: Nar. 50, 21: -beácno, Blickl. Hom. 117, 30.

fōre-beón *to be before* or *over, to preside;* præesse, Scint. 32, 58. v. fōre-eom, fōre-wesan.

fōre-beran; *part.* -berende; *p.* -bær, *pl.* -bǣron; *pp.* -boren *To prefer;* præferre:—He sundorlīf and munuclīf wæs fōreberende eallum ðām weólum and ārum ðæs eorþlīcan rīces *ĕrat vītam prīvātam et mŏnachĭcam cunctis regni dīvĭtiis et hŏnōrĭbus præfĕrens*, Bd. 4, 11; S. 579, 8. v. fōr-beran.

fōre-bētan; *p.* -bētte; *pp.* -bēted [fōre *before, full, entire;* bētan *to make amends*] *To make full amends to* or *for anyone* or *anything;* compensāre prō ălĭquo:—Lādige mid his māgan, ðe fǣhþe mōton mid-beran, oððe fōrebētan *let him clear himself with his kinsmen, who must bear the feud with him, or make full amends for it*, L. Eth. ix. 23; Th. i. 344, 27: L. C. E. 5; Th. i. 362, 23. Gif he nyte hwā him fōrebēte *if he know not who shall make full amends for him*, L. Ed. 9; Th. i. 164, 12: L. Ath. i. 8; Th. i. 204, 8.

fōre-birig; *dat. s. of* fōre-burh *a vestibule*, Ex. 29, 32.

fōre-bodian; *p.* ode; *pp.* od *To* FOREBODE, *announce, declare;* annuntiāre, prōnuntiāre:—Mūþ mīn fōrebodaþ rihtwīsnysse ðīne *os meum annuntiābit justĭtiam tuam*, Ps. Spl. 70, 16. Fōrebodaþ tunge [MS. tunga] mīn spræca ðīne *prōnuntiābit lingua mea elŏquium tuum*, 118, 172.

fōre-breóst, es; *n. The fore-breast, breast, chest;* præcordia, thōrax = θώραξ:—Fōrebreóst *præcordia*, Ælfc. Gl. 73; Som. 71, 23; Wrt. Voc. 44, 9.

fōre-burh; *gen.* -burge; *dat.* -byrig, -birig; *f.* I. *a fore-court, entrance-court, vestibule;* vestĭbŭlum:—Hig etaþ ða hlāfas on ðæs geteldes fōrebirig *comĕdent pānes in tabernācŭli testĭmōnii vestĭbŭlo*, Ex. 29, 32. II. *a wall before a fortification;* pro-mūrāle, mūrus ante mūrum, dictum ex eo quod pro mūnītione sit [*Du Cange*]:—Fōreburh *promūrāle*, Ælfc. Gl. 55; Som. 66, 118; Wrt. Voc. 36, 38.

fōre-bȳsen, e; *f.* [fōre, bȳsen *an example, model*] *A fore-model, an example;* exemplum:—Arcebisceop sceal hālgian and getryman mid gōdan mynegunga and fōrebȳsene *an archbishop shall hallow and strengthen them with good admonitions and example*, Chr. 694; Th. 67, 43.

fōre-ceorfan; *p.* -cearf, *pl.* -curfon; *pp.* -corfen [fōre *fore*, ceorfan *to cut*] *To cut off the front;* præcīdĕre:—Ic fōreceorfe *præcīdo*, Ælfc. Gr. 28, 4; Som. 31, 35.

fōre-ceorfend, es; *m.* [fōre-ceorfende, *part. of* fōre-ceorfan] *A fore-cutter, front tooth;* præcīsor, Wrt. Voc. 282, 73.

fore-costian, -costigan; *p.* ode; *pp.* od [=for-costian] *To profane, pollute;* profānāre:—Gyf rihtwīsnys mīn hī forecostigaþ *si justĭtias meas profānāvĕrint*, Ps. Spl. C. 88, 31.

fōre-cuman; *part.* -cumende; ic -cume, ðū -cumest, -cymest, -cymst, he -cumeþ, -cymeþ, -cymþ, -cimþ, *pl.* -cumaþ; *p.* -com, -cwom, *pl.* -cōmon, -cwōmon; *pp.* -cumen *To come forth, come before, prevent;* prævĕnīre:—Ðæt ðū sī fōrecumende Drihtnes onsȳne in andetnesse *quo præoccupando făciem Dŏmĭni in confessiōne*, Bd. 4, 25; S. 599, 42. God fōrecymeþ me *Deus prævĕniet me*, Ps. Spl. 58, 10. Fōrecymþ *prævĕniet*, 67, 34. Ic fōrecom oððe ic fōrhradode on rīpunga oððe on rīpnysse *prævĕni in matūrĭtāte*, Ps. Lamb. 118, 147. Ðū fōrecōme hine on bletsunge swētnysse *prævĕnisti eum in benedictiōnĭbus dulcēdĭnis*, Ps. Spl. 20, 3. Fōrecōmon eágan mīne to ðē on dægrēd *prævĕnērunt ŏcŭli mei ad te dilūcŭlo*, Ps. Spl. 118, 148: 17, 21. [*Goth.* faura-qīman.] v. fōr-cuman.

fōre-cweðan; *p.* -cwæþ, *pl.* -cwǣdon; *pp.* -cweden *To foresay, predict;* prædīcĕre, propōnĕre:—Hēt he him sillabas and word fōrecweðan *addĭdit et syllăbas ac verba dīcenda illi propōnĕre*, Bd. 5, 2; S. 615, 13. Ealle ðās þing swā se bisceop fōrecwæþ, of endebyrdnysse gelumpon and gefyllede wǣron *quæ cuncta ut prædixĕrat antistes, ex ordĭne complēta sunt*, 3, 15; S. 541, 37. Swā swā we on ðysse ǣrran bēc feáwum wordum fōrecwǣdon *ut præcēdente libro paucis dixĭmus*, 4, 1; S. 563, 18. Sume men eác swylce sægdon, ðæt heó, þurh witedōmes gāst, ða ādle fōrecwǣde [MS. -cwede], ðe heó on forþferde *sunt ĕtiam qui dīcant, quia per prophētīæ spīrĭtum, pestĭlentiam qua ipsa esset mŏrĭtūra, prædixĕrat*, 4, 19; S. 588, 15. Swā hit fōrecweden wæs *ut prædictum ĕrat*, 3, 15; S. 542, 3. [*Goth.* faura-qiþan.] DER. cweðan.

fōre-cwide, es; *m. A foretelling, prophecy;* prædictio, Som. Ben. Lye.

fōre-cymeþ, -cymþ *prævĕniet*, Ps. Spl. 58, 10: 67, 34. v. fōre-cuman.

fōre-cynn; *pl. n. Ancestors, predecessors, progenitors;* antecessōres, prædecessōres, progĕnĭtōres, Som. Ben. Lye.

fōre-cynren, es; *n. A progeny;* progĕnies, Cot. 154.

fored; *part. Broken, fractured;* fractus:—Gif monnes ceácan mon fōrslihþ ðæt hie beón forede *if a man smite another's cheeks that they be broken*, L. Alf. pol. 50; Th. i. 94, 15, note 34. Se foreda fōt [MS. foot] *the fractured foot*, Past. 11, 2; Hat. MS. 15 a, 4. v. forod.

fōre-dūru, e; *f:* -dȳr, es; *n. A fore-door, porch, an entry, hall;* vestĭbŭlum, propȳlæum = προπύλαιον:—Fōredȳre *vestĭbŭla*, Cot. 190.

fōre-eom [fōre *before*, eom *am*] *I am before* or *over, I preside;* præsum:—Ic begīme oððe ic fōre-eom *præsum*, Ælfc. Gr. 32; Som. 36, 32. v. fōre-wesan.

fōre-fæder, fōre-fæderas FOREFATHER, FOREFATHERS; mājōres. v. forþ-fæderas.

fore-feng, -fong, es; *m.* [=for-feng] *A seizing, rescuing;* apprehensio:—Be forstolenes monnes forefonge *of seizing a stolen man*, L. In. 53; Th. i. 134, 15. Be forefonge [forefenge MSS. B, G, H.], 72; Th. i. 148, 5. Be forstolenes ceápes forefonge *of the rescuing of stolen property*, 75; Th. i. 150, 4. v. for-fang.

fōre-fōn, ic -fō; *p.* -fēng, *pl.* -fēngon; *pp.* -fangen *To take before, anticipate;* antĭcĭpāre:—Fōrefēngon wæccan eágan mīne *antĭcĭpāvērunt vigĭlias ŏcŭli mei*, Ps. Spl. C. T. 76, 4. Raðe fōrefō us mildheortnysse ðīne *cĭto antĭcĭpent nos mĭsĕrĭcordiæ tuæ*, Ps. Spl. C. 78, 8.

fōre-gān; *p.* -eóde; *pp.* -gān *To go before, precede;* præcēdĕre:—Mildheortnys and sōþfæstnys fōregāþ ansȳne ðīne *misericordia et vērĭtas præcēdent făciem tuam*, Ps. Spl. C. 88, 15. Ōðer fōre-eóde ða sunnan *ūna sōlem præcēdēbat*, Bd. 5, 23; S. 645, 24. v. fōre-gangan, fōr-gān.

fōre-gangan; *part.* -gangende; *p.* -geóng, -gēng, *pl.* -geóngon, -gēngon; *pp.* -gangen *To go before, precede;* præcēdĕre:—Hī wǣron fōregangende in ðone lēg *they were going before into the flame*, Bd. 3, 19; S. 548, 31. Hine sōþfæstnes fōregangeþ *justĭtia ante eum ambŭlābit*, Ps. Th. 84, 12. Hwæt ðǣr fōregange oððe hwæt ðǣr æfterfylige we ne cunnon *quid autem præcessĕrit quidve sĕquātur ignōrāmus*, Bd. 2, 13; S. 516, 22. [*Ger.* vor-gehen *to precede.*] v. fōre-gān, fōr-gangan.

fōre-gehāt, es; *n. A fore-promise, vow;* prōmissio:—Ðæt fōregehāt forgifenysse, ðe we habbaþ fram Gode *prōmissio remissiōnis, quam hăbēmus a Deo*, Bd. Whelc. 341, 27. On ðīnum fōregehātum *in pro-missiōnĭbus tuis*, 341, 26.

fōre-genga, an; *m.* I. *a fore-goer, fore-runner, predecessor;* prædecessor:—Ðætte swā æðele fōregenga swylcne yrfeweard hæfde *that so noble a predecessor should have such an heir*, Bd. 3, 6; S. 528, 33: 3, 9; S. 533, 12: 4, 30; S. 609, 6. Laurentius bii his fōregengan bebyrged wæs *Lawrence was buried beside his predecessor*, Bd. 2, 7; S. 509, 6. Ða fōregengan, yldran usse *those ancestors, our parents*, Exon. 62 a; Th. 228, 13; Ph. 437. On hiora fōregengena dagum *in diēbus antīquis*, Ps. Th. 43, 2. II. *a fore-runner;* prodrŏmus = πρόδρομος:—Hæfde fōregenga fȳrene loccas *their fore-runner had fiery locks*, Cd. 148; Th. 185, 9; Exod. 120. Ðone fōregengan Fæder ælmihtig gesette *the almighty Father had placed that fore-runner*, Exon. 40 b; Th. 134, 7; Gū. 504. [*Dut.* voor-ganger: *Ger.* vor-gänger *a predecessor.*]

fōre-genge, an; *f. A fore-goer, female servant;* ancilla:—Hyre fōregenge [MS. fōregenga] blāc-hleór ides *her servant, the pale-faced woman*, Judth. 11; Thw. 23, 18; Jud. 127.

fōre-gesettan; *part.* -gesettende; *p.* -gesette; *pp.* -gesett, -geset *To place before;* præpōnĕre:—Fōregesettendum ðām swȳðe hālgan gōdspellum *præpŏsĭtis sacrosanctis evangĕliis*, Bd. 4, 17; S. 585, 27. [*Goth.* faura-gasatjan *to present.*] v. fōre-settan.

fōre-gewītnys, -nyss, e; *f. False witness;* falsum testĭmōnium:—Ðæt heora ǣnig on fōre-gewītnysse sȳ *quod eōrum ălĭquis in falso testĭmōnium sit*, L. Ath. i. 10; Wilk. 58, 22; Lambd. 49, 12, = wōhre gewītnesse, Th. i. 204, 23; *dat. sing. f. of* wōh and gewītnes.

fōre-gilpan; *p.* -gealp, *pl.* -gulpon; *pp.* -golpen *To boast greatly;* valde jactāre:—Ðæt he wǣre cumen to ðām gōdan tīdum ðe Rōmāne eft fōregulpon *that he was come to the good times of which the Romans afterwards boasted greatly*, Ors. cont. 4, 7; Bos. 12, 13.

fōre-gīsel; *gen.* -gīsles; *m.* [gīsel *a hostage*] *A foremost hostage, principal* or *eminent hostage;* præstans *vel* electus obses:—Salde se here him fōregīslas and micle āþas *the army gave him eminent hostages with great oaths*, Chr. 878; Erl. 80, 16: 877; Erl. 79, 24. Norþhymbre and Eást-Engle hæfdon Ælfrēde cyninge āþas geseald, and Eást-Engle fōregīsla vi *the Northumbrians and East-Angles had given oaths to king Alfred, and the East-Angles six principal hostages*, Chr. 894; Erl. 90, 4.

fōre-gleáw; *adj. Very prudent;* provĭdus, præ aliis săpiens:—Fōregleáw *provĭdus*, R. Ben. 64: Homl. Th. ii. 152, 2. Fōregleáwe ealde ūþwitan *very prudent ancient philosophers*, Menol. Fox 328; Men. 165.

fōre-gleáwlīce; *adv. Providently, prudently;* provĭde, R. Ben. interl. 3.

fōre-gleáwnes, -ness, e; *f. Providence, prudence, carefulness;* provĭdentia, Som. Ben. Lye.

fōre-gulpon *boasted greatly*, Ors. cont. 4, 7; Bos. 12, 13; *p. pl. of* fōre-gilpan.

fōre-heáfod *the forehead;* frons, Som. Ben. Lye. v. fōr-heáfod.

fōre-mǣre; *def.* se fōre-mǣra; *sup.* -mǣrost, -mǣrest; *adj. Fore-great, very honourable, illustrious, eminent, famous, celebrated;* præclārus, illustris, excellens, fāmōsus, celeberrĭmus:—Ic nǣfre ne geseah ne gehȳrde nǣnne wīsne mon ðe mā wolde bión wrecca, and earm, and ælþiódig, and forsewen, ðonne wēlig, and weorþ, and rīce, and fōremǣre on his āgnum earde *I never saw nor heard of any wise man who would rather be an exile, and miserable, and foreign, and despised, than wealthy, and honourable, and powerful, and eminent in his own country*, Bt. 39, 2; Fox 212, 17. Is mīn land nū fōremǣre, and me swȳðe unbleó *hærēdĭtas mea præclāra est mihi*, Ps. Th. 15, 6. Hwǣr is nū se fōremǣra and se arǣda Rōmwāra heretoga *where is now the illustrious and the prudent consul of the Romans?* Bt. 19; Fox 70, 6. Hæfde gefohten fōremǣrne blǣd Iudith *Judith had gained illustrious honour*, Judth. 11; Thw. 23, 15; Jud. 122. Fōremǣre Simon and Iudas symble wǣron Drihtne dȳre *the celebrated Simon and Jude were always dear to the Lord*, Menol. Fox 378; Men. 190. Hū he fōremǣrost seó *how he may be most illustrious*, Bt. 33, 2; Fox 122, 34: 18, 3; Fox 64, 35. Se wer se fōremǣresta *the most eminent man*, Bd. 5, 20; S. 641, note 37.

fōre-mǣrlīc; *adj. Eminent;* præclārus:—Hū weorþlīc and hū fōremǣrlīc *how honourable and how eminent*, Bt. 33, 1; Fox 120, 34.

fōre-mǣrnes, fōr-mǣrnes, -ness, e; *f. Greatness, eminence, renown, glory;* clārĭtas:—Weorþscipe and fōremǣrnes *dignity and renown*, Bt. 34, 6; Fox 142, 7: 33, 1; Fox 122, 12.

fōre-manian; *p.* ode; *pp.* od *To fore-warn;* præmŏnēre:—He fōremanod wæs *præmŏnĭtus fuĕrat*, Bd. 5, 10; S. 623, 39.

fōre-meahtig, fōre-mihtig; *adj. Prepotent, most mighty;* præpŏtens:—Ða fōremeahtige folces rǣswan *the prepotent chieftains of the folk*, Cd. 80; Th. 100, 24; Gen. 1669. Ðǣr he ealdordōm onfēhþ, fōremihtig ofer fugla cynn *where it [the phœnix] receives supremacy, most mighty over the race of birds*, Exon. 58 a; Th. 208, 21; Ph. 159: Cd. 208; Th. 257, 33; Dan. 667.

fōre-mearcod; *part. Fore-noted;* prænŏtātus, Cot. 157.

fōre-mihtig; *adj. Prepotent, most mighty;* præpŏtens, Cd. 208; Th. 257, 33; Dan. 667. v. fōre-meahtig.

fōre-mihtiglīce, -mihtlīce; *adv. Most mightily;* strēnue, Cot. 202.

fōre-mūnt, es; *m. A fore-mount, promontory;* promontōrium, Cot. 149.

fōrene? *before;* ante, cītius, Lye:—Gif hine hwā fōrene [MS. A. of the 12th century has fōra] forstande *if any one stand up for him,* L. C. S. 33; Th. i. 396, 17; Wilk. 139, 22, 23. v. Schmid, s. v. forstandan.

fōre-rīm, es; *m. A prologue, preface;* prolŏgus:—Onginneþ fōrerīm *incĭpit prolŏgus,* Mt. Kmbl. Præf. p. 1, 1.

fōre-rynel, fōr-rynel, es; *m.* [fōre, fōr *before;* rynel, es; *m. a runner*] *A fore-runner;* præcursor:—Iohannes his fōrerynel wæs on līfe ge on deáþe *John was his fore-runner both in life and in death,* Ælfc. T. 24, 20: Bt. 36, 1; Fox 170, 28, MS. Cot. v. fōr-rynel.

fore-sacan; *p.* fore-sōc [=for-sacan] *to forbid;* prohĭbēre:—Foresōc oððe forbeád *prohĭbēbat,* Mt. Lind. Kmbl. 3, 14.

fōre-sǣde *foretold, predicted,* Mt. Bos. 24, 25; *p. of* fōre-secgan.

fōre-sægde *foretold, told,* Bd. 3, 15; S. 541, 16: biseno foresægde *parabolam proposuit,* Mt. Kmbl. 13, 24; *p. of* fōre-secgan.

fōre-sēge *should provide;* provĭdēret, Bd. 4, 1; S. 565, 8; *3rd sing. imperf. subj. of* fōre-seōn.

fōre-sændan *to send before,* Ælfc. Gr. 28, 4; Som. 31, 41, MS. D. v. fōre-sendan.

fōre-sāwe *foresawest;* prævīdisti, Ps. Th. 138, 2; *2nd sing. p. of* fōre-seōn.

fōre-sceáwere, es; *m. A foreshewer, foreseer;* prævīsor, Consid. ætātum lunæ in mōdo gĕnĭtis, Lye.

fōre-sceáwian, fōre-sceáwigan, fōr-sceáwian; *p.* ode; *pp.* od *To foreshew, foresee, provide;* præ-ostendĕre, pōnĕre in conspectu, prævĭdēre, provĭdēre:—Ic fōresceáwige *prævĭdeo,* Ælfc. Gr. 26, 5; Som. 29, 3. God fōresceáwaþ him sylf ða offrunge *Deus provĭdēbit sĭbi victĭmam,* Gen. 22, 8. He him fōresceáwode sumne heretogan *he provided them a leader,* Jud. 6, 8. Ðæt he fōresceáwode hū he hig gecīgde *ut vĭdēret quid vŏcāret ea,* Gen. 2, 19. Ic wisce ðæt hig fōresceáwodon hira ende *ūtĭnam nŏvissima provĭdērent,* Deut. 32, 29. Hū hit gebȳreþ to fōre-sceáwigenne *quōmŏdo oporteat provĭdēre,* L. Ecg. P. cont. i. 1; Th. ii. 170, 3. DER. sceáwian.

fōre-sceáwung, fōr-sceáwung, e; *f. A* FORESHEWING, *foreseeing, fore-sight, providence;* provĭdentia:—Beó ðē ān fōresceáwung *let there be one providence to thee,* Basil. admn. 3; Norm. 38, 17. Fōresceáwung Godes *God's providence,* Bt. 39, 4; Fox 216, 30: 39, 5; Fox 218, 21. Com hit mid Godes fōresceáwunge and bletsunge *it came with God's providence and blessing,* Homl. Th. i. 92, 22: Hexam. 8; Norm. 14, 15. On ðara þinga fōresceáwunge *in rērum provĭdentia,* Bd. 4, 10; S. 578, 7. Þurh godcundan fōresceáwunga *through divine providence,* Bt. 39, 13; Fox 234, 6: fōresceāuung *prudentia,* Rtl. 108, 25.

fōre-scyttels, es; *m.* [fōre, scyttels *a bolt, bar*] *A fore-bolt, bar;* repāgŭlum:—Ðæt ǣnig elda meahte swā fæstlīce fōrescyttelsas ō inhebban *that any one should ever raise up such firm bars,* Exon. 12 a; Th. 20, 4; Cri. 312.

fōre-secgan; *p.* -sægde, -sǣde; *pp.* -sægd, -sǣd *To* FORE-SAY, *foretell, predict, announce;* præfāri, prædicĕre, prædĭcāre, pronuntiāre, annuntiāre:—Ic fōresecge oððe bodige *prædīco,* Ælfc. Gr. 47; Som. 48, 40. Ðæt se bisceop Aidan ðām scypfarendum ðone storm toweardne fōresægde *ut episcŏpus Aidan nautis tempestātem fŭtūram prædixĕrit,* Bd. 3, 15; S. 541, 16: Ps. Th. 118, 172: 147, 8. Gerīses to fōresægcane gōdspell *oportet prædĭcari evangelium,* Mk. Skt. Lind. 13, 10. Iosue cwæþ ðā to ðām fōresǣdan ǣrendracum *Joshua then spoke to the aforesaid messengers,* Jos. 6, 22. [*Ger.* vor-sagen *to recite to a person.*]

fōre-sendan; ic -sende; *p.* -sende; *pp.* -sended *To send before;* præmittĕre:—Ic fōresende *præmitto,* Ælfc. Gr. 28, 4; Som. 31, 41.

fōre-seōn, to -seōnne; *p,* ic, he -seah, ðū -sāwe, *pl.* -sāwon; *pp.* -sewen *To see before,* FORESEE, *provide;* prævĭdēre, provĭdēre:—Swylce eác be heora andlyfene is to þenceanne and to fōreseónne *de eōrum quŏque stīpendio cōgĭtandum atque provĭdendum est,* Bd. 1, 27; S. 489, 21. Ðū ealle mīne wegas wel fōresāwe *omnes vias meas prævidisti,* Ps. Th. 138, 2. He fōreseah Godes cyricum and mynstrum micle frēcnesse towearde *he foresaw much peril awaiting God's churches and monasteries,* Bd. 3, 19; S. 549, 46: 3, 15; S. 542, 4. Ðæt he him on his biscopscīre gerisene stōwe fōresǣge and sealde, on ðære ðe he mid his geferum wunian mihte *ut in diœcēsi sua provĭdēret et dăret ei lŏcum, in quo cum suis apte dēgĕre pŏtuisset,* 4, 1; S. 565, 8. [*Ger.* vor-sehen *to foresee, provide.*]

fōre-seōnd, es; *m. One who foresees, a provider;* provisor:—Līcode ðam ārfæstan fōreseónde ūre hǣlo *plăcuit pio provisōri sălūtis nostræ,* Bd. 4, 23; S. 595, 13.

fōre-seōnes, -ness, -nys, -nyss, e; *f. A foreseeing, foresight, providence;* provīsio, provĭdentia:—Heó ða cūþestan andsware ðære upplīcan fōre-seónesse onfēng *accēpit ipsa certissĭmum sŭpernæ provīsiōnis responsum,* Bd. 4, 7; S. 575, 1. Mid ða godcundan fōreseónesse *dīvīna provīsiōne,* 5, 6; S. 619, 21. Mid ða ārfæstan fōreseónysse ūres alȳsendes *pia redemptōris nostri provīsiōne,* 4, 9; S. 576, 26.

fōre-setnes, -ness, -nys, -nyss, e; *f.* I. *a thing proposed, proposition, purpose, intention;* propŏsĭtio, propŏsĭtum:—Wæs seó cwēn lustfulliende ðære gōdan fōresetnesse and willan ðæs iungan *the queen rejoiced at the young man's good purpose and will,* Bd. 5, 19; S. 637, 32: 5, 20; S. 642, 17. Hēredodon hī his gemynd and his fōresetnesse *laudāvērunt ejus prŏpŏsĭtum,* 5, 19; S. 637, 26: 4, 23; S. 593, 15. Ic ontȳne on sealmlofe ingehygdnessa oððe fōresetnysse mīne *ăpĕriam in psaltērio propŏsĭtiōnem meam,* Ps. Lamb. 48, 5. Ic sprece fōresetnyssa fram frymþe *lŏquar propŏsĭtiōnes ab inĭtio,* 77, 2. II. *that which is placed before, a preposition;* præpŏsĭtio:—Præpŏsĭtio mæg beón gecweden on Englisc fōresetnyss *præpŏsĭtio may be called in English a fore-setting,* Ælfc. Gr. 47; Som. 47, 10: 5; Som. 3, 52.

fōre-settan; *p.* -sette, *pl.* -setton; *pp.* -seted, -sett *To set before, propose, shut, close in;* præpōnĕre, propōnĕre, præclūdĕre:—Hī ða ylcan Eald-Seaxan næfdon āgenne cyning, ac ealdormen wǣron heora þeóde fōresette *non hăbent rēgem iidem antīqui Saxŏnes, sed satrăpas suæ genti præpŏsĭtos,* Bd. 5, 10; S. 624, 23. He fōresette on his mōde ðæt he wolde cuman to Rōme *propŏsuit ănĭmo vĕnīre Rōmam,* 5, 19; S. 637, 23. Hī nā fōresetton ðē on gesihþe his *non propŏsuērunt te in conspectu suo,* Ps. Spl. 85, 13: 53, 3. Gemētton [MS. gemettan] we us storme fōresette *invĕnĭmus nos tempestāte præclūsos,* Bd. 5, 1; S. 613, 31.

fōre-settendlīc; *adj. Set before, prepositive;* præpŏsĭtīvus, Som. Ben. Lye.

fore-seuwenes, -ness, e; *f.* [=for-sewennes] *A despising, contempt, dishonour;* contemptus, dedĕcus:—On mīnre unwurþnesse and fore-seuwenesse *on account of my unworthiness and dishonour,* Bt. 5, 1; Fox 10, 23.

fōre-singend, es; *m. A fore-singer, one who pitches tunes, a precentor;* præcentor, Ælfc. Gl. 33; Som. 62, 37; Wrt. Voc. 28, 19.

fōre-sittan, *part.* -sittende; *p.* -sæt, *pl.* -sǣton; *pp.* -seten *To sit before* or *in front, to preside;* præsidēre:—Wæs fōresittende se Arcebiscop Þeodōrus *the Archbishop Theodore was presiding,* Bd. 4, 5; S. 571, 25. Fōresittendum Theodōre *præsĭdente Theodōro,* 4, 17; S. 585, 24. [*Ger.* vor-sitzen *to preside.*]

fōre-smeagan-smeágean *to premeditate;* præmĕdĭtāri:—Ne scyle gē on eówrum heortum fōresmeágean, hū gē andswarion *pōnĭte in cordĭbus vestris non præmĕdĭtāri, quemadmŏdum respondeătis,* Lk. Bos. 21, 14. Foresmeagan *scrutari, investigare,* Hpt. Gl. DER. smeágan.

fōre-smeáung, e; *f. Premeditation;* præmĕdĭtātio, Som. Ben. Lye.

fōre-snotor; *adj. Highly sagacious;* prudentissĭmus:—Fōresnotre men *highly sagacious men,* Beo. Th. 6305; B. 3163.

fore-spæc, e; *f. A speaking for* or *together, an assenting, agreement;* astipŭlātio:—Ðæt eall gelǣst sȳ ðæt on ūre forespæce stænt *that all be fulfilled which stands in our agreement,* L. Ath. v. § 3; Th. i. 232, 8. v. fore-spræc.

fōre-spæc, e; *f. A fore-speech, preface;* præfātio:—Fōrespæc *præfātio,* Ælfc. Gl. 90; Som. 74, 126; Wrt. Voc. 51, 39. v. fōre-spræc.

fore-speca, an; *m.* [=for, speca *a speaker*] *One who speaks for another, a sponsor, an advocate, a patron;* prolŏcūtor, advŏcātus:—Fore-speca [=for-speca] *causĭdĭcus, advŏcātus,* Ælfc. Gl. 48; Som. 65, 67; Wrt. Voc. 34, 2: Th. Diplm. A. D. 997; 539, 33; 540, 15.

fōre-specen; *part. Fore-spoken, aforesaid;* præfātus, prædictus:—Dō ðæt [MS. ðæs] leán to ðām fōrespecenan gōdum *add that reward to the aforesaid goods,* Bt. 37, 2; Fox 190, 2. v. fōre-sprecen.

fore-spræc, -spæc, e; *f.* [=for, spræc *a speech*] *A speaking for, a defence, an assenting, agreement;* defensio, excūsātio, astipŭlātio:—Ic secge ðæt sió forespræc ne dȳge, nāuðer ne ðam scyldigan, ne ðam ðe him foreþingaþ *I say that the defence does no good, neither to the guilty, nor to him who pleads for him,* Bt. 38, 7; Fox 210, 6.

fōre-spræc, fōre-spæc, e; *f.* [fōre- *fore-,* spræc *a speech*] *A fore-speech, preface, introduction, a speaking before for another, a fore-promise;* præfātio, præ-sponsio:—Ðis is seó fōrespræc hū S. Gregorius ðas bōc gedihte, ðe man Pastoralem nemnaþ *this is the preface how St. Gregory made this book which people call Pastoral,* Past. pref; Cot. MS. Beóþ ða ungewittigan- cild gehealdene on ðam fulluhte þurh fōresprǣce ðæs godfæder *unknowing children are saved in baptism by the fore-promise of the godfather,* Bd. Whelc. 180, 44.

fore-spreca, -spræca, an; *m.* [=for-speca] *One who speaks for another, an advocate;* prolŏcūtor, advŏcātus:—Ðæt he beó mīn freónd and forespreca, and ðære [MS. ðara] hālgan stōwe freónd and forespræca *that he be my friend and advocate, and the friend and advocate of the holy place,* Th. Diplm. A. D. 972; 524, 34-525, 1. He gebond feónda foresprecan *he bound the advocate of fiends [the devil],* Exon. 18 b; Th. 46, 6; Cri. 733. Cleopedon feónda foresprecan *the advocates of the fiends cried out,* 36 a; Th. 118, 7; Gū. 236. [*Ger.* für-sprecher, *m. an advocate.*]

fōre-sprecen, -specen, fōr-sprecen; *part.* FORE-SPOKEN, *aforesaid, fore-mentioned;* præfātus, prædictus:—Se fōresprecena here *the fore-mentioned army,* Chr. 896; Erl. 93, 34. Se fōresprecena Godes man *præfātus clērĭcus,* Bd. 1, 7; S. 477, 5. He on ðæt fōresprecene mynster gedōn and geþeóded wæs *he had been put in and joined to the aforesaid monastery,* 5, 19; S. 637. 29.

fōre-stæppan *to step* or *go before, precede,* Ælfc. Gr. 28, 4; Som. 31, 30: Ps. Lamb. 88, 15. v. fōre-steppan.

fōre-stæppend, es; *m.* [fōre-stæppende; *part. of* fōre-stæppan] *A stepper* or *goer before;* præcessor:—Se ðe fōrestæppend ys *qui præcessor est,* Lk. Bos. 22, 26.

fóre-stæppung, e; *f. A stepping before, preventing, anticipation;* præventio, antĭcĭpātio, Som. Ben. Lye.

fóre-stæpþ *steps before, precedes,* Homl. Th. ii. 82, 18; *pres. of* fóre-stapan.

fóre-standan; *p.* -stód, *pl.* -stódon; *pp.* -standen *To stand before, to excel;* præstāre:—Fórestandan *præstāre,* Cot. 149.

fóre-standende; *part. Standing before;* præstans:—Biscop oðđe fóre-standende *antistes,* Ælfc. Gr. 9, 26; Som. 11, 9.

fóre-stapan; he -stæpþ; *p.* ic, he -stóp, đú -stópe, *pl.* -stópon; *impert.* -stape, -stæpe, *pl.* -stapaþ; *pp.* -stapen *To step before, prevent, come* or *go before, precede;* prægrĕdi, prævĕnīre, præīre, præcēdĕre:—Forđan đú fórestópe hine on blætsungum *quŏniam prævēnisti eum in benedictiōnĭbus,* Ps. Lamb. 20, 4. Arís eálā Drihten, fórestæpe oðđe fórhrada hine *exsurge Dŏmĭne, prævĕni eum,* 16, 13. Đa đe fórestópon hine þreádon, đæt he súwode *qui præībant, incrĕpābant eum, ut tăcēret,* Lk. Bos. 18, 39. Fýr ætfóran him fórestæpþ *ignis ante ipsum præcēdet,* Ps. Lamb. 96, 3: Homl. Th. ii. 82, 18. Paulus fórestóp Stephanum *Paul preceded Stephen,* Homl. Th. ii. 82, 22.

fóre-steall, es; *m.* [fóre *before,* steall from stellan *to leap*] *A leaping before, forestalling, rescue;* assultus, interceptio:—Đa Iudéiscan ealdras geornlíce smeádon hú hí Hǣlend Crist acwellan mihton, ondrēdon him swā-đeáh đæs folces fóresteall *the Jewish elders earnestly deliberated how they might slay Jesus Christ, but they dreaded a rescue by the people,* Homl. Th. ii. 242, 14. v. fór-steal.

fóre-steóra, an; *m. A fore-steerer, man at the prow of a ship;* prōrēta, prōræ conductor, Cot. 149.

fóre-steppan, -stæppan, ic -steppe, -stæppe, he -stepþ, *pl.* -steppaþ, -stæppaþ; *p.* -stepede = -stepte? *pp.* -steped = -stept? *To step* or *come before, to prevent, go before, precede;* prægrĕdi, prævĕnīre, antĭcĭpāre, præcēdĕre:—Mín God fórscýt [MS. forscytte] oðđe fórestepþ me *Deus meus prævĕniet me,* Ps. Lamb. 58, 11. Fórhradien oðđe fóresteppen [MS. forhradian oðđe foresteppan] us đíne mildheortnessa *antĭcĭpent nos misericordiæ tuæ,* 78, 8. Ic fórestæppe *præcēdo,* Ælfc. Gr. 28, 4; Som. 31, 30. Mildheortnys and sóþfæstnys fóresteppaþ [Lamb. fórestæppaþ] ansýne đíne *misericordia et vēritas præcēdent făciem tuam,* Ps. Spl. 88, 15.

fóre-stígan; *p.* -stág, -stáh, *pl.* -stigon; *pp.* -stigen *To go before, to excel;* excellĕre:—Ic fórestíge *excelleo,* Ælfc. Gr. 26, 2; Som. 28, 45, MS. C. DER. stígan.

fóre-stihtod, -stihtud; *part.* [stihtian *to dispose, order*] *Fore-appointed* or *ordained, determined;* prædestĭnātus, dēfīnītus:—Fórestihtod, fóre-stihtud *prædestĭnātus,* Scint. de Prædest. Æfter đam đe fórestihtod wæs *sĕcundum quod dēfīnītum est,* Lk. Bos. 22, 22.

fóre-stihtung, e; *f. A fore-appointment;* prædestĭnātio, dispensātio:—Mid fórestihtunge đære godcundan árfæstnesse *by the dispensation of the divine mercy,* Bd. 4, 29; S. 607, note 42: Homl. Th. ii. 364, 29.

fóre-stóp, đú -stópe, *pl.* -stópon *stepped before, prevented, went before, preceded,* Ps. Lamb. 20, 4: Lk. Bos. 18, 39: Homl. Th. ii. 82, 22; *p. of* fóre-stapan.

fóre-swerian; *p.* ic, he -swór, đú -swóre, *pl.* -swóron; *pp.* -sworen *To* FORESWEAR, *declare before;* antejūrāre:—Đæt land, đe ic fóreswór heora fæderum *terram, pro qua* [*ante-*] *jūrāvi patrĭbus eōrum,* Num. 14, 23. Đæt land, đe đú hira fæderum fóreswóre *terram, pro qua* [*ante-*] *jūrasti patrĭbus eōrum,* 11, 12.

fóre-tácen, -tácn, es; *n. A* FORE-TOKEN, *presage, sign, wonder;* præsāgium, prodĭgium:—Fóretácn écra góda *a fore-token of eternal blessings,* Bt. 40, 2; Fox 236, 21: Ps. Spl. 77, 48: 70, 8. Đæt biþ fóretácna mǣst *that shall be the greatest of fore-tokens,* Exon. 21 a; Th. 55, 34; Cri. 893. He sette on him word tácna heora and fóretácna *pŏsuit in eis verba signōrum suōrum et prodigiōrum,* Ps. Spl. 104, 25. He sende fóretácna *emīsit prodĭgia,* 134, 9.

fóre-tácnian; *p.* ode; *pp.* od *To foreshow;* præmonstrāre:—Đætte seó sáwl þrówiende wæs, đætte se líchoma fóretácnode *quod anĭma passa sit căro præmonstrābat,* Bd. 3, 19; S. 549, 17.

fóre-teohung, -teohhung, e; *f. Predestination;* prædestĭnātio:—Sió godcunde fóreteohhung is ánfeald and unawendendlíc *the divine predestination is simple and unchangeable,* Bt. 39, 6; Fox 220, 16. Be đære fóreteohunga Godes *concerning the predestination of God,* Bt. titl. xxxix; Fox xviii. 16. v. fóre-tiohung.

fóre-teón; *p.* -teóde; *pp.* -teód *To pre-dispose, pre-ordain;* prædispōnĕre, præordĭnāre:—Swā đē bearn weorþaþ geboren syđđan, đa ylcan ic ǣr fóreteóde *ecce nātio fíliōrum tuōrum quibus dispŏsui,* Ps. Th. 72, 12. Swā monige swā fóreteóde wǣron to écum lífe *quotquot ĕrant præordĭnāti ad vītam æternam,* Bd. 2, 14; S. 517, 36.

fóre-téþ; *pl. m. The fore-teeth;* præcīsōres, Ælfc. Gl. 71; Som. 70, 101; Wrt. Voc. 43, 30. v. tóþ *a tooth.*

fóre-þanc, es; *m. Forethought, consideration;* consīdĕrātio:—Biþ andgit ǣghwǣr sēlest, ferhþes fóreþanc *understanding is everywhere best, forethought of mind,* Beo. Th. 2124; B. 1060. Náhton fóreþances wísdómes gewitt *they had no sense of wisdom's foresight,* Elen. Kmbl. 712; El. 356. Đa hát-heortan hie mid náne fóreþance nyllaþ gestillan *the furious will not calm themselves with any consideration,* Past. 40, 6; Cot. MS. v. fóre-þonc.

fóre-þanclíce; *adv. Considerately, prudently;* consīdĕrāte, provīde, Past. 15, 5, Lye.

fóre-þancolnes, -ness, e; *f. Forethought, prudence;* prūdentia:—Seó smeáung mínre heortan wile sprecan fóreþancolnesse *medĭtātio cordis mei lŏquētur prūdentiam,* Ps. Th. 48, 3.

fóre-þancul, -þoncol, fór-þoncol; *adj. Forethinking, provident, prudent;* prōvĭdus, prūdens:—Se fóreþancula wer *the provident man,* Past. 41, 5; Hat. MS. 57 b, 16.

fore-þencan; *p.* -þohte, *pl.* -þohton; *pp.* -þoht [= for-þencan] *To distrust, despair;* diffīdĕre, despērāre:—Đý-læs he hine for đære wynsuman wyrde fortrúwige, oðđe for đære rēđan foreþence *lest he on account of pleasant fortune should be arrogant, or on account of the affliction should despair,* Bt. 40, 3; Fox 238, 18.

fóre-þencan, -þencean; *p.* -þohte, *pl.* -þohton; *pp.* -þoht *To* FORETHINK, *consider beforehand;* præcōgĭtāre, præmĕdĭtāri:—Se láreów sceal mid geornfullíce ingehygde fóreþencean *the teacher must consider beforehand with careful meditation,* Past. 15, 5; Hat. MS. 20 a, 1.

fore-þingere, es; *m.* [fore = for, þingere *a pleader*] *One who pleads for another, an intercessor;* intercessor:—Sceolon đa æđelan Godes þeówas beón his folces foreþingeras *the noble servants of God should be the intercessors of his people,* Homl. Th. ii. 224, 11.

fore-þingian, for-þingian; *p.* ode; *pp.* od [fore = for, þingian *to plead*] *To plead for anyone, intercede, defend;* intercēdĕre, defendĕre:—Ic secge đæt sió forespræc ne dýge, náuđer ne đam scyldigan, ne đam đe him foreþingaþ *I say that the defence does no good, neither to the guilty, nor to him who pleads for him,* Bt. 38, 7; Fox 210, 7. Foreþinga for synnum mínum *intercēde pro peccātis meis,* Wanl. Catal. 293, 28, col. 2: 294, 25, col. 1. Ne cweđe ic ná đæt đæt yfel síe đæt mon helpe đæs unscyldigan, and him foreþingie *I do not say that it is wrong that a man should help the innocent, and defend him,* Bt. 38, 7; Fox 210, 4: L. Alf. pol. 21; Th. i. 76, 3: 24; Th. i. 78, 10.

fore-þingiend, es; *m. One who pleads for another, an intercessor;* intercessor:—Us Drihten sealde đē foreþingiend *nobis Dŏmĭnus dĕdit te intercessōrem,* Wanl. Catal. 294, 34, col. 1.

fore-þingrǣden, e; *f. A pleading for anyone, intercession;* intercessio:—Þurh foreþingrǣdena háligra martira đínra *per intercessiōnes sanctōrum martyrum tuōrum,* Wanl. Catal. 294, 16, col. 1. Ic gyrne fultum đínre foreþingrǣdene đú háligoste mægden and þrówystre *implōro auxĭlium tuæ interventiōnis sanctissĭma virgo et martyr,* 294, 6, col. 2.

fore-þingung, e; *f. A pleading for anyone, intercession;* intercessio:—Se Hǣlend hēt gehwilcne óđerne aþweán fram fúlum synnum mid fore-þingunge *the Saviour commanded each to wash the other from foul sins by intercession,* Homl. Th. ii. 242, 33. Þurh foreþingunga ealra háligra đínra gehýr me *per intercessiōnes omnium sanctōrum tuōrum exaudi me,* Wanl. Catal. 294, 20, col. 2. Mid gódum foreþingungum *with good ntercessions,* Bd. 4, 3; S. 568, 21, note, MS. Ca.; Rtl. 49, 34.

fóre-þonc, -þanc, es; *m. Fore-thought, providence;* provĭdentia:—Ananias, Azarias and Misahel þurh fóreþoncas fýr gebýgdon *Hananiah, Azariah and Mishael escaped the fire through providences,* i. e. *through their trust in the provisions of God,* Dei provĭdentiis *vel* provisiōnĭbus ignem supĕrārunt, Exon. 55 b; Th. 197, 16; Az. 191: 118 a; Th. 454, 22; Hy. 4, 37. Se fóreþonc is sió godcunde gesceádwísnes, sió đe eall fórewát *providence is the divine intelligence, which foreknows all,* Bt. 39, 5; Fox 218, 26. Se godcunda fóreþonc headeraþ ealle gesceafta *the divine providence restrains all creatures,* 39, 5; Fox 218, 30: 39, 5; Fox 220, 1, 2: 39, 6; Fox 220, 11. Be đam godcundan fóreþonce,—se godcunda fóreþonc stýreþ đone ródor and đa tunglu *with respect to divine providence,—the divine providence rules the sky and the stars,* Bt. 39, 8; Fox 224, 3-7.

fóre-þoncol; *adj. Sagacious, prudent;* prōvĭdus, prūdens:—Đæt fóre-þoncle men sægdon *what sagacious men said,* Exon. 25 a; Th. 73, 19; Cri. 1192. v. fóre-þancul.

fore-þýstrian; *p.* ede; *pp.* ed *To darken;* obscūrāre:—He sende þýstru and foreþýstrede *mīsit tĕnebras et obscūrāvit,* Ps. Spl. 104, 26. v. for-þeóstrian.

fóre-tíge, es; *m.* [tíge from tígan *to bind*] *A fore-binding place, market;* fŏrum:—Heó ys gelíc sittendum cnapum [MS. cnapun] on fóretíge *sĭmĭlis est puĕris sedentĭbus in fŏro,* Mt. Bos. 11, 16.

fóre-timbrigende; *part. Building before, shutting up;* præclūdens, Bd. 5, 1; S. 613, 31, note.

fóre-tiohung, -tiohhung, -teohung, -teohhung, e; *f. A fore-appointing, predestination;* prædestĭnātio:—Ǣr hit wæs Godes fóretiohung *before it was God's predestination,* Bt. 39, 6; Fox 220, 11: 39, 4; Fox 216, 31. Be đære Godes fóretiohunge *concerning the predestination of God,* 40, 5; Fox 240, 13. Sió godcunde fóretiohhung *the divine predestination,* 40, 6; Fox 242, 9. DER. tiohhian *to determine.*

fóre-týnd; *part. p. Foreclosed;* præclūsus:—Gemēttan we us ǣghwanan gelíce storme fóresette and fóretýnde *invĕnĭmus nos pări tempestāte præclūsos,* Bd. 5, 1; S. 613, 31.

fōre-wæs *was before* or *over*, Bd. 5, 18; S. 635, 35; *p. of* fōre-wesan.

fōre-ward, e; *f. An agreement, compact, treaty;* pactum, fœdus:—His brōđer griþ and fōrewarde eall æftercwæþ *his brother renounced all peace and agreement,* Chr. 1094; Erl. 229, 30, 31. Būton he đa fōrewarda geheólde *unless he kept the agreements,* Erl. 229, 32: Cod. Dipl. 732; A.D. 1016–1020; Kmbl. iv. 10, 16. v. fōre-weard, e; *f.*

fōre-ward; *adj. Forward, fore, former, early;* prōnus, antĕrior, prior:—On fōrewardre đyssere bēc ys awriten be me *in the fore part of this book it is written of me,* Ps. Th. 39, 8. v. fōre-weard; *adj.*

fōre-warde, an; *f. An agreement;* pactum:—Seó fōrewarde ǽr wæs gewroht *the agreement was formerly made,* Chr. 1094; Erl. 229, 34. v. fōre-weard, e; *f.*

fōre-weall, es; *m. A fore-wall, bulwark;* propugnācŭlum:—Syndon đa fōreweallas gestēpte ōþ wolcna hrōf *the fore-walls are raised to the clouds' roof [the water-walls in the Red Sea],* Cd. 158; Th. 196, 25; Exod. 297.

fōre-weard, -ward, fōr-word, -werd, e; *f:* fōre-warde, an; *f. A* FOREWARD, *precaution, contract, agreement, compact, treaty, provision;* præcautio, pactum, fœdus:—Wurdon đa fōrewearda full worhte *the contracts were completed,* Chr. 1109; Erl. 242, 22. To đān ylcan fōreweardum [MS. foreweardan] *with the same provisions,* Cod. Dipl. 731; A.D. 1013–1020; Kmbl. iv. 10, 6. Fōreweard *exordium,* Rtl. 69, 17. DER. weard, e; *f.* [*Dut.* voor-waarde, *f. condition, terms, pre-contract.*]

fōre-weard, es; *m. A forewarder, scout;* antecursor, explōrātor:—Siđđan Scipia geahsode đæt đa fōreweardas wǽron feor đam fæstenne gesette, he đā dȳgellīce gelǽdde his fyrde betuh đām weardum *when Scipio learned that the scouts [forewarders] were set far from the fastness, he then secretly led his army between the warders,* Ors. 4, 10; Bos. 95, 12. v. weard; *m.*

fōre-weard, fōr-weard, -werd, -ward; *adj.* FORWARD, *fore, former, early;* prōnus, antĕrior, prior:—Lǽteþ fōreweard hleór on strangne stān *he shall let his cheek [fall] forward on a strong stone,* Salm. Kmbl. 228; Sal. 113. In fōreweardum Danieles dagum *in the early days of Daniel,* Chr. 709; Erl. 42, 30. On fōreweard Eásterfæsten *in the fore [part of the] Easter-fast;* incipiente Quadragēsĭma, Bd. 5, 2; S. 614, 37. Fōreweard feng đara [MS. đære] lippena togædere *the fore-grasp of the lips together;* rostrum, Ælfc. Gl. 71; Som. 70, 95; Wrt. Voc. 43, 26. Fōreweard fōt *the fore [part of the] foot, the sole of the foot;* planta, Ælfc. Gl. 75; Som. 71, 95; Wrt. Voc. 45, 3. Đa sylfan tiid [= tīd] folc habbaþ fōreweard geár *at the same time people have the fore [part of the] year,* Menol. Fox 12; Men. 6. Fōrewearde heáfod *the forehead;* frons, Wrt. Voc. 70, 28. We sceolon mearcian ūre fōrewearde heáfod mid Cristes rōde tācne *we should mark our foreheads with the sign of Christ's cross,* Homl. Th. ii. 266, 11. Fōreweard lencten *the early spring;* ver nŏvum, Ælfc. Gl. 95; Som. 76, 12; Wrt. Voc. 53, 26. Hit wæs fōreweard middæg *it was the fore [part of] midday;* hōra sĕcunda diei, Bd. 4, 32; S. 612, 5. Wæs fōreweard niht *it was the early [part of] night;* prīma hōra noctis, Bd. 2, 12; S. 513, 19. On fōreweardre niht *in the early [part of] night;* prīmo tempŏre noctis, Bd. 5, 13; Whelc. 412, 15. Fōreweard nōsu *the fore-nose, extremity of the nose;* pirŭla [*q.v.* in Du Cange], Ælfc. Gl. 71; Som. 70, 90; Wrt. Voc. 43, 21. On đæs cyninges rīce fōreweardum *in the fore [part of the] reign of the king;* cujus regni princĭpio, Bd. 5, 2; S. 614, 24: 5, 23; S. 646, 3. Be đisses bisceopes līfes stealle fōreweardum *of the early state of this bishop's life;* de cujus pontĭfĭcis stătu vītæ ad priōra repĕdantes, Bd. 5, 19; S. 637, 2. Drihten đē gesett on fōreweard and nā on æfteweard *constĭtuet te Dŏmĭnus in căput et non in caudam,* Deut. 28, 13. Đū gesetst me on heáfod ođđe on fōreweardne þeóda *constĭtues me in căput gentium,* Ps. Lamb. 17, 44. [*Dut.* voor-waarts; *adv. forward.*]

fōre-werd; *adj. Forward, fore, former, early;* prōnus, antĕrior, prior, prīmus:—On fōrewerdne morgen ic drīfe sceáp mīne to heora lease *in prīmo māne mīno ŏves meas ad pascua,* Coll. Monast. Th. 20, 11. Fōrewerd swira *căpĭtium,* Wrt. Voc. 282, 42. Fōrewerd nāsū *pĭrŭla,* 282, 65. On fōrewerd đære bōc ođđe on heáfde bǽc awriten is be me *in căpĭte libri scriptum est de me,* Ps. Lamb. 39, 9. v. fōre-weard; *adj.*

fōre-wesan; *p.* ic, he -wæs, đū -wǽre, *pl.* -wǽron [fōre *before,* wesan *to be*] *To be before, to preside;* præesse:—Đyssum tīdum fōrewæs Norþan Hymbra rīce se strangesta cyning *his tempŏrĭbus regno Nordanhymbrōrum præfuit rex fortissĭmus,* Bd. 1, 34; S. 499, 18: 5, 18; S. 635, 35. v. wesan *to be.*

fōre-wīs; *adj. Forewise, foreknowing;* præscius, Cot. 149.

fōre-witan, fōr-witan; ic, he -wāt, đū -wāst, *pl.* -witon; *p.* -wiste, *pl.* -wiston; *pp.* -witen *To foreknow;* præscīre:—He eall fōrewāt hū hit geweorþan sceal *he foreknows all how it shall come to pass,* Bt. 39, 5; Fox 218, 27.

fōre-wītigian; *p.* ode, ade; *pp.* od, ad *To foresay, prophesy;* prænuntiāre:—Se mycla hunger, đe wæs fōrewītegad on Actibus Apostŏlōrum *the great famine, which was foretold in the Acts of the Apostles,* Chr. 47; Erl. 7, 24.

fōre-witig-wittig; *adj. Foreknowing;* præscius:—Fōrewitig towerdra þinga *præscius fŭtūri,* Ælfc. Gr. 41; Som. 44, 12; Hpt. Gl.

fōre-witol; *adj.* [witol *knowing*] *Foreknowing;* præscius, Lye.

fōre-witung, e; *f. A foreknowing, foretelling, presage;* præsāgium, Som. Ben. Lye.; Hpt. Gl.

fore-wrēgan; *p.* de; *pp.* ed *To accuse strongly;* valde accūsāre:—He būtan leahtrum wæs clǽne gemēted đara þinga đe hine mon forewrēgde *he was found without crimes clean of the things of which he was accused;* absque crīmĭne accūsātus fuisse inventus est, Bd. 5, 19; S. 639, 30.

fore-wrītan; *p.* -wrāt, *pl.* -writon; *pp.* -writen *To proscribe, banish;* proscrībĕre, Som. Ben. Lye.

fore-writennes, -ness, e; *f. Proscription, banishment, exile;* proscriptio, Som. Ben. Lye.

fore-wyrcan; *p.* -worhte; *pp.* -worht *To work for, do anything for anyone;* făcĕre alĭquid pro alĭquo:—Se man đane ōđerne æt rihte gebrenge, ođđe riht forewyrce *let the man bring the other to justice, or do justice for him,* L. H. E. 15; Th. i. 34, 2.

fōre-wyrd, e; *f.* [fōre, wyrd *an event*] *A deed done before;* antefactum, Som. Ben. Lye.

for-fang, -feng, fore-feng, -fong, es; *m.* I. *a seizing* or *rescuing of stolen* or *lost property;* apprehensio:—Be forstolenes mannes forfenge *of seizing a stolen man,* L. In. 53; Th. i. 134, 15, note 32. Be forstolenes ceápes forfenge *of the rescuing of stolen property,* 75; Th. i. 150, 4, note 7. II. *the reward for rescuing such property;* merces, quæ bŏnōrum surreptōrum restĭtūtōri dătur:—Forfang ofer eall fīftyne peningas *the reward for rescuing stolen property shall be everywhere fifteen pence,* L. Ff; Th. i. 224, 21. Embe forfang, witan habbaþ gerǽdd, đæt man ofer eall Engle-land gelīcne dōm healde; đæt is æt men fīftene peningas, and æt horse eal [MS. heal] swā ... Hwīlon stōd, đæt man æt ǽlcon þeófstolenan orfe ... and be his forfange sylle, đæt is, æt ǽlcon scill. penig, sȳ đæs cynnes orf đe hit sȳ, gyf hit man æt þeófes handa ahret; gyf hit đonne elles on hȳdelse funden sȳ, đonne mæg đæt forfangfeoh leóhtre beón *concerning the reward for rescuing stolen property, the counsellors have determined, that one shall hold like judgment all over England; that is for a man fifteen pence, and for a horse as much ... Formerly it stood, that for all stolen cattle ... and on its rescue one should pay, that is, for every shilling a penny, be the cattle of whatever kind it may, if one rescues it from the hands of the thief; but if otherwise it be found in a hiding-place, then the reward for rescuing may be less,* Th. i. 224, 24–226, 5.

for-fangen *forfeited,* L. Alf. pol. 2; Th. i. 62, note 9; *Seized,* Cd. 205; Th. 254, 19; Dan. 614; *pp. of* for-fōn.

forfang-feoh; *gen.* -feós; *n. The reward for rescuing stolen cattle* or *lost property;* merces, quæ bŏnōrum surreptōrum restĭtūtōri dătur:—Gyf hit đonne elles on hȳdelse funden sȳ, đonne mæg đæt forfangfeoh leóhtre beón *if otherwise it be found in a hiding-place, the reward for rescuing it may be less,* L. Ff; Th. i. 226, 5.

for-faran; *p.* -fōr, *pl.* -fōron; *pp.* -faren [for-, faran *to go*]. I. *to go* or *pass away, perish;* perīre:—Seó scipfyrd [MS. scipfyrde] ælmǽst earmlīce forfōr *almost all the ship-force perished miserably,* Chr. 1091; Erl. 227, 35. Hī mǽst ealle forfōron *they almost all perished,* 910; Erl. 101, 8, 33: 1096; Erl. 233, 22. II. *to cause to pass away, cause to perish, to destroy;* perdĕre:—Forfare hȳ man mid ealle *let a man totally destroy them,* L. E. G. 11; Th. i. 174, 2: L. C. S. 4; Th. i. 378, 9. Đæt man đa sāwla ne forfare đe Crist mid his āgenum līfe gebohte *that a man cause not the souls to perish which Christ bought with his own life,* L. C. S. 3; Th. i. 378, 2. Wæs swīđe feala manna forfaren *very many men were destroyed,* Chr. 1025; Erl. 163, 10. Mycel orfes wæs đæs geáres forfaren *much cattle was destroyed this year,* 1041; Erl. 169, 8. Wearþ micel his heres forfaren *many of his army were destroyed,* 1067; Erl. 204, 9. Fordoes ł forfæras *perdiderit,* Mt. Kmb. Lind. 10, 39.

fōr-faran; *p.* -fōr, *pl.* -fōron; *pp.* -faren [fōr *before,* faran *to go*] *To go before, get in front of;* præīre:—Fōrfōron him đone mūþan fōran on ūter mere *they got in front of them before the mouth [of the river] in the outer sea,* Chr. 897; Erl. 95, 21. [*O. Sax.* furfaran *to precede.*]

for-fēhþ *surprises,* Exon. 20 b; Th. 54, 25; Cri. 874; *3rd sing. pres. of* for-fōn.

for-feng *a seizing of stolen property,* L. In. 75; Th. i. 150, 4, note 7, MS. H. v. for-fang.

for-feran; *p.* de; *pp.* ed [for-, feran *to go*] *To go* or *pass away, perish;* pĕrire:—Fōrneáh ǽlc tilþ on mersclande forferde *very nearly all the tilth in the marsh-land perished,* Chr. 1098; Erl. 235, 13.

for-fleón; *p.* -fleáh, *pl.* -flugon; *subj. pres.* -fleó, *pl.* -fleón; *pp.* -flogen [for-, fleón *to flee*] *To flee away from, escape;* fŭgĕre, effŭgĕre:—Ic forfleó mīne hlǽfdian *a făcie dŏmĭnæ meæ ĕgo fŭgio,* Gen. 16, 8. Đæt gē đās towerdan þing forfleón *that ye escape those future things,* Lk. Bos. 21, 36.

for-fōn; ic -fō, đū -fēhst, he -fēhþ, *pl.* -fōþ; *p.* ic, he -fēng, đū -fēnge, *pl.* -fēngon; *pp.* -fangen, -fongen [for-, fōn *to take*]. I. *to be deprived of anything, forfeit;* ălĭquo prīvāri, amittĕre:—Næbbe his āgne forfongen [hæbbe his āgen forfangen MS. H.] *let him not have forfeited his own [let him have forfeited his own,* MS. H.], L. Alf. pol. 2; Th. i. 62, 6. II. *to take violently* or *by surprise, clutch, arrest, seize;*

vehementer căpĕre, imprōvīso adventu căpĕre, prehendĕre, apprehendĕre, deprehendĕre:—Swā þeóf sorgleáse hæleþ semninga forfēhþ slǣpe gebundne *as a thief suddenly surprises careless mortals bound in sleep*, Exon. 20 b; Th. 54, 25; Cri. 874. Ealle deáþrǣs forfēng *the death-rush clutched them all*, Andr. Kmbl. 1990; An. 997. Ǣr đū đa miclan meaht mīn forfēnge *ere thou didst arrest my great power*, Exon. 73 a; Th. 273, 26; Jul. 522. Forfōh đone frætgan, and fæste geheald *seize the proud one* [*the devil*], *and firmly hold* [*him*], Exon. 69 b; Th. 259, 18; Jul. 284. For đam gylpe gumena drihten forfangen wearþ, and on fleám gewāt *for that boast the lord of men* [*Nebuchadnezzar*] *was seized* [*with madness*], *and in flight departed*, Cd. 205; Th. 254, 19; Dan. 614. [*O. Sax.* farfahan: *Ger.* verfangen.]

for-fōr, *pl.* -fōron *passed away, perished*:—Seó scipfyrd earmlīce forfōr *the ship-force miserably perished*, Chr. 1091; Erl. 227, 35: 910; Erl. 101, 8; *p. of* for-faran.

fōr-fōr, *pl.* -fōron *went before, got in front of*:—Fōrfōron *went before*, Chr. 897; Erl. 95, 21; *p. of* fōr-faran.

for-fylden [fylden = fealden, *pp. of* fealdan *to fold up*] *Filled up, stopped, opposed*; obstructus, Cot. 148.

for-gǣgan; *p.* de; *pp.* ed *To transgress, prevaricate*; transgrĕdi, prætĕrīre, prævārĭcāre:—Ic forgǣge *prætĕreo*, Ælfc. Gr. 30, 5; Som. 35, 2. Hī Godes bebod forgǣgdon *they transgressed God's command*, Homl. Th. i. 112, 14. Đæt he Godes beboda ne forgǣge *that he transgress not God's commandments*, i. 604, 20. Ic geseah ǣslītendras ođđe đa forgǣgendan *vidi prævārĭcantes*, Ps. Lamb. 118, 158.

for-gǣgednys, -nyss, e; *f. A transgression, prevarication, stubbornness*; transgressio, prævārĭcātio, perversĭtas:—Hī wǣron deádlīce for đære forgǣgednysse *they became mortal through the transgression*, Boutr. Scrd. 20, 29. Cain wiste his fæder forgǣgednysse *Cain knew his father's transgression*, 20, 40. Þurh Adames forgǣgednysse *through Adam's transgression*, Homl. Th. ii. 268, 31. We sceolon ūre forgǣgednysse geandettan *we ought to confess our transgressions*, ii. 98, 25. Đæt gē ne beón scildige scamlīcre forgǣgednysse *ne sītis prævarĭcātiōnis rei*, Jos. 6, 18.

for-gæt, *pl.* -gǣton *forgot*, Ps. Lamb. 77, 11: 118, 61, = for-geat, *pl.* -geáton; *p. of* for-gitan.

for-gān, to -gānne; he -gǣþ; *p.* -eóde, *pl.* -eódon; *pp.* -gān *To* FOR-GO, *abstain from, pass over, neglect*; abstĭnēre, transcendĕre, prætĕrīre:—Đæt he smeáge hwæt him sȳ to dōnne and to forgānne *that he meditate what is for him to do and what to forgo*, L. C. S. 85; Th. i. 424, 6. We lǣraþ, đæt man freólsdagum and fæstendagum forgā āþas and ordēla *we enjoin, that a man on feast-days and fast-days forgo oaths and ordeals*, L. Edg. C. 24; Th. ii. 248, 28: 25; Th. ii. 250, 1. He forgǣþ đæs hūses dūru *transcendet ostium dŏmus*, Ex. 12, 23. Se đe đis forgǣþ [MS. forgæiþ], his sāwul losaþ *he who neglects this, his soul shall perish*, Homl. Th. i. 92, 2: pricle ne forgǣs *iota non præteribit*, Mt. Kmbl. Lind. 5, 18.

fōr-gān, fōre-gān; he -gǣþ; *p.* -eóde, *pl.* -eódon; *pp.* -gān *To go before, precede, stand out, project*; præcēdĕre, prōdīre:—Fōrgǣþ swā swā of fætnysse unrihtwīsnys heora *prōdit quasi ex adĭpe inīquĭtas eōrum*, Ps. Spl. 72, 7. [*Dut.* voor-gaan: *Ger.* vor-gehen *to go before.*]

fōr-gangan, fōre-gangan; *p.* -geóng, -gēng, *pl.* -geóngon, -gēngon; *pp.* -gangen *To go before, precede*; præīre, præcēdĕre:—Mildheortnes and sōþfæstnes fōrgangaþ đīnne andwlitan *misericordia et vērĭtas præībunt ante făciem tuam*, Ps. Th. 88, 13. v. fōr-gān.

for-geaf, đū -geáfe, *pl.* -geáfon *forgave, gave, gavest*, Cd. 30; Th. 40, 20; Gen. 642: Gen. 3, 12; *p. of* for-gifan.

for-geald *paid for, repaid*, Job Thw. 168, 17; *p. of* for-gildan.

for-geat, đū -geáte, *pl.* -geáton *forgot, hast forgotten*, Gen. 24, 67: Ps. Lamb. 41, 10: Jud. 3, 7; *p. of* for-gitan: for-geáte *should forget*, Ors. 6, 3; Bos. 118, 4; *p. subj. of* for-gitan.

for-gedōn; *p.* -gedyde, *pl.* -gedydon; *pp.* -gedōn *To do for, destroy*; perdĕre:—Ǣr Rōmaburh abrocen wǣre and forgedōn *ere the city Rome was broken into and done for*, Bd. 1, 11; S. 480, 10, note. v. for-dōn.

for-gef = for-geaf, *the perf. also for* for-gif, *the impert. of* for-gifan *to give, forgive*, Andr. Kmbl. 971; An. 486: Ps. C. 50, 45; Ps. Grn. ii. 277, 45: 50, 63; Ps. Grn. ii. 278, 63: 50, 139; Ps. Grn. ii. 280, 139: 50, 154; Ps. Grn. ii. 280, 154.

for-gefenes, -ness, e; *f. Forgiveness*, Ps. C. 50, 37; Ps. Grn. ii. 277, 37. v. for-gifnes.

for-geldan *to pay for, repay, return, give, render*; reddĕre, retrĭbuĕre:—Ic forgelde heom *retrĭbuam eis*, Ps. Lamb. 40, 11. Twentig scillinga forgelde *let him pay twenty shillings*, L. Ethb. 22; Th. i. 8, 6: 7; Th. i. 4, 9: 12; Th. i. 6, 8: 26; Th. i. 8, 12, 13: 32; Th. i. 12, 2. Hine man forgelde *let a man pay for him*, L. H. E. 4; Th. i. 28, 7: 11; Th. i. 32, 7. Đa māgas healfne leód forgelden *let his kindred pay half the fine* [*for slaying a man*], L. Ethb. 23; Th. i. 8, 8. v. for-gildan.

for-gēman *to neglect*, Prov. 19. v. for-gȳman.

for-gēmeleásian; *p.* ode; *pp.* od *To neglect*; neglĭgĕre:—Swylc gerēfa swylc đis forgēmeleásige *quilibet præfectus qui hoc neglĭgit*, L. Ath. iv. 1; Wilk. 62, 38. v. for-gȳmeleásian.

fōr-gesettenys, -nyss, e; *f. A proposition*; propŏsĭtio:—Ic atȳne on saltere fōrgesettenysse mīne *ăpĕriam in psaltĕrio propŏsĭtiōnem meam*, Ps. Spl. 48, 4. v. fōre-setnes.

for-get *forgets*, Bt. 3, 2; Fox 6, 9, = for-git, -giteþ; *3rd pres. sing. of* for-gitan: for-getst *forgettest*, Ps. Lamb. 43, 24, = for-gitst; *2nd pres. sing. of* for-gitan.

for-gēton *forgot*, Deut. 32, 18: Mt. Bos. 16, 5, = for-geáton; *p. pl. of* for-gitan.

for-giefan; *pp.* -giefen *To give, forgive, bestow, give up*; dăre, dēdĕre, remittĕre, dimittĕre, Exon. 93 a; Th. 348, 25; Sch. 33: 28 a; Th. 85, 33; Cri. 1400: 49 a; Th. 170, 4; Gū. 1106: 39 a; Th. 130, 2; Gū. 432. v. for-gifan.

for-gieldan *to pay for, repay, requite*; reddĕre:—Đæt he hine scolde forgieldan *that he should pay for it*, Past. 63; Hat. MS. We đē nū willaþ womma gehwylces leán forgieldan *we will now pay thee retribution for every crime*, Exon. 41 a; Th. 137, 16; Gū. 560: 117 a; Th. 450, 1; Dōm. 81. Forgield me đīn līf *give me thy life*, 29 b; Th. 90, 20; Cri. 1477. Forgielde he hine *let him pay for him*, L. In. 35, 36; Th. i. 124, 9, 18: 9; Th. i. 108, 5: 11; Th. i. 110, 4: 31; Th. i. 122, 6. v. for-gildan.

for-giémeleásian; *p.* ode; *pp.* od *To neglect*; neglĭgĕre:—Gif hwā adulfe pytt, and forgiémeleásode đæt he hine betȳnde *if anyone dug a pit, and neglected to inclose it*, Past. 63; Hat. MS. v. for-gȳmeleásian.

for-gietan *to forget*; oblīvisci:—Hȳ sceolon forgietan đære gesceafte *they shall forget the world*, Exon. 92 a; Th. 345, 4; Gn. Ex. 183. v. for-gitan.

for-gifan, -gyfan, -giefan; *p.* ic, he -geaf, đū -geáfe, *pl.* -geáfon; *pp.* -gifen. I. *to give, grant, supply, permit, give up, leave off*; dăre, dōnāre, præbēre, indulgēre, dēdĕre, relinquĕre:—Đæt wīf đæt đū me forgeáfe *mŭlier, quam dĕdisti mihi*, Gen. 3, 12. Manegum blindum he gesihþe forgeaf *cæcis multis dōnāvit vīsum*, Lk. Bos. 7, 21. He forgeaf wīd-brādne wēlan *he gave wide-spread bliss*, Cd. 30; Th. 40, 20; Gen. 642. Siđđan đis gedōn wæs, gesceóp God Adam, and him sāwle forgeaf *after this was done, God created Adam, and gave him a soul*, Ælfc. T. 4, 25-5, 1. Đisum men ic forgife hors *huic hŏmĭni do ĕquum*, Ælfc. Gr. 7; Som. 6, 21. Ne biþ đæt forgifen đætte alȳfed biþ *non indulgētur quod lĭcet*, Bd. 1, 27; S. 496, 1. He him his bearn forgeaf *he gave up his child to him*, Cd. 141; Th. 177, 4; Gen. 2924. Hlyst ȳst forgeaf *the storm left off being heard* [*hearing*], Andr. Kmbl. 3171; An. 1588. II. *to* FORGIVE, *remit*; remittĕre, dimittĕre, condōnāre:—Eádige beóþ đa, đe him beóþ heora unrihtwīsnesse forgifene *beāti, quorum remissæ sunt inīquĭtātes*, Ps. Th. 31, 1. Forgifaþ, gif gē hwæt agēn ǣnigne habbaþ *dimittite, si quid hăbētis adversus ălĭquem*, Mk. Bos. 11, 25. Fæder, forgif him *Păter, dimitte illis*, Lk. Bos. 23, 34. He forgifþ hit *he will forgive it*, Cd. 30; Th. 41, 25; Gen. 662. [*Dut.* ver-geven: *Ger.* ver-geben *to forgive, pardon.*]

for-gifenlīc, -gifendlīc, -gyfendlīc, -gyfenlīc; *comp. m.* ra; *f. n.* re; *sup.* ost; *adj.* I. *giving, dative*, or *giving* [*case*]; dātīvus:—Dātīvus is forgifendlīc *dative is giving*: Mid đam casu biþ geswutelod ǣlces þinges gifu *the gift of everything is declared by this case*. Đisum menn ic forgife hors *huic hŏmĭni do ĕquum*, Ælfc. Gr. 7; Som. 6, 19. II. *forgiving, pardonable, bearable*; remissus, tolerābĭlis:—Ic eów secge, đæt Sodom-warum, on đam dæge, biþ forgifenlīcre đonne đære ceastre *dīco vōbis, quia Sŏdŏmis, in die illa, remissius ĕrit quam illi cīvĭtāti*, Lk. Bos. 10, 12.

for-gifnes, -gyfnes, -ness, -nyss, -gifeness, -gyfenes, -gyfennes, -gifeniss, -gifenys, -gefenes, -ness, e; *f.* FORGIVENESS, *remission, indulgence, permission*; remissio, vĕnia, indulgentia:—Sȳ on đære bōte forgifnes [forgyfnes MS. A.] *let there be a remission in the compensation*, L. Edg. ii. 1; Th. i. 266, 5: L. Edg. S. 1; Th. i. 272, 9: 9; Th. i. 276, 3. Dō him his synna forgifenesse *grant him forgiveness of his sins*, Chr. 1086; Erl. 222, 39. Đæt he đa gȳmeleáste to forgyfenesse [forgyfnysse MS. F.] lǣte *that he grant forgiveness of the neglect*, L. Edg. S. 1; Th. i. 270, 17. His forgifnesse gumum to helpe dǣleþ dōgra gehwam Dryhten weoroda *the Lord of hosts dealeth his forgiveness each day for help to men*, Exon. 14 a; Th. 27, 7; Cri. 427. Se næfþ on ēcnysse forgyfenesse *non hăbēbit remissiōnem in æternum*, Mk. Bos. 3, 29. On hyra synna forgyfenesse *in remissiōnem peccātōrum eōrum*, Lk. Bos. 1, 77: 3, 3. On synna forgyfennesse *in remissiōnem peccātōrum*, Mt. Bos. 26, 28. Đæt fīftigođe gēr biþ hālig, and forgifenisse gēr *sanctĭfĭcābis annum quinquāgēsĭmum, et vŏcābis remissiōnem*, Lev. 25, 10. Mīn unrihtwīsnysse is māre đonne ic forgifenysse wyrđe sȳ *mājor est inīquĭtas mea, quam ut vĕniam mĕrear*, Gen. 4, 13. Đis ic cwēđe æfter forgifenysse nalæs æfter bebode *hoc autem dīco sĕcundum indulgentiam, non sĕcundum impĕrium*, Bd. 1, 27; S. 495, 45. To forgefenesse gāste mīnum *for forgiveness to my soul*, Ps. C. 50, 37; Ps. Grn. ii. 277, 37. [*Dut.* ver-giffenis, *f. pardon, forgiveness.*]

for-gifung, e; *f. A giving, gift, donation*; dōnātio:—Forgifung *dōnātio*, Ælfc. Gl. 13; Som. 57, 115; Wrt. Voc. 20, 52.

for-gildan, -gyldan, -gieldan, -geldan; he -gildeþ, -gilt; *p.* ic, he -geald, đū -gulde, *pl.* -guldon; *subj. pres.* -gilde, *pl.* -gilden; *p.* -gulde, *pl.* -gulden; *pp.* -golden *To pay for, make good, repay, requite, recompense*, *reward;* reddĕre, exsolvĕre, compensāre, retrĭbuĕre:—Him wile ēce Ælmihtig forgildan *the eternal Almighty will repay them,* Exon. 62 b; Th. 230, 17; Ph. 473. He him ðære lisse leán forgildeþ *he will pay him a reward for that affection,* Exon. 14 a; Th. 27, 22; Cri. 434. Eall he hit forgilt *he will recompense it all,* Bt. 42; Fox 258, 28. Swā hwæt swā man ðǽr of forstæl, ic hit forgeald *whatsoever has been stolen therefrom, I have repaid it;* quidquid furto pĕrībant, a me exīgēbas, Gen. 31, 39: Job Thw. 168, 17: Beo. Th. 3087; B. 1541: 5929; B. 2968: Cd. 158; Th. 197, 31; Exod. 315: 226; Th. 301, 8; Sat. 578. Ða forguldon yfelu for gōdum *retrĭbuērunt māla pro bŏnis,* Ps. Spl. 37, 21: Chr. 1039; Erl. 167, 20. Forgilde hine be his were *let him pay for him according to his value,* L. In. 11; Th. i. 110, 4, note 14, MS. H: 9; Th. i. 108, 5, note 14, MS. H: L. Ath. i. 1, 3; Th. i. 200, 1, 15: L. Edg. ii. 4; Th. i. 266, 25: Andr. Kmbl. 774; An. 387. Forgildan hȳ hine be his were *let them pay for him according to his value,* L. Ath. i. 1; Th. i. 198, 24. Ðæt hine man forgulde *that a man should pay for him.* L. Ath. v. § 6, 3; Th. i. 234, 11: Ps. Th. 65, 13. Gif ðū gōd dēst, hit biþ ðē mid gōde forgolden; gif ðū ðonne yfel dēst, hit biþ ðē mid yfele forgolden *if thou doest good, it shall be repaid thee with good; but if thou doest evil, it shall be repaid thee with evil,* Gen. 4, 7: Cd. 35; Th. 47, 6; Gen. 756: Beo. Th. 5679; B. 2843: Judth. 11; Thw. 24, 31; Jud. 217: Menol. Fox 302; Men. 152. Him wǽron eft forgoldene feówertyne þūsend sceápa *fourteen thousand sheep were repaid him,* Job Thw. 168, 19. [*Dut.* ver-gelden: *Ger.* ver-gelten *to reward, recompense.*]

for-gīman *to neglect,* Ex. 9, 21. v. for-gȳman.

for-gīmeleásian; *p.* ode; *pp.* od *To neglect entirely;* omnīno neglĭgĕre, neglĭgĕre:—Gif gē forgīmeleásiaþ Drihtnes bebod eówres Godes *if ye neglect the command of the Lord your God,* Deut. 8, 19. v. forgȳmeleásian.

for-gitan, -gytan, -gietan; ic -gite, ðū -gitest, -gitst, he -giteþ, -gitt, -git, *pl.* -gitaþ; *p.* ic, he -geat, -gæt, ðū -geáte, *pl.* -geáton, -gǽton, -gēton, *impert.* -git, *pl.* -gitaþ; *subj. pres.* -gite, *pl.* -giton; *p.* -geáte, *pl.* -geáten; *pp.* -giten; *v. trans. gen. acc.* [for-, gitan *to get*] *To* FORGET, *neglect;* oblīvisci, neglĭgĕre:—Hū lange wilt ðū, Drihten, mīn forgitan *quousque, Dŏmĭne, oblīviscĕris me?* Ps. Th. 12, 1: 118, 109. Ic forgite *oblīviscor,* Ælfc. Gr. 29; Som. 33, 54. Ic forgite [MS. forgeite] *neglĭgo,* 28, 5; Som. 31, 50. Hū lange, eálā Drihten, forgitst ðū me *usquequo, Dŏmĭne, oblīviscĕris me?* Ps. Lamb. 12, 1: Ps. Th. 41, 11. Ðæt man forgitt ða ǽrran geár *that the former years shall be forgotten,* Gen. 41, 30. Ne he ne forgit his wedd *neque oblīviscētur pacti,* Deut. 4, 31: Ps. Th. 9, 32: Bt. Met. Fox 3, 11; Met. 3, 6. Sȳn gecyrrede to helle ealle þeóda ða ðe forgitaþ God *convertantur in infernum omnes gentes qui oblīviscuntur Deum,* Ps. Lamb. 9, 18. Ic forgeat to etanne mīnne hlāf *oblītus sum comĕdĕre pānem meum,* 101, 5: 118, 153, 176. Ǽ ðīne ic ne forgæt *lēgem tuam non sum oblītus,* Ps. Lamb. 118, 61, 109, 141. For hwī forgeáte ðū mīn *quāre oblītus es mei?* 41, 10. Nǽfre nāuht he ne forgeat *he has never forgotten anything,* Bt. 42; Fox 258, 1: Bd. 3, 2; S. 525, 13: Gen. 24, 67: Ps. Spl. 9, 12. Ne we ne forgeáton ðē *nec oblīti sŭmus te,* Ps. Lamb. 43, 18. Gē forgēton Drihten *oblītus es Dŏmĭni,* Deut. 32, 18. Hig his hālgan ǽ forgeáton *they forgot his holy law,* Jud. 3, 7: Ps. Lamb. 105, 21: 118, 139: Cd. 227; Th. 305, 6; Sat. 642. Hig forgǽton his welldǽda *oblīti sunt benefactōrum,* Ps. Lamb. 77, 11. Hig forgēton ðæt hig hlāfas nāmon *oblīti sunt pānes accĭpĕre,* Mt. Bos. 16, 5: Cd. 149; Th. 186, 25; Exod. 144. Ne forgit ðū þearfena *ne oblīviscāris paupĕrum,* Ps. Lamb. second 9, 12: 44, 11: Ps. Th. 73, 18, 22. Gemunaþ and ne forgitaþ, hū swīðe gē gremedon Drihten *mĕmento et non obliviscāris, quōmŏdo ad īrācundiam provŏcāvĕris Dŏmĭnum,* Deut. 9, 7. Óþ-ðæt he forgite ða þing, ðe ðū him dydest *dōnec oblīviscātur eōrum, quæ fēcisti in eum,* Gen. 27, 45. Ðæt gē nǽfre ne forgiton Drihtnes wedd *ne quando oblīviscāris pacti Dŏmĭni,* Deut. 4, 23: 6, 12. Ðæt he hī ðe-læs forgeáte *that he should the less forget them,* Ors. 6, 3; Bos. 118, 4: Cd. 40; Th. 52, 25; Gen. 849. Ðe ðū forgiten hafst *which thou hast forgotten,* Bt. 36, 2; Fox 174, 22: Ps. Lamb. second 9, 11: Ps. Th. 77, 13. Manige licggaþ deáde, mid ealle forgitene *many lie dead, entirely forgotten,* Bt. 19; Fox 70, 13: Bt. Met. Fox 10, 120; Met. 10, 60. Án ðē is forgeten *unum tibi deest,* Mk. Skt. Lind. 10, 21. [*Dut.* ver-geten: *Ger.* ver-gessen *to forget.*]

for-gitel *forgetful, forgetting.* v. for-gytel.

for-gitelnes, -ness, e; *f. Forgetfulness, a forgetting;* oblīvio:—Ne forgitelnes byþ ðæs þearfan *non oblīvio ĕrit paupĕris,* Ps. Lamb. 9, 19. v. for-gytelnes.

for-gitennes, -ness, e; *f. Forgetfulness, oblivion;* oblīvio, Som. Ben. Lye.

for-glendrad; *part. p. Conglūtĭnātus, allectus:*—Gebīged oððe forglendrad oððe gelīmod is to eorþan wambe ūre *conglūtĭnātus est in terra venter noster,* Ps. Lamb. 43, 25.

for-glendran; *p.* ade, ede; *pp.* ad, ed [glendran *to devour*] *To eat greedily, devour voraciously;* lurcāri, devŏrāre:—Forglendrad *lurcātus,* Cot. 124. Ealle heora snytru beóþ yfele forglendred *omnis săpientia eōrum devŏrāta est,* Ps. Th. 106, 26: Blickl. Hom. 99, 9. Forglendred *serviunculus?* Wrt. Voc. 290, 49. Forglendrad *conglūtĭnātus?* = glūtītus *devoured,* vel glūtĭnātus *glued together,* Ps. Lamb. 43, 25.

for-gnād *rubbed together, broke,* Ps. Lamb. 104, 16; *p. of* for-gnīdan.

for-gnagan; *p.* -gnōg, *pl.* -gnōgon; *pp.* -gnagen [for-, gnagan *to gnaw*] *To gnaw* or *eat up;* corrōdĕre, comĕdĕre:—On eallum grōwendum þingon hig forgnagaþ *omnia quæ nascuntur corrōdent, sive comĕdent,* Ex. 10, 5. Gærstapan forgnōgon swā hwæt swā se hagol belǽfde *locusts gnawed up whatsoever the hail had left,* Homl. Th. ii. 194, 1.

for-gnīdan, -gnȳdan, -cnīdan; he -gnīt; *p.* ic, he -gnād, ðū -gnide, *pl.* -gnidon; *pp.* -gniden [for-, gnīdan *to rub*] *To rub together, dash* or *throw down, break;* contĕrĕre, allīdĕre, elīdĕre:—He forgnād oððe he tobrytte treów gemǽru heora *contrīvit lignum fīnium eōrum,* Ps. Lamb. 104, 33, 16: Ps. Spl. 106, 16. Grin forgniden is, and we alȳsde synd *lăqueus contrītus est, et nos lībĕrāti sŭmus,* Ps. Spl. 123, 7. Heorte forgnidene God nā beheóld *cor contrītum Deus non despĭcies,* Ps. Spl. 50, 18. He forgnīt hine *allīdit illum,* Mk. Bos. 9, 18. Forðon ðū forgnide me *quia allīsisti me,* Ps. Spl. 101, 11. Drihten arǽreþ ealle forgnidene *Dŏmĭnus erĭgit omnes elīsos,* Ps. Spl. 144, 15.

for-gnidennys, -nyss, e; *f. Contrition, sorrow;* contrītio:—Tobrytednys oððe forgnidennys and ungesǽlignys [syndon] on wegum heora *contrītio et infēlīcĭtas [sunt] in viis eōrum,* Ps. Lamb. 13, 3.

for-gnīsednys, -nyss, e; *f. Bruisedness, sorrow, contrition;* contrītio, Som. Ben. Lye.

for-gnōg, *pl.* -gnōgon *gnawed up,* Homl. Th. ii. 194, 1; *p. of* forgnagan.

for-gnȳdan; *pp.* -gnyden *To dash* or *throw down;* elīdĕre:—On eorþan forgnyden, fǽmende he tearflode *elīsus in terram, vŏlūtābātur spūmans,* Mk. Bos. 9, 20. v. for-gnīdan.

for-golden *paid for, repaid,* Judth. 11; Thw. 24, 31; Jud. 217; *pp. of* for-gildan.

for-grand *crushed,* Beo. Th. 852; B. 424; *p. of* for-grindan.

for-grāp *grasped,* Beo. Th. 4695; B. 2353; *p. of* for-grīpan.

for-grindan; *p.* -grand, *pl.* -grundon; *pp.* -grunden [for-, grindan *to grind*] *To grind thoroughly, grind to pieces, grind down, crush, pulverize, mangle, consume, destroy;* commōlĕre, contĕrĕre, contundĕre, confringĕre, pulvĕrāre, lăcĕrāre, demōlīri:—Forgrindan *commōlĕre,* Cot. 35. Ic forgrand gramum *I fiercely* (?) *crushed* [*them*], Beo. Th. 852; B. 424. Ðǽr læg secg manig, gārum forgrunden *there lay many a warrior, ground to pieces by javelins,* Chr. 937; Th. 202, 21, col. 2; Æðelst. 18. Billum forgrunden *ground down with swords,* Andr. Kmbl. 826; An. 413. Biþ beorhtast nesta bǽle forgrunden *the brightest of nests is pulverized by the fire,* Exon. 59 a; Th. 213, 20; Ph. 227. Wundum forgrunden *mangled with wounds,* Chr. 937; Erl. 114, 9; Æðelst. 43. Glēdum forgrunden *consumed* or *destroyed by fire,* Beo. Th. 4659; B. 2335: 5347; B. 2677.

for-grīpan; *p.* -grāp, *pl.* -gripon; *subj. pres.* -grīpe, *pl.* -grīpen; *pp.* -gripen [for-, grīpan *to grasp*] *To grasp, snatch away, seize, assail, overwhelm;* corrĭpĕre, comprehendĕre, apprehendĕre, vim afferre, obruĕre:—Âdle forgripen *languōre correptus,* Bd. 5, 7; S. 620, 40, note. He þohte forgrīpan gumcynne *he resolved to overwhelm mankind,* Cd. 64; Th. 77, 14; Gen. 1275. Ðonne fȳr æpplede gold gīfre forgrīpeþ *when fire greedily grasps appled gold,* Exon. 63 a; Th. 232, 15; Ph. 507: Ps. Th. 58, 12. He æt gūþe forgrāp Grendeles mǽgum *he in conflict grasped Grendel's kinsmen,* Beo. Th. 4695; B. 2353. Æbylignes yrres ðīnes hī forgrīpe *indignātio īræ tuæ apprehendat eos,* Ps. Th. 68, 25. Ðonne we hine forgrīpen *when we seize him,* Ps. Th. 70, 10: 138, 9. Ðeáh gē mīnne flǽschoman fȳres wylme forgrīpen *though ye assail my body with fire's heat,* Exon. 38 a; Th. 124, 31; Gū. 346. [*O. Sax.* fargrīpan *to seize for destruction: Ger.* ver-greifen *to take away.*]

fōr-grīpan; *p.* -grāp, *pl.* -gripon; *subj. pres.* -grīpe, *pl.* -grīpen; *pp.* -gripen *To take before, carry off prematurely, pre-occupy;* prærĭpĕre, præ-occŭpāre:—Wæs heó mid deáþe fōrgripen *illa morte prærepta est,* Bd. 3, 8; S. 532, 27: 3, 29; S. 561, 17. Ðȳ-læs hit sī mid deáþe fōrgripen *ne morte præ-occŭpētur,* 1, 27; S. 492, 30, note. [*Ger.* vorgreifen *to anticipate, forestall.*]

for-grōwan; *p.* -greów, *pl.* -greówon; *pp.* -grōwen [for-, grōwan *to grow*] *To grow up, grow into;* increscĕre:—Se ǽr in dæge wæs dȳre, scrīðeþ nū deóp feor, brondhord geblōwen, breóstum in forgrōwen *copper was dear in* [*that*] *day, now it circulates wide and far, an ardent treasure flourishing, grown up in the hearts,* Exon. 94 b; Th. 354, 16; Reim. 46.

for-gulde *should pay for* or *repay,* Ps. Th. 65, 13; *p. subj. of* forgildan. For-guldon *paid for,* Ps. Spl. 37, 21; *p. pl. of* for-gildan.

for-gyfan; *pp.* -gyfen *To give, forgive, supply;* dăre, ministrāre, remittĕre, dimittĕre, Lk. Bos. 7, 48: Mt. Bos. 6, 12: 18, 21: Mk. Bos. 2, 7: Lk. Bos. 6, 37: Bd. 1, 25; S. 486, 29: Exon. 28 a; Th. 85, 9; Cri. 1388. v. for-gifan.

for-gyfendlīc, -gyfenlīc; *adj. Forgiving, pardonable, tolerable;* remissus:—Tyro and Sydone byþ forgyfendlīcre [MS. forgyfendlīcur] on dōmes dæg, ðonne eów *it shall be more pardonable for Tyre and Sidon in the day of judgment, than for you;* Tyro et Sidoni remissius ĕrit in die jūdĭcii quam vōbis, Mt. Bos. 11, 22. Sodomwara lande byþ forgyfenlīcre on dōmes dæg, ðonne ðē *terræ Sŏdŏmōrum remissius ĕrit in die jūdĭcii, quam tĭbi*, Mt. Bos. 11, 24: Lk. Bos. 10, 14. v. for-gifenlīc.

for-gyfenes, -gyfennes, -gyfnes, -ness, -nyss *forgiveness, remission*, Mt. Bos. 26, 28: Lk. Bos. 3, 3: L. Edg. ii. 1; Th. i. 266, 5, MS. A: L. Edg. S. 1; Th. i. 270, 17, MS. F. v. for-gifnes.

for-gyldan; ic -gylde, ðū -gylst; *subj. pres.* -gylde, *pl.* -gylden; the other inflections as in for-gildan *To pay for, repay, requite, recompense, reward*:—Hwī nolde God him forgyldan his bearn be twīfealdum *why would not God repay him his children twofold?* Job Thw. 168, 23: L. Ath. v. § 8, 8; Th. i. 238, 10. Hēht forgyldan *commanded to pay for*, Beo. Th. 2112; B. 1054; Fins. Th. 79; Fin. 39: Lk. Bos. 10, 35: Ps. Th. 88, 29: Ps. Lamb. 141, 8: L. Ethb. 4; Th. i. 4, 3: L. In. 9; Th. i. 108, 5, note 14, MS. B: 11; Th. i. 110, 4, note 14, MS. B: L. Ath. i. 1; Th. i. 198, 17: i. 2; Th. i. 200, 11: L. Edm. S. 1; Th. i. 248, 4: Ps. Th. 141, 9: Beo. Th. 1916; B. 956: L. Ath. i. 6; Th. i. 202, 16: Byrht. Th. 132, 47; By. 32.

for-gyltan *to become guilty, to commit*; committĕre, Scint. Ben. Lye. [*Orm.* forrgilltenn: *A. R.* vorgulte *p. p.*] v. gyltan.

for-gȳman, -gīman; *p.* de; *pp.* ed [for, gȳman *to take care*] *To neglect, pass by, transgress*; neglĭgĕre, prætĕrīre, transgrĕdi:—He ða forþgesceaft forgyteþ and forgȳmeþ *he forgets and neglects the future state*, Beo. Th. 3506; B. 1751. Hwī forgȳmaþ ðīne leorningcnihtas ūre yldrena lage *quāre discĭpŭli tui transgrĕdiuntur tradĭtiōnem sĕniōrum?* Mt. Bos. 15, 2. Hwī forgȳme gē Godes bebod for eówre lage *quāre vos transgrĕdĭmĭni mandātum Dei propter tradĭtiōnem vestram?* 15, 3. Se ðe Drihtnes word forgīmde, he forlēt his men and nȳtenu ūte *qui neglexit sermōnem Dŏmĭni, dimīsit servos suos et jūmenta in agris*, Ex. 9, 21. Ic nǣfre ðīn bebod ne forgȳmde *nunquam mandātum tuum prætĕrĭvi*, Lk. Bos. 15, 29. Hie þegnscipe Godes forgȳmdon *they neglected the service of God*, Cd. 18; Th. 21, 20; Gen. 327. Forgȳmdon hig ðæt *illi neglexĕrunt*, Mt. Bos. 22, 5. Ne forgȳm ðū ðīnes Drihtnes steóre *be not heedless of thy Lord's correction*, Homl. Th. ii. 328, 21. [*O. Sax.* fargūmōn *to neglect.*]

for-gȳmednes, -ness, e; *f. Neglect*; neglĭgentia, Som. Ben. Lye.

for-gȳmeleásian, -gīmeleásian, -giémeleásian, -gēmeleásian; *p.* ode; *pp.* od [for-, gȳmeleásian *to neglect*] *To neglect entirely*; omnīno neglĭgĕre:—Forgȳmeleásian *neglĭgĕre*, Scint. 81: Fulg. 18. Gif he forgȳmeleásaþ his hlāfordes gafol *if he neglect his lord's tribute*, L. Edg. S. 1; Th. i. 270, 15. Swylc gerēfa swylc ðis forgȳmeleásie *such reeve as may neglect this*, L. Ath. iv. 1; Th. i. 222, 2. Forgȳmeleásod beón *neglectus esse, neglĭgi*, R. Ben. 36.

forgȳmeleásnes, -ness, e; *f. Carelessness, neglect*; neglĭgentia, Som. Ben. Lye.

fōr-gyrd, es; *m. A fore-girdle, martingale*; antela, cingŭlum illud quod ante pectus ĕqui tendĭtur, Som. Ben. Lye. v. forþ-gyrd.

for-gytan; ic -gyte, ðū -gytest, -gytst, he -gyteþ, -gyt, *pl.* -gytaþ; *impert.* -gyt, *pl.* -gytaþ; *subj.* -gyte, *pl.* -gytan; *pp.* -gyten *To forget*; oblīvisci:—Nylle ðū forgytan ealle edleánunga oððe edleán his *nōli oblīvisci omnes retrĭbūtiōnes ejus*, Ps. Lamb. 102, 2: Ps. Th. 118, 93: Ps. Lamb. 118, 16, 83, 93: 136, 5: Ps. Th. 43, 25: Beo. Th. 3506; B. 1751: Ps. Lamb. 76, 10: 43, 21: 49, 22: 73, 19, 23: Ps. Th. 136, 5: Ps. Lamb. 77, 7: 58, 12. The other forms as in for-gitan.

for-gytel, -gytol, -gyttol; *adj. Forgetful, forgetting*; oblīviōsus:—He næs forgytel [forgyttol, Homl. Th. ii. 118, 19] *he was not forgetful*, Nat. S. Greg. Els. 5, 11. Forgytele we ne synt ðē *nec oblīti sŭmus te*, Ps. Lamb. 43, 18. He nis forgytol clypunge þearfena *non est oblītus clāmōrem paupĕrum*, 9, 13.

for-gytelnes, -gitelnes, -ness, -nyss, e; *f. Forgetfulness, forgetting, oblivion*; oblīvio:—On lande forgytelnysse *in terra oblīviōnis*, Ps. Lamb. 87, 13. Forgytelnesse geseald ic eom *oblīviōni dătus sum*, 30, 13. Forgytelnesse sȳ geseald seó swīðre mīn *oblīviōni dētur dextĕra mea*, 136, 5.

for-habban; *part.* -hæbbende; *p.* -hæfde, *pl.* -hæfdon; *impert.* -hafa, *pl.* -habbaþ; *pp.* -hæfed, -hæfd; *v. trans. To hold in, restrain, retain, abstain, refrain*; tĕnēre, contĭnēre, cŏhĭbēre, prōhĭbēre, abstĭnēre:—Ne meahte wæfre mōd forhabban in hreðre *he might not retain his wavering courage in his heart*, Beo. Th. 2306; B. 1151: 5211; B. 2609. He ðǣr sum fæc on forhæbbendum līfe lifede *ălĭquandiu contĭnentissĭmam gessit vītam*, Bd. 5, 11; S. 626, 16. Ðæt mynster ōþ gyt to dæge Englisce menn ðǣr on ælþeódignysse hī forhabbaþ *quod vĭdēlĭcet mōnastērium usque hŏdie ab Anglis tĕnētur incŏlis*, 4, 4; S. 571, 17. Forbeód oððe forhafa oððe bewere tungan ðīne fram yfle *prŏhĭbe linguam tuam a mălo*, Ps. Lamb. 33, 14. Hit forhæfed gewearþ ðætte hie sǣdon swefn cyninge *it was denied them that they should say the dream to the king*, Cd. 179; Th. 225, 1; Dan. 147. Hyra eágan wǣron forhæfde *ŏcŭli illōrum tĕnēbantur*, Lk. Bos. 24, 16.

for-hæfedesta; *m. sup. Most continent*; contĭnentissĭmus:—Se hālgesta wer and se forhæfedesta *vir sanctissĭmus et contĭnentissĭmus*, Bd. 4, 3; S. 569, 41; *sup. of* for-hæfed, *pp. of* for-habban.

for-hæfednes, -hæfdnes, -ness, -nys, -nyss, e; *f. Restraint, continence, abstinence*; contĭnentia, abstĭnentia:—Forhæfednyss [MS. -hefednyss] *abstĭnentia*, Ælfc. Gr. 43; Som. 45, 7. He hæfde swȳðe mycle geornnysse sibbe and sōþre lufan and forhæfdnesse and eádmōdnysse *stŭdium vĭdēlĭcet pācis et cārĭtātis, contĭnentiæ et hŭmĭlĭtātis*, Bd. 3, 17; S. 545, 7. Ða fægerestan bȳsne his gingrum forlēt, ðæt he wæs micelre forhæfdnysse and forwyrnednesse līfes *sălūberrĭmum abstĭnentiæ vel contĭnentiæ clērĭcis exemplum relīquit*, 3, 5; S. 526, 21. On forhæfednysse and on eádmōdnysse *in continence and in humility*, 4, 3; S. 569, 1, 37. Lifde se man his līf on mycelre forhæfdnesse *the man lived his life in great continence*, 4, 25; S. 599, 28. Ðæt is wundor ðæt ðū swā rēðe forhæfednesse and swā hearde habban wylt *mīrum quod tam austēram tĕnēre continentiam vĕlis*, 5, 12; S. 631, 33.

for-hæl, -hǣle, -hǣlon; *p. indic. subj. indic. pl. of* for-helan *to conceal*, Glostr. Frag. 4, 20.

for-hǣlde, es; *m?* [for, hǣlde, *p. of* hǣlan *to heal*] *An offence*; offensa, Cot. 148, Lye.

for-hātan; *p.* -hēt, -hēht; *pp.* -hāten [for, hātan *to call*] *To renounce, forswear*; renuntiāre, ejurāre:—Būton he hit forhāten hæbbe *unless he have forsworn it*, L. Ælf. P. 47; Th. ii. 384, 30.

for-hātena, an; *m.* [hātan *to call* or *name*] *An ill-named*, or *a reprobate person*; fāmōsus, perdĭtus:—Ðā se forhātena spræc *then spake the reprobate one*, Cd. 29; Th. 38, 20; Gen. 609.

fōr-heáfod, es; *n. The fore part of the head*, FOREHEAD, *skull*; ancĭput? calvārium:—Fōrheáfod *ancĭput?* Ælfc. Gl. 69; Som. 70, 34; Wrt. Voc. 42, 42. Fōrheáfod *vel* heáfodpanne *calvārium*, 69; Som. 70, 33; Wrt. Voc. 42, 41.

for-healdan *to withhold, keep back, disregard*; detinēre, neglĭgĕre, contemnĕre:—Hæfdon hȳ forhealden helm Scylfinga *they had disregarded the helm of the Scylfings* [*had deserted him*], Beo. Th. 4751; B. 2381: Bt. 29, 1; Fox 102, 17. [*Ger.* ver-halten *to reserve, withhold, conceal.*]

for-healden *polluted*; incestus, Cot. 105.

fōr-heard; *adj. Very hard*; prædūrus;—Wulfmǣr forlēt fōrheardne gār faran eft ongeán *Wulfmær let the piercing dart fly back again*, Byrht. Th. 136, 24; By. 156.

for-heardian; *p.* ode; *pp.* od *To harden, become hard*; indūrāre:—He forheardaþ and fordrugaþ *indūret et arescat*, Ps. Lamb. 89, 6. [*Dut.* ver-harden *to harden*: *Ger.* ver-härten *to grow hard, to harden.*]

for-heáwan; *p.* -heów; *pp.* -heáwen *To hew* or *cut down, cut in pieces, slaughter*; concīdĕre, occīdĕre:—Hȳ forheówan Heaðobeardna þrym *they slaughtered the host of Heathobeards*, Scōp. Th. 99; Wīd. 49: Byrht. Th. 135, 9; By. 115. [*Ger.* ver-hauen *to cut down.*]

for-helan, he -hilþ; *p.* -hæl, *pl.* -hǣlon; *subj. p.* -hǣle, *pl.* -hǣlen; *pp.* -holen *To cover over, hide, conceal*; celāre, occultāre, abscondĕre:—Ðe hit forhelan þenceþ *who seeks to conceal it*, Exon. 91 a; Th. 340, 25; Gn. Ex. 116. Hū mæg ic forhelan Abrahame, ðe ic dōn wille *num celāre potĕro Abraham, quæ factūrus sum?* Gen. 18, 17. Forhele ic incrum Hērran hearmes swā fela *I will conceal from your Lord so much calumny*, Cd. 27; Th. 36, 29; Gen. 579. Gif he hit forhilþ *if he hide it*, Lev. 5, 1. Ne biþ ðǣr wiht forholen *there shall be naught concealed*, Exon. 23 b; Th. 65, 14; Cri. 1054. Ðæt he ðæs hālgan hǣse forhǣle his hlāforde *that he should conceal the saint's command from his Lord*, Glostr. Frag. 4, 20. Ðæt mīne cræftas and ānweald ne wurden forgitene and forholene *that my talents and power should not be forgotten and concealed*, Bt. 17; Fox 60, 9. [*Dut.* ver-helen: *Ger.* ver-hehlen *to conceal.*]

for-hergian, -heregian, to -hergianne; *part.* -hergiende, -hergende; *p.* ode, ade, ede; *pp.* od, ad, ed *To lay waste, destroy, ravage, devastate, plunder*; vastāre, devastāre, depŏpŭlāre:—Ne wile he ealle ða rīcu forsleán and forheregian *will he not slay and destroy all the kingdoms?* Bt. 16, 1; Fox 50, 3. Mid ðȳ se ylca cyning gedyrstelīce here lǣdde to forhergianne Pehta mǣgþe *idem rex, cum tĕmĕre exercĭtum ad vastandam Pictōrum prōvinciam duxisset*, Bd. 4, 26; S. 602, 16. Forhergiende *depŏpŭlans*, 1, 15; S. 483, 44. Forhergende, 4, 7; S. 574, 30. Ceadwala eft forhergode Cent *Ceadwalla again ravaged Kent*, Chr. 687; Erl. 43, 2: 1000; Erl. 137, 2. Ecgfriþ Norþan-Hymbra cyning sende wered and fyrd on Hibernia Scotta eálonde, and hī ða unscæððendan þeóde, and symble Angelcynne ða holdestan earmlīce forhergodon *Ecgfrid rex Nordanhymbrōrum misso Hĭberniam exercĭtu vastāvit mĭsĕre gentem innoxiam et nātiōni Anglōrum ămīcissĭmam*, Bd. 4, 26; S. 602, 7. Ceadwalla and Mul Cent and Wieht forhergedon *Ceadwalla and Mul ravaged Kent and Wight*, Chr. 686; Erl. 40, 25. Fēng to rīce Honorius, twām geárum ǣr Rōma burh abrocen and forhergad wǣre *Honorius succeeded to the sovereignty, two years before the city Rome was broken into and devastated*, Bd. 1, 11; S. 480, 10. Seó hreównes ðæs oft cwedenan wōles feor and wīde eall wæs forheregod and fornumen *tempestas sæpe dictæ clādis lāte cuncta depŏpŭlans*, 4, 7; S. 574, 30, MS. B. Hī forhergode wǣron *they were plundered*, Chr. 1013; Erl. 149, 19. [*Ger.* ver-heeren *to destroy, lay waste.*]

for-hergung, -heriung, e; *f. A molesting, devastation, annoyance, trouble*; vastātio, infestātio:—Mid forhergunge gebysmerad *disgraced by pillage*, Ors. 2, 4; Bos. 45, 1: Cot. 108.

for-hicgan, -higan; *p.* ede, de; *pp.* ed *To neglect, reject, despise, condemn*; despĭcĕre, spernĕre:—Se wæs middangeard forhicgende *he was despising the world*; cum esset contemptu mundi insignis, Bd. 5, 9; S. 623, 25. Se ðe me forhigþ *qui spernit me*, Jn. Bos. 12, 48. We forhicgaþ on arīsendum on us *spernēmus insurgentes in nōbis*, Ps. Spl. 43, 7. Driht nā forhigede and ne forseah bēne þearfena *Dŏmĭnus non sprēvit neque despexit deprecātiōnem paupĕris*, 21, 23. Nā he forhigde bēne heora *non sprēvit prĕcem eōrum*, 101, 18. v. for-hycgan.

for-hilþ *hides*, Lev. 5, 1; *3rd sing. pres. of* for-helan.

for-hogednes, -hogodnes, -hogydnys, -ness, e; *f*: for-hogung, e; *f*. *Contempt, disdain;* contemptus:—Fatu on forhogednysse hæfde *vāsa despectui hăbĭta*, Bd. 3, 22; S. 552, 15. Gefylled we synd forhogodnesse *replēti sŭmus despectiōne*, Ps. Spl. M. C. 122, 4.

for-hogian; *p.* ede, ode; *pp.* ed, od [hogian *to be anxious*] *To neglect, despise, accuse;* neglĭgĕre, spernĕre:—Hwylc wracu him forhogiende æfter fyligde *quæ illos spernentes ultĭo sĕcūtā sit*, Bd. 2, 2; S. 502, 4. Ealle middaneardlīce þing swā swā ælfremede forhogigende *despising all earthly things as entirely foreign ones*, Nat. S. Greg. Els. 35, 4. He forhogaþ, ðæt he hīre uncre lāre *mŏnĭta nostra audīre contemnit*, Deut. 21, 20. Driht nā forhogode and ne forseah bēne þearfena *Dŏmĭnus non sprēvit neque despexit deprecātiōnem paupĕris*, Ps. Spl. C. 21, 23. Forhogedun Drihtnes bebod *contempsistis impĕrium Dŏmĭni*, Deut. 9, 23. Ða Sundor-hālgan forhogodon ðæs Hǣlendes geþeaht *Pharĭsæi consĭlium Dei sprēvērunt*, Lk. Bos. 7, 30. We forhogien on arīsendum on us *spernēmus insurgentes in nōbis*, Ps. Spl. T. 43, 7. Forhogedre āre heora anddetnesse *contempta revĕrentia suæ professiōnis*, Bd. 4, 25; S. 601, 15. Gif he ðonne eów forhogige, sī ðonne he fram eów forhogod *sin autem vos sprēvĕrit, et ipse spernātur a vobis*, 2, 2; S. 503, 12, 13.

for-hogung *contempt*, Ps. Spl. 118, 22. v. for-hogednes.

for-hogydnys *contempt*, Cambr. MS. Ps. 118, 22. v. for-hogednes.

for-holen *concealed, hidden*, Exon. 23 b; Th. 65, 14; Cri. 1054: Lk. Skt. Lind. 8, 17; *pp. of* for-helan.

forhōrwade *was dirty;* obsorduit, Hymn.

fōr-hradian, -hradigan; *p.* ode; *pp.* od *To hasten before, anticipate, prevent;* prævĕnīre, præoccŭpāre:—Utan fōrhradian his ansȳne on andetnesse *prœoccŭpēmus făciem ejus in confessiōne*, Ps. Lamb. 94, 2. Se sylfa deáþ ðære ādle yldinge fōrhradaþ *death itself prevents the tarrying of the disease*, Homl. Th. ii. 124, 12. Fōrhradode Godes mildheortnys us *God's mercy prevented us*, ii. 84, 13. Ðonne hie fōrhradigaþ ðone tīman gōdes weorces *when they anticipate the time of a good work*, Past. 39, 3.

fōr-hraðe; *adv. Very quickly, soon;* cĭto, confestim:—Æfter ðam ðæs fōrhraðe *very soon after that*, Chr. 921; Erl. 107, 6, 24. v. fōr-raðe.

for-hrēred; *part. Annulled, made void;* cassātus:—Forhrēred *cassāta*, Ælfc. Gl. 49; Som. 65, 99; Wrt. Voc. 34, 28. v. hrēran.

forhswebung, e; *f. A storm;* prŏcella, Ps. Spl. T. 106, 25.

FORHT; *adj.* I. *fearful, timid, affrighted;* tĭmĭdus, păvĭdus, terrĭtus, trĕpĭdus:—Ne beó ðū on sefan tō forht *be not thou too fearful in mind*, Andr. Kmbl. 196; An. 98: Beo. Th. 1512; B. 754. Næs he forht *he was not afraid*, 5927; B. 2967: Andr. Kmbl. 2172; An. 1087: Rood Kmbl. 41; Kr. 21. Heó com forht *trĕmens vēnit*, Lk. Bos. 8, 47. To hwī synt gē forhte *quid tĭmĭdi estis?* Mt. Bos. 8, 26: Mk. Bos. 4, 40. We beóþ forhte on ferþþe *we are fearful in soul*, Exon. 70 b; Th. 262, 5; Jul. 328: Ps. Th. 64, 8: Bd. 5, 19; S. 640, 33. He sent on eów forhte heortan *dăbit tĭbi cor păvĭdum*, Deut. 28, 65. Nō ðȳ forhtra wæs Gūþlāces gǣst *the soul of Guthlac was not the more fearful*, Exon. 35 b; Th. 114, 14; Gū. 172. II. *terrible, dreadful, formidable;* terrĭbilis, formīdŏlōsus:—Ne wile forht wesan brōðor ōðrum *a brother will not be formidable to another*, Exon. 112 b; Th. 430, 20; Rā. 44, 11. On ða forhtan tīd *in that dreadful time*, Hy. 10, 56; Hy. Grn. ii. 294, 56. [*O. Sax.* foraht, forht, furht: *O. H. Ger.* forht *tĭmĭdus, tĭmens*: *Goth.* faurhts.] DER. an-forht, ge-, un-.

forht-full; *adj. Fearful;* formīdŏlōsus, Coll. Monast. Th. 22, 21.

forhtian, forhtigan, forhtigean, forhtgean; to forhtianne; *part.* forhtiende, forhtigende; *p.* ode, ede; *pp.* od, ed [forht *affrighted*, and the terminations -an, -anne, -gan]. I. *v. intrans. To be afraid* or *frightened, tremble;* pāvēre, trĕmĕre, trĕpĭdāre, formīdāre:—Ongan he forhtian, and sārgian *cœpit păvēre, et tædēre*, Mk. Bos. 14, 33: Boutr. Scrd, 21, 22. Ongunnon hī forhtigan *they began to be afraid*, Bd. 1, 23; S. 485, 30. Forhtigean, Ps. Th. 113, 7. To heora mōde gelǣddum ðære forhtiendan tīde *reducto ad mentem trĕmendo illo tempŏre*, Bd. 4, 3; S. 569, 25. Flugon forhtigende *trembling they fled*, Cd. 166; Th. 206, 15; Exod. 452; Bd. 4, 7; S. 575, 8. Ic forhtige *formīdo*, Ælfc. Gr. 36; Som. 38, 50. Hie forhtiaþ *they will be afraid*, Rood Kmbl. 227; Kr. 115: Ps. Th. 67, 9. Ðǣr hig forhtodon mid ege *illic trĕpĭdāvērunt tĭmōre*, Ps. Lamb. 52, 6. He bæd ðæt ne forhtedon nā *he bade that they should not be afraid*, Byrht. Th. 132, 25; By. 21. Ne sȳ eówer heorte gedrēfed, ne ne forhtige gē *non turbētur cor vestrum, neque formīdet*, Jn. Bos. 14, 27. Ðæt ōðre forhtian *that others may fear*, Homl. Th. ii. 300, 15. II. *v. trans. To fear, be frightened at, dread;* tĭmēre:—Ic ne forhtige wiht I *fear nothing*, Ps. Th. 61, 2: 54, 2. Ne forhtast ðū on dǣge flān on lyfte *non tĭmēbis a săgitta vŏlante in die*, 90, 6. Ðe Drihten forhtaþ *qui tĭmet Dŏmĭnum*, 127, 5: 60, 4. Ða ðē on feore forhtigaþ, ða me on fægere geseóþ *qui tĭment te, vĭdēbunt me*, 118, 74. Ne nān þing ne forhtgeaþ *fear nothing*, Deut. 1, 20. DER. a-forhtian, on-.

forhtiendlīc, forhtigendlīc; *adj. Timorous, fearful;* metĭcŭlōsus, Cot. 129.

forht-līc; *adj. Timid, fearful, trembling;* trĕpĭdus, terrĭbilis:—Him forhtlīce fǣrspel bodedon *they fearful announced to them the sudden news*, Judth. 12; Thw. 25, 5; Jud. 244. Fleóþ forhtlīce þunres brōgan *they, being afraid, shall flee the terror of [thy] thunder;* a vōce tŏnitrui tui formīdābunt, Ps. Th. 103, 8. On ða forhtlīce sorgum wlītaþ *on which, they, frightened, look sorrowfully*, Exon. 24 a; Th. 68, 15; Cri. 1104. [*O. Sax.* forhtlīk *terrible.*]

forht-līce; *adv. Fearfully, tremblingly;* trĕpĭde:—Ǣghwylc wille feores forhtlīce aþolian *every one will fearfully endure life*, Exon. 27 a; Th. 81, 7; Cri. 1320: R. Ben. interl. 5.

forht-mōd; *adj. Mind-frighted, timid, pusillanimous;* trĕpĭdus anĭmo, păvĭdus:—He forhtmōd wāfode *he was hesitating, being frightened in mind*, Ælfc. T. 35, 23. Ic sceal eaforan mīne forhtmōd fergan *I, being timid, must convey my children*, Exon. 104 b; Th. 397, 1; Rā. 16, 13.

forhtnys, fyrhtnes, -ness, e; *f. Fear, amazement, terror, dread;* tĭmor:—Ðā aforhtode Isaac micelre forhtnisse *expāvit Isaac stupōre vehĕmenti*, Gen. 27, 33.

forhtra *more fearful:*—Ne beóþ gē ðȳ forhtran *be ye not the more fearful*, Cd. 156; Th. 194, 11.

forhtudon = forhtodon *trĕpĭdāvērunt*, Ps. Spl. 13, 9; *p. of* forhtian *to fear, tremble.*

forhtung, e; *f.* [forht, ung] *Fear;* păvor:—Būton blācunge and forhtunge *without paleness and fear*, Homl. Th. i. 72, 28: ii. 560, 15. On forhtunge *in păvōre*, Ps. Lamb. 30, 23.

for-hwǣga, -hwāga; *adv. At least;* saltem:—Forhwǣga on fīf mīlum oððe on syx mīlum fram ðæm feó *at least within five or six miles from the property*, Ors. 1, 1; Bos. 22, 35. Forhwāga on ānre mīle fram ðæm tūne *at least within one mile from the town*, 1, 1; Bos. 22, 30.

for-hwām *wherefore, why.* v. hwā *who; interrog.*

for-hwerfan *To transform, pervert;* transformāre, pervertĕre:—Cnihtas wurdon ealle forhwerfde to sumum dióre *the men were all transformed to some beast*, Bt. Met. Fox 26, 172; Met. 26, 86: Bt. 38, 1; Fox 196, 2. Eówra sāwla mā forhwerfdon ðonne hie gerihton *they have perverted more of your souls than they have directed*, L. Alf. 49; Th. i. 56, 18. v. for-hwyrfan.

for-hwī, -hwig *For why, wherefore;* quāre, cur, Ps. Th. 113, 5; Nicod. 4; Thw. 2, 19.

for-hwon *why;* quāre, Bd. 2, 6; S. 508, 14: 2, 12; S. 513, 37.

for-hwyrfan, -hwerfan; *part.* -hwyrfende; *p.* -hwyrfde; *pp.* -hwyrfed, -hwyrfd. I. *to change for* or *from, transform, transfer, remove;* avertĕre, transformāre:—He forhwyrfþ eów of ðam lande *he will remove you from the land*, Deut. 28, 63. Sī se man awirged, ðe forhwyrfe his freóndes landgemǣro *maledictus hŏmo, qui transfert termĭnos proxĭmi sui*, Deut. 27, 17. II. *to turn aside, pervert, deprave;* subvertĕre, pervertĕre, deprāvāre:—Ðisne we gemētton forhwyrfende ūre þeóde *hunc invēnĭmus subvertentem gentem nostram*, Lk. Bos. 23, 2. Swylce he ðis folc forhwyrfde *as if he perverted this people*, 23, 14. Ðā forhwyrfed wæs *when it was perverted*, Exon. 8 a; Th. 3, 11; Cri. 34. Mid forhwyrfedum forhwyrfed ðū bist *cum perverso pervertēris*, Ps. Spl. T. 17, 28. Hwyrf ðē wið ða forhwyrfdan *cum perverso pervertēris*, Ps. Th. 17, 25.

for-hycgan *To despise, reject;* despicĕre, contemnĕre, spernĕre:—Ðe forhycgeaþ God *who despise God*, Ps. Th. 52, 6. Ðæt ic ne forhycge *I reject it not*, Exon. 63 b; Th. 235, 4; Ph. 552.

for-hȳdan *To hide;* abscondĕre:—Forhȳddan meinwitgyrene *abscondērunt mĭhi lăqueōs*, Ps. Th. 139, 5.

for-hygde-līc; *adj. Despisable;* contemptĭbilis:—Forhygdelīc oððe forsewen *contemptus*, Ps. Lamb. 118, 141.

for-hylman; *p.* de; *pp.* ed *To cover over, conceal;* obdūcĕre, occŭlĕre:—Ne dorste forhylman Hǣlendes bebod *he dared not conceal the Saviour's command*, Andr. Kmbl. 1469; An. 736.

for-hȳnan; *p.* -hȳnde; *pp.* -hȳned, -hȳnd [hȳnan *to humble, put down*] *To cast down, humble, oppress, waste;* hŭmĭliāre, opprĭmĕre, vastāre:—Ðone forhȳndan and þearfan gerihtlǣcaþ *hŭmĭlem et paupĕrem justĭfĭcāte*, Ps. Lamb. 81, 3. Forhȳned *cast down*, Ors. 3, 7; Bos. 62, 10. Wǣron Pene forhȳnde *the Carthaginians were cast down*, Ors. 4, 10; Bos. 95, 30. Mid ðam bryne Rōme burh wæs swīðe forhȳned *the city Rome was brought very low by that burning*, Ors. 6, 1; Bos. 115, 41.

for-hyrdan; *p.* de; *pp.* ed; *v. trans. To harden against, to harden;* obdūrāre:—Nǣfre gē heortan geþanc deorce forhyrden *nolīte obdūrāre corda vestra*, Ps. Th. 94, 8.

for-lācan; *p.* -lēc, -leólc; *pp.* -lācen *To seduce, betray, deceive;* sedūcĕre, decĭpĕre:—Ðū leóda feala forleólce and forlǣrdest *thou hast deceived and seduced many people*, Andr. Kmbl. 2727; An. 1366. Forlēc hie mid ligenum *he seduced her with lies*, Cd. 30; Th. 40, 30; Gen. 647. Hie seó wyrd forleólc *fate deceived them*, Andr. Kmbl. 1227; An. 614. He wearþ on feónda geweald forlācen *he was betrayed into the foes' power*, Beo. Th. 1811; B. 903.

for-lǣdan; *p.* -lǣdde; *pp.* -lǣded, -lǣdd, -lǣd *To mislead, lead astray, seduce;* sedūcĕre:—Forlǣdan and forlǣran *to mislead and pervert*, Cd. 23

Th. 29, 18; Gen. 452: 32; Th. 43, 17; Gen. 692. Ic bepǽce oððe forlǽde *sedūco*, Ælfc. Gr. 47; Som. 48, 53. He ðæs folces ðone mǽstan dǽl mid ealle forlǽdde *he wholly misled the greatest part of the people*, Ors. 1, 12; Bos. 35, 41. Hie forlǽddon swǽse gesíþas *they misled their dear associates*, Beo. Th. 4084; B. 2039. Forlǽdd be ðâm lygenum *misled by lies*, Cd. 28; Th. 37, 31; Gen. 598. Ðeáh heó wurde forlǽd mid ligenum *though she was misled with lies*, 30; Th. 39, 23; Gen. 630: Past. 58; Hat. MS. Men synt forlǽdde *men are misled*, Cd. 33; Th. 45, 18; Gen. 728. [*O. Sax.* farlêdean: *Dut.* ver-leiden: *Ger.* verleiten *to mislead, seduce: Laym.* forledeþ *leads astray.*]

for-lǽge *neglected, disgraced*:—Ðý-læs seó mynegung [MS. mynugung] forlǽge *lest the giving notice should be neglected*, L. Ath. v. § 7; Th. i. 234, 29; *subj. of* forlicgan. v. licgan.

for-lǽran; to -lǽranne; *p.* -lǽrde; *pp.* -lǽred *To misteach, deceive, seduce, corrupt, pervert*; decĭpĕre, sedūcĕre, corrumpĕre:—Forlǽdan and forlǽran *to mislead and pervert*, Cd. 23; Th. 29, 18; Gen. 452: 32; Th. 43, 17; Gen. 692. Handweorc Godes to forlǽranne *to deceive God's handywork*, 33; Th. 44, 3; Gen. 703. Ðû leóda feala forleólce and forlǽrdest *thou hast deceived and seduced many people*, Andr. Kmbl. 2727; An. 1366. Hie seó wyrd forlǽrde *fate mistaught them*, 1227; An. 614: Elen. Kmbl. 415; El. 208. Ðe hig forlǽrdon *who deceived them*, Num. 31, 16. Ðû me forlǽred hæfst *thou hast seduced me*, Cd. 38; Th. 50, 34; Gen. 818: Ex. 14, 11. [*Dut.* ver-leeren *to unteach.*]

for-lǽtan; ic -lǽte, ðû -lǽtest, -lǽtst, he -lǽteþ, -lêteþ, *pl.* -lǽtaþ; *p.* -lêt, -leórt, -leót, *pl.* -lêton; *pp.* -lǽten [for, lǽtan]. I. *to let go, permit, suffer*; permittĕre:—Sum eorþlíc ǽ forlǽtaþ *some earthly law permits*, Bd. 1, 27; S. 491, 2. II. *to relinquish, forsake, omit, neglect*; relinquĕre, omittĕre, prætĕrīre:—Forlǽt se man fæder and môder, and geþeót hine to his wífe *the man shall leave father and mother, and join himself to his wife*, Gen. 2, 24. [*Dut.* ver-laten: *Ger.* ver-lassen *to leave, quit, abandon, forsake.*]

for-lǽtennys, -lǽtnys, -nyss, -ness, e; *f. A leaving, remission, desolation, loss*; intermissio, remissio, desōlātio, perdĭtio:—Þeóstru ne synd nân þing bûton leóhtes forlǽtennyss *darkness is nothing but the departure of light*, Boutr. Scrd. 20, 46. On synna forlǽtnysse bæþe *lavacro peccātōrum remissiōnis*, Bd. 2, 14; S. 518, 10. On synna forlǽtnesse *in remissiōnem peccātōrum*, 5, 6; S. 620, 3. On forlǽtnysse *in desōlātiōnem*, Ps. Spl. 72, 19. On forlǽtennysse *in perdĭtiōne*, 87, 12. Forlǽtnes gôda *loss of goods*, Lchdm. iii. 172, 2.

for-leás *lost*, Beo. Th. 5715; B. 2861; *p. of* for-leósan.

for-lêc *seduced, deceived*, Cd. 30; Th. 40, 30; Gen. 647; *p. of* forlâcan.

for-legen *fornicated, committed fornication*, Gen. 38, 24; *pp. of* forlicgan. [*Orm.* forrleȝenn.]

for-legenes, -legnes, -ness, -nys, -nyss, e; *f. Fornication*; fornĭcātio:—Bûton forlegenysse þingum *excepta fornĭcātiōnis causa*, Mt. Bos. 5, 32. He swylce unalýfeddre forlegnesse and egeslícre wæs besmiten *fornĭcātiōne pollūtus est tāli*, Bd. 2, 5; S. 506, 39.

for-legere, es; *m. A fornicator*; fornĭcātor, Som. Ben. Lye. v. forliger, es; *m.*

for-legis, -legiss, e; *f. A fornicatress, harlot*; mĕretrix:—Ðû hæfst forlegisse andwlitan *frons mĕretrīcis facta est tĭbi*, Past. 52, 2; Hat. MS. Cwæþ Crist be Marian ðære forlegisse *Christ spoke of Mary the harlot*, Past. 52, 9; Hat. MS.

for-legystre, an; *f. A harlot*; mĕretrix, Som. Ben. Lye. v. for-legis.

for-leógan; *p.* -leág, *pl.* -lugon; *pp.* -logen [leógan *to lie*] *To lie greatly, belie*; valde mentīri, ementīri:—Hí mid leásum gewitum forleógan woldon *they would lie with false witnesses*, Homl. Th. ii. 248, 16. Leáse gewitan hine forlugon *false witnesses belied him*, Homl. Th. i. 44, 28. Mænige synd forsworene and swýðe forlogene *permulti sunt perjūri et mendāces*, Lupi Serm. 1, 12; Hick. Thes. ii. 102, 41.

for-leólc *seduced, deceived*, Andr. Kmbl. 1227; An. 614; *p. of* forlâcan.

for-leósan, he -lýst; *p.* ic, he -leás, ðû -lure, *pl.* -luron; *subj. pres.* -leóse, *pl.* -leósen; *p.* -lure, *pl.* -luran, -luren; *pp.* -loren *To lose, let go, destroy*; amittĕre, perdĕre, destruĕre:—He wolde forleósan líca gehwilc *he would destroy each body*, Cd. 64; Th. 77, 26; Gen. 1281. His treówe for feógýtsunge forleósan *fĭdem suam amōre pĕcūniæ perdĕre*, Bd. 2, 12; S. 514, 40. Ic forleóse *amitto*, Ælfc. Gr. 28, 4; Som. 31, 41. Gif he forlýst ân of ðâm *si perdĭdĕrit ūnam ex illis*, Lk. Bos. 15, 4. Ic forleás *perdĭdĕram*, Lk. Bos. 15, 9. Ðû forleóse lâþra gehwylcne *mayest thou destroy every one of my enemies*, Ps. Th. 142, 12. Ðam ðe ǽr his elne forleás *to him who had before lost his courage*, Beo. Th. 5715; B. 2861. Ðû nâne myrhþe ne forlure, ðâ ðâ ðû hie forlure *thou didst lose no pleasure, when thou didst lose them*, Bt. 7, 1; Fox 16, 18. Ðý-læs ic mín gehât forleóse *ne fĭdem mei promissi prævārĭcer*, Bd. 4, 22; S. 592, 2. Hí sylfe þurh ðæt forluran *they ruined themselves through that*, 3, 1; S. 523, 23. Gê eówra yldrena hwetstân forluron *ye have lost the whetstone of your elders*, Ors. 4, 13; Bos. 100, 24. Ðæt he forlure ða gestrión *that he would lose the treasures*, Past. 7, 1; Hat. MS. 12 a, 5. Ðû forloren hæfst ða woruldsǽlþa *thou hast lost the worldly prosperity*, Bt. 7, 1; Fox 16, 7. [*Dut.* ver-liezen: *Ger.* ver-lieren *to lose.*]

for-lêt *left*, Cd. 70; Th. 84, 29; Gen. 1405; *p. of* for-lǽtan.

for-lêtenes, -lêtnes, -ness, e; *f. A leaving, leaving off, end*; intermissio, reliquiæ:—Synd forlêtnesse manna gesibsumum *sunt reliquiæ hŏmĭni pacĭfĭco*, Ps. Spl. T. 36, 39: R. Ben. interl. 15. v. for-lǽtennys.

for-licgan, -liccgan, -ligan; *p.* -læg, *pl.* -lǽgon; *pp.* -legen [licgan *to lie*] *To lie in a forbidden manner, fornicate, commit fornication*; fornĭcāri, adultĕrāre:—Ðâ forlæg heó hý sôna *then she soon committed fornication*, Ors. 3, 6; Bos. 58, 6: 4, 4; Bos. 80, 21. Ðæt nân wíf heó ne forlicge *that no woman commit fornication*, L. C. S. 54; Th. i. 406, 4, 7: 51; Th. i. 404, 22: L. E. G. 3; Th. i. 168, 5: 4; Th. i. 168, 19: L. N. P. L. 63; Th. ii. 300, 20. Gif beweddodu fǽmne hie forlicgge *if a betrothed woman commit fornication*, L. Alf. pol. 18; Th. i. 72, 11. Sceolan þeófas and forlegene lífes ne wênan *thieves and fornicators shall not hope for life*, Exon. 31 b; Th. 98, 21; Cri. 1611: L. Alf. pol. 10; Th. i. 68, 8. Forligende *fornĭcans*, Obs. Lun. § 4; Lchdm. iii. 186, 2.

for-liden; *part.* [for-, liden, *pp. of* líðan *to sail*] *Shipwrecked*; naufrăgus:—Gemildsa me, nacodum, forlidenum *pity me, naked, shipwrecked*, Apol. Th. 11, 19: 14, 1, 9: 15, 11: 21, 7, 13, 14, 15, 20: 22, 1, 22: 24, 16: 25, 9.

for-lidennes, -ness, e; *f. Shipwreck*; naufrăgium:—Hwâr gefôre ðû forlidennesse *where hast thou suffered shipwreck?* Apol. Th. 21, 19.

for-ligenes, -lignes, -ness, -nys, -nyss, e; *f. Fornication, adultery*; fornĭcātio:—Ne wæs acenned of unrihthǽmede ne þurh dyrne forligenysse *non de adultĕrio vel fornĭcātiōne nātus fuĕrat*, Bd. 1, 27; S. 495, 21. Ymb hiora hetelícan forlignessa ic hit eall forlǽte *I pass over all about their hateful adulteries*, Ors. 1, 8; Bos. 31, 38. v. for-legenes.

for-liger, -ligr, es; *pl. nom. acc.* -ligeru, -ligru, -ligra; *n. Fornication, adultery*; fornĭcātio, adultĕrium:—For forligere *ob fornĭcātiōnem*, Mt. Bos. 19, 9: Jn. Bos. 8, 41: Homl. Th. ii. 322, 28: L. Edm. S. 4; Th. i. 246, 5. Se ôðer heáfodleahter is gecweden forliger *the second chief sin is called fornication*, Homl. Th. ii. 220, 3. Innan of manna heortan cumaþ forligeru *ab intus de corde hŏmĭnum procēdunt fornĭcātiōnes*, Mk. Bos. 7, 21. Forligru *fornĭcātiōnes*, Mt. Bos. 15, 19. Ǽnig cristen mann ne ǽnige forligru ne begange *let not any christian man commit fornication*, L. C. E. 7; Th. i. 364, 24. Ascúnige man swíðe fûle forligra *let a man earnestly shun foul fornications*, L. Eth. vi. 28; Th. i. 322, 15.

for-liger, -ligr, -lír, es; *m. A fornicator, adulterer*; fornĭcātor, ădulter:—Ðæt Abraham nǽre forliger [MS. -ligr] geteald *ut Abraham non compŭtātus ădulter esset*, Boutr. Scrd. 22, 21. v. hor-cwên *an adulteress.* Forligr *adulter*, Wrt. Voc. 86, 68. He is forlír *he is an adulterer*, Homl. Th. ii. 208, 17. God fordêmþ ða dyrnan forlíras *God condemns secret adulterers*, ii. 324, 7.

for-liger; *adj. Adulterous*; ădulter:—Yfel cneórys and forliger [μοιχαλίς *adulterous*] sêcþ tâcn *gĕnĕrātio măla et adultĕra signum quærit*, Mt. Bos. 12, 39.

forliger-bed, -bedd, es; *n. A bed of fornication*; fornĭcātiōnis lectus:—On forligerbeddum *in beds of fornication*, Homl. Th. i. 604, 30.

for-liggang, es; *n? Lŭpānar, prostĭbŭlum*, Cot. 194.

for-ligr, es; *m. A fornicator*, Boutr. Scrd. 22, 21. v. for-liger, es; *m.*

for-ligr, es; *n. Fornication*, Mt. Bos. 15, 19. v. for-ligenes; *f.*

for-ligrian; *p.* ode; *pp.* od [for-liger *a fornicator*] *To fornicate*; fornĭcāri:—Ðû forspildest ealle ða ðe forligriaþ fram ðê *perdĭdisti omnes qui fornĭcantur abs te*, Ps. Spl. 72, 26.

for-lír *a fornicator*, Homl. Th. ii. 208, 17: 324, 7. v. for-liger, es; *m.*

for-líðednes, -ness, e; *f.* [líðan *to sail*] *Shipwreck*; naufrăgium, Som. Ben. Lye.

for-logen *lied greatly*, Lupi Serm. 1, 12; Hick. Thes. ii. 102, 41; *pp. of* for-leógan *to lie.*

for-lor, es; *m. Destruction, perdition, loss*; perdĭtio:—Hæleða forlor *men's perdition*, Cd. 33; Th. 45, 4; Gen. 721. Ic ofslôg ðis folc and to forlore gedyde *I slew and destroyed this people*, Past. 37, 2; Hat. MS. 49 b, 23: Andr. Kmbl. 2846; An. 1425. Mid hæleða forlore *with men's perdition*, Cd. 35; Th. 47, 8; Gen. 757. Ðêh ðe he hý mid micle forlore ðæs folces begeáte *though he took it with great loss of the people*, Ors. 3, 9; Bos. 67, 28. [*O. Sax.* farlor.]

for-loren *forlorn, lost*, Bd. 2, 5; S. 507, 41; *pp. of* for-leósan.

for-lorenes, -ness, e; *f.* FORLORNNESS, *destruction*; perdĭtio:—Ic geseó me stôwe gegearwode beón êccre forlorenesse *mihi lŏcum despĭcio æternæ perdĭtiōnis esse præpărātum*, Bd. 5, 14; S. 634, 29. On lyre oððe on forlorenesse *in perdĭtiōne*, Ps. Lamb. 87, 12.

for-lure *hast lost, didst lose*, Exon. 28 a; Th. 85, 30; Cri. 1399; *2nd sing. p. of* for-leósan: for-lure *would lose*, Chr. 81; Erl. 8, 4: Past. 7, 1; Hat. MS. 12 a, 5; *p. subj. of* for-leósan.

for-luron *lost, have lost*, Ors. 4, 13; Bos. 100, 24; *p. pl. of* for-leósan.

fór-lustlíce; *adv. Very willingly, gladly*; libentissime:—Ic wille fórlustlíce, for ðínum lufum *I will gladly* [*do so*], *for love of thee*, Bt. 22, 2; Fox 78, 12. [Cf. beon forrlisst *to be very desirous, Orm.*]

for-lȳst *loses*, Mk. Bos. 9, 41; *3rd sing. pres. of* for-leósan.

FORMA; *m*: forme; *f. n*: *def. adj. The first, earliest;* prīmus:—Se forma ys Simon *the first is Simon*, Mt. Bos. 10, 2: 22, 25: Bt. 15; Fox 48, 22: Cd. 143; Th. 179, 2; Exod. 22: Exon. 18 b; Th. 45, 16; Cri. 720: Beo. Th. 1437; B. 716: Menol. Fox 17; Men. 9: Bt. Met. Fox 8, 109; Met. 8, 55. Hū gesǣlig seó forme eld was đises middangeardes *how happy was the first age of this world*, Bt. 15; Fox 48, 2: Bt. Met. Fox 8, 7; Met. 8, 4: Boutr. Scrd. 21, 8. Đis wæs đæt forme tācn *this was the first miracle*, Jn. Bos. 2, 11. On đone forman dæg *on the first day*, Boutr. Scrd. 19, 4: Bd. de nat. rerum; Wrt. popl. science 4, 12; Lchdm. iii. 238, 15: Cd. 48; Th. 61, 17; Gen. 998: Byrht. Th. 133, 68; By. 77. Forman sīđe *for the first time*, Beo. Th. 4562; B. 2286: Exon. 84 b; Th. 319, 3; Wīd. 6: Cd. 17; Th. 21, 4; Gen. 319. Gebletsode Metod monna cynnes đa forman twā *the Lord blessed the first two of mankind*, Cd. 10; Th. 12, 31; Gen. 194. On forman *at first*, Blickl. Homl. 127, 20. [*Wyc.* forme *in* forme-fadris: *Chauc.* forme: *Laym.* uorme, forme: *Orm.* forrme: *O. Sax.* formo: *O. Frs.* forma: *Goth.* fruma *the first*: *Icel.* frum- in compounds, *the first.*]

fōr-mǣl, fōr-māl, e; *f.* [fōr = fōre, mǣl *a speech, discourse*] *An agreement, a treaty;* fœdus, pactum:—Wiđ đam đe he eall đæt lǣste đæt uncer fōrmǣl wæs *on condition that he fulfil all that was our agreement*, L. O. 1; Th. i. 178, 8. Æfter đām fōrmālum [MS. -mālan] *according to the treaties*, L. Eth. ii. 1; Th. i. 284, 11.

fōr-mǣrnes, -ness, e; *f. Brightness, glory, renown;* clārĭtas:—Fōrmǣrnes and genyht *renown and abundance*, Bt. 34, 6; Fox 140, 23, note 8. v. fōre-mǣrnes.

fōr-maneg, -moni; *adj. Very many;* permultus:—Heora fōrmanega oft fēngon to ānwealde *very many of them often undertook the government*, Jud. Thw. 161, 26.

for-meltan, -myltan; *p.* -mealt, *pl.* -multon; *pp.* -molten; *v. intrans. To melt away, become liquid, liquefy;* lĭquescĕre, lĭquĕfĭeri:—Hēt wǣpen eall formeltan *he commanded the weapons all to melt away*, Andr. Kmbl. 2294; An. 1148. Formealt ođđe hnesce geworden is eorþe *lĭquĕfacta est terra*, Ps. Lamb. 74, 4: Ex. 16, 21. Ealle đa scipu formultan *all the ships were consumed*, Ors. 5, 4; Bos. 105, 14. [*Dut.* versmelten *to melt, dissolve*: *Ger.* ver-schmelzen *to melt away.*]

for-mengan; *p.* de; *pp.* ed *To join together, mingle;* conjungĕre, Past. 21, 1? Lye. [*Dut. Ger.* ver-mengen *to mix, mingle, confuse.*] v. mengan.

formesta; *m*: formeste; *f. n*: *def. adj.* [*sup. of* forma *the first*] *Foremost, first, bēst, most valiant;* primus, strēnuissĭmus:—Wæs he se wer se formesta *ĕrat vir ipse strēnuissĭmus*, Bd. 5, 20; S. 641, 37. v. fyrmest.

fōr-mete, es; *m.* [fōr *a journey*, mete *food*] *Fare-meat, provision for a journey;* cĭbus in itĭnĕre sūmendus, Gr. Dial. 2, 13: Deut. 15, 14.

for-molsnian; *p.* ode, ede; *pp.* od, ed [molsnian *to corrupt*] *To putrefy, corrupt, make rotten, decay;* putrefăcĕre, tabefăcĕre, macĕrāre:—To duste formolsnod *decayed to dust*, Wanl. Catal. 20, 4; Homl. Th. i. 218, 25. Se ylca God, đe ealle þing of nāhte geworhte, mæg arǣran đa formolsnedan līchaman of đam duste *the same God, that wrought all things from naught, can raise up the decayed corpses from the dust*, Homl. Th. ii. 608, 6.

fōr-moni; *adj. Very many;* permultus:—Fōrmoni man *many a man*, Byrht. Th. 138, 52; By. 239. v. fōr-maneg.

for-myltan *to melt*:—Ic formylte *lĭquor*, Ælfc. Gr. 29; Som. 33, 44. v. for-meltan.

for-myrþrian; *p.* ode; *pp.* od *To kill, murder, destroy utterly;* occīdĕre, enĕcāre, perdĕre:—Gif wīf hire cild formyrþrige innan hire *si mŭlier infantem suum intra se perdidĕrit*, L. M. I. P. 10; Th. ii. 268, 5.

FORN, e; *f? A trout?* turnus:—Forn *turnus?* Ælfc. Gl. 102; Som. 77, 72; Wrt. Voc. 55, 76. [*Ger.* fohre, fore, forelle, *f. a trout*: *Ger. Swiss dial.* forne: *M. H. Ger.* vorhen, *f*: *O. H. Ger.* forahana, forhana *trutta*: *Dut.* voorn, *f*; vóren, *m. a roach.*]

fōrn, fōrne; *adv. Before;* cōram:—Gesæt Benedictus fōrn ongeán đam Riggon *Benedict sat opposite to Riggo*, Homl. Th. ii. 168, 15. Óþ-đæt he eft cume hyre fōrne geán *until he again comes opposite to it*, Bd. de nat. rerum; Wrt. popl. science 8, 13; Lchdm. iii. 248, 17. v. fōran; *prep.*

for-nam, *pl.* -nāmon *took away, destroyed, consumed*, Beo. Th. 2415; B. 1205: Ps. Th. 77, 53; *p. of* for-niman.

forne; *prep. acc. For;* pro, propter:—Gif hwā hine forne forstande *if anyone will stand up for him*, L. Eth. i. 4; Th. i. 284, 3, note 8. v. for; *prep.* v. forene.

fōrne; *adv. Before, sooner;* prius, cĭtius:—Se ōđer leorningcniht fōrarn Petrus fōrne *ille ălius discĭpŭlus præcucurrit cĭtius Petro*, Jn. Bos. 20, 4. v. fōran; *adv.* [*O. Sax.* forana.]

fōr-neáh, fōr-neán; *adv. Very nearly, nigh, nearly, almost, about;* prŏpe, fĕre, pæne, paulo mĭnus, circĭter:—Fōrneáh *fĕre*, Ælfc. Gr. 33; Som. 37, 50. Fōrneáh ođđe hwæt-hwega hī fordydon me on eorþan *paulo mĭnus consummāvĕrunt me in terram*, Ps. Lamb. 118, 87: 93, 17. Seó upastīhþ fōrneán ōþ đone mōnan *it extends upwards very nearly to the moon*, Bd. de nat. rerum; Wrt. popl. science 17, 4; Lchdm. iii. 272, 18. Fōrneán *fĕre*, Ælfc. Gr. 38; Som. 41, 45. Mīne fōrneán astyrode synt fēt *mei pæne mōti sunt pĕdes*, Ps. Lamb. 72, 2. Fōrneán þreó þūsend *circĭter tria millia*, Ælfc. Gr. 47; Som. 47, 42, 43.

fōr-nefe, an; *f. A nephew's daughter;* proneptis, Som. Ben. Lye. v. nefe.

Fornētes folm, e; *f. Fornet's palm;* Fornēti palma:—Wyl on eówe meolce Fornētes folm *boil Fornet's palm in ewe's milk*, L. M. 1, 70; Lchdm. ii. 144, 22. Nim Fornētes folm *take Fornet's palm*, 1, 71; Lchdm. ii. 146, 4. The *Icel.* has Fornjótr; *gen.* Fornjóts, the name of an eóten, es; *m. a giant.* Fornjótr's three sons had control over *air, fire*, and *wind.* In the Gl. Cleop. folm is glossed *mănus, the hand* or *palm.* As this refers to the palm only, it leaves us in difficulty what variety is intended by Fornet's palm. It must, however, be one of the chief species, as Fornjótr was a chief god of the heathen Icelanders.

for-niman, -nyman; *p.* -nam, -nom, *pl.* -nāmon, -nōmon; *pp.* -numen; *v. trans. To take away, deform, plunder, destroy, ransack, waste, consume, devour;* rapĕre, perdĕre, extermĭnāre, vastāre, consūmĕre, devŏrāre:—Đū hī eáđe miht forniman *thou mayest easily consume them*, Ps. Th. 72, 16: 118, 36. Eów in beorge bǣl fornimeþ *fire shall consume you upon the hill*, Elen. Kmbl. 1153; El. 578. Se đe fornimþ þearfan on dȳgelnysse *qui devŏrat paupĕrem in abscondĭto*, Cant. Abac. Lamb. fol. 190 b, 14. Hig fornymaþ hyra ansȳna *extermĭnant făcies suas*, Mt. Bos. 6, 16. Hine wyrd fornam *fate took him away*, Beo. Th. 2415; B. 1205: 2877; B. 1436: 4245; B. 2119. Līg eall fornam *the flame consumed all*, Cd. 119; Th. 153, 34; Gen. 2548: Andr. Kmbl. 1988; An. 996: 3061; An. 1533. Swylt ealle fornom secga hlōþe *death destroyed all the band of men*, Exon. 75 b; Th. 283, 5; Jul. 675: 59 b; Th. 216, 15; Ph. 268. Se Brytta þeóde fornom *qui gentem vastāvit Brittōnum*, Bd. 1, 34; S. 499, 20. Him īrenne ecga fornāmon *iron edges had taken them away from him*, Beo. Th. 5649; B. 2828. Fōrneáh hī fornāmon me on lande *paulo mĭnus consummāvĕrunt me in terra*, Ps. Spl. C. 118, 87. Fornōmon [MS. -noman] *have consumed*, Exon. 78 a; Th. 292, 14; Wand. 99. Wylt đū we secgaþ đæt fȳr cume of heofone, and fornime hig *vis dīcĭmus ut ignis descendat de cœlo, et consūmat illos?* Lk. Bos. 9, 54. Đæs mannes wlite wyrþeþ eall fornumen mid onsīgendre ylde *the beauty of man becomes thoroughly destroyed by approaching old age*, Basil admn. 8; Norm. 50, 20. Swā swā sceáp from wulfum and wildeórum beóþ fornumene, swā đa earman ceasterwaran toslitene and fornumene wǣron fram heora feóndum *sicut agni a fĕris, ĭta misĕri cīves discerpuntur ab hostĭbus*, Bd. 1, 12; S. 481, 26, 27: Homl. Th. ii. 416, 12.

for-nȳdan; *p.* -nȳdde; *pp.* -nȳded, -nȳdd *To force greatly, compel;* cōgĕre:—Wydewan syndon wīde fornȳdde on unriht to ceorle *viduæ crebro injuste ad nuptias trăhuntur*, Lupi Serm. i. 5; Hick. Thes. ii. 100, 25.

for-nyman *to take away, deform, disfigure*, Mt. Bos. 6, 16. v. forniman.

forod, forad, fored, forud; *adj. part.* [v. nacod *naked*] *Broken, fractured, violated;* fractus, violātus:—Wæs him gylp forod *their vaunt was broken*, Cd. 4; Th. 5, 10; Gen. 69. Đā wearþ hire mid ānum wyrpe ān ribb forod *then with one throw one of its ribs was broken*, Ors. 4, 6; Bos. 84, 41. Gif se earm biþ forod *if the arm be broken*, L. Alf. pol. 54; Th. i. 94, 24, note 57. Gif monnes ceácan mon forslihþ, đæt hie beóþ forode *if a man smite another's cheeks, so that they be broken*, L. Alf. pol. 50; Th. i. 94, 15: Ps. Th. 30, 12. Foredum sceancum *with broken legs*, H. R. 101, 21.

fōr-oft; *adv. Very often;* persæpe:—Se deófol sǣwþ fōroft mānfullīce geþohtas into đæs mannes heortan *the devil very often sows evil thoughts in the heart of man*, Boutr. Scrd. 20, 16. Swā swā we sylfe fōroft gesāwon *as we ourselves have very often seen*, Bd. de nat. rerum; Wrt. popl. science 12, 9; Lchdm. iii. 260, 2: Wrt. popl. science 11, 8; Lchdm. iii. 256, 16.

fōron *went*, Ps. Spl. 65, 11; *pl. p. of* faran *to go.*

for-pǣran; *p.* de; *pp.* ed *To turn away, pervert, ruin, destroy;* pervertĕre, perdĕre:—He đæs ōđres sāwle forpǣrþ þurh his yfelum tihtingum *he perverts the other's soul by his evil instigations*, Homl. Th. ii. 226, 31: 208, 20. Hie forpǣraþ đæm edleáne *mĕrĭtum pervertunt*, Past. 39, 3; Hat. MS. 53 b, 8. Gif we us sylfe ne forpǣraþ *if we do not destroy ourselves*, Homl. Th. i. 216, 9: ii. 50, 5. Adam us forpǣrde þurh ānes æpples þigene *Adam ruined us by the eating of an apple*, Homl. Th. ii. 330, 32. Đæt he đone man forpǣre *that he may destroy the man*, Boutr. Scrd. 20, 20.

for-pyndan; *p.* de; *pp.* ed *To turn away;* remŏvēre, reprĭmĕre:—Đæt Éuan scyld is eal forpynded *the sin of Eve is all turned away*, Exon. 9 a; Th. 7, 7; Cri. 97. [*Icel.* pynda *prĕmĕre, vexāre.*] v. pynding.

fōr-rād *rode before*:—Fōrrād sió fierd hie fōran *the force rode before them*, Chr. 894; Th. 166, 7; *p. of* fōr-rīdan, *q. v.*

fōr-radian *to hasten before, prevent*, Nat. S. Greg. Els. 23, 4: 24, 6. v. fōr-hradian.

for-rǣdan; *p.* -rǣdde; *pp.* -rǣded; or *p.* -reord, -rēd; *pp.* -rǣden, *v. a. to give counsel against, to condemn, plot against, deprive by* *treachery, wrong*; condemnāre, insĭdias pārāre:—We beódaþ ðæt man Cristene men for ealles tō lytlum to deáþe ne forrǣde *we command that Christian men be not for altogether too little condemned to death*, L. C. S. 2; Th. i. 376, 19. Eádweard man forrǣdde and syððan acwealde *they plotted against Edward and afterwards murdered him*, Lupi Serm. i. 9; Hick. Thes. ii. 102, 10. Ðæt man his hlāford of līfe forrǣde *that a man deprive his lord of life*, Lupi Serm. i. 9; Hick. Thes. ii. 102, 7. [Cf. *Icel.* ráða af dögum *to kill.*] Gif man gehādodne man forrǣde æt feó oððe æt feore *if any one wrong a man in holy orders as to money or as to life*, L. C. S. 40; Th. i. 400, 5: L. E. G. 12; Th. i. 174, 6. [*Ger.* ver-rathen *to betray.*]

fōr-raðe; *adv. Very quickly;* cito:—Hī Godes bebod tobrǣcon fōrraðe *they broke the commandment of God very quickly*, Ælfc. T. 5, 6: Gen. 20, 7.

fōr-rīdan; *p.* -rād, *pl.* -ridon; *pp.* -riden *To ride before, intercept;* præequĭtāre, intercĭpĕre:—Fōrrād sió fierd hie fōran *the force rode before them*, Chr. 894; Erl. 90, 25. Ða men hie fōran fōrrīdan mehton būtan geweorce *the men they might intercept outside the work*, 894; Erl. 93, 11. [*Laym. p.p.* forriden: *Ger.* vor-reiten *to ride before.*]

fōr-rīdel, es; *m. A fore-rider, outrider, harbinger;* præcursor:—Cyning Totilla sende his fōrrīdel cȳðan his tocyme ðam hālgan were *king Totila sent his harbinger to announce his coming to the holy man*, Homl. Th. ii. 168, 10. [*A. R.* vorrideles: *Ger.* vor-reiter *a fore-rider.*]

for-rotian; *p.* ode, ade, ede; *pp.* od, ad, ed [for-, rotian *to rot*] *To become wholly rotten, to rot, putrefy;* computrescĕre:—Ða fixas acwelaþ and ða wæteru forrotiaþ *pisces mŏrientur et computrescent ăquæ*, Ex. 7, 18. Hit forrotode *computruit*, 16, 20. Gemolsnad flǣsc *vel* forrotad *corrupted flesh;* tābes, Ælfc. Gl. 12; Som. 57, 74; Wrt. Voc. 20, 16. Ðæt sió rēþnes ðæs wīnes ða forrotedan wunde clǣnsige *that the harshness of the wine may cleanse the corrupted wound*, Past. 17, 10; Hat. MS. 25 a, 9. [*A. R.* vorrotien: *Dut. Ger.* ver-rotten *to rot, putrefy, mortify.*]

for-rotodnys, -rotednys, -nyss, e; *f. Rottenness, corruption;* putrēdo, pus:—Mīn flǣsc is ymbscrȳd mid forrotodnysse *my flesh is covered with corruption*, Job Thw. 167, 36: Prov. 12: Homl. Th. ii. 282, 11. Ðeós forrotednyss *hoc pus*, Ælfc. Gr. 8; Som. 7, 35.

fōr-rynel, fōre-rynel, es; *m. A forerunner;* præcursor:—Is se fōrrynel fæger and sciéne *the forerunner [morning star] is fair and shining*, Bt. Met. Fox 29, 49; Met. 29, 25. Iohannes wæs Cristes fōrrynel *John was Christ's forerunner*, Homl. Th. i. 484, 34: 356, 21: Bt. 36, 1; Fox 170, 28. Ðæs mǣran fōrryneles *of the great forerunner*, Homl. Th. i. 364, 6.

for-sacan; *p.* -sōc, *pl.* -sōcon; *pp.* -sacen *To declare an opposition, oppose, object to, refuse, give up, forsake;* detrectāre, recūsāre, desĕrĕre:—Gange ān mynet ofer ealne ðæs cynges ānweald, and ðone nān man ne forsace *let one money pass throughout the king's dominion, and that let no man refuse*, L. Edg. ii. 8; Th. i. 270, 1. Forsōc ðæne triumphan *refused the triumph*, Ors. 2, 4; Bos. 42, 43. He ðæt wæs eall forsacende *he was giving up all that*, 1, 12; Bos. 36, 16. v. sacan.

for-sǣcan *to punish*, Exon. 38 a; Th. 125, 2; Gū. 348. v. for-sēcan.

for-sǣde, *pl.* -sǣdon *accused*, Homl. Th. i. 50, 14, 16; *p. of* for-secgan.

for-sæt, *pl.* -sǣton *delayed, deferred, obstructed*, Cd. 138; Th. 173, 10; Gen. 2859: 114; Th. 150, 10; Gen. 2489; *p. of* for-sittan.

for-sāwon *rejected, despised*, Elen. Kmbl. 2633; El. 1318; *p. pl. of* for-seón.

for-scāden *scattered*, Exon. 39 b; Th. 131, 1; Gū. 449; *pp. of* for-scādan. v. for-sceádan.

for-scæncednys, -nyss, e; *f.* [for-, screncednes *supplantātio*] *A supplanting, deceit;* supplantātio, fraus:—Man miclode ofor me hleóhræscnesse oððe forscæncednysse *hŏmo magnĭfĭcāvit sŭper me supplantātiōnem*, Ps. Lamb. 40, 10.

for-scapung, -sceapung, e; *f. A bad action, fault, crime;* perversa actio, scĕlus:—Hī sǣdon ðæt hió wǣre for Fetontis forscapunge *they said that it was for the fault of Phaëton*, Ors. 1, 7; Bos. 30, 35. On mislīcre forsceapunge *by various misdeeds*, 1, 11; Bos. 35, 2.

for-sceádan, -scādan; *p.* -sceód, *pl.* -sceódon; *pp.* -sceáden, -scāden [sceádan *to separate*] *To scatter, disperse;* dispergĕre:—Ðæt ða giemmas wǣren forsceádne [forsceadene, Cot.] æfter ðǣm strǣtum *that the gems were scattered along the streets*, Past. 18, 4; Hat. MS. 26 b, 25. Gē sind forscādene *ye are scattered*, Exon. 39 b; Th. 131, 1; Gū. 449.

for-sceáf *cast down*, Cd. 153; Th. 190, 25; Exod. 204; *p. of* for-scūfan.

for-sceamian, -scamian, -scamigan; *p.* ode; *pp.* od [sceamian *to be ashamed*] *To be greatly ashamed;* erūbescĕre:—Forsceamian *erŭbescĕre*, Scint. 8. Hie forscamige *let it shame them*, Past. 21, 1; Hat. MS. 29 a, 26. [*Orm.* forrshamedd *much ashamed.*]

for-sceap, es; *n.* [*from* sceapen *formed, created; pp. of* sceppan *to create*] What is for- or mis-shapen *a fault, crime;* mălefactum:—Me nædre to forsceape scyhte *the serpent incited me to crime*, Cd. 42; Th. 55, 22; Gen. 898.

fōr-sceáwian; *p.* ode; *pp.* od *To foreshew, foresee;* præ-ostendĕre, pōrĕre in conspectu, provĭdēre:—Ic fōrsceáwode Driht on gesihþe mīnre symble *provĭdēbam Dŏmĭnum in conspectu meo semper*, Ps. Spl. 15, 8. [*Ger.* vor-schauen *to foresee.*] v. fōre-sceáwian.

fōr-sceáwudlīce; *adv. Providently, carefully, prudently;* prōvĭde, Procem. R. Conc.

fōr-sceáwung, e; *f. Providence;* prōvĭdentia:—Þurh Godes fōrsceáwunge *by the providence of God*, Homl. Th. i. 234, 21. v. fōre-sceáwung.

for-scending, e; *f.* [scendan *to confound*] *Confusion;* confūsio:—Mid forscendinge *præ confŭsiōne*, Lk. Skt. Rush. 21, 25.

for-sceóppan; *p.* -scōp, *pl.* -scōpon; *pp.* -sceápen *To re-create, transform, deform;* transformāre:—Sume, hī sǣdon, ðæt hió [Circe] sceolde forsceóppan to león *some, they said, she [Circe] should transform to a lioness*, Bt. 38, 1; Fox 194, 33. v. for-sceppan.

for-sceorfan; *p.* -scearf, *pl.* -scurfon; *pp.* -scorfen [sceorfan *to gnaw, bite*] *To gnaw or eat off;* arrōdĕre:—Gærstapan ǣlc wuht forscurfon, ðæs ðe on ðam lande wæs grōwendes *locusts ate off everything that was growing in the land*, Ors. 5, 4; Bos. 105, 17, notes, p. 24, 7, MS. L.

fōr-sceótan, he -scȳt, *pl.* -sceótaþ; *p.* -sceát, *pl.* -scuton; *pp.* -scoten *To shoot before, anticipate, come before, prevent;* anticĭpāre, prævĕnīre:—Ða ungesǣligan menn ne māgon gebidon hwonne he [deáþ] him to cume, ac fōrsceótaþ hine fōran *unhappy men cannot wait till he [death] comes to them, but anticipate him beforehand*, Bt. 39, 1; Fox 212, 3. Fōrscȳt ðæt hwīlendlīce wīte ða ēcan geniðerunge *the transient punishment will prevent eternal damnation*, Homl. Th. i. 576, 2. Mīn God fōrscȳt [MS. forscytte] oððe fōrestepþ me *Deus meus prævĕniet me*, Ps. Lamb. 58, 11. [*Ger.* vor-schiessen.]

for-sceppan, -sceóppan; *p.* -sceóp, *pl.* -sceópon; *pp.* -scepen *To transform;* transformāre:—Heó alle forsceóp Drihten to deóflum *the Lord transformed them all to devils*, Cd. 16; Th. 20, 14; Gen. 308. Scinnan forscepene [*their*] *beauty transformed*, Cd. 214; Th. 269, 12; Sat. 72.

fōr-scip, es; *n. The forepart of a ship, the prow;* prōra:—Ancersetl [MS. anfer-] *vel* fōrscip *prōra*, Ælfc. Gl. 83; Som. 73, 73; Wrt. Voc. 48, 12.

for-scranc *shrank up, dried up, withered*, Gen. 32, 25: Mt. Bos. 21, 19: Mk. Bos. 4, 6; *p. of* for-scrincan.

for-scrang *shrank up, dried up*, Ps. Spl. 128, 5, = for-scranc; *p. of* for-scrincan.

for-screncan, -scræncan; *p.* -screncte, -scræncte; *pp.* -scrænct, -screnct [screncan *to trip up*] *To supplant, overcome, oppress, cast down;* supplantāre, opprĭmĕre, elīdĕre:—Ða ðe leahtras forscrencaþ belimpaþ to Godes rīce *those who overcome sins belong to God's kingdom*, Homl. Th. i. 198, 23. Forscrænc hine *supplanta eum*, Ps. Lamb. 16, 13. Ðū forscrænctest onarīsende on me *supplantasti insurgentes in me*, 17, 40. Forscrenct *elīsa* vel *dejecta*, Ælfc. Gl. 78; Som. 72, 36; Wrt. Voc. 45, 68. Crist arǣrþ ða forscrenctan *Christ raises the oppressed*, Homl. Th. ii. 414, 23.

for-screncend, es; *m.* [*part. of* forscrencan] *A supplanter;* supplantātor:—Iacob is gecweden, forscrencend *Jacob is interpreted, a supplanter*, Homl. Th. i. 198, 21.

for-scrīfan; *p.* -scrāf, *pl.* -scrifon; *pp.* -scrifen [scrīfan *to judge*]. I. *to condemn, proscribe;* condemnāre, proscrībĕre:—He ðæt scyldige werud forscrifen hefde *he had proscribed the guilty host*, Cd. 213; Th. 267, 5; Sat. 33. Grendel fīfelcynnes eard weardode hwīle, siððan him Scyppend forscrifen hæfde *Grendel inhabited a while the monster-race's abode, after the Creator had proscribed him*, Beo. Th. 213; B. 106. II. *to write* or *cut into, cut down;* incīdĕre, succīdĕre:—Awrīteþ he on his wǣpne wællnota heáp, bealwe bōcstafas bill forscrīfeþ *he writes upon his weapon a heap of fatal marks, baleful letters he cuts into the bill*, Salm. Kmbl. 323–326, note; Sal. 161, 162. Forscrīf hine *succīde illam*, Lk. Skt. Hat. 13, 7, 9. [*Ger.* ver-schreiben *to prescribe.*]

for-scrīhan; *p.* -scrāh, *pl.* -scrigon; *pp.* -scrigen [scrīhan *dĭcāre*] *To abdicate, resign, give up;* abdĭcāre:—Forscrāh *abdĭcāvit*, Cot. 205.

for-scrincan, he -scrincþ; *p.* -scranc, *pl.* -scruncon; *pp.* -scruncen [for-, scrincan *to shrink*] *To shrink up, dry up, dwindle away, wither;* emarcescĕre, exarescĕre, arefiĕri, arescĕre:—He forscrincþ *arescit*, Mk. Bos. 9, 18. Æt-hrān he his sine on his þeó and heó ðǣrrihte forscranc *tĕtĭgit nervum fĕmŏris ejus, et stătim emarcuit*, Gen. 32, 25. Sǣd forscranc *sĕmen exăruit*, Mk. Bos. 4, 6: Lk. Bos. 8, 6. Sōna forscranc ðæt fīctreów *arefacta est contĭnuo fĭculnea*, Mt. Bos. 21, 19. Hig forscruncon *ăruĕrunt*, Mt. Bos. 13, 6. Mīn hȳd is forscruncen *my skin is shrunk up*, Job Thw. 167, 37. Hī gesāwon ðæt fīctreów forscruncen of ðām wyrtruman *vidĕrunt fĭcum arĭdam factam a radĭcĭbus*, Mk. Bos. 11, 20. On ðām porticon læg mycel menigeo forscruncenra *in his portĭcĭbus jăcēbat multĭtūdo magna arĭdōrum*, Jn. Bos. 5, 3.

for-scrufon *ate off*, Ors. 5, 4; Bos. 105, 17, = for-scurfon; *p. pl. of* for-sceorfan.

for-scruncen *shrank up, dried up, withered*, Job Thw. 167, 37: Mk. Bos. 11, 20; *pp. of* for-scrincan.

for-scruncon *dried up*, Mt. Bos. 13, 6; *p. pl. of* for-scrincan.

for-scūfan; *p.* -sceáf, *pl.* -scufon; *pp.* -scofen *To cast down;* amŏvēre, dispellĕre:—Wlance forsceáf mihtig engel *a mighty angel cast down their pride*, Cd. 153; Th. 190, 25; Exod. 204. v. scūfan.

for-scúnian, -scúnigean; *p.* ode; *pp.* od [scúnian *to shun*] *To blush, feel shame;* erŭbescĕre, Scint. 4.

for-scurfon *gnawed* or *ate off*, Ors. 5, 4; Bos. 105, 17, notes, p. 24, 7, MS. L; *p. pl. of* for-sceorfan.

for-scyldigian, -scyldegian, -scyldgian; *p.* ode; *pp.* od [scyldigian *accūsāre*] *To make guilty, to criminate, condemn;* reum făcĕre, damnāre:—Hreówlīce gefærþ se ðe hine sylfne forþ forscyldigaþ *he fares roughly who constantly criminates himself*, L. Pen. 12; Th. ii. 280, 28. Forscyldegod *scĕlĕrātus* vel *făcĭnŏrōsus*, Wrt. Voc. 86, 65. Wurdon hī deádlīce and forscyldegode þurh āgenne cyre *they became mortal and guilty through their own choice*, Homl. Th. i. 112, 16. He wæs forscyldgod *he was guilty*, i. 12, 21. Ne slihþ se dēma ðone forscyldgodan sceaðan, ac he hǣt his underþeóddan hine belifian *the judge slays not the condemned robber, but he commands his subordinates to deprive him of life*, ii. 36, 9. [Cf. *Ger.* ver-schulden *to be guilty*.]

for-scyppan *to transform*. v. for-sceóppan.

fōr-scȳt *shoots before, prevents* or *will prevent*, Homl. Th. i. 576, 2; *pres. of* fōr-sceótan.

fōr-scyttan; *p.* -scytte, *pl.* -scytton; *pp.* -scytted *To shoot before, prevent;* prævĕnīre:—Hī heófodon folces synna, and heora wrace on him sylfum fōrscytton *they bewailed the people's sins, and prevented their punishment on themselves*, Homl. Th. i. 540, 31. Ðæt ða sceortan wītu ðises geswincfullan līfes fōrscytten [MS. forscyttan] ða toweardan, ðe nǣfre ateoriaþ *that the short punishments of this painful life may prevent those to come, which will never fail*, Homl. Th. ii. 328, 34. DER. scyttan.

for-seah, ðū -seáge *despised, thou despisedst*, Exon. 40 b; Th. 134, 23; Gū. 512: Ps. Spl. 88, 37; *p. of* for-seón.

for-seárian; *p.* ode; *pp.* od [seárian *to sear*] *To dry up, wither;* arēre, arescĕre:—Ic forseárige *āreo*, Ælfc. Gr. 26, 2; Som. 28, 44. Se līchama gewyrþeþ to duste and forseáraþ *the body turns to dust and withers*, Basil admn. 8; Norm. 50, 17: Homl. Th. ii. 92, 3. Adruwode oððe forseárode swā swā blȳwnys oððe crocsceard mægen mīn *āruit tamquam testa virtus mea*, Ps. Lamb. 21, 16. Mīn hȳd forseárode *my skin withered*, Job Thw. 167, 37. Ðonne hit forealdod biþ and forseárod *when it is grown old and withered*, Bt. 39, 8; Fox 224, 11.

for-sēcan, -sǣcan; *p.* -sōhte, *pl.* -sōhton; *pp.* -sōht *To afflict, punish;* pœna affĭcĕre:—Ðeáh ðe gē hine sārum forsǣcen *though ye sorely afflict it*, Exon. 38 a; Th. 125, 2; Gū. 348. Sārum forsōht *afflicted with sorrows*, Elen. Kmbl. 1862; El. 933. DER. sēcan.

for-secgan; *p.* -sægde, -sǣde; *pp.* -sægd, -sǣd *To for-say, mis-say, pretend, deny, say against, accuse;* prædīcĕre, diffāmāre, nĕgāre, accūsāre:—Se ðe ōðerne mid wō forsecgan wille *he who shall accuse another wrongfully*, L. C. S. 16; Th. i. 384, 20: L. Edg. ii. 4; Th. i. 266, 22. Se ōðerne to deáþe forsegþ *he traduces another to death*, Homl. Th. ii. 208, 19. Be ðon ðe mon ōðerne forsecgaþ *in case any one accuse another*, L. Edg. ii. 4, titl; Th. i. 266, 21. Swā hwā swā ōðerne forsǣde *whosoever accused another*, Homl. Th. i. 50, 16. Ða leásan gewitan hine forsǣdon *the false witnesses accused him*, i. 50, 14.

for-sēgon *despised, rejected, renounced*, Elen. Kmbl. 778; El. 389; *p. pl. of* for-seón.

for-sendan; *p.* -sende; *pp.* -sended *To send away, send into banishment, banish;* dimittĕre, relēgāre, deportāre:—Sume on wræcsīþ forsende *some he sent away into banishment*, Ors. 3, 7; Bos. 60, 39. He hine siððan forsende *he afterwards banished him*, 3, 7; Bos. 59, 26. He wearþ snūde forsended *he was quickly banished*, Beo. Th. 1812; B. 904. [*Ger.* ver-senden *to send away*.]

fōr-sendan *to send before*. v. fōre-sendan.

for-seón, -sión; ic -seó, ðū -sihst, -sixt, he -sihþ, -syhþ, *pl.* -seóþ; *p.* -ic, he -seah, ðū -sāwe, -seáge, *pl.* -sāwon, -sēgon; *impert.* -seoh; *subj.* he -seó; *pp.* -sewen *To overlook, despise, contemn, scorn, be ashamed of, neglect, reject, renounce;* despĭcĕre, temnĕre, contemnĕre, spernĕre, erūbescĕre, neglĭgĕre, posthăbēre, rejĭcĕre:—We ā sculon īdle lustas forseón *we should ever despise idle lusts*, Exon. 19 a; Th. 47, 18; Cri. 757: Boutr. Scrd. 21, 43. Ōþ-ðæt ðū meahte ǣlc eorþlīc þing forsión *until thou mayest look down upon every earthly thing*, Bt. Met. Fox 24, 14; Met. 24, 7. Ic forseó *temno*, Ælfc. Gr. 28, 4; Som. 31, 17. Ic fracuþe forseó feóndas mīne *ĕgo vĭdēbo inĭmīcos meos*, Ps. Th. 117, 7. Ic forseó *posthăbeo*, Ælfc. Gr. 47; Som. 48, 31. Ðū forsihst [-sixt, Lamb.] on gerecum on gedrēfednysse *despĭcis in ŏpportunĭtātĭbus in trĭbulātiōne*, Ps. Spl. second 9, 1. He forsihþ ðās eorþlīcan gōd *he despises these earthly goods*, Bt. 12; Fox 36, 25: Gen. 16, 5. Se ðe me and mīne spæca forsyhþ, ðone mannes Sunu forsyhþ *qui me erubuĕrit et meos sermōnes, hunc Fīlius hŏmĭnis erubescet*, Lk. Bos. 9, 26: Mk. Bos. 8, 38. Gif gē mīne ǣ and mīne dōmas forseóþ *si sprevĕrĭtis lēges meas et jūdĭcia mea*, Lev. 26, 15. Gūþlāc mān eall forseah *Guthlac despised all sin*, Exon. 34 a; Th. 108, 4; Gū. 67: 40 b; Th. 134, 23; Gū. 512. Ðū forseáge Cristum ðīnne *despexisti Christum tuum*, Ps. Spl. 88, 37. Hie māna gehwylc forsāwon *they rejected every sin*, Elen. Kmbl. 2633; El. 1318. Forsāwon hyra sēllan *they despised their superior*, Exon. 84 a; Th. 317, 5; Mōd. 61. Gē blindnesse bōte forsēgon *ye renounced the remedy of blindness*, Elen. Kmbl. 778; El. 389. Ne forseoh ǣfre, ðæt ðū sylfa ǣr, mid ðīnum handum hēr geworhtest *ŏpĕra manuum tuārum ne despĭcias*, Ps. Th. 137, 8: 54, 1: Ps. Lamb. 26, 9. Gif preóst ōðerne forseó oððe gebismirige *if a priest despise or insult another*, L. N. P. L. 29; Th. ii. 294, 17. Wæs mǣrþa fruma tō swīðe forsewen *the source of marvels was too greatly despised*, Chr. 975; Erl. 126, 16; Edg. 42. Bióþ forsewene heora lāreówas *their teachers are despised*, Bt. Met. Fox 13, 74; Met. 13, 37. Forhygdelīc oððe forsewen *contemptus*, Ps. Lamb. 118, 141. [*Orm.* forrseon *to despise*: *Ger.* ver-sehen *to see wrong*.]

for-seónnes, -ness, e; *f. A looking down upon, contempt;* despectio, contemptus, Som. Ben. Lye. v. for-sewennes.

for-seten *obstructed*, Ors. 4, 6; Bos. 84, 13; *pp. of* for-sittan.

for-settan; *p.* -sette, *pl.* -setton; *pp.* -seted, -sett *To obstruct;* obstruĕre:—Hī ðone heofonlīcan weg forsetton *they obstructed the heavenly way*, Bd. 3, 19; S. 548, 4. [*Ger.* versetzen *to misplace, obstruct*.]

fōr-settan; *p.* -sette, *pl.* -setton; *pp.* -seted, -sett *To set before;* prōpōnĕre:—Gif ic ne fōrsette ðē Hierusalem *si non prŏpŏsuĕro Hierūsălem*, Ps. Th. 136, 6. Hig ne fōrsetton God tofōran ansȳne heora *non prŏpŏsuĕrunt Deum ante conspectum suum*, Ps. Lamb. 53, 5. [*Ger.* vor-setzen *to set before*.]

fōr-settednys, -nyss, e; *f.* [fōrseted, *pp. of* fōrsettan; -nyss] *A proposition;* propŏsĭtio:—Ic sprece fōrsettednyssa of frymþe *lŏquar propŏsĭtiōnes ab inĭtio*, Ps. Spl. 77, 2. v. fōre-setnes.

for-sewen *despised*, Ps. Lamb. 118, 141; *pp. of* for-seón.

for-sewenlīce; *comp.* -līcor; *adv. Contemptibly, ignominiously;* contemptĭbĭlĭter, turpĭter:—Swā he forsewenlīcor biþ gewītnod for Godes naman, swā his wuldor biþ māre fōr Gode *the more ignominiously he is tortured for the name of God, the greater shall his glory be before God*, Homl. Th. i. 486, 23.

for-sewennes, fore-seuwenes, -ness, -nyss, e; *f. A looking down upon, contempt;* contemptus, despectio:—Gefylled we synd forsewennysse *replēti sŭmus despectiōne*, Ps. Spl. 122, 4, 5. For his forsewennesse *out of contempt for him*, Ors. 4, 4; Bos. 81, 13. Forsewennyss *contemptus*, Ælfc. Gr. 28, 4; Som. 31, 17.

for-sewestre, an; *f. She who despises;* contemptrix, Som. Ben. Lye.

for-sihst, -sihþ *despisest, despiseth*, Ps. Spl. second 9, 1: Gen. 16, 5; *2nd and 3rd sing. pres. of* for-seón.

for-singian *to sin greatly*, L. Pen. 12; Wilk. 95, 9. v. for-syngian.

for-sión *to despise*, Past. 32, 1; Hat. MS. 39 b, 27. v. forseón.

for-sīþ, es; *m. A going away, departure, death;* exĭtium, ŏbĭtus, mors:—Sōna æfter his forsīþe wæs ealra witena gemōt on Oxna forda *soon after his death there was a meeting of all the counsellors at Oxford*, Chr. 1036; Erl. 164, 12. v. forþ-sīþ.

for-sīðian; *p.* ode; *pp.* od [sīðian *to journey*] *To perish;* ĭter fātāle inīre:—Hæfde ðā forsīðod sunu Ecgþeówes *Ecgtheow's son had then perished*, Beo. Th. 3104, note; B. 1550.

for-sittan; he -siteþ; *p.* -sæt, *pl.* -sǣton; *pp.* -seten *To mis-sit, to be absent from, neglect, delay, defer, diminish, obstruct, besiege;* abesse a, neglĭgĕre, supersĕdēre, desĕrĕre, præstruĕre, obsĭdēre:—Be ðon ðe gemōt forsitte *of him who is absent from the council*, L. Ath. i. 20; Th. i. 208, 25, 26. Be ðon ðe man fyrde forsitte *in case a man neglect the army*, L. In. 51; Th. i. 134, 7, 8. Ne forsæt he ðȳ sīðe *he delayed not the journey*, Cd. 138; Th. 173, 10; Gen. 2859. Ne he tīd forsæt *he deferred not the time*, Exon. 37 b; Th. 122, 26; Gū. 311. Ðæt eágena bearhtm forsiteþ and forsworceþ *the twinkling of the eyes diminishes and darkens*, Beo. Th. 3538; B. 1767. Hī hæfdon ðone weg forseten *they had blockaded the way*, Ors. 4, 6; Bos. 84, 13. Fearras forsǣton me *tauri obsĕdĕrunt me*, Ps. Spl. 21, 11: Cd. 114; Th. 150, 10; Gen. 2489.

for-sixst *despisest*, Ps. Lamb. second 9, 1, = for-sihst; *2nd sing. pres. of* for-seón.

for-slægen *slain*, Chr. 882; Erl. 82, 13; *pp. of* for-sleán.

for-slæhþ *breaks*, L. Ethb. 50; Th. i. 16, 1; *3rd sing. pres. of* for-sleán.

for-slagen *slain*, Ors. 3, 7; Bos. 62, 10; *pp. of* for-sleán.

for-slāwian; *p.* ode; *pp.* od [slāwian *to be slow*] *To be slow, unwilling;* pĭgēre:—Ic wāt, ðæt ðū nāht nē forslāwodest *I know that thou wouldest not be unwilling*, Bt. 10; Fox 28, 15.

for-sleán, he -slæhþ, -slyhþ, -slihþ; *p.* -slōh, *pl.* -slōgon; *pp.* -slegen, -slægen, -slagen [sleán *to strike*] *To strike with violence, smite, break, slay, kill, destroy;* vehementer fĕrīre, percŭtĕre, frangĕre, occīdĕre, interfĭcĕre:—Se ðe cinbān forslæhþ mid xx scillingum forgelde *let him who breaks the chin-bone pay for it with twenty shillings*, L. Ethb. 50; Th. i. 16, 1. Gif monnes ceácan mon forslihþ [forslyhþ, H] ðæt hie beóþ forode, gebēte mid xv scillinga *if one smite a man's cheeks, that they be broken, let him make amends with fifteen shillings*, L. Alf. pol. 50; Th. i. 94, 14. He ealle ða rīcostan forsleán hēt *he commanded [them] to slay all the most powerful*, Ors. 3, 7; Bos. 60, 38. Ercol hī swīðe forslōh and fordyde *Hercules grievously slew and destroyed them*, Ors. 1, 10; Bos. 33, 34. Forslegen Sodoma folc *the slaughtered people of Sodom*, Cd. 94; Th. 122, 5; Gen. 2022. Hī forslegene wurdon *they were slain*, Ors. 1, 13; Bos. 37, 5. Ða men wǣron forslægene *the men were slain*, Chr. 882; Erl. 82, 13. He hī forslagen hæfde *he had slain them*, Bt. 16, 2; Fox 54, 2: Ors. 3, 7; Bos. 62, 10. [*Ger.* verschlagen.]

for-slegen *slain, slaughtered,* Cd. 94; Th. 122, 5; Gen. 2022; *pp. of* for-sleán.

for-sliet, es; *m.* [sliet = slite *a slit*] *Slaughter, massacre;* internĕcio, Cot. 108.

for-sliþ *smites,* L. Alf. pol. 50; Th. i. 94, 14; *3rd sing. pres. of* for-sleán.

for-slītan; *p.* -slāt, *pl.* -sliton; *pp.* -sliten [slītan *to tear*] *To tear with the teeth, to devour;* mordĭcus lacĕrāre, comĕdĕre:—Lēt [wyrm] hiora wyrta wæstme forslītan *he let [the worm] devour the fruit of their plants,* Ps. Th. 77, 46. [*O. Sax.* farslītan *to tear up, consume.*]

for-slōh *slew,* Ors. 1, 10; Bos. 33, 34; *p. of* for-sleán.

for-slyhþ *smites,* L. Alf. pol. 50; Th. i. 94, 14, MS. H; *3rd sing. pres. of* for-slean.

for-smorian; *p.* ode; *pp.* od; *v. trans. To smother, choke, suffocate, stifle;* suffōcāre:—Hī synd mid heora līfes lustum forsmorode... woruldcara and wēlan forsmoriaþ ðæs mōdes þrotan *they are choked with the pleasures of their life...worldly cares and riches choke the throat of the mind,* Homl. Th. ii. 92, 8-11. On ūrum gāstlīcum fulluhte biþ se deófol forsmorod fram us *in our spiritual baptism the devil is stifled by us,* ii. 200, 19.

for-sōc, *pl.* -sōcon *refused,* Chr. 1070; Erl. 208, 4; *p. of* for-sacan.

for-sogen *sucked* or *drawn out,* L. M. 2, 7; Lchdm. ii. 186, 17; *pp. of* for-sūgan.

fōr-sorged; *part.* [fōr, sorgian *to sorrow*] *Made very sad, grieved, sorrowful;* tristātus, triste factus, Som. Ben. Lye.

for-sōþ; *adv.* FORSOOTH, *truly, certainly;* certe:—Wite ðū forsōþ *know thou assuredly,* Bt. 14, 3; Fox 46, 16. Ic forsōþ wāt *vērum nōvi,* Bd. 3, 13; S. 538, 33. Saga him forsōþ *dic ergo illi,* Bd. 5, 9; S. 622, 37.

for-spanan, he -spaneþ, -spenþ; *p.* -spon, -speón, *pl.* -spōnon, -speónon; *pp.* -spanen, -sponen; *v. trans.* [spanan *to allure*] *To entice, seduce;* illĭcĕre, sedūcĕre:—Gehwā se ðe ōðerne to leahtrum forspenþ is manslaga *every one who entices another to sins is a manslayer,* Homl. Th. ii. 226, 30. Hine his hyge forspeón, ðæt he ne wolde Drihtnes word wurþian *his mind seduced him, that he would not revere the Lord's word,* Cd. 18; Th. 22, 34; Gen. 350. Forspanen beón *seductum esse, sedūci,* Prov. 30, Lye. [*O. Sax.* for-far-spanan *to entice.*]

for-spancg, -spanc *an enticement, allurement.* v. for-spanincg.

for-spanend, es; *m. A seducer;* seductor, Som. Ben. Lye.

for-spanincg, -spanniucg, e; *f. An enticement, allurement;* illĕcebra, Scint. 21, Lye.

for-speca, fore-speca, -spreca, -spræca, an; *m. One who speaks for another, a defender, advocate;* advŏcātus, patrōnus:—Forspeca *vel* mundbora *advŏcātus, patrōnus,* vel *interpellātor,* Ælfc. Gl. 106; Som. 78, 62; Wrt. Voc. 57, 42. Slaga sceal his forspecan on hand syllan, and se forspeca māgum *the slayer shall give pledge to his advocate, and the advocate to the kinsmen,* L. Edm. S. 7; Th. i. 250, 14, 15, 16. Ðe hire forsprecan [-specan MS. B.] synd *who are her advocates,* L. Edm. B. 1; Th. i. 254, 5.

for-specan; *p.* -spæc, *pl.* -spǣcon; *pp.* -specen [for-, specan, sprecan *to speak*] *To speak in vain, speak negatively, deny;* frustra dicĕre, nĕgāre:—Hæbbe he ðæt eall forspecen *let him have spoken that all in vain,* L. C. S. 27; Th. i. 392, 6. Ne sȳ forspecen ne forswīgod *let it not be denied nor concealed,* L. Ath. v. § 8, 9; Th. i. 238, 15.

fōr-spēdian; *p.* ode; *pp.* od *To speed forward, to prosper;* prospĕrāre:—Eálā ðū Driht gehǣl me, eálā ðū Driht wel to fōrspēdienne *O Dŏmĭne salvum me fac, O Dŏmĭne bĕne prospĕrāre,* Ps. Spl. T. 117, 24. v. spēdan.

for-spendan; *p.* de; *pp.* ed [for-, spendan *to spend*] *To spend utterly, to consume;* consūmĕre:—Swīðost ealle hys spēda hȳ forspendaþ *they squander almost all his property,* Ors. 1, 1; Bos. 22, 45.

for-spennen, e; *f. An enticement;* lēnōcĭnium:—Forspennene *lēnōcĭnia,* Mone B. 671. v. for-spenning.

for-spennend, es; *m. A whoremonger;* lēno, Ælfc. Gr. 9, 3; Som. 8, 49: Mone B. 3130. v. for-spanend.

for-spennestre, -spennystre, an; *f. A bawd;* lēna, Ælfc. Gr. 9, 3; Som. 8, 49.

for-spenning, e; *f. An enticement, allurement;* illĕcebra, lēnōcĭnium:—Forspenningce *illĕcebras,* Mone B. 4614. Mid forspenningce *lēnōcĭnio,* 3098. Forspenningce *lēnōcĭnia,* 6013: 6274.

for-spenþ *entices,* Homl. Th. ii. 226, 30; *3rd sing. pres. of* for-spanan.

for-speón *seduced,* Cd. 18; Th. 22, 34; Gen. 350; *p. of* for-spanan.

for-spild, es; *m. Destruction;* perdĭtio:—On forspild *into destruction,* Past. 40, 5; Cott. MS.

for-spildan; *p.* de; *pp.* ed [spild *destruction*] *To bring to naught, destroy;* perdĕre:—Sum sceal on geóguþe, mid Godes meahtum, his earfoþsīþ forspildan *one shall in youth, with God's power, bring to naught his hard lot,* Exon. 88 a; Th. 330, 31; Vy. 59.

for-spillan, -spyllan; *p.* de; *pp.* ed [spillan *to spill, spoil, destroy*] *To spill, lose, waste, destroy, disperse;* perdĕre, disperdĕre, dissĭpāre:—Darfus wolde hine sylfne forspillan *Darius would destroy himself,* Ors. 3, 9; Bos. 65, 40. Alȳfþ reste-dagum wel to dōnne, hwæðer ðe yfele? sāwla gehǣlan, hwæðer ðe forspillan *lĭcet sabbătis benefăcĕre, an mălĕ? anĭmam salvam făcĕre, an perdĕre?* Mk. Bos. 3, 4. Se ðe wyle hys sāwle hāle gedōn, he hig forspilþ; and se ðe wyle hig for me forspyllan, se hig fint *qui vŏluĕrit anĭmam suam salvam făcĕre, perdet eam; qui autem perdĭdĕrit anĭmam suam propter me, invĕniet eam,* Mt. Bos. 16, 25. Ðū forspildest ealle ða ðe forligriaþ fram ðē *perdĭdisti omnes qui fornĭcantur abs te,* Ps. Spl. 72, 26. He his gōd forspilde *dissipasset bŏna ipsīus,* Lk. Bos. 16, 1: 15, 13. Ne forspil ðū sāwle mīne *ne perdas anĭmam meam,* Ps. Spl. 26, 9. Ðæt he fordō oððe forspille of lande gemynd heora *ut perdat de terra mĕmŏriam eōrum,* Ps. Lamb. 33, 17. [*Dut.* ver-spillen *to spend, waste.*]

for-spilledness, -nys, -ness, -nyss, e; *f.* [forspilled, *pp. of* forspillan *to spill;* -nes, -ness] *A spilling, waste, perdition, destruction;* perdĭtio:—Forhwī wæs ðisse sealfe forspilledness geworden *ut quid perdĭtio ista unguenti facta est?* Mk. Bos. 14, 4. Ne forwearþ hyra nān, būton forspillednysse bearn *nēmo ex eis pĕriit, nĭsi fīlius perdĭtiōnis,* Jn. Bos. 17, 12. Se weg is swīðe rūm ðe to forspillednesse gelǣt *spatiōsa via est, quæ dūcit ad perdĭtiōnem,* Mt. Bos. 7, 13.

for-spreca *one who speaks for another, an advocate,* L. Edm. B. 1; Th. i. 254, 5. v. for-speca.

fōr-sprecen; *part. Fore-spoken, fore-mentioned;* præfātus:—Todǣlde se fōrsprecena here on twā *the fore-mentioned army divided into two,* Chr. 885; Erl. 83, 22. v. fōre-sprecen.

for-spyllan *to lose:*—Wyle forspyllan *will lose,* Mt. Bos. 16, 25. v. for-spillan.

for-spyrcan; *p.* te; *pp.* ed [spearca *a spark*] *To dry out, empty;* exarescĕre, arēre:—Forspyrcende synd mīne mearhcōfan *ossa mea aruĕrunt,* Ps. Th. 101, 3.

FORST, es; *m.* FROST; gĕlu:—Se hearda forst *the hard frost,* Exon. 56 b; Th. 201, 19; Ph. 58: 111 a; Th. 425, 11; Rä. 41, 54. Forst *gĕlu,* Ælfc. Gl. 94; Som. 75, 101; Wrt. Voc. 52, 51: 76, 39: Ps. Th. 148, 8. Hwīlum hāra scōc forst of feaxe *sometimes the hoar frost shook from my hair,* Exon. 130 a; Th. 498, 27; Rä. 88, 8. Ān sceal inbindan forstes fetre *one shall unbind frost's fetters,* 90 a; Th. 338, 9; Gn. Ex. 76: Beo. Th. 3222; B. 1609: Salm. Kmbl. 708; Sal. 353. Forste gefeterad *fettered with frost,* Menol. Fox 407; Men. 205: Homl. Th. i. 84, 15. Forstas and snāwas *frosts and snows,* Cd. 192; Th. 239, 31; Dan. 378. [*Chauc.* froste: *Orm.* frosst: *O. Sax.* frost, *m: Frs.* froast: *O. Frs.* frost, forst: *Dut.* vorst, *f: Ger.* frost, *m: M. H. Ger.* vrost, *m: O. H. Ger.* frost, *m: Goth.* frius, *n: Dan.* frost, *m. f: Swed.* frost, *m: Icel.* frost, *n.*] DER. rīm-forst.

for-stæl, *pl.* -stǣlon *stole,* Gen. 27, 36: Mt. Bos. 28, 13; *p. of* for-stelan.

fōr-stæpþ *steps before, goes before,* Ps. Spl. 96, 3; *pres. of* fōr-stapan.

fōr-stal *an assault, fine for an assault,* L. C. S. 12; Th. i. 382, 14. v. fōr-steal.

for-stalian; *p.* ede; *pp.* ed [stalian *to steal*] *To steal away;* aufŭgĕre:—Gif wītepeów hine forstalie *if a penal slave steal himself away,* L. In. 24; Th. i. 118, 6. Gif he hine forstalede *if he should have stolen himself away,* L. Ath. v. § 6, 3; Th. i. 234, 7.

for-standan, -stondan; he -stent; *p.* -stōd, *pl.* -stōdon; *pp.* -standen; *v. trans.* I. *to stand up for, to defend, aid, help, benefit, avail;* defendĕre, prodesse:—Gif hine nelle forstandan *if he will not stand up for him,* L. In. 62; Th. i. 142, 6. Twelfhyndes mannes āþ forstent vi ceorla āþ *a twelve hundred man's oath stands for the oath of six churls,* L. O. 13; Th. i. 182, 19. Ðæt his gewitnes eft nāht ne forstande *that his witness avail again nothing,* L. Ath. i. 10; Th. i. 204, 24. Gif hine hwā forstande *if any one stand up for him,* L. Ath. i. 1; Th. i. 198, 25. Gif hine hwā fōrene forstande *if any one defend him,* v. § 1, 4; Th. i. 230, 4: v. § 8, 2; Th. i. 236, 12: L. Eth. i. 4; Th. i. 284, 3: L. C. S. 33; Th. i. 396, 17. He mihte hord forstandan *he might defend the treasure,* Beo. Th. 5903; B. 2955. Forstond ðu mec *protect thou me,* Exon. 118 b; Th. 455, 31; Hy. 4, 58. Hwā forstandeþ hie, gif ðū hie ne scyldest *who shall defend it, if thou dost not shield it,* Blickl. Homl. 225, 18. Hwæt forstōd ðām betestum mannum—oððe hwæt forstent hit *what did it help the best men—or what does it profit?* Bt. 18, 4; Fox 68, 7, 9. Ne forstent ðæt þweál nāuht *the washing profits nothing,* Past. 54; Hat. MS. II. *to understand;* intellĭgĕre:—Uneáðe ic mæg forstandan ðīne acsunga *I can scarcely understand thy questions,* Bt. 5, 3; Fox 12, 15. Selfe forstōdon his word onwended *they themselves understood his words [to be] perverted,* Cd. 37; Th. 48, 2; Gen. 769. v. under-standan. [Like *Dut.* ver-staan: *Ger.* ver-stehen *to understand.*]

fōr-standan, -stondan; *p.* -stōd, *pl.* -stōdon; *pp.* -standen *To stand before* or *against, withstand, oppose, hinder;* resistĕre, impĕdire:—Ne meahte seó weálāf wīge fōrstandan *the miserable remnant could not withstand in battle,* Bt. Met. Fox 1, 44; Met. 1, 22. Ne māgon gē him ða wīc fōrstondan *to him ye may not hinder the dwellings,* Exon. 42 b; Th. 144, 7; Gū. 674. Ic him ðæt fōrstonde *I hinder them from that,* Exon. 105 a; Th. 398, 15; Rä. 17, 8. Godes engel fōrstōd ðone weg *stĕtit angĕlus Dŏmĭni in via,* Num. 22, 22. v. wiðstandan *to withstand.*

fōr-stapan; he -stæpþ; *p.* -stōp, *pl.* -stōpon; *pp.* -stapen *To step* or go *before, precede;* præcēdĕre:—Fȳr ætfôran him fôrstæpþ [Lamb. fôre-stæpþ] *ignis ante ipsum præcēdet*, Ps. Spl. 96, 3. v. fôre-stapan.

fôr-steal, -steall, -stal, fôre-steall, es; *m.* [fôr, fôre *before;* steal *from* stellan *to leap, spring;* therefore, at least originally, *an assault, consisting in one man springing or placing himself before another, so as to obstruct his progress*, Thorpe's Glos. to A. Sax. Laws]. I. *an assault;* assultus sūper ălĭquem in via rēgia factus, viæ obstructio:—Gif hwâ fôr-steal oððon openne wiðercwyde ongeán lahriht Cristes oððe cyninges gewyrce *if any one commit an assault or open opposition against the law of Christ or of the king*, L. Eth. v. 31; Th. i. 312, 8: vi. 38; Th. i. 324, 21. In L. H. 80, § 2; Th. i. 586, 2, it is said,—'Si in via rēgia fiat assultus sūper ălĭquem, fôrestel est.' II. *the fine for an assault;* mulcta pro assultu:—Ðis syndon ða gerihta ðe se cyning âh ofer ealle men on West-Sexan [MS. Wes-Sexan], ðæt is ... fôrsteal *these are the rights which the king enjoys over all men in Wessex, that is ... the fine for assault*, L. C. S. 12; Th. i. 382, 14, note 27, MS. G. Switelige ic hēr hwæt se eáca is ðe ic ðǣrto ge-unnen hæbbe ... ðæt syndan fôr-steallas *I here declare what the augmentation is which I have thereto granted ... that is the fines for assaults*, Th. Diplm. A. D. 1035; 333, 32: A. D. 1066; 411, 32. See also Schmid Glos. forsteal.

for-stelan, he -steleþ, -stelþ, -stylþ, *pl.* -stelaþ; *p.* -stæl, *pl.* -stǣlon; *pp.* -stolen *To steal with violence, rob, deprive;* fūrāri, surrĭpĕre, prīvāre:—Sēcende forstelan sâwla *quærens fūrāri anĭmas*, Ps. Lamb. fol. 142, 8. Gif ceorl ceáp forstelþ [-stylþ MS. B; -steleþ MS. H.] *if a churl steal property*, L. In. 57; Th. i. 138, 15: L. Alf. 15; Th. i. 48, 5, MS. H. Gif hwâ befæst his feoh to hyrdnysse and hit man forstylþ ðam, ðe hit underfēhþ, gif man ðone þeóf finde, gilde be twîfealdon *si quis com-mendāvĕrit amīco pĕcūniam in custōdiam et ab eo, qui suscēpĕrat, furto ablāta fuĕrit, si invĕnītur fur, duplum reddet*, Ex. 22, 7. Ðǣr þeófas hit delfaþ and forstelaþ *ubi fūres effŏdiunt et fūrantur*, Mt. Bos. 6, 19, 20. Ǣr he ætbræd me mîne frumcennedan and nū ôðre sîþe forstæl mîne bletsunga *prīmogĕnĭta mea ante tŭlit et nunc sĕcundo surrĭpuit benedictiōnem meam*, Gen. 27, 36. Secgeaþ, ðæt hys leorningcnihtas forstǣlon hyne *dīcĭte, quia discĭpŭli fūrāti sunt eum*, Mt. Bos. 28, 13. Gif frigman mannan forstele *if a freeman steal a man*, L. H. E. 5; Th. i. 28, 10: 7; Th. i. 30, 7: L. In. 46; Th. i. 130, 12. Gif hine man forstǣle *if any one should steal him*, L. Ath. v. § 6, § 3; Th. i. 234, 4: L. Alf. 15; Th. i. 48, 5. Iacob niste, ðæt Rachel hæfde ða andlîcnyssa forstolen *Iacob ignōrābat, quod Rachel fūrāta esset idōla*, Gen. 31, 32: Exon. 92 a; Th. 345, 18; Gn. Ex. 190. Ferhþe forstolen *deprived of life*, Cd. 76; Th. 95, 15; Gen. 1579. Gif mon forstolenne ceáp befēhþ *if a man attach stolen cattle*, L. In. 47; Th. i. 132, 4: 75; Th. i. 150, 5. Be forstolenes ceápes forefonge *of the rescuing of stolen property*, 75; Th. i. 150, 4. Be forstolenum flǣsce *of stolen flesh*, 17; Th. i. 114, 1.

for-stent *stands for, avails, profits*, L. O. 13; Th. i. 182, 19: Bt. 18, 4; Fox 68, 9; *3rd sing. pres. of* for-standan. v. standan.

forst-líc; *adj. Frost-like, frozen;* glăciālis:—Forstlîc *glăciālis*, Ælfc. Gl. 94; Som. 75, 104; Wrt. Voc. 52, 54.

for-stôd, *pl.* -stôdon *stood for, availed, profited, understood*, Bt. 18, 4; Fox 68, 7: Cd. 37; Th. 48, 2; Gen. 769; *p. of* for-standan.

fôr-stôd, *pl.* -stôdon *stood before* or *against, withstood*, Num. 22, 22; *p. of* fôr-standan.

for-stolen *stolen*, Gen. 31, 32; *pp. of* for-stelan.

for-stondan *to stand up for, defend, protect*, Exon. 118 b; Th. 455, 31; Hy. 4, 58. v. for-standan.

fôr-stondan *to stand before* or *against, oppose, hinder*, Exon. 42 b; Th. 144, 7; Gū. 674: 105 a; Th. 398, 15; Rä. 17, 8. v. fôr-standan.

fôr-strang; *adj. Very strong;* prævălĭdus:—Fôrstrangne oft wîf hine wrîþ [*though*] *very strong, a woman often binds him*, Exon. 113 a; Th. 434, 2; Rä. 51, 4.

for-stylþ *steals*, Ex. 22, 7; *3rd sing. pres. of* for-stelan.

for-styntan *to break, knock, blunt;* contundĕre, Cot. 48: 177. DER. stintan.

for-sūgan; *p.* -seág, *pl.* -sugon; *pp.* -sogen [sūgan *to suck*] *To suck* or *draw out;* exsūgere:—Wið forsogenum magan oððe aþundenum *for a drawn out or puffed up stomach*, L. M. 2, 7; Lchdm. ii. 186, 17.

for-sūwian, -sūgian; *p.* ode, ade; *pp.* od, ad; *v. trans. To pass over in silence, keep silent;* sĭlentio prætĕrīre, tăcēre, retĭcēre:—We wyllaþ sume forsūwian *we will pass some in silence*, Homl. Th. ii. 138, 26. We woldon iówra Rōmâna bismora beón forsūgiende *we would pass in silence over the shames of you Romans*, Ors. 3, 8; Bos. 63, 23. Gif hî unriht spræcaþ, oððe riht forsūwiaþ *if they speak the wrong, or keep silent the right*, Job Thw. 166, 14: Homl. Th. i. 56, 18. Ic secge ðæt ic ǣr forsūwode *I say that which I before kept silent*, Boutr. Scrd. 18, 27. Iob Godes hērunge ne forsūwade *Job kept not God's praise silent*, Job Thw. 166, 16. Hwî wæs ðæra engla syn forsūgod on ðære bēc Genesis *why was the angels' sin passed over in silence in the book of Genesis?* Boutr. Scrd. 17, 19. Ǣlc cræft biþ forsūgod, gif he biþ būtan wîsdôme *every craft is passed over in silence, if it be without wisdom*, Bt. 17; Fox 60, 10, MS. Cot. v. for-swîgian.

for-swælan; *p.* de; *pp.* ed *To burn, burn up, consume, scorch;* ūrĕre, exūrĕre, combūrĕre, concrĕmāre, exæstuāre:—Ic forswæle oððe forbærne *ūro*, Ælfc. Gr. 28, 4; Som. 31, 11. Hî wendon to Wealinga forda, and ðæt eall forswældon *they turned to Wallingford and burnt it all*, Chr. 1006; Th. 256, 26, col. 1. Fȳr forswælþ wudu, swâ swâ lîget for-swælende dūna *ignis combūrit silvam, sīcut flamma combūrens montes*, Ps. Lamb. 82, 15. Ðâ hit [sǣd] upeóde, seó sunne hit forswælde *when it* [*the seed*] *grew up, the sun scorched* [*burnt up*] *it*, Mk. Bos. 4, 6, quando exortus est sol, exæstuāvit [ἐκαυματίσθη], Vulg. Onleóht breóst and ðinre lufe forswæl *illūmĭna pectŏra tuoque ămōre concrĕma*, Hymn. Surt. 36, 12. Hî wurdon mid swæflenum fȳre forswælede *they were burnt up with sulphurous fire*, Boutr. Scrd. 22, 32: Homl. Th. ii. 496, 27. We sind mid lîgum forswælede *we are scorched up with flames*, Homl. Th. ii. 494, 20. [*Laym. p.* forswælde, *pp.* forswæled.]

for-swâpan; *p.* -sweóp; *pp.* -swâpen *To sweep away;* verrĕre, pro-trūdĕre:—Hie wyrd forsweóp *fate has swept them away*, Beo. Th. 959; B. 477. Hafaþ us God forswâpen on ðâs sweartan mistas *God has swept us into these dark mists*, Cd. 21; Th. 25, 9; Gen. 391. Ealle wyrd forsweóp [MS. forsweof] mîne mâgas *fate has swept away all my kinsmen*, Beo. Th. 5621; B. 2814. [Cf. *O. Sax.* forswîpan *to sweep away*.]

for-swealh, -swealg *swallowed up, devoured*, Ex. 7, 12: Beo. Th. 2249; B. 1122; *p. of* for-swelgan.

for-swealt *died away*, Cot. 65: 190; *p. of* for-sweltan.

for-swelan; *p.* -swæl, *pl.* -swǣlon; *pp.* -swolen [swelan *to burn*] *To burn up, kindle;* combūri:—Hit fǣringa fȳre byrneþ, forsweleþ under sunnan *it suddenly burns with fire, kindles under the sun*, Exon. 63 b; Th. 233, 29; Ph. 532.

for-swelgan, -sweolgan, he -swelgeþ, -swilgeþ, -swelhþ, *pl.* -swelgaþ; *p.* ic, he -swealh, -swealg, ðū -swulge, *pl.* -swulgon; *subj. pres.* -swelge, *pl.* -swelgen; *p.* -swulge, *pl.* -swulgen; *pp.* -swolgen, -swelgen [swelgan *to swallow*] *To swallow up, devour, absorb;* devŏrāre, degluttīre, ab-sorbēre:—Baru sond willaþ rēn forswelgan *the bare sand will swallow up the rain*, Bt. Met. Fox 7, 27; Met. 7, 14: Exon. 35 a; Th. 113, 30; Gū. 164. Wēn is ðæt hî us wyllen forsweolgan *forsĭtan deglūtissent nos*, Ps. Th. 123, 2. Ic forswelge *absorbeo*, Ælfc. Gr. 26, 2; Som. 28, 51. Hit eorþe forswelgeþ *the earth swallows it up*, Ps. Th. 57, 6. Forswilgeþ *devours*, Exon. 113 a; Th. 433, 22; Rä. 50, 11. He forswelhþ hig *absorbet eos*, Ps. Lamb. 57, 10. Ða ðe wudewena hūs forswelgaþ *qui devŏrant dŏmos vĭduārum*, Mk. Bos. 12, 40: Ps. Spl. 13, 8: Exon. 22 b; Th. 62, 4; Cri. 996. Aarones gird forswealh ealle heora girda *devŏrāvit virga Aaron virgas eōrum*, Ex. 7, 12: Cd. 119; Th. 154, 17; Gen. 2557: Ps. Th. 77, 50. Seó eorþe forswealh Dathan and Abiron *Dathan atque Abiron terra absorbuit*, Deut. 11, 6: Ps. Spl. 105, 17. Grendel leófes mannes lîc forswealg *Grendel devoured the beloved man's body*, Beo. Th. 4167; B. 2080: Andr. Kmbl. 3179; An. 1592. Ðe ðū for-swulge *which thou hast swallowed up*, Cd. 43; Th. 57, 34; Gen. 938. We forswulgon hine *devŏrāvĭmus eum*, Ps. Spl. 34, 28: Ps. Lamb. 123, 3. Ne me forswelge deóp *lest the deep swallow me up*, Ps. Th. 68, 15. Wǣnunga wæteru forswulgen us *forsĭtan ăqua absorbuisset nos*, Ps. Lamb. 123, 4. Eall wîsdôm heora forswolgen is *omnis săpientia eōrum devŏrāta est*, 106, 27. Syndon hî æt stâne forswolgene *absorpti sunt juxta petram*, Ps. Th. 140, 8. Heó beóþ forswelgene *they shall be swallowed up*, 57, 8. [*Ger.* ver-schwelgen *to waste in excess*.]

for-swelhþ *swallows up*, Ps. Lamb. 57, 10; *3rd sing. pres. of* for-swelgan.

for-sweltan, he -swilt; *p.* -swealt, *pl.* -swulton; *pp.* -swolten *To die away, perish;* permŏri:—Manig wîf forswilt for hire bearne *many a woman dies because of her child*, Bt. 31, 1; Fox 112, 11, note 17. Forswealt *disparuit*, Cot. 65: 190.

for-sweóf, Beo. Th. 5621, note, = for-sweóp *swept away; p. of* for-swâpan.

for-sweógian; *p.* ode; *pp.* od *To pass over in silence, keep silent;* sĭlentio prætĕrīre:—We ne durron forsweógian ... gif we hit forsweógiaþ *we dare not keep silent ... if we keep it silent*, L. Ælf. P. 1; Th. ii. 364, 11, 13. v. for-swîgian.

for-sweolgan *to swallow up, devour*, Ps. Th. 123, 2. v. for-swelgan.

for-sweóp *swept away*, Beo. Th. 959; B. 477; *p. of* for-swâpan.

for-sweorcan, he -sworceþ; *p.* -swearc, *pl.* -swurcon; *pp.* -sworcen [sweorcan *to dim*] *To be very dark, to darken, obscure;* calīgāre, obscū-rāre:—Eágena bearhtm forsiteþ and forsworceþ *the brightness of the eyes diminishes and darkens*, Beo. Th. 3538; B. 1767. Seó sunne biþ for-sworcen *sol obscūrābĭtur*, Mt. Bos. 24, 29. On forsworcenan *in obscūro*, Prov. 7.

for-swerian; *p.* -swôr, *pl.* -swôron; *pp.* -sworen *To* FORSWEAR, *to swear falsely, perjure;* ejūrāre, pējĕrāre:—He sigewǣpnum forsworen hæfde *he had forsworn martial weapons*, Beo. Th. 1613; B. 804. Ic forswerige *pējĕro*, Ælfc. Gl. 84; Som. 73, 98; Wrt. Voc. 49, 6. Ne forswere ðū *non perjūrābis*, Mt. Bos. 5, 33. Gyf gehâdod man forswerige oððe forlicge, gebēte ðæt be ðæm ðe seó dǣd sȳ *if a man in orders swear falsely or fornicate, let him make amends for it according as the deed may be*, L. E. G. 3; Th. i. 168, 5. Gif hwylc lǣwede man hine forswerige, fæste iv geár *if any layman perjure himself, let him fast four years*,

L. Ecg. P. ii. 24; Th. ii. 192, 6, 14. Forsworen *perjūrus*, Wrt. Voc. 86, 69: Gen. 24, 8. We ne beóþ forsworene *ĕrĭmus mundi ab hoc jūrāmento*, Jos. 2, 20. He hine forsworenne and trȳwleásne clypode *he called him forsworn and faithless*, Chr. 1094; Erl. 229, 32. Ða forsworenan mid forsworenum forwurþaþ *perjurers shall perish with perjurers*, Homl. Th. i. 132, 24. [*Ger.* sich ver-schwören *to conspire.*]

for-swīgian, -sweógian, -swūgian, -sūwian, -sūğian, -sȳgian, to -swīgianne, -swīgienne; *p.* ode, ade, ede; *pp.* od, ad, ed. **I.** *v. trans.* *To pass over in silence, keep silent, conceal;* sĭlentio prætĕrīre:—Betwih ðās þing nis to forswīgianne, hwylc heofonlīc wundor and mægen ætȳwed wæs, ðā his bān gefunden and gemēted wǣron *inter quæ nequaquam sĭlentio prætereundum reor, quid virtūtis ac mīrācŭli cælestis fuĕrit ostensum, cum ossa ejus inventa sunt*, Bd. 3, 11; S. 535, 9. Nis us ðonne se hlīsa to forswīgienne *nec sĭlentio prætereunda opīnio*, 2, 1; S. 501, 1. Forswīged yrfe-bōc [MS. -bec] *suppressum testāmentum*, Ælfc. Gl. 13; Som. 57, 104; Wrt. Voc. 20, 43. **II.** *v. intrans.* *To be silent;* retĭcēre:—He rīcum mannum nō for āre ne for ege nǣfre forswīgian wolde *nunquam dīvĭtĭbus hŏnōris sīve tĭmōris grātia retĭcēbat*, Bd. 3, 5; S. 527, 10. [*Ger.* ver-schweigen *to pass over in silence.*]

for-swilgeþ *swallows up, devours*, Exon. 113 a; Th. 433, 22; Rä. 50, 11; *3rd sing. pres. of* for-swelgan.

for-swilt *dies*, Bt. 31, 1; Fox 112, 11, note 17; *3rd sing. pres. of* for-sweltan.

fōr-swīþ; *adj. Very strong, very great;* prævălĭdus:—Is ðīn meaht fōrswīþ *is thy power very great?* Exon. 92 b; Th. 348, 11; Sch. 26.

for-swīðan; he -swīþ; *p.* ede; *pp.* ed *To overcome;* reprĭmĕre:—Se ðas orsorgnesse ðe he hēr hæfþ ne forswīþ mid ðære gesceádwīsnesse his ingeþonces *he does not overcome the prosperity he has here with prudence of mind*, Past. 50, 1; Hat. MS. Seó him sāra gehwylc symle forswīðede *which constantly overcame each of his pains*, Exon. 46 b; Th. 160, 5; Gū. 939. Forsuīða *confundere*, Rtl. 50, 13; *præcedere*, 32, 21.

fōr-swīðe; *adv. Very strongly, very much, vehemently, utterly;* valde, vehĕmenter:—Hī wurdon gehergode and gehȳnde fōrswīðe eahtatȳne geár *afflicti sunt et vehĕmenter oppressi per annos dĕcem et octo*, Jud. 10, 8: Ps. Th. 84, 8. Næfde se here Angelcyn ealles fōrswīðe gebrōcod *the army had not utterly broken up the English race*, Chr. 897; Erl. 94, 29.

for-swolgen *swallowed up, devoured*, Ps. Lamb. 106, 27; *pp. of* for-swelgan.

for-sworcen *darkened, obscured*, Mt. Bos. 24, 29; *pp. of* for-sweorcan.

for-sworceþ *darkens*, Beo. Th. 3538; B. 1767; *3rd sing. pres. of* for-sweorcan.

for-sworen *forsworn, perjured*, Gen. 24, 8; *pp. of* for-swerian.

for-sworennys, -nyss, e; *f.* [forsworen, *pp. of* forswerian *to forswear;* -nys, -nyss] *False swearing, perjury;* pejĕrātio, perjūrium:—Cȳpmannum gedafenaþ ðæt hī sōþfæstnysse healdon, and lofian heora þing būton lāþre forsworennysse *it is fitting to merchants that they hold truth, and praise their things without hateful perjury*, Homl. Th. ii. 328, 9.

for-swūgian; *p.* ode; *pp.* od *To pass over in silence;* sĭlentio prætĕrīre:—Ælc ānweald biþ forswūgod, gif he biþ būtan wīsdōme *every power is passed over in silence, if it be without wisdom*, Bt. 17; Fox 60, 10. v. for-swīgian.

for-swulge *hast swallowed up* or *devoured*, Cd. 43; Th. 57, 34; Gen. 938; *2nd sing. p. of* for-swelgan.

for-swulgen *would have swallowed up* or *devoured*, Ps. Lamb. 123, 4; *subj. p. pl. of* for-swelgan.

for-swulgon *swallowed up, devoured*, Ps. Spl. 34, 28; *p. pl. of* forswelgan.

for-sȳgian; *p.* ode, ede; *pp.* od, ed *To pass over in silence, conceal;* silentio prætĕrīre:—Hū wēne we hū monegra māran bismra hȳ forsȳgedon *can we think how many greater reproaches they concealed?* Ors. 4, 4; Bos. 80, 27. v. for-swīgian.

for-syhþ *despises*, Lk. Bos. 9, 26; *3rd sing. pres. of* for-seón.

fōr-syngian, -singian; *p.* ode, ade; *pp.* od, ad [syngian *to sin*] *To sin greatly;* multum peccāre:—Ne wurþ ǣnig man on worlde swā swīðe fōrsyngad, ðe he wið Gode gebētan ne mǣge *no man in the world is so very sinful, that he may not make atonement to God*, L. Pen. 12; Th. ii. 282, 1. [Cf. *Ger.* sich versündigen *to sin against.*]

fōr-tācen [=fōre-tācen] *afore-token;* portentum, Ælfc. Gl. 5; Som. 56, 12.

for-teáh *misled, seduced*, Exon. 11 b; Th. 17, 14; Cri. 270; *p. of* for-teón. v. teón.

for-tendan; *p.* -tende [=-tendede], *pl.* -tendon; *pp.* -tended [for-, tendan *to burn*] *To burn off* or *away, sear;* inūrĕre:—Ðǣm mǣdencildum [MS. -cildan], ða wīf fortendon ðæt swȳðre breóst fōran, ðæt hit weaxan ne sceolde, ðæt hī hæfden ðȳ strengran scyte; forðon hī mon hēt on Creácisc Amāzanas, ðæt is on Englisc fortende *from the female children, the women burnt off the right breast so far that it should not grow, that they might have stronger shot; therefore, they are called in Greek* Amazons, *that is in English seared*, Ors. 1, 10; Bos. 33, 10–13. *The Latin of Ors. is,*—fēmĭnas stŭdiōse nutriunt, *inustis* infantium dextĕriōrĭbus mamillis, ne sagittārum jactus impĕdīrentur, unde Amāzŏnes dictæ, *Ors. Hav.* Lib. I. Cap. xv, p. 65, 3–4. [Amazons='Αμάζονες, -όνων, *pl. f.* ἀ- *without*, μαζός *a breast*, or ἀ-, ἀμ- *intensive, and* ἄζω *to dry, parch*, or *sear.*]

Fortende, a; *pl. f.* [*pp. of* fortendan *to burn off* or *away, sear*] *The seared ones, Amazons;* Amāzŏnes, Ors. 1, 10; Bos. 33, 13.

for-teón, -tión; *impert.* -teó, -teoh, *pl.* -teóþ; *subj.* -teó, *pl.* -teón [for-, teón *to draw, lead*] *To mislead, seduce;* sedūcĕre. v. teón, tión.

forþ; *adv.* [faran *to go*] FORTH, *thence, hence, forwards, onwards, henceforth, further, still;* inde, hinc, prorsum, porro, dehinc, deinceps, tămen:—Abraham eóde forþ *Abraham went forth*, Gen. 18, 16: Num. 22, 35: Jud. 16, 30. Alǣdaþ mīne bān forþ mid eów *efferte ossa mea hinc vōbiscum*, Ex. 13, 19: Beo. Th. 1229; B. 612: Cd. 111; Th. 147, 12; Gen. 2438: Exon. 21 b; Th. 57, 20; Cri. 921: Elen. Kmbl. 2207; El. 1105. Forþ on leóht gelǣded *brought forth into light;* prolātum in lūcem, Bd. 4, 19; S. 588, 37. Teáh heora ōðer forþ fægere bōc *one of them drew forth a beautiful book*, Bd. 5, 13; S. 632, 36; 633, 5. Gewāt se dæg forþ *the day was going forth*, Lk. Bos. 9. 12. Hī ne mihton ðanon fleón, ne forþ ne underbæc *they could not flee thence, neither forwards nor backwards*, Jos. 8, 20: Cd. 118; Th. 153, 8; Gen. 2535. Cynrīc rīcsode forþ xxvi wintra *Cynric reigned on for twenty-six years*, Chr. 534; Erl. 14, 33. Swā forþ swā he mihte *as far as he could*, Bd. 3, 17; S. 545, 16: 5, 21; S. 643, 5. Heald forþ tela niwe sibbe *hold well henceforth our new kinship*, Beo. Th. 1901; B. 948: Cd. 22; Th. 28, 17; Gen. 437. Gif ðū forþ his willan gehȳrsum beón wylt *si deinceps voluntāti ejus obsecundāre vŏlŭeris*, Bd. 2, 12; S. 515, 27. He lēt ðæt forþ on his bōsme awunian *he let it still remain in his bosom*, Bd. 3, 2; S. 525, 13: Cd. 17; Th. 21, 7; Gen. 320: Exon. 11 a; Th. 13, 31; Cri. 211. And swā forþ *and so forth, and so on*, Ælfc. Gr. 25; Som. 26, 59: Homl. Th. ii. 198, 18: Bd. de nat. rerum; Wrt. popl. science 8, 26; Lchdm. iii. 250, 7. On cnihthāde and swā forþ eallne ðonne giógoþhād *in childhood and then throughout youth*, Bt. 38, 5; Fox 206, 24. [*O. Sax.* forð: *Frs.* fort, ford: *O. Frs.* forth, ford: *Dut.* voort: *Ger.* fort: *M. H. Ger.* vort.] v. forþon=furþ-um, *dat. of an old adj.* forþ, furþum-līc.

forþ; *prep. Out of, forth;* e, ex: used in composition, Som. Ben. Lye.

for-ða; *adv. For that cause, therefore;* proptĕrea:—Forða bletsode ðē God on ēcnysse *proptĕrea benedixit te Deus in æternum*, Ps. Spl. 44, 3. v. for-ðam; *adv.*

forþ-acīgan; *p.* de; *pp.* ed *To call forth;* provŏcāre:—He monige forþacīgde *he called forth many*, Bd. 5, 14; S. 635, 6.

forþ-agān; *part. Gone forth, passed;* prætĕrĭtus, peractus:—Tīma ys forþagān *hōra prætĕriit*, Mt. Bos. 14, 15: Mk. Bos. 6, 35. Forþagāne ðȳ wintre *peracta hiĕme*, Bd. 4, 28; S. 606, 22.

for-ðam, for-ðæm, for-ðan, for-ðon, for-ðam-ðe, for-ðæm-ðe, for-ðan-ðe, for-ðon-ðe; *conj.* [*for that which*] *For that, for that reason which, for, because;* nam, quia:—Eádige synd ða gāstlīcan þearfan, forðam hyra ys heofena rīce *blessed are the poor in spirit, for theirs is the kingdom of heaven*, Mt. Bos. 5, 3: Ps. Spl. 24, 22: Beo. Th. 301; B. 149: Cd. 167; Th. 209, 30; Exod. 507: Runic pm. 20; Kmbl. 343, 15; Hick. Thes. i. 135, 40. Swīðost he fōr ðyder for ðǣm horshwælum, forðæm hī habbaþ swȳðe æðele bān on hyra tōþum *he went there chiefly for the walruses, because they have very good bone in their teeth*, Ors. 1, 1; Bos. 20, 16, 28: Bt. Met. Fox 5, 76; Met. 5, 38. Me ðæt gelǣrdon leóde mīne ðæt ic ðē sōhte, forðan hie mægenes cræft mīne cūðon *my people counselled me that I should seek thee, because they knew my capacity of strength*, Beo. Th. 840; B. 418: Ps. Spl. 6, 2: Apstls. Kmbl. 93; Ap. 47: Menol. Fox 42; Men. 21. Hī wīte þoliaþ forðon hie þegnscipe Godes forgȳmdon *they suffer torment because they neglected the service of God*, Cd. 18; Th. 21, 19; Gen. 326: Exon. 10 a; Th. 11, 11; Cri. 169: Beo. Th. 4688; B. 2349: Ps. Spl. 11, 1: Bd. 4, 19; S. 587, 30. Eádige synd ða ðe nū wēpaþ, forðamðe hī beóþ gefrēfrede *blessed are they who weep now, for they shall be comforted*, Mt. Bos. 5, 4, 5, 6, 7, 8, 9, 10, 12: Cd. 184; Th. 230, 1; Dan. 226: Bt. Met. Fox 20, 73; Met. 20, 37. Næfþ ðys word [willan] nǣnne imperātīvum, forðanðe se willa sceall beón ǣfre frig *this verb* [*to will*] *has no imperative, for the will must always be free*, Ælfc. Gr. 32; Som. 36, 11: Homl. Th. ii. 290, 1, 3, 25. Forðonðe sió sunne ðǣr gǣþ neár on setl, ðonne on ōðrum lande, ðǣr syndon lȳðran wedera ðonne on Brittannia *because the sun in its setting goes nearer there than in any other land, there are milder weathers than in Britain*, Ors. 1, 1; Bos. 24, 20, 32: Mt. Bos. 7, 13: Ps. Spl. 1, 7: Exon. 25 b; Th. 74, 7; Cri. 1203: Beo. Th. 1010; B. 503.

for-ðam, for-ðæm, for-ðan, for-ðon; *adv. For that cause, consequently;* proptĕrea, idcirco, ĭdeo:—Forðam ic secge eów *ĭdeo dīco vōbis*, Mt. Bos. 6, 25: 12, 27, 31: Cd. 5; Th. 6, 32; Gen. 97. Ne mōst ðū wesan forðæm ormōd *thou must not consequently be dejected*, Bt. Met. Fox 5, 58; Met. 5, 29. He arās of deáþe, and forðan synd ðās wundru gefremode on him *ipse surrexit a mortuis, et ĭdeo virtūtes operantur in eo*, Mt. Bos. 14, 2: Beo. Th. 1362; B. 679: Cd. 217; Th. 276, 25; Sat. 194: Andr. Kmbl. 915; An. 458: Elen. Kmbl. 618; El. 309. Wæs he sōþfæstnysse wer, and he forðon eallum wæs leóf *he was a man of truth, and was consequently dear to all*, Bd. 3, 15; S. 541, 22: Cd. 9; Th. 11, 9; Gen. 172: Exon. 10 a; Th. 10, 7; Cri. 148: Beo. Th. 6035;

B. 3021: Menol. Fox 382; Men. 192: Ps. Th. 54, 20: Salm. Kmbl. 921; Sal. 460.

forþ-arǽsan; *p.* de; *pp.* ed *To rush forth;* prosĭlīre:—Ic forþarǽse *prosĭlio*, Ælfc. Gr. 30, 3; Som. 34, 43. Forþarǽsde of his bedde *prosĭliit ex lecto suo*, Greg. Dial. 1, 2.

forþ-ascúfan; *p.* -sceáf, *pl.* -scufon; *pp.* -scofen *To shove forth, drive forward;* propellĕre, Exon. 129 b; Th. 498, 1; Rä. 87, 6.

forþ-asendan; *p.* -sende; *pp.* -sended, -send *To send forth;* emittĕre:—Binnan þrȳm dagum he mæg đone migþan forþasendan *within three days he may send forth the urine*, Herb. 7, 3; Lchdm. i. 98, 8. Forþasend *emissus*, Greg. Dial. 1, 12.

forþ-asettan; *p.* -sette; *pp.* -seted *To set forth, appoint, make;* propōnĕre, pōnĕre, statuĕre:—Ic đone frumbearn forþasette ofer eorþcyningas ealra heáhstne *ĕgo prīmogĕnĭtum pōnam illum, excelsum præ rēgĭbus terræ*, Ps. Th. 88, 24.

forþ-asliden *passed* or *gone before, tumbled* or *fallen down;* prælapsus, prolapsus, Som. Ben. Lye. DER. a-slīdan.

forþ-ateón; *p.* -teáh, *pl.* -tugon; *pp.* -togen *To draw forth, bring forth, produce;* proferre, prodūcĕre, edūcĕre:—Forþateónde *prodūcens*, Ps. Lamb. 103, 14. Seó eorþe forþateáh grōwende wirte *protŭlit terra herbam vĭrentem*, Gen. 1, 12. God đá forþateáh of đære moldan ǽlces cynnes treów *produxitque Dŏmĭnus Deus de hŭmo omne lignum*, Gen. 2, 9. He forþateáh wæter of stāne *eduxit ăquam de petra*, Ps. Lamb. 77, 16. Forþ-atogen *progenitus*, Hpt. Gl.

forþ-atincg, e; *f. An exhorting, exhortation, encouraging;* exhortātio, Prooem. R. Concord.

forþ-aurnen; *part. Run forth, elapsed;* elapsus:—Nalæs micelre tīde forþaurnenre *non multo elapso tempŏre*, Bd. 4, 6; S. 573, 37.

forþ-bǽro; *f. indecl. A bringing forth, a production;* procreātio, productio:—Forþbǽro tīd *the time of production*, Cd. 6; Th. 8, 31; Gen. 132. Cf. onbǽru. Or is forþ-bǽro *adj. f.*? Cf. *O. H Ger.* frambari *inclytus; Icel.* frábærr *surpassing;* and forþ-genge for similar adjectival forms.

forþ-becuman, -bicuman; *p.* -com, -cwom, *pl.* -cōmon, -cwōmon; *pp.* -cumen *To come forth, proceed;* procēdĕre:—He gesyhþ fram hwylcum wyrttruman seó besmitenes forþbecom *vĭdet a qua rādīce inquĭnātio illa processĕrit*, Bd. 1, 27; S. 497, 8: Ps. Th. 72, 6.

forþ-beran; he -bereþ, -bireþ; *p.* -bær, *pl.* -bǽron; *pp.* -boren *To bear* or *carry forth, bring forth, bring forward, produce;* proferre, perhĭbēre:—Đone æđelan Albanum seó wæstmberende Bryton forþbereþ *Albānum egrĕgium fēcunda Britannia profert*, Bd. 1, 7; S. 476, 34. Đætte ealle openlīce be heora dǽde þurh andetnesse forþbǽron *ut omnes pălam quæ gessĕrant confĭtendo proferrent*, 4, 27; S. 604, 23: Blickl. Homl. 25, 2; 101, 30. Đæt he gewitnesse forþbǽre be đam leóhte *ut testĭmōnium perhĭbēret de lūmĭne*, Jn. Bos. 1, 8.

forþ-berstan; *p.* -bærst, *pl.* -burston; *pp.* -borsten *To burst* or *break forth;* erumpĕre, Som. Ben. Lye.

forþ-beseón; *p.* -beseah, *pl.* -besāwon; *pp.* -besewen *To look forth, look out;* prospĭcĕre:—He forþbeseah of heánnysse hālgan his *prospexit de excelso sancto suo*, Ps. Lamb. 101, 20.

forþ-bicuman; *p.* -bicwom, *pl.* -bicwōmon; *pp.* -bicumen *To come forth*; provĕnīre:—Forþbicwom Godes þegna blǽd *the prosperity of God's servants came forth*, Exon. 18 a; Th. 44, 28; Cri. 709. v. forþ-becuman.

forþ-blǽstan; *p.* te; *pp.* ed [blǽst *a blast*] *To blast forth, puff out, burst out;* insufflāre, erumpĕre, Cot. 74.

forþ-blāwan; *p.* -bleów, *pl.* -bleówon; *pp.* -blāwen *To blow forth, belch out;* eructāre, Cot. 78.

forþ-boren; *part.* [*pp. of* forþ-beran] *Born forth, noble-born, high-born;* clāris parentĭbus ortus, nōbĭlis:—We lǽraþ đæt ǽnig forþboren preóst ne forseó đone læsborenan *we enjoin that no high-born priest despise the lower born*, L. Edg. C. 13; Th. ii. 246, 20.

forþ-brengan; *p.* -brohte; *pp.* -broht [forþ, brengan *to bring*] *To bring forth, produce, fulfil, accomplish;* proferre, prodūcĕre, dedūcĕre, effĭcĕre:—Wel forþbrengeþ hit *it brings forth well*, Bt. Met. Fox 29, 142; Met. 29, 71. Se Metod eallra gesceafta ealle forþbrengþ *the Creator of all things produces them all*, Bt. 39, 13; Fox 234, 19. Forþbrohte *proferret*, Bd. 4, 24; S. 596, 35. He forþbrohte swylce flōd wæteru *deduxit tamquam flūmina ăquas*, Ps. Lamb. 77, 16.

forþ-bringan; *p.* -brang, *pl.* -brungon; *pp.* -brungen [forþ, bringan *to bring*] *To bring forth, produce, fulfil, accomplish;* proferre, prodūcĕre, effĭcĕre:—Gif he đone āþ forþbringan ne mæg *if he cannot bring forth the oath*, L. Ath. iv. 6; Th. i. 224, 17. He ne mæg đæt forþbringan *he cannot accomplish it*, Bt. 18, 3; Fox 64, 29. Yfel man yfel forþbringþ *mălus hŏmo profert mălum*, Lk. Bos. 6, 45: Mt. Bos. 13, 52. Ealle đa wæstmas đe eorđe forþbringeþ *all the fruits that earth produces*, Blickl. Homl. 39, 17. Đe swā manig ungelimp wæs forþbringende *which was bringing forth so many misfortunes*, Chr. 1086; Erl. 220, 23.

forþ-brohte *brought forth*, Ps. Lamb. 77, 16; *p. of* forþ-brengan.

forþ-bylding, e; *f. An instigation, incitement, emboldening;* incĭtātio:—Heora feónda forþbylding *the emboldening of their foes*, Chr. 999; Erl. 135, 38.

forþ-clipung, e; *f. A calling forth, provoking, an appeal;* provŏcātio, evŏcātio, Som. Ben. Lye.

forþ-clypian; *p.* ode; *pp.* od *To call forth, provoke;* provŏcāre:—Forþclypiende us betwynan *provŏcantes invĭcem*, Gal. 5, 26.

forþ-cuman; he -cymeþ, -cymþ, *pl.* -cumaþ; *p.* -com, *pl.* -cōmon; *subj. pres.* -cume, -cyme, *pl.* -cumen, -cymen; *pp.* -cumen, -cymen *To come forth* or *forward, proceed, succeed, arrive;* procēdĕre, pervĕnīre, advĕnīre:—Metod hēht leóht forþcuman *the Creator bade light to come forth*, Cd. 6; Th. 8, 11; Gen. 122. Đonne forþcumaþ fyrenfulra þreát hīge onlīc *cum exŏrientur peccātōres sīcut fēnum*, Ps. Th. 91, 6. Siđđan hit forþcume *after it is come forth;* postquam nātus sit, L. M. I. P. 10; Th. ii. 268, 6. Đæt ǽlc spræc hæbbe āndagan hwænne hit forþcume *that every suit have a term when it shall come forward*, L. Ed. 11; Th. i. 164, 21. Gif se āþ forþcume *if the oath succeed*, L. Eth. i. 1; Th. i. 280, 15; 282, 7. Đæt he forþcume to đǽm gesǽlþum *that he may arrive at the felicities*, Bt. Met. Fox 21, 16; Met. 21, 8. Đonne ic forþcyme *when I come forth*, Exon. 125 a; Th. 480, 28; Rä. 64, 8. Wæs forþcumen geóc æfter gyrne *comfort was come forth after sorrow*, Andr. Kmbl. 3167; An. 1586. Forþcymene, *pp. pl. come forth*, Exon. 104 a; Th. 394, 28; Rä. 14, 10.

forþ-cyme, es; *m. A coming forth, egress;* egressus, effūsio:—On đæra cilda forþcyme *in effūsiōne infantum*, Gen. 38, 28.

forþ-cyme *may come forth* or *forward*, Exon. 125 a; Th. 480, 28; Rä. 64, 8; *subj. pres. of* forþ-cuman.

forþ-cymen *come forth*, Exon. 104 a; Th. 394, 28; Rä. 14, 10; *pp. of* forþ-cuman.

forþ-cȳđan; *p.* de; *pp.* ed *To declare, pronounce;* pronuntiāre, declārāre, Hymn. Lye.

forþ-dōn; *p.* -dyde; *pp.* -dōn *To put forth;* proferre:—Hēt he his tungan forþdōn of his mūþe, and him eówian *linguam proferre ex ōre, ac sibi ostendĕre jussit*, Bd. 5, 2; S. 615, 6.

fōr-þearle; *adv. Very much, greatly;* valde, vehĕmenter:—He behȳdde his swīđran hand, ofsceamod fōrþearle *he hid his right hand, greatly ashamed thereof*, Ælfc. T. 37, 13: Jud. 3, 8.

fōr-þearlīce; *adv. Very severely, strictly;* districte, R. Ben. 2.

for-þencan; *p.* -þohte, *pl.* -þohton; *pp.* -þoht *To misthink, disdain, despise, distrust, despair;* dedignāri, diffīdĕre:—Đæt is nū git đīnre unrihtwīsnesse đæt đū eart fullneáh forþoht; ac ic nolde đæt đū đē forþohtest; forđam se se đe hine forþencþ, se biþ ormōd *it is still thy fault that thou art almost despaired; but I was unwilling that thou shouldest distrust thyself; for he who distrusts himself is without courage*, Bt. 8; Fox 24, 15–18. He lǽrde đæt đa þearfan hȳ ne forþohton *he taught that they should not despise the poor*, Ps. Th. arg. 48. He fela worda spræc, forþoht þearle *he uttered many words, greatly despaired*, Bt. Met. Fox 1, 163; Met. 1, 82. [*Ger.* ver-denken *to think wrong, blame.*] v. fore-þencan.

for-þeón; *p.* -þeóde; *pp.* -þeód *To oppress;* opprĭmere, subĭgĕre:—Scīrne scīman sceadu forþeóde *shadow oppressed the bright splendour*, Rood Kmbl. 108; Kr. 54. [*O. H. Ger.* fardúhian *opprimere.*]

for-þeóstrian; *p.* ode, ade; *pp.* od, ad *To darken, be dark;* obscūrāre:—He asende þeóstru and forþeóstrade ođđe swearc *mīsit tenebras et obscūrāvit*, Ps. Lamb. 104, 28. [*Ger.* ver-düstern *to darken.*] v. a-þȳstrian.

forþ-fæderas; *gen.* a; *dat.* um; *pl. m. Forefathers;* mājōres:—Abrahames forþfæderas *Abraham's forefathers*, Ælfc. T. 7, 26. Forþfæderas *tritavi*, Hpt. Gl. 426. v. fōrefæder.

forþ-faran; *p.* -fōr, *pl.* -fōron; *pp.* -faren *To go forth, depart, die;* discēdĕre, abīre, defungi:—Đætte hī ǽgđer ge forþfaraþ ge eftcumaþ *that they both depart and return*, Bt. 33, 4; Fox 128, 8. On đam ilcan geáre he forþfōr *in the same year he died*, Chr. 571; Erl. 19, 18. Forþfaren *defunctus*, Ælfc. Gr. 41; Som. 44, 31: Wrt. Voc. 85, 58. Đā Hērōdes wæs forþfaren *defuncto Hērōde*, Mt. Bos. 2, 19: Chr. 685; Erl. 41, 34: Homl. Th. ii. 158, 4. Synd forþfarene, đe đæs cildes sāwle sōhton *defuncti sunt, qui quærēbant anĭmam puĕri*, Mt. Bos. 2, 20. [*Laym.* forđfaren *pp. dead.*]

forþ-faru, e; *f. A going forth, departure, death;* ŏbĭtus, Som. Ben. Lye. [*Laym.* forđfare *departure, death.*]

forþ-feran; *p.* de; *pp.* ed *To go forth, depart, die;* decēdĕre, defungi, mŏri, expīrāre:—He đǽr forþferan sceolde *he should die there*, Bd. 3, 29; S. 561, 25: 4, 11; S. 579, 29, 42. Hī đǽr cȳddon hine forþferende *quem ĭbĭdem ŏbiisse narrāvĕrint*, 3, 29; S. 561, 4. Se Hǽlend asende his stefne and forþferde *Iesus emissa vōce magna expīrāvit*, Mk. Bos. 15, 37. Forþferde đæt wīf *mŭlier defuncta est*, Mt. Bos. 22, 27: Lk. Bos. 16, 22: Bd. 3, 29; S. 561, 17: 4, 11; S. 579, 14; 580, 3: Chr. 101; Erl. 9, 10: 534; Erl. 14, 32: 544; Erl. 17, 5. Cūþrēd and Coenbryht on ānum geáre forþferdun *Cuthred and Cenbyrht died in one year*, Chr. 661; Erl. 34, 13. He forþfered wæs *defunctus est*, Bd. 2, 3; S. 505, 3. Hī wurdon fǽrlīce forþferede *they suddenly died*, Homl. Th. ii. 174, 15. Đā mette he đane man forþferedne þe ǽr untrum wæs *then he found the man dead that before was ill*, Blickl. Homl. 217, 18.

forþ-ferednes, -ness, e; *f. A going forth, departure, death;* ŏbĭtus, transmigrātio :—Ongeáton hī on đon, đæt heó to đon đider com, đæt heó hire sǽde đa neáh-tīde hire forþferednesse *ex quo intellexēre quod ipsa ei tempus suæ transmigrātiōnis in proxĭmum nunciāre vēnisset*, Bd. 4, 9; S. 577, 34, MS. C.

forþ-fering, e; *f. A going forth, deceasing, dying;* defunctio, decessio, Scint.

forþ-fleógan; *p.* -fleáh, *pl.* -flugon; *pp.* -flogen *To fly forth;* evŏlāre :—Hie lēton forþfleógan flāna scūras *they let fly forth showers of arrows,* Judth. 11; Thw. 24, 33; Jud. 221.

forþ-flōwan; *p.* -fleów, *pl.* -fleówon; *pp.* -flōwen *To flow forth;* efflŭere :—Genihtsum wæter forþflōweþ *plentiful water flows forth,* Bd. 5, 10; S. 625, 24.

forþ-fōr, e; *f.* [fōr *a going*] *A going forth, departure, death;* exĭtus, ŏbĭtus, mors :—Forđamđe him cūþ forþfōr toweard wǽre *eo quod certus sibi exĭtus esset,* Bd. 3, 19; S. 547, 16. Đæt is gesægd đæt he wǽre gewis his sylfes forþfōre, of đām đe we nū secgan hȳrdon *præscius sui ŏbĭtus exstitisse, ex his quæ narrāvĭmus, vĭdētur,* 4, 24; S. 599, 14: 3, 19; S. 547, 17. He læg æt forþfōre *incĭpiēbat mŏri,* Jn. Bos. 4, 47: Bd. 4, 24; S. 598, 28, 37: 5, 3; S. 616, 17. Be his forþfōre *de ŏbĭtu ejus,* 2, 3; S. 504, 13. Heora gemynde and forþfōre mid mæssesange mǽrsade syndon *their memory and decease are celebrated with mass-song,* 2, 3; S. 504, 41.

forþ-forlǽtan; *p.* -forlēt, *pl.* -forlēton; *pp.* -forlǽten *To let forth, send forth;* emittĕre :—Egeslīcne cwide Weard ofer đæt fǽge folc forþforlǽteþ *the Lord shall send forth a dreadful utterance over the fated people,* Exon. 30 a; Th. 92, 34; Cri. 1518.

forþ-forlǽtenes, -ness, e; *f. A free permission, license, fault;* derelictio :—On đara mānfulra forþforlǽtenesse *on account of the license of the wicked,* Bt. 5, 1; Fox 10, 24.

forþ-framian, -fremian; *p.* ode; *pp.* od [fremian *to advance, avail*] *To grow up, ripen;* pubescĕre :—Forþframiende *pubescens,* Cot. 150.

forþ-fromung, e; *f.* [fromung *a going*] *A going forth, going away, departure;* profectio :—Geblissod is Egypt on forþfromunge heora *lætāta est Ægyptus in profectiōne eōrum,* Ps. Spl. C. 104, 36.

forþ-gān; *p.* -eóde, *pl.* -eódon; *pp.* -gān *To go forth, proceed, go* or *pass by;* exīre, procēdĕre, prætĕrīre, transīre :—Raulf wolde forþgān mid his folce *Ralph would go forth with his people,* Chr. 1075; Erl. 213, 18. Đa hwīle đe ic forþgā *dōnec transeam,* Ex. 33, 22. Þūsend geár befōran eágan đīnum, swā swā dæg estra [= giestra] se forþgǽþ *mille anni ante ŏcŭlos tuos tanquam dies hesterna quæ prætĕriit,* Ps. Spl. 89, 4. Đa þing đe of đam men forþgāþ, þa hine besmītaþ *quæ de hŏmĭne procēdunt illa sunt, quæ commūnĭcant hŏmĭnem,* Mk. Bos. 7, 15. Đā he forþeóde *quo transeunte cōram eo,* Ex. 34, 6. Đa đe forþeódon *qui prætĕrĭbant,* Ps. Spl. C. 128, 7. Hȳ on heora dagum butu forþeōdon *ambo processissent in diebus suis,* Lk. 1, 7.

forþ-gang, es; *m.* I. [gang I. *a going*] *a going forth, progress, advance;* processus, progressus :—Đæs cyninges rīce ge fōreweard ge forþgang *cūjus rēgis regni et princĭpia et processus,* Bd. 5, 23; S. 646, 3. Se hæfþ forþgang fōr Gode and fōr worulde *he shall have progress before God and before the world,* Ælfc. T. 1, 7. II. [gang II. *latrīna*] *a passage, drain, privy;* meātus, secessus, latrīna :—Forþgang *meātus,* Ælfc. Gl. 75; Som. 71, 75; Wrt. Voc. 44, 57. Eall đæt on đone mūþ gǽþ, gǽþ on đa wambe, and byþ on forþgang asend *quod in os intrat, in ventrem vādit, et in secessum emittĭtur,* Mt. Bos. 15, 17: Mk. Bos. 7, 19. [vorđgong *progress, A. R.*]

forþ-gangan, -gongan; *p.* -geóng, *pl.* -geóngon; *pp.* -gangen, -gongen *To go forth, proceed, go before, precede;* procēdĕre, progrĕdi, præcēdĕre :—Hēt hyssa hwæne forþgangan *he commanded each of the youths to go forth,* Byrht. Th. 131, 5; By. 3. Forþgangendre tīde *procēdente tempŏre,* Bd. 3, 19; S. 547, 30. Forđgeonga *prægredi,* Mk. Skt. Lind. 2, 23.

forþ-gebrengan; *p.* -gebrohte; *pp.* -gebroht *To bring forth* or *forward, make known;* edūcĕre, proferre :—Hī se hlīsa ne mæg forþgebrengan *fame cannot bring them forward,* Bt. Met. Fox 10, 124; Met. 10, 62.

forþ-geclypian; *p.* ode; *pp.* od *To call forth, incite, provoke;* provŏcāre, Scint.

forþ-gecȳgan; *p.* de; *pp.* ed *To call forth;* provŏcāre :—He hī to gefeohte forþgecȳgde *he called them forth to battle,* Bd. 1, 16; S. 484, 20.

forþ-gefaran; *p.* -gefōr, *pl.* -gefōron; *pp.* -gefaren *To go forth, go by, pass;* transīre :—Nymne seó clǽnsunge tīd forþgefare *nĭsi purgātiōnis tempus transiĕrit,* Bd. 1, 27; S. 493, 39. Wulfrīc forþgefaren wæs *Wulfric was departed* [*dead*], Chr. 1061; Th. 329, 37: 560; Erl. 17, 16: Nar. 40, 9.

forþ-geferan; *p.* de; *pp.* ed *To go forth, depart, die;* decēdĕre, mŏri :—Đara monige forþgeferdon on Drihten *many of whom died in the Lord,* Bd. 5, 11; S. 626, 34: 2, 14; S. 518, 1.

forþ-gefremman; *p.* ede; *pp.* ed [gefremman *to effect, bring to pass*] *To move forwards, cause to advance;* promŏvēre :—Hine God ofer ealle men forþgefremede *God advanced him above all men,* Beo. Th. 3440; B. 1718.

forþ-gelǽdan; *p.* de; *pp.* ed *To lead* or *bring forth, produce, conduct;* prodūcĕre, provĕhĕre :—He wolde manna rīm forþgelǽdan *he would lead forth a number of men,* Cd. 222; Th. 289, 24; Sat. 402. Se forþgelǽdeþ on muntum hīg *qui prodūcit in montĭbus fœnum,* Ps. Spl. 146, 9. Se đe hine to heánnysse cynerīces forþgelǽdde *qui se ad regni ăpĭcem provĕhĕret,* Bd. 2, 12; S. 514, 19: Blickl. Homl. 205, 32.

forþ-gelang; *adj. Dependent;* pendens, nixus :—On wīsum scrifte biþ swīđe forþgelang forsyngodes mannes nȳdhelp *on wise confession is greatly dependent the needful help to a sinful man,* L. Pen. 1; Th. ii. 278, 2: 9; Th. ii. 280, 12.

forþ-geleoran; *p.* de; *pp.* ed *To pass forth, pass away, depart, die;* transīre, decēdĕre, mŏri :—Monige forþgeleordon on Drihten *many died in the Lord,* Bd. 5, 11; S. 626, 34, MS. T: 2, 14; S. 518, 1, MS. T. Nymne seó clǽnsunge tīd forþgeleore *nĭsi purgātiōnis tempus transiĕrit,* 1, 27; S. 493, 39, MSS. B. T. Đā ongeat he đone mann, and him to gemynde com đæt he his hrægle onfēng đā he forþgeleored wæs *cognōvitque hŏmĭnem, et quia vestīmentum ejus mŏrientis accēpĕrit, ad mĕmŏriam reduxit,* 3, 19; S. 549, 3: Th. Chart. 138, 4.

forþ-genge; *adj. Progressive, increasing, effective;* pŏtens :—Hū mæg se leáfa beón forþgenge, gif seó lār [MS. lare] and đa lāreówas ateoriaþ *how can the faith be increasing if the doctrine and the teachers fail?* Ælfc. Gr. pref; Som. 1, 34. Đæt hit þurh đone fultum sīe forþgenge *that it become effective through help,* Past. 14, 1; Hat. MS. 17 b, 2.

forþ-geong, es; *m. A going forth, progress, process;* processus :—On forþgeonge đæs ǽrendgewrites *in processu epistŏlæ,* Bd. 1, 13; S. 481, 43. v. forþ-gang.

forþ-georn; *adj. Desirous to go forth, impetuous;* vehĕmens :—Swā dyde Æđerīc, fūs and forþgeorn *thus did Ætheric, eager and impetuous,* Byrht. Th. 139, 68; By. 281.

forþ-geótan; *p.* -geát, *pl.* -guton; *pp.* -goten *To pour forth;* profundĕre :—Ongeán đam rǽse đæs forþgotenan streámes *contra impĕtum flŭvii decurrentis,* Bd. 5, 10; S. 625, 7. He, forþgotenum teárum of inneweardre heortan, Drihtne his willan bebeád *profūsis ex imo pectŏre lacrȳmis, Dŏmĭno sua vōta commendābat,* 4, 28; S. 606, 42.

forþ-gesceaft, e; *f.* I. *the created things, creation, world;* creātūra, res creātæ, mundus :—Fyrn forþgesceaft Fæder ealle bewāt *the Father guards all the ancient creation,* Exon. 128 a; Th. 492, 4; Rä. 81, 9: 92 b; Th. 346, 24; Sch. 3. II. *the future world, state,* or *condition;* stătus fūtūrus :—Is seó forþgesceaft dīgol and dyrne *the future condition is dark and secret,* Menol. Fox 584; Gn. C. 61. He đa forþgesceaft forgyteþ and forgȳmeþ *he forgets and neglects the future state,* Beo. Th. 3505; B. 1750: Exon. 80 b; Th. 303, 20; Fä. 56. Đæt ic an forþgesceaft feran mōte *that I may come to a future state,* Ps. C. 50, 52; Ps. Grn. ii. 278, 52.

forþ-geseón; *p.* -geseah, *pl.* -gesāwon; *pp.* -gesewen *To see forth, onward,* or *in front;* providēre :—Hī forþgesāwon līfes lātþeów *they saw the guide of life in front,* Cd. 147; Th. 184, 7; Exod. 103.

forþ-gestapan; *p.* -gestōp, *pl.* -gestōpon; *pp.* -gestapen *To step forth;* progrĕdi :—He to forþgestōp dracan heáfde neáh *he had stept forth near to the dragon's head,* Beo. Th. 4568; B. 2289.

forþ-gestīgan; *p.* -gestāh, *pl.* -gestigon; *pp.* -gestigen *To go forth* or *forwards, to advance, ascend;* prodīre, procēdĕre, ascendĕre :—Đæt ǽnig forþgestīgeþ *that any shall advance,* Exon. 78 b; Th. 294, 24; Crā. 20. Đæt we eáđe māgon upcund rīce forþgestīgan *that we may easily ascend to the realm on high,* 93 a; Th. 348, 28; Sch. 35.

forþ-gestrangian; *p.* ode, ade; *pp.* od, ad *To make very strong, strengthen much;* confortāre :—Ofer me syndon, đa đe me ēhton, forþgestrangad *confortāti sunt sūper me qui me persequuntur,* Ps. Th. 68, 5.

forþ-gesȳne; *adj. Visible;* conspĭcuus :—Fela biþ on foldan forþgesȳnra geongra geofona *there are many early gifts ever visible on earth,* Exon. 78 a; Th. 293, 15; Crā. 1.

forþ-gewāt *went forth, passed,* Ps. Lamb. 89, 4; *p. of* forþ-gewītan.

forþ-gewendan; *p.* de; *pp.* ed *To go* or *turn out;* prodīre :—Đæt ǽlc man đe fere wǽre forþgewende *so that every man who was able to go should turn out,* Chr. 1016; Erl. 153, 31.

forþ-gewītan; *p.* -gewāt, *pl.* -gewiton; *pp.* -gewiten *To go forth, proceed, go by, pass, depart, die;* procēdĕre, transīre, prætĕrīre, decēdĕre, mŏri :—Swā swā brȳdguma forþgewītende of brȳdbūre his *tanquam sponsus procēdens de thălămo suo,* Ps. Spl. 18, 5. Ōþ-đæt forþgewīteþ unriht *dōnec transeat inīquĭtas,* 56, 2. Swylce gysternlīc dæg đe forþgewāt *tanquam dies hesterna quæ prætĕriit,* Ps. Lamb. 89, 4: Bd. 4, 9; S. 577, 35. Forþgewīt and rīce *procēde et regna,* Ps. Spl. 44, 5. Prætĕrĭtum tempus is forþgewiten tīd *prætĕrĭtum tempus is the past tense,* Ælfc. Gr. 20; Som. 23, 7, 10, 12, 13. Se forþgewitena tīma *the past tense,* Som. 23, 14. Đone forþgewitenan tīman, Som. 23, 9.

forþ-gewitenes, -ness, e; *f. A going forth, departure;* profectio :—Blissade đæt þeóstre folc on forþgewitenesse ođđe fære heora *lætāta est Ægyptus in profectiōne eōrum,* Ps. Lamb. 104, 38.

forþ-gongan; *part.* -gongende; *p.* -geóng, *pl.* -geóngon; *pp.* -gongen *To go forth, proceed;* procēdĕre, præcēdĕre :—Forþgongende *going forth,* Exon. 14 a; Th. 27, 5; Cri. 426: Bd. 1, 8; S. 479, 20: 1, 1;

S. 474, 24. Forþgongendre yldo *ævo præcēdente*, 4, 19; S. 587, 32. v. forþ-gangan.

forþ-gyrd, fōr-gyrd, es; *m. A fore-girdle, martingale, the girdle which passes between the fore-legs of a horse from the nose-band to the girth;* antela [ab ante et telon, quod est longum, compōnĭtur, Du Cange, sub voce], cingŭlum illud quod ante pectus ĕqui tendĭtur, crassius lōrum quo pectus, partim ad ornāmentum, partim ad firmandam sellam cingĭtur:—Forþgyrd *antela*, Ælfc. Gl. 20; Som. 59, 53; Wrt. Voc. 23, 14: 84, 4.

forþ-heald, -heold; *adj. Bent forward, inclined downwards, stooping;* incurvus, prōnus, proclīvus:—Hwōn forþheald *paulŭlum incurvus*, Bd. 2, 16; S. 519, 33. He lang fæc forþheald licgende wæs *aliquandiu prōnus jăcens*, 4, 31; S. 610, 14. Forþheold *proclīvus*, Ælfc. Gr. 47; Som. 48, 39. Forđhald ł gebeged *inclinata*, Lk. Skt. Lind. 13, 11.

forþ-healdan; *p.* -heóld, *pl.* -heóldon; *pp.* -healden *To hold to, follow out, maintain;* exsĕqui:—Mid đȳ he đæt langre tīde forþheóld and dyde *quod dum multo tempŏre sēdŭlus exsĕquĕrētur*, Bd. 4, 25; S. 600, 24.

forþ-heold; *adj. Stooping;* proclīvus, Ælfc. Gr. 47; Som. 48, 39. v. forþ-heald.

forþ-here, -herge, es; *m. The front* or *van of an army;* frons exercĭtūs:—Hie getealdon on đam forþherge fēđan twelfe *they numbered twelve bands in their van*, Cd. 154; Th. 192, 1; Exod. 225.

forþ-hreósan, he -hrȳst; *p.* -hreás, *pl.* -hruron; *pp.* -hroren *To rush forth;* proruĕre:—Forþhrȳst *proruit*, Scint. 26.

for-đī, for-đī-đe; *conj. For that, for, because, therefore;* quia, quŏniam, ĭtăque:—Nā forđīđe heó of Moyse sȳ *non quia ex Moyse est*, Jn. Bos. 7, 22: Ps. Lamb. 77, 22. Forđīđe he slōh stān *quŏniam percussit petram*, Ps. Lamb. 77, 20. v. for-đȳ; *conj.*

for-đī, for-đī đonne; *adv. For that cause, consequently, wherefore;* quamobrem, proptĕrea, quapropter, ĭdeo, idcirco:—Forhwī ođđe forđī *quamobrem*, Ælfc. Gr. 38; Som. 40, 58. Forđī đonne *qua propter:* forđī *ĭdeo, idcirco, proptĕrea*, 44; Som. 46, 17, 18. Forđī gehȳrde Drihten *ĭdeo audīvit Dŏmĭnus*, Ps. Lamb. 77, 21: Homl. Th. ii. 288, 22, 25. v. for-đȳ; *adv.*

forþian; *p.* ode; *pp.* od *To further, aid, assist, advance, perform;* promŏvēre:—He ne muge hit forþian *he may not perform it*, Chr. 675; Erl. 38, 11: 1052; Erl. 182, 2. Đæt he Godes circan forþige *ut Dei ecclēsias promŏveat*, L. I. P. 2; Wilk. 147, 34. DER. ge-forþian.

for-đig; *conj. For, because;* ĕnim, etĕnim, quia, quŏniam:—Forđig he āhte ǣgđer ge Engla land ge Normandige *for he owned both the land of the English as well as Normandy*, Chr. 1085; Erl. 218, 3–4. v. for-đȳ; *conj.*

for-đig; *adv. For that cause, consequently;* proptĕrea:—Forđig ic eów sǣde *proptĕrea dixi vōbis*, Jn. Bos. 6, 65. v. for-đȳ; *adv.*

for-þingian; *p.* ode; *pp.* od *To plead for anyone, intercede;* intercēdĕre:—Būton se hlāford đone wer forþingian wille *unless the lord will intercede for the man*, L. Alf. pol. 21; Wilk. 39, 34. v. fore-þingian.

for-þiófan *to thieve, steal;* fūrāri:—Đæt đū ne forstele ođđe ne forþiófe *ne fūrēris*, Mk. Skt. Lind. 10, 19. v. þeófan, þiófan.

forþ-lǣdan; *p.* de; *pp.* ed *To lead* or *bring forth, produce;* prodūcĕre:—Se đe forþlǣdeþ windas of goldhordum his *qui prodūcit ventos de thesauris suis*, Ps. Lamb. 134, 7. Freódrihten hine forþlǣdde to đam hālgan hām *the Lord led him forth to the holy home*, Cd. 226; Th. 300, 18; Sat. 566.

forþ-lǣdnys, -nyss, e; *f. A bringing forth, production;* prolātio, productio:—On đæs tuddres forþlǣdnysse *in prōlis prolātiōne*, Bd. 1, 27; S. 493, 21.

forþ-lǣstan; *p.* -lǣste; *pp.* -lǣsted *To follow out, accomplish, fulfil;* ăgĕre, perăgĕre:—Đæt for intingan đæs godcundan eges ǣne sīþe for his scylde onbyrded ongan, swā he eác eft for intingan đære godcundan lufan lustfulligende đām ēcum mēdum fæstlīce forþlǣste *quod causa dīvīni tĭmōris sĕmel ob reātum compunctus cœpĕrat, jam causa dīvīni ămōris delectātus præmiis indefessus ăgēbat*, Bd. 4, 25; S. 600, 23.

forþ-lǣtan; *p.* -lēt, *pl.* -lēton; *pp.* -lǣten *To let forth, send forth, emit;* emittĕre:—Swylce word he đǣr forþlēt *such words he let forth there*, Nicod. 11; Thw. 6, 5: Blickl. Homl. 133, 29.

forþ-leoran; *part.* -leorende; *p.* de; *pp.* ed *To go forth, proceed;* procēdĕre:—Wuldriende hāligne Gāst forþleorendne of Fæder and of Suna unasecgendlīce *glōrĭfĭcantes Spīrĭtum sanctum, procēdentem ex Patre et Fīlio inenarrābĭlĭter*, Bd. 4, 17; S. 586, 13, note.

forþ-līfan; *p.* -lāf, *pl.* -lifon; *pp.* -lifen [līfan *to leave*] *To stand out, appear;* promĭnēre:—Mid đȳ me of sweoran forþlīfaþ seó reádnes and bryne đæs swyles *dum mihi de collo rŭbor tŭmōris, ardorque promĭneat*, Bd. 4, 19; S. 589, 30.

forþ-lōcian; *p.* ode, ade; *pp.* od, ad *To look forth;* prospĭcĕre:—Dryhten of heofene forþlōcade ofer bearn monna *Dŏmĭnus de cœlo prospexit sŭper fīlios hŏmĭnum*, Ps. Surt. 52, 3: Blickl. Homl. 217, 31; 219, 18.

forþ-lūtan; *p.* -leát, *pl.* -luton; *pp.* -loten *To fall forwards, fall down;* procĭdĕre:—He forþleát on his andwlitan *procĭdĕret in făciem*, Bd. 4, 3; S. 569, 11. Forþloten *prōnus, proclīvis*, Scint. 6: Prov. 29.

forþ-mǣre; *adj. Very great;* præclārus:—Gewīteþ on westrōdor forþmǣre tungol faran *the very great star departs to go into the western sky*, Exon. 93 b; Th. 350, 25; Sch. 69.

forþ-man *one very rich* or *wealthy;* prædīves, Som. Ben. Lye.

for-þoht *despaired*, Bt. 8; Fox 24, 16; *pp. of* for-þencan.

for-þohte, đū -þohtest *despaired, hast despaired*, Bt. 8; Fox 24, 17; *p. of* for-þencan.

for-þolian; *p.* ode; *pp.* od *To be deprived of, want;* prīvāri, cărēre:—Wāt se đe sceal his winedryhtnes lārcwidum longe forþolian *he knows who must long be deprived of his dear lord's lessons*, Exon. 77 a; Th. 288, 29; Wand. 38.

for-đon, for-đon-đe; *conj. For that, for, because;* quia, quŏniam:—Forđon đū ofslōge ealle *quŏniam tu percussisti omnes*, Ps. Spl. 3, 7. Forđonđe wyste Drihten weg rihtwīsra *quŏniam nōvit Dŏmĭnus viam justōrum*, 1, 7. v. for-đam; *conj.*

for-đon = for-đam; *adv. For that cause, consequently, therefore;* proptĕrea, ĭdeo:—Forđon ne arīsaþ đa ārleáse on dōme *ĭdeo non resurgunt impii in jūdĭcio*, Ps. Spl. 1, 6.

forþ-on; *adv.* [= forþ-an, forþ-um = furþ-um] *At first, indeed, also;* prīmo, ĕtiam:—Nō forþon ānlēpe *no, not even* [*also*] *one*, Ps. Th. 13, 2. v. furþ-um.

fōr-þoncol; *adj. Forethoughtful, prudent;* prōvĭdus, prūdens:—Đū ahȳddest đās from snottrum and fōrþonclum *abscondisti hæc a săpientĭbus et prūdentĭbus*, Mt. Kmbl. Rush. 11, 25. v. fōre-þancul.

forþ-onettan; *p.* te; *pp.* ed *To hasten forth;* porro festīnāre:—Fæder on fultum forþonetteþ *the Father hastens forth to his aid*, Exon. 62 b; Th. 229, 15; Ph. 455: 108 a; Th. 412, 9; Rä. 30, 11. He forþonette *he hastened forth*, Exon. 120 a; Th. 461, 26; Hö. 41: Wald. 77; Vald. 2, 10.

forþ-ongangan *to go forth, proceed;* procēdĕre:—Hie gesāwon fyrd Faraonis forþongangan *they saw the host of Pharaoh go forth*, Cd. 149; Th. 187, 25; Exod. 156. v. forþ-gangan.

forþ-onloten; *part.* [forþ *forth, forwards;* onloten, *pp. of* onlūtan *to incline to, bow*] *Fallen forwards, prostrate;* provŏlūtus, Gr. Dial. 1, 8.

forþ-onsendan; *p.* de; *pp.* ed *To send forth;* emittĕre:—He in folc Godes forþonsendeþ of his brægdbogan biterne strǣl *he* [*the devil*] *sends forth, amongst God's people, the bitter arrow from his deceitful bow*, Exon. 19 a; Th. 47, 33; Cri. 764. Hī nædran forþonsendon *they sent forth snakes*, Elen. Kmbl. 240; El. 120. Đæt đū forþonsende wæter *that thou send forth water*, Andr. Kmbl. 3011; An. 1508.

forđor *further, more*, Mt. Kmbl. Lind. 6, 25, 30: Mk. Skt. Lind. 6, 51: Lk. Skt. Lind. Rush. 22, 71. v. furđor.

forþ-rǣsan; *p.* de; *pp.* ed *To rush forth, spring forth, spring up, rise up;* proruĕre, exsĭlīre, sălīre, exsurgĕre:—Biþ on him will forþrǣsendes wæteres on ēce līf *fiet in eo fons ăquæ sălientis in vītam æternam*, Jn. Bos. 4, 14. He đā awearp his reáf, and forþrǣsde and to him com *qui projecto vestīmento suo exsĭliens, vēnit ad eum*, Mk. Bos. 10, 50. Forþrǣsdon of đǣm wītum *exsurrexērunt a supplĭciis*, Martyrol. ad 26, Mart.

for-þrǣstan; *p.* te; *pp.* ed *To entirely bruise, break;* contĕrĕre, Ps. Spl. C. 45, 9: 104, 15, 31: 123, 7. Hpt. Gl. 425; 441. v. þrǣstan.

for-þriccan *to tread under, oppress*, Som. Ben. Lye. v. for-þryccan.

for-þriccednes, -ness, e; *f. A pressing, an oppression, distress, anxiety;* pressūra:—Þeóda forþriccednes *pressūra gentium*, Lk. Bos. 21, 25.

forþ-riht; *adj. Right forth, distinct, plain;* hence, forþriht spræc *plain speech, prose;* prōsa = prorsa, *i. e.* proversa, Som. Ben. Lye.

forþ-rihte; *adv. Distinctly, plainly, manifestly;* expresse, plāne, dīrecte, C. R. Ben. 29. Forþrihte *indeclinabiliter*, Hpt. Gl. 406. [*Orm*, forrþrihht *straightway*.]

for-þringan; *p.* -þrang, *pl.* -þrungon; *pp.* -þrungen [þringan *to crowd, throng, rush upon*] *To snatch from any one, protect from any one;* erĭpĕre ălĭcui, defendĕre ab ălĭquo:—Đæt he ne meahte đa weálāfe wīge forþringan þeódnes þegne *that he might not by war protect the sad remnant from the king's thane*, Beo. Th. 2173; B. 1084. [*Orm.* forrþrungenn *oppressed: Ger.* verdrängen *to push away.*]

for-þryccan, -þrycan; *p.* -þrycte; *pp.* -þrycced, -þryct *To tread under, oppress greatly, suppress, overwhelm;* opprĭmĕre, supprĭmĕre:—Đære wambe flēwsan he forþryceþ *it suppresses the flux of the stomach*, Med. ex Quadr. 6, 9; Lchdm. i. 352, 17. Næs ǣnig đara đæt mec þreám forþrycte *there was not any of them that overwhelmed me with reproofs*, Exon. 73 a; Th. 273, 22; Jul. 520. Þreám forþrycced *oppressed with afflictions*, 50 a; Th. 174, 1; Gū. 1171: Elen. Kmbl. 2551; El. 1277. Gesihst đū nū đæt đa rihtwīsan sint lāđe and forþrycte *seest thou now that the virtuous are hated and oppressed?* Bt. 3, 4; Fox 6, 23.

for-þryct *oppressed*, Bt. 3, 4; Fox 6, 23; *pp. of* for-þryccan.

forþ-ryne, es; *m. An onward course;* procursus:—Heóldon forþryne eástreámas heora *river-streams held their onward course*, Cd. 12; Th. 14, 8; Gen. 215.

for-þrysmian; *p.* ode, ede; *pp.* od, ed [þrysmian *to suffocate*] *To suffocate, choke, strangle;* suffŏcāre:—Eornfullness đisse woruld, and leásung đissa woruldwēlena forþrysmiaþ đæt wurd *sollĭcĭtūdo sæcŭli istīus, et fallācia dīvĭtiārum suffŏcat verbum*, Mt. Bos. 13, 22. Đa þornas hyt forþrysmodon *spīnæ suffōcāvērunt illud*, Lk. Bos. 8, 7. Ða synd forþrysmede *qui suffōcantur*, 8, 14.

forþ-scencan *to drink to;* propīnāre, Cot. 149.

forþ-scrīðan; *p.* -scrāþ, *pl.* -scridon; *pp.* -scriðen *To go forth, pass on, depart;* prōdīre, decēdĕre:—Dagas forþscridon [MS. forþscridun] *days passed on*, Exon. 47 a; Th. 160, 12; Gū. 942. Ðonne dōgor beóþ on moldwege mīn forþscriðen *then my day on earth will be departed*, 48 a; Th. 164, 16; Gū. 1012.

forþ-scype, es; *m. A going forth, growth;* profectus:—For his forþscype onstyred *mōtus ejus profectĭbus*, Bd. 1, 34; S. 499, 28, note.

forþ-sīþ, es; *m.* [sīþ *a journey*] *A going forth, departure, death;* progressus, ăbĭtus, ŏbĭtus:—Forþsīþes georn *glad of departure*, Exon. 123 b; Th. 475, 2; Bo. 41: 124 b; Th. 479, 21; Rä. 63, 2. Æfter Ōswaldes forþsīþe *after Oswald's death*, Chr. 992; Erl. 130, 37: Hy. 7, 72; Hy. Grn. ii. 288, 72. Hreðer innan born, afȳsed on forþsīþ *his spirit burned within, bent on departure*, Exon. 46 b; Th. 158, 19; Gū. 911: 50 a; Th. 173, 2; Gū. 1154: 52 b; Th. 182, 34; Gū. 1320. He wæs ðǣr ōþ Hērōdes forþsīþ *ĕrat ĭbi usque ad ŏbĭtum Hērōdis*, Mt. Bos. 2, 15.

forþ-sīðian; *p.* ode; *pp.* od [sīðian *to journey*] *To go forth, depart, die;* prōdīre, discēdĕre, mŏri, Som. Ben. Lye.

forþ-snoter, -snotter; *adj.* [snoter *wise*] *Very wise;* săpientissĭmus:—Elene hēht gefetian on fultum forþsnoterne *Elene bade to fetch to her aid the very wise* [*man*], Elen. Kmbl. 2104; El. 1053. Forþsnotterne, 2320; El. 1161. Fundon fīfhund forþsnotterra *they found five hundred very wise* [*men*], 758; El. 379.

forþ-spell, es; *n.* [spell *a history*] *A speaking out, saying, intimation;* effātum, dictum:—Be ðissum feáwum forþspellum *by these few intimations*, Exon. 84 a; Th. 316, 11; Mōd. 47.

forþ-spōwnes, -ness, e; *f.* [spōwan *to succeed*] *Great success*, hence *An advance, a growth, prosperity;* profectus:—To forþspōwnesse gedēfenre heánesse *ad profectum dēbĭti culmĭnis*, Bd. 2, 4; S. 505, 17.

forþ-sprecan; *p.* -spræc, *pl.* -sprǣcon; *pp.* -sprecen *To speak forth, speak out;* prolŏqui:—Ic sceal forþsprecan gēn ymbe Grendel *I shall speak forth again about Grendel*, Beo. Th. 4145; B. 2069.

forþ-stæppan; *part.* -stæppende *To step forth, proceed*, Homl. Th. ii. 90, 11. v. forþ-steppan.

forþ-stapan; *p.* -stōp, *pl.* -stōpon; *pp.* -stapen *To step* or *go forth, proceed, to go* or *pass by;* prōgrĕdi, prōdīre, procēdĕre, prætĕrīre:—Forþstōp swylce of rysele heora unrihtwīsnes *prōdiit quăsi ex ădĭpe iniquĭtas eōrum*, Ps. Lamb. 72, 7. Ðā he lyt-hwōn forþstōp *cum prōcessisset paulŭlum*, Mk. Bos. 14, 35. Ða ðe forþstōpon hine gremedon *qui prætervĕrunt blasphēmābant eum*, 15, 29.

forþ-steallian; *p.* ode; *pp.* od *To come to pass;* posthac lŏcum hăbēre:—Sceal seó wyrd swā ðeáh forþsteallian *that event shall yet come to pass*, Cd. 109; Th. 144, 15; Gen. 2390.

forþ-stefn, es; *m.* [stefn *a prow*] *A fore-prow, prow;* prōra:—Forþstefn scipes *prōra nāvis*, Lye.

forþ-steppan, -stæppan; *part.* -stæppende: *p.* -stepede = -stepte? *pp.* -steped = -stept? *To step* or *go forth, proceed;* progrĕdi, prōdīre, procēdĕre:—Of ansȳne ðīnre dōm mīn forþsteppe *de vultu tuo judĭcium meum prōdeat*, Ps. Lamb. 16, 2. He is swā swā brȳdguma forþstæppende of brȳdbūre his *ipse est tamquam sponsus procēdens de thălāmo suo*, Ps. Lamb. 18, 6: Homl. Th. ii. 90, 11. Ða þing ðe forþsteppaþ [MS. forþstappaþ] of mīnum welerum *quæ procēdunt de lăbiis meis*, Ps. Lamb. 88, 35.

forþ-stōp, *pl.* -stōpon *went forth, proceeded, passed by*, Ps. Lamb. 72, 7: Mk. Bos. 14, 35: 15, 29; *p. of* forþ-stapan.

forþ-swebban, -swefian; *p.* -swefede; *pp.* -swefed *To prevail, profit;* profĭcĕre:—Nāht forþswefaþ fȳnd *nĭhil prōfĭciet inĭmĭcus*, Ps. Spl. T. 88, 22.

forþ-tēge, forþ-tīge, -tȳge, es; *m. A fore-court, porch, entrance;* vestĭbŭlum, fŏris:—On ðam forþtēge *in ipsis fŏrĭbus*, Prov. 8. Forþtȳge *vestĭbŭlum, atrium*, Hpt. Gl. 496; Leo A.Sax. Gl. 384, 56. v. fōre-tīge.

forþ-teón; *p.* -teáh, *pl.* -tugon; *pp.* -togen *To lead forth, make known, discover, betray, render up;* prōdĕre, Som. Ben. Lye.

forþ-tīhan; he -tīhþ; *p.* -tāh, *pl.* -tigon; *pp.* -tigen *To draw forth;* protrăhĕre, extrăhĕre:—Meaht forþtīhþ heofoncondelle *his might draweth forth heaven's candle*, Exon. 93 a; Th. 349, 29; Sch. 53. v. tīhan I.

forþ-tihting, e; *f.* [tihting *persuasion*] *An exhortation;* exhortātio, Epil. Reg. Concord.

forþ-tȳge, es; *m. A fore-court;* vestĭbŭlum, Hpt. Gl. 496. v. forþ-tēge.

forþum; *adv. Even, indeed;* quĭdem, saltem:—Nǣnig forþum wæs *none indeed was*, Exon. 46 a; Th. 157, 22; Gū. 895. v. furþum.

for-þunden; *part. p.* [þindan; *p.* þand; *pp.* þunden *to swell*] *Swollen up;* tŭmĭdus:—Gyf seó wund forþunden sȳ *if the wound is swollen up*, Herb. 90, 16; Lchdm. i. 198, 11.

forðung *an armament.* DER. scip-forðung. v. fyrdung.

forþ-weard, es; *m. A forward guard, pilot;* prōrēta:—Forþweard scipes *the pilot of the ship*, Cd. 71; Th. 86, 26; Gen. 1436.

forþ-weard, -werd; *adj.* I. *in a forward direction, forward;* prōnus:—Forþweard *forward*, Exon. 106 a; Th. 403, 25; Rä. 22, 13: 126 b; Th. 487, 4; Rä. 72, 23. Ā swā hit forþwerdre beón sceolde, swā wæs hit lætre *always as it should be more forward, so was it later*, Chr. 999; Erl. 134, 32. II. *tending towards any one;* ălĭquem versus tendens:—Forþweard to ðē *tending towards thee*, Ps. Cot. 50, 79; Ps. Grn. ii. 278, 79. III. *everlasting, continual;* sempĭternus:—Ic forþweardne gefeán hæbbe *I have everlasting joy*, Exon. 64 a; Th. 236, 4; Ph. 569. Fremum forþweardum *with continual benefits*, Cd. 12; Th. 13, 29; Gen. 210.

forþ-weaxan; *p.* -weóx, *pl.* -weóxon; *pp.* -weaxen *To grow* or *break forth;* procrescĕre, prorumpĕre:—Forþweóx his feóndscipe *prorūpit ejus ŏdium*, Gr. Dial. 2, 27.

forþ-weg, es; *m. An onward course, a going forth, departure, journey;* progressus, profectio, ăbĭtus, ŏbĭtus:—Fūs forþweges *desirous of departure*, Exon. 108 a; Th. 412, 20; Rä. 31, 3. Ferede in forþwege *borne on their journey hence*, 77 b; Th. 291, 12; Wand. 81: Rood Kmbl. 247; Kr. 125. He of ealdre gewāt on forþweg *he departed from life on his way forth*, Beo. Th. 5243; B. 2625: Cd. 148; Th. 185, 27; Exod. 129. On forþwegas *on their ways forth*, 160; Th. 200, 1; Exod. 350: 144; Th. 179, 22; Exod. 32.

forþ-werd [= -weard] *Forthward, those who are present;* præsens:—Ðis gemet [imperativus] sprecþ forþwerd *this mood* [*imperative*] *speaketh to those present*, Ælfc. Gr. 21; Som. 23, 23. v. bebeódendlīc gemet.

forþ-wīf, es; *n. A married woman, mother*, hence *A matron;* matrōna, Wrt. Voc. 72, 78.

forþ-wīsian; *p.* ode, ade; *pp.* od, ad *To guide forth, direct;* dirĭgĕre:—Him seleþegn forþwīsade *the hall-thane guided him forth*, Beo. Th. 3595; B. 1795.

for-ðȳ, for-ðȳ-ðe, for-ðī, for-ðī-ðe, for-ðig; *conj. For that, for, because, therefore;* nam, quia, ĭtăque:—Forðȳ ðam cræftegan ne mæg nǣfre his cræft losigan *because to the skilful his skill can never be lost*, Bt. 19; Fox 70, 2. Nān mon forðȳ ne rīt ðe hine rīdan lyste *no man rides because he lists to ride*, Bt. 34, 7; Fox 144, 6, 12.

for-ðȳ, for-ðī, for-ðig; *adv. For that cause, consequently;* proptĕrea, ĭdeo:—Forðȳ Moyses eów sealde ymbsnydenysse *proptĕrea Moyses dĕdit vōbis circumcisiōnem*, Jn. Bos. 7, 22: Bt. 19; Fox 70, 1: Bt. Met. Fox 20, 385; Met. 20, 193. [*Orm.* forrþl = *Laym.* for þl.]

for-þyldian, -þyldigian, -þyldegian, -þylgian; *p.* ode; *pp.* od *To sustain, bear, endure, suffer, be patient, wait patiently;* sustĭnēre, tolĕrāre, păti:—For ðē ic forþyldegode hosp *propter te sustĭnui opprobrium*, Ps. Spl. 68, 10: 54, 12: Homl. Th. ii. 174, 10. Hī forþyldegodon [Lamb. forþyldigodon] sāwle mīne *sustĭnuĕrunt anĭmam meam*, Ps. Spl. 55, 7. Ic forbær ðē oððe forþylgode ðē *sustĭnui te*, 24, 22. Geþola oððe forþyldiga Drihten *sustĭne Dŏmĭnum*, Ps. Lamb. 26, 14.

for-þylman, -þylmian; *p.* de, ode; *pp.* ed, od *To encompass, overwhelm, cover over, obscure;* involvĕre, obvolvĕre, obscūrāre:—He his sylfes ðǣr bān gebringeþ, ða ǣr brondes wylm on beorhstede forþylmde *it* [*the phœnix*] *brings its own bones there, which the fire's rage had before encompassed on the mound*, Exon. 60 a; Th. 217, 23; Ph. 284. Þeóstrum forþylmed *overwhelmed with darkness*, Elen. Kmbl. 1530; El. 767: Judth. 10; Thw. 23, 12; Jud. 118. Þeóstru ne beóþ forþylmode oððe forsworcene to ðē *tĕnebræ non obscūrābuntur a te*, Ps. Lamb. 138, 12.

forþ-yppan; *p.* te; *pp.* ed *To make known, publish, declare;* promulgāre, publicāre, prōdĕre, Cot. 150: Ps. Vos. 16, 3.

forþ-yrnan; *part.* -yrnende; *p.* -arn, *pl.* -urnon; *pp.* -urnen *To run forth* or *before, precede;* præcurrĕre:—Wæs, æfter forþyrnendre tīde, ymb fīfhund wintra and tū and hundnigontig fram Cristes hidercyme *it was, according to the time preceding, about five hundred and ninety-two years from Christ's coming hither*, Bd. 1, 23; S. 485, 18.

for-þyrrian; *p.* ode; *pp.* od [þyr *dry*] *To dry up;* perarescĕre:—Ðæt ða sȳn forþyrrode *that they are dried up*, L. M. 2, 27; Lchdm. ii. 222, 5.

for-þȳstrian *to darken.* v. for-þeóstrian.

for-tīhan; he -tīþ; *p.* -tāh, *pl.* -tigon; *pp.* -tigen *To draw against* or *over, cover over with anything, darken, obscure;* obdūcĕre:—Mid gedwolmiste fortīþ mōd *covers over the mind with the mist of error*, Bt. Met. Fox 22, 67; Met. 22, 34. DER. tīhan I. [*Germ.* vorziehen.]

for-tió *may cover over; subj. pres. of* for-tión.

for-tión; *impert.* -tió, -tióh, *pl.* -tióþ; *subj.* -tió, *pl.* -tión *To draw against* or *over, cover over, obscure;* obdūcĕre:—Ðæt mōd mid ðam gedwol-miste fortió *may cover over the mind with the mist of error*, Bt. 35, 1; Fox 156, 1. v. for-teón.

for-tīþ *covers over, obscures*, Bt. Met. Fox 22, 67; Met. 22, 34; *pres. of* for-tīhan.

for-togen; *part. Tugged* or *drawn together;* contractus:—Fortogen *turmĭnōsus* [= *tormĭnōsus*], Ælfc. Gl. 2; Som. 55, 35; Wrt. Voc. 16, 10.

for-togenes, -ness, e; *f. A tugging, drawing together, griping, cramp, convulsion;* contractio, convulsio; spasmus:—Wið fortogenesse innan *for inward griping* or *colic*, L. M. 2, 33; Lchdm. ii. 236, 32.

for-tredan, ðū -tretst, -trydst, -trytst; *p.* -træd, *pl.* -trǣdon; *pp.* -treden *To tread upon, tread under foot;* conculcāre, calcāre:—Ðæt ðū cunne fortredan ðas woruld *that thou mayest tread down this world*, Homl. Th.

ii. 392, 34. Ic fortrede *conculco*, Ælfc. Gr. 47; Som. 48, 43. Fortretst đū đa woruldlīcan styrunga *thou wilt tread down worldly commotions*, Homl. Th. ii. 392, 25. Đū fortrydst leóna and dracena *thou shalt be a treader down of lions and of dragons*, Ps. Spl. 90, 13. Đū fortrytst eorþan *conculcābis terram*, Cant. Abac. Lamb. fol. 190 a, 12. Wēnunga þeóstru fortredaþ me *forsĭtan tenebræ conculcābunt me*, Ps. Lamb. 138, 11. Wegferende đæt sǣd fortrǣdon *the wayfarers trod the seed down*, Homl. Th. ii. 90, 15: i. 544, 28. Būton đæt hit sȳ fram mannum fortreden *nĭsi ut conculcētur ab hŏmĭnĭbus*, Mt. Bos. 5, 13. Hierusalem biþ fram þeódum fortreden *Jerūsălem calcābĭtur a gentĭbus*, Lk. Bos. 21, 24. Seó fortredene heorte *the trodden down heart*, Homl. Th. ii. 90, 16. [*Chauc.* fortroden *trodden down*: *Ger.* ver-treten *to tread down*.]

for-treding, e; *f. A treading down, crushing*; conculcātio, contrītio, Som. Ben. Lye.

for-trūgadnes *over-confidence, precipitancy*, Ps. Spl. T. 51, 4. v. for-trūwodnes.

for-trūwian, -trūwigan; *p.* ode, ude; *pp.* od, ud *To be over-confident, rash, to presume*; præsūmĕre, præcĭpĭtāre:—Đū đē fortrūwodest [MS. fortrūwudest] for đīnre rihtwīsnesse *thou wast over-confident on account of thy virtue*, Bt. 7, 3; Fox 22, 13. Đȳ-læs he hine for đære wynsuman wyrde fortrūwige *lest he through the pleasant fortune should be presumptuous*, 40, 3; Fox 238, 17. Đa fortrūwodan *the presumptuous*, Past. 32, 1; Hat. MS. 39 b, 25, 26. Đa fortrūwudan, 32, 1; Hat. MS. 40 a, 2, 12. Đǣm fortrūwodum monnum *to presumptuous men*, 49, 5; Hat. MS.

for-trūwodnes, -trūgadnes, -ness, e; *f. Over-confidence, precipitancy, presumption, arrogance*; præcĭpĭtātio, præsumptio, arrŏgantia:—For eówerre fortrūwodnesse *for your presumption*, Past. 32, 1; Hat. MS. 40 a, 25. Đa fortrūwodnesse and đa ānwilnesse an Corinctheum Paulus ongeat swīđe wiđerweardne wiđ hine *the presumption and obstinacy of the Corinthians Paul saw* [*to be*] *greatly opposed to himself*, 32, 1; Hat. MS. 40 a, 16. Đū lufedest ealle word fortrūgadnesse *dīlexisti omnia verba præcĭpĭtātiōnis*, Ps. Spl. T. 51, 4.

for-trūwung, e; *f. Over-confidence, presumption*; præcĭpĭtātio:—On đære fortrūwunga and on đam gilpe *by presumption and by arrogance*, Bt. 3, 1; Fox 6, 4.

for-trydst, -trytst *treadest down*, Ps. Spl. 90, 13: Cant. Abac. Lamb. fol. 190 a, 12; *2nd sing. pres. of* for-tredan.

for-tyhtan; *p.* te; *pp.* ed *To draw away, lead astray, seduce*; sedūcĕre:—Se ealda feónd forlǣrde lygesearwum, leóde fortyhte *the old fiend mistaught with lying snares, led astray the people*, Elen. Kmbl. 416; El. 208.

for-tyllan; *p.* de; *pp.* ed *To draw off from the object, seduce*; sedūcĕre:—Đonan us se swearta gǣst forteáh and fortylde *whence the dark spirit drew away and seduced us*, Exon. 11 b; Th. 17, 14; Cri. 270. v. tillan.

fōr-tymbrian; *p.* ode, ede; *pp.* od, ed *To build before* or *in front of, stop up, obstruct*; obstruĕre:—Fōrtymbred is mūþ sprecendra unrihtu *obstructum est os lŏquentium inīqua*, Ps. Spl. C. 62, 10.

for-tȳnan; *p.* de; *pp.* ed *To shut in, stop, hinder*; interclūdĕre:—Hī mid gelomlīcum oncunningum tiledon đæt hī him đone heofonlīcan weg fōrsetton and fortȳndon *qui crebris accūsātiōnĭbus ĭter illi cœleste interclūdĕre contendēbant*, Bd. 3, 19; S. 548, 4.

forud; *part. Broken, fractured, worn out, decayed*; fractus, contrītus:—Se foruda fōt and sió forude hond *the fractured foot and the fractured hand*, Past. 11, 2; Cot. MS. On đisum þrīm stelum stynt se cynestōl, and gif ān biþ forud, he fylþ adūn sōna *the throne stands on these three pillars, and if one is decayed, it soon falls down*, Ælfc. T. 41, 6. v. forod.

for-ūton; *conj. Without, besides, except*; sĭne, nĭsi:—Se fīr forbearnde ealle đe minstre, forūton feáwe bēc *the fire burnt all the monastery except a few books*, Chr. 1122; Erl. 249, 8. v. būtan; *conj.*

for-wærnan; *p.* de; *pp.* ed *To deny, refuse*; rĕcūsāre:—Gif he byrigan forwærne *if he refuse to give a pledge*, L. H. E. 9; Th. i. 30, 15. v. for-wyrnan.

for-wandian, -wandigan; *p.* ode; *pp.* od [wandian *to fear*]. I. *v. trans. To reverence, have in honour*; vĕrēri, revĕrēri:—Mīnne sunu hig forwandiaþ *revĕrēbuntur fīlium meum*, Mk. Bos. 12, 6: Lk. Bos. 20, 13. II. *v. intrans. To be afraid, be confounded, hesitate*; confundi, cunctāri:—Nellaþ forwandian đæt hī ne syllon sōþfæstnysse wiđ sceattum *they are not afraid to betray truth for money*, Homl. Th. ii. 244, 23. Hig forwandiaþ đæt hig ne dōn mīnum suna swā *they will be afraid to do so to my son*, Mt. Bos. 21, 37. Forwandigaþ đæt hie mid đǣm kycglum hiera worda ongeán hiera ierre worpigen *they hesitate to hurl the darts of their words against their anger*, Past. 40, 5; Hat. MS. 55 b, 4. He forwandode đæt he swā ne dyde *he hesitated to do so*, 49, 5; Hat. MS. Gescamian and forwandian, đe đe sēcaþ sāwle mīne *let them be ashamed and confounded that seek after my soul*, Ps. Spl. T. 69, 2: Ps. Spl. 39, 19. Nā hī forwandian ofer me *non confundantur sŭper me*, 68, 9.

for-wandung, e; *f. Shyness, shame, dishonour*; revĕrentia, ignōmĭnia:—Đū wāst forwandunga mīne *tu scis revĕrentiam meam*, Ps. Spl. 68, 23.

fōr-ward *a fore-ward, precaution*, Chart. ad calc. C. R. Ben. Lye. v. fōre-weard, e; *f.*

for-warþ *perished*, Cd. 213; Jun. 92, 2, = for-wearþ; *p. of* for-weorþan.

for-weallen; *part. Thoroughly boiled*; excoctus, percoctus, Som. Ben. Lye; *pp. of* for-weallan. v. weallan.

fōr-weard; *adj. Forward, fore*; antĕrior:—Is se fugel fæger fōrweard hiwe *the bird is fair of hue in front* [*forward*], Exon. 60 a; Th. 218, 8; Ph. 291. Fōrweard heáfod *the forehead*; frons [obcăput, Wrt. Voc. 64, 26]. Hig beóþ on fōrwearde and gē on æfteweard *ipse ĕrit in căput et tu ĕris in caudam*, Deut. 28, 44. v. fōre-weard; *adj.*

fōr-weard; *adv. Onwards, continually, always*; semper:—Gif hie wolden lāre Godes fōrweard fremman *if they would always perform God's precepts*, Cd. 37; Th. 49, 6; Gen. 788.

for-wearþ *perished*, Cd. 121; Th. 156, 14; Gen. 2588; *1st and 3rd sing. p. of* for-weorþan.

for-weaxan; *p.* -weóx, *pl.* -weóxon; *pp.* -weaxen, -wexen *To overgrow, grow immoderately, swell*; excrescĕre, turgescĕre:—Đȳ-læs hie to đæm forweóxen đæt hie forseáreden *lest they should grow so much that they should wither away*, Past. 40, 3; Hat. MS. 54 b, 17. Wiđ đon đe man on wambe forweaxen sȳ *in case that a man be overgrown in the belly*, Herb. 2, 4; Lchdm. i. 80, 22. Forwexen *overgrown*, 40, 1; Lchdm. i. 140, 16: 53, 1; Lchdm. i. 156, 9: 69, 1; Lchdm. i. 172, 7. [*Ger.* ver-wachsen *to overgrow*.]

for-weddod = for-weddad; *pp.* [wed *a pledge*] *Pledged*; oppignĕrātus:—Forweddod [MS. for-weddad] feoh *pledged property*; fīdūcia, Ælfc. Gl. 14; Som. 58, 13; Wrt. Voc. 21, 8.

for-wegan; *p.* -wæg, *pl.* -wǣgon; *pp.* -wegen *To kill*; interficere:—Đæt se on foldan læg forwegen mid his wǣpne *that he lay slain on the field with his weapon*, Byrht. Th. 138, 30; By. 228.

fōr-wel; *adv. Very well, very*; valde:—Him nǣfre seó gītsung fōrwel ne līcode *covetousness never very well pleased him*, Bt. titl. xvii; Fox xii. 24: Bt. 17; Fox 58, 24. Ōlǣcþ đes middangeard fōrwel menige *this world flatters very many*, Homl. Th. i. 490, 14: ii. 158, 30: Ps. Th. 131, 6. Wurdon geworhte wundra fōrwel fela *very many wonders were wrought*, Homl. Th. ii. 152, 28: 292, 34. Fōrwel oft *very often*; multŏtiens, Ælfc. Gr. 49; Som. 50, 35.

for-wēnan; *p.* de; *pp.* ed *To overween, think too highly of*; nĭmium æstĭmāre:—Forwēned *insŏlens*, Cot. 186. v. wēnan.

for-weoren = for-woren; *part. p.* [for-, woren, *pp. of* forweosan, v. weosan] *Tottering, decayed*; marcĭdus, decrĕpĭtus:—Eorþgrāp hafaþ waldendwyrhtan, forweorene [MS. forweorone], geleorene *earth's grasp* [i. e. *the grave*] *holdeth its mighty workmen, decayed, departed*, Exon. 124 a; Th. 476, 14; Ruin. 7. Forworen *decrĕpĭtus*, Hpt. Gl. 456; Leo A. Sax. Gl. 84, 60.

for-weornan; *p.* de; *pp.* ed *To refuse*; recūsāre:—He forweornde swīđe *he refused vehemently*, Chr. 1046; Erl. 174, 16. Ne forweorn đū me *refuse thou not me*, Hy. 3, 54; Hy. Grn. ii. 282, 54. v. for-wyrnan.

for-weornian; *p.* ode; *pp.* od *To dry up, wither away, fade, grow old, rot, decay*; marcescĕre, sĕnescĕre, tābescĕre:—Eal forweornast, lāmes gelīcnes *thou art all rotting, image of clay!* Exon. 98 a; Th. 368, 8; Seel. 18. Đonne forweornaþ he and adeádaþ *then it decays and dies*, Homl. Th. i. 168, 31. Hȳ forweorniaþ *they wither away*, Salm. Kmbl. 629; Sal. 314. Đæt gē hrædlīce forweornion *that ye may speedily fade*, Homl. Th. i. 64, 15.

for-weorpan; *p.* ic, he -wearp, đū -wurpe, *pl.* -wurpon; *subj. p.* -wurpe, *pl.* -wurpen; *pp.* -worpen *To cast, cast away, reject*; jăcĕre, projĭcĕre, repellĕre:—Se feónd hogode on đæt micle morþ men forweorpan *the foe thought to cast men into that great perdition*, Cd. 32; Th. 43, 16; Gen. 691. Đū forwurpe mīn word *tu projēcisti sermōnes meos*, Ps. Th. 49, 18. Mæg secgan se đe wyle sōþ sprecan đæt he gūþgewǣdu forwurpe *he who will speak the truth can say that he cast away his armour* [*war-garments*], Beo. Th. 5736; B. 2872. Hwī forwurpe đū me ođđe forhwī ūtaþȳgdest đū me *quāre repŭlisti me?* Ps. Lamb. 42, 2. [*Goth.* frawairpan: *Orm.* forrwerrpenn: *O. Sax.* farwerpan: *Ger.* ver-werfen *to reject*.] DER. weorpan.

for-weorþan, -wurþan; ic -weorþe, đū -weorþest, -wyrst, he -weorþeþ, -wyrþ, *pl.* -weorþaþ, -wyrþaþ; *p.* ic, he -wearþ, đū -wurde, *pl.* -wurdon; *pp.* -worden *To become nothing, to be undone, to perish, die*; ad nihĭlum devĕnīre, pĕrīre, intĕrīre, defĭcĕre:—Swā sceal ǣlce sāwl forweorþan æfter đam unrihthǣmede, būton se mon hweorfe to gōde *so shall every soul perish after unlawful lust, unless the man turn to good*, Bt. 31, 2; Fox 112, 27: 34, 9; Fox 148, 12. Sceolon hig ealle samod forweorþan *pĕrĭbunt sĭmul?* Gen. 18, 24: Ps. Th. 118, 176. Đū forwyrst *pĕrĭbis*, Ex. 9, 15. Ōþ-đæt điós eorþe eall forweorþeþ *until this earth shall all perish*, Bt. Met. Fox 11, 170; Met. 11, 85. Sīþfæt ārleásra forwyrþ ođđe losaþ *ĭter impiōrum pĕrĭbit*, Ps. Lamb. 1, 6. Hī forweorþaþ *pĕrĭbunt*, Ps. Spl. 79, 17: Ps. Th. 63, 5: 67, 2: 72, 22. Hig forwyrþaþ ođđe losiaþ *ipsi pĕrĭbunt*, Ps. Lamb. 101, 27. Seó mænegeo forwearþ *the multitude perished*, Cd. 121; Th. 156, 14; Gen. 2588; 213;

Th. 266, 13; Sat. 21: Chr. 655; Erl. 28, 1. Ealle nȳtenu neáh forwurdon *nearly all the cattle died*, Ors. 1, 7; Bos. 30, 31: Chr. 593; Erl. 18, 33. Ðȳ-læs ðū forweorþe *lest thou perish*, Cd. 116; Th. 151, 3; Gen. 2503. Hī forweorþan *ad nihĭlum dēvĕnient*, Ps. Th. 57, 6. Ðā wēnunga ic forwurde on eáþmōdnesse mīnre *tunc forte pĕrissem in hŭmĭlĭtāte mea*, Ps. Lamb. 118, 92. Ðæt hī forwordene weorþen syððan, on worulda woruld and to wīdan feore *ut intĕreant in sæcŭlum sæcŭli*, Ps. Th. 91, 6. v. for-wurþan, wurþan.

for-weorþenes, -ness, e; *f. A coming to nothing, perishing, ruin;* intĕrĭtus:—Ðis wæs swīðe gedeorfsum geár hēr on lande and þurh orfcwealm and wæstma forweorþenesse *this was a very grievous year in the land, both through murrain of cattle and perishing of fruits*, Chr. 1103; Erl. 239, 3. v. for-wordenes.

fōr-weorþfullīc; *adj. Very worthy, very excellent;* præclārus:—Fōrweorþfullīc wēla *very excellent wealth*, Bt. 29, 1; Fox 102, 14.

for-weosnian *to pine, fade* or *wither away;* tābescĕre, languescĕre, marcescĕre, Som. Ben. Lye. v. for-wisnian.

fōr-werd, e; *f. A fore-ward, precaution, contract, agreement;* præcautio, pactum:—Hēr swutelaþ ymb ða fōrwerda ðe Wulfrīc and se arcebisceop geworhton *here is made known concerning the agreements which Wulfric and the archbishop made*, Cod. Dipl. 738; A. D. 1023; Kmbl. iv. 25, 29. v. fōre-weard, e; *f.*

for-werednys, -nyss, e; *f. Old age;* sĕnium:—On ylde and forwerednysse *in sĕnectam et sĕnium*, Ps. Spl. 70, 19.

for-wernan; *p.* de; *pp.* ed *To refuse;* recūsāre:—Se arcebisceop him ānrǣdlīce forwernde *the archbishop constantly refused him*, Chr. 1048; Erl. 177, 24. Hī forwerndon heom ǣgðer ge upganges ge wæteres *they refused them both landing and water*, 1046; Erl. 171, 5. v. for-wyrnan.

fōr-wernedlīce; *adv. Against one's will, very grievously, hardly;* ægre, anguste, Som. Ben. Lye.

fōr-werod, -wered; *part. p.* [werian *to wear*] *Worn out, very old;* attrītus, vĕtus:—Seó endlyfte tīd biþ seó fōrwerode ealdnyss *the eleventh hour is very late* or *very great oldness*, Homl. Th. ii. 76, 22. On fōrwerodre ealdnysse *in very old age*, 76, 26. Næs his reáf hōrig ne tosigen, ne his scōs fōrwerode *his raiment was not dirty nor threadbare, nor his shoes worn out*, i. 456, 21: ii. 94, 11. Nǣron eówre reáf fōrwerede *non sunt attrīta vestīmenta vestra*, Deut. 29, 5. Fōrwerede fetelsas *saccos vĕtĕres*, Jos. 9, 5. [*Laym.* uorwerien *to spend.*]

for-weryþ *shall destroy*, destruet, Ps. Spl. 51, 5, = for-werpþ [Ps. Lamb. towyrpþ *destruet*, 51, 7] for-weorpeþ; *3rd sing. pres. of* forweorpan.

for-wexen *overgrown*, Herb. 69, 1; Lchdm. i. 172, 7, = for-weaxen *pp. of* for-weaxan.

for-wiernan, -wirnan; *p.* de; *pp.* ed *To hinder, prevent, keep from, withhold;* arcēre, rĕtĭnēre:—Ðæt ða Deniscan him ne mehton ðæs rīpes forwiernan *that the Danish might not hinder them from the harvest* Chr. 896; Erl. 94, 7. Ðæt mann forwierne his sweorde blōdes, ðæt hwā forwirne his lāre ðæt he mid ðære ne ofsleá ðæs flǣsces lustas *keeping one's sword from blood is withholding one's instruction, and not slaying with it the lusts of the flesh*, Past. 49; Hat. MS. v. for-wyrnan.

for-wird, e; *f. Loss, destruction, ruin, perdition;* perdĭtio, intĕrĭtio:—Hira forwirde dæg ys gehende *juxta est dies perdĭtiōnis*, Deut. 32, 35. He generode hī of forwirdum heora *erĭpuit eos de intĕrĭtiōnĭbus eōrum*, Ps. Spl. 106, 20. v. for-wyrd.

for-wisnian; *p.* ode, ade; *pp.* od, ad *To wither* or *wizen away, dry up, decay;* marcescĕre, arescĕre, tābescĕre, putrescĕre:—Wyrt forwisnaþ, weorþeþ to duste *herba indūret, et arescat*, Ps. Th. 89, 6: 101, 23. Ðæt biþ forwisnad wraðe sōna, ǣr hit afohten foldan losige *quod priusquam evellātur, arescit*, 128, 4. To hwan drehtest ðū me eal forwisnad *wherefore didst thou torture me all decayed?* Soul Kmbl. 36; Seel. 18.

fōr-witan; *p.* -wiste, *pl.* -wiston; *subj. pres.* -wite; *pp.* -witen *To foreknow, know beforehand;* præscīre:—Ðæs ðe ðū fōrwite hwām ðū gemiltsige *that thou mayest know beforehand whom thou pitiest*, Apol. Th. 11, 21. v. fōre-witan.

fōr-witolnes, -ness, e; *f. Foreknowledge, diligence, industry;* præscientia, industria, R. Ben. interl. 27.

fōr-wlencean; *p.* -wlencte; *pp.* -wlenced [wlenco *pride*] *To exalt, fill with pride, make very proud;* exaltāre, arrŏgantia implēre:—Ðonne hine ne māgon ða wēlan fōrwlencean *when the riches are not able to make him proud*, Past. 26; Hat. MS. 35 b, 2. Forwlencte *proud*, Blickl. Homl. 199, 14.

fōr-word, es; *n. A fore-word, stipulation, agreement;* præcautio, pactum:—Ðæt hire frȳnd ða fōrword habban *that her friends have the stipulations*, L. Edm. B. 7; Th. i. 256, 2. Ðis synd ða fōrword ðe Æðelrēd cyng and ealle his witan wið ðone here gedōn habbaþ *these are the agreements which king Æthelred and all his counsellors have made with the army*, L. Eth. ii. prm; Th. i. 284, 6. cf. fōre-weard, e; *f.*

for-worden *perished*, Ps. Th. 91, 6; *pp. of* for-weorþan.

for-wordenes, -weorþenes, -ness, e; *f.* [*pp.* forworden *perished*] *A coming to nothing, perishing, ruin;* intĕrĭtus:—Ðis wæs swīðe gedyrfsum geár hēr on lande þurh wæstma forwordenessa *this was a very grievous year in the land through the perishing of fruits*, Chr. 1105; Erl. 240, 15.

for-wordenlīc *damnable;* damnabĭlis, Som. Ben. Lye.

fōr-worht *obstructed*, Chr. 901; Erl. 96, 31; *pp. of* fōr-wyrcan.

for-worhta, an; *m.* [*pp. of* for-wyrcan] *A misdoer, malefactor;* scĕlestus, mălefactor:—Ða forworhtan, ða ðe firnedon, beóþ beofigende *the malefactors, they who sinned, shall be trembling*, Cd. 227; Th. 303, 28; Sat. 620.

for-worhte *did wrong, sinned, ruined, convicted, condemned, forfeited*, Cd. 40; Th. 53, 6; Gen. 857: Exon. 21 b; Th. 57, 20; Cri. 921, = *p. of* for-wyrcan.

for-wrecan; *p.* -wræc, *pl.* -wrǣcon; *pp.* -wrecen [wrecan *to drive*] *To drive out, banish, expel;* expellĕre, propellĕre, fŭgāre:—Ðȳ-læs hit ȳþa þrym forwrecan meahte *lest the force of the waves might drive it out*, Beo. Th. 3843; B. 1919. He hine feor forwræc *he banished him far*, 219; B. 109. Hȳ forwrǣcon wīcinga cynn *they expelled the race of the vikings*, Scōp Th. 95; Wīd. 47. Eart ðū āna forwrecen on Hierusalem *tu sōlus peregrīnus es in Jerusalem?* Lk. Bos. 24, 18.

for-wrēgan, fore-wrēgan; *p.* de; *pp.* ed [wrēgan *to accuse*] *To accuse strongly;* vehementer accūsāre:—Brihtrīc forwrēgde Wulfnōþ to ðam cyning *Brihtric accused Wulfnoth to the king*, Chr. 1009; Erl. 141, 29. Ða Wælisce men forwrēgdon ða eorlas *the Welshmen accused the earls*, 1048; Erl. 178, 24. He wæs oft to ðam cyninge forwrēged *he had often been accused to the king*, 952; Erl. 118, 27: 1068; Erl. 206, 33. Se wearþ wið hine forwrēged *hic diffāmătus est ăpud illum*, Lk. Bos. 16, 1.

for-wrītan; *p.* -wrāt, *pl.* -writon; *pp.* -writen [wrītan *to cut, carve, engrave, write*] *To cut asunder;* dissĕcāre:—He forwrāt wyrm on middan *he cut the worm asunder in the middle*, Beo. Th. 5403; B. 2705.

for-wrīðan; *p.* -wrāþ, *pl.* -wridon; *pp.* -wriden *To bind up, stanch;* oblĭgāre, supprĭmĕre:—Gif ðū ne mǣge blōd-dolh forwrīðan *if thou canst not stanch a blood-running wound*, L. M. 3, 52; Lchdm. ii. 340, 19.

for-wūndian; *p.* ode, ede; *pp.* od, ed *To wound badly, ulcerate;* grăvĭter vulnĕrāre:—Gif mon ōðrum ða geweald uppe on ðam sweoran forwūndie [-wūndige MS. H.] *if a man wound the tendons on another's neck*, L. Alf. pol. 77; Th. i. 100, 11. Eall ic wæs mid strǣlum forwūndod *I was all wounded with arrows*, Rood Kmbl. 124; Kr. 62: Cd. 216; Th. 273, 4; Sat. 131. Se læg on his dūra swȳðe forwūndod *qui jăcēbat ad jănuam ejus ulcĕrĭbus plēnus*, Lk. Bos. 16, 20. Forwūnded mid wommum *wounded with sins*, Rood Kmbl. 27; Kr. 14. Ða men wǣron forwūndode *the men were badly wounded*, Chr. 882; Erl. 83, 11: 897; Erl. 96, 13. [*Ger.* ver-wunden *to wound.*]

for-wurdon *perished*, Ors. 1, 7; Bos. 30, 31; *p. pl. of* for-weorþan.

for-wurþan *to perish;* pĕrīre:—Ðæt eall Egipta land mōt forwurþan *quod pĕrierit Ægyptus*, Ex. 10, 7: Mt. Bos. 8, 25: Hy. 7, 112; Hy. Grn. ii. 289, 112. v. for-weorþan.

for-wyrcan, -wyrcean; *p.* -worhte, -wyrhte; *pp.* -worht, -wyrht [for-, wyrcan *to work, do*]. I. *to miswork, do wrong, sin;* măle ăgĕre, delinquĕre, peccāre:—Ðæt ðām forworhtum mannum beó ðe māra ege for ūre gesomnunge *that to the wrong doing men there may be the more fear for our assemblage*, L. Ath. v. § 8, 3; Th. i. 236, 16. He wiste forworhte, ða he ǣr wlite sealde *he knew [they had] done wrong whom he had before gifted with beauty*, Cd. 40; Th. 53, 6; Gen. 857. Iudas hine sylfne ahēng, and rihtlīce gewrāþ ða forwyrhtan þrotan, seó ðe belǣwde Drihten *Judas hanged himself, and justly bound the sinful throat, which had betrayed the Lord*, Homl. Th. ii. 250, 15. II. *to do for, destroy, ruin, convict, condemn;* perdĕre, destruĕre, labefactāre, condemnāre:—Ða Perse ondrēdon ðæt man ða brycge forwyrcean wolde *the Persians dreaded that they would destroy the bridge*, Ors, 2, 5; Bos. 46, 8. Gif hwā hine sylfne forwyrce on mænigfealdum synnum *si quis seipsum multĭfāriis peccātis labefactāvĕrit*, L. M. I. P. 44; Th. ii. 276, 28: L. E. G. 4; Th. i. 168, 22. He biþ egeslīc to geseónne ðām ðǣr mid firenum cumaþ forþ forworhte *he shall be dreadful to see to those who come ever done for with crimes*, Exon. 21 b; Th. 57, 20; Cri. 921. Wā me forworhtum *woe to me ruined!* 75 a; Th. 280, 20; Jul. 632. Se ðe þȳfþe oft forworht wǣre openlīce *he who has often been convicted openly of theft*, L. Ath. v. § 1, 4; Th. i. 228, 25. Ðe forworht wǣre *who has been condemned*, L. E. G. 10; Th. i. 172, 16. Ne dȳde man ǣfre on Sunnan dæges freólse ǣnigne forwyrhtne [forworhtne MS. B.] man *let not a man ever put any condemned man to death on the festival of Sunday*, L. C. S. 45; Th. i. 402, 10: L. E. G. 9; Th. i. 172, 14. III. *to forfeit;* amittĕre:—Ðæt man sceolde ge-earnian ða wununga on heofenan rīce, ðe se deófol forwyrhte mid mōdignysse *that man should merit the dwellings in the kingdom of heaven, which the devil had forfeited through his pride*, Homl. Th. i. 12, 28. Gif hwā freót forwyrce *if any one forfeit his freedom*, L. Ed. 9; Th. i. 164, 10: L. Edg. ii. 2; Th. i. 266, 13: L. In. 5; Th. i. 104, 15. Ic forworht hæbbe hyldo ðīne *I have forfeited thy favour*, Cd. 48; Th. 62, 33; Gen. 1024: Blickl. Homl. 25, 1: L. Alf. pol. 42; Th. i. 90, 20; L. Eth. vii. 16; Th. i. 332, 16. [*Ger.* verwirken *to forfeit.*]

fōr-wyrcan, -wyrcean; *p.* -worhte; *pp.* -worht [fōr *before*, wyrcan *to work, do*] *To work* or *place before, obstruct, barricade;* oppōnĕre, obstruĕre:—Se cing gehāwode hwǣr man mihte ða eá fōrwyrcan [fōrwyrcean, col. 2] *the king observed where the river might be obstructed,* Chr. 896; Th. 173, 36, col. 1. He hæfde ealle ða geatu fōrworht into him *he had barricaded all the entrances against him,* Chr. 901; Erl. 96, 31. Synt ðissa heldōra wegas fōrworhte *the ways of these hell-doors are obstructed,* Cd. 19; Th. 24, 21; Gen. 381.

for-wyrd, -wird, e; *f.* [wyrd *fortune;* for-weorþan *to perish*] *Loss, damage, destruction, perdition, ruin, death;* detrīmentum, intĕrĭtus, intĕrĭtio, perdĭtio, pernĭcies, internĕcio:—Hēr is geswutelod ūre forwyrd *here is made manifest our destruction,* Judth. 12; Thw. 25, 30; Jud. 285. He alȳsde ðīn līf of forwyrde *qui redĭmit de intĕrĭtu vītam tuam,* Ps. Th. 102, 4: 106, 19: Ps. Lamb. 9, 16: Boutr. Scrd. 17, 23: 20, 16. Hwæt fremaþ ǣnegum menn, ðeáh he ealne middaneard gestrȳne, gyf he hys sāwle forwyrd þolaþ *quid prodest hŏmĭni, si mundum ūnĭversum lucrētur, anĭmæ vēro suæ detrīmentum pătiātur?* Mt. Bos. 16, 26: Lk. Bos. 9, 25. Ðā sió wērge sceólu hreósan sceolde in wīta forwyrd *when the wretched crew must fall into the ruin of punishment,* Elen. Kmbl. 1526; El. 765: Frag. Kmbl. 16; Leás. 10: Andr. Kmbl. 3234; An. 1620. Ðæt hī ōþ forwyrd ǣghwǣr fordiligade ne wǣron *ne usque ad internĕciōnem usquequaque delērentur,* Bd. 1, 16; S. 484, 17. Of forwyrdum heora *de intĕrĭtiōnĭbus eōrum,* Ps. Lamb. 106, 20. **2.** for-wyrd, es; *n.* is *neuter* in the following examples:—Ðīn andbīdaþ ðæt ēce forwyrd *the eternal perdition awaits thee,* Homl. Th. i. 598, 9. God forlǣt hī to ðam ēcan forwyrde *God will abandon them to the eternal perdition,* i. 112, 23.

for-wyrht, es; *n. A sin, crime;* peccātum. DER. mān-forwyrht.

for-wyrhta, an; *m.* [for *for,* wyrhta *a workman*] *One who does anything for another, an agent, vicegerent;* instĭtor, procūrātor:—Ðe nǣnne forwyrhtan næfde *who had no agent,* L. Ath. v. 2; Th. i. 230, 20. Se ðe swā geþogenne forwyrhtan næfde, swōre for sylfne *he who had not such a prosperous vicegerent, swore for himself,* L. R. 4; Th. i. 192, 5.

for-wyrhte *destroyed, forfeited,* Homl. Th. i. 12, 28; *p. of* for-wyrcan.

for-wyrnan, -weornan, -wiernan, -wirnan, -wernan; *p.* de; *pp.* ed *To prohibit, deny, refuse, restrain, prevent, hinder;* prohĭbēre, recūsāre, denĕgāre, renuĕre:—Him ðǣr se geonga cyning ðæs oferfæreldes forwyrnan myhte *where the young king might prevent his going over,* Ors. 2, 4; Bos. 45, 9. Se ilca forwyrnþ ðære [MS. ðæræ] sǣ ðæt heó ne mōt ðone þeorscwold oferstæppan ðære eorþan *the same restrains the sea that it may not overstep the threshold of the earth,* Bt. 21; Fox 74, 25. Me ðæs forwyrnde Waldend heofona *the Lord of heaven hath denied it me,* Cd. 101; Th. 134, 3; Gen. 2219: Exon. 34 b; Th. 111, 31; Gū. 135. He ne forwyrnde woroldrǣdenne *he refused not worldly converse,* Beo. Th. 2288; B. 1142. Forwyrnde beón afrēfrod sāwle mīn *renuit consōlāri anĭma mea,* Ps. Spl. 76, 3. Þearfum forwyrndon, ðæt hī under eówrum þæce mōsten ingebūgan *ye prohibited the needy, that they might enter under your roof,* Exon. 30 a; Th. 92, 4; Cri. 1504. Ðæt ðū me ne forwyrne *that thou deny me not,* Beo. Th. 862; B. 429. Ðȳ-læs eów weges forwyrnen to wuldres byrig *lest they prohibit you the way to glory's city,* Exon. 75 b; Th. 282, 18; Jul. 665. Me hwīlum biþ forwyrned willan mīnes *sometimes I am denied my will,* 72 a; Th. 268, 32; Jul. 441. [*O. Sax.* far-wernian *to refuse: Laym. pp.* forwurnen.]

for-wyrnednes, -ness, e; *f. A restraining, continence, forbidding;* contĭnentia:—He wæs micelre forhæfdnysse and forwyrnednesse līfes *he was of great abstinence and continence of life,* Bd. 3, 5; S. 526, 21.

for-wyrpnes, -ness, e; *f. A rejection;* abjectio:—Ic eom forwyrpnes oððe aworpennys folces *ĕgo sum abjectio plēbis,* Ps. Lamb. 21, 7.

for-wyrst, he -wyrþ *shalt perish, perishes,* Ex. 9, 15: Ps. Lamb. 1, 6; *2nd and 3rd sing. pres. and fut. of* for-weorþan.

for-wyrþaþ *perish,* Ps. Lamb. 101, 27, = for-weorþaþ; *pl. pres. of* for-weorþan,

for-yldan; *p.* -ylde; *pp.* -ylded *To put off, defer;* differre, sŭpersĕdēre:—Ne mæg mon foryldan ðone deóran sīþ *no one may put off the severe journey,* Salm. Kmbl. 721; Sal. 360. Ðe he to medmicelre tīde forylde dōn [MS. doan] *quam ad brĕve tempus făcĕre sŭpersēdit,* Bd. 5, 13; S. 633, 23: Blickl. Homl. 213, 24; 95, 25

for-yrman; *p.* de; *pp.* ed [yrman *to afflict*] *To afflict greatly, harass;* vehementer afflīgĕre:—Hī hī ealle foryrmdon *they harassed them all,* Bd. 1, 12; S. 480, 36.

fōr-yrnan; *p.* -arn, *pl.* -urnon; *pp.* -urnen *To run before;* præcurrĕre:—Se ōðer leorningcniht fōrarn Petrus *ille ălius discĭpŭlus præcŭcurrit Petro,* Jn. Bos. 20, 4. [*Ger.* vor-rennen *to run before.*]

fōr-yrnere *a fore-runner;* præcursor, Som. Ben. Lye. v. fōr-rynel.

FŌSTER, fōstor, fōstur; *gen.* fōstres; *n. A* FOSTER*ing, nourishing, rearing, feeding, food, nourishment, provisions;* ēdŭcātio, nutrīcium, pastio, alĭmentum, victus:—Ic gegaderige in to ðē of deórcynne and of fugelcynne gemacan, ðæt hī eft to fōstre beón *I will gather in to thee mates of beast-kind and of bird-kind, that they afterwards may be for food,* Homl. Th. i. 20, 35. Be fundenes cildes fōstre. To fundenes cildes fōstre ðȳ forman geáre geselle vi scillinga, ðȳ æfterran twelf, ðȳ þriddan xxx; siððan, be his wlite *of the fostering of a foundling* [lit. *of a found child*]. *Let six shillings be paid for the fostering of a foundling for the first year, twelve for the second, thirty for the third; afterwards, according to its appearance,* L. In. 26; Th. i. 118, 17–20: 38; Th. i. 126, 5. Mon sceal sellan, to fōstre, x fata hunies, ccc hlāfa, etc. *one shall give, as provisions, ten vats of honey, three hundred loaves, etc.* L. In. 70; Th. i. 146, 16. He gecȳdde hwæðer he mǣnde ðe ðæs mōdes fōster ðe ðæs līchoman *he made known whether he meant the feeding of the mind or of the body;* pastiōnem cordis an corpŏris suādēret, apĕruit, Past. 18, 6; Hat. MS. 27 a, 21. [*Laym.* uoster *a foster-child: Plat.* voedster: *Dut.* voedster, *f. a nurse: Dan. Swed.* foster, *n. embryo, child: Icel.* fóstr, *n. the fostering of a child.*] v. fōda *food.*

fōster-bearn, fēster-bearn, es; *n. A* FOSTER-BEARN *or child;* ălumnus, Cot. 9.

fōster-brōðor; *m. A* FOSTER-BROTHER; collactāneus:—Fōsterbrōðor *ălumnus,* Wrt. Voc. 284, 74.

fōster-cild, es; *n. A* FOSTER-CHILD; ălumnus, Wrt. Voc. 72, 39.

fōster-fæder, fēster-fæder, es; *m. A* FOSTER-FATHER, *nourisher, bringer up;* altor, nutrītor, Wrt. Voc. 72, 37. Fōsterfæder *ălumnus,* Ælfc. Gl. 86; Som. 74, 36; Wrt. Voc. 50, 18. [*Orm.* fossterfaderr.]

fōster-land, fōstor-land, es; *n.* FOSTER-LAND, *land assigned for the procuring of provisions;* fundus cĭbāriis emendis assignātus:—He gean [MS. geun] ðæs landes æt Wihtrīces hamme ðām Godes þeówum, to fōsterlande *he gives the land at Wittersham to God's servants, as foster-land,* Th. Diplm. A. D. 1032; 329, 27. Se cyning ðæt land geaf into Cristes cyrcean ðan hīrēde to fōsterlande *the king gave the land to Christ-church as foster-land for the convent,* Th. Diplm. A. D. 1052; 368, 17.

fōster-leán, fōstor-leán, es; *n. Foster-loan, remuneration for rearing a foster-child;* educatiōnis præmium, nutrīcii merces:—Is to witanne hwām ðæt fōsterleán gebȳrige *it is to be known to whom the remuneration for fostering belongs,* L. Edm. B. 2; Th. i. 254, 8.

fōster-ling *a* FOSTERLING, *foster-child,* Som. Ben. Lye. v. fōstor-ling.

fōster-man *a foster-man, bondsman, security.* v. fēster-man.

fōster-mōdor, -mōder, fōstor-mōdor, fēster-mōdor, -mōdur, fǣster-mōdor; *f. A* FOSTER-MOTHER, *nurse;* altrix, nutrix:—Hwæðer hit oncneówe his fōstermōdor *whether it knew its foster-mother,* Bt. 3, 1; Fox 4, 30. Fōstermōder *altrix* vel *nutrix,* Wrt. Voc. 72, 38. Ic gean mīnre fōstermēder ðæs landes æt Westune *I give to my mother the land at Weston,* Th. Diplm. 560, 25.

fōster-nōþ, fōstor-nōþ, es; *m? A pasturage, pasture;* pascua:—On stōwe fōsternōþes me he gestaðelode *in lŏco pascuæ me collŏcāvit,* Ps. Spl. T. 22, 1.

fōster-sweostor; *f. A* FOSTER-SISTER; collactānea, Som. Ben. Lye.

fōstor *a fostering, nourishing, food, nourishment,* Som. Ben. Lye. v. fōster.

fōstor-land, es; *n. Land assigned for the procuring of provisions:*—Ðæt ylce land hī gefreódon Godes þeówan to brȳce into fōstorlande *they freed the same land for the use of God's servants as foster-land,* Th. Diplm. A. D. 963–975; 227, 33. v. fōster-land.

fōstor-leán, es; *n. Remuneration for fostering;* nutrīcii merces:—Hæfde Nergend fōstorleán fǣmnan forgolden, ēce to ealdre *the Saviour had repaid the virgin the reward for fostering, in eternal life,* Menol. Fox 301; Men. 152. v. fōster-leán.

fōstor-ling, es; *m. A fosterling, foster-child;* ălumnus, verna, vernŭla:—Fōstorling *vernŭla,* Ælfc. Gl. 8; Som. 56, 103; Wrt. Voc. 18, 53. Inberdling *vel* fōstorling *verna* vel *vernăcŭlus,* 86; Som. 74, 34; Wrt. Voc. 50, 17. [*Laym.* fosterling.]

fōstor-mōdor; *f. A foster-mother;* altrix:—Ðæs mǣdenes fōstormōdor into ðam būre eóde *the maiden's foster-mother went into the chamber,* Apol. Th. 2, 7, 11, 12, 15, 19, 23: Nar. 40, 7. v. fōster-mōdor.

fōstor-nōþ, es; *m? A pasture;* pascua:—Sceáp fōstornōþes his *ŏves pascuæ ejus,* Wanl. Catal. 223, 37, col. 2: 291, 23, col. 1. v. fōster-nōþ.

fōstraþ, es; *m. Food, victuals;* esca, cibus:—Met oððe fōstraþ *esca,* Mt. Kmbl. Lind. 3, 4. Hlāf oððe fōstraþ *pānem,* Jn. Lind. War. 6, 31. Fōstraþ *manna,* Jn. Lind. War. 6, 49. Fōstraþas *epimēnia* = ἐπιμήνια *provisions for a month, a month's rations,* Som. Ben. Lye.

fōstre, an; *f. A fosterer, nurse;* altrix, nutrix. DER. cild-fōstre.

fōstrian; *p.* ode; *pp.* od *To* FOSTER, *nourish;* ălĕre, nutrīre, Som. Ben. Lye. v. fēstrian. [*Orm.* fosstrenn *to nourish: Laym.* fostrien.]

fōstur, es; *n. A fostering, feeding, food, nourishment;* educātio, pastio, nutrīcium:—Fōstur feormian *to give food, to foster, cherish,* Ps. Th. 77, 69. v. fōster.

FŌT; *nom. acc: gen.* fōtes; *dat.* fēt, fōte; *pl. nom. acc.* fēt, fōtas; *gen.* fōta; *dat. inst:* fōtum; *m.* **I.** *a* FOOT; pēs, *gen.* pĕdis; *m:*—Gyf ðīn hand oððe ðīn fōt ðē swīcaþ *si mănus tua, vel pēs tuus scandălīzat te,* Mt. Bos. 18, 8. Ne cume me fōt ofermōdignysse *ne vĕniat mihi pēs superbiæ,* Ps. Spl. 35, 12. Swā his fōt gestōp *where his foot stepped,* Andr. Kmbl. 3163; An. 1584. Nāmen ðā ðet fōtspure ðe wæs undernæðen his fōte *then [they] took the footstool, that was underneath his foot,* Chr. 1070; Erl. 209, 8. Ðæt ic heonon nelle fleón fōtes trym *I will not flee hence a footstep,* Byrht. Th. 138, 68; By. 247. On ānum fēt *on one foot,* Exon. 108 b; Th. 415, 5; Rä. 33, 6. On fōte *in the foot,* 108 b; Th. 414, 8; Rä. 32, 17. Mid fōte *pĕde,* Ps. Th. 65, 5. Sylle fōt wið fēt *reddat pĕdem pro pĕde,* Ex. 21, 24: Ps. Spl. 90, 12: Lk. Bos. 4, 11. Standende wǣron fēt ūre on cāfertūnum ðīnum *stantes ĕrant pĕdes nostri in atriis tuis,* Ps.

Spl. 121, 2: Cd. 19; Th. 24, 18; Gen. 379. Sindon fealwe fōtas *the feet are yellow*, Exon. 60 a; Th. 219, 22; Ph. 311: Ps. Th. 121, 2: 131, 7. Ge-eádmēdaþ oððe gebiddaþ fōtsceamol his fōta *adōrāte scabellum pĕdum ejus*, Ps. Lamb. 98, 5: Exon. 107 b; Th. 410, 12; Rä. 28, 15. Ðe-læs hig mid hyra fōtum hig fortredon *ne forte conculcent eas pĕdibus suis*, Mt. Bos. 7, 6. Hæfde gefeormod fēt and folma *he had devoured feet and hands*, Beo. Th. 1494; B. 745. II. *the foot;* pēs, *gen.* pĕdis:—*The foot of a man, a measure of length, was divided into twelve equal parts or inches*, v. ynce, es; *m. inch; and an inch is three barley-corns in length.* In Anglo-Saxon times, the people and their rulers were satisfied with the simplest weights and measures, thus a yard was three feet, of twelve inches each foot, while an inch was in length three barley-corns. In our day, the legislature passed an act so late as July 30, 1855. It is styled, *An Act for legalising and preserving the restored standards of weights and measures.* This Act includes the weights of George the Fourth, 1824, in which the pounds avoirdupois is fixed by a standard weight, kept in the office of the Exchequer, and one equal seven-thousandth part of such pound avoirdupois shall be a grain. Thus our measures and weights are so recently fixed by standards. v. fōt-gemet, eln, ynce, met-geard, geard, gyrd. Nigon fōta, and ix scæfta munda, and ix bere-corna *nine feet, and nine half feet, and nine barley-corns or three inches*, L. Ath. iv. 5; Th. i. 224, 9. [*Wyc. Piers P. Chauc.* foot: *Laym. Orm.* fot: *Plat.* voot, *m*: *O. Sax.* fōt, fuot, *m*: *Frs.* foet: *O. Frs.* fot, *m*: *Dut.* voet, *m*: *Ger.* fusz, *m*: *M. H. Ger.* vuoz, *m*: *O. H. Ger.* fuoz, *m*: *Goth.* fotus, *m*: *Dan.* fod, *m. f*: *Swed.* fot, *m*: *Icel.* fótr, *m*: *Lat.* pēs, *gen.* pĕd-is, *m*: *Grk.* πούς, *gen.* ποδός, *m*: *Pers.* پا pa; *pl.* پایان payan: *Lith.* pádas *sole of the foot*: *Sansk.* पद् pad, पाद् pād, पाद pāda, *m.* from पद् pad *to go.*]

fōt-ādl, e; *f. A foot-disease, the gout;* podagra:—Wæs Mellitus mid fōtādle swīðe gehefigad *ĕrat Mellitus podagra grăvātus*, Bd. 2, 7; S. 509, 12. Wið fōtādle *against gout*, Lchdm. i. 376, 1.

fōt-bred, es; *n. A foot-board, stirrup;* tăbella in qua pĕdes requiescunt, astrăba [*q. v.* in Du Cange]:—Fōtbred [MS. fōtbret] *astrăba*, Ælfc. Gl. 3; Som. 55, 67; Wrt. Voc. 16, 40.

fōt-cops, -cosp, es; *m. A fetter, shackle for the feet;* pĕdĭca, compes:—Fōtcops *compes* vel *cippus*, Wrt. Voc. 86, 31. Hig ge-eádmēttan on fōtcopsum fēt his *humiliāvērunt in compĕdĭbus pĕdes ejus*, Ps. Lamb. 104, 18. Hine ne mihte nān man mid fōtcopsum gehæftan *no man could confine him with fetters*, Homl. Th. ii. 378, 27: Mk. 5, 4. To gewrīðenne cyningas heora on fōtcopsum *ad allĭgandos rēges eōrum in compĕdĭbus*, Ps. Spl. 149, 8.

fōt-cosp, es; *m. A fetter;* compes:—Hī ge-eádmētton on fōtcospum fēt his *humiliāvērunt in compĕdĭbus pĕdes ejus*, Ps. Spl. C. 104, 17. v. fōt-cops.

fōt-cōðu, e; *f. A foot-disease, the gout;* podagra, Hpt. Gl. 471, 472; Leo A. Sax. Gl. 24, 28.

fōt-cypsed; *part. Fettered;* compĕdĭtus, Som. Ben. Lye. DER. ge-fōtcypsed.

fōte; *adj. Provided with feet, footed;* pĕdātus. DER. feðer-fōte, fiðer-, flax-, flohten-, flox-, fyðer-. v. fēte.

fōt-ece, es; *m. Foot-ache, the gout;* pĕdis dŏlor, podagra = πόδαγρα:—Wið fōtece *for foot-ache*, L. M. 1, 27; Lchdm. ii. 68, 12, 19, 20, 23.

fōt-gemearc, es; *n. A foot-mark, length of a foot;* ūnius pĕdis longĭtūdo:—Se lēgdraca wæs fīftiges fōtgemearces lang *the fire-dragon was fifty feet of measure long*, Beo. Th. 6077; B. 3042.

fōt-gemet, es; *n. A foot-measure, foot-band, fetter;* pĕdis mensūra, compes:—Hī ge-eádmētton on fōtgemetum fēt his *humiliāvērunt in compĕdĭbus pĕdes ejus*, Ps. Spl. T. 104, 17.

fōt-gewǣde, es; *n. Foot-clothing;* pĕdum indūmentum, R. Ben. 55.

fōþ *take; pl. impert. of* fōn, *q. v*:—On fōþ hine *accĭpĭte eum*, Bd. 5, 13; S. 633, 14.

FŌÐER, fōður, es; *n.* I. *food, food for cattle, fodder;* ălĭmentum, jūmenti pābŭlum:—Fōðres ne gītsaþ *it is not desirous of food*, Exon. 114 b; Th. 440, 1; Rä. 59, 11. Twentig pūnd-wǣga fōðres *twenty pounds weight of fodder*, L. In. 70; Th. i. 146, 20. Se ceorl, se ðe hæfþ ōðres oxan ahȳrod, gif he hæbbe ealle on fōðre to agifanne, agife ealle. Gif he næbbe, agife healf on fōðre, healf on ōðrum ceápe *the ceorl, who has hired another's oxen, if he have to pay all in fodder, let him give it all. If he have not, let him pay half in fodder, and half in other goods*, 60; Th. i. 140, 8-11. II. that in which food is carried,—*a basket;* cophĭnus = κόφινος:—Genōmon ceawlas *vel* fōðer *tŭlērunt cophĭnos*, Mt. Lind. Stv. 14, 20. III. that in which food for cattle is carried,—*a cart* or *cart-load, about* 19 *or* 20 *cwt.* a heavy weight, as we now use the word for a FOTHER of lead, that is 19½ cwt; vĕhes, plaustrum, nunc massa *vel* vŏlūmen plumbi:—He scolde gife sixtiga fōðra wuda, and twælf fōður græfan, and sex fōður gearda *he should give sixty loads of wood, and twelve loads of gravel, and six loads of faggots*, Chr. 852; Erl. 67, 37: Cod. Dipl. 508; A. D. 963; Kmbl. ii. 398, 20. [*Laym.* iii. 22 uoðere, foðer *a load*: *O. Sax.* fōder, uoðer *vĕhes*: *Dut.* voeder, *n. a cart-load*: *Ger.* fuder, *n. a cart-load, tun*: *M. H. Ger.* vuoder, *n. a cart-load, tun*: *O. H. Ger.* fuotar, *n. thēca, plaustrum.*] v. fōdder.

fōþorn, es; *m.* [fōn *to grasp, catch;* þorn *a thorn*] *A fothorn, surgeon's instrument;* tĕnācŭlum:—Wið ðam niðeran tōþece, slīt mid ðē fōþorne ōþ-ðæt hie blēden *for the nether tooth-ache, slit* [*the gums*] *with the fothorn till they bleed*, L. M. 1, 6; Lchdm. ii. 52, 8.

fōt-lǣst, -lāst, es; *m. A foot-step, foot-trace;* vestīgium pĕdis, trāmes:—Se wyrm onfand feóndes fōtlāst *the worm found the foe's foot-trace*, Beo. Th. 4567; B. 2289. Fōtlǣstas [MS. fōtlǣst] ðīne ne beóþ oncnāwen *vestīgia tua non cognoscentur*, Ps. Spl. 76, 19: Blickl. Homl. 203, 36.

fōt-mǣl, es; *n. A foot-mark* or *print, foot-space;* signum *vel* mensūra pĕdis:—Ic wille nǣfre ðē myntan ne furh ne fōtmǣl *I will never appoint for thee neither furrow nor foot-mark*, L. O. 13; Th. i. 184, 7. He næfde ðā ealles landes būton seofon fōtmǣl *he had not then but seven feet of all his land*, Chr. 1086; Erl. 221, 2. Ðæt he nolde fleógan fōtmǣl landes *that he would not flee a foot-space of land*, Byrht. Th. 139, 57; By. 275. On twentigum fōtmǣlum feor *twenty feet deep*, Elen. Kmbl. 1658; El. 831: Nar. 35, 2; 36, 12.

fōt-mǣlum; *adv. By footsteps, step by step, by degrees;* pĕdĕtentim, grădātim, R. Conc. 5: Cot. 95. v. mǣl, es; *n.* III.

fōt-rāp, es; *m. A rope of a ship which fastens the sail;* prōpes:—Fōtrāp *prōpes*, Ælfc. Gl. 84; Som. 73, 87; Wrt. Voc. 48, 25.

fōt-sceamel, -sceamol, -scamel, -scamul, es; *m. A footstool;* pĕdum scăbellum, subpĕdāneum:—Ōþ-ðæt ic asette ðīne fȳnd to fōtsceamele ðīnra fōta *dōnec pōnam inĭmīcōs tuos scăbellum pĕdum tuōrum*, Lk. Bos. 20, 43: Ps. Lamb. 109, 1. Ge-eádmēdaþ fōtsceamol his fōta *adōrāte scăbellum pĕdum ejus*, Ps. Lamb. 98, 5: Mt. Bos. 22, 44: Mk. Bos. 12, 36. Under ðīnum fōtscamele *under thy footstool*, Homl. Th. i. 314, 32. Seó eorþe ys Godes fōtscamul *terra scabellum est pĕdum Dei*, Mt. Bos. 5, 35. Fōtscamul *scabellum* vel *subpĕdāneum*, Ælfc. Gl. 66; Som. 69, 79; Wrt. Voc. 41, 33. [*O. Sax.* fōt-skamel: *Germ.* fuss-schemel.]

fōt-sīþ-gerif, es; *n. A taking away* or *stoppage of a foot-path;* līmes, Ælfc. Gl. 3; Som. 55, 72; Wrt. Voc. 16, 45.

fōt-sīþ-sticcel, es; *m. A cloak, mantle;* chlămys, ȳdis, *f.* = χλαμύς, ύδος, *f*:—Hacele *vel* fōtsīþsticcel *chlămys*, Ælfc. Gl. 65; Som. 69, 40; Wrt. Voc. 40, 67.

fōt-spor, es; *n. A foot-track, foot-trace;* pĕdis vestīgium:—On ðæt fōtspor *on the foot-track*, Lchdm. iii. 286, 3.

fōt-spure, es; *n. A foot-support, foot-rest;* pĕdum fultūra:—Hī clumben upp to ðe hālge rōde, nāmen ðā ðe kynehelm of ūre Drihtnes heáfod, eall of smeáte golde, nāmen ðā ðet fōtspure ðe wæs undernæðen his fōte, ðæt wæs eall of reád golde *they climbed up to the holy cross, and took the crown, all of beaten gold, from our Lord's head, and took the foot-rest which was underneath his foot, which was all of red gold*, Chr. 1070; Erl. 209, 6-8.

fōt-stān, es; *m. A foot-stone, base, pedestal;* băsis = βάσις, fultūra:—Fōtstān *fultūra*, Ælfc. Gl. 116; Som. 80, 72; Wrt. Voc. 61, 49.

fōt-swæþ; *gen.* -swæðes; *pl. nom. acc.* -swaðu; *n*: fot-swaðu, e; *f. A foot-trace, foot-print;* pĕdis vestīgium:—Ðæt ne sȳn astyrode oððe awende sīþstapla oððe wegas oððe fōtswaðu mīne *ut non mŏveantur vestīgia mea*, Ps. Lamb. 16, 5. Eall ðæt rȳmet, ðe eówer fōtswaðu on bestæpþ, ic eów forgife *omnem lŏcum, quem calcāvĕrit vestīgium pedis vestri, vōbis trādam*, Jos. 1, 3. Ðīne fōtswaða nǣron oncnāwene *vestīgia tua non cognoscentur*, Ps. Lamb. 76, 20.

fōt-swile, -swyle, es; *m. A foot-swelling;* pĕdis tūmor:—Wið fōtswylum *for foot-swellings*, Med. ex Quadr. 4, 3; Lchdm. i. 342, 18. Ðes drænc is gōd wið fōtswilum *this drink is good for foot-swellings*, Lchdm. iii. 50, 12.

fōt-þweál, es; *n. A washing of the feet;* pĕdum lōtio:—Fōtþweál *pedĭlăvium*, Ælfc. Gl. 56; Som. 67, 27; Wrt. Voc. 37, 17. Fōtþweáles fæt *a vessel for washing the feet in;* pellŭviæ, 26; Som. 60, 88; Wrt. Voc. 25, 28.

fōt-wærc, es; *n. A pain in the foot;* pĕdis dŏlor:—Wið fōtwærce [MS. fōtwræce] *for a pain in the foot*, Med. ex Quadr. 3, 15; Lchdm. i. 342, 10.

fōt-welm, -wylm, es; *m*: fōt-wolma, an; *m. The sole of the foot;* pĕdis planta:—Fōtwelm *planta*, Ælfc. Gl. 75; Som. 71, 94; Wrt. Voc. 45, 2. Fōtwylm *planta*, Wrt. Voc. 71, 62. Mid ðære cōðe he wæs ofset fram ðam hnolle ufan ōþ his fōtwylmas neoðan *with which disease he was afflicted from the crown above to the soles of his feet below*, Homl. Th. ii. 480, 12: 508, 20. He hæfde ðæs brōðor fōtwolman on handa *plantam fratris tĕnēbat mānu*, Gen. 25, 25. Ðæt ðū næbbe nān þing hāles fram ðām fōtwolmum ōþ ðone hneccan *sanāri non possis a planta pĕdis usque ad vertĭcem tuum*, Deut. 28, 35.

fōwer *four*:—Cnut hit todǣlde on fōwer *Cnut divided it into four*, Chr. 1017; Th. 285, 19, col. 1. v. feówer.

fox, es; *m. A* FOX; vulpes:—Fox *vulpes*, Ælfc. Gl. 19; Som. 59, 27; Wrt. Voc. 22, 68. Secgaþ ðam foxe *dīcĭte vulpi illi*, Lk. Bos. 13, 32. Foxas habbaþ holu *vulpes fŏveas hăbent*, 9, 58. Foxes dǣlas *vulpis partes*, Ps. Th. 62, 8. [*Laym.* fox, uox: *Orm.* fox: *Plat. Dut.* vos, *m.*

Ger. fuchs, *m*: *M.H.Ger.* vuhs, *m*; vohe, *f*: *O.H.Ger.* fuhs, *m*; foha, *f*: *Goth.* fauho, *f*.]

foxes clâte, an; *f*. *Fox's clote, burdock*; arctium lappa, Lin:—Wið hundes dolge, foxes clâte, etc. *for wound by a hound, burdock, etc.* L. M. 1, 69; Lchdm. ii. 144, 11.

foxes clife, an; *f*. *The greater burdock*; arctium lappa, Lin:—Genim clifwyrt, sume men hâtaþ foxes clife, sume eáwyrt *take burdock, some men call it fox's cliver* or *the greater burdock, some riverwort*, L. M. 1, 15; Lchdm. ii. 58, 3: Lchdm. iii. 74, 10.

foxes fôt, es; *m*. *Fox's foot, bur reed, a water plant*; sparganum simplex, xiphion = ξιφίον:—Genim ðysse wyrte wyrttruman, ðe man *xiphion*, and ôðrum naman foxes fôt, nemneþ *take a root of this plant, which is named* xiphion, *and by another name fox's foot*, Herb. 47, 1; Lchdm. i. 150, 16.

foxes glôfa, an; *m*. [foxes glôfa MS. B.] *Foxglove*; digitālis purpūrea, Lin:—Wið ôman genim ðysse wyrte leáf ðe man στρύχνος μανικός, and ôðrum naman foxes glôfa [MS. foxes clôfa] nemneþ *for inflammatory sores, take leaves of this wort, which is named* sōlānum insānum *or* Sodŏmeum, *and by another name foxglove*, Herb. 144; Lchdm. i. 266, 18. Mr. Cockayne says, in note b on this passage,—'Strychnos manikos is Sōlānum insānum *or* Sodŏmeum fairly drawn, MS. V. fol. 60 a, not an English plant, and certainly not *foxglove*. The leechdoms here recorded seem derived from what Dioskorides says of the στρύχνος κηπαῖος: namely, τὰ φύλλα καταπλασσόμενα ἁρμόζει πρὸς ἐρυσιπέλατα καὶ ἕρπητας; and so on of κεφαλαλγία and στόμαχος καυσούμενος and ὠταλγία [iv. 71].' v. clifwyrt *foxglove*.

fra *from, fro*, Chr. 656; Erl. 31, 10: 963; Erl. 123, 2. v. fram.

fraced *abominable*, Ælfc. T. 34, 25. v. fracoþ; *adj*.

fraced-lîce; *comp.* -lîcor; *adv. Shamefully, disgracefully*; turpĭter:—Hwæt is fracedlîcor *quid est turpius?* Ælfc. Gr. 48; Som. 49, 15. v. fracoþ-lîce.

fraceþ *an insult*, Exon. 66 b; Th. 246, 34; Jul. 71. v. fracoþ, es; *n*.

fracod *vile, abominable, useless*, Coll. Monast. Th. 18, 11: Beo. Th. 3155; B. 1575. v. fracoþ; *adj*.

fracod-lîc *shameful*, L. Eth. vi. 28; Th. i. 322, 14. v. fracoþ-lîc.

fracod-lîce; *adv. Shamefully*; turpĭter:—Hî wyllaþ fracodlîce him betwynan sacian *they will shamefully quarrel among themselves*, Homl. Th. ii. 292, 35. v. fracoþ-lîce.

fracoþ, fracuþ, fracod, fraced; *adj. Vile, filthy, unseemly, hateful, abominable, worthless, useless*; turpis, detestābilis, indĕcōrus:—Is ûser lîf fracoþ and gefrǽge *our life is vile and infamous*, Cd. 189; Th. 235, 10; Dan. 304: Salm. Kmbl. 67; Sal. 34: Exon. 10 b; Th. 12, 33; Cri. 195. Ne wæs ðæt [MS. ðær] hûru fracoðes gealga *that was indeed no vile* [*man's*] *gibbet*, Rood Kmbl. 20; Kr. 10. We bióþ folcum fracoðe *we shall be hateful to the people*, Andr. Kmbl. 817; An. 409. Fracoðest *vilest*, Salm. Kmbl. 702; Sal. 350. Wæs ûre lîf fracuþ and gefrǽge *our life has been vile and infamous*, Exon. 53 a; Th. 186, 23; Az. 24. Hî fracuðe and earme wǽron *they were worthless and wretched*, Bd. 3, 21; S. 551, 26. Hwæt rece we hwæt we sprecan, bûton hit riht spræc sŷ, and behêfe, næs îdel, oððe fracod *quid cūrāmus quid lŏquāmur, nĭsi recta lŏcūtio sit, et ūtĭlis, non ănĭlis, aut turpis?* Coll. Monast. Th. 18, 11. Næs seó ecg fracod hilde rince *the edge was not useless to the warrior*, Beo. Th. 3155; B. 1575. On ðam fracodan gilte *in făcĭnŏre*, Jos. 7, 15. On his fracedum dǽdum *in his abominable deeds*, Ælfc. T. 34, 25.

fracoþ, fraceþ, es; *pl. nom. acc.* fracoðu, fraceðu; *n*. [fracoþ *vile*] *An insult, contumely*; turpĭtūdo, contŭmēlia:—Bûtan fracoðum *without insults*, Ps. Th. 54, 22. Me ða fraceðu sind mǽste weorce *these insults are the greatest trouble to me*, Exon. 66 b; Th. 246, 34; Jul. 71: 73 b; Th. 274, 31; Jul. 541. Fracoþ *abominatio*, Lk. Skt. Lind. 16, 15.

fracoðe, fracuðe; *adv. Shamefully*; turpĭter:—He mæg ûre fŷnd gedôn fracoðe to nâhte *he can shamefully destroy our enemies*, Ps. Th. 59, 11: 88, 28. Ic fracuðe forseó feóndas mîne *I shamefully despise my enemies*, 117, 7: 62, 8.

fracoþ-lîc, fracuþ-lîc, fraceþ-lîc, fracod-lîc; *adj. Heinous, ignominious, shameful*; turpis:—Ðam folctogan fracuþlîc þûhte *it seemed heinous to the chieftain*, Exon. 69 a; Th. 256, 2; Jul. 225. Fracodlîce fitunga *shameful fightings*, L. Eth. vi. 28; Th. i. 322, 14. Ðæt wîte ðæs fracoþlîcostan [fraceþlêcestan MS. Hat.] deáþes he geceás *he chose the punishment of the most ignominious death*, Past. 3, 1; Cot. MS.

fracoþ-lîce, fracuþ-lîce, fracod-lîce, fraced-lîce; *adv. Shamefully, disgracefully, wickedly*; turpĭter:—Biþ us swîðe fracoþlîce [fracuþlîce MS. Cot.] ôðer fôt unscôd *one of our feet is very disgracefully unshod*, Past. 5, 2; Hat. MS. 11 a, 17. Ic fracoþlîce feóndrǽs gefremede *I wickedly committed the fiendish violence*, Cd. 42; Th. 55, 25; Gen. 899.

fracoþ-nes, -ness, e; *f*. *Vileness, obscenity*; turpĭtūdo, obscēnĭtas, Cot. 143.

fracu, e; *f*. *Wickedness, impudence*; protervĭtas. DER. neód-fracu, scyld-.

fracuþ *vile*, Exon. 53 a; Th. 186, 23; Az. 24. v. fracoþ; *adj*.

fracuðe; *adv. Shamefully*, Ps. Th. 62, 8: 117, 7. v. fracoðe.

fracuþ-lîc *heinous*, Exon. 69 a; Th. 256, 2; Jul. 225. v. fracoþ-lîc.

fracuþ-lîce *disgracefully*, Past. 5, 2; Cot. MS. v. fracoþ-lîce.

frǽ- *before, in a greater degree, very, exceedingly*; præ-: found in the compounds frǽ-beorht, -fætt, -mǽre, -micel, -ôfestlîce. v. freá-.

frǽ-beorht *exceedingly bright*; præclārus, Lye. v. freá-beorht.

fræc; *adj. Voracious, greedy*; gŭlōsus:—Fræc [MS. fræt] *gŭlōsa*, Mone B. 3533. v. frec.

frǽcednys, -nyss, e; *f*. *Danger, peril*; perĭcŭlum:—Saca mid frǽcednysse hit getâcnaþ *it betokens disputes with peril*, Somn. 122; Lchdm. iii. 204, 33. v. frêcednes.

frǽcenes, frǽcnes, -ness, -nyss, e; *f*. *Danger, peril*; perĭcŭlum:—On frǽcenesse heora stealles *in perĭcŭlum sui stătus*, Bd. 4, 25; S. 601, 17. Bûtan frǽcnesse *without danger*, Herb. 30, 4; Lchdm. i. 126, 24, MS. B. Bûtan frǽcnysse, 63, 2; Lchdm. i. 166, 7, MSS. B. H. v. frêcennes.

frǽcenful; *adj. Dangerous, perilous*; perĭcŭlōsus:—Môna se þreóteóða frǽcenful ys to angennene þing *the thirteenth moon is perilous for beginning things*, Obs. Lun. § 13; Lchdm. iii. 190, 11: 15; Lchdm. iii. 190, 30: 17; Lchdm. iii. 192, 14. v. frêcenful.

fræc-genga, an; *m*. *A fugitive, apostate*; profŭgus, apostăta, Som. Ben. Lye.

fræclîce; *adv. Greedily*; ăvĭde:—Fræclîce bât *ăvĭde momordit*, Gr. Dial. 1, 4.

fræc-mâse, an; *f*. *The nun bird, titmouse*; pārus cærŭleus:—Fræcmâse *sigatula?* Glos. Brux. Recd. 36, 38; Wrt. Voc. 62, 38. v. frec-mâse.

frǽcne; *adj. Grievous, dire, dangerous*; dīrus, perĭcŭlōsus:—Awend ðîn ansŷne fram mînum frǽcnum firenum *turn thy face from my grievous sins*, Ps. Ben. 50, 10; Ps. Grn. ii. 149, 10. Ðæt hî ne þorftan in swâ frǽcne sîþfætt feran *ne tam perĭcŭlōsam peregrīnātiōnem adīre dēbērent*, Bd. 1, 23; S. 485, 37. v. frêcne; *adj*.

frǽcne; *adv. Fiercely, severely, hardly*; dūre, atrōcĭter, audacter:—Abrahames cwên spræc frǽcne on fǽmnan *Abraham's wife spoke severely against the damsel*, Cd. 103; Th. 136, 22; Gen. 2262: Ps. Th. 64, 3: 90, 12. Ðonne hit ðê frǽcnost þynce *when it seems worst to thee*, Prov. Kmbl. 75. v. frêcne; *adv*.

frǽcnes, -ness, -nyss *danger*, Herb. 30, 4; Lchdm. i. 126, 24, MS. B: 63, 2; Lchdm. i. 166, 7, MSS. B. H. Blickl. Homl. 109, 7. v. frêcennes.

frǽ-fætt; *adj. Very fat*; præpinguis, Cot. 177.

fræfele; *adj. Saucy*; audax, prŏcax, Som. Ben. Lye. [*Scot.* frewall *frivolous*: *Plat.* wrevel, wrewel, *m. obstinacy, impudence*: *O.Frs.* frevelhed *boldness*: *Dut.* wrevel, *m. stubbornness, contumacy*: *Ger.* frevel *bold, frivolous*; frevel, *m. boldness, crime, insolence, impudence*: *M.H.Ger.* vrevel, vrävel *bold, impudent*; vrevele, vrevel, *f. m. boldness, impudence*: *O.H.Ger.* frafali *contŭmax, protervus*; fravali, *f. temĕrĭtas, protervĭtas*: *Lat.* frīvŏlus *empty, trifling, worthless, frivolous*.]

fræfellîce; *adv. Saucily*; procācĭter, Som. Ben. Lye.

fræfelnes, -ness, e; *f*. *Sauciness, faction*; procăcĭtas, factio, Cot. 213.

fræg, ðû frǽge, *pl.* frǽgon *asked, hast asked, inquired*; *p. of* fricgan.

frǽge, frêge *known, famous*. DER. ge-frǽge, -frêge; *adj*.

frǽge, frêge *an inquiring, knowing, hearsay*. DER. ge-frǽge, -frêge, es; *n*.

frægin *asked*, Bd. 2, 1; S. 501, 9: 4, 5; S. 572, 21, = frægn; *p. of* frignan.

frægn *asked*; interrŏgāvit, Bd. 2, 12; S. 513, 37, 38; *p. of* frignan.

frǽ-mǽre, -mêre; *adj. Very great, famous, excellent*; egrĕgius, eximius, Cot. 77. v. freá-mǽre.

fræmde *strange, foreign*, L. Wih. 28; Th. i. 42, 23: Somn. 79; Lchdm. iii. 202, 20. v. fremede.

frǽ-micel; *adj. Very great, famous*; præ-magnus, exĭmius, Cot. 178.

fræm-sum; *adj. Kind*; benignus:—Gedô fræmsume frôfre ðîne *make thy comfort kind*, Ps. C. 50, 130; Ps. Grn. ii. 279, 130. v. frem-sum.

fræng *asked*, Bd. 3, 14; S. 541, 3, = frægn; *p. of* frignan.

frǽ-ôfestlîce; *adv. Very hastily, very quickly*; præprŏpĕre, Cot. 178.

fræt; *adj. Obstinate, proud*; perversus, superbus:—Hâteþ ðæt ðû, on ðis fræte folc, onsende wæter *he commandeth that thou send water upon this obstinate people*, Andr. Kmbl. 3010; An. 1508: Exon. 28 a; Th. 84, 15; Cri. 1374. Frætre þeóde *to the proud people*, Andr. Kmbl. 1141; An. 571.

fræt, ðû frǽte, *pl.* fræton *devoured, devouredst*, Beo. Th. 3167; B. 1581: Ps. Th. 34, 23; *p. of* fretan.

frætewe, frætewa *ornaments*, Bd. 1, 29; S. 498, 10, note. v. frætwe.

frætewung, e; *f*. *An ornament*; ornāmentum:—Heofonas and eorþe and eall heora frætewung *cœli et terra et omnis ornātus eōrum*, Gen. 2, 1. v. frætwung.

frætig; *def.* se frætga; *adj. Proud, perverse, wicked*; superbus, perversus:—Forfôh ðone frætgan *seize the proud one* [*the devil*], Exon. 69 b; Th. 259, 18; Jul. 284.

fræt-læppa, an; *m*. *Dew-lap*; pălear:—Frætlæppa *runia* vel *pălеāre*, Ælfc. Gl. 99; Som. 76, 123; Wrt. Voc. 54, 63.

frættewian, frætwian, fretwian, frætwan; *p.* ode, ede; *pp.* od, ed *To adorn, deck, embroider, trim*; ornāre:—Ða burh timbrum and gyfum eác frættewodon and weorþodon *urbem ædificiis ac donāriis adornārunt*, Bd. 3, 19: S. 547, 24. Ðe ðone sele frætweþ *who adorns the hall*

Exon. 117 a; Th. 450, 24; Dôm. 92. Ic wylle frætwian mec *I will prepare myself*, Exon. 119 a; Th. 456, 23; Hy. 4, 71. Hī oððe hī sylfe frætwiaþ *aut seipsas adornent*, Bd. 4, 25; S. 601, 17. Sāwle frætwaþ hālgum gehygdum *they adorn their souls with holy meditations*, Exon. 44 b; Th. 150, 14; Gū. 778. Ða ðe geolo godwebb geatwum frætwaþ *those who embroider the yellow godly garment with ornaments*, Exon. 109 a; Th. 417, 26; Rä. 36, 10. Ðe mec frætwede *who adorned me*, 124 b; Th. 479, 15; Rä. 62, 8. Folcstede frætwan *to deck a dwelling-place*, Beo. Th. 152, note; B. 76. Brīdels frætwan *to deck the bridle*, Elen. Kmbl. 2396; El. 1199. Hyrstum frætwed *adorned with ornaments*, Exon. 104 a; Th. 395, 22; Rä. 15, 11: 107 b; Th. 411, 1; Rä. 29, 6: 108 b; Th. 414, 15; Rä. 32, 20. [*Chauc.* fret *wrought*: *O. Sax.* fratahōn *to adorn, ornament, decorate*: *Goth.* us-fratwyan *to make ready, to outfit.*] DER. ge-frætewian, -frætwian, ymb-.

frætwe, frætewe, frætuwe, frætwa, frætewa; *gen.* frætwa; *pl. f. Ornaments, adornments, decorations, treasures*; ornāmenta, ornātus, res pretiōsæ:—Holtes frætwe *the decorations of the wood*, Exon. 57 a; Th. 202, 22; Ph. 73. Ða wæstmas, foldan frætwe *the fruits, the treasures of the earth*, 59 b; Th. 215, 22; Ph. 257. Wangas grēne, foldan frætuwe *green fields, the ornaments of the earth*, Menol. Fox 411; Menol. 207. Ic ðara frætwa þanc secge *I say thanks for these ornaments*, Beo. Th. 5580; B. 2794. Frætwa hyrde *the guardian of the treasures*, 6258; B. 3133. Māþma fela frætwa *many treasures, ornaments*, 74; B. 37. Ðām frætwum *to these precious things*, 4332; B. 2163. He ðām frætwum fēng *he received the ornaments*, 5970; B. 2989. On frætewum *in his garnishments, viz. armour*, 1928; B. 962. Secgas bǣron beorhte frætwe *the warriors bare bright arms*, 434, note; B. 214. He frætwe geheóld, bill and byrnan *he held the armour, the falchion and coat of mail*, 5233; B. 2620. Frætwe and fætgold *ornaments and plated gold*, 3846, note; B. 1921. Hafa wunden gold, feoh and frætwa *have the twisted gold, the wealth and ornaments*, Cd. 98; Th. 128, 21; Gen. 2130: 136; Th. 171, 17; Gen. 2829: Exon. 51 b; Th. 179, 3; Gū. 1256: Beo. Th. 1797; B. 896. Cyricean frætewa *ornāmenta ecclēsiæ*, Bd. 1, 29; S. 498, 10, note. Frætwum gefyrðred *furthered by the treasures*, Beo. Th. 5561; B. 2784: 4114; B. 2054. [*O. Sax.* fratahi, *f? ornaments.*] DER. gold-frætwe.

frætwednes, fretwednes, frætwædnys, -ness, -nyss, e; *f. An adorning, ornament, a trifle*; ornātio, ornāmentum, crĕpundia:—He sende cyricean frætwednesse *mīsit ornāmenta ecclēsiæ*, Bd. 1, 29; S. 498, 10. On eorþlīcre frætwædnysse [fretwednesse MS. Ca.] *in earthly adorning*, 3, 22; S. 552, 20: Blickl. Homl. 195, 11; 127, 3; 207, 25. Frætwednessa *crepundia*, Cot. 56. DER. hrægel-gefrætwodnes.

frætwung, frætewung, e; *f. An adorning, adornment, ornament*; ornātus, ornāmentum:—He micele swīðor lufode ðære heortan clǣnnysse ðonne ðæra stāna frætwunge *he much more loved cleanness of heart than the adornment of stones*, Homl. Th. i. 508, 22. On ðisum getelde wǣron forneán unasecgendlīce frætwunga *in this tabernacle were almost unspeakable ornaments*, ii. 210, 11. DER. world-frætwung.

fragendlīc; *adj.* [= framigendlīc, *q. v.*] *Beneficial*; salubris, salūtāris:—Fragendlīc lǣcedōm *a beneficial medicine*, Herb. 159; Lchdm. i. 288, 2, MS. B.

FRAM, from; *prep. dat.* I. FROM; a, ab:—Ic adilige ðone mannan fram ðære eorþan ansīne, fram ðam men ōþ ða nȳtenu, fram ðam slincendum ōþ ða fugelas *delēbo hŏmĭnem a făcie terræ, ab hŏmĭne usque ad anĭmantia, a reptĭli usque ad volucres cœli*, Gen. 6, 7. Gewītaþ fram me *discēdĭte a me*, Ps. Th. 6, 7: Ps. Spl. 30, 15: Mt. Bos. 1, 17, 21, 22. II. with verbs of speaking, *Concerning, about, of*; *cum verbis lŏquendi*, de:—Ðæt he fram Sigemunde secgan hȳrde ellendǣdum *that he, concerning Sigemund, had heard tell of valiant deeds*, Beo. Th. 1754; B. 875. Nō ic fram ðē swylcra searunīða secgan hȳrde *never have I heard speak about thee of such hostile snares*, Beo. Th. 1167; B. 581. III. fram *is sometimes placed after its case*:—He hine forwræc mancynne fram *he banished him from mankind*, Beo. Th. 221; B. 110. [*Chauc.* fra: *Laym.* fram, from: *Orm.* fra: *O. Sax.* fram, vram: *O. H. Ger.* fram: *Goth.* fram: *Dan.* fra: *Swed.* fram *forward, forth*; från *from*: *Icel.* fram *forward*; frá *from.*]

fram; *adj. Valiant, stout, firm*; strēnuus:—Geong and fram *young and valiant*, Bd. 4, 15; S. 583, 25. He wæs fram to Godes compe *he was stout for God's battle*, Andr. Kmbl. 467; An. 234. v. from.

fram-acyrran; *p.* de; *pp.* ed *To turn from* or *away, take from*; avertĕre, auferre:—Framacyr yrre ðīn fram us *averte iram tuam a nōbis*, Ps. Spl. 84, 4. Se brȳdguma him biþ framacyrred *auferētur ab eis sponsus*, Mk. Bos. 2, 20.

fram-adōn, he -adēþ; *p.* -adyde; *pp.* -adōn *To do* or *take from* or *away, cut off*; auferre, abscīdere:—Sōna heó ðone fefer framadēþ *it will soon take away the fever*, Herb. 12, 5; Lchdm. i. 104, 15. Mildheortnesse his he framadēþ *misericordiam suam abscīdet*, Ps. Lamb. 76, 9.

fram-adrīfan, -adrȳfan; *p.* -adrāf, *pl.* -adrifon *To drive from* or *away, expel*; expellĕre:—Gif gē me framadrȳfaþ *si me expellĭtis*, Coll. Monast. Th. 29, 23.

fram-ahyldan; *p.* de; *pp.* ed *To turn from* or *away*; declīnāre:—Hió him framahyldeþ *it will turn from them*, Med. ex Quadr. 1, 2; Lchdm. i. 328, 10.

fram-anȳdan; *p.* -anȳdde; *pp.* -anȳded, -anȳdd *To force from* or *away, drive away*; repellĕre:—Ða feforas beóþ framanȳdde *the fevers will be forced away*, Herb. 143, 4; Lchdm. i. 266, 13.

fram-a-teón; *p.* -ateáh, *pl.* -atugon; *pp.* -atogen *To draw away from*; abstrăhĕre, extrăhĕre:—Framatuge *extraxisti*, Ps. Vos. 21, 8. Framatogen *detractus, ablātus*, Cot. 69. v. teón I.

fram-ateran; *p.* -atær, *pl.* -atǣron; *pp.* -atoren *To tear from* or *asunder, to tear in pieces*; dirĭpĕre:—Ic framatere *dirĭpio*, Ælfc. Gr. 28, 3; Som. 30, 64.

framaþ *does good, avails*, Herb. 146, 2; Lchdm. i. 270, 4, = fremaþ; *3rd sing. pres. of* fremian.

fram-atīhan; he -atīhþ; *p.* -atāh, *pl.* -atigon; *pp.* -atigen *To draw away from*; abstrăhĕre:—Ðonne he framatīhþ hine *dum adtrăhit* [*abstrăhet*, Ps. Surt. 9, 30] *eum*, Ps. Spl. second 9, 11. v. tīhan I.

fram-awendan; *p.* de; *pp.* ed *To turn from* or *away*; avertĕre, Scint. 53.

fram-aweorpan, -wurpan; ic -aweorpe, -awurpe; *p.* -awearp, *pl.* -awurpon; *pp.* -aworpen *To cast from, throw away*; abjĭcĕre:—Ic framawurpe *abjĭcio*, Ælfc. Gr. 28, 6; Som. 32, 39. DER. weorpan.

fram-bringan; *p.* -brang, *pl.* -brungon; *pp.* -brungen *To bring from* or *away*; dedūcĕre:—Gyf he ðone him eáðelīce frambringan ne mǣge *if he cannot easily bring it away from him*, Herb. 158, 2; Lchdm. i. 284, 24.

fram-būgan; *p.* -beáh, *pl.* -bugon; *pp.* -bogen *To turn from* or *away, leave*; deflectĕre, declīnāre:—Ðæt him ða frambugon [MS. frambugan], ðe hī betst getreówodon *that those left them, whom they most trusted*, Ors. 2, 5; Bos. 47, 44.

fram-fleón; *p.* -fleáh, *pl.* -flugon; *subj. p.* -fluge, *pl.* -flugen; *pp.* -flogen *To flee from*; aufŭgĕre:—Ðæt hī him framflugen *that they should flee from them*, Ors. 1, 7; Bos. 30, 10.

fram-gewītan, from-gewītan; *p.* -gewāt, *pl.* -gewiton; *pp.* -gewiten *To go away from, depart from*; discēdĕre:—Hie him framgewītaþ *they depart from him*, Bt. 8; Fox 26, 10.

framian *to avail, profit*; vălēre, prōdesse, R. Ben. 64, 72: R. Conc. 7. v. fremian.

framigendlīc; *adj.* [framigende, *part. of* fremian *and* līc] *Profitable, beneficial*; salubris, salūtāris:—Ðæt sylfe is framigendlīc lǣcedōm ongeán ealle āttru *the same is a beneficial medicine against all poisons*, Herb. 159; Lchdm. i. 288, 2.

framlīce; *adv. Strongly, firmly, stoutly*; fortĭter, strēnue:—Ðes Cāsere framlīce rehte ða cynewīsan *this Cæsar firmly ruled the kingdom*, Bd. 1, 5; S. 476, 7: 4, 10; S. 578, 6. Benedictus ðone sīþfæt framlīce to Rōme geferde *Benedict stoutly went his journey to Rome*, Bd. 5, 19; S. 637, 45. v. from-līce.

fram-scipe, es; *m. A fellowship, association, fraternity*; collēgium:—Framscipe muneca *collēgium monachōrum*, Bd. 3, 5; S. 526, 18, note, MSS. Ca. O.

fram-sīþ *a going from* or *away, departure*, Som. Ben. Lye. v. from-sīþ.

fram-sīðian; *p.* ode; *pp.* od *To go from* or *away, depart*; abscēdĕre, Som. Ben. Lye.

fram-standan; *p.* -stōd, *pl.* -stōdon; *pp.* -standen *To stand away from, stand aloof*; abstāre, Som. Ben. Lye.

fram-swengan; *p.* de; *pp.* ed *To shake from* or *away, shake off*; excŭtĕre:—Framswengde *excussit*, Cot. 179.

fram-weard; *adj. Turned from* or *away, averse, froward, perverse*; aversus, perversus, Som. Ben. Lye. v. from-weard.

fram-wīsum; *adv. Wisely*; săpienter:—Ǣttrene beóþ gegalene framwīsum *venefĭci incantantis săpienter*, Ps. Spl. 57, 5.

fran *asked, inquired*; *p. of* frinan.

franca, an; *m. A javelin, lance*; lancea, frămea, hasta:—He lēt his francan wadan þurh ðæs hysses hals *he let his javelin go through the youth's neck*, Byrht. Th. 135, 59; By. 140. He ðone forman man mid his francan ofsceát *he shot the foremost man with his javelin*, 134, 1; By. 77. Francan wǣron hlūde *the javelins were loud*, Cd. 93; Th. 119, 20; Gen. 1982 [*Icel.* frakka]. v. Grm. Gesch. D. S. p. 359.

Francan; *gen.* Francena, Francna; *dat.* Francum; *pl. m*: France; *gen.* Franca; *pl. m. The Franks*; Franci:—Hēr Ald-Seaxe and Francan gefuhton *in this year* [A. D. 780] *the Old Saxons and the Franks fought*, Chr. 780; Erl. 54, 3; 881; Erl. 82, 5. Of Francena cyningcynne *de gente Francōrum rēgia*, Bd. 1, 25; S. 486, 32. Francena cyning *Francōrum rex*, 3, 19; S. 550, 2. Wið Francena rīce *against the kingdom of the Franks*, 4, 1; S. 565, 1. Cyrdon hī to Pipne Francna cyninge *divertērunt ad Pippinum dūcem Francōrum*, 5, 10; S. 624, 2: Chr. 855; Erl. 68, 29: 885; Erl. 82, 34. Ymb ii geár ðæs ðe he of Francum cōm, he gefōr *two years after he came from the Franks, he died*, Chr. 855; Th. 126, 2, col. 2, 3: 890; Erl. 86, 32. Franca cyng *king of the Franks*, Chr. 1070; Th. 347, 7: 1077; Th. 351, 14. DER. Eást-Francan. v. Grm. Gesch. D. S. cap. xx.

Franc-land, Fronc-land, Frang-land, es; *n. Frank-land, the country* *of the Franks;* Francōrum terra, Francia:—Nāmon [MS. noman] hī him wealhstōdas of Franclande mid *accēpērunt de gente Francōrum interprētes*, Bd. 1, 25; S. 486, 24. On ðam mynstre ðe on Franclande wæs getimbred *in monastērio quod in rĕgiōne Francōrum construc̄tum est*, 3, 8; S. 531, 13. On Francland [Froncland, Th. 150, 23, col. 1; Frangland, 151, 23, col. 2, 3] *into Frank-land*, Chr. 882; Th. 150, 23, col. 2, 3.

Franc-rīce, es; *n. The kingdom of the Franks;* Francōrum regnum:—He hæfde ǽrendo sum to Breotone cyningum of Francrīce *he had an errand to the kings of Britain against the kingdom of the Franks*, Bd. 4, 1; S. 565, 1, MS. B: Chr. 1060; Erl. 193, 32.

FRĀSIAN, freásian; *p.* ade; *pp.* ad *To ask, inquire, tempt;* interrŏgāre, conquirĕre, sciscĭtāri, tentāre:—Frāsiaþ [MS. frasias] *conquīrĭtis*, Mk. Skt. Lind. 9, 16. Wæs mǽst Babilōn burga, ōþ-ðæt Baldazar, þurh gylp, grome Godes freásade [MS. frea sæde] *Babylon was greatest of cities, until Belshazzar, through vain glory, fiercely tempted God*, Cd. 209; Th. 259, 22; Dan. 695. [*O. Sax.* frēsōn *to try, tempt: M. H. Ger.* vreisen *to endanger: O. H. Ger.* freisōn *periclĭtāri: Goth.* fraisan *to try, tempt;* fraistubni, *f. temptation: Dan.* friste *to try, tempt: Swed.* fresta: *Icel.* freista.] DER. ge-frāsian.

frāsung, e; *f. An asking, inquiring, tempting, temptation;* interrŏgātio, tentātio:—Hȳ to Gūþlāces gāste gelǽddun frāsunga fela *they brought many temptations to Guthlac's spirit*, Exon. 35 a; Th. 113, 19; Gū. 160. Mid frāsung *interrogātiōne*, Mt. Kmbl. Præf. p. 19, 9.

FREÁ [=freaha], freó; *gen.* freán; *m. A lord, master, the Lord;* dŏmĭnus:—Freá sceáwode fyrngeweorc *the lord beheld the ancient work*, Beo. Th. 4560; B. 2285. Freá Ælmihtig *the Lord Almighty*, Cd. 1; Th. 1, 9; Gen. 5: 101; Th. 134, 24; Gen. 2229. Freá moncynnes *Lord of mankind*, Bt. Met. Fox 17, 17; Met. 17, 9. Swā neáh wæs sigora Freán þūsend aurnen *so nearly a thousand [winters] of the Lord of victories had elapsed*, Chr. 973; Erl. 124, 23; Edg. 15. Habbaþ we to ðæm mǽran ǽrende Deniga freán *we have an errand to the famous lord of the Danes*, Beo. Th. 547; B. 271. Ðis is hold weorod freán Scyldinga *this is a band attached to the lord of the Scyldings*, 587; B. 291. Wīgheafolan bær freán on fultum *he bore the helmet to bring aid to his lord*, 5316, note; B. 2662. To hire freán sittan *to sit by her lord*, 1287; B. 641. Ic Freán þanc secge, ēcum Dryhtne *I say thanks to the Lord, the eternal Ruler*, 5581; B. 2794. He ðone wísan wordum hnǽgde freán Ingwina *he addressed with words the wise lord of the Ingwines*, 2642; B. 1319. Gūþ nimeþ freán eówerne *war shall take away your lord*, 5068; B. 2537. Ðonne we geferian freán ūserne, leófne mannan *when we bear our lord, the dear man*, 6206; B. 3107. [*O. Sax.* frāho, frōho, frōio, frō, *m: O. H. Ger.* frō, *m. dŏmĭnus: Goth.* frauya, *m. lord: Icel.* Freyr, *m. name of the god Freyr.*] DER. āgend-freá, aldor-, folc-, gūþ-, heáh-, līf-, mān-, sin-.

freá-, frǽ- *before, in a greater degree, very, exceedingly;* præ-: found in the compounds freá-beorht, -bodian, -drēman, -fætt, -gleáw, -hræd, -mǽre, -micel, -ōfestlīce, -reccere.

freá-beorht, -briht, frǽ-beorht; *adj. Exceedingly bright, glorious;* præclārus, clarissĭmus:—Eálā freábeorht folces [MS. folkes] scippend *O! glorious creator of people*, Hy. 2, 1; Hy. Grn. ii. 281, 1. Eálā freábrihta folces Scyppend, Ps. Lamb. fol. 183 b, 15. Blickl. Homl. 229, 28.

freá-bodian; *p.* ode; *pp.* od *To proclaim, declare;* pronuntiāre:—Freábodaþ oððe mǽrsaþ tunge mīn spæce ðīne *pronuntiābit lingua mea elŏquium tuum*, Ps. Lamb. 118, 172.

freá-drēman; *p.* de; *pp.* ed *To rejoice exceedingly, shout for joy;* jubĭlāre:—Fægniaþ oððe freádrēmaþ Gode on stefne wynsumnesse oððe blisse *jubĭlāte Deo in vōce exultatiōnis*, Ps. Lamb. 46, 2; 97, 4.

freá-drihten, freah-drihten; *gen.* -drihtnes; *m. A lord, master, the Lord;* dŏmĭnus:—Wæs his freádrihtnes folc-cūþ nama Agamemnon *his lord's celebrated name was Agamemnon*, Bt. Met. Fox 26, 17; Met. 26, 9. Abraham, ðīn freádrihten *Abraham, thy lord*, Cd. 130; Th. 165, 9; Gen. 2729. Freádrihten mīn *O my Lord*, 42; Th. 54, 29; Gen. 884. He wolde freahdrihtnes feorh ealgian *he would defend his lord's life*, Beo. Th. 1596, note; B. 796.

freá-fætt *very fat.* v. frǽ-fætt.

freá-gleáw; *adj. Very prudent;* prudentissĭmus:—Hie ðǽr fundon freágleáwe æðele cnihtas *they found there very prudent noble youths*, Cd. 176; Th. 221, 15; Dan. 88.

freah-drihten *a lord, master*, Beo. Th. 1596, note; B. 796. v. freádrihten.

freá-hræd; *adj. Very quick, speedy, swift;* prŏpĕrus, expĕdītus, Som. Ben. Lye.

freá-mǽre, frǽ-mǽre; *adj. Very renowned;* celeberrĭmus:—Firum freámǽrne eard weardian *to inhabit a country very renowned to men*, Exon. 95 b; Th. 356, 11; Pa. 10.

freá-micel *very great, famous.* v. frǽ-micel.

freá-ōfestlīce *very hastily, very quickly.* v. frǽ-ōfestlīce.

freá-reccere, es; *m. A chief ruler, prince;* princeps:—Freárecceras oððe ealdras ēhton me būton ge-earnungum *princĭpes persĕcūti sunt me grātis*, Ps. Lamb. 118, 161.

freás, *pl.* fruron *froze; p. of* freósan.

freatewung, e; *f. An adorning, adornment, ornament;* ornātus, ornāmentum, Som. Ben. Lye. v. frætwung.

freáum *to chieftains*, Exon. 94 b; Th. 353, 53; Reim. 32; *dat. pl. of* freá.

freá-wine, es; *m. A dear* or *beloved lord;* dŏmĭnus cārus:—Syððan freáwine folca swealt *when the beloved lord of people perished*, Beo. Th. 4703; B. 2357: 4849; B. 2429. He of hornbogan his freáwine flāne geswencte *he laid low his dear lord with an arrow from his horned bow*, 4867; B. 2438. Cf. Grm. D. M. 82, 192.

freá-wrāsen, e; *f. A noble* or *royal chain, a diadem;* nōbĭlis torquis, diadēma = διάδημα:—Se hwīta helm hafelan werede, since geweorþad, befongen freáwrāsnum *the bright helmet guarded his head, ornamented with treasure, encircled with noble chains*, Beo. Th. 2906; B. 1451.

FREC, fræc; *adj. Desirous, greedy, gluttonous, audacious, bold;* avĭdus, gŭlōsus, audax, temĕrārius:—Gīfere *vel* frec *ambro* [*q. v.* in Du Cange], Ælfc. Gl. 88; Som. 74, 83; Wrt. Voc. 50, 63. Frec *ambro*, Wrt. Voc. 86, 50. Hī firenlusta frece ne wǽron *they were not desirous of luxuries*, Bt. Met. Fox 8, 30; Met. 8, 15. Ðæt hie firendǽda tō frece wurdon *that they were too audacious in wicked deeds*, Cd. 121; Th. 155, 30; Gen. 2580. [*Dut.* vrec, *m. a miser: Ger.* frech *rash, impertinent: M. H. Ger.* vrëch: *O. H. Ger.* frëh, frëch *avārus, cupĭdus, arrŏgans: Goth.* friks in faihu-friks *desirous for money, avaricious: Dan.* fräk: *Swed.* fräck: *Icel.* frekr *greedy, voracious.*] DER. ferhþ-frec, gūþ-.

freca, an; *m.* [frec *bold*] *A bold man, warrior, hero;* bellātor, hērōs = ἥρως:—Gefēng fetelhilt freca Scyldinga *the Scyldings' warrior seized the belted hilt*, Beo. Th. 3131; B. 1563: Andr. Kmbl. 2328; An. 1165. Moyses bebeád frecan arīsan *Moses bade the bold arise*, Cd. 154; Th. 191, 20; Exod. 217. DER. hild-freca, scyld-, sweord-, wīg-.

frēcednes, -ness, -nyss, frǽcednys, -nyss, e; *f. Danger, peril, hazard;* perĭcŭlum, discrīmen:—Ne ða tobeótiendan frēcednesse ðam eágan mennisc hand gehǽlan mihte *human hand could not save the eye from the threatening danger*, Bd. 4, 32; S. 611, 23. Ahred fram frēcednysse *saved from peril*, Homl. Th. ii. 304, 30. Forðam he geþristade ðæt he hine sylfne on geweald sealde swylcere frēcednysse *quod se ille discrīmĭni dăre præsumpsisset*, Bd. 1, 7; S. 477, 16. Frēcednysse helle gemētton me *perīcŭla inferni invēnērunt me*, Ps. Lamb. 114, 3. He ferde fram eallum frēcednyssum ðises lǽnan līfes *he went from all the perils of this frail life*, Homl. Th. ii. 516, 2. v. frēcennes.

frēcelsod; *part. Put in danger, endangered;* periclĭtātus:—Frēcelsod *qui periclĭtātus est*, Cot. 151.

frēcen; *gen.* frēcnes; *n. Peril, danger;* perīcŭlum, discrīmen:—Frēcnes ne wēnaþ *they think not of peril*, Exon. 96 b; Th. 361, 16; Wal. 20. Ðǽr is ealra frēcna mǽste *there is the greatest of all perils*, Cd. 24; Th. 31, 21; Gen. 488.

frēcendlīc; *adj. Dangerous;* perīcŭlōsus:—Hū frēcendlīc ðæt dysig is *how dangerous the error is!* Bt. 32, 3; Fox 118, 6. Ða habbaþ sum yfel frēcendlīcre ðonne ǽnig wīte sīe on ðisse woruldе *they have an evil more dangerous than any punishment in this world is*, 38, 3; Fox 200, 27. v. frēcenlīc.

frēcenful, frǽcenful, -full; *adj. Harmful, dangerous, perilous;* perīcŭlōsus:—Se þunor byþ frēcenfull [MS. P. frēcenful] for ðæs fȳres sceótungum *thunder is harmful from the shootings of the fire*, Bd. de nat. rerum; Lchdm. iii. 280, 14; Wrt. popl. science 19, 27. Of frēcenfulre forliðennysse *perīcŭlōso naufrăgio*, Mone B. 685, 686.

frēcenlīc, frēcendlīc; *adj. Dangerous, perilous;* perīcŭlōsus:—Ðæt ðære tīde blōdlæswu wǽre frēcenlīc *quia perīcŭlōsa sit illīus tempŏris phlebŏtŏmia*, Bd. 5, 3; S. 616, 16. Ðæt is hefig dysig, and frēcenlīc fira gehwilcum *that is a grievous folly, and dangerous to every man*, Bt. Met. Fox 19, 3; Met. 19, 2: Bt. 14, 1; Fox 42, 13.

frēcenlīce; *adv. Dangerously;* perīcŭlōse:—Scipio frēcenlīce gewundod wearþ *Scipio was dangerously wounded*, Ors. 4, 8; Bos. 89, 40: Lchdm. iii. 156, 26.

frēcennes, frǽcenes, frēcednes, frēcenis, frēcnes, -nis, -ness, -niss, -nyss, e; *f. Danger, peril, hazard, mischief, harm;* perīcŭlum, discrīmen, mălum:—Betwuh ða frēcennesse stōwe *inter perīcŭlōsa lŏca*, Cot. 111. For ege māran frēcennesse *mĕtu mājōris perīcŭli*, Bd. 4, 32; Whelc. 365, 18. Būtan mycelre frēcennesse *without much peril*, Ps. Th. 9, 26: Bd. 3, 19; S. 548, 33. Frēcennyssa helle gemētton me *perīcŭla inferni invēnērunt me*, Ps. Spl. 114, 3. He ongon ða frēcenisse onweg adrīfan *cœpit perīculum abĭgĕre*, Bd. 2, 7; S. 509, 25. Ðǽr seó frēcnis mǽst wæs *where the danger was greatest*, 2, 7; S. 509, 24. To swylcre frēcnesse *discrīmĭni*, Bd. 1, 7; S. 477, 16, MS. B: Herb. 30, 4; Lchdm. i. 126, 24. Būtan frēcnysse *without harm*, 63, 2; Lchdm. i. 166, 7. He fōreseah micle frēcnesse *he foresaw much peril*, Bd. 3, 19; S. 549, 46. Mid frēcnysse deáþes *mortis perīcŭlo*, 1, 27; S. 493, 26. He oferwon frēcnessa fela *he overcame many perils*, Exon. 35 a; Th. 113, 3; Gū. 152. Mænige ætberstaþ frēcnyssa *multi evādunt perīcŭla*, Coll. Monast. Th. 25, 1. Se hālga wer in ða ǽrestan ældu gelufade frēcnessa fela *the holy man in his early age loved much mischief*, Exon. 34 a; Th. 108, 31; Gū. 81.

freceo *a glutton;* lurco, Cot. 120. v. frec.

frecgenga? *apostacy;* apostăsia = ἀποστασία, Cot. 16. Lye.

frec-mâse, fræc-mâse, an; *f. The nun bird, titmouse;* pārus cærŭleus:—Frecmâse *sigitula?* Wrt. Voc. 281, 9.

FRÊCNE, frǽcne; *adj. Horrible, savage, audacious, wicked, daring, dangerous, perilous;* dīrus, asper, austērus, atrox, audax, perīcŭlōsus:—Ðǽr ðú findest frêcne feohtan *there thou wilt find a savage contest,* Andr. Kmbl. 2699; An. 1352. Ðæt biþ frêcne wúnd *that is a perilous wound,* Exon. 19 a; Th. 48, 12; Cri. 770. He âna geneðde frêcne dǽde *he alone ventured on the daring deed,* Beo. Th. 1782; B. 889. Be ðære frêcnan côðe *of the dangerous disorder,* L. M. 2, 33; Lchdm. ii. 236, 12. He sceal fleón ðone frêcnan wlite ðises middaneardes *he should avoid the dangerous splendour of this earth,* Bt. 12; Fox 36, 20. On ða frêcnan tīd *tempŏre discrīmĭnis,* Bd. 1, 8; S. 479, 21. Frêcne þúhton egle eálâda *the fearful sea-ways seemed terrible,* Andr. Kmbl. 880; An. 440. Hwonne him Freá frêcenra sīþa reste ageáfe *when the Lord should give him rest from his perilous journeyings,* Cd. 71; Th. 86, 8; Gen. 1427: Ps. Th. 143, 8. To frêcnum þingum *for daring things,* Lchdm. iii. 158, 16. Ðæt he him afirre frêcne geþohtas *that he should banish from him wicked thoughts,* Cd. 219; Th. 282, 10; Sat. 284. He frêcnu gestreón funde *he found dangerous wealth,* Bt. Met. Fox 8, 115; Met. 8, 58. Ðe ða frêcnan deórwurþnessa funde *who found the dangerous treasures,* Bt. 15; Fox 48, 24. [*O. Sax.* frôkan *wild, bold, impudent.*] DER. fela-frêcne: ge-frêcnod.

frêcne, frǽcne; *adv. Horribly, savagely, fiercely, severely, insolently, boldly, dangerously;* atrōcĭter, dūre, audacter, perīcŭlōse:—Se wráða boda fylgde him frêcne *the dire messenger boldly followed him,* Cd. 32; Th. 43, 9; Gen. 688: Beo. Th. 1923; B. 959: 3386; B. 1691. Hie hit frêcne geneðdon *they severely oppressed it,* Cd. 170; Th. 214, 17; Exod. 570: Exon. 105 b; Th. 401, 23; Rä. 21, 16: Ps. Th. 67, 2: 103, 33: 104, 25. Ðæt him hit frêcne ne meahte sceððan *that it might not dangerously wound him,* Beo. Th. 2069; B. 1032: Ps. Th. 114, 3.

frêcnen-spræc, e; *f. An audacious* or *hostile speech;* audax *vel* hostīlis sermo:—Gyf Frysna hwylc frêcnenspræce ðæs morðorhetes myndgiend wǽre *if any of the Frisians, by audacious speech, should call to mind* [lit. *should be a rememberer of*] *this deadly feud,* Beo. Th. 2213, note; B. 1104.

frecnes? *glis,* Cot. 96, Som. Lye: also *clammy earth;* argilla, Som. Ben. Frecnis *glus,* Glos. Epnl. Recd. 157, 25.

frêcnes, -nis, -ness, -nyss *danger, peril,* Bd. 2, 7; S. 509, 24: 3, 19; S. 549, 46: Coll. Monast. Th. 25, 1. v. frêcennes.

frêcne-stīg, e; *f. A dangerous way* or *path, steep place, precipice;* præcĭpĭtium, Som. Ben. Lye.

frêdan; *p.* de; *pp.* ed [frôd *wise, prudent*] *To feel, perceive, know, be sensible of;* sentīre. DER. ge-frêdan.

frêfergende = frêfrigende *comforting; part. of* frêfrian, Cd. 220; Th. 284, 7; Sat. 318.

frêfran; *p.* ede; *pp.* ed *To comfort, console;* consōlāri:—Ic findan meahte ðone ðe mec freóndleásne frêfran wolde *I might find one who would comfort me friendless,* Exon. 76 b; Th. 288, 9; Wand. 28: Andr. Kmbl. 733; An. 367. Hwīlum ic frêfre ða ic ǽr winne on *sometimes I comfort those whom ere I war against,* Exon. 102 b; Th. 389, 13; Rä. 7, 7: 27 b; Th. 82, 19; Cri. 1341. Hī earme frêfraþ *they comfort the poor,* 33 b; Th. 106, 29; Gū. 48. Ðū me frêfredest *tu me consōlātus es,* Ps. Th. 85, 17: Blickl. Homl. 135, 23. Cwæþ he ðæt gewunalīce word ðara frêfrendra *dixit sōlito consōlantium sermōne,* Bd. 5, 5; S. 681, 9. Frêfrede *consōlāti,* Ps. Spl. 125, 1. DER. ge-frêfran. v. frêfrian.

frêfrend, es; *m. A comforter, consoler;* consōlātor:—Mêðra frêfrend *comforter of the weak,* Exon. 62 a; Th. 227, 13; Ph. 422. Frêfrend ic sôhte, findan ic ne mihte *consōlantem me quæsīvi, et non invēni,* Ps. Th. 68, 21: 31, 8: Blickl. Homl. 135, 33: 131, 23. v. frêfriend.

frêfrian; *p.* ode, ade; *pp.* od *To comfort, console;* consōlāri:—Ðæt hig woldon hī frêfrian *ut consōlārentur eas,* Jn. Bos. 11, 19. Hwænne frêfrast ðū me *quando consōlāberis me?* Ps. Spl. 118, 82. Ðæt he frêfrige me *ut consōlētur me,* 118, 76. Ðū frêfrodest me *tu consōlātus es me,* 85, 16: 118, 50: Ps. Th. 118, 82. Frêfra ðīne mæcgas on môde *comfort thy young men in mind,* Andr. Kmbl. 842; An. 421. He hêran ne wolde Fæder frêfergendum [= frêfrigendum] *he would not obey the comforting Father,* Cd. 220; Th. 284, 7; Sat. 318. [*Laym.* uroefrien; *p.* freuerede: *Orm.* froffrenn, frofrenn: *O. Sax.* frôbrean: *O. H. Ger.* flôbarjan, fluobarēn.] DER. a-frêfrian, ge-. v. frôfor.

frêfriend, es; *m. A comforter, the Comforter, the Paraclete;* consōlātor, paraclētus:—Ne cymþ se frêfriend to eów *Paraclētus non vĕniet ad vos,* Jn. Bos. 16, 7: 14, 16: Ps. Th. 134, 14.

frêfrung, e; *f. A comforting, comfort, consolation;* consōlātio:—He nolde nâne frêfrunge underfôn *nōluit consōlātiōnem accĭpĕre,* Gen. 37, 35.

fregn *asked, inquired,* Andr. Kmbl. 2327; An. 1165, = frægn; *p. of* frignan.

fregnan *to inquire,* Mt. Kmbl. Lind. 21, 24: Mk. 11, 29. v. frignan.

fremde *did, effected,* Cd. 181; Th. 227, 11; Dan. 185, = fremede; *p. of* fremman.

fremde *foreign, strange,* Beo. Th. 3387; B. 1691. v. fremede.

fremdian; *p.* ode; *pp.* od *To alienate, estrange;* aliēnāre, R. Ben. 4.

fremdnys, -nyss, e; *f. Strangeness, the condition of a foreigner;* perēgrīnĭtas, Som. Ben. Lye.

freme; *adj. Good, strenuous, bold;* bŏnus, strēnuus:—Fremu folces cwēn *the folk's bold queen,* Beo. Th. 3868; B. 1932. v. fram, from; *adj.*

freme, an; *f. Advantage, profit, benefit, good;* commŏdum, quæstus, emŏlŭmentum, bŏnum:—Hȳþ *vel* freme *commŏdum, quæstus,* Ælfc. Gl. 81; Som. 73, 25; Wrt. Voc. 47, 30. Ðæs we mâgon fremena gewinnan *of what we may gain of advantages,* Cd. 22; Th. 28, 18; Gen. 437. Ðū us unfreóndlīce fremena þancast *thou thankest us unkindly for our benefits,* Cd. 128; Th. 162, 31; Gen. 2689: 89; Th. 110, 24; Gen. 1843: 135; Th. 170, 27; Gen. 2819. Gesǽton land unspêdigran fremena gehwilcre *they inhabited a land more barren of every good,* 46; Th. 59, 13; Gen. 963. v. fremu.

freme *do, effect, perform,* Ps. Th. 68, 17; *impert. of* fremman.

FREMEDE, fremde, fremþe, træmde; *adj. Strange, foreign, estranged from, devoid of;* aliēnus, peregrīnus, aliēnātus, aversus, remōtus, expers:—He biþ fremede Freán ælmihtigum *he shall be estranged from almighty God,* Salm. Kmbl. 67; Sal. 34. Ðonne beó we fremde fram eallum ðām gôdum *then should we be cut off from all those good things,* St. And. 8, 10. Feorcund mon oððe fremde *a far-coming or a strange man,* L. In. 20; Th. i. 114, 15: L. Edg. ii. 7; Th. i. 268, 21: L. C. S. 25; Th. i. 390, 24: Ps. Spl. C. T. 68, 11. Me biþ se ēðel fremde *the land is strange to me,* Exon. 105 a; Th. 398, 6; Rä. 17, 3: Cd. 5; Th. 7, 13; Gen. 105: Beo. Th. 3387; B. 1691: Ps. Th. 136, 4. Ðe ðara gefeána sceal fremde weorþan *who shall be devoid of those joys,* Andr. Kmbl. 1780; An. 892: Hy. 6, 30; Hy. Grn. ii. 286, 30. On fremdes fæðm *into the embrace of a strange* [*man*], Cd. 92; Th. 118, 26; Gen. 1971. Fremdre meówlan *of a strange damsel,* Exon. 80 b; Th. 302, 20; Fä. 39: Bt. Met. Fox 3, 21; Met. 3, 11. On fremedum *in aliēno,* Lk. Bos. 16, 12. Ne lǽne ðīnum brêðer nân þing to hire, ac fremdum menn *non fænĕrābĕris fratri tuo ad ūsūram pĕcūniam, sed aliēno,* Deut. 23, 20. On lande fremdre *in terra aliēna,* Ps. Spl. 136, 5. Ne ðū fremedne god gebiddest *neque adōrābis deum aliēnum,* Ps. Th. 80, 9. Wilt ðū fremdne monnan grêtan *wilt thou address a strange man?* Exon. 92 b; Th. 346, 20; Sch. 1. Him folcweras fremde wǽron *the people were strange to him,* Cd. 89; Th. 110, 31; Gen. 1846. Folca fremdra *of strange people,* Ps. Th. 104, 39. Of fremedum *ab aliēnis,* Mt. Bos. 17, 25, 26. Ðæt ða þing ðīne âgene sīen, ða ðe heora âgene gecynd ðē gedydon fremde *that those things can be thine own, which their own natures have made foreign to thee,* Bt. 14, 1; Fox 40, 32. Gif ðū fremdu godu bigongest *if thou wilt worship strange gods,* Exon. 67 b; Th. 250, 2; Jul. 121. On ða fremdan þīstro *into the strange darkness,* Bt. 3, 2; Fox 6, 10. [*Piers P.* fremmed *strange: Chauc.* fremde, fremed *foreign, strange: Orm.* fremmde *strange, not of kin: Scot.* fremyt, fremmyt: *Plat.* fromd, frömd: *O. Sax.* fremiði, fremethi, fremit: *Frs.* freamd: *O. Frs.* framd, fremed: *Dut.* vreemd: *Ger.* fremd: *M. H. Ger.* vremede, vremde: *O. H. Ger.* framadi, fremidi: *Goth.* framaþs: *Dan.* fremmed: *Swed.* främmande: *Icel.* framandi *a man of distinction, stranger.*] v. Grm. R. A. pp. 396 sqq. Schmid. s. v. fremde.

fremede, *pl.* fremedon *made, did, performed,* Elen. Kmbl. 942; El. 472: Bd. 1, 8; S. 479, 26; *p. of* fremman.

fremednes, -ness, -nyss, e; *f.* [fremed, *pp. of* fremman *and* -ness, -nyss] *An accomplishment, fulfilment;* peractio:—Næfþ ðæt swefen nǽnige fremednesse gôdes ne yfeles *the dream has no accomplishment for good* or *evil,* Lchdm. iii. 154, 17. Nǽnige fremednysse *no fulfilment,* iii. 156, 1.

fremeþ *performs, practises,* Beo. Th. 3406; B. 1701; *3rd sing. pres. of* fremman.

fremfull; *adj.* [freme *good;* ful, full *full*] *Beneficent, profitable;* bĕnĕfĭcus:—Ða ðe ânweald ofer hig habbaþ synd fremfulle genemned *qui pŏtestātem hăbent sŭper eos bĕnĕfĭci vŏcantur,* Lk. Bos. 22, 25.

fremfullīce; *adv. Effectually, beneficially;* efficācĭter, R. Ben. interl. Prol.

fremfulnes, -ness, e; *f. Profitableness, utility;* utĭlĭtas, R. Ben. 53.

fremian, freomian; *part.* fremiende; hit fremaþ; *p.* ode; *pp.* od [fremman] *To profit, do good, be good* or *expedient, avail;* profĭcĕre, prōdesse, expĕdīre, vălēre:—Ne mid seglinge ne mid rôwnesse ôwiht fremian *nĕque vēlo nĕque remĭgio quicquam profĭcĕre,* Bd. 5, 1; S. 613, 26. Biþ heó fremiende to his clǽnsunge *ĕrit in expiatiōnem ejus prōfĭciens,* Lev. 1, 4. Hwæt fremaþ ǽnegum menn *quid prodest hŏmĭni?* Mt. Bos. 16, 26: 15, 5. Gyf se wǽta byþ mâre ðonne ðæt fȳr, ðonne fremaþ hit *if the moisture is more than the fire, then it does good,* Bd. de nat. rerum; Wrt. popl. science 19, 23; Lchdm. iii. 280, 9. Eów fremaþ ðæt ic fare *expĕdit vōbis ut ĕgo vādam,* Jn. Bos. 16, 7: Mt. Bos. 19, 10. Ðæt hyt nâht ne fremode *quia nihil profĭcĕret,* Mt. Bos. 27, 24: Mk. Bos. 5, 26. Ðonne biþ gesȳne, hwæt him his swefn fremion *tunc appārēbit, quid illi prōsint somnia tua,* Gen. 37, 20. [*Orm.* frame *profit: Swed.* främja *to forward, advance: Icel.* frama *to further.*]

FREMMAN, to fremmanne; ic fremme, ðū fremest, he fremeþ, *pl.* fremmaþ; *p.* fremede, fremde, *pl.* fremedon; *impert.* freme, *pl.* fremmaþ;

subj. pres. fremme, *pl.* fremmen; *pp.* fremed. I. *to advance;* promŏvēre:—Ðæt ic eáđe mæg ānra gehwylcne fremman and fyrđran freónda mīnra *that I may easily advance and further every one of my friends,* Andr. Kmbl. 1867; An. 936: Beo. Th. 3669; B. 1832. Sume ic to geflīte fremede *some I have urged to strife,* Exon. 72 b; Th. 271, 18; Jul. 484. II. *to* FRAME, *make, do, effect, perform, commit;* făcĕre, patrāre, effĭcĕre, perfĭcĕre, perpetrāre:—Ðe done unrǣd ongan ǣrest fremman *who first began to frame that evil counsel,* Cd. 1; Th. 3, 4; Gen. 30: Andr. Kmbl. 133; An. 67: Beo. Th. 4991; B. 2499: Exon. 67 b; Th. 250, 27; Jul. 133. Sæcce to fremmanne *to make strife,* Exon. 129 b; Th. 496, 28; Rä. 85, 21. Ic gūþe fremme *I make war,* Exon. 105 b; Th. 402, 5; Rä. 21, 25. Ne fremest đū riht wiđ me *thou doest not right towards me,* Cd. 102; Th. 135, 19; Gen. 2245: Exon. 54 b; Th. 191, 33; Az. 97. He sōþ fremeþ *he performs truth,* Exon. 81 a; Th. 304, 35; Fä. 80. Sume stale fremmaþ *quidam furtum perpetrant,* Bd. 1, 27; S. 490, 9: 491, 36: Exon. 44 b; Th. 150, 17; Gū. 780. Ic andsæc fremede *I made denial,* Elen. Kmbl. 942; El. 472: Exon. 17 a; Th. 40, 23; Cri. 643: Beo. Th. 6004; B. 3006: Andr. Kmbl. 1237; An. 619: Cd. 177; Th. 222, 18; Dan. 106. He fremede swā and Freán hȳrde *he did so and obeyed the Lord,* Cd. 73; Th. 90, 10; Gen. 1493: 130; Th. 165, 21; Gen. 2735. Ne ic firene fremde *I have not committed crimes,* Ps. Th. 58, 3: Cd. 181; Th. 227, 11; Dan. 185. Hī đa godcundan gerȳno clǣnre heortan fremedon *they performed the divine mysteries with a clean heart,* Bd. 1, 8; S. 479, 26: Beo. Th. 6; B. 3: Elen. Kmbl. 1288; El. 646: Menol. Fox 254; Men. 128: Exon. 26 b; Th. 79, 16; Cri. 1291: Cd. 149; Th. 187, 5; Exod. 146. Me help freme *do me help* or *give me help,* Ps. Th. 68, 17. Fremmaþ gē nū leóda þearfe *perform ye now the people's need,* Beo. Th. 5593; B. 2800. Ðæt đū hospcwide ǣfre ne fremme wiđ Godes bearne *that thou never make contemptuous words against God's son,* Elen. Kmbl. 1046; El. 524: Andr. Kmbl. 2708; An. 1356. Fremme se đe wille *let him perform [it] who will,* Beo. Th. 2011; B. 1003. Ǣr gē fremmen yfel *ere ye commit evil,* Cd. 113; Th. 149, 4; Gen. 2469. Nō hwæđre he ofer Offan eorlscype fremede *yet he could not effect supremacy over Offa,* Exon. 85 a; Th. 320, 31; Wīd. 37: Beo. Th. 4274; B. 2134. [*Laym.* fremmen, uremmen *to perform, frame: O. Sax.* fremmian, fremman *to perform, execute: O. Frs.* frema *to commit, effect: O. H. Ger.* ga-fremjan: *Dan.* fremme *to promote: Icel.* fremja *to further: Armor.* framma *to join.*] DER. ge-fremman: ǣ-fremmende, firen-, gōd-, gūþ-, heađo-, mān-, nāht-, ryht-, till-, wōh-.

fremming, e; *f. A framing, an effect, efficacy;* fabrĭcātio, effectus, effĭcācia:—Fremming *effectus,* Ælfc. Gr. 11; Som. 15, 15: Homl. Th. i. 8, 7.

frem-sum, fræm-sum; *adj. Kind, benign, courteous;* benignus:—He þearfum and ellreordigum symble eáþmōd and fremsum and rūmmōd wæs *paupĕrĭbus et pĕrĕgrīnis semper hŭmĭlis, benignus et largus fuit,* Bd. 3, 6; S. 528, 11: Ps. Spl. 68, 20: Ps. Th. 134, 3. Syleþ us fremsum gōd Drihten *Dŏmĭnus dăbit benignĭtātem,* 84, 11.

fremsumlīce; *adv. Kindly, benignly;* benigne:—Đā wæs he fremsumlīce onfangen *cum benigne susceptus,* Bd. 3, 11; S. 536, 12: 1, 25; S. 487, 15.

fremsumnes, -ness, -nys, -nyss, e; *f.* [fremsum, -nes, -ness] *Kindness, benefit, benignity, liberality;* benignĭtas, bĕnĕfĭcium:—For fremsumnysse *pro benignĭtāte,* Bd. 1, 27; S. 493, 7: Ps. Spl. C. 84, 13. Đū geáres hring mid gyfe bletsast, and đīne fremsumnesse wylt folcum dǣlan *bĕnĕdīces cŏrōnæ anni benignĭtātis tuæ,* Ps. Th. 64, 12. Be đām godcundum fremsumnessum *de bĕnĕfĭciis dīvīnis,* Bd. 4, 24; S. 598, 17.

fremþe; *adj. Strange, foreign;* aliēnus, externus:—Ðæt rīce tweógende cyningas and fremþe forluron and towurpon *regnum rēges dŭbii vel externi disperdĭdērunt,* Bd. 4, 26; S. 603, 17. Hī awurpon đa ealdormenn đæs fremþan cyninges *they cast off the aldermen of the strange king,* 3, 24; S. 557, 45: Lk. Skt. Lind. 24, 18: Jn. 10, 5. v. fremede.

FREMU, e; *f. Advantage, profit, gain, benefit;* commŏdum, emŏlŭmentum, quæstus, fructus, benĕfĭcium, sălus:—Hwelc fremu is đē đæt, đæt đū wilnige đissa gesǣlþa *what advantage is it to thee, that thou desirest these goods?* Bt. 14, 1; Fox 42, 8: 26, 3; Fox 94, 12. Ðe đissum folce to freme stondaþ *which for this folk's prosperity stand,* Exon. 67 b; Th. 350, 7; Jul. 123; 54 a; Th. 191; Az. 81: Nar. 39, 18. Ðæt we sceoldon [MS. sceolde] fremena friclan, and us fremu sēcan *that we might desire benefits, and seek to us advantage,* Cd. 89; Th. 110, 25; Gen. 1843. Ne đǣr freme mēteþ fira ǣnig *no man findeth profit there,* Exon. 68 b; Th. 255, 22; Jul. 218. Neorxna wang stōd, gifena gefylled, fremum forþweardum *paradise stood, filled with gifts, with continual benefits,* Cd. 12; Th. 13, 29; Gen. 210: Exon. 113 a; Th. 434, 10; Rä. 51, 8. DER. un-fremu. v. freme, an; *f.*

fremung, freomung, fromung, e; *f. Advantage, profit, good;* commŏdum, profectus, benefĭcium:—Ðæt gē gehycgen ymbe đa fremunge gōdra weorca *that ye meditate on the advantage of good works,* L. E. I. prm; Th. ii. 400, 32. For heora fremunge *for their good,* ii. 400, 36.

Frencisc; *def.* se Frencisca; *adj. Belonging to France;* Francus:—Þurh đone Frenciscan ceorl Hugon *through the French churl Hugo,* Chr. 1003; Erl. 139, 1. Mid mycclum werode Frenciscra manna *with a great multitude of Frenchmen,* Chr. 1052; Erl. 181, 30. Mid đām Franciscum mannum *with the Frenchmen,* Chr. 1052; Erl. 186, 6. Ða Frencisce menn *the Frenchmen,* Chr. 1052; Erl. 187, 7, 26. [*Laym.* frensc.]

Frencisca, an; *m. A Frenchman;* Francus:—Ægebertus, se Frencisca, was gehādod *Ægebert, the Frenchman, was ordained,* Chr. 650; Th. 51, 2, col. 2.

frēnd *friend* or *friends;* amīcus, amīcos:—Ðæt đū swutole mihtest tocnāwan đīne frēnd and đīne fȳnd *that thou mightest clearly distinguish thy friends and thy foes,* Bt. 20; Fox 72, 20, MS. Cot. v. freónd.

FREÓ, frió, freoh, frioh, frig, frī, frȳ; *adj.* FREE, *having liberty* or *immunity, noble, glad, joyful;* līber, sui jūris, ingĕnuus, nōbĭlis, lætus:—Heó đā freó on hire fōta gangum blīđe hām wæs hweorfende *ipsa lībĕro pĕdum incessu dŏmum læta reversa est,* Bd. 4, 10; S. 578, 32. Beó he freó *he shall be free,* L. Alf. 11; Th. i. 46, 3, MS. H: L. In. 3; Th. i. 104, 3, MS. B: Bt. 34, 8; Fox 144, 23. Hū wolde đē līcian, gif hwylc swīđe rīce cyning næfde nǣnne freóne mon on eallon his rīce *how would it please thee, if some very powerful king had not any free man in all his realm?* 41, 2; Fox 24, 25, MS. Cot. Gif he mǣgburg hæbbe freó *if he have a free kindred,* L. In. 74; Th. i. 148, 19. Đǣr freó, mōton eard weardigan *where free, they might inhabit a country,* Andr. Kmbl. 1196; An. 598. Đā wearþ worn afēded freóra bearna *then was a number of noble children brought forth,* Cd. 79; Th. 99, 6; Gen. 1642: 131; Th. 166, 26; Gen. 2753. Lǣt me freó lǣdan, eft on ēđel *let me lead them free, back into their country,* 98; Th. 128, 22; Gen. 2130: Bt. 41, 2; Fox 244, 30; MS. Cot. Ðæt hȳ đȳ freóran hyge gefēngen *that they might receive the gladder spirit,* Exon. 30 a; Th. 92, 22; Cri. 1512. [*Chauc.* fre: *Laym.* freo: *Orm.* freo, fre: *Plat.* fri, frij: *O. Sax.* frī in frī-līk *free-born: Frs.* fry: *O. Frs.* fri: *Dut.* vrij: *Ger.* frei: *M. H. Ger.* vrī: *O. H. Ger.* frī: *Goth.* freis: *Dan. Swed.* fri: *Icel.* frí.] DER. mūþ-freó.

freó; *indecl. m. A lord, master;* dŏmĭnus:—Freó đæt bihealdeþ *my master beholds that,* Exon. 105 a; Th. 399, 3; Rä. 18, 5. v. freá.

freó; *indecl. f. A woman;* mŭlier ingĕnua:—Ōþ-đæt he funde freó fægroste *until he found the fairest woman,* Cd. 23; Th. 29, 28; Gen. 457. [*O. Sax.* frī.] v. Grim. D. M. 279.

freó-bearn, es; *n. One free-born, a noble child;* prōles ingĕnua, fīlius nōbĭlis:—Freóbearn *vel* æđelborene cild *lībĕri,* Ælfc. Gl. 91; Som. 75, 23; Wrt. Voc. 51, 67. Freóbearn Godes *the noble son of God,* Exon. 17 a; Th. 40, 24; Cri. 643. Freóbearn wurdon alǣten līges gange *the noble children were delivered from the course of the flame,* Cd. 187; Th. 232, 19; Dan. 262.

freó-bearn-fæder; *m. A father of noble children;* nōbĭlium fīliōrum păter, Cd. 163; Th. 206, 1; Exod. 445.

freó-borh; *gen.* -borges; *m. A free surety, pledge, bondman;* fidejussus, L. Ed. C. 20; Wilk. 201, 53, col. 2. v. friþ-borh.

freó-brōđor; *m. An own brother;* germānus frāter:—Him frumbearnes riht freóbrōđor ōþ-þah *his own brother took from him his firstborn's right,* Cd. 160; Th. 199, 14; Exod. 338.

freó-burh; *gen.* -burge; *f. A free city;* lībĕra arx:—He scolde gesēcean freóburh *he should seek the free city,* Beo. Th. 1390; B. 693.

freócenness *danger, peril;* perīcŭlum, Som. Ben. Lye. v. frēcennes.

freód, e; *f. Affection, good-will, friendship, peace;* ămor, dilectio, amīcĭtia, pax, grātia:—Næs đǣr māra fyrst freóde to friclan *there was no more time to desire peace,* Beo. Th. 5105, note; B. 2556. Swā đū wiđ me freóde gecȳđdest *as thou hast manifested affection to me,* Andr. Kmbl. 780; An. 390. Freóde ne woldon healdan *they would not hold peace,* Beo. Th. 4946; B. 2476. Ic forworht hæbbe đīne lufan and freóde *I have forfeited thy love and good-will,* Cd. 48; Th. 63, 2; Gen. 1026: Exon. 10 a; Th. 11, 5; Cri. 166: Beo. Th. 3418; B. 1707. Ðæt đū wille syllan sǣmannum feoh wiđ freóde *that thou wilt give treasures to the seamen for their friendship,* Byrht. Th. 132, 60; By. 39.

freód *liberty, privilege,* Th. Diplm. A. D. 970; 243, 20. v. freót.

freóde, *pl.* freódon *freed,* Chr. 777; Erl. 55, 22: 963; Erl. 121, 30; *p. of* freógan, freón.

freó-dōm, frió-dōm, frȳ-dōm, es; *m.* FREEDOM, *liberty;* lībertas, emancĭpātio:—Ðæt is se freódōm, đætte mon mōt dōn đæt he wile *that is freedom, that a man may do what he will,* Bt. 41, 2; Fox 246, 4, MS. Cot. Freódōm *emancĭpātio,* Ælfc. Gl. 112; Som. 79, 93; Wrt. Voc. 60, 2. Đām he geaf micle gife freódōmes *to these he gave the great gift of freedom,* Bt. 41, 2; Fox 246, 1. Be đam freódōme *concerning freedom,* 41, 2; Fox 246, 13. Nis nān gesceádwīs gesceaft đæt næbbe freódōm *there is no rational creature which has not freedom,* 40, 7; Fox 242, 17: 34, 8; Fox 144, 26. Freódōm onfēngon *lībertātem recēpērunt,* Bd. 3, 24; S. 557, 46: 4, 26; S. 602, 31.

freó-drihten, -dryhten, es; *m. A noble lord* or *master;* ingĕnuus *vel* nōbĭlis dŏmĭnus:—Onfōh đissum fulle, freódrihten mīn *accept this cup, my noble lord,* Beo. Th. 2343; B. 1169. Freódrihten hine forþlǣdde to đam hālgan hām, heofna Ealdor *the noble Lord, the Prince of heaven, led him forth to the holy home,* Cd. 226; Th. 300, 17; Sat. 566: 225; Th. 299, 10; Sat. 547. Wāst đū freódryhten, hū đeós ādle scyle ende gesettan *knowest thou, noble master, how this disease shall have an end?* Exon. 47 b; Th. 163, 16; Gû. 994.

frê-ôfestlîce *very hastily, quickly, speedily;* præprŏpĕre, festinanter, expĕdīte, Som. Ben. Lye. v. frǽ-ôfestlîce.

FREÓGAN, freón; ic freó, he freóþ, *pl.* freógaþ, freóþ; *p.* freóde, *pl.* freódon; *impert.* freó; *subj. pres.* freóge; *pp.* freód [freó *free*]. I. *to free, make free;* manumittĕre, lībĕrāre:—Man sceal freógan ǽlcne þeówan *one shall free every slave;* revertētur hŏmo ad possessiōnem suam, Lev. 25, 10. Ic hit freó *I free it*, Chr. 963; Erl. 122, 2. He freóde ðæt mynster [MS. mynstre] *he freed the monastery*, 777; Erl. 55, 22. Hî hit freódon *they freed it*, 963; Erl. 121, 30. Freó hine on ðam seofoðan geáre *free him in the seventh year;* in septĭmo anno dimittes eum lībĕrum, Deut. 15, 12. Ðonne ðû hine freóge *when thou freest him;* quem lībertāte donāvĕris, 15, 13. Ðæt he scolde freón his mynster [MS. mynstre] *that he would free his monastery*, Chr. 777; Erl. 55, 18. II. *to honour, like, love;* honōrāre, dilĭgĕre, ămāre:—Ic ðec for sunu wylle freógan *I will love thee as a son*, Beo. Th. 1900; B. 948. Nǽnig ôðerne freóþ swâ him God bebeád *no one loves another as God commanded him*, Frag. Kmbl. 70; Leás. 37. Ðû ðîn âgen môst mennen ateón swâ ðîn môd freóþ *thou mayest treat thine own servant as thy mind liketh*, Cd. 103; Th. 136, 15; Gen. 2258. Ða gecorenan freógaþ folces Weard *the chosen shall love the Lord of mankind*, Exon. 32 a; Th. 100, 27; Cri. 1648: 114 a; Th. 436, 36; Rä. 55, 12. Freóþ hŷ fremde monnan *strange men love them*, 90 b; Th. 339, 32; Gn. Ex. 103. Fæder and môdor freó ðû *love thou father and mother*, 80 a; Th. 300, 21; Fä. 9. Hit gedêfe biþ ðæt mon his winedryhten freóge *it is fitting that a man love his dear lord*, Beo. Th. 6334; B. 3177. [*Laym.* freoien, freoiȝen, ureoiȝen *to set free: Plat.* frijen *to free, woo: O. Sax.* friohan *to love: O. Frs.* friaia, fraia, fria *to free: Dut.* vrijen *to woo: Ger.* freien *to woo;* be-freien *to free: M. H. Ger.* vrîen, vrîgen *to free: Goth.* friyon, frion *to love: Dan.* frie *to woo, deliver: Swed.* fria *to free, save, court: Icel.* frjá *to pet.*] DER. be-freón, ge-freógan, -freón.

freó-gyld *a free guild* or *society;* lībĕrum sodālĭtium. v. frŷ-gyld.

freoh; *adj. Free;* līber:—Ic neom freoh *non sum līber*, Coll. Monast. Th. 20, 7: Ps. Spl. 87, 4. Gif he freoh sŷ *if he be free*, L. Wg. 8; Th. i. 188, 3: L. Ath. i. 24; Th. i. 212, 14. He gewât freoh fram deáþes sârnysse *he departed free from the pain of death*, Homl. Th. i. 76, 13. v. freó.

freó-lâc, es; *n. A free offering, oblation;* lībĕra oblātio:—Ðû onfêhst onsægdnesse rihtwîsnesse, freólâca and offrunga *acceptābis sacrĭfĭcium justĭtiæ, oblātiōnes et holocausta*, Ps. Lamb. 50, 21.

freó-lǽta, frig-lǽta, an; *m. One made free, a freedman;* libertus:—Freólǽta *libertus*, Ælfc. Gl. 8; Som. 56, 106; Wrt. Voc. 18, 55. Freólǽtan sunu *the son of a freedman;* libertinus, 8; Som. 56, 107; Wrt. Voc. 18, 56.

freólîc, freólêc, frîlîc; *adj. Free, noble, ingenuous, comely, goodly;* liber, ingĕnuus, egrĕgius, dĕcens:—Eádward, Engla hlâford, freólîc wealdend *Edward, lord of the English, a noble ruler*, Chr. 1065; Erl. 196, 25; Edw. 6. Se eafora wæs Enoc hâten, freólîc frumbearn *the offspring was called Enoch, a comely first-born*, Cd. 59; Th. 72, 19; Gen. 1189. Freólîc fyrdsceorp *a goodly war-vest*, Exon. 104 a; Th. 395, 25; Rä. 15, 13: Cd. 55; Th. 67, 29; Gen. 1108. Freólîc wîf *the noble woman*, Beo. Th. 1234; B. 615. Freólîcu meówle *a goodly damsel*, Exon. 124 b; Th. 479, 2; Rä. 62, 1. Freólêcu mǽg *a comely maiden*, Cd. 50; Th. 64, 21; Gen. 1053: 101; Th. 134, 18; Gen. 2226. Freólîcum *lībĕro*, Mone B. 1341. Ðæt he brohte wîf to hâme, fæger and freólîc *that he should bring to his home a wife, fair and goodly*, Cd. 83; Th. 103, 22; Gen. 1722. Bearn freólîcu tû *two comely children*, 82; Th. 102, 30; Gen. 1708. Mid his twegen suno, freólîco frumbearn *with his two sons, comely first-born*, Exon. 112 b; Th. 431, 31; Rä. 47, 4. Fǽmne freólîcast *most noble damsel*, 9 a; Th. 5, 20; Cri. 72. [*O. Sax.* frîlîk.] DER. ful-freólîc.

freólîce, friólîce; *comp.* freólîcor; *adv.* FREELY, *without hindrance, with impunity;* libĕre, impūne:—Ðæt he mihte freólîce Gode þeówian *that he might freely serve God*, Bd. 3, 19; S. 547, 31: Ps. Spl. 93, 1: Cd. 67; Th. 81, 8; Gen. 1342: Andr. Kmbl. 585; An. 293. Seó sâwl færþ swîðe freólîce [friólîce Cott.] to heofonum *the soul goes very freely to the heavens*, Bt. 18, 4; Fox 68, 14. Heó deófla bigængum freólîce þeówedon *dæmŏnĭcis cultĭbus impūne serviēbant*, Bd. 2, 5; S. 507, 38. Ðæt hî for gewillnunge ðara êcra gôda ðŷ freólîcor winnen *pro appĕtītu æternōrum bŏnōrum lībĕrius labōrāre*, 4, 25; S. 601, 7.

FREÓLS, es; *m. sometimes, but rarely, n.* I. *freedom, immunity, privilege;* lībertas, immūnĭtas, privĭlēgium:—Ic ðisne freóls on Rôme gefæstnode *I confirmed this freedom at Rome*, Th. Diplm. A. D. 856; 116, 5. Gif man his mæn an wiofode freóls gefe, se sîe folcfrŷ *if any one give freedom to his man at the altar, let him be folk-free*, L. Wih. 8; Th. i. 38, 15: Cod. Dipl. 925; Kmbl. iv. 263, 27. Ic forgyfe ðisne freóls to ðære hâlgan stôwe æt Scireburnan *I give this immunity to the holy place at Sherborne*, Th. Diplm. A. D. 864; 125, 5. Se arcebisceop spæc to me ymbe Christes circean freóls; ðâ lŷfde ic him ðæt he môste niwan freóls settan; ðâ cwæþ he ðæt he freólsas genôge hæfde; ðâ nam ic ða freólsas *the archbishop spoke to me about the privilege of Christ's church; then I allowed him to institute a new privilege; then he said that he had privileges enough; then I took the privileges*, Cod. Dipl. 731; A. D. 1013–1020; Kmbl. iv. 9, 32, 35; 10, 1, 3. II. *a time of freedom, a holy day, feast, festival, the celebration of a festival;* festum, festi celebrātio:—Ðæt man sceal fæstan ǽlce Frigedæg, bûtan hit freóls sŷ *that a man shall fast every Friday, unless it be a festival*, L. Eth. v. 17; Th. i. 308, 23: L. C. E. 16; Th. i. 368, 26. To ðam eásterlîcan freólse *to the paschal feast*, Lk. Bos. 2, 42: L. Eth. v. 14; Th. i. 308, 14, 16, 17: L. C. E. 16; Th. i. 368, 25. Gif mæsse-preóst folc miswyssige æt freólse and æt fæstene *if a mass-priest misdirect the people about a festival and about a fast*, L. E. G. 3; Th. i. 168, 8. On Sunnan dæges freólse *on the festival of Sunday*, L. E. G. 9; Th. i. 172, 14. Be mæsse-daga freólse *of the celebration of mass-days*, L. Alf. pol. 43; Th. i. 92, 1. Sunnan dæges freóls healde man georne *let a man diligently keep the festival of Sunday*, L. Eth. v. 13; Th. i. 308, 10: vi. 22; Th. i. 320, 11. Freólsa and fæstena healde man rihtlîce *let a man rightly keep festivals and fasts*, L. Eth. v. 12; Th. i. 308, 8: v. 15; Th. i. 308, 18: vi. 22; Th. i. 320, 10: L. C. E. 14; Th. i. 368, 10. [*O. Frs.* frihals, frihelse *freedom: O. H. Ger.* frihalsi *lībertas: Goth.* frei-hals, *m.: Icel.* frelsi, *f. freedom.*] DER. gâl-freólsas, heáh-freóls, sunder-.

freóls; *adj. Free;* liber:—Sŷ ðis land ǽlces þinges freóls *let this land be free of everything*, Cod. Dipl. 923; Kmbl. iv. 263, 5. v. freó.

freóls-ǽfen, es; *m. A festival-eve, vigil;* festi vigilia:—Man môt, freólsǽfenum [MS. freólsǽfenan], faran betweonan Eferwîc and six mîla gemete *one may travel, on festival-eves, between York and a distance of six miles*, L. N. P. L. 56; Th. ii. 298, 26.

freóls-bôc, e; *f. A charter of freedom;* lībertātis charta = $\chi\acute{a}\rho\tau\eta s$:—Ðis is seó freólsbôc to ðan mynstre æt Byrtûne, ðe Æðelrêd cyng ǽfre êcelîce gefreóde *this is the charter of freedom to the monastery at Burton, which king Æthelred for ever freed*, Th. Diplm. A. D. 1002; 548, 29.

freóls-brice, -bryce, es; *m.* [freóls *a feast, festival;* brice, bryce *a breaking, breach*] *A breach* or *violation of a festival;* festi violātio:—On freólsbricum [MS. freólsbricon] *in breaches of festivals*, L. Eth. vi. 28; Th. i. 322, 19. Freôlsbrycas *breaches of festivals*, Wulfst. 109, 152.

freóls-dæg, es; *m. A feast-day, festival-day;* festus dies:—Geneálǽhte freólsdæg azimorum, se is gecweden eástre *appropinquābat dies festus azymōrum, qui dīcĭtur pascha*, Lk. Bos. 22, 1. On ðam freólsdæge *in die festo*, Mt. Bos. 26, 5. Gif hlâford his þeówan freólsdæge nŷde to weorce *if a lord oblige his servant to work on a feast-day*, L. E. G. 7; Th. i. 172, 2. Be freólsdagum and fæstenum *of festivals and fasts*, L. Edg. i. 5; Th. i. 264, 17: L. Eth. v. 18; Th. i. 308, 24: L. C. E. 17; Th. i. 370, 2. Freólsdæg *festīvĭtas, solemnĭtas*, vel *celebrĭtas*, vel *cerēmōnia*, Ælfc. Gl. 56; Som. 67, 23; Wrt. Voc. 37, 13. DER. heáh-freólsdæg.

freóls-dôm, es; *m. Freedom, liberty;* lībertas:—Ciricean freólsdôm [MS. freólsdôme] gafola *to the church freedom from imposts*, L. Wih. 1; Th. i. 36, 15. v. freó-dôm.

freóls-geár, -gêr, es; *n. A feast-year, jubilee;* annus jubĭlæus, Cot. 106.

freóls-gefa, an; *m. A freedom-giver;* manumissor:—Gif man his mæn freóls gefe, freólsgefa âge his erfe *if any one give freedom to his man, let the freedom-giver have his heritage*, L. Wih. 8; Th. i. 38, 16.

freólsian; *p.* ode; *pp.* od [freóls *a holy day*]; *v. trans. To keep holy day, to celebrate;* celebrāre diem festum:—Sce. Eádweardes mæssedæg witan habbaþ gecoren, ðæt man freólsian sceal ofer eal Engla land *the witan have chosen, that St. Edward's mass-day should be celebrated over all England*, L. Eth. v. 16; Th. i. 308, 21: L. C. E. 17; Th. i. 370, 7. Wirc six dagas and freólsa ðone seofoðan *sex diēbus ŏpĕrābĕris, die septĭmo cessābis*, Ex. 34. 21. Freólsiaþ Drihtnes restedæg *sabbătīzes sabbătum Dŏmĭno*, Lev. 25, 2. Beó ðû gemyndig ðæt ðû ðone restendæg freólsige *be thou mindful that thou keep holy the day of rest*, Homl. Th. ii. 198, 4: E. Eth. v. 14; Th. i. 308, 15. [*Orm.* freollsenn.] DER. ge-freólsian.

freólslîce; *adv. Solemnly, freely;* sollennĭter, lībĕre:—Freólslîce *sollennĭter*, R. Concord. 8. In ðæm he freólslîce meahte lifian *in which he might freely live*, Bd. 3, 19; S. 547, note 30. v. freólîce.

freóls-man; *gen.* -mannes; *m. A freeman;* liber:—Ic wylle, ðæt ða ðe to mînre âre fôn ðæt hî fêdon twentig freólsmanna *I will, that those who succeed to my property feed twenty freemen*, Cod. Dipl. 694; Kmbl. iii. 295, 6. v. freó-man.

freóls-stôw, e; *f. A festival-place;* lŏcus in quo festīvĭtas consecrātæ diei celebrāri solēbat:—On freóls-stôwum [MS. -stôwan] *in festival-places*, L. C. S. 38; Th. i. 398, 17.

freóls-tîd, e; *f. A feast-tide;* festīvum tempus:—Æt ðissere freólstîde *at this feast-tide*, Homl. Th. ii. 264, 17. Sce. Marian freólstîda ealle weorþie man georne *let all St. Mary's feast-tides be strictly honoured*, L. Eth. v. 14; Th. i. 308, 13. Freólstîdan and fæstentîdan *at festival-tides and fast-tides*, L. C. S. 38; Th. i. 398, 17. DER. heáh-freólstîd.

freólsung, e; *f. A feasting, celebrating a feast;* sollennĭtas:—On middele freólsunga ðîne *in mĕdio sollennĭtātis tuæ*, Ps. Spl. 73, 5. Healde mon ǽlces Sunnan dæges freólsunge *let a man keep every Sunday's festival*, L. C. E. 14; Th. i. 368, 11: L. Edg. i. 5; Th. i. 264, 18.

freom; *adj. Firm, strong, powerful;* firmus, strēnuus, fortis:—Ðā com Metod freom on fultum *then came the powerful Lord to his aid*, Cd. 134; Th. 169, 1; Gen. 2793: 143; Th. 178, 19; Exod. 14. Se wæs mā on cyriclīcum þeódscypum gelǽred, đonne he freom wǽre in weoroldþingum *măgis ecclesiastĭcis discĭplīnis instĭtūtum, quam in sēcŭli rēbus strēnuum*, Bd. 4, 2; S. 566, 18. v. from.

freó-mǽg, -māg, es; *m. A relation, kinsman;* consanguĭneus, germānus:—Cain freómǽg ofslōh, brōđor sīnne *Cain slew his kinsman, his brother*, Cd. 47; Th. 60, 18; Gen. 983. Ðeáh đū from scyle freómāgum feor gewītan *though thou shalt depart far from thy kindred*, 50; Th. 63, 28; Gen. 1039: 161; Th. 200, 12; Exod. 355. Freómǽgum feor *far from my kindred*, Exon. 76 b; Th. 287, 28; Wand. 21: 85 b; Th. 321, 28; Wīd. 53.

freó-man, frī-man, frig-man, -mann, es; *m. A freeman, free-born man;* līběræ conditiōnis hŏmo, vir ingĕnuus:—Ðæt ǽlc freóman getreówne borh hæbbe *that every freeman have a true surety*, L. Eth. i. 1; Th. i. 280, 7: L. C. S. 20; Th. i. 386, 19. Hwæt gifest đū me freómanna to frōfre *what givest thou me for men's comfort?* Cd. 99; Th. 131, 12; Gen. 2175.

freomian, *part.* freomigende *To profit, be good, avail;* prōdesse, vălēre:—Ðæt đære ylcan stōwe myl wiđ fȳre wæs freomigende *ut pulvis lŏci illīus contra ignem văluĕrit*, Bd. 3, 10; S. 534, 16. v. fremian.

freomlīc; *adj. Profitable, advantageous;* ūtĭlis, commŏdus:—Nerōn nāht freomlīces ongan on đære cynewīsan *Nero began nothing profitable in the state*, Bd. 1, 3; S. 475, 20.

freomung, e; *f. Profit, advantage, good;* profectus:—In đa tīd his bisceophādes swā mycel gāstlīc freomung ongon beón in Angelcynnes cyricum, swā nǽfre ǽr đon beón mihte *tantum profectus spīrĭtālis tempŏre præsŭlātus illīus Anglōrum ecclēsiæ, quantum nunquam antea potuēre, cœpērunt*, Bd. 5, 8; S. 621, 30. v. fremung.

freón; *p.* freóde; *pp.* freód *To free, love;* līběrāre, ămāre, Chr. 777; Erl. 55, 18. v. freógan.

freó-nama, -noma, an; *m. A surname;* cognōmen:—Ðæs fæder wæs hāten Oerīc, wæs his freónama Oesc *cūjus păter Oeric, cognōmento Oisc*, Bd. 2, 5; S. 506, 33: 4, 2; S. 565, 39: 5, 19; S. 637, 39. Se pāpa hine nemde freónaman Clemens *the pope named him by surname Clement*, 5, 11; S. 626, 23.

freónd, friónd, es; *pl. nom. acc.* freóndas, frēnd, frȳnd, freónd; *gen.* freónda; *dat.* freóndum; *m.* [freónde *loving, part. of* freón, v. freógan, freón **II.** *to honour, like, love*] *A* FRIEND; ămīcus:—Se feónd and se freónd *the fiend and the friend*, Elen. Kmbl. 1904; El. 954: Exon. 43 a; Th. 144, 33; Gū. 687. Mānfulra and synfulra freónd *publicānōrum et peccātōrum amīcus*, Mt. Bos. 11, 19: Lk. Bos. 7, 34. He wæs Godes freónd *he was the friend of God*, Chr. 654; Erl. 29, 12: 656; Erl. 32, 28. Se hlāford ne scrīfþ freónde ne feónde *the lord regards not friend nor foe*, Bt. Met. Fox 25, 31; Met. 25, 16: Exon. 105 b; Th. 401, 23; Rä. 21, 16. Gif đū āge freónd ǽnigne *if thou have any friend*, Cd. 116; Th. 150, 30; Gen. 2499: 135; Th. 170, 10; Gen. 2811: Beo. Th. 2774; B. 1385. Hwylc eówer hæfþ sumne freónd *quis vestrum habēbit amīcum?* Lk. Bos. 11, 5: Ps. Th. 90, 2. Me đǽr freóndas gefrunon *friends discovered me there*, Rood Kmbl. 151; Kr. 76. Frȳnd synd hie mīne georne *they are my zealous friends*, Cd. 15; Th. 19, 7; Gen. 287: Exon. 115 b; Th. 443, 21; Kl. 33. Gē synđ mīne frȳnd, gif gē dōþ đa þing, đe ic eów bebeóde *vos amīci mei estis, si fecĕrĭtis quæ ĕgo præcĭpio vōbis*, Jn. Bos. 15, 14: Ps. Spl. 37, 11: Ps. Th. 138, 15. Ðǽr mōtan freónd sēman *there the friends must arbitrate*, L. Ethb. 65; Th. i. 18, 14: L. Eth. ix. 1; Th. i. 340, 7. He wæs freónda gefylled *he was deprived of his friends*, Chr. 937; Erl. 114, 7: Bt. 20; Fox 72, 14. Nāh ic rīcra feala freónda on foldan *I have not many powerful friends on earth*, Rood Kmbl. 261; Kr. 132: Apstls. Kmbl. 182; Ap. 91: Andr. Kmbl. 1868; An. 936: 2257; An. 1130. Hine his freóndum gecȳđe *let notice of him be given to his friends*, L. Alf. pol. 42; Th. i. 90, 16. Ðæt inwitspell Abraham sægde freóndum sīnum *Abram told that tale of woe to his friends*, Cd. 94; Th. 122, 11; Gen. 2025: 79; Th. 97, 12; Gen. 1611. Se hundrēdman sende hys frȳnd to him *mīsit ad eum centŭrio amīcos*, Lk. Bos. 7, 6: 15, 6, 9: Ps. Th. 87, 18. Heorot innan wæs freóndum afylled *Heorot within was filled with friends*, Beo. Th. 2040; B. 1018: 2256; B. 1126. [*Wyc.* frendesse *a female friend: Laym.* freond: *Orm.* freond, frend: *Scot.* frend *a relation: Plat.* frund, fründ, *m: O. Sax.* friund, *m. a friend, relation: Frs.* frjuen: *O. Frs.* friond, friund, *m: Dut.* vriend, vrind, *m: Ger.* freund, *m: M. H. Ger.* vriunt, *m: O. H. Ger.* friunt, friōnt, friant, *m: Goth.* friyonds, *m. a friend*; friyondi, *f. a female friend: Dan.* frende, frænde, *m. f. a cousin, kinsman: Swed.* frände, *m. a relation: Icel.* frændi, *m. a kinsman.*] DER. weoruld-freónd.

freónd-heald; *adj.* [heald *inclined*] *Friend-inclined, friendly;* amīcābĭlis:—Cild biþ freóndheald *a child will be friendly*, Obs. Lun. § 17; Lchdm. iii. 192, 15.

freónd-lār, e; *f.* [lār *instruction*] *Friendly instruction;* fămĭliāris instructio:—He hine on folce freóndlārum heóld *he maintained him among his people with friendly instructions*, Beo. Th. 4744; B. 2377.

freónd-lađu, e; *f. A friendly invitation;* invītātio fămĭliāris:—Him wæs freóndlađu bewægned *a friendly invitation was offered him*, Beo. Th. 2389; B. 1192.

freónd-leás; *adj.* FRIENDLESS; absque amīcis:—Gif freóndleás man geswenced weorþe *if a friendless man be distressed*, L. C. S. 35; Th. i. 396, 22. Ic findan meahte đone đe mec freóndleásne frēfran wolde *I might find one who would comfort me friendless*, Exon. 76 b; Th. 288, 8; Wand. 28: L. Eth. ix. 22; Th. i. 344, 22: L. C. E. 5; Th. i. 362, 18. Be freóndleásan *of the friendless*, L. C. S. 35; Th. i. 396, 22, 26.

freónd-leást, e; *f. Want of friends, indigence;* amīcōrum inŏpia, indĭgentia:—Þurh freóndleáste *through want of friends*, L. C. S. 35; Th. i. 396, 23.

freóndlīc; *adj. Friend-like, friendly;* ămīcus, benignus:—Þurh đa freóndlīcan englas *per ămīcos angĕlos*, Bd. 5, 13; S. 633, 29.

freóndlīce; *adv. Like a friend, kindly;* ămīce, benigne:—We đē freondlīce wīc getǽhton *we kindly assigned to thee a dwelling-place*, Cd. 127; Th. 162, 25; Gen. 2686: 76; Th. 95, 16; Gen. 1579: Past. pref; Hat. MS. Freóndlīcor *more kindly*, Beo. Th. 2058; B. 1027. DER. un-freóndlīce.

freónd-lufu, e; *f. Friendly love, friendship, love, intimacy;* amīcĭtia, cārĭtas, familiārĭtas:—Saga đæt đū sīe sweostor mīn, đonne đē leódweras fricgen, hwæt sīe freóndlufu uncer twega *say that thou art my sister, when the men of the country ask thee what may be the intimacy of us two*, Cd. 89; Th. 110, 7; Gen. 1834.

freónd-mynd, e; *f. An amorous mind;* amātōria mens:—Ic me onēgan [MS. onagen] mæg đæt me wrāþra sum, wǽpnes ecge, for freóndmynde, feore beneóte *I for myself may fear that some enemy, through amorous mind, may deprive me of life with a weapon's edge*, Cd. 89; Th. 109, 31; Gen. 1831.

freónd-rǽden, -rǽdden, -rǽdenn, e; *f. A friend-condition, friendship;* amīcĭtia:—Ðæt heó mīnre ne gȳme freóndrǽdenne *that she cares not for my friendship*, Exon. 66 b; Th. 246, 33; Jul. 71. Hig mihton nāne freóndrǽdene wiđ hine habban *they would have no friendship with him*, Gen. 37, 4. Hie getreówlīce heora freóndrǽdenne healdaþ *they faithfully hold their friendship*, Bt. 21; Fox 74, 39: Exon. 67 a; Th. 249, 5; Jul. 107: Elen. Kmbl. 2413; El. 1208. Gif man wille fulle freóndrǽdene [freóndrǽddene MS. B.] habban *if a man will have full friendship*, L. E. G. 12; Th. i. 176, 2. God gefēgþ mid freóndrǽdenne folc togædere *God joins people together with friendship*, Bt. 21; Fox 74, 37.

freónd-scipe, -scype, es; *m.* FRIENDSHIP; amīcĭtia:—Is nū swā hit nō wǽre freóndscipe uncer *our friendship is now as it had not been*, Exon. 115 a; Th. 443, 4; Kl. 25. Þolige ūre ealra freóndscipes, and ealles đæs đe he āge *let him forfeit the friendship of us all, and all that he has*, L. Ed. 8; Th. i. 164, 4: L. Ath. i. 26; Th. i. 214, 5. Be mīnum freóndscipe *by my friendship*, i. prm; Th. i. 194, 5: L. Edg. S. 1; Th. i. 272, 5. Fram đyssa muneca freóndscipe *by the friendship of these monks*, Bd. 3, 5; S. 526, 18. Man fullne freóndscipe gefæstnode *they confirmed full friendship*, Chr. 1014; Erl. 150, 14: 1016; Erl. 159, 3. Ðæt man friþ and freóndscipe rihtlīce healde *that peace and friendship be lawfully observed*, L. Eth. v. 1; Th. i. 304, 10: vi. 8; Th. i. 316, 28. Git mōston freóndscype fremman *ye might foster friendship*, Exon. 123 a; Th. 473, 21; Bo. 18. Se gefēhþ fela folca tosomne mid freóndscipe *he joins many people together with friendship*, Bt. Met. Fox 11, 179; Met. 11, 90. Freóndscipas niwe *new friendships*, Somn. 203; Lchdm. iii. 210, 2.

freónd-spēd, e; *f. An abundance of friends;* amīcōrum cōpia:—Ic đam magorince sylle freóndspēd *I will give many friends to the youth*, Cd. 106; Th. 140, 19; Gen. 2330.

freónd-spēdig; *adj. Rich in friends;* amīcōrum dīves:—Ðus mæg mihtig man, and freóndspēdig, his dǽdbōte, mid freónda fultume, micelum gelīhtan *thus may a powerful man, and rich in friends, greatly lighten his penance, with the help of his friends*, L. P. M; Th. ii. 286, 13.

freó-noma, an; *m. A surname, noble name;* cognōmen:—Iob Sunu Waldendes freónoman cende *Job gave a noble name to the Lord's son*, Exon. 17 a; Th. 40, 9; Crī. 636. v. freó-nama.

freóra *of free*, Cd. 131; Th. 166, 26; Gen. 2753; *gen. pl. of* freó; *adj.*

freórig; *adj.* **I.** *freezing, chilled, frigid, frozen;* frīgens, frīgŏre rĭgens, frīgĭdus, gĕlĭdus:—Ic wæs mundum freórig *my hands were chilled* [lit. *I was freezing in my hands*], Andr. Kmbl. 982; An. 491. Mec se wǽta wong, wundrum freórig, ǽrist cende *the humid field, wonderously frigid, first brought me forth*, Exon. 109 a; Th. 417, 8; Rä. 36, 1. Land wǽron freórig cealdum cȳlegicelum *the lands were frozen with cold icicles*, Andr. Kmbl. 2520; An. 1261. **II.** *chilled with fear or sorrow, trembling, sad;* trĕmens, tristis:—He gefeóll freórig to foldan *he fell trembling to the ground*, Judth. 12; Thw. 25, 27; Jud. 281. Ongon hygegeómor, freórig and ferþwērig, fūsne grētan *he, sad in mind, trembling and weary of soul, resolved to greet the departing* [*man*], Exon. 49 b; Th. 171, 21; Gû. 1130. Ferþloca freórig *a trembling body*, 76 b; Th. 288, 18; Wand. 33.

freórig-ferþ; *adj. Sad in soul;* tristis ănĭmo:—Cwom freórigferþ ðā seó fǣmne wæs *he, sad in soul, came to where the damsel was*, Exon. 52 b; Th. 182, 30; Gû. 1318.

freórig-mōd; *adj. Sad in mind;* tristis ănĭmo:—He monge gehǣlde, ðe hine ādle gebundne gesōhtun, freórigmōde *he healed many, who, oppressed with malady, sad in mind, sought him*, Exon. 45 b; Th. 155, 14; Gû. 860.

freó-riht, es; *n. A free right, common right, right of a freeman;* lībĕrōrum et ingenuōrum jus:—He ne beó syððan ǣniges freórihtes wyrðe *he shall not afterwards deserve any free right*, L. C. S. 20; Th. i. 386, 22.

FREÓSAN, hit freóseþ, frȳsþ, frȳst; *p.* freás, *pl.* fruron; *pp.* froren *To* FREEZE; gĕlāre:—Forst sceal freósan *frost shall freeze*, Exon. 90 a; Th. 338, 1; Gn. Ex. 72. Men steorran māgon [MS. magan] geseón swā sutole swā on niht ðonne hit swīðe freóseþ *men may see the stars as plainly as at night when it freezes hard*, Homl. Blick. 93, 20. Hit frȳst [frȳsþ MS. D.] *gĕlat*, Ælfc. Gr. 22; Som. 24, 8. [*Wyc.* frees, freesede *froze*: *Plat.* fresen, freren: *Dut.* vriezen: *Ger.* frieren: *M. H. Ger.* vriusen: *O. H. Ger.* friusan, freosan: *Goth.* frius, *n. frost*: *Dan.* fryse: *Swed.* frysa: *Icel.* frjósa.] DER. ge-freósan: ofer-froren.

freót, freód, es; *m. Freedom, liberty, an enfranchisement, a setting a man free;* lībertas, mănūmissio:—Þolie his freótes *let him forfeit his freedom*, L. E. G. 7; Th. i. 170, 17. We scylon todǣlan freót and þeówet *we ought to distinguish between freedom and slavery*, L. C. S. 69; Th. i. 412, 9: L. Ed. 9; Th. i. 164, 10.

freót-gifa, an; *m. A giver of freedom, liberator, emancipator;* manumissor, Ælfc. Gl. 112; Som. 79, 91; Wrt. Voc. 59, 58.

freót-gifu, e; *f. The gift of freedom, emancipation, manumission*, manumissio:—Freótgifu [MS. freótgife] *manumissio*, Ælfc. Gl. 112; Som. 79, 92; Wrt. Voc. 60, 1.

freoða, an; *m. A protector, defender;* tūtor:—Ðū me, God, wǣre freoða *thou, O God, wast a protector to me;* refŭgium meum es tu, Ps. Th. 70, 3.

freoðan; *p.* ede; *pp.* ed *To* FROTH; spūmāre, Som. DER. a-freoðan.

freoðian; *p.* ode, ade; *pp.* od, ad *To care for, maintain, cherish, protect, keep, observe;* consŭlĕre, sustentāre, fŏvēre, tuēri, observāre:—In eallum þingum ðære cirican eahtum and gōdum he freoðode and fultemede *ecclēsiæ rēbus in omnĭbus consŭlĕre ac făvēre cūrāvit*, Bd. 2, 6; S. 508, 32. Ðæt mīnes freán mōdwēn freoðaþ *what my master's mind's thought will maintain*, Exon. 129 b; Th. 498, 3; Rä. 87, 7. God mīn feorg freoðaþ *God will protect my life*, Exon. 36 a; Th. 116, 28; Gû. 214. Hie ælmihtig sigebearn Godes freoðode *the almighty victorious Son of God protected her*, Elen. Kmbl. 2292; El. 1147: Exon. 94 b; Th. 354, 3; Reim. 40: 103 a; Th. 391, 14; Rä. 10, 5. Hine weoruda God freoðade on foldan *the God of hosts protected him on earth*, Exon. 38 a; Th. 126, 6; Gû. 367. Hī ðone heágan dæg healdaþ and freoðiaþ *they keep and observe the high day* [*Sunday*], Hy. 9, 27; Hy. Grn. ii. 291, 27. DER. ge-freoðian. v. friðian.

freoðo, frioðo, freoðu, friðo, fryðo, freðo; *indecl. f:* freoðu, friðu, e; *f. Peace, security, protection, a refuge;* pax, secūrĭtas, tūtēla, asȳlum:—Seó [treów] ðē freoðo sceal in līfdagum weorþan *which* [*faith*] *shall be peace to thee in thy life's days*, Cd. 163; Th. 204, 21; Exod. 422. Wel biþ ðæm ðe mōt Drihten sēcean, and to Fæder fæðmum freoðo wilnian *it shall be well to him who may seek the Lord, and desire peace in his Father's bosom*, Beo. Th. 379; B. 188: Exon. 121 a; Th. 465, 3; Hö. 98. Gif me freoðo Drihten an *if the Lord will grant me protection*, Cd. 89; Th. 110, 15; Gen. 1838: 183; Th. 229, 25; Dan. 222. Ic me freoðu to ðē wilnige *I desire peace from thee*, Ps. Th. 55, 8. Hī ðǣr lifgaþ ā in freoðu Dryhtnes *they shall live there for ever in the Lord's peace*, Exon. 64 b; Th. 238, 1; Ph. 597. Þurh ðē eorþbūende ealle onfōþ freoðo and freóndscipe *through thee all dwellers upon earth shall receive peace and friendship*, Cd. 84; Th. 105, 28; Gen. 1760. Ic eów freoðo healde *I will hold you in protection*, Andr. Kmbl. 672; An. 336. Ne mihte earmsceapen findan freoðe *the poor wretch could not find protection*, 2261; An. 1132. Utan us to Fæder freoða wilnian *let us desire peace from our Father*, Exon. 19 a; Th. 48, 18; Cri. 773. [*O. Sax.* friðu: *O. H. Ger.* fridu.] DER. fenfreoðo. v. friþ.

freoðo-beácen, es; *n. A sign of peace, sign granting safety;* pācis signum, signum incolumĭtātem præbens:—Hine Waldend on tācen sette, freoðobeácen, ðȳ-læs hine feónda hwilc mid gūþ-þræce grētan dorste *the Lord set a token, a sign of peace, upon him* [*Cain*], *lest some enemy durst greet him with hostile force*, Cd. 50; Th. 64, 4; Gen. 1045.

freoðo-burh; *gen.* -burge; *f. A peaceful city, city of refuge, an asylum;* pācis arx, asȳlum:—He gesōhte freoðoburh *he sought the peaceful city*, Beo. Th. 1048; B. 522. v. friþ-burh.

freoðo-leás; *adj. Peaceless;* pāce cărens:—Swylc wæs ðæs folces freoðoleás tācen *such was the people's peaceless token*, Andr. Kmbl. 58; An. 29. v. friþ-leás.

freoðo-scealc, es; *m. A minister of peace;* pācis minister:—Swā se engel, fǣle freoðoscealc, fǣmnan sægde *as the angel, the faithful minister of peace, said to the damsel*, Cd. 105; Th. 138, 33; Gen. 2301. Sprǣcon fǣle freoðoscealcas to Lothe *the faithful ministers of peace spake to Lot*, Cd. 115; Th. 150, 25; Gen. 2497.

freoðo-sibb *protecting peace.* v. friðu-sibb.

freoðo-spēd, friðo-spēd, e; *f. Abundance of peace, protecting power;* pācis cōpia, tutēlāris pŏtestas:—Enoch siððan ealdordōm ahōf, freoðospēd *Enoch then raised his sovereignty, his protecting power*, Cd. 60; Th. 73, 2; Gen. 1198.

freoðo-tācen *a token* or *sign of peace.* v. friðo-tācen.

freoðo-þeáw, es; *m. Peaceful behaviour* or *manner;* pacĭfĭci mōres:—Ðā wæs sibb on heofnum, freoðoþeáwas *then there was agreement in heaven, peaceful manners*, Cd. 4; Th. 5, 29; Gen. 79.

freoðo-wǣr, freoðu-wǣr, frioðo-wǣr, frioðu-wǣr, friðo-wǣr, e; *f. A covenant of peace, an agreement, compact;* pācis fœdus, pactum:—Wæs seó eorla gedriht ānes mōdes, fæstum fæðmum freoðowǣre heóld *the host of men was of one mind, held the covenant of peace in their firm breasts*, Cd. 158; Th. 197, 13; Exod. 306. Hī onfēngon fulwihte and freoðuwǣre *they received baptism and the covenant of peace*, Andr. Kmbl. 3259; An. 1632. v. frīoðo-wār, -waru.

freoðo-weard *a guardian of peace.* v. freoðu-weard.

freoðo-webba *a peace-weaver, an angel.* v. friðo-webba.

freoðo-webbe *a peace-weaver, woman.* v. freoðu-webbe.

freoðo-wong, es; *m. A peaceful plain;* pācis campus:—Freoðowong ðone ofereódon *they went over the peaceful plain*, Beo. Th. 5910; B. 2959.

freoðu *peace, security, protection*, Ps. Th. 55, 8: Exon. 64 b; Th. 238, 1; Ph. 597. v. freoðo.

freoðu-wǣr *a covenant of peace*, Andr. Kmbl. 3259; An. 1632. v. freoðo-wǣr.

freoðu-weard, es; *m. A guardian of peace;* pācis custos:—Him wæs engel neáh fǣle freoðuweard *the angel was near him, a faithful guardian of peace*, Exon. 35 a; Th. 112, 15; Gû. 144.

freoðu-webbe, an; *f. A peace-weaver, woman;* pācis textrix, conciliatrix, mŭlier:—Ne biþ swylc cwēnlīc þeáw, ðætte freoðuwebbe feores onsæce leófne mannan *such is no feminine usage, that a peace-weaver deprive a dear man of his life*, Beo. Th. 3888; B. 1942. Wīdsīþ mid Ealhhilde, fǣlre freoðuwebban, hām gesōhte Eormanrīces *Widsith with Ealhild, faithful peace-weaver, sought the home of Ermanric*, Exon. 84 b; Th. 319, 2; Wīd. 6. v. Grm. And. u. El. 144.

freót-man, -mann, es; *m. A freedman;* lībertus:—Hió hyre an ðara [MS. ðere] manna and ðæs yrfes, būtan ðām freótmannum [MS. -mannon] *she gives her the men and the stock, except the freedmen*, Cod. Dipl. 1290; A. D. 995; Kmbl. vi. 131, 10.

freó-wine, es; *m. A noble friend;* nōbĭlis *vel* princeps āmīcus:—Ðæt ðū me ne forwyrne, freówine folca *that thou deny me not, noble friend of people*, Beo. Th. 864, note; B. 430.

Fresan; *gen.* Fresena, Fresna; *pl. m. The Frisians;* Frisii, Fresōnes:—He mid Wilbrord ðone hālgan bisceop Fresena wæs wuniende *ăpud sanctissĭmum Fresōnum gentis archiepiscŏpum Vilbrordum mŏrābātur*, Bd. 3, 13; S. 538, 8: Beo. Th. 2191; B. 1093. Ðæt Swīþbyrht and Wilbrord biscopas wǣron Fresna þeóde gehālgode *that Swithbyrht and Wilbrord were consecrated bishops of the Frisians' nation*, Bd. 5, 11; S. 625, 28: Exon. 85 a; Th. 320, 11; Wīd. 27: Beo. Th. 5823; B. 2915. v. Frysa.

Fres-cyning, es; *m. A Frisian king;* Fresōnum rex:—Nalles he Frescyninge breóstweorþunge bringan mōste *he could not bring the ornament to the Frisian king*, Beo. Th. 5000; B. 2503.

Fresisc; *adj. Of* or *belonging to Friesland, Frisian;* Frīsĭcus:—Nǣron hī nāwðer ne on Fresisc gescæpene ne on Denisc *they were shapen neither as the Frisian nor as the Danish*, Chr. 897; Erl. 95, 15. Ðǣr wearþ ofslægen Lucumon, and ealra monna, Fresiscra and Engliscra, lxii *there was slain Lucumon, and of all the men, Frisian and English, sixty-two*, Chr. 897; Erl. 96, 4. v. Frysisc.

Fres-lond, es; *n. Friesland;* Frīsia:—Freslondum on Hreðles eafora swealt *Hrethel's offspring perished in the Frieslands*, Beo. Th. 4704; B. 2357. v. Frys-land.

FRETAN, ic frete, ðū fritest, fritst, he freteþ, friteþ, fritt, fryt, *pl.* fretaþ; *p.* ic, he fræt, ðū frǣte, *pl.* frǣton; *pp.* freten [for-, etan *to eat?*]. I. *to eat up, gnaw*, FRET, *devour, consume;* devŏrāre, consūmĕre, comĕdĕre:—Ða ðe wilniaþ fretan mīn folc *qui devŏrant plēbem meam*, Ps. Th. 13, 9: 26, 3: Exon. 127 a; Th. 488, 11; Rä. 76, 5: 87 b; Th. 329, 34; Vy. 44: Beo. Th. 6021; B. 3014: 6220; B. 3114. Swā 'līg freteþ mōrhǣþ *vĕlut flamma incendat montes*, Ps. Th. 82, 10. Friteþ wildne fugol *it eats the wild bird*, Salm. Kmbl. 596; Sal. 297: 808; Sal. 403. Deáþ misfēdeþ oððe fritt hig *mors depascet eos*, Ps. Spl. T. 48, 14. Fȳr fryt land mid his wæstme *ignis devŏrābit terram cum germĭne suo*, Deut. 32, 22. Gærstapan hit fretaþ eall *locustæ devŏrābunt omnia*, Deut. 28, 38: Ps. Th. 52, 5. He fræt fȳftȳne men *he devoured fifteen men*, Beo. Th. 3167; B. 1581: Exon. 112 b; Th. 432, 4; Rä. 48, 1. He fræt uncer wurþ *cŏmĕdit prĕtium nostrum*, Gen. 31, 15: Ps. Spl. 79, 14.

Fugelas hit frǣton *vŏlucres comĕdĕrunt illud*, Mk. Bos. 4, 4; frétun, Rush.: fréton, Mt. Lind. 13, 4: Gen. 37, 20. We hine frǣton *obsorbuĭmus eum*, Ps. Th. 34, 23: 104, 30. Wǣron hie mid meteliéste gewǣgde, and hæfdon miclne dǣl ðara horsa freten *they were distressed for want of food, and had eaten a great part of their horses*, Chr. 894; Erl. 92, 28. Swā hwylcne man swā hȳ gefōþ fretaþ hī hine *quoscunque capiunt comedunt*, Nar. 36, 4. Freotas *devorant*, Mk. Skt. Rush. 12, 40. II. *to break, burst;* frangĕre, rumpĕre:—Heó wǣre frǣton *they brake their covenant*, Cd. 149; Th. 187, 7; Exod. 147. [*Piers P. Chauc.* frete: *Laym.* freten *to gnaw*: *Orm.* freteþþ *fretteth*: *Plat.* freten, vreten: *Dut.* vreten: *Ger.* fressen: *M. H. Ger.* vrëzzen: *O. H. Ger.* farëzzan, firezan, frezzan, frëzan: *Goth.* fra-ītan: *Dan.* fraadse: *Swed.* fräta, fråssa.]

fretere, es; *m. A glutton;* lurco, Som. Ben. Lye.

freðo; *indecl. f. Peace;* pax:—Gewīt on freðo gangan, ūt of earce *go forth in peace, out of the ark*, Cd. 73; Th. 89, 28; Gen. 1487. v. freoðo.

fretnes, -ness, e; *f. A devouring, ravening;* edācĭtas, vŏrācĭtas, Som. Ben. Lye.

fretol, frettol; *adj. Voracious, gluttonous;* ĕdax:—Frettol *ĕdax* vel *glutto*, Ælfc. Gl. 88; Som. 74, 81; Wrt. Voc. 50, 61.

frettan; *p.* te; *pp.* ed *To feed upon, eat up, consume;* depasci:—Hine [wīngeard] wilde deór wēstaþ and frettaþ *singŭlāris fĕrus depastus est eam* [*vīneam*], Ps. Th. 79, 13. Hie ðæt corn forbærndon, and mid hira horsum fretton on ǣlcere efenēhþe *they burned the corn, and with their horses ate it up on every plain*, Chr. 894; Erl. 93, 12. Fretton *comederunt*, Mk. Skt. Lind. 4, 4.

fretwednes, fretwodnes, -ness, e; *f. An adorning, decoration;* ornātio, decŏrāmentum:—On eorþlīcre fretwednesse *in earthly adorning*, Bd. 3, 22; S. 552, 20, note. Beóþ ðonne ūre hrægla fretwodnes on ðam ēcan fȳre wītnode *then our decoration of garments will be punished in the eternal fire*, L. E. I. prm; Th. ii. 394, 11. v. frætwednes.

fretwian; *p.* ode; *pp.* od *To adorn;* ornāre, insignīre:—Ic mǣrsige oððe fretwige *insignio*, Ælfc. Gr. 30; Som. 34, 60. v. frættewian.

fretwung *an adorning;* ornātio, Som. Ben. Lye. v. frætwung.

frī; *adj. Free, noble;* līber, ingĕnuus, nōbĭlis:—Frīes mannes wīf *the wife of a free man*, L. Ethb. 31; Th. i. 10, 6. Ic ðē on folcum frīne Drihten ēcne andete *I acknowledge thee amongst the people, a noble eternal Lord*, Ps. Th. 56, 11. v. freó; *adj.*

friá, an; *m. A lord, master;* dŏmĭnus:—Ðam āgenan frián *to the possessor*, L. Eth. iii. 4; Th. i. 294, 17. v. freá, āgen-frigea.

fría; *p.* ade; *pp.* ad I. *to love:*—Frīende was *complexus esset*, Mk. Skt. Lind. 9, 36. II. *to free:*—Ic fría *liberabo*, Rtl. 9, 40. We sie fríado *liberemur*, 7, 3. v. freógan.

frī-borh; *gen.* -borges; *m. A free surety, pledge, bondman;* fīdejussio, L. Ed. C. 20; Wilk. 202, 11. v. freó-borh.

fric; *adj. Voracious:*—Fric ⁊ étere *vorax*, Mt. Lind. 11, 19. v. frec.

fricca, fryccea, an; *m. A crier, herald;* præco:—Hleówon hornboran, hreópon friccan *trumpeters sounded, heralds shouted*, Elen. Kmbl. 108; El. 54: 1097; El. 550. Hreópon friccan *heralds shouted*, Andr. Kmbl. 2314; An. 1158. Cristes fricca *Christ's crier*, Blickl. Homl. 163, 21. Sylle se friccea his stefne *let the crier give out his voice*, 163, 31.

fricgan, fricgean, fricggan; *part.* fricgende; ic fricge, ðū frigest, frigst, frihst, he frigeþ, frigþ, frihþ, *pl.* fricgaþ; *p.* ic, he fræg, ðū frǣge, *pl.* frǣgon; *impert.* frige; *subj. pres.* fricge, *pl.* fricgen; *pp.* ge-frigen, -fregen, -frægen *To ask, inquire, question, find out, seek after, learn, get information of;* interrŏgāre, sciscĭtāri, pĕtĕre, fando accĭpĕre, compĕrīre:—Wilt ðū fricgan felageongne ymb forþgesceaft *wilt thou ask one who has travelled much about the creation?* Exon. 92 b; Th. 346, 23; Sch. 3. Sceal bearna gehwylc leánes fricgan, ealles ðæs ðe we on eorþan ǣr geworhton [MS. geweorhtan], gōdes oððe yfles *every child shall seek the reward of all that we ere did on earth, of good or evil*, Exon. 116 b; Th. 447, 18; Dōm. 41. Higelāc ongan sīnne geseldan fricgean *Higelac began to question his guest*, Beo. Th. 3974; B. 1985: Cd. 139; Th. 174, 33; Gen. 2887. Ðæs fricggan ongan folces aldor *the prince of the people began to inquire about it*, Elen. Kmbl. 313; El. 157: 1116; El. 560. Gomela Scylding, fela fricgende, feorran rehte *the aged Scylding, learning much, related* [*things*] *from* [*times*] *remote*, Beo. Th. 4218; B. 2106: Exon. 92 b; Th. 347, 17; Sch. 14. Fricge ic ðē, hwæðres biþ hira folgoþ betra *I ask thee, of which of them is the condition better?* Salm. Kmbl. 739; Sal. 369. Hī fricgaþ, hū... *they ask, how...*, Exon. 9 a; Th. 6, 30; Cri. 92. Frige mec frōdum wordum *question me in prudent words*, Exon. 88 b; Th. 333, 8; Gn. Ex. 1. Frige hwæt ic hātte *find out what I am called*, Exon. 104 a; Th. 396, 6; Rä. 15, 19: 105 a; Th. 398, 20; Rä. 17, 10: 107 a; Th. 409, 9; Rä. 27, 26: 107 b; Th. 410, 13; Rä. 28, 15. Ðonne ðē leódweras fricgen *when the men of the country ask thee*, Cd. 89; Th. 110, 6; Gen. 1834. DER. ge-fricgan, un-fricgende. v. frignan.

frician; *p.* ode, ude; *pp.* od, ud *To dance;* saltāre:—Gē ne fricudun *non saltastis*, Mt. Bos. 11, 17.

friclan; *p.* ede; *pp.* ed; *with the gen. To desire, seek for;* appĕtĕre:—Ðæt we sceolden [MS. sceolde] fremena friclan *that we might desire benefits*, Cd. 89; Th. 110, 24; Gen. 1843. Næs ðǣr māra fyrst freóde to friclan *there was no time more to seek for friendship*, Beo. Th. 5105; B. 2556.

friclo; *indecl. f. An appetite;* appĕtītus:—Be ðære ofermiclan friclo, ðonne of ðære selfan cealdan ādle ðæs magan cymþ, ðæt sió ofermiclo friclo and gīfernes arīst *of the excessive appetite, when from the same cold disease of the stomach it comes, that the excessive appetite and greediness arise*, L. M. 2, 16; Lchdm. ii. 196, 1, 2.

frico; *f. Usury;* usura, Mt. Lind. 25, 27. [Cf. *O. H. Ger.* frechí *avaritia.*]

frictrung, frictung; *f. Divination;* ariolatus, Gl. Mett. 10: Gl. Amplon. 45. v. frihtrung, freht.

frīd-hengest, es; *m. A stately horse:*—Hæfdon xi eóredmæcgas frīdhengestas *the horsemen had eleven stately horses*, Exon. 106 a; Th. 404, 7; Rä. 23, 4.

friénd *friend:*—Ne murnþ nāuðer ne friénd ne fiénd *he regards neither friend nor foe*, Bt. 37, 1; Fox 186, 7. v. freónd.

Friesa *a Frisian*, Chr. 897; Erl. 96, 2, 3. v. Frysa.

frig; *def.* se frigea; *adj. Free, noble;* līber, ingĕnuus, nōbĭlis:—Nelle ic gān ūt ne beón frig *non egrĕdiar līber*, Ex. 21, 5. Gif hwā his āgenne geleód bebycgge, þeówne oððe frigne *if any one sell his own countryman, bond or free*, L. In. 11; Th. i. 110, 4: L. Wih. 14; Th. i. 40, 9: L. C. S. 20; Th. i. 388, 3. Gif God næfde on eallum his rīce nāne frige sceaft *if God had not any free creature in all his kingdom*, Bt. 41, 2; Fox 244, 29. Gē beóþ frige *lībĕri ĕrĭtis*, Jn. Bos. 8, 33, 36: Bd. 3, 24; S. 557, 46. Gif se frigea ðȳ dæge wyrce *if a freeman work on that day*, L. In. 3; Th. i. 104, 5: 74; Th. i. 150, 1. Eal swā ǣlcan frigean men gebȳreþ *sīcut omnis līber făcĕre dēbet*, L. R. S. 3; Th. i. 432, 23: L. In. 74; Th. i. 150, 3. v. freó.

frig, frigu? e; *f. Love, affection, favour;* ămor:—Sió weres friga wiht ne cūðe *she knew nothing of the love* [*affections*] *of man*, Exon. 13 b; Th. 26, 19; Cri. 419. Ðæt wæs geworden būtan weres frigum *that was done without the favours of man*, 8 b; Th. 3, 17; Cri. 37.

Frig-dæg, Frige dæg, es; *m.* FRIDAY, *Friga's day, the day on which the heathens worshipped the goddess Friga*, or *Venus*, *the consort of Woden and protectress of matrimony;* dies Vĕnĕris:—Man singe ǣlc Frigdæge æt ǣlcum mynstre, ealle ða Godes þeówan, ān fiftig sealmas for ðone cyng *one shall sing every Friday, at every monastery, all servants of God fifty psalms for the king*, L. Ath. iv. 3; Th. i. 222, 18. Ǣlces Frige dæges fæsten *every Friday's fast*, L. Edg. i. 5; Th. i. 264, 23: L. C. E. 16; Th. i. 368, 25. Fæstan ǣlce Frige dæg *to fast every Friday*, L. Eth. v. 17; Th. i. 308, 23: vi. 24; Th. i. 320, 22. Ðis sceal on Frige dæg ofer twelftan dæg *this* [*Gospel*] *must be* [*read*] *on Friday after the twelfth day*, Rubc. Mt. Bos. 4, 12, 23; Notes. p, 574. For Friga v. Grm. D. M. p. 278; and for names of the days of the week in the several Teutonic dialects pp. 112–115.

frigea, an; *m. A lord, master;* dŏmĭnus:—Se āgena frigea *the possessor*, L. Eth. iii. 4; Th. i. 294, 18. DER. āgen-frigea. v. freá.

Frige ǣfen, es; *m. Thursday evening*, Homl. Th. i. 216, 21.

frigenes, frignes, -ness, -nyss, e; *f.* [frigen *asked, pp. of* fricgan *to ask;* ness, -ness] *An asking, inquiry, a question;* interrŏgātio, quæstio:—Þurh his geornfulle frigenesse *repĕtīta interrŏgātiōne*, Bd. 5, 12; S. 631, 4. Wæs Ēdwine bealdra geworden on ðære frignesse *Edwin was become bolder on that inquiry*, Bd. 2, 12; S. 514, 10. Be monigum frignyssum ða ðe him nȳdþearflīce gesewen wǣron *de eis quæ necessāriæ vĭdēbantur quæstiōnĭbus*, 1, 27; S. 488, 33. DER. ge-frignys.

frigest, frigst, frihst, he frigeþ, frigþ, frihþ *inquirest, inquires;* 2nd and 3rd *pers. pres. of* fricgan.

frig-lǣta, an; *m. One made free, a freedman;* lībertus, Cot. 120. v. freó-lǣta.

frig-man, -mann, es; *m. A freeman;* hŏmo līber:—Gif frigman freólsdæge wyrce *if a freeman work on a festival-day*, L. C. S. 45; Th. i. 402, 12, note 28: 47; Th. i. 402, 21. Gif frigman frēum stelþ *if a freeman steal from a freeman*, L. Ethb. 9; Th. i. 6, 2. v. freó-man.

FRIGNAN; *part.* frignende, ic frigne, ðū frignest, he frigneþ, *pl.* frignaþ; *p.* ic, he frægn, frægen, frægin, fræng, fregen, fregn, ðū frugne, *pl.* frugnon; *impert.* frign, *pl.* frignaþ; *subj. pres.* frigne, *pl.* frignen; *pp.* frugnen *To ask, inquire;* interrŏgāre, sciscĭtāri:—Ic ðē frignan wille hwæt forlǣtest ðū me *I wish to ask thee why hast thou forsaken me*, Andr. Kmbl. 2824; An. 1414. He hine wæs frignende, for hwon he ðæt Godes eówde forlǣtan wolde *illum sciscĭtābātur, quāre grĕgem relinquĕret*, Bd. 2, 6; S. 508, 14: 2, 13; S. 515, 41. Ic fregno(a) *interrogabo*, Mt. Lind. 21, 24: Mk. 11, 29. Swā ðū hine wordum frignest *as thou askest him in words*, Elen. Kmbl. 1175; El. 589: Exon. 50 b; Th. 175, 27; Gū. 1201. Gif ðeós cwēn ūsic frigneþ ymb ðæt treó *if this queen asks us about the tree*, Elen. Kmbl. 1065; El. 534. Frægn gif him wǣre niht getǣse *he asked if he had had an easy night*, Beo. Th. 2643; B. 1319. Eft he frægn hwæt seó þeód nemned wǣre *rursus interrŏgāvit quod esset vocābŭlum illius gentis*, Bd. 2, 1; S. 501, 16: 2, 12; S. 513, 37, 38. He frægen and axode *interrogabat*, Nar. 17, 30. Frægin he of hwylcum lande hī brohte wǣron *interrŏgāvit de qua terra essent adlāti*, Bd. 2, 1; S. 501, 9: 4, 5; S. 572, 21. Ðā fræng hine his mæsse-preóst for hwon he weópe *quem dum presbȳter suus quare lachrymārētur interrogasset*, Bd. 3, 14; S. 541, 3. Fregn freca óðerne *one warrior asked another*, Andr. Kmbl. 2327; An. 1165. Cȳðeras unrehte ða ic nysse frugnon mec *testes iniqui quæ ignōrābam interrŏgābant me*, Ps. Surt. 34, 11: 136, 3. Frign mec *interrŏga me*, Ps. Surt. 138, 23. Ðeáh hine rinca hwilc æfter frigne *though any man inquire about it*, Bt. Met. Fox 22, 91; Met. 22, 46. Gif he frugnen biþ *if he is asked*, 22, 104; Met. 22, 52: Invent. Crs. Recd. 1083; El. 542. [*Piers P.* fraynen: *Chauc.* freyne: *Laym.* fræine, fræinien: *Orm.* fragnenn: *O.Sax.* fregnan, fragōn: *Frs.* freegjen: *O.Frs.* fregia: *Dut.* vragen: *Ger.* fragen: *M.H.Ger.* vragen: *O.H.Ger.* frāgēn: *Goth.* fraihnan: *Swed.* frāga: *Icel.* fregna *to hear, ask*: *Lat.* prĕc-or *I ask*: *Lith.* praszyti: *Sansk.* prać̣h *to ask.*] DER. ge-frignan. v. frinan.

frignes, -ness, e; *f. Freeness, immunity;* lībertas, immūnĭtas, Chr. 796; Th. 102, note 1, 2.

frihtan *to fright, terrify;* terrēre, Som. Ben. Lye. v. fyrhtan.

frihtere, es; *m. A soothsayer, diviner;* hariŏlus:—Ða syndon gefeaxene swā frihteras *quasi dīvīne*, Nar. 37, 2. The translator has read dīvīni for dīvīne.

frihþ *the soul, spirit, mind.* DER. stīþ-frihþ. v. ferhþ.

frihtrung, e; *f. Divination, sooth-saying;* hariŏlātio, Cot. 21. v. frictrung.

frīlīc; *adj. Free, liberal;* līber, lībĕrālis:—Frīlīc gestreón *lībĕrāle fœnus*, Prov. 28. v. freólīc.

frī-man, -mann, es; *m. A freeman;* līber hŏmo:—Gif frīman edorbrecþe gedēþ, vi scillingum gebēte *if a freeman commit house-breaking, let him make amends with six shillings*, L. Ethb. 27; Th. i. 8, 15: 29, 31; Th. i. 10, 3, 6: L. Wih. 11; Th. i. 40, 1: L. N. P. L. 56; Th. ii. 298, 24. v. freó-man.

frimdig, frimdi, frymdi, firmdig; *adj. Inquisitive, asking, desirous;* inquīsītīvus, desīdĕrans, requīrens:—Man him sōna funde, ðæs ðe he frimdig wæs *one soon found for him, what he was desirous*, Ælfc. T. 36, 13. Swā gē frimdie wǣron *sīcut dīcĭtis*, Ex. 12, 31. Hū māge gē ðæs frimdie beón *how can ye be asking for that?* Ex. 10, 10. Ðæt land ðe ðú me firmdig to wǣre ðæt ic ðē lēnde *the land that thou wast desirous I should lease to thee*, Th. Chart. 162, 13.

frinan; *part.* frinnende; ic frine, ðū frinest, he frineþ, *pl.* frinaþ; *p.* ic, he fran, ðū frune, *pl.* frunon, frunnon; *impert.* frin, *pl.* frinaþ; *subj. pres.* frine, *pl.* frinen; *p.* frune, *pl.* frunen; *pp.* frunen *To ask, inquire, consult;* interrŏgāre, sciscĭtāri, consŭlĕre:—Se gesīþ ongan hine frinan, for hwon hine mon gebindan ne mihte *cŏmes eum interrŏgāre cœpit quāre lĭgāri non posset*, Bd. 4, 22; S. 591, 24: Cd. 25; Th. 31, 34; Gen. 495: Beo. Th. 708; B. 351. Me sylfum frinnendum *mihimet sciscĭtanti*, Bd. 4, 19; S. 587, 26. Ne frine ic ðē for tǣle *I ask thee not for blame*, Andr. Kmbl. 1265; An. 633. Ic frine ðē *consŭlo te*, Ælfc. Gl. 86; Som. 74, 15; Wrt. Voc. 49, 38. Hwæt frinest ðū me *what askest thou of me?* Andr. Kmbl. 1257; An. 629. Frineþ he hwǣr se man sīe *he will ask where the man is*, Rood Kmbl. 221; Kr. 112: Salm. Kmbl. 117; Sal. 58. Ða ic nyste hī frunon me *quæ ignōrābam interrŏgābant me*, Ps. Spl. C. 34, 13: Ps. Th. 136, 3. Mid ðȳ hine frunnon his geferan, for hwon he ðis dyde *cum interrŏgārētur a suis, quāre hoc făcĕret*, Bd. 4, 3; S. 569, 16. Ne frin ðū æfter sǣlum *ask thou not after happiness*, Beo. Th. 2648; B. 1322. Frine me *interrŏga me*, Ps. Th. 138, 20. Ðæt heó hī frune hwæt hī sōhton *that she asked them what they sought*, Bd. 3, 8; S. 531, 39: Nar. 28, 22. DER. be-frinan, ge-. v. frignan.

frīnd *friends*, Bt. 20; Fox 72, 20, = frȳnd; *pl. of* freónd.

frió; *adj. Free;* līber:—Frióra ǣghwilc fundie to ðæm ēcum gōde *let every one of the free aspire to the eternal good*, Bt. Met. Fox 21, 3; Met. 21, 2. He gesceóp twā gesceádwīsan gesceafta frió *he created two rational creatures free*, Bt. 41, 2; Fox 244, 30. v. freó.

frió-dōm, es; *m. Freedom, liberty;* lībertas:—Sēce him hræðe fulne frió-dōm *let him quickly seek for himself full freedom*, Bt. Met. Fox 21, 15; Met. 21, 8. v. freó-dōm.

frioh; *adj. Free;* līber:—Beó he frioh *he shall be free*, L. Alf. 11; Th. i. 46, 3: L. In. 3; Th. i. 104, 3. v. freó.

frió-lēta *a freedman*, Som. Ben. Lye. v. freó-lǣta.

friólīce *freely*, Bt. 18, 4; Fox 68, 14, note 4. v. freólīce.

friólsend, friólsiend, es; *m. A deliverer, redeemer;* lĭbĕrātor:—Drihten, friólsend mīn *Dŏmĭnus, lībĕrātor meus*, Ps. Spl. T. 17, 1, 49. Friólsiend mīn *lībĕrātor meus*, Ps. Spl. T. 69, 7. v. freóls.

friónd, es; *m. A friend;* amīcus:—Hine his mǣgum gebodie and his frióndum *let notice of him be given to his kinsmen and to his friends*, L. Alf. pol. 42; Th. i. 90, 9. v. freónd.

frioðo; *indecl. f. Peace, pardon;* pax, vĕnia:—He feóll to foldan, frioðo wilnode *he fell to the earth, implored pardon*, Andr. Recd. 1839; An. 920. v. freoðo.

frioðo-wǣr, frioðu-wǣr, e; *f. A covenant of peace;* pācis fœdus:—Hie getrūwedon fæste frioðuwǣre *they confirmed a firm covenant of peace*, Beo. Th. 2196; B. 1096. v. freoðo-wǣr, friðo-wǣr.

frioðo-waru, e; *f. Protection;* tutela:—He frioðo-wære bæd hlāford sīnne *he prayed his lord for protection*, Beo. Th. 4554; B. 2282. [Cf. *O. Sax.* friðu-wara.]

Frisan; *pl. m. Frisians;* Frīsii:—Ðǣr wǣron Frisan mid *there were Frisians with them*, Chr. 885; Th. 154, 24, col. 1. v. Frysa.

frisca, an; *m. A bittern;* būtio, Som. Ben. Lye.

frist-mearc, e; *f.* [frist = first, fyrst *a space of time*] *An interval of time, intermission, respite;* intercăpēdo:—Fristmearc *intercăpēdo*, Glos. Epnl. Recd. 158, 19. v. fyrst-mearc.

friteþ, fritt *eats*, Salm. Kmbl. 596; Sal. 297: Ps. Spl. T. 48, 14; *3rd pers. pres. of* fretan.

FRIÞ, fryþ, es; *m. n. Peace, freedom from molestation, security guaranteed by law to those under special protection*, e. g. that of the Church, v. cyric-friþ. See Stubbs' Const. Hist. i. 180:—*It seems to have been used for the king's peace or protection in general, and to be the right of all within the pale of the law* [cf. *Icel.* fyrirgöra fé ok friði = *to be outlawed*]: *agreement, truce, league;* pax, tūtēla, refūgium:—Ðæt ðū wille niman friþ æt us: we willaþ eów friþes healdan *that thou wilt accept peace from us: we will keep peace with you*, Byrht. Th. 132, 56–65; By. 37–41. Ðis friþ, *n. this protection*, L. Alf. pol. 5; Th. i. 64, 9. Ðis is ðæt friþ, ðæt Ælfrēd cyning [cynincg MS.] and Gūþrūm [Gyþrum MS.] cyning gecweden habbaþ *this is the peace, that king Alfred and king Guthrum have agreed upon*, L. A. G; Th. i. 152, 2: L. Ath. v. § 8, 9; Th. i. 238, 24. He nam friþ wið ðæt folc *he made peace with the people*, Ors. 5, 2; Bos. 102, 41. Friþes bōt *a compensation or offering of peace, peace-offering, amends for a breach of the peace*, L. Edg. S. 14; Th. i. 278, 2: L. Eth. i. prm; Th. i. 280, 4: L. Eth. v. 26; Th. i. 310, 22: L. C. S. 8; Th. i. 380, 12, 13. Drihten is mīn friþ *Dŏmĭnus est refŭgium meum*, Ps. Th. 143, 2. Ðonne nam mon friþ and griþ wið hī, and nā-ðe-læs for eallum ðissum griþe and gafole, hī ferdon ǣghweder and heregodon ūre earme folc *then they* [*Saxons*] *made truce and peace with them* [*Danes*], *nevertheless for all this peace and tribute, they went everywhere, and harried our miserable people*, Chr. 1011; Th. 266, 14–18, col. 1. Gif we aslaciaþ ðæs friþes *if we get neglectful of the peace*, L. Ath. v. § 8, 9; Th. i. 238, 21. To þearfe and to friþe *for the need and peace*, L. Edg. S. 2; Th. i. 272, 26. To gebeorge and to friþe eallum leódscipe *for security and peace to all the people*, L. Edg. S. 12; Th. i. 276, 21. Eallum folce to friþe *to the peace for all the people*, L. Edg. S. 15; Th. i. 278, 7. [*Piers P.* fryth *an inclosed wood*: *Laym.* frið *concord, amity*: *Orm.* friþþ *love, concord*: *Plat.* frede, free, *m*: *O. Sax.* friðu, *m*: *Frs.* freede, freed: *O. Frs.* fretho, frede, ferd, *m*: *Dut.* vrede, *m*: *Ger.* friede, *m*: *M. H. Ger.* vride, *m*: *O. H. Ger.* fridu, frido, *m*; frida, *f*: *Dan.* fred, *m. f*: *Swed.* frid, fred, *m*: *Icel.* friðr, *m.*] DER. cyric-friþ, un-, woruld-. For the difference in the meanings of friþ, *m. n*; friðo, friðu, *f*; griþ, *n*; and sib, *f*, v. griþ and sib.

frīþ; *adj. Stately, beautiful;* splendĭdus, pulcher:—Seó frīþe mǣg *the stately woman*, Exon. 103 a; Th. 391, 22; Rä. 10, 9. [*Icel.* fríðr *fair, beautiful, handsome.*]

friþ-āþ, es; *m. A peace-oath;* pācis jūrāmentum, Lye.

friþ-bēna, an; *m.* [bēna *a petitioner*] *A peace-petitioner, refugee;* pācis supplex:—Būtan hit friþbēna sȳ *unless it be a peace-petitioner*, L. Eth. v. 29; Th. i. 312, 1. Būtan friþbēnan sindan *unless they are peace-petitioners*, vi. 36; Th. i. 324, 15.

friþ-borh; *gen.* -borges; *m. A peace* or *frank-pledge, peace-surety;* pācis fidejussio, L. Ed. C. 20; Th. i. 450, 24, 29; 451, 2, 4, 7: 21; Th. i. 451, 19, 20: 28; Th. i. 454, 18, 22. v. Stubbs' Const. Hist. i. 87.

friþ-bræc, -brec, e; *f. A peace-breaking, breach of the peace;* pācis violātio:—Gyf binnan byrig gedōn biþ seó friþbræc *if the breach of the peace be committed within a city*, L. Eth. ii. 6; Th. i. 286, 30. Is ðæt friþbrec *that is a breach of the peace*, ii. 5; Th. i. 286, 26.

friþ-burh, freoðo-burh; *gen.* -burge; *dat.* -byrig; *f. A town with which one is at peace, one included in the* 'friþ' *or peace made between two parties;* pācis urbs:—Ðēh hit [the ship] gedriuen beō and hit ætfleō to hwilcre friþbyrig and ða menn ūtætberstan into ðære byrig ðonne habban ða men friþ *though it be driven and it escape to any town with which* 'friþ' *has been made, and the men get away into the town, then let the men have protection*, L. Eth. ii. 2; Th. i. 286, 1. v. Schmid, 204, note.

friþ-candel, e; *f. A peace-candle, the sun;* pācis lucerna, sol:—Folca friþcandel furðum eóde *the peace-candle* [*sun*] *of nations had just mounted*, Cd. 118; Th. 153, 15; Gen. 2539. DER. candel.

friþ-dōm, es; *m. Liberty, freedom;* lībertas, Som. Ben. Lye.

friþe-leás; *adj. Peaceless;* sĭne pāce:—Hǣðene feóllon friðeleáse *the heathen fell without quarter being given them*, Elen. Kmbl. 253; El. 127. v. friþ-leás.

friþ-geár, es; *n. A year of peace* or *jubilee;* pācis annus, jūbĭlæus annus, Som. Ben. Lye.

friþ-geard, es; *m. An inclosed space, habitation of peace;* septum, pācis domĭcĭlium:—Gif friþgeard sī on hwæs lande, abūton stān, oððe treów, oððe wille, oððe swilces ǣnige fleard *if there be an inclosed space on any one's land, about a stone, or a tree, or a well, or any trifles of such kind*, L. N. P. L. 54; Th. ii. 298, 16. Friþgeardum in *in the courts of* *peace* [*in heaven*], Exon. 13 b; Th. 25, 12; Cri. 399. v. Th. L. Gl. s. v.

friþ-gedāl, es; *n. A life* or *spirit-separation, death;* a pāce divortium, ŏbĭtus:—He friþgedāl fremman sceolde *he should effect separation from life*, Cd. 56; Th. 69, 27; Gen. 1142. v. ferþ *vita?*

friþ-gegilda, friþ-gegylda, an; *m.* [friþ-gild *a peace-guild*] *A member of a peace-guild;* congildo, sŏdālis, sŏcius:—Ðis is seó gerǽdnis ðe ða biscopas and ða gerēfan ðe to Lundenbyrig hȳraþ gecweden habbaþ on ūrum friþgegyldum, ǽgðer ge eorlisce ge ceorlisce *this is the ordinance that the bishops and reeves which belong to London have agreed on among the members of our peace-guilds, as well earlish as churlish*, L. Ath. v. prm; Th. i. 228, 6-9. v. ge-gilda.

friþ-georn; *adj. Peace-desirous, peaceable;* pācĭfĭcus:—Sibsume oððe friþgeorne *pacĭfĭci*, Mt. Kmbl. Lind. 5, 9.

friþ-gewrit, es; *n. Peace-writing, an article of peace;* pācis scrĭptum, artĭcŭlus pācis *vel* fœdĕris scripto consignāti:—Bēte be ðam ðe ða friþgewritu sæcgan *let him make amends according as the articles of peace say*, L. Ed. 8; Th. i. 164, 8.

friþ-gild, es; *n. A peace-guild, a society for the maintenance of peace and security;* fœderātōrum sodālĭcium. This name was given to certain guilds or clubs established during, or before, the reign of king Athelstan, for the repression of theft, the tracing of stolen cattle, and the indemnification of persons robbed, by means of a common fund raised by subscription of the members [gegildan]. The statutes of these guilds are contained in the JUDICIA CIVITATIS LUNDONIÆ, set forth, under royal authority, by the bishop and reeves of the city [v. Th. L. Gl.]:—Gif ūre hlāford us ǽnigne eácan geþæncean mǽge to ūrum friþgildum *if our lord should suggest to us any addition to our peace-guilds*, L. Ath. v. § 8, 9; Th. i. 238, 17. v. friþ-gegilda.

friþ-gīsel, es; *m. A peace-pledge, peace-hostage;* obses pācis feriendæ causa dătus:—Ðæt man hūru friþgīslas to heom lǽte *that at least peace-hostages be allowed them*, L. O. D. 9; Th. i. 356, 20.

friþ-hūs, es; *n. A house of peace, refuge, an asylum;* pācis dŏmus, āsȳlum:—Friþhūs *vel* generstede *ăsȳlum*, Ælfc. Gl. 110; Som. 79, 28; Wrt. Voc. 59, 2. [Cf. *O. Sax.* friðu-wīh.]

FRIÐIAN, freoðian; *p.* ode; *pp.* od; *v. a.* [friþ *peace*]. I. *to keep the peace*, 'friþ,' *towards, make peace, to protect, defend, keep;* pācĭfĭcāre protĕgĕre, tuēri:—Ðæt man eall friðige, ðæt se cyng friðian wille *that one shall keep the peace towards all that the king will*, L. Ath. i. 20; Th. i. 210, 2. Ælc ðæra landa, ðe ǽnigne friðige ðæra ðe Ængla land hergie *each of those lands which may keep the peace towards, afford protection to, any of those who ravage England*, L. Eth. ii. 1; Th. i. 284, 17. Man scolde friðian wiþ þonne here *peace should be made with the army*, Chr. 1004: Erl. 138, 22. Ðæt hie eall ðæt friðian woldon ðæt se cyng friðian wolde *that they would protect all that the king would protect*, Chr. 921; Erl. 108, 10, 11. Angunnon hergian ða ðe hȳ friðian sceoldan *they began to pillage those whom they ought to have protected*, Ors. 4, 1; Bos. 79, 1. Ne fūl nāwar friðian ne feormian *that they shall not protect nor harbour a guilty one anywhere*, L. Ed. 7; Th. i. 162, 26. Ðæt hī Godes þeówas friðian and griðian *that they shall protect and defend God's servants*, L. E. B. 1; Th. ii. 240, 6. Hit friðaþ and fyrðraþ *it shelters and furthers*, Bt. 34, 10; Fox 148, 29. Ðæt ic friðian sceal *that I shall protect them*, Exon. 105 a; Th. 398, 14; Rä. 17, 7. Ealle Godes gerihta friðige man georne *one shall diligently keep all God's laws*, L. C. E. 14; Th. i. 368, 9, note 8. [*Piers P.* frythed *wooded: O. Sax.* friðon: *O. Frs.* frethia, frithia, ferdia: *Ger.* frieden *tuēri: M. H. Ger.* vriden: *O. H. Ger.* ga-fridōn *pacāre, protĕgĕre: Goth.* friþōn *to make peace: Dan.* frede: *Swed.* freda *to fence in, protect: Icel.* friða *to pacify.*] DER. ge-friðian: ferþ-friðende.

friþ-land, es; *n. A land with which one is at peace, with which* '*friþ' has been made;* pācis terra:—Hī ðone mǽstan hearm dydon ðe ǽfre here innon friþlande dōn sceolde *they did the greatest harm that ever an army could do in a land with which it was at peace*, Chr. 1097; Erl. 234, 22. [*Icel.* friðland *a friendly country*, v. Cle. and Vig. Dict.]

friþ-leás, friþe-leás, freoðo-leás; *adj. Peaceless, not included in a treaty of peace;* pācis expers:—Gif hwā ðæne friþleásan man healde *if any one keep a peaceless man*, L. C. S. 15; Th. i. 384, 5. [*Icel.* friðlauss, *outlawed.*]

friþlīc; *adj. Peaceable, gentle, mild;* pacĭfĭcus, clēmens, mītis:—Gerǽde man friþlīce steóra *let a man decree mild punishments*, L. Eth. vi. 10; Th. i. 318, 2: L. C. S. 2; Th. i. 376, 19.

friþ-līce; *adv. Peaceably, quietly;* pācĭfĭce, quiēte, Som. Ben. Lye.

friþ-mǽl, -māl, es; *n. An article of peace;* pācis pactio:—Ðis synd ða friþmāl and ða fōrword *these are the articles of peace and the agreements*, L. Eth. ii. prm; Th. i. 284, 6.

friþ-man, fryþ-man, -mann, es; *m. One who is under special protection*, 'friþ:'—Ælc ǽgenra friþmanna friþ hæbbe *let each of those who are in our* '*friþ' be unmolested*, L. Eth. ii. 3; Th. i. 286, 5, 7, 13.

friðo; *indecl. f. Peace;* pax:—On friðo Drihtnes *in the Lord's peace*, Cd. 57; Th. 70, 11; Gen. 1151. He benam his feónd friðo *he deprived his foe of peace*, Cd. 4; Th. 4, 21; Gen. 57. v. freoðo.

friðo-sibb *protecting peace.* v. friðu-sibb.

friðo-spēd, e; *f. Peaceful speed* or *prosperity;* pācis cōpia:—He friðospēde bæd [MS. friþo spebæd] gǽste sīnum *he prayed for peaceful prosperity for his soul*, Exon. 114 b; Th. 440, 16; Rä. 60, 3. v. freoðo-spēd.

friðo-tācen, -tācn, es; *n. A peace-sign;* pācis signum:—Abraham sette friðotācn on his selfes sunu *Abraham set a sign of peace on his own son*, Cd. 107; Th. 142, 29; Gen. 2369. [*Icel.* friðar-tákn.]

friðo-wǽr, e; *f. A covenant of peace;* pācis pactum:—Ic manige geseah men ða ðe noldan heora friðowǽre fæste healdan *vīdi non servantes pactum*, Ps. Th. 118, 158. v. freoðo-wǽr.

friðo-webba, an; *m. A peace-weaver, an angel;* pācis tector, angĕlus:—He up lōcade swā him se ār abeád, fǽle friðowebba *he looked up as the messenger commanded him, the faithful weaver of peace*, Elen. Kmbl. 175; El. 88. v. Grm. And. u. El. pp. 143-5.

friþ-scipe, es; *m. A state of peace;* pax:—To friþscipe *for peace*, L. R. S. 1; Th. i. 432, 5.

friþ-sōcn, e; *f. A peace-refuge, an asylum;* asȳlum:—Ðæt he friþsōcne gesēce *that he may seek a refuge of peace*, L. Eth. ix. 1; Th. i. 340, 8: L. C. E. 2; Th. i. 358, 25.

friþ-splot, -splott, es; *m?* [splot *a spot*] *A peace-spot* or *place;* pācis lŏcus:—On friþsplottum *in peace-spots*, L. Edg. C. 16; Th. ii. 248, 5.

friþ-stōl, fryþ-stōl, es; *m. A peace-stool* or *seat, peace-place, asylum, sanctuary, refuge;* pācis sēdes *vel* lŏcus, asȳlum, refŭgium:—Se here com to his friþstōle [fryþstōle, Th. 256, 18, col. 2; 257, 18, col. 1] *the army came to its secure quarters*, Chr. 1006; Th. 256, 18, col. 1. Gif forworht man friþstōl gesēce *if a man who has forfeited his life seek a sanctuary*, L. Eth. vii. 16; Th. i. 332, 16. Ðū eart friþstōl us, Drihten *Dŏmĭne, refŭgium factus es nōbis*, Ps. Th. 89, 1: 90, 9. Me is geworden Drihten to friþstōle *factus est mihi Dŏmĭnus in refŭgium*, 93, 21. [*Icel.* friðstóll.]

friþ-stōw, e; *f. A peace-place, refuge, asylum;* pācis lŏcus, refŭgium, asȳlum:—Ðæt is seó ān friþstōw *this is the only refuge*, Bt. 34, 8; Fox 144, 29: Bt. Met. Fox 21, 31; Met. 21, 16. Gif he friþstōwe gesēce *if he seek an asylum*, L. Alf. 13; Th. i. 46, 25. v. Grm. R. A. 886 sqq.

friþ-sum; *adj. Peaceful, peace-making, pacific;* pācĭfĭcus:—Sibsume oððe friþsume *pācĭfĭci*, Mt. Kmbl. Rush. 5, 9. [Cf. *O. Sax.* friðu-samo; *adv. in peace: Icel.* friðsamr: *O. H. Ger.* fridu-samo.] DER. gefryþsum.

friðu-sibb, e; *f. Protecting peace;* tūtēla pācis, tūtēla pacĭfica:—Cwēn, friðusibb folca *the queen, the protecting peace of nations*, Beo. Th. 4038; B. 2017.

fritt *eats, devours*, Ps. Spl. T. 48, 14; *3rd sing. pres. of* fretan.

frocga *a frog*, Ps. Spl. 77, 50. v. frogga.

frocx? *A nightingale;* luscĭnia, luscicia? Cot. 121, Lye.

FRŌD; *def.* se frōda, seó, ðæt frōde; *comp. m.* frōdra, *f. n.* frōdre; *adj.* I. *wise, prudent, sage, skilful;* săpiens, prūdens, sciens, perītus:—Þing sceal gehēgan frōd wið frōdne *the wise shall hold counsel with the wise*, Exon. 89 a; Th. 334, 20; Gn. Ex. 19: Menol. Fox 267; Men. 135: Beo. Th. 3693; B. 1844: Cd. 161; Th. 200, 11; Exod. 355: Elen. Kmbl. 685; El. 343. Se frōda *the sage* [*Isaiah*], Exon. 12 b; Th. 20, 32; Cri. 326. Heó hēht gefetigean frōdne on ferhþe *she commanded* [*them*] *to fetch the prudent in mind*, Elen. Kmbl. 2325; El. 1164. Gemyne frōde fæder lāre *remember* [*thy*] *father's wise lore*, Exon. 81 a; Th. 305, 26; Fä. 94. Þurh frōd gewit *through wise mind*, Exon. 25 a; Th. 72, 26; Cri. 1178. Frōdra and gōdra gumena *of wise and good men*, Elen. Kmbl. 1270; El. 637. Frōde men *prudent men*, Salm. Kmbl. 849; Sal. 424. Frige mec frōdum wordum *question me in prudent words*, Exon. 88 b; Th. 333, 8; Gn. Ex. 1. Hȳ beóþ ferþe ðȳ frōdran *they will be the wiser in mind*, 107 a; Th. 408, 32; Rä. 27, 21. II. as wisdom and experience belong to old age, hence,—*Advanced in years, aged, old, ancient;* ætāte provectus, sĕnex, vĕtus, priscus:—Wintrum frōd *advanced in years*, Cd. 107; Th. 141, 31; Gen. 2353: Exon. 58 a; Th. 208, 11; Ph. 154: Beo. Th. 5243; B. 2625: Andr. Kmbl. 1012; An. 506: Menol. Fox 133; Men. 66: Byrht. Th. 141, 4; By. 317. Frōd cyn *the ancient race*, Cd. 143; Th. 179, 15; Exod. 29. Se frōda Constantīnus *the aged Constantine*, Chr. 937; Th. 204, 18; Æðelst. 37: Beo. Th. 5848; B. 2928. Geárum frōdne, *acc. advanced in years*, Exon. 126 b; Th. 485, 25; Rä. 72, 3. [*Plat.* frod, vrood: *O. Sax.* frōd: *Frs.* froed: *O. Frs.* frod: *Dut.* vroed: *M. H. Ger.* vruot *healthy, brave: O. H. Ger.* fruot, frōt: *Goth.* frōþs *prudent: Icel.* fróðr *learned.*] DER. geómor-frōd, hige-, in-, un-.

frōdian; *p.* ade; *pp.* ad *To be wise* or *prudent;* săpĕre:—[Ic] frōdade [*I*] *was wise*, Exon. 94 b; Th. 353, 53; Reim. 32.

frōfer *comfort, solace, consolation*, Hy. 9, 15; Hy. Grn. ii. 291, 15. v. frōfor.

frōfer-bōc, e; *f. A consolation-book;* consōlātiōnis lĭber:—Seó æftre frōferbōc Boētiuses *the second consolation-book of Boëthius*, Bt. 21; Fox 76, 2.

frōfer-gāst, es; *m. The consolation-ghost, the Holy Ghost;* consōlātiōnis Spīrĭtus, Paraclētus:—Frōfergāst *paraclētus*, Wrt. Voc. 75, 47. v. frōfor-gāst.

frōferian, frōfrian; *p.* ode; *pp.* od *To comfort;* consōlāri, Grm. Gr.

ii. 137, 11: Som. Ben. Lye. Ðæt wíf nalde froefra *Rachel noluit consolari*, Mt. Kmbl. Lind. 2, 18. v. frēfrian, frēfran.

fróferni s, se; *f. Consolation;* consōlātio:—Gie babbaþ froefernise, *habetis consolationem*, Lk. Skt. Lind. 6, 24.

FRŌFOR, frōfer, frōfur; *gen.* frōfre; *f:* v. II; but frōfor and frōfer are sometimes *m.* I. *comfort, solace, consolation, help, benefit, profit, refuge;* sōlāmen, sōlātium, consōlātio, auxilium, refūgium:—Sió frōfor *the comfort*, Bt. Met. Fox 21, 32; Met. 21, 16. Wæs frōfor cumen *comfort was come*, Cd. 72; Th. 89, 4; Gen. 1475. Frōfor eft gelamp sārigmōdum *comfort afterwards came to the sad in mind*, Beo. Th. 5875; B. 2941. Sārge gē ne sōhton, ne him swǽslīc word frōfre gē sprǽcon *the sorrowful ye sought not, nor a kindly word spoke ye to them*, Exon. 30 a; Th. 92, 21; Cri. 1512. In me frōfre gǽst ge-eardode *in me the Spirit of comfort hath dwelt*, 10 b; Th. 13, 24; Cri. 207. Folce to frōfre *for comfort to the people*, Beo. Th. 27; B. 14: Menol. Fox 115; Men. 57. Hȳ symle frōfre đǽr fundon *they ever found comfort there*, Exon. 45 b; Th. 155, 15; Gū. 860: Andr. Kmbl. 190; An. 95. Him Dryhten forgeaf frōfor and fultum *to them the Lord gave comfort and succour*, Beo. Th. 1400; B. 698. Frōfra đīne *consōlātiōnes tuæ*, Ps. Spl. 93, 19. Đīne frōfre, Ps. Th. 93, 18. Frōfra Fæder *the Father of consolations*, Hy. 9, 8; Hy. Grn. ii. 291, 8. Hie fuhton đē æfter frōfre *they fought for help to thee*, Cd. 98; Th. 130, 3; Gen. 2154. Frōfor mīn *refūgium meum*, Ps. Spl. 17, 1: 30, 4: 58, 19. II. the following examples are *m:*—Frōfres ic đē bidde *I ask thee for comfort*, Hy. 6, 1; Hy. Grn. ii. 286, 1. He geandbīdode đone frōfer *he awaited the comfort*, Homl. Th. i. 136, 2. Nū behōfige gē đæs đe swīđor đæs bōclīcan frōfres *now need ye so much the more the comfort of books*, ii. 370, 18. Se mann đe biþ dreórig, he behōfaþ sumes frōfres *the man who is sad needs some comfort*, ii. 370, 21. [*Laym.* froure, *dat.* frofre, frouere, froure: *Orm.* frofre, *acc: O. Sax.* frōƀra, frōfra, *f: O. H. Ger.* fluobara, *f.*] DER. hyge-frōfor: frōfer-bōc, -gāst.

frōfor-gāst, frōfer-gāst, es; *m. The Spirit of comfort, the Holy Ghost, Paraclete;* consōlātiōnis Spīrĭtus, Spīrĭtus Sanctus, Paraclētus = Παράκλητος:—Se Hālga Gāst is gehāten on Grēciscum gereorde Paraclitus, đæt is, Frōforgāst, forđīđe he frēfraþ đa dreórian *the Holy Ghost is called in the Greek tongue* Παράκλητος, *that is Spirit of comfort, because he comforts the sad*, Homl. Th. i. 322, 21.

frōfre gāst, es; *m. The Spirit of consolation, the Holy Ghost, Paraclete;* consōlātiōnis Spīrĭtus, Paraclētus:—Se Hālga Frōfre Gāst *Paraclētus Spīrĭtus Sanctus*, Jn. Bos. 14, 26. v. frōfor-gāst.

frōfrung, e; *f. Comfort, consolation;* consōlātio, Som. Ben. Lye. v. frēfrung.

frōfur *comfort, consolation:*—Feoh byþ frōfur fira gehwylcum *money is a consolation to every man*, Runic pm. 1; Kmbl. 339, 1; Hick. Thes. i. 135, 1: 4; Kmbl. 340, 8; Hick. Thes. i. 135, 7. v. frōfor.

FROGGA, froga, frocga, an; *m. A* FROG; rāna:—Frogga *rāna*, Ælfc. Gl. 24; Som. 60, 16; Wrt. Voc. 24, 20: 78, 58. He asende on hig froggan [frocgan, Spl.] *mīsit in eos rānam*, Ps. Lamb. 77, 45. Acende eorþe heora ȳcan ođđe froggan [frogan, Spl.] *edīdit terra eōrum rānas*, 104, 30. He afylde eal heora land mid froggum [MS. froggon] *he filled all their land with frogs*, Homl. Th. ii. 192, 20. [*Wyc.* froggis, *pl: Chauc.* frogges, *pl: R. Glouc.* frogge: *Plat.* pogge: *Dut.* vorsch, *m: Ger.* frosch, *m: M. H. Ger.* vrosch, *m: O. H. Ger.* frosc, *m: Dan.* frö *m. f: Swed.* frö, *n: Icel.* froskr, *m.*] v. frox.

froht; *adj. Timid;* Mk. Skt. Lind. 4, 40. v. forht.

frohtian; *p.* ade, *pp.* ad *To fear, to be in danger:*—From frohtendum, *a periclitantibus*, Mt. Kmbl. p. 15, 18. Frohtende *timidi*, Lind. 8, 26. Frohtade *timuit*, Rush. 14, 30. v. forhtian.

FROM, freom; *comp.* fromra; *sup.* fromest, frommast; *adj.* I. FIRM, *strong, stout, bold, strenuous;* fortis, strēnuus:—Ic eom on mōde from *I am firm in mind*, Beo. Th. 5048; B. 2527: Exon. 46 a; Th. 156, 13; Gū. 874. Ic eom forþsīþes from *I am strenuous of departure*, 124 b; Th. 479, 21; Rä. 63, 2: 126 b; Th. 487, 6; Rä. 72, 24. Hȳ Gūþlāc in Godes willan fromne fundon *they found Guthlac firm in God's will*, 37 b; Th. 123, 9; Gū. 320: Ps. C. 50, 22; Ps. Grn. ii. 277, 22. Đæt wǽron frome folctogan *those were bold leaders*, Andr. Kmbl. 15; An. 8: Elen. Kmbl. 521; El. 261: Ps. Th. 103, 5: Bd. 5, 9; S. 622, 25. Wæs Bassa heora lātteów Ēdwines þeng đæs cyninges se fromesta *vēnit illuc dūce Basso, mīlĭte rēgis Æduini fortissĭmo*, 2, 20; S. 521, 42: 3, 18; S. 546, 27, col. 2. Hió biþ frommast and swīđost *she is most strenuous and most strong*, Exon. 128 a; Th. 493, 1; Rä. 81, 23. II. *rich, abundant, excellent;* über, abundans, præstans:—Swilc biþ mǽgburg menigo đīnre, folcbearnum frome *such shall be the family of thy people, abundant in children*, Cd. 100; Th. 132, 16; Gen. 2194. Fromum feohgiftum *with rich money gifts*, Beo. Th. 41; B. 21. Fromra *præstantior*, Cot. 154. [*Orm.* frame *profit: Plat.* fram, fraam *pious: O. Sax.* from *virtuous;* fruma, *f. benefit: Frs.* froem *useful: O. Frs.* fremo, from *beneficial;* froma *benefit: Dut.* vroom *virtuous, religious: Ger.* fromm *pious: M. H. Ger.* vrum, vrom *useful: O. H. Ger.* frum *efficax;* fruma, *f. benefit: Dan. Swed.* from *pious, meek: Icel.* frómi *honest, guileless.*] DER. dǽd-from, hild-, orleg-, sīþ-, un-.

from; *prep. dat. From;* a, ab:—From eásteweardan *from the eastward*, Bt. 18, 1; Fox 60, 31: 16, 4; Fox 58, 11: Exon. 25 a; Th. 73, 20; Cri. 1192: Cd. 161; Th. 201, 26; Exod. 378: Beo. Th. 3274; B. 1635. v. fram.

from; *adv. Forth;* fōras:—From ǽrest cwom *first came forth*, Beo. Th. 5106; B. 2556.

Frōm, e; *f.* FROME, *Somersetshire;* oppĭdi nōmen in agro Somersetensi:—Hēr forþferde Eádrēd cining on Sc̃e Clementes mæssedæg on Frōme *here king Eadred died on St. Clement's mass-day at Frome*, Chr. 955; Erl. 118, 6.

Frōm, e; *f.* FROME; flūvii nōmen in agro Dorsetensi, Som. Ben. Lye. v. Frōm-mūþa.

fromawælta; *pp.* -ed *To roll away:*—Stan fromawælted *lapidem revolutum*, Lk. Skt. Lind. 24, 2.

fromcerran; *p.* de, *pp.* ed *To turn from, avert:*—Fromcerr iorre đīn from us *averte iram tuam a nobis*, Rtl. 172, 35; 168, 17.

fromcumen; *to be rejected, reprobari*, Lk. Skt. Rush. 9, 22.

from-cyme, es; *m. A coming from, a race, progeny;* prōgĕnies:—Fromcyme folde weorþeþ đīne gefylled *the earth shall be filled with thy race*, Cd. 84; Th. 106, 2; Gen. 1765.

from-cyn, -cynn, es; *n.* I. *a from-kin, offspring, progeny, posterity;* prōgĕnies, prōles:—Gif đū wille habban holdne freónd đīnum fromcynne *if thou wilt have a faithful friend to thine offspring*, Cd. 106; Th. 139, 23; Gen. 2314. Đæt đū hyra fromcynn ȳcan wolde *that thou wouldest increase their offspring*, Exon. 53 b; Th. 187, 19; Az. 33. Fyllaþ eówre fromcynne foldan sceátas *fill the regions of the earth with your offspring*, Cd. 75; Th. 92, 25; Gen. 1534: 100; Th. 133, 1; Gen. 2204. II. *the race from which one springs, ancestry, origin;* gĕnus, ŏrīgo:—Frōd wæs mīn fromcynn *my ancestry was ancient*, Exon. 127 b; Th. 490, 16; Rä. 80, 1: Th. 491, 2; Rä. 80, 8. Nis ǽnig đæs horsc, đe đīn fromcyn mǽge, fira bearnum, sweotule geseđan *there is not any so wise, who may manifestly declare thine origin to the children of men*, Exon. 11 a; Th. 15, 26; Cri. 242.

from-doe:—Gisēne wērun swā fromdoe word đās *visa sunt sicut deleramentum verba ista*, Lk. Skt. Rush. 24, 11.

from-faru, e; *f. An excess:*—Fromfarum *excessibus*, Rtl. 17, 15. v. faru.

from-fēran; *p.* de *To go out, from:*—Fromfoerde of ceastre *egrediebatur de civitate*, Mk. Skt. Lind. 11, 9.

from[-gangan], -geonga, -gonga *To go away;* abire, Jn. Skt. Lind. Rush. 6, 67; Mt. Kmbl. Lind. 11, 7.

from-gebūga; *p.* -beāh, bēg *To turn from:*—Fromgebēg *declinavit*, Jn. Skt. Lind. 5, 15.

from-genimma *to take away;* diripere, Mt. Kmbl. Lind. 12, 29.

from-gewītan; *p.* -gewāt, *pl.* -gewiton; *pp.* -gewiten *To go away from, depart from;* discēdĕre:—Gif hit eallunga fromgewite *if it should altogether depart*, Bt. 33, 4; Fox 130, 35. Ne syndon me fromgewitene *they have not departed from me*, Cd. 63; Th. 76, 11; Gen. 1255. v. fram-gewītan.

from-gibēgan; *p.* de *To turn from:*—Fromgibēgde, Jn. Skt. Rush. 5, 13.

from-hweorfan; *p.* -hwearf, *pl.* -hwurfon; *pp.* -hworfen *To turn from, go* or *depart from;* exīre, discēdĕre:—Freá hēt hie fromhweorfan neorxna wange *the Lord bade them depart from paradise*, Cd. 45; Th. 58, 9; Gen. 943: 50; Th. 64, 9; Gen. 1047. Đonne heó hwām fromhweorfende beóþ *when they are departing from any one*, Bt. 7, 2; Fox 18, 16. Nǽfre ic fromhweorfe *I will never depart from* [*you*], Exon. 14 b; Th. 30, 8; Cri. 476.

fromian; *p.* ode, ade; *pp.* od, ad *To profit, avail;* prōdesse, vălēre:—Đætte seó hālwende onsægednes to ēcre alȳsnesse swīþrade and fromade ge līchoman ge sāwle *quia sacrĭfĭcium sălūtāre ad redemptiōnem vălēret et anĭmæ et corpŏris sempĭternam*, Bd. 4, 22; S. 592, 28. v. fremian.

from-lād, e; *f.* [from, lād *a way*] *A going from, departure, retreat;* discessus, ăbĭtus:—Hwelc gromra wearþ feónda fromlād *what the fierce enemies' retreat had been*, Cd. 97; Th. 126, 20; Gen. 2098.

fromlīce, framlīce; *adv. Strongly, stoutly, boldly, strenuously, promptly, speedily;* audācĭter, strēnue, prŏpĕre:—Gāþ fromlīce đæt gē gūþfreán gylp forbēgan *go boldly that ye may bow the warrior's pride!* Andr. Kmbl. 2666; An. 1334: 2366; An. 1184: Judth. 10; Thw. 22, 1; Jud. 41. Ic sceal fromlīce fēđemundum þurh steápne beorg strǽte wyrcan *I shall strenuously work with my feet a road through a steep mountain*, Exon. 104 b; Th. 397, 9; Rä. 16, 17: Cd. 95; Th. 123, 23; Gen. 2050: Bd. 5, 7; S. 620, 41. Fromlīcor *more stoutly*, Exon. 111 a; Th. 425, 34; Rä. 41, 66. Fromlīcast *most promptly*, 66 a; Th. 245, 5; Jul. 40.

from-lōcian; *p.* ode; *pp.* od *To look from* or *away, look back;* respĭcĕre:—Biþ hit swutol đæt he biþ fromlōciende oferswīđed *it is manifest that he will be overcome on looking back*, Past. 51, 9; Hat. MS.

Frōm-mūþa, Frōmūþa, an; *m. The mouth of the river Frome in Dorsetshire, where the Frome discharges itself into Poole Bay;* Fromi ostium in agro Dorsetensi, ŭbi se in sinum illum ad quem *Poole* oppĭdum assīdet, Fromus exŏnĕrat:—Hēr wende se here eft eástweard into Frōmmūþan, and up eódon swā wīde swā hī woldon into Dorsǽton *here* [A. D. 998] *the army again went eastward into the mouth of the Frome, and they went up as far as they would into Dorsetshire*, Chr. 998; Erl. 134, 16. Cnut cyng com to Frōmmūþan, and heregode đā on Dorsǽtum, and on Wiltūnscīre, and on Sumersǽtum *king Cnut came to the mouth of the Frome, and then ravaged in Dorsetshire, and in Wiltshire, and in Somersetshire*, Chr. 1015; Th. 276, 12. To Frōmūþan, Th. 277, 13.

fromnis, se; *f. Strength, excellence*:—Ic geseah mīne gesǽlinesse and þa fromnisse mīnre iuguđe *ego respiciens felicitatem meam insigni numero juventutis*, Nar. 7, 22. v. from.

fromscipe, -scype, es; *m. Exercise, a proceeding, progress;* exercĭtātio, profectus:—Geunrōtsod ic eom on bigonge ođđe fromscipe mīnum *contristātus sum in exercĭtātiōne mea*, Ps. Spl. C. 54, 2. Wæs for his fromscype onstyred Ǽdon Sceotta cyning *mōtus ĕrat ejus profectĭbus Ædan rex Scottōrum*, Bd. 1, 34; S. 499, 28.

from-sīþ, es; *m. A going from* or *away, departure;* discessus, abĭtus:—Fromsīþ freán *my lord's departure*, Exon. 115 b; Th. 443, 20; Kl. 33.

from-slit[t]nis, se; *f. Desolation;* desolatio, Mk. Skt. Rush. and Lind. 13, 14.

from-swīcan; *p.* -swāc, *pl.* -swicon; *pp.* -swicen *To withdraw, desert;* desciscĕre, desĕrĕre:—Đeáh đe he him fromswice *though he had withdrawn from them*, Cd. 46; Th. 58, 31; Gen. 954. Đa leóde him fromswicon *the nations deserted him*, Cd. 93; Th. 119, 18; Gen. 1981.

fromung, e; *f. Profit, advantage, good;* profectus:—Micel fromung *much good*, Bd. 5, 8; S. 621, 30, note. v. freomung, fremung.

from-weard; *adj. From-ward, turned from* or *away, departing, about to depart;* aversus, abĭtūrus, morĭtūrus:—Ǽlc đara đe đās woruldgesǽlþa hæfþ, he wāt đæt hī [MS. he] him fromwearde beóþ *every one who possesses these worldly goods, knows that they will be departing from him*, Bt. 11, 2; Fox 34, 24. Ādl fǽgum fromweardum feorh ōþ-þringeþ *disease will expel life from the fated, about to depart*, Exon. 82 b; Th. 310, 7; Seef. 71. [*Laym.* from-fram-ward.]

from-weardes; *adv. From-wards, in a direction away from*:—Gif hunta gebīte mannan, sleah þrȳ scearpan neáh fromweardes *if a hunting spider bite a man, strike three scarifications near, in a direction from* [*the bite*], L. M. 1, 68; Lchdm. ii. 142, 19.

from-wendan; *p.* de *To avert*:—Fromwoend *averte*, Rtl. 42, 13.

Fronc-land, -lond, es; *m. Frank-land, the country of the Franks;* Francōrum terra:—On Froncland *into the land of the Franks*, Chr. 920; Erl. 104, 35. On Fronclond, 836; Erl. 64, 32: 880; Erl. 82, 2. v. Franc-land.

frore, es; *m. Frost, ice, icicle;* gĕlu, glăcies, stīria, Wald. 81; Vald. 2, 12. v. hilde-frore. [*O. Nrs.* freri, *pl.* frerar, *m. ice, frozen ground.*]

froren *frozen; pp. of* freósan.

frost, es; *m. Frost, hoar-frost;* gĕlu, pruīna:—On frost *in pruīna*, Ps. Spl. C. T. 77, 52. v. forst.

frostig; *adj. Frosty;* gĕlĭdus, Som. Ben. Lye.

frōuer, e; *f. Comfort;* consōlātio:—On đisum geáre se ārwurþa muneca feder and frōuer, Landfranc arcebisceop, gewāt of đissum līfe *in this year* [A. D. 1089] *the venerable father and comfort of monks, archbishop Lanfranc, departed from this life*, Chr. 1089; Erl. 226, 14. v. frōfor.

frox, es; *m. A frog;* rāna:—To đē and to đīnum folce and in to eallum đīnum þeówum gāþ đa froxas *ad te et ad pŏpŭlum tuum et ad omnes servos tuos intrābunt rānæ*, Ex. 8, 4, 6, 9, 11, 13: Ors. 1, 7; Bos. 29, 25. Ic sende froxas ofer ealle đīne landgemǽro *I will send frogs over all thy borders*, Ex. 8, 2, 5, 8. Đæt flōd awylþ eall froxum *ebulliet flūvius rānas*, 8, 3, 12. v. frogga.

frugnen *asked*, Bt. Met. Fox 22, 104; Met. 22, 52; *pp. of* frignan.

frugnon *interrŏgābant*, Ps. Surt. 34, 11; *p. pl. of* frignan.

frum; *comp.* frumra; *adj. Vigorous, strenuous, prompt, quick, rapid;* strēnuus:—Swift wæs on fōre, fuglum frumra *it was swift in its course, more rapid than birds*, Exon. 113 b; Th. 434, 21; Rä. 52, 4. v. from.

FRUM; *def.* se fruma; *adj. Original, primitive, first;* nātīvus, prīmĭtīvus, prīmus:—Frum, in composition, is used with the preceding meanings:—On đære fruman gecynde *in the original nature*, Bt. 30, 2; Fox 110, 14. Đone fruman sceaft geþencan *to remember the first creation*, Bt. 30, 2; Fox 110, 17, 21. Frūmes *primæ*, Rtl. 35, 13. Æt fruman *at first* [cf. æt ǽrestan], H. R. 103, 34. [*Laym.* frum *first*: *Goth.* fruma *the first*: *Icel.* frum- *the first*: *Lat.* prīmus *the first.*]

FRUMA, an; *m.* [frum *primitive, first*]. I. *a beginning, commencement, origin;* princĭpium, inĭtium, ŏrīgo, prīmordium, exordium:—Hī sendon ǽrendgewrit, wæs se fruma đus awriten *mittunt epistŏlam, cūjus hoc princĭpium est*, Bd. 1, 13; S. 481, 41: 4, 17; S. 585, 17: Ps. Spl. 118, 160: Cd. 1; Th. 1, 10; Gen. 5: Exon. 44 b; Th. 151, 15; Gū. 795: Beo. Th. 4608; B. 2309. Đū eart ealra þinga fruma and ende *thou* [*God*] *art the beginning and end of all things*, Bt. 33, 4; Fox 132, 36: Bt. Met. Fox 20, 549; Met. 20, 275: Andr. Recd. 1116; An. 556. On fruman wæs word *in princĭpio ĕrat verbum*, Jn. Bos. 1, 1: 6, 64: Mt. Bos. 19, 4: Bd. 1, 1; S. 474, 5: 1, 27; S. 489, 13: 4, 17: S. 586, 12: Ps. Spl. C. 73, 2: 76, 11: 101, 26: Boutr. Scrd. 17, 14: Cd. 174; Th. 218, 7; Dan. 35: Exon. 69 b; Th. 258, 33; Jul. 274; Bt. Met. Fox 17, 25; Met. 17, 13. Fram fruman gesceafte *ab inĭtio creātūræ*, Mk. Bos. 10, 6: Chr. 655; Erl. 28, 2: Bt. 33, 4; Fox 128, 7: Exon. 25 a; Th. 73, 20; Cri. 1192: Elen. Kmbl. 2282; El. 1142: Andr. Kmbl. 2969; An. 1487: Ps. Th. 92, 3: 98, 4. Song he be fruman moncynnes *cănēbat de orīgine hūmāni gĕnĕris*, Bd. 4, 24; S. 598, 10: 1, 15; S. 483, 21. Ealle men hæfdon gelīcne fruman *all men had a like beginning*, Bt. 30, 2; Fox 110, 8: Cd. 64; Th. 77, 19; Gen. 1277. Of đæs strȳnde monigra mǽgþa cyningcynn fruman lǽdde *de cūjus stirpe multārum provinciārum rēgium gĕnus orīgĭnem duxit*, Bd. 1, 15; S. 483, 31. Of đam đa fruman aweallaþ Deorwentan streámes *de quo Deruentiōnis flūvii prīmordia erumpunt*, 4, 29; S. 607, 10. Hie sealdon heora wæstma fruman *they should give their first-fruits*, Blickl. Homl. 41, 5. To đǽm frummum *ad initia* Mt. Kmbl. p. 1, 5. II. *an originator, author, founder, inventor;* auctor, inventor:—God is fruma eallra gesceafta *God is the author of all creatures*, Bt. Met. Fox 29, 161; Met. 29, 81. Sigores fruma *the Lord of triumph*, Exon. 12 a; Th. 19, 2; Cri. 294. Fyrnweorca Fruma *the Author of deeds of old*, 16 a; Th. 36, 20; Cri. 579: Chr. 975; Erl 126, 15; Edg. 41: Elen. Kmbl. 1583; El. 793. Ealre synne fruma *the author of all sin*, Elen. Kmbl. 1540; El. 772: Salm. Kmbl. 887; Sal. 443. Tubal Cain sulhgeweorces fruma wæs *Tubal Cain was inventor of plough-work*, Cd. 52; Th. 66, 20; Gen. 1087. Hie leahtra fruman lārum ne hȳrdon *they obeyed not the doctrines of the author of crimes*, Elen. Kmbl. 1674; El. 839. Đæt đū onsægde synna fruman *that thou shouldest sacrifice to the author of crimes*, Exon. 71 a; Th. 264, 10; Jul. 362. Gif hī [MS. he] ne þiówedon hiora fruman *if they served not their author*, Bt. 39, 13; Fox 234, 31: Exon. 8 b; Th. 3, 31; Cri. 44. III. *a chief, prince, ruler, king;* prŏcer, princeps, rex:—Burgwarena fruma *chief of citizens*, Exon. 86 a; Th. 324, 6; Wīd. 90. Filistina fruma *prince of the Philistines*, Salm. Kmbl. 555, 561; Sal. 277, 280. Herga fruma *ruler of hosts*, Exon. 20 a; Th. 53, 4; Cri. 845. Ealles folces fruma *prince of all people*, 120 a; Th. 461, 2; Hö. 29. Upengla fruma *prince of archangels*, Andr. Kmbl. 451; An. 226. Se fruma David *the king David*, Ps. C. 50, 20; Ps. Grn. ii. 277, 20. Melchisedec com fyrdrinca fruman grētan *Melchizedec came to greet the chief of warriors*, Cd. 97; Th. 127, 1; Gen. 2104: Ps. Th. 112, 7. Hie ahēngon herga Fruman *they hung up the Prince of hosts*, Elen. Kmbl. 419; El. 210. [*Laym.* frume *beginning*: *Goth.* frums, *m. beginning.*] DER. dǽd-fruma, eád-, gūþ-, hild-, land-, leód-, leóht-, līf-, ord-, þiód-, tīr-, wīg-.

frum-bearn, es; *n. A firstborn;* primogĕnĭtus:—Frumbearn Godes *the firstborn of God*, Cd. 223; Th. 294, 13; Sat. 470: Exon. 48 a; Th. 166, 17; Gū. 1044. Frumbearnes riht *the firstborn's right*, Cd. 160; Th. 199, 13; Exod. 338. Ic đone [đonne MS.] frumbearn forþasette *ego primogĕnĭtum pōnam illum*, Ps. Th. 88, 24.

frum-byrd, e; *f. Birth, nativity*:—On mīnre frumbyrde dæiæge *on the day of my birth*, Th. Chart. 369, 9.

frum-byrdling, es; *m. Pūbe tĕnus*, Ælfc. Gl. 88; Som. 74, 70; Wrt. Voc. 50, 50. [Frumberdlinges *youths*, O. E. Homl. 2nd series, p. 41.]

frum-cend, e; *f. Origin*:—Frūmes frūmcende (?) *primæ originis*, Rtl. 35, 13.

frum-cenned, -cend; *def.* se -cenneda; *part.* I. *first-begotten, firstborn;* primogĕnĭtus:—Đæt wæs se frumcenneda *that was the firstborn*, Homl. Th. ii. 194, 9. He ofslōh ǽlc þing frumcendes on lande *percussit omne primogĕnĭtum in terra*, Ps. Lamb. 77, 51: 104, 36. Ic frumcendne gesette hine *ego primogĕnĭtum pōnam illum*, 88, 28. He ofslōh ǽlc frumcenned cyld *percussit omne primogĕnĭtum*, Ps. Spl. 77, 56. Ōþ-đæt heó cende hyre frumcennedan sunu *dōnec pĕpĕrit fīlium suum primogĕnĭtum*, Mt. Bos. 1, 25: Lk. Bos. 2, 7. Đe on đæm lande frumcennede wǽron *who were firstborn in the land*, Ors. 1, 7; Bos. 30, 5. He ætbræd me mīne frumcennedan *primogĕnĭta mea tŭlit*, Gen. 27, 36. Frumcendo *primitiæ*, Rtl. 2, 27. II. in grammar, *primitive;* primĭtīvus:—Sume naman sind *primĭtīva*, đæt sind frumcennede ođđe fyrmyste *some nouns are* primĭtīva, *which are primitive or original*, Ælfc. Gr. 5; Som. 4, 7. Hī synd sume *primĭtīva*, đæt synd frumcennede *some of them* [*pronouns*] *are* primĭtīva, *that is primitive*, 15; Som. 17, 32, 33. Frumcynned *primitivus*, Hpt. Gl. 448.

frum-cneów, es; *n. A first generation;* primĭtīva genĕrātio:—Noe hæfde frumcneów gehwæs, fæder and mōder tuddorteóndra *Noah had the first generation of each of* [*those*] *producing offspring, father and mother*, Cd. 161; Th. 201, 12; Exod. 371. v. cneow II.

frum-cyn, -cynn, es; *n.* I. *original kind, lineage, descent, origin;* prosāpia, ŏrīgo:—Đa đe mǽgburge mǽst gefrunon, frumcyn feora *those who most understood kinship, the lineage of men*, Cd. 161; Th. 200, 23; Exod. 361. Ic eówer sceal frumcyn witan *I must know your origin*, Beo. Th. 509; B. 252. II. *a race, tribe;* gĕnus, gens:—Đæt he ahredde frumcyn fira *that he saved the race of men*,

Exon. 8 a; Th. 3, 12; Cri. 35: Cd. 190; Th. 236, 6; Dan. 317. He slôh frumcynnes heora freán *he slew the princes of their race*, Ps. Th. 104, 31. He geceás Iudan him geswæs frumcynn *elēgit trĭbum Jūda*, 77, 67.

frum-cyrr, es; *m.* [cyrr *a turn, space of time*] *A first turn* or *time*; prīmæ vīces:—Beó his weres scyldig æt frumcyrre *let him be liable in his fine* [*for slaying a man*] *for the first time*, L. Ath. i. 3; Th. i. 200, 21.

frum-gâr, es; *m.* **I**: frum-gâra, an; *m.* **II.** [frum *prīmus*; gâr *a spear.*] **I.** *a chieftain, leader, prince, patriarch*; primĭpīlus, prŏcer, dux, princeps, patriarcha:—Geared se frumgâr wæs his freómâgum leóf *Jared the patriarch was dear to his kindred*, Cd. 59; Th. 72, 7; Gen. 1183. Ne meahte he on ðam frumgâre feorh gehealdan *he could not keep life in the chieftain*, Beo. Th. 5704; B. 2856: Exon. 75 b; Th. 283, 24; Jul. 685. Gesamnedon herigeas folces frumgâras *the leaders of the people collected their bands*, Andr. Kmbl. 2137; An. 1070: Cd. 176; Th. 222, 7; Dan. 101: Judth. 11; Thw. 24, 18; Jud. 195. Of ðām frumgârum folc unrīm awōcon *from those patriarchs innumerable people sprang*, Cd. 124; Th. 158, 8; Gen. 2614. **II.** se frumgâra Malalehel *the patriarch Mahalaleel*, Cd. 58; Th. 71, 11; Gen. 1169. Gif ðū ðam frumgâran brȳde wyrnest *if thou deny to the patriarch his wife*, 126; Th. 161, 3; Gen. 2659. Ða frumgâran hâtene wǣron Abraham and Aaron *the patriarchs were called Abram and Haran*, 82; Th. 102, 31; Gen. 1708. [Cf. *O. H. Germ.* proper name Frumigêr.]

frum-gesceap, es; *n.* [frum *first*; gesceap *creation*] *The first creation*; prīma creātio, princĭpium mundi:—Ðǣr biþ ōþȳwed egsa mâra ðonne from frumgesceape gefrægen wurde *there shall be shown greater terror than had been heard of from the first creation*, Exon. 20 a; Th. 52, 27; Cri. 840.

frum-gifu, e; *f. An original gift, privilege, prerogative*; primāria grātia, prærogātīva:—Frumgifu *vel* synder-wurþmynt *prærogātīva*, Ælfc. Gl. 99; Som. 76, 119; Wrt. Voc. 54, 61. Hpt. Gl. 457. [*Icel.* frum-gjöf *first gift*].

frum-gild, -gyld, es; *n. A first payment* or *compensation,—the first payment* or *instalment of the price* [wer] *at which every man was valued, according to his degree, to be paid to the kindred*, or *guild-brethren, of a slain person, as compensation for his murder*; prīma compensātio:—Gylde man ðæs weres ðæt frumgyld *let the first payment of the valuation be paid*, L. E. G. 12; Th. i. 174, 28: L. Edm. S. 7; Th. i. 250, 21.

frum-gripa, an; *m. A first grasper, occupier*; prīmus captor, occŭpātor, Wulfst. par 4: Mann. Lye.

frum-heowung, e; *f. First formation* or *creation*; protoplasma, prīma formātio, Cot. 154.

frum-hrægl, es; *n. A first garment*; prīmus vestītus:—Hêt heora sceome þeccan Freá frumhrægle *the Lord bade them conceal their nakedness with the first garment*, Cd. 45; Th. 58, 8; Gen. 943.

frum-leóht, es; *n. First light, dawn*; prīma lux, aurōra:—To ðē ic wacige of frumleóhte *ad te de lūce vĭgĭlo*, Wanl. Catal. 47, 41.

frum-líc; *adj. Original*, Hpt. Gl. 433. v. frymlíc.

frum-lyhtan; *p.* -lȳhte *to dawn*:—Siððan hit frumlȳhte *after it had dawned*, Blickl. Homl. 207, 35.

frum-meolc, -meoluc, e; *f. The first milk, nectar*; prīmum lac, nectar, Som. Ben. Lye.

frum-rǣd, es; *m. The first* or *primary ordinance*; prīmum consĭlium:—Ðæra biscopa frumrǣd *the primary ordinance of bishops*, L. Eth. vi. 1; Th. i. 314, 4.

frum-rǣden, e; *f. An original, previous ordinance, condition*:—Ðā wæs first agân frumrǣdenne *then was expired the space of time previously fixed*, Andr. Kmbl. 294; An. 147.

frum-rīpa, an; *m.* [rīpa *a handful of corn*] *First-fruits*; prīmĭtiæ:—Ðīne teóðan sceattas, and ðīne frumrīpan gongendes and weaxendes, agyf ðū Gode *thy tithes, and thy first-fruits of moving and growing things, render thou to God*, L. Alf. 38; Th. i. 52, 31.

frum-sceaft, e; *f.* **I.** *the first creation, the creation, beginning, origin, original state* or *condition*; prīma creātio, ŏrīgo, prīmĭtīva *vel* pristīna condĭtio:—Sing me frumsceaft *canta princĭpium creatūrārum*, Bd. 4, 24; S. 597, 16. Moyses awrât ǣrest be frumsceafte *Moses wrote first of the creation*, Homl. Th. ii. 198, 15. Frumsceaft *genesis*, Jn. Skt. p. 1, 12. Gē māgon hwæt-hwego ongitan be eówrum frumsceafte, ðæt is God *ye can in some measure understand concerning your origin, that is God*, Bt. 26, 1; Fox 90, 4. Æt frumsceafte *at the beginning*, Exon. 99 a; Th. 371, 21; Seel. 79: Beo. Th. 89; B. 45: Andr. Kmbl. 1593; An. 798. He cūðe frumsceaft fira feorran reccan *he could relate the origin of men from* [*times*] *remote*, Beo. Th. 182; B. 91. Fȳr clymmaþ on gecyndo, cunnaþ hwænne mōte on his frumsceaft, eft to his ēþle *fire climbeth in its nature, strives when it can towards its origin, back to its home*, Salm. Kmbl. 831; Sal. 415. He forlǣt ǣrest līfes frumsceaft *he first forsakes his original state of life*, Bt. Met. Fox 17, 48; Met. 17, 24. **II.** *a created being, creature*; creātūra:—Hī hēredon līfes Âgend, Fæder frumsceafta *they praised the Lord of life, the Father of all created beings*, Exon. 14 b; Th. 29, 33; Cri. 472: 84 a; Th. 317, 15; Mōd. 66: Cd. 156; Th. 195, 9; Exod. 274.

frum-sceapen; *part. First formed* or *created*; prīmus formātus *vel* creātus:—Ðā ðā he geworhte Adam, ðone frumsceapenan mann *when he wrought Adam, the first created man*, Hexam. 14; Norm. 22, 14.

frum-sceat, -sceatt, es; *m.* [sceat *money, gain*] *First-fruits*; prīmĭtiæ:—He ofslōh frumsceateas ealles geswinces heora on geteldum Chames *percussit prīmĭtias omnis lăbōris eōrum in tăbernăcŭlis Cham*, Ps. Spl. 77, 56. He slōh frumsceattas oððe frumwæstmas ealles geswinces heora *percussit prīmĭtias omnis lăbōris eōrum*, Ps. Lamb. 104, 36.

frum-scepend-sceppend, es; *m. An author, originator, creator*:—Frumscepend *auctor*, Rtl. 16, 19; 123, 10.

frum-scyld, e; *f. Original sin*; princĭpālis *vel* căpĭtālis culpa:—Frumscylda gehwæs fæder and mōdor *father and mother of every original sin*, Salm. Kmbl. 891; Sal. 445.

frum-setnes, se; *f. Authority*; auctoritas, Rtl. 123, 15.

frum-setnung, e; *f. Original formation*:—Middengeordes frumsetnung *constitutio mundi*, Jn. Skt. Rush. 17, 24.

frum-slǣp, e; *f. First sleep*; prīmus somnus:—On frumslǣpe *in the first sleep*, Ors. 2, 8; Bos. 51, 9: Cd. 177; Th. 222, 22; Dan. 108.

frum-spræc, e; *f. An original speech, a promise, covenant*; prædictum, promissum:—Fyl nū frumspræce *fulfil now thy promise*, Cd. 190; Th. 236, 24; Dan. 326: Exon. 53 b; Th. 188, 7; Az. 42.

frum-staðol, es; *m. An original station*; prīmĭtīva sēdes:—Ic mīnum gewunade frumstaðole fæst *I dwelt fast in my original station*, Exon. 122 b; Th. 471, 18; Rä. 61, 3.

frum-stemn, es; *m. The fore-part of a ship, prow*; prōra, Glos. Brux. Recd. 37, 41; Wrt. Voc. 63, 55.

frum-stōl, es; *m. An original seat, mansion-house, a proper residence* or *station*; sēdes princĭpālis:—Se frumstōl, ðe hie of adrifen wurdon *the original seat* [*paradise*] *from which they were driven*, Cd. 46; Th. 59, 14; Gen. 963. Habbaþ ða feówer frumstōl hiora, ǣghwilc hiora âgenne stede *the four* [*elements*] *have their proper station, each of them its own place*, Bt. Met. Fox 20, 126; Met. 20, 63. Ðæs fȳres frumstōl *the fire's proper station*, 20, 250; Met. 20, 125. Healden ða mǣgas ðone frumstōl *let the kindred hold the paternal mansion*, L. In. 38; Th. i. 126, 6. [v. note in Schmid.] In ðam frumstōle, ðe him Freá sette *in the first seat, which the Lord placed for them*, Exon. 93 a; Th. 349, 24; Sch. 51.

frum-talu, e; *f.* [talu *a tale, story*] *First words of witnesses, first accusation*; prīma testium dicta, prīma delāta:—We willaþ ðæt frumtalu fæste stande *we will that first words of witnesses stand fast*, L. N. P. L. 67; Th. ii. 302, 6.

frumþ, es; *m*: e; *f. A beginning*; princĭpium:—Ic frumþa God fōresceáwode *I saw the eternal God* [lit. *God of beginnings*] *face to face*, Elen. Kmbl. 689; El. 345. v. frymþ.

frum-tīhtle, -tȳhtle, an; *f.* [frum *original, primitive, first*; tīhtle *an accusation, charge*] *A first accusation, first charge*; prīma accūsātio, prīma calumnĭa:—Ðæt he borh næbbe æt frumtȳhtlan *that he have no surety at the first accusation*, L. C. S. 35; Th. i. 396, 24.

frum-wæstm, es; *m*: e; *f.* [wæstm *fruit*] *First-fruits*; prīmĭtiæ:—Frumwæstmas *prīmĭtiæ*, Ælfc. Gr. 13; Som. 16, 17. Heora frumwæstme fulle syndon *promptuāria eōrum plēna*, Ps. Th. 143, 16. He ofslōh frumwæstmas [-wæstme, Th.] ealles geswinca heora *percussit prīmĭtias omnis lăbōris eōrum*, Ps. Lamb. 77, 51: 104, 36.

frum-weorc, es; *n. An ancient work, the work of the creation*; ŏpus priscum, res in princĭpio creāta:—Woldon hie ædre gecȳðan frumweorca fæder *they would at once proclaim the father of creation's works*, Andr. Kmbl. 1607; An. 805.

frum-wyrhta, an; *m. An author, creator*; auctor:—Léhtes frumwyrhte *lucis auctor*, Rtl. 37, 7.

frum-yldo, e; *f. The first age*; prīma ætas:—Frumyldo *prīmævus?* Cot. 3: Som. Ben. Lye.

frune *asked*, Bd. 3, 8; S. 531, 39; *p. s. subj. of* frinan: frunon, frunnon *asked*, Ps. Th. 136, 3: Bd. 4, 3; S. 569, 16; *p. pl. of* frinan.

fruron *froze*; *p. pl. of* freósan.

frȳ; *adj. Free*; līber:—Betwyx deádum frȳ *inter mortuos līber*, Ps. Lamb. 87, 6. Gif hwylc swīðe rīce cyning næfde nǣnne frȳne mon on eallon his rīce *if some very powerful king had not any free man in all his realm*, Bt. 41, 2; Fox 244, 25. v. freó.

fryccea, an; *m. A crier, preacher, herald*; præco:—Se dumba fryccea *the dumb herald*, Past. 15, 3; Hat. MS. 19 a, 28. v. fricca.

frȳ-dōm, es; *m. Freedom, liberty*; lībertas:—Se frȳdōm *the freedom*, Bt. 41, 2; Fox 246, 4. Ða men habbaþ simle frȳdōm *men have always freedom*, 40, 7; Fox 242, 25, 27, 28: 41, 2; Fox 244, 16, 21. v. freó-dōm.

frȳ-gyld, es; *n. A free guild* or *society*; lībĕrum sodālĭtium *vel* collēgium, Som. Ben. Lye. v. friþ-gild.

fryhtendo; *pres. part. Trementes*, Rtl. 122, 16. v. fyrhtian.

fryhtu, e; *f. Fright, terror*, Rtl. 59, 19. v. fyrhtu.

frymdi; *adj. Inquisitive, asking, desirous, suppliant*; inquīsītīvus, requīrens, desīdĕrans, supplex:—Ic eom frymdi to ðē *I am suppliant to thee*, Byrht. Th. 137, 1; By. 179 v. frimdig.

frymetling, e; *f.* [frum *original, first, primitive*] *A youngling, young* *cow; jŭvenca*:—Cūhyrde gebȳreþ ðæt he hæbbe ealdre cū meolc, vii niht syððan heó nige cealfod hæfþ, and frymetlinge bȳstinge xiv niht *it belongs to a cowherd that he have the milk of an old cow, seven nights after she has newly calved, and the biestings of a young cow fourteen nights*, L. R. S. 13; Th. i. 438, 19.

frymlíc; *adj.* [frym = frum *first*] *Primitive, first*; prīmĭtīvus:—Ongunnon hī ðæt apostolíce līf ðære frymlīcan cyricean onhȳrigean *cœpĕrunt apostŏlĭcam prīmĭtīvæ ecclēsiæ vītam imĭtāri*, Bd. 1, 26; Whelc. 78, 22. v. frymþelíc.

frymþ, e; *f. A harbouring, an entertainment*; susceptio, receptio:—Ælc mon mōt onsacan frymþe *every man may deny entertainment*, L. In. 46; Th. i. 132, 1. v. fyrmþ.

frymþ, frumþ, es; *m*: e; *f.* [frum *original, first*] *A beginning, foundation, origin, first-fruits*; inĭtium, princĭpium, constĭtūtio, ŏrīgo, prīmĭtiæ:—Næs his frymþ ǣfre *his origin never was*, Exon. 65 a; Th. 240, 12; Ph. 637. Ic sprece fōresetnyssa fram frymþe *lŏquar prŏpŏsĭtiōnes ab inĭtio*, Ps. Lamb. 77, 2: Ps. Spl. 101, 26: Mt. Bos. 19, 8: Lk. Bos. 1, 2. Sceal seó wyrd swā ðeáh forþsteallian, swā ic ðē æt frymþe gehēt *that event shall yet come to pass, as I promised thee at the beginning*, Cd. 109; Th. 144, 16; Gen. 2390: 6; Th. 8, 30; Gen. 132: 174; Th. 218, 6; Dan. 35: Bt. Met. Fox 11, 75; Met. 11, 38: 13, 25; Met. 13, 13: Ps. Th. 70, 4: 104, 24. Of middangeardes frymþe *a constĭtūtiōne mundi*, Mt. Bos. 25, 34: Bd. de nat. rerum; Wrt. popl. science 13, 29; Lchdm. iii. 264, 10. Heó of ðære ylcan mǣgþe Eást-Engla līchoman frymþe lǣdde *de provincia eōrumdem Orientālium Anglōrum ipsa carnis orīgĭnem duxĕrat*, Bd. 4, 19; S. 590, 8. Frymþas *prīmĭtiæ*, Scint. Lye. Gefreoða ūsic, frymþa Scyppend *protect us, Creator of beginnings!* Exon. 65 a; Th. 239, 32; Ph. 630: 44 b; Th. 151, 9; Gū. 792: Elen. Kmbl. 1002; El. 502. [*Orm.* frummþe.]

frymþelíc; *adj.* [frymþ *a beginning*] *Primitive, first*; prīmĭtīvus:—Ongunnon hī ðæt apostolíce līf ðære frymþelīcan cyricean onhȳrigean *cœpĕrunt apostŏlĭcam prīmĭtīvæ ecclēsiæ vītam imĭtāri*, Bd. 1, 26; S. 487, 32: 4, 23; S. 593, 41. On frymþelīcum synne *originali peccato*, Rtl. 101, 20. Of ðam frymþlīcan *from the original*, Blickl. Homl. 107, 5.

frymþ-yldo, e; *f. An early, original age*, Hpt. Gl. 462. Cf. frumyldo.

frȳnd *friends*, Jn. Bos. 15, 14: Lk. Bos. 7, 6; *pl. nom. acc. of* freónd.

Frysa, Friesa, an; *pl. nom. acc.* Frysan, Frisan, Fresan; *gen.* Frysena, Frysna; *dat.* Frysum; *m. A Frisian*; Frīsius, Freso:—Se Frysa hine gewrāþ *the Frisian bound him*, Homl. Th. ii. 358, 19, 22: Chr. 897; Th. 176, 32, 33, col. 2; 177, 32, 33. Sealde se ealdorman hine sumum Frysan of Lundene *the alderman sold him to a Frisian of London*, Homl. Th. ii. 358, 18. Be norþan-westan him syndon Frysan *to the north-west of them are the Frisians*, Ors. 1, 1; Bos. 18, 35: Bd. 5, 9; S. 622, 15: Chr. 886; Th. 154, 24, col. 2, 3; 155, 23, col. 1. He com on Frysena land *he came to the land of the Frisians*, Bd. 5, 9; S. 623, 27: 5, 10; S. 623, 35: 5, 11; S. 626, 18, 21: 5, 19; S. 639, 20. Gyf Frysna hwylc ðæs morðorhetes myndgiend wǣre *if any of the Frisians should be a rememberer of this deadly feud*, Beo. Th. 2212; B. 1104. Ic wæs mid Frysum *I was with the Frisians*, Exon. 85 b; Th. 322, 24; Wīd. 68: Beo. Th. 2418; B. 1207: 5816; B. 2912: Bd. 5, 11; S. 625, 42. He ge-eóde ða fyrran Frysan *he had overcome the farther Frisians*, Bd. 5, 10; S. 624, 3.

Frys-cyning *a Frisian king*. v. Fres-cyning.

Frysisc, Fresisc; *adj. Of* or *belonging to Friesland. Frisian*; Frīsĭcus:—Nǣron hie nāðor ne on Frysisc gesceapen ne on Denisc *they were shapen neither as the Frisian nor as the Danish*, Chr. 897; Th. 176, 2, col. 2; 177, 2. Ðǣr wearþ ofslegen Lucuman, and ealra manna, Frysiscra and Engliscra, lxii *there was slain Lucuman, and of all the men, Frisian and English, sixty-two*, 897; Th. 176, 34, col. 2; 177, 34.

Frys-land, Fres-lond, es; *n. Friesland*; Frīsia:—Be westan Eald-Seaxum is Ælfe mūþa ðære eá and Frysland *to the west of the Old Saxons is the mouth of the river Elbe and Friesland*, Ors. 1, 1; Bos. 18, 36. Gewiton him wīgend Frysland geseón *the warriors departed to see Friesland*, Beo. Th. 2277; B. 1126.

frȳst, frȳsþ *freezes*, Ælfc. Gr. 22; Som. 24, 8; *3rd sing. pres. of* freósan.

fryt *eats up, devours, consumes*, Deut. 32, 22; *3rd sing. pres. of* fretan.

fryþ, es; *n. m? Peace*; pax:—Seó lāf [MS. lafe] wið ðone here fryþ nam *the remainder made peace with the army*, Chr. 867; Erl. 73, 16: 1036; Th. 294, 9, col. 2. Ðæt he ne beó nānes fryþes weorðe *that he be not worthy of any peace*, L. Eth. iii. 15; Th. i. 298, 12. v. friþ.

fryþ-gegylda *a member of a peace-guild*, L. Ath. v. prm; Wilk. 65, 5. v. friþ-gegilda.

fryþing *a furthering, furtherance*, L. E. I. 21; Th. ii. 414, 23, = fyrþring. v. fyrþrung.

fryþ-man, -mann. v. friþ-man.

fryðo; *indecl. f. Peace*; pax:—Brūcaþ mid gefeán fryðo *enjoy peace with delight*, Cd. 74; Th. 91, 16; Gen. 1513. v. freoðo.

fryþ-stōl *an asylum, refuge*, Chr. 1006; Th. 256, 18, col. 2; 257, 18, col. 1. v. friþ-stōl.

FUGEL, fugol, fugul; *gen.* fugeles, fugles; *m. A bird*, FOWL; ăvis, āles:—Ðes fugel *hæc ăvis*, Ælfc. Gr. 9, 28; Som. 11, 54: Lk. Bos. 13, 34: Cd. 72; Th. 88, 5; Gen. 1460: Exon. 17 a; Th. 40, 27; Cri. 645: Salm. Kmbl. 507; Sal. 254: Judth. 11; Thw. 24, 25; Jud. 207. Fugel *āles*, Ælfc. Gr. 10; Som. 14, 59. Ne wirce gē nāne andlīcnissa ne nānes nȳtenes ne fugeles *make no images of any beast or bird*, Deut. 4, 17. Wæs ðæs fugles flyht dyrne and dēgol *the bird's flight was hidden and secret*, Exon. 17 a; Th. 40, 15; Cri. 639: 57 b; Th. 206, 12; Ph. 125: Salm. Kmbl. 451; Sal. 226. Ic spearuwan swā some gelīce gewearþ, ānlīcum fugele *factus sum sicut passer ūnĭçus*, Ps. Th. 101, 5: Exon. 108 a; Th. 413, 18; Rä. 32, 7. Fugle gelīcost *most like to a bird*, Beo. Th. 442; B. 218. Ðone fugel hātaþ Filistina fruman uasa mortis *the princes of the Philistines call the bird* vāsa mortis, Salm. Kmbl. 559; Sal. 279: Exon. 17 a; Th. 40, 10; Cri. 636. Fugelas ǣton of ðam *ăves comĕdĕrunt ex eo*, Gen. 40, 17, 19: Ps. Spl. 103, 13: Mk. Bos. 4, 4, 32: Lk. Bos. 9, 58: Exon. 61 a; Th. 222, 22; Ph. 352: Fins. Th. 9; Fin. 5: Ps. Th. 77, 27. Heofenan fuglas habbaþ nest *volucres cœli nīdos hăbent*, Mt. Bos. 8, 20: 13, 4: Cd. 200; Th. 248, 2; Dan. 507: Exon. 55 a; Th. 194, 16; Az. 140: Ps. Th. 104, 35. Ðæt hī gehīran ōðerra fugela stemne *that they hear the sounds of other birds*, Bt. 25; Fox 88, 21: Gen. 7, 21. Hēr wæs ðæt micle fugla wæl *in this year* [A. D. 671] *was the great destruction of birds*, Chr. 671; Erl. 34, 33. Ofer fugla cynn *over the race of birds*, Exon. 58 a; Th. 208, 22; Ph. 159: 60 b; Th. 221, 6, 16; Ph. 330, 335. Gif seó offrung biþ of fugelum *si de ăvĭbus oblātio fuĕrit*, Lev. 1, 14: Deut. 28, 26: Ps. Lamb. 78, 2. He spyraþ æfter fuglum *he seeks after birds*, Bt. 39, 1; Fox 210, 29: Exon. 126 b; Th. 487, 16; Rä. 73, 3: Judth. 12; Thw. 25, 37; Jud. 297: Ps. Th. 78, 2. Ða fugelas he ne todǣlde *ăves non divīsit*, Gen. 15, 10: Ps. Spl. 8, 8: 49, 12: 77, 31: Bt. Met. Fox 13, 95; Met. 13, 48. Behealdaþ heofonan fuglas *respĭcĭte volătĭlia cœli*, Mt. Bos. 6, 26: Cd. 65; Th. 78, 26; Gen. 1299. [*Piers P.* fowel: *Chauc.* foule: *Wyc.* foulis *fowls*: *Laym.* foȝel, fuȝel, fowel: *Plat.* vagel, *m*: *O. Sax.* fugal: *Frs.* fugil, foeggel: *O. Frs.* fugel: *Dut. Ger. M. H. Ger.* vogel, *m*: *O. H. Ger.* fogal, fugal, *m*: *Goth.* fugls, *m*: *Dan.* fugl, *m. f*: *Swed.* fågel, *m*: *Icel.* fugl, fogl, *m.*] DER. brim-fugel, carl-, cwēn-, dop-, fen-, gūþ-, hen-, heofon-, here-, nē-, treó-, wudu-.

fugel-bana, -bona, an; *m. A bird-killer, fowler*; auceps:—Sum biþ fugelbona, hafeces cræftig *one is a fowler, skilful with the hawk*, Exon. 79 b; Th. 298, 5; Crä. 80.

fugel-cyn, fugol-cyn, -cynn, -cinn, es; *n.* FOWL-KIND; vŏlucrium gĕnus:—Eallum nȳtenum and eallum fugelcynne *cunctis anĭmantĭbus terræ omnique vŏlucri cœli*, Gen. 1, 30: 7, 8. Nim of fugelcinne seofen and seofen ǣgðres gecyndes *tolle de volătĭlĭbus septēna et septēna, mascŭlum et fēmĭnam*, Gen. 7, 3.

fugel-doppe, es; *m? A dipping-fowl, water-fowl*; mergŭlus, Ælfc. Gl. 36; Som. 62, 118; Wrt. Voc. 29, 14. v. dop-fugel.

fugeleran = fugelerum *with fowlers*, Ors. 1, 1; Bos. 20, 5; *dat. pl. of* fugelere.

fugelere, fuglere, es; *m. A* FOWLER; auceps:—Fugelere *auceps*, Wrt. Voc. 73, 45: Coll. Monast. Th. 25, 9. Ðǣr gewīcodon fisceras oððe fugeleras *where fishers or fowlers encamped*, Ors. 1, 1; Bos. 20, 9. Fugelerum [MS. fugeleran] *with fowlers*, 1, 1; Bos. 20, 5.

fugeles leác, es; *n. Viumum?* Glos. Brux. Recd. 42, 30; Wrt. Voc. 68, 45.

fugeles wīse, fugeles wȳse, an; *f. The plant larkspur*; delphīnium = δελφίνιον:—Fugeles wīse *delphin*, Cot. 211, Som. Ben. Lye. Fugeles wȳse *delphinion*, Glos. Brux. Recd. 41, 69; Wrt. Voc. 68, 4.

fugel-hǣlsere, es; *m.* [hǣlsere *a diviner*] *A diviner by birds, soothsayer*; augur, Som. Ben. Lye. v. fugel-weohlere.

fugel-hwata, an; *m. A diviner by birds*; augur:—Fugelhwata *caragius*, Ælfc. Gl. 48; Som. 65, 69; Wrt. Voc. 34, 4. v. Du Cange *sub vōce* Caragus.

fugelian, fuglian; *p.* ode; *pp.* od *To fowl, catch birds*; aucŭpāri:—Ic fugelige *aucŭpor*, Ælfc. Gr. 25; Som. 27, 12, MS. D.

fugel-līm, es; *m. Bird-lime*; viscum, Cot. 194.

fugel-net, -nett, es; *n. A bird-net*; aucŭpātōrium rēte:—Fugelnet [MS. fugelint] *pendera* [= *panthēra* = πανθήρα], Wrt. Voc. 288, 77.

fugel-noþ, es; *m? Bird-catching, fowling*; aucŭpium:—On fugelnoþum *in fowlings*, Cod. Dipl. 715; A. D. 1006; Kmbl. iii. 350, 9.

fugeloþ *bird-catching, fowling*. v. fugoloþ.

fugel-timber, es; *n.* [timber *a frame, structure*] *A young bird*; avicŭla, pullus:—Biþ fæger fugeltimber *it is a fair young bird*, Exon. 59 a; Th. 214, 8; Ph. 236.

fugel-tras? *pl. m. Poles* or *forks for spreading nets*; ămĭtes, Cot. 13.

fugel-weohlere, es; *m.* [fugel *a bird*, weohlere = wiglere *a soothsayer*] *A diviner by birds*; augur, auspex, Ælfc. Gl. 4; Som. 56, 4; Wrt. Voc. 17, 13.

fugel-wylle *abounding in birds*. v. fugol-wylle.

fuglere, es; *m. A fowler;* auceps, Wrt. Voc. 285, 15. v. fugelere.

fugles *of a bird* or *fowl*, Exon. 17 a; Th. 41, 11; Cri. 654; *gen. of* fugel.

fugles beán, e; *f. Vetch*, Gl. Mett. 919.

fuglian *to fowl;* aucŭpāri:—Ic fuglige *aucŭpor*, Ælfc. Gr. 25; Som. 27, 12. v. fugelian.

fuglung, e; *f. Fowling, bird-catching;* aucŭpium, Wrt. Voc. 285, 19.

fugol, es; *m. A bird, fowl;* ăvis:—Friteþ wildne fugol *it eateth the wild bird*, Salm. Kmbl. 597; Sal. 298. Fugole gelīcost *most like to a bird*, Andr. Kmbl. 994; An. 497. God gelǽdde ðære lyfte fugolas to Adame *Deus volātĭlia cœli adduxit ad Adam*, Gen. 2, 19: Cd. 200; Th. 248, 14; Dan. 513. v. fugel.

fugol-cyn, -cynn, -cinn, es; *n. Fowl-kind;* vŏlucrium gĕnus:—Micel fugolcyn *much fowl-kind*, Ex. 16, 13. Fisccinn and fugolcinn *fish and fowl*, Ælfc. T. 8, 26. v. fugel-cyn.

fugoloþ, es; *m? Bird-catching, fowling;* aucŭpium:—Būton huntoþe and fugoloþe *besides hunting and fowling*, Homl. Th. ii. 576, 34. v. fugelnoþ.

fugol-wylle; *adj. Bird-springing, producing birds, abounding in birds;* ăvĭbus ăbundans:—Hit is fiscwylle and fugolwylle *it is abounding in fish and fowl*, Bd. 1, 1; S. 474, 41.

fugul, es; *m. A bird, fowl;* ăvis, vŏlucris:—Ne wæs ðæt nā fugul āna *it was not a bird only*, Exon. 109 b; Th. 418, 23; Rä. 37, 9. Heofones fugulas hit frǽton *vŏlucres cœli comēdērunt illud*, Lk. Bos. 8, 5. Fugulum *volātĭlĭbus*, Ps. Spl. 78, 2. v. fugel.

fuhlas *birds, fowls*, Mt. Bos. 13, 32, = fuglas; *pl. nom. acc. of* fugel.

FŪHT; *adj. Moist, damp;* hūmĭdus:—Ðeós wyrt biþ cenned on fūhtum and on wæteregum stōwum *this herb is produced in damp and watery places*, Herb. 9, 1; Lchdm. i. 98, 25: 39, 1; Lchdm. i. 140, 5: 52, 1; Lchdm. i. 154, 26. [*Plat.* fucht: *Dut.* vocht, *n. moisture;* vochtig *damp, humid: Ger.* feucht: *M. H. Ger.* viuhte: *O. H. Ger.* fiuhti: *Dan.* fugtig: *Swed.* fukt, *m. moisture;* fuktig *moist.*]

fūhtiende; *part. Moist, damp;* hūmĭdus, Som. Ben. Lye.

fuhton *fought*, Chr. 449; Erl. 12, 4; *p. pl. of* feohtan.

ful; *adj. Full, filled, complete, entire;* plēnus:—Ealra fūla ful *full of all foulness* [*impurities*], Elen. Kmbl. 1534; El. 769: 1875; El. 939: Cd. 166; Th. 206, 11; Exod. 450: Exon. 74 b; Th. 279, 12; Jul. 612: 78 b; Th. 294, 33; Crä. 24: 84 a; Th. 316, 4; Mōd. 43. Ǽfþancum ful *filled with grudges*, Salm. Kmbl. 992; Sal. 497. Ðā beád Swegen ful gyld and metsunge to his here ðone winter *Sweyn then commanded full tribute and provisions for his army during the winter*, Chr. 1013; Erl. 149, 24. v. full.

ful, full; *adv. Full, perfectly, very, well;* plēne, perfecte, valde:—Wyrd ne ful cūðe *he knew not well her destiny*, Exon. 66 a; Th. 244, 26; Jul. 33.

ful, full, es; *n.* I. *a cup;* pōcŭlum:—He ðæt ful geþah *he partook of the cup*, Beo. Th. 1261; B. 628. Him wæs ful boren *to him the cup was borne*, Beo. Th. 2388; B. 1192. Onfōh ðissum fulle *accept this cup*, Beo. Th. 2342; B. 1169. Full *the cup*, Exon. 106 b; Th. 406, 8; Rä. 24, 14. Drince þreó ful fulle nistig *let him drink three cups full fasting*, Herb. 3, 6; Lchdm. i. 88, 13. II. what contains liquids, *A collection of water, the sea, clouds;* receptācŭlum liquĭdi, măre, nūbes:—He ða frætwe wæg ofer ȳða ful *he carried the ornament over the sea* [lit. *the cup of the waves*], Beo. Th. 2421; B. 1208. Ic wīde toþringe lagustreáma full *I widely disperse the clouds* [lit. *the collection of water-streams*], Exon. 102 a; Th. 385, 1; Rä. 4, 38. [*O. Sax.* ful, *n. a goblet: Icel.* full, *n. a goblet full of drink.*] DER. medo-ful, meodu-sele-.

ful-, full-, in composition, denotes the *fulness, completeness* or *perfection* of the meaning of the word with which it is joined. [Cf. *Goth.* fulla-.] v. full.

-ful, -full, e; *f. -ful*, as in būc-ful *a bucketful*, hand-ful, -full *a handful*, q. v.

-ful, -full, the termination of many adjectives, as,—Bealo-ful, -full *baleful:* Car-ful, cear-full *careful:* Ege-full *fearful*, etc.

FŪL; *adj.* FOUL, *dirty, impure, corrupt, rotten, stinking, guilty, convicted of a crime;* fœdus, immundus, sordĭdus, obscœnus, spurcus, pūtĭdus, fœtĭdus, culpæ conscius, crīmĭne convictus:—Byrgen ūtan fæger, and innan fūl *a sepulchre fair without, and foul within*, Ps. Th. 13, 5. On ðīnne fūlan mūþ *in thy foul mouth*, 49, 17. In fūle wyllan *to the foul spring*, Cod. Dipl. 724; A. D. 1016; Kmbl. iii. 367, 13: 366, 31. Þurh fūle synne *through foul sin*, Exon. 29 b; Th. 90, 33; Cri. 1483. Ne nāht fūles ne þicge *nec immundum quidquam comĕdas*, Jud. 13, 4. Wið fūlne gālscipe *against foul lasciviousness*, L. C. E. 24; Th. i. 374, 9. Ascūnige man swīðe fūle forligra *let foul fornications be earnestly shunned*, L. Eth. vi. 28; Th. i. 322, 15. Swā fūle swā gǽt *as foul as goats*, Exon. 26 a; Th. 75, 34; Cri. 1231. Fūl wīn *spurcum vīnum*, Ælfc. Gl. 32; Som. 61, 127; Wrt. Voc. 27, 54. Ic eom wyrslicre ðonne ðes wudu fūla *I am viler than this rotten wood*, Exon. 111 a; Th. 424, 33; Rä. 41, 48. Fūl fȳr of heora mūþe blāwende *de ōre ignem pūtĭdum efflantes*, Bd. 5, 12; S. 628, 41: 5, 12; S. 630, 12. Ic fūlre eom ðonne ðis fen swearte, ðæt hēr yfle adelan stinceþ *I am fouler than this black fen, that here smells badly of filth*, Exon. 110 b; Th. 423, 32; Rä. 41, 31. Gif se mynetere fūl wurþe *if the minter be guilty*, L. Ath. i. 14; Th. i. 206, 20: v. § 1, 1; Th. i. 228, 14. Gif he ðonne fūl wurþe *if he then be convicted*, L. Eth. i. 1; Th. i. 280, 19: i. 2; Th. i. 282, 21: L. C. S. 30; Th. i. 394, 6. [*Piers P. Chauc. R. Glouc.* foul: *Laym.* ful, fule: *Orm.* fule: *Plat.* vuul, ful, fuul: *Frs.* fuwle, fule: *O. Frs.* ful: *Dut.* vuil: *Ger.* faul: *M. H. Ger.* vūl: *O. H. Ger.* fūl: *Goth.* fuls: *Dan.* fuul: *Swed.* ful: *Icel.* fúll: *Lat.* pŭter *foul, putrid: Lith.* pú-lei *putrid matter: Sansk.* pūti *putrid;* from the root pūy *to become foul* or *putrid.*]

FŪL, es; *n. Foulness, impurity, guilt, offence, fault;* illŭvies, impūrĭtas, culpa:—Fūl and wydel *illŭvies*, Cot. 105. Ealra fūla ful *full of all foulness* [*impurities*], Elen. Kmbl. 1534; El. 769. Ðār ǽnig þing fūles neáh ne cume *where nothing foul* [*of foulness*] *may come near*, L. Edg. C. 42; Th. ii. 252, 25. Se ðe ðæs fācnes and ðæs fūles gewita sȳ *he who is privy to the crime and the guilt*, L. Ath. v. § 1, 2; Th. i. 228, 22. Sleá man of ða hand ðe he ðæt fūl mid worhte *let the hand be struck off with which he wrought that offence*, i. 14; Th. i. 206, 21. v. fūl *foul; adj.*

fūl, es; *m. A convicted offender;* reus, qui scĕlĕris damnātus est:—Ðæt hȳ ne fūl nāwār friðian ne feormian *nor that they anywhere protect or harbour a convicted offender*, L. Ed. 7; Th. i. 162, 25. Be ðon ðe fūl friðiaþ *concerning those who protect a convicted offender*, 8 titl; Th. i. 164, 1. v. fūl; *adj.*

fūl, e; *f:* fūle, an; *f. A foul, common* or *unconsecrated place, a highway where criminals were buried;* lŏcus profānus:—Sleá mon hine and on fūl lecge *let him be slain and be laid in a common place*, L. Eth. i. 4; Th. i. 284, 2. Hine man on fūlan lecge *let one lay him in a common place*, L. C. S. 33; Th. i. 396, 17. v. Th. L. Gl.

ful-æðele *full noble, very noble.* v. full-æðele.

ful-bealdlīce, -baldlīce; *adv. Full boldly, very boldly;* audācissĭme:—Ðe ðīnes sīþes fulbealdlīce biddaþ *who full boldly pray for thy coming*, Ps. Th. 68, 7. He fulbaldlīce beornas lǽrde *he exhorted the warriors full boldly*, Byrht. Th. 140, 60; By. 311.

fūl-beám; *gen.* fūlan beámes; *m. The black alder;* alnus nigra, rhamnus frangŭla:—Wyl on wætere fūlan beámes rinde *boil in water black alder rind*, L. M. 1, 32; Lchdm. ii. 78, 12.

ful-berstan; *p.* -bærst, *pl.* -burston; *pp.* -borsten; *v. intrans. To burst fully* or *thoroughly;* plēne rumpi, Off. Reg. 3.

ful-bētan, full-bētan; *p.* -bētte; *pp.* -bēted *To make full amends, give satisfaction;* pĕnĭtus compensāre, sătisfăcĕre:—Ðæt he fulbēte *till he make full amends*, L. Pen. 12; Th. ii. 280, 29.

ful-blāc; *adj.* [blāc I. *bright, shining*] *Full bright, very bright;* prælūcĭdus:—On fulblācne beám *on the very bright tree*, Exon. 116 b; Th. 449, 4; Dōm. 66.

ful-blīðe *full glad, very joyful.* v. full-blīðe.

ful-boren; *part. Full-born, noble-born;* nōbĭlis nātu:—Mid eahta and feówertig fulborenra þegena *with eight and forty noble-born thanes*, L. Ath. iv. 7; Th. i. 228, 4.

ful-bōt *full amends;* plēna compensātio, Som. Ben. Lye.

ful-brecan; *p.* -bræc, *pl.* -brǽcon; *pp.* -brocen *To break entirely, violate;* pĕnĭtus frangĕre, violāre:—Se ðe āðor fulbrece *he who violates either*, L. C. E. 2; Th. i. 358, 21.

ful-brice, -bryce, es; *m.* [ful *full*, brice *a breaking, breach*] *A full* or *entire breach of the peace;* plēna pācis violātio:—Gif fulbrice wyrþe *si plēna pācis violātio fĭeret*, L. E. B. 4, 6, 7; Th. ii. 240, 17, 23; 242, 3. Fulbryce, 5, 8; Th. ii. 240, 20; 242, 6.

ful-cāflīce *full quickly, very eagerly.* v. full-cāflīce.

ful-clǽne; *adj. Full clean, very pure;* purissĭmus:—Ic ðīne gewitnesse wāt fulclǽne *I know thy testimonies* [*are*] *very pure*, Ps. Th. 118, 14.

ful-cūþ, full-cūþ; *adj. Full known, well known, famous, public;* bĕne nōtus, insignis, publĭcus:—On fulcūþum gemynde *in famous memory*, Ælfc. T. 21, 1. Bī fulcūþum strǽtum *juxta publĭcos viārum transĭtus*, Bd. 2, 16; S. 520, 4, note, MS. T: Nar. 2, 15.

ful-cyrten; *adj. Very beautiful;* pulcherrĭmus:—Fulcyrtenu ceorles dōhtor *a churl's very beautiful daughter*, Exon. 106 b; Th. 407, 16; Rä. 26, 6.

ful-dōn; *p.* -dyde, *pl.* -dydon; *pp.* -dōn *To do fully, satisfy;* plēne ăgĕre, satisfăcĕre, R. Ben. 44.

ful-dysig *very foolish* or *ignorant.* v. full-dysig.

ful-dyslīce; *adv. Very foolishly;* stultissĭme:—Se Godes cunnaþ fuldyslīce *he tempteth God very foolishly*, Salm. Kmbl. 455; Sal. 228.

ful-earmlīce; *adv. Full miserably, very wretchedly;* miserrĭme:—Sum sceal fulearmlīce ealdre linnan *one shall full miserably lose his life*, Exon. 88 a; Th. 330, 20; Vy. 54.

ful-eáðe, full-eáðe; *adv. Full easily, very easily;* facillĭme:—Ða men ðe habbaþ unhāle eágan ne māgon fuleáðe lōcian ongeán ða sunnan *the men who have weak eyes cannot very easily look at the sun*, Bt. 38, 5; Fox 204, 27.

ful-endian *to end fully, complete.* v. full-endian.

ful-fealdan; *p.* -feóld, *pl.* -feóldon; *pp.* -fealden *To explain;* explĭcāre:—Ic fulfealde *explĭco*, Ælfc. Gr. 24; Som. 25, 52.

ful-fleón *to flee fully* or *completely, flee away.* v. full-fleón.

ful-fremedlíce, full-fremedlíce; *adv. Fully, completely, perfectly;* perfecte:—Ne mæg nān gesceaft fulfremedlíce understandan ymbe God *no creature can perfectly understand about God*, Homl. Th. i. 10, 2, 4.

ful-fremednys, full-fremednes, -ness, -nyss, e; *f. Fulfilment, perfection;* perfectio:—Hwǣr is đīnra dǣda fulfremednys *ubi est perfectio viārum tuārum?* Job Thw. 167, 16. Lifde he his līf on sōþfæstnysse and on fulfremednysse *duxit vītam in justĭtiæ perfectiōne*, Bd. 3, 27; S. 559, 29.

ful-fremman, full-fremman, to -fremmanne; he -fremeþ; *p.* -fremede; *pp.* -fremed *To fulfil, perfect, practise;* perfĭcĕre:—Đīnre unrihtgītsunga gewill to fulfremmanne *to fulfil the desire of thine evil covetousness*, Bt. 7, 5; Fox 24, 10. Ic fulfremme *perfĭcio*, Ælfc. Gr. 28, 6; Som. 32, 37. He his mōd went to đām yflum and hī fulfremeþ *he turns his mind to the vices and practises them*, Bt. 35, 6; Fox 170, 20. Of mūþe cildra and sūcendra đū fulfremedest lof *ex ōre infantium et lactentium perfēcisti laudem*, Ps. Lamb. 8, 3: Ps. Spl. 39, 9. Heáhsetl his [biþ] swā swā mōna fulfremed on ēcnysse *thrŏnus ejus [erit] sīcut lūna perfecta in æternum*, Ps. Spl. 88, 36. Beóþ fulfremede *estōte vos perfecti*, Mt. Bos. 5, 48. DER. un-fulfremed.

ful-freólic; *adj. Very liberal;* pĕnĭtus lībĕrālis:—Đa yldestan Chus and Cham hātene wǣron, fulfreólīce feorh, frumbearn Chames *the eldest were called Cush and Canaan, most liberal beings, Ham's firstborn*, Cd. 79; Th. 97, 25; Gen. 1618.

ful-fyllan *to fulfil, accomplish.* v. full-fyllan.

ful-gān, full-gān; he -gǣþ; *p.* -eóde, *pl.* -eódon; *pp.* -gān; *with the dat. To fulfil, perform, carry out, follow, accomplish;* adimplēre, perfĭcĕre, perăgĕre, obsĕqui, patrāre:—Đæt hī mǣgen hiora wīsdōme fulgān *that they can fulfil their wisdom*, Bt. 39, 2; Fox 212, 19. Đe hiora willan fulgǣþ *which fulfils their will*, 39, 8; Fox 224, 18. Se ne hwyrfþ his mōd æfter īdlum geþohtum, and him mid weorcum [ne] fulgǣþ *he turns not his mind after vain thoughts, and does [not] carry them out with works*, Ps. Th. 23, 4. He fulgǣþ his lustum and his plegan *he follows his lusts and his pleasure*, Homl. Th. i. 66, 11.

ful-gangan, -gongan, full-gangan; *p.* -geóng, *pl.* -geóngon; *pp.* -gangen *To fulfil, perfect, follow, accomplish, finish;* complēre, perfĭcĕre, obsĕqui, fīnīre:—God bǣdon đæt hie his hearmsceare habban mōsten fulgangan *they prayed God that they might have to fulfil his punishment*, Cd. 37; Th. 48, 27; Gen. 782. Gif we him fulgangan wyllaþ *if we will follow him*, Ors. 5, 1; Bos. 101, 15. Hit is riht đæt đū heora þeáwum fulgange *it is right that thou follow their manners*, Bt. 7, 2; Fox 18, 35.

ful-geare, -gearwe, -gere; *adv. Full well, very well, fully, thoroughly;* sătis bĕne, plēne, pĕnĭtus:—Ic nāt fulgeare ymbe hwæt đū gyt tweóst *I know not full well about what thou still doubtest*, Bt. 5, 3; Fox 12, 12: Ps. Th. 117, 28. Hió ne fulgeare cūđon gesecggan be đam sigebeácne *they could not fully tell about the victorious sign*, Elen. Kmbl. 334; El. 167. Ic fulgearwe wāt đæt he byþ wīs and mildheort *I know full well that he is wise and merciful*, Ps. Th. 135, 1: Exon. 127 b; Th. 491, 1; Rä. 80, 7. Judas ne fulgere wiste be đam sigebeáme *Judas did not thoroughly know about the victorious tree*, Elen. Kmbl. 1717; El. 860.

ful-gegān; *p.* -ge-eóde, -geóde, *pl.* -ge-eódon, -geódon; *pp.* -gegān; *with the dat. To fulfil, perform, carry out, follow;* complēre, perfĭcĕre, perăgĕre, obsĕqui:—Đā đū lustgryrum eallum fulgeódest *when thou didst follow all horrid lusts*, Soul Kmbl. 47; Seel. 24. v. ful-gān.

ful-gehende; *prep. Full nigh, very near;* valde prŏpe:—Hine man byrigde đam stȳple fulgehende, on đam sūþ-portice *he was buried very near the steeple, in the south porch*, Chr. 1036; Erl. 165, 38; Ælf. Tod. 19.

ful-gemæc; *adj. Very suitable;* aptissĭmus:—Đā ic me fulgemæcne monnan funde *when I found a man very suitable for me*, Exon. 115 a; Th. 442, 25; Kl. 18.

ful-genihtsum; *adj. Very abundant, quite sufficient;* sătis abundans, omnīno amplus:—Fulgenihtsum is munuce *suffĭcit monacho*, R. Ben. 55.

ful-geódest *didst fulfil, didst follow*, Soul Kmbl. 47; Seel. 24; *2nd sing. p. of* ful-gegān.

ful-geómor; *adj. Full sad, very sad;* valde tristis:—Ic đis giedd wrece bī me fulgeómorre *I recite this lay of myself very sad*, Exon. 115 a; Th. 441, 19; Kl. 1.

ful-georne, full-georne; *adv. Full earnestly, very diligently, full well;* diligentissĭme, optĭme:—He wiste fulgeorne đæt God hine lufode *he knew full well that God loved him;* qui optĭme nōvĕrat Dŏmĭnum esse cum eo, Gen. 39, 3.

ful-gere *full well, fully, thoroughly*, Elen. Kmbl. 1717; El. 860. v. ful-geare.

ful-getreów *full true, very true.* v. full-getreów.

ful-gewēpned *fully weaponed, fully armed.* v. full-gewēpned.

ful-gleáwlīce *full wisely, very prudently.* v. full-gleáwlīce.

fulgon *entered*, Chr. 755; Erl. 50, 27; *p. pl. of* felgan.

ful-gongan *to fulfil, perfect;* perfĭcĕre:—Đæt he wīslīce woruld fulgonge *that he wisely perfect the world*, Exon. 92 b; Th. 348, 3; Sch. 22. v. ful-gangan.

ful-hār; *adj. Full hoary, gray-haired;* cānus, albescens senectūte, Cot. 54.

ful-heálīce; *adv. Full highly, very highly;* altissĭme:—Hȳ singaþ fulheálīce hlūdan stefne *they sing full highly with loud voice*, Exon. 13 b; Th. 24, 23; Cri. 389.

ful-hearde *full strongly, very firmly* or *tightly.* v. full-hearde.

ful-hræde *full quickly, immediately*, Bt. 22, 1; Rawl. 47, 7, note *f.* v. ful-rađe.

fulhtere, es; *m. A baptizer, baptist;* baptista:—To đæm dæge Seint Iohannes đæs fulhteres *on the day of Saint John the baptist*, L. Ath. i. prm; Th. i. 196, 19. v. fulluhtere.

fūlian; *p.* ode, ede; *pp.* od, ed; *v. n. To become foul, putrefy, rot, decay;* putrescĕre, computrescĕre, corrumpi:—Đǣr is mid Eástum ān mǣgþ, đæt hī māgon cȳle gewyrcan; and đȳ đǣr licgaþ đa deádan men swā lange, and ne fūliaþ, đæt hī wyrcaþ đone cȳle hine on *there is among the Esthonians a tribe that can produce cold; and, therefore, the dead men lie there so long, and decay not, because they bring the cold into them*, Ors. 1, 1; Bos. 23, 7. Mīne wunda rote an and fūledon *computruērunt et deteriorāvērunt cicātrīces meæ*, Ps. Th. 37, 5: Ps. Surt. 37, 6. DER. a-fūlian.

fūlīce; *adv. Foully;* sordĭde, R. Ben. 82.

FULL, ful; *gen. m. n.* fulles, *f.* fulre: *def.* se fulla; seó, đæt fulle: *comp. m.* fulra, *f. n.* fulre; *sup.* fullost; *adj.* FULL, *filled, complete, entire;* plēnus, sătiātus, confertus, intĕger:—Đæt se weorþig full sǣte *that the street was* [lit. *sat*] *full*, Bd. 3, 6; S. 528, 18. Be-yrnþ se mōna hwīltīdum đonne he full byþ on đære sceade ufeweardre *the moon, when it is full, sometimes enters into the upper part of the shadow*, Bd. de nat. rerum; Wrt. popl. science 5, 14, 20; Lchdm. iii. 240, 22; 242, 1. He wæs full cyng ofer eall Engla land *he was complete king over all England*, Chr. 1036; Erl. 165, 10. Mildheortnysse Drihtnes full is eorþe *misericordia Dŏmĭni plēna est terra*, Ps. Spl. 32, 5: Exon. 8 b; Th. 4, 24; Cri. 57: Cd. 18; Th. 21, 33; Gen. 333: Beo. Th. 4816; B. 2412: Ps. Th. 140, 1: Salm. Kmbl. 63; Sal. 32. Đes fulla mann *hic sătur*, Ælfc. Gr. 8; Som. 7, 26. Mīn fulla freónd *my full friend*, Th. Diplm. A. D. 972; 524, 35. Se fulla mōna *the full moon*, Bt. 39, 3; Fox 214, 29. Hwā is đæt ne wundrige fulles mōnan *who is there that wonders not at the full moon?* Bt. Met. Fox 28, 81; Met. 28, 41. Hī gebrohton hie on fullum fleáme *they put them to full flight*, Chr. 917; Erl. 102, 18. On fullum mōnan *at full moon*, Bd. de nat. rerum; Wrt. popl. science 15, 13; Lchdm. iii. 268, 10. He gewende sūþweard mid fulre fyrde *he went southward with the entire army*, Chr. 1013; Erl. 148, 4: 1014; Erl. 151, 4, 22: 1022; Erl. 161, 35. Be fullan *abundanter*, Ps. Th. 30, 27: Past. pref; Hat. MS. Man đā fullne [fulne, Erl. 150, 32], freóndscipe gefæstnode *they then confirmed full friendship*, Chr. 1014; Erl. 150, 14: 1052; Erl. 187, 23: 1013; Erl. 148, 19, 36: Bt. Met. Fox 21, 15; Met. 21, 8. Sceolon đone ryhtan dōm ǣnne geæfnan, egsan fulne *they shall suffer the one righteous doom, full of terror*, Exon. 28 a; Th. 84, 8; Cri. 1370. Hāteþ đonne heáhcyning helle betȳnan, fȳres fulle *then the mighty king shall command [them] to close hell, full of fire*, Salm. Kmbl. 349; Sal. 174. He geseah unrihte eorþan fulle *he saw the earth filled with unrighteousness*, Cd. 64; Th. 78, 13; Gen. 1292. Moises hēt nyman đæt gemetfæt full, and settan befōran Drihtne *Moses commanded [them] to take the measure full, and to set [it] before the Lord*, Ex. 16, 33. Gōd gemet, and full hig syllaþ on eówerne bearm *mensūram bŏnam, et confertam dăbunt in sīnum vestrum*, Lk. Bos. 6, 38. Beád đā Swegen full gild *Sweyn then commanded full tribute*, Chr. 1013; Erl. 149, 2. Gif hī fulle ne beóþ *si non fuĕrint satŭrāti*, Ps. Th. 58, 15: Ps. Spl. 143, 16. Hig fyldon twelf wylian fulle đæra brytsena *they filled twelve baskets full of the fragments*, Jn. Bos. 6, 13. Đār hig wǣron seofon dagas fulle *they were there seven full days*, Gen. 50, 10. Of đære tīde, Paulinus, syx geár fulle, on đære mǣgþe Godes word bodade and lǣrde *Paulīnus ex eo tempŏre sex annis contĭnuis, verbum Dei in ea provincia prædĭcābat*, Bd. 2, 14; S. 517, 33. Hit is gecyndelīc đæt ealle eorþlīce līchaman beóþ fulran on weaxendum mōnan đonne on wanigendum *it is natural that all earthly bodies are fuller at the increasing moon than at the waning*, Bd. de nat. rerum; Wrt. popl. science 15, 11; Lchdm. iii. 268, 8. Hwenne đæt flōd byþ fullost *when the tide is fullest*, Chr. 1031; Erl. 162, 6, 16. [*Chauc.* ful, full: *R. Glouc.* ful: *Laym.* ful, uul, uule, fulle, uulle: *Orm.* full: *Plat.* vull, full: *O. Sax.* ful, fol: *Frs.* fol: *O. Frs.* ful, fol: *Dut.* vol: *Ger.* voll: *M. H. Ger.* vol: *O. H. Ger.* foll, fol, full: *Goth.* fulls: *Dan.* fuld: *Swed.* full: *Icel.* fullr: *Lat.* plēnus: *Grk.* πλήρης: *Lith.* pilnas: *Sansk.* pūrṇa *filled, full.*]

full; *adv. Fully, perfectly, entirely;* plēne, perfecte, omnīno:—Þurh tyn winter full *for fully ten winters*, Bd. 1, 6; S. 476, 25. He sæt đǣr tyn winter full *he remained there fully ten winters*, Bt. Met. Fox 26, 33; Met. 26, 17. v. ful; *adv.*

full, es; *n. A cup;* pōcŭlum:—Gedrinc his þreó full fulle *drink three cups full of it*, Herb. 1, 9; Lchdm. i. 74, 2. v. ful; *n.*

-full *-ful.* v. -ful, the termination of many adjectives.

ful-lǣst, -lēst, -lāste (?) es; *m. Help, aid, support;* auxĭlium, subsĭdium:—Is mægenwīsa trum, fullēsta mǣst, se đas fare lǣdeþ *he is a firm army-*

leader, the greatest of supports, who leads this expedition, Cd. 170; Th. 213, 18; Exod. 554. Ðæt we hæfdon æt ðæm fȳre leóht and fullāste *that we might have light and help from the fire*, Nar. 13, 3. [*O. Sax.* fullēsti; *O. H. Ger.* folleist.]

ful-lǽstan, -lēstan; *p.* te; *pp.* ed *To help, aid, support;* opĭtŭlāri:—Ic ðē fullǽstu *I will support thee*, Beo. Th. 5330; B. 2668. ᚠ [ōs] fullēsteþ [*the mind*] *gives aid*, Exon. 106 b; Th. 407, 1; Rä. 25, 8. Him men fullēstaþ *men aid them*, 119 a; Th. 457, 31; Hy. 4, 92. [*O. Sax.* fullēstian: *O. H. Ger.* folleistian.]

full-æðele; *adj. Full noble, very noble;* valde nōbĭlis:—Manege beóþ ǽgðer ge fullæðele ge fullwēlige, and beóþ ðeáh fullunrōte *many are both very noble and very wealthy, and yet are very unhappy*, Bt. 11, 1; Fox 32, 3.

Fullan-ham, -hom; *gen.* -hammes, -hommes; *m.* [*Asser* Fullonham: *Hunt.* Fulenham: *Sim. Dun.* Fulanham: *Brom.* Fullenham] FULHAM, *Middlesex;* lŏci nōmen in agro Middlesexiensi, ad rīpam Tămēsis flūmĭnis:—Æt Fullanhamme be Temese *at Fulham on the Thames*, Chr. 879; Th. 150, 3. On Fullanhomme *at Fulham*, 880; Th. 150, 12, col. 1.

full-bētan; *p.* te; *pp.* ed *To make full satisfaction;* sătisfăcĕre:—Ic fullbēte oððe behreówsige *sătisfăcio*, Ælfc. Gr. 37; Som. 39, 40. v. ful-bētan.

full-bliðe; *adj. Full glad, very joyful;* lætissĭmus:—Ða Philistei fullbliðe wǽron *the Philistines were very joyful*, Jud. 16, 23.

full-cāflīce; *adv. Full quickly, very eagerly;* velocissĭme:—Se fullcāflīce bræd of ðæm beorne blōdigne gār *he very eagerly plucked the bloody dart from the chief*, Byrht. Th. 136, 19; By. 153.

full-cūþ; *adj. Full known, well known;* bĕne nōtus:—On cyninga bōcum ys fullcūþ be ðām *in the books of the kings it is well known about them*, Jud. Thw. 161, 20.

full-dysig; *adj. Very foolish* or *ignorant;* perfecte stultus:—Fulldysig biþ se mann *the man is very foolish*, Hexam. 2; Norm. 4, 6.

full-eáðe; *adv. Very easily;* facillĭme:—Ne meht ðū fulleáðe cweðan ðæt ðū earm sē *thou canst not very easily say that thou art miserable*, Bt. 8; Fox 24, 22. v. ful-eáðe.

full-endian; *p.* ode; *pp.* od *To end fully, complete, finish;* complēre, fīnīre:—He bæd Cynebill ðæt he ða ārfæstan ongunnennesse fullendode *pĕtiit Cynibillum pia cœpta complēre*, Bd. 3, 23; S. 554, 39, note. [*Ger.* vollenden.]

full-eóde, *pl.* -eódon *went after, followed, aided*, Beo. Th. 6230, note; B. 3119: Cd. 98; Th. 130, 1; Gen. 2153; *p. of* full-gān.

fullere, es; *m. A* FULLER, *bleacher;* fullo:—His reáf wurdon glitinende swā hwīte swā snāw, swā nān fullere ōfer eorþan ne mæg swā hwīte gedōn, Mk. Bos. 9, 3; *vestīmenta ejus facta sunt splendentia et candĭda nĭmis vĕlut nix, quālia fullo non pŏtest sŭper terram candĭda făcĕre*, Vulg; his clothis ben maad schynynge and white ful moche as snow, and which maner clothis a fullere, *or walkere of cloth* may not make white on erthe, Wyc. Fulleras *fullōnes*, Ælfc. Gl. 9; Som. 57, 1; Wrt. Voc. 19, 12.

full-fleón, ic -fleó; *p.* -fleáh, *pl.* -flugon; *pp.* -flogen *To flee fully* or *completely, flee away;* perfŭgĕre:—Ic fullfleó *perfŭgio*, Ælfc. Gr. 28, 6; Som. 32, 49.

full-fremedlīce; *comp.* -līcor; *adv. Fully, completely, perfectly;* perfecte:—Nān man ne mæg fullfremedlīce secgan embe ðone sōþan God *no man is able to speak perfectly about the true God*, Hexam. 3; Norm. 4, 26. Ne eart ðū fullfremedlīce gefullod *non es perfecte baptīzātus*, Bd. 5, 6; S. 620, 6: 618, 38. Ǽrðon ðe he be ðām forþgewitenum gȳmeleásnyssum his fullfremedlīcor of ðære tīde geclǽnsade *priusquam prætĕrĭtas neglĭgentias perfectius ex tempŏre castīgāret*, 3, 27; S. 559, 6. [*Orm.* fullfremeddlike.] v. ful-fremedlīce.

full-fremednes, -ness, -nyss, e; *f. Fulfilment, perfection;* perfectio:—Ðæt ic hæbbe manege men gelǽd to ðæm stæðe fullfremednesse on ðæm scipe mīnes mōdes *that I have brought many men to the shore of perfection in the ship of my mind*, Past. 65; Hat. MS. Ðæt he fullfremednysse hæbbe *that it may have fulfilment*, Ælfc. Gr. 21; Som. 23, 27. DER. un-fullfremednes. [*Orm.* fullfremeddness.] v. ful-fremednys.

full-fremman, to -fremmenne; *p.* -fremede; *pp.* -fremed *To do fully, fulfil, finish, perfect, practise;* perfĭcĕre, perăgĕre, patrāre:—Syððan he ne mæg ðæne grundweall fullfremman *posteaquam fundāmentum non potuĕrit perfĭcĕre*, Lk. Bos. 14, 29. Hwæðer he hæbbe hine to fullfremmenne *si hăbeat ad perfĭciendum*, 14, 28. Ðæt ic fullfremme his weorc *ut perfĭciam ŏpus ejus*, Jn. Bos. 4, 34. Ðæt he hī eft fullfremme *that he practise them* [*the vices*] *again*, Bt. 35, 6; Fox 170, 18. Swā eówer heofonlīca fæder is fullfremed *sīcut păter vester cœlestis perfectus est*, Mt. Bos. 5, 48: Ælfc. Gr. 20; Som. 23, 12, 13. Ðeáh hī on manegum þingum sīen fullfremede *though they are perfect in many things*, Past. 65; Hat. MS. [*Orm.* fullfremedd.] v. ful-fremman.

full-fyllan; *p.* -fylde; *pp.* -fylled *To fulfil, accomplish;* complēre:—Ic fullfylle *compleo*, Ælfc. Gr. 26; Som. 28, 29.

full-gān; he -gǽþ; *p.* -eóde, *pl.* -eódon; *pp.* -gān; *with the dat. To fulfil, perform, go after, follow, aid;* perfĭcĕre, perăgĕre, sĕqui, adjŭvāre:—We ne mōton fullgān ūres Scippendes willan *we cannot perform our Maker's will*, Bt. 7, 5; Fox 24, 8. Se lyðra man fullgǽþ deófles willan *the wicked man fulfils the devil's will*, Homl. Th. i. 172, 18. Sceaft flāne fulleóde *the shaft went after the arrow*, Beo. Th. 6230, note; B. 3119. Hie me fulleódon *they well aided me*, Cd. 98; Th. 130, 1; Gen. 2153. v. ful-gān.

full-gangan; *p.* -geóng, *pl.* -geóngon; *pp.* -gangen; *with the dat. To fulfil, accomplish, finish;* perfĭcĕre, fīnīre:—Ðæt hī mōstan ðam gewinne fullgangan *that they might finish the war*, Ors. 3, 1; Bos. 54, 21. v. ful-gangan.

full-georne; *adv. Full earnestly, very diligently;* diligentissĭme:—Ic mīne earfeðu ealle fullgeorne fōre him sæcge *I tell all my troubles very diligently before him*, Ps. Th. 141, 2. v. ful-georne.

full-getreów; *adj. Full true, altogether true;* pĕnĭtus vērax:—We synd fullgetreówe *sŭmus pĕnĭtus vērāces*, Gen. 42, 31.

full-gewēpned; *part. Fully weaponed, fully armed;* perfecte armātus:—Hī cōmon onuppon ða munecas fullgewēpnede *they came upon the monks fully armed*, Chr. 1083; Erl. 217, 11.

full-gleáwlīce; *adv. Full wisely, very prudently;* sapientissĭme, prudentissĭme:—Ic mīne sāwle symble wylle fullgleáwlīce Gode underþeódan *I will always very prudently subject my soul to God*, Ps. Th. 61, 1: 72, 13: 106, 42.

full-hearde; *adv. Full strongly, very firmly* or *tightly;* firmissĭme, artissĭme:—He ðone fullhearde geband *he bound it very tightly*, Cd. 23; Th. 29, 3; Gen. 444.

fullian, fulligan, fulwian, to fullianne; *part.* fulligende; ic fullige, ðū fullast, he fullaþ, *pl.* fulliaþ; *p.* fullode, ede; *pp.* fullod, ed; *v. trans. To* FULL or *make white as a fuller* [fullere, *q.v.*], *to baptize;* albāre, candĭdum făcĕre, baptīzāre = βαπτίζειν. A word of doubtful origin. It is by some connected with the verb which appears in Gothic as weihan *to sanctify*. See fulluht. Ongunnon hī men lǽran and fullian *ipsi prædĭcāre et baptīzāre cœpērunt*, Bd. 1, 26; S. 488, 4: 1, 27; S. 493, 25. Se ðe me sende to fullianne on wætere *qui mīsit me baptīzāre in ăquam*, Jn. Bos. 1, 33. Iohannes wæs on wēstene fulligende *fuit Joannes in deserto baptīzans*, Mk. Bos. 1, 4. Ic fullige on wætere *ĕgo baptīzo in ăqua*, Jn. Bos. 1, 26. Hwī fullast ðū *quid baptīzas?* 1, 25. Se ðe fullaþ on Hālgum Gāste *qui baptīzat in Spīrĭtu Sancto*, 1, 33: 3, 26: L. C. E. 4; Th. i. 360, 30. Iohannes fullode ða ðe him to cōmon *John baptized those who came to him*, Homl. Th. i. 352, 16: Jn. Bos. 1, 28, 31: 3, 22, 23: 4, 2: 10, 40. Lǽraþ ealle þeóda, and fulligeaþ hig *dŏcēte omnes gentes, baptīzantes eos*, Mt. Bos. 28, 19. Ðæt he hine fullode *that he might baptize him*, 3, 13. Iohannes se Fulluhtere cwæþ, witodlīce ic eów fullige on wætere, to dǽdbōte; se ðe æfter me towerd ys... he eów fullaþ on Hālgum Gāste, Mt. Bos. 3, 11; *Joon Baptist saide, forsothe Y cristene* [= *waische*] *ȝou in water, in to penaunce; forsothe he that is to cumme after me... he shal baptise, or cristen ȝow in the Holy Goost*, Wyc: Joannes Baptista dixit, ĕgo quĭdem baptīzo vos in ăqua in pœnĭtentiam; qui autem post me ventūrus est... ipse vos baptīzābit in Spīrĭtu Sancto, Vulg. 'In Anturs of Arther, end of 13th century, we find, st. xviii. lines 4, 5:—*pp.* Fulled *whitened, baptized: R. Glouc.* A.D. 1297; 3 *p.* Follede; *pp.* y-fulled, fulled; s. fullynge: *Piers P.* 1362, *Wrt. small* 8vo. *London, Pickering*, 1842, pp. 244, 322, fullynge *baptizing, whitening:* 398, fullynge *baptizing*. After this, we do not find fulled, y-fulled, fullynge; yet in *A. Sax.* Mk. Bos. 9, 3, we have fullere: *Wyc.* 1389, fullere [*or walkere of cloth*, note]: *Tynd.* 1526 and *Eng. version* 1611, fuller. Baptem and Baptym with the verb Baptise is used by Wycliffe, and Baptyme and Baptyzyn by the compiler of the Promptorium. Wycliffe also uses the 1st person of the verb I waisch in Mt. 3, 11; and the two forms of the *pp.* waischen, waischun, in Mt. 3, 6, and Mk. 10, 38, 39. The form Bapteme seems to have been introduced into the language, through the French, by Robert Manning, called de Brunne, from Bourne, near Depyng in Lincolnshire, in his translation of Peter Langtoft's Chronicle, and to have been current, with slight variation in the orthography, till nearly the middle of the 16th century = 1550. Thus the forms Baptim and Baptime appear in the version of the N. T. by Tyndale in 1526, and Baptym, Baptyme in that by Cranmer in 1539. In the version made by Coverdale and other Protestant exiles at Geneva in 1559, in the Anglo-Rhemish version made by Cardinal Allen and other Romanists at Rheims in 1559, and in the authorized version of 1611, the word is written Baptisme. This last form is also found in *Piers P.* p. 398. Ormin only uses the verb *to dip*, once:—Unnderr waterr dippesst, H. 1551. In *Goth.* and in other divisions of the Teutonic as well as in the *Swed.* and *Dan.* divisions of the Scandinavian branch of the Gothic language, a noun and verb are used expressive of *dipping*, e.g. *Goth.* daupyan, daupeins: *O. H. Ger.* doufan, doufa: *Dut.* doopen, doop: *Ger.* taufen, taufe: *Swed.* döpa, döpelse: *Dan.* döbe, daab.' Orm. ii. 626, 627. Dyppan is also used in the Rushworth Gloss. v. fulwian. DER. ge-fullian, -fulwian: un-gefullod.

fullian; *p.* ode; *pp.* od *To fulfil, perfect;* exsĕqui:—Gif gē bebodu willaþ mīn fullian *if ye will fulfil my commandments*, Cd. 106; Th. 139, 29; Gen. 2317. Ðonne sceal he ðæt mid mildheortum weorcum fullian *then shall he perfect that with works of mercy*, Blickl. Hom. 37, 19. Fullade 213, 16. [*O. Sax.* fullōn: *O. H. Ger.* fullén.] DER. lust-fullian, ge-lustfullian, wist-fullian: un-gefullod. v. fyllan.

fūl-līc; *adj. Foul, base;* fœdus, turpis:—Gārclifan etan ǣrende fūllīc getācnaþ *to eat agrimony betokens a disagreeable message*, Lchdm. iii. 198, 25. Ansīne fūllīce habban *to have a dirty face*, iii. 204, 10, 26.

fullīce; *comp.* -līcor; *adv. Fully, perfectly, completely;* plēne, perfecte:—Se ðe Englisc fullīce ne cūðe *qui Anglōrum linguam perfecte non nōvĕrat*, Bd. 3, 3; S. 525, 39: 2, 3; S. 504, 32. Fullīcor *plēnius*, 4, 25; S. 600, 10.

fūl-līce; *comp.* -līcor; *adv. Foully, shamefully;* fœde, sordĭde, turpĭter:—Gif hwā fūllīce hine sylfne besmīte *si quis fœde seipsum polluĕrit*, L. M. I. P. 40; Th. ii. 276, 7: C. R. Ben. 44: Scint. 24.

fulligan, to fulligenne *To baptize;* baptīzāre:—Diāconus mōt fulligan cild *a deacon may baptize children*, L. Ælf. C. 16; Th. ii. 348, 14. Gif cild biþ to fulligenne *if there be a child to baptize*, 29; Th. ii. 352, 30. v. fullian.

fulligenne *to baptize*, Th. L. ii. 352, 30. v. fulligan.

full-mannod, -monnad; *part. Full manned, well peopled;* vĭris instructus, pŏpŭlo frĕquens:—Ðæt he hæbbe his land fullmannod [Cot. fullmonnad] *that he have his land well peopled*, Bt. 17; Fox 58, 32.

full-neáh; *adj. Full nigh, very near;* valde propinquus:—Wæs se feónd fullneáh *the foe was very near*, Cd. 32; Th. 43, 10; Gen. 688.

full-neáh; *adv. Full nearly, very nearly, almost;* fĕre:—Ðū eart fullneáh forþoht *thou art almost despairing*, Bt. 8; Fox 24, 16: Chr. 897; Th. 175, 39, col. 1. v. ful-neáh; *adv.*

fullnes, -ness, -nyss, e; *f.* FULNESS; plenĭtūdo, Som. Ben. Lye.

fūllnes, -ness, e; *f. Foulness, stench;* fætor:—Seó wundriende swētnes ðæs miclan swæcces sōna ealle ða fūllnessa ðæs þȳstran ofnes on weg aflȳmede *omnem mox fætōrem tenebrōsæ fornācis effūgāvit admīrandi hūjus suāvĭtas ŏdōris*, Bd. 5, 12; S. 629, 21. v. fūlnes.

fulloc, es; *n. Baptism;* baptismus:—We willaþ ðæt fulloc fæste stande *we will that baptism stand fast*, L. N. P. L. 67; Th. ii. 302, 6. v. fulluht.

full-oft; *adv. Full oft, very often;* sæpissĭme:—We beóþ fulloft geneádode *we are very often compelled*, Greg. Dial. pref; Hat. MS. 1 a, 19. Fulloft fyrwit frineþ *curiosity inquires very often*, Salm. Kmbl. 116; Sal. 57. v. ful-oft.

ful-longe; *adv. Full long, very long;* diutissĭme:—Ða gyldnan geatu ðe fullonge ǣr bilocen stōdon *the golden gates which very long before stood locked*, Exon. 11 b; Th. 16, 12; Cri. 252.

full-recen; *adj. Full quick, very quick;* citissĭmus:—Ðū meahtest ðē fullrecen on ðæm rōdere ufan siððan weorþan *thou, very quick, mayest afterwards advance into the sky above*, Bt. Met. Fox 24, 33; Met. 24, 17.

full-slāw; *adj. Full slow, very slow;* persegnis, Off. Reg. 15.

full-sōþ *full sooth, most truly*, L. Ælf. C. 6; Lambd. 128, 29. v. ful-sōþ.

full-strong; *adj. Full strong, most rigid;* valde sĕvērus *vel* rĭgĭdus:—Wæs ðæt eall fullstrong *that was all most rigid*, Cd. 220; Th. 284, 16; Sat. 322. v. ful-strang.

fulluht, fulwiht, fullwiht, fulwuht, es; *n.* [v. Grimm And. u. El. pp. 136-7] *Baptism;* baptismus:—Hwæðer wæs Iohannes fulluht? Mt. Bos. 21, 25; *of whennes was the baptem of Joon?* Wyc; baptismus Joannis unde ĕrat? Vulg: Mk. Bos. 11, 30: Lk. Bos. 20, 4: Ælfc. Gr. 9, 1; Som. 8, 22. Ðæt fulluht us aþwehþ fram eallum synnum *baptism washes us from all sins*, Homl. Th. ii. 48, 29: 46, 24, 33: 48, 18, 20: i. 94, 2. Fram gyfe ðæs hālgan fulluhtes *a sacri baptismătis gratia*, Bd. 1, 27; S. 493, 10. Fulluhtes bæþ *the bath of baptism*, 2, 14; S. 518, 4. Māge gyt beón gefullod on ðam fulluhte, ðe ic beó gefullod *pŏtestis baptismo, quo ego baptīzor, baptīzāri?* Mk. Bos. 10, 38, 39: Mt. Bos. 3, 7: Lk. Bos. 7, 29: 12, 50: L. C. E. 22; Th. i. 374, 3: L. Ælf. C. 27; Th. ii. 352, 19: L. Ælf. P. 20; Th. ii. 370, 32: Chr. 601; Erl. 21, 11: 942; Erl. 116, 20: Ps. Th. arg. 22. Se yfela preóst ne mæg nǣfre Godes þēnunge gefīlan, nāðer ne ðæt fulluht, ne ða mæssan *the evil priest cannot ever defile God's ministry, nor baptism, nor the mass*, L. Ælf. P. 41; Th. ii. 382, 14: L. Alf. 49; Th. i. 58, 25: Homl. Th. i. 208, 11: 306, 1: 312, 21: ii. 48, 1, 3, 4, 5: Lk. Bos. 3, 3. [*Orm.* fulluhht: *Laym.* fulluht.]

fulluht-bæþ, fulwiht-bæþ, es; *n.* [full, wiht, e; *f:* bæþ, es; *n.*] *A bath* or *font of baptism;* baptismi fons, baptistērium = βαπτιστήριον:—Ðæt gerȳne onfōn fulluhtbæþes *to receive the sacrament of the baptismal font*, Bd. 1, 27; S. 492, 31. Fulluhtebæþes, 3, 3; S. 525, 30. Ðā onfēng Eádwine cyning fulluhtebæþe *then king Edwin received the bath of baptism*, 2, 14; S. 517, 23: 1, 27; S. 491, 29.

fulluht-ere, fulwiht-ere, es; *m.* [ful, full; uht, wiht; ere; es; *m.*] *A baptizer, the Baptist;* baptista:—On ðām dagum com Iohannes se Fulluhtere *in diēbus illis vēnit Joannes Baptista*, Mt. Bos. 3, 1: 14, 2: Mk. Bos. 6, 14: Lk. Bos. 7, 20, 28, 33: Homl. Th. i. 356, 7: 358, 22: 478, 1, 30. Syle me on ānum disce Iohannes heáfod ðæs Fulluhteres *da mihi in disco căput Joannis Baptistæ*, Mt. Bos. 14, 8: Mk. Bos. 6, 24: Homl. Th. i. 350, 31: 352, 23: 364, 6. Be Iohanne ðam Fulluhtere *de Joanne Baptista*, Mt. Bos. 17, 13: Homl. Th. i. 356, 19: 476, 27: 484, 22. Sume secgeaþ Iohannem ðone Fulluhtere *ălii dīcunt Joannem Baptistam*, Mt. Bos. 16, 14: Mk. Bos. 8, 28.

fulluht-nama, an; *m. The baptismal* or *christian name;* nōmen tempŏre baptīzandi impŏsĭtum:—Hēr Godrum se norþerna cyning forþferde, ðæs fulluhtnama wæs Æðelstān *here* [A. D. 890] *Guthrum the Northern* [i. e. *Danish*] *king died, whose baptismal name was Æthelstan*, Chr. 890; Erl. 86, 27.

fulluht-stōw *a baptism-place, baptistery.* v. fulwiht-stōw.

fulluht-þeáw, es; *m. The rite of baptism;* baptismi mos:—Cyning onfēng fulluhtþeáwum *the king received the rite of baptism*, Bt. Met. Fox 1, 65; Met. 1, 33.

fulluht-tīd *time of baptism, baptismal time.* v. fulwiht-tīd.

fullunga; *adv. Fully*:—Fullunga *peramplius*, Rtl. 21, 8: Jn. Skt. Lind. note in the margin.

full-unrōt; *adj. Full sad, very unhappy;* valde tristis:—Manege beóþ ǣgðer ge fullæðele ge fullwēlige, and beóþ ðeáh fullunrōte *many are both very noble and very wealthy, and yet are very unhappy*, Bt. 11, 1; Fox 32, 3.

full-wēlig; *adj. Full wealthy, very rich;* valde dīves, ditissĭmus:—Manege beóþ fullwēlige *many are very wealthy*, Bt. 11, 1; Fox 32, 3.

full-weorþlīce *full worthily, very honourably*, Chr. 1036; Th. 294, 21, col. 2. v. ful-wurþlīce.

fullwiht, es; *n. Baptism;* baptismus:—Hū hī hine bǣdan fullwihtes bæþes *how they had asked him for a font of baptism*, Ors. 6, 34; Bos. 130, 30: Bd. 2, 14; S. 518, note 10: Andr. Kmbl. 3279; An. 1642. Mid ðȳ fullwihte *with baptism*, Exon. 121 b; Th. 467, 9; Hö. 136. v. full-uht.

full-wīte, es; *n. Full fine;* plēna mulcta:—Gylde fullwīte [fulwīte MS. B.] *let him pay full fine*, L. C. S. 49; Th. i. 404, 7, 9: L. In. 43; Th. i. 128, 18, note 48, MSS. B. H. v. ful-wīte.

fullwon, e; *f. Baptism?* baptismus?—Fullwona bearn *children of baptism, christians*, Cd. 92; Th. 117, 9; Gen. 1951. v. fulluht.

full-wyrcan; *p.* -worhte; *pp.* -worht *To do fully, commit, accomplish, complete;* perfĭcĕre, complēre:—Se godcunda ānweald hī tostencte ǣr hī hit fullwyrcan mōston *the divine power dispersed them before they could complete it*, Bt. 35, 4; Fox 162, 25. [*Orm.* fullwrohht *finished.*] v. fulwyrcan.

ful-mannod *full manned, well peopled.* v. full-mannod.

ful-moneg; *adj. Full many, very many;* permultus:—To fulmonegum dæge men synt forlǣdde *men are seduced for full many a day*, Cd. 33; Th. 45, 17; Gen. 728.

ful-neáh *full nigh, very near.* v. full-neáh; *adj.*

ful-neáh, full-neáh, ful-nēh; *adv. Full nearly, very nearly, almost;* prŏpe, fĕre:—Steorran hie ætiéwdon fulneáh [fulnēh, Th. 29, 12, col. 1] healfe tīd ofer undern *stars shewed themselves very nearly half an hour after nine o'clock* [*a. m.*], Chr. 540; Th. 28, 13; 29, 12, col. 2. Fulneáh [fullneáh, Th. 175, 39, col. 1] tū swā lange *very nearly twice as long*, Chr. 897; Th. 174, 42; 175, 39, col. 2. Se yfela willa unrihthǣmedes gedrēfþ fulneáh ǣlces libbendes monnes mōd *the evil desire of unlawful lust disquiets the mind of almost every living man*, Bt. 31, 2; Fox 112, 25: 4; Fox 8, 18: 11; Fox 30, 18: Bt. Met. Fox 18, 8; Met. 18, 4.

fūlnes, fūllnes, fȳlnes, -ness, e; *f.* FOULNESS, *impurity, stench;* fœdĭtas, sordes, fætor:—Fūlnes [fȳlnes, Exon. 98 a; Th. 368, 7] eorþan, eal forwisnad *foulness of earth, all decayed*, Soul Kmbl. 35; Seel. 18. Unarǣfnendlīce fūlnes wæs upp aweallende *fætor incompărābĭlis ebulliens ĕrat*, Bd. 5, 12; S. 628, 25.

ful-oft, full-oft; *adv. Full oft, very often;* sæpissĭme:—Hie ablændaþ fuloft wīsra monna geþoht *they very often blind the thought of wise men*, L. Alf. 46; Th. i. 54, 18. Sió wyrd fuloft dereþ unscyldegum *fate very often injures the guiltless*, Bt. Met. Fox 4, 71; Met. 4, 36: Beo. Th. 964; B. 480: Exon. 81 b; Th. 307, 16; Seef. 24: Cd. 216; Th. 274, 11; Sat. 152: Salm. Kmbl. 695; Sal. 347.

ful-raðe, -ræðe, -hræðe; *adv. Full quickly, immediately;* cĭtissĭme:—Fulraðe [Cott. fulræðe] ðæs ic clipode *immediately thereupon I spoke*, Bt. 22, 1; Fox 76, 8. Fulraðe yrnende *running very quickly*, Ors. 1, 1; Bos. 17, 21.

ful-recen *full quick, very quick.* v. full-recen.

ful-ricene; *adv. Full quickly, very quickly, immediately;* citissĭme:—Gif he mūntas hrīneþ, hī fulricene reócaþ *if he touches the mountains, they immediately smoke*, Ps. Th. 103, 30.

ful-riht; *adj. Full right, most right* or *direct;* valde rectus, directissĭmus:—Ðū ne mihtest gyt fulrihtne weg arēdian *thou hast not yet been able to find the most direct way*, Bt. 22, 2; Fox 78, 8.

ful-rihte; *adv. Full rightly, very rightly;* rectissĭme, Solil. 5.

ful-sārlīce; *adv. Full sorely, very harshly* or *violently;* tristissĭme, acerbissĭme, gravissĭme:—Ðæt mīn sylfes fōt fulsārlīce asliden wǣre *that my own foot had very violently slipped*, Ps. Th. 93, 17.

ful-scrid; *adj. Full quick, very swift;* velocissĭmus:—Is ðes bāt fulscrid, fugole gelīcost glīdeþ on geofone *this boat is very quick, it glideth on the ocean most like to a bird*, Andr. Recd. 996; An. 496.

ful-séfte; *adj. Full soft, very soft;* valde mollis:—Ic geworhte fulséfte seld, ðæt hí sǽton on *I made a very soft seat, which they sat on,* Ps. Th. 88, 3.

ful-sláw *full slow, very slow.* v. full-sláw.

ful-sméðe; *adj. Full smooth, very smooth;* levissĭmus:—Ðe fulsméðe spræce habbaþ *who have very smooth speech,* Frag. Kmbl. 20; Leás. 12.

ful-sóþ, full-sóþ; *adv. Full sooth, very truly;* verissĭme:—Fulsóþ hý secgaþ *they say very truly,* L. Ælf. C. 6; Th. ii. 344, 22.

fúl-stincende; *part. Foul-stinking;* fœde ŏlens:—Ðú fúlstincendiste hell, geopena ðíne gatu *thou most foul-stinking hell, open thy gates,* Nicod. 27; Thw. 16, 3.

ful-strang, -strong, full-strong; *adj. Full strong, very severe* or *overwhelming;* valde sĕvērus *vel* rĭgĭdus:—Wæs him eall fulstrang *it was all very severe to them,* Cd. 218; Th. 278, 23; Sat. 226. Is ðeós þrag fulstrong *this moment is very overwhelming,* Exon. 72 b; Th. 270, 13; Jul. 464.

ful-swíðe; *adv. Very much, very;* valde:—Wéne ic fulswíðe *I think very much,* Exon. 120 a; Th. 461, 4; Hö. 30.

fulteman, fultemian *to assist, help, support;* jŭvāre, auxĭlĭāri:—Sió womb sceal fulteman ðǽm hondum *the belly must support the hands,* Past. 34, 3; Hat. MS. 44 a, 21. For ðæm ánwalde ðe ánra gehwilc fultemaþ *through the power which each one supports,* Bt. Met. Fox 25, 42; Met. 25, 21. v. fultuman.

ful-þiclíce; *adv. Full thickly, very often, very frequently;* persæpe, frequentissĭme:—Heó spræc to Adame fulþiclíce *she spoke to Adam very frequently,* Cd. 33; Th. 44, 6; Gen. 705.

ful-þungen; *part. Full grown, high, lofty;* celsus, R. Ben. 73.

fultom, es; *m. Help, aid, support;* auxĭlium, adjūtōrium:—Ðæt he ðone hálgan heáp bidde friþes and fultomes *that he implore the holy troop for peace and support,* Apstls. Kmbl. 181; Ap. 91. To fultome *for aid,* Chr. 601; Erl. 20, 12. v. fultum.

fultomian; *part.* fultomiende *To help, aid;* auxĭlĭāri:—Sóna eft, Gode fultomiendum, he meahte geseón and sprecan *soon after, God helping, he could see and speak,* Chr. 797; Erl. 58, 15. v. fultuman.

ful-trum; *adj. Full strong, very firm;* valde firmus:—Sécaþ gé Drihten, and gé beóþ fultrume *quærĭte Dŏmĭnum, et confirmāmĭni,* Ps. Th. 104, 4.

ful-trúwian; *p.* ode; *pp.* od *To trust fully in, confide in;* pĕnĭtus confīdĕre:—Ic nát, hwí gé fultrúwiaþ ðam hreósendan wélan *I do not know, why ye confide in these perishable riches,* Bt. 26, 2; Fox 94, 7.

fultum, fultom, es; *m.* I. *help, aid, assistance, support, succour;* auxĭlium, adjūtōrium, adjūmentum:—Him wæs fultum neáh *support was nigh to him,* Exon. 35 a; Th. 113, 20; Gú. 160. Fultum mín *adjūtōrium meum,* Ps. Lamb. 7, 11. Bæd fultumes wǽrfæst hæleþ *the righteous man sought their aid,* Cd. 94; Th. 122, 12; Gen. 2025: Ors. 3, 7; Bos. 59, 38: 3, 7; Bos. 60, 32. Hie Mæcedoniam on fultume wǽron *they had helped the Macedonians,* 2, 5; Bos. 46, 16: 2, 5; Bos. 47, 14, 33: 3, 7; Bos. 59, 35. Syle us nú on earfoðum æðelne fultum *da nōbis auxĭlium de trĭbŭlātiōne,* Ps. Th. 59, 10: 83, 6: Ps. Lamb. 19, 3. Him Drihten forgeaf frófor and fultum *the Lord gave to them comfort and succour,* Beo. Th. 1400; B. 698: 3674; B. 1835: Salm. Kmbl. 882; Sal. 440: Bt. Met. Fox 31, 15; Met. 31, 8. Óðer ǽhte heóld fæder on fultum *the other kept cattle in aid of his father,* Cd. 47; Th. 59, 35; Gen. 974: 95; Th. 125, 1; Gen. 2072: Exon. 62 b; Th. 229, 14; Ph. 455: Ors. 2, 5; Bos. 47, 27: 3, 7; Bos. 58, 29. Mid godcunde fultume *by divine aid,* 1, 5; Bos. 28, 5. II. *a helper, an army, forces;* adjūtor, cōpiæ:—Fultum mín and alýsend mín beó ðú *adjūtor meus et lĭbĕrātor meus es tu,* Ps. Spl. 69, 7: 70, 8: Ps. Lamb. 18, 15. He gegaderode ðone fultum ðe he ðá mihte *he gathered what forces he then could,* Ors. 1, 12; Bos. 36, 1: 2, 5; Bos. 46, 27. He mid his fultume næs *he was not with his army,* 2, 5; Bos. 48, 15, 22: 3, 7; Bos. 59, 18. DER. feorm-fultum, mann-.

fultuman, fultumian, fultomian, fulteman, fultemian; *p.* ode, ede; *pp.* od, ed *To help, assist, aid, support;* jŭvāre, adjŭvāre, auxĭlĭāri, făvēre:—Hí woldon me má fultumian *me pŏtius jŭvāre vellent,* Bd. 2, 13; S. 516, 9: Ps. Th. 118, 114. Ic fultumige *auxĭlior,* Ælfc. Gr. 25; Som. 26, 61: *făveo,* 26, 5; Som. 28, 66. Me God fultumeþ *Deus adjŭvat me,* Ps. Th. 53, 4: 88, 18. We eów fultumiaþ *we will aid you,* Chr. Erl. 3, 12. Him náuðer ne fét ne fiðeras ne fultumaþ *neither feet nor wings support them,* Bt. 41, 6; Fox 254, 26. Me ðíne dómas dǽdum fultumiaþ *jūdĭcia tua adjŭvābunt me,* Ps. Th. 118, 175. Fultumode Beorhtríc Offan *Beorhtric assisted Offa,* Chr. 836; Erl. 64, 32. Ðet hí him fultumedon *that they would aid them,* 868; Erl. 73, 22. DER. gefultuman, -fultumian, to-, to-ge-.

fultumend, fultumiend, es; *m.* [fultumende, fultumiende, *part. of* fultuman, fultumian] *A helper, assistant, co-operator;* adjūtor, coŏpĕrātor:—Ðe his gefera wæs and fultumend ðæs godcundan wordes *qui cŏmes ĭtĭnĕris illi et co-ŏpĕrātor verbi,* Bd. 3, 30; S. 562, 12. Ðonne biþ eádig ðe him ǽror wæs Iacobes God geára fultumiend *beātus, cūjus Deus Iacob adjūtor ejus,* Ps. Th. 145, 4: 70, 3: Ps. Lamb. 70, 7: Bd. pref; S. 471, 22.

fultum-leás; *adj. Without help, helpless;* sĭne auxĭlio:—Ðæt hí tó raðe woldon fultumleáse beón æt hiora bearnteámum *that they would very soon be without help from their posterity,* Ors. 1, 14; Bos. 37, 18.

ful-unrót *full sad, very unhappy.* v. full-unrót.

ful-wacor; *adj. Full watchful, very watchful;* pervĭgil, vĭgĭlans, Off. Reg. 5.

ful-wærlíc; *adj. Full wary, very cautious* or *prudent;* valde circumspectus vel cautus, prudentissĭmus:—Ys hit fulwærlíc *it is very prudent,* Gen. 41, 33.

ful-wélig *full wealthy, very rich.* v. full-wélig.

fulwere, es; *m. A baptist;* baptista, Menol. v. fulluhtere.

fulwian; *p.* ode, ade; *pp.* od, ad *To baptize;* baptīzāre:—Fulwiaþ folc under róderum *baptize the people under the firmament,* Exon. 14 b; Th. 30, 23; Cri. 484. Hwæt fulwastu *quid baptizas,* Jn. Sk. Rush. 1, 25. Fulwande, fulwende *baptizans,* Lind. and Rush. 3, 23. Fulwad beón *baptīzāri,* Bd. 1, 27; S. 492, 28. Fulwod beón, 1, 27; S. 493, 2, note. [*Laym.* fulwen.] v. fullian.

ful-wíde; *adv. Full widely, all around, round about;* circumcirca:—Lóca fulwíde ofer londbúende *look all around over the land-dwellers,* Cd. 228; Th. 307, 23; Sat. 684: Exon. 115 b; Th. 444, 13; Kl. 46. Wælhreówes [Nerónes] gewéd wæs fulwíde cúþ *the madness of the cruel [Nero] was full widely known,* Bt. Met. Fox 9, 10; Met. 9, 5.

fulwiht, es; *n. Baptism;* baptismus:—Wæs mid ðý folce fulwiht hæfen *baptism was raised up among the people,* Andr. Kmbl. 3285; An. 1645. Fulwihtes bæþ *the bath of baptism,* Bd. 2, 5; S. 507, 17: Chr. 604; Erl. 20, 18: Cd. 225; Th. 299, 8; Sat. 546: Elen. Kmbl. 978; El. 490. Bútan fulwihte *without baptism,* L. In. 2; Th. i. 102, 20: Chr. 601; Erl. 20, 13: 661; Erl. 34, 16. Ceadwalla fór to Róme, and fulwihte onféng from ðam pápan *Ceadwalla went to Rome, and received baptism from the pope,* Chr. 688; Erl. 42, 6: 878; Erl. 80, 18: Exon. 99 b; Th. 372, 3; Seel. 86: Andr. Kmbl. 3258; An. 1632: Elen. Kmbl. 383; El. 192. Iohannes wæs bodiende dǽdbóte fulwiht *fuit Joannes prædĭcans baptismum pœnĭtentiæ,* Mk. Bos. 1, 4: Chr. 565; Erl. 19, 6: 606; Erl. 20, 26: 661; Erl. 34, 18: Andr. Kmbl. 3268; An. 1637. Þurh fulwihte *through baptism,* Elen. Kmbl. 344; El. 172. Fulwihta calica *baptismata calicum,* Mk. Skt. Lind. 7, 4. v. fulluht.

fulwiht-bæþ, es; *n.* [MS. ful-wihte; bæþ, es; *n.*] *A bath* or *font of baptism;* baptismi fons:—Mon ðæt cild brohte to ðam hálgan þweále fulwihtebæþes *they brought the child to the holy washing of the baptismal font,* Guthl. 2; Gdwin. 10, 18.

fulwiht-ere, es; *m. A baptizer, the Baptist;* baptista:—Ne arás mára Iohanne Fulwihtere *non surrexit mājor Joanne Baptista,* Mt. Bos. 11, 11. Iohannes Fulwihteres *Joannis Baptistæ,* 11, 12. v. fulluhtere.

fulwiht-fæder, es; *m. A baptizer:*—Sancte Iohannes, Cristes fulwihtfæder *St. John, Christ's baptizer,* Blickl. Homl. 205, 17.

fulwiht-hád, es; *m. A baptismal vow:*—Ðæt hie heora fulwihrhádas wel gehealdan *that they keep well their baptismal vows,* Blickl. Homl. 109, 26.

fulwihðe *baptism,* L. Wih. 6; Th. i. 38, 9. v. fulluht.

fulwiht-stow, e; *f. A baptism-place, baptistery;* baptismătis lŏcus, baptistērium:—Ne wǽron cyrican getimbrede, ne fulwihtstowe *churches were not built, nor baptism-places* [baptistēria], Bd. 2, 14; S. 518, 16.

fulwiht-tíd, e; *f. Time of baptism, baptismal time;* baptismătis tempus:—Fulwiht-tíd [MS. -tiid] éces Drihtnes to us cymeþ *the baptismal time of the eternal Lord comes to us,* Menol. Fox 22; Men. 11.

fulwiht-wer, es; *m. A baptist:*—Seó gebyrd Sancte Iohannes ðæs fulwiht-weres *the birthday of St. John the Baptist,* Blickl. Homl. 161, 6.

ful-wíte, full-wíte, es; *n. A full fine;* plēna mulcta:—Gielde he fulwíte [fullwíte MSS. B. H.] *let him pay the full fine,* L. In. 43; Th. i. 128, 18: 72; Th. i. 148, 8: L. C. S. 49; Th. i. 404, 9, note 18, MS. G.

fulwod *baptized,* Bd. 1, 27; S. 493, 2, note; *pp. of* fulwian.

ful-wrætlíce; *adv. Full wondrously, very wonderfully;* mirissĭme:—Ðæt me on gescyldrum scínan mótan fulwrætlíce wundne loccas *that on my shoulders curled locks may shine very wonderfully,* Exon. 111 b; Th. 428, 6; Rä. 41, 104.

fulwuht, es; *n. Baptism;* baptismus:—Hér Birínus bisceop bodude West-Seaxum fulwuht *in this year* [A. D. 634] *bishop Birinus preached baptism to the West-Saxons,* Chr. 634; Erl. 24, 9. v. fulluht.

ful-wurþlíce, full-weorþlíce; *adv. Full worthily, very honourably;* dignissĭme:—Hine man byrígde fulwurþlíce [fullweorþlíce, Th. 294, 21, col. 2], swá he wyrðe wæs *they buried him very honourably, as he was worthy,* Chr. 1036; Th. 294, 22, col. 1.

ful-wyrcan, full-wyrcan; *p.* -worhte; *pp.* -worht *To do fully, accomplish, commit;* perfĭcĕre:—Gif hwá griþbryce fulwyrce *if any one commit a breach of the peace,* L. C. S. 62; Th. i. 408, 22.

ful-yrre; *adj. Full angry, very angry;* valde īrātus:—He fulyrre wód *he rushed forth very angry,* Byrht. Th. 139, 13; By. 253.

funde, *pl.* fundon; *pp.* funden *Found,* Cd. 72; Th. 87, 6; Gen. 1444: 122; Th. 156, 27; Gen. 2595: 174; Th. 220, 5; Dan. 66; *p. and pp. of* findan.

fundian, ic fundige; *p.* ode, ade, ede; *pp.* od, ad, ed *To endeavour to* *find, tend to, aspire to, strive, go forward, hasten, intend, desire;* nīti, tendĕre, intendĕre, propĕrāre:—Ic wylle fundian sylf to ðam sīþe *I will hasten myself to the journey,* Exon. 119 a; Th. 456, 24; Hy. 4, 71: 89 b; Th. 336, 21; Gn. Ex. 52. Fundigende of ðissere worulde *hastening from this world,* Homl. Th. ii. 360, 2. Ic fundige to ðē *I hasten to thee,* Exon. 118 b; Th. 454, 28; Hy. 4, 40. Hwider fundast ðū *whither art thou hastening?* Cd. 103; Th. 137, 5; Gen. 2269. He fundaþ to ðæm weorþscipe ðæs folgoþes *he aspires to the honour of rule,* Past. 8, 2; Hat. MS. 12 b, 25: 11, 3; Hat. MS. 15 a, 9. Hī to ðē hionan fundiaþ *they tend hence to thee,* Bt. 33, 4; Fox 132, 25, 38. Gif twegen men fundiaþ to ānre stowe *if two men are going to the same place,* 36, 4; Fox 178, 10: Past. 18, 1; Hat. MS. 25 b, 6. Nū ðū mōst feran ðider ðū fundadest *now thou mayest go whither thou desiredst,* Exon. 32 b; Th. 102, 12; Cri. 1671. Fundode wrecca of geardum *the stranger hastened from the dwellings,* Beo. Th. 2279; B. 1137. Hwæðer ðū nū ongite forhwȳ ðæt fȳr fundige up *dost thou understand why fire tends upwards?* Bt. 34, 11; Fox 150, 19. Frióra ǣghwilc fundie to ðæm ēcum gōde *let every one of the free aspire to the eternal good,* Bt. Met. Fox 21, 4; Met. 21, 2. Swā hie fundedon *as they desired,* Cd. 115; Th. 150, 17; Gen. 2493: Exon. 106 a; Th. 404, 11; Rä. 23, 6. [*Laym.* fondien *to seek, try: O. Sax.* fundōn *to strive: O. H. Ger.* fundjan, fundēn *subīre.*] DER. tofundian.

fundung, e; *f. A going, departure;* abĭtus, decessus:—He nolde on his fundunge ofer sǣ hīrēd healdan *he would not hold a court on his departure over sea,* Chr. 1106; Erl. 241, 2.

furan; *sulcare, scribere,* Hpt. Gl. 465, 507. v. furh.

FURH; *nom. gen. acc; dat.* fyrh; *dat. pl.* furum; *f. A* FURROW; sulcus:—Furh *sulcus,* Ælfc. Gl. 1; Som. 55, 17; Wrt. Voc. 15, 17: 289, 80. Ne furh ne fōtmǣl *neither furrow nor foot-mark,* L. O. 13; Th. i. 184, 7. Andlang ðære furh *along the furrow,* Cod. Dipl. 554; A. D. 969; Kmbl. iii. 38, 34. Andlang weges to ðære gedrifenan fyrh; andlang fyrh *along the way to the driven furrow; along the furrow,* 1172; A. D. 955; Kmbl. v. 332, 22: Cod. Dipl. Apndx. 441; A. D. 956; Kmbl. iii. 437, 21. On ða furh *on the furrow,* 356; Kmbl. iii. 409, 5: 441; A. D. 956; Kmbl. iii. 437, 23. Ðām drīum furum *in the dry furrows,* Bt. 5, 2; Fox 10, 31. [*Wyc.* forewis, forowis *furrows: Piers P.* furwe: *Plat.* fore, fare, *f: Frs.* furch, furge: *O. Frs.* furch, *f: Dut.* vōre, *f: Ger.* furche, *f: M. H. Ger.* vurch, *f: O. H. Ger.* furh, furuh, *f: Dan.* fure, *m. f: Swed.* fåra, *f: Icel.* furask *to be furrowed.*]

furh-wudu; *m. Fir-wood, a fir-tree;* pīnus, Gl. C. fol. 48 d; Lchdm. iii. 327, 39, col. 1.

furlang, furlung, es; *n. A* FURLONG; stădium:—On ðæt lange furlang *to the long furlong,* Cod. Dipl. 578; A. D. 973; Kmbl. iii. 97, 32. Bethania ys gehende Hierusalem ofer fȳftyne furlang *ĕrat Bethania juxta Ierosŏlȳmam quăsi stădiis quindĕcim,* Jn. Bos. 11, 18. Twentig furlanga *stădia vĭginti,* 6, 19: Lk. Bos. 24, 13. Se is þreóra furlunga brād *qui est latitūdĭnis circĭter trium stădiōrum,* Bd. 1, 25; S. 486, 20.

furþ-an, furþ-on, furþ-um; *adv.* [furþ = forþ *forth,* furþan, furþon, furþum, forþum, *dat.*] *Also, too, even, indeed, further, at first;* etiam, quĭdem, prīmo:—Ic secge eów sōþlīce, ðæt furþon Salomon on eallum hys wuldre næs oferwrigen swā swā ān of ðyson *dico autem vobis, quoniam nec Salomon in omni gloria sua coopertus est sicut unum ex istis,* Mt. Bos. 6, 29. He wēneþ furþon ðæt he man ne sȳ *he even thinks that he is not man,* Blickl. Homl. 179, 5. Ic furþum ongan būgan *I first* [prīmo] *began to dwell,* Exon. 50 b; Th. 176, 21; Gū. 1213.

FURÐOR, furður; *adv.* FURTHER, *more, forwards;* ultĕrius, ultra, amplius, porro:—Ne gang ðū ānne stæpe furðor *go not thou one step further,* Jos. 10, 12: Cd. 223; Th. 292, 24; Sat. 445. Siððan he ðone fintan furðor cūðe *when he further knew the sequel,* Exon. 74 b; Th. 278, 32; Jul. 606: Cd. 21; Th. 26, 3; Gen. 401. Eóde se sæster hwǣtes to lv penega, and eác furðor *the sester of wheat went to fifty-five pence, and even further,* Chr. 1039; Erl. 167, 22. Ðæt he ā furðor wǣre ðonne ōðre brōðor *that he was always more than the other brethren,* Past. 17, 6; Hat. MS. 23 b, 1. Ic wille furðor gān *I will go forwards,* Byrht. Th. 139, 1; By. 247. Furðor dōn *to prefer, esteem,* Past. 17, 7; Hat. MS. 23 b, 14. [*O. Sax.* furðor *further: O. Frs.* furthor, furdur *further: Ger.* fürder *moreover: M. H. Ger.* vürder *further: O. H. Ger.* furdir *ultĕrius.*]

furðra, *m;* furðre, *f. n: comp. adj.* FURTHER, *greater, superior;* ultĕrior, mājor, prior:—Nys se þeówa furðra ðonne se hlāford *non est servus mājor dŏmĭno suo,* Jn. Bos. 13, 16. Hwilc cræft ðē geþūht betwux ðās furðra wesan *quæ ars tĭbi vĭdētur inter istas prior esse?* Coll. Monast. Th. 30, 13.

furðrung *a furthering, promoting, forwarding,* Somn. 2: 17, Lye. v. fyrðrung.

furþ-um; *adv.* [*dat. of* forþ?] *Also, even, indeed, at first;* prīmo, ĕtiam:—Ne furþum nǣnig nǣre on heofenum *nor was there any even in heaven,* Blickl. Homl. 117, 27. He furþum ongan *he also began,* Cd. 63; Th. 75, 11; Gen. 1238. Ic furþum ongan *I first began,* Exon. 50 b; Th. 176, 21; Gū. 1213. v. furþum-līc.

furþum-līc; *adj.* [furþ = forþ *forth, onwards;* furþum = forþum, *dat.* to *onwards, excessive?* līc] *Luxurious, indulgent;* luxŭriōsus, mollis, ventrĭcōsus:—Sarðanapālus [MS. -olus] se sīþmesta cyningc, wæs swīðe furþumlīc man *Sardanapālus the last king was a very luxurious man,* Ors. 1, 12; Bos. 35, 15.

furður; *adv. Further, more;* ultĕrius, ultra:—Ǣr gē on land furður feran *ere ye proceed further into the land,* Beo. Th. 513; B. 254: 1527; B. 761: Exon. 73 b; Th. 274, 30; Jul. 541: Cd. 94; Th. 121, 22; Gen. 2014: Andr. Kmbl. 2976; An. 1491. Ðæt ðē cyning engla gefrætwode furður micle ðonne eall gimma cynn *that the king of angels adorned thee much more than all the kinds of gems,* 3035; An. 1520. v. furðor.

furum *in furrows,* Bt. 5, 2; Fox 10, 31; *dat. pl. of* furh.

FŪS; *adj. Ready, prepared, prompt, quick, eager, hastening, prone, inclined, willing, ready for death, dying;* promptus, cĕler, părātus, prōnus, cŭpĭdus, propĕræ morti devōtus, mŏrĭbundus:—Se ðe stōd fūs on faroþe *he who stood ready on the beach,* Andr. Kmbl. 509; An. 255: Exon. 126 b; Th. 487, 7; Rä. 72, 24: Byrht. Th. 139, 68; By. 281. He ferde siððan swīðe fūs to Rōme *he, being very quick, afterwards went to Rome,* Ælfc. T. 30, 8: Cd. 23; Th. 28, 28; Gen. 443: 147; Th. 184, 6; Exod. 103. Ic eom sīþes fūs *I am ready for the journey,* Beo. Th. 2955; B. 1475: Elen. Kmbl. 2436; El. 1219: Exon. 58 b; Th. 212, 10; Ph. 208. Is him fūs hyge *their mind is ready for death,* Andr. Kmbl. 3327; An. 1666. Ealle ða gemoniaþ mōdes fūsne *all these admonish the prompt of mind,* Exon. 82 a; Th. 309, 1; Seef. 50: Andr. Kmbl. 3307; An. 1656. Ðū me fūsne frignest *thou askest me dying,* Exon. 50 b; Th. 175, 27; Gū. 1201: 49 b; Th. 171, 22; Gū. 1130. Geseah ic ðæt fūse beácen wendan wǣdum and bleóm *I saw the hastening beacon change in hangings and colours,* Rood Kmbl. 42; Kr. 21. Gesāwon randwīgan segn ofer sweóton, fūs on forþweg *the warriors saw the sign over the bands, hastening on its onward way,* Cd. 148; Th. 185, 27; Exod. 129. Wǣron æðelingas eft to leódum fūse to farenne *the nobles were ready to go again to their people,* Beo. Th. 3614; B. 1805: Cd. 151; Th. 190, 9; Exod. 196. Ic of fūsum rād *I rode from the ready* [*men*], Exon. 130 a; Th. 498, 28; Rä. 88, 8. [*Orm.* fus *eager: Laym.* fuse, *pl. prompt, ready: O. Sax.* fūs *inclined, ready: O. H. Ger.* funs *prōnus, promptus: Dan.* fuse *to rush forth: Icel.* fúss *willing, wishing for.*] DER. bealo-fūs, ellor-, grund-, hell-, hin-, ūt-, wæl-.

fūs, es; *n. A hastening, progress;* festīnātio, progressus:—Se ðe leófra manna fūs feor wlātode *who beheld afar the dear men's progress,* Beo. Th. 3836; B. 1916.

fūse; *adv. Readily, promptly;* părāte, prompte, Th. Anlct.

fūs-leóþ, es; *n. A parting-song, death-song, dirge;* mŏrientis cantus, fūnebris nēnia:—Ðǣr wæs ȳþfynde innan burgum fūsleóþ galen *there was easy to be found within the dwellings the death-song sung,* Andr. Kmbl. 3097; An. 1551. Ðū scealt fūsleóþ galan *thou shalt sing the death-song,* Exon. 17 a; Th. 39, 17; Cri. 623: 52 b; Th. 183, 1; Gū. 1320.

fūslīc; *adj. Ready, prepared;* părātus:—Him Onela forgeaf his gædelinges gūþgewǣdu, fyrdsearu fūslīc *Onela gave him his companion's battle-garments, ready martial gear,* Beo. Th. 5229; B. 2618. He geseah beorhte randas, fyrdsearo fūslīcu *he saw bright shields, a war-equipment ready,* 469; B. 232.

fūslīce; *adv. Readily, promptly, gladly;* prompte, lĭbenter:—Ðæt hī, fūslīce gehȳrdon, ða ðe him gelǣrde wǣron *ut lĭbenter ea, quæ dīcĕrentur, audīrent,* Bd. 4, 27; S. 604, note 17, MS. T.

fūs-trendel; *focus,* Hpt. Gl. 439.

fȳfteógeða *the fifteenth:*—Forþferde he ðȳ fȳfteógeðan dæge Kalendarum Martiarum *qui defunctus die dĕcĭma quinta Kalendārum Martiārum,* Bd. 4, 5; S. 571, 36. v. fīfteóða.

fȳftyne *fifteen;* quindĕcim:—Ofer fȳftyne furlang *over fifteen furlongs,* Jn. Bos. 11, 18. v. fīftyne.

fyht *a fight, battle,* Som. Ben. Lye. v. feoht.

fyhte-horn, es; *m. A fighting* or *battle-horn;* pugnātōrium cornu:—Ealra fyrenfulra fyhtehornas ic bealdlīce gebrece snióme *omnia cornua peccātōrum confringam,* Ps. Th. 74, 9.

fyhtling, es; *m. A fightling, soldier;* prælĭātor, Gr. Dial. 2, 3.

fyht-wīte, fiht-wīte, es; *n. A fine for fighting;* pugnæ mulcta:—Ðæt fyht-wīte *the fine for fighting,* L. E. G. 13; Th. i. 174, 27.

fyl, es; *m. A fall, ruin, destruction;* cāsus, intĕrĭtus:—Hȳ ðam feore fyl gehēhton *they threatened destruction to his life,* Exon. 40 b; Th. 135, 7; Gū. 520: Byrht. Th. 133, 57; By. 71: 139, 35; By. 264. DER. hrā-fyl. v. fyll, es; *m.*

fȳlan; *p.* de; *pp.* ed *To foul, defile;* inquĭnāre, fœdāre, contāmĭnāre. DER. a-fȳlan, be-, ge-. v. fūlian.

fylc, es; *n. A company, troop, tribe, country, province;* agmen, caterva, trĭbus, provincia. [*Icel.* fylki, *n. a county* or *shire.*] DER. æl-fylc, bī-, ge-.

fylcian; *p.* ade *To arrange troops:*—Harald his liþ fylcade *Harold drew up his force,* Chr. 1066; Erl. 200, 33. [*Icel.* fylkja.]

fyld, es; *m. A fold, volume;* vŏlūmen, Som. Ben. Lye. Hpt. Gl. 494.

fylde, *pl.* fyldon *filled,* Andr. Kmbl. 1046; An. 523: Jn. Bos. 6, 13; *p. of* fyllan.

FYLGEAN, fylgan, fylgian, fyligean, fylian, filian, feligean; *p.* de; *pp.* ed; *v. trans. dat. acc. To follow, attend, follow* or *carry out;* sĕqui, insĕqui, exsĕqui:—Ðæt hearma swā fela fylgean sceolde monna cynne *that so many ills must follow to mankind*, Cd. 33; Th. 44, 15; Gen. 709: L. Eth. ii. 9; Th. i. 288, 29. Ongon se wīsdōm his gewunan fylgan *wisdom began to follow his custom*, Bt. Met. Fox 7, 2; Met. 7, 1: Exon. 122 a; Th. 468, 6; Phar. 3: Judth. 10; Thw. 21, 24; Jud. 33. Ðe him fylgian wolde *who would follow him*, Hy. 10, 39; Hy. Grn. ii. 293, 39. He ne lēt him ǣnig ne fyligean *non admīsit quemquam se sĕqui*, Mk. Bos. 5, 37: 8, 34. Ða he on his weorcum wæs geornlīce fyligende *which he was diligently carrying out in his works*, Bd. 3, 28; S. 560, 17. We wǣron þē fylgende *we were following thee*, St. And. 2, 20. Him fyliende *sĕquentes se*, Jn. Bos. 1, 38. Ic fylige *sĕquor*, Ælfc. Gr. 36; Som. 38, 24. Ðū gedwolan fylgest *thou followest error*, Exon. 68 b; Th. 254, 25; Jul. 202. Gūþmecga him fylgeþ *the warrior pursues him*, Salm. Kmbl. 186; Sal. 92. Ic fylgde gōdnysse *sĕquēbar bonĭtātem*, Ps. Spl. 37, 21: Bt. Met. Fox 26, 108; Met. 26, 54. Se wrāđa boda fylgde him *the fell messenger followed him*, Cd. 32; Th. 43, 9; Gen. 688. Ðe he ǣr fyligde [fylgde, MS. B.] *whom he before followed*, L. Ed. 10; Th. i. 164, 16. Gē gedwolan fylgdon *ye followed error*, Elen. Kmbl. 742; El. 371: Exon. 29 a; Th. 88, 16; Cri. 1441. Twegen leorningcnihtas fyligdon đam Hǣlende *duo discĭpŭli sĕcūti sunt Jēsum*, Jn. Bos. 1, 37. Fyle [fylge MS. C.] đū đam *persĕquĕre eam*, Ps. Spl. 33, 14. Ðæt we Godes lage fylgean [fylgian MS. B.] *that we follow God's law*, L. C. S. 85; Th. i. 424, 7. Ðæt hī georne heora bōcum and gebēdum fylgean *that they strictly attend to their books and prayers*, L. Eth. vi. 41; Th. i. 326, 3. [*Wyc.* foleweden, *p. pl: Piers P.* folwe, folwen: *Chauc.* folwe: *Laym.* folien, foluen, fulien: *Orm.* follȝhenn: *O. Sax.* folgōn: *Frs.* folgjen: *O. Frs.* folgia, fulgia, folia: *Dut.* volgen: *Ger.* folgen: *M. H. Ger.* volgen: *O. H. Ger.* folgēn, folkēn: *Dan.* fölge: *Swed.* följa: *Icel.* fylgja.] DER. æfter-fylian, æt-fyligan, be-filgan, ge-fylgan, under-fylgan. v. folgian.

fylgend, es; *m. One who follows* or *carries anything out, a performer;* exsĕcūtor:—Ðara þinga đe he ōđre lǣrde to dōnne, he sylfa wæs se wilsumesta fylgend *eōrum quæ agenda dŏcēbat ĕrat exsĕcūtor devōtissĭmus*, Bd. 5, 22; S. 644, 4, note, MSS. B. C.

fylgestre; *f. sectatrix*. Hpt. Gl. 435.

fylging, e; *f. A following:*—Miþ fylginge *sectando*, Rtl. 16, 23; 56, 5.

fylging, e; *f. That which follows, a harrow;* occa, Cot. 143.

fylian *to follow:*—Fyle đū đam *persequere eam*, Ps. Spl. 33, 14. Fylidon, Mt. Kmbl. C. C. 4, 22. v. fylgean.

fyligean *to follow, attend, follow* or *carry out*, Mk. Bos. 5, 37: 8, 34: Bd. 3, 28; S. 560, 17. v. fylgean.

fylignes, -ness, e; *f. A following, completing, executing;* successio, exĕcūtio:—Ðæt to gōdra dǣda fylignessum he hī aweahte *ut eos ad ŏpĕrum bŏnōrum exĕcūtiōnem excitāret*, Bd. 3, 5; S. 526, 33.

FYLL, fill, fyllu, fyllo, e; *f. The* FILL, *fulness, plenty;* plēnĭtūdo, satŭrĭtas:—Drinc nū đīne fylle *drink now thy fill*, Ors. 2, 4; Bos. 45, 36. Gē etaþ to fylle *comĕdētis in satŭrĭtāte*, Lev. 26, 5. Fylle gefrægnod *known by its plenteousness*, Beo. Th. 2670, note; B. 1333. Fylle gefǣgon *they rejoiced in the plenty*, 2032; B. 1014. Næs hie đære fylle gefeán hæfdon *they had no joy of that plenty*, 1128; B. 562. Ic sylle heora hungrium hlāf to fylle *paupĕres ejus satŭrābo pānibus*, Ps. Th. 131, 16. [*Ger.* fülle, *f: M. H. Ger.* volle, *f. m;* vülle, *f: O. H. Ger.* folla, follī, fullī, *f: Goth.* fullei, fullo, *f: Dan.* fylde, *m. f: Swed.* fylle, *n: Icel.* fylli, fyllr, *f.*] DER. wist-fyll.

FYLL, fyl, fell, fiell, es; *m.* I. *a* FALL, *ruin, destruction, death;* cāsus, intĕrĭtus:—Crist is ofermōdigra fyll *Christ is the fall of the high-minded*, Ors. 3, 2; Bos. 55, 6. Æfter his fylle *after his death*, 6, 5; Bos. 119, 22. Mīne innoþas on đam fylle tolocene wǣron *interānea essent ruendo convulsa*, Bd. 5, 6; S. 619, 31. Se bisceop sārgode be đam fylle and mīne forwyrde *episcŏpus de cāsu et intĕrĭtu meo dŏlēbat*, 5, 6; S. 619, 32. Æt fylle *at the fall*, L. M. 1, 4; Lchdm. ii. 48, 14, note. II. *a* FALL, *case, inflection in grammar;* cāsus, inflectio:—Cāsus, đæt is fyll odde gebīgedniss *case, that is a declining or inflection*, Ælfc. Gr. 14; Som. 17, 23. [*Orm.* fall: *O. Sax.* fal, *m: Frs. O. Frs.* fal, fel, *m: Dut.* val, *m: Ger.* fall, *m: M. H. Ger.* val, *m: O. H. Ger.* fal, *m: Dan.* fald, *n: Swed.* fall, *n: Icel.* fall, *n. lapsus, cāsus*, Rask Hald. Egils.] DER. wæl-fyll.

FYLLAN; ic fylle, đū fyllest, fylst, he fylleþ, fylþ, *pl.* fyllaþ; *p.* fylde, fyllde, *pl.* fyldon; *impert.* fyl, *pl.* fyllaþ; *pp.* fylled, fyld; *v. trans. To* FILL, *replenish, satisfy, cram, stuff, finish, complete, fulfil;* implēre, replēre, sātŭrāre, farcīre, supplēre, complēre:—Ðæt sceolon fyllan firengeorne men *sinful men shall fill that*, Exon. 31 b; Th. 98, 11; Cri. 1606: 124 b; Th. 479, 16; Rä. 62, 8. Ðæt he fyrngewyrht fyllan sceolde *that he should finish his former deeds*, 47 a; Th. 160, 16; Gū. 944. Ic crammige odde fylle *farcio*, Ælfc. Gr. 30, 2; Som. 34, 36. Ic fylle *suppleo*, 26, 1; Som. 28, 29. Ðū fyllest [fylst Spl.] ealra wihta gehwam bletsunga *tu imples omne anĭmal bĕnĕdictiōne*, Ps. Th. 144, 17. He heáhgetimbro fylleþ fȳres egsan *he shall fill the high structures with fire's horror*, Exon. 22 a; Th. 60, 25; Cri. 975. Se đe fylþ on gōdum gewilnunge đīne *qui replet in bŏnis desīdĕrium tuum*, Ps. Spl. 102, 5. Hī fyllaþ mid feore foldan gesceafte *they shall fill earth's creation with their spirit*, Exon. 22 a; Th. 59, 15; Cri. 953: Ps. Th. 64, 5. He fylde hig *sătŭrāvit eos*, Ps. Spl. 104, 38. He wuldres fylde beorhtne boldwēlan *he filled the bright dwelling of wealth with glory*, Andr. Kmbl. 1046; An. 523; Hy. 10, 19; Hy. Grn. ii. 293, 19. Moises spræc đās word befōran Isrēla folce and hig fyllde ōþ ende *lŏcūtus est Moyses audiente ūnĭverso cœtu Israel verba carmĭnis hūjus et ad fīnem usque complēvit*, Deut. 31, 30. Hig fyldon twelf wylian fulle *implēvērunt duodĕcim cophĭnos*, Jn. Bos. 6, 13. Fyl nū đa frumspræce *fulfil now the saying of old!* Exon. 53 b; Th. 188, 7; Az. 42: Cd. 190; Th. 236, 24; Dan. 326. Tudre fyllaþ eorþan ælgrēne *fill the all-green earth with progeny*, 10; Th. 13, 2; Gen. 196: 75; Th. 92, 24; Gen. 1533. Beóþ đīne feldas fylde mid wæstmum *campi tui replēbuntur ūbertāte*, Ps. Th. 64, 12. Ðonne heofon and hel hæleđa bearnum fylde weorþeþ *when heaven and hell shall be filled with the sons of men*, Exon. 31 a; Th. 97, 20; Cri. 1593. [*Wyc.* fill, fille: *Piers P.* fillen: *Chauc.* filled, *pp: Laym.* fulle, iuullen: *Orm.* fillenn: *Plat.* vullen: *O. Sax.* fullian: *Frs.* folljen: *O. Frs.* fullia, folla, fella: *Dut.* vullen: *Ger.* füllen: *M. H. Ger.* vüllen: *O. H. Ger.* fulljan: *Goth.* fullyan: *Dan.* fylde: *Swed.* fylla: *Icel.* fylla.] DER. a-fyllan, be-, ge-, ongeán-, samod-: ǣ-fyllende.

FYLLAN = fellan; ic fylle, đū fyllest, he fylleþ, *pl.* fyllaþ; *p.* fylde, *pl.* fyldon; *pp.* fylled; *v. trans. To fell, cut down, cast down, throw down, destroy;* prosternĕre, cædĕre, dejĭcĕre, destruĕre:—Đā us man fyllan ongan ealle to eorþan *then they began to fell us all to the ground*, Rood Kmbl. 146; Kr. 73. Fyllan, Judth. 11; Thw. 24, 17; Jud. 194. Gif đū wylt đa firenfullan fyllan mid deáþe *if thou wilt fell the wicked with death*, Ps. Th. 138, 16. Ic beámas fylle *I fell trees*, Exon. 101 a; Th. 381, 11; Rä. 2, 9. Se grimmesta hungor hī fylde *fămes acerbissĭma eos prostrāvit*, Bd. 4, 13; S. 582, 29: Cd. 35; Th. 46, 20; Gen. 747. Ða synsceađan Godes tempel fyldon *the sinful cast down God's temple*, Exon. 18 a; Th. 44, 27; Cri. 709. Fyll đa oferhydigan *cast down the proud*, Ps. Th. 73, 22. Hergas fyllaþ *cast down the idols*, Exon. 14 b; Th. 30, 27; Cri. 486. [*Chauc.* felle: *Laym.* fallen: *O. Sax.* fellian: *Frs.* fellen: *O. Frs.* falla, fella: *Dut.* vellen: *Ger.* fällen: *M. H. Ger.* falljan, fellen: *Dan.* fælde: *Swed.* fälla: *Icel.* fella.] DER. a-fyllan, be-, ge-, of-, to-.

fyllend, es; *m. A fulfiller, performer;* exsĕcūtor:—Ðara þinga đe he ōđre lǣrde to dōnne, he sylfa wæs se wilsumesta fyllend *eōrum quæ agenda dŏcēbat ĕrat exsĕcūtor devōtissĭmus*, Bd. 5, 22; S. 644, 4.

fylle-seóc; *adj. Falling sick, epileptic, lunatic;* ĕpĭleptĭcus = ἐπιληπτικός, lunātĭcus:—Ðȳ-læs cild sȳ fylleseóc *lest the child be epileptic*, Med. ex Quadr. 5, 12; Lchdm. i. 350, 12. He ys fylleseóc *lunātĭcus est*, Mt. Bos. 17, 15. Wiđ fylleseócum men *for an epileptic man*, Med. ex Quadr. 8, 9; Lchdm. i. 358, 21. Heó fylleseócum helpeþ *it helpeth the epileptic*, Herb. 143, 1; Lchdm. i. 266, 5.

fylle-seócnys, -nyss, e; *f. The falling sickness, epilepsy;* ĕpĭlepsia = ἐπιληψία:—Wiđ fylleseócnysse *for the falling sickness*, Herb. 61, 3; Lchdm. i. 164, 9.

fylle-wærc, felle-wærc, es; *n. The falling sickness, epilepsy;* ĕpĭlepsia = ἐπιληψία:—Of đæs magan ādle cumaþ hramma and fyllewærc *from the disease of the stomach come cramps and epilepsy*, L. M. 2, 1; Lchdm. ii. 174, 25.

fyllnis, se; *f. Fulness, that which makes full or complete, a supplement:*—Fyllniss *plenitudo*, Mt. Kmbl. Lind. 9, 16; Rtl. 100, 13. Fyllnis *supplementum*, Mk. Skt. Lind. 2, 21. Fylnis *perfectio*, p. 1, 13.

fyllu, e; *f:* fyllo; *indecl. f. Fulness;* plēnĭtudo:—Anfēng fǣmne fyllo *the woman received fulness*, Exon. 112 a; Th. 429, 15; Rä. 43, 5. v. fyll, e; *f.*

fyllung, e; *f. A fulfilling, performing;* perfectio, Som. Ben. Lye.

fylmen, es; *n. A film, thin skin, prepuce;* præpūtium, omentum:—Gē emsnīdaþ đæt flǣsc eówres fylmenes *circumcīdētis carnem præpūtii vestri*, Gen. 17, 11. Se werhādes man, đe ne byþ ymsniden on đam flǣsce hys fylmenes, his sāwul biþ adilegod of his folce *mascŭlus, cūjus præpūtii căro circumcīsa non fuĕrit, delēbĭtur ănĭma illa de pŏpŭlo suo*, 17, 14: Homl. Th. i. 94, 32. Fylmena *films; omenta vel membrānæ*, Ælfc. Gl. 31; Som. 61, 93; Wrt. Voc. 27, 23: Cot. 133. Fylmen *omentum*, 74; Som. 71, 61; Wrt. Voc. 44, 43. On đam fylmene *in præpūtio*, Homl. Th. i. 94, 13. Feóllon swylce fylmena of his eágum *there fell as it were films from his eyes*, Homl. Th. i. 386, 31.

fȳlnes, -ness, e; *f. Foulness;* fœdĭtas, fœtor, fūlīgo:—Eorþan fȳlnes, eal forweornast *foulness of earth, thou art all rotting*, Exon. 98 a; Th. 368, 7: Cot. 83. v. fūlnes.

fylst, he fylþ *fillest, he fills*, Ps. Spl. 144, 17: 102, 5; *2nd and 3rd sing. pres. of* fyllan.

FYLST, e; *f. Help, assistance;* auxĭlium:—Mid Godes fylste *with God's help*, Bt. Met. Fox 23, 14; Met. 23, 7: Ors. 1, 12; Bos. 35, 20. [*Laym.* fulste, vulste *aid, help: O. Frs.* fulliste, folliste, folste, *aid.* [Cf. fullǣst.]

fylstan, filstan, ic fylste, he fylsteþ; *p.* [fylstede =] fylste, *pl.* fylston; *subj. pres.* fylste, *pl.* fylsten, fylston; *pp.* fylsted; *v. trans. dat.* [fylst e;

f. help] *To help, give help, aid, protect;* adjūvāre, auxĭliāri, protĕgĕre:—Ongan him fylstan *began to give help to them,* Byrht. Th. 139, 37; By. 265. Hig bĭcnodon hyra geferan, ðæt hī him fylston *annuĕrunt sŏciis, ut adjūvārent eos* [*that they should give help to them*], Lk. Bos. 5, 7. Him fylste Drihten *the Lord helped him,* Cd. 124; Th. 159, 8; Gen. 2631. Pirrus him fylste *Pyrrhus helped him,* Ors. 3, 11; Bos. 75, 28. Hī him fylston wel *they helped him well,* Cd. 114; Th. 149, 34; Gen. 2484. Arīson and fylston eów *surgant et vos protĕgant,* Deut. 32, 38. [*Laym.* fulsten.] DER. ge-fylstan, to-: ge-fylsta. Cf. fullǽstan.

fylþ *falls,* Mt. Bos. 21, 44; *3rd pers. pres. of* feallan.

FYLÞ, e; *f.* FILTH, *impurity, rottenness;* spurcĭtia, putrēdo:—Hig synt innan fulle ealre fȳlþe *intus plēna sunt omni spurcĭtia,* Mt. Bos. 23, 27. Wiđ āne cwēnan fȳlþe adreógaþ *cum ūna meretrīce spurcĭtiem ăgunt,* Lup. Serm. 1, 11; Hick. Thes. ii. 102, 27, 29: Scint. 9. [*O. Sax.* fūlitha, *f*: *O. H. Ger.* fūlida, *f*.]

fyl-wērig; *adj. Slaughter-weary;* cæde defessus:—Ðū hine geseón mōste fylwērigne *thou mightest have seen him slaughter-weary,* Beo. Th. 1929; B. 962.

fȳnd *a fiend, an enemy,* Ps. Spl. 40, 12. v. feónd.

fȳnd, *pl.* of fēond: Lev. 26, 8, 16: Bt. 20; Fox 72, 21: Mt. Bos. 5, 44: Lk. Bos. 6, 27, 35.

fynde; *adj. Able to be found.* DER. eáþ-fynde, ēþ-, ȳþ-.

fyne, es; *n? Moisture, mould;* ūlīgo:—Fyne allugo [*=ūlīgo*], Ælfc. Gl. 106; Som. 78, 47; Wrt. Voc. 57, 28.

fynegian; *p.* ode; *pp.* od [fynig *mouldy*] *To become mouldy* or *musty;* mūcescĕre:—Ðæt ðæt hālige hūsel sceole fynegian *that the holy housel should become mouldy,* L. Ælf. C. 36; Th. ii. 360, 7.

fynel, es; *m. Fennel;* fēnĭcŭlum, Ælfc. Gl. 39; Som. 63, 68; Wrt. Voc. 30, 20. v. finol.

fynig, fini; *adj. Mouldy, musty, damp;* mūcĭdus, ulĭgĭnōsus:—Gyf ðæt hūsel byþ fynig *if the housel be mouldy,* L. Ælf. C. 36; Th. ii. 360, 8, 13. Fynig *alluginatus* [*=ulĭgĭnōsus*], Ælfc. Gl. 106; Som. 78, 48; Wrt. Voc. 57, 29.

fyorh; *gen.* fyores; *dat.* fyore; *n. Life;* vīta:—Fīf and hundteontig on fyore lifde wintra *he passed a hundred and five years in life,* Cd. 59; Th. 72, 10; Gen. 1184. v. feorh I.

fyr, fyrr, fier; *adv.* [*comp. of* feor; *adv. far,* q. v.] *Farther;* ultĕrius, longius:—Ðeáh ðū fyr sēo ðonne ðū wǽre *though thou art farther than thou wast,* Bt. 5, 1; Fox 8, 33, note 7, MS. Bod. Ǽr gē fyr heonan feran *ere ye proceed farther hence,* Beo. Th. 510; B. 252: 288; B. 143. Fyr faran *longius īre,* Lk. Bos. 24, 28. Fyr fleón *to flee farther,* Ors. 1, 12; Bos. 36, 4.

FȲR, fīr, es; *n.* FIRE, *a fire, hearth;* ignis, fŏcus:—Būton he hæbbe swā scearp andget swā ðæt fȳr *unless he have an understanding as sharp as the fire,* Bt. 39, 4; Fox 216, 28. Fȳr *ignis,* Wrt. Voc. 284, 11: Mk. Bos. 9, 44, 46: Ex. 22, 6: Lev. 10, 2: Ps. Spl. 49, 4. Fȳr *ignis* vel *fŏcus,* Wrt. Voc. 82, 51. Him befōran fōron fȳr and wolcen *fire and cloud journeyed before him,* Cd. 146; Th. 183, 18; Exod. 93: 169; Th. 212, 9; Exod. 536: 192; Th. 239, 22; Dan. 374. Ðæs fȳres gecynd is hāt and drīe *the nature of fire is hot and dry,* Boutr. Scrd. 18, 22, 23. In fȳres fæđm *into the fire's embrace,* Beo. Th. 372; B. 185. Fȳres feng *grasp of the fire,* 3532; B. 1764. Lāgon ða ōđre fȳnd on ðam fȳre *the other fiends lay in the fire,* Cd. 17; Th. 21, 10; Gen. 322: 24; Th. 31, 19; Gen. 487: 117; Th. 152, 17; Gen. 2521. Sȳ hyt forcorfen, and on fȳr aworpen *excīdētur, et in ignem mittētur,* Mt. Bos. 7, 19: 17, 15: Mk. Bos. 9, 43: Lk. Bos. 3, 9: Jn. Bos. 15, 6. Ne onæle gē nān fȳr on ðam dæge *non succendētis ignem per diem sabbăti,* Ex. 35, 3: 22, 6. Mid fȳre *with fire,* Bt. 39, 4; Fox 216, 25. He sweartade fȳre and āttre *he blackened with fire and venom,* Cd. 214; Th. 269, 26; Sat. 79: 220; Th. 284, 21: Sat. 325: Beo. Th. 5183; B. 2595. [*Wyc.* fyr, fire: *Piers P.* fir: *Chauc.* fire: *R. Glouc.* fyur: *Laym.* fur: *Orm.* fir: *Scot.* fyre: *Plat.* vür, vüer, füer, *n*: *O. Sax.* fiur, *n*: *Frs.* fjoer: *O. Frs.* fior, fiur, *n*: *Dut.* vuur, *n*: *Ger.* feuer, *n*: *M. H. Ger.* viur, viuwer, viwer, *n*: *O. H. Ger.* fiur, *n*: *Dan.* fyr, *m. f*: *Swed.* fyr, *m. a lighthouse, beacon*: *Icel.* fúrr, *m. fire*: *Lat.* prūna, *f. a burning coal*: *Grk.* πῦρ, *n.*] DER. ād-fȳr, æled-, bǽl-, heáh-, heađo-, helle-, līg-, wæl-, wælm-, wan-, won-.

fyran; *p.* fyrde *To go;* īre:—Ine fyrde to Sce. Petres *Ine went to St. Peter's,* Text Rof. 61, 15. v. feran.

fȳran; *adj. Fiery;* ignītus:—God gelogode fȳran swurd *God placed a fiery sword,* Boutr. Scrd. 20, 30. v. fȳren.

fȳran; *p.* de; *pp.* ed *To castrate;* castrāre:—Bāras fȳran *apros castrāre,* Obs. Lun. § 3; Lchdm. iii. 184, 19. DER. a-fȳran.

fyras; *gen.* fyra; *pl. m. Men;* hŏmĭnes:—Freá sceáwode fyra fyrngeweorc *the lord beheld the ancient work of men,* Beo. Th. 4561; B. 2286: 4007; B. 2001. Ǽnig ne wæs fyra cynnes *there was not any of the race of men,* Exon. 47 a; Th. 161, 19; Gū. 961: 63 a; Th. 231, 20; Ph. 492: 92 a; Th. 345, 22; Gn. Ex. 194. v. firas.

fȳr-bǽr; *adj. Igniferus,* Hpt. Gl. 509.

fȳr-bæþ; *gen.* -bæđes, -bađes; *n. A fire-bath;* igneum balneum:—On fȳrbæđe *in the fire-bath,* Elen. Kmbl. 1895; El. 949. In fȳrbađe *in the fire-bath,* Exon. 20 a; Th. 52, 10; Cri. 831: 22 b; Th. 61, 18; Cri. 986.

fȳr-bend, es; *m. A fire-band;* vincŭlum igne dūrātum:—Dūru onarn fȳrbendum fæst *the door fast with fire-bands yielded,* Beo. Th. 1448; B. 722.

fȳr-bēta, an; *m.* [bētan II. *to light* or *make a fire, kindle*] *One who looks after the fire;* fŏcārius, Ælfc. Gl. 30; Som. 61, 74; Wrt. Voc. 27, 3.

fȳr-bryne, es; *m. A fire burning;* incendium:—Wearþ ungemetlīc fȳrbryne mid Rōmānum *an immense fire happened among the Romans,* Ors. 4, 7; Bos. 87, 18.

fyrclian; *p.* ode; *pp.* od *To flash, flicker;* fulgēre:—Swilce se beám ongeán weardes wiđ ðæs steorran ward fyrcliende wǽre *as if the beam were flashing towards the star from an opposite direction,* Chr. 1106; Erl. 240, 34. v. flicerian.

fȳr-clom; *gen.* -clommes; *m.* [clom *a band, bond*] *A fire-bond;* vincŭlum ignītum vel igne dūrātum:—Ðis is þeóstre [đeostræ MS.] hām, þearle gebunden fæstum fȳrclommum *this is a dark home, strongly bound with fast fire-bonds,* Cd. 213; Th. 267, 16; Sat. 39.

fȳr-cruce *a fire-cruse* or *pot, kettle;* cŭcŭma, Som. Ben. Lye. DER. cruce.

fȳr-cyn, -cynn, es; *n. A kind of fire;* igneum gĕnus:—Mycel fȳrcyn and mycel bryne *a great kind of fire and a great burning,* Ors. 6, 1; Bos. 115, 36.

FYRD, fyrdung, e; *f.* I. *an army, the military array of the whole country;* exercĭtus, expĕdītio. To take part in the *fyrd* was the general duty of every freeman, even of the mere churl, but as forming one branch of the *trinoda necessitas* it belonged especially to owners of land. 'Every owner of land was obliged to the *fyrd* or expeditio; the owner of bookland as liable to the *trinoda necessitas* alone; the occupier of folkland as subject to that as well as to many other obligations from which bookland was exempted.' Stubbs' Const. Hist. i. 190, q. v. *By the simple appellation of* fyrd *the land-force was to be understood.* The naval armament was denominated the scip-fyrd. v. folc-land I [*c*]:—Be ðon đe gesīþcund man fyrde forsitte. Gif gesīþcund mon, landāgende, forsitte fyrde, geselle cxx scillinga and þolie his landes; unlandāgende lx scillinga; cierlisc xxx scillinga; to fyrd-wīte [MS. fierd-wīte] *in case a* gesithcund *man neglects the* fyrd. *If a* gesithcund *man owning land, neglect the* fyrd, *let him pay* 120 *shillings and forfeit his land; one not owning land,* 60 *shillings; a churlish man,* 30 *shillings; as a fine for neglecting the* fyrd, L. In. 51; Th. i. 134, 7-10. II. *an army;* agmen, exercĭtus:—Fyrd sceal wiđ fyrde sacan *army shall strive against army,* Menol. Fox 565; Gn. C. 52: Cd. 146; Th. 183, 8; Exod. 88. On Faraones fyrde *in Pharaoh's army,* Exon. 122 a; Th. 468, 3; Phar. 2. Claudius, se cāsere, fyrde gelǽdde on Breotone *Claudius, the emperor, led an army into Britain,* Bd. 1, 3; S. 475, 11: Cd. 145; Th. 181, 17; Exod. 62. Gesomnade he his fyrd wiđ West-Seaxum *he assembled his army against the West Saxons,* Bd. 2, 9; S. 512, 2: Cd. 149; Th. 187, 24; Exod. 156. Fōr fyrda mǽst *the greatest of armies marched,* Elen. Kmbl. 69; El. 35. Hī heora fyrd gesomnedon *they assembled their armies,* Bd. 3, 14; S. 539, 36. III. *an expedition;* expĕdītio:—Ðæt ic of ðisse fyrde feran wille *that I will flee out of this expedition,* Byrht. Th. 138, 16; By. 221. Ðeáh ðū mid us ne fare on fyrd *though thou go not with us in the expedition,* Ps. Th. 43, 11. Onginnaþ ymb ða fyrde þencean *they begin to think about the expedition,* Cd. 21; Th. 26, 18; Gen. 408: 32; Th. 43, 11; Gen. 689: 92; Th. 118, 7; Gen. 1961. IV. *a camp;* castrum:—Fyrd *castrum,* Ælfc. Gl. 7; Som. 56, 76; Wrt. Voc. 18, 28. [*Laym.* ferde, uerde, *f. an army*: *Orm.* ferd *an army*: *Scot.* ferde *an army, host*: *O. Sax.* fard, *f. an expedition*: *Frs.* feard: *O. Frs.* ferd, *f. an expedition*: *Ger.* fahrt, fart, *f. ĭter*: *M. H. Ger.* vart, *f*: *O. H. Ger.* fart, *f. ĭter*: *Dan.* fart, færd, *m. f. an expedition*: *Swed.* fart, *m. a passage*: *Icel.* ferð, *f. travel.*]

fyrd *a ford,* found in the compound Twȳ-fyrd *Twyford.* v. ford.

fyrd-cræft *an expedition.* v. fird-cræft.

fyrderung, e; *f. A preparation* or *provision for an expedition;* expedītiōnis appărātus, Som. Ben. Lye.

fyrd-esne, es; *m. A warlike youth* or *man, warrior;* bellĭcōsus jŭvĕnis, bellātor:—In ðam ylcan gefeohte, Ōsfriþ his ōđer sunu, ǽr him gefeóll, se hwatesta fyrdesne *in quo bello, ante illum ūnus fīlius ējus Osfrid, jŭvĕnis bellĭcōsus, cĕcĭdit,* Bd. 2, 20; S. 521, 15.

fyrd-færeld, es; *n.* [fyrd *an army;* færeld *a journey*] *A military expedition* or *service;* mīlĭtāris expedītio:—Būtan ðysum þrīm þingum, ðæt is, fyrdfærelde, and brigcgewurce, and burhbōte *except these three things, that is, military service, bridge-work, and reparation of fortresses,* Cod. Dipl. 715; A. D. 1006; Kmbl. iii. 350, 10. Ðæt he þreó þing of his lande dō, fyrdfæreld, and burhbōte, and brycgeweorc *ut ĭta făciat pro terra sua, scilĭcet, expĕdītiōnem, burhbōtam, et brigbōtam,* L. R. S. 1; Th. i. 432, 2.

fyrd-faru, ferd-faru, e; *f. A military expedition* or *service;* mīlĭtāris expĕdītio:—Gif hwā burhbōte, ođđe bricgbōte, ođđe fyrdfare forsitte *if any one neglect reparation of fortresses, or reparation of bridges, or military service,* L. C. S. 66; Th. i. 410, 8.

fyrd-geatwe, -geatewe; *gen.* a; *pl. f.* [geatwe *arms, trappings*] *Warlike trappings* or *arms;* bellĭcōsus appărātus:—Yr byþ fyrdgeatewa [fyrdgeacewa MS.] sum *a bow is a part of warlike arms*, Runic pm. 27; Hick. Thes. i. 135, 54.

fyrd-gemaca, an; *m.* [gemaca *a companion*] *A companion in war, fellow-soldier;* commīlĭto:—Tytus asende bodan to hys fyrdgemacan, đe wæs genemned Uespasianus *Titus sent messengers to his fellow-soldier, who was named Vespasian*, Nathan. 5.

fyrd-gestealla, an; *m. A comrade in arms, martial comrade;* expĕdītiōnis bellĭcæ sŏcius, commīlĭto:—Nealles folc-cyning fyrdgesteallum gylpan þorfte *the people's king needed not to boast of his comrades in arms*, Beo. Th. 5739; B. 2873. Wurdon Sodomware leófum bedrorene fyrdgesteallum *the inhabitants of Sodom were deprived of their beloved martial comrades*, Cd. 93; Th. 120, 23; Gen. 1999.

fyrd-getrum, es; *n.* [getrum *a band*] *A martial band, company of soldiers;* agmen, cŏhors:—Fūs fyrdgetrum *the prompt martial band*, Cd. 147; Th. 184, 6; Exod. 103. Hēht his herecist healdan georne, fæst fyrdgetrum *he bade his warlike band, the firm company, bear them boldly*, 151; Th. 189, 1; Exod. 178.

fyrd-hom, es; *m.* [hom *a covering, garment*] *A war-covering;* bellĭca vestis, lōrīca:—Đæt heó đone fyrdhom þurhfōn ne mihte *that she might not pierce through the war-covering*, Beo. Th. 3012; B. 1504.

fyrd-hrægl, es; *n.* [hrægel, hrægl *a garment*] *A war-garb;* bellĭca vestis, lōrīca:—Helm oft gescær, fǣges fyrdhrægl *it often slashed the helmet, the war-garb of the fated*, Beo. Th. 3058; B. 1527.

fyrd-hwæt; *adj. Bold in warfare, warlike, brave;* bellĭcōsus:—Đæt wǣron mǣre men ofer eorþan, and fyrdhwate *those were famous men throughout the earth, and bold in warfare*, Andr. Kmbl. 16; An. 8: Elen. Kmbl. 2356; El. 1179: Apstls. Kmbl. 23; Ap. 12: Beo. Th. 3286; B. 1641.

fyrdian, fierdian, feordian; *p.* ode, ede; *pp.* od, ed [fyrd *an army*] *To go with an army, march, be at war;* profĭcisci, bellum gĕrĕre:—Fyrdode him togeánes *he marched against him*, Chr. 835; Th. 117, 18, col. 1, 2: 894; Th. 166, 17, col. 2; 167, 16, col. 1. Hī fyrdedon wiđ Ætlan Hūna cyninge *they were at war with Attila, king of the Huns*, 443; Th. 18, 30, col. 1.

fyrding, firding, e; *f.* I. *an army, army prepared for war;* exercĭtus, procinctus:—Fyrding [MS. fyrdingc] *procinctus*, Ælfc. Gl. 87; Som. 74, 42; Wrt. Voc. 50, 24: 72, 71. Mid ormǣtre fyrdinge *with an immense army*, Homl. Th. ii. 66, 2: 194, 13. II. *an expedition;* expĕdītio:—Geswicon đǣre fyrdinge *they withdrew from the expedition*, Chr. 1016; Erl. 153, 29. v. fyrdung.

fyrdinga; *adv. In companies* or *flocks, by bands* or *multitudes;* catervātim, Som. Ben. Lye.

fyrdleás, fierdleás; *adj. Without an army* or *force;* exercĭtu cărens:—Hit đonne fyrdleás wæs *it was then without a force*, Chr. 894; Th. 164, 29, col. 2; 165, 29, col. 1, 2.

fyrd-leóþ, es; *n. A war-song;* mīlĭtāre carmen:—Fyrdleóþ agōl wulf on walde *a wolf sang a war-song in the wood*, Elen. Kmbl. 54; El. 27: Cd. 171; Th. 215, 3; Exod. 577.

fyrdlīc; *adj. Military, martial;* mīlĭtāris:—Hire fær is wiđmeten fyrdlīcum truman *her course is compared to a martial band*, Homl. Th. i. 444, 5: Jos. 11, 10.

fyrd-man, ferd-mon; *pl.* -men; *m. A military man, a soldier;* mīles:—He sceal hæbban fyrdmen *he must have soldiers*, Bt. 17; Fox 58, 33.

fȳr-draca, an; *m. A fire-dragon, fire-drake;* ignĭvŏmus drăco:—Frēcne fȳrdraca *a fell fire-dragon*, Beo. Th. 5371; B. 2689.

fyrd-rinc, ferd-rinc, es; *m. A man of arms, warrior, soldier;* bellātor, mīles:—Frōd wæs se fyrdrinc *skilful was the man of arms*, Byrht. Th. 135, 58; By. 140. Fyrdrincas frome *bold soldiers*, Elen. Kmbl. 521; El. 261. Se com fyrdrinca fruman grētan *who came to greet the chief of warriors*, Cd. 97; Th. 127, 1; Gen. 2104.

fyrdringnes *an exalting, promoting, advancing* or *furthering;* exaltātio, promōtio, Som. Ben. Lye. v. fyrđringnes.

fyrd-sceorp, es; *n. A war-vest;* bellĭcus ornātus:—Hwīlum hongige on wage freólīc fyrdsceorp *sometimes I hang on the wall a goodly war-vest*, Exon. 104 a; Th. 395, 25; Rä. 15, 13.

fyrd-scip, es; *n. A ship of war;* bellĭca nāvis:—Gif hwā fyrdscip awyrde *if any one injure a ship of war*, L. Eth. vi. 34; Th. i. 324, 5. Đæt man fyrdscipa gearwige *that ships of war be made ready*, vi. 33; Th. i. 324, 4.

fyrd-searu, -searo; *gen.* -wes; *n. A war-equipment;* bellĭcus appărātus:—Him Onela forgeaf fyrdsearu fūslīc *Onela gave him a ready war-equipment*, Beo. Th. 5229; B. 2618. Fyrdsearo, 469; B. 232.

fyrd-sōcn, e; *f.* [sōcn *the seeking*] *The seeking of the army, military service;* mīlĭtia:—Đæt hit sȳ gefreód ealra þeówdōma, būton fyrdsōcne, and burhgeweorce and bryggeweorce *that it shall be freed from all services, except military service, castle-building, and bridge-work*, Th. Diplm. A. D. 1061; 389, 30.

fyrd-stemn *an army-corps.* v. fird-stemn.

fyrd-tiber, es; *n.* [tiber *a sacrifice*] *A military sacrifice;* mīlĭtāris hostia:—Fyrdtiber [MS. fyrdtimber] *hostia exercĭtūs*, Cot. 103.

fyrd-truma, an; *m. A martial band, an army;* exercĭtus:—Swā egeslīc swā fyrdtruma *as terrible as a martial band*, Homl. Th. i. 442, 34.

fyrdung, e; *f.* I. *an army prepared for war, armament;* exercĭtus:—Beó man georne ymbe fyrdunga *let the armaments be diligently attended to*, L. Eth. v. 26; Th. i. 310, 24: vi. 32; Th. i. 322, 32. II. *an expedition;* expĕdītio:—On fyrdunge *in the expedition*, L. C. S. 79; Th. i. 420, 14. III. *a camp;* castra:—Fyrdunga ođđe fyrdwīcu *castra*, Ps. Lamb. 26, 3. v. fyrd.

fyrd-wǣn, es; *m. A military waggon;* essĕdum, Th. Diplm. A. D. 1050–1073; 430, 2.

fyrd-weard, e; *f. An army-guard, a military watch;* mīlĭtāris custōdia:—Sǣweard and heáfodweard and fyrdweard *sea-guard and head-guard and army-guard*, L. R. S. 1; Th. i. 432, 5.

fyrd-werod, -weord, es; *n. An army-host, phalanx;* turma, phălanx = φάλαγξ, Cot. 140. Micel stefn fyrdweorodes getrymnesse *a great sound of the arraying of a host*, Blickl. Homl. 91, 35.

fyrd-wīc, es; *n. An army-station, a camp;* castra:—Đis ys Godes fyrdwīc *castra Dei sunt hæc*, Gen. 32, 2: Ælfc. Gl. 7; Som. 56, 77; Wrt. Voc. 18, 29. Fyrdunga ođđe fyrdwīcu *castra*, Ps. Lamb. 26, 3. Hī feóllon on middele fyrdwīca heora *cĕcĭdērunt in mĕdio castrōrum eōrum*, Ps. Spl. C. 77, 32. To đām fyrdwīcum *to the camps*, Judth. 11; Thw. 24, 33; Jud. 220.

fyrd-wīsa, an; *m. A leader of an expedition;* expĕdītiōnis dux:—Sum biþ heretoga, fyrdwīsa from *one is a general, a bold leader*, Exon. 79 b; Th. 297, 32; Crä. 77.

fyrd-wīse, an; *f. A military manner:*—Se mon se ne wǣre mid his wǣpnum æfter fyrdwīson gegered *qui non legitimis indutus insignibusque armis*, Nar. 9, 28.

fyrd-wīte, ferd-wīte, es; *n. A fine for neglecting the* fyrd, L. C. S. 12; Th. i. 382, 14: 15; Th. i. 384, 3: Th. Diplm. A. D. 1066; 411, 31.

fyrd-wyrđe; *adj. Famous in war;* bello clārus:—Gang æfter flōre fyrdwyrđe man *the man famous in war went along the floor*, Beo. Th. 2637; B. 1316.

fyren, e; *f. A sin, crime;* peccātum, crimen:—Deorce fyrene *dark sins*, Ps. Th. 108, 14. He đǣre mǣgþe fleáh fyrene *he avoided the crimes of the people*, Cd. 92; Th. 116, 24; Gen. 1941: Exon. 48 a; Th. 166, 18; Gū. 1044. v. firen.

fȳren, fȳran; *def.* se fȳrena, seó, đæt fȳrene; *adj. Fiery, burning, flaming;* ignītus, igneus, flammeus:—Is đīn āgen spræc innan fȳren, sylf swīđe hāt *ignītum elŏquium tuum vehementer*, Ps. Th. 118, 140. Sió fȳrene sunne *the fiery sun*, Bt. 39, 13; Fox 232, 27. Swylce eal Finns buruh fȳrenu wǣre *as if all Fin's castle were on fire*, Fins. Th. 73; Fin. 36. Đæt fȳrene swurd *the fiery sword*, Boutr. Scrd. 20, 33. Under đam fȳrenan hrōfe *under the fiery roof*, Cd. 185; Th. 230, 27; Dan. 239. God hēt him fȳrenne beám befōran wīsian *God commanded a pillar of fire to point out the way before them*, Ps. Th. 104, 34. Fȳren swurd *flammeum glădium*, Gen. 3, 24. Fȳrene sweorde *with a fiery sword*, Cd. 45; Th. 58, 17; Gen. 947: 76; Th. 95, 8; Gen. 1575. Fȳrnum clommum *with fiery fetters*, Andr. Kmbl. 2756; An. 1380: Exon. 18 b; Th. 46, 7; Cri. 733. [*Orm.* firen: *Laym.* furen.]

fȳren cylle, an; *f. A fiery torch;* ignea fax, Bd. 5, 23; S. 645, 29, note, MS. B. v. fȳren þecelle.

fyren-dǣd, e; *f. A wicked deed;* scĕlestum făcĭnus:—He is mildheort, and manþwǣre hiora fyrendǣdum *ipse est mĭsericors, et prŏpĭtius fit peccātis eorum*, Ps. Th. 77, 37: Beo. Th. 2006; B. 1001: Cd. 191; Th. 237, 30; Dan. 345. v. firen-dǣd.

fyren-earfeđe, es; *n. A sinful woe;* scĕlestum mălum:—Heó nyste đæt swā fela fyrenearfeđa fylgean sceolde *she knew not that so many sinful woes must follow*, Cd. 33; Th. 44, 14; Gen. 709.

fyren-full; *adj. Sinful, unjust, wicked;* inīquus:—Fyrenfulle men geworhton *wicked men have wrought*, Soul Kmbl. 179; Seel. 90. Used as a noun, *One who is sinful, a sinner;* peccātor:—Swā đa fyrenfullan frēcne forweorþaþ *sic pĕreant peccātōres a făcie Dei*, Ps. Th. 67, 2: 54, 2: 57, 9. v. firen-full.

fȳrenfull; *adj. Fiery;* ignītus:—Is fȳrenfull spæc đīn swīđlīce *est ignītum elŏquium tuum vehementer*, Ps. Lamb. 118, 140.

fyrenfulnes, -ness, e; *f. Luxury, riot;* luxŭria, tŭmultus, Som. Ben. Lye.

fyrenian, fyrnian; *p.* ede; *pp.* ed *To sin, commit adultery;* peccāre, mœchāri:—Fyrnaþ đus đæt flǣschord *thus will the body sin*, Soul Kmbl. 203; Seel. 103. Ne fyrena đū *non mœchābĕris*, Lk. Bos. 18, 20. DER. ge-fyrnian. v. firenian.

fyrenlīce; *adv. Vehemently, rashly;* vehementer:—Đæt đū tō fyrenlīce feohtan sōhtest *that thou soughtest to fight too rashly*, Wald. 35; Vald. 1, 20.

fyren-ligerian; *p.* ede; *pp.* ed *To commit fornication;* fornĭcāri:—Hī fyrenligeredon on begīmingum his *fornĭcāti sunt in adinventiōnibus suis*, Ps. Spl. 105, 36.

fyren-lust, es; *m. Luxury;* luxŭria:—Ne gēmdon hie nānes fyrenlustes *they cared not for any luxury,* Bt. 15; Fox 48, 7. v. firen-lust.

fyren-þearf, e; *f. Dire distress;* nĭmia mĭsĕria:—Fyrenþearfe ongeat *he perceived the dire need,* Beo. Th. 28; B. 14.

fȳren þecelle, an; *f. A fiery torch;* ignea fax, Bd. 5, 23; S. 645, 29. v. þecelle.

fyrenum; *adv.* [*dat. pl. of* fyren *a sin, crime*] *Sinfully, criminally;* măle, sceleste:—Bona of flānbogan fyrenum sceóteþ *the slayer wickedly shoots from his arrow-bow,* Beo. Th. 3493; B. 1744. Fyrenum gesyngad *criminally perpetrated,* 4874; B. 2441.

fyren-wyrcende; *part. Evil-doing, committing sin;* mălum făciens, peccans:—Ic fyrenwyrcende oft elnade *I often emulated evil-doing* [*men*], Ps. Th. 72, 2. v. firen-wyrcende, firen.

fyren-wyrhta, an; *m. An evil-doer, sinner;* măli actor, peccātor:—Hū lange fyrenwyrhtan foldan wealdaþ *how long shall evil-doers rule the earth?* Ps. Th. 93, 3. Ðæt ic on wrāþne seáþ mid fyrenwyrhtum feallan sceolde *that I should fall with sinners into the horrible pit,* 87, 4.

fyres *furze,* Wrt. Voc. 285, 48. v. fyrs.

fyrest; *adj. First, front;* prīmus:—Æt ðām feówer tōþum fyrestum *for the four front teeth,* L. Ethb. 51; Th. i. 16, 2. v. fyrst; *adj.*

fȳr-feaxe; *adj.* [feaxe *having hair*] *Fiery-haired;* ignĭcŏmus:—Fȳrfeaxe [MS. -feaxa] *ignĭcŏmus,* Cot. 170.

fȳr-gearwunge; *pl. f. Fire-preparation, fuel;* fōmes, focŭlāria, Cot. 83.

fȳr-gebræc, es; *n. A fire-crash;* ignis frăgor *vel* strĕpĭtus:—Ðæt fȳrgebræc *the fire-crash,* Cd. 119; Th. 154, 24; Gen. 2560.

fyrgen, es; *n. A mountain, mountain-woodland;* mons, saltus:—Flet [MS. fled] Þor on fyrgen hæfde *Thor had a dwelling on the mountain,* Lchdm. iii. 54, 17. DER. fyrgen-beám, -holt, -streám. v. firgen.

fyrgen-beám, es; *m. A mountain-tree;* saltuensis arbor:—He fyrgenbeámas ofer hārne stān hleónian funde *he found mountain-trees leaning over the hoar rock,* Beo. Th. 2833; B. 1414.

fyrgen-holt, es; *n. A mountain-wood;* montāna silva:—On fyrgenholt *into a mountain-wood,* Beo. Th. 2791; B. 1393.

fyrgen-streám, es; *m. A mountain-stream;* montānum flūmen:—Ðǣr fyrgenstreám niđer gewīteþ *where the mountain-stream flows downward,* Beo. Th. 2723; B. 1359. v. firgen-streám.

fȳr-gnāst, es; *m. A fire-spark;* scintilla:—Flugon fȳrgnāstas *fire-sparks flew,* Andr. Kmbl. 3090; An. 1548.

fyrh *to a furrow,* Cod. Dipl. 1172; A. D. 955; Kmbl. v. 332, 22; *dat. sing. of* furh.

fȳr-hāt; *adj. Fire-hot;* ut ignis ardens:—Fȳrhāt lufu *a fire-hot love,* Elen. Kmbl. 1871; El. 937.

fȳr-heard; *adj. Fire-hard;* igne dūrātus:—Eoforlīc scionon fāh and fȳrheard *boar's likenesses shone variegated and fire-hard,* Beo. Th. 615; B. 305.

fȳr-hole; *f. Catasta,* Hpt, Gl. 310. 'Catastæ, genus tormenti, i. e. lecti ferrei, quibus impositi Martyres, ignis supponebatur.' Du Cange.

fyrht, firht, freht, es; *n? A divining, divination, augury;* auspĭcium, hariolātio, augŭrium:—Ođđe on blōte ođđe on fyrhte *either by sacrifice or by divination,* L. C. S. 5; Th. i. 378, 22. On firhte, L. N. P. L. 48; Th. ii. 296, 28. Ǣristum ođđe frumum frehtum *prīmis auspĭciis,* Rtl. 97, 16. v. frihtrung.

fyrht; *adj. Timid;* tĭmĭdus:—On his sōþfæstnesse swylce dēmeþ on folce fyrhte þearfan *in sua justĭtia jūdĭcābit paupĕres hujus pŏpŭli,* Ps. Th. 71, 4. DER. god-fyrht. v. forht.

fyrhtan; *p.* fyrhte; *pp.* fyrhted *To* FRIGHTEN, *terrify, tremble;* terrēre tremere:—Gif līgette and þunorrāde eorþan and lyfte brēgdon and fyrhton *si corusci ac tonitrua terras et aëra terrērent,* Bd. 4, 3; S. 569, 13. Ðū dōest đa fyrhta *facis eam tremere,* Rtl. 102, 21. DER. afyrhtan.

fyrhþ, es; *m. n.* I. *the soul, spirit, mind;* ănĭmus, mens:—Biþ fyrhþ afrēfred *the spirit is comforted,* Andr. Kmbl. 1275; An. 638. Ic ne can đæt ic nāt findan on fyrhþe *I cannot find what I know not in my mind,* Elen. Kmbl. 1278; El. 641: 391; El. 196. II. *life;* vīta:—Đū God Dryhten wealdest wīdan fyrhþ *thou Lord God rulest for ever,* Elen. Kmbl. 1518; El. 761. DER. stærced-fyrhþ, wīde-. v. ferhþ.

fyrhþ-gleáw; *adj. Wise-minded, prudent;* prūdens, săpiens, Elen. Kmbl. 1758; El. 881. v. ferhþ-gleáw.

fyrhþ-loca, an; *m. The soul-inclosure, breast;* mentis clausūra, pectus:—Wæs Cristes lof on fyrhþlocan fæste bewunden *Christ's praise was steadfastly enclosed within his breast,* Andr. Kmbl. 115; An. 58: 3138; An. 1572. v. ferhþ-loca.

fyrhþ-lufe, an; *f. Love of the soul, mental love;* anĭmi ămor:—Ic to ānum đē stađolige fæste fyrhþlufan *I keep the steadfast love of my soul firmly fixed to thee only,* Andr. Kmbl. 165; An. 83.

fyrhþ-sefa, an; *m. The mind;* mens:—Gē fyrhþsefan mīnne cunnon *ye know my mind,* Elen. Kmbl. 1066; El. 534. v. ferhþ-sefa.

fyrhþ-wērig; *adj. Soul-weary, sorrowful;* mæstus:—Seó cwēn ongan fricggan fyrhþwērige, ymb fyrngewritu *the queen began to ask them, sorrowful, concerning the old scriptures,* Invent. Crs. Recd. 1119; El. 560. v. ferþ-wērig.

fyrhtnes, -ness, e; *f. Fear;* tĭmor:—Mid micelre fyrhtnesse *with great fear,* Ors. 6, 30; Bos. 126, 14; Mt. Kembl. Lind. 14, 26. v. forhtnys.

FYRHTO; *indecl. in sing.* fyrhtu, e; *f. Fear,* FRIGHT, *dread, terror, trembling;* tĭmor, păvor, formīdo, terror, trĕmor:—Us fyrhto gegrāp *fear seized us,* Nicod. 21; Thw. 10, 32: Cant. Moys. Ex. 15, 19; Thw. 30, 19. Fyrhto ođđe bifung *trĕmor,* Ps. Lamb. 47, 7. Đeós firhtu [fyrhtu, MS. D.] *hæc formīdo,* Ælfc. Gr. 36; Som. 38, 50: Ps. Th. 54, 4. Egsa me and fyrhtu forcwōmon *tĭmor et trĕmor vēnĕrunt sŭper me,* Ps. Th. 54, 5. On mīnre fyrhto *in păvōre meo,* 30, 25. Geblissiaþ him on fyrhto [fyrhtu, Lamb.] *exultāte ei in trĕmōre,* Ps. Spl. 2, 11. Hī mycle fyrhto onstyredon đām monnum đe hī sceáwodon and gesāwon *they stirred up much fear in the men who beheld and saw them,* Bd. 5, 23; S. 645, 23: Exon. 119 a; Th. 457, 21; Hy. 4, 87. Ne him Godes fyrhtu georne ondrǣdaþ *non tĭmuĕrunt Deum,* Ps. Th. 54, 20: 77, 53. [*O. Sax.* forhta, *f: O. Frs.* fruchta: *Dut. Kil.* vrucht, vurcht: *Ger.* furcht, *f: M. H. Ger.* vorhte, *f: O. H. Ger.* forhta, *f: Goth.* faurhtei, *f: Dan.* frygt, *m. f: Swed.* fruktan, *f.*]

fȳr-hūs, es; *n. A* FIRE-HOUSE, *furnace;* cămīnus = κάμινος, fornax:—Fȳrhūs *camīnātum?* Ælfc. Gl. 107; Som. 78, 92; Wrt. Voc. 58, 7. Fȳrhūses hlȳwing *caumenæ* (?) *refŭgium,* R. Concord. 11.

fyrian; *p.* ode; *pp.* od *To make a furrow, to plough, till;* proscindĕre aratro, Scint. 32.

fȳrian; *p.* ode; *pp.* od *To make a fire, give warmth, to cherish;* fŏcum præbēre:—Fēde þearfan and scrȳde and hūsige and fȳrige *let him feed the needy, and clothe, and house, and fire them,* L. Pen. 14; Th. ii. 282, 16.

fyrlen, feorlen; *adj. Far off, distant, remote;* longinquus, distans, remōtus:—Đeáh đe he fyrlen sȳ *though he be far off,* Homl. Th. ii. 444, 9. For đære fyrlenan heáhnysse *for its remote elevation,* Bd. de nat. rerum; Lchdm. iii. 232, 15, note 7. Sum æđelboren man ferde on fyrlen land *hŏmo quidam nōbĭlis abiit in rĕgiōnem longinquam,* Lk. Bos. 19, 12: Homl. Th. ii. 122, 14. To fyrlenum eardum *to distant lands,* Gen. 20, 13. Mid fulluhte aþwagen fram his fyrlenum dǣdum *with baptism washed from his former deeds,* H. R. 107, 14.

fyrlen, es; *n. Distance;* distantia:—For đam mycclan fyrlene *on account of the great distance,* Boutr. Scrd. 18, 43.

fȳr-leóht, es; *n. A fire-light;* igneum lūmen:—He fȳrleóht geseah *he saw a fire-light,* Beo. Th. 3037; B. 1516.

fȳr-leóma, an; *m.* [leóma *a ray of light, beam*] *A fire-beam;* igneus splendor:—Fȳrleóma stōd geond đæt atole scræf *a fire-beam stood through that horrid den,* Cd. 216; Th. 272, 32; Sat. 128.

fyrlīce *suddenly,* Num. 16, 35. v. fǣrlīce.

fȳr-loca, an; *m. A fire-bond;* igneum claustrum:—Eart tū in fȳrlocan feste gebunden *thou art fast bound in fire-bonds,* Cd. 214; Th. 268, 20; Sat. 58.

fyrm, e; *f. A feast;* ĕpŭlæ:—Đa Philistei micele fyrme geworhton *the Philistines made a great feast,* Jud. 16, 25. v. feórm.

fȳr-mǣl, es; *m. A fire-mark;* măcŭla igne inusta:—Fȳrmǣlum fāg *variegated with marks of fire,* Andr. Kmbl. 2269; An. 1136.

fyrmest, formest; *def.* se fyrmesta, seó, đæt fyrmeste; *sup. adj.* FOREMOST, *first;* prīmus:—Se đe wyle betweox eów beón fyrmest, sȳ he eówer þeów *qui vŏluĕrit inter vos prīmus esse, ĕrit vester servus,* Mt. Bos. 20, 27: Mk. Bos. 9, 35: Boutr. Scrd. 21, 35. Se fyrmesta and se betesta *the foremost and the best;* præstantissĭmus, Cot. 153. Se fyrmesta is easterne wind *the first is the east wind,* Bd. de nat. rerum; Wrt. popl. science 17, 22; Lchdm. iii. 274, 13. Đis ys đæt mǣste and đæt fyrmeste bebod *hoc est maxĭmum et prĭmum mandātum,* Mt. Bos. 22, 38. Agynn fram đam ȳtemestan ōþ đone fyrmestan *begin from the last to the first,* 20, 8. Manega fyrmeste beóþ ȳtemeste, and ȳtemeste fyrmeste *multi ĕrunt prīmi novissĭmi, et novissĭmi prīmi,* 19, 30: Mk. Bos. 10, 31: Lk. Bos. 13, 30. Đa fyrmestan *prīmi,* Mt. Bos. 20, 16. Fyrmest manna *first of men;* summas, prīmas, Ælfc. Gr. 9, 25; Som. 10, 58, 59: Chr. 1086; Erl. 221, 39. Fyrmeste [MS. fyrmyste] naman *prīmĭtīvan ōmĭna,* 5; Som. 4, 8.

fyrmest; *sup. adv. At first, most, very well, best;* prīmo, maxĭme, optĭme:—Hie feónda gefær fyrmest gesǣgon *they first saw the enemies' march,* Elen. Kmbl. 136; El. 68: Cd. 158; Th. 197, 21; Exod. 310. Swā he fyrmest meahte *as much as ever he could,* Bd. 2, 6; S. 508, 32: Elen. Kmbl. 632; El. 316: Ps. Th. 72, 6: 106, 29: 121, 7. Swā forþ swa we fyrmest leornian māgon *as far as ever we can learn,* Bd. 5, 21; S. 643, 5: L. C. S. 11; Th. i. 382, 6: L. Eth. vi. 40; Th. i. 324, 28.

fyrmþ, frymþ, e; *f.* I. [feormian I. *to feed, support, entertain*] *A receiving to food, harbouring, an entertainment;* receptio ad vĭctum, susceptio:—Đis syndon đa gerihta đe se cyning āh ofer ealle men; đæt is . . . and flȳmena fyrmþe *these are the rights which the king possesses over all men; that is . . . and* [*the penalty for*] *the harbouring of fugitives,* L. C. S. 12; Th. i. 382, 14. Ǣlc mon mōt onsacan fyrmþe *every man* *may deny entertainment*, L. In. 46; Th. i. 132, 1, note 3, MSS. B, H. III. [feormian III. *to cleanse*] *A cleansing, washing;* ablūtio, baptisma = βάπτισμα:—Calica fyrmþa *călīcum baptismăta*, Mk. Bos. 7, 4: Hpt. Gl. 420.

FYRN; *adj. Ancient, old;* antīquus, priscus:—Fyrn forþgesceaft *the ancient creation*, Exon. 128 a; Th. 492, 4; Rä. 81, 9. [*O. Sax.* fern: *Ger.* firn, firne: *M. H. Ger.* virne: *O. H. Ger.* firni: *Goth.* fairneis: *Swed.* forn *only in compounds;* as, forn-ålder, *m. antiquity: Icel.* forn: *Lith.* pernay *anni priōris.*]

fyrn; *adv. Formerly, long ago, of old;* ōlim, prīdem, antīquĭtus:—Hū mæg ic ðæt findan ðæt swā fyrn gewearþ *how can I find that which happened so long ago?* Elen. Kmbl. 1261; El. 632: 1279; El. 641. Ðæt he bibūgan mǽge ðone bitran drync ðone Eue fyrn Adame geaf *that he may escape the bitter drink which Eve of old gave to Adam*, Exon. 45 b; Th. 154, 11; Gū. 841: 47 a; Th. 160, 20; Gū. 946: Cd. 128; Th. 163, 11; Gen. 2696. [*O. Sax.* forn, furn: *O. H. Ger.* forn *prius, ōlim.*] DER. ge-fyrn, un-.

fyrn-dagas; *gen.* a; *dat.* um; *pl. m. Days of old, ancient days;* priscæ dies:—Ðis is se ilca God ðone on fyrndagum fæderas cūðon *this is the same God whom your fathers knew in days of old*, Andr. Kmbl. 1503; An. 753: 1951: An. 978: Cd. 223; Th. 293, 31; Sat. 463. Swā hine fyrndagum worhte wǽpna smiþ *as the armourer wrought it in ancient days*, Beo. Th. 2907; B. 1451. [*Laym.* i furn daȝen: *O. Sax.* an furndagun.]

fyrn-geár, es; *n. A former* or *by-gone year;* priscus *vel* prætĕrĭtus annus:—Fyrngeárum frōd *old with by-gone years*, Exon. 59 a; Th. 213, 3; Ph. 219: Menol. Fox 483; Gn. C. 12. [*Piers P.* fernyere.]

fyrn-geára; *adv.* [*gen. pl. of* -geár] *In by-gone years, of old time;* ōlim, antīquĭtus, Ps. Th. 94, 9.

fyrn-geflīt, es; *n. An ancient strife, old conflict;* vĕtus lis *vel* rixa:—Þurh fyrngeflīt *through the old conflict*, Elen. Kmbl. 1804; El. 904. Hī guldon hyra fyrngeflītu fāgum swyrdum *they requited their ancient strifes with stained swords*, Judth. 12; Thw. 25, 17; Jud. 264.

fyrn-geflīta, an; *m. An enemy of old;* antīquus inĭmīcus:—Būtan his fyrngeflītan *except to his enemy of old*, Exon. 96 a; Th. 357, 25; Pa. 34.

fyrn-gemynd, es; *n. An ancient reminiscence;* antīqua mĕmŏria:—Ða ðe fyrngemynd mid Iudēum gearwast cūðon *they who best knew the old memories among the Jews*, Elen. Kmbl. 654; El. 327.

fyrn-gesceap, es; *n. A decree of old;* ōlim constĭtūtum:—Ne wāt ǽnig hū ða wīsan sind wundorlīce, fæger fyrngesceap, ymb ðæs fugles gebyrd *not any knows how the conditions are wondrous, the fair decree of old, concerning the bird's birth*, Exon. 61 a; Th. 223, 15; Ph. 360.

fyrn-gesetu; *pl. n. Ancient seats, a former dwelling-place;* pristīnum dŏmĭcĭlium:—Ōþ-ðæt fyrngesetu eft gesēceþ *till it again seeks its ancient seats*, Exon. 59 b; Th. 216, 5; Ph. 263.

fyrn-gestreón, es; *n. An ancient treasure;* antīquus thesaurus:—Full fyrngestreóna *full of ancient treasures*, Salm. Kmbl. 64; Sal. 32, MS. B.

fyrn-geweorc, es; *n. An ancient work;* priscum *vel* jam diu perfectum ŏpus:—Ǽr ðon endige frōd fyrngeweorc *before his wise ancient work shall end*, Exon. 57 a; Th. 203, 14; Ph. 48: 57 a; Th. 204, 9; Ph. 95: Andr. Kmbl. 1473; An. 738. Freá sceáwode fyra fyrngeweorc *the lord beheld the ancient work of men*, Beo. Th. 4561; B. 2286.

fyrn-gewinn, es; *n. An ancient war;* vĕtus pugna:—On ðæm wæs ōr writen fyrngewinnes *on which was engraved the origin of the ancient war*, Beo. Th. 3382; B. 1689.

fyrn-gewrit, -gewryt, es; *pl. nom. acc.* -gewritu, -gewrito; *n. An ancient writing, old scripture;* vĕtus *vel* prisca scriptūra:—Ðȳ-læs toworpen sīen frōd fyrngewritu *lest the wise old scriptures should be overturned*, Elen. Kmbl. 861; El. 431. Ða ðe fyrngewritu sēlest cunnen *those who best know the ancient writings*, 746; El. 373: 1117; El. 560. Þurh fyrngewrito *through ancient writings*, 309; El. 155. On eallum ðām fyrngewrytum *in all the ancient writings*, Salm. Kmbl. 15; Sal. 8.

fyrn-gewyrht, es; *n. A former work;* ōlim factum:—Ðæt he fyrngewyrht fyllan sceolde *that he should finish his former work*, Exon. 47 a; Th. 160, 15; Gū. 944.

fyrn-gid, -gidd, es; *n. An old prophecy;* vĕtus prŏphētia:—Fyrngidda frōd *prudent in old prophecies*, Elen. Kmbl. 1079; El. 542.

fyrnian, he fyrnaþ; *p.* ede; *pp.* ed *To revile;* calumniāri:—Fyrnaþ ðus ðæt flǽschord *thus it* [*the soul*] *shall revile the flesh*, Soul Kmbl. 203; Seel. 103. v. firenian.

fyrn-man, -mann, es; *m. A man of yore;* qui ōlim vixit:—Geseah he fyrnmanna fatu *he saw vessels of men of yore*, Beo. Th. 5515; B. 2761.

fyrn-sceaða, an; *m. An old enemy* or *fiend;* antīquus inĭmīcus:—Fāh fyrnsceaða *a hostile fiend*, Andr. Kmbl. 2691; An. 1348.

fyrn-streámas; *pl. m. Ancient streams, the ocean;* prisca fluenta, oceănus:—Fyrnstreáma geflotan *to the ocean-floater*, Exon. 96 b; Th. 360, 17; Wal. 7.

fyrn-syn, -synn, e; *f. A sin of yore;* priscum peccātum:—Fyrnsynna fruma *the author of sins of yore*, Exon. 70 b; Th. 263, 9; Jul. 347.

fyrnum; *adv. With horror, horribly, intensely;* horrĭbĭlĭter:—Ðonne cymþ forst fyrnum cald *then cometh frost intensely cold*, Cd. 17; Th. 20, 28; Gen. 316: 38; Th. 50, 16; Gen. 809. v. firnum.

fyrn-weorc, es; *n. An ancient work, the creation;* priscum ŏpus, creātio:—Fyrnweorca Freá *Lord of creation*, Andr. Kmbl. 2819; An. 1412: Exon. 16 a; Th. 36, 20; Cri. 579.

fyrn-wita, -wiota, -weota, an; *m. An ancient sage, old counsellor, prophet;* antīquus săpiens:—Frōd fyrnwiota *a wise old counsellor*, Elen. Kmbl. 875; El. 438. Dauid cyning, frōd fyrnweota *king David, the prudent prophet*, 685; El. 343. Wæs frōdan fyrnwitan feorh ūþgenge *life was departed from the wise old counsellor*, Beo. Th. 4252; B. 2123. Frōde fyrnweotan *wise ancient sages*, Andr. Kmbl. 1567; An. 785. Wæs se wītedōm þurh fyrnwitan sungen *the prophecy was sung by old seers*, Elen. Kmbl. 2305; El. 1154.

fȳr-panne, an; *f.* [fȳr *fire*, panne *a pan*] *A fire-pan, chafing-dish, pan for burning odoriferous herbs;* batillum, Ælfc. Gl. 26; Som. 60, 95; Wrt. Voc. 25, 35.

fyrr; *adv.* [*comp. of* feor; *adv. far*, q. v.] *Farther;* ultĕrius, longius:—We usse gesihþ fyrr upp ahōfan *longius vīsum lĕvāvĭmus*, Bd. 5, 1; S. 613, 32: Bd. de nat. rerum; Wrt. popl. science 3, 11; Lchdm. iii. 236, 9: Cd. 122; Th. 156, 23; Gen. 2593. v. fyr.

fyrra, firra, *m;* fyrre, firre, *f. n. adj.* [*comp. of* feor; *adv. far*, q. v.] *Farther;* ultĕrior:—He ge-eóde ða fyrran Frysan *he had overcome the farther Frisians*, Bd. 5, 10; S. 624, 3.

fyrrest; *adv.* [*sup. of* feor; *adv. far*, q. v.] *Farthest;* longissĭme:—Se mōna wæs ðære sunnan fyrrest *the moon was farthest from the sun*, Ors. 6, 2; Bos. 117, 14: Bt. 39, 7; Fox 222, 21.

fyrs, es; *n. A verse;* versus, Ælfc. Gr. 37; Som. 39, 3. v. fers.

FYRS, es; *m.* FURZE, *furze-bushes;* genista, rhamnus, ulex eurōpæus, Lin:—Fyrs *rhamnus*, Wrt. Voc. 80, 21. Fyrses berian *arciotidas* [= ἀρκευθίδες *juniper-berries*], Glos. Brux. Recd. 43, 15; Wrt. Voc. 69, 30. Ǽr-ðan undergǽton eówre þornas fyrs *priusquam intellĭgĕrent spīnæ rhamnum*, Ps. Lamb. 57, 10: Lchdm. iii. 86, 17. Swā hwā swā wille sāwan westmbǽre land, atió ǽrest of ða þornas, and ða fyrsas *whosoever will sow fertile land, let him first draw out the thorns, and the furze*, Bt. 23; Fox 78, 22: Bt. Met. Fox 12, 6; Met. 12, 3. [*Wyc.* firse, frijse *gorst, furze: Piers P.* firses, *pl.*]

fȳr-scofl, e; *f? A fire-shovel;* batilla, Cot. 24.

fyrsian; *p.* ode; *pp.* od *To put far, remove, separate;* elongāre:—Ða ðe fyrsiaþ hig fram ðē losiaþ *qui elongant se a te pĕrĭbunt*, Ps. Lamb. 72, 27. DER. a-fyrsian.

fȳr-smeortende; *part. Fire-smarting;* ignītus:—Gnættas cōmon ofer ðæt land mid fȳrsmeortendum bītum *gnats came over the land with fire-smarting bites*, Ors. 1, 7; Bos. 29, 30.

fyrsn, e; *f. The heel;* calx, calcăneum, Cot. 38. v. fiersn.

fȳr-spearca, an; *m. A fire-spark;* scintilla:—Būton īsene fȳrspearcan *nĭsi ferreas scintillas*, Coll. Monast. Th. 31, 5.

FYRST, first, fierst, es; *m.* I. *the first entrance, a threshold, door;* limen, Cot. 118. II. *the first in height, the top, ridge, the inward roof, ceiling of a chamber;* culmen, lăquear:—Fyrst *lăquear*, Ælfc. Gl. 29; Som. 61, 43; Wrt. Voc. 26, 42: 82, 15. [*Ger.* first, *m. f. a gable, summit: M. H. Ger.* virst, *m: O. H. Ger.* first, *m. culmen, pinna.*]

FYRST, first, fierst, es; *m. A space of time, time, respite, truce;* spătium tempŏris, tempus constĭtūtum, intercăpēdo:—Næs hit lengra fyrst *it was not a longer space of time*, Beo. Th. 269; B. 134: 5104; B. 2555. Ne wæs se fyrst micel *the respite was not great*, Exon. 37 a; Th. 121, 32; Gū. 297. Æfter miclum fyrste *post multum tempŏris*, Mt. Bos. 25, 19: 26, 73: Ex. 17, 4: Boutr. Scrd. 18, 32: 20, 19. Hæfde nȳdfara nihtlangne fyrst *the fugitive had a night-long space*, Cd. 154; Th. 191, 2; Exod. 208: Andr. Kmbl. 1668; An. 836: 2620; An. 1311. Fyrst næfdon ðæt hī ǽton *nec spătium mandūcandi hăbēbant*, Mk. Bos. 6, 31: Chr. 1004; Erl. 139, 22. Ðȳ fyrste *in the time*, Beo. Th. 5139; B. 2573. [*Laym.* first, uirst, urist, feorst: *Orm.* fresst: *Plat.* ferst, *f: O. Sax.* vrist, *f: O. Frs.* ferst, first, frist, *n: Dut. Kil.* verste, verst, frist, virst *dilātio: Ger.* frist, *f: M. H. Ger.* vrist, *f: O. H. Ger.* frist, *f. mŏra, spătium: Dan.* frist, *m. f: Swed.* frist, *m.*] DER. lang-fyrst.

FYRST, first, fyrest; *adj.* FIRST; prīmus:—Fyrst ferhþ-bana *the first life-destroyer*, Cd. 162; Th. 203, 5; Exod. 399. [*Wyc. R. Glouc.* firste: *Piers P.* furste, ferste: *Orm.* firrste: *Plat.* foorste *a prince: O. Sax.* furisto *first: Frs.* foarste: *O. Frs.* ferost: *Dut.* vorst, *m. a prince: Ger.* fürst, *m. a prince: M. H. Ger.* vürst *first: O. H. Ger.* furisto: *Dan. Swed.* först, förste: *Icel.* fyrstr *first, foremost.*]

fyrst; *adv.* At FIRST; primo:—Se biscop com fyrst to Ēlīg *the bishop came first to Ely*, Chr. 963; Erl. 121, 20: 123, 2.

fyrstan [fyrst *a space of time, respite*] *To give respite;* indūcias facere, Som. Ben. Lye.

fȳr-stān, es; *m. A fire-stone, flint;* pȳrītes = πυρίτης:—Fȳrstān *pȳrītes vel fŏcāris lăpis*, Ælfc. Gl. 58; Som. 67, 105; Wrt. Voc. 38, 29.

fyrst-gemearc, es; *n. An appointed time, space of time;* tempus constĭtūtum, tempŏris spătium:—Ne biþ ðæs lengra swice sâwelgedâles ðonne seofon niht fyrstgemearces *there will be no longer evasion of the soul-separation than seven nights of time's space*, Exon. 47 b; Th. 164, 9; Gû. 1009: Andr. Kmbl. 1861; An. 933.

fyrstig; *adj.* [forst *frost*] *Frosty*; gĕlĭdus:—Ðæt se winter wǽre ceald and fyrstig *that the winter was cold and frosty*, Bd. 3, 19; S. 549, 27.

fyrst-mearc, frist-mearc, e; *f.* [mearc *a mark*] *Marked* or *appointed time, a space of time, interval*; tempus constĭtūtum, tempŏris spatium, intercăpēdo:—Sunne oncneów fyrstmearc his *the sun knew his appointed time*, Ps. Spl. T. 103, 20. Him eft-cymeþ æfter fyrstmearce feorh *life returns to it after a space of time*, Exon. 59 a; Th. 213, 11; Ph. 223: Andr. Recd. 269; An. 133: Elen. Kmbl. 2065; El. 1034. Ymb geára fyrstmearc *after a space of years*; *interjecto tempŏre aliquanto*, Bd. 3, 17; S. 543, 47: Cd. 202; Th. 251, 8; Dan. 560. Bûtan fyrstmearce ǽnigre reste *sĭne ulla quiētis intercăpēdĭne*, Bd. 5, 12; S. 628, 3.

fȳr-sweart; *def.* se -swearta; *adj. Fire-swart, blackened with fire*; igne obscūrātus:—Færeþ æfter foldan [se] fȳrswearta lêg *the fire-swart flame shall pass along the earth*, Exon. 22 a; Th. 61, 14; Cri. 984.

fȳr-tang *fire-tongs*; forceps igniāria, Som. Ben. Lye.

fȳr-þolle? *An oven*; clībănus:—Ðû setst hig swâ swâ fȳrþolle fȳres þônes *eos ut clībānum ignis*, Ps. Spl. T. 20, 9.

fyrþran, fyrþrian; *p.* ede, ode; *pp.* ed, od [furðor *further*] *To further, support, advance, promote*; provehere, promŏvēre:—Ðæt ic eáðe mæg ânra gehwylcne fremman and fyrþran freónda mînra *that I may easily advance and further every one of my friends*, Andr. Kmbl. 1867; An. 936. Ðæt hî mâgen hênan ða yflan, and fyrþrian ða gôdan *that they may humiliate the evil, and further the good*, Bt. 39, 2; Fox 212, 22. Friðaþ and fyrþraþ *protects and supports*, Bt. 34, 10; Fox 148, 29. Ealle Godes gerihto fyrþrie man georne *let every one zealously further all God's dues*, L. E. G. 5; Th. i. 168, 25, note 28, MS. B. DER. gefyrþran.

fyrþringnes, -ness, e; *f. A furthering, furtherance, promotion*; promōtio, L. I. P. 3; Th. ii. 306, 21.

fyrþrung, e; *f. A furthering, furtherance, promotion*; promōtio:—Ceápes fyrþrung *furtherance of trade*, Somn. 167; Lchdm. iii. 208, 6.

fȳr-tor, -torr, es; *m. A fire-tower, light-house*; phărus = φάρος, Cot. 93.

FYRWET, -wit, -wyt, es; *n. Curiosity*; cūriōsĭtas:—Hyne fyrwet bræc *curiosity urged him*, Beo. Th. 5562; B. 2784: 3975; B. 1985. Mec ðæs on worulde full oft fyrwit frineþ *my curiosity enquireth very often about this in the world*, Salm. Kmbl. 117; Sal. 58. Hine fyrwyt bræc *curiosity urged him*, Beo. Th. 470; B. 232. He his fyrwites ganges gylt forgeaf *he forgave him the guilt of his walk of curiosity*, Homl. Th. ii. 138, 24. Þurh fyrwet *through curiosity*, Exon. 9 a; Th. 6, 30; Cri. 92. [*O. Sax.* firiwit, *m. n*: *O. H. Ger.* firiwizzî, *f. cūriōsĭtas, portentum*: *Icel.* fyrir-wissa, *f. a foreboding*.]

fyrwet-georn, firwet-georn; *adj. Curious, inquisitive*; cūriōsus:—Fela biþ fyrwetgeornra *there are many inquisitive*, Exon. 90 b; Th. 339, 31; Gn. Ex. 102.

fyrwet-geornnes, se; *f. Curiosity*:—For fyrwetgeornnesse ðæs wundres *for curiosity on account of the miracle*, Blickl. Homl. 69, 22.

fyrwit, -witt, -wytt; *adj. Curious, inquisitive*; cūriōsus:—Menn ða ða fyrwytte [fyrwite, MS. L.] beóþ *men who are inquisitive*, Bd. de nat. rerum; Wrt. popl. science 15, 9; Lchdm. iii. 268, 5.

fyrwit *curiosity*, Salm. Kmbl. 117; Sal. 58. v. fyrwet.

fyrwitnys, -nyss, e; *f. Curiosity*; cūriōsĭtas:—Hefigtyme leahter is ungefôh fyrwitnys *immoderate curiosity is a grave sin*, Homl. Th. ii. 374, 3. Ðæt he his fyrwitnysse fæderlîce miltsode *that he would paternally compassionate his curiosity*, ii. 138, 19.

fȳr-wylm, es; *m. A fire-boiling, raging flame*; flamma æstuans:—Wyrm cwom ôðre sîþe, fȳrwylmum fâh *the dragon came a second time, coloured with raging flames*, Beo. Th. 5335; B. 2671.

fyrwyt *curiosity*, Beo. Th. 470; B. 232. v. fyrwet.

fȳryn, es; *n. A fire*; ignis:—On fȳrynes midlene *de mĕdio ignis*, Deut. 5, 24. v. fȳr.

FȲSAN; *p.* de; *pp.* ed [fûs *ready, prompt, quick*]. I. *v. intrans. To hasten*; festīnāre:—He ongan fȳsan to fôre *he began to hasten for the way*, Cd. 138; Th. 173, 12; Gen. 2860: Elen. Kmbl. 451; El. 226. II. *v. reflex. To speed oneself, make haste, take oneself away, hasten away*; se festīnāre, propĕrāre, se abrĭpĕre:—He ongan hine fȳsan and to flote gyrwan *he began speedily to prepare* [lit. *to speed himself and to prepare*] *for sailing*, Andr. Kmbl. 3392; An. 1700. Gǽst hine fȳseþ on ēcnegeard *the soul hasteneth to an eternal mansion*, Exon. 51 a; Th. 178, 7; Gû. 1240. He fȳsde hine *he hastened himself*, 120 a; Th. 461, 9; Hö. 33. III. *v. trans. To incite, stimulate, to send forth, drive away*; stĭmŭlāre, incĭtāre, accĕlĕrāre, emittĕre:—Ðû here fȳsest to gefeohte *thou excitest the host to a battle*, Andr. Kmbl. 2376; An. 1189. He fȳsþ ðē of getelde *emigrābit te de tabernācŭlo*, Ps. Lamb. 51, 7. He fȳsde forþ flâna genehe *he sent forth arrows abundantly*, Byrht. Th. 139, 44; By. 269. Fȳse hî man ût of ðysan earde *let them be driven out of this country*, L. Eth. vi. 7; Th. i. 316, 22: L. C. S. 4; Th. i. 378, 8. [*Laym.* fusen, fuse, ifusen *to proceed, rush, drive*: *O. Sax.* fûsian *to incline, strive*: *Icel.* fýsa *to exhort*.] DER. a-fȳsan: ge-fȳsed.

fȳsian, fêsian *to send forth, to drive away*; relēgāre:—Ðonne fȳsie hî man of earde *let them then be driven from the country*, L. E. G. 11; Th. i. 174, 1. v. fȳsan.

FȲST, e; *f. A* FIST; pugnus:—Fȳst *pugnus*, Ælfc. Gl. 72; Som. 71, 3; Wrt. Voc. 43, 57. Gif men cídaþ and hira ôðer hys nēxtan mid ȳste slicþ *si rixāti fuĕrint vĭri et percussĕrit alter proxĭmum suum pugno*, Ex. 21, 18. On ðone eádgan andwlitan helfûse men hondum slôgun, folmum areahtum, and fȳstum eác *wicked men struck on the blessed visage with their hands, with outstretched palms, and with fists also*, Exon. 24 a; Th. 69, 24; Cri. 1125; Blickl. Homl. 23, 33; Mk. Bos. 14, 65. [*Piers P.* fust: *Chauc.* fest: *R. Glouc.* fustes, *pl*: *Laym.* uustes, fustes, *pl. fists*: *Plat.* fuust, fust, *f*: *Frs. O. Frs.* fest, *f*: *Dut.* vuist, *f*: *Ger.* faust, *f*: *M. H. Ger.* vûst, *f*: *O. H. Ger.* fûst, *f*: *Dan.* pust, *n. a blow*: *Swed.* pust, *m. a blow with the fist, box on the ear*: *Icel.* pústr, *m. a box on the ear*.]

fȳst-gebeát, es; *n. A blow with the fist*; pugni ictus, Past. 1, 3, 6? Lye.

fȳst-slægen; *part. Struck with the fist*; pugno cæsus:—Fȳstslægenu wæs *exalapārētur, pugno cæsus erat*, Cot. 79.

fyðer-, fiðer-, feðer- *four-*, found only in the compounds,—fyðer-dǽled, -fête, -hiwe, -ling, -rîca, -rîce, -scȳte. v. feówer.

fyðera, fyðeru, fyðru, *pl. nom. acc*; *gen.* fyðera, fyðerena; *dat. inst.* fyðerum; *n*: also *pl. nom. acc.* fyðeras; *m. Wings*; ālæ, pennæ:—Fyðera [Lamb. fyðeras] culfran ofersylfrede *pennæ cŏlumbæ deargentātæ*, Ps. Spl. 67, 14. Sunu manna on wǽfelse fyðera ðînra hihtaþ *fīlii hŏmĭnum in tegmĭne ālārum tuārum spērābunt*, Ps. Spl. 35, 8: 56, 2: 60, 4: 62, 8. Under sceade fyðerena ðînra gescyld me *sub umbra ālārum tuārum protĕge me*, Ps. Lamb. 16, 8. Under his fyðerum ðû trûwast oððe ðû gehihtest *sub pennis ejus spērābis*, Ps. Lamb. 90, 4. Hwilc silþ me fyðera swâ swâ culfran *quis dăbit mihi pennas sĭcut cŏlumbæ?* Ps. Spl. 54, 6. Seó henn hyre cicenu under hyre fyðeru gegaderaþ *gallīna congrĕgat pullos suos sub ālas*, Mt. Bos. 23, 37. Ofer fyðeru [Lamb. fyðeras] winda *sŭper pennas ventōrum*, Ps. Spl. 103, 4. He fleáh ofer fyðru winda *vŏlāvit sŭper pennas ventōrum*, Ps. Lamb. 17, 11. v. fiðere, es; *n*: but generally *pl.*

fyðer-dǽled; *part. Divided into four, quartered*; quadripartītus, Leo. 151.

fyðered *having wings, winged*; ālātus, Som. Ben. Lye.

fyðer-fête, -fôte; *adj. Four-footed*; quadrūpes:—Fyðerfête nȳten *a four-footed animal*, Med. ex Quadr. 1; Lchdm. i. 326, 11. Fyðerfête *quadrŭpes*, Ælfc. Gr. 9, 26; Som. 11, 6. Ne on fyðerfôtum ne on creópendum *neither among the four-footed nor the creeping*, Homl. Th. i. 486, 28. v. feówer-fête.

fyðer-hiwe; *adj. Four-formed*; quadriformis, Leo. 151.

fyðerling, es; *m. The fourth part of a number* or *measure, a farthing*; quadrans, Som. Ben. Lye. v. feórþling.

fyðer-rîca, an; *m. A ruler over a fourth part, tetrarch*; tetrarches, tetrarcha, æ; *m.* = τετράρχης, ου; *m*:—Ða sind gecwedene tetrarche, ðæt sind, fyðerrîcan; fyðerrîca biþ se ðe hæfþ feórþan dǽl rîces *who are called tetrarchs, that is, rulers over a fourth*; *a tetrarch is he who has a fourth part of a kingdom*, Homl. Th. i. 478, 21.

fyðer-rîce, es; *n. A tetrarchy*; tetrarchia, Som. Ben. Lye.

fyðer-scȳte; *adj. Four-cornered, quadrangular*; quadrangŭlus:—Se arc wæs fyðerscȳte *the ark was quadrangular*, Boutr. Scrd. 21, 3. v. feówer-scȳte.

fȳtung, e; *f. A fighting, quarrelling*; rixa:—Ascūnige man swȳðe fracodlîce fȳtunga *turpes rixæ admŏdum evītentur*, L. Eth. vi. 28; Wilk. 122, 23. v. fītung, feohtan *to fight*.

fyxum *fishes*, Hexam. 11; Norm. 20, 5, = fixum, fiscum; *dat. pl. of* fisc.

G

WHEN *g* is the last radical letter of an Anglo-Saxon word, and follows a long vowel or an *r*, it is often changed into *h*, but then the *g* is resumed when followed by a vowel; as,—Beáh *a ring*; *gen.* es; *m.* beáges *of a ring*; *pl.* beágas *rings*; burh *a town*; *gen.* e; *f.* burge *of a town*; beorh *a hill*; *gen.* es; *m.* beorges *of a hill*; *pl.* beorgas *hills*. The same change takes place after a short vowel in wah *a wall*; *gen.* wages. In the conjugation of verbs, in some cases, *h* is found taking the place of *g*; thus from belgan *to be angry*, bilhst, bilhþ; from âgan *to own*, âhte. **2.** *g* is generally inserted between the vowels *-ie*, making -ige, -igende, *etc.* the first sing. *pres.* and part of verbs in -ian. Thus, from lufian *to love*, bletsian *to bless*, *etc.* are formed ic lufige *I love*, ic bletsige *I bless*, lufigende *loving*, bletsigende *blessing*. **3.** In later English the place of the earlier *g* is often taken by *y*, sometimes by *w*; as,—Geár *a year*, dæg *a day*, dagas *days*. *etc*; morg(en) *morrow*, sorg = *sorrow*, *etc.* **4.** The Anglo-Saxon Rune ᚷ not only stands for the letter *g*, but for gifu *a gift*; because gifu is the Anglo-Saxon name of this Rune. v. gifu **II.** and **RŪN**.

gá *go, come*:—Gá hider neár *come hither near*; accēde huc, Gen. 27, 21; *impert. of* gán.

gaad *a goad*, Som. Ben. Lye. v. gád, e; *f.*

gaar-leece *garlic*, Som. Ben. Lye. v. gár-leác.

gaast, es; *m. A ghost, spirit*; spīrĭtus:—Gaast is God *spīrĭtus est Deus*, Jn. Lind. Skt. 4, 24. v. gást.

gabban; *p.* ede; *pp.* ed *To scoff, mock, delude, jest*; hence, perhaps, GABBLE, GIBBERISH; derīdēre, lūdĕre, illūdĕre, Som. Ben. Lye. [*Prompt.* gabbin *mentiri*: *Piers P.* gabbe *to lie*: *Chauc. to chatter, lie*: *Scot.* gab *to mock, prate*: *Icel.* gabba *to mock.*]

gabbung, e; *f. A scoffing, mocking*, GIBING, *jesting*; derīsio, irrīsio, illūsio, Som. Ben. Lye. [*Prompt*, gabbinge *mendacium*: *Piers P.* gabbynge *lying*: *Scot.* gabbing *mockery, jeering.*]

gabere, es; *m. An enchanter, a charmer*; incantātor, Som. Ben. Lye. v. galere.

gabote, an; *f. A platter, small dish, dessert-dish*; paropsis = παροψίς, Wrt. Voc. 290, 22.

gabul-roid? *a line, rod, staff, compass*; rădius, circĭnus = κίρκινος, Som. Ben. Lye. v. gafol-rand.

GÁD, e; *f. A point of a weapon, spear* or *arrow-head, sting, prick*, GOAD; cuspis, acūleus, stĭmŭlus:—Gád *cuspis*, Wrt. Voc. 288, 23. Gád *stĭmŭlus*, Wrt. Voc. 75, 1. Se yrþling ná gáde hæfþ, búton of cræfte mínum *ărātor nec stĭmŭlum hăbet, nĭsi ex arte mea*, Coll. Monast. Th. 30, 31. Hafaþ gúþmecga gyrde lange, gyldene gáde *the warrior has a long rod, a golden goad*, Salm. Kmbl. 183: Sal. 91. [*Goth.* gazds, *m. a prick, sting*: *Swed.* gadd, *m. a sting*: *Icel.* gaddr, *m. a goad, spike, sting.*] DER. gád-ísen.

GÁD, gǽd, es; *n? A lack, want, desire*; defectus, pēnūria, desīdĕrium, appĕtītus:—Ðæt ðám gēngum þrým gád ne wǽre wiste ne wǽde *that there should be no lack of food or clothing to the three youths*, Cd. 176; Th. 222, 10; Dan. 102: Elen. Kmbl. 1981; El. 992. Ne biþ ðé ǽnigra gád wilna *there shall not be to thee a lack of any pleasures*, Beo. Th. 1903; B. 949. Ne wæs me in healle gád *there was not a want to me in the hall*, Exon. 94 a; Th. 353, 20; Reim. 15. Ne wyrþ inc wilna gǽd *there shall not be to you two a lack of pleasures*, Cd. 13; Th. 15, 21; Gen. 236. Nis him wilna gád, ne meara, ne máþma, gif he ðín beneah *there is not to him a desire for pleasures, nor horses, nor treasures, if he lacks thee*, Exon. 123 b; Th. 475, 6; Bo. 43. [*O. Sax.* gēdea, *f. a want*, in meti-gēdea *lack of food*: *Goth.* gaidw, *n. a want.*]

gada *a companion, an associate.* DER. ge-gada.

GADERIAN, gadorigean, gadrian, gadrigean, gæderian, gædrian; to gaderigenne, gadrienne, gadrigenne; ic gaderie, gaderige, gadrige, ðú gaderast, gadrast, he gaderaþ, gadraþ, *pl.* gaderiaþ, gadriaþ; *p.* gaderode; *pp.* gaderod *To* GATHER, *gather together, collect, store up*; lĕgere, collĭgĕre, congrĕgāre:—Næs nán heáfodman ðæt fyrde gaderian wolde *there was not a chief man who would gather together a force*, Chr. 1010; Erl. 144, 10. Ðá án ongann folc gadorigean *then one began to gather the people*, Andr. Kmbl. 3111; An. 1558. Ic wolde eác gadrian sum gehwǽde andgyt of ðære béc *I would also gather some little information from the book*, Bd. de nat. rerum; Lchdm. iii. 232, 2. Gadrigean, Andr. Kmbl. 1562; An. 782. Ðá ongan se æðeling Eádmund to gaderigenne [gadrigenne, Th. 276, 33, col. 2: gadrienne, 277, 33, col. 1] fyrde *then the etheling Edmund began to gather a force*, Chr. 1016; Th. 276, 33, col. 1. Ic gaderige ðyder eall ðæt me gewexen ys *illuc congrĕgābo omnia, quæ nāta sunt mihi*, Lk. Bos. 12, 18. Ic gadrige [gaderie, MS. D.] *lĕgo*, Ælfc. Gr. 37; Som. 39, 22. Se ðe ne gaderaþ mid me, se hit tostret *qui non collĭgit mecum, dispergit*, Lk. Bos. 11, 23. Hý gaderiaþ feoh, and nyton hwám hý hyt gadriaþ *they store up wealth, and know not for whom they store it up*, Ps. Th. 38, 8: Lk. Bos. 6, 44: Mt. Bos. 6, 26. Ðæt folc gaderode mid micle menio ðæra fugela *the people gathered together a great number of the birds*, Num. 11, 32: Chr. 1015; Th. 277, 16, col. 1: Bd. de nat. rerum; Wrt. popl. science 1, 2; Lchdm. iii. 232, 4. Ic næbbe hwyder ic míne wæstmas gadrige *non hăbeo quo congrĕgem fructus meos*, Lk. Bos. 12, 17. [*Wyc.* gadre, geder, gedere: *Chauc.* gadred *gathered*: *R. Glouc.* gedere *gathered*: *Laym.* gædere, gaderen: *Orm.* gaddrenn: *Scot.* gadyr: *Plat.* gadern, gaddern: *Frs.* gearjen: *O. Frs.* gaduria, gaderia, gadria, garia: *Dut.* gaderen: *Ger.* gattern: *M. H. Ger.* gatern, getern: *Icel.* gadda *coarctāre*, Rask Hald.] DER. ge-gaderian.

gaderigendlíc, gadrigendlíc; *adj. Collective, congregative*; collectīvus, congrĕgātīvus, Som. Ben. Lye.

gaderscype, es; *m. Matrimonium*, Hpt. Gl. 438.

gader-tang, gæder-tang, gæder-teng; *adj. Continuous, connected with, united*; contĭnuus, assŏcius, consŏcius:—Biþ sum corn sǽdes gehealden symle on ðære sáule sóþfæstnysse, þenden gadertang wunaþ gást on líce *some grain of the seed of truth will be always retained in the soul, while the spirit dwells in the body united to it*, Bt. Met. Fox 22, 77; Met. 22, 9: Scint. 1.

gader-tangnys, gæder-tangnys, -nyss, e; *f. A continuation*, Scint. 12.

gader-tengan, gæder-tengan; *p.* de; *pp.* ed *To continue, join*; contĭnuāre, Som. Ben. Lye.

gaderung, e; *f. A* GATHERING, *congregation, joining, council, assembly, crowd*; congrĕgātio:—Cyrce oððe geleáfful gaderung *a church or faithful gathering*; ecclēsia, Wrt. Voc. 80, 72. DER. ge-gaderung.

gadinca? *Mūtĭnus, fascĭnum obscēnum*; membrum vĭrīle:—Gadinca *vel* hnoc *mūtĭnus*, Ælfc. Gl. 22; Som. 59, 83; Wrt. Voc. 23, 49.

gád-ísen, es; *n. A gad-iron, goad*; acūleus, stĭmŭlus:—Sticel *vel* gádísen *acūleus*, Ælfc. Gl. 1; Som. 55, 15; Wrt. Voc. 15, 15. Ic hæbbe sumne cnapan þýwende oxan mid gádísene *hăbeo quendam puĕrum minantem bŏves cum stĭmŭlo*, Coll. Monast. Th. 19, 27.

gadorigean *to gather*, Andr. Kmbl. 3111; An. 1558. v. gaderian.

gador-wist, e; *f. A dwelling together, companionship, intercourse*; contubernium, Ælfc. Gl. 116; Som. 80, 59; Wrt. Voc. 61, 42: Cot. 43. DER. ge-gadorwist.

gadrian, gadrigean *to gather*, Bd. de nat. rerum; Lchdm. iii. 232, 2: Andr. Kmbl. 1562; An. 782. v. gaderian.

gadrigendlíc *collective*; collectivus, Som. Ben. Lye. v. gaderigendlíc.

gæ *yea, yes*, Mt. Kmbl. Rush. 17, 25. v. gea.

gǽc, es; *m. A cuckoo, gawk*; cŭcūlus:—Gǽces súre *cuckoo-sorrel, wood-sorrel*; acētōsa, acĭdŭla, Som. Ben. Lye. v. geác.

gæd, es; *n. A being together, fellowship, union*; sŏcĭĕtas:—Nolde gæd geador in Godes ríce, eádiges engles and ðæs ofermódan *there would not [be] any fellowship in God's kingdom, of the blessed angel and the proud together*, Salm. Kmbl. 899; Sal. 449.

gǽd *a lack, want*, Col. 13; Th. 15, 21; Gen. 236. v. gád, es; *n.*

gædeling, es; *m. A companion*; cŏmes:—His gædelinges gúþ-gewǽdu *his companion's battle-garments*, Beo. Th 5227; B. 2617: Cd. 193; Th. 242, 20; Dan. 422. [*Piers P. Chauc. R. Glouc.* gadeling *an idle vagabond*: *Laym.* gadelinges, *pl. men of base degree*: *O. Sax.* gaduling, *m. a relation, kinsman*: *M. H. Ger.* geteling, *m. a relation, fellow*: *O. H. Ger.* gataling, *m. consanguĭneus, părens*: *Goth.* gadiliggs, *m. a cousin, relation.*]

gædere; *adv. Together.* DER. æt-gædere, to-. v. geador.

gæderian, gædrian *to gather*, Ps. Spl. 38, 10: Exon. 58 b; Th. 211, 6; Ph. 193. v. gaderian.

gæf *gave*, Bd. 3, 24; S. 557, 34, = geaf; *p. of* gifan.

gæfe, e; *f. Grace*; Mid Godes gæfe *by God's grace*, Th. Chart. 459, 2. v. gifu.

gæfel, es; *n. A gift, offering, tribute*; hostia, trĭbūtum, Lk. Skt. Rush. 2, 24: Mt. Kmbl. Lind. 17, 25: Mt. Kmbl. Rush. 9, 9. v. gafol.

gæfel-geroefa, -gehrēfa, -hroefa; *m. A publican*, Mt. Kmbl. Rush. 5, 46; 9, 11, 10.

gægl *wanton*; lascīvus, Lye. v. gagol.

gægl-bǽrnes, bērnes, -ness, e; *f. Wantonness, luxury, riot*; lascivia, Cot. 118.

gælæþ, gæleþ? *A cage to sell or punish bondmen in*; catasta, Som. Ben. Lye:—Gæleþ *catasta*, Wrt. Voc. 288, 24.

GǼLAN; *p.* de; *pp.* ed. I. *v. trans. to hinder, delay, impede, keep in suspense*; retardāre, mŏrāri, impĕdīre:—Hú lange gǽlst ðú úre líf *quousque anĭmam nostram tollis?* Jn. Bos. 10, 24. Swá mon oft lett fundiendne monnan, ond his færelt gǽlþ, swá gǽlþ se líchoma ðæt mód *as a man hastening forward is often hindered, and his journey impeded, so the body impedes the mind*, Past. 256, 6; Hat. MS. 48 a, 16. Ðeáh hine singale gēmen gǽle *though perpetual care impede him*, Bt. Met. Fox 7, 101; Met. 7, 51. He men gǽleþ ǽlces gódes *he hinders men in respect to every good thing*, Blickl. Homl. 179, 11: 191, 20. II. *v. intrans. to hesitate, delay*; cunctāri:—Scealcas ne gǽldon *the servants delayed not*, Elen. Kmbl. 1381; El. 692: 1999; El. 1001. DER. a-gǽlan.

gældan *to pay, depend, suspend*; pendēre, dependēre, suspendēre, Som. Ben. Lye. v. geldan, gildan.

gæle? *Saffron*; crŏcus:—Gæle, geolo *crŏcus*, Wrt. Voc. 288, 47.

gæleþ, ðú gælest *sings, thou singest*, Beo. Th. 4912; B. 2460; *3rd and 2nd pers. pres. of* galan.

gǽlnys, -nyss, e; *f. Wearisomeness, tediousness, loathing, disgust*; tædium:—Slǽpþ sáwel mín for gǽlnysse *dormĭtāvit ănĭma mea præ tædio*, Ps. Spl. 118, 28. v. gálnes.

gǽlsa, an; *m. Luxury, extravagance*; luxus, luxŭria:—Lust oððe gǽlsa *luxus*, Ælfc. Gr. 11; Som. 15, 10. Lybbende on his gǽlsan *vivendo luxŭrĭōse*, Lk. Bos. 15, 13. Þurh fulne folces gǽlsan *propter pŏpŭli luxum consummātum*, Lupi Serm. i. 21; Hick. Thes. ii. 105, 39. Ic him monigfealde módes gǽlsan ongeánbere *I present manifold mind's extravagances to him*, Exon. 71 a; Th. 264, 19; Jul. 366: Homl. Th. i. 544, 28. Gælso *sollicitudo*, Mt. Kmbl. Lind. 13, 22. DER. hyge-gælsa.

gælþ, ðú gælst *sings, thou singest*; *3rd and 2nd pers. pres. of* galan.

gæmnian; *p.* ode; *pp.* od *To play, game*; lūsĭtāre:—Ðæt man ungemetlíce gæmnige *that a man immoderately play*, Homl. Th. ii. 590, 26. v. gamenian.

gængang; *adj. Pregnant?* prægnans?—Gif hió gængang weorþeþ *if she becomes pregnant*, L. Ethb. 84; Th. i. 24, 7. v. Schmid, p. 9, note to c. 84.

gǽn-hwyrft, es; *m.* [gǽn = geán, ongeán *again*] *A turning again*; conversio:—On gecerringe oððe on gǽnhwyrfte Drihten gehæftnesse oððe hæftnunge Siones *in convertendo Dŏmĭnus captĭvĭtātem Sion*, Ps. Lamb. 125, 1.

gǣn-ryne, es; *m. A running against, meeting;* occursus:—Arīs on mīnum gǣnryne *exsurge in occursum meum*, Ps. Lamb. 58, 6. v. geán-ryne.

Gænt *Ghent in Flanders*, Chr. 881; Th. 150, 13, col. 3. v. Gent.

gæp; *adj. Cautious, shrewd, subtle;* săgax, cautus, Ben. Lye. v. geap, II.

gǣr, geár, es; *n. A year;* annus:—Ūre gǣr beóþ asmeáde *anni nostri medĭtābuntur*, Ps. Lamb. 89, 9. v. geár.

gærcian; *p.* ode; *pp.* od *To prepare;* părāre:—Ðū gærcodest on ðīnre swētnysse ðam þearfan *părasti in dulcēdĭne tua paupĕri*, Ps. Lamb. 67, 11. Hī gærcodon flāna heora on cocere [MS. kokere] *părāvērunt săgittas suas in pharetra*, 10, 3. v. gearcian.

gærcung, e; *f. A preparation, practice;* exercĭtātio:—Gedrēfed oððe geunrōtsod ic eom on mīnre gærcunge [MS. gærcuncge] *contristātus sum in exercĭtātiōne mea*, Ps. Lamb. 54, 3. v. gearcung.

gǣr-getal, es; *n.* [gǣr = geár *a year;* getæl, getel *a number*] *A tale of years, number of years;* annōrum sĕries:—Hit cymþ æfter fiftigum wintra his gǣrgetales *it comes after fifty winters of his number of years*, L. M. 2, 59; Lchdm. ii. 284, 22.

GÆRS, gers, græs, es; *n.* GRASS, *a blade of grass, herb, hay;* grāmen, herba, fænum:—Gærs *vel* wyrt *herba*, Ælfc Gr. 4; Som. 3, 20: Jn. Bos. 6, 10. Hīg and gærs *hay and grass*, Andr. Kmbl. 76; An. 38: Bt. Met. Fox 20, 196; Met. 20. 98. Gyf he māran gærses beþyrfe *if he need more grass*, L. R. S. 4; Th. i. 434, 17. Seó eorþe wæstm beraþ, ǣrest gærs, syððan ear, syððan fulne hwǣte on ðam eare *terra fructĭfĭcat, prīmum herbam, deinde spīcam, deinde plēnum frumentum in spīca*, Mk. Bos. 4, 28: Gen. 1, 11: Num. 22, 4. Ðā he hēt ða menegu ofer ðæt gærs hī sittan *cum jussisset turbam discumbĕre sŭper fænum*, Mt. Bos. 14, 19: Ps. Spl. 105, 20. Ofer gærsa cīþas *sŭper grāmĭna*, Deut. 32, 2. [*R. Brun.* gres: *Laym.* græs, gras: *Orm.* gresess *herbs: Scot.* gers, gerss, gyrs: *O. Sax.* gras, *n: Frs.* gerz: *O. Frs.* gers, gres, *n: Dut. Ger.* gras, *n: M. H. Ger. O. H. Ger.* gras, *n: Goth.* gras, *n: Dan.* græs, *n: Swed.* gräs, *n: Icel.* gras, *n.*]

gærsama, gersuma, an; *m. Treasure;* ŏpes:—He lēt nyman of hire ealle ða betstan gærsaman *he caused all the best treasures to be taken from her*, Chr. 1035; Th. 292, 22, col. 2. Gif he ne sealde ðe māre gersuman *if he had not given the greater treasures*, Chr. 1047; Erl. 177, 7. v. gærsum.

gærs-bed, -bedd, es; *n. A grass-bed, grave;* sub cæspĭte lectus, sepulcrum:—Ðonne he gāst ofgifeþ, syððan hine (?) gærsbedd sceal wunian *when he gives up his spirit, then must he inhabit a grave*, Ps. Th. 102, 15.

gærs-cīþ, es; *m. A blade of grass;* grāmĭnis germen:—Gærstapan cōmon and frǣton ealle ða gærscīþas *locusts came and ate up all the blades of grass*, Ors. 1, 7; Bos. 29, 42.

gærs-grēne *grass-green;* grāmĭneus, herbĭdus, vĭrĭdis, Som. Ben. Lye.

gærs-hoppa, an; *m. A grass-hopper, locust;* lŏcusta, cĭcāda:—He cwæþ and com gærshoppa *dixit et vēnit lŏcusta*, Ps. Lamb. 104, 34: 108, 23. Cwōmón gærshoppan *grass-hoppers came*, Ps. Th. 104, 30: 77, 46. [*Orm.* gress hoppe *locusts.*]

gærs-molde *grass-land.* v. græs-molde.

gærs-stapa, gærstapa, an; *m. A* GRASS-STEPPER, *locust;* lŏcusta:—Gærstapa *lŏcusta*, Wrt. Voc. 78, 61. He sǣde and com gærstapa *dixit et vēnit lŏcusta*, Ps. Spl. 104, 32: 108, 22. He sealde geswinc heora gærstapan *dĕdit lăbōres eōrum lŏcustæ*, Ps. Lamb. 77, 46. Gærstapan cōmon and frǣton ealle ða gærscīþas *locusts came and ate up all the blades of grass*, Ors. 1, 7; Bos. 29, 42: Homl. Th. ii. 192. 35. Gærstapan hit fretaþ eall *lŏcustæ devŏrābunt omnia*, Deut. 28, 38: Num. 13, 33: Ex. 10, 12: Jud. 6, 5: Mt. Bos. 3, 4. Se byrnenda wind brohte gærstapan *ventus ūrens levāvit lŏcustas*, Ex. 10, 13, 19: 10, 4.

gærs-swȳn, es; *n. A pasturage swine;* herbāgii porcus:—He sceal syllan gærs-swȳn *dēbet dăre porcum herbāgii*, L. R. S. 2; Th. i. 432, 9.

gærst *green like grass;* herbeus, Som. Ben. Lye.

gærs-tūn, es; *m. A grass-enclosure, a meadow;* prātum, pascuum: hence GERSTON, now used in Surrey and Sussex, in the same sense:—Be ceorles gærstūne: gif ceorlas gærstūn hæbben gemǣnne, oððe ōðer gedālland to tȳnanne *of a churl's meadow: if churls have a common meadow or other partible land to fence*, L. In. 42; Th. i. 128, 5. Prātum quod Saxŏnice Garstūn appellātur, Cod. Dipl. 350; A. D. 930; Kmbl. ii. 166, 6: Cod. Dipl. Apndx. 461; A. D. 956; Kmbl. iii. 449, 19.

gærs-tūn-dīc, es; *m. A grass-meadow-dike;* vallum circa prātum ductum:—On gærstūndīc sūðeweardne *to the south of the grass-meadow-dike*, Cod. Dipl. Apndx. 441; A. D. 956; Kmbl. iii. 438, 4.

gærsum, gersum, es; *m. n. Treasure, riches;* thēsaurus, ŏpes:—He lēt niman of hyre ealle ða betstan gærsuma *he caused all the best treasure to be taken from her*, Chr. 1035; Erl. 164, 23: 1090; Erl. 226, 25. Hī betǣhtan ðǣr ealla ða gærsume *they deposited there all the treasures*, 1070; Erl. 209, 17, 27, 33. Hī nāmen manega gersumas *they took many treasures*, Chr. 1070; Erl. 209, 13. For his mycele gersuma *for his great treasures*, 1090; Erl. 226, 38. [*Laym.* gærsume *treasure: Scot.* gersome *a sum paid by a tenant to a landlord on the entry of a lease.* The word seems to have been introduced from the Scandinavian, cf. *Icel.* gör-semi, ger-semi *a costly thing, jewel;* and see Cl. and Vig. Dict. for etymology.]

gærs-wong *a field of grass, grassy plain.* v. græs-wong.

gærs-yrþ, e; *f. Grass-land, pasturage;* herbāgium:—To gærsyrþe *de herbāgio*, L. R. S. 4; Th. i. 434, 17. See Schmid, p. 374, note.

gæruwe, an; *f. Yarrow;* millefōlium:—Gæruwe *millefŏlium*, Ælfc. Gl. 40; Som. 63, 82; Wrt. Voc. 30, 32. v. gearwe.

gǣsne, gesne, geásne, gēsine; *adj. Barren, sterile, empty, wanting, void of, lifeless;* stĕrĭlis, inānis, ĕgēnus, destĭtūtus, expers, exănĭmis:—Ðæt we gǣstes wlite, on ðās gǣsnan tīd, georne biþencen *that we earnestly consider, in this barren time, the spirit's beauty*, Exon. 20 a; Th. 53, 13; Cri. 850. Ðis geár wæs gǣsne on mæstene *this year was barren in mast-fruit*, Chr. 1116; Th. 371, 16. Hirdas lǣgon gǣsne on greóte *the keepers lay lifeless on the sand*, Andr. Kmbl. 2169; An. 1086. v. Grm. Andr. Elen. p. 124, 1085: Graff. IV. 267. [*Piers P.* gesen: Halliw. Dict. geson *scarce.*]

gæst, gest, gist, giest, gyst, es; *pl. nom. acc.* gastas; *m.* I. *a* GUEST; hospes, sŏcius:—Gæst inne swæf *the guest slept within*, Beo. Th. 3605; B. 1800. Biþ symle gæst *will ever be a guest*, Exon. 84 c; Th. 318, 9; Mod. 80. Gārsecges gæst *the ocean's guest*, 97 a; Th. 301, 33; Wal. 29. Ferende gæst *a journeying guest*, 103 a; Th. 390, 12; Rä. 8, 9. Gæst ne grētte *he greeted not the guest*, Beo. Th. 3790; B. 1893. Gasta werode *with the multitude of guests*, Cd. 67; Th. 81, 16; Gen. 1346. Gif hine sǣ byreþ gæsta [gasta?] fulne *if the sea shall bear it* [*the vessel*] *full of guests*, Exon. 101 b; Th. 384, 20; Rä. 4, 30. II. *a stranger, an enemy;* vir ălienĭgĕnus, hostis:—Wæs se grimma gæst Grendel hāten, wonsǣlig wer *the grim enemy was called Grendel, the unblest man*, Beo. Th. 204; B. 102: 4158; B. 2073. Ða se gæst ongan glēdum spīwan *then the fiend* [*the dragon*] *began to vomit fire*, 4613; B. 2312. Hwonne gæst cume to dūrum mīnum, him biþ deáþ witod *when a stranger comes to my doors, death is decreed to him*, Exon. 104 b; Th. 396, 26; Rä. 16, 10. [*Piers P.* gest: *Wyc.* geste: *Chauc.* gest: *Laym.* gesst: *O. Sax.* gast, *m: Plat. Dut. Ger. M. H. Ger. O. H. Ger.* gast. *m: Goth.* gasts, *m: Dan.* giest, *m. f: Swed.* gäst, *m: Icel.* gestr, *m.*] DER. beód-gæst, brim-, nīþ-, wæl-.

gǣst, es; *m. The soul, spirit, mind;* spīrĭtus, anĭmus:—Him wæs gǣst geseald *a spirit was given to him*, Cd. 201; Th. 249, 21; Dan. 533. Nyle he ǣngum ānum ealle gesyllan gǣstes snyttru *he will not give all wisdom of mind to any one man*, Exon. 17 b; Th. 43, 5; Cri. 684. Gūþlāc in gǣste bær heofoncundne hyht *Guthlac bare heavenly hope in his spirit*, Exon. 35 a; Th. 112, 10; Gū. 141. Ðeáh ðe him onwrige wuldres cyning wīsdōmes gǣst *though the king of glory revealed to them the spirit of wisdom*, Exon. 73 a; Th. 273, 15; Jul. 516. v. gāst.

gǣst *goest, walkest*, Gen. 3, 14; *2nd pers. pres. of* gān.

gæst-ærn, -ern *a guest-place, guest-chamber, an inn.* v. gest-ærn.

gǣstan; *p.* te; *pp.* ed [gāst, gǣst *a spirit, ghost*] *To gast, frighten, afflict, torment;* terrēre, crŭciāre, affligĕre:—Hī gǣston Godes cempan gāre and līge *they afflicted God's champions with spear and flame*, Exon. 66 a; Th. 243, 27; Jul. 17. [*Wyc.* gaste *to make greatly afraid: Piers P.* gaste *to scare* [*birds*]. Cf. *Goth.* us-gaisjan, and v. Dief. ii. pp. 397–8.]

gǣst-berend, es; *pl. nom. acc.* -berend; *m. A spirit-bearer, man;* is qui spīrĭtum *vel* ănĭmum fert, hŏmo:—Ðās gǣstberend gīman nellaþ *these spirit-bearers will not heed*, Exon. 31 a; Th. 97, 33; Cri. 1600: 78 a; Th. 293, 17; Crä. 2. Ic gǣstberend cwelle compwǣpnum *I kill the living with battle-weapons*, 105 b; Th. 401, 8; Rä. 21, 8.

gǣst-cund; *adj. Spiritual;* spīrĭtālis:—Seó lufu in monnes mōde getimbreþ gǣstcunde gife *love builds up spiritual grace in man's mind*, Exon. 44 a; Th. 148, 11; Gū. 743.

gǣst-cwalu, e; *f. Torment of soul;* ănĭmæ tormentum:—Ðǣr eów is hām sceapen, grim gǣstcwalu *there a home is made for you, bitter torment of soul*, Exon. 42 b; Th. 142, 28; Gū. 651.

gǣst-gedāl, es; *n. Separation of soul and body, death;* ănĭmæ et corpŏris divortium, mors:—Ne he sorge wæg gǣstgedāles *he sorrowed not for his soul's separation*, Exon. 49 a; Th. 170, 14; Gū. 1111. v. gāst-gedāl.

gǣst-gehygd, es; *n. Thought of mind;* ănĭmi cōgĭtātio:—Him seó unforhte ageaf andsware, þurh gǣstgehygd, Iuliana *the fearless Juliana gave him answer through her mind's thought*, Exon. 67 b; Th. 251, 20; Jul. 148. v. gāst-gehygd.

gǣst-gemynd, es; *n. Thought of mind* or *spirit;* ănĭmi cōgĭtātio:—Ic him gǣstgemyndum wille wesan underþȳded *I will be subjected to him in my spirit's thoughts*, Exon. 41 a; Th. 138, 11; Gū. 574.

gǣst-genīþla, an; *m. A persecutor* or *foe of souls, the devil;* anĭmārum insectātor *vel* hostis, diabŏlus:—Hæfde engles hiw gǣstgenīþla, helle hæftling *the foe of souls, the captive of hell, had an angel's form*, Exon. 69 a; Th. 257, 11; Jul. 245.

gǣst-gerȳne, es; *n. A ghostly* or *spiritual mystery, a mystery of the mind;* spīrĭtāle mystērium, ănĭmi mystērium:—In godcundum gǣstgerȳnum *in divine spiritual mysteries*, Exon. 36 a; Th. 117, 5; Gū. 219: 49 a; Th. 168, 31; Gū. 1086. Bī ðon Salomon song, giedda snottor, gǣstgerȳnum *of whom Solomon, wise in song, sang in spiritual mysteries*, Exon. 18 a; Th. 45, 3; Cri. 713: 14 a; Th. 28, 2; Cri. 440. v. gāst-gerȳne.

gǽst-gewinn, es; *n. Torment of soul;* ănĭmæ tormentum:—In ðam grimmestan gǽstgewinne *in the bitterest torment of soul*, Exon. 41 a; Th. 137, 19; Gú. 561.

gǽst-hálig; *adj. Spirit-holy, holy in spirit;* in spīrĭtu sanctus:—Wǽr is ætsomne Godes and monna, gǽst-hálig treów *there is a compact together of God and men, a spiritual holy covenant*, Exon. 16 a; Th. 36, 31; Cri. 584. He fond fúsne on forþsíþ freán unwemne, gǽst-hálig*ne he found his blameless master bent on departure, holy in spirit*, 49 b; Th. 171, 5; Gú. 1122. Gǽst-hálge guman *men holy in spirit*, 95 b; Th. 356, 33; Pa. 21: 45 b; Th. 154, 19; Gú. 845. v. gást-hálig.

gæst-, gast-, gest-, gyst-hús, es; *n. A guest-house, guest-chamber;* hospĭtium:—Gæst-hus *hospĭtium*, Wrt. Voc. 86, 44. [*Orm.* gessthus: *Ger.* gasthaus *inn.*]

gæst-hof *a guest-house*, v. gast-hof.

gæstlíc *hospitable, ready for guests.* v. gastlíc.

gǽstlíc; *adj. Ghostly, spiritual;* spīrĭtālis:—Giofu gǽstlíc *spiritual grace*, Exon. 8 b; Th. 3, 26; Cri. 42: 18 a; Th. 44, 7; Cri. 699: 71 a; Th. 265, 26; Jul. 387. Þurh gǽstlícu wundor *through spiritual miracles*, Exon. 34 b; Th. 111, 14; Gú. 126. Mid gǽstlícum wǽpnum *with spiritual weapons*, 35 a; Th. 114, 24; Gú. 148. v. gástlíc.

gǽstlíce; *adv. Spiritually;* spīrĭtālĭter:—Ðeáh he gódes hwæt onginne gǽstlíce *though he attempt aught of good spiritually*, Exon. 71 b; Th. 266, 15; Jul. 398. v. gástlíce.

gæst-líðe *kind to guests, hospitable.* v. gist-líðe.

gæst-líðnes, gest-líðnes, giest-líðnys, -nyss, e; *f. Hospitableness, hospitality, entertainment of guests;* hospĭtālĭtas:—We willaþ eów on gæstlíðnesse onfón *we will receive you in hospitality*, Bd. 1, 25; S. 487, 15. Ðætte ælþeódige bisceopas sýn þoncfulle heora gæstlíðnesse and feorme *ut episcŏpi peregrīni contenti sint hospitālĭtātis mūnĕre oblāto*, Bd. 4, 5; S. 573, 3.

gǽst-lufe, an; *f. Soul's love, spiritual love;* spīrĭtālis ămor:—For gǽstlufan *for spiritual love*, Exon. 55 b; Th. 196, 11; Az. 172. Mid gǽstlufan *with spiritual love*, 55 b; Th. 197, 11; Az. 188.

gæst-mægen. v. gist-mægen.

gæst-sele *a guest-hall.* v. gest-sele.

gǽst-sunu; *gen.* -suna; *m. A spiritual son, Christ:*—Godes gǽstsunu *God's spiritual Son*, Exon. 17 b; Th. 41, 23; Cri. 660: 20 b; Th. 53, 35; Cri. 861. v. gást-sunu.

gæt, es; *n. A gate:*—Æt ðam gæte *ad ostium*, Bd. 3, 11; S. 536, 17: Mt. Lind. Stv. 7, 13. v. geat.

gǽt *goats*, Exon. 26 a; Th. 75, 34; Cri. 1231; Rtl. 119, 16; *pl. nom. acc. of* gát.

gǽtan; *p.* de, te; *pp.* ed *To grant, to confirm:*—Ic gǽte *I confirm*, Chr. 675; Th. 59, 30. v. geátan.

gǽten; *adj.* [gát *a goat*] *Of* or *pertaining to goats;* caprīnus:—Gǽten smeoro *goat's grease*, Med. ex Quadr. 6, 15; Lchdm. i. 354, 8. Gǽten roc [MS. rooc] *a garment made of goat-skins;* mēlōtes = μηλωτή, Ælfc. Gl. 63; Som. 68, 117; Wrt. Voc. 40, 27.

gǽþ *goes:*—He gǽþ *he goes*, Beo. Th. 4075; B. 2034; *3rd pers. pres. of* gán.

GAF; *adj. Base, vile, lewd;* turpis, vīlis, lŏquax:—Hwǽr biþ his gaf spræc *where will be his wanton discourse?* Basil admn. 8; Norm. 50, 28. [*Scot.* gaff *to talk loudly and merrily* (?)]. DER. ge-gaf; and cf. gaffetung.

gaf *gave*, Salm. Kmbl. 114, note; Sal. 56; *p. of* gifan.

gafel, es; *n. Tax, tribute;* vectīgal, trĭbūtum:—Ðæt he mǽge cyninges gafel forþbringan *that he can bring forth the king's tribute*, L. Wg. 7; Th. i. 186, 14, note 17. Hí Godes gafel lǽston *they rendered God's tribute*, L. Eth. ix. 43; Th. i. 350, 8. Gafeles andfengend *numĕrārius, numŭlārius, vectīgālis, receptor*, Cot. 142. v. gafol.

gafelian; *p.* ode; *pp.* od *To rent;* condūcĕre:—Ic geann ðárto twegra hída ðe Eádríc gafelaþ *I give thereto two hides which Eadric rents*, Cod. Dipl. 699; A. D. 997; Kmbl. iii. 305, 6. DER. ge-gafelod.

gafellíc; *adj. Tributary;* trĭbūto sive fisco pertĭnens, Cot. 85.

gafeluc, es; *m. A spear, javelin;* hastīle:—Gafelucas *hastīlia*, Ælfc. Gl. 52; Som. 66, 54; Wrt. Voc. 35, 41. [*R. Brun.* gauelokes *javelins: M. H. Ger.* gabilôt, gabylôt, *n. a javelin: Icel.* gaflok, *n. spīcŭli gĕnus*, Rask Hald: *Fr.* javelot, *m. a javelin: It.* giavelotto, *m: Wel.* gaflach, *m. a fork, bearded spear: Ir.* gabhla *a spear, lance: Gael.* gobhlach *forked: Armor.* gavlod, *m. a javelin.*]

gaffetung, gafetung, e; *f. A scoffing, mocking;* dērīsio:—Of ðisum leahtre beóþ acennede módes unstæððignys and ýdel gaffetung *of this sin are born unsteadiness of mind and idle scoffing*, Homl. Th. ii. 218, 33. He forlǽt derigendlíce gaffetunga *he forsakes injurious scoffings*, Homl. Th. i. 306, 2. Ða wélegan on heora gebeórscipe begáþ derigendlíce gafetunge *the wealthy in their feasting practise pernicious scoffing*, i. 330, 33. v. gaf.

gaflas; *pl. m. Forks, props, spars of a building, a gallows;* furcæ, patĭbŭlum, Som. Ben. Lye. [*O. H. Ger.* gabala *furca:* and v. Dief. ii. 402.]

gafol, gafel, gaful, es; *n.* [gifan *to give*] *Tax, tribute, rent, interest;* vectīgal, trĭbūtum, census, ūsūra:—Hyra ár is mǽst on ðæm gafole, ðe ða Finnas him gyldaþ: ðæt gafol biþ on deóra fellum, and on fugela feðerum *their revenue is chiefly in the tribute, which the Finns pay them: the tribute is in skins of beasts, and in feathers of birds*, Ors. 1, 1; Bos. 20, 32–34. To gafle gesettan *to let out for rent*, Chr. 1100; Erl. 236, 6. Gafol ūsūra, Ælfc. Gr. 43; Som. 45, 4. Ætýwaþ me ðæs gafoles mynyt *ostendĭte mihi numisma census*, Mt. Bos. 22, 19: L. Edg. S. 1; Th. i. 270, 19: Exon. 16 a; Th. 35, 16; Cri. 559. Cyninges gafoles bígerdel *a king's tribute-purse;* saccus *vel* fiscus, Ælfc. Gl. 65; Som. 69, 35; Wrt. Voc. 40, 63. Hí ðone fíftan dǽl ealra hiora eorþwæstma ðæm cyninge to gafole gesyllaþ *they give the fifth part of all their fruits of the earth to the king for tribute*, Ors. 1, 5; Bos. 28, 31: Byrht. Th. 133, 6; By. 46. Ic náme ðæt mín ys mid ðam gafole *ego recēpissem quod meum est cum ūsūra*, Mt. Bos. 25, 27. Se ðe feoh his ne sealde to gafole *qui pĕcūniam suam non dĕdit ad ūsūra..*, Ps. Lamb. 14, 5. Ðæt him leófre wǽre wið hine to feohtanne, ðonne gafol to gyldenne *that they would rather fight against him, than pay him tribute*, Ors. 1, 10; Bos. 32, 24, 28: L. Edg. S. 1; Th. i. 270, 16: L. O. D. 9; Th. i. 356, 18: Chr. 991; Erl. 130, 21: 994; Erl. 132, 31. Ða dæt gafol námon *qui didrachma accipiēbant*, Mt. Bos. 17, 24, 25: 22, 17: Lk. Bos. 20, 22: 23, 2. Gafol sellan *to give tribute*, Cd. 93; Th. 119, 12; Gen. 1978. Ðæt gé ðisne gárrǽs mid gafole forgyldon *that ye buy off this warfare with tribute*, Byrht. Th. 132, 47; By. 32. Freólsdóm gafola *freedom from imposts*, L. Wih. 1; Th. i. 36, 15. [*M. Lat.* gablum: *Fr.* gabelle: *It.* gabella: *Span.* gabela *tax.* A Celtic origin has been suggested for this word, v. Dief. ii. 400–1.] DER. bere-gafol, ealu-, feoh-, hunig-, land-, mete-, neád-, rǽde-.

Gafol-, Gaful-ford; *gen.* -fordes; *dat.* -forde, -forda; *m.* [gafol *tribute*, ford *a ford: the tributary ford*] *Camelford, Cornwall;* lŏci nōmen in agro Cornubiensi:—Hér wæs Weala gefeoht and Defna æt Gafolforda [Gafulforda, Th. 110, 111, 17, col. 1] *here* [A. D. 823] *there was a battle of the Welsh and Devonians at Camelford*, Chr. 823; Th. 110, 17, col. 2; 111, 17, col. 2, 3.

gafol-bere, es; *m. Barley paid as rent:*—Threó pund gauolbæres, Th. Chart. 145, 2.

gafol-, gaful-gylda, -gilda, -gelda, an; *m.* I. *a tribute-payer, tributary, debtor;* trĭbūti reddĭtor, dēbĭtor:—Rómáne hý to gafol-gyldum gedydon *the Romans made them tributaries*, Ors. 3, 8; Bos. 63, 38: Bd. 2, 5; S. 506, 20. Beón hig ealle gesunde and þeówion ðé and beón ðíne gafolgildan *cunctus pŏpŭlus salvābĭtur et serviet tĭbi sub trĭbūto*, Deut. 20, 11. Twegen gafolgyldan wǽron sumum lǽnende *duo dēbĭtōres ĕrant cuidam fænĕrātōri*, Lk. Bos. 7, 41: 16, 5. II. *a rent-payer, a renter of land as opposed to the owner:* qui censum annum pendit, conductor:—Wealh gafolgelda [gafolgylda MSS. B. H.] *a foreign* [*i. e.* of British race] *tenant*, L. In. 23; Th. i. 118, 3. Gif he on gafolgeldan [gafolgildan MS. H.] húse gefeohte, cxx scillinga to wíte geselle *if he fight in a tenant's house, let him pay cxx shillings as fine*, 6; Th. i. 106, 7.

gafol-gyldere, es; *m. A tribute-payer, tributary;* trĭbūti reddĭtor:—Ða Indiscan willaþ beón eówere gafolgylderas, and mid ealre sibbe eów underþeódan *the Indians will be your tributaries, and with all peace submit to you*, Homl. Th. ii. 482, 31.

gafol-heord, e; *f.* [gafol *a tax*, heord *a herd, flock*] *A taxable stock* or *hive of bees;* grex ad censum:—Beóceorle gebýreþ, gif he gafolheorde healt, ðæt he sylle ðonne lande gerǽd beo. Mid us is gerǽd ðæt he sylle v sustras huniges to gafole *it behoves a keeper of bees, if he hold a taxable hive* [*stock of bees*], *that he then shall pay what shall be ordered in the country. With us it is ordered that he shall pay five* sustras *of honey for a tax;* 'bochero, id est, ăpum custōdi, pertĭnet, si gavelheorde, id est, grĕgem ad censum tĕneat, ut inde reddat sīcut ĭbi mos [MS. moris] ĕrit. In quibusdam lŏcis est instĭtūtum, reddi V. [MS. VI] mellis ad censum,' L. R. S. 5; Th. i. 434, 36–436, 2.

gafol-hwitel, es; *m. A tribute-whittle* or *blanket, a legal tender instead of coin for the rent of a hide of land;* trĭbūtāria săga:—Gafolhwitel sceal beón æt híwisce vi pæninga weorþ *a tribute-whittle from a hide* [*of land*] *shall be worth six pence*, L. In. 44; Th. i. 130, 5. Cf. Grm. R. A. p. 378. Perhaps híwisc in the above passage should be translated 'family;' cf. Th. Chart. 144, 31.

gafolian *to rent.* v. gafelian.

gafol-land, es; *n. Tribute-land, land let for rent* or *services;* trĭbūtāria terra:—Búton ðam ceorle ðe on gafollande sit *except the churl who resides on tribute-land*, L. A. G. 2; Th. i. 154, 2. Cf. Th. Chart. p. 144–5. [*Scot.* gaffol-land *land rented*, or *liable to taxation.*]

gafollíc *of* or *belonging to tribute, tributary.* v. gafellíc.

gafol-mǽd, e; *f. A meadow, the mowing of which was part of the* gafol *due from the churls on an estate:*—Healfne æcer gauolmǽde, Th. Chart. 145, 3.

gafol-penig, es; *m. A tribute-penny;* trĭbūtārius dēnārius:—He sceal syllan on Michaeles mæssedæg x gafolpenigas *he shall give on Michael's mass-day ten tribute-pennies;* dăre dēbet in festo Sancti Michaelis x dēnārios de gablo, L. R. S. 4; Th. i. 434, 10.

gafol-, gaful-rǽden, -rǽdenn, e; *f.* [gafol *tribute*, -rǽden *state, condition*] *Tribute;* trĭbūtum:—On sumum landum gebýreþ máre gafolrǽden *in quibusdam lŏcis plus gabli reddĭtur*, L. R. S. 5; Th. i. 436, 3.

gafol-rand? *A pair of compasses;* circīnus = κίρκινος, Cot. 54, Som. Ben. Lye. v. gabul-roid.

gafol-swân, es; *m. A tribute-swain, a swine-herd, paying a tribute* or *part of his stock, for permission to feed his pigs on the land;* porcārius ad censum:—Gafolswâne gebȳreþ, ðæt he sylle his slyht be ðam ðe on lande stent. On manegum landum stent, ðæt he sylle ǽlce geáre xv swȳn to sticunge, x ealde, and v gynge; hæbbe sylf ðæt he ofer ðæt arǽre *gafolswāne, id est, ad censum porcārio, pertĭnet, ut suam occīsiōnem det secundum quod in patria stătūtum est. In multis lŏcis stat, ut det singŭlis annis xv porcos ad occīsiōnem, x vĕtĕres, et v juvĕnes; ipse autem hăbeat superaugmentum*, L. R. S. 6; Th. i. 436, 11–14.

gafol-tîning, e; *f. Material for fencing due as* gafol:—XVI gyrda gauoltîninga, Th. Chart. 145, 8.

gafol-wydu, a; *m. Wood furnished as* gafol:—IIII foðera aclofenas gauolwyda, Th. Chart. 145, 6.

gafol-yrþ, e; *f. The cultivation of tribute-land;* tribūtāriæ terræ arātio:—His gafolyrþe [MS. gauolyrþe] iii æceras erige, and sâwe of his âgenum berne *de arātūra gabli sui arābit iii acras, et semĭnābit de horreo suo*, L. R. S. 4; Th. i. 434, 18.

gaful, es; *n. Tax, tribute, rent;* vectīgal, trĭbūtum:—Gaful *vectīgal*, Ælfc. Gr. 9, 5; Som. 9, 2. Alȳfþ gaful to syllanne ðam Câsere *lĭcet dări trĭbūtum Cæsări?* Mk. Bos. 12, 14: Exon. 68 a; Th. 251, 27; Jul. 151. v. gafol.

Gaful-ford *Camelford, Cornwall*, Chr. 823; Th. 110, 111, 17, col. 1. v. Gafol-ford.

gaful-gylda, an; *m. A tribute-payer, tributary;* trĭbūti reddĭtor:—He hî to gafulgyldum gesette on Angelþeódde *he made them tributaries among the English*, Bd. 1, 34; S. 499, 24. v. gafol-gylda.

gaful-rǽden, -rǽdenn, e; *f. A tax, tribute;* census, trĭbūtum:—Ða byre onguldon gafulrǽdenne *the children paid the tax*, Exon, 47 a; Th. 161, 16; Gû. 959: 73 b; Th. 274, 7; Jul. 529: Andr. Kmbl. 591; An. 296. v. gafol-rǽden.

gagâtes; *indecl. m. The agate* or *jet, a precious stone;* găgātes = γαγάτης:—Hêr biþ eác gemêted gagâtes, se stân biþ blæc-gym *here is also found the agate, the stone is a black gem*, Bd. 1, 1; S. 473, 24. Sceaf gagâtes dǽl ðæs stânes on ðæt wîn *shave off a part of the stone agate into the wine*, L. M. 2, 65; Lchdm. ii. 296, 11. Be ðam stâne ðe gagâtes hâtte, is sǽd ðæt he viii mægen hæbbe *of the stone which is called agate, it is said that it hath eight virtues*, 2, 66; Lchdm. iii. 296, 29.

gagel, es; *m?* gagelle, gagille, gagolle, an; *f. Gale, sweet gale;* myrica gale, Lin:—Genim gagel *take gale*, L. M. 1, 36; Lchdm. ii. 86, 10: iii. 22, 21. Nim þrê leáf mgageles *take three leaves of gale*, Lchdm. iii. 6, 17. Genim gagéllan ... dô of ða gagellan *take gale ... remove the gale*, L. M. 2, 51; Lchdm. ii. 264, 27: 2, 53; Lchdm. ii. 274, 10. Genim gagollan *take gale*, 3, 14; Lchdm. ii. 316, 15. [*Prompt.* gawl *myrtus: Scot.* gale, gaul *a myrtle: Dut.* gagel, *m. a wild myrtle: Ger.* gagel *a myrtle-bush.*]

gagel-croppan; *pl. m.* [croppa *the top of a flower* or *herb*] *Catkins of gale;* myricæ panĭcŭlæ:—Genim gagelcroppan *take catkins of gale*, L. M. 1, 36; Lchdm. ii. 86, 20.

gagol, gægl, geagl; *adj. Lascivious, wanton;* lascīvus:—Gagol *lascīva*, Ælfc. Gl. 106; Som. 78, 46; Wrt. Voc. 57, 27. [*M. H. Ger.* gogel *licentious.*] v. gâl.

gagol-bǽrnes, gægl-bǽrnes, -bērnes, -ness, e; *f. Wantonness, luxury, riot;* lascīvia, luxŭria, Cot. 118.

gagul-suillan *to gargle;* gargarīzāre, Som. Ben. Lye.

-gal, -gil, -gel, *as* sin-gal *perpetual, continual:* wîd-gal, wîd-gil, wîd-gel, *wide-spread*, March. 38; p. 27, 8. v. wîd-gil, wîd-gal.

GÂL, es; *n. Lust, wantonness, lightness, folly;* lascīvia, lĭbīdo, luxŭria, lĕvĭtas:—Hie hyra gâl beswâc *their folly deceived them*, Cd. 18; Th. 21, 21; Gen. 327. Gôdes oððe gâles *of good or evil*, Exon. 23 a; Th, 64, 9; Cri. 1035. [Cf. *Icel.* gáll, *m. a fit of gaiety.*]

gâl; *adj. Light, pleasant, wanton, licentious, wicked;* lĕvis, libīdĭnōsus, luxŭriōsus, mălus:—Ðam unstæððigan and ðam gâlan, ðû miht secggan, ðæt he [MS. hi] biþ winde gelîcra, ðonne gemetfæstum monnum *to the inconstant and the light* [*man*], *thou mayest say that he is more like the wind, than modest men*, Bt. 37, 4; Fox 192, 23, note 20, MS. Cott. Ðæt he gesâwe ungelîce bêc him berende beón þurh ða gôdan gâstas oððe þurh ða gâlan *ut cōdĭces diversos per bŏnos sīve mălos spīrĭtus sĭbi vĭdĕrit offerri*, Bd. 5, 13; S. 633, 25. Gecunnian hwæðer he wǽre gôd oððe gâl *to try whether he were good or bad*, Gu. 17; Gdwn. 74, 6. [*Orm.* gal *wanton: O. Sax.* gêl *merry: Dut. Ger.* geil *lustful: M. H. Ger.* geil *licentious: O. H. Ger.* geil *lætus, elātus, fĕrox, libīdĭnōsus: Dan.* geil *wanton:* and cf. *Icel.* gáli *a wag.*] DER. ealo-gâl, hyge-, medu-, rûm-, symbel-, wîn-.

GALAN; *part.* galende, ic gale, ðû gælest, gælst, he gæleþ, gælþ, *pl.* galaþ, *p.* gôl, *pl.* gôlon; *pp.* galen *To sing, enchant, call;* cănĕre, incantāre, insŏnāre, clāmāre:—Seó ne geherþ stemne galendra, and âtterwyrhtan galendes wîslîce *quæ non exaudiet vōcem incantantium, et venĕfĭci incantantis săpienter*, Ps. Lamb. 57, 6. Sorh-leóþ gæleþ *he sings a sad lay*, Beo. Th. 4912; B. 2460. Se wîsdôm gôl gyd *wisdom sung a lay*, Bt. Met. Fox 7, 3; Met. 7, 2. Wîf fyrd-leóþ gôlon [MS. galan] *the women sang a martial song*, Cd. 171; Th. 215, 3; Exod. 577. Ða ðe gehȳrdon gryreleóþ galan Godes andsacan *those who heard the adversary of God sing the horrid lay*, Beo. Th. 1576; B. 786. Ðâ wæs sigeleóþ galen *then was the song of triumph sung*, Elen. Kmbl. 248; El. 124: Andr. Kmbl. 3097; An. 1551. [*Chauc.* gale: *Scot.* gale *to cry: O. Sax.* galan: *O. H. Ger.* galan *cănĕre: Dan.* gale *to crow: Swed.* gala *to crow: Icel.* gala *to crow, sing.*] DER. a-galan, be-, on-: nihte-gale. See Grm. D. M. pp. 987, 1173.

galder-cræftiga *one crafty* or *skilful in enchantments, an enchanter*, L. Alf. 30; Th. i. 52, 9; MS. H. v. galdor-cræftiga.

galdere, es; *m. An enchanter, a charmer, sorcerer, diviner, soothsayer;* incantātor, augur, haruspex, Som. Ben. Lye. DER. wyrm-galdere. [Cf. *O. H. Ger.* kalstarari *incantator.*] v. galan.

galdor, gealdor, es; *pl. nom. acc.* galdor, galdru; *gen.* galdra; *dat.* galdrum; *n.* [galan *to sing, enchant*, q. v.] *An incantation, divination, enchantment, a charm, magic, sorcery;* incantātio, cantio, carmen, fascĭnātio:—Þurh heora galdor *per incantātiōnes*, Bd. 4, 27; S. 604, 9. Sing ðæt galdor *sing the charm*, Lchdm. iii. 38, 3. Galdre bewunden *encircled by enchantment*, Beo. Th. 6097; B. 3052. Ne sceal nân man mid galdre wyrte besingan *no man shall enchant a herb with magic*, Homl. Th. i. 476, 8. Galdra fela *many sorceries*, Bt. Met. Fox 26, 106; Met. 26, 53: Deut. 18, 11. Nis ðê ende feor, ðæs ðe ic on galdrum ongieten hæbbe *thy end is not far off, from what I have understood by* [*thy*] *divinations*, Exon. 50 a; Th. 174, 19; Gû. 1180. Ðâs galdor mon mæg singan on wunde *a man may sing these charms over a wound*, L. M. 3, 63; Lchdm. ii. 352, 5. Hig worhton ôðer swilc þing þurh hira drȳcræft and þurh Egiptisce galdru *fecērunt etiam ipsi per incantātiōnes Ægyptiacas et arcāna quædam simĭlĭter*, Ex. 7, 11. Galdrum cȳdan *to inform by divination*, Elen. Kmbl. 321; El. 161. [*Laym.* galdere, *dat. magic: Icel.* galdr, galðr, *m. a song, charm, spell, witchcraft, sorcery.*] DER. ceargaldor-, gealdor-cræftiga, an; *m. One crafty* or *skilful in enchantments, an enchanter;* incantātor:—Ða fǽmnan, ðe gewunniaþ [MS. gewunniah] onfôn galdorcræftigan, ne lǽt ðû ða libban *the women, who are wont to receive enchanters, suffer thou not to live*, L. Alf. 30; Wilk. 31, 26. gealdor, heáh-galdor.

galdor-cræft, gealdor-cræft, es; *m. The art of enchanting, magic art, incantation;* incantandi ars, măgĭca ars, incantātio:—On galdorcræftum *per incantātiōnes*, L. M. I. P. 39; Th. ii. 274, 32. He Iudêa galdorcræftum wiðstôd *he withstood the magic arts of the Jews*, Andr. Kmbl. 332; An. 166. Ða ðe galdorcræftas begangaþ *those that practise magical arts*, Blickl. Homl. 62, 23.

galdor-cwide, es; *m. A magic saying, song;* măgĭcus sermo, cantus, Exon. 113 a; Th. 432, 28; Rä. 49, 7.

galdor-galere, es; *m. An enchanter, soothsayer;* incantātor, Cot. 118: 193.

galdor-leóþ, es; *n. A magic song, an enchantment, charm, spell;* incantātio, carmen, incantāmentum, Cot. 188.

galdor-word, es; *n. A magic word, word of incantation;* cantātiōnis verbum:—Ic galdorwordum gôl *I sang in magic words*, Exon. 94 b; Th. 353, 37; Reim. 24.

galdra *of enchantments, of sorceries*, Bt. Met. Fox 26, 106; Met. 26, 53; *gen. pl. of* galdor.

galdru *enchantments*, Ex. 7, 11; *pl. nom. acc. of* galdor.

galdrygea, an; *m. An enchanter;* incantātor, Cot. 108.

galere, es; *m. An enchanter;* incantātor:—Galere *incantātor*, Wrt. Voc. 74, 38. DER. galdor-, wyrm-galere.

gâl-ferhþ; *adj. Mind-lustful, licentious;* libīdĭnōsus, lascīvus:—Gewât ðâ se deófulcunda gâlferhþ his beddes neosan *then the devilish* [*man*] *went lustful in mind to seek his bed*, Judth. 10; Thw. 22, 14; Jud. 62.

gâl-freólsas; *pl. m. Licentious festivals;* lascīva festa, Lupercālia, Som. Ben. Lye.

gâlfull; *adj. Lustful, licentious, luxurious;* libīdĭnōsus, luxŭriōsus, Scint. 21: 28: 58.

gâlfullîce; *adv. Lustfully, luxuriously;* libīdĭnōse, luxŭriōse, Scint. 13.

GALGA, gealga, an; *m. A gallows, gibbet, cross;* arbor infēlix, patĭbŭlum, crux:—Galga *patĭbŭlum*, Ælfc. Gl. 15; Som. 58, 30; Wrt. Voc. 21, 24. He of galgan his gǽst onsend *he sent forth his soul from a gallows*, Exon. 70 a; Th. 261, 4; Jul. 310: 72 b; Th. 271, 15; Jul. 482: Beo. Th. 4883; B. 2446. He his blôd ageát on galgan *he shed his blood on the cross*, Cd. 225; Th. 299, 15; Sat. 550: Menol. Fox 170; Men. 86: Elen. Kmbl. 957; El. 480. On galgum *on the cross*, Cd. 224; Th. 297, 3; Sat. 511. [*Chauc. R. Brun.* galwes, *pl: Plat.* galge: *O. Sax.* galgo, *m: O. Frs.* galga, *m: Dut.* galg, *f: Ger.* galgen, *m: M. H. Ger.* galge, *m: O. H. Ger.* galgo, *m: Goth.* galga, *m. a cross: Dan.* galge, *m. f: Swed.* galge, *m: Icel.* gálgi, *m.*] See Grm. R. A. pp. 682–4.

galga-trê, es; *n. A gallows-tree, cross:*—Ðîn rôdes galgatrê *tuum crucis patibulum*, Rtl. 23, 36. On rôdes galgatree *in crucis patibulo*, 124, 1. v. galg-treów. [*Havel.* galwetre: *Icel.* gálga-trê.]

galg-môd; *adj.* [galg = gealh *sad;* môd *mind*] *Sad in mind, gloomy;* tristis anĭmo:—His môdor, gîfre and galg-môd, gegân wolde sorhfulne sīþ *his mother, greedy and gloomy, would go a sorrowful journey*, Beo. Th. 2558; B. 1277. v. gealg-mōd.

galg-treów, gealg-treów, es; *n. A gallows-tree, cross;* crŭcis lignum, crux:—He wolde sume on galgtreówum [MS. galgtreówu] *he would* [*hang*] *some on gallows-trees*, Beo. Th. 5873; B. 2940.

Galilēa *Galilee*:—Sǣ Galilæs *măre Galilææ*, Mk. Skt. Lind. 1, 16. Galiles, Jn. Skt. Lind. 6, 1. Of Galilēam ðæm lande, Blickl. Homl. 123, 21. Witga of Galilēum *a prophet from Galilee*, 71, 16.

Galilēisc, Galilēsc; *adj. Galilean;* Galilæus:—Pilatus acsode hwæðer he wǣre Galileisc man *Pīlātus interrŏgāvit si hŏmo Galilæus esset*, Lk. Bos. 23, 6: 22, 59: Mk. Bos. 14, 70: Jn. Bos. 7, 52. Of ðære Galileiscan Bethsaida *a Bethsaida Galilææ*, Jn. Bos. 12, 21. Wið da Galileiscan sǣ *juxta măre Galilææ*, Mt. Bos. 4, 18: 15, 29: Mk. Bos. 1, 16. Wēne gē, wǣron ða Galileiscan synfulle tofōran eallum Galileiscum *pŭtātis quod hi Galilæi præ omnĭbus Galilæis peccātōres fuĕrint?* Lk. Bos. 13, 2. On Galileisce dǣlas *in partes Galilææ*, Mt. Bos. 2, 22. Hwæt bīdaþ gē Galilēsce guman on hwearfte *why abide ye Galilean men about?* Exon. 15 a; Th. 32, 11; Cri. 511: Blickl. Homl. 123, 20.

Galleas *Gauls, the French*, Bd. 5, 11; S. 626, 27. v. Gallias.

Gallia rīce *the kingdom of the Gauls, France*, Bd. 4, 1; S. 564, 16: 5, 8; S. 621, 39. v. Gallias.

Gallias, Gallie, Galleas; *gen.* Gallia; *pl. m. The Gauls, the Franks;* Galli, ōrum; Galliæ, ārum; *pl. m*:—Ðǣr wæs Gallia ofslagen twā-hund þūsenda *ducenta millia Gallōrum interfecta sunt*, Ors. 5, 8; Bos. 107, 33; Hav. 329, 8: 4, 7; Bos. 89, 7. Gefeaht wið Gallie *adversum Gallos conflixit*, 4, 7; Bos. 89, 8; Hav. 251, 2. Hū sceolan we dōn mid Gallia and Brytta bisceopum *quālĭter dēbēmus cum Galliārum Brittaniārumque episcŏpis ăgĕre?* Bd. 1. 27; S. 492, 10. Biscop Gallia rīces *bishop of the kingdom of the Gauls* [Galliārum], Bd. 5, 8; S. 621, 39. Galleas nemnaþ Trajectum *the Gauls call it Utrecht*, Bd. 5, 11; S. 626, 27. Monige gewunedon sēcan Francna mynstro and Gallia *multi Francōrum vel Galliārum Monastĕria adīre sŏlēbant*, Bd. 3, 8; S. 531, 17. Adrianus se abbad ða dǣlas Gallia rīces geferde and gesōhte *Adrian the abbot went and visited the parts of the kingdom of the Gauls;* partes Galliārum [regni] adiisset, Bd. 4, 1; S. 564, 16. Gallia rice *the kingdom of the Gauls*, Bd. 5, 23; S. 645, 31.

gāl-līc; *adj. Lustful*:—Ælc gāllīc ontendnys wearþ adwæsced *every lustful fervour was extinguished*, Th. Homl. ii. 156, 35. [*O. Eng. Homl.* galiche dede, i. 149, 16.]

Gallie; *gen.* a; *pl. m. The Gauls;* Galli:—Gallie oferhergodon land *the Gauls overran the lands*, Ors. 3, 4; Bos. 56, 9: 4, 7; Bos. 89, 8. v. Gallias.

Gallisc; *adj. Gaulish, belonging to Gaul;* Gallĭcus:—Ðǣr gefeaht Mallius wið ānne Galliscne mann *there Manlius fought with a man of Gaul*, Ors. 3, 4; Bos. 56, 16.

galluc, galloc, gallac, es; *m. The plant comfrey;* symphȳtum officĭnāle, Lin:—Ðeós wyrt, ðe man *confirmam*, and ōðrum naman galluc nemneþ, biþ cenned on mōrum and on feldum, and eác on mǣdum *this herb, which is called confirma, and by another name comfrey, is produced on moors and in fields, and also in meadows*, Herb. 60, 1; Lchdm. i. 162, 10–12. Galluces moran *roots of comfrey*, Lchdm. iii. 6, 10. Genime galluc gesodenne *take sodden comfrey*, L. M. 1, 27; Lchdm. ii. 68, 15: 1, 31; Lchdm ii. 74, 11: 3, 73; Lchdm. ii. 358, 23. Galluc *adriatica* vel *mālum terræ*, Ælfc. Gl. 39; Som. 63, 70; Wrt. Voc. 30, 22: 79, 17. Galloc *galla*, Glos. Brux. Recd. 41, 46; Wrt. Voc. 67, 61. Gallac *symphȳtum*, 42, 14; Wrt. Voc. 68, 29.

Galmanhō, Galmahō? *An Anglo-Saxon abbey at York, afterwards St. Mary's;* abbātiæ nōmen ăpud Eborācum:—On ðysum geáre forþferde Sīward eorl on Eoforwīc, and his līc līþ binnan ðam mynstre æt Galmanhō [Galmahō, Th. 324, 10, col. 2], ðe he sylf ǣr getimbrade, Gode to lofe and eallum his hālgum *in this year* [A. D. 1055] *earl Siward died at York, and his body lies within the monastery of Galmanho, which he himself had before built, to the glory of God and all his saints*, Chr. 1055; Th. 324, 8–12, col. 1.

gāl-mōd; *adj. Light-minded, licentious;* libīdĭnōsæ mentis, lascīvus:—Se galmōda *the licentious* [*Holofernes*], Judth. 12; Thw. 25, 12; Jud. 256. [*O. Sax.* gēl-mōd.]

gālnes, -ness, -nyss, e; *f. Lustfulness, lust, luxury, wantonness;* lascīvia, lĭbīdo, luxŭria, petulantia, Cot. 150: Scint. 12: 21: 81. He cnihtlice gālnysse næs begangende *he was not addicted to boyish levity*, Guthl. 2; Gdwn. 12, 16. [*Orm.* galness.]

gāl-scipe, es; *m.* [gāl *lust*, -scipe *-ship*] *Luxury, lustfulness, lasciviousness, wantonness, lewdness;* luxŭria, lĭbīdo, lascīvia, petulantia, satȳriăsis = σατυρίασις:—He begǣþ unǣtas and oferdrincas and gālscipe *comessatiōnĭbus văcat et luxŭriæ atque conviviis*, Deut. 20, 21. We lǣraþ, ðæt man wið fūlne gālscipe warnige symle *we instruct, that one always guard himself against foul lasciviousness*, L. C. E. 24; Th. i. 374, 9. For gālscipe *for wantonness*, Cd. 18; Th. 22, 15; Gen. 341. Synwrēnnys *vel* gālscipe *satȳriasis*, Ælfc. Gl. 11; Som. 57, 49; Wrt. Voc. 19, 51.

gālsere, es; *m. A lustful man;* libīdĭnōsus, Off. Reg. 15.

gāl-smerc; *adj.* [smercian *to smirk, smile*] *Light, laughing, giggling;* pĕtŭlans:—Gyf se munuc ne biþ gālsmerc, and eáðe and hræde on hleahtre *si mŏnăchus non sit pĕtŭlans, et făcĭlis et proclīvis ad ridendum*, R. Ben. 7.

galung, e; *f. Incantation*, Hpt. Gl. 519.

Galwalas, galwealas, *nom. acc; gen.* a; *dat.* um; *pl. m.* [wealh *foreign;* cf. Bryt-walas] *Gauls, Frenchmen, people of Gaul in a body*, and as the name of a people is often used where according to later usage the name of their country would be found, the word may be translated *Gaul, France;* Galli, Gallia:—Hēr wæs Brihtwald gehālgod to ærcebiscope fram Godune Galwala biscop *in this year* [A. D. 693] *Brihtwald was consecrated archbishop by Godun bishop of the Gauls*, Chr. 693; Erl. 43, 17. He gewāt into Galwalum *he went into Gaul*, Chr. Erl. 5, 5, 14. Hēr Ægelbryht of Galwalum [Galwealum, Th. 50, 2, col. 2, 3] onfēng Wesseaxna bisceopdōme *in this year* [A. D. 650] *Ægelbyrht of Gaul received the bishopric of the West Saxons*, Chr. 650; Th. 50, 2, col. 1: 660; Th. 54, 16. He fōr in Galwalas *he went into Gaul*, 380; Erl. 11, 2. v. Gallias.

gāl-wrǣne; *adj. Luxurious, lecherous;* luxŭriōsus, Som. Ben. Lye.

gamel, gamol; *adj. Old, aged;* sĕnex, vĕtustus:—Wolde beddes neósan gamela Scylding *the aged Scylding would visit his bed*, Beo. Th. 3588; B. 1792. Wæs gylden hilt gamelum rince gyfen *the golden hilt was given to the aged warrior*, 3359; B. 1677: Elen. Kmbl. 2491; El. 1247. Gamele ne mōston hāre heaðorincas hilde onþeón *the aged hoary chieftains might not prosper in battle*, Cd. 154; Th. 193, 3; Exod. 240. Ǣr he on weg hwurfe, gamol, of geardum *ere he, old, departed on his way from his courts*, Beo. Th. 535; B. 265: 115; B. 58. v. gomel. [*Icel.* gamall.]

gamelīc; *adj. Theatralis, ridiculosus*, Hpt. Gl. 459, 508.

GAMEN, gomen, es; *n.* GAME, *joy, pleasure, mirth, sport, pastime;* jŏcus, oblectāmentum, gaudium, jūbĭlum, lætĭtia, lūdus:—Gamen eft astāh *pastime rose again*, Beo. Th. 2325; B. 1160. Wynsum gamen *a pleasant game;* sāles, Ælfc. Gl. 16; Som. 58, 67; Wrt. Voc. 21, 54. Næs ðæt hērlīc dǣd, ðæt hine swelces gamenes gilpan lyste *that was not a glorious deed, that he should wish to boast of such sport*, Bt. Met. Fox 9, 37; Met. 9, 19. Him to gamene *for his sport*, 9, 17; Met. 9, 9: 9, 91; Met. 9, 46. Ic mæg swegles gamen gehȳran on heofnum *I can hear the joy of the firmament in heaven*, Cd. 32; Th. 42, 18; Gen. 675. Bǣdon hig sume, ðæt Samson mōste him macian sum gamen *præcēpērunt ut vocārētur Samson et ante eos lūdĕret*, Jud. 16, 25. Gamena *lūdōrum:* gamene *jŏco*, Mone B. 2807, 2808. [*Piers P.* gamen *a play: Laym.* game *a play: Scot.* gamyn *a game, play: O. Sax.* gaman, *n: Frs.* gammen: *O. Frs.* game, gome, *f: M. H. Ger.* gamen, *m. n: O. H. Ger.* gaman, *gaudium, jŏcus, lūdus: Dan.* gammen, *m. f: Icel.* gaman, *n. game, sport, pleasure, amusement.*] DER. glig-gamen, heal-.

gamenian, gamnian, gæmnian; *p.* ode; *pp.* od [gamen *game*] *To joke, play;* jŏcŭlāri, jŏcāri:—Gregorius gamenode mid his wordum *Gregory played with his words*, Homl. Th. ii. 122, 4. [*Icel.* gamna *to amuse, divert.*]

gamenlīce; *adv. Sportingly, deceitfully;* jŏcōse, callĭde:—Hī gamenlīce rǣddon *they counselled deceitfully*, Jos. 9, 3.

gamenung, e; *f. A gaming, jesting, playing;* lūsus, jŏcus:—Hwǣr biþ his gaf spræc and ða īdelan gamenunga *where will be his wanton discourse, and the idle jestings?* Basil admn. 8; Norm. 50, 28.

gamen-wāðu *a joyous path*. v. gomen-wāðu.

gamen-wudu *pleasure-wood, glee-wood, a musical instrument, harp*. v. gomen-wudu.

gamian *to game, play, sport*, Som. Ben. Lye v. gamenian.

gaming, e; *f. A* GAMING, *playing, gesticulation;* lūsus, gannātūra, *sive* mīmĭca, gestĭcŭlātio, Cot. 203.

gamnian; *part.* gamnigende; *p.* ode; *pp.* od *To play;* lūdĕre:—Wæs him geþūht, swilce he gamnigende sprǣce *vīsus est eis quăsi lūdens lŏqui*, Gen. 19, 14. v. gamenian.

gamol *old, aged*, Beo. Th. 115; B. 58: 535; B. 265. v. gomel.

gamol-feax; *adj. With hoary locks, grey-haired;* cānus:—Gamolfeax hæleþ *a hoary-headed hero*, Chr. 975; Erl. 126, 20; Edg. 46: Beo. Th. 1220; B. 608. v. gomel-feax.

gamol-ferhþ; *adj. Advanced in age, aged;* ætāte provectus:—Gamolferhþ goldes brytta *the aged dispenser of gold*, Cd. 138; Th. 173, 26; Gen. 2867.

gān *yawned;* hiāvit; *p. of* gīnan.

GĀN, to gānne; ic gā, ðū gǣst, he gǣþ; *pl.* gāþ; *p.* ic he eóde, ðū eódest; *pl.* eódon; *imp.* gā, *pl.* gāþ; *pp.* gān; *v. n.* [the conjugation is formed from two roots, the past tense being from root i; cf. Gothic iddja]; *To go, come, walk, happen;* īre, grădi, evĕnīre:—Uton gān and feligean fremdum godum *cāmus et sequāmur deos aliēnos*, Deut. 13, 1. Gearo to gānne *ready to go*, Homl. Th. ii. 32, 7. Ðū gǣst on ðīnum breóste *sŭper pectus tuum grădiēris*, Gen. 3, 14. He on flet gǣþ *he walks in the court*, Beo. Th. 4075; B. 2034. Gǣþ ā wyrd swā hió sceal *fate goes ever as it must*, Beo. Th. 915; B. 455. Hī gāþ *they go*, Andr. Kmbl. 3328; An. 1667. Gif gē gāþ æfter fremdum godum *if ye go after strange gods*, Deut. 11, 28. He sǣde unc eall swā hit siððan ā eóde [*or* a-eode?] *he told us all as it always afterwards happened;* audīvĭmus quidquid **postea**

rei prōbāvit eventus, Gen. 41, 13. Eóde eall seó ceasterwaru togeánes đam Hǣlende *tōta cīvĭtas exiit obviam Jesu*, Mt. Bos. 8, 34: Bd. 1, 7; S. 478, 12. Sume for hungre heora feóndum on hand eódon *some for hunger went into the hands of their foes*, 1, 15; S. 484, 5. Gā hider *come hither*, Gen. 27, 21. Gāþ eów into đære cyrcan unforhtlīce *go into the church fearlessly*, Homl. Th. i. 508, 1. [*Wyc.* gon, goon, goo: *Piers P.* goon: *Chauc.* gon, goon: *R. Glouc.* goon: *Laym. Orm.* gan: *Plat.* gan. gaan; gaen: *O. Sax.* gân: *Frs.* gean: *O. Frs.* gan: *Dut.* gaan: *Ger.* gehen, gehn: *M. H. Ger.* gân, gên: *O. H. Ger.* gân: *Dan.* gaae: *Swed.* gå: *Zend.* gâ, gê *to go*: *Sansk.* gā *to go.*] DER. a-gân, æfter-, be-, bi-, for-, fōre-, forþ-, ful-, ge-, in-, of-, ofer-, ōþ-, þurh-, to-, under-, up-, upp-, ūt-, wiđ-, ymb-. v. gangan.

gancgan *to go*, Ps. Th. 85, 10. v. gangan.

Gandis, Gandes; *indecl. f. The river Ganges;* Ganges = Γάγγης:— Đǣr licgeþ se mūþa ūt on đone gârsecg đære eá, đe man hāteþ Gandis *there the mouth of the river, which is called Ganges, opens out into the ocean*, Ors. 1, 1; Bos. 16, 13, 17. Gandes seó eá is eallra ferscra wætera mǣst, būtan Eufrate *the river Ganges is the greatest of all fresh waters, except the Euphrates*, 2, 4; Bos. 43, 45. Æt Gande đære eá, Nar. 3, 22.

GANDRA, ganra, an; *m.* A GANDER; anser:—Gandra *anser, m.* Ælfc. Gr. 9, 18; Som. 9, 59. [*Eng.* gander, *m*: *Ger.* gänserich, *m*: *Ger. dial.* gandert: *M. H. Ger.* ganzer, ganze, *m*: *O. H. Ger.* ganzo, *m*: *Icel.* gassi, *m. a gander.*]

ganet, es; *m. A gannet, sea-fowl, water-fowl, swan;* fūlĭca, cygnus:— Ganet *cygnus*, Glos. Prudent. Recd. 144, 32. Ofer ganetes bæþ [MS. baþ] *over the sea-fowl's bath*, Chr. 975; Erl. 125, 21. Ganetes hleóđor *the gannet's cry*, Exon. 81 b; Th. 307, 8; Seef. 20. Cōmon of gârsecge ganetas fleógan *sea-fowls came flying from the ocean*, Ps. Th. 104, 35. v. ganot.

GANG, geng, gong, gung, es; *m.* I. GANG, *going, journey, step, way, path, passage, course* (*of time*); ĭter, grădus, gressus, incessus, ambŭlātio, sēmĭta:—Beswīcan gangas [MS. M. stepas] mīne *supplantāre gressus meos*, Ps. Spl. C. 139, 5. Mīnne gang *gressum meum*, Ps. Th. 139, 5. Ganges, Beo. Th. 1940; B. 968. Him tǣcean līfes weg and rihtne gang *to heofonum to teach them the way of life and the right path to heaven*, Blickl. Homl. 109, 18. Đīne gangas *gressus tui*, Ps. Th. 67, 23. Fōta gangas *pedum gressus*, 72, 1. Mīne gangas *meæ sēmĭtæ*, 138, 2. On đære eá gang *in the river's course*, Ors. 2, 4; Bos. 44, 13. Heó freó on hira fōta gangum blīđe hâm wæs hweorfende *ipsa lībĕro pĕdum incessu dŏmum læta reversa est*, Bd. 4, 10; S. 578, 33. Heora geára gang *anni eorum*, Ps. Th. 77, 32. Geára gongum *in the course of years*, Elen. Kmbl. 1292; El. 648. II. *a passage, drain, privy;* latrīna, secessus:— Gang *latrīna, secessus*, Ælfc. Gl. 108; Som. 78, 121; Wrt. Voc. 58, 33. Đonne him to gange lyst *when he desires the privy*, Hexam. 20; Norm. 28, 23: L. Ælf. C. 3; Th. ii. 344, 6: Homl. Th. i. 290, 19. [*Orm.* gang *a journey*: *Prompt.* gong *latrina*: *Scot.* gang *a journey*: *O. Sax.* gang, *m*: *O. Frs.* gong, gung, *m*: *Dut. Ger.* gang, *m*: *M. H. Ger.* ganc, *m*: *O. H. Ger.* gang, *m*: *Goth.* gaggs, *m*: *Dan.* gang, *m. f*: *Swed.* gång, *m. time*: *Icel.* gangr, *m*; göng, *n. pl. a passage.*] DER. be-gang, -gong, bi-, eder-, embe-, fēđe-, forþ-, ge-, hin-, hlāf-, hūsel-, in-, on-, setl-, stal-, stepe-, to-, up-, ūt-, wæfer-, ymb-, ymbe-.

gang *go, come*, Cd. 228; Th. 308, 32; Sat. 701: Gen. 27, 26; *impert. of* gangan.

gang *went*, Beo. Th. 2595; B. 1295; *p. of* geongan.

GANGAN, gongan, gancgan; *part.* gangende, gongende; ic gange, gonge, đū gangest, gongest, he gangeþ, gongeþ, *pl.* gangaþ, gongaþ; *p.* geóng, gióng, giéng, gēng, *pl.* geóngon, gióngon, giéngon, gēngon; *imp.* gang, gong; *pp.* gangen, gongen *To go, walk, turn out;* ire, meāre, vādĕre, ambŭlāre, ingrĕdi, tendĕre, evĕnīre:—Ic gange *ambŭlo*, Ælfc. Gr. 19; Som. 22, 41. Gáng hider *accēde*, Gen. 27, 26: Num. 11, 21. He heonon gangeþ [gangaþ MS.] *he goes from hence*, Andr. Kmbl. 1782; An. 893. He of worulde gangende wæs *he was going from the world*, Bd. 4, 24; S. 598, 30. He ealle đa tīd mihte ge sprecan ge gangan *tōto eo tempŏre et lŏqui et ingrĕdi pŏtuit*, Bd. 4, 24; S. 598, 30. He to healle geóng *he went to the hall*, Beo. Th. 1855, note; B. 925. He ofer willan gióng *he went against his will*, 4810, note; B. 2409. Heó giéng [gien MS.] to Adame *she went to Adam*, Cd. 29; Th. 39, 15; Gen. 626. Ic to đam grunde gēnge *I would go to the abyss*, Cd. 39; Th. 51, 29; Gen. 834. Forþ gangan *to go forward, to continue*:—Gange se teám forþ *let the warranty go forward*, L. Ed. 1; Th. i. 158, 13: Exon. 14 a; Th. 27, 5; Cri. 426. Ic ongitan mihte hu đis gewinn wolde gangan *I should be able to know how this labour would turn out*, Ps. Th. 72, 13: 88, 3. [*Piers P.* gange, gangen: *Orm.* ganngenn: *Scot.* gang: *O. Sax.* gangan: *O. Frs.* gunga: *M. H. Ger.* gangen: *O. H. Ger.* gangan: *Goth.* gaggan: *Swed.* gånga: *Icel.* ganga.] DER. a-gangan, -gongan, æt-, be-, bi-, fōr-, fōre-, forþ-, ful-, ge-, in-, of-, ofer-, on-, ongeán-, þurh-, to-, under-, up-, ūt-, wiđ-, ymb-, ymbe-.

gang-dagas, gong-dagas; *pl. m.* [dæg *a day*] *Perambulation days, the three days before Ascension day* or *Holy Thursday, Rogation days, when the boundaries of parishes and districts were traversed;* dies perambŭlātiōnes *vel* processiōnis, rogātiōnum dies:—Betweox gang-dagum and middum sumera *betwixt Rogation days and Midsummer*, Chr. 913; Erl. 102, 3: 1063; Erl. 195, 7. Ofer gang-dagas *after Rogation days*, L. Ath. i. 13; Th. i. 206, 15. Đys Gōdspel sceal to Gang-dagon *this Gospel must be on the Rogation days* [*Gang-days*], Rubc. Mt. Bos. 7, 7-14, notes, p. 575. Đis sceal to Gang-dagon đæge twegen dagas, *this* [*Gospel*] *must be on the two days of the Rogation days*, Rubc. Lk. Bos. 11, 5-13? notes, p. 578. [*Icel.* gangdagar.]

gangel *going.* v. gongel. [*Icel.* göngull *strolling.*]

gangel-wæfre *a ganging weaver, spider*, Som. Ben. Lye. v. gongel-wæfre.

gangere, es; *m. A ganger, footman;* pedester, Som. Ben. Lye.

gang-ern, es; *n.* [gang II. *a privy*, ern *a place*] *A privy;* latrīna:— Goldhordhūs, dīgle gangern *hypodrŏmum* vel *spondoromum?* [= *spidromum*, q. v. in Du Cange], Ælfc. Gl. 107; Som. 78, 81; Wrt. Voc. 57, 57.

gange-wifre, -wæfre, geonge-wifre, gonge-wifre, gongel-wæfre, an; *f. A ganging weaver, spider;* viātica arānea:—Đū gedēst đæt he aswint on his mōde, and wyrþ swā tedre swā swā gangewifran nett *thou causest that he dwindles away in his mind, and becomes as frail as a spider's web*, Ps. Th. 38, 12. Swindan đū dydest swā swā gangewæfre [āttercoppan MS. T.] sāwle his *tabescĕre fēcisti sīcut arāneam anĭmam ejus*, Ps. Spl. 38, 15.

gang-feormere, es; *m. A jakes-farmer, privy-cleanser;* fīmārius, cloācārius, Som. Ben. Lye.

gang-geteld, es; *n. A travelling-tent, tent, pavilion;* tentōrium ambŭlātōrium, pāpĭlio:—Gang-geteld *pāpĭlio*, Ælfc. Gl. 110; Som. 79, 40; Wrt. Voc. 59, 12.

gang-here, es; *m. A foot-army, infantry;* pedester exercĭtus:—Pirrus him com to mid đam mǣstan fultume, ǣgđer ge on ganghere, ge on rādhere *Pyrrhus came to them with the greatest force, both in infantry, and in cavalry*, Ors. 4, 1; Bos. 76, 40.

gang-pyt, -pytt, es; *m. A privy;* latrīna:—On đære nyđemestan flēringe wæs heora gangpyt and heora myxen *on the lowermost flooring* [*of the ark*] *was their privy and their dunghill*, Boutr. Scrd. 21, 7. v. gang II.

gang-setl, es; *n. A privy;* latrīna, Som. Ben. Lye. v. gang II.

gang-tūn, es; *m. A privy;* latrīna, Som. Ben. Lye. v. gang II.

gang-weg, es; *m. A gang-way, way, road;* via:—Anes wǣnes gangweg *a road for one vehicle;* actus, Ælfc. Gl. 56; Som. 67, 50; Wrt. Voc. 37, 38. Twegra wǣna gangweg *a road for two vehicles;* via, 56; Som. 67, 51; Wrt. Voc. 37, 39.

gang-wuce, an; *f. Rogation week, the week of holy Thursday;* perambŭlātiōnis septĭmāna:—Đis sceal on Þunres dæg, innan đære Gang-wucan *this* [*Gospel*] *must be on Thursday in the Rogation week*, Rubc. Mk. Bos. 16, 14-20, notes, p. 578. Đys Gōdspel gebȳraþ on Wōdnes dæg, on đære Gang-wucan to đam uigilian *this Gospel belongs to the vigil on Wednesday, in the Rogation week*, Rubc. Jn. Bos. 17, 1-10, notes, p. 580.

GĀNIAN; *p*, ode; *pp.* od *To* YAWN, *gape, open;* hiāre, oscĭtāre, apĕrīre:—Gāniende *oscĭtans*, Cot. 147. Đeáh đe me synfulra, inwitfulra, mūþas on gānian *though the mouths of the sinful* [*and*] *deceitful yawn upon me*, Ps. Th. 108, 1. [*Plat.* janen: *Dut.* geeuwen: *Ger.* gähnen: *M. H. Ger.* gēnen: *O. H. Ger.* geinōn, ginōn, ginēn, giēn: *Icel.* gína: *Lat.* hiāre: *Grk.* χαίνειν *to yawn, gape.*]

GANOT, ganet, es; *m. A gannet, sea-fowl, water-fowl, fen-duck;* ăvis mărīna, fūlix, fūlĭca:—Ganot *fūlix*, Wrt. Voc. 62, 7: 280, 13. Đā wearþ adrǣfed deórmōd hæleþ, Ōslāc of earde, ofer ȳþa gewealc, ofer ganotes bæþ *then the brave man, Oslac, was driven away from the land, over the billows' roll, over the gannet's bath* [*the sea*], Chr. 975; Erl. 126, 20; Edg. 46: Beo. Th. 3727; B. 1861. Āc fereþ gelōme ofer ganotes bæþ *a ship* [lit. *oak*] *often saileth over the gannet's bath* [*the sea*], Runic pm. 25; Kmbl. 344, 19; Hick. Thes. i. 135, 49. [*Plat.* gante: *Dut.* gent, *m. a male goose, gander*: *O. H. Ger.* ganazo, ganzo, *m. anetus.*]

ganra, an; *m. A gander;* anser, Ælfc. Gl. 36; Som. 62, 121; Wrt. Voc. 29, 17: 77, 33. v. gandra.

gānung, e; *f. A yawning;* oscĭtātio, Ælfc. Gl. 78; Som. 72, 59; Wrt. Voc. 46, 18.

GĀR, es; *m. A dart, javelin, spear, shaft, arrow, weapon, arms;* jacŭlum, pīlum, hasta, hastæ cuspis, săgitta, tēlum, arma:—Se gār *the dart*, Beo. Th. 3697; B. 1846. Fleág giellende gār on grome þeóde *the yelling shaft flew on the fierce nation*, Exon. 86 b; Th. 326, 13; Wīd. 128. Lǣtaþ gāres ord in gedūfan in fǣges ferþ *let the javelin-point plunge into the life of the doomed one*, Andr. Kmbl. 2662; An. 1332: Cd. 75; Th. 92, 2; Gen. 1522. Sende se sǣrinc sūþerne gār *the sea-chief sent a southern dart*, Byrht. Th. 135, 47; By. 134: 138, 48; By. 237. Gāre wunde *wounded by a dart*, Beo. Th. 2154; B. 1075: Exon. 66 a; Th. 243, 28; Jul. 17. Hī gewurdon scearpe gāras *ipsi sunt jăcŭla*, Ps. Th. 54, 21: 90, 6. Gāra ordum *with javelin-points*, Andr. Kmbl. 64; An. 32: Cd. 94; Th. 121, 32; Gen. 2019. Hȳ togædre gāras hlǣndon *they had inclined their weapons together*, Exon. 66 b; Th. 246, 8; Jul. 63: Elen. Kmbl. 235; El. 118. Gārum gehyrsted *adorned with javelins*, Andr. Kmbl. 90; An. 45: 2287; An. 1145: Chr. 937; Erl. 112, 18; Æđelst. 18. [*Chauc.* gere, *pl*: *Laym.* gar, gare, gære *a dart, spear,* *weapon: Plat.* gere *a wedge: Kil.* gheer *fuscĭna cuspĭdĭbus horrens, quibus pisces căpiuntur: O. Sax.* gêr, *m: Ger. M. H. Ger. O. H. Ger.* gĕr, *m. hastīle, jăcŭlum, tēlum: Icel.* geirr, *m. a spear.*] DER. æt-gâr, bon-, frum-, hyge-, tite-, wæl-.

gâra, an; *m. A spear-man.* v. frum-gâra *in* frum-gâr.

gârà, an; *m.* [gâr *a dart, point*] *An angular point of land, a promontory, corner of land;* ōra prōmĭnens, angŭlus:—Ispania land is þrýscýte . . . ân ðæra gârena lîþ sûþ-west, ongeán ðæt îgland, ðe Gades hâtte *the country of Spain is three-cornered . . . one of the corners lies south-west, opposite the island which is called Cadiz,* Ors. 1, 1; Bos. 24, 5.

gâr-beám, es; *m. The wood* or *handle of a javelin, a spear-shaft;* cuspĭdis hasta:—Gârbeámes feng *a spear-shaft's grasp,* Cd. 155; Th. 193, 14; Exod. 246.

gâr-berend, es; *m. A javelin-bearer, soldier;* hastĭfer, tēlĭfer:—Grame gârberend *the incensed javelin-bearers,* Byrht. Th. 139, 30; By. 262. Gârberendra x hund *ten hundred javelin-bearers,* Cd. 154; Th. 192, 13; Exod. 231.

gâr-cêne; *adj. Spear-bold, bold in arms;* hastâ audax:—Offa wæs gârcêne man *Offa was a man bold in arms,* Beo. Th. 3921; B. 1958.

gâr-clife, an; *f. Agrimony;* agrĭmōnia eupătōria:—Genim ðas wyrte, ðe man agrimoniam, and ôðrum naman gârclife nemneþ *take this herb, which is named agrimony, and by another name garclive,* Herb. 32, 1; Lchdm. i. 130, 3. Genim gârclifan *take garclive,* L. M. 2, 51; Lchdm. ii. 266, 8. Gârclifan etan ǽrende fûllîc getâcnaþ *to eat agrimony betokens a disagreeable message,* Somn. 20; Lchdm. iii. 198, 24. v. agrimonia.

gâr-cwealm, es; *m. Spear-slaughter;* nex tēlo patrāta, clādes:—Se ðe eall gemân gârcwealm gumena *who all remembers the slaughter of men,* Beo. Th. 4092; B. 2043.

Gâr-Dene; *gen.* a; *dat.* um; *pl. m. The spear-Danes, Danes who fought with spears, armed* or *warlike Danes;* hastāti Dāni:—We Gâr-Dena, in geárdagum, þeódcyninga þrym gefrunon *we have heard of the renown of the Gar-Danes' great kings in days of yore,* Beo. Th. 1; B. 1. He sæcce ne wêneþ to Gâr-Denum *he expects not warfare from the Gar-Danes,* 1206; B. 601: 3717; B. 1856: 4982; B. 2494.

gare *yare, ready, finished;* paratus, effectus:—Wæs ðæt mynstre gare *the monastery was finished,* Chr. 656; Erl. 30, 19. v. gearo.

gâr-faru, e; *f. A martial expedition,* v. faru III; turma hastifera:—Þûfas wundon ofer gârfare *the standards fluttered over the martial band,* Cd. 160; Th. 199, 23; Exod. 342. Ne þearf him ondrǽdan deófla strǽlas, gromra gârfare *he need not dread the shafts of devils, the armed band of the hostile,* Exon. 98 a; Th. 49, 5; Cri. 781. [*Or* gârfaru *flight of spears,* cf. hægelfaru.]

gâr-getrum, es; *n. A troop armed with spears, javelins:*—Gârgetrum ofer scild-hreádan sceótend sendaþ flacor flángeweorc *the spear-troop, the archers, send over the shields the quivering arrows,* Exon. 17 b; Th. 42, 18; Cri. 674.

gâr-gewinn, es; *n. Spear-war;* hastātōrum pugna:—Wǽron þearle gelyste gârgewinnes *they were very desirous of the spear-war,* Judth. 12; Thw. 26, 3; Jud. 308. Ne lǽt ðê ahweorfan grim gârgewinn *let not the fierce javelin-strife turn thee away,* Andr. Kmbl. 1915; An. 960.

gâr-heáp, es; *m. A spear-band, armed band;* hastĭfēra turma:—Hæfdon him beácen arǽred in ðam gârheápe *they had a signal reared in the armed band,* Cd. 160; Th. 198, 11; Exod. 321.

gâr-holt, es; *n.* [holt *lignum*] *A javelin-shaft, javelin;* hastæ lignum, hasta:—Ðæt ic ðê to geóce gârholt bere *that I may bear the javelin-shaft for thy succour,* Beo. Th. 3673; B. 1834.

gâr-leác, es; *n.* [gâr *a spear,* leác *a leek:* from its tapering acute leaves] GARLIC; allium:—Gârleác *allium,* Ælfc. Gl. 41; Som. 63, 111; Wrt. Voc. 30, 59: 286, 6. Genim gârleáces þreó heáfdu *take three heads of garlic,* L. M. 2, 32; Lchdm. ii. 234, 19. Gârleáces iii clufe *three cloves of garlic,* 3, 62; Lchdm. ii. 350, 8. Nim gârleáces gôdne dǽl *take a good deal of garlic,* Lchdm. iii. 12, 15. Nim gârleác *take garlic,* L. M. 1, 47; Lchdm. ii. 118, 12: 1, 58; Lchdm. ii. 128, 10: 1, 63; Lchdm. ii. 138, 3: 2, 56; Lchdm. ii. 276, 15. Wið gârleác gemenged *mingled with garlic,* L. M. 1, 31; Lchdm. ii. 72, 4. [*Icel.* geirlaukr.]

gâr-mitting, -mittung, e; *f. A meeting of spears* or *javelins, a battle:*—Ðæt hî beadoweorca beteran wurdon, on campstede, cumbolgehnâstes, gârmittinge [gârmittunge, Th. 207, 3, col. 2] *that they were the better [the victors] in works of war, on the battle-field, at the conflict of banners, at the meeting of javelins,* Chr. 937; Th. 207, 3, col. 1; Æðelst. 50.

gâr-nîþ, es; *m. A spear-battle, spear-war;* hastātōrum pugna:—Gerîseþ gârnîþ werum *spear-war is fitting for men.* Exon. 91 a; Th. 341, 19; Gn. Ex. 128.

gâr-rǽs, es; *m. A rush of spears, battle, war, warfare;* hastārum impĕtus, prœlium:—Ðæt gê ðisne gârrǽs mid gafole forgyldon *that ye buy off this warfare with tribute,* Byrht. Th. 132, 46; By. 32.

gâr-secg, -sæcg, es; *m.* [gâr *a spear,* secg *man*]. I. *a spear-man, the ocean;* hŏmo jăcŭlo armātus, oceănus. The myth of an armed man,—a spear-man is employed by the Anglo-Saxons as a term to denote the Ocean, and has some analogy to the personification of Neptune holding his trident. Spears were placed in the hands of the images of heathen gods, as mentioned by Justin.—Per ea adhuc tempŏra rēges hastas pro diadēmăte habēbant, quas Græci sceptra dixēre. Nam et ab orĭgĭne rērum, pro diis immortālĭbus vĕtĕres hastas coluēre; ob cujus religiōnis memŏriam adhuc deōrum simulacris hastæ adduntur, l. xliii: c. iii:—Ûre yldran ealne ðysne ymbhwyrft ðyses middangeardes, cwæþ Orosius, swâ swâ Oceanus ymbligeþ ûtan, ðone man gârsecg hâteþ, on þreó todǽldon *our forefathers, said Orosius, divided into three parts, all the globe of this mid-earth, which the ocean that we call Garsecg, surrounds,* Ors. 1, 1; Bos. 15, 2-4. Asia is befangen mid Oceanus—dæm gârsecge—sûþan, and norþan, and eástan *Asia is encompassed by the ocean—the garsecg—on the south, and north, and east,* 1, 1; Bos. 15, 8. Be norþan ðæm beorgum, andlang ðæs gârsecges, ôþ ðone norþ-eást ende ðyses middangeardes, ðǽr Bore seó eá scýt ût on ðone gârsecg *to the north of the mountains, along the ocean to the north-east end of this mid-earth, there the river Bore shoots out into the ocean,* Ors. 1, 1; Bos. 18, 5-7. Gârsecges deóp *the ocean's deep,* Cd. 157; Th. 195, 24; Exod. 281. Gârsecges begang *the circuit of ocean,* Andr. Kmbl. 1059; An. 530. II. *a sea;* măre:—And norþ ôþ ðone gârsecg, ðe man Cwên-Sǽ hǽt *and north to the sea, which is called the White Sea,* Ors. 1, 1; Bos. 18, 27. Fuglas cômon of gârsecge *ăves ex mări vēnērunt,* Ps. Th. 104, 35. Ût on gârsæcge *out in the sea,* 96, 1.

gâr-þræc, e; *f. Attack of javelins, battle;* hastōrum impĕtus, pugna:—Æt gârþræce *in the attack of javelins,* Elen. Kmbl. 2369; El. 1186.

gâr-þrîst; *adj. Spear-bold, daring with a spear;* hastâ audax:—Gûþheard, gârþrîst *warlike, spear-bold,* Elen. Kmbl. 407; El. 204.

gâr-torn, es; *m.* [torn *anger*] *Spear-anger, rage of darts;* īra tēlis manifestāta:—Hî gârtorn geótaþ gîfrum deófle *they shall pour the rage of darts upon the greedy devil,* Salm. Kmbl. 291; Sal. 145.

garuwe, an; *f. Yarrow;* millefōlium, Herb. 90; Lchdm. i. 194, 4, MS. B. v. gearwe.

garwan *ready, prepared,* Chr. 1006; Erl. 140, 17, = gearwan; *dat. def. of* gearo, *q. v.*

gâr-wîga, an; *m. A spear-fighter, warrior;* hastātus bellātor:—Byrne ne meahte geongum gârwîgan geóce gefremman *the corslet could not afford aid to the young warrior,* Beo. Th. 5341; B. 2674: 5614; B. 2811.

gâr-wîgend, es; *m. A spear-fighter, warrior;* hastātus bellator:—He ûsic gârwîgend gôde tealde *he accounted us warriors good,* Beo. Th. 5275; B. 2641.

gâr-wudu; *gen.* -wuda; *m. Spear-wood, a javelin;* hastæ lignum, hasta:—Hie to gûþe gârwudu rǽrdon *they raised the spear-wood to battle,* Cd. 160; Th. 198, 20; Exod. 325.

gast *a guest;* hospes, Cot. 102. DER. gast-hof, -hûs, -lîc. v. gæst.

GÂST, gǽst, es; *m.* I. *the breath;* hālĭtus, spīrāmen:—Ne ne is gâst on mûþe heora *there is not breath in their mouth,* Ps. Spl. 134, 17. Ðæt ic ofsleá eall flǽsc, on ðam ðe ys lîfes gâst *that I may slay all flesh, in which is the breath of life,* Gen. 6, 17. Mid gâste mûþes his *with the breath of his mouth,* Ps. Lamb. 32, 6. Blǽde odðe gâste *spīrāmĭne,* Hymn Surt. 43, 36. II. *the spirit, soul,* GHOST; spīrĭtus, anĭmus, ănĭma:—Gâst *spīrĭtus,* Wrt. Voc. 76, 31. Se gâst is hræd *spīrĭtus promptus est,* Mt. Bos. 26, 41: Gen. 45, 27: Num. 11, 25, 26: Soul Kmbl. 17; Seel. 9. Nô man scyle his gâstes lufan wið Gode dǽlan *a man ought not to divide his spirit's love with God,* Cd. 173; Th. 217, 11; Dan. 21: Andr. Kmbl. 310; An. 155: Salm. Kmbl. 131; Sal. 65. Hwyder ic gange fram gâste ðînum *quo ībo a spīrĭtu tuo?* Ps. Spl. 138, 6: Num. 11, 17, 25: Elen. Kmbl. 939; El. 471: Exon. 35 a; Th. 113, 18; Gû. 159. Bidde ic weoroda God, ðæt ic gâst mînne agifan môte *I pray [thee] God of hosts, that I may give up my spirit,* Andr. Kmbl. 2831; An. 1418; Salm. Kmbl. 110; Sal. 54: Menol. Fox 340; Men. 171: Elen. Kmbl. 958; El. 480. Gâstas hwurfon, sôhton engla êðel *souls departed, sought the home of angels,* Andr. Kmbl. 1280; An. 640: Exon. 100 a; Th. 375, 6; Seel. 134. Gâsta weardas *the guardians of spirits,* Cd. 2; Th. 3, 25; Gen. 41. Gâsta helm *the protector of spirits, God,* Cd. 86; Th. 107, 22; Gen. 1793. Arâs Metodes þeów gâstum togeánes *the Lord's servant [Lot] arose towards the spirits [angels],* 111; Th. 140, 30; Gen. 2430. Folc wæs afǽred, flôdegsa becwom gâstas geómre *the folk was affrighted, the flood-dread seized on the sad souls,* 166; Th. 206, 5; Exod. 447. Se hâlga Gâst *the holy Ghost;* Spīrĭtus sanctus, Mk. Bos. 13, 11: Lk. Bos. 1, 15, 35: 2, 25, 26: Jn. Bos. 20, 22: Elen. Kmbl. 2287; El. 1145. Se unclǽna gâst *the unclean spirit,* Mt. Bos. 12, 43: Mk. Bos. 1, 23: 5, 13: Lk. Bos. 4, 36: Elen. Kmbl. 603; El. 302. Se werega gâst *the accursed spirit, the devil,* Cd. 216; Th. 272, 27; Sat. 126. Werige gâstas *accursed spirits, devils, demons,* Cd. 227; Th. 304, 15; Sat. 630. [*Piers P.* goost: *Chauc.* gost, goste: *R. Brun.* gaste: *Laym.* gæst, gast, gost: *Orm.* gast: *Scot.* gest *a ghost, spirit: Plat.* geest, *m: O. Sax.* gêst, gâst, geist, *m: Frs.* gæst: *O. Frs.* gast, iest, *m: Dut.* geest, *m: Ger. M. H. Ger. O. H. Ger.* geist, *m: Goth.* gaisyan *to be frightened: Dan.* geist, *m. f: Swed.* gast, *m. an evil spirit, ghost.*] DER. ǽrend-gâst, cear-, ellen-, ellor-, geósceaft-, heáh-, helle-, wuldor-.

gást-berend *a spirit-bearer, soul-bearer, living person, man.* v. gǽst-berend.

gást-bona, an; *m. The soul-killer, the devil;* anĭmi destructor, diăbŏlus:—Ðæt him gástbona geóce gefremede *that the spirit-slayer would afford them help,* Beo. Th. 356; B. 177.

gást-cófa, an; *m. The spirit's chamber, breast;* anĭmi cŭbīle, pectus:—Hī habbaþ in gástcófan grimme geþohtas *they have fierce thoughts in their breast,* Frag. Kmbl. 22; Leas. 13.

gást-cund *spiritual.* v. gǽst-cund.

gást-cwalu *torment of soul.* v. gǽst-cwalu.

gást-cyning, es; *m. A spirit-king, God;* spīrĭtālis rex, Deus:—Siððan wit ǽrende gástcyninge agifen habbaþ *after we two have performed the errand to the king of spirits* [*God*], Cd. 139; Th. 174, 24; Gen. 2883.

gást-gedál, gǽst-gedál, es; *n. Separation of soul and body, death;* anĭmæ et corpŏris divortium, mors:—Ðá he ðas woruld þurh gástgedál ofgyfan sceolde *when he must give up this world through death,* Cd. 55; Th. 68, 33; Gen. 1127: Exon. 45 a; Th. 153, 32; Gú. 834.

gást-gehygd, gǽst-gehygd, es; *n. Thought of mind* or *spirit;* anĭmi cōgĭtātio:—Ðæt ðú sylfa miht ongitan gleáwlíce gástgehygdum *that thou thyself mayest prudently understand it with the thoughts of thy spirit,* Andr. Kmbl. 1722; An. 863.

gást-gemynd *thought of mind* or *spirit.* v. gǽst-gemynd.

gást-geníþla *a persecutor* or *foe of souls, the devil.* v. gǽst-geníþla.

gást-gerýne, gǽst-gerýne, es; *n. A ghostly* or *spiritual mystery, a mystery of the mind;* spīrĭtāle mystērium, ănĭmi mystērium:—Him ða æðelingas ondsweorodon gástgerýnum *the princes answered him in spiritual mysteries,* Andr. Kmbl. 1716; An. 860: Elen. Kmbl. 378; El. 189: 2294; An. 1148.

gást-gewinn *torment of soul.* v. gǽst-gewinn.

gást-hálig, gǽst-hálig; *adj. Spirit-holy, holy in mind;* anĭmi sanctus:—Witgan sungon, gast-halíge guman, be Godes bearne *prophets, men holy in spirit, sung of the son of God,* Elen. Kmbl. 1120; El. 562.

gast-hof, es; *n. A guest-house, guest-chamber;* hospĭtium:—In ðam gast-hofe *in the guest-house,* Exon. 19 b; Th. 21, 24; Cri. 821. [*Ger.* gasthof *inn.*]

gast-hús, es; *n. A guest-house, guest-chamber;* hospĭtium:—On heora gast-húsum is gramlíc inwit *nēquĭtia est in hospĭtiis eōrum,* Ps. Th. 54, 15. v. gæst-hús.

gást-leás; *adj. Lifeless, dead;* exănĭmis, mortuus:—Geíærenne man brohton on bǽre, gingne, gástleásne *they brought a dead man on a bier, young, lifeless,* Elen. Kmbl. 1746; El. 875.

gastlíc; *adj. Hospitable, ready for guests;* hospĭtālis:—Neorxna wang stód gód and gastlíc *paradise stood good and ready for guests,* Cd. 11; Th. 13, 27; Gen. 209.

gástlíc, gǽstlíc; *adj. Ghostly, spiritual;* spīrĭtālis:—Gástlíc hreám *a cry of spirits, ghostly cry,* Nicod. 27; Thw. 15, 5. Leoðolíc and gástlíc *the bodily and the ghostly,* Andr. Kmbl. 3254; An. 1630. Gé gástlícne god-dreám forségon *ye despised spiritual joy divine,* Exon. 41 b; Th. 139, 32; Gú. 602. Ðæt he healde gástlíce lufe *that he hold spiritual love,* Frag. Kmbl. 74; Leás. 39. Ðæt gástlíce folc *pŏpŭlus spīrĭtālis,* Bd. 1, 27; S. 496, 28. Eádige synd ða gástlícan þearfan, forðam hyra ys heofena ríce *beāti sunt paupĕres spīrĭtu, quoniam ipsōrum est regnum cælōrum,* Mt. Bos. 5, 3.

gástlíce, gǽstlíce; *adv. Spiritually;* spīrĭtālĭter:—Ðæt hálige húsel is gástlíce Cristes líchama *the holy housel is spiritually Christ's body,* Homl. Th. i. 34, 19. Ðæt húsel is Cristes líchama, ná líchamlíce, ac gástlíce *the housel is Christ's body, not bodily, but spiritually,* L. Ælf. C. 36; Th. ii. 360, 16: Bd. de nat. rerum; Wrt. popl. science 19, 25; Lchdm. iii. 280, 11: Cd. 220; Th. 283, 7; Sat. 301.

gást-lufe *soul's love, spiritual love.* v. gǽst-lufe.

gást-sunu, gǽst-sunu; *gen.* a; *dat.* a, u; *acc.* u; *pl. nom. acc.* a, o, u; *gen.* a, ena; *dat.* um; *m. A spiritual son, Christ;* spīrĭtālis fīlius, Christus:—Ahangen wæs on Caluarie Godes gástsunu *the spiritual Son of God was hanged up on Calvary,* Elen. Kmbl. 1342; El. 673.

gat, es; *pl. nom. acc.* u, a, o; *n. A* GATE; porta:—Ðá se Hǽlend geneálǽhte ðære ceastre gate *when the Saviour approached the gate of the city,* Lk. Bos. 7, 12: Exon. 12 b; Th. 20, 15; Cri. 318: Ps. Spl. 117, 19: Ps. Th. 126, 6. v. geat.

GÁT; *nom. acc; gen.* gáte, gǽte; *dat.* gǽt; *pl. nom. acc.* gǽt, gét; *gen.* gáta; *dat.* gátum; *f. A she-*GOAT; capra:—Ic blǽte swá gát *I bleat as a goat,* Exon. 106 b; Th. 406, 17; Rä. 25, 2. Gát *capra* vel *capella,* Wrt. Voc. 78, 33: 287, 36: 288, 16. Gáte blód *goat's blood,* Med. ex Quadr. 6, 4; Lchdm. i. 352, 3. Gáte flǽsc *goat's flesh,* L. M. 1, 31; Lchdm. ii. 72, 8. Gáte horn *a goat's horn,* Med. ex Quadr. 6, 1; Lchdm. i. 350, 17. Gǽte meolc *goat's milk,* L. M. 1, 7; Lchdm. ii. 52, 13. Genim ðæt wæter ðe innan gǽt byþ *take the water which is inside a goat,* Med. ex Quadr. 6, 10; Lchdm. i. 352, 19. Geoffra me áne þríwintre gát *sūme mihi capram trīmam,* Gen. 15, 9: Lev. 3, 12: 4, 28: 5, 6. Hý beofiaþ fóre Freán, swá fúle swá gǽt *they shall tremble before the Lord, as foul as goats,* Exon. 26 a; Th. 75, 34; Cri. 1231. He asyndrode twáhund gáta *sepărāvit capras ducentas,* Gen. 32, 14. Gáta hús *a goat-house;* caprīle, Ælfc. Gl. 108; Som. 78, 112; Wrt. Voc. 58, 27. Gáta loc *an enclosure for goats,* Wrt. Voc. 288, 20. Gáta hierde *a goat-herd,* 288, 21. Gif seó offrung beó of gátum *si oblātio est de capris,* Lev. 1, 10. Drihten toscǽt hí on twá, swá swá scéphyrde toscǽt scép fram gátum: gelogaþ he ða scép on his swíðran hand, and ða gǽt on his wynstran *the Lord will part them into two, as a shepherd parts sheep from goats: he will place the sheep on his right hand, and the goats on his left,* Homl. Th. ii. 106, 27-29. Buccan oððe gét geseón ferþrunge getácnaþ *to see bucks or goats betokens advancement,* Somn. 126; Lchdm. iii. 206, 2. Gif ðú gesihst manega gét, ýdel getácnaþ *if thou seest many goats it betokens vanity,* 273; Lchdm. iii. 214, 1. Wæterbuca vel gát *tippŭla* [=*an insect that runs swiftly over the water, the water-spider, water-spinner*], Ælfc. Gl. 23; Som. 60, 10; Wrt. Voc. 24, 14. [*Chauc.* gat: *Laym.* gat, got: *Orm.* gat: *Dut.* geit, *f*: *Ger.* geisz, *f*: *M. H. Ger. O. H. Ger.* geiz, *f*: *Goth.* gaits, *f*: *Dan.* ged, *m. f*: *Swed.* get, *f*: *Icel.* geit, *f*: *Lat.* hædus, *m. a young goat, kid*: *Wel.* gid, giten, *f. a she-goat, young goat.*] DER. firgen-gát.

gát-bucca, an; *m. A he-goat;* căper:—Gát-buccan hyrde *a keeper of a he-goat,* Ælfc. Gl. 20; Som. 59, 37; Wrt. Voc. 22, 78.

Gátes héued, es; *n.* [*Goat's head*] GATESHEAD, *near Newcastle, Durham;* oppĭdi nōmen juxta Nŏvum Castrum in agro Dunelmensi, *capræ căput* signĭficans, Som. Ben. Lye: Bd. 3, 21; S. 125, note 37. v. Hrége-heáfod.

gáte-treów, es; *n. A cornel tree?* cornus sanguinea? Lin:—Genim bircean, elebeám, gátetreów, ǽlces treówes dǽl *take birch, olive-tree, cornel-tree, a part of each tree,* L. M. 1, 36; Lchdm. ii. 86, 8.

gáþ *go,* Deut. 11, 28: Mt. Bos. 9, 13; *pl. pres. indic. and impert. of* gán.

gaðerian *to gather,* Som. Ben. Lye. v. gaderian.

gát-hyrde, es; *m. A* GOAT-HERD; caprārius:—Be gát-hyrde: gát-hyrde gebýreþ his heorde meolc ofer Martinus mæssedæg, and ǽr ðam his dǽl hwǽges, and anticcen of geáres geógoþe, gif he his heorde wel begýmeþ *de caprario: caprārio convĕnit lac grĕgis sui post festum Sancti Martini, et antea pars sua mesguii, et caprĭcum annĭcŭlum, si bĕne custōdiat grĕgem suum,* L. R. S, 15; Th. i. 438, 26-29.

gauel *a tribute,* Ps. Spl. T. 54, 11. v. gafol.

gauel-sester, es; *m. A measure of rent ale;* sextārius vectīgālis cerevisiæ, Som. Ben. Lye. v. gafol, sester.

ge; *conj. And, also;* et:—Ánra gehwylc, sóþfæst ge synnig, séceþ Meotudes dóm *every one, just and sinful, shall seek the Creator's doom,* Exon. 63 b; Th. 233, 11; Ph. 523: Bt. Met. Fox 26, 171; Met. 26, 86: Ps. Th. 66, 6. Ge ... ge *both ... and;* et ... et. He bebýt ge windum ge sǽ *et ventis et mări impĕrat,* Lk. Bos. 8, 25; Jn. Bos. 2, 15: Bt. 41, 3; Fox 248, 28: Chr. 835; Erl. 64, 28: Bt. Met. Fox 9, 3; Met. 9, 2: 20, 25, 26; Met. 20, 13: Andr. Kmbl. 1083; An. 542. Ge mid býsenum heofonlíces lífes ge eác mid monungum *et exemplis vitæ cælestis et monitis,* Bd. 4, 19; S. 588, 3: 2, 12; S. 512, 30, 31. Ge ... and *both ... and,* Cd. 35; Th. 46, 30-33; Gen. 752, 753. Ge eác swá same *and in like manner,* Bt. Met. Fox 11, 19; Met. 11, 10. Ge swylce *and also,* Beo. Th. 4508; B. 2258. Ǽghwæðer ge ... ge *either ... or;* vel ... vel, Bd. 2, 12; S. 513, 14, 15. Ǽghwæðer ge on mete, ge on hrægl, ge on ǽghwilcum ðinge *both in meat, and in dress, and in every thing,* Blickl. Homl. 219, 29. Ǽgðer ge ... ge *both ... and,* Bt. 41, 2; Fox 246, 5. Ǽgðer ge on spræce, ge on þeáwum, ge on eallum sidum *both in speech, and in manners, and in all customs,* Bt. 18, 2; Fox 62, 29: 41, 5; Fox 254, 19-21. [*O. Sax.* ge, gi, ja *and.*]

ge-, or ǽg-, prefixed to pronouns. v. ǽg-.

ge-, a preposition, originally meaning *with,* but found only as a prefix. v. Schleicher, Die Deutsche Sprache, p. 224. In accordance with this meaning it often gives a collective sense to nouns to which it is prefixed, as, ge-bróðor *brothers;* ge-húsan *housefolk;* ge-magas *kinsmen;* ge-macan *mates;* ge-gylda *a member of a corporation* or *guild;* ge-wita *a witness, accomplice;* ge-fera *a companion, attendant;* gescý *shoes.* Ge- sometimes gives to a neuter verb an active signification, as winnan *to fight,* ge-winnan *to win by fighting:*—Wið God winnan *to fight* [*war*] *with God,* Cd. 18; Th. 22, 26; Gen. 346. Sige on him ge-wann *he gained* [*won*] *a victory over him,* Num. 21, 1. Rídan *to ride;* ge-rídan *to reach by riding, arrive at:*—Ic on wicge ríde *I ride on a horse,* Exon. 127 a; Th. 489, 14; Rä. 78, 7. Ge-rád Æðelwold ðone hám æt Winburnan *postea invāsit Æthelwaldus villam ăpud Winburnam,* Gib. 99, 37: Chr. 901; Erl. 97, 11. On this power of ge-, Mr. Earle, in Chr. p. 321, remarks:—'A strong instance is ge-winnan [1090] = *to win;* which sense, now so intimately identified with this root, is not in the simple verb winnan, until compounded with ge-. Winnan *is to toil, fight, contend;* ge-winnan *is to get by striving, fighting, contending,* i. e. *to win,*' A. D. 685; p. 40, 16: p. 4, 25. Ge- often seems void of signification; as, ge-sǽlþ *bliss;* ge-líc *like;* ge-súnd *sound, healthy.* In verbs it seems sometimes to be a mere augment, e. g. in the following:—Ðæt wíf genam ðá of ðæs treówes wæstme and geæt and sealde hire were: he æt ða *mŭlier tŭlit de fructu illīus et comĕdit dĕditque vĭro suo, qui comĕdit,* Gen. 3, 6. It often changes the signification from literal to figurative; as, healdan *to hold;* ge-healdan *to observe, preserve;* fyllan *to fill;* ge-fyllan *to fulfil*; biddan *to bid, require*; ge-biddan *to pray*. In the Rushworth Gloss. the prefix is often gi-. [*Wyc. Piers P. Chauc.* y-: *Laym.* i-: *O. Sax.* gi-: *O. Frs.* ge-, gi-, ie-: *Dut. Ger.* ge-: *M. H. Ger.* ge-, gi-: *O. H. Ger.* ga-, ka-, gi-, ki-, ge-, ke-: *Goth.* ga-: *Dan. Swed.* ge-.]

gē *ye, you*; vos, ὑμεῖς; *gen.* eówer [iwer] *your, of you*; vestrum *vel* vestri, ὑμῶν; *dat.* eów [iów, iu, iuh, iuih, iwh] *to you*; vobis, ὑμῖν; *acc.* eów [iów, iu, iuh, iuih, iwh], eówic *you*; vos, ὑμᾶς; *pl. of pers. pron. 2nd pers.* ðū *thou*:—Ne ondrǣde gē *fear ye not*, Mt. Bos. 10, 28. Gē ðe on hūse standaþ *you who stand in the house*; tu qui stātis in dŏmo, Ps. Th. 133, 2. Gebīde gē on beorge *abide you on the mount*, Beo. Th. 5051; B. 2529. Hwylc eówer *quis vestrum?* Mt. Bos. 6, 27. Ān eówer *ūnus vestrum*, 26, 21. Ic sylle eów *dăbo vobis*, Ex. 6, 8. Ic secge eów *dīco vobis*, Mt. Bos. 6, 16: 7, 7. Gyf gē ða lufiaþ ðe eów lufiaþ *si dīlĭgĭtis eos qui vos dīlĭgunt*, Mt. Bos. 5, 46. On eów becymþ Godes rīce *pervĕnit in vos regnum Dei*, Mt. Bos. 12, 28. Eówic grētan hēt *bade to greet you*, Beo. Th. 182; B. 3095. Hwanon eágorstreám eówic brohte *whence hath the ocean-stream brought you?* Andr. Kmbl. 518; An. 259: 1764; An. 884. Sibb sȳ mid eówic *peace be with you*, Exon. 75 b; Th. 282, 25; Jul. 668. [*Wyc.* ȝee, ȝe: *Piers P.* ye: *Chauc. Orm.* ȝe: *O. Sax.* gi, ge: *O. Frs.* gi, i: *Ger.* ihr: *M. H. Ger.* ir: *O. H. Ger.* īr: *Goth.* yus: *Dan. Swed.* i: *Icel.* ér.]

GEÁ; *adv.* YEA; ĕtiam:—'Quod est, lingua Anglōrum, verbum adfirmandi et consentiendi,' Bd. 5, 2; S. 183, 35. Geá, Drihten, ðū wāst ðæt ic ðē lufige, *yea, Lord, thou knowest that I love thee*, Jn. Bos. 21, 15, 16; ĕtiam, Dŏmĭne, Vulg. Cweþ [cwæþ MS.] nū geá *say now yea*, Bd. 5, 2; S. 615, 9. [*Wyc.* ȝea, ȝhe: *Piers P.* ye: *Chauc.* ya, ye, yhe: *Orm.* ȝa: *O. Sax.* jā: *Frs.* ja: *O. Frs.* ie, ge: *Dut. Ger.* ja: *M. H. Ger. O. H. Ger.* jā: *Goth.* ya, yai: *Dan. Swed.* ja, jo: *Icel.* já *yes, yea.*]

GEÁC, es; *m. A cuckoo, gawk*; cŭcūlus:—Geác *cŭcūlus*, Ælfc. Gl. 37; Som. 63, 16; Wrt. Voc. 29, 38: 63, 3: 281, 31. Geác monaþ geómran reorde, singeþ sumeres weard *the cuckoo exhorts with mournful voice, summer's warden sings*, Exon. 82 a; Th. 309, 6; Seef. 53. Siððan ðū gehȳrde galan geómorne geác on bearwe *when thou hast heard the sad cuckoo sing in the grove*, 123 b; Th. 473, 30; Bo. 22. Geácas geár budon *cuckoos announced the* [*time of*] *year*, Exon. 43 b; Th. 146, 27; Gū. 716. ¶ Geáces sūre, an; *f. Cuckoo-sorrel, wood-sorrel*; oxălis acetōsella, Lin:—Geáces sūre *vel* þrīlēfe *trifŏlium*, Ælfc. Gl. 39; Som. 63, 72; Wrt. Voc. 30, 24. Genim geáces sūran *take cuckoo-sorrel*, L. M. 1, 2; Lchdm. ii. 38, 14: 1, 38; Lchdm. ii. 96, 22: 3, 48; Lchdm. ii. 340, 2: iii. 12, 30. [*Scot.* gowk: *Dut.* koekoek, *m*: *Ger.* kuckuk, kukuk, gauch, *m. a cuckoo, gawk, simpleton*: *M. H. Ger.* gouch, *m*: *O. H. Ger.* gouch, gauch, *m. cŭcūlus, stultus*: *Dan.* giøg, *m. f*: *Swed.* gök, *m*: *Icel.* gaukr, *m*: *Fr.* coucou, *m*: *It.* cuculo, *m*: *Span.* cuco, cuclillo, *m*: *Lat.* cŭcūlus, *m*: *Grk.* κόκκυξ, *m*: *Sansk.* kokila, *m.*] v. Grm. D. M. pp. 640 sqq.

ge-aclian; *p.* ode, ade; *pp.* od, ad *To frighten, excite*; terrēre, terrōre percellĕre:—Ðā ðæt folc gewearþ egesan geaclod *then was the people terrified with fear*, Andr. Kmbl. 1609; An. 805: Elen. Kmbl. 2255; El. 1129. Cyning wæs egsan geaclad *the king was excited with terror*, 113; El. 57: Exon. 69 b; Th. 258, 20; Jul. 268.

geácnod *increased*, Elen. Kmbl. 681; El. 341, = ge-eácnod; *pp. of* ge-eácnian.

geácnung *a conceiving*; conceptio, Som. Ben. Lye. v. ge-eácnung.

ge-acsian, -acsigan; *p.* ode, ade; *pp.* od, ad *To find out by asking, discover, learn, hear*; resciscĕre, discĕre, agnoscĕre, audīre:—Ic wolde geacsigan and gewitan hwæt be ðē ðōn sceolde *I would find out and know what should be done about thee*, Bd. 5, 12; S. 630, 30. Gyf se dēma ðis geacsaþ *si hoc audītum fuĕrit a præsĭde*, Mt. Bos. 28, 14. Ðā se pāpa ðæt geacsade *when the pope heard it*, Bd. 2, 17; S. 520, 15: 5, 10; S. 625, 20. We geacsodan *agnōvĭmus*, Bd. pref; S. 472, 16. Gif hine mon geacsige *if he be discovered*, L. In. 39; Th. i. 126, 9, MS. B. v. ge-ascian.

geacsung *an asking, inquiry*; inquīsītio, Som. Ben. Lye. v. ge-ascung.

ge-ādlian; *p.* ode, ede; *pp.* od, ed [ādlian *to be sick, to languish*] *To be sick, to languish, become impotent*; languescĕre:—On ðām porticon læg mycel menigeo geādledra *in his portĭcis jăcēbat multĭtūdo magna languentium*, Jn. Bos. 5, 3. Ðæt ūre mōd þurh wærscipe wacole beón, ðæt hī þurh orsorhnysse ne asleacion, ne þurh nytennysse geādlion *that our minds may be vigilant through heedfulness, that through security they slacken not, nor through ignorance become impotent*, Homl. Th. i. 610, 17.

geador; *adv. Together, altogether*; ūna, sĭmul:—Þenden gǣst and līc geador sīðedan *while soul and body journeyed together*, Exon. 76 a; Th. 285, 15; Jul. 714: Bt. Met. Fox 13, 98; Met. 13, 49: Salm. Kmbl. 899; Sal. 449. Gecyre ic ætsomne S. R. geador *I turn at once S and R together*, Exon. 123 b; Th. 475, 16; Bo. 48. Geátmæcgum geador ætsomne *for the Gothic warriors altogether*, Beo. Th. 987; B. 491. DER. eal-geador, on-geador. v. eador.

ge-æbiligan; *p.* de; *pp.* ed *To make angry, offend*; irrītāri:—Ðone ðe he ǣr mid forseweunysse geæbiligde *whom he had before angered by negligence*, Homl. Th. ii. 592, 16. Gif hī us geæbiligdon *if they have offended us*, ii. 100, 33.

ge-ǣfenian, -ǣfnian; *p.* ode, ede; *pp.* od, ed [ǣfen *evening*] *To draw towards evening, become evening*; vesperascĕre, advesperascĕre:—Geǣfnaþ me vesperasco, Ælfc. Gr. 35; Som. 38, 10. Geǣfenedan dæge *advesperascente die*, Prov. 7.

ge-æfenlǣcan *to imitate*, Ben. Lye. v. ge-efenlǣcan.

ge-æfēstian *to envy*:—Giæfīstiaþ *invidet*, Rtl. 122, 1. v. æfēstian.

ge-æfnan; *p.* de; *pp.* ed [æfnan *to perform, execute*]. I. *to perform, execute, perpetrate, accomplish, complete, make*; perfĭcĕre, patrāre, præstāre, făcĕre:—He nele lāþes wiht ǣngum geæfnan *he will not perpetrate aught of harm to any*, Exon. 96 a; Th. 357, 23; Pa. 33: 95 b; Th. 356, 28; Pa. 18. Se eádga wer mægen unsōfte elne geæfnde *the blessed man with difficulty strenuously exerted his power*, 49 a; Th. 168, 21; Gū. 1081. We ðæt geæfndon swā *we thus accomplished it*, Beo. Th. 1081; B. 538. Sīe sió bǣr gearo ædre geæfned *let the bier be quickly made ready*, 6203; B. 3106: 2218; B. 1107. II. *to stir up, excite*; excĭtāre:—Ic nolde þurh gielpcwide ǣfre geæfnan æbylg Godes *I would not through vaunting speech ever excite the anger of God*, Exon. 50 b; Th. 176, 16; Gū. 1211. III. *to bear, suffer, endure*; sufferre, sustĭnēre:—Hī sceolon ðone ryhtan dōm ǣnne geæfnan *they shall suffer the one righteous doom*, Exon. 27 b; Th. 84, 7; Cri. 1370. Ic yrmþu geæfnde *I suffered miseries*, 28 b; Th. 87, 24; Cri. 1430. v. ge-efnan.

ge-æhtan, -æhtian; *p.* te, ode; *pp.* ed, od [æht *valuation, estimation*] *To value, prize*; æstĭmāre:—Wæs gifu Hrōþgāres oft geæhted *the gift of Hrothgar was often prized*, Beo. Th. 3774; B. 1885. Gebēte swā hit mon geæhtie *let him make amends as it may be valued*, L. Alf. 26; Th. i. 50, 26, MS. H. v. ge-eahtian.

ge-æhtendlīc; *adj. Valuable, estimable*; æstĭmābĭlis, Som. Ben. Lye.

ge-æhtle, an; *f.* [æht *valuation, estimation*] *Estimation, consideration*; æstĭmātio, delĭbĕrātio:—Hȳ, on wīggetawum, wyrðe þinceaþ eorla geæhtlan, *they, in their war-equipments, appear of the estimation of earls*, Beo. Th. 743; B. 369. Grein and Heyne give geǣhtla *persecutor*; cf. ēhtan; then eorla geǣhtlan would mean *warriors*.

ge-æhtung, e; *f. Deliberation, counsel*; consĭlium:—Nā hī wel syððan his geæhtunge āhwǣr heóldan *non sustĭnuērunt consĭlium ejus*, Ps. Th. 105, 11.

ge-ælged; *part. Coloured, painted, tanned, sunburnt*; cŏlōrātus, sōle fuscātus, Som. Ben. Lye.

ge-æmtian, -æmettigian, -æmtogian; *p.* ode; *pp.* od [æmtian *to be at leisure*] *To be unoccupied, be at leisure, be void*; văcuum esse, văcāre:—Ðe hie selfe geæmettigian sceoldon *who ought to keep themselves unoccupied*, Past. 18, 4; Swt. 134, 5; Cot. MS.; Swt. 4, 3. Geæmtiaþ eów, and geseóþ ðæt ic eam God *văcāte, et vĭdēte quŏniam ĕgo sum Deus*, Ps. Lamb. 45, 11. He wæs geæmtogod *he was void*, Homl. Th. i. 290, 21.

ge-ændung, e; *f. An end, a finish*; consummātio:—On graman geændunge *in īra consummātiōnis*, Ps. Lamb. 58, 14. v. ge-endung.

ge-ænged; *part.* [ænge *narrow, troubled, anxious*] *Troubled, anxious*; anxius:—Ge-ængedu anxia, Cot. 18.

ge-ǣrendian, -ērendian, -ǣrndian; *p.* ode; *pp.* od [ǣrendian *to go on an errand*] *To go on an errand, to ask, tell, intercede*; mandātum deferre, nuntiāre, interpellāre:—Se ðe him mǣge geǣrendian [ge-ērendian MS. B: geǣrndian MS. H.] *who can do his errands*, L. In. 33; Th. i. 122, 13. Ðæt he him sceolde Gaiuses miltse geǣrendian *that he might ask the mercy of Caius for them*, Ors. 6, 3; Bos. 117, 36. He geǣrendaþ [geǣrndaþ MSS. A. G.] to Gode sylfum ymbe ǣlce neóde ðe man beþearf *he intercedes to God himself about every need a man may have*, L. C. E. 22; Th. i. 372, 29. Him geǣrndode Blyþþryþ his cwēn, ðæt he him wunonesse stōwe sealde on sumum ēalande bī Rīne *qui, interpellante Blithrydæ conjuge sua, dĕdit ei lŏcum mansiōnis in insŭla quādam Rheni*, Bd. 5, 11; S. 626, 13. [*O. Sax.* habda giārundid *had performed his business.*] v. ǣrendian.

ge-ærnan, he -ærneþ; *p.* de; *pp.* ed. I. *v. intrans. To run*; currĕre:—Ðā geærndon hī sume þrage and efthwurfon *then they ran for some time and returned*, Bd. 5, 6; S. 619, 9. II. *v. trans. To run for, to gain by running*; cursu certāre, propalma cursu contendĕre:—He nimþ ðone læstan dǣl, se nȳhst ðæm tūne ðæt feoh geærneþ *he takes the least part, who nearest the town, gains* [*by running*] *the property*, Ors. 1, 1; Bos. 22, 40. DER. ærnan, yrnan, irnan.

ge-ærnian; *p.* ode; *pp.* od *To earn, deserve*; mĕrēri, promĕrēri:—Hī geærnian māgen *illi promĕrēri pŏtĕrint*, L. Alf. pol. 39; Wilk. 44, 42. v. ge-earnian.

ge-ærwe; *adj.* [arg *wicked, depraved*] *Perverse, wicked*; prāvus:—Nā tocleofode me heorte geærwe *non adhæsit mihi cor prāvum*, Ps. Spl. T. 100, 4.

ge-ǣswīcod; *part. Offended, scandalized*; scandălĭzātus, Som. Ben. Lye. DER. ǣ-swīcian.

ge-æt *ate*, Gen. 3, 6; *p. of* ge-etan.

ge-ǣðed; *part.* [āþ *an oath, a swearing*] *Sworn*; jūrātus:—Swā geǽðedra manna sȳn twegen oððe þrȳ to gewitnysse *of such sworn men let there be two or three as witness*, L. Edg. S. 6; Th. i. 274, 18.

ge-æðele; *adj. Congenial, in accordance with one's nature, race* [v. æðelo]; congĕnĭtus:—Swā him geæðele wæs from cneómǽgum *as was to them natural from their kindred*, Chr. 937; Erl. 112, 7; Æðelst. 7. v. on-æðele. cf. gecynde.

ge-æðelian; *p.* ode; *pp.* od; *v. trans. To render celebrated, renowned, excellent, to ennoble, improve*; nobĭlĭtāre:—Ðū geæðelodest ealle gesceafta *thou ennobledst all creatures*, Hy. 7, 64; Hy. Grn. ii. 288, 64. Ðū eart geæðelod geond ealle world *thou art renowned throughout all the world*, 7, 26; Hy. Grn. ii. 287, 26. [*Laym.* i-æðelien *to honour*.]

ge-ǽtred, -ǽttred, -ǽttrad, -ǽttrud; *part.* [ātor *poison, venom*] *Poisoned, envenomed, poisonous*; infectus, toxĭcātus, vĕnēnātus:—Forwearþ micel heres for geǽtredum gescotum *many of the army died from poisoned arrows*, Ors. 3, 9; Bos. 68, 38. Geǽttred *infectus*, Cot. 104. Hæfde he twigecgede handseax geǽttred *hăbēbat sīcam bicipĭtem toxĭcātam*, Bd. 2, 9; S. 511, 15. Geǽttrad flaa *a poisoned arrow*, Ælfc. Gl. 53; Som. 66, 65; Wrt. Voc. 35, 51. Geǽttrude nȳtenu *vĕnēnāta anĭmālia*, Scint. 7.

ge-ǽwnod; *part.* [ǽwnian *to marry, wed*] *Married*; nuptus:—Ruth wearþ geǽwnod Iessan ealdan fæder *Ruth was married to the grandfather of Jesse*, Ælfc. T. 12, 17.

geaf *gave*:—He nallas beágas geaf *he gave no rings*, Beo. Th. 3443; B. 1719; *p. of* gifan.

geafel, es; *m? A fork*:—Hine ufan mid īsenum geaflum ðydon *from above pierced him with iron forks*, Homl. Th. i. 430, 5. [Gaffle *a dung-fork*, Halliwell: *Ger.* gabel: cf. *O. H. Ger.* isarngabala, *f. tridens.*] v. gaflas.

geafia; *p.* ode, ade; *pp.* od, ad *To glorify*:—Geafade hine *glorificavit eum*, Rtl. 78, 32.

geaflas; *pl. m. The jaws*; fauces:—Geaflas *fauces*, Cot. 91. Ðæt nebb lixeþ swā glæs oððe gim, geaflas scȳne innan and ūtan *the beak* [*of the Phœnix*] *glitters like glass or gem, the jaws comely within and without*, Exon. 60 a; Th. 219, 1; Ph. 300. Biþ ðæt heáfod tohliden, geaflas toginene *the head shall be split open, the jaws distended*, Exon. 99 b; Th. 373, 17; Seel. 110. Ðam ða geaflas beóþ nǽdle scearpran *whose jaws are sharper than a needle*, 100 a; Th. 373, 32; Seel. 118.

geafle ? *a lever*; palanga, vectis, Som. Ben. Lye.

geafol-monung, e; *f*:—Sittende to geafol-monunge *sedens ad teloneum*, Mk. Skt. Rush. 2, 14.

ge-aforud; *part.* [aforud *exalted*] *Lifted up*; sublīmātus, Som. Ben. Lye.

geafu, e; *f. A gift*; dōnum:—Ic mōt meorda hleótan, gingra geafena *I may obtain rewards, new gifts*, Exon. 48 a; Th. 164, 21; Gū. 1015. v. gifu.

ge-āgen; *adj. Own*:—His geāgenes ðances *of his own accord*, Th. Chart. 159, 5. v. āgen.

ge-āgennud; *part.* [āgen *own*] *Adopted*; adoptīvus:—Geāgennud bearn *an adopted child*; filius adoptīvus. Som. Ben. Lye.

geagl, geahl, es; *m.* [also *n.* v. the last example] *The jowl, jaw*; mandĭbŭla, rictus, fauces:—Geagl *mandĭbŭla*, Cot. 128. Geagl *rictus* Procem. R. Concord. On ðam geagle *in the jowl*, L. M. 1, 4; Lchdm. ii. 46, 8. To swillanne ðone geagl *to swill the jowl*, 1, 1; Lchdm. ii. 24, 10: 1, 4; Lchdm. ii. 48, 15, 19. Biþ ðæt heáfod tohliden, geaglas toginene *the head shall be split open, the jaws distended*, Soul Kmbl. 215; Seel. 110: 229; Seel. 118. Ðæt geagl to swillanne *to swill the jowl*, L. M. 1, 1; Lchdm. ii. 24, 12, 22, 26, 29.

geagl *light, frolicsome, lascivious*, Bd. 5, 6; Whelc. 390, 39, MS. C. v. gagol.

geaglisc, geglesc; *adj. Light, frolicsome, lascivious*; lĕvis, lascīvus:—Ic wæs mid geaglisce [geglescum MS. B: geagle MS. C.] mōde oferswȳðed *I was overcome with a frolicsome mood*; lascīvo supĕrātus anĭmo, Bd. 5, 6; Whelc. 390, 39. v. gagol.

geagl-swile, es; *m. A swelling of the jowl*; faucium tŭmor:—Lǽcedōm wið geaglswile *a remedy for jowl-swelling*, L. M. 1, 4; Lchdm. ii. 46, 7. Wið geaglswile [MS. gealhswile] *for jowl-swelling*, 1, 4; Lchdm. ii. 44, 8.

geagn-cwide, es; *m. A reply, answering again*; responsum:—Grimme geagncwide *with grim response*, Elen. Kmbl. 1047; El. 525. v. gegn-cwide.

ge-āgnian, -āhnian; to -āgnianne, -āhnianne; *p.* ode, ade, ede; *pp.* od, ad, ed *To own, possess, inherit, appropriate to one's self, claim as one's own*; possĭdēre, herēdĭtāre, vindicāre sibi:—Hwī sceal he him ānum geāgnian ðæt him bām is forgifen *why should he appropriate to himself only that which is given to both?* Homl. Th. ii. 102, 29: Ors. 5, 4; Bos. 104, 17: Cd. 86; Th. 109, 27; Gen. 1829. Nān man hit nāh to geāhnianne [geāgnianne MS. A.] *no man ought to claim possession of it*, L. C. S. 24; Th. i. 390, 13. Ic geāhnige *possĭdeo*, Ælfc. Gr. 26, 5; Som. 29, 5. He his gecorenan on ðisum middanearde geāgnaþ *he owns his chosen in this world*, Homl. Th. ii. 72, 28. Ða geyrfweardiaþ oððe geāhniaþ land *ipsi herēdĭtābunt terram*, Ps. Lamb. 36, 9. Ðū geāgnadest, Ps. Th. 79, 16. Parthe him ðæt rīce geāhnedon *the Parthians took the kingdom to themselves*, Ors. 5, 4; Bos. 104, 35. Ōþ-ðæt se āgenfrigea him ðæt orf geāhnige *till the proprietor claims the cattle for his own*, L. Edg. S. 11; Th. i. 276, 16. Sceal monna gehwilc wesan geāgnod me *every man shall be appropriated to me*, Cd. 106; Th. 140, 1; Gen. 2321. [*Goth.* ga-āiginōn: *Laym.* iahnien.]

ge-āgniendlīc, -āgnigendlīc; *adj. Owning, possessive*; possessīvus:—Genitivus is gestrȳnendlīc oððe geāgniendlīc *the genitive* [*case*] *is producing or possessive*, Ælfc. Gr. 7; Som. 6, 17. Sume synd geāgnigendlīce, ða geswuteliaþ ða þing ðe beóþ geāgnode *some are possessive, which make known the things which are owned*, 5; Som. 4, 55.

geagninga; *adv. Clearly, truly, certainly*; plāne, prorsus, certe:—Ðū scealt geagninga wīsdōm onwreon *thou shalt truly display wisdom*, Elen. Kmbl. 1343; El. 673. v. gegninga.

geahl, es; *m. The jowl, jaw*; fauces:—God forbriteþ tēþ, heora on mūþe heora, tuxlas oððe geahlas leóna tobrycþ Drihten *Deus contĕret dentes eōrum in ōre ipsōrum, mŏlas leōnum confringet Dŏmĭnus*, Ps. Spl. 57, 6. v. geagl.

ge-āhnian *to own, possess, appropriate to one's self*:—Ic geāhnige *possĭdeo*, Ælfc. Gr. 26, 5; Som. 29, 5: Ors. 5, 4; Bos. 104, 35: L. Edg. S. 11; Th. i. 276, 16. v. ge-āgnian.

ge-āhnung, e; *f. An appropriation, possession, owning*; appropriātio, possessio, Som. Ben. Lye.

ge-ahsian; *p.* ode; *pp.* od *To find out by asking, discover, learn, hear*; fando accĭpĕre, resciscĕre, discĕre:—Ðā Latinus hyre wer geahsode *when Collatinus her husband heard it*, Ors. 2, 2; Bos. 41, 32: 3, 11; Bos. 75, 26. We geahsodon ðæt ūre gefēran sume to eów cōmon *we have heard that some of our fellows have come to you*, L. Alf. 40; Th. i. 56, 14, MS. G: Ors. 3, 11; Bos. 74, 41. Gif hine mon geahsige *if he be discovered*, L. In. 39; Th. i. 126, 10. Hæbbe ic geahsod, ðæt . . . *I have heard that . . .*, Beo. Th. 870; B. 433. v. ge-ascian.

geal, *pl.* gullon *yelled*; *p. of* gellan.

geal-ādl, e; *f.* [gealla *gall, bile*] *Gall-disease, the jaundice*; ictĕrus = ἴκτερος, aurūgo:—Of gealādle cymeþ greát yfel . . . se līchoma ageolwaþ swā gōd seoluc *from jaundice comes great evil . . . the body becomes yellow like good silk*, L. M. 1, 42; Lchdm. ii. 106, 19–22.

gealchattan ? *p.* te; *pp.* ed *To ordain, frame, devise*; concinnāre:—Tunge ðīn gealchatte oððe gereónode fācnu *lingua tua concinnābat dŏlos*, Ps. Lamb. 49, 19.

geald *possibly, perhaps*; forte, forsĭtan, Jos. 9, 8. v. weald; *adv.*

geald *paid*, Beo. Th. 2099; B. 1047; *p. of* gildan.

gealdor, es; *n. An incantation, a charm, lore*; incantātio:—Be ðam gealdre *through that lore*, Exon. 83 a; Th. 313, 26; Mōd. 6. Sing ðis gealdor *sing this charm*, L. M. 3, 63; Lchdm. ii. 350, 28: 3, 24; Lchdm. ii. 322, 6. v. galdor.

gealdor-cræft, es; *m. The art of enchanting, incantation*; incantātio:—On ǽniges cynnes gealdorcræftum *per alĭcūjus gĕnĕris incantātiōnes*, L. Ecg. P. iv. 18; Th. ii. 208, 32. v. galdor-cræft.

gealdor-cræftiga, an; *m. One crafty* or *skilful in enchantments, an enchanter*; in arte incantandi perītus, incantātor:—Ða fǽmnan, ðe gewuniaþ onfōn gealdorcræftigan ne lǽt ðū ða libban *the women, who are wont to receive enchanters, suffer thou them not to live*, L. Alf. 30; Th. i. 52, 9. v. galdor-cræftiga.

gealewe *yellow*; flāvus, Som. Ben. Lye. v. geolo.

gealga, an; *m. A gallows, gibbet, cross*; patĭbŭlum, crux:—Fracoðes gealga *a malefactor's gibbet*, Rood Kmbl. 20; Kr. 10. Ðone ōðerne he hēt hōn on gealgan *altĕrum suspendit in crŭcem*, Gen. 40, 22: Deut. 21, 22: Past. 3, 1; Swt. 33, 20; Hat. MS. 8 b, 7: Apstls. Kmbl. 44; Ap. 22: Rood Kmbl. 80; Kr. 40. v. galga.

ge-algian, -ealgian; *p.* ode; *pp.* od *To protect, defend*; tuēri, defendĕre:—Hēr stynt eorl, ðe wile gealgian ēðel ðysne *here stands an earl, who will defend this land*, Byrht. Th. 133, 18; By. 52. Ðæt hī, æt campe, wið lāþra gehwæne, land gealgodon *that they, in conflict, should defend the land against every foe*, Chr. 937; Th. 203, 4, col. 2; Æðelst. 9. v. ealgian.

gealg-mōd, galg-mōd, gealh-mōd; *adj.* [gealg = gealh *sād*; mōd *mind*] *Sad in mind, gloomy, furious*; tristis anĭmo, furiōsus:—Gealgmōd guma *the furious man*, Exon. 73 b; Th. 274, 10; Jul. 531: 74 b; Th. 278, 15; Jul. 598. Hie eágena gesihþ aguton gealgmōde gāra ordum *they, furious, thrust out the eyesight with javelins' points*, Andr. Kmbl. 63; An. 32: 1125; An. 563.

gealg-treów, es; *n. A gallows-tree, cross*; crux:—Dryhten þrōwode on ðam gealgtreówe for guman synnum *the Lord suffered on the cross for the sins of man*, Rood Kmbl. 289; Kr. 146. v. galg-treów.

gealh; *adj. Sad, angry*; tristis:—Unrōt *vel* gealh *tristis*, Ælfc. Gl. 88; Som. 74, 88; Wrt. Voc. 51, 1. Se ðe biþ ungeðyldig, and mid gealgum mōde ceoraþ ongēan Gode *he who is impatient and passionately murmurs against God*, Homl. Th. i. 472, 8.

gealh-mōd; *adj. Sad in mind, gloomy*; tristis anĭmo:—Grim and gealhmōd *grim and gloomy*, Cd. 184; Th. 230, 8; Dan. 230. v. gealg-mōd.

gealh-swile *a swelling of the jowl*, L. M. 1, 4; Lchdm. ii. 44, 8. v. geagl-swile.

GEALLA, ealla, an; *m.* I. GALL, *bile;* fel, bīlis:—Gealla *fel* vel *bīlis*, Ælfc. Gl. 76; Som. 71, 111; Wrt. Voc. 45, 17. Ðe cymeþ of togotennysse ðæs geallan *which cometh of effusion of the gall*, Herb. 141, 2; Lchdm. i. 262, 12, MS. O: 146, 2; Lchdm. i. 270, 4, MS. H. Hig sealdon hym wīn drincan mid geallan gemenged *dĕdĕrunt ei vīnum bĭbĕre cum felle mistum*, Mt. Bos. 27, 34: Exon. 29 a; Th. 88, 13; Cri. 1439. Wiđ seóndum geallan *for straining out bile*, L. M. 3, 11; Lchdm. ii. 314, 7. II. *a gall, fretted place on the skin;* intertrīgo:—Wiđ horses geallan *for a horse's gall*, L. M. 1, 88; Lchdm. ii. 156, 21. Lācna đone geallan mid *cure the gall therewith*, 1, 88; Lchdm. ii. 156, 21. [*Orm.* galle: *O. Sax.* galla, *f: Dut.* gal, *f: Ger. M. H. Ger.* galle, *f: O. H. Ger.* galla, *f: Dan.* galde, *m. f: Swed.* galle, *m: Icel.* gall, *n: Lat.* fel, *n: Grk.* χολή, *f;* χόλος, *m.*]

gealled; *part. Galled, fretted;* intertrīgĭnōsus:—Gif hors geallede sīe *if a horse be galled*, L. M. 1, 88; Lchdm. ii. 156, 18.

geallig; *adj. Acris, tristis*, Hpt. Gl. 456.

gealp *boasted*, Beo. Th. 5160; B. 2583; *p. of* gilpan.

ge-an ic, he *I give, he gives*, Th. Diplm. 560, 24; *1st and 3rd pres. of* ge-unnan.

geán; *prep. Against, over against, on the opposite side;* contra:—Mōnaþ is đonne se mōna gecyrþ niwe fram đære sunnan, ōþ-đæt he eft cume hyre fōrne geán *a month is when the moon returns new from the sun, until it [the moon] again comes opposite it [the sun]*, Bd. de nat. rerum; Wrt. popl. science 8, 13; Lchdm. iii. 248, 17, note 30. On đæm clife on đæm is geán bearwum *on the cliff which is over against the woods*, Blickl. Homl. 209, 35. [*Orm.* ȝæn.] v. on-geán.

geána; *adv. Yet, still;* adhuc:—Get geána *adhuc*, Mt. Kmbl. Lind. 15, 16. v. gén.

ge-anbīdian; *part.* -anbīdiende, -anbīdigende; *p.* ode; *pp.* od [anbīdian *to abide*] *To abide, await, wait for, expect;* expectāre, sustĭnēre:—Ðes man wæs ōþ Israhēla frōfor geanbīdiende *hŏmo iste expectans consōlātiōnem Israel*, Lk. Bos. 2, 25. Ðæt folc wæs Zachariam geanbīdigende *ĕrat plebs expectans Zachariam*, 1, 21. Hī þrȳ dagas me geanbīdiaþ *jam trīduo sustĭnent me*, Mk. Bos. 8, 2. Geanbīda Drihten, werlīce dō đū, and sȳ gestrangod heorte đīn, and geanbīda Drihten *expecta Dŏmĭnum, virīlĭter āge, et confortētur cor tuum, et sustĭne Dŏmĭnum*, Ps. Spl. 26, 20.

ge-anbyrdan, ge-onbyrdan; *p.* de; *pp.* ed *To strive against, resist;* repugnāre, resistĕre:—Gif he gewyrce đæt man hine afylle þurh đæt đe he ongeán riht geanbyrde *if he act so that he be killed because he strove against right*, L. C. S. 49; Th. i. 404, 13. v. anbyrdnys.

ge-ancsumian; *p.* ode; *pp.* od *To make anxious, vex;* anxiāre:—Wæs geancsumod mīn heorte *anxiārētur cor meum*, Ps. Lamb. 60, 3. v. ge-angsumian.

geán-cyme, es; *m. A coming against, meeting;* occursus:—Ðæt đū yfele geáncymas ne ondrǣde *ut occursus mălos ne formīdes*, Herb. 111, 3; Lchdm. i. 224, 19.

geán-cyr, -cyrr, es; *m. A turning against, coming against, meeting;* occursus:—Fram heán heofone is ūtgang his, and geáncyr his ōþ to heáhnesse his *a summo cœlo est egressio ejus, et occursus ejus usque ad summum ejus*, Ps. Spl. 18, 7.

ge-āndagian; *p.* ode; *pp.* od; *v. a. To appoint a day* or *term;* diem dīcĕre:—Ðæt he him geándagode of đam folclande *that he should give him a term respecting the folk-land*, L. Ed. 2; Th. i. 160, 12. v. āndagian.

ge-andettan, -ondettan; *p.* te; *pp.* ed *To confess;* confĭtēri:—Se seóca sceal geandettan đam sacerde *the sick must confess to the priest*, L. Ælf. C. 32; Th. ii. 354, 28: L. Alf. pol. 14; Th. i. 70, 15, note 38. Gif he hine geandette *if he confess himself*, L. Alf. pol. 5; Th. i. 64, 22: L. In. 71; Th. i. 148, 3, note 4. v. andettan.

ge-andswarian; *p.* ode; *pp.* od *To answer;* respondēre:—Ðā ne geandswarode he hyre *qui non respondit ei verbum*, Mt. Bos. 15, 23. v. and-swarian.

ge-andwerdian; *p.* ode; *pp.* od [andweard *present*] *To present, bring before one;* præsentāre:—Ða hēt he đone biscop mid his preōstum samod geandwerdian *then commanded he to bring the bishop together with his priests before [him]*, Homl. Th. i. 416, 4. Geandweardod beōn *præsentātus esse, præsentāri*, R. Ben. 7. Giondweardad *præsentātus*, Rtl. 4, 28.

ge-andwyrdan, -andwerdan; *p.* -andwyrde; *pp.* -andwyrded, -andwyrd *To answer;* respondēre:—Ne mihton hig agēn đis him geandwyrdan *non pŏtĕrant ad hæc respondēre illi*, Lk. Bos. 14, 6: Bt. 41, 2; Fox. 244, 23. Geandwyrde [geandwerde MS. G.] he đam ōđrum swā hundrēde riht þence *let him answer to the other as shall seem right to the hundred*, L. C. S. 27; Th. i. 392, 6. Him wæs geandwyrd đus *he was answered thus*, Gen. 19, 21.

ge-āned; *part.* [ān *one*] *Made one, united;* adūnātus:—Oþ-đæt đe hī wǣron on ǣnne unmǣtne lēg geānede *usque ad in immensam adūnāti sunt flammam*, Bd. 3, 19; S. 548, 21. [Cf. *Ger.* vereint: *O. H. Ger.* gaeinōn *adunare.*]

geán-fær, es; *n. A going again, returning, return;* rĕdĭtus:—Him wiđcwæþ se cyng ǣlces geánfæres [MS. geánfares] to Engla lande *the king prohibited him from all return to England*, Chr. 1119; Erl. 247, 34.

ge-angsumian, -ancsumian, -anxsumian; *p.* ode; *pp.* od *To vex, make anxious* or *uneasy;* angĕre, anxiāre:—Ic geangsumige *ango*, Ælfc. Gr. 28, 5; Som. 31, 56.

geán-hweorfan; *p.* -hwearf, *pl.* -hwurfon; *pp.* -hworfen *To turn again, return;* rĕdīre, Hpt. Gl. 409; Leo A. Sax. Gl. 229, 21.

geán-hworfennis, se; *f. A return;* obvia quæque, ad propria limina reversio, Hpt. Gl. 470.

geán-hwyrft *a turning again.* v. gǣn-hwyrft.

ge-ānlǣcan; *p.* -lǣhte; *pp.* -lǣht *To make one, join, unite;* unāre, unīre:—Ic geānlǣce [MS. -lace] *ūno, ūnio*, Ælfc. Gr. 37; Som. 39, 29. Þurh đæs Hālgan Gāstes tocyme wurdon ealle gereord geānlǣhte *through the advent of the Holy Ghost all languages became united*, Homl. Th. i. 318, 24. Geānlǣcan *adsciscere, miscere*, Hpt. Gl. 504.

ge-anlīcian; *p.* ode; *pp.* od [līc *like*] *To make like, liken;* assĭmĭlāre:—For hwam geanlīcie we heofena rīce *cui assĭmĭlābĭmus regnum Dei?* Mk. Bos. 4, 30.

ge-anmētan; *p.* -anmētte; *pp.* -anmēted, -anmētt *To encourage;* anĭmāre:—He him to fultume com, and hine swīđe geanmētte *he came to his help and greatly encouraged him*, Ors. 3, 10; Bos. 70, 45. Wæs Demetrias swīđe þearle geanmētt *Demetrius was very greatly encouraged*, 3, 11; Bos. 75, 25.

geánnis, se; *f. A meeting;* obviam itio, Hpt. Gl. 513.

geán-ryne, gǣn-ryne, es; *m. A running against, meeting;* occursus:—Arīs on geánryne mīnne *exurge in occursum meum*, Ps. Spl. 58, 5.

geán-þingian; *p.* ode, ade; *pp.* od, ad [þingian *to address, speak*] *To speak again, answer, reply;* respondēre:—Him brego engla geánþingade *the Lord of angels replied to him*, Cd. 48; Th. 62, 5; Gen. 1009.

geánunga; *adv. Directly:*—Geánunga foron đa sunnan *directly before the sun*, Bd. de nat. rerum; Wrt. popl. science 5, 29; Lchdm. iii. 242, 12, note. v. gegnunga.

ge-anwyrde; *adj. Known, manifest, confessed;* professus:—Ic eom geanwyrde monuc *professus sum monachus*, Coll. Monast. Th. 18, 23. He đæs geanwyrde wæs ætfōran eallum đām mannum *he confessed it before all the men*, Chr. 1055; Erl. 189, 5. v. note where the Latin is given, ipse ante cognovit ita esse.

ge-anxsumian; *p.* ode, ade; *pp.* od, ad *To make anxious, vex;* anxiāre:—Geanxsumad is ofer me gāst mīn *anxiātus est sŭper me spĭrĭtus meus*, Ps. Lamb. 142, 4. v. ge-angsumian.

geap, gæp; *comp. m.* geappra, *f. n.* geappre; *adj.* I. *crooked, bent, curved;* curvus, pandus:—Geap *curvus*, Cot. 50. Geap stæf *a crooked letter*, Salm. Kmbl. 250; Sal. 124: 269; Sal. 134. Geapum, gebīgedum *pando*, Mone B. 90. II. *not straightforward, deceitful, crafty, cunning, shrewd, astute;* fallax, callĭdus, astūtus:—Geap *callĭdus*, Wrt. Voc. 49, 11. Seó næddre wæs geappre đonne ealle đa ōđre nȳtenu *serpens ĕrat callĭdior cunctis animantĭbus terræ*, Gen. 3, 1. Cild geap *an astute child*, Obs. Lun. § 2; Lchdm. iii. 184, 14: § 9; Lchdm. iii. 188, 11. DER. hinder-geap. Grein writes geáp, in support of which may be noticed ȝæp in the Ormulum. Layamon also has the word, and it occurs in Piers P.

geáp *took*, Exon. 106 b; Th. 405, 29; Rä. 24, 9; *p. of* geópan.

GEÁP; *adj. Open, spread out, extended, broad, roomy, spacious, wide;* pătens, pătŭlus, amplus, lātus:—Gim sceal on hringe standan, steáp and geáp *a gem shall stand in a ring, prominent and broad*, Menol. Fox 505; Gn. C. 23. Steáp and geáp *high and wide*, Salm. Kmbl. 827; Sal. 413. Reced hlīfade, geáp and goldfāh *the mansion towered, spacious and golden-hued*, Beo. Th. 3604; B. 1800. Munt is hine ymbūtan, geáp gylden weal *a mountain is about him, a lofty golden wall*, Salm. Kmbl. 511; Sal. 256. Sum sceal on geápum galgan rīdan *one shall ride on the extended gallows*, Exon. 87 b; Th. 239, 12; Vy. 33. Under geápne hrōf *under the spacious roof*, Beo. Th. 1677; B. 836. [Cf. *Icel.* gaupn *both hands held together* in the form of a bowl; geypna *to encompass.*] DER. horn-geáp, sǣ-.

geáp, geápu, e; *f.* [geáp *roomy, spacious*] *Expanse, room;* latĭtūdo, spătium:—Ðās hofu dreórgiaþ, and đæs teáfor geápu *these courts are dreary, and its purple expanse* [?], Exon. 124 a; Th. 477, 27; Ruin. 31.

geápan, geapian; *p.* te, ode; *pp.* ed, od *To* GAPE, *open;* pandĕre, Cot. 158.

geápes; *adv.* [*gen. of* geáp *broad, spacious, roomy*] *In width, wide;* lāte:—Strūdende fȳr, steápes and geápes, forswealh eall eador *the ravaging fire swallowed all together, high and wide*, Cd. 119; Th. 154, 16; Gen. 2556. So Bouterwek takes it, but the word is rather a neuter genitive after 'eall;' cf. vv. 2548–9.

geaplīc; *adj. Crafty, cunning, deceitful;* subdŏlus, callĭdus:—Hī mid geaplīcre fare ferdon to Iosue *they went to Joshua with deceitful expedition*, Jos. 9, 6.

geaplīce; *adv. Deceitfully, boldly;* subdŏle, procācĭter, Prov. 21.

geap-neb; *adj.* [geap *crooked;* neb *the head, face, beak, nib*] *Crooked-*

nibbed, with a bent beak, arched; curvātus:—Standeþ me hēr on eaxelum Ælfheres lāf, gôd and geapneb *Ælfhere's legacy stands here on my shoulders, good and crooked-nibbed*, Wald. 94; Vald. 2, 19.

geap-scipe, es; *m. Craft, cunning, deceit, fraud;* astūtia, fraus:—Eall heora geapscipe wearþ ameldod Israhēla bearnum *all their deceit was made known to the children of Israel*, Jos. 9, 16. Þurh his geapscipe he begeat đone castel *through his cunning he obtained the castle*, Chr. 1090; Erl. 226, 25.

geápung, e; *f. A heaping, heap, pile;* cŭmŭlus:—Fôþ him on, and on geápunga eówre niđerunge gelǣdaþ *acc˘pĭte, et in cŭmŭlum damnātiōnis vestræ dūcĭte*, Bd. 5, 13; S. 633, 14, note 13, MS. B. v. heápung.

gear, *pl.* gurron *sounded, creaked; p. of* georran.

GEÁR, gēr, gǣr, es; *n. A* YEAR; annus:—Ōđer com geár *another year came*, Beo. Th. 2272; B. 1134. Đis wæs feorþes geáres his rīces *this was in the fourth year of his reign*, Chr. 47; Th. 10, 13, col. 1. On geáre *in the year*, Menol. Fox 218; Men. 110. Đrīwa on gére *thrice a year*, Thw. Exod. 23, 17. Hæfde me ēce geár ealle on mōde *annos æternos in mente hăbui*, Ps. Th. 76, 5: Lk. Bos. 2, 36. Þreó and þritig geára *three and thirty years*, Cd. 224; Th. 296, 16; Sat. 503. Geárum frōd *old in years*, 109; Th. 143, 19; Gen. 2381. Men hâtaþ đysne dæg geáres dæg, swylce đes dæg fyrmest sȳ on geáres ymbryne *men call this day [new] year's day, as if this day were the first in the year's circuit*, Homl. Th. i. 98, 16. [*Wyc.* ȝeer, ȝer, ȝeers, ȝerys *years: Piers P.* yere: *Chauc.* yer, yere: *R. Brun.* ȝere: *Laym. Orm.* ȝer: *Plat.* jaar, jar, *n: O. Sax.* gēr, jār, *n: Frs.* jier: *O. Frs.* ier, iar, ger, *n: Dut.* jaar, *n: Ger.* jahr, jar, *n: M. H. Ger.* jār, *n: O. H. Ger.* jār, *n: Goth.* yér, *n: Dan.* aar, *n: Swed.* år, *n: Icel.* ár, *n: Bohem.* gar, *m. f. spring: Zend.* yāre, *n. year.*] DER. freóls-geár, fyrn-. v. Grm. D. M. p. 715.

geara; *adv.* [gearo? *ready*] *Utterly, altogether, well, enough, very much;* pĕnĭtus, prorsus, bĕne, sătis, valde:—He hēt geara forbærnan Rōmāna burig *he [Nero] commanded utterly to burn up the city of the Romans*, Bt. Met. Fox 9, 18; Met. 9, 9. Đū geara canst *tu bĕne nosti*, Bd. 1, 27; S. 439, 2: Ps. Th. 75, 1: 81, 5. Đonne mon me geofe geara þūsende goldes and seolfres *sŭper millia auri et argenti*, 118, 72.

geara; *gen. pl. of* geare, q. v. *furniture, gear for horses.*

geára; *adv.* [*gen. pl. of* geár *a year*] YORE, *formerly, of old, long since, once;* ōlim, antīquĭtus, quondam:—Se geára hider fram đam eádigan Gregorie sended wæs *qui olim huc a beato Gregorio directus fuit*, Bd. 2, 3; S. 504, 44. Ic þeódenmādmas geára forgeáfe *I princely treasures gave of old*, Cd. 22; Th. 26, 21; Gen. 410. Đū on geóguþfeore geára gecwǣde *thou in youthful life long since didst say*, Beo. Th. 5322; B. 2664: Ps. Th. 73, 12: 80, 10: 104, 6: 118, 152. Geára iū, Exon. 76 b; Th. 287, 30; Wand. 22: 84 a; Th. 316, 31; Mōd. 57: Bt. Met. Fox 1, 1; Met. 1, 1. [*Laym.* ȝære, ȝare: *Chauc.* yore.] DER. ǣr-geára, fyrn-, geó-, iū-, un-.

gearcian, gærcian; *p.* ode; *pp.* od [gearo *ready*] *To prepare, make ready, procure, furnish, supply;* părāre, præpărāre, appărāre, exhĭbēre, præbēre:—Ic gearcige *exhĭbeo, præbeo*, Ælfc. Gr. 26, 2; Som. 28, 35, 36: 47; Som. 48, 43. On lāfum đīnum đū gearcast [MS. gearcost] andwlitan heora *in relĭquiis tuis præpărābis vultum eōrum*, Ps. Spl. 20, 12. On him gearcode fæt deáþes *in eo părāvit vāsa mortis*, 7, 14: Gen. 19, 3. [*Piers P.* yarken *to make ready: R. Glouc.* yarkede, *p. prepared: Laym.* ȝarkien, ȝarekien, ȝeorkien *to get ready: Orm.* ȝarrkenn *to prepare, make ready.*] DER. ge-gearcian.

gearcung, e; *f. A preparation, preparing;* præpărātio, appărātus:—Gearcunge heortan heora gehȳrde eáre đīn *præpărātiōnem cordis eōrum audīvit auris tua*, Ps. Spl. second 9, 20: 32, 14. Gearcung *appărātus*, Ælfc. Gl. 87; Som. 74, 44; Wrt. Voc. 50, 26. [*Orm.* ȝarrking.]

gearcung-dæg, es; *m. A preparation-day, day before the Sabbath;* præpărātionis dies, parascēve = παρασκευή, dies azȳmōrum:—On đam forman gearcungdæge *prīma die azymōrum*, Mt. Bos. 26, 17.

geár-cyning, es; *m. A year-king, consul;* consul, Cot. 48. v. consul.

geár-cyningdōm, es; *m. A year-kingdom, a consulate;* consŭlātus, Som. Ben. Lye.

GEARD, es; *m. An inclosure, inclosed place,* YARD, GARDEN, *court, dwelling, home, region, land;* septum, lŏcus septus, hortus, ārea, habĭtācŭlum, domĭcĭlium, rēgio:—Se Godes cwide is weorþmynda geard *the word of God is the garden of worship*, Salm. Kmbl. 168; Sal. 83. On gearde deáþes sceade *in rēgiōne umbræ mortis*, Mt. Bos. 4, 16. Đæt ǣlc cōme to his āgenum gearde *that each should come to his own land*, Ors. 5, 14; Bos. 114, 18. On geard *at home*, Menol. Fox 215; Men. 109. In ēcne geard *into the eternal home*, Exon. 44 a; Th. 149, 17; Gū. 763: 51 a; Th. 178, 8; Gū. 1241. Geard ymbtynde *sepem circumdedit*, Mt. Kmbl. Rush. 21, 33. Brāde synd on woruld grēne geardas *in the world are broad green regions*, Cd. 25; Th. 32, 30; Gen. 511. Ǣr he on weg hwurfe of geardum *ere he went away from his courts*, Beo. Th. 535; B. 265: Exon. 64 a; Th. 236, 23; Ph. 578. In geardum *at home*, Exon. 10 b; Th. 13, 11; Cri. 201: 50 b; Th. 175, 13; Gū. 1194: 61 a; Th. 223, 5; Ph. 355: Beo. Th. 25; B. 13. Wit forlēton on heofonrīce gōdlīce geardas *we two have lost in the heavenly kingdom goodly courts*, Cd. 35; Th. 46, 6; Gen. 740: Beo. Th. 2272; B. 1134. On Fæder geardas *in the dwellings of the Father*, Salm. Kmbl. 832; Sal. 415: Exon. 105 b; Th. 401, 7; Rä. 21, 8. [*Wyc.* ȝerd *a field, garden: Piers P.* yerd *habitation: Chauc.* yerde: *O. Sax.* gard, *m: O. Frs.* garda, *m: Dut. Kil.* gærde, gærd *hortus: Ger.* garten, *m: M. H. Ger.* garte, *m: O. H. Ger.* garto, gart, *m. hortus, dŏmus: Goth.* gards, *m. house: Dan.* gaard, *m. f: Swed.* gård, *m: Icel.* garðr, *m: Lat.* hortus, *m: Grk.* χόρτος, *m. an inclosed place, feeding-place: Slav.* grad, gorod *a fence.*] DER. eador-geard, eard-, fæder-, friþ-, leód-, middan-, ort-, wīn-, wyrm-, wyrt-.

geard, e; *f. A staff, rod, stake, fagot;* băcŭlum, virga, pālus, fascis:—He scolde gifan [MS. gife] sex fōđur gearda *he should give six loads of fagots*, Chr. 852; Erl. 67, 38. DER. cyne-geard. v. gyrd.

geár-dagas; *pl. m.* [geár, dæg] YORE-DAYS, *days of yore, days of years, time of life;* dies antīqui, annōrum dies:—In [on] geardagum *in days of yore*, Exon. 11 b; Th. 16, 11; Cri. 251: 77 a; Th. 289, 6; Wand. 44: Cd. 21; Th. 287, 16; Sat. 368: Beo. Th. 2; B. 1: 2712; B. 1354: 4458; B. 2233. In geárdagan, Menol. Fox 231; Men. 117. Ūre geárdagas *dies annōrum nostrōrum*, Ps. Th. 89, 10. Scyle gumena gehwylc on his geárdagum georne biþencan *every man should in the days of his years well consider*, Exon. 19 b; Th. 51, 26; Cri. 822: 61 a; Th. 225, 4; Ph. 384: Elen. Grm. 1267: L. Eth. vii. 24; Th. i. 334, 21. [*Icel.* í árdaga *in days of yore*. Cf. Gen. 47, 9, 'The days of the years of my pilgrimage are an hundred and thirty years.']

geár-dagum; *adv.* [*dat. pl. of* geárdæg, *nom. pl.* -dagas] *In days of yore, formerly;* ōlim, antīquĭtus:—Hie gesetton đā Sennar geárdagum *then they occupied Shinar in days of old*, Cd. 80; Th. 99, 36; Gen. 1657: Exon. 16 a; Th. 35, 17; Cri. 559: Andr. Kmbl. 3036; An. 1521: Elen. Grm. 291: 834.

geardlīc; *adj. Worldly, mundane;* mundiālis, mundānus, Som. Ben. Lye.

geare; *pl. f. Furniture,* GEAR *for horses;* appărātus:—Geara feng *the grasp of the gear, the bit;* harpax *vel* lŭpus, Ælfc. Gl. 3; Som. 55, 69; Wrt. Voc. 16, 42: 105; Som. 78, 32; Wrt. Voc. 57, 14. v. gearwe; *pl. f.*

geare, gearwe, gearuwe, gearewe, gere; *adv.* [gearo? *ready*] *Entirely, clearly, certainly, well, very well, enough;* pĕnĭtus, prorsus, plāne, certe, bĕne, valde, optĭme, sătis:—Ic wāt geare *I well know*, Beo. Th. 5306; B. 2656: Bt. Met. Fox 20, 188; Met. 20, 94. Ic cann swā geare *I so well know*, Cd. 27; Th. 37, 1; Gen. 583. Nū gē geare cunnon *now ye well know*, Exon. 16 a; Th. 36, 9; Cri. 573. Hī wiston geare *certi sunt*, Lk. Bos. 20, 6. Swīđe geare, Ps. Th. 101, 5. Gearor, *comp.* Ors. 5, 14; Bos. 114, 11. [*O. Sax.* garo *quite, entirely: O. H. Ger.* garo, garawo *penitus, prorsus: Ger.* gar: *Icel.* görva, gerva *quite.*]

geáre; *adv. Formerly, of old;* ōlim:—Geáre ic đæt ongeat *jam ōlim intellexĕram*, Bd. 2, 13; S. 516, 29. DER. geó-geáre. v. geára; *adv.*

gearewe; *adv. Entirely, well, very well;* pĕnĭtus, prorsus, bĕne, optĭme, Ps. Th. 55, 4, 11: 68, 3: 118, 118. v. geare; *adv.*

gearewe, an; *f. Yarrow;* millefŏlium, Glos. Brux. Recd. 41, 45; Wrt. Voc. 67, 60. [*O. Sax.* gare: *O. H. Ger.* garawa *millefolium: Ger.* schaf-garbe *common yarrow;* ȝarow, Wrt. Voc.] v. gearwe.

ge-arfoþ, es; *n. Trouble;* molestia:—He sceal geþolian manige gearfođu *he shall suffer many troubles*, Bt. 31, 1; Fox 110, 26. DER. earfoþ, es; *n.*

ge-arfođe; *adj. Difficult;* diffĭcĭlis, molestus:—Hū gearfođe đis is to gereccanne! *how difficult this is to explain!* Bt. 39, 4; Fox 216, 33. DER. earfeđe; *adj.*

geár-gemearc, es; *n. A year's limit* or *space;* anni defīnītio *vel* spătium:—Siđđan ic ongon on đone ānseld būgan geárgemearces *after I had dwelt in the hermitage for a year's space*, Exon. 50 b; Th. 176, 24; Gū. 1215.

geár-geriht, es; *n. A yearly due;* annuum dēbĭtum:—Gif preóst geárgerihta unmynegode lǣte, gebēte đæt *if a priest let the yearly dues pass unreminded, let him make amends for it*, L. N. P. L. 43; Th. ii. 296, 15.

geár-gerīm, es; *n. A year-number, number of years, numbering by years;* annōrum nŭmĕrus:—Ymb þritig geárgerīmes *after thirty, numbering by years*, i. e. *after thirty years*, Bt. Met. Fox 28, 59; Met. 28, 30. v. geár-rīm.

geár-getal *a tale of years, number of years.* [Cf. *O. Sax.* gér-tal: *O. H. Ger.* jár-zala *a full year.*] v. gǣr-getal.

ge-ārian; *p.* ode; *pp.* od; *v. trans. with the dat.* I. [ār I. *honour*] *To give honour, to honour;* honōrāre, honorĭfĭcāre:—Onsegdnis lofes geāraþ mec *sacrĭfĭcium laudis honorĭfĭcābit me*, Ps. Surt. 49, 23. Hȳ beóþ geārode and uppahefene *honōrāti et exaltāti fuĕrint*, Ps. Th. 36, 19. II. [ār. II. *kindness, favour, mercy*] *To have mercy* or *compassion upon any one, be merciful to, pity, pardon;* propĭtium esse, misĕrēri, parcĕre:—Þolige he landes and līfes, būton him se cyning geārian wylle *let him forfeit land and life, unless the king will be merciful to him*, L. C. E. 2; Th. i. 358, 21: L. C. L. 60; Th. i. 408, 15: L. Eth. vii. 16; Th. i. 332, 18. Geāra me, ēce Waldend! *have compassion upon me, eternal Ruler!* Hy. 1, 2; Hy. Grn. ii. 280, 2. Đæt se Dēma us geārige *that the Judge may have compassion on us*, Homl. Th. ii. 126, 13. Wæs Abrahame leófre đæt he Godes hǣse gefylde, đonne he his leófan bearne geãrode *it was dearer to Abraham to fulfil God's command, than to have compassion on his beloved son*, Boutr. Scrd. 23, 5: Ps. Th. arg. 34. III. [ãr III. *property*] *To endow*:—Ðurh ðone tocyme we wǣron geweorðode and gewelgade and geãrode *through that advent we were honoured and enriched and endowed*, Blickl. Homl. 105, 24.

geárlíc; *adj. Yearly, annual*; annuus:—Ðes geárlîca ymryne *this yearly course*, Homl. Th. ii. 98, 23. Ge ðæs libbendes yrfes, ge ðæs geárlîces westmes *both of live stock and of yearly fruit*, L. Ath. i. prm; Th. i. 194, 17. Geárlîcne tîman *annuum tempus*, Hymn. Surt. 106, 33. Geárlîc wuldor *annuam glōriam*, 79, 34. Geárlîce tîda gesette wǣron *the yearly seasons were fixed*, Bd. de nat. rerum; Wrt. popl. science 7, 25; Lchdm. iii. 246, 23.

geárlîce; *adv. Yearly, from year to year*; annuātim, Cot.

geár-mǣlum; *adv.* [mǣlum, *dat. pl. of* mǣl, es; *n.*] *Yearly*; quotannis:—Rîce geármǣlum weóx *the kingdom increased year by year*, Bt. Met. Fox 1, 10; Met. 1, 5.

GEARN, gern; es; *n.* YARN, *spun wool*; pensum, lāna nēta:—Gearn *pensum, stāmen, lāna*, Cot. 85. Unwunden gearn *unwound yarn, a ball or clew of yarn*; glŏmus, Ælfc. Gl. 111; Som. 79. 67; Wrt. Voc. 59, 36. [*Dut.* garen, *n. thread, yarn*: *Ger. M.H.Ger. O.H.Ger.* garn, *n. fīlamen*: *Dan. Swed.* garn, *n*: *Icel.* garn, *n.*] DER. nett-gern.

gearnfull; *adj. Anxious*; sollĭcĭtus:—Gearnfulle *sollĭcĭti*, Lk. Skt. Lind. 12, 11. Gearnfull *austerus*, 19, 22. v. geornful.

ge-arnian; *p.* ode; *pp.* od [earnian *to earn*] *To earn, merit*; mĕrēri:—Sceal mon lofes [MS. leofes] gearnian *a man shall merit praise*, Exon. 91 a; Th. 342, 9; Gn. Ex. 140. v. ge-earnian.

ge-arnung, e; *f.* [earnung *an earning*] *Merit, reward*; mĕrĭtum:—Nǣnig efenlîc ðam, ǣr ne siððan, in worlde gewearþ, wîfes gearnung *no woman's reward in the world was equal to that, before nor after*, Exon. 8 b; Th. 3, 23; Cri. 40. v. ge-earnung.

gearn-winde, gern-winde, es; *m?* [windan *to wind*] *A yarn-winder, reel*; rhombus = ῥόμβος:—Gearn-winde *conductum*, Wrt. Voc. 66, 19.

GEARO, gearu; *gen. m. n.* -wes, -owes; *f.* -re, -rwe; *def.* se gearwa; *adj.* YARE, *ready, prepared, equipped, complete*; promptus, părātus, instructus, perfectus:—Gearo wyrde on gespræce *factus est lŏquēla promptus*, Bd. 5, 2; S. 615, 29. Gearo is mîn heorte *părātum est cor meum*, Ps. Th. 56, 9. Gearo ic eom *părātus sum*, 118, 60: Ps. Spl. 16, 13: 107, 1. Wes tû gearo *părātus esto*, Bd. 5, 19; S. 640, 44. He wæs gearo gûþe *he was ready for war*, Andr. Kmbl. 467; An. 234. Ic beó gearo sôna *I shall be ready at once*, Beo. Th. 3655; B. 1825: 6202; B. 3106. Ðâ wæs gearo gyrnwræce Grendeles môdor *then was Grendel's mother ready with vengeance for wrongs*, 4242; B. 2118. Swâ gearwe swâ seó leó *sicut leo părātus*, Ps. Th. 16, 11. Óþ-ðæt he Adam gearone funde *until he found Adam ready*, Cd. 23; Th. 29, 25; Gen. 455: Bt. Met. Fox 7, 67; Met. 7, 34. Gearwe, *acc. s. f.* Beo. Th. 2017; B. 1006: Exon. 45 b; Th. 155, 17; Gû. 861. Ðæt hŷ grim helle fŷr gearo to wite seóþ *that they shall see hell's grim fire ready for punishment*, 26 b; Th. 78, 7; Cri. 1270. Beornas gearwe on stefn stigon *the warriors ready* [or *equipped*] *stept on the prow*, Beo. Th. 428; B. 211: Ps. Th. 124, 5: 141, 4. Ealle þing synt gearwe *omnia sunt părāta*, Mt. Bos. 22, 4. Ða flotan stôdon gearowe wîcinga fela *the pirates stood ready, many Vikings*, Byrht. Th. 133, 59; By. 72: 134, 47; By. 100. Searwum gearwe *equipped with arms*, Beo. Th. 3631; B. 1813. Geseah Metod geofonhûsa mǣst gearo hlifigean *the Creator saw the greatest of sea-houses arise complete*, Cd. 66; Th. 79, 35; Gen. 1321. Geofum biþ gearora *with gifts is more prepared*, Exon. 128 b; Th. 493, 15; Rä. 81, 31. [*Chauc.* yare: *R. Glouc.* ȝare: *Laym.* ȝaru, ȝæru: *O. Sax.* garu: *Ger.* gar *ready*: *M.H.Ger.* gar, gare: *O.H.Ger.* garo, garaw.] DER. ânwîg-gearo, eal-, un-.

gearo, gearu; *adv. Promptly, readily, entirely, altogether*; prompte, omnīno, prorsus:—Ðæt ic goldǣht gearo sceáwige *that I may promptly behold the gold-treasure*, Beo. Th. 5490; B. 2748. Gê ða fægran gesceaft gearo forsêgon *ye utterly despised the fair creation*, Exon. 41 b; Th. 139, 33; Gû. 602: 9 b; Th. 7, 31; Cri. 109. Se mec gearo [or geáro; see next word] on bende legde *he who altogether laid me in bonds*, 105 b; Th. 402, 14; Rä. 21, 29. v. geare; *adv.*

geáro; *adv. Of yore, formerly, of old*; ōlim:—Be ðam wealle, ðe geáro Rômâne Breotone eálond begyrdon *juxta mūrum, quo ōlim Rōmāni Brittaniam insŭlam præcinxēre*, Bd. 3, 22; S. 552, 30. v. geára.

gearo-brygd, e; *f.* [bregdan *to vibrate*] *A prompt vibration*; prompta pulsātio:—Âh he gleóbeámes gearobrygda list *he has skill in prompt vibrations of the harp*, Exon. 79 a; Th. 296, 13; Crä. 50.

gearod *clothed, endowed*, Bt. 14, 3; Fox 46, note 7, MS. Cott. = gearwod; *pp. of* gearwian.

gearo-folm; *adj.* [folm *a hand*] *Ready-handed*; promptus mănu:—He grâpode gearofolm *he ready-handed grasped* [*me*], Beo. Th. 4176; B. 2085.

gearo-gongende *going quickly* or *swiftly*. v. gearu-gongende.

gearolîce; *adv. Readily, clearly*; prompte, plāne:—Ic ðæt gearolîce ongiten hæbbe *I have clearly understood that*, Elen. Kmbl. 575; El. 288: Exon. 100 a; Th. 378, 2; Deór. 10. [*O. Sax.* garolîko: *O. H. Ger.* garalîhho.]

gearo-snotor, -snottor, gearu-snottor; *adj. Very wise*; valde săpiens:—Gidda gearosnotor *very wise in songs*, Elen. Kmbl. 835; El. 418. Giedda gearosnottor, Exon. 18 a; Th. 45, 2; Cri. 713.

gearo-þoncol; *adj. Very considerate* or *prudent*; valde consīdĕrātus vel provĭdus:—Hî ðæt idese ageáfon gearoþoncolre *they gave it to the very prudent woman*, Judth. 12; Thw. 26, 23; Jud. 342.

gearowe *prepared, ready*, Jud. 4, 13; *dat. s. f. of* gearo.

gearo-wita, an; *m. Intellect, understanding*; intelligentia, intellectus:—Ðeáh we fela smeán, we habbaþ litelne gearowitan bûton tweón *though we contemplate many things, we have little understanding free from doubt*, Bt. 41, 5; Fox 254, 10: 39, 8; Fox 224, 4.

gearo-wyrdig, gearu-wyrdig; *adj. Ready in words, speaking with ease* or *fluency, eloquent*; verbis promptus, fācundus:—Se wîtga song, gearowyrdig guma ðæt gyd awræc *the prophet sang, the eloquent man recited the lay*, Exon. 84 a; Th. 316, 19; Môd. 51.

geár-rîm, es; *n. A year-number, a year* [?], *number of years*; annōrum nŭmĕrus:—Seó tîd gegǣþ, geár-rîmum, ðæt ða geongan leomu geloden weorþaþ *the time passes, in a number of years* [or *by years*], *that the young limbs be grown*, Exon. 87 a; Th. 327, 17; Vy. 5. [Cf. *O. Sax.* gêr-tal *a year*.]

geár-þênung, e; *f. A yearly service, annual service*; annuum ministērium:—Gif preóst misendebirde ciriclîce geárþênunga, dæges oððe nihtes, gebête ðæt *if a priest misorder the annual services of the church, by day or by night, let him make amends for it*, L. N. P. L. 38; Th. ii. 296, 7.

geár-torht; *adj. Yearly bright, every year glorious*; quotannis splendĭdus:—Ðâ him wæstmas brohte, geártorhte gife, grêne folde *when the green earth should bring fruits to him, yearly-bright gifts*, Cd. 76; Th. 94, 13; Gen. 1561.

gearu; *adj. Yare, ready, prepared*; promptus, părātus, Beo. Th. 2223; B. 1109: Cd. 178; Th. 223, 32; Dan. 128: Ps. Th. 61, 2, 7: Andr. Kmbl. 2716; An. 1360: 3157; An. 1581: Jn. Bos. 7, 6: Ps. Th. 107, 1: Elen. Grm. 604. v. gearo; *adj.*

gearu-gongende; *part. Going quickly* or *swiftly*; expĕdīte incēdens:—Ic eom to ðon bleáþ, ðæt mec mæg gearugongende grîma abrêgan *I am so timid, that a phantom going swiftly may frighten me*, Exon. 110 b; Th. 423, 6; Rä. 41, 17.

gearu-snottor; *adj. Very wise*; valde săpiens:—Hie ǣnne betǣhton giddum gearusnottorne *they gave up one very skilled in songs*, Elen. Kmbl. 1168; El. 586. v. gearo-snotor.

gearuwe *prepared, ready*, Bd. 4, 2; S. 565, 34; *acc. pl. of* gearu. v. gearo; *adj.*

gearuwe, an; *f. Yarrow*; millefŏlium:—Seó reáde gearuwe *the red yarrow*, Lchdm. iii. 24, 2. v. gearwe.

gearuwe; *adv. Entirely, well, very well*; pĕnĭtus, prorsus, bĕne, optĭme, Ps. Th. 53, 2: 61; 11: 62, 1: 70, 1: 118, 21: 138, 11: 139, 12. v. geare; *adv.*

gearu-wyrdig; *adj. Ready in words, eloquent*; verbis promptus:—Sum biþ gearu-wyrdig *one is eloquent*, Exon. 78 b; Th. 295, 21; Crä. 36. v. gearo-wyrdig.

gearwa *prepared*; părātus; *nom. m. def. of* gearo; *adj.*

gearwe; *comp.* gearwor; *sup.* gearwost, gearwast; *adv. Entirely, well, very well, enough*; pĕnĭtus, prorsus, bĕne, optĭme, sătis, Cd. 52; Th. 67, 10; Gen. 1098: 107; Th. 141, 10; Gen. 2342: Beo. Th. 536; B. 265: Exon. 48 a; Th. 164, 28; Gû. 1018: Bd. 5, 6; S. 618, 30: Ps. Th. 142, 9. Gearwor, Andr. Kmbl. 1864; An. 934: Exon. 73 b; Th. 275, 27; Jul. 556: Beo. Th. 6141; B. 3074: Elen. Grm. 945. Gearwost, Beo. Th. 1435; B. 715. Gearwast, Elen. Grm. 329. v. geare.

gearwe *prepared*; părāta:—Ealle mîne þing synt gearwe *omnia părāta sunt*, Mt. Bos. 22, 4; *nom. pl. n. of* gearo; *adj.*

gearwe, an; *f. Clothing, attire*; vestītus, hăbĭtus:—Ic on his gearwan geseó ðæt he is ǣrendsecge uncres Hearran *I see by his attire that he is the messenger of our Lord*, Cd. 30; Th. 41, 16; Gen. 657. v. gearwe; *pl. f.*

gearwe; *pl. f. Clothing, attire*, GEAR, *adornment, arms, armour*; vestītus, hăbĭtus, arma:—Enoch cwic gewât mid Cyning engla of ðyssum lǣnan lîfe, on ðâm gearwum ðe his gâst onfêng, ǣr hine to monnum môdor brohte *Enoch alive departed with the King of angels from this frail life, in the vestment which his soul received, ere his mother brought him amongst men*, Cd. 60; Th. 73, 29; Gen. 1212: Menol. Fox 150; Men. 76. Óþ-ðæt hie on Gûþmyrce gearwe bǣron *till they bore their arms against the Æthiopians*, 145; Th. 181, 11; Exod. 59: 151; Th. 190, 3; Exod. 193. [*O. Sax.* garuwi, *f*: *O. H. Ger.* garawi, *f.*] DER. feðer-gearwe.

gearwe, gearuwe, gearewe, gæruwe, garuwe, an; *f.* YARROW; millefŏlium, achillæa millefŏlium, Lin:—Ðas wyrte man *millefŏlium* and on ûre geþeóde gearwe nemneþ *this plant is named* millefŏlium *and in our language yarrow*, Herb. 90, 1; Lchdm. i. 194, 6: Wrt. Voc. 79, 23. Wylle gearwan on buteran *boil yarrow in butter*, L. M. 1, 60; Lchdm. ii. 130, 22: 2, 56; Lchm. ii. 276, 19: 3, 30; Lchdm. ii. 324, 25. Wyl on meolcum ða reádan gearwan *boil in milk the red yarrow*, L. M. 3, 65; Lchm. ii. 354, 9. v. gearewe.

ge-ârweorþian, -ârwurþian; *p.* ode, ede; *pp.* od, ed *To honour*; honorĭfĭcāre:—Me swīðe geārweorþede syndon freónd ðīne *mihi nĭmis honorĭfĭcāti sunt amĭci tui*, Ps. Lamb. 138, 17.

gearwian, gerwian, getwan, girwan, gierwan, gyrwan, gyrian, girian, gierian; *p.* ode, ade, ede; *pp.* od, ad, ed *To make ready, prepare, procure, supply, put on, clothe*; părāre, præpărāre, præstāre, induĕre, vestīre:—Ðū gǣst befōran Drihtnes ansȳne, his wegas gearwian *præibis ante faciem Dŏmĭni, părāre vias ejus*, Lk. Bos. 1, 76: Exon. 58 b; Th. 210, 21; Ph. 189: 119 a; Th. 456, 27; Hy. 4, 73: Elen. Kmbl. 1997; El. 1000. Wīsdōm oððe snytro gearwiende lytlingum *săpientiam præstans parvŭlis*, Ps. Spl. 18, 8. Ōþ on ēcnysse ic gearwie sǣd ðīn *usque in æternum præpărābo sēmen tuum*, 88, 4. He līfes weg gǣstum gearwaþ *he prepares life's way for souls*, Exon. 34 a; Th. 108, 11; Gū. 71: 117 a; Th. 450, 21; Dōm. 91. Ic gearwode leóhtfæt cyninge mīnum *părāvi lucernam Christo meo*, Ps. Spl. 131, 18. Ðū gearwodest wlite mīnum mægn *præstĭtisti dĕcōri meo virtūtem*, 29, 8. Grinu hī gearwodon fōtum mīnum *laqueum părāvērunt pĕdibus meis*, Ps. Spl. 56, 8. Sumum wundorgiefe þurh goldsmiþe gearwad weorþeþ *to one a wondrous skill in goldsmith's art is provided*, Exon. 88 a; Th. 331, 25; Vy. 73. Gearwian us togēnes grēne strǣte up to englum *let us prepare before ourselves a green path to the angels above*, Cd. 219; Th. 282, 15; Sat. 287. Hū gē eówic gearwige *quid induamini*, Mt. Kmbl. Rush. 6, 25: 27, 29. Ðæt selfe wæter ðegnunge gearwode beforan his fōtum *the very water did reverence before his feet*, St. And. 22, 19. [*Piers P.* gare: *R. Brun.* ȝared, *pp. prepared*: *Laym.* ȝærwen *to make ready*: *O. Sax.* garuwian, gerwean, girwian *to make ready, prepare*: *O. H. Ger.* garawēn, garwēn, garawjan.] v. Grm. D. M. 984. DER. a-gearwian, ge-.

gearwung, e; *f. A making ready, preparation*; præpărātio:—Of gearwunge eardunge his *de præpărāto habĭtācŭlo suo*, Ps. Spl. T. 32, 14. Gearwunga dæg *parasceue*, Jn. Skt. Lind. 19, 31. DER. ge-gearwung.

ge-ârwurþian; *p.* ode; *pp.* od *To honour*; honorĭfĭcāre:—Ðæt hī sīn geārwurþode fram mannum *ut honorĭfĭcentur ab hŏmĭnĭbus*, Mt. Bos. 6, 2: Ps. Lamb. 36, 20. v. ge-ârweorþian.

gearwutol; *adj. Austere*:—Gearwutol *austerus*, Lk. Skt. Lind. 19, 21, 22.

ge-ascian, -acsian, -ahsian, -axian; *p.* ode, ade; *pp.* od, ad [acsian *to ask*] *To find out by asking, learn, hear*; fando accipĕre, discĕre, audīre:—Geascode he ðone cyning on Meran tūne *he learnt* [*that*] *the king* [*was*] *at Merton*, Chr. 755; Erl. 48, 28. Ðā geascade se cyng ðæt ðæt hie ūt on hergaþ fōron *then the king heard that they were gone out to ravage*, 911; Erl. 100, 24. We geascodon ðæt ūre geferan sume to eów cōmon *we have heard that some of our fellows have come to you*, L. Alf. 49; Th. i. 56, 14: Exon. 100 a; Th. 378, 24; Deór. 20. Habbaþ we geascad ðæt se Ælmihtiga worhte wer and wīf *we have heard that the Almighty created man and woman*, 61 b; Th. 225, 22; Ph. 393.

ge-ascung, e; *f.* [acsung *asking*] *An asking, inquiry*; interrogātio, inquīsītio:—Būton be gemynde and be geascunga *except by memory and by inquiry*, Bt. 42; Fox 256, 25.

ge-asmirian; *p.* ode, ede; *pp.* od, ed [smyrian, smirian *to smear*] *To smear, anoint*; ungĕre, inungĕre:—Bring clǣne ofenbacene hlāfas mid ele geasmirede būtan beorman *pānes scĭlĭcet absque fermento conspersos ŏleo*, Lev. 2, 4.

geásne; *adj. c. gen. Deprived of, void of*; expers:—He sceal gōdra gum-cysta geásne hweorfan *he shall pass away, deprived of good blessings*, Exon. 71 a; Th. 265, 15; Jul. 381. Ða sind geásne gōda gehwylces *those are void of every good*, 68 b; Th. 255, 18: Jul. 216. v. gēsne, gǣsne.

ge-asyndrod; *part. Sundered, separated*; sequestrātus, R. Ben. interl. 43. v. a-syndran.

geat, *pl.* geáton *got*; *p. of* gitan.

GEAT, gat, es; *pl. nom. acc.* u, a, o; *n. A gate, door*; porta, ostium, jānua:—Ic eom sceápa geat *ego sum ostium ŏvium*, Jn. Bos. 10, 7, 9: 10, 1, 2. Gangaþ inn þurh ðæt nearwe geat, forðonðe ðæt geat is swȳðe wīd *intrāte per angustam portam, quia lāta porta est*, Mt. Bos. 7, 13, 14. Ðǣr is geat gylden *there is the golden gate*, Cd. 227; Th. 305, 19; Sat. 649. Þurh ðæs wealles geat *through the gate of the wall*, Judth. 11; Thw. 23, 32; Jud. 151: Exon. 71 b; Th. 266, 21; Jul. 401. Ðā he geneálǣhte ðære ceastre gate *cum appropinquāret portæ cĭvĭtātis*, Lk. Bos. 7, 12. Heó ðæt geat ðæs mynstres ontȳnde *illa apĕruit jānuam Monastĕrii*, Bd. 3, 11; S. 536, 18. Ða gyldnan geatu hāt ontȳnan *bid open the golden gates*, Exon. 11 b; Th. 16, 10; Cri. 251: 16 a; Th. 36, 15; Cri. 576. Opnyaþ me gatu rihtwīsnysse *apĕrīte mihi portas justĭtiæ*, Ps. Spl. 117, 19: Exon. 12 b; Th. 20, 15; Cri. 318. On gaton *in portis*, Ps. Th. 126, 6. [*Piers P.* yates, *pl. gates*; gate *a way*: *Chauc.* yate *a gate*; gate *a street, way*: *Laym.* ȝæt: *Orm.* ȝate *a gate*; gate *a way*: *Scot.* yet, yett *a gate*: *O. Sax.* gat, *n. a hole*: *Frs.* gat: *O. Frs.* gat, iet, *n. a hole*: *Dut.* gat, *n. a hole*: *Ger.* gasse, *f. a thoroughfare, narrow road*: *M. H. Ger.* gat, *n. a hole*; gazze, *f. a narrow road*: *O. H. Ger.* gaza, *f. vicus, plătea*: *Goth.* gatwo, *f. plătea*: *Dan.* gat, *m. f. an aperture, opening*: *Swed.* gata, *f. a street, lane*: *Icel.* gat, *n. a hole*; gata, *f. a way.*] DER. ben-geat, burh-, fæsten-, hord-, weall-.

Geát, es; *m. Geat*, Exon. 100 a; Th. 378, 13; Deór. 15. See Grimm D. M. 341–5.

geát *poured out*, Bd. 2, 6; S. 508, 9; *p. of* geótan.

GEÁTAN, gǣtan, gētan; *p.* de te; *pp.* ed *To grant, confirm, assent to*; concēdĕre, confirmāre, assentīri:—Ic geáte ðē *I grant to thee*, Chr. 656: Th. 53, 38: 675; Th. 59, 33. Ic Ædgār geáte and gife tō dæi *I Edgar grant and give to-day*, 963; Th. 220, 33. Se æðeling hit him geátte *the ætheling granted it to them*, 1066; Th. 337, 30. Ealle hit geátton *all confirmed it*, 963; Th. 221, 25. [*Laym.* ȝetten *to grant*: *Orm.* ȝatenn *to grant, allow*: *O. Frs.* gēta, gāta *confirmāre*: *Icel.* játa, játta *to say 'yes,' assent.*] v. geá.

GEÁTAS, Iótas, Iútas, Eótenas [v. eóten, II.]; *gen.* a; *dat.* um; *pl. m.* I. *the Jutes, the ancient inhabitants of Jutland, who, with the Angles and Saxons, colonized Britain*; Jutæ, pŏpŭlus Chersŏnēsi Cymbrĭcæ, qui relicta patria ūna cum Saxŏnĭbus Anglisque Britanniam occupāvērunt. Though the Jutes are now regarded as Danes, they were, in the earliest times, distinguished as a separate people, and were probably the descendants of earlier Gothic settlers in Jutland, while the Danes = Dene, were an invading nation. Thus Hengest was a Jute, and Healfdene, his lord, a Dane. The Eótenas = Jötnar, were apparently a still earlier Finnish race, from whom the Gothic conquerors probably derived their *trolls* and *giants*. Both Jóti; *pl.* Jótar, and iötunn; *pl.* iötnar, are rendered in *A. Sax.* by eóten; *pl.* eótenas. From the Ynglinga-Saga, c. 5, we learn that before the time of Skiold, the seat of the Danish kings was in Reitgothland = Jutland, but Skiold transferred it to Lethra in Seeland, of which he was the founder:—Cōmon hī of þrīm folcum ðām strangestan Germanie, ðæt [is,] of Seaxum, and of Angle, and of Geátum. Of Geáta fruman syndon Cantware, and Wihtsǣtan, ðæt is seó þeód ðe Wiht ðæt Eálond oneardaþ . . . And of Engle cōman Eást-Engle and Middel-Engle, and Myrce, and eall Norþhembra cynn, is ðæt land ðe Angulus is nemned betwyh Geátum and Seaxum *advĕnĕrant autem de trĭbus Germāniæ pŏpŭlis fortiōrĭbus, id est, Saxŏnĭbus, Anglis, Jutis. De Jutārum orīgĭne sunt Cantuārii et Victuārii, hoc est, ea gens, quæ Vectam tĕnet Insŭlam . . . De Anglis vēnēre Orientāles Angli, Mediterrānei Angli, Merci,* [*et*] *Nordanhymbrōrum prōgĕnies, id est, de illa patria quæ Angŭlus dĭcĭtur inter provincias Jutārum et Saxŏnum*, Bd. 1, 15; S. 483, 20–26. II. *the* GAUTS, *the inhabitants of the south of Sweden*, which in ancient times comprehended nearly the whole of South-Sweden = *A. Sax.* Geát-land, *Icel.* Gautland *the land of the Gauts*, which must be distinguished from *Icel.* Gotar, and *A. Sax.* Gotland *the land of the Goths*, q. v; Gauti in Suecia = Γαυτοί, Procopius Bell. Goth. 2, 15:—We synt gumcynnes Geáta leóde *we are of the race of the Gauts' nation*, Beo. Th. 526; B. 260: 730; B. 362. Ic wæs mid Hrēþ-Gotum, mid Sweóm and mid Geátum, and mid Sūþ-Denum *I was with the Hreth-Goths, with the Swedes, and with the Gauts, and with the South-Danes*, Exon. 85 b; Th. 322, 4; Wid. 58: Beo. Th. 392; B. 195: 2347; B. 1171: 4391; B. 2192. Beó wid Geátas glæd *be cheerful towards the Gauts*, Beo. Th. 2350; B. 1173. DER. Gūþ-Geátas, Sǣ-, Weder-. See Grimm Geschichte d. D. S. pp. 512, 312.

ge-atelod; *part.* [ge, atol, atel *dire, terrible*] *Misshapen, deformed, hideous*; deformis, deformātus:—Geatelod *deformis*, Cot. 66: *deformātus*, 202.

geáþ, e; *f. Foolishness, lightmindedness, luxury, mockery*; stultĭtia, lascīvia, luxŭria, ludibrium:—Ðū, on geáþe, hafast ofer witena dōm wīsan gefongen *thou, in foolishness, hast taken thy course against wise men's judgment*, Exon. 67 a; Th. 248, 16; Jul. 96. Þeódum ȳwaþ wīsdōm weras, siððan geóguþe geáþ gǣst afliĥþ *men manifest wisdom to people, when the spirit puts to flight the lightmindedness of youth*, 40 a; Th. 132, 19; Gū. 475. Ðȳ-læs ðæt wundredan weras and idesa, and on geáþ gutan *lest men and women should wonder thereat, and pour it forth in mockery*, 50 b; Th. 176, 8; Gū. 1206. [Gɫác *a cuckoo*: *Icel.* gaúð, *f. a barking.*]

geatolic; *adj. Ready, prepared, equipped, stately*; părātus, instructus, ornātus:—Ðǣr wæs on eorle geatolīc gūþscrūd *there was on the man a prepared war-dress*, Elen. Kmbl. 515; El. 258: Beo. Th. 435; B. 215: 4314; B. 2154. Wīsa fengel geatolīc gengde *the wise prince went stately*, 2806; B. 1401.

geat-torr, es; *m. A* GATE-TOWER; portam hăbens turris:—Sind geat-torras berofen *the gate-towers are despoiled*, Exon. 124 a; Th. 476, 7; Ruin. 4.

geatwan; *p.* ede; *pp.* ed *To make ready, equip, adorn*; părāre, ornāre:—Frætwed, geatwed *adorned, equipped*, Exon. 107 b; Th. 411, 1; Rä. 29, 6.

geatwe; *gen.* a; *dat.* um; *acc.* a; *pl. f. Arms, trappings, garments, ornaments*; armāmenta, vestimenta ornāmenta:—Twegen englas gesceldode and gesperode and mid heora geatwum gegyrede, efne swā hie to campe fēran woldon *two angels with shields and spears and with their equipments, just as if they meant to go to battle*, Blickl. Homl. 221, 28. Freólīce in geatwum [MS. geotwum] *in trappings goodly*, Chr. 1066;

Th. 334, 35, col. 1; Edw. 22. Geatwum *with ornaments*, Exon. 109 a; Th. 417, 26; Ra. 36, 10. Ic geondseah recedes geatwa *I looked over the ornaments of the house*, Beo. 6167; B. 3087. DER. eóred-geatwe, fyrd-, gryre-, gûþ-, here-, hilde-. v. ge-tawe.

geat-weard, es; *m. A gate-ward, door-keeper, porter;* ostiārius:—Ðæne se geatweard lǽt in *huic ostiārius apĕrit*, Jn. Bos. 10, 3. Geatweard *januārius*, Wrt. Voc. 81, 16.

ge-aurnen; *part.* [aurnen *run out, pp. of* a-yrnan] *Over-run, overtaken;* cursu apprehensus, Som. Ben. Lye.

ge-aworpen; *part.* [ge, and *pp. of* a-weorpan *to throw away*] *Cast* or *thrown away;* abjectus, Som. Ben. Lye.

ge-axian; *p.* ode; *pp.* od [acsian *to ask*] *To find out by asking, learn, hear;* exquīrĕre, resciscĕre, audīre:—Swā hwā swā ðæt geaxaþ, he hlihþ eác mid me *quicumque audiĕrit, corrīdēbit mihi*, Gen. 21, 6. Æfter ðære tíde ðe he geaxode fram ðām tungelwītegum *sĕcundum tempus exquīsiĕrat a māgis*, Mt. Bos. 2, 16. Geaxodon ða cynegas *audiērunt rēges*, Jos. 5, 1: L. Alf. 49; Th. i. 56, 14, MS. H. Geaxode dōmas *responsa*, Ælfc. Gl. 14; Som. 57, 131; Wrt. Voc. 20, 68. v. ge-ascian, ge-acsian.

ge-bacen; *part.* BAKED; coctus:—Gesoden, gebacen *coctus*, Ælfc. Gl. 31; Som. 61, 86; Wrt. Voc. 27, 16; 82, 71. DER. bacan; *p.* bōc, *pl.* bōcon; *pp.* bacen *to bake*.

ge-bād *abode, dwelt, remained*, Jn. Bos. 8, 9; *p. of* ge-bīdan.

ge-bæc, es; *n.* [bacan *to bake*] *Anything baked;* quod est tostum:—Ic geseah swefen, ðæt ic hæfde þrī windlas mid meluwe ofer mīn heáfod, and on ðam ufemystan windle wǽre manegra cynna gebæc *ego vīdi somnium, quod tria canistra fărīnæ habērem sŭper căput meum, et in ūno canistro, quod ĕrat excelsius, portāre me omnes cĭbos, qui fiunt arte pistōria*, Gen. 40, 17.

ge-bæcu; *pl. n. Back parts, hinder parts;* postĕriōra:—Synd gebæcu hire hrycges on blācunge goldes *sunt postĕriōra dorsi ejus in pallōre auri*, Ps. Lamb. 67, 14. He slōh heora fȳnd on gebæcum *percussit inĭmīci suos in postĕriōra*, 77, 66. v. bæc.

ge-bæd *prayed*, Ps. Th. 108, 3; *p. of* ge-biddan.

ge-bǽdan; *p.* -bǽdde; *pp.* -bǽded [bǽdan *to compel*] *To compel, constrain, force, impel, urge, oppress;* compellĕre, cōgĕre, persuādēre, impellĕre, urgēre, prĕmĕre:—Mid rihtre nȳdþearfnysse gebǽded *justa necessĭtāte compulsus*, Bd. 2, 2; S. 502, 27. Mid nȳde gebǽded *necessĭtāte cōgente*, 3, 24; S. 556, 7: Exon. 70 b; Th. 263, 2; Jul. 343: Bt. Met. Fox 6, 28; Met. 6, 14. Nīþa gebǽded *constrained by hatred*, Exon. 68 b; Th. 254, 27; Jul. 203. Mon sceal gebīdan ðæs he gebǽdan ne mæg *a man ought to wait for what he cannot hasten* [*compel to come*], 90 b; Th. 340, 2; Gn. Ex. 105. Hie gecwǽdon ðæt ne hie to ðam gebēde he mihte gebǽdan *they said that he could not force them to that prayer*, Cd. 182; Th. 228, 15; Dan. 202. Strǽla storm strengum gebǽded, scōc ofer scyld-weall *a storm of shafts, impelled from strings, rushed over the shield-wall*, Beo. Th. 6226; B. 3117. Bȳsigum gebǽded *oppressed with labour*, 5153; B. 2580; 5644; B. 2826. [*Goth.* gabaidjan.]

ge-bælded; *part.* [ge-, *pp. of* bældan *to animate*] *Made bold, animated;* anĭmātus:—Wæs Laurentius mid ðæs apostoles swingum and trymenessum swīðe gebælded *apostŏli flagellis sĭmul et exhortatiōnĭbus anĭmātus ĕrat Laurentius*, Bd. 2, 6; Wilk. 124, 7.

ge-bændan; *p.* de; *pp.* ed [ge, *and* bænd *a band*] *To bind;* vincīre:—Ic hine gebændan hēt *I commanded* [*them*] *to bind him*, Salm. Kmbl. 551; Sal. 275.

ge-bær *bare, bore*, Gen. 39, 19; *p. of* ge-beran *to bear, bring forth.*

ge-bǽran; *p.* de; *pp.* ed [ge-, *and* bǽru *bearing, habit*] *To bear one's self, behave* or *conduct one's self;* se gerere:—Ne gefrægn ic ða mǽgþe sēl gebǽran *never have I heard of the tribe bearing themselves better*, Beo. Th. 2029; B. 1012: 5640; B. 2824: Fins. Th. 77; Fin. 38. Ne scule gē wið hine gebǽran swā swā wið feónd *ye must not behave to him as to an enemy*, Past. 46, 8; Swt. 356, 7; Hat. MS. 68 a, 14. We gebǽraþ swelce we hit nyten *we behave as though we know it not*, 28, 4; Swt. 194, 4; Hat. MS. 37 a, 25. Ðæt hī gebǽrdon wel *that they should bear themselves well*, Judth. 10; Thw. 21, 20; Jud. 27: Bd. 4, 25; S. 600, 32: Ps. Th. 113, 6. [*Laym.* i-bere: *O. Sax.* gi-bārian: *O. H. Ger.* ga-baran.]

ge-bærd *natural quality, nature;* indōles, Som. Ben. Lye. v. ge-byrd, II.

gebærd-stān, es; *m. Calcisvia?* Ælfc. Gl. 58; Som. 67, 102; Wrt. Voc. 38, 27: *forte* gebærn-stān *vel* gebærned stān *calx viva*, Som. 67, 102.

ge-bærmed; *part.* [ge, *and pp. of* byrman *to ferment with barm* or *leaven*] *Fermented, leavened;* fermentātus:—Gebærmed hlāf *leavened bread;* pānis fermentātus, Som. Ben. Lye. v. ge-byrman.

ge-bærnan; *p.* -bærnde; *pp.* -bærned [ge, *and* bærnan *to burn*] *To burn;* ūrĕre:—Ne ðē sunne on dæge gebærne *per diem sol non ūret te*, Ps. Th. 120, 6.

gebærn-līm *quicklime;* calx vīva, Som. Ben. Lye.

gebǽr-scipe, es; *n. A feast*, Lk. Skt. Lind. 14, 13. v. gebeór-scipe.

ge-bǽru, *gen.* e; *acc.* e, u; *f:* ge-bǽro; *f. indecl.* Or ge-bǽre; *n; pl.* u. See the cognate words at the end. [baero, bǽru *a bearing*] BEARING, *state, habit* or *disposition of body* or *mind, manner, conduct, behaviour, demeanour, manners in society, society;* gestus, hăbĭtus, mōres, consortium, consuētūdo:—Biþ swā fæger fugles gebǽru *the bird's bearing* [*demeanour*] *is so pleasing*, Exon. 57 b; Th. 206, 12; Ph. 125. We on gewritu setton þeóda gebǽru *we have set in writing the conduct of the people*, Elen. Kmbl. 1314; El. 659. Gehȳrde beornes gebǽro *she heard of the conduct of the man*, 1416; El. 710. Ðæt he sceáwode monna gebǽru *that he might behold men's behaviour*, Exon. 38 b; Th. 127, 17; Gū. 387: Ors. 4, 10; Bos. 92, 37. Swylce habban sceal blīðe gebǽro *shall such have a blithe demeanour?* Exon. 115 b; Th. 444, 8; Kl. 44: 115 a; Th. 442, 31; Kl. 21. On gebǽrum *ex hăbĭtu ejus*, Bd. 4, 22; S. 591, 33: Ps. Th. 34, 15. He swīðor lufade wīfa gebǽra, ðonne wǽpnedmanna *he loved the society of women more than of men*, Ors. 1, 12; Bos. 35, 16. On ðæs wīfes gebǽrum onfundon ðæs cyninges ðegnas ða unstilnesse *by the woman's cries* [?] *the king's thanes discovered the disturbance*, Chr. 755; Erl. 100, 2. Cf. *Laym.* wide me mihte iheren Brutten iberen, iii. 125. [*O. Sax.* gi-bāri, *n: O. H. Ger.* ga-bāri, *n.*]

ge-bǽtan; *p.* -bǽtte; *pp.* -bǽted, -bǽt [ge, *and* bǽtan *to bridle*] *To bit, bridle, curb;* frēnum ĕquo *vel* ăsĭno injĭcĕre, frēnāre:—Ðā wæs Hrōþgāre hors gebǽted *then a horse was bitted for Hrothgar*, Beo. Th. 2803; B. 1399. He gebǽtte his āgen weorc *he curbed his own work*, Bt. Met. Fox 11, 152; Met. 11, 76. Hæfþ se Alwealda ealle gesceafta gebǽt mid his bridle *the Almighty has restrained all creatures with his bridle*, Bt. Met. Fox 11, 45; Met. 11, 23.

ge-bǽte, -bǽtel, es; *n.* [ge, *and* bǽte *a bit of a bridle*] *A bit of a bridle, a bridle, trappings;* lŭpātum, cāmus, frēnum:—Ðæt gebǽtel of ateáh *he took the bridle off*, Bd. 3, 9; S. 533, 34. Mid ðām gebǽtum *with the trappings*, Bd. 3, 14: S. 540, 22.

ge-ban, -bann, -benn, es; *n.* I. *a command, ordinance, decree, proclamation;* mandātum, stătūtum, decrētum:—Brād is ðīn gebann *lātum est mandātum tuum*, Ps. Th. 118, 96. Ðīne ealle gebann *omnia mandāta tua*, 118, 86. Ðīnre ǽ geban *lēgis tuæ mandātum*, 58, 10: Elen. Grm. 556. Þurh hlāfordes geban *by his lord's decree*, L. Edg. H. 7; Th. i. 260, 14. Gif preóst biscopes geban forbūge *if a priest decline* [*to obey*] *the bishop's edict*, L. N. P. 4; Th. ii. 290, 20. II. ge-bann, -bonn, es; *n. the indiction;* indictio, edictum. The indiction is a cycle or revolution of 15 years, like the date of the year from the Birth of our Saviour. Indiction was introduced by Augustine, through the influence of Gregory the Great. It was used by the Roman emperors in the solemn *Edictum* or *Indictio*, relative to the taxes, and adopted by the Church to denote the cycle of 15 years. The number of the Indiction was thus easily ascertained, add 3 to the year of our Lord and divide by 15, and the remainder will be the year of Indiction. If there be no remainder the Indiction will be 15. Bede, in his *De Rătiōne Tempŏrum*, says plainly,—Si vis scīre quŏta sit Indictio, sūme annos Dŏmĭni, et adjĭce tria, partīre per xv, et quod remansĕrit, ipsa est Indictio anni præsentis, *Cap. xiv.* Indiction is useful in ascertaining the exact year in a reign, *etc:*—Ðam mildestan cyninge Cantwara, Wihtrǽde, rīxigendum, ðē fīftan wintra his rīces, ðȳ niguþan gebanne, in ðære stōwe ðy hātte Berghāmstyde, ðǽr wæs gesamnad eádigra geþeahtendlīc ymcyme *in the reign of the most mild king of the Kentish-men, Wihtræd, in the fifth year of his reign, the ninth indiction, in the place which is called Berham, where was assembled a deliberative assembly of the great men*, L. Wih. pref; Th. i. 36, 4-7. Thus, Wihtrǽd began to reign A. D. 691; add 5 years, this gives A. D. 696 for the deliberative assembly; add 3 by rule, the sum, 699, divided by 15, leaves 9 remainder after the division, or the year of the Indiction as in the preceding example. Rīxiendum ussum Dryhtene ðæm Hǽlendan Crist. Æfter ðon ðe agān wæs ehta hund wintra and syx and hundnigontig efter his acennednesse, and ðȳ feówerteóðan gebonn-gēre; ðā, ðȳ gēre, gebeón [*p. of* gebannan] Æðelrēd ealderman alle Mercna weotan tosomne to Gleaweceastre *under the rule of our Lord Jesus Christ. When 896 winters were passed after his birth, and in the 14th indiction-year; then, in that year, alderman Æthelred assembled all the witan of the Mercians together at Gloucester*, Th. Diplm. A. D. 896; 139, 4-13. Thus, Æthelred assembled the witan at Gloucester in the year 896; 896 + 3 = 899; this after division by 15 leaves a remainder 14, or the year of Indiction, as stated in the foregoing example. Geban *edictum*, Ælfc. Gl. 87; Som. 74, 43; Wrt. Voc. 50, 25. [*O. Sax.* ban, *n. mandātum: O. Frs.* ban, bon, *n: Dut.* ban, *m: Ger.* bann, *m. edictum, interdictum, proscriptio: M. H. Ger.* ban, *m: O. H. Ger.* pan, *m. scītum, anathēma: Dan.* band, *m. f: Swed.* bann, *n: Icel.* bann, *n. interdictum, excommunĭcātio, prohĭbĭtio.*]

ge-band *bound*, Gen. 22, 9; *p. of* ge-bindan.

ge-bannan, -bonnan; *p.* -beónn, *pl.* -beónnon; *pp.* -bannen [ge, *and* bannan *to summon*]. I. *to command, order, proclaim;* jŭbēre, mandāre, edīcĕre:—Ðā ic gefrægn weorc gebannan manigre mǽgþe *then I heard* [*him*] *command the work to many a tribe*, Beo. Th. 149; B. 74. II. *to summon, call together;* cĭtare, convŏcāre:—Folc biþ gebonnen ealle to spræce *all people shall be summoned to judgment*, Exon. 117 b; Th. 451, 8; Dōm. 100. Ðā gebeón Æðelrēd ealderman alle Mercna weotan tosomne *then alderman Æthelred summoned all the 'witan' of the Mercians together*, Th. Diplm. 139, 11. [*Laym.* i-bannen *to summon.*]

ge-barn *burned*, Beo. Th. 5388; B. 2697; *p. of* ge-beornan.

ge-bâsnian; *p.* ade; *pp.* ad [ge, *and* bâsnian *to expect*] *To expect;* exspectāre:—Gebâsnade rîc Godes *expectābat regnum Dei*, Lk. Skt. Lind. 23, 51.

ge-bâtad, -bâtod; *part. Abated;* mitīgātus, Cot. 135.

ge-beácnian, -bēcnian, -bîcnian; *p.* ode; *pp.* od [ge, *and* beácnian *to beckon*] *To point out, indicate, make signs;* indīcāre, nuntiāre, innuere:—Đâ him gebeácnod wæs *then it was indicated to him*, Beo. Th. 283; B. 140. We woldon mid gebeácnian đa sôþfæstnesse *we would therewith point out the truth*, Bt. 35, 5; Fox 166, 16. Gebēcnadon feder his *innuebant patri ejus*, Lk. Skt. Lind. 1, 62. [*O. Sax.* gi-bōknian *to shew, indicate*: *O. H. Ger.* ga-bauhnjan *adnuere, figurare.*]

ge-beácnung, -bîcnung, e; *f.* [ge, *and* beácnung *a beckoning*] *A presage, sign, a speaking by tropes* or *figures, predicament;* præsāgium, catēgŏria = κατηγορία:—Gebeacnunge *catēgŏriæ*, Cot. 57.

ge-beád *offered*, Chr. 755; Erl. 50, 5, 15; *p. of* ge-beódan.

ge-beág, -beáh *bowed*, Beo. Th. 2487; B. 1241: 3085; B. 1540: 5128; B. 2567; *p. of* ge-bûgan.

ge-beágian, -bēgian; *p.* ode; *pp.* od *To crown*:—Mid lawere gebeágod *crowned with laurel*, Blickl. Homl. 187, 28. Gebēgde, 203, 30.

ge-bealg, -bealh [ge, *and* bealg *was angry*, *p. of* belgan *to be angry*] *made angry, irritated, enraged*, Bt. 27, 1; Fox 94, 32: Lk. Bos. 15, 28.

ge-bearg, -bearh *secured, protected*, Beo. Th. 5134; B. 2570: 3101; B. 1548; *p. of* ge-beorgan.

gebeár-scipe *a feast*, Lk. Skt. Lind. 9, 14. v. gebeór-scipe.

ge-beát, es; *n. A beating, blow*:—Drihten worhte âne swipe of râpum, and hî ealle mid gebeáte ûtascynde *the Lord made a scourge of ropes and hurried them all out with beating*, Homl. Th. i. 406, 8. [*Laym.* i-beat *beating, striking*: *M. H. Ger.* gebôz.] DER. fŷst-gebeát.

ge-beátan; *p.* -beót, *pl.* -beóton; *pp.* -beáten *To beat, strike;* tundĕre, fĕrīre:—Hređles eafora swealt, bille gebeáten *Hrethel's offspring perished, beaten by the falchion*, Beo. Th. 4707; B. 2359. Gebeáten fisc *mĭnūtal*, Ælfc. Gl. 31; Som. 61, 98; Wrt. Voc. 27, 27. Gebeáten flæsc *martisia* vel *baptitura*, 31; Som. 61, 99; Wrt. Voc. 27, 28.

ge-bécan [ge, *and* bôcian *to book* or *charter*] *to grant by book* or *charter, to charter*, Hem. p. 480.

ge-bécnend, es; *m. A discoverer, discloser, informer;* index:—Gebēcnend mîn *index meus*, Ps. Surt. 72, 14. v. ge-beácnian.

ge-bécnendlîce, -bēcniendlîce; *adv. Figuratively;* allēgŏrĭce, Cot. 1.

ge-béd, -bēdd; *gen.* es; *pl. nom. acc.* -bēd, -bēdu, -bēdo; *n.* [The other dialects seem to point to 'gebed:' *O. Sax.* gibed: *O. H. Ger.* gabet: *Ger.* gebet.] I. *a prayer, petition, supplication;* ōrātio, prĕces, supplĭcātio:—Gebēd mîn on bôsme mînum sŷ gecyrred *ōrātio mea in sĭnum meum convertĕtur*, Ps. Spl. 34, 16. Gehŷr mîn gebēd *exaudi ōrātiōnem meam*, Ps. Th. 54, 1. Đû mînes gebēdes bêne gehŷrdest *exaudīvisti vōcem ōrātiōnis meæ*, 114, 1: 129, 1. Beald in gebēde *bold in prayer*, Exon. 71 a; Th. 265, 28; Jul. 388. Wæs wacigende on Godes gebēde *ĕrat pernoctans in ōrātiōne Dei*, Lk. Bos. 6, 12. Hie to gebēde feóllon *they fell to prayer*, Cd. 37; Th. 48, 18; Gen. 777. Hŷ gebēdu sēcaþ *they seek prayers*, Exon. 44 b; Th. 150, 20; Gû. 781: Cd. 181; Th. 227, 24; Dan. 191. Đæt hî bêna and gebēdu sendan and geótan *qui prĕces fundant*, Bd. 1, 27; S. 492, 8. His gebēdo mihte gesēcan *ad deprecandum Dŏmĭnum advĕnīre dēbēret*, 3, 23; S. 554, 11. Mid đŷ he đâ đæt gebēdd gefylde *cum ōrātiōnem complēret*, Bd. 5, 1; S. 614, 7. Wesan đîne eáran eác gehŷrende and beheldende on eall gebēdd esnes đînes *fiant aures tuæ intendentes in ōrātiōnem servi tui*, Ps. Th. 129, 2. II. *a religious service, an ordinance;* verbum legĭtĭmum, cærĭmōnia:—Gehealdaþ đis gebēd on ēcnysse *custōdi verbum istud legĭtĭmum in æternum*, Ex. 12, 24. DER. bēd, *q. v. for cognates.*

gebed-clŷfa [ge, bed *a bed*, clŷfa, II. *a cave, den*] an; *m. A den;* spēlunca:—Swâ swâ leo on gebedclŷfan *quăsi leo in spēlunca*, Ps. Spl. C. second 9, 10: 103, 23. v. bed-clŷfa.

ge-bedda, -bedde [(?) cf. heals-gebedda, Beo. 63], an; *f. A bed-fellow, consort, wife;* consors tŏri, uxor:—His gebedde [MS. gebedda] wæs gecîged Elisabeth *his wife was named Elizabeth*, Wanl. Catal. 4, 13: Cd. 86; Th. 109, 25; Gen. 1828. Wolde wîgfruma sēcan cwēn to gebeddan *the martial leader would seek the queen as bed-companion*, Beo. Th. 1334; B. 665: Runic pm. 29; Kmbl. 345, 16; Hick. Thes. i. 135, 58. Sægde Lameh leófum gebeddum unârlîc spel *Lamech told a wicked tale to his dear consorts*, Cd. 52; Th. 66, 29; Gen. 1091. Gebed wîf *uxor*, Mt. Kmbl. pp. 14, 16. [*O. Sax.* gi-beddio: *O. H. Ger.* ga-betti or -betta *a bed-fellow.*]

ge-bēd-dagas; *pl. m. Prayer-days;* Lītānia mājor: this *greater Litany* is for St. Mark's day, and the *Less Litany*, Lītānia mĭnor, is for gangdagas *the Rogation days*:—In Letānia mājōre: đas dagas synd gehâtene Letāniæ, đæt sint, Gebēd-dagas *on the greater Litany: these days are called Litāniæ, that is, Prayer-days*, Homl. Th. i. 244, 11.

ge-béded *compelled, driven*, Chr. 937; Erl. 112, 33, = ge-bæ̂ded; *pp. of* ge-bæ̂dan.

ge-beden *demanded, intreated*, Lk. Bos. 1, 63; *pp. of* ge-biddan.

gebed-giht, e; *f. Bed-time;* contĭcĭnium:—Cwyltîd *vel* gebedgiht *contĭcĭnium*, Ælfc. Gl. 16; Som. 58, 63; Wrt. Voc. 21, 50.

ge-béd-hûs, es; *n. A prayer-house, an oratory, house of prayer;* ōrātōrium, dŏmus ōrātiōnis:—Habbaþ đa wîc gebēd-hûs *the dwellings have a prayer-house*, Bd. 5, 2; S. 614, 33. Mîn hûs biþ genemned gebēd-hûs *dŏmus mea dŏmus ōrātiōnis vŏcābitur*, Mk. Bos. 11, 17. Godes cyrce is ûre gebēd-hûs *God's church is our prayer-house*, Homl. Th. ii. 584, 3. [*O. H. Ger.* gabethûs.]

ge-bédian, bēdigan; *p.* ode; *pp.* od *To pray, pray to, worship;* ōrāre, adōrāre:—Đæt he wolde Rôme gesēcan, and him đǣr gebēdigan *that he would visit Rome, and worship there*, Bd. 5, 9; S. 622, 21, note, MS. T. DER. ge-bēd, ge-biddan.

ge-béd-man, -mannes; *m. A prayer-man, one whose duty it is to pray, one of the clergy, worshipper;* ōrātor, adōrātor:—He sceal hæbban gebēdmen and fyrdmen and weorcmen *he must have prayer-men and soldiers and workmen*, Bt. 17; Fox 58, 33. Sôþe gebēd-men gebiddaþ fæder on gâste and on sôþfæstnesse *vēri adōrātōres adōrābunt Patrem in spīrĭtu et vērĭtāte*, Jn. Bos. 4, 23.

ge-béd-rǣden, -rǣddenn, -rēddenn, e; *f. The office of prayer, prayer;* precātiōnis offĭcium, prēces:—Heó hî ealle eádmôdlîce heora gebēdrǣddenne bæd *se omnium prĕcĭbus humĭlĭter commendāvit*, Bd. 3, 8; S. 531, 34: R. Ben. 52. Hî beóþ on ealdra eorþlîcra gebēdrǣdenne đe Cristene wǣron *they shall be in the prayers of all earthly folk who have been Christians*, Blickl. Homl. 45, 37. He nelle gehŷran đæs gîmeleásan mannes gebēdrǣdene *he will not listen to the prayers of the negligent man*, 57, 4.

gebed-scipe, es; *m. Bed-fellowship, cohabitation, marriage;* cohabĭtātio:—Þurh đone gebedscipe *through cohabitation*, Exon. 9 a; Th. 5, 29; Cri. 76: Cd. 57; Th. 70, 4; Gen. 1148: 100; Th. 133, 25; Gen. 2216.

ge-béd-stôw, e; *f. A prayer-place, place where prayers have been offered, an oratory;* ōrātiōnis lŏcus, ōrātōrium:—In đære gebēdstôwe æfter đon monige mægen and hǣlo tâcen gefremede wǣron *in cūjus lŏco ōrātiōnis innŭmĕræ virtūtes sanĭtātum noscuntur esse patrātæ*, Bd. 3, 2; S. 524, 28. He ne mæg lenge gewunian in gebēdstôwe *he may not longer remain in the place of prayer*, Exon. 71 a; Th. 265, 4; Jul. 376. On heora gebēdstôwe *in their place of prayer*, Blickl. Homl. 133, 19.

ge-bégan; *p.* de; *pp.* ed; *v. trans. To cause to bow, bend, bow down, recline, press down, humble, crush;* flectĕre, incurvāre, humiliare, deprimĕre:—Gebēgdon sâwle mîne *incurvāvĕrunt anĭmam meam*, Ps. Surt. 56, 7: Lk. Skt. Lind. 9, 58. Se đe hine ahefeþ he biþ gebēged and se đe hine gebēges he ahæfen biþ *qui se exaltaverit humiliabitur et qui se humiliaverit exaltabitur*, Mt. Kmbl. Lind. 23, 12. Heó sceáf in đæt neowle genip, nearwe gebēged *thrust them into that deep darkness, closely pressed down*, Cd. 223; Th. 292, 26; Sat. 446. Burga fîfe wǣran under Norþmannum nŷde gebēgde on hǣđenra hæfteclommum lange þrage *five towns were under the Northmen by necessity bowed down in the bonds of the heathen for a long space*, Chr. 941; Th. 210, 7, col. 1; Edm. 9. DER. bēgan *to bow*, ge-bŷgan.

ge-bégnes, -bēgednes, -ness, e; *f. Crookedness;* aduncĭtas, oblīquĭtas, Som. Ben. Lye.

ge-bégendlîc; *adj. Bending, flexible;* flexĭbĭlis, Som. Ben. Lye. v. ge-bŷgendlîc.

gebéldan; *p.* de:—Eđiluald hit [the book] ûta giđryde and gibēlde *Ethelwald made it firm on the outside and covered it*, Jn. Skt. p. 188, 3. See note 8, p. viii. Or is it the verb gebeldan [from bald] used in the sense of 'strengthen?' cf. note 7, on giđryde and the connection suggested with đryþ.

ge-belg, -belh, es; *m. Anger, offence;* īra, offensio:—Us is acumendlîcere eówer gebelh, đonne đæs Ælmihtigan Godes grama *your displeasure is more tolerable to us than the anger of the Almighty God*, Homl. Th. i. 96, 6. Bd. de Sapientibus, Som. Ben. Lye. DER. belgan.

ge-belgan, he -bylgþ, -bilhþ; *p.* -bealg, -bealh, *pl.* -bulgon; *pp.* -bolgen. I. *v. reflex. acc.* [ge, *and* belgan *to irritate*] *To make one angry, irritate, enrage;* īra se tumefăcĕre, irrītāre, exaspĕrāre:—Se wîsa Catulus hine gebealg *the wise Catulus made himself angry*, Bt. 27, 1; Fox 94, 32. Đâ gebealh he hine *tunc ille indignātus est*, Lk. Bos. 15, 28: 13, 14: Ors. 4, 4; Bos. 81, 12. Gebulgon đa tyne hî be Iacōbe and Iohanne *dĕcem coepērunt indignāri de Jacobo ēt Joanne*, Mk. Bos. 10, 41. II. *trans. dat. To anger, incense;* irrītāre, exaspĕrāre:—Đæt he ēcean Dryhtne bitre gebulge *that he had bitterly incensed the eternal Lord*, Beo. Th. 4651; B. 2331. Đâ wæs Herodes swŷđe gebolgen *tunc Hērōdes irātus est valde*, Mt. Bos. 2, 16: 26, 8: Cd. 4; Th. 4, 16; Gen. 54. Torne gebolgen *swollen with anger*, Beo. Th. 4794; B. 2401. Mid gebolgne hond *with wrathful hand*, Exon. 37 a; Th. 120, 19; Gû. 274. III. *intrans. To be angry;* indignāri, irasci:—Gebulgon wiđ đa twegen gebrôđru *indignāti sunt de duŏbus fratrĭbus*, Mt. Bos. 20, 24.

ge-belimpan; *p.* -belamp, *pl.* -belumpon; *pp.* belumpen *To happen, occur, befall;* evĕnīre, accĭdĕre, contingĕre:—Hit gebŷraþ đæt hit gebelimpe *oportet hæc fiĕri*, Mk. Bos. 13, 7. DER. be-limpan, II.

ge-bēn *a praying, prayer;* prĕces, Ben. Lye. Hiora ēcelīcum giboene *eorum perpetua supplicatione*, Rtl. 73, 38: 74, 12. v. bēn.

ge-bend, es; *n. A band;* vinculum:—Gebend tungæs his *vinculum linguæ ejus*, Mk. Skt. Lind. 7, 35.

ge-bendan, -bændan; *p.* -bende; *pp.* -bended, -bend. I. *to bend;* flectĕre, tendĕre:—He hornbogan hearde gebendaþ *confrēgit cornua arcuum*, Ps. Th. 75, 3. He gebende his bogan *he bent his bow*, Homl. Th. i. 502, 15. Of gebendum bogan *from a bended bow*, Guthl. 4; Gdwin. 28, 2. II. *to bind, fetter;* vincīre:—Swā gebend he wæs wuniende, ōþ he his līf forlēt *he remained so bound until he gave up his life*, Ors. 5, 2; Bos. 103, 1. Hieremias se wītega wearþ oft gebend *Jeremiah the prophet was often in bonds*, Ælfc. T. 18, 23. DER. bendan.

ge-bēnlīc *prayer-like, nun-like;* vestālis, Som. Ben. Lye.

ge-benn, es; *n. A command, edict*, Cot. 79. v. ge-ban.

ge-bennian; *p.* ode; *pp.* od, ad *To wound;* vulnĕrāre:—Bille gebennad *wounded with a sword*, Exon. 102 b; Th. 388, 3; Rä. 6, 2. DER. ben, benn *a wound.*

ge-bēnsian *to pray:*—Gi-boensandum đīnum *supplicibus tuis*, Rtl. 51, 29. v. bēnsian.

ge-beod, es; *n. A prayer, supplication;* prĕces:—Dæghwamlīce Drihtne bēna and gebeoda borene beón sceoldan *cotīdie Domino prĕces offerri dēbērent*, Bd. 3, 14; S. 540, 6. Gebeodo đīna *deprecatio tua*, Lk. Skt. Lind. 1, 13: Rtl. 14, 36. v. ge-bēd.

ge-beódan; p. -beád, *pl.* -budon; *pp.* -boden [ge-, beódan *to command*]. I. *to command, order, summon;* jŭbēre, mandāre:—Hēt gebeódan byre Wihstānes hæleđa monegum boldāgendra, đæt hie bǣlwudu feorran feredon *Wihstan's son bade command many house-owning men, that they should convey pile-wood from afar*, Beo. Th. 6211; B. 3110: Elen. Kmbl. 551; El. 276. II. *to announce, proclaim;* annuntiāre:—Hit beó seofon nihtum geboden ǣr *let it be announced seven days before*, L. Ath. i. 20; Th. i. 208, 27: Cd. 183; Th. 229, 27; Dan. 223. III. *to offer, propose, give, grant;* offerre, præbēre:—Hiera se æđeling gehwelcum feoh and feorh gebeád *to each of them the noble offered money and life*, Chr. 755; Erl. 50, 5, 15. Gebudon him Perse đæt hī hæfdon iii winter sibbe wiđ hī *the Persians proposed that they should have peace with them for three years*, Ors. 3, 1; Bos. 52, 27. [*O. Sax.* gibiodan: *O. H. Ger.* ga-biutan, -piotan: *Ger.* gebieten.]

ge-beón, -beónn *commanded, assembled*, Cod. Dipl. 1073; A. D. 896; Kmbl. v. 140, 8: Th. Diplm. A. D. 896; 139, 11; *p. of* ge-bannan.

ge-beón *been*, Chr. 1096; Erl. 233, 3. v. beón.

ge-beór, es; *m. A guest;* hospes, convīva:—Đā đæt đa gebeóras gesāwon *quod cum convīvæ conspĭcĕrent*, Bd. 3, 10; S. 534, 33. Gebeór *conviva*, Ælfc. Gr. 7; Som. 6, 45: Scint. 63: Homl. Th. i. 484, 1; 528, 9. DER. beór.

ge-beoran, to -beoranne [ge-, beoran *to bear*] *To bear, bring, offer;* ferre, prōferre:—Đām đe se deáþ tobeótaþ, būtan ǣnigre yldinge is to gebeoranne *his quĭbus mors inmĭnet, sĭne ulla dilātiōne prōfĕrenda est*, Bd. 1, 27; S. 493, 30.

ge-beorc, es; *n? A barking;* latrātus:—Gemenged stemn is đe biþ būtan andgite, swylc swā is hryđera gehlōw, and horsa hnǣgung, hūnda gebeorc, treówa brastlung, et cætera *confused voice is what is without understanding, such as is the lowing of oxen, and the neighing of horses, the barking of dogs, the rustling of trees, etc*, Ælfc. Gr. 1; Som. 2, 34–36.

ge-beorg, es; *m. A mountain;* mons. v. ge-beorh.

ge-beorg, -beorh, -berg; *gen.* -beorges, -beorhges; *n.* [ge-, *and* beorg *a protection, refuge*] *A defence, protection, safety, refuge;* præsĭdium, refŭgium, tutāmen, tuĭtio:—Leófsunu ahōf bord to gebeorge *Leofsunu raised up his buckler for defence*, Byrht. Th. 138, 64; By. 245: 135, 40; By. 131. Britwalum to gebeorge *for the protection of the Brito-Welsh*, Chr. 189; Erl. 9, 26: Bd. 1, 12; S. 480, 32.

ge-beorgan, to -beorganne; *p.* ic, he -bearg, -bearh, đū -burge, *pl.* -burgon; *pp.* -borgen [ge-, beorgan *to save*] *To save, protect, defend, secure, spare, preserve;* servāre, salvāre, tuēri, defendĕre, arcēre, parcĕre:—Ne mæg nān man ōđerne wyrian and him sylfum gebeorgan *no man may curse another and save himself*, Homl. Th. ii. 36, 3: Gen. 19, 19, 20: Boutr. Scrd. 22, 3. Āge he þreóra nihta fierst him to gebeorganne *let him have a space of three days to save himself*, L. Alf. pol. 2; Th. i. 62, 2. Đū him yfele dagas ealle gebeorgest *mītĭges eum a diēbus mālis*, Ps. Th. 93, 12. Scyldweall gebearg līf and līce *the shield-wall secured life and body*, Beo. Th. 5134; B. 2570. Đæt gebearh feore *which protected his life*, 3101; B. 1548: Cd. 197; Th. 246, 6; Dan. 475. Gebeorh đē on đam munte *in monte salvum te fac*, Gen. 19, 17: Homl. Th. i. 416, 17. Đæt hī him gebeorgen bogan and strǣle *ut fŭgiant a făcie arcus*, Ps. Th. 59, 4. Ne biþ us geborgen *we shall not be secure*, Homl. Th. i. 56, 18. [*O. Sax.* gi-bergan: *O. H. Ger.* ga-pergan.]

ge-beorglīc *safe, cautious, prudent, becoming*, L. Edg. ii. 1; Th. i. 266, 6, note 12, MS. G. v. ge-beorhlīc.

ge-beorh; *gen.* -beorges; *m.* [ge-, *and* beorh *a hill, mountain*] *A mountain;* mons:—Gebeorh Godes *mons Dei*, Ps. Th. 67, 15. [*Ger.* gebirge]

ge-beorh; *gen.* -beorges, -beorhges; *n. A defence, protection, refuge;* tuĭtio, refŭgium:—Dryhten ys ūre gebeorh *Deus noster refŭgium est*, Ps. Th. 45, 1: Ps. Spl. C. 9, 9: 17, 1. To gebeorhge đæs sǣs *for the sea's protection*, Bd. 1, 12; S. 481, 12. Wolde he đām gebeorh gewarnian đe he heora lāre onfēng *vŏlens scĭlĭcet tuĭtiōnem eis, quos et quōrum doctrīnam suscēpĕrat, præstāre*, 2, 5; S. 506, 30, MS. B. DER. ge-beorg.

ge-beorhlīc, -beorglīc; *adj. Safe, cautious, prudent, becoming;* tūtus, circumspectus, dĕcens:—Gebeorhlīcre ys me faran to eá, mid scype mȳnum, đænne faran mid manegum scypum, on huntunge hranes *tūtius est mihi īre ad amnem, cum nāve mea, quam īre cum multis nāvĭbus, in venātiōnem bālænæ*, Coll. Monast. Th. 24, 21. Gebeorhlīc *circumspectus*, R. Ben. 64. Swilce hit fōr Gode gebeorhlīc sȳ and fōr weorulde aberendlīc *as it may be becoming before God and tolerable before the world*, L. Edg. ii. 1; Th. i. 266, 6: L. C. S. 2; Th. i. 376, 14.

ge-beorhnys, -nyss, e; *f. A refuge;* refŭgium:—On hūse gebeorhnysse *in dŏmum refŭgii*, Ps. Spl. C. 30, 3.

gebeorh-stōw, e; *f. A place of refuge;* refŭgium:—Đū eart mīn gebeorhstōw on mīnum earfođum *tu es mihi refŭgium a pressūra*, Ps. Th. 31, 8.

ge-beorhtian; *p.* ode; *pp.* od [ge-, beorhtian *to shine, brighten*] *To make bright, brighten, glorify;* clārĭfĭcāre:—Đū Fæder, gebeorhta me mid đē sylfum *clārĭfĭca me tu, Pater, ăpud temetipsum*, Jn. Bos. 17, 5. [*Goth.* ga-bairhtjan.]

ge-beornan; *p.* -barn, *pl.* -burnon; *pp.* -bornen, -burnen [ge-, beornan *to burn*]. I. *v. intrans. To burn, be on fire, be consumed;* ardēre, combūri:—Sió hand gebarn mōdiges mannes *the hand of the bold man burned*, Beo. Th. 5388; B. 2697. II. *v. trans:*—Seó eorþe wæs to axsan geburnen *the earth was burnt to ashes*, Ors. 4, 2; Bos. 79, 19.

ge-beór-scipe, -scype, es; *m.* [ge-, beór *beer*, -scipe *-ship*] BEER-SHIP, *convivial society, a drinking party, feast, an entertainment;* pōtātio, compōtātio, coena, convīvium:—Hig lufigeaþ đa fyrmestan setl on gebeórscypum *ămant prīmos recŭbĭtus in coenis*, Mt. Bos. 23, 6: Jn. Bos. 12, 2; 21, 20. Dyde mycelne gebeórscype *fēcit convīvium magnum*, Lk. Bos. 5, 29: Gen. 21, 8: 40, 20. In gebeórscipe *in convīvio*, Bd. 4, 24; S. 597, 4. On gebeórscipe *at a feast*, L. In. 6; Th. i. 106, 11.

ge-beorþor; *g.* -beorþres; *n.* [ge-, beorþor *child-birth*] *A birth;* nātus:—Þurh đa burþran we wǣron gehǣlde, and þurh đæt gebeorþor we wurdon alȳsde *through the issue we were saved, and through the birth we were redeemed*, Homl. Blickl. 105, 21.

ge-beót, es; *n.* [ge-, beót *a threatening*]. I. *a threatening, threat, boast;* comminātio, mĭnæ:—Alȳs us, Drihten, fram his gebeóte and mihte *redeem us, Lord, from his threatening and might*, Homl. Th. i. 568, 22. Swā fela þeóda wurdon todǣlede æt đære wundorlīcan byrig đe đa entas woldon wircean mid gebeóte æfter Noes flōde, ǣr đan đe hī toferdon *so many [of] nations were divided at the wonderful city which the giants would build with boasting after the flood of Noah, before they parted*, Ælfc. T. 39, 10–12. II. *a promise;* promissum:—Ofer eald gebeót *contrary to the old promise*, Exon. 123 b; Th. 475, 13; Bo. 47. [*Laym.* ibeot.] DER. word-gebeót.

ge-beótian; *p.* ode, ede; *pp.* od, ed [ge-, beotian, II. *to boast, vow, promise*] *To promise in a boastful manner, to vow;* glōriōse pollĭcēri:—Gebeótode ān þegena, đæt he mid sunde đa eá oferfaran woldon *one of the officers vowed that he by swimming would cross over the river*, Ors. 2, 4; Bos. 44, 2, 4. Antigones and Perþica gebeótedan, đæt hȳ woldan him betweonum gefeohtan *Antigonus and Perdiccas vowed that they would fight with one another*, Ors. 3, 11; Bos. 72, 41. Wit gebeótedon, đæt wit on gārsecg ūt aldrum nēđdon *we two vowed that we would venture our lives out on the ocean*, Beo. Th. 1076; B. 536: 964; B. 480.

ge-beótung, e; *f.* [ge-, beótung *a threatening*] *A threatening;* comminātio:—Gebeótung *fascĭnātio?* Cot. 90.

ge-beran; he -bireþ, -byreþ, -byrþ; *p.* -bær, *pl.* -bǣron; *pp.* -boren [ge-, beran *to bear*] *To bear, bring forth;* ferre, pārĕre:—Ne mihton nānuht libbendes geberan *they could not bring forth anything alive*, Ors. 4. 1; Bos. 78, 22: Exon. 10 b; Th. 13, 19; Cri. 205. Rachel gebær Beniamin *Rachel bare Benjamin*, Gen. 35, 19. Him wīf sunu gebær *his wife bare a son to him*, Cd. 132; Th. 167, 31; Gen. 2774. Đā wearþ Abrahame Ismael geboren *then Ishmael was born to Abraham*, 105; Th. 138, 26; Gen. 2297: Andr. Kmbl. 1379; An. 690.

geberbed; *pp. Vermiculatus:*—Giberbedo sulfere *vermiculatas argento*, Rtl. 4, 5. [Cf. *O. H. Ger.* furbēn, furbian *mundare, purgare.*]

ge-bered; *part. Vexed, oppressed, crushed;* vexātus, mācĕrātus, elīsus:—Gebered beón *mācĕrāri*, Cot. 136. Gebered wæs *vexābātur*, Mk. Skt. Lind. 5, 15, 18. Geberede *vexāti*, Mt. Kmbl. Lind. 9, 36. Gebered *elīsus*, Mk. Skt. Lind. 9, 20. Beren gebered corn *tipsane* [= *ptĭsăna* = πτισάνη *barley, crushed and cleaned from the hulls*], Ælfc. Gl. 12; Som. 57, 86; Wrt. Voc. 20, 27.

ge-berg, es; *n. A defence, refuge;* refŭgium:—Geworden is Dryht geberg þearfena *factus est Dŏmĭnus refŭgium pauperum*, Ps. Surt. 9, 10: 58, 17: 89, 1. v. ge-beorg.

ge-berhtan, -byrhtan, -birhtan; *p.* te; *pp.* ed [ge-, berhtan *to shine*] *To make bright, brighten, enlighten;* illūmināre, clārĭfĭcāre:—Đe wuhta gehwæs wlite geberhteþ *which brightens the beauty of everything*, Bt. Met. Fox 21, 64; Met. 21, 32.

ge-berian; *p.* ede; *pp.* ed [ge-, berian *to happen*] *To happen;* evĕnīre, accĭdĕre:—Geberian *compĕtĕre*, C. R. Ben. 37. Geberede hit dæt Ercules com to him *it happened that Hercules came to him*, Bt. 16, 2; Fox 52, 34, note 10, MS. Cot: Bt. Met. Fox 25, 61; Met. 25, 31.

ge-bernan [ge-, bernan *to burn*] *To burn;* combūrere:—Geberneþ *combūret*, Lk. Skt. Lind. 3, 17.

ge-berst, es; *m?* *A bursting, eruption;* eruptio:—Wiđ ōmena geberste *against bursting of erysipelas*, L. M. 1, 39; Lchdm. ii. 100, 2.

ge-bésmed; *part. Bosomed, bent, crooked;* sĭnuātus, Som. Ben. Lye. v. ge-bōsmed.

ge-bētan, he -bēteþ, *pl.* -bētaþ; *p.* bētte, *pl.* bētton; *pp.* -bēted, -bētt; *v. trans.* [ge-, bētan *to amend*]. I. *to make better, improve, mend, amend, repair;* emendāre, repărāre:—Gimmas ne scearpnesse gebētaþ *gems do not improve sharpness*, Bt. 34, 8; Fox 144, 33. Đæt hī gebētton *that they repaired*, Ors. 3, 1; Bos. 54, 15: Bt. 20: Fox 70, 35. Geboeton netta hiora *reficientes retia sua*, Mt. Kmbl. Lind. 4, 21. Geboeta *curare*, 4, 24. Giboeted wæs đā fȳr *accenso autem igni*, Lk. Skt. Rush. 22, 55. II. *to make strong, fortify, surround with a wall;* confirmāre, mūnīre, mūrāre:—Sceáwiaþ đæt land hwæđer hit wæstmbǽre sī, and đa burga gebētte ođđe būtan weallum *consīdĕrāte terram, quālis sit, hūmus pinguis, et urbes quāles, mūrātæ an absque mūris*, Num. 13, 20. III. *to make amends, reparation*, 'bōt' *for, repent:*—Đonne sceolan we mid ūre ānre sāule forgyldan and gebētan ealle đa đing đe we ǽr ofor his bebod gedydon *then must we with our soul alone make recompence and amends for all things that we have previously done against his command*, Blickl. Homl. 91, 16; 63, 34; 57, 27: Ors. 1, 1; Bos. 23, 5; H. R. 107, 4. Hea geboeton *pæniterent*, Lk. Skt. Lind. 10, 13. IV. *to obtain a remedy against, to get* 'bot' *from, avenge:*—Đū wille cweđan đæt đa welgan habban mid hwam hī mǽgen đæt [*hunger, thirst, cold*] gebētan *you will say that the rich have wherewith they can remedy that*, Boeth. 26, 2; Fox 92, 37. Ne meahte on đam feorh-bonan fǽhþe gebētan *could not avenge the feud on the murderer*, Beo. Th. 4922; B. 2465. [*Goth.* ga-bōtjan: *O. Sax.* gi-bōtean: *O. H. Ger.* ga-bōzian.]

ge-beterian, -betrian; *p.* ode; *pp.* od [ge-, beterian *to make better*, betera *better*] *To better, make better;* meliōrāre, emendāre:—Đe mid đære lāre gebeterode wǽron *who were bettered by that instruction*, Homl. Th. i. 406, 32. Đa scamfæstan beóþ oft mid gemetlīcre lāre gebetrode *the modest are often improved with moderate instruction*, Past. 31, 1; Swt. 205, 23; Hat. MS. 39 b, 5.

ge-beterung *an amending, bettering, making better;* emendātio, instauratio, Som. Ben. Lye.

ge-beđian; *p.* ode, ede; *pp.* od, ed; *v. trans.* [ge-, beđian *to bathe*] *To wash, bathe, foment, cherish, warm;* lăvāre, fŏvēre:—Mid đam wætere đa eágan gebeđa *bathe the eyes with the water*, Herb. 88; Lchdm. i. 192, 5. Wearþ his lǽcum geþūht đæt hī on wlacum ele hine gebeđedon *it seemed good to his physicians that they should bathe him in lukewarm oil*, Homl. Th. i. 86, 23. Byþ langum ǽrđamđe heó eft gebeđod sȳ *it is long before it is again warmed*, Bd. de nat. rerum; Wrt. popl. science 9, 21, 22; Lchdm. iii. 252, 8, 10. Of đam wīne sȳn đa lyđu gebeđede *let the joints be bathed with the wine*, Herb. 89, 5; Lchdm. i. 192, 25.

ge-bētt *amended, reformed*, Bd. 1, 21; S. 485, 8: 1, 27; S. 492, 17; *pp. of* ge-bētan.

ge-bētung, -bēttung, e; *f.* [gebētan *to better*] *A bettering, amending, repairing, renewing, restoring;* emendātio, instaurātio:—Be ciricena gebētunge *of the repairing of churches*, L. Edm. E. 5; Th. i. 246, 9. Be burga gebēttunge *of repairing of fortresses*, L. Ath. i. 13; Th. i. 206, 13.

ge-bicgan, -bicgean *to buy, purchase*, Exon. 90 a; Th. 338, 22; Gu. Ex. 82: L. Edg. ii. 3; Th. i. 266, 18: L. Eth. ii. 1; Th. i. 284, 13. v. ge-bycgan.

ge-bīcnian, -bȳcnian; *p.* ode, ede; *pp.* od, ed [ge-, bīcnian *to beckon, nod*]. I. *to beckon, nod;* innuĕre:—Ic gebīcnige [gebȳcnige MS. D.] *innuo*, Ælfc. Gr. 28, 3; Som. 30, 48. II. *to point out, shew, indicate, betoken;* indĭcāre, signĭfĭcāre, portendĕre:—Ic gebīcnige [gebȳcnige MS. D.], Ælfc. Gr. 37; Som. 39, 40. Hī gebīcniaþ sum þing niwes *they betoken something new*, Bd. de nat. rerum; Wrt. popl. science 16, 23; Lchdm. iii. 272, 7. Pirrus gebīcnede eft hū him se sige gelīcode *Pyrrhus afterwards shewed how the victory pleased him*, Ors. 4, 1; Bos. 77, 35. Gebȳcna hit eal me *tell it all to me*, St. A. 44, 12. v. ge-beácnian.

ge-bicnigendlīc; *adj. Pointing out, shewing, indicative;* indĭcātīvus:—Gebīcnigendlīc gemet *indĭcātīvus mŏdus*, Ælfc. Gr. 21; Som. 23, 18.

ge-bīcnung, e; *f.* [ge-, bīcnung *a sign*] *A presage, sign;* præsāgium:—Þurh heofenlīcere gebīcnunge *through a heavenly sign*. Hom. Th. ii. 306, 7. v. ge-beácnung.

ge-bīdan, he -bīdeþ, -bīt; *p.* -bād, *pl.* -bidon; *pp.* -biden [ge-, bīdan *to bide, abide*] *To abide, tarry, remain, await, look for, expect, meet with, experience, endure;* mănēre, remănēre, expectāre, consĕqui, sustĭnere, tŏlĕrāre:—Đæt feorhdaga on woruldrīce worn gebīde *that he may abide many life-days in the world's realm*, Cd. 107; Th. 142, 10; Gen. 2359. Gebīdaþ hēr *sustĭnēte hic*, Mt. Bos. 26, 38. Dreámleás gebād *he continued joyless*, Beo. Th. 3445; B. 1720. He gebād đār sylf *remansit sōlus Jēsus*, Jn. Bos. 8, 9. Ne mæg feónd gebīdan *foe may not await him*, Exon. 30 a; Th. 93, 23; Cri. 1530. Hig gebidon his *erant expectantes eum*, Lk. Bos. 8, 40. He đæs frōfre gebād *he from that [time] met with comfort*, Beo. Th. 14; B. 7: Exon. 41 b; Th. 140, 11; Gū. 608. Ōđres ne gȳmeþ to gebīdanne yrfeweardes *he cares not to wait for another heir*, Beo. Th. 4895; B. 2452. Fela sceal gebīdan leófes and lāþes *much shall he experience of loved and hated*, 2125; B. 1060. [*Laym.* i-biden: *Goth.* ga-beidan *to abide, endure: O. Sax.* gi-bīdan *to experience.*]

ge-biddan; *p.* -bæd, *pl.* -bǽdon; *pp.* -beden; *often followed by a reflexive dative* [ge-, biddan *to ask, pray*] *To pray, pray to, worship, adore;* ōrāre, adōrāre, cŏlĕre:—Uton gebiddan us *let us pray*, Homl. Blick. 139, 30. Đonne we us gebiddaþ *when we pray*, Bt. 41, 2; Fox 246, 21. Đonne gē eów gebiddon *cum ōrātis*, Mt. Bos. 6, 5. Đonne đū đē gebidde *cum orāvĕris*, 6, 6. Lǽr us us gebiddan *dŏce nos ōrāre*, Lk. Bos. 11, 1. For đē gebitt *ōrābit pro te*, Gen. 20, 7. Ic him ā gebæd *ego autem ōrābam*, Ps. Th. 108, 3. Ne đū fremedne god gebiddest *neque adōrābis deum aliēnum*, 80, 9. Gebiddaþ him đǽr to *adōrant eum*, Ex. 32, 8. Gebiddaþ on gesihþe his *adōrābunt in conspectu ejus*, Ps. Spl. 21, 28. Ic me to him gebidde *eum cŏlo*, Bd. 1, 7; S. 477, 34. Gebiddande *orans*, Mt. Kmbl. 26, 39.

ge-bierde; *adj. Inborn, natural;* innātus, natūrālis, Cot. 106. v. gebyrde.

ge-biesgian *to occupy, afflict, overcome*, Exon. 96 a; Th. 358, 2; Pa. 39. v. ge-bȳsgian.

ge-bīgan; *p.* de; *pp.* ed; *v. trans.* [ge-, bīgan *to bow, bend*] *To bow, bend, turn, inflect or decline a part of speech, twist, bow down, humble, bring under, subdue, crush;* flectĕre, inflectĕre, declīnāre, humiliāre:—He hī to fulluhte gebīgde *he brought them to baptism*, H. R. 101, 26. Se sceal heán wesan niđer gebīged *he shall be low bowed down*, Exon. 84 a; Th. 316, 28; Mōd. 55: Bd. 4, 10; S. 578, 28: Gen. 27, 29. Ealle naman beóþ gebīgede on fīf declīnungum *omnia nōmĭna quinque declīnātiōnĭbus inflectuntur*, Ælfc. Gr. 7; Som. 6, 2: 14; Som. 16, 56: Exon. 24 a; Th. 69, 26; Cri. 1126: Ors. 3, 9; Bos. 64, 15: Ælfc. T. 30, 5. Ps. Th. 106, 15. v. ge-bȳgan.

ge-bīgednys, -nyss, e; *f. A bending, inflection, declining, declension, case;* declīnātio, cāsus:—Gebīgednys *cāsus*, Ælfc. Gr. 15; Som. 17, 30. Cāsus, đæt is fyll ođđe gebīgedniss *a case, that is a fall or inflection*, Ælfc. Gr. 14; Som. 17, 23. Đa pronōmĭna đe habbaþ vŏcātīvum, đa habbaþ six casus, and đa ōđre ealle nabbaþ būton fīf gebīgednyssa *the pronouns which have a vocative have six cases, and all the other have but five cases*, Ælfc. Gr. 18; Som. 20, 55. Nemnigendlīc gebīgednys *vel* nemnigendlīc cāsus *Nominative case*, Ælfc. Gr. 7; Som. 6, 16. Gestrȳnendlīc, geāgniendlīc *Genitive*, 6, 17: Forgifendlīc *Dative*, 6, 19: Wrēgendlīc *Accusative*, 6, 22: Clipigendlīc, ođđe gecīgendlīc *Vocative*, 6, 24, 25: Ætbredendlīc *Ablative* and *Instrumental*, 6, 27, *q. v.*

ge-bīgendlīc; *adj. Bending, flexible, declined with cases;* flexĭbĭlis, căsuālis:—Be đām six gebīgendlīcum hiwum *de sex casuālibus formis*, Ælfc. Gr. 14; Som. 17, 19.

ge-bigeþ, -bigþ *buys*, L. Ethb. 77; Th. i. 22, 1: Mt. Bos. 13, 44, = ge-bygeþ; *pres. of* ge-bycgan.

ge-bihþ, e; *f.* [cf. byht *a dwelling, abode*] *An abode, habitation;* domĭcĭlium:—On mislīcum monna gebihþum *in the various abodes of men*, Exon. 45 b; Th. 154, 22; Gū. 846.

ge-bild; *adj. Bold, brave, confident;* audax, fortis, fīdens:—He mid gebildum mōde hine ealne gedranc *he drank it all with a bold mind*, Homl. Th. i. 72, 25. v. gebyldan.

ge-bilegan *to make angry, to be angry*, Som. Ben. Lye. v. ge-belgan.

ge-bilod; *pp.* [bile *a bill, beak*] *Having a bill or beak;* rostrātus:—Đa fugelas, đe be flǽsce lybbaþ, syndon clyferfēte and scearpe gebilode *the birds which live by flesh are cloven-footed and sharp-billed*, Hexam. 9; Norm. 14, 19.

ge-bind, es; *n. A binding, fastening;* ligātūra, strictūra:—Ofer wađema gebind [or wađema-gebind, cf. ȳþ-gebland] *over the watery band*, i. e. *the surface of the water*, Exon. 76 b; Th. 288, 1; Wand. 24: 77 a; Th. 289, 32; Wand. 57. Gebynd *strictura*, Ælfc. Gl. 11; Wrt. Voc. 19, 50. [Cf. *Goth.* ga-binda, -bindi *a band.*] v. īs-gebind.

ge-bindan; ic -binde, đū -bintst, -binst, he -bint, *pl.* -bindaþ; *p.* ic, he -band, -bond, đū -bunde, *pl.* -bundon; *pp.* -bunden [ge-, bindan *to bind, tie*]. I. *to bind, tie up;* lĭgāre, allĭgāre, vincīre, constringĕre:—Hine nān man ne mihte gebindan *neque quisquam pŏtĕrat eum lĭgāre*, Mk. Bos. 5, 3: 6, 17; Cd. 184; Th. 230, 6; Dan. 229: Salm. Kmbl. 556; Sal. 277. Sorg and slǽp earmne ānhogan oft gebindaþ *sorrow and sleep often bind a poor lone-dweller*, Exon. 77 a; Th. 288, 33; Wand. 40. Đū mec fæste fetrum gebunde *thou didst bind me fast with fetters*, Exon. 72 a; Th. 268, 17; Jul. 433: 98 a; Th. 368, 28; Seel. 31. He geband đā his sunu *cum alligasset filium suum*, Gen. 22, 9: Homl. Th. ii. 414, 18: Cd. 23; Th. 29, 3; Gen. 444: Beo. Th. 845; B. 420. Đære moldan sumne dǽl he gebond on his sceáte *a part of the mould he tied* *up in his clothing*, Bd. 3, 10; S. 524, 23: Exon. 18 b; Th. 46, 5; Cri. 732. Hie handa gebundon *they bound the hands*, Andr. Kmbl. 96; An. 48: 2446; An. 1224. Ceácan heora gewrîþ oðđe gebind *maxillas eōrum constringe*, Ps. Spl. 31, 12. Gif he hî ne gebunde *if he had not bound them*, Bt. 35, 2; Fox 158, 1, note, MS. Cot. Se wæs gebunden *qui ĕrat vinctus*, Mk. Bos. 15, 7: Bd. 1, 27; S. 497, 31, 32: Cd. 35; Th. 45, 30; Gen. 734: Exon. 13 a; Th. 23, 7; Cri. 365: Andr. Kmbl. 2792; An. 1398: Bt. Met. Fox 5, 78; Met. 5, 39: Judth. 10; Thw. 23, 11; Jud. 115: Beo. Th. 3490; B. 1743. Wæs his gewuna đæt he him forgeáfe ǽnne gebundenne *sŏlēbat dimittĕre illis ūnum ex vinctis*, Mk. Bos. 15, 6: Bd. 1, 27; S. 497, 33: Chr. 796; Erl. 58, 12: Exon. 102 b; Th. 387, 20; Rä. 5, 8. He gehýrde heáh gnornunge đæra đe gebundene bitere wǽron *audīvit gĕmĭtum vincŭlātōrum*, Ps. Th. 101, 18: Cd. 19; Th. 24, 18; Gen. 379: Andr. Kmbl. 1893; An. 949. II. *to deceive* [?]; fallĕre:—He hine on đære wēnunge [wenunge Thorpe] geband *he deceived him in that hope*, Ors. 3, 7; Bos. 59, 25. [*Goth.* ga-bindan: *O. Sax.* gi-bindan.]

ge-bîraþ *becomes*, L. Edg C. 64; Th. ii. 258, 8. v. ge-bӯrian.

ge-bird, e; *f. Birth, origin*:—Forđam sîn ealle men ânra gebirda *because all men are of one origin*, L. Edg. C. 13; Th. ii. 246, 22. v. ge-byrd.

gebirg, es; *n. Taste*:—On gebirge *in gustu*, Rtl. 116, 5.

ge-birhtan, he -birht; *p.* -birhte; *pp.* -birhted, -birht *To make bright, brighten, illuminate*; illūmĭnāre:—Đe ealle þing gebirht *which brightens all things*, Bt. 34, 8; Fox 144, 37. Ealle steorran weorþaþ onlîhte and gebirhte of đære sunnan *all stars are lighted and made bright by the sun*, 34, 5; Fox 140, 5. v. ge-berhtan.

ge-bîrigan *to taste*, Mt. Kmbl. Hat. 27, 34. v. ge-bӯrgan.

ge-bisgian *to occupy, afflict, agitate*, Exon. 50 a; Th. 173, 34; Gū. 1170. v. ge-bӯsgian.

ge-bismerian, -bismrian, -bysmerian, -bysmrian; *p.* ode, ede; *pp.* od, ed [ge-, bismerian *to mock*] *To mock, laugh at, deride, provoke*; illūdĕre, irrīdēre, derīdēre, exacerbāre:—Draca đes đe đū hywodest to gebismrienne him *drăco iste quem formasti ad illūdendum ei*, Ps. Lamb. 103, 26. Se đe eardaþ on heofenum gebismeraþ oðđe hyscþ hig *qui hăbĭtat in cœlis irrīdēbit eos*, 2, 4. Đū, Drihten, gebysmerast hî *tu, Domine, derīdēbis eos*, 58, 9. Hî heánne God gebysmredon [MS. gebysmredan] *exacerbāvērunt Deum excelsum*, Ps. Th. 77, 56.

ge-bisnere, es; *m. An imitator*:—Gibisnere *imitator*, Rtl. 45, 14.

ge-bisnian *to inform, imitate*:—Gibisnendo *informanda*, Rtl. 103, 30. We gibisnia *imitemur*, 52, 3. Gebisened *imitandam*, Lk. Skt. p. 6, 20. v. gebysnian.

ge-bisnung *an example*; exemplum, Som. Ben. Lye. v. ge-bysnung.

ge-bit, -bitt, es; *n.* [ge-, biten, *pp. of* bîtan *to bite*] *A biting, biting together, grinding, gnashing*; morsus, strīdor:—Đǽr biþ wōp and tōþa gebitt *there shall be weeping and gnashing of teeth*, Homl. Th. 126, 20.

ge-bîtan *to bite*:—Gebîtes ł to-slîtes *adlidit*, Mk. Skt. Lind. 9, 18.

ge-biterian; *p.* ode; *pp.* od [ge-, biterian *to embitter*] *To make bitter*; amarefacere:—Hî sealdon him gebiterod wîn *dăbant ei myrrhātum vīnum* [*amarefactum vīnum, vīnum myrrha imbūtum*], Mk. Bos. 15, 23.

ge-bitt *prays* or *will pray*; ōrābit, Gen. 20, 7; *3rd pres. of* ge-biddan.

ge-blǽd, es; *m.* [ge-, blǽd I. *a blast, blowing*] *A blowing out in the skin, blister*; vēsīca in cŭte. DER. þorn-geblǽd, þystel-, wæter-, wyrm-, ӯs-.

ge-blǽdfæst; *adj.* [blǽd *fruit*] *Fruitful*; fertĭlis:—Beorht and geblǽdfæst *bright and fruitful*, Cd. 5; Th. 6, 15; Gen. 89.

ge-bland, -blond, es; *n.* [ge-, bland *a mixture, confusion*] *A mixture, mingling, commotion*; commixtio, turba:—Ofer æra gebland *over the mingling of the waves*, Chr. 937; Erl. 112, 26; Æđelst. 26. Árӯþa geblond *commotion of the oar-waves*, Andr. Kmbl. 1063; An. 532. DER. âr-gebland, ear-, snāw-, sund-, ӯþ-. v. bland.

ge-blandan, -blondan; *p.* -bleónd, -blēnd, *pl.* bleóndon, -blēndon; *pp.* -blanden, -blonden [ge-bland]. I. *to blend, mix, mingle*; miscēre, turbāre:—Hî me geblēndon unswētne drync *they mixed for me an unsweet drink*, Exon. 29 a; Th. 88, 10; Cri. 1438: Andr. Kmbl. 65; An. 33. Wurman geblonden *mixed with scarlet*, Exon. 60 a; Th. 218, 14; Ph. 294. Hie him sealdon attor drincan đæt mid myclen lybcræfte wæs geblanden *they gave them poison to drink mixed by powerful magic*, Blickl. Homl. 229, 12. [Cf. *O. Sax.* baluwes gi-blandan.] II. *to stain, colour, corrupt*; inficĕre:—Geblēnde *infēcit*, Cot. 112. Wæs seó hǽwene lyft heolfre geblanden *the azure air was corrupted with gore*, Cd. 166; Th. 208, 1; Exod. 476.

ge-blann *ceased*, Mk. Skt. Lind. 6, 51; *p. of* ge-blinnan.

ge-blâwan; *p.* -bleów, *pl.* -bleówon; *pp.* -blâwen [ge-, blâwan *to blow*] *To blow*; flāre, sufflāre:—Gebleów *sufflāvit*, Jn. Skt. Lind. 20, 22.

ge-blecte [?] *destroyed*; extermĭnāvit, Ps. Spl. C. 79, 14.

ge-bledsian; *p.* ode; *pp.* od [ge-, bledsian *to bless*] *To bless*; benedīcĕre:—Gebledsod wearþ engla ēđel *the dwelling of the angels was blessed*, Andr. Kmbl. 1048; An. 524: 1079; An. 540: 1873; An. 939: 3434; An. 1721.

ge-blēgenad; *part.* [ge-, blēgen *a blain, blister*] *Blistered*; ulcĕrātus, Som. Ben. Lye.

ge-blēnd, *pl.* -blēndon *mixed*, Exon. 29 a; Th. 88, 10; Cri. 1438; *p. of* ge-blandan.

ge-blendan; *p.* -blende; *pp.* -blended, -blend [ge, blendan *to blind*] *To blind, make blind*; cœcāre:—Gē habbaþ eówre heortan geblende *ye have your hearts blinded*, Mk. Bos. 8, 17. [*Goth.* ga-blindjan.]

ge-bleód, -blíód; *part.* [ge-, bleoh, bleó *a colour, hue, complexion*] *Coloured, of different colours, variegated, gifted with beauty, beautiful in countenance*; colōrātus, versĭcŏlor, spĕcie prædĭtus, aspectu formātus:—Đa wyrta greówon, mid menigfealdum blōstmum mislîce gebleóde *the plants grew, diversely coloured with manifold blossoms*, Hexam. 6; Norm. 10, 36. Ōþӯweþ Cristes onsӯn, on sefan swēte sînum folce, gebleód wundrum *Christ's countenance shall appear, sweet in mind to his people, wondrously gifted with beauty*, Exon. 21 a; Th. 56, 32; Cri. 909.

ge-bleoh, -bleó; *gen.* -bleós; *n.* [ge-, bleoh *a colour*] *A colour*; cŏlor:—Mid swā wlitigum blōstmum hî oferstîgaþ ealle eorþlîce gebleoh *with such beautiful blossoms they excel all earthly colours*, Homl. Th. ii. 464, 9.

ge-bleów *blew*, Jn. Skt. Lind. 20, 22; *p. of* ge-blâwan.

ge-bletsian, -bledsian; *p.* ode, ade; *pp.* od, ad [ge-, bletsian *to bless*] *To bless, consecrate*; benedīcĕre, consecrāre:—Ic đē gebletsige *benedīcam tibi*, Gen. 12, 2, 3: 17, 16. Ic wât, đæt se biþ gebletsod, đe đū gebletsast *nōvi ĕnim, quod benedictus sit, cui benedixĕris*, Num. 22, 6. Gebletsode Romulus mid his brōđor blōde đone weall *Romulus blessed* [*consecrated*] *the wall* [*of Rome*] *with his brother's blood*, Ors. 2, 2; Bos. 41, 5. God gebletsode đone seofeđan dæg and hine gehālgode *Deus benedixit diei septĭmo et sanctĭfĭcāvit illum*, Gen. 2, 3: 5, 2: 24, 1. Đū gebletsadest bearn Israhēla *benedixit dŏmui Israel*, Ps. Th. 113, 21. Miltsa us mihtig Drihten, and us on mōde eác gebletsa nū *Deus misereātur nostri, et benedicat nōbis*, 66, 1. Đæt ǽnig preóst ne forlǽte đa circan đe he to gebletsod wæs *that no priest forsake the church to which he was consecrated*, L. Edg. C. 8; Th. ii. 246, 8. Sӯ gebletsod se đe com on Drihtenes naman *benedictus qui vēnit in nōmĭne Domĭni*, Mt. Bos. 21, 9: 23, 39. Đū gebletsad eart *thou art blessed*, Cd. 192; Th. 241, 18; Dan. 406: 83; Th. 105, 13; Gen. 1752.

ge-blinnan; *p.* -blann, *pl.* -blunnon; *pp.* blunnen [ge-, blinnan *to cease*] *To cease, desist*; cessāre, desistēre:—Geblann đæt wind *the wind ceased*, Mk. Skt. Lind. 6, 51.

ge-blíód; *part. Coloured, variegated*; colōrātus, variegātus:—Geblíód reáf *vestis variegāta*, Prov. 31. v. ge-bleód.

ge-blissian; *part.* -blissiende; *p.* ode, ade; *pp.* od, ad [ge-, blissian *to rejoice*]. I. *v. intrans. To rejoice, be glad*; lætāri, gaudēre:—Đē gebӯrede gewistfullian and geblissian *epŭlāri et gaudēre oportēbat*, Lk. Bos. 15, 32: Jn. Bos. 5, 35. Geblissiaþ on Drihtne *lætāmĭni in Dŏmĭno*, Ps. Spl. 31, 14: Mt. Bos. 5, 12. II. *v. trans. To make to rejoice, gladden, fill with bliss, bless*; lætĭfĭcāre, benedīcĕre:—Rihtwîsnyssa Drihtnes rihte synt, geblissiende heortan *justĭtiæ Dŏmĭni rectæ sunt, lætĭfĭcantes corda*, Ps. Lamb. 18, 9. Đū geblissast hine *lætĭfĭcābis eum*, 20, 7. Pater Noster hālige geblissaþ *the Pater Noster gladdens the holy*, Salm. Kmbl. 80; Sal. 40: Ps. Spl. 45, 4. Frōfra đîne geblissodon sāwle mîne *consōlātiōnes tuæ lætĭfĭcāvērunt anĭmam meam*, 93, 19. Đū đisne middangeard milde geblissa *do thou kindly bless this mid-earth*, Exon. 11 b; Th. 16, 7; Cri. 249. Iudas wæs miclum geblissod *Judas was greatly rejoiced*, Elen. Kmbl. 1749; El. 876: 2249; El. 1126. Đā wæs Gūþlâces gǽst geblissad *then was Guthlac's spirit gladdened*, Exon. 43 a; Th. 145, 14; Gū. 694: 56 a; Th 198, 9; Ph. 7. Eálā! heofoncund Þrӯnes, brāde geblissad geond brytenwongas *oh! heavenly Trinity, widely blessed over the spacious world!* 13 a; Th. 24, 5; Cri. 380. [*Laym.* i-blissed.]

ge-blissung, e; *f. A rejoicing, joyousness, hilarity*; hĭlărĭtas, Procem. R. Conc.

ge-blōdegian, -blōdgian; *p.* ode, ade; *pp.* od, ad [ge-, blōdegian *to make bloody*] *To make bloody, cover with blood*; cruentāre:—He geblōdegod wearþ sāwuldrióre *he was made bloody with life-gore*, Beo. Th. 5378; B. 2692. Swilce đǽr lǽge on đam disce ānes fingres liþ eal geblōdgod *as if there lay in the dish the joint of a finger all covered with blood*, Homl. Th. ii. 272, 27; Wanl. Catal. 43, 16. Gif đæt flet geblōdgad wyrþe *if the dwelling be covered with blood*, L. H. E. 14; Th. i. 32, 14.

ge-blond *a mixture*, Andr. Kmbl. 1063; An. 532. v. ge-bland.

ge-blondan; *pp.* -blonden *To blend, mix, mingle*; miscēre:—Âttre geblonden *mixed with venom*, Cd. 216; Th. 272, 34; Sat. 129. v. geblandan.

ge-blōt, es; *n.* [ge-, blōt *a sacrifice*] *A sacrifice*; sacrifĭcium:—Būtan geblōte *without sacrifice*, Ors. 5, 2; Bos. 102, 14. Hî swylc geblōt and swylc morþ dōnde wǽron *they made such sacrifices and such murders*, 1, 8; Bos. 31, 8.

ge-blōwan; *p.* -bleów, *pl.* -bleówon; *pp.* -blōwen [ge-, blōwan *to blow*] *To blow, flourish, bloom, blossom*; flōrēre, efflōrēre:—Wyrt geblōweþ *herba flōreat*, Ps. Th. 89, 6. Đæt gē on his wîcum wel geblōwan *in atriis dŏmus Dei nostri flōrēbunt*, 91, 12. Se ædela feld wrîdaþ under wolcnum, wynnum geblówen *the noble field flourishes under the skies, blooming with delights*, Exon. 56 a; Th. 199, 18; Ph. 27: 56 b; Th. 200, 27; Ph. 47. Geseh he geblówene bearwas, blǽdum gehrodene *he saw blooming groves, adorned with blossoms*, Andr. Kmbl. 2894; An. 1450: Exon. 51 a; Th. 178, 25; Gú. 1249. He geseah geblówen treów wæstm-berende *he saw a full-blown tree bearing fruit*, Blickl. Homl. 245, 8.

ge-bócian; *p.* ode; *pp.* od [ge-, bócian *to give by charter*]. I. *to give* or *grant by book* or *charter, to charter*; libro *vel* charta dōnāre:—Ðis is seó bóc, đe Æđelstán cing gebócode Friþestáne bisceope *this is the charter which king Athelstan chartered to bishop Frithestan*, Th. Diplm. A. D. 938; 187, 19: 966; 218, 12. Gebócode Æđelwulf [MS. Adelwulf] cing teóđan dǽl his landes, ofer ealle his ríce, Gode to lofe *king Æthelwulf chartered the tenth part of his land over all his kingdom for the glory of God*, Chr. 856; Th. 124, 22, col. 3: Text. Rof. 115, 22. II. *to furnish with books*; libris instruĕre:—Gé preóstas sculon beón gebócode *ye priests shall be furnished with books*, L. Ælf. P. 44; Th. ii. 382, 36.

ge-bod, es; *n.* [ge-, bod *a command*] *A command, order, mandate*; jussum, mandātum:—Is đæt þeódnes gebod *it is God's command*, Exon. 56 b; Th. 202, 12; Ph. 68: Menol. Fox 457; Men. 230. Be đæs cyninges gebode *by the king's command*, Bt. 39, 13; Fox 234, 13. Gif preóst ofer arcediácones gebod mæssige *if a priest celebrate mass against the archdeacon's command*, L. N. P. L. 7; Th. ii. 290, 25: Chr. 901; Erl. 98, 3. Ðú gebod Godes læstes *thou hast performed God's mandate*, Cd. 27; Th. 36, 14; Gen. 571: 33; Th. 43, 29; Gen. 698: Ps. Th. 118, 87. Hí woldon onwendan eall đa gebodu *they would change all the orders*, Ors. 6, 10; Bos. 120, 33. [*O. Sax.* gi-bod: *O. H. Ger.* ga-pot: *Ger.* gebot.]

ge-boden *announced*, L. Ath. i. 20; Th. i. 208, 27; *pp. of* ge-beódan.

ge-bodian; *p.* ode, ade; *pp.* od, ad [ge-, bodian *to tell*] *To tell, make known, announce, proclaim*; nuntiāre, annuntiāre:—Se đæt láþspell æt hám gebodode *who made known the sad story at home*, Ors. 2, 4; Bos. 43, 37: Hy. 10, 13; Hy. Grn. ii. 293, 13. Ðæt đǽr nán to láfe ne wearþ đæt hit to Róme gebodade *so that there was none left to tell it at Rome*, Ors. 4, 11; Bos. 97, 30: Exon. 10 b; Th. 13, 14; Cri. 202. [*Laym.* i-boded.]

gebod-scipe, es; *m.* [gebod *a command*] *A commandment*; mandātum:—Gif hie brecaþ his gebodscipe *if they break his commandment*, Cd. 22; Th. 28, 3; Gen. 430. [*O. Sax.* gi-bodskepi, *n.*]

ge-bogen *submitted*, Chr. 1013; Erl. 148, 2, 21; *pp. of* ge-búgan.

ge-bógian; *p.* ode; *pp.* od [ge-, bógian *to inhabit*] *To inhabit*; incŏlĕre:—Hí gebógodon eástdǽl middaneardes *they inhabited the east part of the earth*, Boutr. Scrd. 21, 30, 31, 32. v. ge-búgian.

ge-boht *bought*, Ælfc. Gl. 86; Som. 74, 33; Wrt. Voc. 50, 16; *pp. of* ge-bycgan: ge-bohte, *pl.* -bohton *bought, redeemed*, Gen. 39, 1: L. C. E. 18; Th. i. 370, 28: Chr. 1016; Erl. 159, 23; *p. of* ge-bycgan.

ge-bolged; *part. Caused to swell, made angry*; tumĭdus, indignātus, Som. Ben. Lye.

ge-bolgen *offended, angry*, Mt. Bos. 2, 16; *pp. of* ge-belgan.

ge-bolstrod; *part.* [ge-, bolster *a bolster*] *Guarded, environed, defended, supported* or *bolstered up*; stīpātus, Som. Ben. Lye.

ge-bond *bound, tied up*, Bd. 3, 10; S. 543, 23; *p. of* ge-bindan.

ge-boned; *part. Polished, burnished*; pŏlītus:—He hæfþ điderynn gedón ii mycele gebonede róda, and ii mycele Cristes béc gebonede, and iii gebonede scrín, and i geboned altare *he has placed therein two large burnished crosses, and two large Christ's books* [= *Gospels*] *polished, and three burnished shrines, and one burnished altar*, Th. Diplm. A. D. 1050–1073; 429, 11–18. Ic gean Sc̄e Eádmunde twegea gebonedra horna *I give to St. Edmund two polished horns*, Th. Diplm. A. D. 1046; 564, 12. [*Swed.* bona *to polish with wax, to rub*: *Dan.* bone *to cleanse, make clean, to burnish, polish.*]

ge-bonn, es; *n. The indiction*; indictio, Th. Diplm. A. D. 896; 139, 10: Cod. Diplm. 1073; Kmbl. v. 140, 8. v. ge-ban II.

ge-bonnan; *pp.* bonnen *To summon, call together*:—Folc biþ gebonnen *mankind shall be summoned*, Exon. 117 b; Th. 451, 8; Dóm. 100. v. ge-bannan.

ge-bonn-gér, es; *n.* [gebonn *indiction*; gér, geár *a year*] *The indiction-year*; indictiōnis annus, Cod. Dipl. 1073; A. D. 896; Kmbl. v. 140, 8: Th. Diplm. A. D. 896; 139, 10. v. ge-ban II.

ge-boren *born*, Chr. 381; Erl. 10, 2; *pp. of* ge-beran.

ge-borga *a protector, guardian*; tūtor. DER. lind-geborga.

ge-borgen *defended, safe, secure*, Homl. Th. i. 56, 18; *pp. of* ge-beorgan.

ge-borhfæstan; *p.* te; *pp.* ed [ge-, borhfæstan *to fasten by pledge* or *surety*] *To determine* or *fasten by a surety*; intertiāre [q. v. in Du Cange], ăpud sequestrum depōnĕre, Cot. 107.

ge-borsnung, e; *f. Corruption*; corruptio:—Ne đú ne selst háligne đínne geseón geborsnunga *nec dābis sanctum tuum vĭdēre corruptiōnem*, Ps. Spl. 15, 10. v. ge-brosnung.

ge-bósmed; *part.* [ge-, bósum, bósm *the bosom*; sĭnus] *Bosomed, bent, crooked*; sĭnuātus:—Gebósmed segelbósmas *sinuāta carbăsa*, Cot. 185.

ge-bótad; *part. Bettered, mended*; resartus:—Ðá him gebótad wæs *when he was better*, Chr. 1093; Erl. 228, 30. v. ge-bétan.

ge-bræc, đú -brǽce, *pl.* -brǽcon *broke, didst break*, Bd. 3, 2; S. 525, 2: Ps. Th. 73, 13; *p. of* ge-brecan.

ge-bræc, es; *n.* [ge-, bræc *a breaking*] *A breaking, crashing, noise*; fractio, frăgor, strĕpĭtus:—Ðá wearþ borda gebræc *then there was a crashing of shields*, Byrht. Th. 140, 28; By. 295: Beo. Th. 4510; B. 2259. [*O. Sax.* gi-brak: *O. H. Ger.* ka-preh *fragor.*] v. ge-brec.

ge-bræceo; *indecl. n. A cough*; tussis:—Wiđ gebræceo *for cough*, Herb. 124, 2; Lchdm. i. 236, 15: 126, 1; Lchdm. i. 236, 24. Heó gebræceo útatyhþ *it draweth out cough*, 124, 1; Lchdm. i. 236, 12.

ge-bræcseóc, -bræcsióc; *adj.* [ge-, bræcseóc *epileptic, lunatic*] *Epileptic, lunatic*; epilepticus = ἐπιληπτικός, lunātĭcus:—Gebræcsióce *epileptĭci, comĭtiāles*, Cot. 46.

ge-bræcseócnes, -ness, e; *f.* [ge-, bræcseócnes *epilepsy*] *The falling sickness, epilepsy*; morbus comĭtiālis, epilepsia, Som. Ben. Lye.

ge-bræd *drew, brandished*, Beo. Th. 5118; B. 2562; *p. of* ge-bredan.

ge-brǽdan; to -brǽdenne; *p.* de; *pp.* ed [ge-, brǽdan *to make broad*] *To make broad, broaden, extend, spread*; dilātāre, ampliāre, extendĕre, expandĕre, sternere:—Merestreám ne dear ofer eorþan sceát eard gebrǽdan *the sea-stream dares not extend its province over the region of the earth*, Bt. Met. Fox 11, 132; Met. 11, 66. Ðæt mód wilnaþ to gebrǽdenne his ǽgen lof *the mind desires to extend its own praise*, Past. 65, 4; Swt. 463, 36; Hat. MS; Bt. 18, 2; Fox 64, 15. He his cyricean wundorlícum weorcum gebrǽdde *ecclesiam suam mīrĭfĭcis ampliāvit opĕrĭbus*, Bd. 5, 20; S. 641, 40. Ealle đa telgan đú æt sǽstreámas sealte gebrǽddest *extendisti palmĭtes ejus usque ad măre*, Ps. Th. 79, 11. Ðreátas gebrǽdon wēdo hiora *turba straverunt vestĭmenta sua*, Mt. Kmbl. Lind. 21, 8. Miþ stáne gebrǽded *lapide stratus*, Jn. Skt. Lind. 19, 13.

ge-brǽdan; *p.* -brǽdde; *pp.* -brǽded, -brǽdd, -brǽd [ge-, brǽdan *to roast*] *To roast, broil*; torrēre, assāre:—Eton ealle đæt flǽsc on fýre gebrǽdd *ĕdent carnes assas igni*, Ex. 12, 8. Ne ne eton gé of đam nán þing hreówes, ne mid wætere gesoden, ac sig hit eall on fýre gebrǽdd *non comĕdētis ex eo crūdum quid, nec coctum ăqua, sed tantum assum igni*, 12, 9. Hig brohton him dǽl gebrǽddes fisces *illi obtŭlērunt ei partem piscis assi*, Lk. Bos. 24, 42. Genime đysse ylcan wyrte wyrttruman gebrǽde on hátan axan *let him take roots of this same herb roasted on hot ashes*, Herb. 60, 3; Lchdm. i. 162, 17.

ge-brægd *drew*, Beo. Th. 3133; B. 1564; *p. of* ge-bregdan.

ge-brægd, es; *m.* [ge-, brægd *deceit*] *Deceit, fraud*; fraus, fallācia:—Gebrægdas ođđe leásunga đæra wlenca *fallācia divĭtiārum*, Mt. Kmbl. Lind. 13, 22. [Cf. *Icel.* bragð *a trick.*]

ge-brægdnys, -nyss, e; *f. Craft, deceit*; astus, Cot. 18.

ge-breadian; *p.* ode; *pp.* od, ad [= ge-bredian] *To restore the flesh* or *body*:—Ðonne [Fénix] þurh briddes hád gebreadad weorþeþ eft of ascan *then* [*the Phœnix*] *through youth's state is restored again from ashes*, Exon. 61 a; Th. 224, 8; Ph. 372.

ge-brec, -bræc, es; *n.* [ge-, brec *a breaking, crash*] *A breaking, crashing, clamour, noise*; fractio, frăgor, strĕpĭtus:—Se dæg biþ dæg gebreces *the day will be a day of clamour*, Past. 35, 5; Swt. 245, 5; Hat. MS. 46 a, 17. He gehýrde đæt gebrec đara storma *audīto frăgōre procellārum*, Bd. 5, 1; S. 614, 3. Gebrecu feraþ ofer dreohtum [MS. dreontum] *the crashes go over multitudes*, Exon. 102 a; Th. 385, 14; Rä. 4, 44. Se biþ gebreca hlúdast *that is loudest of crashes*, 102 a; Th. 385, 6; Rä. 4, 40.

ge-brecan, he -breceþ, -bryceþ; *p.* -bræc, đú -brǽce, *pl.* -brǽcon; *pp.* -brocen; *v. trans.* [ge-, brecan *to break*] *To break, bruise, crush, destroy, shatter, waste*; frangĕre, confringĕre, contrībŭlāre, contĕrĕre, conquassāre, attĕrĕre:—Ealra fyrenfulra fyhtehornas ic bealdlíce gebrece snióme *omnia cornua peccātōrum confringam*, Ps. Th. 74, 9. Heáfod he gebreceþ hæleđa mæniges *conquassābit căpĭta multa*, 109, 7. Se snáw gebryceþ burga geatu *the snow destroys the gates of towns*, Salm. Kmbl. 613; Sal. 306. Ðú gebrǽce đæt dracan heáfod deópe wætere *tu contrībŭlasti căpĭta drăcōnum sŭper ăquas*, Ps. Th. 73, 13. He him on fæđm gebræc *he crushed them into his grasp*, i. e. *subdued them*, Cd. 4; Th. 4, 32; Gen. 62: 97; Th. 127, 15; Gen. 2111: Bd. 3, 2; S. 525, 2. He đa mǽgþe mid grimme wæle and herge gebræc *provinciam illam sæva cæde ac depopŭlātiōne attrivit*, 4, 15; S. 583, 26, MS. C. Se þuma gebrocen wæs *the thumb was broken*, 5, 6; S. 619, 24: Andr. Kmbl. 2944; An. 1475. [*Goth.* ga-brikan: *O. H. Ger.* ga-brechan.]

gebrec-drenc, es; *m. A drink for epilepsy*; epilepticus pōtus, arteriaca? Cot. 14. v. ge-bræcseóc.

ge-bredan; *p.* -bræd, *pl.* -brudon; *pp.* -broden [ge-, bredan *to draw*] I. *to draw, unsheath, brandish*; stringĕre, evagĭnāre, vibrāre:—He sweord gebræd *he drew his sword*, Beo. Th. 5118; B. 2562. Sweord gebrudon đa synfullan *glădium evagĭnāvērunt peccātōres*, Ps. Spl. 36, 14. Gif hwá his wǽpn gebrede *if any one draw his weapon*, L. Alf. pol. 7; Th. 66, 9. Ic đý wǽpne gebræd *I brandished the weapon*, Beo. Th. 3333; B. 1664. Cyning wælseaxe gebræd *the king brandished his deadly knife*, 5400;

B. 2703. II. *to draw breath, take breath, inspire;* inspīrāre:—Ðeáh he late meahte oreþe gebredan *though he could slowly take breath,* Exon. 49 b; Th. 172, 4; Gū. 1138. III. *to weave, plait;* nectĕre, plectĕre:—Spyrte biþ of rixum gebroden *a basket is plaited of rushes,* Homl. Th. ii. 402, 8. Herebyrne hondum gebroden *a martial corslet woven with hands,* Beo. Th. 2891; B. 1443. IV. *to feign, pretend;* simŭlāre:—Gebræd he hine seócne *he feigned himself sick,* Chr. 1003; Erl. 139, 9.

ge-bredian; *p.* ode; *pp.* od, ad *To restore the flesh* or *body;* pulpōsum reddere:—Him folgiaþ fuglas scȳne, beorhte gebredade, blissum hrēmige *beautiful birds follow him, brightly restored, blissfully exulting,* Exon. 64 b; Th. 237, 18; Ph. 592. v. ge-breadian.

ge-brēgan; *p.* de; *pp.* ed [ge-, brēgan *to give fear*] *To frighten, terrify;* terrēre, perterrēre:—Wæs his mōd mid ðām beótungum gebrēged *his mind was frightened by the threats,* Bd. 2, 12; S. 513, 14. Ic wæs mid ðysse ongrislīcan wæfersȳne gebrēged *I was terrified by this horrible sight,* 5, 12; S. 628, 9. We sind gebrēgede *we are terrified,* Homl. Th. i. 578, 27.

ge-bregd, -brægd, es; *m. Craft, cunning;* astūtia:—Dryhten dǣleþ sumum tæfle cræft, bleóbordes gebregd *the Lord allots to one skill at the table, cunning at the coloured board,* Exon. 88 a; Th. 331, 20; Vy. 71.

ge-bregd, es; *n.* [ge-, bregdan *to move to and fro*] *A moving to and fro, agitation, tossing;* vibrātio, agĭtātio, jactātio:—Nis ðǣr on ðam londe wedra gebregd hreóh under heofonum, ne se hearda forst *there is not in that land tossing of tempests rough under heaven, nor the hard frost,* Exon. 56 b; Th. 201, 17; Ph. 57.

ge-bregdan; *p.* -brægd, *pl.* -brugdon; *pp.* -brogden [ge-, bregdan *to vibrate, draw*]. I. *to draw, unsheath;* stringĕre, exĭmĕre:—He hringmǣl gebrægd *he drew the ringed sword,* Beo. Th. 3133; B. 1564. He gebrægd his sweord *exēmit gladium suum,* Mt. Kmbl. Rush. 26, 51. II. *to feign, pretend:*—Se ðe ða gebregdnan dōmas dēmde *he who hath judged false judgments,* Blickl. Homl. 99, 32. [v. brægden.] v. gebredan.

ge-brēgdnes, -ness, e; *f. Fear, dread;* tĭmor, terror, Som. Ben. Lye.

gebregd-stafas; *pl. m.* [gebregd *craft, cunning;* stafas, *pl. of* stæf *a letter*] *Literary arts;* artes litĕrārum:—Ic īglanda eallra hæbbe bōca onbȳrged þurh gebregdstafas *I have tasted the books of all islands through literary arts,* Salm. Kmbl. 4; Sal. 2.

ge-brehtnian; *p.* ade, ode; *pp.* ad, od *To become bright:*—Ðætte he gebrehtnige *se clarificari,* Jn. Skt. p. 6, 17. Gibrehtnad [gebereht-nad, Lind.] is *clarificatus est,* Jn. Skt. Rush. 13, 31.

ge-brehtnis, se; *f. Brightness:*—Gebrehtnis *clarificatio,* Jn. Skt. p. 6, 15.

ge-brēman; *p.* de; *pp.* ed [ge-, brēman *to celebrate*] *To celebrate, make famous, honour;* celebrāre, honōrāre:—He wolde gebrēman ða Iudēiscan *he would honour the Jews,* Som. Lye.

ge-brengan; *p.* -brohte, *pl.* -brohton; *pp.* -broht; *v. trans.* [ge-, brengan *to bring*] *To bring, lead, produce, bear;* ferre, dūcĕre, produ-cĕre:—He wēnþ ðæt ðone mon ǣr mǣge gebrengan on fǣrwyrde *that he thinks may bring the man earlier to a terrible fate,* Past. 62; Swt. 457, 11; Hat. MS: Salm. Kmbl. MS. A. 176; Sal. 87: 296; Sal. 147. Gif ðū gebrengest *if thou bringest,* Salm. Kmbl. MS. A. 178; Sal. 88. Iudith gebrohte heáfod on ðam fætelse *Judith put the head into the sack,* Judth. 11; Thw. 23, 17; Jud. 125. Ðū us to eádmēdum gebrohtest *thou broughtest us to humility;* nos humiliasti, Ps. Th. 89, 17. Hȳ hit gebrohton burgum in innan *they brought it within the towns,* Exon. 75 b; Th. 284, 2; Jul. 691: 40 b; Th. 135, 24; Gū. 529. On þeówote gebroht *brought into slavery,* Ors. 3, 9; Bos. 66, 20. Ðǣr wæs gebroht wīn *there was wine brought,* Chr. 1012; Th. 269, 21, col. 1. [*O. Sax.* gi-brengean.]

ge-brengnis, -niss, e; *f. Food, support;* victus, Mk. Skt. Lind. 12, 44.

ge-brice, -bryce, es; *m.* [ge-, brice *a breaking*] *A breaking, breach;* confractio:—Gyf nā Moyses gecoren his stōde on gebrice [Lamb. gebryce] on gesihþe his *si non Moyses electus ejus stetisset in confractiōne in conspectu ejus,* Ps. Spl. 105, 22.

ge-bridlian, -bridligan; *p.* ode; *pp.* od [ge-, bridlian *to bridle*] *To bridle, restrain;* frēnāre:—He ða gesceafta nū gebridlod [MS. gebridlode] hæfþ *he has now bridled the creatures,* Bt. 21; Fox 74, 32. Ðæt hī hira mōd gebridligen *that they bridle their mind,* Past. 33, 1; Swt. 215, 7; Hat. MS. 41 a, 8.

ge-brihtan; *p.* te; *pp.* ed [ge-, brihtan *to brighten*] *To brighten, make beautiful;* illumināre, pulchrum reddĕre:—Gebrihted *beautiful,* Menol. Fox 272; Men. 137.

gebringan, he -bringeþ, -brincþ; *p.* -brang, -brong; *pp.* brungen [ge-, bringan *to bring*] *To bring, lead, adduce, produce, bear;* ferre, dūcĕre, addūcĕre, prodūcĕre, offerre:—He mæg ðone lāðan gāst fleónde gebringan *he may bring the evil spirit to flight,* Salm. Kmbl. 176; Sal. 87: Bt. 32, 1; Fox 114, 4. Gif ðū mec gebringest *if thou bring me,* Salm. Kmbl. 31; Sal. 16. Storm oft holm gebringeþ *the sea often brings a storm,* Exon. 89 b; Th. 336, 19; Gn. Ex. 51. Ðe hine gebrincþ to ðære byrig *which brings him to the city,* Homl. Th. i. 164, 9: 198, 20. Ða hine on yrre gebringaþ *they bring him to anger;* in īra provŏcant, Ps. Th. 65, 6. Ðæt he hine on orwēnnysse gebringe *that he may bring him to despair,* Boutr. Scrd. 20, 17: Homl. Th. i. 8, 13: Rood Kmbl. 275; Kr. 139. Ðæt we ðone gebringen [MS. gebringan] on ādfære *that we bring him on the way to the pile,* Beo. Th. 6010; B. 3009: Homl. Th. i. 164, 11.

ge-britnod; *part.* [ge-, brytnian *to dispense*] *Bestowed;* impensus, Som. Ben. Lye.

ge-brittan *to exhibit, give, to crumble, break small;* exhĭbēre, impendēre, friāre, Som. Ben. Lye.

ge-broc, es; *n.* [ge-brocen, *pp. of* ge-brecan *to break*] *A breaking, broken piece, fragment;* fractio, fragmentum:—Sum biþ mid ðæs innoþes gebrocum gemenged *some is mingled with fragments of the inwards,* L. M. 2, 56; Lchdm. ii. 276, 26. Ðara gebroca *fragmentorum,* Mt. Kmbl. Rush. 14, 20: 15, 37. [*Goth.* ga-bruka *a fragment.*]

ge-brōc, es; *n.* [ge-, brōc *affliction*] *Affliction, sorrow;* dŏlor:—Ðēh eów lytles hwæt swelcra gebrōca on become *though only a little of such sorrows comes upon you,* Ors. 3, 7; Bos. 62, 26.

ge-brocen *broken,* Bd. 5, 6; S. 619, 24; *pp. of* ge-brecan.

ge-brocen *enjoyed,* Exon. 38 b; Th. 127, 29; Gū. 392; *pp. of* ge-brūcan.

ge-brōcod, -brōcad, -brōced, -brōcud [or -brocod?]; *part. p.* [ge-, brōcod; *pp. of* brōcian *to oppress, vex*] *Afflicted, broken up, injured;* afflictus, confractus:—Gif se synfulla biþ gebrōcod *if the sinful be afflicted,* Homl. Th. i. 472, 3: 474, 19. Næfde se here Angelcyn ealles fōrswīðe gebrōcod *the army had not all too much afflicted the English race,* Chr. 897; Erl. 94, 30. Sume gebrōcode wǣron *some were injured,* 978; Erl. 127, 12: Homl. Th. i. 476, 19. Ða ōðre gebrōcade aweg cōmon *the others came away afflicted,* Ors. 4, 1; Bos. 78, 1. Hie wǣron gebrōcede *they were afflicted,* Chr. 897; Erl. 94, 30. We ealle on hǣðenum folce gebrōcude wǣron *we were all afflicted by the heathen folk,* Cod. Dipl. 314; A. D. 880-885; Kmbl. ii. 113, 16. [Cf. *O. H. Ger.* ga-brochōn *confringere.*]

ge-brocseóc; *adj. Lunatic, frantic;* phreneticus:—Sum gebrocseóc man *phreneticus quidam,* Bd. 4, 3; S. 570, 10. v. ge-bræcseóc.

ge-broden *drawn, unsheathed; pp. of* ge-bredan.

ge-brogne, an; *n. A bush:*—Gistīgeþ swoelce gibrogne *ascendet sicut virgultum,* Rtl. 19, 33.

ge-broht *brought,* Ors. 3, 9; Bos. 66, 20; *pp. of* ge-brengan.

ge-broiden *entwined,* Chr. 1104; Erl. 239, 19. v. ge-bredan III. *to weave.*

ge-brosnod, -brosnad; *part. p.* [ge-, brosnod, *pp. of* brosnian *to corrupt*] *Corrupted, decayed;* corruptus:—Gebrosnad is hūs under hrōfe *the house is decayed under the roof,* Exon. 8 a; Th. 2, 3; Cri. 13: 9 a; Th. 6, 15; Cri. 84. Rotudon and gebrosnode sȳnd dolhswaðo mīne *putruērunt et corruptæ sunt cicātrīces meæ,* Ps. Spl. 37, 5. Ða gebrosnodan bān *the corrupted bones,* Hy. 7, 88; Hy. Grn. ii. 289, 88.

ge-brosnodlīc; *adj. Corrupted:*—Ðeós world is gebrosnodlīc *this world is corrupted,* Blickl. Homl. 115, 3.

ge-brosnung, -borsnung, e; *f.* [ge-, brosnung *corruption*] *A decaying, corruption;* corruptio:—Hī hire līchoman gemētton swā ungewemmedne and swā gesundne, swā swā heó wæs fram gebrosnunge līcumlīcre willnunge clǣne and unwemme *intĕmĕrātum corpus invĕnēre, ut a corruptiōne concŭpiscentiæ carnālis ĕrat immūne,* Bd. 3, 8; S. 532, 36: 3, 19; S. 550, 15.

ge-brot, es; *n.* [ge-, brot *a fragment*] *A fragment;* fragmentum:—Of ðam gebrote hig nāmon seofon wilian fulle *de fragmentis tūlērunt septem sportas plēnas,* Mt. Bos. 16, 37. Man nam ða gebrotu ðe ðǣr belifon, twelf cȳpan fulle *sublātum est quod superfuit illis, fragmentōrum cophĭni duodĕcim,* Lk. Bos. 9, 17.

ge-brot, es; *m. A barn-keeper;* granatārius, frumenti præfectus, N. Som. Ben. Lye.

ge-brōðor, -brōðer, -brōðra, -brōðru, -brōðro *brethren, used as the pl. of* brōðor, brōðer *for brothers collectively;* fratres conjuncti:—Begen ða gebrōðor *both the brethren,* Andr. Kmbl. 2053; An. 1029: Ps. Th. 98, 6. Ic seah vi gebrōðor *I saw six brethren,* Exon. 104 a; Th. 394, 12; Rä. 14, 2: 98 a; Th. 366, 12; Reb. 11. Ða gebrōðer begen ætsamne *the brothers both together,* Chr. 937; Th. 206, 17, col. 1; Æðelst. 57. Wyt sind gebrōðra *we two are brethren;* nos duo fratres sūmus, Gen. 13, 8. Gē synt ealle gebrōðru *omnes vos fratres estis,* Mt. Bos. 23, 8: Mk. Bos. 10, 29. Twegen ǣwe gebrōðro *duo germāni fratres,* Bd. 1, 27; S. 490, 28. Be ðǣm gebrōðrum twǣm *by the two brethren,* Beo. Th. 2387; B. 1191: Andr. Kmbl. 2027; An. 1016. [*Laym.* i-broðeren: *O. Sax.* gi-broðar: *O. H. Ger.* ga-pruoder: *Ger.* gebrüder.] v. brōðor.

ge-brōðorscipe, es; *m. Brothership, brotherhood, fraternity;* fraternitas:—Ðyllīcne gebrōðorscipe hȳ heóldon [MS. healdan] him betweonum *such brotherhood they had among them,* Ors. 3, 11; Bos. 76, 6.

ge-brotu *fragments,* Lk. Bos. 9, 17; *pl. nom. acc. of* ge-brot.

ge-browen *brewed,* Ors. 1, 1; Bos. 22, 17: Homl. Th. i. 352, 7; *pp. of* breówan.

ge-brūcan; *p.* -breác, *pl.* -brucon; *pp.* -brocen [ge-, brūcan *to use, enjoy*] *To enjoy, eat;* perfrui, edere, manducare:—Hī ðæs blǣdes gebrocen hæfdon *they had enjoyed the success,* Exon. 38 b; Th. 127, 29; Gū. 393.

Miđđȳ sacerdhâd gebrêce *cum sacerdotio fungeretur*, Lk. Skt. Lind. 1, 8. Đætte hia gebrêcon *manducarent*, Jn. Skt. Lind. 18, 28: 6, 58.

ge-brudon *drew, unsheathed*, Ps. Spl. 36, 14; *p. pl. of* ge-bredan.

ge-bryce *a breaking, breach*, Ps. Lamb. 105, 23. v. ge-brice.

ge-bryceþ *breaks, destroys*, Salm. Kmbl. 613; Sal. 306; *3rd sing. pres. of* ge-brecan.

ge-brȳcgan *to use*:—Gibrȳcgende *utenda*, Rtl. 97, 33. v. brȳcian.

ge-brȳcsian; *p.* ade, ode; *pp.* ad, od *To use, enjoy*:—Gebrȳcsiaþ *utuntur*, Rtl. 118, 39. Gebrȳcsade *functus est*, 195, 1. v. brȳcian, brîcsian.

ge-bryddan; *p.* de; *pp.* ed *To frighten, terrify;* terrēre:—Gif đū mec gebringest, đæt ic sī gebrydded þurh đæs cantices cwide Cristes līnan *if thou wilt bring me, that I may be frightened through the word of the canticle of Christ's discipline*, Salm. Kmbl. 32; Sal. 16. v. broddetan.

ge-bryidan; *p.* de; *pp.* id [ge-, bryidan *to take*] *To take;* tollĕre, sūmĕre:—Đonne mon hæfþ his ǣhte gebryid *when a man has taken* [Th. *discovered*] *his property*, L. O. 2; Th. i. 178, 11.

ge-brȳsed; *part. p.* [ge-, brȳsed, *pp. of* brȳsan *to bruise*] *Bruised;* contrītus:—Đæt he his preósta ǣnne of horse fallende and gebrȳsedne gelīce gebiddende and bletsigende fram deáþe gecyrde *ut clĕrĭcum suum cadendo contrītum, æque ōrando ac benedīcendo a morte revocāvĕrit*, Bd. 5, 6; S. 618, 24.

ge-brȳsednes, -ness, e; *f. A bruising;* contūsio, Som. Ben. Lye.

ge-brytan; *p.* te; *pp.* ed [ge-, brytan *to break*] *To break up, destroy;* confringĕre, extermĭnāre:—Gebrytte hine eofor of wuda *extermĭnāvit eam ăper de sylva*, Ps. Spl. C. 79, 14. Gebryted wiđ ecede *broken up with vinegar*, Med. ex Quadr. 5, 1; Lchdm. i. 348, 3.

ge-būan; *p.* -būde, *pl.* -būdon; *pp.* -būen, -būn [ge-, būan *to dwell*]. I. *intrans. To dwell, abide;* habĭtāre, versāri alīquo lŏco:—Hī gebūdon betweoh Capadotiam and Pontum *they abode between Cappadocia and Pontus*, Ors. 1, 10; Bos. 32, 36. II. *v. a. acc. To inhabit, occupy;* inhabĭtāre, incŏlĕre:—Hū hit [đæt hūs] Hring-Dene gebūn hæfdon *how the Ring-Danes had occupied it* [*the house*], Beo. Th. 235; B. 117. Ne sceal đes wong gebūen weorþan *nor shall this field be occupied*, Exon. 37 a; Th. 120, 24; Gū. 276: Blickl. Homl. 121, 33.

ge-budon *proposed*, Ors. 3, 1; Bos. 52, 27; *p. pl. of* ge-beódan.

ge-būdon *abode*, Ors. 1, 10; Bos. 32, 36; *p. pl. of* ge-būan.

ge-būgan; *p.* ic, he -beág, -beáh, đū -buge, *pl.* -bugon; *impert.* -būh, *pl.* -būgaþ; *pp.* -bogen [ge-, būgan *tō bow*]. I. *v. intrans. To bow or bow down oneself, bend, submit, turn, turn away, revolt;* se flectĕre *vel* inclīnāre, curvāre, declīnāre, transfŭgĕre:—He cwæþ đæt he wolde to fulluhte gebūgan *he said that he would submit to baptism*, Homl. Th. ii. 26, 10: Boutr. Scrd. 22, 43: Bt. Met. Fox 25, 128; Met. 25, 64. Heó on flet gebeáh *she bowed to the floor*, Beo. Th. 3085; B. 1540: 5953; B. 2980. Se wyrm gebeáh snūde tosomne *the worm quickly bent together*, 5128; B. 2567. Hī gebugon to Iosue and to Israhēla bearnum *transfŭgĕrit ad Iosue et ad filios Israel*, Jos. 10, 4. Ne đū ne gebūh fram đære ǣ on đa swīđran healfe ne on đa wynstran *ne declīnes ab lēge ad dextĕram vel ad sinistram*, 1, 7. Đæt đū to sǣmran gebuge *that thou should bow to worse*, Exon. 71 a; Th. 264, 9; Jul. 361. Eall folc him to gebogen wæs *all people submitted to him*, Chr. 1013; Erl. 148, 2, 21: L. Edm. S. 4; Th. i. 250, 1. Đe ǣr fram him gebogene wǣron *who had formerly turned from them*, Ors. 2, 5; Bos. 45, 44. II. *v. trans. acc. To bow to, turn towards;* inclīnāre ad:—Sum fletreste gebeág *one bowed to his domestic couch*, Beo. Th. 2487; B. 1241. Monig snellīc sǣrinc selereste gebeáh *many a keen seaman bowed to his hall-couch*, 1385; B. 690. DER. in-gebūgan.

ge-būgian, -bōgian; *p.* ode; *pp.* od; *v. trans.* [ge-, būgian II. *to inhabit, occupy*] *To inhabit, occupy;* inhabĭtāre, incŏlĕre:—Hȳ hit ne māgon ealle gebūgian *they cannot inhabit it all*, Bt. 18, 1; Fox 62, 10.

ge-būh *turn from*, Jos. 1, 7; *impert. of* ge-būgan.

ge-būn *inhabited*, Ors. 1, 1, § 13; Bos. 20, 2, 3, 7; *pp. of* ge-būan, q. v.

ge-bunden *bound*, Mk. Bos. 15, 7; *pp. of* ge-bindan.

gebundennes, -ness, e; *f.* [ge-bunden, *pp. of* ge-bindan *to bind*] *A binding, an obligation;* oblīgātio:—Gibundennises *ligandi*, Rtl. 59, 11. Đa abūgendan on gebundennesse ođđe to bændum *declīnantes in oblīgātiōnes*, Ps. Lamb. 124, 5.

GEBŪR, es; *m. A dweller, husbandman, farmer, countryman*, BOOR; incŏla, agricŏla, cŏlōnus:—Gif he on gebūres hūse gefeohte *if he fight in a boor's house*, L. In. 6; Th. i. 106, 8. Gebūres gerihte *rights of the boor*, Th. i. 434, 3. See the section to which this heading belongs for an account of the relation of the 'gebur' to his lord. [Cf. *Icel.* búi [in compounds] and bónde [v. Cl. and Vig. Dicty. s. v.], and see Kemble's Saxons in England, i. 131: *Plat.* buur, *m;* in earlier time *a neighbour, a citizen;* now *a farmer, a peasant: Dut. Frs.* boer, *m: Ger.* bauer, *m:* in *Silesia* gebaur, *m.* The *Old Franc.* and *Al.* writers designate by puarre, buara *an inhabitant*, and by gibura, giburo *a peasant, a farmer*. From the *A.-S.* būan *to dwell, inhabit.*] DER. neáh-gebūr.

gebūr-gerihta; *pl. n. A boor's* or *farmer's rights* or *dues;* cŏlōni consuetūdines:—Gebūrgerihta sȳn mislīce, gehwār hȳ sȳn hefige, gehwār eác medeme *geburi consuetudines inveniuntur multimode, et ubi sunt onerose et ubi sunt leviores aut medie*, Th. i. 434, 4.

ge-burh-scipe, es; *m. A township;* municipium, municipatus:—On đam ylcan geburhscipe [MS. B. gebūrscipe] *in the same township*, L. Ed. 1; Th. i. 158, 21. v. burh-scipe.

ge-burnen *burnt*, Ors. 4, 2; Bos. 79, 19; *pp. of* beornan.

ge-būr-scipe, es; *m.* [ge-būr *a dweller;* scipe *state, condition*] *A neighbourhood, an association of the dwellers in a certain district acknowledged by the state;* colonia, vicinia, consociatio:—On đam ylcan gebūrscipe *in the same neighbourhood*, L. Ed. 1; Th. i. 158, 21 [MS. B].

ge-bȳa; *p.* -bȳde *To dwell*:—Gibȳaþ miþ đǣm *habitabit cum eis*, Rtl. 71, 3. Gebȳde *habitavit*, Mt. Kmbl. Lind. 1, 23; 4, 13. Gibȳe *posside*, Rtl. 165, 20. v. gebūgian.

ge-bycgan, -bicgan, -bicgean; ic -bycge, -bicge, đū -bygest, -bigest, he -bygeþ, -bigeþ, -bigþ, *pl.* -bycgaþ, -bicgaþ; *p.* -bohte, *pl.* bohton; *pp.* -boht *To buy, procure, purchase, redeem;* emere, redimere:—Hī meahton hefonrīce gebycgan [MS. gebycggan] *they could buy the kingdom of heaven*, Past. 59, 2; Swt. 449, 15; Hat. MS. Cyning sceal mid ceápe cwēne gebicgan *a king shall buy a queen with goods*, Exon. 90 a; Th. 338, 22; Gn. Ex. 82. [For this use of the verb see Grimm R. A. pp. 421 sqq. where similar phrases in other dialects are given.] Đæt hȳ mōston friþ gebicgean *that they might buy peace*, L. Eth. ii. 1; Th. i. 284, 13. Ic gebycge bât *I buy a boat*, Exon. 119 a; Th. 458, 11; Hy. 4, 99. Đæt hī man beágum gebycge *that one may buy her with bracelets*, Menol. Fox 551; Gn. C. 45: L. H. E. 16; Th. i. 34, 3: L. C. S. 15; Th. i. 384, 11. Būtan he hine æt đam cynge gebicge *unless he buys it of the king*, L. Edg. ii. 3; Th. i. 266, 18. Gif mon hwelcne ceáp gebygeþ *if a man buy any kind of cattle*, L. In. 56; Th. i. 138, 10. Gif man mægþ gebigeþ *if a man buy a maiden*, L. Ethb. 77; Th. i. 22, 1. Se man gebigþ đone æcer *homo emit agrum illum*, Mt. Bos. 13, 44. Hine gebohte Putifar *emit eum Putiphar*, Gen. 39, 1: Cd. 149; Th. 187, 15; Exod. 151: Beo. Th. 1951; B. 973: 4956; B. 2481. God us deópum ceápe gebohte *Deus redemit nos alto pretio*, L. C. E. 18; Th. i. 370, 28: Exon. 29 a; Th. 89, 27; Cri. 1463: 98 a; Th. 368, 25; Sēel. 30. Đū blōde gebohtest bearn Israēla *thou hast redeemed the children of Israel with thy blood*, Hy. 8, 26; Hy. Grn. ii. 290, 26. Lundenwaru him friþ gebohton *the Londoners bought themselves peace*, Chr. 1016; Erl. 159, 23. Nǣnig usic miđ leáne gebohte *nemo nos conduxit*, Mt. Kmbl. Rush. 20, 7. Geboht þeówa *emptitius*, Ælfc. Gl. 86; Som. 74, 33; Wrt. Voc. 50, 16: Gen. 17, 12.

ge-bȳcnian *to beckon, shew, indicate*, St. A. 44, 12: Evan. Nic. 4, 13: Ælfc. Gr. 28, 3; Som. 30, 48, MS. D: 37; Som. 39, 40, MS. D. v. gebīcnian.

gebȳdan *to abide, wait.* v. gebīdan.

ge-bȳgan, -bīgan, -bȳgean, -bīgean, -bēgan; *p.* de; *pp.* ed; *v. trans. To bow, bend, turn, inflect* or *decline a part of speech, recline, twist, bow down, humble, abase, bring under, subdue, crush;* flectere, incurvare, inflectere, declinare, reclinare, torquere, humiliare, confringere:—Gebīgdum cneówum *flexis genibus*, Bd. 4, 10; S. 578, 28. Hȳ gebȳgdon sāwle mīne *incurvaverunt animam meam*, Ps. Spl. 56, 8: Gen. 27, 29. Đā hī hwæsne beág ymb mīn heafod gebȳgdon *then they twisted a sharp crown around my head*, Exon. 29 a; Th. 88, 25; Cri. 1445. Hȳ ealle to him gebīgde *he brought them all under him*, Ors. 3, 9; Bos. 64, 15: 5, 3; Bos. 104, 11. Đæt hig ealle leóda sceoldan gebīgan to geleáfan *that they should subdue all nations to the faith*, Ælfc. T. Lisle 30, 5. Īserne steng gebīgeþ *vectes ferreos confringit*, Ps. Th. 106, 15: 72, 17; 143, 18. v. bȳgan.

ge-bȳgean, -bīgean; *v. trans. To bow, bend, turn, bow down, subdue, crush*:—Đū miht leon and dracan liste gebȳgean *conculcabis leonem et draconem*, Ps. Th. 90, 13. Gebīgean to synnum *adigere ad peccata*, Alb. resp. 68 [Lye]. v. ge-bȳgan.

ge-bȳgednys, -nyss, e; *f. A bending, declining, declension, case.* v. gebīgednys.

ge-bȳgel; *adj. Subject, submissive, obedient;* subjectus:—Gebȳgle to dōnne *to make obedient*, Chr. 1091; Th. 358, 38: 1105; Th. 367, 22.

ge-bȳgendlīc; *adj. Bending, flexible, declined with cases.* v. gebīgendlīc.

ge-bygeþ *buys*, L. In. 56; Th. i. 138, 10; *pres. of* ge-bycgan.

ge-byld, e; *f.* [byld *boldness*] *Boldness, courage;* audācia:—Calep hig gestilde and cwæþ mid gebylde *Caleb quieted them and said with courage*, Num. 13, 31: Jos. 4, 9.

gebyld; *adj. Bold, courageous;* audax:—Gebyld swīđe đurh God, Jud. 4, 14.

ge-bylded, -bælded, -byld; *part.* [ge-, byldan *to make bold*] *Emboldened, encouraged, animated;* corrōbŏrātus, anĭmātus:—Wæs Laurentius mid đæs apostoles swingum and trymnessum swīđe gebylded *apostŏli flagellis sĭmul et exhortatiōnibus anĭmātus ĕrat Laurentius*, Bd. 2, 6; S. 508, 22. He wiđ mongum stōd ealdfeónda elne gebylded *he stood against many of the old fiends, emboldened with courage*, Exon. 39 b; Th. 130, 31; Gū. 446. Se Barac, gebyld swīđe þurh God, feaht him togeánes *Barak, much encouraged by God, fought against them*, Jud. 4, 14. Hȳ wǣron gebylde *they were encouraged*, Ors. 4, 1; Bos. 77, 25. We us bletsiaþ gebylde đurh God *we bless ourselves emboldened by God*, H. R. 105, 17.

ge-bylgan; *p.* de; *pp.* ed *To cause to swell, to make angry*:—Leóhtlíce gebylged *leviter indignata*, Bd. 4, 9; S. 577, 24. v. ge-belgan.

ge-bylged *made angry; pp. of* ge-bylgan.

ge-byrd; *gen. dat.* -byrde; *acc.* -byrde, -byrd; *pl. nom. gen. acc.* a; *dat.* um; *f*: ge -byrdo; *indecl. in s*; *f*: found in both *s.* and *pl.* without any apparent difference of meaning. I. *birth, origin, beginning, parentage, family, lineage*; nativitas, origo, stirps, genus:—Bearnes þurh gebyrde *through the birth of a child*, Exon. 9 a; Th. 5, 28; Cri. 76. Þurh bearnes gebyrd *through child-birth*, 8 b; Th. 3, 18; Cri. 38. On dæg gebyrde *die natalis*, Mt. Kmbl. Rush. 14, 6. Wītgan cýþdon Cristes gebyrd *prophets announced Christ's birth*, 8 b; Th. 5, 5; Cri. 65. Bearnes gebyrda *the infant's birth*, 13 b; Th. 45, 24; Cri. 724: L. Edg. C. 13; Th. ii. 246, 22. Cennan bearn mid gebyrdum *to bring forth children by birth*, Exon. 89 a; Th. 334, 32; Gn. Ex. 25. Wæs he līchomlīcre gebyrde æđeles cynnes *erat carnis origine nobilis*, Bd. 2, 7; S. 509, 15. Of đære cynelīcan gebyrdo *de stirpe regiâ*, 5, 7; S. 621, 8, note 8. Be đam gebyrdum *concerning parentage*, Bt. 30, 1; Fox 108, 19. II. *nature* [*what a man is* natu *by birth, or to what he is* natus *born*], *quality, state, condition, lot, fate*; natura, qualitas, conditio, sors, fatum:—God āna wāt ymb đæs fugles gebyrd *God alone knows concerning the bird's nature*, Exon. 61 a; Th. 223, 16; Ph. 360. Ic cann engla gebyrdo *I know the nature of the angels*, Cd. 27; Th. 37, 2; Gen. 583. Æghwilc gylt be hys gebyrdum *every one pays according to his condition*, Ors. 1, 1; Bos. 20, 35. Nāh seó mōdor geweald bearnes blǣdes, ac sceal on gebyrd faran ān æfter ānum *the mother hath not power over her child's happiness, but according to his fate* [*what he is born to*] *one shall go after another*, Salm. Kmbl. 770; Sal. 384. Hie on gebyrd hruron gāre wunde *they fell according to their fate, wounded by the spear*, Beo. Th. 2153; B. 1074. Or in the last two instances may 'gebyrd' be referred to 'gebyrian' *to happen*? [*O. Sax.* gi-burd, *f. nativitas, genus*: *Ger.* geburt, *f*: *Goth.* ga-baurþs, *f.*] DER. eág-gebyrd, eorl-, sib-, weoruld-. v. beran.

ge-byrd; *part. p.* [beard *a beard*] *Bearded*; barbātus:—Gebyrd *barbātus*, Ælfc. Gr. 43; Som. 45, 11. Gebyrdne hine he gesihþ *he sees himself bearded*, Lchdm. iii. 200, 4.

ge-byrd; *part. p. Burdened*:—Gebyrde sindun *onerati estis*, Mt. Kmbl. Rush. 11, 28.

ge-byrd-dæg, es; *m. A birth-day*; natalis dies:—On Herodes gebyrddæge *die natalis Herodis*, Mt. Bos. 14, 6.

ge-byrde, -bierde; *adj. Inborn, innate, natural*; innatus, ingenitus, naturalis:—Ne him nis gebyrde đæt hī đē folgien *it is not natural to them that they should follow thee*, Bt. 14, 1; Fox 40, 34. Him gebyrde is đæt he gēncwidas gleáwe hæbbe *to him it is natural that he should have prudent replies*, Elen. Kmbl. 1183; El. 593.

ge-byrdelīce; *adv. Suitably, orderly*:—Ymbsittaþ đa burg swīđe gebyrdelīce *ordinabis adversus eam obsidionem*, Past. 21, 5; Swt. 160, 19.

ge-byrdo *birth, nature, condition.* v. ge-byrd.

ge-byrd-tīd, e; *f. Birth-tide, time of birth*; natale tempus:—Se dæg com Herodes gebyrdtīde *dies accidit Herodis natalis*, Mk. Bos. 6, 21: Gen. 40, 20. Fram gebyrdtīde brēmes cyninges *from the birth-tide of the glorious king*, Chr. 973; Th. 224, 36; Edg. 12.

ge-byrd-wiglære, es; *m. A birth-diviner*; ex natalibus divinator, astrologus, Ælfc. Gl. 4; Wrt. Voc. 17, 14.

ge-byrd-wītega, an; *m. A birth-prophet, an astrologer*; ex natalibus propheta, astrologus, mathematicus, Ælfc. Gl. 112; Wrt. Voc. 60, 12.

ge-byre, es; *m. The time at which anything happens, a favourable time, an opportunity*; occasio, opportunitas:—Hwonne him eft gebyre weorþe, hām cymeþ *when there shall again be an opportunity to him he will come home*, Exon. 90 b; Th. 340, 3; Gn. Ex. 105. [*O. H. Ger.* gaburi, *f. eventus, casus.*] v. byre, ge-byrian.

ge-byredlīc; *adj. Suitable, fitting, due*; debitus, congruus:—Herenissa gibyredlīco *laudes debitas*, Rtl. 165, 22. Gibyredlīcre worđunge *congruo honore*, 78, 10; 8, 23.

ge-byredlīce; *adv. Conveniently*; convenienter, Rtl. 16, 31.

ge-byrelic beón:—Ne sint gebyrelīco Iudea to Samaritaniscum *non coutuntur Iudæi Samaritanis*, Jn. Skt. Lind. 4, 9.

ge-byreþ *bears, produces*, L. Ethb. 78; Th. i. 22, 4. v. ge-beran.

ge-byreþ, ge-byraþ *happens, becomes, behoves.* v. ge-byrian.

ge-byrgan; *p.* de; *pp.* ed *To bury*; sepelire:—Wæs on helle gebyrged *sepultus est in inferno*, Lk. Bos. 16, 22. v. byrgan.

ge-býrgan; *p.* de; *pp.* ed *To taste*; gustare:—Nō he fōddor þigeþ, nemne mele-deáwes dǣl gebýrge *it touches not food, except that of honey-dew it tastes a portion*, Exon. 59 b; Th. 215, 30; Ph. 261: Cd. 24; Th. 31, 10; Gen. 483. v. býrgan.

ge-byrhtan; *p.* te; *pp.* ed *To make bright, brighten*; illūmināre, clārificāre:—Ys his nama fōr him neóde gebyrhted *præclārum nōmen eōrum cōram ipso*, Ps. Th. 71, 14. v. ge-berhtan.

gebyrhte *declared.*

ge-býrian, -býrigan, -bīrian; *3rd sing.* eþ; *p.* ede; *pp.* ed; *3rd sing.* aþ; *p.* ode; *pp.* od. [The cognate words point to a short vowel.] I. *v. intrans. To happen, to fall out, to pertain to, belong to*; evenire, accidere, contingere, pertinere ad:—Đonne hit gebýrigan mæg *when it may happen*, Bt. Met. Fox 4, 22; Met. 4, 11. Syle me mīnne dǣl mīnre ǣhte, đe me to gebýreþ *da mihi portionem substantiæ quæ me contingit*, Lk. Bos. 15, 12. Hit nis náuht đæt mon cwiþ đæt ǣnig þing weás gebýrige *it is naught* [*nothing*] *that men say that anything happens by chance*, Bt. 40, 5; Fox 240, 28: Ps. Th. 4, 5. Đās đing gebyrigeaþ ǣryst *oportet primum hæc fieri*, Lk. Bos. 21, 9. Men cwǣdon gió đonne him hwæt unwēnunga gebýrede, đæt đæt wære weás gebýred *men said formerly, when anything happened to them unexpectedly, that it happened by chance*, Bt. 40, 6; Fox 242, 4: 16, 2; Fox 54, 3. Gebýrode, Ex. 14, 28. And feng to ealle đam landum đe đǣr-to gebýredon *and took to all the lands which thereto belonged*, Chr. 910; Erl. 101, 6. II. *v. impers. It pertains to, it is fitting* or *suitable, it becomes, it behoves*; pertinet ad, convenit, oportet, decet:—Swā gebýreþ ælcum Cristnum men *as it becometh every Christian man*, Ps. Th. 39, Arg. Swā đǣr-to gebýrige *as may thereto be becoming*, L. Eth. vi. 22; Th. i. 320, 11: L. Ath. v. 1, 4; Th. i. 230, 3. Ne gebýraþ hit swā *non ita convenit*, Gen. 48, 18. Him ne gebýraþ to đām sceāpum *non pertinet ad eum de ovibus*, Jn. Bos. 10, 13. Him gebýrode to đām þearfum *de egenis pertinebat ad eum*, 12, 6. Hine man byrigde swā him wel gebýrede *they buried him as well became him*, Chr. 1036; Th. 294, 22. On ealle þeóda gebýraþ beón đæt gōdspel gebodod *in omnes gentes oportet prædicari evangelium*, Mk. Bos. 13, 10. [*Orm. 3rd pres.* birrþ *it becomes*, *3rd p.* birrde: *Havl. p.* birde: *R. Brun.* burd: *Gaw. gloss.* burde: *O. Sax.* giburian *accidere, evenire, contingere*: *Ger.* gebühren: *O. H. Ger.* gaburjan *pertinere, contingere*: *O. Nrs.* byrja *incipere, inchoare, decere.*] v. býrian.

ge-byrigednes, -ness, e; *f. A burial*; sĕpultūra:—Æfter monigum geárum his gebyrigednesse *post multos sĕpultūræ annos*, Bd. 4, 32; Whelc. 365, 31.

ge-byrman; *p.* de; *pp.* ed *To ferment with* BARM, *to leaven*; fermentare:—Bryđen wæs ongunnen đætte Adame Eue gebyrmde *the drink was prepared which Eve fermented for Adam*, Exon. 47 a; Th. 161, 6; Gū. 954. Þrymme gebyrmed *fermented with greatness*, 84 a; Th. 316, 2; Mōd. 42. Ne beó nān beorma on eówrum hūsum; swā hwilc man swā ytt gebyrmed, forwyrþ *non erit fermentum in domibus vestris; quicumque comederit fermentatum, peribit*, Ex. 12, 15: 12, 19. v. beorma.

ge-byrmed BARMED, *fermented, leavened*; fermentatus, Ex. 12, 15, 19. v. ge-byrman.

ge-byrnod; *part. p.* [byrne *a coat of mail*] *Furnished with a coat of mail*; lōrīcātus:—Gebyrnod *lōrīcātus*, Ælfc. Gr. 43; Som. 45, 12. [*Laym.* i-burned.]

ge-byr-tīd, e; *f. Birth-tide*; natale tempus, Chr. 1087; Th. 353, 34. v. ge-byrd-tīd.

ge-býsgian [or - bysgian?], -bīsgian, -býsigan, -biesgian; *p.* ode, ade; *pp.* od, ad [ge, býsgian *occupare, affligere, tribulare*] *To occupy, busy, afflict, trouble, vex, oppress, overcome, agitate, weaken, destroy*; occupare, affligere, turbare, vexare, opprimere, corripere, conficere:—He mid gýmeleáste hūru us gebýsgaþ *saltem negligentia nos occuparet*, Bd. Whelc. 310, 20. Đonne hī hī gebýsgiaþ mid woruldlīcum hordum *when they busy themselves with worldly treasures*, Homl. Th. i. 524, 14. Ic eom lēg býsig, fȳre gebýsgad *I am a busy flame, with fire occupied*, Exon. 108 a; Th. 412, 21; Rä. 31, 3. Mōde gebýsgad *in mind afflicted*, Exon. 87 b; Th. 328, 20; Vy. 20: 47 b; Th. 162, 34; Gū. 985. Is mōdigra mægen miclum gebýsgod *the strength of the valiant is much troubled*, Andr. Kmbl. 790; An. 395. Moyses wearþ gebýsgad for heora yfelum *vexatus est Moyses propter eos*, Ps. Th. 105, 25: 76, 6. Wintrum gebýsgad *oppressed with years*, Exon. 58 a; Th. 208, 28; Ph. 162: 62 a; Th. 227, 25; Ph. 428. Ādle gebýsgad *with disease oppressed*, 49 a; Th. 170, 10; Gū. 1109. Slǣpe gebiesgad *with sleep overcome*, Exon. 96 a; Th. 358, 2; Pa. 39. Ne đǣr wæter fealleþ, lyfte gebýsgad *water falls not there, agitated in air*, Exon. 56 b; Th. 201, 26; Ph. 62. Wearþ mōdgeþanc miclum gebīsgad, þurh đæs þeódnes word, ombehtþegne *the mind of the disciple was greatly agitated through his lord's words*, 50 a; Th. 173, 34; Gū. 1170. Sceađa biþ gebýsigod, swīđe gestilled *the fiend shall be destroyed, made very still*, Salm. Kmbl. 234; Sal. 116.

ge-býsigan *to occupy, afflict, overcome*, Salm. Kmbl. 234; Sal. 116. v. ge-býsgian.

ge-bysmerian *to deride*, Ps. Lamb. 58, 9. v. ge-bismerian.

ge-bysmrian *to mock, deride, provoke*, Ps. Th. 77, 56. v. ge-bismerian.

ge-býsnian [or -bysnian; cf. *Goth.* busns]; *p.* ode; *pp.* od *To give* or *set an example*; exemplum dare:—Se man biþ hērigendlīc, đe ōđrum gebýsnaþ *the man is praiseworthy who sets an example to others*, Homl. Th. ii. 406, 17. v. býsnian.

ge-býsnung, e; *f.* [býsnung *an example*] *An example*; exemplum:—He sealde sōþe gebýsnunge *he gave true example*, Ælfc. T. Lisle 38, 3. Mā manna beóþ gecyrrede þurh his gebýsnunge to Godes hērunge *more* [*of*] *men will be turned through his example to the praise of God*, Homl.

Th. i. 494, 23. Ne dō ge nā be his gebȳsnungum *do ye not according to his examples*, Homl. Th. ii. 48, 35.

ge-bȳtlian [*or rather* -bytlian, cf. botl]; *p.* ode; *pp.* od [bȳtlian *to build*] *To build;* ædificare:—Eal Godes gelaðung is ofer ðam stāne gebȳtlod *all God's church is built on that stone*, Homl. Th. i. 368, 18.

ge-bytlu; *indecl. f. A building:*—Man bytlode āne gebytlu, and ða wyrhtan worhton ða gebytlu on ðam Sæternes-dæge, and wæs ðā forneán geendod *they were building a building, and the workmen were making the building on the Saturday, and it was then very nearly finished*, Homl. Th. ii. 580, 32; 172, 23; 580, 21. He gȳmþ grǣdelīce his gafoles, his gebytlu *he attends greedily to his rent, his buildings*, i. 66, 11; 68, 2. He eów sylþ micle burga and ða sēlustan gebytlu *he will give you great cities and the best buildings*, Deut. 6, 10. v. botl.

ge-bytlung, e; *f.* [bytlung *a building*] *A building;* ædificium:—Ic inc ealle ða gebytlunge gewisslīce tǣhte *I shewed you two plainly all the building*, Homl. Th. ii. 172, 27; 16.

ge-cǣlan; *p.* de; *pp.* ed; *v. trans. To cool;* refrigerare:—Send Lazarum, ðæt he dyppe his fingeres liþ on wætere, and mīne tungan gecǣle *mitte Lazarum, ut intingat extremum digiti sui in aquam, ut refrigeret linguam meam*, Lk. Bos. 16, 24.

ge-cælcian; *p.* ode; *pp.* od *To whiten;* dealbare:—Gecælcad *dealbatus*, Mt. Kmbl. Lind. 23, 27.

ge-cænenis, gecænes *a calling, vocation.* v. gecigednes. [Cf. gecænnan?]

ge-cænnan *to declare, clear, prove;* advocare, purgare, manifestare:—Hine gecænne ðæt he ðane banan begeten ne mihte *let him prove that he could not obtain the slayer*, L. H. E. 2; Th. i. 28, 2: 4; Th. i. 28, 8. DER. cennan *to declare*, q. v. and cf. *Goth.* ga-kannjan *to make known.*

ge-cafstrian; *p.* ode; *pp.* od [cæfester *a halter*] *To bridle, restrain;* frænare, restringere:—Swelce sió geþyld hæbbe ðæt mōd gecafstrod *as if patience has restrained the mind*, Past. 33, 4; Swt. 218, 22; Cot. MS. 42 a.

ge-camp, -comp, es; *m.* [camp *a contest, war*] *Warfare, a contest, battle;* milĭtia, certāmen, pugna:—Gecampes feld *certāmĭnis campus*, Greg. Dial. 2, 3. On gecampe *in warfare*, Byrht. Th. 136, 18; By. 153. Iosue com mid gecampe to him mid eallum his here *vēnit Iosue et omnis exercĭtus cum eo adversus illos*, Jos. 11, 7. In gecomp *in agonia*, Lk. Skt. Lind. 22, 44.

ge-campian, -compian; *p.* ode; *pp.* od *To fight:*—He wolde gecompian wiþ ðone awerigdan gāst *he wished to fight with the accursed spirit*, Blickl. Homl. 29, 17.

ge-canc, es; *n.* [?] *A mock, gibe;* ludibrium, vituperium, Som: Hpt. Gl. 441, 510. [Cf. *Icel.* kank, *n*; kank-yrði *gibes;* kankast *to jeer, gibe;* cank *to talk of anything, to cackle, Halliwell: Scot.* cangle *to quarrel.*]

ge-ceápian; *p.* ode; *pp.* od [ceápian *to bargain*] *To buy, purchase, trade;* ĕmĕre, negotiari:—He sǣde, ðæt man nāne burh ne mihte ȳþ mid feó geceápian *he said that no city could be more easily bought with money*, Ors. 5, 7; Bos. 106, 16. Geoweorþa geceápode mid his feó æt ðam consule *Jugurtha bribed the consul with his money*, 5, 7; Bos. 106, 10, 12. Ðone māndrinc geceápaþ *he buys the deadly drink*, Exon. 106 b; Th. 406, 7; Rä. 24, 13. Gif he hit næbbe befōran gōdum weotum geceápod *if he have not bought it before good witnesses*, L. In. 25; Th. i. 118, 14: L. Ethb. 77; Th. i. 22, 1: Gen. 43, 21. Hū feolu ēghwelc geceápad wēre *quantum quisque negotiatus ĕsset*, Lk. Skt. Rush. 19, 15.

ge-cearfan, -ceorfan; *p.* earf *To kill, cut off or up;* interficere, decollare:—Gie soecas mec gecearfa *quaeritis me interficere*, Jn. Skt. Lind. 8, 37; 40. Ðone ic gecearf *quem ego decollavi*, Mk. Skt. Lind. 6, 16.

ge-ceás *chose*, Bd. 1, 6; S. 476, 17; *p. of* ge-ceósan.

ge-cēgan *to call, to call upon*, Ps. Spl. 48, 11: 49, 1. v. ge-cīgan.

ge-cēgung, -cīgung, e; *f. A calling;* invocatio:—Giceigingcum ūsum *invocationibus nostris*, Rtl. 97, 37.

ge-cēlan; *p.* de; *pp.* ed. I. *v. trans. To make cold, to cool, allay;* refrigerare:—Ðæt man ne mæge wæterseóces þurst gecēlan *that any one might not allay the thirst of a watersick* [*dropsical*] *man.* II. *v. intrans. To become cold, to be refreshed;* refrigerari:—Forlǣt me ðæt ic gecēle ǣrðam ðe ic gang *remitte mihi ut refrigerer priusquam abeam*, Ps. Spl. 38, 18. v. cēlan, calan.

gecele *an icicle.* v. gicel.

ge-celf; *adj. Great with calf:*—Ðæt ic hæbbe hnesce litlingas, and gecelfe cȳ mid me *that I have tender children and incalving cows with me*, Gen. 33, 13; quod parvŭlos hăbeam tĕnĕros, et boves fetas mecum, Vulg. Gen. 33, 13.

ge-cēlnes, -nys, -nyss, e; *f. Coolness;* refrigerium:—For wegferendra gecēlnysse *ob refrigerium viantium*, Bd. 2, 16; S. 520, 6. v. cēl-nes.

ge-cenenis, se; *f. A delight*, Som.

ge-cennan; *p.* de; *pp.* ed. I. *to beget, bring forth, produce:*—Gicende *edidit*, Rtl. 108, 29. From forleigere ne aru we gecenned *ex fornicatione non sumus nati*, Jn. Skt. Lind. 8, 41. [Cf. *O. H. Ger.* kichennan, *gignere.*] II. *to clear, declare, prove;* purgare, advocare, manifestare:—Gif he gecenne *if he prove*, L. Eth. ii. 8; Th. i. 288, 17. Ic ðē ēcne God ǣnne gecenne *I confess thee the only everlasting God*, Grn. Hy. 10, 4. DER. cennan. v. gecænnan.

ge-cennice, an [?]; *f. Genetrix*, Rtl. 68, 39.

ge-ceolan; *p.* de; *pp.* ed; *v. trans. To make cold, to cool;* refrigerare, Lk. Skt. Lind. 16, 24. v. gecēlan, calan.

ge-ceósan; to geceósanne, geceósenne; ic -ceóse, ðū -ceósest, -cȳst, -cīst, he -ceóseþ, -cȳsþ, -cȳst, *pl.* -ceósaþ; *p.* -ceás, *pl.* -curon; *pp.* -coren *To elect, choose, decide, prove, approve;* eligere, præeligere, seligere, asciscere, petere, nancisci:—Nū monna gehwylc geceósan mōt swā helle hiénþu swā heofones mǣrþu *now every man may choose either hell's humiliations or heaven's glories*, Exon. 16 b; Th. 37, 9; Cri. 590. He wolde geceósan *he would choose*, Bd. 4, 11; S. 579, 9: Salm. Kmbl. 780; Sal. 389. Swā ðē leófre biþ to geceósanne *ut tibi placeat eligere*, Elen. Kmbl. 1210; El. 607. To geceósenne *to choose*, Beo. Th. 3706; B. 1851. Gif ðū ða swīðran healfe gecīst *si tu dextĕram elēgĕris*, Gen. 13, 9. Eall ðæt folc heom ðæt gecuron *all the people approved for themselves of that plan*, St. And. 36, 14. He hyht geceóseþ *he chooseth hope*, Frag. Kmbl. 77; Leas. 40: Exon. 79 b; Th. 298, 21; Crä. 88: Ps. Th. 64, 4: Exon. 61 a; Th. 225, 1; Ph. 382. Ðonne hine man to gewitnysse gecȳsþ *when he is chosen as witness*, L. Edg. S. 6; Th. i. 274, 15. Hȳ wīc geceósaþ *they choose a habitation*, Exon. 97 a; Th. 362, 16; Wal. 37: 95 a; Th. 354, 36; Reim. 56: Ps. Th. 136, 7. Se geceás Maximianum to fultume his rīces *he chose Maximianus to the help of his kingdom*, Bd. 1, 6; S. 476, 17: Ex. 18, 25. Cain geceás wīc *Cain chose a dwelling*, Cd. 50; Th. 64, 17; Gen. 1051: 91; Th. 115, 29; Gen. 1927: 129; Th. 164, 3; Gen. 2709: Beo. Th. 2407; B. 1201: 4930; B. 2469: 5270; B. 2638: Exon. 45 b; Th. 154, 34; Gū. 852: 46 b; Th. 158, 12; Gū. 907: Elen. Kmbl. 2076; El. 1039: 2330; El. 1166: Apstls. Kmbl. 38; Ap. 19: Ps. Th. 77, 67: 131, 14: Byrht. Th. 135, 5; By. 113. Gecuron hīg ða gōdan on hyra fatu *elegerunt bonos in vasa*, Mt. Bos. 13, 48: Gen. 6, 2: Ors. 1, 14; Bos. 37, 26: Ps. Th. 105, 27. Ðē wīc geceós on ðissum lande *choose thee a habitation in this land*, Cd. 130; Th. 164, 30; Gen. 2722: Beo. Th. 3523; B. 1759: Exon. 80 b; Th. 303, 3; Fä. 47. Ðeáh hī gecure būtan cræftum cyninga dysegast *though the most foolish of kings chose them without skill*, Bt. Met. Fox 15, 21; Met. 15, 11. Se foresprecena wer for hine in bisceop-hāde wæs gecoren *the aforesaid man was chosen into bishophood for him*, Bd. 4, 23; S. 594, 29: 4, 1; S. 564, 12. Ðætte eallra heora dōme gecoren wǣre *ut universorum judicio probaretur*, Bd. 4, 24; S. 597, 31. Ðā Abraham gewāt Drihtne gecoren *then Abraham, the chosen of the Lord, departed*, Cd. 86; Th. 109, 5; Gen. 1818: 179; Th. 225, 7; Dan. 150: 212; Th. 261, 35; Dan. 736: Andr. Kmbl. 647; An. 324: Exon. 108 a; Th. 413, 23; Rä. 32, 10. He wiste ðone lāreów gecorenne *he knew the teacher chosen*, Exon. 47 b; Th. 162, 18; Gū. 977. Witodlīce manega synt gelaðode, and feáwa gecorene *multi enim sunt vocati, pauci vero electi*, Mt. Bos. 22, 14: Ælfc. Gl. 7; Som. 56, 64. Torhte twelfe wǣron, Dryhtne gecorene *bright were the twelve, chosen unto the Lord*, Apstls. Kmbl. 10; Ap. 5: Elen. Kmbl. 2115; El. 1059: Cd. 83; Th. 104, 12; Gen. 1734: 176; Th. 221, 23; Dan. 92: Hy. 7, 53; Hy. Grn. ii. 288, 53: Ps. Th. 131, 5: Exon. 25 b; Th. 75, 19; Cri. 1224: 15 a; Th. 31, 18; Cri. 497: 12 b; Th. 21, 7; Cri. 331: 64 b; Th. 237, 21; Ph. 593: 63 b; Th. 234, 16; Ph. 541: 74 b; Th. 279, 13; Jul. 613: 66 a; Th. 243, 26; Jul. 16: 74 b; Th. 278, 29; Jul. 605: 33 a; Th. 105, 29; Gū. 30: 44 a; Th. 149, 29; Gū. 769. He hæfde cempan gecorone *he had chosen champions*, Beo. Th. 417; B. 206. Simon sacan ongon wið ða gecorenan Cristes þegnas *Simon began to strive against the chosen ministers of Christ*, Exon. 70 a; Th. 260, 18; Jul. 299: 31 b; Th. 100, 1; Cri. 1635: Ps. Th. 104, 38: 107, 5: Hy. 9, 42; Hy. Grn. ii. 292, 42. Ic mīnum gecorenum cūðe gesette *deposui testamentum electis meis*, Ps. Th. 88, 3: 105, 5: 131, 18: Exon. 61 b; Th. 225, 12; Ph. 388. [*Goth.* ga-kiusan *to test, approve: O. H. Ger.* gi-chiosan *discernere, probare, approbare, eligere.*] v. ceósan.

ge-ceówan; *p.* -ceáw, *pl.* -cuwon; *pp.* -cowen [ceówan *to chew*] *To chew;* rūmĭnāre:—Sume dweorgedwostlan geceówaþ *some chew pennyroyal*, L. M. 2, 32; Lchdm. ii. 236, 11. Lege dweorgedwostlan gecowene on ðone nafolan *lay chewed pennyroyal on the navel*, 2, 30; Lchdm. ii. 228, 20.

ge-cēpan; *p.* -cēpte; *pp.* -cēpt *To buy;* ĕmĕre:—Hī ðæt rīce hæfdon dióre gecēpte *they had dearly bought that kingdom*, Bt. Met. Fox 26, 37; Met. 26, 19. v. ge-cȳpan.

ge-cerran; *p.* de; *pp.* ed *To turn, return:*—Ic gecyrre on mīn hūs *revertar in domum meam*, Mt. Bos. 12, 44. Gecerreþ ðæt folc *commovet populum*, Lk. Skt. Lind. 23, 5. Gecerre hine *let him turn*, Bt. 35, 1; Fox 156, 10. From wind gecerred *a vento motus*, Lk. Skt. Lind. 7, 24. v. cerran.

ge-cerring, e; *f. A turning, conversion;* conversio:—On gecerringce oððe on gǣnhwyrfte *in convertendo*, Ps. Lamb. 125, 1.

ge-cīaþ *call*, Ps. Lamb. 19, 8, = ge-cīgaþ, *pres. pl. of* ge-cīgan.

ge-cīd, es; *m. n? Strife;* lis:—Gecīid *lis*, Rtl. 162, 28.

ge-cīdan; *p.* -cīdde, *pl.* -cīddon, -cīdon; *pp.* -cīded, -cīdd *To chide, quarrel, strive;* litigare, rixari:—Gecīdon oððe getugon Iudēas bituih *litigabant Judæi adinvicem*, Jn. Skt. Lind. 6, 52. Gif on gebeórscipe hie gecīden *if they quarrel in a feast*, L. In. 6; Th. i. 106, 11.

ge-cīgan, -cīgean, -cȳgan, -cēgan; *p.* -cīgde, -cȳgde, -cēgde; *pp.* -cīged, -cȳged, -cȳgd, -cēged [ge, cīgan *to call*]; *v. trans. To call, name, call upon, invoke, call forth, provoke, incite;* vocare, nominare, invocare, provocare, incitare:—Ne com ic rihtwīse to gecīgeanne, ac đa synnfullan *non veni vocare justos, sed peccatores*, Mt. Bos. 9, 13. Đū gecīgst his naman Ysmaēl *vocabis nomen ejus Ismael*, Gen. 16, 11. Him Dryhten gecȳgþ *the Lord calls him*, Exon. 62 b; Th. 229, 13; Ph. 454. Drihten gecēgde eorþan *Dominus vocavit terram*, Ps. Spl. 49, 1. Hī gecēgdon naman heora *vocaverunt nomina sua*, Ps. Spl. 48, 11. Se wæs gecīged Godwine *he was called Godwine*, Chr. 984; Erl. 130, 3: Ælfc. Gr. 22; Som. 24, 4: Bd. 1, 7; S. 477, 31: 4, 19; S. 588, 30. Hī gewunedon to gebēdum gecīgde beón *they were accustomed to be called to prayers*, 4, 23; S. 595, 41. On đam þeódlande đe is gecȳged Ēlīge *in regione quæ vocatur Elge*, Bd. 4, 19; S. 588, 1: 4, 23; S. 593, 20, 35. Seó is gecȳgd Solente *quod vocatur Solvente*, 4, 16; S. 585, 2. Đū, Drihten, [eart] wynsum eallum gecȳgendum đē *tu, Domine, [es] suavis omnibus invocantibus te*, Ps. Spl. 85, 4. On dagum mīnum ic gecȳge hine *in diebus meis invocabo eum*, Ps. Lamb. 114, 2. He gecȳgde me *invocavit me*, Ps. Spl. 88, 26. Hine hī gecȳgdon *eum provocaverunt*, Ps. Spl. 77, 4. Đa to yrre beóþ gecīgde *they shall be provoked to anger*, Ps. Th. 7, 7. Folc gecȳgde naman đīnne *populus incitavit nomen tuum*, Ps. Spl. 73, 19.

ge-cīgednes, -cȳgednes, -ness, e; *f. A calling;* vŏcātio:—Ōþ đone dæg his gecīgednesse of middangearde *usque ad diem suæ vŏcātiōnis*, Bd. 5, 12; S. 631, 34. Gecīgednes *vocatio, vocabulum, nomen*, Hpt. Gl. 441, 466.

ge-cīgendlīc; *adj.* [cīgan *to call, invoke*] *Calling, addressing;* vocativus:—Vocativus is clipigendlīc ođđe gecīgendlīc *vocative is calling or invoking*, Ælfc. Gr. 7; Som. 6, 25. v. clipigendlīc.

ge-cīgnes, se; *f. A calling, entreaty:*—Ofer mīnre gecīgnesse đū gesettest ealle đīne apostolas to mīnre byrgenne *without my entreaty thou hast appointed all the apostles to be present at my burial*, Blickl. Homl. 143, 29.

ge-cind, es; *n: also*, e: *f. A kind, nature, sort;* generatio, genus, conditio:—And of fugelcinne seofen, and seofen ǣgþres gecindes *et de volatilibus caeli septena, et septena cujuslibet generationis*, Gen. 7, 3. Fram gecinde *a generatione*, Ps. Spl. T. second 9, 7. v. ge-cynd.

ge-cīst *choosest*, Gen. 13, 9; *2nd sing. pres. of* ge-ceósan.

ge-clāded; *part. Clothed, clad;* vestitus:—Hī gesēgon hine geclāded ođđe gegerelad *vident illum vestitum*, Mk. Skt. Lind. 5, 15.

ge-clǣman; *p.* de; *pp.* ed *To smear;* linere:—Geclǣm ealle đa seámas mid tyrwan, *smear all the seams with tar*, Homl. Th. i. 20, 33. v. O. Engl. Homl. i. 225, 17, i-clem.

ge-clǣne; *adj. Clean, pure:*—Giclǣno heart innwardo *pura cordis intima*, Rtl. 163, 1.

ge-clǣnsian, -clǣnsigan, -clǣsnian, -clānsian; *p.* ode, ede; *pp.* od, ed [clǣnsian *to cleanse*] *To cleanse, purify;* mundāre, purgāre:—Gyf đū wylt, đū miht me geclǣnsian *si vis, pŏtes me mundāre*, Mt. Bos. 8, 2: Mk. Bos. 1, 40: Elen. Kmbl. 1352; El. 678. Saul ne meahte his wambe geclǣnsigan *Saul could not purify his stomach*, Past. 28, 6; Swt. 197, 24; Hat. MS. 38 a, 9. Geclǣnsa ođđe afeorma me *munda me*, Ps. Lamb. 50, 4. Ic beó geclǣnsod *mundābor*, 50, 9: Mt. Bos. 8, 3: Mk. Bos. 1, 40, 41: Bt. 38, 4; Fox 202, 29. Geclǣnsedra *castīgātior*, Bd. 4, 31; S. 611, 1.

ge-clǣnsung, e; *f. A cleansing, purifying;* purĭfĭcātio:—Æfter Iudēa geclǣnsunge *sĕcundum purĭfĭcātiōnem Judæorum*, Jn. Bos. 2, 6.

ge-clǣsnian; *p.* ode; *pp.* od *To cleanse, purify;* mundāre, purgāre:—Saul ne meahte his wambe geclǣsnian *Saul could not purify his stomach*, Past. 28, 6; Swt. 196, 24; Cot. MS. Ōđer dǣl sceal beón geclǣsnod *the other part shall be cleansed*, Bt. 38, 4; Fox 202, 29, MS. Cot. v. ge-clǣnsian.

ge-clānsian; *p.* ode; *pp.* od *To cleanse:*—Geltas geclānsa, đa đe ic gefremede *cleanse the sins which I have committed*, Ps. C. 50, 39; Ps. Grn. ii. 227, 39: 50, 112, 127; Ps. Grn. ii. 279, 112, 127. v. ge-clǣnsian.

ge-cleofian; *p.* ode, ede; *pp.* od, ed [clifian, cleofian *to cleave, adhere*] *To cleave, adhere, stick;* adhærēre:—Geþeódde ođđe gecleofede on flōre sāwle mīn *adhæsit pāvimento anĭma mea*, Ps. Lamb. 118, 25.

ge-clibs, -cleps, -clebs, -clysp *a clamour, outcry;* clamor:—Ne wend đū đē on đæs folces geclysp *turn thou not thyself to the people's cry*, L. Alf. 41; Th. i. 54, 7. [Cf. clypian.]

ge-cliht; *part. Collectus:*—Hand gecliht [or hand-gecliht?] *manus collecta* vel *contracta, pugnus*, Som. [Cf. *Scot.* cleik *to seize as by a hook: A.R.* clahte [*p. tense*] *seized;* clech *unguis: Mod. Engl.* clutch.]

ge-clungen *dried up, shrivelled;* contractus, *pp. of* geclingan:—Hȳ beóþ cealde geclungne *they are shrivelled with cold*, Salm. Kmbl. 609; Sal. 304: Exon. 59 a; Th. 213, 17; Ph. 226.

ge-clūtod; *adj.* [clūt *a patch*] CLOUTED, *patched, nailed;* consutus, clavatus:—Geclūtode bytta *patched bottles* [A. V. *wine bottles old, and rent, and bound up*], Jos. 9, 5. Gesceód mid geclūdedum scōn *shod with clouted shoes*, Dial. 1, 4.

ge-clypian, -clipian; *p.* ode, ede; *pp.* od, ed [clypian, clipian *to call*] *To call, call upon, invoke;* vŏcāre, invŏcāre:—He his naman geclipode *invŏcāvit nōmen ejus*, Gen. 12, 8. Manega synt geclypede *multi sunt vŏcāti*, Mt. Bos. 20, 16. [*Still retained in* y-clept.]

ge-cnǣwe; *adj. Knowing, conscious, aware, acknowledging;* cognoscens, conscius:—Se synfulla stōd feorran, gecnǣwe his misdǣda *the sinful stood afar off, conscious of his misdeeds*, Homl. Th. ii. 428, 27. Se cwellere bæd forgifenysse, gecnǣwe his mānes *the murderer prayed for forgiveness, acknowledging his crime*, 510, 20. We sind gecnǣwe đæt . . . *we are aware that* . . . , 378, 9. Hīg ealle wǣron đæs gecnǣwe *omnes testimonium illi dabant*, Lk. Bos. 4, 22.

ge-cnāwan; ic -cnāwe, đū -cnāwest, -cnǣwst, he -cnāweþ, -cnǣwþ, *pl.* -cnāwaþ; *p.* -cneów, *pl.* -cneówon; *pp.* -cnāwen *To know, perceive, understand, recognise;* noscere, agnoscere, sentire, cognoscere:—Ne meahton [meahtan MS.] đa đæs fugles flyht gecnāwan *they might not know the bird's flight*, Exon. 17 a; Th. 41, 12; Cri. 654: Bt. Met. Fox 12, 46; Met. 12, 23; Beo. Th. 4101; B. 2047. Đonne đæt gecnāweþ flāh feónd gemāh *when the deceitful impious fiend knows that*, Exon. 97 a; Th. 362, 17; Wal. 38. Heonon-forþ ge hyne gecnāwaþ *henceforth ye shall know him*, Jn. Bos. 14, 7. He đæt gecneów *he knew that*, Exon. 46 b; Th. 159, 22; Gū. 930: Mk. Bos. 14, 69. Đā he đa lāc gecneów *qui agnitis muneribus*, Gen. 38, 26. Đæt đū gecnāwe đæt đis is sōþ *that thou may know that this is true*, Exon. 70 b; Th. 263, 27; Jul. 356. Hī hine gecneówon *cognoverunt eum*, Mk. Bos. 6, 54. Gif mīn fæder me handlaþ and me gecnǣwþ *if my father handleth me and knows me*, Gen. 27, 12. Ic đæt gecneów *I perceived that*, Exon. 72 a; Th. 269, 1; Jul. 443. Ge māgon sōþ gecnāwan *ye may know the truth*, Andr. Kmbl. 3115; An. 1560: 3032; An. 1519: Elen. Kmbl. 1413; El. 708. Đæt geđeóde đe we ealle gecnāwan mægen *the language that we can all understand*, Past. Swt. 6, 8. Ic hafu gecnāwen đæt đū Hǣlend eart middangeardes *I have perceived that thou art the Saviour of the world*, Elen. Kmbl. 1613; El. 808. Đū miht đa sōđan gesǣlþa gecnāwan *thou mayest recognise the true goods*, Bt. 23; Fox 78, 32; 80, 2.

ge-cnedan; *p.* -cnæd, *pl.* -cnǣdon; *pp.* -cneden *To mix, mingle, spread, knead;* depsere:—Gecned nū hrædlīce þrī sestras smedeman *depse nunc tres mensuras similaginis*, Gen. 18, 6. Gecned hine mid meocle *knead it with milk*, Th. An. 119, 5. Ōđđæt sie gecnoeden all *donec fermentaretur totum*, Lk. Skt. Lind. 13, 21. Gecneden sealf *cataplasma*, Cot. 209.

ge-cneord; *adj. Diligent, intent;* intentus, sollers:—Wæs he on wilsumnesse hāligra gebēda gecneord and geornfull *ĕrat ōrātiōnum dēvōtiōni sollertissĭme intentus*, Bd. 4, 28; S. 606, 34.

ge-cneordlǣcan *to study, be diligent*, Hpt. Gl. 412, 432. v. cneordlǣcan.

ge-cneordlīc; *adj. Diligent:*—Swilce hī swuncon on wīngeardes biggencge mid gecneordlīcere teolunge *as if they had laboured in the cultivation of the vineyard with diligent tilling*, Homl. Th. ii. 74, 33.

ge-cneordlīce; *adv. Diligently;* studiose:—Đa đe woldon woruldwisdom gecneordlīce leornian *those who wished diligently to learn philosophy*, Homl. Th. i. 60, 27.

ge-cneordnys, -nyss, e; *f.* [cneordnys *diligence*] *Diligence, study, an invention;* dīligentia, stūdium, adinventio:—Gecneordnysse *stūdium*, Greg. Dial. 2, 8. Gremedon hine on gecneordnyssum his *irrītāvērunt eum in adinventiōnibus suis*, Ps. Spl. 105, 28.

ge-cneórednis, se; *f. Genealogy;* genealogia, Hpt. Gl. 552.

ge-cneów *knew, perceived*, Gen. 38, 26: Elen. Kmbl. 2278; El. 1140; *p. of* ge-cnāwan.

ge-cneówian; *p.* ode; *pp.* od. [cneówian *to kneel*] *To bend the knee, kneel;* genuflectĕre:—He on dīglum stōwum gecneówige gelōme *let him frequently kneel in secret places*, L. Pen. 16; Th. ii. 282, 30.

ge-cnocian *to beat, pound*, Herb. 64; Lchdm. i. 168, 6, MS. B. v. ge-cnucian.

ge-cnoden *given, dedicated*, Bt. Met. Fox 1, 63; Met. 1, 32. v. cnōdan.

ge-cnucian, -cnocian; *p.* ode, ede, ude; *pp.* od, ed, ud [cnucian *to beat*] *To beat, pound;* tundĕre, pertundĕre:—Gecnuca hȳ mid swīnenum gōre *pound it with swine dung*, Herb. 9, 3; Lchdm. i. 100, 11. Mid gecnucedum [MS. gecnucedon] ele *ŏleo tūso*, Ex. 29, 40. Genim đa wyrte gecnucude [gecnocode MS. B.] *take the herb pounded*, Herb. 64; Lchdm. i. 168, 6.

ge-cnycc, es; *n. A bond;* nexus:—Gicnyccum *nexibus*, Rtl. 59, 13; 66, 25. v. gecnyttan.

ge-cnyrdlæcan *to study*. v. cneordlæcan.

ge-cnyssan, -cnysan; *p.* ede, de; *pp.* ed [cnyssan *to press, trouble*] *To press, trouble, strike, beat, overcome;* prĕmĕre, trĭbŭlāre, pulsāre, īcĕre:—Unsōþfæstne wer yfel gecnysseþ *vĭrum injustum māla căpient*, Ps. Th. 139, 11. Gecnyssed *ictus*, Ælfc. Gr. 43; Som. 44, 55. Wurdon Rōmāne gecnysede *the Romans were overcome*, Ors. 3, 11; Bos. 71, 19.

ge-cnyttan, -cnyhtan; *p.* -cnytte; *pp.* -cnytted, -cnytt, -cnyt [cnyttan *to tie*] *To tie* or *fasten to, to annex;* adnectĕre, alligāre:—Gecnyttan *adnectĕre*, Cot. 4. Bende gicnyhtest *vinculo nexius ti*, Rtl. 108, 21. Betere him ys ðæt ān cwyrnstān sī to hys swyran gecnytt *expĕdit ei ut suspendātur mŏla asĭnāria in collo ejus*, Mt. Bos. 18, 6. Gecnyt, Mk. Bos. 9, 42: Lk. Bos. 17, 2. Gicnyht, Rtl. 109, 41; Jn. Skt. Lind. 11, 44. [*Laym.* i-cnutten; *p. pl. knotted.*]

ge-cǽlan; *p.* de; *pp.* ed; *v. trans.* *To cool, refresh, revive;* refrigerare:—Forlētaþ me ðæt ic sie gecǽled ǽrðon ic gewīte *remitte mihi ut refrigerer prius quam abeam*, Ps. Surt. 38, 14. v. cǽlan, calan.

ge-cope; *adj. Fit, proper;* congruus, opportūnus:—We sculon geleornian ðæt we gecope tīd [MS. tiid] arēdigen *we must learn to arrange a proper time*, Past. 38, 5; Swt. 277, 1; Hat. MS. 51 b, 8. Hwæt him gecopust sié *what is most fit for them*, 13, 2; Swt. 77, 26; Hat. MS. 17 a, 1; Swt. 275, 18.

ge-coplīce; *adv. Fitly, well, readily;* apte, congrue:—Ic geó hwīlum gecoplīce funde *I formerly readily invented*, Bt. 2; Fox 4, 9.

ge-copsende; *part.* [cops *a fetter*] *Fettered;* compĕdītus:—Ðæt he gehērde geomrunga gecopsendra oððe gefōtcypstra *ut audīret gĕmĭtus compĕdītōrum*, Ps. Lamb. 101, 21.

ge-coren; *pp. of* geceósan *Chosen, choice, fit, good, beloved, dear:*—Mīn gecorena *dilectus meus*, Mt. Bos. 12, 18. Ðone gicoren *Christum*, Rtl. 4, 36; 82, 36. Ðe gecorena *Messias*, Jn. Skt. Lind. 4, 25. Gecoren is to rīc godes *aptus est regno dei*, Lk. Skt. Lind. 9, 62. Ðū gecorene *optime*, Lk. Skt. Lind. 1, 3; 8, 15. Sanctus Iohannes eallum Godes hālgum is gecorenra *St. John is more beloved than all God's saints*, Blickl. Homl. 167, 26. Ða gecorenistan dune *the goodliest mountain*, Deut. 3, 25.

ge-corenes, -corennes, -ness, -nys, -nyss, e; *f.* [corenes *an election*] *An election, choice, choiceness, goodness;* electio, electus, probĭtas:—Seó gecorennys stent on Godes fōresceáwunge *the election stands in God's providence*, Homl. Th. ii. 524, 25. Ne ic on heora gecorenesse becume ǽfre *non commĭnābor cum electis eōrum*, Ps. Th. 140, 6. Ðe gelȳfedre yldo wǽron oððe on gecorenesse heora þeáwa māran and beteran wǽron *quæ vel ætāte provectæ vel probĭtāte ĕrant mōrum insigniōres*, Bd. 3, 8; S. 531, 33: Mk. Skt. p. 2, 1.

ge-corenlīc; *adj. Choice, elegant;* elĕgans, Cot. 74.

ge-corenlīce; *adv. Choicely, elegantly;* elĕganter, Cot. 77.

ge-corenscipe, es; *m. Election, excellence;* electio, excellentia:—Gecorenscip *electio*, Mt. Kmbl. p. 12, 11: Rtl. 2, 27. Gicorenscipe *excellentia*, Rtl. 54, 21.

ge-corōnian; *p.* ode; *pp.* od *To crown:*—Ðū us gecorōnadest *coronasti nos*, Ps. Th. 5, 13.

ge-cosped; *part. p.* [cosp *a fetter*] *Fettered;* compĕdītus:—Drihten tolȳsþ gecospede oððe ða gefōtcypstan *Dŏmĭnus solvit compĕdītos*, Ps. Lamb. 145, 8.

ge-cost; *adj.* [cost *tried*] *Tried, proved, chosen;* probātus:—Til mon, tiles and tomes meares, cūþes and gecostes *a good man has care for a good and tame horse. known and tried*, Exon. 91 a; Th. 342, 14; Gn. Ex. 143. Heápe gecoste *with a chosen company*, Elen. Kmbl. 538; El. 269. Swyrd ecgum gecoste *swords tried in their edges*, Judth. 11; Thw. 24, 39; Jud. 231. Ða ðe seolfres beóþ since gecoste *qui probāta sunt argento*, Ps. Th. 67, 27. Ðæt sind ða gecostan cempan *these are the proved champions*, Exon. 33 b; Th. 107, 21; Gū. 62. [Cf. *Goth.* ga-kusts; *f. trial, test: O. H. Ger.* gi-costōt *proved.*] v. gecostian.

ge-costian, -costnian; *p.* ode; *pp.* od. [costian *to tempt*] *To tempt, try, prove;* tentāre, probāre:—He gecostaþ wildeóra worn *it tryeth the multitude of beasts*, Salm. Kmbl. 610; Sal. 304. Ne eart ðū clǽne gecostad *thou art not thoroughly proved*, Exon. 41 a; Th. 136, 36; Gū. 552: 40 b; Th. 134, 13; Gū. 507. [*O. Sax.* gi-kostōn: *O. H. Ger.* gi-costót *proved, tried.*]

ge-costnes, -ness, e; *f.* [costnes *a temptation*] *A temptation, trial, proving;* probātio:—Se wæs of dæghwamlīcre gecostnesse ðæs mynstres becom to āncerlīfe *qui de monastērii probātiōne ad heremītĭcam pervĕnĕrat vitam*, Bd. 3, 19; S. 549, 42.

ge-costnian; *p.* ode; *pp.* od *To try;* tentare:—Gecostna me *tenta me*, Ps. Lamb. 25, 2. He wæs fram Satane gecostnod *tentabatur a Satane*, Mk. Bos. 1, 13.

ge-costung, e; *f. Tribulation, trial;* tribulatio, Mk. Skt. Lind. 13, 24.

ge-cræftan; *p.* -cræfte; *pp.* -cræfted, cræft [cræftan *to build;* cræft *art*] *To contrive, build;* molīri, machināri:—Ic gecræfte, ðæt se cempa ongon Waldend wundian *I contrived that the soldier did wound the Lord*, Exon. 70 a; Th. 259, 30; Jul. 290. Ðæt Godes tempel wæs wundorlīce gecræft *the temple of God was wonderfully contrived*, Homl. Th. ii. 574, 29.

ge-cræftgian; *p.* ade; *pp.* ad [cræft I. *power, strength*] *To strengthen, make powerful;* firmare, roborare:—Ða rīcu of nānes mannes mihtum gecræftgade ne wurdon *the kingdoms were not strengthened by the powers of any man*, Ors. 2, 1; Bos. 39, 2.

ge-crāwan *to crow:*—Hona gesang ł gecrāwæ *gallus cantavit*, Mt. Kmbl. Lind. 26, 74.

ge-crincan; *p.* -cranc, *pl.* -cruncon; *pp.* -cruncen *To yield, fall;* occumbere, ruere:—He under rande gecranc *he fell beneath his shield*, Beo. Th. 2423; B. 1209: Byrht. Th. 139, 7; By. 250: 141, 19; By. 324. v. crincan.

ge-cringan; *p.* -crang, -crong, *pl.* crungon; *pp.* crungen *To sink, fall, die;* occumbere, mori:—Heó on flet gecrong *on the ground she sank*, Beo. Th. 3141; B. 1568: 5003; B. 2505: 2679; B. 1337: Apstls. Kmbl. 120; Ap. 60: Exon. 124 b; Th. 477, 30; Ruin 32. Gārulf gecrang *Garulf fell*, Fins. Th. 63; Fin. 31: Exon. 77 b; Th. 291, 9; Wand 79. Stīðmōd gecrang *firm of mind he died*, Apstls. Kmbl. 144; Ap. 72. v. cringan.

ge-cristnian; *p.* ode, ade; *pp.* od, ad [cristnian *to christianize*] *To christianize, catechize;* catechīzāre:—He ðone cyning gecristnade, and hine eft æfter fæce mid fulluhtbæþe aþwōgh mid his þeóde *cum rex ipse catechīzātus, fonte baptism, cum sua gente abluĕrētur*, Bd. 3, 7; S. 329, 13. Syððan he gecristnad wæs *cum catechīzārētur*, 2, 14; S. 517, 27: Blickl. Homl. 211, 29: 213, 15: 215, 22. Ne mōt gefullod inne mid ðam gecristnedan etan *non licet baptizato cum catecumeno comedere*, Th. Lg. ii. 144, 25.

ge-croced; *adj. Croceus, coccineus*, Hpt. Gl. 528.

gecrod, es; *n. A crowd;* turba. v. hlōþ-gecrod, lind-: creódan.

ge-cuman, -cyme; *p.* -com, *pl.* -cōmon; *pp.* -cumen *To come, go;* venire, ire:—Seueriana gecom to ðæra hālgena byrgenum *Severiana came to the graves of the saints*, Homl. Th. ii. 312, 27. Gecum to mīnum þeówan Saulum *go to my servant Saul*, Homl. Th. i. 386, 19. Of nānum ōðrum gecumen *come from none other*, Ælfc. T. 2, 26. Æfter meh gecyme *post me venire*, Mt. Kmbl. Lind. 16, 24; 17, 10: Jn. Skt. Lind. 5, 40; 7, 27. [*Goth.* ga-kwiman: *O. H. Ger.* ka-queman.]

ge-cundelīc; *adj. Natural;* natūrālis:—Gē wēnaþ ðæt gē nān gecundelīce gōd ne gesǽlþa in eów selfum nabbaþ *ye think ye have no natural good or happiness within yourselves*, Bt. 14, 2; Fox 44, 16. v. ge-cyndelīc.

ge-cunnan; *p.* -cūðe *To know:*—Huu alle bispello gie gecunnas ł giecunna gie māgon [Rush. gicunniga] *quomodo omnes parabolas cognoscetis*, Mk. Skt. Lind. 4, 13. Ic ðē gecūðe ǽr ðan ðe ic ðē gesceōpe *I knew thee ere I created thee*, Ælf. Test; Swt. Rdr. 70, 433. [*Goth.* ga-kunnan *to know.*]

ge-cunnian; *p.* ode, ade; *pp.* od, ad *To try, enquire, experience;* probare, explorare, experiri:—Ðæt hi mōstan gecunnian hwylc heora swiftost hors hæfde *that they should try which of them had the swiftest horse*, Bd. 5, 6; S. 618, 42: Nar. 25, 29. Ðe ðone wīgend aweccan dorste oððe gecunnian, hū *who dared to awake the warrior or to enquire how…*, Judth. 12; Thw. 25, 14; Jud. 259. Ic hæbbe gecunnad cearselda fela *I have experienced many places of sorrow*, Exon. 81 b; Th. 306, 9; Seef. 5. v. cunnian.

gecure, gecuron *chose;* gecoren *chosen.* v. geceosan.

ge-cūþ, *known.* v. gecunnan.

ge-cwæþ, ðū -cwǽde, *pl.* -cwǽdon *Said, spoke, pronounced*, Cd. 202; Th. 251, 10; Dan. 561: Beo. Th. 5322; B. 2664: Chr. 1014; Erl. 150, 16; *p.* of ge-cweðan.

ge-cweccan:—Gecwecton ðegnas his ða croppas *vellebant discipuli ejus spicas*, Lk. Skt. Lind. 7, 1.

ge-cwed, -cwid, -cwyde *a word, command.* v. cwide.

ge-cweden *spoken, called, ordained*, Chr. 456; Th. 22, 5, col. 2, 3: L. Ath. v. § 12, 1; Th. i. 240, 32; *pp. of* ge-cweðan.

ge-cwednis, se; *f. Vocabulum, nomen*, Hpt. Gl. 441.

ge-cwed-rǽden, ne; *f. An agreement*, Ors. 5, 12; Bos. 111, 23.

ge-cwellan *to kill:*—Ða suno gecuoellas hia *filii morte adficient eos*, Mk. Skt. Lind. 13, 12. Ðætte hia woere gecuelledo *ut interficerentur*, Lk. Skt. Lind. 23, 32. [*O. H. Ger.* ge-quelit *cruciatus.*]

ge-cwelman *to destroy.* v. ge-cwylman.

ge-cwelmbǽran *to be tortured;* extorqueri, cruciari, Hpt. Gl. 470.

ge-cwēman; *p.* de; *pp.* ed [cwēman *to please*] *To please, satisfy, propitiate;* plăcēre, satisfăcĕre:—He ne mihte ðām folcum mid gifum gecwēman *he had not power to satisfy the people with rewards*, Ors. 3, 7; Bos. 60, 45. Pilatus wolde ðam folce gecwēmam *Pilātus vŏlens pŏpŭlo satisfăcĕre*, Mk. Bos. 15, 15. Gif ðū godum ussum gecwēmest *if thou wilt propitiate our gods*, Exon. 68 a; Th. 252, 27; Jul. 169. Ðe him dǽdum gecwēmde *who pleased him by deeds*, 46 b; Th. 159, 6; Gū. 922. Sume gecwēmdon englum *some have given pleasure to angels*, Homl. Th. ii. 286, 12. God, ðū ðe mid hreōwnisse gicuoemes ł gicōmed biþ *Deus qui pœnitentia placaris*, Rtl. 8, 33. [*Laym.* i-quemen *to please.*]

ge-cwēmdun *pleased*, Exon. 21 a; Th. 57, 14; Cri. 918, = gecwēmdon; *p. pl. of* gecwēman.

ge-cwēme; *adj.* [cwēme *pleasant, pleasing*] *Pleasant, pleasing, grateful, acceptable, fit;* jŏcundus, grātus, plăcĭtus, complăcĭtus, acceptus:—Noe wæs Gode gecwēme and gife ætfōran him gemētte *Noe invĕnit grātiam coram Domĭno*, Gen. 6, 8. Seó wæs Criste gecwēme *she was acceptable to Christ*, Exon. 69 b; Th. 258, 2; Jul. 259: Elen. Kmbl. 2097; El. 1050. Gecwēme sȳ him spræc mīn *jŏcundum sit ei elŏquium meum*, Ps. Spl. 103, 35. Forðam hyt wæs swā gecwēme beforan ðē *quoniam sic fuit plăcĭtum ante te*, Mt. Bos. 11, 26: Jn. Bos. 8, 29. Ðǽr is brāde land in heofonrīce Criste gecwēmra *there is a spacious land in heaven's kingdom of the grateful to Christ*, Cd. 218; Th. 278, 5; Sat. 217. Gecwēmre *complăcĭtior*, Ps. Spl. 76, 7. Swā him gecwēmast wæs as was most pleasing to him, H. R. 103, 6. [*Laym, A. R.* i-queme *pleasing*. Cf. *O. H. Ger.* biquâme: *Ger.* bequem.]

ge-cwêmedlîc; *adj. Well pleased;* beneplăcĭtus:—Gecwêmedlîc is Drihtne *beneplăcĭtum est Dŏmĭno*, Ps. Lamb. 146, 11. Ne ne on glywcum weres gecwêmedlîce ođđe welgecwême biþ him *nec in tibiis viri beneplăcĭtum ĕrit ei*, 146, 10. v. ge-cwêmlîc.

ge-cwêmednes, -ness, -nys, -nyss, e; *f. Satisfaction, pleasure, contentment;* beneplăcĭtum:—Gode to gecwêmednesse *to the pleasure of God*, L. Ælf. C. 33; Th. ii. 376, 38. Gode to gecwemednysse *to God's contentment*, Homl. Th. i. 180, 10. v. ge-cwêmnes.

ge-cwêming, e; *f. A pleasing;* beneplăcĭtum:—On gecwêminge đînre *in beneplăcĭto tuo*, Ps. Spl. 88, 17.

ge-cwêmlîc; *adj. Agreeable, well pleased;* placitus, placatus, complacatus, congruus, beneplăcĭtus:—Gecwêmlîc *congruus*, R. Ben. interl. 43. Gecwêmlîc is Drihtne on his folce *beneplăcĭtum est Dŏmĭno pŏpŭlo suo*, Ps. Lamb. 149, 4. In tîde gicuoemlîcum *in tempore placito*, Rtl. 19, 7; 18, 29. Gicuoemlîce *placatus*, 43, 17; 35, 43. Gicuoemlîc *complacatus*, 69, 11. Gicuǽmlîc *supplex*, 166, 5.

ge-cwêmlîce; *adv. Agreeably, acceptably*:—Hû fela wîtegan under đære ǽ Gode gecwêmlîce drohtnodon *how many prophets under the old law passed their life acceptably to God*, Homl. Th. ii. 78, 33; 576, 4.

ge-cwêmnes, -nys, -ness, -nyss, e; *f. A pleasing, satisfaction, appeasing;* plăcātio, beneplăcĭtum:—He ne selþ Gode gecwêmnesse his *non dăbit Deo plăcātiōnem suam*, Ps. Lamb. 48, 8. On gecwêmnesse folces đînes *in beneplăcĭto pŏpŭli tui*, 105, 4. Tîma gecwêmnysse *tempus beneplăcĭti*, Ps. Spl. 68, 16. Martha wæs geornful đæt heó đon Hǽlende to gecwêmnesse đegnode *Martha was desirous to minister to the Saviour to his satisfaction*, Blickl. Homl. 67, 29. Gicuoemnise hæbbendo *sufficentiam habentes*, Rtl. 13, 15.

ge-cwêmsum; *adj. Illibatus*, Hpt. Gl. 520.

ge-cweđan; he -cweđeþ, -cwyþ; *p.* ic, he -cwæþ, đû -cwǽde, *pl.* -cwǽdon; *pp.* -cweden *To say, speak, call, pronounce, agree, resolve, order;* dīcĕre, lŏqui, profāri, pronunciāre, pangĕre, stătuĕre:—Se nǽfre nǽnig word gecweđan mihte *qui ne ūnum quĭdem sermōnum unquam profāri pŏtĕrat*, Bd. 5, 2; S. 614, 43. He đæt word gecwæþ *he spake the word*, Elen. Kmbl. 687; El. 344: 878; El. 440: Andr. Kmbl. 1791; An. 898: 2600; An. 1301. Đe Drihten wiđ eów gecwæþ *quod pĕpĭgit vobiscum Dŏmĭnus*, Deut. 9, 9. Hî ǽfre ǽlcne Deniscne cyng ûtlah of Engla lande gecwǽdon *they pronounced every Danish king an outlaw from England for ever*, Chr. 1014; Erl. 150, 34. On đære stôwe đe is gecweden Creacan ford *in the place which is called Crayford*, Chr. 456; Th. 22, 5, col. 2, 3: H. R. 105, 9. Êce Drihten gecwyþ *the Lord eternal shall speak*, Cd. 227; Th. 304, 9; Sat. 627. Đû gecwǽde đæt đû ne alǽte dôm gedreósan *thou saidst that thou wouldst not let thy greatness sink*, Beo. Th. 5322; B. 2664. Swâ seó stefn gecwæþ *thus spake the voice*, Cd. 202; Th. 251, 10; Dan. 561: 203; Th. 252, 22; Dan. 582. Iulianus se câsere gecwæþ to gefeohte *the emperor Julian gave order for a battle*, Homl. Th. ii. 502, 4. Swâ hit gecweden wæs *as it was agreed*, L. Ath. v. § 12, 1; Th. i. 240, 32: L. A. G. prm; Th. i. 152, 4. Đa deófolgildan gecwǽdon đæt hî woldon đone apostol to heora hǽđenscipe geneádian *the idolaters agreed to force the apostle to their idolatry*, Homl. Th. i. 70, 24; H. R. 101, 20. [*Laym.* i-queđen: *Goth.* ga-kwithan *to agree*: *O. Sax.* gi-queđan *to speak, declare*: *O. H. Ger.* gi-quedan *dicere*.]

ge-cwician, -cwycian; *p.* ode, ude; *pp.* od, ud [cwician *to quicken*] *To quicken, create;* vivĭfĭcāre, creāre:—Dô me æfter đînum wordum wel gecwician *vivĭfĭca me secundum verbum tuum*, Ps. Th. 118, 25. Heortan clǽne gecwica in me God *cor mundum crea in me Deus*, Ps. Surt. 50, 12. Đæt đû me on rihtes rǽd gecwycige *in æquĭtāte tua vivĭfĭca me*, Ps. Th. 118, 40. He bebeád and gecwicode synd *ipse mandāvit et creāta sunt*, Ps. Spl. C. 32, 9: 101, 19. Hî bîþ gecwicude *creābuntur*, Ps. Spl. C. 103, 31. [*Goth.* ga-kwiujan *to quicken, make alive*: *O. H. Ger.* ki-chuuichan.]

ge-cwide, v. cwide, p. 180, col. 2. [Cf. *O. H. Ger.* ka-qhuit, kechuiti, *f. sententia*.]

ge-cwid-rǽdden, -cwid-rǽden, -cwyd-rǽden, -cwed-rǽden, -rǽdenn, e; *f. An agreement, a contract, statute, conspiration;* ratio, pactorum, conventio, conspiratio:—He oferbræc heora gecwidrǽdenne *he broke through their agreement*, Ors. 3, 6; Bos. 57, 40. Gewordenre gecwydrǽdene *conventione facta*, Mt. Bos. 20, 1. Gecwidrædden *conspiratio*, Ælfc. Gl. 49; Som. 65, 87: Wrt. Voc. 34, 19. Đæt wæs seó gecwydrǽden *that was the agreement*, Ors. 5, 12; Bos. 111, 26.

ge-cwis *a conspiracy, consent;* conspiratio, Cot. 46: Hpt. Gl. 519. [*Goth.* ga-kwiss *consent*.]

ge-cwyd-rǽden *agreement*, Ors. 5, 12; Bos. 111, 21, 26: Mt. Bos. 20, 2. v. ge-cwidrǽden.

ge-cwylman; *p.* de; *pp.* ed [cwelman, cwylman *to torment*] *To afflict, torment, punish, destroy, kill;* pūnire, trucīdāre, mortĭfĭcāre:—Nâ đæt ân me, ac eác swylce mîne geféran mid ânum slege he mæg gecwylman *non sōlum me, sed etiam meos sŏcios ūno ictu pŏtĕrat mortĭfĭcāre*, Coll. Monast. Th. 24, 33. Đæt hî gecwylmen rihte heortan *ut trucīdent rectos corde*, Ps. Spl. C. 36, 15. Đæt he byþ gecwylmed *ut pūniētur*, Ps. Lamb. 36, 13. Mid ormǽtre angsumnysse gecwylmed *afflicted with excessive pain*, Homl. Th. i. 88, 6.

ge-cwylmful; *adj. Pernicious;* perniciosus, Hpt. Gl. 428.

ge-cwyþ *speaks*, Cd. 227; Th. 304, 9; Sat. 627; *3rd sing. pres. of* ge-cweđan.

ge-cŷgan *to call, call upon, invoke, provoke, incite*, Exon. 62 b; Th. 229, 13; Ph. 454: Ps. Spl. 73, 19: 77, 64: 85, 4. v. ge-cîgan.

ge-cygd *strife, contention, debate;* jurgium, Bd. 1, 14; S. 482, 26. v. gecîd.

ge-cŷgednes, -ness, e; *f. A calling;* vŏcātio:—On đam dæge đe geneálǽhte hyre gecŷgednesse of đyssum lîfe *immĭnente die suæ vŏcātiōnis*, Bd. 3, 8; S. 531, 31. v. ge-cîgednes.

ge-cyn, -cynn, es; *n. Nature;* natura:—Đæt is of untrumnisse đæs gecynnes *ex infirmitate naturæ est*, Bd. 1, 27; S. 494, 15.

ge-cynd, ge-cind, *acc.* ge-cynd, ge-cynde; *f. also* ge-cynd, ge-cynde, *nom. acc*; *gen.* -cyndes; *dat.* -cynde; *pl. nom. acc.* -cyndu, -cyndo, -cynd; *gen.* -cynda; *dat.* -cyndum; *n.* I. *nature, kind, manner, condition, gender;* natura, indoles, ingenium, proprietas, modus, qualitas, conditio, genus:—For his âgenre gecynde *from its own nature*, Bt. 13; Fox 38, 7. On swîđe lytlon hæfþ seó gecynd genôg *with very little nature has enough*, Bt. 14, 1; Fox 42, 10. Is sió þridde gecynd betere *the third nature is better*, Bt. Met. Fox 20, 373; Met. 20, 187. On đa beteran gecynd *into the better nature*, Andr. Kmbl. 1176; An. 588. Hû his gecynde biþ *what its nature [sex] is*, Exon. 61 a; Th. 223, 8; Ph. 356. Wæstma gecyndu *kinds of fruits*, 33 a; Th. 104, 30; Gû. 15. Cristes gecyndo *the natures of Christ*, Salm. Kmbl. 819; Sal. 409. On feówer gecynd *in four kinds*, 996; Sal. 499. Æfter gecynde *de genere*, Ælfc. Gr. 6; Som. 5, 27. II. *generation, nakedness;* generatio, natales, partes, genitales, verenda:—Đurh clǽne gecynd *by pure generation*, Hy. 9, 11; Hy. Grn. ii. 291, 11: 9, 52; Hy. Grn. ii. 292, 52. Beheledon heora fæderes gecynd *operuerunt verenda patris sui*, Gen. 9, 23. III. *offspring;* proles:—Hyra gecynda on weorold bringaþ *prolem reddunt*, Nar. 35, 26. [Cf. *O. Sax.* kind: *O. H. Ger.* kint: *Ger.* kind.]

ge-cynd-bôc, e; *f. Genesis*:—Seó bôc ys gehâten Genesis đæt ys gecyndbôc *the book is called Genesis, that is the book of generation*, Thw. Hept. p. 2, 33.

ge-cynde; *adj.* [cynde *natural*] *Natural, innate, inborn, genial;* natūrālis, innātus, ingĕnĭtus, ingĕnuus:—Gif se weorþscipe đam wêlan gecynde wǽre *if dignity were natural to wealth*, Bt. 27, 3; Fox 98, 25. Swâ him gecynde wæs *as was natural to him*, Beo. Th. 5386; B. 2690: Bt. 36, 4; Fox 178, 12. Gecynde riht *jus naturāle*, Ælfc. Gl. 12; Som. 57, 90; Wrt. Voc. 20, 31. Gefrægn ic hebrêos in Hierusalem cyningdôm habban, swâ him gecynde wæs *I have heard that the Hebrews had kingly sway in Jerusalem, as was natural to them*, Cd. 173; Th. 216, 8; Dan. 3. Þurh gecyndne cræft *through natural virtue*, Chr. 975; Erl. 126, 9; Edg. 35. Cêne men gecynde rîce *bold men [have] inborn sway*, Exon. 89 b; Th. 337, 3; Gn. Ex. 59. Hæfdan him gecynde cyningas twegen *they had two kings of their own race*, Bt. Met. Fox 1, 11; Met. 1, 6.

ge-cyndelîc; *adj.* [cyndelîc *natural*] *Natural, according to nature;* natūrālis:—Hit is gecyndelîc đæt ealle eorþlîce lîchaman beóþ fulran on weaxendum mônan, đonne on wanigendum *it is natural that all earthly bodies are fuller at the increasing moon than at the waning*, Bd. de nat. rerum; Wrt. popl. science 15, 11; Lchdm. iii. 268, 7. Gecyndelîce dohtor *filia natūrālis*, Bd. 3, 8; S. 531, 21. Gecyndelîces gôdes *of natural good*, Bt. 27, 3; Fox 100, 4. Hî nân gecyndelîc gôd on him selfum nabbaþ *they have no natural good in themselves*, Bt. 27, 3; Fox 98, 30: 27, 4; Fox 100, 18. Ne forlêton hî nô đæt gecyndelîce gôd *they would not lose the natural good*, 27, 3; Fox 100, 6.

ge-cyndelîce; *adv. Naturally;* natūrālĭter:—Ealle gesceafta gecyndelîce fundiaþ to cumanne to gôde *all creatures naturally desire to come to good*, Bt. 35, 4; Fox 160, 15.

gecynde-spræc, e; *f. A natural speech, an idiom;* proprietas linguæ, idioma, Ælfc. Gl. 101; Som. 77, 41.

ge-cynd-lim, es; *n. A birth-limb, womb;* vulva:—Gecyndlim ontŷnende *vulvam aperiens*, Lk. Bos. 2, 23: Hpt. Gl. 441.

ge-cyndnys, -nyss, e; *f. A nation;* nātio:—Gecyndnys bearna dînra ic ascunode *nātiōnem filiōrum tuōrum reprobāvi*, Ps. Spl. 72, 15.

ge-cŷpan, -cêpan; *p.* -cŷpte; *pp.* -cŷpt [cŷpan *to sell*] *To buy, purchase;* ĕmĕre:—Wyrsan wîgfrecan gecŷpan *to buy a worse warrior*, Beo. Th. 4986; B. 2496. Đæt ic đê gecŷpte *which I bought for thee*, Exon. 29 b; Th. 90, 11; Cri. 1472.

ge-cŷpe; *adj. For sale*:—Đǽr wǽron gecŷpe hryđeru *there were oxen for sale*, Homl. Th. i. 402, 17.

ge-cypsed; *part. p. Fettered;* compĕdītus:—Ingâ on gesyhþe đîne geómrunga gecypsedra *introeat in conspectu tuo gĕmĭtus compĕdītōrum*, Ps. Spl. 78, 11. Driht tolŷseþ gecypsede *Dŏmĭnus solvit compĕdītos*, Ps. Spl. 145, 6.

ge-cyrnlad; *adj. Having kernels*:—Gecyrnlade appla *pomegranates*, Hpt. Gl. 496.

ge-cyrran; *p.* de; *pp.* ed. I. *to turn, convert*; vertere, convertere:—We sceolan ða wundor gecyrran on sōðfæstnesse geleáfan *we must apply those wonders to the belief in the truth*, Blickl. Homl. 17, 10. Ic gecyrre feónd mīnne *converto inimicum meum*, Ps. Spl. 9, 3. Manega israhela bearna he gecyrþ to drihtne *multos filiorum israel convertet ad dominum*, Lk. Bos. 1, 16. Gif hē ðæt Cristene folc mid lufan ne mehton gecyrron *if they could not by love convert Christian people*, Blickl. Homl. 45, 22. Ðīne heortan to rǣde gecyr *turn thy heart to counsel*, Blickl. Homl. 113, 27: Ps. Th. 114, 7; 84, 5. Heora līf he hæfþ to gefeán gecyrred *their life he hath turned to joy*, Blickl. Homl. 85, 24; 57, 30; 59, 13. II. *to turn* [*one's self*], *go, return*; verti, reverti, ire:—Ic wille ðæt he libbe and to Gode gecyrran *I will that he live and turn to God*, Blickl. Homl. 97, 34; 101, 15. Gecyrraþ to me ðonne gecyrre ic to eów. He ðonne gecyrde to us *turn to me then will I turn to you. He turned to us then*, Blickl. Homl. 103, 1. Ðū ne gecyr from ðīnre ðeówene *turn not from thy servant*, 89, 12: Ps. Th. 58, 14: Andr. Kmbl. 2158; An. 1080. Hī symle sculon ðone ylcan ryne eft gecyrran *they ever must go again the same course*, Bt. Met. Fox 11, 74; Met. 11, 37. Ðā gecyrdon ða twā and hund-seofontig *reversi sunt septuaginta duo*, Lk. Bos. 10, 17. Hwænne he sȳ fram gyftum gecyrred *quando revertatur a nuptis*, Lk. Bos. 12, 36.

ge-cyrred-nes, -ness, e; *f. A turning, conversion*:—Æfter his gecyrrednysse, Gregorius þēnode þearfum *after his conversion Gregory ministered to the poor*, Homl. Th. ii. 118, 35. v. acyrrednes.

ge-cyrring, e; *f. Converting, changing*; conversio, C. R. Ben. 62: Ps. Spl. T. 9, 3.

ge-cyspyd *fettered*, Ps. Spl. 78, 11. v. cyspan.

ge-cyssan; *p.* -cyste; *pp.* -cyssed [cyssan *to kiss*] *To kiss*; oscŭlāri:—Gecyste cyning þegn betstan *the king kissed the best of thanes*, Beo. Th. 3744; B. 1870. Gecyste foet his *osculabatur pedes ejus*, Lk. Skt. Lind. 7, 38.

ge-cȳð, -cȳðð, e; *f. A country, native country*; patria, natale solum:—On hiora āgenre gecȳþþe *in their own country*, Bt. 27, 3; Fox 100, 1. v. cȳð.

ge-cȳðan; *p.* -cȳðde, -cȳdde; *pp.* -cȳðed, -cȳd. I. *to make known, tell, relate, proclaim, announce, inform*; nuntiare, annuntiare, referre, effari, monēre:—Ða andsware gecȳðan *to make known the answer*, Beo. Th. 714; B. 354: 4638; B. 2324: Ps. Spl. 101, 24. Gecȳð *make known*, Exon. 50 a; Th. 173, 4; Gū. 1155. Sōþ gecȳðan *to tell the truth*, Elen. Kmbl. 1173; El. 588. Se ðæt orleg-weorc ðam ebriscan eorle gecȳðde *who announced that fatal work to the Hebrew leader*, Cd. 94; Th. 122, 4; Gen. 2021: Andr. Kmbl. 1568; An. 785: 1718; An. 861. Swā hie gecȳðde wǣron *as they were informed*, Cd. 195; Th. 243, 9; Dan. 433. Him wæs gecȳðed *nuntiatum est illi*, Lk. Bos. 8, 20. Ðā wearþ hit Constantine gecȳd *it was told to Constantine*, H. R. 3, 11. II. *to declare, reveal, manifest, shew, perform, confirm, testify, prove*; declarare, revelare, edocere, manifestare, monstrare, perhibere, testari, probare:—Ðæt wille ic gecȳðan, ðæt ða rīcu of nānes mannes mihtum swā gecræftgade ne wurdon *that will I declare, that the kingdoms were not strengthened by the powers of man*, Ors. 2, 1; Bos. 39, 1. God wolde gecȳðan hwylcre geearnunge se hālga wer wǣre *Deus qualis meriti vir fuerit demonstrare voluit*, Bd. 1, 33; S. 499, 8; H. R. 15, 31. Se inlīca dēma mannum gecȳdde *internus arbiter edocuit*, 3, 15; S. 541, 19. He gecȳðeþ ðē wisdōmes gife *he will shew thee the gift of wisdom*, Elen. Kmbl. 187; El. 595. Swā ðū hyldo wið me gecȳðdest *as thou hast manifested grace to me*, Andr. Kmbl. 780; An. 390. Ðæt ðīne leóde gecȳðdon *that thy people shewed*, Salm. Kmbl. 654; Sal. 326. Wundor wæs gecȳðed *the miracle was manifested*, Cd. 208; Th. 257, 6; Dan. 653: 212; Th. 263, 11; Dan. 760. Gecȳðan mid āþe *to prove or declare on oath*, L. In. 16; Th. i. 112, 7: 17; Th. i. 114, 2: L. Ed. 1; Th. i. 160, 5. Tree of wæstm his gecȳðed biþ *arbor fructu suo cognoscitur*, Lk. Skt. Lind. 6, 44. III. *to make celebrated, renowned, famed*; notum facere, inclytum reddere:—Cyning cystum gecȳðed *the king for virtues famed*, Beo. Th. 1850; B. 923: 530; B. 262: Exon. 41 a; Th. 137, 3; Gū. 553. [*O. Sax.* gi-kūðian: *O. H. Ger.* ga-chundan.] v. cȳðan, cūð.

ge-cȳðelic; *adj. Manifest, made known*; manifestatus, Alb. resp. 10. v. cȳðlic.

ge-cȳðig; *adj. Knowing, cognizant*:—Gicȳðig *cognitor*, Rtl. 41, 23. [Cf. *Ger.* kundig *acquainted with.*]

ge-cȳðnes, -ness, -nys, -nyss, e; *f. Testimony, testament, manifestation*; testimonium, testamentum:—Manega sǣdon leáse gecȳðnysse *multi testimonium falsum dicebant*, Mk. Bos. 14, 56. Ðes calic is niwe gecȳðnes on mīnum blōde *hic est calix novum testamentum in sanguine meo*, Lk. Bos. 22, 20: Ps. Spl. 49, 6, 17. Drihten, ðīne gecȳðnessa sindon swīðe geleáflīce *Lord, thy testimonies are very faithful*, Homl. Th. ii. 42, 14. Seó ealde gecȳðnis *the Old Testament*, Thw. Hept. p. 2, 14. Nū neálǣceþ ǣgðer ge ðīn onwrigennes ge uncer gecȳðnes *now approaches both the discovery of thee* [*as false*] *and the manifestation of us two* [*as true*], Blickl. Homl. 187, 23. v. cȳðnes.

ged, gedd, es; *n. A song, proverb, poem*, Bt. Met. Fox 2, 10; Met. 2, 5. Gedd *proverbium*, Jn. Skt. Lind. 10, 6; 16, 25. v. gid.

ge-dæftan; *p.* -dæfte; *pp.* dæft *To put in order, make ready, prepare*:—Ða ðe mid ðām [treowum] Cristes weig gedæfton *those who with the* [*trees*] *prepared Christ's way*, Homl. Th. i. 212, 34. He eów betǣcþ mycele healle gedæfte *ipse vobis ostendet cenaculum magnum stratum*, Lk. Bos. 22, 12: Mk. Bos. 14, 15. v. dæftan.

ge-dæfte; *adj. Mild, gentle, meek*:—Ðīn cyning cymþ to ðē, gedæfte *rex tuus venit tibi, mansuetus*, Mt. Bos. 21, 5. [Cf. *Orm.* daffte *humble, quiet.*] The later sense of 'daft' *foolish, stupid*, may be compared with the slang sense of 'soft.'

ge-dæftlīce, -dæftelīce, -deftlīce; *adv. Fitly, seasonably*; opportūne, commŏde:—Ic ðē beóde ðæt ðū stande on ðissum wordum, and hie lǣre ǣgðer ge gedæftlīce ge ungedæftlīce *I charge thee to abide by these words, and teach them both seasonably and unseasonably*, Past. 15, 6; Swt. 96, 15; Hat. MS. 20 a, 21. Gedæftelīce *seasonably*, 15, 6; Swt. 96, 17; Hat. MS. 20 a, 22.

ge-dǣlan; *p.* de; *pp.* ed *To divide, part, impart, separate, distribute, share, partake*:—Seoððan se līchoma and se gāst gedǣlde beóþ *after the body and the spirit shall be separated*, Blickl. Homl. 111, 30. Ic gedǣle bā Sicimam et convallem, ða ǣr samod wǣron *dividam Sichimam et convallem*, Ps. Th. 59, 5. Hine gedǣlaþ *dividet eum*, Mt. Kmbl. Rush. 24, 51. He sceole wiþ ðæm līchomon hine gedǣlon *he must separate himself from the body*, Blickl. Homl. 97, 21. He hine wiþ ðas world gedǣleþ *he separates himself from the world*, 125, 11; 21, 26: Exon. 10 b; Th. 102, 6; Cri. 1668: Beo. Th. 4836; B. 2422: Exon. Th. 115, 32; Gū. 198. Ne mæg mīn līchoma wiþ deáþ ge-dǣlan *my body cannot separate* [*itself*] *from* [i. e. *avoid*] *death*, Exon. Th. 124, 25; Gū. 343; 146, 19; Gū. 712. Gedaelde woeron ł todǣldon woedo mīno *partiti sunt vestimenta mea*, Jn. Skt. Lind. 19, 24. Gif he ǣr nele ðone sēlestan dǣl Gode gedǣlan *if he will not before give the best part to God*, Blickl. Homl. 195, 7. Ðæt we gedǣlan ðone teóþan dǣl *that we distribute the tenth part*, 39, 19. Gedǣled ðearfendum mannum *given to the poor*, 69, 8; 75, 23; Beo. Th. 143; B. 71: Exon. Th. 371, 19; Seel. 78: Past. 63; Swt. 459, 12. Sceolde he worc ðæs gewinnes gedǣlan *he should get pain on account of that struggle*, Cd. Th. 19, 24; Gen. 296. [*Goth.* ga-dailjan: *O. Sax.* gi-dēlian: *O. H. Ger.* ki-teilan *to divide, impart, distribute.*]

ge-dǣledlīce; *adv. Apart, separately*: separatim, Cot. 201.

ge-dæman *to obstruct, dam*; obstruere, Serm. Creat.

ge-dærsted; *part.* [dærst *leaven*] *Leavened, fermented*; fermentatus:—Gedærsted is all *fermentatum est totum*, Mt. Kmbl. Lind. 13, 33. Ōþ-ðæt sié gedærsted oððe gecnoeden all *donec fermentaretur totum*, Lk. Skt. Lind. 13, 21.

ge-dafen; *part.* [dafen *becoming*] *Becoming, fit, suitable*; dĕcens, congruus, convĕniens:—Gif ðē gedafen þince *if it seem becoming to thee*, Exon. 67 a; Th. 247, 32; Jul. 87. This points to a verb 'ge-dafan,' corresponding to the Gothic 'gadaban;' *convenire, decere*. [Cf. gedafenian.]

ge-dafenian, -dafnian, -dæfnia; *p.* ode; *pp.* od *To be becoming* or *fit, to behove*; decere, convĕnīre: chiefly used impersonally, *it behoves, it is becoming* or *fit, ought*; dĕcet, oportet:—Ic axige hwæðer hit mihte gedafnian Abrahame *I will ask whether it was becoming to Abraham*, Boutr. Scrd. 21, 47. Lāreówum gedafenaþ ðæt hī mid wīsdōmes sealte geleáffulra manna mōd sylton *it befits teachers that they salt the minds of believing men with the salt of wisdom*, Homl. Th. ii. 536, 16: L. E. I. 24; Th. ii. 420, 32. Me gedæfnaþ *me oportet*, Jn. Skt. Lind. 9, 4. Ðē gedæfneþ *te oportet*, 3, 7. Ðē gedafenaþ *te dĕcet*, Ps. Th. 64, 1: 92, 7: Ælfc. Gr. 33; Som. 37, 20: Andr. Kmbl. 633; An. 317. Me gedafenaþ ōðrum ceastrum Godes rīce bodian *aliis cīvĭtātibus oportet me evangelizāre regnum Dei*, Lk. Bos. 4, 43: Ælfc. Gr. 33; Som. 37, 21. Gedafenode *dĕcuit*, 33; Som. 37, 21: Bd. 4, 11; S. 579, 11. Hit gedafnode ðæt se Ælmihtiga ǣrest ðæt hwīlendlīce leóht geworhte *it was becoming that the Almighty first created the temporary light*, Boutr. Scrd. 19, 4: 21, 39. Gedæfnad is ūs *decet nos*, Mt. Kmbl. Lind. 3, 15.

ge-dafenigendlīce; *adv. Consequently*; consequenter, Scint. 11.

ge-dafenlīc, -dæfenlīc; *adj.* [ge-dafen *becoming*] *Becoming, fit, decent, convenient, agreeable*; dĕcens, congruus, convĕniens, hăbilis:—Ðæt is gedafenlīc ðæt ðū Dryhtnes word on hyge healde *it is fit that thou shouldst keep in mind the word of the Lord*, Elen. Kmbl. 2333; El. 1168: Bt. Met. Fox 31, 42; Met. 31, 21: Bd. 4, 23; S. 594, 43. Hit gedafenlīc is ðæt his reáf ne beó hōrig *it is becoming that his vestment be not dirty*, L. Ælf. C. 22; Th. ii. 350, 20. Gedafenlīc þeódnes [MS. seodnys] *hăbĭlis conjunctio*, Ælfc. Gl. 99; Som. 76, 118; Wrt. Voc. 54, 60. Us dæg endebyrdnysse mid gedafenlīcre cymþ *nōbis dies ordĭne congruo vĕnit*, Hymn. Surt. 38, 3. Nis nā gedafenlīc ðæt ðes man āna beó *it is not fitting that this man be alone*, Homl. Th. i. 14, 17. Uæs gedæfenlīc [gidæfendlic, Rush.] *oportebat*, Jn. Skt. Lind. 4, 4.

ge-dafenlīce; *adv. Fitly, properly, justly*; dĕcenter, convenienter, juste :—God gewræc swíðe gedafenlíce on ðam árleásan men his árleáse geþoht *God very justly avenged his wicked thought on this wicked man*, Ors. 6, 31; Bos. 128, 33.

ge-dafenlícnes, -nys, -ness, -nyss, e; *f. Decency, convenience, an opportunity*; dĕcentia, convĕnientia, opportūnĭtas :—Eton mid gedafenlícnysse *juxta convĕnientiam comēdāmus*, Bd. Whelc. 228, 43. On gedafenlícnessum *in opportūnĭtātĭbus*, Ps. Lamb. 9, 10: second 9, 1.

ge-daflíc; *adj. Convenient, fitting*; conveniens, congruus, Hpt. Gl. 415.

ge-dafniendlíc; *adj. Suitable*, Hpt. Gl. 433, 497.

ge-dǽl, es; *n. A division, separation, parting, distribution*; dīvīsio, sēpărātio, dīvortium, distrĭbūtio :—Ðé is gedǽl witod líces and sáwle *a separation of body and soul is decreed to thee*, Cd. 43; Th. 57, 19; Gen. 930: Beo. Th. 6128; B. 3068. Ic uncres gedáles onbád earfoþlíce *I awaited our parting in sorrow*, Soul Kmbl. 74; Seel. 37: Bd. 1, 15; S. 483, 37. Se hæfde heortan unhneáweste hringa gedáles *he had the most liberal heart in the distribution of rings*, Scóp Th. 148; Wíd. 73. Æfter ðæs líchoman gedále and ðære sáwle *after the separation of the body and soul*, Bt. 18, 4; Fox 68, 12. Ðú ondrǽtst ðé on ðam gedále *thou fearest to distribute*, Homl. Th. ii. 104, 25. Se todǽlde sǽ reáde on gedǽl *qui dīvīsit măre rubrum in dīvīsiōnes*, Ps. Spl. 135, 13. [Cf. *O. Eng. Homl.* elmes i-dal *almsgiving*.] DER. deáþ-, ealdor-, feorh-, friþ-, gást-, híw-, líf-, nýd-, sáwel-, ðeóden-, woruld-gedǽl.

ge-dǽl-land, -dæl-land, es; *n. Partible land, land belonging to several proprietors*; sepărābĭlis terra :—Gif ceorlas gærstún hæbben gemǽnne, oððe gedǽlland to týnanne *if churls have a common meadow or partible land to fence*, L. In. 42; Th. i. 128, 6. v. note. Híd gedǽllandes, Kmbl. Cod. Dipl. iii. 6, 11.

geddian; *p.* ode; *pp.* od *To sing*; cantare :—Ðá ongan he geddian *then began he to sing*, Bt. 31, 2; Fox 112, note 25. Se scóp geddode *the poet sang*, 35, 5; Fox 166, 8. v. giddian.

geddung, giddung, e; *f. A similitude, parable, riddle*; similitudo, parabola :—In geddungum *in parabolis*, Lk. Skt. Lind. 8, 10. Geddung *parabola*, 18, 9; 19, 11. Geddung ł onlícnis *similitudo*, 13, 6. v. gidding.

ge-deágod *dyed, coloured*. DER. twi-gedeágod. v. deágian.

ge-deápian; *p.* ade, ode; *pp.* ad, od *To deepen, become deep* [?] :—Gideópadon niólnisso *preruperunt abyssi*, Rtl. 81, 24. [Cf. *Goth.* gadiupjan *to deepen, dig deeply*.]

ge-deáðian; *p.* ode; *pp.* od *To kill*; mortificare :—Gedeáða ðú *mortifica*, Rtl. 48, 14. v. ge-dēðan.

ge-deccan; *imp.* -dec. [deccan *to cover*] *To cover*; tĕgĕre :—Gedec ánne cláþ ðǽr mid *cover a cloth therewith*, Herb. 78, 2; Lchdm. i. 182, 3. Gedeced mid wyrtum *covered with spices*, Homl. Th. ii. 260, 35. v. Leo 607, 39. v. ge-þeccan.

GE-DÉFE, -doefe; *comp.* -ra; *superl.* -est, -ust; *adj. Becoming, fit, proper, seemly, convenient, agreeable, decent, quiet, mild, meek, gentle, kind, benevolent*; congruus, convĕniens, dĕcens, opportūnus, hŏnestus, quiētus, mansuētus, bĕnignus :—Swá hit gedéfe wæs *as it was fit*, Beo. Th. 3345; B. 1670: Ps. Th. 60, 6: 117, 13. Ne biþ ðæt gedéfe deáþ *that is not a seemly death*, Exon. 91 a; Th. 340, 26; Gn. Ex. 117. Beóþ gé gedoefe *estote vos perfecta*, Mt. Kmbl. Rush. 5, 48. Noe wæs dómfæst and gedéfe *Noah was just and meek*, Cd. 64; Th. 78, 2; Gen. 1287: Exon. 41 a; Th. 136, 34; Gú. 551: Beo. Th. 2458; B. 1227. Gedéfe is ðín milde mód *bĕnigna est misĕrĭcordia tua*, Ps. Th. 68, 16. Gedéfe sacerd *sacerdos quietus*, Nar. 37, 25. Eart ðú on lifigendra lande se gedéfa dǽl *tu es portio mea in terra vīventium*, 141, 5. On tíde gedéfre *in tempŏre opportūno*, Ps. Spl. C. 144, 16: Bd. 4, 1; S. 564, 3. Þurh gedéfne dóm *with fitting judgment*, Exon. 41 b; Th. 138, 26; Gú. 582: Bd. 4, 1; S. 564, 4. Dó gedéfe mid me. Drihten, tácen *fac mecum, Dŏmĭne, signum in bŏno*, Ps. Th. 85, 16. Ða synd líðe and gedéfe *they are meek and gentle*, Homl. Th. i. 550, 20. Sýn hí adilgad of gedéfra eác ðæra lifigendra leófra bócum *deleantur de libro vīventium*, Ps. Th. 68, 29. Wuna mid us ðæt ðú us gedéfra gedó *stop with us to improve us*, St. And. 24, 8. Deórust and gedéfust *dearest and fittest*, 102, 16. Ealra démena ðam gedéfestan *to the most benevolent of all judges*, Exon. 93 a; Th. 350, 4; Sch. 58. [*Goth.* ga-dōbs *fitting*.] DER. lǽr-gedéfe.

ge-défe; *adv. Becomingly, decently*; dĕcenter :—Ic eom on ðínum dómum gedéfe glæd *jūdĭcia tua jŭcunda*, Ps. Th. 118, 39: 124, 4.

ge-défelíc; *adj. Fit, becoming, decent, honest*; honestus :—Ðǽr syndon gedéfelíce menn *sunt ibi homines honesti*, Nar. 37, 32.

ge-défelíce; *adv. Becomingly, fitly, decently, properly*; dĕcenter, opportūne :—Sóna ðæs ðe gehálgod wæs, ða dyde mon his líchoman in, and on ðære cyricean norþ-portice gedéfelíce wæs bebyriged *mox vēro ut dedĭcāta est, intro inlātum, et in portĭcu illĭus aquĭlōnālis dĕcenter sepultum est*, Bd. 2, 3; S. 504, 34. He symle gedéfelíce æftercwæþ *he always repeated [them] properly*, 5, 2; S. 615, 15.

ge-defen; *part. Fit, proper, due*; dēbĭtus :—Gedefen *dēbĭtus*, Cot. 61: Th. An. 101, 10. To forþspównesse gedefenre heánesse *ad profectum dēbĭti culmĭnis*, Bd. 2, 4; S. 505, 17. v. gedafen.

ge-defenlíc; *adj. Fit, proper, due*; dēbitus :—Mid gedefenlícre ege *dēbĭto cum tĭmōre*, Bd. 4, 3; S. 569, 28. v. gedafenlíc.

ge-défnes, -ness, e; *f. Quietness, mildness, gentleness*; mansuētūdo :—Oferbecymþ gedéfnes *sŭpervĕnit mansuētūdo*, Ps. Lamb. 89, 10.

ge-deftlíce; *adv. Fitly, moderately*; dĕcenter :—Gif ðú wile hál beón, drinc ðé gedeftlíce *if thou wilt be healthy, drink in moderation*, Prov. Kmbl. 61. v. ge-dæftlíce.

ge-dégan, ge-dégean *to pass through, escape*; pertransīre :—Oft úre sáwl swýðe frécne hlimman gedégde hlúdes wæteres; wéne ic forðon ðæt heó wel mǽge ðæt swýðre mægen sáwel usser wæteres wénan ðæs wel gedégean *torrentem pertransivit anima nostra; forsitan pertransisset anima nostra aquam intolerabilem*, Ps. Th. 123, 4. Gif he wille sylf Godes dómas gedégan *if he himself wish to be uncondemned*, Blickl. Homl. 43, 12. v. gedígan.

ge-dégled *hidden*; absconditus, Lk. Skt. Lind. 12, 2. v. ge-díglian.

ge-delf, es; *n. A delving, the act of digging, a trench*; fossio, fossa :—Mid gedelfe *by digging*, Ors. 2, 4; Bos. 44, 12. He lét delfon an mycel gedelf *he had a great trench dug*, Cod. Dipl. Kmbl. iv. 58, 5.

ge-delfan; *p.* -dealf, *pl.* -dulfon; *pp.* dolfen *To dig, delve*; fodere, effodere :—Wæs ðǽr sum hláw ðone men gedulfon *there was a mound which men had dug*, Guthl. 4; Gdwin. 26, 6. Ðé wearþ helle seáþ niðer gedolfen *the pit of hell was dug beneath for thee*, Exon. 71 b; Th. 267, 30; Jul. 423.

ge-déman; *p.* de; *pp.* ed *To deem, judge, determine, ordain, decree, doom, condemn*; jūdĭcāre, decernĕre, sancīre, condemnāre :—He wile gedéman dǽda gehwylce *he will judge each deed*, Exon. 15 b; Th. 33, 13; Cri. 525. Ðæt he ǽghwelcne on riht gedémeþ *that he judge every one righteously*, L. Alf. 49; Th. i. 56, 30: Ps. Th. 57, 10. He gedémde úrne Drihten to deáþe *he condemned our Lord to death*, Ors. 6, 3; Bos. 117, 42. Gedémdon [MS. gedémden] *sanxērunt*, Mone B. 1940. Se ðe undóm gedéme *he who shall doom unjust doom*, L. C. S. 15; Th. i. 384, 7. Swá gedémed is *as is ordained*, Exon. 58 a; Th. 207, 26; Ph. 147. He gedémed hæfde ðæt Ceólwulf æfter him cyning wǽre *successōrem fore Ceoluulfum decrēvisset*, Bd. 5, 23; S. 646, 1: Cd. 186; Th. 231, 11; Dan. 245. Fýnd syndon eówere gedémed to deáþe *your enemies are condemned to death*, Judth. 11; Thw. 24, 19; Jud. 196. [*Goth.* ga-dōmjan.]

ge-deóful-geld *idolatry*. v. deófolgeld.

ge-deorf, es; *n. Labour, trouble, tribulation*; lābor, trībŭlātio :—Micel gedeorf ys hit *magnus lăbor est*, Coll. Monast. Th. 20, 5, 7. Byþ mycel gedeorf *ĕrit trībŭlātio magna*, Mt. Bos. 24, 21. Hæfst ðú ǽnig gedeorf *hăbestu ălĭquem lābōrem?* Coll. Monast. Th. 20, 9. For his micclum gedeorfum *for his great labours*, Homl. Th. ii. 522, 3: 82, 33.

ge-deorfan; *p.* -dearf, *pl.* -durfon; *pp.* -dorfen *To labour* :—Micel ic gedeorfe *multum laboro*, Coll. Monast. Th. 20, 25. *In* Ors. 4, 6; Bos. 86, 3, Heora scipa gedurfon L and C *perhaps we should read* gedufon *sank*, cf. 85, 38, gedeáf [gedráf], *and* Ors. 1, 7; Bos. 30, 24, Ðá gedufon hí ealle and adruncon. [*A. R.* i-dorven; *pp. grieved, injured*.]

ge-deorfleás; *adj.* This word in Glos. Prudent. Recd. 151, 73 is explained *nil prosperum*. The natural meaning would be *without labour, trouble*, which hardly agrees with that given above. Leo 230, 38, to connect the two, suggests the meaning *without effort*, so *without result, success*.

ge-deorfnys, -nyss, e; *f. Trouble, tribulation*; trībŭlātio :—God is úre fultum on gedeorfnyssum oððe on gedréfednyssum *Deus est noster adjūtor in trībŭlātiōnĭbus*, Ps. Lamb. 45, 2.

ge-deorfsum; *adj. Troublesome, grievous*; mŏlestus, grăvis :—Ðis wæs swíðe gedeorfsum geár *this was a very grievous year*, Chr. 1103; Erl. 239, 1.

ge-derian; *p.* ode, ede; *pp.* od, ed *To injure, hurt*; lædĕre :—Ðyssum wordum ðá gecwedenum, hine sóna se wind onwearp fram ðære byrig, and dráf ðæt fýr on ða ðe hit ǽr onbærndon, swá ðæt hí sume mid ðam fýre gederede wǽron *quo dicto, stātim mūtāti ab urbe venti, in eos qui accendĕrant flammārum incendia retorsērunt, ĭta ut ălĭquot læsi*, Bd. 3, 16; S. 543, 7–12, col. 1.

ge-dícian; *p.* ode; *pp.* od. *To make a dike* or *mound*; vallum facere :—Eardædon Bryttas binnan ðam díce, ðe we gemynegodon ðæt Severus hét þwyrs ofer ðæt eálond gedícian *habitabant Brittones intra vallum, quod Severum trans insulam fecisse commemoravimus*, Bd. 1, 11; S. 480. v. dícian.

ge-dieglan *To hide, cover*; velare :—He wolde ðara scamfæstna giemelieste mid líðelícum wordum gedieglan *he would cover* [velare] *the negligence of the modest with gentle words*, Past. 31, 2; Swt. 207, 23; Hat. MS. 39 b, 23. v. ge-díglan.

ge-diernan; *p.* de; *pp.* ed *To conceal*; cēlāre :—Se ðe þiéfþe gedierne, forgielde ðone þeóf be his were *let him who conceals the theft pay for the thief according to his value*, L. In. 36; Th. i. 124, 17. v. ge-dyrnan.

ge-dígan, -dýgan, -dégan, ic -díge, ðú -dígest, he -dígeþ, *pl.* -dígaþ; *p.* de; *pp.* ed *To endure, carry through, tolerate, overcome, escape*; ēti, perpĕti, perferre, tolerāre, superāre, evadere :—Swá mæg unfæge gedígan weán so *an undoomed* [*man*] *may escape calamity*, Beo. Th. 4572; B. 2291. Ðú aldre gedígest *thou escapest with life*, 1327; B. 661. He gedígeþ *he escapes*, 606; B. 300. He feore gedígde *he escaped with life*, 1161; B. 578. Feore gedýged *escaped with life*, Exon. 39 a; Th. 128, 21; Gú. 407. Ðæt wíf ne gedígþ hyre feore *the woman will not escape with her life*, Nar. 50, 10. Ðara monna hit ǽlc gedígde *hominibus idem morsus non usque ad interitum nocebant*, Nar. 16, 11. Sume hit ne gedýgdan mid ðam lífe *some did not escape with life*, Chr. 978; Erl. 127, 12. v. dýgan, gedégan.

ge-dígl[i]ian, -déglan, -dýglan; *p.* ode, ede; *pp.* od, ed, ad *To hide, conceal, cover;* abscondere, operire:—Gedeigla *abscondere*, Mt. Kmbl. Lind. 5, 14. Gedeigeldes *abscondisti*, 11, 25. Gedégled *opertum*, 10, 26. Gidéglad [delgad] *abscondita*, Rtl. 25, 7. Helme gedýgled *concealed by a covering*, Hy. 11, 13. [Cf. *O. H. Ger.* tougilian *to hide*.]

ge-díhligean *to hide, make private, detach, separate;* velare, secernere, separare:—Eádgár, mid rýmette gedíhligean hét ða mynstra *Edgar commanded the monasteries to be made private* or *detached*, Th. Diplm. A.D. 963–975; 231, 4. v. ge-díglan.

ge-diht, es; *n. A composition:*—Fela fægere godspel we forlǽtaþ on ðisum gedihte *many excellent gospels we omit in this composition*, Homl. Th. ii. 520, 1. [Cf. *Ger.* gedicht.]

ge-dihtan; *p.* -dihte; *pp.* -dihted, -diht. I. *to put in order, dispose, compose, arrange, conspire;* disponere, componere, conspirare:—Nú sindon twá béc gesette on endebyrdnisse to Salomones bócum, swilce he híg gedihte *now two books are set in order after Solomon's books, as if he composed them*, Ælfc. T; Swt. A. S. Rdr. 69, 402. Béda ðe ðas bóc gedihte *Bede who composed this book*, Swt. A. S. Rdr. 102, 224. Ðá gedihton ða Iudeas *jam conspiraverant Judæi*, Jn. Bos. 9, 22. Gediht *digestus, ordinatus*, Hpt. Gl. 409. II. *to order, direct, appoint;* dirigere, dictare:—Híg dydon swá, swá swá him gedihte Iosue *they did as Joshua directed them*, Josh. 6, 23. Ðis gewrit wæs to ánum menn gediht *this writing was directed to a particular man*, Ælfc. T; Swt. A. S. Rdr. 56, 1. [*Laym.* to dæðe idihte.] v. dihtan.

ge-dihtnung *a disposing*. v. dihtnung.

ge-dilgian; *p.* ede, ode; *pp.* ed, od *To blot out:*—Gidilge *dele*, Rtl. 168, 19: 19, 1.

ge-dirnan; *p.* de; *pp.* ed *To conceal, keep secret;* céláre:—Se ðe forstolen flǽsc findeþ and gedirneþ *he who finds stolen flesh and keeps it secret*, L. In. 17; Th. i. 114, 2, note 1. v. ge-dyrnan.

ge-dofung, e; *f. Dotage;* deliramentum, Hpt. Gl. 416.

ge-dolgian; *p.* ode; *pp.* od *To wound;* vulneráre:—Deópe gedolgod *deeply wounded*, Exon. 113 b; Th. 435, 25; Rä. 54, 6.

ge-dón; ic -dó, ðú -dést, he -déþ, *pl.* -dóþ; *p.* -dyde, *pl.* -dydon; *pp.* -dén, -dón *To do, make, put, cause, effect, reach a place;* facere:—Ic sceal cunnan hwæt ðú gedón wille *I shall know what thou wilt do*, Andr. Kmbl. 684; An. 343. Ðú ne miht ǽnne locc gedón hwítne *non potes unum capillum album facere*, Mt. Bos. 5, 36. Gedó dé hálne *salvum te fac*, Lk. Bos. 23, 37: 8, 48. Ðæt gefeoht wæs gedón mid micelre geornfulnesse *the battle was fought* [*done*] *with much earnestness*, Ors. 3, 9; Bos. 64, 45. Ðæt hit gedón wǽre *that it was done*, Andr. Kmbl. 1530; An. 766. Swá fela wundra swá we gehýrdon gedóne *quanta audivimus facta*, Lk. Bos. 4, 23. Ðæt he us ðæt cúþ gedó *that he make that known to us*, Blick. Homl. 139, 31. Hie gedóþ ðæt ǽgðer biþ ofer froren *they cause each to be frozen over*, Ors. 1, 1; Bos. 23, 9: Past. Swt. 7, 8: Ps. Th. 82, 12. Ðone eádigan Matheum he gedyde gangan *he caused the blessed Matthew to go*, St. And. 14, 13. We syndon niwe to ðissum geleáfan gedón *we are newly turned to this faith*, 24, 9. Streównesse him under gedón *to put litter under him*, Blickl. Homl. 227, 12. On cweartern gedón *to put in prison*, Jn. Bos. 3, 24. Fóron óð ðæt hie gedydon æt Sæferne *they went until they reached the Severn*, Chr. 894; Erl. 92, 14; 93, 5: 895; Erl. 94, 2, 15. Fóron ðæt hie gedydon innan Sæferne múðan *they went so as to get within the mouth of the Severn*, Chr. 918; Erl. 102, 24. [*O. Sax.* gi-dón.] DER. dón.

ge-drǽfan; *p.* de; *pp.* ed *To drive, push, urge, trouble;* pellere, urgere, perturbare:—Wód-þrag gedrǽfþ sefan ingehygd *lust urges the thoughts of mind*, Bt. Met. Fox 25, 83; Met. 25, 42: 18, 5; Met. 18, 3. v. dræfan, gedrífan.

ge-drǽfnes, ness, e; *f. A disturbance;* perturbatio, Bt. Met. Fox 22, 121; Met. 22, 61.

ge-dræg, ge-dreag, es; *n. A dragging, band, multitude, tumult;* tractus, turma, tumultus:—He wolde sécan deófla gedræg *he would seek the band of devils*, Beo. Th. 1516; B. 756. Eác ðon breost-ceare sin-sorgna gedreag sý æt him *even when care of breast, multitude of constant sorrows be at him*, Exon. 115 b; Th. 444, 10; Kl. 45. Ðǽr wæs fordénera gedræg *there was a tumult of undone men*, Andr. Kmbl. 85; An. 43. Ðǽr wæs wíde gehýred earmlíc ylda gedræg *then was widely heard the wretched tumult of mortals*, 3108; An. 1557.

ge-dráf *drove, was wrecked*, Ors. Cot. MS. 4, 6; Bos. Notes, p. 20, col. 2, § 10. v. ge-drífan.

ge-dreag *multitude, tumult*, Exon. 22 b; Th. 62, 11; Cri. 1000: 103 a; Th. 389, 19; Rä. 7, 10. v. gedræg.

ge-dreccan; *p.* -drehte; *pp.* -dreht, -dreaht *To vex, afflict, torment, oppress;* vexare, affligere, tribulare, opprimere:—He hæfþ on slǽpe ðýn wýf gedreht *he hath vexed thy wife in her sleep*, Nicod. 6; Thw. 3, 15. Beornas, gretaþ hýgegeómre hreówum gedreahte *men sad in mind with griefs afflicted shall wail*, Exon. 22 b; Th. 61, 34; Cri. 994. Hí scondum gedreahte *they shamefully tormented*, Exon. 26 b; Th. 79, 32; Cri. 1299: 30 a; Th. 92, 15; Cri. 1509. For meteleáste gedrehte *for want of food oppressed*, Andr. Kmbl. 78; An. 39. Of unclǽnum gástum gedrehte *vexati a spiritibus immundis*, Lk. Bos. 6, 18: 7, 6.

ge-dreccednys, se; *f. Tribulation, affliction:*—Ðonne beóþ swilce gedreccednyssa swilce nǽron ǽr *then shall be such tribulations as were not before*, Homl. Th. i. 4, 1. Líchamlíc gedreccednys *bodily affliction*, 454, 26.

ge-drecte *oppressed*. v. gedreccan

ge-dréfan; *p.* de; *pp.* ed *To disturb, trouble, vex, offend;* turbare, conturbare, confundere, scandalizare:—Hwí gedréfe gyt me *quare* [*vos duo*] *conturbatis me*, Ps. Th. 41, 5. Se Hǽlend gedréfde hyne sylfne *Jesus turbavit seipsum*, Jn. Bos. 11, 33: Lk. Bos. 24, 37. Ðú gedréfest deópe wǽlas *tu conturbas profundos vortices*, Ps. Th. 64, 7. Ðú gedréfst grúnd sǽs *tu confundas profundum maris*, Ps. Spl. 64, 7. Beóþ gedréfde þeóda *turbabuntur gentes*, Ps. Spl. 64, 8. Swá hwá swá gedréfþ ǽnne of ðyssum lytlingum *whosoever shall offend one of these little ones*, Mk. Bos. 9, 42. [*O. Sax.* ge-drôbian.] v. dréfan.

ge-dréfedlíc; *adj. Troublesome;* turbulentus, Ors. 1, 7; Bos. 30, 4.

gedréfednes, -drófednes, se; *f. Trouble, disturbance, confusion, vexation, tribulation, offence, scandal;* perturbatio, conturbatio, confusio, tribulatio, scandalum:—Bútan gedréfednesse ðe menn þrówiaþ *a conturbatione hominum*, Ps. Th. 30, 22. For gedréfednesse sǽs swéges and ýða *præ confusione sonitus maris et fluctuum*, Lk. Bos. 21, 25: Mt. Bos. 13, 21: Lk. Bos. 17, 1.

ge-dréfnis, niss, e; *f. Disturbance, confusion;* perturbatio:—To ætécte ðisse gedréfnisse storm Sæberhtes deáþ *auxit procellam hujusce perturbationis mors Sabercti*, Bd. 2, 5; S. 507, 6: Hpt. Gl. 463. v. gedréfednes, ge-drǽfnes.

ge-dreht, *oppressed, afflicted*. v. gedreccan.

ge-dréme, -drýme; *adj. Melodious, harmonious, joyous;* cānōrus, consŏnus, lætus:—Beóþ on heora húsum blíðe gedréme *lætābuntur in cubīlibus suis*, Ps. Th. 149, 5. Hí ealle samod mid gedrémum sange Godes wuldor hleoðrodon *they all together celebrated God's glory with melodious song*, Homl. Th. i. 38, 7. On gedrémum lofsangum *in harmonious hymns*, 600, 9.

ge-drencan; *p.* -drencte; *pp.* -drenced *To drench, drown;* submergere, demergere:—Se wǽg gedrencte [-drecte MS.] dugoþ Egypta *the wave drowned the army of the Egyptians*, Cd. 167; Th. 209, 16; Exod. 500. Deáþe gedrenced *drenched with death*, 144; Th. 179, 25; Exod. 34. Ðú [bist] to helle gedrencged *tu ad infernum demergeris*, Lk. Skt. Lind. 10, 15.

ge-dreog, es; *n. A rubbing:*—Swínes rysl his scón to gedreoge *swine's fat for rubbing his shoes*, Homl. Th. ii. 144, 29.

ge-dreóg, es; *n. A retiring, modesty;* modestia, R. Ben. 8.

ge-dreógan; *p.* -dreág, -dreáh, *pl.* -drugon; *pp.* -drogen *To perform, finish, bear, suffer;* perficere, tolerare, pati:—Gedrogen hæfde *had finished*, Beo. Th. 5446; B. 2726. Wíf gedróg *mulier patiebatur*, Mt. Kmbl. Lind. 9, 20. v. dreógan.

ge-dreóh; *adj. Sober:*—We lǽraþ ðæt man, æt ciric-wæccan, swíðe gedreóh sí *we teach that man, at the church wakes, be very sober*, L. Edg. 28; Th. ii. 250, 12.

ge-dreóhlíce; *adv. Discreetly, modestly, cautiously;* patienter, modeste, prudenter, L. C. S. 76; Th. i. 418, 6.

ge-dreósan; *p.* -dreás, *pl.* -druron; *pp.* -droren; *v. intrans. To fall together, disappear, fail;* cadere, corruere, deficere, Beo. Th. 3513; B. 1754: 5325; B. 2666: Ps. Th. 101, 9: Exon. 77 a; Th. 288, 25; Wand. 36. [*Goth.* gadriusan.]

ge-drep, es; *n. A stroke;* ictus:—Þurh daroþa gedrep *through the stroke of darts*, Andr. Kmbl. 2886; An. 1446.

ge-drettan; *p.* -drette; *pp.* -drett *To consume;* consūmĕre:—Beóþ gedrette eác gescende *confundantur et deficiant*, Ps. Th. 70, 12. [*Or does* gedrette = gedrehte?]

ge-drif, e; *f. A fever;* febris, Mk. Skt. Rush. 1, 31. v. drif.

ge-dríf, -drif [?], es; *n. What is driven, stubble;* stipula:—Gesete hí swá swá gedríf ætforan ansýne windes *pone illos sicut stipulam ante faciem venti*, Ps. Spl. T. 82, 12. [Cf. *Icel.* drif *driven snow*.]

ge-dríf, es; *n. A driving, movement:*—Ðæs lyftes gedríf ðæs wæteres gedríf *the regions of air and water*, Salm. Kmbl. 186, 22. [Cf. *Icel.* drífa *a fall of snow*.]

ge-drífan, *p.* -dráf, *pl.* -drifon; *pp.* -drifen *To drive, go adrift, be driven, cast away* or *lost;* agere, agi, ventis jactari, naufragare:—Ðéh scyp gedrifen [MS. gedriuen] beó *though a ship be driven*, L. Eth. ii. 2; Th. i. 286, 1. Rōmāne oferhlæstan heora scipa ðæt heora gedráf [gedeaf *Laud.*] cc and xxx, and lxx wearþ to láfe, and uneáðe genered *the Romans overloaded their ships, so that 230 of them were lost, and 70* *were left, and with difficulty saved*, Ors. 4, 6; Th. 400, 20. Ðæt scip gedrifen wæs *naviculo jactabatur*, Mt. Kmbl. Lind. 14, 24.

ge-driht, -dryht, e; *f. A host, company;* turma, cohors:—Wæs seó eorla gedriht ânes môdes *the host of men was of one mind*, Cd. 158; Th. 197, 10; Exod. 304: Exon. 22 b; Th. 63, 3; Cri. 1014.

ge-drîhþ, e; *f. Forbearance, sobriety;* patientia, sobrietas, L. T. P. 9; Th. ii. 314, 34.

ge-drinc, -drync, es; *n. A drinking;* compotatio, convivium:—We lǽraþ ðæt man ǽnig gedrinc, and ǽnig unnit ðǽr ne dreóge *we teach that man suffer not there any drinking nor any vanity*, L. Edg. 28; Th. ii. 250, 12: Exon. 88 a; Th. 330, 27; Vy. 57: Ors. 1, 1; Bos. 22, 25.

ge-drincan; *p.* -dranc, *pl.* -druncon; *pp.* -druncen *To drink;* bibere:—Grûndleás gîtsung gilpes and ǽhta gedrinceþ to dryggum dreósendne wēlan *the bottomless avarice of glory and possessions drinks to the dregs perishable wealth*, Bt. Met. Fox 7, 31; Met. 7, 16. Ðæt wîn is gedruncen *bibitur vinum*, Ælf. Gr. 19; Som. 22, 47: Bd. 5, 5; S. 618, 13: Gen. 27, 25.

ge-dripan *to drip.* v. gedrypan.

ge-drôf; *adj. Dirty, muddy;* turbĭdus, lŭtōsus:—On ðæm gedrôfum wætere *in the muddy water*, Past. 54, 1; Swt. 421, 8; Hat. MS.

ge-drôfednys *trouble*, Scint. 50. v. ge-drēfednys.

ge-drôfenlîc; *adj. Troublous:*—Ðeós world is gedrôfenlîc *this world is troublous*, Blickl. Homl. 115, 3.

ge-drugian; *p.* ode, ade; *pp.* od, ad *To become dry, wither;* arescere:—Ficbeám gedrugade *ficus aruit*, Mk. Skt. Lind. 11, 21; 4, 6: Ps. Th. 68, 22. Gedrugad wæs *arefacta est*, Mt. Kmbl. Lind. 21, 19. v. drugian.

ge-druncen *drunk*, Bd. 5, 5; S. 618, 13; *pp. of* ge-drincan.

ge-druncnian; *p.* ode, ade; *pp.* od, ad *To sink, drown:*—Gedruncnadon *mergerentur*, Lk. Skt. Lind. 5, 7.

ge-drygan; *p.* de; *pp.* ed *To dry:*—Gedrygde his foet *extersit pedes ejus*, Jn. Skt. Lind. 11, 2. Gidrygedo *abstersa*, Rtl. 98, 24.

ge-dryht, -driht, e; *f. A host, company, band of retainers:*—Engla gedryht *a company of angels*, Exon. 22 b; Th. 63, 3; Cri. 1014: 60 b; Th. 222, 13; Ph. 348. Ðǽr cyninges giefe brûcaþ eádigra gedryht *there the band of the blessed enjoy the king's grace*, Exon. 32 a; Th. 101, 26; Cri. 1664. Ðînra secga gedryht *the band of thy men*, Beo. Th. 3349; B. 1672. v. dryht.

ge-dryhta, an; *m. A comrade;* commilito, Grm. ii. 736, 40.

ge-dryhtu; *pl. n. Elementa, sidera, fortunæ*, Hpt. Gl. 462. [Cf. droht?]

ge-drŷme; *adj. Melodious, joyous;* lætus:—Drihta gedrŷmost *most joyous of multitudes*, Cd. 146; Th. 182, 21; Exod. 79: Hpt. Gl. 513, 519. v. ge-drēme.

ge-drync *drinking*, Ors. 1, 1; Bos. 22, 25. v. ge-drinc.

ge-drypan; *p.* -drypte; *impert.* -dryp, -drype; *pp.* -dryped *To drop;* stillāre:—Beolonan seáw on eáre gedryp *drop juice of henbane on the ear*, L. M. 1, 3; Lchdm. ii. 40, 14. Gedrype on *drop [it] on*, 1, 3; Lchdm. ii. 40, 7.

ge-drysnan; *p.* ade, ede; *pp.* ad, ed *To put out, quench, extinguish, vanish;* extinguĕre, evanescĕre:—Ðæt fŷr ne biþ gedrysned *ignis non extinguĭtur*, Mk. Skt. Lind. 9, 44, 48. He gedrysnade from ēgum hiora *ipse evanuit ex oculis eorum*, Lk. Skt. Lind. 24, 31.

ge-dûfan, he -dŷfþ; *p.* -deáf, we -dufon; *pp.* -dofen; *v. intrans. To plunge, to duck, sink, dive, be drowned;* mergi:—Heó gedûfan sceolun in ðone deópan wælm *they must dive into the deep fire*, Cd. 213; Th. 266, 30; Sat. 30: Exon. 41 a; Th. 137, 6; Gû. 555. Gedeáf *sank*, Ors. 4, 6; Bos. 85, 38. Ðæt ðæt sweord gedeáf *so that the sword dived*, Beo. Th. 5394; B. 2700: Cd. 228; Th. 306, 27; Sat. 670. Ðā gedufon hî ealle and adruncon *then they all sank and were drowned*, Ors. 1, 7; Bos. 30, 24. He wearþ gedofen *coepit mergi*, Mt. Bos. 14, 13.

ge-dugan; *p.* -deáh *To thrive*, Shrn. 13, 1.

ge-dwǽlan; *p.* -dwǽlde *To seduce, lead astray:*—Ðæt is hefig dysig, ðæt ða earman men mid ealle gedwǽleþ of ðæm rihtan wege *that is a grievous folly that altogether seduces the miserable men from the right way*, Bt. Met. Fox 19, 6; Met. 19, 3. [*Or* gedwæleþ = gedweleþ *from* gedwellan.]

ge-dwǽs; *adj. Foolish, dull, stupid:*—Gedrēfede syndon, hearde onhrērede her anlîcast, hû druncen hwylc gedwǽs spyrige *turbati sunt et moti sunt ut ebrius*, Ps. Th. 106, 26. v. dwǽs.

ge-dwelian, -dweligan. I. *to deceive, lead astray:*—Ðæt his me nān man gedweligan mæg *that no man can seduce me from it*, Bt. 23, 3; Fox 126, 18. Ne weorðe ic ðînra dôma gedweled ǽfre *judicia tua non sum oblitus*, Ps. Th. 118, 30. II. *to err:*—Ic gedwelede swā ðæt dysige scēp *erravi sicut ovis*, Ps. Th. 118, 176. v. dwelian *and* ge-dwellan.

ge-dwellan; I. *to deceive, lead astray*, Bt. 23, 3; Fox 126, 18, note 6. Dysge and gedwealde *foolish and led astray*, Exon. 24 b; Th. 69, 29; Cri. 1128. II. *to err:*—Gedwellas *erratis*, Mt. Kmbl. Lind. 22, 29. v. dwellan *and* ge-dwelian.

ge-dweola, -dweolda, an; *m. Error, heresy;* error, hærĕsis:—Se gedweola wæs on ðam Nyceniscan sinoþe geniðerad *the error was put down in the Nicene synod*, Bd. 1, 8; S. 479, 36. Gē gedweolan lifdon *ye lived in error*, Invent. Crs. Recd. 623; El. 311. Se Arrianisca gedweolda *Arriāna hærĕsis*, Bd. 1, 8; S. 479, 27. v. ge-dwola.

ge-dwild, -dwyld, es; *n. Error, heresy;* error, hærĕsis:—On ðâm tîdum arâs Pelaies gedwild geond middangeard *in those times the heresy of Pelagius arose throughout the world*, Chr. 380; Erl. 11, 6. On gedwilde *into error*, Cd. 1; Th. 2, 22; Gen. 23. Ðū scealt þrôwian ðînra dǽda gedwild *thou shalt expiate the error of thy deeds*, 43; Th. 57, 2; Gen. 922. Dyrnra gedwilda *of dark errors*, Exon. 71 a; Th. 264, 22; Jul. 368. Deorcum gedwildum *by dark errors*, 72 b; Th. 270, 4; Jul. 460.

ge-dwimere, -dwomere; *m. A juggler, sorcerer;* nebulo, Hpt. Gl. 514, 515.

ge-dwimor, -dwimer, -dwymer, es; *n. An illusion, delusion, apparition, phantom;* error, fallācia, phantasma = φάντασμα, phantăsia = φαντασία:—Gedwimor *phantasma* vel *phantăsia*, Ælfc. Gl. 78; Som. 72, 54; Wrt. Voc. 46, 14: 77, 7. Hî wēndon ðæt hit sum gedwimor wǽre *they thought that it was an apparition*, Homl. Th. ii. 388, 24: Jud. 15, 19. Hine drehton nihtlîce gedwimor *nightly phantoms tormented him*, Homl. Th. i. 86, 18. Swylcra gedwimera *of such illusions*, L. C. S. 5; Th. i. 378, 22. On manegum mislîcum gedwimerum *with many various delusions*, L. Edg. C. 16; Th. ii. 248, 7.

ge-dwimorlîce; *adv. Illusorily, fantastically*, Homl. Th. ii. 140, 16.

ge-dwînan; *p.* -dwân, *pl.* -dwinon; *pp.* -dwinen *To dwindle* or *vanish away, disappear;* evanescere, disparere:—Ðæt hâlige sǽd gedwân and gewât *the holy seed has wasted away and departed*, Blickl. Homl. 55, 29. His drýcræftas gedwinon *his magic vanished*, Shrn. 135, 1.

ge-dwola, -dweola, an; *m.* I. *error, madness, heresy;* error, errātum, vesānia, hærĕsis:—Se mennisca gedwola *human error*, Bt. 33, 2; Fox 122, 22. Se Arrianisca gedwola *Arriāna hærĕsis*, Bd. 1, 8; S. 479, 33: Bt. Met. Fox 1, 81; Met. 1, 41. Ôþ ða tîde ðæs Arrianiscan gedwolan *usque ad tempŏra Arriānæ vesāniæ*, Bd. 1, 8; S. 479, 18. Gē gedwolan fylgdon *ye followed error*, Elen. Kmbl. 742; El. 371: Bt. Met. Fox 26, 108; Met. 26, 54. Ðæt ða beóþ on gedwolan gelǽdde *ut in errōrem indūcantur*, Mt. Bos. 24, 24: Gen. 21, 14: 37, 15: Bt. Met. Fox 26, 78; Met. 26, 39. Þurh deópne gedwolan *through deep error*, Andr. Kmbl. 1221; An. 611: Exon. 70 a; Th. 260, 22; Jul. 301. Gedwolena rîm *a number of errors*, 71 a; Th. 264, 23; Jul. 368. For mînum gedwolum *pro meis errātĭbus*, Bd. 4, 25; S. 601, 3. II. *a heretic;* hærĕtĭcus:—Begeat se gedwola ðæs cāseres fultum to his gedwylde *the heretic got the emperor's support to his heresy*, Homl. Th. i. 290, 11, 17, 28. Done ealdan gedwolan *the old deceiver*, Blickl. Homl. 7, 12.

ge-dwol-cræft, es; *m. A deceptive art, deception:*—Mid heora gedwolcræftum *with their deceptions*, Blickl. Homl. 61, 25. Ða ðe gedwolcræftas begangaþ *those who practise divination*, 63, 14.

ge-dwolen [*pp. of strong verb* ge-dwelan. v. dwelan]; *adj. Erroneous, wrong, perverse:*—Dǽdum gedwolene *in deeds perverse*, Cd. 91; Th. 116, 14; Gen. 1936: Exon. 66 a; Th. 243, 19; Jul. 13: 103 b; Th. 393, 8; Rä. 12, 7. [Cf. *O. H. Ger.* ki-tiuolin *sopitus*.]

ge-dwol-godas; *pl. m. False gods, idols;* falsi dei, īdōla:—To gedwolgoda weorþunge *īdōlōrum cultui*, Lupi Serm. i. 4; Hick. Thes. ii. 100, 3. Ne dear man gewanian on hǽðenum ǽnig ðæra þinga ðe gedwolgodum [MS. -an] broht biþ *ne ausus est quispiam e păgānis eōrum quidquam commĭnuĕre quæ deōrum simulacris allāta fuĕrant*, i. 4; Hick. Thes. ii. 100, 6, 11.

ge-dwolian; *p.* ede; *pp.* ed *To err:*—Ic gedwolede swâ swâ sceáp ðæt forwearþ *I have erred as the sheep that perished*, Blickl. Homl. 87, 30. Gē swîðe gidwoligas *vos multum erratis*, Mk. Skt. Rush. 12, 27: Mt. Kmbl. Lind. 18, 12.

ge-dwol-man, gedwol-mon, es; *m. An erring man, a heretic, impostor;* hæreticus:—Arrius hâtte ân gedwolman *there was a heretic called Arius*, Homl. Th. i. 290, 3, 5, 25: 110, 6.

gedwol-mist, es; *m. Mist of error;* errōris nĕbŭla:—Mid ðam gedwolmiste *with the mist of error*, Bt. 35, 1; Fox 156, 1: Bt. Met. Fox 22, 65; Met. 22, 33.

ge-dwolsum; *adj. Erroneous;* errōneus:—Hit biþ swîðe gedwolsum *it is very erroneous*, Ælf. Pref. Gen. 4, 10.

ge-dwol-þing *an erroneous thing, deceit, imposture.*

ge-dwomer, es; *n. Necromancy*, Hpt. Gl. 515.

ge-dwyld, es; *n. Error, heresy;* error, hærĕsis:—Ðæt æftere gedwyld *novissĭmus error*, Mt. Bos. 27, 64. Ic wille him dôn edleán heora gedwyldes *I will give them a reward for their error*, Boutr. Scrd. 22, 37. Forwearþ ðes gedwola mid his gedwylde *this heretic perished with his heresy*, Homl. Th. i. 290, 29: ii. 506, 27: Boutr. Scrd. 18, 30. Ðæt he mid his hâlgan lâre middaneardlîc gedwyld adwæscte *that he might extinguish worldly error by his holy doctrine*, Homl. Th. ii. 90, 13: Deut. 4, 19. v. ge-dwild.

ge-dwymer, es; *n. An illusion;* error:—Swylcra gedwymera *of such illusions*, L. C. S. 5; Th. i. 378, 22, note 66. v. ge-dwimor.

ge-dwymorlîc; *adj. Illusive;* phantasticus, Dial. 2, 10.

ge-dýgan; *p.* de; *pp.* ed *To escape*:—Hwæðer mǽge wunde gedýgan *which may escape from wound*, Beo. Th. 5056; B. 2531: 5091, note; B. 2549. Gedýgdon *escaped*, Exon. 55 b; Th. 197, 17; Az. 191. Gedýged, 39 a; Th. 128, 21; Gú. 407. v. ge-dígan.

ge-dyn, es; *m. A din, noise*; frăgor, clangor:—Se dæg biþ dæg gedynes ofer ealle [MS. ealla] truma ceastra *the day will be a day of din over all strong cities*, Past. 35, 5; Swt. 245, 6; Hat. MS. 46 a, 17. Gedyne micle *with a great din*, Exon. 102 a; Th. 385, 16; Rä. 4, 45.

ge-dyngan; *p.* ede; *pp.* ed *To dung, manure*; stercŏrāre:—Hit ðonne mid ðam gedynged wearþ *then it was thus manured*, Ors. 1, 3; Bos. 27, 23.

ge-dyppan, -deppan *to dip, baptize*:—Ðā gedeped [wæs] *baptizatus*, Mt. Kmbl. Rush. 3, 16.

ge-dýran; *p.* de; *pp.* ed *To glorify, endear*; glorĭfĭcāre:—Dreámum gedýrde *endeared by joys*, Exon. 32 a; Th. 100, 21; Cri. 1645.

gedýre, es; *n.* [*or* -dyre, y *from* u; cf. *Goth.* daur] *A door-post*; postis ad fores:—On ǽgðrum gedýre *in utro poste*, Ex. 12, 23. On ǽgðer gedýre *on each door-post*, Ex. 12, 7. Hí mearcodon mid blóde on heora gedýrum Tau, ðæt is, rōde tācen *they marked on their door-posts* Tau, *that is, the sign of the cross*, Homl. Th. ii. 266, 8: 264, 1. v. ofer-gedýre.

ge-dyrfsum; *adj. Afflictive*; calamitosus, Lye.

ge-dyrnan, -diernan, -dirnan; *p.* de; *pp.* ed *To conceal, hide, keep secret*; cēlāre, occultāre:—Se ðe forstolen flǽsc findeþ and gedyrneþ *he who finds stolen flesh and keeps it secret*, L. In. 17; Th. i. 114, 2. Se ðe ða þýfþe gedyrne, forgylde ðone þeóf be his were *let him who conceals the theft pay for the thief according to his value*, 36; Th. i. 124, 17, note 40, MS. B. Ðonne hit gedyrned weorþeþ *when it is hidden*, Exon. 91 a; Th. 340, 27; Gn. Ex. 117.

ge-dýrsian; *p.* ode; *pp.* od *To glorify*; glorĭfĭcāre:—Dóme gedýrsod, Judth. 12; Thw. 25, 40; Jud. 300.

ge-dyrst, e; *f. Tribulation*; tribulatio? [Th]:—Ic ðē hālsie deópe in gedyrstum, ðæt ðū us gemiltsie *I beseech thee deeply in tribulations, that thou us pity*, Exon. 121 a; Th. 465, 22; Hö. 108. [*O. H. Ger.* gaturst, *f. audacia.*]

ge-dyrste-líce; *adv. Boldly, daringly, rashly*; temere, audaciter, Bd. 4, 26; S. 602, 16. v. dyrste-líce.

ge-dyrstig; *adj. Bold*; audax, protervus, Exon. 72 a; Th. 268, 12; Jul. 431: Past. 32, 1; Swt. 209, 15; Hat. MS. 40 a, 8: Guthl. 20; Gdwn. 84, 20. v. un-gedyrstig, dyrstig.

ge-dyrstigan; *p.* ede; *pp.* ed *To dare, presume*; audēre, præsumĕre:—Ðe gedyrstigedon ðæt hí Eástran heóldan būtan heora rihtre tíde *qui Pascha non suo tempŏre observāre præsumĕrent*, Bd. 5, 21; S. 642, 40.

ge-dyrstig-nes, -ness, e; *f. Boldness*; audacia, Past. 13, 2; Swt. 79, 17; Hat. MS. 17 a, 15: Nar. 19, 11. v. dyrstignes.

ge-dyrst-lǽcan; *p.* -lǽhte; *pp.* -lǽht *To dare*; audere:—He ne gedyrstlǽcþ ðæt he furðon orðige oððe sprece *he dare not even breathe or speak*, Homl. Th. i. 456, 9: Ælfc. Gr. 41; Som. 43, 29. v. dyrst-lǽcan.

ge-dysig; *adj. Foolish.* v. dysig.

gee *yea, yes.* v. gea.

ge-eácnian, ic -eácnige, ðū -eácnigast, he -eácnaþ, *pl.* -eácniaþ; *p.* ode; *pp.* od *To increase, conceive, become pregnant*; augēri, concipĕre, augēre:—Ic hine bletsige and geeácnige *benedīcam ei et augēbo eum*, Gen. 17, 20. Efnenū geeácnode unrihtwísnesse *ecce partūri injustĭtia*, Ps. Lamb. 7, 15. Hí geeácnodon unrihtwísnysse *augēbant injustĭtiam*, Jud. 4, 1: Elen. Grm. 342. Elizabeþ his wíf geeácnode *Elizabeth his wife conceived*, Lk. Bos. 1, 24. Ðū on innoðe geeácnast *thou shalt conceive in thy womb*, 1, 31. In synnum geeácnod wæs *he was conceived in sins*, Ps. C. 50, 61; Ps. Grn. ii. 278, 61. DER. to-geeácnian. v. eácnian.

ge-eácnung, e; *f. A conceiving, conception*; conceptio, conceptus:—Ðæt he bodige hire geeácnunge *to proclaim her* [*Maria*] *conception*, Blickl. Homl. 143, 24. Ic gemenigfilde ðíne yrmþa and ðíne geeácnunga *multiplicabo ærumnas tuas et conceptus tuos*, Gen. 3, 16. v. eácnung.

ge-eádgian; *p.* ode, ade; *pp.* od, ad *To bless*:—Gieadgade hine *beatificavit illum*, Rtl. 88, 26.

ge-eádmēdan, -eaþmēdan, he -eádmēdeþ; *p.* -mēdde, -mētte; *pp.* -mēded, -mēt; *v. a. To humble, humiliate, subdue, submit one's self, humble one's self, deign, condescend, adore, worship*; humiliare, dignari, condescendere, adorare:—Se gehnysta gāst and geeádmēded ingeþancum *the bruised heart and humbled by reflections*, Ps. C. 50, 128; Ps. Gen. ii. 279, 128. Ic geeádmēded eom *humiliatus sum*, Ps. Th. 141, 6. Hí hí geeádmētte *he humiliated* [*subdued*] *them*, Jud. 11, 33. Se ðe hyne sylfne geeaþmēt *qui se humiliaverit*, Mt. Bos. 23, 12: 18, 4. Hine to him geeaþmēdde *he submitted himself to him*, 8, 2: Bd. 5, 3; S. 616, 9. We cōmon us him to ge-eádmēdenne *venimus adorare eum*, Mt. Bos. 2, 2. Geeámēdun ðē ealle mǽgþa *may all nations adore thee*, Gen. 27, 29: Ex. 11, 8; Mt. Bos. 20, 20. v. ge-eáþmēdan, eádmēdan.

ge-eádmōdian, -eáþmōdian *to humiliate, deign*:—Se ðe ne wyle geeádmōded ingangan *qui non vult humiliatus ingredi*, Bd. 5, 14; S. 634, 19. Ðæt he ge-eádmōdige *ut ipse dignetur*, 2, 2; S. 502, 19. v. eád-mōdan.

ge-eádmōdlíce; *adv. Humbly*; humiliter, Bd. 2, 2; S. 503, 11. v. eádmōdlíce.

ge-eæd-leǽnian, ic -eædleǽnige *to repay, reward*, Ps. Spl. T. 17, 22. v. ed-leǽnian.

ge-eærfoðod *troubled.* v. eærfoðian.

ge-eahtian, -ehtian, -æhtian; *p.* ode; *pp.* od *To estimate, value*; æstĭmāre:—Gebēte swā hit mon geeahtige *let him make amends as it may be valued*, L. Alf. 26; Th. i. 50, 26: L. Alf. pol. 32; Th. i. 82, 2.

ge-ealdian; *p.* ode; *pp.* od, ad *To grow old*; senescere:—Geealdad biþ *is become old*, Exon. 62 a; Th. 227; 23; Ph. 427. v. ealdian.

ge-ealgian *to defend*, R. Ben. 69, Lye. v. ge-algian.

ge-eán; *adj. Yeaning*; enītens, pariens:—Ðū wāst ðæt ic hæbbe hnesce litlingas, and ge-eáne eówa mid me *thou knowest that I have tender infants and yeaning sheep with me*, Gen. 33, 13; tu scis [MS. nosti = novisti], quod parvŭlos hăbeam tĕnĕros et oves fētas mecum, Vulg. Gen. 33, 13. v. gecelf. DER. eánian [?].

ge-eardian; *p.* ode; *pp.* od *To dwell*; inhabitāre:—In me gǽst geeardode *the spirit dwelt in me*, Exon. 11 a; Th. 13, 25; Cri. 208: Ps. Lamb. 26, 4.

ge-earfoþ, es; *n. Trouble*; trībŭlātio:—He sceal geþolian manige geearfoðu [MS. gearfoðu] *he shall suffer many troubles*, Bt. 31, 1; Fox 110, 26.

ge-earnian, -igan; *p.* ode; *pp.* od *To earn, deserve, enjoy*; mereri, promereri, frui:—Ic ge-earnige *mereor*, ðū ge-earnast *mereris*, he geearnaþ *meretur*, ic ge-earnode *merui* vel *meritus*, Ælfc. Gr. 27; Som. 29, 64, 65: 33; Som. 36, 49. Ðæt heó ðý ēþ meahte ðæt ēce ríce in heofonum geearnian *quo facilius perpetuam in cœlis patriam posset mereri*, Bd. 4, 23; S. 593, 12. Ðæt se man sceolde ða myrhþe geearnian *that man should enjoy the pleasure* [gaudium], Hexam. 17; Norm. 24, 23. Hie ne māgon geearnigan ðæt gē heora wundrigen *they cannot deserve that ye should admire them*, Bt. 13; Fox 40, 8. He geearnode *meruit*, Bd. 4, 23; S. 593, 6. He hí hæfþ geearnod mid his hearpunga *he has earned her by his harping*, Bt. 35, 6; Fox 170, 7.

ge-earnung, e; *f. Earning, desert, merit*; meritum:—For heora lífes geearnunge *for their life's earning* [*desert*]; præ merito virtutum, Bd. 3, 8; S. 531, 23. Nū ic ongite ðæt sió sōþe gesǽlþ stent on gōdra monna geearnunga *now I understand that true happiness stands on the merit of good men*, Bt. 39, 2; Fox 212, 12. Be geearnunge *de merito*, Ps. Lamb. 7, 5. Geearnunga *merita*, Cot. 129. Būtan geearnungum *sine merito, immerito, gratis*, Ps. Lamb. 34, 7; 68, 5: 108, 3: 118, 161: 119, 7. DER. earnung.

ge-eáþmēdan *to humiliate, submit one's self, condescend, vouchsafe, deign*, Mt. Bos. 8, 2: Bd. 5, 3; S. 616, 9. v. ge-eádmēdan.

ge-eáþmōdian *to humiliate, condescend, vouchsafe, deign*:—Drihten wæs geeáþmōdad to onwreónne *dominus revelare dignatus est*, Bd. 4, 23; S. 595, 35. v. ge-eádmōdian.

ge-eáwan; *p.* de; *pp.* ed; *v. trans. To shew, manifest, bestow*; ostendere, manifestare, præbere:—Geeáude him alle rícas middangeardes *ostendit ei omnia regna munda*, Mt. Kmbl. 4, 8. Him wæs wunden gold ēstum geeáwed *on him was twisted gold kindly bestowed*, Beo. Th. 2392; B. 1194: Exon. 60 b; Th. 221, 14; Ph. 334: 66 b; Th. 246, 29; Jul. 69: Bt. 39, 8; Fox 224, 12: Elen. Grm. 102: Elen. Kmbl. 1570; El. 787. DER. eáwan, ýwan.

ge-ebbian; *p.* ode, ade; *pp.* od, ad *To ebb*; recedere, refluere:—Ðā ðæt wæter wæs geebbod fram ðām scipum *when the water had ebbed from the ships*, Chr. 897; Th. 176, 26, col. 2. v. ebbian.

ge-ebolsian, -eofulsian; *p.* ode, ade; *pp.* od, ad *To blaspheme*, Mk. Skt. Lind. and Rush. 15, 29: Mt. Kmbl. Lind. 27, 39.

ge-ēcan *to add, increase*:—His sylfes synna geēceþ *increases his own sins*, Blickl. Homl. 97, 9; 37, 17; 121, 32. v. ge-ícan.

ge-edbyrdan; *p.* de; *pp.* ed *To cause to be born again, to regenerate*; facere ut aliquis renascatur, regenerare:—Ðonne he unc hafaþ geedbyrded ōðre síðe *when he hath caused us two to be born again a second time*, Exon. 99 b; Th. 372, 30; Seel. 100.

ge-edcēgan; *p.* de; *pp.* ed *To recall*; revŏcāre:—Ne geedcēg ðū me on midlunge mínra daga *ne revŏces me in dimĭdio diērum meōrum*, Ps. Lamb. 101, 25.

ge-edcenned *regenerated*; regeneratus, Jn. Bos. 3, 5.

ge-edcucian, -cwician; *p.* ode, ede; *pp.* od, ed *To requicken, revive*; revīviscĕre:—Ic geedcucige *revivisco*, Ælfc. Gr. 35; Som. 38, 9. Ðes mín sunu wæs deád, and he geedcucode *hic filius meus mortuus ĕrat, et revixit*, Lk. Bos. 15, 24, 32: Homl. Th. ii. 26, 27: 28, 5. His cealdan limu geedcucodon *his cold limbs requickened*, i. 534, 35. He wearþ ðā geedcucod æfter lytlum fyrste *he then after a little space revived*, ii. 504, 27: 28, 8. Geedcuced *redivivus*, Ælfc. Gl. 35; Som. 62, 91; Wrt. Voc. 28, 68. His gāst wearþ geedcwicod *revixit spirĭtus ējus*, Gen. 45, 27. Geedcwycode *brought to life again*, Nicod. Thw. p. 18, 15.

ge-edhiwod; *part. p. Conformatus*, Som.

ge-edhyrt; *adj. Recreatus*, Gl. Prud. 201.

ge-edlǽcan; *p.* -lǽhte; *pp.* -lǽht *To repeat*:—Ðonne mōt he geornlíce warnian, ðæt he eft ðām yfelum dǽdum ne geedlǽce *then must he* *diligently take heed that he do not afterwards repeat those evil deeds,* Homl. Th. ii. 602, 24. Geedlǽcend, geedlǽht, *reciprocus,* Hpt. Gl. 450, 460, 481, 484.

ge-edlæsian; *p.* ode; *pp.* od *To restore;* restituere:—Ðú ðe geedlæsast *qui restitues,* Ps. Lamb. 15, 5.

ge-edleánend, es; *m. A rewarder,* Som.

ge-edlian *to renew,* Som.

ge-edniwian, -edneowian; *p.* ode, ade; *pp.* od, ad *To restore, renew, renovate, change;* restĭtuĕre, renŏvāre, innŏvāre:—Helias geedniwaþ ealle þing *Elias restĭtuet omnia,* Mt. Bos. 17, 11: Mk. Bos. 9, 12. Geedniwod eald hrægel *renovāta antīqua vestis,* Ælfc. Gl. 63; Som. 68, 105. Se móna biþ þreottyne síðon geedniwod [MS. geedniwad] *the moon is thirteen times changed [renewed],* Lchdm. iii. 248, 24. Biþ geedniwad moncyn *mankind shall be renewed,* Exon. 23 a; Th. 64, 20; Cri. 1040: Ps. Th. 103, 28. Se firdstemn hie geedneowade *the army-corps renovated it,* Chr. 921; Erl. 107, 33. Gást riht geedneowa on innoþum mínum *spīrĭtum rectum innŏva in viscĕrĭbus meis,* Ps. Lamb. 50, 12. Se man ðe æfter dǽdbóte his mánfullan dǽda geedniwaþ *the man who after repentance renews his sinful deeds,* Homl. Th. ii. 602, 25.

ge-edstaðelian; *p.* ode; *pp.* od *To restore;* instaurare, suscitare:—Ða hǽr beóþ ealle geedstaðelode *the hairs shall be all restored,* Homl. Th. ii. 542, 35: i. 62, 11, 12. Se cyng férde and ða burh geædstaðelede *the king went and restored the town,* Chr. 1092; Erl. 228, 15: Th. Apol. 27, 5: Hpt. Gl. 456.

ge-edstaðelung, e; *f. A renewing;* repărātio, C. R. Ben. 48.

ge-edstaðolian. v. ge-edstaðelian.

ge-edðrawen; *part. p. Twisted again* or *back;* retortus, Som.

ge-edwistian; *p.* ode; *pp.* od *To feed, support:*—He geedwistode me *educavit me,* Ps. Lamb. 22, 2.

ge-edwyrpan; *p.* te; *pp.* ed *To recover, revive;* revīviscĕre:—Ðá æt nýhstan onféng he gáste and wearþ geedwyrped *tandem recepto spīrĭtu revixit,* Bd. 4, 22; S. 590, 36.

ge-efenlǽcan; *p.* -lǽhte; *pp.* -lǽht, -lǽced; *v. trans. To be like, equal, to imitate;* æquāre, assĭmĭlāri, imĭtāri:—Nellen ge eornostlíce him geefenlǽcan *nolīte ergo assĭmĭlāri eis,* Mt. Bos. 6, 8. Hwylc biþ geefenlǽced drihtne *quis æquālĭtur Domino,* Ps. Spl. 88, 7: Wanl. catal. 5, 1. Ongann Augustinus mid his munecum to geefenlǽcenne ðæra apostola líf *Augustine with his monks began to imitate the life of the apostles,* Homl. Th. ii. 128, 32. Ðæt hí ðám flæsclícum geefenlǽcon *that they imitate the fleshly,* 82, 15. v. efenlǽcan.

ge-efenlæcestre, an; *f. A female imitator,* Scint. 13, Lye.

ge-efenlǽcung, e; *f. Imitation:*—To geefenlǽcunge ðæra eádigra apostola *in imitation of the blessed apostles,* Homl. Th. ii. 148, 23.

ge-efenlíc; *adj. Equal,* Bd. 4, 29; S. 608, 3, note, MS. Ca. See next word.

ge-efenlícad; *part. p. Made equal;* æquātus:—Ðæt he swá geefenlícad wǽre mid ða gife his þingeres *quātĕnus æquātus grātia suo intercessōri,* Bd. 4, 29; S. 608, 3.

ge-efesian, -efsian; *p.* ode; *pp.* od *To cut in the form of eaves, to round, shear, clip, crop;* tondēre:—Ne he næs geefesod ne bescoren *he was not clipped nor shorn,* Homl. Th. ii. 298, 20. Ic næs nǽfre geefsod ne nǽfre bescoren *ferrum nunquam ascendit super caput meum,* Jud. 16, 17. DER. efesian.

ge-efnan; *p.* ede; *pp.* ed *To do, perform, carry out, sustain:*—Eft geblóweþ and geefneþ swá óþ ðæt ǽfen cymeþ *it blows again, and does so until even comes,* Ps. Th. 86, 6. Hió geefenede swá *she did so,* Elen. Kmbl. 2028; El. 1015. Hwá gedéþ ǽfre, ðæt he ðæt geefne *quis sustinebit?* Ps. Th. 129, 3. Ealdor geefnan *to spend [one's] life,* Salm. Kmbl. 711; Sal. 355. v. efnan, ge-æfnan.

ge-efn[i]an; *p.* ade, [e]de; *pp.* ed *To make even, liken, compare:*—Byrgennum ða ilco geefnade *monumentis eos comparans,* Mt. Kmbl. p. 19, 12. Giefndes *coequasti,* Rtl. 57, 13. Geefnad *æquatus,* Bd. 4, 29; S. 608, 3, note. Geefned biþ *assimilabitur,* Mt. Kmbl. 7, 24. [*O. H. Ger.* ge-ebanōn *explanare, æquare.*]

ge-ēfstan; *p.* -ēfste; *impert.* -ēfst; *pp.* -ēfsted, -ēfst *To hasten, make haste, be quick;* festīnāre, accĕlĕrāre:—Geēfst oððe hrada ðæt ðú alýse me *accĕlĕra ut eruas me,* Ps. Lamb. 30, 2. DER. ēfstan.

ge-egesian; *p.* ode; *pp.* od *To frighten;* terrēre:—Hí wurdon geegesode *they were frightened,* Ors. 5, 3; Bos. 104, 5. v. ge-egsian.

ge-eggian; *p.* ede *To egg on, urge, excite:*—Ða biscobas geeggedon ðone ðreát *Pontifices concitaverunt turbam,* Mk. Skt. Lind. 15, 11.

ge-eglan, -eglian; *p.* de, ede, ode; *pp.* ed *To trouble, injure;* mŏlestāre:—Hyra líce ne wæs ówiht geegled *their bodies were not injured aught,* Cd. 191; Th. 237, 27; Dan. 344: Shrn. 99, 9: 154, 4.

ge-egsian, -egesian; *p.* ode; *pp.* od *To frighten;* terrēre:—He hý mid his wordum geegsode *he frightened them with his words,* Ors. 2, 3; Bos. 42, 13: Jud. 7, 22. Geegsod *frightened,* 4, 17.

ge-ehtian; *p.* ode; *pp.* od *To estimate, value;* æstĭmāre:—Ðæt hie mon ná undeórran weorþe móste lésan ðonne hie mon be ðam were geehtige *which must not be redeemed at any cheaper rate than it is estimated at according to his value,* L. Alf. pol. 32; Th. i. 82, 2, note 8. v. geeahtian.

ge-elnian; *p.* ode; *pp.* od *To strive with zeal after another;* zēlāre:—Ic geelnode ofer ða unrihtwísan *zēlāvi sŭper ĭnĭquos,* Ps. Spl. T. 72, 3.

ge-embehtan; *p.* ade *To minister;* ministrare:—Geembehta *ministrare,* Lk. Skt. Lind. 10, 40. He geembihtæs *ministrat,* Mt. Kmbl. p. 15, 15. Ðætte he geembehtade *ut ministraret,* Mk. Skt. Lind. 10, 45: 15, 41.

ge-emnettan, -emnittan, -emnyttan; *p.* te; *pp.* ed *To make even* or *level, compare;* æquāre, exæquāre:—Deáþ geemnet ða rícan and ða heánan *death levels the rich and the poor,* Bt. 19; Fox 68, 34. Gif we úre unþeáwas geemnettaþ be his hǽsum *if we level our vices by his commands,* Homl. Th. ii. 316, 1. Heó hí sylfe to hwelpum geemnette *she compared herself to the whelps,* 114, 10. Geemnittan *exæquāre,* Scint. 9. Ðæt heó ðone dæg and ða niht geemnytte *that it might make even the day and the night,* Bd. de nat. rerum; Lchdm. iii. 238, 24. Geemnettan *quadrare, congruere,* Hpt. Gl. 506.

ge-emnian; *p.* ode; *pp.* od *To make even, match;* adæquare, Som. [Cf. ge-efnian.]

ge-encgd; *part. p. Anxious, careful,* Som. [Cf. ange, enge.]

ge-endadung, e; *f. Finishing, consummation:*—Giendadunge *consummatu,* Rtl. 105, 28.

ge-ende, es; *m. An end,* Som.

ge-endebredian; *p.* ade; *pp.* ad *To set in order,* Rtl. 69, 4: 109, 4.

ge-endebrednian; *p.* ade; *pp.* ad *To set in order;* ordinare:—Ðætte hia geendebrednadon *ordinare,* Lk. Skt. Lind. 1, 1. Geendebrednege *ordinare,* Mt. Kmbl. p. 7, 2.

ge-endebyrdan; *p.* -byrde; *pp.* -byrded, -byrd *To set in order, arrange, dispose;* ordĭnāre, dispōnĕre:—Manega þohton ðæra þinga race geendebyrdan *multi cōnāti sunt ordĭnāre narrātiōnem rērum,* Lk. Bos. 1, 1. Heó ðæt sóna mid reogollíce lífe gesette and geendebyrde *she soon settled and ordered it with regular life,* Bd. 4, 23; S. 593, 28. Rihte Godes dóme geendebyrded wæs æfter synne ðæs ǽrestan mannes *est digno Dei jūdĭcio post culpam ordĭnātum,* 1, 27; S. 494, 13. Gif heora mód wǽre geendebyrd *if their minds were ordered,* Bt. 21; Fox 76, 1: Bt. Met. Fox 11, 199; Met. 11, 100.

ge-endian, -endigan, to -endianne; *p.* ode, ade; *pp.* od, ad. I. *v. trans. To end, finish, complete, accomplish;* fīnīre, consummāre, perfĭcĕre:—Ðes man agan timbrian, and ne mihte hit geendian *hic hŏmo cœpit ædĭfĭcāre, et non pŏtuit consummāre,* Lk. Bos. 14, 30. Ǽr heó hit geendigan móste *ere she might end it,* Bd. 3, 8; S. 532, 28. Se cyning mid árleásre cwale ofslegen wæs, and ðæt ylce geweorc his æfterfyligende Oswalde forlét to geendianne *rex ipse impio nece occīsus, ŏpus ĭdem successōri suo Osualdo perfĭciendum relĭquit,* 2, 14; S. 517, 33. Ic geendige *finio,* Ælfc. Gr. 30, 5; Som. 34, 57. Man ðæt geendaþ on ǽfynne *man ends it in the evening,* Ps. Th. 103, 22. Oþoniél geendode his dagas *mortuus est Othoniel,* Jud. 3, 11: Chr. 189; Erl. 9, 27. Hyt ys geendod *consummātum est,* Jn. Bos. 19, 30: Mk. Bos. 13, 4. Ðe nó geendad weorþeþ *which shall not be ended,* Exon. 32 a; Th. 100, 12; Cri. 1640: 63 a; Th. 232, 1; Ph. 500. II. *to come to an end:*—Ðá geendode se gebeorscipe *then the feast came to an end,* Th. Apol. 18, 8. Siððan Eádgár geendode *since Edgar died,* Swt. A. S. Rdr. 106, 44: 68, 365. Geendiaþ ealle on ans *they all end in -ans,* Ælfc. Gr. Som. 43, 46.

ge-endung, -ændung, e; *f. An end, finish, death;* fīnis, consummātio, mors:—Geendung ealles flǽsces *finis ūnĭversæ carnis,* Gen. 6, 13. Ðonne cymþ seó geendung *tunc vĕniet consummātio,* Mt. Bos. 24, 14. Óþ ðisre worulde geendunge *until the end of this world,* Boutr., Scrd. 17, 18: 20, 20; Homl. Th. ii. 74, 10. On geendunga *in consummātiōne,* Ps. Spl. 58, 14. Æfter geendunge ðæra ealdra manna *after the death of the old men,* Jud. Thw. 153, 20: Homl. Th. ii. 122, 18.

ge-engd, -enged; *past p. Anxious, sad.* v. ange.

ge-eofot, es; *n. A debt;* dēbĭtum:—Gif mon on folces gemóte geeofot uppe *if a man declare a debt at a folk-moot,* L. Alf. pol. 22; Th. i. 76, 6, MS. H. v. eofot.

ge-eorsian; *p.* ode; *pp.* od *To be angry;* īrasci:—Wæs geeorsod on hát-heortnesse Drihten on folce his *īrātus est fŭrōre Dŏmĭnus in pŏpŭlo suo,* Ps. Lamb. 105, 40. v. ge-yrsian.

ge-eówan *to shew, discover;* ostendere:—He hit eft gehýt and eft geeówþ *it [the divine providence] again hides it and again discovers it,* Bt. 39, 8; Fox 224, 12. v. ge-eáwan, eówan.

ge-ērendian *to go on an errand,* L. In. 33; Th. i. 122, 13, note 37, MS. B. v. ge-ǽrendian.

ge-erfeweardian; *p.* ade *To inherit:*—Gierfeueardade *hereditavit,* Rtl. 45, 35: 84, 37.

ge-erian; *p.* ede, ode, ade; *pp.* ed, od, ad *To ear, plough;* arare:—Geerod [geered MS. C; geerad MS. D.] *aratus,* Ælfc. Gr. 19; Som. 22, 45. Ðæt land is geerod [geered MS. C.] *aratur terra,* 19; Som. 22, 46: Heming, p. 134.

gees *geese,* L. In. 70; Th. i. 146, 18, = gēs; *pl. of* gōs.

ge-etan; *p.* ic, he ge-æt, ðú ge-ǽte, *pl.* ge-ǽton; *pp.* ge-eten *To eat together, to eat, to consume;* comedere, edere:—Elnung húses ðínes geet mec [me æt, Bos.] Jn. Skt. Lind. 2, 17. Ðæt híg ǽton: ðá híg geeten hæfdon, hīg wunedon ðǽr *ut ederunt: cum comedissent, manserunt ibi*, Gen. 31, 54. Gif ðū ðæs treówes wæstm geetst *if thou eatest the fruit of this tree*, Homl. Th. i. 14, 2.

ge-éðan; *p.* de; *pp.* ed [ēðe *easy*] *To make easy* or *light, alleviate*; lĕvāre:—Ðæt ðū hygesorge heortan mīnre geēðe *that thou alleviate the sorrow of my heart*, Exon. 50 a; Th. 174, 17; Gū. 1179.

ge-eþcucigan *to revive.* v. ge-edcucian.

gef, *pl.* gēfon *Gave*:—Ge him hleoþ gēfon *ye gave them shelter*, Exon. 27 b; Th. 83, 11; Cri. 1354; *p. of* gifan.

gef *if*, Bt. 36, 4; Fox 178, 27. v. gif.

ge-fā [= ge-faa], ān; *m.* [fāh *a foe*] *A foe, an enemy*; inimicus, adversarius:—Gif se man [MS. mon] his gefān wite *if the man know his foe*, L. Alf. pol. 42; Th. i. 90, 2, 4, 14. Ðā mētte hine his eald-gefāna sum, and hine ofstang *then one of his old foes met him, and stabbed [killed] him*, Ors. 3, 7; Bos. 62, 22. To bismere his gefān [MS. gefaan = gefān = gefāum = gefāhum] *in mockery to his foes*, Homl. Th. i. 226, 28. v. fāh, fā.

ge-fadian; *p.* ode, ade, ede; *pp.* od, ad, ed *To set in order, dispose, arrange, regulate*; ordĭnāre, dispōnĕre:—Se ðe awent of Ledene on Englisc sceal gefadian hit swā ðæt ðæt Englisc hæbbe his āgene wīsan *he that translates from Latin into English must arrange it so that the English have its own manner*, Thw. Hept. p. 4, 9. Se Fæder gefadaþ ealle þing *the Father disposes all things*, Homl. Th. ii. 606, 3. He gefadode wið ða burhware *he arranged with the townsfolk*, Chr. 1052; Erl. 184, 21: Homl. Th. i. 278, 19. Hī ða gebytlunge gefadedon *they arranged the building*, ii. 172, 30. Gefadige [gefadie MS. B.] man ða steóre swā hit fōr Gode sȳ gebeorhlīc and fōr worulde aberendlīc *let the correction be regulated so that it be becoming before God and tolerable before the world*, L. C. S. 2; Th. i. 376, 13. Gefadad *disposed*, Th. Diplm. A. D. 972; 522, 12.

ge-fadung, e; *f. A disposing, arranging*; dispŏsĭtio:—He nǽre nā ælmihtig, gyf him ǽnig gefadung earfoðe wǽre *he would not be almighty if any arranging were difficult to him*, Bd. de nat. rerum; Wrt. popl. science 19, 6; Lchdm. iii. 278, 14.

ge-fæd, es; *n? Order, decorum*; dĕcōrum:—Mid gefæde *with decorum*, L. Edg. C. 4; Th. i. 244, 15.

ge-fæd; *adj.* [ge-fadian *to set in order*] *Orderly*; dispŏsĭtus:—Ðæt preósta gehwilc to sinoþe hæbbe gefædne man to cnihte *that every priest at the synod have an orderly man for servant*, L. Edg. C. 4; Th. ii. 244, 14.

ge-fædera, an; *m. A godfather*; compater:—Mauricius wæs his gefædera *Mauricius was his godfather*, Homl. Th. ii. 122, 24. [*O. H. Ger.* geuatero *compater*: *Ger.* gevatter.] v. cumpæder.

ge-fæderan, *pl.* v. suhtor-gefæderan.

ge-fædere, ge-federe, an; *f. A godmother*; commater, susceptrix:—Ǽfre ne geweorþe, ðæt Cristen man gewīfige on his gefæderan *let it never be that a Christian man marry with his godmother*, L. Eth. vi. 12; Th. i. 318, 17: L. C. E. 7; Th. i. 364, 22. [*O. H. Ger.* gi-uatara; *Ger.* gevatterin.]

ge-fædlīce; *adv. Orderly, quietly*; quiēte, Glos. Prudent. Recd. 145, 78.

ge-fædred; *part. Fathered*, Ors. 3, 7; Bos. 60, 19. v. ge-fædrian.

ge-fædrian; *p* ede; *pp.* ed *To* FATHER, *to adopt* or *to ascribe to any one as a son* or *daughter*; adeptare, patri filium vel filiam ascribere:—Ða þrȳ gebrōþra nǽron nā Philippuse gemēdred, ac wǽron gefædred *the three were not brothers of Philip by their mother [mothered], but they were by their father [fathered]*, Ors. 3, 7; Bos. 60, 19.

ge-fægen, -fagen; *adj. Glad, rejoiced*; lætus:—Ic bió swīðe gefægen *I shall be very glad*, Bt. 40, 5; Fox 240, 25, MS. Cot. Hie ðæs gefægene wǽrun *they were rejoiced thereat*, Chr. 855; Erl. 68, 31: 878; Erl. 80, 11.

ge-fægerian; *p.* ode; *pp.* od *To adorn*; ornare, Som.

ge-fægnian, -fagnian, -fagenian; *p.* ode; *pp.* od *To rejoice, be glad, exult*; gaudēre, exultāre:—Ic geblissige and ic gefægnige on ðē *lætābor et exultābo in te*, Ps. Lamb. 9, 3. Geblissiaþ, and gefægniaþ on ðām dagum *gaudēte in illa die et exultāte*, Lk. Bos. 6, 23. Blissian and gefægnian þeóda *lætentur et exultent gentes*, Ps. Spl. 66, 4.

ge-fægnung, e; *f. Exultation*; exultātio:—Ðon gefylled is tunge ūre gefægnunge *tunc repleta est lingua nostra exultātiōne*, Ps. Spl. 125, 2: 104, 41: 44, 17. v. fægnung.

ge-fǽgon *rejoiced.* v. gefeón.

ge-fælan, -fællan; *p.* de; *pp.* ed *To overturn, overthrow, throw down*; prosternere, Ps. Vos. 105, 25: Lk. Skt. Lind. 20, 18. v. a-fælan.

ge-fællnis, -fælnis, se; *f. A fall*, Lk. Skt. Lind. 2, 34; *transmigration*, Mt. Kmbl. Lind. 1, 12.

ge-fælsian; *p.* ode, ade; *pp.* od, ad *To cleanse, purify, expiate*; lustrāre, pūrĭfĭcāre, expiāre:—He wolde gefælsian foldan mǽgþe *he would purify the race of earth*, Exon. 10 a; Th. 9, 33; Cri. 144: 12 b; Th. 20, 19; Cri. 320. Heorot is gefælsod *Heorot is purified*, Beo. Th. 2357; B. 1176: 3245; B. 1620: Apstls. Kmbl. 132; Ap. 66. Fȳre gefælsad *purified with fire*, Exon. 127 b; Th. 490, 21; Rä. 80, 5.

ge-fær, es; *n. A going, journey, course, march, expedition*; profectio, expĕdītio:—Ðisses fugles gefær *this bird's course*, Exon. 62 a; Th. 227, 20; Ph. 426. On gefære *in profectiōne*, Ps. Spl. 104, 36. Ðæs ðe hie feónda gefær fyrmest geségon *after they first saw the enemies' march*, Elen. Kmbl. 135; El. 68.

ge-fǽran [= ge-fēran]; *p.* de; *pp.* ed *To lead, bring*:—Ic eów hebbe hām gefǽrde alle *I have brought you all home*, Cd. Th. 270, 18; Sat. 92. [Cf. *O. Sax.* gi-fōrian *to bring*.]

ge-færnys, se; *f. A transmigration*, Som.

ge-fǽrrǽden, ge-fǽrscipe. v. gefērrǽden, gefērscipe.

ge-fæstan; *p.* -fæste; *pp.* -fæsted *To place*; locare:—Monn gefæste ða *homo locavit eam*, Mk. Skt. Lind, 12, 1. v. fæstan.

ge-fæstan; *p.* -fæste *To fast*:—Gefæsta *jejunare*, Lk. Skt. Lind. 5, 34: Mt. Kmbl. Lind. 4, 2; 6, 16.

ge-fæsten, es; *n. A fast*; jejunium, Rtl. 16, 41.

ge-fæstnian; *p.* ode, ade; *pp.* od, ad *To fix, fasten, secure, confirm, betroth*; figere, firmare, confirmare, infigere, despondere:—Iulius him mid gewritum gefæstnod *Julius secured it to him by writings*, Ors. 5, 13; Bos. 112, 31. Gefæstnade *secured*, Bd. 1, 5; S. 476, 10. Gefæstnode, 4, 28; S. 605, 24. Gefæstnode synd þeóda *infixæ sunt gentes*, Ps. Spl. 9, 15. Gifæstnad *desponsata*, Lk. Skt. Rush. 1, 27.

ge-fæstnung, e; *f. A fastening, securing, defence*; munimen, Rtl. 37, 15.

ge-fætan; *p.* -te *To pack up*; convasare:—Ðæt gold hī gefætaþ on ða myran *the gold they pack on the mares*, Nar. 35, 12. v. fæt.

ge-fætian *to fetch, send for*, Cd. Th. 297, 22; Sat. 521. v. gefetian.

ge-fætnian; *p.* ode; *pp.* od *To fatten, anoint*; impinguare, unguere:—Ðū amæstest oððe ðū gefætnodest on ele heáfod mīn *impinguasti in oleo caput meum*, Ps. Lamb. 22, 5. v. fætnian.

ge-fættian; *p.* ode; *pp.* od *To fatten, anoint*; impinguare, pinguefieri, Ps. Vos. 19, 3. Gefætted *incrassatum*, Mt. Kmbl. Rush. 13, 15. v. ge-fætnian.

ge-fagen; *adj. Glad, joyful*; lætus:—Gefagen biþ, gif hit ǽfre to cuman mæg *it will be joyful if it ever may come thereto*, Bt. 25; Fox 88, 29. v. ge-fægen.

ge-fagnian, -fagenian; *p.* ode; *pp.* od *To rejoice, be glad, exult*; gaudēre, exultāre:—Manega on his acennednysse gefagniaþ *multi in nativitāte ejus gaudēbunt*, Lk. Bos. 1, 14. Gefagnode ðæt cild on hyre innoþe *exultāvit infans in utĕro ejus*, 1, 41. Ic blissie and ic gefagenie on ðē *lætābor et exultābo in te*, Ps. Spl. T. 9, 2. v. ge-fægnian.

ge-fāh, ge-fāhmon *an enemy.* v. fāh, fāhman.

ge-fana, an; *m. A standard*, Som.

ge-fandod, -fondad; *past. p.* Beo. Th. 4900; B. 2454: 4592; B. 2301. [*Laym.* i-fonded.] v. fandian.

ge-fangennes, se; *f. A taking, laying hold of, apprehension*, Som.

ge-fara, an; *m. A companion*; sŏcius:—Ic eom fyrdrinces gefara *I am a soldier's companion*, Exon. 127 a; Th. 489, 3; Rä 78, 2. Hī heora wǽpen hwyrfdon wið heora gefaran *in sŏcios arma vertĕre incipiunt*, Bd. 1, 15; S. 483, 5. v. ge-fēra.

ge-faran; *p.* fōr; *pl.* -fōron, -fōran; *pp.* faren. I. *intrans. To go, proceed, reach by going, arrive*; ire, proficisci, meare:—[He] walde gefara *voluit exire*, Jn. Skt. Lind. 1, 43. Swā feor swā man on ānum dæge gefaran mæg *as far as one can journey in a day*, Thw. Num. 11, 31. Eall under hrōf gefōr *all came under the roof*, Gen. 1360. Óþ ðæt drihtweras gefōran ðǽr is botlwela bethlem hāten *until the men arrived where is a village called Bethel*, Cd. Th. 107, 33; Gen. 1798. II. *to depart, die*:—His fæder gefærþ *his father dies*, Blickl. Homl. 131, 25. Bearn hraðe gefaraþ *[their] children soon die*, Boeth. 11, 1; Fox 32, 10. Ne wēne ic ðæt ǽnig wǽre ðe ðæt atellan mihte, ðæt on ðam gefeohte gefōr *I do not suppose that anybody could reckon [the number] that died in that battle*, Ors. 3, 11; Bos. 75, 9. Gefōr Ǽðerēd cyning *king Ethelred died*, Chr. 871; Erl. 76, 1. Hȳ æt nȳhstan ne ahsedan hwæt ðæra gefarenra wǽre *at last they did not ask how many there were dead*, Ors. 4, 4; Bos. 80, 12. III. *to proceed, get on, fare*:—Hū se mānscaða gefaran wolde *how the wicked spoiler meant to proceed*, Beo. Th. 1481; B. 738. Eustatius cȳdde hū hī gefaren hæfdon *Eustace told how they had fared*, Chr. 1048; Erl. 178, 6. We nyton hwæt Moises gefaren hafþ *we know not what has become of Moses*, Exod. Thw. 32, 1, 23. IV. *v. trans. To get by going, experience, occupy, reach, obtain, go against*:—Hū mæg ic hit on ðrim dagum gefaran *how can I perform the journey in three days*, Blickl. Homl. 231, 23: 235, 35. Hie wræcstōwe gefōran *they had reached the place of exile*, Cd. Th. 6, 20; Gen. 91. Ic wisce ðæt ic eft forlidennesse gefare *I wish that I may again suffer shipwreck*, Th. Apol. 12, 10: 21, 19. Ðænne gefærþ he sige on ǽghwylcum gefeohte *then shall he obtain victory in every battle*, H. R. 17, 10. Twegen æðelingas gefōran ðæt lond *two princes occupied that land*, Ors. 1, 10; Bos. 32, 35. Philippus gefōr heora burh *Philip took their town*, 3, 7; Bos. 60, 6. Ne dorste he genēðan ðæt he hie mid firde gefōre *he dare not venture to attack them with an army*, 1, 10; Bos. 33, 31. Cf. gerīdan. [*O. Sax.* gifaran *takes an accusative.*]

gefe *a gift*, Bd. 2, 13; S. 516, 6: Mt. Kmbl. Lind. 23, 18, 19. v. gifu.

ge-feá, an; *m. Joy, gladness, glory, favour;* gaudium:—Ðes mīn gefeá is gefylled *this my joy is fulfilled*, Jn. Bos. 3, 29. Mid gefeán *with joy;* gaudio, 3, 29. Bodan cȳþdon sōþne gefeán *messengers announced real joy*, Exon. 14 a; Th. 28, 23; Cri. 451. Se biþ gefeána fægrast *that shall be the fairest of joys*, 32 b; Th. 102, 1; Cri. 1666: 15, 11. On gefean *with joy*, Ps. Spl. 20, 6.

ge-feagan, -feān. v. ge-feohan, -feōn.

ge-feaht, es; *n. A battle;* prælium:—Ðǣr nān hefilīc gefeaht ne wearþ *there was no hard battle there*, Chr. 868; Erl. 73, 26. Mycclum gefeahtum *in great battles*, 755; Erl. 49, 26. v. ge-feoht.

ge-feald, es; *n. A fold, inclosure, field;* septum, ăger:—Þurh fīfela gefeald forþonette *he hastened forth through the field of the monsters*, Wald. 76; Vald. 2, 10.

ge-fealdan; *p.* -feóld, *pl.* -feóldon; *pp.* -fealden *To fold up, wrap;* plĭcāre, involvĕre:—Ne læg hyt nā mid līnwǣdum, ac onsundron gefealden on ānre stōwe *non cum linteamĭnĭbus pŏsĭtum, sed sepărātim invŏlūtum in ūnum lŏcum*, Jn. Bos. 20, 7. Miđđȳ gefeáld đæt bōc *cum plicuisset librum*, Lk. Skt. Lind. 4, 20.

ge-feálīc; *adj. Pleasant, joyous, delightful;* lætus:—Ðǣr is ēđellond fæger and gefeálīc *there is a country fair and joyous*, Exon. 42 a; Th. 141, 18; Gū. 628: 44 b; Th. 151, 18; Gū. 797.

ge-feallan; *p.* -feól, -feóll, *pl.* -feóllon; *pp.* feallen *To fall;* cadere, decidere:—Ic gefealle be gewyrhtum fram feóndum mīnum *decidam merito ab inimicis meis*, Ps. Spl. 7, 4. Ðǣr Pharaon gefeól, on đam Reádan Sǣ *et excussit Pharaonem in Mari Rubro*, Ps. Th. 135, 15. He eorþan gefeóll *he fell to earth*, Beo. Th. 5661; B. 2834: 4207; B. 2100. Me fela đīnra edwīta on gefeóllon *opprobria exprobantium tibi ceciderunt super me*, Ps. Th. 68, 9. Ðā gefeól hire mōd on his lufe *then she fell in love with him*, Th. Apol. 17, 18: 1, 13. Sōđlīce đīn dōhtor gefeól on swēgcræft, ac heó næfþ hine nā wel geleornod *thy daughter indeed has attempted* [?] *music, but she has not learnt it well*, 16, 23. v. feallan.

ge-fearh-sugu, e; *f.* [fearh *a farrow*] *A farrowing sow;* prægnans sus, forda:—Gefearhsugu *forda*, Wrt. Voc. 286, 49.

ge-fearrian; *p.* ade; *pp.* ad *To remove to a distance, go away;* avellere, discedere, abscedere:—He gefearrad wæs from him *ipse avulsus est ab eis*, Lk. Skt. Lind. 22, 41. Gifearria *abscedat*, Rtl. 98, 22; *discedat*, 120, 31. v. feorran, afyrran.

ge-feastian; *p.* ode, ade; *pp.* od, ad *To entrust, commit;* commendare:—Gefeastadon *commendaverunt*, Lk. Skt. Lind. 12, 48. v. gefæstan.

ge-feaxe; *adj.* [feax *hair*] *Having hair;* cŏmātus:—Wǣron men æđelīce gefeaxe *the men had beautiful hair* [lit. *the men were beautifully haired*], Bd. 2, 1; S. 501, 8.

ge-feaxen; *adj. Having hair, haired;* cŏmātus:—Ða syndon gefeaxene swā frihteras *they have hair as soothsayers have*, Nar. 37, 1. v. gefeaxode.

ge-feaxode, -fexode; *adj. Having hair, haired;* cŏmātus:—Ða wǣron hwītes līchaman and fægres andwlitan men, and æđelīce gefeaxode [gefexode, Homl. Th. ii. 120, 19] *they were men of white complexion and fair countenance, and having noble hair*, Nat. S. Greg. Els. 12, 1. v. feaxede.

ge-feccan, -feccean; *p.* -feahte, -fehte; *pp.* -feaht, -feht *To fetch, bring to;* addūcĕre:—He mæg đa sāwle gefeccan under foldan *it can fetch back the soul under the earth*, Salm. Kmbl. 139; Sal. 69. He him hēt to wīfe gefeccean Cleopatran *he commanded [them] to bring Cleopatra to him for a wife*, Ors. 5, 13; Bos. 112, 44: Blickl. Homl. 187, 15.

ge-fecgan; *p.* -feah *To seize;* arrĭpĕre:—He wolde đæs beornes beágas gefecgan *he would seize the chieftains gems*, Byrht. Th. 136, 33; By. 160.

ge-fēdan; đū -fēdst; *p.* -fēdde; *pp.* -fēded, -fēdd, -fēd *To feed, nourish;* pascĕre, enutrīre:—Ðū gefēdst me *enutries me*, Ps. Lamb. 30, 4. Ic eom gefēd *pascor*, Ælfc. Gr. 33; Som. 36, 44, MS. D.

ge-federe, an; *f. A godmother;* susceptrix, L. C. E. 7; Th. i. 365, note 18. v. ge-fædere.

ge-fēg, -feig, es; *n. A joining, juncture;* commissura, junctura, Cot. 43: Ælfc. Gl. 62; Som. 68, 82; Wrt. Voc. 39, 65: Compago, 70; Som. 70, 57; Wrt. Voc. 42, 65. Gefeig *formula*, Lye. Gefēg borda *a joining of boards*, Ælfc. Gl. 62; Som. 68, 82. Mennisce handa hit ne mihton towurpan, for đam fæstum gefēge đæs feóndlīcan temples *human hands could not overthrow it because of the fast joining of the devilish temple*, Homl. Th. ii. 510, 14. [*Ger.* gefüge.]

ge-fēgan, -fēgean; *p.* de; *pp.* ed; *v. trans. To join, unite, compact, compose;* jungĕre, conjungĕre, compingĕre, compōnĕre:—Con he sīdne ræced fæste gefēgan *he can firmly compact the spacious dwelling*, Exon. 79 a; Th. 296, 8; Crä. 48: 79 a; Th. 297, 10; Crä. 66. Ic đa ged ne mæg gefēgean *I cannot compose the songs*, Bt. Met. Fox 2, 11; Met. 2, 6. Ic gefēge *compōno*, Ælfc. Gr. 28, 3; Som. 30, 57. Conjunctio gefēgþ togædere ǣgđer ge naman ge word *a conjunction joins together both nouns and verbs*, 5; Som. 3, 48, 51: Bt. 21; Fox 74, 37. Se gefēhþ fela folca tosomne *he joins many people together*, Bt. Met. Fox 11, 177; Met. 11, 89. Gefēg đās bricas *join these fragments*, Homl. Th. i. 62, 7. Ne weorþaþ hī nǣfre tosomne gefēged *they are never united together*, Bt. 16, 63; Fox 56, 7: Bt. Met. Fox 20, 231; Met. 20, 116: 20, 241; Met. 20, 121. Gifoega *sociare, conciliare*, Rtl. 104, 12: 74, 18.

ge-fēge; *adj. Fit, adapted;* aptus, Grm. i. 735, 5. [*Ger.* gefüge *flexible.*] v. ungefēge.

ge-fēgednes, se; *f. Figure, shape, a joining*, Som.

ge-fegian *to rejoice.* v. gefeón.

ge-fēgincg, -fēgung, e; *f. A joining, composing, conjunction;* compositio, conjunctio:—Seó geþeódnys ođđe gefegincg is conjunctio *the joining is a conjunction*, Ælfc. Gr. 5; Som. 3, 47. v. ge-þeódnes.

ge-fēgniss, e; *f. Companionship;* societas, Rtl. 109, 25: 106, 4.

gefēhst *catchest;* capis, Coll. Monast. Th. 23, 7.

gefēhþ *seizes*, Bt. 39, 1; Fox 212, 1. v. ge-fōn.

ge-fēlan; *p.* de; *pp.* ed *To feel, perceive;* sentīre:—Ðæt hit man gefēlan mihte *that it might be felt*, Ors. 1, 7; Bos. 30, 4: Exon. 24 b; Th. 69, 33; Cri. 1130: 25 a; Th. 72, 28; Cri. 1179. Gefēleþ fācnes cræftig đæt him đa fērend on fæste wuniaþ *the skilled in guile feels that the voyagers firmly rest on him*, 97 a; Th. 361, 23; Wal. 24. Gefēlde ic me beótiende and wyrpende *me mĕlius hăbēre sentīrem*, Bd. 5, 6; S. 620, 12. Gefēlde he his līchoman healfne dǣl mid đa ādle geslægene beón *sensit dimĭdiam corpŏris sui partem languōre depressam*, 4, 31; S. 610, 15: 3, 2; S. 525, 15: 3, 9; S. 534, 11. He đæs wītes worn gefēlde *he felt the force of the torment*, Cd. 214; Th. 269, 23; Sat. 77.

ge-felgan; *p.* -fealh, *pl.* -fulgon; *pp.* -folgen *To stick to;* inhærēre:—He đære godspellīcan lāre georne gefealh *he earnestly stuck to the gospel lore*, Bd. 3, 22; S. 552, 43. v. felgan.

ge-fellan; *p.* -felde; *pp.* -felled *To fill, fulfil:*—Se gefelde xx daga *he had fulfilled twenty days*, St. And. 4, 23. v. gefyllan.

ge-fellan; *p.* -felde; *pp.* -feld *To cause to fall, fell, kill:*—Hie gefēlde wurdon fram Alexandre *they were killed by Alexander*, Nar. 38, 11. v. gefyllan.

ge-fēlniss, e; *f. A feeling, perception, sense;* sensus:—Būtan ǣnigre gefēlnisse *without any feeling*, Bd. 4, 11; S. 580, 2. DER. fēlnyss.

ge-felsode *expiated.* v. gefælsian.

gefend, es; *m. A giver:*—Gefend *largitor*, Rtl. 108, 16. v. gifend.

ge-feng, es; *n. A taking, capture, captivity;* captura, captivitas:—On gefeng *in capturam*, Lk. Skt. Lind. 5, 4. On gefeng fiscana *in captura piscium*, 5, 9. Gefeng *captivitas*, Rtl. 83, 3. v. feng.

gefeó *take*, Coll. Monast. Th. 21, 31, = gefō; *pres. of* gefōn, *q. v.*

ge-feógan *to hate.* v. ge-fīa.

ge-feohan *to rejoice:*—Gefeoh nū on ferþe *rejoice now in mind*, Hy. 11, 1; Hy. Grn. ii. 294, 1. v. gefeón.

ge-feoht, -fioht, -feht, es; *n. A fight, battle, contest, war, preparation for war;* prælium, pugna, congressio, bellum, procinctus:—Ðæt ungemetlīce mycle gefeoht *the very great battle*, Ors. 1, 9; Bos. 32, 1: Homl. Th. ii. 538, 14: Chr. 603; Erl. 20, 15: 868; Erl. 72, 28. Gefeoht *congressio*, Ælfc. Gl. 14; Som. 57, 125; Wrt. Voc. 20, 62. On dæge gefeohtes *in die belli*, Ps. Lamb. 139, 8. Ðū here fȳsest to gefeohte *thou incitest a host to battle*, Andr. Kmbl. 2377; An. 1190: 2393; An. 1198: Elen. Kmbl. 2365; El. 1184. To gefeohte *in procinctu*, Ælfc. Gl. 101; Som. 77, 35; Wrt. Voc. 55, 40. Gē gehȳraþ gefeoht and sace *ye shall hear of battle and strife*, Homl. Th. ii. 538, 2, 13: Bt. 15; Fox 48, 15. Ðonne gē geseóþ gefeoht and twȳrǣdnessa *cum audiĕritis prœlia et sedĭtiōnes*, Lk. Bos. 21, 9: Mt. Bos. 24, 6: Ps. Lamb. 139, 3. Ðonne gē gehȳraþ gefeohtu and gefeohta hlīsan, ne ondrǣde gē eów *cum audiĕritis bella et opiniōnes bellōrum, ne timuĕritis*, Mk. Bos. 13, 7: Mt. Bos. 24, 6. Miclum gefeohtum *in great battles*, Chr. 755; Erl. 48, 25: L. In. 6; Th. i. 106, 1, note 1. Gefehto and woeno gefehtana *prœlia et opiniones prœliorum*, Mt. Kmbl. Lind. 24, 6. [*Laym.* i-fiht.]

ge-feohtan; *p.* -feaht, *pl.* -fuhton; *pp.* -fohten. I. *to fight;* pugnare:—And gif he đonne wiđ hine gefeohtan ne mæg *and if he may not fight against him*, Lk. Bos. 14, 32. Ðe teáh mine fingras to gefeohtanne *qui docet digitos meos ad bellum*, Ps. Th. 143, 1. He wel gefeaht *he fought well*, Ors. 5, 13; Bos. 112, 34. Margareta wiþ đone deófol gefæht *Margaret fought with the devil*, Nar. 39, 28. Gif hwā gefeohte on cyninges huse, sié [sy MSS. B. H.] he scyldig ealles his ierfes [yrfes MSS. B. H.] *if any one fight in the king's house, let him be liable in all his property*, L. In. 6; Th. i. 106, 2. Ðeáh hit sié on middum felda gefohten *though it be fought on mid-field*, L. In. 6; Th. i. 106, 10: Judth. 11; Thw. 23, 15; Jud. 122. II. *to obtain by fighting;* pugnando acquirere:—Ðæt he ne meahte wiht gefeohtan *that he could not gain aught by fighting* [lit. *to fight*], Beo. Th. 2171; B. 1083. Dōm gefeohtan *to gain glory by fighting*, Bryht. Th. 135, 37; By. 129. Hæfde đā gefohten foremǣrne blǣd Judith *Judith had gained exceeding great glory*, Judth. 11; Thw. 23, 15; Jud. 122. [*Cf. Ger.* erfechten.] v. feohtan.

gefeoht-dæg, es; *m. A fight-day, day of battle;* dies belli:—On gefeohtdæge, Ps. Th. 139, 7.

ge-feolan; *p.* -fæl, *pl.* -fǣlon; *pp.* -folen, -feolen *To stick to, persist;*

insistere:—Ðæt he ðám hálwendum ongynnessum georne gefeole *ut cœptis salutaribus insisteret*, Bd. 5, 19; S. 637, 11. v. feolan.

ge-feón, -feohan, -feagan, -feagian; ic -feó, ðú -fehst, he -fehþ, -fiþ, -feaþ, *pl.* -feóþ; *p.* -feah, -feh, *pl.* -fǽgon; *pp.* -fegen [The Northern Gospels have weak forms] *To be glad, rejoice, exult;* lætari, delectari, gaudere, exultare:—Ic gefeó *gaudeo*, Jn. Skt. Lind. 11, 15. Gefeaþ *gaudebit*, 16, 20, 22. Manige on his gebyrd gefeóþ *many shall rejoice at his birth*, Blickl. Homl. 165, 10. Míne weleras gefeóþ *gaudebunt labia mea*, Ps. Th. 70, 21. Gefeah blíðe-mód ðæs ðe . . . *glad of mind rejoiced that*..., Cd. 72; Th. 88, 21; Gen. 1468. Bona weorces gefeah *the destroyer rejoiced at the work*, Exon. Th. 464, 17; Hö. 88: Elen. Kmbl. 220; El. 110. Secg weorce gefeh *the warrior in the work rejoiced*, Beo. Th. 3143; B. 1569: 3253; B. 1624. Fylle gefǽgon *they rejoiced at the plenty*, Beo. Th. 2032; B. 1014. Leóhte gefégun *they rejoiced in the light*, Exon. Th. 31, 32; Cri. 504. Gefeade *exaltavit* [misread by the translator *exultavit*], Jn. Skt. Lind. 3, 14. Gefeade *exultavit*, 8, 56. Gefeoh *rejoice*, Hy. 11, 1; Hy. Grn. ii. 294, 1. Gefeóþ mid me *rejoice with me*, Blickl. Homl. 191, 22. Gefeaþ *gaudete*, Mt. Kmbl. Lind. 5, 12. Eal rihtgelýfed folc sceal gefeón on ðone his tocyme *all right-believing folk ought to rejoice at his advent*, Blickl. Homl. 167, 14. Ðonne mótan we in ðære engellícan blisse gefeón *then may we in angelic bliss rejoice*, 83, 3. Gefeage *exultare*, Jn. Skt. Lind. 5, 35: 3, 14. Gifeaga *gaudere*, Rtl. 34, 3. Gifeagia *gaudere*, 69, 30. Gefeónde for Paules eáðmódnesse *rejoicing on account of Paul's humility*, Blickl. Homl. 141, 4. He wæs gefeónde myclum gefeán *he was rejoicing with great joy*, 233, 2. Hio wǽron gefeónde mycle gefeán, 249, 16. Gefeándo woeron *gavisi sunt*, Mk. Skt. Lind. 14, 11. Gefagen wéron *gavisi sunt*, Mt. Kmbl. Lind. 2, 10.

ge-feormian; *p.* ode; *pp.* od. *v. a.* I. *to entertain, harbour, receive as a guest, feed, cherish, support;* suscipere, hospitio suscipere, epulare, fovere, curare:—Sanctus Albanus for ðam cuman, ðe he gefeormode [MS. gefeormade] gegyrede hine *Saint Alban arrayed himself for the stranger whom he entertained*, Bd. 1, 7; S. 477, 9. Ðæt se, ðe hine feormode, and se, ðe gefeormod wæs, sýn hí begen bisceopes dóme scyldig *that he who entertained him, and he who was entertained, be both liable to excommunication;* susceptor et is qui susceptus est excommunicationi subjacebit, 4, 5; S. 573, 1. Búton ðæs bisceopes leáfe, ðe hí on his scíre gefeormode [MS. gefeormade] sín *without the bishop's leave, in whose diocese they may be entertained*, 4, 5; S. 573, 5. We ðé gefeormedon *we entertained thee*, Cd. 127; Th. 162, 24; Gen. 2686. Ðonne mon mothan betýhþ ðæt he ceáp forstele, oððe forstolenne gefeormie *when a man charges another that he steal cattle, or harbour the stolen*, L. In. 46; Th. i. 130, 13. Geóca mihtig Dryhten mínre sáwle, gefreoða hyre and gefeorma hý *save my soul, O mighty Lord, protect it and cherish it*, Exon. 118 b; Th. 456, 3; Hy. 4, 61. II. *to feed on, devour;* vesci, comedere:—Hie ða behlidenan him to lífnere gefeormedon *they feed on the dead* [mortuos] *to* [*save*] *their lives*, Andr. Kmbl. 2181; An. 1092. Grendel unlifigendes gefeormod fét and folma *Grendel devoured the feet and hands of the lifeless*, Beo. Th. 1493; B. 744. III. *to cleanse, farm* or *cleanse out, Provncl;* mundare:—Ðæt hí ða bán woldon upádón, and onþweán and gefeormian *that they would take up the bones to wash and cleanse*, Bd. 4, 19; S. 589, 11. Hát gefeormian mín blód *bid* [*them*] *wipe away my blood*, Blickl. Homl. 183, 26. v. feormian.

ge-fér, es; *n. A company, society;* cōmĭtātus:—Eart ðú úres geféres ðe úre wiðerwinna *noster es an adversāriōrum* [?], Jos. 5, 13. Wéndon ðæt he on heora geférе wǽre *existĭmantes illum esse in cŏmĭtātu*, Lk. Bos. 2, 44.

ge-féra, an; *m. A companion, comrade, associate, fellow, colleague, fellow-disciple, man, servant;* sŏcius, contŭbernālis, cŏmes, condiscĭpŭlus, vir, puer:—Geféra *contŭbernālis* vel *sŏcius*, Ælfc. Gl. 116; Som. 80, 63; Wrt. Voc. 61, 41: Ælfc. Gr. 5; Som. 5, 20. Geféran áþ *a companion's oath*, L. O. 6; Th. i. 180, 17. Ðæt wíf ðæt ðú me forgeáfe to geféran *mŭlier quam dĕdisti mihi sŏciam*, Gen. 3, 12: Exon. 76 b; Th. 288, 13; Wand. 30. He geseh swǽsne geféran *he saw his dear comrade*, Andr. Kmbl. 2018; An. 1011: 2040; An. 1022. Æðele geféran Philippus and Iacob feorh agéfan for Meotudes lufan *the noble companions Philip and James gave their lives for the love of God*, Menol. Fox 158; Men. 80: Gen. 14, 10: Chr. 755; Erl. 50, 25. Bæd se gesíþ hine ðæt he eóde in to ánum his geféréna *rogātus est ab eodem cŏmĭte intrāre ad unum de puĕris ejus*, Bd. 5, 5; S. 617, 36: 1, 7; S. 476, 29. Cwæþ Thomas to hys geférum *dixit Thomas ad condiscĭpŭlos*, Jn. Bos. 11, 16: Bd. 2, 3; S. 504, 29: 3, 21; S. 551, 9. Ceós ðé geféran and feoht ongén Amalech *elĭge vĭros et pugna contra Amalec*, Ex. 17, 9. Wordes geféra *a verb's companion, an adverb;* adverbium, Ælfc. Gr. 5; Som. 3, 34. Gefoera *condiscipulus*, Jn. Skt. Lind. 11, 16. [*Laym: A. R.* i-vere.]

ge-féran; *p.* -férde; *pp.* -féred. I. *v. intrans. To go, travel, go on, behave, fare, get on, come, get to a place:*—He geférde óð ðæt he Adam funde *he journeyed until he found Adam*, Cd. 23; Th. 29, 20; Gen. 453. Frécne geférdon *daringly they behaved*, Beo. Th. 3386; B. 1691. Ðá ðis cúþ wæs hú ða óðre geférdon *when this was known how the others had fared*, Chr. 1009; Erl. 142, 8: Cd. 214; Th. 268, 29; Sat. 62. Ne mæg ðǽr unwitfull ǽnig geféran *no deceitful man can get there*, Cd. 45; Th. 58, 19; Gen. 948. Ic eom hider feorran geféred *I have come hither from far*, 25; Th. 32, 4; Gen. 498. II. *v. trans. To perform a journey, reach* or *get by going, obtain, attain, experience, suffer:*—Ðú scealt ða fóre geféran *thou shalt perform that journey*, Andr. Kmbl. 431; An. 215; 388; An. 194. Se hit mæg hrædlícor geféran *who can perform the journey more speedily*, Blickl. Homl. 231, 24, 25. Ðe ðæt upplíce ríce geférdon *who reached the realm on high*, Homl. Th. i. 542, 26: Chr. 988; Erl. 131, 10; Beo. Th. 6119; B. 3063. Ðæs siges ðe hie geféred hæfdon *for the victory that they had obtained*, Blickl. Homl. 203, 33. Ðá férdon ða Pyhtas and geférdon ðis land norðanweard *then the Picts went and got the north part of this land*, Chr. Erl. 3, 13. Hafast ðú geféred ðæt ðé weras ehtigaþ *thou hast attained* [*this*] *that men will esteem thee*, Beo. Th. 2446; B. 1221. Hí ðǽr geférdon máran hearm ðonne hí ǽfre wéndon *they there suffered greater hurt than they ever expected*, Chr. 994; Erl. 132, 21: Andr. Kmbl. 2801; An. 1403.

ge-fercian; *p.* ode; *pp.* od *To support, sustain;* sustentāre:—Úre hwílendlíce líf biþ mid mettum gefercod *our transitory life is sustained by meats*, Homl. Th. ii. 462, 20.

ge-fére; *adj. Easy of access;* făcĭlis accessu:—Nis se foldan sceát mongum gefére *the tract of earth is not easy of access to many*, Exon. 55 b; Th. 198, 3; Ph. 4. [Cf. *O. H. Ger.* kifuari *apta*, Grff. iii. 600.] v. fére.

ge-ferian, -fergan; *p.* ode, ede; *pp.* od, ed *To carry, convey, bear, lead, conduct;* ferre, vehĕre, dūcĕre:—Feówer scoldon geferian to ðæm goldsele Grendles heáfod *four must convey Grendel's head to the gold-hall*, Beo. Th. 3281; B. 1638: Andr. Kmbl. 793; An. 397. He geferode hine mid mycclum wurþscipe to Scæftes byrig *he conveyed it with great honour to Shaftesbury*, Chr. 980; Erl. 129, 33. Ðæt he úsic geferge in Fæder ríce *that he convey us into his Father's kingdom*, Exon. 12 b; Th. 22, 1; Cri. 345. Ðonne we geferian freán úserne ðǽr he longe sceal on ðæs Waldendes wære geþolian *then we bear our lord to where he shall long endure in the All-powerful's care*, Beo. Th. 6205; B. 3107. Ðæt hie út geferedon dýre máþmas *that they might convey out the precious treasures*, 6252; B. 3130. Godes gást wæs geferod ofer wæteru *spīrĭtus Dei fĕrēbātur sŭper ăquas*, Gen. 1, 2: Boutr. Scrd. 19, 2: Nicod. 31; Thw. 18, 10. Feorran gefered *conveyed from afar*, Salm. Kmbl. 357; Sal. 178: Andr. Kmbl. 529; An. 265: Elen. Kmbl. 1982; El. 993. Se arc wæs geferud ofer ða wæteru *arca fĕrēbātur sŭper aquas*, Gen. 7, 18.

gefér-lǽcan; *p.* -lǽhte; *pp.* -lǽht *To keep company* or *fellowship, accompany, associate;* assŏciāre:—Ic gefērlǽce *associo?* Ælfc. Gr. 30, 5; Som. 34, 52. He hí gefērlǽcþ on ánnysse his gelaðunge *he associates them in the unity of his church*, Homl. Th. i. 496, 24. He biþ gemǽnscipe ðære hálgan gelaðunge gefērlǽht *he is associated in the communion of the holy church*, i. 494, 19. Ðǽr beóþ gefērlǽhte on ánre súsle, ða ðe on lífe on mándǽdum geþeódde wǽron *there shall be associated in one torment those who in life were united in evil deeds*, Homl. Th. i. 132, 20: 414, 34.

ge-fēr-rǽden, -rēden, -rēdin, -rǽdenn, e; *f.* I. *companionship, fellowship, congregation, church;* societas, comitatus, ecclesia, synagoga:—Hwá wolde on ðære gefērrǽddene [MS. B. gefērǽdene] beón ðe he wǽre *who would be in that fellowship that he was*, L. Ed. 4; Th. i. 162, 5: Ors. 5, 12; Bos. 111, 23. He hæfde on his gefērrǽdene cratu and rídende men *habuit in comitatu currus et equites*, Gen. 50, 9. Smerede ðē God ðín mid ele blysse for gefērrēdinum ðínum *unxit te Deus tuus, oleo lætitiæ præ consortibus tuis*, Ps. Spl. C. 44, 9. Gyf he híg ne gehýrþ, sæge hyt gefērrǽdene *quod si non audierit eos: dic ecclesiæ*, Mt. Bos. 18, 17: Jn. Bos. 9, 22. II. *familiarity, friendship;* familiaritas, amicitia:—Ðæs cyninges gefērrǽden mæg nǽnigne mon gedón weligne *the king's familiarity can make no man wealthy*, Bt. 29, 3; Fox 102, 2. v. ge-fēr-scipe.

ge-fēr-rǽdnes, -ness, e; *f. Society;* societas, Lye.

ge-fēr-scipe, -scype, es; *m. Society, fellowship, brotherhood;* sŏcĭĕtas, cŏmĭtātus, clērus:—To healfum fó se cyng, to healfum se gefērscipe *let the king take half, half the fellowship*, L. Ath. v. § 1, 1; Th. i. 228, 18. Þolige ǽgðer ge gefērscipes ge freóndscipes *let him forfeit both their society and friendship*, L. Eth. ix. 27; Th. i. 346, 11: L. C. E. 5; Th. i. 362, 32: L. N. P. L. 45; Th. ii. 296, 19. Of gefērscipe ðæs bisceopes Deosdedit *de clēro Deusdedit episcŏpi*, Bd. 3, 29; S. 561, 12: 4, 1; S. 564, 18: 5, 6; S. 618, 28: 5, 19; S. 639, 3: L. E. B. 12; Th. ii. 242, 18. For lufan ðínre and gefērscype *for thy love and fellowship*, Exon. 51 a; Th. 177, 24; Gú. 1232: Nicod. 11; Thw. 6, 3. Wið ðone gefērscipe *with the fellowship*, L. Ath. v. § 1, 1; Th. i. 228, 20. Se cræftga gefērscipas fæste gesamnaþ *the artificer firmly unites societies*, Bt. Met. Fox 11, 185; Met. 11, 93. Of hiora gefoerscipe *de eorum societate*, Rtl. 75, 28.

ge-fērscipian *to unite, accompany:*—Gifoerscipia *unitare*, Rtl. 110, 18. Gifoerscipeþ *comitentur*, 93, 13.

ge-festnian; *p.* ode; *pp.* od *To fasten, make fast, confirm, shut up, imprison;* firmāre, confirmāre, inclūdĕre:—He ðæt mid āþe gefestnode *he confirmed that with oath,* Chr. 1091; Erl. 228, 4. Se cyng genam Roger eorl his mǽg, and gefestnode hine *the king took earl Roger his kinsman and imprisoned him,* 1075; Erl. 214, 5. Ðe be swylcre gewittnesse gefestnod is *which is confirmed by such witness,* Th. Diplm. A. D. 856; 117, 18. v. ge-fæstnian.

ge-fetelsod; *adj.* [fetel *a girdle, belt*] *Polished, trimmed, ornamented;* perpŏlītus, adornātus:—Twā sweord gefetelsode *two swords trimmed; duos glădios optĭme adornātos,* Text. Roff. 110, 15.

ge-feterian, -fetrian; *p.* ode, ade; *pp.* od ad *To fetter, bind; compĕdīre,* vincīre:—He ða strangan mæg streámas gefeterian *he can fetter the strong streams,* Ps. Th. 65, 5. He gefeteraþ fǽges monnes handa *he fetters the hands of the doomed man,* Salm. Kmbl. 317; Sal. 158. He gefeterode fēt and honda bearne sīnum *he fettered the feet and hands of his child,* Cd. 140; Th. 175, 27; Gen. 2902. Ða wǽron gefeterade fæste togædre *who were fettered fast together,* Exon. 113 b; Th. 435, 7; Rä. 53, 4.

ge-fēðe; *adj. Lying at the feet,* Gl. Prud. 1046. *Contentus, conscriptus,* Hpt. Gl. 499.

ge-feðeran, -feðran; *p.* ede; *pp.* ed *To feather, give wings to;* ālas addĕre:—Ic sceal ǽrest ðīn mōd gefeðeran *I shall first give wings to thy mind,* Bt. 36, 1; Fox 172, 31, MS. Cot. Gefeðran, Bt. Met. Fox 24, 8; Met. 24, 4. v. ge-fiðerian.

ge-fetian, -fetigan, -fetigean; *p.* -fetode, -fetede, -fette; *pp.* -fetod *To fetch, bring;* addūcĕre, accīre, afferre:—Elene hēht gefetian on fultum forþsnoterne hæleða gerǽdum *Elene bade [them] fetch to her aid the very wise in the councils of men,* Elen. Kmbl. 2103; El. 1053: Beo. Th. 4387; B. 2190. Gefetigan, Exon. 66 b; Th. 246, 11; Jul. 60. Hēt heó sōna hire þīnenne gān and ða cyste hire to gefetigean *stătim jussit ire ministram et capsellam addūcĕre,* Bd. 3, 11; S. 536, 27: Elen. Kmbl. 2319; El. 1161. Swā strang ðæt ǽs him gefetede *so strong that it got prey for itself,* Chr. 975; Erl. 125, 29. He of helle hūþe gefette sāwla manega *he from hell fetched spoils, many souls,* Hy. 10, 30; Hy. Grn. ii. 293, 30: Gen. 24, 11. Ða men of Lundenbyrig gefetodon ða scipu *the men of London brought away the ships,* Chr. 896; Erl. 94, 17. Hȳ gefetton Escolāfius ðone scīnlācan *they fetched Æsculapius the magician,* Ors. 3, 10; Bos. 70, 30. Hwænne me Dryhtnes rōd gefetige *when the Lord's cross shall fetch me,* Rood. Kmbl. 274; Kr. 138. Gefetod *accītus,* Cot. 7. Gefotad *accersitus,* Mk. Skt. Lind. 15, 44.

ge-fetrian; *p.* ode, ade, ede; *pp.* od, ad, ed *To fetter, bind;* compĕdīre, vincīre:—Ðone he gefetrade fȳrnum teágum *whom he fettered with fiery shackles,* Exon. 96 a; Th. 359, 9; Pa. 60. Drihten ða gefetredan alȳseþ *Dŏmĭnus solvit compĕdītos,* Ps. Th. 145, 7. v. ge-feterian.

ge-fettan. v. gefetian.

ge-fette, *pl.* -fetton *Fetched, brought,* Gen. 24, 11: Ors. 3, 10; Bos. 70, 30; *p. of* ge-fetian.

ge-fexode *having hair, haired,* Homl. Th. ii. 120, 19. v. ge-feaxode.

ge-fīa, -fiáge *to hate*:—Gefiáge *odisse,* Jn. Skt. Lind. 7, 7. Gefīeþ *odit,* 3, 20: 12, 20. Gefīweþ *odiet,* Lk. Skt. Lind. 16, 13. Gefīadon *oderant,* 19, 14. v. gefeógan.

ge-fic, es; *n. Fraud, deceit;* fraus:—Mid fǽcne gefice *with fraudulent deceit,* Elen. Kmbl. 1150; El. 577.

ge-fiht *a fight, battle,* Chr. 1128; Erl. 257, 1. v. ge-feoht.

ge-filce. v. gefylce.

ge-filde, es; *n. A field, plain;* campus:—Be norþan Capadocia is ðæt gefilde ðe man hǽt Temeseras *to the north of Cappadocia is the plain which is called Themiscyra,* Ors. 1, 1; Bos. 17, 7.

ge-fillan; *p.* -filde; *pp.* -filled, -fild *To fulfil, finish, complete;* implēre, complēre:—Ðū gefilst Godes hǽse and his bebodu *implēbis impĕrium Dei et præcepta ejus,* Ex. 18, 23. God gefilde on ðone seofeðan dæg his weorc *complēvit Deus die septĭmo ŏpus suum,* Gen. 2, 2: Deut. 31, 24. Gefild *fulfilled,* Chr. 605; Erl. 21, 27. v. ge-fyllan.

ge-findan; *p.* -fand, -fond, *pl.* -fundon; *pp.* -funden *To find;* invĕnīre:—His bān gefunden and gemēted wǽron *ossa ejus inventa sunt,* Bd. 3, 11; S. 535, 10: Chr. 963; Erl. 121, 36.

ge-findig; *adj. Finding, receiving, capable;* capax:—Numol oððe gefindig *capax,* Ælfc. Gr. 9, 60; Som. 13, 42.

ge-finegod; *part. p.* [fynegian *to become mouldy*] *Mouldy;* mūcĭdus:—Ðe nū sind gefinegode *which are now mouldy,* Jos. 9, 12.

ge-fioht, es; *n. A battle;* prælium:—Aulixes to ðam gefiohte fōr *Ulysses went to the battle,* Bt. 38, 1; Fox 194, 6. v. ge-feoht.

ge-firenian, -firnian; *p.* ode; *pp.* od *To sin;* peccāre:—We gefirenodon mid fæderum ūrum *peccāvĭmus cum patrĭbus nostris,* Ps. Spl. C. 105, 6. Ic gefirnode *I sinned,* St. And. 10, 19: Mt. Kmbl. Rush. 27, 4. v. gefyrenian.

ge-firn; *adv. Long ago,* Th. Apol. 19, 25. v. gefyrn.

ge-firnian. v. ge-firenian.

ge-fiðerhamod; *part. p. Provided with a covering of feathers*:—He wæs egeslīce gefiðerhamod *he was frightfully feather-clad,* Homl. Th. i. 466, 27. [Cf. Thorpe's North. Myth. i. 52.]

ge-fiðerian, -fiðerigan, -fiðrian, -fyðerian; *p.* ode, ade; *pp.* od, ad *To give wings to, provide with wings;* ālas addĕre, pennis instruĕre:—Ic sceal ǽrest ðīn mōd gefiðerian *I must first give wings to thy mind,* Bt. 36, 1; Fox 172, 31. Gefiðerigan, 36, 2; Fox 174, 6. Gefiðrade [MS. gefriðade] fugelas *vŏlātĭlia pennāta,* Ps. Th. 77, 27.

ge-flǽman; *p.* de; *pp.* ed *To cause to flee, put to flight*:—Ðū fiónd geflǽmdest *thou didst put to flight the enemy,* Hy. 8, 25; Hy. Grn. ii. 290, 25. v. ge-flȳman.

ge-flǽschamod; *part. p. Incarnate;* incarnātus:—Se wearþ geflǽschamod *who was incarnate,* Homl. Th. ii. 596, 32: i. 40, 24: 284, 22.

ge-flǽscnes, -ness, e; *f. Incarnation;* incarnātio:—Ǽr Cristes geflǽscnesse *before Christ's incarnation,* Chr. Erl. 4, 22.

ge-fleard, es; *n. A trifling, nonsense, madness*:—Gefleard *deliramentum,* Hpt. Gl. 416.

ge-flēman; *p.* de; *pp.* ed *To cause to flee, to rout*:—Hæfde ðā Drihten seolf feónd geflēmed *then the Lord himself had routed the foe,* Cd. 223; Th. 293, 30; Sat. 463: Chr. 938; Th. 204, 9, col. 1; Ædelst. 32. v. ge-flȳman.

ge-flēme; *adj. Fugitive;* fugitivus, Rtl. 147, 15.

ge-fleógan; *p.* -fleág, -fleáh, *pl.* -flugon; *pp.* -flogen *To fly, fly over;* volare, transvolare:—He hēht his heáhbodan hider gefleógan *he commanded his archangel to fly hither,* Exon. 12 a; Th. 19, 4; Cri. 295. Ne mæg ǽnig ðone mearcstede fugol gefleógan *nor may any bird fly over the boundary place,* Salm. Kmbl. 435; Sal. 218.

ge-fleón, -fleóhan; *p.* -fleáh, *pl.* -flugon *To flee, escape*:—Gefleá *fugere,* Mt. Kmbl. Lind. 3, 7. Se to ānre ðara burga gefliéhþ *who to one of those cities escapes,* Past. 21, 7; Swt. 167, 20; Hatt. MS. Geflēg *fugit,* Rtl. 147, 15. Alle geflugun *omnes fugerunt,* Mt. Kmbl. Lind. 26, 56. Ðætte giflēga *ut fugiant,* Rtl. 118, 31. Ǽr he on ða wēstenu middangeardes gefluge *antequam in desertas orbis terrarum abiret solitudines,* Nar. 6, 6.

ge-fleów *overflowed,* Ors. 1, 3; Bos. 27, 28; *p. of* ge-flōwan.

ge-fliéman; *p.* de; *pp.* ed *To cause to flee, to drive away;* fugare, Past. 61, 2; Hat. MS. v. ge-flȳman.

ge-flit *a fan to clean corn;* vannus, Cot. 33.

ge-flīt, -flȳt, es; *n. Contention, strife, contest, dispute, discussion;* contentio, lis, certāmen, concertātio, rixa:—Agoten is geflīt ofer ealderas *effūsa est contentio sŭper princĭpes,* Ps. Lamb. 107, 40: Bd. 1, 1; S. 473, 30. Ðis geflīt *hæc lis,* Ælfc. Gr. 9, 29; Som. 11, 62. Sume ic to geflȳte fremede *I have urged some to strife,* Exon. 72 b; Th. 271, 18; Jul. 484; Bd. 5, 6: S. 619, 4. On geflīt *in contest,* Beo. Th. 1734; B. 865. We on geflītum sǽton *we sat in discussion,* Salm. Kmbl. 862; Sal. 430: H. R. 9, 3. Uton towurpan hwætlīcor ðās geflītu *dissolvāmus cĭtius has contentiones,* Coll. Monast. Th. 31, 23: Elen. Kmbl. 884; El. 443: 1905; El. 954. Heó gehȳrde martyra geflītu *she heard of the struggle of martyrs,* Nar. 40, 13. To geflītes *emulously, eagerly,* Apol. Th. 10, 5.

ge-flīta. v. fyrn-geflīta.

ge-flītan, -flȳtan; *p.* -flāt, *pl.* -fliton; *pp.* -fliten *To strive, fight, dispute;* contendĕre, certāre:—Cynewulf and Offa gefliton ymb Benesingtūn *Cynewulf and Offa fought at Benson,* Chr. 777; Th. 93, 11, col. 1. Ne geflītes *non contendet,* Mt. Kmbl. Lind. 12, 19. Geflioton *disputaverant,* Mt. Skt. Lind. 9, 34. Geflītan [-flīta, Lind.] *contendere,* Mt. Kmbl. Rush. 5, 40.

ge-flītful; *adj. Contentious;* contentiōsus:—Geflītful *contentiōsus,* Ælfc. Gl. 85; Som. 74, 10; Wrt. Voc. 49, 33: 74, 31: Hpt. Gl. 502.

ge-flītfullīc; *adj. Contentious;* contentiōsus:—Wæs geflītfullīc senoþ æt Cealchȳþe *there was a contentious synod at Chalk,* Chr. 785; Erl. 56, 7.

ge-flītgeorn; *adj. Contentious;* contentiōsus, R. Ben. 71.

ge-flītlīce; *adv. Contentiously, emulously;* certātim:—Ðæt ge wēpned ge wīfmen geflītlīce dydon *quod vĭri et fēmĭnæ certātim făcĕre consuērunt,* Bd. 5, 7; S. 621, 15.

ge-flītmǽlum; *adv. Contentiously, emulously;* certātim, R. Ben. interl. 72.

ge-flota, an; *m. A floater, swimmer*:—Fyrnstreáma geflotan *to the ocean's floater [the whale],* Exon. 96 b; Th. 360, 17; Wal. 7. v. flota.

ge-flōwan; *p.* -fleów, *pl.* -fleówon; *pp.* -flōwen *To overflow;* inundāre:—Swā hit ðære eá flōd ǽr gefleów *as the flowing of the river formerly flowed over it,* Ors. 1, 3; Bos. 27, 28.

ge-flȳman, -flǽman, -flēman; *p.* de; *pp.* ed *To cause to flee, put to flight, drive away, banish;* fugare, in fugam vertere, expellere:—His ēhtendas ealle geflȳme *odientes eum in fugam convertam,* Ps. Th. 88, 20: Ors. 1, 10; Bos. 32, 25. Feónd wæs geflȳmed *the fiend was put to flight,* Exon. 34 b; Th. 110, 13; Gū. 107: Cd. 187; Th. 232, 17; Dan. 261. v. flȳman.

ge-flȳt, es; *n. Contention, strife, schism;* contentio, lis, schisma:—Geflȳt *schisma,* Ælfc. Gr. 9, 1; Som. 8, 23. v. ge-flīt.

ge-flȳtan; *p.* -flāt, *pl.* -flytor; *pp.* -flyten *To strive, fight;* contendĕre, certāre:—Cynewulf and Offa geflyton ymb Benesingtūn *Cynewulf and Offa fought at Benson,* Chr. 777; Erl. 55, 1. v. ge-flītan.

ge-fnæd, es; *n. A hem*:—Gif ic huru his reáfes gefnædu hreppe *if I only touch the hems of his garment*, Homl. Th. ii. 394, 10. v. fnæd.

ge-fnēsan *to sneeze*; sternūtāre:—Ðæt he gelōme gefnēse *that he often sneezes*, L. M. 2, 59; Lchdm. ii. 282, 27.

ge-fōg, es; *n. A joining, joint*:—Ðæt ðū gesomnige sīde weallas fæste gefōge *that thou unite the spacious walls with a fast juncture*, Exon. 8 a; Th. 1, 10; Cri. 6. From eallum heora gefōgum *from all their joints*, Blickl. Homl. 101, 4. [Cf. *Ger.* gefüge.] v. fōg.

ge-folc *people, a troop*. v. folc.

ge-fole; *adj. Having a foal, milch*:—Ðrītig gefolra olfend-myrena mid heora coltum *thirty milch camels* [*camelos fœtas*] *with their colts*, Gen. 32, 15.

ge-fōn, ic ge-fō; ðū ge-fēhst; he ge-fēhþ, *pl.* ge-fōþ; *imp.* ge-fōh; *p.* ge-fēng, *pl.* ge-fēngon; *pp.* ge-fangen *To take, seize, catch*; capere:—Ic sylle cync swā hwæt swā ic gefō *ego do regi quicquid capio*, Coll. Monast. Th. 22, 27. He gefēhþ ðæt ðæt he æfter spyreþ *he seizes that which he tracks*, Bt. 39, 1; Fox 212, 1. Ðū byst men gefōnde *homines eris capiens*, Lk. Bos. 5, 10. Ðonne ðū hīg gefangen hæbbe *quando tu illos cepisti*, Gen. 44, 4. Hū gefēhst ðū fixas? *quomodo capis pisces?* Coll. Monast. Th. 23, 7.

ge-fōr *died*, Ors. 6, 3; Bos. 126, 40; *p. of* ge-faran.

ge-forht *timid*. v. forht.

ge-forþian; *p.* -forþode; *pp.* forþod *To carry out, perform, accomplish, further, promote*:—His feónd ne mihten nā geforþian heora fare *his enemies could not carry out their expedition*, Chr. 1085; Erl. 218, 14. He hæfde geforþod ðæt he his freán gehēt *he had performed what he promised his lord*, Byrht. Th. 140, 16; By. 289: Hy. 9, 24; Hy. Grn. ii. 291, 24. He ðæt mynster wel geforþode ða hwīle ðe he ðǽr wæs *he advanced the monastery while he was there*, Chr. 1045; Erl. 171, 17. [*Laym.* i-forðed.] v. forþian.

ge-forwearþan *to perish*. v. forweorþan.

ge-fōrword; *part. Agreed upon, covenanted, bargained*; compactus:—Gif hit swā gefōrword biþ *if it be so agreed*, L. Edm. B. 4; Th. i. 254, 14: L. Eth. ii. 4; Th. i. 286, 19.

ge-fōtcypsed, -cypst; *part.* [cops *a fetter*] *Bound with fetters*; compĕdītus:—Infare on ðīnre gesihþe geómrung gefōtcypsedra *introeat in conspectu tuo gĕmĭtus compedĭtōrum*, Ps. Lamb. 78, 11: Ps. Spl. 101, 21. Drihten tolȳsþ gecospede odde ða gefōtcypstan *Dŏmĭnus solvit compĕdĭtos*, Ps. Lamb. 145, 8.

ge-frǽge, -frēge, es; *n. An inquiring, a knowing, knowledge, information, hearsay*; percontātio, cognĭtio, audītio:—Mīne gefrǽge *in my knowledge, as I have heard, as I am informed*, Beo. Th. 1557; B. 776: 1679; B. 837: Cd. 58; Th. 71, 20; Gen. 1173: 161; Th. 201, 7; Exod. 368: Chr. 975; Erl. 126, 10; Edg. 36.

ge-frǽge, -frēge; *adj. Known, renowned, celebrated, remarkable, noted, famous, notorious, infamous*; nōtus, mānĭfestus, celĕber, fāmōsus:—Hæbbe ic gefrugnen ðætte is eástdǽlum on æðelast londa, firum gefrǽge *I have heard tell that in eastern parts there is a land most noble, renowned among men*, Exon. 55 b; Th. 197, 22; Ph. 3: 44 b; Th. 151, 8; Gū. 792. Ic eom folcum gefrǽge *I am noted among people*, 130 b; Th. 500, 7; Rä. 89, 3: Beo. Th. 109; B. 55. Wæs ūre līf fracuþ and gefrǽge *our life was vile and infamous*, Exon. 53 a; Th. 186, 23; Az. 24: Cd. 189; Th. 235, 10; Dan. 304. Hæleðum gefrǽgost *most famous among men*, 162; Th. 202, 27; Dan. 394. [*O. Sax.* gi-frāgi: *Icel.* frægr.]

ge-frægen, -fregen [*part. p. of* gefragan [?]; cf. gefragian] *Heard of, known*:—Egsa māra, ðonne from frumgesceape gefrægen wurde ǽfre on eorðan *greater terror than was ever heard of on earth since the creation*, Exon. 20 a; Th. 52, 28; Cri. 840. Ðara ðe ic ofer foldan gefrægen hæbbe *of those that I have heard of on earth*, Exon. 85 a; Th. 319, 25; Vīd. 17: Beo. Th. 2397; B. 1196: Andr. Kmbl. 1374; An. 687: 2122; An. 1062. Gefregen, Exon. 53 b; Th. 188, 14; Az. 45. [Cf. *Icel.* freginn.] v. gefragian.

ge-frægnan, -fraignan, -fregnan, -frægnian; *p.* -frægn, -fraign, -frægnade, *pl.* -frugnon *To ask, inquire*:—Gifrægna *interrogare*, Jn. Skt. Lind. Gifregna, Rush. 21, 12. Gefraigne, Mk. Skt. Lind. 12, 34. Gefraign *interrogavit*, Lind. Gifrægn, Rush. 8, 5; 9, 16. Gefrægnade *interrogavit*, Lind. 15, 2. Gefraignade *sciscitabatur*, Mt. Kmbl. Lind. 2, 4. Gefrugnun *interrogaverunt*, 17, 10: Jn. Skt. Lind. 5, 12. Gefrugnon *interrogarent*, Jn. Skt. Lind. 1, 19. Gefraignaþ *interrogate*, Jn. Skt. Lind. 9, 21. Gefraignes *interrogate*, Mt. Kmbl. Lind. 10, 11: 2, 8. v. gefrignan.

ge-frǽgnian; *p.* ode; *pp.* od *To make famous*:—Gefrǽgnod, Beo. Th. 2670. [*Thorpe* gefrēfrod.]

ge-fræpi[g]an; *p.* ede. I. *to accuse*:—Gefræpgedon *accusarent*, Mt. Kmbl. Lind. 12, 10. II. *to reverence*:—Gefræppegedon *reverebuntur*, Mk. Skt. Lind. 12, 6.

ge-frætewian, -frætwian, -fretwian; *p.* ode, ade, ede; *pp.* od, ad, ed *To adorn, deck, trim*; ornāre, redimīre:—Ic gefrætwige *orno*, Ælfc. Gr. 24; Som. 25, 41. Ic gefretwige *redimio*, 30; Som. 34, 58. Ðē Cyning engla gefrætwode *the King of angels adorned thee*, Andr. Kmbl. 3034; An. 1520. He gefrætwade foldan sceátas *he adorned earth's regions*, Beo. Th. 192; B. 96. He æfter fæce mid ōðrum gāstlīcum mægenum gefrætewod ætȳwde *postmŏdum cætĕris virtūtibus ornātus appăruit*, Bd. 3, 5; S. 527, 44: 3, 11; S. 535, 32. Ðǽr is geat gylden, gimmum gefrætewod *there is a golden gate decked with gems*, Cd. 227; Th. 305, 20; Sat. 649: 220; Th. 283, 21; Sat. 308. Fiðrum gefrætwad *adorned with wings*, Elen. Kmbl. 1482; El. 743: Exon. 59 a; Th. 214, 14; Ph. 239. Fægre gefrætwed *neatly adorned*, 59 b; Th. 217, 2; Ph. 274: 64 a; Th. 237, 4; Ph. 585.

ge-frætwodnes *an ornament*. v. frætwednes, hrægel-gefrætwodnes.

ge-fragian; *p.* ade *To learn by asking*:—Gefragade *exquisierat*, Mt. Kmbl. Lind. 2, 16.

ge-frāsian; *p.* ade; *pp.* ad *To ask, inquire*; interrŏgāre, sciscĭtāri:—He gefrāsade þegnas his *interrŏgābat discĭpŭlos suos*, Mt. Kmbl. Lind. 16, 13. Geascade odde gefrāsade *sciscitābātur*, Mt. Kmbl. Lind. 2, 4.

ge-freán *to free*; liberare, Ps. Spl. C. 43, 29.

ge-frēcnod; *part.* [frēcne *savage, wicked*] *Savage, evil, wicked, corrupted*; atrox, scĕlestus:—Mōde gefrēcnod *corrupted in mind*, Cd. 181; Th. 227, 10; Dan. 184.

ge-frēdan, ic -frēde, ðū -frēdest, he -frēdeþ, frēt, *pl.* -frēdaþ; *p.* -frēdde; *pp.* -frēded *To feel, perceive, know, be sensible of*; sentīre:—Sió gefrēdnes hine mæg gegrāpian, and gefrēdan ðæt hit līchoma biþ, ac hió ne mæg gefrēdan hwæðer he biþ ðe blac ðe hwīt *the feeling may touch it, and feel that it is a body, but cannot feel whether it be black or white*, Bt. 41, 4; Fox 252, 10, 11. Ðeáh ðe we hit gefrēdan ne māgon *though we cannot perceive it*, Boutr. Scrd. 18, 44. Ic gefrēde *sentio*, Ælfc. Gr. 30; Som. 34, 39: 37; Som. 39, 8. Se līchama awent eorþan and anbīdaþ æristes, and on ðam fyrste nān þing ne gefrēt *the body turns to earth and awaits the resurrection, and in that space feels nothing*, Homl. Th. ii. 232, 25. Stānas ne gefrēdaþ *stones have not sense*, i. 302, 14, 18. Heó on hire gefrēdde ðæt heó of ðam wīte gehǽled wæs *sensit corpŏre quia sanāta esset a plāga*, Mk. Bos. 5, 29. He gefrēdde his deáþes neálǽcunge *he was sensible of his death's approach*, Homl. Th. i. 88, 8: 574, 16. Hī swurdes ecge ne gefrēddon *they felt not the sword's edge*, 544, 22. Ðæt he gefrēde *that he has sense*, 302, 21.

ge-frēdendlīc; *adj. Sensible, perceptible*; sensĭbĭlis:—Stemn is geslagen lyft, gefrēdendlīc on hlyste *the voice is struck air, perceptible to the hearing*, Ælfc. Gr. 1; Som. 2, 29.

ge-frēdmǽlum; *adv. Sensim, paulatim*, Hpt. Gl. 482.

ge-frēdnes, -ness, e; *f. A feeling, sense, perception*; sensus:—Gesiht, and gehērnes, and gefrēdnes ongitaþ ðone līchoman ðæs monnes *sight, and hearing, and feeling perceive the body of the man*, Bt. 41, 4; Fox 252, 7, 10.

ge-frēfran; *p.* ede; *pp.* ed *To comfort, console*; consolari:—Ðæt hīg hira fæder gefrēfredon *ut lenirent dolorem patris*, Gen. 37, 35. Heó nolde beón gefrēfred *noluit consolari*, Mt. Bos. 2, 18. Gefroefred, Mt. Kmbl. Lind. 5, 5. v. frēfran.

ge-frēfrian; *p.* ode; *pp.* od *To comfort, console*; consolari:—Ic gefrēfrige *consolor*, Ælfc. Gr. 25; Som. 26, 64. Nū ys ðes gefrēfrod *nunc hic consolatur*, Lk. Bos. 16. 25. v. frēfrian.

ge-frēge, es; *n. A knowing, knowledge, hearsay*; cognĭtio, audītio:—Mīne gefrēge *in my knowledge, as I have heard*, Andr. Kmbl. 3251; An. 1628: Apstls. Kmbl. 50; Ap. 25. v. ge-frǽge, es; *n.*

ge-frēge; *adj. Known, celebrated, famous*; nōtus, cĕlĕber, fāmōsus:—Lǽt ðē on gemyndum hū ðæt manegum wearþ fira gefrēge *keep in thy mind how that was known among many men*, Andr. Kmbl. 1921; An. 963: 2240; An. 1121. v. ge-frǽge; *adj.*

ge-fremednes, -ness, e; *f. An accomplishment, fulfilment, effect*; perfectio, effectus:—He hraðe ða gefremednesse ðære ārfestan bēne wæs fylgende *mox effectum piæ postulātiōnis consĕcūtus est*, Bd. 1, 4; S. 475, 31.

ge-fremian; *p.* ode; *pp.* od; *v. a. To finish, effect, bring to pass, accomplish, commit*; effĭcĕre, perfĭcĕre, patrāre, committĕre:—Se gefremode fēt [MS. fōt] mīne swā swā heortes *qui perfēcit pĕdes meos tanquam cervōrum*, Ps. Spl. 17, 35. Ðe he gefremode *quod patrārat*, Gen. 2, 2: Jos. 7, 17. Ic ne gemune nānra his synna ðe he gefremode *I will remember none of his sins which he has committed*, Homl. Th. ii. 602, 19. Forðan synd ðās wundru gefremode on him *ĭdeo virtūtes ŏpĕrantur in eo*, Mt. Bos. 14, 2. Ārleásnes ða scilde on me gefremode *impiety perpetrated that guilt against me*, Th. Apol. 2, 19.

ge-fremman; *p.* -fremede; *pp.* -fremed *To promote, perfect, perform, commit*:—Hie mihtan ǽghwæt gefremman *they could accomplish anything*, Blickl. Homl. 137, 1. Ðæt weorc to gefremmenne *to perform that work*, Homl. Th. ii. 122, 10. Ic hǽla gefremme *sanitates perficio*, Lk. Bos. 13, 32. Ðās ongunnenan ðing ðurh Godes fultum gefremmaþ *perform the things begun with God's help*, Homl. Th. ii. 128, 4. Swā hwæt swā he on mycclum gyltum gefremede *whatsoever he hath committed in great sins*, Blickl. Homl. 107, 14: 189, 22. Seó stihtung wæs gefremed *the arrangement was completed*, 81, 29. Hine mihtig God ofer ealle men forþ gefremede *him mighty God advanced above all men*, Beo. Th. 3440; B. 1718. Ðæt hire mægen on untrumnesse gefremed and getrymed wǽre *ut virtus ejus in infirmitate perficeretur*, Bd. 4, 23; S. 595, 16. Ðæt gefremede mān *the perpetrated crime*, Th. Apol. 2, 5. v. fremman.

ge-fremniss, e; *f. Effect;* effectus, Rtl. 16, 41: 41, 11.

ge-fremđian *to curse;* anathematizare, Mk. Skt. Lind. 14, 71.

ge-freógan, -freón; *p.* -freóde; *pp.* -freód *To free, make free:*—Đonne mōt hine se hlaford gefreógan *then must the lord free him*, L. In. 74; Th. i. 148, 18: L. Ælfc. C. 20; Th. i. 48, 25: Ps. Th. 93, 1. Gefreóde *freed*, Exon. 16 a; Th. 37, 4; Cri. 588. Gefreó us wiþ yfela *free us from evils*, Hy. 6, 31; Hy. Grn. ii. 286, 31. Gefreouad *liberatus*, Lk. Skt. Lind. 1, 74. v. freógan.

ge-freólsian; *p.* ode; *pp.* od *To liberate, deliver, set free:*—He wolde Adam gefreólsian *he would deliver Adam*, Blickl. Homl. 29, 20, 35. Ic đē gefreólsige of ealre frēcennesse *I will deliver thee from all danger*, 231, 3. Ūre Drihten us gefreólsode *our Lord delivered us*, 83, 25. Đurh Cristes sige ealle hālige wǣron gefreólsode *through Christ's victory all holy men were set free*, 31, 35.

ge-freođian; *p.* ode; *pp.* od *To protect, guard, free, keep:*—We wǣron gefreođode feónda gafoles *we were freed from devils' tribute*, Blickl. Homl. 105, 23. Se đe his ānum her feore gefreođade *he who here protected only his life*, Exon. 39 a; Th. 128, 32; Gū. 413. Gefreođa hyre *protect it* [*the soul*], Exon. 118 b; Th. 456, 3; Hy. Grn. ii. 284, 61. Gefreóde and gefreođade folc *freed and protected the people*, Exon. 16 a; Th. 37, 4; Cri. 588. Gefreođode, Andr. Kmbl. 2083; An. 1043. He lȳfde đæt friþ wiþ hȳ gefreođad wǣre *he allowed that peace should be kept towards them*, Exon. 38 b; Th. 127, 7; Gū. 382. Đæt lond Gode gefreođode *he kept that land for God*, 34 b; Th. 111, 7; Gū. 123. v. gefriđian.

gefrett *consumed;* devorāvit, Lk. Skt. Lind. 15, 30. v. fretan.

ge-fricgan, -fricgean; *p.* -fræg, *pl.* -frǣgon; *pp.* -frigen *To learn by asking* or *by inquiry, hear of:*—Syđđan hie gefricgeaþ freán ūserne ealdorleásne *when they learn that our lord is lifeless*, Beo. Th. 5996; B. 3002. Gif ic đæt gefricge *if I learn that*, 3656; B. 1826. Syđđan æđelingas feorran gefricgean fleám eówerne *after nobles from afar shall hear of your flight*, 5770; B. 2889. Đæt đæt folca fela gefrigen habbaþ *that which many peoples have heard of*, Cd. 190; Th. 236, 31; Dan. 329: Bt. Met. Fox 9, 54; Met. 9, 27. Đa đe snyttrocræft đurh fyrngewritu gefrigen hæfden *they who had learned wisdom through ancient writings*, Elen. Kmbl. 310; El. 155. We feor and neáh gefrigen habbaþ Moyses dōmas hæleđum secgan *we far and near have heard that Moses gave laws to men*, Cd. 143; Th. 177, 28; Exod. 1.

ge-frige, es; *n. Inquiry, knowledge resulting from inquiry:*—Gefreogum gleáwe *men wise from the knowledge obtained by their inquiries*, Exon. 56 a; Th. 199, 22; Ph. 29.

ge-frigian *to embrace*, Mk. Skt. Lind. 10, 16.

ge-frignan, -fringan; *p.* -frægn, -fregn, *pl.* -frugnon; *pp.* -frugnen. I. *to ask;* interrogare:—Đā Euan gefrægn ælmihtig God *then almighty God asked Eve*, Cd. 42; Th. 54, 34; Gen. 887. II. *to learn by asking, hear of:*—Đā gefrægn Higelāces đegn Grendles dǣda *when Hygelac's thane heard of Grendel's deeds*, Beo. Th. 390; B. 194: 1155; B. 595. Eác we đæt gefrugnon *also we have heard that*, Exon. 12 a; Th. 19, 15; Cri. 301: 100 a; Th. 378, 11; Deór. 14: Elen. Kmbl. 343; El. 172. Swā guman gefrungon *as men have heard*, Beo. Th. 1337; B. 666. Hæbbe ic gefrugnen *I have heard*, Exon. 55 b; Th. 197, 18; Ph. 1. Đā ic nēđan gefrægn hæleþ to hilde *then I heard that heroes went daringly to war*, Cd. 95; Th. 124, 9; Gen. 2060: 92; Th. 118, 4; Gen. 1960: Beo. Th. 148; B. 74: 4961; B. 2484. Gefregn, Cd. 224; Th. 298, 1; Sat. 526. Gefregen, 218; Th. 278, 21; Sat. 225. Ne gefrægen ic đa mǣgđe sēl gebæran *never have I heard of the tribe bearing itself better*, Beo. Th. 2026; B. 1011. [*O. Sax.* gifregnan.] v. ge-frægnan.

ge-frignys, -nyss, e; *f. Inquiry, questioning:*—Đis syndon andsware to geđeahtunge and to gefrignysse Sct. Augustinus *responsiones ad consulta Augustini*, Bd. 1, 27; S. 497, 44.

ge-frinan, ic -frine, đū -frinst, he -frinþ, *pl.* -frinaþ; *p.* -fran, *pl.* -frunon; *pp.* -frunen *To learn by asking, find out, hear of:*—Đā gefran Ioseph đæt Archelaus rixode on Iudea lande *then Joseph learned that Archelaus reigned in Judea*, Homl. Th. i. 88, 19. We đeódcyninga đrym gefrunon *we have heard of the glory of the great kings*, Beo. Th. 4; B. 2: Andr. Kmbl. 1; An. 1: Cd. 184; Th. 230, 19; Dan. 235. Me đǣr dryhtnes đegnas gefrunon *the Lord's servants found me there*, Rood Kmbl. 151; Kr. 76. Hie hæfdon gefrunen *they had learned*, Beo. Th. 1392; B. 694: 4797; B. 2403. v. ge-frignan.

ge-friólīc; *adj. Free;* liber, Rtl. 32, 9.

ge-friđian; *p.* ode; *pp.* od *To guard, protect, defend, deliver:*—He hie gefriđode *he protected her*, Judth. 9; Thw. 21, 3; Jud. 5: Bt. 39, 10; Fox 228, 11. Đæt hys yrþ sī gefriđod *that its produce be protected*, Th. An. 118, 20. He me gefriđode *eripuit me*, Ps. Th. 33, 4. Alȳs me and gefriđa me *libera me et eripe me*, 7, 1. Gefriđie *protegat*, 19, 1: Exod. 19, 4. v. ge-freođian.

ge-froefred *comforted;* consolatus, Mt. Kmbl. Lind. 5, 5, = ge-frēfred; *pp. of* ge-frēfran.

ge-frohtian *to be afraid;* expavescere, Mk. Skt. Lind. 16, 6. v. forhtian.

ge-froren *frozen.* v. freósan.

ge-frunon *asked, understood.* v. gefrinan.

ge-frygnys *a question.* v. gefrignys.

ge-frȳnd *friends:*—On đam dæge wurdun Herodes and Pilatus gefrȳnd *facti sunt amici Herodes et Pilatus in ipsa die*, Lk. Bos. 23, 12. v. freónd.

ge-fryþsum; *adj. Safe, fortified;* salvus, mūnītus:—On stōwe [MS. stōwum] gefryþsumre *in lŏcum mūnītum*, Ps. Spl. 70, 3. v. friþsum.

Gefđas, Gifđas, *pl. The Gepidæ:*—Mid Gefđum ic wæs *I was among the Gefths*, Exon. 85 b; Th. 322, 8; Vīd. 60. Gifđum, Beo. Th. 4981; B. 2494. v. Grm. Gesch. D. S. 324.

ge-fullan *to fill:*—Đū gefullest me of blisse mid andwlitan đīnum *adimplēbis me lætĭtia cum vultu tuo*, Ps. Spl. 15, 11. v. ge-fyllan.

ge-fullǣstan; *p.* -lǣste; *pp.* -lǣst *To help, give aid, assist;* auxĭliāri:—Weoruda God gefullǣste, đæt seó cwēn begeat willan in worulde *the Lord of Hosts gave aid, that the queen obtained her will in this world*, Elen. Kmbl. 2299; El. 1151.

ge-fullfremman *to perfect.* v. fulfremman.

ge-fullian; *p.* ode; *pp.* od *To become full, perfect:*—Gē geseóþ nū todæge mīnra gewinna wæstm gefullian *ye see now to-day the fruit of my toils come to perfection*, Blickl. Homl. 191, 23.

ge-fullian; *p.* ode; *pp.* od *To baptize;* baptizāre:—He gefullode đone sunu *he baptized the son*, Homl. Th. i. 352, 20. Gyt beóþ gefullode đam fulluhte, đe ic beó gefullod *baptismo, quo ego baptizor, baptizari*, Mk. Bos. 10, 39. Gefullod, Mt. Bos. 3, 14, 16: Mk. Bos. 1, 9: 10, 38, 39: 16, 16: Lk. 3, 21. v. fullian.

ge-fultuma, an; *m. A helper;* adjūtor:—Driht gefultuma mīn and alȳsend mīn *Dŏmĭne adjūtor meus et redemptor meus*, Ps. Spl. 18, 16.

ge-fultuman, -fultumian, -fultmian; *p.* ode, ede; *pp.* od, ed *To help, assist, help to, supply:*—Đæt hie sceoldan Martine gefultmian *that they should help St. Martin*, Blickl. Homl. 221, 31. Gefultumian *subministrare, concurrere, suppeditare*, Hpt. Gl. 446. Of đem ærfe đe me God forgef and mīne friónd to gefultemedan *of the inheritance that God gave me and my friends helped me to*, Th. An. 127, 21: 24. Būton him seó sōþe hreów gefultmige *unless true penitence succour them*, Blickl. Homl. 101, 8: 159, 34. Nymđe me drihten gefultumede *unless the Lord had helped me*, Ps. Th. 93, 16. Gefultuma me *adjuva me*, 69, 6. Đū gefultuma ūrum misdǣdum *impietatibus nostris tu propitiaberis*, 64, 3. He wæs godcundlīce gefultumad *divinitus adjutus*, Bd. 4, 24; S. 596, 41.

ge-fultumend, es; *m. A helper:*—Đū eart mīn alȳsend, and mīn gefultumend *liberator meus, adjutor meus*, Ps. Th. 17, 2.

ge-fulwian, -fulgwian; *p.* ode, ade; *pp.* od, ad *To baptize:*—Gefulwia *baptizari*, Mt. Kmbl. Lind. 3, 14. Gefulwas *baptizabit*, Mk. Skt. Lind. 1, 8. Se đe gefulguas *qui baptizat*, Jn. Skt. Lind. 1, 33. Hine man gefulwade *he was baptized*, Blickl. Homl. 219, 1. Gefulguade *baptizabat*, Jn. Skt. Lind. 3, 22. Gefulwad, Blickl. Homl. 213, 14: Elen. Kmbl. 2085; El. 1044. Gifulgwado *baptizati*, Rtl. 26, 9.

ge-funden *found*, Bd. 3, 11; S. 535, 10; *pp. of* ge-findan.

ge-fȳlan; *p.* ede; *pp.* ed; *v. a. To foul, defile, pollute;* inquinare, foedare, contaminare:—Đæt hī willaþ mid gegaf-sprǣcum Godes hūs gefȳlan *so that they will with idle speeches defile God's house*, L. Ælfc. C. 35; Th. ii. 356, note 2, line 22. Đæt man mid flǣsc-mete hine sylfne gefȳle *that any one should defile himself with flesh-meat*, L. C. S. 47; Th. i. 402, 24, note 57.

ge-fylce, -filce, es; *n. A collection of people, army, troop, division:*—Đa Wylisce menn gewinn up ahōfon and syđđan heora gefylce weóx hī hī on mā todǣldon *the Welshmen raised war . . . and after their number had increased they separated into more* [*bands*], Chr. 1094; Erl. 230, 36. Hī fērdon mid miclum gefilce *they marched with a great army*, Thw. Hept. 162, 38. Send đærto gefylcio *send troops against it*, Past. 21, 5; Swt. 161, 6; Hatt. MS. Hie wǣrun on twǣm gefylcum *they were in two divisions*, Chr. 871; Erl. 74, 16, 30: Nar. 19, 22. v. fylc.

ge-fylced *collected as an army.* v. fylcian.

ge-fylgan; *p.* -fylgde; *pp.* -fylged *To follow, attend upon, reach by following:*—Đæt him gefylgan ne mæg drȳmendra gedryht *so that the flock of rejoicing ones cannot follow him*, Exon. 60 b; Th. 222, 12; Ph. 347. Gif gē đisum leáse leng gefylgaþ *if ye pursue this falsehood longer*, Elen. Kmbl. 1149; El. 576. Đa ilco gefylgdon him *illi secuti sunt eum*, Mt. Kmbl. Lind. 4, 20. Gefylgend wæs ł gefylgede *sequebantur*, Jn. Skt. Lind. 18, 15. Gifylge *assequi*, Rtl. 4, 20. Đætte eestes gefe we gifylga *ut resurrectionis gratiam consequamur*, 23, 40.

ge-fyllan; *p.* -fylde; *pp.* -fylled *To fell, cut down, cast down, destroy, deprive of;* cædere, destruere:—Đā wolde he đæt gyld gefyllan *then he determined to cast down the idol*, Blickl. Homl. 221, 21, 32: Beo. Th. 5303; B. 2655. He gefylde đone ealdan feónd *he cast down the old fiend*, Blickl. Homl. 87, 19: 221, 2, 4, 33. Freónda gefylled *deprived of friends*, Chr. 937; Erl. 114. 7; Ædelst. 41. Seó nædre gefylled wæs *the serpent was destroyed*, Ors. 4, 6; Bos. 84, 45.

ge-fyllan; *p.* ede, de; *pp.* ed; *v. a. To fill, fulfil, make a total, complete, finish, accomplish, satisfy;* implere, saturare:—Đus unc gedafenaþ ealle rihtwisnisse gefyllan, Mt. 3, 15. We sceolon đone geleáfan mid gōdum dǣdum gefyllan *we must complete the belief with good deeds*,

Blickl. Homl. 23, 10. Hí ne mâgon ealle đíne bletsunge gefyllan *they do not complete the sum of all thy blessings*, 157, 20. Ealle stówa he gefylleþ *he fills all places*, 23, 20. Míne geornnesse mid góde đú gefyldest *thou didst satisfy my longing with good*, 89, 5. He him gehêt his æriste swâ he mid sóđe gefylde *he promised them his resurrection as he truly performed*, 17, 4. Hí heofon-hláfe hálige gefylde *pane cæli saturavit eos*, Ps. Th. 104, 35. Đú gefyldest foldan and rodoras wuldres đínes *thou hast filled earth and skies with thy glory*, Exon. 13 b; Th. 25, 29; Cri. 408. Ôđ đæt đú gefylle đíne đegnunge *until thou fulfil thy business*, Blickl. Homl. 233, 28, 12: Guthl. 5; Gdwn. 40, 25. On hire wæs gefylled đætte on Cantica Canticorum wæs gesungen *in her was fulfilled what was sung in the Song of Songs*, Blickl. Homl. 11, 15: 13, 26. Gefylde, 15, 8. Æfter đon đe đa mæssan wǽron gefyllede *after the masses were finished*, 207, 29: Lk. Bos. 4, 13. Đæt hús wæs gefylled of đære sealfe swæces *domus impleta est ex odore ungenti*, Jn. Bos. 12, 3. Gifena gefylled fremum forđweardum *filled with gifts with continual benefits*, Cd. 11; Th. 13, 28; Gen. 209. Gefylled *consumtus, finitus*, Hpt. Gl. 457. Wel gefylde *bene pastos*, Th. An. 20, 31.

ge-fylledness, -ness, -nys, -nyss, e; *f. A fulness, satiety, completion, finishing, end*; plēnĭtūdo, sătŭrĭtas, consummātio:—Astyrod biþ sǽ and gefyllednys hyre *commŏveātur, măre et plēnĭtūdo ejus*, Ps. Spl. 95, 11: 97, 7. Cherubin is gereht gefyllednyss ingehydes *cherubin is interpreted the fulness of the mind*, Boutr. Scrd. 20, 33. On graman gefyllednysse *in īra consummātĭōnis*, Ps. Spl. C. 58, 15. Of his gefyllednesse we ealle onfêngon *de plēnĭtūdĭne ejus nos omnes accēpĭmus*, Jn. Bos. 1, 16. He asende gefyllednysse on sâwlum heora *mīsit sătŭrĭtātem in anĭmas eōrum*, Ps. Spl. 105, 15. Ôþ đissere worulde gefyllednysse *until the end of the world*, Homl. Th. i. 600, 18.

ge-fyllendlíc; *adj. Filling*; explētīvus, complētīvus:—Sume syndon gehâtene *explētīvæ* ođđe *complētīvæ*, đæt synd gefyllendlíce *some are called* explētīvæ *or* complētīvæ, *that is filling*, Ælfc. Gr. 44; Som. 45, 57.

ge-fylnes, -ness, e; *f. Fulness, fulfilment, performance, completion*:—On gefylnesse Godes beboda *in the performance of God's commands*, Blickl. Homl. 29, 9. For gefyllnesse đæs heofonlícan eđles *for the perfection of the heavenly country*, 81, 29. Đe hie swâ mycle gefylnesse hæfdon *of which they had so great fulness*, 135, 24. Gifylnisse *plenitudinis*, Rtl. 83, 18.

ge-fylst *help*. v. fylst.

ge-fylsta, an; *m. A helper, an assistant*; adjūtor:—God mín gefylstâ is *Deus meus adjūtor est*, Ps. Spl. 17, 2: 27, 9. He him to gefylstan gesette *he appointed him his assistant*, Homl. Th. ii. 120, 13: Job Thw. 166, 39.

ge-fylstan; ic -fylste; *subj. pres.* -fylste; *p.* [-fylstede], -fylste, *pl.* -fylston; *pp.* -fylsted *To help, give help*; adjuvare:—Đæt heó him gefylste *that she might assist them*, Ors. 3, 11; Bos. 73, 45. God gefylsteþ me *Deus adjuvat me*, Ps. Spl. 53, 4. Driht, to gefylstane me efste *Domine, ad adjuvandum me festina*, 69, 1. DER fylstan.

ge-fýnd *foes, enemies*:—Híg wǽron ǽr gefýnd him betwynan *antea inimici erant adinvicem*, Lk. Bos. 23, 12. v. feond.

ge-fyndig; *adj. Capable*; capax, Ælf. gr. 9, 60. v. gefindig.

ge-fyrenian, -fyrnian; *p.* ode, ede; *pp.* od, ed *To sin*; peccāre:—Ic gefyrenode *I have sinned*, Blickl. Homl. 235, 32, 34. We gefyrnedan mid úrum fæderum *peccāvĭmus cum patrĭbus nostris*, Ps. Th. 105, 6. v. ge-firenian.

ge-fyrht, ge-fyrhted; *part. p. Terrified, affrighted*:—Đâ wæs se dêma swýđe gedrêfed and gefyrhted *then was the judge very much troubled and frightened*, Bd. 1, 7; S. 478, 44. Hie wǽron to đæs swýđe gefyrhte *they were so greatly terrified*, Blickl. Homl. 221, 34. [Cf. fyrhtan, gefyrhtian.]

ge-fyrhtian; *p.* ade; *pp.* ad *To frighten*:—Wífo sume gefyrhtadon úsig *mulieres quædam terruerunt nos*, Lk. Skt. Lind. 24, 22. Miþ fyrhto gefyrhtad *timore exterriti*, Mk. Skt. Lind. 9, 6.

ge-fyrhto; *p. Fear, doubt*:—Be đære cennendre gefyrhtum đæs bearnes weorđe ongyten wǽre *by the mother's fears the child's worth might be understood*, Blickl. Homl. 163, 27.

ge-fyrn; *adv.* [fyrn *formerly*] *Formerly, long ago, of old, of yore*; olim, pridem:—Hú ne wǽran đâs gefyrn forþgewitene *were not these long ago departed?* Bt. 19; Fox 70, 9. Đú mid Fæder đínne gefyrn wǽre efenwesende *thou with thy father of old was co-existent*, Exon. 12 b; Th. 22, 10; Cri. 349: 12 a; Th. 19, 16; Cri. 301. Gefyrn hí dydun dǽdbôte on hǽran and on axan *olim cĭlĭcio et cĭnĕre pænĭtentiam egissent*, Mt. Bos. 11, 21: Lk. Bos. 10, 13: Ælfc. Gr. 38; Som. 39, 57. Gefyrn *pridem*, 38; Som. 39, 56. Gefyrn ǽr *formerly*, Bt. 33, 3; Fox 126, 30: 37, 1; Fox 186, 25: Chr. 892; Erl. 89, 1.

ge-fyrþran; *p.* ede; *pp.* ed *To further, advance, promote, improve*; promovere, prosperare:—Heora síþfæt wæs fram Drihtne sylfum gefyrþred [MS. gefyrþrad], *their journey was furthered by the Lord himself*, Bd. 4, 19; S. 588, 34. Wæs eftsíđes georn, frætwum gefyrþred *was desirous of return, furthered by the treasures*, Beo. Th. 5561; B. 2784. Ânrǽd oretta elne gefyrþred *the steadfast champion advanced with valour*, Andr. Kmbl. 1966; An. 985. Ic đê gefyrþrede *I improved thee*, Bt. 8; Fox 24, 29. DER. fyrþran.

ge-fýsan; *p.* -fýsde; *pp.* -fýsed *To make ready, cause to hasten*:—Werod wæs gefýsed *the band was made ready*, Cd. 154; Th. 191, 28; Exod. 221. Gefýsed to fæder ríce *ready to depart to his father's kingdom*, Exon. 14 b; Th. 30, 5; Cri. 475. Winde gefýsed *hurried on by the wind*, Beo. Th. 440; B. 217. Secgas wǽron síđes gefýsde *the men were ready for the journey* [cf. síđes fús, B. 1475], Elen. Kmbl. 520; El. 260. v. fýsan.

ge-fystlian; *pp.* -lad *To beat with the fists, buffet*; pugnis impetere, Scint. 2.

ge-fyđerian; *p.* ode, ade, ede; *pp.* od, ad, ed *To feather, give wings to, provide with wings*; ālas addĕre, pennis instruĕre:—Gefyđerad flaa *săgitta* vel *spĭcŭlum*, Ælfc. Gl. 53; Som. 66, 64; Wrt. Voc. 35, 50. Fugelas gefyđerede *vŏlātĭlia pennāta*, Ps. Spl. 77, 31. v. ge-fiđerian.

ge-gada, an; *A fellow-traveller, a companion, associate*; comes, complex, conspirans, Ælfc. Gl. 86; Som. 74, 27, 28. He feóll đâ adún and ealle his gegadan into helle wíte *he fell down then and all his companions into hell torment*, Swt. A. S. Rdr. 59, 93, 87. Afeóll se deófoll mid his gegadum *the devil fell with his companions*, Hexam. 10; Norm. 16, 18. v. gædeling.

ge-gaderian; *p.* ode; *pp.* od *To gather, unite*; colligere, conjungere:—Se fela folca fæste gegadraþ *he unites many people*, Bt. Met. Fox 11, 180; Met. 11, 90. Gegaderade *conjuncti*, Ps. Th. 67, 24: Chr. 973; Th. 224, 32. v. gadorian, ge-gæderian.

ge-gaderscype, -gæderscype, es; *m. A joining, union, matrimony*; jugalitas, Hpt. Gl. 411, 416.

ge-gaderung, e; *f. A gathering, congregation, assembly, crowd*; congregatio, turba:—Se Hǽlend beáh fram đære gegaderunge *Iesus declinavit a turba*, Jn. Bos. 5, 13: Ps. Spl. 39, 14; Ælfc. Gl. 87; Som. 74, 47. Gegaderung líchoman *copula carnis*, Bd. 1, 27; S. 495, 30. Gegaderung *congregatio*, Th. An. 30, 7. Rihtwísra manna gegaderung is gecweden heofenan ríce *a gathering of righteous men is called the kingdom of heaven*, Homl. Th. ii. 72, 25. v. gaderung.

ge-gador-wist, e; *f. An assembly for feasting*; contubernium, Ælfc. Gl. 93; Som. 75, 87. v. gador-wist.

ge-gæde *a collection, congregation*; congregatio, R. Ben. interl. 2. v. gæd.

ge-gæderian, -gaderian; *p.* ode, ade; *pp.* od, ad *To gather, join*; colligere, congregare:—Searwum gegædraþ bân gebrosnad *he gathers skilfully the perished bones*, Exon. 59 b; Th. 216, 17; Ph. 269. Beóþ gegædrad gǽst and bân-sele *soul and body shall be joined*, 117 b; Th. 451, 11; Dôm. 102. Wyt beóþ gegæderode *we two shall be gathered*, 100 a; Th. 376, 23; Seel. 159. Đam biþ gæst gegæderad Godes þearn *God's child will be a guest associated with him*, 84 b; Th. 318, 9; Môd. 80. v. gæderian, gegaderian.

ge-gælen, -galen, *enchanted*, Ps. Spl. 57, 5. v. galan.

ge-gæncg, es; *m. A society, meeting, an assembly*; cœtus:—Đe wæs on đam gegæncge đâr man Crist bænde *who was in the company where Christ was bound*, Ælf. ep. 1st, 50; Th. ii. 386, 23.

ge-gærwan *to prepare*. v. gegerwan.

ge-gaf; *adj. Base, wanton, lewd*:—He wæs gegaf spræce *he was wanton in talk*, Homl. Th. i. 534, 2. [*Or* gegaf-spræce; *adj.* (?).]

ge-gafelian; *p.* ode; *pp.* od *To impose a fine, proscribe*, Hpt. Gl. 517.

ge-gafelod *confiscated*; infiscatus, Cot. 108, 194. v. gegafelian.

ge-gaf-sprǽc, e; *f. Idle, wanton, scoffing speech*:—Đâ wæs seó tunge teartlícor gewítnod for his gegafspræce *then was the tongue more sharply punished for his wanton speech*, Homl. Th. i. 330, 34. Men willaþ bysmorlíce plegian and mid gegafspræcum Godes hús gefýlan *men will play shamefully and defile God's house with wanton speeches*, L. Ælfc. C. 35; Th. ii. 357 note, 3. v. gaf.

ge-gân; *p.* -eóde, -ióde; *pp.* -gân. I. *to go, go or pass over, come to pass, happen*; ire, præterire, evenire:—Heó mihte gegân ofer eall đis eálond *vellet totam perambulare insulam*, Bd. 2, 16; S. 520, 2. Se đe gryre-síþas gegân dorste *who durst go ways of terror*, Beo. Th. 2929; B. 1462. Swâ geostran-dæg gegân wǽre *sicut dies hesterna quæ præteriit*, Ps. Th. 89, 4. Hú đæt geeóde, đæt . . . *how that came to pass, that . . .*, Exon. 14 a; Th. 28, 7; Cri. 443. Eall đâs wundor geeódon in ussera tída tíman *all these wonders happened in the period of our times*, 43 b; Th. 147, 11; Gú. 725. II. *to occupy, overcome, overrun, subdue*; occupare, vincere, subigere:—Đæt đú hâm on us [hus MS.] gegân wille *that thou wilt occupy a home with us*, Exon. 36 b; Th. 118, 21; Gú. 243. Eádmund cyning Myrce geeóde *king Edmund subdued Mercia*, Chr. 942; Th. 208, 33; Edm. 2: Bd. 1, 2; S. 475, 4: 2, 5; S. 506, 20: Ors. 3, 7; Bos. 58, 39: 3, 9; Bos. 65, 44. Ne geeódon úre foregengan nâ đas eorđan mid sweorda ecgum *non enim in gladio suo possidebunt terram*, Ps. Th. 43, 4. Seo burh wæs gegân *civitas capta erat*, Jos. 8, 21. III. *to observe, practise, exercise, effect, accomplish*; observare, exercere, perficere, efficere:—Gif gê đæt tâcen gegâþ *if ye observe that sign*, Cd. 106; Th. 140, 8; Gen. 2324. Đæt se hálga þeów elne geeóde *which the holy minister* *zealously practised*, Exon. 34 b; Th. 111, 19; Gû. 129: Ps. Th. 118, 40. Hie elne geeódon *they effected by strength*, Beo. Th. 5826; B. 2917. IV. used with an adjective [cf. such an expression as 'to go lame'] :—He wæs wêrig gegân *fatigatus ex itinere*, Jn. Bos. 4, 6.

ge-gang *an event, a fate*. v. gegong.

ge-gangan, -gongan; *pp.* -gangen, -gongen. I. *to go, happen, take place, befal, to fall to one's share, to come in*; ire, evenire, accidere :—Ne mâgon hî ofer gemǣre mâre gegangan *non transgredientur terminum*, Ps. Th. 103, 9. Ful oft đæt gegongeþ *full oft it happens*, Exon. 87 a; Th. 327, 9; Vy. 1: 117 a; Th. 451, 3; Dôm. 98. Đâ wæs gegongen gumum unfrôdum, đæt . . . *then it had befallen the youthful man, that* . . . , Beo. Th. 5634; B. 2821. Ealles đæs andlyfenes đe him gegonge *of all the livelihood which comes in to them*, Bd. 1, 27; S. 489, 6. II. *to exercise, effect, accomplish*; exercere, perficere, efficere :—Ic đîne bebodu bealde gegange *exercebor in mandatis tuis*, Ps. Th. 118, 78. He hæfde elne gegongen, đæt . . . *he had effected by his valour, that* . . . , Beo. Th. 1791; B. 893. III. *to go against with hostile intention, to pass over, overcome, subdue, conquer, obtain, acquire*; aggredi, transgredi, superare, subigere, oblinere, adipisci, possidere :—Gif frîman edor gegangeþ *if a freeman pass over a fence*, L. Ethb. 29; Th. i. 10, 3. Hî þohton Italia ealle gegongan *they thought to conquer all Italy*, Bt. Met. Fox 1, 24; Met. 1, 12. Ic mid elne sceal gold gegangan *I shall with valour obtain the gold*, Beo. Th. 5065; B. 2036: 6162; B. 3085: Ps. Th. 78, 12. v. gân.

ge-geafian; *p.* ede, ode; *pp.* ed, od *To bestow gifts upon* :—Ic hine mid deórweorđum gyfum gegeafede *dignis eum muneribus honoravi*, Nar. 8, 16. Gigeafiga *præstolari* [= *præstare?*], Rtl. 20, 15. v. gegifod.

ge-gealt = ge-healt, Deut. 7. 12. v. gehealdan.

ge-gearcian; *p.* ode; *pp.* od *To prepare* :—Đâ hêt se cyngc scipa gegearcian and him æfter faran, ac hit wæs lang ǣr đam þe đa scipa gegearcode wǣron *then the king bade prepare ships and go after him, but it was long before the ships were ready*, Th. Ap. 7, 16-7: Homl. Th. ii. 84, 16. v. gearcian.

ge-gearcung-dæg, es; *m. Preparation-day*; parasceve = παρασκευή :—Hit wæs eástra gegearcung-dæg *erat parasceve Paschæ ἦν παρασκευὴ τοῦ πάσχα*, Jn. Bos. 19, 14, 31. v. gearcung.

ge-gearnian, Blickl. Homl. 35, 36. v. ge-earnian.

ge-gearwian, -gearwigean; *p.* ode, ede; *pp.* od, ad *To prepare, make ready, provide with, endue* :—Đa lâreowas sceolan Drihtnes weg gegearwian to heora môdum *the teachers ought to prepare the Lord's way for their minds*, Blickl. Homl. 81, 7. Gegearwigean, Cd. 23; Th. 29, 30; Gen. 458. Đa âne đe mid clǣnum geleáfan hie to đæm gegearwiaþ *those only who with pure belief prepare themselves for it*, Blickl. Homl. 185, 10. Gegearwode he đǣm êce forwyrde *he prepared for them eternal perdition*, 159, 19: 233, 33. Gegearewadest, Ps. Th. 64, 10. Gegearwiga we *paremus*, Mk. Skt. Lind. 14, 12. Đâ wearþ werod gegearewod to campe *then was the band made ready for battle*, Judth. 11; Thw. 24, 21; Jud. 199. Đæt his lîf đæm his naman wæs gelîce gegearwod *his life was ordered like to his name*, Blickl. Homl. 167, 32. Gâste gegearwod *endued with spirit*, Cd. 10; Th. 12, 17; Gen. 187: Elen. Kmbl. 1774; El. 889. v. gearwian.

ge-gearwung, e; *f. A preparation*; præparatio :—Gegearwung setles đînes *præparatio sedis tuæ*, Ps. Spl. 88, 14. v. gearwung.

ge-gearwungness, e; *f. A preparation*; præparātio :—Gearcunga ođđe gegearwungnessa heortan gehŷrde *præparātio cordis audīvit*, Ps. Lamb. second 9, 17.

ge-gegnian; *p.* ode, ade; *pp.* od, ad *To meet*; obviare, Rtl. 45, 23.

ge-gêman; *p.* de; *pp.* ed *To heal, cure, amend, treat* [*as a patient*] :—Đæt hea gegême all unhǣlo *ut curarent omnem languorem*, Mt. Kmbl. Lind. 10, 1: Mk. Skt. Lind. 3, 2. Gegêmde ł gehǣlde *curavit*, 6, 5. Gegêma *corrigere*, Mt. Kmbl. p. 1. 9. Gegêmed, L. Ǣđelb. 62; Th. i. 18, 8. [See the note, and also Schmid, p. 8, note.]

ge-geótan; *p.* -geát; *pp.* -goten *To found, cast* :—He of golde geseát and geworhte *he cast and wrought them of gold*, Nar. 19, 29. Đa gelîcnessa wǣron gegotene *the images were cast*, 32.

ge-gerela, -gyrela, -girla, an; *m. Clothing, apparel, habit, garment, robe*; amiculum, stola :—Hwǣr agylte he ǣfre on his gegerelan *where trespassed he ever in his clothing?* Blickl. Homl. 169, 1. His gegirla hine geswutelaþ *his garment betrays him*, Th. Ap. 14, 3: 12, 8. Bringaþ rađe đæne sêlestan gegyrelan, Lk. Bos. 15, 22: Mk. Bos. 12, 38.

ge-gerelad, -gerlad; *part. Clothed*; indutus :—Gegerlad is Drihten mid stræncþe *indutus est Dominus fortitudinem*, Ps. Lamb. 92, 1. Gegerelad *vestitus*, Mk. Skt. Lind. 1, 6.

ge-gerwan, -gærwan, -girwan, -gierwan, -gyrwan; *p.* -gerede; *pp.* -gered, -gerwed *To prepare, make ready, clothe, array, adorn, furnish* :—Ne hŷrde ic cymlîcor ceól gegyrwan hilde wǣpnum *I never heard of furnishing a comelier vessel with weapons of war*, Beo. Th. 76; 13, 38. Đǣr đû scealt âd gegærwan *there shalt thou prepare a pile*, Cd. 138; Th. 173, 3; Gen. 2855. Ic his sacerdas mid hǣlu gegyrwe *sacerdotes ejus induam salutare*, Ps. Th. 131, 17. Heó alegde hire hrægl đe heó mid gegyred wæs and hie gegyrede mid đon sêlestan hrægle *she laid aside the garment that she was clothed with, and arrayed herself with the finest garment*, Blickl. Homl. 139, 6, 7: 89, 35: 103, 3. Đǣr weofod inne wlitelîce geworhtan and gegyredon *therein they wrought and adorned an altar beautifully*, 205, 6: Beo. Th. 6265; B. 3137. Gegyre đû hine *clothe him*, Blickl. Homl. 37, 21. Mid heora geatwum gegyrede *equipped*, 221, 29: Nar. 4, 13. Golde gegyrwed *adorned with gold*, Beo. Th. 1110; B. 553. Ymb frætwum ûtan gegyrede *circumornatæ*, Ps. 143, 15. Sió wæs orđoncum eall gegyrwed diófles cræftum *it was all cunningly prepared with devilish arts*, Beo. Th. 4181; B. 2087. Heardum tôþum and miclum hit wæs gegyred *duris munitum dentibus*, Nar. 21, 1.

ge-gifod; *part. Enriched with gifts* :—Se cyng him wel gegifod hæfde on golde and on seolfre *the king had bestowed many gifts of gold and silver on him*, Chr. 1001; Erl. 136, 17. v. gegeafian.

ge-gild, ge-gyld, es; *n. A guild, society, or club*; societas, fraternitas :—We for his lufon đis gegyld gegaderodon *for love of him we have gathered this guild*, Th. Diplm. 608, 7. v. gild.

ge-gilda, -gylda, an; *m. A person who belongs to a guild, club, or corporation, a guild-brother, a companion, fellow* [v. Kmbl. Sax. Eng. i. 262, 259]; congildo, socius, sodalis :—Gieldan đa gegildan healfne *let his guild-brethren pay half*, L. Alf. pol. 27; Th. i. 78, 24: 28; Th. i. 80, 3: L. In. 16; Th. i. 112, 8: 21; Th. i. 116, 6: L. Ath. v. § 8, 6; Th. i. 236, 36: Hick. Thes. ii. Dis. Epist. pp. 20-21. v. gild; and Schmid, s. v.

ge-gild-heall, e; *f. A guild-hall* :—Orc hæfþ gegyfen đæ gegyldhealle đam gyldscipe to âgenne *Orc hath given the guild-hall for the guild to own*, Kmbl. Cod. Dipl. iv. 277, 21.

ge-giwian; *p.* ade, ode; *pp.* ad, od *To demand, ask*; postulare, petere :—Swǣ hwæt đû gegiuas *quidquid petieris*, Mk. Skt. Lind. 6. 23. Gegiwade *postulans*, Lk. Skt. Lind. 1, 63.

ge-gladian; *p.* ode; *pp.* od *To make glad, gladden, appease*; lætĭfĭcāre, exhĭlărāre, plācāre :—Flódes ryne gegladaþ burg Godes *flūmĭnis impĕtus lætĭfĭcat cīvĭtātem Dei*, Ps. Lamb. 45, 5; Homl. Th. i. 288, 8. Cûþbertus hit mid cossum gegladode *Cuthbert gladdened it with kisses*, ii. 134, 21. Đæt he gegladie ansêne on ele *ut exhĭlăret făciem in ŏleo*, 103, 15. Đæt he đê mid his lâcum gegladige *that he appease thee with his gifts*, Gen. 32, 20. Gegladan *mitigare, repropitiare*, Hpt. Gl. 515.

ge-glêded; *part.* [glêd *a burning coal*] *Kindled*; accensus :—Wæs geglêded fŷr on Iacobe *ignis accensus est in Iacob*, Ps. Th. 77, 23.

ge-glendrian; *p.* ade, ode; *pp.* ad, od *To precipitate* :—Đætte hia geglendradon hine *ut præcipitarent eum*, Lk. Skt. Lind. 4, 29.

ge-glengan, -glencan, -glæncan, -glencgan, -glengcan; *p.* -glengde, -glencde; *pp.* -glenged, -glencged, -glengd, -glend *To adorn, embellish, set in order, compose*; ornāre, cōmĕre, compōnĕre :—Gê preóstas sculon eówerne hâd healdan ârwurþlîce, and mid gôdum þeáwum symle geglæncan *ye priests should religiously observe your order, and always adorn it with good habits*, L. Ælf. P. 5; Th. ii. 366, 2. Ic geglenge *cōmo*, Ælfc. Gr. 28, 4; Som. 31, 13. Ic smicere geglencge *orno*, Ælfc. Gl. 99; Som. 76, 116; Wrt. Voc. 54, 58. Nerôn hine mid ǣlces cynnes gimmum geglengde *Nero adorned himself with gems of every kind*, Bt. 28; Fox 100, 27: Bt. Met. Fox 15, 7; Met. 15, 4. Đæt he æfter medmiclum fæce in sceópgereorde mid đa mǣstan swêtnesse and inbrydnesse geglencde, and in Englisc gereorde wel gehwǣr forþbrohte *hoc ipse post pūsillum verbis poētĭcis maxĭma suāvĭtāte et compunctiōne compŏsĭtis, in sua, id est, Anglōrum lingua proferret*, Bd. 4, 24; S. 596, 35. Đæt hit wǣre geglenged mid gôdum stânum and gôdum gifum *quod bŏnis lăpĭdĭbus et dōnis ornātum esset*, Lk. Bos. 21, 5: Elen. Kmbl. 179; El. 90. Geglenged *discrīmĭnātus*, Ælfc. Gl. 61; Som. 68, 48; Wrt. Voc. 39, 32. Godes gelađung is geglencged mid deórwurþre frætewunge *God's church is adorned with precious ornament*, Homl. Th. ii. 586, 17. Heó wæs geglengd þurh Godes wundra *it was embellished by the miracles of God*, Th. Diplm. A. D. 970; 241, 6. Đa bióþ sweordum and fetelum swîđe geglende *who are greatly adorned with swords and belts*, Bt. Met. Fox 25, 20; Met. 25, 10.

ge-glengendlîc; *adj. Splendid, brilliant*; pomposus, delicatus, Hpt. Gl. 435.

geglesc *light, frolicsome, lascivious*, Bd. 5, 6; Whelc. 390, 39, MS. B. v. geaglisc.

ge-glîdan; *p.* -glâd, *pl.* -glidon; *pp.* -gliden *To glide, fall*; labi :—Đâ he sceolde into geglîdan Nergendes nîþ *when he must fall into the Saviour's hate*, Cd. 221; Th. 288, 6; Sat. 376. v. glîdan.

gegn, geagn, geán, gên; *adv. Again*; contra :—Brego geán þingade *the Lord spoke again*, Cd. 48; Th. 62, 5; Gen. 1009.

gegn-cwide, es; *m. A reply, answering again*; responsum :—Đînra gegncwida [MS. -cwida] *of thy replies*, Beo. Th. 739; B. 367.

Gegnes-burh *Gainsborough, Lincolnshire*, Chr. 1013.

ge-gnîdan; *p.* -gnâd, *pl.* -gnidon; *pp.* -gniden *To rub, rub together, comminute*; fricare, defricare, fricando comminuere, planare, levigare :—Nim đas ylcan wyrte dryg he đonne and gegnîd to duste *take this same wort, then dry it, and rub it to dust*, Herb. 90, 10; Lchdm. i.

196, 12. Genim ðas wyrte on wætre gegnidene *take this wort rubbed in water*, Herb. 84, 1; Lchdm. i. 188, 1. Ic gegnîde *plano* vel *levigo*, Ælfc. Gl. 36; Som. 62, 8. v. gnîdan.

gegninga, -nunga; *adv. Plainly, wholly, altogether, certainly, directly;* omnino :—Ðǽr ðû gegninga gûðe findest *there wilt thou straightway find war*, Andr. Kmbl. 2697; An. 1351. Ðæt hit gegnunga from Gode côme *that it came directly from God*, Cd. 32; Th. 42, 35; Gen. 683: Exon. 44 b; Th. 150, 27; Gû. 785.

gegn-pæþ, es; *m. A path along which one goes to oppose another*, Exon. 104 b; Th. 397, 27; Rä. 16, 26.

gegn-slege, es; *m. A striking back again, exchange of blows, battle*, Andr. Kmbl. 2711; An. 1358.

gegnum; *adv. Forward;* obviam :—For hwam ne môton we ðonne gegnum gangan *why then may we not go forward?* Salm. Kmbl. 705; Sal. 352. Eódon ðâ gegnum ðanonne *they thence went on forward*, Judth. 11; Thw. 23, 21; Jud. 132: Beo. Th. 633; B. 314: 2813; B. 1404. [Cf. *Icel.* gegnum *through*.]

ge-gnysan *to dash against*, Ps. 136, 12. v. forgnidan.

ge-góded. v. gegôdian.

ge-gôdian; *p.* ode; *pp.* od *To bestow goods upon, enrich*:—Ða mynstru he genihtsumlîce to dæghwomlîcum bigleofan gegôdode *he abundantly enriched those minsters for daily subsistence*, Homl. Th. ii. 118, 30; H. R. 105, 6: Chr. 1086; Erl. 220, 39. Ðonne ðû Hierusalem gegôdie *in die Hierusalem*, Ps. Th. 136, 7. Apollonius ðe ðurh us gegôdod is *Apollonius who is enriched by us*, Th. Ap. 18, 20. Ða sîn gegôded *utuntur*, Hpt. Gl. 447, 494. Gegôded *fretus*, 503; *acquisitus, adeptus*, 513. v. gôdian.

ge-gogud *relying on;* fretus, R. Conc. v. ge-gôded [?].

ge-golden; *part. Paid, performed;* præstitus, L. In. 71.

ge-gong, -gang *fate, a falling out, an accident;* fatum, Cot. 48.

ge-gongan *to go over, conquer*, Bt. Met. Fox 1, 24; Met. 1, 12. v. gegangan.

ge-goten *poured out, molten, melted*, Kmbl. Sal. and Sat. 61; Sat. 31. v. ge-geótan.

ge-græppian; *p.* ade; *pp.* ad *To seize*, Mt. Kmbl. Lind. 14, 31.

ge-grâpian; *p.* ode; *pp.* od *To grope, touch;* palpāre :—Sió gefrêdnes hine mæg gegrâpian *the feeling may touch it*, Bt. 41, 4; Fox 252, 10: Ps. Th. 113, 15: 134, 18. Hand hî habbaþ and hîg ne gegrâpiaþ *mănus hăbent et non palpābunt*, Ps. Lamb. second 113, 7. Ðâ he hyne ggrâpod hæfde *palpāto eo*, Gen. 27, 22.

ge-gremian, -gremman; *p.* ode, ede; *pp.* od, ed *To irritate, provoke, excite, incense, inflame;* exaspĕrāre, provŏcāre, exăcerbāre :—Ðe in eorre [hine] gegremmaþ *qui in ira* [*eum*] *provŏcant*, Ps. Surt. 67, 7. Hwæt hit swîður gehierste and gegremige *what more scorches and excites it?* Past. 21, 6; Swt. 165, 2; Hat. MS. 32 a, 15. Gegremod wearþ se gûþrinc *the chief was incensed*, Byrht. Th. 135, 54; By. 138. Hî wǽron gûþe gegremede *they were made fierce by battle*, Judth. 12; Thw. 26, 2; Jud. 306: Cd. 4; Th. 4, 29; Gen. 61.

ge-grêtan; he -grêt, *pl.* -grêtaþ; *p.* -grêtte, *pl.* -grêtton; *pp.* -grêted *To approach, come to, address, greet, welcome;* adire, alloqui, salutare :—Wîf sceal eodor æþelinga [MS. e] ǽrest gegrêtan *the wife shall the nobles' chief first greet*, Exon. 90 a; Th. 339, 7; Gn. Ex. 90. Holdne gegrêtte meaglum wordum *he addressed his faithful friend in powerful words*, Beo. Th. 3964; B. 1980. Hie ðâ gegrêtte *he then addressed them*, Andr. Kmbl. 507; An. 254. Ðæt we mâgon ûre frŷnd geseón and ûre siblingas gegrêtan *that we may see our friends and greet our kinsmen*, Homl. Th. ii. 526, 33. Man tǽleþ and mid yfle gegrêteþ ða ðe riht lufiaþ *men blame and insult those that love right*, Swt. A. S. Rdr. 110, 164. v. grêtan.

ge-grêwþ *grows*, Bt. 34, 10; Fox 148, 27; *3rd sing. pres. of* gegrôwan.

ge-grin *a snare*, Ps. Spl. T. 24, 16. v. grin.

ge-grinan; *p.* ode; *pp.* od *To ensnare;* illaqueare, Prov. 6.

ge-grind, es; *n. A grinding* or *rubbing together, a noise, whizzing, clashing, commotion;* collîsio, contrîtio, frăgor :—Grîmhelma gegrind *the crashing of helmets*, Cd. 160; Th. 198, 29; Exod. 330: 95; Th. 124, 15; Gen. 2063. Geótende gegrind grund eall forswealg *the abyss swallowed up the pouring commotion*, Andr. Kmbl. 3178; An. 1592.

ge-grindan; *p.* -grand, *pl.* -grundon; *pp.* -grunden *To grind together, sharpen, grind to powder;* commolere, pertricare :—Gegrindæs *comminuet*, Lk. Skt. Lind. 20, 18. Gegrunden [MS. gegrunde] *commolitus*, Ælfc. Gl. 36; Wrt. Voc. 28, 78. Gegrundene gâras *the sharpened arrows*, Byrht. Th. 134, 64; By. 109. DER. grindan.

ge-grip *a gripe, seizing*. v. gripa.

ge-grîpan; *p.* -grâp, *pl.* -gripon; *pp.* -gripen *To gripe, grasp, seize;* capere, rapere, prehendere, apprehendere, comprehendere, arripere, corripere, eripere :—Mâran ðonne ðû in hreðre mǽge môde gegrîpan *too great for thee to comprehend in thy breast with thy mind*, Exon. 92 b; Th. 348, 10; Sch. 26: Bt. Met. Fox 10, 138; Met. 10, 69. Feónd sâwle mîne gegrîpeþ *inimicus animam meam comprehendat*, Ps. Spl. 7, 5: Salm. Kmbl. 226; Sal. 112. Us fyrhto gegrâp *fear seized us*, Nicod. 21; Thw. 10, 33: Cd. 140: Th. 175, 32; Gen. 2904: Cant. Moys. Surt. 188, 15: Nar. 44, 13. Ðâ gegripon ða unclǽnan gâstas ǽnne of ðâm mannum *then the unclean spirits seized one of the men*, Bd. 3, 19; S. 548, 47: Ps. Spl. 39, 16: Cant. Moys. Ex. 15, 17. Gegrîp wǽpn and scyld *apprehende arma et scutum*, Ps. Spl. 34, 2. Êhtaþ gê and gegrîpaþ hine *persequimini et comprehendite eum*, Ps. Spl. 70, 12. Ðî læs âhwænne gegrîpe swâ swâ leó sâwle mîne *ne quando rapiat ut leo animam meam*, Ps. Spl. 7, 2. Ðâ wæs he fram deófle gegripen *then he was seized by a devil*, Bd. 3, 11; S. 536, 13: Ps. Spl. 17, 31. On tintregum gegripene *tormentis comprehensos*, Mt. Bos. 4, 24. Geneálǽcende he hî upahôf, hyre handa gegripenre *accedens elevavit eam, apprehensa manu ejus*, Mk. Bos. 1, 31. Hî wurdon gegripene fram môderlicum breóstum *they were snatched from their mothers' breasts*, Homl. Th. i. 84, 8. v. grîpan.

ge-gripennis, -niss, e; *f. A taking, seizing, snare;* correptio, captio :—Gegripennis ðone ðe he behŷdde togegrîpe hine *captio quam abscondit apprehendat eum*, Ps. Spl. T. 34, 9.

ge-griþian; *p.* ode, ede; *pp.* od, ed. I. *v. intrans. To make peace;* pācĭfĭcāre :—Ealle Eást-Centingas gegriþedan wið hî *all the East Kentians made peace with them*, Chr. 1009; Th. 261, 20, col. 2. II. *v. trans. To protect;* tuēri :—Syndon cyrcan wâce gegriþode *churches are weakly protected*, L. I. P. 25; Th. ii. 340, 11.

ge-grôwan; *p.* -greów, *pl.* -greówon; *pp.* -grówen *To grow;* succrescere :—Ne gegrêwþ hit ðǽr *it will not grow there*, Bt. 34, 10; Fox 148, 27. v. grôwan.

ge-grunded *grounded, founded*.

ge-grundon *ground*. v. ge-grindan.

ge-grundweallian; *p.* ode; *pp.* od *To found;* fundāre :—He ofer sǽs gegrundweallode hine *ipse sŭper măria fundāvit eum*, Ps. Spl. 23, 2.

ge-grynd, es; *n. A plot of ground* :—Aðelwold gesealde twâ gegrynd *Æthelwold gave two plots of ground*, Thorpe Chart. 231, 22.

ge-gryndan; *p.* de; *pp.* ed *To found*, Mt. Kmbl. Lind. 7, 25 [MS. gewrynded].

ge-gyddian; *p.* ode; *pp.* od *To sing;* cantāre :—Ic ðâs word gegyddode *I sang these words*, Nicod. 27; Thw. 15, 40. v. giddian.

ge-gyfan *to bestow*. v. gifan.

ge-gyld, es; *n. A guild, society* or *club*. v. ge-gild.

ge-gyld; *adj. Golden, gilded;* deaurātus :—On gyrlan gegyldum *in vestītu deaurāto*, Ps. Spl. 44, 11. Gyldena, *vel* gegylde fatu *gilded vessels*, Ælfc. Gl. 67; Som. 69, 97; Wrt. Voc. 41, 48. v. gylden.

ge-gylda, an; *m. A member of a guild, club,* or *corporation, a companion, fellow*. v. ge-gilda.

ge-gyldan; *p.* -geald *To yield, pay, give, requite;* reddere, tribuere, retribuere :—Him God wolde æfter ðrowinga ðonc gegyldan *to him God would, after sufferings, requite favour*, Exon. 39 b; Th. 130, 23; Gû. 442. v. gildan.

ge-gyld-scipe, es; *m. A guild-ship, society;* sodalitas, L. Ath. v. § 8, 6; Th. i. 236, 35. v. gild-scipe.

ge-gyltan; *p.* -gylte; *pp.* -gylt *To become guilty, to offend, sin;* peccāre :—Deáh ðe he self gegyltan ne meahte *although he himself could not sin*, Past. 49; Swt. 385; 17; Hat. MS. Ðeáh ðe hwâ gegylte *though any one become guilty*, Ors. 1, 12; Bos. 36, 44.

ge-gymmod; *part. Gemmed, set with gems;* gemmātus :—Gegymmod *gemmātus*, Ælfc. Gr. 43; Som. 45, 16.

ge-gyrdan; *p.* -gyrde; *pp.* -gyrded, -gyrd *To gird;* præcingĕre :—Eaxle gegyrde *girded shoulders*, Exon. 126 b; Th. 486, 14; Rä. 72, 14.

ge-gyrela, -gyryla *a garment*. v. gegerela.

ge-gyrian; *p.* ode; *pp.* od, wed; *v. a. To clothe, put on, adorn, endow;* vestire :—Ðû gegyrydist, Ps. Spl. C. 103, 2. Ðone lîchoman gegyredon *clothed the body*, Bd. 4, 30; S. 609, 21. Gegyrewod *endowed*, Bt. 14, 3; Fox 46, 12. v. gegerwian.

ge-gyrnan; *p.* de; *pp.* ed [gyrnan *to yearn*] *To desire, seek;* desīdĕrāre, pĕtĕre :—Ic friþ wille æt Gode gegyrnan *I will desire peace from God*, Exon. 36 a; Th. 117, 24; Gû. 229. Ðonne ðæt gegyrnaþ ða ðe him Godes egsa hleónaþ ofer heáfdum *when they, over whose heads the fear of God impendeth, desire that*, 33 b; Th. 106, 18; Gû. 43.

ge-gyrnendlic; *adj. Desirable;* desiderabilis, Ps. Spl. T. 18, 11.

ge-gyrwan. v. ge-gerwan.

ge-habban; ðû -hæfst, -hafast, *pl.* -habbaþ; *p.* -hæfde; *pp.* -hæfed, -hæfd *To hold, be* [*ill*]; habere, tenere :—Gehafa geþyld on me *patientiam habe in me*, Mt. Bos. 18, 26: Exon. 105 a; Th. 398, 19; Rä. 17, 10. Ðara synna gê gihabbaþ *quorum peccata retinuerites*, Jn. Skt. Lind. 20, 23: Past. 51, 9; Swt. 401, 32; Hat. MS. Æfter ðisum wordum wearþ gemôt gehæfd *after these words a meeting was held*, Homl. Th. ii. 148, 1. Ðǽr ðǽr wǽron gehæfde hâte baþu *where hot baths were kept*, i. 86, 21. Mîn cneów is yfele gehæfd *my knee is diseased*, 134, 33: 150, 7.

ge-haccod *hacked, cut*. v. haccan.

ge-hâda, an; *m. One of the same state* or *order;* qui ejusdem stātus *vel* ordĭnis est :—Mid twâm his gehâdan *with two of his fellow ecclesiastics*, L. Eth. ix. 19, 20; Th. i. 344, 14, 16: L. C. E. 5; Th. i. 362, 12, 15.

ge-hâdian; *p.* -hâdode; *pp.* -hâdod *To ordain, consecrate;* consecrare :—Hêr Vitalianus se pâpa gehâdode Theodorus to arcebiscop *in* *this year pope Vitalianus consecrated Theodore archbishop*, Chr. 668; Erl. 35, 27: 1070; Erl. 208, 2. Hēr Paulinus wæs gehādod Norþhymbrum to biscepe *in this year Paulinus was consecrated bishop of Northumbria*, 625; Erl. 22, 11. Mauricius hine gehādian hēt *Mauricius ordered that he should be ordained*, Homl. Th. ii. 122, 32: Bd. 3, 7; S. 530, 30. v. hādian.

ge-hādod, -hāded; *def.* se ge-hādoda; *part. In holy orders;* ordĭnātus:—Nū, gē habbaþ gehīred be gehādodum mannum *now ye have heard concerning men in orders*, L. Ælf. P. 41; Th. ii. 382, 16; Wilk. 169, 23. Se gehādoda *one in holy orders;* ordĭnātus, 42; Th. ii. 382, 23; Wilk. 169, 34. Be gehādedum mannum *concerning men in holy orders;* de ordinatis, Th. ii. 364, 7; Wilk. 161, 1. He ǽlces mannes gehādodes and lǽwedes yrfenuma beón wolde *he wanted to be the heir of every man, cleric and lay*, Chr. 1100; Erl. 236, 7.

ge-hæft; *adj.* [-hæft; *pp. of* ge-hæftan] *Bound, captive;* captus:—Ōþ ðære gehæftan wylne *to the captive slave*, Ex. 12, 29. Nyle he gehæfte nā forhycgan *vinctos suos non sprevit*, Ps. Th. 68, 34. Ða gehæftan *vinctos*, 67, 7. Gehæftum *captivis*, Lk. Bos. 4, 18.

ge-hæftan, he -hæft; *p.* -hæftede, -hæfte; *pp.* -hæfted, -hæft *To take, take captive, cast into prison, detain, bind;* captare, captivare, vincire:—Swā hwæt swā hīg gehæftaþ *quicquid ceperint*, Th. An. 23, 11. Hī gehæftaþ on sāwle rihtwīses *captabunt in animam justi*, Ps. 93, 21. Abraham geseah ānne ramm be ðām hornum gehæft *Abraham saw a ram caught* [*captus*] *by his horns*, Gen. 22, 13. On ēcnesse gehæft *for ever binds*, Bt. 19; Fox 70, 18. Mid ðȳ me God hafaþ gehæfted be ðam healse *with which God hath fastened me by the neck*, Cd. 19; Th. 24, 29; Gen. 385: Judth. 10; Thw. 23, 11; Jud. 116. He hæfde ǽnne ðeófman gehæftne *habebat vinctum*, Mt. Bos. 27, 16. Handa synt gehæfte *my hands are manacled*, Cd. 19; Th. 24, 19; Gen. 380: Exon. 16 a; Th. 35, 22; Cri. 562. Hīg mycelum ege gehæfte wǽron *timore magno tenebantur*, Lk. Bos. 8, 37. Drihten hīg gehȳrde ðæt hīg gehæfton wiþ hine, Josh. 11, 20 [?].

ge-hæftednes, -ness, e; *f. A captivity;* captīvĭtas:—Gecyr Drihten gehæftednesse ūre *converte Dŏmĭne captīvĭtātem nostram*, Ps. Lamb. 125, 4.

ge-hæftfæst; *adj. Captive;* captivus, Hpt. Gl. 434.

ge-hæftnan, -hæftnian; *p.* ede, ade; *pp.* ed, ad *To take, lay hold of, take captive;* comprehendĕre, captīvāre:—Ðū me gehæftnedest [gehæftnadest, Exon. 98 a; Th. 368, 29] *thou didst take me captive*, Soul Kmbl. 63; Seel. 32. Sȳ ēhtende oððe ēhte feónd mīne sāwle and gehæftnige hī oððe gegrīpe hī *persĕquātur inĭmīcus anĭmam meam et comprehendat*, Ps. Lamb. 7, 6. Ða ðe ǽr gehæftnede wǽron *who before were held captive*, Blickl. Homl. 87, 7: 89, 29.

ge-hæftnys, -nyss, e; *f. Captivity;* captīvĭtas:—Ðonne awent oððe acyrreþ God gehæftnysse oððe hæftnōde folces his *cum convertit Deus captīvĭtātem plēbis suæ*, Ps. Lamb. 52, 7. v. ge-hæftednes.

ge-hæft-world, e; *f. A captive world:*—Ðeós gehæftworld, Blickl. Homl. 9, 4.

ge-hægan; *pp.* -hæged *To surround as with a hedge:*—Folc wæs gehæged *the people was hemmed in*, Cd. 151; Th. 188, 17; Exod. 169. [Cf. *Icel.* hegna *to hedge, fence* (?); and see Grein, gehǽgan.]

ge-hæge, es; *n. Land hedged in, a paddock, garden;* hortus, pratum, Mone B. 618: Hpt. Gl. 419, 439.

ge-hǽlan; *p.* -hǽlde; *pp.* -hǽled *To heal, cure, save;* sanare, salvare:—Untrume gehǽlan *to heal the sick*, Lk. Bos. 9, 2. He gehǽlde manega folc *he saved much people*, Gen. 50, 20. Ðæt gē him sāra gehwylc hondum gehǽlde *that ye should heal with hands each of his sores*, Exon. 42 b; Th. 144, 12; Gū. 677.

ge-hæld *a keeping, regarding;* observatio, Bd. 4, 23; S. 594, 16. v. ge-heald.

ge-hǽled; *comp.* gehǽledra, gehǽldra, gehāldre; *adj. Safe, secure, good;* tutus, Bd. 2, 2; S. 503, 39.

ge-hǽman; *p.* de; *pp.* ed *To lie with, cohabit, commit fornication;* concumbĕre:—Gif he mid gehǽme *if he lie with her*, L. Alf. pol. 11; Th. i. 68, 16.

ge-hǽnan *to accuse, condemn*, Jn. Skt. Lind. 8, 6; 8, 10. v. gehēnan.

ge-hǽnan; *p.* de; *pp.* ed *To stone:*—Ic gemētte ðǽr Archelaus gehǽnedne *I found there Archelaus stoned*, St. And. 44, 18. v. hǽnan.

ge-hæp; *adj. Fit:*—On stōwe gehæppre *in loco apto*, Th. An. 21, 13.

ge-hǽre; *adj. Hairy:*—Wǽron hie swā gehǽre swā wildeór *pilosus in modum ferarum*, Nar. 22, 5.

ge-hǽt; *part. Made warm, heated;* călĕfactus:—Ðæt sȳ gehǽt *let it be heated*, Herb. 23, 2; Lchdm. i. 120, 8.

ge-hǽtan *to promise;* promittere, Bt. 20; Fox 70, 33. v. ge-hātan.

ge-hafa *have*, Mt. 18, 26; *imp. of* ge-habban.

ge-hafen *raised up, fermented*, Ælfc. Gl. 66; Wrt. Voc. 41, 15. v. ge-hebban.

ge-hagian; *p.* ode; *pp.* od; *v impers. To please:*—Swā hwylc swā ðæt sió ðæt hine to ðan gehagige ðæt he ða ōðoro lond begeotan wille *whoever it be that is ready to take the other lands*, Kmbl. Cod. Dipl. ii. 120, 24, v. onhagian.

ge-hāl; *adj. Entire, whole, healthy;* intĕger, sānus:—Gemētte he ðæt fæt swā gehāl, ðæt ðǽr nān cīnu on næs gesewen *he found the vessel so whole that no chink was visible in it*, Homl. Th. ii. 154, 22: 166, 11: Bt. 34, 12; Fox 152, 27. On gehālum þingum *in health*, Homl. Th. ii. 352, 22.

ge-haldan; *pp.* -halden *To keep, preserve, hold;* servāre, recondĕre, tĕnēre:—On ðam heó wilnode gehaldan ða ārwurþan bān hire fæderan *in quo desīdĕrābat hŏnōranda patrui sui ossa recondĕre*, Bd. 3, 11; S. 535, 16. Mid ðȳ hine ðā nǽnig man ne gehaldan ne gebindan mihte *cum a nullo vel tĕnēri vel ligāri pŏtuisset*, 3, 11; S. 536, 16. Ðǽr hī nū gehaldene syndon *in qua nunc servantur*, 3, 11; S. 535, 11: 3, 6; S. 528, 29. v. ge-healdan.

ge-halding, e; *f. A holding, keeping;* custōdia:—On gehaldinge sprǽca ðīne *in custōdiendo sermōnes tuos*, Ps. Spl. C. 118, 9.

ge-hālgegend, es; *m. One who hallows;* dicator, Hymn. Surt. 64, 19.

ge-hālgian; *p.* ode, ade; *pp.* od, ad *To consecrate, dedicate, initiate, ordain, hallow, make holy, sanctify;* consecrāre, dedĭcāre, sacrāre, inĭtiāre, ordĭnāre, sanctĭfĭcāre:—Hēt se pāpa hine to bisceope gehālgian *the pope commanded to consecrate him bishop*, Bd. 3, 7; S. 529, 9: 3, 24; S. 556, 19. Ðæt hīg woldon hīg sylfe gehālgian *ut sanctĭfĭcārent seipsos*, Jn. Bos. 11, 55. Siððan ðū gehālgast hira handa *postquam inĭtiāvĕris mănus eōrum*, Ex. 29, 9, 35. Ðū gehālgast ðæt gehālgode anribb and ðone bōh *sanctĭfĭcābis et pectuscŭlum consecrātum et armum*, 29, 27, 36. He gehālgode wīn of wætere *he hallowed wine from water*, Andr. Kmbl. 1171; An. 586: 3298; An. 1652. Wælhreów Criste gehālgode offrunge *tȳrannus Christo sacrāvit victĭmam*, Hymn. Surt. 52, 11. Gif preóst on treowenan calice hūsl gehālgige *if a priest consecrate housel in a wooden chalice*, L. N. P. L. 14; Th. ii. 292, 20. Ðis hūs ðē gehālgod ys *hæc dŏmus tibi dedĭcāta est*, Hymn. Surt. 141, 18: L. Ælf. C. 25; Th. ii. 352, 13. Sȳ ðīn nama gehālgod *hallowed be thy name*, Homl. Th. ii. 596, 5: Hy. 6, 3; Hy. Grn. ii. 286, 3: 7, 18; Hy. Grn. ii. 287, 18. He wæs gehālgod fram Scottum *ordĭnātus a Scottis*, Bd. 3, 24; S. 557, 22. On gehālgodre cirican *in a consecrated church*, L. Edg. C. 30; Th. ii. 250, 19.

ge-hālgung, e; *f. A consecration, sanctification, sanctuary;* consecrātio, sanctĭfĭcātio, sanctuārium:—He ingelǽdde hie in munt gehālgunge his *induxit eos in montem sanctĭfĭcātiōnis suæ*, Ps. Surt. 77, 54: 131, 8. On gehālgunge hys *in sanctĭfĭcātiōne ejus*, Ps. Spl. C. T. 95, 6.

ge-hālsian; *p.* ode; *pp.* od *To adjure, exorcise:*—Ic gihālsige *adjuro*, Rtl. 113, 24. Gihālsad *adjuratus*, 120, 35. Gihālsia *exorcizare*, 119, 7. Ic gihǽlsiga *exorcizo*, 120, 21.

ge-hāmettan; *p.* te; *pp.* ed *To appoint a home, domicile;* dŏmum assignāre:—Ðæt hī hine to folcryhte gehāmetten *that they domicile him to folk-right*, L. Ath. i. 2; Th. i. 200, 7.

ge-hāmian; *p.* ode, ade; *pp.* od, ad *To make* [*one's self*] *familiar with* (?):—Aldred hine gihāmadi mið ðæm ðriim dǽlum *Aldred made himself familiar with the three parts*, Jn. Skt. 188, 7. [See p. ix. note 1.]

gehāt, es; *n. A promise, vow;* promissum, votum:—Gemunde heofonweardes gehāt *he remembered the promise of heaven's guardian*, Cd. 86; Th. 107, 28; Gen. 1796. He ðam gehāte getrūwode *he trusted to the promise*, 33; Th. 44, 9; Gen. 706. Ðæt ic mīn gehāt hēr agylde *ut reddam vota mea*, Ps. Th. 60, 6. Gehāt gehēt *votum vovit*, 131, 2: Bd. 3, 27; S. 559, 8. [*O. H. Ger.* ki-heiz. v. Grm. R. A. p. 893.] DER. ge-hātan.

ge-hata *a hater, an enemy;* inimicus, Cot. 74.

ge-hātan, -hǽtan, he -hǽt, -hǽt; *p.* -hēt, *pl.* -hēton, -hēht, *pl.* -hēhton; *pp.* -hāten. I. *to call, name;* vocare, nominare:—Swā ðū gehāten eart *as thou art called*, Exon. 8 b; Th. 4, 26; Cri. 58. Crist wæs on ðȳ eahteoþan dæg Hǽlend gehāten *Christ was on the eighth day named Jesus*, Menol. Fox 7; Men. 4. Is gehāten Saturnus *is called Saturn*, Bt. Met. Fox 28, 48; Met. 28, 24. Ðæt land ðe ys gehāten Euilaþ *omnem terram Hevilath*, Gen. 2, 11: Jud. 4, 2, 6. II. *to call, command, promise, vow, threaten;* vocare, accessere, jubere, spondere, promittere, vovere:—Fōre waldende gǽþ bī noman gehātne *they shall go before the Lord, called for by name*, Exon. 23 b; Th. 66, 16; Cri. 1072. Him ðæt eall gehǽt his rēcelēst *his security commands all that to him*, Bt. Met. Fox 25, 104; Met. 25, 52. Him sibbe gehāteþ *he shall promise peace to them*, Exon. 27 b; Th. 82, 16; Cri. 1339. Ic ðē gehāte *I vow to thee*, Cd. 98; Th. 129, 5; Gen. 2139. Gehātaþ Drihtne *vovete Domino*, Ps. Th. 75, 8. Ðeáh ðe gē me deáþ gehāten *though ye have threatened death to me*, Exon. 36 a; Th. 116, 23; Gū. 211: 40 b; Th. 135, 7; Gū. 520. v. hātan.

ge-haðerian; *p.* ode; *pp.* od *To restrain;* cohĭbēre:—Wambe sār gehaðeraþ *it restraineth sore of stomach*, Med. ex Quadr. 2, 2; Lchdm. i. 334, 8. Ðā ðæt ðā geseah se ðe hine gebohte, ðæt he mid bendum ne mihte gehaðerod beón *cumque vīdisset qui emērat, vincŭlis eum non pŏtuisse cohĭbēri*, Bd. 4, 22; S. 592, 9. Ic am gehaðrad *coarctor*, Lk. Skt. Lind. 12, 50. v. ge-heaðerian.

ge-hāthyrt; *adj. Irritated, angry:*—Ðā wearþ se hālga wer gehāthyrt *the holy man was irritated*, Homl. Th. ii. 176, 18.

ge-hāthyrtan; *p.* te; *v. reflex. To become angry:*—Se Godes wiðersaca hine ðā gehāthyrte *the adversary of God then became angry*, Homl. Th. i. 450, 9.

ge-hātian; *p.* ode, ude; *pp.* od, ud *To become* or *be hot;* concălescĕre:—Gehātude heorte mīn on in me *concăluit cor meum intra me*, Ps. Spl. 38, 4.

ge-hāt-land, es; *n. Land of promise*:—Be inngonge ðæs gehātlondes *about the entrance of the promised land*, Bd. 4, 24; S. 598, 12.

ge-hāwian; *p.* ode, ade; *pp.* od, ad *To look at, view, observe, examine, survey, inspect;* intuēri, aspĭcĕre, circumspĭcĕre:—Se cing gehāwode [gehāwade, col. 1] hwǽr man mihte ða eá forwyrcean *the king observed where the river might be obstructed*, Chr. 896; Th. 172, 35, col. 2; 173, 35: Shrn. 178, 7: 179, 21.

ge-heád; *adj.* [heáh *high*] *Lifted up, exalted;* exaltātus:—Wæs Bryten swȳðe geheád *Britain was very much exalted*, Bd. 1, 6; S. 476, 27, MS. B. [*A. R.* i-heied.]

ge-heald, -hæld, es; *m.* [?] *n.* [?] I. *a holding, keeping, guard, observing;* observantia:—He sende him stafas and gewrit be gehealde rihtra Eástrana *he sent him a letter and epistle about the holding of right Easters*, Bd. 5, 21; S. 643, 8. Habbaþ gē gehæld *habetis custodiam*, Mt. Kmbl. Lind. 27, 65: Rtl. 123, 31: Shrn. 36, 30. II. *a keeper, guardian, protection;* custos, tūtēla:—Willelm eorl sceolde beón [MS. ben] his geheald *earl William was to be his guardian*, Chr. 1070; Th. 347, 7. Ælfgār eorl gesōhte Griffines geheald on Norþwealan *earl Ælfgar sought Griffith's protection in North Wales*, 1055; Th. 325, 20. He beó ðǽrto geheald and mund under me *let him be thereto guardian and patron under me*, Thorpe Chart. 391, 17. v. ge-hyld.

ge-heald; *adj.* v. ge-hyldra.

ge-healdan, -haldan, to -healdenne; ic -healde, ðū -healdest, -hiltst, he -healdeþ, -healt, -helt, -hylt, *pl.* -healdaþ; *p.* -heóld, -hióld, ðū -heólde, *pl.* -heóldon, -hióldon; *impert.* -heald, *pl.* -healdaþ; *subj. pres.* -healde, *pl.* -healden; *p.* -heólde, *pl.* -heólden; *pp.* -healden. I. *to keep, hold, observe, keep in, retain, reserve, preserve, save, defend, protect;* custodīre, servāre, observāre, contĭnēre, reservāre, salvāre, defendĕre:—Ðæt ic ðīne word mihte wel gehealdan *ut custōdiam verbum tuum*, Ps. Th. 118, 101: Andr. Kmbl. 426; An. 213. Se ðe him God syleþ gumena rīce to gehealdenne *to whom God gives an empire over men to hold*, Scōp Th. 269; Wíd. 134. Ic gehealde wegas mīne *custōdiam vias meas*, Ps. Lamb. 38, 2. Gif ðū hīg gehiltst *si custōdiĕris ea*, Deut. 7, 12: Ex. 34, 6. Drihten gehealdeþ dōme ða lytlan *custōdiens parvŭlos Dŏmĭnus*, Ps. Th. 114, 6. Se stranga gewǽpnod his cāfertūn gehealt *fortis armātus custōdit atrium suum*, Lk. Bos. 11, 21: Ps. Lamb. 120, 5. God hine gehelt ǽghwonan *God preserves him everywhere*, Bt. 12; Fox 36, 37. Drihten gehylt ðē fram ǽlcum yfele *Dŏmĭnus custōdit te ab omni mălo*, Ps. Lamb. 120, 7. Ic ðē forðig geheóld *ideo custōdīvi te*, Gen. 20, 6. Ðū eágan mīne wið teárum geheólde *thou hast kept mine eyes from tears*, Ps. Th. 114, 8. Hī ðæt word geheóldon betwux *verbum contĭnuērunt ăpud se*, Mk. Bos. 9, 10. Hie sibbe innan bordes gehióldon *they preserved peace at home*, Past. pref.; Swt. 3, 7; Hat. MS. Geheald ðū, mīn folc, mīne fæste ǽ *attendĭte, pŏpŭle meus, lēgem meam*, Ps. Th. 77, 1. Ðec ā wið firenum geheald *preserve thyself ever from sins*, Exon. 81 a; Th. 305, 27; Fä. 94. Fæder alwalda mid ārstafum eówic gehealde *may the all-ruling Father hold you with honour*, Beo. Th. 640; B. 317. Ðæt he cōme and ða burh geheólde *that he would come and defend the city*, Jos. 10, 6. Ðæt sǽd sī gehealden ofer ealre eorþan brādnisse *ut salvētur sēmen sŭper făciem ūnĭversæ terræ*, Gen. 7, 3: Jos. 2, 13: Mt. Bos. 9, 17. Gehealdne, *pp. pl.* Exon. 23 b; Th. 65, 26; Cri. 1060. Mid gehealdan *to satisfy*, Bt. 13; Fox 38, 34. Wel gehealden *well contented, satisfied*, Bt. 18, 3; Fox 64, 27: Basil admn. 9; Norm. 52, 22. II. *to hold, occupy, possess;* tĕnēre, possĭdēre:—On eówrum geþylde gē gehealdaþ eówre sāwla *in pătientia vestra possĭdēbĭtis anĭmas vestras*, Lk. Bos, 21, 19. He frætwe geheóld fela missera *he held the armour many years*, Beo. Th. 5253; B. 2620.

ge-heald-dagas; *pl. m. Kalends*:—Gehealddagas *vel* hālige dagas *kalendæ*, Ælfc. Gl. 96; Som. 76, 26; Wrt. Voc. 53, 35.

ge-healden; *part. p. Satisfied*:—Beó gehealden on ðīnum gecynde ðonne hæfst ðū genōh *be satisfied in thy kind, then hast thou enough*, Kmbl. Sal. 264, 21. v. gehealdan.

ge-healdnys, -nyss, e; *f. A keeping;* custōdia:—On gehealdnysse ðara *in custōdiendis illis*, Ps. Lamb. 18, 12.

ge-healdsum; *adj. Keeping, sparing, frugal;* parcus:—Ðæt he sīe gehealdsum on ðæm ðe he healdan scyle oððe dǽlan *that he is frugal in what he ought to keep or give away*, Past. 20, 2; Swt. 149, 18; Hat. MS. 29 b, 9.

ge-healdsumnys, -nyss, e; *f. A keeping, observance, preservation, abstinence;* custōdia, observātio, conservātio, abstĭnentia:—We rǽdaþ on bōcum, ðæt ðeós gehealdsumnys wurde arǽred on ðone tīman ðe gelamp on ānre byrig ðe Uigenna is gecweden micel eorþstyrung *we read in books, that this observance was established at the time when a great earthquake happened in a city which is called Vienna*, Homl. Th. i. 244, 15. Ðæt he wǽre on gehealdsumnysse ðæs bebodes his Scyppende underþeód *that he was subject to his Creator in the keeping of the commandment*, Boutr. Scrd. 17, 29. For gehealdsumnysse sōþre eádmōdnysse beóþ fōrwel oft Godes gecorenan geswencte *for preservation of true humility God's chosen are very often afflicted*, Homl. Th. i. 474, 10. Mid ðære gehealdsumnysse *with abstinence*, i. 318, 8.

ge-heálgian; *p.* ode; *pp.* od *To consecrate, hallow;* consecrāre, sacrāre:—Theodōr bisceop on Hrōfes ceastre Quichelm to bisceope geheálgode *Theodōrus in cĭvĭtāte Hrofi Cuichelmum consecrāvit episcŏpum*, Bd. 4, 13; S. 581, 8. Ðǽr se bisceop towearp and fordyde ða wigbed ðe he sylf ǽr geheálgode *ubi pontĭfex polluit et destruxit eas quas ipse sacrāvĕrat āras*, 2, 13; S. 517, 18. v. ge-hālgian.

ge-healt *keeps, guards, protects*, Lk. Bos. 11, 21: Ps. Lamb. 120, 5; *3rd sing. pres. of* ge-healdan.

ge-healtsumnys *captivity*.

ge-heáne *servire*, Rtl. 42, 40. v. gehȳnan.

ge-heápod; *part. Heaped* or *piled up;* coacervātus:—Gōd gemet, and full, and geheápod, and oferflōwende hīg syllaþ on eówerne bearm *mensūram bŏnam, et confertam, et coagĭtātam, et sŭpereffluentem dăbunt in sĭnum vestrum*, Lk. Bos. 6, 38: Blickl. Homl. 175, 17. v. ge-hȳpan.

ge-heaðorian, -heaðerian, -heaðrian; *p.* ode, ade; *pp.* od, ad *To restrain, control, compress;* cohĭbēre, coartāre, coangustāre:—Hafaþ geheaðorad heofona Wealdend ealle gesceafta *the Ruler of the heavens has controlled all creatures*, Bt. Met. Fox 13, 11; Met. 13, 6: Bt. 21; Fox 74, 9: 25; Fox 88, 5. Ðæt se secg wǽre hergum geheaðerod *that the man should be restrained with harryings*, Beo. Th. 6136; B. 3072. He eft semninga swīge gewyrþeþ, in nēdcleofan nearwe geheaðrod *it* [*the wind*] *again suddenly becomes silent, narrowly compressed in its close bed*, Elen. Kmbl. 2550; El. 1276.

ge-heáw, es; *n. A striking together, a gnashing, grinding;* concussio, stridor:—Tōþa geheáw *a gnashing of teeth*, Cd. 221; Th. 285, 18; Sat. 339.

ge-heáwan; *p.* -heów; *pp.* -heáwen *To hew, cut, cut in pieces;* dolare, cædere, concidere:—Wicg hornum geheáweþ *heweth the war-horse with his horns*, Salm. Kmbl. 313; Sal. 156: Beo. Th. 1368; B. 682: Judth. 10; Thw. 22, 33; Jud. 90: 12; Thw. 25, 36; Jud. 295: Bd. 4. 19; S. 588, 27. Ðæt wæs geheáwen of carre *quod erat excisum de petra*, Mk. Skt. Lind. 15, 46. DER. heáwan.

ge-hebban; *p.* -hōf; *pp.* -hafen *To heave up, raise up, ferment;* elevare, fermentare:—Gehafen hlāf *fermentatus panis*, Ælfc. Gl. 66; Wrt. Voc. 41, 15. Gehebbes ða ilco *levabit eam*, Mt. Kmbl. Lind. 12, 11. Gehefen biþ *exaltabitur*, Lk. Skt. Lind. 14, 11. v. hebban.

ge-hēdan; *p.* de; *pp.* ed. I. *to hide, conceal;* condĕre, abscondĕre:—Is ðæt fȳr on stānum gehēded *fire is hidden in stones*, Bt. Met. Fox 20, 302; Met. 20, 151. II. *to acquire, obtain, seize;* obtĭnēre, deprehendĕre:—Ǽr he gehēde ðæt he ǽr æfter spȳrede *until he seizes that which he before sought after*, Bt. Met. Fox 27, 29; Met. 27, 15. Forðonðe he ne ūðe ðæt ǽnig ōðer man ǽfre mǽrþa mā gehēdde under heofenum ðonne he sylfa *because he would not grant that any other man had ever obtained more glories under heaven than himself*, Beo. Th. 1014; B. 505. v. ge-hȳdan.

ge-hēed; *adj.* [=ge-heád] *Exalted;* exaltātus:—Wæs Bryten gehēed *Britain was exalted*, Bd. 1, 6; S. 476, 27.

ge-hefigian, -hefegian, -hefgian; *p.* ode; *pp.* od, ad; *v. trans. To make heavy* or *sad, to load, burden, weigh down, increase the weight of, aggravate;* gravare, contristare, vexare, deprimere, aggravare:—He handa gehefegaþ *he makes the hands heavy*, Salm. Kmbl. 319; Sal. 159. Ðonne biþ gehefgad haswig-feðra, gomol, geárum frōd *then the variegated-feathered* [*phœnix*] *becomes sad, old, advanced in years*, Exon. 58 a; Th. 208, 9; Ph. 153. Ðē-læs eówer heortan gehefegode sȳn on oferfyllē *ne forte graventur corda vestra in crapula*, Lk. Bos. 21, 34. Swā swā hefig byrðen mīn unriht synt gehefegode ofer me *sicut onus grave iniquitates meæ gravatæ sunt super me*, Ps. Th. 37, 4. Wæs mid swā mycelre untrumnesse his līchoman gehefigad *tanta erat corporis infirmitate depressus*, Bd. 4, 23; S. 594, 26: Lk. Bos. 9, 32: Num. 11, 17. Heora synn ys swīðe gehefegod *peccatum eorum aggravatum est*, Gen. 18, 20.

ge-hēgan; *p.* -hēgde, -hēde *To do, perform, effect, hold*:—Ðing gehēgan *to have a meeting*, Beo. Th. 855; B. 425: Andr. Kmbl. 1859; An. 932: Exon. 89 a; Th. 334, 19; Gn. Ex. 18. Seonoþ gehēgan *to hold a synod*, 63 a; Th. 231, 23; Ph. 493: 116 a; Th. 445, 17; Dōm. 9. Hie ðing gehēgdon *they held a meeting*, Andr. Kmbl. 314; An. 157: 2100; An. 1051: 2991; An. 1498. [*See* heyja *in Cl. and Vig. Icel. Dict; Grimm writes* gehegan = *sepire*, And. u. El. 101.]

ge-helan; he -heleþ, -hileþ; *p.* -hæl, *pl.* -hǽlon; *pp.* -holen *To conceal, hide, cover up;* cēlāre, occŭlere, tĕgĕre:—Se ðe dearnenga bearn gestriéneþ and gehileþ [geheleþ MSS. B. H.] *he who secretly begets a child and conceals it*, L. In. 27; Th. i. 120, 2. Ic ðē hāte ðæt ðū hī gehele and gehealde, ōþ-ðæt ic wite hwæt God wylle *te sĭlentio tĕgĕre vŏlo, dōnec sciam quid vĕlit Deus*, Bd. 5, 19; S. 640, 37. Woldon hī and wēndon dæt hī ðǽr mihton dīgle and geholene beón fram andsȳne ðæs unholdan cyninges *occŭlendos se a făci rēgis victōris crēdĭdissent*, 4, 16; S. 584, 25.

ge-hēlan; *p.* de; *pp.* ed *To heal, save;* sānāre, salvum făcĕre:—Gehēl me of eallum ǽhtendum *salvum me fac ex omnĭbus persĕquentĭbus*, Ps. Lamb. 7, 2. v. ge-hǽlan.

ge-helian; *p.* ede; *pp.* ed *To conceal, hide, cover over;* cēlāre, claudĕre:—Se pitt wæs geheled mid ânum stâne *os ejus grandi lăpĭde claudēbātur*, Gen. 29, 2.

ge-helmian; *p.* ode, ede; *pp.* od, ed *To cover with a helmet, crown;* gălеāre, cŏrōnāre:—Đû gehelmodest us *cŏrōnasti nos*, Ps. Spl. 5, 15. Of wuldre and weorþmynt đû gehelmedest hine *de glōria et hŏnōre cŏrōnasti eum*, Ps. Spl. T. 8, 6. Gehelmod *gălеātus*, Ælfc. Gr. 43; Som. 45, 11. [*Laym.* i-helmed: *O. H. Ger.* gehelmot.]

ge-helpan; *p.* -healp, -heolp, *pl.* -hulpon; *pp.* -holpen; *gen. dat. To assist, preserve, to be sufficient;* adjuvare, subvenire, suppetere. I. *cum gen*:—Đonne hie mâgon đîn gehelpan *when they can help thee*, Bt. 14, 1; Fox 42, 10. Đû gehelpest đysses menniscan cynnes *thou shalt help this human race*, Blickl. Homl. 9, 8. Đû mîn hæfst geholpen *thou hast assisted me*, Bt. 41, 4; Fox 250, 18. II. *cum dat*:—Him đâ Ioseph gehealp *then Joseph helped them*, Ors. 1, 5; Bos. 28, 6. Đæt wîf, đe eówrum lîfe geheolp *the woman who preserved your life*, Jos. 6, 22. He wolde gehelpan đearfum *he wished to help needy people*, Swt. A. S. Rdr. 102, 226. v. helpan.

ge-helt *preserves*, Bt. 12; Fox 36, 37; *3rd sing. pres. of* ge-healdan.

ge-hên; *adj. Fallen, low*:—Đa gehēno *kaduca*, Rtl. 189, 31. v. heán.

ge-hênan; *p.* de; *pp.* ed *To humble, accuse, condemn, despise;* humiliare, accusare, condemnare, spernere:—Gehēned ic eom *humiliatus sum*, Ps. Vossii, 37, 8. Hine gehēnan [MS. gehena] *illum accusare*, Lk. Skt. Lind. 23, 2. He gehēned wæs *he was condemned*, Cd. 217; Th. 276, 18; Sat. 190. Gehēneþ mec *spernit me*, Lk. Skt. Lind. 10, 16. v. hēnan.

ge-hendan; *p.* de; *pp.* ed *To hold;* tĕnēre:—Me đîn seó swîđre đǣr gehendeþ *tĕnēbit me dextĕra tua*, Ps. Th. 138, 8.

ge-hende; *adj. Neighbouring, next;* vicinus:—On gehende tûnas *in proximos vicos*, Mk. Bos. 1, 38: 6, 36. Đâ fērdon hî to gehendre byrig *then they went to a neighbouring city*, Homl. Th. i. 456, 5. Đæt hŷ đǣr gehendaste wǣron on gehwylc land đanon to winnanne *that they there should be most handy for waging war thence on every land*, Ors. 3, 7; Bos. 61, 5.

ge-hende; *adv. Near, at hand;* prope:—Sumor is gehende *æstas est prope*, Lk. Bos. 21, 30. Godes rîce is gehende *Dei regnum est prope*, 21, 31: Gen. 19, 20: Exod. 2, 12: Deut. 31, 14. Hî wǣron swâ gehende đet ǣgđer heora on ôđer hâwede *they were so near that each of them looked on the other*, Chr. 1003; Erl. 139, 8. Đa mynstra gehendor đam wæterscipe timbrian *to build the monasteries nearer to the water*, Homl. Th. ii. 160, 32: i. 106, 19.

ge-hende; *prep. dat. Nigh, near:* juxta:—Me gehende *juxta me*, Gen. 45, 10: 12, 11. He wæs gehende đam scype *he was near the ship*, Jn. Bos. 6, 19. He læg đeódne gehende *he lay by his prince*, Byrht. Th. 140, 27; By. 294: Ælfc. Gr. 47; Som. 47, 34.

ge-hendnys, -nyss, e; *f. Nearness, proximity, vicinity;* proxĭmĭtas, vĭcīnĭtas:—Gehendnys *vĭcīnĭtas*, Glos. Prudent. Recd. 139, 47. Đa geswuteliaþ gehendnysse *they express vicinity*, Ælfc. Gr. 5; Som. 4, 50. On gehendnysse his mynstres *in the neighbourhood of his monastery*, Homl. Th. ii. 174, 5.

ge-hentan; *p.* te; *pp.* ed *To take, seize;* căpĕre, prehendĕre:—Hió abît hæleđa gehwilcne đe hió gehentan mæg *she devours every man whom she can seize*, Bt. Met. Fox 13, 64; Met. 13, 32. Eall đæt hie gehentan mehton *all that they could seize*, Chron. 905; Erl. 98, 17.

ge-heofegian; *p.* ode, ede; *pp.* od, ed; *v. trans. To make heavy, load, weigh down;* gravare, Mt. Kmbl. Hat. 26, 43. v. ge-hefigian.

ge-heold, es; *m? A keeping, observing;* custōdia, observātio:—Hî sôþfæstnysse and ârfæstnesse and clǣnnesse, and ôđra gâstlîcra mægena geheold, and swýđost sibbe and Godes lufan geornlîce lǣrde *justĭtiæ, pĭetātis et castĭmōniæ, cætĕrārumque virtūtum, sed maxime pācis et cārĭtātis custōdiam dŏcuit*, Bd. 4, 23; S. 593, 40. On geheoldum [MS. geheoldan] unrihta Eástrena *in the keeping of unright Easters*, 5, 24; S. 646, 39. v. geheald.

ge-heóld, đû -heólde; *pl.* -heóldon *kept, observed*, Gen. 20, 6: Ps. Th. 114, 8: Andr. Kmbl. 691; An. 346; *p. of* ge-healdan: ge-heólde, *pl.* -heólden *would save*, Jos. 10, 6; *p. subj. of* ge-healdan.

ge-heolp *preserved*, Jos. 6, 22; *p. of* ge-helpan.

ge-heóran; *p.* de; *pp.* ed *To hear;* audire:—Geheór nû *hear now*, Bt. 35, 5; Fox 116, 21. Ne geheórþ *hears not*, Bt. 18, 2; Fox 64, 3. Ne geheórdon *heard not*, 18, 2; Fox 64, 12. v. gehŷran, hŷran.

ge-heordnes, -ness, -nys, -nyss, e; *f. A keeping, guard, watch;* custōdia:—On geheordnesse đara edieán manige [is] *in custōdiendis illis retrĭbūtio multa* [*est*], Ps. Spl. T. 18, 12. Gesete Driht geheordnysse mûþes mînes *pōne Dŏmĭne custōdiam ōri meo*, Ps. Spl. 140, 3. v. gehyrdnes.

ge-heordung, e; *f. A keeping, guard, watch;* custōdia:—Ic sette mûþe mînum geheordunga *pŏsui ōri meo custōdiam*, Ps. Spl. T. 38, 2.

ge-heort; *comp.* ra; *adj. Hearty, animated, courageous;* anĭmæquus:—On geheortum hyge *in a courageous soul*, Exon. 81 a; Th. 305, 14; Fä. 86. Beó geheortra *anĭmæquior esto*, Mk. Bos. 10, 49.

ge-heowian; *p.* ode, ade; *pp.* od, ad *To form;* formāre:—Dracan đû đysne geheowadest *drăco iste, quem formasti*, Ps. Th. 103, 25: Blickl. Homl. 87, 32: 31, 16. v. ge-hiwian.

ge-heowung. v. gehiwung.

geher *an ear of corn*, Mk. Skt. Rush. 4, 28. v. ear.

ge-hêran; *p.* de; *pp.* ed *To hear;* audire:—Ic ne sceal ǣfre gehēran đære byrhtestan bēman stefne *I shall never hear the brightest trumpet's sound*, Cd. 216; Th. 275, 14; Sat. 171: 220; Th. 284, 27; Sat. 328. Ic gehēre helle scealcas grundas mǣnan *I hear hell's ministers bemoaning the gulfs*, 216; Th. 273, 7; Sat. 133. We gehērdon wuldres swēg *we heard the sound of glory*, 218; Th. 279, 13; Sat. 237. Gehēr ân spell *hear a discourse*, Bt. 37, 1; Fox 186, 1: 35, 5; Fox 166, 21, note 24. Đâ sió stefn gewearþ gehēred of heofenum *then the voice was heard out of heaven*, Andr. Kmbl. 335; An. 168. v. ge-hŷran.

ge-hercnian; *p.* ode; *pp.* od *To hear*:—Gehercnadon *audientes*, Mt. Kmbl. Lind. 22, 22.

ge-hergian; *p.* ode, ade; *pp.* od, ad *To ravage, plunder, afflict, harrow, take captive;* vastāre, spŏliāre, afflīgĕre, captīvum dūcĕre:—He on đam fyrste helle gehergode *he harrowed hell in that space of time*, Homl. Th. ii. 608, 1. Đe hie gehergod hæfdon *which they had plundered*, Chr. 895; Erl. 93, 19. Gehergad *ravaged*, Ors. 3, 11; Bos. 72, 22. Đæt ûre wîf and ûre cild wurdon gehergode *ut uxōres ac lĭbĕri nostri dūcantur captīvi*, Num. 14, 3: Jud. 10, 8: Gen. 31, 26: Shrn. 96, 12.

ge-hêrian [*or* -herian; cf. *Goth.* hazjan]; *p.* ode, ede; *pp.* od, ed [hērian *to praise*] *To praise, honour, glorify;* laudāre, hŏnōrāre, celebrāre:—Unlǣde biþ se ne can Crist gehērian *wretched is he who cannot honour Christ*, Salm. Kmbl. 48; Sal. 24. On Gode byþ gehērod mîn sâwl *in Dŏmĭno laudābĭtur anĭma mea*, Ps. Th. 33, 2. Đeáh he seó ânum gehēred *though it be praised in one*, Bt. 30, 1; Fox 108, 14: Blickl. Homl. 71, 16. On Gode we beóþ gehērode *in Dŏmĭno laudābĭmur*, Ps. Lamb. 43, 9. He wæs gehiered *he was praised*, Blickl. Homl. 165, 1.

ge-hêring, e; *f. A hearing, hearsay, tidings;* audītio:—Fram gehēringe yfelre he ne ondrǣt *ab audītiōne māla non tĭmēbit*, Ps. Lamb. 111, 7.

gehêr-nes, -ness, e; *f. Hearing;* auditus:—In gehērnesse *audiendo*, Bd. 4, 24; S. 598, 6. Dryhten ic gehērde gehērnisse [gehîrnesse, Ps. Trin. Camb. fol. 244, 7] đîne *Domine audivi auditum tuum vocem tuam*, Cant. Abac. Surt. 189, 2: Jn. Skt. Rush. 12, 38. v. ge-hŷrnes.

ge-hêt *promised*. v. ge-hâtan.

Gehhol, Gehhel, es; *n. Yule, Christmas*, L. Alf. pol. 5; Th. i. 64, 23: 43; Th. i. 92, 3. v. geól.

ge-hicgan, -hicggan, -hicgean, -higgan *to study, search out*. v. gehycgan.

ge-hîdan; *p.* de; *pp.* ed *To hide, conceal;* condĕre, abscondĕre:—Đe ic hafa on stânfate gehîded *which I have hidden in a stone chest*, Wald. 63; Vald. 2, 3. v. ge-hŷdan.

ge-hiénan *to humble*. v. ge-hŷnan.

ge-hiéran. v. ge-hŷran.

ge-hierstan *to fry*. v. ge-hyrstan.

ge-hiérsum; *adj. Obedient;* obēdiens:—Hie him alle gehiérsume dydon *they made all obedient to him*, Chr. 853; Erl. 68, 11. v. ge-hŷrsum.

ge-hiérsumian *to make obedient*, Chr. 853; Th. 122, 22, col. 1. v. ge-hŷrsumian.

ge-higd, e; *f*: es; *n. Thought, meditation;* cōgĭtātio:—Sende mihtig God his milde gehigd *mīsit Deus mĭsĕrĭcordiam suam*, Ps. Th. 56, 4. Heortan gehigdum *in the heart's thoughts*, Elen. Kmbl. 2445; El. 1224. v. ge-hygd.

ge-hihtan, -hyhtan; *p.* -hihte; *pp.* -hihted. I. *to hope, trust;* spērāre:—Betere is gehihtan on Drihtne đonne gehihtan on ealdrum *bŏnum est spērāre in Dŏmĭno quam spērāre in princĭpĭbus*, Ps. Lamb. 117, 9. On hys naman đeóda gehyhtaþ *in nōmĭne ejus gentes spērābunt*, Mt. Bos. 12, 21. II. *to rejoice;* exultāre:—Muntas gehihtaþ swâ swâ rammas *montes exultasti sīcut arietes*, Ps. Spl. 113, 6.

ge-hild, es; *n. A secret place*:—On gehildum *in abditis*, Ps. Spl. T. 16, 13.

ge-hileþ *conceals*, L. In. 27; Th. i. 120, 2; *3rd sing. pres. of* ge-helan.

ge-hilt, es; *n. A hilt, handle;* căpŭlus:—He gegrâp sweord be gehiltum *he seized the sword by the hilt*, Cd. 140; Th. 176, 1; Gen. 2905. [*O. H. Ger.* gehilze.]

ge-hiltst *keepest*, Ex. 34, 6; *2nd sing. pres. of* ge-healdan.

ge-hînan *to oppress*, Ex. 5, 9: L. Alf. 35; Th. i. 52, 23, note 64. v. ge-hŷnan.

ge-hindred, -hindrad, -hyndred; *part. Hindered;* impĕdītus:—Biþ eall se here swîđe gehindred [gehindrad, 252, 33, col. 1; gehyndred, col. 2] *all the army will be greatly hindered*, Chr. 1003; Th. 253, 32.

ge-hióld, *pl.* -hióldon *kept, preserved*, Past. pref; Swt. 3, 7; Hat. MS; *p. of* ge-healdan.

ge-hióran; *p.* de; *pp.* ed *To hear;* audīre:—Đa [MS. đe] eáran ongitaþ đæt hî gehióraþ *the ears perceive that which they hear*, Bt. 41, 4; Fox 252, 8. v. ge-hŷran.

ge-hiowian; *p.* ade; *pp.* ad *To form, fashion;* formāre:—Ðú gehiowades mec *formasti me,* Ps. Surt. 138, 5: 103, 26. v. ge-hiwian.

ge-hîran; *p.* -hîrde; *pp.* -hîred *To hear;* exaudire:—Gehîr, God! mîn gebed *exaudi, Deus! orātionem meam.* Ðys is gebed, and ná hǽs *this is a prayer, and not a command,* Ælfc. Gr. 33; Som. 37, 52. v. ge-hŷran, hŷran.

ge-hîrness, e; *f. Hearing;* auditus:—Ic gehîre gehîrnesse ðîne *audivi auditum tuum* [*vocem tuam*], Ps. Trin. Camb. fol. 244, 7. v. ge-hērnes.

ge-hîrsumnes, se; *f. Obedience:*—For his gehîrsumnisse ðe he hæfde to Gode *for his obedience to God,* Swt. A. S. Rdr. 62, 181.

ge-hiscan *to hate;* abominari:—Ðæne wer gehiscþ drihten *virum abominabitur dominus,* Ps. Lamb. 5, 8.

ge-hiwad; *p. part. Coloured;* purpuratus, Lk. Skt. p. 9, 2. [*A. R.* i-heouwed.]

ge-hiwian, -hywian, -heowian, -hiowian; *p.* ode, ade, ede; *pp.* od, ad, ed. **I.** *to form, fashion, make, transform, transfigure;* formāre, plasmāre, fingĕre, fīgūrāre, transfīgūrāre:—Ðú ðe gehiwast sārnesse on bebode *qui fingis lăbōrem in præcepto,* Ps. Lamb. 93, 20. Sió godcunde fōreteohhung eall þing gehiwaþ *the divine predestination fashions everything,* Bt. 39, 6; Fox 220, 17. Ðú gehiwadest me *formasti me,* Ps. Th. 138, 3. Handa me ðîne geworhton and gehiwedan *mănus tuæ fēcērunt me et plasmāvērunt me,* 118, 73. He wæs gehiwod beforan him *transfīgūrātus est ante eos,* Mt. Bos. 17, 2. Seó heáfodstōw gescrepelîce gehiwad ætȳwde to ðam gemete hyre heáfdes *lŏcus căpĭtis ad mensūram căpĭtis illīus aptissĭme fīgūrātus appāruit,* Bd. 4, 19; S. 590, 2. **II.** *to seem, appear, pretend;* sĭmŭlāre:—Ðeáh ðe he hit swá gehiwige *though he may so pretend,* Homl. Th. i. 6, 18. Seó gehiwode anlîcnys getiðode ðám toslitenum mannum hwîlendlîc lîf *the apparent likeness imparted to the torn men transitory life,* ii. 240, 17. Gehiwed *dissimulatus,* Hpt. Gl. 517. Ne lufa ðú ðînne broðor mid gehiwodre heortan *do not love thy brother with a dissembling heart,* Basil admn. 5; Norm. 46, 4.

ge-hîwian, -hiewian; *p.* ode; *pp.* od *To marry:*—Forðæm hit is awriten ðæt hit sîe betere ðæt mon gehiewige ðonne he birne, forðæm būtan synne he mæg gehîwian *for it is written that it is better to marry than to burn, because a man may marry without sin,* Past. 51, 9; Swt. 401, 33; Hat. MS.

ge-hiwung, -hywung, -heowung, e; *f. A form, fashion, shape, position, predicament;* figmentum, cătēgŏria:—He oncneów gehywunge ūre *ipse cognōvit figmentum nostrum,* Ps. Spl. C. 102, 13. Gehiwunge *cătēgŏriæ,* Cot. 57. Drihten, ðú wâst mîne geheowunga *Lord, thou knowest my fashioning,* Blickl. Homl. 89, 15.

ge-hladan; *p.* -hlōd, -hleód, *pl.* -hlōdon; *pp.* -hladen, -hlæden. **I.** *to load, burden, freight, heap up;* onĕrāre, impōnĕre, congĕrĕre, cūmŭlāre:—Ðe he on foldan on his gǽste gehlōd *which he on earth loaded on his soul,* Exon. 23 a; Th. 64, 10; Cri. 1035. He sǽbât gehleód *he loaded the sea-boat,* Beo. Th. 1795, note; B. 895, note. Hî gehlōdon werum and wîfum wǽghengestas *they loaded the ocean-stallions with men and women,* Elen. Kmbl. 467; El. 234: Cd. 174; Th. 220, 2; Dan. 65. Biþ seó mōdor wistum gehladen *the mother is laden with provisions,* Exon. 128 a; Th. 492, 16; Rä. 81, 16. Ða wǽron ofætes gehlædene *which were laden with fruit,* Cd. 23; Th. 30, 4; Gen. 461. **II.** *to draw* [*water*]; haurire:—To gehladanne *haurire,* Jn. Skt. Lind. 4, 15.

ge-hlǽg, es; *n. Scorn, ridicule:*—Hî gehlǽges tilgaþ *they strive after scorn,* Exon. 116 a; Th. 446, 1; Dōm. 15. [Cf. *Icel.* hlægi *ridicule,* and hlihan.]

ge-hlǽnian *to make lean, thin.* v. lǽnian.

ge-hlæstan; *p.* -hlæste; *pp.* -hlæsted, -hlæst *To load, adorn:*—Mid ðȳ hî þæt scyp gehlæsted hæfdon *when they had freighted the ship,* Bd. 5, 9; S. 623, 17: Exon. 52 a; Th. 182, 8; Gú. 1307. Ða eádigan mægþ beágum gehlæste *the blessed maid adorned with rings,* Judth. 10; Thw. 21, 30; Jud. 36.

ge-hlaðen *invited.* v. ge-laðian.

ge-hleápan; *p.* -hleóp, *pl.* -hleópon; *pp.* -hleápen *To leap, dance;* salire, saltare:—Meotud gehleápeþ heá dūne *the Creator shall leap the high downs,* Exon. 18 a; Th. 45, 10; Cri. 717. He gehleóp ðone eoh *he leaped upon the horse,* Byrht. Th. 137, 20; By. 189.

ge-hleód *loaded,* Beo. Th. 1795, note; B. 895, note; *p. of* ge-hladan.

ge-hleodu *vaults,* Exon. 21 a; Th. 56, 23; Cri. 905; *pl. nom. acc. of* ge-hlid.

ge-hleótan; *p.* -hleát, *pl.* -hluton; *pp.* -hloten *To share* or *appoint by lot, to get, receive;* sortiri, nancisci:—He ðæs weorc gehleát *he got pain for this,* Cd. 131; Th. 166, 10; Gen. 2745: Ps. Th. 105, 24. Se eádiga Matheus gehleát to Marmadonia *St. Matthew was allotted to Mermedonia,* Blickl. Homl. 229, 6. Gehluton [MS. gehlutan] *they obtained,* Ps. Th. 113, 2. Gehloten, Exon. 95 a; Th. 355, 18; Reim. 79. Hit wæs gehloten to Iosepes bearna lande *it was allotted to the land of the children of Joseph,* Jos. 24, 32. Ic wæs gehloten mid ânum wîfe in ânes ceorles ðeówdōme *I was allotted with a woman to the service of a certain man,* Shrn. 38, 13. [*Laym.* i-leoten *to fall to one's lot.*] v. hleótan.

ge-hleóþ; *adj. Harmonious;* consonus:—Ðæt hî ðysne letanîan and antefn gehleóþre stæfne sungan *quia hanc litaniam consona voce modularentur,* Bd. 1, 25; S. 487, 24.

ge-hleów *a lowing.* v. gehlōw.

ge-hleow; *adj. Sheltered, warm:*—Ond ðá on gehliúran dene and on wearmran we gewîcodon *in apriciore valle sedem castrorum inveni,* Nar. 23, 4. [Cf. *Icel.* hlýr *warm.*] v. unhleow.

ge-hlēða, an; *m.* [hlōþ] *A companion, comrade;* sŏcius:—Wulf sang ahōf, holtes gehlēða *the wolf uplifted his song, the companion of the forest,* Elen. Kmbl. 225; El. 113. Se ðe ǽr bær wulfes gehlēðan *who ere bore the wolf's companion,* Exon. 130 b; Th. 499, 30; Rä. 88, 23. DER. wil-gehlēða.

ge-hlid, es; *pl. nom. acc.* -hlidu, -hleodu; *n. A lid, covering, roof, an inclosure, a vault;* tectum, clausūra, septum:—Ic cann ealle heáh-heofona gehlidu *I know all the roofs of the high heavens,* Cd. 27; Th. 37, 3; Gen. 584: Exon. 15 a; Th. 32, 25; Cri. 518. Ðonne bearn Godes þurh heofona gehleodu ōþȳweþ *when the son of God shall appear through heaven's vaults,* 21 a; Th. 56, 23; Cri. 905.

ge-hlidad; *part.* [ge-hlid *a lid*] *Lidded, covered with a lid;* opercŭlo tectus:—Seó wæs gerisenlîce gehlidad mid gelîce stāne *operculo sĭmĭlis lăpĭdis aptissĭme tectum,* Bd. 4, 19; S. 588, 32.

ge-hlihan; *p. pl.* gehlogun *to deride.* v. hlihan.

ge-hlioran *to pass over.* v. leoran.

ge-hliþ, es; *pl. nom. acc.* -hliðo; *n. A lid, covering, roof;* tectum:—Sceolde he sēcan helle gehliðo *he must seek the roofs of hell* [or *gates of hell:* cf. *Icel.* hlið *a gate*], Cd. 36; Th. 47, 21; Gen. 764. v. ge-hlid.

ge-hlōd, *pl.* -hlōdon *loaded,* Exon. 23 a; Th. 64, 10; Cri. 1035: Elen. Kmbl. 467; El. 234; *p. of* ge-hladan.

ge-hlot, es; *n. A lot;* sors:—Ðæt gehlot *sors,* Jos. 7, 14, 17.

ge-hloten *appointed by lot.* v. ge-hleótan.

gehlot-land, es; *n. Land appointed by lot, an inheritance;* terra sorte assignāta, possessio:—Hîg hine bebirigdon on his gehlotland *sepĕliērunt eum in fīnĭbus possessiōnis suæ,* Jos. 24, 30.

ge-hlōw, -hleów *a lowing of beasts;* mugitus:—Hryðera gehlōw *lowing of oxen,* Ælfc. Gr. 1; Som. 2, 35.

ge-hluttrad; *part.* [hluttran *to purify*] *Purified, made clear;* defæcātus:—Gehluttrad wîn *defæcātum vinum,* Ælfc. Gl. 32; Som. 62, 6; Wrt. Voc. 27, 60.

ge-hlȳd; *part. Covered;* tectus:—Of flȳsum mînra sceápa wǽron gehlȳde þearfena sîdan *the sides of the poor were covered with the fleeces of my sheep,* Job Thw. 165, 2. v. ge-hlywan.

ge-hlȳd, -hlȳde, es; *n. A cry, clamour, noise, tumult, murmuring;* clāmor, tumultus, murmur:—Mycel gehlȳd wæs on ðære menigeo be him *murmur multum ĕrat in turba de eo,* Jn. Bos. 7, 12: Mt. Bos. 27, 24: Homl. Th. ii. 336, 18. Gehlȳde mîn to ðē become *clāmor meus ad te pervĕniat,* Ps. Th. 101, 1. He geseah mycel gehlȳd *vĭdet tumultum multum,* Mk. Bos. 5, 38: Bd. 5, 12; S. 628, 30: Homl. Th. ii. 252, 17: 546, 16: Basil admn. 2; Norm. 34, 15. Mid ânþræcum gehlȳde *with a horrible clamour,* Homl. Th. ii. 508, 17.

ge-hlyn, es; *n. A noise, din;* clangor:—Ðá wæs on healle wælslihta gehlyn *then was in the hall the din of slaughters,* Fins Th. 57; Fin. 28.

ge-hlyst, es; *n. Hearing;* auditus, R. Ben. 67. DER. hlyst.

ge-hlystan; *p.* -hlyste; *pp.* -hlysted. **I.** *to listen, hear;* auscultare, audire:—Gehlyste me *audiat me,* Mk. Bos. 7, 16. Beornas gehlyston *men listened,* Byrht. Th. 134, 31; By. 92. **II.** *to obey;* obedire:—On hlyste eáran gehlyste me *in auditu auris obediunt mihi,* Ps. Spl. 17, 46. DER. hlystan.

ge-hlystfull; *adj. Exorable, gracious;* audire volens, deprecabilis, Ps. Lamb. 89, 13. DER. hlyst.

ge-hlyta, an; *m. A companion;* consors:—Fōr gehlytum ðînum *præ consortĭbus tuis,* Ps. Spl. 44, 9.

ge-hlytto *fellowship;* consortium, Rtl. 38, 43.

ge-hlyttrod; *part. Purified, pure;* mĕrăcus:—Gehlyttrod wîn *mĕrăcum vinum,* Ælfc. Gl. 32; Som. 62, 7; Wrt. Voc. 27, 61. v. ge-hluttrad.

ge-hlywan; *p.* de; *pp.* ed *To cover, shelter:*—Of flȳsum mînra sceápa wǽron gehlywde ðearfena sîdan *the sides of the needy were covered with the fleeces of my sheep,* Homl. Th. ii. 448, 18. v. hleow.

ge-hnâd, es; *n. A conflict, fight;* immanitas, Chr. 937; Erl. 114, 15. v. ge-hnǽst.

ge-hnǽcan; *p.* te; *pp.* ed *To check, restrain, bruise, destroy;* reprīmĕre, contĕrĕre, allīdĕre:—Heó gehnǽceþ ða anginnu *it checketh the beginnings,* Herb. 148, 1; Lchdm. i. 272, 15: 163, 6; Lchdm. i. 292, 19. Ðú me ahōfe and gehnǽctest eft *elĕvans allīsisti me,* Ps. Th. 101, 8.

ge-hnǽgan, -hnǽgean, -hnēgan; *p.* -hnǽgde, -hnǽde; *pp.* -hnǽged, -hnǽgd; *v. trans. To bend down, humble, cast down, subdue;* declīnāre, hūmĭliāre, dejĭcĕre, subĭgĕre:—Ðú miht oferhydige eáðe mid wunde heáne gehnǽgean *tu hŭmĭliasti sīcut vulnĕrātum sŭperbum,* Ps. Th. 88, 9. Ðú hî mid fȳre fǽcnes gehnēgest *in ignem dejĭcies eos,* 139, 10. He fyrenfulle wið eorþan nider ealle gehnēgeþ *hŭmĭliat peccātōres usque ad terram,* 146, 6. Hie on wætere wicg gehnǽgaþ *they cast down the horse in the water,* Salm. Kmbl. 312; Sal. 155. Ðú goda ussa gilp gehnǽgdest *thou humbledst the glory of our gods,* Andr. Kmbl. 2640; An. 1321:

Ps. Th. 118, 71. He gehnǽgde helle·gâst *he subdued the spirit of hell*, Beo. Th. 2552; B. 1274: Andr. Kmbl. 2383; An. 1193. Mîn Drihten ðe gehnǽde in helle *my Lord hath trodden thee down in hell*, Blickl. Homl. 241, 5. Hyne Hetware hilde gehnǽgdon *the Hetwaras subdued him in war*, Beo. Th. 5825; B. 2916. Ðæt gê wiðerfeohtend gehnǽgan *that ye may subdue your adversary*, Andr. Kmbl. 2368; An. 1185. Blǽd is gehnǽged *glory is humbled*, Exon. 82 b; Th. 311, 7; Seef. 88: Ps. Th. 142, 3. Wǽron ða mǽgþe mid hefigran þeówdôme gehnǽgde *provincia grăviōre servĭtio subacta*, Bd. 4, 15; S. 583, 30.

ge-hnǽst, -hnâst, es; *n. A conflict, slaughter;* conflictus, prœlium:—Æfter ðæm gehnǽste *after the battle*, Cd. 94; Th. 121, 24; Gen. 2015: Chr. 937; Erl. 114, 15, note 9. DER. cumbol-, hôp-, wolcen-. v. hnîtan.

ge-hnêgan *to humble, cast down*, Ps. Th. 139, 10: 146, 6. v. ge-hnǽgan.

ge-hnesctun, -hnescod *softened*. v. hnescian.

ge-hnîgan; *p.* -hnâh, -hnâg, *pl.* -hnigon; *pp.* -hnigen *To bow, bow the head;* inclinare, inclinare se:—Heán sceal gehnîgan *the humble shall bow*, Exon. 91 a; Th. 340, 28; Gn. Ex 118. v. hnîgan.

ge-hnyscan *to crush;* conterere, Mt. Kmbl. Rush. 21, 44. [Cf. hnesc.]

ge-hnyst; *part. p. Contrite:*—Se gehnysta gâst *the contrite spirit*, Ps. C. 50, 127; Ps. Grn. ii. 279, 127. [Cf. hnossian *and* cnyssan (?).]

ge-hoered *heard*. v. ge-hýran.

ge-hoferod; *part. Hump-backed;* gibbĕrōsus:—Ðe wǽron gehoferode *who were hump-backed*, Homl. Th. ii. 586, 23.

ge-hogde, -hogode. v. ge-hycgan.

ge-hola, an; *m. A protector:*—Ðam ðe him lyt hafaþ leófra geholena *to him who has for himself few dear protectors*, Exon. 76 b; Th. 288, 15; Wand. 31.

ge-holen *hidden*, Bd. 4, 16; S. 584, 25; *pp. of* ge-helan.

ge-hôn, -hongian; *pp.* -hongen, -hoen *To hang, hang with:*—Ðætte he gehongiga *that he hang*, Mt. Kmbl. Lind. 18, 6. He sē gehoen *crucifigatur*, 26, 2. Wudu biþ blêdum gehongen *the wood will be hung with fruits*, Exon. 56 a; Th. 200, 9; Ph. 38: 566; Th. 202, 18; Ph. 71.

ge-honge; *adj. Having an inclination to:*—Teala gehonge *inclined to good*, Exon. 94 b; Th. 354, 8; Reim. 42.

ge-hopp *a little bag;* folliculus, Cot. 87.

ge-horian; *pp.* ad *To spit:*—Gehorogæ *conspuere*, Mk. Skt. Lind. 14, 65. Gehoræd biþ *conspuetur*, Lk. Skt. Lind. 18, 32. v. horu.

ge-hornian; *p.* ade *To insult* [?]:—Mid sceofmum miclum gehornadon *contumeliis affecerunt*, Mk. Skt. Lind. 12, 4. v. gehornung.

ge-hornung, e; *f. Sadness, grief*, Som.

ge-horsian; *p.* ode, ade, ude; *pp.* od, ad, ud *To horse, to set* or *mount on a horse, to supply with a horse;* equitem facere, equo instruere *vel* imponere: *as yet found only as pp:*—Here gehorsode wurdon *the army was horsed* [*mounted*], Chr. 867; Th. 130, 28, col. 3: Gehorsade, 130, 28, col. 2: 131, 28, col. 1, 2: Gehorsude, 130, 27, col. 1. Ælfrêd æfter ðam gehorsodan [gehorsudan, col. 1; -sedum, 147, 3, col. 1; sedun, col. 2] here mid fyrde râd ôþ Exancester *Alfred with his force rode after the mounted army to Exeter*, Chr. 877; Th. 146, 1, col. 3. Ða Denan wurdon gehorsode *the Danes were horsed* [*mounted*], Chr. 1010; Th. 264, 2, col. 2. DER. horsian.

ge-horsod [*pp. of* ge-horsian] *Horsed, mounted;* equo impositus *vel* instructus:—Ðâ com him ðǽr ongeán twâ hund þûsenda gehorsodes [MS. gehorsades] folces *then came against him* [*Alexander*] *two hundred thousand horsemen* [*horsed folk, cavalry*], Ors. 3. 9; Bos. 67, 43. v. ge-horsian.

ge-hradian; *p.* ode; *pp.* od *To hasten;* accelerare:—Sôna wôl ealra monna gehradode *continuo omnium lues scelerum adceleravit* Bd. 1, 14; S. 482, 23: 4, 19; S. 588, 33. v. ge-radod.

ge-hræcan *to set in order, direct;* dirigĕre:—Weorc handa ussera gehræce *ōpus mănuum nostrārum dirige*, Ps. Lamb. 89, 17. v. ge-reccan

ge-hrædnys, -nyss, e; *f. What passes swiftly, swiftness, fewness;* paucitas, Ps. Spl. 101, 24.

ge-hrân *touched*, Exon. 47 b; Th. 163, 28; Gû. 1000; *p. sing. of* ge-hrînan.

ge-hreás *rushed*. v. ge-hreósan.

ge-hrec, es; *n. Government, management:*—Mid mycele gehrece *sedulo moderamine*, Bd. 3, 7; Whelc. 179, 8. v. ge-rec.

ge-hrêfan; *p.* de; *pp.* ed [hrôf *a roof*] *To roof, cover;* tĕgĕre:—Gehrêf hit eall *roof it all*, Homl. Th. i. 20, 32. Holme gehrêfed *covered with water*, Exon. 101 a; Th. 381, 12; Rä. 2, 10.

ge-hrehte *corrected;* correxi, Bd. 5, 24; S. 648, 25. v. ge-rehte.

ge-hrêman; *p.* de *To cry, implore:*—Gihrêmaþ and woepaþ gê *plorabitis et flebitis vos*, Jn. Skt. Rush. 16, 20. Gihrême we *imploramus*, Rtl. 37, 3.

ge-hremmed; *part. Hindered;* impĕdītus:—Gehremmed beón *impĕdīri*, R. Ben. 52.

ge-hreónis, se; *f. Repentance*, Rtl. 102, 45.

ge-hreósan; *p.* -hreás, *pl.* -hruron; *pp.* -hroren *To rush, fall, glide away, to fail;* ruere, cadere, labi, deficere:—Hrôfas sind gehrorene *the roofs are fallen*, Exon. 124 a; Th. 476, 5; Ruin. 3. Ðâ cômon hî to sumre ceastre gehrorenre *venerunt ad civitatulam quandam desolatam*, Bd. 4, 19; S. 588, 29. Ic ðus gehroren eom ond aweg gewiten *I* [*Babylon*] *am thus fallen and passed away*, Ors. 2, 4; Bos. 44, 35. Môna niðer gehreóseþ *the moon shall fall down*, Exon. 21 b; Th. 58, 22; Cri. 939. Swîðe oft se micla anweald ðara yfelena gehrîst swîðe fǽrlîce *very often the great power of the wicked falls very suddenly*, Bt. 38, 2; Fox 198, 8. Gehreósaþ *labuntur*, Exon. 95 a; Th. 354, 34; Reim. 55. DER. hreósan.

ge-hreóðan *to adorn*. v. ge-hroden.

ge-hreów, es; *n. A lamenting;* lamentatio:—Ðǽr biþ gehreów and hlûd wôp *there shall be lamenting and loud weeping*, Exon. 22 b; Th. 62, 9; Cri. 999. DER. hreów.

ge-hreówan; *p.* -hreáw, *pl.* -hruwon; *pp.* -hrowen *To rue, repent, grieve, pity;* pœnitere, dolere, miserere:—Mec his bysgu gehreáw *his affliction grieved me*, Exon. 43 a; Th. 144, 31; Gû. 686. Generally *impers.* hit-hreóweþ, -hrýwþ; *p.* hit-hreáw *It rues, it repents, it grieves, it pities;* pœnitet, dolet, miseret; hit-hreáw *it grieved:*—Him ðæt gehreówan mæg *that may rue them*, Cd. 225; Th. 298, 29; Sat. 540. Mec æt heortan gehreáw *I repented at heart* [lit. *it repented me at heart*], Exon. 29 b; Th. 91, 18; Cri. 1494: Cd. 221; Th. 288, 2; Sat. 374. DER. hreówan.

ge-hrepod [*pp. of* ge-hrepian *to touch*] *touched;* tactus:—He wæs gehrepod mid heortan sârnisse wiðinnan *tactus dolore cordis intrinsecus*, Gen. 6, 6. Gehrepod *tactus*, Ælfc. Gr. 43; Som. 44, 56.

ge-hrêran; *p.* de *To move:*—Mægen heofunas bióþ gehroered *virtutes cœlorum commovebuntur*, Mt. Kmbl. Lind. 24, 29.

ge-hrespan *to tear:*—Hý him sylfum gehrespaþ *diripiebant sibi*, Ps. Th. 43, 12.

ge-hrifan; *p.* ede; *pp.* ed [hrif *the womb*] *To bring forth;* părĕre:—Gecende sârnessa and gehrifede oððe acende unrihtwîsnesse *concēpit dolōrem et pĕpĕrit inīquītātem*, Ps. Lamb. 7, 15.

ge-hrînan, -rînan; he -hrîneþ, -hrînþ; *p.* -hrân, *pl.* -hrinon; *pp.* -hrinen *To touch, take hold of, seize, affect;* tangĕre, contingĕre, răpĕre, affectāre:—Ne ofer ðæt syððan hine ôwiht gehrînan dorste *neque umquam exinde eum audēret contingĕre*, Bd. 3, 12; S. 537, 14, MS. B: 3, 17; S. 544, 28. Ða mǽran tungl áuðer ôðres rene â ne gehrîneþ *these splendid stars never touch each other's course*, Bt. Met. Fox 29, 20; Met. 29, 10. Hî gehrînþ hêr sumu wracu *some punishment affects them here*, Past. 55; Swt. 429, 19; Hat. MS. Me sâr gehrân *pain hath touched me*, Exon. 47 b; Th 163, 28; Gû. 1000. Heó sôna wæs gehrinen and genumen of middanearde *rapta confestim de mundo*, Bd. 4, 19; S. 589, 5: 4, 8; S. 575, 30. Hia gehrînadon ł gehrînad hæfde *tetigerunt*, Mt. Kmbl. Lind. 14, 36.

ge-hrinenes, -ness, e; *f. A touch;* tactus:—Mid ðý gehrinenesse ðæra [MS. ðære] ilcena gegyrlena *tactu indūmentōrum eōrumdem*, Bd. 4, 19; S. 589, 32.

ge-hrîst *falls*. v. hreósan.

ge-hroden [*pp. of* ge-hreóðan *to adorn*] *adorned;* ornatus:—Biþ seó môdor hordum gehroden *the mother is adorned with treasures*, Exon. 128 a; Th. 492, 17; Rä. 81, 17. Eoforlîc gehroden golde *a boar's likeness adorned with gold*, Beo. Th. 614; B. 304. Grêne stondaþ gehroden hyhtlîce beorhtast bearwa *the brightest of groves stands green, gloriously adorned*, Exon. 57 a; Th. 203, 4; Ph. 79. Ðec gemêtte, meahtum gehrodene *he found thee adorned with virtues*, 12 b; Th. 21, 6; Cri. 330: Judth. 10; Thw. 21, 27; Jud. 37. Geseh he bearwas blǽdum gehrodene *he saw groves adorned with blossoms*, Andr. Kmbl. 2896; An. 1451: Exon. 97 b; Th. 364, 21; Wal. 74.

ge-hror, es; *n. A fall, ruin, death:*—Ðonne ðæt gelumpe ðæt hî of middangearde genumene wǽron ðý ylcan gehrore ðe hî ôðre gesâwon *cum eas eodem quo cæteros exterminio raptari e mundo contingeret*, Bd. 4, 7; S. 574, 38. v. gehreósan, *and* cf. *Icel.* hrör *cadaver*.

ge-hroren *fallen*, Exon. 124 a; Th. 476, 5; Ruin. 3; *pp. of* gehreósan.

ge-hrorenes, -ness, e; *f. Affliction, ruin;* ærumna:—Gecerrod oððe gewend ic eom on gehrorenesse oððe yrmþum mînum *conversus sum in ærumna mea*, Ps. Lamb. 31, 4.

ge-hruron, -hroren *rushed down, destroyed, was desolate*. v. gehreósan.

ge-hruxl *a noise, disturbance;* tumultus, Dial. 2, 10.

ge-hrýne, es; *n. A mystery, sacrament;* mystērium:—Ðǽr Godes nama gelôme gecýged biþ, and ðæt [MS. ða] hâlige gehrýne on mæssesange geoffrod, nis nǽnig tweó ðæt ðǽr biþ Godes engla andweardnes *where God's name is frequently invoked, and the holy mystery offered in the mass service, there is no doubt that the presence of God's angels is there*, L. E. I. 10; Th. ii. 408, 24. v. ge-rýne.

ge-hrysed *shaken*. v. hrysian.

gehþ *a station*, Ex. MS. Conb. p. 233. v. giht.

gehðo, gehðu, geohðu, geoðu, giohðo, giðu, e; *f. Care, anxiety;* cura, solicitudo:—Gomol on gehðo eówic grêtan hêt *the aged* [*prince*] *in sadness commanded to greet you*, Beo. Th. 6181; B. 3095. Gehðo mǽnan *to bemoan misery*, Andr. Kmbl. 3095; An. 1550. Iudas cwæþ ðæt he ðæt on gehðu gespræ̆ce *Judas said that he spoke that in trouble*, Elen. Kmbl. 1331; El. 667. Ne meahte he ða gehðu bebūgan *he could not avoid the sorrow*, 1215; El. 609. Ic sceal gehðu mǽnan *I must lament my cares*, Exon. 71 b; Th. 266, 1; Jul. 391. Oft mec gehða gemanode *often sorrow hath admonished me*, 50 a; Th. 174, 22; Gū. 1181. Sceal se gǽst cuman gehðum hrēmig *the ghost shall come moaning with anxiety*, 98 a; Th. 367, 18; Seel. 9: 9 a; Th. 6, 27; Cri. 90: Elen. Kmbl. 643; El. 322: 1059; El. 531. Geohðo mǽnaþ *they lament their grief*, Andr. Kmbl. 3329; An. 1667. Ic þurh geohða sceal dǽda fremman *I must do deeds with sorrow*, Andr. Kmbl. 132; An. 66. Sceal se gāst cuman geohðum hrēmig *the spirit shall come sadly lamenting*, Soul Kmbl. 18; Seel. 9. He ðǽr āna sæt geoðum geómor *he sat there alone sad with sorrows*, Andr. Kmbl. 2015; An. 1010. Gomel on giohðe gold sceáwode *the aged [man] beheld the gold in sorrow*, Beo. Th. 5578; B. 2793. Giohðo mǽnde *he bewailed his afflictions*, 4527; B. 2267. Geómrian on gihða *to mourn in spirit*, Salm. Kmbl. 701; Sal. 350. Ēðelleáse ðysne gyst-sele gihðum healdeþ *the homeless held in memory this guest-hall*, Cd. 169; Th. 212, 5; Exod. 534. v. Grm. And. u. El. p. 97.

ge-hū; *adv. In any manner*:—He is gecweden hlāf ðurh getācnunge and lamb and leó and gehū elles *he is called bread typically and lamb and lion and in any other way*, Homl. Th. ii. 268, 17. Ðeáh ðe heó sȳ gebȳged gehū *though it be bent anyhow*, Hexam. 6; Norm. 10, 30.

ge-hugod; *part. p. Minded, disposed*:—Boda bitre gehugod *the messenger bitter of purpose*, Cd. 33; Th. 45, 11; Gen. 725.

ge-huntian; *p.* ode; *pp.* od *To hunt*:—Hī gehuntigaþ *venantur*, Nar. 38, 6.

ge-hūsan; *pl. m. Housefolk, those of the household*; dŏmestĭci:—Mannes fȳnd, hys gehūsan *inĭmīci hŏmĭnis, dŏmestĭci ejus*, Mt. Bos. 10, 36.

ge-hūsed; *part. Housed, having a house*; dŏmum hăbens:—Gehūsed snægl *a housed* or *shelled snail*; testūdo, Ælfc. Gl. 23; Som. 60, 1; Wrt. Voc. 24, 5.

ge-hūslian; *p.* ode; *pp.* od *To give the eucharist, housel*:—He hēt ðǽr hine gehūslian *he commanded them to give him the eucharist*, Homl. Th. ii. 186, 29. Se hālga sacerd Iustinus him eallum gemæssode and gehūslode *the holy priest Justin said mass to them all and houseled them*, i. 430, 29. Gehūslod beón *communicari*, R. Conc. 5.

ge-hūsscype, es; *m. A house, household, family, race*; dŏmus:—Gehūsscype Israhel bletsiaþ Driht *dŏmus Israhel benedĭcĭte Dŏmĭno*, Ps. Spl. C. 134, 19.

ge-hwā; *m.* -hwæt; *n. g.* -hwæs; *pron. Every one, whoever, who*; quisque, quis. This word is often found with a genitive:—Forðī sceal gehwā on his Drihtne wuldrian *therefore shall every man glory in his Lord*, Homl. Th. ii. 526, 12. Hwæt gehwā nāme *quis quid tolleret*, Mk. Bos. 15, 24. Fæder-æðelo gehwæs *the ancestry of each*, Cd. 161; Th. 200, 24; Exod. 361. Ðonne fēran sceal ānra gehwæs sāwl of līce *when the soul of each one shall go from the body*, Exon. 54 b; Th. 191, 24; Az. 93: 64 b; Th. 238, 3; Ph. 598. Ðec sōþfæstra gehwæs sāwle and gāstas lofiaþ *the souls and spirits of all the just praise thee*, Cd. 192; Th. 240, 31; Dan. 395. He ðeóda gehwam hefonrīce forgeaf *he to every people gave heaven's kingdom*, 30; Th. 40, 19; Gen. 641. Ic leófra gehwone lǽran wille *I will teach each dear one*, Exon. 19 b; Th. 51, 14; Cri. 816. Hāteþ cuman to gemōte moncynnes gehwone *bids come to the meeting every man*, 23 a; Th. 63, 30; Cri. 1027. Ðæt fȳr nimeþ ðurh foldan gehwæt *the fire shall seize everything on earth*, 22 b; Th. 62, 18; Cri. 1003. [*O. Sax.* gi-hwe *quisque.*]

ge-hwǽde; *adj. Little, moderate, scanty*:—Hī wǽron gehwǽde acwealde *they were killed while little*, Homl. Th. i. 84, 21: ii. 162, 2: Gen. 19, 20. Ūre gehwǽda wæstm *our little fruit*, Homl. Th. 526, 22. Seó gehwǽde oferflōwendnys *the slight superfluity*, i. 332, 14: Mt. Bos. 6, 30: Bd. de nat. rerum; Wrt. popl. science 1, 1; Lchdm. iii. 232, 1.

ge-hwǽdnes, -hwēdnes, se; *f. Sparingness, paucity, fewness, subtilty*; parcitas, paucitas:—Gehwǽdnis *humilitas, mediocritas*, Hpt. Gl. 403, 467. Gehwǽdnysse dagena mīnra gecȳþ me *paucitatem dierum meorum nuntia mihi*, Ps. Spl. 101, 24.

ge-hwæmlīc; *adj. Each, every*:—Dæge gehwæmlīce *cotidie*, Lk. Skt. Lind. 9, 23.

ge-hwǽr, -hwār; *adv. On every side, everywhere*; undique, ubique:—Se symle lēofaþ gehwǽr on unrīm gōdum *qui innumeris semper vivit ubique bonis*, Bd. 2, 1; S. 500, 23. His gebyrd and goodnys sind gehwǽr cūþe *his birth and goodness are known everywhere*, Homl. Th. i. 2, 16. Nemnaþ men ðæne mōnaþ gehwǽr Iulius *men name that month everywhere July*, Chr. 975; Erl. 124, 33; Edg 25: Elen. Kmbl. 2364; El. 1183. Wel wīde gehwǽr *everywhere far and wide*, Menol. Fox 118; Men. 59. Ðeáh ðū heaðorǽsa gehwǽr dohte *though thou hast in martial exploits everywhere succeeded*, Beo. Th. 1057; B. 526: Elen. Kmbl. 1092; El. 548. Gehwār hī syn hefige gehwār eác medeme *in some places they are heavy, in others moderate*, Th. Ll. i. 434, 4. [*Laym.* i-hwær, i-war: *A. R.* i-hwar.]

ge-hwæðer; *pron. Both, each, either*; uterque, promiscuus:—Wæs gehwæðer ōðrum lāþ *each was hateful to the other*, Beo. Th. 1633; B. 814. Gehwæðer incer *either of you two*, 1173; B. 584. He biþ him self gehwæðer fæder and sunu *it is to itself both father and son*, Exon. 61 a; Th. 224, 12; Ph. 374. Se willa bēga gehwædres ge . . . ge . . . *her will in both respects both . . . and . . .*, Elen. Kmbl. 1925; El. 964: Beo. Th. 2091; B. 1043. Ðǽr wearþ monig mon ofslægen on gehwæðre hond *there was many a man slain on each side*, Chr. 853; Erl. 68, 19: 871; Erl. 74, 12.

ge-hwæðere; *adv. Yet, however*:—Weorðeþ heó ðeáh oft niða bearnum to helpe and to hǽle gehwæðere *it becomes oft however help and safety nevertheless to the children of men*, Runic pm. 10; Kmbl. 341, 12. v. hwæðere.

ge-hwæðeres; *adv. Anywhere, on every side, every way*; undique:—Wæs gehwæðeres waa *there was woe on every side*, Bt. Met. Fox 1, 50; Met. 1, 25. v. ge-hwæðer.

ge-hwanon; *adv. From all sides*:—Fela ðearfan gehwanon cumene *many needy come from all sides*, Swt. A. S. Rdr. 97, 78.

ge-hwearf, -hwyrf, es; *n. A change, exchange*; commūtātio, permūtātio:—Gehwearf *commūtātio*, Ælfc. Gl. 81; Som. 73, 26; Wrt. Voc. 47, 31.

ge-hwearf *returned.* v. ge-hweorfan.

ge-hweled; *part. Inflamed*; inflammātus:—Ðæt ðǽrinne gehweled biþ *which is inflamed therein*, Past. 38, 3; Swt. 273, 22; Hat. MS. 51 a, 12: Swt. 275, 5.

ge-hweorf; *adj.* I. *versed, practised, clever*; versutus:—Sum biþ ðegn gehweorf on meoduhealle *one is a thane familiar in the mead-hall*, Exon. 79 a; Th. 297, 15; Crä. 68. v. hwearf. II. *converted*:—Nymðe gē gewerfe beón *nisi conversi fueritis*, Mt. Kmbl. Rush. 18, 3. [Cf. *Goth.* ga-hwairbs.]

ge-hweorfan; *p.* -hwearf, *pl.* -hwurfon; *pp.* -hworfen. I. *act. To turn*; convertere:—Manige sindon ðe ðū gehweorfest to heofonleóhte *there are many whom thou shalt turn to the light of heaven*, Andr. Kmbl. 1947; An. 976. Gehweorf ūre hæftnēd *converte captivitatem nostram*, Ps. Th. 125, 4. Gehweorf us, mægena God *Domine Deus virtutum, converte nos*, 79, 4. Gehweorf nū ðīne ansȳne *turn now thine eye*, 79, 14. II. *intrans. To turn, go away, depart, die, pass as property, fall as a lot*; verti, abire, redire, excidere:—Ymb ofn ūtan alet gehwearf *the fire turned round about the oven*, Cd. 186; Th. 232, 3; Dan. 254. Mān eft gehwearf ðǽr *their sin turned again thither*, Andr. Kmbl. 1388; An. 694: Lk. Bos. 8, 55: 17, 7: 24, 52. Siððan to reste gehwearf *after he had gone to rest*, Cd. 177; Th. 222, 23; Dan. 109. Ǽr ic of ðysum līfe gehweorfe *ere I depart from this life*, Hy. 3, 53; Hy. Grn. ii. 284, 53. Hit on ǽht gehwearf Denigea freán *it passed into the possession of the Danes' lord*, Beo. Th. 3363; B. 1679: 2424; B. 1210: 4422; B. 2208. Ðā se tān gehwearf ofer ǽnne ealdgesīþa *then the lot fell on one of the old comrades*, Andr. Kmbl. 2208; An. 1105. v. hweorfan.

ge-hwerfnes *a conversion.* v. ge-hwyrfednes.

ge-hwettan; *p.* te; *pp.* ed *To whet, excite*; excītāre:—He gehwette and tihte ðæra Iudēiscra manna heortan *he whetted and instigated the hearts of the Jews*, Homl. Th. i. 26, 31.

ge-hwider; *adv. Whithersoever, anywhere, everywhere*; alicubi:—Ðonon eóde gehwyder ymb *inde circumquaque exire consueverat*, Bd. 3, 17; S. 543, 26: Bt. Met. Fox 25, 26; Met. 25, 13.

ge-hwylc, -hwelc, -hwilc; *pron. Each, every one, all, whoever, whatever*; quisque, unusquisque:—Gē gehwilce uncōðe gehǽldon *ye healed every disease*, Homl. Th. i. 64, 23. Of gehwilcum burgum *from every city*, 86, 29. Nū smeádon gehwilce men *now some men have enquired*, ii. 268, 7. Dǽda gehwylcra *of all deeds*, Elen. Kmbl. 2563; El. 1283. Hāteþ arīsan folc ānra gehwylc *bids each folk arise*, Exon. 23 a; Th. 63, 28; Cri. 1026. Ðæt he wiste hū mycel gehwylc gemangode *ut sciret quantum quisque negotiatus esset*, Lk. Bos. 19, 15. Sió gesceádwīsnes sceal on gehwelcum waldan *reason shall rule in each one*, Bt. Met. Fox 20, 394; Met. 20, 197. Ongan ānra gehwylc cweðan *cœperunt singuli dicere*, Mt. Bos. 26, 22: Deut. 24, 16. Lifigendra gehwylc *every one living*, Cd. 219; Th. 282, 12; Sat. 285. And hiera se æðeling gehwelcum feoh and feorh gebeád *and the atheling offered each of them money and life*, Chr. 755; Erl. 50, 5. He beheóld heora ānra gehwilcne *he observed each one of them*, Th. Ap. 12, 24.

ge-hwyrf, es; *n. Exchange*; permūtātio:—Be gehwyrfe *of exchange*, L. Ath. i. 10; Th. i. 204, 16, 21, note 23, 31. v. ge-hwearf.

ge-hwyrfan, -hwerfan, -hwirfan, -hwierfan; *p.* de; *pp.* ed *To change, turn, convert*; mutare, convertere:—Hyra woruld wæs gehwyrfed *their world [life] was changed*, Cd. 17; Th. 21, 3; Gen. 318. Flōd gehwerfde ða ceastre *a flood overturned the city*, Shrn. 77, 12. Hwylc ðonne gēna gehwyrfed byþ *quoadusque justitia convertatur in judicium*, Ps. Th. 93, 14. Hī gehwyrfde synd *conversi sunt*, Ps. Spl. 77, 46: Exon. 10 b; Th. 12, 20; Cri. 188. Mīn drihten, ðū ðe gehwyrfest ealle sāule *my Lord, thou who convertest all souls*, Blickl. Homl. 249, 14. Manige Israhela bearna he gehwyrfþ to heora drihtne *many of the children of Israel he shall turn to their Lord*, 165, 13. Ic ðē bidde for ðīnum naman ðæt ðū gehwyrfe on me ealle eáþmōdnesse ðīnra beboda *I beseech* *thee for thy name that thou devolve on me all submission to thy commands,* 147, 11. Paulinus gehwerfde Ēdwine Norþhymbra cyning to fulwihte *Paulinus converted Edwin king of Northumbria to christianity,* Chr. 601; Erl. 20, 12. Hēr wæs Paulus gehwierfed *in this year Paul was converted,* 34; Erl. 6, 14: 30; Erl. 6, 9. His word bióþ gehwirfdo to unnytre ofersprǣce *his words will be perverted to useless loquacity,* Past. 21; Swt. 164, 18; Cot. MS. Hī wurdon gehwyrfede to deórwurđum gimmum *they were turned into precious stones,* Homl. Th. i. 64, 5: Th. An. 28, 35. On heáf gehwyrfede *turned to mourning,* Blickl. Homl. 195, 17: 233, 5. Ic wæs gehwyrfed on mīnne līchoman *I was restored to my body,* 155, 25.

ge-hwyrfednes, -hwyrfenes, -ness, e; *f. A conversion, change;* conversio:—Đara geleáfan and gehwyrfednesse *quōrum fīdei et conversiōni,* Bd. 1, 26; S. 488, 13. In đa tīd heora gehwyrfenesse *tempŏre suæ conversiōnis,* 4, 5; S. 572, 39.

ge-hwyrftnian *to tear* (?):—His æfterfolgeras hit siđđan totugon and totǣron đam gelīcost đonne seó leó bringaþ his hungregum hwelpum hwæt to etanne hȳ đonne gecȳđaþ on đam ǣte hwylc heora mǣst mæg gehwyrftnian *his successors afterwards rent and tore it most like to when the lion brings its hungry whelps something to eat, then they show in that food which of them can tear it most,* Ors. 3, 11; Bos. 71, 39, note.

ge-hycgan, -hicgan; *p.* -hogde, -hogede, -hogode; *pp.* -hogod [see March, § 222] *To think, conceive, consider, devise, reflect, be mindful, think about, care, intend, resolve:*—Ne mæg ic đeáh gehycgan hwȳ him on hige đorfte ā đȳ sǣl wesan *I cannot, however, conceive why it need be the better in mind for them,* Bt. Met. Fox 15, 17; Met. 15, 9. Sceal gehycgan hæleđa ǣghwilc đæt he ne abælige bearn wealdendes *every man must be mindful that he offend not the son of the powerful,* Cd. 217; Th. 276, 25; Sat. 195: 219; Th. 282, 7; Sat. 283. Đū gehycgan meaht đæt gē willaþ đa on wuda sēcan *you may consider that you will seek them in the wood,* Bt. Met. Fox 19, 34; Met. 19, 17. Sum in mæđle mæg folcrǣdenne gehycgan *one in council can devise a nation's law,* Exon. 79 a; Th. 295, 33; Crā. 42: Cd. 203; Th. 252, 29; Dan. 586. Gehyge on đīnum breóstum đæt đū inc bām meaht wīte bewarigan *reflect in thy breast that thou from you both mayest ward off punishment,* Cd. 27; Th. 35, 29; Gen. 562. Fela gē fore monnum mīđaþ đæs đe gē in mōde gehycgaþ *much ye before men conceal of what ye in mind devise,* Exon. 39 a; Th. 130, 11; Gū. 436. Hū đū yfle gehogdes *how thou didst devise evilly,* 28 a; Th. 85, 29; Cri, 1398. Đā đū gehogodest sæcce sēcean *when thou didst resolve to seek conflict,* Beo. Th. 3981; B. 1988: Cd. 209; Th. 259, 5; Dan. 687: Andr. Kmbl. 857; An. 429. Hæfde on ān gehogod đæt he gedǣde swā hine drihten hēt *his purpose had continually been to do as the Lord commanded him,* Cd. 140; Th. 175, 9; Gen. 2892. Đæt hió đæs niwan taman nāuht ne gehicgge *that she care nothing about the new tameness,* Bt. Met. Fox 13, 52; Met. 13, 26. On drihten helpe gehogedan *speravit in domino,* Ps. Th. 113, 18: Exon. 33 a; Th. 105, 5; Gū. 18. [*Goth.* ga-hugjan: *O. Sax.* gi-huggian.]

ge-hȳd, e; *f*: es; *n. A thought;* cōgĭtātio:—In sefan gehȳdum *in the mind's thoughts,* Cd. 212; Th. 261, 27: Dan. 732. DER. mis-gehȳd. v. ge-hygd.

ge-hȳd; *part. p. Exalted;* exaltatus, Hpt. Gl. 440. v. geheád.

ge-hȳd; *part. p. Provided with a skin,* Nar. 50, 5.

ge-hȳdan, -hīdan, -hēdan; he -hȳdeþ, -hȳt, *pl.* -hȳdaþ; *p.* -hȳdde; *pp.* -hȳded, -hȳdd. I. *to hide, conceal;* condĕre, abscondĕre:—He hit gehȳt and gehelt *it hides and preserves it,* Bt. 39, 8; Fox 224, 11: 39, 13; Fox 234, 19. Sumne dreórighleór in eorþscræfe eorl gehȳdde *a man sad of countenance has hidden one in an earth-grave,* Exon. 77 b; Th. 291, 19; Wand. 84: Beo. Th. 4463; B. 2235. Hī wiston đæt hine gehȳddan hæleþ Iudēa *they knew that the men of Judea had hidden him,* Exon. 119 b; Th. 460, 6; Hö. 13. Læg mīn flǣschoma niþre gehȳded, in byrgenne *my body lay hidden beneath, in the sepulchre,* 29 a; Th. 89, 34; Cri. 1467: Elen. Kmbl. 2182; El. 1092. Heofona rīce is gelīc gehȳddum goldhorde on đam æcere *sĭmĭle est regnum cælōrum thēsauro abscondĭto in agro,* Mt. Bos. 13, 44. Fint he đǣr đa ryhtwīsnesse gehȳdde mid đæs līchoman hæfignesse *he will there find the wisdom concealed by the heaviness of the body,* Bt. 35, 1; Fox 156, 11. Sticiaþ gehȳdde beorhte cræftas *bright virtues lie hid,* 4; Fox 8, 15: 32, 3; Fox 118, 23. II. *to watch, guard, heed;* observāre:—Đæt heó gehȳden hǣlan [MS. hælun] mīne *calcāneum meum observābunt,* Ps. Th. 55, 6. III. *to bring into safety, make firm, fasten;* allĭgāre:—Hȳ gehȳdaþ heáhstefn scipu to đam unlonde oncyrrāpum *they fasten the high-prow'd ships to the false land with anchor-ropes,* Exon. 96 b; Th. 361, 1; Wal. 13. v. hēdan *and* hȳdan.

ge-hȳdnes, se; *f. Comfort, security* (?):—Đȳlæs hie gedwelle sió gehȳdnes and đa getǣsu đe hie on đæm wege habbaþ *lest the comfort and pleasures that they have on the way seduce them,* Past. 50, 1; Swt. 387, 13; Hat. MS. See the note on this passage, Swt. 491–2. Or is the word connected with gehȳdan? cf. gehȳdan III. and the *subsidia itineris* of the original Latin.

ge-hygd, -higd, -hȳd, e; *f*: es; *n. Thought, cogitation, meditation, deliberation, consultation;* cōgĭtātio, mĕdĭtātio, consilium:—Sceal on leóht cuman heortan gehygd *his heart's thought shall come into light,* Exon. 23 a; Th. 64, 17; Cri. 1039: 77 b; Th. 290, 28; Wand. 72. On mīnre gehygde heortan ealre *in tōto corde meo,* Ps. Th. 137, 1: 118, 58: 54, 20. Þurh deóp gehygd *through deep thought,* Exon. 72 a; Th. 268, 13; Jul. 431: Cd. 221; Th. 285, 28; Sat. 344. Sete on Drihten đīn sōþ gehygd *jacta in Deum cōgĭtātum tuum,* Ps. Th. 54, 22. Ne biþ đǣr wiht forholen monna gehygda *there shall be naught of men's cogitations concealed,* Exon. 23 b; Th. 65, 15; Cri. 1055. On sefan gehygdum *in the mind's thoughts,* 39 b; Th. 130, 27; Gū. 444: 81 a; Th. 305, 14; Fä. 88. Eálā đæt we nū māgon geseón on ussum sāwlum synna wunde, mid līchoman leahtra gehygdu eágum *alas that we now may see in our souls wounds of sin, with the body's eyes wicked cogitations!* 27 a; Th. 80, 32; Cri. 1315. Đū āna canst ealra gehygdo *thou alone knowest the thoughts of all men,* Andr. Kmbl. 136; An. 68: 399; An. 200. Hī sāwle frætwaþ hālgum gehygdum *they adorn their souls with holy meditations,* Exon. 44 b; Th. 150, 15; Gū. 779: 62 b; Th. 229, 22; Ph. 459. Landāgende men ic lǣrde đæt hie heora gafol mid gehygdum aguldon *I taught landowners to pay their taxes carefully,* Blickl. Homl. 185, 22. [*Goth.* ga-hugds; *f*: *O. Sax.* gi-hugd; *f.*] DER. breóst-, gāst-, in-, inn-, mōd-gehygd.

ge-hyht, es; *m. A hope, comfort, refuge;* refūgium:—Drihten trumnes mīn and gehyht mīn *Dŏmĭnus firmāmentum meum et refūgium meum,* Ps. Spl. T. 17, 1.

ge-hyhtan; *p.* te *To hope, trust:*—We sceolan gehyhtan on godes đa gehālgodan cyricean *we must trust in God's holy church,* Blickl. Homl. 111, 8. On his naman đeóda gehyhtaþ *in nomine ejus gentes sperabunt,* Mt. Bos. 12, 21. On hine gehyhtton *trusted in him,* Blickl. Homl. 103, 12: 159, 18. Đæt on đīnum upstige geblissian and gehyhton ealle đīne gecorenan *that in thy ascension all thine elect may rejoice and trust,* 87, 25. v. ge-hihtan.

ge-hyhtlīc; *adj. Seasonable, fit, commodious;* opportunus, R. Ben. 53. v. hihtlīc.

ge-hylced; *part. p. Divaricatus,* Gl. Prud. 758.

ge-hyld, es; *n. Regard, observation, keeping, concealing;* observantia, custodia:—In gehylde rihtra Eástrana *in the keeping of right Easter,* Bd. 2, 4; S. 505, 25. Ic wæs on đīnum gehylde begangen *in observationibus tuis exercebor,* Ps. Th. 76, 10. [Him] hālige heápas on gehyld bebeád *commended to his protection the holy bands,* Cd. 161; Th. 202, 3; Ex. 382. Lǣdan on gehyld Godes *to lead into God's protection,* Andr. Kmbl. 2091; An. 1047: 234; An. 117. Hāligra gehyld *the preservation of the holy ones,* Exon. 55 b; Th. 196, 4; Az. 169. He is manna gehyld *he is the protection of men,* Beo. Th. 6104. On heofona gehyld *into the protection* [?] *of the heavens,* Exon. 15 b; Th. 34, 20; Cri. 545. Thorpe translates *into heaven's vault,* Grein has *recessus, arcanum?* Or could the word have the sense of *space,* cf. *Ger.* gehalt, gehaltig? Cf. *also* geheald *subst. and adj. and* gehild.

ge-hyldan; *p.* -hylde; *pp.* hylded *To keep, hold, forbear;* custodire, conservare, differe:—Gehylde *forbore;* distulit, Ps. Spl. 77, 25.

ge-hyldan *to bend, incline:*—To gehyldanne *declinare,* Ps. Lamb. 16, 11.

ge-hyldig; *adj. Patient;* patiens, Ps. Spl. 7, 12.

ge-hyldness, e; *f. Keeping, observance:*—On heora gehyldnesse *in custodiendis illis,* Ps. Th. 18, 10.

ge-hyldra; *m.* e; *f. n; compar. of* geheald (?) *Safer:*—Đǣm gehyldrum wegum *tuta itinera,* Nar. 6, 3. Đohtan đæt him wīslīcre and gehyldre wǣre *they thought that it would be wiser and safer for them,* Bd. 1, 23; S. 485, 31. On gehældran stowe *in tutiore loco,* Bd. 2, 2; S. 503, 39.

ge-hylmd, -hylmed; *adj. Galeatus,* Cot. 97. *Frondosus,* 89.

ge-hylt *keeps,* Ps. Lamb. 120, 7; *3rd sing. pres. of* ge-healdan.

ge-hȳnan, -hēnan, -hīnan; *p.* de; *pp.* ed *To humble, oppress, waste, destroy;* humiliare, opprimere, damnare:—Uton gehȳnan hit *opprimamus eum,* Ex. 1, 10. Eágan ofermōdra đū gehȳnyst *oculos superborum humiliabis,* Ps. Spl. C. 17, 29. Gehȳnyþ *humiliat,* Ps. Spl. C. M. 74, 7. Hīg gehȳndon *eos oppresserunt,* Ex. 1, 11. Gehȳned *damnatus,* C. R. Ben. 58. Gehēned, Ps. Vos. 37, 8. v. ge-hīnan, hȳnan.

ge-hyndred; *part. Hindered;* impĕdītus:—Biþ eall se here swȳđe gehyndred *all the army will be greatly hindered,* Chr. 1003; Th. 252, 33, col. 2. v. ge-hindred.

ge-hyngran; *p.* -hyngerde *To be hungry:*—Mec gehyncgerde *esurivi,* Mt. Kmbl. Lind. 25, 42. Ic gehwyncgerde *esurivi,* 25, 35. Hine gehyngerde *esuriit,* 12, 3. Gihyñcrede *esuriit,* Mk. Skt. Rush. 11, 12. Eádgo đa đe nū gehyncres *beati qui nunc esuritis,* Lk. Skt. Lind. 6, 21. Gehyngrede hundas *hungry dogs,* Shrn. 145, 3.

ge-hȳpan; *p.* de; *pp.* ed *To heap:*—Đonne hit gehȳpþ yfel ofer yfele *when it heaps evil upon evil,* Homl. Th. i. 410, 21.

ge-hȳran, -hīran, -hēran; to -hȳranne, -hȳrenne; *part.* -hȳrende; ic -hȳre, -đū -hȳrest, -hȳrst, he -hȳreþ, -hȳrþ, *pl.* -hȳraþ; *p.* ic, he -hȳrde, đū -hȳrdest, *pl.* -hȳrdon; *impert.* -hȳr, *pl.* -hȳre, -hȳraþ; *subj. pres.* -hȳre, *pl.* -hȳron; *p.* -hȳrde, *pl.* -hȳrden; *pp.* -hȳred. I. *v. trans. To hear, give ear to;* audire, exaudire:—Forđamđe gē ne māgon gehȳran mīne spæce *quia non pŏtestis audīre sermonem meum*, Jn. Bos. 8, 43: Bd. 3, 5; S. 527, 22, 35. To eallum ðe ðis ylce stǽr becyme ūres cynnes to rǽdanne oððe gehȳranne *omnes ad quos hæc eadem histŏria pervĕnīre potĕrit nostræ natiōnis lĕgentes sīve audientes*, 5, 24; S. 649, 6. Ic ðæt gehȳre, ðæt ðis is hold weorod *I hear that this is a friendly band*, Beo. Th. 585; B. 290: Exon. 72 b; Th. 270, 6; Jul. 461. Gehȳrest ðū uncerne earne hwelp *hearest thou our active whelp?* 101 a; Th. 380, 30; Rä. 1, 16. Georne gehȳreþ heofoncyninga hȳhst hæleða dǽde *the highest of heaven's kings will earnestly hear men's deeds*, 117 b; Th. 451, 22; Dōm. 107: 19 b; Th. 50, 9; Cri. 797. Ðænne hī ðæt word gehȳraþ *qui cum audiĕrint verbum*, Mk. Bos. 4, 16, 18, 20. Ic gehȳrde hine ðīne dǽd and word lofian *I heard him praise thy deed and words*, Cd. 25; Th. 32, 23; Gen. 507: 26; Th. 33, 23; Gen. 524. Ðū gehȳrdest me *exaudisti me*, Ps. Spl. 118, 26: Ps. Th. 114, 1, 2. We ðis nǽfre gehȳrdon hæleðum cȳðan *we have never heard this declared to men*, Elen. Kmbl. 1317; El. 660: 727; El. 364: Apstls. Kmbl. 125; Ap. 63. Gāþ and cȳðaþ Iohanne ða þing ðe gē gehȳrdon and gesāwon *euntes renunciāte Ioanne quæ audistis et vīdistis*, Mt. Bos. 11, 4: Lk. Bos. 7, 22: Jn. Bos. 14, 24. Gehȳr me Drihten God mīn *exaudi me Dŏmĭne Deus meus*, Ps. Spl. 12, 3: 68, 17: 142, 7. Gehȳre gē ðæs sāwendan bigspell *vos audīte parăbŏlam sēmĭnantis*, Mt. Bos. 13, 18. Gehȳraþ me *audīte me*, Ps. Th. 65, 14. Ǽr he dōmdæges dyn gehȳre *before he shall hear doomsday's din*, Salm. Kmbl. 546; Sal. 272: Exon. 13 a; Th. 22, 31; Cri. 360. Wearþ Stephanes bēn gehȳred *Stephen's prayer was heard*, Homl. Th. i. 52, 32, 33. **II.** *v. intrans. To hear;* audīre:—Gehȳran mæg ic rūme *I can hear from far*, Cd. 32; Th. 42, 14; Gen. 673. Se ðe hæbbe eáran to gehȳrenne, gehȳre *qui hăbet aures audiendi, audiat*, Mt. Bos. 13, 9. Geworden ic eom swā swā man nā gehȳrende *factus sum sīcut hŏmo non audiens*, Ps. Spl. 37, 15: Mt. Bos. 13, 13. Ic gehȳre *audio;* ðū gehȳrst *audis;* he gehȳrþ *audit*, Ælfc. Gr. 30; Som. 33, 57, 58. Deáfe gehȳrdon *the deaf heard*, Andr. Kmbl. 1154; An. 577. Ðē-læs hīg mid eárum gehȳron *nequando aurĭbus audiant*, Mt. Bos. 13, 15: Mk. Bos. 4, 12. **III.** *to obey;* obēdīre:—Hie Drihtne gehȳrdon *they obeyed the Lord*, Cd. 196; Th. 245, 2; Dan. 456: Exon. 62 a; Th. 228, 26; Ph. 444: Ps. Th. 17, 42.

ge-hȳran; *p.* de; *pp.* ed *To hire;* conducere, locare:—Ðæs hīredes ealdor gehȳrde wyrhtan *the chief of the household hired workmen*, Homl. Th. ii. 74, 7. Behīring *vel* gehȳred feóh *locatio*, Ælfc. Gl. 13; Som. 57, 123; Wrt. Voc. 20, 60. v. be-hīring.

ge-hyrdan; *p.* de; *pp.* ed; *v. trans. To harden, to strengthen;* durare, indurare, Exon. 88 a; Th. 331, 26; Vy. 74. v. hyrdan.

ge-hyrde. v. ge-hyrwan.

ge-hyrdnes, -ness, e; *f. A keeping, guard, watch;* custōdia:—Sete gehyrdnessa mūþe mīnum *pōne custōdiam ōri meo*, Ps. Lamb. 140, 3.

ge-hyrned; *part. Horned;* cornūtus:—Gehyrned *cornūtus*, Ælfc. Gr. 43; Som. 45, 17: Ex. 34, 29, 30. Byþ he ymlīce gehyrned *he is equally horned*, Bd. de nat. rerum; Wrt. popl. science 15, 2; Lchdm. iii. 266, 22.

ge-hȳrnes, se; *f. A hearing, report;* auditus:—Of gehȳrnysse gē gehȳraþ, and gē ne ongytaþ *audietis, et non intelligetis*, Mt. Bos. 13, 14: Blickl. Homl. 55, 31. DER. hȳrnes.

ge-hyrst, e; *f. An ornament;* ornāmentum:—Man reliquias rēran onginneþ, hāliga gehyrste *man begins to elevate relics, holy ornaments*, Menol. Fox 146; Men. 74. Gehyrsto *phaleræ*, Lye.

ge-hȳrst *hearest*, Ælfc. Gr. 30; Som. 33, 57, 58; *2nd sing. pres. of* ge-hȳran.

ge-hyrstan; *p.* -hyrste; *pp.* -hyrsted, -hyrst *To adorn, ornament, decorate;* adornāre, ornāre, dĕcōrāre:—He gehyrsteþ wēl *he adorns the metal work*, Exon. 88 a; Th. 331, 27; Vy. 74. Golde gehyrsted *adorned with gold*, Elen. Kmbl. 662; El. 331: Andr. Kmbl. 90; An. 45. Ða bióþ mid fetlum gehyrste *who are adorned with belts*, Bt. 37, 1; Fox 186, 6.

ge-hyrstan, -hierstan; *p.* -hyrste; *pp.* -hyrsted, -hyrst *To fry, roast;* frīgĕre:—Hī cōcas gehyrstan *cooks roasted them*, Ps. Th. 101, 3. Gehyrsted sīe *frīgētur*, Cot. 87. Gehyrst hlāf *frixius pānis*, Ælfc. Gl. 66; Som. 69, 69; Wrt. Voc. 41, 23. Et ðas sīdan ðe gehirsted is *eat this side that is roasted*, Shrn. 116, 6. [*O. H. Ger.* giharstit *frixus*.]

ge-hyrstan; *p.* te *To murmur:*—Gehyrston *murmurabant*, Lk. Skt. Lind. 15, 2.

ge-hȳrsum, -hiérsum; *adj. Obedient, obliging, ready to serve;* obēdiens, offĭciōsus:—Wæs Abraham Gode gehȳrsum *Abraham was obedient to God*, Boutr. Scrd. 23, 4: Homl. Th. ii. 162, 26: Mt. Bos. 6, 24. Ēstful *vel* gehȳrsum *offĭciōsus*, Ælfc. Gl. 115; Som. 80, 54; Wrt. Voc. 61, 32. Hī woldon him beón gehȳrsume *they would be obedient to him*, Chr. 1083; Erl. 217, 6. [*O. H. Ger.* and *Ger.* gehōrsam.]

ge-hȳrsumian, -hiérsumian; *p.* ode, ade; *pp.* od, ad. **I.** *to obey, be obedient to;* obēdīre, pārēre:—Ic gehȳrsumige *obēdio*, Ælfc. Gr. 30, 5; Som. 34, 56: *pāreo*, 26, 2; Som. 28, 43. Ðe heora lustum gehȳrsumiaþ *who obey their lusts*, Homl. Th. ii. 82, 13. **II.** *to make obedient, bring into subjection;* subjĭcĕre:—Ðæt he him Norþ-Wealas gehȳrsumode [gehiérsumade, col. 1] *that he might make the North Welsh obedient to him*, Chr. 853; Th. 122, 22, col. 2. [*O. H. Ger.* gihōrsamōn *to obey*.]

ge-hȳrsumlīce; *adv. Obediently;* obēdienter, Som. Ben. Lye.

ge-hȳrsumnys, -nyss, e; *f. Obedience, subjection;* obĕdientia:—God wolde fandian Abrahames gehȳrsumnysse *tentāvit Deus Abraham*, Gen. 22, 1: Boutr. Scrd. 19, 26: Chr. 1091; Erl. 228, 3.

ge-hyrtan; *p.* -hyrte; *pp.* -hyrted, -hyrt [hyrtan *to hearten, encourage;* heorte *the heart*] *To encourage, animate, refresh;* confortare, animare, refrigerare:—Beó ðū hūru gehyrt, and hicg þegenlīce *be thou only encouraged, and strive nobly*, Jos. 1, 18. Ðæt ðīnre wylne sunu sȳ gehyrt *that the son of thy slave may be refreshed;* ut refrigeretur filius ancillæ tuæ, Ex. 23, 12. Drihten us gehyrte *the Lord encouraged us*, Homl. Th. ii. 538, 12. Mīn werod gehyrted wæs *my army was encouraged*, Nar. 8, 17. Gehyrtan *refocillare, confortare*, Hpt. Gl. 478. Se læg dæg and niht geswōgen. He wearþ ðā gehyrt *he lay day and night senseless. He then revived*, Homl. Th. ii. 356, 27.

ge-hȳrþ *hears*, Ælfc. Gr. 30; Som. 33, 58; *3rd sing. pres. of* ge-hȳran.

ge-hyrwan; *p.* de; *pp.* ed *To make game of, despise, disparage, traduce, vex, oppress;* cavillāri, contemnĕre, detrăhĕre:—Elene ne wolde ðæs wilgifan word gehyrwan *Elene would not despise the dear prince's word*, Elen. Kmbl. 442; El. 221: Exon. 39 b; Th. 131, 27; Gū. 462. He gehyrweþ fuloft hālge lāre *he very often traduces holy lore*, 117 a; Th. 449, 12; Dōm. 70. Hȳ ðæs lāreowes word ne gehyrwdon *they despised not the teacher's words*, 14 b; Th. 29, 8; Cri. 459. Beóþ ða gehyrwede *they are despised*, Ps. 52, 6; Ps. Grn. ii. 150, 6. Seó langung hine swīðe gehyrde and ðreáde *that longing much oppressed and afflicted him*, Blickl. Homl. 113, 14. Hī wurdon gehergode and gehyrde *they were wasted and oppressed*, Jud. 10, 8. [*O. H. Ger.* harwjan *exasperare*.]

ge-hyscan; *p.* te *To mock, deride:*—Ūre fȳnd gehyscton us *inimici nostri subsannauerunt nos*, Ps. Lamb. 79, 7. Gehiscþ *abominabitur*, 5, 8.

ge-hyspan; *p.* de, te *To deride, mock, scoff;* insultare, exprobare, Hpt. Gl. 441. Se god ðe on heofonum ys hīg gehyspþ *qui habitat in cœlis irridebit eos*, Ps. Th. 2, 4.

ge-hyspendlīc; *adj. Despicable, abominable:*—Hī syndon gehyspendlīc geworden *sunt abominabiles facti*, Ps. Lamb. 13, 1.

ge-hȳt *hides*, Bt. 39, 8; Fox 224, 11; *3rd sing. pres. of* ge-hȳdan.

ge-hyðegod; *part. p:*—Gehyðegode *expedita*, Gl. Prud. 229.

ge-hyðelīc; *adj. Favourable, seasonable;* opportunus, Ps. Spl. 31, 7; Hpt. Gl. 470.

ge hyþnes, se; *f. Opportunity.*

ge-hȳwan; *p.* de; *pp.* ed; *v. trans. To shew;* ostendere:—Ðū gehȳwdest ðam eorle bān Iosephes *thou shewest the man the bones of Joseph*, Elen. Kmbl. 1570; El. 787. v. geȳwan.

ge-hywian; *p.* ode; *pp.* od. **I.** *to form, fashion;* fingĕre:—Se ðe gehywode synderlīce heortan heora *qui finxit singillātim corda eōrum*, Ps. Lamb. 32, 15. **II.** *to seem, pretend;* sĭmŭlāre:—Ðeáh ðe hit swā gehywod wǽre *though it seemed so*, Job Thw. 166, 6. Mid gehywedan mōde *with feigned mind*, Th. Ap. 3, 2. v. ge-hiwian.

ge-hywung *a form, fashion, shape*, Ps. Spl. C. 102, 13. v. ge-hiwung.

ge-īcan, -īcean, -ȳcan, -iécan; *p.* -īcte, -īhton; *pp.* -īced, -īct *To eke, increase, add, enlarge;* augere, extendere:—Heó ongan his mǽg-burge geīcean sunum and dohtrum *she began his kindred to increase with sons and daughters*, Cd. 56; Th. 69, 8; Gen. 1132. Eall geīceaþ *increase all things*, 74; Th. 91, 18; Gen. 1514. Ofer eall ðæt geīcte *adjecit hoc supra omnia*, Lk. Bos. 3, 20. Æðelinga rīm feorum geīcte *he increased the number of men with lives*, 58; Th. 70, 33; Gen. 1162. Bizantium wæs fram Constantino geiéced *Byzantium was enlarged by Constantine*, Ors. 3, 7; Bos. 61, 10: Th. Diplm. A. D. 864; 125, 19. v. ēcan.

ge-īcendlīc; *adj. Added to, adjective;* adjectivus:—Geīcendlīc nama *a noun adjective*, Som.

ge-īchte, -īhton *added; p. of* ge-īcan.

ge-īdlian; *p.* ade *To make* or *become vain, empty:*—Giīdladest *vacuasti*, Rtl. 33, 3. Giīdlege *vanescat*, 98, 24.

ge-iermed, -irmed; *adj. Afflicted*, Past. 28, 1; Swt. 188, 16.

ge-iéwan; *p.* de; *pp.* ed; *v. trans. To shew;* ostendere:—He ðæt beácen geseah ðæt him on heofonum ǽr geiéwed wearþ *he saw the beacon which to him before in heaven was shewn*, Elen. Grm. 102. v. ȳwan, eāwan.

ge-īhtnyss, e; *f. An addition, epact*, Lye.

ge-illerocaþ *surfeited;* crapulatus, Ps. Spl. C. 77, 71.

ge-incfullian; *p.* ade; *pp.* ad *To offend, scandalize:*—We ðonne ðyles geincfulligæ hiæ *ut autem non scandalizemus eos*, Mt. Kmbl. Rush. 17, 27. Se ðe ne biþ in me geincfullad *qui non fuerit scandalizatus in me*, 11, 6: 15, 12.

ge-inlagian; *p.* ode; *pp.* od [ge, inlagian] *To inlaw, to restore to the protection of the law;* inlagare, intra legum protectionem accipere:—Man geinlagode Swegen eorl *Earl Sweyn was inlawed*, Chr. 1050; Erl. 176, 6. Willem se cyng Eádgār geinlagode and ealle his men *William the king inlawed Edgar and all his men*, 1074; Erl. 212, 5.

ge-innian; *pp.* -innod *To bring in, include, to fill, supply, charge;* præstare, includere:—Wolde God geinnian ðone lyre *God would supply the loss,* Homl. Th. i. 12, 24: 180, 18: L. In. 62; Th. i. 142, 4: Th. Apol. 23, 7. Súsle geinnod *with sulphur filled,* Cd. 2; Th. 3, 28; Gen. 42. He hæfþ geinnod ðat ǽr geútod wæs *he has included what before was excluded,* Cod. Ex. p. 1.

ge-inseglian, -insegelian; *p.* ode; *pp.* od, ud *To seal, to impress with a seal;* signare, obsignare:—Hú nǽron ðás geinseglude on mínum goldhordum? *whether these thingis ben seelid in myn tresouris?* Wyc; nonne hæc signata in thesauris meis? Deut. 32, 34. Annas and Caiphas ðæt loc geinseglodon *Annas et Caiphas illud claustrum obsignarunt,* Nicod. 14; Thw. 7, 2. Lá hú ne ðás þingc geinseglode on goldhordum mínum *nonne hæc signata in thesauris meis,* Cant. Moys. Isrl. Lamb. 194 a, 34: Th. Apol. 20, 10: 21, 2.

ge-irgan; *p.* de; *pp.* ed *To make cowardly, terrify,* Jos. 2, 9. v. ge-yrgan.

ge-irman; *p.* de; *pp.* ed *To afflict;* affligere:—Ðæt hie elles ne síen geirmed *that they be not altogether afflicted,* Past. 28, 1; Swt. 189, 16; Hat. MS. 36 b, 5. v. ge-yrman.

ge-iukod; *part. p. Yoked:*—Geiukodan oxan *junctis bobus,* Th. An. 19, 19.

ge-lác, es; *n.* [lácan *to move as* e. g. *the waves do, to sport, play*] *Motion, commotion, tumultuous assembly, play:*—Sealtýða gelác *the tossing of the salt waves,* Exon. 82 a; Th. 308, 5; Seef. 35: 115 a; Th. 442, 3; Kl. 7: Ps. Th. 118, 136: Bt. Met. Fox 20, 345; Met. 20, 173: 26, 57; Met. 26, 29. Sweorda gelác *the play of swords,* i. e. *battle,* Beo. Th. 2084; B. 1040: 2340; B. 1168. Gelác engla and deófla *hosts of angels and devils,* Exon. 21 a; Th. 56, 5; Cri. 896. Ðurh heard gelác *through hard fortune,* Andr. Kmbl. 2185; An. 1094. v. bord-, lind-, lyft-, scín-gelác.

ge-lácan; *p.* -léc *To play a trick on, delude:*—On hý geléc ðæt hý mid him wunnon *he deluded them into making war with him,* Ors. 3, 7; Bos. 60, 2. [Cf. *Icel.* leika á *to play a trick on.*]

ge-lácian, ic, he -lácige; *p.* ode; *pp.* od [lác *a gift*] *To give, bestow, present one with a thing;* munerare, munerare aliquem aliqua re:—Gelácige mid eádigum gifum *donis beatis munerabit.* Mid écum dó, mid hálgum ðínum, wuldre beón gelácod *eternâ fac, cum sanctis tuis, gloriâ munerari,* Te Deum, 21; Lamb. 195 b, 21.

ge-lácnian, -lácnigan; *p.* ode; *pp.* od *To heal, cure;* sánáre, méderi:—Gif hine mon gelácnian mæge *if he can be healed,* L. Alf. pol. 69; Th. i. 98, 8. His sáwle wunda dǽdbétende gelácnian *to heal the wounds of his soul by doing penance,* Homl. Th. i. 124, 14. Gelácnigan, Exon. 27 a; Th. 80, 19; Cri. 1309. Ic gelácnige *mĕdeor,* Ælfc. Gr. 27; Som. 29, 56. Gelácna ðú hý *heal thou them,* Hy. 1, 5; Hy. Grn. ii. 280, 5. He wæs gelácnod *he was cured,* Ors. 3, 7; Bos. 61, 44. Mon geseah hine laman gelácnian *people saw him healing the lame,* Blickl. Homl. 177, 16. Hine gelácnode *curam ejus egit,* Lk. Skt. 10, 34, note.

ge-lád, es; *n. A way, path, road, course;* via, trāmes:—Oferfór he uncúþ gelád *he traversed an unknown way,* Cd. 145; Th. 181, 9; Exod. 58: 158; Th. 197, 27; Exod. 313. Ofer deóp gelád *over the deep way,* i. e. *ocean,* Andr. Kmbl. 380; An. 190: Exon. 51 b; Th. 179, 23; Gú. 1266. v. fen-gelád. See Kmbl. Cod. Dipl. iii. xxvi.

ge-ládian; *p.* ode; *pp.* od *To clear, vindicate, excuse;* purgare, exculpare, excusare:—Gelādige hine *let him clear himself,* L. C. S. 44; Th. i. 402, 5: 29; Th. i. 392, 16. Ðonne biþ he self gelādod wiþ hine selfne *then shall he himself be acquitted towards himself,* Past. 21; Swt. 151, 18; Hat. MS.

ge-læccan, -læccean; he -læcþ; *p.* he -læhte, *pl.* -læhton; *pp.* -læht *To take, catch, seize, apprehend, comprehend;* capere, arripere, comprehendere:—Ðæt híg woldon hine gelæccean and to cyninge dón, Jn. Bos. 6, 15. Híg gelæhton hys hand, Gen. 19, 16: Mk. Bos. 9, 18. Ða Englisce men gelæhton of ðám mannon má . . . *the English men captured of those men more . . . ,* Chr. 1087; Erl. 225, 26. Hwæt gelæhtest ðú *quid cepisti,* Th. An. 22, 5. Germanus gelæhte ðone pistol æt Gregories ǽrendracan and hine totær *Germanus took the letter from Gregory's messenger and tore it to pieces,* Homl. Th. ii. 122, 29. Hét sóna gelæccan Stranguilionem *he bade seize Stranguilio at once,* Th. Apol. 25, 25. Ðis þing ic gelæhte *I have comprehended this thing;* hanc rem apprehendi, Ælfc. Gr. 7; Som. 6, 24.

ge-lǽdan, -lédan; *part.* -lǽdende; he -lǽdeþ, -lǽdt, -lǽt, *pl.* -lǽdaþ; *p.* ic, he -lǽdde, ðú -lǽddest, *pl.* -lǽddon; *impert.* -lǽd, *pl.* -lǽdaþ; *subj. pres.* -lǽde, *pl.* -lǽden; *pp.* -lǽded, -lǽdd, -lǽd *To lead, conduct, bear, bring, derive, bring out, bring forth, produce, bring up;* dūcĕre, dedūcĕre, ăgĕre, indūcĕre, deferre, perferre, derivāre, edūcĕre, prodūcĕre, edūcāre:—He wile folc gelǽdan in dreáma dreám *he will lead the people into joy of joys,* Exon. 16 a; Th. 36, 21; Cri. 579: 73 b; Th. 274, 13; Jul. 532. Gelǽdende híg nítenum *prodūcens fœnum jumentis,* Ps. Spl. 103, 15. Ic gelǽde *derivo,* Ælfc. Gl. 61; Som. 68, 46; Wrt. Voc. 39, 30. Me engel to ealle gelǽdeþ spówende spéd *an angel will bring to me all prosperous success,* Exon. 36 a; Th. 117, 15; Gú. 224: 33 b; Th. 107, 9; Gú. 56. Ðe to lífe gelǽdt *quæ dūcit ad vītam,* Mt. Bos. 7, 14. Ðe to forspilled-nesse gelǽt *quæ dūcit ad perdĭtiōnem,* 7, 13. Ða ðe feorran ðider feorh gelǽdaþ *they who lead their life thither from afar,* Andr. Kmbl. 564; An. 282. Ðú gelǽddest me *deduxisti me,* Ps. Spl. 60, 3: Ps. Th. 114, 8. Moyses fyrde gelǽdde *Moses led the march,* Cd. 145; Th. 181, 17; Exod. 62: 162; Th. 203, 2; Exod. 397. He gelǽdde me *edŭcāvit me,* Ps. Spl. C. 22, 2. Ðæt gé on fára folc feorh gelǽddon *that ye would lead your life among a hostile people,* Andr. Kmbl. 860; An. 430. Gelǽd me on rihtwísnesse ðínre *deduc me in justĭtia tua,* Ps. Lamb. 5, 9: 138, 23. Ne gelǽd ðú us on costnunge *ne nos indūcas in tentātiōnem,* Mt. Bos. 6, 13. Ðæt ðú gelǽde hláf of eorþan *ut edūcas pānem de terra,* Ps. Spl. 103, 16. His líchoma wæs to Turnum gelǽded *corpus Turōnis delātum,* Bd. 4, 18; S. 587, 9, 12. He wæs gelǽdd óþ ða þriddan heofonan *he was led to the third heaven,* Bd. de nat. rerum; Wrt. popl. science 2, 4; Lchdm. iii. 232, 26. He wæs fram Háligum Gástum gelǽd on sumum wéstene *ăgēbātur a spīrĭtu in desertum,* Lk. Bos. 4, 1: Chr. 693; Erl. 43, 19.

ge-lǽdenlíc; *adj. What is easily led* or *beaten out, malleable;* ductilis:—On býman gelǽdenlícum *in tubis ductilibus,* Ps. Spl. M. 97, 6.

ge-lǽfa, an; *m. Belief, faith;* fides:—He wolde ðone Cristes gelǽfan gerihtan *he would set right the faith of Christ,* Chr. 680; Erl. 41, 14. v. ge-leáfa.

ge-lǽfa, an; *m. Leave, permission;* permissio:—Be ðæs cynges gelǽfan *by the king's leave,* Chr. 1043; Erl. 170, 1.

ge-lǽfan *to believe.* v. ge-lýfan.

ge-lǽfan; *p.* de; *pp.* ed *To leave;* derelinquĕre:—Ðé gelǽfed is se þearfa *tibi derelictus est pauper,* Ps. Lamb. second 9, 14. Ðæt gelǽfed wæs *quod superfuit,* Mt. Kmbl. Lind. 15, 37.

ge-læht, *pl.* ge-læhte; *pp. Taken;* captus, comprehensus:—Híg beóþ gelæhte *comprehenduntur,* Ps. Lamb. second 9, 2; *pp. of* ge-læccan.

ge-læmed; *part. Lamed;* claudus factus:—Gif eaxle gelæmed weorþeþ *if a shoulder be lamed,* L. Ethb. 38; Th. i. 14, 2.

ge-længed, -længd; *part. Lengthened, drawn out:*—Eardbegengnes mín afeorrad ođđe gelængd is *incolatus meus prolongatus est,* Ps. Lamb. 119, 5. v. langian.

ge-lǽr; *adj. Void, empty;* vacuus, Som. [*Laym.* i-lær.]

ge-lǽran; ic -lǽre, ðú -lǽrest, -lǽrst, he -lǽreþ, -lǽrþ, *pl.* -lǽraþ; *p.* -lǽrde; *pp.* -lǽred, -lǽrd *To teach, educate, instruct, advise, persuade, induce;* dŏcēre, ērudīre, persuādēre:—We ðé mágon eáðe sélre gelǽran *we may easily teach thee better,* Andr. Kmbl. 2706; An. 1355: Beo. Th. 562; B. 278. Se gelǽrde peohtas to fullwihte *he brought the Picts by his teaching to baptism,* Shrn. 89, 33. Gif he ða cwéne gespannan and gelǽran mihte ðæt heó brúcan wolde his gesynscipes *si reginæ posset persuādēre ejus ūti connūbio,* Bd. 4, 19; S. 587, 30. Nǽfre ðú gelǽrest, ðæt ic dumbum and deáfum deófolgieldum gaful onháte *never shalt thou induce me, that I promise tribute to dumb and deaf idols,* Exon. 67 b; Th. 251, 22; Jul. 149. Ðæt gebrócode flǽsc gelǽrþ ðæt upahæfene mód *the afflicted flesh teaches the proud mind,* Past. 36, 7; Swt. 257, 14; Hat. MS. 48 a, 22. Hí á sibbe gelǽraþ *they shall ever teach peace,* Exon. 89 a; Th. 334, 23; Gn. Ex. 20. He gelǽrde ealle Crécas ðæt hý Alexandre wiðsócon *he persuaded all the Greeks to strive against Alexander,* Ors. 3, 9; Bos. 64, 6: Cd. 222; Th. 290, 10; Sat. 413: Th. Apol. 10, 18. Ðú us gelǽrdest ðæt we Hélende héran ne sceoldon *thou persuadest us that we should not obey the Saviour,* 214; Th. 268, 10; Sat. 53. Me gelǽr *dŏce me,* Ps. Th. 118, 68. Gelǽred *doctus,* Ælfc. Gr. 8; Som. 7, 41: 39; Som. 42, 47, 56. Ic eom gelǽred *dŏceor;* ðú eart gelǽrd *dŏcēris;* he is gelǽrd *dŏcētur,* 27; Som. 29, 21. Beóþ gelǽrede gé ðe démaþ eorþan *ērŭdīmĭni qui judĭcātis terram,* Ps. Spl. 2, 10.

ge-lǽred; *part. p. Learned;* doctus:—Albinus wæs betst gelǽred *Albinus was most learned,* Bd. Pref; S. 471, 23. He is gleáwest úre gelǽred *he is the most skilfully instructed of us,* H. R. 11, 9. Mid gelǽredre handa he swang ðone top *with skilful hand he whipped the top,* Th. Apol. 13, 13.

ge-lǽrednes, -ness, -nys, -nyss, e; *f. Learning, knowledge, skill;* ērŭdītio, pĕrītia:—Wæs Cúþberhte swá mycel getýdnes and gelǽrednes to sprecanne *Cudbercto tanta ĕrat dīcendi pĕrītia,* Bd. 4, 27; S 604, 19. Ðá se cyning his gelǽrednesse geseah *cujus ērŭdĭtiōnem vidēns rex,* 3, 7; S. 529, 46. On gelǽrednysse *in ērŭdĭtiōne,* 3, 21; S. 551, 13.

ge-lǽstan; to -lǽstenne; he -lǽsteþ, -lǽst; *p.* -lǽste; *pp.* -lǽsted, -lǽst. I. *to do, perform, accomplish, fulfil, discharge, execute, pay;* făcĕre, perfĭcĕre, patrāre, præstāre, persolvĕre:—Ic náuht ne tweóge ðat ðú hit mæge gelǽstan *I doubt not that thou canst perform it,* Bt. 36, 3; Fox 174, 31: Elen. Kmbl. 2329; El. 1166. Ic ða wǽre sóþe gelǽste *I will truly execute the compact,* Cd. 106; Th. 139, 11; Gen. 2308. Gif we sóþ and riht symle gelǽstaþ *if we always perform truth and right,* Hy. 7, 75; Hy. Grn. ii. 288, 75. Beót eal wið ðé he sóþe gelǽste *he truly fulfilled all his promise to thee,* Beo. Th. 1053; B. 524: Byrht. Th. 132, 13; By. 15. Ðe ǽr Godes hyldo gelǽston *who ere executed God's pleasure,* Cd. 17; Th. 21, 9; Gen. 321: Chr. 878; Erl. 81, 16: Ors. 4, 9; Bos. 91, 17. Hwænne man ðæt gelǽste *when it shall be fulfilled,* L. Edg. H. 7; Th. i. 260, 13: L. In. 4; Th. i. 104, 10: L. E. G. 6; Th. i. 170, 4. He hæfde wordbeót leófum gelǽsted *he had performed* *his promise to the beloved*, Cd. 132; Th. 167, 7; Gen. 2762: 109; Th. 144, 25; Gen. 2395. Ðæt gafol wæs gelǽst *the tribute was paid*, Chr. 1012; Erl. 146, 10: 1007; Erl. 141, 13. II. *to accompany, follow, attend, serve;* cŏmĭtāri, sĕqui, persĕqui:—He wolde gelǽstan freán to gefeohte *he would accompany his lord to the fight*, Byrht. Th. 132, 5; By. 11. Mec mīn gewit gelǽsteþ *my intellect attends me*, Exon. 38 a; Th. 125, 1; Gū. 347. Swā lange swā me līf gelǽst *as long as life attends me*, L. Edg. S. 12; Th. i. 276, 19: 16; Th. i. 278, 12. Ðæt hȳ him æt ðām gewinnum gelǽston *that they would serve him in the wars*, Ors. 4, 9; Bos. 91, 30. Ðæt hine ðonne wīg cume leóde gelǽsten *that the people serve him when war comes*, Beo. Th. 47; B. 24. III. *v. intrans. To continue, remain, last, endure;* mănēre, dūrāre:—Ne mæg hūs on munte lange gelǽstan *a house cannot long remain on a mountain*, Bt. Met. Fox 7, 37; Met. 7, 19. Ðæt eówre blǽda gelǽston *ut fructus vester măneat*, Jn. Bos. 15, 16.

ge-læswian; *p.* ode; *pp.* od [læswian *to feed*] *To feed:*—Gilesua *pasce*, Jn. Skt. Lind. 21, 17. Ic eom gelæswod *pastus sum*, Ælfc. Gr. 33; Som. 36, 44.

ge-lǽt *leads*, Mt. Bos. 7, 13; *3rd sing. pres. of* ge-lǽdan.

ge-lǽtan, -lētan; *p.* -leórt; *pp.* -lǽten *To allow, make over to any one:*—Eádgār æðeling wearþ belandod of ðām ðe se eorl him ǽror to handa gelǽten hæfde *Edgar Atheling was deprived of those lands which the earl had before made over to him*, Chr. 1091; Erl. 227, 24. Ðū gelētas *permittas*, Rtl. 59, 5. Ne geleórt ǽnigne monno to fylganne *non admisit quemquam sequi*, Mk. Skt. Rush. 5, 37. Ðū gileórtest *concessisti*, Rtl. 76, 36.

ge-lǽte, es; *pl.* -lǽtu; *n.* [lǽtan *to let go, leave*] *A going out, ending, meeting;* exitus, occursus:—To wega gelǽtum *to the meetings of ways*, Mt. 22, 9. Twegra wega gelǽtu *meetings of two ways*, Cot. 110. Æt ðæra wæga gelǽte, Gen. 38, 21. v. weggelǽte.

ge-lafian; *p.* ode, ede; *pp.* od, ed *To wash, lave, refresh;* refĭcĕre:—He winedryhten his wætere gelafede *he laved his liege lord with water*, Beo. Th. 5438; B. 2722.

ge-lagian; *p.* ode; *pp.* od *To establish by law, constitute, decree;* lēge sancīre:—Ðe Eádgār cyningc gelagode *which king Edgar decreed*, L. Eth. ix. 7; Th. i. 342, 13. Hū hit gelagod wæs *how it was constituted*, L. Ælf. P. 41; Th. ii. 382, 17. Ðe gelagod is to gedwolgoda weorðunge *that is appointed for the worship of false gods*, Swt. Rdr. 105, 27.

ge-lagu; *n.* (?) *A collection of water:*—Ofer holmą gelagu *over ocean's flood*, Exon. 82 a; Th. 309, 28; Seef. 64. v. lagu.

ge-landa. v. ge-londa.

ge-landian; *p.* ode; *pp.* od. I. *to land, arrive;* accedere ad terram, Som. [Cf. ge-lendan.] II. *to enrich with lands or possessions;* terris locupletare:—Ðe gelandod sȳ *who has lands*, L. Lund. 11. Opposed to be-landian. v. ge-lendan.

ge-lang, -long; *adj. Along* (*in the phrase* along of), *belonging, depending, consequent:*—Æt ðē is ūre lȳf gelang *our life is along of thee* (*thou hast saved our lives*, A. V.), Gen. 47, 25. Seó gescyldnys is æt ūrum Fæder gelang *protection comes from our Father*, Homl. Th. i. 252, 4: Ps. Th. 61, 1: Beo. Th. 2757; B. 1376. Nis me wiht æt eów leófes gelong *I am not dependent upon you for anything dear*, Exon. 37 a; Th. 121, 5; Gū. 284: 115 b; Th. 444, 11; Kl. 45. Ðæt wæs swīðor on ðam gelang *that was rather owing to this reason*, Ors. 4, 10; Bos. 94, 35. Gif hit on preóste gelang sȳ *if it be along of the priest*, L. M. I. P. 42; Th. ii. 276, 15: Bd. 3, 10; S. 534, 37. On heofonum sind lāre gelonge *instruction comes from heaven*, Exon. 36 a; Th. 117, 12; Gū. 223. Frægn se Scipio hine on hwȳ hit gelang wǽre *Scipio asked him to what it was owing*, Ors. 5, 3; Bos. 103, 42. Ðǽr is help gelong *help comes from there*, Exon. 75 a: Th. 281, 13; Jul. 645: 83 a; Th. 313, 8; Seef. 121. [*Laym.* ilong: *O. Sax.* gilang.]

ge-langian, -langian; *p.* ode; *pp.* od; *v. trans.* [ge, lang'an *to long for*] *To call for, send for, deliver, liberate;* convocare, arcessere, accersire, liberare:—Ðū gelangast to ðē ðīne leófostan frȳnd *thou shalt call to thee thy most beloved friends*, Jos. 2, 18. Gelangode to him ða brōðru *convocavit ad se fratres*, Greg. Dial. 2, 3. He hēt gelangian ðone hālgan lāreów *he ordered the holy teacher to be sent for*, Homl. Th. ii. 308, 5. He gelangode him to his swustur *he sent for his sister*, i. 86, 30. He bæd ðæt him man sumne mæsse-preóst gelangode *he asked them to send for a priest*, ii. 26, 9. Ic gelangige *arcesso* [MS. *acccrso*], Ælfc. Gr. 28, 1; Som. 30, 35. Wearþ ðā eft gelangod se geleáffulla apostol of ðam īglande *so was the faithful apostle liberated from that island*, Ælfc. T. Grn. 16, 28.

ge-lāst, es; *n.* [v. ge-lǽstan] *Duty, due;* officium:—To ǽlcum ðara gelāste *to each of those duties*, L. Æðelst 5, 3; Th. i. 230, 23: 232, 5. Gelāst *votum*, Ps. 64, 2, Blickl. Gl. [Cf. fullǽst, *and O. Sax.* gilēsti *an act, deed.*]

ge-lāstfull; *adj. Helpful, officious:*—Ðæt ǽlc man wǽre ōðrum gelāstfull *that every man should be helpful to other*, L. Æðelst. 5, 4; Th. i. 232, 11.

ge-lāþ; *adj. Hostile:*—Gelāþe *the foes*, Cd. 153; Th. 190, 28, note; Exod. 206, v. lāðe, 207, 3; Exod. 461; *and* cf. ge-fȳnd. [*Owl and Night.* ilað.]

ge-laðian; *p.* ode, ade, ede; *pp.* od, ad, ed *To invite, bid, call, summon, assemble, congregate;* invītāre, vŏcāre, arcessĕre, ciere, congrĕgāre:—Māgon we Ioseph to us geladian *can we invite Joseph* [*to come*] *to us*, Nicod. 20; Thw. 10, 3: Bd. 4, 1; S. 563, 34. Ic gelangige oððe gelaðige *cieo*, Ælfc. Gr. 37; Som. 39, 26: 30, 5; Som. 34, 52. Sum man worhte mycele feorme, and manega gelaðode *hŏmo quīdam fēcit cœnam magnam, et vocavit multos*, Lk. Bos. 14, 16: Chr. 449; Erl. 13, 2. He to Bethania his þegna gedryht gelaðade *he assembled his band of disciples in Bethany*, Exon. 14 b; Th. 29, 5; Cri. 458. Gelaðede se gesīþ hine to his hāme *the earl invited him to his home*, Bd. 3, 22; S. 553, 29. Ðonne ðū byst to gyftum gelaðod *cum invītātus fuĕris ad nuptias*, Lk. Bos. 14, 8. Ða ðe gelaðode wǽron, ne synt wyrðe *qui invītāti ĕrant, non fuĕrunt digni*, Mt. Bos. 22, 8: Jn. Bos. 2, 2. Wǽron ealle ða wīf befōran Rōmāna witan gelaðode *all the women were summoned before the Roman senators*, Ors. 3, 6; Bos. 58, 21.

ge-laðung, e; *f. A congregation, assembly, church;* congrĕgātio, convŏcātio, ecclēsia:—Gelaðung *convŏcātio*, Ælfc. Gl. 30; Som. 61, 51; Wrt. Voc. 26, 50. On middele gelaðunge ic hērige ðē *in mĕdio ecclēsiæ laudābo te*, Ps. Spl. 21, 21. On Godes gelaðunge *in God's church*, Homl. Th. i. 412, 1, 21: 502, 6. Ic gelȳfe on ða hālgan gelaðunge *I believe in the holy church*, ii. 596, 21: 598, 11. On gelaðunga hāligra *in ecclēsia sanctōrum*, Ps. Spl. 88, 6. On gesamningum oððe on gelaðungum ic bletsige ðē *in ecclēsiis bĕnĕdīcam te*, Ps. Lamb. 25, 12.

ge-laured *of* or *belonging to laurels;* laureus, Som.

geld, es; *n. A payment, society, worship, service*, Ælfc. Gl. 35; Som. 62, 76: Cot. 76: Prov. 22. v. gild.

geldan, ic gelde, ðū geltst, gelst, he gelt, *pl.* geldaþ; *p.* geald, *pl.* guldon; *pp.* golden *To pay, restore, render, make an offering, serve, worship:*—Geld ðæt ðū āht to geldanne *redde quod debes*, Mt. Kmbl. Lind. 18, 28: Bt. 41, 3; Fox 248, 22, note 27: L. Wih. 12; Th. i. 40, 4, 6: L. H. E. 10; Th. i. 32, 2. v. gildan.

gelde; *adj. That has yeaned, brought forth;* effeta, Cot. 75.

gelden *golden*. v. gylden.

ge-leáf *leave, license*. v. leáf.

ge-leáfa, an; *m.* [leáfa *belief*] *Belief, faith, confidence, trust;* fīdes, fīdūcia:—Se rihta geleáfa us tǽcþ, ðæt we sceolon gelȳfan on ðone Hālgan Gāst *the right faith teaches us that we should believe in the Holy Ghost*, Homl. Th. i. 280, 22: Elen. Kmbl. 2070; El. 1036. Geleáfa *fīdes*, Ælfc. Gr. 12; Som. 15. 54. Dæges ōr onwōc leóhtes geleáfan *the dayspring of bright belief awoke*, Apstls. Kmbl. 131; Ap. 66: Elen. Kmbl. 1928; El. 966. On rihtum geleáfan *in right faith*, Bt. 6; Fox 14, 31. Hī monige hrǽdlīce fram deófolgyldum to Cristes geleáfan gecyrdon *multos in brĕvi ab idōlătria ad fīdem convertĕrent Christi*, Bd. 5, 10; S. 624, 9: Chr. 565; Erl. 17, 21. Ðū ðone geleáfan hæfst *thou hast the belief*, Bt. 5, 3; Fox 12, 11. Nū we wyllaþ secgan eów ðone geleáfan ðe on ðam crēdan stent *we will now declare to you the faith which stands in the creed*, Homl. Th. i. 274, 23: 292, 9, 10: 294, 8. Habbaþ geleáfan *habēte fīdūciam*, Mt. Bos. 14, 27. Ic hæbbe me fæstne geleáfan up to ðam ælmihtegan Gode *I have firm trust in the Almighty God above*, Cd. 26; Th. 34, 26; Gen. 543: 205; Th. 256, 19; Dan. 643: Andr. Kmbl. 670; An. 335. Eom ic leóhte geleáfan fægre gefylled *I am fairly filled with bright belief*, Exon. 42 a; Th. 141, 8; Gū. 624: 62 b; Th. 230, 28; Ph. 479: 75 a; Th. 281, 28; Jul. 653. [*O. Sax.* gi-lōbo: *O. H. Ger.* ki-lauba: *Ger.* glaube: *and* cf. *Goth.* ga-laubeins.]

ge-leáfful, -full; *adj. Full of belief, believing, faithful, holy;* fĭdēlis, crēdŭlus:—Heó wundrade hū he swā geleáfful, on swā lytlum fæce, and swā uncȳdig, ǽfre wurde gleáwnysse þurhgoten *she wondered how he, so full of belief, in so short a space, and so ignorant, could ever be saturated with prudence*, Elen. Kmbl. 1916; El. 960. Getreówe, oððe geleáfful *fĭdēlis*, Wrt. Voc. 74, 27. Cyrce, oððe geleáfful gaderung *a church or faithful gathering;* ecclēsia, 80, 72. Wyrd gescreāf ðæt he, swā geleáfful, weorþan sceolde Criste gecwēme *fortune ordained that he, so full of faith, should become accepted of Christ*, Elen. Kmbl. 2093; El. 1048. Ne geleáffulle gecwēme synd on cȳðnesse his *nec habĭti sunt in testāmento ejus*, Ps. Spl. 77, 41. On geleáffullum bōcum *in holy books*, Ælfc. T. 13, 22. Ealle þing synd ðam geleáffullum acumendlīce *omnia sunt possĭbĭlia crēdenti*, Boutr. Scrd. 20, 26. Ofer geleáffulle eorþbūgende *super fĭdēles terræ*, Ps. Th. 100, 6. Ða beorhtan steorran getācniaþ ða geleáffullan on Godes gelaðunge *the bright stars betoken the faithful in God's church*, Bd. de nat. rerum; Wrt. popl. science 4, 4; Lchdm. iii. 238, 4.

ge-leáffulnes, -ness, -nys, -nyss, e; *f. Faithfulness, belief, trust;* fīdēlĭtas, crēdŭlĭtas:—Geleáffulnys *crēdŭlĭtas*, Ælfc. Gr. 9, 25; Som. 10, 64. We sceolan andettan ða sōðan geleáffulnesse on ūrne Drihten *we must confess the true belief in our Lord*, Blickl. Homl. 111, 6.

ge-leáfhlystend, es; *m. A catechumen;* catechumenus, Hpt. Gl. 457, 458.

ge-leáfleás; *adj. Unbelieving:*—Ðone geleáfleásne ent *the unbelieving giant*, Swt. Rdr. 66, 323.

ge-leáfleást, -leáflȳst, e; *f. Want of faith, unbelief, infidelity, unfaith-*

fulness; infīdēlĭtas, incrēdŭlĭtas:—For hyra geleáfleáste *on account of their unbelief,* Basil admn. 4; Norm. 42, 1. Drihten Hǣlend þreáde mid wordum ðæra Iudeiscra þwyrnysse and geleáfleáste *the Lord reproved with words the perversity and unbelief of the Jews,* Homl. Th. ii. 110, 4. Nū sind adwæscede ealle geleáflȳstu *now all infidelities are extinguished,* i. 226, 2: Deut. 1, 40.

ge-leáflíc; *adj. To be believed, credible, faithful;* crēdĭbĭlis:—Nis hit nā geleáflīc ðæt se wurm Euan bepǣhte, and se deófol spræc þurh ða næddran *it is not to be believed that the serpent deceived Eve, but the devil spoke through the serpent,* Boutr. Scrd. 19, 40. Ðīne gecȳðnyssa sindon swīðe geleáflīce *thy testimonies are very faithful,* Homl. Th. ii. 43, 15. Ðīne gecȳdnyssa [MS. -kyðnyssa] geleáflīce gewordene synt swīðe *testĭmōnia tua crēdĭbĭlia facta sunt nimis,* Ps. Lamb. 92, 5.

ge-leáfnes-word, es; *n. A pass-word,* Beo. Th. 496.

ge-leáfsum; *adj. Faithful, credible, credulous;* fĭdēlis, credĭbĭlis:—Ðīn gewitnes is weorcum geleáfsum *testĭmōnia tua credĭbĭlia facta sunt,* Ps. Th. 92, 6. Wǣron forþgongende ða cristenan men and ða geleáfsuman *the christian men and the faithful went forth,* Bd. 1, 8; S. 479, 20. Seó ætȳwnys heofonlīces wundres geopnode hū ārwyrþlīce hī wǣron to onfōnne eallum geleáfsumum *mīrācŭli cælestis ostensio, quam revĕrenter eæ suscĭpiendæ a cunctis fĭdēlibus essent, patĕfēcit,* 3, 11; S. 535, 34, note: 5, 24; S. 646, 32.

ge-leáh; *p. of* ge-leógan.

ge-leahtrian; *p.* ode, ade; *pp.* od, ad *To accuse, complain of, rebuke;* crīmĭnāri, accūsāre:—He wæs geleahtrad from Gode *he was rebuked by God,* Past. 46, 6; Swt. 355, 1; Hat. MS. 67 b, 14.

ge-leánian; *p.* ode; *pp.* od *To reward, repay, recompense;* reddĕre, trĭbuĕre, rependĕre:—Ne māgon we geleánian him mid lāþes wihte *we may not reward him with aught of hostility,* Cd. 21; Th. 25, 15; Gen. 394. Him ðæt geleánaþ līfes Waldend *the Lord of life will repay him that,* Exon. 117 a; Th. 450, 9; Dōm. 85. Biþ hiora yfel geleánod be heora gewyrhtum *their wickedness is recompensed according to their deserts,* Bt. 38, 3; Fox 202, 4.

ge-leás; *adj. False;* falsus:—Ne underfō geleáse gewitnysse *non suscĭpies vōcem mendācii,* Ex. 23, 1.

ge-leást, e; *f. Carelessness, negligence;* incuria, Som.

ge-leaðian; *p.* ade; *pp.* ad *To invite:* invītāre:—Hengest and Horsa, from Wyrtgeorne geleaðade Bretta kyninge, gesōhton Bretene *Hengest and Horsa, invited by Vortigern, king of the Britons, sought Britain,* Chr. 449; Erl. 12, 1. v. ge-laðian.

ge-leccan; *part.* -leccende; ic -lecce, ðū -lecest, -lecst, he -leceþ, -lecþ, *pl.* -leccaþ; *p.* -lehte; *pp.* -leht *To moisten, wet;* hūmectāre, rĭgāre:—Geleccende muntas ofer ðām uferum his *rĭgans montes de sŭpĕriōrĭbus suis,* Ps. Spl. 103, 14. Mid mīnum teárum strecednysse mīne oððe mīne beddinge ic beþweá oððe ic gelecce *lacrĭmis meis strātum meum rĭgābo,* Ps. Lamb. 6, 7. Sió mildheortnes ðæs lāreówes geþwǣnþ and gelecþ ða breóst ðæs gehiérendes *the kindness of the teacher softens and moistens the breast of the hearer,* Past. 18, 5; Swt. 137, 8; Hat. MS. 27 a, 12. For ðam sȳpe heó biþ geleht *by the moistening it becomes wet,* Bt. 33, 4; Fox 130, 6. Ðā sōna mīnne ðurst gelehte *I then at once slaked my thirst,* Nar. 12, 11.

ge-lecgan; *p.* -legde; *pp.* -leged, -legd, -lēd *To lay;* pōnĕre:—Hī ðec gelegdon on lāþne bend *they laid on thee the loathsome band,* Cd. 225; Th. 298, 26; Sat. 539. Hwār he gelēd wǣre *ubi pōnĕrētur,* Mk. Bos. 15, 47. He wæs unscyldig ðæs ðe him gelēd wæs *he was guiltless of that which was laid to him,* Chr. 1053; Erl. 187, 21.

ge-lēcnian, -leicnian *to cure,* Mt. Kmbl. Lind. 12, 10, 22. v. gelācnian.

ge-lēdan; *p.* -lēdde; *pp.* -lēded, -lēdd *To lead;* dūcĕre:—Ðe ic hebbe to helle hām gelēdde *which I have led home to hell,* Cd. 215; Th. 270, 11; Sat. 88. v. ge-lǣdan.

ge-lēdd; *part. p. Malleable, ductile;* ductilis:—On bȳman gelēddon *in tubis ductilibus,* Ps. Spl. T. 97, 6.

ge-lēfan *to allow, permit,* Mt. Kmbl. Lind. 12, 10: Mk. Skt. Lind. 11, 16. v. ge-lȳfan.

ge-lēfan; *p.* de; *pp.* ed *To believe, confide, trust;* crēdĕre, confīdĕre:—Gif gē willaþ mīnre mihte gelēfan *if ye will believe my power,* Cd. 219; Th. 280, 6; Sat. 251. Gelēfst ðū ðæt seó wyrd wealde disse worulde *dost thou believe that fortune governs this world?* Bt. 5, 3; Fox 12, 1. v. ge-lȳfan.

ge-lēfed; *part.* [lēf *infirm, weak*] *Corrupted, injured;* putrĭdus:—Se milte wyrþ gelēfed *the milt becomes corrupted,* L. M. 2, 36; Lchdm. ii. 244, 10. Hēr sindon ðurh synnleáfa sāre gelēfede to manege *here through impunity in sin too many are injured,* Swt. Rdr. 110, 174. v. ge-lȳfed.

ge-lēfenscipe, es; *m. Permission, excuse;* excusatio, Jn. Skt. Lind. 15, 22.

ge-leht *wet,* Bt. 33, 4; Fox 130, 6; *pp. of* ge-leccan.

ge-lend; *part. p. Provided with land:*—Gyf he wel gelend biþ *si bonam terram habeat,* L. R. S. 5; Th. i. 436, 5. [Cf. belendan, gelandian.]

ge-lend, e; *f. Fat, lard;* adeps, axungia, Ælfc. Gl. 73; Som. 71, 35. v. gelynd.

gelenda, an; *m. A man of landed property, a rich man;* dives, Som: Hpt. Gl. 480.

ge-lendan, he -lent; *p.* -lende; *pp.* -lended, -lend *To approach, come, arrive, go, proceed;* applĭcāre, accēdĕre, procēdĕre:—Ic gelende mid scipe *applĭco,* Ælfc. Gr. 24; Som. 25, 53. Ðæt scip gelent mid ðȳ streáme *the ship goes with the current,* Past. 58; Swt. 445, 13; Hat. MS. Conon gelende to Ahtene *Conon came to Athens,* Ors. 3, 1; Bos. 54, 12: Chr. 886; Erl. 85, 10. He wæs on hergaþ gelend on ðæt ilce rīce *he had arrived on a plundering expedition in the same kingdom,* 894; Erl. 92, 3. Heo on Norþhumbrelond gelændon mid æscum *they came to Northumbria with their boats,* Th. An. 120, 17: Shrn. 191, 15.

ge-lendan; *p.* de *To endow with land:*—Ða seofon mynstru he gelende mid his ǣgenum *those seven monasteries he endowed with his own lands,* Homl. Th. ii. 118, 29. v. ge-lend, ge-lendian, be-lendan.

ge-lēned; *part. p. Lent:*—Gelēned feoh *res credita,* Ælfc. Gl. 14; Som. 58, 2; Wrt. Voc. 20, 70. v. lǣnan.

ge-lengan; *p.* de; *pp.* ed *To prolong, lengthen;* prolongāre, protēlāre:—Heora unriht gelengdon *prolongāvērunt inīquĭtātem suam,* Ps. Th. 128, 2. Eówre dagas sīn gelengede *protēlentur dies vestræ,* Deut. 5, 33: Homl. Th. ii. 576, 26.

ge-lenge; *adj. Belonging, related;* pertinens, pertingens:—Ða ðe ðurh geleáfan us gelenge beóþ *those who through belief are related to us,* Homl. Th. ii. 314, 14. Yrfeweard līce gelenge *an heir of my body,* Beo. Th. 5457; B. 2732. Leahtrum gelenge *attached to vices,* Exon. 71 a; Th. 264, 28; Jul. 371. v. ge-lang.

ge-lent *goes,* Past. 58; Swt. 445, 113; Hat. MS; *3rd sing. pres. of* ge-lendan.

ge-leód, es; *m. One of a nation, a fellow-countryman, compatriot;* conterraneus, compatriota:—Gif hwā his āgenne geleód bebycgge *if any one sell his own countryman,* L. In. 11; Th. i. 110, 3.

ge-leódan; *p.* leád, *pl.* -ludon; *pp.* -loden *To spring, grow, descend;* crescere, germinare:—From ðām gumrincum folc geludon *nations grew from these patriarchs,* Cd. 75; Th. 93, 28; Gen. 1553. Ōþðæt ða geongan leomu geloden weorþaþ *till the young limbs be grown,* Exon. 87 a; Th. 327, 20; Vy. 6: Elen. Kmbl. 2451; El. 1227: Runic pm. 18; Kmbl. 343, 1; Hick. Thes. i. 135. DER. leódan.

ge-leofian; *p.* ode, ade; *pp.* od, ad *To live;* vīvĕre:—Ne geleofaþ man nāht miriges, ða hwīle ðe mon deáþ ondrǣt *there is no mirth in life when there is dread of death,* Prov. Kmbl. 16. Gyf swā biþ geleofad *si sic vīvĭtur,* Cant. Ezech. Lamb. fol. 185 a, 16. v. ge-lifian.

ge-leófst *believest,* Bt. 5, 3; Fox 14, 10, = ge-lȳfst; *2nd sing. pres. of* ge-lȳfan.

ge-leógan; *p.* -leáh, *pl.* -lugon; *pp.* -logen *To lie, belie, deceive;* mentīre, fallĕre:—Be ðām ðe hiora gewitnessa befōran bisceope geleógaþ *of those who belie their testimonies before a bishop,* L. In. 13; Th. i. 110, 10, MS. B. Him seó wēn geleáh *hope deceived him,* Beo. Th. 4636; B. 2323: Andr. Kmbl. 2150; An. 1076. Gelugon hȳ him *they deceived themselves,* Exon. 118 b; Th. 455, 27; Hy. 4, 56.

ge-leómod, -leómad; *part.* [leóma *a ray of light*] *Rayed, furnished with rays;* rădiātus:—Comētæ synd geleómade [MSS. R. P. L. geleómode] *comets are furnished with rays,* Bd. de nat. rerum; Wrt. popl. science 16, 20; Lchdm. iii. 272, 4.

ge-leoran; *p.* de; *pp.* ed *To go, depart, emigrate, die;* īre, migrāre, emigrāre, defĭcĕre:—Mec geleoran lǣt *let me depart,* Exon. 118 b; Th. 455, 3; Hy. 4, 44: Bd. 4, 23; S. 596, 11. Ic nā geleore *non emigrābo,* Ps. Spl. C. 61, 6. Seó rēdelse, and ðæt geþeaht ūrra feónda geleorde [MS. geleorode], ðā hī hit endian sceoldon *inĭmīci defĕcērunt frāmeæ in finem,* Ps. Th. 9, 6. Ðonne heora hwylc of weorulde geleored wæs *cum quis eōrum de sæcŭlo fuisset evŏcātus,* Bd. 4, 23; S. 595, 41, note. Sægde Hilde of weorulde geleoran *nunciavit Hild migrasse de sæculo,* 596, 11. Ne gelioraþ *non præteribit,* Mt. Kmbl. Lind. 24, 34. Dōhter mīn geliored is *filia mea defuncta est,* 9, 18.

ge-leorednes, -ness, -nys, -nyss, e; *f. A going, removing, transmigration;* transĭtus, transmigrātio:—Fram Dauide ōþ Babilōnis geleorednysse, and fram Babilōnis geleorednesse ōþ Crist *a David usque ad transmigrātiōnem Babȳlōnis, et a transmigrātiōne Babȳlōnis usque ad Christum,* Mt. Bos. 1, 17. v. ge-leornes.

ge-leoren; *part. Gone away, departed;* defunctus:—Eorþgrāp hafaþ waldendwyrhtan, forweorene [MS. forweorone], geleorene *earth's grasp* [i. e. *the grave*] *holds its powerful workmen, decayed, departed,* Exon. 124 a; Th. 476, 14; Ruin. 7.

ge-leorendlíc, -liorendlīc; *adj. Transitory;* transiens, Rtl. 28, 1.

ge-leornes, -ness, e; *f. A going, removing, departure, death;* transĭtus, transmigrātio:—Wæs gemēted ðætte hire geleornes wæs in ða ilcan tīd ðe hire þurh ða gesihþe ætȳwed wæs *inventum est eadem hōra transĭtum ejus illis ostensum esse per visiōnem,* Bd. 4, 23; S. 596, 22. Ongeáton hī on ðon, ðæt heó to ðon ðider com, ðæt heó hire sǣde ða neáhtīde hire geleornesse *ex quo intellexēre quod ipsa ei tempus suæ transmigrātiōnis in proxĭmum nunciāre venisset,* 4, 9; S. 577, 34. In geliornisse *in transmigratione*, Mt. Kmbl. Lind. 1, 11. To geliornisse herodes *ad obitum Herodis*, 2, 15. In dālum geliornesse *in partes Galileæ*, 2, 22. This gloss is to be explained by the old interpretation of the Hebrew name, according to which *Galilea = transmigratio.*

ge-leornian; *p.* ode, ede; *pp.* od, ed *To learn, inquire*; discĕre, disquīrĕre:—Swā swā heó æt gelǽredum wǽpnedmonnum geleornian mihte *prout a doctis viris discĕre pŏtĕrat*, Bd. 4, 23; S. 593, 28: 4, 18; S. 587, 1. He nǽfre ǽnig leóþ geleornode *nil carmĭnum alĭquando dĭdĭcĕrat*, 4, 24; S. 597, 4: Ps. Th. 118, 7. Hū hī ðās þing geleornodon *quomŏdo hæc dĭdĭcissent*, Bd. 4, 23; S. 596, 20. Geleornedon his byrelas him betweónum, hū hȳ him mihton ðæt līf ōþþringan *his cupbearers inquired among themselves how they might take away his life*, Ors. 3, 9; Bos. 69, 9.

GE-LES, -lis, es; *n. Reading, study, learning*; studium, lectura:—Gelis *studium*, Nar. 1, 20. On gelesum hāligra gewrita gelǽred *in studiis scripturarum institutus*, Bd. 5, 20; S. 641, 33. Betweoh geleoso ðære godcundan leornunge *inter studia divinæ lectionis* Bd. 3, 13; S. 538, 29. [Cf. *O. Sax.* lesan: *Icel.* lesa: *O. H. Ger.* lesan, ga-lesan *to read.*]

ge-lēsan; *p.* de; *pp.* ed *To redeem, save, spare*:—Gilēsdes usig *redemisti nos*, Rtl. 29, 19. Ic gilēse scīp mīno *ego parcam oves meas*, 10, 3. Gilēseno *redemti*, 24, 38.

ge-lēsniss, e; *f. Redemption*, Rtl. 12, 33.

ge-leswian *to feed*; pascere, Jn. Skt. Lind. 21, 17.

ge-lēt *an ending, a meeting.* v. ge-lǽte.

ge-leðran; *p.* ede; *pp.* ed *To lather*; saponem illinere, sapone bullas excitare:—Ðæt heó sȳ eall geleðred *so that it may be all lathered*, Lchdm. iii. 2, 3. v. lyðran.

ge-lettan; ðū -letest; *p.* -lette; *pp.* -lett, -let; *v. a. To hinder, delay, let, stop*; retardare, impedire:—Hī hine māgon gelettan *they may delay it*, Bt. 41, 2; Fox 246, 9. Hine seó eá lange gelette ðæs oferfæreldes *the river long hindered him from passing over*, Ors. 2, 4; Bos. 43, 45. Ðū geletest lāþ werod *thou shalt stop the hostile force*, Elen. Kmbl. 187; El. 94. To hraðe hine gelette lidmanna sum ðā he ðæs eorles earm amyrde *too soon one of the seamen hindered him when he disabled the earl's arm*, Byrht. Th. 136, 40; By. 164. Ne lǽt ðec sīðes getwǽfan lāde gelettan lifgendne monn *let not living man divert thee from the course, hinder thee from the way*, Exon. 123 b; Th. 474, 3; Bo. 24: 37 b; Th. 123, 29; Gū. 330. Ac hit wæs ðā ðurh Eádrīc ealdorman gelet swā hit ðā ǽfre wæs *but matters were hindered by alderman Eadric as they always were then*, Chr. 1009; Erl. 143, 1. He wearþ gelet *he was hindered*, 1075; Erl. 213, 17. v. lettan.

gelew; *adj. Yellow, bay*; flāvus:—On horse gelewum sittan hȳnþe getācnaþ *to sit on a bay horse betokens humiliation*, Lchdm. iii. 202, 29. v. geolo.

ge-lēwan; *p.* de; *pp.* ed *To betray, deceive, weaken, injure*; prodere:—Gelēwend *prodens*, Lye. Gif hit byþ deád oððe gelēwed *if it is dead or hurt*, Exod. 22, 10, 14. (*Or does* gelēwed *here* = gelēfed? cf. alēuaþ and geuntrumaþ, Homl. Th. i. 4, 22; *and* Swt. Rdr. 110, 174, note.) [*Goth.* ga-lēwjan *to betray.*]

ge-līc [-līce?], es; *n. Likeness, similitude*; sĭmĭlĭtūdo:—Næfdon hī māre monnum gelīces ðonne ingeþonc *they had no more likeness to men than the mind*, Bt. Met. Fox 26, 186; Met. 26, 93. [Cf. *Goth.* ga-leiki.]

ge-līc; *comp. m.* -līcra; *f. n.* -līcre; *superl.* -līcost, -līcast, -līcust; *adj. Like, alike, similar, equal*; sĭmĭlis, æquālis:—Næs se wæstm gelīc *the fruit was not alike*, Cd. 23; Th. 30, 13; Gen. 466: Bt. 38, 6; Fox 208, 17: Exon. 89 a; Th. 334, 21; Gn. Ex. 19. Heofena rīce is geworden gelīc senepes corne *sĭmĭle est regnum cœlōrum grāno sinăpis*, Mt. Bos. 13, 31, 33: 22, 2: Lk. Bos. 13, 18, 19, 20, 21: Ps. Spl. 48, 12, 21. Ealle men hæfdon gelīcne fruman *all men had a like beginning*, Bt. 30, 2; Fox 110, 7: Andr. Kmbl. 988; An. 494. Ic ðē mæg andreccan sprǽce gelīce [MS. gelīcne] *I can relate to thee a similar tale*, Bt. Met. Fox 26, 4; Met. 26, 2. Ic ǽnig ne mētte wið ðē gelīc *I have not met any like unto thee*, Exon. 73 b; Th. 275, 13; Jul. 549. Ealle hī beóþ gelīce acennede *they are all born alike*, Bt. 30, 2; Fox 110, 9: Beo. Th. 4334; B. 2164. Wirc ðē twā stǽnene tabulan ðām ōðrum gelīce *præcīde tibi duas tăbŭlas lăpĭdeas instar priōrum*, Ex. 34, 1: Ps. Th. 65, 5. Se līchoma wæs slǽpendum men gelīcra ðonne deádum *the body was more like a sleeping than a dead man*, Bd. 4, 19; S. 589, 16: Ps. Th. 88, 5. Gelīcre *sĭmĭlior*, Ælfc. Gr. 5; Som. 5, 5. Slǽp biþ deáþe gelīcost *sleep is most like death*, Salm. Kmbl. 624; Sal. 311: Bt. Met. Fox 25, 36; Met. 25, 18: 26, 176; Met. 26, 88. Rēce hī gelīcast ricene geteoriaþ *sīcut dēfĭcit fūmus, dēfĭciant*, Ps. Th. 67, 2: 102, 5. Īs byþ gimmum gelīcust *ice is most like gems*, Runic pm. 11; Hick. Thes. i. 135, 21; Kmbl. 341, 17. Didimus ðæt ys Gelȳcost on ure geðeóde *Didimus, that is in our language twin*, Jn. 20, 24: 21, 2. [*Chauc.* ilik: *Goth.* ga-leiks: *O. Sax.* gi-līk: *O. Icel.* glíkr: *O. H. Ger.* ge-lich: *Ger.* gleich.]

ge-līca, an; *m*: *also* ge-līce, an; *f. An equal*; æqualis, par, æqualitas:—Nān man nis his gelīca on eorþan *non sit ei similis in terra*, Job. Thw. 164, 17. Micel is ðæt ongin ðīnre gelīcan *great is the attempt for thy equal* [cf. *Ger.* für Deinesgleichen; *colloquial English* for the like of you], Exon. 67 b; Th. 250, 16; Jul. 128. Nān þing nis ðīn gelīca *no thing is thine equal*, Bt. Met. Fox 20, 74; Met. 20, 37: Homl. Th. ii. 576, 22. [*Laym.* (his) iliche: *O. H. Ger.* (min) gilicho.]

ge-līcan *to liken, imitate*:—To gelīcanne *ad imitandum*, Rtl. 22, 36. Gelīced biþ *assimilabitur*, Mt. Kmbl. Lind. 7, 24. [*Goth.* ga-leikon: *O. H. Ger.* ki-lihhan: *Ger.* gleichen.]

ge-līcbisnung, e; *f. Imitation*; imitatio, Rtl. 76, 1.

ge-liccettan; *p.* te; *pp.* ed *To flatter, dissemble*; assentari, simulare, Som.

gelīce; *adv. Likewise, also, as*; pariter, Ps. Spl. 67, 7: Mt. Bos. 27, 44. Gelīce swā swā heó bebeád *likewise as she commanded*, Bd. 4, 19; S. 588, 19: Blickl. Hom. 17, 4. He dyde swā gelīce *fecit similiter*, Mt. Bos. 20, 5. Elpendes hȳd wyle drincan wætan gelīce ān spinge deþ *an elephant's hide will imbibe water as a sponge doth*, Ors. 5, 7; Bos. 107, 11. Ðǽm biscopum ðe hēr on worlde syndon swȳðe gelīce gegange ðæm biscope ðe Paulus geseah *it shall happen to those bishops that are in this world as it did to the bishop that St. Paul saw*, Blickl. Homl. 45, 4: 59, 4. Nis ðæt nō be eallum dēmum gelīce to secgenne *that is not to be said of all judges alike*, 63, 16. Ne wǽron ðās ealle gelīce lange *these were not all alike long*, 119, 3. His līf ðæm his naman wæs gelīce gegearwod *his life was ordered in accordance with his name*, 167, 32. Gelīce sē lēg hie cwylmde gelīce ða Cristenan him mid heora wǽpnum hȳndon *they were killed alike by the lightning and laid low by the weapons of the Christians*, 203, 16: Nar. 14, 10. Ðon gelīcost ðe ðǽr sum mon gestōde *just as if a man had stood there*, Blickl. Homl. 203, 35. Emne ðon gelīcost ðe he ne cūðe *just as if he didn't know*, Cd. 92; Th. 116, 28; Gen. 1943. Efne ðæm gelīcost swylce *just as if*, Blickl. Homl. 221, 14.

ge-licgan, -licgean; *p.* -læg, *pl.* -lǽgon; *pp.* -legen. I. *to lie, lie near, together*; jacere, adjacere, conjacere:—Mægen-stān him on middan geligeþ *a huge stone lies in the middle of it*, Bt. Met. Fox 5, 32; Met. 5, 16. Stedewangas strǽte gelicgaþ *fixed plains lie near the road*, Andr. Kmbl. 668; An. 334. On ðæm gelæg *in quo jacebat*, Lk. Skt. Lind. 5, 25. Ðā heó ðǽr on gelegen wæs *when she had lain down there*, Ors. 5, 13; Bos. 113, 23. II. *to lie down, fail, cease, loiter, delay*; deficere, cessare:—Windblond gelæg *the wind-storm ceased*, Beo. Th. 6284; B. 3146. Ne mihte se nīþ betwux him twām gelicgean *the strife between the two could not be appeased*, Ors. 3, 11; Bos. 75, 36.

ge-līc-gemaca, an; *m. An equal*; compar, Ælfc. Gr. 9, 51.

ge-līchamod, -homod; *part. p. Incarnate*:—Drihten wæs gelīchomod *the Lord became incarnate*, Blickl. Homl. 33, 15.

ge-līcian; *p.* ode; *pp.* od; *with dat.* I. *to please, delight*; placere, acquiescere, delectare:—Ic gelīcie *placebo*, Ps. Th. 114, 8. Gelīcaþ [gelīcige, Lamb. 14; Spl. 18] ðē Dryhten *complaceat tibi Domine*, Ps. Surt. 39, 14. Ðæt ðē gelīciaþ *ut te complaceant*, Ps. Spl. 18, 15. On ðē ic gelīcode *in te complacui*, Mk. Bos. 1, 11. II. *impers. it pleases*; placet:—Me gelīcaþ *placet mihi*, Ælfc. Gr. 33; Som. 37. 17. v. līcian.

ge-līclīc; *adj. Likely, fit*; aptus:—Swīþor ðonne hit gelīclīc sīe *more strongly than is proper*, L. M. 2, 16: Lchdm. ii. 194, 14: Hpt. Gl. 506.

ge-līclīce; *adv. Equally*:—Gelīclīc *æqualiter*, Jn. Skt. p. 4, 10.

ge-līcnes, -ness, e; *f.* I. *a likeness, image, resemblance*; similitudo, imago:—Uton wircean man to andlīcnisse, and to ūre gelīcnisse *faciamus hominem ad imaginem, et similitudinem nostram*, Gen. 1, 26. Ǽlc man hæfþ þreó þing on him sylfum untodǽledlīce and togædere wyrcende, swā swā God cwæþ, ðāðā he ǽrest mann gesceóp. He cwæþ, 'Uton gewyrcean mannan to ūre gelīcnysse.' And he worhte ðā Adam to his anlīcnysse. On hwilcum dǽle hæfþ se man Godes anlīcnysse on him? On ðære sāwle, nā on ðam līchaman *every man has three things in himself indivisible and working together, as God said when he first created man. He said, 'Let us make man in our own likeness.' And he then made Adam in his own likeness. In which part has man the likeness of God in him? In the soul, not in the body*, Homl. Th. i. 288, 11–17. He worhte of seolfre ǽnne heáhne stȳpel on stānweorces gelīcnysse *he wrought a high tower of silver in the form of stone-work*, H. R. 99, 23. Uton gewyrcan mannan to ūre anlīcnysse and to ūre gelīcnysse *faciamus hominem ad imaginem nostram et similitudinem nostram*, Hexam. 11; Norm. 18, 15. II. *a parable, proverb*; parabola, proverbium:—Arecce us gelīcnisse ðas *edissere nobis parabolam istam*, Mt. Kmbl. Rush. 15, 15. Gē secgaþ me ðas gelīcnesse, Eálā lǽce, gehǽl ðē sylfne *dicetis mihi hanc similitudinem* [*proverbium*], *Medice, cura teipsum*, Lk. Bos. 4. 23. [*O. H. Ger.* gelīhnessi *parabola*: *Ger.* gleichniss.]

ge-līcung, e; *f. A liking.* v. līcung.

ge-liden *sailed*, Exon. 20 b; Th. 53, 30; Cri. 858; *pp. of* ge-līðan.

ge-liese *care, learning.* v. ge-les.

ge-līfan, -liéfan; *p.* de; *pp.* ed *To believe. trust*; crēdĕre, confīdĕre:—Gif hie willen geliéfan ðætte Godes rīce hiera sīe *if they will believe that God's kingdom is theirs*, Past. 36, 5; Swt. 253, 9; Hat. MS. 47 b, 8. Se ðe him to ðam hālgan helpe gelīfeþ, he ðǽr gearo findeþ *he who trusteth himself to the holy one for help, he findeth it there readily*, Wald. 111; Vald. 2, 27. Abram gelīfde Gode *crēdĭdit Abram Deo*, Gen. 15, 6. Ðæt hie geliéfon on ðīnne naman *that they may believe on thy name*, Blickl. Homl. 247, 25. v. ge-lȳfan.

ge-līfedlīce *lawfully.* v. ge-lȳfedlīce.

ge-līffæstan; *p.* -līffæste; *pp.* -līffæsted, -līffæst *To make alive, quicken; vivificāre*:—God geworhte ǽnne mannan, and hine gelīffæste, and he wearþ đā mann gesceapen on sāwle and on līchaman *God made one man, and made him alive, and he then became man with soul and body,* Homl. Th. i. 12, 29. Se sunu gelīffæst đa de he wyle *filius quos vult vivificat,* Jn. Bos. 5, 21. He wolde swā synfulle sāwle gelīffæstan *he would quicken so sinful a soul,* Homl. Th. i. 496, 15: ii. 206, 17. Mid gesceádwīsre sāwle gelīffæst *quickened by a rational soul,* 270, 20.

ge-lifian; *p.* ode; *pp.* od *To live* [cf. *Ger.* erleben]:—Gif he hit gelifode *if he had lived,* Chr. 1093; Erl. 229, 8. v. ge-leofian.

ge-līgenod; *part. p. Convicted of lying*:—Se apostol Paulus ne biþ gelīgenod *the apostle Paul is not shewn to be false,* Homl. Th. i. 54, 1.

ge-liger, es; *n. A lying with, fornication, adultery;* concŭbĭtus, conjŭgium, fornicātio, adultĕrium:—He sǽde đæt his nama wǽre spiritus fornicationis đæt is dernes geligeres gāst *he said that his name was spiritus fornicationis, that is, spirit of fornication,* Shrn. 52, 27: 130, 14. To geligere *concubitu,* Ors. 1, 2; Bos. 27, 13. Æt geligere *de conjŭgio,* Bos. 27, 15. Geligre *fornicatiōni,* Bos. 27, 9. [*Goth.* ga-ligri. Cf. forliger.]

ge-ligernes, ness, e; *f. Fornication, adultery;* fornicātio, libīdo:—For hyre geligernesse *for her lustfulness,* Ors. 1, 2; Bos. 27, 11.

ge-līhtan; *p.* -līhte *To lighten, mitigate, assuage;* alleviare:—Mid ānre mæssan man mæg alȳsan xii daga fæsten and mid x mæssan man mæg gelīhtan iiii monđa fæsten and mid xxx mæssan man mæg gelīhtan xii monđa fæsten *with one mass a man may redeem a xii days' fast, and with x masses a man may lighten a iiii months' fast; and with xxx masses a man may lighten a xii months' fast,* L. Pen. 19; Th. ii. 286, 6-9: 14. Đonne hie willaþ him selfum đæt yfel đæt hie đurhtugon to swīđe gelīhtan *when they wish to make too light of the evil they have done,* Past. 21; Swt. 159, 20; Hat. MS. Ic mīnne đurst gelēhte [?] *I assuaged my thirst* [or gelehte *from* geleccan], Nar. 12, 11. [*A. R.* i-lihted *alleviated: O. H. Ger.* gi-līhten *lenire.*]

ge-līhtan; *p.* -līhte *To alight, approach, come*:—Gelīht of his horse *desiliit ab equo suo,* Gr. Dial. 1, 2. Đā gelīhte se cuma *then the stranger alighted,* Homl. Th. ii. 134, 34. He gelīhte to đæm hearge *propiabat ad fanum,* Bd. 2, 13; S. 517, 11. Segde đætte sealfa god wolde helwarum hām gelīhtan *said that God himself would come home to the dwellers in hell,* Cd. 222; Th. 291, 16; Sat. 431.

ge-līhtan; *p.* -līhte *To shine, grow light;* lucere, lucescere:—Đæt he gelīhte allum *ut luceat omnibus,* Mt. Kmbl. Rush. 5, 15. Gelihted *lucescit,* Lind. 28, 1. v. gelȳhtan.

ge-līman; *pp.* ed *To glue* or *join together, connect;* conglutinare:—Gelīmþ đa friénd togædere *joins the friends together,* Bt. 24, 3; Fox 84, 1. Gelīmed fæste tosomne *joined fast together,* Bt. 35, 2; Fox 156, 35. Gelīmod *conglūtinatus,* Ps. Lamb. 43, 25.

ge-limp, es; *n. An event, accident, a chance;* accĭdens, cāsus:—Đara in gelimpe līfe weóldon *of those who in chance possessed life,* Exon. 36 b; Th. 118, 13; Gū. 239. Is ǽnig ōđer on eallum đām gelimpum būton godes yrre ofer đas đeóde swutol and gesȳne *is there anything else plain and visible in these events but God's anger over this people?* Swt. A. S. Rdr. 109, 137. Đā forhtede đe biscop for đam fǽrlīce gelimpe *then the bishop was afraid on account of that dangerous case,* Th. An. 121, 5: Th. Ap. 1, 12. Đū woldest witan his naman and his gelimp *you wanted to know his name and what had befallen him,* 16, 4: 15, 20, 26.

ge-limpan; he -limpeþ, -limpþ; *p.* -lamp, -lomp, *pl.* -lumpon; *subj. p.* -lumpe, *pl.* -lumpen; *pp.* -lumpen *To happen, occur, befall, come to pass, take place;* accĭdĕre, evĕnīre, contingĕre:—Đæt gelimpan sceal đætte lagu flōweþ ofer foldan *it shall happen that water shall flow over the earth,* Exon. 115 b; Th. 445, 1; Dōm. 1: 117 b; Th. 452, 5; Dōm. 116. Hit eft gelimpeþ đæt se līchoma lǽne gedreóseþ *it afterwards befalls that the body miserably sinks,* Beo. Th. 3511; B. 1753. Gyf hyt gelimpþ đæt he hyt fint *si contĭgĕret ut invĕniat eam,* Mt. Bos. 18, 13. Đā gelamp hit *then it happened,* Gen. 40, 1: Homl. Th. ii. 120, 14. Frōfor eft gelamp sārigmōdum *comfort afterwards came to the sad of mood,* Beo. Th. 5875; B. 2941. Đā sió tīd gelomp *when the time came,* Bt. Met. Fox 26, 34; Met. 26, 17: Bt. 18, 4; Fox 66, 27. Ealle đās ungesǽlþa us gelumpon þurh unrǽdas *all these calamities befell us through evil counsels,* Chr. 1011; Erl. 145, 1. Gif đē đæt gelimpe *if that befall thee,* Elen. Kmbl. 879; El. 441: Beo. Th. 1862; B. 929. Geseón hwæt us gelumpe *vidēre quid nōbis accĭdĕret,* Bd. 5, 1; S. 614, 3: Exon. 35 a; Th. 113, 32; Gū. 165. Gregorius Gode þancode đæt Angelcynne swā gelumpen wæs, swā swā he sylf geornlīce gewilnode *Gregory thanked God that it had so happened to the English nation, as he himself had earnestly desired,* Homl. Th. ii. 130, 28: Beo. Th. 1653; B. 824.

ge-limpfull; *adj. Fit, suitable*:—Đæt he gedō đisne weig gelimpfulran *that he make this way better,* Shrn. 163, 25.

ge-limplīc; *adj. Fit, seasonable, suitable, meet, ordered by fate, fatal;* compĕtens, congruus, opportūnus, fātālis:—Gelimplīc *fātālis,* Cot. 89. On gelimplīcre tīde *in tempŏre opportūno,* Ps. Spl. 144, 16: Bd. 4, 24; S. 597, 10. Swā hwǽr swā he gelimplīce stōwe findan mihte *wheresoever he could find a suitable place,* 3, 19; S. 547, 5: 5, 3; S. 616, 25.

ge-limplīce; *comp.* -līcor; *adv. Fitly, seasonably, opportunely;* opportūne:—Đæt hī oncnāwen hū gelimplīce ūre God đa ānwaldas and đa rīcu sette *that they might know how seasonably our God settled the empires and the kingdoms,* Ors. 2, 1; Bos. 40, 7. Gelimplīce he us lǽrde hū we us gebiddan sceoldan *fortunately he hath taught us how we ought to pray,* Blickl. Homl. 19, 35. Gelimplīcor *opportūnius,* Bd. 3, 29; S. 561, 29.

ge-limpwīse, an; *f. An event;* eventus, quod evenit, Hpt. Gl. 457.

ge-lióma, an; *m. A light;* lumen, Mone B. 174.

ge-lioran *to pass over.* v. ge-leoran.

ge-liornes *a going, death.* v. ge-leornes.

ge-lirde *emigrated.* v. ge-leoran.

ge-lis *study, learning.* v. ge-les.

ge-līsian *to slip, slide*:—Be đæm is awriten se đe nylle onscūnian his lytlan scylda đæt he wille gelīsian to māran *it is written that he who will not shun his little sins will glide into greater,* Past. 57, 2; Swt. 437, 20; Hat. MS. v. note.

ge-lisþelīcnis, se; *f. Opportunity;* opportunitas, Ps. Spl. T. 9, 9.

ge-līđan; *p.* -lāþ, *pl.* -lidon; *pp.* -liđen, -liden *To go, move, sail, advance, proceed, come;* īre, meāre, advĕhi, profĭcisci, vĕnīre:—Mænig tungul māran ymbhwyrft hafaþ on heofonum, sume hwīle eft læsse gelīđaþ, đa đe lācaþ ymb eaxe ende *many a star has a greater circuit in the heavens; sometimes again, they move in a less, that sport about the end of the axis,* Bt. Met. Fox 28, 43; Met. 28, 22. Ǽr đon we to lande geliden hæfdon *ere that we had sailed to land,* Exon. 20 b; Th. 53, 30; Cri. 858: Elen. Kmbl. 498; El. 249. Đæs đe lencten geliden hæfde werum *after spring had come to men,* Menol. Fox 57; Men. 28.

ge-līđewǽcan; *p.* -wǽhte; *pp.* -wǽht *To soften, calm, appease;* lēnīre:—Ic gelīđewǽce *lēnio,* Ælfc. Gr. 30, 5; Som. 34, 56. His afyrhte mōd swīđe fægerlīce mid his frōfre he gelīđewǽhte *he gently appeased his troubled mind with his comfort,* Ælfc. T. 37, 24.

ge-līđian, -līđegian; *p.* ode; *pp.* od *To soothe, soften, mitigate, relieve, appease;* lēnīre, mītĭgāre, plācāre:—Styrunge ȳþa hire đū gelīđegast [gelīđegost MS.] *mōtum fluctuum ejus tu mītĭgas,* Ps. Lamb. 88, 10. Gāte cȳse niwe ongelegd đæt sār gelīđegaþ *a new goat's cheese laid on relieveth the sore,* Med. ex Quadr. 6, 7; Lchdm. i. 352, 9. Đū gelīđegodest ealne đīnne graman *mītĭgasti omnem īram tuam,* Ps. Lamb. 84, 4. Drihtnes yrre wearþ gelīđegod ongēn đæt folc *plācātus est Dŏmĭnus adversus pŏpŭlum suum,* Ex. 32, 14. His đurst wæs gelīþad *his thirst was appeased,* Shrn. 130, 5. Forđæm is swīđe micel nēđđearf đæt mon mid micelre gemetgunge swelcra scylda đreáunga gelīđige *therefore it is very necessary that the chiding of such sins be tempered with great moderation,* Past. 21; Swt. 159, 3; Hat. MS.

ge-litlian; *p.* ode; *pp.* od *To diminish, lessen;* mĭnōrāre:—Nȳtenu heora he ne gelitlode ođđe he ne gewanode *jūmenta eōrum non mĭnōrāvit,* Ps. Lamb. 106, 38. Ic beóde mīnum erfeweardum đæt heo nǽfre đis feoh gelitlian *I enjoin my heirs that they never diminish this money,* Th. Chart. 168, 22. v. ge-lytlian.

gellan, gillan, giellan, gyllan; *part.* gellende, gillende, giellende, gyllende; ic gelle, gille, gielle, gylle, đū gilst, gielst, gylst; he gilleþ, gilþ, gielþ, gylleþ, gylþ, *pl.* gellaþ, gillaþ, giellaþ, gyllaþ; *p.* geal, *pl.* gullon; *pp.* gollen *To yell, sing, chirp;* stridere, sonare:—Gellende *yelling,* Exon. 94 b; Th. 353, 40; Reim. 25. Ic seah searo giellende *I saw a yelling machine,* 108 b; Th. 415, 1; Rä. 33, 4. Gyllende gryre *with yelling horror,* Cd. 167; Th. 208, 26; Exod. 489. Ic gielle swā hafoc *I yell as a hawk,* Exon. 106 b; Th. 406, 19; Rä. 25, 3. Gilleþ geómorlīce *he yelleth sadly,* Salm. Kmbl. 535; Sal. 267. Gylleþ grǽghama *the cricket chirps,* Fins. Th. 10; Fin. 6. Gielleþ ānfloga *the lone-flier yells,* Exon. 82 a; Th. 309, 25; Seef. 62. Hī gullon *they sung,* Andr. Kmbl. 253; An. 127. [*Plat.* gillen *to shriek*: *Frs.* galljen: *Dut.* galmen *to sound*: *Ger.* gellen, gällen *to sound, from* gal, gall *a sound*: *O. H. Ger.* calm, galm: *Icel.* gella.] DER. bi-gellan.

gellet, es; *n? A large vessel* or *cup, basin;* alveus, pōcŭlum mājus:—Gescearfa đās wyrto tosomne, dō on gellet *scrape these herbs together, put them into a basin,* L. M. 3, 48; Lchdm. ii. 340. 3.

GELM, gilm, es; *m. A* YELM, *handful;* manĭpŭlus:—Genim grēne mintan, ǽnne gelm *take green mint, a handful,* L. M. 1, 48; Lchdm. ii. 120, 22: iii. 74, 18.

gelo; *adj. Saffron, yellow;* crocus, Som.

ge-loccian *to stroke gently;* demulcere, Som. [*O. H. Ger.* gi-locchon *mulcere.*]

ge-lōcian; *p.* ode; *pp.* od *To look, behold, see;* respĭcĕre, aspĭcĕre:—Driht of heofonum on eorþan gelōcaþ *Dŏmĭnus de cœlo in terram aspexit,* Ps. Spl. 101, 20. Eágan his ofer þeóda gelōciaþ *ŏcŭli ejus sŭper gentes respĭciunt,* 65, 6. Gelōca on cȳđnysse đīne *respĭce in testāmentum tuum,* Ps. Spl. C. 73, 20.

ge-loda; *pl. Joints of the back*:—Geloda *vel* gelyndu *spondilia,* Ælfc. Gl. 74; Som. 71, 51; Wrt. Voc. 44, 34.

ge-loda, an; *m. A brother;* frater:—Gebrođru *vel* gelodan *fratres,* Ælfc. Gl. 92; Som. 75, 42; Wrt. Voc. 52, 3.

gelodr, e; *f. A part of the body about the chest, the backbone* or *spine?* pars corporis circa thoracem *vel* spinam?—Se maga biþ neáh đære heortan and ðære gelodre *the stomach is near the heart and the spine*, L. M. 2, 1; Lchdm. ii. 176, 3.

ge-lod-wyrt, e; *f. Silverweed;* potentilla anserina:—Gelodwyrt *heptaphyllon*, Recd. 42, 75; Wrt. Voc. 68, 10: Lchdm. ii. 78, 1: 98, 16.

ge-logian; *p.* ode; *pp.* od *To place, lodge, dispose, regulate;* ponere, disponere, reponere, collocare:—God gelogode ðone man *Deus posuit hominem*, Gen. 2, 8: Homl. Th. i. 12, 33. Ða geleáfullan folc hig sylfe gelogiaþ and heora líf for Gode *the faithful folk dispose themselves and their life for God*, Ælfc. T. Lisle 28, 13. Gelogaþ his ágen líf *regulates his own life*, Tract. de Spir. Septif: Homl. Th. i. 168, 11. Godes ðeów se ðe hǽd underféhþ sceal beón on ða wísan gelogod ðe God tǽhte *the servant of God who takes orders must be disposed in the manner that God has taught*, ii. 48, 31: i. 286, 13. Ðæt mynster he gelogode mid wellybbendum mannum *that monastery he filled with men of good life*, 506, 15. Ðá ðwóh man ða hálgan bán and gelogodon hí up *then the holy bones were washed and laid up*, Swt. Rdr. 100, 158. Hí gelogodon sc̄e Ælfeáges hálgan líchaman on norþhealfe weofodes *they placed S. Ælfeg's holy body on the north side of the altar*, Chr. 1023; Erl. 163, 33. He begeat má castelas and ðǽr inne his ríderas gelogode *he got more castles and lodged his knights therein*, 1090; Erl. 226, 30. Geloga híg on ðære sélostan stówe *in the best of the land make them to dwell*, Gen. 47, 6. Ðás lamb ðe ðú gelogast on sundron *these lambs which thou hast set by themselves*, 21, 9. Ðone wudu gelogode *laid the wood in order*, 22, 9. He wæs gelogod to his folcum *he was gathered to his people*, Deut. 32, 50.

ge-logod; *part. p. Arranged;* appositus:—For ðære gelícnisse his gelogodan sprǽce *for the likeness of his disposed speech* or *style*, Ælfc. T. Lisle 17, 12.

GE-LÓMAN; *pl. m. Household stuff, furniture, utensils, tools;* supellex, instrumenta:—Ísern-gelóman *ferramenta ruralia*, Bd. 4, 28; S. 605, 32: Shrn. 146, 15. Ða men hwílum ða íren-gelóman liccodan *milites nunc ferramenta lambendo*, Nar. 9, 19. v. andlóman.

ge-lóme; *adv. Often, frequently, continually, repeatedly;* sæpe, frĕquenter, contĭnuo, crebro:—Fregn gelóme freca óðerne *one warrior often asked the other*, Andr. Kmbl. 2327; An. 1165: Beo. Th. 1122; B. 559: Ps. Th. 54, 13: 62, 4. Ðonne hí gelóme sáwon swíðlíce rénas *when they frequently saw severe showers*, Boutr. Scrd. 21, 22: 17, 11. Wæs he se mon ǽfest on his dǽdum and gelóme on hálgum gebedum *ĕrat relĭgiōsis actĭbus, crebris prĕcĭbus*, Bd. 4, 11; S. 579, 6. Oft and gelóme *very frequently*, Bt. Met. Fox 30, 10, 14; Met. 30, 5, 7: Chr. 887; Erl. 86, 11: 959; Erl. 119, 25. Oft gelóme *full oft, very often*, Cd. 75; Th. 93, 2; Gen. 1539. [*O. H. Ger.* ki-lômo *frequenter*.]

ge-lómed; *part. p. Having rays;* radiatus. v. ge-leómed.

ge-lómelic *frequent*, Bd. 2, 7; S. 509, 32. v. ge-lómlíc.

ge-lómlǽcan; *p.* -lǽhte; *pp.* -lǽht *To frequent, to use often;* frequentare:—Gelómlǽcende word *frequentative verb*, Ælfc. Gr. 36; Som. 38, 14. Mid gelómlǽcendum hryrum *with frequent destructions*, Homl. Th. i. 578, 34: ii. 350, 19.

ge-lómlǽcing, -lómlǽcung, e; *f. Frequency, a frequenting, a common resort;* frequentatio, Ælfc. Gr. 36; Som. 38, 15.

ge-lómlǽcnys, -lómlícnes, ness, e; *f. A frequented* or *public place;* locus condensus, Ps. Spl. 117, 26.

ge-lómlíc, -lómelíc; *adj. Frequent, repeated;* frĕquens, crēber:—Mid gelómlícra wundra wyrcnysse *virtūtum frĕquentium opĕrātiōne*, Bd. 3, 13; S. 538, 39. Mid gelómlícum oncunningum *by frequent accusations*, 3, 19; S. 548, 3. Mid his gelómlícum bedum *crebris ōrātiōnĭbus*, 2, 7; S. 509, 32.

ge-lómlíce; *comp.* -lícor; *superl.* -lícost; *adv. Often, frequently, repeatedly;* sæpe, frĕquenter, crebro:—Gelómlíce *sæpe*, Ælfc. Gr. 38; Som. 39, 52. Hwí fæste we and ða Sundor-hálgan gelómlíce *quare nos et Pharisæi jejūnāmus frĕquenter?* Mt. Bos. 9, 14: Bd. 3, 22; S. 552, 9: 3, 23; S. 554, 11. Búton hí hyra handa gelómlíce þweán *nisi crebro lāvĕrint mănus*, Mk. Bos. 7, 3: Bd. 3, 13; S. 538, 8: Hymn. Surt. 116, 14. Gelómlícor *oftener;* sæpius, Ælfc. T. 22, 22: Ælfc. Gr. 38; Som. 39, 53. Gelómlícost *most frequently;* sæpissĭme, Ors. 4, 4; Bos. 81, 3: Ælfc. Gr. 38; Som. 39, 53.

ge-lómlícian; *p.* ode; *pp.* od *To become frequent:*—Manig yfel we geaxiaþ hér on lífe gelómlícian and wæstmian *many an evil we learn has become frequent in this life and flourishes*, Blickl. Homl. 109, 2.

ge-lomp *happened*, Bt. 18, 4; Fox 66, 27; *p. of* ge-limpan.

ge-londa, an; *m. A fellow-countryman;* compatriota:—Be ðám monnum ðe hiora gelondan bebycgaþ *of those men who sell their countrymen*, L. In. 11; Th. i. 110, 1. Cf. ge-leód. [*O. H. Ger.* gi-lante *patriota*.]

ge-long. v. ge-lang.

ge-lósian; *p.* ode, ade; *pp.* od, ad *To lose, perish:*—We bíðn gelósoad *perimus*, Mt. Kmbl. Lind. 8, 25. Gelósiga *perdet*, 16, 25. Ðæt gelósade *quod perierat*, 18, 11. [*Laym.* i-losed.]

ge-lostr *a gathering to form matter, imposthume;* suppuratio, Som.

ge-loten dæg oððe ofernón *latter part of the day;* suprema, Ælfc. Gl. 95; Som. 75; Wrt. Voc. 53, 14. v. lútan.

gelp, es; *m. Glory, vain-glory, pride;* glōria, vāna glōria:—Ne gýtsung, ne ídel gelp him on ne rícsode *neither avarice nor vain-glory reigned in him*, Bd. 3, 17; S. 545, 9. Gif he unnýtne gelp ágan wille *if he will possess unprofitable glory*, Bt. Met. Fox 10, 3; Met. 10, 2. v. gilp.

gelpan *to boast;* glōriāri:—Gif hwá ðæs gelpþ *if any one boast of it*, Bt. 30, 1; Fox 108, 19, MS. Bod. v. gilpan.

gelp-scaða, an; *m. A boastful foe:*—Ðone gelpscaðan ríces berǽdan *to deprive that boastful foe of his power*, Bt. Met. Fox 9, 99; Met. 9, 49. v. gielp-sceaða.

gelsa. v. gælsa.

gelt, es; *m. A sin, crime, fault, debt;* delictum, dēbĭtum:—Geltas geclǽnsa ða ðe ic gefremede *cleanse the sins which I have committed*, Ps. C. 50, 39; Ps. Grn. ii. 277, 39. Gelt *dēbĭtum*, Prov. 24. v. gylt.

ge-lúcan; *p.* -leác, *pl.* -lucon; *pp.* -locen *To shut, lock, fasten, weave;* claudĕre, nectĕre:—Ðé gelúcaþ ríce heofona *quia clauditis regnum cœlorum*, Mt. Kmbl. Rush. 23, 13. He geseah segn eallgylden, hondwundra mǽst, gelocen leóðo-cræftum [*or* leoðo-cræftum?] *he saw an all-golden ensign, greatest of hand-wonders, woven by arts of song* [*by magic*], Beo. Th. 5531; B. 2769. [Cf. hand-locen.]

ge-ludon *descended*. v. geleódan.

ge-lufian; *p.* ode, ade; *pp.* od, ad *To love, esteem;* ămāre, dilĭgĕre:—Ne sceal se Dryhtnes þeów máre gelufian eorþan ǽhtwelan *nor shall the Lord's servant love more of earth's riches*, Exon. 38 a; Th. 125, 23; Gú. 358: 119 b; Th. 458, 26; Hy. 4, 106. Se hálga wer, in ða ǽrestan ældu, gelufade frécnessa fela *the holy man, in his first age, loved much mischief*, 34 a; Th. 108, 30; Gú. 80: 39 b; Th. 130, 25; Gú. 443: 43 a; Th. 144, 23; Gú. 682. Ic eom gelufod *ămor*, Ælfc. Gr. 25; Som. 26, 1, 6, 9, 12, 16. Ðú eart mín gelufoda sunu *tu es fīlius meus dilectus*, Mk. Bos. 1, 11. Hí wǽron gelufode *ămāti sunt*, Ælfc. Gr. 25; Som. 26, 8, 11, 13, 16.

ge-luggian *to pull, lug;* vellere, Som.

ge-lugon *deceived*, Exon. 118 b; Th. 455, 27; Hy. 4, 56; *p. pl. of* ge-leógan.

ge-lumpe, *pl.* -lumpen *would happen*, Bd. 5, 1; S. 614, 3: Exon. 35 a; Th. 113, 32; Gú. 165; *subj. p. of* ge-limpan: ge-lumpen *happened*, Homl. Th. ii. 130, 28; *pp. of* ge-limpan: ge-lumpon *befell*, Chr. 1011; Erl. 145, 1; *p. pl. of* ge-limpan.

ge-lustfullian; *p.* ode; *pp.* od. I. *v. intrans. To be delighted, be pleased, rejoice;* delectāri, lætāri:—Hí gelustfulliaþ on mycelnysse sybbe *delectābuntur in multĭtūdĭne pācis*, Ps. Spl. 36, 11. Gelustfulla on Drihtne *delectāre in Dŏmĭno*, 36, 4. For ðysum gelustfullod is heorte mín *propter hoc lætātum est cor meum*, 15, 9. Ðe gelustfullaþ on yfelum lustum *that delights in evil pleasures*, Homl. Th. i. 496, 13. II. *v. trans. To delight, please;* delectāre, jŭvāre:—Me gelustfullaþ *jŭvat me*, Ælfc. Gr. 33; Som. 37, 12. Gelustfullodon ðé dóhtra cyninga *delectāvērunt te filiæ rēgum*, Ps. Spl. 44, 10. Ða welan gelustfulliaþ *riches afford pleasure*, Homl. Th. ii. 88, 20: 130, 9.

ge-lustfullíce; *comp.* -lícor; *adv. Willingly, earnestly, studiously;* stŭdiōse:—Nǽnig ðínra þegna neódlícor [MS. -lucor] ne gelustfullícor hine sylfne underþeódde to úra goda bigange ðonne ic *nullus tuōrum stŭdiōsius quam ĕgo cultūræ deōrum nostrōrum se subdĭdit*, Bd. 2, 13; S. 516, 5.

ge-lustfulling, e; *f. That which delights* or *pleases;* oblectamentum, Scint. 81.

ge-lustfulnys, -nyss, e; *f. Delight, pleasure;* delectātio:—Gelustfulnyssa [synd] on swíðran ðíne óþ on ende *delectātiōnes* [*sunt*] *in dextĕra tua usque in fīnem*, Ps. Spl. 15, 11.

ge-lútan; *p.* -leát *To bow:*—Se bisceop eádmódlíce to ðam Godes were geleát *the bishop humbly bowed to the man of God*, Guthl. 17; Gdwin. 72, 17.

ge-lútian; *p.* ode; *pp.* od *To lie hid;* lătēre:—Ðæt ic gelútian ne mæg on ðyssum sídan sele *that I may not lie hid in this wide hall*, Cd. 216; Th. 273, 2; Sat. 130.

ge-lýcost *a twin;* gemellus:—Didymus, ðæt is gelýcost, Jn. 20, 24: 21, 2.

ge-lýfan, -lífan, -léfan; to -lýfanne, -lýfenne; *part.* -lýfende; ic -lýfe, ðú -lýfest, -lýfst, he -lýfeþ, -lýfþ, *pl.* -lýfaþ; *p.* ic, he -lýfde, ðú -lýfdest, *pl.* -lýfdon; *impert.* -lýf, *pl.* -lýfe, -lýfaþ; *subj. pres.* -lýfe, *pl.* -lýfon; *pp.* -lýfed *To believe, confide, trust, hope;* crēdĕre, confīdĕre, spērāre:—We sceolon on hine gelýfan *we should believe in him*, Homl. Th. i. 274, 27: 280, 22: 290, 31. To gelýfanne [-lýfenne, col. 1] to ðan leófan Gode *to trust in the beloved God*, Chr. 1036; Th. 294, 10, col. 2. Of ðyssum lytlingum on me gelýfendum *ex his pusillis crēdentĭbus in me*, Mk. Bos. 9, 42. Se Hǽlend wiste hwæt ða gelýfendan wǽron *sciebat Jesus qui essent credentes*, Jn. Bos. 6, 64. Ne gelýfe ic nó, ðæt . . . *I do not believe that* . . . , Bt. 5, 3; Fox 12, 4: Exon. 82 a; Th. 309, 33; Seef. 66. Gif ðú sóþne God lufast and gelýfest *if thou lovest and believest the true God*, 66 b; Th. 245, 21; Jul. 48: Cd. 203; Th. 252, 14; Dan. 578. Gelýfst ðú ðyses *crēdis hoc?* Jn. Bos. 11, 26. He his Hláfordes hyldo gelýfeþ *he believes his Lord's kindness*, Exon. 120 b; Th. 463, 9; Hö. 67: 81 b; Th. 307, 21; Seef. 27. He gelýfþ on God *confīdit in Deo*, Mt. Bos. 27, 43: Jn. Bos. 11, 25. Ðe on me gelýfaþ *qui in me crēdunt*, Mt. Bos. 18, 6. Ic ðín bebod gelýfde *mandātis tuis crēdĭdi*,

Ps. Th. 118, 66: Bt. 38, 1; Fox 194, 14. Ðū mīnum wordum ne gelȳfdest *non crēdidisti verbis meis*, Lk. Bos. 1, 20: Jn. Bos. 1, 50. Hī nō gelȳfdon ðæt he God wǣre *they believed not that he was God*, Andr. Kmbl. 1123; An. 562: Elen. Kmbl. 1034; El. 518. Aarones hūs on Dryhten leófne gelȳfdan *dŏmus Aaron spērāvit in Dŏmĭno*, Ps. Th. 113, 19. Gelȳf me *crēde mihi*, Jn. Bos. 4, 21. Gelȳfe gyt, ðæt ic inc mæg gehǣlan *crēdĭtis quia hoc possum făcĕre vōbis?* Mt. Bos. 9, 28. Gelȳfaþ for ðām weorcum *propter ŏpĕra ipsa crēdĭte*, Jn. Bos. 14, 11. Ne bepǣce nān man hine sylfne, swā ðæt he secge oððe gelȳfe ðæt þrȳ Godas syndon *let no man deceive himself, so as to say or believe that there are three Gods*, Homl. Th. i. 284, 16. Ðæt gē gelȳfon, ðæt se Hǣlend ys Crist *ut crēdātis, quia Jesus est Christus*, Jn. Bos. 20, 31: Ex. 4, 5. Ne gelȳfe ic me nū ðæs leóhtes furðor *I have no longer now any hope for myself of that light*, Cd. 21; Th. 26, 3; Gen. 401. [*Goth.* ga-laubjan: *O. Sax.* gi-lōƀian: *O. H. Ger.* gi-louban: *Ger.* glauben.]

ge-lȳfan; *p.* de; *pp.* ed *To make dear* [leóf]:—Dryhtne gelȳfde *endeared to the Lord* [*faithful to the Lord*, Th.], Exon. 32 a; Th. 100, 22; Cri. 1645.

ge-lȳfan; *p.* de; *pp.* ed *To allow, permit*; concēdĕre, permittĕre:—Wæs him seó rōw gelȳfed þurh lytel fæc *repose was allowed them for a little time*, Exon. 35 b; Th. 115, 5; Gū. 185.

ge-lȳfed; *part. p.* [*pp. of* ge-lȳfan *to believe*] *One who believed, faithful*; religiosus, fidus, fidelis:—His [Constantīnes] mōdor wæs cristen, Elena gehāten, swīðe gelȳfed mann, and þearle eáwfæst *his* [*Constantine's*] *mother was a christian, called Helena, a very faithful person, and very pious*, Homl. Th. ii. 306, 3: i. 60, 13. Com se ārwurþa Swīþhun to sumum gelȳfedan smiþe on swefne *the venerable Swithun came to a certain religious* [lit. *faithful*] *artisan in a dream*, Glostr. Frag. 2, 5. Wæs sum cyning gelȳfed swīðe on God *there was a king firmly believing on God*, Swt. Rdr. 95, 2: H. R. 101, 13. Hie wurdan hraðe gelȳfde *they immediately believed*, Blickl. Homl. 155, 5. Ealle ðing synd gelȳfedum mihtlīce *omnia possibilia credenti*, Mk. Bos. 9, 23.

ge-lȳfed; *part. p. Weakened, advanced* [*in age*]:—Ðara ðe gelȳfedre yldo *earum quæ ætate provectæ*, Bd. 3, 8; S. 531, 33: 4, 24; S. 597, 3.

ge-lȳfedlīc; *adj.* [ge-lȳfan *to allow*] *Allowable, permissible*; licĭtus, permissus:—Nis hit nāht gelȳfedlīc *it is not allowable*, L. E. I. 39; Th. ii. 436, 35.

ge-lȳfedlīce; *adv. Faithfully, confidently*; confīdenter:—Xersis swīðe gelȳfedlīce his þegene gehȳrde *Xerxes very confidently listened to his general*, Ors. 2, 5; Bos. 48, 9: 3, 1; Bos. 53, 15.

ge-lȳhtan; *p.* -lȳhte; *pp.* -lȳhted, -lȳht *To illumine, give light to*:—He blynde gelȳhte *he enlightened the blind*, St. And. 44, 34: Nic. 34; Thw. 20, 2. [*Goth.* ga-liuhtjan: *O. Sax.* gi-liuhtian.] v. ge-līhtan.

ge-lymp *an accident*. v. ge-limp.

ge-lymplīcnys, se; *f. Opportunity, occasion*; opportunitas, Ps. Spl. C. 9, 9.

ge-lynd, -lend, e; *f.* [lynd*fat*] *Grease, fat, fatness*; adeps, pinguedo:—Ys sāwl mīn swētes gefylled, swā seó fætte gelynd fægeres smeoruwes *sicut adipe et pinguedine repleatur animea mea*, Ps. Th. 62, 5. Gelynde *ex adipe*, 72, 6. Bringon gelynde *offerent adipem*, Lev. 3, 10. Nim león gelynde *take lion's fat*, Med. ex Quadr. 10, 2; Lchdm. i. 364, 24: 10, 4; Lchdm. i. 366, 4. DER. lynd.

ge-lyndu; *n. pl. Joints of the backbone*:—Geloda *vel* gelyndu *spondilia* [*Gk.* σπόνδυλος], Ælfc. Gl. 74; Som. 71, 51; Wrt. Voc. 44, 34.

ge-lȳsan; *pp.* ed *To redeem, loosen, dissolve, break*:—Eall his līchama wæs gelȳsed *all his body was broken*, Blickl. Homl. 241, 30. [Cf. to-lȳsan *and* ge-lēsan.]

ge-lȳsednes *redemption*. v. alȳsednys.

ge-lystan; *p.* -lyste; *pp.* -lysted, -lyst; *v. impers. with acc. of pers., gen. of thing; To please, cause a desire for anything*:—Ðegnas ðearle gelyste gārgewinnes *the thanes were very eager for the struggle*, Judth. 12; Thw. 26, 3; Jud. 307: Exon. 97 a; Th. 361, 22; Wal. 23. Gūðe gelysted *desirous for war*, Bt. Met. Fox 1, 18; Met. 1, 9. [*O. Sax.* gilustean: *O. H. Ger.* gi-lusten (*with the same government*): *Ger.* gelüsten.]

ge-lytfullīce; *adv. Prosperously*; prospere, Ps. Spl. C. 44, 5.

ge-lyðen; *part. p. Travelled*:—Se ylca Nathan wæs swā gelyðen ðæt he hæfde gefaren fram ǣlcum lande to ōðrum *this Nathan was so travelled that he had gone from every land to the other*, St. And. 26, 13. v. ge-līðan.

ge-lytlian, -litlian; *p.* ode, ade; *pp.* od, ad *To diminish, lessen, humble*; minuĕre, hūmĭliāre:—Ǣghwilc ælmesriht ǣlc man gelytlaþ oððe forhealdeþ *every almsright every man lessens or withholds*, Swt. Rdr. 106, 59. Ealle hire wæstmbǣro he gelytlade *he lessened all her* [*the earth's*] *fruitfulness*, Ors. 2, 1; Bos. 38, 8. Mīn līf gelytlad is *hūmĭliāvit vītam meam*, Ps. Th. 142, 3.

ge-maad *mad*. v. ge-mǣd.

ge-maca, an; *m. and f. A mate, an equal, companion*; par, socius:—Gemaca *hic et hæc par*, Ælfc. Gr. 9; Som. 9, 50. Of eallum nȳtenum ealles flǣsces twegen gemacan *of all beasts two of the same kind, male and female*, Gen. 6, 19. [*Laym.* i-maken: *O. Sax.* ge-maco: *O. H. Ger.* ka-mahho *socius*.] DER. fyrd-, heáfod-gemaca. [Cf. ge-mæcca.]

ge-macian; *p.* ode; *pp.* od *To make, cause*:—Hī heora lufigendne gemaciaþ weligne ēcelīce *they make the lover of them rich eternally*, Homl. Th. ii. 88, 29. Ðone ðe he ǣr martyr gemacode *whom he had before made a martyr*, 82, 24. Hī ðæra cinga sehte gemacedon *they made peace between the two kings*, Chr. 1091; Erl. 228, 2. Ðæt landfolc gemacodon ðæt he nāht ne dyde *the folk of the country prevented him from doing anything*, 1075; Erl. 213, 20: Exod. 5, 21. He lēt castelas gemakian *he had castles built*, Chr. 1097; Erl. 234, 8. Eác is mōdsorg gode gemacod *also grief of mind is caused to God*, Cd. 35; Th. 47, 3; Gen. 755.

ge-mæc; *adj. Equal, like, well-matched, suited*:—Hī wīf habbaþ him gemæc *they are well-matched in marriage*, Bt. 11, 1; Fox 32, 4. Gemæcca ł gelīco *æquales* [*or* v. ge-mæcca?], Lk. Skt. Lind. 20, 36. Ic me ful gemæcne monnan funde *I found a man fully equal to me*, Exon. 115 a; Th. 442, 25; Kl. 18. [Cf. Grff. ii. 632.]

ge-mæcca, -mæccea, an; *m. and f. A companion, mate, consort, husband* or *wife*:—Twegen turturan gemæccan *a pair of turtle doves*, Blickl. Homl. 23, 27. Ne eart ðū ðon leófre nǣngum lifigendra menn to gemæccan ðonne se swearta hrefn *thou art not any dearer to any living man as mate than the swart raven*, Exon. 99 a; Th. 370, 6; Seel. 53. Boga sceal strǣle sceal mon to gemæccan *a bow must have an arrow, a man must to his mate*, Exon. 91 b; Th. 343, 10; Gn. Ex. 155. Gemæcca *conjunx*, Ælfc. Gr. 28; Som. 31, 54. Gif wīf wiþ ōðres gemæccan hǣmþ *si mulier cum alterius conjuge adulteraverit*, L. Ecg. P. iii. 10; Th. ii. 186, 7. Be Euan his gemæccan *by Eve his wife*, Gen. 4, 1: 28, 1: Homl. Th. ii. 498, 26. He onfēng hys gemæccean *accepit conjugem suam*, Mt. Bos. 1, 24. [*O. H. Ger.* gi-mahha *conjux*.] Cf. ge-maca.

ge-mæclīc; *adj. Relating to a wife, conjugal*; conjugalis, Scint. 58.

ge-mæcnes, -ness, e; *f. A companionship, mixture*; commixtio:—On ðæs līchoman gemæcnesse biþ willa *in carnis commixtiōne voluptas est*, Bd. 1, 27; S. 493, 20, MS. B.

ge-mæcscipe, es; *m. Fellowship, connection, cohabitation*; consortium, conjŭgium, concŭbĭtus:—Þurh gemæcscipe *through cohabitation*, Exon. 10 b; Th. 13, 7; Cri. 199.

ge-mǣd; *adj.* [cf. *O. Sax.* ge-mēd *foolish*: *O. H. Ger.* ka-meit *stultus*: *or* ge-mæd? v. Leo 29] *Troubled in mind, mad*; amens, Cot. 10, 169.

ge-mǣdan; *p.* de; *pp.* ed *To madden, make foolish*:—Swā gemǣdde mōde bestolene dǣde gedwolene *so foolish bereft of mind erring in deed*, Exon. 103 b; Th. 393, 6; Rä. 12, 6. Gemǣded *vecors*, Lye. [Cf. *Laym.* Of witten heo weoren amadde (*later* MS. awed).] v. ge-mǣd.

ge-mædla, an; *m. Talk*:—Wiþ wīf-gemædlan geberge on neaht nestig rædices moran ðȳ dæge ne mæg ðē se gemædla sceððan *against a woman's chatter; taste at night fasting a root of radish, that day the chatter cannot harm thee*, L. M. 3, 57; Lchdm. ii. 342, 11. v. ge-maðel.

ge-mǣg, es; *m. A kinsman*:—Wit synt gemǣgas *we two are kinsmen*, Cd. 91; Th. 114, 14; Gen. 1904. v. mǣg.

ge-mægened; *part. p. Established, confirmed, strengthened*; confirmatus:—Gemægenad and gestrongad beón *to be confirmed and strengthened*, Bd. 4, 16; S. 584, 4.

ge-mægfæst; *adj. Gluttonous*; cibi deditus, Lye.

ge-mægnan. v. ge-mengan.

ge-mægþ, e; *f. Power, greatness*; pŏtentia:—Me nǣfre seó gemægþ ðisses eorþlīcan anwealdes fōrwel ne līcode *the greatness of this earthly power never too well pleased me*, Bt. 17; Fox 58, 23.

ge-mǣgþ, e; *f. A family, tribe*; fămĭlia, trĭbus:—Twā gemǣgþa *two families*, Ors. 3, 5; Bos. 57, 33.

ge-mǣhþ, e; *f. Greediness*:—Ic wolde witan hwæðer ðīn ealde gȳtsung and seó gemǣhþ eallunga of ðīnum mōde astȳfcod wēre *I wanted to know whether thine old covetousness and greediness were altogether eradicated from thy mind*, Shrn. 184, 2. v. ge-māh.

ge-mǣl; *adj. Marked, stained*:—Earh ǣttre gemǣl *the arrow stained with poison*, Andr. Kmbl. 2663; An. 1333.

ge-mǣlan; *p.* de; *pp.* ed *To mark, stain*:—Seó hālge stōd ungewemde wlite næs hyre feax ne fel fȳre gemǣled *the saint stood with spotless aspect, neither her hair nor skin was marked by the fire*, Exon. 74 a; Th. 278, 2; Jul. 591.

ge-mǣlan; *p.* de; *pp.* ed *To speak, harangue*:—Adam gemǣlde and to Euan spræc *Adam spoke and to Eve said*, Cd. 37; Th. 49, 10; Gen. 790. Offa gemǣlde *Offa spake*, Byrht. Th. 138, 34; By. 230: 53; By. 244.

gēmæn. v. gēmen.

ge-mǣnan; *p.* de; *pp.* ed [ge-mǣne *communis*]. I. *to* MEAN, *to signify*; sibi velle, significare:—Hwæt gemǣnaþ ðās lamb *quid sibi volunt agnæ istæ?* Gen. 21, 29. Ic wēne ðæt ðū nyte hwæt ðis gemǣne *I expect that thou wilt not know what this means*, Btwk. Scrd. 18, 26. Hwæt gemǣnaþ ða ðreó ūtfaru? Ðæt getācnaþ . . . *what do the three outgoings mean? They indicate* . . ., 21, 40. II. *to communicate, announce, pronounce, utter*; communicare, pronuntiare:—Hwīlum ic glidan reorde mūþe gemǣne *sometimes in a kite's voice I utter with my mouth*, Exon. 106 b; Th. 406, 24; Rä. 25, 6. III. *to give expression to one's feelings*, as, *of pain, to* MOAN, *to groan*; ingemiscere, plangere, Mk. Skt. Lind. 8, 12: Lk. Skt. Lind. 23, 27. IV. *to commune with oneself about anything, to consider*; colloqui, considerare:—

Se fæder hit gemǽnde stille *pater rem tacitus considerabat*, Gen. 37, 11. V. [gemǽne *vilis, scelestus*] *to make common, contaminate, defile, violate;* communicare, coinquinare, violare:—Ðæt ðǽr ǽnig mon wordum ne worcum wǽre ne brǽce, ne þurh inwit-searo ǽfre gemǽnden *that there not any man by words or works should break the compact, nor through guileful art should ever violate it*, Beo. Th. 2207, note; B. 1101. [*Goth.* ga-mainjan *communicare alicui; κοινῶν vel κοινωνεῖν τινί τι*, etiam, *coinquinare* vel *communicare aliquid; κοινῶν τι: O. Sax.* gi-mênian *to make known: O. H. Ger.* gi-meinen *dicere, monstrare, judicare.*] v. mǽnan.

ge-mæncgan, -mængan; *p.* -mænced *To mix.* v. ge-mengan.

ge-mǽne; *adj. Common, general, mutual, in common;* communis:—Reord wæs ðá gieta eorþ-búendum án gemǽne *there was yet one common language to the dwellers upon earth*, Cd. 79; Th. 98, 27; Gen. 1636. Sib sceal gemǽne englum and ældum á forþ heonan wesan *a common peace shall be to angels and men henceforth for ever*, Exon. 16 a; Th. 36, 25; Cri. 581. Hwæt ys ðé and us gemǽne *what is common to thee and us?* Mt. Bos. 8, 29. Ne beó ðé nán þing gemǽne ongén ðisne rihtwísan *ne quid tibi sit commune adversus hunc justum*, 27, 19: Nicod. 6; Thw. 3, 11. Se ðe oferhogie ðæt he Godes bodan hlyste, hæbbe him gemǽne ðæt wið God sylfne *he who scorns to listen to God's preacher, let him have that between him and God himself*, L. C. E. 26; Th. i. 374, 27: Kmbl. Cod. Dipl. iii. 22, 27. Ðæt hí sceoldon habban sunu him gemǽne *that they should have a son common to them [between them]*, Jud. 13, 3: Cd. 100; Th. 133, 26; Gen. 2216. Gemǽne win *communis labor*, Bd. 2, 2; S. 502, 9. Gemǽne læs *compascuus ager*, Ælfc. Gl. 96; Wrt. Voc. 53, 54. Him eallum wǽron eall gemǽne *erant eis omnia communia*, Bd. 1, 27; S. 489, 15: Jos. 8, 2. Unc sceal worn fela máðma gemǽnra *to us two shall be a great many common treasures*, Beo. Th. 3572; B. 1784. Ðá wæs synn and sacu Sweóna and Geáta, wróht gemǽne *then was sin and strife of Swedes and Goths, mutual dissension*, Beo. Th. 4938; B. 2473. Ðæt sceal Geáta leódum and Gár-Denum sib gemǽnum *so that there shall be peace to the Goths' people and to the Gar-Danes in common*, 3718; B. 1857. Hand gemǽne *a joined hand [in conflict]*; manus conserta, 4281; B. 2137. [*Laym.* i-mæne: *O. Sax.* gi-mêni *communis, generalis, solitus: O. Frs.* ge-mêne: *O. H. Ger.* ga-meini: *Goth.* ga-mains *communis; κοινός, συγκοινωνός.*]

ge-mǽne-líc; *adj. Common, general;* communis, generalis:—Swá swá man geræ̂de for gemǽnelícre neóde *so that the common need may be consulted for*, L. Eth. vi. 32; Th. i. 324, 1. Hí arísaþ on ðam gemǽnelícum dóme *they shall arise at the judgment of all*, Homl. Th. i. 84, 22, 24. Mid ða getýdnesse ge cyriclícra gewrita ge eac gemǽnelícra *cum eruditione litterarum vel ecclesiasticarum vel generalium*, Bd. 5, 23; S. 645, 15. Gemǽnelíce naman *appellative* or *common nouns;* appellativa nomina, Ælfc. Gr. 9, 3; Som. 8, 31.

ge-mǽnelíc nama, an; *m. A common noun;* appellativum nomen, Ælfc. Gr. 9; Som. 8, 31. v. ge-mǽnelíc.

ge-mǽne-líce; *adv. Commonly, in common, generally, mutually, in turn, one amongst another;* communiter, generaliter, invicem:—Ðæt hý ðæt feoh mihton him eallum gemǽnelíce to nytte gedón *that they might apply that wealth to the use of all in common*, Ors. 2, 4; Bos. 43, 24: Bt. 39, 13; Fox 234, 28. Iohannes ðá beád ðreóra daga fæsten gemǽnelíce *John then ordered a general fast of three days*, Homl. Th. i. 70, 8. Þurh hí sende gemǽnelíce ða þing eall ða ðe to cyrican bigange and þénunge nýdþearflíco wǽron *misit per eos generaliter universa quæ ad cultum erant ac ministerium ecclesiæ necessaria*, Bd. 1, 29; S. 498, 8. Ðæt gé lufion eów gemǽnelíce, swá ic eów lufode *ut diligatis invicem, sicut dilexi vos*, Jn. Bos. 15, 12, 17.

ge-mænigfealdian; *p.* ode; *pp.* od *To multiply:*—Gemænigfealdige ðis mihtig Dryhten ofer eów ealle *adjiciat Dominus super vos*, Ps. Th. 113, 22.

ge-mænigfyldan; *p.* de *To multiply, enlarge;* multiplicare:—Ðú gemænigfyldest sunú manna, Ps. Spl. 11, 9: 17, 16. Gemænigfylde beón, Ex. 1, 7.

ge-mǽn-nes, -ness, e; *f.* [ge-mǽne *communis*] *A communion, fellowship, connection;* communio, consortium, admixtio:—Hí sealdon hí ðǽr on ðara fǽmnena gemǽnnesse *they gave her up there to the society of the women*, Shrn. 127, 11. Ne ic ǽfre mid mannum mán-fremmendum gemǽnnesse micle hæbbe *cum hominibus operantibus iniquitatem non comminabor* [Vulg. *communicabo*, Ps. Surt. *conbinabor*], Ps. Th. 140, 6: R. Ben. proœm. Gemencgnyss [MS. B. gemǽnnes] wífes *admixtio conjugis*, Bd. 1, 27; S. 495, 18. Ðurh flǽsces gemǽnnysse *per carnis contubernium*, Hymn. Surt. 31, 32. [Hence the Kentish word *mennys* a large common.]

ge-mǽnnung, e; *f. Communion, fellowship;* communio, contubernium, Som.

ge-mǽn-scipe, es; *m. Communion, fellowship;* communio:—Ic gemǽnscipe getreówe ðínra háligra *I believe in the communion of thy saints*, Hy. 10, 52; Hy. Grn. ii. 294, 52: Wanl. Catal. 49, 16.

ge-mǽn-sumian, -mǽn-suman; *p.* ode, ade; *pp.* od, ad [ge-mǽne *communis*] *To do or have anything in common with another, to communicate to* or *share with another, to marry;* communicare, nubere:—Wylladon us ða þing gemǽnsuman [MS. gemǽnsumian] *ea nobis communicare desiderastis*, Bd. 1, 25; S. 487, 14. Gemǽnsumad *nuptus*, Mk. Skt. Lind. 12, 25. [*O. H. Ger.* ga-meinsamôn *communicare, participare.*] v. mǽn-sumian.

ge-mǽnsumnys, -nyss, e; *f. A communion, a participation*, also *the Sacrament of the Holy Communion;* communio:—Ne syndon hí for ðysse wísan to bescyrianne gemǽnsumnysse Cristes líchoman and blódes *non pro hac re sacri corporis ac sanguinis Domini communione privandi sunt*, Bd. 1, 27; S. 491, 27. Ðam gerýne onfón ðǽre hálgan gemǽnsumnysse *sacræ communionis sacramentum* vel *mysterium percipere*, Bd. 1, 27; S. 492, 35: 1, 27; S. 494, 23.

ge-mǽn-sumung, e; *f. A communion;* communio, R. Ben. 38.

ge-mǽran *to fix limits, determine:*—Gimǽrende *diterminans*, Rtl. 164, 38.

ge-mǽran; *p.* de; *pp.* ed [mǽre] *To celebrate, divulge, spread abroad:*—Ðá ðeós gesyhþ wæs gemǽred *qua divulgata visione*, Bd. 4, 25; S. 601, 25: 3, 10; S. 535, note 2. Gemǽred wæs word ðis mið Iudeum *divulgatum est verbum istud apud Judæos*, Mt. Kmbl. Rush. 28, 15. Hiæ gemērdon hine *illi diffamaverunt eum*, 9, 31.

ge-mǽran; *p.* de; *pp.* ed [mǽra] *To enlarge:*—He merce gemǽrde wiþ Myrgingum *he enlarged his marches towards the Myrgings* [or gemǽrde *from* gemǽran *to determine?*], Exon. 85 a; Th. 321, 6; Víd. 42.

ge-mǽre, es; *pl. nom.* a, o, u; *n. An end, boundary, termination, limit;* finis:—Gemǽro *limes*, Ælfc. Gr. 9; Som. 11, 16. Gemǽre ðú settest *terminum posuisti*, Ps. Spl. 103, 10. Ne mágon hí ofer gemǽre gegangan *terminum non transgredientur*, Ps. Th. 103, 10. On Hwicna gemǽre and West-Sexna *in confinio Huicciorum et occidentalium Saxonum*, Bd. 2, 2; S. 502, 7: 5, 23; S. 646, 25: Exon. 93 a; Th. 349, 28; Sch. 53. Gemǽro eorðan *terminos terræ*, Ps. Spl. 2, 8. Óþ gemǽru *usque ad terminos*, 71, 8 Ðis sind ðæs londes gemǽra *these are the land's boundaries*, Kmbl. Cod. Dipl. iii. 78, 20. He ða gemǽro his rynes gefylde *metas sui cursus implevit*, Bd. 3, 20; S. 550, 25. Eall eorðan gemǽru *omnes fines terræ*, Ps. Th. 66, 6: 73, 16. Mycel sǽ and on gemǽrum wíd *mare magnum et spatiosum*, 103, 24. On gemǽru *in finibus eorum*, 104, 27: Bt. Met. Fox 29, 17; Met. 29, 9: Th. Apol. 9, 14. Cýð ðis folc ðæt híg ne gán ofer ða gemǽro *tell this people not to cross the bounds*, Exod. 19, 21, 12. v. Kmbl. Cod. Dipl. iii. viii sqq.

ge-mǽrsian, ic -mǽrsige; *p.* ode; *pp.* od *To magnify, glorify, celebrate;* magnĭfĭcāre, glorĭfĭcāre, celebrāre:—Ðinne naman ic gemǽrsige *magnĭfĭcābo nomen tuum*, Gen. 12, 2. Ðú Sunnan dæg sylf hálgodest and gemǽrsodest hine manegum to helpe *thou thyself didst sanctify Sunday and didst glorify it for help to many*, Hy. 9, 26; Hy. Grn. ii. 291, 26. On ðam dæge gemǽrsode se mihtiga Drihten Iosue ðone æðelan ætfóran Israhéla folce *in die illo magnĭfĭcāvit Dŏmĭnus Josue coram omni Israel*, Jos. 4, 14. Is ðín nama miltsum gemǽrsod *thy name is magnified with mercies*, Andr. Kmbl. 1087; An. 544: Hy. 7, 44; Hy. Grn. ii. 288, 44. He wæs fram eallum gemǽrsod *ipse magnĭfĭcābātur ab omnĭbus*, Lk. Bos. 4, 15. Ic beó gemǽrsod on Pharaone *glorĭfĭcābor in Pharaōne*, Ex. 14, 17. He wæs gemǽrsod ofer ealle óðre cyningas *he was celebrated above all other kings*, Ors. 4, 1; Bos. 76, 41.

ge-mǽrsung, -mērsung, e; *f. Magnificence;* magnĭfĭcentia:—Ðæt hí cúðe wyrcan wuldor gemǽrsunge ríces ðínes *ut nōtam făciant glōriam magnĭfĭcentiæ regni tui*, Ps. Spl. 144, 12. Gimērsung *celebritas*, Rtl. 48, 20.

ge-mæssian; *p.* ode; *pp.* od *To say mass to:*—Iustinus him eallum gemæssode *Justin said mass to them all*, Homl. Th. i. 430, 29.

ge-mæst; *part. p. Fat, fattened;* altilis. v. ge-mæstan.

ge-mæstan; *pp.* -mæsted, -mæst *To fatten;* saginare, pinguefacere, impinguare:—Híg wǽron gemæste *erant impinguati*, Deut. 32, 15. Gemæstra fugela *of fatted fowls*, Homl. Th. ii. 576, 34: Bd. Whelc. 378, 19. v. amæstan, mæstan.

ge-mǽtan; *p.* -mǽtte; *pp.* -mǽted; *v. impers. acc. To dream;* somniare, somnium videre:—Hwæt hine gemǽtte *what he had dreamed*, Cd. 178; Th. 223, 20; Dan. 122: Rood. Kmbl. 3; Kr. 2. Swá his man-drihten gemǽted wearþ *as his lord had dreamed*, Cd. 179; Th. 225, 21; Dan. 157. v. mǽtan.

ge-mǽte; *adj. Moderate, meet, fit;* modicus, aptus, Mod. Conf. 1; C. R. Ben. 55. [*O. H. Ger.* ge-mâzer: *Laym.* i-mete.] v. mǽte.

ge-mæt-fæstan; *p.* -fæste; *pp.* -fæsted, -fæst [gemet *a measure*, fæst *fast*] *To compare;* comparare, Ps. Lamb. 48, 21. v. ge-met-festan.

ge-mǽtgan; *p.* ede; *pp.* ed; *v. trans.* [mǽte *moderate*] *To make moderate, to limit, diminish;* moderare, moderari, minuere:—Ful oft hit eác ðæs deófles dugoþe gemǽtgeþ *full oft it also limits the devil's power*, Salm. Kmbl. 800; Sal. 399.

ge-mǽðian, -mǽðegian, -mǽðrian, -mēðrian; *p.* ode; *pp.* od *To honour, bestow something with honour upon one;* hŏnōrāre, bĕnigne conferre:—Búton he hwæne furðor gemǽðrian [gemǽðian, MS. B.] *unless he will more amply honour any one*, L. C. S. 12; Th. i. 382, 15: 15; Th. i. 384, 4. For ðære micclan mǽrþe ðe he hine gemǽðegode *for the great glory which he honourably bestowed upon him*, Ælfc. T. 4, 11.

ge-mǽt-líc; *adj. Moderate;* modicus. v. un-ge-mǽt-líc.

ge-mâgas; *pl. m. Kinsmen, relations;* consanguinei:—Wit synt gemâgas *we two are kinsmen,* Cd. 91; Th. 114, 14; Gen. 1904. God hî gesceóp to gemâgum *God created them as relations,* Bd. 24, 3; Fox 82, 31. v. mǽg.

ge-mâglic; *adj. Importunate, pertinacious:*—Mid gemâglîcum wôpum *with importunate weeping,* Homl. Th. ii. 126, 1. v. ge-mâhlîc.

ge-mâglîce; *adv. Urgently, importunately:*—He tiht ǽlcne swîđe gemâglîce to gebedum *he exhorts everybody very urgently to prayers,* Homl. Th. i. 158, 13. v. ge-mâhlîce.

ge-mâgnys, se; *f. Perseverance, importunity, petulance:*—Sôđlîce gemâgnys is đam sôđan Dêman gecwême *truly importunity is pleasing to the true judge,* Homl. Th. ii. 126, 2. Asolcennys acenþ gemâgnysse *slothfulness gives birth to petulance,* 220, 26.

ge-mâh; *adj. Shameless, obstinate, stubborn, impious, wicked, importunate;* prŏcax, pervĭcax, pertĭnax, imprŏbus, importūnus:—Gemâh *prŏcax* vel *pervĭcax,* Ælfc. Gl. 88; Som. 74, 84; Wrt. Voc. 50, 64: 86, 52. Flâh feónd gemâh *the deceitful impious fiend,* Exon. 97 a; Th. 362, 19; Wal. 39: 64 b; Th. 237, 24; Ph. 595. Gemâh *importūnus,* Ælfc. Gl. 101; Som. 77, 45; Wrt. Voc. 55, 50.

ge-mâh *made water;* minxit, Med. ex Quadr. 9, 13; Lchdm. i. 364, 1; *p. of* ge-mîgan.

ge-mâhlic; *adj. Shameless, wanton, greedy;* prŏcax, ăvĭdus:—Đæt hit gemâhlîc wǽre and unrihtlîc *that it was greedy and unjust,* Ors. 1, 10; Bos. 32, 20. v. ge-mâglîc.

ge-mâhlîce; *adv. Importunately, peremptorily, boldly, pertinaciously:*—Se cyng hêt swýđe gemâhlîce ofer eall đis land beódan *the king very peremptorily ordered it to be proclaimed over all this land,* Chr. 1095; Erl. 232, 22. Ân blac đrostle flicorode ymbe his neb swâ gemâhlîce *a black throstle flitted about his face so boldly,* Homl. Th. ii. 156, 23: Gr. Dial. 1, 8. v. ge-mâglîce.

ge-mâhlicnes, se; *f. Importunity, perverseness, dishonesty;* importunitas:—Se forhwierfeda gewuna gemâlîcnesse *the perverse habit of wantonness,* Past. 13, 2; Swt. 79, 19; Hat. MS

ge-mâhnes, -nys, -ness, -nyss, e; *f. Shamelessness, stubbornness;* prŏcăcĭtas, pervĭcācia:—Gemâhnes *prŏcăcĭtas,* Wrt. Voc. 86, 53. Gemâhnys *prŏcăcĭtas* vel *pervĭcācia,* Ælfc. Gl. 88; Som. 74, 85; Wrt. Voc. 50, 65. v. ge-mâgnys.

ge-mâleca *importunate;* importunus, Cot. 2.

ge-mâlîce; *adv. Importunately;* importune, Cot. 189.

ge-mal-mægen *an assembly.* v. al-mægen.

ge-man *the hollow of the hand, sole of the foot;* vola, Cot. 198.

ge-man, ic, he *I remember, he remembers,* Beo. Th. 5259; B. 2633: Jn. Bos. 16, 21; *pres. of* ge-munan.

gêman; *p.* de; *pp.* ed *To care for, regard, heed, cure;* cūrāre:—Ne gêmdon hie nânes fyrenlustes *they cared not for any luxury,* Bt. 15; Fox 48, 7: Bd. 2, 6; S. 508, 39. Nǽnig mon ne sceal lufian ne ne gêman his gesibbes gif he hine ǽrost agælde Godes đeówdômes *no man shall love or care about his relatives if he first have devoted himself to God's service,* Blickl. Homl. 23, 17: 67, 30. Hî nystan ne ne gêmdon *they neither knew nor cared,* 99, 30. Ic cymo and gêmo hine *ego veniam et curabo eum,* Mt. Kmbl. Lind. 8, 7: Lk. Skt. Lind. 10, 9. Nallaþ gie gêma *nolite solliciti esse,* 12, 11. Ne gêmes đû *non curas,* Mk. Skt. Lind. 12, 14. Gêmende *solliciti,* Mt. Kmbl. Lind. 6, 25. v. gýman.

ge-mâna, an; *m.* [ge-mæne *communis*] *Companionship, society, fellowship, familiarity, marriage, intercourse, commerce, conjunction;* communio, societas, consortium, contubernium, commercium, concubitus:—Gifeôn we on đone gemânan Godes and manna and on đone gemânan đæs brýdguman and đære brýde *let us rejoice in the union of God and men and in the union of the bridegroom and the bride,* Blickl. Homl. 11, 5. Đonne he wæs mid his âgnum cynne đonne he wæs on đare ryhtwîsera gemânan *he was then with his own kin when he was in the company of the righteous,* Bt. 5, 1; Fox 10, 12. Engla gemâna *the society of angels,* Exon. 42 a; Th. 142, 10; Gû. 642: Ps. Th. 56, 4: Bd. 4, 23; S. 596, 13. Đysse fǽmnan gemânan bæd *hujus virginis consortium petebat,* 2, 9; S. 510, 23, 26: Exon. 67 b; Th. 250, 14; Jul. 127: Jn. Skt. p. 1, 3: Rtl. 109, 31. Hrêman ne þorfte mǽcan gemânan *he needed not to exult in the falchion's intercourse,* Chr. 937; Th. 204, 24; Ædelst. 40. Wiđ dam đe đû mînes gemânan brûce *ut fruaris concubitu meo,* Gen. 38, 16: Med. ex Quadr. 5, 11; Lchdm. i. 350, 10. [*Goth.* ga-mainei: *O. H. Ger.* gameinî *f.*]

ge-mane, -mone; *adj. Having a mane:*—Đara hǽfda beóþ gemona swâ leóna hǽfdo *their heads have manes like lions' heads,* Nar. 35, 29. [Cf. *O. H. Ger.* mana: *Icel.* mön *a mane.*]

ge-mang, -mong, es; *n.* I. *a mingling together, mixture, crowd, throng, company, multitude, an assemblage, a congregation;* commixtio, turba, cœtus, sŏcietas:—Ic bebeóde wundor geweorþan on wera gemange *I command a miracle to be done in the midst of men,* Andr. Kmbl. 1460; An. 730. God mihtig stôd godum on gemange *Deus stĕtit in synăgōga deōrum,* Ps. Th. 81, 1. In heora gemange *in their congregation,* L. Wih. 23; Th. i. 42, 6: Nicod. 6; Thw. 6, 8. Gâras sendon in heardra gemang *they sent their darts into the throng of the brave,* Judth. 11; Thw. 24, 36; Jud. 225. On clǽnra gemang *in the company of the pure,* Elen. Kmbl. 191; El. 96: 216; El. 108: 236; El. 118. II. *an assembly for legal or other business:*—Ne miltsa đû þearfan on gemange *pauperis non misĕrēbĕris in jūdĭcio,* Ex. 23, 3. Ne mæg ic âna eówre gemang acuman *non văleo sōlus nĕgōtia vestra sustĭnēre,* Deut. 1, 12: Shrn. 40, 30.

ge-mang; *prep.* [ge-mang *a mixture*] AMONG; inter, in medio. I. *dat:*—Đeós sprǽc com ût gemang brôþrum *exiit sermo iste inter fratres,* Jn. Bos. 21; 23. Arîs gemang him *surge in medium,* Mk. Bos. 3, 3. Gemang đâm *interim,* Gen. 43, 1. Gemang đâm arâs micel murcnung *interea ortum est murmur,* Num. 11, 1. II. *acc:*—Ic eów sende swâ sceáp gemang wulfas *ego mitto vos sicut oves in medio luporum,* Mt. Bos. 10, 16. DER. a-mang, on-.

ge-mangcennyss, e; *f. A mingling, confection;* confectio, debilitatio, Hpt. Gl. 450: Mone B. 1846.

ge-mangian; *p.* ode; *pp.* od *To traffic, trade;* nĕgōtiāri:—Đæt he wiste hû mycel gehwilc gemangode *ut scīret quantum quisque nĕgōtiātus esset,* Lk. Bos. 19, 15. Hwæt forstent ǽnegum men, đeáh he gemangige đæt he ealne đisne middangeard âge, gif he his sâule forspildeþ *what profits it any man, though he trade so as to obtain all this world, if he destroy his soul?* Past. 44, 10; Swt. 332, 9; Cot. MS.

ge-mangnys, se; *f. A mingling, confection;* commixtio. Som.

ge-manian, -monian, -monigan; *p.* ode, ade; *pp.* od, ad *To admonish, exhort, prompt, remind, remember;* admonere, hortari, suggerere, in memoriam rei reducere, recordari:—Seó sâwl đurh đæt gemynd gemanþ *the soul through the memory reminds,* Homl. Th. i. 288, 28. Oft mec geómor sefa gemanode *oft my sad spirit has admonished me,* Exon. 50 a; Th. 174, 22; Gû. 1181. Se ânwealda hæfþ ealle his gesceafta mid his bridle getogene and gemanode *the Ruler has with his bridle restrained and admonished all his creatures,* Bt. 21; Fox 74, 7: Bt. Met. Fox 11, 47; Met. 11, 24. Gemanad *admonished,* Exon. 102 a; Th. 386, 23; Râ. 4, 66: Exon. 88 b; Th. 333, 19; Gn. Ex. 6: Cd. 49; Th. 63, 9; Gen. 1029. v. manian.

ge-mânna, an; *m. Fellowship,* Wanl. Catal. 23, 47. v. ge-mâna.

ge-mannian; *p.* ode; *pp.* od *To man, supply with men, garrison;* vĭris *vel* mīlĭtibus instruĕre:—He hêt đa burg gemannian *he commanded to man the city,* Chr. 923; Erl. 110, 2, 5: 924; Erl. 110, 13.

ge-martyrian, -martirian, -martrian; *p.* ode, ade, ede; *pp.* od, ad, ed *To martyr;* martўrem făcĕre:—He hine gemartirode *he martyred him,* Homl. Th. ii. 478, 21. Hî Petrus and Paulus gemartredan *they martyred Peter and Paul,* Ors. 6, 5; Bos. 119, 21. He wæs for sôþfæstnysse gemartyrod *he was martyred for truth,* Homl. Th. i. 484, 33: Boutr. Scrd. 18, 8, 10. Wæs heáfde beslegen and gemartyrad se mon *decollātus est mīles,* Bd. 1, 7; S. 478, 39. Đus wearþ gemartirod se mǽra apostol *thus was martyred the great apostle,* Homl. Th. ii. 300, 24: 478, 22: 496, 22.

ge-mađel, es; *n. Speech, conversation, talking, harangue;* sermo, ōrātio, sermōcĭnātio:—Ûre heofenlîca Hlâford nolde đæra deófla gemađeles nâ mâre habban *our heavenly Lord would not have any more of the devil's harangue,* Nicod. 29; Thw. 16, 39.

ge-mearc, es; *n. A boundary, limit;* lŏcus designātus:—Gewât him se æđeling to đæs gemearces đe him Metod tǽhte *the man departed to the limit which the Lord had shewn him,* Cd. 139; Th. 174, 28; Gen. 2885. DER. fôt-gemearc, fyrst-, geár-, mîl-, þing-, word-.

ge-mearcan; to -mearcenne; *p.* ede; *pp.* ed *To mark, observe, keep;* observāre:—Getâcna me đǽr sêlast sý sâwle mînre to gemearcenne Meotudes willan *signify to me where it be best for my soul to observe the Creator's will,* Exon. 118 a; Th. 453, 7; Hy. 4, 11.

ge-mearcian; *p.* ode, ade; *pp.* od, ad *To mark, point out, describe, assign, appoint, determine;* nŏtāre, signāre, designāre, assignāre, constĭtuĕre, decernĕre:—He gemet ne con gemearcian his mûđe môde sîne *he cannot set bounds to his mouth with his mind,* Exon. 87 b; Th. 330, 18; Vy. 53. Ic wolde gesecgan hû Crêca gewinn, đe of Lacedemonia đære byrig ǽrest onstæled wæs, and, mid spellcwydum gemearcian *I wished to tell how the war of the Greeks was first raised from the city of the Lacedæmonians, and, in the language of history, to describe it,* Ors. 3, 1; Bos. 54, 34. Đû him mete sylest, mǽla gehwylce, and đæs tîdlîce tîd gemearcast *tu das escam illis in tempŏre opportūno,* Ps. Th. 144, 16. Symle he twelf sîþum tîda gemearcaþ dæges and nihtes *it ever marks the hours of day and night twelve times,* Exon. 58 a; Th. 207, 24; Ph. 146. Se Hǽlend gemearcode ôđre twâ and hundseofentig *designāvit Dŏmĭnus et alios septuaginta duos,* Lk. Bos. 10, 1: Bd. 3, 9; S. 534, 2. Hæfde hire wâcran hige Metod gemearcod *to her the Creator had appointed a weaker mind,* Cd. 28; Th. 37, 17; Gen. 591: 38; Th. 50, 25; Gen. 814. Getâcnod ođđe gemearcod is ofor us leóht andwlitan đînes *signātum est sŭper nos lūmen vultus tui,* Ps. Lamb. 4, 7. He is wuldre gemearcad *it is marked with glory,* Exon. 60 b; Th. 220, 11; Ph. 318. Hî hæfdon ǽlce scire on West-Sexum stîđe gemearcod mid bryne and mid hergunge *they had severely marked every shire of Wessex with burning and harrying,* Chr. 1006; Erl. 141, 2. Gemearca hû hý ǽr stôdon *mark how they stood before,* Lchdm. i. 398, 5. v. ge-mercian.

ge-mearcod; *part. Marked;* signatus:—On đa gemearcodan lindan *on the marked linden* or *lime tree*, Cod. Dipl. 1317; A.D. 1033; Kmbl. vi. 182, 2: 1102; A.D. 931; Kmbl. v. 195, 14.

ge-mearcund. v. ge-mercung.

ge-meare *an end*, Ps. Lamb. 58, 14. v. ge-mǣre.

ge-mearr, es; *n. A hindrance, error*:—Đonne se Godes điów on đæt gemearr đære woruldsorga befēhþ *when the servant of God accepts the hindrance of worldly cares*, Past. 51, 7; Swt. 401, 20; Hat. MS. Đa gemearr đe man drīfþ on mislīcum gewiglungum *the erroneous practices which are carried on with various spells*, L. Can. Edg. 16; Th. ii. 248, 4. Gemear *nugæ, errores*, Gl. Prud. 662. [Cf. *Goth.* ga-marzeins *a stumbling-block*.] v. myrran.

ge-mearr; *adj. Wicked, fraudulent*:—Gif hwā gemearra manna wǣre *if there were any wicked man*, L. Edw. 1; Th. i. 160, note 2. v. gemearr.

ge-mec; *adj. Equal, suited, matched*:—Ođđe wīf habbaþ him gemæc ođđe him gemece nabbaþ *either they are well-matched in marriage or have not wives suited to them*, Bt. 11, 1; Fox 32, 5. v. ge-mæc.

ge-mecca, an; *m. and f. A consort, an equal*:—Ic Oswulf aldormonn ond Beorndryþ mīn gemecca *I Oswulf alderman and Beornthryth my wife*, Th. Dipl. 459, 3: 469, 30. Gemecca *conjunx*, Ælfc. Gl. 3; Wrt. Voc. 72, 9. Clippende to heora gemeccum *clamantes coæqualibus*, Mt. Kmbl. Rush. 11, 16. v. ge-mæcca.

ge-mēd *mad*. v. ge-mǣd.

ge-mēde, es; *n. That which pleases, satisfies, due observance*:—Maga gemēdu *the due observances of kinsmen*, Beo. Th. 499; B. 247. [*O. Sax.* gimōdi:—Đemu manne te gimōdea *to satisfy the man*: *O. H. Ger.* gi-muati.] v. ge-mēde; *adj.*

ge-mēde; *superl.* -mēdost; *adj. Agreeable, pleasing*; acceptus, grātus:—Swā him gemēdost wæs *as was most agreeable to them*, Andr. Kmbl. 1188; An. 594. Gemēde *agreeable*, Bt. 11, 1; Bt. Fox 32, note 1. Gimoedo ł wala middangeardes *prospera mundi*, Rtl. 50, 6. [*O. H. Ger.* gi-muati: cf. *O. Sax.* gi-mōdi, *n.*] DER. un-gemēde.

ge-medemian; *p.* ode; *pp.* od [medeme] *To deign, deem worthy, honour, vouchsafe, moderate, humiliate, humble*:—Ic gemedemige đē to đam đinge *dignor te illa re*, Ælfc. Gr. 41; Som. 44, 5. Đætte hia mildelīce miđ woere hire gisomnia đū gimeodomiga *ut eam propitius cum viro suo copulare digneris*, Rtl. 108, 42: 36. Ic đancige mīnum Gode đe me gemedemode to his hālgum *I thank my God that has deemed me worthy to be among his saints*, Homl. Th. i. 424, 15. Đū eart on ēcnesse gemedemod *thou art honoured for ever*, Blickl. Homl. 147, 12. Godes sunu gemedemode hine sylfne đæt he wolde beón acenned of Marian *God's Son condescended to be born of Mary*, Homl. Th. 32, 7: Blickl. Homl. 39, 17: Nicod. 20; Thw. 10, 9. Crist sylf gemedemode đæt he wolde gebīgan his hālige heáfod to his đeówan handum *Christ himself deigned to bow his head to his servant's hands*, Homl. Th. i. 40, 25. He wæs gemedomad on rōde beón ahangen *he suffered the humiliation of being hung on the cross*, L. E. I. 21; Th. ii. 416, 28: Blickl. Homl. 179, 9: 139, 26. Gemedemud *temperatus*, Scint. 12.

ge-medemlīce, -meodomlīce; *adv. Worthily*; digne, Rtl. 18, 33: dignanter, 34, 18.

ge-mēder; *f. A godmother*; commater, Som.

ge-medmicel; *adj. Small, mean, weak*:—Gimetomicla *infirma*, Rtl. 50, 11.

ge-mēdred; *part. Mothered, of the same mother*; uterinus, Ors. 3, 7; Bos. 60, 19. v. ge-mēdrian.

ge-mēdrian; *p.* ede, ode; *pp.* ed, yd *To* MOTHER, *to adopt* or *to have as a son* or *daughter*; adoptare, habere sibi filium *vel* filiam:—Đa þrȳ gebrōđra nǣron nā Philippuse gemēdred *the three were not brothers of Philip by their mother* [*mothered*], Ors. 3, 7; Bos. 60, 19. Geseah hys gemēdrydan brōđor Beniamin *vidit Benjamin fratrem suum uterinum*, Gen. 43, 29.

ge-mēdryd; *def.* se ge-mēdryda; *part. p. Mothered, of the same mother*, Gen. 43, 29: 44, 20. v. ge-mēdrian.

ge-meldian; *p.* ode, ade; *pp.* od, ad *To announce*; nuntiare, adnuntiare:— Blōd-gyte weorđeþ mongum gemeldad *bloodshed shall be announced to many*, Exon. 116 b; Th. 448, 20; Dōm. 37: Ps. Th. 61, 11.

gême-leás; *adj. Negligent*; neglīgens, C. R. Ben. 54. v. gȳme-leás.

gême-leáslīce; *adv. Negligently*; neglīgenter:—For hwon sǣdest đū Ecgbyrhte swā gēmeleáslīce and swā wlætlīce đa þing đe ic đē bebeád him to secganne *quāre tam neglīgenter ac tĕpĭde dixisti Ecgbercto quæ tibi dīcenda præcēpi?* Bd. 5, 9; S. 623, 9. Đa đe unwærlīce and gēmeleáslīce Gode hȳraþ *those who heedlessly and carelessly serve God*, Blickl. Homl. 63, 22. v. gȳme-leáslīce.

gême-leásniss, e; *f. Negligence*; negligentia, Rtl. 178, 11. v. gȳmeleásness.

gême-lēst, e; *f. Negligence, carelessness*; neglĭgentia, incūria:—Þurh đīne āgene gēmelēste *through thine own negligence*, Bt. 5, 1; Fox 10, 2. Þurh heora gēmelēst *through their carelessness*, Chr. 1070; Erl. 209, 34. v. gȳme-leást.

ge-meltan, -myltan; *p.* -mealt, *pl.* -multon; *pp.* -molten *To melt, digest*:—Beorgas gemeltaþ *the hills shall melt*, Exon. 22 a; Th. 61, 2; Cri. 978. Gif his mete gemyltan nelle *if his meat will not digest*, Herb. i. 90, 9; Lchdm. i. 196, 6: 1, 19; Lchdm. 76, 15. Đæt sweord eal gemealt īse gelīcost *the sword all melted just like ice*, Beo. Th. 3220; B. 1608: 3235; B. 1615. Ne gemealt him se mōdsefa *his courage did not fail*, 5249; B. 2628. On hyre bryne gemultan ealle đa anlīcnessa togædere *in its burning all the statues melted together*, Ors. 5, 2; Bos. 101, 21. Eorđe is gemolten *liquefacta est terra*, Ps. Th. 74, 3. Me wearþ gemolten mōd on hredre *defectio animo tenuit me*, 118, 53.

ge-men; *nom. pl*: *gen.* -manna *Men*:—Wǣron đǣrin gemanna hund twelftig đūsenda *there were therein a hundred and twenty thousand men*, Salm. and Sat. Kmbl. 186, 1.

gêmen; *gen.* gēmenne; *f. Care*; cūra:—Ǣlc mon'mæg witan hū hefig sorg men beoþ seó gēmen his bearna *every one may know how heavy a trouble to a man is the care of his children*, Bt. 31, 1; Fox 112, 17: 12; Fox 36, 38. Be đære hæfegan gēmenne bearna *concerning the heavy care of children*, 31, 1; Fox 112, 19. Mid micle gēmænne and gewinne *cum magna cura ac labore*, Bd. 2, 7: S. 509, 11. v. gȳmen.

ge-mencgan *to mingle*, Ælfc. Gr. 28, 6; Som. 32, 33. v. ge-mengan.

ge-mencgednys, -nyss *a mingling together*, Bd. 1, 27; S. 495, 29. v. ge-mengednys.

ge-mend *a memorial*. v. ge-mynd.

gêmend, es; *m. A keeper*; custos, Mt. Kmbl. p. 20, 4.

ge-mendful, -full; *adj.* [ge-mend = ge-mynd *the mind, memory*] *Of good memory, mindful*; mĕmor:—Cild biþ gemendful *a child will be of good memory*, Lchdm. iii. 186, 24.

ge-mēnelic; *adj.* [ge-mēne = ge-mǣne *common*] *Common*; commūnis:—For gemēnelīcre neóde *for the common need*, L. C. S. 10; Th. i. 382, 2, MS. A. v. ge-mǣnelīc.

ge-mēnelīce; *adv. In common, commonly*; commūnĭter:—We mynegiaþ eów ealle gemēnelīce *we admonish you all in common*, Wanl. Catal. 111, 25, col. 2. v. ge-mǣnelīce.

ge-mengan, -mencgan; *p.* de; *pp.* ed *To mingle, commingle, mix, blend, confuse, unite, join, combine*; miscēre, commiscēre, confundĕre, consŏciāre, infĭcĕre:—Đæt he wīsdōm mǣge wiđ ofermetta gemengan *that he may mingle wisdom with sensuality*, Bt. Met. Fox 7, 16; Met. 7, 8. Ic gemencge *confundo*, Ælfc. Gr. 28, 6; Som. 32, 33. Ic gemenge *confĭcio*, Ælfc. Gl. 36; Som. 62, 99; Wrt. Voc. 28, 76. Đū hī on đisse worulde gemengest *thou unitest them in this world*, Bt. 33, 4; Fox 132, 24. He gemengeþ đæt fȳr wiđ đam cīle *he mingles the fire with the cold*, 39, 13; Fox 234, 11: Bt. Met. Fox 11, 182; Met. 11, 91. Ic me to đam plegan gemengde *lūdentĭbus me miscui*, Bd. 5, 6; S. 619, 11. Đæt we hit gemengen to đam ǣrran *that we mix it with the preceding*, Bt. 34, 5; Fox 140, 13. Eorþe wearþ eall mid blōde māne gemenged *infecta est terra in sanguinĭbus eōrum*, Ps. Th. 105, 28. Đæt wæter and seó eorþe wǣron gemengede ōþ đone þriddan dæg *the water and the earth were commingled unto the third day*, Hexam. 4; Norm. 8, 15. Đǣr gemengde beóþ onhǣlo gelāc engla and deófla *there shall be mingled the whole assemblage of angels and of devils*, Exon. 21 a; Th. 56, 4; Cri. 895: Bd. 5, 23; S. 646, 4. Se ryhtwīsa Dēma se đe hine on ūrne gefērscipe đurh flǣsces gecynd gemengde *the righteous Judge who joined himself to our fellowship through fleshly nature*, Past. 21; Swt. 167, 23; Hat. MS.

ge-menged, -mencged; *part. p. Mixed, mingled, confused*; mixtus, commistus, confusus:—God sende rēnscūr mid swefle gemenged *God sent a shower of rain mingled with brimstone*, Gen. 19, 24. Gemencged *mixtus*, Ps. Spl. 74, 7. Gemencged hund and wulf *commistus canis et lupus*, Wrt. Voc. 77, 79. Gemenged stemn is, đe biþ būtan andgite, swylc swā is hryþera gehlōw, hunda gebeorc, treówa brastlung *confused voice is what is without understanding, such as lowing of oxen, barking of dogs, rustling of trees, etc*, Ælfc. Gr. 1; Som. 2, 34, 3.

ge-mengednys, -mengdnys, -mencgednys, -mencgdnys, -mencgnys, -nyss, e; *f. A mingling together, mixing, mixture, connection*; commixtio, admixtio:—Seó gemengdnys đæs flǣsces *carnis commixtio*, Bd. 1, 27; S. 495, 31. Se willa mā waldeþ on đam weorce đære gemengdnysse *vōluntas dŏmĭnātur in ŏpĕre commixtiōnis*, 1, 27; S. 495, 38. On đæs līchoman gemengednysse biþ willa *in carnis commixtiōne vŏluptas est*, 1, 27; S. 493, 20: 1, 27; S. 495, 39. Ǣfter his wīfes gemengednysse *post admixtiōnem conjŭgis*, 1, 27; S. 496, 17. Hwæđere on đām wordum is sweotol đæt he wōnysse nemde nalæs đa gemencgdnysse đæs gesinscypes, ac đone sylfan willan đære gemencgednysse *in quĭbus tămen verbis non admixtiōnem conjŭgium inīquĭtātem nōmĭnat, sed ipsam videlĭcet vŏluptātem admixtiōnis*, 1, 27; S. 495, 28, 29. Seó alȳfede gemencgnyss *ipsa lĭcĭta admixtio*, 1, 27; S. 495, 18. Ǣfter gemencgnysse āgenes wīfes *post admixtiōnem propriæ conjŭgis*, 1, 27; S. 495, 15. Būtan womme ođđe gemencgednysse đwyrlīces weorces *without blemish or admixture of perverse work*, Homl. Th. i. 544, 17. Đære sǣ gemengednyssa *the minglings of the sea*, 610, 11: 608, 20. [Cf. Lk. 21, 25.]

ge-mengung, e; *f. A mixing, confusing*; mixtura, Cot. 35.

ge-menigfealdan, -menigfildan; *p.* de [menig *many*, feald *a fold, plait*] *To multiply, increase, extend*; multiplicare, Ex. 32, 13: Gen. 9, 27: 32, 12.

gêmenis, gêmnis, se; *f. Care;* cura, Mt. Kmbl. Lind. *and* Rush. 22, 16.

ge-meodniss, e; *f. Worthiness, dignity;* dignitas, Rtl. 192, 37.

ge-meotu *boundaries, limits,* Andr. Kmbl. 907; An. 454, = ge-metu. v. ge-met.

ge-mercian; *p.* ode; *pp.* od *To mark out;* signâre:—Man hæfde ða buruh mid stacum gemercod *the city was marked out with stakes,* Ors. 5, 5; Bos. 105, 28. Gemercadon ðone stân *signantes lapidem,* Mt. Kmbl. Lind. 27, 66. Ðæt gemercad wêre all ymb-hyrft *ut describeretur universus orbis,* Lk. Skt. Lind. 2, 1. v. ge-mearcian.

ge-mercung, e; *f. A description;* descriptio, Lk. Skt. Lind. 2, 2.

ge-mêre, es; *n. A boundary, end;* fînis:—Fram gemērum eorþan *a finibus terræ,* Ps. Spl. 60, 2. v. ge-mǽre.

ge-merran *to mar, spoil,* Lk. Skt. Lind. 13, 7. v. ge-myrran.

ge-mêrsian, Mt. Kmbl. Lind. 9, 31; 28, 15. v. ge-mǽrsian.

ge-met, es; *nom. acc. pl.* -u, -a; *n.* I. *a measure, space, distance;* mensura, spatium, intervallum:—Gefylle gē ðæt gemet eówra fædera *vos implete mensuram patrum vestrorum,* Mt. Bos. 23, 32. On ðam ylcan gemete ðe gē metaþ *qua mensura mensi fueritis,* Mt. Bos. 7, 2: Mk. Bos. 4, 24: Lk. Bos. 6, 38: Cd. 80; Th. 101, 4; Gen. 1677. Betweonan Eferwîc and six mîla gemete *between York and a distance of six miles,* L. N. P. L. 56; Th. ii. 298, 27. II. *that by which anything is measured, a measure;* mensura, modius, satum:—Gemeta and gewihta rihte man georne *let measures and weights be carefully rectified,* L. C. S. 9; Th. i. 380, 24. Hæbbe ǽlc man rihte gemetu *modius æqualis et verus erit tibi,* Deut. 25, 15: Lev. 6, 20: 19, 36. On þrîm gemetum melwes *in farinæ satis tribus,* Mt. Bos. 13, 33: Lk. Bos. 13, 21. III. *measure, capacity, ability, power, etc;* mensura, facultas, potestas, vis:—Ne sceal se Dryhtnes þeów in his môd-sefan mâre gelufian eorþan ǽhtwelan, ðonne his ânes gemet, ðæt he his lîchoman lâde hæbbe *the Lord's servant shall not in his mind love more of earth's riches than his own measure, that he may have support for his body,* Exon. 38 a; Th. 125, 25; Gû. 359. Nis ðæt monnes gemet *it is not man's ability,* 92 b; Th. 348, 12; Sch. 27. Næs ðâ monna gemet, ne mægen engla, ðæt eów mihte helpan *there was then no power of men, no angel's might, that could help you,* Cd. 224; Th. 295, 22; Sat. 490. Ofer mîn gemet *above my power,* Beo. Th. 5750; B. 2879: 5059; B. 2533: Ps. Th. 59, 11: 107, 12. IV. *a fit* or *proper measure, and so* metaph. *measure, proportion, moderation, bounds, limit, boundary, means, way, manner;* mensura, modus, finis, terminus, limes, ratio:—Ðý læs he of gemete hweorfe *lest he turn from moderation,* Exon. 78 b; Th. 294, 35; Crä. 25: 83 a; Th. 312, 18; Seef. 111. He gemet ne con gemearcian his mûþe môd sîne *he cannot set bounds to his mouth by his understanding,* 88 a; Th. 330, 17; Vy. 52. Gytsung gemet nât *avarice knows no bounds,* Scint. 25. Ðâs miclan gemetu middan-geardes *these great boundaries of middle-earth,* Exon. 20 a; Th. 52, 1; Cri. 827: Andr. Kmbl. 617; An. 309. Eal ic hit arǽfnede ðæt ic eów æteówe hwylcum gemete gē sceolan arǽfnan *I suffered it all to shew you how you ought to suffer,* Blickl. Homl. 237, 12. Ealle gemete *omni modo,* Bd. 1, 27; S. 491, 9. Ðysses gemetes *hujusmodi,* 2, 1, S. 500, 18: 4, 9; S. 577, 7: 4, 19; S. 589, 18. On ðam gemete *quemadmodum,* Ps. Spl. 36, 2, 21: 32, 22. V. *a rule, order, law;* norma, regula, lex:—Fram ðâm he ðæt gemet leornode regollîces þeódscipes *a quibus normam disciplinæ regularis didicerat,* Bd. 3, 23; S. 554, 35. Gemetu *normulæ,* Cot. 138: Exon. 93 a; Th. 349, 14; Sch. 46. Ðînes mûþes gemet *lex oris tui,* Ps. Th. 118, 72. VI. 1. *a mood, the inflection of a verb expressing the mode* or *manner of action* or *being, abstracted from time—tense* tîd *q. v. and person* hâd IV. *q. v: such as, indicative* gebîcnigendlîc, *q. v: imperative* bebeódendlîc, *q. v. subjunctive* under-þeódendlîc, *q. v: infinitive* unge-endigendlîc, *q. v;* modus:—Modus is gemet oððe ðare sprǽce wîse *a mood is mode [manner] or the manner [wise] of speaking,* Ælfc. Gr. 21; Som. 23, 17. 2. *a poetical measure, metre;* metrum:—And ðâm wordum sôna monig word in ðæt ylce gemet Gode wyrðes songes to geþeódde *et eis mox plura in eundem modum verba Deo digni carminis adjunxit,* Bd. 4, 24; S. 597, 26. [*O. Sax.* gi-met: *O. H. Ger.* ki-mez.] DER. eln-gemet, un-. v. metan.

ge-met; *adj.* [ge-met IV. *a fit* or *proper measure*] *Fit, meet, proper;* aptus, congruus, conveniens:—Wearþ him hýrra hyge ðonne gemet wǽre *he had a loftier soul than were meet,* Cd. 198; Th. 247, 5; Dan. 492: 186; Th. 231, 21; Dan. 250: Andr. Kmbl. 2358; An. 1180. Swâ him gemet þince *as to him may seem fit,* Beo. Th. 1379; B. 687: 6107; B. 3057. Ðæt hit gemet wǽre *that it were fit,* Ps. Th. 143, 4: Bt. Met. Fox 29, 86; Met. 29, 42. DER. un-ge-met.

ge-mêt, es; *n. A meeting, assembly;* conventus:—Hî hæfdon ǽlce dæge heora witena gemêt *they had their meeting of counsellors every day,* Jud. Thw. 161, 31. v. ge-môt.

ge-meta *measures,* L. C. S. 9; Th. i. 380, 24. v. ge-met.

ge-metan; *p.* -mæt *and* -mette, *pl.* -mǽton; *pp.* -meten; *v. trans.* I. *to measure, measure back* or *again;* metiri, remetiri:—On ðam ylcan gemete ðe gē metaþ, eów byþ gemeten *qua mensura mensi fueritis, remetietur vobis,* Mt. Bos. 7, 2: Mk. Bos. 4, 24: Lk. Bos. 6, 38. God ðû ðe heofen mid honda gemettest and eorðan on ðînre fyst betýndest *God thou who has meted heaven with thy hand and enclosed the earth in thy fist* [cf. Isaiah 40, 12], St. And. 47, 2. II. *to measure by traversing* or *going over;* metiri transeundo:—And his cwēn mid him medo-stîg gemæt *and his queen with him measured the mead-way [way to the mead-hall],* Beo. Th. 1852; B. 924. v. metan.

ge-metan; *p.* -mette; *pp.* -mett, -met *To paint;* pingere, depingere:—Swylce hî gemette wǽron *as if they were painted,* Chr. 1104; Th. 367, 1: Lchdm. iii. 206, 18: Prov. 7. Gē sind gelîce gemettum ofergeweorcum *ye are like painted sepulchres,* Homl. Th. ii. 404, 17. v. metan *to paint.*

ge-mêtan; he -mēteþ, -mētt, -mēt; *p.* -mētte, *pl.* -mētton; *pp.* -mēted, -mētod, -mētt, -mēt *To find, find out, discover, come upon, meet with;* invĕnîre, compĕrîre:—Ic gemēte *invĕnio,* Ælfc. Gr. 30, 4; Som. 34, 49: 37; Som. 39, 6. He holtes hleó heáh gemēteþ *he finds the wood's lofty shelter,* Exon. 62 a; Th. 227, 27; Ph. 429: Ps. Th. 54, 24: 87, 12. Gemoetaþ *invenerit,* Lk. Skt. Lind. 12, 43. Ealc ðæra, ðe me gemētt, me ofslyþ *omnis qui invĕnĕrit me, occîdet me,* Gen. 4, 14. Se ðe gemēt hys sâwle, se forspilþ hîg *qui invĕnit anĭmam suam, perdet illam,* Mt. Bos. 10, 39: 24, 46: Lk. Bos. 12, 37, 38, 43. Gē gemētaþ ân cild hræglum bewunden, and on binne alēd *invĕniētis infantem pannis invŏlūtum, et pŏsĭtum in præsēpio,* 2, 12: Mt. Bos. 11, 29: Mk. Bos. 11, 2. Ðæs bisceopes lîf ic gemētte biscope wyrðe beón *vītam episcŏpi episcŏpo dignam esse compĕri,* Bd. 5, 6; S. 618, 30. Ðû gemēttes Meotod alwihta *thou hast met the Lord of all things,* Cd. 228; Th. 308, 23; Sat. 697. He gemētte stapul ǽrenne *he found a brazen pillar,* Andr. Kmbl. 2123; An. 1063: 481; An. 241. Geswinc and angnys gemētton me *trĭbŭlātio et angustia invĕnĕrunt me,* Ps. Spl. 118, 143: 75, 5. Gemēte gē hine *invĕnies eum,* Deut. 4, 29. Gif ic gemēte fîftig rihtwîsra wera *si invĕnĕro quinquaginta justos,* Gen. 18, 26, 28. Gif hwâ þeóf gemēte *if any one find a thief,* L. C. S. 29; Th. i. 392, 14: L. In. 49; Th. i. 132, 12. Ðæt we ðîne onsýne milde gemēten *that we may find thy countenance mild,* Exon. 76 a; Th. 286, 13; Jul. 731. Swâ hwylce swâ gē gemēton *quoscumque invĕnĕrĭtis,* Mt. Bos. 22, 9. Hî hæfdon neowne gefeán gemēted *they had met with new joy,* Elen. Kmbl. 1738; El. 871: 2447; El. 1225. He is gemēt *inventus est,* Lk. Bos. 15, 24, 32. Gif ðǽr beóþ gemētte feówertig rihtwîsra *sin quadraginta ibi inventi fuĕrint,* Gen. 18, 29: 2, 12. Gif we gemēte sîn on moldwege oððe feor oððe neáh fundne weorðen *if we are met on earth's way or far or near are found,* Exon. 70 b; Th. 262, 17; Jul. 334. Gif hwilc mon sî gemētod on ðînum ðam egeslîcan dôme *if any man be found at thy awful judgment,* St. And. 47, 8.

ge-mete; *adv. Fitly, meetly, in a proper manner;* apte, congruenter, convenienter, Exon. 40 a; Th. 132, 13; Gû. 472: Bt. Met. Fox 13, 36; Met. 13, 18. DER. un-gemete.

ge-meted = ge-mett *painted,* Som. 143? v. ge-metan.

ge-mêtednes, -ness, e; *f. An invention, a discovery;* inventio, adinventio:—Syle heom æfter nearoþancnysse oððe mâne gemētednessa oððe heora afundennysse *da illis sĕcundum nequĭtiam adinventiōnum ipsōrum,* Ps. Lamb. 27, 4.

ge-metegian; *p.* ode; *pp.* od *To measure, moderate,* Ps. Spl. 38, 7. v. ge-metgian.

ge-meten; *part. Measured, measured back* or *again;* remensus, Mt. Bos. 7, 2. v. ge-metan.

ge-mêteng *a meeting.* v. ge-mêting.

ge-met-fæst; *adj. Moderate, modest;* moderatus, modestus:—Ne hie ðâm geþyldegum and ðâm gemetfæstum simble ne wuniaþ *neither do they always dwell with the patient and moderate,* Bt. 11, 1; Fox 34, 3. Sió is swîðe gemetfæst *she is very modest,* 10; Fox 28, 20. Man gemetfæst *vir modestus,* Bd. 1, 16; S. 484, 18: 4, 28; S. 606, 33: Exon. 48 b; Th. 168, 19; Gû. 1080: 95 b; Th. 357, 19; Pa. 31.

ge-met-fæstlîce; *adv. Modestly;* modeste:—He swâ gemetfæstlîce hine sylfne beheóld *ita se modeste gerebat,* Bd. 5, 19; S. 637, 4.

ge-met-fæstnys, -nyss, e; *f. Moderation, modesty;* moderatio, moderamen, modestia:—Mycelre monþwǽrnysse and ǽrfæstnysse and gemetfæstnysse mon *summæ mansuetudinis et pietatis ac moderaminis vir,* Bd. 3, 3; S. 525, 32: 3, 14; S. 540, 13. Petrus tihte geleáffulle wîf to eádmôdnesse and gemetfæstnysse *Peter exhorted faithful women to humility and modesty,* Homl. Th. i. 98, 3. Gimetfæstnisse *modestiam,* Rtl. 13, 33.

gemet-fæt, es; *nom. acc. pl.* -fatu; *n. A measuring-vessel, a measure;* metatorium vas, mensura quævis definita:—Ân gemetfæt full, ðe hîg Gomor hēton, Ex. 16, 16, 33.

ge-met-festan; *p.* -feste; *pp.* -fested, -fest *To compare;* comparare:—Gemetfest *comparatus,* Ps. Spl. T. 48, 21.

ge-metgian, -metegian, -metigian; *p.* ode; *pp.* od. I. *v. trans. To measure, moderate, temper, regulate, order, govern, restrain;* mensurare, temperare, moderare, regere:—Heora wîte biþ gemetegod ǽlcum be his gearnungum *their punishment shall be measured to every one by his deserts,* Homl. Th. i. 294, 6. Efne gemetegode ðû settest dagas mîne *ecce mensurabiles posuisti dies meos,* Ps. Spl. 38, 7. Hine se'fne of dûne astīgende he cūđe gemetgian his hiéremonnum *se auditoribus condescendendo noverat temperare*, Past. 16, 2; Swt. 101, 15; Hat. MS. 21 a, 2: 35, 1; Swt. 237, 23; Hat. MS. 45 a, 4. Ā sceal đæt wiđerwearde đæt ōđer wiđerwearde gemetgian *ever must the contrary moderate the other contrary*, Bt. 21; Fox 74, 19: 40, 3; Fox 238, 25: Bt. Met. Fox 11, 107; Met. 11, 54. Gif đū ne gemetgodest cēle and hǣto *if thou didst not moderate cold and heat*, Bt. Met. Fox 20, 224; Met. 20, 112: Salm. Kmbl. 879; Sal. 439. Beorhte steorran mōna gemetgaþ *the moon tempers the bright stars*, Bt. Met. Fox 4, 17; Met. 4, 9. Se gemetgaþ đone bridel *he regulates the bridle*, Bt. 36, 2; Fox 174, 18. God gemetgaþ ealla gesceafta *God regulates all creatures*, Bt. 39, 13; Fox 234, 9: Bt. Met. Fox 13, 10; Met. 13, 5: 24, 78; Met. 24, 39. II. *to measure in the mind, to deliberate, meditate on*; deliberare, meditari:—Ic on đīnum bebodum mōte gemetgian rǣd *meditabor in mandatis tuis*, Ps. Th. 118, 47. III. *v. intrans. To become moderate, to moderate one's self*; moderari, temperari:—Him gemetgaþ eall ēđles leóma *to them shall all the bright fire of their home moderate itself*, Elen. Kmbl. 2584; El. 1293. v. metgian.

ge-metgung, e; *f. Moderation, temperance, a fit* or *proper measure, a direction, a regulation*; moderatio, temperantia, modus, moderamen:—Wīsdōm is se hēhsta cræft, and se hæfþ on him feówer ōđre cræftas, đara is ān wærscipe, ōđer gemetgung, þridde is ellen, feórþe rihtwīsnes *wisdom is the highest virtue, and it has in it four other virtues, of which one is prudence, another temperance, the third is fortitude, and the fourth justice*, Bt. 27, 2; Fox 96, 34, note. Ealla gesceafta onfōþ æt Gode endebyrdnesse, and andwlitan, and gemetgunge *all creatures receive from God order, and form, and measure*, Bt. 39, 5; Fox 218, 15, 20, 33. Mid đam gemetgunge đæs gesceádes gefrætewod *moderamine discretionis ornatus*, Bd. 3, 5; S. 527, 42. Swylce monige gemetgunge đara rihtgelȳfedra gehælde đære Rōmaniscan cyricean Angel-cynnes cyricum mid his lāre brohte *perplura Catholicæ observationis moderamina ecclesiis Anglorum sua doctrina contulit*, 3, 28; S. 560, 37. Hī būton gemetgunge đæt wīn drincende wǣron *they drank the wine without moderation*, Ors. 2, 4; Bos. 45, 19. v. metgung.

ge-mēđgian; *p.* ode, ade; *pp.* od, ad [mēđig *wearied*] *To weary, fatigue, impair*; fătīgāre:—Wæs Gūþlāce mægen gemēđgad *Guthlac's strength was impaired*, Exon. 47 a; Th. 160, 27; Gū. 950.

ge-mēđrian; *p.* ode; *pp.* od *To honour*; hŏnōrāre:—Būton he hwæne furđor gemēđrian wylle *unless he will more amply honour any one*, L. C. S. 15; Th. i. 384, 4, MS. A. v. ge-mǣđian.

ge-mēting, e; *f. A meeting, an assembly, association, a society*; conventus, conventio, conventĭcŭlum, congrĕgātio:—Is undyrne uncer gemēting *our meeting is not secret*, Beo. Th. 4006; B. 2001. Gemētingc *conventus* vel *conventio*, Wrt. Voc. 72, 75. Đū bewruge me fram gemētinge awyrgedra *protexisti mea conventu mălignantium*, Ps. Spl. 63, 2: Ps. Th. 105, 16. On gemētingum *in congrĕgātiōne*, 110, 1. Ne ic ne gederige gemētinga heora *non congrĕgābo conventĭcŭla eōrum*, Ps. Spl. 15, 4. To gemoetingum *conciliis*, Mk. Skt. Lind. 13, 9.

ge-metlǣcan; *p.* -lǣhte; *pp.* -lǣht *To moderate*:—We hit eft gemetlǣcaþ *we afterwards moderate it*, Past. 16, 2; Swt. 101, 12; Hat. MS.

ge-met-līc; *adj. Moderate, temperate, measurable, fit*; moderatus, temperatus, mensurabilis, aptus:—Hæle wīsfæst and gemetlīc *a man wise and moderate*, Exon. 81 a; Th. 305, 12; Fä. 87. Him gemetlīc seó *may be suitable for him*, Bt. 14, 2; Fox 44, 21: 40, 3; Fox 238, 21; Ps. Lamb. 38, 6. [*O. H. Ger.* ki-mezlih *mediocris*.]

ge-met-līce; *adv. Moderately, fitly*; moderate, modeste, apte:—To đon gemetlīce *adeo moderate*, Bd. 4, 24; S. 598, 26. Gemetlīcost *most fitly*, Bt. Met. Fox 8, 32; Met. 8, 16. [*O. H. Ger.* ki-mezliho *commode*.]

ge-met-līcung, e; *f. Due measure, moderation*; moderatio, Som.

ge-mētnes, -ness, e; *f. A finding, discovery*; inventio:—Se dæg heora þrōwunga ge heora līchoman gemētnesse mid ārwurþre weorþunge on đām stōwum mǣrsode syndon *dies passiōnis vel inventiōnis eōrum congrua illis in lŏcis vĕnĕrātiōne celebrātur*, Bd. 5, 10; S. 625, 18. v. ge-mētednes.

ge-metsian; *p.* ode; *pp.* od *To furnish with provisions*:—Đæt scip đe Swegen eorl hæfde him silfum ǣr gegearcod and gemetsod *the ship that Earl Sweyn had before prepared and provisioned for himself*, Chr. 1052; Erl. 181, 14. v. metsian.

ge-mett *measure, manner*, Bd. 4, 9; S. 577, 7. v. ge-met.

ge-mettan; *pl. m. Eaters, partakers*; comestōres:—Đa gemettan ne mōston đæs lambes bān scǣnan *the partakers might not break the bones of the lamb*, Homl. Th. ii. 282, 7. Đām gemettum *to the partakers*, 282, 2.

ge-mette *painted*, Chr. 1104; Th. 367, 1. v. ge-metan.

ge-metu *measures, boundaries, laws*, Deut. 25, 15: Andr. Kmbl. 617; An. 309: Exon. 93 a; Th. 349, 14; Sch. 46. v. ge-met.

ge-miclian, -myclian; *p.* ode, ade; *pp.* od, ad *To enlarge, magnify, extol, glorify*:—Se Mǣđa rīce swīđe gemiclade *who greatly enlarged the kingdom of the Medes*, Ors. 1, 12; Bos. 35, 28: Ps. Th. 147, 3. Se đe reorda gehwæs ryne gemiclaþ *he who enlargeth the course of every speech*, Exon. 8 b; Th. 4, 4; Cri. 47. Swīđe gemiclade se drihten miltheortnisse his *magnificavit dominus misericordiam suam*, Lk. Skt. Lind. 1, 58. Gemycla mīne sāuwle *magnify my soul*, Blickl. Homl. 159, 2. Gemycclige mīn sāul Drihten *my soul magnify the Lord*, 13, 5. Gemicliaþ hine *glorificate eum*, Ps. Spl. 21, 22. Đū gemiclast me *honorificabis me*, 49, 16.

ge-miclung, e; *f.* [mycel *much, great*] *Greatness, magnificence, glory*; magnificentia, Ps. Spl. 144, 5: 70, 21.

ge-midlian, -middlian; *p.* ode; *pp.* od [middel *middle*] *To divide, separate in the middle*; dimidiare:—Fācenfulle nā gemidliaþ dagas heora *dolosi non dimidiabunt dies suos*, Ps. Spl. C. 54, 27.

ge-midlian; *p.* ode; *pp.* od [medl *a bridle*] *To bridle, restrain*:—Gif hwā nyle gemidlian his tungan *if a man will not bridle his tongue*, Past. 38, 8; Swt. 281, 3; Hat. MS: 38, 1; Swt. 271, 13; Hat. MS.

ge-midlige *a bridle*, Lye. v. midl.

ge-mieltan *to melt, digest*:—Suā suā sió wamb gemielt đone mete suā gemielt đæt mōd mid đære gescādwīsnesse his geþeahtes his sorga *as the belly digests food so does the mind digest its sorrows with wise reflection*, Past. 36, 8; Swt. 259, 6; Hat. MS. v. ge-myltan.

ge-mīgan; *p.* -māh, *pl.* -migon; *pp.* -migen *To water, pass water*; mingere:—Gif hwā ne mǣge gemīgan *if one cannot pass water*, Herb. 7, 3; Lchdm. i. 98, 5: 12, 1; Lchdm. i. 102. 19: 80, 1; Lchdm. i. 182, 12. Đǣr se hund gemāh *where the hound watered*, Med. ex Quadr. 9, 13; Lchdm. i. 364, 1.

ge-milcian; *p.* ode, ade; *pp.* od, ad *To give milk, suckle*; lactare, Lk. Skt. Lind. 23, 29.

ge-mildscad; *part. p. Mixed with honey*; mulsus:—Gemildscad wæter *melicraton*, i. e. *mellis mistura, sc. cum aqua*: *hydromeli*. Gemildscad wīn *mulsum*, i. e. *mellis mistura cum vino*, Cot. 137; Lye. v. milisc.

ge-mildsian; *p.* ode; *pp.* od *To shew mercy, to pity*; mĭsĕrēri:—Nemne God me earmum and unwyrđum gemildsian wylle *unless God will shew mercy to me wretched and unworthy*, Bd. 3, 13; S. 538, 35. v. ge-miltsian.

ge-mildsiend, -miltsiend, es; *m. A pitier*; mĭsĕrātor:—Đū Driht God gemildsiend *tu Dŏmĭne Deus mĭsĕrātor*, Ps. Spl. 85, 14. Đū gōda cyngc and earmra gemiltsigend *thou good king and pitier of the poor*, Th. Apol. 18, 11.

ge-miltan; *p.* -milte; *pp.* -milted *To melt, soften, subdue*; liquefăcĕre, emollīre:—Woldon āninga ellenrōfes mōd gemiltan *they would entirely subdue the bold man's mood*, Andr. Kmbl. 2785; An. 1395. v. ge-myltan.

ge-miltsian, -mildsian, -milsian; *p.* ode; *pp.* od. I. *to shew mercy, have compassion, to pity, pardon*; mĭsĕrēri, propĭtiāri:—Ic gemiltsige đysse menegu *mĭsĕreor sŭper turbam*, Mk. Bos. 8, 2: Ælfc. Gr. 27; Som. 29, 56. Ārleásnyssum ūrum đū gemiltsast *impietātibus nostris tu propĭtiābĕris*, Ps. Spl. 64, 3: 24, 12. Gemiltsode se Hǣlend him *mĭsertus eōrum Jēsus*, Mt. Bos. 20, 34. Gemiltsa me God, gemiltsa mīn *mĭsĕrēre mei Deus, mĭsĕrēre mei*, Ps. Spl. 56, 1: 50, 1: Ps. Th. 118, 132. Đæt đū gemiltsige me *that thou pardon me*, Hy. 3, 49; Hy. Grn. ii. 282, 49. Đæt đū us gemiltsie *that thou pity us*, Exon. 121 b; Th. 465, 24; Hö. 109. Gimildsa *propitiare*, Rtl. 89, 40. Đætte he gimilsage *miserere*, 40, 19. II. *to make mild, make kind, soften*; propĭtium reddĕre, mītĭgāre:—Đæt Pater Noster Metod gemiltsaþ *the Pater Noster makes mild the Lord*, Salm. Kmbl. 81; Sal. 41.

ge-miltsiend. v. ge-mildsiend.

ge-miltsung, e; *f. Favour, mercy, pardon*; propĭtiātio:—Forđonđe mid đē gemiltsung is *quia ăpud te propĭtiātio est*, Ps. Spl. 129, 4.

ge-mimor; *adj. Existing in the memory* or *mind* [?], *known*; notus:—Leden him wæs swā cūþ and swā gemimor swā swā Englisc đæt him gecyndelīc wæs *linguam Latinam non minus quam Anglorum, quæ sibi naturalis est, noverit*, Bd. 5, 20; S. 641, 35. v. Grm. D. M. 352–3.

ge-mimorlīce; *adv. By heart*; memoriter, R. Ben. Inter. 13.

ge-mincged *mixed*. v. ge-mengan.

ge-mind, es; *n. A remembrance, memorial*; mĕmŏriāle:—Đū Driht on ēcnysse þurhwunast, and gemind đīn on cynrine and cynrine *tu Dŏmĭne, in æternum permănes, et mĕmŏriāle tuum in generātiōne et generātiōnem*, Ps. Spl. C. 101, 13. [*Goth.* ga-minþi *remembrance*.] v. ge-mynd.

ge-mindblīđe [blīđe *cheerful*] *A grateful remembrance, a memorial*; memoriale, Ps. Spl. T. 101, 13.

ge-mindig; *adj. Mindful*; mĕmor:—Gemindig biþ on worulde gecȳđnysse his *mĕmor ĕrit in sæcŭlum testāmenti sui*, Ps. Spl. 110, 5: 8, 5. Gif he sī gemindig mīnum [?] naman and đīnes *if he be mindful of my name and thine*, Nar. 47, 9. v. ge-myndig.

ge-mindiglīcnys, -nyss, e; *f. A remembrance, memorial*; mĕmŏriāle:—Đū Driht on ēcnysse þurhwunast, and gemindiglīcnys đīn on cynrine and cynrine *tu Dŏmĭne in æternum permănes, et mĕmŏriāle tuum in generātiōnem et generātiōnem*, Ps. Spl. 101, 13.

ge-mittan; *p.* -mitte; *pp.* -mitted *To find, meet*; invĕnīre, obviam hăbēre:—On hwan mæg se iunga, on gōdne weg, rihtan ne rǣdran rǣd gemittan *in quo corrĭgit Jūnior viam suam?* Ps. Th. 118, 9. Gif đū đyslícne þegn gemittest *if thou meetest such a man*, Exon. 84 a; Th. 316, 8; Môd. 45. Hý gemittaþ mearclonde neáh heá hlincas *they meet lofty hills near the border-land*, 101 b; Th. 384, 5; Rä. 4, 23: 117 b; Th. 451, 15; Dôm. 104. Hine gemitte ân man *invēnit eum vir*, Gen. 37, 15: Cd. 103; Th. 137, 2; Gen. 2267. Efne we đás eall on Eufraten sæcgean gehýrdon, syđđan gemittan fôrwel manegu, on wudu-feldum *ecce audīvimus ea in Euphrata, invēnimus ea in campis silvæ*, Ps. Th. 131, 6: Cd. 80; Th. 101, 24; Gen. 1687. Hie æt burhgeate beorn gemitton *they found the chief at the town-gate*, 111; Th. 146, 23; Gen. 2426. Gif gê gemitton Esau mînne brôđur *si obvium hăbuĕris fratrem meum Esau*, Gen. 32, 17.

ge-mitting, -mittung, e; *f. A meeting, an assembly;* congressus:—Heora gemitting wæs æt Trefia đære eá *their meeting was at the river Trebia*, Ors. 4, 8; Bos. 90, 2: 5, 7; Bos. 106, 20, 43. Æt heora gemittinge *in their meeting*, 4, 6; Bos. 85, 26. Wega gemittung *a meeting of ways;* compitum, Ælfc. Gl. 100; Som. 77, 5; Wrt. Voc. 55, 8.

gemme *a* GEM; gemma:—Sweor-gemme *a neck-gem* or *-lace;* monile, Cot. 170.

gêmnis, se; *f. Care, anxiety;* cura:—Ne is đê gêmnise *non est tibi curæ*, Lk. Skt. Lind. 10, 40: 34: Mt. Kmbl. Lind 9, 12. Gêmnisse *sollicitudo*, 13, 22.

ge-môd; *adj.* [môd *mind*] *Of one mind, agreed;* concors:—Đîne freónd næfst đê swâ gemôde swâ swâ đû woldest *thou hast not thy friends in such agreement with thee as thou wouldest*, Shrn. 182, 5. Wæs đû gemôd đînum đæm weđerwearde *esto consentiens adversario tuo*, Mt. Kmbl. Rush. 5, 25. Gemôde *conjurati*, Cot. 36. [Cf. gemêde.]

ge-môdod; *part.* [môd *the mind*] *Minded, disposed;* prōnus, proclīvis:—Sume beóþ þwyrlîce gemôdode *some are perversely minded*, Homl. Th. i. 524, 18.

ge-môdsumian; *p.* ode; *pp.* od *To agree;* concordāre:—We geþiédaþ and gemôdsumiaþ to đæra yfelena freóndscipe *we associate and agree in the friendship of the wicked*, Past. 46, 6; Swt. 355, 7; Hat. MS. 67 b, 18. [*O. H. Ger.* ki-môtsamôn *consacrare*.]

ge-môdsumnes, -ness, e; *f. Agreement, concord;* concordia:—He cýđde đæt he nolde habban nâne gemôdsumnesse wiđ đa yfelan *he proclaimed that he would have no concord with the wicked*, Past. 46, 5; Swt. 353, 4; Hat. MS. 67 a, 21. [Cf. *O.H. Ger.* ki-môtsam *commodus*.]

ge-molsnian; *p.* ode, ade; *pp.* od, ad *To corrupt, decay, wither;* putrefacere, tabefacere, macerare, marcescere:—He đǽr on moldan gemolsnaþ *he shall there rot in the earth*, Blickl. Homl. 109, 32. Mîne herewîc syndon gebrosnode and gemolsnode *my dwellings are decayed and perished*, 113, 26. Gemolsnad flǽsc *tabes*, Ælfc. Gl. 12; Wrt. Voc. 20, 16: Solil. 2. Swâ gemolsnad wyrt *as a withered herb*, Ps. Th. 89, 6. v. molsnian.

ge-molten *molten, melted*. v. ge-meltan.

ge-mon ic, he *I remember, he remembers*, Exon. 74 b; Th. 280, 5; Jul. 624: Beo. Th. 3407; B. 1701. v. ge-munan.

ge-monan *to remember:*—Gemona *recordare*, Lk. Skt. Lind. 16, 25. Seó leó gemonþ [= geman] đæs wildan gewunan hire eldrena [MS. eldrana] *the lioness remembers the wild manner of her parents*, Bt. 25; Fox 88, 12. v. ge-munan.

ge-mone. v. ge-mane.

ge-mong, es; *n. A mixture, crowd, throng, company;* commixtio, turba, cætus:—Đǽr is sib bûtan nîþe hâlgum on gemonge *there is amity without envy among the holy*, Exon. 32 a; Th. 101, 19; Cri. 1661: 59 b; Th. 216, 9; Ph. 265. On gemonge *in the throng*, Beo. Th. 3290; B. 1643. On clǽnra gemong *in the company of the pure*, Exon. 71 b; Th. 267, 24; Jul. 420: Judth. 11; Thw. 24, 17; Jud. 193: 12; Thw. 26, 1; Jud. 304. Wyrta gemong *aromata*, Lk. Skt. Lind. 23, 56. Đæt gemong *mixtura*, Jn. Skt. Lind. 19, 39. v. ge-mang.

ge-mong *among*. v. ge-mang.

ge-monian, -monigan; *p.* ode, ade; *pp.* od, ad *To admonish, exhort, remind:*—Ealle đa gemoniaþ môdes fûsne fêran to sîþe *all these admonish the prompt of mind to go on a journey*, Exon. 82 a; Th. 308, 25; Seef. 50: 88 b; Th. 333, 19; Gn. Ex. 6: 52 a; Th. 182, 22; Gû. 1314: Cd. 49; Th. 63, 9; Gen. 1029. v. ge-manian.

ge-monige *may remind*, Cd. 49; Th. 63, 9; Gen. 1029. v. ge-monian.

ge-monigfealdian; *p.* ode *To increase, multiply;* amplificare:—Đætte gemonigfaldade ꝉ gewôxe *quod abundabat*, Mk. Skt. Lind. 12, 44. Gimonigfalda *multiplica*, Rtl. 8, 90. Gemonigfealdode *multiplied*, Blickl. Homl. 107, 25: Bd. 5, 20; S. 641, 40. v. ge-mænigfealdian.

ge-monnad *manned, supplied with men*. v. ge-mannian.

ge-môt, es; *n. A meeting, coming together,* MOOT, *assembly, council;* conventus, congregatio, concursus:—Gârmitting gumena gemôt wǽpengewrixl *the meeting of spears, concourse of men, exchange of weapons*, Chr. 937; Erl. 114, 16; Æđelst. 50: Exon. 72 a; Th. 268, 3; Jul. 426. Gif he leng bide lâđran gemôtes *if he should longer await a more hostile meeting*, 36 a; Th. 116, 15; Gû. 207: Byrht. Th. 140, 40; By. 301. Híg hæfdon mycel gemôt *they held a great council*, Mt. Bos. 26, 4: 26, 59: 28, 12. Se gedwola cwæþ gemôt ongeán đone bisceop *the heretic proclaimed a council against the bishop*, Homl. Th. i. 290, 12. Đû me oft aweredest wyrigra gemôtes *protexisti me a conventu malignantium*, Ps. Th. 63, 2: Andr. Kmbl. 2120; An. 1061: Exon. 34 a; Th. 109, 31; Gû. 98. Đǽr monig beoþ on gemôt lǽded fore onsýne êces dêman *there many a one shall be brought to the assembly before the face of the eternal Judge*, 19 b; Th. 50, 5; Cri. 795: 21 b; Th. 58, 30; Cri. 943: 23 a; Th. 63, 29; Cri. 1027. On gemôt cuman *to come to the assembly*, Elen. Kmbl. 558; El. 279. Gif hwâ gemôt forsitte *if any one fail to attend the 'gemot,'* L. Athelst. 20; Th. i. 208, 26. Hwî biþ elles ǽlce dæge swelc seófung and swelce geflîtu and gemôt and dômas *why else is every day such sorrow and such contentions and assemblies and judgments*, Bt. 26, 2; Fox 92, 16. ¶ Witena gemôt *an assembly of the wise* [sapientum conventus, Bd. 3, 5; S. 527, 23]; *the supreme council of the Anglo-Saxon nation or parliament.* Mr. Kemble, in his 'Saxons in England,' vol. ii. page 203, A. D. 1849, says—'The proper [Anglo-] Saxon name for these assemblies was Witena gemôt, literally *the meeting of the witan* [or *the wise* or *experienced*]; but we also find,—Micel gemôt *the great meeting;* Sinoþlîc gemôt *the synodal meeting;* Seonoþ *the synod.* The Latin names are Concĭlium, Conventus, Synŏdus, Synŏdāle concĭliābŭlum, and the like. Although synŏdus and seonoþ might more properly be confined to ecclesiastical conventions, the Saxons do not appear to have made any distinction; probably because ecclesiastical and secular regulations were made by the same body, and at the same time. . . . It is very probable that the . . . system of separate houses for the clergy and laity prevailed . . . , and that merely ecclesiastical affairs were decided by the king and clergy alone. It is probable that even in strictly ecclesiastical synods, the king had a presidency at least, as head of the church in his dominions, Cod. Dipl. 116; A. D. 767; Kmbl. i. 142, 143. There are some acts [of the Witena Gemôt], in which the signatures are those of clergymen only, others in which the clerical signatures are followed and, as it were, confirmed by those of the laity; and in one remarkable case of this kind, the king signs at the head of each list, as if he had in fact affixed his mark successively in the two houses, as president of each.' See above, Cod. Dipl. 116. Se cyng hæfde đǽr [MS. đæs] on morgen witena gemôt *on the morrow the king* [*Edward*] *had there a meeting of the wise*, Chr. 1052; Erl. 181, 9. Wæs đâ witena gemôt *then there was a meeting of the wise*, 1052; Erl. 184, 35. Hæfde Eádwerde cing witena gemôt on Lunden *king Edward had a meeting of the wise in London*, 1050; Erl. 176, 9. See also Stubbs' Const. Hist. i. cap. vi. Bisceopa gemôt *a meeting of bishops*, Bd. 1, 14: S. 482, 35. Be gemôtum *of moots*. And sêce man hundred-gemôt swâ hit ǽr geset wæs; hæbbe man þrîwa on geáre burh-gemôt; and tûwa, scir-gemôt, and đǽr beó on đære scire biscop and se ealdorman, and đǽr ǽgđer tǽcan ge Godes riht ge woruld-riht *and let the hundred-moot be attended as it was before fixed; and thrice in the year let a city-moot be held; and twice a shire-moot; and let there be present the bishop of the shire and the alderman, and there each expound both God's law* [*right*] *and the world's law*, L. Edg. ii. 5; Th. i. 268, 1-5. Đâs gemôt *these moots*, ii. 7; Th. i. 268, 15. See Schmid A. S. Gesetz. 595-6. DER. burh-gemôt, folc-, halle-, hundred-, scir-.

gemôt-ærn, -ern, es; *n.* [gemôt; ærn, ern *a place*] *A meeting-place, senate-house, hall;* conveniendi locus, aula:—Ahleópon đâ ealle, and hine mid heora metseaxum ofsticedon on heora gemôtærne [MS. gemôterne] *then* [*the consuls and the senate*] *all jumped up, and stabbed him* [*Julius Cæsar*] *with their daggers in their senate-house*, Ors. 5, 12; Bos. 112, 25. Gemôtern *in pretorio*, Mt. Kmbl. Lind. 27, 27.

ge-môtod *discussed*, Th. Chart. 172, 10. v. môtian.

gemôt-stede, es; *m. A meeting-place;* convĕniendi lŏcus:—On gemôtstede manna and engla *in the meeting-place of men and angels*, Soul. Kmbl. 296; Seel. 152.

gemôt-stôw, e; *f.* [gemôt, stôw *a place*] *A meeting-place, council;* conveniendi locus, concilium:—Gemôtstôw *vel* ceorla samnung *a meeting-place* or *a meeting of freemen;* compita, Ælfc. Gl. 55; Som. 66, 110; Wrt. Voc. 36, 32. Ic ne sæt mid gemôtstôwe ydelnyssa *non sedi cum concilio vanitatis*, Ps. Spl. T. 25, 4.

ge-mun; *adj. Mindful, having a recollection:*—Swâ gemune menn wǽron ǽlces brôces *men had such a recollection of every trouble*, Ors. 1, 10; Bos. 34, 2. v. ge-myne.

ge-munan; ic, he -man, -mon, *pl.* -munon; *also* ic -mune, he -monþ, *pl.* -munaþ; *p.* -munde; *pp.* -munen [*a verb whose present tense is the past tense of a lost strong verb, cf. Lat.* memini]; *with gen. and acc. To remember, bear in mind, consider;* recordari, memorari, meminisse, meditari:—Gemunan his hâlegan cýđnesse *memorari testamenti sui sancti*, Lk. Bos. 1, 72. Gif he ne wile mid inneweardre heortan gemunan and geþencean *if he will not with sincere heart bear in mind and consider*, Blickl. Homl. 55, 11. Hie nellaþ gemunan đone dæg heora forþfôre *they will not remember the day of their departure*, 61, 4. Ne geman heó đære hefinysse *non meminit pressuræ*, Jn. Bos. 16, 21. Gif he đæt eal gemon *if he remembers that all*, Beo. Th. 2375; B. 1185. Ic đê đæs leán geman *I will remember a reward for thee for it*, 2445; B. 1220. Ic gemune đê *recordor tui*, Ælfc. Gr. 41; Som. 44, 2. Ic gemuna *meditabor*,

Ps. Spl. 62, 7. Seó leó gemonþ ðæs wildan gewunan hire eldrana *the lioness remembers the wild manner of her parents*, Bt. 25; Fox 88, 12. Hie ðæt eall gemunan and ðurh ðæt leóht gemanode beóþ *they remember all that and are admonished by the light*, Blickl. Homl. 129, 21: Bt. 16, 1; Fox 48, 30. Hie gemunaþ ða mycclan eádmōdnesse *they recollect his great humility*, Blickl. Homl. 129, 10. Ðonne gē gemunaþ Drihten eówerne God *when ye remember the Lord your God*, Deut. 4, 29. Ðā gemunde God sunu Lameches *then God remembered Lamech's son*, Cd. 71; Th. 84, 33; Gen. 1407: 121; Th. 156, 8; Gen. 2585. Hīg gemundon his worda *recordati sunt verborum ejus*, Lk. Bos. 24, 8. Gemundon weardas wīg-leóþ *the watchmen remembered the war-song*, 154; Th. 191, 26; Exod. 220. Gemun ðīn mann-weorod *memento congregationis tui*, Ps. Th. 73, 2. Gemune ðū manigra bearna ðe on Edom synt *memento filiorum Edom*, 136, 7: 118, 49: Ps. Spl. 24, 6. Gemunaþ mīnre sprǣce *mementote sermonis mei*, Jn. Bos. 15, 20. Gemunaþ ðæt gē silfe wǣron þeówe on Egipta lande *remember that ye yourselves were slaves in Egypt*, Deut. 5, 15; Exon. 75 a; Th. 281, 4; Jul. 641. Gemunon we ūre dæghwamlīcan synna *let us be mindful of our daily sins*, Blickl. Homl. 25, 14: Cd. 217; Th. 277, 11; Sat. 202. Gif hī ða geearnunga ealle gemundon *if they had remembered all the benefits*, Byrht. Th. 137, 35. Ne biþ gemunen *non memoretur*, Ps. Spl. 82, 4. v. munan.

ge-mund *meditation;* meditatio, Som.

ge-mundbyrdan; *p.* de; *pp.* ed [mundbyrd *protection*] *To protect, defend, patronize;* protĕgĕre, tuēri:—Ða ic fōr God wille gemundbyrdan *whom I will protect before God*, Cd. 113; Th. 149, 11; Gen. 2473. Ðæt he hine gemundbyrde *that he would protect him*, Bt. 35, 6; Fox 168, 21.

ge-mundian *to protect:*—Mildheortnys āna gemundaþ us on ðam micelum dōme *mercy alone will protect us at the great doom*, Homl. Th. ii. 102, 5. Gemunde ðisne heáp *protect this assembly*, H. R. 103, 31.

gēmung, e; *f. A marriage;* nuptiæ:—Ðe worhte gēmunge sunu his *qui fecit nubtias filio suo*, Mt. Kmbl. Rush. 22, 2: 3: 25, 10. Se ðe worhte gīmungo bearne his *qui fecit nuptias filio suo*, Rtl. 107, 15. Gīmungana *nuptiarum*, 108, 19: 109, 23. [Cf. [?] *O.H.Ger.* gauma *epulæ; and* farmum ꝉ gereordum *nuptias*, Mt. Kmbl. p. 19, 4.] v. gȳmung.

gēmungian *to marry:*—Gimungia *nubat*, Rtl. 109, 35.

gēmunglīc; *adj. Belonging to a marriage, nuptial;* nuptialis:—Hrægl gēmunglīc *vestis nubtialis*, Mt. Kmbl. Rush. 22, 12: 11. Gīmungalīc *nuptialis*, Rtl. 108, 1.

ge-myltan, -miltan, -mieltan; *pp.* ed *To cause to melt, soften:*—Gold ðæt biþ ðurh ofnes fȳr gemylted *gold that is melted by the fire of the furnace*, Elen. Kmbl. 2621; El. 1312. Gemyltyd is eorðe *liquefacta est terra*, Ps. Spl. C. 74, 3. Woldon ellenrōfes mōd gemiltan *they wished to subdue the bold man's courage*, Andr. Kmbl. 2785; An. 1395. v. gemieltan.

ge-mynan; *p.* de *To remember, remind:*—Dryhten gemynest ðū ðæt se forlǣrd cwæþ *sir, dost thou remember that that deceiver said?* Mt. Kmbl. Rush. 27, 63. Ðū nū gemyndest ða word ðe ic ðē sǣde *thou now rememberest the words that I said to thee*, Bt. 35, 2; Fox 156, 21. Ðæt he mec bī noman mīnum gemyne *that he remember me by name*, Exon. 76 a; Th. 215, 28; Jul. 721. Gie gemynan *reminiscamini*, Jn. Skt. Lind. 16, 4. Gemyne ðū ðæt ðū ðisne ele send on ða sǣ *tu memento ut hoc oleum mittas in mare*, Bd. 3, 15; S. 541, 33. Gemyne ðē sylfne hū mycel yfel ðē gelamp *remember how great an evil befell thee*, Blickl. Homl. 31, 12. Gemyne ðis *remember this*, 113, 23, 24: 225, 21: Exon. 81 a; Th. 305, 25; Fä. 93: Beo. Th. 1322; B. 659. God gemyne ðū Eádfriþ *O God, remember Eadfrith*, Mk. Skt. p. 1, 4. Gemynas gie *mementote*, Jn. Skt. Lind. 15, 20. v. ge-munan.

ge-mynd, es; *n:* e; *f. Mind, memory, memorial, memento, remembrance, commemoration:*—He fæste on gemynde hæfde *he had fast in mind;* memoriter retinuit, Bd. 4, 24; S. 597, 26. Gecerre hine to his gemynde *let him have recourse to his memory*, Bt. 35, 1; Fox 156, 10. Ðæs mannes sāwl hæfþ on hire þreó þing, ðæt is gemynd and andgit and willa. Ðurh ðæt gemynd se man geþencþ ða þing ðe he gehȳrde oððe geseah oððe geleornode *man's soul has in it three things, that is memory and understanding and will. By the memory a man recollects the things that he has heard or seen or learned*, Homl. Th. i. 288, 18–21: 28. Tubal Cain ðurh mōdes gemynd sulh-geweorces fruma wæs *Tubal Cain was the originator of plough-work by thought of mind*, Cd. 52; Th. 66, 16; Gen. 1085: Exon. 17 b; Th. 41, 33; Cri. 665: Bt. Met. Fox 22, 115; Met. 22, 58. Ðǣr se wīsdōm ā wunaþ on gemyndum *there wisdom ever dwells in mind*, 7, 79; Met. 7, 39. Me hæfþ ðeós gnornung ðære gemynde benumen *this grief has deprived me of the recollection*, Bt. 5, 3; Fox 12, 20. We witon swīþe lytel ðæs ðe ǣr us wæs būton be gemynde and be geacsunge *we know very little of that which was before us except by memory and by inquiry*, 42; Fox 256, 25. Heora gemynd is forgiten *the memory of them is forgotten*, Swt. A. S. Rdr. 57, 13. Ic wilnode ðǣm monnum to lǣfanne ðe æfter me wǣren mīn gemynd on gōdum weorcum *I desired to leave to the men that should be after me my memory in good works*, Bt. 17; Fox 60, 16; Blickl. Homl. 197, 5. Ðīn gemynd *memoriale tuum*, Ps. Th. 101, 10: Blickl. Homl. 171, 32. Ðis wæs gedōn on mīn gemynd *this was done in remembrance of me*, 69, 20. Ðæs hālgan biscopes gemynd *the commemoration of the holy bishop*, Shrn. 78, 23: 86, 29: 105, 30. Mannum to ēcre gemynde *for a perpetual remembrance to men*, 127, 22; 189, 15. Ðis to gemyndum habban *to have this as a memento*, 113, 34: Beo. Th. 5600; B. 2804. Ne cwæþ he ðæt nā forðon ðe him wǣre ǣnig gemynd ðearfendra manna *he did not say that because he minded about the needy*, Blickl. Homl. 69, 10: 61, 25: 83, 16. Swā ic ðīn gemynd rihte begange *sic memor fui tui*, Ps. Th. 62, 6: 108, 16. Us is mid mycelre gemynde to geþencenne *we must bear well in mind*, Blickl. Homl. 29, 2. Gimynd *commemoratio*, Rtl. 62, 21. In gemyndum to habbanne *to be had in mind*, Nar. 4, 9: 2, 8. [*Goth.* gamunds; *f. remembrance: O.H.Ger.* gi-munt; *f.*]

ge-mynd-benimming, e; *f. Lethargy*, Lye.

ge-mynd-dæg, es; *m. A commemoration day, day of birth* or *of death:*—Ðære abbudissan gemynd-dæg *cujus natalis*, Bd. 3, 8; S. 532, 39. Ðȳ dæge ðe his gemynd-dæg wǣre *die depositionis ejus*, Bd. 4, 30; S. 608, 35: Th. Chart. 496, 4.

ge-mynd-drepen, e; *f. A mind stroke, a swoon, delirium;* mentis percussio:—On gemynd-drepen *in his mind's swoon*, Cd. 76; Th. 94, 34; Gen. 1571. Grn. *has*,—On gemynd drepen; *pp. of* drepan. DER. drepen.

ge-myndelīc; *adj. Belonging to memory, memorable;* mĕmŏriālis, mĕmŏrābilis:—Gemyndelīc *mĕmŏriālis*, Ælfc. Gr. 9, 28; Som. 11, 35. Ðyssum tīdum wæs sum gemyndelīc wundor, and ealdum wundrum gelīc on Breotone geworden *his tempŏrĭbus mīrācŭlum mĕmŏrābĭle, et antīquōrum simĭle in Britannia factum est*, Bd. 5, 12; S. 627, 4: 3, 16; S. 542, 14.

ge-myndelīce; *adv. By memory, without book;* mĕmŏrĭter, sĭne libro:—Lǣraþ ðisne cantic Israēla bearn, ðæt hīg hine gemyndelīce singon, and sī me to tācne ðis leóþ gemang Israēla folce *cantĭcum istud dŏcēte fīlios Israel, ut mĕmŏrĭter tĕneant et ore decantent, et sit mihi carmen istud pro testĭmōnio inter fīlios Israel*, Deut. 31, 19.

ge-myndig, -mindig; *adj. Mindful, remembering;* mĕmor:—Wæs he gemyndig his bebodes *ipsi mĕmor præcepti ejus*, Bd. 4, 25; S. 600, 14: Ps. Spl. 118, 52. Wæs heó þearle gemyndig, hū heó ðone atolan eáðost mihte ealdre benǣman *she was very mindful how she might easiest deprive the fell one of life*, Judth. 10; Thw. 22, 23; Jud. 74: Ps. Th. 73, 21: 82, 4. Hȳ nǣron gemyndige manigfealdnesse mildheortnesse ðīnre *non fuērunt mĕmŏres multĭtūdĭnis mĭsĕrĭcordiæ tuæ*, Ps. Lamb. 105, 7. Beóþ hyra geóca gemyndge *they are mindful of their safety*, Exon. 33 b; Th. 107, 18; Gū. 60: 39 a; Th. 129, 7; Gū. 417. Gemyndigra monna *of mindful men*, 34 b; Th. 111, 11; Gū. 125.

ge-myndigian; *p.* ode, ade; *pp.* od, ad *To remember, be mindful of, call to mind:*—Gemyndga cȳðnise *memorari testamenti*, Lk. Skt. Lind. 1, 72. Ic gemyndige ða mǣran Raab and Babilonis *memor ero Rahab et Babylonis*, Ps. Th. 86, 2. Ðæt ðū ne gemyndgast æfter mandreáme ne gewittes wāst būtan wildeóra ðeáw *that thou shalt not understand after the manner of the joy of man, nor know aught but the manner of wild beasts*, Cd. 203; Th. 251, 29; Dan. 571. Cwoen sūðerne gemyndgade *reginam austri commemorans*, Mt. Kmbl. p. 16, 19. Ic God gemyndgade *memor fui Dei*, Ps. Th. 76, 3: 135, 24: 142, 5. Gemyndga mīnes *memineris mei*, Mt. Kmbl. p. 4, 9. Gemyndgad biþ *memoratur*, p. 16, 15: Lk. Skt. Lind. 1, 54. [*O. H. Ger.* gi-muntigōn *to remember.*]

ge-myndleás; *adj. Senseless, witless;* amens:—Sum gemyndleás wīf *a witless woman*, Homl. Th. ii. 188, 14. Gemyndleás *demens*, Ælfc. Gr. 47; Som. 48, 38.

ge-mynd-stōw, e; *f. A monument:*—Gemyndstōwa *monumenta*, Mt. Bos. 23, 29.

ge-myne; *adj. Mindful:*—Gif ðū ðǣr gemyne bist *si ibi recordatus fueris*, Mt. Kmbl. Rush. 5, 23.

ge-mynegian; *p.* ode; *pp.* od *To call to mind, remember, mention, admonish:*—He eall ða he in gehērnesse geleornian mihte mid hine gemynegode *ipse cuncta quæ audiendo discere poterat rememorando secum*, Bd. 4, 24; S. 598, 6. We gemynegodon *commemoravimus*, 1, 11; S. 480, 18. Ne gemynega ðū me mīnra firena ðe ic geong dyde *delicta juventulis meæ ne memineris*, Ps. Ben. 24, 6. Ðā wearþ he on swefne gemynegod *then was he admonished in a dream*, Homl. Th. i. 88, 22. Gemyngad *admonitus*, Mt. Kmbl. Rush. 2, 22: Mt. Bos. 14, 8. Seó gemynegode cyninges dōhter *memorata regis filia*, Bd. 3, 24; S. 557, 3. v. mynegian.

ge-myntan; *p.* -mynte; *pp.* -mynted, -mynt *To determine, resolve;* stătuĕre, decernĕre:—Gregorius gemunde hwæt he gefyrn Angel-cynne gemynte *Gregory remembered what he of old had determined for the English race*, Homl. Th. ii. 126, 25. He befran hwam ða gebytlu gemynte wǣron. Him wæs gesǣd ðæt hī wǣron gemynte ānum sutere *he asked for whom those buildings were intended. He was told that they were meant for a shoemaker*, 354, 35. Hæfdon hie gemynted to ðam *they had resolved thereon*, Cd. 153; Th. 190, 10; Exod. 197. Ic hæfde gemynt ðē to ārwurþienne on ǣhtum and on feó *decrēvĕram quidem* *magnĭfĭce hŏnŏrāre te*, Num. 24, 11: Gen. 18, 33: Bd. 3, 9; S. 534, 3: Homl. Th. ii. 548, 31.

ge-myrran; *p.* de; *pp.* ed *To hinder, obstruct, force, trouble;* impedire, turbare, obstruere:—Mōde gemyrde *disturbed in mind*, Andr. Kmbl. 1491; An. 747: Ps. Th. 62, 9: Exon. 71 b; Th. 267, 8; Jul. 412. v. myrran.

ge-mȳþ; *pl. n. The mouth of a river;* ostium fluminis:—Æt ðām gemȳðum Tyne streámes *juxta ostium Tini fluminis*, Bd. 5, 6; S. 618, 28: Cod. Dipl. Kmbl. iii. 48, 26. [*O. H. Ger.* ge-mundi *ostia.*]

GĒN, gién; *adv. Again, moreover, besides, at length, yet, hitherto;* iterum, denuo, adhuc, insuper, denique:—Ðǽr he gēn ligeþ *there he still lies*, Exon. 18 b; Th. 46, 9; Cri. 734. Swā he nū gēn dēþ *as he still does*, Beo. Th. 5711; B. 2589: Exon. 29 a; Th. 89, 17; Cri. 1458. Bidon ealle ðǽr tyn niht ðā gēn *all waited there yet ten nights*, 15 b; Th. 34, 15; Cri. 542. Ðā gién wæs yrre God *God was yet angry*, Cd. 131; Th. 166, 1; Gen. 2741. Wæs Iustus ðā gēn lifigende *Iustus adhuc superstes*, Bd. 2, 7; S. 509, 10. Ðæs gēn to tācne is *of that further is as proof*, 6; S. 508, 42. Ic sceal forð sprecan gēn ymb Grendel *I shall go on to speak further about Grendel*, Beo. Th. 4146; B. 2070: Exon. 96 b; Th. 360, 5; Wal. 1: Elen. Kmbl. 2434; El. 1218. Gién ðē sunu weorðeþ *yet there shall be a son to thee*, Cd. 100; Th. 132, 19; Gen. 2195. Gēn ic ðē feores unnan wille *yet will I grant thee life*, Exon. 68 b; Th. 254, 3; Jul. 191. Ðā gēn Abrahame eówde heáhcyning *again the high king appeared to Abraham*, Cd. 98; Th. 130, 23; Gen. 2164. Ðā gién seó fǽmne spræc *then again spoke the woman*, Exon. 71 b; Th. 267, 19; Jul. 417. Geornor ðonne he gēn dyde *more eagerly than yet he had done*, 67 a; Th. 249, 12; Jul. 110. Gēn strengre is *it is yet harder*, 10 b; Th. 12, 28; Cri. 192: 95 b; Th. 357, 14; Pa. 28: 97 a; Th. 363, 8; Wal. 50.

gēn, gegn [?]; *adj. Direct, short, near* [*of a road*]:—Ðe ða gēnran wegas cūðan ðara sīðfato *qui brevitates itinerum noverant*, Nar. 6, 7. [*O. E.* gein, v. Stratmann: *North E.* and *Scot.* gane, 'the ganest way:' *Icel.* gegn, 'hinn gegnsta vegr.']

gēna; *adv. Yet, still, further*:—Ðafodest ðū gēna ðæt me þeówmennen drehte *thou hast still permitted the slave-woman to vex me*, Cd. 102; Th. 135, 21; Gen. 2246. Næbbe ic synne wiþ hie gefremed gēna *I have not committed sin against her yet*, 125; Th. 160, 17; Gen. 2651. Nū gēna *still at the present time*, Exon. 34 b: Th. 111, 13; Gū. 126. Ic eom gēna swētran *I am yet sweeter*, 111 a; Th. 425, 19; Rä. 41, 58. Ic wille ðē ānre nū gēna bēne biddan *I will of thee one more boon require*, Andr. Kmbl. 950; An. 475. Mycel is nū gēna lād ofer lagustreám *great is now still our voyage over the lake-stream*, 844; An. 422. Cwico wæs ðā gēna *was still living*, Beo. Th. 6178; B. 3093. v. gēn, geóna.

ge-nacian; *p.* ode, ede, *pl.* odon, edon; *pp.* od, ed *To make naked* or *bare;* nudare, nudum facere:—Menigo genacedon ðæt hūs *turba nudaverunt tectum*, Mk. Skt. Lind. 2, 4. DER. nacian.

ge-nacodian; *p.* ode, ade; *pp.* od, ad *To make bare, naked, to strip;* nudare:—He hine middangeardes þingum ongyrede and genacodade [genacode?] *he unclothed and stripped himself of worldly things*, Bd. 4, 3; S. 567, 24. DER. nacodian, nacod.

ge-næfd; *part. p. Not had*:—Ðonne sint hie ðē pleólīcran gehæfd ðonne genæfd *then are they more dangerous to thee had than not had*, Bt. 14, 1; Fox 42, 22.

ge-nǽgan, -nēgan; *p.* de; *pp.* ed; *c. acc. pers: gen. inst. rei To approach one with anything, address, approach, assail, assault;* adire aliquem aliqua re, appellare, instare alicui, urgere, tribulare:—Hio sió cwēn ongan wordum genēgan *the queen began to address them with words*, Elen. Kmbl. 769; El. 385. Þeóf ðe eorlas ungearwe yfles genǽgeþ *the thief who assaults with evil unprepared men*, Exon. 20 b; Th. 54, 28; Cri. 875. Ðā hyne gesōhton Heaðoscylfingas, nīða genǽgdon [MS. gehnægdan] *when the martial Scylfings him sought* [*and*] *assailed* [*him*] *in the wars*, Beo. Th. 4418; B. 2206. Nearwum genǽged nȳd-costingum *assailed with painful troubles*, Exon. 49 b; Th. 171, 13; Cri. 1126.

ge-nǽged [= gehnǽged]; *part. p. Subdued, humbled;* subactus, Mt. Kmbl. Rush. 23, 12.

ge-nægled; *part. p. Nailed*:—Genæglad on rōde *nailed on the cross*, Mt. Kmbl. Lind. 27, 22, 26, 31: Exon. 90 b; Th. 339, 14; Gn. Ex. 94. Genæglod, Homl. Th. i. 82, 25.

ge-næs, -nǽson *saved.* v. ge-nesan.

ge-nǽstan; *p.* te *To contend*:—Se ðe wiþ mægenðisan mīnre genǽsteþ *he that contends against my main force*, Exon. 107 b; Th. 410, 3; Rä. 28, 10. [Cf. ge-nǽtan.]

ge-nǽtan; *pp.* -nǽt *To afflict, trouble*:—Ða underðiéddan mon sceal lǽran ðæt hie elles ne sién genǽt ne geirmed *illos ne subjectio conterat*, Past. 28, 1; Swt. 189, 16; Hat. MS. Ðonne genǽt he hine *humiliabit eum*, Ps. Th. 9, 30. [*Goth.* ga-naitjan *to maltreat.*]

ge-nāg *or* **-nag** [?] *incumbens* [Grn.], *urgens* [Ettm.], Exon. 95 a; Th. 354, 38, 40; Reim. 57, 58.

ge-namian; *p.* ode; *pp.* od [nama *a name*] *To name, call, appoint;* appellare, vocare:—And Adam ðā genamode ealle nȳtenu heora namum *and Adam then named all cattle by their names;* appellavitque omne jumentum nominibus suis, Gen. 2, 20. Hī wurdon genamode to ðam ylcan gewinne ðe heora fæderas on wǽron *they were nominated to the same warfare in which their fathers were*, Homl. Th. ii. 500, 4: i. 88, 3. Būtan ðære mægðe Leui ðe næs genamod ðǽr *to besides the tribe of Levi that was not named amongst them*, Swt. Rdr. 63, 224: Homl. Th. i. 282, 20. DER. namian, nama. v. ge-nomian.

ge-namne = ge-numne [?]. v. ge-niman.

ge-nāp *darkened; p. of* ge-nīpan.

ge-nāpan; *p.* -neóp, *pl.* -neópon; *pp.* -nāpen *To overwhelm;* incumbere, obrepere, supervenire:—Se ðe feóndum geneóp *who overwhelmed the foes*, Cd. 166; Th. 207, 32; Exod. 475. v. nāpan.

gēn-cyme, es; *m. A meeting;* conventus, Ps. Spl. T. 63, 2.

gende = gengde, Beo. Th. 2806; B. 1401. Grein however compares *Icel.* gana *to rush.*

ge-neádian, -nēdian; *p.* ode; *pp.* od *To compel*:—Nolde swā-ðeáh nǽnne to cristendōme geneádian *he would not however compel any one to christianity*, Homl. Th. ii. 130, 14: i. 70, 25. Næs Iohannes mid ēhtnysse geneádod ðæt he Criste wiðsōce *John was not compelled by persecution to deny Christ*, i. 484, 31: 88, 1. Geneádige *urgent*, Ps. Lamb. 68, 16. We bióþ genēdode *we are forced*, Past. 53; Swt. 417, 30; Hat. MS.

ge-neah, es; *n. f.* [?] *Sufficiency, abundance*:—Mid geneahe *abundantly*, Vercel. Kmbl. ii. 81, 68; Leás. 36. [Cf. *Goth.* ga-nauha *sufficiency: O. H. Ger.* gi-nogi, Grff. ii. 1008.]

ge-neah *it is sufficient;* sufficit, Exon. 93 a; Th. 348, 29; Sch. 35. v. ge-nugan.

ge-neahhe, -neahe, -nehhe, -nehe; *adv. Enough, sufficiently, abundantly, frequently, very much, earnestly, instantly;* satis, sufficienter, frequenter, valde, sedulo, instanter:—Ðara ðe geneahhe noman scyppendes hergan willaþ *of those who sufficiently will praise the creator's name*, Exon. 8 b; Th. 4, 5; Cri. 48: Elen. Kmbl. 2313; El. 1158: Beo. Th. 1570; B. 783. Nū ic his geneahhe neósan wille *now I will frequently visit him*, Exon. 43 a; Th. 145, 7; Gū. 691: 100 b; Th. 379, 13; Deór. 32: 77 a; Th. 289, 31; Wand. 56. He wyscte geneahhe, ðæt . . . *he wished earnestly, that* . . . , 100 b; Th. 378, 33; Deór. 25: Ps. Th. 62, 8: 63, 1: 65, 13: 87, 3: 114, 4: 137, 7: 149, 1. Swīðe genehhe *very frequently*, Hy. 3, 42; Hy. Grn. ii. 282, 42; L. E. I. 10; Th. ii. 408, 25. Geneahe *sufficiently*, Cd. 137; Th. 172, 12; Gen. 2843. Genehe *abundantly*, Byrht. Th. 139, 45; By. 269. Ðǽr genehost brægd eorl Beówulfes ealde lāfe *then very frequently drew a warrior of Beowulf's an ancient relic* [i. e. *very many of Beowulf's warriors*, etc.], Beo. Th. 1593; B. 794. DER. swīð-geneahhe.

ge-neahhie, -neahhige, -nehhige; *adv. Enough, sufficiently, abundantly, frequently, very much, earnestly, instantly;* satis, sufficienter, frequenter, valde, sedulo, instanter, Ps. Th. 55, 7: 67, 4: 118, 25: 65, 3: 70, 5: 85, 3. DER. swīð-geneahhige.

ge-neáhsen; *adj. Near*:—Hwīlum mōna sunnan sīnes leóhtes bereáfaþ ðonne hit gebyrigan mæg ðæt swā geneáhsne weorðaþ *sometimes the moon deprives the sun of its light when it happens that they get so near*, Bt. Met. Fox 4, 23; Met. 4, 12.

ge-neálǽcan, -lǽcean; *p.* -lǽhte; *pp.* -lǽht *To approach, draw near, adhere* [*with dat. and acc.*]:—Ne dorstan hie ðære stōwe geneálǽcan *they durst not approach the place*, Blickl. Homl. 199, 26. Hī ne dorston hine geneálǽcan *they durst not approach him*, 243, 13. Geneálǽcean, 77, 11: Shrn. 76, 29. Nū geneálǽceþ mīnum gebedum ðæt ic bidde on ðīnre gesihþe *appropiet oratio mea in conspectu tuo*, Ps. Th. 118, 169. Geneálǽcþ *adhæret*, Ps. Spl. C. 93, 20. He him geneálǽhte *he drew near to him*, Blickl. Homl. 15, 24: 67, 2. Geneáhlǽhte *adhæsit*, Ps. Spl. C. 101, 6. Me geneálǽhton *me appropinquaverunt*, Ps. Spl. 37, 11. Hī geneálæhton *acceleraverunt*, Ps. Lamb. 15, 4. Folce geneálǽcendum *populo appropinquanti*, Ps. Spl. 148, 14.

ge-neálǽcing, e; *f. An approach*:—Toforan ðære geneálǽcincge ðæs fefores *before the access of the fever*, Herb. 160; Lchdm. i. 288, 11.

ge-neán *to draw near, cleave, adhere*:—Gineá ðū dōast *inherere facias*, Rtl. 34, 28. Ðes cwom ł geneó *hic accessit*, Mt. Kmbl. Lind. 27, 58. v. ge-nēhwian.

ge-near, -ner *a refuge, protection;* refugium:—Genear [gener, Lamb.] mīn eart ðū *refugium meum es tu*, Ps. Spl. 90, 2. v. ge-ner.

ge-nearwian; *p.* ode, ade; *pp.* od, ad, ot *To narrow, straiten, constrain, confine, oppress, afflict*:—Hwīlum mec mīn freá fæste genearwaþ *sometimes my master fast confines me*, Exon. 101 b; Th. 382, 24; Rä. 4, 1. Swā hit is genearwed *so is it narrowed*, Bt. 18, 1; Fox 62, 24. Fæste genearwad *fast confined*, Exon. 126 a; Th. 484, 8; Rä. 70, 4. Mid eofer-spreótum hearde genearwod *hard pressed with boar-spears*, Beo. Th. 2881; B. 1438. Mid weres egsan hearde genearwod *with the fear of man sorely oppressed*, Cd. 43; Th. 56, 32; Gen. 921: 123; Th. 157, 9; Gen. 2603. Genearwad biþ heorte mīn *anxiaretur cor meum*, Ps. Spl. 60, 2. v. ge-nyrwian.

ge-neát, es; *m. A companion, associate, vassal*:—Big-standaþ me strange geneátas ða ne willaþ me æt ðam strīðe geswīcan *strong companions stand by me who will not fail me at the strife*, Cd. 15; Th. 18, 36;

Gen. 284. Geneát *inquilinus*, Cot. 108: *parasitus*, 152. Byrhtwold wæs eald geneát [or eald-geneát, *q. v.*] Be cynínges geneáte *of a king's 'geneat,'* L. In. 19; Th. i. 114, 9: Chr. 897; Erl. 96, 3. Be ðon ðe monnes geneát stalige *in case a man's 'geneát' steal*, L. In. 22; Th. i. 116, 9. [*Icel.* nautr: *O. H. Ger.* ganōz, Grff. ii. 1125: *Ger.* genoss.] v. Stubbs' Const. Hist. i. 149; Kemble's 'Saxons in England,' i. c. vii; Schmid A. S. Ger. s. v. DER. beód-, heorþ-geneát.

ge-neát-land, es; *n. Land granted for services* or *rent*:—Ǽgðer ge of ðegnes inlande ge of geneát-lande *both from a thane's inland and from 'geneát-land,'* L. Eádg. I, 1; Th. i. 262, 8. v. in-land.

ge-neát-man, -mann, es; *m.* [v. ge-neát] *A tenant, one holding land on payment of rent, '* gafol':'—Gif geneátmanna hwilc forgȳmeleásaþ his hlāfordes gafol *if any 'geneat-man' neglect the tribute due to his lord*, L. Eádg. Suppl; Th. i. 270, 16.

ge-neát-riht, es; *n. The conditions regulating the tenure of the 'geneát-land*:'—Geneát-riht is mistlic be ðam ðe on lande stænt. On sumon he sceal land-gafol syllan . . . *villani rectum est varium et multiplex secundum quod in terra statutum est. In quibusdam terris debet dare land-gablum* . . . , LL. Th. i. 115, note.

ge-neát-scōlu, e; *f. A band of companions*:—Ða ðegnas seó geneát-scōlu, Exon. 75 b; Th. 283, 22; Jul. 684.

ge-nec *a light ship, a frigate*; liburnica, Cot. 120. v. naca.

ge-nēdan, -niedan, -nȳdan; *p.* de; *pp.* ed *To compel, force, urge*:—Ðū tunglu genēdest ðæt hí ðē to hēraþ *thou compellest the stars to obey thee*, Bt. Met. Fox 4, 9; Met. 4, 5: 4, 30; Met. 4, 15. Seðe ðec genēdes *quicunque te angariaberit*, Mt. Kmbl. Lind. 5, 41. Sihhem geniédde ðæt mǣden *Sichem forced the maiden*, Past. 53, 5; Swt. 415, 22; Hat. MS. Genēddon Simon *angariaverunt Simonem*, Mk. Skt. Lind. 15, 21. Ealle Asiam hȳ genȳddon ðæt hí him gafol guldon *they compelled all Asia to pay them tribute*, Ors. 1, 10; Bos. 32, 28. He næs nō genēded *he was not compelled*, Blickl. Homl. 29, 15. Ðæt Bryttas mid ðȳ mǣrran hungre genēdde ða elreordian adrifan *ut Brittōnes fame famosa coacti barbaros pepulerint*, Bd. 1, 14; S. 482, 12.

ge-nēdedlīc; *adj. Compulsory, forced*; coactus:—He geleornade ðæt Cristes þeówdōm sceolde beón wilsumlīc, nalæs genēdedlīc *didĭcērat servĭtium Christi voluntārium, non coactitium esse debēre*, Bd. 1, 26; S. 488, 18.

ge-nefa, an; *m. A nephew*; nepos:—Caius his [Agustuses] genefa nolde gebiddan to ðam ælmihtigum Gode *Caius his [Augustus's] nephew would not worship the almighty God*, Ors. 6, 1; Bos. 116, 18.

ge-nēgan; *p.* de; *pp.* ed *To approach one with anything, to address*, Elen. Kmbl. 769: El. 385. v. ge-nǣgan.

ge-neh; *adv. Enough, sufficiently, abundantly*:—Ðonne sceolon we geneh geþencean emb ūre sāula ðearfa *then ought we to consider very much about our souls' needs*, Blickl. Homl. 101, 32. v. ge-neahhe.

ge-nehhe, -nehe *enough, frequently*, L. E. I. 10; Th. ii. 408, 25. v. ge-neahhe.

ge-nehige, -nehge; *adv. Enough, very much, frequently*:—Hie genehge mid gebedum sēceaþ *seek it frequently with prayers*, Blickl. Homl. 207, 3. v. ge-neahhie.

ge-nehlīce; *adv. Sufficiently, abundantly, frequently*:—Gē sceolon myngian eówre hȳremen ðæt hīg hyra gebedu genehlīce begān *ye shall admonish your parishioners that they sufficiently cultivate their prayers*, L. E. I. 29; Th. ii. 424, 39.

ge-nēhlīce; *adv. Near*:—Ðæt reáf ðe he genēhlīce on him hæfde *the garment that he wore next his skin*, Guthl. 16; Gdwin. 68, 17.

ge-nēhwian; *p.* ode, ade; *pp.* od, ad *To approach, draw near, adhere*:—Monn genēhwas wīfe his *homo adhærebit uxori suæ*, Mt. Kmbl. Lind. 19, 5. Ānum genēhwaþ *uni adhærebit*, Lk. Skt. Lind. 16, 13. Genēhwade ānum *adhæsit uni*, 15, 15. [Cf. ge-neálǣcan.]

ge-nemnan; *p.* -nemde; *pp.* -nemned, -nemnod *To name*; nominare:—On ðære ceastre, ðe is genemned Nazareth *in civitate, quæ vocatur Nazareth*, Mt. Bos. 2, 23: 5, 19: Mk. Skt. Lind. 15, 7: Cd. 6; Th. 8, 27; Gen. 130: 217; Th. 277, 16; Sat. 205: 221; Th. 287, 13; Sat. 366. Ðā genemde ðæra scypmanna ān Scs. Martynus *then one of the sailors named St. Martin*, Shrn. 147, 8. Hī beóþ Godas genemnede [Cot. genemde] *they are named gods*, Bt. 37, 4; Fox 192, 9. Hī Angle genemnode wǣron *they were named Angles*, Homl. Th. ii. 120, 29.

ge-neósian; *p.* ode; *pp.* od [neósian *to visit*] *To visit, come to*; visĭtāre, adire:—Beheald holdlīce, hū ðū hraðe wylle geneósian niða bearna ealra þeóda *intende ad visĭtandas omnes gentes*, Ps. Th. 58, 5. Hī ne mihton hine for ðære manegu geneósian *non potĕrant adire eum præ turba*, Lk. Bos. 8, 19. Ðū geneósast hine *visĭtas eum*, Ps. Spl. 8, 5. Se gesǣliga his ealdcȳþþe eft geneósaþ *the blessed [bird] again visits its old country*, Exon. 61 a; Th. 222, 20; Ph. 351. Forðam ðe he geneósode, and his folces alȳsednesse dyde *quia visĭtāvit, et fecit redemptiōnem plebis suæ*, Lk. Bos. 1, 68, 78. Us mid hǣlo hēr geneósa *visĭta nos in salutāri tua*, Ps. Th. 105, 4. Ðæt ic geneósige temple his *ut visĭtem templum ejus*, Ps. Spl. 26, 8.

ge-neósung, e; *f. A visiting, visitation*; visitatio:—Forðam ðe ðū ne oncneówe ða tīde ðīnre geneósunge *eo quod non cognoveris tempus visitationis tuæ*, Lk. Bos. 19, 44: Scint. 21: Greg. Dial. 2, 35. v. neósung.

ge-neoðerian *to condemn*. v. ge-niðerian.

ge-ner, -near, es; *n. A refuge*; refugium, asylum, sanctuarium:—Ðū eart gener mīn *tu es refugium meum*, Ps. Spl. 31, 9: Ps. Lamb. 90, 2. Hī ōðer gener næfdon *they had not another refuge*, Ors. 1, 12; Bos. 36, 10. Ongin ðē generes wilnian *desire a refuge for thyself*, Exon. 36 b; Th. 119, 28; Gū. 261. v. ner, feorh-gener.

ge-nerenes, -ness, e; *f. A taking away, deliverance*; ereptio:—For generenesse heora freónda, ðara ðe of weorulde leordan *pro ereptiōne suōrum qui de sæcŭlo migrāvĕrant*, Bd. 4, 22; S. 592, 26. Ginerenis *ereptio*, Rtl. 30, 5.

ge-nerian, -nergan, -nerigan; *p.* ede, ode; *pp.* ed, od *To save, deliver, take away, set free, preserve, defend*; servare, redimere, liberare, eripere, salvum facere, defendere:—Se mec wile wiþ ðām nīðum genergan *he will protect me against that malice*, Exon. 36 a; Th. 116, 24; Gū. 212. We māgon feorh generigan *we may save life*, Cd. 117; Th. 152, 22; Gen. 2524. Ic hine generige *eripiam eum*, Ps. Th. 90. 16. He generaþ hīg *eripiet eos*, Ps. Spl. 33, 7. Oswio his ðeóde generede *Osuiu suam gentem liberavit*, Bd. 3, 24; S. 557, 14. Abraham Loth generede *Abraham saved Lot*, Cd. 121; Th. 156, 12; Gen. 2587. Ðū hī generedest *liberavisti eos*, Ps. 105, 8: Exon. 98 a; Th. 369, 28; Seel. 48. He hīg generode of Egipta lande *he delivered them out of the land of the Egyptians*, Ex. 18, 9. Alȳs me and genere *eripe me et libera me*, Ps. Th. 143, 8: 139, 1. Ðæt ðū generige oððe alȳse me *ut eruas me*, Ps. Lamb. 39, 14: Ps. Th. 88, 41. Generigende *eripiens*, Ps. Spl. 34, 11. Genered *liberatus*, Bd. 4, 31; S. 610, 24. Genered *saved*, Beo. Th. 1658; B. 827. Hī sind fram graman generode *they are saved from wrath*, Homl. Th. ii. 120, 35. [Cf. ge-nesan.]

ge-nerwde *vexed*. v. ge-nyrwian.

ge-nesan; *p.* -næs, *pl.* -nǣson; *pp.* -nesen *To be saved, preserved, escape from*:—Se biþ hāl and geneseþ on ēcnesse *he shall be safe and shall be preserved to eternity*, Blickl. Homl. 171, 26. Hrōf āna genæs ealles ānsūnd *the roof alone was saved wholly sound*, Beo. Th. 2003; B. 999. Se ða sæcce genæs *who had come safely from the conflict*, 3959; B. 1977: 4844; B. 2426: Cd. 94; Th. 121, 33; Gen. 2019. Ða ðe ða frēcennesse and yrmðo genǣson *those who had survived the danger and misery*, Blickl. Homl. 203, 20: Ors. 4, 8; Bos. 90, 8: Fins. Th. 95; Fin. 47. Hȳ ðurh miltse meotudes genǣson *they have been saved through the Lord's mercy*, Exon. 26 a; Th. 77, 12; Cri. 1255. He nīða gehwane genesen hæfde *he had survived every struggle*, Beo. Th. 4786; B. 2397. Ðæt hīg mihton ða frǣcnesse genesan *that they might escape the danger*, Shrn. 38, 2. [*Goth.* ga-nisan *to be saved*: *O. Sax.* gi-nesan: *O. H. Ger.* ge-nesan: *Ger.* ge-nesen *to get well*.]

Gēnesburuh *Gainsborough*. v. Gegnesburh.

ge-nēsta, an; *m. A neighbour*; proximus:—Mið ðǣm ginēstum sīnum *apud proximos suos*, Rtl. 84, 37.

ge-nēðan; *p.* de; *pp.* ed *To venture, attempt, strive*:—Ne dorste he genēðan ðæt . . . *he durst not venture to* . . . , Ors. 1, 10; Bos. 33, 30. Nū ðū Andreas scealt genēðan in gramra gripe *now shalt thou Andrew venture into the grasp of foes*, Andr. Kmbl. 1900; An. 952: 2702; An. 1353. Sió sunne uncūðne weg nihtes genēðeþ *the sun ventures on an unknown way by night*, Bt. Met. Fox 13, 117; Met. 13, 59: Exon. 100 a; Th. 374, 1; Seel. 119. He genēðde under ānne elpend *he ventured under an elephant*, Ors. 4, 1; Bos. 77, 20: 8; 90, 8. He āna genēðde frēcne dǣde *he alone ventured on the daring deed*, Beo. Th. 1781; B. 889: 3317; B. 1656. Ðæt ic ealdre genēðde *that I should venture my life*, 4273; B. 2133: Apstls. Kmbl. 34; Ap. 17: 100; Ap. 50. Hie hit frēcne genēðdon under wætera hrōfas *they boldly ventured it under the waters' roofs*, Cd. 170; Th. 214, 17; Exod. 570: Beo. Th. 1923; 959. v. nēðan.

geng *a privy*; latrina, Cot. 123. v. gang.

geng; *adj. Young*; jŭvĕnis:—Ðām gengum þrȳm *to the three young men*, Cd. 176; Th. 222, 9; Dan. 102. v. geong.

gengan; *p.* de, *pl.* don; *pp.* ed *To go, pass*; ire, meare, currere, ferri, converti:—Forhwī gengdest ðū on bæcling *quare conversus es retrorsum*, Ps. Th. 113, 5. He feára sum beforan gengde wong sceáwian *he with a few went before to view the plain*, Beo. Th. 2829; B. 1412. Him oft betwuh gnornword gengdon *words of sadness passed oft between them*, Cd. 37; Th. 47, 27; Gen. 767. Beornas cōmon wicgum gengan *the men came riding on horses*, Andr. Kmbl. 2192; An. 1097. v. gān, gangan.

gengdon *passed*, Cd. 37; Th. 47, 27; Gen. 767; *p.* of gengan.

genge; *f. A* GANG, *flock, company*; grex:—Ðæt wæs Hereweard and his genge *that was Hereward and his followers*, Chr. 1070; Erl. 207, 29. [*Laym. Orm.* genge *a host, retinue*.]

gēnge ic *I would go*, Cd. 39; Th. 51, 29; Gen. 834; *p. subj. of* gangan.

genge; *adj. Going, current, prevalent, valid*:—Ðeáh ðe ðæs cyninges bēne mid hine swīðode and genge wǣre *preces regis illius multum valere apud eum*, Bd. 3, 12; S. 537, 19. Ðæt his sōþ fore us genge weorðe *that his truth be current before us*, Exon. 43 b; Th. 147, 35; Gū. 737.

Á ðín dóm sý gód and genge *ever be thy judgment good and valid*, 54 b; Th. 192, 20; Az. 109. Gód biþ genge and wiþ God lenge *good prevails and lasts before God*, 91 a; Th. 341, 4; Gn. Ex. 121. [*O. H. Ger.* gengi *usual: Ger.* gäng.]

ge-nídde, Ps. Vos. 58, 14: ge-níded *compelled;* coactus, Cot. 59: 106. v. ge-nēdan.

ge-niédde *compelled, forced.* v. ge-nēdan.

ge-nierede, -wod *vexed.* v. ge-nyrwian.

ge-niht, -nyht, es; *n:* e; *f. Abundance, fulness, sufficiency;* abundantia, ūbertas:—Wénst ðú ðæt se ánweald and ðæt geniht seó to forseónne *thinkest thou that power and abundance are to be despised?* Bt. 33, 1; Fox 120, 22, 24, 26. Hý beóþ oferdrencte on ðære genihte ðínes húses *inebriābuntur ab ūbertāte dŏmus tuæ*, Ps. Th. 35, 8. To genihte *in abundantia*, Ps. Th. 77, 25, 27: 84, 6: Menol. Fox 364; Men. 183. Ðú sealdest me wilna geniht *thou gavest me the fulness of my desires*, Soul Kmbl. 285; Seel. 146: Cd. 90; Th. 113, 21; Gen. 1890: Ps. Th. 4, 8. [*O. H. Ger.* ge-nuht *copia, abundantia.*]

ge-nihtlíce; *adv. abundantly;* abunde, Cot. 6.

ge-nihtsum, -nyhtsum; *adj.* I. *abundant, abounding, copious, rich, plentiful, fruitful;* abundans, ūber, cōpiōsus, affluus, profluus:—Genihtsum *ūber*, Ælfc. Gr. 9, 18; Som. 10, 7. Genihtsum wæter forþflóweþ *plentiful water flows forth*, Bd. 5, 10; S. 625, 24: Ps. Th. 85, 4: 143, 17. On ylde genihtsumre *in sĕnecta ūbĕri*, Ps. Spl. 91, 14. Ðæt hí wǽron genihtsume *ut essent proflui*, Hymn. Surt. 94, 5. Hladungum genihtsumum *haustĭbus affluis*, 58, 12. II. *satisfied;* sātiābĭlis:—Se ðe ǽr ne wæs níþes genihtsum *who ere was not satisfied with slaughter*, Cd. 93; Th. 120, 15; Gen. 1995. [*O. H. Ger.* ge-nuhtsam *abundans.*]

ge-nihtsumian, -nyhtsumian; *part.* -nihtsumigende; *p.* ode; *pp.* od *To abound, suffice;* abundāre, suffĭcĕre:—Hí synfulle and genihtsumigende on worulde, hí begeáton welan *ipsi peccātōres et abundantes in sæcŭlo, obtĭnuērunt dīvĭtias*, Ps. Spl. 72, 12: 127, 3. Ic genihtsumige *abundo*, Ælfc. Gr. 38; Som. 41, 10. Se ungesǽliga gýtsere wile máre habban ðonne him genihtsumaþ *the unhappy miser wishes to have more than suffices him*, Homl. Th. i. 64, 34. Ánes engles geearnung ne genihtsumode to alýsednysse ealles mancynnes *the merit of an angel was not sufficient for the redemption of all mankind*, Boutr. Scrd. 17, 37.

ge-nihtsumlíce, -nyhtsumlíce; *comp.* -lícor; *adv. Abundantly, plentifully, copiously, sufficiently;* abundanter, abunde, ūbertim, suffĭcienter:—He agylt genihtsumlíce ðám wyrcendum ofermódignysse *retrĭbuet abundanter făcientibus sŭperbiam*, Ps. Spl. 30, 30: Bd. 5, 19; S. 637, 48. Genihtsumlíce *abunde*, Ælfc. Gr. 38; Som. 41, 10. Ðǽr genihtsumlíce is sǽd *ubi ūbertim indĭcātum est*, Bd. 1, 27; S. 494, 36: 4, 28; S. 605, 12. Genihtsumlícor *abundantius*, 3, 27; S. 559, 7.

ge-nihtsumnes, -nyhtsumnes, -ness, -nys, -nyss, -nis, -niss, e; *f. Abundance, plenty, copiousness, sufficiency;* abundantia, ūbertas, cōpia:—Genihtsumnys *abundantia* vel *cōpia*, Wrt. Voc. 83, 40. Genihtsumnys *ūbertas*, Ælfc. Gr. 9, 18; Som. 10, 7. Gemynd genihtsumnesse wynsumnesse ðínre hí bylcettaþ *mĕmŏriam abundantiæ suāvĭtātis tuæ eructābunt*, Ps. Lamb. 144, 7. On genihtsumnysse mínre *in abundantia mea*, 29, 7: 77, 25. Híg beóþ gedrencte for genihtsumnisse húses ðínes *inebriābuntur ab ūbertāte dŏmus tuæ*, 35, 9. Ðære eorþan wæstmbǽrnysse and genihtsumnysse we nellaþ habban us to lífes brícum, ac to oferflówednyssum *the fruitfulness and abundance of the earth we will not have for the uses of life, but as superfluities*, Homl. Th. ii. 540, 10: 64, 35.

ge-niman, -nyman, -nioman; he -nimeþ, -nimþ; *p.* -nam, -nom, *pl.* -námon, -nómon; *imp.* -nim, *pl.* -nimaþ; *subj. p.* -náme, *pl.* -námen; *pp.* -numen *To take, take up, take away, assume, receive, accept, obtain, comprehend, enter into;* sūmĕre, tollĕre, auferre, assūmĕre, accĭpĕre, nancisci, comprehendĕre, inīre:—Forlǽt mec englas geniman on ðínne neáwest *let angels take me into thy presence*, Exon. 118 b; Th. 455, 13; Hy. 4, 49. Ðæt hí woldon his bán geniman *ut tollĕrent ossa illius*, Bd. 4, 30; S. 608, 28. He genimeþ hraðe ðære rósan wlite *it taketh away the beauty of the rose*, Bt. Met. Fox 6, 24; Met. 6, 12: Cd. 60; Th. 73, 23; Gen. 1209. Wintres dæg sigelbeorhtne genimþ hærfest *winter's day takes away the sun-bright autumn*, Menol. Fox 404; Men. 203. Hú lange démaþ gé unrihtwísnysse, and ansýne synfulra genimaþ *usquequo jūdĭcātis iniquĭtātem, et făcies peccātōrum sūmĭtis?* Ps. Spl. 81, 2. Heó genam cúðe folme *she took the well known hand*, Beo. Th. 2609; B. 1302: 4850; B. 2429. He his folc genam swá fǽle sceáp *abstŭlit sicut oves pŏpŭlum suum*, Ps. Th. 77, 52, 69. Ðe ic to swá myclum cyninge genom *quod cum tanto rēge inii*, Bd. 2, 12; S. 513, 25. He feówer túnas genom *he took four towns*, Chr. 571; Erl. 18, 13: 584; Erl. 18, 24. On ðam ilcan ðú eard genáme *in quo hăbĭtas in idipsum*, Ps. Th. 73, 3: 72, 19. Genámon me ðǽr strange feóndas *strong enemies took me there*, Rood. Kmbl. 60; Kr. 30: 120; Kr. 60: Cd. 210; Th. 260, 10; Dan. 707. Þýstro ðæt ne genámon *tenebræ eam non comprehendĕrunt*, Jn. Bos. 1, 5. Hí genómon unlytel *they took not a little*, Chr. 921; Erl. 106, 14. Ðú ðé ánne genim to gesprecan *take thou one to thee for counsellor*, Exon. 80 a; Th. 301, 25; Fä. 24: Cd. 67; Th. 80, 27; Gen. 1335. Genimaþ eów árlíce lác *tollite hostias*, Ps. Th. 95, 8. Búton hwá þurh flánes flyht fyl genáme *unless any one through an arrow's flight obtained his fall*, Byrht. Th. 133, 57; By. 71. Hét se kásere ðæt he genáme on ðam biscope ealle godes béc *the emperor ordered him to take from the bishop all God's books*, Shrn. 123, 24. Án byþ genumen *ūnus assūmētur*, Mt. Bos. 24, 40, 41: Gen. 2, 23. Geniman friþ *to make peace*, Chr. 865; Erl. 71, 12: Ors. 5, 7; Bos. 106, 21.

ge-nioman *to take, receive, obtain;* sūmĕre, nancisci:—Ðǽr gé to genihte geniomaþ wæstme *where ye shall obtain fruits in abundance*, Ps. Th. 67, 16. v. ge-niman.

ge-nip, es; *pl. nom. acc.* -nipu; *n. A mist, cloud, darkness, obscurity;* nĕbŭla, cālīgo, nūbes, tĕnebræ:—Mist *vel* genip *nĕbŭla*, Ælfc. Gl. 94; Som. 75, 111; Wrt. Voc. 52, 61. Wearþ genip, and ofersceadede híg *facta est nūbes, et obumbrāvit eos*, Lk. Bos. 9, 34. Ðæt genip stód æt ðæs geteldes dura *the cloud stood at the door of the tabernacle*, Ex. 33, 10: Cd. 8; Th. 9, 9; Gen. 139. Moises eóde to ðam genipe *Moyses accessit ad calīgĭnem*, Ex. 20, 21. Com stefen of ðam genipe *vox facta est de nūbe*, Lk. Bos. 9, 35. On ðæt genip *in nūbem*, 9, 34. In ðæt neowle genip *into the deep darkness*, Cd. 223; Th. 292, 25; Sat. 445: 217; Th. 275, 31; Sat. 180: Exon. 93 b; Th. 351, 12; Sch. 79. Ofer flóda genipu *over the mists of floods*, Beo. Th. 5608; B. 2808: 2724; B. 1360. Ðú ðe gesetst genipu upastínesse ðínne oððe ðínne upstíge *qui pōnis nūbem ascensum tuum*, Ps. Lamb. 103, 3: Ps. Spl. 77, 27. Sweart wolcen and genip *atra nubes*, Nar. 23, 23. [Cf. *Ger.* nebel: *Icel.* nifl.]

ge-nípan; *p.* -náp, *pl.* -nipon; *pp.* -nipen. I. *to darken, become dark;* cālīgāre, obnūbilāri:—Hú seó þrag gewát, genáp under niht-helm, swá heó nó wǽre *how the time has passed, has darkened under the veil of night, as if it had not been*, Exon. 77 b; Th. 292, 8; Wand. 96. II. *to rise as a cloud, to creep up* or *come suddenly upon one;* obrēpĕre, sŭpervĕnīre alĭcui:—Him ongén genáp atol ýþa gewealc *the terrible rolling of the waves rose as a cloud against them* [*came suddenly upon them*], Cd. 166; Th. 206, 20; Exod. 454.

ge-nirwed *vexed.* v. ge-nyrwian.

ge-niðerian, -niðrian, -neðerian, -nyðerian; *p.* ode, ade; *pp.* od, ad *To put down, bring low, subdue, humiliate, condemn:*—Nelle gé genyðerian and gé ne beóþ genyðerude *nolite condemnare et non condemnabimini*, Lk. Bos. 6, 37. Ne ic ðech geniðro *nec ego te condemnabo*, Jn. Skt. Lind. 8, 11. Eágan ofermódra ðú genyðerǽst *oculos superborum humiliabis*, Ps. Spl. 17, 29. Útan cumene men eów genyðriaþ *strangers shall bring you low*, Deut. 28, 43. Ðú genyðerodest *tu humiliasti*, Ps. Spl. 88, 11. He ðurh his ðrowunga deófles ríce geneðerode *he through his passion put down the devil's kingdom*, Blickl. Homl. 7, 13. Alle geniðradon hine *omnes condemnaverunt eum*, Mk. Skt. Lind. 14, 64. On Godes dóme geniðerod *condemned at God's judgment*, Homl. Th. i. 60, 33. Geniðrad *damnatus*, Mt. Kmbl. Lind. 27, 3: Mk. Skt. Lind. 16, 16. Se ðe hyne upaheſþ se byþ genyðerud *qui se exaltaverit humiliabitur*, Mt. Bos. 23, 12. Simon ne aríseþ nǽfre forðon ðe he is sóðlíce deád and on écum wítum genyðerod *Simon will never arise for he is really dead and sunk in eternal punishments*, Blickl. Homl. 189, 20; Judth. 10; Thw. 23, 9; Jud. 113. Ðurh Cristes sige ealle hálige wǽron gefreólsode; swá ðonne beóþ ða synfullan genyðerade mid heora ordfruman swá he genyðerad wearþ *through Christ's victory all holy people were set free; so then the sinful shall be subdued with their chief as he was subdued*, Blickl. Homl. 33, 1: Chr. 1075; Erl. 214, 17.

ge-niðerung, -nyðerung, e; *f. Condemnation, humiliation, laying low:*—Ða ýttran ðeóstru is seó swearte niht ðære écan geniðerunge *the outer darkness is the black night of eternal condemnation*, Homl. Th. i. 530, 23. Ðæt he onfó ðære écan genyðerunga *that he receive the everlasting condemnation*, Blickl. Homl. 61, 32. For deófles genyðerunge *for the casting down of the devil*, 67, 3.

ge-níðla, an; *m. An enemy, a foe:*—Nǽfre ðú gelǽrest ðæt ic dumbum and deáfum deófolgieldum gǽste geníðlum gafol onháte *never shalt thou induce me to promise tribute to dumb and deaf idols, foes to the spirit*, Exon. 68 a; Th. 251, 26; Jul. 151. DER. eald-, feorh-, gást-, láþ-, mán-, sweord-, torn-geníðla.

ge-níðle, an; *f.* [or a, an; *m?*] *Enmity, hate, fierceness:*—Fram hungres geníðlan *from the fierceness of hunger*, Elen. Kmbl. 1398; El. 701: 1216; El. 610. Ic onféng feonda geníðlan *I received the hate of foes*, Exon. 29 a; Th. 88, 15; Cri. 1440.

ge-niwian; *p.* ode; *pp.* od, ad *To renew, make new, change;* renovare, innovare:—Gást rihtne geniwa *spiritum rectum innova*, Ps. Spl. 50, 11. Biþ geniwod *renovabitur*, 102, 5. On sumum geáre byþ se móna twelf síðon geniwod fram ðære hálgan Eáster-tíde óþ eft Eástron; and on sumum geáre he biþ þreóttyne síðon geedniwad *in some years the moon is twelve times changed* [*renewed*] *from the holy Easter time till Easter again; and in some years it is thirteen times changed* [*renewed*], Lchdm. iii. 248, 22. Heáf wæs geniwad *the wail was renewed*, Cd. 144; Th. 179, 28; Exod. 35: Exon. 15 b; Th. 33, 22; Cri. 529: 60 a; Th. 217, 13; Ph. 279: Andr. Kmbl. 2020; An. 1012. v. niwian.

ge-niwung, e; *f. A renewing, recovering;* renovatio, Som.

gén-lád, e; *f. An arm of the sea, into which a river discharges itself;* brachium oceani, Som. v. lád.

gennelung, e; *f. Greatness;* magnificentia, Ps. Spl. 67, 37. v. gemiclung [?]

ge-nōg, -nōh; *adj.* ENOUGH, *sufficient, abundant;* satis, sufficiens, abundans:—He hæfþ on his āgenum genōh *he has of his own enough,* Bt. 24, 4; Fox 86, 8. Ðǣr wæs genōg drinc sōna gearu *there was soon drink enough ready,* Andr. Kmbl. 3067; An. 1536. Hwæt druge ðū dugeða genōhra *what madest thou of the abundant blessings,* Cd. 42; Th. 55, 3; Gen. 888. Hī māgon geseón on him selfum synne genōge *they may see in themselves sins enough,* Exon. 26 a; Th. 77, 32; Cri. 1265. Ðū hæfst ǣlces gōdes genōh *thou shalt have abundance of every good thing,* Deut. 28, 11: Exon. 93 b; Th. 352, 8; Sch. 94: Cd. 29; Th. 39, 4; Gen. 619. [*Orm. Laym.* inoh: *Plat.* nog, genog: *O. Sax.* ginōg: *O. Frs.* enoch, anog, noch: *Dut.* genoeg: *Ger.* genug: *M. H. Ger.* genuoc, gnuoc: *O. H. Ger.* ginuog: *Goth.* ganōhs: *Dan.* nok: *O. Nrs.* gnogr.]

GE-NŌG, -nōh; *adv. Sufficiently, abundantly,* ENOUGH; satis, abunde:—Genōg sweotol hit is *it is sufficiently manifest,* Bt. 36, 3; Fox 176, 27. Genōg riht ðū segst *rightly enough thou sayest,* Bt. 33, 1; Fox 120, 17. Ðæt hīg habbon līf and habbon genōh *ut vitam habeant et abundantius habeant,* Jn. Bos. 10, 10. Cwǣdon ðæt we fundon sumne swīðe micelne mere in ðæm wǣre fersc wæter and swēte genōg *dixerunt ingens nos stagnum dulcissime aque inventuros,* Nar. 11, 27.

ge-nōgan *to multiply;* multiplicare, Lye. [*O. H. Ger.* gi-nuogan.]

ge-nōh; *adj. Sufficient, abundant;* abundans. v. ge-nōg.

ge-nōh *sufficiently,* Bt. 13; Fox 38, 22. v. ge-nōg; *adv.*

ge-nom, *pl.* -nōmon *took:*—Weard genom *the guardian took,* Exon. 11 a; Th. 14, 22; Cri. 223: Chr. 921; Erl. 106, 14; *p. of* ge-niman.

ge-nomian, -namian; *p.* ode; *pp.* od *To name, point out;* nominare, indicere, Exon. 24 a; Th. 68, 10; Cri. 1101.

ge-notian; *p.* ode; *pp.* od, ud *To use, consume:*—Hie hæfdon hiora mete genotudne *they had consumed their provisions,* Chr. 894; Erl. 90, 31. [Cf. ge-nyttian.]

Gent, Gænt, Gend *Ghent, in Flanders;* Gandavum, Chr. 880; Erl. 83, 2.

ge-nugan; *pres.* hit -neah [*Goth.* ganah] *To suffice, to be sufficient, not to be wanting;* sufficere:—Gif us on ferðe geneah *if in our soul we be not wanting* [*if it is sufficient to us in our soul*], Exon. 93 a; Th. 348, 29; Sch. 35: 90 a; Th. 337, 26; Gn. Ex. 70. Nǣnig mennisc tunge ne geneah ðæs acendan engles godcund mægen to gesecgenne *no human tongue is sufficient to tell the divine virtue of that begotten messenger,* Blickl. Homl. 165, 5. v. be-nugan, nugan.

ge-numen *taken,* Mt. Bos. 24, 40, 41; *pp. of* ge-niman.

ge-nycled, -cnycled *knuckled, crooked;* obuncus, Som.

ge-nȳdan, -nēdan, -niédan, he -nȳt; *p.* de; *pp.* ed *To compel, force, press;* cogere, compellere, expellere:—Alexander ðæt folc to him genȳdde *Alexander forced the people to him,* Ors. 3, 9; Bos. 65, 18, 19, 20. Genȳddon, Mk. Bos. 15, 21. Genȳt, Mt. Bos. 5, 41. Gāst hine on wēsten genȳdde *spiritus expulit eum in deserto,* Mk. Bos. 1, 12. Wǣron genȳdde *were forced,* Ors. 3, 6; Bos. 58, 21. v. ge-nēdan.

ge-nȳd-magas; *pl. m. Near relations:*—Gif twegen genȳdmagas *if two near relations,* L. E. and G. 4; Th. i. 168, 19, MS. B. v. nȳdmaga.

ge-nȳh; *adj. Near:*—Gif twegen genȳhe magas [genȳhe-magas, Th. cf. neáh-mæg] *if two near kinsmen,* L. E. and G. 4; Th. i. 168, 19.

ge-nyht, es; *n:* e; *f.* [*O. H. Ger.* ganuht, *f.*] *An abundance, plenty, sufficiency, fulfilment;* abundantia, ubertas:—Ðeáh mon nū anweald and genyht to twǣm þingum nemne *though any one call power and abundance two things,* Bt. 33, 1; Fox 120, 20. Ðætte genyht wǣre gesǣlða *that sufficiency was happiness,* 35, 3; Fox 158, 13. v. ge-niht.

ge-nyht-ful, -full; *adj. Plentiful;* profusus, prodigus, Lye.

ge-nyhtlīce; *adv. Abundantly;* abunde, Cot. 6.

ge-nyhtsum; *adj. Plentiful, abundant;* abundans, uber, copiosus:—Feoh genyhtsum sældun ðǣm kempum *they gave much money to the soldiers,* Mt. Kmbl. Rush. 28, 12. v. ge-nihtsum.

ge-nyhtsumian, -nihtsumian; *p.* ode; *pp.* od *To suffice, abound;* abundare:—Gemǣru and dene genyhtsumiaþ hwǣte *convalles abundabunt frumento,* Ps. Surt. 64, 14. Genyhtsumegende *abundantes,* Ps. Surt. 72, 12. v. ge-nihtsumian.

ge-nyhtsumlīce; *adv. Abundantly, plentifully;* abunde, abundanter:—Ða genyhtsumlīce dóeþ oferhygd *qui abundanter faciunt superbiam,* Ps. Surt. 30, 24. v. ge-nihtsumlīce.

ge-nyhtsum-nes, -ness, -nis, -niss, e; *f. An abundance, plenty;* abundantia:—In mīnre genyhtsumnisse *in mea abundantia,* Ps. Surt. 29, 7: 64, 12. v. ge-nihtsumnes.

ge-nyman *to take;* assūmĕre:—Ðū genymest gecȳðnysse mīne þurh mūþ ðīnne *tu assūmis testāmentum meum per os tuum,* Ps. Spl. 49, 17. v. ge-niman.

ge-nyrwian, -nyrwan; *p.* ede, ode; *pp.* ed, od *To make narrow, compress, oppress:*—Ic genyrwige *co-arto,* Ælfc. Gr. 47; Som. 48, 56. Ðīne fȳnd ðē genyrwaþ *inimici tui coangustabunt te,* Lk. Bos. 19, 43. Ne genyrwe ofer me pyt mūþ his *neque urgeat super me puteus os suum,* Ps. Spl. 68, 19. Genyrwyd [C], geniered [T] is ofer me gāst mīn *anxiatus est super me spiritus meus,* 142, 4. Swā genyrwod so *narrowed,* Btwk. Scrd. 21, 5. Hearde genyrwad *hardly constrained,* Exon. 13 a; Th. 23, 6; Cri. 364.

ge-nȳt *compels.* v. ge-nȳdan.

ge-nyðerian, -nyðrian; *p.* ode; *pp.* od, ad, ud *To humble, condemn,* Ps. Spl. 17, 29: Lk. 6, 37. v. ge-niðerian.

ge-nyðerung *humiliation, condemnation.* v. ge-niðerung.

ge-nyttian; *p.* ode; *pp.* od *To use, enjoy:*—He hæfde eorþ-scrafa ende genyttod *he had enjoyed the last of his earth-dens,* Beo. Th. 6085; B. 3046. [Cf. ge-notian.]

GEÓ, gió; *adv. Formerly, of old, before;* quandam, olim, pridem:—Ða lióþ ðe ic, wrecca, geó lustbǣrlīce song, ic sceal nū heófiende singan *the lays which I, an exile, formerly with delight sung, I shall now mourning sing,* Bt. 2; Fox 4, 7: Bt. Met. Fox 10, 68; Met. 10, 34. Ðū wið Criste geó wunne *thou of old didst strive against Christ,* Exon. 71 b; Th. 267, 25; Jul. 420: 19 b; Th. 51, 11; Cri. 814: Cd. 106; Th. 139, 12; Gen. 2308: Menol. Fox 34; Men. 17. Wæs ðis eálond geó gewurþad mid æðelestum ceastrum *this island was formerly adorned with the noblest cities,* Bd. 1, 1; S. 473, 25. Geþenc se snottra fengel hwæt wit geó sprǣcon *do thou, sagacious prince, bear in mind what we have before spoken,* Beo. Th. 2957; B. 1476. Geó ǣr *long before,* Bd. 4, 19; S. 589, 17. Geó dagum *in days of old, formerly,* 4, 27; S. 605, note 2. Geó geāra *formerly,* Bt. 31, 1; Fox 112, 15. Geó hwīlum *in times of old, formerly,* 2; Fox 4, 9. [*Goth.* ju: *O. Sax.* giu: *O. H. Ger.* giu.]

geoc, gioc, geoht, gōc, ioc, es; *n: pl.* geocu. I. *a* YOKE; jugum:—Nimaþ mīn geoc ofer eów *tollite jugum meum super vos,* Mt. Bos. 11, 29. Mīn geoc ys wynsum *jugum meum suave est,* 11, 30. We weorpan fram us geoc heora *projiciamus a nobis jugum ipsorum,* Ps. Spl. 2, 3. Utan aweorpan heora geocu of us *projiciamus a nobis juga ipsorum,* Ps. Th. 2, 3. II. *a yoke of oxen;* boum jugum, boves jugo juncti:—Se ceorl hæfþ ōðres geoht [geoc: B. oxan] ahȳrod *the ceorl has hired another's yoke,* L. In. 60; Th. i. 140, 8. Be hȳr-geohte [hyrgeoce: B. hȳr-oxan] *of a hired yoke,* 60; Th. i. 140, 7. III. *conjux:*—Gebede ł geoc *conjugem,* Mt. Kmbl. Lind. 1, 20. [*Goth.* juk: *O. H. Ger.* joh: *Ger.* joch.]

geóc, gióc, eóc, e; *f. Safety, help, aid, succour, comfort, consolation;* salus, auxīlium, subsīdium, consōlātio:—Mec geóc cyme *safety shall come to me,* Exon. 102 b; Th. 388, 9; Rä. 6, 5: Andr. Kmbl. 3618; An. 1587. Geóce gefēgon *they rejoiced in the aid,* Exon. 43 b; Th. 146, 16; Gū. 710. Ne miht ðū me ofer ðisne dæg ǣnige helpe ne geóce gefremman *non mihi aliquid utilitatis aut salutis potes ultra conferre,* Bd. 5, 13; S. 632, 30. Nū we cunnon hyhtan ðæt we heofones leóht uppe mid englum āgan mōton, gāstum to geóce *now we can hope that we may possess the light of heaven above with the angels, for the comfort of our spirits,* Frag. Kmbl. 88; Leás. 46: Elen. Kmbl. 2491; El. 1247. Gnyrna to geóce *for a consolation of sorrows,* 2275; El. 1139. Se hālga his God geóce bæd *the holy one prayed to his God for aid,* Andr. Kmbl. 2060; An. 1032: 2132; An. 1569. Ðæt him gāstbona geóce gefremede *that the spirit-slayer would afford them succour,* Beo. Th. 357; B. 177: 5342; B. 2674: Cd. 77; Th. 95, 31; Gen. 1587: 184; Th. 230, 14: Dan. 233. Beóþ hyra geóca gemyndge *they are mindful of their safety,* Exon. 33 b; Th. 107, 18; Gū. 60.

geocboga, an; *m. A yoke.* v. geoc.

geócend, es; *m. A preserver, Saviour;* servator, salvator:—Wīs biþ se ðe con ongytan ðone geócend *he is wise who can understand the preserver,* Exon. 54 a; Th. 191, 14; Az. 88. Gǣsta geócend *Saviour of souls,* 10 b; Th. 13, 5; Cri. 198: 49 a; Th. 170, 3; Gū. 1106: Andr. Kmbl. 1095; An. 548: 1801; An. 903: Elen. Kmbl. 1360; El. 682: 2151; El. 1077.

geócian; *p.* ode; *pp.* od; *gen. dat. To preserve, save;* servare, salvare. I. *with the gen:*—Geóca ūser *preserve us,* Cd. 188; Th. 234, 14; Dan. 292. Geóca mīnes gǣstes *save my soul,* Exon. 118 b; Th. 455, 5; Hy. 4, 45. II. *with the dat:*—Geóca us *preserve us,* Exon. 53 a; Th. 185, 23; Az. 12. Geóca mīnre sāwle *save my soul,* 118 b; Th. 455, 34; Hy. 4, 59.

geócor [*or* geocor? cf. geocsa]; *adj. Strong, fierce, harsh, dire, sad:*—Geócor sefa, geómrende hyge *sad spirit, mourning mind,* Exon. 48 a; Th. 164, 33; Gū. 1021: 49 a; Th. 170, 13; Gū. 1111. On ða geócran tīd *in that grievous time,* 47 a; Th. 160, 26; Gū. 949. Hȳ sceolon forgietan ðara geócran gesceafte habban him gomen *they shall forget the harsh fate and have pleasure,* 92 a; Th. 345, 4; Gn. Ex. 183. Wiste his fingra geweald on grames grāpum ðæt he wæs geócor *he* [*Grendel*] *knew that his fingers' power was in the gripe of the fierce one, so that he was sad,* Beo. Th. 1535. v. B. 765 for a different reading. Geócrostne sīþ *a very sad journey,* Cd. 205; Th. 254, 25; Dan. 617. [Cf. *Goth.* juka *strife, anger.*] v. Grm. And. u. El. 119.

geócre; *adv. Harshly, roughly:*—Ðā Babilone weard yrre andswarode eorlum onmǣlde grimme ðām gingum and geócre oncwæþ *then the lord of Babylon angrily answered to the men, announced fiercely to the youths, and harshly spoke,* Cd. 183; Th. 229, 3; Dan. 211.

geocsa, an; *m. A sobbing;* singultus:—Ðiós siccetung ðes geocsa *this sighing, this sobbing,* Bt. Met. Fox 2, 9; Met. 2, 5.

geoc-stecca, -sticca, an; *m. A bolt of a door, a bar;* obex, Cot. 145.

geocsung, e; *f. Sobbing;* singultus, Ælfc. Gl. 99; Wrt. Voc. 54, 64.

geofa *a giver.* v. gifa.

geofan; *p.* geaf, *pl.* geáfon; *pp.* gifen *To give;* dare:—Nymþ đū me rǣd geofe *unless thou mayest give me counsel,* Ps. Th. 58, 1: 118, 72. v. gifan.

geofen *the ocean,* Exon. 89 b; Th. 336, 20; Gn. Ex. 52. Geofenes *of the ocean,* Beo. Th. 729; B. 362. v. geofon.

ge-offrian; *p.* ode; *pp.* od *To offer, sacrifice:*—He hēt hine his leófan sunu geoffrian Gode to lāce *he bade him offer his dear son as a sacrifice to God,* Btwk. Scrd. 23, 3. Abel geoffrode đa sēlostan lāc Gode *Abel offered the best sacrifices to God,* 18, 5: 22, 9: Gen. 8, 20. Đæt hī be hreówsunge Gode geoffrodon *that they should sacrifice to God by penitence,* Homl. Th. i. 68, 17. Geoffrod *sacrificed,* Lev. 4, 15.

geofian, *p.* ode; *pp.* od *To give, to endow;* dare, donare:—He mæg me geofian mid gōda gehwilcum *he can endow me with every good,* Cd. 26; Th. 34, 31; Gen. 546. DER. geofu. v. gifian.

geofon, geofen, gifen, gyfen, es; *n. The sea, ocean;* mare, oceanus:—On geofones streám *on the ocean's wave,* Andr. Kmbl. 1704; An. 854: Exon. 57 b; Th. 205, 25; Ph. 118. Geofon geótende *a gushing ocean,* Andr. Kmbl. 3014; An. 1510. [*O. Sax.* gebano.] v. Grm. D. M. 219.

geofon-flōd, es; *m.* [geofon *a sea, ocean;* flōd *a flood*] *A sea* or *ocean flood;* maris fluctus:—Dryhtnes bibod geofonflōda gehwylc georne bihealdeþ *each ocean flood strictly observes the Lord's command,* Exon. 54 b; Th. 193, 21; Az. 125.

geofon-hūs, es; *n. A sea-house, vessel:*—Geofonhūsa mǣst *greatest of sea-houses,* Cd. 66; Th. 79, 34; Gen. 1321.

geofon-ȳþ, e; *f. A sea-wave, billow;* maris unda, Beo. Th. 1035; B. 515.

geofu, e; *gen. pl.* -a, -ena, -ona; *f. A gift, grace;* donus, gratia:—Beó geofena gemyndig *be mindful of gifts,* Beo. Th. 2351; B. 1173. Đæt he dryhtnes mōt geofona neótan *that he may partake of the Lord's gifts,* Exon. 61 a; Th. 225, 5; Ph. 384. Ne biddan we ūrne Drihten đyssa eorđlīcra geofa *let us not ask our Lord for these earthly gifts,* Blickl. Homl. 21, 11. He hī mid missenlīcum geofum gewelgode *ille eam [ecclesiam] diversis donis ditavit,* Bd. 1, 33; S. 499, 1: Exon. 18 a; Th. 43, 10; Cri. 686: 128 b; Th. 493, 15; Rä. 81, 31. Geofu wæs mid Gūþlāc *grace was with Guthlac,* 40 a; Th. 134, 1; Gū. 501. v. gifu.

geó-geára; *adv. Of old;* olim, antiquitus, Ps. Th. 42, 3. v. geó, geára; *adv.*

geó-geáre; *adv. Of old;* olim, antiquitus:—Swā swā we geógeáre hȳrdon *so as we of old have heard,* Ps. Th. 47, 7. v. geó, geáre.

geógelere, es: *m. A juggler;* præstigiator, Som. Geógulere *magus, haruspex, hariolus,* Hpt. Gl. 500, 502, 510. [*O. H. Ger.* gougulari: *Icel.* kuklari: *Ger.* gaukler.] v. Grff. iv. 134: Grm. D. M. 990.

geógoþ-feorh *youthful life, youth,* Beo. Th. 1078; B. 537. v. geóguþ-feorh.

geógoþ-hād *youth,* Cd. 74; Th. 91, 4; Gen. 1507. v. geóguþ-hād.

geógoþ-lust, es; *m. Youthful pleasure, lust:*—Se līchoma geunlustaþ đa geógoþlustas to fremmenne *the body loathes to perform those youthful lusts,* Blickl. Homl. 59, 9.

geóguþ, geógeþ, giógoþ, geógaþ, gīgoþ, iūguþ, e; *f.* I. YOUTH, *the state of being young;* juventus, juvenilis ætas *vel* status:—Ūre cnihthād is swylce undern-tīd, on đam astīhþ ūre geógoþ swā swā sunne dēþ ymbe đære đriddan tīde *our boyhood is as it were the third hour in which arises our youth as the sun does about the third hour,* Homl. Th. ii. 76, 15: Elen. Kmbl. 2528; El. 1265. Of mīnre geóguþe *a juventute mea,* Mk. Bos. 10, 20: Blickl. Homl. 211, 26. Đǣr is geógoþ būton ylde *there is youth without age,* 65, 17: Exon. 32 a; Th. 101, 6; Cri. 1654. On geóguþe *in youth,* 34 a; Th. 108, 19; Gū. 75: Ps. Th. 70, 4. Hie on geógoþe bu wlitebeorht wǣron on woruld cenned *they both in youth beautiful were born into the world,* Cd. 10; Th. 12, 18; Gen. 187: Ps. Th. 118, 141. On geógoþe *in youth,* Beo. Th. 4843; B. 2426. From gīgoþe mīnum *a juventute mea,* Mk. Skt. Lind. 10, 20: Lk. Skt. Lind. 18, 21. Se fērde on his iūgoþe fram his freóndum *he went in his youth from his friends,* Swt. A. S. Rdr. 95, 3. II. *the youth, young persons;* juventus, juvenes:—Eall sió gióguþ đe nū is on Angelcynne *all the youth now in England,* Past. Pref; Swt. 7, 10; Hat. MS. Đā wearþ iafeđe geógoþ afēded *then to Japhet was a youthful offspring born,* Cd. 78; Th. 96, 34; Gen. 1604. Ōđđæt seó geógoþ geweóx *until the youth grew up,* Beo. Th. 133; B. 66. Hyre byre Hrēđrīc and Hrōđmund and hæleđa bearn giógoþ ætgædere *her sons Hrethric and Hrothmund and children of warriors, the youth together,* 2384; B. 1189: Cd. 176; Th. 220, 34; Dan. 81. Helpe gefremman gumena geógoþe *to give help to the young men of the people,* Andr. Kmbl. 3228; An. 1617. Duguþe and geógoþe *to old and young,* 304; An. 152: Beo. Th. 323; B. 160. Heora geóguþ *juvenes eorum,* Ps. Th. 77, 64. Ic geseah mīne gesǣlinesse and mīn wuldor and đa fromnisse mīnre iūguþe *ego respiciens felicitatem meam insigni numero juventutis,* Nar. 7, 22. [*O. Sax.* jugud: *O. H. Ger.* jugund: *Ger.* jugend.]

geóguþ-cnōsl, es; *n.* [geóguþ *youth;* cnōsl *progeny, a family*] *A youthful family, young progeny;* novella famīlia, libĕri:—Ic bīde đǣr mid geóguþcnōsle *I abide there with my young progeny,* Exon. 104 b; Th. 396, 25; Rä. 16, 10.

geóguþ-feorh, geógoþ-feorh; *gen.* -feores; *dat.* -feore; *n.* [geóguþ *youth,* feorh *life*] *Youthful life, youth;* juventus:—Sumum đæt gegongeþ on geóguþfeore, đæt se endestæf weálīc weorþeþ *it happens to one in youthful life that the end is miserable,* Exon. 87 a; Th. 328, 1; Vy. 10: Beo. Th. 5321; B. 2664. On geógoþfeore *in youthful life,* 1078; B. 537.

geóguþ-hād, geógoþ-hād, es; *m. The state of youth, youth;* jŭventūtis stātus, jŭventus:—Đū hafast geóguþhādes blǣd *thou hast youth's prosperity,* Exon. 68 a; Th. 252, 25; Jul. 168: Elen. Kmbl. 2531; El. 1267. Đū me lǣrdest of geóguþhāde *dŏcuisti me a jŭventūte,* Ps. Th. 70, 16. On geógoþhāde *in youth,* Cd. 74; Th. 91, 4; Gen. 1507: Blickl. Homl. 59, 5: 211, 22.

geóguþ-hādnes, -ness, e; *f. The state of youth, youth;* ădŏlescentia:—On đa ǣrestan tīd mīnre geóguþhādnesse *cum prīmævo ădŏlescentiæ tempŏre,* Bd. 5, 6; S. 618, 36.

geóguþ-līc; *adj. Youthlike, youthful;* jŭvĕnīlis:—Ic ne wæs mīn mōd fullfremedlīce bewerigende đām geóguþlīcum unalȳfednessum *non anĭmum perfecte a jŭvĕnīlibus cohĭbens inlĕcebris,* Bd. 5, 6; S. 618, 39.

geóguþ-myru, we; *f. Youthful joy?* Exon. 109 b; Th. 419, 23; Rä. 39, 2.

Geóhel-, geóhhel-dæg, es; *m. Yule-day, a day at Yule-tide:*—On đone forman dæig on geáre đæt is on đone ǣrestan geóheldæig eall cristen folc wurđiaþ cristes acennednesse *on the first day of the year, that is, on the first day of Yule all christian folk honour Christ's birth,* Shrn. 29, 26. On đone eahteþan geóhheldæig biþ đæs mōnþes fruma đe mon nemneþ ianuarius *on the eighth day of Yule is the beginning of the month that is called January,* 47, 13.

Geóhol, Geóhhol, es; *n. Yule, Christmas:*—Đȳ twelftan dæge ofer geóhol *on the twelfth day after Yule,* Bd. 4, 19; S. 588, 8: L. Alf. pol. 5; Th. i. 64, 23, note. v. geól.

geoht, es; *n. A yoke,* L. In. 60; Th. i. 140, 8: 60; Th. i. 140, 7. v. geoc.

geohđu. v. gehđu.

GEÓL, giúl, iūl, geóhol, es; *n.* YULE, *Christmas;* festum nativitatis Domini:—On geól *at Christmas,* L. Alf. pol. 5; Th. i. 64, 23, note: Menol. Fox 59, note a. Đȳ twelftan dæge ofer geóhol *Epiphaniæ,* Bd. 4, 19; S. 588, 8. Feówertig daga ǣr eástran and feówertig daga ǣr Cristes acennisse đæt is ǣr geólum *fourty days before Easter and fourty days before Christ's birth, that is, before Christmas,* Shrn. 82, 11. [*Dan.* juul: *Swed.* jul, *m*: *O. Nrs.* jōl, *n. pl. festum jolense, festum natalitiorum Christi, festum quodvis, convivium.*] For this and the next word v. Grm. Gesch. D. S. c. vi, and Cl. and Vig. Icel. Dict. jól.

Geóla, Iūla, an; *m.* [geól *Yule*] *The* YULE or *Christmas month,* that is, *December:*—Se ǣrra geóla *the ere,* or *former yule, December.* Se æftera geóla *the after yule, January.* Se mōnaþ is nemned on Leden *Decembris,* and on ūre geþeóde se ǣrra geóla, forđan đa mōnþas twegen syndon nemde ānum naman, ōđer se ǣrra geóla [*December*], ōđer se æftera *mensis* [*Januarius*] *hic vocatur Latine* December, *nostra vero lingua prior Geola, quoniam duo sunt menses qui uno nomine gaudent, alter Geola prior* [December], *alter posterior* [January], Hick. Thes. i. 212, 56; Shrn. 153, 23-6. [*Goth.* jiuleis, *m.*]

geolca, gioleca, geoloca, an; *m. A* YOLK; ovi vitellus:—Sceáwa nū on ānum æge, hū đæt hwīte ne biþ gemenged to đam geolcan, and biþ hwæđere ān æg *look now on an egg, how the white is not mingled with the yolk, and yet it is one egg,* Homl. Th. i. 40, 28. On æge biþ gioleca on middan *in an egg the yolk is in the middle,* Bt. Met. Fox 20, 339; Met. 20, 170. Genim geolocan *take the yolk,* L. M. 1, 2; Lchdm. ii. 38, 7.

geold, es; *n. Charge, impost:*—Ne gafle ne geold *neither tax nor charge,* Chr. 675; Erl. 38, 1. Strange geoldes *heavy imposts,* 1124; Erl. 253, 21. v. gild.

ge-ōleccan; *v. a. To allure;* blandiri:—Đā hī đē mǣst geōleccan *when they most allure thee,* Bt. 7, 2; Fox 18, 1.

geole-wearte *a nightingale;* luscinus, Ælfc. Gl. 38; Som. 63, 37; Wrt. Voc. 29, 55.

geolhstor, geolstor, es; *m? Matter, corruption, poison, venom;* sanies:—Hire geolhstor ūt fleów *the matter flowed out from her,* Bd. 4, 19; S. 589, note 3. Geolster *virus, tabum,* Hpt. Gl. 517, 490.

geolna, an; *m. A kind of Egyptian stork;* ibis, Ælfc. Gl. 38; Som. 63, 30; Wrt. Voc. 29, 49.

geolo, geolu; *gen. m. n.* geolwes; *dat.* geolwum; *def.* se geolwa; *adj.* YELLOW; flavus:—Geolo godwebb *the yellow silk,* Exon. 109 a; Th. 417, 25; Rä. 36, 10. Geolwe linde [*acc. f.*] *yellow shield,* 5213; B. 2610. Him beóþ đa eágan geolwe *his eyes will be yellow,* L. M. 3, 62; Lchdm. ii. 348, 12. Geolo *flavus, fuscus,* Hpt. Gl. 510. Mid geolewere fāhnisse *crocea qualitate,* 419.

geolo-ādl, e; *f. The jaundice,* Lye.

geolo-blāc; *adj. Pale yellow,* Lye.

geoloca, an; *m. A yolk;* ovi vitellus:—Genim hænne æges geolocan *take the yolk of a hen's egg,* L. M. 1, 2; Lchdm. ii. 38, 7. v. geolca.

geolo-hwît; *adj. Yellow-white;* mellinus, color stramineus, Lye.

geolo-rand, es; *m. A yellow disk, shield,* Beo. Th. 880; B. 438: Elen. Kmbl. 235; El. 118. v. Grm. A. u. E. 145.

geolo-reád; *adj. Yellow-red;* croceus, Lye.

geolstrig; *adj. Poisonous;* virulentus, Hpt. Gl. 450, 453. Geolstru? Som.

geolwian; *p.* ode; *pp.* od *To become yellow;* flavescere. DER. a-geolwian.

geó-man, gió-man, -mann, es; *m. A man of old;* qui olim vixit. v. gió-man.

geómeleáslîce *carelessly.* v. gýmeleáslîce.

geómen *care.* v. gýmen.

geómerian *to groan, mourn, murmur,* Boutr. Scrd. 20, 43: Homl. Th. i. 142, 17. v. geómrian.

geómer-môd *sad of mind, sorrowful,* Cd. 40; Th. 53, 9; Gen. 858. v. geómor-môd.

geómerung *a groaning, moaning, lamentation,* Ps. Spl. 6, 6: Homl. Th. i. 142, 18: ii. 86, 16. v. geómrung.

geómian *to take care of.* v. gýman.

geómor, geómur, giómor; *adj. Sad, sorrowful, mournful, murmuring, miserable, wretched;* tristis, mæstus, quĕrŭlus, mĭser:—Him wæs geómor sefa *his mind was sad,* Elen. Kmbl. 1251; El. 627: Beo. Th. 98; B. 49. He đǽr âna sæt, geođum geómor *he sat there alone, sad of mind,* Andr. Kmbl. 2015; An. 1010. Ic of grundum to đē geómur cleopode *de profundis clāmāvi ad te,* Ps. Th. 129, 1. Đæt wæs geómuru ides *that was a mournful woman,* Beo. Th. 2155; B. 1075. Đeós geómre lyft *this murmuring air,* Cd. 163; Th. 205, 4; Exod. 430. Dust ne mæg andsware ǽnige gehâtan geómrum gâste *the dust cannot give any answer to the sad spirit,* Soul Kmbl. 211; Seel. 108: Apstls. Kmbl. 178; Ap. 89. Siđđan đû gehýrde galan geómorne geác on bearwe *when thou hast heard the sad cuckoo sing in the grove,* Exon. 123 b; Th. 473, 29; Bo. 22. He wæg hyge geómurne *he bare a mournful spirit,* 52 a; Th. 182, 15; Gû. 1310. In đas geómran woruld *in this sad world,* 57 b; Th. 207, 10; Ph. 139: 63 a; Th. 232, 35; Ph. 517. Geómran stefne *with mournful voice,* Andr. Kmbl. 122; An. 61: 2254; An. 1128. Geómre gâstas *sad spirits,* Cd. 4; Th. 5, 9; Gen. 69: 166; Th. 206, 5; Exod. 447. Geómrum to geóce *for salvation to the sad,* Exon. 9 b; Th. 8, 27; Cri. 124. [*Laym.* ȝeomere *doleful, miserable: O. Sax.* jâmar *depressed, sad, sorrowful: Dut.* jammer, *n. misery: Ger.* jammer, *m. misery: M. H. Ger.* jâmer, âmer, *m. pity: O. H. Ger.* jâmar, âmar, *m. mĭsĕria.*] DER. fela-geómor, hyge-, môd-, sîþ-, wine-.

geómor-frôd; *adj.* [geómor *sad,* frôd *old*] *Old with sadness;* mĭsĕre ætate provectus:—Ic eom geómorfrôd *I am old with sadness,* Cd. 101; Th. 134, 14; Gen. 2224.

geómor-gid, -gidd, -gyd, es; *n. A mournful song, dirge, lamentation;* lūgubris cantus, nēnia, lāmentātio:—Wæs geómorgidd wrecen *a mournful song was sung,* Andr. Kmbl. 3094; An. 1550. Geómorgyd, Beo. Th. 6291; B. 3150.

geómor-lîc; *adj. Sad, sorrowful;* mæstus, flēbĭlis:—Biþ geómorlîc gomelum eorle to gebîdanne, đæt his byre rîde giong on galgan *it is sad for an aged man to experience that his child hang young on the gallows,* Beo. Th. 4879; B. 2444: Ors. 4, 5; Bos. 81, 31. [*O. Sax.* jâmarlîk: *O. H. Ger.* jâmarlîh: *Ger.* jämmerlich.]

geómor-lîce; *adv. Sadly;* lūgubre:—He gilleþ geómorlîce *he yelleth sadly,* Salm. Kmbl. 535; Sal. 267.

geómor-môd, geómer-môd, giómor-môd; *adj. Sad of mind, sorrowful;* mæstus animo:—Ongan geómormôd to Gode cleopian *he sad of mind began to cry to God,* Andr. Kmbl. 2795; An. 1400: Beo. Th. 4094; B. 2044: Gen. 27, 34. Hie engel Drihtnes gemitte geómormôde *an angel of the Lord met her sad in mood,* Cd. 103; Th. 137, 3; Gen. 2268. Heó wǽron geómormôde *they were sorrowful,* Elen. Kmbl. 1107; El. 555: 825; El. 413. Gewitan him gangan, geómermôde *they retired, sad of mind,* Cd. 40; Th. 53, 9; Gen. 858. [*O. Sax.* jâmar-môd.]

geómrian, geómerian, geómran; *part.* geómrigende, geómriende, geómerigende, geómrende; *p.* ode; *pp.* od [geómor *sad, sorrowful*] *To be sad, to sigh, groan, murmur, mourn, sorrow, lament, bewail;* gĕmĕre, murmŭrāre, ingĕmĕre, ingĕmiscĕre, lūgēre, querī:—Se đe â wile geómrian on gihđa *who for ever will mourn in spirit,* Salm. Kmbl. 701; Sal. 350. Bēna geómrigende we asendaþ *prĕces gĕmentes fundĭmus,* Hymn. Surt. 21, 13. Gâþ geómriende weras wîf samod *men and women together go sorrowing,* Andr. Kmbl. 3328; An. 1667: Bd. 1, 27; S. 497, 35: Gen. 42, 38: Mk. Bos. 5, 38: 8, 12. Geómerigende *mourning,* Boutr. Scrd. 20, 42. Gē, geómrende, gehđum mǽnaþ *ye, murmuring, grieve in spirit,* Exon. 9 a: Th. 6, 26; Cri. 90: 48 a; Th. 164, 34; Gû. 1021. Ic geómrige *gĕmo,* Ælfc. Gr. 28, 3; Som. 30, 58. Hî murcniaþ ođđe geómriaþ *murmŭrābunt,* Ps. Spl. 58, 17. Hî geómeriaþ *they murmur,* Homl. Th. i. 142, 17. Ides geómrode giddum *the lady bewailed in songs,* Beo. Th. 2240; B. 1118. On đone heofon behealdende, geómrode *suspĭciens in cœlum, ingĕmuit,* Mk. Bos. 7, 34: Jn. Bos. 11, 33, 38. Ne geómra đû *be not thou sad,* Cd. 100; Th. 132, 25; Gen. 2198.

geómrung, geómerung, e; *f. A groaning, moaning, lamentation;* gĕmĭtus, lāmentum:—Brytta geómerung *gĕmĭtus Brittanōrum,* Bd. 1, 13; S. 481, 42. Fram geómrunga heortan mînre *a gĕmĭtu cordis mei,* Ps. Spl. 37, 8. On geómerunga mînre *in gĕmĭtu meo,* 6, 6: Bd. 5, 6; S. 619, 14. Hî getâcniaþ hâligra manna geómerunge *they betoken the groaning of holy men,* Homl. Th. i. 142, 18. Deáþes geómerunga me beeódon *the moanings of death surrounded me,* ii. 86, 16. On geómrungum *in gĕmĭtĭbus,* Ps. Spl. 30, 12. On geómrunga *in lamentation,* Blickl. Homl. 89, 14. For đære geómrunga đæs ôđres deáđes *for sorrow at the other's death,* 113, 11.

geómur *sad, sorrowful,* Ps. Th. 129, 1. v. geómor.

geóna; *adv. Hitherto, yet;* adhuc:—Hwædd geóna me gwona is *quod adhuc mihi deest?* Mt. Kmbl. Lind. 19, 20. Geóna hlifigende *adhuc vivens,* 27, 63. Đâ geóna [geone, Lind.] *athuc,* Jn. Skt. Rush. 11, 30: Mk. Skt. Rush. 5, 35. Ne đâ geóna *nondum,* Jn. Skt. Rush. 7, 39: 8, 57. v. gêna.

ge-onbyrdan; *p.* de; *pp.* ed *To bear against, strive against, resist:*—Gif he on đone geonbyrde đe hine slôg *if he strove against him who slew him,* L. In. 76; Th. i. 150, 18: L. E. G. 6; Th. i. 170, 13: L. Eth. v. 31; Th. i. 312, 11. v. ge-anbyrdan.

geonc *young,* Bt. 8; Rawl. 15, 13, note m. v. geong.

geond, giond; *prep. acc. Through, throughout, over, as far as, among, in, after, beyond;* per, trans, inter, post, ultra; κατά:—He gǽđ geond drige stôwa *ambulat per loca arida,* Mt. Bos. 12, 43: 14, 35. Đâ eôde geond Hiericho *tum perambulabat Jericho,* Lk. Bos. 19, 1. Beóþ mycele eorþan styrunga geond stôwa *terræ motus magni erunt per loca,* 21, 11. Geond eorþan *throughout the earth,* Beo. Th. 538; B. 266: Cd. 227; Th. 305, 10; Sat. 644. Geond gehwilce weras *viritim,* Ælfc. Gr. 38; Som. 41, 5. Hî ealle beweópon Aarones forđsîþ geond đrîtig daga *they all mourned Aaron's death during thirty days,* Num. 20, 29. Đē we þanciaþ geond ungeendode worulde *we will thank thee to all eternity,* Homl. Th. i. 76, 7. Geond to dæg *usque hodie,* Bd. 1, 1; S. 474, 28. Đǽr se hâlga stenc wunaþ geond wynlond *there a holy fragrance rests over the pleasant land,* Exon. 57 a; Th. 203, 10; Ph. 82. Geond sîdne grund *over the wide abyss,* Cd. 6; Th. 8, 35; Gen. 134. Đû geond holt wunast *thou shalt dwell among the groves,* Cd. 203; Th. 252, 6; Dan. 574. Geond đa þeóda *among the people,* Andr. Kmbl. 49; An. 25. Môdes snyttru seów and sette geond sefan monna *he sowed and set the wisdom of mind in the minds of men,* Exon. 17 b; Th. 41, 30; Cri. 663. Mân wridode geond beorna breóst *wickedness blossomed in the breast of men,* Andr. Kmbl. 1535; An. 769. Geond feówertig daga *post quadraginta dies,* Num. 13, 22. Fæder folca gehwæs us fêran hêt geond ginne grund *the father of every nation bids us depart beyond the abysmal deep,* Andr. Kmbl. 661; An. 331. Sittaþ yfele men giond eorþrîcu *wicked men sit in earthly kingdoms,* Bt. Met. Fox 4, 74; Met. 4, 37. Giond đas wîdan woruld *through this wide world,* 11, 89; Met. 11, 45. [*Laym.* ȝond *per.*] v. geondan, be-geondan.

geond; *adv. Yond, yonder, thither, beyond;* illuc:—Hider and geond *hither and thither,* Lye. Hyder geond *yonder,* Mt. Bos. 26, 36. [*Chauc.* yond: *Goth.* jaind *there.* Cf. *Orm.* ȝond *in* o ȝond half.]

geondan; *prep. acc. Beyond;* trans:—Đâ sône com Willelm eorl fram geondan sǽ *then earl William soon came from beyond sea,* Chr. 1052; Erl. 181, 29: 1048; Erl. 177, 28. v. geond, be-geondan.

geond-brǽdan; *p.* -brǽdde; *pp.* -brǽded [geond *over,* brǽdan *to spread*] *To overspread;* supersternĕre:—Hit geondbrǽded wearþ beddum and bolstrum *it was overspread with beds and bolsters,* Beo. Th. 2483; B. 1239.

ge-ondbyrde *strove against, resisted,* L. C. S. 49; Th. i. 404, 13, note 30. v. ge-onbyrdan.

ge-ondettan; *p.* te; *pp.* ed *To confess;* confĭtēri:—Đe geondettaþ *that confess,* Blickl. Homl. 57, 27. Gif he hit geondette *if he confess it,* L. In. 71; Th. i. 148, 3. v. ge-andettan.

geond-faran; *part.* -farende; *p.* -fôr, *pl.* -fôron; *pp.* -faren [geond *through,* faran *to go*] *To go through, pervade;* perambŭlāre, pervăgāri:—He langre tîde ealle heora mǽgþe mid gewêde wæs geonfarende *multo tempŏre totas eorum provincias debacchando pervăgātus,* Bd. 2, 20; S. 521, 27. Fram mangunge geondfarendre on þýstrum *a negŏtio perambŭlante in tenebris,* Ps. Lamb. 90, 6. Wæter wynsumu bearo ealne geondfaraþ *pleasant waters pervade all the grove,* Exon. 56 b; Th. 202, 10; Ph. 67.

geond-felan, -feolan: *p.* -fæl, *pl.* -fǽlon; *pp.* -folen [cf. (?) *Goth.* filhan: *Icel.* fela *to hide;* hence *to give into one's keeping;* so geondfolen fýre = *utterly given up to fire. Or may* folen *be taken from the literal meaning and so* geondfolen *compare with the preceding participle* geinnod? The meaning of the verb in any case seems to be] *To fill throughout;* mplere, Cd. 2; Th. 3, 29; Gen. 43.

geond-féran; *p.* -férde; *pp.* -féred [geond *through,* féran *to go*] *To go through, traverse;* pertransire, peragrāre:—Ne môstan đē geondféran foldbûende *earth's inhabitants may not traverse thee,* Exon. 121 a; Th. 465, 8; Hö. 101. Gewunede he swýđost đa stôwe geondféran, and in đâm tûnum godcunde lâre bodian, đa đe in heágum môrum and in hrêđum feor gesette wǽron *solēbat autem ea maxĭme lŏca peragrāre, illis prædĭcāre in vicŭlis, qui in arduis aspĕrisque montĭbus procul posĭti,*

Bd. 4, 27; S. 604, 26. Ic geondférde fela fremdra londa *I traversed many foreign lands*, Exon. 85 b; Th. 321, 22; Wíd. 50: 84 b; Th. 318, 23; Wíd. 3.

geond-flôwan; *p.*-fleów, *pl.*-fleówon; *pp.*-flôwen *To flow through*; pertransfluere:—Nales ðú geondflôwan foldbûende *thou flowest not through earth's inhabitants*, Exon. 121 a; Th. 465, 16; Hö. 105. v. flôwan.

geond-folen *filled throughout*, Cd. 2; Th. 3, 29; Gen. 43. v. geondfelan.

geond-geótan; *p.* -geát, *pl.* -guton; *pp.* -goten *To pour, pour out*; perfundĕre:—Ic geondgeóte *perfundo*, Ælfc. Gr. 28, 6; Som. 32, 33. Heó mid wôpe and mid teárum wæs swýðe geondgoten *flētuque ac lacrymis perfūsa*, Bd. 4, 23; S. 596, 10.

geond-hweorfan; *p.* -hwearf; *pp.* -hworfen *To turn* or *pass through, go about, traverse*; pertransire, peragrare, perlustrare:—Ðonne maga gemynd môd geondhweorfeþ *when remembrance of friends passes through his mind*, Exon. 77 a; Th. 289, 21; Wand. 51. Hwîlum cwēn flet eall geondhwearf *at times the queen went about all the hall*, Beo. Th. 4039; B. 2017. Ðonan ic ealne geondhwearf ēðel Gotena *thence I traversed all the country of the Goths*, Exon. 86 b; Th. 325, 9; Wíd. 109. Land eal geondhwearf *he travelled over all the land*, Salm. Kmbl. 372; Sal. 185. DER. hweorfan.

geond-hyrdan; *p.* de; *pp.* ed *To harden thoroughly*, Salm. Kmbl. 150, 28.

geond-innan; *prep. acc. Throughout*; per:—Geond woruld innan *throughout the world*, Exon. 14 b; Th. 29, 28; Cri. 469. Geond Bryten innan *throughout Britain*, 45 b; Th. 155, 5; Gû. 855: 95 b; Th. 355, 43; Pa. 4.

geond-lâcan; *p.* -lēc; *pp.* -lâcen *To go through* or *over, flow over*; pertransīre, transfluĕre:—Ðætte ðæt tírfæste lond geondlâce laguflôda wynn *that the joy of water-floods sports over the glorious land*, Exon. 56 b; Th. 202, 15; Ph. 70.

geond-leccan; *part.* -leccende; *p.* -lehte; *pp.* -leht *To wet through, moisten, water*; rīgāre:—Geondleccende muntas of heora uferum dǽlum *rīgans montes de sŭpĕriōrĭbus suis*, Ps. Lamb. 103, 13.

geond-lîhtan; *p.* -lîhte; *pp.* -lîhted; *v. a.* [lýhtan, lîhtan *to shine*] *To enlighten*; illūmĭnāre:—Sunne endemes ne mæg ealle [gesceafta] geondlîhtan innan and ûtan *the sun cannot equally enlighten all* [*creatures*] *within and without*, Bt. Met. Fox 30, 24; Met. 30, 12.

geond-mengan; *p.* de; *pp.* ed [mengan *to mingle*] *To mingle, confuse*; perturbāre:—Mec ðæs full oft fyrwit frineþ, môd geondmengeþ *about this my curiosity full oft enquireth, it confuses my mind*, Salm. Kmbl. 119, MS. B; Sal. 59.

geond-sâwan; *p.* -seów, *pl.* -seówon; *pp.* -sâwen *To sow, scatter, spread abroad*; serere, spargere, disseminare:—Deáw-driás winde geondsâwen *the dew-fall is scattered by the wind*, Cd. 188; Th. 233, 19; Dan. 278. DER. sâwan.

geond-sceáwian; *p.* ode; *pp.* od [sceáwian *to look*] *To look at, survey*; perlustrāre ocŭlis:—Georne geondsceáwaþ *earnestly surveys*, Exon. 77 a; Th. 289, 23; Wand. 52. Geondsceáwode he ða þing ðe to ðære stôwe belumpon *he looked about at the things which appertained to the place*, Guthl. 3; Gdwin. 22, 17.

geond-scînan, -scân; *pp.* -scinen *To shine upon, illuminate*; collustrare, illuminare:—Hit seó ēce ne môt geondscînan sunne *the eternal sun cannot shine on it*, Bt. Met. Fox 5, 88; Met. 5, 44: Salm. Kmbl. 678; Sal. 339: Bt. 41, 1; Fox 244, 9. Sió sunne hine geondscînþ *the sun shines upon him*, Bt. 34, 5; Fox 140, 8.

geond-scînþ *shines upon*, Bt. 34, 5; Fox 140, 8; *3rd pres. of* geondscînan.

geond-sêcan; *p.* -sôhte, *pl.* -sôhton; *pp.* -sôht *To search thoroughly, pervade*; pervestigare:—Se gifra gæst grundas geondsēceþ *the greedy guest shall pervade earth*, Exon. 22 a; Th. 60, 22; Cri. 973. His intinga wæs geondsôhte *his business was thoroughly searched*, Bd. 5, 19; S. 639, 28. DER. sêcan.

geond-sendan; *p.* -sende; *pp.* -sended *To overspread*; perfundere:—Wæs gûþ-hergum wera ēðel-land wîde geondsended *the people's native-land was widely overspread with hostile bands*, Cd. 92; Th. 118, 21; Gen. 1968: 119; Th. 154, 6; Gen. 2551.

geond-seón; *p.* -seáh *To see beyond* or *through*; perspicere, in conspectu habere, Beo. Th. 6166; B. 3087.

geond-smeágan; *p.*-smeáde; *pp.* -smeád *To search through, examine, discuss*; perscrūtāri, discŭtĕre:—Ðæt we geondsmeáge ða dīgolnysse ûre heortan *that we search through the secrets of our heart*, Bd. 4, 3; Whelc. 266, 43, MSS. B. C.

geond-spǽtan; *p.*-spǽtte; *pp.*-spǽt *To spit* or *squirt through, syringe through, to squirt water as through a syringe* or *pipe*; sīphonĭbus āquam exprĭmĕre:—Ðú hie ǽlce dæge mid pîpan geondspǽt *do thou syringe through it every day with a tube*, L. M. 2, 22; Lchdm. ii. 208, 26.

geond-sprengan; *p.* de; *pp.* ed *To sprinkle over*; perspergere, perfudere:—Se awyrgeda gâst ðæs ylcan preóstes heortan and geþanc mid his searwes âttre geondsprengde [-spregde, MS.] *the accursed spirit sprinkled over with the poison of his deceit the heart and mind of the same priest*, Guthl. 7; Gdwin. 44, 13. Me fugles wyn geond [-sprengde] spēd-dropum *the bird's delight* [*feather*] *sprinkled me over with copious drops*, Rä. 27, 8.

geond-spreót *sprouted through* or *over, pervaded*; pergerminavit, pervasit, Exon. 8 b; Th. 3, 27; Cri. 42. v. spreótan.

geond-, gend-springan *percrebrescere, multiplicari*, Hpt. Gl. 473.

geond-stredan; *p.* -stredde; *pp.* -streded, -stred *To scatter about, sprinkle*; spargĕre:—Ic geondstrede *spargo*, Ælfc. Gr. 28, 4; Som. 31, 37. Geondstred *scattered over*, Homl. Th. ii. 536, 18.

geond-styrian; *p.* ede; *pp.* ed [geond, styrian *to move, stir*] *To move* or *stir violently, to agitate*; per omnes partes commovere, agitare:—Geondstyred *agitated*, Bt. Met. Fox 6, 29; Met. 6, 15.

ge-ond-swarian; *p.* ode; *pp.* od *To answer*; respondere, Lk. Skt. Lind. 10, 28. v. and-swarian.

geond-þencan; *p.* -þohte; *pp.* -þoht [þencan *to think*] *To think over, consider, contemplate*; anĭmo lustrāre, contemplāri:—Ðonne ic eorla lîf eal geondþence *when I consider all the chieftains' life*, Exon. 77 a; Th. 290, 5; Wand. 60. Se ðis deorce lîf deópe geondþenceþ *he profoundly contemplates this dark life*, 77 b; Th. 291, 29; Wand. 89.

ge-ond-weardan, -wardan; *p.* de *To answer*, Blickl. Homl. 21, 21: Mt. Kmbl. Lind. 3, 15: 8, 8. v. ge-and-wyrdan.

ge-ond-weardian *to present*, Blickl. Homl. 181, 2: Rtl. 4, 28, 30. v. ge-and-werdian.

geond-wlîtan; *p.* -wlât, *pl.* -wliton; *pp.* -wliten. I. *v. trans. To look through, see through, look over*; perspĭcĕre, ŏcŭlis lustrāre:—He selfa mæg sǽ geondwlîtan *he can himself look through the sea*, Cd. 213; Th. 265, 18; Sat. 9: Beo. Th. 5335; B. 2771. Sunne woruld geondwlîteþ *the sun looks over the world*, Exon. 59 a; Th. 212, 16; Ph. 211. Ðæt ic ingehygd eal geondwlite *that I can see through all his inward thoughts*, 71 b; Th. 266, 17; Jul. 399. II. *v. intrans. To look about, look around*; circumspectāre:—Sioh sylfa ðē geond ðas sîdan gesceaft geondwlîtan *see thyself look around this wide creation*, Exon. 8 b; Th. 4, 30; Cri. 60.

geond-yrnan; *p.* -arn, *pl.* -urnon; *pp.* -urnen *To run about*; discurrĕre:—Ic geondyrne *discurro*, Ælfc. Gr. 47; Som. 48, 51.

ge-onet; *part. p. Hastened*; festinatus, Lye.

ge-ōnētan [?] *To make useless*:—Giōnētaþ ł gemerras *occupat*, Lk. Skt. Lind. 13, 7. Geōnēt *occupatus*, Lye. [Cf. (?) *Icel.* ū-nýta *to make useless, destroy*.]

ge-onfenge; *adj. Taken*:—Ân geonfenge biþ *una assumetur*, Lk. Skt. Lind. 17, 35. v. onfenge.

geong, es; *m. A course, passage, journey*; cursus, meātus, iter:—Ongunnon him on ûhtan æðelcunde mægþ gierwan to geonge *the noble women resolved ere dawn to prepare for a journey*, Exon. 119 b; Th. 459, 19, note; Hö. 2. Geong *iter*, Lk. Skt. Lind. 2, 44: 8, 1.

geong *sighs*; gemitus:—Hēr is Brytta geong [gnornung, B.] and geómerung *gemitus Brittanorum*, Bd. 1, 13; S. 481, 42.

GEONG, giong, geng, ging, giung, iung, gung; *def.* se geonga, seó, ðæt geonge; *comp.* geongra, gingra, gyngra; *superl.* gingest, gingst; *adj.* YOUNG, *youthful, new, recent, fresh*; jŭvĕnis, adolescens, nŏvellus, rĕcens:—Ðeáh ðe he geong sý folces hyrde *although he be a young shepherd of his folk*, Beo. Th. 3667; B. 1831: Rood Kmbl. 77; Kr. 39. Mǽden, oððe geong wîfman *puella*, Wrt. Voc. 73, 5. Se geonga mann *adolescens*, Mt. Bos. 19, 22: Lk. Bos. 7, 14: Ors. 2, 4; Bos. 45, 12: Chr. 871; Erl. 75, 23. Ymb ðæs geongan feorh *about the young man's life*, Andr. Kmbl. 2236; An. 1119. On swâ geongum feore *in so young a life*, Beo. Th. 3690; B. 1843. Me eáden wearþ, geongre *it was granted to me young*, Exon. 10 b; Th. 13, 11; Cri. 201. Ic ðē geongne gelǽrde *I taught thee young*, Bt. 8; Fox 24, 27: Andr. Kmbl. 1101; An. 551: 2222; An. 1112. Cýse geongne onfôn gestreón getācnaþ *to accept new cheese betokens gain*, Lchdm. iii. 200, 29. Ðǽr geonge wiste wîc weardian *where he knew the young* [*woman*] *to be abiding*, Exon. 67 a; Th. 248, 6; Jul. 91. Ðæt he feorh geong eft onfôn môte *that it may again receive a new spirit*, 62 a; Th. 228, 4; Ph. 433: 58 b; Th. 211, 3; Ph. 192. Sint geþreáde geonge gûþrincas *my young warriors are rebuked*, Andr. Kmbl. 783; An. 392: 1715; An. 860: 3060; An. 1533. Ða geongan leomu *the young limbs*, Exon. 87 a; Th. 327, 18; Vy. 5. Geongra gyfena *of recent gifts*, 65 a; Th. 239, 20; Ph. 624: 78 a; Th. 293, 16; Crä. 2. Geongum and ealdum *to young and old*, Beo. Th. 144; B. 72. He hēht hine geonge twegen men mid sîþian *he bade two young men accompany him*, Cd. 138; Th. 173, 27; Gen. 2867: Beo. Th. 4040; B. 2018. Geongra ic wæs, witendlîce ic ealdode *jūnior fui, etenim sĕnui*, Ps. Spl. C. 36, 26. Gingra brôðor *a younger brother*, Exon. 130 a; Th. 499, 2, note; Rä. 88, 9. Seó gingre *the younger*, Cd. 123; Th. 158, 5; Gen. 2612. Ic gyngra wæs *jūnior fui*, Ps. Spl. 36, 26. Gingran brôðor *younger brothers*, Exon. 129 a; Th. 496, 10; Rä. 85, 12. Ioseph gingst wæs hys gebrôðra *Joseph was the youngest of his brethren*, Ors. 1, 5; Bos. 28, 7. Se gingsta ys mid ûrum fæder *mĭnĭmus cum patre nostro est*, Gen. 42, 13, 32. Fram ðam yldestan ôþ ðone gingestan *a mājōre usque ad mĭnĭmum*, 42, 12. [*Wyc.* ȝong: *Chauc.* yong: *Laym.* ȝunge, ȝenge, ȝeonge: *Orm.* ȝung, ȝunng: *Plat.* jung, junk: *O. Sax.* jung: *Dut.* jong: *Frs.* jong: *O. Frs.* jung, jong:

Ger. jung: *M. H. Ger.* junc: *O. H. Ger.* jung: *Goth.* yuggs: *Dan. Swed.* ung: *Icel.* ungr: *Lat.* jŭvĕnis: *Sansk.* yuvan *young.*] DER. cild-geong, cniht-, ed-, fela-, heađo-, magu-.

geóng *went,* Beo. Th. 1855, note; B. 925; *p. of* gangan.

geongan, ic geonge, đú geongest, he geongeþ; *p.* gang, *pl.* gungon *To go;* ire:—He com to sele geongan *he came to go* [= *he came* or *went*] *to the hall,* Andr. Kmbl. 2624; An. 1313. Wutun geonga *eamus,* Mk. Skt. Lind. 14, 42: 12, 3, Geongende *ambulans,* 16, 12: Jn. Skt. Lind. 1, 36. Ic giungo, geongo, geonga *vado,* 13, 36, 33: 16, 7. Ic geonge *I go,* Exon. 106 a; Th. 403, 4; Rä. 22, 4. Heó to fenne gang *she went to the fen,* Beo. Th. 2595; B. 1295: 2022; B. 1009: 2636; B. 1316. Wyt on godes húse gungan [gangan, MS.] *in domo Dei ambulavimus,* Ps. Th. 54, 13. Geonge for đē care *intret in conspectu tuo gemitus,* Ps. Th. 78, 11. Nú đú lungre geong hord sceáwian *now go thou quickly and view the treasure,* Beo. Th. 5480; B. 2743. Geong *vade,* Jn. Skt. Lind. 8, 11. v. gân, gangan.

geongerdôm *subjection,* Cd. 14; Th. 18, 3; Gen. 267. v. geongordôm.

geonge-wifre, an; *f. A ganging-weaver, spider;* viātĭca arānea:—Wǽron ânlícast úre winter geongewifran, đonne hió geornast biþ, đæt heó afǽre fleógan on nette *our years* [lit. *winters*] *were most like to a spider when it is most eager to terrify flies into its net;* anni nostri sīcut arānea medĭtābuntur, Ps. Th. 89, 10. v. gange-wifre.

geong-líc; *adj. Youthful, young;* juvĕnīlis:—Geonglíc *juvĕnīlis,* Ælfc. Gr. 9, 28; Som. 11, 39. On geonglícum geárum *in his young years,* Homl. Th. ii. 118, 23. [*O. H. Ger.* junglich.]

geong-lícnys, -nyss, e; *f. Youth;* jŭventus, Scint. 32.

geong-ling, es; *m. A youngling, youth;* jŭvĕnis:—Đæt hí tǽcon sum geråd heora geonglingum *that they teach some prudence to their younglings,* Ælfc. Gr. pref; Som. 1, 30. [*O. H. Ger.* jungeling: *Ger.* jüngling.]

geongor-dôm, geonger-dôm, es; *m. Youngership, minority, subjection, obedience, service, vassalage;* juvĕnīlis status, obsĕquium, obēdientia, ministĕrium:—Hwý sceal ic búgan him swilces geongordômes *why shall I submit to him in such vassalage?* Cd. 15; Th. 18, 34; Gen. 283. Unc wearþ God yrre forđon wit him noldon hnígan mid heáfdum þurh geongordôm *God was angry with us two because we two would not bow to him with our heads in subjection,* 35; Th. 46, 12; Gen. 743: 30; Th. 41, 26; Gen. 662. Đæt he Gode wolde geongerdôme þeówian *that he would serve God in subjection,* 14; Th. 18, 3; Gen. 267. [*O. Sax.* jungar-dôm.]

geongor-scipe *youngership, service.* v. giongor-scipe.

geongra, giongra, gingra, gyngra, giungra, an; *m. A junior, disciple, vassal, subject, follower, attendant, servant;* jūnior, adŏlescentŭlus, discĭpŭlus, assecla, sectātor, mĭnister:—Geongra ic eom *adŏlescentŭlus sum ego,* Ps. Spl. 118, 141. Ne wille ic leng his geongra wurþan *I will no longer be his vassal,* Cd. 15; Th. 19, 15; Gen. 291: 15; Th. 18, 23; Gen. 277. Þurh ǽnne đara apostola geongrena *through one of the followers of the apostles,* Ors. 6, 11; Bos. 121, 8. He wolde Drihtnes geongran beswícan *he would deceive the subjects of the Lord,* Cd. 23; Th. 29, 15; Gen. 450.

geongre *a female servant, maid-servant.* v. gingre.

geónian; *part.* geóniende; *p.* ode; *pp.* od *To yawn;* hiāre:—Fore openre wunde and geóniendre *pro aperto et hiante vulnĕre,* Bd. 4, 19; S. 589, 19. Hí todydon heora múþ ongeán me swā swā leó đonne he geónaþ *aperuerunt in me os suum, sicut leo rapiens,* Ps. Th. 21, 11. v. gýnian.

geonlíc [= geonglíc?]; *adj. Youthful:*—For geonlíces mægdenes plegan *for a young maiden's play,* Shrn. 123, 7.

geonre; *adv. There, yonder;* illuc, Som. [Cf. *Goth.* jainar *there.*]

geónung, e; *f. A* YAWNING, *braying, chattering;* oscitatio, barritus, Cot. 95.

geópan, ic geópe, đú gýpst, he gýpþ, *pl.* geópaþ; *p.* geáp, *pl.* gupon; *pp.* gopen *To take up, take to oneself, receive;* accĭpĕre:—Ôþ-đæt ic spǽte eal-felo âttor, đæt ic ǽr geáp *until I spit the very baleful venom which I took up before,* Exon. 106 b; Th. 405, 29; Rä. 24, 9. [Cf. *Scot.* gowpen *to lift* or *lade out with the hands: Icel.* gaupn: *O. H. Ger.* coufan *both hands held together in the form of a bowl.*]

ge-openian; -openigean; *p.* ode; *pp.* od, ad. I. *trans. To open, manifest, shew, reveal:*—He bæd him engla weard geopenigean uncúđe wyrd *he prayed the guardian of angels to reveal to him the unknown fate,* Elen. Kmbl. 2201; El. 1102. Se anweald geopenaþ his yfel and gedēþ hit sweotol *power reveals his evil and makes it plain,* Bt. 16, 3; Fox 56, 20: Salm. Kmbl. 266, 2. He his godcundnysse mihta mid đam tâcne geopenode *he revealed the powers of his divinity with that miraclé,* Homl. Th. ii. 54, 31: Gen. 18, 20. He heofonan ríces infær geopenode *he opened an entrance to the kingdom of heaven,* Homl. Th. ii. 128, 24: 260, 11: i. 78, 27. Geopena ongeán me lífes geat *open to me the gate of life,* 76, 3. Đæt he geopenige *that he shew,* Past. 21; Swt. 159, 24; Hat. MS. God hine onwrýhþ đeáh đe wit hine ne geopenian *God will reveal it though we two do not make it manifest,* Blickl. Homl. 187, 17. Geopenod *opened,* 9, 8. II. *intrans. To open:*—Đá geopenode seó sǽ togeánes Moysen *the sea opened before Moses,* Swt. A. S. Rdr. 63, 228.

ge-orettan, -oretan, -orrettan; *p.* te; *pp.* ted *To disturb, confound;* perturbare, confundere:—Ealle beóþ georette eác gescende *omnes confundantur et conturbentur,* Ps. Th. 82, 13. Georetan *confundere, conturbare,* Gl. Prud. 735. Georrettan *infamare,* Cot. 111.

georman-leaf, es; *n. Mallow* [?] L. Med. 1, 27; Lchdm. ii. 68, 12: 33; 80, 9.

GEORN; *comp. m.* geornra; *f. n.* geornre; *sup.* geornast; *adj. Desirous, eager, anxious, ardent, zealous, studious, intent, careful, diligent;* cupĭdus, appĕtens, sollĭcĭtus, studiōsus, intentus, dīlĭgens:—Cyning biþ anwealdes georn *a king is desirous of power,* Exon. 89 b; Th. 337, 4; Gn. Ex. 59. Georn wísdômes *desirous of wisdom,* 81 a; Th. 305, 15; Fä. 88. Forđam đe ǽgđer đæra folca wæs đæs gefeohtes georn *because the people on both sides were eager for the fight,* Ors. 3, 8; Bos. 63, 35. Dǽda georn *zealous in deeds,* Cd. 188; Th. 233, 27; Dan. 282. Teónum georn *anxious for mischiefs,* 27; Th. 36, 34; Gen. 581. Azarias, dǽdum georn, Dryhten herede *Azariah, ardent in deeds, praised the Lord,* Exon. 53 a; Th. 185, 5; Az. 3. Ic beó lâreów georn *I am a diligent instructor,* 71 b; Th. 267, 3; Jul. 409. Mǽrþa georne *eager for glory,* Cd. 80; Th. 101, 5; Gen. 1677. Micle hý wǽron geornran đæt hí him fram flugen *they were much more eager that they should go from them,* Ors. 1, 7; Bos. 30, 9. Geornast *most eager,* Ps. Th. 89, 10. [*Piers P.* yerne *eagerly: Chauc.* yerne *brisk, quick: R. Brun.* ȝerne *earnestly: Laym.* ȝeorne, ȝeornen *earnestly, eagerly: Orm.* ȝeorne, ȝeorrne, ȝerne, ȝerrne, *willingly, earnestly: O. Sax.* gern *desirous: Frs.* jearn: *O. Frs.* ierne gerne *willingly: Dut.* gaarne *willingly: Ger.* gerne, gern *willingly: M. H. Ger.* gërne, gërn *desirous: O. H. Ger.* gern, gerni *intentus, cupĭdus, stŭdiōsus, prōnus: Goth.* gairns *yearning for: Dan.* gjerne *gladly: Swed.* gerna *fain, willingly: Icel.* gjarn *eager, willing.*] DER. ælmes-georn, clǽn-, dôm-, firen-, firwet-, fyrwet-, gilp-, glig-, ídel-, lof-, slâp-, weorþ-.

ge-orn *rose;* exortus est, surrexit, Bd. 4, 28; S. 605, 40; *p. of* ge-yrnan.

geornan, giornan, giornian; *p.* de, ade, ede; *pp.* ed *To desire, beg;* desīdĕrāre:—Gē geornaþ đæt gē woldon eówerne naman tobrǽdan geond ealle [eallne, MS.] eorþan *ye desire that ye should spread your name over all the earth,* Bt. 18, 2; Fox 64, 4. Se cyng and his witan georndon friþes *the king and his witan desired peace,* Chr. 1011; Erl. 144, 21. To geornanne *mendicare,* Lk. Skt. Lind. 16, 3. Giornade, giornede, giornde *begged,* Mk. Skt. Lind. 10, 46: 1, 40: Jn. Skt. Lind. 9, 8. v. gyrnan.

georne, giorne, gyrne; *comp.* geornor; *superl.* geornost, geornast; *adv. Eagerly, earnestly, diligently, carefully, zealously, willingly, readily, gladly, well;* cŭpĭde, enixe, dīlĭgenter, stŭdiōse, prompte, lĭbenter, bĕne:—Đæt fýr georne asēceþ innan and útan eorþan sceátas *the fire shall eagerly seek within and without the tracts of earth,* Exon. 22 b; Th. 62, 20; Cri. 1004: Cd. 29; Th. 38, 15; Gen. 606. Ic him georne đæs unrihtes andsæc fremede *I earnestly made denial to their injustice,* Elen. Kmbl. 940; El. 471: 1197; El. 600: Cd. 103; Th. 137, 4; Gen. 2268: 137; Th. 172, 19; Gen. 2846. He sōhte georne æfter grunde *he sought diligently along the ground,* Beo. Th. 4577; B. 2294: Exon. 44 b; Th. 150, 11; Gú. 777: 57 a; Th. 204, 4; Ph. 92. He befran hí georne hwænne se steorra him æteówde *dīlĭgenter dĭdĭcit ab eis tempus stellæ, quæ appāruit eis,* Mt. Bos. 2, 7: Ps. Th. 76, 6: 131, 5. Hæleþ hinfúse hýrdon to georne wrâđum wǽrlogan *the death-devoted men too readily listened to the furious pledge-breaker,* Andr. Kmbl. 1224; An. 612: Exon. 34 a; Th. 109, 24; Gú. 95. Ongan Dryhtnes ǽ georne cýđan *he began gladly to proclaim the Lord's law,* Elen. Kmbl. 398; El. 199: Cd. 32; Th. 42, 26; Gen. 679. Hit gōdode georne *it prospered well,* Chr. 959; Erl. 119, 13, 16: Bt. Met. Fox 20, 61; Met. 20, 31: 21, 39; Met. 21, 20. Geornor we woldon iówra Rômâna bismora beón forsúgiende *we would more willingly be silent about the shame of you Romans,* Ors. 3, 8; Bos. 63, 22: 3, 1; Bos. 53, 14. Swâ he geornost mǽge *as he best may,* Bt. Met. Fox 27, 58; Met. 27, 29. Geornast *most diligently,* Exon. 37 b; Th. 123, 25; Gu. 328.

geornes, geornys, gyrnes, gyrnys, -ness, -nyss, e; *f. Earnestness, diligence, industry, care, endeavour;* industria, stŭdium:—Mid đysses cyninges geornesse *hujus industria rēgis,* Bd. 3, 6; S. 528, 30. He hæfde swýđe mycle geornysse sibbe *stŭdium vĭdēlĭcet pācis hăbuit,* Bd. 3, 17; S. 545, 7: 3, 28; S. 560, 31. Míne geornnesse mid gōde đú gefyldest *thou didst satisfy my longing with good,* Blickl. Homl. 89, 4.

georneste; *adj. Earnest, serious:*—Georneste *seria,* Cot. 195. v. eorneste.

georn-ful, -full; *comp.* -fulra; *adj. Full of desire, eager, solicitous, anxious, strenuous, zealous, intent, diligent;* sollĭcĭtus, stŭdiōsus, anxius, sēdŭlus, intentus, dīlĭgens:—On orde stôd Eádweard, gearo and geornful *Edward stood in the array, ready and eager,* Byrht. Th. 139, 54; By. 274. Geornfull đú eart *sollĭcĭta es,* Lk. Bos. 10, 41. Wæs he on willsumnesse hâligrâ gebeda gecneord and geornfull *erat ōrātiōnum dĕvōtiōni sollertissĭme intentus,* Bd. 4, 28; S. 606, 34. Đæt he swâ geornfulle gýmenne dyde him đa hǽla úre þeóde *tam sēdŭlam erga sălūtem nostræ gentis cūram gessĕrit,* 2, 1; S. 501, 3: Hymn. Surt. 49, 21. Geornfulle men *diligent men,* Bt. 32, 3; Fox 118, 10. Se is yfla gehwæs geornfulra đonne ic *who is more zealous than I for every evil,* Exon. 70 b; Th. 261, 33; Jul. 324. He wiste đæt hý woldon geornfulran beón ðære wrace, ðonne ôðre men *he knew that they would be more eager for revenge than others*, Ors. 2, 5; Bos. 47, 3.

geornful-lîce; *comp.* -lîcor; *adv.* [geornful *eager*] *Anxiously, diligently, earnestly;* stŭdiōse, dīlĭgenter, sēdŭlo:—He hûsulfatu and leóhtfatu geornfullîce gegearwode *vasa sancta et lumĭnāria stŭdiōsissĭme părāvit*, Bd. 5, 20; S. 642, 4. Swâ he geornfullîcor ðæs êcan lîfes gewilnode *he the more earnestly desired the eternal life*, Homl. Th. ii. 120, 8.

geornful-nes, giornful-nes, -nys, -ness, -nyss, e; *f. Eagerness, diligence, earnestness, zeal, fervour, devotion;* sollertia, dīlĭgentia, industria, fervor, devōtio:—Sió geornfulnes [giornfulnes, MS. Hat.] eorþlîcra þinga ablent ðæs môdes eágan mid ðære costunga *the eagerness for earthly things blinds the eyes of the mind with temptation*, Past. 18, 2; Swt. 128, 15; Cot. MS. Ðeós geornfulnyss *hæc dīlĭgentia*, Ælfc. Gr. 43; Som. 45, 6. He geornlîce gŷmde ðæt he to lufan and to geornfulnesse awehte gôdra dǽda *ad dilectiōnem vero et sollertiam bŏnæ actiōnis excitāre cūrābat*, Bd. 4, 24; S. 598, 19: 5, 13; S. 632, 8. Ðâ he ðâ se cyning his gelǽrednysse and his geornfulnysse geseah *cujus ērudītiōnem atque industriam videns rex*, 3, 7; S. 529, 46. Mid mycelre geornfulnesse *devōtiōne magna*, 3, 30; S. 562, 3: L. Edg. i. 5; Th. i. 264, 22. Ðone pipor ða næddran healdaþ on heora geornfulnysse *piper quod serpentes servant sua industria*, Nar. 34, 22.

geornlîc; *adj. Desirable*:—Hit biþ geornlîc ðæt ... *it is desirable that* ..., Ors. 4, 13; Bos. 100, 28.

geornlîce; *comp.* -lîcor; *superl.* -lîcost; *adv. Earnestly, diligently, zealously, strenuously, carefully, willingly;* dīlĭgenter, stŭdiōse, obnixe, sollĭcĭte, lĭbenter:—Faraþ and axiaþ geornlîce be ðam cilde *īte, et interrŏgāte dīlĭgenter de puĕro*, Mt. Bos. 2, 8: Bd. 3, 11; S. 535, 28: 3, 19; S. 547, 14, 15: 4, 9; S. 576, 21: 5, 14; S. 634, 30. Ongan geornlîce on sefan sêcean weg to wuldre *she began earnestly in her mind to seek the way to glory*, Elen. Kmbl. 2293; El. 1148: Salm. Kmbl. 169; Sal. 84. He geornlîce on gebede hleóþrede *obnixius ōrātiōni incumbĕret*, Bd. 4, 3; S. 569, 11: 3, 28; S. 560, 17. Hî bǽdon hyne geornlîce *rŏgābant eum sollĭcĭte*, Lk. Bos. 7, 4. Geornlîce Cyriacus on Caluarie hleór onhylde *Cyriacus willingly bent down his cheeks on Calvary*, Elen. Kmbl. 2192; El. 1097. Ðæt he wolde Paulinus ðone bisceop geornlîcor gehŷran be ðam Gode sprecende ðe he bodade *quia vellet ipsum Paulīnum dīlĭgentius audīre de Deo quem prædĭcābat, verbum făcientem*, Bd. 2, 13; S. 516, 26, 30: 4, 9; S. 576, 34. Ðæt he geornlîcost God weorþige *that he most zealously worship God*, Exon. 14 a; Th. 27, 19; Cri. 433.

geornung, gyrning, e; *f. A yearning, desire, diligence*:—Ic haue geheórd seo kyninges Æðelrêdes geornunge *I have heard king Ethelred's desire*, Chr. 675: Erl. 37, 21. Geornung *industria*, Lye.

georran, girran, gyrran; ic georre, gyrre, ðû gyrst, he gyrþ, *pl.* georraþ; *p.* gear, *pl.* gurron; *pp.* gorren *To chatter, sound, creak;* sonare, stridere, garrire:—Ic gyrre *garrio*, Ælfc. Gr. 36; Som. 38, 29. Strengas gurron *the ropes creaked*, Andr. Kmbl. 748; An. 374. [Cf. *Laym.* ȝurren þa stanes 28358: garryng Morr. and Skt. Spec. 241, 163.]

ge-orsod *enraged*, Ps. Lamb. 105, 37. v. geyrsian.

georst *heath.* v. gorst.

georstan-dæg *yesterday.* v. gyrstan-dæg.

ge-ortrêwan; *p.* de; *pp.* ed [trêwan *to trust*] *To despair;* dēspērāre:—Ða þreó ðê ne lǽtaþ geortrêwan be ðam êcan lîfe *these three suffer thee not to despair of the everlasting life*, Bt. 10; Fox 30, 9. v. ge-ortrûwian.

ge-ortrûwian, -trŷwian; *p.* ode; *pp.* od [or *without*, treówian, trûwian *to trust*] *To distrust, despair;* diffīdĕre, dēspērāre:—Ða ðê ne lǽtaþ geortrûwian be ðis andweardan lîfe *they suffer thee not to despair of this present life*, Bt. 10; Fox 30, 7. Se man lôcaþ underbæc, ðe geortrûwaþ Godes mildheortnysse *the man looks behind who despairs of God's mercy*, Homl. Th. i. 252, 10. Ðæt ûre nân be his nêxtan ne geortrûwige *that none of us despair of his neighbour*, ii. 82, 27. Nis ðæt to geortrŷwianne *nec diffīdendum est*, Bd. 4, 19; S. 587, 32. Ðæt ðû ne geortrŷwe nânes gôdes on nânre wiðerweardnesse *that thou despair not of any good in any adversity*, Bt. 6; Fox 14, 35.

ge-orwênan; *p.* de; *pp.* ed [wên *hope*] *To despair, to be out of hope;* despērāre:—Georwened *despērātus*, Ælfc. Gr. 47; Som. 48, 38. Ðæt he ðŷ earmlîcor georwênedre hǽlo hêr nû forwurde *quo mĭsĕrābĭlius ipse despērāta sălūte pĕrīret*, Bd. 5, 14; S. 635, 3.

ge-orwyrþed *disgraced;* traductus, Cot. 171. v. onwurðe.

geó-sceaft, e; *f. That which has been determined of old, fate*:—Weras wyrd ne cûðon geósceaft grimme [MS. grimne] *men knew not their destiny, their grim fate*, Beo. Th. 2472; B. 1234. [Cf. frumsceaft, gesceaft.]

geó-sceaft-gást, es; *m. A fatal, dire spirit* [?] or *ancient spirit* [?]:—Ðanon wôc fela geósceaftgâsta wæs ðæra Grendel sum *thence arose many dire spirits, Grendel was one of them*, Beo. Th. 2536; B. 1266.

geosterlîc; *adj. Of yesterday;* hesternus. v. gysternlic.

geostra, giestra [estra, Ps. Spl: 89, 4] gystra, gyrsta; *adj. Of yesterday;* hesternus:—Geostran dæg *dies hesterna*, Ps. Th. 89, 4. Giostor doeg *heri*, Jn. Skt. Lind. 4, 52. Giestron *yesterday*, Exon. 111 a; Th. 424, 24; Rä. 41, 44. Gystran niht *yesternight*, Beo. Th. 2672; B. 1334. Gyrstan dæg *heri*, Jn. Bos. 4, 52: Th. An. 22, 1. [*Laym.* ȝerstendæi (o, u): *Goth.* gistra dagis *to-morrow*, with which meaning the *Icel.* i gör occurs, v. Cl. and Vig. Dict. gær: *O. H. Ger.* gestre, gesteren *heri;* gestren *hesternum*: *Ger.* gestern: *Lat.* heri, hesternus.]

geot *yet*, Bt. 5, 3. v. gyt.

GEÓTAN; ic geóte, ðû gŷtst, he gŷt, *pl.* geótaþ; *p.* geát, gêt, *pl.* guton; *pp.* goten; *v. a.* I. *to pour, pour out, shed;* fundere, effundere, profundere:—Teáras geótan *to shed tears*, Exon. 10 b; Th. 11, 19; Cri. 173. Geát teáras *shed tears;* fundebat lachrymas, Bd. 2, 6; S. 508, 9. He gêt ðæt blôd uppan ðæt weofod *fudit sanguinem super altare*, Lev. 8, 24: Ex. 24, 6. Swâ man gute wæter *as one would pour water*, Ps. Th. 78, 3. Ðŷ læs weras and idesa on geáþ gutan *lest men and women should pour it forth in mockery*, Exon. 50 b; Th. 176, 8; Gû. 1207. Ofer hleór goten *poured over the cheek*, Elen. Kmbl. 2264; El. 1133. II. *to flow, stream;* profluere, *v. n*:—He hâte lêt teáras geótan *he let hot tears flow*, Exon. 48 a; Th. 165, 16; Gû. 1029. Geofon geótende *the flowing sea*, Andr. Kmbl. 785; An. 393: 3014; An. 1510; Ps. Th. 17, 4. Mid geótendan here *with an overwhelming army*, Chr. 1052; Erl. 184, 17. III. *to found, cast*:—Gold and seolfur ðe hêr geótaþ menn *gold and silver that men here found*, Ps. Th. 134, 15. Hîg guton him hǽðenne god *they have made them a molten image*, Deut. 9, 12. [Cf. *Orm.* Moyses shollde ȝetenn himm a neddre: *Laym.* ȝeoten *to pour*: *Goth.* giutan: *O. Sax.* giotan: *Dan.* gyde: *Swed.* giuta *to cast*: *O. H. Ger.* giozan: *Ger.* giessen.] DER. a-geótan, be-, ge-, ofer-, on-, þurh-, to-.

geótende *arteries, veins;* arteriæ, Cot. 8.

geótere, es; *m. A pourer, melter, founder;* fūsor, flātor:—Se geótere *the founder*, Ors. 1, 12; Bos. 36, 27, 35. DER. âr-geótere.

geôtton *confirmed*, Chr. 656; Th. 53, 32; *for* geâtton. v. geâtan.

Geoweorþa *Jugurtha*, Ors. 5, 7.

ge-oweðan *to subdue;* subjugare:—He bæd his twâm sunum ðæt hî ðæs rîces ðriddan dǽl geoweðan sculdon *he ordered his two sons to subdue the third part of the kingdom*, Som. ge-ðeówan [?]

geoxa, geoxung *a sobbing, hiccup*, Cot. 109. v. geocsa.

gep *sly, cunning*, Scint. 3, 24, 65. v. geap.

ge-palmtwîged; *def.* se -twîgeda, seó, ðæt -twîgede; *part.* [palm-twîg *a palm-twig*] *Palm-twigged, adorned with palm-twigs;* palmæ rāmis ornātus:—Se gepalmtwîgeda Pater Noster *the palm-twigged Pater Noster*, Salm. Kmbl. 23; Sal. 12. Ðæt gepalmtwîgede Pater Noster, 77; Sal. 39.

ge-pilod *heaped* or *piled up*, Ex. 16, 14.

ge-pîned; *part. p. Punished*:—Ðætte hia wêre gepîned *puniri*, Lk. Skt. p. 9, 4.

ge-plægde *danced*, Mt. Kmbl. Lind. 14, 6. v. plægan.

ge-plantod; *part.* [plantian *to plant*] *Planted;* plantātus:—Sum man hæfde ân fîctreów geplantod on his wîngearde *arbŏrem fīci hăbēbat quīdam plantātam in vīnea sua*, Lk. Bos. 13, 6.

ge-portian; *p.* ode; *pp.* od *To beat, pound;* contundĕre:—Geporta ða wyrta tosomne *pound the herbs together*, Lchdm. iii. 4, 10. v. portian.

ge-pôs, es; *n. The* POSE, *a cold in the head, catarrh;* grăvēdo:—Wið gepôsu *for colds in the head*, Herb. 46, 1; Lchdm. i. 148, 12. Wið gepôsum *for poses*, L. M. 1, 10; Lchdm. ii. 54, 17.

ge-price *a point* or *comma;* comma, Som.

ge-punian; *p.* ode, ude; *pp.* od, ud *To pound, beat, bray;* contĕrĕre, contundĕre:—Gepuna eall tosomne *pound all together*, Herb. 101, 3; Lchdm. i. 216, 13. Genim ðas ylcan wyrte gepunude [gepunode, MS. B.] *take this same herb pounded*, 129, 3; Lchdm. i. 240, 15: 75, 1; Lchdm. i. 176, 20.

ge-pyndan; *p.* -pynde; *pp.* -pynded, -pynd *To pound, impound, shut up;* circumclūdĕre:—Nellaþ hie gehæftan and gepyndan hiora môd *they will not restrain and shut up their mind*, Past. 39, 1; Swt. 283, 13; Hat. MS. 52 b, 26. Ðæt wæter biþ gepynd *the water is shut up*, 38, 6; Swt. 277, 6; Hat. MS. 51 b, 13.

gêr, es; *n.* I. *a year;* annus:—Hærfest biþ hreðeádegost, hæleðum bringeþ gêres wæstmas *autumn is most joyous, [it] bringeth the fruits of the year to men*, Menol. Fox 477; Gn. C. 9. Wintras oððe gêr *winters or years*, Glos. Prudent. Recd. 139, 23. II. *the Anglo-Saxon Rune* ᛄ = *g*, the name of which letter in Anglo-Saxon is gêr *a year*, hence, this Rune not only stands for the letter *g*, but for gêr *a year*, as,—ᛄ [gêr] byþ gumena hiht, ðonne God lǽteþ hrusan syllan beorhte blǽda beornum and þearfum *the year is the hope of men, when God letteth the earth give her bright fruits to rich and poor*, Runic pm. 12; Kmbl. 341, 20; Hick. Thes. i. 135. v. geár *winter*, II.

ge-râd. v. ge-rîdan.

ge-râd, es; *n. Consideration, account, condition, reason, wisdom, prudence, manner;* ratio, conditio:—Ðâ he ðæt gerâd sette *cum coepisset rationem ponere*, Mt. Bos. 18, 24. Se hlâford dyhte hym gerâd *dominus posuit rationem cum eis*, 25, 19. Ðâm ealdum gedafenaþ ðæt hî tǽcon sum gerâd heora geonglingum *ad senes spectat juvenes prudentia erudire*, Ælfc. Gr. pref; Som. 1, 33. On ðæt gerâd ðet he gesylle ǽlce geáre *on the condition that he give every year*, Th. Chart. 147, 31: Chr. 945:

Erl. 116, 31. To ðam geráde ðe . . . *on the condition that* . . . , Th. Chart. 168, 13. On ða ylcan geràd *under the same conditions*, Ps. Th. 9, argument 3. Crist awende úre stuntnysse to geráde *Christ turned our folly to wisdom*, Homl. Th. i. 208, 19. ¶ On ðæt geràd *for that reason*, Ors. 1, 12; Bos. 36, 4. On ða geràd *on the condition* or *account*, Bt. 7, 3; Fox 22, 7: Chr. Erl. 3, 15: 1093; Erl. 229, 25.

ge-râd; *adj. Considered, instructed, learned, skilful, expert, prudent, suited, conditioned;* consultus, consideratus, instructus, peritus, prudens, elegans, concinnus:—Gif ic ðé gerâdne gemête *if I find thee instructed* [*skilful*], Bt. 5, 1; Fox 10, 16. Hí wurdon gerâde wígcræfta *they became skilful in the arts of war*, Ors. 1, 2; Bos. 26, 29. Sió is swíðe wel gerâd and swíðe gemetfæst *she is very prudent and very modest*, Bt. 10; Fox 28, 20: Beo. Th. 1751; B. 873. Ic him rûmne weg and gerâdne tǽhte *I might shew him a spacious and direct road*, Guthl. prol; Gdwn. 6, 3. On gerâde sprǽce *into prose*, Bd. 5, 24; S. 648, 22. Gerâd beón wiþ his wyrd *to be suited to his fortune*, Bt. 11, 1; Fox 32, 11. ¶ Ðus gerâd, swâ gerâd *such, of such sort*, Jn. Bos. 8, 5: Deut. 4, 32: Basil admn. 2; Norm. 36, 30: Guthl. 3; Gdwn. 22, 2: Bt. 39, 11; Fox 230, 16. Hû gerâd *of what kind*, Guthl. 17; Gdwn. 72, 2. [*Laym.* i-rad: *Goth.* ga-raids.] DER. un-ge-râd.

ge-râdegian; *p.* ode; *pp.* od *To reckon with*:—Anlíc ðam cyninge ðe hys ðeówas gerâdegode *adsimilatum regi qui voluit rationem ponere cum servis suis*, Mt. Bos. 18, 23. [Cf. ge-râdian.]

ge-râdian; *p.* ode; *pp.* od *To arrange, reason, argue;* disponere, rationem conferre, supputare cum aliquo:—Wiðerwearda gesceafta wǽron gegaderode and gerâdode *contrary creatures were united and arranged*, Bt. 35, 2; Fox 156, 36. v. ge-rǽdan.

ge-râdnes, -ness, e; *f. An agreement, a conspiracy;* conjuratio, Cot. 209.

ge-radod; *part. p. Quick;* citatus, Obs. Lun. 26; Lchdm. iii. 196, 7. v. ge-hradian.

ge-râdscipe, es; *m.* [gerâd *consideration*, scipe *condition*] *Prudence;* prudentia:—He âwuht nafaþ on his môdsefan rihtwísnesses ne gerâdscipes *he has not aught in his mind of wisdom or prudence*, Bt. Met. Fox 22, 96; Met. 22, 48.

ge-rǽc, es; *m? Opportunity;* opportunitas:—In gerǽcum *in opportunitatibus*, Ps. Spl. 9, 9.

ge-rǽcan, -rǽcean; *p.* -rǽhte; *pp.* -rǽht *To reach, obtain, seize, get, lay hold on, attain, reproach, present, offer*:—Sió fird hie gerǽcan ne mehte *the* [*English*] *force could not reach them*, Chr. 895; Erl. 93, 22: 894; Erl. 90, 11: Cd. 216; Th. 275, 10; Sat. 169. Gerǽcean, Blickl. Homl. 207, 22. Ne ðû ðé ǽfre ne lǽt wlenca gerǽcan *never do thou let pride lay hold on thee*, Bt. Met. Fox 5, 61; Met. 5, 31. Ðæs landes mâre gerǽcan *to obtain more of the land*, Chr. 921; Erl. 106, 21. Sige gerǽcan *to get the victory*, Ors. 3, 1; Bos. 53, 30: 9; 68, 11, 12. Andlifne gerǽcan *to get* [*one's*] *living*, Cd. 43; Th. 57, 26; Gen. 934. Of eágum teáras gerǽcan *to draw tears from the eyes*, L. Edg. C. iv; Th. ii. 288, 5. Ðæt he þence ðone sélestan hwet-stân on to gerǽcanne *that he think of applying the best whetstone*, Ors. 4, 13; Bos. 100, 30. To freán hond gerǽcan *to present to the lord's hand*, Exon. 90 b; Th. 339, 10; Gn. Ex. 92. Siððan ic ðurh hylles hrôf gerǽce *when I reach through the hill's summit*, 104 b; Th. 397, 30; Rä. 16, 27. Ðe gerǽcaþ wǽpen *whom weapons reach*, 102 a; Th. 386, 7; Rä. 4, 58. Ðû me gerǽhtest mid handa *extendisti manum tuam*, Ps. Th. 137, 7. Hyne Wulf wǽpne gerǽhte *Wolf reached him with his weapon*, Beo. Th. 5923; B. 2965: 1117; B. 556: Byrht. Th. 135, 63; By. 142: 136, 29; By. 158. He ða burh gerǽhte *he took the town*, Ors. 2, 4; Bos. 44, 14. He hǽlu gerǽhte écan lífes *he obtained the salvation of eternal life*, Exon. 35 a; Th. 112, 12; Gû. 142. Ða scipo alle gerǽhton *seized all the ships*, Chr. 885; Erl. 82, 29: Cd. 119; Th. 154, 13; Gen. 2555. Hí ðæt ríce gerǽht hæfdon *they had got that kingdom*, Bt. Met. Fox 26, 36; Met. 26, 18. Æfter ðæm ðe ða wíf hí swâ scandlíce gerǽht hæfdon *after the women had so reproachfully addressed them*, Ors. 1, 12; Bos. 36, 12.

ge-rǽd *elegans*, Cot. 80.

ge-rǽd *advised; p. of* ge-rǽdan; *p.* -reórd.

ge-rǽdan; *p.* -reórd, -rêd, -rǽd *To give counsel, advise, bring about by advice;* consilium dare:—Ðe him ðone teónan gerǽd *who brought that injury upon them by his counsel*, Cd. 37; Th. 48, 12; Gen. 774: 37; Th. 49, 25; Gen. 797. [Cf. *O. Sax.* Siu bad, that he iru helpa gerêdi.] v. rǽdan; *p.* -reórd.

ge-rǽdan; *p.* de; *pp.* ed, -rǽdd, -rǽd. I. *to arrange, dispose, direct, advise, determine, ordain, consult for, provide for;* decernere, statuere, edicere, consulere, providere:—Gerece and gerǽd ða rihtwísan *diriges justum*, Ps. Th. 7, 10: 24, 4. Gerǽdes *dispensas*, Rtl. 71, 11. Ðæne rǽd gerǽdde Síric arcebisceop *that counsel advised archbishop Sigeric*, Chr. 991; Th. 238, 28: 1052; Th. 320, 13, col. 1. Gyf ðû ðæt gerǽdest *if thou decidest on that*, Byrht. Th. 132, 54; By. 36: Exon. 92 a; Th. 344, 24; Gn. Ex. 178. Ðâ witan gerǽddan *the counsellors ordained*, L. E. G. 4; Th. i. 168, 15. Heó hire feax gerǽdde *crines composuit*, Bd. 3, 9; S. 534, 13. [Cf. *Icel.* greiða hâr *to dress the hair.*] Biðon girǽded *disponentur*, Rtl. 86, 24. Ic ðone friþ gerǽdd hæbbe *I have ordained the peace*, L. Ath. v. § 11; Th. i. 240, 14. Gerǽd *ordained*, § 10; Th. i. 240, 2: L. Eth. vi. 32; Th. i. 324, 1. [*Goth.* ga-raidjan *to enjoin*: *Icel.* greiða *to arrange.*] II. *to read;* legere:—Sý gerǽd *sit lectus*, C. R. Ben. 22. Hit is gerǽd on gewyrdelícum racum *it is read in historical narratives*, Homl. Th. i. 58, 9. Ðonne gerǽde gê ðâs word beforan him ðæt híg gehíron *then read these words before them that they may hear*, Deut. 31, 11. [Cf. ge-râdian.]

ge-rǽde, es; *n*: ge-rǽdu, e; *f? A housing, harness, trappings, equipage;* phaleræ, apparatus:—Ða here-geata medemra þegna syndon hors and his gerǽda *the heriots of the medial thanes are a horse and his trappings*, L. C. S. 72; Th. i. 414, 12, MS. G: Bd. 3, 14; S. 540, 22, MS. B. Folc féreþ herega gerǽdum *the nation marches with martial equipage*, Cd. 209; Th. 259, 29; Dan. 699: Elen. Kmbl. 2105; El. 1054: 2213; El. 1108. v. ge-rêde, ge-rǽþle.

ge-rǽde; *adj. Ready, swift, prompt, easy, plain, simple;* paratus, celer, promptus, expeditus, planus, simplex:—He gedyde míne fét swâ gerǽde swâ swâ heorotum *qui perfecit pedes meos* [*celeres*] *tanquam cervi*, Ps. Th. 17, 32. Ge meterfers, ge gerǽdre sprǽce *et versibus heroicis, et simplici oratione*, Bd. 4, 28; S. 605, 13: 5, 18; S. 636, 6; Bd. 5, 24; S. 648, 27. [*Icel.* greiðr *ready, free*: cf. *North. E.* gradely.] v. rǽde, ge-râd.

ge-rǽden, ne; *f. A proposal, purpose, condition;* propositum, Rtl. 92, 36. On ða gerǽdene *on the condition*, Th. Chart. 484, 29.

ge-rǽdend, es; *m. A disposer;* dispositor, Rtl. 108, 16.

ge-rǽding, es; *m. A decree;* consultum, Cot. 59; Lye.

ge-rǽdnes, -rǽdnis, -rǽdnys, -ness, e; *f. An ordinance, a decree, purpose, an intention, a resolution, condition;* consultum:—Ðis is seó gerǽdnys ðe Eádgâr cyng gerǽdde *this is the ordinance that king Eadgar ordained*, L. Edg. i. pref; Th. i. 262, 2: L. E. G. pref; Th. i. 166, 5: L. Ath. v. pref; Th. i. 228, 6: L. Eth. vi. 1, 2, 3; Th. i. 314, 2, 12, 19: Cod. Dipl. ii. 150, 33: Th. Chart. 168, 27. In ðas gerêdnisse *on this condition*, 104, 20. [Cf. *Goth.* ga-raideins *an ordinance.*]

ge-rǽdod; *part. p. Furnished with trappings, harnessed*:—Ân gerǽdod hors *a harnessed horse*, Ælfc. T. Lisle 36, 12: Th. Chart. 501, 5. v. ge-rǽde; *subst.*

ge-rǽf; *adj. Fixed;* fixus:—Gif mon folc-leásunge gewyrce and hió on hine gerǽf weorðe *if a man commit folk-leasing and it be fixed upon him*, L. Ælf. 32; Th. i. 80, 21, note.

ge-rǽft *torn, distracted;* discerptus, Bt. 37, 1; Fox 186, 21.

ge-rǽpan *to bind*, Bt. Met. Fox 13, 15; Met. 13, 8: 25, 73, 96; 25, 37, 48. v. rǽpan.

ge-rǽsan; *p.* de; *pp.* ed [rǽsan *to rush*] *To rush;* irrûere:—Ðe wið swâ miclum mægne gerǽsde *who rushed against so great a power*, Cd. 97; Th. 126, 15; Gen. 2095: Beo. Th. 5671; B. 2839. Hí gerǽsdon *they rushed*, Chr. Erl. 5, 7: Shrn. 130, 22, 23.

ge-ræstan *to rest, sit;* quiescere:—Geræstun mid þone Hæland *discumbebant cum Jesu*, Mt. Kmbl. Lind. 9, 10: Mk. Skt. Lind. 2, 15: Jn. Skt. Lind. 21, 20. v. ræstan.

ge-rǽswa, an; *m.* [rǽswa *a chief*] *A chief, prince;* dux, princeps:—Cymeþ engla gerǽswa *the prince of angels cometh*, Salm. Kmbl. 223; Sal. 111.

ge-rǽþle, an; *n. A harness, trappings;* phaleræ:—Hors and his gerǽþlan *a horse and his trappings*, L. C. S. 72; Th. i. 414, 12. v. ge-rǽde.

ge-rǽwen, -rǽwud *set in rows, plaited, embroidered;* segmentatus:—Gerǽwen hrægel *segmentata vestis*, Ælfc. Gl. 63; Som. 68; Wrt. Voc. 40, 10.

ge-rafende, -rawende RIFTING, *cleaving;* infindens, Cot. 181.

Geransingas; *gen.* a; *pl. The Gergesenes*:—In lond Geransinga *in regionem Gerasenorum*, Mt. Kmbl. Rush. 8, 28.

ge-rár *a roaring, howling;* boatus, ululatus, Shrn. 50, 10.

ge-rás. v. ge-rísan.

GERD, e; *f. A yard, rod, reed, twig, young shoot;* virga, arundo, Mt. Kmbl. Lind. 11, 7: 12, 20. Sex foður gerda *six fothers of faggots*, Th. Chart. 104, 27.

gerdel *a girdle*, Prov. 31. v. gyrdel.

gere; *adv. Entirely, well, very well;* penitus, bene, optime, Cd. 158; Th. 196, 14; Exod. 291. v. geare; *adv.*

ge-reǽpan *to bind.* v. ge-rǽpan.

ge-reáfa, an; *m. A reeve, judge, count;* præfectus, judex, comes:—Ic bebeóde eallum mínum gereáfum *I command all my reeves*, L. Ath. i. prm: Th. i. 194, 14. v. ge-réfa.

ge-reáfian; *p.* ode; *pp.* od *To rob, steal, spoil*:—Gereófage *diripere*, Mk. Skt. Lind. 3, 27. Secgaþ ðæt his ðegnas gereáfodan his líc on us and forstǽlan *say that his disciples robbed his body from us and stole it away*, Blickl. Homl. 177, 29. Gereáfydon *diripiebant*, Ps. Spl. C. 43, 12. Ðone deórwyrþan gym ðone ðe deófol wolde gereáfian *the precious jewel that the devil would steal*, Shrn. 155, 21.

ge-reahte, -reaht *related, explained, denoted, directed, ruled, reproved*, Exon. 34 b; Th. 110, 12; Gû. 106: Bt. Met. Fox 11, 197; Met. 11, 99; *p. and pp. of* ge-reccan.

ge-rec, es; *n. Rule, government, management, order, direction, explanation;* regimen, moderamen, ratio, directio, expositio:—On ðara ôðra mǽgþa gerece awunode *in illarum provinciarum regimine permansit*, Bd. 4, 12; S. 581, 28: 4, 23; S. 593, 26. Ðone bisceophâd mid mycele gerece heóld and rihte *episcopatum sedulo moderamine gessit*, 3, 7; S. 530, 35: Bt. 21; Fox 74, 29: Bt. Met. Fox 22, 2; Met. 22, 1. Be efen-nihte æfter Anatholius gerece *concerning even-night* [*the equinox*] *after the explanation of Anatolius*, Bd. 5, 23; S. 648, 19, note.

ge-rec, es; *n. A tumult:*—Gerec *tumultus*, Mt. Kmbl. Lind. 27, 24. [Cf. (?) *O. H. Ger.* ungareh *tumultus*.]

ge-reca, an; *m. A governor, ruler, prefect;* præfectus:—Heáh gereca *summus præfectus*, Nat. S. Greg. Els. 21, 1.

ge-reccan, -recan, -reccean; ic -recce, ðú -reccest, -recest, he -receþ, -recþ; *imp.* -rece; *p.* -reahte, -rehte; *pp.* -reaht, -reht; *v. trans.* I. *to put forth, shew, relate, express, denote, explain, interpret, translate;* exponere, demonstrare, narrare, referre, disserere, exprimere, interpretari, reddere:—Ic gereccan mæg *I can shew*, Bt. Met. Fox 25, 74; Met. 25, 37. Ic eów mæg gerecan [MS. Cot. gereccan] *I can shew you*, Bt. 11, 2; Fox 34, 7. Gé ðæt cunnon gereccan *ye know how to relate that*, Elen. Kmbl. 1294; El. 649: Homl. Th. ii. 118, 3. Nemn nú gif ðú hit gereccean mǽge *declare it now if thou art able to shew it*, Blickl. Homl. 181, 14. Aristoteles hit gerehte *Aristotle has explained it*, Bt. 40, 6; Fox 242, 2. Wordum gereccan *to express in words*, 20; Fox 70, 28. Ðæt is gereht Crist *quod est interpretatum Christus*, Jn. Bos. 1, 38, 41, 42: Exon. 9 b; Th. 9, 12; Cri. 133. Emanuhél, ðæt ys gereht on úre geþeóde, God mid us *Emanuel, which is, translated into our speech, God with us*, Mt. Bos. 1, 23: Mk. Bos. 5, 41: 15, 22. Gereccean þancas *referre gratias*, Procem. R. Conc. II. *to set forth, extend, direct, order, rule, control, reprove, correct, subdue, reduce to subjection;* exponere, extendere, dirigere, regere, corripere, corrigere, subigere, sub imperium redigere:—Sý on ðínre gesihþe mínes sylfes gebed gereht swá rícels byþ *dirigatur oratio mea sicut incensum in conspectu tuo*, Ps. Th. 140, 2. Sǽd heora on worulda biþ gereht *semen eorum in seculum dirigetur*, Ps. Spl. 101, 29. He hie gereceþ to eallum gódum *he will direct them to all good*, Blickl. Homl. 79, 33. Ne biþ se ofer eorþan gereaht *non dirigetur super terram*, Ps. Th. 139, 11. Gerece on gesihþe ðíne weg mínne *dirige in conspectu tuo viam meam*, Ps. Spl. 5, 9: 24, 5: 39, 3: Ps. Th. 118, 133. Hú Gúþlác his in Godes willan mód gerehte *how Guthlac directed his mind to God's will*, Exon. 34 a; Th. 108, 3; Gú. 67. Óþ-ðæt ðæs gewinnes God ende gereahte *until God directed an end of the strife*, 34 b; Th. 110, 12; Gú. 106. Ða witan gerehton Eádgife ðæt heó sceolde hire fæder hand geclǽnsian *the witan directed Eadgifu to clear her father's hand*, Chart. Th. 201, 33: 70, 31. Míne fét to heofenum gereahte *my feet* [*shall be*] *directed to heaven*, Blickl. Homl. 191, 7. Gif hiora mód-sefa meahte weorþan staðol-fæst, gereaht þurh ða strongan meaht *if their mind might become stable, ruled by strong might*, Bt. Met. Fox 11, 197; Met. 11, 99. Me sóþfæst symble gerecce and mildheorte móde þreáge *corripiet me justus in misericordia et increpabit me*, Ps. Th. 140, 7: Exon. 66 b; Th. 247, 4; Jul. 73. To gereccanne ðone gedwolan *ad corrigendum errorem*, Bd. 3, 30; S. 562, 9. In anwald gerehton *they reduced to subjection*, Bt. 1; Fox 2, 5. Mon gerehte ðæt yrfe cinge *the property was confiscated to the king*, Th. Chart. 173, 1. v. reccan.

ge-recce-líc; *adj. Stretched out, extended, strict, firm, steadfast;* extensus, strictus, firmus, Som.

ge-recednys, -recednes, -recenes, -nyss, e; *f. A narration, history, report, an interpretation, a direction, correction;* narratio, relatio, historia, interpretatio, directio, correctio:—Ðæt gódspell æfter Matheus gerecednysse *the gospel according to the narration of Matthew*, Mt. Bos. titl: Mk. Bos. titl: Greg. Dial. 2, 15: Th. Apol. 1, 1. To mǽgwlite andgytes and gástlícra gerecenessa ic to ætýcte *ad formam sensus et interpretationis eorum superadjeci*, Bd. 5, 23; S. 647, 35. Ðú gearwodest gerecednyssa, dóm and rihtwísnysse on Iacobe ðú dydest *tu parasti directiones, judicium et justitiam in Iacob tu fecisti*, Ps. Spl. 98, 4: 96, 2.

ge-recenian; *p.* ode; *pp.* od *To explain;* exponere, explanare, interpretari:—Rún biþ gerecenod *a mystery shall be explained*, Cd. 169; Th. 211, 12; Exod. 525.

ge-rec-líce; *adv. In a direct course, directly, extensively, strictly, firmly;* extenso cursu *vel* modo, directe, stricte, firme:—Gereclíce rihte flóweþ *flows in a direct course straight along*, Bt. Met. Fox 5, 27; Met. 5, 14: 24, 16; Met. 24, 8: Bt. 35, 4; Fox 162, 1.

ge-réde, an; *n. Harness, trappings;* phaleræ:—Hors and his gerédan *a horse and his trappings*, L. C. S. 72; Th. i. 414, 12, note 39. [Cf. ge-rǽde.]

GE-RÉFA, ge-reáfa, groefa, an; *m. A prefect, steward, fiscal officer of the shire* or *county, judge, reeve* or *sheriff, count;* præpŏsĭtus, villĭcus, jūdex, præfectus, cŏmes:—Fóreset *vel* geréfa *præpŏsĭtus*, Ælfc. Gl. 87; Som. 74, 37; Wrt. Voc. 50, 19. Cwæþ se geréfa *ait villĭcus*, Lk. Bos. 16, 3. Gif man biscopes esne tihte oððe cyninges, cænne hine on geréfan hand, oððe hine geréfa clénsie, oððe selle to swinganne *if any one accuse a bishop's servant or that of the king, he shall clear himself before the judge, either the judge shall clear him or give him up to be scourged*, L. Wih. 22; Th. i. 42, 4. Ðæs cynges geréfa *the king's reeve*, L. Eth. i. 4; Th. i. 282, 31: L. C. S. 33; Th. i. 396, 14. Gif hit se geréfa ne amanige mid rihte *if the reeve do not lawfully exact it* [*the fine*], L. Ed. 5; Th. i. 162, 12. Ðæt ǽlc geréfa náme ðæt wedd on his ágenre scire, ðæt hí ealle ðæt friþ healdan woldan *that each reeve should take a pledge in his own shire, that they would all hold the peace*, L. Ath. v. § 10; Th. i. 240, 1. Ðæt ǽlc geréfa fylste óðrum to úre ealra friþe *that every reeve may help another for the common peace of us all*, v. § 8, 4; Th. i. 286, 27. Ðæs landrícan and ðæs biscopes geréfa *the landlord's and the bishop's reeve*, L. Eth. ix. 8; Th. i. 342, 16: L. C. E. 8; Th. i. 366, 7. Iosep, se æðela geréfa, of Arimathia *Ioseph ab Arimathæa, nōbĭlis decŭrio*, Mk. Bos. 15, 43. Sum wæs ǽhtwelig æðeles cynnes, ríce geréfa *there was a wealthy man of noble race, a powerful count*, Exon. 66 a; Th. 243, 31; Jul. 19. Se geréfa hét Iulianan *the count commanded Juliana*, 73 b; Th. 274, 9; Jul. 530. Geréfa mín *my steward*, Cd. 100; Th. 131, 25; Gen. 2181. Ealdorman oððe geréfa *cōmes*, Wrt. Voc. 72, 61. Geréfa *consul*, Ælfc. Gl. 6; Som. 56, 49; Wrt. Voc. 18, 4. Nán man ne hwyrfe nánes yrfes bútan ðæs geréfan gewitnesse *let no man exchange any property without the witness of the reeve*, L. Ath. i. 10; Th. i. 204, 17, 18. On ǽlces geréfan manunge *in every reeve's district*, iv. 1; Th. i. 222, 9. Iohanna, Chuzan wíf, Herodes geréfan *Ioana, uxor Chusae, procŭrātōris Herōdis*, Lk. Bos. 8, 3. He cwæþ to his geréfan *præcēpit dispensātōris dŏmus suæ dīcens*, Gen. 43, 16. Gecýðe cyninges geréfan *let them declare it to the king's reeve*, L. Alf. pol. 34; Th. i. 82, 17: 22; Th. i. 76, 5. Swá hie geþingian mǽgen wið cyning and his geréfan *as they can agree with the king and his reeve*, L. In. 73; Th. i. 148, 12. Gif man ðone geréfan teó *if any accuse the reeve*, L. C. S. 8; Th. i. 380, 19. On Lindcolene ceastre geréfan *pertingens ad præfectum Lindocolinæ civitatis*, Bd. 2, 16; S. 519, 20: Shrn. 120, 12: 123, 24. He sende his geréfan *mīsit præfectum suum*, 4, 1; S. 564, 42. Míne ealdormen and míne geréfan *my aldermen and my reeves*, L. Ath. i. prm; Th. i. 194, 10. Ic wille, ðæt bisceop and ða geréfan hit beódan *I will that the bishop and the reeves command it*, i. prm; Th. i. 194, 10. Ic wille, ðæt míne geréfan gedón, ðæt man agife da ciricsceattas and sáwlsceattas *I will that my reeves cause that a man shall give the church-scots and the soul-scots*, i. prm; Th. i. 196, 8. Ic Æðelstán cyningc cýðe [MS. cýð] ðám geréfan to hwilcere birig *I, Æthelstan king, make known to the reeves at each town*, i. prm; Th. i. 194, 3. Eádwerd cyning být ðám geréfum eallum, ðæt ge déman swá rihte dómas swá ge rihtoste cunnon, and hit on ðære dómbéc stande *King Edward commands all the reeves, that ye pass the most righteous sentences you can, and as it stands in the doom book*, L. Ed. prm; Th. i. 158, 3: L. Eth. ix. 32; Th. i. 346, 29. Se sette geréfan geond eall ðæt ríce *qui constĭtuat præpŏsĭtos per cunctas regiones*, Gen. 41, 34. He hét sécan síne geréfan *he commanded to seek his officers*, Cd. 176; Th. 220, 31; Dan. 79. We ðǽr settan and geendebyrdedon úre geréfan *ordinarios proprætoresque nostros proposuimus*, Nar. 3, 25. From ðen groefæ *a præside*, Mt. Kmbl. Lind. 28, 14: Mk. Skt. Lind. 15, 5: Jn. Skt. Lind. 19, 1, 4. See Stubbs' Const. Hist. and Schmid A. S. Gesetz. *s. v;* Kemble's Saxons in England, ii. c. 5; Grm. R. A. 752-4.

ge-réf-ærn, es; *n. A court-house:*—Urbanus eode to his geréfærne *Urbanus went to his court-house*, Shrn. 106, 16.

ge-réf-land, es; *n. Tributary land;* tributarium territorium, Cot. 106.

ge-réflang, es; *m. A minister:*—Ða geréflanges of Cristes circean *the ministers of Christchurch*, Chart. Th. 317, 32.

ge-réf-mǽd, e; *f.* '*The meadow which the reeve owned " ex officio," or over which, as common pasture, he exercised the right of superintendence*,' Cod. Dipl. Kmbl. iii. xxxiv.

ge-réf-scipe, es; *m. Office of a* geréfa:—Ne heora nán geréfscipe ne drífe *let none of them practise any reeveship*, Homl. Th. ii. 94, 33.

ge-réf-scir or -scire, e; *f. Stewardship;* villicatio:—Mín hláford míne geréfscire fram me nymþ *dominus meus aufert a me vilicationem*, Lk. Bos. 16, 3. Geréfscyre *præfectura*, Hpt. Gl. 438. v. scir, ge-sciran.

ge-regnian, -rénian; *p.* ode; *pp.* od, ad *To put, dispose, adorn:*—Geregnian, *inficere*, Cot. 112. Hwæðer him leófre wǽre ðe he hý ealle acwealde ðe hý libbende to bismre gerénian héte *whether he would rather that he should kill them all or should order them to be put to shame while living*, Ors. 3, 8; Bos. 63, 14. Lii hit oftræd and hie to loman gerénode ðæt hie mec ǽnigre note nytte beón ne meahton 52 *it trode down and made them cripples so that they could be of no use to me;* calcatos inutiles fecit, Nar. 15, 26. Ðonne hangaþ ðǽr eác búfan ðǽm lástum geregnod swíðe mycel leóhtfæt *moreover there hangs, placed above the footsteps, a great lamp*, Blickl. Homl. 127, 29. Ðæs geregnedan *concinnati*, Cot. 57. Ne ðæt ne beoþ on ðý fægerre ðæt mid elles hwam gerénod biþ ðeáh ða gerénu fægeru síen ðe hit mid gerénod biþ *nor will that be the fairer which is adorned with something else though the ornaments be fair with which it is adorned*, Bt. 74, 3; Fox 46, 14: 27, 1; Fox 96, 1. Golde geregnad *adorned with gold*, Beo. Th. 1558; B. 777. Gerénod *adorned*, Byrht. Th. 136, 35; By. 161: Judth. 12; Thw. 26, 21; Jud. 339. Girínad *ornatum*, Lk. Skt. Rush. 21, 5. [Cf. *Goth.* garaginon.]

ge-regnong *a making up;* confectio, Cot. 44.

ge-rehtad *made straight, set up;* erectus, Lk. Skt. Lind. 13, 13.

ge-rehte, -reht *related, explained, interpreted, directed*, Bt. 40, 6; Fox 242, 2: Ps. Th. 140, 2: Jn. Bos. 1, 38, 41, 42; *p. and pp. of* ge-reccan.

gerela, gierela, an; *m. Apparel:*—Gif ðú wénst ðætte wundorlíc[e] gerela hwelc weorðmynd síe *if you suppose that wonderful apparel is any* *honour*, Bt. 14, 1; Fox 42, 18. Wynna gierelan gielplîces *the pleasures of pompous apparel*, Exon. 35 a; Th. 112, 3; Gû. 138: 38 b; 127, 22; Gû. 390. v. ge-gerela.

ge-rên, es; *n. An ornament*:—Ðeáh ða gerênu fægru sîen ðe hit mid gerênod biþ *though the ornaments be fair with which it is adorned*, Bt. 14, 3; Fox 46, 15. Ða gerêno *the ornaments*, Exon. 107 a; Th. 408, 20; Rä. 27, 15. Girîno ł glencas *ædificationes*, Mk. Skt. Rush. 13, 2.

ge-rêne, es; *pl. nom. acc.* -u, -o, -a; *n. A mystery*; mysterium, Hy. 8, 11; Hy. Grn. ii. 290, 11. v. ge-rŷne.

ge-rênian. v. ge-regnian.

gereófage. v. ge-reáfian.

ge-reohnung, e; *f. A making up*; confectio, Cot. 171. v. ge-regnong.

ge-reónian; *p.* ode; *pp.* od *To conspire, ordain, frame, devise*; conspirare, concinnare:—Ic gereónige *conspiro*, Ælfc. Gr. 47; Som. 48, 42. Tunge ðîn gereónode fâcnu *lingua tua concinnabat dolos*, Ps. Lamb. 49, 19; thy tongue frameth deceit; *thi tunge ordeynde treccheries*, Wyc. Æfter manegum dagum gereónodon ða Iudeiscan hû hî done Godes cempan acwellan sceoldon *after many days the Jews conspired how they were to kill that champion of God*, Homl. Th. i. 388, 5.

ge-reónung, e; *f. A conspiracy, confederacy*; conjuratio:—Ne understenst ðû ðisra twegra manna gereónunge ongeán me *dost thou not understand the plot of these two men against me?* Homl. Th. i. 380, 7. Gereónung *fictio, mendacium*, Hpt. Gl. 459.

ge-reord, -reorde, es; *n. Language, speech, tongue, voice*:—Hî cunnon eall mennisc gereord *nationum linguis loquentes*, Nar. 37, 4: Bd. 1, 1; S. 474, 2: Hy. Grn. ii. 287, 19: 293, 43. Ðæt ys on ûrum gereorde *that is in our language*, Thw. Hept. 155, 37: Swt. A. S. Rdr. 97, 55. To Norþhymbriscum gereorde *to the Northumbrian speech*, 58. Weorþlîce getŷd ge on Ledenisc gereorde ge on Grecisc *Græcæ pariter et Latinæ linguæ peritissimus*, Bd. 4, 1; S. 563, 33: 2; 565, 28: Th. An. 18, 29. Ðâ wǽron ða apostolas cweðende to him hwonon him ða wundorlîcan gereordo côman *then the apostles were saying to him whence came to him those wonderful speeches*, Blickl. Homl. 153, 9. Hwîlum ic gereordum rincas laðige to wîne *sometimes with voices I invite men to wine*, Exon. 104 a; Th. 395, 31; Rä. 15, 16. v. reord.

ge-reord, -reorde, es; *n. A meal, refection, food*:—Sæt se Hǽlynd æt gereorde *discumbebat Iesus*, Mt. Bos. 26, 20. Hwǽr is mîn gereord *ubi est refectio mea*, Mk. Bos. 14, 14. Ǽr his gereorde *ante prandium*, Lk. Bos. 11, 38: Gen. 19, 3. Be ðam liflîcum gereorde *concerning the vital refection*, Homl. Th. ii. 262, 24. Ôððæt ðæt gereorde gefylled wæs *until the meal was finished*, Bd. 5, 4; S. 617, 26. Cyninga gereordo *regum convivia*, Cot. 93. Him beád reste and gereorda *offered them rest and refreshment*, Cd. 112; Th. 147, 17; Gen. 2441: Exon. 96 a; Th. 357, 29; Pa. 36: Mt. Kmbl. Lind. 26, 7. Heofonlîcu gereordu *heavenly food*, Shrn. 30, 28: 64, 2. Giriord *cœna, alimentum prandium, cibus*, Rtl. 70, 37: 99, 11: 107, 19: 116, 5. Gehriord *epula*, 116, 34. To gereordum ł farmum *ad nuptias*, Mt. Kmbl. p. 19, 4.

ge-reordan, -reordian; *p.* ode; *pp.* ad, od *To give food to, feed, take food, satisfy, refresh, feast*; cibare, saturare, satiare, epulari:—Ic gereordige *prandeo*, Ælfc. Gr. 26; Som. 29, 8. Ic gereordige *vescor*, 29; Som. 33, 50. Ic gereordige *reficio*, ic eom gereordod *reficior*, 37; Som. 39, 2. He hine gereordode mid ðam papan *he dined with the pope*, Chr. 1022; Erl. 161, 34. Giriordade hine *cibavit illum*, Rtl. 46, 9. He gereordode hî *saturavit eos*, Ps. Spl. C. 80, 15. Crist gereorde fîf þûsenda wera *Christ fed five thousand men*, Shrn. 48, 30. Ðæt gê ców gereordian *that ye may refresh yourselves*, Gen. 18, 5. Ǽr mǽle hine gereordige *that one take refection before the time*, Homl. Th. ii. 590, 25. Giriordiga we *epulemur*, Rtl. 25, 17. Giriord *satia*, 146, 17. Unbindaþ hî and gereordigaþ *unbind her and give her to eat*, Homl. Th. i. 458, 19. We willaþ mid ðŷ hlâfe gereorde beón *pane illo refici volumus*, Bd. 2, 5; S. 507, 22. Ðâ wæs flet-sittendum fægere gereorded *then were the sitters in the hall nobly feasted*, Beo. Th. 3581; B. 1788. Hûsle gereorded *refreshed with the eucharist*, Exon. 51 b; Th. 180, 4; Gû. 1274. Gereordod, Andr. Kmbl. 770; An. 385. Ða ilco bîðon geriorded *saturabuntur*, Mt. Kmbl. Lind. 5, 6: 14, 20. Hia sîe giriordado *reficiantur*, Rtl. 15, 5.

ge-reord-hûs, es; *n. A dining-room*; refectorium, triclinium, Ælfc. Gl. 107; Som. 78, 74; Wrt. Voc. 57, 51.

ge-reordig-hûs *a dining-room*; refectorium, Lye.

ge-reording, -ung, e; *f. A meal, refection*; prandium, refectio:—Gearca us gereordunge *prepare us a meal*, Homl. Th. i. 60, 18. On gereorduncge *in prandio*, Th. An. 28, 9. On ânre gereordinge *in una refectione*, 34, 37. Ofer wæteru gereordunga *super aquam refectionis*, Ps. Spl. 22, 2. Giriording *a meal*, Lk. Skt. Rush. 12, 19, 37.

ge-reordnes, -nys, se; *f. A repast, dinner, fulness*; refectio, Ps. Spl. C. 22, 2: Bd. 4, 28; S. 606, 1.

ge-reósan; *p.* -reás, *pl.* -ruron; *pp.* -roren *To fall*; cadere, Ps. Spl. second 9, 12. v. ge-hreósan.

ge-resp *convicted*; convictus, L. Alf. pol. 28; Th. i. 80, 21.

ge-rest, es; *n. A resting-place, couch*; accubitus, Rtl. 4, 11.

ge-resta, an; *f. One who rests with another, consort*:—Seó wæs Eádwardes cynges geresta *she was king Edward's consort*, Chr. 1076; Erl. 214, 32. Heó Balan sealde Iacobe to gerestan *Bilham dedit Iacobo quacum concumberet*, Gen. 30, 4.

ge-restan; *p.* te; *pp.* ed *To rest, remain, rest [one's self]*:—Ðæt he hine gerestan meahte *ad quiescendum membra*, Bd. 2, 6; S. 508, 9. Forðon ic ǽfre ne mæg ðære môd-ceare mînre gerestan *for I can never rest from my mind's sorrow*, Exon. 115 b; Th. 444, 1; Kl. 40. Templ Hâliges Gâstes snytro on to gerestenne *a temple for the wisdom of the Holy Ghost to dwell in*, Blickl. Homl. 163, 15. Ic me gereste *quiesco*, Ælfc. Gr. 28; Som. 30, 30. Mîn hige geresteþ nô *my mind resteth not*, Elen. Kmbl. 2164; El. 1083: Exon. 8 b; Th. 4, 16; Cri. 53. On ðone seofoðan ðû gerestest *on the seventh thou didst rest*, Hy. 9, 23; Grn. ii. 291, 23. Gif ic on ðunwange gereste *si dedero requiem temporibus meis*, Ps. Th. 131, 4. Gerest ðê *requiesce*, Lk. Bos. 12, 19: Homl. Th. ii. 104, 20. Girestun [Rush.] gehræston [Lind.] *requieverunt*, Lk. Skt. 12, 19.

ge-restscipe, es; *m.* I. *rest, ease*; quies, ôtium, Som. Ben. Lye. II. *a cohabitation*; concŭbĭtus:—To hyre gerestscipe hire wer ne sceal gangan *ad ejus concŭbĭtum vir suus accēdĕre non dēbet*, Bd. 1, 27; S. 493, 32.

ge-rêtan; *p.* -rêtte; *pp.* -rêted, -rêt *To restore, refresh, set right*; recreāre, refĭcĕre:—Wæs heó semninga mid gâstlîcre gesyhþe gerêted *sŭbĭto vīsiōne spīrĭtāli recreāta*, Bd. 4, 9; S. 577, 19: 5, 1; S. 613, 22. Ðû me hæfst gerêtne mid ðînre gesceadwîsnesse *thou hast comforted me with thy reasoning*, Bt. 22, 1; Fox 76, 12.

ge-rêþra, an; *m. A sailor, rower*; nauta:—Gerêþra [MS. gerêþru] *nauta*, Ælfc. Gl. 103; Wrt. Voc. 56, 15. v. rêþra.

ge-rêþru; *pl. n. Rudder, helm* [the steering was done by means of an oar]:—Ða men ða ðe beóþ winnende in sciplîcum gewinne hîg ðonne begâþ ǽrost ða gerêþru in ðære hŷþe *qui in nauali prœlio demicaturi sunt ante in portu inflectant gubernacula*, Shrn. 35, 8: 9. Gerêþru *vel* scipgetawu *aplustre*, Ælfc. Gl. 103; Wrt. Voc. 56, 19. Gerêþra *aplustra*, Gl. Mett. 15. On ânum bâte bûtan ǽlcum gerêþrum *in a boat without any means of steering*, Chr. 891; Erl. 88, 6, see note on this passage. 'Gerêþrum' can however hardly be a case of 'gerêþra' *nauta*, as the singular number would be used with 'ǽlc;' it is rather a plural like 'geatwe' or 'frætwe.'

gêr-hwamlîce; *adv. Yearly*; annuatim, Som.

gerian; *p.* ede; *pp.* ed *To clothe*; vestîre:—Ðâm ðe ðone lîchoman Cûþberhtes geredon *quibus corpus Cudbercti vestierant*, Bd. 4, 31; S. 611, 5, MS. B. v. gyrian.

ge-rîcsian; *p.* ode; *pp.* od *To rule, govern*; regere, dominari, gubernare, Rtl. 8, 7: 26, 43: 38, 41.

ge-rîdan; *p.* -râd; *pp.* -riden *To ride, reach* or *obtain by riding, get into one's power, subject*:—Ðâ he gerâd to Ecgbryhtes stâne *then he rode to Brixton*, Chr. 878; Erl. 80, 8. Se ðe næs gerâd *he who rode to the ness*, Beo. Th. 5789; B. 2898. Ðâ gerâd he ða burg æt Tameworþige *then he rode and took the town at Tamworth*, Chr. 922; Erl. 108, 24: 901; Erl. 96, 26. Se here geridon Wesseaxna lond and gesǽton micel ðæs folces ofer sǽ adrǽfdon and ðæs ôðres ðone mǽstan dǽl hie geridon *the [Danish] army rode to Wessex and occupied it; much of the folk they drove over sea and most part of the rest they got into their power*, 878; Erl. 78, 29-32. He gerâd eall Norþhymbra land him to gewealde *he got all Northumberland into his power*, 948; Erl. 117, 9. Se cing lêt gerîdan ealle ða land ðe his môdor âhte him to handa *the king caused all the lands that his mother owned to be brought under his own control*, 1043; Erl. 168, 8.

ge-rîd-men *horsemen, knights*; equites, Cot. 212.

ge-rif, es; *n. A seizing, taking away, a catching—as of fish*, also *that which is caught*; raptura, captura:—Ân gerif fisca, oððe ân snǽs fisca oððe ôðra þinga *one taking of fish, or one spear of fish, or of other things*; una sorta, Mone A. 141; Recd. 37, 77; Wrt. Voc. 64, 9: Ælfc. Gl. 98; Wrt. Voc. 54, 40. DER. fôt-sîþ-gerif.

ge-rifled, -riflod; *part. p. Wrinkled*; rugatus, Som.

ge-rifod; *part. p. Wrinkled*:—On ealdlîcum geárum biþ ðæs mannes neb gerifod *in the years of old age man's face is wrinkled*, Homl. Th. i. 614, 14.

ge-riht, es; *n. What is right, a right, due, last office of the church, direction*; rectum, jus, ratio, officium:—Gif hwâ ǽnigra godcundra gerihto forwyrne *if any one refuse any divine dues*, L. E. G. 6; Th. i. 170, 7. Godes gerihto *God's dues*, 5; Th. i. 168, 25: Homl. Th. i. 74, 22: Swt. A. S. Rdr. 105, 39: L. Eth. 5, 11; Th. i. 306, 30: Shrn. 208, 28. Ðis syndon ða gerihta ðe se cyning âh ofer ealle men on Wessexan *these are the rights which the king has over all men in Wessex*, L. C. S. 12; Th. i. 382, 12. Cynescipes gerihta *rights of royalty*, L. Edg. S. 2; Th. i. 272, 27: Chr. 1085; Erl. 218, 28. Ealla ða gerihta ðe ðǽr of arîsaþ *all the rights arising therefrom*, 1031; Erl. 162, 4: 1074; Erl. 212, 6. Geriht *ratio*, Mt. Kmbl. Rush. 23, 23, 24. Heó to cyrcean eóde and hire gerihtan underfeng *she went to the church and received her rites*, Chr. 1093; Erl. 229, 11: Homl. Th. ii. 142, 9. Fôron to gefeohte forþ on gerihte *marched straight on to battle*, Judth. 11; Thw. 24, 23; Jud. 202. Man âna gǽþ mid his andwlitan up on gerihte *man alone walks with his face erect*, Bt. Met. Fox 31, 34; Met. 31, 17. On geryhte ongeán ðæne mûþan *in a direction opposite the mouth*, Ors. 1, 1; Bos. 24, 8. On gerihte fram ðam scipe to ðam ancre *right from the ship to the anchor*, Shrn. 175, 19: Cod. Dipl. ii. 172, 20. DER. ald-, cyric-, geár-, woruld-geriht.

ge-riht; *adj.* RIGHT, *direct;* directus:—Ðweoru beóþ on gerihte *erunt prava in directa*, Lk. Bos. 3, 5. [*Goth.* ga-raihts.]

ge-rihtan, -ryhtan; *p.* -rihte; *pp.* -rihted, -riht *To set right* or *straight, to direct, correct;* dirĭgĕre, corrĭgĕre, emendāre:—He wolde ðone Cristes gelǽfan gerihtan *he would set right the faith of Christ*, Chr. 680; Erl. 41, 14. Ða þing ðe he unfullfremed gemētte, mid heora fultume he ða gerihte and bētte *ea quæ mĭnus perfecta repĕrit, his quoque juvantĭbus corrĭgēbat*, Bd. 4, 2; S. 566, 3. Gerihtaþ Drihtnes weg *dirĭgĭte viam Dŏmĭni*, Jn. Bos. 1, 23. Fram sumum ungetýddum gerihted *a quodam impĕrĭto emendātum*, Bd. 5, 24; S. 648, 24. Mīn mundbyrd is geriht to ðære rōde *my protection is directed to the cross*, Rood Kmbl. 259; Kr. 131. [*Goth.* garaihtjan.]

ge-riht-lǽcan; *p.* -lǽhte; *pp.* -lǽht *To justify, correct, direct, rectify, reprove;* rectificare, corrigere, arguere:—Se Hǽlend wolde ða synfullan gerihtlǽcan *the Healer* [*Saviour*] *would correct the sinful*, Homl. Th. ii. 470, 14. Ðæt hys weorc ne sȳn gerihtlǽhte *ut non arguantur opera ejus*, Jn. Bos. 3, 20: Ps. Lamb. 36, 24. He ðǽrbinnan wunode gerihtlǽcende ðæt folc mid lāre to geleáfan *he dwelt therein directing the people by teaching to belief*, Swt. A. S. Rdr. 98, 113. Menn be his lāre heora līf gerihtlǽton *men by his instruction rectified their lives*, Homl. Th. ii. 146, 8. Gif we beóþ fram ūrum ðwyrnyssum gerihtlǽhte *if we be corrected from our perversities*, 124, 35.

ge-rihtnes, -ness, e; *f. A setting right, correction;* correctio:—Be heora gerihtnesse *de illōrum correctiōne*, Bd. 5, 22; S. 644, 45. He wæs firena forgifnes and gerihtnes hǽþenra þeóda *he was forgiveness of sins and the setting right of heathen peoples*, Blickl. Homl. 163, 23.

ge-rihtreccan *to direct:*—Ðē to gerihtrecenne ðæt ðū gesyhst myd ðīnes mōdes eágan god *to direct thee to see God with thy mind's eye*, Shrn. 177, 25.

ge-riht-wīsian; *p.* ode; *pp.* od; *v. a. To justify;* justificare:—He wolde hine sylfne gerihtwīsian *ille vŏlens justĭfĭcāre seipsum*, Lk. Bos. 10, 29. Ðū eart se ðe me gerihtwīsast *thou art he who justifieth me*, Ps. Th. 4, 1. Ða ðe he him to clypode, ða he gerihtwīsode, and ða ðe he gerihtwīsode, ða he gemǽrsode *those whom he called unto him he justified, and those whom he justified he glorified*, Homl. Th. ii. 366, 2. Hī synt gerihtwīsode *justĭfĭcāta sunt*, Ps. Th. 18, 8. Gerihtwisud *justificatus*, Mt. Bos. 11, 19,

ge-rīm, es; *n. A number, computation, calendar, diary;* nŭmĕrus, compŭtātio, ephēmĕris = ἐφημερίς:—Ðæs næs nā gerīm *cujus non ĕrat nŭmĕrus*, Ps. Spl. 104, 32. Feówer and twentig wintra gerīmes *twenty four winters in number*, Chr. 1065; Erl. 196, 26, 40; Edw. 7, 21: Cd. 224; Th. 296, 15; Sat. 502. Ofer gerīm *sŭper nŭmĕrum*, Ps. Spl. 39, 8: 38, 6. Ic ne mæg gerīm witan heardra heteþonca *I cannot know the number of cruel enmities*, Exon. 70 a; Th. 261, 13; Jul. 314: Hy. 3, 17; Hy. Grn. ii. 281, 17. Gerīm *ephēmĕrĭdes, nŭmĕrus quotĭdiānus*, Ælfc. Gl. 82; Som. 73, 51; Wrt. Voc. 47, 55. On getal gerīmes *by reckoning of numbers*, Salm. Kmbl. 184, 7. On gerīme *by number*, 192, 10. DER. dōgor-gerīm, geár-, heáfod-, niht-, þūsend-, un-, winter-.

ge-rīman, to -rīmenne; *p.* de; *pp.* ed [rīman *to number*] *To number, reckon;* nŭmĕrāre:—He āna mǽge ealle gerīman *he alone can number all*, Cd. 163; Th. 205, 22; Exod. 439: Exon. 121 b; Th. 466, 4; Hö. 116. Ðonne mæg he eác swilce gerīman ðīnne ofspring *sēmen quŏque tuum nŭmĕrāre pŏtest*, Gen. 13, 16: Ps. Th. 104, 30. To gerīmenne *to reckon*, Ors. 2, 5; Bos. 46, 39. Sceáwa heofon, hyrste gerīm *behold the heaven, number its ornaments*, Cd. 100; Th. 132, 7; Gen. 2189. Ðæm feówer bearn, forþ gerīmed, in worold wōcon *to him four children, numbered forth, were born into the world*, Beo. Th. 118; B. 59.

ge-rīmcræft, es; *m. Arithmetic, art of numbering:*—Ðe sēlost cunnon on gerīmcræfte *that are best acquainted with arithmetic*, Bd. de nat. rerum; Wrt. popl. science 11, 1; Lchdm. iii. 256, 7: Hexam. 4: Norm. 8, 5.

ge-rīmtæl, es; *n. A number, reckoning:*—Bión on ðæm gerīmtæle mid mīnum brōþor *to be of the number with my brother*, H. R. 13, 11. [Cf. rīmgetæl.]

ge-rīnan; *pp.* -rinen *To touch, take hold of, grip;* tangĕre, contingĕre, arrĭpĕre:—Ne ofer ðæt syððan hine ō gerīnan dorste *neque unquam exinde eum audēret contingĕre*, Bd. 3, 12; S. 537, 14. Wæs he sōna gerinen līchomlīce untrumnysse *confestim languōre corpŏris tactus est*, 4, 3; S. 568, 37. Wæs he semninga fram deofle gerinen *sŭbĭto a diăbŏlo arreptus*, 3, 11; S. 536, 13, MS. B. v. ge-hrīnan.

ge-rīne, es; *pl. nom. acc.* -u, -o, -a; *n. A mystery;* mysterium:—Eów is geseald to witanne Godes rīces gerīnu *vobis datum est nosse mysteria regni Dei*, Mk. Bos. 4, 11. v. ge-rȳne.

ge-rinelīc; *adj. Prosperous*, Hpt. Gl. 466.

ge-rinnan; *p.* -ran; *pp.* -runnen *To run, run together, congeal, join;* coagulare, coagulari:—Nis nā gerunnen togædere seó Godcundnys and seó menniscnys *the divinity and the humanity are not mingled together*, Homl. Th. ii. 8, 5. Gerunnen is swā swā meolc heorte heora *coagulatum est sicut lac cor eorum*, Ps. Lamb. 118, 70. Munt gerunnen, dūne fæt, to hwȳ wēne gē muntas gerunnene *mons coagulatus, mons pinguis, ut quid suspicamini montes coagulatos*, Ps. Spl. 67, 16. Gerunnen *coagulatus*, Ælfc. Gl. 33; Som. 62, 17; Wrt. Voc. 28, 1. Gerunnen blōd *viscum*, 78; Som. 72, 52; Wrt. Voc. 46, 12. [*Goth.* ga-rinnan *to run together: O. H. Ger.* gi-rinnan *coagulare.*]

ge-rīno *buildings;* ædificationes, Mk. Skt. Rush. 13, 2. v. ge-rēn.

ge-rīp, es; *n.* [rīp *harvest*] *A reaping, harvest;* messis:—Ðæt gerīp is micel *the reaping is great*, Homl. Th. ii. 530, 16. Gerīp *messis*, Ælfc. Gr. 9, 28; Som. 11, 56: Wrt. Voc. 74, 69: Gen. 8, 22. Biddaþ ðæs gerīpes hlāford, ðæt he asende wyrhtan to his gerīpe *pray to the lord of the reaping, that he send workmen to his reaping*, Homl. Th. ii. 530, 20. On Godes gerīpe *in God's reaping*, 530, 19. Hwā gemenigfylt ðæt gerīp of feáwum cornum *who multiplies the harvest from a few grains of corn*, i. 184, 31.

ge-rīpan; *p.* -rāp, *pl.* -ripon; *pp.* -ripen *To reap;* mĕtĕre:—Hie heora corn geripon *they reaped their corn*, Chr. 896; Th. 172, 32, col. 2. On ðæt gerād ðe he ǽlce geáre gerīpe *on the condition that each year he reap*, Cod. Dipl. ii. 398, 21.

ge-rīpian; *p.* ode, ede; *pp.* od, ed [rīpian *to ripen*] *To ripen, grow old;* mātūrāri, sĕnescĕre:—Nǽron hī gerīpode to slege *they were not ripe for slaughter*, Homl. Th. i. 84, 5. On wintrum gerīpod *ripe in years*, ii. 24, 23. Mīn hlāford gerīpod ys *dŏmĭnus meus vĕtŭlus est*, Gen. 18, 12. Gerīped *mātūrus*, C. R. Ben. 43.

ge-rīsan; *3rd sing. pres.* -rīseþ, -rīst, *pl.* -rīsaþ; *p.* -rās, *pl.* -rison; *pp.* -risen *To behove, become, befit, suit;* dĕcēre, convĕnīre: generally used impersonally:—Gold gerīseþ on guman sweorde *gold is fitting on a man's sword*, Exon. 91 a; Th. 341, 14; Gn. Ex. 126. Ðē gerīseþ lofsang *te dĕcet hymnus*, Ps. Spl. 64, 1: 92, 7. Cyninge gerīst rihtwīsnys *righteousness becomes a king*, Homl. Th. ii. 318, 32: i. 418, 8. Ðe him betst gerīst *which suits him best*, Bt. 34, 10; Fox 148, 20: Menol. Fox 117; Men. 58. Wera gehwylcum wīslīcu word gerīsaþ *to every man wise words are fitting*, Exon. 91 b; Th. 343, 34; Gn. Ex. 166. Swā ðam þeódne gerās *as was fitting to the master*, 49 a; Th. 168, 34; Gū. 1087. Ðæt ðæm weorce nānum men ne gerīse bēt to fandienne, ðonne ðam wyrhtan ðe hit worhte *that it became no man better to prove the work than the workman who made it*, Ors. 1, 12; Bos. 36, 37.

ge-rīsan; *pp.* -risen *To seize, take;* rapere:—Gerīseþ *rapit*, Mt. Kmbl. Rush. 13, 19. Gerīsaþ *rapiunt*, 11, 12. Sōna wæs gerisen and genumen of middanearde *rapta confestim de mundo*, Bd. 4, 19; S. 589, 5, note.

ge-risen, -risne [?], es; *n. A seizing;* rapina:—Ne begitest ðū nā ðæt rīce on gerisne woruldlīcra þinga *non in præda, nec in rapina regnum tibi dabitur*, Guthl. 19; Gdwin. 78, 5. v. ge-rīsan *to seize.*

ge-risene, -risne, -rysne; *adj. Fit, convenient, proper;* congruus, decens, conveniens:—He sealde his lāreowum gerisene stōwe and ēþel heora hāde *doctoribus suis locum sedis eorum gradui congruum donaret*, Bd. 4, 26; S. 488, 19. Æfter gerisenre āre swā myclum B' *juxta honorem tanto Pontifici congruum*, 5, 19; S. 636, 45. Ða gerisno digna, Lk. Skt. Lind. 12, 48. Ðis þinceþ gerisne *this seems fitting*, Cd. 114; Th. 149, 17; Gen. 2476. Swā gerysne ne wæs *as was not seemly*, 76; Th. 94, 22; Gen. 1565: 9; Th. 11, 2; Gen. 169: Beo. Th. 5299; B. 2653. Hit is ealles gerisnost *it is most fitting*, Blickl. Homl. 205, 24.

ge-risene, -risne, -rysne, es; [seems to occur only in *pl.*] *n. What is fitting, decent:*—Godes hūs sindon innan bestrȳpte ǽlcra gerisna *God's houses are stripped within of everything seemly*, Swt. A. S. Rdr. 106, 43: Th. Chart. 511, 4. Ðæt heora gerisna nǽre ðæt hȳ swā heáne hȳ geþohtan ðæt hȳ heora gelīcan wurdan *that it was not fitting for them* [*the Romans*] *to think themselves so low as to be their* [*the Carthaginians'*] *equals*, Ors. 4, 6; Bos. 86, 27: Cd. 93; Th. 242, 17; Dan. 420. Ne fremest ðū gerysnu and riht wiþ me *thou dost not do what is fitting and right towards me*, 102; Th. 135, 19; Gen. 2245: 111; Th. 146, 4; Gen. 2432. Gif he mōt ðǽr rihtes and gerysena onbrūcan *if he can there enjoy what is right and fitting*, Runic pm. 23; Kmbl. 344, 6. Ryhtum gerisnum *right fittingly*, Exon. 80 b; Th. 302, 2; Fā. 30.

ge-risenlīc; *comp. m.* -līcra, *f. n.* -līcre; *adj. Convenient, suitable, befitting;* convĕniens, aptus:—Ne þuhte hit me nāuht gerisenlīc *I should not think it at all suitable*, Bt. 41, 2; Fox 244, 27. Ægðer ðara is swīðe nyt weorc and gerisenlīc *either is a very useful and befitting work*, Prov. Kmbl. 60. On ðæm gerisnlīcan hēhsetle *on that seemly throne*, Blickl. Homl. 9, 26. Gerisenlīc me to wosanne *oportet me esse*, Lk. Skt. Lind. 2, 49. Ðē is gerisenlīcre ðæt ðū sī mid rihte ofersteled, ðonne ðū oferstele ōðerne man mid wōge *it is more befitting thee to be overruled with right than to overrule another with wrong*, Prov. Kmbl. 8: Bd. 2, 13; S. 516, 23.

ge-risenlīce; *comp.* -līcor; *adv. Becomingly, fitly;* apte:—Seó wæs gerisenlīce gehlidad mid gelīce stāne *opercŭlo sĭmĭlis lăpĭdis aptissĭme tectum*, Bd. 4, 19; S. 588, 32: 3, 17; S. 544, 4, col. 1. Gerisenlīcor *aptius*, 2, 13; S. 517, 2: 3, 29; S. 561, 29.

ge-risennes, -risnes, se; *f. Conveniency, agreeableness, congruity;* convenientia, Cot. 58.

ge-rislīc; *adj. Convenient*, Bd. 5, 19; S. 636, 34, note. v. ge-risenlīc.

ge-risnian *to agree, accord;* convenire, Cot. 38.

ge-rīxian *to rule;* regnare, Lk. Skt. Lind. 19, 14. v. ge-rīcsian.

gerla, an; *m. Tribute:*—To sellanne đone gerlo *dare tributum*, Lk. Skt. Rush. 20, 22.

gērlīc; *adj. Yearly;* annuus, Rtl. 49, 25: Shrn. 208, 28.

Germania, e [=æ]; *f. Germany.* The Germania of Alfred extended from the Don on the east to the Rhine and the German Ocean on the west; and from the Danube on the south to the White Sea on the north; it therefore embraced nearly the whole of Europe north of the Rhine and the Danube. Its great extent will be seen by the countries mentioned in the notes from 5 to 39, and in the text of Ors. Bos. pp. 35–40. See also Cluverii Introductionis in universam Geographiam, Libri vi. Amstelædami, 4to. 1729, Lib. iii. Cap. 1. De veteri Germania, pp. 183–186, and the map of Europe, p. 72. Also the very learned work, Cluverii Germania antiqua, Lugd. Batavorum, Elzevir, Fol. 1616: Lib. 1: Cap. xi. De magnitudine Germaniæ antiquæ, pp. 94–98, also Lib. iii. Cap. xxxviii. pp. 157–162, and the map, p. 3. Also Cellarii Geographia Antiqua, Cantab. 4to. 1703, pp. 309–313. Warnefried's Hist. Longob. Lib. i. Cap. 1:—Nū wille we ymb Europe land-gemǣre reccan, swā mycel swā we hit fyrmest witon.—Fram đære eá Danais, west ōþ Rīn đa eá, [seó wylþ of đæm beorge đe man Alpis hǣt, and yrnþ đonne norþ-ryhte on đæs gārsecges earm, đe đæt land ūtanymblīþ, đe man Bryttannia hǣt];—and eft sūþ ōþ Donua đa eá, [đære ǣwylme is neáh đære eá Rīnes, and is siđđan eást yrnende wiđ norþan Crēca land ūt on đone Wendel-Sǣ];—and norþ ōþ đone gārsecg, đe man Cwēn-Sǣ hǣt: binnan đǣm syndon manega þeóda; ac hit man hǣt eall, GERMANIA *now we will speak, as much as we know, about the boundaries of Europe.—From the river Don, westward to the river Rhine, [which springs from the Alps, and then runs right north into the arm of the ocean, that lies around the country called Britain];—and again south to the river Danube, [whose spring is near the river Rhine, and which afterwards runs east by the country north of Greece into the Mediterranean Sea];—and north to the ocean, which is called the White Sea: within these are many nations, but it is all called* GERMANIA, Ors. 1, 1; Bos. 18, 20–28. Cōmon hī of þrīm folcum đām strangestan Germanie đæt of Seaxum, and of Angle, and of Geátum *advenerunt de tribus Germaniæ populis fortioribus, id est Saxonibus, Anglis, Jutis*, Bd. 1, 15; S. 483, 20.

gern *yarn, spun wool.* DER. nett-gern. v. gearn.

gernan; *p.* de; *pp.* ed *To desire;* desīdērāre:—He đæs biscophādes gernde *he desired episcopal ordination*, Chr. 1048; Erl. 177, 23. v. gyrnan.

gern-winde, es; *m? A yarn-winder, reel;* conductum [ăpud textōres], Wrt. Voc. 282, 2. v. gearn-winde.

ge-rora. v. ge-hror.

ge-rōsod *rosy, belonging to roses;* rosaceus, Som.

ge-rostod *roasted;* assus, Som.

ge-rōtsian [=geunrōtsian?] *to make sad;* contristare, Rtl. 56, 20.

ge-rōwen *rowed.* v. rōwan.

gers, es; *n. Grass;* herba:—Se đe forþatȳhþ wyrtcynren ođđe gers þeówdōmes manna *qui prodūcit herbam servĭtūti, hŏmĭnum*, Ps. Lamb. 146, 8: Mk. Skt. Lind. 4, 28. v. gærs.

GERST; GRIST, *pearled barley;* frumentum quodvis tritum, Lye.

gersum, es; *m. n:* gersuma, an; *m. Treasure;* thēsaurus, Chr. 1070; Erl. 209, 13: 1090; Erl. 226, 38: 1047; Erl. 177, 7. v. gærsum, gærsama; and see Grm. D. M. 840.

ge-rūm, es; *n.* [rūm *space*] *Room, space;* spătium:—Hī nāuđer ne gestillan ne mōton, ne eác swīđor styrian, đonne he him đæt gerūm his wealdleđeres toforlǣt *they neither can be still, nor yet move farther, than he allows to them the space of his rein*, Bt. 21; Fox 74, 8. Eódon on gerūm eorlas āglēwe *the men learned in law went apart*, Elen. Kmbl. 639; El. 320. Cyning healdeþ me on heáđore, hwīlum lǣteþ eft on gerūm sceacan *the king holds me in restraint, sometimes again lets me go at large*, Exon. 105 b; Th. 401, 20; Rä. 21, 14.

ge-rūma, an; *m.* [rūm *room*] *A room, place, space;* lŏcus, spătium:—Ic his bīdan ne dear rēđes on gerūman *I dare not await him fierce in my place*, Exon. 104 b; Th. 397, 7; Rä. 16, 16.

ge-rūme; *adj. Ample, roomy, expanded, made open;* amplus, spătiōsus, dīlātus, pătĕfactus:—Is mīn mōd gehǣled, hyge ymb heortan gerūme *my mind is healed, the thoughts around my heart expanded*, Cd. 35; Th. 47, 11; Gen. 759. Syndon đīne willan rihte and gerūme *thy wishes are right and great*, 188; Th. 234, 12; Dan. 291. [*Ger.* geraum *spacious: O. H. Ger.* kirūmo *opportunus.*]

ge-rumpen *rough, wrinkled;* rugosus:—Gerumpenu nædre *cerastes, coluber*, Cot. 38.

ge-rūna, an; *m. A counsellor:*—Gerūna *sinmistes* vel *consecretalis*, Ælfc. Gl. 7; Som. 56, 66; Wrt. Voc. 18, 18. Gerūna *a secretis*, vel *principis consiliarius*, 113; Som. 79, 127; Wrt. Voc. 60, 32.

ge-runnen *run together, congealed, joined;* coagulatus, Ps. Lamb. 67, 16: 118, 70: Ælfc. Gl. 33; Som. 62, 17; Wrt. Voc. 28, 1: 78; Som. 72, 52; Wrt. Voc. 46, 12; *pp. of* ge-rinnan.

gerwan, gerwian, gerwigan; *p.* ede, ode; *pp.* ed, od *To make ready prepare, make, construct;* părāre, præpărāre, făcĕre, construĕre:—Ciricean getimbran, gerwan Godes tempel *to build a church, to construct a temple of God*, Andr. Kmbl. 3266; An. 1636. Gerwigan wīfe hūs wexinge getācnaþ *to prepare [one's] house for a wife betokens increase*, Som. 205; Lchdm. iii. 210, 3. v. gearwian.

ge-ryd, -rid; *adj. Prepared, ready, usual;* paratus:—Đeáh se graf geryd sī *though the grave be prepared*, Lchdm. iii. 355, 2, col. 1; Shrn. 184, 20. Moises dyde on geryde orcas *Moses put it into the usual basons*, Ex. 24, 6.

ge-ryht. v. ge-riht.

ge-ryhtan *to set right;* dirĭgĕre:—He wolde đone Cristes geleáfan geryhtan *he would set right the faith of Christ*, Chr. 680; Erl. 40, 12. v. ge-rihtan.

ge-rȳman; *p.* de; *pp.* ed [rȳman *to make room*] *To extend, enlarge, make room, open, manifest, expand;* dīlātāre, amplĭfĭcāre, lŏcum dāre, apĕrīre, expandĕre:—Ongyn đē scip wyrcan, on đam đū monegum scealt reste gerȳman *begin thou to make a ship, in which thou shalt make room for resting-places to many*, Cd. 65; Th. 78, 36; Gen. 1304. Ic gerȳme đīne gemǣro *dīlātāvĕro termĭnos tuos*, Ex. 34, 24. He ōđrum gerȳmeþ wyrmum to wiste *he clears the way for other worms' repast*, Exon. 100 a; Th. 374, 9; Seel. 123. Ic him līfes weg gerȳmde *I opened the way of life to them*, Rood Kmbl. 175; Kr. 89: Elen. Kmbl. 2496; El. 1249. Đū me gerȳmdes *dīlātasti mihi*, Ps. Th. 4, 1. Octauianus gerȳmde Rōmāna rīce *Octavianus extended the Roman empire*, Homl. Th. i. 32, 18. Đæt hie him ōđer flet eal gerȳmdon *that they would wholly open to him another dwelling*, Beo. Th. 2177; B. 1086. Se weg biþ us gerȳmed *the way is open to us*, Boutr. Scrd. 20, 32: Andr. Kmbl. 3159; An. 1582: Bt. Met. Fox 1, 37; Met. 1, 19: Homl. Th. i. 564, 18: 28, 12. Se đe his godcundnesse mid sōþum wīsum gerȳmeþ *who truly manifests his divinity*, Blickl. Homl. 179, 24. Gif him swā byþ gerȳmed *if he has opportunity*, Basil admn. 9; Norm. 52, 28. On đam rȳmette đe se cing hēt gerȳmen into ealdan mynstre *in the space that the king ordered to cede to the old monastery*, Ch. Th. 231, 26.

ge-rȳne, -rīne, -rēne, es; *pl. nom. acc.* -u, -o, -a; *n. A mystery, a sacrament;* mysterium:—Đæt dēgol wæs Dryhtnes gerȳne *that was a secret mystery of the Lord*, Exon. 8 b; Th. 3, 25; Cri. 41. Đæt monnum nis cūþ gerȳne *that mystery is not known to men*, 9 a; Th. 7, 2; Cri. 95. Dryhtnes gerȳne *the mystery of the Lord*, 49 a; Th. 169, 14; Gū. 1094: Lk. Bos. 8, 10. Đæt word đæs heofonlīcan gerȳnes *the word of the heavenly mystery*, Blickl. Homl. 17, 9: 7. Eów is geseald to witanne heofena rīces gerȳnu *vobis datum est nosse mysteria regni cælorum*, Mt. Bos. 13, 11. Đa gerȳnu Cristes menniscnysse *the mysteries of Christ's humanity*, Homl. Pasc. Lisle 12, 17. Hit forhæfed gewearþ đætte hie sǣdon swefn cyninge, wyrda gerȳnu *it was denied that they should tell the dream to the king, the mysteries of the fates*, Cd. 179; Th. 225, 4; Dan. 149. Engel Drihtnes wrāt in wāge worda gerȳnu *the angel of the Lord wrote on the wall mysteries of words*, 210; Th. 261, 9; Dan. 723. On đē wrāt wuldres God gerȳno *on thee the God of glory wrote [his] mysteries*, Andr. Kmbl. 3020; An. 1513. Đæt hie đæt hālige gerȳne ārwurþlīce breman mǣgen *that they may reverently celebrate the holy mystery*, L. E. I. 4; Th. ii. 404, 27: Bd. 1, 27; S. 496, 23, 43: 497, 2, 5. [*Goth.* ga-rūni *counsel: O. Sax.* gi-rūni *mystery: O. H. Ger.* ki-rūni *mysterium, sacramentum.*] DER. gāst-gerȳne, gǣst-, word-. v. rȳne, rūn, ge-rȳno, ge-rȳnu.

ge-rȳnelīc; *adj. Mystical;* mysticus:—Gerȳnelīco word sprecende *mystica verba loquens*, Bd. 2, 1; S. 500, 26. Of gerȳnelīcum gāste *ex mystico spiramine*, Hymn. Surt. 43, 36. Đās gerȳnelīcan þing *hæc mystica*, 94, 17: Blickl. Homl. 165, 35.

ge-rȳnelīce *mystically;* mystice, Cot. 131.

ge-rȳno; *indecl. n. A mystery:*—Đis Eástorlīce gerȳno us æteóweþ đæs ēcean līfes sweotole bysene *this Easter mystery [Christ's resurrection] shews us a clear example of the life eternal*, Blickl. Homl. 83, 7. v. gerȳne.

ge-rȳnu; *indecl. f. A mystery:*—Đeós gerȳnu is wedd *this mystery is a pledge*, Homl. Th. ii. 272, 6. Þurh gāstlīcere gerȳnu *through a spiritual mystery*, 268, 29: 260, 12: 262, 22: Bd. de nat. rerum; Wrt. popl. science 14, 1; Lchdm. iii. 264, 11. [*O. H. Ger.* gi-riuna, *f.*] v. ge-rȳne.

ge-rypon *reaped*, Chr. 896; Th. 172, 33, col. 1; = ge-ripon; *p. pl. of* ge-rīpan.

ge-rysene *fit.* v. ge-risene.

gēs *geese*, L. In. 70; Th. i. 146, 18, MS. H; *pl. nom. acc. of* gōs.

ge-saca, an; *m. An adversary;* adversarius:—Geþafedon đæt his gesacan *concesserunt id adversarii*, Bd. 2, 2; S. 502, 24. On gesacum *on his adversaries*, Cd. 4; Th. 4, 25; Gen. 59: Beo. Th. 3551; B. 1773. Gesaca *æmulus*, Ælfc. Gl. 114; Som. 80, 17; Wrt. Voc. 60, 51. v. sacan.

ge-sacan? *p.* -sōc, *pl.* -sōcon; *pp.* -sacen *To oppose, strive against;* adversari:—Gesacan sceal sāwl-berendra, niđđa bearna, gearwe stōwe *shall strive against the place prepared for those having souls, for the children of men*, Beo. Th. 2012, note; B. 1004. v. sacan.

ge-sacu, e; *f. Contention, hostility;* contentio, hostilitas, Beo. Th. 3479; B. 1737. v. sacu.

ge-sadelod, -sadolod; *part.* [sadelian *to saddle*] *Saddled;* strātus:—Twā hors, ān gesadelod and ōđer ungesadelod *two horses, one saddled* *and the other unsaddled*, L. C. S. 72; Th. i. 414, 17. Eahta hors, feówer gesadelode [gesadolode, MS. A.] and feówer ungesadelode *eight horses, four saddled and four unsaddled*, 72; Th. i. 414, 5, 10. DER. un-gesadelod.

ge-sadian; *p.* ode, ade; *pp.* od *To satisfy, fill*; saturare:—Beóþ gesadode oðđe gefyllede treówa feldes *saturabuntur ligna campi*, Ps. Lamb. 103, 16. Drihten đé gesadade mid đý sēlestan hwǽtecynnes holde lynde *Dominus adipe frumenti satiat te*, Ps. Th. 147, 3. v. sadian.

ge-sæccan *to dispute, discuss*; disserere, Mt. Kmbl. p. 11, 2.

ge-sæcgan *to say, tell*, Ps. Th. 77, 8. v. ge-secgan.

ge-sǽd *said, told, proved*, Ors. 1, 8; Bos. 31, 33, 34; *pp. of* ge-secgan.

ge-sǽgan; *p.* de; *pp.* ed [sǽgan *to cause to sink*] *To lay low, cast down*; prosternĕre, incurvāre:—Hæfdon ealfela Eótena cynnes sweordum gesǽged *they had laid low full many of the Jutes' race with their swords*, Beo. Th. 1772; B. 884: Judth. 12; Thw. 25, 36; Jud. 294. Ic eom gesǽged, *incurvātus sum*, Ps. Th. 37, 8.

ge-sægde, -sǽde, *pl.* -sægdon *said, told*, Beo. Th. 4321; B. 2157: Bd. 4, 18; S. 587, 2: 1, 12; S. 481, 3; *p. of* ge-secgan.

ge-sægdnis, e; *f. A mystery*; mysterium, Mt. Kmbl. Lind. 13, 11.

ge-sægen *a saying, telling, tradition*, Bd. pref; S. 472, 8, 20, 25, 30: 5, 23; S. 647, 17: Blickl. Homl. 55, 26. v. ge-segen, ge-sagun.

ge-sæhtlian; *p.* ode, ade; *pp.* od, ad [sæhtlian *to reconcile*] *To reconcile*; reconcĭliare:—Wearþ Eádgār wiđ đone cyng gesæhtlad *Edgar was reconciled with the king*, Chr. 1091; Erl. 228.

ge-sæhtniss. v. ge-sehtniss.

ge-sǽlan; *p.* de; *pp.* ed [sǽlan *to bind, tie*] *To bind, tie*; lĭgāre:—Đa folan hý gesǽlaþ *they tie the foals*, Nar. 35, 11. Đæt is se ealda feónd đone he gesǽlde *that is the ancient fiend whom he bound*, Exon. 96 a; Th. 359, 7; Pa. 59. He ligeþ synnum gesǽled *he lies bound with sins*, 18 b; Th. 46, 12; Cri. 736: Beo. Th. 5521; B. 2764: Cd. 37; Th. 47, 23; Gen. 765: 200; Th. 248, 30; Dan. 251. Đonne gemēte gyt đǽr eoselan gesǽlede *then shall ye find there an ass tied*, Blickl. Homl. 69, 36: Mt. Kmbl. Rush. 21, 2.

ge-sǽlan; hit -sǽleþ, -sǽlþ; *p.* de; *pp.* ed [sǽl *an occasion*] *To happen, come to pass, befall*; accĭdĕre, evĕnīre:—Hū gesǽleþ đæt *how doth that happen?* Salm. Kmbl. 698; Sal. 348: Andr. Kmbl. 1021; An. 511: 1029; An. 515. Gif hit ǽfre gesǽlþ, đæt . . . *if it ever happen that* . . . , Bt. Met. Fox 13, 43; Met. 13, 22: Th. Ch. 472, 4: 166, 20. Me gesǽlde đæt ic mid sweorde ofslōh niceras nigene *it befell me that I slew with my sword nine monsters*, Beo. Th. 1152; B. 574: 1784; B. 890: 2504; B. 1250. Đeáh eów nū gesǽle, đæt . . . *though it now happen to you that* . . . , Bt. Met. Fox 10, 47; Met. 10, 24. Uncūþ hū him æt ǽhtum gesǽle *it is unknown how it may befall him in the matter of property*, Prov. Kmbl. 20.

ge-sǽlan; *p.* de *To be successful, succeed*:—Đam đe eahtan wile sāwla gehwylcre đǽr he gesǽlan mæg *to him who will persecute every soul if he can manage it*, Exon. 37 b; Th. 123, 6; Gū. 318.

ge-sǽlge; *adv. Happily*; fauste, Cot. 89.

ge-sǽli; *adj. Happy*; fēlix:—Hweđer micel feoh mǽge ǽnigne mon dōn swā gesǽline, đæt he nānes þinges māran ne þurfe *can much money make any man so happy that he may need nothing more?* Bt. 26, 1; Fox 90, 13. v. ge-sǽlig.

ge-sǽlig, es; *m. One who carries a standard*; signifer, Hpt. Gl. 495.

ge-sǽlig, -sǽli; *comp.* ra; *superl.* ost, ust; *adj.* [sǽlig *happy*] *Happy, prosperous, blessed, fortunate*; fēlix, beatus, fortūnātus:—Seth wæs gesǽlig *Seth was happy*, Cd. 56; Th. 69, 19; Gen. 1138: 130; Th. 165, 28; Gen. 2738: Bt. Met. Fox 23, 3; Met. 23, 2. Se gesǽliga hlīsa *fēlix rūmor*, Bd. 4, 23; S. 594, 41: Exon. 61 a; Th. 222, 17; Ph. 350. Đæt gesǽlige weorud *the blessed company*, 26 a; Th. 76, 33; Cri. 1249. Wǽron swīđe gesǽlige *they were very happy*, Cd. 1; Th. 2, 12; Gen. 18: 220; Th. 282, 33; Sat. 296. Hī fram gesǽlgum tīdum gilpaþ *they boast of happy times*, Ors. 5, 2; Bos. 103, 11: Exon. 32 a; Th. 101, 1, 17; Cri. 1652, 1660. Mǽrþa gesǽligost *most blessed of glories*, Salm. Kmbl. 136; Sal. 67. Cild gesǽligust *a very prosperous child*, Lchdm. iii. 196, 21. Se gesǽlgosta *the happiest*, Bt. 26, 1; Fox 90, 10.

ge-sǽlig-līc, -sǽl-līc; *adj. Happy, fortunate*; fēlix, fortūnātus:—Đam đe līf forgeaf gesǽliglīc *to him who gave him a happy life*, Cd. 137; Th. 172, 14; Gen. 2844: Exon. 23 b; Th. 66, 29; Cri. 1079. v. ge-sǽlig.

ge-sǽlig-līce, -sǽli-līce, -sǽl-līce; *adv. Happily*; fēlīcĭter:—Gesǽliglīce *fēlīcĭter*, Scint. 1. Manige habbaþ genōg gesǽlilīce [gesǽllīce, MS. Cot.] gewīfod *many have married happily enough*, Bt. 11, 1; Fox 32, 5. Gesǽlilīce *fēlīcĭter*, Bd. 5, 19; S. 639, 27.

ge-sǽlignes, -nys, -ness, -nyss, e; *f. Happiness*; fēlīcĭtas:—Đǽr biþ engla dreám, sib and gesǽlignes *there is joy of angels, peace and happiness*, Exon. 32 b; Th. 102, 23; Cri. 1677. Gif đū wille đysses līfes gesǽlignysse mid us brūcan *si vis pĕrennis vītæ fēlīcĭtāte perfrui*, Bd. 1, 7; S. 477, 35.

gesǽli-līce *happily*; fēlīcĭter, Bd. 5, 19; S. 639, 27. v. ge-sǽlig-līce.

ge-sǽl-līc; *adj. Happy*; fēlix:—Gesǽllīc mon *a happy man*, Bt. Met. Fox 2, 34; Met. 2, 17. v. gesǽlig-līc.

gesǽl-līce *happily*, Bt. 11, 1; Fox 32, 5, MS. Cot. v. gesǽlig-līce.

ge-sæltan; *pp.* -sælted, -sælt *To salt*, Mt. Kmbl. Lind. 5, 13: Mk. Skt. Lind. 9, 49.

ge-sǽlþ, e; *f.* [sǽlþ *happiness*] *Happiness, felicity, prosperity, wealth, good, advantage*; fēlīcĭtas, prospĕrĭtas, bŏnum:—Sió sōđe gesǽlþ *the true happiness*, Bt. 23; Fox 78, 30: 34, 2; Fox 134, 32: 34, 4; Fox 138, 21, 24. God is full ǽlcere gesǽlþe *God is full of all happiness*, 34, 3; Fox 136, 20. Sōþra gesǽlþa *of true felicities*, Bt. Met. Fox 21, 49; Met. 21, 25. To đǽm gesǽlþum *to the felicities*, 21, 7, 17; Met. 21, 4, 9. He selþ đa gesǽlþa đǽm gōdum *he gives felicities to the good*, Bt. 39, 2; Fox 214, 2, 5: 34, 1; Fox 134, 7. Đū miht đa sōđan gesǽlþa gecnāwan *thou mayest discover the true goods*, 23; Fox 78, 32.

ge-sǽlþ *happens*, Bt. Met. Fox 13, 43; Met. 13, 22; *3rd sing. pres. of* ge-sǽlan.

ge-sǽman. v. ge-sýman.

ge-sæt, *pl.* -sǽton *sat, sat down*, Beo. Th. 5427; B. 2717: Elen. Kmbl. 1732; El. 868; *p. of* ge-sittan.

ge-sætnys. v. ge-setnes.

ge-sagian *to say, tell*; dicere:—Gesaga him *tell them*, Beo. Th. 781; B. 388: Bd. 1, 7; S. 477, 30. v. sagian.

ge-sagu *a narration*, Lk. Skt. Lind. 1, 1.

ge-sagun, e; *f. A narration*, Lk. Skt. Rush. 1, 1.

ge-salde *sold*; tradidit, Cd. 226; Th. 301, 2; Sat. 575, = ge-sealde; *p. of* ge-sellan.

ge-saldniss, e; *f. A giving*:—Ic berhtwulf rex đas mīne gesaldnisse trymme *I, king Berhtwulf, confirm this my gift*, Cod. Dipl. Kmbl. ii. 5, 32.

ge-sam, in composition, denotes *together, with*; simul, con. v. sam.

ge-sam-hīwan; *gen.* -hīwena, *pl. m. Married persons*; conjugati, conjugia:—Unriht gewuna is arisen betwih gesamhīwum *prava in conjugatorum moribus consuetudo surrexit*, Bd. 1, 27; S. 493, 34, note: Bd. 4, 5; S. 573, 14, note. v. gesinhīwan.

ge-samnian, -somnian; *p.* ode, ade, ede; *pp.* od, ad, ed. I. *to gather, collect*; congrĕgāre, collĭgĕre:—Se āncenneda ealle gesamnaþ *the only begotten one shall gather all*, Soul Kmbl. 102; Seel. 51. Valentinianus gesamnode weorod *Valentinian gathered an army*, Chr. 380; Erl. 11, 4: Cd. 174; Th. 219, 9; Dan. 52. He hī of sīdfolcum gesamnade *de regiōnĭbus congrĕgāvit eos*, Ps. Th. 106, 2. Gesamnedon sīde hērigeas folces frumgāras *the leaders of the people collected their wide bands*, Andr. Kmbl. 2135; An. 1069: Ps. Th. 125, 6. Us gesamna of wīdwegum *congrĕga nos de nātiōnĭbus*, 105, 36. Wæs eall-geador to đam þingstede þeód gesamnod *the people was collected together in the public place*, Andr. Kmbl. 2198; An. 1100: Elen. Kmbl. 563; El. 282. Mycle mænigeo wǽron gesamnode to hym *congrĕgātæ sunt ad eum turbæ multæ*, Mt. Bos. 13, 2: 26, 3. II. *to unite, join*; consŏcĭāre, jungĕre:—Geférscipas fæste gesamnaþ *firmly unites societies*, Bt. Met. Fox 11, 186; Met. 11, 93: Bt. 21; Fox 74, 38. Se gesamnade sāwle to līce *he united the soul to the body*, Bt. Met. Fox 17, 23; Met. 17, 12. III. *v. intrans. To collect, come together*; congrĕgāri, convĕnīre:—Hī gesamniaþ *congrĕgāti sunt*, Ps. Th. 103, 21. Gesamnadon weras *the men collected together*, Andr. Kmbl. 3270; An. 1638.

ge-samning *a synagogue*; sўnăgōga, Ps. Th. 85, 13. v. ge-samnung.

ge-samnung, -somnung, -samning, -somning, e; *f. A meeting, assembly, council, union, congregation, synagogue, church*; conventus, conventio, concĭlium, congrĕgātio, sўnăgōga, ecclēsia:—Gesamnung *conventus, conventio*, Ælfc. Gl. 87; Som. 74, 48; Wrt. Voc. 50, 30. Se wæs đære gesamnunge ealdor *ipse princeps sўnăgōgæ ĕrat*, Lk. Bos. 8, 41. Fram gesamnunge mycelre *a concĭlio multo*, Ps. Spl. C. 39, 14. Ealra heora eágan on đære gesamnunge wǽron on hyne behealdende *omnium in sўnăgōga ŏcŭli ĕrant intendentes in eum*, Lk. Bos. 4, 20: 8, 49: Jn. Bos. 6, 59: 18, 20. He eóde on reste-dæge on đa gesamnunge æfter his gewunan *intrāvit sĕcundum consuetūdĭnem die sabbăti in sўnăgōgam*, Lk. Bos. 4, 16. He lǽrde hīg on hyra gesamnungum *dŏcēbat eos in sўnăgōgis eōrum*, Mt. Bos. 13, 54: 23, 6: Mk. 1, 39: 12, 39: Lk. Bos. 4, 44: 11, 43: 20, 46. On gesamnunga *in sўnăgōgas*, Lk. Bos. 21, 12. On gesamnunga hāligra *in ecclēsia sanctōrum*, Ps. Lamb. 149, 1. Þurh đa gesamnunga we wǽron gefreoþode feónda gafoles *through that union we were freed from devils' tribute*, Blickl. Homl. 105, 22.

ge-samodlǽcan *to put together*; conlocare, Blickl. Gl. 112, 8.

ge-sanco; *pl. n. Suckers*:—Gesanco *exigia*, Wrt. Voc. 287, 35.

ge-sārgian; *p.* ode, ade; *pp.* od, ad [sārgian *to afflict*] *To afflict, trouble, damage*; affligĕre, trĭbŭlāre:—Biþ untreó gesārgad *the faithless shall be afflicted*, Exon. 22 a; Th. 59, 34; Cri. 962: 22 a; Th. 60, 18; Cri. 971. Ne sceal nān mon siócne monnan gesārgodne swencan *no one ought to afflict a sick troubled person*, Bt. 38, 7; Fox 210, 20. Wǽron hie gesārgode *they were damaged*, Chr. 897; Erl. 96, 8.

ge-sāwan; *pp.* -sāwen *To sow*; seminare, Mt. Kmbl. Lind. 13, 3. DER. sāwan.

ge-sāweled; *part. p. Provided with a soul*; animatus, Mk. Skt. p. 1, 11.

ge-scād *distance, reason*, Exon. 94 a; Th. 353, 16: Reim. 13. v. gesceád.

ge-scādenlīce; *adv. Separately, distinctly*; separatim, Cot. 198.

ge-scādwīs *reasonable, intelligent*. v. ge-sceádwīs.

ge-scádwíslíce; *comp.* or; *adv. Wisely, prudently, clearly;* prudenter, Ors. 1, 10; Bos. 32, 20: 2, 1; Bos. 38, 29.

ge-scádwyrt, e: *f. Oxeye*, Lchdm. ii. 274, 18; see the glossary at the end of the volume, and also iii. 328.

ge-scæft, e; *f. Creation;* creātio:—On ða beorhtan gescæft *on the bright creation*, Cd. 216; Th. 273, 20; Sat. 139. v. ge-sceaft.

ge-scǽnan, -sceánan, -scēnan; *p.* de; *pp.* ed *To diminish, break, bruise, shake, shatter;* contĕrĕre, confringĕre, conquassāre:—God heora tóþas gescǽneþ *Deus contĕret dentes eōrum*, Ps. Th. 57, 5: 67, 21. Ðú ðæs myclan dracan heáfod gescǽndest *tu confrēgisti căput dracōnis magni*, 73, 14. Ða he sylfa oft gebræc and gescǽnde *quas ipse ălĭquando contrīvĕrat*, Bd. 5, 12; S. 631, 27. Gesceányþ heáfda *conquassabit capita*, Ps. Spl. C. 109, 7.

ge-scænctest *thou hast given drink;* potasti, Ps. Lamb. 59, 3.

ge-scǽned, -scæned [?]; *part. p. Ornamented* [?]:—Sweord swíðe gescǽned, Salm. Kmbl. 444; Sal. 222. Cf. on ðæm scennum scíran goldes, Beo. Th. 3392; B. 1694. Grein compares with *O. H. Ger.* giskeinan, and translates *made bright;* Kemble, again, translates *sheathed.*

ge-scǽnednes, -scǽningnes, se; *f. A dashing together, a breaking;* collisio, Cot. 59.

ge-scæp. v. ge-sceap.

ge-scafan, -sceafan; *p.* -scóf; *pp.* -scafen *To shave, scrape, plane;* radere, complanare:—Wið innoðes flēwsan gāte horn gesceafen [gescafen, MS. B.] *for flux of inwards a goat's horn shaven*, Med. ex Quadr. 6, 9; Lchdm. i. 352, 15: 4, 12; Lchdm. i. 344, 23. v. scafan.

ge-scaldwyrt, e; *f. Talumbus*, Wrt. Voc. 289, 40.

ge-scamian; *p.* ode; *pp.* od. I. *v. intrans. To be ashamed, to blush;* erūbescĕre:—Sýn gecyrred underbæc and gescamian, ða ðe wyllaþ me yfelu *avertantur retrorsum et erūbescant, qui vŏlunt mihi măla*, Ps. Spl. 69, 3. II. *v. trans. impers. To shame, cause or bring shame to;* pŭdēre:—Sceal gescamian ða unrihtwísan *it shall shame the wicked;* erūbescant impii, Ps. Th. 30, 20. Gescamige hí *let it shame them;* erūbescant, Ps. Spl. 82, 16. v. ge-sceamian.

ge-scapennys, -nyss, e; *f. A creation, creating, formation;* creātio, figmentum:—Se emnihtes dæg is se feórþa dæg ðysse worulde gescapennysse *the day of the equinox is the fourth day of the creation of this world*, Bd. de nat. rerum; Wrt. popl. science 4, 14, 16; Lchdm. iii. 238, 18, 20. He sylf oncneów hiwunga oððe gescapennysse úre *ipse cognōvit figmentum nostrum*, Ps. Lamb. 102, 14. v. ge-sceapennys.

ge-scapu *pudenda*. v. ge-sceap.

gescea *a sobbing;* singultum, Wrt. Voc. 289, 35.

ge-sceád, -scád, es; *n.* I. *separation, distinction, difference:*—Ðæt gesceád *separatio*, Lk. Skt. Lind. 12, 51. Gesceád *distinctio*, Mt. Kmbl. p. 3, 3: Mk. Skt. Rush. 4, 12. Eálā mid hú micle gesceáde God todǽlde betwih leóht and ðýstru *O quam grandi distantia divisit deus inter lucem et tenebras*, Bd. 5, 14; S. 634, 37. He sceal geþencan ðæt gedál and ðæt gesceád *he must consider the distinction and the difference*, L. de Cf. 1; Th. ii. 260, 13. Gescád, Exon. 94 a; Th. 353, 16; Reim. 13. II. *power of distinguishing, reason, discretion, discrimination, an account, a reckoning, argument:*—Gē habbaþ gesceád ǽgðer ge gōdes ge yfeles *ye can distinguish between good and evil*, Homl. Th. i. 176, 24. Fordý sealde God mannum gesceád *therefore has God given reason to men*, 96, 13: 7: Bt. Met. Fox 20, 436; Met. 20, 218: 22, 88; Met. 22, 44. On gesceád witan *to understand*, Exon. 83 b; Th. 314, 3; Mód. 8. Gesceád witan, cunnan [with *gen;* cf. the same phrase in *O. Sax.* wissun thingo giskēd; and the *Ger.* bescheid wissen] *to be able to distinguish between things, to understand them*, Homl. Th. 186, 4: Beo. Th. 582; B. 288. Gesceád *discretio*, Bd. 1, 27; S. 496, 35. Gesceád agyldan *to render an account*, Mt. Bos. 12, 36: Homl. Th. i. 96, 20: ii. 50, 1. Dæt he mid gesceáde hine betealde unsynninne *that he proved himself sinless with reasoning*, 226, 11: Chr. 1070; Erl. 208, 17. For hwylcum gesceáde *propter quam rationem, quapropter*, Ælfc. Gr. 44; Som. 46, 16. Myd gewyssum gesceáde *propter certam rationem*, Nicod. 3; Thw. 2, 6. [*O. Sax.* gi-skēd: *O. H. Ger.* ga-skeit *distinctio, discretio, distantia.*]

ge-sceádan, -scádan; *p.* -scēd, -sceód; *pp.* -sceáden [in the Northern Gospels weak forms occur] *To separate, distinguish, discern, decide:*—Wēron gesceádad from *exceptis*, Mt. Kmbl. Lind. 14, 21. Ðú ðe gesceádest *qui separasti*, Rtl. 182, 31: 36, 27. Gisceád *distingue*, 36, 29. Wolde hilde gesceádan *would decide the war*, Cd. 167; Th. 209, 25; Exod. 504: Elen. Kmbl. 298; El. 149. Rodera rǽdend hit on riht gescēd *the ruler of the firmament decided it aright*, Beo. Th. 3115; B. 1555. He biþ on ðæt wynstre weorud gesceáden *he will be assigned at the separation to the band on the left hand*, Exon. 117 a; Th. 449, 23; Dōm. 75. [*Goth.* ga-skaidan *to separate:* *O. H. Ger.* gi-sceidan.]

ge-sceáden; *adj. Rational:*—Nān nýten næfde nān gesceádne sáwle *no beast had a rational soul*, Btwk. Scrd. 19, 35.

ge-sceádlíce; *adv. Reasonably, rationally;* rationabiliter:—Ful gesceádlíce ðú me andswarast and fulrihte *thou answerest me very rationally and rightly*, Shrn. 184, 17: 165, 21. Man sceal gesceádlíce tosceádan ylde and geógupe *we must discreetly distinguish between age and youth*, L. de Cf. 4; Th. ii. 262, 4. Gesceádlícor *more rationally*, Bt. 39, 2; Fox 214, 7.

ge-sceádwís; *adj. Reasonable, rational, discriminating, intelligent, prudent, cautious;* rationalis:—God gesceóp twā gesceádwísan gesceafta *God created two rational creatures*, Bt. 41, 2; Fox 244, 30: 42, 1; Fox 256, 9. Ǽlce dǽde sceal gesceádwís dēma wíslíce tosceádan hú heó gedōn sí and hwǽr and hwænne *in each deed an intelligent judge must distinguish how it be done, and where and when*, L. de Cf; Th. ii. 260, 27: Past. 21; Swt. 151, 6: Bt. Met. Fox 15, 27; Met. 15, 14. Mid gesceádwísum mægne *with intelligent power*, 20, 16; Met. 20, 8.

ge-sceádwíslíc; *adj. Reasonable;* rationalis, R. Ben. Interl. 2.

ge-sceádwíslíce; *adv. Rationally, prudently, sagaciously, discreetly, distinctly;* rationabiliter:—Ðú ðe gesceádwíslíce heora welst *thou that rulest them rationally*, Bt. 33, 4; Fox 128, 6: 21; Fox 74, 20. Hý him ðā gescádwíslíce andwyrdon *they answered him discreetly*, Ors. 1, 10; Bos. 32, 20. Ic wille gescádwíslícor gesecgan *apertissime expedire curabo*, 2, 1; Bos. 38, 29.

ge-sceádwísnes, ness, e; *f. Reason, discretion;* ratio:—Gelēf ðínre āgenre gesceádwísnesse *believe thine own reason*, Shrn. 199, 12: Bt. 33, 4; Fox 132, 9: Past. 11, 2; Swt. 65, 21; Hat. MS. 14 b, 27: Bt. Met. Fox 20, 375; Met. 188: 393; Met. 20, 197.

ge-sceafan *to shave, plane*, Med. ex Quadr. 6, 9; Lchdm. i. 352, 15: 4, 12; Lchdm. i. 344, 23. v. ge-scafan.

ge-sceaft, -scæft, -sceft, e; *f:* es; *n.* I. *the creation, a created being or thing, creature, an element;* creātio, creātūra, plasma, ĕlĕmentum:—Eall ðeós mǽre gesceaft *all this great creation*, Rood Kmbl. 24; Kr. 12: 162; Kr. 82: Salm. Kmbl. 60; Sal. 30. Gesceaft *plasma*, Ælfc. Gr. 9, 1; Som. 8, 22. Fram fruman gesceafte *ab initio creātūræ*, Mk. Bos. 10, 6: Cd. 9; Th. 11, 7; Gen. 171. On ðisse lǽnan gesceafte *in this perishable creation*, Salm. Kmbl. 653; Sal. 326: 737; Sal. 368. Þurh ða ilcan gesceaft *through the same creature*, Elen. Kmbl. 365; El. 183: 2061; El. 1032. Ða wiðerweardan gesceafta betwux him winnaþ *contrary creatures strive with each other*, Bt. 21; Fox 74, 13: Exon. 68 a; Th. 253, 21; Jul. 183. Ealle gesceafte forhte geweorþaþ *all creatures shall tremble*, Andr. Kmbl. 2997; An. 1501: Cd. 191: Th. 239, 11; Dan. 368: Bt. Met. Fox 11, 16; Met. 11, 8. Hí wuldriaþ æðelne ordfruman ealra gesceafta *they glorify the noble origin of all creatures*, 13 b; Th. 25, 18; Cri. 402: 21 b; Th. 57, 29; Cri. 926: Andr. Kmbl. 652; An. 326: Elen. Kmbl. 1785; El. 894: Bt. 21; Fox 72, 29. Eallum his gesceaftum *to all his creatures*, 21; Fox 74, 2, 21: Salm. Kmbl. 672; Sal. 335. He gemetgaþ ða feówer gesceafta *he regulates the four elements*, Bt. 39, 8; Fox 224, 8: 33, 4; Fox 128, 29: Boutr. Scrd. 18, 20: 30, 7. Ofer ealle gesceafte *over all creatures*, Exon. 28 a; Th. 84, 33; Cri. 1388: 43 b; Th. 147, 25; Gú. 732. Biþ ðæt gesceaft swíðe nearu geþuht *the creation will appear very narrow*, Homl. Th. ii. 186, 7. He awende ðæt gesceaft *he changed the creature*, ii. 72, 10: i. 276, 8, 10, 14, 15, 20. Ða gescæfta tācnedon ðæt he wæs sōþ god *created things shewed that he was very God*, Shrn. 67, 16. Bodigaþ ēlce gescæfte *prædicate omni creaturæ*, Mk. Skt. Rush. 16, 15: Rtl. 97, 12. Giscæf[t] *sexus*, 51, 7. Ðú ðe gimetgaþ gescæfta wrixla *qui temperas rerum vices*, 164, 12. II. *a decree, destiny, fate, condition;* destĭnāta, sors, fātum, condĭtio:—Ðæt is eald gesceaft *that is the ancient fate*, Salm. Kmbl. 772; Sal. 385. Nǽni eft cymeþ hider, ðe mannum secge hwylc sý Meotodes gesceaft *no one returns hither who may reveal to men what is the condition of the Creator*, Menol. Fox 592; Gn. C. 65. In gesceaft Godes *by God's decree*, Exon. 93 b; Th. 351, 3; Sch. 74. He sægde him wereda gesceafte *he told him the fates of peoples*, Cd. 180; Th. 225, 27; Dan. 160. [*Goth.* ga-skafts *creation, creature:* *O. Sax.* gi-skefti *decree of fate:* *O. H. Ger.* ga-skaft *creatura, elementum, habitus, fatum.*] DER. ealdor-gesceaft, eorþ-, forþ-, hand-, heáh-, land-, líf-, mǽl-, metod-, woruld-.

ge-sceamian, -sceomian, -scamian, -scomian; *p.* ode; *pp.* od. I. *v. intrans. To blush, be ashamed, be confounded;* erubescĕre, confundi:—Gesceamian [MS. gesceaman] oððe gescende sýn ða sēcendan sáwle míne *confundantur quærentes animam meam*, Ps. Spl. 34, 4. Gesceomadon alle fióndas his *erubescebant omnes adversari ejus*, Lk. Skt. Lind. 13, 17: 9, 26. II. *v. trans. To shame, cause or bring shame to, confound;* pŭdēre, confundĕre:—Nú mæg ðám Cristenan gescomian *now may the Christians blush*, Ors. 4, 12; Bos. 99, 12. Ne gesceamaþ hý *it shall not confound them;* non confundentur, Ps. Th. 36, 18: 30, 1. Gesceamige heom *erubescant*, Ps. Lamb. 6, 11: Ps. Th. 30, 19. Gisceomiga *confundas*, Rtl. 125, 15. [*Goth.* ga-skaman sik *to be ashamed.*]

ge-sceandnys, -nyss, e; *f. A confusion;* confūsio:—Ðú wāst gesceandnysse míne *tu scis confūsiōnem meam*, Ps. Spl. 68, 23: 131, 19. v. ge-scendnys.

ge-sceánon. v. ge-scǽnan.

ge-sceap, -scæp, -scep, es; *pl. nom. acc.* -sceapu, -sceapo; *gen.* -sceapa, -sceapena; *n.* I. *a creation, created being or thing, creature;* creātio, creātūra:—Song he be middangeardes gesceape *cănēbat de creātiōne mundi*, Bd. 4, 24; S. 598, 9. Þurh ðæt beorhte gesceap *through that bright creature*, Elen. Kmbl. 1576; El. 790. Ðisses gisceppes *hujus creationis*, Rtl. 21, 10. II. *a decree, fate, destiny, condition, nature, form, shape;* fātum, destĭnāta, condĭtio, nātūra, indōles, forma, spĕcies:—Ðæt ic sceolde wiđ gesceape mīnum on bonan willan būgan *that I must submit to a murderer's will against my nature*, Exon. 126 b; Th. 486, 2; Rä. 72, 6. Ðeós woruld gesceap dreógeþ *this world fulfils its destiny*, 122 b; Th. 469, 25; Hy. 11, 7: Beo. Th. 6160; B. 3084. Swā mīn gesceapu wǣron *such were my decrees*, Exon. 103 a; Th. 391, 19; Rä. 10, 7: 110 a; Th. 421, 26; Rä. 40, 24: Cd. 76; Th. 95, 4; Gen. 1573. Ðæt đīn līchoma leóhtra wurde, đīn gesceapu scēnran *that thy body would become brighter, thy form more beauteous*, 25; Th. 32, 14; Gen. 503. God gesceapo ferede ǣghwylcum on eorþan eormencynnes *God has borne his decrees to every one of the human race on earth*, Exon. 88 b; Th. 333, 1; Vy. 95. Sineweałt gesceap *volūbĭle schēma*, Ælfc. Gl. 100; Som. 77, 14; Wrt. Voc. 55, 18. Giscæp *habitus*, Rtl. 103, 32. III. *the privy members;* vĕrenda, pūdenda:—Sumne dǣl đæs felles æt foreweardan his gesceape *part of the foreskin*, Homl. Th. i. 94, 1. His gesceapu mađan weóllon *his members swarmed with vermin*, 86, 10: ii. 512, 4: Gen. 9, 22. Wiđ gicþan đæra gesceapa *against itch of the veranda*, Herb. 94, 4; Lchdm. i. 204, 22: 123, 1; Lchdm. i. 234, 19. Ðæra gesceapena *of the verenda*, 103, 1; Lchdm. i. 218, 7. [*O. Sax.* gi-skap *creature;* gi-skapu, *pl. decrees of fate*, v. Grm. D. M. 817.] DER. frum-gesceap, fyrn-, heáh-.

ge-sceapen; *part. p. Formed, created:*—Adam wearþ đā mann, gesceapen on sāwle and on līchaman *Adam then became man, formed with soul and body*, Homl. Th. i. 12, 30. v. sceppan *to create.*

ge-sceapennys, -sceapenys, -scapennys, -nyss, e; *f. A creation, creating, formation;* creātio:—God geswāc đære niwan gesceapennysse *God ceased from the new creation*, Boutr. Scrd. 17, 17. On đæs mannes gesceapennysse *in the creating of man*, 19, 7. Se man đe deófle geefenlǣcþ, se biþ deófles bearn, nā þurh gecynd ođđe þurh gesceapenysse, ac þurh đa geefenlǣcunge and yfele gearnunga *the man who imitates the devil is a child of the devil, not by nature nor by creation, but by that imitation and evil deserts*, Homl. Th. i. 260, 13, 15.

ge-sceap-hwīl, e; *f. The time appointed by fate for dying:*—To gescæphwīle *at the appointed time*, Beo. Th. 52; B. 26. v. Grm. D. M. 817.

ge-sceaplīce; *adv. Properly, fitly, well;* apte:—Seó heáfodstōw gesceaplīce gehiwad to đam gemete hyre heáfdes *locus capitis ad mensuram capitis illius aptissime figuratus*, Bd. 4, 19; S. 590, 1, note.

ge-scearfan *to cut off;* succidere, Lk. Skt. Lind. 13, 9.

ge-sceát *shot forward, darted*, Beo. Th. 4628; B. 2319; *p. of* ge-sceótan.

ge-sceátaþ *fall to, shall fall to* or *be allotted to*, Ex. 29, 28, = gesceótaþ; *pres. pl. of* ge-sceótan.

ge-sceaþan. v. ge-sceþþan.

ge-sceaþian; *p.* ode; *pp.* od *To injure, harm, scathe:*—Hū he on manna sāulum mǣst gesceaþian mǣge *how he can most injure the souls of men*, L. C. E. 26; Th. i. 374, 31. [Cf. ge-sceþþan.]

ge-sceáwian; *p.* ode; *pp.* od. I. *act. To shew, manifest, exhibit;* exhibere, monstrāre, manifestāre:—Āre ne wolde gesceáwian *would not shew reverence*, Cd. 76; Th. 95, 19; Gen. 1581. Wile đonne gesceáwian wlitige and unclǣne *then will he manifest the fair and the foul*, 227; Th. 303, 7; Sat. 609. Eorle monegum āre gesceáwaþ *to many a man he shews honour*, Exon. 100 b; Th. 379, 15; Deor. 33. He him wolde ārlīc bisceop-setl gesceáwian *he would shew* [*provide for*] *him an honourable bishop's-seat*, Bd. 3, 7; S. 530, 2. II. *act. To see, behold, view, look round upon;* videre, perspicere, circumspicere:—Heó endestæf gesceáwiaþ *they shall behold their end*, Cd. 225; Th. 298, 31: Sat. 541. Ðæt deáþ ne gesceáwige *qui non videbit mortem*, Ps. Th. 88, 41. Mīnre heortan gehygd gesceáwa *view the thoughts of my heart*, 138, 20. Hord ys gesceáwod *the hoard has been seen*, Beo. Th. 6161; B. 3084. Ðæt đū đa bisne sweotole gesceáwige *that thou mayest clearly view the example*, Bt. 22, 2; Fox 78, 15. Him eallum gesceáwodum *iis omnibus circumspectis*, Lk. Bos. 6, 10. III. *intrans. To see, consider;* videre, considerare:—And he scearpe ne mǣge gesceáwian *non considerat?* Ps. Th. 93, 9.

ge-sceft, e; *f. The creation, a creature;* creātio, creātūra:—In đære ēcan gescefte [MS. gesceft] *in the eternal creation*, Cd. 228; Th. 306, 15; Sat. 664. Ealra gescefta *of all creatures*, 226; Th. 301, 20; Sat. 584: 217; Th. 277, 13; Sat. 203. v. ge-sceaft.

ge-sceldod; *part. p. Provided with a shield:*—Twegen englas gesceldode *two angels with shields*, Blickl. Homl. 221, 28.

ge-scēnan; *p.* de; *pp.* ed *To break, bruise, wound;* contĕrĕre, vulnĕrāre:—Hī woldon ǣninga heafolan gescēnan *they would at once wound the head*, Andr. Kmbl. 2286; An. 1144. Forđon he ǣren dōr gesceeneþ *quia contrivit portas æreas*, Ps. Th. 106, 15. v. ge-scǣnan.

ge-scendan, -scindan, -scyndan; *p.* de; *pp.* ed *To shame, put to shame, confound, corrupt:*—Drihten hȳg gescent *Dominus subsannabit eos*, Ps. Th. 2, 4. Gescendes *corrumpit*, Lk. Skt. Lind. 12, 33. Ðæt đū hīg gescindest *that thou didst shame her*, Gen. 20, 6. He us gescende and ūre weorc *he hath put us and our deeds to shame*, Blickl. Homl. 243, 11. Hwā biþ gescended đæt me forđæm ne scamige *who is shamed and I am not ashamed?* Past. 21, 6; Swt. 165, 5; Hat. MS. Ne gescend me *non confundas me*, Ps. Th. 118, 116. Ðæt ic ne wese gescended *ut non confundar*, 80: 87, 15: 126, 6. Beóþ gescende mīne fȳnd *confundantur inimici mei*, 69, 2: 82, 13. Ne wylt đū me gescyndan *noli me confundere*, 118, 31. Ne beó ic gescynded *non confundar*, 6.

ge-scendnys, -scyndnys, se; *f. A confounding;* confusio:—Gescendnys, Ps. Spl. 43, 17: 34, 30. Ðone deófol đe đa synfullan gelǣt to gescyndnysse. Babilonia seó Chaldeisca burh is gereht gescyndnys *the devil that leads the sinful to confusion. Babylon, the Chaldean city, is interpreted 'confusion,'* Homl. Th. ii. 66, 21.

ge-sceó *shoes;* calceamenta, Mt. Kmbl. Lind. 3, 11. v. ge-scȳ.

ge-sceód; *part. p. Provided with shoes, shod:*—Gesceóde [gescōed, Lind.] mid calcum *calciatos sandalis*, Mk. Bos. 6, 9: Homl. Th. ii. 264, 9.

ge-sceón; *p.* de *To happen, come upon;* accidere, contingere:—Him nīþ godes gesceóde *God's enmity came upon him*, Cd. 206; Th. 255, 7; Dan. 620. [Cf. Cod. Ex. Th. 226, 4; Ph. 400.] Him bonena hand hearde gesceóde [Kmbl. gesceód] *the hand of slayers had been hard upon him*, Andr. Kmbl. 36; An. 18. Egyptum wearþ đæs dægweorces deóp leán gesceód *to the Egyptians for that day's work a deep requital was given*, Cd. 167; Th. 209, 29; Ex. 506.

ge-sceorf, es; *n. Scurf, the fur of the mucous membrane;* mucus intestinorum, L. M. 2, 35; Lchdm. ii. 240, 23. v. sceorf.

ge-sceorpan; *p.* -scearp *To scrape, carve in pieces;* conscindere minutatim, Herb. 57, 1; Lchdm. i. 160, 4. v. sceorfan, screpan.

ge-sceortian; *p.* ade *To fall short, fail:*—Miđđȳ đæt wīn gesceortade *vino deficiente*, Jn. Skt. Lind. 2, 3.

ge-sceot, -scot, es; *n.* I. *the collection of weapons necessary for shooting, a weapon that is shot* or *hurled, an arrow, dart:*—Nim đīn gesceot đīnne cocur and đīnne bogan *take thy weapons, thy quiver and thy bow*, Gen. 27, 3. Ðū of heofenum dōm mid gescote sendest *de cœlo judicium jaculatum est*, Ps. Th. 75, 6. Ðǣr forwearþ micel Alexandres heres for geǣtredum gescotum *there much of Alexander's army perished by poisoned arrows*, Ors. 3, 9; Bos. 68, 38. [*O. H. Ger.* gascoz *jaculum: Ger.* geschoss.] II. *an advance* [*of money*], *a contribution, tribute* [cf. *Ger.* vorschiessen]. v. corn-, Rōm-gesceot. III. *a part of a building shut off from the rest* [v. Cl. and Vig. Icel. Dict. skot, III; *and cf. Ger.* geschoss *story of a house*]:—Gesceot bæftan đæm heáhweofode *propitiatorium*, vel *sanctum sanctorum*, vel *secretarium*, vel *pastoforum*, Ælfc. Gl. 109; Som. 79, 26; Wrt. Voc. 59, 1. v. selegesceot.

ge-sceót, es; *n.* I. *shooting, hurling:*—Ge mid gesceótum [*or* gesceotum? v. gesceot] ge mid stāna torfungum *both with shootings and flingings of stones*, Ors. 3, 9: Bos. 68, 19. II. *rapid movement as of anything shot:*—Ða wǣmna flugon mid swiftum gesceóte on heora fȳnd *the weapons flew with swift movement on to their enemies*, Jud. c. 16; Thw. 162, 8. v. sceót.

ge-sceótan; he -scȳt, -scītt, *pl.* -sceótaþ; *p.* -sceát, *pl.* -scuton; *subj.* ic, đū, he -sceóte, *pl.* -sceóten; *pp.* -scoten. I. *to shoot forward, to rush* or *dart forward with a quick motion, send forth, expend, pay, to fall to any one's share, be allotted to;* cum impetu movere *vel* ruere, expendere, cedere in partem alicujus:—Draca hord eft gesceát, dryhtsele dyrne *the dragon again darted to his hoard, his secret hall*, Beo. Th. 4628; B. 2319. Ðæt feoh đe ic for hyre āre gescoten [MS. gesceoten] hæbbe *the money which I have paid for her honour*, Th. Diplm. 558, 19. Ðū nāst hwām hit [wela] gescȳt *thou knowest not to whom it* [*wealth*] *shall fall*, Homl. Th. ii. 104, 9. Hit gescītt to his dǣle *it shall fall to his share*, Ex. 29, 26 Hīg gesceótaþ [MS. gesceataþ] to Aarones dǣle and his suna ēcre lage fram Israhēla bearnum *cedent in partem Aaron et filiorum ejus jure perpetuo a filiis Israel*, 29, 28. Ðeáh sumum men gesceóte læsse dǣl *though a less part be allotted to one man*, Homl. Th. ii. 272, 2: Jos. 9, 7. II. *to bring before* or *refer to any one;* referre ad aliquem:—We lǣraþ, đæt nān sacu đe betweóx preostan sī, ne beó gescoten to worldmanna sōme *we enjoin that no dispute that be between priests be referred to the adjustment of secular men*, L. Edg. C. 7; Th. ii. 246, 4.

ge-sceppan, -scippan, -scyppan; *p.* -sceóp, -scōp, *pl.* -sceópon, -scōpon; *pp.* -scæpen, -sceapen, -sceopen, -sceapen *To form, create;* formare, disponere, creare:—Ic gescippe *creo*, Ælfc. Gr. 26; Som. 29, 16. God gescypþ symle edniwan *God creates ever anew*, Boutr. Scrd. 18, 18. Ðā gesceóp Adam naman his wīfe *then Adam made a name for his wife*, Gen. 3, 20: Boutr. Scrd. 19, 32. Hēr ǣrest gesceóp ēce Drihten heofon and eorþan *here the Lord eternal first created heaven and earth*, Cd. 5; Th. 7, 26; Gen. 112: 12; Th. 14, 16; Gen. 219. God đas world gescōp *God created this world*, Exon. 17 b; Th. 41, 22; Cri. 659: Salm. Kmbl. 936; Sal. 467. Hwæt! đū ēce God! ealra gesceafta wundorlīce wel gesceópe *O! eternal God! thou hast made all creatures wonderfully well*, Bt. Met. Fox 20, 10; Met. 20, 5: Exon. 117 b; Th. 452, 14; Hy. 4, 1. Ǣr đæt đec ic gesceópe *prius quam te formarem*, Rtl. 55, 4. Nǣron nāwđer ne on Fresisc gescæpene ne on Denisc *they were formed neither on a Frisian nor on a Danish model*, Chr. 897; Erl. 95, 15. Ðā đā hīg wǣron gesceopene *when they were created*,

Gen. 2, 4. Mon wæs to Godes anlícnesse ǽrest gesceapen *man was to God's image first created*, Cd. 75; Th. 92, 16; Gen. 1529. Gesceapene híg synt *creata sunt*, Ps. Lamb. 32, 9: Ps. Th. 148, 5. Gescype scylfan on scipes bósme *make shelves in the ship's bosom*, Cd. 65; Th. 79, 4; Gen. 1306. God wolde þurh his ágene handa hine gescyppan *God would form him with his own hands*, Boutr. Scrd. 19, 10. To gescippenne *in order to create*, 3.

ge-sceppend, -scyppend, es; *m. A creator*:—Fram ðæm heáhsetle úre gescyppendes *from the throne of our Creator*, Blickl. Homl. 11, 29.

ge-sceran; *p.* -scer, -scær; *pp.* -scoren *To cut, cleave*; secare, dissecare:—He him on heáfde helm gescer *he clave the helmet on his head*, Beo. Th. 5939; B. 2973. Helm gescær *he cut the helmet*, 3057; B. 1526. v. sceran.

ge-scerian, -scyrian, -scyrigan; *p.* ede; *pp.* ed. I. *to bestow, appoint, provide, ordain, destine*; tribuere, providere, ordinare, destinare:—He sceolde his Drihtne þancian ðæs leánes, ðe he him on ðam leóhte gescerede *he should thank his Lord for the reward which he bestowed on him in that light*, Cd. 14; Th. 17, 11; Gen. 258. Ic biddan wille ðæt ðú me ne gescyrige mid scyldhetum *I will pray that thou appoint me not among the guilty ones*, Andr. Kmbl. 169; An. 85 Is se rǽd gescyred monna cynne *this counsel is ordained for mankind*, Cd. 22; Th. 27, 28; Gen. 424. II. *to number, reckon*; numerare:—Se me beág forgeaf, on ðam siexhund wæs, smǽtes goldes, gescyred sceatta *he gave me a bracelet, on which six hundred sceats of beaten gold were numbered*, Exon. 86 a; Th. 324, 9; Wíd. 92. Ic wéne ðæt ðǽr screoda wǽre gescyred ríme siexhundreda *I believe that there were six hundred chariots reckoned by number*, 122 a; Th. 468, 10; Phar. 5. [*O. Sax.* gi-skerian *to ordain, arrange*.]

ge-scerpan, -scirpan, -scierpan; *p.* te *To sharpen*; acuere:—Ic gescirpe mín swurd *I will sharpen my sword*, Deut. 32, 41. Ðære culfran bilwitnesse gescierpan [-scirpan, Hat. MS.] *to sharpen the simplicity of the dove*, Past. 35, 1; Swt. 236, 23; Cot. MS.

ge-scerpan, -scirpan, -scyrpan; *p.* te *To clothe, furnish, adorn, deck*; vestire, ornare:—Ðeáh Neron hine gescerpte wlitegum wǽdum *though Nero clothed himself in beautiful garments*, Bt. Met. Fox 15, 4; Met. 15, 2. Gescyrpte, Bt. 28; Fox 100, 26. Ele andwlitan gescyrpeþ *oleum faciem exhilarat*, Ps. Th. 103, 15. Ðá ðæt folc hine geseah swá gescyrpedne *when the people saw him so furnished* [i. e. *with sword and spear, and riding on the king's horse*], Bd. 2, 13; S. 517, 10: 5, 19; S. 638, 9, 10. Fugla cynn fiðerum gescyrped *volucres pennatæ*, Ps. Th. 148, 10. Ða ðe gescirped sind *qui vestiuntur*, Mt. Kmbl. Lind. 11, 8.

ge-sceððan [with the same form in the infinitive are to be found, apparently, two verbs, one belonging to the strong, the other to the weak conjugation. Corresponding to the *Gothic* verb skaþjan, skóþ *is* sceððan, scód; [cf. sceppan, scóp.] The infinitive 'sceaðan' also occurs. Corresponding to *Icel.* skeðja, skaddi *is* sceððan, sceðede. There is besides the weak verb 'sceaðian,' which corresponds to *Icel.* skaða, skaðaði, *or O. H. Ger.* scadón, scadota. With regard to the form 'scód' instead of 'skóþ,' see Grm. And. u. El. 93] *To injure, hurt, oppress, be an enemy to*; nocere, adversari:—Gisceðeþ *nocebit*, Rtl. 8, 29. Ða ðe hríppum usum gesceððaþ and gefrettaþ *quæ messibus nostris adversantur et comedunt*, 147, 7. Ðæt him bám gescód *that injured them both*, Exon. 45 b; Th. 154, 14; Gú. 842: 38 b; Th. 127, 35; Gú. 396: 61 b; Th. 226, 4; Ph. 400. He manegum gesceód *it proved a foe to many*, Cd. 167; Th. 208, 25; Exod. 488: 198; Th. 247, 1; Dan. 490: 209; Th. 258, 20; Dan. 678. Him hettende oft gescódan *enemies oft oppressed them*, Exon. 62 a; Th. 228, 23; Ph. 442. Him gesceðe scyldignis *ei noceat reatus*, Rtl. 103, 15. Gáste gesceððan *to injure the soul*, Andr. Kmbl. 1834; An. 919: Beo. Th. 2899; B. 1447. Gesceðded *læsus*, Lye.

ge-sceððendlíc; *adj. Hurtful*:—Alle gesceððendlíca *omnia nociva*, Rtl. 118, 33.

ge-scierpan *to sharpen*. v. ge-scerpan.

ge-scild, es; *n. A refuge*; refugium, Ps. Spl. T. 70, 4.

ge-scildan, -scyldan; *p.* de; *pp.* ed *To shield, cover, protect, defend*; protegere, tueri:—Ic gescilde ðé mínre swýðran handan *I will cover thee with my right hand*, Ex. 33, 22. Ic ðé gescilde on drihtenes name *I will protect thee in the name of the Lord*, Shrn. 15, 19. Gif ðé man scotaþ to ðú gescylst ðé *if you are shot at you shield yourself*, Homl. Th. ii. 538, 10. Giscildes *protegis*, Rtl. 62, 14. Us gescyldeþ scyppend engla *the Creator of angels protects us*, Andr. Kmbl. 867; An. 434: Exon. 68 b; Th. 255, 14; Jul. 214. He us gesceldeþ wiþ eallum feóndum *he will shield us from all enemies*, Blickl. Homl. 51, 14. Siððan hie heofonríces weard wið ðone hearm gescylde *after heaven's guardian had protected them against that hurt*, Cd. 196; Th. 245, 6; Dan. 458: Shrn. 90, 7: Mt. Kmbl. p. 7, 9. Giscilde *protegat*, Rtl. 49, 34. Wiþ egesan yfeles feóndes míne sáwle gescyld *a timore inimici eripe animam meam*, Ps. Th. 63, 1. Gescildan wið *to protect against*, Exon. 40 b; Th. 135, 23; Gú. 528. Heó is gescyld *she is protected*, Ors. 2, 4; Bos. 45, 3. Gescylded *protected*, Exon. 58 b; Th. 210, 4; Ph. 180: Bd. 3, 23; S. 555, 35.

ge-scildend, -scyldend, es; *m. A protector*:—Mín gescyldend *protector meus*, Ps. Th. 27, 8: Andr. Kmbl. 2583; An. 1293.

ge-scildnes, -scyldnes, -scildness, e; *f. Protection, defence, shielding*; tuitio, tutamen, tutela, defensio:—Þurh his gescildnisse synd ða fýnd on dínum handum oferwunnene *through his protection are the enemies overcome in thy hands*, Gen. 14, 20: Homl. Th. ii. 140, 27. For heora gescyldnysse *ob eorum defensionem*, Bd. 1, 12; S. 481, 4: 2, 5; S. 506, 30. Gescyldnysse *protectionem*, Ps. Spl. 17, 37. Giscildniss *protectio, tuitio, defensio*, Rtl. 17, 9: 62, 8: 145, 30.

ge-scínan; *p.* -scán; *pp.* -scinen *To shine, shine upon, illuminate*; fulgere, collustrare, illuminare:—Ne mæg heó ealle gesceafta gescínan, ne ða gesceafta ðe heó gescínan mæg, ne mæg hió ealle endemest gescínan *she cannot shine upon all creatures, nor those creatures which she may shine upon can she shine upon all equally*, Bt. 41, 1; Fox 244, 7-9: Bt. Met. Fox 30, 17; Met. 30, 9: 30, 22; Met. 30, 11. Wuldres gim grund gescíneþ *the gem of glory illuminates the ground*, Exon. 57 b; Th. 205, 26; Ph. 118. Swá sió sunne hine gescínþ *as the sun shines upon him*, Bt. 34, 5; Fox 140, 8. Gescíneþ *lucet*, Jn. Skt. Lind. 1, 5. Giscína *fulgere*, Rtl. 67, 10: 86, 34. Gisceán *innituit* [= *enituit*], 45, 16.

ge-scincio; *pl. n. The fat about the kidneys*. v. Lchdm. iii. 361.

ge-scindan. v. ge-scendan.

ge-scipian; *p.* ode; *pp.* od *To provide with ships*:—Se micla here wurdon gescipode *the great army got ships*, Chr. 893; Erl. 88, 23.

ge-scippan. v. ge-sceppan.

ge-sciran *to act as a steward*; vilicare, Lk. Skt. Lind. 16, 2.

ge-scirpan. v. ge-scerpan.

ge-scirpla, -scyrpla, an; *m. Clothing, clothes*; vestitus:—Wǽron hie on gescirplan scipférendum onlíce *they were in clothing like seafarers*, Andr. Kmbl. 499; An. 250. Hwǽr beóþ ðonne his ídlan gescyrplan *where shall his vain garments be then?* Blickl. Homl. 111, 35.

ge-scítt *shoots forward, falls to, is allotted to*, Ex. 29, 26; *pres. of* ge-sceótan.

ge-scód, -scóed. v. ge-sceód.

ge-scóe, Mk. Skt. Rush. 1, 7: Lk. Skt. Rush. 10, 4: Jn. Skt. Rush. 1, 27. v. ge-scý.

ge-scola, an; *m. A fellow-debtor*; condebitor, Cot. 208. [*M. H. Ger.* geschol.] v. sculan.

ge-scomian. v. ge-sceamian.

ge-scot. v. ge-sceot.

ge-scotfeoht, es; *n. A fight with arrows* or *darts*:—Eft gewurdon on gescotfeohta scearpe gáras *ipsi sunt jacula*, Ps. Th. 54, 21: 75, 3.

ge-scræpe, -screope, -scroepe; *adj. Convenient, meet, fit for, accommodated*; aptus:—Breoton is gescræpe on læswe sceápa and neáta *Brittannia est apta alendis pecoribus ac jumentis*, Bd. 1, 1; S. 473, 13, 22. Giscroepo *aptas*, Rtl. 117, 14: Bd. 5, 6; S. 618, 41. DER. un-gescræpe. v. ge-screpelíce, ge-scropenys, ge-screope.

ge-screádian; *p.* ode, ede; *pp.* od, ed *To cut off, trim, prune*; sarpere:—Gif se wíngeard ne biþ onriht gescreádod *if the vineyard be not rightly pruned*, Homl. Th. ii. 74, 14. Gescreáded wíngeard *sarpta vinea*, Ælfc. Gl. 99; Som. 76, 125; Wrt. Voc. 54, 65. DER. screádian.

ge-screncan; *p.* te *To cause to shrink, to destroy, supplant*:—Wéron gescrencde *aruerunt*, Mt. Kmbl. Lind. 13, 6. Ðú gescrenctyst onarísende on me *supplantasti insurgentes in me*, Ps. Spl. C. 17, 41.

ge-screncednes, -ness, e; *f. A supplanting, an overturning*; supplantatio, Ps. Spl. C. 40, 10.

ge-screngce; *adj. Withered, shrunken, dry*; aridus, Lk. Skt. Lind. 6, 8.

ge-screope; *adj. Fit for, apt*; aptus:—Fela óðera gescreopa and gesynto he onceneów heofonlíce him forgifen beón *alia commoda et prospera cœlitus sibi fuisse data intellexit*, Bd. 4, 22; S. 592, 20: Bd. 4, 19; S. 589, 42, note. v. ge-scræpe.

ge-screpelíce; *adv. Aptly, conveniently, fitly*; apte:—Gescrepelíce gehiwad *aptissime figuratus*, Bd. 4, 19; S. 590, 1. v. ge-scræpe.

ge-scrif, es; *n. A judgment, command, ceremony*; censura, edictum, ceremonia, Cot. 59: 79: 56. [Cf. *O. H. Ger.* gi-scrip *scriptura, forma*.] v. ge-scrífan.

ge-scrífan; *p.* -scráf, -screáf; *pp.* -scrifen. I. *to judge, deem, assign, impose, appoint*; judicare, assignare, imponere, designare:—Se ðe him gescráf weán *who to him had assigned misery*, Cd. 148; Th. 186, 16; Exod. 139. Swá him wyrd gescráf *so fate assigned to him*, Beo. Th. 5142; B. 2574: Elen. Grm. 1047: Bt. Met. Fox 1, 58; Met. 1, 29. Hió me lytle læs láðe woldan ðisses eorþweges ende gescrífan *paulo minus consummaverunt me in terra*, Ps. Th. 118, 87. Siððan gé agifen habbaþ sceattas gescrifene *when you have given the appointed sum*, Andr. Kmbl. 593; An. 297. II. *to shrive, impose penance, censure*; pœnitentiam imponere, reprehendere:—Manna sáwla lǽce sceal geþencan, hú he mannum heora dǽda gescríſe and hí þeáh-hwæðere ne fordéme *the physician of men's souls must consider how he shall shrive their deeds and yet not condemn them*, L. de. Cf. 1; Th. ii. 260, 14.

ge-scrincan; *p.* -scranc; *pp.* -scruncen *To shrink, dry up*:—Giscrinca hia *arrescunt*, Rtl. 125, 35. For ðæm ciéle him gescruncan ealle ða ǽdra ðæt him mon ðæs lífes ne wénde [*cum in præfrigidum amnem descen-*

disset] *obriguit, contractuque nervorum proximus morti fuit*, Ors. 3, 9; Bos. 64, 38. Gescriungon *aruerunt*, Mt. Kmbl. Lind. 13, 6. Mengo giscrungenra *multitudo aridorum*, Jn. Skt. Rush. 5, 3. Ða gescruncenan *marcida*, Cot. 133.

ge-scroepe. v. ge-scræpe.

ge-scropelīce *fitly, meetly*, Som. v. ge-screpelice.

ge-scropenys, -nyss, e; *f. An applying, a fitting, accommodation;* accommodatio, Som. DER. un-ge-screpnes. v. ge-scræpe.

ge-scrȳdan, -scrīdan; *p.* -scrȳdde; *pp.* -scrȳd, -scȳrd *To clothe;* induere, vestire:—God gescrīdde hī *God clothed them*, Gen. 3, 21. Mann hnescum gyrlum gescrȳdne; nū ða ðe synt hnescum gyrlum gescrȳdde synt on cyninga hūsum *hominem mollibus vestitum? ecce qui mollibus vestiuntur in domibus regum sunt*, Mt. Bos. 11, 8. Mid wlite gescȳrd is gescȳrd is driht strangnysse *decore indutus est, indutus est dominus fortitudinem*, Ps. Spl. 92, 1. Myrce gescȳrded *shrouded in darkness*, Andr. Kmbl. 2628; An. 1315.

ge-scryfu *ceremonies;* ceremoniæ, Som. v. ge-scrif.

ge-sculdre, -sculdru; *pl. n. The shoulders;* humeri:—Gesculdre *palæ*, Ælfc. Gl. 74; Som. 71, 45; Wrt. Voc. 44, 28. Middel gesculdru *interscapilium*, 74; Som. 71, 46; Wrt. Voc. 44, 29. Mid his gesculdrum *scapulis suis*, Ps. Th. 90, 4.

ge-scȳ, es; *n. A pair of shoes;* calceamentum, tegmentum pedis, caliga:—Gif he [man] ðonne cwiþ 'Nelle ic hīg habban to wīfe,' gā ðæt wīf to him and nyme his gescȳ of his fōtum beforan ðām ealdrum and spǣte on his nebb and nemne hine ǣlc man on Israēla folce 'unsceóda' *if he* [*the man*] *then say 'I will not have her to wife,' let the woman go to him and take his shoes off his feet before the elders and spit in his face, and let every man amongst the people of the Israelites call him 'the unshod,'* Deut. 25, 8–10. In Idumea lande ic aþenige gescȳ mīn *in Idumæam extendam calceamentum meum*, Ps. Spl. 59, 9; Ps. Th. 59, 7 *has* On Idumea mīn gescy sende. Gescȳ *calceamentum*, Ps. Spl. 107, 10: Ps. Th. 107, 8. Ðæs gescȳ neom ic wyrþe to berenne *non sum dignus calceamenta portare*, Mt. Bos. 3, 11: Lk. Bos. 15, 22. Hwæt sind gescȳ būton deádra nȳtena hȳda *what are shoes but the hides of dead cattle*, Homl. Th. ii. 280, 29. [*Goth.* ga-skohi: *O. Sax.* gi-skohi: *O. H. Ger.* gi-scuohi; *n.*] v. ge-scóe.

ge-scȳfan; *pp.* -scyfen *To eject;* ejicere, Mt. Kmbl. p. 16, 4. [Cf. scūfan.]

ge-scyftan; *pp.* -scyft *To share, distribute:*—Beó seó ǣht gescyft swȳðe rihte *let the property be very fairly distributed*, L. C. S. 71; Th. i. 414, 1.

ge-scyld, es; *n. Guilt, debt;* reatus, debitum:—Gescyldum *reatibus*, Rtl. 79, 22. All gescyld *universum debitum*, Mt. Kmbl. Lind. 18, 34.

ge-scyldan. v. ge-scildan.

ge-scyldend. v. ge-scildend.

ge-scyldigian, -scyldegian; *p.* ode; *pp.* od *To prove guilty, charge with guilt, deserve punishment in consequence of guilt:*—Ðæt hīg hine gescyldegodon *ut caperent eum in sermone*, Lk. Bos. 20, 20. Þurh ðæt gescildgade wīte *per debitam pœnam*, Bd. 3, 19: S. 548, 30. [Cf. *O. H. Ger.* sculdigon: *Ger.* schuldigen.]

ge-scyldnes. v. ge-scildnes.

ge-scyldru; *pl. n. The shoulders:*—Me on gescyldrum *on my shoulders*, Exon. 111 b; Th. 428, 4; Rä. 41, 103: 125 b; Th. 483, 17; Rä. 69, 4.

ge-scyndan. v. ge-scendan.

ge-scyndan; *p.* de. I. *to hasten:*—Heofon-torht swegl gescyndeþ *the heaven-bright sun hastens*, Exon. 93 b; Th. 351, 2; Sch. 74. II. *to cause to hasten, to drive:*—Ða twegen drȳmen wurdon gescynde of ðam earde *the two wizards were driven from the land*, Homl. Th. ii. 476, 8. [Cf. a-, ge-, fȳsan.]

ge-scyndnys *a confusion;* confusio, Ps. Spl. 70, 14. v. ge-scendnys.

ge-scȳnian *to fear;* metuere, Rtl. 32, 9. [Cf. scūnian.]

ge-scyppan. v. ge-sceppan.

ge-scȳrd. v. ge-scrȳdan.

ge-scyrian *to ordain, number, reckon*, Cd. 22; Th. 27, 28; Gen. 424: Exon. 86 a; Th. 324, 9; Wid. 92: 122 a; Th. 468, 10; Phar. 5. v. ge-scerian.

ge-scyrigan *to appoint*, Andr. Kmbl. 169; An. 85. v. ge-scerian.

ge-scyrpan. v. ge-scerpan.

ge-scyrtan; *p.* -scyrte; *pp.* -scyrted, -scyrt; *v. a.* [scyrt *short*]. I. *to shorten, contract, lessen;* abbreviare, minuere:—Ða spell ic sceal gescyrtan *I must shorten the stories*, Ors. 1, 8; Bos. 31, 29. Ðū his dagena tīd gescyrtest *minorasti dies temporis ejus*, Ps. Th. 88, 38. Gif drihten ðās dagas ne gescyrte... he gescyrte ða dagas *nisi breviasset dies ... breviavit dies*, Mk. Bos. 13, 20. Būton ða dagas gescyrte wǣron ... ða dagas beóþ gescyrte, Mt. Bos. 24, 22. Heáp wæs gescyrted *the crowd was diminished*, Elen. Kmbl. 282; El. 141. II. *to become short, be lessened, fail:*—Ðætte gescyrte *deficere*, Jn. Skt. p. 3, 12: Lind. 2, 3.

ge-scȳt *shoots forward, falls* or *is allotted to*, Homl. Th. ii. 104, 9; *pres. of* ge-sceótan.

GESE, gise, gyse [ge + se = geá + sī]; *adv.* YES; immo, etiam:—Gise, lā gese, *yes, oh yes*, Bt. 16, 4; Fox 58, 15. v. geā.

ge-sealdniss. v. ge-saldniss.

ge-seáw; *adj.* [seáw *juice*] *Juicy;* sūci plēnus:—Geseáwe pȳsan *juicy peas*, L. M. 2, 43; Lchdm. ii. 254, 15.

ge-sēcan, -sēcean; to -sǣcanne, -sēcenne; *part.* -sēcende, ic -sēce, ðū -sēcest, -sēcst, he -sēceþ, -sēcþ, *pl.* -sēcaþ; *p.* -sōhte, *pl.* -sōhton; *pp.* -sōht; *v. a.* I. *to seek, inquire, ask for;* quærere, requirere, inquirere:—Ne mæg ic aldornere mīne gesēcan *I cannot seek my life's safety*, Cd. 103; Th. 136, 30; Gen. 2514. Gif he gesēcean dear wīg *if he dare seek war*, Beo. Th. 1373; B. 684. Heó mynster gesōhte *monasterium petiit*, Bd. 4, 19; S. 588, 5. Hie ðæs cnihtes cwealm gesōhton *they sought the young man's death*, Andr. Kmbl. 2244; An. 1123: Ps. Th. 70, 22. Ðæt ealra witegena blōd sȳ gesōht fram ðysse cneórysse *ut inquiratur sanguis omnium prophetarum a generatione ista*, Lk. Bos. 11, 50. II. *to seek, go to, approach, look for, visit, come to;* adire, ire *vel* proficisci, aliquo *vel* ad aliquem, visitare, venire, pervenire aliquo:—Wile nū gesēcan sāwla nergend gǣsta giefstōl *now the saviour of souls will seek the spirits' throne of grace*, Exon. 16 a; Th. 36, 4; Cri. 571: Bd. 1, 23; 23; S. 485, 33: 3, 23; S. 554, 11. Nǣnig heora þohte ðæt he scolde eft eardlufan ǣfre gesēcean *not one of them thought that he should ever seek his loved home again*, Beo. Th. 1389; B. 692. Land swīðe feor to gesēcanne *the land is very far to seek*, Andr. Kmbl. 847; An. 424: Beo. Th. 3848; B. 1922. Ðonne ic ðas ilcan ōðre sīþe wīc gesēce *when I seek this same dwelling a second time*, Cd. 109; Th. 144, 23; Gen. 2394. He ōðer līf eft gesēceþ *he shall seek another life hereafter*, Cd. 218; Th. 277, 30; Sat. 212: Salm. Kmbl. 316; Sal. 157: Exon. 97 a; Th. 361, 34; Wal. 29. Nales Dryhtnes gemynd siððan gesēcaþ *they shall not seek the Lord's remembrance afterwards*, 30 b; Th. 94, 10; Cri. 1538. He gesōhte Sūþ-Dena folc *he sought the people of the South-Danes*, Beo. Th. 930; B. 463: Cd. 128; Th. 163, 13; Gen. 2697: Andr. Kmbl. 759; An. 380. Hie gesōhton Sennera feld *they sought the plains of Shinar*, Cd. 80; Th. 100, 22; Gen. 1668: 111; Th. 146, 20; Gen. 2425. Ðæt land gesēc ðe ic ðē ȳwan wille *seek the land which I will show to thee*, 83; Th. 105, 9; Gen. 1750: Cot. 3. III. *to seek with hostile intention, to persecute, afflict, invade;* hostiliter aggredi, invadere, corripere:—Gif ūre fȳnd us mid gefeohte gesēcaþ *if our enemies make war upon us*, Ex. 1, 10. Eorringa gesēceþ bōcstafa brego *the prince of letters shall angrily seek him*, Salm. Kmbl. 198; Sal. 98: Beo. Th. 5024; B. 2515. Ðæt he ðone wīd-flogan weorode gesōhte *that he should seek the dragon* [*wide-flier*] *with a host*, 4682; B. 2346. Geáta leóde gesōhton Gūþscilfingas *the people of the Goths sought the warlike Scylfings*, 5845; B. 2926: 4414; B. 2204. Gesōht; *pp.* Exon. 47 b; Th. 163, 11; Gū. 992: 49 b; Th. 170, 27; Gū. 1118. Hī scyndan sārum gesōhte *they hastened forth sought with wounds*, Exon. 72 b; Th. 271, 30; Jul. 490: 46 b; Th. 159, 21; Gū. 930: 47 b; Th. 163, 33; Gū. 1003. IV. *to seek, go to, visit;* ire, proficisci:—Ðū scealt sīþe gesēcan ðǣr sylfǣtan eard weardigaþ *thou shalt seek in a journey where the cannibals defend the land*, Andr. Kmbl. 349; An. 175. We ðē willaþ ferigan freólīce to ðam lande ðǣr ðē lust myneþ to gesēcanne *we will freely convey thee to the land which desire urges thee to seek*, 589; An. 295. Ðǣr mīn hyht myneþ to gesēcenne *there my hope thinketh to visit*, Exon. 48 b; Th. 167, 18; Gū. 1062. Ðæt him to mōde sorg gesōhte *that to his mind should come care*, 37 b; Th. 123, 19; Gū. 325. V. *to appoint, dispose, beset;* exigere, disponere:—Hæfdon æglǣcan sæcce gesōhte *the wretches had appointed hostilities*, Andr. Kmbl. 2265; An. 1134. Ðæt he mid āþsware to Abrahame, and to Isaac, eác gesōhte *quod disposuit ad Abraham, et juramenti sui ad Isaac*, Ps. Th. 104, 9. Synne gesōhte *beset with sin*, Exon. 74 b; Th. 280, 4; Jul. 624. DER. sēcan.

ge-seccan = ge-sēcean [?] *or* ge-feccan [?]:—Ides sceal dyrne cræfte hire freónd geseccan gif heó nelle on folce geþeón ðæt hī man beágum gebycge *a woman must by secret art get herself a friend if she do not wish publicly to succeed in being bought with rings*, Menol. Fox 548; Gn. C. 44.

ge-sēcednes, -ness, e; *f. A search, an inquiry, appeal;* inquisitio, Som.

ge-secgan, -sæcgan, -secgean; to -secganne, -secgenne; *p.* -sægde, -sǣde, *pl.* -sægdon, -sǣdon; *impert.* -sege; *pp.* -sægd, -sǣd *To say, tell, relate, declare, prove;* dicere, narrare, indicere:—Mec Dryhten hēht gesecgan *the Lord commanded me to say*, Exon. 42 b; Th. 144, 10; Gū. 676: 102 b; Th. 387, 29; Rä. 5, 12. Nelle ic ðē gesecgan *I will not tell thee*, Exon. 88 b; Th. 333, 11; Gn. Ex. 2: Elen. Kmbl. 1966: El. 985. Ic ðē sceal Meotudes mægenspēd *I shall relate to thee the Creator's power*, Exon. 92 b; Th. 348, 7; Sch. 24. Him sceolde se yldra eall gesæcgan *narrabunt eam filiis suis*, Ps. Th. 77, 8. Ic wille mīne leahterfulle þeáwas gesecgean *I will confess my wicked ways;* vitiosos mores corrigere, Bd. 3, 13; S. 538, 32. To gesecganne *to say*, Exon. 109 b; Th. 419, 1; Rä. 37, 13: Cd. 202; Th. 250, 9; Dan. 544. To gesecgenne *to say*, Cd. 163; Th. 205, 17; Exod. 437. Gif he hit gesēgþ *if he saith it*, Exon. 27 a; Th. 80, 22; Cri. 1310. Andreas þeódne þanc gesægde *Andrew said thanks to his Lord*, Andr. Kmbl. 768; An. 384: Beo. Th. 4321; B. 2157. He gesǣde swefen cyninge *he said the dream to the king*, Cd. 180; Th. 226, 2; Dan. 165: B. 4, 18; S. 587, 2. Ðā gesægdon Rōmāne Bryttum *then the Romans said to the Britons*, Bd. 1, 12; S. 481, 3. Gesege me *dicito mihi*, Bd. 2, 12; S. 514, 1. Ðæt ðū gesecge sweostor mīnre *that thou mayest say to my sister*, Exon. 50 a; Th. 172, 31; Gū. 1152: Bd. 4, 3; S. 568, 27. Wæs gesǣd hwām ðæt sweord geworht wǣre *it was said for whom that sword was wrought*, Beo. Th. 3396; B. 1696. Ic sceall ealle forlǣtan ða ðe of Perseo and of Cathma gesǣde syndon *I must pass over all things that are said of Perseus and Cadmus*, Ors. 1, 8; Bos. 31, 33, 34. Ðæt is gesǣd *that is proved*, Bt. 34, 9; Fox 146, 25, 27. DER. secgan.

ge-secggan *to say, tell;* dicere, narrare:—Hio him ne meahton gesecggan be ðam sigebeácne *they could not tell him about the victorious sign*, Elen. Kmbl. 335; El. 168. v. ge-secgan.

ge-sēclod; *part. Taken sick, ill;* ægrōtus:—Warþ se cyng gesēclod *the king was taken sick*, Chr. 1093; Erl. 228, 22. v. ge-sīclian.

ge-sedian *to satisfy;* satiare, Ps. Th. 106, 8.

ge-sēfte; *adj. Soft, mild;* mītis:—Wǣron hyra gongas smēðe and gesēfte *their ways were smooth and soft*, Exon. 43 a; Th. 146, 3; Gū. 704. Swā him ēðost biþ, sylfum gesēftost *as to them may be easiest, softest to themselves*, Elen. Kmbl. 2587; El. 1295.

ge-sege *say, tell*, Bd. 2, 12; S. 514, 1; *impert. of* ge-secgan.

ge-segen, -sægen, -segn, e; *f. A saying, telling, conversation, relation, tradition;* dictum, narratio, relatio, traditio:—Mid gesegenum unrīm geleáffulra witena *by the sayings of innumerable faithful witnesses*, Bd. pref; S. 472, note 25: Nar. 2, 6. Þurh gesegene ðæs ārwurþan biscopes Cynebyrhtes *through the conversation of the reverend bishop Cynebyrht*, Bd. pref; S. 472, 21. Mid Isses gesægene [gesegnum, MS. B.] ðæs ārwurþan Abbudes *by the conversation of the reverend abbot Isi*, 472, 20. Þurh swīðe getreówra manna gesægene *through the telling of very true men*, 472, 30: Bd. 5, 12; S. 631, 5, 11: 5, 23; S. 647, 17. v. segen.

ge-seglian; *p.* ode, ede; *pp.* od, ed. I. *to sail;* vēlĭfĭcāri:—Ðyder he cwæþ, ðæt nān man ne mihte geseglian on ānum mōnþe *thither he said that a man could not sail in a month*, Ors. 1, 1; Bos. 21, 19. II. *to furnish with sails;* vēlis instruĕre:—Se ðe nafaþ gesegled scip *who hath not a ship furnished with sails*, Salm. Kmbl. 450; Sal. 225.

ge-segn *a saying, telling, conversation*, Bd. pref; S. 472, note 20. v. ge-segen.

ge-segnian, -sēnian; *p.* ode, ade; *pp.* od, ad [segnian, sēnian *to sign*] *To mark with the sign of the cross, to sign, bless;* crŭcis signo signāre, bĕnĕdīcĕre:—Fæder mancynnes hie gesegnaþ *the Father of mankind shall bless them*, Cd. 221; Th. 286, 30; Sat. 360: Salm. Kmbl. 807; Sal. 403. He heó gesēnaþ mid his swīðran hond *he shall bless them with his right hand*, Cd. 227; Th. 303, 18; Sat. 615. Se bisceop me gebletsode and gesegnode *the bishop blessed me and signed me*, Bd. 5, 3; S. 616, 33. Gesēnode, 5, 3; S. 616, 25. His wuduwan ic wordum bletsige and gesegnade *vĭdŭam ejus bĕnĕdīcens bĕnĕdīcam*, Ps. Th. 131, 16. Gesēnige hine *let him sign himself*, L. E. I. 29; Th. ii. 426, 9, 16. Gif heó gesegnod biþ *if it hath been blessed*, Salm. Kmbl. 812; Sal. 405. Gesunde and gesēnade *safe and blessed*, Exon. 27 b; Th. 82, 22; Cri. 1342.

ge-sehtian; *p.* ode; *pp.* od [sehtian *to settle*] *To settle, reconcile;* rĕconcĭlĭāre:—Ða heáfodmen ða brōðra gesehtodan *the chief men reconciled the brothers*, Chr. 1101; Erl. 237, 26.

ge-sehtness, e; *f. Reconciliation:*—To sibbe and to gesehtnesse *for peace and reconciliation*, Cod. Dipl. Kmbl. iii. 129, 22.

ge-selda, an; *m. One of the same dwelling, a companion, comrade;* contŭbernālis, sŏcius:—Ic eom cyninges geselda *I am a king's companion*, Exon. 127 a; Th. 489, 5; Rä. 78, 3. Higelāc ongan sīnne geseldan fricgean *Hygelac began to question his comrade*, Beo. Th. 3972; B. 1984: Exon. 77 a; Th. 289, 24; Wand. 53

ge-sele, es; *m.* [sele] *A tabernacle;* tăbernācŭlum:—On gesele ðīnum *in tăbernācŭlo tuo*, Ps. Spl. T. 14, 1.

ge-selenis, -niss, e; *f. A handing over, giving, tradition:*—Æfter gimett giselenisse Cristes *secundum mensuram donationis Christi*, Rtl. 83, 1. Æfter geselenise *juxta traditionem*, Mk. Skt. Lind. 7, 5. v. selenis.

ge-sēlig; *adj. Happy;* fēlix:—Gebed dōn gesēligran tīman getācnaþ *to be repeating prayers betokens a happier time*, Lchdm. iii. 208, 23. v. ge-sǣlig.

ge-sēlignes. v. ge-sǣlignys.

ge-sellan, -syllan; *p.* -sealde, -salde; *pp.* -seald *To give, give up, betray, sell;* dare, tradere, vendere:—Ōðrum gesellan *to give to others*, Beo. Th. 2063; B. 1029. Ic ðē geselle *I will give thee*, Cd. 228; Th. 307, 25; Sat. 685. Me ða blǣda Eue gesealde *Eve gave me the fruits*, 42; Th. 54, 27; Gen. 883: Exon. 100 b; Th. 379, 31; Deór. 41. Ðū me gesealdest sweord *thou gavest me a sword*, 120 b; Th. 463, 18; Hö. 72. Ðe feorh gesealdon *who gave up life*, Andr, Kmbl. 3231; An. 1618: 865; An. 433. Inc is feoh geseald *cattle is given to you*, Cd. 10; Th. 13, 14; Gen. 202: 74; Th. 91, 23; Gen. 1516. Iudas gesalde Drihten Hǣlend *Judas sold [tradidit] the Lord Saviour*, 226; Th. 301, 2; Sat. 575. Ælfnōþ and Wulfmǣr feorh gesealdon *Ælfnoth and Wulfmær gave up their lives*, Byrht. Th. 137, 11; By. 184. DER. sellan.

ge-sēlþ, e; *f. Happiness;* fēlĭcĭtas:—Gesēlþe tīman hit getācnaþ *it betokens a time of happiness*, Lchdm. iii. 202, 10: 204, 23. We gyt næfdon ða gesēlþa *we had not yet the happiness*, Chr. 1009; Erl. 141, 25. v. ge-sǣlþ.

ge-sēm, es; *n. Reconciliation, an agreement, a compromise;* reconcĭlĭātio, comprōmissum:—Siððan āne neaht ofer ðæt gesēm bīe *postquam ūna nox supra comprōmissum prætĕriit*, L. H. E. 10; Wilk. 8, 49.

ge-sēman; *p.* de; *pp.* ed *To compose, settle, make peace with, reconcile, satisfy;* compōnĕre, concĭlĭāre, reconcĭlĭāre, satisfăcĕre:—Ðæt he hȳ gesēman wolde *that he would make peace with them*, Ors. 3, 7; Bos. 60, 33. Ðæt hī scioldon Wynflǣde and Leófwine gesēman *that they should reconcile Wynflæd and Leofwine*, Th. Diplm. A. D. 995; 288, 31: Past. 46, 4; Swt. 349, 12; Hat. MS. 66 b, 13: Byrht. Th. 133, 35; By. 60. Ðæt me gesēme snoterra mon *that a wiser man shall reconcile me*, Salm. Kmbl. 501; Sal. 251. Ðæt he hȳ ymbe ðæt rīce gesēmde *that he would satisfy them about the kingdom*, Ors. 3, 7; Bos. 60, 23. Siððan sió sace gesēmed sió *after the suit is settled*, L. H. E. 10; Th. i. 30, 19: Ors. 1, 12; Bos. 35, 39. Hī gesēmede beón ne mihtan *they could not be reconciled*, Chr. 1094; Erl. 230, 1: Homl. Th. ii. 338, 1.

ge-sencan; *p.* -sencte; *pp.* -senct *To sink, drown;* submergĕre:—Hī gesencte [synt] on ðære [MS. ðere] reádan sǣ [MS. sea] *they are drowned in the Red sea*, Cant. Moys. Ex. 15, 4; Thw. 15, 4.

ge-sendan; *p.* -sende; *pp.* -sended, -send *To send:*—Middȳ gesende stefne *emissa voce*, Mk. Skt. Lind. 15, 37. Ðā wæs gesended *then was sent*, Blickl. Homl. 9, 28: Mt. Kmbl. Lind. 5, 13: 15, 17. Gesend *missus*, Ps. Lamb. 33, 8.

ge-sēne; *adj.* v. ge-sȳne.

ge-sēne; *adv. Clearly;* manifeste, Jn. Skt. Lind. 11, 14.

ge-sēnelic; *adj. Visible:*—Se gesēnelīca līchama *the visible body*, Blickl. Homl. 21, 24.

ge-sēnelīce; *adv. Visibly;* visibiliter, Rtl. 103, 30.

ge-sēnian *to mark with the sign of the cross, to sign, bless*, Cd. 227; Th. 303, 18; Sat 615: Bd. 5, 3; S. 616, 25: L. E. I. 29; Th. ii. 426, 9, 16: Exon. 27 b; Th. 82, 22; Cri. 1342. v. ge-segnian.

ge-seón, -sión, ic -seó, ðū -sihst, he -syhþ; *p.* -seah, ðū -sāwe, *pl.* -sāwon, -sēgon; *imp.* -syh, -seoh; *subj. pres.* ic -sāwe; *pp.* -sawen *To see;* videre, conspicere. I. *used absolutely* or *with acc:*—Ic geseóm menn *video homines*, Mk. Skt. Lind. 8, 24. He hēr gesihþ *he here seeth*, Apol. Th. 14, 26. Ða līðende land gesāwon *the voyagers saw land*, Beo. Th. 448; B. 221. Ðā heó Isaac geseah *when she saw Isaac*, Gen. 24, 64. Ðā he beseah, ðā geseah he olfendas *when he looked about then he saw the camels*, Gen. 24, 63. Abraham beseah upp and geseah þrī weras *Abraham looked up and saw three men*, Gen. 18, 2. Hie ðone heora scyppend gesēgon *they saw their creator*, Blickl. Homl. 121, 28: Exon. 15 b; Th. 35, 7; Cri. 554. Manega rihtwīse gewilnudon ða þing to geseónne ðe gē geseóþ and hīg ne gesāwon *multi justi cupierunt videre quæ videtis et non viderunt*, Mt. Bos. 13, 17. Hwī fērde gē geseón . . . hwī fērde gē to geseónne *quid existis videre*, Lk. Skt. 7, 24, 25, note. Ðæt hī geseónde ne geseón *ut videntes non videant*, 8, 10. Cum and geseoh *veni et vide*, Jn. Bos. 1, 46. Ðīne gangas wǣron gesewene *visi sunt gressus tui*, Ps. Th. 67, 23: Shrn. 97, 30. Him wæs gesewen ðæt . . . *it seemed to him that* . . . , 111, 27: Blickl. Homl. 195, 20. Hie wurdon gesawene *they appeared*, 173, 25. Ic ðē gesāwe *that I saw thee*, Wald. 21; Vald. 1, 13. II. *with predicative adj.* or *part:*—Ic geseó mīnne Crist cīgendne me *I see my Christ calling me*, Blickl. Homl. 187, 23: 59, 2. Hie Drihten gesāwon upastīgendne *they saw the Lord ascending*, 121, 22: 123, 25. Gesyhþ wīnsele wēstne *he sees the wine-hall deserted*, Beo. Th. 4901; B. 2455: Cd. 37; Th. 48, 30; Gen. 783: 64; Th. 78, 12; Gen. 1292. Geseah līfes weard drige stōwe wīde æteówde *life's guardian saw the dry place widely displayed*, 8; Th. 10, 28; Gen. 163. III. *with acc. and infin:*—Ða ðe he gesyhþ to Gode higian *those that he sees hurry to God*, Blickl. Homl. 29, 22. Hie ðæt leóht geseóþ scīnan *they see the light shine*, 129, 7: Cd 5; Th. 7, 20; Gen. 108: 32; Th. 42, 4; Gen. 669. Gesēgun ða dumban gesceaft gefēlan *they saw the dumb creation feel*, Exon. 24 b; Th. 69, 30; Cri. 1128. IV. *with infin:*—Geseah weard beran beorhte randas *the warder saw bright shields borne*, Beo. Th. 463; B. 229: 2051; B. 1023. V. *followed by a clause:*—Hie geseóþ hū God ða stōwe geweorðaþ *they see how God honours the place*, Blickl. Homl. 129, 25: 229, 22: 41, 28: Ps. Th. 73, 19. He gesāwe ðæt he wǣre getogen *he saw that he was pulled*, Blickl. Homl. 43, 26: 145, 8. Ic mæg geseón hwǣr he sylf siteþ *I can see where he himself sits*, Cd. 32; Th. 41, 34; Gen. 666. v. seón.

ge-seóred; *part. p. Leavened:*—Geseorid hlāf *acrizimus panis*, Ælfc. Gl. 66; Som. 69, 62; Wrt. Voc. 41, 18.

ge-set, es; *n. A sitting, lying in wait, ambush;* insidiæ:—Giseto *insidias*, Rtl. 37, 19. [Cf. *O. H. Ger.* gisez *obsidio.*]

ge-sete, *pl.* -setu, -seotu; *n. A seat, habitation, house;* sedes, domicilium, habitatio:—Ofer eall beorht gesetu *over all bright habitations*, Exon. 117 b; Th. 452, 7; Dōm. 117: 121 b; Th. 466, 3; Hö. 115. Sun-beorht gesetu *dwellings bright with the sun*, 59 b; Th. 217, 10;

Ph. 278: 62a; Th. 228, 10; Ph. 436. On sēllan gesetu *to better dwellings*, 51a; Th. 178, 10; Gū. 1242. Ofer burga gesetu *over the cities' dwellings*, 26a; Th. 76, 16; Cri. 1240. Gesetu, Cd. 227; Th. 302, 20; Sat. 602. Ða cynelīcan burh porres and his cynelīcan geseto *ipsam urbem regiam pori domumque*, Nar. 4, 20. To heora gesetum *to their lairs*, Blickl. Homl. 199, 7. [Cf. *O. H. Ger.* gesaze *habitatio, sedes, domicilium: O. Sax.* hōh-gisetu.]

ge-setednes, -nys, -ness, -nyss, e; *f. A constitution, law, ceremony, religion;* constĭtūtio, lex, cērĕmōnia, relĭgio:—Hwæt ys ðeós gesetednys *quæ est ista relĭgio?* Ex. 12, 26. Fram middaneardes gesetednesse *a constĭtūtiōne mundi*, Mt. Bos. 13, 35. Begȳmaþ ðisse gesetednysse *observābĭtis cērĕmōnias istas*, Ex. 12, 25. To gesetednisse *for a law*, Gen. 47, 26. v. ge-setnes.

ge-setenes, -ness, e; *f. A constitution, an appointment;* constĭtūtio:—Ða gesetenes he lǣt standan *he allows this appointment to stand*, Bt. 21; Fox 74, 30. v. ge-setnes.

ge-sēðan; *p.* de; *pp.* ed [sēðan *to affirm*] *To state as true, declare, prove, show, affirm;* effāri, testĭfĭcāri, vērĭfĭcāre, contestāri, prōbāre:—Nis ǣnig ðæs horsc, ðe ðīn fromcyn mǣge fira bearnum sweotule gesēðan *none is so wise who may manifestly declare thy origin to the children of men*, Exon. 11b; Th. 15, 18; Cri. 243. Ne māgon gē ða word gesēðan *ye cannot prove the words*, Elen. Kmbl. 1160; El. 582: Bt. 7, 3; Fox 20, 7. Ic gesweotelige oððe gesēðe ðē God *testĭfĭcābor tibi Deus*, Ps. Lamb. 49, 7. Gehȳr folc mīn and ic gesēðe ðē *audi pŏpŭlus meus et contestābor te*, Ps. Spl. 80, 8. Hī gesēðaþ and sprecaþ unrihtwīsnysse *effābuntur et lŏquentur inĭquĭtātem*, 93, 4. Ðære gesyhþe sōþ wæs gecȳðed and gesēðed *cujus vērĭtas prŏbāta est*, Bd. 4, 8; S. 576, 10: Cd. 208; Th. 257, 7; Dan. 254. Gesēðde, *pp. pl. proved*, Ps. Th. 118, 160. Ða wurdon mid manegum tācnum gesēðde *which were proved by many miracles*, Homl. Th. ii. 130, 11.

ge-sēðung, e; *f. Assertion, affirmation;* assertio, affirmatio, Hpt. Gl. 455.

ge-setl, es; *n. A seat, settle:*—Ða foerþmestu gisedla æt feormum *primos discubitos in cenis*, Mk. Skt. Rush. 12, 39. v. setl.

ge-setnes, -setenes, -setednes, -ness, -nis, -niss, -nys, -nyss, e; *f. Position, foundation, tradition, an institution, constitution, composition, ordinance, decree, law;* pŏsĭtio, sĭtus, fundātio, trādĭtio, instĭtūtio, constĭtūtio, compŏsĭtio, lex, pactum:—Cūþ is gehwilcum snotterum mannum, ðæt seó ealde ǣ wæs eáðelīcre ðonne Cristes gesetnys sȳ *it is known to every intelligent man that the old law was easier than the institute of Christ is*, Homl. Th. i. 358, 28, 30. Wæs se cyning becumen on swā mycle lufan ðære Rōmāniscan cyricean gesetnysse and ðære Apostolīcan *rex tĕnēbātur ămōre Rōmānæ et Ăpŏstŏlĭcæ instĭtūtiōnis*, Bd. 4, 5; S. 571, 32: 5, 20; S. 642, 13. Be gesetnysse Breotene *de sĭtu Brĭtanniæ*, 1, 1; S. 473, 6: Nar. 1, 5. Ǣr middaneardes gesetnysse *before the foundation of the world*, Homl. Th. ii. 364, 27: Mk. Bos. 7, 5. Be Godes gesetnysse *by God's ordinance*, Bd. de nat. rerum; Wrt. popl. science 11, 22; Lchdm. iii. 258, 7: Ælfc. T. 17, 24. Ðū cwǣde ðæt ǣlc wuht his rihte gesetnesse fuleóde, būtan menn ānum *thou saidst that every creature fulfilled its right institution, except man alone*, Bt. 5, 3; Fox 12, 9: Homl. Th. ii. 330, 35. Rǣdaþ sume men ða leásan gesetnysse *some men read the false composition*, Homl. Th. ii. 332, 22: i. 358, 14. Israhēl syngode and ða gesetnisse gewemde *peccāvit Israel et prævārĭcātus est pactum meum*, Jos. 7, 11. Sint heora gesetnessa swīðe mislīca *their institutions are very various*, Bt. 18, 2; Fox 64, 22. Healdende hira yldrena gesetnessa *tĕnentes trādĭtiōnem sĕniōrum*, Mk. Bos. 7, 3. Ða gesetnessa sigora Wealdend lǣt geond ðas mǣran gesceaft mearce healden *the Lord of victories permits these constitutions to keep their limits over this great creation*, Bt. Met. Fox 11, 141; Met. 11, 71. Be gesetnessum and gemētum sprǣccynna *de fĭgūris mōdisque lŏcūtiōnum*, Bd. 5, 24: S. 648, 42. Be heofenes gesetenissum *de statu cœli*, Nar. 1, 16.

ge-setnian; *p.* ode, ade *To lie in wait;* insidiari:—Herodia gesetnade him *Herodias insidiabatur illi*, Mk. Skt. Lind. 6, 19.

ge-settan; *p.* -sette; *pp.* -seted, -set, -sett *To set, put, fix, confirm, restore, appoint, decree, settle, possess, occupy, place together, compose, make, compare, expose, allay:*—Ða apostolas hie gesetton on ðæm fægran neorxna wange *the apostles placed her in the fair paradise*, Blickl. Homl. 143, 25: Exon. 28a; Th. 85, 13; Cri. 1390: Ps. Spl. 18, 5. Hie on God ǣnne heora hyht gesetton *they should put their trust in God alone*, Blickl. Homl. 185, 15. Naman gesettan *to give a name*, 197, 29. He wæs to bōclīcre lāre gesett *he was put to book-learning*, Shrn. 12, 16. Ðǣr is dryhtnes folc geseted to symle *there is the Lord's folk set to the feast*, Rood Kmbl. 279; Kr. 141. Ðæt hī hine Gode gesettan *to present him to God*, Lk. Bos. 2, 22. Under anweald gesett *sub potestate constitutus*, 7, 8: 3, 13. Hwonne he ðisse worlde ende gesettan wolde *when he meant to fix the end of this world*, Blickl. Homl. 119, 9: 27, 24. Ǣnne of heora aldormannum to bisceope he him gesette *he appointed one of their chief men as their bishop*, 247, 31: Chr. 604; Erl. 20, 21. He Isaace wīf gesette *he fixed upon a wife for Isaac*, Gen. 24, 11. Heora gewinn mid ðam swīðe gesettan *therewith greatly confirmed their hostility*, Ors. 5, 10; Bos. 109, 5, note. Wilt ðū on ðas tīd gesettan Israhēla folca rīce *si in tempore hoc restitues regnum Israel?* Blickl. Homl. 117, 11. Gesete *restitue*, Ps. Spl. 34, 20. Hī him gesetton ðæt hyra ān lātteów wǣre *they decreed for themselves that there should be one leader of them*, Ors. 2, 4; Bos. 42, 26: Shrn. 112, 18: Blickl. Homl. 193, 3: 61, 27. Dōm gesettan *to judge*, Gen. 18, 25. Gesette ȳðum heora onrihtne ryne *he appointed the waves their proper course*, Cd. 8; Th. 10, 34; Gen. 166. He gefōr ða burg and hēt hie gesettan ǣgðer ge mid Engliscum mannum ge mid Deniscum *he gained the town and ordered it to be occupied by both English and Danes*, Chr. 922; El. 108, 31: 886; Erl. 84, 26: Mt. Bos. 21, 33, 41: Ors. 3, 5; Bos. 56, 35. Ealne norþdǣl ðysses eálondes genōman and gesetton *omnem aquilonalem insulæ partem capessunt*, Bd. 1, 12; S. 481, 18: Blickl. Homl. 79, 26. Heora ēðel on heofenum sceolde eft gebūen and geseted weorðan mid hālgum sāwlum *their home in heaven should again be inhabited and peopled with holy souls*, 121, 33. Seó landbūnes is swīðost cȳpemonnum geseted *hæc colonia est maxime negotiatorum*, Nar. 33, 15. Gesettaþ *possidebit*, Ps. Spl. C. 68, 42: 78, 12: 82, 11. Of lāme ic ðē leoðe gesette *of loam I formed thee limbs*, Exon. 28a; Th. 84, 31; Cri. 1380: 33a; Th. 105, 12; Gū. 22. Ðū gesettest sunnan and mōnan *tu fecisti solem et lunam*, Ps. Th. 73, 16. Ic ðē gesette manegra þeóda fæder *a father of many nations have I made thee*, Gen. 17. 5: Homl. Th. ii. 136, 23. Ðæt tempel towearp æfter feówer hund geárum ðæs ðe hit gesett wæs *he destroyed the temple four hundred years after it was built*, Swt. A. S. Rdr. 68, 374. Swā hwæt swā ic ðē gehēt eal ic hit gesette *whatsoever I have promised thee I will do it all*, Blickl. Homl. 147, 8. Seó tunge ðe swā monig hālwende word on ðæs scyppendes lof gesette *illa lingua quæ tot salutaria verba in laudem conditoris composuerat*, Bd. 4, 24; S. 599, 11: Bt. 2; Fox 4, 7. Ða bōc ic gesette *I composed the book*, Guthl. prol; Gdwin. 2, 8: Homl. Th. i. 70, 7: Th. Apol. 28, 13. Hiora birhto ne biþ to gesettanne wiþ ðære sunnan leóht *their brightness is not to be compared with the sun's light*, Bt. Met. Fox 6, 13; Met. 6, 7. Ðæt ðis ǣfre gesett sprǣc wǣre *that this should be a suit finally settled*, Th. Ch. 203, 4. Ðone storm he gesette and gestilde *tempestatem sedaverit*, Bd. 5, 1; S. 613, 8. Ðæt he ðæt yrre gesette *to allay their anger*, Ors. 4, 11; Bos. 98, 2: Beo. Th. 4062; B. 2029. Ða earman ceasterwaran wǣron to hungre gesette *the miserable citizens were exposed to famine*, Bd. 1, 12; S. 481, 28. Ðæt land sum hit is to gafole gesett *some of the land is let*, Cod. Dipl. Kmbl. iii. 450, 19, 12.

ge-settnys, -nyss, e; *f. Constitution, statute;* stătūtum:—Ða ðe ða reogollīcan gesettnysse hāligra fædera gelufedon and cūðon *qui cănŏnĭca patrum stătūta et dīlĭgĕrent et nossent*, Bd. 4, 5; S. 571, 40. v. ge-setnes.

ge-setu *seats*, Th. 76, 16. v. ge-sete.

ge-séuling *a servant;* minister, Lye.

ge-séunes *the sea;* æquor, Lye.

ge-sewenlīc; *adj. Visible:*—Ðīne gesceafta gesewenlīce and eác ungesewenlīce *thy creatures visible and also invisible*, Bt. 33, 4; Fox 128, 5: Bd. de nat. rerum; Wrt. popl. science 1, 12; Lchdm. iii. 232, 14: Bt. Met. Fox 20, 13; Met. 20, 7: 253; Met. 20, 127.

ge-sewenlīce; *adv. Visibly:*—Ðū miht sōþlīce and gesewenlīce ðīne mihte gecȳðan on Marian *thou canst truly and visibly make thy power known on Mary*, Blickl. Homl. 157, 3.

ge-sib, -sibb, -syb; *adj. Peaceable, near, related, familiar;* pācĭfĭcus, cognātus, prŏpinquus, fămĭliāris:—Ne bearh nū for oft gesibb gesibbum ðȳ mā ðe fremdum *too often now has a kinsman no more protected a kinsman than a stranger*, Swt. A. S. Rdr. 107, 75. Sylle swā gesibre handa swā fremdre *give to a relation or to a stranger*, Cod. Dipl. Kmbl. ii. 114, 7. Nǣnig mon ne sceal lufian ne gēman his gesibbes gif . . . *no man shall love or be mindful of his relative if . . .*, Blickl. Homl. 23, 17. Gisibbe *cognatos*, Lk. Skt. Rush. 14, 12. Tǣlende dīgellīce gesibne his *dētrăhentem sĕcrēto proxĭmo suo*, Ps. Spl. 100, 5. Ðe him gesibbe wǣron *who were related to him*, Job Thw. 167, 3. Gesibbe ǣrendracan *cādūcĕātōres* vel *pācĭfĭci*, Ælfc. Gl. 53; Som. 66, 79; Wrt. Voc. 36, 6. Hȳ habbaþ freónda ðȳ mā swǣsra and gesibbra *they will have more friends dear and near*, Exon. 107a; Th. 408, 34; Rä. 27, 22: 84a; Th. 317, 21; Mōd. 69. Snotor mid gesibbum sēcean wolde Cananea land *the sagacious would seek the Canaanites' land with his kinsfolk*, Cd. 83; Th. 104, 8; Gen. 1738: 79; Th. 97, 13; Gen. 1612. Gesibbra ærfeweard *a nearer heir*, Th. Chart. 483, 16. Sweolcum swelce him ðonne gesibbast wǣre *to such as may then be nearest of kin to him*, 105, 29. [*O. H. Ger.* gisibbo *consanguineus.*]

ge-sibbian; *p.* ode, ade, ede; *pp.* od, ad, ed [sibbian *to pacify*] *To make peaceful, pacify, appease, gladden;* pācāre, pācĭfĭcāre, concĭliāre, lætĭfĭcāre:—Ic gesibbige *concĭlio*, Ælfc. Gl. 76; Som. 74, 18; Wrt. Voc. 50, 2. He gesibbade ða cyningas betwih and ða folc *pācātis altĕrūtrum rēgĭbus ac pŏpŭlis*, Bd. 4, 21; S. 590, 22. Gesibbedan sāwle mīne *lætĭfĭcāvērunt anĭmam meam*, Ps. Th. 93, 18. Ðā he hæfde ðone hīred gesibbodne *when he had reconciled the household*, Blickl. Homl. 225, 10. [*Goth.* ga-sibjon *to reconcile: O. H. Ger.* ge-sippot *united.*]

ge-sibbsum; *adj. Peaceful;* pācātus:—Salomon is gecweden gesibbsum on Englisc *Salomon is in English 'peaceful,'* Swt. A. S. Rdr. 67, 353. Sint to manienne ða gesibbsuman *the peaceful are to be admonished*, Past. 46, 5; Swt. 351, 3; Hat. MS. 66b, 27. v. ge-sibsum.

ge-sibbsumnys, -nyss, e; *f. Peacefulness;* pax:—For gesibbsumnysse *for peacefulness*, Lev. 7, 32. v. ge-sibsumnes.

ge-siblîce; *adv. Peaceably;* pācĭfĭce:—Fæste gebunden gesiblîce togædere *fast bound peaceably together*, Bt. Met. Fox 20, 135; Met. 20, 68.

ge-sibling, es; *m.* [sibling *a relation*] *A relation;* prŏpinquus:—Mǽg *vel* gesibling *prŏpinquus*, Ælfc. Gl. 92; Som. 75, 39; Wrt. Voc. 51, 81.

ge-sibness, e; *f. Relationship;* affinitas, Lye.

ge-sibsum, -sybsum, -sibbsum; *adj.* [sibsum *peaceable*] *Peaceable, peaceful, loving peace;* pacatus, pācĭfĭcus:—Se ðe of Gode cymþ he biþ gôdes willan and gesibsum *that which comes from God is of good will and peaceful*, Past. 46, 3; Swt. 349, 1; Hat. MS. 66 b, 5, 7. On ôðre wîsan sint to manigenne ða gesibsuman *the peaceful are to be admonished in one way*, 46, 1; Swt. 345, 6; Hat. MS. 65 b, 22: 46, 5; Swt. 351, 3; Hat. MS. 67 a, 12: 46, 7; Swt. 355, 9; Hat. MS. 67 b, 19: 47, 1; Swt. 357, 15; Hat. MS. 68 a, 18, 19.

ge-sibsumian; *p.* ode; *pp.* od *To make peaceable, reconcile*:—Ðê to him gesibsuma *reconcile thyself to him*, Homl. Th. i. 54, 20: Mt. Bos. 5, 24.

ge-sibsumlîce, -sybsumlîce; *adv.* [sibsumlîce *peaceably*] *Peaceably, peacefully;* pācĭfĭce:—Ða fuglas gesibsumlîce faraþ *the birds fly peacefully*, Past. 46, 4; Swt. 349, 22; Hat. MS. 66 b, 22. Forðamðe me witedlîce gesybsumlîce hî sprǽcon *quŏniam mihi quĭdem pācĭfĭce lŏquēbantur*, Ps. Spl. 34, 23: Nicod. 20; Thw. 10, 15.

ge-sibsumnes, -sibbsumnes, -ness, -nys, -nyss, e; *f.* [sibsumnes *peacefulness*] *Peacefulness, concord, reconciliation;* pax, concordĭa, rĕconcĭlĭātio:—We mâgon gecnâwan on ðara ungesceádwîsra nîétena gesibsumnesse, hû micel yfel sió gesceádwîslîce gecynd þurh ða ungesibsumnesse gefremeþ *we can understand from the peacefulness of irrational animals how great a sin the rational race of man commits in being quarrelsome*, Past. 46, 4; Swt. 349, 25; Hat. MS. 66 b, 24; Lev. 7, 32.

ge-sibsumung, e; *f. A making peace, conciliation;* consiliatio, Ælfc. Gl. 86; Som. 74, 16; Wrt. Voc. 49, 39.

ge-sîcan; *p.* te; *pp.* ed [sîcan *to give suck*] *To wean;* ablactāre:—Swâ swâ gesîced ofer môdor his *sīcut ablactatus sŭper matre sua*, Ps. Spl. 130, 4.

ge-sîclian, -sŷclian; *p.* ode; *pp.* od [seóc *sick*] *To be taken sick* or *ill, to be infirm;* ægrōtāre, infirmāri:—Ðæt his fæder wǽre gesîclod *quod ægrōtāret pāter suus*, Gen. 48, 1: Chr. 1003; Erl. 139, 10. Sum undercyning wæs, ðæs sunu wæs gesŷclod on Capharnaum *ĕrat quĭdam rēgulus, cujus fīlius īnfirmābātur Capharnaum*, Jn. Bos. 4, 46. Ðâ wearþ his hors gesîclod *his horse became ill*, Swt. A. S. Rdr. 100, 169.

ge-sîda. v. heort-gesîda.

ge-sie *to be;* esse, Mt. Kmbl. Lind. 6, 31.

ge-siehþ *sight*, Bt. 5, 3; Fox 14, 18. v. ge-sihþ.

ge-siftan; *p.* -sifte; *pp.* -sifted, -sift *To sift*:—Gesyft [*or* gesyfl?] melu *fine meal*, Ex. 12, 34.

ge-sig; *n. Victory*:—Ðæt gesig *victoria*, Rtl. 28, 3.

ge-sîgan; *p.* -sâh, *pl.* -sigon; *pp.* -sigen [sîgan *to sink*] *To sink, fall, set as the sun;* cadere, labi, occĭdĕre ut sol:—Ǽr heó [sunne] fullîce gesîgan onginne *before it* [*the sun*] *begin fully to sink*, Herb. 19, 5; Lchdm. i. 112, 21. Ðæt he âna scyle gesîgan æt sæcce *that he alone should sink in conflict*, Beo. Th. 5311; B. 2659. Ðonne me ylde tîd on gesîge *in tempore senectutis*, Ps. Th. 70, 8. Ðâ to ðam wage gesâg *then to the wall he sank*, Exon. 51 a; Th. 178, 13; Gû. 1243.

ge-sigefæstan; *p.* -fæste; *pp.* -fæsted, -fæst [sige *victory*] *To make triumphant, crown;* corrōbŏrāre, cŏrōnāre:—He ðê gesigefæste sôþre miltse *qui coronat te in mĭsĕrātiōne*, Ps. Th. 102, 5. Hî synne geswencton and gesigefæston *they outwearied sin and triumphed*, Exon. 55 b; Th. 197, 13; Az. 189. We gesigefæstan ðîne bǽre *let us crown thy bier*, Blickl. Homl. 149, 19: 151, 9. Ðæt ic mid Criste gesigefæsted wǽre *ipse cum Cristo coronandus*, Bd. 2, 6; S. 508, 21. Twegen cynelîce cnihtas mid syndriglîcre Godes gyfe wǽron gesigefæste *dŭō rēgii pueri fratres spĕciāli sunt Dei grātia cŏrōnāti*, 4, 16; S. 584, 21. Siendon ðînne ðômas gesigefæste *thy decrees are triumphant*, Cd. 188; Th. 234, 8; Dan. 288: Exon. 53 a; Th. 185, 18; Az. 9: Shrn. 146, 11. Drihten gesigefæsted *the Lord triumphant*, Blickl. Homl. 67, 14.

ge-sigfæstnian; *p.* ode; *pp.* od *To triumph, crown*:—He gesigfæstnade *triumphans*, Mt. Kmbl. 13, 3. Gesigfæstnad *coronandus*, Jn. Skt. 8, 12.

ge-siht, -sihþ, -siehþ, -syhþ, -sihtþ, e; *f. Sight, power of seeing, vision, something seen, aspect, respect;* visus, acies oculorum, visio, aspectus, conspectus, respectus:—Se ord on here oððe scearp gesihþ *acies*, Ælfc. Gr. 5; Som. 4, 14. Yfel gesihþ *oculus malus*, Mk. Bos. 7, 22. Bodian blindum gesihþe *prædicare cæcis visum*, Lk. Bos. 4, 18: Homl. Th. i. 64, 22: Blickl. Homl. 155, 5. Ðû wâst ðæt gesiht and gehêrnes ongitaþ ðone lîchoman ðæs monnes *thou knowest that sight and hearing perceive the body of a man*, Bt. 41, 4; Fox 252, 6. Eágena gesihþ *eye-sight*, Andr. Kmbl. 60; An. 30: Ps. Th. 93, 9. Forhwan woldest ðû ðînre gesihþe me wyrnan *quid avertis faciem tuam a me?* 87, 14. He wundrode æfter ðære gesihþe *he wondered at the sight*, Blickl. Homl. 153, 36: 215, 31. Forht ic wæs for ðære fægran gesyhþe *terrified I was at the fair sight*, Rood Kmbl. 41; Kr. 21. Ðæt he sume gesihtþe geseah *quod visionem vidisset*, Lk. Bos. 1, 22. Engla gesihþe *visionem angelorum*, 24, 23. Þurh nihtlîce gesihþ *in a vision of the night*, Shrn. 63, 16: Lchdm. iii. 204, 31. Ðære uplîcan sibbe gesiehþ *the sight of the peace above*, Past. 21; Swt. 161, 16; Hat. MS. On ealles ðæs folces gesihþe *in the sight of all the people*, Homl. Th. i. 60, 25: Blickl. Homl. 121, 17: 201, 5. On ðînre gesyhþe *in conspectu tuo*, Ps. Th. 55, 7: 137, 1: Cd. 49; Th. 63, 20; Gen. 1035 Of heora gesihþum *from their sight*, Jud. 16, 3. Bûtan gesyhþe ǽrfæstnesse *sine respectu pietatis*, Bd. 4, 12; S. 580, 41.

ge-sincan; *p.* -sanc, -sonc, *pl.* -suncon; *pp.* -suncen *To sink;* delābi:—Him in gesonc flacor flânþracu *the flickering arrow's force sank into him*, Exon. 49 b; Th. 170, 22; Gû. 1115. Ðâ ne meahton hi on ðæm wætere gesincan *then they could not sink in the water*, Shrn. 103, 19.

gêsine; *adj. Void, destitute;* expers:—Môdum tǽcan ðæt we gêsine ne sŷn godes þeódscipes *to teach our minds that we be not destitute of God's communion*, Cd. 169; Th. 211, 18; Exod. 528. v. gêsne, gǽsne.

ge-sîne. v. ge-sŷne.

ge-singalian; *p.* ode, ade *To continue, perpetuate*:—Gesyngalade *continui*, Ps. Spl. C. 88, 49.

ge-singallîcode *continually;* continuatim, V. Ps. 140, 7. v. singallîce.

ge-singan; *p.* -sang, *pl.* -sungon; *pp.* -sungen *To sing;* cănĕre:—Sceal mon leóþ gesingan *a man shall sing songs*, Exon. 91 a; Th. 342, 8; Gn. Ex. 140: Menol. Fox 140; Men. 70. David þurh Godes gâst Gode to lofe gesang *David through God's spirit sang to the praise of God*, Swt. A. S. Rdr. 67, 332. Mæssan gesingan *to sing mass*, Blickl. Homl. 45, 31: 207, 5. Ðætte on Cantica Canticorum wæs gesungen *what was sung in the Song of Songs*, 11, 15.

ge-singe [= ge-sinhîge (?) v. ge-sinîg], an; *f. A wife*:—Ne meaht ðû habban mec ðê to gesingan *thou mayest not have me for thy wife*, Exon. 66 b; Th. 245, 34; Jul. 54. [Cf. ge-sinhîwan.]

ge-singian; *p.* ode; *pp.* od *To sin;* peccāre:—We habbaþ swîðe gesingod *we have greatly sinned*, Hy. 7, 115; Hy. Grn. ii. 289, 115. v. ge-syngian.

ge-sinhîwan, -hîgan; *pl. m. Married persons;* conjuges, conjugati, conjugia:—Unriht gewuna is arisen betwih gesinhîwum *prava in conjugatorum moribus consuetudo surrexit*, Bd. 1, 27; S. 493, 34. Gesinhîwan *conjuges* vel *conjugales*, Ælfc. Gl. 86; Som. 74, 25; Wrt. Voc. 50, 7. Ðæt lîf ðara gesinhîwena oferstîgþ ðæt lîf ðæs mægþhâdes *the life of the married surpasses the life of virginity*, Past. 52, 8; Swt. 409, 29; Hat. MS. Tu gesinhîwan sprǽcon ymbe hine ealle niht *two married people were talking about him all night*, Shrn. 90, 2. Ealla ðara monna hûs bûtan ðara gesinhîgna *all men's houses except the two married people's*, 5. Ðara hâligra gesinhîna tîd *the holy man and wife's tide*, 55, 31. Wit sŷn swâ swâ gesinhîna [?] *we be as married people*, 40, 20. For gesinhîwum *pro conjugiis*, Bd. 4, 5; S. 573, 14. v. sin-hîwan.

ge-sinîg [= sin-hîg, -hîw?], e; *f. Marriage;* connubium:—Fore hâlgum gesinîge ǽ *pro sacra connubii lege*, Rtl. 108, 14.

ge-sinîgan *to marry;* nubere:—Gesinîgaþ *nubunt*, Lk. Skt. Lind. Gisinnîgo, Rush. 20, 34. v. ge-sinîg.

ge-sinîgscipe, es; *m. Marriage;* connubium, Rtl. 108, 23. v. sinhîgscipe.

ge-sinlîce; *adv. Curiously, strictly;* curiose, R. Ben. 58.

ge-sinscipe, es; *m. Marriage, wedlock, matrimony; in pl. Married people;* connubium, Bd. 4, 5; S. 573, 14: 19; S. 587, 30: Shrn. 60, 2. Se mægþhâd is hîrra ðonne se gesinscipe *virginity is more exalted than marriage*, Past. 52, 8; Swt. 409, 24; Hat. MS. He wæs seofan geár on gesinscipe geseted ǽr his biscopdôme *he was married for seven years before he was a bishop*, Shrn. 110, 1. Eác is gesynscipum micel þearf *for those married also there is much need*, L. E. I. 42; Th. ii. 440, 2.

ge-sinscipîc; *adj. Conjugal, matrimonial;* conjugalis, L. E. I. 43; Th. ii. 440, 7.

ge-sión *to see, behold;* videre:—Wênaþ ða dysgan ðæt ǽlc mon sîe blind swâ hî sint; and ðæt nân mon ne mǽge seón [gesión, note] ðæt hî gesión ne mâgon *the foolish think that every man is blind as they are; and that no man is able to see what they cannot see*, Bt. 38, 5; Fox 206, 21. v. ge-seón.

ge-siowed *sewed together*. v. ge-siwed.

ge-sirwan, -serwan, -syrwan; *p.* ede; *pp.* ed. I. *to plot, contrive, conspire, deliberate*:—Se se ðe ða synne gesireþ *he who designs the sin*, Past. 56, 6; Swt. 435, 6; Hat. MS. Ðonne ne gesirede hit nô ðæt hit þurhtuge swelce synne *then would it not have designed to carry out such sin*, Swt. 435, 4. Ic gesyrede *I plotted*, Exon. 72 b; Th. 270, 20; Jul. 468. Ðŷ ne wricþ Dryhten nô gelîce ða gesiredan synne and fǽrlîce þurhtogenan forðæm sió gesirede syn biþ ungelîc eallum ôðrum synnum *so the Lord does not punish equally the deliberate sin and the suddenly perpetrated, for the deliberate sin is unlike all other sins*, Past. 56, 7; Swt. 435, 13; Hat. MS. II. *to furnish with arms, equip*:—Gesyrwed secg *an armed man*, Byrht. Th. 136, 30; By. 159. v. ge-syrwan.

ge-sîþ, es; *m.* [cf. ge-fêra] *A companion, fellow, companion* or *follower of a chief* or *king;* socius, comes:—Gif mon elþeódigne ofsleá gif he mǽgleás sîe healf kyningc [âh] healf se gesîþ *if one slay a foreigner, if he be kinless, half the king* [*has*], *half the companion*, L. In. 23; Th. i. 116, 16. Gif gesîþcund mon þingaþ wiđ cyning for his inhîwan, nâh he nâne wîterǽdenne, se gesîþ *if a 'gesithcund' man compound a suit with the king for his household, he, the 'gesith,' shall not have any fee*, 50; Th. i. 134, 5. Se gesîþ geladede đone cyning to his hâme *rex, rogatus a comite*, Bd. 3, 22; S. 553, 29. Him se gesîþ fultumade and ealle đa neáhmenn *juvante cŏmĭte ac vicĭnis omnĭbus*, 4, 4; S. 571, 14. Wæs sum gesîþ on neáweste *erat cŏmes in proximo*, 4, 10; S. 578, 18. Đâ bæd se gesîþ hine, đæt he eóde on his hûs *rŏgāvit cŏmes eum in dŏmum suam ingrĕdi*, 5, 4; S. 617, 10: 5, 5; S. 617, 40. Daniel deóra gesîþ *Daniel, the beasts' associate*, Cd. 208; Th. 251, 24; Dan. 662. Hyre wæs hâlig gǽst singal gesîþ *to her the Holy Spirit was a constant companion*, Exon. 69 a; Th. 257, 4; Jul. 242. To hâm his gesîþes *in dŏmo cŏmĭtis*, Bd. 3, 14; S. 539, 43. He on đæs gesîþes hûs ineóde *dŏmum cŏmĭtis intrāvit*, 5, 4; S. 617, 16. Wæs se bisceop geladod sumes gesîþes cyricean to hâlgianne *episcopus vocātus est ad dedicandam Ecclesiam comĭtis*, 5, 5; S. 617, 34: Shrn. 69, 32: 70, 23: 122, 18. On gesîþes hâd *in the condition of a comrade*, Beo. Th. 2598; B. 1297. Fram đam ylcan gesîþe *ab eōdem comĭte*, Bd. 5, 4; S. 617, 9. To his treówum gesîþe *to his faithful companion*, Exon. 51 b; Th. 179, 29; Gû. 1269. He hæfde him to gesîþþe sorge and longaþ *he had for his companion sorrow and longing*, 100 a; Th. 377, 13; Deór. 3. Swǽse gesîþas *his dear companions*, Beo. Th. 57; B. 29: 4086; B. 2040: 5029; B. 2518. Frôde gesîþas, ealde ǽgleáwe hit getealdon *wise fellows, elders skilled in law computed it*, Menol. Fox 36; Men. 18. Đa gesîþas *the comrades*, Salm. Kmbl. 693; Sal. 346. Mec gesîþas sendaþ æfter hondum *comrades send me from hand to hand*, Exon. 108 a; Th. 412, 24; Rä. 31, 5. Hûþe feredon seccas and gesîþþas *warriors and allies carried away the spoil*, Cd. 95; Th. 124, 23; Gen. 2067: Judth. 11; Thw. 24, 22; Jud. 201. Gesîþa đa sǽmestan *the worst of companions*, Exon. 86 b; Th. 326, 7; Wîd. 125. Nǽnig swǽsra gesîþa *no one of the dear companions*, Beo. Th. 3872; B. 1934. Ǽđele cempa mid gesîþum *the noble champion with his companions*, 2630; B. 1313: 3852; B. 1924: 5257; B. 2632: Exon. 14 b; Th. 30, 1; Cri. 473. Đæt wæs Satane and his gesîþum mid gegearwad *that was prepared for Satan and his associates with him*, 30 a; Th. 93, 7; Cri. 1522: 123 b; Th. 474, 21; Bo. 33: 89 b; Th. 337, 2; Gn. Ex. 58: Salm. Kmbl. 907; Sal. 453. Þeóda þrymfæste þegnum and gesîþþum *famous nations with vassals and allies*, Cd. 91; Th. 114, 23; Gen. 1908. [For the technical meaning of 'gesith' see Stubbs' Const. Hist. under 'comitatus' and 'gesith;' Kemble's Saxons in England, i. 168; and Schmid's A. S. Gesetz. 'gesîþ.' *Goth.* ga-sinþja: *O. Sax.* gi-sîđ: *O. H. Ger.* gi-sindo.]

ge-sîþ, -sîþþ, es; *n. Company, fellowship;* comitatus:—Sweotol is đæt đe sôþ metod on gesîþþe is *it is plain that the true Lord is with thee*, Cd. 135; Th. 170, 3; Gen. 2807: 109; Th. 145, 5; Gen. 2401. [*O. H. Ger.* gi-sindi; *n. comitatus: O. Sax.* ge-sîþi; *n.*]

ge-sîþcund; *adj. Of the rank of a 'gesith:'*—Gif gesîþcund mon landâgende forsitte fyrde, geselle cxx scillinga and þolie his landes *if a 'gesithcund' man, owning land, neglect the 'fyrd,' let him pay 120 shillings and forfeit his land*, L. In. 51; Th. i. 134, 8. Gif gesîþcund man fare, þonne môt he habban his gerêfan mid him, and his smiþ and his cildfêstran *if a 'gesithcund' man go away, then may he have his reeve with him, and his smith and his child's fosterer*, 63; Th. i. 144, 2: 45; Th. i. 130, 9: 54; Th. i. 136, 12: 68; Th. i. 146, 7: L. Wih. 5; Th. i. 38, 4.

ge-sîþcundlîc, -sîþlîc; *adj. Pertaining to a companion:*—Swâ swâ he wǽre gesîþcundlîcre [MS. Ca. gesîþlîcre, MS. B.] gegaderunga *quasi comes copulæ carnalis*, Bd. 2, 9; S. 511, 1, note.

gesîþ-mægen; *gen.* -mægnes; *n. A multitude of companions;* comitum turba:—For gesîþmægen, Exon. 90 a; Th. 339, 4; Gn. Ex. 89.

ge-sîþman, -mon; *gen.* -mannes, -monnes; *m. A 'gesith;'* comes:—Se gesîþmon [gesîþmon, MSS. B. H.] *the 'gesith,'* L. In. 30; Th. i. 122, 1. v. ge-sîþ.

ge-sîþscipe, es; *m. A fellowship, society;* societas:—Nam he twegen bisceopas of Britta þeóde on gesîþscipe đære hâlgunge *adsumtis in societatem ordinationis duobus de Brittonum gente episcopis*, Bd. 3, 28; S. 560, 27. Sum swîþe eald wîfman wæs in his gesîþscipe *a very old woman lived with him*, Shrn. 36, 9. [*O. Sax.* gi-sîđskepi.]

ge-sîþwîf, es; *n. A woman of the class to which the 'gesith,' 'comes' belongs:*—Sca anastasiam đære hâlegan gesîþwîfes seó wæs swîþe ædele for worulde *St. Anastasia's the holy lady; she was very noble with respect to this world*, Shrn. 30, 20. All đa gesîþwîf and đa ædelan fǽmnan *all the ladies and noble women*, 87, 21. [Cf. ge-sîþman.]

ge-sittan; *p.* -sæt, *pl.* -sǽton; *pp.* -seten. I. *to sit, sit down, settle, lean, recline;* sĕdēre, consĭdēre, discumbĕre:—Ic gesitte *I sit*, Exon. 73 a; Th. 272, 6; Jul. 495. Hî gesittaþ him on gesundum þingum *they sit in sound condition*, 89 b; Th. 337, 1; Gn. Ex. 58. He wiđ earm gesæt *he leaned on his arm*, Beo. Th. 1503; B. 749: Cd. 223; Th. 291, 18; Sat. 432. Đâ eóde he into đæs Fariseiscan hûse, and gesæt *ingressus dŏmum Pharisæi discŭbuit*, Lk. Bos. 7, 36. Alexander æt Somnite gemǽre and Rômâna gesæt *Alexander posted himself on the boundary of the Samnites and the Romans*, Ors. 3, 7; Bos. 58, 28. Gesǽton searuþancle sundor to rûne *the wise of thought sat apart in council*, Andr. Kmbl. 2323; An. 1163: Elen. Kmbl. 1732; El. 868. Twegen iunge men gesǽton æt me *two young men sat by me*, Bd. 5, 13; S. 632, 35. Him cierde eall đæt folc to, đe on Mercna lande geseten wæs *all the people who were settled in the Mercians' land submitted to him*, Chr. 922; Erl. 108, 34. Hie hæfdon heora stemn gesetenne *they had sat out their time of service*, Chr. 894; Erl. 90, 31. II. *to occupy, possess, inhabit;* possĭdēre, hăbĭtāre:—Đeáh đe wyrigcwydole Godes rîce gesittan ne mâgon *quamvis maledĭci regnum Dei possĭdēre non possint*, Bd. 4, 26; S. 602, 11. Sume sêcaþ and gesittaþ hâmas on heolstrum *some seek and occupy houses in caverns*, Exon. 33 b; Th. 107, 3; Gû. 53: Cd. 170; Th. 213, 34; Exod. 562. Paulinus gesæt đæt biscepsetl on Hrôfes ceastre *Paulinus occupied the bishop's see at Rochester*, Chr. 633; Erl. 24, 7: 890; Erl. 87, 27: Beo. Th. 1270; B. 633. Hî folca gewinn fremdra gesǽton *lābōres pŏpŭlōrum possēdērunt*, Ps. Th. 104, 39: 77, 56: Cd. 46; Th. 59, 9; Gen. 961. Bûtan ôđrum manegum gesetenum îglandum *besides many other inhabited islands*, Ors. 1, 1; Bos. 16, 25. Us is alêfed heofena rîce to gesittenne *we are permitted to occupy heaven's kingdom*, Blickl. Homl. 137, 15: Ors. 6, 34; Bos. 130, 23.

ge-siwed, -siwod, -siwud, -siuwed; *part. Sewed, patched;* sutus, assutus, consutus:—Gediht ođđe gesiwed hrægel *acupicta vel Phrygia vestis*, Ælfc. Gl. 63; Som. 68, 107; Wrt. Voc. 40, 18. Mid golde gesiwud bend *nimbus*, 64; Som. 69, 13; Wrt. Voc. 40, 47. v. siwian.

ge-slǽpan, -slêpan, -slêpian [in the Northern glosses of the Gospels the verb is weak] *to sleep:*—He geslêpde *dormiebat*, Mt. Kmbl. Lind. 8, 24. Geslêpedon alle and geslêpdon *dormitaverunt omnes et dormierunt*, 25, 5.

ge-sleán; *p.* -slôg, -slôh, *pl.* -slôgon; *pp.* -slagen, -slægen, -slegen *To strike, pitch* [*a tent*], *smite, slay, quell, forge, fight, obtain by fighting:*—Hî lâgon swylce hî wǽron deáþe geslegene *they lay as if they were stricken by death*, Judth. 10; Thw. 21, 23; Jud. 31. Se geslagena biþ mid deáþe gegripen *the man stricken* [*by disease*] *is seized by death*, Homl. Th. ii. 124, 12. Đǽr he geslôh his geteld *he pitched his tent there*, Gen. 12, 8. Wulfheard aldorman micel wæl geslôg and sige nom *alderman Wulfhard made a great slaughter and got the victory*, Chr. 837; Erl. 66, 5: 845; Erl. 66, 24: 823; Erl. 62, 17: 867; Erl. 72, 15: Bd. 1, 16; S. 484, 23. He geslôg xxv dracena *he slew xxv dragons*, Salm. Kmbl. 417; Sal. 214. Geslôh đîn fæder fǽhþe mǽste *thy father quelled the greatest feud*, Beo. Th. 922; B. 459. Geslægene grindlas *forged bars*, Cd. 19; Th. 24, 26; Gen. 383. Of đære tîde hwîlum Bryttas hwîlum Seaxena sige geslôgan *ex eo tempore nunc cives nunc hostes vincebant*, Bd. 1, 16; S. 484, 22. Offa geslôg cynerîca mǽst *Offa won the greatest of kingdoms*, Exon. 85 a; Th. 320, 32; Vîd. 38: Th. 321, 11; Vîd. 44. Hûþe đe ic æt hilde geslôh *spoil that I gained in war*, Cd. 98; Th. 129, 25; Gen. 2149: Chr. 937; Erl. 112, 4; Æthelst. 4: Beo. Th. 5985; B. 2996. Dariun we ofercwômon and oferswŷđdon and us in onweald geslôgon eal his londrîce *dario superato acceptaque in conditiones omni ejus regione*, Nar. 3, 24. Đâ þohte ic hwæđer ic meahte ealne middangeard me on onweald gesleán *cogitabam si devicto orbe terrarum*, 29, 2. Ôþ đæt up gewât lîg and þurh lust geslôh *until the flame went up and at will smote*, Cd. 186; Th. 231, 19; Dan. 249.

ge-sleccan; *p.* -slæhte *To make slack, enfeeble, weaken:*—Sûslum geslæhte *weakened by torments*, Exon. 10 a; Th. 10, 8; Cri. 149. [Cf. *O. Sax.* an siuni gislekit.]

ge-slêfed; *pp. Having sleeves;* manicatus, manuleātus:—Geslêfed *manuleātus* vel *manicātus*, Ælfc. Gl. 3; Som. 55, 74; Wrt. Voc. 16, 47. DER. slêfan.

ge-sleht; *n.* v. bil-gesleht, ge-slyht.

ge-slit, es; *n. A bite, tearing:*—Đæra næddrena geslit wæs deádlîc *the bite of those serpents was deadly*, Homl. Th. ii. 238, 30. Þurh deóra geslit *by the tearing of beasts*, 544, 2.

ge-slîtan; *p.* -slât; *pp.* -sliten *To tear, rend, break:*—Midđŷ geslitten wêron đa bendo *ruptis vinculis*, Lk. Skt. Lind. 8, 29.

ge-slôh *struck.* v. ge-sleán.

ge-slyht, -sleht, -sliht, es; *n. Battle, fight, conflict:*—Swâ he nîþa gehwane genesen hæfde slîþra geslyhta *so he had come safely out of every enmity, every fierce conflict*, Beo. Th. 4787; B. 2398. v. bil-gesleht.

ge-smeágan, -smeán; *p.* -smeáde; *pp.* -smeád *To search, examine, consider;* scrutari, cogitare:—Hia gesmeádon miþ him *illi cogitabant secum*, Mk. Skt. Lind. 11, 31. Gismeáþ wegas ûsra *scrutemur vias nostras*, Rtl. 20, 21. Gismeága *excogitare*, 170, 5. Gesmeád sprǽc *sermo commentitius*, Ælfc. Gl. 100; Som. 77, 21; Wrt. Voc. 55, 25.

ge-smeáh; *gen.* -smeáges [?]; *n. Intrigue:*—Đǽr wearþ se cyng of France þurh gesmeáh gecyrred *there the king of France was turned back by intrigue*, Chr. 1094; Erl. 230, 23.

ge-smecgan; *p.* ede; *pp.* ed [smæccan *to taste*] *To taste;* gustāre:—Ic gesmecge *gusto*, Ælfc. Gl. 5; Som. 56, 33; Wrt. Voc. 17, 37.

ge-smēđan; *p.* de; *pp.* ed; *v. a. To make smooth* or *even, to soothe, soften;* complanare:—Se ele gesmēđ đa wunda *the oil sooths the wounds*, Past. 17, 10; Swt. 125, 10; Hat. MS.

ge-smicerad [smicere *elegant*]; *part. p. Worked, neatly made;* fabrefactus, Cot. 88, 184.

ge-smirian *to anoint*, Ex. 29, 29. v. ge-smyrian.

ge-smiten; *part. p. Anointed, smeared, smutted;* litus, unctus, Som. [*Goth.* ga-smeitan.]

ge-smiđian; *p.* ede; *pp.* ed; *v. trans. To forge, to make as a smith does;* fabricare:—Bend agimmed and gesmiđed *diadema*, Ælfc. Gl. 64; Wrt. Voc. 40, 46. [*Goth.* ga-smiþon: *O. H. Ger.* gi-smidon *cudere.*]

ge-smyltan; *p.* te; *pp.* ed [smylt *serene*] *To appease, quiet;* plācāre:—He đone aþundenan sǣ gesmylte *tŭmĭda æquŏra plācāvit*, Bd. 5, 1; S. 614, 8.

ge-smyrian, -smirian; *p.* ode, ede; *pp.* od, ed [smyrian *to smear*] *To smear, anoint;* ungēre:—Hī word hira wel gesmyredon, ele anlīcast *mollĭĕrunt sermōnes suos sŭper ŏleum*, Ps. Th. 54, 21. Forđon gesmiride meç *propter quod unxit me*, Lk. Skt. Lind. 4, 18. Đætte gesmiredon hine *ut ungerent eum*, Mk. Skt. Lind. 16, 1. Đæt hīg sīn gesmirode on đam and hira handa gehālgode *ut ungantur in ea et consecrentur mănus eōrum*, Ex. 29, 29. Đæt nǣfre ne afūlaþ đæt mid hire gesmered biþ *that never becomes foul that is anointed with it*, Blickl. Homl. 73, 23. Gesmearuad oele hālgum *unctus oleo sancto*, Rtl. 198, 31.

gēsne; *adj. Lacking, wanting, destitute, lifeless;* expers, egenus, destitutus, exanimis:—Læg se fūla leáp gēsne *the foul corpse lay lifeless*, Judth. 10; Thw. 23, 8; Jud. 112. He funde đā on bedde his goldgifan gǣstes gēsne, līfes belidenne *he then found his goldgiver void of spirit, deprived of life*, 12; Thw. 25, 26; Jud. 279. v. gǣsne.

ge-snid, es; *n. A killing, slaughter;* occisio:—Swā swā sceáp to gesnide *sicut oves occisionis*, Ps. Lamb. 43, 23.

ge-snīþan; *p.* -snāþ; *pp.* -sniden *To cut, cut off:*—Summ monn gesnāþ him đa eárelipprica *quidam amputavit illi auricula*, Mk. Skt. Lind. 14, 47. Gif đū stǣnen weofod me wyrce ne tymbra đū đæt of gesnidenum stānum *if thou wilt make me an altar of stone, thou shalt not build it of hewn stone*, Ex. 20, 25.

ge-snīđan [?] *to lie down:*—Đætte gesniđa [Rush. gesnide] gedydon alle *ut accumbere facerent omnes*, Mk. Skt. Lind. 6, 39.

ge-snīþung, e; *f. A cutting;* dolatio, Som.

ge-snot *snot*. v. snot.

ge-snyttro; *f. n.* [?] *Wisdom:*—Gūþlāc wæs ealra gesnyttra goldhord *Guthlac was a treasure of all wisdom*, Guthl. 20; Gdwn. 92, 17.

gesoc, es; *m? Suck;* suctus:—Đæt Sarra sceolde lecgan cild to hyre breóste to gesoce *quod Sara lactāret fīlium*, Gen. 21, 7.

ge-sod, es; *n? A cooking, boiling;* coctio, coctūra:—Gesod *coctio*, Wrt. Voc. 82, 70.

ge-soden; *part.* [soden, *pp. of* seóđan *to seethe*] *Seethed, sodden, cooked, boiled;* coctus, elixus:—Gesoden, gebacen *coctus*, Ælfc. Gl. 31; Som. 61, 86; Wrt. Voc. 27, 16: 82, 71. Gesoden mæt on wætere *elixus cĭbus*, 31; Som. 61, 87; Wrt. Voc. 27, 17. Gesoden wīn *defrūtum vīnum*, 32; Som. 62, 8; Wrt. Voc. 27, 62.

ge-soecan *to seek, follow*, Jn. Skt. Lind. 13, 37. v. ge-sēcan.

ge-sōm; *adj. Unanimous, united, peaceable;* concors, pācĭfĭcus:—Wǣron gesōme đa đe swegl būan *those that inhabit the firmament were unanimous*, Cd. 5; Th. 6, 1; Gen. 82. Wit wǣron gesōme *we two were united*, Exon. 129 b; Th. 496, 27; Rä. 85, 21: Gen. 45, 24. Gesōme and to đam geþwǣre đæt heora nān ne mæg ōđerne mid ælle fordōn *in union and in such accord that none can entirely destroy another*, Shrn. 165, 33.

ge-somnian; *p.* ode; *pp.* od *To assemble, collect;* congregare, colligere:—He us to dæge wolde on đisse tīde gesomnian *he wished to assemble us to-day at this time*, Blickl. Homl. 139, 31. Gesomna cūe mesa *collect cow's dung*, L. M. I, 38; Lchdm. ii. 98, 5. v. ge-samnian.

ge-somning, e; *f. A congregation;* congrĕgātio:—Seó Godes circe, þurh gesomninga sōđes and ryhtes, beorhte blīceþ *the church of God, through congregations of truth and right, brightly gleameth*, Exon. 18 a; Th. 44, 9; Cri. 700. v. ge-samnung.

ge-somnung, e; *f. A congregation, synagogue, church;* congrĕgātio, sy̆năgōga, ecclēsia:—He com into hyra gesomnunge *vēnit in sy̆năgōgam eōrum*, Mt. Bos. 12, 9. On gesomnunge ingongan *ecclēsiam intrāre*, Bd. 1, 27; S. 495, 7. Justus reahte đa gesomnunge *Justus rĕgēbat ecclēsiam*, 2, 7; S. 509, 10. Gesomnunga folca ymbtrymdon đē *sy̆năgōga pŏpŭlōrum circumdăbit te*, Ps. Spl. 7, 7. Beferde se Hǣlend ealle Galileam, lǣrende on hyra gesomnungum *circumībat Iesus tōtam Gălilæam, dŏcens in sy̆năgōgis eōrum*, Mt. Bos. 4, 23: 6, 2, 5: 9, 35. v. ge-samnung.

ge-somodlǣcan. v. ge-samodlǣcan.

ge-sōđ *a soother, flatterer;* parasitus, Cot. 152.

ge-sōþfæstian; *p.* ode, ade; *pp.* od, ad *To justify:*—Bærsynnig gesōþfæstadon god *publicani justificaverunt deum*, Lk. Skt. Lind. 7, 29. He wolde gesōþfæstiga hine seolfne *ille volens justificare seipsum*, 10, 29. Gesōþfæstad is snytro *justificata est sapientia*, Mt. Kmbl. Lind. 11, 19: 12, 37.

ge-sōþian; ic -sōþige; *p.* ode; *pp.* od *To prove the truth of, bear witness;* probare, testari:—Gif man đæt gesōþige *if that be proved*, L. E. G. 6; Th. i. 170, 13. Menigo of hlāfe and līchoma his gesōþade *plurima de pane et carne sua testatur*, Jn. Skt. p. 5, 2.

ge-sotig; *adj. Dirty*, Gl. Prud. 579.

ge-spænning, e; *f. An incitement, a provocation;* incitamentum, Som.

gespan *the tamarisk tree;* myrica, Cot. 131.

ge-span, -spon, es; *n. A prompting, enticing, persuasion, seduction;* suggestio, illectatio, persuasio, seductio, Past. 53, 7; Swt. 417, 20; Hat. MS: Cd. 33; Th. 45, 2; Gen. 720.

ge-span, -spann, -spon, es; *n. A joining, fastening together;* nexus:—Wīra gespann *joining of wires*, Andr. Kmbl. 604; An. 303. Wīra gespon, Elen. Kmbl. 2267; El. 1135. He is on helle hæft mid hringa gesponne *he is in hell bound with the clasping of rings*, Cd. 35; Th. 47, 17; Gen. 762. Searo-rūna gespon *the web of mysteries*, Exon. 92 b; Th. 347, 20; Sch. 15. v. ge-spannan, eaxle-gespan.

ge-spanan; *p.* -spōn, -speón, *pl.* -spōnon, -speónon; *pp.* -spanen, -sponen; *v. trans. To allure, entice, incite, persuade, induce, draw;* allicere, illicere, incitare, persuadere, inducere:—Đe hine to dæm unfriđe gespōn *who had allured him to a violation of the peace*, Chr. 905; Th. 182, 7, col. 1. Gif he đa cwēne gespanan [gespannan, MS.] and gelǣran mihte, đæt heó brūcan wolde his gesynscipes *si reginæ posset persuadere ejus uti connubio*, Bd. 4, 19; S. 587, 29. Gespeón *persuadebat*, 2, 15; S. 518, 26. Swȳđost gesponen [gesponnen, MS.] to onfōnne Cristes geleáfan *maxime persuasus ad percipiendam Christi fidem*, 3, 21; S. 551, 5. Wæs hām gelađad and gesponen [gesponnen, MS.] *was called and drawn home*, 4, 23; S. 593, 17.

ge-spang, -spong, es; *n. A clasp, binding:*—Me habbaþ hringa gespong sīþes amyrred *the rings' clasps have hindered me from going*, Cd. 19; Th. 24, 14; Gen. 377.

ge-spannan, -sponnan; *p.* -speón; *pp.* -spannen *To join, span, clasp, fasten:*—Gūþweard grīmhelm gespeón *the leader clasped his helm*, Cd. 151; Th. 188, 27; Exod. 174. Đā hēht cāsere gesponnan fiówer wildo hors to scride *then the emperor ordered to harness four wild horses to a chariot*, Shrn. 71, 34. [*O. H. Ger.* gi-spannan *tendere, conjungere.*] v. spannan.

ge-sparian; *p.* ede *To spare:*—Ne gisperede *non pepercit*, Rtl. 22, 17.

ge-sparrian; *p.* ode, ade; *pp.* od, ad *To shut;* claudere:—Gesparrado dure đīn *clauso ostio tuo*, Mt. Kmbl. Lind. 6, 6.

ge-spearn. v. ge-speornan.

ge-speca, an; *m. A speaker.* DER. eár-gespeca. v. ge-spreca.

ge-spēdan; *p.* -spēdde; *pp.* -spēded, -spēdd *To speed, prosper, succeed;* progredi, prosperare, succedere:—Đæs đe blōdgyte, wæll-fyll weres, wæpnum gespēdeþ *because that bloodshedding, slaughter of man, speedeth by means of weapons*, Cd. 75; Th. 92, 12; Gen. 1527. Ac hī nāht nā gespēddan *but they succeeded naught*, Chr. 1036; Th. 293, 23, col. 2. Ac man đǣr ne gespǣdde *but they didn't succeed there*, 1096; Erl. 233, 29. Ealle þinge swā hwæt swā he dēþ beóþ gespēdde *omnia quæcunque faciet prosperabuntur*, Ps. Lamb. 1, 3.

ge-spēdiglīce; *adv. Prosperously, successfully;* prospĕre:—Gesundfullīce ođđe gespēdiglīce forþstæpe and rīxa *prospĕre procēde et regna*, Ps. Lamb. 44, 5.

ge-spēdsumian *to prosper, succeed;* prosperari, Hpt. Gl. 491.

ge-spelia, an; *m.* [spelian *to represent*] *A substitute, deputy, vicegerent;* vicārius:—Cristen cyning is Cristes gespelia geteald on cristenre þeóde *a christian king is accounted Christ's vicegerent among christian people*, L. Eth. ix. 2; Th. i. 340, 12. Wiđ Cristes gespelian *against Christ's vicegerent*, ix. 42; Th. i. 350, 3. He wæs Æþelstānes b' gespelian siđđan he unfere wæs *he was bishop Athelstane's substitute after he was unable to move*, Chr. 1055; Erl. 191, 12.

ge-spellian *to speak, tell:*—Miđđȳ gespelledon *dum fabularentur*, Lk. Skt. Lind. 24. 15. [*Goth.* ga-spillon.]

ge-speoftad; *part. p. Spit upon:*—Gespeoftad biþ *conspuetur*, Lk. Skt. Lind. 18, 32. [Cf. speowian.]

ge-speón. v. ge-spanan, ge-spannan.

ge-speornan, -spornan; *p.* -spearn, *pl.* -spurnon; *pp.* -spornen *To tread upon, to perch, spurn;* calcare:—Đæt heó fōtum ne meahte land gespornan *so that she might not perch on land with her feet*, Cd. 72; Th. 87, 33; Gen. 1458: 72; Th. 87, 11; Gen. 1447. Đæt se hearn-flota sond-lond gespearn *so that the floater of the surge spurned the sandy land*, Exon. 52 a; Th. 182, 11; Gū. 1308.

ge-speów *prospered*, Judth. 11; Thw. 24, 7; Jud. 175; *p. of* gespōwan.

ge-sperod; *part.* [spere *a spear*] *Armed with a spear;* hastātus:—Gesperod *hastātus*, Ælfc. Gr. 43; Som. 45, 13: Blickl. Homl. 221, 28.

ge-spillan; *p.* de *To destroy, dissipate:*—Đēr ne hrust gespilleş *ubi neque ærugo demolitur*, Mt. Kmbl. Lind. 6, 20. Gespilleþ *perdiderit*,

Lk. Skt. Lind. 17, 33. Alle gespilde *omnes perdidit*, 29: Rtl. 107, 29. Ðǽr wǽron manege mid micel unrihte gespilde *there were many very wrongfully destroyed*, Chr. 1124; Erl. 253, 16: Mt. Kmbl. Lind. 6, 19. Erfwardniso gispilledo *hereditates dissipatas*, Rtl. 21, 1.

ge-spittan; *pp.* ed *To spit upon;* conspuere:—Gispitted biþ *conspuetur*, Lk. Skt. Rush. 18, 32. Gispittendum on mec *conspuentibus in me*, Rtl. 19, 17.

ge-spon, es; *n. An enticing, persuasion, artifice;* illectatio, persuasio, seductio:—Deófles gespon *the devil's artifice*, Cd. 33; Th. 45, 2; Gen. 720. v. ge-span.

ge-spon. v. ge-span.

ge-spôn *allured, incited*, Chr. 905; Th. 182, 7, col. 1. v. ge-spanan.

ge-spong. v. ge-spang.

ge-sponnen *persuaded, drawn*, Bd. 3, 21; S. 551, 5: 4, 23; S. 593, 17. For ge-sponen; *pp. of* ge-spanan.

ge-spornan. v. ge-speornan.

ge-spôwan; *p.* -speów, *pl.* -speówon; *pp.* -spôwen [spôwan *to succeed*] *To succeed, prosper;* succēdĕre, prospĕrāre:—Hū hyre æt beaduwe gespeów *how she prospered in battle*, Judth. 11; Thw. 24, 7; Jud. 175: Andr. Kmbl. 2688; An. 1346. Him æt ðære byrig ne gespeów *he did not succeed at the city*, Ors. 4, 5; Bos. 82, 8.

ge-sprǽc, es; *n. Speech, discourse, conversation, advice:*—Se cyning wæs on gesprǽce wynsum *erat rex affatu jucundus*, Bd. 3, 14; S. 540, 8. Ic wæs mid his gesprǽce wel gerēted *allocutione ejus refecti*, 5, 1; S. 613, 22. Gearo on gesprǽce *loquela promptus*, 2; S. 615, 29. Ðā hæfde he gesprǽce and geþeaht *habito consilio*, 2, 13; S. 515, 40. Com for gesprǽce Finano ðæs biscopes *pervenire propter conloquium Finani episcopi*, 3, 22; S. 552, 41. Wæs gemyndig ðæs apostoles gesprǽces *was mindful of what the apostle said*, Shrn. 39, 5. Gesprǽcu, gesprēcu *oracula*, Cot. 143, Lye. [*O. H. Ger.* ge-sprâche; *n.*]

ge-sprǽce; *adj. Eloquent, affable;* eloquens, affabilis:—Næs ic nǽfre gesprǽce *non sum eloquens*, Ex. 4, 10. He wæs eallum gesprǽce *erat affabilis omnibus*, Bd. 4, 28; S. 606, 34. [*O. H. Ger.* ge-sprâche *facetus, affabilis, disertus, orator.*] v. sprǽce.

ge-sprǽcelic; *adj. Loquelaris:*—Ðās synd gehātene loquelares, loquela is sprǽc and loquelares synd gesprǽcelīce forþan ðe ðās syx prepositiones ne beóþ nā hwār āna ac beóþ ǽfre to sumum ōðrum worde gefēgede, Ælfc. Gr. 47; Som. 48, 49. [*O. H. Ger.* ki-sprachlich *rhetoricus, urbanus.*]

ge-sprǽdan; *p.* de; *pp.* ed *To spread out, extend;* extendere:—Gesprǽd hond ðīn *extende manum tuam*, Mt. Kmbl. Lind. 12, 13. Gesprǽde hond *extendens manum*, 8, 3.

ge-sprec, es; *n. The power of speech:*—He him sealde monnes gesprec *he should give him human speech*, Shrn. 76, 23. Sealde he dumbum gesprec *he gave speech to the dumb*, Andr. Kmbl. 1153; An. 577.

ge-spreca, an; *m. One who talks with another, a counsellor:*—Abraham wæs Godes gespreca *Abraham was one who talked with God*, Homl. Th. ii. 190, 12. Ðū ðē ānne genim to gesprecan symle spella and lāra rǽd-hycgende *always take as thy counsellor one sagacious in discourses and doctrines*, Exon. 80 a; Th. 301, 26; Fä. 25.

ge-sprecan, -specan; *p.* -spræc, *pl.* -sprǽcon; *pp.* -sprecen *To speak, speak with, agree;* sometimes takes an accusative of the person spoken to:—Gif ðū him wuht hearmes gesprǽce *if thou hast said to him aught injurious*, Cd. 30; Th. 41, 24; Gen. 661. Feala worda gespæc se engel *many words spake the angel*, 15; Th. 18, 11; Gen. 271. Adam gespræc *Adam spoke*, 27; Th. 36, 31; Gen. 580. Ðe git on ǽrdagum oft gesprǽcon *which ye two in former days oft agreed upon*, Exon. 123 a; Th. 476, 16; Bo. 15: 123 b; Th. 475, 24; Bo. 52. Feówer ða strengestan þeóda hȳ him betweonum gesprǽcan *the four strongest peoples agreed with one another*, Ors. 3, 10; Bos. 69, 33: 6, 10; Bos. 120, 32. Mid ðȳ ðe hie ðis gesprecen hæfdon *when they had said this*, Blickl. Homl. 143, 14: 191, 23: Elen. Kmbl. 2568; El. 1285. God hī gespræc ðā *God addressed them then*, Homl. Th. ii. 456, 26: 156, 16. Ðā wæs ic gesprecende ðone man *then was I conversing with the man*, Shrn. 36, 19. Plato hæfde hine gesprecen *Plato had conversed with him*, Swt. A. S. Rdr. 70, 443.

ge-sprengan; *p.* de; *pp.* ed *To sprinkle;* conspergere:—Ðū nymst ānne hlāf mid ele gesprengedne *tolles unum panem oleo conspersum*, Ex. 29, 23.

ge-spring, es; *n. A spring;* fons, scaturigo:—Ðǽr wæs on blōde brim weallende, atol ȳða gespring [geswing, Th.] eal gemenged *there was the surge boiling with blood, the foul spring of waves all mingled*, Beo. Kmbl. 1689. v. spring.

ge-springan; *p.*-sprang, -sprong, *pl.*-sprungon; *pp.*-sprungen. I. *v. intrans. To spring, bound, arise, go out, go forth;* prosilire, exoriri, abire, procedere:—Swā ðæt blōd gesprang *as the blood sprang*, Beo. Th. 3339; B. 1667. Sigemunde gesprong æfter deáþ-dæge dōm unlytel *to Sigemund sprang after his death-day no little glory*, 1773; B. 884: Exon. 92 a; Th. 345, 27; Gu. Ex. 196: Mt. Kmbl. Lind. 4, 24: Mk. Skt. Lind. 1, 28. II. *v. trans. To get by going* [?], *to cause to spring;* eructare:—Wīd-gongel wīf word gespringeþ *a rambling woman gets words* [= *a bad reputation*, or *reproofs?*] *by wandering*, Exon. 90 a; Th. 337, 15; Gn. Ex. 65. [Or has gespringan the same meaning as in the following?] Fēwor streámas neirxna wong gesprang *quattuor flumina paradisi instar eructans*, Mt. Kmbl. p. 8, 5. Gisprunt [?] word *eructavit verbum*. Jn. Skt. p. 187, 26.

ge-sprucg *discord, strife;* seditio, Som. 171; Lye.

ge-spryng *a spring.* v. ge-spring.

ge-spunnen *spun;* netus, Som.

ge-spyrian; *p.* ede; *pp.* ed *To track, search, seek:*—Gif man spor gespirige *if one trace a track*, L. Æðelst. 5, 8; Th. i. 236, 20. Loca nū hwæðer ðū wille ðæt wit gespyrigen æfter ǽnigre gesceádwīsnesse further *look now whether you wish us two to seek further after any argument*, Bt. 35, 5; Fox 162, 30, note.

GEST, es; *m.* GUEST, *stranger;* hospes:—For feorme and onfangenysse gesta *propter hospitalitātem atque susceptiōnem hospĭtum*, Bd. 1, 27; S. 489, 8: Exon. 106 a; Th. 404, 30; Rä. 23, 15. Gest hine clǽnsie sylfes āþe on wiofode *let a stranger clear himself with his own oath at the altar*, L. Wih. 20; Th. i. 40, 19. DER. fēðe-gest, inwit-, wil-. v. gæst.

gēst *a ghost, spirit.* v. cear-gēst, gāst.

gestæf-lǽred; *part.* [stæf *a letter;* lǽred *learned; pp. of* lǽran] *Versed in letters, literate, learned, booklearned;* lītĕrātus:—Cild biþ gestæflǽred *a child will be booklearned*, Lchdm. iii. 184, 3: 192, 15: 194, 12.

ge-stælan; *p.* de; *pp.* ed *To set up, put upon, impute, accuse;* statuere, imponere in, imputare, arguere, accusare:—Ge feor hafaþ fǽhþe gestæled *and moreover* [*she*] *hath a deadly feud set up*, Beo. Th. 2685; B. 1340. Ne mæg on me fācnes frum-bearn fyrene gestælan *may not deceit's firstborn* [*the devil*] *impute crime to me*, Exon. 48 a; Th. 166, 18; Gū. 1044. He us ne mæg ǽnige synne gestælan *he cannot accuse us of any sin*, Cd. 21; Th. 25, 10; Gen. 391. Ðȳ læs on me mǽge īdel spellung oððe scondlīc leágung beón gestæled *ne aut fabulæ aut turpi mendacio dignus efficiar*, Nar. 2, 21. v. stælan. [Cf. (?) ge-stal.]

ge-stællan *to stall, stable:*—Ðā hēt he on ðæs pāpan ciericean gestællan his blancan and monig ōðer neát *he ordered his horse and many other cattle to be stabled in the pope's church*, Shrn. 51, 22.

ge-stǽn, es; *n. A groaning:*—Mīn geár wǽron on sīcetunga and on gestǽne *anni mei in gemitibus*, Ps. Th. 30, 11. [Cf. *Ger.* stöhnen.]

ge-stǽnan; *p.* de; *pp.* ed *To stone:*—Stephanus for Godes geleáfan wæs gestǽned *Stephen was stoned for belief in God*, Homl. Th. ii. 82, 21. In ǽ Moises bebeád us duslīc gestǽna *in lege Moses mandavit nobis hujusmodi lapidare*, Jn. Skt. Lind. 8, 5. Forðætt ðætte hiora werc mec gestǽnas *propter quod eorum opus me lapidatis*, Rush. 10, 32. Ðæt folc all gestǽnaþ usig *plebs universa lapidabit nos*, Lk. Skt. Lind. 20, 6. Ōðer gestǽndon *alium lapidaverunt*, Mt. Kmbl. Lind. 21, 35.

ge-stænce. v. ge-stence.

ge-stæppan *to step, go;* ire, ingredi:—Ðǽr nǽnig fira ne mæg fōtum gestæppan *where no man may step with feet*, Salm. Kmbl. 420; Sal. 210: Bt. Met. Fox 20, 279; Met. 20, 140. v. ge-steppan.

gest-ærn, -ern, gyst-ern, es; *n. A guest-place, guest-chamber, an inn;* hospĭtālis aula, hospitium, diversōrium:—Eódon hī on sumes tūngerēfan gestærn *qui intrāvērunt hospĭtium cujusdam villĭci*, Bd. 5, 10; S. 624, 20: Lk. Skt. Lind. Rush. 22, 11.

ge-stæððig; *adj.* [stæðig *firm*] *Steadfast, firm;* stăbĭlis, firmus:—Se ān dēma is gestæððig and beorht *the only judge is steadfast and bright*, Bt. 36, 2; Fox 174, 20: Bt. Met. Fox 24, 84; Met. 24, 42: 29, 171; Met. 29, 87. Ealle gesceafta onfōþ æt ðam gestæððigan Gode, endebyrdnesse, and andwlitan, and gemetgunge *all creatures receive from the steadfast God order, and form, and measure*, Bt. 39, 5; Fox 218, 14.

ge-stæððignes, -stæððines, -ness, -nys, -nyss, e; *f. Gravity, consistency, steadiness, maturity;* grăvitas, constantia, mātūrĭtas:—Wæs he mycelre gestæððignysse wer *multæ grăvĭtātis ac vērĭtātis vir*, Bd. 3, 15; S. 541, 21. On līfes gestæððignesse *in consistency of life*, Past. 13, 1: Swt. 77, 14; Hat. MS. 16 b, 18. Ongan se bisceop lustfullian gestæððinesse his geþohta *dēlectābatur antistes constantia ac mātūrĭtāte cōgĭtātiōnis*, 5, 19; S. 637, 47. v. ge-stæððines.

ge-stæððines *consistency*, Bd. 5, 19; S. 637, 47: Shrn. 168, 2: 175, 28. v. ge-stæððignes.

ge-stal *an obstacle, objection;* objectio, Cot. 144, Lye.

ge-stala, an; *m. A thief;* fur:—Ðæt he ne gestala nǽre *that he was not a thief*, L. In. 25; Th. i. 118, 15.

ge-stalian; *p.* ode; *pp.* od *To steal;* fūrāri:—Gyf gehādod man gestalige *if a man in orders steal*, L. E. G. 3; Th. i. 168, 4, MS. B.

ge-stalu, e; *f.* [stalu *theft*] *Theft;* furtum:—Ylce gestale *for every theft*, L. Ath. iv. 3; Th. i. 222, 22. Oft gē in gestalum stondaþ *oft ye are engaged in thefts* [or gestalum *from* gestala?], Exon. 40 a; Th. 132, 31; Gū. 481.

ge-standan, -stondan; *p.* -stōd, *pl.* -stōdon; *pp.* -standen. I. *to stand, stand still, remain, last, exist, be;* stāre, mānēre, existĕre, esse:—Heó mihte Gode willsumra wīfmonna lāreów and fēster-mōdur gestandan ipsa Deo dēvōtārum māter ac nutrix posset existĕre fēmĭnārum, Bd. 4, 6; S. 574, 17: Ps. Th. 118, 114. Eádig byþ se wer, se ðe him ege Drihtnes, on ferhþcleofan, fæste gestandeþ *beatus vir, qui tĭmet Dŏmĭnum*, 111, 1: 113, 20. He fór eaxlum gestód Deniga freán *he stood before the shoulders of the Danes' lord*, Beo. Th. 722; B. 358: 813; B. 404: Andr. Kmbl. 1414; An. 707. Æðelinga bearn ymbe gestódon *sons of nobles stood around*, Beo. Th. 5188; B. 2597: Rood Kmbl. 126; Kr. 63. His fōtas ǽr fæste gestódan *stĕtĕrunt pĕdes ejus*, Ps. Th. 131, 7: 93, 18. Wese ðín milde mód geswíðed, and me to frófre fæste gestande *fiat nunc mīsĕrĭcordia tua, ut consōlētur me*, 118, 76. Ahsige hú lange seó sibb gestóde *let him ask how long the peace lasted*, Ors. 4, 7; Bos. 88, 6; Bd. 4, 23; S. 594, 40. Ðæt gestód lytle leng ðonne vii hund wintra *that lasted a little longer than seven hundred years*, Ors. 6, 1; Bos. 115, 28, 20. Ðá gestód seó cweorn *the mill stopped*, Shrn. 145, 28. Hǽlend ðá gestód *the Saviour then stood still*, Blickl. Homl. 15, 23: 219, 10. Æfter ðære béne gestóden him mæssan *after the prayer they attended mass*, Homl. Th. ii. 272, 15. Hie on eallum heora lífe orleahtre gestódan *they continued blameless in all their life*, Blickl. Homl. 163, 17, 4. Hie mon to his andweardnesse héht gestandan *they were ordered to stand in his presence*, 173, 11. Siððan hyt gestanden beó *when it be stood*, Herb. 1, 4; Lchdm. i. 72, 8. II. *to stand against any one, oppose, oppress, attack, urge, seize*; insurgĕre, ingruĕre, urgēre, corrĭpĕre:—He á wile ealra feónda gehwone fæste gestandan *he ever will firmly stand against every foe*, Salm. Kmbl. 196; Sal. 97. Forðam me fremde oft fácne gestódon *quŏniam ălieni insurrexĕrunt in me*, Ps. Th. 53, 3. Ne mæg hús náht lange standan on ðam heán múnte, gif hit full ungemetlíc wind gestent *a house cannot long stand on the high mountain if a violent wind press on it*, Bt. 12; Fox 36, 16: 38, 1; Fox 194, 10. Búton ðú gestande ðone unrihtwísan and him his unrihtwísnysse secge *unless thou oppose the unrighteous man and tell him his unrighteousness*, Homl. Th. ii. 340, 23: i. 6, 24. Ðá gestód hine swá micel líchamlíc costung *then so great a temptation of the body assailed him*, ii. 156, 25: 122, 17: Guthl. 20; Gdwn. 80, 5. Wæs heó gestanden mid hefigre untrumysse líchoman *she was seized with a heavy illness*, Bd. 4, 23; S. 595, 16: 5, 13; S. 632, 17: Blickl. Homl. 227, 6. [*Goth.* ga-standan: *O. Sax.* gi-standan.]

ge-stapan; *p.* -stóp, *pl.* -stópon; *pp.* -stapen *To step, go*; gradi, ire, ingredi:—Ðá gestóp he to ánes wealles býge *then he stepped to a bend of a wall*, Ors. 3, 9; Bos. 68, 22: Andr. Kmbl. 3163; An. 1584. DER. stapan.

ge-starian; *p.* ode; *pp.* od [starian *to stare*] *To stare*; rectis ŏcŭlis intuēri:—He gestarode ðǽr gestaðelad wæs æðelíc ingong *he gazed where a noble entrance was placed*, Exon. 12 a; Th. 19, 27; Cri. 307.

gestaðel-fæstan; *p.* -fæste; *pp.* -fæsted [staðel *a foundation*, fæstan *to make fast*] *To found, establish*; stăbĭlīre:—Ic gestaðelfæste *stăbĭlio*, Ælfc. Gr. 30, 5; Som. 34, 54.

ge-staðelian, -staðolian; *p.* ode, ade; *pp.* od, ad [staðelian *to found, establish*] *To found, establish, build, erect, place, settle, strengthen, confirm, fortify, repair, restore*; fundāre, stăbĭlīre, ædĭfĭcāre, collŏcāre, lŏcare, confortāre, confirmāre, restaurāre:—Ðe Eádgár cyng hét Aðelwold gestaðelian *which king Edgar commanded Æthelwold to found*, Chr. 975; Erl. 127, 7: Shrn. 138, 1. Ðæt hí woldan his bán on ðære ylcan stówe búfan eorþan mid gedafenlícre árwurþnesse gesettan and gestaðolian *ut ossa illīus in eodem quĭdem lŏco, sed supra păvīmentum dignæ vĕnĕrātiōnis grātia lŏcārent*, Bd. 4, 30; S. 608, 32. Ðú ná gestaðolast hí *non ædĭfĭcābis eos*, Ps. Lamb. 27, 5: Mt. Bos. 18, 15. Meotud him ðæt mód gestaðelaþ *the Creator strengthens his mind*, Exon. 83 a; Th. 312, 11: Seef. 108. He gestaðolaþ and gemetgaþ ealle gesceafta *he establishes and regulates all creatures*, Bt. 25; Fox 88, 4. Gestrangaþ hý and gestaðeliaþ staðolfæstne geþoht *they strengthen and confirm the steadfast thought*, Salm. Kmbl. 477; Sal. 239. Ic geseó mónan and steorran, ða ðú gestaðelodest *vĭdēbo lunam et stellas, quæ tu fundasti*, Ps. Spl. 8, 4: Ps. Th. 89, 8. Se þe middangeard gestaðelode *he who established the earth*, Andr. Kmbl. 323; An. 162: Cd. 6; Th. 7, 32; Gen. 115: Bd. 3, 23; S. 555, 4: Chr. 920; Erl. 104, 33. Ðǽr me he gestaðelode *ibi me collŏcāvit*, Ps. Spl. 22, 1: Bd. 4, 4; S. 570, 42. Þe wuldres blǽd gestaðolade *who established the increase of glory*, Andr. Kmbl. 1071; An. 536: Exon. 83 a; Th. 312, 3; Seef. 104. Ðe hit gestaðelod wæs *qua fundāta est*, Ex. 9, 18: Ps. Th. 121, 5. Ðǽr gestaðelad wæs æðelíc ingong *where a noble entrance was placed*, Exon. 12 a; Th. 19, 28; Cri. 307: 67 a; Th. 249, 6; Jul. 107. Ðú wǽre gestaðolod þurh me *thou wast confirmed through me*, Soul Kmbl. 90; Seel. 45. Hí ðǽr gestaðelode wǽron *they were settled there*, Bd. 4, 4; S. 571, 1: Ps. Th. 138, 20.

ge-staðolfæstnian *to make firm*; solidare, Rtl. 22, 5.

ge-staðolian *to found, establish, strengthen, confirm*, Bd. 4, 30; S. 608, 32: Ps. Lamb. 27, 5: Bt. 25; Fox 88, 4: Andr. Kmbl. 1071; An. 536: Soul Kmbl. 90; Seel. 45. v. ge-staðelian.

ge-staðolung, e; *f. Firmness, stability*; stăbĭlĭtas:—Ðú ðe staðelodest eorþan ofer gestaðolung his *qui fundasti terram sŭper stăbĭlĭtātem suam*, Ps. Spl. T. 103, 6.

ge-steal, -steall, es; *n. Constitution, frame*:—Eal ðis eorþan gesteal *all this earth's frame*, Exon. 78 a; Th. 293, 2; Wand. 110. [Cf. *O. H. Ger.* gistelli: *Ger.* gestell.]

ge-stealla, an; *m. A companion*; socius. DER. eaxl-, folc-, fyrd-, hand-, lind-, nýd-, will-gestealla. v. steal, steallian.

ge-steald, es; *n. A settled place, a station, dwelling-place, an abode*; stătio, dŏmĭcilium:—He lífes gesteald sceáwode *he beheld life's dwelling-place*, Exon. 12 a; Th. 19, 22; Cri. 304. Ðæt he walde wídanferhþ écra gestealda *that he shall rule for ever the eternal abodes*, Elen. Kmbl. 1601; El. 802.

gestéd-hors, es; *n.* [stéda *a steed*] *A stallion*; ĕquus admissārius *vel* ēmissārius:—He ðone cyng bæd ðæt he him wǽpen sealde and gestédhors *rŏgāvit sibi rēgem arma dăre et ĕquum ēmissārum*, Bd. 2, 14; S. 517, 5.

ge-stefnan; *p.* de; *pp.* ed [stefnian *to institute*] *To institute, place, fix*; instĭtuĕre:—Freá engla héht wesan wæter gemǽne, stówe gestefnde *the lord of angels bade the waters to be common, and their places fixed*, Cd. 8; Th. 10, 21; Gen. 160.

ge-stelan *to steal*; furari, Jn. Skt. Lind. 10, 10.

ge-stenc, es; *n. Odour, smell*; odor:—Svoetnisse gistencs *suavitatem odoris*, Rtl. 3, 20: 12, 15.

ge-stence, -stænce; *adj. Fragrant, odorous*:—He hafaþ hwítne wyrtruman and swýðe gestencne [-stæncne, MS. B.] *it has a white and very fragrant root*, Herb. 156, 1; Lchdm. i. 282, 19.

ge-stencniss, e; *f. Odour*; odor, Rtl. 3, 22.

ge-steóran; *p.* de; *pp.* ed *To steer, direct, control, correct*; contĭnēre, corrĭgĕre:—Híg wistan ðæt híg ne mihton manegum gesteóran *they knew that they might not control many*, L. E. G. prm; Th. i. 116, 14. Ðú his ýþum miht ána gesteóran *mōtum fluctuum ejus tu mītĭgas*, Ps. Th. 88, 8: Bt. 16, 4; Fox 58, 15. v. ge-stýran.

ge-stépan; *p.* -stépte; *pp.* -stépt [stépan *to raise*]. I. *to set erect, raise*; ērĭgĕre:—Syndon ða fóreweallas fægre gestépte *the forewalls are fairly raised*, Cd. 158; Th. 196, 26; Exod. 297. II. *to assist, sustain, support, help*; sublĕvāre, sustentāre, fulcīre, auxĭlĭāri:—He gestépte sunu Ohtheres *he supported Ohthere's son*, Beo. Th. 4766; B. 2393.

ge-steped *stepped, introduced*; initiatus, Cot. 108; *pp. of* ge-steppan. v. steppan.

ge-steppan, -stæppan; *p.* -stepede = -stepte? *pp.* -steped = -stept? *To step, go*; gradi, ire, incedere:—Ðǽr nǽnig fira ne mæg fótum gestæppan *where no man may step with feet*, Salm. Kmbl. 420; Sal. 210: Bt. Met. Fox 20, 279; Met. 20, 140. For hwí geunrótsod gesteppe ic oððe gá ic *quare contristatus incedo*, Ps. Lamb. 42, 10. Gistepe ue *gradiamur*, Rtl. 51, 9. Gesteped *initiatus*, Cot. 108.

gest-ern, es; *n. A guest-place, guest-chamber*:—Ðæt gestern *dĭversōrium*, Lk. Skt. Lind. Rush. 22, 11. v. gest-ærn.

gest-hús, es; *n. A guest-house, guest-chamber*; hospĭtium:—Gán we sécan úre gesthús *let us go and seek our hostel*, Th. Apol. 18, 16. In gest-húsum *in hospitiis*, Ps. Surt. 54, 16. v. gæst-hús.

ge-stician, -sticcian; *p.* ode, ede; *pp.* od, ed [stician *to stick*] *To stick, pierce, transfix*:—Hét mon me ðæt ic ðone swile gesticode *jussĕrunt me incīdĕre tŭmōrem illum*, Bd. 4, 19; S. 589, 1. Gebýreþ ðæt ðæt mód wierþ gesticced mid ðære scylde gielpes *it happens that the mind is pierced by the sin of boasting*, Past. 33, 2; Swt. 217, 6; Hat. MS. 41 b, 1.

ge-stiéran; *p.* de; *pp.* ed *To correct*; corrĭgĕre:—He him nolde gestiéran *he would not correct him*, L. In. 50; Th. i. 134, 5. v. ge-stýran.

gestig; *adj. Strange*:—Huonne ðec we ségon gestig *quando te vidimus hospitem*, Mt. Kmbl. Lind. 25, 38.

ge-stígan; *p.* -stág, -stáh, *pl.* -stigon; *pp.* -stigen *To mount, ascend, descend*:—He me wolde on gestígan *he would mount upon me* [*the cross*], Rood Kmbl. 68; Kr. 34. In écne geard up gestígan *to mount up to the eternal abode*, Exon. 44 a; Th. 149, 18; Gú. 763. Ðonne gestíge ic ofer ðone *then will I ascend upon it*, Blickl. Homl. 183, 4. Ðætte gestíge *ut descendat*, Rtl. 98, 10. Of dúne gestígdes ðú *descendes*, Mt. Kmbl. Lind. 11, 23. Ðæt we to ðam hýhstan hrófe gestígan *that we may mount to the highest roof*, Exon. 18 b; Th. 47, 3; Cri. 749. Ðá ic on holm gestáh *when I went on the main*, Beo. Th. 1269; B. 632: Cd. 69; Th. 82, 29; Gen. 1369. Mihtig god on hira ánne gestág *the mighty God mounted on to one of them* [*trees*], Exon. 25 a; Th. 72, 13; Cri. 1172. Siððan ðú gestígest steápe dúne *after thou dost mount the lofty hills*, Cd. 137; Th. 172, 32; Gen. 2853: 227; Th. 303, 14; Sal. 612. Beddreste gestáh *mounted the couch*, 102; Th. 135, 25; Gen. 2248. Ród ðe ic ǽr gestág *the cross which I mounted before*, Exon. 29 b; Th. 91, 15; Cri. 1492. Ic ðis lond gestág *I have reached this land*, 37 a; Th. 120, 28; Gú. 278: 15 a; Th. 32, 18; Cri. 514. [*Goth.* ga-steigan *to ascend, descend*: *O. Sax.* gi-stígan *with acc. and with prepositions.*]

ge-stihtian, -stihtan, -stitian; *p.* ode, ade, ede; *pp.* od, ad, ed [stihtian *to dispose*] *To dispose, order, determine*; dispōnĕre, appōnĕre:—Sunu unrihtwísnesse ne geýcþ oððe ne gestihteþ derian hine *fīlius inīquĭtātis non appōnet nŏcēre eum*, Ps. Lamb. 88, 23. Ic gestihtode *dispŏsui*, Ps. Vos. 72, 25. Gestihtade he and funde ðæt he wolde land-fyrde ðider gelǽdan *terrestri quĭdem ĭtĭnĕre illo vĕnīre dispōnēbat*, Bd. 3, 15; S. 541,

26. Mellitus and Justus gestihtedon ðæt heó ðǽr wolden ðære wīsan ende gebīdan *Mellitus ac Justus ibi rērum finem expectāre dispōnentes*, 2, 5; S. 507, 35. Ðæt cūþ is ðæt ðæt mid Drihtnes mihte gestihtad wæs *quod Dŏmĭni nūtu dispŏsĭtum esse constat*, 1, 14; S. 482, 41: Ors. 6, 21; Bos. 123, 31.

ge-stihtung, e; *f.* [stihtung *a disposing*] *A dispensing, disposing, providence*; dispŏsĭtio, prōvĭdentia:—Fram Godes gestihtunge *by God's providence*, Ors. 2, 1; Bos. 39, 3.

ge-stillan, -styllan; *p.* de; *pp.* ed [stillan *to rest*]. **I.** *v. intrans. To rest, cease, be still, quiet, mute*; quiescĕre, sēdāri, sĭlēre, obmutescĕre, rĕtĭcēre:—Hī ne mōten ǽfre gestillan *they may not ever be still*, Bt. Met. Fox 11, 51; Met. 11, 26. Seó gecyndelīce hǽtu gestilleþ on ðē *the natural heat shall be quiet in thee*, Blickl. Homl. 7, 28. Se wuldor-maga worda gestilde *the illustrious man ceased from words*, Exon. 48 b; Th. 167, 29; Gū. 1067: Andr. Kmbl. 1064; An. 532. On Sæterdæg hīg gestildon *sabbăto sĭluērunt*, Lk. Bos. 23, 56. Tantalus gestilde *Tantalus became quiet*, Bt. 35, 6; Fox 170, 2. Sūwa, and gestil *tăce obmūtesce*, Mk. Bos. 4, 39. He bebeád ðæm winde ðæt he gestilde *he commanded the wind to be still*, Blickl. Homl. 235, 8. Ic bebeóde ðē ðæt ðū fram ðisse ungeþwǽrnysse gestille *I command thee to cease from this troubling*, Guthl. 8; Gdwn. 48, 17. **II.** *v. trans. To restrain, still, stop, stay, calm, keep in*; compescĕre, cŏhĭbēre, sēdāre, mītĭgāre, rĕtĭnēre:—Hilde calla hēht ða folctogan fyrde gestillan *the herald of war bade the folk-leaders make the army still*, Cd. 156; Th. 194, 2; Exod. 254. Ða hāt-heortan hie mid nāne fōreþonce nyllaþ gestillan *the furious will not calm themselves with reflection*, Past. 40, 6; Swt. 297, 4; Hat. MS. 55 b, 7. Hwā gestilleþ ðæt *who shall still that?* Exon. 101 b; Th. 384, 30; Rä. 4, 35. Hī ðone storm gestildon *tempestātem sēdārent*, Bd. 3, 15; S. 541, 17. Hæfde Metod regn gestilled *the Creator had stilled the rain*, Cd. 71; Th. 85, 18; Gen. 1416: Salm. Kmbl. 236; Sal. 117.

ge-stincan; *p.* -stanc, *pl.* -stuncon; *pp.* -stuncen *To perceive by the sense of smelling*; olfacere aliquid, odorare, odorari:—Nas-þeorlu oððe nōsa hī habbaþ, and hīg ne gestincaþ *nostrils or noses they have, and they smell not*, Ps. Lamb. second 113, 6. Hī nōse habbaþ nāwiht gestincaþ *they have a nose [and] smell naught*, Ps. Th. 134, 17. Sume māgon gehīran, sume gestincan *some can hear, some smell*, Bt. 41, 5; Fox 252, 24. Ðonne gē ða swētan stencas gestincaþ *when ye smell the sweet odours*, Blickl. Homl. 59, 3. Hī ðæs landes lyft gestuncon *they smelt the air of the land*, Bd. 1, 1; S. 474, 35. Hī nā gestingcaþ [= gestincaþ] *they smell not*, Ps. Spl. 113, 14.

ge-stióran; *p.* de; *pp.* ed *To correct, restrain, direct, guide*; corrĭgĕre:—Wēnst ðū ðæt se anwald eáðe ne meahte Godes Ælmihtiges him his yfeles gestióran *thinkest thou that the power of Almighty God could not keep him from his evil*, Bt. Met. Fox 9, 104; Met. 9, 52. v. ge-stȳran.

ge-stir, -stirian. v. ge-styr, -styrian.

ge-stīran; *p.* de; *pp.* ed *To correct, restrain*; corrĭgĕre, cŏhĭbēre:—Forðæm ðæt ða wītu gestīrdon [gestīrden, MS. Cot.] ōðrum ðæt hī swā dōn ne dorsten *in order that the punishments might restrain others from daring to do so*, Bt. 39, 11; Fox 230, 7. v. ge-stȳran.

ge-stīðian; *p.* ode, ude; *pp.* od, ud *To become hard, strong*; indurare:—Gistīðia *induratam*, Rtl. 102, 41. Mægen on him weōx and gestīðode *his power waxed and was strengthened*, Guthl. 2; Gdwn. 12, 26. Ðā dā he gestīðod wæs *when he was grown up*, Homl. Th. ii. 38, 3.

ge-stitian; *p.* ode; *pp.* od *To dispose, order*; dispōnĕre:—Ða he gestitode to Abrahame *quod dispŏsuit ad Abraham*, Ps. Spl. C. 104, 8: Ps. Spl. T. 102, 12. v. ge-stihtian.

gest-līð; *adj. Hospitable*; hospitalis, Som.

gest-līðnes, -ness, -nyss, e; *f. Hospitableness, hospitality*; hospĭtālĭtas:—Ðā se fōresprecena Godes man fela daga mid him wæs on gestlīðnesse *cum prǽfātus clērĭcus alĭquot diēbus ăpud eum hospĭtārētur*, Bd. 1, 7; S. 477, 6. On gestlīðnysse *in hospitality*, 1, 7; S. 476, 37: 477, 16: 1, 27; S. 489, 26. v. gæst-līðnes.

ge-stondan. v. ge-standan.

ge-stōp *stepped, went*, Ors. 3, 9; Bos. 68, 22; *p. of* ge-stapan.

gestor-dæge *yesterday*; heri, Jn. Skt. Rush. 4, 52.

gestran-dæg *yesterday*; hesterna dies, Ps. Vos. 89, 4. v. gyrstan-dæg.

ge-strangian, -strongian; *p.* ode, ade; *pp.* od, ad [strangian *to strengthen*] *To make strong, strengthen, confirm, establish*; rōbŏrāre, corrōbŏrāre, confortāre, confirmāre:—Ðā wolde he heora geleáfan gestrangian and getrymman *then would he strengthen and confirm their belief*, Homl. Th. i. 152, 34. Ic gestrangige *confirmo*, Cod. Dipl. Kmbl. iii. 349, 26: 350, 34. Ic heortan mannes gestrangie *ego cor hominis confirmo*, Th. Anal. 29, 1. Earm mīn gestrangaþ hine *brachium meum confortābit eum*, Ps. Spl. 88, 21: Salm. Kmbl. 477; Sal. 239. He gestrangode hī *illos confortāvĕrit*, Bd. 1, 23; S. 485, 16. Bebeód Iosue and gestranga hine *prǽcĭpe Iosue et corrōbŏra eum*, Deut. 3, 28. Ne biþ gestrangod man *non confortēmur hŏmo*, Ps. Spl. 9, 20: Ps. Th. 138, 4, 15. Wes ðū gestrangad and ne ondrǽd ðū ðē *be thou strengthened and fear not*, Blickl. Homl. 231, 2: Lk. Bos. 1, 80. Israēla folc wǽron swȳðe gestrangode *filii Israel sunt rōbŏrāti nĭmis*, Ex. 1, 7: Ors. 6, 35; Bos. 131, 1.

ge-streágung, e; *f. Vegetatio*, Hpt. Gl. 440.

ge-streáwian, -streówian; *p.* ode; *pp.* od *To strew*:—Swylc hit eall gestreáwod wǽre mid wynsume blōstmen and wyrtgemangum *as if it all were strewed with pleasant flowers and spices*, Shrn. 15, 31.

ge-streccan; *p.* -streahte, -strehte; *pp.* -streaht, -streht *To stretch, spread*; sternere:—Wel gestreht bed *a well spread bed*, Lchdm. iii. 208, 4. v. streccan

ge-stredd; *part. p. Sprinkled*; sale conditus, Lye.

ge-streht *spread*; *pp. of* ge-streccan.

ge-strengan; *pp.* ed *To strengthen*; confortare:—Se cnæht gestrenced wes *puer confortebatur*, Lk. Skt. Lind. 1, 80.

ge-streón, -strión, es; *n. Gain, product, emolument, wealth, riches, treasure, usury, business*; merces, mercātus, quæstus, lucrum, ēmŏlŭmentum, ōpes, thesaurus, ūsūra, nĕgōtium:—Gestreón *quæstus* vel *lucrum*, Ælfc. Gl. 114; Som. 80, 6; Wrt. Voc. 60, 42. Swunce māre se ðe unriht gestreón on his handa stōde *he should toil more, in whose hands lay the unjust gain*, L. Eth. ii. 9; Th. i. 290, 5. Sunu gestreónes wæstm innoðes *filii mercis fructus ventris*, Ps. Spl. 126, 4. Fæderes gestreónes *patrĭmōnii*, Mone B. 3568. Ic hit witodlīce mid gestreóne onfēnge *cum ūsūris ŭtĭque exegissem illam*, Lk. Bos. 19, 23. Fram gestreóne *a nĕgōtio*, Ps. Spl. 90, 6. Mathusal magum dǽlde æðelinga gestreón *Mathuselah distributed the chieftains' treasure to his brethren*, Cd. 52; Th. 65, 24; Gen. 1071: Bt. Met. Fox 8, 115, Met. 8, 58. Gestreóne *mercātu*, Mone B. 2588. Hȳ beóþ rūmmōde ryhtra gestreóna *they are liberal of just gains*, Exon. 33 b; Th. 106, 31; Gū. 49: 105 b; Th. 402, 18; Rä. 21, 31: 107 b; Th. 410, 23; Rä. 29, 3. Ðæt he æfter him to eallum his gestreónum fēnge *that he should take all his riches after him*, Ors. 5, 13; Bos. 112, 32. Æfter filiende gestreón *sĕcūtūra ēmŏlŭmenta*, Mone B. 623. Gehlōdon him hordwearda gestreón *they loaded on themselves the riches of the treasure-wards*, Cd. 174; Th. 220, 3; Dan. 65: 208; Th. 257, 31; Dan. 666: 209; Th. 260, 4; Dan. 704. Gestreón *usura*, Blickl. Gloss. Fram gestreóne gangendum *a negotio perambulante*, id. Ic wylle heora cȳpan hēr luflīcor ðonne ic gebicge ðǽr ðæt sum gestreón me ic begyte *volo vendere hic carius quam emi illic ut aliquod lucrum mihi adquiram*, Th. Anal. 27, 21. [*O. Sax.* gi-striuni: *O. H. Ger.* ki-striuni *lucrum*.]

ge-streónan; *p.* de; *pp.* ed *To gain, get, obtain, acquire*; lucrāri, acquīrĕre:—Heora Criste sāule gestreónan *suas Christo anĭmas lucrāri*, Hymn. Surt. 73, 7. Ðǽr is cūþre līf ðonne we on eorþan mǽgen ǽfre gestreónan *there is a life more glorious than we may ever obtain on earth*, Cd. 226; Th. 302, 11; Sat. 597. Ðæt he manige þeóde ūrum Drihtne þurh his lāre gestreónde *so that he gained many a nation for our Lord by his teaching*, Blickl. Homl. 121, 10.

ge-streónful; *adj. Full of riches, copious, expensive, precious, sumptuous*; sumptuōsus:—Gestreónfulre *sumptuōsā*, Mone B. 3566. Gestreónful *copiosus, fructuosus*, Hpt. Gl. 443, 452, 491. His ða leófan and ða gestreónfullan bearn *his beloved and precious children*, Blickl. Homl. 131, 27.

ge-stric, es; *m? Strife, mutiny, sedition*; sēdĭtio:—Gesihþ león wēdan feóndes gestric getācnaþ *the sight of a mad lion betokens sedition of an enemy*, Lchdm. iii. 206, 33.

ge-strician; *p.* ede *To knit*:—Gestricedon netta hiora *reficiebant retia sua*, Mt. Kmbl. Lind. 4, 21. [Cf. *Ger.* stricken.]

ge-strīnan, -striénan; *p.* de; *pp.* ed *To obtain, get, acquire, beget, procreate*; acquīrĕre, gignĕre, procreāre:—Ðæt gē me mid rihte gestrīnan māgon *what ye may justly acquire for me*, L. Ath. i. prm; Th. i. 196, 16. Se ðe bearn gestriéneþ *he who begets a child*, L. In. 27; Th. i. 120, 2: L. Alf. pol. 8; Th. i. 66, 19. Ðe hit on fruman gestrīndon *who first acquired it*, 41; Th. i. 88, 19. v. ge-strȳnan.

ge-strión, es; *n. Gain, wealth*; merces, ōpes:—Gió-monna gestrión sealdon unwillum ēðelweardas *the country's guardians unwillingly gave up the wealth of men of old*, Bt. Met. Fox 1, 46; Met. 1, 23. v. ge-streón.

ge-strod, es; *n. Banishment*; proscriptio, Cot. 194.

ge-strod, es; *n. Plunder* [?], *wealth*:—Ðæt hī ðȳ ēþ mǽgen heora unriht gewitt forþbringan hī sind mid gifum and mid gestreónum [Cot. gestrodum] gefyrðrode *flagitiosum facinus ad efficiendum præmiis incitari*, Bt. 3, 4; Fox 6, note 7. [Cf. ge-strūdan.]

ge-strogdniss, e; *f. A sprinkling*; conspersio, Rtl. 25, 15.

ge-strongian; *p.* ode, ade; *pp.* od, ad *To strengthen*; corrōbŏrāre:—Ceadwala wæs gestrongad *Ceadwalla was strengthened*, Bd. 4, 16; S. 584, 4. v. ge-strangian.

ge-strūdan; *p.* -streád, *pl.* -strudon; *pp.* -stroden *To destroy, plunder*; rapere, spoliare:—Godes cwide helle gestrūdeþ *God's word destroyeth hell*, Salm. Kmbl. 148; Sal. 73. Feoh gestrūdaþ *they destroy the cattle*, Salm. Kmbl. 310; Sal. 154. Ða wīgan gestrudon [MS. gestrudan] gestreóna *the warriors plundered the treasures*, Cd. 174; Th. 219, 27; Dan. 61. v. strūdan.

ge-strȳnan, -streónan, -strīnan, -striénan; *p.* de; *pp.* ed [gestreón *gain*] *To gain, get, obtain, acquire, beget, procreate*; lucrāri, acquīrĕre, gignĕre, procreāre:—Ðæs ðe ic mōste mīnum leóde swylc gestrȳnan *because I have been able to acquire such for my people*, Beo. Th. 5589; B. 2798: L. Ath. i. prm; Th. i. 196, 18: Homl. Th. ii. 46, 14. Ic gestrȳne *gigno*, Ælfc. Gr. 28, 3; Som. 30, 57. Nǣnig fira tō fela gestrȳneþ *no man gains too much*, Exon. 91 a; Th. 342, 17; Gn. Ex. 144: L. C. S. 85; Th. i. 424, 13. Ðæt hȳ mid rihte gestrȳnaþ *what they lawfully acquire*, L. Edg. S. 2; Th. i. 274, 3: Exon. 61 b; Th. 225, 21; Ph. 392. Ðīn pund gestrȳnde tyn pund *mna tua dĕcem mnas acquīsīvit*, Lk. Bos. 19, 16, 18: Mt. Bos. 25, 16, 17, 20: Ps. Spl. 77, 59. He worn gestrȳnde suna and dōhtra *he begat several sons and daughters*, Cd. 62; Th. 74, 11; Gen. 1220: Mt. Bos. 1, 2–16. Ðeáh he ealne middaneard gestrȳne *si mundum ūnĭversum lucrētur*, 16, 26: Mk. Bos. 8, 36. Ic hæbbe gestrȳned ōðre twā *alia duo lucrātus sum*, Mt. Bos. 25, 22.

ge-strȳnedlīc, -strȳnendlīc; *adj. Producing, genitive;* genitivus:—Gestrȳnendlīc oððe geāgniendlīc *genitive or possessive*, Ælfc. Gr. 7; Som. 6, 17.

ge-strynge, es; *m. A wrestler, champion;* athleta:—Gestrynga plegstōw *a place of wrestlers, a theatre;* athletarum locus, Cot. 151. [Cf. strang.]

gest-sele, gyst-sele, es; *m. A guest-hall;* hospĭtālis aula:—Ðe gestsele gyredon *who prepared the guest-hall*, Beo. Th. 1992; B. 994.

ge-stun, es; *n.* [stunian *to stun*] *A noise, stun, crash, whirlwind;* strĕpĭtus, frăgor, turbo:—Ðæt gestun and se storm brecaþ brāde gesceaft *the stun and the storm shall break the broad creation*, Exon. 22 b; Th. 61, 27; Cri. 991. Of gestune *from the whirlwind*, 102 a; Th. 386, 3; Rä. 4, 56. Þurh gestun *per turbĭnem*, Cot. 157.

ge-stuncon *smelt*, Bd. 1, 1; S. 474, 35; *p. pl. of* ge-stincan.

ge-stund, es; *n. A noise, din:*—Hī swā ungemetlīcum gestundum fōron ðæt him þūhte ðæt hit eall betweox heofone and eorþan hleóðrode ðām egeslīcum stefnum *they came with such immoderate noises that it seemed to him that between heaven and earth it all resounded with their voices*, Guthl. 5; Gdwn. 36, 28.

ge-stungen; *part.* [stungen, *pp. of* stingan *to pierce*] *Pierced;* transfixus:—He wæs mid spere on his sȳdan gestungen *he was pierced in his side with a spear*, L. E. I. 21; Th. ii. 416, 31.

ge-styllan; *p.* de; *pp.* ed *To still, calm;* sēdāre:—Se eorl gestylde ðæt folc *the earl stilled the people*, Chr. 1052; Erl. 187, 3. v. ge-stillan II.

ge-styllan; *p.* de *To spring, move rapidly:*—Hwīlum he to eorþan gestylde *at times he descended to earth*, Exon. 17 a; Th. 40, 34; Cri. 648. Cyning engla munt gestylleþ gehleápeþ heá dūne *the king of angels shall mount a hill, shall leap the high downs*, 18 a; Th. 45, 9; Cri. 716. [Cf. a-stellan.]

ge-styltan; *p.* te *To be astonished, to be silent from astonishment:*—Gestylton ɫ gesuīgdon alle *stupebant omnes*, Mt. Kmbl. Lind. 12, 23. Folc gestylte [gistylted wæs, Rush.] *populus stupefactus est*, Mk. Skt. Lind. 9, 15. Gestyldon aldro *stupuerunt parentes*, Lk. Skt. Lind. 8, 56. v. ge-stillan [?].

ge-styr, -stir, es; *n. Movement, action:*—Gestir *actio*, Rtl. 187, 15.

ge-stȳran, -stīran, -steóran, -stióran, -stiéran; *p.* de; *pp.* ed [stȳran *to steer, rule*] *To steer, direct, rule, correct, restrain, withhold;* rĕgĕre, corrĭgĕre, cŏhĭbēre, rĕtĭnēre:—Meaht ðū Adame eft gestȳran *thou mightest afterwards rule Adam*, Cd. 27; Th. 36, 8; Gen. 568: Ors. 3, 1; Bos. 52, 36. Hām cymeþ nefne him holm gestȳreþ *he will come home unless the ocean restrains him*, Exon. 90 b; Th. 340, 5; Gn. Ex. 106. Gif him Scipio ne gestȳrde *if Scipio had not withheld them*, Ors. 4, 9; Bos. 91, 18: Judth. 10; Thw. 22, 13; Jud. 60. Forstond ðū mec and gestȳr him *protect thou me and correct them*, Exon. 118 b; Th. 455, 31; Hy. 4, 58.

ge-styreniss, e; *f. Trouble, tribulation;* tribulatio, Rtl. 40, 39.

ge-styrian, -stirian; *p.* ede; *pp.* ed [ge, styrian *to move, stir*] *To move, remove, excite, agitate;* amovere, agitare:—Nælle ðū gestyrege hine *noli vexare illum*, Lk. Skt. Lind. 8, 49. Biþ gestyred hiora orsorgnes [MS. orsorgnesse] *their prosperity will be removed*, Bt. 38, 2; Fox 196, 23. Ðū wǣre stronge gestyred *thou wast strongly excited*, Exon. 98 a; Th. 369, 22; Seel. 45. Ðā wearþ swīðe gestired se here ongeán ðone biscop forðan ðe he nolde heom nān feoh behāten *then was the [Danish] army very much excited against the bishop because he would not promise them any money*, Chr. 1012; Erl. 146, 12. Mægna ða ðe sint in heofnum gestyred bīþon *virtutes quæ sunt in cælis movebuntur*, Mk. Skt. Lind. 13, 25. Forhuon arogie gestyred *quid turbamini*, 5, 39: Mt. Kmbl. Lind. 24, 6: Jn. Skt. Lind. 12, 27. Dōhter mīn from diwble is gestyred *filia mea a dæmonio vexatur*, Mt. Kmbl. Lind. 15, 22.

ge-sufel; *adj.* A word of uncertain meaning, but descriptive of a certain kind of bread:—Ǣlc gegilda gesylle ǣnne gesufelne hlāf *let each gild-brother give a 'gesufel' loaf*, L. Æthelst. 5, 8; Th. i. 236, 36. Mon geselle cxx gesufira hlāfa *let cxx 'gesufel' loaves be given*, Th. Ch. 460, 32: 469, 3. v. sufel.

ge-sūgian; *p.* ode; *pp.* od *To be silent;* tăcēre:—Gif ðū gesūgian meahte *if thou mightest be silent*, Bt. 18, 4; Fox 68, 4, MS. Cot. Gesūgode he *he was silent*, 17; Fox 58, 21, MS. Cot. v. ge-swīgian.

ge-suirfed *polished, filed;* politus, Som.

ge-sund; *adj. Sound, healthy, entire, unhurt, safe, favourable, prosperous;* sanus, integer, salvus, incolumis, prosper, felix:—Ðæs ðe hī hyne gesundne geseón mōston *for that they might see him sound*, Beo. Th. 3260; B. 1628: Exon. 74 a; Th. 276, 19; Jul. 568: 42 b; Th. 144, 4; Gū. 673: 23 b; Th. 66, 21; Cri. 1075. Beó gesund *ave, salve:* Beóþ gesunde *avete, salvete*, Ælfc. Gr. 33; Som. 37, 42, 43. He cwæþ 'Wel gesund hlāford apolloni' *he said 'All hail, lord Apollonius*,' Th. Apol. 7, 21. Ðā cwæþ he to ānum cnapan 'Swā ðū gesund sȳ sege me' *then said he to a boy 'So be thou in health, tell me*, 6, 19. Hīg cōmon gesunde to hȳde *they came to port safe and sound*, Shrn. 147, 10. Hȳ beóþ ðȳ gesundran *they will be the healthier*, Exon. 107 a; Th. 408, 28; Rä. 27, 19. Ðæt ic ðē lǣte brūcan since gesundne *that I will let thee enjoy wealth uninjured*, Cd. 126; Th. 161. 14; Gen. 2665. Ðonne beón hīg ealle gesunde *cunctus populus salvabitur*, Deut. 20, 11. On ðære stōwe we gesunde māgon bīdan *in that place we may abide safe*, Cd. 117; Th. 152, 20; Gen. 2523: Exon. 27 b; Th. 82, 21; Cri. 1342: Beo. Th. 641; B. 318. Eálā ðū, Dryhten mīn, dō us gesunde *fac, O Domine, bene prosperare*. Ps. Th. 117, 23: Elen. Grm. 996: 1005. [*O. Sax.* gi-sund: *O. H. Ger.* ge-sunt: *Ger.* ge-sund.] DER. sund.

ge-sund-ful, -full; *adj. Full* or *quite sound, prosperous, successful;* prospĕrus:—Gesundfull sīþfæt dō us, God *prospĕrum ĭter făciet nōbis Deus*, Ps. Spl. 67, 21. His swīðre hand is gesundfull ōþ ðis *his right hand is sound to this day*, Swt. A. S. Rdr. 98, 85.

ge-sundfullian; *p.* ode; *pp.* od *To be made prosperous, to be successful;* prosperari:—Swā hwæt swā he dēþ beóþ gesundfullode *quæcumque faciet prosperabuntur*, Ps. Lamb. 1, 3. Gesundfulla *prosperare*, Ps. Spl. C. 117, 24.

ge-sundfullīc; *adj. Safe, sound:*—Ne biþ ǣfre ōwiht gesundfullīces in ðam deófle *there is never aught sound in the devil*, Shrn. 38, 35.

ge-sundfullīce; *superl.* -līcost; *adv. Safely, securely, successfully, prosperously;* tūte, prospĕre:—Hī to ðisum īglande gesundfullīce becōmon *they came safely to this island*, Homl. Th. ii. 128, 16. Begȳm gesundfullīce *intende prospĕre*, Ps. Spl. 44, 5. Hió færþ gesundfullīcost *it goes most securely*, Bt. 39, 7; Fox 222, 22.

ge-sundfulnes, -fullnes, -ness, -nys, -nyss, e; *f. Soundness, healthiness, prosperity;* sānĭtas corpŏris, prospĕrĭtas:—On ðīnre gesundfulnesse *in thy health*, Bt. 6; Fox 14, 35. Se oferdrenc fordēþ untwīlīce ðæs mannes sāwle and his gesundfullnysse *over-drinking surely destroys a man's soul and his soundness*, Ælfc. T. 43, 16. Ne breác se ārleásа Herodes his cynerīces mid langsumere gesundfullnysse *the impious Herod did not enjoy his kingdom in long health*, Homl. Th. i. 84, 34.

ge-sundig; *adj. Prosperous, favourable;* prospĕrus, sĕcundus:—Gesundige windas *sĕcundi venti*, Bd. 5, 1; S. 614, 9. v. ge-sundlīce.

ge-sundlīce; *adv. Prosperously;* prospere:—Gesundlīce *prosperare* [= *prospere?*], Ps. Spl. 117, 24. We ða niht on ðære wīcstōwe gesundlīce wīcodon *we stopped safely in the camp that night;* quieta nox fuit usque ad lucem, Nar. 21, 30.

ge-sundrian; *p.* ode; *pp.* od [sundrian, syndrian *to sunder*] *To separate, divide, sunder;* sēpărāre, discēdĕre, disjungĕre:—Gesundrode sigora Waldend leóht wið þeóstrum *the Lord of triumphs sundered light from darkness*, Cd. 6; Th. 8, 18; Gen. 126: 8; Th. 9, 13; Gen. 141. Gesundrod wæs lago wið lande *water was separated from land*, 8; Th. 10, 26; Gen. 162. Of sceádes ɫ gesundras *definiens*, Mt. Kmbl. p. 12, 13. Ðū ðe gesundradest *qui destinasti*, Rtl. 56, 31.

ge-sūpan; *p.* -seáp, *pl.* -supon; *pp.* -sopen *To sup, sip, suck up, absorb;* absorbēre:—Wēn is ðæt hī us woldan wætre gelīce sōna gesūpan *forsĭtan vĕlut aqua absorbuissent nos*, Ps. Th. 123, 3.

ge-suppan *to taste:*—Hia ðæt gebirigdon ɫ gesupedon *gustaturos*, Mk. Skt. p. 4, 3. v. suppan.

ge-sūwian *to be silent.* v. ge-swīgian.

ge-swāc *ceased, rested from*, Mt. Bos. 14, 32: Gen. 2, 3; *p. of* ge-swīcan.

ge-swælan; *p.* de; *pp.* ed, ud *To light, kindle;* inflammare, accendere:—Geswælud spoon [= spōn, *q. v.*] *vel* tynder *kindled chips* or *tinder;* fomes, Ælfc. Gl. 60; Som. 68, 35; Wrt. Voc. 39, 21.

ge-swæncan; *p.* te; *pp.* ed *To afflict, oppress;* afflīgĕre, opprĭmĕre:—Ða he gelomlīce geswæncte *whom he repeatedly oppressed*, Chr. 1105; Erl. 240, 11. v. ge-swencan.

ge-swǣpa, -swǣpo; *pl. n. Sweepings;* peripsema, sordes, Cot. 149, 169. Geswāpa *ruina* vel *rudera*, Ælfc. Gl. 17; Som. 58, 96; Wrt. Voc. 22, 12. v. æsce-geswāp.

ge-swǣre, es; *n. Heaviness, affliction:*—Gisuoere *afflictionem*, Rtl. 41, 37. [Cf. *O. H. Ger.* swāri: *Ger.* schwere *weight*.]

ge-swǣre; *adj. Heavy, oppressed, afflicted:*—He lǣrde ǣlcne man ðe geswǣre and ofercumen, and eft gefriþod byþ, ðæt he swā ylce Gode þancode *he taught every man that is oppressed and overcome, and afterwards is saved, that he in the same way should thank God*, Ps. Th. 47, argument. [*O. H. Ger.* ge-swar.] v. ge-swǣre, *subst; and* swǣr.

ge-swǣs; *adj. Dear, familiar, kind;* cārus, fămĭlĭāris, blandus:—He geceás Iudan him, geswǣs frumcynn *elēgit trĭbus Juda*, Ps. Th. 77, 67.

Iohannes mid geswǽsum wordum ðæt folc tihte *John exhorted the people with kind words*, Homl. Th. i. 70, 34.

ge-swǽslǽcan; *p.* -lǽhte; *pp.* -lǽht *To flatter*; blandīri :—Ic geswǽslǽce *blandior*, Ælfc. Gr. 31; Som. 35, 49.

ge-swǽsnys, se; *f. A sweet word, a compliment, an enticement, allurement, a dainty*; blanditia :—Geswǽsnyssa *blanditiæ*, Ælfc. Gr. 13; Som. 16, 17.

ge-swǽtan; *p.* te *To sweat* :—Heó nā ne geswǽtte *she did not sweat*, Shrn. 150, 2.

ge-swæþian; *p.* ode; *pp.* od *To track out, investigate* :—Geswæþodes *investigasti*, Ps. Spl. T. 138, 2. v. swæþ, swaþu.

ge-swædrung, e; *f. A failing, a want*; delīquium :—Se mon geswōgunga þrōwaþ and mōdes geswædrunga *the man suffers swoonings and failings of the mind*, L. M. 2, 21; Lchdm. ii. 206, 9. v. ge-sweđerian.

ge-swāp. v. æsce-geswāp.

ge-sweccan; *p.* te; *pp.* ed [sweccan *to smell*] *To smell*; odōrāri :—Næsþyrlu hī habbaþ and nā gesweccaþ *nāres hăbent et non odōrābunt*, Ps. Spl. M. 113, 14.

ge-swefian, ic -swefige; *p.* ode; *pp.* od [swefan *to sleep*] *To cause to sleep, cast asleep, lull, appease*; sōpīre, sōpōrāre :—Ic geswefige *sōpio*, Ælfc. Gr. 30, 5; Som. 34, 57. MS. D. God geswefode đone Adam *God caused Adam to sleep*, Homl. Th. i. 14, 20. Drihten on rōde mid deáþe wæs geswefod *the Lord was put to sleep by death on the cross*, ii. 260, 18: i. 496, 12: Boutr. Scrd. 19, 37. Ic eom geswefod *sōpōrātus sum*, Ps. Lamb. 3, 6.

ge-swēge; *adj.* v. ungeswēge.

ge-swēgsumlīce; *adv. Harmoniously, with one voice* :—Dā sǽde eall se þeódscipe geswēgsumlīce *then all the people agreed in saying*, Shrn. 36, 17.

ge-swel, -swell, es; *n.* [swellan *to swell*] *A swelling, tumour*; tŭmor :—Wiđ ǽlcum heardum swile odđe geswelle *for every hard tumour or swelling*, L. M. 1, 31; Lchdm. ii. 70, 20: Herb. 86, 1; Lchdm. i. 188, 20: 90, 1; Lchdm. i. 194, 19: 109, 3; Lchdm. i. 222, 14. Hyt đæt geswel gelīđigaþ *it relieves the swelling*, 109, 3; Lchdm. i. 222, 14: 76, 1; Lchdm. i. 178, 20: iii. 8, 28. Wiđ geswell *for a swelling*, Herb. 90, 4; Lchdm. i. 194, 18. Wiđ ealle geswell *for all swellings*, 130, 1; Lchdm. i. 240, 18. Đā wolde se heofenlīca lǽce đæt geswell heora heortan gelăcnian *then would the heavenly leech cure the swelling of their heart*, Homl. Th. i. 338, 23. Mislīce geswel and blǽdran *divers boils and blisters*, ii. 192, 30.

ge-swelgan; *p.* -swealg, -swealh, *pl.* -swulgon; *pp.* -swolgen [swelgan *to swallow*] *To swallow, devour*; devŏrāre, deglutīre :—Đa mægenþreátas meredeáþ geswealh *the sea-death swallowed those mighty bands*, Cd. 169; Th. 210, 9; Exod. 512.

ge-swelge, es; *n. An abyss, gulf*; vorago, barathrum, charybdis, Hpt. Gl. 421, 513.

ge-swelgend; es; *m. An abyss, chasm*; vorago, Hpt. Gl. 507.

ge-sweltan; *p.* -swealt, *pl.* -swulton; *pp.* -swolten [sweltan *to die*] *To die, perish*; mŏri :—Men gesweltaþ *hŏmĭnes moriemini*, Ps. Spl. 81, 6. Geswolten, Bd. 5, 6; S. 619, 18.

ge-swenc, es; *n. Labour, trouble* :—Þurh đæt geswenc to ēce reste becom *through that suffering came to the eternal rest*, Nar. 40, 2. v. ge-swinc.

ge-swencan, -swæncan; *p.* -swencte; *pp.* -swenced, -swenct [swencan *to disturb, vex*] *To disturb, agitate, trouble, vex, fatigue, outweary, afflict, harass, oppress*; pulsāre, agitāre, trĭbŭlāre, vexāre, fătīgāre, affligĕre, afficĕre, opprĭmĕre :—Herodes cyning wolde geswencan sume of đære gelađunge *Herod the king would afflict some of the church*, Homl. Th. ii. 380, 25: Salm. Kmbl. 299; Sal. 149. Hīg eów to deáþe geswencaþ *morte afficient ex vobis*, Lk. Bos. 21, 16: 8, 45. Sarai hīg đā geswencte and heó sōna fleáh ūt to đam wēstene *affligiente igĭtur eam Sarai fŭgam iniit*, Gen. 16, 6. Hī synne geswencton *they outwearied sin*, Exon. 55 b; Th. 197, 12; Az. 189: Chr. 1116; Erl. 245, 35. Ūtancumene and elþeódige ne geswenc đū nō *vex thou not comers from without and strangers*, L. Alf. 33; Th. i. 52, 14. Ic geswenced sȳ *trĭbŭlor*, Ps. Th. 101, 2, 4: Bd. 4, 9; S. 576, 27. Synnum geswenced *oppressed with sins*, Beo. Th. 1954; B. 975: 2741; B. 1368: Andr. Kmbl. 788; An. 394. He wæs geswenced mid grimmum gefeohte *he was wearied with fierce fighting*, Chr. Erl. 5, 30. He biþ geswenct ōþ geár seofone *he will be troubled for seven years*, Lchdm. iii. 188, 12: 192, 4: 204, 14. Hī wurdan geswencte *vexāti sunt*, Ps. Th. 106, 38: 43, 23: Ors. 1, 7; Bos. 30, 30.

ge-swencednes, -swincednes, -swenctnes, -nis, -nys, -ness, -niss, -nyss, e; *f.* [geswencan, *pp. of* geswencan *to disturb, trouble, afflict*] *Sorrow, affliction, tribulation*; afflictio, tribŭlātio :—Hī fōrecōmon me on đæge geswencednysse mīnre *prævenērunt me in die afflictiōnis meæ*, Ps. Spl. 17, 21: Homl. Th. ii. 456, 11. Æfter đære geswencednysse *post trĭbŭlātiōnem illam*, Mk. Bos. 13, 24: Ps. Spl. 54, 2. For đam hwīlwendlīcum geswenctnessum [MS. e] *for the temporal afflictions*; temporales afflictiones, Bd. 4, 9; S. 577, 12. Nān đyssera geswencednyssa ne becom on đam ende đæs eardes đe đæt godes folc on eardode *none of these afflictions came into that part of the country in which the people of God dwelt*, Homl. Th. ii. 192, 25.

ge-sweógian; *p.* ode; *pp.* od *To be silent*; tăcēre :—Gesweógode he āne hwīle *he was silent for some time*, Bt. 39, 2; Fox 212, 10. v. geswīgian.

ge-sweopornes, -swiopernis, -ness, -niss, e; *f. Cunning, craftiness, hypocrisy*; astutia, Mk. Skt. Rush. 12, 15. v. ge-swipornis.

ge-sweorc, -sworc, es; *n.* [sweorcan *to darken*] *A cloud, mist, smoke*; nūbes, nĕbŭla, cālīgo :—Gif hēr wind cymþ gesweorc upfæreþ *if wind comes here a cloud ascends*, Cd. 38; Th. 50, 12; Gen. 807. Cining geseah deorc gesweorc *the king saw a dark cloud*, 5; Th. 7, 19; Gen. 108. [*O. Sax.* gi-swerk: *O. H. Ger.* gi-swerc.]

ge-sweorcan, he -swyrcþ; *p.* -swearc, *pl.* -swurcon; *pp.* -sworcen *To become dark, be darkened, saddened, angry* :—Rōdor eal geswearc *the heavens all grew dark*, Elen. Kmbl. 1709; El. 856: Beo. Th. 3583; B. 1789: Cd. 166; Th. 207, 4; Exod. 461. Seó eorþe wæs gesworcen and aþȳstrod under his fōtum *caligo sub pedibus ejus*, Ps. Th. 17, 9. Đā geswearc se Godes man semninga and ongan heardlīce and bitterlīce wēpan *then suddenly the man of God became sad and began to weep sorely and bitterly*; solutus est in lacrymis vir Dei, Bd. 4, 25; S. 600, 29: Exon. 77 a; Th. 290, 3; Wand. 59. Geswearc đā sweor *the father-in-law then grew angry*, 67 a; Th. 247, 13; Jul. 78. Cf. asweorcan. [*O. Sax.* gi-swerkan *to become dark, literally and metaphorically as in English*: *O. H. Ger.* ge-sworcen; *part. p. turbulentus, nubilus.*]

ge-sweorcnes, -ness, e; *f. Cloudiness, gloom, horror, affliction*; obscūrĭtus, horror, afflictio :—Ne đǽr nǽfre biþ biternes, ne gesweorcnesse stōw gemēted *nor is bitterness ever there, nor a place found for gloom*, L. E. I. prm; Th. ii. 400, 9.

ge-sweorf, es; *m. n.* [?] *Filings*; limatura. DER. ār-gesweorf. v. geswyrf.

ge-sweorfan; *p.* -swearf, *pl.* -swurfon; *pp.* -sworfen *To file* or *rub off, to polish off*; expolire :—To āsworfenum ōran, to gesworfenum ōran *sub expolita*, Glos. Prudent. Recd. 142, 19. v. sweorfan.

ge-sweoru, -swiru, -swyru; *pl. n. Hills*; colles :—Wurdan gesweoru swā on seledreáme swā on sceápum beóþ sceóne lambru *colles vĕlut agni ŏvium*, Ps. Th. 113, 6. Mid wynngrāfe weaxaþ geswiru [MS. gespiru] *exultātiōne colles accingentur*, 64, 13. Muntas and geswyru *montes et omnes colles*, 148, 9: 71, 3: 113, 4.

ge-sweostor, -sweostra, -sweostro, -swustra, -swystra *sisters*; sorores; *used as the pl. of* sweostor :—His twā dōhtor, swāse gesweostor *his two daughters, own sisters*, Exon. 112 b; Th. 431, 29; Rä. 47, 3. Đǽr wǽron twā cwēna đa wǽran gesweostra *there were two queens who were sisters*, Ors. 1, 10; Bos. 33, 36. Hwæđer mōtan twegen ǽwe gebrōđro twā gesweostro on gesinscipe onfōn *si debeant duo germani fratres singulas sorores accipere*, Bd. 1, 27; S. 490, 28. Đara eádigra gesweostra gemynd *the commemoration of the blessed sisters*, Shrn. 69, 18. [*O. Sax.* gi-swester: *O. H. Ger.* gi-suester.] DER. will-gesweostor. v. sweostor.

ge-sweotulian, -sweotlian; *p.* ode, ade; *pp.* od, ad *To manifest*; mănĭfestāre :—Gesweotula nū đīn sylfes weorc *manifest now thine own work*, Exon. 8 a; Th. 1, 16; Cri. 9. Biþ meaht gesweotlad *her might is manifested*, 128 a; Th. 492, 20; Rä. 81, 18. v. ge-swutelian.

ge-swerian, ic -swerige, -swerge; *p.* -swōr, -sweór, *pl.* -swōron; *pp.* -sworen [swerian *to swear*] *To swear, take an oath*; jūrāre :—Ic đæt geswerige þurh sunu Meotudes *this I swear by the son of the Creator*, Elen. Kmbl. 1368; El. 686. Ic geswerge *I swear*, Exon. 67 a; Th. 247, 17; Jul. 80. Swā ic geswōr wiđ Drihten *sīcut jūrāvit Domĭno*, Ps. Th. 131, 2. Đū geswōre Apollonio *thou didst swear to Apollonius*, Apol. Th. 23, 5. He befōran his fæder gesweór, đæt he nǽfre ne wurde Rōmāna freónd *he swore before his father that he would never become a friend of the Romans*, Ors. 4, 8; Bos. 89, 25. Him betweonum geswōran *they took an oath among themselves*, 1, 11; Bos. 34, 37: 1, 14; Bos. 37, 16.

ge-swētan; *p.* -swētte; *pp.* -swēted, -swēt [swēte *sweet*] *To make sweet, sweeten, season*; condīre, indulcāre, indulcōrāre :—Ic geswēte synna lustas *I sweeten the delights of sins*, Exon. 71 a; Th. 264, 24; Jul. 369. His bodunga mid sōþre lufe symle geswētte *he ever sweetened his preachings with true love*, Homl. Th. ii. 148, 28. Ic genam đa reliquias and mid swōtum wyrtum gesweótte *I took the relics and sweetened with sweet herbs*, Nar. 49, 8. Geswēted wīn *sweetened wine*; defrucatum, Wrt. Voc. 290, 58. Geswēt wīn *mĕlicrātum* = μελίκρατον, Ælfc. Gl. 32; Som. 61, 113; Wrt. Voc. 27, 42. Geswēt eced *sweetened vinegar*; oximellum, 32; Som. 61, 115; Wrt. Voc. 27, 44. On geswēttum wætere *in sweetened water*, Herb. 103, 3; Lchdm. i. 218, 3: 33, 2; Lchdm. i. 132, 13: 111, 2; Lchdm. i. 224, 17.

ge-sweđerian, -swedrian; *p.* ode; *pp.* od *To weaken, destroy* :—Gesweđerad wæs se swyle *fuga tumoris secuta est*, Bd. 5, 3; S. 616, 39. Đonne beoþ mīn sorg geswedrad *my sorrow will be stilled*, Exon. 48; Th. 164, 17; Gū. 1013. v. swedrian, ge-swiđrian, ge-swædrung.

ge-swētlēht; *part. p. Made sweet* [?] :—Onsægnessa geswētlēhte *holocausta medullata*, Blickl. Gloss.

ge-swic, es; *n. An offence;* scandalum, Ps. Spl. T. 118, 165: 49, 21. v. ǽ-, be-swic.

ge-swícan; ic -swíce, ðú -swícest, -swícst, he -swíceþ, -swícþ, *pl.* -swícaþ; *p.* -swác, *pl.* -swicon; *pp.* -swicen *To leave off, desist, stop, cease, rest from, turn from, withdraw, relinquish, fail, deceive, betray;* intermittere. desistere, cessare, quiescere, requiescere, deserere, discedere, relinquere, deficere, fallere, prodere. I. *v. n:*—He nolde geswícan *he would not cease,* L. Ælfc. C. 3; Th. ii. 344, 5. Ne wolde ic fram ðínum bebodum geswícan *a mandatis tuis non erravi,* Ps. Th. 118, 110. Ic gedó, ðæt hira gemynd geswícþ of eallum mannum *cessare faciam ex hominibus memoriam eorum.* Deut. 32, 26. Geswác se wind *cessavit ventus,* Mt. Bos. 14, 32: Lk. Bos. 5, 4: 11, 1: Gen. 8, 22. Ic geswíce oððe ic forlǽte oððe ic me reste *quiesco,* Ælfc. Gr. 28, 1; Som. 30, 28. Geswác æt sæcce Beówulfes sweord *Beowulf's sword failed in the conflict,* Beo. Th. 5355; B. 2681. Gesuícas *mentientes,* Mt. Kmbl. Lind. 5, 11. II. *with the genitive:*—Wile heó ðæs síðes geswícan *it will desist from its course,* Salm. Kmbl. 647; Sal. 323. Gif he unrǽdes ne geswíceþ *if he desist not from mischief,* Exon. 107 b; Th. 410, 7; Rä. 28, 12. Bútan he ðæs yfles geswíce *except he desist from evil,* Ps. Lamb fol. 183 b, 20. Hí ðæs gefeohtes geswicon *they stopped the fight,* Ors. 3, 1; Bos. 54, 29. Ðæs fixnoþes geswícan *to cease from fishing,* Homl. Th. ii. 516, 11. Gif ðú unrǽdes ne geswícest *if thou cease not from evil counsel,* Exon. 67 b; Th. 250, 1; Jul. 120. Gif we ðæs unrihtes geswícaþ *if we cease from evil,* Elen. Kmbl. 1030; El. 516. Gerǽddon [gerædden, MS.] ða witan ðæt man ǽlces yfeles geswác *the witan decreed that men should cease from every kind of evil,* Chr. 1048; Erl. 178, 33: Ps. Th. 58, 4. Hí nǽfre heora yfeles geswicon *they never ceased from their evil,* Chr. 1001; Erl. 137, 20. He geswác hys weorces *he rested from his work,* Gen. 2, 3. Gé hellfirena sweartra geswícaþ *ye turn from black hell-crimes,* Exon. 98 a; Th. 366, 4; Reb. 7. Geswícaþ ðære synne *turn from that sin,* Cd. 113; Th. 149, 1; Gen. 2468. Geswíc ðisses setles *relinquish this seat,* Exon. 36 b; Th. 119, 3; Gú. 249. III. *with the dative:*—Hí ðære heregunge geswicon *they ceased the ravaging,* Chr. 994; Erl. 132, 32. Hí geswicon ðære fyrdinge *they withdrew from the expedition,* 1016; Erl. 153, 29. Ðæt hí woldon [woldan, MS.] Rómánum geswícan *that they would relinquish the Romans,* Ors. 5, 10; Bos. 108, 29. Ðæt ic ðínum lárum geswíce *that I relinquish thy doctrines,* Andr. Kmbl. 2582; An. 1292. Wélandes geworc ne geswíceþ monna ǽnigum *Weland's work deceiveth not any [of] men,* Wald. 3; Vald. 1, 2. Seó ecg geswác þeódne *the edge failed its Lord,* Beo. Th. 3053; B. 1524. Earm biþ se him his frýnd geswícaþ *miserable is he whom his friends betray,* Exon. 89 a; Th. 335, 22; Gn. Ex. 37. Ne ǽnig iuih giswíca *nemo vos seducat,* Rtl. 13, 29. Hine manoden ðæt he ne geswice Godes word to bodigenne *admonished him not to cease preaching God's word,* Shrn. 13, 33.

ge-swicennes, -swicenes, -ness, -nys, -nyss, e; *f. A ceasing, cessation, abstaining, repentance;* cessātio, resīpiscentia:—Búton geswicennesse *without abstaining,* L. N. P. L. 63; Th. ii. 300, 22. Mid geswicennysse yfelra dǽda *with cessation from evil deeds,* Homl. Th. ii. 48, 27: Ælfc. T. 29, 18. Þurh geswicenysse yfeles *by cessation from evil,* Homl. Th. ii. 332, 3. Búton ǽlcere geswicenesse *sĭne ulla resīpiscentia,* L. M. I. P. 20; Th. ii. 270, 21.

ge-swicn, e; *f. A cleansing, clearance;* purgātio:—Nâh he ða geswicne *he shall not have the clearance,* L. In. 15; Th. i. 112, 5, MSS. B. H. [Cf. *Goth.* swiknei *purity: Icel.* sykna *blamelessness.*]

ge-swicnan; *p,* ede; *pp.* ed *To cleanse, clear;* purgāre:—Geswicne se hine be cxx hída *let him clear himself with cxx hides,* L. In. 14; Th. i. 110, 16: 15; Th. i. 112, 3: 52; Th. i. 134, 12. [Cf. *Goth.* swikns *innocent, pure: Icel.* sykn *free from guilt, innocent.*]

ge-swicneful; *comp.* -fulra; *adj. Treacherous, deceitful, harmful:*—Sint hie ðé geswicnefulran *they are more harmful to thee,* Bt. 14, 1; Fox 42, 22.

ge-swícung, e; *f. A ceasing, an intermission;* cessatio, R. Conc. pref. Mon. Angl.

ge-swígian, -swúgian; *p.* ode; *pp.* od. I. *to be silent:*—Monig mon hæfþ ðone unþeáw, ðæt he ne can nyt sprecan ne ne can geswígian *many a man has the bad habit, that he can say nothing to the purpose, nor yet hold his peace,* Prov. Kmbl. 47. Gif ðú geswúgian mihtest *if thou couldst be silent,* Bt. 18, 4; Fox 68, 4. He gesuígde *obmutuit,* Mt. Kmbl. Lind. 22, 12. Gesuígdon alle *stupebant omnes,* 12, 23. Ðá for ðæs bysceopes hálignysse geswígdon eall ða deófolgyld *then on account of the bishop's holiness all the idols were silent,* Shrn. 151, 31. II. *to pass over in silence; with the genitive:*—Nelle ic lofes ðínes geswígian *I will not pass over thy praise in silence,* Ps. Th. 108, 1. Sóþes geswúgedon *were silent about the truth,* Swt. A. S. Rdr. 111, 202. Eác ic wille geswígian Tontolis and Philopes ðara scondlicestena spella *nec mihi nunc enumerare opus est Tantali et Pelopis facta turpia, fabulas turpiores,* Ors. 1, 8; Bos. 31, 24. III. *to silence:*—Fugol biþ geswíged *the bird is hushed,* Exon. 58 a; Th. 207, 22; Ph. 145. [*O. H. Ger.* gi-suígan, Grff. vi. 859–60: *Ger.* ge-schweigen *to pass over in silence.*]

ge-swígung *silence,* Lye.

ge-swin, -swins [?], es; *n. Melody;* modulatio:—Geswin *melody,* Exon. 57 b; Th. 207, 5; Ph. 137.

ge-swinc, -swing, es; *n.* [swinc *labour, trouble*] *Labour, exercise, inconvenience, fatigue, trouble, affliction, tribulation, torment, temptation, banishment;* lăbor, exercĭtātio, incommŏdum, afflictio, trĭbŭlātio, tentātio, exsĭlium:—Geswinc *lăbor,* Ælfc. Gr. 9, 21; Som. 10, 27. Com ðis geswinc ofer us *vĕnit sŭper nos ista trĭbŭlātio,* Gen. 42, 21: Ps. Surt. 21, 12. On tíd geswinces *in tempŏre trĭbŭlātiōnis,* 36, 39: 17, 19. Ðú eall þing birest búton geswince *thou bearest all things without labour,* Bt. Met. Fox 20, 553; Met. 20, 277: Chr. 1016; Erl. 155, 3. On geswince *in exercĭtātiōne,* Ps. Spl. 54, 2. Sum heard geswinc habban sceoldon *they must have some hard torment,* Cd. 17; Th. 20, 30; Gen. 317: Chr. 1085; Erl. 218, 10. Eallra geswinca *of all labours,* Bt. Met. Fox 21, 20; Met. 21, 10: 21, 28; Met. 21, 14. On mínum geswincum *in tentātiōnĭbus meis,* Lk. Bos. 22, 28: Homl. Th. ii. 82, 23. Gé eodon on hyra geswinc *in lăbōres eōrum introistis,* Jn. Bos. 4, 38. Geswinc *exsĭlium,* Cot. 73.

ge-swinc-dæg, es; *m. A labour-day, day of toil;* tribulationis dies, Exon. 81 b; Th. 306, 4; Seef. 2.

ge-swincednes, -nis, -ness, -niss, e; *f. Tribulation;* trĭbŭlātio:—On geswincednisse *in trĭbŭlātiōne,* Ps. Spl. C. 9, 9. v. ge-swencednes.

geswinc-ful, -full; *adj. Full of labour, laborious, troublesome, wearisome;* lăbōriōsus, incommŏdus:—Hit biþ swíðe geswincful *it is very laborious,* Past. 60; Swt. 453, 10; Hat. MS: Lchdm. iii. 188, 19: 192, 2, 23. Ðis wæs geswincfull *this was troublesome,* Chr. 1097; Erl. 234, 24. Sint hí ðé geswincfulran *they are more troublesome to thee,* Bt. 14, 1; Fox 42, 22, MS. Cot.

geswincfulnys, -nyss, e; *f. Sorrow, affliction, tribulation;* trĭbŭlātio:—Of eallum geswincfulnyssum he gehǽlde hine *de omnĭbus trĭbŭlātiōnĭbus ejus salvābit eum,* Ps. Lamb. 33, 7.

ge-swincg, es; *n. Labour, toil;* lăbor:—Léton ealles þeódscipes geswincg ðus leohtlíce forwurðan *they let the toil of all the nation thus lightly perish,* Chr. 1009; Erl. 142, 12. v. ge-swinc.

ge-swing, es; *n. Labour;* lăbor:—Geswing is beforan me *lăbor est ante me,* Ps. Spl. 72, 16: 89, 11. v. ge-swinc.

ge-swing, es; *n. A vibration;* vibrātio, fluctuātio:—Ofer ýða geswing *over the vibration of the waves,* Andr. Kmbl. 703; An. 352: Beo. Th. 1700; B. 848: Exon. 95 b; Th. 356, 7; Pa. 8.

ge-swingan; *p.* -swang, *pl* -swungon; *pp.* -swungen *To scourge, beat;* flagellare, verberare:—Hia geswingas iuih *flagellabunt vos,* Mt. Kmbl. Lind. 10, 17. God geswang Farao ðone cining mid ðám mǽstum wítum *flagellavit Dominus Pharaonem regem plagis maximis,* Gen. 12, 17: Jn. Skt. Lind. 19, 1. Ic wæs ealne dæg geswungen *fui flagellatus tota die,* Ps. Th. 72, 11: Andr. Kmbl. 2791; An. 1398. Gie bíþon geswinged *vapulabitis,* Mk. Skt. Lind. 13, 9. Gesuungun ł gesuincged biþ *flagellabitur,* Lk. Skt. Lind. 18, 32. Hia geþurscon ł geswungdon [MS. gesumgdon] *cædebant,* Mt. Kmbl Lind. 21, 8.

ge-swins. v. ge-swin.

ge-swip, es; *n. A scourge, whip;* flagellum, Som. v. swip.

ge-swip; *adj. Cunning, crafty;* astutus:—Geswippre múþe *ore astuto,* Bd. 2, 9; S. 511, 19.

ge-swiporlíce; *adv. Cunningly;* astute, V. Ps. 82, 3.

ge-swiporness, -swiforness, -swioporness, e; *f. Craft, cunning, art:* versutia:—Ðæs deófles geswipornysse syndon swíðe unasecgendlíce *the devil's arts are quite indescribable,* Shrn. 38, 35. Ðæs ealdan feóndes geswifornis *the old enemy's cunning,* 37, 14. Se ðe wiste geswipernise [-swiopornisse, Rush.] hiora *qui sciens versutiam eorum,* Mk. Skt. Lind. 12, 15.

ge-swiria, an; *m. A sister's son;* sororis filius, Cot. 35.

ge-swiru; *pl. n. Hills;* colles, Ps. Th. 64, 13. v. ge-sweoru.

ge-swíðan, -swýðan; *p.* de; *pp.* ed *To make strong, confirm, comfort:*—Mín earm hine mid mycle mægene geswýðeþ *brachium meum confortabit eum,* Ps. Th. 88, 18. He twelf apostolas mid his gástes gife geswíðde *he strengthened twelve apostles with the gift of his spirit,* Cd. 226; Th. 300, 29; Sat. 572. Hæfde he ðá geswíðed sóþum cræftum werodes aldor *he had then strengthened with true powers the chief of the band,* 143; Th. 179, 17; Exod. 30: 188; Th. 234, 7; Dan 288: Andr. Kmbl. 1394; An. 697: 1402; An. 701: Salm. Kmbl. 91; Sal. 45: Ps. Th. 118, 76: Exon. 13 a; Th. 24, 16; Cri. 385. Geswýðede, Ps. Th. 118, 77.

ge-swiðrian; *p.* ode, ade; *pp.* od, ad *To weaken, destroy;* imminuere, debilitare, conficere:—Mægen wæs geswiðrod *the might was destroyed,* Elen. Kmbl. 1393; El. 698: 1833; El. 918: 2526; El. 1264: Judth. 12; Thw. 25, 18; Jud. 266. Ne mót innan geondscínan sunne for ðæm sweartum mistum ǽr ðæm hí geswiðrad weorþen *the sun cannot shine through from within for the black mists before they are dissipated,* Bt. Met. Fox 5, 90; Met. 5, 45. Ðæt helle fýr wæs siððan geswiðrad *that hell-fire was afterwards mitigated,* Ors. 2, 6; Bos. 50, 20. v. ge-sweðrian.

ge-swógen; *part. p. Senseless, inanimate, swooned:*—Se læg geswógen betwux ðám ofslegenum *he lay in a swoon amongst the slain,* Homl. Th. ii. 356, 27: Swt. A. S. Rdr. 66, 324. v. ge-swówung.

ge-swógung, -swówung, e; *f. Swooning*, Lchdm. ii. 176, 13: 194, 3.

ge-sworc, es; *n. A cloud, mist;* nĕbŭla:—Gesworc swâ swâ ahsan he tostredeþ *nĕbŭlam sīcut cĭnĕrem spargit*, Ps. Spl. C. 147, 5. v. ge-sweorc.

ge-sworfen *rubbed off, polished off*, Glos. Prud. Recd. 142, 19. v. ge-sweorfan.

ge-swúgian. v. ge-swígian.

ge-swungen *scourged, beaten*, Andr. Kmbl. 2791; An. 1398; *pp. of* ge-swingan.

ge-swurdod [sweord, swurd *a sword*] *armed with a sword;* glădio cinctus:—Geswurdod *glădiātus*, Ælfc. Gr. 43; Som. 45, 13.

ge-swustra, -swustru *sisters*, Mk. Bos. 10, 29: Homl. Th. ii. 458, 29. To mînre mêder and mînum geswustrum *to my mother and my sisters*, Nar. 3, 8. v. ge-sweostor.

ge-swutelian, -swuteligan, -swytelian, -sweotulian, -sweotlian; *p.* ode, ade, ude; *pp.* od, ad, ud [sweotol *manifest, clear, open*] *To declare, publish, make known, explain, prove, manifest, show, glorify;* monstrāre, demonstrāre, publĭcāre, exprĭmĕre, manĭfestāre, signāre, explānāre, prŏbāre, clārĭfĭcāre:—Ic wolde mid ðære gebîcnunge geswutelian ðæt ic eom ðære stôwe hyrde *I would manifest by that sign that I am the guardian of the place*, Homl. Th. i. 504, 1: L. C. E. 22; Th. i. 372, 26: Ps. Spl. 79, 2: Jn. Bos. 14, 22. He wolde God geswutelian *clārĭfĭcātūrus esset Deum*, 21, 19. Ic geswutelige *exprĭmo*, Ælfc. Gr. 28, 4; Som. 31, 16: Jn. Bos. 14, 21. He inc geswutelaþ mycele healle gedæfte *ipse vobis demonstrābit cœnācŭlum grande strātum*, Mk. Bos. 14, 15. Geswutelaþ *prŏbat*, Glos. Prudent. Recd. 139, 25. He him lîfes weig geswutelode *he manifested to them the way of life*, Homl. Th. ii. 118, 16: Boutr. Scrd. 20, 28: 22, 2. Moses geswutelude ða æ̂ *cœpit Moyses explānāre lēgem*, Deut. 1, 5. Geswutelie mid gewitnysse *let him show by witness*, L. Eth. ii. 9; Th. i. 290, 10. Nis nân þing dîgle, ðæt ne sý geswutelod *non est occultum, quod non manĭfestētur*, Lk. Bos. 8, 17. Is geswutelod *signātum est*, Ps. Th. 4, 7. Nû ys mannes sunu geswutelod, and God ys geswutelod on him *nunc clārĭfĭcātus est fīlius hŏmĭnis, et Deus clārĭfĭcātus est in eo*, Jn. Bos. 13, 31, 32.

ge-swutelung, e; *f. A making clear, plain, a manifestation, declaration:*—Ðæt sum tâcn wǽre on heora lîchaman to geswutelunge ðæt hî on God belýfdon *that there might be some token on their body as a manifestation that they believed on God*, Homl Th. i. 92, 32: Cod. Dipl. Kmbl. ii. 300, 9. Hêr is siú geswitelung ðære gerǽdnisse ðe ðiús geférrǽden gerǽd hæfþ *here is the declaration of the ordinance that this society has decided upon*, Th. Chart. 610, 27.

ge-swyrf, es; *m. Filings;* limatum:—Genim ânre yntsan gewihte geswyrfes of seolfre *take the weight of one ounce of the filings of silver*, Herb. 101, 3; Lchdm. i. 216, 12.

ge-swyrfan *to file off, to polish;* elimare, Cot. 71. v. ge-sweorfan.

ge-swyru; *pl. n. Hills;* colles, Ps. Th. 71, 3: 113, 4: 148, 9. v. ge-sweoru.

ge-swystra *sisters:*—Geswystrena bearn *sisters' children*, Bt. 35, 4; Fox 162, 10. To mînre mêder and geswystrum *to my mother and sisters*, Nar. 1, 12. v. ge-sweostor.

ge-swytelian; *p.* ode; *pp.* od *To make known, manifest, show;* manĭfestāre:—Ðæt he ðæt sôþeste geswytelie *that he make manifest what is most true*, L. Ath. iv. 7; Th. i. 226, 30. v. ge-swutelian.

ge-syb *peaceable, related*, Soul Kmbl. 107; Seel. 54. v. ge-sib.

ge-sybsum; *adj Peaceable;* pācĭfĭcus:—Eádige synd ða gesybsuman *beati pācĭfĭci*, Mt. Bos. 5, 9. v. ge-sibsum.

ge-sybsumlîce *peaceably*, Ps. Spl. 34, 23. v. ge-sibsumlîce.

ge-sýcan, -sîcan; *p.* -sýhte *To give suck to, to suckle:*—Ða breóst ðe swylce gesîhton *the breasts that gave such suck*, Homl. Th. i. 84, 16.

ge-sýclian *to be infirm*, Jn. Bos. 4, 46. v. ge-sîclian.

ge-syd, es; *n. A place in which to wallow, mud:*—Sol *vel* gesyd *volutabrum*, Ælfc. Gl. 56; Som. 67, 32; Wrt. Voc. 37, 22.

ge-syflan *to provide 'sufol,' q. v.* Salm. Kmbl. 807; Sal. 403.

ge-syfled hlâf *panis lacticinio et ovorum luteo maceratus*, Lye. v. ge-sufel.

ge-syfl-melu; *n. Dough:*—Ðæt folc nam gesyflmelu [gesyft melu, Thw.] ǽr ðam hit gebyrmed wǽre *the people took their dough before it was leavened*, Exod. 12, 34.

ge-syft. v. ge-syfl-melu.

ge-syhð. v. ge-siht.

ge-sylhð *a plough;* aratrum, Som.

ge-syllan; *p.* -sealde; *pp.* -seald *To give, deliver, betray, sell, give up;* dare, donare:—Mycel feoh to gesyllanne *to give much money*, Bd. 4, 19; S. 587, 29: Ps. Th. 110, 4: 104, 10: 117, 18. Gesyllon ðone oxan and todǽlon ðæt wurþ *let them sell the ox and divide the price*, Ex. 21, 35. v. ge-sellan, sellan.

ge-sylt *salted;* sale conditus:—Gyf ðæt sealt awyrþ, on ðam ðe hit gesylt biþ *if the salt be insipid, with what shall it be salted?* Mt. Bos. 5, 13: Mk. Bos. 9, 49; *pp. of* ge-syltan. v. syltan.

ge-sýlð *happiness*. v. ge-sǽlð.

ge-sýman, -sêman, -sǽman; *p.* de; *pp.* ed *To load:*—Se cyning gesýmde gold and seolfor uppan olfendas *the king loaded gold and silver upon camels*, Homl. Th. i. 458, 23. Ða wǽron gesýmed mid feó and mid hrægle *that were laden with money and raiment*, Gen. 45, 23. Ealle ðe gesýmede synt *omnes qui onerati estis*, Mt. Bos. 11, 28. Ðeáh ðe we gesǽmde beón mid ðare berdene ðæs deádlîces lîues *licet mortalis vitæ pondere pressi*, Th. Chart. 317, 3.

ge-syndlîc; *adj. Prosperous, healthy, happy;* prosperus:—On ðâm gesyndlîcan þingum . . . and on ðâm wiðerweardum þingum *in prosperous . . . and in adverse circumstances*, Bd. 4, 23; S. 595, 21.

ge-syndrian *to separate:*—Gesyndrod sî he fram beodes dǽlnimunge *let him be separated from sharing in the table*, R. Ben. interl. 24, Lye. On ðære gesyndredan hîde *in the separate hide*, Cod. Dipl. Kmbl. iii. 4, 8.

ge-sýne, -sêne, -siêne; *adj. Visible, seen, evident, plain:*—Ne mihte ic hire bedyrnan mînes môdes unrôtnesse for ðan hit wæs on mînum andwlitan gesýne *I could not hide from her the disquiet of my mind for it was evident in my face*, Shrn. 41, 25: Ors. 1, 7; Bos. 30, 28: Blickl. Homl. 93, 35. Ða fôtlâstas wǽron swutole and gesýne *the footsteps were plain and visible*, 203, 36: Andr. Kmbl. 1129; An. 565: Beo. Th. 2811; B. 1403: 4622; B. 2316: Elen. Kmbl. 527; El. 264. Ðǽr wæs gesýne his seó sôþe spêd *videbitur in majestate sua*, Ps. Th. 101, 14. Wæs gesýne ðæt . . . *it was evident that* . . . , Blickl. Homl. 207, 11: Beo. Th. 2515; B. 1255: Andr. Kmbl. 1051; An. 526: 1097; An. 549: Elen. Kmbl. 487; El. 244. On me syndon ða dolg gesiéne *the wounds are visible on me*, Rood Kmbl. 92; Kr. 46. Gesêne, Cd. 135; Th. 170, 1; Gen. 2806: 218; Th. 278, 30; Sat. 230: Chr. 1121; Erl. 248, 39. Ðæt hia gesêne sîe *ut videantur*, Mt. Kmbl. Lind. 6, 5, 16.

ge-sýnelîce; *adv. Visibly:*—Ðæt tâcen gesýnelîce bær *bore that token visibly*, Bd. 3, 19; S. 549, 15.

ge-syngian, -singian; *p.* ode, ade; *pp.* od, ad *To sin, perpetrate crime, commit adultery;* peccāre, mæchāri:—Ðæt ǽlc ðæra ðe wîf gesyhþ and hyre gewilnaþ, eallunga ðæt se gesyngaþ on hys heortan *quia omnis, qui vīdĕrit mŭlĭĕrem ad concŭpiscendum eam, jam mœchātus eam in corde suo*, Mt. Bos. 5, 28. Nû is gesêne ðæt we gesyngodon *now it is seen that we have sinned*, Cd. 218; Th. 278, 31; Sat. 230. Ðæt wæs feohleás gefeoht, fyrenum gesyngad *that was a priceless fight, criminally perpetrated*, Beo. Th. 4874; B. 2441.

ge-synlîce; *adv. More frequently;* sæpius, R. Ben. 56.

ge-synto; *indecl. in sing; gen. pl.* -synta, -synto; *dat. pl.* -syntum; *f. Health, welfare, safety, prosperity, success, advantage, profit, benefit;* sānĭtas, sospĭtas, sălus, prospĕrĭtas:—Hî ðære gefeán ðære willendan gesynto onfôþ *cŭpĭtæ sospĭtātis gaudia redĭbunt*, Bd. 4, 3; S. 570, 22. For heora gesynto *for their health*, 3, 15; S. 541, 29. Ðe on eallum þingum mâron gesynto hæfdon *qui măgis prospĕrantur in omnĭbus*, 2, 13; S. 516, 8. Geunne me mînra gesynta *grant me my health*, Judth. 10; Thw. 22, 34; Jud. 90: Exon. 37 a; Th. 122, 9; Gû. 303. Fela ôðera gescreopa and gesynto *many other advantages and benefits*, Bd. 4, 22; S. 592, 21. He hêt hine leóde swǽse sêcean on gesyntum *he bade him seek his own people in safety*, Beo. Th. 3742; B. 1869: Ps. Th. 114, 5. Him wǽre mîn gesynto leófre ðonne hiora seolfra hǽlo *magis pro mea salute mori paratos*, Nar. 30, 17: 8, 6.

ge-syrwan; *p.* -syrede; *pp.* -syrwed. I. *to arm* [v. searu *armour*]:—Eode ða gesyrwed secg to ðam eorle *then went an armed man to the earl*, Byrht. Th. 136, 30; By. 159. [*Or* gesyrwed *wily*, searu *a wile;* cf. gelýfed *having belief.*] II. *to plot, machinate* [searu *artifice*]:—Wom-dǽda ðe [MS. ðy] ic gesyrede *the ill-deeds that I have devised cunningly*, Exon. 72 b; Th. 270, 20; Jul. 468.

get, geta. v. git, gita.

gêt *she-goats*, Som. 126; Lchdm. iii. 206, 2; *acc. pl. of* gât.

get *a gate*. v. geat.

gêt *poured out:*—He gêt ðæt blôd uppan ðæt weofod *fudit sanguinem super altare*, Lev. 8, 24; *p. of* geótan.

ge-tâcnian; *p.* ode, ade, ude; *pp.* od, ad, ud [tâcen, tâcn *a sign, token*]. I. *to denote by a sign, signify, betoken, show, instruct;* signāre, signĭfĭcāre, denŏtāre, insĭnuāre, monstrāre, instruĕre:—Ic getâcnige *signĭfĭco*, Ælfc. Gr. 37; Som. 39, 36. Wæter getâcnaþ on ðyssere stôwe mennisc ingehýd *water in this place betokens human knowledge*, Homl. Th. ii. 280, 1: Boutr. Scrd. 21, 42: Lchdm. iii. 198, 6, 7. Ða alecgendlîcan word getâcniaþ dǽde *the deponent verbs signify action*, Ælfc. Gr. 19; Som. 22, 56. Eua getâcnode Godes gelaðunge *Eve betokened God's church*, Ælfc. T. 6, 11, 13: 7, 1. Adam getâcnude ûrne Hǽlend Crist *Adam betokened our Saviour Christ*, 6, 8. Ðû me sôþfæstnysse weg getâcna *viam justĭfĭcātiōnum tuārum insĭnua mihi*, Ps. Th. 118, 27. Him gedafenaþ ðæt hî cunnon hwæt heó gâstlîce getâcnige *it is fitting that they know what it betokens spiritually*, Homl. Th. ii. 264, 27. Mid ðý is getâcnod, ðæt . . . *by that is signified that* . . . , Bt. Met. Fox 31, 35; Met. 31, 18: Boutr. Scrd. 19, 27, 28. II. *to sign, mark, witness, seal;* signāre, insignîre, obsignāre:—He getâcnaþ ðæt God is sôþfæstnes *signāvit quia Deus vērax est*, Jn. Bos. 3, 33. Ðone God Fæder getâcnode *hunc Păter signāvit Deus*, 6, 27. Is eall heáhmægen tîre getâcnod *all the lofty power is marked with glory*, Elen. Kmbl. 1504; El. 754. Godes þeówas getâcnade beón sceoldan *clēricos insignīri deceret*, Bd. 5, 21; S. 642, 42.

ge-tâcniendlîc, -tâcnigendlîc; *adj. Bearing a sign, significative, typical;* significātīvus:—Ðæt getâcniendlîce [getâcnigendlîce, Homl. Th. ii. 278, 14] lamb wæs geoffrod æt heora Eáster-tîde *the typical lamb was offered at their Easter-tide*, Homl. Pasc. Lisle 11, 18.

ge-tâcnung, e; *f.* [tâcnung *a sign*] *A sign, signification, token, type;* significātio:—Ðæt unscæððige lamb hæfde getâcnunge Cristes þrówunge *the innocent lamb was a token of Christ's passion*, Homl. Th. ii. 264, 29: 266, 1: 276, 4: 278, 7: Jud. 16; Thw. 161, 6. Sume þing sind gecwedene be Criste þurh getâcnunge *some things are said of Christ typically*, Homl. Th. ii. 268, 13, 16.

ge-tǽcan, -tǽcean, -tǽcan; *p.* -tǽhte; *pp.* -tǽht [tǽcan *to teach*] *To teach, instruct, show, declare, assign;* dŏcēre, instruĕre, ostendere, assignāre, offerre:—Ic hit ðé wille getǽcan *I will teach it thee*, Bt. 34, 9; Fox 146, 13: 36, 1; Fox 172, 28. He cwæþ ðæt he mihte óðerne getǽcan [getǽcnan, MS. T.] *ostendĕre posse se dixit alium*, Bd. 4, 1; S. 564, 2. Getǽcean, Ps. Th. 105, 25. Ðe ic ðé getǽce *which I will show thee*, Cd. 137; Th. 173, 1; Gen. 2854. Ðú me róde rôdera cining ryhte getǽhtest *thou hast rightly shown me the cross of heaven's king*, Elen. Kmbl. 2148; El. 1075. Ðæt hie us fersc wæter and swéte getǽhton *ut dulcem aquam demonstrarent*, Nar. 10, 20: Guthl. 3; Gdwn. 20, 24. Him Dryhten hlyt getǽhte *God assigned to them a lot*, Andr. Kmbl. 12; An. 6: Beo. Th. 4031; B. 2013: Cd. 136; Th. 171, 32; Gen. 2837. We ðé wîc getǽhton *we assigned to thee a dwelling-place*, 127; Th. 162, 27; Gen. 2687. Weg rihtwîsnyssa ðînra getǽc me *viam justĭfĭcātiōnum tuārum instrue me*, Ps. Spl. 118, 27. Ðæt ðú me getǽhte *that thou teach me*, Andr. Kmbl. 969; An. 485. Ðæt he riht getǽhte *that he should declare the truth*, Elen. Kmbl. 1199; El. 601.

ge-tæl, -tel, -teal, es; *pl. nom. acc.* -talu; *n.* I. *a number, series, reckoning, computation;* numerus, series, computus, computatio:—Ðæra etendra getæl wæs fîf þûsenda wera *manducantium fuit numerus quinque millia virorum*, Mt. Bos. 14, 21. Seó Abbudisse hét hine [Cædmon] lǽran ðæt getæl ðæs hâlgan stǽres and spelles *the Abbess commanded [them] to teach him [Cædmon] the series of the holy story and narrative;* Abbatissa jussit illum [Cædmonem] seriem sacræ historiæ doceri, Bd. 4, 24; S. 598, 5: Homl. Th. ii. 222, 3. Getel is *numerus*, Ælfc. Gr. 13; Som. 15, 56: Num. Pref. Âgene naman habbaþ ânfeald getel, and nabbaþ mænigfeald; eác sunne and môna syndon ânfealdes geteles *proper names have a singular number and have not a plural; the sun and moon are also of the singular number*, 13; Som. 16, 1. Sume naman synd óðres cynnes on ânfealdum getele, and óðres cynnes on mænigfealdum getele *some nouns are of one gender in the singular number, and of another gender in the plural number*, 13; Som. 16, 25, 26. On fulfremedra hâlgena geteal *in the number of perfect saints*, Nat. S. Greg. Els. 9, 2. God geíce fela þûsenda to ðison getale *Deus addat ad hunc numerum multa millia*, Deut. 1, 11. Twelf pund be getale *twelve pounds by tale*, Chart. Th. 577, 19. II. *a company, race, tribe;* centuria, tribus:—Getalu *vel* heápas *vel* hundredu *centurias*, Ælfc. Gl. 96; Som. 76, 25; Wrt. Voc. 53, 34. All getalu oððe cynn *omnes tribus*, Mt. Kmbl. Rush. 24, 30. Hie gemitton getalum myclum *they met in many tribes*, Cd. 80; Th. 101, 27; Gen. 1688. III. *a book of reckoning, a register, catalogue;* laterculum, catalogus = κατάλογος:—Getæl *laterculum*, Cot. 119: *catalogus*, 31, 37, 104. DER. bold-getæl, -getel, folc-, rîm-, rinc-, tigol-, winter-.

ge-tǽlan, -tǽlan; *p.* ede; *pp.* ed *To accuse, reprove;* accusare, exprobrare, calumniari, reprehendere:—Ne meaht ðú nó getǽlan ðîne wyrd *thou canst not accuse thy fortune*, Bt. 10; Fox 28, 1. Ic mǽge getǽlan *I may reprove*, 32, 3; Fox 118, 27. Word his getǽla *verbum ejus repræhendere*, Lk. Skt. Lind. 20, 26. Óðerne getǽleþ *alterum contemnet*, Mt. Kmbl. Lind. 6, 24. Nǽfre getǽldon gé ða unsuinnigo *numquam condemnassetis innocentes*, 12, 7. Ðætte hé getǽldon him *ut accusarent eum*, 10: Mk. Skt. Lind. 3, 2. Ða ðé getǽled aron *quæ tibi objiciuntur*, 14, 60. DER. tǽlan.

getæl-fæst; *adj. Measurable;* mensūrābĭlis:—Efne gemetelîce oððe getælfæste oððe ametendlîce ðú asettest dagas mîne *ecce mensūrābĭles pŏsŭisti dies meos*, Ps. Lamb. 38, 6.

getæl-rîme, es; *n.* [getæl *a number*] *Succession;* successio:—On getælrîme *in succession*, Salm. Kmbl. 76; Sal. 38.

ge-tænge; *adj. Incident;* incĭdens:—Gif hwylcum men sý ðæs feórþan dæges fefer getænge *if to any man there be a quartan fever incident*, Herb. 2, 12; Lchdm. i. 84, 5, MS. B. v. ge-tenge.

ge-tǽsan; *p.* de; *pp.* ed [tǽsan *to tease*] *To pluck, tease;* carpĕre:—Nim wǽte wulle wel getǽsede *take wet wool well teased*, Herb. 178, 6; Lchdm. i. 312, 13.

ge-tǽse, es; *n. An advantage;* commodum:—Ac geþenc ðæt ðú hym forwyrndest ǽlcra getǽsa ðá git becgen on lîchaman wǽron and ðú hæfdest ǽlc good and he hefde ǽlc yfel ne mót he ðé nú ðý mâre dón to getǽsan ðe ðú ðá hym woldest *but remember that thou didst refuse him every advantage when ye were both in the body and thou hadst every good and he had every evil; he cannot now do more for thy advantage than thou wouldest then do for his*, Shrn. 202, 31–4. Hió an Æþelflede ealra ðera getǽsa ðet ðǽr binnan beóþ *she gives to Æthelfled all the desirable things that are there within*, Th. Chart. 538, 37. Getǽse *commodum*, Cot. 59, Lye.

ge-tǽse; *adj. Meet, convenient, suitable, mild, easy;* accommodus, placidus, lenis:—Gif him wǽre niht getǽse *if he had had an easy night*, Beo. Th. 2645; B. 1320. Swá hit getǽsost wæs *as was most fitting*, Bt. Met. Fox 20, 22; Met. 20, 11. [*O. H. Ger.* ki-zeso *dextrum*. v. Grff. v. 708–10.]

ge-tǽsnes, se; *f. An opportunity, a saving, placing;* commoditas, Cot. 55.

ge-tal; *adj. Quick, ready, active;* agilis, velox, expeditus:—Wǽron hyra tungan getale teónan gehwylcre and to yfele gehwâm ungemet scearpe *their tongues were swift to every wrong and to every evil exceeding sharp;* lingua eorum machæra acuta, Ps. Th. 56, 5. [*O. H. Ger.* ge-zal *agilis, rapidus, alacer.*]

ge-talian; *p.* ode, ade; *pp.* od, ad, ed *To tell, number, reckon, consider:*—Getalade *reputans*, Lk. Skt. Lind. 11, 38. Héras heáfdes alle getalad aron *capilli capitis omnes numerati sunt*, Mt. Kmbl. Lind. 10, 30. Ueras getaled suelce fîfo þûsendo *viri numero quasi quinque milia*, Jn. Skt. Lind. 6, 10. Miþ unrehtwîsum getaled wæs *cum iniquis reputatus est*, Mk. Skt. Lind. 15, 28. v. ge-tellan.

getal-scipe, es; *m. Number;* numerositas:—Getalscipes and tîdes *numerositatis et temporis*, Mt. Kmbl. p. 12, 14.

ge-talu *tribes;* tribus, Mt. Kmbl. Rush. 24, 30; *pl. nom. of* ge-tæl, II.

getan; *p.* de, te; *pp.* ed *To* GET, *take, obtain;* adipisci, capere, assequi:—Cwæþ he on mergenne méces ecgum getan wolde *said he in the morning would take them with the edges of the sword*, Beo. Th. 5872; B. 2940. DER. a-getan. v. -gitan.

gêtan; *p.* de, te; *pp.* ed *To grant, to confirm, assent to:*—Geáfon and gêtton *gave and granted*, Chr. 675; Th. 59, 20. Gêtton hit ælle ða óþre *all the others assented to it*, 656; Th. 53, 27. v. geátan.

ge-tang *lying, prostrate;* prostratus, C. R. Ben. 34, Lye.

ge-tanned; *part. Tanned;* cortĭce mācĕrātus:—Getannede hýd *subacta cŏrĭa*, vel *mĕdĭcāta*, vel *confecta*, Ælfc. Gl. 17; Som. 58, 104; Wrt. Voc. 22, 19.

ge-targed; *part. Provided with a shield;* scutatus, Hpt. Gl. 459. v. targe.

ge-tawa; *pl. f. Instruments;* instrumenta:—Mannes getawa *instrumenta genitalia*, L. M. 1, 29; Lchdm. ii. 70, 7. Ðis syndon ða getawa *these are the instruments*, L. E. I. 2; Th. ii. 404, 3. [*O.H.Ger.* gizawa *suppellex, stipendium.*] DER. gúþ-getawe, wîg-. v. taw, e; *f.*

ge-tawian; *p.* ode, ade; *pp.* od, ad [tawian *to prepare*] *To prepare, reduce* or *bring to;* părāre, redūcĕre ad:—Getawian to yrmþe *redūcĕre ad mĭsĕrĭam*, Nathan. 7; St. And. 34, 18. Hý se æðeling to ðam bismre getawade *the prince brought them to shame*, Ors. 3, 8; Bos. 63, 15. To bysmere beóþ itawode ðæs earman lond-leódæ *to shame are brought this miserable people*, Th. An. 121, 9. v. tawian.

ge-teág, -teáh *drew, led, gave*, Cd. 162; Th. 203, 22; Exod. 407: Bd. 5, 18; S. 636, 4: Beo. Th. 2093; B. 1044. v. ge-teón.

ge-teágan, -têgan; *p.* -têde; *pp.* -teád *To make, prepare:*—Ðæt land mid to teágenne. Ðá ðæt land ðá geteád wæs *to prepare the land with. When then the land was prepared;* preparata terra, Bd. 4, 28; S. 605, 33. Ðone ilcan mete ðe he hí ǽror mid tame getêde *the same food with which before he had made them tame* [*the prose has* ða ilcan mettas ðe hí ǽr tame mid gewenedon, Fox 88, 18], Bt. Met. Fox 13, 87; Met. 13, 44. [Cf. ge-tawian.]

ge-teal -teall *a number*, Nat. S. Greg. Els. 9, 2; Chr. 1014; Erl. 151, 16. v. ge-tæl, I.

ge-teald, es; *n. A tent, tabernacle;* tabernācŭlum:—God afærþ ðé of getealde ðînum *Deus emigrābit te de tabernācŭlo tuo*, Ps. Spl. 51, 5. v. ge-teld.

ge-teáma, -týma, an; *m. An advocate, avoucher, a warranter;* advŏcātus, qui rei emptæ fîdem præstat:—Ic wille ðæt gehwilc man hæbbe his geteáman *I will that every man have his warranter*, L. Ed. 1; Th. i. 158, 9: L. Eth. ii. 8; Th. i. 288, 16. v. teám, ge-têman.

ge-têcan *to show:*—Is þearf ðæt ic ðé hí selfe getêce *it is necessary that I show thee itself*, Bt. 33, 1; Fox 120, 1. v. ge-tǽcan.

ge-têde. v. ge-teágan.

ge-têh *drew*, Nicod. 30; Thw. 17, 31. v. ge-teón.

ge-tehhod *determined, decreed*, Bt. 7, 3; Fox 20, 30 = ge-teohhod; *pp. of* ge-teohhian.

ge-tel *a number;* numerus:—Gemænigfylde hí synt ofer getele *multiplicati sunt super numerum*, Ps. Lamb. 39, 6: Ælfc. Gr. 13; Som. 15, 56. v. ge-tæl, I.

ge-têlan. v. ge-tǽlen.

getel-cræft, es; *m. Arithmetic*, Hpt. Gl. 479.

ge-teld, -tæld, -teald, es; *n.* [teld *a tent*] *A tent, tabernacle, pavilion,* TILT, *cover;* tentōrium, tabernācŭlum:—Geteld *tentōrium* vel *tabernācŭlum*, Wrt. Voc. 85, 84: *scēna* vel *tabernācŭlum*, Ælfc. Gl. 56; Som. 67, 25; Wrt. Voc. 37, 15. God æteówde Abrahame on ðam dene Mambre, ðǽr ðǽr he sæt on his geteldes ingange *appāruit Abraham in convalle Mambre, sĕdenti in ostio tabernācŭli sui*, Gen. 18, 1: Ps. Spl. 26, 9. Hwylc eardaþ on getelde ðînum *quis habĭtābit in tabernācŭlo tuo?* 14, 1. Hí aslógan ân geteld *tĕtendĕrunt tentōrium*, Bd. 3, 17; S. 543, 34. On sunnan gesette getelda his *in sōle pŏsuit tabernācŭlum suum*, Ps. Spl. 18, 5.

ge-teldung, e; *f. A tent, tabernacle;* tabernācŭlum:—On sunnan gesette geteldunge his *in sōle pŏsuit tabernācŭlum suum*, Ps. Spl. T. 18, 5: 26, 9.

geteld-wurþung, e; *f. A celebration of tents, the feast of tabernacles;* scēnŏpēgia = σκηνοπηγία:—Getimbra hālgung *vel* geteldwurþung *scēnŏpēgia*, Ælfc. Gl. 3; Som. 55, 77; Wrt. Voc. 16, 50.

ge-telged *coloured, dyed;* coloratus, Cot. 49, 81. v. tælg.

ge-tellan, ic -telle, ðú -telest, he -teleþ, *pl.* -tellaþ; *p.* -tealde, *pl.* -tealdon; *pp.* -teald, -teled *To tell, number, reckon, esteem, consider, ascribe, assign;* numerare, computare, reputare, comparare, dinumerare:—Ruben and Simeon beóþ mid me getealde *Ruben et Simeon reputabuntur mihi*, Gen. 48, 5: Ps. Spl. C. 43, 25: Ps. Th. 118, 119. Hit getealdon ealde ǽgleáwe *elders skilled in laws reckoned it*, Menol. Fox 34; Men. 17: Cd. 154; Th. 191, 33; Exod. 224. Hwylc can getellan *quis novit dinumerare*, Ps. Spl. 89, 13. Ðá getealdon hie ðæt ðǽr wæs eác syx hund manna acweald *then they reckoned that there were six hundred men slain*, Blickl. Homl. 203, 27. Seó bōc ðe ys genemned on Englisc getel for ðam ðe Israhēla bearn wǽron on ðære getealde *the book that is called in English Numbers because in it the children of Israel were numbered*, Num. Pref: Ps. Th. 89, 11: Andr. Kmbl. 1765; An. 885: Mt. Bos. 10, 30. Ðæt is geteald ðæs læssan mīlgetæles ðe stadia hātte ccc and þreó twentig *it is, reckoned by the smaller measure of distance that are called stadia, three hundred and twenty-three*, Nar. 36, 16: 34, 27. Se biþ geteald Godes feónd *he will be accounted God's enemy*, Homl. Th. i. 162, 22. Ān eórod is geteald to six þūsendum *a legion is reckoned at six thousand*, ii. 378, 29: i. 68, 35. Ðæt Mæcedonisce gewinn ðæt mon mæg to ðām mǽstan gewinnum getellan *the Macedonian war which may be reckoned amongst the greatest wars*, Ors. 4, 11; Bos. 98, 18. Ðonne biþ he geteald to ðære fȳrenan eá *then shall he be assigned to the fiery river*, Blickl. Homl. 43, 24. Ðæt hī hiora āgnum godum getealde wǽron *that they might be ascribed to their own gods*, Ors. 1, 5; Bos. 28, 27. Ðá ðis Constantine geteald wæs *when this was told to Constantine*, H. R. 5, 27. Geteled rīmes *reckoned by number*, Cd. 67; Th. 80, 30; Gen. 1336: 107; Th. 141, 14; Gen. 2344: Elen. Kmbl. 4; El. 2. Geteled rīme, Cd. 64; Th. 76, 27; Gen. 1263: 161; Th. 201, 15; Exod. 372: Andr. Kmbl. 2070; An. 1037. Tyn hund geteled *ten hundred in number*, Cd. 154; Th. 192, 15; Exod. 232: Andr. Kmbl. 1329; An. 665: Ps. Th. 90, 7. v. ge-talian.

ge-têman, -tȳman; *p.* de; *pp.* ed *To vouch to warranty;* vocare ad warrantum. "Vouching to warranty. A process by which a person, in whose possession lost or stolen property was found, was compelled to show from whom he bought or had it, which latter was, in like manner, obliged to declare how it came into his hands, and so on to a third holder, beyond whom, provided he could prove lawful possession, the tracing might not proceed. The person from whom the accused party had the property, and who came forth as his warranter, was called the 'getȳma' or 'geteáma,' and the process itself 'teám,'" LL. Th. Glos. v. L. H. E. 7; Th. i. 30, 8: L. In. 35; Th. i. 124, 10.

ge-temesed, -temsud; *part. Sifted;* cribratus:—Hlāfas getemeseda *panes propositionis*, Mt. Kmbl. Lind. 12, 4: Lk. Skt. Lind. 6. 4. Nim getemsud melu *take sifted meal*, Lchdm. iii. 134, 20.

ge-temian; *p.* ede; *pp.* ed *To tame;* domare:—Ic gewylde oððe temige [getemige, MS. C.] *domo*, Ælfc. Gr. 36; Som. 38, 19. Ða getemedon *domitos*, Th. An. 26, 7, 13. Se getemeda assa hæfde getācnunge ðæs Iudēiscan folces, ðe wæs getemed under ðære ealdan ǽ *the tamed ass betokened the Jewish people that was tamed under the old law*, Homl. Th. i. 208, 20. v. temian.

ge-temprian; *p.* ode; *pp.* od *To temper, moderate, govern, cure;* temperare:—Seó sunne ða eorþan getempraþ *the sun tempers the earth*, Bd. de nat. rerum; Wrt. popl. Scienc. 9, 3; Lchdm. iii. 250, 14. Getemprie seó bilewitnys ðæt fȳr ðæt hit to rēðe ne sȳ *let the meekness temper the fire that it be not too fierce*, Homl. Th. ii. 46, 8. Ān is ðæt gehwā hine sylfne getemprige mid gemete on ǽte and on wǽte *one is, that every one govern himself with moderation in food and drink*, i. 360, 12. Mōt se ðe wile mid sōþum lǽcecræfte his līchaman getemprian *he who will may cure his body with true leechcraft*, 474, 35.

ge-temsud *sifted.* v. ge-temesed.

ge-tengan; *p.* de; *pp.* ed [tengan *to hasten, rush upon*] *To hasten, join, devote one's self to;* injungĕre, dēdĕre:—Hine sylfne getengde in Godes þeówdōm *he devoted himself to God's service*, Elen. Kmbl. 400; El. 200. Ðá getengde se Aristodemus to ðam heáhgerēfa *then Aristodemus hastened to the prefect*, Homl. Th. i. 72, 18. He sōna getengde wiþ ðæs drȳs *he at once hastened towards the magician*, 374, 4. Se þeign ðá ðǽr to geteingde *the servant then hastened thither*, Shrn. 14, 27.

ge-tenge; *adj. Near to, close to, pressing upon, oppressing;* propinquus, incumbens, gravis, molestus:—Geseah gold glitnian grunde getenge *he saw gold glitter lying on the ground*, Beo. Th. 5510; B. 2758: Elen. Kmbl. 2226; El. 1114: 456; El. 228: Bt. Met. Fox 31, 14; Met. 31, 7. Cyningas on heáhsetlum hrōfe getenge *kings high-raised* [lit. *close to the roof*] *on thrones*, 25, 10; Met. 25, 5: Cd. 38; Th. 50, 14; Gen. 808: Runic pm. Kmbl. 343, 2; Rūn. 18. Hundas deórum getenge *dogs pressing upon the animals*, Homl. Th. ii. 514, 25: Shrn. 37, 14. Swā fela gāsta wǽron getenge ðam ānum men *so many spirits were oppressing that one man*, 378, 30. Heora þurst ðe him getenge wæs *their thirst that was oppressive to them*, Ors. 5, 8; Bos. 107, 28: 6, 4; Bos. 119, 4: Nar. 8, 24: Bt. 5, 1; Fox 10, 24: 10; Fox 30, 5. Brōhþreá Cananēa wearþ cynne getenge hunger se hearda *terrible calamity came upon the race of the Canaanites the hard famine*, Cd. 86; Th. 108, 31; Gen. 1814: 149; Th. 187, 9; Exod. 148: 206; Th. 255, 25; Dan. 629: 229; Th. 309, 18; Sat. 711. [Cf. *O. Sax.* bi-tengi: and v. *O. H. Ger.* gi-zengi, Grff. v. 680.] v. ge-tengan, ge-tingan.

getenys, gytenes, se; *f. A procuring, attaining,* GETTING, *instruction, education;* adeptio, institutio, Lye. Getenis *historia*, Hpt. Gl. 459.

ge-teód *determined, decreed*, Bd. 3, 24; S. 556, 12; *pp. of* ge-teón.

ge-teóde *formed, decreed, assigned*, Cd. 182; Th. 228, 19; Dan. 204: Exon. 88 b; Th. 333, 17; Gn. Ex. 5; *p.* of ge-teón.

ge-teóh; *gen.* -teóges; *n. Matter, material; pl. instruments, implements, utensils:*—Se ðis leóht onwrāh and ðæt torhte geteóh tillīce onwrāh *who this light displayed and the bright matter* [*the universe*] *revealed*, Exon. 94 a; Th. 352, 32; Reim. 2. Sulh-geteógo *ploughing implements*, Th. An. 118, 12. [*O. H. Ger.* ge-ziug *materia, suppellex, instrumentum: Ger.* ge-zeug.]

ge-teohhian, -teohian, -tiohhian, -tihhian; *p.* ode, ade; *pp.* od, ad *To appoint, determine, decree, assign;* stătuĕre, decernĕre, assignāre:—Ðá heó Gode ānum geteohode þeówian *cum Deo sōli servīre decrēvisset*, Bd. 4, 23; S. 593, 7. Wæs ōðer in geteohhod mǽrum Geáte *another dwelling had been assigned to the renowned Goth*, Beo. Th. 2605; B. 1300. Geteohod, Bd. 5, 14; S. 634, 31, note. Ðē sind heardlīcu wītu geteohhad *stern torments are determined for thee*, Exon. 69 b; Th. 258, 13; Jul. 264: Blickl. Homl. 25, 25. Ðe his sylfes sāwle hafaþ deáþe geteohhad *who hath assigned his own soul to death*, 183, 33. Eall ðæt yfel, ðæt hī him geteohod hæfdon *all the evil that they had determined against him*, Ps. Th. 9, argument: 14: 16, 13. Ðæt hī toweorpen ðæt God geteohhad hæfþ to wyrcanne *to destroy what God had determined to do*, 10, 3.

ge-teolod; *part. Gained;* lucrifactus:—Ðonne sceal gehwā him æteówian hwæt he mid ðam punde geteolod hæfþ *then shall every one show to him what he has gained with the pound*, Homl. Th. ii. 558, 10. v. ge-tilian.

ge-teón, ic -teó, ðú -tȳhst, he -tȳhþ, *pl.* -teóþ; *p.* -teáh, -teág, -tēh, *pl.* -tugon; *pp.* -togen. I. *to draw, lead, incite, excite, constrain, restrain, bring up, instruct, bring to an end, complete, draw* or *bind together, string a musical instrument;* trahere, ducere, perducere, stringere, evaginare, excitare, constringere, educare, instituere, ad finem perducere, complere, nervis aptare *vel* instruere:—Woldon hine geteón in orwēnnysse *would draw him into despair*, Exon. 41 a; Th. 136, 24; Gū. 546. Ðás wīf wuna geteþ *has mulieres consuetudo constringit*, Bd. 1, 7; S. 494, 11. Ðū getīhst his heáhnisse *consummabis summitatem ejus*, Gen. 6, 16. He Adam fram helle getēh *he drew Adam from hell*, Nicod. 30; Thw. 17, 31. He monige to rihtre weorþunge ðǽre Drihtenlīcan Eástrana geteáh and gelǽdde *multos ad Catholicam Dominici Paschæ celebrationem perduxit*, Bd. 5, 18; S. 636, 4. Ðá hī hæfdon getogen eall Creáca folc to ðǽm gewinnum *when they had drawn all the people of Greece to the wars*, Ors. 1, 14; Bos. 37, 14, 35. He geteág ealde lāfe *he drew an ancient relic* [i. e. *a sword*], Cd. 162; Th. 203, 22; Exod. 407. Getogene ðȳ wǽpne *evaginata sica*, Bd. 2, 9; S. 511, 21. Folc to mānum getogen *excitatum ad scelera vulgus*, 2, 5; S. 507, 42. Hæfþ ealle gesceafta getogen *he has restrained all creatures*, Bt. Met. Fox 11, 48; Met. 11, 24. Ða ðe wǽron on rīm-cræfte rihte getogene *those who were rightly instructed in the art of numbers*, Chr. 975; Th. 226, 31; Edg. 27. Swā getogen mann *a man so well instructed*, Homl. Th. ii. 122, 13: Th. Ap. 17, 18. Heós fyrd wæs getogen ðȳ feorþan geáre his rīces *hoc bellum quarto imperii sui anno complevit*, Bd. 1, 3; S. 475, 15. Wæs heó mid micle sāre getogen *illa erat multo dolore constricta*, 5, 3; S. 616, 22. Wamb getogen *alvus constricta*, Med. ex Quadr. 6, 11; Lchdm. i. 352, 24. Mid tyn strengum getogen hearpe *a harp strung with ten strings*, Ps. Th. 143, 10. Ða organa wǽron getogene *the organs were played*, Th. Ap. 25, 15. II. *to bring as an offering* or *gift, contribute, bestow, give;* conferre:—Onweald geteáh wicga and wǽpna *gave possession of war-horses and weapons*, Beo. Th. 2093; B. 1044: 4337; B. 2165. Nō ðū him wearne geteóh *do not give them a denial*, 738; B. 366.

ge-teón, -tión; *p.* -teóde; *pp.* -teód *To make, form, frame, appoint, determine, decree, ordain, assign;* făcĕre, stătuĕre, constĭtuĕre, decernĕre:—Ðe him to gode geteóde *which he had formed to himself for a god*, Cd. 182; Th. 228, 19; Dan. 204. He us æt frymþe geteóde līf *he assigned life to us at the beginning*, Exon. 88 b; Th. 333, 17; Gn. Ex. 5: 90 a; Th. 337, 28; Gn. Ex. 71: Andr. Kmbl. 28; An. 14. He hine gegyrede mid grame wyrgþu, swā he hine wǽdum wrǽstum geteóde *induit se mălĕdictiōne sīcut vestīmento*, Ps. Th. 108, 18. Hū woruld wǽre wundrum geteód *how the world was wondrously framed*, Cd. 177; Th. 222, 28; Dan. 111. Se ðe geteód hæfde *qui decrēvĕrat*, Bd. 3, 24;

S. 556, 12: Blickl. Homl. 19, 35. Geteód to ðǽm ēcan wītum *destined to eternal torments*, 37, 4: 31, 22. Ðonne biþ ðam heard dōm geteód *a hard sentence will be the lot of that man*, 95, 36. Þurh hwelces monnes hond mīn ende wǽre getiód *by what man's hand my death was determined;* cujus mortem percussoris manu cavendam habeam, Nar. 31, 19: Th. Ch. 483, 15.

ge-teorian, -teorigan, -teorigean; *p.* ode, ude; *pp.* od, ud, ad; *v. intrans. To fail, faint, be weary, languish, cease, perish;* deficere, fatigari, languere, exterminari:—Geteoriaþ *deficiant*, Ps. Th. 67, 2: 103, 27: Ps. Spl. 17, 39. Ic geteorode *ego defeci*, Ps. Spl. 38, 14: 54, 11. Ðā se mete geteorude ðe hig of Egipta lande brohton *when the food was consumed that they brought from Egypt*, Gen. 43, 2: 47, 15: Jn. Bos. 2, 3. Hī geteorodon *defecerunt*, Ps. Spl. 72, 19. Ūre dagas ealle geteorudun *omnes dies nostri defecerunt*, Ps. Th. 89, 9. Ðē læs hig on wege geteorian *ne deficiant in via*, Mt. Bos. 15, 32. Me is heorte geteorad *defecit cor meum*, Ps. Th. 72, 21. He sent on eów geteorigende eágan and mōdes gnornunge *he shall send on you failing eyes and sorrow of mind*, Deut. 28, 65. Geteorigende ateoraþ *deficientes deficient*, Ps. Spl. 36, 21. Be wege hī geteorigeaþ *deficient in via*, Mk. Bos. 8, 3. For swīðlīcre hǽtan geteorud *wearied by the excessive heat*, Herb. 114, 1; Lchdm. i. 226, 23. Beóþ geteorode *exterminabuntur*, Ps. Spl. 36, 9. Sume sceufon sume tugon and swīðe swǽtton ōþ ðæt hig geteorode wǽron *some shoved, some pulled and sweated exceedingly until they were exhausted*, Shrn. 154, 27.

ge-teorung, e; *f. A failing, fainting, languishing, weariness;* defectio, languor, fatigatio:—Geteorung nam me for synnullum *defectio tenuit me præ peccatoribus*, Ps. Spl. 118, 53: 141, 3.

ge-teóþian; *p.* ode; *pp.* od *To tithe, give a tenth part:*—Ic ealle ða landāre ðe ic on Angla þeóde hæfde Gode into hālgan stōwon geteóðode *I gave a tenth part of all my landed property to God for holy places*, Chart. Th. 116, 27. v. teóðian.

ge-ter, es; *n. A tearing;* dilaceratio, Hpt. Gl. 499.

ge-teran *to tear:*—Getearende *discerpens*, Mk. Skt. Lind. 9, 26.

ge-tēse. v. ge-tǽse.

ge-tete *pomp, show, ostentation, magnificence.* v. ge-tot.

ge-tēung. v. ofer-bæc-getēung.

ge-þaca, an; *m. A thatcher, coverer;* tector:—Sceal ðis sāwel-hūs fǽge flǽschoma leomu lāmes geþacan wunian wælreste *this soul-house, the doomed flesh-covering, the limbs, coverers of the earth [lying upon the earth], must inhabit the mortal resting-place*, Exon. 47 b; Th. 164, 1; Gū. 1005.

ge-þæf; *adj.* [geþafian *to agree, consent*] *Agreeing, content;* consentiens:—He his nō geþæf wæs *he was not a consenting party to it*, Cod. Dipl. 183; A.D. 803; Kmbl. i. 222, 35: R. Ben. 7.

ge-þæht, e; *f:* es; *n. Counsel, consultation;* consĭlium:—Ðæt he wolde mid his freóndum sprǽce and geþæht habban *that he would have a conference and consultation with his friends*, Bd. 2, 13; S. 515, 37. Giþæht *consilium*, Rtl. 1, 9. v. ge-þeaht.

ge-þæslǽcan *to fit, to be fit, to become;* aptare, quadrare, congruere, R. Ben. interl. 2: Hpt. Gl. 506; 523.

ge-þæslīc; *adj.* [þæslīc *fit*] *Fit, proper;* dĕcens, opportūnus:—Geþæslīc [MS. geþæsliic] *dĕcens*, Ælfc. Gr. 14; Som. 16, 44. On tīman geþæslīcum oððe on gedafenlīcre tīde *in tempŏre opportūno*, Ps. Lamb. 31, 6.

ge-þafa, an; *m.* [geþafian *to consent*] *A favourer, supporter, helper, assenter, consenter;* fautor, adjūtor:—He biþ ryhtes geþeahtes geþafa *he is the supporter of good designs*, Past. 42, 1; Swt. 306, 14; Hat. MS. 58 a, 17: Cd. 22; Th. 127, 8; Gen. 414. Hwī ne eart ðū his geþafa *why art thou not an assenter to this?* Bt. 26, 2; Fox 92, 13: L. De Cf. 7; Th. ii. 262, 30. Ic eom geþafa *I am convinced, I am an assenter*, Bt. 35, 2; Fox 156, 13: 36, 5; Fox 180, 16: 38, 2; Fox 196, 16. Gif ðē mon for rihtre scylde brōcie, geþola hit wel and beó his wel geþafa *if thou art afflicted for a just cause, bear it well and assent to it readily*, Prov. Kmbl. 45. Ðā næs Æðelm nā fullīce geþafa *then Æthelm did not fully assent*, Th. Ch. 171, 4. We sceolon beón geþafan *we must necessarily be consenters*, Bt. 34, 12; Fox 154, 7.

ge-þafian, -þafigan, -þafigean; *p.* ode, ude; *pp.* od, ud [þafian *to permit, allow, consent*] *To favour, support, permit, allow, admit, assent, consent, agree, approve, obey, submit to;* fāvēre, sustĭnēre, sĭnĕre, admittĕre, permittĕre, assentīre, consentīre, obēdīre, concēdĕre:—Ðū deáþe sweltest gif ðū geþafian nelt mōdges gemānan *thou shalt perish by death if thou wilt not consent to the proud one's fellowship*, Exon. 67 b; Th. 250, 12; Jul. 126: 41 a; Th. 138, 7; Gū. 572: Judth. 10; Thw. 22, 12; Jud. 60: L. Alf. pol. 6; Th. i. 66, 5. He nolde geþafigan ðæt man hys hūs underdulfe *non sĭnĕret perfŏdi dŏmum suam*, Mt. Bos. 24, 43. Geþafigean, Bd. 2, 2; S. 502, 14. Ic geþafige *consentio*, Ælfc. Gr. 30, 2; Som. 34, 39: 37; Som. 39, 9: Ps. Th. 130, 3. He ne geþafode ðæt hig ǽnig þing sprǽcon *non sĭnēbat ea lŏqui*, Lk. Bos. 4, 41: 12, 39. Se eádega wer idese lārum geþafode *the blessed man assented to the woman's counsels*, Cd. 101; Th. 134, 31; Gen. 2233: Bd. 3, 23; S. 555, 2. Nā hī geþafudon geþeaht his *non sustĭnuērunt consĭlium ejus*, Ps. Spl. 105, 13. Ðīnum mǽge mān ne geþafa *approve not wickedness in thy kinsman*, Exon. 80 a; Th. 301, 12; Fä. 18. Ne gē in ne gāþ, ne gē ne geþafiaþ ðæt ōðre ingān *vos non intrātis, nec introeuntes sĭnĭtis intrāre*, Mt. Bos. 23, 13. Ðās hwīlwendlīcan gedrefednyssa we sceolon mid gefeán for Cristes naman geþafian *but these transitory tribulations we ought to submit to with joy for Christ's name*, Homl. Th. i. 556, 10: Prov. Kmbl. 9: Past. 21, 1; Swt. 151, 15; Hat. MS. Beágmund geþafie and mid wrīte *I, Beagmund, approve and consign*, Th. Ch. 475, 16.

ge-þafsum; *adj. Agreeing;* consentiens:—Wæs ðū geþafsum *esto consentiens*, Mt. Kmbl. Lind. 5, 25.

ge-þafsumniss, e; *f. Agreement, consent*, Mt. Kmbl. p. 14, 14.

ge-þafung, e; *f. Permission, allowance, assent, consent;* permissio, assensus, consensus:—Mid Earnulfes geþafunge *with Arnulf's permission*, Chr. 887; Erl. 86, 3. Be his geþafunge gecyrde se apostol *by his permission the apostle returned*, Homl. Th. i. 60, 6: Th. Ch. 526, 21. On hūse Godes we eodon mid geþafunge *in dŏmo Dei ambulāvĭmus cum consensu*, Ps. Spl. C. 54, 15: Bd. 1, 27; S. 497, 25. Ðyssum wordum ōðer ðæs cyninges wita and ealdormann geþafunge sealde, and to ðære sprǽce fēng *cujus suasiōni verbisque prudentĭbus alius optĭmātum trĭbŭens assensum, contĭnuo subdĭdit*, Bd. 2, 13; S. 516, 12: 4, 8; S. 576, note 5.

ge-þanc, -þonc, -þang, es: generally *m.* but sometimes *n.* [þanc *will*] *Mind, will, opinion, thought;* mens, animus, cogitatio:—Þincþ on his geþance *thinks in his mind*, R. Ben. 65. Ðone fǽlan geþanc frine *interroga me*, Ps. Th. 138, 20. Se Hǽlend geseh hyra heortan geðancas *Iesus videns cogitationes cordis illorum*, Lk. Bos. 9, 47: Ps. Th. 91, 4: 93, 11: 128, 3: 139, 8; all *m;* but the following three are *n:*—Sōþlīce ðæt geþanc eode on hig, hwylc hyra yldest wǽre *intravit autem cogitatio in eos, quis eorum major esset*, Lk. Bos. 9, 46: Byrht. Th. 132, 9; By. 13. Geþancu and geþeahtu *thoughts and plans*, Lchdm. iii. 214, 23. Ðone ilcan geþang ic ðē ǽr sǽde *the same thought I have told thee before*, Blickl. Homl. 179, 28. Geþanges *mentis*, Ps. Spl. 67, 29.

ge-þancian, -þoncian; *p.* ode, ede; *pp.* od, ed [þancian *to thank*] *To thank, give thanks, reward;* grātias agĕre:—Geþance ðē þeóda Waldend, ealra ðæra wynna ðe ic on worulde gebād *I thank thee, Lord of the nations, for all the delights which I have experienced on earth*, Byrht. Th. 136, 57; By. 173. He geþancode Gode his sande *he thanked God for what he had sent*, Homl. Th. ii. 136, 18. We sceolon geþancian Gode ðæt he wolde asendan his āncennedan Sunu *we ought to thank God that he was willing to send his only-begotten Son*, 23, 2. We him his geswinces geþancedon, of ūrum gemǽnum feó *we would reward him for his labour out of our common money*, L. Ath. v. § 7; Th. i. 234, 27. We giþoncia *gratulamur*, Rtl. 74, 7: 31, 1.

geþanc-metian; *p.* ode; *pp.* od *To deliberate, consider;* consĭdĕrāre:—Geþancmeta ðīne mōde, on hwilce healfe ðū wille hwyrft dōn *deliberate in thy mind on which side thou wilt depart*, Cd. 91; Th. 115, 9; Gen. 1917.

ge-þancol, -þancul, -þoncol; *adj.* [þanc *the mind, thought*] *Mindful, thoughtful, considerate, suppliant;* mĕmor, cōgĭtābundus, supplex:—Ic wæs gemyndig mǽrra dōma ðīnra geþancol, þeóden Dryhten *mĕmor fui judĭciōrum tuōrum a sĕcŭlo, Dŏmĭne*, Ps. Th. 118, 52: Ps. C. 50, 6; Ps. Grn. ii. 276, 6. Swā hleóðrode hālig cempa, þeáwum geþancul *thus spake the holy champion, in all his ways thoughtful*, Andr. Kmbl. 923; An. 462. Giþoncolo *intenti*, Rtl. 16, 31. Giþoncle *supplices*, 4, 24.

ge-þancol, -þoncol; *adj. Thankful, grateful:*—Giþoncolo wosaþ gie *grati estote*, Rtl. 13, 39.

ge-þang. v. ge-þanc.

ge-þang, es; *n. Growth:*—Gyfe pund, ðanon him wæs geseald se fæt and geþang *a pound of grace, thence was given him the fat and growth*, Salm. Kmbl. 180, 12.

ge-þawenian; *p.* ode, ede; *pp.* od, ed *To moisten;* humectāre:—Hió mid ðæm wætere weorþeþ [weorþaþ, MS.] geþawened *it is moistened with the water*, Bt. Met. Fox 20, 204; Met. 20, 102.

ge-þeáh *thrived*, L. R. 3; Th. i. 190, 18; *p. of* ge-þeón.

ge-þeád. v. ge-þeód.

ge-þeaht, -þæht, e; *f:* es; *n.* I. *counsel, consultation, deliberation, advice, thought, a determination, resolution, device, plan, purpose;* consĭlium, cōgĭtātio:—Geþeaht Drihtnes on ēcnysse wunaþ *consĭlium Dŏmĭni in æternum mănet*, Ps. Spl. 32, 11: Ps. Th. 88, 6. Ðæt geþeaht *the counsel*, Ps. Th. 9, 6. Hie ðære geþeahte wǽron *they were of the resolution*, Cd. 182; Th. 228, 21; Dan. 205. Hī nyllaþ geþafan beón ōðerra monna geþeahtes *they will not be supporters of the plan of other men*, Past. 42, 1; Swt. 305, 15; Hat. MS. 58 a, 2. On ānre geþeahte *consĭlium fēcērunt in ūnum*, Ps. Th. 70, 9 [MS. geþeaht] eodan togædere. On geþeahte *in consĭlio*, Ps. Spl. 1, 1: Ps. Th. 105, 32. Būtan geþeahte *without advice;* inconsulte, Bd. 3, 1; S. 523, 31. Of hiera āgnum geþeahte *from their own determination*, Past. 42, 1; Swt. 305, 18; Hat. MS. 58 a, 4. Ealle geþeaht ðīn he getrymþ *omne consĭlium tuum confirmet*, Ps. Spl. 19, 4. Þurh monnes geþeaht *through man's device*, Cd. 29; Th. 38, 12; Gen. 605: Elen. Kmbl. 2117; El. 1060. Hī forhogodon ðæs Hǽlendes geþeaht *consĭlium Dei sprēvērunt*, Lk. Bos. 7, 30: Bd. 2, 13; S. 515, 32, 40. Hī ān geþeaht ealle ymbsǽtan *cōgĭtāvērunt consensum in ūnum*, Ps. Th. 82, 5. Ðæt he him geþeaht sealde *ut consĭlium sibi dăret*, Bd. 4, 25; S. 599, 38. Ðū [God] eal gōd [MS. good] ānes geþeahte ðīnes geþohtest *thou [God] didst conceive all good* *by the counsel of thyself alone*, Bt. Met. Fox 20, 78; Met. 20, 39: Bt. 33, 4; Fox 128, 20. Mid geþeahte ðínum *with thy counsel*, Bt. Met. Fox 20, 173; Met. 20, 87. Geþancu and geþeahtu *thoughts and plans*, Lchdm. iii. 214, 24. He wiðcwyþ geþeaht ealdrum *reprŏbat consĭlia princĭpum*, Ps. Spl. 32, 10: Ps. Th. 55, 5. II. *a council, an assembly;* concĭlium:—Geþeaht awyrgedra ofsǽton me *cŏncĭlium mălignantium obsēdit me*, Ps. Spl. 21, 15. Ic ne sæt mid geþeahte ýdelnyssa *non sēdi cum concĭlio vānĭtātis*, 25, 4. On ðam geþeahte *in the council*, Homl. Th. i. 46, 5. DER. rǽd-geþeaht.

ge-þeaht *covered*, Cd. 73; Th. 90, 8; Gen. 1492; *pp. of* ge-þeccan.

ge-þeahta, an; *m. A counsellor;* consiliarius:—Hæfst ðú ǽnigne wísne geþeahtan *habes aliquem sapientem consiliarium*, Coll. Monast. Th. 30, 5.

ge-þeahtend, es; *m. A counsellor;* consĭliārius:—Se geþeahtend andswaraþ *consĭliārius respondit*, Coll. Monast. Th. 30, 37: 31, 21.

ge-þeahtendlíc; *adj. Deliberative:*—Geþeahtendlíc ymcyme *a deliberative convention*, L. Wih. pref; Th. i. 36, 7.

ge-þeahtere, es; *m. A counsellor;* consĭliārius:—Se wæs geþeahtere ðæs apostolícan pápan *qui consĭliārius ĕrat ăpostŏlĭci pāpæ*, Bd. 5, 19; S. 638, 14. DER. þeahtere.

ge-þeahtian; *p.* ode; *pp.* od *To take counsel, consult;* consĭliāri:—Geniman sáwle míne hí geþeahtodon *accĭpĕre anĭmam meam consĭliāti sunt*, Ps. Lamb. 30, 17.

ge-þeahting, -þeahtung, -þæhtung, e; *f. Counsel, consultation, deliberation, agreement;* consĭlium, consultātio, consultum, consensus:—Ic Ælfrēd cingc mid geþeahtunge Æþerēdes ercebisceopes *I, king Alfred, with the counsel of archbishop Athered*, Th. Ch. 484, 11. Hú egesfullíc he is in geþeahtingum ofer monna bearn *quam terrĭbĭlis in consĭliis sŭper fīlios hŏmĭnum!* Bd. 4, 25; S. 601, 36. Se geþeahtingum hafaþ in hondum heofon and eorþan *who by his counsels holdeth in his power heaven and earth*, Exon. 43 a; Th. 140, 31; Gú. 618. To geþeahtunge *ad consulta*, Bd. 1, 27; S. 497, 43. Mid geþeahtunge *cum consensu*, Ps. Th. 54, 13. Geþæhtung *consilium*, Mt. Kmbl. Lind. 12, 14: 22, 15.

ge-þearf, ic, he; *I have*, or *he has need* or *necessity*. v. ge-þurfan.

ge-þearfian; *p.* ode; *pp.* od *To impose necessity;* necessitatem imponere:—Ðá him swá geþearfod wæs *as necessity thus was imposed upon them*, Beo. Th. 2211; B. 1103. v. þearfian.

ge-þeccan; *p.*-þeahte *To cover;* tegere:—Lago hæfde geþeahte ēðel *the water had covered the country*, Cd. 73; Th. 90, 8; Gen. 1492. DER. þeccan.

ge-þecgan; *p.* ede *To consume:*—Þurste geþegede *consumed with thirst*, Exon. 30 a; Th. 92, 17; Cri. 1510. v. a-, of-þecgan. *But cf. also* ge-þēwan.

ge-þegnian, -þēnian; *p.* ode; *pp.* od [þegnian *to serve*] *To minister, serve;* ministrāre:—Ðú hæfst to þance geþēnod ðínum hearran *thou hast served thy lord so as to please him*, Cd. 25; Th. 32, 20; Gen. 506.

ge-þencan, -þencean, ic -þence, ðú -þencest, -þencst, he -þenceþ, -þencþ, *pl.* -þencaþ, -þenceaþ; *p.* ic, he -þohte, ðú -þohtest, *pl.* -þohton; *pp.* -þoht. I. *to think, conceive, perceive, reflect upon, weigh;* meditari, considerare, pensare:—Hwylc eówer mæg sóþlíce geþencan ðæt he geeácnige áne elne to hys anlícnesse *quis autem vestrum cogitans potest adjicere ad staturam suam cubitum unum*, Mt. Bos. 6, 27: Exon. 77 a; Th. 289, 34; Wand. 58: 100 a; Th. 378, 6; Deor. 12. Ðú meaht sweotole geþencean *thou mayest clearly perceive*, Bt. Met. Fox 5, 2; Met. 5, 1. To geþencanne *to think*, Exon. 112 a; Th. 429, 3; Rä. 42, 8. Ðú [God] eal gōd [MS. good] ánes geþeahte ðínes geþohtest, and hí ðá worhtest *thou* [*God*] *didst conceive all good by the counsel of thyself alone, and then didst create it*, Bt. Met. Fox 20, 79; Met. 20, 40. Snyttro geþencaþ weras wísfæste *think prudence, oh ye wise men!* Elen. Kmbl. 626; El. 313. II. *to think about, remember, consider maturely, to take to heart;* recogitare, iterum cogitare, reminisci:—He sceal geþencan gǽstes þearfe *he shall think about the need of his soul*, Exon. 23 b; Th. 65, 20; Cri. 1057. Geþenceþ *thinketh*, 117 a; Th. 449, 27; Dóm. 77. Ic geþence *reminiscor*, Ælfc. Gr. 29; Som. 33, 54. Ic ánne ánlēpne ne mæg geþencean *I cannot remember a single one*, Past. pref; Swt. 3, 18; Hat. MS. Ðæt he ne mæg ende geþencean *that he cannot consider his end*, Beo. Th. 3473; B. 1734. Gif he hit geþencan can *if he can consider it*, Salm. Kmbl. 814; Sal. 406: Exon. 115 b; Th, 445, 8; Dóm. 4. Hwæt! ðú lyt geþohtest *lo! thou didst consider little*, Soul Kmbl. 45; Seel. 23. III. *to think of, bear in mind, remember;* recordari, cogitare, memor esse:—Mæg geþencan, ðæt geond ðas woruld witig Dryhten wendeþ geneahhe *he may bear in mind that throughout this world the sagacious Lord alternates abundantly*, Exon. 100 b; Th. 379, 10; Deór. 31: 83 b; Th. 314, 5; Mód. 9. Ðe his synna geþenceþ *who bears in mind his sins*, 117 a; Th. 450, 6; Dóm. 83. Sóþfæste beót geþenceaþ *the righteous think of the promise* [*of God*], Ps. Th. 106, 41: 118, 74. Ic ealde dagas geþohte *cogitavi dies antiquos*, 76, 5. Geþenc se snottra fengel hwæt wit sprǽcon *let the sagacious prince bear in mind what we have spoken*, Beo. Th. 2952; B. 1474: Exon. 13 a; Th. 23, 18; Cri. 370. IV. *to excogitate, devise, invent, conceive;* excogitare, struere, invenire:—Ðú meaht rǽd geþencan *thou mayest devise counsel*, Cd. 27; Th. 35, 28; Gen. 561. Mid swilcum mæg man rǽd geþencean *with such one may devise counsel*, 15; Th. 19, 4; Gen. 286. He worn geþenceþ hinderhóca *he devises a number of stratagems*, Exon. 83 b; Th. 315, 19; Mód. 33. Se geréfa hēt ða hálgan margaretan on karcerne betýnan óþ ðæt he geþohte hú he hire mægþhád forspilde *the prefect ordered the holy Margaret to be shut up in prison until he had devised how he might destroy her virginity*, Nar. 41, 17. He cwæþ ðæt he nán ryhtre geþencan ne meahte *he said he could conceive nothing more right*, Th. Ch. 171, 15. Hý grófon ǽghwylcne stán swá se cásere geþohte *they carved every stone as the emperor devised*, Shrn. 146, 17. V. *to resolve, intend, wish;* intendere, velle:—Uton geþencan Hǽlende hēran *let us resolve to obey the Saviour*, Cd. 227; Th. 305, 9; Sat. 644. Se awyrgda geþohte ðæt he heofencyninge hēran ne wolde *the accursed one resolved that he would not obey heaven's king*, 220; Th. 284, 4; Sat. 316: 217; Th. 276, 11; Sat. 187. Ðú geþohtest ðæt ðú ðíne mægþhád Meotude sealdes *thou didst resolve that thou wouldest give to the Lord thy maidenhood*, Exon. 12 a; Th. 18, 23; Cri. 288. DER. þencan.

ge-þenian; *p.* ede; *pp.* ed *To stretch out, extend:*—Geþenede *extendens*, Mt. Kmbl. Lind. 12, 49: 14, 31.

ge-þēnsum; *adj. Obsequious, obliging, serviceable;* officiosus:—He wearþ geset cumena þēn ðæt he mynsterlícum cumum geþēnsum wǽre *he was appointed servant of guests that he might attend upon the monastic guests*, Homl. Th. ii. 136, 24. Gif hwilc sibling ðē biþ swá geþēnsum swilce ðín ágen fōt *if any kinsman be as serviceable to thee as thy own foot*, i. 516, 15.

ge-þeód; *part. p. Captive;* captivus:—Geþeódo *captivi*, Lk. Skt. Lind. 21, 24. Fore geþeádum *pro captivis*, Rtl. 177, 19. v. ge-þeón.

ge-þeódan, he -þeót; *p.* -þeódde; *pp.* -þeóded, -þeód *To join, connect, unite, associate, apply, adjust, translate;* jungĕre, adjungĕre, conjungĕre, cŏpŭlāre, sŏciāre, aptāre:—Ic geþeóde *conjungo*, Ælfc. Gr. 47; Som. 48, 42. Forðam forlǽt se man fæder and móder and geþeót hine to his wífe *quamobrem relinquet hŏmo patrem suum et matrem et adhærēbit uxōri suæ*, Gen. 2, 24: Mt. Bos. 19, 5. Ðe hí hie oftost to geþeódaþ *to whom they most frequently join themselves*, Bt. 16, 3; Fox 56, 34. He ðám wordum sóna monig word to geþeódde *eis mox plūra verba adjunxit*, Bd. 4, 24; S. 597, 27. Ðæt us Gode ðú geþeóddest *ut nos Deo conjungĕres*, Hymn. Surt. 31, 29. Ðonne mihte he ðara ríme geþeóded beón *posset eōrum nŭmĕro sŏciāri*, Bd. 5, 13; S. 633, 36: Ps. Th. 61, 5. Mihte swýðe well beón to him geþeóded se cwide ðe Iacob se heáh-fæder cwæþ *cui mĕrĭto pŏtĕrat illud quod Patriarcha dīcēbat aptāri*, Bd. 1, 34; S. 499, 25. Ðá wæs geþeóded hefig gefeoht *conserto grăvi prælio*, 2, 20; S. 521, 10: 4, 21; S. 590, 12. Ðæt bearn fæderlícum setle ys geþeód *quod partus pāternæ sēdi jungĭtur*, Hymn. Surt. 89, 32. Of hwylce cneórysse sculon cristene men mid heora mágum him betwih on gesinscipe geþeódde beón *usque ad quŏtam generātiōnem fĭdēles dēbeant cum propinquis sibi conjŭgio cŏpŭlāri?* Bd. 1, 27; S. 490, 35: 2, 3; S. 504, 17. He hēt ðisne regul of læden-gereorde on englisc geþeódan *he ordered to translate this rule from Latin into English*, Lchdm. iii. 440, 28. v. ge-þýdan.

ge-þeóde, es; *n. Language, speech, idiom, translation;* lingua:—Nis nán mennisc geþeóde *non sunt sermones*, Ps. Th. 18, 3. Ðǽr ðǽr hine nán man ne can ne he nǽnne mon ne furðum ðæt geþeóde ne can *where no man knows him nor he any man, nor does he know even the language*, Bt. 27, 3; Fox 98, 23. Ðæt ys gereht on úre geþeóde *quod est interpretatum*, Mt. Kmbl. 1, 23: Mk. Skt. 5, 41: 15, 22: Homl. Th. i. 194, 1: Past. pref; Swt. 5, 13; Hat. MS. Ða Finnas and ða Beormas sprǽcon neáh án geþeóde *the Finns and the Permians spoke nearly one language*, Ors. 1, 1; Bos. 20, 15. Hēr sind fíf geþeóde Englisc and Brittisc and Wilsc and Scyttisc and Pyhtisc and Bóc Leden *there are five languages here, English, British, Scotch, Pictish, and Latin*, Chr. Erl. 3, 2. Hí mihton sóna sprecan on ǽghwelc ðara geþeóda ðe under heofonum is *they could at once speak in every language under heaven*, Shrn. 85, 16: Bt. 35, 4; Fox 162, 26. Ðæt hēr ðý mára wísdóm on londe wǽre ðý we má geþeóda cúþon *that there might be the more wisdom in the land the more languages we knew*, Past. pref; Swt. 5, 25; Hat. MS. Hát todǽlan heora geþeóde *divide linguas eorum*, Ps. Th. 54, 8. Ic ðá geþeóde to micclan gesceáde telede *I reckoned then a translation to make much difference*, Lchdm. iii. 442, 4. [Cf. *O. H. Ger.* ge-diuti, Grff. v. 131.]

ge-þeóde. v. ingeþeóde.

ge-þeódendlíc; *adj. Conjunctive, joining;* copulativus:—Copulativæ ðæt synd geþeódendlíce *copulativæ, that is, joining together*, Ælfc. Gr. 44; Som. 45, 36.

ge-þeódnes, -ness, -nyss, e; *f.* [ge, þeódnes, -nys *a joining*]. I. *a joining, juncture, joint;* junctio, junctura, compages:—Seó geþeódnes ðæs heáfdes tobrocen wæs *the joining of the head was broken*, Bd. 5, 6; S. 619, 24. He wæs býgendlíc on ðám geþeódnessum his liþa *he was flexible in the joints of his limbs*, 4, 30; S. 608, 38. Monigra monna mód to geþeódnesse ðæs heofonlícan lífes onbærnde wǽron *multorum animi appetitum sunt vitæ cœlestis accensi*, 4, 24; S. 596, 37. II. *a conjunction:*—Conjunctio mæg beón gecweden geþeódnyss *conjunctio may be called 'geþeódnyss*,' Ælfc. Gr. 44, 2; Som. 45, 24: 5, 26; Som. 3, 50. III. *conjugation:*—Conjugatio verborum is worda geþeódnyss . . . Conjugatio mæg beón gecweden geþeódnyss forðan ðe on ðære beóþ manega word geþeódde on ânre declînunge, Ælfc. Gr. 24; Som. 24, 19–23. IV. *a translation*:—Ðeáh ða scearpþanclan witan ðisse engliscan geþeódnesse ne behôfien *though the acute wise men need not this English translation*, Lchdm. iii. 440, 32.

ge-þeódrǽden, e; *f. Fellowship, society*:—Ðonne biþ ðê sêlre ðæt ðû heora geþeódrǽdene forbuge *then it will be better for thee that thou avoid their society*, Homl. Th. i. 516, 17.

ge-þeódsumness, e; *f. Assent, consent, agreement*, Lk. Skt. p. 8, 1.

ge-þeófian; *p.* ode, ade: *pp.* od, ad *To steal, thieve*; furâri:—Gif hwâ on cirican hwæt geþeófige *if any one thieve aught in a church*, L. Alf. pol. 6; Th. i. 66, 2. Ðæt he hæbbe ǽr geþeófad *that he had before thieved*, L. In. 48; Th. i. 132, 8, MSS. B. H.

ge-þeón, ic -þeó, *pl.* -þeóþ; *p.* -þeáh, *pl.* -þugon; *pp.* -þogen *To grow, grow up, increase, thrive, flourish, prosper*; crescĕre, profĭcĕre, vĭgēre:—Lofdǽdum sceal man geþeón *a man shall flourish by praiseworthy deeds*, Beo. Th. 50; B. 25: 1825; B. 910: Homl. Th. i. 12, 26. Erigende ic geþeó *arando proficio*, Ælfc. Gr. 24; Som. 25, 18. Ic strangige oððe geþeó *vĭgeo*, 26, 3; Som. 28, 47. Fela rîccra manna geþeóþ Gode *many rich men thrive to God*, Homl. Th. i. 130, 33: ii. 22, 15. Gif þegen geþeáh ðæt he þênode cynge *if a thane thrived so that he served the king*, L. R. 3; Th. i. 190, 18: 5, 6; Th. i. 192, 7, 9. Wæs his fæder ǽrest cyninges þegn and ðâ æt nêhstan geþeáh ðæt he wæs cininges þegna aldorman *his father was first a king's thane, and at last rose to be chief of the king's thanes*, Blickl. Homl. 211, 21. Ðe Gode geþugon þurh gehaltsumnysse his beboda *who throve to God through observance of his commandments*, Homl. Th. ii. 280, 32: i. 444, 16. Geþeóh tela *thrive well!* Beo. Th. 2441; B. 1218: Exon. 122 a; Th. 469, 13; Hy. 11, 1. Ðæt ic ðê geþeó þinga gehwylce *that I may thrive to thee in everything*, 118 a; Th. 453, 9; Hy. 4, 12: L. Wg. 7, 10; Th. i. 188, 1, 8. Se ðe for wîsdôme wende to Scottum ðæt he ælþeódig on lâre geþuge *who for the sake of wisdom had gone to Scotland that in a foreign land he might increase in learning*, Homl. Th. ii. 148, 19. Ðâ ðâ he geþogen wæs *when he was grown up*, 38, 9: L. Ælf. P. 40; Th. ii. 380, 27. Se ðe swâ geþogenne forwyrhtan næfde *he who had not so prosperous a vicegerent*, L. R. 4; Th. i. 192, 5. Wæl geboren and yfele geþogen *degĕner*, Ælfc. Gr. 9, 18; Som. 10, 6. Geþogen [geþogend, MS.] on mægne *mactus virtūte*, 41; Som. 44, 14.

ge-þeón, -þeówan; *p.* -þeóde, -þeówde; *pp.* -þeód *To tame, oppress*; dŏmāre, opprimĕre:—Se mec âna mæg êcan meahtum geþeón *who alone can tame me by his eternal powers*, Exon. 111 b; Th. 427, 14; Rä. 41, 91. Me ðînes yrres egsa geþeówde *the terror of thine anger oppressed me*, Ps. Th. 87, 16. v. ge-þýwan *and* ge-þeód *captive.*

ge-þeón; *p.* -þeóde *To do, commit, perform*; perficere, patrare:—Ðæt we siððan forþ ða sêllan þing symle môten geþeón *that henceforth we may ever do those better things*, Exon 13 a; Th. 23, 31; Cri. 377. v. þeón.

ge-þeót, es; *n. Howling*:—Wulfa geþeót *howling of wolves*, Guthl. 8; Gdwn. 48, 4.

ge-þeót *shall join*, = *3rd pres. sing. of* ge-þeódan.

ge-þeówan *to oppress*, Ps. Th. 87, 16. v. ge-þeón, -þýwan.

ge-þeówian; *p.* ode, ade; *pp.* od, ad *To make a slave, enslave*; servĭtūti subjĭcĕre, in servĭtūtem redĭgĕre:—Ǽr hine mon geþeówode *before he was made a slave*, L. In. 48; Th. i. 132, 9. Gif hwelc man biþ niwan geþeówad *if any man be newly made a slave*, 48; Th. i. 132, 7: Th. Chart. 553, 9. Syndon cradolcild geþeówode *infantes e cūnābŭlis sunt mancĭpāti*, Lupi Serm. i. 5; Hick. Thes. ii. 100, 30; Swt. A. S. Rdr. 106, 50.

ge-þersc *a stripe, blow*; verber, Dial. 1, 2.

ge-þerscan; *p.* -þearsc, *pl.* -þurscon *To strike, beat, thrash*:—Geþearsca *cædere*, Mk. Skt. Lind. 14, 65. To geþearscanne, 15, 15. Geþurscon *cederunt*, 12, 3: Mt. Kmbl. Lind. 21, 35.

ge-þêwan; *p.* -þêwde; *pp.* -þêwed, -þêwd *To oppress*; opprĭmĕre:—He sârig folc, geþêwde þurste, blissade *he gladdened the sorrowful people, oppressed with thirst*, Ps. Th. 106, 32. v. ge-þýwan.

ge-þicfyldan; *p.* de *To make thick*; densare, Gl. Prud. 970.

ge-þicgan, -þicgean; *p.* -þah *To take, accept, receive*; sumere, accipere:—Waldon ða swângerêfan ða læswe forður gedrîfan and ðone wudu geþicgan ðonne hit aldgeryhto wêron *the swainreeves wanted to push the pasturage and take the wood further than the old rights extended*, Th. Ch. 70, 22. And hiera se æþeling gehwelcum feoh and feorh gebeád and hiera nǽnig hit geþicgean nolde *the atheling offered every one of them money and life and none of them would accept it*, Chr. 755; Erl. 50, 6. Hit on mete oððe on drince to geþicganne *to take it* [*poison*] *in meat or drink*, Ors. 3, 6; Bos. 58, 16. He ðæt ful geþeah æt Wealþeón *he took the cup from Waltheow*, Beo. Th. 1261; B. 628: 1241; B. 618: Cd. 42; Th. 54, 30; Gen. 885. Ðǽr ic beág geþah *there I received a bracelet*, Exon. 85 b; Th. 322, 19; Vîd. 65: 84 b; Th. 318, 24; Vîd. 3. Londryht geþah *he received the land-right*, 100 b; Th. 379, 29; Deór. 40: Cd. 161; Th. 200, 10; Exod. 354. Boitius se hæle hâtte se ðone hlîsan geþah *Boethius the man was named who got that fame*, Bt. Met. Fox 1, 106; Met. 1, 53. Geþǽgon medoful manig *they took many a mead-cup*, Beo. Th. 2033; B. 1014.

ge-þicgan; *pp.* -þiged *To take*:—Seoððan wæs mêce geþiged [Th. geþinged] *afterwards was the sword taken*, Beo. Th. 3881; B. 1938. v. þicgan *wk.*

ge-þiédan. v. ge-þeódan.

ge-þiéfian; *p.* ode, ede; *pp.* od, ed *To steal*; fūrāri, L. In. 48; Th. i. 132, 8. v. ge-þeófian.

ge-þîhan; *p.* -þâh, -þâg, -þǽh *To thrive, prosper, grow*; vigere, proficere, crescere:—Ǽlc ðæra ðe Gode geþîhþ *every one that thrives to God*, Homl. Th. ii. 454, 29. Eádig biþ se ðe in his êðle geþîhþ *happy is he who thrives in his country*, Exon. 89 a; Th. 335, 21; Gn. Ex. 37. Alexandreas monna cynnes mǽst geþâh *Alexandreas prospered most of the race of men*, Exon. 85 a; Th. 319, 23; Wid. 16: 40 b; Th. 134, 16; Gû. 508: Cd. 149; Th. 186, 24; Exod. 143. [Cf. ge-þeón.] DER. þîhan.

ge-þincð. v. ge-þingþu.

ge-þind. v. ge-þynd.

ge-þinde; *pl. m. Rivals*; æmulatores, Hpt. Gl. 429. [Cf. þindan.]

ge-þing, es; *n.* I. *a council, an assembly*; concilium, concio:—Ðâ se þeóden ongan geþinges wyrcan *then did the prince form a council*, Cd. 197; Th. 245, 25; Dan. 468. Hêt hie upastandan to Godes geþinge *he bade them arise to God's assembly*, Andr. Kmbl. 1588; An. 795I. II. *a compact, an agreement, a condition*; pactum:—Be diernum geþinge *concerning a private compact*, L. In. 52; Th. i. 134, 11, 12: 50; Th. i. 134, 1: L. Ath. v. § 11; Th. i. 240, 16: Th. Ch. 465, 12. Hig him geþingo budon ðæt hie him ôðer flet eal gerýmdon *they offered him conditions that they would wholly yield to him another dwelling*, Beo. Th. 2175; Th. 1085. v. Grm. R. A. 600. III. *what is impending over one, what is awaiting one, what is certainly to be expected* or *hoped for, fate, destiny*; quod est imminens *vel* expectandum, fatum, sors:—Bâd beadwa geþinges *he awaited the fate of the battle*, Beo. Th. 1423; B. 709: 802; B. 398. Wêndon hie þearlra geþinga þræge hnâgran *they expected a worse period of severe fates*, Andr. Kmbl. 3194; An. 1600: 1512; An. 757.

ge-þingan; *p.* -þang, *pl.* -þungon; *pp.* -þungen *To thrive, grow, become excellent*:—Metode geþungon Abraham and Loth *Abraham and Lot throve to the Lord* [cf. ge-þeón], Cd. 82; Th. 103, 7; Gen. 1714: Bt. Met. Fox 1, 14; Met. 1, 7. Ǽghwæðer heora wæs ælþeódig ðǽr and hwæðere for heora lîfes gearnunge geþungon ðæt hî bûtâ wǽron Abbudissan on ðam mynstre *quæ utraque cum esset peregrina, præ merito virtutum ejusdem monasterii est abbatissa constituta*, Bd. 3, 8; S. 531, 23. Wât ic ðæt ðû wǽre on woruldrîce geþungen þrymlîce *I know that thou wert in this world exalted gloriously*, Soul Kmbl. 328; Seel. 168. v. ge-þungen.

ge-þingan; *pp.* ed *To determine, fix, destine*:—Gif him ðonne Hrêðrîc to hofum Geáta geþingeþ [MS. -ed] he mæg ðǽr fela freónda findan *if then Hrethric determine to come to the Goths' courts he can find there many friends*, Beo. Th. 3678; B. 1857. Hafaþ him geþinged hider þeóden usser *our prince hath determined to come hither*, Exon. 115 b; Th. 445, 9; Dôm. 5. [Cf. ge-þingian, II.] Wiste hilde geþinged *he knew war was destined*, Beo. Th. 1299; B. 647: Menol. Fox 326; Men. 164: 14; Men. 7.

ge-þingelic; *adj. Concerning a council*, Cot. 179.

ge-þingere, es; *m. An intercessor*:—We biddaþ ðætte fore us geþingere astonde *quesumus ut pro nobis intercessor existat*, Rtl. 44, 36.

ge-þingian; *p.* ode; *pp.* od, ad. I. [ge-þing, **II.**] *to make terms with a person for one's self* or *for another, to be reconciled, to come to an agreement, to reconcile, settle a dispute, intercede, mediate*:—Swâ hie geþingian mǽgen wið cyning and his gerêfan *according to the terms they can make with the king and his reeve*, L. In. 73; Th. i. 148, 11: 62; Th. i. 142, 3: Cod. Dipl. ii. 58, 26. Ðâ geþingadun wið ðǽm wyrhtum *conventione facta cum operariis*, Mt. Kmbl. Rush. 20, 2: Chr. 694; Erl. 42, 15: 628; Erl. 24, 4. Ðǽr genam Hettulf Honoriuses sweostor and siððon wið hine geþingode *there Ataulf took the sister of Honorius and afterwards made an agreement with him*, Ors. 6, 38; Bos. 133, 15. Bûtan ðû ǽr wið hî geþingige *unless thou first be reconciled to them*, Exon. 68 b; Th. 254, 16; Jul. 198. Geþinge wið ðînum brôðer *reconciliare fratri tuo*, Mt. Kmbl. Rush. 5, 24. Swâ beóþ þeóda geþwǽre ðonne hý geþingad habbaþ *so are peoples in concord when they have made a treaty*, Exon. 89 b; Th. 336, 29; Gn. Ex. 57. Goda bæd ðæt se kynincg him geþingude wið Eádgife his bôca edgift *Goda asked that the king would arrange for him with Eadgifu the restoration of his charters*, Th. Ch. 202, 32. He geþingade fǽhþa mæste *he settled the greatest feud*, Exon. 16 b; Th. 39, 2; Cri. 616: Blickl. Homl. 9, 6. Nâ ðê geþingodre *none the more settled*, L. In. 22; Th. i. 116, 12, MS. B. Gehwilces mannes dǽda hine gewrêgaþ oððe geþingiaþ *every man's deeds accuse him or reconcile him* [*to God*], Boutr. Scrd. 20, 38. Ðæt me seó hâlge wið ðone hýhstan cyning geþingige *that the holy one intercede for me to the most high king*, Exon. 76 a; Th. 285, 20; Jul. 717. Giþingage *intercedat*, Rtl. 66, 13: *intervenire*, 60, 42. Ðæt hî to ðam mildheortan Hǽlende hire geþingodon *that they would intercede for her to the merciful Saviour*, Homl. Th. ii. 112, 22: 528, 14: Past. 10, 2: Swt. 63, 2, 10:

Hat. MS. Geþinga us *intercede for us*, Exon. 12 b; Th. 21, 29; Cri. 342. II. *to determine:*—Hafaþ nū geþingod to us þeóden mǣra *the great prince hath determined* [*to come*] *to us*, Cd. 226; Th. 302, 12; Sat. 598. [Cf. ge-þingan.]

ge-þingio *a provision;* apparatio, Cot. 8, Lye.

geþing-sceat, es; *m. Ransom:*—He ne sealde Gode nǣnne geþingsceat wiđ his miltse *he gave God no ransom for his mercy*, Past. 45; Swt. 339, 10; Hat. MS.

ge-þingþu, -þingcþu, -þincþ, -þyncþ, e; *f.* I. *honour, dignity, rank;* honor, dignitas;—He becom to đære cynelīcan geþincþe *he arrived at the royal dignity*, Homl. Th. i. 82, 1. Eal folc đone eádigan Gregorius to đære geþincþe geceás *all folk chose the blessed Gregory to that dignity*, ii. 122, 22. Hū micelre geþincþe sȳ đæt hālige mǣden Maria *of how great dignity is the holy maiden Mary*, 22, 21. Godes gecorenan scīnaþ on heofonlīcum wuldre ǣlc be his geþingcþum; nū is geleáflīc đæt seó eádige cwēn mid swā micclum wuldre and beorhtnysse ōđre oferstīge, swā micclum swā hire geþincþu ōđra hālgena unwiđmetenlīce sind *God's elect shine in heavenly glory each according to his rank; now it is credible that the blessed queen excels others with so much brightness and glory, as much as her rank is not comparable with that of other saints*, i. 446, 2–5: Jud. Thw. p. 161, 21: Swt. A. S. Rdr. 98, 93: Homl. Th. ii. 450, 2. Sum geþungen lāreow wæs on Engla lande Albin gehāten and hæfde micele geþincþa *there was a certain distinguished teacher in England named Albin and he had great honour*, Boutr. Scrd. 17, 6. Him to wǣron witode geþingþo *to him were destined honours*, Cd. 23; Th. 30, 31; Gen. 475. Geþyncþum *honourably*, Exon. 41 b; Th. 138, 16; Gū. 577. II. *a court, legal assembly:*—Đæt griþ đæt se ealdormann on fīf-burhga geþincþe sylle and đæt griþ đæt man sylleþ on burh-geþincþe bēte man *for the 'grith' which the alderman in the assembly of the five-burghs may give and for the 'grith' that is given in a burgh-assembly, let 'bōt' be made*, L. Eth. iii. 1; Th. i. 292, 6. [Cf. ge-þungen *and* ge-þing (?).]

ge-þingung, e; *f. Intercession:* — Giþingunge *intercessione*, Rtl. 71, 17: 124, 36.

ge-þinnian, -þinngian, -þynnian; *p.* ode; *pp.* od *To thin, lessen, diminish, dispel;* attenuāre:—Ic hie sceal ǣrest geþinnian [geþinngian, MS. Bod.] *I must first dispel them*, Bt. 5, 3; Fox 14, 19.

ge-þióđe *speech.* v. ge-þeóde.

ge-þióstrian; *p.* ode; *pp.* od *To obscure;* obscūrāre: — Seó sunne oferlīht ealle ōđre steorran, and geþióstraþ mid hire leóhte *the sun outshines all other stars, and obscures* [*them*] *with her light*, Bt. titl. ix; Fox xii. 2. Sunna biþ geþióstrod *sol contenebrabitur*, Mk. Skt. Lind. 13, 24.

ge-þīwan; *p.* de; *pp.* ed *To threaten, rebuke, oppress:* — Simon me mid his englum geþīwde *Simon threatened me with his angels*, Homl. Th. i. 378, 2. Óþ-đæt hio ōđer folc egsan geþīwdan *until they oppressed other people with fear*, Ps. Th. 104, 11. v. ge-þȳwan.

ge-þofta, an; *m. A companion, comrade;* sōdālis, contŭbernālis: — Onbræd se his geþofta and lōcade to him *expergefactus sōdālis respexit eum*, Bd. 3, 27; S. 559, 17. Đe ǣr his geþofta wæs *who was formerly his companion*, Ors. 3, 7; Bos. 61, 18: 3, 11; Bos. 74, 45. Geþofta *contŭbernālis*, Ælfc. Gr. 49; Som. 65, 80; Wrt. Voc. 34, 12. Đæt đū sī gemyndig đīnes getreówan geþoftan *tui mĕmor sis fīdissimi sŏdālis*, Bd. 4, 29; S. 607, 25. Gemētte he đone his geþoftan slǣpendne *invēnit sŏdālem dormientem*, 3, 27; S. 559, 14. Hé gesomnode wered his geþoftena *he collected a band of his companions*, Guthl. 2; Gdwn. 14, 2: Shrn. 196, 20. Geþofta *cliens*, Wrt. Voc. 291, 33.

ge-þoftian; *p.* ode, ade, ede; *pp.* od, ad, ed *To associate, join, to enter into an agreement;* assŏciāre, societātem inīre:—Geþoftade he wiđ Ptholomeus *he joined with Ptolemy*, Ors. 3, 11; Bos. 74, 26. Seleucus and Demetrias him togædere geþoftedan *Seleucus and Demetrius joined together*, 3, 11; Bos. 75, 14.

ge-þoftrǣden, e; *f. Companionship, fellowship, converse;* consortium:—God to him genam geþoftrǣdene *God held converse with him*, Homl. Th. i. 90, 20.

ge-þoftscipe, es; *m. Companionship, society;* consortium:—Đȳlæs he sīe innan asliten from đæm geþoftscipe đæs incundan dēman *lest he be inwardly cut off from the society of the internal judge*, Past. 46, 5; Swt. 351, 24; Hat. MS. 67 a, 16, 20: Swt. 353, 3.

ge-þogen *grown up*, Homl. Th. ii. 38, 9; *pp. of* ge-þeón.

ge-þoht, es; *m. n.* [ge-þoht, *pp. of* ge-þencan *to think*] THOUGHT, *thinking, mind, determination;* cōgĭtātio, mens:—Đæt wæs þreālīc geþoht *that was a guilty thought*, Elen. Kmbl. 851; El. 426: Exon. 115 b; Th. 444, 6; Kl. 43. Forđonđe mannes geþoht mægen andetteþ *quia cōgĭtātio hŏmĭnis confĭtēbĭtur tibi*, Ps. Th. 75, 7: 32, 10. Manna cynnes [MS. kynnes] costere hafaþ acenned on đē đa unablinnu đæs yfelan geþohtes *the tempter of mankind* [lit. *of the race of men*] *hath begotten in thee the unrest of this evil thought*, Guth. 7; Gdwn. 46, 10: Bd. 1, 27: S. 496, 32: Exon. 73 b; Th. 275, 14; Jul. 550. Mīnne gehȳraþ ānfealdne geþoht *hear my simple thought*, Beo. Th. 517; B. 256: 1225; B. 610: Salm. Kmbl. 478; Sal. 239. Hwīle mid geþohte *sometimes with thought*, Hy. 3, 45; Hy. Grn. ii. 282, 45: Exon. 77 b; Th. 291, 27; Wand. 88. Đæt geþohtas sȳn awrigene of manegum heortum *ut revēlentur ex multis cordĭbus cōgĭtātiōnes*, Lk. Bos. 2, 35: Ps. Th. 138, 2. Gē sind earmra geþohta *ye are of poor thoughts*, Andr. Kmbl. 1488; An. 745: Bd. 2, 12; S. 513, 31. On geþohtum *in cōgĭtātiōnĭbus*, Ps. Th. 138, 17. Đæt he him afirre frēcne geþohtas *that he banish from him wicked thoughts*, Cd. 219; Th. 282, 10; Sat. 284: 217; Th. 277, 18; Sat. 206. The following examples are neuter:—Þurh dyrne [*or* = dyrnne?] geþoht *through dark counsel*, Exon. 115 a; Th. 442, 13; Kl. 12: Ps. Th. 139, 2.

ge-þohte *thought*, Cd. 217; Th. 276, 11; Sat. 187; *p. of* ge-þencean.

ge-þolian, to -þolianne, -þolienne, -þoligenne; *p.* ode, ade, ede; *pp.* od, ad, ed [þolienne *to bear, suffer*]. I. *to bear, suffer, endure, sustain;* sufferre, păti, sustĭnēre: — Hea geþolas *patiuntur*, Mt. Kmbl. Lind. 5, 10: Mk. Skt. Lind. 9, 12. Hie geþolian sceolon earmlīc wīte *they shall suffer miserable torment*, Cd. 227; Th 304, 26; Sat. 636: Elen. Kmbl. 2582; El. 1292. Đæt Andrea þūhte þeódbealo þearlīc to geþolianne *that seemed to Andrew a general evil hard to bear*, Andr. Kmbl. 2274; An. 1138: Beo. Th. 2842; B. 1419: Exon. 48 a; Th. 166, 7; Gū. 1039. To geþolienne, Andr. Kmbl. 3375; An. 1691. To geþoligenne, 3317; An. 1661. We hēnþo geþoliaþ *we shall suffer punishment*, Cd. 222; Th. 289, 18; Sat. 399: Exon. 70 b; Th. 262, 30; Jul. 340. He feala wīta geþolode *he endured a multitude of torments*, Andr. Kmbl. 2979; An. 1492: Beo. Th. 297; B. 147. Ic đæt for worulde geþolade *I suffered that for the world*, Exon. 28 b; Th. 87, 13; Cri. 1424: 29 a; Th. 88, 21; Cri. 1443. Geþoledan, Ps. Th. 145, 6. Geþola Drihtnes willan *sustĭne Dŏmĭnum*, 26, 16: Andr. Kmbl, 213; An. 107. II. *to have patience, endure, wait, remain;* perdūrāre, mănēre:—Đū scealt geþolian sume hwīle *thou must bear* [*with me*] *for some time*, Bt. 39, 4; Fox 218, 8. Gif he inne geþolian wille *if he will remain within*, L. Alf. pol. 42; Th. i. 90, 6: Beo. Th. 6210; B. 3109. Se đe geþolas on ende *qui sustinuerit in finem;* Mk. Skt. Lind. 13, 13: 14, 34. III. *with the gen. To suffer loss of, forfeit, lose;* cărēre:—Ic geþolian sceal þinga ǣghwylces *I must forfeit everything*, Cd. 219; Th. 281, 17; Sat. 273.

ge-þonc, es; *m. n. Thought, mind, understanding;* cōgĭtātio, mens:—Gleáw on geþonce *cunning in thought*, Judth. 9; Thw. 21, 11; Jud. 13. Þurh glædne geþonc *through benign thought*, Exon. 12 b; Th. 20, 10; Cri. 315. Đæt ic him monigfealde ongeánbere grimra geþonca *that I present manifold dire thoughts to him*, 71 a; Th. 264, 21; Jul. 367: 31 a; Th. 97, 1; Cri. 1584. Ic onsende in breóstsefan bitre geþoncas *I send into his mind bitter thoughts*, 71 b; Th. 266, 29; Jul. 405. He us geþonc syleþ, missenlīcu mōd *he gives us understandings, various minds*, 89 a; Th. 334, 7; Gn. Ex. 13. Breóst innan weóll þeóstrum geþoncum *his breast boiled within with dark thoughts*, Beo. Th. 4653; B. 2332: Exon. 54 a; Th. 190, 4; Az. 68. v. ge-þanc.

ge-þracen; *part. p. Prepared, decked;* ornatus:—Geþracen hors *mannus* vel *brunnicus*, Ælfc. Gl. 5; Som. 56, 18; Wrt. Voc. 17, 22. [Cf. ge-þræc *apparatus*, Lye.]

ge-þræc, -þrec, es; *n. Press, crowd, crush, tumult:*—Ac wæs flōd to deóp atol ȳđa geþræc *but too deep was the flood, the fierce press of the waves*, Exon. 106 a; Th. 404, 13; Rä. 23, 7: 101 a; Th. 381, 26; Rä. 3, 2. Þurh þreáta geþræcu [?], 109 a; Th. 417, 17; Rä. 36, 6. Beorna geþrec *press of men*, Elen. Kmbl. 228; El. 114: Ps. C. 50, 44; Ps. Grn. ii. 277, 44: Exon. 102 a; Th. 386, 13; Rä. 4, 61. Geþrec *clangor*, Cot. 59, Lye.

ge-þræc *apparatus, adjutorium*, Cot. 1, Lye.

ge-þrǣstan; *p.* -þrǣste; *pp.* -þrǣst *To twist, hurt, torment, afflict;* contĕrĕre, afflīgere:—Gefeóll he semninga on his earm ufan, and đone swȳđe geþrǣste and gebræc *repente corrŭens brachĭum contrīvit*, Bd. 3, 2; S. 525, 2. Se hǣleþ heortan geþrǣste *qui sānat contrītos corde*, Ps. Th. 146, 3. Weorþen hī swā geþrǣste mid hungre đæt hi eton swȳnen flǣsc *may they be so tormented with hunger as to eat swine-flesh*, Ps. Th. 16, 14. On đām dagum đe ic geþrǣsted wæs *in die afflictionis meæ*, 17, 19. Godes engel hī geþrǣste *angelus Domini adfligens eos*, 34, 6.

ge-þrǣstian *adducere, præjudicare*, Hpt. Gl. 440.

ge-þrǣstnes, -ness, e; *f. Affliction, contrition;* contrītio: — On swā mycelre geþræstnesse *in tanta contrītiōne*, Bd. 5, 12; S. 627, 27.

ge-þrāfod *corrected, chastised.* v. þrāfian.

ge-þrang, es; *n. A throng, crowd, tumult;* turba, tumultus: — On geþrang *in the throng*, Byrht. Th. 140, 36; By. 299. [Cf. *O. H. Ger.* ge-threngi: *Ger.* ge-dränge.]

ge-þrāwan, -þrǣwan; *p.* -þreów, *pl.* -þreówon; *pp.* -þrāwen, -þrǣwen *To twist;* torquere:—Đæt geþrǣwene [geþrāwene, MS. Cot.] twīn *byssus torta*, Past. 14, 6; Swt. 87, 11; Hat. MS. 18 b, 15. Geþrāwan *torquere*, Hpt. Gl. 435.

ge-þreán; *p.* -þreáde; *pp.* -þreád *To reprove, rebuke, afflict, vex, constrain, compel;* corripere, increpare, arguere, cogere, affligere, coartare, urgere, vexare:—Se đe him sylfum leofaþ rihtlīce he is ȳdel geþreád *he who lives for himself is rightly reproved as idle*, Homl. Th. ii. 78, 5.

Huelc from iúh geþreáþ mec *quis ex vobis arguit me?* Jn. Skt. Lind. 8, 46: 16, 18. He geþreáde ðæt wind *ille increpavit ventum*, Lk. Skt. Lind. 8, 24: 9, 55. Geþreá hine *increpa illum*, 17, 3. Ne geþreá me *neque corripias me*, Ps. Surt. 37, 2. From giþreándum *ab increpantibus*, Rtl. 19, 15. Hū beó ic geþreád *quomodo coarctor*, Lk. 12, 50. Ic wæs geþreád ðæt ic ðē sōhte *I was compelled to seek thee*, Exon. 70 b; Th. 263, 3; Jul. 344. Egsan geþreád *afflicted with terror*, 30 b; Th. 95, 28; Cri. 1564: 33 b; Th. 106, 22; Gū. 45: Cd. 90; Th. 112, 4; Gen. 1865: 126; Th. 161, 21; Gen. 2668: Andr. Kmbl. 781; An. 391. He nāhte his līchoman geweald ac he wæs mid godcundum mægene geþreád *he had no power over his body, but was afflicted by the divine might*, Blickl. Homl. 223, 12.

ge-þreátian; *p.* ode, ade; *pp.* od, ad [þreátian *to urge, press*] *To urge, oppress, threaten, rebuke, compel, restrain, afflict, torment;* urgēre, cōgĕre, afflīgĕre, trībŭlāre:—Ne meaht ðū mec geþreátian ðē to gesingan *thou canst not compel me to be thy wife*, Exon. 66 b; Th. 245, 33; Jul. 54. On yrre ðū folc geþreátast *in ira populos confringes*, Ps. Th. 55, 6: Exon. 68 a; Th. 253, 6; Jul. 176. Se snāw hȳ geþreátaþ *the snow oppresseth them*, Salm. Kmbl. 607; Sal. 303. Geþȳd and geþreátod *rebuked and threatened*, Andr. Kmbl. 871; An. 436: 2231; An. 1117: Elen. Kmbl. 1387; El. 695. Hungre geþreátad *oppressed by hunger*, Exon. 46 a; Th. 157, 8; Gū. 888. Ðæt geþreátade mōd biþ suīðe raðe gehwierfed to fióunga *the rebuked mind will very soon be turned to hatred*, Past. 21; Swt. 167, 13; Hat. MS. Hie hine hæfdon geþreátodne mid fȳrenum racentum ðæt he ne mōste gecweðan 'Miltsa me God' *they had restrained him with fiery chains from saying 'Have mercy on me, O God!'* Blickl. Homl. 43, 30: 221, 15. Geþreátad *coactus*, Mt. Kmbl. p. 8, 1. Petrus ongan giþreátiga hine *Petrus coepit increpare eum*, Mk. Skt. Rush. 8, 32: Mt. Kmbl. Lind. 8, 26: 20, 31. Sōna geþreátade þegnas his *statim coegit discipulos suos*, Mk. Skt. Rush. 6, 45.

ge-þrec. v. ge-þræc.

ge-þrēstan, Ps. Surt. 146, 3. v. ge-þrǣstan.

ge-þring, es; *n.* [ge-þringan *to press*] *A press, tumult, crowd, throng;* tŭmultus, turba:—Ofer wætera geþring *over the throng of waters*, Chr. 975; Erl. 126, 21; Edg. 47: Andr. Kmbl. 736; An. 368: Beo. Th. 4271; B. 2132. Wæs giþring *there was a throng*, Lk. Skt. Rush. 8, 42. [*O. Sax.* ge-þring.] Cf. ge-þrang.

ge-þringan; *p.* -þrang, -þringde [North. Gospels], *pl.* -þrungon; *pp.* -þrungen *To press, oppress;* comprimere, contendere, opprimere. I. *v. intrans*:—Ceól up geþrang *the keel pressed up*, Beo. Th. 3829; B. 1912. Deáþ in geþrong *death pressed in*, Exon. 45 a; Th. 153, 34; Gū. 835. Hū he þurh ðæt folc geþrang *how he pressed through the people*, Ors. 3, 9; Bos. 68, 30. Geþringas to ingeonganne *contendite intrare*, Lk. Skt. Lind. 13, 24. Hæfde ðā se æþeling in geþrungen *then had the noble one pressed in*, Andr. Kmbl. 1980; An. 992. Wæs ðā ende-dōgor neáh geþrungen *the final day had come near*, Exon. 46 b; Th. 158, 10; Gū. 906. Ðære tīde ys neáh geþrungen *it is close upon the time*, Judth. 12; Thw. 25, 31; Jud. 287: Cd 116; Th. 151, 15; Gen. 2509. II. *v. trans*:—Woldon Rōmwara rīce geþringan *they would oppress the power of the Romans*, Elen. Kmbl. 80; El. 40 Me firenlustas ðīne geþrungon *me thy sinful lusts oppressed*, Exon. 98 b; Th. 369, 2; Seel. 35: Bt. Met. Fox 1, 5; Met. 1, 3. Geþringdon hine *comprimebant eum*, Mk. Skt. Lind. 5, 24. From ðæm here wæs geþringed ł geþrungen *a turba comprimebatur*, Lk. Skt. Lind. 8, 42. Calde geþrungen wǣron mīne fēt *pinched with cold were my feet*, Exon. 81 b; Th. 306, 16; Seef. 8. Wombe geþrungne *a swollen belly*, 129 a; Th. 485, 3; Rä. 84, 2.

ge-þrīstian; *p.* ode, ade; *pp.* od, ad [þrīst, þrīste *bold*] *To dare, presume;* audēre, præsūmĕre:—Ic ne geþrīstige *ego non audeo*, Coll. Monast. Th. 25, 5. Forðam he geþrīstade *quod se præsumpsisset*, Bd. 1, 7; S. 477, 15.

ge-þrīstlǣcan; *p.* -lǣhte, -lǣcte *To dare, presume, excite;* provocare:—Ne geþrīstlǣcaþ hī ō ðæt hī mānswergen on his noman *they never dare to sware falsely in his name*, Shrn. 109, 17. Þurh Albinus swīðost ic geþrīstlǣhte ðæt ic dorste ðis weorc ongynnan *hortatu præcipue ipsius Albini ut hoc opus adgredi auderem provocatus sum*, Bd. pref; S. 472, 11. Eádrēd biddeþ ðet nān man geþrīstlīce his cynelīcan gefe gewonian *Eadred prays that no man will presume to diminish his royal gift*, Cod. Dipl. Kmbl. ii. 304, 26. We geþrīstlǣcton *provocavimus*, Cot. 154.

ge-þrowian, -þrowigan; *p.* ode, ade; *pp.* od, ad *To suffer*:—Feolo geþrowia *multa pati*, Lk. Skt. Lind. 9, 22. Gē ondspyrnise geþrowiges *vos scandalum patiemini*, Mt. Kmbl. Lind. 26, 31. On hwylcre þeóden engla geþrowode *on which the prince of angels suffered*, Elen. Kmbl. 1714; El. 859. Se cyle geþrowode wið ða hǣto *the cold should suffer by the heat*, Bt. 33, 4; Fox 128, 33. Geþrowade, 1123; El. 563. Twegen mid him geþrowedon *two suffered with him*, 1706; El. 855. Sunu monnes geþrowend biþ *Filius hominis passurus est*, Mt. Kmbl. Lind. 17, 12. Ðū bist geþrouad *tu cruciaris*, Lk. Skt. Lind. 16, 25. He swā micel for ūre lufan geþrowode *he has suffered so much for love of us*, Blickl. Homl. 25, 3: 91, 12. Geþrowade, Elen. Kmbl. 1035; El. 519. Deáþ he geþrowode for us *he suffered death for us*, Blickl. Homl. 85, 2: Cd. 228; Th. 306, 18; Sat. 666. He æt ðǣm unlǣdum Iudēum manig bysmor geþrowade *he suffered many contumelies at the hands of the wicked Jews*, Blickl. Homl. 23, 31.

ge-þruen [= ge-þuren]; *part. p.* *Pressed together, compact*:—Eorþe is hefigre ōðrum gesceaftum þicre geþruen *earth is heavier than the other elements, more closely compact*, Bt. Met. Fox 20, 267; Met. 20, 134. v. ge-þweran.

ge-þryccan, -þrycgan; *p.* -þrȳde *To press, compress, bind a book* [?], *restrain, express;* premere, comprimere, exprimere, operire:—Ōðer geþrȳde ł awrāt *alius expressit*, Mt. Kmbl. p. 3, 6. Eþiluald hit ūta giþrȳde *Ethewold bound* [?] *it*, Jn. Skt. p. 188, 3. See note, p. viii. Ðone fiónd ūserne geþrycg *hostem nostrum comprime*, Rtl. 180, 18.

ge-þrȳde. v. ge-þryccan.

ge-þryle *an assembly, a meeting;* frequentia:—For þæs folces geþryle *for the folk's assembly*, Hom. 8, Cal. Jan. p. 18, Lye.

ge-þryscan; *p.* te; *pp.* ed *To press, oppress, press down, depress;* premere, deprimere:—Ðæt hine ne geþrysce nān wiðermōdnes to ormōdnesse *non aspera ad desperationem premant*, Past. 14, 3; Swt. 83, 18; Hat. MS. 17 b, 26. Ðonne sió þreáung biþ ungemetgad ðonne biþ ðæt mōd ðæs agyltendan mid ormōdnesse geþrysced *cumque increpatio immoderate accenditur, corda delinquentium in desperatione deprimuntur*, 21, 7; Swt. 165, 19; Hat. MS.

ge-þryþian; *p.* ede; *pp.* ed [þryþ *power, strength*] *To strengthen, arm;* corroborare:—Deáþ nimeþ wīga wælgīfre wǣpnum geþryþed ealdor ānra gehwæs *death, the blood-greedy warrior, armed with weapons, takes the life of every one*, Exon. 62 b; Th. 231, 9; Ph. 486.

ge-þūf *growing, luxuriant;* luxurians, Cot. 123, 198. v. þūf, þūfian.

ge-þugon *throve*, Homl. Th. ii. 280, 32; *p. pl. of* ge-þeón.

ge-þuhtsum; *adj. Abundant*:—Hit wæs ǣr ðǣr singal druwung and sōna æfter ðam com geþuhtsum rēn on eorþan *there had been there before continual drought, and directly after that came abundant rain on the earth*, Shrn. 113, 20. [Cf. þyhtig, ge-þyht.]

ge-þuild *patience*, Lk. Skt. Lind. 18, 7. v. ge-þyld.

ge-þun, es; *n. A noise;* clangor:—Us þūhte for þam geþune ðæt sió eorþe eall cracode *it seemed to us from the noise that the earth all cracked*, Ps. Th. 45, 3.

ge-þungen; *part. p. Grown, thriven, advanced* [*morally, mentally*, etc.], *excellent, pious, noble, perfect*:—Leomum geþungen *perfect in its limbs*, Exon. 64 a; Th. 241, 1; Ph. 649. On geþungenum wæstme *in mature growth*, Homl. Th. ii. 76, 25. Geþungen *emeritus, provectus*, Ælfc. Gl. 82; Som. 73, 52; Wrt. Voc. 47, 56. Ðæt nǣnig þing ne gedafenade swā æþelum cyninge and swā geþungenum *quia nulla ratione conveniat tanto regi*, Bd. 2, 12; S. 514, 38: 2, 1; 501, 34: Homl. Th. ii. 122, 14: 126, 28. Gōdne wer and geþungenne to biscophāde *virum bonum et aptum episcopatu*, Bd. 3, 29; S. 561, 11: 4, 23; S. 594, 6. Sum ǣfast mann and geþungen *veracem ac religiosum hominem*, 3, 19; S. 549, 24. Sum geþungen and gedēfe sacerd *sacerdos quietus*, Nar. 37, 25. Mōd geþungen *mens sobria*, Ps. Stev. ii. 202, 7. Wæs he swīðe geþungen on his þeáwum *he was very excellent in his conduct*, Blickl. Homl. 217, 6: Judth. 11; Thw. 23, 19; Jud. 129. Cwēn mōde geþungen *the queen excellent of mind*, Beo. Th. 1252; B. 624. Þegen geþungen *an illustrious minister*, Andr. Kmbl. 1055; An. 528: Exon. 69 b; Th. 258, 8; Jul. 262. Ic ða geþungnestan nemde *I have named the most distinguished*, Chr. 897; Erl. 95, 6: 905; Erl. 98, 30. Hafa ðū me to ðan geþungennestan wīfe *have me as the most excellent wife*, Shrn. 40, 17. [*O. Sax.* gi-þungan.]

ge-þungenlīce; *adv. Soberly;* sobrie, Ps. Stev. ii. 201, 21.

ge-þungennes, -ness, e; *f. Increase, growth, piety, excellence, gravity*:—Ðæt wæs ðæt templ ðære geþungennesse and ealre clǣnnesse *that was the temple of piety and all purity*, Blickl. Homl. 5, 20: Shrn. 40, 2: 44, 9. Geþungennis *incrementum*, Mk. Skt. p. 2, 6. Geþungennes *perfectio*, Mone Gl. 365.

ge-þurfan, ic -þearf; *p.* -þorfte *To have need* or *necessity;* indigere, necesse habere:—Ðȳlæs ðē geþearfe to ōðres mannes ǣhtum *lest thou have need of another man's goods*, Prov. Kmbl. 73. v. þurfan.

ge-þwǣnan; *p.* de; *pp.* ed *To moisten, wet, soften;* irrigare, emollire:—Gif þat wæter hī ne geþwǣnde *if the water moisten it not*, Bt. 33, 4; Fox 130, 7. Ða adrugodan heortan geþwǣnan mid ðǣm flōwendan ȳðon [ȳðum, MS. Cot.] his lāre *corda arentia doctrinæ fluentis irrigare*, Past. 10, 1; Swt. 61, 19; Hat. MS. 14 a, 15: 18, 5; Swt. 137, 8; Hat. MS. 27 a, 12. His lǣcas tiloden and ðone swile mid sealfum and mid beþenum geþwǣnan woldon *curabant medici tumorem adpositis pigmentorum fomentis emollire*, Bd. 4, 32; S. 611, 20.

ge-þwǣran *mansuescere, respirari*, Gl. Prud. 644, 714.

ge-þwǣre, -þwēre; *adj. United, agreeing, consonant, harmonious, accordant, concordant, mild, gentle, peaceful;* concors, congruus, consŏnus, mansuētus, pācĭfĭcus, plăcĭdus:—Geþwǣre *concors*, Ælfc. Gr. 9, 44; Som. 13, 4, MSS. C. D. Geþwǣre sang *harmŏnĭa*, Ælfc. Gl. 34; Som. 62, 59; Wrt. Voc. 28, 39. Ðū noldest on eallum þingum beón geþwǣre ðæs unrihtwīsan cyninges willan *thou wouldest not in all things be conformable* *to the will of the unrighteous king*, Bt. 27, 2; Fox 96, 16. Sum hafaþ mōd and word monnum geþwǣre *one has mind and words agreeable to men*, Exon. 79 b; Th. 298, 15; Crä. 85. Þegnas syndon geþwǣre *the thanes are united*, Beo. Th. 2464; B. 1230: Exon. 9 b; Th. 8, 33; Cri. 127: 89 b; Th. 336, 29; Gn. Ex. 57. Wurdon ealle gereord geānlǣhte and geþwǣre *all languages became united and concordant*, Homl. Th. i. 318, 24. Ða geþwǣran yrfweardiaþ eorþan *mansuēti hæreditabunt terram*, Ps. Spl. 36, 11. On geþwǣrum limum *in agreeing limbs*, Bt. 33, 4; Fox 130, 39. Ðonne hit ǣfre geþwǣrust sȳ ondrǣt ðē ðonne ungeþwǣrnisse *when things go most smoothly, then expect trouble*, Prov. Kmbl. 75.

ge-þwǣrian, -þwērian; *p.* ode, ede; *pp.* od. I. *to cause to agree, to make accordant, mild*:—He geþwǣrede ða ðe ǒþ ðæt ungeþwǣre wǣron *he brought those to agree who until then had disagreed*, Bd. 3, 6; S. 528, 31. God gemetgaþ ealla gesceafta and geþwǣraþ ðā hē betwuh him wuniaþ *God regulates all creatures and makes them agree when they exist together*, Bt. 39, 13; Fox 234, 10: 8; Fox 224, 9, Cot. MS. Geþwēraþ [geþweraþ?] Bt. Met. Fox 29, 94; Met. 29, 47. Ðū geþwēras *tu mitigas*, Ps. Spl. T. 88, 10. Geþwiǣrodes *mitigasti*, 84, 3. II. *to be or become in accord, to agree, consent, be agreeable*; consentire, concordare, congruere, convenire:—Se eorl nolde nā geþwǣrian ðære infare *the earl would not consent to the entrance*, Chr. 1048; Erl. 178, 11. Uton geþwǣrian mid ðam yrþlinge *conveniamus apud aratorem*, Coll. Monast. Th. 31, 27. Gif twegen of eów geþwǣriaþ be ǣlcum þinge *si duo ex vobis consenserint de omni re*, Mt. Bos. 18, 19. Ðes ne geþwǣrode hyra geþeahte *hic non consenserat consilio eorum*, Lk. Bos. 23, 51. Hī geþwǣredon *sibi concordant*, Bd. 2, 2; S. 502, 16. Ða þing ðe geþwǣredon ǣnnysse ðære cyriclīcan sibbe *ea quæ unitati pacis ecclesiasticæ congruerent*, 4, 5; S. 571, 42. Ðū ðe wǣre geþwǣrigende ðam Hǣlende *thou that wast consenting to the Saviour*, Nicod. Thw. 6, 24.

geþwǣr-lǣcan, -lēcan; *p.* -lǣhte; *pp.* -lǣht *To agree, assent to*; concordāre, assentīre:—He sǣde ðæt heora þeáwas ne mihton his dihte geþwǣrlǣcan *he said that their manners could not accord with his disposition*, Homl. Th. ii. 158, 7. Se ðe sōþlīce God lufaþ nele he wiðerian ongeán his bebodum ac hī geþwǣrlǣhþ *he that truly loves God will not resist his commands but comply with them*, 522, 19. Seó sǣ and se mōna geþwǣrlǣcaþ *the sea and the moon agree*, Bd. de nat. rerum; Wrt. popl. science 15, 15; Lchdm. 268, 12. Ða hǣðengyldan ðisum cwide geþwǣrlǣhton *the idolaters assented to this proposal*, Homl. Th. i. 70, 34. Geþwǣrlēcan *to agree*, Boutr. Scrd. 21, 1.

ge-þwǣrlīce, -þwǣrelīce; *adv. Harmoniously, in accord*:—Sió sunne and se mōna rīcsiaþ swīðe geþwǣrelīce *the sun and moon rule very harmoniously*, Bt. 39, 13; Fox 234, 6. Geþwǣrlīce *consonanter*, Bd. 4, 17; S. 585, 35.

ge-þwǣrnes, -ness, niss, -e; *f. Concord, agreement, mildness*; concordia, mansuetudo:—Mid fægerre geþwǣrnesse *pulchra concordia*, Bd. 4, 23; S. 596, 23. Sibb and geþwǣrnyss *pax et concordia*, Coll. Monast. Th. 31, 25: Blickl. Homl. 109, 16. He ðæt rīce heóld on gōdre geþwǣrnesse and on micelre sibsumnesse *he held the kingdom in great peace and tranquillity*, Chr. 860; Erl. 70, 23: 827; Erl. 64, 8. Geþwǣrnysse *mansuetudinem*, Ps. Spl. 44, 6: Prov. Kmbl. 23.

ge-þweán; *p.* -þwōh, *pl.* -þwōgun; *pp.* -þwagen, -þwegen, -þwogen, -þwǣn *To wash*:—Ongann geþuoá foet his *coepit rigare pedes ejus*, Lk. Skt. Lind. 7, 38. Geþuōgon ðæt nett *lavabant retiam*, 5, 2. Būta oftor geþuōgon hondo *nisi crebro lavarent manus*, Mk. Skt. Lind. 7, 3. Būton hī geþwegene beón *nisi baptizentur*, Mk. Bos. 7, 4. Se ðe geþuǣn is *qui lavatus est*, Jn. Skt. Lind. 13, 10. Hwī he geþwogen nǣre *quare non baptizatus esset*, Lk. Bos. 11, 38.

ge-þweor, es; *n. Curd, what is coagulated*; coagulum, Coll. Monast. Th. 28, 19. v. buter-geþweor.

ge-þweran; *p.* -þwær, *pl.* -þwǣron; *pp.* -þworen, -þuren *To stir, beat or mix together, to churn, make thick* [*as butter from cream*], poetically, *to forge*; cudere:—Genim cū meoluc būtan wætere lǣt weorþan to flētum geþwer to buteran *take cow's milk, without water, let it become cream, churn it to butter*, L. M. 1, 44; Lchdm. ii. 108, 22. Geþworen [Lye], geþrofen [Wrt.] fliéte *churned cream*; lactudiclum, Wrt. Voc. 290, 28. Heoru hamere geþuren *the sword forged with the hammer*, Beo. Th. 2575; B. 1285: Exon. 129 b; Th. 497, 16; Rä. 87, 1. Eorþe is hefigre ōðrum gesceaftum þicre geþruen *earth is heavier than the other elements, more closely compacted*, Bt. Met. Fox 20, 267; Met. 20, 134. [Cf. þwiril *verberaturium*; *O. H. Ger.* ga-dweran *confundere, miscere*, Grff. v. 278.]

ge-þwēre; *adj. United, agreeing*; concors, Ælfc. Gr. 9, 44; Som. 13, 4: Shrn. 182, 5. v. ge-þwǣre.

ge-þwerian, -þweorian; *p.* ode, ede; *pp.* od, ed *To mix, mingle*:—Geþwere *mix*, L. M. 2, 51; Lchdm. ii. 264, 25. Geþweorod sint þegnas togædere *the ministers are mingled together* [cf. v. 66], Bt. Met. Fox 20, 143; Met. 20, 72. [Cf. ge-þweran, ge-þwǣrian; *and O. H. Ger.* tuaron, Grff. v. 278.]

ge-þwin [-þwing? Grn: cf. *O. Sax.* ge-þwing: *O. H. Ger.* ge-dwing], es; *n. Torment*; tormentum. v. hell-geþwin.

ge-þwinglod; *part. p. Compressed, fastened up*:—Ða Ismaheli hæfdon geþwinglode loccas *the Ishmaelites had their hair fastened up* [?], Shrn. 38, 5.

ge-þwit, es; *n. What is cut* or *shaved off, shavings, cuttings, chips*; assulæ:—Heo of ðǣre ilcan styþe spōnas þweoton ond sceafþan [ðæt geþwit, MS. B.] nōmon ond in wæter sendon *they cut off chips from the very stud* [*prop*] *and threw the cuttings into the water*, Bd. 3, 17, MS. T; S. 544, 44, col. 2, note. DER. þwītan.

ge-þȳan; *p.* de; *pp.* ed *To press*; premere:—Geþȳþ hȳ *presses them*, Salm. Kmbl. 607; Sal. 303: Salm. Kmbl. p. 150, 34. v. þȳan.

ge-þȳdan; *p.* de; *pp.* ed *To join, associate*; sŏciāre:—Monige to ðære ānnesse hī geþȳddan þurh geleáfan ðære hālgan Cristes cyrican *plūres ūnītāti se sanctæ Christi ecclēsiæ crēdendo sŏciare*, Bd. 1, 26; S. 488, 12. Saga hū ðū ðec geþȳde on clǣnra gemong *say how thou associatest thyself in the company of the pure!* Exon. 71 b; Th. 267, 22; Jul. 419. Us is swīðe mycel nēdþearf ðæt we us geþȳdon to ūrum hālgum gebedum *there is very great need for us to betake ourselves to our holy prayers*, Blickl. Homl. 133, 8. Wit sceoldan beón tosamne geþȳdde *we had to be joined together*, Shrn. 39, 19. He wæs Gūþlāce neáh geþȳded *he was nearly associated to Guthlac*, 47 a; Th. 162, 6; Gū. 971. v. ge-þeódan.

ge-þȳde; *adj. Good*:—Sum biþ ārfæst and ælmes-georn þeáwum geþȳde *one is pious and charitable, morally good*, Exon. 79 a; Th. 297, 14; Crä. 68. [Cf. *Goth.* þiuþ.]

ge-þyht; *adj. Good, advantageous*, Exon. 94 a; Th. 353, 25; Reim. 18. [Cf. þyhtig, ge-þuhtsum.]

ge-þylan *succumbere, consentire*, Hpt. Gl. 482.

ge-þyld, e; *f. Patience, resignation*; patientia:—Ðū me eart fǣle geþyld *tu es patientia mea*, Ps. Th. 70, 4: Ps. Spl. 61, 5: Job Thw. 167, 16. Sum þafaþ in geþylde ðæt he sceal *one allows what he must with patience*, Exon. 79 a; Th. 297, 20; Crä. 71. On geþylde *in patientia*, Lk. Bos. 8, 15. Gehafa geþyld on me *patientiam hăbe in me*, Mt. Bos. 18, 26: Exon. 79 b: Th. 298, 3; Crä. 79: Beo. Th. 2795; B. 1395. Mid geþylde *with patience*, L. In. 6; Th. i. 106, 12: Ps. Th. 91, 13. Eal ðū hit geþyldum gehealdest *thou supportest it all patiently*, Beo. Th. 3415; B. 1705. Forber oft ðæt ðū wrecan mǣge geþyld biþ middes eádes *often forbear when vengeance is in your power, patience is half happiness*, Prov. Kmbl. 25. [*O. Sax.* gi-þuld: *O. H. Ger.* ge-dult: *Ger.* ge-duld.]

ge-þyldelīc; *adj. Patient*:—Crist us onstealde geþyldelīce bysene *Christ has set us an example of patience*, Blickl. Homl. 75, 29.

ge-þyldelīce; *adv. Patiently, quietly*; patienter:—Drihten deófles costunga geþyldelīce abær *the Lord bore the temptation of the devil patiently*, Blick. Homl. 33, 28: Bd. 1, 7; S. 477, 46.

ge-þyldig; *adj. Patient, long-suffering, quiet*; patiens, longănĭmis:—Þeáwfæst and geþyldig *upright and patient*, Cd. 126; Th. 161, 8; Gen. 2662: 92; Th. 116, 26; Gen. 1942. Geþyldig and swȳðe mildheort *patiens et multum misĕrĭcors*, Ps. Spl. 144, 8: Ps. Th. 85, 14: 102, 8. Geþyldige hī beóþ *patientes ĕrunt*, Ps. Spl. C. 91, 14. Ða geþyldigan *sustĭnentes*, Ps. Spl. 36, 9. [*O. H. Ger.* ge-dultig: *Ger.* geduldig.]

ge-þyldigean, -þyldgian, -þyldian; *p.* ode; *pp.* od *To be patient, to bear patiently, endure, to bear, endure, sustain*; sustinere, patientiam habere, tolerare, pati:—He ne mæg geþyldgian ðæt he ðæt forhele *he cannot bear to conceal it*, Past. 33, 2; Swt. 216, 6, 8. Geþyldega *patientiam habe*, Mt. Bos. 18, 29. Ðē ic geþyldgode ealne dæg *te sustinui tota die*, Ps. Spl. 24, 5. Geþyldigendum *patientibus*, 102, 6. Geþyldiendium, Ps. Spl. T. 145, 5. [*O. H. Ger.* ge-dultian: *Ger.* gedulden.]

ge-þyldiglīce. v. ge-þyldelīce.

ge-þyll, es; *n. A breeze, air*:—Giþyll scendende *aura corrumpens*, Rtl. 121, 38.

ge-þylmēdan *to make patient, bring down*:—Hī geþylmēde synt *ipsi obligati sunt*, Ps. Lamb, 19, 9.

ge-þylmōd; *adj. Patient*; patiens, Lye.

ge-þylmōdness, e; *f. Patience*; patientia, Lye.

ge-þȳn = ge-þȳan *to press*:—He mæg ealla gesceafta on ānes weaxæpples [MS. -æples] onlīcnisse geþȳn *he can press all creatures into the likeness of a wax apple*, Salm. Kmbl. p. 150, 34.

ge-þyncan; *p.* -þūhte; *pp.* -þūht *To seem, appear*:—Ðǣr him wlitebeorhte wongas geþūhton *where appeared to them plains beautifully bright*, Cd. 86; Th. 108, 11; Gen. 1804. Se ðe to-dæg is ūre folgere geþūht *he who to-day seems our follower*, Homl. Th. ii. 80, 20. His loccas and his beard wǣron gylden geþūht *his hair and his beard seemed of gold*, Nar. 43, 14: Homl. Th. ii. 80, 12. Ðonne wǣre geþūht swilce . . . *then it would have seemed as if* . . . , i. 578, 3. Is me geþūht *it seems to me*, Exon. 47 b; Th. 163, 6; Gū. 989: 49 a; Th. 169, 18; Gū. 1096. v. þyncan.

ge-þyncþ. v. ge-þincþ.

ge-þynd, es; *n. A swelling*:—Wið geþind *against a swelling*, Herb 46, 4; Lchdm. i. 150, 1. [Cf. to-þunden.]

ge-þynge, es; *n. Growth, increase, advancement, honour*:—Ðætte he hæbbe forþgeong and geþyngo *that he may have advancement and honour*, Jn. Skt. p. 188, 11. Giþynge *provectum*, Rtl. 50, 21. [Cf. ge-þungen.]

ge-þynnian; *p.* ode; *pp.* od *To thin, lessen, diminish*; attenuāre:—Geþynnode synt eágan míne *attenuāti ŏcŭli mei*, Cant. Ezech. Lamb. fol. 185 a, 14. v. ge-þinnian.

ge-þyrst; *adj. Thirsty*:—Se geþyrsta mon meolcode ða hinde *the thirsty man milked the hind*, Shrn. 130, 4.

ge-þýwan, -þýan, -þíwan, -þēwan, -þeón, -þeówan; *p.* -þýwde, -þýde; *pp.* -þýd *To press, impel, urge, force, impress, rebuke, oppress*; prĕmĕre, trūdĕre, urgēre, compellĕre, imprĭmĕre, incrĕpāre, opprĭmĕre:—Se snáw geþýþ hý and geþreátaþ *the snow presses and afflicts them*, Salm. Kmbl. 607; Sal. 303. Ðú Reádne Sǽ ricene geþýwdest *incrĕpāvit Măre Rubrum*, Ps. Th. 105, 9. He Ægypti egesan geþýwde mid feala tácna *pŏsuit in Ægypto signa sua*, 77, 43. Hí mec þingum geþýdan *they pressed me violently*, Exon. 123 a; Th. 472, 10; Rä. 61, 14. Geþýd and geþreátod *rebuked and threatened*, Andr. Kmbl. 871; An. 436. Gesáwon hí swilce mannes fótlǽsta fæstlíce on ðam stáne geþýde *they saw as it were a man's footsteps firmly impressed on the stone*, Homl. Th. i. 506, 12.

ge-þýwe; *adj. Customary, usual*:—Him geþýwe wæs ðæt he oft ðǽr wunode [*other version has* his gewuna wæs] *sæpius ibidem diverti ac manere consueverat*, Bd. 3, 17; S. 543, 24. Swá him geþýwe ne wæs *as was not usual with him*, Beo. Th. 4654; B. 2332. v. ungeþeáwe.

ge-tídan, -týdan; *p.* de; *pp.* ed [tídan *to betide*] *To betide, happen*; contingere:—Getídeþ oft *it often happens*, Bt. 33, 2; Fox 124, 13. Ðē-læs ðe ðē on sumum þingum wyrs getíde *ne deterius tibi ălĭquid contingat*, Jn. Bos. 5, 14. Getýdde hit, ðæt . . . *it happened that* . . . , Bt. 16, 2; Fox 52, 34.

ge-tígan; *pp.* -tíged *To tie, bind*:—Forhwon fealleþ se snáw wæstmas getígeþ *why does the snow fall, bind up the fruits?* Salm. Kmbl. 606; Sal. 302. Ðǽr stód án ramm getíged be ðam hornum *there stood a ram tied by the horns*, Homl. Th. ii. 62, 3: i. 206, 10: Lk. Bos. 19, 30: Mt. Bos. 21, 2.

ge-tigþian *to grant*, Cd. 131; Th. 166, 23; Gen. 2752. v. ge-tíðian.

ge-tihhian; *p.* ode, ade; *pp.* od, ad *To appoint, determine, assign*; stătuĕre, decernĕre, assignāre:—Swá he æt fruman getihhod hæfde *as he at the beginning had determined*, Bt. 39, 3; Fox 220, 26. Hafast ðē ánum eall getihhad land and leóde *thou hast brought all the land and people on thyself*, Andr. Kmbl. 2642; An. 1322. v. ge-teohhian, -tiohhian.

ge-tihtan; *p.* te *To incite, urge, persuade*:—Ic getihte hundas míne *instigo canes meos*, Coll. Monast. Th. 21, 15. Getiht *suasum*, Ælfc. Gr. 26; Som. 28, 53. Getiht *instigatus, præmonitus, compunctus*, Hpt. Gl. 420.

ge-tíhtlod, -tíhtled, -týhtlod, -týhtled; *part.* [tíhtlian *to accuse*] *Accused*; accūsātus:—Gif se getíhtloda man máran werude beó ðonne twelfa sum *if the accused man be of a larger company than twelve*, L. Ath. i. 23; Th. i. 212, 8. Nán man ne tǽce his getíhtledan man fram him, ǽr he hæbbe ryht geworhte *let no one dismiss his accused man from him before he has done what is right*, i. 22; Th. i. 210, 23.

ge-tilian, -tilgan; *p.* ode; *pp.* od. I. *to strive after, to get by striving, to obtain, procure, acquire*; acquīrĕre:—Ne ic máran getilige to haldænne *nor do I strive to have more*, Shrn. 183, 3. Se ðe hit dēþ him seluan ēce hellewíte ungesǽliglíce getilaþ *he who does it will miserably get for himself everlasting hell torment*, Th. Chart. 117, 24. Hæbbe ic þearfe ðæt ic ðíne hyldo getilge *I have need that I acquire thy grace*, Exon. 118 a; Th. 454, 8; Hy. 4, 29. [*Goth.* ga-tilon *to obtain.*] II. *to treat a patient*; curāre:—Ic wát hú ðín man getilian sceal *I know how you must be treated*, Bt. 5, 3; Fox 12, 32.

ge-tillan; *p.* de; *pp.* ed *To touch, reach, attain*; tangere, attingere:—Astrece ðíne hand and getill ealle ða þing ðe he áh *extende manum tuam et tange cuncta quæ possidet*, Job Thw. 165, 15. Weras blóda and fácenfulle ná healfe getillaþ *viri sanguinei et dolosi non dimidiabunt*, Blickl. Gl.

ge-tilþ, e; *f. Gain*; mercimonia, Hpt. Gl. 439.

ge-timbernes, -ness, e; *f. A building, edification*; ædĭfĭcātio:—To gemynde and to getimbernesse ðara æfterfyligendra *ad mĕmŏriam ædĭfĭcātiōnemque sĕquentium*, Bd. 4, 7; S. 574, 25. Gitimbernise *ædificatio*, Rtl. 82, 36: 83, 13.

ge-timbran, -timbrian, -timbrigean; *part.* -timbriende; *p.* ode, ade, ede; *pp.* od, ad, ed [timbrian *to build*]. I. *to make of wood, to build, to build up, construct*; ædĭfĭcāre, construĕre, exstruĕre:—Ciricean getimbran *to build a church*, Andr. Kmbl. 3265; An. 1635. He hēt getimbrian cyrican of treówe *he commanded a church of wood to be built*, Chr. 626; Erl. 23, 40: Bd. 2, 3; S. 504, 23. Getimbrigean, Mt. Bos. 26, 61. Getimbriende Hierusalem Drihten *ædĭfĭcans Hierusalem Dŏmĭnus*, Ps. Spl. 146, 2. Ic getimbre hús *I will build a house*, Exon. 36 a; Th. 117, 9; Gú. 221. Ic getimbrie, Mk. Bos. 14, 58. Ofer ðisne stán ic getimbrige míne cyrcan *over this stone I will build my church*, Homl. Th. ii. 390, 2, 10, 11, 12. Ná ðú getimbrast hí *non ædĭfĭcābis eos*, Ps. Spl. 27, 7. He getimbreþ eardwíc niwe *he builds a new dwelling-place*, Exon. 62 a; Th. 227, 28; Ph. 430: Salm. Kmbl. 150; Sal. 74. Wá, ðæt ðes towyrpþ Godes templ, and on þrím dagum hyt eft getimbraþ *vah qui destruis templum Dei, et in trĭduo illud reædĭfĭcas*, Mt. Bos. 27, 40: Mk. Bos. 15, 29. On ðam seáþe ufan se eádiga wer, Gúthlác, him hús getimbrode *over the cistern the blessed man, Guthlac, built himself a house*, Guthl. 4; Gdwin. 26, 9: Gen. 4, 17: Ex. 24, 4. Ðe Róme burh getimbredon *who built Rome*, Ors. 2, 1; Bos. 38, 41. Naman mínne on ferhþlocan fæste getimbre *fast build up my name within their hearts*, Andr. Kmbl. 3339; An. 1673. Ðeáh ðe ðæt port beó trumlíce on ǽlce healfe getimbrod *though the gate be firmly constructed on every side*, Homl. Th. ii. 432, 3. Ðǽr getimbred wæs tempel Dryhtnes *where the temple of the Lord was built*, Andr. Kmbl. 1333; An. 667: Ors. 2, 1; Bos. 39, 30. Beóþ byrig mid Iudēum eft getimbrade *ædĭfĭcābuntur cīvĭtātes Judæ*, Ps. Th. 68, 36: Bd. 1, 1; S. 473, 27. II. *to build up the mind, instruct, edify*; instruĕre:—Ic getimbrige ðē on wege *instrŭam te in via*, Ps. Spl. C. 31, 10.

ge-timbru, -timbro; *pl. gen.* -timbra; *n. An edifice, a building, structure*; ædĭficium, structūra:—Gē geseóþ ealle ða fægernessa ðissa getimbra . . . ealle ðás getimbro beóþ toworpene *ye see all the beauties of these buildings . . . all these buildings shall be destroyed*, Blickl. Homl. 77, 34-6: Mt. Kmbl. Lind. Rush. 24, 1. Ðæt sind ða getimbru ðe nó [MS. nú] tydriaþ *these are the structures which shall not decay*, Exon. 32 b; Th. 103, 5; Cri. 1683: 39 b; Th. 131, 16; Gú. 456: Bd. 3, 8; S. 532, 30. Hruran and feóllan cynelíco getimbro and ánlípie *ruēbant ædĭfĭcia publĭca sĭmul et prīvāta*, Bd. 1, 15; S. 483, 45: 3, 8; S. 532, 32: Cd. 15; Th. 18, 20; Gen. 276. Getimbra hálgung *scenophegia* [=*scēnŏpēgia*], Ælfc. Gl. 3; Som. 55, 77; Wrt. Voc. 16, 50. [*O. H. Ger.* gi-zimbri; *n. materia, ædificium*: *Ger.* ge-zimmer; *n. timber-work*: and cf. *Goth.* ga-timrjo; *f. a building.*]

ge-timbrung, e; *f.* I. *an edifice, a structure, building*; ædĭfĭcium, ædĭfĭcātio, structūra:—Getimbrung *ædĭfĭcium*, Ælfc. Gl. 81; Som. 73, 12; Wrt. Voc. 47, 19: 86, 26. Hí geswicon ðære getimbrunge *they ceased from the building*, Homl. Th. i. 318, 21. Ðæt hí him ætýwdon ðæs temples getimbrunge *ut ostendĕrent ei ædĭfĭcātiōnes templi*, Mt. Bos. 24, 1: Homl. Th. ii. 390, 13. Lóca hwylce getimbrunga *aspĭce, quāles structūræ*, Mk. Bos. 13, 1. II. *a definition*; definītio:—Getimbrung *definītio*, Cot. 69.

ge-tímian, -týmian; *p.* ode; *pp.* od [tíma *time*] *To happen, befall*; accĭdĕre:—Getímian *to happen*, Jud. 5; Thw. 156, 8. Getímode hit ðæt he becom to heora byrig ðe wæs Gaza gehāten *it befell that he came to their city which was called Gaza*, Homl. Th. i. 226, 24: 318, 15. Him getímode swíðe rihtlíce *it happened very justly to them*, 88, 29: ii. 160, 14: 304, 24. Getímige ðē swá swá ðú gelýfdest *be it to thee as thou hast believed*, i. 126, 21.

ge-ting, -tincg, e; *f. Condition, state*:—Missenlícræ yldo and getincge men *homines conditionis diversæ et ætatis*, Bd. 1, 7: S. 478, 6.

ge-tingan; *p.* -tang *To press upon, throng*:—Corþer óðrum getang *one troop pressed on the other*, Andr. Kmbl. 276; An. 138.

ge-tingcræft, es; *m. Mechanics*, Hpt. Gl. 479.

ge-tinge, -tynge *eloquence*; lepor, Lye.

ge-tinge, -tingce, -tynge; *adj. Skilful with the tongue, eloquent*:—Getinge *disertus*, Ælfc. Gr. 47; Som. 48, 51. Getingce *lepida* vel *facunda*, Ælfc. Gl. 100; Som. 76, 129; Wrt. Voc. 55, 1. Gif se Hǽlend gecure æt fruman getinge láreówas *if the Saviour had chosen at first eloquent teachers*, Homl. Th. i. 578, 1. Wer getinge *vir linguosus*, Ps. Spl. C. 139, 12. v. ge-tynge.

ge-tingelic, -tyngelíc; *adj. Pleasant in speech, affable, eloquent*; lepidus, affabilis:—Getyngelíc *rhetoricus*, Hpt. Gl. 485: Cot. 179.

ge-tingelíce; *adv. Eloquently*:—Ðæt cild getingelíce spræc *the child spoke eloquently*, Homl. Th. ii. 490, 32.

ge-tingness, -tyngness, e; *f. Eloquence, ease of speech*; facundia:—Dumbum he forgeaf getingnysse *to the dumb he gave eloquence*, Homl. Th. i. 26, 12. Of woruldlícre getingnysse *from worldly eloquence*, 578, 4: ii. 140, 30: Swt. A. S. Rdr. 69, 403. Metcundlíc getyngnis *metrica facundia*, Hpt. Gl. 409.

ge-tióde *appointed, determined, decreed*, Bt. Met. Fox 11, 76; Met. 11, 38: 13, 26; Met. 13, 13; *p. of* ge-tión.

ge-tiohhian; *p.* ode; *pp.* od *To appoint, determine, ordain*; stătuĕre, decernĕre:—Ðú ðǽm winterdagum wundrum sceorta tída getiohhast *thou appointest wondrously short times to winter-days*, Bt. Met. Fox 4, 41; Met. 4, 21. Swá him æt frymþe Fæder getiohhode *as the Father appointed to them at the beginning*, 29, 78; Met. 29, 38. Swá he getiohhod habbe *as he has ordained*, Bt. 41, 2; Fox 244, 20. v. geteohhian.

ge-tión, ic -tió, *pl.* -tióþ; *impert.* -tió, *pl.* -tióþ; *subj. pres.* -tió, *pl.* -tión *To draw, to attract*; trăhĕre, attrahere:—Hwæðer nú gimma wlite eówre eágan to him getió *does now the beauty of gems attract your eyes to them?* Bt. 13; Fox 40, 2: 38, 1; Fox 196, 15.

ge-tión; *p.* -tióde; *pp.* -tiód *To appoint, determine, ordain*; stătuĕre, decernĕre :—Swā him æt frymþe Fæder getióde *as the Father appointed to it at the beginning*, Bt. Met. Fox 24, 28; Met. 24, 14: 13, 26; Met. 13, 13: 11, 76; Met. 11, 38. v. ge-teón.

ge-tiorian. v. ge-teorian.

ge-titelian; *p.* ode; *pp.* od *To entitle, ascribe*:—Twā bēc for ðære gelīcnisse his gelogodan sprǣce man getitelode him *two books from the likeness to his style are ascribed to him*, Swt. A. S. Rdr. 69, 404.

ge-tīþ *draws, constrains*, Bd. 1, 27; S. 494, 11. v. ge-teón.

ge-tīðian, -tȳðian, -tigðian; *p.* ode; *pp.* od *To grant, allow*:—Him nolde Alexander ðæs getīðian *Alexander would not grant him that*, Ors. 3, 9; Bos. 65, 7. Ðæs him getīðaþ Drihten Crist *the Lord Christ grants him that*, Homl. Th. i. 76, 22. Ðū bǣde me and ic ðē ne getīðode *you asked me and I did not grant thee*, Swt. A. S. Rdr. 57, 16: Bd. 3, 3; S. 525, 30. Gif he eów ðises ne getīðode *if he has not granted you this*, Homl. Th. ii. 144, 17. Hȳ him ðære bēne getigðedon *they granted him the request*, Ors. 2, 5; Bos. 47, 43: Cd. 131; Th. 166, 23; Gen. 2752. Getīða me *grant me*, Hy. 3, 2: 55. Ic wille ðæt gē ealle getīðe mīne worde *I will that ye all allow my words*, Chr. 656; Erl. 31, 3. Hī his bēnum getīðodon *they should grant his prayers*, Swt. A. S. Rdr. 96, 42. Him wearþ ðæs getīðod *that was granted him*, 44: Beo. Th. 4558; B. 2284.

ge-toge, es; *n. A tugging, contraction, cramp, convulsion, spasm*; contractio, convulsio, spasmus:—Wið sina getoge *for spasm of sinews*, Med. ex Quadr. 6, 23; Lchdm. i. 356, 3. v. ge-teón.

ge-togen *drawn, incited, restrained, educated, brought to an end, drawn together, strung*, Ors. 1, 14; Bos. 37, 14: Bd. 2, 5; S. 507, 42. v. ge-teón.

ge-togennes, -ness, e; *f. Cramp, convulsion*; contractio, convulsio, Som.

ge-toht, es; *n. A warlike expedition, battle*; expĕditio bellĭca, pugna:—Æt getohte *at the battle*, Byrht. Th. 134, 54; By. 104. v. tohte.

ge-torfian; *p.* ode; *pp.* od *To stone*:—Hig wǣron myd stānum getorfode *they were stoned with stones*, St. And. 36, 19. v. torfian, of-torfian.

ge-tot, es; *n. Pomp, splendour*; pompa:—Īdel-wuldor ðæt is gylp oððe getot *vain-glory, that is pride or pomp*, Homl. Th. ii. 220, 28. Riggon ðe mid ðam leáslīcum getote inneode *Riggo who entered with the false pomp*, 168, 16. Getote *pompa*, R. Ben. 7, Lye.

ge-trahtian, -trahtnian; *p.* ode; *pp.* od *To treat, explain, expound, consider*; tractāre, expōnĕre, consīdĕrāre:—Sume ðas race we habbaþ getrahtnod on ōðre stōwe *some of this narrative we have expounded in another place*, Homl. Th. ii. 264, 23. Ðā cwæþ Pilatus Hū clypedon hig and hū byþ hit getrahtnod on Hebreisc *then said Pilate 'How did they call out and how is it explained in Hebrew,'* Nicod. 4; Thw. 2, 31. Getrahtad *interpretatum*, Jn. Skt. Lind. 1, 38, 41: 9, 7. Huætd on woeg gie getrahtade *quid in via tractabatis*, Mk. Skt. Lind. 9, 33. Habbaþ word gearu wið ðam æglǣcan eall getrahtod *we have words ready all considered against the wretch*, Andr. Kmbl. 2718; An. 1361.

ge-tredan *to tread down*; conculcare:—Ðȳ læs hia getrede ða ilco miþ fōtum hiora *ne forte conculcent eas pedibus suis*, Mt. Kmbl. Lind. 7, 6. Getreden biþ *conculcetur*, 5, 13: Lk. Skt. Lind. 8, 5.

ge-tregian, *to despise*; despicere:—Þū ne getregedest mǣdenes innoþ *tu non despexisti virginis uterum*, Te Deum, Lye.

ge-treminc *a fort, fortress*; munimentum, Prov. 12, Lye.

ge-tremman; *p.* -tremede; *pp.* -tremed *To strengthen, establish, confirm*; firmāre, confirmāre:—Eall ūre līf he getremede *he strengthened all our life*, Blickl. Homl. 9, 36. Hwā hine heálīce torhtne getremede tungolgimmum *who had established it bright on high with starry gems*, Exon. 24 b; Th. 71, 5; Cri. 1151. Me gāste ðīne, God, getreme *strengthen me, O God, with thy spirit*, Ps. C. 50, 102; Ps. Grn. ii. 279, 102. Getremed *confirmed*, 50, 133; Ps. Grn. ii. 279, 133: Blickl. Homl. 17, 6: 119, 14. v. ge-trymman.

ge-treówan, -triówan, -triéwan; *p.* de; *pp.* ed. I. *to trust, believe, have confidence, hope*; confidere, credere, sperare:—Ic gemǣnscipe getreówe ðīnra hāligra *I believe the communion of thy saints*, Hy. Grn. ii. 294, 52, 55: Ps. Th. 118, 15. Ic on ðīn word getreówe *in verbum tuum speravi*, 114: 62, 1, 7: 129, 5: 124, 1: 129, 6. Ic on ðīnum wordum getreówde *I trusted in thy words*, 5. Ic ðīnum wordum getreówde *in verbum tuum speravi*, 118, 74. Ðū in ēcne god ðīnne getreowdes *thou hast trusted in thy eternal God*, Exon. 72 a; Th. 268, 21; Jul. 435. Gūþlāc sette hyht in heofonas hǣlu getreówde *Guthlac put his hope in heaven, trusted in salvation*, 39 a; Th. 128, 19; Gū. 406. II. *to make true* or *credible*:—Ðīn gewitnes is weorcum geleáfsum and mid sōþe is swīðe getreówed *testimonia tua credibilia facta sunt nimis*, Ps. Th. 92, 6. III. *to persuade, suggest*:—We getrēwaþ him *nos suadebimus ei*, Mt. Kmbl. Lind. 28, 14: 27, 20. Ðe hālig gāst gitrióweþ iówih alle ða ðe swā hwæt ic cweðo iów *spiritus sanctus suggeret vobis omnia quæcumque dixero vobis*, Jn. Skt. Rush. 14, 26. IV. *to make one's self out to be true, to clear one's self*:—Getrióẃe hine fācnes se ðe hine fēde *let him who brings him up clear himself of treachery*, L. Alf. 17; Th. i. 72, 5. Getriéwe hine ðæs sleges *let him clear himself of the slaying*, L. In. 34; Th. i. 122, 17. v. getreówian, ge-treówsian, ge-trūwan.

ge-treówe, -trȳwe, -trūwe, -trēwe; *def.* se -treówa; *comp.* -treówra; *superl.* -treówest; *adj. True, trusty, faithful*; fīdus, fīdēlis:—Getreówe oððe geleáfful *fĭdēlis*, Wrt. Voc. 74, 27: Ps. Lamb. 144, 14. Ǣlc getreówa man *every true man*, L. C. S. 23; Th. i. 388, 9, note 12, MS. B. Mid fulre gewitnesse and getreówre *with full and true witness*, L. Ath. v. § 10; Th. i. 240, 9. Gif þegen hæbbe getreówne man *if a thane have a true man*, L. C. S. 23; Th. i. 388, 16, MS. B. Ic wille him syllan mīne gewitnesse weorþe and getreówe *servabo testāmentum meum fĭdēle ipsi*, Ps. Th. 88, 25: 118, 111. Hwæðer gē getreówe synd *whether ye are true*, Gen. 42, 33. Hȳ habbaþ freónda ðȳ mā tilra and getreówra *they will have the more of excellent and faithful friends*, Exon. 107 a; Th. 409, 2; Rä. 27, 23. Beó getreówra *be more trusty*, Prov. Kmbl. 76. Ðe he, getreóweste, gelufade *whom, most faithful, he loved*, Exon. 43 a; Th. 144, 21; Gū. 681. DER. un-getreówe.

ge-treówfæstnian *to be faithful, firm, strong*:—Ðū getreówfæstnig *valeas*, Mt. Kmbl. p. 4, 9.

ge-treówfull; *adj. Faithful*; fīdēlis:—Getreówfull *fĭdēlis*, Ælfc. Gr. 9, 28; Som. 11, 38. Gecȳðnys getreówfull *testĭmōnium fĭdēle*, Ps. Spl. 18, 8. Ðū gōda þeów and ðū getreówfulla *thou good servant and faithful*, Blickl. Homl. 63, 26.

ge-treówfullīce; *adv. Faithfully, confidently*; fīdūciālĭter:—Getreówfullīce ic dēme on ðam *fīdūciālĭter ăgam in eo*, Ps. Spl. 11, 6.

ge-treówian, -triówian; *p.* ode, ede; *pp.* od, ed. I. *to trust, confide, hope*:—Nelle gē on ealdurmenn getreówian *nolite confide in principibus*, Ps. Th. 145, 2. Ic on ðīn sōþfæst word getreówige *I will trust to thy true word*, Ps. Th. 118, 80, 43, 48: 130, 5. Ic me on mīnne Drihten getreówige *ego in te sperabo Domine*, 54, 24: 70, 13. II. *to make a treaty, be confederate* [v. ge-treówþ]:—Ða beorn getreówedon betwuh him and sieredon ymbe ðone fæder *the children were confederates and plotted against the father*, Bt. 31, 1; Fox 112, 13. Getreówod *fæderatus*, Cot. 85, Lye. III. *to clear one's self*:—Getriówie hine *let him clear himself*, L. Alf. 36; Th. i. 84, 15. v. ge-treówan, ge-trūwian.

ge-treówleás, -trȳwleás; *def.* se -leása; *adj. Without faith, unfaithful, perfidious*; perfīdus:—Se getreówleása cyning *rex perfĭdus*, Bd. 3, 24; S. 556, 11.

ge-treówleásnes, -ness, -nys, -nyss, e; *f. Infidelity, perfidy*; perfidia:—Hī þrowedon heora getreówleásnesse *suæ perfĭdiæ pœnas luēbant*, Bd. 5, 23; S. 645, 34. For heora getreówleásnysse *for their perfidy*, 2, 2; S. 504, 9: 1, 8; S. 479, 34.

ge-treówlīc; *adj. Faithful*; fīdēlis:—Getreówlīcu oððe getrȳwe ealle bebodu his synd *fĭdēlia omnia mandāta ejus sunt*, Ps. Lamb. 110, 8. Us is swīðe uncūþ hwæt ūre yrfeweardas getreówlīces dōn willon æfter ūrum līfe *it is quite unknown to us how faithfully our heirs will act after our life*, Blickl. Homl. 51, 36.

ge-treówlīce, -triówlīce, -trīwlīce, -trȳwlīce; *adv. Faithfully*; fīdēlĭter:—Ðe him getreówlīce þeówdon *qui illi fĭdēlĭter serviĕrunt*, Bd. 3, 13; S. 538, 36: 3, 23; S. 554, 13: Swt. A. S. Rdr. 107, 81: Blickl. Homl. 185, 24, 28. Getrīwlīce, Th. Ch. 202, 26.

ge-treówsian, -trȳwsian; *p.* ode; *pp.* od *To justify one's self, clear one's self, prove one's self innocent*; se justĭfĭcāre, se purgāre:—Getreówsie hine fācnes *let him prove himself innocent of the treachery*, L. Alf. pol. 17; Th. i. 72, 5, note 8, MS. H: 36; Th. i. 84, 15, note 36, MS. B.

ge-treówþ, -trȳwþ, e; *f. A covenant, treaty, pledge*; fædus, pignus:—He gemunde ðara getreówþa *recordātus est fœdĕris*, Ex. 2, 24. v. ge-trȳwþ.

ge-trēwe; *adj. True, faithful*; fīdus, fīdēlis, Cot. 85. v. ge-treówe.

ge-tricce; *adj. Faithful* [?]:—Gif he biþ eáþhylde and ðære stōwe getricce *si contentus fuerit consuetudine loci*, R. Ben. 61, Lye. v. ge-tryccan.

ge-triéwan, -triówan. v. ge-treówan.

ge-trifulian *to rub down*; triturare:—Genim ða reádan netlan getrifula *take the red nettle, bruise it*, L. M. 1, 1; Lchdm. ii. 20, 15.

ge-trimmed; *part.* [ge-trymman *to draw up*] *Drawn up*; instructus:—Getrimmed fēða *cuneus*, Ælfc. Gl. 7; Som. 56, 79; Wrt. Voc. 18, 31.

ge-triówlice; *adv. Faithfully*; fīdēlĭter, Prov. 10. v. ge-treówlīce.

ge-trīwe; *def.* se -trīwa; *adj. True, faithful*; fīdus, fīdēlis:—Ǣlc getrīwa man *every true man*, L. C. S. 23; Th. i. 388, 9, note 12, MS. A. v. ge-treówe.

ge-trucian *to fail*; deficere:—Ðā ðæt wīn getrukede *deficiente vino*, Jn. Skt. 2, 3, col. 2.

ge-trudend, es; *m. A seizer*; raptor, Cot. 170, Lye.

ge-trūgung, e; *f. A certainty, defence, refuge*; confidentia, Ps. Vos. 88, 18.

ge-trum, es; *n. A knot, band, mass, company, company of soldiers*; nodus, caterva, cohors, exercitus:—Getrum *nodus, inter militāria*, Ælfc.

Gl. 7; Som. 56, 81; Wrt. Voc. 18, 33. Fyrd sceal ætsomne, tírfæstra getrum *the army shall be assembled, a band of warriors*, Menol. Fox 523; Gn. C. 32. Under tungla getrumum *under the troops of stars*, Salm. Kmbl. 285; Sal. 142. He eft gewát getrume micle *he returned with a great company*, Andr. Kmbl. 1413; An. 707: Beo. Th. 1849; B. 922: Exon. 90 a; Th. 337, 12; Gn. Ex. 63. DER. ân-getrum, folc-, fyrd-, gár-.

ge-truma, an; *m. A company, troop of soldiers;* cohors, exercitus:—Wið ðara cyninga getruman *with the kings' troop*, Chr. 871; Erl. 74, 19, 21. Ðeáh hí wyrcen getruman wið me *si consistant adversum me castra*, Ps. Th. 26, 4. v. ge-trum.

ge-trumian; *p.* ode, ade; *pp.* od, ad. I. *to grow strong, to recover, to gain strength;* convălescĕre:—Ðá he getrumad wæs *ut convăluit*, Bd. 4, 22; S. 592, 3. II. *to make strong, confirm;* confirmāre:—Ðone ðú getrumodest *quem confirmasti*, Ps. Spl. 79, 16, 18. Getrummade *exortans*, Lk. Skt. Lind. 3, 18. Getrumade *firmavit*, 9, 51.

ge-trúwa, an; *m. Confidence;* confīdentia:—Ælcum getrúwan ic gyrne fultum ðínre foreþingrǽdene *omni confidentia implōro auxĭlium tuæ interventiōnis*, Wanl. Catal. 294, 4, col. 2.

ge-trúwian; *p.* ode, ede; *pp.* od, ed. I. *to trust, hope;* confīdere, sperare:—Ða ðe on heora feó getrúwigeaþ *confidentes in pecuniis*, Mk. Bos. 10, 24. He getrúwade ðæt he hine beswícan mihte *he trusted that he could circumvent him*, Ors. 2, 4; Bos. 45, 10: 4, 1; Bos. 78, 44. Ðǽm he getrúwode ðæt hie his giongorscipe fulgân wolden *of whom he expected that they would perform his service*, Cd. 14; Th. 16, 25; Gen. 248. Ðú mínum wordum getrúwodest *thou hast trusted my words*, 29; Th. 38, 28; Gen. 613: 33; Th. 44, 9; Gen. 706: Beo. Th. 3071; B. 1533: 5074; B. 2540. Beorges getrúwode wíges and wealles *in his hill he trusted, in his war and his wall*, 4634; B. 2322. Ic on ðínum wordum getrúwade *in verba tua speravi*, Ps. Th. 118, 147: 51, 6. II. *to make a treaty;* sancire:—Hie getrúwedon on twá healfa fæste frioðuwǽre *they confirmed on both sides a fast compact of peace*, Beo. Th. 2194; B. 1095. v. ge-treówian.

ge-trúwung, e; *f. Confidence, trust:*—Getrúwung úre *assumptio nostra*, Ps. Spl. C. 88, 18.

ge-tryccan *to trust:*—Getryccaþ *confidite*, Jn. Skt. Lind. 16, 33.

ge-trym, es; *m. n? A support;* firmāmentum:—Æðele getrym eorþan weardaþ, biþ se beorht ahafen ofer beorgas *ĕrit firmāmentum in terra, in summis montium*, Ps. Th. 71, 16.

ge-trymman, -trymian, -trymigan, -tremman; he -trymmeþ, -trymþ; *p.* -trymde, -trymede; *pp.* -trymed, -trymmed, -trymd. I. *to confirm, strengthen, encourage, establish, found, set in order, arrange, draw up;* firmāre, confirmāre, mūnīre, confortāre, hortāri, fundāre, instruĕre:—Ic Wærferþ bisceop mid mínre ágenre handa ðas sylene getrimme and gefæstnie *I, bishop Wærferth, with my own hand confirm and ratify this donation*, Th. Ch. 169, 3. Ða ðé mágon getrymian [getrymigan, MS. Bod.] *which may encourage thee*, Bt. 36, 1; Fox 172, 27. Ic getrymme ofer ðé eágan míne *firmābo sŭper te ŏcŭlos meos*, Ps. Lamb. 31, 8: Ps. Th. 74, 3. Getrymmeþ rihtwíse Drihten *confirmat justos Dŏmĭnus*, Ps. Spl. 36, 18. Ealle geþeaht ðín he getrymþ *omne consĭlium tuum confirmet*, 19, 4: Ps. Lamb. 36, 18. Ðú getrymdest ofer me hand ðíne *confirmasti sŭper me manum tuam*, Ps. Spl. 37, 2. Ðú me getrymedest *exhortātus es me*, Ps. Th. 70, 20: 79, 14, 16. He ða ymbhwyrft eorþan getrymede *firmāvit orbem terræ*, 92, 2: 104, 20: 131, 11. He beforan ðam geate his folc getrymede *he drew up his army before the gate*, Ors. 4, 10; Bos. 92, 41. Getrym me *confirma me*, Ps. Spl. 50, 13. Ðín weorc on us getryme *confirma hoc quod opĕrātus es in nobis*, Ps. Th. 67, 26. Eall ðín geþeaht he getrymie *omne consĭlium tuum confirmet*, 19, 4. Byþ his heorte getrymed *confirmātum est cor ejus*, 111, 7: 116, 2. Hit wæs ofer ðæne stân getrymed *fundāta ĕrat sŭper petram*, Lk. Bos. 6, 48. He hæfde ðæt folc getrymmed *he had drawn up the troops*, Byrht. Th. 132, 27; By. 22. Worde [MS. word] Drihtnes heofonas [MS. heofones] getrymde synd *verbo Dŏmĭni cæli firmāti sunt*, Ps. Spl. 32, 6. II. *v. reflex. To grow strong, gain strength, recover;* convălescĕre:—Ecbyrht hine ðære ádle getrymede *Ecgberct ægrĭtudĭnis convăluit*, Bd. 3, 27; S. 559, 23.

ge-trymnes, -ness, e; *f. An exhortation, persuasion, a setting in order, an arraying;* hortātus:—Mid his getrymnesse *ejus hortātu*, Bd. 1, 33; S. 498, 35. Gitrymniso *ortamenta*, Rtl. 56, 4. Fyrdweorodes getrymnes *the arraying of a host*, Blickl. Homl. 91, 36.

ge-trýwan; *p.* de *To trust, hope:*—Ða ðe noldan on hine getrýwan *those who would not trust in him*, Blickl. Homl. 159, 11. Ic getrýwe in ðone torhtestan þrýnesse þrym *I believe in the most glorious virtue of the Trinity*, Exon. 42 a; Th. 140, 28; Gú. 617. Mín sáwel on ðé swíðe getrýweþ *in te confidit anima mea*, Ps. Th. 56, 1. Mægene getrýweþ *trusts in its strength*, Frag. Kmbl. 65; Leás. 34: Cd. 27; Th. 36, 10; Gen. 569. Getrýwde hweðre on Ælmihtiges Godes miht *he trusted however in the power of Almighty God*, Blickl. Homl. 217, 23. v. ge-treówan.

ge-trýwe; *def.* se -trýwa; *adj.* TRUE, *faithful;* fīdus, fīdēlis:—Beó blíðe, ðú góda þeów and getrýwa; forðamðe ðú wǽre getrýwe ofer lytle þing, ic gesette ðé ofer mycle *euge, serve bŏne et fīdēlis; quia sŭper pauca fuisti fīdēlis, sŭper multa te constĭtuam*, Mt. Bos. 25, 21, 23: 24, 45: L. C. S. 23; Th. i. 388, 9. He wearþ Criste getrýwe *he became faithful unto Christ*, Elen. Kmbl. 2068; El. 1035: Beo. Th. 2461; B. 1228. He eallum mannum sǽde and bodode ðæt wuldor his getrýwan þeówes *omnĭbus fīdēlis sui fămŭli glōriam prædĭcābat*, Bd. 3, 13; S. 539, 10. Gif þegen hæbbe getrýwe man *if a thane have a true man*, L. C. S. 23; Th. i. 388, 16. Twegen getrýwe men *two true men*, 30; Th. i. 392, 26: 394, 21. Ðam getrýwestan witan *to the most faithful senator*, Ors. 5, 4; Bos. 105, 7. v. ge-treówe.

ge-trýwian; *p.* ode. I. *to trust:*—Ic on ðínum wordum wel getrýwade *in verbum tuum supersperavi*, Ps. Th. 118, 1. II. *to clear one's self:*—Getrýwie hine ðæs sleges *let him clear himself of the slaying*, L. In. 34; Th. i. 122, 15, MS. B. v. ge-treówian.

ge-trýwleás; *adj. Perfidious;* perfĭdus, Greg. Dial. 2, 14. v. ge-treówleás.

ge-trýwlíce; *adv. Faithfully, confidently;* fīdēlĭter, fīdūciālĭter:—Ðæt flǽsclícnysse úres Drihtnes Hǽlendes Cristes getrýwlíce he gelýfe *ut incarnātiōnem Dŏmĭni nostri Iēsu Christi fīdēlĭter crēdat*, Ps. Lamb. fol. 201 b, 29: 202 b, 42. Getrýwlíce oððe baldlíce ic dó on him *fīdūciālĭter ăgam in eo*, Ps. Lamb. 11, 6. v. ge-treówlíce.

ge-trýwsian; *p.* ode; *pp.* od *To justify one's self;* se justĭfĭcāre:—Ðæt he hine ðæs getrýwsige *that he may justify himself thereof*, L. Ed. 6; Th. i. 162, 18. v. ge-treówsian.

ge-trýwþ, e; *f. A covenant, treaty, pledge, faith, fidelity;* fœdus, pignus:—Ofer ealle ða getrýwþa ðe he him geseald hæfde *against all the pledges which he had given him*, Chr. 1001; Erl. 136, 15: 1093; Erl. 229, 19. Lytle getrýwþa wǽron mid mannum *there has been little faith amongst men*, Swt. A. S. Rdr. 104, 8: 107, 74; 111, 220. v. ge-treówþ.

ge-tucian; *p.* ode; *pp.* od *To torment, vex, punish;* pūnīre:—Swilce he for his synnum swá getucod wǽre *as if he was so tormented for his sins*, Job Thw. 167, 14. v. tucian.

ge-tucian; *p.* ode; *pp.* od *To adorn, dress* [?]:—Ðǽr stent cwén ðé on ða swýðran hand mid golde getucode, and mid ǽlcere mislícre fægernysse gegyred *adstitit regina a dextris tuis in vestitu deaurato circumamicta varietate*, Ps. Th. 44, 11.

ge-twǽfan; *p.* de; *pp.* ed *To separate, divert, detain, hinder, deprive:*—Ne lǽt ðú ǽc síðes getwǽfan láde gelettan lifgendne monn *do not thou let any living man divert thee from thy course, hinder thy journey*, Exon. 123 b; Th. 474, 2; Bo. 23: Beo. Th. 3820; B. 1908: 963; B. 479. Sóna biþ ðæt ǽc ádl oððe ecg eafoþes getwǽfeþ *soon will it be that disease or sword will deprive thee of vigour*, 3531; B. 1763. Sumne Geáta leód feores getwǽfde *one the Goths' prince separated from life*, 2871; B. 1433. Gúþ wæs getwǽfed *the contest was parted*, 3320; B. 1658. Swelaþ sǽ-fiscas sundes getwǽfde *the sea-fishes shall burn cut off from the ocean*, Exon. 22 b; Th. 61, 20; Cri. 987. Hiin se mǽra mód getwǽfde *the great one took courage from them*, Cd. 4; Th. 4, 14; Gen. 53: 148; Th. 185, 8; Exod. 119 [?].

ge-twǽman, -twéman; *p.* de; *pp.* ed [twǽman *to separate*] *To cut off, separate, divide;* sepărāre, sejungĕre, dīvĭdĕre:—Ic hine ne mihte ganges getwǽman *I could not cut him off from his course*, Beo. Th. 1940; B. 968: L. N. P. L. 65; Th. ii. 300, 28. Ðá man getwǽmde ðæt ǽr wæs gemǽne Criste and cynincge *then was separated what was before in common to Christ and the king*, L. Eth. ix. 38; Th. i. 348, 20: Wald. 88; Vald. 2, 16. Ne getwǽme nán mann ða ðe God gesomnode *quod Deus conjunxit, hŏmo non sepăret*, Mt. Bos. 19, 6. Beó ǽlc sacu getwǽmed *let every strife be appeased*, L. Eth. v. 19; Th. i. 308, 30. Getwéman *to alienate*, Basil admn. 4; Norm. 40, 29, note p.

ge-twancg, es; *n. Fraud, deception;* colludium, fraus, deceptio, Hpt. Gl. 442.

ge-tweó; *gen.* -tweón; *m. Doubt, ambiguity:*—In gituiá *in ambiguitate*, Rtl. 105, 9.

ge-tweógan, -tweón; *p.* -tweóde; *pp.* -tweód; *v. pers. and impers. To doubt, hesitate;* dŭbĭtāre:—Ne getweóge ic náwuht be godes ǽcnessa *I do not at all doubt about God's eternity*, Shrn. 195, 4. Nó him treów getweóde *his faith doubted not in him*, Exon. 37 b; Th. 122, 25; Gú. 311: 40 b; Th. 134, 27; Gú. 515. Getuíga *hæsitare*, Mk. Skt. Lind. 11, 23. Forhwon getwiódes tú *quare dubitasti*, Mt. Kmbl. Rush. 24, 31: Lind. 28, 17. Ðá gehreów him ðæt hyne ǽfre swá on his geþohte getweóde *then he repented that he had ever so doubted in his mind*, Shrn. 155, 19.

ge-tweónian; *p.* ode; *pp.* od; *v. impers. To seem doubtful to any one;* dŭbium vĭdēri alĭcui:—Getweónode hí hwæðer . . . *it seemed doubtful to them whether* . . . , Ors. 1, 14; Bos. 37, 28.

ge-twífealdad; *part. Doubled;* duplĭcĭtus:—Biþ ðæt ǽfengyfel getwífealdad *the evening refection will be doubled*, L. E. I. 38; Th. ii. 436, 30.

ge-twífyldan, -twýfyldan *to double:*—Seó eahteoðe præteritum getwýfylt ðæt æftre stæfgefég *the eighth preterite doubles the second syllable*, Ælfc. Gr. 28, 8; Som. 33, 1. Hí beóþ getwyfylde *they are doubled*, Homl. Th. ii. 372, 35.

ge-twin, es; *m. A twin*:—Geminus ðæt is on úre geþeóde getwyn *geminus, that is in our language twin*, Shrn. 155, 30. Hí wǽron getwinnas *they were twins*, 92, 22: 134, 23: Salm. Kmbl. 729; Sal. 364: 216; Sal. 107 [?]. [Cf. *O. H. Ger.* zwinal, ge-zuinele *geminus*.]

ge-twis; *adj. Germanus*, Hpt. Gl. 477. Getwise *fratres germani*, Gl. M. 392.

ge-twisa, an; *m. A twin*:—Twegen getwisan *two twins*, Gen. 38, 27: Swt. A. S. Rdr. 62, 197. Getwisan *gemini*, Ælfc. Gr. 13; Som. 16, 13: Bd. de nat. rerum; Wrt. popl. science 7, 5; Lchdm. iii. 244, 24.

ge-týan; *p.* de; *pp.* -týd *To instruct, teach, imbue*; instruere, imbuere, docere:—He Sanctus Martinus fulfremedlíce on Godes ǽ and on Godes þeówdóm getýde and lǽrde *he perfectly instructed and taught St. Martin in God's law and service*, Blickl. Homl. 217, 5. Ðín lár getýde me *disciplina tua ipsa edocuit me*, Ps. Th. 17, 34: Bt. 8; Fox 24, 25: Ors. 5, 13; Bos. 112, 33. Gregorius wæs fram cildháde on bóclícum lárum getýd *Gregorius was from childhood instructed in book learning*, Homl. Th. ii. 118, 17: Bd. 1, 27; S. 489, 10: Guthl. 2; Gdwin. 18, 11: Nar. 1, 14. On snytrum sýn swýðe getýde *eruditos corde in sapientia*, Ps. Th. 89, 14: Elen. Kmbl. 2034; El. 1018.

ge-týd; *part. p. Skilful, learned*; peritus:—Wæs he se getýdesta sangere *cantator erat peritissimus*, Bd. 5, 20; S. 642, 11. v. ge-týan.

ge-týdan; *p.* -týdde [v. (?) ge-týd] *To make learned, skilled, to instruct*:—Dysine and ungelǽredne ic ðé underféng and ðá ðé getýdde and gelǽrede *foolish and ignorant I received thee, and then made thee wise and taught thee*, Bt. 7, 3; Fox 20, 10. Ic þohte ealra swíðost ymb ðone abbud ðe me getýdde *I thought most of all of the abbot that had instructed me*, Shrn. 46, 33. [*Or* ge-týdde = ge-týde?]

ge-týdan; *p.* de; *pp.* ed *To happen*; contingĕre:—Getýdde hit, ðæt ... *it happened that* ..., Bt. 16, 2; Fox 52, 34.

ge-tyddrian; *p.* ode; *pp.* od *To produce, bring forth*:—Swilce he swá fela wínboga getyddrode *as if it so many vine-branches brought forth*, Homl. Th. ii. 74, 7.

ge-týdnes, -ness, e; *f. Learning, knowledge, skill*; erŭdītio, pĕrītia:—Wæs Cúþberhte swá mycel getýdnes and gelǽrednes to sprecanne *Cudbercto tanta ĕrat dīcendi pĕrītia*, Bd. 4, 27; S. 604, 19. Mid ða getýdnesse ge cyriclícra gewrita ge eác gemǽnelícra *cum ĕrŭdītiōne lĭtĕrārum vel ecclēsiastĭcārum vel gĕnĕrālium*, 5, 23; S. 645, 15.

ge-tyhtan; *p.* te; *pp.* ed *To educate, teach, instruct*; ĕrŭdīre, dŏcēre, instruĕre:—Ðe ðú hine getyhtest *quem tu ĕrŭdiĕris*, Ps. Th. 93, 12. Byþ his heorte getrymed and getyhted *confirmātum est cor ejus*, 111, 7.

ge-týhtlod, -týhtled; *part. Accused*; accūsātus:—Ðe oft getýhtlod wǽron *who have often been accused*, L. Ath. i. 7; Th. i. 202, 25, note 48. Se getýhtleda man *the accused man*, i. 23; Th. i. 212, 8, note 19. v. ge-tíhtlod.

ge-týma, an; *m. An advocate, avoucher, a warranter*; advŏcātus:—Be getýmum. Ðæt ǽlc man wite his getýman *of warranters. That every man know his warranter*, L. A. G. 4; Th. i. 154, 12, 13. v. geteáma.

ge-tymbrian; *p.* ode; *pp.* od *To build*; ædĭfĭcāre:—Ðæt sýn getymbrod weallas *ædĭfĭcentur mūri*, Ps. Spl. 50, 19. v. ge-timbrian.

ge-týme, es; *n. A team, yoke*; jŭgum:—Ic bohte án getýme oxena *jŭga boum ēmi quinque*, Lk. Bos. 14, 19. Fýf hund getýmu oxena *quingenta jŭga boum*, Job. Thw. 164, 5: Homl. Th. ii. 372, 23.

ge-týnan; *p.* de; *pp.* ed *To shut up, hide*; ŏpĕrīre, inclūdĕre:—Se Hǽlend me in ðam engan hám oft getýnde *the Saviour often shut me up in the narrow dwelling*, Elen. Kmbl. 1839; El. 921. Foldan getýned *hidden in earth*, 1441; El. 722. Ēgo hiora getýndon *oculos suos clauserunt*, Mt. Kmbl. Lind. 13, 15. Getýned wæs ðe dura *clausa est janua*, 25, 10.

ge-týne, es; *n. A court*; atrium:—On his getýnum ðe ymb Dryhtnes hús deóre sindan *in atriis dŏmus Dŏmĭni*, Ps. Th. 115, 8. [Cf. tún.]

ge-tynge; *adj. Talkative*:—Se getynga wer *vir linguosus*, Ps. Th. 139, 11. [Cf. *O. H. Ger.* ge-zungel *loquax, facundus*; gi-zungili *verbositas*.] v. ge-tinge.

ge-tyrflan. v. ge-torfian.

ge-tyrian; *p.* ode; *pp.* od *To grow weary*; fătīgāre:—Ðeáh ðú getyrige *if thou shouldest grow weary*, Bt. 40, 5; Fox 240, 23. v. geteorian.

ge-uferian; *p.* ode; *pp.* od *To exalt, elevate, delay, put off*:—Ðæt he mid ðæs wurþmyntes wuldre geuferod wǽre *to be exalted with the glory of that honour*, Homl. Th. ii. 122, 26. Ic geseah árleásne geuferodne *vidi impium elevatum*, Ps. Lamb. 36, 35. Wæs ðá þurh his langsume fær ðæra cildra slege geuferod *the children's slaying was delayed by his long journey*, Homl. Th. i. 80, 28.

ge-unárian *To dishonour*:—Hí hys cyn geunáredon *they dishonoured his race*, Ors. 1, 5; Bos. 28, 31. Sýn geunárode *may they be dishonoured*, Ps. Spl. 34, 4.

ge-unclǽnsian *to make unclean, to pollute*; fœdare:—Romulus hiora angin geunclǽnsode mid his bróðor slege *Romulus polluted their undertaking with his brother's murder*, Ors. 2, 2; Bos. 40, 30.

ge-ungewlitegian; *p.* ode; *pp.* od *To deprive of beauty*:—Óðre hwíle gegiereþ mid ðám winsumestum wlitum óðre hwíle eft geungewlitegaþ *at one time adorns with the most delightful beauty, at another again deprives of beauty*, Shrn. 195, 11.

ge-unlustian *to loathe*:—Se líchoma geunlustaþ ða geógoþlustas to fremmenne *the body loathes to do the pleasures of youth*, Blickl. Homl. 59, 8.

ge-unlybba, an; *m. Poison [particularly when used in witchcraft]*:—Ne lǽt ðú lybban ða ðe geunlybban wyrcon *thou shalt not suffer a witch to live*, Ex. 22, 18. v. unlybba, lyblác.

ge-unnan; ic, he -an; ðú -unne, *pl.* -unnon; *p.* -úðe, *pl.* -úðon; *subj.* -unne, *pl.* -unnen; *p.* -úðe, *pl.* -úðen; *pp.* -unnen *To give, grant, allow, concede*; concedere, indulgere, permittere, largiri:—Gif he us geunnan wile, ðæt we hine grétan móton *if he will grant to us that we may greet him*, Beo. Th. 698; B. 346: Chr. 1095; Erl. 231, 25. Se cyning nolde him his feores geunnan *the king would not grant him his life*, Bt. 29, 2; Fox 104, 22: Andr. Kmbl. 358; An. 179: L. C. E. 2; Th. i. 358, 26. Hér sit mín mǽge ðe ic geann ǽgðer ge mínes landes ge mínes goldes ge ealles ðe ic áh æfter mínon dæge *here sits my kinswoman, to whom I give both my land and my gold and all that I own, after my day*, Th. Chart. 337, 30: 560, 9, 11, 15. Ǽrðon me geunne éce dryhten, ðæt *until to me shall grant the eternal Lord, that*, Salm. Kmbl. 499; Sal. 250. Me geúðe ylda waldend, ðæt *the Ruler of men granted me, that*, Beo. Th. 3326; B. 1661. Ðú geúðest his bearne his cyneríces *thou hast given his kingdom to his child*, Homl. Th. ii. 576, 14. Ðæt ðæt him góde menn geúðon *that which good men have given them*, Swt. A. S. Rdr. 106, 56. Hú Cnut cyncg and Ælfgifu seó hlǽfdige geúðan heora preóste ðæt he móste ateón ðæt land swá him sylfan leófast wǽre *how king Cnut and the lady Ælfgifu granted their priest that he might dispose of the land as he liked best*, Th. Chart. 328, 20: Homl. Th. ii. 152, 15. God him geunne ðæt ... *God grant him that* ..., Chr. 959; Erl. 121, 5. Ðæra þinga wurðe ðe se cyng him geunnen hæfde *worthy of those things that the king had granted him*, 1046; Erl. 173, 3. [*O. Sax.* gi-unnan; *p.* -onsta: *O. H. Ger.* gunnen; *p.* gi-onsta, *both with the same cases as the English verb*: *Ger.* gönnen.]

ge-un-ret *saddened*; *pp. of* ge-un-rétan.

ge-un-rétan; *p.* -rétte; *pp.* -réted, -rét *To make sorrowful, sadden, trouble*; contristare:—Ðá wæs se engel cweðende 'Ne beó ðú Maria geunréted' *then the angel said 'Be not sorrowful, Mary,'* Blickl. Homl. 139, 15. Hý wurdon geunrétt mid manncwealme *they were troubled with pestilence*, Ors. 3, 10; Bos. 70, 27. Ðá wearþ se cyning geunrét for ðam áðe and for ðám ðe him mid sǽton nolde ðeáh hí geunrétan *et contristatus est rex propter jusjurandum et propter simul discumbentes noluit eam contristare*, Mk. Bos. 6, 26: Mt. Bos. 14, 9: Lk. Bos. 18, 23.

ge-un-rótsian, -un-rótsigean; *p.* ode; *pp.* od. I. *to make sorrowful, to offend*; contristare, contribulare, scandalizare:—Ðæt we hí ne geunrótsigeon *ut non scandalizemus eos*, Mt. Bos. 17, 27. Ne sý úre nán geunrótsod *let none of us be sad*, Blickl. Homl. 149, 19: Mt. Kmbl. Rush. 14, 9. Geunrótsade swíðe *contristati valde*, Lind. 26, 22: Mk. Skt. Lind. 10, 22. II. *to become troubled, discontented*:—Ðæt se man geunrótsige ongeán God for ungelimpum ðises andwerdan lífes *so that a man becomes discontented with God for the mishaps of this present life*, Homl. Th. ii. 220, 16. Gást geunrótsod *spiritus contribulatus*, Ps. Spl. T. 50, 18.

ge-unsóþian; *p.* ode; *pp.* od *To disprove, refute, prove false*; refellĕre:—Gif se óðer ðæt geunsóþian mǽge ðæt him man onsecgan wolde *if the other can disprove that which any one would charge to him*, L. Edg. ii. 4; Th. i. 266, 24: L. C. S. 16; Th. i. 384, 22.

ge-unstillian; *p.* ode; *pp.* od *To disquiet, disturb*; inquiētāre:—Ðætte ða mynster ða ðe Góde gehálgode syndon nǽnigum bisceope alýfed sí in ǽnigum þinge hí geunstillian *ut quæque monastēria Deo consecrāta sunt, nulli episcŏpōrum lĭceat ea in alĭquo inquiētāre*, Bd. 4, 5; S. 572, 35.

ge-unþwǽrian, -unþwǽrigan; *p.* ode; *pp.* od *To disagree, differ*; dissentīre, discordāre:—Ic geunþwǽrige *dissentio*, Ælfc. Gr. 37; Som. 39, 9. Ðætte hie selfe ne geunþwǽrigen [geunþwǽrien, MS. Cot.] ðǽm wordum ðe hie lǽraþ, mid ðý ðæt hie óðer dón, óðer hie lǽraþ *that they themselves differ not from the words they teach, by doing one thing and teaching another*, Past. 48, 4; Swt. 371, 12; Hat. MS.

ge-untreówsian, -untrýwsian; *p.* ode; *pp.* od *To be offended*; scandălĭzāri:—Ðeáh ðe hig ealle geuntreówsion on ðé, ic nǽfre geuntreówsige *si omnes scandălĭzāti fuĕrint in te, ĕgo nunquam scandălĭzābor*, Mt. Bos. 26, 33. Ealle gé wurþaþ geuntreówsode on me *omnes vos scandălum pătiemĭni in me*, 26, 31: 13, 21.

ge-untrumian; *p.* ode; *pp.* od. I. *v. trans. To enfeeble, make weak or sick*; infirmāre, debĭlĭtāre:—Deófol geuntrumaþ ða hálan *the devil enfeebles the healthy*, Homl. Th. i. 4, 22. Ðe God sylf ǽr geuntrumode *whom God himself had before enfeebled*, i. 4, 27. Þurh ðæs dracan blǽd eal seó menigu micclum wearþ geuntrumod *all the multitude were greatly sickened by the dragon's breath*, ii. 294, 23: 296, 9: 516, 17. Ðe wǽron geuntrumode *qui infirmābantur*, Jn. Bos. 6, 2: Ps. Spl. 17, 38. II. *v. intrans. To be enfeebled, be sick*; infirmāri, ægrōtāre:—

Hī geuntrumiaþ *infirmābuntur*, Ps. Spl. 9, 3. Ða geuntrumade he mid ðære mettrymnesse podagre *then he was ill with the gout*, Shrn. 100, 18.

ge-untrȳwsian; *p.* ode; *pp.* od *To be offended;* scandălīzāri:—Hig wǣron geuntrȳwsode on him *scandălīzābantur in eo*, Mt. Bos. 13, 57. v. ge-untreówsian.

ge-unwendness, e; *f. Unchangeableness:*—Ðeós ungewendnes *hæc immutatio*, Ps. Th. 76, 9.

ge-unwurđod *dishonoured.* v. unweorđian.

ge-upped; *part. Revealed:*—Ne mihte Scs Neotus behȳdd beón đā đā God hine geupped habben wolde *St. Neot could not be hid when God would have him revealed*, Shrn. 12, 15. v. ge-yppan.

ge-ūđe; *p. of* ge-unnan.

ge-ūtian; *p.* ode; *pp.* od *To eject, banish, alienate;* ejĭcĕre, expellĕre:—Se cyng hine geūtode of earde *the king banished him from the country*, Chr. 1002; Erl. 137, 29. Wæs Ōslāc geūtod of Angelcynne *Oslac was banished from England*, 975; Erl. 127, 8. He beád đæt nāđer ne đære stōwe bisceop ne nānes bisceopes æftergenga đæt land nǣfre of đære stōwe geūtode *he ordered that neither the bishop of the place nor any bishop's successor should ever alienate that land from the place*, Cod. Dipl. Kmbl. iii. 112, 9: iv. 72, 27, 32. Cwǣdon hī đæt hit betere wǣre đæt ic đa preóstas of Cristes cyrcean geūtode *they said it would be better that I should expel the priests from Christchurch*, iii. 349, 14. Ic nelle geþafian đæt ǣni man geūtige ān æker landes *nolo permittere ut quis unum jugerum excludat*, iv. 202, 15. Geūtian *exiliare*, Hpt. Gl. 517.

ge-ūtlagian; *p.* ode; *pp.* od *To outlaw;* proscrībĕre:—Man geūtlagode Ælfgār eorl *earl Ælfgar was outlawed*, Chr. 1055; Erl. 188, 27: 1020; Erl. 161, 22.

ge-wācian; *p.* ode; *pp.* od *To grow weak* or *lose energy, to flinch;* languescere, obtorpescere:—Gif hȳ đǣr ne gewācodan [gewīcadon, Laud] *if they had not there lost energy* [*stopped*], Ors. 3, 4; Bos. 56, 11. v. wācian, wīcian.

ge-wacsan. v. ge-wascan.

ge-wadan; *p.* -wōd; *pp.* -waden. I. *v. intrans. To wade, go;* vadere, ire:—Sār gewōd ymb đæs beornes breóst *pain went around the man's breast*, Andr. Kmbl. 2494; An. 1248. Ord in gewōd *the point entered*, Byrht Th. 136, 26; By. 157: Exon. 47 b; Th. 163, 29; Gū. 1001. Wundenstefna gewaden hæfde đæt đa līđende land gesāwon *the ship had gone* [*so far*] *that the sailors saw land*, Beo. Th. 446; B. 220. II. *v. trans. To pervade, go through:*—Flōd blōd gewōd *blood pervaded the flood*, Cd. 166; Th. 207, 6; Exod. 462: Elen. Kmbl. 2378; El. 1190. v. wadan.

ge-wǣcan, -wǣcean; *part.* -wǣcende; *p.* -wǣcte, -wǣhte; *pp.* -wǣct, -wǣht *To weaken, affect, trouble, vex, afflict, oppress;* afficĕre, affligĕre:—Heó nele đa andweardan myrhþe gewǣcan mid nānre care đære toweardan ungesǣlþe *it will not trouble the present joy with any care for the future unhappiness*, Homl. Th. i. 408, 21. Beóton hig đone, and mid teónum, gewǣcende, hine forlēton īdelne *illi hunc cædentes, et afficientes contŭmēlia, dimīserunt inānem*, Lk. Bos. 20, 11. Hī mid deáþe hī gewǣceaþ *morte afficient eos*, Mk. Bos. 13, 12: Homl. Th. ii. 542, 17. Hig eall đæt rīce myd forspyllednysse gewǣhton *they destroyed all that kingdom*, St. And. 32, 32. Mid fefore gewǣht *suffering from fever*, Homl. Th. ii. 516, 30. Gewǣht ic eom *afflictus sum*, Ps. Spl. 37, 8. Ðe mid đȳ hungre gewǣcte wǣron *who were oppressed with the hunger*, Bd. 4, 13; S. 582, 31. Gelomp us đæt we wurdon earfoþlīce mid þurste geswencte and gewǣcte *accidit nobis siti laborare*, Nar. 7, 30. We on đīnum yrre synt swīđe gewǣhte *in īra tua defēcimus*, Ps. Th. 89, 9: Jud. 6, 2: Homl. Th. ii. 396, 28.

ge-wæccan *to watch:*—Ne mæhtes đū ān huīl gewæccæ *non potuisti una hora vigilare*, Mk. Skt. Lind. 14, 37. Gewaccas *vigilate*, 13, 35. Ðætte we giuæcge *ut vigilemus*, Rtl. 124, 23.

ge-wǣcedyss, e; *f. Weakness:*—Him nān þing ne eglaþ ǣnigre brosnunge odđe gewǣcednysse *nothing pains him of any corruption or weakness*, Homl. Th. ii. 552, 29.

ge-wǣde, -wēde, es; *n. A garment, clothing;* vestimentum:—Saga hwæt đis gewǣde [gewædu, MS.] sȳ *say what this vestment is*, Exon. 109 a; Th. 418, 5; Rä. 36, 14. He nywolnessa him to gewǣde woruhte *abyssus amictus ejus*, Ps. Th. 103, 7. Mīne gewǣda *vestimentum meum*, 68, 11: Homl. Th. ii. 148, 30. Wǣpen and gewǣdu *arms and clothing*, Beo. Th. 589; B. 292. Gewēde *vestimentum*, Mt. Kmbl. Lind. 3, 4. Mid his gewēdum *vestimentis ejus*, 27, 31. He onfēng cynegewǣdum *purpuram sumpsit*, Bd. 1, 6; S. 476, 19. Ongon me gewēdum þeccan *he began to deck me with weeds*, Exon. 103 a; Th. 391, 13; Rä. 10, 4. [*O. Sax.* gi-wādi: *O. H. Ger.* gi-wāti *vestimentum, vestis.*]

ge-wǣdian, -wēdian; *p.* ode; *pp.* od *To dress, clothe, equip:*—Giwoedes *induite*, Rtl. 13, 31. Gewǣdod *equipped*, Chr. 992; Erl. 131, 34. Gewēded *vestitus*, Mt. Kmbl. Lind. 11, 8. Woere gewoedad *vestiebatur*, Lk. Skt. Lind. 12, 27.

ge-wǣdod; *part. Prepared, equipped;* appărātus, instructus:—Hī đæt scip genāmon eall gewǣpnod and gewǣdod *they took the ship all armed and equipped*, Chr. 992; Erl. 131, 34. v. ge-wǣdian.

ge-wæg *bore, carried*, Bd. 3, 16; S. 542, 22; *p. of* ge-wegan.

ge-wǣgan; *p.* ede; *pp.* ed. I. *to affect, weigh down, oppress;* afficere, deprimere, vexare:—Wīne gewǣged *affected by wine*, Exon. 84 a; Th. 315, 34; Mōd. 41. Wōpe gewǣged *oppressed with weeping*, Bt. Met. Fox 2, 5; Met. 2, 3. Mid meteliéste gewǣgde *oppressed with lack of food*, Chr. 894; Erl. 92, 27. II. *to frustrate;* frustrari, irritum facere:—Cūþ sceal geweorþan đæt ic gewǣgan ne mæg *that which I may not frustrate shall become manifest*, Exon. 117 b; Th. 452, 3; Dōm. 115. v. wǣgan, a-wǣgan.

ge-wæge, es; *n. A weight, measure:*—Gewæge *weight*, Herb. 1, 15; Lchdm. i. 74, 21: 16; Lchdm. i. 76, 1. Gewege, 2; Lchdm. i. 70, 15, note. Gewæge [giwege, Rush.] *mensura*, Mk. Skt. Lind. 4, 24. Gewoege ł gemet *mensura*, Lk. Skt. Lind. 6, 38. v. ge-wegan.

ge-wǣgnian; *p.* ode; *pp.* od *To frustrate, deceive, disappoint;* frustrari, Cot. 83.

ge-wǣlan *to vex, afflict:*—Hie wēron gewǣlde *erant vexati*, Mt. Kmbl. Rush. 9, 36. v. wǣlan, be-wǣlan.

ge-wæltan *to roll:*—Gewælteno *provolutus*, Mt. Kmbl. 17, 14. He gewælte stān micel to duru đæs byrgennes *advolvit saxum magnum ad ostium monumenti*, 27, 60.

ge-wæmnednes, se; *f. A corruption;* corruptio:—Ānes wordes gewæmnednys *a corruption of a word, a barbarism;* barbarismus, Som. v. ge-wemmedness.

ge-wǣmnod *armed;* Ælfc. T. 36, 22, *q.* ge-wǣpnod. v. ge-wǣpnian.

ge-wænian; *p.* ede; *pp.* ed. I. *to accustom;* assuefacere:—Folc to ælmessan gewænian *to accustom the people to alms*, L. Edg. C. 55; Th. 256, 9. II. *to wean;* ablactare, Gen. 21, 8. v. gewenian.

ge-wǣpnian, -wēpnian; *p.* ode; *pp.* od *To arm, furnish with weapons;* armāre:—Ic gewǣpnige *armo*, Ælfc. Gr. 24; Som. 25, 41: 36; Som. 38, 36, 37. He mid rōdetācne his mūþ and ealne his līchaman gewǣpnode *he armed his mouth and all his body with the sign of the cross*, Homl. Th. i. 72, 23. Se stranga gewǣpnod his cāfertūn gehealt *fortis armātus custōdit atrium sum*, Lk. Bos. 11, 21: Ælfc. Gr. 43; Som. 45, 15. Hī đæt scip genāmon eall gewǣpnod and gewǣdod *they took the ship all armed and equipped*, Chr. 992; Erl. 131, 34.

ge-wær; *adj. Aware;* conscius:—Hī his gewær wurdon *they were aware of him*, Chr. 1095; Erl. 231, 39.

ge-wærlǣcan; *p.* -lǣhte, -lēhte; *pp.* -lǣht, -lēht *To remind, admonish;* commonefăcĕre:—Cain wiste his fæder forgǣgednysse, and næs þurh đæt gewærlēht *Cain knew his father's transgression, and was not admonished by it*, Boutr. Scrd. 20, 40.

ge-wærlan; *p.* de *To go, pass:*—Ēghuoelc on weg his giwærlde *quisque in viam suam declinavit*, Rtl. 19, 39. v. wærlan.

ge-wæsc *a washing up* or *overflow of water;* alluvio:—Wætera gewæsc *aquarum alluvio*, Ælfc. Gl. 100; Wrt. Voc. 55, 26. v. wætergewæsc.

ge-wǣtan, -wētan; *p.* -wǣtte; *pp.* -wǣted, -wǣtt *To wet, to make wet:*—Onsend Ladzarus đætte he gewǣte his ȳtemestan finger on wættre *send Lazarus, that he may wet the tip of his finger in water*, Past. 43, 1; Swt. 309, 6; Hat. MS. • Strengas gurron wædo gewǣtte *the ropes creaked wet with the waters*, Andr. Kmbl. 749; An. 375: Ps. Th. 104, 36.

ge-wæterian, -wætrian; *p.* ode; *pp.* od *To water, irrigate;* adăquāre, irrīgāre:—Ðæt mǣge and cunne ōđerra monna ingeþonc giendgeótan and gewæterian [gewætrian, MS. Cot.] *that he may be able and know how to irrigate and water the minds of others*, Past. 18, 5; Swt. 137, 10; Hat. MS. 27 a, 14. Ic betǣce hig đam yrþlincge, wel gefylde and gewæterode *adsigno eos arātōri, bĕne pastos et adăquātos*, Coll. Monast. Th. 20, 31. Teóh đū forþ rēnscūras gif đū miht and gewætera đīne æceras *bring forth rain-showers, if thou canst, and water thy fields*, Homl. Th. ii. 104, 1.

ge-wald, es; *m. n. Power, mastery, sway:*—Ða Denescan āhton wælstōwe gewald *the Danes had the mastery of the battle-place*, Chr. 833; Th. 116, 7, col. 1: Cd. 214; Th. 268, 15; Sat. 55. v. ge-weald.

ge-waldan *to have power over.* v. ge-wealdan.

ge-walden. v. ge-wealden.

gewald-leđer *a power-leather, a rein*, Bt. Met. Fox 24, 77; Met. 24, 39. v. geweald-leđer.

ge-wana, -wona, an; *m. A lack, want:*—Huædd me gwona is *quid mihi deest*, Mt. Kmbl. Lind. 19, 20, v. wana.

ge-wand *turned*, Beo. Th. 2007; B. 1001; *p. of* ge-windan.

ge-wanian, -wonian; *p.* ode; *pp.* od. I. *to lessen, diminish:*—Se lāreow ne sceal đa inneran giémenne gewanian for đære ūterran abisgunge *the teacher is not to diminish his care of inner things for outer occupations*, Past. 18, 1; Swt. 127, 8; Hat. MS. His cynelīcan gefe gewonian *to diminish his royal gift*, Cod. Dipl. Kmbl. ii. 304, 27. Ðone hryre đe se feallenda deófol on engla werode gewanode *the loss that the falling devil caused in the host of angels*, Homl. Th. i. 32, 23: 214, 24. He his godcundnesse nān wiht ne gewanode *he did not at all diminish* *his divinity*, Blickl. Homl. 91, 9. Gewanude, Th. Chart. 203, 36. Gewonade, Exon. 44 a; Th. 148, 19; Gû. 747. Bûton he his flǽsclîcan lustas gewanige *unless he diminish his fleshly lusts*, Homl. Th. i. 96, 3: Past. 48, 1; Swt. 127, 12; Hat. MS. Ne gē nān þing ne gewanion *ye shall not diminish ought*, Ex. 5, 8. Gewonige, Cod. Dipl. Kmbl. ii. 100, 27. Is mîn flet-werod gewanod *my band of retainers is lessened*, Beo. Th. 958; B. 477: Cd. 24; Th. 31, 6; Gen. 481: Gen. 8, 1. Đā wæs đǽm tunglum gewonad heora beorhtnes *then had the stars their brightness diminished*, Shrn. 64, 22. **II.** *to be wanting*:—Giwonia deesse, Rtl. 71, 37.

ge-waran; *gen.* -warena; *pl. m*; used as a termination to denote *inhabitants, dwellers*; incolæ:—Đa Rōmāniscan ceastergewaran noldon geþafian đæt Gregorius đa burh forlēte *the Roman citizens would not consent that Gregory should leave the city*, Homl. Th. ii. 122, 13. v. waran.

ge-wardod *seen*; visus:—Þat he sȳ gewardod fram him *ut videatur ab illo*, R. Ben. interl. 49.

ge-warenian; *p.* ode; *pp.* od *To warn, guard*; cavere:—Ǽlc gleáw mōd hit gewarenaþ *every prudent mind guards itself*, Bt. 7, 2; Fox 18, 24. v. warenian.

ge-warian *to protect*; protegere, Hpt. Gl. 489, 500.

ge-warnian; *p.* ode; *pp.* od *To warn*:—God on swefne hî gewarnode *God warned them in a dream*, Homl. Th. i. 78, 29. Đā gewarnode man hî đæt đǽr wæs fyrd æt Lundene *then they had notice that there was a force at London*, Chr. 1009; Erl. 143, 12. Đā wearþ Godwine gewarnod *then was earl Godwin warned*, 1052; Erl. 183, 2. Gebeorh gewarnian *tuitionem præstare*, Bd. 2, 5; S. 506, 30, note.

ge-wascan, -wacsan; *p.* -wōcs *To wash*:—Ic hine mid mînen handen gewōchs *I washed him with my hands*, Cod. Dipl. Kmbl. iv. 261, 1.

ge-wât *departed*; *p. of* ge-wîtan.

ge-wealc, es; *n. A rolling, motion, an attack*; volutatio, impetus:—Ȳđa gewealc *a rolling of waves*, Ap. Th. 11, 1: Cd. 166; Th. 206, 21; Exod. 455: Exon. 81 b; Th. 306, 11; Seef. 6: 82 a; Th. 308, 28; Seef. 46: Beo. Th. 932; B. 464: Chr. 975: Erl. 126, 19; Edg. 45: Andr. Kmbl. 517; An. 259. Togeánes đan he manega gewealc and gewinn hæfde *against which he had many a struggle and contest*, Chr. 1100; Erl. 237, 9. v. ge-wilcþ, ge-wylc.

ge-wealcan; *p.* -weólc; *pp.* -wealcen *To roll*; volvere, revolvere:—Fām biþ gewealcen *the foam is rolled*, Exon. 101 a; Th. 382, 1; Rä. 3, 4.

ge-weald, -wald, es; *m. n.* **I.** *power, strength, might, efficacy*; potestas:—Þurh geweald Godes *through the power of God*, Cd. 1; Th. 1, 21; Gen. 11. Geweald hafaþ *shall have power*, Exon. 32 a; Th. 100, 29; Cri. 1649. Wiste his fingra geweald *knew the power of his fingers*, Beo. Th. 1533; B. 764. Gif hit geweald āhte *if it possessed power*, Bt. Met. Fox 22, 72; Met. 22, 36. Gif mon ōþrum đa geweald forsleá uppe on đam sweoran *if a man rupture the powers* [*tendons*] *on another's neck*, L. Alf. pol. 77; Th. i. 100, 10. **II.** *power over any thing, empire, rule, dominion, mastery, sway, jurisdiction, government, protection, keeping, a bridle-bit*; potestas, facultas, imperium, ditio, arbitrium, jus, camus:—Đæt he nāge đæra geweald *that he has no power over them*, L. Alf. pol. 77; Th. i. 100, 12: Jud. Thw. p. 153, 9. Đonne he his geweald hafaþ *when he has power over it*, Cd. 30; Th. 40, 7; Gen. 635: Bt. Met. Fox 9, 126; Met. 9, 63. Gesealde wǽpna geweald *gave power over weapons*, Cd. 143; Th. 178, 31; Exod. 20. Āhte bega geweald, lîfes and deáđes *he had power of both, of life and death*, Exon. 40 a; Th. 133, 24; Gû. 494: Beo. Th. 3459; B. 1727: Shrn. 150, 13. On geweald gehwearf worold-cyninga *it passed into the power of worldly kings*, Beo. Th. 3372; B. 1684: Andr. Kmbl. 2547; An. 1275. His gewealdes *of his own accord*, L. Alf. 13; Th. i. 46, 21. Đæt se Gode mōte in geweald cuman *that he may come into God's dominion*, Exon. 32 b; Th. 103, 27; Cri. 1694; Cd. 10; Th. 13, 14; Gen. 202. Werþeóda geweald *the sway of nations*, 161; Th. 202, 4; Exod. 383. Wînærnes geweald *jurisdiction over the wine-hall*, Beo. Th. 1312; B. 654. Đū scealt wǽpned-men wesan on gewealde *thou shalt be in subjection to man*, Cd. 43; Th. 56, 30; Gen. 920. Đæt mîn sāwul to đē sîđian mōte on đîn geweald *that my soul may proceed to thee, into thy keeping*, Byrht. Th. 136, 66; By. 178. Ic đǽ lǽte habban đis land to gewealde *I will let you rule this land*, H. R. 101, 33. Ic hine sealde to đînum gewealde *I have given him into thy power*, Num. 21, 34. Đæt is God đe ealle þing on his gewealdum hafaþ *that is God, that hath all things in its power*, Salm. Kmbl. 178, 11: Blickl. Homl. 63, 3. Siđđan ic đā me hæfde đās þing ealle be gewealdum *quibus in potestatem redactis*, Nar. 5, 17. Under hāligra hyrda gewealdum *under the protection of holy guardians*, Exon. 38 b; Th. 127, 15; Gû. 386: Ps. Spl. 31, 12. [*O. Sax.* gi-wald; *f. potestas, facultas, imperium*: *Ger.* gewalt; *f*: *M. H. Ger.* gewalt; *f*: *O. H. Ger.* gawalt; *m. f.*] DER. hand-geweald, ǽht-, nȳd-. v. ge-wealdes.

ge-weald, -wald, es; *m. n. Pudenda, inguen*:—Neáh đam gewealde *prope inguinem*, Herb. 104, 2; Lchdm. i. 218, 23: 5, 5; Lchdm. i. 94, 22, 24. Đæt geweald, Lchdm. ii. 388, 9. v. ge-weald *power*.

ge-wealdan; *p.* -weóld; *pp.* -wealden *To wield, rule, have power over, command, control, cause.* **I.** *with gen*:—Ic gewealde ealles middaneardes *I rule all the world*, Homl. Th. ii. 308, 21. Gregorius đæs pāpan setles geweóld *Gregory ruled the papal see*, 132, 18. Būton đū eác ūre gewelde *except thou make thyself altogether a prince over us*, Num. 16, 13. Gif he abilhþe āhwām on unriht āhwār geweólde gebēte hit georne and gif him abulge ǽnig man swîđe forgife đæt *if he anywhere have wrongly been the cause of offence to any man, let him diligently make amends; and if any man have much offended him, let him forgive it*, L. Pen. 16; Th. ii. 284, 7. Wǽpna gewealdan *to wield weapons*, Beo. Th. 3022; B. 1509. Swā heó đæs unlǽdan eáđost mihte wel gewealdan *so she most easily might have complete power over the wretch*, Judth. 10; Thw. 23, 3; Jud. 103. **II.** *with acc*:—Se đe gewylt đa đe he gesceóp *he who rules those whom he created*, Homl. Th. ii. 72, 27: Th. Chart. 239, 37. Đe ealne middangeard geweóld *who ruled all the world*, Homl. Th. i. 80, 7. Hālig God geweóld wîgsigor *holy God controlled victory in battle*, Beo. Th. 3112; B. 1554. **III.** *with instr*:—Nū leng ne miht gewealdan đȳ weorce *now canst thou no longer control the work*, Andr. Kmbl. 2729; An. 1367: Exon. 50 b; Th. 175, 24; Gû. 1199. Cyning geweóld his gewitte *the king got command of his senses*, Beo. Th. 5399; B. 2703.

ge-wealden; *part. Subject, under the power* or *control of any one, inconsiderable, small*:—God gedēþ him gewealdene worolde dǽlas sîde rîce *God puts under his power parts of the world, spacious realms*, Beo. Th. 3468; B. 1732. Hond biþ gelǽred wîs and gewealden *the hand is instructed, wise and under control*, Exon. 79 a; Th. 296, 4; Cra. 46; 91 a; Th. 341, 7; Gn. Ex. 122. Meahtig dryhten scyreþ sumum gūþe blǽd gewealdenne wîgplegan *the mighty Lord assigns to one glory in war, battle under his control*, i. e. *successful*, 88 a; Th. 331, 16; Vy. 69. Drincan gewealden wînes for eówres magan mettrymnesse *modico vino utere propter stomachum*, Past. 43, 9; Swt. 319, 6; Hat. MS. Đā næfdon hî nān wîn būton on ānum gewealdenum butruce *in uno parvissimo vasculo*, Lchdm. iii. 362, col. 1. Būton swîđe gewaldenum dǽle eásteweardes đæs folces *except a small part of the people of the east of England*, Chr. 894; Erl. 91, 11: Ors. 4, 9; Bos. 92, 1. He myd us [wyrcþ] swā swā myd sumum gewealdum tōlum *he works with us as with some insignificant tools* [or *tools under his control, over which he has complete command?*], Shrn. 179, 28. v. Lchdm. iii. 361, col. 1. [Cf. ge-wealden-mōd.]

ge-wealdende; *adj. Powerful, mighty*; potens, validus:—Mid his gewealdendre hand *with his mighty hand*, Ps. Th. 113, 8. v. wealdende.

ge-wealdendlîce; *adv. Powerfully, mightily*; potenter, valide, Ps. Th. 135, 16.

ge-wealden-mōd; *adj. Subdued in mind, having the mind under control, self-controlled*:—Sum gewealdenmōd þafaþ in geþylde đæt he đonne sceal *one, self-controlled, suffers in patience what then he must* [cf. Luke 21, 19], Exon. 79 a; Th. 297, 19; Cra. 70. v. ge-wealden.

ge-wealdes; *adv.* [*gen. of* ge-weald *power*] *Of one's power, of one's own accord, willingly*; sponte:—Gif man hine sylfne gewealdes ofslihþ *si quis sponte seipsum occiderit*, L. M. I. P. 13; Th. ii. 268, 15. Se đe his gewealdes monnan ofsleá *he who slays a man of his own accord*, L. Alf. 13; Th. i. 46, 21, 26. Eówres gewealdes *quod ex vobis est*, Past. 46, 7, 8; Swt. 355, 19, 20, 25; Hat. MS.

ge-weald-leđer, ge-wald-leđer, es; *n.* [ge-, weald-leđer *a directing-leather*] *A power-leather, a directing-leather, a rein*:—Đonne he đæt gewealdleđer forlǽt đara bridla *when he shall let go the rein of the bridles*, Bt. 21; Fox 74, 31: Bt. Met. Fox 11, 55; Met. 11, 28: 11, 149; Met. 11, 75: 24, 77; Met. 24, 39: 29, 155; Met. 29, 78.

ge-weallan *to boil, be hot*; fervescere, fervere, Rtl. 101, 26: 105, 3.

ge-weallod, -wealled; *part.* [weall *a wall*] *Walled, surrounded with a wall, fortified*; mūrātus, mūnîtus:—Đa strengestan weras wuniaþ on đam lande and micele burga đǽr sind and mǽrlîce geweallode *cultōres fortissimos habet et urbes grandes atque mūrātas*, Num. 13, 29. On ceastre gewealledre *in cîvitāte mūnîta*, Ps. Spl. 30, 27.

ge-weardian. v. ge-weardod.

ge-wearmian; *p.* ode; *pp.* od *To become warm*; calere, calescere, Ælfc. Gr. 26, 2, 36.

ge-wearnian; *p.* ode; *pp.* od *To guard against, avoid*:—Hwǽr him wǽre fultum to sēcanne to gewearnienne swā rēđre hergunge *ubi quærendum est præsidium ad evitandas tam feras inruptiones*, Bd. 1, 14; S. 482, 37.

ge-wearþ *was, became, happened*, Beo. Th. 6115; B. 3061: Exon. 11 b; Th. 13, 30; Cri. 210: Andr. Kmbl. 613; An. 307; *1st and 3rd sing. p. of* ge-weorþan.

ge-weaxan; *p.* -weóx; *pp.* -weaxen *To grow, grow up*; crescere:—Gūþ sceal geweaxan *war shall grow*, Exon. 90 a; Th. 338, 27; Gn. Ex. 85. Moises geweóx *Moises creverat*, Ex. 2, 11. Geweaxen *auctus*, Exon. 99 b; Th. 372, 22; Seel. 96: Gen. 38, 11. Đǽm landbūendum is beboden, đæt ealles đæs đe him on heora ceápe geweaxe, hig Gode đone teóđan dǽl agyfen *to farmers it is commanded that of all which increases to them of their cattle, they give the tenth part to God*, L. E. I.

35; Th. ii. 432, 29. Gyf hit geweaxen man sȳ fæste 1 geár *if he be a grown man let him fast one year*, L. Ecg. P. iv. 52; Th. ii. 218, note 11, line 9.

ge-wéd, es; *n. A raging, madness;* fŭror insānus, răbies:—Wælhreówes [Nerōnes] gewēd wæs fulwīde cūþ *the madness of the cruel [Nero] was full widely known*, Bt. Met. Fox 9, 9; Met. 9, 5. He langre tīde ealle heora mǣgþe mid gewēde wæs geondfarende *multo tempŏre tōtas eōrum provincias debacchando pervăgātus*, Bd. 2, 20; S. 521, 27.

ge-weddian *to weed;* herbis noxiis purgare, Cot. 178, 188, Lye.

ge-weddian *to betroth*:—Gewoedded *desponsata*, Lk. Skt. Lind. 1, 27.

ge-wēded. v. ge-wǣdod.

ge-weder, -wider, -wyder, es; *pl. nom. acc.* -wederu; *n.* [weder *weather*] *Weather, the temperature of the air;* tempestas, cæli tempĕries:—Se sceortigenda dæg hæfþ līðran gewederu ðonne se langienda dæg *the shortening day hath milder weather than the lengthening day*, Bd. de nat. rerum; Wrt. popl. science 9, 21; Lchdm. iii. 252, 9. Godes miht gefādaþ ealle gewederu *God's power ordereth all weathers*, 19, 4; Lchdm. iii. 278, 13.

ge-wefan *to weave;* texere, Exon. 95 a; Th. 355, 1; Reim. 70 [v. Grmm. D. M. p. 387]: 111 b; Th. 427, 2; Rä. 41, 85: Ælfc. Gl. 63; Som. 68, 100, 101; Wrt. Voc. 40, 11, 12.

ge-wef[e], -wife, es; *n. A web;* textura. The word gets the meaning *fate, fortune*, from the spinning, which is the occupation of the Fates. Cf. Wyrd gewæf, Exon. 95 a; Th. 355, 1; Reim. 70. See Grmm. D. M. 387:—Gewife *fatum, fortuna*, Cot. 88; Lye. Him Dryhten forgeaf wīgspēda gewiofu *the Lord gave him the webs of success in war*, i. e. *he was successful in war*, Beo. Th. 1398; B. 697.

ge-wegan; *p.* -wæg, *pl.* -wǣgon; *pp.* -wegen. I. *to bear, carry, move, go, proceed;* vehere, ire, procedere:—He to ðære byrig gewæg mycelne aad *advexit illi urbi plurimam congeriem*, Bd. 3, 16; S. 542, 22. To ðǣm readorlīcum blīðe ic sȳ gewegen rīces coelnesse *ad ethera letus vehar regni refrigeria*, Wanl. Catal. 304, 49. He wið ðam wyrme gewegan sceolde *he must proceed against the worm [dragon]*, Beo. Th. 4792; B. 2400. [Cf. *Icel.* vega *to fight*.] II. *to weigh, measure*:—Gewihþ *weighs*, L. M. 2, 67; Lchdm. ii. 298, 16–25. Gewegen biþ *remetietur*, Mt. Kmbl. Lind. 7, 2: Mk. Skt. Lind. 4, 24. [Cf. a-wegan.]

ge-wēlan; *pp.* ed *To bind together*:—Þurh ðas þeóde gewēlede togædere *through this people banded together*, Swt. A. S. Rdr. 108, 131.

ge-weldan *to rule, restrain;* regere, cohibere:—Ðæt he hit ðonne [ne, MS. Cot.] mǣge to his willan gewealdan [geweldan, MS. Cot.] *so that he then cannot restrain it according to his will*, Past. 17, 8; Swt. 119, 17; Hat. MS. 24 a, 6. DER. wealdan.

ge-welgian, -welegian; *p.* ode, ade; *pp.* od, ad *To enrich, make wealthy, endow;* ditāre, dōtāre:—Ðū gemænifyldest gewelgian hine *multĭplĭcasti lŏcuplētāre eam*, Ps. Spl. 64, 9. Mid hire gestreóne he gewelgode Rōme burh *he enriched Rome with its wealth*, Ors. 5, 13; Bos. 113, 36: Bd. 1, 33; S. 499, 1. Ic gewelegode Abram *ĕgo dĭtāvi Abram*, Gen. 14, 23. Hī nalæs mid deófolcræfte, ac mid godcunde mægene gewelgade cōman *illi non dæmonĭca, sed divīna virtūte prædĭti vĕniēbant*, Bd. 1, 25; S. 487, 2: 4, 13; S. 582, 39. Ða ðe geára on sacerdhāde æðellīce gewelegode wǣron *quos ōlim sacerdōtii grădu non ignobĭlĭter potītos*, 3, 19; S. 548, 38.

ge-welhwǣr; *adv. Everywhere;* ŭbīque:—Is wīde cūþ þeódum gewelhwǣr *it is well known to people everywhere*, Menol. Fox 61; Men. 30: Swt. A. S. Rdr. 105, 33.

ge-welhwilc; *adj. Every*:—On gewelhwilcum ende *on every side*, Swt. A. S. Rdr. 106, 68: 108, 121.

ge-welt-leðer, es; *n. A power-leather, a rein*, Bt. Met. Fox 29, 155; Met. 29, 78. v. ge-weald-leðer.

ge-wēman; *p.* de; *pp.* ed [ge-, wēman *to persuade, entice*] *To turn, incline, seduce;* inclīnāre, sedūcĕre:—Hī næfdon ðone lāreów ðe cūþe hī to sōþfæstnysse wege gewēman *they had not the teacher who could incline them to the way of truth*, Homl. Th. ii. 400, 30: i. 498, 18. Hine wolde se deófol fram Gode gewēman *the devil would seduce him from God*, ii. 448, 28: 478, 34: 542, 19. Seó costnung gewēmþ ðone man to syngienne *the temptation seduces the man to sin*, Boutr. Scrd. 23, 9. Hī eów to ōðrum Gode gewēmaþ *they will seduce you to another God*, Homl. Th. ii. 494, 9. Ðæt we ne sceolon nā geþafian ðæt deófol us gewēme fram Cristes brōðorrǣdene *we should not allow the devil to seduce us from the brotherhood of Christ*, i. 260, 11.

ge-wemman; *p.* -wemde; *pp.* -wemmed, -wemd *To stain, defile, pollute, profane, corrupt, vitiate, mar, injure;* coinquĭnāre, turpāre, pollŭere, profānāre, corrumpĕre, vĭtiāre, contāmĭnāre, viŏlāre:—Ne mihte heora wlite gewemman wylm ðæs wæfran līges *the heat of the flickering flame might not corrupt their beauty*, Cd. 185; Th. 231, 1; Dan. 240. Ic gewemme *corrumpo*, Ælfc. Gr. 28, 6; Som. 32, 21. Ðyder þeóf ne geneálǣcþ, ne moþþe ne gewemþ *quo fur non apprŏpiat, neque tĭnea corrumpit*, Lk. Bos. 12, 33. Hī on ðam temple gewemmaþ ðone restedæg *in templo sabbătum viŏlant*, Mt. Bos. 12, 5. Ic honda gewemde *I have polluted my hands*, Cd. 52; Th. 672; Gen. 1094. Ðū gewemdest his hālignesse on eorþan *profānasti in terra sanctĭtātem ejus*, Ps. Th. 88, 32: Exon. 29 b; Th. 91, 5; Cri. 1487. Ða ðīn fǣle hūs ealh hālige gewemdan *coinquĭnāvērunt templum sanctum tuum*, Ps. Th. 78, 1. Næs him gewemmed wlite *his beauty was not injured*, Andr. Kmbl. 2940; An. 1473: Cd. 4; Th. 5, 13; Gen. 71: Bd. 2, 12; S. 513, 15: Ps. Spl. 13, 2. He geseah sīde sǣlwongas widlum gewemde *he saw the wide fertile plains defiled with pollutions*, Cd. 64: Th. 78, 16; Gen. 1294.

ge-wemmednys, se; *f. Defilement, pollution*:—Ælfremed fram līchamlīcere gewemmednysse *exempt from bodily defilement*, Homl. Th. i. 76, 15: 90, 2: ii. 478, 10: 552, 24: Blickl. Homl. 75, 6. Gewemmednyssa *prævaricationes*, Ps. Spl. 100, 3.

ge-wemming, -wemmincg, e; *f. A corruption, violation, profanation;* corruptio:—Be reste daga gewemminge *with regard to the profanation of sabbaths*, Nicod. 10; Thw. 5, 22.

ge-wemmodlīce; *adv. Corruptly, impurely*:—Gewæmmodlīce we sprecaþ *corrupte loquimur*, Coll. Monast. Th. 18, 8.

ge-wēn, e; *f. Hope;* spes. v ge-wēne.

ge-wēnan; *p.* de; *pp.* ed *To hope, expect, suppose, think, esteem*:—Ne þurfon hī to meotude miltse gewēnan *they need expect no mercy from the Lord*, Exon. 27 b; Th. 83, 35; Cri. 1366. Nellaþ gē gewēnan welan unrihte *nolite sperare in iniquitatem*, Ps. Th. 61, 10. On ǣrmergen ic on ðē gewēne *in matutinis meditabor in te*, 62, 6. Ic on God mīnne gewēne *spero in Deum meum*, 68, 3: 51, 7. Se sōþfæsta bōte gewēneþ *justus sperabit*, 63, 9. On his milde mōd gewēnaþ *sperant super misericordia ejus*, 146, 12: 144, 16. Ic me ðyslīcre ǣr þrage ne gewēnde *I before expected not such a time for myself*, Exon. 72 a; Th. 269, 21; Jul. 453. Gewēned ic eom *æstimatus sum.* Ps. Spl. 87, 4; 43, 25. Ðās beóþ men gewēnede *hi putantur homines fuisse*, Nar. 35, 33.

ge-wend, es; *n. A spiral shell, snail-shell;* coclea, Ælfc. Gl. 49; Som. 65, 81; Wrt. Voc. 34, 13. [Cf. ge-wind, windan.]

ge-wendan; *p.* -wende; *pp.* -wended, -wend. I. *v. trans. To turn, change, translate, incline, bring about*:—Gif hit eówer ǣnig mǣge gewendan ðæt . . . *if any of you can bring it about that . . .*, Cd. 22; Th. 27, 35; Gen. 428. He cwæþ ðætte ǣghwilc ungemyndig rihtwīsnesse hine hræðe sceolde eft gewendan in to sīnum mōdes gemyndo *he said that every one unmindful of righteousness should speedily turn again to his mind*, Bt. Met. Fox 22, 113; Met. 22, 57. Wicg gewende *he turned his steed*, Beo. Th. 635; B. 315. Gewend *conversus*, Lk. Bos. 22, 32. Ðis folc eall to yfele gewend ys *this people is all inclined to evil*, Ex. 32, 22. Him ðæt heáfod wæs adūne gewended *his head was turned down*, Blickl. Homl. 173, 4. Ne biþ ðē nō līf afyrred ac biþ gewenden [?] in ðæt betere *life is not taken from thee but changed to the better*, Shrn. 119, 29. Ðonne weorþeþ sunne sweart gewended *then shall the sun be turned black*, Exon. 21 b; Th. 58, 14; Cri. 935. II. *v. intrans. To turn [one's self], change, go, return*:—Wā biþ ðam ðe sceal frōfre ne wēnan wihte gewendan *woe to the man that must expect no comfort, who must change [his condition] in nothing [whose state is hopeless and unchangeable?]*, Beo. Th. 374; B. 186. He gewendeþ on ða wyrsan hand *he turns to the worse side*, Salm. Kmbl. 997; Sal. 500. Hwīlum hie gewendaþ on wyrmes līc *sometimes they turn into the body of a snake*, 305; Sal. 152. Siððan nǣfre to unrihtum ne gewendaþ *never afterwards do they turn to iniquity*, Blickl. Homl. 193, 24: Elen. Kmbl. 1230; El. 617. Drusiana hām gewende *Drusiana went home*, Homl. Th. i. 60, 20. Drihten gewende to heofenum *the Lord returned to heaven*, 74, 19. Gewendon ealle heom hām *they all went home*, Chr. 1052; Erl. 183, 11, 6, 12, 15. Ðā wæs se cyng gewend ofer Temese *then the king was gone over the Thames*, 1006; Erl. 140, 29: 1052; Erl. 183, 18.

ge-wēne; *adv. Perhaps;* forte:—Gewoene *forte*, Mk. Skt. Rush. 14, 2.

ge-wenge, es; *n. The cheek;* maxilla:—And ðam ðe ðē slihþ on ðīn gewenge *et qui te percutit in maxillam*, Lk. Bos. 6, 29; and to him that schal smyte thee on o cheke, *Wyc.* Ān strǣl hyne gewundode on hys ōðer gewenge *an arrow wounded him in one of his cheeks*, Shrn. 97, 14. Gewenge *maxilla*, Ælfc. Gl. 71; Som. 70, 80; Wrt. Voc. 43, 13. v. wenge.

ge-wenian; *p.* ede; *pp.* ed. I. *to accustom, to accustom any one to one's self;* assuefacere:—Gewenede hine sylfne to heora synlīcum þeáwum *he accustomed himself to their sinful manners*, Ælfc. T. Lisle 34, 20: Bt. Met. Fox 29, 11; Met. 29, 6. Heora lāreówas him bióðan ða ilcan mettas ðe hī ǣr tame mid gewenedon *their teachers offer them the same meats which they before accustomed the tame with* or *with which they before accustomed them to be tame*, Bt. 25; Fox 88, 18: L. Edg. C. 55; Th. ii. 256, 9. II. *to wean, to separate;* ablactare, a lacte depellere, depellere, seducere:—Ðæt cild wearþ gewened *puer ablactatus est*, Gen. 21, 8. Se deófol wolde hine fram Gode gewenian *the devil would wean him from God*, Job. Thw. 165, 11. [*O. H. Ger.* ge-wenian *assuefacere.*] v. wenian.

ge-weold. v. ge-wild.

ge-weorc, -worc, -werc, es; *n.* [ge-, weorc *a work*]. I. *work;* ŏpus, ŏpuscŭlus:—Eue wæs geweorc Godes *Eve was God's work*, Cd. 38; Th. 51, 6; Gen. 822: Exon. 9 b; Th. 8, 4; Cri. 112. Ðæt ðam þeódne wæs sīþes sigehwīl, sylfes dǣdum, worlde geweorces *that was a victorious moment to the prince of his enterprise, by his own deeds, of his worldly* *work*, Beo. Th. 5415; B. 2711. He geseah eald enta geweorc *he saw the antique work of giants*, Andr. Kmbl. 2988; An. 1497: 2155; An. 1079. On ðæt geweorc *in ŏpus*, Bd. 1, 23; S. 485, 40. Ne wāciaþ ðās geweorc *these works fail not*, Exon. 93 b; Th. 351, 26; Sch. 86. Mǣre wurdon his wundra geweorc *great were his wondrous works*, 45 b; Th. 155, 2; Gū. 854: 40 a; Th. 133, 35; Gū. 500. Of geweorcum ārwurþra fædera *ex ŏpuscŭlis venerābĭlium patrum*, Bd. 5, 24; S. 647, 33. II. *a fort, fortress;* arx:—He of ðam geweorce wæs winnende wiđ ðone here *he warred on the army from the fortress*, Chr. 878; Erl. 80, 5: 896; Erl. 94, 3, 21. He worhte him geweorc æt Middeltūne *he wrought him a fortress at Middleton*, 892; Erl. 89, 14: 894; Erl. 92, 4, 11. Ðe æt hām æt ðǣm geweorcum wǣron *who were at home in the fortresses*, 894; Erl. 92, 18. Hī worhton tū geweorc *they wrought two forts*, 896; Erl. 94, 11. Geweorc *arx, figmentum, māchĭna*, Scint. 62: Cot. 85: 128, Lye. [*Goth.* ga-waurki: *O. Sax.* gi-werk: *O. H. Ger.* ga-werk.] DER. ǣr-geweorc, eald-, flān-, fyrn-, gold-, gūþ-, hand-, heáh-, land-, nīþ-, sulh-.

ge-weorht, es; *n. Work, deed, merit, desert;* ŏpus, făcĭnus, mĕrĭtum:—Ðætte rinca gehwylc ōđrum gulde edleán on riht be geweorhtum *that every man should render rightly to other a reward proportionable to his deserts*, Bt. Met. Fox 27, 53; Met. 27, 27. v. ge-wyrht.

ge-weorhta, an; *m. One working with another, accomplice:*—Gif mæsse-preóst þeófa gewita and geweorhta beó *if a mass-priest be an accessory and accomplice of thieves*, L. Eth. ix. 27; Th. i. 346, 9. v. ge-wyrhta.

ge-weorp, es; *n. A throwing, tossing, dashing, what is thrown up, a heap;* jactus, jactātio, projectio:—Ofer waroþa geweorp *over the dashing of the waves*, Andr. Kmbl. 611; An. 306. Ðǣr ðū geseó tord-wifel on eorþan up weorpan ymbfō hine mid twām handum mid his geweorpe *when you see a dung-beetle in the earth throwing up mould, catch it with both hands along with his casting up*, L. M. iii. 18; Lchdm. ii. 318, 17. v. winter-geweorp, ge-wyrp.

ge-weorpan, -worpan; *p.* -wearp, *pl.* -wurpon; *pp.* -worpen. I. *to throw, cast;* jacere, projicere:—Hī habbaþ ingang swā mycelre brǣdo, swā mon mæg mid liđeran geworpan *they have an entrance of so much breadth, as one can throw with a sling*, Bd. 4, 13; S. 583, 11. Drihten hī gewyrpþ mid grine *the Lord will cast a snare upon them;* pluet super peccatores laqueos, Ps. Th. 10, 7. Miđđȳ gewearp woedo his *projecto vestimento suo*, Mk. Skt. Lind. 10, 50. Gewurpon būta *ejecerunt extra*, 12, 8, 41. Honda gewurpon on hine *manus injecerunt in eum*, 14, 46. Swā gewundade wrāđe slǣpe, sȳn ðonne geworpene on wīdne hlǣw *sicut vulnerati dormientes, projecti in monumentis*, Ps. Th. 87, 5. II. *to turn one's self away, go away, depart, pass by;* averti, abire, transire:—Winter sceal geweorpan, weder eft cuman, sumor hāt *winter shall pass by, fair weather again shall come, hot summer*, Exon. 90 a; Th. 338, 11; Gn. Ex. 77. DER. weorpan.

ge-weorþ, es; *n. Value, worth, price*, Th. Chart. 159, 1. v. ge-wyrþe.

ge-weorþan, -wiorþan, -wurþan, -wyrþan; he -weorþeþ, -weorþ, *pl.* -weorþaþ; *p.* ic, he -wearþ, ðū -wurde, *pl.* -wurdon; *subj. pres.* -weorþe, *pl.* -weorþen; *p.* -wurde, *pl.* -wurden; *pp.* -worden. I. *to be, be made, become, happen;* fĭĕri:—Hū māgon ðās þing ðus geweorþan *quomŏdo possunt hæc fĭĕri?* Jn. Bos. 3, 9: Elen. Kmbl. 909; El. 456. Ne sēc ðū þurh hlytas hū ðē geweorþan scyle *seek not by lots how it is to happen to thee*, Prov. Kmbl. 32. Hū geweorþeþ ðæt *how happeneth that?* Salm. Kmbl. 684; Sal. 341: Andr. Kmbl. 2872; An. 1439. Gif feaxfang geweorþ *if there be a taking hold of the hair*, L. Ethb. 33; Th. i. 12, 3. Ealle gesceafte forhte geweorþaþ *all creatures shall tremble*, Andr. Kmbl. 2298; An. 1502. He gewyrþ micelre mǣgþe *he shall become a great nation*, Gen. 21, 18. Ðes sige gewearþ Punicum *this victory happened to the Carthaginians*, Ors. 4, 6; Bos. 85, 23. Ic his mōdor gewearþ *I have become his mother*, Exon. 11 a; Th. 13, 30; Cri. 210: 9 a; Th. 6, 33; Cri. 93. Ðū đissum hysse hold gewurde *thou hast been gracious to this man*, Andr. Kmbl. 1100; An. 550. Sió fǣhþ gewearþ gewrecen wrāþlīce *the quarrel was wrothfully avenged*, Beo. Th. 6115; B. 3061: Exon. 33 b; Th. 107, 26; Gū. 64; Chr. 592; Erl. 19, 34. Gewurdon manige wundor on manegum landum *many wonders happened in many lands*, Ors. 5, 10; Bos. 108, 16 Ðæt me Meotud moncynnes milde geweorþe *that the Lord of mankind be merciful to me*, Exon. 75 b; Th. 282, 23; Jul. 667: 78 b; Th. 294, 19; Cra. 17. Ðeáh mīn bān and blōd būtū geweorþen eorþan to eácan *though my bones and blood both become an increase to earth*, 38 a; Th. 125, 9; Gū. 351. Saga, hū ðæt gewurde *say how that happened*, Andr. Kmbl. 1115; An. 558: Exon. 11 a; Th. 15, 19; Cri. 238. Ðæt word wæs flǣsc geworden *verbum căro factum est*, Jn. Bos. 1, 14: Homl. Th. i. 40, 17: Cd. 219; Th. 282, 5; Sat. 282: 223; Th. 293, 10; Sat. 453. Wæs onlīce bī hig geworden [swā bī Zachariam] gewearþ and bī Elizabeþ his wīfe *it had happened with them as it happened with Zacharias and his wife Elizabeth*, Shrn. 36, 12. We gesēgon windas and wǣgas forhte gewordne *we saw winds and waves become fearful*, Andr. Kmbl. 913; An. 457. II. *v. impers. cum acc. To happen, come to pass, befall, come together, agree, be agreeable;* contingĕre, evĕnīre, convĕnīre, plăcēre:—Ne mihte hī betwih him geþwǣrian and geweorþan *they might not accord and agree among themselves*, Bd. 4, 4; S. 571, 2: Cd. 81; Th. 101, 32; Gen. 169, 1. Hū gewearþ ðē ðæs *how doth this befall thee?* Andr. Kmbl. 613; An. 307: Jud. 16, 21. Me gewearþ *convĕnior*, Ælfc. Gr. 37; Som. 39, 6. Hȳ gewearþ, ðæt hȳ woldan to Rōmānum friþes wilnian *they agreed that they would seek peace from the Romans*, Ors. 4, 6; Bos. 86, 17: 5, 10; Bos. 108, 29: 6, 30; Bos. 126, 24: Gen. 20, 13. Ðā hī nānre sibbe gewearþ *when they could not agree upon any terms of peace*, Ors. 4, 11; Bos. 97, 19. Ðeáh ðe Rōmāne hæfde geworden ðæt . . . *though the Romans had agreed that* . . ., 4, 12; Bos. 98, 43. Hū ðone cumbolwīgan hæfde geworden *how it had befallen the warrior*, Judth. 12; Thw. 25, 15; Jud. 260. III. *cum dat:*—Ðā gewearþ ðam hlāforde and ðām hȳrigmannum wiþ ānum peninge *then the lord and the labourers agreed on a penny*, Th. An. 73, 29: 74, 21 [*or acc.*]. Gewearþ him and ðam folce on Lindesīge ānes ðæt hī hine horsian sceolde *it was agreed between him and the people of Lindsey that they should provide him with horses*, Chr. 1014; Erl. 151, 1: Thw. 161, 30. Wyn ðū ongeán ðone wuldres cyning and gewurþe ðē and him *fight against the king of glory and let there be an agreement between thee and him*, Nicod. 27; Thw. 15, 14. [Cf. *O. Sax.* thea gumon alle giwarth that . . .: *Goth.* ga-wairþi *peace?*]

ge-weorþian, -wurþian, -wyrþian; *p.* ode, ade, ude; *pp.* od, ad, ud. I. *to set a price on, value:*—Ðone ðe wæs ǣr geweorþod *quem appretiaverunt*, Mt. Kmbl. 27, 9, note. II. *to distinguish, honour, dignify, adorn, worship, adore, celebrate, praise;* insignīre, hŏnōrāre, ornāre, instruĕre, mactāre, adōrāre, celebrāre:—Ðū hine gewuldrast and geweorþast *glōria et hŏnōre cŏrōnasti eum*, Ps. Th. 8, 6. Ðē beorht Fæder geweorþaþ wuldorgifum *the bright Father dignifies thee with glorious gifts*, Andr. Kmbl. 1875; An. 940: Bt. 14, 3; Fox 46, 13. Me geweorþode wuldres Ealdor *the Prince of glory honoured me*, Rood Kmbl. 177; Kr. 90: 185; Kr. 94. He Abrahames cynn geweorþude *he honoured Abraham's race*, Ps. Th. 104, 6. Geweorþie wuldres Ealdor eall ðeós eorþe, ēcne Drihten *omnis terra adōret te, Deus*, 65, 3. Gē wēnaþ ðæt ǣnig mæg mid fræmdum welum beón geweorþod *ye think that one can be made honourable by external riches*, Bt. 14, 3; Fox 46, 10, 11. Wæs ēþfynde Afrisc meówle, golde geweorþod *the African maid was easy to be found, adorned with gold*, Cd. 171; Th. 215, 9; Exod. 580: 174; Th. 218, 18; Dan. 41: Elen. Kmbl. 2384; El. 1193. Wuldre geweorþad *honoured with glory*, Exon. 63 b; Th. 235, 2; Ph. 551: Beo. Th. 2904; B. 1450. Wīde is geweorþod hāligra tīd *the time of the saints is widely celebrated*, Menol. Fox 237; Men. 120: 306; Men. 154.

ge-weoton *went, departed*, Bd. 2, 5; S. 507, 34; *p. pl. of* ge-wītan.

ge-wēpan; *p.* -weóp, *pl.* -weópon; *pp.* -wōpen *To weep, lament;* flere:—Petrus geweáp bitterlīce *Petrus flevit amare*, Lk. Skt. Lind. 22, 62. Giweópun alle *flebant omnes*, Rush. 8, 52. Gewōpen *fletum*, Ælfc. Gr. 26, 1; Som. 28, 28.

ge-werc, es; *n. A fort, fortress;* arx:—Hie ðǣr gewerc worhton *they there wrought a fortress*, Chr. 896; Erl. 94, 16. v. ge-weorc.

ge-werdan; *p.* de; *pp.* ed *To hurt, injure;* lædere, nocere:—Gif hwā on ceáse wīf gewerde *if any one in strife hurt a woman*, L. Alf. 18; Th. i. 48, 17: 26; Th. i. 50, 24. v. ge-wyrdan.

ge-weredlǣht, -werodlǣht *sweetened, made sweet;* indulcoratus, Scint. 64. v. werod.

ge-werged; *part. Accursed:*—Ðara gewergedra *maledicorum*, Mt. Kmbl. p. 1, 11.

ge-wērgian, -wērigan; *p.* ode, ade; *pp.* od, ad *To weary, fatigue;* fatīgāre:—He gewērgad sæt *he sat wearied*, Beo. Th. 5697; B. 2852: Exon. 51 a; Th. 178, 12; Gū. 1243. Mauritanie wǣron mid ðam gewērgode *the Mauritanians were wearied by it*, Ors. 5, 7; Bos. 107, 7. Ðe on lengtenādle gewērigade wǣron *who were wearied with ague*, Bd. 4, 6; S. 574, 7.

ge-werian; *p.* ode, ede; *pp.* od, ed *To put on, cover, clothe;* induĕre, vestīre:—Giwoeria *to cover, conceal*, Rtl. 103, 3. Ðe he mid gewered wæs *quĭbus indūtum ĕrat*, Bd. 4, 30; S. 608, note 39, 41. Gewered mid wæstme *covered with fruit*, Cd. 23; Th. 30, 5; Gen. 462. In hwītum hræglum gewerede englas ne ōþeówdun *angels appeared not clad in white robes*, Exon. 14 a; Th. 28, 16; Cri. 447: 15 b; Th. 35, 3; Cri. 552. [*Goth.* ga-wasjan.]

ge-werian; *p.* ede, ode; *pp.* ed, od. I. *to defend, protect, take care of, make* [*land*] *free from claims;* defendĕre, procurare:—Ic gewerige *defendo*, Ælfc. Gr. 28, 6; Som. 32, 29. Se ðe land gewerod hæbbe *he who has defended land*, L. C. S. 80; Th. i. 420, 19. Þēr of is gewerod ān and tuenti hīde *twenty-one hides of it are held in undisputed possession*, Schmid. A. S. Ges. p. 614, col. 1. See also p. 677. Ðonnæ his ðæs londæs hundseofontig hīda and is nū eall gewæred and ðā hit æst mīn lāford mæ to lǣt ðā wæs hit ierfelǣás *hujus terræ sunt lxx hidæ, et est modo tota bene procurata, quæ quando dominus meus michi eam tradidit omni peccunia caruit*, Th. Chart. 162, 26. Gange [ðæt land] into ðære stōwe swā gewered swā hit stande mid mete and mid mannum and mid ǣlcum þingan *let the land go afterwards to that place so provided as it may then be, with meat and with men and with everything*, 519, 3: Cod. Dipl. Kmbl. ii. 300, 10. II. *to associate with for the cause of defence.*

to make a treaty with; assŏciāre defensiōnis causa, jungere fœdĕre:—Nalæs æfter micelre tīde ðæt hī geweredon wið him, and heora wǣpen hwyrfdon wið Bryttas heora gefaran *non multo post juncto cum his fœdĕre, in sŏcios arma vertĕrit,* Bd. 1, 15; S. 483, 4, 35. v. werian.

ge-wesan *to be together, converse, discuss:*—Ic flītan gefrægn mōdgleáwe men gewesan ymbe hyra wīsdōm *I have learnt that wise men had disputes and discussions about their wisdom,* Salm. Kmbl. 363; Sal. 181. Grein writes 'gewēsan; *p.* -weós,' and compares 'ymbweoson' in the Northumbrian Gospels. But this word is wrongly written by Bouterwek, it should be 'ymbwoeson,' see Mk. Skt. p. 1. The Durham Ritual glosses 'conversatio' by 'giwosa,' and this may throw light on the meaning of 'gewesan.' Both *Goth.* and *O. H. Ger.* have the word 'gawisan, gi-wesan,' in the sense *to remain, abide;* restare.

ge-wēsan; *p.* de; *pp.* ed *To soak:*—Mid ecede gewēsed *soaked with vinegar,* Herb. 116, 3; Lchdm. i. 228, 24. Gewēsan *inficere, miscere, fucare,* Hpt. Gl. 524. v. wōs.

ge-wēstan *to lay waste;* desolare:—Gewoested biþ *desolabitur,* Mt. Kmbl. Lind. 12, 25.

ge-wēðnis, se; *f. Mildness;* lenitas:—Giwoeðnis *lenitas,* Rtl. 105, 1. v. wēðe.

ge-wīcan; *p.* -wāc, *pl.* -wicon; *pp.* -wicen *To give way, fail, depart, retire;* cedere, deficere, recedere:—To hwȳ, Driht, gewic [gewite, Sur.] ðū feor *ut quid, Domine, recessisti longe,* Ps. Spl. second 9, 1. Ne his mægenes [mǣges?] lāf gewāc æt wīge *his kinsman's legacy failed not in the contest,* Beo. Th. 5251; B. 2629: 5148; B. 2577. v. wīcan.

ge-wīcian; *p.* ode; *pp.* od *To dwell, lodge, encamp;* hospitare, castra metari:—Hȳ landes hæfdon ðæt hȳ mihton on gewīcian *they had land on which they could encamp,* Ors. 2, 5; Bos. 46, 36. Ic on fægerum scūan fiðera ðīnra gewīcie *in umbra alarum tuarum spero,* Ps. Th. 56, 1. Se wilda fugel hūs getimbreþ and gewīcaþ ðǣr *the wild bird builds a house and dwells there,* Exon. 58 b; Th. 212, 1; Ph. 203. Ðonne gewīceaþ faroþ-lācende on ðam eálonde *then the seafarers camp on that island,* 96 b; Th. 361, 13; Wal. 19. Ðā gewīcode he neáh ānre eá *then he encamped near a river,* Ors. 4, 6; Bos. 84, 31: Chr. 894; Erl. 90, 8: Blickl. Homl. 79, 14. v. wīcian.

ge-wider, -widor, es; *pl. nom. acc.* -wideru, -widera, -widru; *n. Weather, the temperature of the air, a tempest;* tempestas, cæli tempĕries:—Hī monige dagas windes and gewidor abidon *opportūnos alĭquot dies ventos exspectārent,* Bd. 5, 9; S. 623, 19. Se sceortigenda dæg hæfþ līðran gewideru [gewidera, MS. R.] ðonne se langienda dæg *the shortening day hath milder weather than the lengthening day,* Bd. de nat. rerum; Lchdm. iii. 252, 9, MS. L: Bt. Met. Fox 11, 121; Met. 11, 61. On ðæm dæge eall godes folc sceal god biddan ðæt he him forgefe smyltelīco gewidra and genihtsume wæstmas *on that day all God's folk are to pray God to give them fair weather and abundant harvests,* Shrn. 74, 11. Ðonne wind styreþ lāþ gewidru *when the wind stirs hateful tempests,* Beo. Th. 2754; B. 1375. [Cf. *O. Sax.* un-giwideri: *O. H. Ger.* gi-witri *temperies, tempestas: Ger.* ge-witter.] v. ge-weder.

ge-widlian, -widligan; *p.* ede; *pp.* ed *To defile, contaminate, make common:* coinquinare, contaminare, Mk. Skt. Lind. 7, 15. v. widl.

ge-wīdmǣrsian; *p.* ode; *pp.* od *To publish, spread abroad, divulge, celebrate;* divulgare:—Ofer ealle Iudēa munt-land wǣron ðās word gewīdmǣrsode *super omnia montana Iudææ divulgabantur omnia verba hæc,* Lk. Bos. 1, 65: Mt. Bos. 28, 15. Iosep nolde hī gewīdmǣrsian *Joseph nollet eam traducere,* 1, 19.

ge-wif, es; *n. An affection of the eye, web:*—Wið ǣlces cynnes brōc on eágon wið gewif *for every sort of malady in the eyes, for web,* Lchdm. iii. 290, 3. v. Hall. Dict. pin-and-web.

ge-wife *fortune, destiny;* fatum, Cot. 88. v. ge-wef.

ge-wīfian; *p.* ode, ade; *pp.* od, ad [wīfian *to take a wife*] *To take a wife, marry;* uxōrem dūcĕre:—Gewīfodon *duxĕrunt uxōres,* Jud. 3, 6. Ðæt cristen man gewīfige *that a christian man marry,* L. Eth. vi. 12; Th. i. 318, 13, 18: L. C. E. 7; Th. i. 364, 23. Manige habbaþ genōg gesǣlilīce gewīfod *many have married happily enough,* Bt. 11, 1; Fox 32, 5. Gewīfad, Bd. 4, 22; S. 591, 7.

ge-wifsǣlig; *adj. Fortunate;* fato *vel* fortuna felix, Cot. 88, 194, 196, Lye [Cf. ge-wef.]

ge-wiglung, e; *f. Soothsaying, divination, spell:*—Ða gemearr ðe man drīfþ on mislīcum gewiglungum *the erroneous practices that are carried on with various spells,* L. Edg. C. 16; Th. ii. 248, 4. v. wiglian.

ge-wiht, -wyht, -wihte, es; *n. Weight;* pondus:—Twegra pundra gewiht *two pounds' weight;* dupondius, Ælfc. Gl. 59; Som. 67, 114; Wrt. Voc. 38, 37: Th. Chart. 522, 22: Salm. Kmbl. p. 180, 5. Gange ān gemet and ān gewihte *let one measure and one weight pass,* L. Edg ii. 8; Th. i. 270, 2. Nū hæbbe we hit broht ongēn be ðam ylcan gewihte *quam nunc eodem pondĕre reportāvĭmus,* Gen. 43, 21: 23, 16: Lev. 26, 26. False gewihta *false weights,* L. Eth. v. 24; Th. i. 310, 13: vi. 28; Th. i. 322, 14. Gemeta and gewihta rihte man georne *let measures and weights be carefully rectified,* vi. 32; Th. i. 322, 30: L. C. S. 9; Th. i. 380, 24. Gē etaþ hlāf be gewihte *ye shall eat bread by weight,* Lev. 26, 26. Mid twām hundred mancosan goldes be gewihte and mid v. pundan be gewihte seolfres *for two hundred mancuses of gold by weight and for five pounds by weight of silver,* Th. Chart. 557, 28. See Turner's Hist. Anglo-Sax. ii. Appendix ii. [*Ger.* gewicht.]

ge-wil, -will, -wile, -wyle, es; *n. A will, wish, pleasure;* vŏluntas, arbitrium, vōtum:—Ne wend ðū ðē nō on ðæs folces unriht gewil *turn thou not thyself to the unjust wish of the people,* L. Alf. 41; Th. i. 54, 7: Hy. 7, 78; Hy. Grn. ii. 288, 78. On yfelra manna gewill *according to the will of evil men,* Bt. 4; Fox 8, 19: Exon. 13 a; Th. 23, 2; Cri. 362: Ors. 1, 10; Bos. 34, 1: 1, 12; Bos. 36, 33. Hit næs ne his gewile [-wyle, MS. A.] *it was not his will,* L. C. S. 76; Th. i. 418, 11.

ge-wilcþ, e; *f. Rolling, motion* [*of waves*]:—Gewilcþ ȳðe *motum fluctuum,* Ps. Spl. M. 88, 10.

ge-wilcumian; *p.* ode; *pp.* od *To welcome;* salutare:—Se cāsere hig gewilcumode *the emperor welcomed them,* L. Ælf. P. 23; Th. ii. 372, 30.

ge-wild, -weold, es; *n. Power, control:*—Æfter ðæm ðe Alexander hæfde ealle Indie him to gewildon gedōn *perdomita Alexander India,* Ors. 3, 9; Swt. 132, 9. Geweoldum sylfes willum *spontaneously, of his own accord,* Beo. Th. 4446; B. 2222. [Cf. ge-weald, ge-wealdes, ge-wylde.]

ge-wildan *to exercise power over, rule over,* Gen. 3, 16: Ps. Spl. 105, 38. v. ge-wyldan.

ge-wile, es; *n. A will;* vŏluntas, L. C. S. 76; Th. i. 418, 11. v. ge-wil.

ge-willnung *a wish, appetite,* Bd. 4, 25; S. 601, 7. v. ge-wilnung.

ge-willsum; *adj. Desirable;* desīdĕrābilis:—Hī hæfdon eorþan gewillsum *hăbuĕrunt terram desīdĕrābilem,* Ps. Spl. C. 105, 23.

ge-wilnian, -wilnigan, to -wilnienne; *p.* ode; *pp.* od [wilnian *to desire*] *To wish, desire, expect. seek, strive for;* cŭpĕre, concŭpiscĕre, desīdĕrāre, expĕtĕre, ambīre:—Reáflācum nylle gē gewilnian *răpinas nōlite concŭpiscĕre,* Ps. Spl. 61, 10: Ps. Spl. 118, 20. Gōdes þegenas sceolon to ðam ēcan līfe ǣfre gewilnian *God's servants must ever strive after the life everlasting,* Boutr. Scrd. 21, 44. He ne sceal gewilnian ða woruldlīcan þingc *he must not desire the things of this world,* 22, 44. Ðæt sum sume swīðe ondryslīcu, and eác to gewilnienne secgende wæs *ut quidam multa et trĕmenda, et desīdĕranda narrāvĕrit,* Bd. 5, 12; S. 627, 3. Ic gewilnige [gewilnie, MS. D.] *cŭpio,* Ælfc. Gr. 35; Som. 38, 8: 28, 1; Som. 30, 39. Ic gewilnige *ambio,* 30, 5; Som. 35, 8. Ǣlc ðæra ðe wīf gesyhþ and hyre gewilnaþ *omnis, qui vidĕrit mŭliĕrem ad concupiscendum eam,* Mt. Bos. 5, 28. Ic nānes eorþlīces gestreónes ne flǣsclīces lustes ne gewilnige *I desire no earthly treasure nor fleshly pleasure,* Homl. Th. i. 458, 31: 512, 13. Gif hwā gewilnigeþ to gewitanne *if any one desires to know,* Chr. 1086; Erl. 221, 10. Gewilnod *ambĭtus,* Ælfc. Gr. 30, 5; Som. 35, 10.

ge-wilnigendlīc, -wilniendlīc, -wilnindlīc; *adj. Desirable;* desiderābilis:—For nāht hī hæfdon eorþan gewilnigendlīce *pro nihĭlo hăbuĕrunt terram desiderābĭlem,* Ps. Spl. 105, 23. Gewilniendlīc *desīderābĭlis,* Prov. 21. Gewilnindlīc, Prov. 8.

ge-wilnung, -willnung. e; *f. A wish, desire, longing, seeking, appetite. will, vow;* concŭpiscentia, desīdĕrium, ambĭtus, appĕtītus, affectus, vōtum:—Gewilnung *ambĭtus,* Ælfc. Gr. 30, 5; Som. 35, 10. Of gewilnunge ic gewilnode etan mid eów ðās eástron *desīdĕrio desīdĕrāvi hoc pascha mandūcāre vobiscum,* Lk. Bos. 22, 15. Hȳ fērdon on gewilnunge heortan *transiĕrunt in affectum cordis,* Ps. Spl. 72, 7: Homl. Th. i. 136, 9, 31. For gewillnunge ðara ēcra gōda *pro appĕtītu æternōrum bonōrum,* Bd. 4, 25; S. 601, 7. Ōðra gewilnunga *relĭqua concŭpiscentiæ,* Mk. Bos. 4, 19: Num. 11, 34. Mid eallum gewilnungum *with all desires,* Homl. Th. ii. 118, 25. Ðæt ic agylde gewilnunga of dæge to dæge *ut reddam vōta mea de die in diem,* Ps. Spl. 60, 8.

ge-win, -winn, es; *n.* [winnan *to fight*]. I. *a battle, contest, war, strife, quarrel, hostility, tumult;* certāmen, pugna, bellum, tŭmultus:—On ða tīde Troiāna gewin wearþ *the Trojan war happened at that time,* Bt. Met. Fox 26, 24; Met. 26, 12. Sceolde he worc ðæs gewinnes gedǣlan *he must get pain on account of that struggle,* Cd. 15; Th. 19, 24; Gen. 296: 17; Th. 21, 12; Gen. 323: Bt. Met. Fox 25, 101; Met. 25, 51. On ðam gewinne *in the contest,* Bt. 37, 1; Fox 186, 31: 38, 1; Fox 194, 8: Rood Kmbl. 129; Kr. 65. Hie gewin drugon *they fought,* Beo. Th. 1601; B. 798: 1758; B. 877. Heora gewinn mid ðam swīðe geiécton *their quarrel was thus much strengthened,* Ors. 5, 10; Bos. 109, 4: 5, 13; Bos. 112, 43. He his mōdsefan wið ðam fǣrhagan fæste trymede feónda gewinna *he firmly strengthened his mind against the peril of the fiends' hostilities,* Exon. 46 b; Th. 159, 29; Gū. 934. II. *labour, toil, sorrow, agony;* lăbor, trĭbŭlātio, ăgōnia:—Ðis gewin *hic lăbor,* Bd. 2, 1; S. 500, 29. Gewinn and sār *lăbor et dŏlor,* Ps. Th. 89, 11: 72, 13. Wæs gewinnes endedōgor neáh geþrungen *the final day of his labour was near at hand,* Exon. 46 a; Th. 158, 6; Gū. 904: Ps. Th. 127, 2. Ðū scealt wunian in gewinne *thou shalt continue in toil,* Exon. 16 b; Th. 39, 14; Cri. 622: 32 a; Th. 101, 10; Cri. 1656: Bd. 1, 23; S. 485, 17. He wæs on gewinne *factus in ăgōnia,* Lk. Bos. 22, 44. Þurh mycel gewinn *with much toil,* Guthl. 16; Gdwin. 68, 5. On gewinnum *in lăbōrĭbus,* Ps. Th. 106, 11: 72, 4. III. *fruit of labours, gain, profit;* fruc'us lăbōrum, lucrum, quæstus:—Hī folca gewinn fremdra gesǣton *lăbōres pŏpŭlōrum possēdĕrunt,* Ps. Th. 104, 39: 77, 46. Gif hwilc man leóht dēþ on mīnum cirican of his gewinne *if any man* *puts a light in my church* [*bought*] *out of his gain,* Nar. 47, 6, 15. [*O. Sax.* ge-win *strife: O. H. Ger.* ga-win *labor, certamen, quæstus: Ger.* ge-winn *gain.*]

ge-wind, es; *n.* [windan *to bend*] *A winding, circuitous ascent,* Ælfc. Gl 55; Som. 67, 6; Wrt. Voc. 37, 4.

gewin-dæg, es; *m. A labour* or *trouble-day, battle-day;* laboris *vel* tribulationis dies, pugnæ dies:—On gewindæge *in the day of trouble,* Ps. Th. 77, 42. Of gewindagum weorþan sceolde līf alȳsed *her life should be released from days of trouble,* Exon. 74 b; Th. 279, 9; Jul. 611: Cd. 205; Th. 254, 24; Dan. 616. Đonne cumbulgebrec on gewinndagum weorþan scoldun *when there should be crashings of banners in days of battle,* Ps. C. 50, 12; Ps. Grn. ii. 227, 12. v. win-dæg.

ge-windan; *p.* -wand, *pl.* -wundon; *pp.* -wunden. I. *v. trans. To twist, weave, bend, wind;* torquēre, plectere, implĭcāre:—Đa þegnas gewundun ðæt sigbēg of þornum *milites plectentes coronam de spinis,* Jn. Skt. Lind. 19, 2. Ne hafu ic in heáfde hwīte loccas, wrǣste gewundne *I have not white locks on my head, delicately wound,* Exon. 111 b; Th. 427, 30; Rä. 41, 99. II. *v. intrans. To go, turn, turn about, revolve, roll;* ire, se vertĕre, volvĕre:—He meahte wīdre gewindan *he might more widely turn about,* Beo. Th. 1530; B. 763. Se aglǣca on fleám gewand *the miserable being turned to flight,* 2007; B. 1001: Homl. Th. i. 290, 19. Se līg gewand on lāđe men *the flame rolled on to the hostile men,* Cd. 186; Th. 231, 22; Dan. 251.

ge-winde; *adj*:—Đā hit wæs wel gewinde on ða burh *when the wind was in the right quarter* [*for blowing the flames*] *on to the town;* ventum opportunum, Bd. 3, 16; S. 542, 25.

ge-windwian; *p.* ode; *pp.* od *To blow*:—Seó onblāwnes ðære heofonlīcan onfæđmnesse sȳ gewindwod on ðē *let the inspiration of the heavenly embrace be blown into thee,* Blickl. Homl. 7, 27.

ge-winful, -full; *adj. Full of labour, laborious, troublesome;* labōriōsus:—Agustinus ðysses gewinfullan geflītes ende gesette *Augustinus hunc lābōriōsi certāminis finem fēcit,* Bd. 2, 2; S. 502, 17.

ge-winfullīc, -winnfullīc; *adj. Laborious, toilsome;* laboriōsus:—Đæt hī ne þorftan in swā frǣcne sīþfætt, and on swā gewinfullīcne, and on swā uncūþe ællþeódignysse fēran *ne tam periculōsam, tam incertam peregrīnātiōnem adīre dēbērent,* Bd. 1, 23; S. 485, 37. Đæt hī nō mā ne mihton swā gewinnfullīcum fyrdum swencte beón *non se ultra tam labōriōsis expedītiōnibus posse fatīgāri,* 1, 12; S. 481, 4.

ge-winfullīce; *adv. Laboriously, with difficulty;* laboriōse:—Đæt eahta and twentig wintra gewinnfullīce he heóld *id per annos viginti octo labōriōsissĭme tĕnuit,* Bd. 3, 14; S. 539, 17.

ge-winna, an; *m. An enemy, adversary, a foe, rival;* hostis, inĭmīcus, æmŭlus:—Cwom semninga hæleþa gewinna *the foe of men suddenly came,* Exon. 69 a; Th. 257, 7; Jul. 243. Gesaca *vel* gewinna *æmŭlus,* Ælfc. Gl. 114; Som. 80, 17; Wrt. Voc. 60, 51. Lǣddon leóde lāþne gewinnan to carcerne *the people led their hated foe unto the prison,* Andr. Kmbl. 2500; An. 1251: 2603; An. 1303. Beóþ ðē hungor and þurst hearde gewinnan *hunger and thirst will be hard adversaries to thee,* Exon. 36 b; Th. 118, 28; Gū. 246. Heora gewinnan hī ēhtan *insĕquĭtur hostis,* Bd. 1, 12; S. 481, 23: 1, 23; S. 483, 13. Đa ǣrran gewinnan *priores inimici,* S. 1, 12; S. 480, 33.

ge-winnan; *p.* -wan, -won, -wann, *pl.* -wunnon; *pp.* -wunnen. I. *to make war, fight, contend;* pugnare, bellum gerere:—He āna gewon *he fought alone,* Exon. 39 a; Th. 129, 15; Gū. 21: Bd. 3, 19; S. 548, 2. Hū hie wiđ ðæm drȳ gefliton and gewunnon *how they contended and strove against the sorcerer,* Blickl. Homl. 173, 3. II. *to obtain by fighting, to conquer, gain, win;* pugna consequi, obtinere, subjugare:—Hū he mihte Normandige of him gewinnan *how he might conquer* [*win*] *Normandy from him,* Chr. 1090; Erl. 226, 25. Ne māgon we ðæt on aldre gewinnan *we cannot ever obtain that,* Cd. 421; Th. 26, 6; Gen. 402. Ǣnig ne mæg friþ gewinnan *no one may gain peace,* Exon. 22 b; Th. 62, 14; Cri. 1001. Đæs đe he heora sāulum to hǣle and to rǣde gewinnan mihte *provided that he could win their souls to salvation and counsel,* Blickl. Homl. 227, 4. He hit gewan mid wisdōme *he gained it by wisdom,* Th. Ap. 4, 19. Chananēus đā wann wiđ Israēla bearn and sige on him gewann *the Canaanite fought against the children of Israel and gained a victory over them,* Num. 21, 1. Đone cyning đe hie ǣr mid unrihte gewunnen hæfde *the king that had before unjustly conquered them,* Bt. 16, 2; Fox 52, 22. On āgenum hwīlum mid earfeþum gewunnen *laboriously gained in their own time,* Swt. A. S. Rdr. 106, 55. Đā wæs Rōmāna rīce gewunnen *then the empire of the Romans was conquered,* Bt. Met. Fox 1, 34; Met. 1, 17. [*O. Sax.* ge-winnan: *O. H. Ger.* ga-winnan: *Ger.* ge-winnen *to gain, obtain.*]

gewin-stōw, e; *f. A place to contend in, battle-place, wrestling-place;* certāminis lŏcus, pălæstra, Ælfc. Gl. 29; Som. 61, 49; Wrt. Voc. 26, 48.

ge-wintred, -wintrad; *part. Grown to full age, full-aged, aged;* adultus:—Ōþ-ðæt hit gewintred sīe *until it be of age,* L. In. 38; Th. i. 126, 7. Midđȳ đū bist gewintrad *cum senueris,* Jn. Skt. Lind. 21, 18. Đeáh he gewintred wǣre *though he was aged,* Ors. 6, 31; Bos. 128, 7. Đæs gewintredan monnes *of a full-aged man,* L. Alf. pol. 26; Th. i. 78, 18. [*Cf. M. H. Ger.* ge-jāret.] DER. un-gewintred.

gewin-woruld, e; *f. A world of toil;* trībŭlātiōnis plēnus mundus:—Hȳ scofene wurdon on gewinwōruld *they were thrust into a world of toil,* Exon. 45 a; Th. 153, 21; Gū. 829.

ge-wīred; *part. p. Made of wire*:—Hyre ealdan gewīredan preón an vi. mancussum *her old brooch made of* [*gold or silver*] *wire, worth six mancuses,* Th. Chart. 537, 34. v. wīr.

Gewis, Giwis, es; *m. Gewis, the great grandfather of Cerdic*:—Se Cerdic wæs Elesing, Elesa Esling, Esla Gewising, Gewis Wiging *Cerdic was the son of Elesa, Elesa the son of Esla, Elsa the son of Gewis, Gewis the son of Wig,* Chr. 495; Erl. 2, 5: 597; Erl. 20, 7. Giwis, 552; Erl. 16, 19. According to Asser it was from this name that the term Gevissæ, applied by Bede to the West Saxons, was derived. 'Gewis, a quo Britones totam illam gentem Gegwis nominant,' see Grmm. Gesch. D. S. 458. For the use by Bede, see Bd. 3, 7—'Gens Occidentalium Saxonum qui antiquitus Gevissæ vocabantur . . . primum Gevissorum gentem ingrediens,' where the translation has 'West Seaxna þeód . . . Đā com he ǣrest upp on West Seaxum.' See also 4. 15, 16. Smith's note on the word is 'Gevissæ. Saxonicum est pro Occidentalium. Sic Visigothi, præposita tantum Saxonica expletiva *Ge*.' See Thorpe's Lappenberg i. 109, note.

ge-wis, -wiss; *adj. Certain, sure, knowing, foreknowing;* certus:—Gewis be heora gerihtnesse *certus de illorum correctione,* Bd. 5, 22; S. 644, 45. Đæt is gesægd ðæt he wǣre gewis his sylfes forþfōre *qui præscius sui obitus exstitisse videtur,* 4, 24; S. 599, 14. Wite ðæt ǣrest gewiss ðæt ðæt mōd byþ ðære sāwle ǣge *know first that as certain, that the mind is the soul's eye,* Shrn. 178, 2. Gewis is *constat,* Hpt. Gl. 419. Đa ūþwitan đe sǣdon ðæt nǣfre nān wiht gewisses nǣre būton twæónunga *the philosophers that said that there was no certainty without doubt,* Shrn. 174, 25. Swā litel gewis funden *found so little certain,* Bt. 41, 4; Fox 250, 20. Gewis andgit *intelligence,* 5; Fox 252, 20, 30. We syndon gewisse đīnes līfes *we are acquainted with thy life,* Guthl. 5; Gdwin. 30, 18. He hī gewisse gedyde and gelǣrde be ingonge ðæs ēcan rīces *de ingressu regni æterni certos reddidit,* Bd. 4, 16; S. 584, 35. On gewissum tīdum *at certain times,* R. Ben. interl. 48. Of gewissum intingan *of certain causes,* R. Ben. interl. 63. Myd gewyssum gesceáde *with certain reason, wherefore;* propter certam rationem, quapropter, Nicod. 3; Thw. 2, 6. [*O. H. Ger.* giwis: *Ger.* gewiss *certus.*]

ge-wīscan, etc. v. ge-wȳscan, etc.

ge-wisfullīce; *adv. Knowingly, expertly;* scienter, Greg. pref. lib. 2, Dial.

ge-wīsian; *p.* ode; *pp.* od *To direct, teach, shew*:—Bǣdon ðæt him gewīsade waldend se gōda hū hie libban sceolden *prayed the good Ruler to direct them how they were to live,* Cd. 40; Th. 52, 27; Gen. 850.

ge-wislīce, -wisslīce; *adv. Certainly, exactly, truly, especially, besides;* videlicet, scilicet, sane, utique, porro:—Gewisslīce *sane,* Ælfc. Gr. 38; Som. 41, 45. Gyf sōþlīce gewislīce rihtwīsnysse sprecaþ *si vere utique justitiam loquimini,* Ps. Spl. C. 57, 1. Gewislīce ān þing is neád-behēfe *porro unum est necessarium,* Lk. Bos. 10, 42. Đū miht blissigan gewisslīce *thou mayest certainly rejoice,* Homl. Th. ii. 132, 1. Se wītegode be Criste swīđe gewislīce swilce he godspellere wǣre *he prophesied about Christ with great exactness, as if he had been an evangelist,* Swt. A. S. Rdr. 69, 414. Gewislīce ic hæbbe *certe habeo,* Coll. Monast. Th. 30, 7. Ic nāt nāht gewislīce hwæđer ðæs feós swā micel is *I do not know for certain whether there is so much money,* Th. Chart. 490, 15. Seó lencten-līce emniht is gewislīce on duodecima kl. April *the spring equinox is certainly on the twelfth day before the kalends of April,* Bd. de nat. rerum; Wrt. popl. science 11, 1; Lchdm. iii. 256, 8. Ic cweđe nū gewislīcor *I say now more exactly,* 8, 23; Lchdm. iii. 250, 4: Th. Ap. 15, 24. Đæs đe hie gewislīcost gewitan meahton *to the best of their knowledge,* Beo. Th. 2704; B. 1350.

ge-wiss, -wisslīce. v. ge-wis, ge-wislīce.

ge-wissend, es; *m. A director, ruler;* præceptor, rector, Hymn. Lye.

ge-wissian; *p.* ode, ade; *pp.* od *To make* or *cause to know, to instruct, inform, direct, command, govern;* docere, edocere, regere, præcipere, dirigere:—Đæt he đone iungan cniht gewissian sceolde *that he should instruct the young boy,* Ælfc. T. Lisle, 34, 3. To đam lande đe ic đē gewissige *unto a land that I will shew thee,* Boutr. Scrd. 21, 42. On đam regole đe us gewissaþ be ðære hālgan Eástertīde *in the rule that directs us about the holy Eastertide,* Lchdm. iii. 256, 10. Heó gewissaþ and gescylt and gelǣt *it directs and protects and guides,* Homl. Th. i. 52, 15. Se đe gewylt and gewissaþ Israhēla folc *qui reget populum Israhel,* 78, 16. Swā swā him Gregorius ǣr gewissode *as Gregory had before directed him,* ii. 130, 22: Swt. A. S. Rdr. 64, 241. Se wītega hine gewissode ðæt he cūđe gelȳfan *the prophet directed so that he was able to believe,* 70, 444. Đū gewissa đa sacerdas *tu præcipe sacerdotibus,* Jos. 3, 8. Ic gean đara vi. punda đe ic 'Eádmunde mīnon brēđer gewissod hæbbe *I give the six pounds that I have indicated to my brother Edmund,* Th. Chart. 559, 6. Gif đū nelt beón gewissod *if thou wilt not be directed,* Ælfc. T. Lisle, 40, 12.

ge-wissung, e; *f. Direction, instruction, guidance*:—For fela gewissungum đe seó ān bōc hæfþ toforan đām ōđrum *for many directions which that one book has above the others,* Swt. A. S. Rdr. 65, 295.

ge-wistfullian; *p.* ode; *pp.* od *To feast*:—Gewistfullian *epulari,* Lk.

Bos. 15, 23. Et drinc and gewistfulla *eat, drink, and feast*, Homl. Th. ii. 104, 21. Gewistfullien *epulentur*, Blickl. Gl. Ðæt ic mid mínum freóndum gewistfullode *ut cum amicis meis epularer*, Lk. Bos. 15, 29.

ge-wistian *to feast:*—Et drinc and gewista *comede bibe epulare*, Lk. Bos. 12, 19.

gewist-lǽcan; *p.* -lǽhte; *pp.* -lǽht *To feast;* epulari:—Ðá ongunnon hig gewistlǽccan *cœperunt epulari*, Lk. Bos. 15, 24.

ge-wísung, e; *f. Direction:*—Be Godes sylfes gewísunge *by the direction of God himself*, Jud. pref. Thw. 153, 6.

ge-wit, -witt, es; *n.* I. *wits, senses, [right] mind, mind, intellect:*—Wíndruncen gewit *a mind stupefied with wine*, Cd. 212; Th. 262, 32; Dan. 753. Ðenden mec mín gewit gelǽsteþ *whilst my intellect attends me*, Exon. 38 a; Th. 125, 1; Gú. 347. He eft onhwearf wódan gewittes *he recovered from madness*, Cd. 206; Th. 255, 22; Dan. 628. Seó gedrēfednes ðæt mód ne mæg his gewittes bereáfian *trouble cannot rob the mind of its faculties*, Bt. 5, 3; Fox 12, 25. Nú bidde ic ðē ðǽt ðú hí on gewitte gebringe *now I beseech thee bring her to her wits*, Homl. Th. i. 458, 11: Exon. 67 b; Th. 251, 12; Jul. 144: 74 b; Th. 278, 13; Jul. 597. Sió wyrd cymþ of ðam gewitte ðæs ælmihtigan Godes *fate comes from the mind of the almighty God*, Bt. 39, 5; Fox 220, 1: Exon. 120 b; Th. 463, 30; Hö. 78: 78 b; Th. 294, 10; Crä. 13: Andr. Kmbl. 631; An. 316: 1344; An. 672. Bútan gewitte *irrational*, Salm. Kmbl. 46; Sal. 23. Se Hǽlend wódum monnum gewitt forgeaf *the Saviour gave reason to the insane*, Homl. Th. i. 480, 14: H. R. 105, 3: Andr. Kmbl. 69; An. 35: Bt. Met. Fox 26, 200; Met. 26, 100. He him gewit forgeaf *he gave him intelligence*, Cd. 14; Th. 16, 29; Gen. 250: Exon. 25 a; Th. 72, 26; Cri. 1178. Ic wát ðæt ðæt lýf á byþ and ðæt gewit *I know that life and mind will always exist*, Shrn. 199, 30, 26. Gehǽlde gewitte *sanato sensu*, Bd. 4, 3; S. 570, 13. II. *knowledge, understanding, consciousness:*—To syllenne his folce hys hǽle gewit *ad dandam scientiam salutis plebi ejus*, Lk. Bos. 1, 77. Lǽran sceal mon geongne monnan . . . sylle him wist and wǽdo óþ ðæt hine mon on gewitte alǽde *a young man must be taught . . . give him food and clothing until he be brought to understanding*, Exon. 89 b; Th. 336, 13; Gn. Ex. 47. Hwá meahte me swelc gewit gifan gif hit God ne onsende *who could give me such understanding if God did not send it*, Cd. 32; Th. 42, 10; Gen. 671. Cyning geweóld his gewitte *the king recovered consciousness*, Beo. Th. 5399; B. 2703. [*O. Sax.* gi-wit: *O. H. Ger.* ge-wizzi.]

ge-wita, an; *m. One who is cognisant of anything, a witness, an accessory;* testis, conscius:—Gewita *testis*, Wrt. Voc. 76, 21. Ælmihtig drihten ðe is ealra þinga gewita *the Lord Almighty that is cognisant of all things*, Lchdm. iii. 436, 20. Ðisæs is Oda gewita *of this is Oda witness*, Th. Chart. 510, 5. God sylf his is gewita *God is his own witness*, Homl. Th. ii. 126, 9: i. 84, 4: Ps. Th. 88, 31. Ða leásan gewitan *the false witnesses*, Homl. Th. i. 50, 14, 29: Swt. A. S. Rdr. 72, 497. Geweotan, Th. Chart. 480. 16. We þissa wundra gewitan sindon *we are witnesses of these wonders*, Exon. 43 b; Th. 147, 10; Gú. 724. Gif heó clǽne sý and ðæs fácnes gewita nǽre *if she be innocent and were not an accessory to the crime*, L. Ath. v. § 1, 1; Th. i. 228, 17. Ðæt ðú sý wommes gewita *that thou art an accessory to the crime*, Exon. 80 a; Th. 301, 14; Fä. 19: Frag. Kmbl. 12; Leás. 7. Wildeóra gewita *one who has the same knowledge [wit] as the beasts* [Grein and Bouterwek write gewíta = socius], Cd. 206; Th. 255, 14; Dan. 624. [*O. Sax.* ge-wito: *O. H. Ger.* ki-wizo *conscius.*]

ge-witan; *p.* -wiste *To understand, know;* scire:—Hí woldon gewitan hwæt ðæt wǽre *dignoscere quid esset*, Bd. 3, 8; S. 532, 7; 4, 18; S. 587, 1; Beo. Th. 2705; B. 1350. Giuta *scire*, Rtl. 5, 18. Gif hwá gewilnigeþ to gewitane hú gedón mann he wæs *if any one wants to know what sort of man he was*, Chr. 1086; Erl. 221, 10. Ðone woeg giwutun *viam scitis*, Jn. Skt. Rush. 14, 4. Gewiste *sciens*, Mt. Kmbl. Lind. 16, 8: Exon. 108 a; Th. 412, 14; Rä. 30, 14. Embihtmen giwistun *ministri sciebant*, Jn. Skt. Rush. 2, 9. Ðæt ne sē gewitten *quod non scietur*, Mt. Kmbl. Lind. 10, 26. Gá and gewite *go and get to know*, Ap. Th. 13, 24.

ge-wítan; ic -wíte, ðú -wítest, -wítst, he -wíteþ, -wít, *pl.* -wítaþ; *p.* ic, he -wát, ðú -wite, *pl.* -witon; *pp.* -witen. I. [wítan, I. *to see*] *to see, behold;* videre, spectare:—Gewíte and beseoh wíngeard ðisne *vide et visita vineam istam*, Ps. Th. 79, 14. II. *to turn one's eyes in any direction with the intention of taking that direction, to set out towards, start, pass over, to go, depart, withdraw, go away, retreat, retire, die;* transire, discedere. [*a*] *with the infin. of a verb of motion:*—Gewíteþ on weg faran engel *the angel departeth away*, Salm. Kmbl. 1003; Sal. 503. Gewát fleógan mid lácum hire *flew off with her offerings*, Cd. 72; Th. 88, 27; Gen. 1471: 8; Th. 9, 1; Gen. 135: Andr. Kmbl. 2496; An. 1249: Beo. Th. 1710; B. 853. Geweotan, Andr. Kmbl. 1602; An. 802. Gewít ðú nú féran *go now*, Cd. 83; Th. 104, 36; Gen. 1746. Gewát him hám síðian *went off home*, Cd. 98; Th. 130, 17; Gen. 2161: Beo. Th. 3930; B. 1963. [*b*] *with other infinitives:*—Ic gewíte sēcan gársecges grund *I go and seek the ocean's bottom*, Exon. 101 a; Th. 381, 24; Rä. 3, 1. Heó on síþ gewát wésten sēcan *she on her journey went seeking the desert*, Cd. 103; Th 136, 29; Gen. 2265: 93; Th. 120, 24; Gen. 1999: Beo. Th. 230; B. 115: 3811; B. 1903.. Him Noe gewát eaforan lǽdan *Noah went leading his offspring*, Cd. 67; Th 82, 2; Gen. 1356: 96; Th. 126, 21; Gen. 2098. [*c*] *followed by a clause:*—Gewát ðæt he in temple gestód wuldres aldor *the prince of glory went so as to stop in the temple*, Andr. Kmbl. 1411; An. 707: Exon. 52 a; Th. 181, 31; Gú. 1301. [*d*] *with prep. or adv. or adj:*—Hí forþ gewítaþ for ðǽs sumores hǽton *they shall fade away for the summer's heat*, Blickl. Homl. 59, 4. He forþ gewát *he died*, Cd. 52; Th. 65, 19: Rood Kmbl. 262; Kr. 133: Beo. Th. 2962; B. 1479. Ðá gewát se dæg forþ *dies cœperat declinare*, Lk. Bos. 9, 12. Fyrst forþ gewát *the time went on*, Beo. Th. 425; B. 210: Cd. 47; Th. 59, 36; Gen. 974: Exon. 49 a; Th. 170, 6; Gú. 1107. Se to forþ gewát þurh ðone æþelan *it [the dart] reached and pierced the noble man*, Byrht. Th. 136, 13; B. 150. Gif we gewítaþ fram ðē *if we depart from thee*, Blickl. Homl. 233, 31: 21, 12: Exon. 36 b; Th. 119, 1; Gú. 248. Ne syndon me from gewitene *they have not departed from me*, Cd. 63; Th. 76, 11; Gen. 1255. Me lǽrdon Rómáne ðæt ic gewát heonon onweg *the Romans advised me to depart away hence*, Blickl. Homl. 191, 14. Hwyder gewiton ða welan *whither has the wealth gone?* 99, 24. Ðonne gewitan ða sáula niðer *then down went the souls*, 211, 4: Exon. 97 a; Th. 361, 32; Wal. 28. Gewít of ðam menn *depart from the man*, Homl. Th. i. 458, 5: Blickl. Homl. 139, 13. Ðá he of lífe gewát *when he departed this life*, Beo. Th. 4934; B. 2471. Ǽr ðam ðæt óðer of gewíteþ *before the other goes away*, Bt. Met. Fox 29, 22; Met. 29, 11. Gewát ofer wǽgholm *went o'er the ocean*, Beo. Th. 439; B. 217. On fleám gewát *fled*, Cd. 205; Th. 254, 20; Dan. 614. He nǽfre onweg ne gewát *he has never departed*, Blickl. Homl. 117, 1: Ors. 2, 4; Bos. 44, 36. Gewiten under waðeman *retired under ocean*, Exon. 57 a; Th. 204, 13; Ph. 97. In ðæt ēglond up gewítaþ *they go up into that island*, 96 b; Th. 361, 8; Wal. 16. Ðonon ne gewát *he departed not thence*, Blickl. Homl. 121, 31. Ðæt us ðás tída ídle ne gewítan *that these times do not pass away without profit for us*, 129, 36. Seó deorce niht won gewíteþ *the dark night passes away murky*, Exon. 57 a; Th. 204, 17; Ph. 99. [*e*] *used absolutely:*—Gyf ðes calic ne mǽge gewítan *si non potest hic calix transire*, Mt. Bos. 26, 42. Nacode we wǽron acennede and nacode we gewítaþ *naked we were born and naked we depart*, Homl. Th. i. 64, 28. Heofon and eorþe mæg gewítan mín word nǽfre ne gewítaþ *heaven and earth may pass away; my words shall never pass away*, Blickl. Homl. 245, 5: 91, 21: 57, 30: Elen. Kmbl. 2552; El. 1277. Gif ðú gewítest *if you depart*, 225, 17. Hí ðǽrrihte æfter ðam drence gewiton *they died directly after the drink*, Homl. Th. i. 72, 21: Cd. 62; Th. 75, 7; Gen. 1236. Ðæt leóht gewát *the light vanished*, Elen. Kmbl. 188; El. 94. Gif he gewíte ēr ðonne hia *if he depart before she does*, Th. Chart. 465, 30. Ðæt wuldor ðysses middangeardes is sceort and gewítende *the glory of this world is short and transitory*, Blickl. Homl. 65, 15. Ðare gewítendre ǽhte ðises middaneardes *labentibus hujus seculi possessionibus*, Th. Chart. 317, 6: Bd. 3, 22; S. 552, 20. Dagas sind gewitene *days are passed away*, Exon. 82 b; Th. 310, 26; Seef. 80.

ge-wítendlic; *adj. Transitory;* transitorius:—Hwæt is ðiós gewítendlíce sibb *what is this transitory peace*, Past. 46, 5; Swt. 351, 24; Hat. MS. 67 a, 17. Mín mód forhogode ealle ðás gewítendlícan þing *my mind despised all these transitory things*, Greg. Dial. Hat. MS. fol. 1 b, 14. Ðis lǽnelíce líf and ðis gewítendlíce *this poor and transitory life*, Blickl. Homl. 73, 9. Yrfenuma to wítendlícum ǽhtum *heir to transitory possessions*, Homl. Th. i. 56, 13.

ge-wítendnes, se; *f. Departure:*—Sǽdon his gewítendnesse *dicebant excessum ejus*, Lk. Bos. 9, 31.

ge-witennes, se; *f. Departure:*—Ðá ðære tíde neálǽhte his gewitenesse *propinquante hora sui decessus*, Bd. 4, 24; S. 598, 24. On ðone ylcan dæg byþ ðæs bisceopes gewytennys se wæs nemned scs Cassius *on the same day is the bishop's departure who was named St. Cassius*, Shrn. 97, 36.

ge-witfæst; *adj. Of sound mind:*—Nǽnig deófolseóc ðæt he eft wel gewitfæst nǽre *no possessed person that was not in his right mind again*, Guthl. 15; Gdwin. 66, 17.

ge-wiðerworded; *part. p. Opposed;* adversatus, Rtl. 114, 1.

ge-witig. v. ge-wittig.

ge-wítigian, -wítgian; *p.* ode; *pp.* od *To prophesy:*—Wel gewítgade Esaias *bene prophetavit Esaias*, Mt. Kmbl. Lind. 15, 7: 11, 13. Swá hit gewítgod wæs *as it was prophesied*, Blickl. Homl. 93, 29: 83, 28.

gewit-leás; *adj. Witless, foolish, mad;* insanus, amens, stultus:—Gewitleás *amens*, Ælfc. Gr. 47; Som. 48, 35. Wurde ðú ðæs gewitleás ðæt ðú waldende þonc ne wisses *thou wast so witless that thou wast not grateful to the Lord*, Exon. 29 b; Th. 90, 12; Cri. 1473: Bt. Met. Fox 19, 92; Met. 19, 46.

ge-wit-leást, -witt-leást, e; *f. Folly, madness, phrensy;* stultitia:—On ðínre gewitleáste *in thy folly*, Homl. Th. i. 424, 16: Ælfc. T. Lisle 32, 24. Wið ða ádle ðe grēcas frenēsis nemnaþ ðæt is on úre geþeóde gewitlēst ðæs módes *for the disease which the Greeks call φρένησις, that is, in our language, witlessness of the mind*, Herb. 96, 4; Lchdm. i. 210, 1.

gewit-loca, an; *m. A container of intelligence, the mind;* intelligentiæ clausura, animus, mens, pectus, Bt. Met. Fox 12, 52; Met. 12, 26: Exon. 123 a; Th. 473 13; Bo. 14.

ge-witnes, -ness, e; *f.* I. *knowledge, cognisance, witness, testimony*:—Ođđe đeós gewitness weorđeþ on heágum *si est scientia in excelso*, Ps. Th. 72, 9. Būton Godes willan and būton his gewitnesse *without God's will and without his knowledge*, Bt. 39, 9; Fox 212, 33: Gen. 31, 27, 31. Gif he stalie on gewitnesse ealles his hīrēdes *if he steal with the cognisance of all his household*, L. In. 7; Th. i. 106, 16: L. C. S. 76; Th. i. 418, 12. Wundorlīc is đīn gewitnes *mirabilia testimonia tua*, Ps. Th. 118, 129, 24. He wearþ gemyndig his gewitnesse *memor erit testamenti sui*, 110, 4. Ne yfel gewitnes ne wrēgde *nor had evil witness accused them*, Blickl. Homl. 163, 1. Be leásre gewitnesse *of false witness*, L. C. S. 37; Th. i. 398, 9: L. Ath. i. 10; Th. i. 204, 22. On hyra gewitnesse *they being witnesses*, Gen. 23, 9. On Moyses bōca gewitnesse *by the testimony of the books of Moses*, Blickl. Homl. 153, 5. Đæt is to gewitnesse đæt hit him ne līcode *that is for a testimony that they did not like it*, Past. 21, 6; Swt. 165, 13; Hat. MS. In gewitnisse hiora *in testimonium eorum*, Mt. Kmbl. Lind. 10, 14. Iohannes cȳþ gewitnesse be him *Iohannes testimonium perhibet de ipso*, Jn. Bos. 1, 15. At đis gewitnesse wæs seo kining Offa *at this witnessing was king Offa*, Chr. 777; Erl. 55, 12. II. *used of persons*:—Ic Æthelmǣr gewitnys *I Æthelmær am witness*, Cod. Dipl. Kmbl. iii. 351, 12–18: iv. 206, 6–9. Wynflæd gelǣdde hyre gewitnesse đæt wæs Sigerīc arcebiscop, etc. *Wynflæd brought her witnesses, they were archbishop Sigeric, etc.*, Th. Chart. 288, 3: 539, 31. Here ealre đe hēr bē gewitnesse *of all those that here are witnesses*, Chr. 675; Erl. 39, 21. Ymb huæd we willnias gewitnesa *quid desideramus testes*, Mk. Skt. Lind. 14, 63. Fordam arison ongeán me leáse gewitnessa *quoniam insurrexerunt in me testes iniqui*, Ps. Th. 26, 14: Hy. 7, 94; Hy. Grn. ii. 289, 94. Beforan gewitnessum *before witnesses*, L. In. 25; Th. i. 118, 13. [See Grm. R. A. pp. 608, 779.]

ge-wītnian; *p.* ode; *pp.* od *To punish, chastise*:—Se đe mihte hine sōna on helle gewītnian *he that could at once punish him in hell*, Blickl. Homl. 33, 30: Homl. Th. ii. 124, 22. Ic gewītnige *punio*, Ælfc. Gr. 30; Som. 34, 57. Hwī wurdon đa synfullan mid wætere gewītnode? On Noes dagum gewītnode God manna gālnysse mid wætere . . . *why were the sinful punished with water? In Noah's days God punished men's wantonness with water* . . ., Boutr. Scrd. 22, 30: Gen. 20, 18. Se man wæs stranglīce gewītnad *the man was severely punished*, Shrn. 73, 13: Beo. Th. 6138; B. 3073.

ge-wītnung, e; *f. Punishment*:—On đære Sodomitiscra gewītnunge forbearn seó eorþe *in the punishment of the people of Sodom the earth was burnt*, Boutr. Scrd. 22, 33.

ge-witodlīce *truly*; certe, sane, Ps. Spl. T. 57, 1. v. witodlīce.

gewit-scipe, es; *m. A testimony, witnessing*; testimonium, Bd. 1, 27, resp. 6; S. 492, 5, 6. [*O. Sax.* ge-wit-skepi *witness*: *O. H. Ger.* gi-wiz-scaf *testimonium.*]

gewit-seóc; *adj. Mind-sick, lunatic, demoniac*; energumenus, Ælfc. Gl. 78; Som. 72, 35; Wrt. Voc. 45, 67: 75, 52.

gewit-seócnes, -ness, e; *f. Insanity*; insanitas, Som.

ge-wittig, -witig; *adj. Wise, knowing, sane, conscious*; intelligens:—Heó đǣrrihte wearþ gewittig *she straightway became sane*, Homl. Th. ii. 24, 12: 142, 19. Ne forlǣt đē nān đe gewityg byt *nor does any one forsake thee that is wise*, Shrn. 166, 28. Sum biþ gewittig æt wīnþege beórhyrde gōd *one is expert at feasting, a good keeper of beer*, Exon. 79 b; Th. 297, 26; Crä. 74: Beo. Th. 6179; B. 3094.

ge-wixlan. v. ge-wrixlian.

ge-wlacian; *p.* ode; *pp.* od *To make lukewarm*; tepefacere:—Ic eom gewlacod *tepefio*, Ælfc. Gr. 37; Som. 39, 38.

ge-wlǣtan; *p.* -wlǣtte; *pp.* -wlǣted, -wlǣt *To defile, debase*; fœdare:—Gif đū swā gewlǣtne mon mētst *if thou shouldest meet a man so debased*, Bt. 37, 4; Fox 192, 12. DER. wlǣtan.

ge-wleccan, -wlecian; *pp.* -wleht, -wleced *To make lukewarm*:—Genim đysse ylcan wyrte seáw gewlæht [gewleht, MS. H. B.] *take of this same herb the juice made lukewarm*, Herb. 19; Lchdm. i. 114, 2: 80; Lchdm. i. 184, 1. Gewleced *made lukewarm*, L. M. 1, 3; Lchdm. ii. 40, 21, 29. [Cf. ge-wlacian, wleccan.]

ge-wlencan; *pp.* ed *To make proud, rich, to exalt*:—Ic Æþelrǣd eldorman gewelegod and gewlenced mid sume dǣle Mercna rīces *I Ethelred alderman enriched and exalted with a part of the Mercians' realm*, Th. Chart. 129, 26. Wīrum gewlenced *adorned with wires*, Elen. Kmbl. 2525; El. 1264. [*O. Sax.* gi-wlenkid.]

ge-wlitegian; *p.* ode; *pp.* ad, od *To form, adorn, make beautiful*; formare, decorare, exornare, speciosum *vel* pulchriorem reddere:—Giwlitga *decorare*, Rtl. 105, 28. He gewlitegaþ ealle gesceafta *he adorns all creatures*, Shrn. 198, 12: Salm. Kmbl. 793; Sal. 396. Hand his gewlitegodon *manus ejus formaverunt*, Ps. Spl. 94, 5. Wel gewlitegod *formosus*, Wrt. Vōc. 72, 15. Wuldre gewlitegad *with glory beautified*, Exon. 55 b; Th. 197, 8; Az. 187: 57 b; Th. 205, 23; Ph. 117: 108 a; Th. 413, 7; Rä. 32, 2: 128 b; Th. 493, 22; Rä. 81, 35: Andr. Kmbl. 1337; An. 669.

ge-wlō; *adj. Adorned*; ornatus:—Seó eorþe wæstmum gewlō *the earth with fruits adorned*, Cd. 85; Th. 107, 14; Gen. 1789. v. wlō.

ge-wonian. v. ge-wanian.

ge-wōpen *wept, lamented*, Ælfc. Gr. 26, 1; Som. 28, 28; *pp. of* ge-wēpan.

ge-worc, es; *n. A work*; factūra:—On geworce đīnum *in factūra tua*, Ps. Spl. 91, 4. v. ge-weorc.

ge-worpan *to throw, cast*, Bd. 4, 13; S. 583, 11. v. ge-weorpan.

ge-worpen *thrown, cast*; projectus, Ps. Th. 87, 5; *pp. of* ge-weorpan.

ge-woruht = ge-worht *wrought*; *pp. of* ge-wyrcan, Runic pm. 11; Kmbl. 341, 18.

ge-wosa, -wesa *a being together, conversation*; conversatio:—Ǣrfæst giwosa we gifylga bisene *piæ conversationis sequamur exempla*, Rtl. 51, 1: 32, 32: 74, 35.

ge-wrǣstan *to writhe, twist, join*; intorquere, Cot. 4.

ge-wrǣđan *to be wroth, savage*:—Beran to him gewrǣđan gesihþ *if he sees a bear savage at him*, Lchdm. iii. 212, 4.

ge-wrāđian; *p.* ede *To make angry*:—Đā gewrāđede hine Landfranc *then Lanfranc was angry*, Chr. 1070; Erl. 208, 5.

ge-wrecan; *p.* -wræc, *pl.* -wrǣcon; *pp.* -wrecen *To wreak, avenge, revenge, punish*; ulcisci, vindīcāre, pūnīre:—Gebeótode Cirus đæt he his þegen gewrecan wolde *Cyrus threatened that he would avenge his officer*, Ors. 2, 4; Bos. 44, 4: Cd. 64; Th. 77, 13; Gen. 1274. Ic heora unriht gewrece egsan gyrde *visitābo in virga iniquitātes eorum*, Ps. Th. 88, 29. Se gewrycþ mynne teónan on đē *he will avenge on thee my wrong*, Shrn. 96, 16. God gewrecþ on đæm were *God will take vengeance on the man*, Blickl. Homl. 185, 25. Nā đū ūre gyltas egsan gewrǣce *avertisti ab ira indignātiōnis tuæ*, 84, 3: 98, 9. Ic đæt eall gewræc *I have avenged all that*, Beo. Th. 4015; B. 2005: 215; B. 107. Đæt mǣgwinas mīne gewrǣcon *my kinsmen avenged that*, 4952; B. 2479: Cd. 94; Th. 123, 1; Gen. 2038. Hine hafaþ his heofonlīca Fæder swīđe gewrecen *his heavenly Father has amply avenged him*, Chr. 979; Erl. 129, 14: Ors. 1, 14; Bos. 37, 17. Seó his unsynnige cwalu wæs gewrecen *his undeserved death was avenged*, Shrn. 93, 13.

ge-wrēgan; *p.* -wrēgde; *pp.* -wrēged, -wrēht [wrēgan *to accuse*]. I. *to accuse*; accūsāre:—Đa þwyran hǣđengyldan đone apostol to đam cyninge gewrēgdon *the perverse idolaters accused the apostle to the king*, Homl. Th. i. 470, 6: Gen. 37, 2. Đæt hī hine gewrēgdon *ut accūsārent illum*, Mk. Bos. 3, 2. Secgaþ wyrdwrīteras đæt Herodes wearþ gewrēged to đam Rōmāniscan cāsere *historians say that Herod was accused to the Roman emperor*, Homl. Th. i. 80, 6. Gytsung is gewrēht wiđ God *covetousness is accused before God*, 256, 22. II. *to stir up, excite, impel*; concĭtāre:—Gifen biþ gewrēged *the sea is impelled*, Exon. 101 a; Th. 381, 29; Rä. 3, 3.

ge-wreot. v. ge-writ.

ge-wređian; *p.* ede; *pp.* ed *To support*:—Mid his crycce hine gewređede *supported himself with his crutch*; baculo innitens, Bd. 4, 31; S. 610, 18, note.

ge-wrid, es; *n. A place where shrubs grow, thicket*:—Betwyx đa fenlīcan gewrido đæs wīdgillan wēstenes *amongst the fenny thickets of the wide wilderness*, Guthl. 3; Gdwin. 22, 10. Betwux đa þiccan gewrido đara bremela *amongst the dense thickets of brambles*, 5; Gdwin. 36, 12. Gewrid *glomulus*, Cot. 95: *fruticetum*, 90, Lye. [Cf. wrīđan.]

ge-wridian; *p.* ode; *pp.* od *To flourish*:—Unarīmed mengeo on manigfealdum ceápum geweóx and gewridode *the innumerable multitude of all sorts of cattle grew and flourished*, Blickl. Homl. 199, 2.

ge-wrinclod; *part. p. Wrinkled, crooked, winding*:—Đe gewrincloda dīc *the winding dike*, Cod. Dipl. Kmbl. iv. 34, 9.

ge-wring, es; *n.* [ge-wringan *comprimere*, wringan *to wring*, torquere] *What one can wring* or *press out, drink, strong drink*; potus, sicera = σίκερα:—*Sicera* ælces cynnes [MS. kynnes] gewring būtan wīne and wætere *what one can press out of every kind, except wine and water*, Ælfc. Gl. 32; Som. 61, 120; Wrt. Voc. 27, 48.

ge-wringan; *p.* -wrang, *pl.* -wrungon; *pp.* -wrungen *To wring*; comprimere, constringere:—Gewring đa wōs of hyre leáfon *wring the juice from its leaves*, Th. An. 116, 22. Munt gewrungen *mons coagulatus*, Ps. Lamb. 67, 16. Gewrungan *wrung*, Herb. 72, 2; Lchdm. i. 174, 11.

ge-writ, es; *n. Something written, writing, scripture, inscription, a writing, letter, treatise, writ, charter, book*:—Ōþ đone first đe hie wel cunnen Englisc gewrit arǣdan *until such time as they can read English writing well*, Past. pref. Swt. 7, 13, 17. Ne rǣdde gē đis gewrit *nec scripturam hanc legistis*, Mk. Bos. 12, 10. Đæt gewrit swā be him cwæþ *the Scripture thus spake about him*, Blickl. Homl. 167, 15: 123, 6. Mid đon worde đæs godcundan gewrites *with the word of divine Scripture*, 33, 20. Đæs hālgan gewrites *of holy writ*, Homl. Th. i. 82, 13. Đis gewrit *inscribtio*, Mk. Bos. 12, 16. Đā hēht he rǣdan đæt gewrit *then he ordered to read the letter*, Blickl. Homl. 177, 4, 35. Awrītaþ eówre naman on gewrite đonne asænde ic đa gewrita mīnre dōhtor . . . se cyngc nam đa gewrita and geinseglode hī *write your names in a letter, then I will send the letters to my daughter* . . . *The king took the letters and sealed them*, Th. Ap. 20, 6–10: Chr. 627; Erl. 25, 11. Se pāpa seonde his gewrite to Engla lande *the pope sent his bull to England*, 675; Erl. 37, 15. Mid đæs cynges gewrite *with the king's writ*, 1048; Erl. 177, 19. Ān oxe ne ān cū ne ān swīn đæt næs gesæt on his gewrite and ealle đa gewrita wǽron gebroht to him syđđan *there was not an ox nor a cow nor a swine that was not put in his book [Doomsday Book], and all the writings were brought to him afterwards*, 1085; Erl. 218, 37: Homl. Th. i. 30, 2. Đis gewrit *this treatise*, Swt. A. S. Rdr. 56, 1. Đeáh đe gewrita oft nemnan ealle đa land Media *though books often call all those lands Media*, Ors. 1, 1; Bos. 16, 30. Đæs gewritu secgaþ *as books say*, Exon. 60 a; Th. 220, 1; Ph. 313: Chr. 973; Erl. 124, 22; Edg. 14: 109 b; Th. 420, 9; Rä. 40, 1. Swā wītgan us on gewritum cȳđaþ *as sages tell us in books*, 56 a; Th. 199, 24; Ph. 30: Elen. Kmbl. 1651; El. 827. We rǽdaþ on hālgum gewritum *we read in holy writings*, Homl. Th. ii. 356, 19. On gewritum *in scripturis*, Ps. Th. 86, 5. Us gewritu secgaþ *the Scriptures tell us*, Cd. 55; Th. 68, 23; Gen. 1121: 79; Th. 98, 15; Gen. 1630: 119; Th. 154, 30; Gen. 2563: Elen. Kmbl. 1345; El. 674. Đa hālgan gewreotu *the holy Scriptures*, Blickl. Homl. 15, 8: 17, 21. On gewritu settan *to record in books*, Elen. Kmbl. 1305, 1313; El. 654, 658. Tuegen hleáperas Ælfrēd cyning sende mid gewritum *king Alfred sent two couriers with letters*, Chr. 889; Erl. 86, 24. Ūre biscepas to me gewreoto sende *our bishops sent me letters*, Blickl. Homl. 187, 4. Ic hæfde ǽr on ōđre wīsan awriten ymbe mīn yrfe and hæfde monegum mannum đa gewritu ōđfæst *I had previously written in another way about my inheritance and had entrusted the writings to many men*, Chart. Th. 490, 29: 541, 22. DER. ǽrend-, erfe-, firn-, hand-, mæg-, ofer-, riht-, yrfe-gewrit.

ge-wrītan; *p.* -wrāt; *pp.* -writen *To write, to give* or *bestow by writing, to write along with others*; conscribere:—He lētt gewrītan hū mycel landes his arceb's hæfdon *he had written how much land his archbishops had*, Chr. 1085; Erl. 218, 29: Th. Chart. 296, 10. Werfriþ bisceop and seó heórēdden æt Weogerna ceastre syllaþ and gewrītaþ æþelrǽde and æþelflǽde heora hlāfordum *bishop Werfrith and the society at Worcester give and convey by writing to their lords Ethelred and Ethelfled*, Cod. Dipl. Kmbl. ii. 150, 4. Æþrēd aldorman and æþelflæd mercna hlāfordes mid us hit gewriotan *Ethelred alderman and Ethelfled, lords of the Mercians, joined with us in writing this*, 151, 2: Chr. 656; Erl. 32, 20. Seo kyning gewrāt *the king signed*, 23. Đes writ wæs gewriton *this writing was written*, 33, 9. Hwæt is gewriten *quid scribtum est*, Lk. Bos. 10, 26: Ps. Spl. 39, 11. Gewriten yrfe *legatum*, Ælfc. Gl. 13; 57, 96; Wrt. Voc. 20, 37. Gewriten yrfe-weard *legatarius*, Lye.

ge-wrītere, es; *m. A writer*:—Gewrīteres *scribæ*, Ps. Spl. T. 44, 2. v. wrītere.

ge-wrīđan; *part.* -wrīđende; *p.* -wrāđ, *pl.* -wriđon; *pp.* -wriđen *To bind, restrain, tie, tie together*; coartare, alligare:—Lim gewrīđan *to bind the limb*, Homl. Th. ii. 136, 2. Đa myhta to gewrȳđenne *potestatem ligandi*, Th. Chart. 334, 7. Engel gewrīđende ođđe geswencende hig ođđe genyrwiende *angelus coartans eos*, Ps. Lamb. 34, 5. Se heora unrōtnesse gewrīđeþ *qui alligat contritiones eorum*, Ps. Th. 146, 3. Gewrīđ *alligat*, Ps. Spl. 146, 3. Seó godcundnys gewrāđ đone ealdan deófol *the divinity bound the old devil*, Homl. Th. i. 216, 28: ii. 416, 3. Iudas hine sylfne aheng mid grine and rihtlīce gewrāđ đa forwyrhtan þrotan *Judas hung himself with a noose and rightly bound that wicked throat*, 250, 15. He his wunda gewrāđ *he bound up his wounds*, 356, 28. Đonne gewrīđ đū hȳ *then bind it*, Th. An. 116, 13. Ānra gehwilc manna is gewriđen mid rāpum his synna *every man is bound with the ropes of his sins*, Homl. Th. i. 208, 3: 456, 9: 462, 1.

ge-wrixl, -wrixle, es; *n. A change, interchange, vicissitude, turn, course*:—Hwylc gewrixl sylþ se mann for hys sāwle *quam dabit homo commutationem pro anima sua?* Mt. Bos. 16, 26: Mk. Bos. 8, 37. Cēpena þinga gewrixle *commercium*, Ælfc. Gl. 16; Som. 58, 53; Wrt. Voc. 21, 41. Ne wæs đæt gewrixle til đæt hie on bā healfa bicgan scoldon freónda feorum *nor was the exchange good, that they on both sides must buy with the lives of friends*, Beo. Th. 2613; B. 1304. Nū hæfþ God swīđe gesceádwīslīce geset đæt gewrixle eallum his gesceaftum *God hath very wisely appointed change to all his creatures*, Bt. 21; Fox 74, 21: Bt. Met. Fox 11, 111; Met. 11, 56: Shrn. 168, 11. On hys gewrixles endebyrdnesse *in ordine vicis suæ*, Lk. Bos. 1, 8. Benedictus hæfde Paulus gewrixle *Benedictus tenuit Pauli vices*, Gr. Dial. 2, 17, Lye: Blickl. Homl. 91, 24. [Cf. wæpen-gewrixle.]

ge-wrixl; *adj. Changing, vicarious*; vicarius, alternans, aptus, Hpt. Gl. 460, 476, 506.

ge-wrixlian, -wixlian; *p.* ede; *pp.* ed. I. *to change*:—Gewixla *mutare*, Mt. Kmbl. p. 2, 17. II. *to get by exchange, obtain*:—Hie hæfdon gewrixled wīta unrīm *they had got punishments innumerable*, Cd. 18; Th. 22, 3; Gen. 335. III. *to give in exchange, grant*:—Swā sceal gewrixled đām đe ǽr wel heóldon meotudes willan *so shall be granted to those that before well kept the Creator's will*, Exon. 26 a; Th. 77, 23; Cri. 1261.

ge-wuldorbeágian; *p.* ode; *pp.* od *To crown*:—Se gewuldorbeágaþ đē *qui coronat te*, Ps. Spl. 102, 4. Đū gewuldorbeágodest hine *tu coronasti eum*, 8, 6. Stephanus is on Leden coronatus đæt we cweđaþ on Englisc gewuldorbeágod *Stephen is in Latin 'coronatus,' which we express in English by crowned*, Homl. Th. i. 50, 12; 52, 20.

ge-wuldrian; *p.* ode; *pp.* od *To glorify*:—Ic hine gewuldrige *glorificabo eum*, Ps. Th. 90, 16. Gewuldradon *glorificaverunt*, Mt. Kmbl. Lind. 9, 8. Hie gesāwon đæt heó wæs gewuldrod *they saw that she was glorified*, Blickl. Homl. 139, 25. Đū eart gewuldrad *mirificatus es*, Ps. Th. 138, 12. Đū gewuldroda cyning *thou glorified king*, Blickl. Homl. 147, 35.

ge-wun; *adj. Accustomed, usual*:—Gewune drenceas *usual drinks*, Herb. 68; Lchdm. i. 172, 6. Gewune *assuetæ*, Mone Gl. 435. [*O. H. Ger.* gi-won *solitus, suetus, adsuetus*, Grff. i. 869.] v. ge-wuna; *adj.*

ge-wuna, an; *m. A custom, wont, manner, use, rite*; consuetudo:—Næs đīn gewuna đæt đū būtan đīnum diácone geoffrodest *it was not thy wont to offer without thy deacon*, Homl. Th. i. 418, 1. Wæs his gewuna đæt he sægde *referre erat solitus*, Bd. 4, 19; S. 588, 42. Đǽr wæs gewuna đæm folce đæt . . . *the people there were accustomed to* . . . , Blickl. Homl. 209, 6. Swā hit gewuna is *ut adsolet*, Ors. 3, 3; Bos. 55, 20. [*Or do the two last belong to* ge-wuna, *adj.?* (cf. ge-wunelīc.)] Is nū geworden to full yfelum gewunan đæt menn swīđor scamaþ nū for gōddǽdum đonne for misdǽdum *it has now become the very bad custom for men to be more ashamed of good deeds than of bad ones*, Swt. A. S. Rdr. 109, 161. Mid đon gewunon đære heofogoston gewemmednesse *by the practices of the most grievous impurity*, Blickl. Homl. 75, 6. Heó gemonþ đæs wildan gewunan hire eldrana *she remembers the wild manner of her parents*, Bt. 25; Fox 88, 12: Bt. Met. Fox 13, 53; Met. 13, 27. Gewuna *ritus*, Ælfc. Gr. 38; Som. 41, 44. Æfter gewunan *after the custom*, Lk. 1, 9: 2, 27, 42: Blickl. Homl. 207, 18: Chr. 1070; Erl. 208, 2. Æfter ūron gewunon *nostro more*, Coll. Monast. Th. 33, 13. Of gewunan *from custom*, R. Ben. interl. 7. Ofer mīne gewunan *contrary to my custom*. Ælf. T. Lisle 43, 7. [*O. Sax.* gi-wono: *O. H. Ger.* gi-wona *consuetudo*.]

ge-wuna; *indecl. adj. Accustomed*:—Dydon eall swā hī ǽr gewuna wǽron *they did just as they were wont to before*, Chr. 1006; Erl. 140, 6. Suǽ đætte he gewuna wæs *sicut consueverat*, Mk. Skt. Lind. 10, 1. Gewuna wæs se groefa *consueverat præses*, Mt. Kmbl. Lind. 27, 15: Cd. 166; Th. 207, 27; Gen. 473. [*O. Sax.* gi-wono.] v. ge-wun, -wuna, *subst.*

ge-wunden *wound*, Exon. 111 b; Th. 427, 30; Rä. 41, 99; *pp. of* ge-windan.

ge-wundian; *p.* ode; *pp.* ed, od *To wound*:—And eft he hym sende ōđerne þeów and hī đone on heáfde gewundodon, Mk. 12, 4. Hī hine mid spere gewundedon *they wounded him with a spear*, Homl. Th. i. 216, 23. Se swīđe gewundod wæs *he was sore wounded*, Chr. 755; Erl. 50, 8. v. wundian.

ge-wundorlǽcan *to make wonderful*; mirificare, Ps. Spl. 16, 8.

ge-wunelīc, -wunolīc; *adj. Accustomed, wonted, usual, ordinary*; consuetus:—Þam folce wæs gewunelīc đæt . . . *it was usual with the people to* . . . , Jud. 7, 8. Đæm eádberhte wæs gewunelīc đæt he wunode on dȳgolre stōwe *that Eadberht was in the habit of dwelling in a secret place*, Shrn. 82, 9: 88, 1. Eall đæt wæs gewunelīc on đisan lande *all that was usual in this land*, Chr. 1100; Erl. 236, 13: Blickl. Homl. 85, 29. Gewunelīcre mildheortnyssa *solita clementia*, Hymn. Surt. 11, 25. On ūre wīsan us to spræcþ swā đæt we þurh đa gewunelīcan sprǽce đa þing oncnāwan đe us uncūþe wǽron *speaks to us in our manner so that through the speech to which we are accustomed we may understand those things that were unknown to us*, Boutr. Scrd. 21, 2. [*O. H. Ger.* gewonelich *consuetus*: *Ger.* ge-wöhnlich.]

ge-wunelīce; *adv. According to custom, ordinarily, commonly*; rite:—Swīđe gewunelīce *very commonly*, Ælf. T. Lisle 17. Gewunelīce *rite*, Ælfc. Gr. 38; Som. 41, 44. Đæt mynster đe gewunelīce is Magigeo nemned *monasterium quod Muigeo consuete vocatur*, Bd. 4, 4; S. 571, 18. Heó oft gewunolīce cwǽde *solita sit dicere*, 4, 19; S. 589, 24.

ge-wunian; *p.* ode; *pp.* od. I. *to dwell, inhabit*:—Ne māgon đǽr gewunian wīdfērende ne đǽr elþeódige eardes brūcaþ *there may not dwell wide wandering men, nor there do strangers enjoy a home*, Andr. Kmbl. 557; An. 279: Cd. 220; Th. 284, 24; Sat. 326. Nǽfre gewurþe đæt đǽr on gewunige āwiht lifigendes *non sit qui inhabitet*, Ps. Th. 108, 7. Đū in đære stōwe stille gewunadest *in that place didst thou dwell quietly*, Exon. 121 a; Th. 465, 7; Hö. 100. Ic mīnum gewunade frumstaþole fæst *I dwelt fast in my original station*, 122 b; Th. 471, 17; Rä. 61, 2. Siđđan gāst wīc gewunode in đæs weres breóstum *since the spirit inhabited a dwelling in the man's breast*, Elen. Kmbl. 2073; El. 1038. Him on đæt wēsten gewunode *dwelt in the wilderness*, Blickl. Homl. 199, 8. Him aspidas under welerum is gewunad fæste *venenum aspidum sub labiis eorum*, Ps. Th. 139, 3: Cd. 215; Th. 271, 9; Sat. 103. II. *to remain, stay, abide, continue*:—He leng on đam lande gewunian ne mihte *he could not stop any longer in the country*, Blickl. Homl. 113, 11: Ap. Th. 7, 4. Hȳ ealdrihta ǽlces mōsten wyrđe gewunigan *they should remain in the enjoyment of every ancient right*, Bt. Met. Fox 1, 73; Met. 1, 37: 2, 38; Met. 2, 19. Þurh đīnra dǽda spēd dagas hēr gewuniaþ *ordinatione tua perseverat dies*, Ps. Th. 118, 91. He on đæs lāreówes wære gewunade *he continued in the teacher's protection*, Exon. 37 b; Th. 123, 31; Gū. 331. III. *c. acc. To stop, live, associate with, continue in* or *with*:—Hie se leódfruma leng ne wolde gewunian *with them the prince no longer would abide*, Andr. Kmbl. 3320; An. 1636. Ne gewuna wyrsan [MS. wyrsa] *do not associate with an* *inferior*, Exon. 80 a; Th. 301, 22; Fã. 23. Ðæt hine on ylde eft gewunigen wilgesíðas *that with him in his age remain his loved comrades*, Beo. Th. 44; B. 22. Ðæt hý ðis lǽne líf long gewunien *that they continue long in this poor life*, Exon. 62 b; Th. 230, 33; Ph. 481. IV. *to be accustomed, wont*:—Se árwyrþa bisceop gewunade oft secgan *reverentissimus antistes solet referre*, Bd. 3, 13; S. 538, 7: 4, 23; S. 594, 38: 24; S. 596, 31: 5, 2; S. 614, 26. Ðá sǽde Sompeius ðæt Ioseph gewunode monige wundor to wyrcenne *Sompeius said that Joseph used to work many miracles*, Ors. 1, 5; Bos. 28, 12. Him gewunode ðæt he wæs geond ðæt wésten sundorgenga *was accustomed to go through the desert by itself*, Blickl. Homl. 199, 5. Swá swá he gewunode *sicut consueverat*, Mk. Bos. 10, 1. Ðes hálga wer wæs gewunod ðæt he wolde gán on niht to sǽ *this holy man was accustomed to go at night to the sea*, Homl. Th. ii. 138, 3. His mód to ðám woruldsǽlþum gewunod wæs *his mind was accustomed to worldly prosperity*, Bt. 1; Fox 4, 2. [*O. Sax.* gi-wonon: *O. H. Ger.* gi-wonan *manere, solere, consuescere*: *Ger.* ge-wohnen *to be accustomed.*]

ge-wunsum; *adj. Pleasant*:—Swíðe gewunsum hit biþ ðæt mon wíf hæbbe and bearn *it is very pleasant to have wife and children*, Bt. 31, 1; Fox 112, 8. [Cf. wynsum.]

ge-wurde *wast, hast been*, Andr. Kmbl. 1100; An. 550; *2nd sing. p. of* ge-weorþan: ge-wurde *happened*, Andr. Kmbl. 1115; An. 558; *p. subj. of* ge-weorþan: ge-wurdon *happened*, Ors. 5, 10; Bos. 108, 16; *p. pl. of* ge-weorþan.

ge-wurms; *adj. Full of matter, suppurated*; purulentus, Cot. 185, Lye. v. wyrmsig, wyrms.

ge-wurþan; he -wurþ; *subj. pres.* -wurþe, *pl.* -wurþon. I. *to be, become*; fiěri:—Ne mæg nán þinc gewurþan bútan godes willan *nothing can happen without God's will*, Th. Ap. 22, 7: 9, 5. Hit gewurþ him of mínum fæder, ðe on heofonum ys *fiet illis a patre meo, qui in cælis est*, Mt. Bos. 18, 19. Ic ðé háte ðæt ðú hí gehele and gehealde óþ-ðæt ic wite hwæt God wylle, hwæt be me gewurþe *quam te silentio tĕgĕre vŏlo, donec sciam quid de me fiĕri velit Deus*, Bd. 5, 19; S. 640, 38. Ðæt ðás stánas to hláfe gewurðon *ut lăpĭdes isti pānes fiant*, Mt. Bos. 4, 3: 5, 18. II. *v. impers. cum acc. To happen, come to pass, come together, agree*; evĕnīre, convĕnīre:—Ne meahte hie gewurþan *they might not agree*, Cd. 81; Th. 101, 32; Gen. 1691. v. ge-weorþan.

ge-wurþian; *p.* ode, ade; *pp.* od, ad *To distinguish, honour, adorn, celebrate, praise*; insignīre, honōrāre, ornāre, celebrāre:—Ðæt gé gewurþien wuldres Aldor *that ye honour the chief of glory*, Cd. 156; Th. 195, 1; Exod. 270. On Dryhtnes naman se dæg is gewurþod *the day is celebrated in the Lord's name*, Hy. 9, 30; Hy. Grn. ii. 292, 30: 7, 59; Hy. Grn. ii. 288, 59. Hæfde he gewurþodne werodes aldor *he had honoured the prince of the multitude*, Cd. 143; Th. 179, 19; Exod. 31. Wæs ðis eálond gewurþad mid ðám æðelestum ceastrum *insŭla ĕrat civitātĭbus nobilissĭmis insignīta*, Bd. 1, 1; S. 473, 26. v. ge-weorþian.

ge-wyder, es; *pl. nom. acc.* -wyderu, -wydera; *n. Weather, the temperature of the air*; tempestas, cæli tempĕries:—Bringþ sumor wearme gewyderu *summer brings warm weather*, Menol. Fox 177; Men. 90. Godes miht gefadaþ ealle gewydera *God's power ordereth all weathers*, Bd. de nat. rerum; Lchdm. iii. 278, 13, MS. R. Of untýdlícan gewyderum *from unseasonable weather*, Ors. 3, 3; Bos. 55, 20. v. ge-weder.

ge-wyht, es; *n. A weight*; pondus:—Gewyht *vel* pund *pondus*, Ælfc. Gl. 59; Som. 67, 113; Wrt. Voc. 38, 36. v. ge-wiht.

ge-wyld, -wild, es; *n. Power, dominion*:—Æfter ðam ðe Alexander hæfde ealle Inde him to gewyldon gedón *perdomita Alexander India*, Ors. 3, 9; Bos. 67, 21. [Cf. ge-weald *in pl.*]

ge-wyldan, -wildan; he -wyld, -wild, -wylt; *p.* -wylde; *pp.* -wyld; *v. a. To exercise power over, to tame, subdue, conquer, temper, seize, take*; dominari, domare, subigere, prehendere, capere:—Hí gewildon heora *dominati sunt eorum*, Ps. Spl. 105, 38. He gewild ðé *ipse dominabitur tibi*, Gen. 3, 16. Dauid gewylde ðone wildan beran, and his ceaflas totær *David subdued the wild bear, and tore apart his jaws*, Ælfc. T. Lisle 13, 26: 14, 1. Hine nán man gewyldan ne mihte *nemo poterat eum domare*, Mk. Bos. 5, 4: Homl. Th. ii. 192, 25. Gewylt ealle þeóda *will subdue all the nations*, Deut. 31, 3. Heora flǽsclícan gewilnunga gewyldaþ *they subdue their fleshly desires*, Homl. Th. i. 552, 24. Gewyld mid ðam ele ðe sý of lawer treówe gewrungan *temper with the oil which is wrung out of laurel*, Herb. 72, 2; Lchdm. i. 174, 11. Gewildaþ ða eorþan *subjicite terram*, Gen. 1, 28. Gewylde man hine *prehendat aliquis eum*, L. C. S. 25; Th. i. 390, 20: L. E. G. 4; Th. i. 168, 22. Seó burh wearþ gewyld *the city was taken*, Ælfc. T. Lisle 42, 20: Jud. 16, 7. Ðonne he hine hæfþ gewyldne *dum dominabitur pauperi*, Ps. Th. 9, 30. He hæfþ nú gewyld to mínum anwealde Scottas and Cumbras and eác swylce Bryttas *subditis nobis sceptris Scottorum, Cumbrorumque, ac Brittonum*, Th. Chart. 240, 3. Alexander hine [Poros] gewildne gedyde *Porus captus est*, Ors. 3, 9; Bos. 67, 35: Guthl. 12; Gdwin. 56, 23. Mid ele wel gewylde *well tempered with oil*, Herb. 12, 3; Lchdm. i. 104, 6. Ic me gedó allophilas ealle gewylde *mihi allophyli subditi sunt*, Ps. Th. 59, 7.

ge-wylde; *adj. Subject, under one's power* or *control, in one's possession*:—Him wæs gelíce gewylde his wynstre and his swíðre *utraque manu pro dextra utebatur*, Jud. 3, 15. Nis us nán lim swá gewylde to ǽlcum weorce swá us sind úre fingras *we have no limb so at our disposal for every work as are the fingers*, Homl. Th. ii. 204, 7. Seó gewylde gleáwnes *consummata prudentia*, Nar. 2, 1. He hit eft gedyde unc swá gewylde swá hit ðá wæs ðá we hit him óðfæstan *he should put it again as much under our control as it was when we entrusted it to him*, Th. Chart. 484, 30: Cod. Dipl. Kmbl. v. 120, 19. He ne funde nán máre landes ðe ðiderynn gewylde wǽre ðonne twá hída landes *he found no more land belonging thereto than two hides*, Th. Chart. 429, 3. Swá he swíðor syngaþ swá he deófle gewyldra biþ *the more he sins the more he will be in the devil's power*, Homl. Th. i. 268, 24. v. un-gewylde.

ge-wyldor, es; *m. A ruler, governor*; rector, gubernator, Som.

ge-wyle, es; *n. A will*; vŏluntas, L. C. S. 76; Th. i. 418, 11, MS. A. v. ge-wil.

ge-wyllan; *pp.* ed *To boil*:—Gewyll *boil*, Herb. 12, 1; Lchdm. i. 102, 21. Wel gewyllede *well boiled*, 12, 3; Lchdm. i. 104, 6, MS. O. v. a-wyllan.

ge-wylwed *wallowed, rolled*; volutatus, Dial. 2, 2.

ge-wynsumian *to exult*; exultare, Rtl. 1, 17: 13, 37.

ge-wynsumlíc; *adj. Pleasant*; acceptus, desiderativus, Hpt. Gl. 412, 446.

ge-wyrcan, -wyrcean; *p.* -worhte, ðú -worhtest; *pp.* -worht. I. *to work, make, build, form, dispose, do, perform, celebrate, commit*:—Úre Drihten wolde mannan gewyrcan *our Lord would make man*, Hexam. 10; Norm. 16, 16: 11; Norm. 18, 14. Gewyrcean mycelne tor *to build a great tower*, Blickl. Homl. 187, 12: Beo. Th. 139; B. 69. Ðú miht wundor gewyrcean *tu facis mirabilia*, Ps. Th. 76. 11. Gif ic godes meahte willan gewyrcean *if I could do God's will*, Cd. 39; Th. 51, 31; Gen. 835. Ne meahte ic æt hilde mid Hruntinge wiht gewyrcean *I could not perform aught with Hrunting in fight*, Beo. Th. 3324; B. 1660. Ða noldon fleám gewyrcan *they would not fly*, Byrht. Th. 134, 9; By. 81. Hí woldon hyra Eástron gewyrcan *they would celebrate Easter*, Lk. Bos. 22, 7. God wille ðisse worlde ende gewyricean *God will put an end to this world*, Blickl. Homl. 109, 33. He nest gewyrceþ *it makes a nest*, Exon. 62 b; Th. 230, 9; Ph. 469. Hie gewyrcaþ ǽnne líchoman *they form one body*, Bt. 34, 6; Fox 142, 16. Crist him to cwæþ 'Ic ðé geworhte' *Christ said to him 'I made thee,'* Blickl. Homl. 231, 28. Ðú eall geworhtest þing þearle gód *thou didst make every thing exceeding good*, Bt. Met. Fox 20, 88; Met. 20, 44. For úres lífes dǽdum ðe we geworhtan *for our life's deeds that we have done*, Blickl. Homl. 63, 32. Geworhton me him to wæfersýne *made me a spectacle for themselves*, Rood Kmbl. 61; Kr. 31. Mycel yfel gewrohtan *did much harm*, Chr. 993; Erl. 133, 3. Þeáh we æbylgþ wið hine oft gewyrcen *though we oft offend against him*, Elen. Kmbl. 1024; El. 513. Sió wund ðe him se eorþdraca ǽr geworhte *the wound that the dragon had before given him*, Beo. Th. 5418; B. 2712. Hie geweorc geworht hæfdon *they had made a fort*, Chr. 894; Erl. 90, 2. He hæfþ mon geworhtne *he hath made man*, Cd. 21; Th. 25, 18; Gen. 395. Synna ðe we wið Godes willan geworht habbaþ *the sins that we have done against God's will*, Blickl. Homl. 25, 15: 125, 4. Heora ciningas hæfdon sige geworht on heora feóndum *their kings had got victory over their foes*, 67, 9. Of glæse geworht *made of glass*, 127, 33. He nys swá wel wið me geworht swá he wæs *he is not so well disposed to me as he was*, Gen. 31, 5. II. *to get by working, gain, obtain, merit*:—Ic me mid Hruntinge dóm gewyrce *I with Hrunting will gain myself glory*, Beo. Th. 2986; B. 1491. Lof se gewyrceþ hafaþ heáhfæstne dóm *he gains praise, hath undying glory*, Exon. 97 a; Th. 327, 6; Víd. 142. Se ðe gewyrceþ ðæt him wuldorcyning milde geweorþeþ *he who obtains that the king of glory becomes mild to him*, 63 b; Th. 234, 8; Ph. 536. Hú geworhte ic ðæt *how did I merit this?* Cd. 127; Th. 162, 3; Gen. 2675. III. *with gen.* [cf. wyrcan *with gen.*]:—For hwam nele mon him georne gewyrcan dryhtscipes *why will not man earnestly gain himself worship*, Salm. Kmbl. 774; Sal. 386.

ge-wyrd, e; *f. Event, fate, destiny, condition*:—Ðeós æþele gewyrd *this noble event* [*the crucifixion*], Elen. Kmbl. 1291; El. 647. Sume cwǽdon ðæt se steorra his gewyrd wǽre. Gewíte ðis gedwyld fram geleáffullum heortum ðæt ǽnig gewyrd sý búton se ælmihtiga scyppend *some said that the star was his destiny. Let this error depart from believing hearts, that there is any destiny except the Almighty Creator*, Homl. Th. i. 110, 11. Fore giwyrd líchomes *pro conditione carnis*, Rtl. 66, 37. Gewyrd *vel* gecwide *conditio*, Ælfc. Gl. 13; Som. 57, 117; Wrt. Voc. 20, 54. Hit is of ðæra bisceopa gehlote and of heora ágenre gewyrde ðæt ðæt hý secgaþ *in potestate esse antistitis quid velit fingere*, Ors. 3, 9; Bos. 65, 34. Gewyrd *fatum, parca, fortuna*, Hpt. Gl. 529, 467. Binnan ðam wendun gewyrda and gewát Eádrǽd cyng *meanwhile matters changed and king Eadred died*, Th. Chart. 207, 22. [Cf. wyrd, ge-weorþan; *and see* ge-wyrde.]

ge-wyrdan, -werdan; *p.* de; *pp.* ed; *v. trans. To hurt, injure*; lædere, nocere:—Gif hwá on ceáse wíf gewerde [gewyrde, MS. G.] *if any one in strife hurt a woman*, L. Alf. 18; Th. i. 48, 17. Gif hwá gewerde [gewyrde, MS. G.] óðres monnes wíngeard *if any one injure another* *man's vineyard*, 26: Th. i. 50, 24. Ne mæg đǣr rēn ne snāw gewyrdan *neither rain nor snow can there injure*, Exon. 56 a; Th. 199, 1; Ph. 19. Hæfde hī hungor and þurst heard gewyrded *esurientes et sitientes*, Ps. Th. 106, 4.

ge-wyrde, -wyrd [?], es; *n. Speech, conversation, collection of words, sentence, rule* [?]:—Đæt ic mǣge sum rust on weg adrīfan of mīnre tungan đæt ic mǣge becuman to brǣddran gewyrde *that I may clear some rust away from my tongue, so that I may attain to more copious speech*, Shrn. 35, 22. Wīsra gewyrdum *by the rules of wise men*, Menol. Fox 132; Men. 66. Gewyrd *verbositas*, Hpt. Gl. 439. [*Goth.* ga-waurdi: *O. H. Ger.* ga-wurti *comma, brevis dictio*, Grff. i. 1023.] Cf. andwyrde; *and see* ge-wyrd.

ge-wyrdelic; *adj. Historical, fortuitous*:—On gewyrdelīcum racum *in historical narratives*, Homl. Th. i. 58, 9. Gewyrdelīc *historialis*, Hpt. Gl. 506; *fortuitus*, 410, 495. [Cf. *Ger.* geschichtlich *and* geschehen.]

ge-wyrdelīce; *adv. Accurately*, Swt. A. S. Rdr. 69, 414.

ge-wyrdlian; *p.* ede; *pp.* ed *To hurt, injure*; lædere, nocere, Bd. 3, 16; S. 543, 11, col. 2. v. wyrdan.

ge-wyrht, es; *n. Work, deed, merit, desert*:—Deág đīn gewyrhtu *if thy deeds are good*, Exon. 80 a; Th. 300, 11: Fä. 4. Đa heálīcan gewyrhto Sancte Iohannes *the exalted deeds of St. John*, Blickl. Homl. 167, 5. Rǣcaþ ǣghwilcum men āgen gewyrhta *give to every man his deserts*, Hy. Grn. 7, 16. Be heora gewyrhtum *secundum opera eorum* Ps. Th. 27, 5: 102, 10. Be gewirhton we þoliaþ đās þing *deservedly do we suffer these things*, Gen. 42, 21. Ǣlcum men wrecan be his gewyrhtum *to punish every man according to his deeds*, Bt. 35, 6; Fox 168, 26. Būton gewyrhtum *undeservedly*, 22, 1; Fox 76, 15: 38, 3; Fox 202, 3. Wæs him forgolden æfter his āgenum gewyrhtum *he was requited according to his own deeds*, Blickl. Homl. 45, 2. For heora gewyrhtum *for their deeds*, 125, 2: Swt. A. S. Rdr. 108, 112. Mid gewyrhtum *deservedly*, Blickl. Homl. 89, 7. Seóþ đonne on ēce gewyrht *they shall look then on an everlasting state* [*one whose character is determined by their deeds*], Exon. 116 b; Th. 448, 29; Dōm. 61. [*O. Sax.* gi-wurhti *deed*: *O. H. Ger.* ka-wuruht, Grff. i. 975.]

ge-wyrhta, an; *m. A worker, doer, fellow-worker, accomplice*:—Ǣlc đe gewita odđe gewyrhta sī *every one who is cognisant or co-operating*, L. O. D. 6; Th. i. 354, 28. Þeófa gewita and geweorhta *an accessory and accomplice of thieves*, L. Eth. 9, 27; Th. i. 346, 9: L. O. 3; Th. i. 180, 1. Nū gē māgon oncȳđdǣda wrecan on gewyrhtum *now may ye wreak on the doers* [*their*] *grievous deeds*, Andr. Kmbl. 2361; An. 1182. [Cf. *Goth.* ga-waurstwa *a fellow-worker*.]

ge-wyrman *to warm*:—To gewyrmenne, Lchdm. i. 116, 1.

ge-wyrp, es; *n. A heap thrown up* [?]:—Andlang gewyrpes, Cod. Dipl. Kmbl. v. 78, 29. v. ge-weorp, sand-gewurp.

ge-wyrpan; *p.* -wyrpte; *pp.* -wyrped *To recover*; verti, recuperare:—Gif se seóca man eft gewurpþ *if the sick man recovers*, L. Ælfc. P. 47: Th. ii. 384, 29. Godwine gesīclode and eft gewyrpte *Godwin fell sick and got better again*, Chr. 1052; Erl. 186, 13. He eft gewyrpte, and đam orþe onfēng *he recovered again and got his breath*, Guthl. 20; Gdwin. 86, 17. He hyne gewyrpte, đeáh đe him wund hrine *he recovered, though the wound had touched him*, Beo. Th. 5944; B. 2976. He đā befrān on hwilcere tīde he gewyrpte *he then enquired at what hour he recovered*, Homl. Th. i. 128, 12. Sōna đæt him bet wæs, and gewyrpte fram đære untrumnysse *melius habere cœpit, et convalescens ab infirmitate*, Bd. 3, 13; S. 539, 7.

ge-wyrsmed, -wyrmsed; *part. p. Full of matter, suppurated*:—Gewyrsmed, *saporatus*, Wrt. Voc. 289, 20. v. wyrmsan, ge-wurms.

ge-wyrþan; *p.* ede; *pp.* ed *To estimate, value*:—Ōđre ungesawene þing mon mōt mid āþe gewyrþan and syđđan be đam gyldan *other unseen things may be estimated on oath, and then paid for accordingly*, L. O. D. 7; Th. i. 356, 7. Swā hit man gewyrþe *as it may be valued*, L. A. G. 3; Th. i. 154, 11.

ge-wyrþan; he -wyrþeþ, -wyrþ *To be, become, happen*; fĭeri:—Hū mihte đæt gewyrþan *how might that happen?* Andr. Kmbl. 1145; An. 573. Cūþ đæt gewyrþeþ *it shall be known*, Elen. Kmbl. 2381; El. 1192: 2548; El. 1275. Hū gewyrþ đis *quomŏdo fiet istud?* Lk. Bos. 1, 34. v. ge-weorþan.

ge-wyrđe, es; *n. Amount, content*:—Swā micel đæt sȳ iii ægscylla gewyrđe *as much as three eggshells full*, Lchdm. iii. 14, 23. Ānes æges gewyrđe greátes sealtes *of rock salt the content of one egg*, 40, 10. [Cf. *Goth.* andwairþi *price, value*.]

ge-wyrþian; *p.* ode; *pp.* od *To distinguish, honour, dignify*; insignīre, hŏnōrāre:—Đone sōþfæst cyning mid his sylfes miht gewyrþode *whom the just king honoured with his own power*, Cd. 143; Th. 178, 11; Exod. 10. Sigore gewyrþod *honoured with victory*, Andr. Kmbl. 232; An. 116. Đa đe beóþ mid cræftum gewyrþode *who are dignified with virtues*, Bt. 30, 1; Fox 108, 25. v. ge-weorþian.

ge-wyrtian; *p.* ode; *pp.* od *To season with herbs, to spice, perfume*:—Gewyrtad mid hyra weldǣdum *perfumed with their good deeds*, Exon. 63 b: Th. 234, 20; Ph. 543. Gewyrtod wīn [cf. *O. H. Ger.* der gewurzeto win] *factitium vinum*, Cot. 268, Lye. Sele him etan gewyrtodne hen fugel *give him to eat a fowl dressed with herbs*, L. M 3, 12; Lchdm. ii. 314, 15.

ge-wyrtrumian *to root up, eradicate*; eradicare, Rtl. 65, 25.

ge-wyrtūn, es; *m. A garden*:—Đǣr wæs fæger gewyrtūn *ubi erat hortus*, Jn. Skt. Lind. 18, 1.

ge-wȳscan; *p.* te; *pp.* ed. I. *to wish, desire*; optare, desiderare:—Ic wolde gewȳscan đæt hī næfdon đa heardsǣlþa đæt hī mihton yfel dōn *I would wish that they had not the unhappiness of being able to do evil*, Bt. 38, 2; Fox 198, 3. II. *to adopt*:—Him to gāstlīcum bearnum gewīscede *adopted as his spiritual children*, Homl. Th. i. 520, 31.

ge-wȳscednys, se; *f. Adoption*; adoptio, R. Ben. interl. 2, Lye.

ge-wȳscendlīc; *adj. Optative*:—Gewīscendlīc gemet *modus optativus*, Ælfc. Gr. 21; Som. 23, 28. Gewīscendlīce *optativa*, 38; Som. 40, 25.

ge-wȳscendlīce; *adv. By adoption*:—God Fæder Ælmihtig hæfþ ǣnne Sunu gecyndelīce and menige gewīscendlīce *God, the Father Almighty has one Son naturally and many by adoption*, Homl. Th. i. 258, 26.

ge-wȳscing, e; *f. Adoption*, R. Ben. 2, Lye.

ge-ȳcan, -ȳcean; *p.* te *To increase, add, eke*:—Se đe đisne freóls geȳcean wille geȳce God his gesynta *qui hanc libertatis dapsilitatem augere voluerit, augeat dominus ejus prosperitatem*, Cod. Dipl. Kmbl. iii. 138, 14. Swā swā sorge and ymbhogan geȳceþ monnes mōd, swā geȳcþ se cræft his āre *as sorrow and cares increase a man's mind so a craft increaseth his honour*, Prov. Kmbl. 59. Đā geȳhte he sum bigspell *he added a parable*, Lk. Skt. 19, 11, MS. A. v. ge-īcan.

ge-yde *subdued, conquered*, Chr. 617; Erl. 23, 16. v. ge-gān.

ge-yflian; *p.* ode, ede; *pp.* od, ed. I. *to injure*:—Gif hine mon geyflige *if one injure him*, L. Alf. pol. 2; Th. i. 62, 3. Gif se cristena mann đē geyfelode *if the christian man hath done thee wrong*, Homl. Th. i. 54, 25. Næs heora neáta nān geyfelad *jumenta eorum non sunt minorata*, Ps. Th. 106, 37. Mid fræcedo geyfled *contumelia adfectos*, Mt. Kmbl. Lind. 22, 6. II. *to become ill*:—Hine geyflade *he fell sick*, Th. Chart. 272, 29. Him geyfelade and đæt him stranglīce eglade *he fell sick and it afflicted him severely*, Chr. 1086; Erl. 220, 33. Lazarus wæs geyfled *Lazarus infirmabatur*, Jn. Skt. 11, 2.

ge-ylca; *prn. The same*:—Eall đæ geylcan gerihta *all the same rights*, Th. Chart. 433, 36.

ge-ymnyttan. v. ge-emnettan.

ge-yppan; *p.* -ypte; *pp.* -ypped, -yped, -ypt *To open, reveal, declare, manifest, disclose*:—Ic geyppe *promo*, Ælfc. Gr. 28, 4; Som. 31, 12. Wit wēndon đæt đæt sand uncre swađe geypte *we expected that the sand would discover our track*, Shrn. 42, 19. Se geypte hǣđenum dēman đæt đæs tiburtius wæs cristen *he disclosed to the heathen judge that this Tiburtius was a christian*, 116, 23. Him wæs on swefne geyped *it was revealed to him in a dream*, 112, 6. Hit þurh ǣnne þeówne mann geypped wearþ *it was discovered by a slave*, Ors. 3, 6; Bos. 58, 20: Nicod. 17; Thw. 8, 25. Gipped sē *manifestetur*, Rtl. 13, 3: 102, 43. Biþ geypped *sciatur*, Lk. Skt. Lind. 12, 2: Andr. Kmbl. 2447; An. 1225: Menol. Fox 311; Men. 159. Þurh hine wurdon manege geypte *through him were many discovered*, Chr. 1095; Erl. 232, 20.

ge-yrfian; *p.* ode; *pp.* od *To stock with cattle*:—Swā geirfad swā hit nū stent *so stocked as it now stands*, Th. Chart. 158, 10.

ge-yrfweardian *to inherit*, Ps. Lamb. 24, 14. v. yrfweardian.

ge-yrgan, -irgan; *p.* de; *pp.* ed *To make cowardly, terrify*:—Ealle synd geyrgede đe eardiaþ on đisum lande *all the inhabitants of the land do faint because of us*, Jos. 2, 24: 8, 6: Swt. A. S. Rdr. 108, 123. v. earg.

ge-yrman; *p.* de; *pp.* ed *To afflict, make miserable*:—Đū mīne cūþe geyrmdest *thou didst afflict mine acquaintance*, Ps. Th. 87, 18.

ge-yrnan; *p.* -arn, -orn, *pl.* -urnon; *pp.* -urnen *To run, arise*; exoriri, surgere:—Đā georn đǣr sōna upp genihtsumlīc yrnþ and wæstm *then an abundant crop and grain* [*fruit*] *soon rose* [*ran*] *up there*, Bd. 4, 28; S. 605, 40.

ge-yrsian; *p.* ode; *pp.* od. I. *to anger, make angry*:—Hȳ geyrsedon *irritaverunt*, Ps. Lamb. 105, 7. Irtacus đā wearþ swīđe geyrsod *Irtacus then became very angry*, Homl. Th. ii. 476, 34. II. *to be angry*:—He nele swā micclum swā we geearniaþ us geyrsian *he will not be angry with us so much as we deserve*, 126, 6. v. yrsian.

ge-ȳwan, -eáwan, -eówan, -iéwan; ic -ȳwe; đū -ȳwest, -ȳwst; he -ȳweþ, -ȳwþ, *pl.* -ȳwaþ; *p.* de; *pp.* ed; *v. trans. To shew, manifest, reveal*; ostendĕre, præbēre, manifestāre, monstrāre:—Þeóden engla his þegnum seolfne geȳwde *the king of angels revealed himself to his disciples*, Elen. Kmbl. 974; El. 488. Me đīn dōhtor hafaþ geȳwed orwyrđu *thy daughter has shewn me indignity*, Exon. 66 b; Th. 246, 29; Jul. 69: Elen. Kmbl. 1570; El. 787. DER. ȳwan.

gi-; for most words beginning with this prefix see ge-.

giccan *to itch*; prurire:—Wiđ giccendre wombe *for an itching stomach* [Cockayne prefers to translate the verb *to hiccup*, v. his Glossary], Lchdm. iii. 50, 13. Wiđ ōđrum giccendum blece *for other itching blotch*, 70, 27. [*Prompt. Parv.* ȝichin *prurire*: *A. R.* ȝicchen: *Chauc.* icche: *O. H. Ger.* iuchian *prurire, scalpere*: *Ger.* jucken *to itch*.]

giccig; *adj. Putrid*; putridus, purulentus, Hpt. Gl. 453.

GICEL, es; *m. An icicle*:—Īses gicel *stiria, stillicidia*, Ælfc. Gl. 16;

Som. 58, 68; Wrt. Voc. 21, 55. [*Icel.* jökull.] DER. Cyle-, hilde-, hrīm-, īs-gicel.

gicelig; *adj. Icy;* glacialis, Hpt. Gl. 454, 465.

gicel-stān, es; *m. A piece of ice, hailstone:*—He sent gicelstān *mittit chrystallum,* Blickl. Gl.

gicenes, se; *f. An itch,* or *burning in the skin;* prurigo, Cot. 156.

gicþa, gyhþa, an; *m. Itch, itching:*—Gicþa *pruritus,* Ælfc. Gl. 11; Som. 57, 62: Wrt. Voc. 20, 6: Past. 11; Swt. 70, 19; Cot. MS. Wiđ gicþan *against itch,* Herb. 21, 3; Lchdm. i. 116, 23: L. M. 2, 41; Lchdm. ii. 252, 19, 24: 2, 65; Lchdm. ii. 296, 6. [*Prompt. Parv.* ȝikthe *prurigo: O. H. Ger.* iuchido *prurigo, scabies.*] v. gihþa.

gicþa *hiccup,* Lchdm. ii. 4, 27.

gid, gidd, gied, giedd, gyd, gydd, ged, es; *n.* I. *a song, lay, poem;* cantus, cantilena, carmen, poema:—Gid oft wrecen *a song oft sung* [*recited*], Beo. Th. 2135; B. 1065. Gidda gemyndig *mindful of songs,* Beo. Th. 1741; B. 868. Đǣr wæs gidd and gleó *there was song and glee,* Beo. Th. 4216; B. 2105. Gliówordum gōl gyd æt spelle *sung in metre a lay in his discourse,* Bt. Met. Fox 7, 4; Met. 7, 2. Gerīseþ gleōmen gied *a song is proper for a gleeman,* Exon. 91 b; Th. 344, 1; Gn. Ex. 167. Cūþ gyddum *known in lays* [*songs*], Beo. Th. 304; B. 151. Se wītga song and đæt gyd awræc *the prophet sang and recited the poem,* Exon. 84 a; Th. 316, 20; Mōd. 51. Đæt ic đa ged ne mæg gefēgean *that I cannot compose the poems* [*songs*], Bt. Met. Fox 2, 10; Met. 2, 5. II. as Old English or Saxon proverbs, riddles, and particular speeches were generally metrical, and their historians were bards, hence, *A speech, tale, sermon, proverb, riddle;* sermo, dictum, loquela, proverbium, ænigma:—Gyd æfter wræc *the speech afterwards recited,* Beo. Th. 4315; B. 2154. Mæg ic be me sylfum sōþ gied wrecan *of myself I can relate a true tale,* Exon. 81 b; Th. 306, 2; Seef. 1. On gewunon gyddes gehwyrfed *in consuetudinem proverbii versum,* Bd. 3, 12; S. 537, 27. On gydde *into a proverb,* 3, 12; 537, 30. Nū me đisses gieddes onsware ȳwe *now shew me an answer of this riddle,* Exon. 114 a; Th. 437, 28; Rä. 56, 14. v. Grmm. D. M. 853.

giddian, gieddian, gyddian, giddigan; *p.* ode; *pp.* od *To sing, recite, speak:*—Ongan he giddian *he began to sing,* Bt. 31, 2; Fox 112, 24. Giddigan, 16, 4; Fox 56. 36: 21; Fox 72, 27. Se hiora cyning ongan đā singan and giddian *Tyrtæi ducis composito carmine et pro concione recitato,* Ors. 1, 14; Bos. 37, 29. Ongan đā gyddigan þurh gylp micel *began then to speak through great pride,* Cd. 205; Th. 253, 21; Dan. 599. Se wīsdōm geoddode đus *wisdom recited this song,* Bt. 12; Fox 36, 6: Bt. Met. Fox 1, 168; Met. 1, 84. Wīga gyddode Beówulf mađelode *the warrior spake, Beowulf said,* Beo. Th. 1264: B. 630; Cd. 97; Th. 127, 6; Gen. 2106. Waldere gyddode wordum, Wald. 83; Vald. 2, 13. Đus frōd guma in fyrndagum gieddade *thus sang a wise man in days of old,* Exon. 64 a; Th. 236, 8; Ph. 571. Gyddedon hæleþ in healle hwæt seó hand write *heroes in hall discussed what did the hand write,* Cd. 210; Th. 261, 18; Dan. 728.

gidding, giedding, e; *f. Song, saying, discourse:*—Iobes gieddinga *Job's songs,* Exon. 63 b; Th. 234, 32; Ph. 549. Mid gieddingum *with songs,* 92 b; Th. 347, 13; Sch. 12. To đyssere gereccednysse genam se apostol menigfealde gyddunga and gewitnyssa heáhfædera and wītegena *for this narrative the apostle took manifold sayings and testimonies of patriarchs and prophets,* Homl. Th. ii. 420, 11. Giddung *divinatio, cantus,* Hpt. Gl. 466. [*Chauc.* ȝedding.] v. gid.

gidig; *adj.* GIDDY; vertiginosus, Som.

gied, giedd, es; *n. A song, lay, riddle,* Exon. 91 b; Th. 344, 1: 114 a; Th. 437, 28; Rä. 56, 14: 18 a; Th. 45, 2; Cri. 713. v. gid.

giefa *a giver.* v. gifa.

giefan; *p.* geaf, *pl.* geáfon; *pp.* gifen *To give;* dare:—Ic eów meaht giefe *I will give you might,* Exon. 14 b; Th. 30, 11; Cri. 478. He us ǣt giefeþ *he giveth us food,* 16 b; Th. 38, 9; Cri. 604: 87 a; Th. 327, 23; Vy. 8. Đū us freódōm gief *do thou give us freedom,* Hy. 5, 10; Hy. Grn. ii. 286, 10. v. gifan.

giefernes, -ness, e; *f. Gluttony;* gula:—Gemidliaþ hiera giefernesse [gīfernesse, MS. Cot.] *refrenant gulam,* Past. 46, 2; Swt. 345, 23; Hat. MS. 66 a, 9. v. gīfernes.

gief-stōl, es; *m. A gift-seat, throne of grace;* donorum thronus, gratiæ thronus:—Wile nū gesēcan sāwla Nergend gǣsta giefstōl *now will the Saviour of souls seek the spirits' throne of grace,* Exon. 16 a; Th. 36, 6; Cri. 572: 77 a; Th. 289, 7; Wand. 44. v. gif-stōl.

giefu, e; *gen. pl.* -end; *f. A gift, grace, favour;* donum, munus, gratia:—To giefe *as a gift,* or *freely, gratuitously,* Exon. 65 b; Th. 241, 19; Ph. 658: 96 b; Th. 359, 32; Pa. 71. God-bearn on grundum his giefe bryttaþ *the divine Child on earth his grace dispenseth,* 17 b; Th. 43, 2; Cri. 682. Us giefe sealde uppe mid englum *gave us favour above with angels,* 17 b; Th. 41, 24; Cri. 660: 32 a; Th. 101, 24; Cri. 1663. v. gifu.

gield, es; *n. A payment of money, recompense, substitute, offering, worship, service, a heathen deity:*—Sāwlum to gielde *for a recompense to their souls,* Exon. 23 b; Th. 66, 30; Cri. 1079. Wæs Abeles gield *was Abel's substitute,* Cd. 55; Th. 67, 32; Gen. 1109: 5; Th. 7, 5; Gen. 101: 47; Th. 60, 5; Gen. 977: Exon. 67 b; Th. 251, 17; Jul. 146: 58 a; Th. 253, 3; Jul. 174. v. gild.

gieldan, ic gielde, đū gieltst, gielst, he gieldeþ, gielt, *pl.* gieldaþ; *p.* geald, *pl.* guldon; *pp.* golden *To yield, pay, render, repay, requite:*—Sceoldon gombon gieldan *they must pay homage,* Cd. 93; Th. 119, 11; Gen. 1978. Werum gieldeþ gaful *pays tribute to men,* Exon. 108 b; Th. 415, 15; Rä. 33, 11: 34 a; Th. 109, 24; Gū. 95: 39 a; Th. 130, 9; Gū. 435. He đē mid wīte gieldeþ *he will requite thee with punishment,* 80 a; Th. 301, 15; Fä. 19: Bt. 41, 3; Fox 248, 22. v. gildan.

gieldra *older,* Th. Diplm. A. D. 901–909; 162, 18. v. ieldra.

giellan *to yell,* Exon. 106 b; Th. 406, 19; Rä. 25, 3: 82 a; Th. 309, 25; Seef. 62. v. gellan.

gielp. v. gilp.

gielpan *to glory, boast, vaunt;* gloriāri, jactāre:—Đæt hȳ gielpan ne þorftan dǣdum *that they should not boast of deeds,* Exon. 36 a; Th. 116, 21; Gū. 210: 114 b; Th. 440, 4; Rä. 59, 12. v. gilpan.

giéman. v. gȳman.

gién, giéna *again, still, yet.* v. gēn. gēna.

giéng *went,* Cd. 29; Th. 39, 15; Gen. 626; *p. of* gangan.

gierian; *p.* ede; *pp.* ed *To clothe, deck, adorn;* induĕre, vestīre, ornāre:—Hæleþ gierede mec mid golde *a man adorned me with gold,* Exon. 107 a; Th. 408, 16; Rä. 27, 13. v. gearwian, gyrian.

gierstandæg *yesterday.* v. gyrstandæg.

gierwan; *p.* ede; *pp.* ed *To make ready, prepare, put on, clothe, adorn;* părāre, induĕre, vestīre:—Ongunnon him on uhtan æđelcunde mægþ gierwan to geonge *the noble women resolved to prepare for journey at dawn,* Exon. 119 b; Th. 459, 19; Hö. 2. Bearn fæder and mōdor gierwaþ *father and mother adorn the child,* Exon. 87 a; Th. 327, 23; Vy. 8. v. gearwian.

giest, es; *m. A guest:*—Mid giestum *with the guests,* Cd. 112; Th. 148, 11; Gen. 2455: 112; Th. 147, 15; Gen. 2440: Exon. 94 a; Th. 353, 11; Reim. 11. DER. gryre-giest, hilde-, ryne-, stæle-. v. gæst.

giest-līđnys, -nyss, e; *f. Hospitality, entertainment;* hospĭtālĭtas:—Him se æđela geaf giestlīđnysse *the noble* [*man*] *gave them entertainment,* Cd. 112; Th. 147, 28; Gen. 2446. v. gæst-līđnes.

giestron *yesterday;* hesterus:—Ic giestron wæs acenned *I was yesterday brought forth,* Exon. 111 a; Th. 426, 24; Rä. 41, 44. v. geostra.

giet, gieta *yet.* v. git, gita.

gietan. v. gitan.

gif, e; *f: nom. acc.* gif [*as* tīd, dǣd] *A gift, grace;* donum, gratia:—Hū he his gif cȳđde geond woruld *how he shewed his grace throughout the world,* Andr. Kmbl. 1150; An. 575.

gif, gief, gyf, gib; *conj. with indic. or subj. If, though, whether:*—For đȳ me þyncþ betre gif iów swǣ þyncþ *therefore it seems to me better, if it seems so to you,* Past. pref; Swt. 7, 6. Gif hie brecaþ his gebodscipe *if they break his commandment,* Cd. 22; Th. 28, 3; Gen. 434. Gif ic ǣnegum þegne þeóden-mādmas forgeáfe *if to any follower I gave princely treasures,* 22; Th. 26, 19; Gen. 409. Gif đū him wuht hearmes gesprǣce he forgifþ hit đeáh *though thou didst speak to him aught of harm yet will he forgive it,* 30; Th. 41, 23; Gen. 661. Frægn gif him wǣre niht getǣse *asked whether the night had been pleasant to him,* Beo. Th. 2643; B. 1319. Đū wāst gif hit is swā we secgan hȳrdon *thou knowest if it is as we heard say,* 550; B. 272. [*Laym.* ȝif: *Orm.* ȝiff: *Piers P. Chauc.* ȝif, if: *O. Frs.* jef.]

gifa, gyfa, giefa, geofa, an; *m. A giver, bestower;* dator, largitor:—Me þincþ betere đæt ic forlēte đa gyfe and folgyge đam gyfan *it seems to me better to leave the gift and follow the giver,* Shrn. 176, 19. Used in the following compounds:—ār-gifa, æt-, beáh-, beág-, blǣd-, eád-, feorh-, gold-, hyht-, lāc-, māđđum-, rǣd-, sinc-, symbel-, wil-, will-. [*Laym.* rædȝive *counsellor: O. Sax.* mēđom-gibo: *O. H. Ger.* gebo *dator.*]

gifan, gyfan, giefan, geofan, giofan; ic gife; đū gifest, gifst; he gifeþ, gifþ, *pl.* gifaþ; *p.* geaf, gæf, gaf, gef, đū geáfe, gēfe, *pl.* geāfon, gēfon; *pp.* gifen, giefen, gyfen *To give;* dare, impertire:—Hwā meahte me swelc gewit gifan *who could give to me such perception?* Cd. 32; Th. 42, 10; Gen. 672. Ic gife *impertior,* Ælfc. Gr. 37; Som. 39, 13. Gife ic hit đē *I will give it thee,* Cd. 32; Th. 42, 26; Gen. 679. Us drincan gifest *potum dabis nobis,* Ps. Th. 79, 5. Hwæt gifst đū me *quid dabis mihi,* Gen. 15, 2. God gifeþ gleáw word godspellendum *dominus dabit verbum evangelizantibus,* Ps. Th. 67, 12: Hy. 7, 102; Hy. Grn. ii. 289, 102: Ælfc. Gr. 7; Som. 6, 22: Ps. Th. 68, 27. He nallas beágas geaf *he gave no rings,* Beo. Th. 3443; B. 1719. Gæf wæstm his *dedit fructum suum,* Ps. Spl. T. 66, 5. Him scippend geaf [gaf, MS. A.] wuldorlīcne wlite *the Creator gave it wondrous beauty,* Salm. Kmbl. 114; Sal. 56. Gē him hleoþ gēfon *ye gave them shelter,* Exon. 27 b; Th. 83, 11; Cri. 1354 Weoruda waldend đē wist gife heofonlīcne hlāf *the Lord of hosts grant to thee food, heavenly bread,* Andr. Kmbl. 776; An. 388. On Moyses hand wearþ wīg gifen *into Moses' hand martial force was given,* Cd. 173; Th. 216, 11; Dan. 5. Đǣr wurdon đa āđas geswōrene his dōhter đam Cāsere to gifene *oaths were then sworn there to give* [*in marriage*] *his daughter to the emperor,* Chr. 1109; Erl. 242, 23. [*Laym.*

Orm. Chauc. Piers P. ȝiven: *O. Sax.* geƀan: *Goth.* giban: *Icel.* gefa: *O. Frs.* jeva: *O. H. Ger.* geban.] DER. a-, æt-, ed-, for-, of-gifan.

gifen *the sea*, Exon. 101 a; Th. 381, 29; Rä. 3, 3. v. geofon.

gifende *giving, giving in marriage*, Cot. 216. v. gifan, gift.

gîfer, es; *m. A glutton*:—Gîfer hâtte se wyrm *the worm's name is glutton*, Exon. 99 b; Th. 373, 31; Seel. 118. v. gîfre.

gîferlîce; *adj. Greedily, eagerly*; avide:—Ongan gîferlîce ðæt gærs etan *virecta herbarum avidius carpere cœpit*, Bd. 3. 9; S. 533, 41. Gîferlîce *pertinaciter*, Hpt. Gl. 424. [Cf. *Icel.* gîfrliga *savagely: Mod. Icel. exorbitantly.*]

gîfer-nes, -ness, e; *f. Greediness, avarice, voracity, gluttony*; aviditas, gula:—Gîfernys biþ ðæt se man ǽr tîman hine gereordige oððe æt his mǽle to micel þicge mid oferflôwendnysse ǽtes oððe wǽtes *greediness is a man's eating before the time, or taking too much at his meal with superfluity of meat or drink*, Homl. Th. ii. 218, 29. Him wæs metes micel lust ac ðeáh mid nânum ǽtum his gŷfernysse gefyllan ne mihte *he had great craving for food but yet could he not with any viands satisfy his voracity*, i. 86, 6: 168, 12. Ða niétenu for ðære gewilnunge hiera gîfernesse simle lôcigeaþ to ðære eorþan *beasts because of their greedy desires ever look to the earth*, Past. 21; Swt. 154, 20; Cot. MS. Ðæt rîce ðæt ða ǽrestan men forworhtan þurh heora gîfernesse *the kingdom that the first persons forfeited through their greediness*, Blickl. Homl. 25, 1: Num. 11, 4: Bt. 35, 6; Fox 170, 2. [*Orm.* gifernesse: *Laym.* ȝivernesse.]

gifeðe, es; *n. What is granted by fate, lot, fortune, fate*:—Wæs ðæt gifeðe to swîð ðe ðone ðyder ontyhte *too strong was the fate that impelled him thither*, Beo. Th. 6163; B. 3085. On gifeðe *by chance*, Andr. Kmbl. 977; An. 489. v. Grmm. And. u. El. p. 108. [Cf. *Laym.* swulc ȝifueðe, 2nd MS. so moche god, v. 8118: *Icel.* gipta *good luck.*] v. next word.

gifeðe, gyfeðe; *adj. Given, granted* [*by fate*]; datus, concessus:—Gief ðæt biþ him gifeðe *if that be granted him*, Cod. Dipl. Kmbl. iii. 50, 2: Th. Chart. 470, 1: 472, 3. Nô gifeðe wearþ Abrahame ðæt him yrfeweard wlitebeorht ides on worulde brohte *it was not granted to Abraham that the beautiful woman brought him an heir into the world*, Cd. 83; Th. 103, 31; Gen. 1726: 101; Th. 134, 13; Gen. 2224: Beo. Th. 5454; B. 2730. Gyfeðe, 1115; B. 555. Him ðæt gifeðe ne wæs *it was not granted him*, 3658; B. 2682. Hwæt him gûðweorca gifeðe wurde *what work of war should be assigned him*, Andr. Kmbl. 2134; An. 1068: Beo. Th. 4976; B. 2491: 604; B. 299. v. Grmm. D. M. 843. [*Laym.* ȝifveðe: *O. Sax.* giƀiðig: *O. H. Ger.* gibedig.] v. ungifeðe, and preceding word.

gif-fæst; *adj. Gifted with, capable of, fitted for*; capax:—Sum biþ wôþbora giedda giffæst *one is a poet gifted with song*, Exon. 78 b; Th. 295, 20; Crä. 36: Cot. 57.

gif-heal, -heall, e; *f. A gift-hall, hall in which gifts are distributed*; aula in qua dominus dona distribuit:—Ymb ða gifhealle *around the gift-hall*, Beo. Th. 1680; B. 838.

giflan; *p.* ode, ede; *pp.* od, ed *To bestow gifts*:—Se cyng him cynelîce gifode *the king bestowed gifts upon him royally*, Chr. 994; Erl. 133, 32. Hió ðâ gifede mycele þinc ðam biscope *she gave great gifts to the bishop*, H. R. 17, 12.

gifl, giefl, gifel, gyfl, es; *n. Food, meat, piece of food*:—Lîc biþ wyrmes giefl *the body shall be the worm's food*, Exon. 100 a; Th. 374, 15; Seel. 126. Ðû wyrma gifl *thou food for worms*, 98 b; Th. 368, 16; Seel. 22. Hî ðæt gyfl þêgun *they ate that food*, 61 b; Th. 226, 24; Ph. 410: 45 a; Th. 153, 8; Gû. 822. Hûsle gereorded ðŷ æþelan gyfle *fed with the Eucharist, with the noble food*, 51 b: Th. 180, 5; Gû. 1275. Lytlum gieflum *with the little bits of meat*, 88 b; Th. 332, 23; Vy. 89. v. ǽfen-gifl.

gifnes, -ess, e; *f. A favour, grace*; beneficium, gratia:—Ealle we beþurfon Godes gifnesse *we all have need of God's grace*, Hy. 7, 114, 110: Hy. Grn. ii. 289, 114, 110. DER. for-gifnes.

gifol, giful; *adj. Generous, bountiful, liberal*; largus:—He swâ gifol is and swâ rûmedlîce gifþ *he is so liberal and gives so abundantly*, Bt. 38, 3; Fox 202, 14.

gifre; *adj. Useful, salutary*:—Niðum to nytte hæleþum gifre *of advantage to men, useful to warriors*, Exon. 107 b; Th. 409, 12; Rä. 27, 28: 113 a; Th. 433, 6; Rä. 50, 3. v. ungifre, and cf. *Icel.* gæfr.

gîfre; *adj. Greedy, covetous, voracious, eager, desirous*; avidus:—Gîfre *gulosus*, Wrt. Voc. 86, 51. Gîfere *vel* frec *ambro*, Ælfc. Gl. 88; Som. 74, 83; Wrt. Voc. 50, 63. Tantalus se cyning ðe ungemetlîce gîfre wæs *Tantalus the king who was immoderately greedy*, Bt. 35, 6; Fox 170, 1. Ða faraseî ða ðe gîfre wǽron *pharasæi qui erant avari*, Lk. Skt. 16, 14. Lîg gold gîfre forgrîpeþ grǽdig swelgeþ *the flame voracious lays hold on gold, greedy devours it*, Exon. 63 a; Th. 232, 15; Ph. 507: 38 a; Th. 124, 32; Gû. 346. Gîfrum grâpum *with greedy clutches*, 38 b; Th. 126, 28; Gû. 378: Andr. Kmbl. 2671; An. 1337. Gesyhst ðû nû ða sweartan helle grǽdige and gîfre *seest thou now the black hell greedy and ravenous?* Cd. 37; Th. 49, 16; Gen. 793: 213; Th. 267, 2; Sat. 82: 217; Th. 276, 21; Sat. 192: Exon. 82 a; Th. 309, 24; Seef. 62. Se gîfra gǽst *the greedy spirit*, 22 a; Th. 60, 21; Cri. 973. Ic heora eom swîðe gîfre *I am very desirous for them*, Bt. 22, 1; Fox 76, 20. Lîg gǽsta gîfrost *flame, most ravenous of spirits*, Beo. Th. 2250; B. 1123. Gîfrost and grǽdgost *most rapacious and most greedy*, Exon. 128 a; Th. 493, 2; Rä. 81, 24. [*Orm.* giferr: *Laym.* ȝifer: cf. *Icel.* gífr; *n. pl. fiends.*]

gif-sceatt, es; *m. A gift-treasure, present*; donum pretiosum, munus:—Sǽlîðende gifsceattas Geátum feredon *sea-voyagers bore gift-treasures for the Gauts*, Beo. Th. 761; B. 378.

gif-stôl, gief-stôl, es; *m. A gift-seat, seat from which gifts are distributed, throne, throne of grace*; donorum thronus, solium, gratiæ thronus:—Ðone gifstôl grêtan *to greet the throne*, Beo. Th. 338; B. 168. Brynewylmum mealt gifstôl Geáta *the gift-chair of the Goths was consumed by flames of fire*, Beo. Th. 4643; B. 2327: Exon. 16 a; Th. 36, 6; Cri. 572. Sceal gifstôl gegierwed stondan *a throne shall stand prepared*, Exon. 90 a; Th. 337, 23; Gn. Ex. 69: 77 a; Th. 289, 7; Wand. 44.

gift, gyft, e; *f.* I. *a gift*; as a technical term, *the amount to be given by a suitor in consideration of receiving a woman to wife*:—Gif mon wîf gebycgge and sió gyft forþ ne cume *if a man buy a wife and the sum agreed upon be not forthcoming*, L. In. 31; Th. i. 122, 5. See the note. That matrimony in the olden times was a bargain may be seen by the words used in connection with it, e. g. gebycgan, in the passage above; see also ge-ceápian, ceáp. For an account of such a bargaining see Njál Saga, c. 2. See also Th. i. 254–6, Cl. and Vig. Icel. Dict. mundr, and Grmm. R. A. pp. 419 sqq. II. in *pl. f.* and *n.* gifta, giftu *marriage*; nuptiæ:—Giftu *nuptiæ*, Ælfc. Gr. 13; Som. 16, 22: 28, 4; Som. 31, 20: Mone Gl. 433 a. On ðam þriddan dæge wǽron gifta gewordene *die tertia nuptiæ factæ sunt*, Jn. Bos. 2, 1: Mt. Bos. 22, 3. Crist wearþ to his gyftum gelaðod *Christ was invited to his marriage*, Homl. Th. i. 58, 10, 11: Hy. 10, 17; Hy. Grn. ii. 293, 17. Æt ðǽm giftan sceal mæssepreóst beón *at the nuptials there shall be a mass-priest*, L. Edm. 13, 8; Th. i. 256, 6. Wîfigende and gyfta syllende *nubentes et nubtum tradentes*, Mt. Bos. 24, 38: Lk. Bos. 20, 34. Gifta dôn hearm getâcnaþ *to keep a wedding betokens harm*, Lchdm. iii. 208, 21: L. Alf. 12; Th. i. 46, 17. [*Laym. Piers P.* ȝift *gift*: *O. Frs.* jeft: *O. H. Ger.* gift *gift*: *Goth.* fra-gifts *espousal*: *Icel.* gipt *a gift, wedding*.]

gift-bûr, es; *m. A wedding-chamber, bride-chamber*:—Swâ swâ brŷdguma forþ gewîtende of giftbûre his *tanquam sponsus procedens de thalamo suo*, Ps. Spl. T. 18, 5.

gifte, an; *f. Dowry*:—Gilde be ðære giftan mǽþe *reddat pecuniam juxta modum dotis quam virgines accipere consueverunt*, Ex. 22, 17. [Cf. L. Alf. 29; Th. i. 52, 8; *and see* gift.]

giftelic; *adj. Belonging to a wedding*; nuptialis, Cot. 139.

gift-hûs, es; *n. A wedding-house*; nuptiarum domus:—Ðâ wǽrun ða gyfthûs mid sittyndum mannum gefyllede *impletæ sunt nubtiæ discumbentium*, Mt. Kmbl. 22, 10. v. gift-lîc.

giftian; *p.* ode; *pp.* od *To give a woman in marriage*:—Ne wîfiaþ hî ne ne gyftigeaþ *neque nubent neque nubentur*, Mk. Skt. 12, 25. Ne giftigeaþ hî ne wîf ne lǽdaþ *neque nubunt neque ducunt uxores*, Lk. Skt. 20, 35. [Cf. *Icel.* gipta *to give a woman in marriage*; giptask *to marry*: *O. H. Ger.* gi-gift *venundatus, deditus.*]

gift-leóþ, es; *n. A marriage-song*; epithalamium, carmen nubentium, Ælfc. Gl. 82; Som. 73, 53; Wrt. Voc. 47, 57.

gift-lîc; *adj. Nuptial, belonging to a marriage*; nuptialis:—Ðâ geseah he ðǽr ǽnne man ðe næs mid gyftlîcum reáfe gescrŷd *vidit ibi hominem non vestitum veste nubtiali*, Mt. Kmbl. 22, 11, 12. Ðæt gyftlîce hûs *the house where the marriage was*, Homl Th. ii. 70, 16. Giftlîc *sponsalis*, Hpt. Gl. 525; *nuptialis*, 491. Giftlîce *sponsalia*, Mone Gl. 354 a.

giftu. v. gift.

gifu, gyfu, giefu, giofu, geofu, gif, e; *pl. nom. acc.* -a, -e; *gen.* -a, -ena; *f.* I. *a gift, grace, favour*; donum, munus, beneficium, gratia, virtus, facultas:—Wæs gifu Hrôþgâres oft geæhted *the gift of Hrothgar was often prized*, Beo. Th. 3773; B. 1884. Ðâm he geaf micle gife freódômes *to these he gave the great gift of freedom*, Bt. 41, 2; Fox 246, 1. Ðæt hie ælmihtiges gife ânforlêten *that they the Almighty's gift might lose*, Cd. 32; Th. 43, 19; Gen. 693. Ic ðam mago-rince mîne sylle godcunde gife *I will give to the youth my divine grace*, 106; Th. 140, 17; Gen. 2329. We onfêngon gife for gife *we have received grace for grace*, Jn. Bos. 1, 16. Heó gefylled wæs wîsdômes gife *she was filled with the gift of wisdom*, Elen. Kmbl. 2285; El. 1144. Ðâ him wæstmas brohte geártorhte gife grêne folde *when to him the verdant earth should bring fruits, yearly-bright gifts*, Cd. 76; Th. 94, 13; Gen. 1561. Sâulum on heofonum selest weorþlîca gifa *to souls in heaven thou wilt give worthy gifts*, Bt. Met. Fox 20, 453; Met. 20, 227. Næs hió to gnêþ gifa *she was not too sparing of gifts*, Beo. Th. 3864; B. 1930. Neorxna wang stôd gifena gefylled *paradise stood filled with gifts*, Cd. 11; Th. 13, 28; Gen. 209: Exon. 41 b; Th. 138, 18; Gû. 578. Ðîn môd trymeþ godcundum gifum *strengtheneth thy mind with divine gifts*, Cd. 135; Th. 170, 8; Gen. 2810. Brŷdlîce gife *nuptialis dos*, Hpt. Gl. 511. Hlâfordes gifu *impost due to the Lord*, L. Eth. 3, 3; Th. i. 292, 16: L. C. S. 82; Th. i. 422, 1: L. N. P. L. 67; Th. ii. 302, 7. See Thorpe's Glossary. To gifes *gratis*, Hpt. Gl. 478. Gâ hire ût to gife bûtan feó *let her go out free without money*, Ex. 21, 11: Num. 11, 5. To gife *gratis*, Gen. 29, 15. Gifum *gratis*, Ps. Spl. T. 34, 8. II. *the Anglo-Saxon Rune* X = *g*, the name of which letter in Anglo-Saxon is gifu *a gift*,—hence, this Rune not only stands for the letter *g*, but for gifu *a gift*, as:—X [Gifu] gumena byþ gleng and herenys *a gift is the honour and praise of men*, Runic. pm. 7; Kmbl. 340, 23; Hick. Thes. i. 135. [*Orm.* gife: *Laym.* geve: *R. Brun.* give: *Kath.* geoven, *pl*: *Piers P.* yeves: *O. Sax.* geƀa; *f. donum*: *O. Frs.* jeve: *O. H. Ger.* geba: *Goth.* giba: *Icel.* gjöf; *f. donum, munus.*] DER. beáh-gifu, brýd-, eád-, feorh-, freót-, frum-, hyht-, máððum-, morgen-, sinc-, sundor-, sundur-, sweord-, wóþ-, wuldor-, wundor-.

gifung, gyfung, e; *f. A giving, granting, assent, consent*:—Mid gyfunge ðære synne *peccati consensu*, Bd. 1, 27; S. 497, 11.

gigant, gygant, es; *m. A giant*; gigas:—Untydras onwócon, eotenas, swylce gigantas *unnatural progenies sprang forth, monsters, also giants*, Beo. Th. 226; B. 113. Swá swá gigant yrnþ on his weg *ut gigas ad currendam viam*, Ps. Th. 18, 6. Ne se gigant ne wyrþ ná gehæled *nec gigas salvus erit*, 32, 14. He ðone gigant ofwearp *he struck down the giant*, Blickl. Homl. 31, 18. [*Lat.* gigas; *gen.* gigantis.]

gigant-mæcg, es; *m. Giant progeny*; filius gigantis, Cd. 64; Th. 76, 36; Gen. 1268.

gi-hrínian, Jn. Skt. p. 188, 4. v. ge-regnian.

gihsinga *exugia*, Cot. 73, Lye. v. Lchdm. i. lxx, note 6.

gihþa, an; *m. Itch, itching*:—Unaberendlíc gyhþa ofereode ealne ðone líchaman *an unbearable itching overspread the whole body*, Homl. Th. i. 86, 12. [The word used in the passage of Josephus describing Herod's condition is κνησμός.] v. gicþa.

gihþig, giþig; *adj. Lymphaticus, vecors*, Hpt. Gl. 520.

gihþu. v. gehþo.

gild, geld, gield, gyld. es; *n*. I. *a payment of money, a tribute, compensation, retribution, substitute*; solutio, tributum, compensatio, remuneratio, retributio:—Beád ðá Swegen full gild *then Sweyn commanded a full contribution*, Chr. 1013; Th. 273, 6. Ðis wæs swíðe hefigtýme geár þurh mænigfealde gylda *this was a very grievous year on account of manifold taxes*, Chr. 1096; Erl. 233, 25. Menn guldon him gyld *men paid him tribute*, 1066; Erl. 203, 8. On Abeles gyld *in compensation for Abel*, Cd. 55; Th. 67, 22; Gen. 1104: 153; Th. 190, 15; Exod. 199. On ðære sunnan gyld *in the sun's stead*, Exon. 24 a; Th. 68, 14; Cri. 1103. IX gylde forgylde *let him pay nine[-fold] for compensation*, L. Ethb. 4; Th. i. 4, 3. II. *a* GUILD, *society*, or *club, to which payments were made for mutual protection and support, more extensive than our friendly societies*; societas, fraternitas. The members of the A.-Sax. guild were answerable for each other's conduct, and thus character was made of the very greatest importance. v. Kmbl. Sax. Eng. i. 251–253; Th. Chart. p. xvi; pp. 605–17: Stubbs' Const. Hist. s. v. III. *a payment to God, worship, service, sacrifice, offering*; cultus, sacrificium:—Ðú goda ussa gield forhogdest *thou hast despised the service of our gods*, Exon. 67 b; Th. 251, 17; Jul. 146. To ðam gielde *for that sacrifice*, Cd. 74; Th. 90, 26; Gen. 1501. His Waldende gilde onsægde *dedicated an offering to his Lord*, 137; Th. 172, 11; Gen. 2842: Bd. 2, 1; S. 501, note 12. IV. *a heathen deity*; numen:—Gif ðú onsecgan nelt sóþum gieldum *if thou wilt not sacrifice to true deities*, Exon. 68 a; Th. 253, 3; Jul. 174. V. *a visible object of worship, an idol*; idolum:—He sum gild bræc *he was destroying an idol*, Blickl. Homl. 223, 4: 221, 8, 20. Gyld of golde gumum arǽrde *reared up for the people an idol of gold*, Cd. 180; Th. 226, 22: Dan. 175: 182; Th. 228, 18; Dan. 204. [*O. Sax.* geld; *n. retributio, tributum, cultus divinus, sacrificium*: *O. Frs.* jeld; *n*: *O. H. Ger.* gelt; *n*: *Goth.* gild; *n. tributum, census, multa*: *Icel.* gildi, gjald; *n. tributum, pœna, præmium, multa cædis.*] DER. æftergild, [-geld, -gield, -gyld], án-, bryne-, deófol-, ed-, feónd-, friþ-, frum-, god-, hǽðen-, leód-, sceucc-, þeóf-, un-, wer-, wig-, wiðer-. v. Grmm. D. M. 34: R. A. 601, 649. [Cf. friþ-gild.]

gilda, gylda, an; *m. A member of a guild*:—Se gylda ðe óðerne misgrét *the guildbrother that insults another*, Th. Chart. 606, 22: 609, 10. v. ge-gilda.

gildan, geldan, gieldan, gyldan, ic gilde, gielde, gylde, ðú giltst, gieltst, gyltst, gilst, he gildeþ, gilt, gielt, gylt, *pl.* gildaþ; *p.* geald, *pl.* guldon; *pp.* golden; *v. a*; *n. To yield, pay, restore, requite, give, render, make an offering, serve, worship*; reddere, solvere, tribuere, retribuere, rependere, restituere, servire, colere:—Gafol gyldan *to pay tribute*, Ors. 1, 10; Bos. 32, 24, 28: Mt. Bos. 17, 24. Ic mín gehat Dryhtne gylde *vota mea Domino reddam*, Ps. Th. 115, 8: 78, 13: 93, 22. Se gylt ǽlcum be his gewyrhtum *he requites each according to his works*, Bt. 40, 7; Fox 244, 1: Ors. 1, 1; Bos. 20, 35. Gilde ðæt ilce wíte ðæt se óðer sceolde gif he him ryhtes wyrnde *let him pay the like penalty that the other should if he had denied him justice*, L. Ath. i. 3; Th. i. 200, 18. Drihtne guldon gód *they paid good to the Lord*, Cd. 111; Th. 146, 9; Gen. 2419. Gilde be twífealdon *duplum restituet*, Ex. 22, 4, 7. Gilde twífealdon, 22, 9. Gilde ðone byrst *reddet damnum*, 22, 6, 12. Gild ðínum esne góde dǽde *retribue servo tuo*, Ps. Th. 118, 17. Heaðo-rǽsas geald mearum and máðmum *requited war-attacks with horses and treasures*, Beo. Th. 2099; B. 1047. Ðæt ǽlc gulde óþrum edleán ǽlces weorces *that each should render to another recompense for every work*, Bt. 39, 1; Fox 212, 5: Bt. Met. Fox 27, 51; Met. 27, 26. Mín sceal mid grimme gryre golden wurþan fyll and feorh-cwealm *my fall and murder shall be requited with grim horror*, Cd. 55; Th. 67, 18; Gen. 1102. Sceuccgyldum swýðe guldan *servierunt sculptilibus eorum*, Ps. Th. 105, 26. Bebeád se cásere ðæt cristne men guldan deófolgeldum *the emperor ordered that christian men should worship idols*, Shrn. 88, 14, 22: 74, 26. Deóflum geldan *to worship devils*, 110, 18. [*Laym. Orm.* ȝelden: cf. *Shakspere's* God ild you: *O. Sax.* geldan *reddere, retribuere, solvere, præstare*: *O. Frs.* jelda: *O. H. Ger.* geltan *reddere, solvere, retribuere, sacrificare*: *Goth.* -gildan, fra-gildan; *p.* -gald, *pl.* -guldum; *pp.* -guldans *to repay, requite*: *Icel.* gjalda.] DER. a-gildan, an-, on-, for-, ge-, to-.

gildan *to gild*. v. gyldan.

gilden. v. gylden.

Gild-ford, Gyldford, Guldeford [Gild *a fraternity*; ford *a ford*: *Domesd.* Gilda ad vadum] GUILDFORD, *a town in Surrey, on the river Wey*, Lye.

gild-rǽden, gyld-rǽden, -rǽdenn, e; *f. The relation involved in membership of a guild*:—Gif he nele to bóte gebúgan þolige he ðære geférrǽdene and ǽlcere óðre gyldrǽdene *if he will not submit to make amends let him forfeit the fellowship and every other interest in the guild*, Th. Chart. 606, 31. Ðæt byþ rihtlíce gecweden gyldrǽdene ðæt we ðus dón *that is very properly agreed upon as a part of guild-membership, that we do thus*, 607, 24.

gild-scipe, gyld-scipe, es; *m. A guild-ship, society*; sodalitas:—Án gildscipe is gegaderod on Wudeburg lande *a guild-ship is gathered at Woodbury land*, Th. Diplm. 608, 30: 605, 8: L. Edg. C. 9; Th. ii. 246, 12. v. gild.

gild-sester, es; *m. A measure belonging to a guild*; sextarius:—Sceóte ǽlc gegylda ǽnne gyldsester fulne clǽnes hwǽtes *let each guild-brother contribute one guild-measure full of clean wheat*, Th. Chart. 606, 7: 611, 4.

gillan *to yell*, Salm. Kmbl. 535; Sal. 267. v. gellan.

Gillinga, Gillinga-hám GILLINGHAM, *in Dorsetshire, on the river Stour*, Chr. 1016; Erl. 156, 1, 18.

gillister, es; *n. Phlegm*, L. M. 1, 1; Lchdm. ii. 24, 18.

gillistre, an; *f. Phlegm, matter*, L. M. 1, 1; Lchdm. ii. 18, 17: 72; 148, 6.

gilm, es; *m. A yelm, a handful of reaped corn, bundle, bottle*; manipulus:—Eówre gilmas stódon *your sheaves stood*, Gen. 37, 7. v. gelm.

gilp *powder, dust*; scobs, Cot. 181.

GILP, gelp, gielp, gylp, es; *m. Glory, ostentation, pride, boasting, arrogance, vain-glory, haughtiness*; gloria, ostentatio:—Se seofoþa heáfod-leahter is ídelwuldor ðæt is gylp *the seventh chief sin is vain-glory, that is pride*, Homl. Th. ii. 220, 27: 218, 22. He nolde nán þing dón mid gylpe forðon ðe se gylp is án heáfod-leahter *he would do nothing in pride, for pride is a deadly sin*, i. 170, 24. Geþenc be ðám gebyrdum' gif hwá ðæs gilpþ hú ídel and hú unnyt se gilp biþ *consider birth*; *if any one boast of that how vain and how useless is the boast*, Bt. 30, 1; Fox 108, 20: Cd. 219; Th. 280, 12; Sat. 254: 4; Th. 5, 10; Gen. 69: Blickl. Homl. 243, 9. Gilpes ðú girnest *thou desirest glory*, Bt. 32; Fox 114, 18. Hú Orosius spræc ymb Rómána gylp hú hí manega folc oferwunnan *how Orosius spoke of the glory of the Romans, how they overcame many peoples*, Ors. Bos. 12, 42. Is ðæt unnet gelp *that is useless glory*, Bt. Met. Fox 10, 34, 26; Met. 10, 17, 13. Nǽfre gielpes to georn *never too eager for fame*, Exon. 77 b; Th. 290, 22; Wand. 69. On ídel gylp *in vanitate sua*, Ps. Th. 51, 6. For ðínum ídlan gilpe *for thine idle boasting*, Blickl. Homl. 31, 14. [*Laym.* ȝælp, ȝelp: *Orm.* ȝellp: *O. Sax.* gelp: *O. H. Ger.* gelf *jactantia*, [*inanis*] *gloria*.]

gilpan, gielpan, gylpan, ic gilpe, gielpe, gylpe, ðú gilpst, gielpst, gylpst, he gilpþ, gielpþ, *pl.* gilpaþ, gielpaþ, gylpaþ; *p.* gealp, *pl.* gulpon; *pp.* golpen *To glory, boast, desire earnestly*; gloriari:—Gif ðú gilpan wille, gilp Godes *if thou wilt glory, glory in God*, Bt. 14, 1; Fox 40, 24. Nó ðæs gilpan þearf synfull sáwel *the sinful soul need not boast of this*, Exon. 116 b; Th. 449, 9; Dom. 68. Ðæt hine swelces gamenes gilpan lyste *that he liked to boast of such sport*, Bt. Met. Fox 9, 38; Met. 9, 19. Ðæt ðú wile gilpan *that thou wilt boast*, Salm. Kmbl. 409; Sal. 205. Ic wundrige forhwí hí gilpan swelces anwealdes *I wonder why they boast of such power*, Bt. 29, 1; Fox 104, 1. Gelpan ne þorfte *had no cause to boast*, Chr. 937; Erl. 114, 10; Æðelst. 44. Gylpan, Beo. Th. 4016; B. 2006: 5740; B. 2874. Ná ic ðæs gylpe *I boast not of that*, 1177; B. 586: 4116; B. 2055. Hú lange mánwyrhtan morðre gylpaþ *usquequo peccatores gloriabuntur?* Ps. Th. 93, 3: 73, 4. He gealp, ðæt him nówiht wiðstandan mihte *nihil resistĕre posse jactābat*, Bd. 3, 1; S. 524, 8. Hrêþsigora ne gealp *he boasted not of glorious victories*, Beo. Th. 5160; B 2583. Burga aldor gramlíce gealp *the ruler of towns angrily boasted*, Cd. 210; Th. 260, 23; Dan. 714. Swíðe gulpon *they exceedingly boasted*, 210; Th. 260, 20; Dan. 712. Sigore gulpon *they boasted of victory* Cd. 94; Th. 121, 29; Gen. 2017. Firenum gulpon they wickedly boasted, Exon. 36 b; Th. 118, 8; Gú. 236. Ðæt hí ne gulpan ðæs that they may not boast of it, Ps. Th. 74, 4. [Laym. ȝælpen, ȝelpen: Orm. ȝellpenn, ȝillpenn: Chauc. yelpe to boast.]

gilp-cwide, es; m. A boastful speech:—Ðam wífe ða word wel lícodon gilpcwide Geátes well did those words please the woman, the boastful speech of the Gaut. Beo. Th. 1284; B. 640: Exon. 50 b; Th. 176, 12; Gú. 1209. [O. Sax. gelp-quidi.]

gilpen; adj. Boastful:—Ne mæg he geþyldgian ðæt he ðæt forhele ac wierþ donon gilpen he cannot bear to conceal it, but becomes boastful on account of it, Past. 33, 2; Swt. 216, 9: Cot. MS. Wát ic ðæt wǽron Caldéas gúðe ðæs gilpne I knew that the Chaldeans were so boastful in war; Salm. Kmbl. 413; Sal. 207.

gilp-georn; adj. Desirous of glory:—Se strangesta cyning and se gilpgeornesta rex fortissimus et gloriæ cupidissimus, Bd. 1, 34; S. 499, 19.

gilp-hlæden; part. p. Vaunt-laden:—Cyninges þegn guma gilp-hlæden gidda gemyndig a king's thane, a man filled with lofty themes, with memory rich in songs, Beo. Th. 1740; B. 868.

gilplíc; adj. Ostentatious, pompous, proud, vain-glorious:—Ðæt wǽre swíðe gilplíc dǽd gif Crist scute ðá adún it would have been a very vain-glorious act if Christ had thrown himself down then, Homl. Th. i. 170, 21. Gierelan gielplíces of pompous garb, Exon. 35 a; Th. 112, 3; Gú. 138: 38 b; Th. 127, 22; Gú. 390.

gilp-líce; adv. Proudly, vauntingly; arroganter, Cot. 1, Lye. [O. H. Ger. gelfligho jactanter.]

gilpna, an; m. A boaster; jactator:—Betra biþ se geþyldega wer ðonne se gilpna melior est patiens arrogante, Past. 33, 2; Swt. 216, 14; Cot. MS: 20; Swt. 148, 19.

gilp-plega, an; m. Play of which one may boast [war]:—Gylpplegan gáres, Cd. 154; Th. 193, 2; Exod. 240.

gilp-sceaða, an; m. An arrogant, boasting criminal:—Gielpsceaðan boastful and wicked ones [the fallen angels], Cd. 5; Th. 6, 29; Gen. 96. Ðone gelpscaðan that proud and wicked man [Nero], Bt. Met. Fox 9, 98; Met. 9, 49.

gilp-spræc, e; f. Boastful speech, Beo. Th. 1966; B. 981

gilp-word, es; n. A boastful word, a boast, vaunt:—Hí him to gylpworde hæfdon 'ðæt him leófre wǽre ðæt hí hæfdon healtne cyning ðonne healt ríce' their boast was 'that they had rather have a halting king than a halting kingdom,' Ors. 3, 1; Bos. 53, 26. Gylpword boastful words, Cd. 14; Th. 17, 23; Gen. 264; Beo. Th. 1355; B. 675: Byrht. Th. 139, 55; By. 274.

gilte, an; f. A GILT, a young sow:—Gilte suilla vel sucula, Ælfc. Gl. 20; Som. 59, 34; Wrt. Voc. 22, 75. [Ȝelte scropha, Wrt. Voc. 177, 7: gilt Hall. Dict: Icel. gilta a young sow: O. H. Ger. galza, gelza sucula.]

GIM, gimm, gym, gymm; gen. gimmes; m. I. a GEM, jewel; gemma:—Se stán bið blæc gym the stone is a black gem, Bd. 1, 1; S. 473, 24. Ðæt nebb líxeþ swá glæs oððe gim the beak glitters like glass or gem, Exon. 60 a; Th. 218, 25; Ph. 300. Gim sceal on hringe standan steáp the gem shall stand prominent in the ring, Menol. Fox 504; Gn. C. 22: Salm. Kmbl 570; Sal. 284. Gimmas líxton jewels glittered, Elen. Kmbl. 180; El. 90. Seó gesomnung ðara deórwyrþra gimma the collection of the precious gems, Blickl. Homl. 99, 28. Se ðe wæs gescríd mid golde and mid gimmum he that was clad with gold and with gems, Chr. 1086; Erl. 221, 3: Cd. 227; Th. 305, 20; Sat. 649. Hí wurdon gehwyrfede to deórwurþum gimmum they were turned to precious gems, Homl. Th. i. 64, 5. II. used metaphorically of the eye, the sun, stars, etc. [cf. Icel. fagr-gim = sun]:—He his eágan ontýnde hálge heáfdes gimmas he unclosed his eyes, the head's holy gems, Exon. 51 b; Th. 180, 7; Gú. 1276. Hluttor heofenes gim the clear jewel of heaven, i. e. the sun, 58 b; Th. 210, 9; Ph. 183: 63 a; Th. 232, 33; Ph. 516: Beo. Th. 4151; B. 2072: Andr. Kmbl. 2538; An. 1270. Iunius on ðam gim astíhþ on heofenas up hýhst on geáre June in which the gem [sun] rises in the heavens highest in the year, Menol. Fox 216; Men. 109. Hálge gimmas heofontungol sunne and móna holy gems, stars of heaven, sun and moon, Exon. 18 a; Th. 43. 22, 27; Cri. 692, 695. [Laym. ȝim: later MS. gim: Icel. [poetry] gim; n: O. H. Ger. gimma; f.]

gíman. v. gýman.

gimbǽre; adj. Gemmifer, bullifer, Hpt. Gl. 417.

gim-cyn, gym-cyn, -cynn, es; n. A gem-kind, a precious stone, a gem; genus gemmarum, gemma:—Se forma feohgítsere gróf æfter gimcynnum the first miser delved after precious stones, Bt. Met. Fox 8, 114; Met. 8, 57: 15, 8; Met. 15, 4. On ðære ēðyltyrf niððas findaþ gold and gymcynn in that country men find gold and gems, Cd. 12; Th. 14, 29; Gen. 226; Elen. Kmbl. 2046; El. 1024.

gíme-. v. gýme-.

gíming. v. gēmung.

gimmisc; adj. Jewelled; gemmeus:—Monige fatu gimmiscu gemmea vasa, Nar. 5, 13. [O. H. Ger. gimmisc gemmarius.]

gim-reced, es; m. n. A hall adorned with gems:—Ne hí gimreced & setton searolíce nor with art did they build palaces, Bt. Met. Fox 8, 50; Met. 8, 25.

gim-rodor, es; m. A precious stone; draconites, dracontia, Cot. 63, Lye: Hpt. Gl. 431.

gim-stān, es; m. A gem, jewel, precious stone:—Gimstān gemma, Wrt. Voc. 85, 23. Ðás gymstánas synd tocwýsede these jewels are crushed, Homl. Th. i. 62, 6, 13, 15, 21. Hí behwyrfdon heora áre on gymstánum they turned their property into jewels, 60, 28, 24. [Laym. ȝimston: Icel. gim-steinn.]

gim-wyrhta, an; m. A worker in gems, jeweller:—Ðás gymwyrhtan secgaþ ðæt hí nǽfre swá deórwurþe gymstánas ne gemēttou the jewellers say that they never met with such precious jewels, Homl. Th. i. 64, 9.

GIN, es; n. A gap, an opening, abyss; hiatus:—Gārsecges gin ocean's expanse, Cd. 163; Th. 205, 3; Exod. 430. [Icel. gin the mouth of beasts.]

gin; adj. Wide, spacious, ample:—Beligeð úton ginne ríce encompasseth ample realms, Cd. 12; Th. 15, 7; Gen. 230: 46; Th. 59, 2; Gen. 957. Eall ðes ginna grund all this spacious earth, Exon. 116 a; Th. 445, 23; Dōm. 12: 85 b; Th. 321, 24; Víd. 51: Beo. Th. 3106; B. 1551: Judth. 9; Thw. 21, 1; Jud. 2. [Cf. Icel. ginn-; and see Grmm. D. M. 297.]

gínan, ic gēne, ðú gínest, gínst, he gíneþ, gínþ, pl. gínaþ; p. gān, pl. ginon; pp ginen To yawn; hiare, Cot. 23. [Icel. gína; p. gein to yawn.] Cf. ginian. DER be-gínan, to-.

gind. v. geond.

gin-fæst; adj. Very fast or lasting; firmissimus:—Onfōn ginfæstum gifum to receive very fast gifts, Cd. 141; Th. 176, 28: Gen. 2919; Beo. Th. 2546: B. 1271: 4370; B. 2182: Exon. 68 a: Th. 252, 24; Jul. 168: Bt. Met. Fox 20, 453; Met. 20, 227. [Grein renders by amplus; see gin.]

ging; adj. Young; jŭvĕnis:—Ic up ahóf eaforan gingne I raised up a young offspring, Elen. Kmbl. 706; El. 353: 1746; El. 875. v. geong.

gingifer, gingiber, gingifere, an; f. Ginger:—Gingifer ginger, L. M. 1, 14; Lchdm. ii. 56, 11: 23; Lchdm. ii. 66, 3. Gingiber, Lchdm. iii. 92, 15. Gingifran broþ broth of ginger, L. M. 1, 18; Lchdm. ii. 62, 6. Genym gingiferan take ginger, Lchdm. iii. 136, 17. [Laym. gingiuere. Cf. French gingembre: O. French gingibre: Lat. zingiber: Gk. ζιγγίβερις.]

gingra, an; m. A disciple, vassal, follower; discĭpŭlus, assecla:—He and his gingran awyrdaþ manna líchaman he and his disciples injure men's bodies, Homl. Th. i. 4, 24: Cd. 217; Th. 276, 20; Sat. 191: 224; Th. 298, 2; Sat. 526. His gingrum to his disciples, Bd. 3, 5; S. 526, 21. He his gingran sent he sendeth his vassal, Cd. 25; Th. 33, 5; Gen. 515: 26; Th. 34, 32; Gen. 546. v. geongra.

gingre, an; f. A female servant, maid-servant; fămŭla:—Gingran sínre to her maid-servant, Judth. 11; Thw. 23, 21; Jud. 132.

ginian, geonian, gynian; p. ode To yawn, gape:—Ic gynige hio, Ælfc. Gr. 24; Som. 25, 39. Gewíte seó sáwul út ne mæg se múþ clypian ðeáh ðe he gynige if the soul depart the mouth cannot cry, though it gape, Homl. Th. i. 160, 9. Mid gynigendum múþe with gaping mouth, ii. 176, 21: 510. 33. Seó eorþe swá giniende bád the earth remained gaping so, Ors. 3, 3; Bos. 56, 3. [Wick. p. pl. ȝeneden: O. H. Ger. ginen, ginon hiare.] v. geonian.

ginnan. v. a-, an-, be-, on-, under-ginnan.

gínung, e; f. A yawning; hiatus, Cot. 23. [Cf. geonung.]

gin-, gynn-wísed; part. p. Well-directed, wise:—Nǽnig monna wæs godes willan ðæs georn ne gynnwísed no man was so eager for God's will nor so wise, Exon. 45 a; Th. 154, 8; Gú. 839.

gió; adv. Formerly, of old, before; quondam, olim, pridem:—Se wæs gió cyning who was formerly king, Bt. Met. Fox 26, 70; Met. 26, 35: 28, 60; Met. 28, 30: Bt. 16, 1; Fox 50, 7, Cot. MS: 38, 1; Fox 194, 3: Elen. Kmbl. 871; El. 436: Beo. Th. 5036; B. 2521. Ǽror gió before, Bt. Met. Fox 20, 490; Met. 20, 245. v. geó.

gioc, es; n. A yoke; jugum:—Ðæt swǽre gioc the heavy yoke, Bt. Met. Fox 10, 39; Met. 10, 20: 9, 110; Met. 9, 55. v. geoc.

gióc. v. geóc.

giofan; p. geaf, pl. geáfon; pp. gifen To give; dare:—Ne meahte se sunu Wonredes hond-slyht gifan [MS. giofan] nor could the son of Wonred give a hand-stroke, Beo. Th. 5937; B. 2972. v gifan.

giofolnes, se; f. Munificence, liberality; munificentia, Past. 44, 2; Swt. 321, 22; Hat. MS.

giofu, e; f. A gift, grace; donum, gratia:—Ðē cyning engla gefrætwode giofum thee the king of angels adorned with gifts, Andr. Kmbl. 3036; An. 1521. Ðæt wæs giofu gǽstlíc that was a ghostly grace, Exon. 8 b; Th. 3, 26; Cri. 42. v. gifu.

giógoð, giógað youth. v. geóguð.

gioleca, an; m. A yolk; ovi vitellus, Bt. Met. Fox 20, 339; Met. 20, 170. v. geolca.

giolu. v. geolewe.

gió-man, -mann, es; m. A man of old; qui olim vixit:—Giómonna gestrión the wealth of men of old, Bt. Met. Fox 1, 46; Met. 1, 23. v. iú-man.

giómor; *adj. Sad, sorrowful;* mæstus:—Nū sceal ic wreccea giómor, singan sârcwidas *now shall I, a sad wretch, sing mournful songs*, Bt. Met. Fox 2, 6; Met. 2, 3. v. geómor.

gióṁor-mōd; *adj. Sad of mind;* mæstus anĭmo:—He, giómormōd, giohðo mǣnde *he, sad of mind, bewailed his afflictions*, Beo. Th. 4526; B. 2267. v. geómor-mōd.

giond; *prep. acc. Through, throughout, over, in;* per, in:—Waldeþ giond werþióda *he rules throughout nations*, Bt. Met. Fox 24, 70; Met. 24, 35: 11, 126; Met. 11, 63: 4, 74; Met. 4, 37: 11, 89; Met. 11, 45. v. geond.

giong; *def.* se gionga; *adj. Young;* jŭvĕnis:—Se æðeling biþ giong in geardum *the noble [bird] is young in its dwelling*, Exon. 61 a; Th. 223, 5; Ph. 355: Beo. Th. 4883; B. 2446. Se gionga cyning *the young king*, Ors. 2, 4; Bos. 45, 15. v. geong.

gióng *went*, Beo. Th. 4810, note; B. 2409; *p. of* gangan.

giongor-scipe, es; *m. Youngership, service;* juvĕnīlis status, minis-tĕrium:—Ðæt hie his giongorscipe fyligan woldan *that they would follow his service*, Cd. 14; Th. 16, 26; Gen. 249. [*O. Sax.* jungar-skepi.]

giongra, an; *m. A vassal, follower, attendant;* assecla, sectātor:—Môton we hie us to giongrum habban *we may have them as our vassals*, Cd. 21; Th. 26, 16; Gen. 407. v. geongra.

giorne; *adv. Diligently;* dīligenter:—Gif ðū wilnige weoruldrihtnes heáne anwald ongitan giorne *if thou desirest diligently to behold the high power of the world's Lord*, Bt. Met. Fox 29, 5; Met. 29, 3. v. georne.

giornfulnes *earnestness*, Past. 18. 2; Hat. MS. 25 b, 21. v. geornfulnes.

giow, es; *m? A griffin;* gryps, gryphus:—Giow *gryphus*, Wrt. Voc. 62, 3. v. giw.

giowian. v. giwian.

Gipeswīc *Ipswich*, Chr. 993; Erl. 132, 4.

gipung, e; *f. Gaping;* os patulum, Gl. Prud. 991.

gird *a staff*, Ex. 4, 2. v. gyrd.

giren, girn *a snare*, Ps. Vos. 17, 6: 24, 16: 58, 6: 65, 10. v. grin.

girian; *p.* ðū giredost' *To prepare*, Ps. Spl. 146, 8. v. gearwian.

girnan *to yearn, seek for, require*, Ex. 21, 22. v. gyrnan.

girran *to chatter;* garrire. v. georran.

girwan; *p.* ede; *pp.* ed *To prepare;* părāre:—Girwan up swǣsendo *to prepare a feast*, Judth. 9; Thw. 21, 7; Jud. 9. v. gearwian.

giscian *to sob, sigh;* singultire, Bt. 2; Fox 4, 9.

gise *yes;* immo, etiam:—Gise, lā gese *yes, O yes*, Bt. 16, 4; Fox 58, 15. v. gese.

gisel, gȳsel; *gen.* gīsles; *dat.* gīsle; *m. A pledge, hostage;* obses:—Gȳsel *obses*, Wrt. Voc. 72, 63: Byrht. Th. 139, 36; By. 265. Būtan ānum Bryttiscum gīsle *except one British hostage*, Chr. 755; Erl. 50, 8. Ecgferþ wæs to gīsle geseald *Ecgfrid obses tenebatur*, Bd. 3, 24; S. 556, 26. Ðū eádige Maria God ðē hafaþ to gīsle on middangearde geseted *thou blessed Mary, God hath placed thee on earth as a surety*, Blickl. Homl. 9, 5. Hió genam ðone ǣnne to gīsle *she took the one as hostage*, Elen. Kmbl. 1196; El. 600. He him āðas swōr and gīslas salde *he swore oaths to them and gave hostages*, Chr. 874; Erl. 76, 28. Ðā gyrnde he griðes and gīsla *then he required protection and hostages*, 1048; Erl. 180, 6. [*Laym.* ȝisles, *pl: Icel.* gīsl: *Dan.* gidsel, gissel: *Swed.* gislan: *Ger.* geissel: *O. H. Ger.* kīsal *obses.* v. Grm. R. A. 619.]

gīslian; *p.* ode, ade; *pp.* od *To give hostages* or *security;* obsides dare:—He gīslode and hine man deáhhwæðere ofslōh *he gave hostages and yet he was slain*, Chr. 1016; Erl. 154, 11. Man gīslade ða hwīle in to ðām scipum *hostages were sent to the ships during the time*, 994; Erl. 133, 29. Seó burhwaru gīslode *the town's people gave hostages*, 1013; Erl. 148, 8. Ða weasternan þægnas gīslodon *the western thanes gave hostages*, 17: 1015; Erl. 153, 1. [*Icel.* gīsla *to give as hostage*].

gi-sprunt. v. ge-springan.

GIST, gyst, es; *m.* YEAST, *barm, froth;* spuma cerevisiæ, Herb. 21, 6; Lchdm. i. 118, 10. Niwne gist *new yeast*, L. M. ii. 51, 1; Lchdm. ii. 266, 1. [*Prompt. Parv.* ȝeest *spuma.*]

gist, es; *m. A guest:*—Fundode gist of geardum *the guest hastened from the dwellings*, Beo. Th. 2280; B. 1138: 3049: B. 1522: Cd. 113; Th. 149, 9; Gen. 2472: 115; Th. 150, 20; Gen. 2494. v. gæst.

gist *a storm.* v. yst.

gist-. v. gæst-, gest-.

gist-līðe; *adj. Kind to guests, hospitable;* hospes:—Būton cræft mīn gistlīðe him beó *nĭsi ars mea hospĭta ei fuĕrit*, Coll. Monast. Th. 28, 11: Shrn. 129, 26.

gist-mægen, es; *n. A force composed of guests:*—Ðǣr frome wǣron godes spellbodan hæfde gistmægen strengeo *there were bold messengers of God, the band of guests [the angels visiting Lot] had strength*, Cd. 115; Th 150, 20; Gen. 2494.

git, gyt; *nom. You two,* vos duo, σφῶϊ, σφώ; *gen.* incer *of you two,* vestrûm duorum, σφῶϊν, σφῷν; *dat.* inc *to you two,* vobis duobus, σφῶϊν, σφῷν; *acc.* inc. incit *you two,* vos duos, σφῶϊ, σφώ; *personal pron. dual of* ðū *thou:*—Gif git ðæt fæsten fȳre willaþ forstandan *if you two will protect that fastness from fire*, Cd. 117; Th. 152, 16; Gen. 2521. Git me freóndscipe cȳðaþ *you two will shew friendship to me*, 117; Th. 152, 3; Gen. 2514. Gȳt nyton hwæt gyt biddaþ. Māge gyt drincan ðone calic ðe ic to drincenne hæbbe? Ðā cwǣdon hig, Wyt māgon [*vos duo*] *nescitis quid* [*vos duo*] *petatis. Potestis* [*vos duo*] *bibere calicem quem ego bibiturus sum? Dicunt ei,* [*nos duo*] *possumus*, Mt. Bos. 20, 22. Hwæt wylle gyt ðæt ic inc dō *quid vultis* [*vos duo*] *ut faciam vobis* [*duobus*]? 20, 32. Gelȳfe gyt ðæt ic inc mæg gehǣlan [*vos duo*] *creditis, quia hoc possum facere vobis* [*duobus*]? 9, 28. Incer twega *of you two;* vestrûm duorum, Exon. 123 b; Th. 475, 14; Bo. 47. Ne gehwæðer incer *nor either of you two*, Beo. Th. 1173; B. 584. Sȳ inc *fiat vobis* [*duobus*], Mt. Bos. 9, 29. Restaþ incit hēr *rest your two selves here*. Cd. 139; Th. 174, 19; Gen. 2880. Git Iohannis *thou and John*, Exon. 121 b; Th. 467, 7; Hö. 135. [*Laym.* ȝit: *Orm.* ȝitt: *O. Sax.* git; *dat. acc.* inc: *Goth. gen.* igkwara; *dat. acc.* igkwis: *Icel.* it; *gen.* ykkar; *dat. acc.* ykkr.]

git, giet, get, gyt; *adv. Still, yet:*—Hēr mon mæg giet gesión hiora swæþ *their track may still be seen here*, Past. pref; Swt. 5, 15; Hat. MS. Be ðiosum git is swīðe ryhtlīce gecweden to ðæm wītegan *about which further is very rightly said to the prophet*, Swt. 162, 22; Cot. MS. And git hit is māre and eác manigfealdre ðæt dereþ ðisse þeóde *and yet there are greater and more manifold things that hurt this people*, Swt. A. S. Rdr. 108, 106. Gyf heó gyt lyfaþ *if she yet lives*, Beo. Th. 1893; B. 944. Metod eallum weóld gumena cynnes swā he nū git dēþ *the Lord ruled all of the race of men as he yet does now*, 2121; B. 1058. He nyste ne ic ðā git *he did not know, nor I as yet*, Pref. Ælfc. Thw. 2, 2: Gen. 8, 8: Beo. Th. 1077; B. 536. Ðā gyt, Cd. 6; Th. 7, 35; Gen. 1160. Ðā giet, 63; Th. 75, 25; Gen. 1245. He abād ðā git ōðre seofon dagas *he waited then yet other seven days*, Gen. 8, 10. Abraham cwæþ ðā git *Abraham said further*, 18, 29. He sende to eallum ðām cynegum ðe cuce ðā git wǣron *he sent to all the kings that were still alive*, Jos. 11, 1: Homl. Th. i. 72, 9. Ðā get ic furðor gefregen *I yet further learned*, Cd. 218; Th. 278, 21; Sat. 225. Ðā giet, Chr. 921; Erl. 108, 3. Alwalda ðec gōde forgylde swā he nū gyt dyde *may the Almighty repay thee with good as he has done until now*, Beo. Th. 1917; B. 956. Ā ic ðæt heóld nū giet *I have ever held that until now*, Exon. 120 b; Th. 463, 21; Hö. 73. Ic wille mid giddum get gecȳðan hū *I will further make known in songs how . . .*, Bt. Met. Fox 13, 2; Met. 13, 1. Gif giet lǣst mīna lāra *if even now he obey my counsels*, Cd. 29; Th. 39, 2; Gen. 618. Ne wæs ðā giet wiht geworden *there was as yet nothing made*, 5; Th. 7, 8; Gen. 103. Nǣfre git *never yet*, Beo. Th. 1171; B. 583. Swȳðor gyt *yet more*, Judth. 11; Thw. 24, 11; Jud. 182.

gita, gieta, geta, gyta; *adv. Yet, still:*—Dōþ gieta swā *yet do they so*, Cd. 48; Th. 61, 7; Gen. 993. Gita *yet*, Bt. Met. Fox 23, 13; Met. 23, 7. Ne wearþ wæl māre ǣfer gieta folces gefylled *never yet was greater slaughter of people made*, Chr. 937; Erl. 115, 15; Ædelst. 66: Cd. 113; Th. 148, 34; Gen. 2466. Reord wæs ðā gieta eorþbūendum ān gemǣne *there was as yet one speech common to dwellers on earth*, 79; Th. 98, 25; Gen. 1635. Hiora nǣnig næs ðā gieta *as yet none of them existed*, Bt. Met. Fox 8, 24; Met. 8, 12. [*O. Frs.* jeta.]

GITAN, ic gite, gyte, giete, ðū gitst, he git, *pl.* gitaþ gytaþ, gietaþ; *p.* geat, *pl.* geáton; *pp* giten *To* GET, *take, obtain;* adipisci, capere, assequi. Only found in the following compounds:—a-gitan, an-, and-, be-, bi-, for-, ofer-, on-, under-: and-git; andgit, -ful. -fullīce, -ol, -tācen: forgitol, ofergitol, -nes: ongitful, -līce. [*O. Sax.* -getan; bi-getan *invenire, assequi*, far-getan, for-getan *perdere e memoria. oblivisci: O. Frs.* jeta; for-jeta *oblivisci: O. H. Ger.* gezan *adipisci: Goth.* -gitan; *p.* -gat, *pl.* -gētum; *pp.* -gitans *adipisci: O. Nrs.* geta *adipisci, assequi, gignere, dare, præbere.*]

giþcorn, es; *n. Spurge laurel:*—Ðeós wyrt ðe man lactyridem and ōðrum naman giþcorn nemneþ *this plant which is called lacterida and by another name githcorn*, Herb. 113; Lchdm. i. 226, 12: L. M. ii. 65, 1; Lchdm. ii. 292, 9: v. glossary. [Hall. Dict. gith *corn-cockle: Palladius on Husbandrie* gith *cockle*, x. 155.]

giþrife, gitrife, an; *f. Cockle;* agrostemma githago:—Gyþrife, L. M. i. 38, 4; Lchdm. ii. 92, 22. Giþrife, 5; Lchdm. ii. 92, 27. Genim gitrifan, 1, 5; Lchdm. ii. 18, 23.

gītsere, es; *m. An avaricious, a covetous person, miser:*—Ða ðe wēron gītsaras *qui erant avari*, Lk. Skt. Lind. 16, 14. Se ungesǣliga gȳtsere wile māre habban ðonne him genihtsumaþ *the miserable covetous man wants to have more than suffices him*, Homl. Th. i. 64, 33, 35: Bt. 16, 3; Fox 56, 16. He wæs se wyresta gītsere ðe he gesealde wið feó heofcones hlāford *he was the worst covetous man because he sold for money the lord of heaven*, Blickl. Homl. 69, 13, 10. Gītseras ðe on mannum heora ǣhta on wōh nimaþ *covetous men who take their property from men wrongfully*, 61, 21. [*A. R.* ȝissare: *M. H. Ger.* gitesære.]

gītsian; *p.* ode; *pp.* od *To covet, desire:*—Ða ðe ðæs welan gītsiaþ hī biþ symle wædlan on hyra mōde *those who covet [worldly] wealth will ever be poor in their mind*, Prov. Kmbl. 50. Gȳtsaþ *covets*, Beo. Th. 3502; B. 1749. Fōþres ne gītsaþ *it craves not food*, Exon. 114 b;

Th. 440, 1; Rä. 51, 11: Bt. 26, 2; Fox 92, 17. Ðá ðú gîtsiende blǽda náme *when thou coveting didst take the fruit*, Cd. 42; Th. 55, 7; Gen. 890. Ðú gîtsigenda and ðú welega *thou covetous and wealthy man*, Blickl. Homl. 51, 1. Gýtsiendre heortan *insatiabili corde*, Ps. Spl. 100, 6. Mid gîtsigendum eágum *with covetous eyes*, Homl. Th. i. 68, 26. Gýtsian *concupiscere*, Ps. Spl. 61, 10. [*A. R.* ȝiscen: *M. H. Ger.* gitsen.]

gîtsung, e; *f. Covetousness, avarice, cupidity, desire*:—Ða ðe ne sécaþ heora ágen gestreón þurh gýtsunge *those who do not seek their own gain through covetousness*, Homl. Th. ii. 74, 34. Se þrydda heáfodleahter is gýtsung *the third chief sin is avarice*, 218, 21: 592, 6. Hí ongunnan gîtsunge begán *concupierunt concupiscentias*, Ps. Th. 105, 12. Gîtsung *avaritia*, 118, 36: Mk. Skt. 7, 22. Þurh ða ungefyldan gîtsunge woruldmonna *through the unsatisfied covetousness of worldly men*, Bt. 7, 3; Fox 20, 26. Grundleás gîtsung gilpes and ǽhta *the boundless desire for glory and possessions*, Bt. Met. Fox 7, 29; Met. 7, 15: Bt. 16, 3; Fox 56, 2. Nales he giémde þurh gîtsunga lǽnes lîfwelan *he cared not from covetousness for the frail wealth of this world*, Exon. 34 b; Th. 111, 4; Gú. 121. Þurh his ágene gîtsunga he ǽfre ðas leóde mid ungylde tyrwigende wæs *through his own avarice he was ever harassing this nation with bad taxes*, Chr. 1100; Erl. 236, 1: 1086; Erl. 222, 24. From ðisse worlde gîtsungum *from the desires of this world*, Blickl. Homl. 57, 23. [*Laym.* ȝitsung: *Orm.* ȝittsunng: *A. R.* ȝissung.]

giú. v. geó.

giuan. v. giwian.

Giúl *Yule, Christmas.* v. geól.

giung; *def.* se giunga; *adj. Young, youthful*; jŭvĕnis, adolescens:—Wæs sum giung mon *ĕrat quidam adolescens*, Bd. 4, 32; S. 611, 17. Se giunga *the young man*, Cd. 224; Th. 297, 3; Sat. 511. Ic ðé giungne underfêng *I took thee young*, Bt. 8; Fox 24, 23. v. geong.

giungra, an; *m. A junior, disciple, follower*; discipŭlus, assecla:—He ðæt rîce forlêt and his giungrum bebeád *ipse relicto regno ac jŭvĕniōrĭbus commendāto*, Bd. 5, 7; S. 621, 10. v. geongra.

giw, giow, eow, es; *m? A griffin, a four-footed bird*; gryps = γρύψ, griphus:—Giw *griphus*, Wrt. Voc. 280, 5.

giwian, giowian, giwan; *p.* ode; *pp.* de *To ask*; petere, postulare:—Wælde giwiga ł giuiade *postulasset*, Mt. Kmbl. Lind 17, 7. Giuiga *petere*, Rtl. 179, 34. Ic giuge wælle *petam*, Mk. Skt. Lind. 6, 24. Huu giues ðú *quomodo poscis*, Jn. Skt. Lind. 4, 9. Se ðe giuæþ *qui petit*, Mt. Kmbl. Lind. 7, 8. We giugaþ *poscimus*, Rtl. 52, 10. Giude *mendicans*, Mk. Skt. p. 4, 16. Ðæt hia giudon *ut peterent*, Mt. Kmbl. 27, 20. Giwig *pete*, Mk. Skt. Lind. [Rush. giowa] 6, 22. Giwas *petite*, Mt. Kmbl. Lind. 7, 7. Giuwende *petentes*, Mk. Skt. p. 4, 14. Giuendo *postulata*, 18. Giuiendum *petentibus*, Mt. Kmbl. Lind. 7, 11.

giwung, e; *f. An asking, a petition*; postulatio, petitio:—Fîfo giunga *quinque petitionum*, Lk. Skt. p. 7, 2. Giwunges, Rtl. 39, 23.

glad. v. glæd.

glâd *glided, slid*, Beo. Th. 4152; B. 2073; *p. of* glîdan.

Glademuð *Gledmouth.* v. Cledemúð.

gladian; *p.* ode. I. *to be glad*; exultare:—Ða gladia worhtest *quos lætari fecisti*, Rtl. 94, 15. Ða ðe gedrêfaþ me gladiaþ *qui tribulant me exultabunt*, Ps. Lamb. 12, 5. Abraham gladade ł glæd wæs *Abraham gavisus est*; *Wick.* Abraham gladide, Jn. Skt. Rush. 8, 56. Glada and blissa *be glad and rejoice*, Apol. Th. 7, 2. Ne gladige on ðæt cyning *let no king rejoice at that*, Lchdm. iii. 442, 35. II. *to make glad*:—Ic gladige *gratificor*, Ælfc. Gr. 37; Som. 39, 3. Drihten mid to gladienne *to make glad the Lord therewith*, Lev. 1, 3. Gladigan *demulcere*, Hpt. Gl. 476. [*Icel.* gleðja *to gladden*; gleðjask *to become bright, glad.*]

glæd, es; *n. Gladness, joy*:—Swá missenlîce meahtig dryhten eallum dǽleþ sumum earfeþa dǽl sumum geógoþe glæd *thus diversely does the mighty Lord allot to all, to one a share of troubles, to one the gladness of youth*, Exon. 88 a; Th. 331, 14; Vy. 68. *Perhaps here the form given by Lye* ǽr sun gó to glade, v. Grm. D. M. 702–3. [Cf. *Icel.* gleði; *f*: *Dan.* glæde *gladness, merriment*: *and A. R.* gledful.]

GLÆD; *adj.* I. *shining, bright*:—Glæd mid golde *bright with gold*, Exon. 125 a; Th. 480, 16; Rä. 64, 3. Wyrþ heó ungladu ðeáh heó ǽr gladu wǽre on to lôcienne *it* [*the sea*] *becomes turbid though before it was bright to look at* [cf. glæshlutru on to seónne, 24], *and the Latin* sordida visibus obstat], Bt. 6; Fox 14, 26: Bt. Met. Fox 5, 21; Met. 5, 11. Godes condelle glædum gimme *God's candle, the bright jewel* [*the sun*], Exon. 57 a; Th. 204, 3; Ph. 92: 64 b; Th. 237, 20; Ph. 593. Glæd seolfor *shining silver*, Cd. 129; Th. 164, 24; Gen. 2719. Óðer biþ golde glædra óðer biþ grundum sweartra *one is brighter than gold, the other darker than the depths*, Salm. Kmbl. 975; Sal. 488. Gimma gladost *brightest of jewels*, Exon. 60 a; Th. 218, 3; Ph. 289. II. *glad, cheerful, joyous, bright*:—Ðá wærþ he swíðe glæd *then he was very glad*, Chr. 656; Erl. 30, 20. Glæd wæs *gavisus est*, Jn. Skt. Lind. 8, 56. Wosaþ glæd *exultate*, Lk. Skt. Lind. 6, 23. Glædman *hilaris*, Ælfc. Gl. 88; Som. 74, 87; Wrt. Voc. 50, 67. Ǽfre he biþ ânes môdes and glæd þurhwunaþ *he is ever of one mind and continues cheerful*, Homl. Th. i. 456, 25: 72, 27. He wearþ glæd on his ansýne *he was bright of face*, Guthl. 2; Gdwin. 12, 20. Wînes glæd *merry with wine*, Exon. 117 a; Th. 449, 28; Dóm. 78. Glæd gumena weorud *a joyous band of men*, 32 a; Th. 101, 5; Cri. 1654. Nolde gladu ǽfre syððan ætýwan, *she, joyous, would not ever afterwards appear*, Cd. 72; Th. 89, 14; Gen. 1480. Iacob byþ on glædum sǽlum *exultabit Jacob*, Ps. Th. 52, 8. Sefa wæs ðé glædra *her mind was the gladder*, Elen. Kmbl. 1909; El. 956. III. *pleasant, kind, mild, courteous*:—Glæd man *jucundus homo*, Ps. Th. 111, 5. Glade fǽmnan *virgines*, 148, 12. Glædman Hróþgâr *courteous Hrothgar*, Beo. Th. 740; B. 367. Beó wið Geátas glæd geofena gemyndig *be kind to the Gauts, mindful of gifts*, 2350; B. 1173: 1730; B. 863. Mîn Drihten hine gedó glædne wiþ eów *may my Lord make him kind towards you*, Gen. 43, 14. Ðæt we ðone Hǽlend hæbben us glædne *that we may have the Saviour propitious to us*, Th. Chart. 240, 26: Exon. 12 b; Th. 20, 10; Cri. 315. [*Icel.* glaðr *bright, glad*: *Dan.* glad *glad*: *O. H. Ger.* glat *limpidus, candidus*: *Ger.* glatt.]

glædene, an; *Gladden.* v. Lchdm. ii. Glossary.

glædlîc; *adj. Bright, pleasant, kind*:—Scîneþ ðé leóht glædlîc ongeán *the light shineth bright over against thee*, Cd. 29; Th. 38, 31; Gen. 615. Hú glædlîc biþ and gôd swylce *quam bonum et quam jucundum*, Ps. 132, 1. Me gúþhere forgeaf glædlîcne máþþum *Guthhere gave me a splendid jewel*, Exon. 85 b; Th. 322, 31; Vîd. 66.

glædlîce; *adv. Gladly, pleasantly, kindly, cheerfully*:—He glædlîce fram heom eallum onfangen wæs *he was gladly received by them all*, Chr. 1014; Erl. 150, 17. He frǽfrode hig and spræc glædlîce *he comforted them and spake kindly* [*unto them*], Gen. 50, 21. He glædlîce all eorþlîc þing wæs oferhleápende *alacriter terrena quæque transiliens*, Bd. 2, 7; S. 509, 13. Nú ðú ðus rôtlîce and ðus glædlîce to us sprecende eart *qui tam hilariter nobiscum loqueris*, 4, 24; S. 598, 38: Cd. 109; Th. 143, 18; Gen. 2381.

glædman, Beo. Th. 740; B. 367. Thorpe and Kemble take this word as the oblique case of a noun = *gladness, pleasure*; but see 'glæd.'

glæd-môd; *adj. Glad-minded, cheerful, of good cheer, joyous, pleasant, kind, courteous*:—Glædmôd wes ðú *animæquior esto*, Mk. Skt. Rush. 10, 49. Geát wæs glædmôd *the Gaut was glad of mind*, Beo. Th. 3574; B. 1785: Exon. 62 b; Th. 229, 28; Ph. 462: Andr. Kmbl. 2119; An. 1061. Guman glædmôde god wurðedon *the men with cheerful mind worshipped God*, Cd. 187; Th. 232, 14; Dan. 260. Gongaþ glædmôde *go with gladsome mind*, Exon. 16 a; Th. 36, 14; Cri. 576. He biþ ðám gôdum glædmôd on gesihþe *he shall be to the good pleasant of countenance*, 21 a; Th. 56, 36; Cri. 911. Glædmôd *kind*, 48 a; Th. 165, 27; Gú. 1035. [*O. Sax.* glad-môd.] v. glæd.

glædmôdnes, se; *f. Gladness, cheerfulness, joyfulness, kindness*:—Ac ðonne ðæt mennisce môd Godes glædmôdnesse mid gôdum weorcum ne geandsworaþ *sed cum largientem Deum humana mens boni operis responsione non sequitur*, Past. 50, 3; Swt. 391, 6.

glædnes, se; *f. Gladness, joy, cheerfulness*:—Ongan se bisceop lustfullian glædnesse his dǽda *delectabatur antistes alacritate actionis*, Bd. 5, 19; S. 637, 47. Glædnisse miclo *gaudio magno*, Mt. Kmbl. 2, 10: 13, 20: 25, 21. Glædniso *lætitia*, Rtl. 57, 2.

glædscipe, es; *m. Gladness, joy*:—Crist is mid ealles môdes gledscype to herienne *Christ is to be praised with joy of all the mind*, Lchdm. iii. 436, 19. Glædscip mîn *gaudium meum*, Jn. Skt. Rush. 3, 29. [*Laym.* gladscipe: *Orm.* gladdshipe: *A. R.* gledschipe.]

glǽdsted. v. glêdstede.

glǽm, es; *m. Brightness, splendour, radiance*:—Se æðela glǽm *the noble brightness* [*the sun*], Exon. 51 b; Th. 178, 31; Gú. 1252: Th. 179, 18; Gú. 1263. Sunnan glǽm *the sun's radiance*, 59 b: Th. 215, 15; Ph. 253. Mîn se swêtesta sunnan scîma hwæt ðú glǽm hafast *my sweetest sunshine ah! thou hast radiant beauty*, 68 a; Th. 252, 23; Jul. 167. Ðé ofsihþ glǽmes grêne folde *the green earth shall deny thee her beauty*, Cd. 48; Th. 62, 22; Gen. 1018. [*O. H. Ger.* gleimo *nitor.*]

glær, es; *n. Amber*; electrum, succinum, Ælfc. Gl. 51; Som. 66, 6; Wrt. Voc. 34. 66: Wrt. Voc. 286, 68: [Cf. *Icel.* gler *glass*; and see Grm. Gesch. D. S. 499.]

GLÆS, es; *n. Glass*:—Glæs *vitrum*, Ælfc. Gl. 51; Som. 66, 5; Wrt. Voc. 34, 65. Beorhtre ðonne glæs *brighter than glass*, Homl. Th. ii. 518, 10. Ðæt scîre glæs *the clear glass*, Exon. 26 b; Th. 78, 33; Cri. 1283. Ðæt nebb lîxeþ swá glæs oððe gim *the beak glitters like glass or gem*, 60 a; Th. 218, 25; Ph. 300. Biþ ðonne se flǽschoma ascýred swá glæs *then shall the body be as transparent as glass*, Blickl. Homl. 109, 36. Of glæse geworht *made of glass*, 127, 33. Mid glase geworht *wrought with glass*; comptos vitro parietes, Bt. 5, 1; Fox 10, 16. [*O. H. Ger.* glas, clas *vitrum, electrum*: *Icel.* gler.]

glæsen; *adj. Made of glass, grey*; vitreus:—Glæsen *vitreus*, Ælfc. Gr. 5; Som. 4, 60. Ðǽr is ahangen sum glæsen fæt *there is hung a glass vessel*, Homl. Th. i. 510, 1: ii. 158, 16: Blickl. Homl. 209, 4, 7. Hî toslôgon his glæsenne calic *they broke his glass chalice*, Shrn. 114, 25. Sǽ glæsen *mare vitreum*, Mt. Kmbl. p 10, 3. [*Piers P.* glasen: *Prompt. Parv.* glasyne: *O. H. Ger.* glesin.]

glæs-fæt, es; *n. A glass vessel, a glass:*—He sende him glæsfæt full wînes *misit ei calicem vini*, Bd. 5, 5; S. 618, 12. [*Laym.* glæsfat: *O. H. Ger.* glasfaz.]

glæs-hluttor; *adj. Clear as glass:*—Ða sǽ ðe ǽr wæs glæshlutru *the sea that before was clear as glass*, Bt. 6; Fox 14, 24: Bt. Met. Fox 5, 15; Met. 5, 8. Îs glisnaþ glæshluttur *ice glistens clear as glass*, Runic pm. Kmbl. 341, 16; Rún. 11.

Glæstinga-burh; *gen.* burge; *dat.* byrig; Glestinga-byrig, Glasting-byri; *f.* GLASTONBURY, *Somerset:*—He getymbrade ðæt menster æt Glæstingabyrig *he built the monastery at Glastonbury*, Chr. 688; Erl. 42, note.

glæterian *to glitter, shine;* splendescere, Hpt. Gl. 419.

glǽw. v. gleáw.

glappe, an; *f. Buckbean* [?], Lchdm. i. 398, 9: iii. 292, 7.

glas. v. glæs.

glauwnes. v. gleáwnes.

GLEÁM, es; *m. A joyous noise, jubilation, joy:*—Hæfdon gleám and dreám engla þreátas *the hosts of angels had joy and delight*, Cd. 1; Th. 2, 1; Gen. 12. [*Icel.* glaumr; *m. a merry noise, merriment, joy;* gleym-ask *to be merry*.]

GLEÁW; *adj. Clear-sighted, wise, skilful, sagacious, prudent, good;* sagax, prudens, astutus, sapiens, gnarus:—Gleáw *expertus*, i. e. *multum peritus*, Ælfc. Gl. 18; Som. 58, 121; Wrt. Voc. 22, 35. Gleáw *sagax* vel *gnarus*, Wrt. Voc. 76, 9. Gleáw þeów *servus prudens*, Mk. Skt. 24, 45: 25, 2, 4. Ic gehîrde secgan ðæt ðû wǽre gleáw ðǽron *I heard say that thou wast skilled therein*, Gen. 41, 15. Sumne wîsne man and glǽwne *a discreet and wise man*, 33. Ðâ ongan he mid gleáwe môde þencean and smeágean *cœpitque sagaci animo conjicere*, Bd. 3, 10; S. 534, 20. Nis nǽnig swâ gleáw *there is none so skilful*, Cd. 221; Th. 286, 10; Sat. 350: Exon. 11 a; Th. 14, 17; Cri. 220: 120 b; Th. 463, 27; Hö. 76: Andr. Kmbl. 2992; An. 1499. Sum biþ leóþa gleáw *one is skilled in songs*, Exon. 79 a; Th. 296, 16; Crä. 52: 79 b; Th. 298, 33; Crä. 94: Bt. Met. Fox 1, 103; Met. 1, 52. Ǽcraftig gleáw ge-þances *cunning in the law, wise of thought*, Cd. 212; Th. 262, 13; Dan. 743. Swâ him se gleáwa bebeád Gregorius *as the wise Gregory commanded him*, Menol. Fox 198; Men. 100. Þurh gleáwne geþanc *by skilful thought*, Cd. 52; Th. 66, 3; Gen. 1078: Ps. Th. 67, 12: Elen. Kmbl. 1185; El. 594. Ic andette êcne Drihten ðæne goodan God forðan ic hine gleáwne wât *confitemini Domino quoniam bonus*, Ps. Th. 106, 1: 117, 1. Ioseph se ðe gingst wæs hys gebrôðra and eác gleáwra ofer hî ealle *Joseph who was youngest of his brethren and wise beyond them all*, Ors. 1, 5; Bos. 28, 8. He wæs on ðâm dagum gleáwast to wîge *he was in those days the most expert man in war*, 4, 1; Bos. 77, 8. On gecynde se gleáwesta man *vir natura sagacissimus*, Bd. 2, 9; S. 512, 13. Hwilc ðære geógoþe gleáwost wǽre *which of the youth were most skilful*, Cd. 176; Th. 221, 1; Dan. 81. [*Laym.* glæuest *most skilful*: *O. Sax.* glau: *Goth.* glaggwus *diligent*: *Icel.* glöggr: *Scot.* gleg *quick of perception*: *O. H. Ger.* glaw: *Ger.* glau.]

Gleáw-ceaster, Gleáwan-ceaster, Glêu-cester, Glêw-cæster, Glêw-cester, Glôu-cester, Glôwe-ceaster; *gen. dat.* -ceastre GLOUCESTER, *a county town in the west of England:*—Æþelflæd lîð binnan Gleáwceastre *Ethelfleda lies buried at Gloucester*, Chr. 918; Erl. 109, 7.

gleáwe; *adv. Wisely, prudently, well:*—Efne me God gleáwe fultumeþ *ecce Deus adjuvat me*, Ps. Th. 53, 4. Ðæt byþ secga gehwam snytru on frymðe, ðæt he Godes egesan gleáwe healde *initium sapientiæ timor Domini*, 110, 7: 142, 11. Gleáwast, 118, 99.

Gleáwe-cestre-scir *Gloucestershire*, Chr. 1122; Erl. 249, 15.

gleáw-ferhþ; *adj. Of a wise mind, sagacious:*—Gleáwferhþ hæleþ *a man wise of mind*, Cd. 57; Th. 70, 12; Gen. 1152: 112; Th. 147, 27; Gen. 2446.

gleáw-hycgende; *adj. Thinking wisely:*—Gif ðû onsecgan nelt gleáwhycgende *if thou, wisely considering, wilt not sacrifice*, Exon. 69 a; Th. 257, 24; Jul. 252.

gleáw-hýdig; *adj. Wise of thought, heedful, prudent, sagacious:*—Gleáwhýdig wîf *the woman wise of thought*, Judth. 11; Thw. 23, 30; Jud. 148: Elen. Kmbl. 1866; El. 935. Glæd man gleáwhýdig seteþ sôðne dôm þurh his sylfes word *jucundus homo disponet sermones suos in judicio*, Ps. Th. 111, 5.

gleáwlic; *adj. Wise, wary, astute:*—On sprǽcum gleáwlîce *in loquelis astuti*, Coll. Monast. Th. 32, 29.

gleáwlîce; *adv. Prudently, wisely, clearly, well:*—Forþam ðe he gleáwlîce dyde *quia prudenter fecisset*, Lk Bos. 16, 8. Gleáwlîce *astute*, Blickl. Gloss. Gleóulîce *clare*, Mk. Skt. Lind. 8, 25. Ðâ ðæra bæcistra ealdor gehîrde hû glǽwlîce he ðæt swefen rehte *when the chief baker heard how well he explained the dream*, Gen. 40, 16: Exon. 9 b; Th. 9, 6; Cri. 130: 27 a; Th. 81, 24; Cri. 1328: Andr. Kmbl. 853; An. 427: Elen. Kmbl. 377; El. 189. Ic mîne sâwle wylle full gleáwlîce Gode underþeódan *nonne Deo subdita erit anima mea?* Ps. Th. 61, 1. Ic gewitnesse wîse ðîne ongeat gleáwlîce *initio cognovi de testimoniis tuis*, 118, 152: 106, 42: Andr. Kmbl. 1721: An. 863.

gleáw-môd; *adj. Of wise mind:*—Frôd guma gleáwmod *a wise man sagacious in mind*, Exon. 64 a; Th. 236, 8: Ph. 571: 47 a; Th. 162, 13; Gû. 975: Andr. Kmbl. 3156; An. 1581: Cd. 193; Th. 243, 22; Dan. 440.

gleáwnes, glauwnes, se; *f. Prudence, skill, wisdom, ability, sagacity, acuteness:*—Gleáwnys *argutiæ*, Ælfc. Gl. 115; Som. 80, 48; Wrt. Voc. 61, 26. Gleáwnysse *prudentiam*, Ps. Spl. 48, 3: 104, 20. He hæfde ða gleáwnysse Godes beboda to healdenne and to lǽranne *industriam faciendi et docendi mandata cælestia*, Bd. 3, 17; S. 545, 9. Twegen geonge æðelingas mycelre glauwnesse men of Angelþeóde *duo juvenes magnæ indolis, de nobilibus Anglorum*, 3, 27; S. 558, 29. Wer well gelǽred and scearpre gleáwnysse *vir doctissimus atque excellentis ingenii*, 4, 23; S. 594, 35. Þeód is bûton geþeahte and bûtan glǽwnisse *the nation is void of counsel and of understanding*, Deut. 32, 28. Beheald ðas sunnan mid gleáwnysse *behold this sun intelligently*, Homl. Th. i. 284, 34. Seó orþonce glâunes *the ingenious skill*, Blickl. Homl. 99, 31. Mid gleáwnesse feónd oferfeohtaþ *with prudence they overcome the fiend*, Exon. 44 a; Th. 150, 6; Gû. 774: Elen. Kmbl. 1920; El. 962.

gleáwscipe, es; *m. Sagacity, wisdom:*—To rihtwîsra gleáwscype *ad prudentiam justorum*, Lk. Skt. 1, 17: 2, 47.

GLÉD, e; *f. Burning coal, live coal, gleed, ember, fire, flame;* pruna, carbo, flamma:—Glêd *pruna*, Ælfc. Gl. 30; Som. 61, 75; Wrt. Voc. 27, 5: 82, 53. Glêda fýres *carbones ignis*, Ps. Spl. 17, 14: Ps. Th. 17, 12. Swâ rîcels byþ ðonne hit glêda bærnaþ *sicut incensum*, 140, 2: 119, 4. Ða þegnas stôdon æt ðâm glêdon *stabunt ministri ad prunas*, Jn. Skt. 18, 18: 21, 9. Gloedo *scintillæ*, Rtl. 86, 34. Me is leófre ðæt mînne lîchaman glêd fæðmie *I would rather that fire should embrace my body*, Beo. Th. 5298; B. 2652: 6220; B. 3114: Exon. 87 b; Th. 330, 4; Vy. 46: 108 a; Th. 412, 23; Rä. 31, 4. Goldfrætwe glêda forswelgaþ *flames shall devour the gold ornaments*, 22 b; Th. 62, 4; Cri. 996. Biþ eal ðes ginne grund glêda gefylled *all this spacious earth shall be filled with gleeds*, 116 a; Th. 445, 24; Dôm. 12: Elen. Kmbl. 2601; El. 1302. Glêdum spîwan *to spit forth flames*, Beo. Th. 4614; B. 2312: 4659; B. 2335. [*O. Frs.* glêd: *Icel.* glóð; *f. red-hot embers*: *O. H. Ger.* gluot *pruna*: *Ger.* gluth: *and* cf. *O. Sax.* glôd-welo.]

gleddian; *p.* ode *To spatter:*—Gledda, Lchdm. iii. 292, 14.

glêd-egesa, an; *m. Terror caused by fire*, Beo. Th. 5293; B. 2650.

glêd-fæt, es; *n. A fire-vat, chafing-dish:*—Dô glêda an glêdfæt *put live coals in a chafing dish*, L. M. 3, 62; Lchdm. ii. 346, 3.

glêd-stede, es; *m. A place for a fire, an altar:*—On ðam glêdstyde *at the altar*, Cd. 86; Th. 108, 22; Gen. 1810. On ðæm glǽdstede gild onsægde *made an offering on the altar*, 137; Th. 172, 10; Gen. 2842.

glemm *a spot, blemish;* macula, Off. Reg. 15, Lye. [Cf. glam *a wound, sore*, Halliwell; *and see* headu-glem.]

glenc, glencg. v. glenge.

glendran *to devour, swallow;* devorare:—Monn glendrende ł swelgande *homo vorax*, Mt. Kmbl. Rush. 11, 19. Olbendu glendrende *camelum glutientes*, 23, 24. v. for-glendran.

gleng, e; *f. An ornament, honour;* ornamentum, decus:—Gifu gumena byþ gleng *gift is an ornament of men*, Runic pm. Kmbl. 340, 24; Run. 7. Alege nû ðîne glenga *now put off thine ornaments*, Ex. 33, 5, 6. Gebyrdne hine gesihþ glæncge getâcnaþ *if he sees himself bearded, it betokens honour*, Lchdm. iii. 200, 5.

glengan, glengcan; *p.* de; *pp.* ed; *v. a. To adorn, trim, deck, compose, set in order;* ornare:—Þeódnes cynegold sôþfæstra gehwone glengeþ *the prince's crown shall adorn each of the just*, Exon. 64 b; Th. 238, 19; Ph. 606. Glengdon heora leóhtfatu *ornaverunt lampades suas*, Mt. Skt. 25, 7: Exon. 94 a; Th. 353, 14; Reim. 12. Glenged *adorned*, 352, 30; Reim. 3. Glengede word *composita verba*, Lye.

glenge, es; *m. An ornament:*—Hwǽr beóþ ðonne ða glengeas and ða mycclan gegyrelan ðe he ðone lîchoman ǽr mid frætwode *where shall then be the ornaments and the grand apparel with which he before decked his body?* Blickl. Homl. 111, 35. Glengas, 99, 24, 19: 115, 2. Gesih ðâs glencas *vide has ædificationes*, Mk. Skt. Lind. 13, 2.

glengista [?]:—To ðon ðæt hwæt hwygo to ðære ongietenisse ðissa mînra þinga ðîn gelis and glengista geþeóde *ut aliquid per novarum rerum cognitionem studio et ingenio possit accedere*, Nar. 1, 20.

glenglic; *adj. Full of pomp;* pompa plenus, Cot. 154.

gleó-, glig-beám, es; *m. A glee-beam, harp;* musicum lignum, harpa:—Nis hearpan wyn, gomen gleóbeámes *there is no joy of harp, the mirth of the glee-beam*, Beo. Th. 4518; B. 2263. Sum mæg hearpan stirgan, gleóbeám grêtan *one can awake the harp, touch the glee-beam*, Exon. 17 b; Th. 42, 9; Cri. 670. Gligbeám *tympanum*, Blickl. Gloss.

gleó-, glig-cræft, es; *m. Glee-craft, art of music, minstrelsy, playing;* ars musica, histrionia, mimica gesticulatio, Greg. Dial. 1, 9. [*Laym.* gleo-cræft.]

gleó-dreám, es; *m. Glee-joy, pleasure caused by music;* jubilum:—Nû se herewîsa hleahtor alegde, gamen and gleódreám *now the martial leader has ceased from laughter, sport and joy of music*, Beo. Th. 6034; B. 3021. [*Laym.* gleo-drem.]

gleó-gamen, -gomen, es; *n. Glee-pleasure, merriment, sport;* jocus, ludus jocularis. v. gleó, gamen.

gleó-hleóþriend *a glee-sounder, musician, minstrel.* v. gliw-hleóþriend.

gleó-mæ̂den *a glee-maiden.* v. gliew-mēden.

gleó-man, glī-man, glii-man, gliig-man, glig-man, -mann, es; *m. A glee-man, musician, minstrel, jester, player, buffoon;* musicus, cantor, joculator, histrio, scurra, mimus, pantomimus:—Leóþ wæs asungen, gleómannes gyd *the lay was sung, the gleeman's song*, Beo. Th. 2324; B. 1160. Wera gehwylcum wīslīcu word gerīsaþ, gleómen gied *to every man wise words are fitting, song to the gleeman*, Exon. 91 b; Th. 344, 1; Gn. Ex. 167: 87 a; Th. 326, 29; Wīd. 136. Gligman *mimus, jocista, scurra, pantomimus*, Ælfc. Gl. 61; Som. 68, 59, 60; Wrt. Voc. 39, 42, 43. Gligman *mimus* vel *scurra*, 73, 69: *sophista, parasitus*, Hpt. Gl. 406, 483, 504: *seductor*, Gl. Prud. Gif preóst glīman wurþe *if a priest become a gleeman*, L. N. P. L. 41; Th. ii. 296, 11. Monige welige menn fēdaþ yfle gliigmen [gliimen, Cot. MS.] *nonnulli divites nutriunt histriones*, Past. 44, 6; Swt. 327, 7; Hat. MS. See Turner's History of the Anglo-Saxons, Bk. 7, c. 7.

gleomu, e; *f. Splendour:*—Gleoma gefrætwed *splendidly adorned*, Exon. 124 b; Th. 478, 1; Ruin. 34.

gleó-, gliw-stæf, es; *m. Joy:*—Gliwstafum *joyously*, Exon. 77 a; Th. 289, 22; Wand. 52. [Cf. *other compounds with* stæf, e. g. ǣr-, sār-stæf.]

gleow, gleó, gliw, glig, es; *n.* GLEE, *joy, music, musical accompaniment of a song, mirth, jesting, sport;* gaudium, musica, facetiæ, mimus, ludibrium:—Ðǣr wæs gidd and gleó *there was song and glee* [*music*], Beo. Th. 4216; B. 2105. And gegaderade, gleowe sungon, on ðæra manna midle geongra, on tympanis, togenum strengum *conjuncti psallentibus, in medio juvenum tympanistriarum*, Ps. Th. 67, 24: Cot. 84. v. Grm. D. M. 854. [*O. Nrs.* glȳ; *n. lætitia, gaudium.*] v. gliw, glig.

gleowian, gliowian, gliwian, glywian; *p.* ode; *pp.* od *To play on an instrument, sing, joke, jest, act the gleeman* or *buffoon;* fidicinare, jocari, scurrari, scurram agere:—Ðā ongan se wīsdōm gliowian *then wisdom began to sing*, Bt. 12; Fox 36, 6. Ðæt ǣnig preóst ne gliwige *that no priest act the gleeman*, L. Edg. C. 58; Th. ii. 256, 16. He sumu þing ætgædere mid him sprecende and gleowiende wæs ðe ðǣr ǣr inne wǣron *cum ibidem positi aliqua, una cum eis qui ibidem ante inerant, loquerentur ac jocarentur*, Bd. 4, 24; S. 598, 34. Mādena glywiendra *juvencularum tympanistriarum*, Ps. Spl. 67, 27. [*Laym.* gleowien *to chant, play: A. R.* gleowede *was merry.*]

gleów-līce. v. gleáw-līce.

gleó-, glió-word, es; *n. A musical strain, a song*, Bt. Met. Fox 7, 3; Met. 7, 2.

gleow-stōl, es; *m. A glee-stool, seat of joy;* lætitiæ sedes *vel* sella:—Þone gleowstōl [MS. gleáw- *prudens, gnarus*] brōðor mīn āgnade *my brother possessed the seat of joy*, Exon. 130 a; Th. 499, 1; Rä. 88, 9.

glēsan *to gloss, explain;* interpretari. v. next word.

glēsing, glēsincg, e; *f. A* GLOSSING, *interpretation, explanation;* glossa:—Ðæt is glēsincg ðonne mann glēsþ ða earfoðan word mid eáðran Lēdene *that is glossing when one explains the difficult words with easier Latin*, Ælfc. Gr. 50; Som. 51, 43.

glēw. v. gleáw.

glid; *adj. Slippery, ready to glide;* lubricus, Ps. Spl. C. 34, 7.

glida, an; *m. A kite, glede:*—Glida *milvus*, Ælfc. Gl. 38; Som. 63, 29; Wrt. Voc. 29, 48: 77, 14. Se ðe þurh reáflāc gewilnaþ ða þing ðe he mid his eágum widūtan sceáwaþ se is glida nā culfre *he who by rapine desires the things that he sees with his eyes without, he is a kite, not a dove*, Homl. Th. i. 586, 6: Exon. 106 b; Th. 406, 23; Rä. 25, 5. [*Icel.* gleða.]

GLĪDAN, he glīdeþ, glīt; *p.* glād, *pl.* glidon; *pp.* gliden *To* GLIDE, *slip, slide;* labi:—Sunne gewāt to sete glīdan *the sun went gliding to its setting*, Andr. Kmbl. 2610; An. 1306: 2498; An. 1250: Exon. 57 a; Th. 204, 24; Ph. 102: Ps. C. 50, 145; Ps. Grn. ii. 280, 145. Ðeós bāt glīdeþ on geofene *this boat glideth over the ocean*, Andr. Kmbl. 995; An. 498: Bt. Met. Fox 20, 340; Met. 20, 170: 29, 54; Met. 29, 27. Seó sunne glīt abūtan *the sun glides round it*, Lchdm. iii. 258, 6. Heofenes gim glād ofer grundas *heaven's gem had glided over the earth*, Beo. Th. 4152; B. 2073: Homl. Th. i. 78, 23: Exon. 94 a; Th. 353, 15; Reim. 13: Andr. Kmbl. 741; An. 371: Chr. 937; Erl. 112, 15; Æðelst. 15: Ors. 4, 6; Bos. 84, 37. Ðā git glidon ofer gārsecg *when ye glided over the ocean*, Beo. Th. 1034; B. 515. DER. a-glīdan, be-, bi-, ge-, ōþ-, to-.

glidder; *adj. Slippery;* lubricus.

gliddrian *to slip, totter;* nutare, Hpt. Gl. 503.

gliew-mēden, es; *n. A glee-maiden, female musician;* tympanistria, Ps. Spl. T. 67, 27.

glig, gligg, es; *n. Glee, music, minstrelsy, jesting, sport;* gaudium, musica, facetiæ, ludibrium:—Mid ðæm glige [MS. Cot. ðam gligge] *with the music*, Past. 26, 2; Swt. 183, 25; Hat. MS. 35 b; 8. Hī hæfdon him to glige his hālwende mynegunge *habebant inter se ludibrio salutarem ejus admonitionem*, Basil. admn. 9; Norm. 54, 20. v. gleó, gliw.

glig-beám, es; *m. A glee-beam, timbrel, tabret;* tympanum, Ps. Spl. 80, 2: 150, 4. v. gleó-beám.

glig-cræft. v. gleó-cræft.

glig-gamen, -gomen *glee-pleasure.* v. gleó-gamen.

glig-georn; *adj. Glee-loving, fond of sport;* gaudii cupidus, joci amans, Off. Episc. 3.

glī-man, glii-man, gliig-man, glig-man. v. gleó-man.

gliowian. v. gleowian.

glisian *to shine, glisten:*—Se glisigenda wibba *cicindela, the glow-worm*, Ælfc. Gl. 23; Som. 59, 123; Wrt. Voc. 23, 77. [*Laym.* cliseden *glittered: O. Frs.* glisa *splendere.*]

glisnian; *p.* ode; *pp.* od *To glisten, shine:*—Īs glisnaþ glæshluttur *ice glistens bright as glass*, Runic pm. Kmbl. 341, 16; Rūn. 11. Se engel hæfde twegen beágas on hys handa ða glysnodon swa rōsan blōsman *the angel had two rings on his hand, they shone like roses*, Shrn. 149, 29. [*Laym.* glissenede: *p. part. pl: Wick.* glisninge.]

glitenung, e; *f. A flash, gleam:*—Mid glitenungum *coruscationem*, Ps. Spl. 143, 8.

glitinian, glitenian; *p.* ode; *pp.* od *To glitter, glisten, shine:*—Geseah gold glitinian *he saw gold glisten*, Beo. Th. 5509; B. 2758. Heó glytenode on ðæra engla mydle swā scȳnende sunne *she glittered amid the angels as the shining sun*, Shrn. 149, 7. His reáf wurdon glitiniende *vestimenta ejus facta sunt splendentia*, Mk. Skt. 9, 3. [Cf. *Goth.* glitmunjan: *O. H. Ger.* glizinon.]

gliw, es; *n. Glee, joy, minstrelsy, mirth, jesting, drollery;* gaudium, musica, facetiæ, mimus:—Ðȳ læs ðe him con leóða worn, oððe mid hondum con hearpan grētan, hafaþ him his gliwes giefe *unless he knows many songs, or with hands can greet the harp, has his gift of glee*, Exon. 91 b; Th. 344, 11; Gn. Ex. 172. Glæd wæs ic gliwum *glad was I in glee*, 94 a; Th. 352, 29; Reim. 3. Gumum to gliwe *for delight to men*, 57 b; Th. 207, 9; Ph. 139. Ðæt geára iú gliwes cræfte mid gieddingum guman oft wrecan *what of yore, by art of minstrelsy, with their lays men oft related*, 92 b; Th. 347, 12; Sch. 11. Wynsum gliw *facetiæ*, Ælfc. Gl. 115; Som. 80, 39; Wrt. Voc. 61, 19: Cot. 132: 214. v. gleow.

gliw-beám, es; *m. A glee-beam, timbrel, tabret;* tympanum, Ps. Spl. 149, 3. v. glig-beám, gleó-.

gliwere, es; *m. A jester, player, one who aims at pleasing with a view to gain, a flatterer;* parasitus, assentator, scurra, Hpt. Gl. 422: Gl. Prud. 618.

gliw-hleóþriend, es; *m. A glee-sounder, musician, minstrel;* musicus, fidicen, Cot. 134. v. gleó-hleóþriend.

gliwian. v. gleowian.

gliwian; *p.* ede *To adorn* [?]:—Me gliwedon wrætlīc weorc smiþa, Exon. 107 a; Th. 408, 17; Rä. 27, 13.

gliw-stæf, es; *m.* v. gleó-stæf.

gloed. v. glēd.

gloed-scof *a fire-shovel, warming-pan*, Lye.

glof, es; *n. A cliff:*—Hafuc sceal on glofe wilde gewunian *the hawk shall dwell wild on the cliff*, Menol. Fox 494; Gn. C. 17. [Cf. *Icel.* gliufr; *n. an abrupt descent.*]

glōf, e; *a weak pl.* glōfan *occurs; f. A* GLOVE; chirothēca = χειροθήκη:—Glōf hangode, sió [glōf] wæs gegyrwed dracan fellum *his glove hung, it was made with dragon's skins*, Beo. Th. 4177; B. 2085. Glōf *mantium?* Ælfc. Gl. 27; Som. 60, 118; Wrt. Voc. 25, 58. Wilfriþ cwæþ ðæt he forlēte his twā glōfan on ðam scipe *Wilfrid said that he had left his two gloves in the ship*, Guthl, 11; Gdwin. 54, 14, 9, title. He mid gyrde of ðam hūses hrōfe ða glōfe gerǣhte *he reached the glove from the house-roof with a stick*, 22: 56, 4. Earnian mid ðam glōfa him sylfum *deserviat per id cirotecas sibi*, L. R. S; Th. i. 438, 15. Foxes glōfa *buglosse*, Wrt. Voc. 67, 24: Herb. 144; Lchdm. i. 266, 16. [*Laym.* gloven; *pl: Icel.* glōfi; *m.*]

glōfung, e; *f. A providing with gloves:*—Glōfung him gebyreþ *he is to be provided with gloves*, L. R. S; Th. i. 438, 6.

glōf-wyrt, e; *f.* I. *lily of the valley;* convallāria mājālis, Lin:—Ðeós wyrt ðe man *Apollĭnārem*, and ōðrum naman glōfwyrt nemneþ *this plant which is called* Apollĭnāris, *and by another name glovewort*, Herb. 23, 1; Lchdm. i. 120, 3: L. M. 1, 40; Lchdm. ii. 106, 7: Wrt. Voc. 66, 62. II. *hound's tongue;* cynoglossum offĭcĭnāle, Lin:—Ðeós wyrt ðe Engle glōfwyrt, and ōðrum naman hundes tunge hātaþ *this plant, which the English call glovewort, and by another name hound's tongue*, Herb. 42; Lchdm. i. 144, 3.

glōm, es; *m* [?] *Gloom, twilight, darkness:*—Glōm ōðer *a second twilight*, i. e. *the twilight of evening, the first being that of morning* [?], Exon. 93 b; Th. 350, 30; Sch. 71. DER. ǣfen-, mist-, niht-glōm.

glōmung, glōmmung, e; *f. Twilight, gloaming;* crepusculum, Lye.

glōwan *to glow like a coal of fire;* candere, Lye.

glydering, glyderung, e; *f. What glides away, a vision, an illusion;* visio, Cot. 84.

glywian *to play on an instrument; part.* glywiende, Ps. Spl. 67, 27. v. gleowian.

GNÆT, gnætt; *gen.* gnættes; *m.* GNAT; culex:—Gedrehnigeaþ ðone gnæt aweg *ye strain out the gnat*, Mt. Bos. 23, 24. Com hundes fleógan and gnættas *venit cœnomyia et cinipes*, Ps. Spl. 104, 29. Aaron slóh mid ðære girde on ða eorþan, and gnættas wǽron gewordene on mannum and on yrfe; and ealle ðære eorþan dust wæs gewurden to gnættum ofer eall Egipta land *Aaron percussit pulverem terræ, et facti sunt sciniphes* [*gnats*] *in hominibus, et in jumentis; omnis pulvis terræ versus est in sciniphes per totam terram Ægypti*, Ex. 8, 17, 16: Ps. Th 104, 27. Gnættas cōmon ofer eall ðæt land *gnats came over all the land*, Or. 1, 7; Bos. 29, 29.

GNAGAN, ic gnage, ðū gnægest, gnægst, gnæhst, he gnægeþ, gnægþ, gnæhþ, *pl.* gnagaþ; *p.* gnóh, *pl.* gnógon; *pp.* gnagen, gnægen *To* GNAW, *bite;* rodere:—Ic gnage *rodo*, Ælfc. Gr. 28, 4; Som. 31, 24. Ðæt gewrit beó geworpen mūsen to gnagene *illiusmodi litteraturæ membranula suricum morsibus corrodenda*, Chart. Th. 318, 29. [Gnagan = ge-nagan: *Icel.* gnaga, naga: *O. H. Ger.* nagan, gi-nagan.] DER. be-gnagan, for-.

gnāst, es; *m. A spark.* [*O. E. Hom.* gnast: *Icel.* gneisti: *O. H. Ger.* gneisto.] DER. fȳr-gnāst.

gneáð, gnēð; *adj. Sparing, frugal, stingy, scanty, small;* parcus:—Næs hió to gneáð gifa *she was not too sparing of gifts*, Beo. Th. 3864; B. 1930. He self lifde on gneáðum woroldlīfe ān tunece wæs his gegerela and ðæt wæs hǽren and beren hlāf wæs his gereorde *he himself lived a frugal life in the world, one tunic was his raiment, and barley bread was his food*, Shrn. 110, 4: 77, 4. He ðām ðe on scearan māran wǽron on ðām mægnum eáðmōdnesse and hȳrsumnesse nōhte ðon læssa ne gnēðra wæs *eis quæ tonsura majores sunt virtutibus, humilitatis et obedientiæ, non mediocriter insignitus*, Bd. 5, 19; S. 637, 18. Of gnēðum, of lytlum *parcis*, Gl. Prud. 227. [Gnede *scanty, O. E. Misc. Morris.*]

gneáðlīcnis *frugality*, Hpt. Gl. 463.

gnēðelīce; *adv. Sparingly, frugally;* parce, Greg. Dial. 1, 7, Lye. [Cf. *A. R.* al þet mon wilneþ more þen heo mei gnedeliche leden hire lif bi, al his giscunge.]

gnēðen, gnēðn; *adj. Moderate, temperate, modest, low;* mediocris, modestus, Cot. 129, Lye.

gnēðenes, gnēðnes, se; *f. Frugality, care;* parcimonia, Cot. 81, 149, Lye.

GNĪDAN, ic gnīde, ðū gnīst, he gnīt, *pl.* gnīdaþ; *p.* gnād, *pl.* gnidon; *pp.* gniden *To rub, break, rub together, comminute;* fricare, comminuere:—Hys leorningcnihtas ða eár mid hyra handum gnidon *his disciples rubbed the ears with their hands*, Lk. Bos. 6, 1. Gif ðū gang ofer his æcer brec ða eár and gnīd *if thou go across his field pluck the ears and rub them*, Deut. 23, 25. Nim ǽnne sticcan and gnīd to sumum þinge *take a stick and rub it against something*, Lchdm. iii. 274, 3. Gnīd ða þungana and on ufan ðæt hēfd *rub the temples and the top of the head*, 292, 23. Gnīd swīðe smale to duste *rub very small, to dust*, Herb. 1, 2; Lchdm. i. 70, 14. [*Dan.* gnide: *O. H. Ger.* gnītan *fricare.*] DER. for-gnīdan, ge-.

gnidennys, -nyss, e; *f. A rubbing, contrition.* v. for-gnidennys, Ps. Lamb. 13, 3.

gnidill *a pestle;* pistillum, Som.

gnīding *a rubbing;* frictio, Som.

gnīst, he gnīt *rubbest, rubs; 2nd and 3rd pers. pres. of* gnīdan.

gnōh, *pl.* gnōgon *gnawed, bit; p. of* gnagan.

gnorn, es; *m. Sorrow, sadness, affliction;* mæstitia:—Ne biþ ðǽr ǽngum gōdum gnorn ætȳwed *no sorrow shall there be shewn to any good man*, Exon. 31 a; Th. 96, 19; Cri. 1576. Gnorn þrowian *to suffer sadness*, Beo. Th. 5310; B. 2658.

gnorn; *adj. Sorrowful, sad, dejected, complaining;* mœstus:—Leónhwelpas grymetigaþ gnorne *catuli leonum rugientes*, Ps. Th. 103, 20. Flugon forhtigende gylp wearþ gnornra *they fled in terror, their boast became more sorrowful*, Cd. 166; Th. 206, 19; Ex. 454.

gnornan, gnornian; *p.* ede, ode; *pp.* ed, od *To grieve, mourn, be sad, bewail, lament;* mœrere:—Ic gnornige *mereo*, Ælfc. Gr. 33; Som. 36, 49: Ps. Th. 54, 2. Ic cūþlīce wāt for hwon ðū gnornast *scio certissime quare mœres*, Bd. 2, 12; S. 513, 42. Gnornaþ *he grieves*, Exon. 82 b; Th. 311, 14; Seef. 92: 51 a; Th. 178, 6; Gū. 1240. Gif hī fulle ne beóþ fela gnorniaþ *si non fuerint saturati, et murmurabunt*, Ps. Th. 58, 15. Ðæt wīf gnornode *the woman mourned*, Cd. 37; Th. 48, 4; Gen. 770: Beo. Th. 2239; B. 1117: Elen. Kmbl. 2518; El. 1260. Swā gnornedon godes andsacan *thus lamented God's adversaries*, Cd. 219; Th. 282, 1; Sat. 280: Exon. 38 b; Th. 128, 7; Gū. 400. Ne scyle nān wīs monn forhtigan ne gnornian *no wise man ought to fear or lament*, Bt. 40, 3; Fox 238, 8: Cd. 219; Th. 281, 19; Sat. 274. Sceoldon wræcmæcgas ofgiefan gnornende grēne beorgas *the exiles, sorrowing, must give up the green hills*, Exon. 35 b; Th. 116, 6; Gū. 203: 42 b; Th. 142, 29; Gū. 651. He fērde gnornigende *abiit mœrens*, Mk. Skt. 10, 22. Geómor and gnorngende *sad and sorrowing*, Blickl. Homl. 113, 29: Cd. 39; Th. 52, 9; Gen. 841. Gnorniende cynn *a mourning race*, 216; Th. 273, 9; Sat. 134: Ps. Th. 101, 4. Geonge for ðē gnornendra care ðara ðe on feterum fæste wǽran *intret in conspectu tuo gemitus compeditorum*, 78, 11. [*O. Sax.* gnornon.]

gnorn-cearig; *adj. Sad, sorrowful*, Exon. 73 b; Th. 274, 6; Jul. 529.

gnorn-hof, es; *n. A house of grief, a prison*, Andr. Kmbl. 2016; An. 1010: 2087; An. 1045.

gnorn-scendende; *part. Hurrying away in sorrow*, Ps. Th. 89, 10.

gnorn-sorh, -sorg, e; *f. Care, sorrow*, Exon. 52 a; Th. 182, 13; Gū. 1309: Elen. Kmbl. 1307; El. 655: 1951; El. 977.

gnornung, e; *f. Grief, lamentation, mourning;* mœstitia:—Gnornung *meror*, Ælfc. Gr. 33; Som. 36, 51. Hēr is Brytta gnornung *gemitus Brittanorum*, Bd. 1, 13; S. 481, 42, note. Me hæfþ ðeós gnornung ðære gemynde benumen *this grief hath deprived me of the remembrance*, Bt. 5, 3; Fox 12, 20: 7, 2; Fox 18, 10. Mid mycelre gnornunge ymbe ðæs cyninges slege *with great grief for the king's death*, Ors. 2, 4; Bos. 45, 24: Chr. 975; Erl. 126, 13; Edg. 39. Seó ārleáse helwarena stefn wæs gehȳred and heora gnornung *the impious voice of the dwellers in hell was heard, and their lamentation*, Blickl. Homl. 87, 4: 91, 30: Cd. 220; Th. 285, 8; Sat. 334: Exon. 40 b; Th. 134, 29; Gū. 516. DER. heáh-gnornung.

gnorn-word, es; *n. A word of sadness, mournful discourse:*—Him oft betuh gnornword gengdon *oft mournful words passed between them*, Cd. 37; Th. 47, 27; Gen. 767. [Cf. *O. Sax.* gorn-word.]

gnyran [?] *to creak;* stridere:—Gnyrende *stridentes*, Lchdm. iii. 210, 12. See Skt. Etymol. Dict. gnarl.

gnyrn, es; *m. n* [?] *Grief, sorrow, evil, wrong:*—Lāc weorþade ðe hire brungen wæs gnyrna to geóce *the gift she honoured that was brought to her as a consolation of sorrows*, Elen. Kmbl. 2275; El. 1139. Þeóda waldend eallra gnyrna [MS. gnyrnra] leás *the ruler of nations, free from all evils*, 843; El. 422. Wlance drihtne guldon gōd mid gnyrne *arrogant, they repaid good to the Lord with evil*, Cd. 111; Th. 146, 10; Gen. 2420. [Cf. gyrn.]

gnyrn-wracu, e; *f. Revenge for injury* or *grief, enmity, hate*, Elen. Kmbl. 718; El. 359. [Cf. gyrn-wracu.]

GOD, es; *m. God, the Deity, a god.* The following epithets occur:—dryhten, wealdend, nergend, hǽlend, sōþ, hālig, mihtig, ælmihtig, lifgende, ealwealda, heáhengla, heofona, heofonengla, heofonrīces, gǽsta, mihta, mægena, weoruda, wuldres, sigores, sigora. Ān God ys gōd, Mt. 19, 17. Nys nān man gōd, būton God āna, Lk. 18, 19. Hū gōd Israhēl God, Ps. Spl. 72, 1. Hēr is Godes lamb, Jn. 1, 29. Enoch fērde mid Gode, Gen. 5, 24. Ða leásan godas *false gods*, Blickl. Homl. 201, 30. Rachel forstæl hire fæder hǽðenan godas *Rachel furata est idola patris sui*, Gen. 31, 19. Hwī forstæle ðū me mīne godas *cur furatus es deos meos*, 31, 30. Hǽðenan godas *heathen gods*, 31, 32. Hēðenan godas *heathen gods*, 31, 33. Ne wirc ðū ðē agrafene godas *work not thou for thyself graven gods*, Ex. 20, 4. Drihten sylf ys Goda God, mǽre God, and mihtig, and egefull *the Lord himself is God of Gods, a great God, a mighty and a terrible*, Deut. 10, 17. Ne wyrc ðū ðē gyldne godas oððe seolfrene *make thou not to thyself golden or silver gods*, L. Alf. 10; Th. i. 44, 21: Ex. 32, 31: 23, 32: Jn. Skt. 10, 34, 35. Ða hǽðenan noldon beón gehealdene on feáwum godum. . . . Mānfullan men wǽron ða mǽrostan godas *the heathens would not be contented with few gods. . . . Guilty men were the mightiest gods*, Salm. Kmbl. p. 121, 40. [*Goth.* guþ; *m: O. Sax. O. Frs.* god: *Icel.* guð; *m. pl.* guðir *dii: O. H. Ger.* got; *m: Ger.* gott.] v. Grm. D. M. pp. 12 sqq. and cf. god; *n.*

god, es; *n. A god:*—Hiora godu syndon drȳcræfta lāreówas *their gods are teachers of magical arts*, Ors. 1, 5; Bos. 28, 28. He wolde gesēcan helle godu *he would visit the gods of hell*, Bt. 35, 6; Fox 168, 13. Goddo [godo, Rush.] gie aron *dii estis?* Jn. Skt. Lind. 10, 34. God *deos*, Rush. 35. Godu, Ps. Th. 81, 6: 94, 3. Syndon ealle hǽðene godu hilde deóful *omnes dii gentium dæmonia*, 95, 5, 4: Exon. 74 b; Th. 278, 16; Jul. 598. Gif ðū fremdu godu forþ bigongest *if thou dost continue to worship strange gods*, 67 b; Th. 250, 2; Jul. 121. [*Goth.* guþa; *n. pl: Icel.* goð; *n. pl.*]

gōd; *adj.* GOOD; bonus:—Þæs gōdan gōdnes biþ his āgen gōd *the goodness of the good is his own good*, Bt. 37, 3; Fox 190, 14. Gōd mann sōþlīce of gōdum goldhorde bringþ gōd forþ *bonus homo de bono thesauro profert bona*, Mt. Bos. 12, 35. Mæg ǽnig þing gōdes beón of Nazareth *a Nazareth potest aliquid boni esse?* Jn. Bos. 1, 46. Crist, seðe ǽfre is gōd ðeáh ðe we wāce sindon *Christ who is ever good, though we are weak*, Homl. Th. ii. 48, 20. Ðǽr wearþ Heáhmund bisceop ofslægen and fela gōdra monna *there was bishop Heahmund slain and many good men*, Chr. 871; Erl. 74, 34. Þa men hie gefliémdon and hira gōdne dǽl ofslōgon *the men put them to flight and slew a good part of them*, 921; Erl. 106, 24: 913; Erl. 102, 7. Genim giþcornes leáfa gode handfulle *take good handfuls of leaves of githcorn*, L. M. ii. 65, 1; Lchdm. ii. 292, 10. Me is on gōmum gōd and swēte ðīn āgen word *quam dulcia faucibus meis eloquia tua*, Ps. Th. 118, 103. Gōd is ðæt man Drihtne andette *bonum est confiteri domino*, 91, 1: 132, 1. Cyning and cwēn sceolon geofum gōd wesan *a king and queen shall be liberal*, Exon. 90 a; Th. 338, 35; Gn. Ex. 84. Nis mon his gifena ðæs gōd *there is no man so good in his qualities*, 82 a; Th. 308, 15; Seef. 40. He is to freónde gōd *he is good as a friend*, 67 a; Th. 248, 28; Jul. 102. We ðǽr gōde hwīle stōdon *we stood there a good while*, Rood Kmbl. 140; Kr. 70. Him ðæt geleánaþ līfes waldend gōdum dǽdum *the ruler of life will repay them that with benefits*, Exon. 117 a; Th. 450, 13; Dōm. 87. Þurh gōde dǽda Gode līcian *to please God by good deeds*, Blickl. Homl. 129,

34. Ðám ðe gódes willan sýn *to those who are of goodwill*, 93, 10: 37, 27. Gódes lífes bysene onstellan *to set an example of good life*, 81, 6. Wæs he swíðe æþelra gebyrda and gódra *he was of very noble and good birth*, 211, 19. Góde saugeras *good singers*, 207, 31. [*Goth.* góds, góþs: *O. Sax. O. Frs.* gód: *O. H. Ger.* guot: *Ger.* gut: *Icel.* góðr.]

gód, es; *n. Good, good thing, good deed, benefit, goodness, welfare*:—Ǽghwylc man sceal on worlde gearnian ðæt him ðæt gód móte to écum médum gegangan, ðæt him his freónd æfter gedéþ. Se getreówa man sceal syllan his gód on ða tíd ðe hine sylfne lyste his brúcan *each man must in this world deserve that the good that his friend does for him afterwards may conduce to eternal rewards. The true man must give his wealth at the time that it best pleases him to enjoy it himself*, Blickl. Homl. 101, 17. Hwæðer him yfel ðe gód under wunige *whether evil or good dwell in it* [*the heart*], Exon. 27 a; Th. 82, 3; Cri. 1333. Gód dóend *qui faciat bonum*, Ps. Th. 52, 4: Gen. 2, 9: Bt. 37, 3; Fox 192, 1. His gód wæs swíðe gecýðed *his goodness was very famous*, Blickl. Homl. 217, 3: Bt. Met. Fox 20, 57; Met. 20, 29. Ðæt héhste gód *the supreme good*, 90; Met. 20, 46: Bt. 32, 1; Fox 114, 5. Swá hwæt swá we to góde dóþ *whatever good we do*, Blickl. Homl. 29, 8: 215, 26: Ors. 6, 8; Bos. 120, 12. On óðres góde beón gefeónde *to rejoice at another's good*, Blickl. Homl. 75, 20. Se ðe gód onginneþ *he who attempts good*, 21, 34. He Godes good on ðære his dǽde ongeat, *he perceived in that deed of his the goodness of God*, 215, 33. He mid góde gyldan wille uncran eaferan *he will repay our offspring with good*, Beo. Th. 2372; B. 1184. Alwalda ðec góde forgylde *may the Omnipotent reward thee with good*, 1916; B. 956. Him sylfum nǽnige góde beón *to be of no good to themselves*, Blickl. Homl. 45, 16. For eallum ðám gódum ðe he me dyde *pro omnibus quæ retribuit mihi*, Ps. Th. 115, 3: 102, 2: Cd. 15; Th. 19, 14; Gen. 291: Homl. Th. i. 76, 7: Blickl. Homl. 29, 11. Búton he mid óðrum gódum hit geéce *unless he add thereto other good deeds*, Blickl. Homl. 37, 25. Ic gaderige ðyder míne gód *illuc congregabo bona mea*, Lk. Skt. 12, 18: Gen. 24, 10: Bd. 4, 24; S. 598, 4. He forsihþ eorþlícu gód *he despises earthly goods*, Bt. Met. Fox 7, 84; Met. 7, 42.

Goda, an; *m. A deity, god;* deus:—Ealra godena God *Deus deorum*, Ps. Th. 135, 2, 28. God godana *Deus deorum*, Rtl. 101, 10.

god-æpple *a quince apple;* cydonium, Cot. 34, 93.

god-bearn, es; *n.* I. *a divine child, the Son of God;* divinus filius, Dei Filius:—Ahangen wæs Godbearn on galgan *God's Son was hanged on the cross*, Elen. Kmbl. 1434; El. 719. Geségon hí on heáhþu hláford stígan Godbearn of grundum *they saw the Lord, the Son of God, ascend on high from earth*, Exon. 15 a; Th. 31, 21; Cri. 499: Andr. Kmbl. 1279; An. 640. II. *a god-child, a god-son;* filius lustricus, ex sacro fonte baptismi jam primum susceptus:—Godbearn to fela man forspilde *god-children, too many of them have been destroyed*, Swt. A. S. Rdr. 107, 94.

god-borh; *gen.* -borges; *m.* A word of uncertain meaning occurring only in L. Ælf. pol. 33; Th. i. 82, 4–8. q. v.

god-bót, an; *f. An atonement made to the church*, L. Æthel. 6, 51; Th. i. 328, 4.

godcund; *adj. Of the nature of God, divine, religious, sacred*:—Seó godcunde ǽ *lex divina*, Bd. 1, 1; S. 474, 2. Wiotan ǽgðer ge godcundra háda ge woruldcundra *wise men both of religious and secular orders*, Past. Pref; Swt. 3, 3, 8; Hat. MS. Hér sende Gregorius pápa wel monige godcunde láreówas *in this year pope Gregory sent very many religious teachers*, Chr. 601; Erl. 20, 11. In godcundum mægne *in divine power*, Exon. 40 a; Th. 134, 2; Gú. 501: 17 a; Th. 40, 13; Cri. 638. Godcunde béc *sacred books*, Cd. 123; Th. 158, 4; Gen. 2612. [*O. Sax.* god-kund: *O. H. Ger.* gotchund: *Orm. Laym.* godcund.]

godcundlíc; *adj. Divine*:—Búton yldinge him becom seó godcundlíce wracu *without delay the divine vengeance came upon him*, Homl. Th. i. 86, 1. Ðá ongeat he ðæt ðǽr wæs godcundlíc mægen ondweard *then he perceived that there was divine power present*, Blickl. Homl. 217, 29.

godcundlíce; *adv. Divinely, from heaven, by inspiration;* divinitus:—Godcundlíce *divinitus*, Ælfc. Gr. 38; Som. 42, 5. Ðeáh he sé godcundlíce gesceádwís *though he be divinely rational*, Bt. 14, 2; Fox 44, 18: Bd. 4, 3; S. 567, 10: 4, 24; S. 596, 41.

godcundnys, se; *f. Divine nature, Deity, Divinity, Godhead, divine service*:—Se God wunaþ on þrýnnysse untodǽledlíc and on ánnysse ánre Godcundnysse *the Deity exists in Trinity indivisible, and in unity of one Godhead*, Homl. Th. i. 276, 24. Seó hrepaþ swýðost ymbe Cristes godcundnysse *that* [*book*] *treats chiefly of Christ's divinity*, 70, 1. Ðeós wyrt hæfþ mid hire sume wundorlíce godcundnesse *this plant has in it a certain wonderful divine quality*, Herb. 50, 1; Lchdm. i. 152, 24. Ond Wærferþ bisceop and se heóréd habbaþ geseted ðas godcundnysse *and bishop Werferth and the convent have established this divine office*, Chart. Th. 137, 28: Cod. Dipl. Kmbl. v. 218, 32.

gód-dǽd, e; *f. A good deed, a benefit*:—Menn swíðor scamaþ nú for góddǽdum ðonne for misdǽdum *men are now more ashamed of good deeds than of misdeeds*, Swt. A. S. Rdr. 109, 161: Exon. 26 b; Th. 79, 7; Cri. 1287: 65 b; Th. 242, 6; Ph. 669. Ealra góddǽda hí forgiten hæfdon *obliti sunt benefactorum ejus*, Ps. Th. 77, 13.

god-dóhtor; *f. A* GODDAUGHTER:—Ic geann mínre goddóhtor ðæt land æt Strǽttúne *I grant to my goddaughter the land at Stretton*, Chart. Th. 548, 5.

gód-dónd, -dénd, es; *m. One who does good, a benefactor*, Elen. Kmbl. 717; El. 359.

god-dreám, es; *m. A heavenly joy*, Exon. 41 b; Th. 139, 32; Gú. 602: 51 b; Th. 180, 1; Gú. 1273.

god-fæder; *m.* I. *a* GODFATHER; baptizati susceptor, patrinus:—Gif hwá óþres sleá godfæder *if any one slay another's godfather*, L. In. 76; Th. i. 150, 13. Hit wæs mínes godfæder gyfu *it was my godfather's gift*, Chart. Th. 545, 21. II. *God the Father, the Divine Father;* Deus ille Pater, Divinus Pater:—Crist ys word and tunge God-Fæder; þurh hine synt ealle þincg geworht *Christ is the word and tongue of God the Father; through Him are all things made*, Ps. Th. 44, 2. Ic eom Crist ... ic ðé fullwie on mínne godfæder and on mec his efenécne sunu and on ðone hálgan gáste *I am Christ ... I baptize thee in the name of my heavenly Father and of me his co-eternal Son and of the Holy Ghost*, Shrn. 106, 13: 118, 6. Ðú sitest on ða swíþran hand ðínum God-Fæder *thou sittest on the right hand of thy Divine Father*, Hy. 8, 31; Hy. Grn. ii. 290, 31. [*O. Sax.* god-fader *God the Father*.]

gód-fremmende; *part. pres. used as a noun. One doing good, acting bravely*, Beo. Th. 603; B. 299.

God-fyrht, -ferht, -friht; *adj. God-fearing*:—To oft man godfyrhte leahtraþ *too often the god-fearing are reviled*, Swt. A. S. Rdr. 110, 163. Ic haue hére godefrihte muneces *I have here godfearing monks*, Chr. 656; Erl. 32, 1. Ðá ongan Andreas grétan godfyrhtne *then began Andrew to greet the godfearing man*, Andr. Kmbl. 2043; An. 1024: 3030; An. 1518. Godferhte, Ps. C. 14; Grn. ii. 277, 14.

god-gesprǽce, es; *n. An oracle*:—Wæs ðis Godgesprǽce ðysses gemetes *erat oraculum hujusmodi*, Bd. 2, 12; S. 513, 1.

god-gild, -gield, -geld, -gyld, gode-gild, es; *n. An idol*:—He hét wyrcan gyldeno godgeld and seolfrene ... ðá abræc ðæt mægden ðæt gold and ðæt seolfor of ðǽm godgeldum *he bade make golden idols and silver ... then the maiden broke the gold and the silver off the idols*, Shrn. 106, 2–4: 122, 9: L. Alf. 32; Th. i. 52, 12. Ðæt he gulde ðǽm hǽðnum godgyldum *that he should sacrifice to heathen idols*, Shrn. 101, 1: Bd. 1, 7; S. 477, 13. He heora godgieldum eallum wiðsóc *he renounced all their idols*, Ors. 2, 5; Swt. 78, 4. Hí on Choreb cealf ongunnan him to godegylde georne wyrcean *fecerunt vitulum in Choreb, et adoraverunt sculptile*, Ps. Th. 105, 17. [Cf. deófol-gild.]

god-gildlíc; *adj. Phanaticus*, Cot. 152, Lye.

god [**gód-?**] **-gim**, es; *m. A heavenly* [*an excellent?*] *gem*, Elen. Kmbl. 2225; El. 1114.

god-gyld. v. god-gild.

gódian; *p.* ode, ede; *pp.* od, ed. I. *to be* or *become good, to improve, get better*:—Ðonne gódiaþ ðæra lendena sár and ðæra þeóna swýðe hræðe *then the pains in the loins and thighs will very speedily get better*, Herb. 1, 28; Lchdm. i. 80, 1. On his dagum hit gódode *in his days things improved*, Chr. 959; Erl. 119, 13: Swt. A. S. Rdr. 105, 19. Gif his hreófla gódigende wǽre *if his leprosy were getting better*, Homl. Th. i. 124, 27. Þurh ðæt hit sceal on earde gódian to áhte *by that means matters must somewhat improve in the land*, L. C. S. 11; Th. i. 382, 8. II. *to do good, make good, improve, endow, enrich*:—Mid eallum þingum gódode *enriched* [*the place*] *with all things*, Lchdm. iii. 438, 10: Chr. 963; Erl. 123, 28. Gyf ǽnig sý ðe hit mid ǽnigan þingan geécean wylle oððe gódian *si quis autem hanc nostram donationem largioribus amplificare muneribus studuerit*, Cod. Dipl. Kmbl. iv. 72, 29: Lchdm. iii. 442, 14: L. Pen. 14; Th. ii. 282, 9. Hig bǽdan ðone bisceop ðæt hig móstan ðæt mynster gódian *they asked the bishop that they might endow the monastery*, Cod. Dipl. Kmbl. iv. 290, 9: L. Pen. 14; Th. ii. 282, 8.

goding, es; *m. The son of God*:—Ðe hǽlend seðe wæs goding *the Saviour who was the Son of God*, Lk. Skt. Rush. 4, 1.

gód-leás; *adj. Without good, miserable, wretched*:—Ðis ungesǽlige geár and ðæt gódleáse *infaustus ille annus et omnibus bonis exosus*, Bd. 3, 1; S. 523, 33.

gódlíc, -lec; *adj. Goodly, good*:—Gódlíc gumrinc *a goodly man*, Exon. 129 a; Th. 495, 7; Rä. 84, 4. Gódlíce geardas *goodly dwellings*, Cd. 35; Th. 46, 6; Gen. 740. Gódlecran stól *a goodlier throne*, 15; Th. 18, 31; Gen. 281. [*Laym.* godlich: *O. Sax.* gódlík: *O. Frs.* gódlík: *O. H. Ger.* guotlíh.]

god-mægen, es; *n. A divine power, divinity;* numen:—Ic bæd ða godmægen *orabam numina*, Nar. 24, 22. Hie ondrédon ðæt hie hiora godmægne sceoldon beón benumene *they feared that they should be deprived of their divinity;* de numinum suorum statu timentes, 28, 13.

god-módor; *f. A* GODMOTHER:—Æt ðam fulwihte hyre onféng sum godes þeów ðære noma wæs rómána ... heó slép æt ðære godmódor húse *a certain servant of God, whose name was Romana, was her sponsor at baptism ... she slept at the godmother's house*, Shrn. 140, 24.

Godmundingahâm *Goodmanham*, between Pocklington and Beverley, a place a little to the east of York, beyond the river Derwent, where a famous Witena-gemót was convened by Edwin, king of Northumbria, in A. D. 625, to consider the propriety of receiving the Christian faith. The speeches were so much in favour of Christianity that the creed was at once received; these speeches are particularly worthy of notice, Bd. 2, 13; S. 517, 17.

gôdnes, -ness, e; *f. Goodness*:—Se hâlga hî eft alŷsde and lēt hî forþgân for his gôdnysse *the holy man loosed them again, and let them proceed through his goodness*, Homl. Th. ii. 508, 22: Ps. Th. 24, 8. Ðæs gôdan gôdnes biþ his âgen gôd and his âgen edleán *the goodness of the good is his own good and his own reward*, Bt. 37, 3; Fox 190, 14: 33, 4; Fox 128, 15.

god-sǽd, es; *n. The fear of God, piety*:—Æþele cnihtas and ǽfæste ginge and gôde in godsǽde *noble youths and pious, young and good in the fear of God*, Cd. 176; Th. 221, 19; Dan. 90.

godscipe, es; *m. Goodness*:—Godscipe *bonitas*, Rtl. 100, 11: 12, 23.

god-scyld, e; *f. A sin against a god, impiety*:—Ic nŷde sceal godscyld wrecan *I needs must avenge impiety*, Exon. 68 b; Th. 254, 29; Jul. 204.

god-scyldig; *adj. Guilty against God*, Exon. 45 a; Th. 153, 31; Gû. 834.

god-sibb, es; *m. A sponsor*:—Godsibbas and godbearn *sponsors and godchildren*, Swt. A. S. Rdr. 107, 94. [*Ayenb.* godzyb: *Piers P. Chauc.* gossib.]

gôd-spêdig; *adj. Rich in good*, Cd. 48; Th. 62, 4; Gen. 1009.

god-spell, es; *n. Gospel*:—Gôdspel *evangelium, id est, bonum nuntium*, Ælfc. Gl. 8; Wrt. Voc. 75, 9. Hēr ys godspellys angyn *initium euangelii*, Mk. Skt. 1, 1. Gelŷfaþ ðam godspelle *credite euangelio*, 15. Matheus ongan godspell ǽrest wordum wrîtan *Matthew began first to write the gospel in words*, Andr. Kmbl. 24; An. 12. [*Laym. Orm.* goddspell: *Piers P.* godspel, gospel: *Chauc.* gospel: *O. Sax.* god-spell: *Icel.* guð-spjall: *O. H. Ger.* gotspel.]

gôdspell-bôc, e; *f. A copy of the gospels*:—Saltere and pistolbôc and godspellbôc *a psalter, a copy of the epistles, and a copy of the gospels*, L. Ælf. C. 21; Th. ii. 350, 13. [*Orm.* goddspellboc: *Icel.* guðspjallabók.]

godspellere, es; *m. An evangelist*:—Iohannes se godspellere *John the evangelist*, Homl. Th. i. 58, 3, 27: Chr. 84; Erl. 8, 6. [*A. R. Ayenb* godspellere: *Chauc.* gospellere.]

godspellian; *p.* ode; *pp.* od *To declare the gospel*; evangelizare:—Ic godspellige *evangelizo*, Ælfc. Gr. 24; Som. 25, 45. Godspellian [MS. A. godspel secgan] Salm. Kmbl. 132; Sal. 65. God gifeþ gleáw word godspellendum *Dominus dabit verbum evangelizantibus*, Ps. Th. 67, 12.

godspellîc; *adj. Evangelical*:—He fylgde ðæt weorc ðæt him gewunelîc wæs ðæt he godspellîce lâre lǽrde *solitum sibi opus evangelizandi exsequens*, Bd. 3, 19; S. 547, 9: Homl. Th. ii. 586, 3. Mid ðysum wordum ða godspellîcan gesetnysse ongan *with these words began the gospel narrative*, i. 70, 11, 18.

godspellisc; *adj. Evangelical*:—Ðæs godspellesca bodes *euangelicæ prædicationis*, Mk. Skt. p. 1, 11.

god-sprǽce, es; *n. An oracle*:—Wæs sum godsprǽce and heofonlîc onwrigenes *oraculum cæleste*, Bd. 2, 12; S. 512, 23. v. god-gesprǽce.

god-sprec, es; *n. An oracle*:—We neáh stôdan ðǽm godsprecum *we stood near to the oracles*, Nar. 28, 32.

god-sunu, a; *m. A* GODSON:—Ðâ onfêng he him and æt fulluhtbæþe nam æt ðæs B' handa him to godsuna *then he accepted him and took him from the font at the bishop's hand as his godson*, Bd. 3, 7; S. 529, 18. Hiora wæs ôðer his godsunu ôðer Æþerêdes ealdormonnes *one of them was his godson, the other was alderman Ethelred's*, Chr. 894; Erl. 91, 29: L. In. 76; Th. i. 150, 13.

god-þrym; *gen.* -þrymmes; *m. Divine majesty*:—He geseah ðone hǽlend silfne standan on his godþrimme *he saw the Saviour himself stand in his divine majesty*, Shrn. 32, 2. Melchisedech godþrym onwrâh êces alwaldan *Melchizedec revealed the divine majesty of the eternal ruler of all*, Exon. 10 a; Th. 9, 24; Cri. 139.

god-web, gode-web, -webb; *gen.* -webbes; *n. A divine* or *very precious web, purple cloth, excellently woven material*:—Mid golde and mid godewæbbe gefrætewod *auro et purpura compositum*, Bd. 3, 11; S. 535, 32: Homl. Th. i. 62, 26. Godweb mid golde gefâgod *a purple garment variegated with gold*, Blickl. Homl. 113, 20. Weofod bewrigen mid baswe godwebbe *an altar covered with a purple pall*, 207, 17. Twegea bleó godwebb *fine cloth of two colours*; ex duplici tinctura, Past. 14, 6; Swt. 87, 9; Hat. MS. Heó bewand sce adrianes hand on godwebbe *she wrapped up St. Adrian's hand in fine linen*, Shrn. 59, 35. Gold and godweb iosepes gestreón *gold and purple, Joseph's treasures*, Cd. 171; Th. 215, 22; Exod. 587: Bt. Met. Fox 8, 49; Met. 8, 25. Geolo godwebb *yellow silk*, Exon. 109 a; Th. 417, 25; Rä. 36, 10. Godwebba cyst *choicest of textures* [*the veil of the temple*], Exon. 24 b; Th. 70, 8; Cri. 1135. [*O. Sax.* godu-webbi: *O. Frs.* god-wob; *Icel.* guð-vefr: *O. H. Ger.* gota-, goto-, gotu-, cota-, coti-weppi *sericum, purpura, polymitum, byssus*, Grff. i. 646-8.]

god-webben; *adj. Purple*:—Nâ mid golde ne mid godwebbenum hræglum *not with gold nor with purple raiment*, Blickl. Homl. 95, 19. [*O. H. Ger.* gotaweppin *carbaseus, hyacinthinus, purpureus, coccineus, sericus.*]

godweb-wyrhta, an; *m. A weaver of godweb*:—To ðâm diólgum godwebwyrhtum *ad abditos seres*, Nar. 6, 15.

god-wrac, -wrec; *adj. Impious*:—Crist forlēt mid him beón ðone godwracan þeóf *Christ let that impious thief* [*Judas*] *be with him*, Blickl. Homl. 75, 26. Ðâ æfēstgodon ðæt sume godwrece men *then certain wicked men were envious of that*, Shrn. 74, 28. Gangaþ ût git godwrecan and gongaþ ût git rôdewyrðan *come out ye two wretches that deserve to be hanged*, 43, 8.

god-wrecnis, -niss, e; *f. Wickedness, impiety*:—Hefig mân is and godwrecnis ðæt mon hine menge mid his steópmêder *cum noverca miscere grave est facinus*, Bd. 1, 27; S. 491, 10.

gold, es; *n. Gold*:—Ðæs landes gold ys golda sēlost *the gold of that land is the best of all gold*, Gen. 2, 12: Cd. 12; Th. 14, 29; Gen. 226. Abram wæs swîðe welig on golde *Abram was very rich in gold*, Gen. 13, 6. Cnihtas cûþ gedydon ðæt hie him ðæt gold to gode noldon habban *the youths made known that they would not have that gold* [*the golden image*] *as their god*, Cd. 182; Th. 228, 4; Dan. 197: 183; Th. 229, 9; Dan. 216. Reád gold *aurum obrizum*, Ælfc. Gl. 58; Som. 67, 110; Wrt. Voc. 38, 33. Ealle ðâs goldsmiþas secgaþ ðæt hî nǽfre ǽr swâ clǽne gold ne swâ reád ne gesâwon *all these goldsmiths say that they never before saw such pure and such red gold*, Homl. Th. i. 64, 9. Eall mid reádum golde his cynestôl geworhte *he wrought his throne all with red gold*, H. R. 101, 2. Hundtwelftig mancæs reádes goldes *a hundred and twenty mancuses of red gold*, Th. Chart. 232, 10: 375, 28: Bt. Met. Fox 19, 11; Met. 19, 6: Cd. 109; Th. 145, 11; Gen. 2404. Wunden gold *twisted gold*, 91; Th. 116, 4; Gen. 1931: Beo. Th. 2391; B. 1193. *Other epithets applied to gold are* æpled, beorht, fæted, fætt, hyrsted, scîr, smǽte. Gearo gumum gold brittade *Jared dispensed gold to men*, Cd. 59: Th. 72, 4; Gen. 1181. Goldes brytta *a dispenser of gold*, 137; Th. 173, 26; Gen. 2867. [*Goth.* gulth: *O. Sax. O. Frs. O. Ger.* gold: *Icel.* gull.] DER. cyne-, fæt-, heáfod-gold.

gold-ǽht, e; *f. A possession* or *treasure of gold*, Beo. Th. 5489; B. 2748.

gold-beorht; *adj. Bright with gold*; auro splendens:—Beorn monig goldbeorht scân *many a warrior shone bright with golden ornaments*, Exon. 124 b; Th. 477, 33; Ruin. 34.

gold-bleoh; *gen.* -bleós; *n. A golden colour*; crisoletus, auricolor, Ælfc. Gl. 49; Som. 65, 89; Wrt. Voc. 34, 21.

gold-blôma, an; *m. A golden mass*:—Se hâlga Gâst wunode on ðam gecorenan hordfæte . . . se goldblôma on ðas world becom and menniscne lîchoman onfêng æt Sancta Marian *the Holy Ghost dwelt in the chosen treasury . . . the golden mass came into this world and received a human body from St. Mary*, Blickl. Homl. 105, 18. [*Or* blôma = *bloom, blossom*; cf. *Goth.* blôma: *Icel.* blômi?] v. blôma.

gold-burh; *gen.* -burge; *f. A town where gold is distributed* or *which is ornamented with gold*, Andr. Kmbl. 3308; An. 1657: Cd. 119; Th. 154, 2; Gen. 2549. v. Grm. A. u. E. xxxviii.

gold-fæt, es; *n. A golden vessel*:—Godes goldfatu *God's golden vessels*, Cd. 212: Th. 262, 36; Dan. 755. [*O. Sax.* gold-fat: *O. H. Ger.* golt-faz.]

gold-fæt [-fatu?], es; *n. A thin plate of gold*; bractea, lamina aurea:—Stâne gelîcast gladum gimme ðonne in goldfate smiþa orþoncum biseted weorþeþ *to a stone most like to a bright jewel when by the smiths' art it has been set in a bracelet*, Exon. 60 a; Th. 219, 7; Ph. 303.

gold-fâh; *adj. Variegated* or *adorned with gold*:—Hió becwiþ him hyre goldfâgan treówenan cuppan *she bequeaths to him her wooden cup ornamented with gold*, Th. Chart. 536, 17: Beo. Th. 621; B. 308: 5615; B. 2811. Goldfâg scinon web æfter wagum *the hangings along the walls shone interwoven with gold*, 1993; B. 994. [*Laym.* gold-fah, -faȝe, -fawe.]

gold-fell, es; *n. Gold skin, gold leaf*; bractea, Cot. 24, Lye.

gold-finc, es; *m. A gold-finch*; auricinctus, florentius, Ælfc. Gl. 37; Som. 62, 126; Wrt. Voc. 29, 21: 38; Som. 63, 36; Wrt. Voc. 29, 54.

gold-finger, es; *m. The ring-finger*:—Goldfinger *me[di]cus* vel *annularis*, Ælfc. Gl. 73; Som. 71, 21; Wrt. Voc. 44, 7: L. Alf. pol. 59; Th. i. 96, 5: L. Eth. 54; Th. i. 16, 12.

gold-frætwe; *pl. f. Gold ornaments*, Exon. 22 b; Th. 62, 3; Cri. 996.

gold-geweorc, es; *n. Gold-work, what is made of gold*:—Ðǽr wæs ðære sunnan anlŷcnys geworht of golde and heó wæs on gyldenum scryd and æt ðam wǽron gyldene hors . . . ðâ eode ðǽr egeslîc deóful ût of ðam goldgeweorce and ðæt goldgeweorc eall todreás swâ swâ weax gemylt æt fŷre *there was an image of the sun made of gold, and it was on a golden chariot, and there were golden horses to the chariot . . . then came there a horrible devil out of the goldwork, and the goldwork all fell away as wax melts at the fire*, Shrn. 156, 10-16.

gold-gifa, an; *m. A giver of gold, a liberal lord* or *chief*:—Funde ðâ on bedde blâcne licgan his goldgifan *he found then his lord lying pale on the bed*, Judth. 12; Thw. 25, 26; Jud. 279. Goldgyfan, Beo. Th. 5297; B. 2652. Cyningas ne câseras ne goldgiefan *neither kings nor emperors nor lords*, Exon. 82 b; Th. 310, 31; Seef. 83. *See other compounds under* gifa.

gold-hama, an; *m. A gilded* or *golden coat of mail*, Elen. Kmbl. 1980; El. 992.

gold-hilted; *adj. Having a golden hilt*, Exon. 114 a; Th. 437, 27; Rä. 56, 14.

gold-hladen; *adj. Adorned with gold*, Fins. Th. 26; Fin. 13.

gold-hord, es; *m. n. A treasure, treasury*; thesaurus:—Nellen gê goldhordian eów goldhordas on eorþan . . . goldhordiaþ eów goldhordas on heofenan . . . đǽr đîn goldhord is đǽr is đîn heorte *nolite thesaurizare vobis thesauros in terra . . . thesaurizate vobis thesauros in cælo . . . ubi est thesaurus tuus, ibi est cor tuum*, Mt. Kmbl. 6, 19-21: 2, 11: 13, 44, 52: Exon. 19 b; Th. 49, 18; Cri. 787. Goldhord dǽlan *to distribute treasure*, Cd. 173; Th. 216, 16; Dan. 2. Đæt goldhord, đæt yldum wæs lange behýded *the treasure that was long hidden from men*, Elen. Kmbl. 1578; El. 791. Goldhord *thesaurarium*, Ælfc. Gl. 109; Som. 79, 23; Wrt. Voc. 58, 63. He gesette đone gârsecg on his goldhorde *ponens in thesauris abyssos*, Ps. Th. 32, 6. Đe forþlǽdeþ fægere windas of his goldhordum *qui producit ventos de thesauris suis*, Ps. Th. 134, 8.

gold-hord-hûs, es; *n. A privy*; ypodromum, Ælfc. Gl. 107; Som. 78, 80; Wrt. Voc. 57, 57, see note.

gold-hordian; *p.* ode; *pp.* od *To hoard, lay up treasure*; thesaurizare. Mt. Kmbl. 6, 19, 20.

gold-hroden; *adj. Adorned with gold*:—Cwên goldhroden *the queen adorned with gold*, Beo. Th. 1232; B. 614: 1285; B. 640: 3900; B. 1948: 4054; B. 2025: Exon. 86 a; Th. 324, 29; Vîd. 102.

gold-hwæte; *adj. Greedy for gold*, Beo. Th. 6140; B. 3074.

gold-læfra, an; *m. Gold-leaf*; bractea, Cot. 207, Lye.

gold-mæstling, -mæslinc, es; *n. Brass, latten*; auricalcum, Ælfc. Gr. 8; Som. 7, 65: Wrt. Voc. 85, 8.

gold-mâđum, es; *m. A precious thing made of gold, treasure*, Beo. Th. 4820; B. 2414.

gold-sele, es; *m. A hall in which gold is distributed*, or *one adorned with gold*, Beo. Th. 1434; B. 715: 2510; B. 1253: 3282; B. 1639: 4172; B. 2083. [Cf. gold-burh.]

gold-siowod *auro satus, acupictus, segmentatus*, Cot. 178, Lye.

gold-smiþ, es; *m. A goldsmith, worker in gold*; aurifex:—Tubalcain wæs êgđer ge goldsmiþ ge îsensmiþ *Tubalcain was a worker both in gold and in iron*, Gen. 4, 22. Goldsmiþ *aurifex*, Coll. Monast. Th. 29, 35: Homl. Th. i. 64, 8. Đe Eádrêd cyng gebôcode Ælfsige his goldsmiþe *which king Edred gave by charter to his goldsmith Ælfsig*, Cod. Dipl. Kmbl. iii. 431, 24: vi. 211, 7: Bt. Met. Fox 10, 67; Met. 10, 34.

gold-smiþu, e; *f. The art of the goldsmith*, Exon. 88; Th. 331, 24; Vy. 73.

gold-spêdig; *adj. Wealthy*, Exon. 66 a; Th. 245, 3; Jul. 39.

gold-þeóf, es; *m. One who steals gold*, L. Alf. pol. 9; Th. i. 68, 5.

gold-torht; *adj. Bright like gold*, Exon. 93 b; Th. 351, 11; Sch. 78.

gold-weard, es; *m. A guardian of gold* [*a dragon*], Beo. Th. 6154; B. 3081.

gold-wine, es; *m. A liberal and kindly prince*, Judth. 10; Thw. 21, 17; Jud. 22: Beo. Th. 2346; B. 1171: 2956; B. 1476: 4829; B. 2419: 5161; B. 2584: Elen. Kmbl. 401; El. 201: Exon. 77 a; Th. 288, 23; Wand. 35: 76 b; Th. 287, 31; Wand. 22.

gold-wlanc, -wlonc; *adj. Splendidly adorned with gold*, Beo. Th. 3766; B. 1881: Salm. Kmbl. 414; Sal. 207.

gold-wlencu, e; *f. A golden ornament*:—Đonne ne gefultumiaþ đære sâule đara gimma frætwednes, ne đara goldwlenca nân *then the adornment of the gems does not help the soul, nor any of the golden ornaments*, Blickl. Homl. 195, 11.

GÔMA, an; *m. The palate; in pl. the fauces*:—Gôma *vel* hrôf đæs mûþes *palatum* vel *uranon*, Ælfc. Gl. 71; Som. 70, 107; Wrt. Voc. 43, 35. Gôma *palatum*, Wrt. Voc. 70, 53. Đes gôma *hæc faux*, Ælfc. Gr. 9, 71; Som. 14, 15. Ic eom on gôman swêtra đonne đû beóbreád blende mid hunige *sweeter am I on the palate than didst thou blend honeycomb with honey*, Exon. 111 a; Th. 425, 18; Rä. 41, 58: 113 a; Th. 433, 11; Rä. 50, 6. Ic dô đæt đîn tunge clifaþ to đînum gôman *linguam tuam adherescere faciam palato tuo*, Homl. Th. ii. 530, 28. Me syndan gôman hâse *raucæ factæ sunt fauces meæ*, Ps. Th. 68, 3: Soul Kmbl. 216; Seel. 110. Me is on gômum gôd and swête đîn âgen word *quam dulcia faucibus meis eloquia tua*, Ps. Th. 118, 103: 136, 5: 149, 6. He đa grimman gôman bihlemmeþ fæste togædre *he clashes fast together the fierce jaws*, Exon. 97 b; Th. 364, 26; Wal. 76. [*Prompt. Parv.* gome *gingiva*: *Icel.* gômr *the palate*: *O. H. Ger.* guomo, gaumo, giumo *guttur, faux, palatum*: *Ger.* gaum, gaumen *the palate*.]

gombe, an; *f. Tribute*:—Niéde sceoldon gombon gieldon and gafol sellan *needs must they pay tribute and tax*, Cd. 93; Th. 119, 11; Gen. 1978. Gomban gyldan, Beo. Th. 21; B. 11. [Cf. *O. Sax.* gambra, *used with* geldan.]

gomel, gomol, gamel, gamol; *adj. Advanced in age, aged, old, ancient*; ætâte provectus, sĕnex, vĕtustus, vĕtus:—Se fugel weorþeþ gomel *the bird becomes old*, Exon. 59 b; Th. 215, 24; Ph. 258: Beo. Th. 5578; B. 2793. Ahleóp se gomela *the aged* [*man*] *leapt up*, 2798; B. 1397: 5695; B. 2851. Biþ geómorlîc gomelum eorle *it is sad for an aged man*, 4880; B. 2444. Gomele ymb gôdne ongeador sprǽcon *the old spake together about the good* [*warrior*], 3194; B. 1595. He on him gyrdeþ gomelra lâfe *he girds on him the relic of the ancients*, 4079; B. 2036. Forbærst sweord Beówulfes, gomol and grǽgmǽl *Beowulf's sword burst asunder, ancient and grey-marked*, 5357; B. 2682. Se gomola eald ûþwîta *the ancient old sage*, Exon. 81 a; Th. 304, 5; Fä. 65.

gomel-feax, gomol-feax, gamol-feax; *adj. Hoary-locked, grey-haired*; cânus:—Gomelfeax gnornaþ *the hoary-locked grieves*, Exon. 82 b; Th. 311, 14; Seef. 92.

gomel-ferhþ *aged*. v. gamol-ferhþ.

gomen, es; *n. Game, joy, mirth, sport*; jŏcus, jūbĭlium, lætĭtia, lūdus:—Nis đǽr gomen in geardum *there is no mirth in the courts*, Beo. Th. 4909; B. 2459: 4518; B. 2263: 3554; B. 1775. v. gamen.

gomen-wâđu, e; *f. A joyous path*; lætum ĭter:—Gewiton ealdgesîþas of gomenwâđe *the old comrades departed from the joyous path*, Beo. Th. 1713; B. 854.

gomen-wudu; *gen.* -wuda; *m. Pleasure-wood, glee-wood, a musical instrument, harp*; lætitiæ lignum, harpa = ἅρπη:—Đǽr wæs sang and swêg samod ætgædere, gomenwudu grêted *there were song and sound at once together, the glee-wood* [*was*] *touched*, Beo. Th. 2134; B. 1065. Đǽr wæs gidd and gleó, hwîlum he hearpan wynne, gomenwudu grêtte *there was song and glee, at times he touched the joy of harp, the wood of mirth*, 4222; B. 2108.

gomol *old, ancient*, Beo. Th. 5357; B. 2682: Exon. 81 a; Th. 304, 5; Fä. 65. v. gomel.

gomol-feax; *adj. Hoary-locked, grey-haired*; cânus:—Gomolfeax hæleþ *a hoary-locked hero*, Chr. 975; Th. 228, 27, col. 2, 3. v. gomel-feax.

Gomorringas; *pl.* a *The people of Gomorrha*:—Eorþe gomorringa *terra Gomorræorum*, Mt. Kmbl. Rush. 10, 15.

gond. v. geond.

gong. v. gang.

gongan. v. gangan.

gongel, *found in composition as in* fæst-gongel, wîd-. v. gangel-, gongel-wæfre.

gongel-wæfre, an; *f. A ganging weaver, a spider*; arānea viātica:—Wiđ gongelwæfran bîte *for the bite of a spider*, L. M. 2, 65; Lchdm. ii. 296, 17: 2. 48; Lchdm. ii. 142. 23. v. gange-wifre.

gonge-wifre, an; *f. A ganging weaver, a spider*; arānea viātica:—Wiđ gongewifran bîte *against the bite of a spider* [*gangweaver*], L. M. 3, 35; Lchdm. ii. 328, 10. v. gange-wifre.

good. v. gôd.

gop, es; *m. A captive, slave* [?]. Cf. geópan *and Icel.* hergopa; *f. one taken in war, a bondwoman. Or is the word connected with* geap *crafty?*—Þurh gopes hond, Exon. 113 a; Th. 433, 5; Rä. 50, 3.

gor, es; *n. Dung, dirt*; fimus. lutum, coenum:—Đæs cealfes flǽsc, and fell, and gor đû bærnst ûte bûtan fyrdwîcon *carnes vituli, et corium, et fimum combures foris extra castra*, Ex. 29, 14. Đæs gores sunu, đone we wifel nemnaþ *son of the dung, which we call* [*dung-*] *beetle*, Exon. 111 a; Th. 426, 11; Rä. 41, 72. Mid swînenum gore *with swine dung*, Herb. 9, 3; Lchdm. i. 100, 11. Feares gor *bull's dung*, Med. ex Quadr. 11, 10, 11, 12; Lchdm. i. 368, 5, 7, 9. Gor *sordem*, Wrt. Voc. 65, 34. [*Prompt. Parv.* gore *limus*: *Icel.* gor: *O. H. Ger.* gor *fimus*.]

gorst, gost, es; *m.* GORSE, *furze, bramble*:—Đeós wyrt đe man tribulus and ôđrum naman gorst nemneþ *this plant, which is named tribulus, and by another name gorse*, Herb. 142, 1; Lchdm. i. 262, 16. Of gorstum *de tribolis*, Mt. Kmbl. Rush. 7, 16. Ne wînberian on gorste ne nimaþ *neque de rubo vindemiant uvam*, Lk. Skt. 6, 44. Đâ hêt ualerianus gebindan đysne ypolitum on wildu hors đæt hyne drôgon on gorstas and on þornas *then bade Valerian to bind this Hypolitus on wild horses that they might drag him into the brambles and thorns*, Shrn. 117, 13. Iuniperi đæt is gorst *juniper that is gorse*, L. M. i. 31, 3; Lchdm. ii. 72, 10. Gost *accidenetum*, Wrt. Voc. 33, 32. [*Prompt. Parv.* fyrrys or gorstys tre *ruscus*, p. 162, v. note.]

gorst-beám, es; *m. A bramble*; rubus:—Ofer đone gorstbeám *super rubum*, Mk. Skt. 12, 26.

GÔS; *gen.* gôse; *dat.* gês; *acc.* gôs; *pl. nom. acc.* gês, gees; *gen.* gôsa; *dat.* gôsum; *f. A* GOOSE; anser:—Gôs *auca*, Ælfc. Gl. 36; Som. 62, 119; Wrt. Voc. 29, 15: 77, 32. Grǽg gôs *a grey goose*, Cot. 99, Lye. Hwîlum ic grǽde swâ gôs *sometimes I cry as a goose*, Exon. 106 b; Th. 406, 18; Rä. 25, 3. Gees [gês, MS. H.] *geese*, L. In. 70; Th. i. 146, 18. [*Icel.* gâs: *O. H. Ger.* gans: *Lat.* anser: *Gk.* χήν.]

gôs-fugol, es; *m. A goose*, Th. Chart. 471, 31.

gôs-hafoc, es; *m. Goshawk*; aucarius, Ælfc. Gl. 36; Som. 62, 120; Wrt. Voc. 29, 16. [*Chauc.* gos-hauk: *Icel.* gâs-haukr: *O. H. Ger.* gans-hapich.]

gost. v. gorst.

gôst, Shrn. 152, 35. v. gâst.

Gota, an; *m. A Goth;* Gothus; chiefly used in the *pl; nom. acc.* Gotan; *gen.* Gotena; *dat.* Gotum; *m. The Goths:*—Unrîm mânes se Gota fremede *the Goth perpetrated an excess of wickedness,* Bt. Met. Fox 1, 89; Met. 1, 45. **I.** VISIGOTHS or *West Goths, under Alrîca,* q. v. A. D. 382–410, etc:—Đa [MS. đe] Gotan of Sciđđiu mǽgþe, wiđ Rômâna rîce gewin upahôfon; and miđ heora cyningum, Rǽdgota and Eallerîca [Alrîca] wǽron hâtne, Rômâne burig abrǽcon *the Goths, from the country of Scythia, made war against the empire of the Romans; and with their kings, who were called Rhadgast and Alaric, sacked the Roman city* [A. D. 410], Bt. 1; Fox 2, 1. Seó hergung wæs þurh Alarîcum [*acc. Lat.*] Gotena cyning geworden *hæc inruptio per Alaricum regem Gothorum facta est,* Bd. 1, 11; S. 480, 11. Đa Gotan coman of đâm hwatestan mannan Germania *the Goths came from the bravest men of Germany,* Ors. 1, 10; Bos. 34, 5, 11. **II.** OSTROGOTHS, or *East Goths, under Ermanric,* Þeódric, q. v. A. D. 475–526, etc:—Gotan eástan of Sciđđia sceldas lǽddon *Goths from the east led their army from Scythia,* Bt. Met. Fox 1, 2; Met. 1, 1. Hû Gotan gewunnon Rômâna rîce *how the Goths conquered the empire of the Romans,* Bt. titl. i; Fox x. 2. Eormanrîc âhte wîde folc Gotena rîces *Ermanric possessed the wide nations of the kingdom of the Goths,* Exon. 100 b; Th. 378, 28; Deor. 23: 86 a: Th. 324, 3; Wid. 89: 86 b; Th. 325, 10; Wid. 109. Weóld Eormanrîc Gotum *Ermanric ruled the Goths,* Exon. 85 a; Th. 319, 27; Wid. 18. [*Icel.* Goti, *pl.* Gotnar.] v. Grmm. Gesch. D. S. c. xviii.

Got-land GOTHLAND; Gothia, Ors. 1, 1; Bos. 22, 2.

gôt-woþe, an; *f. Goatweed;* ægopodium podagraria, L. M. i. 31, 7; Lchdm. ii. 74, 19: 38, 3; Lchdm. ii. 92, 7.

goung, e; *f. A sighing, sobbing, mourning;* gemitus:—On đæs tuddres forþlǽdnysse biþ goung and sâr *in prolis prolatione gemitus,* Bd. 1, 27 resp. 8; S. 493, 21. [Cf. [?] *Gk.* γοᾶν *to sigh.*]

grad, es; *m.* [*Lat.* gradus] *A* GRADE, *step, order, degree, rank;* gradus, ordo:—Seofon stapas sindon ciriclîcra grada and hâligra hâda *seven are the degrees of ecclesiastical ranks,* L. E. B. 1; Th. ii. 240, 2. Blôd com uppon þâm gradan and of þâm gradan on þa flôre *blood came upon the steps and from the steps on the floor,* Chr. 1083; Erl. 217, 28. Æt sumum sǽle ætslâd se hâlga wer on đâm heálîcum gradum æt đam hâlgum weofode *on one occasion the holy man slipped on the tall steps at the holy altar,* Homl. Th. ii. 512, 11.

grǽd, es; *m. Greed, rapacity;* aviditas:—Fuglas hungrige grǽdum gîfre *birds hungry, greedily voracious,* Exon. 43 a; Th. 146, 15; Gû. 710. [*Goth.* grêdus: *Icel.* grâðr *hunger, greed.*]

grǽdan; *p.* de *To cry, call out;* clamare:—Ic grǽde swâ gôs *I cry like a goose,* Exon. 106 b; Th. 406, 18; Rä. 25, 3. Đonne grǽt se lâreów swâ swâ kok on niht *prædicator clamat quasi gallus cantat in nocte,* Past. 63; Swt. 459, 32; Hat. MS. Hine mon sceal swîđe hlûde hâtan grǽdan odđe singan *he must be bidden to cry out or sing very loud,* L. M. 2, 5; Lchdm. ii. 182, 26. [*A.R. Piers P.* greden: *Laym.* grædde; *p.*]

grǽde, es; *m. Grass, a herb;* gramen:—Grǽde *ulva,* Ælfc. Gl. 42; Som. 64, 23; Wrt. Voc. 31, 33. Grǽdas *gramina,* Cot. 95, Lye.

grǽdig; *adj.* GREEDY, *covetous;* avidus:—Grǽdig *vorator,* Ælfc. Gl. 88; Som. 74, 82; Wrt. Voc. 50, 62. Đa fŷnd heora grîpende wǽron swâ swâ grǽdig wulf *the devils were seizing them like the ravening wolf,* Blickl. Homl. 211, 1. Lîg grǽdig swelgeþ londes frætwe *flame, greedy, swallows the land's treasures,* Exon. 63 a; Th. 232, 16; Ph. 507: Beo. Th. 242; B. 121: 3002; B. 1497. Sum to lyt hafaþ gôdes grǽdig *one hath too little, eager for goods,* Salm. Kmbl. 689; Sal. 344. Đâ getîmode swâ dê ꝥ đam grǽdigan fisce đe gesihþ đæt ǽs and ne gesihþ đone angel đe on đam ǽse sticaþ *then it befel as it does to the greedy fish that sees the bait but sees not the hook which sticks in the bait,* Homl. Th. i. 216, 10. Helle grǽdige and gîfre *hell greedy and ravenous,* Cd. 37; Th. 49, 16; Gen. 793: 217; Th. 276, 21; Sat. 192. León-hwelpas sêcaþ đæt him grǽdigum ǽt God gedême *catuli leonum ... quærant a Deo escam sibi,* Ps. Th. 103, 20. Gîfrost and grǽdgost *most rapacious and most greedy,* Exon. 128 a; Th. 493, 2; Rä. 81, 24. [*Goth.* grêdags: *O. Sax.* grâdag: *Icel.* grâðugr: *O.H. Ger.* grâtag.] DER. heoro-, hilde-, wæl-grǽdige.

grǽdig-, grǽdi-, grǽde-lîce; *adv.* GREEDILY, *covetously;* avidè:—He gŷmþ grǽdelîce his teolunge *he attends greedily to his gain,* Homl. Th. i. 66, 10. Đâs fugelas habbaþ feónda gelîcnysse đe gehwilce menn beswîcaþ and grǽdelîce grîpaþ to grimre helle *these birds are like the fiends, that deceive some men, and greedily snatch them to grim hell,* ii. 516, 10. Đonne him hingraþ he yt grǽdilîce *when he is hungry he eats greedily,* Hexam. 20; Norm. 28, 21.

grǽdignes, se; *f.* GREEDINESS, *covetousness;* aviditas:—Grǽdinesse he lufode *covetousness he loved,* Chr. 1086; Erl. 222, 25. Eorþlîcan grǽdignysse *greediness after earthly things,* Boutr. Scrd. 20, 11.

græf, graf, es; *n. A grave, trench:*—Æt openum græfe *at the open grave,* L. Æthelb. 22; Th. i. 8, 5: L. Eth. 5, 12; Th. i. 308, 4: 6, 20; Th. i. 320, 4: Exon. 82 b; Th. 311, 24; Seef. 97: 91 b; Th. 342, 29; Gn. Ex. 149. Ic ongyte đeáh đæt đa worlde lustas ne sint eallunga awyrtwalode of đînum môde đeáh se graf geryd sî *I perceive however that worldly pleasures are not entirely rooted out of thy mind, though the trench be sufficient,* Shrn. 184, 20. [*O. Sax.* graf: *O. Frs.* greb: *O. H. Ger.* grab: *Ger.* grab; *n: Goth.* graba: *Icel.* gröf; *f.*] DER. eorþ-, fold-, mold-græf.

græf, es; *n. A graving instrument, a style:*—Græf *graffium,* Ælfc. Gl. 8; Wrt. Voc. 75, 17: *graphium* vel *scriptorium,* Ælfc. Gl. 80; Som. 72, 114; Wrt. Voc. 46, 71.

græfa, græfe [?], an:—Twælf fôđur græfan, Chr. 852; Erl. 67, 38. Earle in his note on this word, p. 300, suggests a translation other than that given by previous editors. By them it has been translated 'coal,' he suggests 'gravel.' The word may be of Celtic origin, and so may be compared with Old French *grave,* of which *gravel* is a diminutive. Celtic forms are *Bret.* grouan *gravel: Corn.* grow *gravel, sand: W.* gro *pebbles.*

grǽfa, grêfa, an; *m. A pit, cave, hole:*—Grǽfe *speluncam,* Mt. Kmbl. Lind. 21, 13. See Cod. Dipl. Kmbl. iii. xxvii. [Cf. *Goth.* grôba; *f. a hole: Icel.* grôf; *f. a pit: O.H.Ger.* grôba; *f. fovea, scrobs, barathrum: Ger.* grube.]

græfere, grafere, es; *m. A graver, an engraver:*—Græfere *sculptor* vel *celator,* Ælfc. Gl. 81; Som. 72, 121; Wrt. Voc. 47, 4.

græf-hûs, es; *n. A grave-house, house of the dead:*—Hell grim græfhûs *hell the grim house of the dead,* Cd. 228; Th. 309, 11; Sat. 708.

græf-seax, -sex, es; *n. A graving knife:*—Græfsex *scalprum* vel *scalpellum* vel *cælum,* Ælfc. Gl. 81; Som. 72, 125; Wrt. Voc. 47, 7.

græft, es; *m:* græft, e; *f.* [?] *Carving, graving, a carved* or *graven image:*—Græft *sculptura,* Ælfc. Gl. 81; Som. 72, 122; Wrt. Voc. 47, 5. Ealle đa đe gebiddaþ græftas *omnes qui adorant sculptilia,* Ps. Lamb. 96, 7: Ps. Spl. C. 105, 19: Homl. Th. i. 464, 27. Îrene græfta *ferrea sculptilia, carpenta,* Cot. 38, Lye. [*O. H. Ger.* graft, grefti; *f. cælatura, sculptura, sculptile.*]

græft-geweorc, es; *n. Carved* or *graven work, a graven image:*—Ne wirce đû græftgeweorc *thou shalt not make any graven image,* Deut. 5, 8.

grǽg, grêg; *adj. Grey:*—Grêg *glaucus,* Ælfc. Gl. 79; Som. 72, 90; Wrt. Voc. 46, 47. Deorce grǽg *elbus,* Wrt. Voc. 46, 48. Grǽg hwǽte *far,* Ælfc. Gr. 9, 17; Som. 9, 52. Se grǽga mǽw *the grey mew,* Andr. Kmbl. 742; An. 371. Wulf se grǽga *the grey wolf,* Exon. 91 b; Th. 343, 3; Gn. Ex. 151: Chr. 937; Erl. 115, 13; Ædelst. 64. Sǽ grǽge glashluđre *the sea grey and clear as glass,* Bt. Met. Fox 5, 15; Met. 5, 8. Grǽgan sweorde *with a grey sword,* Cd. 138; Th. 173, 22; Gen. 2865: Beo. Th. 665; B. 330: 673; B. 334. [*Icel.* grâr: *O. Frs.* grê: *O. H. Ger.* grâw: *Ger.* grau.]

grǽg-, grǽ-gôs *a grey goose, wild goose:*—Grǽg-gôs *canta,* Wrt. Voc. 280, 15: 62, 11: Mone Gl. 314. [*Icel.* grâ-gâs.]

grǽg-hama, an; *m. A corslet, coat of mail:*—Gylleþ grǽghama *the corslet rattles,* Fins. Th. 10; Fin. 6. [Cf. grǽge syrcan, Beo. Th. 673; B. 334; *and* gullon gûþ searo, Andr. Kmbl. 253; An. 127. Grein takes the word as an adjective = *grey-coated, the grey-coated one,* i. e. *the wolf.* In support of this cf. scîrham, and the passages given under 'grǽg,' in which that adjective is applied to the wolf.]

grǽg-hiwe, -hæwe; *adj. Of a grey hue* or *colour,* Lye.

grǽg-mǽl; *adj. Of a grey colour,* Beo. Th. 5357; B. 2682. See under 'grǽg,' the passage in which that adjective is applied to weapons.

græp *a grip, furrow, ditch;* sulcus, Som.

græs, es; *n. Grass, plant;* grâmen:—On grêne græs *on the green grass,* Cd. 56; Th. 69, 17; Gen. 1137. Đa đe of græses deáwe geworht wǽron *those that were made of the dew of grass,* Shrn. 66, 3. Sume hió twiccedan đa grasu mid hiora mûþe *some of them pulled the grass with their mouth,* 41, 2: Past. 23, 1; Swt. 173, 20. v. gærs.

græs-hoppa, an; *m. A grass-hopper, locust:*—Græs-hoppa *locustæ,* Mt. Kmbl. Rush. 3, 4. Hŷ habbaþ fêt swylce græs-hoppan *pedes quasi locuste,* Nar. 35, 7. v. gærs-hoppa.

græs-molde, an; *f. Grassland, greensward;* campus graminibus viridis:—Beówulf græs-moldan træd *Beowulf trod the greensward* [*grassy mould*], Beo. Th. 3767; B. 1881.

græs-wang, -wong, es; *m. A grassy plain,* Exon. 57 a; Th. 203, 2; Ph. 78: 65 b; Th. 243, 5; Jul. 6.

grǽtan *to bewail.* v. grêtan.

grætta GRITS, *groats, bran;* farina crassior, furfur, Som. v. gryt.

graf. v. græf.

grâf, es; *m. n. A grove:*—Heó hæbbe đa wudurǽddenne in đæm wuda đe đa ceorlas brûcaþ and êc ic hire lête to đæt ceorla grâf *let her have right of pasturage in the wood which the 'ceorls' use, and besides I leave to her the 'ceorls'' grove,* Cod. Dipl. Kmbl. ii. 100, 14. Andlang đære lytlan dîc æt đæs grâfes ende *along the little ditch at the end of the grove,* 249, 29. Forþ be đam grâfe *along past the grove,* iii. 18, 31. Đone grâf, 52, 23. Eác we wrîtaþ him đone grâf đærto. Đis syndon đa gemǽru đe to đæm grâfe gebyriaþ *also we assign to him in addition the grove. These are the boundaries that belong to the grove,* 261, 5–7. [*Laym.* groue: *Prompt. Parv.* grove *lucus.*]

grafan, ic grafe, græfe, ðú græfest, græfst, he græfeþ, græfþ, *pl.* grafaþ; *p.* grôf, *pl.* grôfon; *pp.* grafen. I. *to dig, delve, dig up;* fodere, effodere:—Ic be grunde græfe *I dig along the ground,* Exon. 106 a; Th. 403, 3: Rä. 22, 2. Ðæt fýr græfeþ grimlíce eorþan sceátas *the fire shall fiercely delve the tracts of earth,* Exon. 22 b; Th. 62, 19; Cri. 1004: 95 a; Th. 354, 55; Reim. 66. Se forma feohgítsere grôf æfter golde *the first miser delved after gold,* Bt. Met. Fox 8, 113; Met. 8, 57: Exon. 109 a; Th. 416, 4; Rä. 34, 6: 130 a; Th. 498, 24; Rä. 88, 6. Ðæt ic grôfe græf *that I may dig a grave,* Exon. 95 a; Th. 355, 3; Reim. 71. II. *to* GRAVE, *engrave, carve;* sculpere, cælare:—Ic grafe *sculpo,* Ælfc. Gr. 28, 4; Som. 31, 20. Ðonne hí wôhgodu worhtan and grôfun *in sculptilibus suis emulati sunt eum,* Ps. Th. 77, 58. Ac hý grôfon ǽghwylcne stân swâ se câsere geþohte *they carved each stone as the emperor designed,* Shrn. 146, 16. [*Laym.* graven: *Prompt. Parv.* gravin *sculpere: O. Sax.* (bi-)graban: *Goth.* graban: *Icel.* grafa: *O. H. Ger.* graban.] DER. a-grafan, be-, bi-.

grafet, es; *n. A trench* [?]:—On ðæt lange grauet of ðam lange grafette, Cod. Dipl. Kmbl. v. 193, 33: 195, 5, 7. Leo takes the word as a diminutive of 'grǽf.'

gram, grom; *adj.* [grama *anger*] *Furious, fierce, wroth, angry, offended, incensed, hostile, troublesome:*—He swâ grom wearþ on his môde *he became so incensed;* rex iratus, Ors. 2, 4; Swt. 72, 32: 6, 4; Swt. 260, 23. Drihten wæs ðam folce gram *the Lord was angry with the people,* Deut. 1, 37: Cd. 16; Th. 20, 2; Gen. 302. Wearþ se cyng swíðe gram wið ða burhware *the king was very angry with the citizens,* Chr. 1048; Erl. 178, 6. He wæs on his gâste gram *exacerbaverunt spiritum ejus,* Ps. Th. 105, 25. Ic eom nalæs grames môdes *non sum turbatus,* 118, 60. Of gramum folce *de populo barbaro,* 113, 1. Ðín ðæt grame yrre *thy fierce anger,* 68, 25: 84, 1: 108, 18. Seó eádge biseah ongeán gramum *the blessed maid looked on the fierce one* [*the devil*], Exon. 75 a; Th. 280, 12; Jul. 628: Cd. 27; Th. 36, 35; Gen. 582. Ða graman Gydena ðe folcisce men hâtaþ Parcas *the fierce goddesses whom common people call Parcæ,* Bt. 35, 6; Fox 168, 24. Grame gûþfrecan *fierce warriors,* Judth. 11; Thw. 24, 35; Jud. 224: Andr. Kmbl. 1833; An. 919: Ps. Th. 104, 30. Grame me forhogedon *my enemies despised me,* 118, 141: 104, 15: Judth. 12; Thw. 25, 2; Jud. 238. Grame manige fremde þeóda *many hostile and strange nations;* alienigenæ, Ps. Th. 82, 6: 118, 138: Exon. 126 b; Th. 485, 26; Rä. 72, 3. Ðǽr ða graman wunnon *where the fierce ones struggled,* Bëo. Th. 1559; B. 777. In gramra gripe *into the grasp of foes,* Andr. Kmbl. 433; An. 217: 1901; An. 953. Gromra, Cd. 114; Th. 150, 2; Gen. 2485. Deófla strǽlas gromra gârfare *the shafts of devils, the spears of fierce spirits,* Exon. 19 a; Th. 49, 5; Cri. 781. Ne beó ðú ælþeódegum gram *thou shalt not . . . oppress a stranger,* Ex. 23, 9. Ne beó ðú me gram *noli mihi molestus esse,* Lk. Skt. 11, 7: 18, 5. [*Laym.* gram: *Orm.* gramm: *O. Sax.* gram, the gramo *the devil: Icel.* gramr *wroth; pl.* gramir, gröm *fiends, demons;* see Grmm. D. M. 942–3: *O. H. Ger.* gram *iratus: Ger.* gram.]

GRAMA, an; *m. Anger, rage, fury, indignation, wrath, trouble;* ira, furor, molestia:—On graman ðínum *in ira tua,* Ps. Spl. 6. 1: 7, 6. Drihten wearþ yrre mid graman his folce *iratus est furore Dominus in populo suo,* Swt. A. S. Rdr. 73, 54–6: Gen. 19, 25. Ic ondrêd his graman and his yrre *I was afraid of his anger and hot displeasure,* Deut. 9, 19. Ðæne úre yldran for graman to deáþe gedêmdon *whom our elders for anger doomed to death,* H. R. 9, 23. Wel hí sind Dere gehâtene forðan ðe hí sind fram graman generode *well are they named Dere* [= *de ira*], *for they are saved from wrath,* Homl. Th. ii. 120, 35: 124, 9. Se upplíca grama *the wrath of heaven,* 538, 28. Æppla gaderian graman getâcnaþ *to gather apples betokens trouble,* Lchdm. iii. 212, 21. [*Laym.* grome, grame: *A. R.* grome *anger: Chauc.* grame: cf. *O. H. Ger.* grame; *f. exacerbatio: Ger.* gram; *m. grief.*]

gramatisc-cræft, es; *m. The art of grammar,* Bd. 4, 2; S. 565, 26.

gram-bǽre; *adj. Angry, passionate;* iracundus, Past. 40, 1; Swt. 289, 5; Hat. MS.

grame, grome; *adv. Fiercely, cruelly, hostilely,* Ps. Th. 57, 5: 68, 3: 93, 2: 123, 7. Grome, Cd. 64; Th. 76, 21; Gen. 1260: 184; Th. 230, 15; Dan. 233: Exon. 89 b; Th. 336, 21; Gn. Ex. 52.

gramfærnys, se; *f. Anger, fury:*—Ǽlc gramfærnys cymþ of deófle *omnis furor venit a diabolo,* L. Ecg. P. 4, 66; Th. ii. 226, 25.

gram-heort; *adj. Having a fierce, hostile heart* or *mind,* Beo. Th. 3368; B. 1682: Exon. 31 a; Th. 136, 14; Gû. 541: 102 b; Th. 387, 17; Rä. 5, 6. [*O. Sax.* gram-hert.]

gram-hycgende; *part. Having fierce, hostile thought* or *purpose,* Ps. Th. 68, 25.

gram-hygdig, -hýdig; *adj. Fierce-minded, hostilely disposed:*—Gramhegdig, Ps. C. 50, 49; Ps. Grn. ii. 278, 49. Gromhýdig guma, Exon. 55 b; Th. 196, 6; Az. 170: 18 b; Th. 46, 8; Cri. 734: Beo. Th. 3502; B. 1749. Ðǽr nǽfre feóndes ne biþ gâstes gramhýdiges gang *where never shall be fiend's or fierce spirit's walk,* Andr. Kmbl. 3384; An. 1696: Ps. Th. 73, 4. Gramhýdige me oft onginnaþ *injusti insurrexerunt in me,* 85, 13. Gromhýdge, Exon. 38 a; Th. 124, 31; Gû. 346: 116 a; Th. 445, 27; Dôm. 14. [*O. Sax.* gram-hugdig.]

gramlíc; *adj. Fierce, hostile, cruel:*—He hig betǽhte sumum gramlícan cininge Iabin gehâton *he gave them into the hands of a fierce king named Jabin,* Jud. 4, 2. Oñ heora gasthúsum is gramlíc inwit *nequitia in hospitiis eorum,* Ps. Th. 54, 15. [*Icel.* gramligr *vexatious.*]

gramlíce; *adv. Hostilely, evilly, fiercely:*—Gramlíce be Gode sprǽcan *male locuti sunt de Deo,* Ps. Th. 77, 20: 105, 12: Cd. 210; Th. 260, 23; Dan. 714.

gram-môd; *adj. Of fierce* or *cruel mind:*—Hine nǽnig man grammôdne ne funde *no one found him cruel,* Blickl. Homl. 223, 33.

gram-word, es; *n. A word* or *speech expressing anger, wrath, hate, evil:*—Ne gê wið gode ǽfre gramword sprecan *nolite loqui adversus deum iniquitatem,* Ps. Th. 74, 5.

grandor-, grondor-leás; *adj. Guileless:*—Geong grondorleás *young and guileless,* Exon. 69 b; Th. 258, 26; Jul. 271. [Cf. *Icel.* grandlauss, grandvarr *guileless.*]

grânian; *p.* ode; *pp.* od *To groan, lament, murmur:*—Grânude *lamentatæ,* Ps. Spl. C. 77, 69. Hí grânedan *murmuraverunt,* Ps. Th. 105, 20. [*Laym.* granien, gronie: *A. R.* gronen: *Prompt. Parv.* gronin *gemere:* cf. *O. H. Ger.* grînan *mutire: Ger.* greinen *to cry.*]

Grantabrycgscir *Cambridgeshire.*

Granta-ceaster GRANTCHESTER, *a village near Cambridge,* Bd. 4, 19; S. 588, 30.

Grantan-brycg, e; *f:* Grante brycg, e; *f:* Granta-brycg, e; *f.* [*Hunt.* Grantebrige: *Dunel.* Grantabric, Grantnebrige, Grantebryge: *Hovd.* Grauntebrigge] CAMBRIDGE, *the chief town in Cambridgeshire, and seat of the University;* Cantābrigia, agri Cantabrigiensis oppidum primarium:—To Grantanbrycge *to Cambridge,* Chr. 875; Th. 144, 9, col. 2: 145, 9, col. 2: 921; Th. 195. 29. To Grante brycge *to Cambridge,* Chr. 875; Th. 144, 9, col. 1, 3. Forbærndon Granta-bricge *they burned down Cambridge,* Chr. 1000; Th. 264, 5, col. 1: 264, 8, col. 2: 265, 7, col. 1.

grânung, e; *f.* GROANING, *lamentation;* gemitus:—Me ymbhringdon sâr and sorga and grânung *circumdederunt me gemitus mortis,* Ps. Th. 17, 4. Mín grânung ðê nis na forholen *gemitus meus a te non est absconditus,* 37, 9. Wununga on ðâm ne ablinþ grânung *dwellings in which groaning ceases not,* Homl. Th. i. 68, 7: L. E. I; Th. ii. 400, 7.

grâp, e; *f. Grasp, clutch:*—Me fæste hæfde on grâpe *fast had me in his grasp,* Beo. Th. 1114; B. 555: 881; B. 438. Hond earm and eaxle Grendles grâpe *hand, arm, and shoulder, Grendel's grasp,* 1676; B. 836. On grâpum *in the clutches,* 1534; B. 765: 3088; B. 1542: Andr. Kmbl. 2671; An. 1337: Exon. 38 b; Th. 126, 28: 47 a; Th. 162, 1. [*Icel.* greip; *f. the space between the thumb and the fingers, a grasp: O. H. Ger.* greifa; *f. bidens.*]

GRÂPIAN, grôpian; *p.* ode; *pp.* od *To grope, touch, feel with the hands:*—Ic grôpige *palpo,* Ælfc. Gr. 24; Som. 25, 42. Grâpige, 36; Som. 38, 46. Handa hí habbaþ and hí nâ grâpiaþ *manus habent et non palpabunt,* Ps. Spl. 113, 15. Se cuma his cneów grâpode mid his hâlwendum handum *the stranger felt his knee with his healing hands,* Homl. Th. ii. 134, 35. Hire wið healse heard grâpode bânhringas bræc *the hard blade touched her neck, broke the bone-rings,* Beo. Th. 3137; B. 1566: 4176; B. 2085. On ðæt bânleáse brýd grâpode hondum *touched with hands that boneless bride,* Exon. 112 b; Th. 431, 20; Rä. 46, 3. Hie wurdon sôna ablinde and grâpodan mid heora handum on ða eorþan *they at once became blind and groped on the ground with their hands,* Blickl. Homl. 151, 6. Grâpiaþ *palpate,* Lk. Skt. 24, 39. Þýstro swâ þicce ðæt hig grâpion *darkness that may be felt,* Ex. 10, 21. Ðæt ðú grâpie on midne dæg swâ se blinda dêþ on þístrum *thou shalt grope at noonday, as the blind gropeth in darkness,* Deut. 28, 29. Ðone líchoman he æteówde to grâpigenne *he shewed the body to be touched,* Homl. Th. i. 230, 24. [*O. H. Ger.* greifon *palpare.*]

grâpigendlíc; *adj. Tangible:*—His líchama wæs grâpigendlíc . . . he æteówde hine grâpigendlícne *his body was tangible . . . he shewed himself tangible,* Homl. Th. i. 230, 25, 26.

grasian *to graze:*—Oxan grasiende gesihþ *if he sees oxen grazing,* Lchdm. iii. 200, 9. [*Icel.* gresja *to graze.*]

grâtan; *pl. Groats, the grain of oats without the husks:*—Nim âtena grâtan *take groats of oats,* Lchdm. iii. 292, 24. [Cf. *Icel.* grautr *porridge.*]

Greácas. v. Grêcas.

GREÁDA, an; *m. A bosom;* sinus, gremium:—On Habrahames greádan *in sinum Abrahæ,* Lk. Skt. 16, 22, 23. Ða ðe beraþ on hira greádum ða â libbendan fatu *those who bear in their bosoms the ever-living vessels,* Past. 13, 1; Swt. 77, 6; Hat. MS. [*Ayenb.* greade: *Alis.* grede.]

GREÁT; *adj. Great, large, thick, coarse:*—Greát *grossus,* Ælfc. Gl. 89; Som. 74, 101; Wrt. Voc. 51, 14. Swâ swâ greát beám *like a great tree,* Bt. 38, 2; Fox 198, 9. Ǽðelword Ǽðelmǽres sunu ðæs grǽtan *Ethelward son of Ethelmer the great,* Chr. 1017; Erl. 161, 7. Tú hund greátes hlâfes and þridde smales *two hundred great loaves and a third of small,* Th. Chart. 158, 25. God him send ufan greáte hagolstânas *God cast down upon them great hailstones,* Jos. 10, 11: Cd. 19; Th. 24, 27; Gen. 384. Ða wǽron unmetlíce greáte heáhnisse *ingenti grossitudine* *atque altitudine*, Nar. 4, 22. Wǣron hie swā greáte swā columnan ge eác sume grȳttran *serpentes columnarum grossitudine aliquantulum proceriores*, 14, 15. Greáte swā stǣnene sweras micle *vastitudine columnarum*, 36, 12. Mid greátan sealte *with coarse salt*; cum sale marino, Herb. 37, 5; Lchdm. i. 138, 14. Mid scearpum pīlum greátum *with sharp and large stakes*, Chr. Erl. 5, 10. [*Orm.* græt: *Laym.* græt, great: *Chauc.* gret, greet: *O. Sax.* grōt: *O. Frs.* grāt: *O. H. Ger.* grōz: *Ger.* gross.]

Greátan leag, leá, e; *f. Probably Greatley, near Andover, Hants;* Greatanleagensis:—Ealle ðis wæs gesetted on ðam miclan synoð æt Greátanleage, on ðam wæs se ærcebisceop Wulfhelme, mid eallum ðǣm æðelum mannum, and wiotan [and Æðelstāne cyninge] *all this was established in the great synod at Greatley, in which was the archbishop Wulfhelm, with all the noblemen and witan [and King Athelstan]*, L. Ath. i. 26; Th. i. 214, 7. To-ēcan ðām dōmum ðe æt Greátanleá and æt Exanceastre gesette wǣron, and æt Þunresfelda *in addition to the dooms which were fixed at Greatley, and at Exeter, and at Thunresfeld*, v. pref; Th. i. 228, 9.

greáte wyrt, e; *f. Meadow saffron;* colchicum autumnale:—Ðeós wyrt ðe man hieribulbum and ōðrum naman greáte wyrt nemneþ *this plant which is called ἱερόβολβος and by another name great wort*, Herb. 22, 1; Lchdm. i. 118, 14: L. M. ii. 52, 1; Lchdm. ii. 268, 22.

greátian; *p.* ode; *pp.* od *To* GREATEN, *to become great* or *large;* grandescere, grossescere:—On ðæs siwenīgean eágum beóþ ða æpplas hāle, ac ða brǣwas greátigaþ *in lippi oculis pupillæ sanæ sunt, sed palpebræ grossescunt*, Past. 11, 4; Swt. 69, 2; Hatt. MS. 15 a, 18. [*A. R.* greaten *to grow great: O. H. Ger.* grōzen *grossescere.*]

greátnes, se; *f.* GREATNESS; magnitudo, R. Ben. 55, Lye.

Grēc *Greek:*—Cwæþende in Grēc *saying in Greek*, Mt. Kmbl. Rush. 27, 46.

Grēcas, Greácas; *gen.* a; *dat.* um; *pl. m. The Greeks;* Græci:—Ðā gefēlde he his līchoman healfne dǣl mid ða ādle geslægene beón, ðe Grēcas nemnaþ paralysis, we cweðaþ lyft-ādl *then felt he that the half of his body was struck with the illness which the Greeks call paralysis, we call lift-ill*, Bd. 4, 31; S. 610, 16. Of Grēcum *from the Greek*, Ors. 5, 11; Bos. 109, 30. Ðā fōron hī on Greácas *then they went against the Greeks*, Ors. 5, 12; Bos. 110, 38. Greáca land *land of the Greeks*, 5, 11; Bos. 109, 28.

Grēcisc, Grēccisc; *adj. Greek, Grecian:*—Heora discipulas wǣron well gelǣrede ge on Grēcisc gereorde ge on Lēdennisc *eorum discipuli Latinam Græcamque linguam æque ut propriam in qua nati sunt norunt*, Bd. 4, 2; S. 565, 27: 4, 1; S. 563, 33. Grēccisc, 5, 8; S. 622, 2. Grecus grēcisc of ðam grecisso and grecor ic leornige grēcisc *Grecus Greek of which grecisso and grecor I learn Greek*, Ælfc. Gr. 36; Som. 38, 32. On grēcisc *in Greek*, Jn. Skt. Lind. 21, 2. On indisc and on grēcisc sprecende *indice et grece loquentes*, Nar. 25, 16. Ða grēciscan onginnaþ hyra geár æt ðam sunnstede *the Greeks begin their year at the solstice*, Lchdm. iii. 246, 18. [*Laym.* grickisc: *O. H. Ger.* grecisc: *Ger.* griechisch.]

Grēc-land, es; *n. Greece:*—Dionisius gewende on ðam tīman fram Grēclande *Dionysius returned at that time from Greece*, Homl. Th. i. 558, 33. [*Laym.* griclond.]

grēdig. v. grǣdig.

Gregorius; *gen.* Gregories; *dat.* Gregorie; *acc.* Gregorium; *m. Gregory the Great, Pope* A. D. 590–604, *who sent Augustine and other missionaries to England in* 597; Gregōrius:—Gregorius se hālga pāpa, Engliscre þeóde apostol, wæs of æðelborenre mǣgþe acenned. . . . Felix, se eáwfæsta pāpa, wæs his fifta fæder. . . . Gregorius is Grēcisc nama [= Γρηγόριος *watchful*, from γρηγορέω *I watch*], se sweigþ on Lēdenum gereorde, *Uigilantius*, ðæt is on Englisc *Wacolre. Gregory the holy pope, the apostle of the English, was born of a noble family. . . . Felix, the pious pope, was his fifth father. . . . Gregorius is a Greek name which in the Latin tongue signifies* Vigilantius, *that is in English* Watchful, Homl. Th. ii. 116, 24; 118, 8, 12. Æt Gregories ǣrendracan *from Gregory's messenger*, Homl. Th. ii. 122, 29. Augustīnus cȳdde ðam eádigan Gregorie, ðæt Angelcynn cristendōm underfēng *Augustine announced to the blessed Gregory, that the English nation had received Christianity*, 130, 24. Ðæt ðæt folc Gregorium to pāpan gecoren hæfde *that the people had chosen Gregory for pope*, 122, 31. Gregorius asende ǣrendracan to ðisum īglande. . . . Ðæra ǣrendracena naman synd,—Agustinus, Mellitus, Laurentius, Petrus, Iohannes, Iustus. Ðās lāreówas asende se eádiga pāpa Gregorius, mid manigum ōðrum munecum, to Angelcynne. . . . Agustīnus ðā mid his gefērum ðæt synd gerehte feówertig ðe fērdon be Gregories hǣse, ōððæt hī becōmon gesundfullīce to ðisum īglande *Gregory sent messengers to this island. . . . The names of these messengers are,—Augustinus, Mellitus, Laurentius, Petrus, Johannes, Justus. These teachers the blessed pope Gregory sent, with many other monks, to the English nation. . . . Augustine then with his companions, who are reckoned at forty men, journeyed by Gregory's command, till they came safely to this island*, Nat. S. Greg. Els. 28, 10–13; 28, 19–29, 6; 31, 15–32, 5.

gremettan *to rage, roar:*—Ic gremette *fremo*, Ælfc. Gr. 28; Som. 30, 60. [*O. H. Ger.* gremizon *fremere, rugire.*] v. grimetian.

gremetunc, gremetung, e; *f. A raging, roaring, murmuring;* fremitus, Prov. 19, Lye. v. grimetung.

gremian; *p.* ede; *pp.* ed *To provoke, irritate, exasperate, vex, revile:*—He ða ōðre elpendas gremede *it irritated the other elephants*, Ors. 4, 1; Bos. 77, 23. Gremedon *exacerbaverunt*, Blickl. Gl. Hig me gremedon *they provoked me*, Lev. 26, 40: Num. 11, 20: Deut. 9, 7, 8. Ða ðe forþstōpon hine gremedon *prætereuntes blasphemabunt eum*, Mk. Skt. 15, 29: Lk. Skt. 23, 39. [*Laym.* gromien, gramie *irritare: A. R.* gremeþ *irritat: Goth.* gramjan: *Icel.* gremja: *O. H. Ger.* gremian *irritare, objurgare: Ger.* grämen.]

Grēna-wīc, Grēne-wīc, es; *n.* GREENWICH, *near London*, Chr. 1013; Erl. 149, 4.

Grendel; *gen.* Grendles GRENDEL, *a monster destroyed by Bēowulf:*—Grendel mǣre mearcstapa, se ðe mōras heóld, fen and fæsten *Grendel the great traverser of the march, that ruled [held] the moors, the fen and fastness*, Beo. Th. 205–208; B. 102–104. [Grendel] reste genam þrītig þegna: gewāt to hām mid ðære wælfylle [*Grendel*] *took thirty thanes in their rest: departed to his home with the slaughtered corpses*, 245–250; B. 122–125. Grendles mōdor *Grendle's mother*, Beo. Th. 3078–3085; B. 1537–1540: 3139–3141; B. 1567–1568.

GRĒNE; *adj. Green;* viridis:—Grēne *viridis*, Ælfc. Gl. 79; Som. 72, 80; Wrt. Voc. 46, 37. Wende man ðæt grēne to ðan weofode *let the green [side of the sods] be turned to the altar*, Lchdm. i. 398, 17. Grēne folde *the green earth*, Cd. 76; Th. 94, 14; Gen. 1561. Of grēnum āre geworht *wrought of green copper*, Blickl. Homl. 127, 7. On grēnum treówe *in viridi ligno*, Lk. Skt. 23, 31. Grēne eorþan *green earth*, Cd. 91; Th. 115, 18; Gen. 1921. Grēne bearwas *green groves*, 72; Th. 89, 13; Gen. 1480. Genim ðære ylcan wyrte leáf ðonne heó grēnost beó *take the leaves of the same plant when it is greenest*, Herb. 1, 4; Lchdm. i. 72, 7. [*O. Sax.* grōni: *O. Frs.* grēne: *Icel.* grænn: *O. H. Ger.* gruoni: *Ger.* grün.]

grēnian *to become green, to flourish;* virescere, Bt. Met. Fox 11, 114; Met. 11, 57. [*A. R.* greneþ; *pres. indic: Ayenb.* greni: *Prompt. Parv.* grenyn *vireo; Icel.* grōna: *O. H. Ger.* gruonan *virescere: Ger.* grünen.]

grēnnes, se; *f.* GREENNESS; viriditas, Bd. 3, 10; S. 534, 21.

grennian; *p.* ode *To grin, shew the teeth as an expression of pain, anger, etc;* ringere:—Ic grennige *ringo*, Ælfc. Gr. 28; Som. 31, 63. He grennade and gristbitade *he grinned and gnashed his teeth*, Exon. 74 b; Th. 278, 11; Jul. 596. Grenniendum welerum hleahter forþbringan *ringentibus labiis risum proferre*, Scint. 55, Lye. [*Laym. A. R.* grennen: *Prompt. Parv.* grennyn *ringo: Icel.* grenja *to howl: O. H. Ger.* grennat *mutiet.*]

grennung, e; *f.* GRINNING; rictus, Som. [*A. R.* grennung: *Prompt. Parv.* grennynge *rictus.*]

greofa, greaua *a pot;* olla, Cot. 146, 173, Lye.

greósan, ic greóse, ðū grȳst, he grȳst, *pl.* greósaþ; *p.* greás, *pl.* gruron; *pp.* groren *To frighten.* DER. be-greósan.

GREÓT, es; *n.* GRIT, *sand, dust, earth, gravel;* pulvis:—Hēt ðæt greót ūtawegan *he ordered the earth to be removed*, Homl. Th. i. 74, 24. Ðū scealt greót etan *dust shalt thou eat*, Cd. 43; Th. 59, 9; Gen. 909. Ic gewīte in greótes fæðm *I depart into dust's bosom*, Exon. 64 a; Th. 235, 13; Ph. 556; Andr. Kmbl. 1587; An. 795; Beo. Th. 6315; B. 3168. Of greóte *from the earth*, Exon. 59 b; Th. 216, 13; Ph. 267; Andr. Kmbl. 3246; An. 1626. Sand is geblonden grund wið greóte *the sand is mixed together, the abyss with the strand*, 849; An. 425: 475; An. 238: 508; An. 254: Exon. 52 a; Th. 182, 12; Gū. 1309. Hēr līþ ūre ealdor on greóte *here lies our chief in the dust*, Byrht. Th. 140, 68; By. 315: Andr. Kmbl. 2169; An. 1086: Judth. 12; Thw. 26, 4; Jud. 308. Ðeáh ðe hit sȳ greóte beþeaht līc mid lāme *though with dust it be covered, the body with clay*, Exon. 117 a; Th. 451, 4; Dōm. 98: Elen. Kmbl. 1666; El. 835. [*A. R.* greot: *Wick.* greet: *O. Sax.* griot; *n. sand, strand: Icel.* grjót; *n. stones, rubble: O. H. Ger.* grioz *glarea, arena: Ger.* gries *gravel, grit.*]

greótan, ic greóte, ðū grȳtest, grȳtst, he greóteþ, grȳt, *pl.* greótaþ; *p.* greát, *pl.* gruton; *pp.* groten *To weep;* flere, lacrimare:—Heó sceal oft greótan *she shall often weep*, Salm. Kmbl. 753; Sal. 376. Se ðe on sefan greóteþ *who weeps in spirit*, Beo. Th. 2689; B. 1342. [*O. Sax.* griotan *to weep.*]

greót-hord, es; *n.* [greót *grit, dust, earth;* hord *hoard, treasure*] *An earthen treasure*, i. e. *the body:*—Greóthord gnornaþ gǣst hine fȳseþ on ēcne geard *the body mourns, the spirit hastens to an eternal dwelling*, Exon. 51 a; Th. 178, 6; Gū. 1240.

grep *a furrow, burrow* [*Prompt. Parv.* gryppe *or a* gryppel *where watur rennythe away in a londe:* grip *a drain, ditch, trench*, Hall. Dict.] v. græp.

grētan, grǣtan; *p.* grēt, *pl.* grēton; *pp.* grēten, grǣten *To bewail, deplore, weep;* plorare, deplorare, flere:—Lāþsīþ grētan *to bewail the dire journey*, Cd. 145; Th. 180, 13; Exod. 44. Beornas grētaþ *men shall wail*, Exon. 22 b; Th. 61, 30; Cri. 992. Hū ða womsceaðan hyra eald-gestreón grēten *how the wicked doers shall bewail their works* *of old*, Exon. 31 a; Th. 96, 10; Cri. 1572. [*Goth.* grētan: *O. Nrs.* grāta *plorare.*] DER. be-grētan.

grētan, he grēt, *pl.* grētaþ; *p.* grētte, *pl.* grētton; *pp.* grēted. I. *to approach, come to, visit, touch, attack, treat* or *use in any way, know carnally*; appropinquare, adire, visitare, tangere, hostiliter aggredi, afficere, cognoscere:—Đē wyrmas gyt gīfre grētaþ *the greedy worms yet come to thee*, Exon. 100 a; Th. 375, 14; Seel. 138. Đonne hine engel grētte *when the angel visited him*, 37 b; Th. 123, 25; Gū. 328. Nō he đone gifstōl grētan mōste *he might not touch the throne* [*gift-seat*], Beo. Th. 339; B. 168. Sum mid hondum mæg hearpan grētan *one may touch the harp with hands*, Exon. 79 a; Th. 296, 11; Crä. 49. Siđđan wæs eallum đām ōđrum swā mycel ege fram him, đǣt hī hine grētan ne dorstan *afterwards the others were in so much fear of him, that they durst not attack him*, Ors. 5, 2; Bos. 102, 3. On sceortne -as geendiaþ grēcisce naman ac we ne grētaþ nū đa *Greek nouns end in short -as, but we shall not treat them now*, Ælfc. Gr. 9, 24; Som. 10, 57. Se dǣl se đæt flōd ne grētte *the part that the water did not touch*, 1, 3; Bos. 27, 29. Gomen-wudu grēted wæs *the glee-wood was touched*, Beo. Th. 2134; B. 1065. Đæt he ne grētte goldweard đone *that he should not assail that gold-ward* [*that dragon*], Beo. Th. 6154; B. 3081: Bd. 3, 11; S. 536, 41. Gif đe ǣnig mid weán grēteþ *if any one entreat thee evil*, Cd. 83; Th. 105, 18; Gen. 1755. He ne grētte hī *non cognoscebat eam*, Mt. Bos. 1, 25. II. *to speak to, call upon, hail, greet, welcome, salute, take leave of, bid farewell to*; alloqui, invocare, ciere, salutare, lætari de, valedicere:—Gomol eówic grētan hēt *the aged* [*prince*] *commanded to greet you*, Beo. Th. 6182; B. 3095: Past. Pref. Swt. 3, 1; Hat. MS. Ælfrīc munuc grēt Æđelwærd ealdorman *Ælfric the monk greets alderman Ethelward*, Pref. Thw. 1, 1. Đonne he on gaton grēteþ his grame feondas *cum loquetur inimicis suis in porta*, Ps. Th. 126, 6. Gif man mannan mid bismær wordum scandlīce grēte *if a man address another shamefully with abusive words*, L. H. E. 11; Th. i. 32, 5. Hȳ grētte blīđum wordum *he addressed her with kind words*, Exon. 68 a; Th. 252, 17; Jul. 164. His God grētte *addressed his God*, Andr. Kmbl. 2059; An. 1032. Ongunnon hine grētan *cœperunt salutare eum*, Mk. Bos. 15, 18. Cwēn grētte guman on healle *the queen greeted the men in the hall*, Beo. Th. 1232; B. 614. Wulfas hilde grētton *the wolves hailed the battle*, Cd. 151; Th. 189, 8; Exod. 181. Wāc ne grētton in đæt rinc-getæl *the weak they welcomed not into that martial number*, Cd. 154; Th. 192, 18; Exod. 233. Hrōþgār grētte Beówulf *Hrothgar took leave of Beowulf*, Beo. Th. 1308; B. 652. [*Orm.* gretenn: *Laym.* græten *to accost, greet*; *p.* grætte: *O. Sax.* grōtian: *N. Frs.* groetjen: *O. Frs.* grēta: *N. Dut.* groeten: *N. Ger.* grüszen: *M. H. Ger.* grüezen: *O. H. Ger.* gruoȝan.] DER. ge-grētan.

grēting, e; *f. A greeting, salutation, present in acknowledgment of a favour done*; salutatio:—Hwæt seó grēting wǣre *qualis esset ista salutatio*, Lk. Bos. 1, 29. Đīnre grētinge stefn *vox salutationis tuæ*, 1, 44. Lufiaþ grētinga on strǣtum *diligitis salutationes in foro*, 11, 43. Pāpa sende Eádwine grētinge *the pope sent to Edwin greeting*, Bd. 2, 10; S. 512, 20. Sendaþ mīn heáfod ān to grētinge and bringaþ mīnre mēder đæt heó đæt cysse *send my head only in greeting and bring it to my mother that she may kiss it*, Shrn. 139, 28. Đā brohte seó sc̄e damiane medmicle grētinge gewritu secgaþ đæt đæt wǣre þreó ægero *then she brought St. Damian a slight acknowledgment; books say that it was three eggs*, 135, 17, 23.

gretta. v. gryt.

grīg-hund *a greyhound*, Cot. 173, Lye.

grillan; *p.* de *To provoke, offend*:—Hie willaþ grillan [griellan, Hat. MS.] ōđre men *they like to provoke other men*, Past. 40, 4; Swt. 292, 19; MS. Cot. [*A. R.* gruellen *to make sad*: *O. E. Homl.* igruld, 2, 259, 30; and see other instances in Stratmann: cf. *Icel.* grellskapr *spite*: *Ger.* groll *rancour.*]

GRIM; *adj. Sharp, bitter, severe, fell, fierce, dire, savage, cruel,* GRIM, *horrible*; acer, immanis, sævus, crudelis, atrox, dirus:—He him æt his ende grim geweorþeþ and hine gelǣdeþ on ēce forwyrd *he* [*the devil*] *will become cruel to him at his end, and will lead him into eternal perdition*, Blickl. Homl. 25, 13: Cd. 184; Th. 230, 8; Dan. 230. Đæt wæs grim cyning *that was a fierce king*, Exon. 100 b; Th. 378, 29; Deór. 23. Grim and grǣdig *savage and greedy*, Beo. Th. 242; B. 121. Mycel wōl and grim *acerba pestis*, Bd. 1, 14; S. 482, 29. Se grimma wītedōm *dira præsagia*, 3, 14; S. 541, 9. Wæs se winter to đæs grim đæt manig man his feorh for cȳle gesealde *the winter was so severe that many a man lost his life with the cold*, Blickl. Homl. 213, 31: Chr. 1005; Erl. 139, 37. Mid grimmun gefeohte *with severe fighting*, 5, 3: Byrht. Th. 133, 36; By. 61. On đam grimmun dæge dōmes đæs miclan *on the terrible day of the great doom*, Exon. 25 b; Th. 74, 12; Cri. 1205. Đæt wæter wæs biterre and grimre to drincanne đonne ic ǣfre ǣnig ōđer bergde *amariorem elleboro fluminis aquam gustavi*, Nar. 8, 29. Cȳle đone grimmestan *the most severe cold*, Blickl. Homl. 61, 35. Đeáh đū wǣre wyrmcynna đæt grimmeste *though thou hadst been of serpents the fiercest*, Soul Kmbl. 167; Seel. 83. [*O. Sax. O. Frs. O. H. Ger.* grim *acerbus, austerus, atrox, sævus, ferus*: *Icel.* grimmr: *Ger.* grimm.]

grīma, an; *m.* I. *a mask, visor, helmet*:—Gylden grīma *a golden helm*, Elen. Kmbl. 249; El. 125. Grīma *a mask*, Gl. Mett. 504. He mīne sāwle swylce gehealde wiđ ehtendra egsan grīman *ut salvam faceret a persequentibus animam meam*, Ps. Th. 108, 30. [*Icel.* grīma *a sort of hood* or *cowl.*] See Grmm. D. M. 218-9. DER. beadu-, here-grīma. II. *a spectre*; larva:—Mec mæg grīma abrēgan *a spectre can terrify me*, Exon. 110 b; Th. 423, 7; Rä. 41, 17. v. eges-grīma in Appendix.

grimena, grimenæ *a caterpillar*; bruchus, Ps. Spl. T. 104, 32.

grimetan, grymetan, grimetian; *p.* ode, ede *To rage, roar, make a loud noise, grunt*; fremere, rugire, grunnire:—Synfull tōþum torn þolaþ teónum grimetaþ *peccator dentibus suis fremet*, Ps. 111, 9. Grimme grymetaþ *fiercely roars*, Exon. 128 a; Th. 491, 22; Rä. 81, 3. Leónhwelpas grymetigaþ *catuli leonum rugientes*, Ps. Th. 103, 20. Đā awēdde he and grymetede *he went mad and cried aloud*, Th. Anal. 125, 8: Ps. Spl. 37, 8. Ecg grymetode *loud rang the blade* [*as it was drawn from the sheath*], Cd. 162; Th. 203, 24; Exon. 408. He gristbitade and grymetade *he gnashed his teeth and raged*, Exon. 74 b; Th. 278, 15; Jul. 598. Sume sceoldan bión eaforas and đonne hī sceoldan hiora sār siófian đonne grymetodan hī *some had to be boars and when they should lament their misfortune then they grunted*, Bt. 38, 1; Fox 194, 35. Grymetedon, Bt. Met. Fox 26, 163; Met. 26, 81. Forhwon grymetedon þeóda *quare fremuerunt gentes?* Ps. Spl. C. T. 2, 1. Grymetigan *to roar*, Bt. Met. Fox 13. 58; Met. 13, 29. Fīf manna sāwla hreówlīce gnorniende and grimetende *five men's souls miserably wailing and crying out*, Homl. Th. ii. 350, 28. Grimetende *rugientes*, Ps. Spl. 103, 22. Swīđe grymetende *cum ingenti murmure*, Nar. 14, 27. Brim grymetende *the roaring ocean*, Exon. 95 b; Th. 356, 6; Pa. 7. Swā grymetigende leó *as a roaring lion*, Guthl. 4; Gdwin. 26, 22. v. gremettan.

grimetung, grymetung, e; *f. Raging, roaring, grunting, loud noise*; murmur, fremitus, rugitus:—Swȳnes grymetunge *swine's grunting*, Guthl. 8; Gdwin. 48, 3: 46, 20. Leóna grymetunge *roaring of lions*, Shrn. 50, 9.

grīm-helm, es; *m. A helmet with a visor*; galea larvata, Cd. 151; Th. 188, 27; Exod. 174: 160; Th. 198, 29; Exod. 330: Elen. Kmbl. 516; El. 258: Beo. Th. 674; B. 334. See Grmm. A. E. xxviii; and grīma.

grīming *witchcraft*; veneficium, Som.

grimlīc; *adj. Grim, fierce, cruel, sharp, severe, bloody*; atrox, dirus, cruentus, crudelis:—Đone grimlīcan gārsecg *the fierce ocean*, Homl. Th. i. 454, 15. Hit wyrþ đonne egeslīc and grimlīc *things will then become awful and terrible*, Swt. A. S. Rdr. 104, 5. Đa Crētense hæfdon đone grimlecan sige *cruentiorem victoriam Cretenses exercuerunt*, Ors. 1, 9; Swt. 42, 28. Se lēgdraca grimlīc gryre *the fire-drake, that fierce horror*, Beo. Th. 6074; B. 3041. Đa gewin wǣron grimlīcran đonne hȳ nū sȳn *struggles were more bloodthirsty than they now are*; quod crudelius graviusque erat quam nunc est, Ors. 1, 2; Swt. 30, 23.

grimlīce; *adv. Fiercely, severely, cruelly*:—Đām mannum sceolan đa dēman grimlīce stȳran *those men must the judges severely restrain*, Blickl. Homl. 63, 15. Oft hī grimlīce Godes costodan *tentaverunt Deum*, Ps. Th. 77, 41. Spreceþ grimlīce *speaketh fiercely*, Soul Kmbl. 31; Seel. 16: Exon. 22 b; Th. 62, 19; Cri. 100, 4.

grimman, ic grimme, đū grimst, he grimmeþ, grimþ, *pl.* grimmaþ; *p.* gram, grom, *pl.* grummon; *pp.* grummen. I. *to rage, roar, make a loud noise*; fremere:—Đū hie grimman meaht gehȳran *thou mayest hear it* [*hell*] *rage*, Cd. 37; Th. 49, 17; Gen. 793. Hwæl-mere hlūde grimmeþ *the whale-mere* [*the sea*] *rages loudly*, Exon. 101 a; Th. 382, 3; Rä. 3, 5. [Cf. *O. Sax.* grimmid the grōto séo.] II. *to run with haste, hasten*; properare, currere, festinare:—Gūþmōde grummon *the warlike of mind hastened*, Beo. Th. 617; B. 306. [So Grein translates the verb, but may not the word be taken more nearly in the sense of the preceding passages '*loud and fierce was their shout?*']

grimme; *adv. Grimly, fiercely*:—Hȳ him æfter đæm grimme forguldon đone wīgcræft đe hȳ æt him geleornodon *they afterwards gave him grim requital for the military skill they learnt from him*, Ors. 1, 2; Bos. 26, 30: Cd. 64; Th. 77, 15; Gen. 1275: 183; Th. 229, 2; Dan. 211: Beo. Th. 6017; B. 3012.

grimnes, se; *f.* GRIMNESS, *severity, fierceness, cruelty*; ferocitas, atrocitas:—Se deófol wile hit him mid grimnesse and mid yfele eall forgyldan *the devil will requite it all to him with cruelty and with evil*, Blickl. Homl. 55, 24. Hī sceoldan đǣm unriht-dōndum mid grimnesse stēran *they should restrain with severity all evil-doers*, 63, 12. On grimnesse *in exacerbatione*, Ps. Th. 94, 9. Cwǣdon to gūđlāce mid grimnysse *fiercely they* [*evil spirits*] *spake to Guthlac*, Exon. 41 a; Th. 136, 33: Gū. 550. [*Prompt. Parv.* grymnesse *austeritas, rigor, horror, horribilitas.*]

grimsian; *p.* ede *To be fierce, cruel, to rage*; sævire:—Đā đara treówleásra cyninga beboda wiđ cristenum monnum grimsedon *cum perfidorum principum mandata adversum Christianos sævirent*, Bd. 1, 7; S. 476, 36. He grimsigende forleás *sæviens disperderet*, 3, 1; S. 523, 29. Wōl mid grimme wæle lange feor and wīde grimsigende *pestilentia acerba clade diutius longe lateque desæviens*, 27; S. 558, 15: 4, 25; S. 601, 20.

grimsung, e; *f. Fierceness, roughness*:—Mid ungemetlīce grimsunge *multa asperitate*, Past. 17, 11; Swt. 125, 14; Hat. MS.

grin, gryn, e; *f*: es; *n*. *A snare, gin, noose;* laqueus:—Swâ swâ grin he becymþ on ealle *tanquam laqueus superveniet in omnes*, Lk. Skt. 21, 35: Ps. Th. 123, 7. Grines *laquei*, Ps. Lamb. 34, 7. Of grames huntan grine *de laqueo venantium*, Ps. Th. 123, 6: 90, 3. Geheald me wið ðare gryne *custodi me a laqueo*, 140, 11. On grine *in laqueum*, 68, 23. Gryne, 65, 10. Ic fô mid grine *laqueo*, Ælfc. Gr. 26; Som. 29, 17. Iudas fêrde and mid gryne hyne sylfne ahêng *Iudas wente awey and goyinge awey he hangide hym with a grane*, Wyc; laqueo se suspendit, Mt. Bos. 27, 5: Homl. Th. ii. 30, 22. Mid ðý ilcan grine *in laqueo isto*, Ps. Th. 9, 14. He rîneþ ofer ða synfullan grinu *pluet super peccatores laqueos*, Ps. Lamb. 10, 7: Ps. Th. 17, 5: 34, 9. Fôtum heó mînum grine gearwodon *laqueos paraverunt pedibus meis*, 56, 7: 141, 4. Mid grinum *laqueis*, Coll. Monast. Th. 25, 13. [*Ayenb.* gryn *snare.*]

GRINDAN, gryndan; *part.* grindende, ic grinde, grynde, ðû grintst, grinst, he grint, *pl.* grindaþ; *p.* ic, he grand, grond, ðû grunde, *pl.* grundon; *pp.* grunden To GRIND, *grind together, rub, rub together;* molere, commolere, terere, frendere, allidi, collidi:—Ic seah searo grindan wið greóte *I saw a machine grind against the dust*, Exon. 108 b; Th. 414, 30; Rä. 33, 4. Ic grynde *molo*, Ælfc. Gr. 28, 3; Som. 31, 3. Ic grinde *commolo*, Ælfc. Gl. 36; Wrt. Voc. 28, 77. Ðû grinst *thou grindest*, Homl. Th. i. 488, 25. Se hæruflota grond wið greóte *the floater of the surge* [*the ship*] *ground against the gravel*, Exon. 52 a; Th. 182, 12; Gû. 1309. Hî grundon ofer me mid tôðum heard *frenduerunt super me dentibus suis*, Ps. Spl. 34, 19: Andr. Kmbl. 746; An. 373. Twâ beóþ æt cwyrne grindende, ân byþ genumen, and ôðer byþ lǽfed *duæ molentes in mola, una assumetur, et una relinquetur*, Mt. Bos. 24, 41: L. Ethb. 11; Th. i. 6, 6. Sume ðara munecena cômon to grindanne *some of the nuns came to grind*, Th. Chart. 447, 1. DER. be-, for-, ge-grindan.

grindel, es; *m*. *A bar, bolt;* in *pl. lattice-work, hurdle;* crates:—Geslægene grindlas greáte *forged large gratings*, Cd. 19; Th. 24, 27; Gen. 384. Guest, English Rhythms, ii. 40, note 1, observes:—'As far as we can judge from the drawing which accompanies the description, the *grindel* was a kind of heavy iron grating, which rather encumbered the prisoner by its weight, than fixed him in its grasp.' [*O. H. Ger.* grintil *temo, repagulum, pessulum, obex, vectis:* cf. *Icel.* grind *a lattice-door.*]

grindere, es; *m*. *A grinder;* molitor, Som.

grind-tôðas *grinding teeth, the grinders*, Som.

gring, es; *n?* *Slaughter;* clades, Elen. Kmbl. 230; El. 115. v. gringan.

gringan, ic gringe, ðû gringest, gringst, he gringeþ, gringþ, *pl.* gringaþ; *p.* grang, *pl.* grungon; *pp.* grungen *To sink down, perish;* occumbere, prosterni:—On herefelda hǽðene grungon *the heathen sank down upon the battle-field*, Elen. Kmbl. 252; El. 126. [Cf. cringan.]

gring-wracu, e; *f*. *Deadly punishment*, Exon. 69 b; Th. 258, 14; Jul. 265.

grinian, grynian; *p.* ode; *pp.* od [grin *a snare*] *To ensnare;* ligare, illaqueare. DER. be-, ge-grinian.

grînu; *adj. Avidius*, Ælfc. Gl. 79; Som. 72, 85; Wrt. Voc. 46, 42.

griósn *a pebble stone;* calculus, Prov. 20, Lye.

gripa, an; *m*. *A handful, a sheaf;* manipulus, pugillus:—Gripa *pugillus*, Hpt. Gl. 497. Genim ðysse ylcan wyrte gôdne gripan *take a good handful of this same plant*, Herb. 36, 4; Lchdm. i. 136, 4: 81, 5; Lchdm. i. 184, 18. Berende gripan heora *portantes manipulos suos*, Ps. Spl. 125, 8.

grîpan, ic grîpe, ðû grîpest, grîpst, he grîpeþ, grîpþ, *pl.* grîpaþ; *p.* grâp, *pl.* gripon; *pp.* gripen; *v. a.* To GRIPE, *grasp, seize, lay hold of, apprehend;* capĕre, rapĕre, prehendĕre, apprehendere:—Ic on Lothe gefrægn hǽþne heremæcgas handum grîpan *I heard that the heathen leaders seized on Lot with their hands*, Cd. 114; Th. 149, 32; Gen. 2483: 219; Th. 281, 9; Sat. 269. Ôþ ðæt ðê heortan grîpeþ âdl unlîðe *until severe disease gripeth thee at heart*, Cd. 43; Th. 57, 31; Gen. 936: Exon. 107 a; Th. 407, 19; Rä. 26, 7. Hwîlum flotan grîpaþ *sometimes they seize the sailor*, Salm. Kmbl. 304; Sal. 151. Grîpaþ lâre *apprehendite disciplinam*, Ps. Spl. 2, 12. Grâp on wrâðe *laid hands on his enemies*, Cd. 4; Th. 4, 30; Gen. 61: 69; Th. 83, 18; Gen. 1381: 95; Th. 125, 1; Gen. 2072: 119; Th. 153, 28; Gen. 2545: Beo. Th. 3006; B. 1501: Exon. 129 a; Th. 495, 8; Rä. 84, 4. Ðû ðe samod mid me swête gripe metas *qui simul mecum dulces capiebas cibos*, Ps. Spl. 54, 15: Cd. 42; Th. 55, 8; Gen. 891. Scearpe gâras gripon *the sharp arrows griped*, Cd. 95; Th. 124, 16; Gen. 2063. Swâ swâ leó hreáfiende oððe grîpende oððe gyrretynde and grymetende *sicut leo rapiens et rugiens*, Ps. Lamb. 21, 14: Blickl. Homl. 211, 1. [*Goth.* greipan: *O. Sax.* grîpan: *O. Frs. Icel.* grîpa. *O. H. Ger.* grîfan.] DER. be-, for-, ge-, to-ge-, ôþ-, wið-grîpan.

grîpe, es; *m*. *A gripe, vulture;* gryps, vultur. [*Laym.* gripes, *pl: Icel.* grîpr: *O. H. Ger.* grîf: *Prompt. Parv.* grype *vultur*, p. 212, note 4: Wrt. Voc. 252, 28 grype *vultur:* and see Nares' Glossary.]

gripe, es; *m*. *Gripe, grip, grasp, hold, clutch, seizure:* pugillus, prehensio, captus:—Se gripe ðære hand *pugillus*, Ælfc. Gl. 72; Som. 71, 1; Wrt. Voc. 43. Gripe *pugilla*, Recd. 38, 72; Wrt. Voc. 64, 75. Eorþgrâp heard gripe hrusan *earth's grasp, the fast hold of the ground*, Exon. 124 a; Th. 476, 15; Ruin. 8. Gripe mêces oððe gâres fliht *the falchion's clutch or the javelin's flight*, Beo. Th. 3534; B. 1735: Andr. Kmbl. 373; An. 187: Exon. 67 b; Th. 250, 10; Jul. 125. Of gromra gripe *from the cruel ones' clutch*, Exon. 68 b; Th. 255, 16; Jul. 215: 71 b; Th. 265, 34; Jul. 391: Salm. Kmbl. 97; Sal. 48: Elen. Kmbl. 2601; El. 1302: Andr. Kmbl. 433; An. 217: 1901; An. 953. For mînum gripe *for my grasp*, Exon. 126 a; Th. 484, 11; Rä. 70, 6: Beo. Th. 2300; B. 1148. Staþole strengra ðonne ealra stâna gripe *stronger in position than the hold of all stones*, Salm. Kmbl. 154; Sal. 76. [*Laym.* gripen; *pl. grasps:* cf. *O. H. Ger.* grif: *Ger.* griff.] DER. fǽr-, mund-, nîð-, stân-, sweord-gripe.

gripennis, se; *f*. *Captivity;* captivitas, Som.

gripu, e; *f*. *A cauldron:*—Seó ǽrene gripu *the brazen cauldron*, Salm. Kmbl. 94; Sal. 46.

grîsan, ic grîse, ðû grîsest, grîst, he grîseþ, grîst, *pl.* grîsaþ; *p.* ic, he grâs, ðû grise, *pl.* grison; *pp.* grisen *To shudder, to be frightened;* horrere. [Me grises, A. R. 366, 7, note: gros, *p. King Horn.* 1314: his herte gros, *Man.* ed. Furn. 8532: him gros, Handl. Synne 7875.] DER. a-grîsan, grislîc, an-grislîc, -grisenlîc.

grislîc, gryslîc; *adj.* GRISLY, *horrible, dreadful, horrid;* horridus, horrendus, horribilis. [*Laym.* grislich: *Orm.* grissliȝ: *A. R.* grislich: *Ayenb.* grislich: *O. Frs.* gryslik: cf. *O. H. Ger.* grisenlich, Grff. iv. 301: *Ger.* grässlich.] This word seems to belong to 'grîsan' rather than to 'greósan,' so should be written with *i* rather than with *y*. The spelling in the Ormulum supports the short vowel. v. grîsan.

grist, es; *m*. [?] *Grist, corn for grinding:*—Grist *molitura*, Ælfc. Gl. 50; Som. 65, 107; Wrt. Voc. 34, 36. v. gyrst.

gristbâtian *to gnash the teeth:*—Gristbâtaþ mid his tôþum *fremet dentibus suis*, Ps. Th. 36, 12, note. [Gristbeatien, *Juliana*, 69, 17: *A. R.* gristbatede; and cf. *Laym.* gristbating.]

gristbâtung, e; *f*. *A grinding, gnashing:*—Gristbâtung tôþa *stridor dentium*, Mt. Kmbl. Rush. 8, 12. [*Laym. O. E. Homl.* grisbating.]

gristbitian; *p.* ode, ede *To gnash or grind the teeth;* frendere, stridere:—Ic cearcige oððe gristbitige *strideo* vel *strido*, Ælfc. Gr. 26; Som. 29, 7. Tôþum gristbitaþ [gristbitteþ, Lind.] *stridet dentibus*, Mk. Skt. 9, 18. He grennade and gristbitade *he grinned and ground his teeth*, Exon. 74 b; Th. 278, 12; Jul. 596. Gristbitedon mid heora tôþum ongeán me *striderunt in me dentibus suis*, Ps. Th. 34, 16. He ongan mid his tôþum gristbitian *cœpit dentibus frendere*, Bd. 3, 11; S. 536, 14: Judth. 12; Thw. 25, 21; Jud. 271.

gristbitung, e; *f*. *A gnashing of the teeth:*—Tôþa gristbitung [gristbiottung, Lind.] *stridor dentium*, Mt. Kmbl. 8, 12: 13, 42, 50: Blickl. Homl. 185, 7: Cd. 220; Th. 285, 7; Sat. 334. Gristbiotung, Mt. Kmbl. Lind. 25, 30. Gristbittung, Lk. Skt. Lind. 13, 28.

gristel, gristl, es; *m*. *Gristle;* cartilago, Ælfc. Gl. 72; Som. 71, 8.

gristel-bân, es; *n*. *A gristle bone;* cartilageum os.

gristian *to grind, grate, gnash*, Hpt. Gl. 513.

gristlung, grystlung, e; *Gnashing, grinding:*—Tôþa grystlung *stridor dentium*, Lk. Skt. 13, 28.

gristra, an; *m*. *A baker of dough made from grist, a baker;* cerealis pistor, Ælfc. Gl. 50; Som. 65, 108; Wrt. Voc. 34, 37.

grið, es; *n*. I. *peace limited to place or time, truce, protection, security, safety.* [The word comes into use during the struggles with the Danes. *Icel.* grið (v. Cl. and Vig. Dict.) means first *home, domicile*, then in *pl. truce, peace, pardon;* friðr is the general word, grið the special, deriving its name from being limited in time or space (asylum)]:—Leófsig ealdorman grið wið hî gesætte *alderman Leofsig made a truce with them*, Chr. 1002; Erl. 137, 25. Ðonne nam man grið and frið wið hî *then was truce and peace made with them*, 1011; Erl. 145, 3, 4. We willaþ wið ðam golde grið fæstnian *for the gold we will make a truce*, Byrht. Th. 132, 53; By. 35. Heó gesôhte Baldwines grið *she sought the protection of Baldwin*, Chr. 1037; Erl. 167, 3: 1048; Erl. 178, 34: 180, 17, 19. Ðâ gyrnde he griðes and gîsla *then he required security and hostages*, 180, 6: 1095; Erl. 231, 25. Sette man him iv nihta grið *his safety was secured for four days*, 1046; Erl. 173, 4. Godes grið *protection belonging to the church*, Swt. A. S. Rdr. 107, 99. II. for the passages in which the word occurs as a technical term in the laws, see Thorpe, index to vol. i. of 'Ancient Laws and Institutes,' s. v. Schmid, p. 585, arranges the several 'griths' under the following heads:—(1) Place; churches, private houses, the king's palace and precincts; (2) Time; fasts and festivals, coronation days, days of public gemots and courts, times when the fyrd is summoned; (3) Persons; clergy, widows, and nuns. On this word, Stubbs, i. 181, says—'The *grith* is a limited or localized peace, under the special guarantee of the individual, and differs little from the protection implied in the *mund* or personal guardianship which appears much earlier; although it may be regarded as another mark of territorial development. When the king becomes the lord, patron, and *mundborh* of his whole people, they pass from the ancient national peace of which he is the guardian into the closer personal or territorial relation of which he is the source. The peace is now the king's peace; . . . the *frith* is enforced by the national officers, the *grith* by the king's personal servants: the one is official, the other personal; the one the business of the country, the other that of the court. The special peace is further extended to places where the national peace is not fully provided for: the great highways . . . are under the king's peace.' [*A. R. Laym.* griþ: *Orm.* griþþ.] DER. cyric-, hǽlnes-, hád-, hand-grið.

grið-brice, -bryce, es; *m.* [grið *peace;* brice, bryce *a breach, violation*] *A breach of the peace;* pacis infractio *vel* violatio:—Griðbrice *infractio pacis,* L. Th. ii. 531, 12. Bēte man ðone griðbryce *let a man make amends for a breach of the peace,* L. Eth. ix. 4; Th. i. 340, 21: L. C. E. 3; Th. i. 360, 12.

griðian; *p.* ode, ede; *pp.* od, ed. I. *to make peace:*—Lundene waru griðede wið ðone here *the people of London made peace with the army,* Chr. 1016; Erl. 159, 9. Griðode, 1046; Erl. 172, 6: 1070; Erl. 207, 19. Griðedon, 1068; Erl. 207, 2. Griðodon, 1087; Erl. 225, 15. II. *to protect, give 'grith:'*—Hwīlum heálīce hādas griðian mihton ða ðe ðæs beþorf *once those of high rank could extend protection to those that needed it,* L. Eth. 7, 3; Th. i. 330, 7. Godes þeówas griðedan *protected God's servants,* 24; Th. i. 334, 24: Swt. A. S. Rdr. 105, 37. Griðian and friðian, L. Eth. 6, 42; Th. i. 326, 16: L. C. E. 2; Th. i. 358, 11: 4; Th. i. 360, 28. [*Laym.* griðien.]

grið-lagu, e; *f. Law concerning 'grith,'* L. Eth. 7, 9; Th. i. 330, 22.

griðleás; *adj. Without 'grith'* or *protection, unprotected,* Swt. A. S. Rdr. 106, 41.

gritta *grit, bran;* furfur:—Ðās gritta *hic furfur,* Ælfc. Gr. 9, 22; Som. 10, 47. v. gryt.

groene *green,* Lk. Skt. Lind. Rush. 23, 31. v. grēne.

groetan *to greet;* groeting *a greeting.* v. grētan, grēting.

grōf, *pl.* grōfon *carved,* Bt. Met. Fox 8, 113; Met. 8, 57; *p. of* grafan.

grom. v. gram.

grōpian. v. grāpian.

grorn, es; *m* [?] *Grief, sadness;* luctus, mœror, Exon. 94 b; Th. 354, 22; Reim. 49.

grorne; *adv. Sadly, mournfully,* Exon. 25 b; Th. 74, 11; Cri. 1205.

grorn-hof, es; *n. A house of sadness, of woe,* Exon. 70 b; Th. 261, 32; Jul. 324.

grornian; *p.* ode *To mourn, murmur:*—Grornaþ eal middangeard *all the earth shall mourn,* Exon. 22 a; Th. 60, 18; Cri. 971. Grornadun *murmurabant,* Mt. Kmbl. Lind 20, 11.

grornung, e; *f. Complaint, mourning:*—Būta grornunge *sine quærella,* Lk. Skt. Lind. Rush. 1, 6.

grot, es; *n. A particle, an atom;* particula:—Nān grot rihtwīsnesse *no particle of wisdom,* Bt. 35, 1; Fox 156, 6. Nān grot andgites *no particle of sense,* 41, 5; Fox 252, 22. Uneáþe ǽnig grot staþoles aðstōd *hardly any particle of foundation remained,* Ors. 6, 1; Swt. 252, 23. [*A. R.* of al þe brode eorðe ne moste he habben a grot forte deien uppon, 260, 20: *Havel.* karf hem al to grotes, 472.]

GRŌWAN; *part.* grōwende; ic grōwe, ðū grōwest, grēwst, he grōweþ, grēwþ, *pl.* grōwaþ; *p.* greów, *pl.* greówon; *pp.* grōwen *To* GROW, *increase, spring, sprout, spring up;* crescere, frondere, virere, germinare, florere:—Lǽteþ hió ða blōwan and grōwan *it lets these blow and grow,* Exon. 109 a; Th. 417, 6; Rä. 35, 9: 90 a; Th. 338, 3; Gn. Ex. 73: Bd. 1, 27; S. 491, 5: Bt. Met. Fox 22, 84; Met. 22, 42: Salm. Kmbl. 969; Sal. 484. Spritte seó eorðe grōwende gærs *germinet terra herbam virentem,* Gen. 1, 11: Ps. Spl. 64, 11: Cd. 5; Th. 6, 13; Gen. 88. Ic grōwe *frondeo,* Ælfc. Gr. 26, 2; Som. 28, 42. Ic grōwe *vireo,* 26, 2; Som. 28, 44: Mk. Bos. 4, 27. Leáf and gærs geond Bretene blōweþ and grōweþ *leaves and grass blow and grow over Britain,* Bt. Met. Fox 20, 198; Met. 20, 99: 29, 140; Met. 29, 70: Ps. Th. 91, 11: 146, 8: Exon. 91 b; Th. 343, 19; Gn. Ex. 159: Hy. 35; Hy. Grn. ii. 292, 35. Eall se dǽl ðæs treówes upweardes grēwþ *all that part of the tree grows upwards,* Bt. 34, 10; Fox 150, 2. Hī grōwaþ geára gehwilce on lencten tīd *they grow every year in spring time,* Bt. Met. Fox 29, 133; Met. 29, 67: Ps. Th. 103, 12: 64, 11. Greów *grew,* Beo. Th. 3441: B. 1718. Ða greówon [MS. greowan] and blōsmodon [MS. blosmodan] *the lands grew and blossomed,* Bd. 4, 13; S. 582, 35: Ps. Th. 106, 36, 37. Forhwī ǽlc sǽd grōwe innon ða eorþan? *why should every seed grow in the earth?* Bt. 34, 10; Fox 148, 31. Hwæt druge ðū grōwendra gifa? *what madest thou of the growing gifts?* Cd. 42; Th. 55, 6; Gen. 890. [*O. Frs.* grōwa: *Icel.* grōa: *O. H. Ger.* grōen, grūen *virescere.*] DER. a-, for-, ge-grōwan.

grōwnes, se; *f. Growth:*—Grōwnys hreódes *viror calami,* Bd. 3, 23; S. 554, 23. Ne com ðǽr nǽnig grōwnes up ne wæstmas ne furþan brordas *nil omnino, non dico spicarum, sed ne herbæ quidem ex eo germinare contigit,* 4, 28; S. 605, 34.

gruncan *prurire,* Gl. Prud. 595.

GRUND, es; *m.* I. *ground, bottom, foundation;* fundus, fundamentum:—Grund *fundamentum,* Lk. Skt. Lind. 14, 29: 6, 48: Rtl. 82, 34. Ǽlc sǽ ðeáh heó deóp sȳ hæfþ grund on ðære eorþan *every sea, though it be deep, hath its bottom in the earth,* Lchdm. iii. 254, 20. Hordweard sōhte georne æfter grunde *the keeper of the hoard sought eagerly along the floor* [*of the cave*], Beo. Th. 4577; B. 2294: 5523; B. 2765: 5510; B. 2758. Grunde getenge *deep in the earth, i. e. lying, as it were, at the bottom of a hole,* Elen. Kmbl. 2226; El. 1114. Me to grunde teáh *he drew me to the bottom* [*of the sea*], Beo. Th. 1111; B. 553: Cd. 39; Th. 51, 29; Gen. 834. Ufan to grunde *from top to bottom,* 228; Th. 309, 2; Sat. 703: 229; Th 310, 15; Sat. 726: Salm. Kmbl. 61; Sal. 31. Sió gītsung ðe nǽnne grund hafaþ *avarice which hath no bottom,* Bt. Met. Fox 8, 92; Met. 8, 46. Mid fōtum ne mæg grund gerǽcan *cannot reach the bottom with his feet,* Salm. Kmbl. 453; Sal. 227: Beo. Th. 2739; B. 1367: Exon. 97 a; Th. 361, 34; Wol. 29. II. *ground, earth, land, country, plain;* terra, solum, campus:—Hie ðæt gild gebrǽcan and gefyldan eal ōð grund *they broke the idol to pieces and cast it all to the ground,* Blickl. Homl. 221, 33. Eal ðes ginna grund *all this spacious earth,* Exon. 116 a; Th. 445, 23; Dōm. 12: Cd. 5; Th. 7, 11; Gen. 104. Eall eorþan grund *all the earth,* 192; Th. 240, 5; Dan. 382. We men on grunde *we men on the earth,* Hy. Grn. ii. 292, 39; Hy. 9, 39. Neól ic fēre and be grunde græfe *prone I go and along the ground dig,* Exon. 106 a; Th. 403, 3; Rä. 22, 2: 128 a; Th. 491, 23; Rä. 81, 3. Geond ealne yrmenne grund *through all the earth,* 14 b; Th. 30, 20; Cri. 481: 66 a; Th. 243, 14; Jul. 10: Cd. 6; Th. 8, 35: Gen. 134: 69; Th. 83, 31; Gen. 1388: Exon. 57 b; Th. 205, 26; Ph. 118. He grund gesōhte *he fell to the ground,* Byrht. Th. 140, 13; By. 287: Andr. Kmbl. 3199; An. 1602. Grund and sund *earth and sea,* 1494; An. 748. Geond grunda fela *through many lands,* Exon. 87 a; Th. 326, 30; Vīd. 136. On grundum *on earth,* 17 b; Th. 43, 1; Crī. 682: 18 b; Th. 46, 28; Cri. 744. Of grundum, 18 a; Th. 44, 13; Cri. 702. Rūme grundas swilce eác rēðe streámas *spacious plains and fierce streams,* Judth. 12; Thw. 26, 30; Jud. 349. Grēne grundas, Andr. Kmbl. 1551; An. 777: Beo. Th. 2812; B. 1404: 4152; B. 2073: Chr. 937; Erl. 112, 15; Ædelst. 15. III. *a depth, sea, abyss, hell;* profundum, abyssus:—On sǽs grund *in profundum maris,* Mt. Kmbl. 18, 6. On grund *in abissum,* Lk. Skt. 8, 31. Grund eall forswealg *the abyss swallowed up all,* Andr. Kmbl. 3179; An. 1592. Sǽs sīdne grund *the sea's spacious depth,* Exon. 93 a; Th. 349, 2; Sch. 40: Menol. Fox 323; Men. 113: Andr. Kmbl. 786; An. 393: 849: An. 425: Beo. Th. 3106: B. 1551. Wese ic earmum gelīc ðe on sweartne grund syððan astīgaþ *ero similis descendentibus in lacum,* Ps. Th. 142, 7. Ic of grundum cleopode *de profundis clamavi,* 129, 1. Ofer deópnesse ealra grunda *above the depth of all abysses,* Blickl. Homl. 141, 9. Deorce grundas *in abyssis,* Ps. Th. 134, 6: Cd. 213; Th. 265, 19; Sat. 10. Of grunde brymmes *de profundo pelagi,* Rtl. 61, 33. Of helle grunde *from the depth of hell,* Blickl. Homl. 67, 21: 85, 4: 33, 19: 65, 14. On helle grunde *in the depth of hell,* Th. Chart. 309, 8. Hēt hine ðære sweartan helle grundes gȳman *bade him rule the black hell's abyss,* Cd. 18; Th. 22, 25, 31; Gen. 346, 349. To grunde *to hell,* 219; Th. 281, 9; Sat. 269: 227; Th. 304, 21; Sat. 633. Grīp wið ðæs grundes *stretch forth thy hands towards the abyss* [*hell*], 228; Th. 308, 31; Sat. 701. Ðone deópan grund *the deep abyss,* Blickl. Homl. 103, 15. Hātne grund, Cd. 224; Th. 295. 13; Sat. 485. Grimne grund, Exon. 30 a; Th. 93, 16; Cri. 1527. Sūsla grund, Elen. Kmbl. 1885; El. 944. Ðās grimman grundas *these grim depths,* Cd. 21; Th. 26, 15; Gen. 407: Cd. 219; Th. 280, 23; Sat. 260. On ðām grundum helle tintreges *in profundis tartari,* Bd. 5, 14; S. 634, 25: Salm. Kmbl. 976; Sal. 488. [*O. Sax. O. Frs.* grund: *Icel.* grunnr *the bottom* [*of the sea,* etc.]: *O. H. Ger.* grunt *fundus, profundum: Ger.* grund: cf. *Goth.* afgrundiþa *abyss;* grundu-waddjus *a foundation.*] DER. bryten-, sǽ-, wæter-grund; un-grund.

grund-bedd, es; *n. The ground;* solum, Exon. 128 a; Th. 493, 3; Rä. 81, 24.

grund-būende; *pl. Inhabitants of the earth,* Beo. Th. 2016; B. 1006; Salm. Kmbl. 578; Sal. 288.

grunde-hirde, es; *m. A guard of the deep,* Beo. Th. 4279; B. 2136.

grunde-swelge, -swelige, -swilige, -swylige, -swulie, -an; *f.* GROUNDSEL; senecio:—Ompre, grundeswelge, ontre *dock, groundsel, radish,* L. M. 1, 32; Lchdm. ii. 78, 25. Grundeswylige *groundsel,* Herb. 77, 1; Lchdm. i. 180, 5. Genīm grundeswelgean *take groundsel,* L. M. 1, 22; Lchdm. ii. 64, 19: 1, 2; Lchdm. ii. 32, 5: 1, 51; Lchdm. ii. 124, 15.

grund-fūs; *adj. Ready for hell, hastening to hell:*—Ðæt biþ feóndes bearn hafaþ grundfūsne gǽst *that is a child of the devil, hath a spirit hastening hellwards,* Exon. 84 a; Th. 316, 15; Mōd. 49.

grundleás; *adj.* GROUNDLESS, *bottomless, boundless, immense, unbounded, interminable, endless;* fundo carens, profundissimus, immensus:—Se grundleás seáþ gǽsta giémeþ *the bottomless pit holds the spirits,* Exon. 30 b; Th. 94, 26; Cri. 1546: Bt. 9, 4; Fox 22, 32, Grundleás gītsung *boundless greed,* Bt. Met. Fox 7, 29; Met. 7, 15: Exon. 97 a: Th. 362, 34; Wal. 46: Cd. 21; Th. 25, 7; Gen. 390. Wurdon grundleáse Geátes frige ðæt him seó sorglufu slǽp binom *Geat's loves were boundless so that anxious love took from him sleep,* Exon. 100 a; Th. 378, 12; Deór. 15.

grundleás-līc; *adj. Bottomless, unbounded, boundless, immense:*—Swā grundleáslīcu costung *such immense temptation,* Past. 53, 6; Swt. 417, 10.

grundlinga, -lunga; *adv. From the very bottom* or *root, entirely, totally*:—Grundlunge oððe mid stybbe mid ealle *stirpatus*: grundlunga *funditus*: grundlinga oððe mid wyrttruman mid ealle *radicitus*, Ælfc. Gr. 38; Som. 42, 3, 4. Hī tobrǽcon ða burh grundlinga *they destroyed the city to its very foundations*, Homl. Th. ii. 66, 3; i. 72, 5. Grundlunge, ii. 164, 16.

grund-sceát, es; *m. A region of earth*, Exon. 8 b; Th. 3, 27; Cri. 42: 17 a; Th. 41, 2; Cri. 649.

grundsōpa *ground soap;* saponaria officinalis:—Cartilago, Gl. C. Lchdm. iii. 329, col. 1.

grund-stān, es; *m. A foundation-stone*:—Grundstānas *cementum*, Ælfc. Gl. 116; Som. 80, 70; Wrt. Voc. 61, 47. [*Ger.* grund-stein.]

grund-wæg, es; *m. A foundation, the earth*:—He on grundwæge men of deáþe worde awehte *he* [*Christ*] *on this earth raised men from death by his word*, Andr. Kmbl. 1163; An. 582. [Cf. *Goth.* grunduwaddjus *foundation.*]

grund-wang, -wong, es; *m. The bottom, ground, floor, the earth*:—He ðone grundwong ongytan mihte *he could perceive the bottom* [*of the lake*], Beo. Th. 2996; B. 1496: 5533; B. 2770. Grundwong ofgyfan *to give up the earth, to die*, 5169; B. 2588.

grund-weall, es; *m. A foundation*:—Ðes grundweall *hoc fundamentum*, Ælfc. Gr. 8; Som. 7, 60. Ic lecge grundweall *fundo*, 37; Som. 39, 20. Se cræft is eallra bōclīcra cræfta ordfruma and grundweall *that art is the beginning and foundation of all literary arts*, 50; Som. 51, 2: Wrt. Voc. 81, 6. Se grundweall ðara munta *fundamenta montium*, Ps. Th. 17, 7: Lk. Skt. 6, 48, 49: Homl. Th. ii. 588, 20: Chr. 654; Erl. 29, 11: Bt. Met. Fox 7, 67; Met. 7, 34. [*Orm.* grunndwall: cf. *Ger.* grundmauer.] v. grund-wæg.

grund-wela, an; *m. Earthly wealth*:—Him grundwelan ginne sealde hēt ðām sinhīwum sǽs and eorþan tuddorteóndra teohha gehwilcre wæstmas fēdan *he gave them ample riches of earth, bade for the man and wife each of sea's and land's productive tribes bring forth fruits*, Cd. 46; Th. 59, 1; Gen. 957.

grund-wyrgen, ne; *f. A wolf of the deep* [*Grendel's mother*], Beo. Th. 3041; B. 1518.

grunian; *p.* ode *To make a loud noise, grunt*:—Swȳn grunaþ *sus grunnit*, Ælfc. Gr. 22; Som. 24, 10. [Cf. *O. H. Ger.* grun, grunni, Grff. iv. 328.]

grunung, e; *f. A crying out, roaring;* rugitus, barritus, mugitus, Hpt. Gl. 462, 508.

grut *vorago*, Hpt. Gl. 423, 507; grutte *abyssus*, 529.

grūt; *indecl.* but also *dat.* grȳt, Lchdm. iii. 28, 9; *f.* GROUT, *the wet residuary materials of malt liquor;* condimentum cerevisiæ:—Wyrc clam of sūrre rigenre grūt oððe dāge *work a paste of sour rye grout or of dough*, L. M. 3, 59; Lchdm. ii. 342, 17. Grūt mealtes, i. 31, 7; Lchdm. ii. 74, 9. Genim ealde grūt *take old grout*, i. 39, 2; Lchdm. ii. 100, 1: 28; Lchdm. ii. 68, 26: Lchdm. iii. 42, 28. [*Worte* siromellum, sed *growte* dicas agromellum, Wrt. Voc. 178, 3. Growtt *hoc idromellum*, 233, 33. Growte for ale *granomellum*, Prompt. Parv. 217, 3, where see note. *Mod. Engl.* grouts *grounds, dregs.*] Cf. next word; *also* cf. *Icel.* grautr; *m. porridge.*

grūt; *pl. n. Fine meal*:—Grūt *pollis*, Wrt. Voc. 290, 63: L. M. i. 61, 1; Lchdm. ii. 132, 15. VI ambra grūta *six measures of meal*, Th. Chart. 471, 13. [Cf. grytta, grot, greót, and the preceding word.]

grym. v. grim.

grymede *glyppus*, Ælfc. Gl. 76; Som. 71, 128; Wrt. Voc. 45, 31.

grymetan. v. grimetan.

grymetung v. grimetung.

gryn, es; *m. n* [?] *Lamentation, grief, affliction, evil*:—Fela ic lāðes gebād grynna æt Grendel *much evil have I experienced, many a grief at Grendel's hands*, Beo. Th. 1864; B. 930. [Cf. *O. H. Ger.* grun; *m.* grunni; *f.* Grff. iv. 328; *and see* grunian, gyrn. *Or does* gryn = grin?]

gryndan; *pp.* ed. I. *to found.* [*Ger.* gründen.] v. ge-gryndan. II. *to come to the ground, to descend*:—Gryndende *descendens*, Cot. 68, Lye. v. agryndan.

grynde, es; *n. An abyss*, Cd. 220; Th. 285, 2; Sat. 331. v. æfgrynde (Appendix), un-grynde.

grynel, es; *m. Kernel;* toles, Mone Gl.

grynian *to ensnare.* v. grinian.

gryn-smiþ, es; *m. One causing grief, affliction, evil* [gryn, q. v.], Andr. Kmbl. 1833; An. 919.

gryre, es; *m. Horror, terror, dread, something horrible, dreadful*:—Ōdrum on gryre wǽron to neósienne *aliis horrori erant visendum*, Bd. 4, 27; S. 604, 27. Him ðæs egesa stōd gryre fram ðam gāste *terror was upon him therefore, horror from the spirit*, Cd. 201; Th. 249, 6; Dan. 526: Exon. 116 a; Th. 446, 12; Dōm. 21: 116 b; Th. 447, 22; Dōm. 43. Wæs se gryre læssa *the horror was less*, Beo. Th. 2569; B. 1282. Se lēgdraca grimlīc gryre *the firedrake, a fierce terror*, 6074; B. 3041: Cd. 195; Th. 243, 20; Dan. 439. Wið ðæs egesan gryre *against the terror of that fear*, 197; Th. 245, 22; Dan. 467: 223; Th. 293, 13; Sat. 454. Ðæt he in ðone grimman gryre gongan sceolde *that he should go into that fell and fearful place*, Exon. 41 a; Th. 136, 18; Gū. 543. Hie wyrd forsweóp on Grendles gryre *fate has swept them off into the terrible power of Grendel*, Beo. Th. 960; B. 478: Cd. 143; Th. 178, 32; Exod. 20. Mid gryrum ecga *with the terrors of swords*, Beo. Th. 971; B. 483: 1187; B. 591. [*Laym.* grure: *A. R.* grure: *O. Sax.* gruri.] DER. fǽr-, helle-, hinsīð-, leód-, wæl-, wēsten-, wīg-gryre.

gryre-brōga, an; *m. Terror, horror*, Exon. 20 a; Th. 53, 12; Cri. 849.

gryre-fæst; *adj. Terribly fast*, Elen. Kmbl. 1516; El. 760.

gryre-fāh; *adj. Terribly hostile* or *terrible in its variegated colouring*, Beo. Th. 5146; B. 2576.

gryre-gæst, es; *m. A dreadful guest*, Beo. Th. 5113; B. 2560.

gryre-geatwe; *pl. f. Terrible, warlike equipments*, Beo. Th. 653; B. 324.

gryre-hwīl, e; *f. A time of terror*, Andr. Kmbl. 935; An. 468.

gryre-leóþ, es; *n. A song of terror*, Beo. Th. 1576; B. 786: Byrht. Th. 140, 8; By. 285.

gryre-līc; *adj. Horrible, terrible*, Andr. Kmbl. 3101; An. 1553: Exon. 108 b; Th. 415, 27; Rä. 24, 3: Beo. Th. 2886; B. 1441: 4278; B. 2136.

gryre-sīð, es; *m. A terrible way*, Beo. Th. 2928; B. 1462.

grystlung. v. gristlung.

gryt *grues*, Wrt. Voc. 287, 25.

grȳto; *f. Greatness;* grossitudo:—Ungemetlīcre grȳto and micelnysse *vincens grossitudine*, Nar. 8, 22.

grytta *and* **gryttan**; *pl. f. Grits, groats, coarse meal*:—Ðās gritta *hic furfur*, Ælfc. Gr. 9, 22; Som. 10, 47. Gretta *furfures*, Wrt. Voc. 83, 21. Beren mela oððe grytta *barley meal or grits*, L. M. 2, 26; Lchdm. ii. 220, 8: 39; Lchdm. ii. 250, 2. Grytte, 18; Lchdm. ii. 200, 9. Of berenum gryttum *of barley grits*, 19; Lchdm. ii. 202, 7: 22; Lchdm. ii. 206, 19, Hwǽte gryttan *apludes* vel *cantabra*, Ælfc. Gl. 50; Som. 65, 124; Wrt. Voc. 34, 53. [Cf. *A. R.* gruttene brede, 186, 11: *O. H. Ger.* gruzze *furfur*: *Ger.* grütze; *f. grit, groats.*]

gū-dǽd, e; *f. A deed done in the past*, Exon. 64 a; Th. 235, 12; Ph. 556. v. iú-dǽd.

guma, an; *m. A man;* vir, homo:—Grētte ðā guma ōðerne *then one man took leave of another*, Beo. Th. 1309; B. 652. God ealle cann guman geþancas *Dominus novit cogitationes hominum*, Ps. Th. 93, 11. Wiste ferhþ guman *knew the man's mind*, Cd. 134; Th. 169, 2; Gen. 2793. Guman God wurþedon *the men worshipped God*, 187; Th. 232, 14; Dan. 260. Gumena aldor *ruler of men*, 89; Th. 111, 30; Gen. 1863. God gumena weard *God, the guardian of men*, 184; Th. 230, 22; Dan. 237. Gumena gehwylc *each man*, Exon. 19 b; Th. 51, 25; Cri. 821: 32 a: Th. 101, 5: Cri. 1654. Gumena bearn *the children of men*, Beo. Th. 1760; B. 878. Geared gumum gold brittade *Jared distributed gold to the people*, Cd. 59; Th. 72, 3; Gen. 1181. [*Laym.* gume, gome: *Piers P.* gome: *O. Sax.* gumo; *m. vir, homo*: *O. Frs.* goma: *O. H. Ger.* goma: *Goth.* guma: *O. Nrs.* gumi; *m. homo, vir, primipilus*: *Lat.* homo.] DER. brȳd-, dryht-, þeód-guma.

gū-mann, es; *m. A man of old*:—Ðǽm gūmonnum *antiquis*, Mt. Kmbl. Rush. 5, 27. v. gió-man.

gum-cynn, es; *n. Mankind, men, a race, nation;* humanum genus, gens, natio:—He þohte forgrīpan gumcynne *he resolved to destroy mankind*, Cd. 64; Th. 77, 14; Gen. 1275. Eom ic gumcynnes ānga ofer eorþan *amongst men on the earth I am unique*, Exon. 129 a; Th. 496, 11; Rä. 85, 12: Beo. Th. 5524; B. 2765. Swā hwylc mægþa ðone magan cende æfter gumcynnum *whatever matron brought forth this son amongst men*, Beo. Th. 1892; B. 944. We synt gumcynnes Geáta leóde *we are of the race of the Gauts' people*, 525; B. 260. [*O. Sax.* gumkunni.]

gum-cyst, e; *f. Manly virtue* or *excellence, munificence, liberality*:—Ðū ðē lǽr be ðon gumcyste ongit *learn from that, understand liberality*, Beo. Th. 3450; B. 1723. He siððan sceal gōdra gumcysta geásne hweorfan *afterwards shall he pass away wanting in all noble virtues*, Exon. 71 a; Th. 265, 14; Jul. 381. Nū is þearf micel ðæt we gumcystum georne hȳran *now is it very needful that we with virtuous zeal attend*, Andr. Kmbl. 3210; An. 1608. Abraham gumcystum gōd golde and seolfre gesǽlig *Abraham, noble in his munificence, blessed with gold and silver*, Cd. 85; Th. 106, 10; Gen. 1769: 86; Th. 108, 23; Gen. 1810: Beo. Th. 2976; B. 1486. Gumcystum gōd *brave* [or *munificent?*], 5079; B. 2543. *See the use of* cystum *under* cyst III.

gum-dreám, es; *m. The joys of men, this life*:—He gumdreám ofgeaf Godes leóht geceás *he gave up the joy of men, chose God's light*, Beo. Th. 4929; B. 2469.

gum-dryhten, es; *m. A lord of men;* virorum dominus, Beo. Th. 3289; B. 1642.

gum-fēða, an; *m. A troop of men*, Beo. Th. 2807; B. 1401.

gum-man, -mann, es; *m. A famous man, a man;* vir clarus, homo, Beo. Th. 2061; B. 1028.

gum-rīce, es; *n. Power, rule over men, a kingdom, the earth*:—**Nis** ðē goda ǽnig on gumrīce efne gelīc ēce Drihten *non est similis tibi in* diis, Domine, Ps. Th. 85, 7. On ðam gumrîce *in that kingdom*, Elen. Kmbl. 2439; El. 1221. Gumrîces weard *the king*, Cd. 180; Th. 226, 25; Dan. 176.

gum-rinc, es; *m. A man* :—Gôdlîc gumrinc *a goodly man*, Exon. 129 a; Th. 495, 7; Rä. 84, 4. Dysiges folces gumrinca gyden *a goddess of the foolish people, of men*, Bt. Met. Fox 26, 105; Met. 26, 53: Cd. 75; Th. 93, 27; Gen. 1552.

gum-stôl, es; *m. A throne*, Beo. Th. 3908; B. 1952.

gum-þegen, es; *m. A man*, Exon. 79 b; Th. 298, 11; Crä. 83.

gum-þeód, e; *f. A nation, people* :—Gumþeóda bearn *the children of men*, Cd. 12; Th. 15, 1; Gen, 226.

gund, es; *m. Matter, corruption*; pus, L. M. 1, 4: 2, 3; Lchdm. ii. 44, 23, 26. [*Prompt. Parv.* gownde of eye *ridda, allugo*. See note, and v. Hall. Dict. gound. *O. H. Ger.* gund, gunt *virus, pus, tabum, tabes.*] DER. heals-gund.

gung; *adj. Young, youthful*; jŭvĕnis, adolescens:—Ic eom gungre yldo *adolescentior sum*, Bd. 4, 25; S. 600, 3. Hî ofslôgon ǽnne gungne Brytiscne man *they slew a young Briton*, Chr. 501; Erl. 15, 16. v. geong.

gungling *a youngling.*

GŪÞ, e; *f.* [*a poetical word*] *War, battle, fight*; bellum :—Gûþ nimeþ freán eówerne *war shall take away your lord*, Beo. Th. 5066; B. 2536: 4960; B. 2483: 3320; B. 1658: 2251; B. 1123. Sumne sceal gûþ abreótan *war shall crush one*, Exon. 87 a; Th. 328, 12; Vy. 16: 88 a; Th. 331, 15; Vy. 68. Bîdan Grendles gûþe *to await Grendel's attack*, Beo. Th. 970; B. 483. Gûþe gefŷsed *ready for battle*, 1265; B. 630: Byrht. Th. 137, 27; By. 192: 140, 30; By. 296: Andr. Kmbl. 467; An. 234. He gûþe rǽs fremman sceolde *he had to perform a war-onslaught*, Beo. Th. 5245; B. 2626: 4712; B. 2356. Grimre gûþe *in fierce fight*, 1058; B. 527. Ðonne hie to gûþe gârwudu rǽrdon *when to battle they reared the spearshaft*, Cd. 160; Th. 198, 19; Exod. 325: Beo. Th. 880; B. 438: 2948; B. 1472: Byrht. Th. 132, 8; By. 13: 134, 34; By. 94: Elen. Kmbl. 45; El. 23. Ðe ðê æsca tîr æt gûþe forgeaf *who gave thee martial glory in fight*, Cd. 97; Th. 127, 11; Gen. 2109: Judth. 11; Thw. 23, 15; Jud. 123: Exon. 17 b; Th. 42, 17; Cri. 674: Beo. Th. 3074; B. 1535; Byrht. Th. 140, 9; By. 285; Chr. 937; Erl. 114, 10; Ædelst. 44: Andr. Kmbl. 2661; An. 1332. Æt ðære gûþe Gârulf gecrang *at the battle fell Garulf*, Fins. Th. 62; Fin. 31. Ðǽr ðû gûþe findest *there wilt thou find conflict*, Andr. Kmbl. 2698; An. 1351. Ǽr ðû gûþe fremme *before thou do battle*, 2708; An. 1356: Exon. 105 b; Th. 402, 5; Rä. 21, 25. Se ða gûþe genæs *he had come safe out of the battle*, Cd. 94; Th. 121, 33; Gen. 2019. Ðe ða gûþe forbeáh *who turned aside from the battle*, Byrht. Th. 141, 21; By. 315. Gûþe spôwan *to thrive in battle*, Cd. 97; Th. 127, 23; Gen. 2115: Exon. 71 b; Th. 266, 4; Jul. 393: Salm. Kmbl. 249; Sal. 124. Ic genēþde fela gûþa *I dared many a conflict*, Beo. Th. 5017; B. 2512: 5080; B. 2543. Guma gûþum cûþ *a man distinguished in battles*, 4362; B. 2178: 3920; B. 1958. [*Icel.* gunnr, gûðr *war* (only used in poetry): *O. H. Ger.* gund, Grff. iv. 219.] See Grmm. D. M. 393.

gûþ-beorn, es; *m. A man of war, warrior*; vir bellicosus, bellator :—Gûþbeorna sum wicg gewende *one of the warriors turned his charger*, Beo. Th. 634; B. 314.

gûþ-bil, -bill, es; *n. A war-bill, a sword*, Beo. Th. 5162; B. 2584: 1610; B. 803.

gûþ-bord, es; *n. A warlike board, a shield*, Exon. 92 a; Th. 346, 11; Gn. Ex. 203: Cd. 128; Th. 163, 5; Gen. 2693. [*Icel.* gunn-borð *shield.*]

gûþ-byrne; *f. A coat of mail*, Beo. Th. 648; B. 321.

gûþ-cearu, e; *f. The care which is caused by battle*, Beo. Th. 2520: B. 1258.

gûþ-cræft, es; *m. Warlike power* or *skill*, Beo. Th. 254; B. 127.

gûþ-cwên, e; *f. A warrior queen*, Elen. Kmbl. 507; El. 254: 661; El. 331.

gûþ-cyning, es; *m. A warlike king*, Cd. 97: Th. 128, 8; Gen. 2123: Beo. Th. 401; B. 199: 3942; B. 1969: 4660; B. 2335: 5119; B. 2563: 5348; B. 2677.

gûþ-cyst, e; *f. Warlike excellence, bravery* :—Sunu simeones sweótum cômon þridde þeódmægen gûþcyste onþrang *the sons of Simeon came in troops, a third great force bravely pressed on* [or cyst = *troop, band, and* gûþcyste onþrang = *pressed on in phalanx*, cf. sweótum cômon], Cd. 160; Th. 199, 24; Exod. 343. [Cf. hilde-cyst.]

gûþ-deáþ, es; *m. Death got in fight*, Beo. Th. 4491; B. 2249.

gûþ-fana, -fona, an; *m. A military standard, ensign, banner*; signum vexillum :—Ðǽr wæs se gûþfana genumen ðe hî ræfen hêton *there was the banner taken that they called the Raven*, Chr. 878; Erl. 81, 3. Ðæt heofonlîce tâcn ðære hâlgan rôde is ûre gûþfana wiđ ðone gramlîcan deófol *the heavenly sign of the Holy Rood is our banner against the fierce devil*, H. R. 105, 16: 52. Ða gûþfonan *signa*, Ors. 6, 4; Swt. 260, 1. Ðǽr wǽron vii hund gûþfanena genumen *there were seven hundred standards taken*, 4, 1; Bos. 77, 29: Th. Chart. 430, 1. Under gûþfanum *under the standards*, Judth. 11; Thw. 24, 32; Jud. 219. [*Icel.* gunn-fani: *O. H. Ger.* gund-fano. Adopted in the French and Italian from the German, *O. Fr.* gun-fanon: *Ital.* gonfalone: hence *Mid. E.* gon-fanoun: *and* gun-faneur *a standard-bearer*, *A. R.* 300, 17.]

gûþ-flân; *m. f*: or gûþ-flâ; *f. A war-dart*, Cd. 95; Th. 124, 15; Gen. 2063.

gûþ-floga, an; *m. One that flies to battle, a dragon*, Beo. Th. 5049; B. 2528.

gûþ-freá, an; *m. A warlike lord* or *prince*, Andr. Kmbl. 2667; An. 1335.

gûþ-frec; *adj. Bold in war* :—Gûþfrec guma *man bold in war*, Andr. Kmbl. 2235; An. 1119.

gûþ-freca, an; *m. A warrior*, Exon. 61 a; Th. 223, 1; Ph. 353 [or perhaps this passage should be put under the preceding word]. Grame gûþfrecan gâras sendon *fierce warriors hurled spears*, Judth. 11; Thw. 24, 35; Jud. 224. v. freca.

gûþ-fremmende; *part. pres. One doing battle* or *fighting*, Cd. 154; Th. 192, 14; Exod. 231: Beo. Th. 497; B. 246.

gûþ-fruma, an; *m. A warlike chief*, Beo. Th. 39; B. 20.

gûþ-fugel, es; *m. A bird of war, eagle*, Exon. 106 b; Th. 406, 22; Rä. 25, 5.

Gûþ-geátas; *pl. The warlike Gauts*, Beo. Th. 3080; B. 1538.

gûþ-geatwe; *pl. f. Warlike dress* or *equipments*, Beo. Th. 796; B. 395.

gûþ-gelâca, an; *m. A companion, comrade in war, a warrior*, Elen. Kmbl. 86; El. 43.

gûþ-gemôt, es; *n. A battle-meeting, battle, fight*, Cd. 95; Th. 124, 1; Gen. 2056: Exon. 104 b; Th. 397, 28; Rä. 16, 25.

gûþ-getawa; *pl. f. War-equipments*, Beo. Th. 5265; B. 2636.

gûþ-geþingu; *pl. n. The lot to be expected from impending war*, Andr. Kmbl. 2044; An. 1024: 2088; An. 1045. v. ge-þing III.

gûþ-gewǽd, es; *n. A martial dress, war-weeds*, Beo. Th. 5228; B. 2617: 5453; B. 2730: 5694; B. 2851: 5735; B. 2871: 459; B. 227: 5240; B. 2623.

gûþ-geweorc, es; *n. A warlike work* or *deed*, Beo. Th. 1360; B. 678: 1967; B. 981: 3654; B. 1825.

gûþ-gewinn, es; *n. Battle, warlike contest*, Andr. Kmbl. 434; An. 217: Exon. 102 b; Th. 388, 10; Rä. 6, 5.

gûþ-hafoc, es; *m. A war-hawk, eagle* :—Earn grǽdigne gûþhafoc *the eagle, greedy war-hawk*, Chr. 937; Erl. 115, 13; Ædelst. 64. [Cf. *Icel.* gunnar-haukr.]

gûþ-heard; *adj. Stout in war*, Elen. Kmbl. 407; El. 204.

gûþ-helm, es; *m. A helm*, Beo. Th. 4967; B. 2487.

gûþ-here, es; *m. A martial band, an army*, Cd. 92; Th. 118, 18; Gen. 1967.

gûþ-horn, es; *m. A war-horn, trumpet*, Beo. Th. 2868; B. 1432.

gûþ-hrêþ, es; *m. Glory in war*, Beo. Th. 1642; B. 819.

gûþ-hwæt; *adj. Active, vigorous in war, valiant*, Apstls. Kmbl. 113; Ap. 57. [*Icel.* gunn-hvatr.]

Gûþ-lâc, es; *m. The hermit* or *saint of Crowland* [v. Crûland] *died at the age of* 41, *in* A. D. 714 :—Gûþlâc se nama ys on Rômânisc, Belli munus *the name Guthlac is in Latin, Belli munus*, Guthl. 2; Gdwin. 10, 23. Se hâlga Gûþlâc ðâs word gehŷrde *the holy Guthlac heard these words*, 4; Gdwin. 30, 9. Onginne ic nû be ðam lîfe ðæs eádigan weres, Gûþlaces *I begin now concerning the life of the blessed man Guthlac*, Guthl. 4; Gdwin. 26, 2: Exon. 34 b; Th. 110, 15; 113, 17; 115, 29. Hæfde Gûþlâc ðâ on ylde six and twentig wintra ðâ he ǽrest on ðam wêstene [Crûlande] gesæt *then Guthlac was six and twenty years of age when he first settled in the desert* [*Crowland*], Guthl. 3; Gdwin. 24, 3. Gûþlâc æfter ðon fiftyne geár ðe he lǽdde his lîf, ðâ wolde God his þeów gelǽdan to ðǽre êcan reste ðæs heofoncundan rîces *after Guthlac had led his life for fifteen years, then God would lead his servant to the eternal rest of his heavenly kingdom*, Guthl. 20; Gdwin. 78, 19–22. A. D. 714, Hēr, forþferde Gûþlâc se hâlga *here*, A. D. 714, *the saint Guthlac died*, Chr. 714; Erl. 44, 5. On ðone ændleftan dæg ðæs mônðes biþ sce gûþlâces geleornes ðæs anceran on brytone *on the eleventh day of the month is the departure of St. Guthlac the anchorite in Britain*, Shrn. 71, 2.

gûþ-leóþ, es; *n. A war-song*, Beo. Th. 3048; B. 1522.

gûþ-mæcga, an; *m. A warlike man*; bellicosus vir, Salm. Kmbl. 181; Sal. 90 [MS. A].

gûþ-maga, an; *m. A warlike man*; bellicosus vir, Salm. Kmbl. 181; Sal. 90 [MS. B].

gûþ-môd; *adj. Of warlike mind*, Beo. Th. 617; B. 306.

Gûþ-myrce; *pl. The Ethiopians*, Cd. 145; Th. 181, 10; Exod. 59. [Cf. Ælmyrca.]

gûþ-plega, an; *m. War-play, battle*, Byrht. Th. 133, 35; By. 61: Exon. 16 a; Th. 36, 8; Cri. 573: Apstls. Kmbl. 43; Ap. 22: Andr. Kmbl. 2737; An. 1371.

gûþ-rǽs, es; *m. A warlike attack*, Andr. Kmbl. 3061; An. 1533: Beo. Th. 5974; B. 2991: 3159; B. 1577: 4844; B. 2426.

gûþ-reáf, es; *n. A warlike dress, armour*, Exon. 71 a; Th. 265, 26; Jul. 387.

gúþ-reów; *adj. Fierce in fight*, Beo. Th. 115; B. 58.

gúþ-rinc, es; *m. A man of war, warrior*, Beo. Th. 1681; B. 838: 3007; B. 1501: 3766; B. 1881: Byrht. Th. 135, 55; By. 138: Andr. Kmbl. 309; An. 155: 783; An. 392.

gúþ-róf; *adj. Famous in war*, Beo. Th. 1220; B. 608: Elen. Kmbl. 545; El. 273.

gúþ-sceaða, an; *m. One who harms by warlike attack*, Beo. Th. 4625; B. 2318.

gúþ-scear, es; *m. War-shearing, slaughter in battle*, Beo. Th. 2430; B. 1213. v. scear, inwit-scear.

gúþ-sceorp, es; *n. War-clothing*; vestitus *vel* ornatus bellicus, Judth. 12; Thw. 26, 15; Jud. 329.

gúþ-scrúd, es; *n. War-clothing*, Elen. Kmbl. 515; El. 258.

gúþ-searo; *n. Arms, armour*, Beo. Th. 435; B. 215: 661; B. 328: Andr. Kmbl. 253; An. 127.

gúþ-sele, es; *m. A war-hall, hall in which warriors sit*, Beo. Th. 890; B. 443.

gúþ-spell, es; *n. War-tidings*, Cd. 97; Th. 126, 18; Gen. 2097.

gúþ-sweord, es; *n. A sword*, Beo. Th. 4314; B. 2154.

gúþ-þræc; *gen.* -þræce; *pl. nom. gen. acc.* -þraca; *f. War-force*; vis bellica:—Mid gúþþræce *with war-force*, Cd. 50; Th. 64, 6; Gen. 1046: 93; Th. 119, 2; Gen. 1973.

gúþ-þreát, es; *m. A martial band*, Cd. 151; Th. 190, 2; Exod. 193.

gúþ-weard, es; *m. A war-guard, a king*, Cd. 151; Th. 188, 26; Exod. 174: Elen. Kmbl. 27; El. 14.

gúþ-weorc, es; *n. A warlike work* or *deed*, Andr. Kmbl. 2133; An. 1068.

gúþ-wérig; *adj. Weary with battle*, Beo. Th. 3176; B. 1586.

gúþ-wíga, an; *m. A warrior*, Beo. Th. 4230; B. 2112.

gúþ-wine, es; *m. A comrade, friend in war*, Beo. Th. 3624; B. 1810: 5463; B. 2735.

gúþ-wudu, a; *m. War-wood, a spear*, Fins. Th. 11; Fin. 6.

gycel-stán. v. gicel-stán.

gyd, gyddian. v. gid, giddian.

gyden, e; *f*: gydene, an; *f. A goddess*; dea:—Iuno wæs swíðe heálíc gyden *Juno was a very lofty goddess*, Salm. Kmbl. 121, 32. Sceolde bión gydene *was said to be a goddess*, Bt. 38, 1; Fox 194, 19: Bt. Met. Fox 26, 105; Met. 26, 53. Óþ he geméтte ða graman gydena *until he met the fierce goddesses*, 35, 6; Fox 168, 24. Seó hæfde gehâten heora gydenne Dianan ðæt heó wolde hiere líf on fǽmnháde alibban *she had promised their goddess Diana that she would live her life in virginity*; virgo vestalis, Ors. 3, 6; Swt. 108, 17. [Cf. *Icel.* guðja: *O. H. Ger.* gutin, gutenna: *Ger.* göttin.]

gydenlíc; *adj. Nunlike, vestal*; vestalis, Cot. 179, Lye.

gyf. v. gif.

gyfa. v. gifa.

gyfan. v. gifan.

gyfen, es; *n. Ocean*:—Ne on gyfenes grund *not in ocean's bed* [*ground*], Beo. Th. 2792, note; B. 1394. v. geofon.

gyfl. v. gifl.

gyft. v. gift.

gyfu, e; *gen. pl.* -ena; *f. A gift, grace*; donum, gratia:—Gyfu gif hwylc is of me *donum quodcumque ex me*, Mk. Bos. 7, 11. Godes gyfu wæs on him *gratia Dei erat in illo*, Lk. Bos. 2, 40: Cd. 212; Th. 262, 5; Dan. 739. v. gifu.

gyfung. v. gifung.

gy-fylness, e; *f. Completion, end*:—Óþ ða gyfylnesse ðisse worlde *until the end of the world*, Blickl. Homl. 145, 16. v. ge-fylness.

gyhþa. v. gihþa.

gyhþu. v. gehþo.

gyld, gyldan. v. gild, gildan.

gylda. v. gilda.

gyldan; *p.* ede *To gild*, Chr. 1052; Th. 321, 25. [*Icel.* gylla: *O. H. Ger.* uber-guldete; *p.*]

gylden, gilden; *adj. Golden*; aureus:—Gylden wed *vel* feoh *arra*, Ælfc. Gl. 14; Som. 58, 11; Wrt. Voc. 21, 6. Gylden læfr *bractea*, 58; Som. 67, 111; Wrt. Voc. 38, 34. Gylden fel *bractea*, Cot. 27, Lye. Gyldena *vel* gegylde fatu *crisendeta*, Ælfc. Gl. 67; Som. 69, 97; Wrt. Voc. 41, 48. Ðá stód ðǽr gyldenu onlícnes *then stood there a golden image*, Shrn. 88, 22. Ðǽr is geat gylden *there is a golden gate*, Cd. 227; Th. 305, 19; Sat. 649. On sumum gyldenum wecge *to a golden wedge*, Homl. Th. i. 60, 29. Under gyldenum beáge *under a golden crown*, Beo. Th. 2330; B. 1163. To ðam gyldnan gylde *to the idol of gold*, Cd. 182; Th. 228, 18; Dan. 204. Hring gyldenne *a golden ring*, Beo. Th. 5611; B. 2809. [*Laym.* gulden: *Orm.* gilden: *O. Sax.* guldin: *O. Frs.* gulden, golden, gelden: *Icel.* gullinn: *O. H. Ger.* guldin: *Ger.* gülden, golden.] DER. eal-gylden.

gylden-beáh, -beág, es; *m. A crown*:—Mid gehálgodon gildenbeáge *with the hallowed crown*, Lev. 8, 9.

gylden-feaxa; *adj. Having golden hair*; auricomus, Cot. 11, Lye. [Cf. ge-feaxe.]

gylding-wecg *a gold mine, a vein of gold*; aurifodina, Cot. 16, 167, Som.

gylian; *p.* ede *To yell, shout out*:—Styrmde and gylede *shouted and yelled*, Judth. 10; Thw. 21, 19; Jud. 25. v. gellan.

gyllan *yell, chirp*, Cd. 167; Th. 208, 26; Exod. 489: Fins. Th. 10; Fin. 6. v. gellan.

gylm. v. gilm.

gylp, and its compounds. v. gilp, etc.

GYLT, gilt, gelt, gielt, es; *m. Guilt, crime, sin, offence, fault, wrong, debt, fine, forfeiture*:—Gylt *facinus* vel *culpa*, Wrt. Voc. 86, 67. Adames gylt *Adam's guilt*, Blickl. Homl. 9, 5: 23, 5: Exon. 61 b; Th. 226, 19; Ph. 408. For ðam gylte ðe hig worhton ðæt gildene celf *for the sin of making the golden calf*, Ex. 32, 35; Deut. 9, 21. Eustatius hæfde gecýdd ðam cynge ðet hit sceolde beón máre gylt ðære burhwaru ðonne his *Eustace had told the king that it was more the citizens' fault than his*, Chr. 1048; Erl. 178, 9. Man geútlagode Ælfgár bútan ǽlcan gylte *Ælfgar was outlawed without any crime* [*being proved against him*], Chr. 1055; Erl. 188, 28: 189, 35. Æt ðam forman gylte ðære fiohbóte onfón *on the first offence to accept pecuniary compensation*, L. Alf. 49; Th. i. 58, 8: L. Alf. pol. 7; Th. i. 66, 12: L. In. 73; Th. i. 148, 11: L. Ath. 1, 11; Th. i. 206, 3: L. Edg. S. 2, 2; Th. i. 266, 13. Gif he ðǽr gylt gewyrce *if he there do wrong*, L. Ath. 1, 8; Th. i. 204, 8. Gylt ceápes *crime in business*, Lchdm. iii. 198, 10. Þurh forman gylt *through the first sin*, Cd. 48; Th. 61, 17; Gen. 998. Forgyf us úre gyltas *demitte nobis debita nostra*, Mt. Kmbl. 6, 12: Ps. Th. 84, 3. Gyltas *delicta*, Ps. Spl. 18, 13. Geltas, Ps. C. 50, 39; Ps. Grn. ii. 277, 39. Gieltas, Exon. 62 b; Th. 229, 26; Ph. 461. Forgifnesse ealra heora gylta *forgiveness of all their sins*, Blickl. Homl. 193, 24: Elen. Kmbl. 1631; El. 817. Gyltum forgiefene *given up to sins*, Exon. 39 a; Th. 130, 2; Gú. 432. Forgeaf him ðone gylt *debitum dimisit ei*, Mt. Kmbl. 18, 27, 32. Ealle ða gyltes ða belimpeþ to míne kinehelme *omnes forisfacturas que pertinent ad regiam coronam meam*, Th. Chart. 423, 3. [*Laym. A. R.* gult: *Orm.* gillt: *Ayenb.* gelt.] Cf. scyld.

gyltan; *p.* gylte; *pp.* gylt *To commit guilt* or *sin, to be guilty*:—Ðara gyltendra scylda *the sins of the guilty*, Past. 21; Swt. 167, 6; Hat. MS. [*Orm.* gilltenn: *Wicl.* gilten: *O. E. Homl.* gulte; *p.*] v. gylting, gyltend, a-, for-gyltan.

gylte GELT, *gelded*; castratus, Som.

gyltend, es; *m. A debtor, an offender*; debitor:—Gyltend *lapsus*, Rtl. 189, 25. Swá swá we forgyfaþ úrum gyltendum *sicut nos dimittimus debitoribus nostris*, Mt. Bos. 6, 12. v. gyltende.

gyltende. v. gyltan.

gyltig; *adj.* GUILTY, *liable, bound*; reus:—Swá hwylc swá swereþ on ðære offrunge ðe ofer ðæt weofud ys, se ys gyltig *quicumque juraverit in dono quod est super illud, debet*, Mt. Kmbl. 23, 18. [*A. R.* Heo is gulti of the bestes deaðe, 58, 17: *Chauc.* gulty.]

gylting, e; *f. Sinning, sin*:—Gyiltincg *prævaricatio*, Rtl. 109, 41. Gultingum *delictis*, 66, 29. Gyltingum, 124, 42.

gyltlíc *wicked, sinful*:—Gé gehýrdon gyltlíce sprǽce *audistis blasphemiam*, Mt. Kmbl. 26, 65.

gym *a gem*. v. gim.

GÝMAN, géman, gíman, gíeman; *p.* de *To care for, take care of, take heed to, heed, observe, regard, keep*; cum gen. acc:—Ic gýme mín wedd *I will keep my covenant*, Lev. 26, 42. Ic geornor gýme ymb ðæs gǽstes forwyrd ðonne ðæs líchoman *I care more earnestly about the spirit's destruction than the body's*, Exon. 71 b; Th. 267, 12; Jul. 414. Ic ne gýme ðæs compes *I care not for the strife*, 105 b; Th. 402, 26; Rä. 21, 35: Lev. 26, 43. Egesan ne gýmeþ *heeds not terror*, Beo. Th. 3519; B. 1757. Dryhten mín gýmþ *Deus curam habet mei*, Ps. Th. 39, 20. Óðres ne gýmeþ to gebídanne yrfeweardes *he cares not to wait for another heir*, Beo. Th. 4894; B. 2451. Se deópa seáð giémeþ gǽsta *the deep pit keeps the spirits*, Exon. 30 b; Th. 94, 26; Cri. 1546. Se ðe ne giémeþ hwæðer his gǽst síe earm ðe eádig *who heeds not whether his spirit be miserable or blessed*, Th. 95, 6; Cri. 1553. Swíðe geornlíce giémaþ ðæt hie ða eorþlícan heortan gelǽren *they take very diligent heed to instruct the wordly hearts*, Past. 21; Swt. 161, 15; Hat. MS. Gýmaþ, Ps. Th. 118, 122. Ðæt he ðone stán nime hláfes ne gýme *to take the stone and neglect the bread*, Elen. Kmbl. 1229; El. 616: Exon. 66 b; Th. 246, 32; Jul. 70. He ǽtes ne gímde *he did not care for food*, Swt. A. S. Rdr. 60, 110. Giémde, Exon. 34 b; Th. 111, 3; Gú. 121. Ðæt hig gímdon ðæs dæges and ðære nihte *to rule the day and the night*, Gen. 1, 18. Moises and Aaron and hira bærn gímdon ðæs temples *Moses and Aaron and their children took charge of the temple*, Num. 3, 38. Rihtes ne gýmdon *cared not for right*, Andr. Kmbl. 278; An. 139: Cd. 113; Th. 148, 20; Gen. 2459: Exon. 18 a; Th. 44, 22; Cri. 706. Hí gýmdon hwæðer . . . *observabant si . . .*, Mk. Skt. 3, 2: Lk. Skt. 6, 7. Ne gím ðú drýcræfta *regard not the arts of wizards*, Lev. 19, 31, 26: Deut. 18, 10: Beo. Th. 3525; B. 1760. Gém *observe*, Bt. Met. Fox 29, 6; Met. 29, 3. Gýmaþ and warniaþ *intuemini et cavete*, Mt. Kmbl. 16, 6. Sceal ic nú ǽniges lustes gíman *shall I care now for any pleasure*, Gen.

18, 12. Ða ðe bet cunnon sceolon gýman óðra manna *those who know better are to take care of other men*, Homl. Th. ii. 282, 1: Ps. Th. 77, 10: Exon. 31 a; Th. 96, 5; Cri. 1569. Gif his ðé gêman lyst *if you pleased to care about it*, Bt. Met. Fox 31, 2; Met. 31, 1. Gýman ðæs grundes *to take charge of the abyss*, Cd. 18; Th. 22, 31, 25; Gen. 349, 346. [*Laym. A. R.* ȝemen: *Orm.* ȝemenn: *Piers P.* ȝeme: *Goth.* gaumjan: *O. Sax.* gômean: *Icel.* geyma: *Dan.* gjemme: *Swed.* gömma: *O. H. Ger.* goumon.] DER. for-, ge-, ofer-gýman. v. gêman.

gýme, an; *f. Care*:—Hý ðæs wealles nâne gýman [giéman, Swt. 134, 21] ne dydan *they took no care of the wall*, Ors. 3, 9; Bos. 68, 24. [*Orm.* gom: *Laym. A. R.* ȝeme: *O. Sax.* gôma; *f*: *Icel.* gaumr; *m.* gaum; *f. heed, attention*: *O. H. Ger.* gouma; *f.* Grff. iv. 203.] Cf. gýmen.

gýmeleás; *adj. Careless, negligent, uncared for, wandering, stray*; negligens:—Gýmeleás feoh [giémeleás fioh] *stray cattle*, L. Alf. 42; Th. i. 54, 9: Ps. Th. 70, 10. Ða gîmeleasan men ðe heora lîf adrugon on ealre îdelnisse *careless men who passed their life in all frivolity*, Swt. A. S. Rdr. 56, 11. Gýmeleáse *heedless*, Exon. 73 a; Th. 271, 33; Jul. 491: Blickl. Homl. 55, 30.

gýmeleásian; *p.* ede *To neglect, be careless, despise*; negligere:—Monige gýmeleásedon ðám gerýnum ðæs hâlgan geleáfan *aliqui, neglectis fidei sacramentis*, Bd. 4, 27; S. 604, 6. DER. a-, for-gýmeleásian.

gýmeleáslîce, gêmeleáslîce; *adv. Carelessly*; negligenter, R. Ben. 44, Lye.

gýmeleásnys, se; *f. Carelessness*; negligentia:—Forþgewitenum gýmeleásnyssum *præteritas negligentias*, Bd. 3, 27; S. 559, 5.

gýmeleást, gîmelîst, gêmelêst, e; *f. Carelessness, negligence, neglect*; negligentia:—Hit gelamp þurh gýmeleáste *evenit per culpam incuriæ*, Bd. 3, 17; S. 544, 27. For giémelêste *for negligence*, Past. 21; Swt. 165, 6. Gîmeleáste, Swt. A. S. Rdr. 68, 376. On heora âgenre gýmeleáste *from their own carelessness*, Chr. 1016; Erl. 156, 11: Bt. 5, 1; Fox 10, 2. Þurh preósta gýmelêste *through the negligence of priests*, Cod. Dipl. Kmbl. iii. 349, 6. Se Hǽlend ne forlêt to gýmeleáste his gelufedan apostol *the Saviour did not leave his beloved apostle to neglect*, Homl. Th. i. 58, 33. [*Orm.* ȝemelæste.]

gýmen, gêmen; *f. Care, heed, solicitude, diligence, superintendence, rule*; cura:—Se rêða rên sumes ymbhogan ungemet gêmen *the fierce rain of some anxiety, immoderate care* [cf. se rên ungemetlîces ymbhogan, Fox 36, 19], Bt. Met. Fox 7, 56; Met. 7, 28: 101; Met. 7, 51. Ðînre gýmenne ic wæs beboden *in te jactatus sum*, Ps. Th. 21, 8. Hêr onfêng Pilatus gýmene ofer ða Iudêas *in this year Pilate received the government of Judæa*, Chr. 26; Erl. 7, 6: to gýmenne, Erl. 6, 7. Of his bisceoplîcan gýmenne *cura pastorali*, Cod. Dipl. Kmbl. iii. 348, 35. Se stæf getâcnaþ gýmene and hyrdrǽdene *the staff is a symbol of care and guardianship*, Homl. Th. ii. 280, 35. Man sceal healdan ðæt hâlige hûsl mid mycelre gýmene *the holy eucharist must be kept with great care*, L. Ælf. C. 36; Th. ii. 360, 11. He swâ geornfulle gýmenne dyde ymb ða hǽla ûre þeóde *tam sedulam erga salutem nostræ gentis curam gesserit*, Bd. 2, 1; S. 501, 3. Weoruldsorge and gýmenne forlǽtan *sæculi curas relinquere*, 4, 19; S. 587, 38. Gýmene dô se Abbod *curam gerit abbas*, R. Ben. interl. 27, Lye. DER. be-, un-gýmen.

gýmend, es; *m. A governor*; gubernator, Scint. 32.

gymmian *jugulare, occidere, perfodere*, Hpt. Gl. 495.

gýmung, e; *f. A marriage, nuptial*:—To gýmungum ðæs heofonlîcum brýdguman eádig fǽmne ineode *ad nuptias sponsi cælestis virgo beata intravit*, Bd. 3, 24; S. 557, 6. v. gêmung.

GYNAN *to* GAIN; lucrari, Lye.

gynd *beyond*. v. geond.

gyngra *younger*, Ps. Spl. 36, 26; *comp. of* geong.

gyngra, an; *m. A junior*; adōlescentŭlus:—Gyngra ic eom *adōlescentŭlus sum ego*, Ps. Spl. M. 118, 141. v. geongra.

gynian. v. ginian.

gynnan. v. ginnan.

gypigend *yawning*; hiulcus, Gl. Prud. 703.

GYR *a fir tree*; abies, Lchdm. iii. 328, col. 1. v. gyrtreów.

gyr, gyra; *m.* gyru; *f. Mud, fen, marsh*:—Gyr *lætamen*, Hpt. Gl. 516. On gyran torr [?], Cod. Dipl. Kmbl. iii. 412, 8. Gyrwe fenn *palus*, Ælfc. Gr. 9, 33; Som. 12, 29. Gyran, gyras *paludes*, Lye. [Cf. *O. Frs.* cere, gere *dirty water*.] v. gor, Gyrwas.

GYRD, gird, gerd, e; *f. A staff, rod, twig*, as a measure of distance, *a yard*, as a measure of area, *the fourth part of a hide*; virga, virgata:—Gyrd *virga*, Wrt. Voc. 80, 3. Ðîn gyrd and ðîn stæf *virga tua et baculus tuus*, Ps. Th. 22, 5. Ðû ðînes yrfes gyrde alýsdest *liberasti virgam hæriditatis tuæ*, 73, 3. Hit ys gird *it is a rod*, Ex. 4, 2. Ber Aarones girde into ðam getelde *bear Aaron's rod into the tabernacle*, Num. 17, 10: Mt. Kmbl. 10, 10: Homl. Th. ii. 8, 11: i. 62, 34. He gebletsode ða grênan gyrda *he blessed the green twigs*, 64, 1. Fiórþe half gird *three yards and a half*, Lchdm. iii. 362, col. 2. Landes sumne dǽl ðæt is ân gyrd *a certain portion of land, that is the fourth part of a hide*, Cod. Dipl. Kmbl. iii. 260, 32: 263, 7. Ðis synd ðære ânre gyrde landgemǽro *these are the boundaries of the one rood*, ii. 208, 18: L. In. 67; Th. i. 146, 1, 2: L. R. S. 4; Th. i. 434, 24. Swâ swýðe nearwelîce he hit lêtt ût aspyrian ðæt næs ân ǽlpig hîde ne ân gyrde landes ðæt næs gesæt on his gewrite *so very narrowly did he have things searched out that there was not a single hide nor a rood of land that was not put down in his book*, Chr. 1085; Erl. 218, 35. [*Orm.* ȝerrd: *A. R. Chauc. Piers P.* ȝerd: *O. H. Ger.* gardea, garda, gerta, kirta: *Ger.* gerte.]

gyrdan, girdan; *p.* gyrde; *pp.* gyrded *To* GIRD, *bind round*; cingere:—Ðâ ðû gingra wǽre ðû gyrdest ðé ... ðonne ðû eldast óðer ðé gyrt *cum esses junior cingebas te . . . cum senueris alius te cinget*, Jn. Skt. 21, 18. Se ðe hine man gelome gyrt *qua semper præcingitur*, Ps. Th. 108, 19. He girde hine *he girded him*, Lev. 8, 7. Hine se hâlga wer gyrde grǽgan sweorde *the holy man girded himself with a grey sword*, Cd. 138; Th. 173, 22; Gen. 2865: Fins. Th. 27; Fin. 13. Gyrd nû ðîn sweord ofer ðîn þeóh *accingere gladium tuum circa femur*, Ps. Th. 44, 4: Lk. Skt. 17, 8. Gyrded cempa *a belted warrior*, Beo. Th. 4162; B. 2078. [*Icel.* gyrða: *O. H. Ger.* gurten: *Ger.* gürten.] DER. be-, ge-, ymb-gyrdan.

gyrdel, es; *m. A* GIRDLE, *belt, zone, purse*; cingulum:—Gyrdel *zona* vel *zonarium* vel *brachile* vel *redimiculum*, Ælfc. Gl. 64; Som. 69, 28; Wrt. Voc. 40, 57. Gyrdel *cingulum* vel *zona* vel *cinctorium*, Wrt. Voc. 81, 47. Gyrdel *stropheum*, Hymn. Surt. 103, 33. Fellenne gyrdel *zonam pelliciam*, Mt. Kmbl. 3, 4: Mk. Skt. 1, 6. We hâtaþ on lêden quinque zonas ðæt synd fîf gyrdlas *we call them in Latin quinque zonas, that is five girdles*, Lchdm. iii. 260, 20. Him bebeád ðæt hî ne nâmon feoh on heora gyrdlum *præcepit ne tollerent in zona æs*, Mk. Skt. 6, 8. [*Icel.* gyrðill; *m. a girdle, purse*: *O. H. Ger.* gurtil; *m. cingulum, cinctorium, strophium, balteum*: *Ger.* gürtel.] v. gyrdels.

gyrdel-bred, es; *n. Pugillar*, Lye.

gyrdel-hring, es; *m. Ligula*, Lye.

gyrdels, es; *m. A girdle*:—Gyrdels *cingulum*, Recd. 40, 27; Wrt. Voc. 66, 35. Gyrdils *zonam*, Mt. Kmbl. Lind. Rush. 3, 4: 10, 9: Mk. Skt. Lind. Rush. 1, 6: 6, 8: Rtl. 79, 7. Gelîc gyrdelse *sicut zona*, Ps. Th. 108, 19: Exon. 113 b; Th. 436, 21; Rä. 55, 4: 114 a; Th. 436, 34; Rä. 55, 11. v. gyrdel.

gyrd-weg, es; *m. A road with a fence on either side* [?], Cod. Dipl. Kmbl. iii. 412, 21.

gyrd-wîte, es; *n. Punishment with a rod, the punishment that came upon the Egyptians through Moses' rod*, Cd. 143; Th. 178, 22; Exod. 15.

gyren = grin, Ps. Th. 118, 110.

gyrian, gyrigan; *part.* gyrigende; *p.* ede, *pl.* gyredon. I. *to prepare*; preparare:—Gyrigende dûna *præparans montes*, Ps. Spl. 64, 7. Gyrede setl his *paravit sedem suam*, 102, 19. II. *to clothe*; vestire, amicire:—Swylce eác ða gegyrelan ðone lîchoman Cûþbertes gyredon *sed et indumenta quibus corpus Cudbercti vestierant*, Bd. 4, 31; S. 611, 5. v. gearwian.

gyrla. v. gerela.

gyrman; *p.* de *To cry out, roar*:—Ic gyrmde *rugiebam*, Ps. Lamb. 37, 8.

gyrn, es; *n. Grief, affliction, trouble, evil, calamity, injury*:—Me biþ gyrn witod *grief will be appointed me*, Exon. 104 b; Th. 396, 18; Rä. 16, 6. Gyrn æfter gomene *grief after joy*, Beo. Th. 3554; B. 1775. Alýsed of leódhete of gyrme *rescued from the popular hate, from calamity*, Andr. Kmbl. 2301; An. 1152: 3168; An. 1587. He gilleþ geómorlîce and his gyrn sefaþ *mournfully he cries out, sighs forth his grief*, Salm. Kmbl. 536; Sal. 267. Gyrn þurh gâstgedâl *affliction through death*, Exon. 45 a; Th. 153, 31; Gû. 834. Gyldaþ nû mid gyrne ðæt heó goda ussa meaht forhogde *requite now with evil her contempt of our gods' might*, 74 b; Th. 279, 25; Jul. 619. Ðæs ða byre siððan gyrne onguldon *for that the children greviously paid*, 61 b; Th. 226, 23. Wita unrîm grimra gyrna *torments numberless, grim troubles*, 68 a; Th. 252, 34; Jul. 173: 39 a; Th. 129, 7; Gû. 417. [Cf. *O. Sax.* gornword.] v. gryn.

gyrnan, girnan; *p.* de *To desire, beg, yearn*:—Ic ne me micles gyrne *I do not desire much for myself*, Exon. 37 a; Th. 121, 20; Gû. 291. Glædmôd gyrneþ ðæt he gôdra mǽst dǽda gefremme *joyous is eager to perform very many good deeds*, 62 b; Th. 229, 28; Ph. 492. Ðæt mǽden hire deáþes girnde *the maiden desired to die*, Apol. Th. 2, 24: 3, 8. Ne gyrne gê ðæt eów man Lâreówas nemne *vos nolite vocari Rabbi*, Mt. Kmbl. 23, 8. Gyrnende *orantes*, Mk. Skt. 11, 24. [*Laym.* ȝeornen, ȝernen, ȝirnen: *Orm.* ȝeornenn, ȝeonenn: *Piers P.* ȝerne: *Goth.* gairnjan: *O. Sax.* girnean, gernean: *Icel.* girna.] v. geornan.

gyrne; *adv. Earnestly*; enixe:—Hí gyrne cleopedon to Gode *they earnestly cried to God*, Chr. 1083; Erl. 217, 22. v. georne.

gyrnes, gyrnys, -ness, -nyss, e; *f. Diligence, industry*; industria:—Þurh Ôsþryþe gyrnysse *per industriam Osthrydæ*, Bd. 3, 11: S. 535, 12. v. geornes.

gyrning. v. geornung.

gyrn-stæf, es; *m. Affliction, trouble*:—Gleáw gyrn-stafa *skilled in afflicting*, Exon. 68 a; Th. 257, 10; Jul. 245.

gyrn-wracu; *f. Vengeance for trouble* or *injury*:—Gearo gyrnwræce *ready to revenge her grief*, Beo. Th. 4242; B. 2118: 2281; B. 1138.

Mārum sārum gyldan gyrnwræce *with greater pains to revenge their trouble*, Exon. 39 a; Th. 128, 16; Gū. 405.

gyrran. v. georran.

gyrretynde *roaring;* rugiens, Ps. Lamb. 21, 11. v. gyrran.

gyrst *gnashing, grinding;* stridor, Hpt. Gl. 513. v. grist.

gyrst; *adj. Grinding, grating;* stridulus, Hpt. Gl. 513.

gyrstan-dæg, gestran-dæg, gysternlīc-dæg YESTERDAY; heri:—Gyrstandæg *heri*, Ælfc. Gr. 38; Som. 39, 57. Swā he wæs gyrstan-dæg and ǣran dæg *sicut erat heri et nudius tertius*, Gen. 31, 5.

gyr-treów, es; *n. A spruce fir;* abies, Ælfc. Gl. 46; Som. 64, 128; Wrt. Voc. 32, 62. v. gyr.

gyrwan; *p.* ede; *pp.* ed *To prepare, make ready, make, put on, clothe, adorn;* părāre, făcĕre, vestīre, ornāre:—Angan hine gyrwan *he began to prepare himself*, Cd. 23; Th. 28, 26; Gen. 442: Andr. Kmbl. 1590; An. 796. Ic hæbbe geweald micel to gyrwanne gōdlecran stōl on heofne *I have great power to form a better throne in heaven*, Cd. 15; Th. 18, 30; Gen. 281. Cyning mec gyrweþ since and seolfre *the king adorns me with treasure and silver*, Exon. 105 b; Th. 401, 10; Rä. 21, 9. Wer and wīf bearn mid bleóm gyrwaþ *man and wife adorn their child with colours*, 87 a; Th. 327, 14; Vy. 3. v. gearwian.

Gyrwas; *pl. The people of a district in which Peterborough was situated:*—Se wæs of Gyrwa mǣgđe *de provincia Gyrviorum*, Bd. 3, 20; S. 550, 22. Abbud đæs mynstres đe gecweden is Medeshāmstyde on Gyrwa[n] lande *Abbas monasterii quod dicitur Medeshamstedi in regione Gyrviorum*, 4, 6; S. 573, 41. v. gyr *a marsh.*

gyse *yes:*—Hig cwǣdon,—Eówer lāreów, ne gylt he gafol? Đā cwæþ he, Gyse he dēþ *they said,—Your master, doth he not pay tribute? He said, Yes, he does;* dixerunt,—Magister vester, non solvit didrachma? Ait, Etiam, Vulg. Mt. Bos. 17, 25. v. gese.

gyst, es; *m. A guest:*—Ic wæs gyst mōdor cildum *factus sum hospes filiis matris meæ*, Ps. Th. 68, 8: Cd. 114; Th. 150, 1; Gen. 2485. DER. sele-gyst. v. gæst.

gyst-ern, es; *n. A guest-place, guest-chamber:*—To đam gysterne *to the guest-chamber*, Judth. 10; Thw. 21, 29: Jud. 40. v. gest-ærn.

gysternlīc-dæg *yesterday:*—Swylce gysternlīc dæg, đe forþgewāt *tanquam dies hesterna quæ præteriit*, Ps. Lamb. 89, 4. v. gyrstan-dæg.

gyst-hūs, es; *n. A guest-house, guest-chamber;* hospitium:—Hwār is mīn gyst-hūs *where is my guest-house?* Mk. Bos. 14, 14. v. gæst-hūs.

gystigan *to lodge, to abide as a guest;* hospitari, Scint. 47.

gyst-sele, es; *m. A guest-hall;* hospĭtālis aula:—Ēđelleáse đysne gystsele gihþum healdaþ [MS. healdeþ] *the homeless hold this guest-hall in memory*, Cd. 169; Th. 212, 4; Exod. 534. v. gest-sele.

gyt *you two;* vos duo:—Gyt nyton hwæt gȳt biddaþ [*vos duo*] *nescitis quid* [*vos duo*] *petatis*, Mt. Bos. 20, 22. v. git.

GYT, gyta. v. git, gita.

gytan. v. gitan, and its compounds.

gyte, es; *m. A pouring, shedding, inundation, flood:*—Beó his blōdes gyte ofer ūrum bearnum *his bloodshed be upon our children*, Homl. Th. ii. 252, 20. Gyte *inundatio*, Cot. 108, Lye. Ne mihton hī for đam ormǣtan gyte heora fēt of đære cytan astyrian *they could not move their feet from the cottage for the excessive flood*, Homl. Th. ii. 184, 6. Martyrdōm biþ gefremmed nā on blōdes gyte ānum *martyrdom is effected not by bloodshed only*, i. 544, 24: Mt. Kmbl. 23, 30. Mid teára gytum *with sheddings of tears*, Blickl. Homl. 61, 20. [*O. H. Ger.* gussi *diluvium;* gussa *inundatio;* guz *fusio*, Grff. iv. 285: *Ger.* guss.]

gytenes. v. getenys.

gyte-sǣl, es; *m. Joy at the pouring out of wine:*—Đā wæs Olofernus on gytesālum *then was Holofernes joyous in feasting*, Judth. 10; Thw. 21, 17: Jud. 22. [Cf. Đā wæs on sālum sinces brytta, Beo. Th. 1218; B. 607 and 2345; B. 1171.]

gyte-streám, es; *m. A current, flowing stream:*—Ebbe *vel* gytestreám *reuma*, Ælfc. Gl. 105; Som. 78, 38; Wrt. Voc. 57, 20: Recd. 37, 65; Wrt. Voc. 63, 78.

gyt-feorm [?], L. R. S. 21; Th. i. 440, 26.

gȳtsere. v. gītsere.

gȳtsian. v. gītsian.

gȳtsung. v. gītsung.

H

IN Anglo-Saxon the letter *h* represents the guttural aspirate and the pure spirant. In later English the guttural *h* is generally represented by *gh*, e. g. leóht *light*, heáh *high*. Under certain circumstances *h* takes the place of *c* and *g*, see those letters. In some cases it is dropped, e. g. bleó for bleoh; seón, *p.* seah; nabban = ne habban. In the Northumbrian specimens the use of the initial *h*, especially in the combinations *hl, hn, hr*, is uncertain, e. g. eorta = heorta, haald = ald, hlīf = līf, lysta = hlysta, hnett = nett, nesc = hnesc, hræst = ræst, ræfn = hræfn. The name of the Runic letter was hægl *hail:*—Hægl byþ hwītust corna, Runic pm. 9; Kmbl. 341, 4; the forms accompanying the poem and given by Kemble are these, ᚺ, ᚻ, ᚺ.

ha ha; *interj. Ha ha!*—Ha ha and he he getācniaþ hlehter on lēden and on Englisc *ha ha and he he denote laughter in Latin and in English*, Ælfc. Gr. 48; Som. 49, 17.

habban, tō habbanne, hæbbene; *pres. part.* hæbbende; *pres. indic.* ic hæbbe, hafa, đū hæfst, hafast, he hæfþ, hafaþ, *pl.* habbaþ, hæbbaþ; *p.* hæfde; *subj.* hæbbe, *pl.* hæbben, habban; *imper.* hafa, *pl.* habbaþ; *pp.* hæfed. I. *cum acc. To* HAVE, *possess, hold, keep:*—Swylce getrȳwþa swā se cyng æt him habban wolde *such pledges as the king wished to have from him*, Chr. 1093; Erl. 229, 19. Būton se biscop hie mid him habban wille *unless the bishop want to have it with him*, Past. Pref. Swt. 9, 6. Đa lǣwedan willaþ habban đone mōnan be đam đe hī hine geseóþ and đa gelǣredan hine healdaþ be đisum foresǣdan gesceáde *laymen will have the moon according as they see it, and the learned hold of it according to the aforesaid distinction*, Lchdm. iii. 266, 10. Hē đa word nel on his heortan habban and healdan *he will not have and hold those words in his heart*, Blickl. Homl. 55, 8. Đonne māgon wē ūs God ælmihtigne mildne habban *then may we have God Almighty merciful to us*, 107, 17. Hāt twelf weras nyman twelf stānas and habban forþ mid eów *bid twelve men take twelve stones and have them along with you*, Jos. 4, 3. Đā hēt ic eald hrægl tōslītan and habban wiđ đæm fȳre and sceldan mid *jussi ergo scissas vestes opponere ignibus*, Nar. 23, 30. Hwilce gerihtæ hē āhte tō habbanne *what dues he ought to have*, Chr. 1085; Erl. 218, 28: Cd. 15; Th. 18, 26; Gen. 279. Swā đa hālgan dydon đe nāht ne gyrndon tō hæbbenne *as the saints did who did not desire to have anything*, Blickl. Homl. 53, 25. Se deáda byþ uneáđe ǣlcon men on neáweste tō hæbbene *it will be a hard matter for any one to have the dead man in his neighbourhood*, 59, 15. Eall đæt him wæs leófost tō āgenne and tō hæbbene *all that he liked best to own and to have*, 111, 27. Ic hæbbe geweald micel *I have much power*, Cd. 15; Th. 18, 29; Gen. 280. Ic hafo, Beo. Th. 4307; B. 2510. Ic hafu, Exon. 48 a; Th. 166, 10; Gū. 1040. Ic hæbbe đē tō secgenne sum þing *habeo tibi aliquid dicere*, Lk. Skt. 7, 40. Se hafaþ in hondum heofon and eorþan *who hath in his hands heaven and earth*, 42 a; Th. 140, 32; Gū. 619. Đis leóht wē habbaþ wiđ nȳtenu gemǣne *this light we have in common with beasts*, Blickl. Homl. 21, 13. Wē habbaþ nēdþearfe đæt wē ongyton *we have need to perceive*, 23, 1. Đa his mǣre word habbaþ and healdaþ *qui facitis verbum ejus*, Ps. Th. 102, 19. Æfter đisum hæfde se cyng mycel geþeaht *after this the king held a great council*, Chr. 1085; Erl. 218, 22: St. And. 32, 29: Chr. 1050; Erl. 176, 9. Hēr hæfde se cyng his hīrēd æt Gleáweceastre *in this year the king held his court at Gloucester*, 1094; Erl. 229, 27. Penda hæfde xxx wintra rīce and hē hæfde l wintra đā đā hē tō rīce fēng *Penda reigned thirty years, and he was fifty years old when he came to the throne*, 626; Erl. 22, 14. Đæt cilde hæfde læsse đonne þrȳ mōnđas đæs þriddan geáres *the child was not quite two years and three months old*, Shrn. 104, 18: Cd. 55; Th. 68, 14: Gen. 1117. Iudas hæfde onlīcnesse đara manna đe willaþ Godes cyricean yfelian *Judas was like those men that desire to do evil to God's church*, Blickl. Homl. 75, 23. Hæfde cista gehwilc gārberendra x hund *each troop contained a thousand warriors*, Cd. 154; Th. 192, 11; Exod. 230. Hē ongan đa cnyhtas tō āxienne for hwig đæt folc đone Hǣlend swā yfele hæfde. Hig cwǣdon Hig habbaþ andan tō hym *he asked the men why the people treated the Saviour so ill. They said, 'They bear malice to him,'* Nicod. 8; Thw. 4, 18. Hē sceal bión stræc wiđ đa đe āgyltaþ ond for ryhtwīsnesse hē sceal habban andan to hira yfele *contra delinquentium vitia per zelum justitiæ erectus*, Past. 12; Swt. 75, 13. Ōđ đet hē đone castel hæfde *until he got the castle*, Chr. 1102; Erl. 238, 14. Hine se mōdega mǣg Higelāces hæfde be honda *the proud kinsman of Hygelac held him by the hand*, Beo. Th. 1632; B. 814. Æđelwulf his dōhtor hæfde him tō cuēne *Ethelwulf had his daughter for his queen*, Chr. 885; Erl. 84, 5. Heó hyt for Crystes andwlytan ǣfre hæfde *she ever considered it as Christ's countenance*, St. And. 38, 4. Eal þeódscype hine hæfde for fulne cyng *all the nation considered him as full king*, Chr. 1013; Erl. 148, 36: Bt. Met. Fox 26, 87; Met. 26, 44: Mt. Kmbl. 14, 5. Đa Seaxan hæfdun sige *the Saxons got the victory*, Chr. 885; Erl. 84, 8: 909; Erl. 101, 20. Hī hæfdon hine mid heom ōþ đēt hī ofslōgon hine *they had him with them till they slew him*, 1046; Erl. 174, 20. Hī on gewunan hæfdon *they have been accustomed*, L. Eth. 9, 31; Th. i. 346, 28. Hine grame hæfdon tō hæfte *fierce men held him captive*, Ps. Th. 104, 15. Đa hæfdon monige unwīse menn him tō worde and tō leásungspelle *quidam ridiculam fabulam texuerunt*, Ors. 1, 7; Swt. 40, 7. Gif cniht wǣpn brede gilde se hlāford ān pund and hæbbe se hlāford æt đæt hē mǣge *if a follower draw a weapon, let the lord pay one pound, and let the lord get from him what he can*, Th. Chart. 612, 25. Đæt ǣrest is đæt man tō ōđrum lǣđđe hæbbe *the first kind* [*of murder*] *is for a man to bear enmity to another*, Blickl. Homl. 63, 36. Se đe forhogaþ đæt hē ǣnig gemynd hæbbe Drihtnes eáđmōdnesse *he that neglects to have any recollection of the Lord's meekness*, 83, 16. Ǣghwilcum men biþ leófre swā hē hæbbe holdra freónda mā *the more friends every man has the better he likes it*, 123, 1. Be đam sacerde đonne hē mæssaþ hwæt hē on him hæbbe *of the priest when he says mass what he is to have on*, L. Edg. C; Th. ii. 128, 19. Āwriten is đæt đīne englas đē on hondum habban *it is written that thine angels shall take thee in their hands*, 27, 14. Đa hwīle đe wē đæt līf on ūrum gewealde habban *while we have the life in our power*, 101, 11. Uton geþencean hwylc handleán wē him forþ tō berenne habban *let us consider what recompense we have to produce for him*, 91, 14. Hafa đē wunden gold *take for thyself the twisted gold*, Cd. 97; Th. 128, 18; Gen. 2128. Gif man frigne man æt hæbbendre handa gefō *if a freeman be taken with stolen goods upon him*, L. Wiht. 26; Th. i. 42, 15: L. Ath. 1, 1; Th. i. 198, 16: 4, pref. Th. i. 220, 11. Wē beóþ hæbbende đæs đe wē ǣr hopedon *we shall be in possession of that which before we hoped for*, Homl. Th. i. 250, 34. Is seó stōw on micelre ārwurþnysse hæfed *in magna veneratione habetur locus ille*, Bd. 3, 2; S. 524, 12. Mid đȳ hē mid đone gesīþ hæfed wæs *dum apud comitem teneretur*, 4, 22; S. 591, 32. Adam and Eva on bendum wǣron hæfde *Adam and Eve were held in bonds*, Blickl. Homl. 87, 26. II. *with partitive gen*:—Hæbbe ic his on handa *I have some of it in my hand*, Cd. 32; Th. 42, 23; Gen. 678. Se đe đara mihta hæbbe ārǣre ciricean *he who has the means let him erect a church*, L. Pen. 14; Th. ii. 282, 5: L. E. I. 3; Th. ii. 404, 22. Hē ne mōste đæs fyrstes habban đe hē gewilnode *he might not have any of the respite that he desired*, Homl. Th. i. 414, 28. III. *with the gerundial infin. to express the future*:—Đone calic đe ic tō drincenne hæbbe *calicem quem ego bibiturus sum*, Mt. Kmbl. 20, 22 [cf. the formation of the future tense in the Romance languages]. IV. *with an uninflected participle*:—Đū mē forlǣred hæfst *thou hast seduced me*, Cd. 38; Th. 50, 34; Gen. 818. Đæs līfes đe đū hafast ofslegen *the life that thou hast slain*, Exon. 29 b; Th. 90, 25; Cri. 1479. For đissum ælþeódigum đe wē on đissum carcerne betȳned hæbbaþ *on account of this stranger whom we shut up in this prison*, Blickl. Homl. 245, 36. Gē habbaþ ūs gedōn lāđe Pharaone *ye have made us hateful to Pharaoh*, Ex. 5, 21. V. *with an inflected participle, sometimes also with an uninflected participle as well*:—Ic mīnes þeódnes hafa hyldo forworhte *I have forfeited my prince's favour*, Cd. 39; Th. 52, 1; Gen. 836. Đū hæfst đē wiđ dryhten dȳrne geworhtne *thou hast made thyself dear to the Lord*, 25; Th. 32, 22; Gen. 507. Đū hafast helle bereáfod and đæs deáþes aldor gebundenne *thou hast despoiled hell, and bound the prince of death*, Blickl. Homl. 87, 22. Đīn āgen geleáfa đē hæfþ gehǣledne *thine own faith hath saved thee*, 15, 27: 85, 23. Đās þing wē habbaþ be him gewritene *we have written these things about him*, Chr. 1086; Erl. 222, 40. Đā cwæþ Iacob Bearnleásne gē habbaþ mē gedōnne *then said Jacob, Ye have made me childless*, Gen. 42, 36. Hie hine ofslægenne hæfdon *they had slain him*, Chr. 755; Erl. 50, 1: 867; Erl. 72, 9. [*Laym.* habben, han: *Orm.* habbenn, hafenn: *A. R.* habben: *Goth.* haban: *O. Sax.* hebbian: *O. Frs.* hebba, habba: *Icel.* hafa: *O. H. Ger.* haben.] DER. ā-, æt-, be-, for-, ge-, of-, on-, wiđ-, wiđer-, ymb-habban: nabban: bord-, daroþ-, dreám-, eard-, lind-, rand-, searo-hæbbende.

haca, an; *m. A hook* [?], *bolt* or *bar of a door*; pessulus, Gl. Mett. 658. [*Icel.* haki: *Dan.* hage: *Swed.* hake *a hook*: *O. H. Ger.* hako, hakko *uncinus, furca*: *Ger.* haken *a hook, clasp*: and cf. *Icel.* haka *the chin*.] See Skeat's Dict. hake, hatch, hackle.

haccian; p. ode; pp. od *To hack*; concidere, secando comminuere, Lye. [*A. R.* hackede; *p*: *Chauc.* hakke: *O. Frs.* (to-)hakkia: *Dut.* hakken *to hew, chop*: *Dan.* hakke *to hack, hoe*: *Ger.* hacken *to chop, cleave*.] v. tō-haccian.

hacele, an; *f*: hæcla, an; *m* [?] *A cloak, mantle, upper garment, coat, cassock*. Lye gives the following meanings *lacerna, subucula, capsula, mantilia, pl*:—Hacele *clamis*, Ælfc. Gl. 65; Som. 69, 40; Wrt. Voc. 40, 67: 110; Som. 79, 51; Wrt. Voc. 59, 22: 284, 65. Đā bewrāh se ārleása gerēfa his ansȳna mid his hacelan *then the impious count covered his face with his cloak*, Nar. 42, 24. Đā gegyrede heó hȳ mid hǣrenre tunecan and mid byrnan đæt is mid lytelre hacelan *she dressed herself in a tunic of hair and in a byrnie, that is in a little cassock*, Shrn. 140, 30. Đā sende him mon āne blace hacelan angeán *a black mantle* [sagum] *was sent to him*, Ors. 5, 10: Swt. 234, 22. Saulus heóld ealra đæra stǣnendra hacelan *Saul held the garments of all those who were stoning* [*Stephen*], Homl. Th. ii. 82, 22: i. 48, 1. Hæcla *pallium*, Mt. Kmbl. Lind. 5, 40. [*Goth.* hakuls; *m. a cloak*: *O. Frs.* hexil [=hekil (?)]: *Icel.* hekla; *f. a kind of cowled* or *hooded frock*: hökull; *m. a priest's cope*: *O. H. Ger.* hachul *cuculla, casula*.] See Grmm. D. M. 873 ff. DER. mæsse-hacele. 'In the West of England the word *hackle* is specially used of the conical straw roofing that is put over bee-hives. Also, of the "straw covering of the apex of a rick," says Mr. Akerman, *Glossary of Wiltshire words*, v. Hackle.'—Earle's Chronicle, p. 338.

hacine *pusta*, Ælfc. Gl. 33; Som. 62, 21; Wrt. Voc. 28, 4.

hacod, es; *m. A pike*:—Hacod *lucius*, Ælfc. Gl. 102; Som. 77, 69; Wrt. Voc. 55, 72; 77, 73. Hacodas *lucios*, Coll. Monast. Th. 23, 33. [Haked *a large pike* (Cambridgeshire): *O. H. Ger.* hachit, hechit, hæcid *lucius, mugil*: *Ger.* hecht *a pike*.] v. haca.

HĀD, es; *m.* I. *person*; persona:—Đū ne besceáwast nānes mannes hād *non respicis personam hominum*, Mt. Bos. 22, 16. Cyninges naman hæfde and wæs đæs hādes well wyrþe *regis nomine ac persona dignissimus*, Bd. 3, 21; S. 550, 40, MS. B. Weorþian wē đa clāþas his hādes *let us honour the clothes of his person*, Blickl. Homl. 11, 9. Hē wæs on ānum hāde twegra gecynda *he was of two natures in one person*, 33, 33. On þrȳm hādum efnespēdelīcum *in tribus personis consubstantialibus*, Bd. 4, 17; S. 585, 38: Homl. Th. ii. 42, 26. Þrȳ hādas synd worda. Se forma hād is đe sprecþ be him sylfum āna . . . Se ōđer hād đe se forma sprecþ tō . . . Se þridda hād is be đam đe se forma hād sprecþ tō đam ōđrum hāde *there are three persons of verbs. The first person is he who speaks about himself alone . . . The second person is he whom the first speaks to . . . The third person is he about whom the first person speaks to the second person*, Ælfc. Gr. 22; Som. 23, 49–53. Hād đæt is *persona*, 15; Som. 17, 30. II. *sex*:—Gewuldrad is se heánra hād *the humbler sex is glorified*, Exon. 9 a; Th. 7, 10; Cri. 99. Ōđre monige ǣghwæđeres hādes *alii utriusque sexus*, Bd. 1, 7; S. 479, 12. Ǣlcere yldo and hāde *omni ætati et sexui*, 1, 1; S. 473, 22. Đæt hē ne forđon wīflīce hāde ārede *ut ne sexui quidem miliebri parceret*, 2, 20; S. 521, 25. III. *degree, rank, order, condition*:—Hād *gradus*, Ælfc. Gr. 11; Som. 15, 17. Gehwylces hādes menn *men of every degree*, Blickl. Homl. 47, 34: L. Ecg. C. 32; Th. ii. 156, 19. Sundor ānra gehwilc herige in hāde *let each one separately praise thee in their degree*, Cd. 192; Th. 239, 16; Dan. 371: 28; Dan. 377: Th. 240, 27; Dan. 393. Fore ǣlcum hāde ciricelīca *pro omni gradu æcclesiastico*, Rtl. 175, 25: 193, 37. Wer on lǣwedum hāde *vir in laico habitu*, Bd. 5, 13; S. 632, 7: 4, 11; S. 579, 19. Hē on lǣwedum hāde beón sceolde *he had to lead the life of a layman*, Blickl. Homl. 213, 9. Heárra on hāde *higher in rank*, L. Eth. 6, 52; Th. i. 328, 14. Þurh hāligne hād gecȳded *made known by clerks*, Exon. 34 a; Th. 107, 27; Gū. 65. Seofon hādas syndon gesette on bōcum tō Godes þēnungum intō Godes circan *seven orders are appointed in books for God's ministries in God's church*, L. Ælfc. P. 34; Th. ii. 378, 1: L. Ælfc. C. 10; Th. ii. 346, 25. Monige sindon hādas under heofenum *many are the conditions under the heavens*, Exon. 33 a; Th. 104, 3; Gū. 2. Biscopes ođđe ōđera hāda *episcopi vel reliquorum ordinum*, Bd. 2, 5; S. 506, 30. Wiotan ǣgđer ge godcundra hāda ge woruldcundra *wise men both clerks and laymen*, Past. Pref. Swt. 3, 3. Būtan hālgum hādum *extra sacros ordines*, Bd. 1, 27; S. 489, 16. Mid myclum hādum biscopas and cyningas *those of high degree, as bishops and kings*, Blickl. Homl. 109, 23: Homl. Th. ii. 122, 27. Swā wē settaþ be eallum hādum ge ceorle ge eorle *so we ordain for all degrees both gentle and simple*, L. Alf. pol. 4; Th. i. 64, 3. Đām đe heora hādas mid clǣnnesse healdan *to those who keep their orders with purity*, Blickl. Homl. 43, 4. Gemǣnes hādes man *clericus*, L. Ecg. P. 2, 24; Th. ii. 192, 8: 16; Th. ii. 186, 31. Tō hāde fōn *to take orders*, 4, 8; Th. ii. 206, 7. IV. *state, condition, kind, nature, form* [*having the meaning which is preserved in the suffix* -hood, -head]:—Leóht hafaþ hād hāliges gāstes *light hath the nature of the holy spirit*, Salm. Kmbl. 817; Sal. 408. Se heáþrym đæs Godes hādes *the excellent glory of the Godhead*, Blickl. Homl. 131, 18. Onsȳn yldran hādes *the aspect of an older state* [*a more advanced age*], Exon. 40 a; Th. 132, 12; Gū. 471. Wæs se sūþduru hwæthwega hāde māre *the south door was somewhat greater in form*, Blickl. Homl. 201, 15. On weres hāde *in the form of a man*, Elen. Kmbl. 144; El. 72. Onwendan heora wuldor on đæne wyrsan hād hǣđenstyrces *mutaverunt gloriam suam in similitudinem vituli*, Ps. Th. 105, 17. Hād oferhogedon hālgan līfes *they despised the state of a holy life*, Cd. 188; Th. 235, 2; Dan. 300. Fǣmnan hād *virginity*, Exon. 9 a; Th. 6, 31; Cri. 92: 14 a; Th. 28, 10; Cri. 444. Cildes hād, Exon. 65 a; Th. 240, 15; Ph. 639: 61 a; Th. 224, 7; Ph. 372. Þurh cnihtes hād onsȳne wearþ *he became visible in the form of a youth*, Andr. Kmbl. 1824; An. 914. Hæleþa leófost on gesīþes hād *dearest of men as a comrade*, Beo. Th. 2598; B. 1297. Næs sinc-māđđum sēlra on sweordes hād *there was no better treasure among swords*, 4393; B. 2193. Þurh hǣstne hād *by violence*, Beo. Th. 2674; B. 1335: Exon. 8 b; Th. 4, 7; Cri. 49. Þurh monigne hād *in many a form*, 54 b; Th. 191, 34. Blis manigra hāda cwicera cynna *the joy of many kinds of living creatures*, Menol. Fox 182; Men. 92: Exon. 33 a; Th. 105, 15; Gū. 23. [*Laym.* hād, hōd: *Orm.* hād: *A. R.* hōd: *Ayenb.* hōd: *Goth.* haidus *manner, way*: *O. Sax.* hēd: *Icel.* heiđr *honour*: *O. H. Ger.* heit *persona, sexus, ordo, gradus*.]

-hād *a suffix forming abstract nouns*, e. g. bisceop-, cild-, man-, wer-hād, etc. In the oldest English it is found combined only with nouns, while in the later stages of the language, as in *O. Sax. O. Frs. O. H. Ger.* words are formed with it from adjectives. An early instance occurs in the Laud MS. of the Chronicle 'druncenhed,' 1070; Erl. 209, 35. In later English it takes two forms, -hode, -hede; in modern times, -hood, -head. [*O. Sax.* hēd: *O. Frs.* -hēd, -hēde, -heid: *O. H. Ger.* -heit, -heiti: *Ger.* -heit: *Dan.* -hed.] v. hād.

hād-bōt, e; *f. A recompence, compensation*, or *atonement for injury done to persons in holy orders*, or hād-bryce; sacri ordinis violati compensatio, L. E. B. 4; Th. ii. 240, 17: L. O. 12; Th. i. 182, 13.

hād-breca, an; *m. A violator of holy orders*; sacri ordinis violator:—Hād-brēcan *violators of holy orders*, L. C. S. 6; Th. i. 380, 2: Lupi Serm. i. 19; Hick. Thes. ii. 105, 3; Swt. A. S. Rdr, 110, 178.

hâd-brice, -bryce, es; *m.* [hâd II. *holy orders in the church; brice a violation, breach*] *An injury done to persons in holy orders, a violation of holy orders;* ordinis infractura, sacri ordinis violatio :—Gif hwâ hâdbryce gewyrce, gebête ðæt be hâdes mǽðe *if any one do an injury to a person in holy orders, let him make amends for it according to the degree of the order*, L. C. S. 50; Th. i. 404, 16. On hâdbricum [MS. hâdbrican] *in breaches of holy orders*, L. Eth. vi. 28; Th. i. 322, 19: v. 25; Th. i. 310, 18: Swt. A. S. Rdr. 109, 148.

hâdelîce; *adv. Personaliter*, Hymn. Surt. 29, 13.

haderung [=hâd-ârung?] *Personarum acceptio*, Som.

hâd-griþ, es; *n. Peace, security*, or *privilege of holy orders;* sacri ordinis pax, L. Eth. vii. 19; Th. i. 332, 25.

hâdian; *p.* ode; *pp.* od *To ordain:*—Tô ðan ðet hê hine hâdian sceolde *in order that he might ordain him*, Chr. 1048; Erl. 177, 20. Lêton hig hâdian tô bisceopum *they got themselves ordained bishops*, 1053 Erl. 188, 14. Ealdorlîcnys ðæt hê bisceopas hâdian môste *ordinandi episcopos auctoritas*, Bd. 2, 8; S. 510, 5. Hine hâdigean tô bysceope *in episcopatus consecrare gradum*, 3, 7; S. 529, 9, note. Sende hê hine tô hâdiganne *misit eum ordinandum*, 3, 28; S. 560, 8. Hâdigenne, L. Ælf. C. 17; Th. ii. 348, 26. Hêr mon hâdode Byrnstân bisceop tô Wintanceastre *in this year Byrnstan was ordained to the bishopric of Winchester*, Chr. 931; Erl. 110, 22. Ne hâdige man ǽfre wudewan tô hrædlîce *never let a widow take the veil too hastily*, L. C. S. 74; Th. i. 416, 15. [*Laym.* hoded; *pp: Orm.* hædedd.]

hâd-notu, e; *f. The employment, ministry, office belonging to holy orders:*—Bûton hê forworhte ðæt hê ðære hâdnote notian ne môste *unless he should do amiss so that he might not exercise the office which belongs to his orders*, L. R. 7; Th. i. 192, 16.

hâdod; *part. p. used as adj. Ordained, in orders, clerical as opposed to lay:*—Ða witan ge hâdode ge lǽwede *the 'witan,' both clerical and lay*, Chr. 1014; Erl. 150, 4: 1023; Erl. 162, 46: L. Edm. S. pref: Th. i. 246, 20.

hâdor, es; *m. n* [?] *The clear, serene sky;* serenum:—Under heofenes hâdor *under heaven's serene*, Beo. Th. 832; B. 416. [Cf. *O. H. Ger.* heiteri *serenum: Icel.* heið *the brightness of the sky.*] Cf. rodor, *and see* hâdor; *adj.*

hâdor, hǽdor; *adj. Clear [applied both to light and to sound], bright, serene:*—Hâdor heofonleóma *the clear heaven-light*, Andr. Kmbl. 1675; An. 840: 2918; An. 1458: 178; An. 89: Bt. Met. Fox 22, 47; Met. 22, 24. Scôp hwîlum sang hâdor on Heorote *at times the poet sang clear-voiced in Heorot*, Beo. Th. 998; B. 497. Seó sunne on hâdrum heofone scîneþ *the sun shines in the clear sky*, Bt. 9; Fox 26, 15: Bt. Met. Fox 28, 95; Met. 28, 48. Hǽdre heofontungol *the bright stars of the sky*, Exon. 18 a; Th. 43, 23; Cri. 693. Hâdrum nihtum *in clear nights*, Bt. Met. Fox 20, 463; Met. 20, 232. Se ðe heofen þeceþ hâdrum wolcnum *qui operit cœlum nubibus*, Ps. Th. 146, 8. Singaþ hǽdrum stefnum *they sing with clear voices*, Elen. Kmbl. 1492; El. 748. [*O. Sax.* hêdor: *O. H. Ger.* heitar *clarus, splendidus, serenus, micans: Ger.* heiter: *Icel.* heiðr *bright (of the sky, stars).*]

hâdre, hǽdre; *adv. Clearly [of light and of sound]:*—Hâdre scîneþ rodores candel *the lamp of the firmament [the sun] shines brightly*, Beo. Th. 3147; B. 1571. Hǽdre blîcan, scînan *to shine brightly*, Exon. 57 b; Th. 205, 20; Ph. 115: 120 b; Th. 462, 17; Hö. 53: 51 b; Th. 179, 6; Gû. 1257. Swêga mǽste hǽdre *clearly with loudest melody*, 64 b; Th. 239, 10; Ph. 619: 54 a; Th. 190, 26; Az. 79. Ðonne sió sunne sweotolost scîneþ hâdrost of hefone *when from heaven shines the sun most clearly and brightly*, Bt. Met. Fox 6, 7; Met. 6, 4. [*O. Sax.* hêdro.]

hâd-swǽpa *pronuba*, Ælfc. Gl. 93; Som. 75, 79; Wrt. Voc. 52, 29. v. next word.

hâd-swâpe, -swǽpe, an; *f. A bridesmaid;* pronuba, paranymphus = παράνυμφος, Ælfc. Gl. 87; Som. 74, 56, 58; Wrt. Voc. 50, 38, 40: 288, 80. [*Ettmüller compares* hâd *in this word with Gothic*, hêþjo *a chamber.*]

hâdung, e; *f. Ordination:*—On ðare smyrunge biþ lǽcedôm and ne biþ nâ hâdung *in the unction is healing and there is not ordination*, L. Ælfc. P. 48; Th. ii. 384, 33. Bisceopum gebyreþ ðæt hî ne beón tô feohgeorne æt hâdunge *it is fitting for bishops not to be too eager after money at ordination*, L. I. P. 10; Th. ii. 316, 32. On ǽlcere hâdunge se ðe gehâdod biþ hê biþ gesmyrod mid gehâlgodum ele *at every ordination he that is ordained is anointed with consecrated oil*, Homl. Th. ii. 14, 25: 124, 2. Ðæt hê ne hâding ne hâleging ne dô *not to ordain nor consecrate*, Chr. 675; Erl. 38, 4. [*Orm.* hading.]

hæbbendlîc; *adj. Habilis:*—Sume habbaþ sceortne i *amabilis* lufigendlîc, *habilis* hæbbendlîc, Ælfc. Gr. 9, 28; Som. 11. 41.

hæbbenga; *adv. With constraint, constrainedly.* [Somner gives this word and explains it by *cohibitio*, but it appears to be an adverb like eallenga, etc.]

hæbern. v. hæfern.

hæc; *gen.* hæcce; *f. A hatch, grating, a gate made of lattice-work* [?]:—Of ðare ealdan hæcce, Th. Chart. 394, 15, 21: 395, 10, 22, 28: 396, 4, 5, 14. [*Prompt. Parv.* hec, hek, or hetche, or a dore *antica.* On this word the following note is given:—'"Antica, a gate, or a dore, or hatche *est antica domus ingressus ab anteriori*," Ortus. "An heke *antica*," Cath. Ang. "*Ostiolum* hek," Roy. MS. 17 c. xvii. f. 27. "Hatche of a dore *hecq*," Pals. "*Guichét*, a wicket, or hatch of a doore," Cotg. Forby gives "hack, half-hack, a hatch, a door divided across." In the North, a heck-door is one partly latticed and partly panelled.' See also Skeat's Dict. *hatch.*] Cf. haca.

hæca *pessulus*, Som. v. haca.

hæcce, e; *f. A crosier:*—Ðis mycel is gegolden of ðære cyricean W. cyninge . . . of ðam candelstæfe x pund and of dære hæcce xxxiii marca *this much has been paid by the church [of Worcester] to king William . . . from the candlestick x pounds, and from the crosier xxxiii marks*, Th. Chart. 440, 4. Ðæt hæcce wæs eall of gold and of seolfre *the crosier was all of gold and silver*, Chr. 1070; Erl. 209, 9. Eall ðæt ðider com ðæt wæs ðone hæcce and sume scrîne and sume rôden *all that came there was the crosier and some shrines and some crucifixes*, 32. [Cf. haca.]

hæced. v. hacod.

hæcele. v. hacele.

hæcewol *exactor*, Ælfc. Gl. 8; Som. 56, 94; Wrt. Voc. 18, 44.

hæc-wer, es; *m. A weir with a grate to take fish*, Cod. Dipl. Kmbl. iii. 450, 15, 22. ['A salmon-*heck*, a grate to take them in,' English Dialect Society, No. 30, p. 82. v. hæc.]

hæðern. v. hêddern.

hædre; *adv. Straitly, hardly, oppressively, anxiously;* arcte, anxie:—Hyge hædre [hearde, A.] wealleþ *my mind is agitated with anxiety*, Salm. Kmbl. 126; Sal. 62. [Mîne sâwle] hædre gehogode hǽl *save [my soul] oppressed by anxious thoughts*, Exon. 118 b; Th. 456, 5; Hy. 4, 62.

hǽdre. v. hâdre.

hæfd. v. heáfod.

hæfdling. v. efen-hæfdling, heáfodling.

hæfe, es; *m. Leaven;* fermentum:—Warniaþ fram herodes hæfe *cavete a fermento herodis*, Mk. Skt. 8, 15. [Cf. *O. H. Ger.* hefo; *m. fæx: Ger.* hefen *yeast.*] v. ge-hafen.

Hæfeldan *the name of a Slavonic people:*—Wylte ðe man Hæfeldan hǽt, Ors. 1, 1; Bos. 18, 39: 19, 18. In explanation of this double naming, Bosworth, p. 36 (translation), quotes 'Wilsos, Henetorum gentem ad *Havelam* trans Albim sedes habentem.' v. note 12.

hæfen, e; *f. Having, property, possession:*—Be his âgenre hæfene *according to his own property*, Homl. Th. i. 582, 28: 580, 22:, ii. 400, 2. [*Icel.* höfn; *f. a holding, possession:* cf. *O. H. Ger.* haba *possessio: Ger.* habe.]

hæfen, e; *f:* hæfene, an; *f. A haven, harbour, port:*—Of ǽiðre healfe ðare hæfene *from either side of the harbour*, Chr. 1031; Erl. 162, 5. Ic ann ða hæuene on Sandwîc *I grant the port of Sandwich*, Th. Chart. 317, 21. Ða hæfenan on Sandwîc *the port of Sandwich*, Chr. 1031; Erl. 162, 3: 1090; Erl. 226, 26. [*Icel.* höfn; *f: Dan.* havn: *Ger.* hafen.]

hæfen-blǽte, es; *m. A haven-bleater* [?], *a sea-gull;* bugium, Ælfc. Gl. 37; Som. 62, 128; Wrt. Voc. 29, 23.

hæfenleás; *adj. Without property, poor, needy*, Ps. Lamb. 11, 5. v. hafenleás.

hæfenleást, e; *f. Poverty, penury:*—Þurh hæfenleáste *through poverty*, Lchdm. iii. 442, 19: Ps. Lamb. 43, 27. v. hafenleást.

hæfer, es; *m. A he-goat, buck;* caper:—Hæfer *caper*, Wrt. Voc. 288, 17. Nim hæferes smera *take goat's grease*, Lchdm. iii. 14, 8. [*Icel.* hafr: *Lat.* caper.]

hæferbîte, es; *m. Forceps*, Som.

hæferblǽte, es; *m. Bicoca*, Ælfc. Gl. 16; Som. 58, 54; Wrt. Voc. 21, 42: 280, 28. [Cf. hammer-bleat *the snipe*, English Dialect Society, No. 20, p. 42.]

hæfern, es; *m. A crab;* cancer, Wrt. Voc. 281, 63. Hæfern *concern = cancer* [?], 291, 31. v. wæter-hæfern.

hæft, es; *m.* I. *one seized* or *taken, a captive:*—Hê licgan geseah hæftas in hylle *he saw captives lying in hell*, Cd. 229; Th. 309, 27; Sat. 717: 217; Th. 277, 10; Sat. 202: Exon. 10 a; Th. 10, 18; Cri. 154: Andr. Kmbl. 2142; An. 1072. Wê ðê biddaþ ðæt ðû gehýre hæfta stefne *we beseech thee to hear the voice of the captives*, Exon. 13 a; Th. 22, 32; Cri. 360. Under hæftum *amid the captives*, Cd. 220; Th. 284, 9; Sat. 319. II. *one taken and enslaved, a slave, servant:*—Ðâ bebohtan bearn Iacobes Ioseph ðǽr hine grame hæfdon tô hæfte *in servum venumdatus est Ioseph*, Ps. Th. 104, 15. Hweorfon ða hǽðenan hæftas fram ðâm hâlgan cnihton *the heathen slaves went from the holy youths*, Cd. 187; Th. 232, 28; Dan. 267. Gearwe stôdun hæftas heársume *ready stood the slaves obedient*, Exon. 43 a; Th. 145, 19; Gû. 697. [*Icel.* haftr *a prisoner, bondman:* cf. *Goth.* hafts *joined: O. Sax.* haft: *O. H. Ger.* haft *vinctus, captivus.*]

hæft, es; *m.* I. *a bond, fetter;* vinculum:—Bûtan hæftum *without bonds*, Salm. Kmbl. 823; Sal. 411: Cd. 222; Th. 291, 8; Sat. 427. Tô hæftum geferian *to bring into bonds*, 216; Th. 274, 2; Sat. 148: 215; Th. 270, 17; Sat. 92. Of hæftum lǽdan *to bring out of captivity*,

224; Th. 296, 20; Sat. 505: 225; Th. 299, 21; Sat. 553. II. *captivity, bondage, imprisonment, keeping;* captivitas, custodia:—Is ðes hæft tō ðan strang *this imprisonment is so severe*, Elen. Kmbl. 1403; El. 703: Cd. 171; Th. 215, 15; Exod. 583. Hē betǣhte hine on ðam hæfte sixtyne cempum tō healdenne *he committed him to the keeping of sixteen soldiers to hold*, Homl. Th. ii. 380, 29. Hē of hæfte āhlōd folces unrīm *from captivity he drew forth people numberless*, Exon. 16 a; Th. 35, 34; Cri. 568: Andr. Kmbl. 2797; An. 1401: 2938; An. 1472. Him on hæft nimeþ *takes into bondage to him*, 11 b; Th. 16, 29; Cri. 260: 41 a; Th. 138, 1; Gū. 569: Cd. 189; Th. 235, 16; Dan. 307: Chr. 1036; Erl. 164, 31. In hæftum *in custodias*, Lk. Skt. Lind. 21, 12. [*Icel.* haft, hapt; *n. a bond, chain: O. H. Ger.* haft; *m: Ger.* haft; *m. clasp, rivet:* haft; f. *imprisonment.*]

hæft, hæfte, es; *n. A haft, handle;* manubrium:—Hæft and helfe *manubrium*, Ælfc. Gl. 52; Som. 66, 31; Wrt. Voc. 35, 20. Nim ðæt seax ðe ðæt hæfte sīe fealo hryðeres horn *take a knife, the handle of which is yellow ox-horn*, L. M. 2, 65; Lchdm. ii. 290, 22: 52; Lchdm. ii. 272, 21. Folc Ebrēa fuhton hæfte guldon hyra fyrngeflītu fāgum sweordum *the Hebrew folk fought with the haft* [=sword, a part put for the whole, cf. ord, ecg?], *with stained swords repaid their quarrels of old*, Judth. 12; Thw. 25, 16; Jud. 263. [*Prompt. Parv.* heft *manubrium: Icel.* hepti; *n. a haft* or *hilt: O. H. Ger.* hefti *capulum, manubrium: Ger.* heft *haft, handle.*]

hæftan; *p.* hæfte; *pp.* hæfted, hæft *To seize, bind, arrest, make captive, imprison*:—Gif hē nite hwā hine āborgie hæfton hine *if he knows not who will be his surety let them arrest him*, L. Ath. i. 20; Th. i. 210, 8. Seó stōw ðe ðū nū on hæft eart *the place in which you are now imprisoned*, Bt. 11, 1; Fox 32, 27. Hæft mid hringa gesponne *bound with the clasp of rings*, Cd. 25; Th. 47, 17; Gen. 762. Hringan hæfted *confined with rings*, Exon. 102 b; Th. 387, 8; Rä. 5, 2. Tō bodanne hæftedum *prædicare captivis*, Lk. Skt. Rush. 4, 18. [*Goth.* haftjan: *O. Sax.* heftian *to bind, fetter: O. H. Ger.* heftan: *Ger.* heften.] DER. be-, gehæftan. v. hæft.

hæfte-clomm, es; *m. Fetter, bond*:—On hǣðenra hæfteclommum *in the fetters of heathen men*, Chr. 942; Erl. 116, 16.

hæfte-dōm, es; *m. Captivity, service*, Bt. Met. Fox 25, 129; Met. 25, 65.

hæften, e; *f. Captivity, custody*:—Ða betste of ðes eorles hīrēde innan ānan fæstene gewann and on hæftene gedyde *he took the best of the earl's household within a fortress and placed them in custody*, Chr. 1095; Erl. 231, 29.

hæft-encel, -incel, es; *m. A slave;* emptītius, Cot. 74, Lye.

hæfte-neód, e; *f. Custody, prison* [?]:—Ūre bān syndon tōworpene be helwarena hæfteneódum *dissipata sunt ossa nostra secus infernum*, Ps. Th. 140, 9. [Grein gives as the meaning of the word *studium captandi* vel *tribulandi;* but is not *infernum* here paraphrased as the 'prison of the dwellers in hell?']

hæfting, e; *f. A fastening*:—Belūcaþ ða ǣrenan gatu and ða hæftinga gehealdaþ ðæt wē ne beón gehæfte *close the brazen gates and keep the fastenings that we be not captured*, Nicod. 27; Thw. 15, 16. [Cf. *Ger.* heftung.]

hæftling, es; *m. A captive*:—Hæftling *captivus*, Ælfc. Gr. 28; Som. 32, 41. Ðā āxode se ealdorman ðone hæftling hwæðer hē þurh drȳcræft his bendas tōbrǣce *then the alderman asked the captive whether he broke his bonds by witchcraft*, Homl. Th. ii. 358, 10. Nabochodonosor hergode on Iudēiscre leóde and hī hæftlingas tō Babilone gelǣdde *Nebuchadnezzar warred on the Jewish people and led them captives to Babylon*, 58, 6: i. 108, 21: Gen. 31, 26.

hæft-mēce, es; *m. A hilted sword*, Beo. Th. 2918; B. 1457.

hæft-nēd, -niéd, -nȳd, e; *f. Captivity, thraldom, custody*:—Israhēla folc on hæftnēde Babiloniscum cyninge þeówde *the people of Israel served the king of Babylon in captivity*, Homl. Th. ii. 84, 27. Lȳsan of hæftnēde *to release from captivity*, Elen. Kmbl. 593; El. 297. On hæftnēde habban *to hold in captivity*, Blickl. Homl. 85, 23. On hæftnȳde gelǣdan *to lead into captivity*, Ps. Th. 14, argument: L. Ecg. C. 26; Th. ii. 152, 4. All Angelcyn ðæt būton Deniscra monna hæftniéde wæs *all the English that were not held in subjection by the Danish men*, Chr. 886; Erl. 84, 28. On hæftnēd lǣdan, Blickl. Homl. 79, 22. Gehweorf ūre hæftnēd *converte captivitatem nostram*, Ps. Th. 125, 4. Se Drihten ðe ūs fram deófles hæftnēdum ālȳsde *the Lord who redeemed us from the devil's thraldom*, Homl. Th. i. 546, 34. Twegen gerēfan on ðæra hæftnēdum wæs se apostol gehæfd *two counts in whose custody the apostle was held*, ii. 294, 21.

hæftnian; *p.* ede; *pp.* ed *To seize, capture*:—Hī hæftniaþ *captabunt*, Ps. Lamb. 93, 21. Hæftned lǣdde ða on hæftnēde lange lifdon *capitivam duxit captivitatem*, Ps. Th. 67, 18.

hæft-noþ, -neþ, es; *m. Custody, keeping, imprisonment*:—On hæftnoþe biþ gehæfd *he will be imprisoned*, Lchdm. iii. 200, 34. On hæftneþe gebringan *to imprison*, Chr. 1095; Erl. 232, 21. Ðǣr hē on hæftneþe wæs *where he was imprisoned*, 1101; Erl. 237, 40.

hæftnung, e; *f. Captivity, fastening, confinement*:—Hē hine gewrāþ gelomlīce ac hine ne mihte nānes cynnes hæftnung gehealdan *he often bound him, but no kind of fastening could hold him*, Homl. Th. ii. 358, 20. On hæftnunge *in captivity*, 86, 3: Ps. Spl. 13, 11. Ǣr hē forðfērde hē beád ðæt man sceolde unlēsan ealle ða menn ðe on hæftnunge wǣron *ere he departed he ordered that all those men who were in confinement should be released*, Chr. 1086; Erl. 223, 39. Dōn on hæftnunge *to put into confinement, imprison*, 1087; Erl. 225, 36.

hæft-nȳd. v. hæft-nēd.

hægel, hægl, es; *m.* I. *hail*:—Fȳr, forst, hægel and gefeallen snāw *ignis, glacies, grando, nix*, Ps. Th. 148, 8. Hægl, Exon. 56 b; Th. 201, 22; Ph. 60. Cymeþ hægles scūr *a shower of hail cometh*, Cd. 38; Th. 50, 13; Gen. 808. Hæglas and snāwas *hails and snows*, Bt. 39, 13; Fox 234, 16. Heora wīngeardas wrāðe hægle nēde fornāmon *occidit in grandine vineas eorum*, Ps. Th. 79, 47. Sealde heora neát hæglum *tradidit grandini jumenta eorum*, 77, 48. II. the Anglo-Saxon rune ᚻ = *h*, the name of which letter is *hægl*:—ᚻ byþ hwītust corna *hail is whitest of grains*, Hick. Thes. 135; Runic pm. 9; Kmbl. 341, 4. Hægelas twegen *two H's*, Exon. 112 a; Th. 429, 27; Rä. 43, 11. v. hagal.

hæghāl; *adj. Safe, uninjured;* incolumis:—Eftgiondwearda ūsig ārmorgenlīcum tīdum hæghāle *representa nos matutinis horis incolomes*, Rtl. 124, 15: 98, 39: 174, 37.

hægl-faru, e; *f. A hailstorm*, Exon. 78 a; Th. 292, 26; Wand. 105.

hægl-scūr, es; *m. A shower of hail, hailstorm*, Andr. Kmbl. 2515; An. 1259. v. hagal-scūr.

hæg-steald, hæge-, heh-, es; *m: e; f*[?] *One living in the lord's house, not having his own household, an unmarried person, a young person, bachelor, virgin;* mansionarius, cælebs, juvenis, virgo:—Hwæðer hē sig hægsteald ðe hǣmedceorl *utrum cælebs sit an uxoratus*, L. Ecg. C. 1; Th. ii. 132, 28. Hegsteald *cælebs*, 14; Th. ii. 142, 13. Hægsteald mōdige wīgend unforhte *youths courageous, warriors fearless*, Cd. 160; Th. 198, 24; Exod. 327. His hægstealdas *his young warriors*, Fins. Th. 81; Fin. 40. Hægestealdas and fǣmnan *juvenes et virgines*, Ps. Th. 148, 12. Swilce geongum hægstealde *ut ephebo hircitallo*, Mone B. 3434. Hehstald *virgo*, Mt. Kmbl. Lind. 1, 23: Lk. Skt. Lind. 1, 27. Hehstaldo *virgines*, Rtl. 47, 36. Hehstaldun *virginibus*, Mt. Kmbl. Lind. 25, 1. Of heghstalde *de virgine*, Rtl. 126, 3. v. hago-steald.

hæg-steald; *adj. Unmarried, young*:—Hægstealdra, Cd. 89; Th. 111, 28; Gen. 1862: Beo. Th. 3782; B. 1889. See the preceding word.

hægsteald-hād, es; *m. The unmarried state, bachelorhood, virginity*:—Hehstaldhād *virginitas*, Rtl. 105, 19: Lk. Skt. Lind. 2, 36. Hægstealdhād *cælibatus*, Mone B. 1419.

hægsteald-līc; *adj. Virgin;* virginalis, Rtl. 66, 1.

hægsteald-man = hægsteald, *q. v.*, Cd. 151; Th. 190, 1; Exod. 192: Exon. 113 b; Th. 436, 18; Rä. 55, 3.

hægstealdnis, e; *f. Virginity*:—Hehstaltnisse *virginitatis*, Jn. Skt. p. 1, 3.

hægtesse, an; *f. A witch, hag, fury*:—Helle-rūne *vel* hægtesse *pythonissa*, Ælfc. Gl. 112; Som. 79, 102; Wrt. Voc. 60, 10. Hægtesse *Tissiphona*, 113; Som. 79, 115; Wrt. Voc. 60, 22. Gif hēr inne sȳ īsenes dǣl hægtessan geweorc hit sceal gemyltan . . . gif hit wǣre ylfa gescot oððe hit wǣre hægtessan gescot nū ic wille ðīn helpan *if herein there be a bit of iron, a witch's work, it shall melt . . . if it were an elf's shot or it were a witch's shot, now will I help thee*, Lchdm. iii. 54, 1-12. v. Grmm. D. M. 992.

hæg-þorn, es; *m. Hawthorn*:—Hægþorn *alba spina*, Ælfc. Gl. 48; Som. 65, 50; Wrt. Voc. 33, 46. Genim hægþornes leáf *take leaves of hawthorn*, Herb. 37, 6; Lchdm. i. 138, 17. Of ðam mappuldre tō ðam hægþorne *from the maple to the hawthorn*, Cod. Dipl. Kmbl. iii. 424, 3. [*Icel.* hagþorn: *M. H. Ger.* hagedorn.]

hæg-weard, hæcg-, es; *m. A hayward, the keeper of cattle in a common field, who prevented trespass on the cultivated ground*, L. R. S. 20; Th. i. 440, 11, 12. [*A. R.* heiward: *Prompt. Parv.* heyward *agellarius.* The following note is given on this word, p. 234:—'Bp. Kennett observes that there were two kinds of *agellarii*, the common herdward of a town or village, called *bubulcus*, who overlooked the common herd, and kept it within bounds; and the heyward of the lord of the manor, or religious house, who was regularly sworn at the court, took care of the tillage, paid the labourers, and looked after trespasses and encroachments: he was termed fields-man or tithing-man, and his wages in 1425 were a noble. "*Inclusarius* a heyewarde." "*Inclusorius* a pynner of beestes." "Haiward, haward *qui garde au commun tout le bestiail d'un bourgade.*"']

hǣl, es; *n. Omen, auspice*:—Hǣl sceáwedon *they observed the favourable omen* (*for Beowulf's undertaking*), Beo. Th. 414; B. 204. [*Icel.* heill; *n. omen, auspice: O. H. Ger.* heil *omen, auspicium.*]

hǣl, e; *f. Health, safety, salvation, happiness;* salus:—Seó hǣl cymeþ symle fram Gode *salus a domino*, Ps. Th. 36, 38. Tō-dæg ðisse hīwrǣdene ys hǣl geworden *this day is salvation come to this house*, Lk. Bos. 19, 9: Homl. Th. i. 582, 5. Cristes þēnung is ūre hǣl and folca ālȳsednys

Christ's service is our salvation and the redemption of peoples, ii. 586, 32. Him cymþ gōd hǣl *good health will come to them*, Lchdm. i. 342, 9. Sȳ him hǣl *Osanna*, Mt. Kmbl. 21, 9. Hrædlīce heora hǣle brūcaþ *speedily they enjoy their health*, Homl. Th. i. 510, 8. Brūc ðisses beáges mid hǣle *use this collar with good fortune*, Beo. Th. 2438; B. 1217. Hēht hē Elenan hǣl ābeódan *he bade them greet Elene*, Elen. Kmbl. 2004; El 1003: Beo. Th. 1311; B. 653. Ðīne hǣle syle *salutare tuum da*, Ps. Th. 84, 6. [*Laym.* heal: *O. Sax.* hēli; *f: Icel.* heill; *f. good luck happiness: O. H. Ger.* heili; *f. salus.*] Cf. hǣl; *n. and* hǣlu.

hǣl; *adj. Hale, safe, whole, sound*:—Hǣle and trume *safe and sound*, Blickl. Homl. 171, 30. v. hāl.

hǣla. v. hēla.

hǣlan; *p.* de; *pp.* ed *To heal, make whole, cure, make safe, save*; sanare, salvare:—Ys hyt ālȳfed tō hǣlenne on restedagum *si licet sabbatis curare*, Mt. Bos. 12, 10. Earm heora ne hǣlþ hig *brachium eorum non salvavit eos*, Ps. Spl. 43, 4. Sweord mīn ne hǣlþ mē *gladius meus non salvabit me*, 43, 8. Hǣl ūs on heánessum *Hosanna in the highest*, Blickl. Homl. 72, 12: Jn. Skt. Rush. 12, 13. Hǣlaþ untrume *heal the sick*, Mt. Bos. 10, 8. Ic offrige mīne lāc Hǣlendum Criste *I will present my offerings to Jesus Christ*, Homl. Th. i. 416, 17. Hī hrædlīce hǣlde wǣron *sanavit eos*, Ps. Th. 106, 19. [*Goth.* hailjan: *O. Sax.* hēlean: *O. Frs.* hēla: *O. H. Ger.* heilan *sanare, curare, salvare*: *Ger.* heilen.]

hǣl-bǣre; *adj. Salutary*, Lye.

hæle, es; *m. A man, brave man, hero* [a word occurring only in poetry]:—Frōd hæle *the aged man*, Cd. 62; Th. 74, 14; Gen. 1222. Boitius se hæle hātte *that man was called Boethius*, Bt. Met. Fox 1, 105; Met. 1, 53: Cd. 74; Th. 90, 28; Gen. 1502: 112; Th. 147, 27; Gen. 2446: 121; Th. 156, 16; Gen. 2589: Andr. Kmbl. 287; An. 144. [*Icel.* (in poetry only), halr *a man.*]

hǣle, an; *f. Health, safety*:—On gode standeþ mīn gearu hǣle *in Deo salutare meum*, Ps. Th. 61, 7.

hǣlend, hēlend, es; *m. A healer, Saviour, Jesus*:—Se Hǣlend ðe is genemned Crist *Iesus qui vocatur Christus*, Mt. Bos. 1, 16. Ðū nemst hys naman Hǣlend. Hē sōþlīce hys folc hāl gedēþ fram hyra synnum *vocabis nomen ejus Iesum; ipse enim salvum faciet populum suum a peccatis eorum*, 1, 16. Iesus is on Lēden Saluator and on Englisc Hǣlend *Jesus is in Latin Salvator and in English healer*, Homl. Th. ii. 214, 22: i. 94, 27: Shrn. 47, 28. Hǣlend Crist *Jesus Christ*, Homl. Th. i. 420, 32. Ðū eart sōþ hēlend *thou art the true Saviour*, Hy. Grn. 8, 16. [*Laym.* hælend (2nd MS. helare): *Orm.* hælennde: *O. Sax.* hēliand: *O. H. Ger.* heilant: *Ger.* heiland.]

hǣlendlīc; *adj. Healthy, salutary*; salvans, prosperus, Hpt. Gl. 442, 511. [*O. H. Ger.* heilantlih *salubris.*]

hǣletend. v. hālettend.

hæleþ, heleþ, es; *m. A man, warrior, hero* [a word occurring only in poetry, but there frequently]:—Gleáwferhþ hæleþ *the man wise of mind*, Cd. 57; Th. 70, 12; Gen. 1152: 59; Th. 72, 6; Gen. 1182, 94; Th. 122, 13; Gen. 2026: Beo. Th. 383; B. 190: 668; B. 331. Hæleþas heardmōde *warriors stern-minded*, Cd. 15; Th. 19, 2; Gen. 285. Hæleþ hātene wǣron Sem and Cham Iafeþ þridde *the heroes were named Shem and Ham, the third Japhet*, Cd. 75; Th. 93, 22; Gen. 1550. Hæleþa scyppend *creator of men*, Exon. 11 b; Th. 17, 7; Cri. 266: Cd. 98; Th. 129, 6; Gen. 2139: Andr. Kmbl. 41; An. 21. Hæleþa bearn *the children of men*, Cd. 35; Th. 46, 30; Gen. 752. Heleþa sceppend *creator of men*, Hy. Grn. 8, 34. [*Laym.* hæleþ, heleþ: *O. Sax.* helið: *O. H. Ger.* helid (appears first in 12th cent. v. Graff. iv. 544): *Ger.* held.]

hæleþ-helm, es; *m. A helm which makes the wearer invisible*, Cd. 23; Th. 29, 2; Gen. 444. [*O Sax.* helið-helm: *O. H. Ger.* helot-, helant-helm *latibulum.*] v. Grm. D. M. 432, and cf. heoloþ-helm.

hǣletoþ, es; *m. Greeting, Hosanna*, Hpt. Gl. 467.

hǣlettung, e; *f. A greeting, salutation*:—Hǣlettungæ on gemōte *salutationes in foro*, Mt. Kmbl. Rush. 23, 7.

hælftre, e; *f. A halter*:—Hælftre *capistrum*, Wrt. Voc. 84, 8. On hælftre *in camo*, Ps. Spl. C. 31, 12. Hælftra *chamos*, Coll. Monast. Th. 28, 1. [*O. H. Ger.* halftra *brachiale, capistrum*: *Ger.* halfter.]

hǣlig; *adj. Slippery, easily moved, fickle, inconstant*; levis:—Ðam ungestæþþegan and ðam hǣlgan ðū miht secggan ðæt hē biþ winde gelīcra oððe unstillum fugelum *levis, atque inconstans studia permutat? nihil ab avibus differt*, Bt. 37, 4; Fox 192, 23. [Cf. *Icel.* hāll *slippery: O. H. Ger.* hāli *lubricus, caducus.*]

hǣling, e; *f. Healing*:—Ic nān yfel on hym næbbe gemēt be hǣlinge *I have found no evil in him with regard to healing*, Nicod. 10; Thw. 5, 21. [*Prompt. Parv.* heelinge: *O. H. Ger.* heilunga *sanatio*: *Ger.* heilung.]

hǣlnes, se; *f.* I. *haleness, salvation*:—Nū sint hǣlnesse dagas *now are the days of salvation*, Past. 36, 1; Swt. 246, 14. II. *a sanctuary*:—On circan and on hǣlnessan *in churches and sanctuaries*, L. Eth. 7, 25; Th. i. 334, 26. v. hālignes.

hǣlnes-griþ, es; *n. Privilege of security belonging to a sanctuary*, L. Eth. 7, 19; Th. i. 332, 25.

hǣlo. v. hǣlu.

hǣlsend, es; *m. An augur*, Cot. 73, Lye.

hǣlsere, es; *m. A soothsayer, diviner*; aruspex, augur, extispex, Cot. 190: exorcista, Lye. v. hālsere.

hǣlsian *to foretell*; augurari, ariolari, auspicari, Cot. 14, 17, Lye. v. hālsian.

hǣlsung, e; *f. Divination, augury*; augurium, Cot. 11, Lye.

hǣlþ, e; *f. Health, healing, cure*:—Ðām ārīst rihtwīsnysse sunne and hǣlþ is on hyre fiðerum *to them shall arise the sun of righteousness, and healing is on its wings*, Lchdm. iii. 236, 31. Ðes þegen bæd for his þeówan hǣlþe *this officer prayed for the health of his servant*, Homl. Th. i. 128, 1. For hǣlþe heora untrumra *for the healing of their sick*, ii. 396, 21. Ūre līchamana hǣlþe wē āwendaþ *we pervert the health of our bodies*, 540, 9. Ealle ða wundra and hǣlþa āwrītan *to write down all the miracles and cures*, 28, 10. [*O. H. Ger.* heilida *sanitas, salus.*]

hǣlu, hǣlo; *indecl. f. Health, safety, salvation*:—Æt him is hǣlu mīn *ab ipso salutare meum*, Ps. Th. 61, 1. Sȳ hǣlu ūrum Gode ðe sitt ofer his þrymsetle *salvation be to our God that sitteth on his throne*, Homl. Th. i. 538, 18. Hǣlo, Exon. 13 b; Th. 26, 1; Cri. 411. Hǣlu būtan sāre *health without pain*, 32 a; Th. 101, 8; Cri. 1655. Tō hǣlo hȳðe *to a haven of safety*, 20 b; Th. 53, 33; Cri. 860. For heora sāwla hǣlu *for the salvation of their souls*, Homl. Th. ii. 344, 1. Hǣlo, L. M. Th. i. 102, 7. Uton hǣlu sēcan *let us seek salvation*, Exon. 97 b; Th. 365, 11; Wal. 87. Drihten ūs sealde hǣlu and ēce ālȳsednysse *the Lord gave us salvation and eternal redemption*, Homl. Th. ii. 248, 25. Heó forstæl hire hǣlu *she stole her health*, 394, 12. Gif gie hǣlo beádas *si salutaveritis*, Mt. Kmbl. Lind. 5, 47. v. hǣl.

hǣlu-bearn, hǣlo-, es; *n. A child who brings salvation, the Saviour*, Exon. 16 a; Th. 37, 1; Cri. 586: 19 a; Th. 47, 12; Cri. 754.

hǣman; *p.* de; *pp.* ed *To lie with, have intercourse with, to marry*; concumbere, coire, nubere:—Wit wǣron swīðe unrōte geworden for ðȳ hǣmede ðe wē wēndon ðæt wit hǣman sceoldon *we became very sad on account of the intercourse that we expected we should be obliged to have*, Shrn. 39, 21. Mid ðām hæleþum hǣman wolden, Cd. 112; Th. 148, 18; Gen. 2458. Gif hwylc man wið ōðres riht-ǣwe hǣmþ *if any man lie with the lawful wife of another*, L. Ecg. P. ii. 8; Th. ii. 184, 21. Hē hǣmþ unrihtlīce *he commits adultery*, Homl. Th. ii. 208, 16. Ðām mannum ðe deófol mid hǣmþ *for those women with whom the devil hath carnal commerce*, L. M. 3, 61; Lchdm. ii. 344, 8. Ne hǣmeþ ne hǣmde bióþ *neque nubent neque nubentur*, Mt. Kmbl. Rush. 22, 30: 19, 10. Gif hwilc carlman hǣmde wið wimman hire unþances *if any man lay with a woman against her will*, Chr. 1086; Erl. 222, 7: Num. 25, 1. Ne hǣm ðū unrihtlīce *commit not adultery*, Homl. Th. ii. 198, 7. Gif ǣnig man hǣme mid ōðres wīfe *if a man be found lying with a woman married to an husband*, Deut. 22, 22: L. Alf. pol. 10; Th. i. 98, 9.

hǣmed, es; *n. A lying with, sexual intercourse, marriage*; coitus:—Ða ðe rihtlīce healdaþ hyra ǣwe and for bearnes gestreóne hǣmed begāþ *those who rightly observe their marriage and for procreation of children have carnal intercourse*, Homl. Th. i. 148, 22. Mægþhād biþ forloren on hǣmede *maidenhead is lost in intercourse*, ii. 10, 5: 220, 4. Be hǣmede *de coitu*, L. Ecg. C; Th. ii. 128, 26. On unrihton hǣmede *in adulterio*, Jn. Skt. 8, 4: Shrn. 132, 6. Ic wið brȳde ne mōt hǣmed habban *with a bride I may not have intercourse*, Exon. 105 b; Th. 402, 11; Rä. 21, 28. Hǣmed *connubium*, Mone Gl. 340. Hǣmeda *connubii convenientia*, 417. Hǣmeða *himeneas*, Ælfc. Gl. 9; Som. 56, 119; Wrt. Voc. 19, 2. Hǣmdo *nubtiæ*, Jn. Skt. Lind. Rush. 2, 1.

hǣmed-ceorl, es; *m. A married man*:—Hwæðer hē sig hægsteald ðe hǣmedceorl *utrum cælebs sit an uxoratus*, L. Ecg. C. 1; Th. ii. 132, 28.

hǣmed-gemāna, an; *m. Matrimony, marriage*; matrimonium, Cot. 129, Lye.

hǣmed-gifta, *pl. f. Nuptials*; hymenæi, Cot. 102, Lye.

hǣmed-lāc, es; *n. Sexual intercourse*; coitus, Exon. 112 a; Th. 429, 11; Rä. 43, 3.

hǣmed-scipe, es; *m. Marriage, matrimony*; connubium, Hpt. Gl. 482: lenocinium, seductio, 521.

hǣmed-þing, es; *n. Carnal intercourse, venery, matrimony*:—Sió lufu ðæs hǣmedþinges biþ for gecynde *the desire of intercourse is from nature*, Bt. 34, 11; Fox 152, 14: Blickl. Homl. 59, 16. Be hǣðenra manna hǣmedþincge *de gentilium hominum matrimonio*, L. Ecg. C; Th. ii. 128, 27. Gif hī him betwynan hǣmedþing fremmen *si inter se fornicationem commiserint*, 16; Th. ii. 144, 9. Be hǣmedþingum: eallum þyrrum līchomum hǣmedþing ne dugon *of venery: venery does not do for all dry constitutions*, L. M. 2, 27; Lchdm. ii. 222, 28: 36; Lchdm. ii. 244, 4.

hǣmed-wīf, es; *n. A married woman*; uxor, matrona, Cot. 136, Lye.

hǣmere, es; *m. One who lies with another*; concubinus, Lye.

hæn, hen, henn, e; *f. A hen*:—Hæn *gallina*, Recd. 36, 56; Wrt. Voc. 63, 10. Seó henn *gallina*, Mt. Kmbl. 23, 37: Lind. Rush. henne. Hænne æges geolocan *the yolk of a hen's egg*, L. M. 1, 2, 23; Lchdm

ii. 38, 6: 3, 2; Lchdm. ii. 40, 10. [*Icel.* hæna: *O. H. Ger.* henna: *Ger.* henne.]

hǽnan; *p.* de; *pp.* ed *To stone*:—For hwylcum ðæra weorca wylle gē mē hǽnan . . . ne hǽne wē ðē for gōdum weorce *propter quod eorum opus me lapidatis . . . de bono opere non lapidamus te*, Jn. Skt. 10, 32, 33: 11, 8. Ðū ðe ða wītegan hǽnst *quæ prophetas lapidas*, Lk. Skt. 13, 34. Eall folc ūs hǽnþ *plebs universa lapidabit nos*, 20, 6. Hǽne hine man mid stānum *let him be stoned with stones*, Lev. 20, 2. v. hān.

hænep, henep, es; *m. Hemp*:—Henep, hænep, Herb. 27, 1; Lchdm. i. 124, 1, 3: Lchdm. iii. 22, 31. [*Icel.* hampr: *O. H. Ger.* hanaf: *Ger.* hanf: *Lat.* cannabis: *Grk.* κάνναβις. 'Grimm and Kuhn both consider the Greek word borrowed from the East, and the Teutonic one from the Latin *cannabis*, which certainly made its way to them.' Curtius, i. 173.]

hæn-fugul, hen-, es; *m. A hen*: — Henfugel *gallina*, L. Ecg. C. 40; Th. ii. 164, 21. Gewurp tō sumum hen [hæn, MS. B.] fugule *throw it to a hen*, Herb. 4, 10; Lchdm. i. 92, 16. iiii hænfugulas *four hens*, Th. Chart. 509, 18. Ðǽr æfter swulten ða henne fugeles *after that the hens died*, Chr. 1130; Erl. 259, 25.

hænne-belle, an; *f. Henbane*; hyoscyamus, Lchdm. iii. 60, 7. Henne-belle, Herb. 5, 1; Lchdm. i. 94, 3, 6. Henne-belle *simphoniaca*, Ælfc. Gl. 40; Som. 63, 96; Wrt. Voc. 30, 42.

hænnewol; *n. m. Henbane*, Lchdm. iii. Gloss.

hæplīc; *adj. Equal*; compar, Cot. 35, Lye. v. ge-hæp.

hæpse, an; *f. A hasp, clasp, fastening*:—Hæpse *sera*, Wrt. Voc. 81, 20: *clustella*, Hpt. Gl. 500. Sum slōh ða hæpsan *one struck the hasps* [*of the door*], Th. An. 124, 14. [*Prompt. Parv.* hespe of a dore *pessulum*: *Icel.* hespa *a hasp, fastening*: *Ger.* haspe.]

hæpsian; *p.* ode; *pp.* od *To hasp, fasten with a bolt*:—Ic scitte sum loc oððe hæpsige *sero*, Ælfc. Gr. 37; Som. 39, 21.

hǽr, hēr, es; *n. Hair, a hair*:—Hǽr *capillus*, Wrt. Gl. 70, 30: *pilus*, Recd. 38, 21; Wrt. Voc. 64, 30. Hǽr *pili*, Ælfc. Gl. 70; Som. 70, 54; Wrt. Voc. 42, 62. Loccas *vel* unscoren hǽr *comæ*, 70, 56; Wrt. Voc. 42, 64. Gif hǽr tō þicce sīe *if the hair be too thick*, L. M. i. 87, 3; Lchdm. ii. 156, 8. Ne sceal eów beón forloren ān hǽr of eówrum heáfde *there shall not a hair of your head be lost*, Homl. Th. i. 236, 22. Ðū ne miht wyrcan ān hǽr ðīnes feaxes hwīt oððe blacc *thou canst not make one hair of thy locks white or black*, 482, 19. His reáf wæs geworht of oluendes hǽre *his raiment was wrought of camel's hair*, ii. 38, 9. Ðæt īren ne cume on hǽre ne on nægle *that iron come not on hair, nor on nail*, L. Pen. 10; Th. ii. 280, 20. Ne losaþ ðæt heáfod ðonne ða hǽr beóþ ealle geedstaðelode *the head perishes not when the hairs are all restored*, Homl. Th. ii. 542, 35. Wið wiðerweard hǽr onweg tō ādōnne *for contrarious hairs, to remove them*, Lchdm. i. 362, 8. Hēras heáfdes *capilli capitis*, Mt. Kmbl. Lind. 10, 30. Hiora is mycle mā ðonne ic mē hæbbe on heáfde nū hǽra feaxes *multiplicati sunt super capillos capitis mei*, Ps. Th. 68, 4. Mið hērum oððe fæx hire *capillis suis*, Jn. Skt. Lind. 11, 2. Se eádiga wæs blīðe on andwlitan mid hwītum hǽrum *the blessed man was cheerful in aspect, with white hair*, Homl. Th. ii. 186, 20. Mid olfendes hǽrum gescrȳd *clothed with camel's hair*, i. 330, 2: Mt. Kmbl. 3, 4. Ic beleás hērum ðām ðe ic hæfde *I lost the hairs that I had*, Exon. 107 a; Th. 407, 36; Rä. 27, 5. [*O. Sax.* hār: *O. Frs.* hēr: *Icel.* hār: *O. H. Ger.* hār: *Ger.* haar.] For notices as to the importance attached to the hair in early times, see Grimm R. A. pp. 146, 240, 283, 339, 702; and see *feax* and its compounds. DER. hrycg-, tægl-hǽr.

hǽre, an; *f. Hair-cloth, sack-cloth*; cilicium, saccus:—Gefyrn hī dydun dǽdbōte on hǽran and on axan *olim in cilicio et cinere pœnitentiam egissent*, Mt. Kmbl. 11, 21. Mid hǽran gescrȳdd *clad in sackcloth*, Homl. Th. ii. 312, 27: Ps. Spl. 34, 15. Se cyning dyde hǽran tō his līce *the king put sackcloth next to his skin*, Homl. Th. i. 568, 13. Ðū slite hǽran mīne *conscidisti saccum meum*, Ps. Spl. 29, 13. [*Laym.* ane ladliche here: *A. R.* here, heare, 'Iudit werede heare:' *Prompt. Parv.* hayre *cilicium*. *Cilicium, velamen factum de pilis caprarum* a heere. An haire *cilicium*: *Icel.* hæra; *f*: *O. H. Ger.* hārra, hāra; *f. cilicium, saccus.*]

hærean-fagol [?] *a hedge-hog*:—Stān gener hæreanfagol *petra refugium herinaciis*, Ps. Spl. 103, 19. v. hatte-fagol.

hærelof. v. herelof.

hǽren; *adj. Made of hair*; cilicius:—Hē hine ðā gegyrede mid hǽrenum hrægle swīðe heardum and unwinsumum *he clothed himself then with a garment of hair very hard and unpleasant*, Blickl. Homl. 221, 24. Wring þurh hǽrenne clāþ *wring through a hair cloth*, Lchdm. i. 382, 21. Reáf hǽren *vestimentum cilicium*, Ps. Lamb. 68, 12. [*Wick.* heeren: *M. H. Ger.* hǽrin: *Ger.* hären.]

hærenes. v. herenes.

hærfest, es; *m. Harvest, autumn*:—Hærfest *autumnus*, Ælfc. Gl. 95; Som. 76, 9; Wrt. Voc. 53, 23. Autumnus is hærfeste, Lchdm. iii. 250, 11. Se hærfest welig on wæstmum *the autumn rich in fruits*, Bt. 14, 1; Fox 40, 27: 21; Fox 74, 22; Bt. Met. Fox 29, 123; Met. 29, 62. Hærfest *æstatem*, Ps. Spl. 73, 18. Ðæt gewrixle ðara feówer tȳda ðæt is lencten and sumer and herfest and winter *the change of the four seasons, that is spring and summer and autumn and winter*, Shrn 168, 12. Ðæs ilcan hærfestes *in the course of the same autumn*, Chr. 921; Erl. 107, 13. Foran tō hærfestes emnihte *ante æquinoctium autumnale*, L. Ecg. P. 11; Th. ii. 208, 2: Th. Chart. 151, 11. On hærfæste *in autumno*, Coll. Monast. Th. 26, 5. Ðis wæs on hærfest *this was in autumn*, Chr. 918; Erl. 104, 16. [*Prompt. Parv.* herueste *autumpnus*: *Icel.* haust; *n. autumn*: *O. H. Ger.* herbist; *m. autumnus*: *Ger.* herbst *autumn.*]

hærfest-handful *a due belonging to the husbandmen on an estate*:—Eallum ǽhte-mannum gebyreþ hærfesthandful *omnibus ehtemannis jure competit manipulus Augusti*, L. R. S. 9; Th. i. 436, 1.

hærfestlīc; *adj. Autumnal*:—Hærfestlīc dæg *autumnalis dies*, Ælfc. Gl. 95; Som. 76, 19; Wrt. Voc. 53, 29. On ðæs hærfestlīcan emnihtes ryne *in the course of the autumnal equinox*, Lchdm. iii. 238, 28: 252, 1.

hærfest-mōnaþ, es; *m. September*, Ælfc. Gr. 9, 18; Som. 9, 54. [Cf. *Robt. of Glouc.* Þe nexte moneþ afturward, þat heruest moneþ ys, He let clepe aftur hym August ywys. *Icel.* haust-mānuðr: *O. H. Ger.* herbist-manoþ: *Ger.* herbst-monat *September.*]

hærfest-wǽta, an; *m. Autumnal wet*; humor æstatis, Ors. 3, 3; Swt. 102, 7.

hǽriht; *adj. Hairy*; crinitus, setosus, Cot. 186, Lye.

hæring, es; *m. A herring*:—Hwæt fēhst ðū on sǽ? Hæringcas *quid capis in mari? Aleces*, Coll. Monast. Th. 24, 9. Ðes hæring *hoc allec*, Ælfc. Gr. 9; Som. 14, 22. Hæring *allec vel jairus* vel *taricius* vel *sardina*, Ælfc. Gl. 102; Som. 77, 80; Wrt. Voc. 56, 3. Hærinc *taricus* vel *allec*, Wrt. Voc. 77, 62. xxx þūsenda hæryngys ǽlce eáre 30 *thousand herrings every year*, Cod. Dipl. Kmbl. iv. 172, 3. [*O. Frs.* hereng: *O. H. Ger.* harinc: *Ger.* häring.]

hæring-tīma, an; *m. Herring-season*:—Twegen hæringc-tīman *two herring-seasons*, Th. Chart. 338, 34.

hǽrlīc. v. hērlīc.

hǽr-loccas; *m. pl. Locks of hair, curls*; cincinni, crines, Hpt. Gl. 526.

hærn, e; *f. The tide, waves, sea*:—Hærn *æstus, flustrum*, Cot. 81, Lye. Hærn eft onwand *back went the waves*, Andr. Kmbl. 1062; An. 531. [*Icel.* hrönn *a wave.*]

hærn *or* hærne [?], es; *m. n? The brain*:—It gæde tō ðe hærnes *it went to the brains*, Chr. 1137; Erl. 262, 6. [*Prompt. Parv.* hernys *or* brayne *cerebrum*; herne panne of þe hed *craneum*: *Icel.* hjarni; *m*: *O. H. Ger.* hirni; *n. cerebrum*: *Ger.* hirn; *n.*]

hǽr-nǽdl, e; *f. A hair-pin*; calamistrum, Lye.

hærn-flota, an; *m. A wave-floater, ship*, Exon. 52 a; Th. 182, 9; Gū. 1307.

hær-sceard, es; *n. Hare-lip*:—Wið hærscearde *for hare-lip*, L. M. 1, 13; Lchdm. ii. 56, 5. [Cf. *Frs.* haskerde *hare-lipped*: *Icel.* skarði *hare-lip* (a nickname): *Ger.* hasenscharte *hare-lip.*]

hærþan. v. herþan.

hǽs, e; *f. A command, hest, behest*:—Hǽs *jussio*, Ælfc. Gr. 9; Som. 8, 40. Gehīr God mīn gebed *exaudi Deus orationem meam*. On ðysum is gebed and nā hǽs *hear my prayer, O God. In this there is a prayer, not a command*, Ælfc. Gr. 33; Som. 37, 52: Cd. 6; Th. 8, 14; Gen. 124. Be his hlāfordes hǽse *by his lord's command*, Gen. 24, 10: Ex. 18, 23: Cd. 46; Th. 59, 18; Gen. 965: 69; Th. 82, 31; Gen. 1370: 85; Th. 106, 35; Gen. 1781. Būton ǽnigre hǽse *abs quolibet jussu*, Ælfc. Gr. 47; Som. 47, 54. Under abbodes hǽsum *under the commands of an abbot*, Homl. Th. ii. 118, 29. [*Orm.* hæs: *Laym. A. R.* hest: cf. *Goth.* haiti.] DER. be-hǽs.

hæsel *galerus*, Lye.

hæsel, es; *m. The hazel*:—Hæsel *corilus*, Ælfc. Gl. 45; Som. 64, 95; Wrt. Voc. 32, 30. Hæsles ragu *the lichen of hazel*, L. M. i. 38, 8; Lchdm. ii. 96, 2: L. M. 2, 52; Lchdm. ii. 270, 22. Hwīt hæsel *wich hazel*; ulmus montana: saginus, Ælfc. Gl. 45; Som. 64, 96; Wrt. Voc. 32, 31. [*Prompt. Parv.* hesyl *corulus, colurnus*: *Icel.* hasl; *m*: *O. H. Ger.* hasal; *m*: hasala; *f. corylus, amygdalus*: *Ger.* hasel; *f.*] For special virtue of the hazel see Grmm. D. M. 927, and cf. hæslen. Cf. also the *Icel.* hasla völl *to challenge to a duel on a field marked out by hazel-poles.*

hæsel-hnutu, e; *f. A hazel-nut*: — Hæsl *vel* hæsel-hnutu *abellanæ*, Ælfc. Gl. 47; Som. 65, 43; Wrt. Voc. 33, 40. [*O. H. Ger.* hasal-nuz: *Ger.* hasel-nuss.]

hæsel-wrid, es; *n. m* [?] *A hazel-thicket*:—Tō ðam miclan hæslwride *to the great hazel-thicket*, Cod. Dipl. Kmbl. ii. 250, 34. v. gewrid.

hæsel-wyrt, e; *f. Asarabacca, asarum Europæum*, Lchdm. iii. 329, col. 2.

hǽsere, es; *m. A commander, one who orders, commands, a master, lord*:—Hǽsere *præceptor*, Lk. Skt. Lind. 8, 24, 45: 9, 49: 17, 13: 21, 7. Hǽsere *imperator*, Rtl. 192, 39.

hæslen; *adj. Of hazel*: — Genim æt fruman hæslenne sticcan oððe ellenne wrīt ðīnne naman on āsleah þrȳ scearpan on gefylle mid ðȳ blōde ðone naman weorp ofer eaxle on yrnende wæter and stand ofer ðone man ða scearpan āsleá ðæt eall swīginde gedō *take, to begin with, a hazel or an elder stick, cut thy name thereon, cut three scores on the place, fill the* *name with the blood, throw it over thy shoulder into running water and stand over the man. Strike the scores, and do all that in silence*, L. M. 1, 39; Lchdm. ii. 104, 6–11. Lǽt ðæt blôd on grêne sticcan hæslenne weorp ðonne ofer weg âweg ðonne ne biþ nân yfel *let the blood run into a green spoon of hazel-wood, then throw it away over the road; then no harm will come of the bite*, 68; Lchdm. ii. 142, 19–21.

hǽst, hêst, e; *f. Violence, fury:*—Ic þurh hêst hrîno lâðgewinnum *I violently touch my foes*, Exon. 104 b; Th. 397, 31; Rä. 16, 28. Fære ne môston wætres brôgan hǽste hrînan *the terrors of the water might not with violence touch the vessel*, Cd. 69; Th. 84, 11; Gen. 1396. [Hǽste may also be taken either as *adj.* agreeing with brôgan (v. next word), or as an adverb.] Grein compares with *Goth.* haifsts.

hǽst, hǽste [?]; *adj. Violent, vehement, impetuous:*—Ðû Grendel cwealdest þurh hæstne hâd heardum clammum *thou didst kill Grendel violently with hard grasps*, Beo. Th. 2674; B. 1335. Nǽfre ðû ðæs swîðlîc sâr gegearwast þurh hǽstne nîþ ðæt ðû mec onwende worda ðissa *never shalt thou, through vehement hate, pain so violent prepare as to turn me from these words*, Exon. 66 b; Th. 246, 3; Jul. 56. Ðæt sceal wrecan swefyl and sweart lîg sâre and grimme hât [Junius hâte] and hǽste hǽðnum folce *sulphur and swart flame, sorely and fiercely, hot and vehement shall avenge it on the heathen folk* [Junius' reading might be taken and hǽste would then be an adverb parallel with sâre *and* grimme: v. preceding word], Cd. 110; Th. 146, 2; Gen. 2416. [Cf. Grff. iv. 969, '*Si quis in curte episcopi armatus contra legem intraverit, quod alamanni* haistera hanti *dicunt:*' and for similar expressions, v. Grmm. R. A. 4.]

hǽste; *adv.* [?] See two preceding words.

Hæstingas, Hestingas, Hæstinga ceaster *Hastings:*—And ða hwîle com Willelm eorl upp æt Hestingan *and that time Earl William landed at Hastings*, Chr. 1066; Erl. 203, 3. Ðâ fêrde se cyng tô Hæstingan *then the king went to Hastings*, 1094; Erl. 229, 35. Hî heafdon ofergân Sûþseaxe and Hæstingas [Hæsting, l. 36] *they had overrun Sussex and Hastings*, 1011; Erl. 144, 27. Tô Hæstinga ceastre *at Hastings*, L. Ath. 1, 14; Th. i. 208, 2.

hǽstlîce; *adv. Violently, vehemently, fiercely*, Exon. 67 b; Th. 250, 33; Jul. 136. [Cf. *O. H. Ger.* heistigo biscoltan, Grff. iv. 1063.]

hǽswalwe *astur*, Som.

hæt, hætt, es; *m. A hat, covering for the head;* pileus, mitra, tiara:—Fellen hæt *galerus* vel *pileus*, Ælfc. Gl. 18; Som. 58, 111; Wrt. Voc. 22, 26. Hæt *calamanca*, Wrt. Voc. 41, 8; *capitium*, 74, 57. Terrentius bær hæt on his heáfde, for ðon Rômânê hæfdon gesett ðæt ða ðe hæt beran môston môston ǽgþer habban ge feorh ge freódôm *Terentius pileatus, quod indultæ sibi libertatis insigne fuit*, Ors. 4, 10; Swt. 202, 25–29. [*Icel.* höttr *a hood, cowl: Dan.* hat.]

hǽtan; *p.* te; *pp.* ed *To heat, make hot:*—Ðæt fŷr ðe man ðæt ordâl mid hǽtan sceal *the fire with which the ordeal is to be heated*, L. Ath. 4, 7; Th. i. 226, 11: 14. Tô hǽtanne magan *to heat the stomach*, L. M. 2, 10; Lchdm. ii. 188, 16. Hit gelamp sume dæige ðæt ðæs swânes wîf hǽtte hire ofen and se king ðǽr big set *it happened one day that the herdsman's wife heated her oven, and the king sat by*, Shrn. 16, 15. Hǽt scenc fulne wînes *heat a cup full of wine*, Lchdm. i. 370, 26: ii. 24, 25. [*Icel.* heita: *Ger.* heizen.]

hǽte, an; *f. Heat:*—Cîle and hǽte ne geswîcaþ *frigus et æstus non requiescent*, Gen. 8, 22. Ðâ ðâ seó hǽte com ðâ forscranc hit *when the heat came then it withered away*, Homl. Th. ii. 90, 30. On ðære hǽtan ðæs dæges *in the heat of the day*, Gen. 18, 1: Mt. Kmbl. 20, 12. For sunnan hætan *on account of the heat of the sun*, Herb. 100, 8; Lchdm. i. 214, 24: 114, 1; Lchdm. i. 226, 23. Wið eágena hǽtan *for heat of the eyes*, Lchdm. i. 352, 5. Eówre glêda nâne hǽtan mînum lîchaman ne gedôþ *your embers cause no heat to my body*, Homl. Th. i. 430, 12. Ðæt hellîce fŷr hæfþ unâsecgendlîce hǽtan and nân leóht *the fire of hell has heat unspeakable, but no light*, 532, 2. Ongan mid monegum hǽtum geswenced beón *multis cœpit æstibus affici*, Bd. 2, 12; S. 513, 31. Wið wunda hâtum *for inflammations of wounds*, Herb. 2, 16; Lchdm. i. 84, 20. [Cf. *Icel.* heita *brewing*.] v. hǽtu.

hætera, hæteru, *pl. Garments:*—Hê hæfde ne hǽlþe ne hætera *he had neither health nor garments*, Homl. Th. i. 330, 14. Se hund tôtær his hæteru sticmǽlum of his bæce *the dog tore his garments to pieces off his back*, 374, 8. Sume hî cuwon heora hætera *some of them chewed their garments*, 404, 5. Gâ hê ût mid his hætron swyclon hê in com *let him go out with his garments such as he came in with*, Ex. 21, 4. [*Laym.* alle his hateren weoren totoren: *A. R.* hateren; *dat. pl: Piers P.* I have but one hatere: *Prompt. Parv.* hatyr, rent clothe *scrutum, pannucia: O. H. Ger.* hadarum; *dat. pl. pannis, mastrugis: Ger.* hader *rag, clout.*]

hǽþ, e; *f. A heath, waste, desert, uncultivated land:*—Hâr hǽþ *the hoar heath*, Cd. 148; Th. 185, 5; Exod. 118. Bera sceal on hǽþe *the bear shall* [*live*] *on the heath*, Menol. Fox 518; Gn. C. 29. [*Goth.* haiþi: *Icel.* heiðr *a low barren heath* or *fell: Ger.* heide (12th cent: Grff. iv. 809).]

hǽþ, e; *f. Heath, heather:*—Hǽþ *marica* vel *brogus*, Ælfc. Gl. 46; Som. 65, 3; Wrt. Gl. 33, 3. Smeóce mid hǽþe *smoke with heath*, Lchdm. i. 354, 24. v. Gloss. iii. 329, col. 2. [*Prompt. Parv.* hethe or lynge *bruarium: O. H. Ger.* heida *thymus, mirice: Ger.* heide, heidekraut.]

hǽþ-berige, an; *f. Heath-berry, bilberry;* vaccinium:—Hǽþbergean wîsan *heath-berry plants*, L. M. 3, 61; Lchdm. ii. 344, 10.

hæþ-cole *Cassis, galea*, Cot. 32, 36, Lye.

hæðen. v. heden.

hǽðen; *adj.* Heathen, *pagan, gentile;* and *subst. a heathen:*—Twâ folc ðæt is Iudêisc and hǽðen *two peoples, that is Jew and gentile*, Homl. Th. i. 206, 32. Ðes wæs hǽðen *hic erat samaritanus*, Lk. Skt. Rush. 17, 16. Gif ungefullod cild fǽrlîce biþ gebroht tô ðam mæssepreóste hê hit môt fullian sôna ðæt hit ne swelte hǽðen *if an unbaptized child be brought to the mass-priest suddenly, he must baptize it at once, that it die not heathen*, L. Ælfc. 26; Th. ii. 352, 17: L. M. I. P. 42; Th. ii. 276, 15. Hêr sæt hǽðen here on Tenet *in this year a heathen* [*Danish*] *army sat in Thanet*, Chr. 865; Erl. 70, 31. Ôð ðone hǽðenan byrgels *up to the heathen tomb*, Cod. Dipl. Kmbl. ii. 250, 13. (The same phrase often occurs in the charters in the descriptions of boundaries.) Se hæfde wununge on hǽðenum byrgenum *he had his dwelling among the tombs*, Homl. Th. ii. 378, 26. Hêr hǽðne men ǽrest ofer winter sǽtun *in this year heathen* [*Danish*] *men first remained through the winter*, Chr. 855; Erl. 68, 23: 851; Erl. 66, 26. Bachsecg and Halfdene ða hǽðenan cyningas *Bachsecg and Halfdene the heathen kings*, 871; Erl. 74, 17. Ða ealdan Rômânî on hǽðenum dagum ongunnon ðæs geáres ymbryne on ðysum dæge *the old Romans, in heathen days, began the circuit of the year on this day*, Homl. Th. i. 98, 20. *Used substantively:*—Ðæt hê forgeáfe gôdne willan ðam seócan hǽðenan *that he would grant good will to the sick heathen*, ii. 24, 33. Sume ða hǽðenan *some of the heathens*, i. 562, 28: 560, 8. Ða hǽðenan on Norþhymbrum hergodon *the heathens harried in Northumbria*, Chr. 794; Erl. 39, 19. Ðyssera hǽðenra fǽrlîcan deáþ *sudden death from these heathens*, Homl. Th. ii. 494, 31. Hǽðinra *gentium*, Lk. Skt. Lind. 21, 25. Hǽðenra þeównêd *thraldom under the heathen*, Cd. 189; Th. 235, 17; Dan. 307. Hê hî on handgeweald hǽðenum sealde *tradidit eos in manus gentium*, Ps. Th. 105, 30. Hie fêrdon ongeán ðǽm hêðnum *they marched against the heathens*, Blickl. Homl. 203, 3. [Cf. *Goth.* haiþno; *f. a heathen, gentile woman: O. Sax.* hêðin: *O. Frs.* hêthen: *Icel.* heiðinn: *O. H. Ger.* heidan *ethnicus, gentilis, paganus, samaritanus: Ger.* heide *a heathen.*] v. Grmm. D. M. 1198.

hǽðena, an; *m. A heathen, gentile:*—Hǽðnana *gentium*, Lk. Skt. Rush. 21, 25. See preceding word.

hǽðen-cyning, es; *m. A heathen king:*—Herige hǽðencyninga *a band of heathen kings*, Cd. 174; Th. 219, 13; Dan. 54.

hǽðen-cynn, es; *n. A heathen race*, Cd. 119; Th. 153, 29; Gen. 2546.

hǽðen-dôm, es; *m. Heathendom, paganism:*—Hî gecwǽdon ðæt hî ǽnne God lufian woldon and ǽlcne hǽðendôm georne âweorpan *they agreed that they would love one God and zealously put away every kind of heathendom*, L. E. G. pref; Th. i. 166, 12. Wê lǽraþ ðæt preósta gehwilc cristendôm geornlîce ârǽre and ǽlcne hǽðendôm mid ealle âdwæsce *we enjoin that every priest zealously promote Christianity, and totally extinguish every kind of paganism*, L. Edg. C. 16; Th. ii. 248, 2: Cd. 183; Th. 229, 23; Dan. 221. [*Orm.* hæþenndom 'and tatt [*the death of the soul with the body*] iss mikell hæþenndom to lefenn and to trowenn:' *Icel.* heiðin-dômr: *O. H. Ger.* heidan-tuom: *Ger.* heidenthum.]

hǽðen-feoh, *gen.* -feós; *n. A heathen sacrifice*, Exon. 66 b; Th. 245, 31; Jul. 53.

hǽðen-gild, -gield, -gyld, es; *n. Heathen worship, idolatry;* also *an idol:*—Ðis hǽðengyld deófles biggeng is *this idolatry is worship of the devil*, Homl. Th. i. 72, 4. Hǽðengield, Exon. 66 a; Th. 243, 23; Jul. 15. Tô ðam hǽðengilde bugon *they turned to the idol* [*Baal-peor*], Num. 25, 2: 31, 16. Hê bæd hig georne ðæt hig bûgan ne sceoldon fram Godes bigengum tô ðam bysmorfullum hǽðengilde *he prayed them earnestly not to turn from the worship of God to degrading idolatry*, Jos. 23, 7. Iulianus ðâ ongann tô lufigenne hǽðengyld *Julian then began to love idolatry*, Homl. Th. i. 448, 30. Ealle ða hǽðengyld ðe ðâs Indiscan wurðiaþ *all the idols that these Indians worship*, 454, 14. Hǽðengield, Exon. 66 a; Th. 244, 4; Jul. 22. v. gild.

hǽðen-gilda, -gylda, an; *m. A heathen worshipper, heathen, an idolater:*—Hê is gehiwod tô cristenum men, and is earm hǽðengylda *he is in appearance a Christian, and is a miserable heathen*, Homl. Th. i. 102, 16. Se yldesta hǽðengylda *the chief idolater*, 72, 9. Se ofslôh ðæs hǽðengyldan sunû *which slew the idolater's son*, ii. 294, 19. Se ealdorman wolde ða hǽðengildan forbærnan *the general then wanted to turn the idolaters*, 484, 8. v. gilda.

hǽðenisc; *adj. Heathenish, pagan:*—Heora biscepas sǽdon ðæt heora godas bǽdon ðæt him man worhte anfiteatra ðæt mon mehte ðone hǽðeniscan plegan ðǽrinne dôn *suasere pontifices, ut ludi scaenici diis expetentibus ederentur*, Ors. 3, 3; Swt. 102, 12. [*O. H. Ger.* heidanisc *gentilis: Ger.* heidnisch.]

hǽðen-mann, -monn, es; *m. A heathen:*—Hǽðinmonn *samaritanus*, Lk. Skt. Lind. 10, 33.

hǽðen-nes, se; *f. Heathenism, paganism;* gentilitas:—Ðá ongunnon monige hǽðennysse þeáw forlǽtan *relicto gentilitatis ritu*, Bd. 1, 26; S. 488, 12. Hé tó hǽðennysse wæs gehwyrfed *ad apostasiam conversus est*, 3, 30; S. 561, 39. [*Laym.* hæðenesse: *Chauc.* 'as wel in Cristendom as in hethenesse,' Prol. 49: *Piers P.* 'al was hethenesse some tyme Ingelond and Wales, 15, 435.]

hǽðen-scipe, es; *m. Heathenism, paganism:*—Wé forbeódaþ eornostlíce ǽlcne hǽðenscipe. Hǽðenscipe biþ ðæt man ídola weorðige ðæt is ðæt man weorðige hǽðene godas and sunnan oððe mónan fýr oððe flód wæter-wyllas oððe stánas *we earnestly forbid all heathenism: heathenism is to worship idols, that is to worship heathen gods, and sun or moon, fire or water, springs or stones*, L. C. S. 5; Th. i. 378, 17, 20. Ðæt ys mycel hǽðenscype *id magnus est paganismus*, L. Ecg. P. 4, 20; Th. ii. 210, 19: L. N. P. L. 48; Th. ii. 296, 27: Chr. 634; Erl. 25, 31. Ða tungelwítegan ðe wǽron on hǽðenscipe wunigende hæfdon getácnunge ealles hǽðenes folces *the astrologers, who were yet heathens, betokened all heathen people*, Homl. Th. i. 106, 9: 70, 25, 28. [*Laym.* hæðenescipe]

hǽðen-styrc, es; *m. A heathen stirk, calf used in heathen worship, the golden calf made by the Israelites:*—Hí on Choreb swylce cealf ongunnon him tó godegylde georne wyrcean; onwendan heora wuldor on ðæne wyrsan hád hǽðenstyrces hig etendes *fecerunt vitulum in Choreb, et adoraverunt sculptile; et mutaverunt gloriam suam in similitudinem vituli comedentis fœnum*, Ps. Th. 105, 17.

Hǽðfeld *Hatfield in Hertfordshire:*—Hér gesæt Þeodorius ærcebiscop senoþ on Hǽðfelda *in this year archbishop Theodore presided over a synod at Hatfield*, Chr. 680; Erl. 40, 11.

hǽðiht; *adj. Heathy:*—In ða hǽðihtan lége *to the heathy lea*, Cod. Dipl. Kmbl. iii. 121, 21: 262, 22.

hǽð-stapa, an; *m. A heath-stepper, an animal which wanders over heaths* or *uncultivated country:*—Ðeáh ðe hǽðstapa hundum geswenced heorot holtwudu séce *although the heath-wanderer, the hart by the hounds wearied, seek that wood*, Beo. Th. 2740; B. 1368. Wulf hár hǽðstapa *the wolf, the grey wanderer of the heath*, Exon. 87 a; Th. 328, 6: Vy. 13.

Hǽðum, æt *Slesvig*, Ors. 1, 1; Bos. 21, 30, 39. [Cf. Ethelweard 'Anglia vetus sita est inter Saxones et Giotos, habens oppidum capitale, quod sermone Saxonico Sleswic nuncupatur, secundum vero Danos Haithaby.' *Icel.* Heiðabær.]

hǽðung [= hǽtung], e; *f. Heating, warming:*—Belimpþ seó hǽðung tó ðære hǽtan and seó onlíhting belimpþ tó ðære beorhtnysse *the heating belongs to the heat and the illumination to the brightness*, Homl. Th. i. 286, 3.

hǽting, e; *f. Calipeatum*, Wrt. Voc. 290, 43.

hætsan *to drive, urge, impel* [?]:—Hwílum mec mín freá hætst on enge *sometimes my lord drives me into a narrow place*, Exon. 101 b; Th. 383, 3; Rä. 4, 5.

hættian; *p.* ode; *pp.* od *To take the hair and skin from a person's head:*—Ðonne dó man út his eágan and ceorfan of his nóse and eáran and uferan lippan oððe hine hættian *then let his eyes be put out and his nose and ears and upper lip be cut off; or let him have the hair and skin of his head pulled off*, L. C. S. 30; Th. i. 394, 14. [The Latin version here has 'aut corium capitis cum capillis (auferatur) quod Angli vocant behættie.' Another translation has 'vel decapilletur.'] Sume man hættode, Chr. 1036; Erl. 164, 39. In the note Earle quotes Florence of Worcester 'cute capitis abstracta.' Cf. Grmm. R. A. 703, where he quotes an explanation of the punishment by which the hair was dragged from a person's head, 'man windet im die haar mit einer kluppen oder knebel aus dem heupt.' He thinks the form hettian [hættian] has no sense, but may it not be connected with *hæt*, as it was just that part of the head which the hat covered that was affected? It was giving the victim the appearance of wearing a hat of a most ghastly kind.

hǽtu, hǽto; *indecl; f. Heat:*—Hǽtu *calor*, Ælfc. Gr. 4, 26. Þridde ágennys is seó hǽtu *the third property is the heat*, Homl. Th. ii. 606, 13, 18. Þýstro and hǽto *darkness and heat*, Cd. 21; Th. 25, 6; Gen. 389: Bt. Met. Fox 20, 146; Met. 20, 73. Hǽto *æstus*, Mt. Kmbl. Lind. 20, 12. Gif se líchoma hwǽr mid hefiglícre hǽto sý gebysgod *if the body be troubled anywhere with heavy inflammation*, Herb. 2, 6; Lchdm. i. 82, 8. Unácumendlíce hǽtu þrowiaþ and unásecgendlíce cýle *they suffer intolerable heat and unspeakable cold*, Homl. Th. i. 532, 1. [*O. Frs.* héte; *f: O. H. Ger.* heizi, heiz; *f. æstus, fervor: O. Sax.* hét; *n.*] v. hǽte.

hǽtung. v. hǽðung.

hǽwen; *adj. Blue, azure, purple, discoloured:*—Hǽwen *glaucus*, Cot. 96: *jacinthina*, 185: *fulvus*, Lye. Ádó in ǽren fæt lǽt ðǽr in óð ðæt hit hǽwen sý *put into a brazen vessel, leave it therein until it be turned colour*, Lchdm. iii. 20, 18. Gyf ðæt húsl byþ fynig oððe hǽwen *if the housel be mouldy or discoloured*, L. Ælf. C. 36; Th. ii. 360, 9. Seó hǽwene lyft *the azure air*, Cd. 166; Th. 207, 33; Exod. 476. Genim ðás wyrte ðe grécas brittanice and engle hǽwen hydele, Herb. 30; Lchdm. i. 126, 6. Hǽwene hnydele, iii. 24, 8. Ðeós wyrt hafaþ lange leáf and hǽwene *this plant hath long leaves and purple*, Herb. 133, 1; Lchdm. i. 248, 18: 150, 1; Lchdm. i. 274, 16. Seó heall wæs getymbred ynnan and útan myd grénum and myd hǽwenum and myd hwýtum *the hall was built within and without with green and with purple and with white*, Shrn. 156, 6. Hǽwen-grén *cæruleus*, Cot. 53, Lye. Hǽwendeáge *hyacinthinus*, Lye.

hafa *and forms as from* hafian. v. habban.

hafecere, es; *m. A hawker:*—Wé lǽraþ ðæt preóst ne beó hunta ne hafecere *we enjoin that a priest be not a hunter, nor a hawker*, L. Edg. C. 64; Th. ii. 258, 7.

hafela, hafala, heafela, heafola, an; *m. The head;* caput; κεφαλή:—Se hwíta helm hafelan werede *the bright helm guarded the head*, Beo. Th. 2901; B. 1448: 2658; B. 1327: 3564; B. 1780. Of ðæs hǽlendes heafelan *from the Saviour's head*, Exon. 15 a; Th. 31, 34; Cri. 505. Heafolan, Beo. Th. 5352; B. 2679. Hafalan, 896; B. 446.

hafe-leást, e; *f. Want of means, indigence:*—For haueléste *from lack of means*, Chr. 675; Erl. 38, 12. v. hafen-leást.

hafen. v. hebban.

hafenian; *p.* ode; *pp.* od *To grasp, hold:*—Wǽpen hafenade heard be hiltum *he grasped the weapon hard by the hilt*, Beo. Th. 3151; B. 1573. Bord hafenode *he grasped his shield*, Byrht. Th. 132, 67; By. 42: 140, 57; By. 309. [*O. H. Ger.* hebinon, hefinon, Grff. iv. 737, 828.]

hafen-leás; *adj. Lacking means, poor, indigent;* inops:—Hafenleás *inops*, Wrt. Voc. 74, 20. Hé wæs swíðe welig wædlum and þearfum and symle him sylfum swíðe hafenleás *he was very wealthy for the poor and needy, and ever very indigent for himself*, Homl. Th. ii. 148, 34. Sum hafenleás man sceolde ágyldan healf pund ánum menn *a certain indigent man had to pay a man half a pound*, 176, 34. Se hafenleása 178, 6. Se ðe spéda hæfþ and ða áspendan nele hafenleásum bréðer *he that hath riches and will not expend them for his brother who lacks*, 318, 11: 484, 33: 178, 19. v. hæfen-leás.

hafen-leást, e; *f. Lack of means, indigence;* inopia:—Wé ne sceolon ða wannspédigan for heora hafenleáste forseón *we ought not to despise those who are without means for their indigence*, Homl. Th. i. 128, 23. Fela sind þearfan þurh hafenleáste and ná on heora gáste. Sind eác óðre þearfan ná þurh hafenleáste ac on gáste *many are poor from want of wealth, and not in spirit. There are also other poor, not from want of wealth, but in spirit*, 550, 3-5, 11, 12, 17. Úre sáule hafenleáste *the indigence of our souls*, ii. 88, 26. Ðá getímode swá micel hafenleást ðæt ða gebróðra næfdon búton fíf hláfas tó heora ealra gereorde *then there befell so great a lack that the brethren had but five loaves for the refection of them all*, 170, 33. v. hæfen-leást.

hafetian *to clap* [*as a bird with its wings*, or *a man with his hands*], *applaud:*—Ic hafetige *plaudo*, Ælfc. Gr. 28; Som. 31, 28. Flódas hafettaþ handum *flumina plaudent manu*, Ps. Spl. 97, 8. Ǽrðan ðe se hana hafitigende cráwe *before the cock clapping its wings crow*, Homl. Th. ii. 246, 4.

hafoc, hafuc, heafoc, es; *m. A hawk;* accipiter:—Heafuc *accipiter*, Wrt. Voc. 77, 15. Mid hafoce *accipitre*, Coll. Monast. Th. 25, 15, 17, 31, 37. Gód hafoc *a good hawk*, Beo. Th. 4519; B. 2263. Sum sceal wildne fugol átemian heafoc *one shall tame the wild bird, the hawk*, Exon. 88 b; Th. 332, 16; Vy. 86. [*Laym.* havek: *Icel.* haukr: *O. H. Ger.* hapuh, habich: *Ger.* habicht.] DER. gós-, gúþ-, mús-, spear-, wealh-hafoc. The word is found in many names of places, see Cod. Dipl. Kmbl. vi. index.

hafoc-cynn, es; *n. The hawk species:*—Ne ete gé nán þing hafoccynnes ne earncynnes *eat nothing of the hawk-kind or the eagle-kind*, Lev. 11, 13.

hafoc-fugel, es; *m. A hawk:*—Ðeáh hafucfugel ábite *etiamsi accipiter momorderit*, L. Ecg. C. 38; Th. ii. 162, 19.

hafoc-wyrt, e; *f. Hawk-weed* [?]; hieracium, L. M. 1, 14; Lchdm. ii. 56, 11.

hafud. v. heáfod.

hafud-æcer, es; *m* [?]:—Tióþa hafudæcer *decumanus*, Ælfc. Gl. 57; Som. 67, 78; Wrt. Voc. 38, 4.

hafud-land, es; *n. A headland, boundary:*—Hafudland *limites*, Ælfc. Gl. 57; Som. 67, 77; Wrt. Voc. 38, 3. ['*Headland*, the upper portion of a field, generally left unploughed for convenience of passage,' Cod. Dipl. Kmbl. iii. xxix. '*Adlands*, those butts in a ploughed field which lie at right angles to the general direction of the others; the part close against the hedge. Salop,' Halliwell. So in Surrey, Engl. Dial. Soc. No. 12, p. 91. '*Headland*, that is which is ploughed overthwart at the ends of the other lands,' No. 30, p. 82.]

haga, an; *m. A place fenced in, an enclosure, a haw, a dwelling in a town:*—Haga *sæpem*, Mk. Skt. Lind. 12, 1. Se haga binnan port ðe Ægelríc himsylfan getimbrod hæfde *the messuage within the town that Ægelric had built himself*, Cod. Dipl. Kmbl. iv. 86, 26: Th. Chart. 569, 2, 5: 514, 13: Cod. Dipl. ii. 150, 5, 11. Ðis syndon ðæs hagan gemǽru *these are the boundaries of the messuage* [in the previous part of the charter the gift is spoken of as *unam curtem*], iii. 240, 18. Ða hagan ealle đe hē be westan cyrcan hæfde *all the messuages that he had west of the church*, Th. Chart. 303, 10. Ǽnne hagan on porte *curtem unum in supradicta civitate*, Cod. Dipl. Kmbl. iv. 72, 27: iii. 213, 13. Quandam hospicii portionem in præfata civitate sitam, quæ patria lingua *haga* solet appellari, vi. 134, 24; cf. 135, 14, 25. Tō hagan þrungon *they pressed to the entrenchment*, Beo. Th. 5913; B. 2960: Beo. Th. 5777; B. 2892. [*Chauc.* hawe *yard*: in *Kentish dialect* haw *a yard*, or *enclosure*: *Icel.* hagi *a hedged field, a pasture.*] DER. bord-, cumbol-, fǣr-, swīn-, turf-, wīg-haga.

haga, an; *m. A haw, berry of the hawthorn;* also *used to signify any thing of no value* [?], [cf. Chaucer's 'not worth an hawe']:—Hagan *gignalia*, Ælfc. Gl. 47; Som. 65, 24; Wrt. Voc. 33, 24. Hagan *quisquilia*, 285, 31. [*Prompt. Parv.* hawe, frute *cinum, cornum, ramnum.*]

hagal, hagol, es; *m. Hail*; grando:—Hagol *grando*, Ælfc. Gl. 94; Som. 75, 100; Wrt. Voc. 52, 50: Homl. Th. ii. 192, 32. Hagol cymþ of đām rēndropum đonne hī beóþ gefrorene *hail comes of the raindrops when they are frozen*, Lchdm. iii. 278, 19. Rēn hagal and snāw hrusan leccaþ *rain, hail, and snow moisten the earth*, Bt. Met. Fox 29, 127; Met. 29, 64. Mid hagole *with hail*, Homl. Th. ii. 350, 8. Gesihþ hreósan hrīm and snāw hagle gemenged *sees rime and snow fall mingled with hail*, Exon. 77 a; Th. 289, 15; Wand. 48. [*Laym.* haȝel: *Icel.* hagl; *n. hail;* Hagall; *m. the name of the rune* h: *O. H. Ger.* hagal; *m*: *Ger.* hagel.] v. hægel.

hagalian; *p.* ode *To hail*:—Hit hagalade stānum ofer ealle Rōmāne *saxea de nubibus grando descendens*, Ors. 3, 5; Swt. 104, 20. [*Icel.* hagla: *M. H. Ger.* hagelen.]

hagal-scūr, hagol-, es; *m. A shower of hail*, Ps. Spl. M. 104, 30: Menol. Fox 71; Men. 35. v. hægel-scūr.

haga-þorn, es; *m. Hawthorn*:—Of hagaþornum *de tribolis*, Mt. Kmbl. Lind. 7, 16. v. hæg-þorn.

hagian. v. on-hagian.

hagol-stān, es; *m. A hailstone*:—God him sende ufan greáte hagolstānas *God sent down upon them great hailstones*, Jos. 10, 11. Betwux đām greátum hagolstānum *amid the great stones*, Homl. Th. i. 52, 18. [*Icel.* hagl-steinn: *M. H. Ger.* hagel-sten: *Ger.* hagel-stein.]

hago-spind, heago-, hecga-, es; *m. n? The cheek*:—Hagospind *genæ*, Wrt. Voc. 64, 41. Heagospind, 282, 56. Hecgaspind, Ælfc. Gl. 71; Som. 70, 78; Wrt. Voc. 43, 11. Heortes heagospind *a hart's cheek*, Lchdm. i. 336, 12. [Somner, Lye, and Wright print *swind* for *spind*, the form which occurs in the transcript by Junius; see note to passage quoted above from Lchdm. i. *Eágospind* occurs, Guthl. 20; Gdwin. 82, 4.] v. spind.

hago-steald, es; *m. One living in the lord's house, not having his own household, an unmarried person, a young person, young warrior*:—Hagosteald onwōc mōdig from moldan *the young warrior* [*Christ*] *was roused exulting from earth*, Exon. 120 a; Th. 460, 23; Hö. 21. Heafoc weorþeþ tō hagostealdes honda gelǣred *the hawk becomes trained to the youth's hand*, 88 b; Th. 332, 28; Vy. 92. [*O. Sax.* haga-stald, -stold *a servant, young man*: *O. H. Ger.* haga-stalt, -stolt *mercenarius, cœlebs*: *Ger.* hagestolz *old bachelor.*] v. Grmm. R. A. 484, *and* hæg-steald.

hago-steald, es; *n. Celibacy*, Exon. 105 b; Th. 402, 17; Rä. 21, 31.

hago-stealdmonn, es; *m.*=hago-steald, q. v. Exon. 104 a; Th. 395, 3; Rä. 15, 2.

Hagustaldes eá, eé, hām *Hexham*, Chr. 681: 685: 766: 780: 789: 806: Bd. 5, 23; S. 646, 30. [*Dun.* Hestaldesham, Hestaldeshige: *Ric.* Hestalasham: *Gerv.* Hestoldesham: *Kni.* Exseldesham.]

hagu-swind. v. hago-spind.

hal, es; *n. A secret place, a corner*:—Đā gemētte hē hine hleonian on đam hale his cyrcan wiđ đam weofode *he found him leaning in the corner of his church against the altar*, Guthl. 20; Gdwin. 82, 22. On halum *in abditis*, Ps. Spl. 16, 13. [Cf. we beth honted from hale to hurne, Pol. Songs. Wrt. 150, 17. In one swiþe diȝele hale, O. and N. 2.] v. helan.

hāl; *adj. Whole, hale, well, in good health, sound, safe, without fraud, honest;* often used in salutation:—Iosep āxode hwæđer hira fæder wǣre hāl *Joseph asked whether their father were well*, Gen. 43, 27. Se man wæs sōna hāl *statim sanus factus est*, Jn. Skt. 5, 9. Se biþ hāl geworden *he shall be saved*, Blickl. Homl. 21, 36. Hē þurh đæt sōna wearþ hāl geworden *he was at once by that restored to health*, 223, 26. Gif hie mon gelācnian mǣge đæt hie hāl sīe *if it* [*the broken sinew*] *can be cured so that it be sound*, L. Alf. pol. 75; Th. i. 100, 4. Mannes sunu com sēcean and hāl dōn đæt forwearþ *venit filius hominis quærere et saluare quod perierat*, Lk. Skt. 19, 10. Gedō mē hālne *salvum me fac*, Mt. Kmbl. 14, 30: Mk. Skt. 5, 34. Hine đǣm mannum hālne and gesundne āgeaf *restored him to the men safe and sound*, Blickl. Homl. 219, 21: 107, 17. Đū mē behēte hāl and clǣne đæt đæt đū mē sealdest *thou didst declare to me that what thou didst sell me was sound and clean*, L. O. 7; Th. i. 180, 22: 9; Th. i. 182, 4. Hē hyne hālne onfēng *he hath received him safe and sound*, Lk. Skt. 15, 27. Ic geaf hit on mīnon hālan līfe intō Cristes cyrcean *I gave it while of sound body to Christ's church*, Cod. Dipl. Kmbl. iv. 305, 12. Đā betǣhte Ecgferþ on hālre tungan land and bōc Dunstāne *then Ecgferth in plain, unequivocal language delivered land and charter to Dunstan* [cf. *Icel.* međ heilum hug *sincerely*], Th. Chart. 208, 11. Hāl wes đū Iudēa cyning *Haue rex Iudæorum*, Mt. Kmbl. 27, 29: Lk. Skt. 1, 28: Andr. Kmbl. 1827; An. 916: Beo. Th. 818; B. 407. Hāle wese gē *Havete*, Mt. Kmbl. 28, 9. Sȳ đū hāl leóf Iudēiscre leóde cyning *hail sir, king of the Jewish people*, Homl. Th. ii. 252, 28. Hāl beó đū *Have*, Mt. Kmbl. 26, 49. Beó đū hāl and sig gebletsod se đe on Dryhtnes naman com *Osanna benedictus qui venit in nomine Domini*, Nicod. 4; Thw. 2, 32. [*Laym.* hal, hæl, hæil, hail, hol: Lauerd king wæs hæil [wassayl, later MS.], 14309: *Orm.* hal: *A. R.* hol: *Prompt. Parv.* hool: *Goth.* hails: *O. Sax. O. Frs.* hēl: *Icel.* heill: *O. H. Ger.* heil: *Ger.* heil.] v. ge-, un-hāl.

halan [*or* hamlan] *afterbirth*:—Gāte geallan on wīne gedruncen wīfa halan him ofādēþ *goat's gall, drunken in wine, removes women's afterbirth for them*, Lchdm. i. 356, 8. v. Gloss: Lchdm. ii.

hāl-bǣre; *adj. Wholesome, salutary;* salutaris, Scint. 32, 78, Lye.

hald. v. heald.

hālettan; *p.* te *To salute, greet, hail*:—Sum man hine hālette and grētte and hine be his naman nemde *quidam eum salutans ac suo appellans nomine*, Bd. 4, 24; S. 597, 12: 2, 12; S. 514, 31: Blickl. Homl. 155, 20. Iohannes hālette on hie mycelre stefne *John greeted her with a loud voice*, 143, 15. Hie hāletton on hie *they greeted her*, 139, 25.

hālettend, es; *m. The middle finger, the finger by which a sign of greeting is made*:—Hālettend midemesta finger *salutarius*, Wrt. Voc. 283, 21. Hǣletend *salutaris*, Recd. 38, 72; Wrt. Voc. 64, 81.

hālettung, e; *f. Greeting, salutation*:—Æfter đæs engles bletsunga and hālettunga swīgende þohte hwæt seó hālettung wǣre *after the angel's blessing and greeting she considered in silence what the greeting might be*, Blickl. Homl. 7, 16. Hālettunge, 3, 21. Hǣlettungæ *salutationes*, Mt. Kmbl. Rush. 23, 7.

half. v. healf.

hāl-fæst; *adj. Salutary;* qui potest sanare, Lye.

hālga, an; *m. A saint*:—Biþ gesmyrod ealra hālgena hālga *the saint of all saints shall be anointed*, Homl. Th. ii. 14, 16. Đæt wundor gelamp þurh đæs hālgan mihte *that miracle happened through the saint's might*, 28, 28; Swt. A. S. Rdr. 102, 212. Fram đam rihtwīsan Abel ōþ đam endenēxtan hālgan *from righteous Abel to the last saint*, Homl. Th. ii. 74, 5. Godes hālgan sind englas and men *God's saints are angels and men*, i. 538, 23: 574, 22: ii. 112, 31. Hālgena līchaman ārison *the bodies of saints arose*, 258, 5. On đone dæg æfter ealra hālgena mæssedæg *on the day after All Saints' day*, Chr. 1083; Erl. 217, 32. November se mōnaþ onginþ on ealra hālgena mæssedæg *the month of November begins on All Saints' day*, Ælfc. Gr. 9; Som. 9, 55. [*Chauc.* halwe: *Mod. E.* in All Hallows: *Ger.* heilige *a saint.*] v. hālig.

hālgawaras; *pl. Holy people, saints*:—Gisungan hālgawaras *cantabant sancti*, Rtl. 47, 26. Hālgawara đīnra *sanctorum tuorum*, 62, 12. Hālgawæra, Mt. Kmbl. Lind. 27, 52. [Cf. hālig-waras.]

hālgian; *p.* ode; *pp.* od *To hallow, make holy, consecrate, sanctify*:—Hweđer hie đa ciricean hālgian dorston on ōđre wīsan *whether they durst consecrate the church otherwise*, Blickl. Homl. 205, 21, 24. Ne miht đū on ōđre wīsan bisceop hālgian būton ōđrum bisceopum *ordinare episcopum non aliter nisi sine episcopis potes*, Bd. 1, 27; S. 492, 3. Đū scealt hālgian hīrēd đīnne *thou shalt hallow thy family*, Cd. 106; Th. 139, 15; Gen. 2310. Hēr man hālgode Ælfēhg tō arcebiscope *in this year Ælfheah was consecrated archbishop*, Chr. 1006; Erl. 138, 2: 1050; Erl. 176, 22. Nis eów þearf đæt gē đa ciricean hālgian *there is no need for you to consecrate the church*, Blickl. Homl. 207, 1. Hweđer hie đa ciricean hālgedon *whether they should consecrate the church*, 205, 11. Hālgig ođđe hālga đū *sanctifica*, Jn. Skt. Lind. 17, 17. Hālgiaþ eówer fæsten *sanctify ye a fast*, Blickl. Homl. 37, 32. Sȳ hālgad noma *hallowed be thy name*, Exon. 122 a; Th. 468, 19; Hy. 5, 2. [*Laym.* halȝien: *Orm.* hallȝhenn: *Prompt. Parv.* halwin *consecrare*: *O. Sax.* hēlagōn: *Icel.* helga: *O. H. Ger.* heilagōn: *Ger.* heiligen.]

Hālgo-land, es; *n. A district* [fylki] *of Norway, Hålogaland*:—Ōhthere sǣde đæt sió scīr hātte Hālgoland đe hē on būde. Hē cwæþ đæt nān mann ne būde be norþan him *Ohthere said that the district was called Halogaland that he lived in. He said that no one lived north of him*, Ors. 1, 1; Bos. 21, 16. See Aall's translation of the Heimskringla, p. 24, note.

hālgung, hālegung, e; *f. Hallowing, consecration, sanctification*:—Getimbra hālgung *scenophegia*, Ælfc. Gl. 3; Som. 55, 78; Wrt. Voc. 16, 50. Niuæs hūses hālgung ł cirica hālgung *encenia*, Jn. Skt. Lind. 10, 22. Geworden is Iudēa hālgung *facta est Iudæa sanctificatio*, Ps. Spl. 113, 2: 77, 59. Biscopes hālgung *episcopi ordinatio*, Bd. 1, 27; S. 492, 5. Đeáh ealle circan habban hālgunge gelīce *though all churches have like consecration*, L. Eth. 9, 5; Th. i. 340, 27. Seđe đa hālgunge ođđe đa lectionem ne mæg æfter þeáwe gefyllan *qui consecrationem vel lectionem non potest rite implere*, L. Ecg C. 3; Th. ii. 160, 16. Hē ne hāding ne hāleging ne dō *let him not ordain nor consecrate*, Cod. Dipl. Kmbl. v. 28, 34. [*Prompt. Parv.* halwynge of holy placys *consecracio, dedicacio*: *O. H. Ger.* heilagunga *sanctificatio*: *Ger.* heiligung.]

hālgung-ram; *m. A consecrated ram*:—For đam hit ys hālgungram *for it is a ram of consecration*, Ex. 29, 22.

hâli-. v. hâlig-.

hâlian; *p.* ode *To become hale, whole, to heal, to get well*:—Lege tô ðam sâre hyt sceal berstan and hâlian *lay to the sore; it shall burst and heal*, Herb. 148, 2; Lchdm. i. 272, 21. Hê ðâ ongan trumian and hâligan *ubi sanescere cœpit*, Bd. 4, 22; S. 591, 10. Ðonne hâlaþ ðæt heáfod swýðe hraðe *the head will heal very quickly*, Herb. 1, 2; Lchdm. i. 70, 16: 2, 6; Lchdm. i. 82, 10. [*O. H. Ger.* heilen *sanescere.*]

hâlig; *adj. Holy*; sanctus, sacer:—Hâlig *sanctus, almus*, Ælfc. Gr. 8; Som. 7, 41. Ðæt hâlige gewrit *scribtura*, Jn. Skt. 17, 12. Se hâliga frôfre gâst *paracletus sanctus spiritus*, 14, 26. Hâlig sealt *holy salt*, L. M. 3, 62; Lchdm. ii. 346, 30; 344, 14. Hâliges wæteres *some holy water*, 348, 2. Woroldlîcra weorca on ðam hâlgan dæge geswîce man georne *let people carefully abstain from worldly works on that holy day* [*Sunday*], L. Eth. 6, 22; Th. i. 320, 13. On ðone hâlgan Ðunresdæg *on holy Thursday*, L. Alf. pol. 5; Th. i. 64, 24. Ða hâlgan hâdas *the clergy*, L. Edm. E. 1; Th. i. 244, 9. Hê spræc þurh hys hâlegra wîtegena mûþ *locutus est per os sanctorum prophetarum ejus*, Lk. Skt. 1, 70. Ðâm hâlgum tîdum *at those holy times*, L. C. S. 17; Th. i. 370, 9. Hâlige bêc *sacros libros*, L. Ecg. P. 3, 4; Th. ii. 196, 27. [*Laym.* hali, holy: *Orm.* haliȝ: *Wick.* hooli: *O. Sax.* hêlag: *O. Frs.* hêlich: *Icel.* heilagr: *O. H. Ger.* heilag: *Ger.* heilig.]

hâlig-dæg, es; *m. A holy day, Sunday*:—Be hâlidæiges freólse *of the festival of Sunday*, L. C. S. 45; Th. i. 402, 8. On hâligdagum *sabbatis*, Mk. Skt. Lind. 3, 2. [*A. R.* halidei: *Piers P.* halidai.]

hâlig-dôm, es; *m.* I. *holiness, sanctity*; sanctimonia:—Hâligdôm *sanctimonia*, Rtl. 100, 11. Mycel is se hâligdôm and seó weorþung sancte Iohannes *great is the sanctity and worthiness of St. John*, Blickl. Homl. 167, 16. Bûton ða heánesse ðæs hâligdômes *nisi excellentia sanctitatis*, Past. 18, 3; Swt. 133, 14: 57; Swt. 439, 23. II. *holy things, relics, holy work, a sacrament*:—Hâligdôm *sacramentum*, Mk. Skt. p. 5, 11. On ðone Drihten ðe ðes hâligdôm is fore hâlig *by the Lord, before whom these relics are holy*, L. O. 1; Th. i. 178, 3, 12. Wê sceolon on ðissum dagum fyligan ûrum hâligdôme ût and inn *on these days we ought to follow our relics out and in*, Homl. Th. i. 246, 28. Ðæt hig bereáfodan æt hâligdome and æt eallon þingan *they plundered the monastery of the relics and of every thing*, Chr. 1055; Erl. 188, 40. On ðam hâligdôme swerian *to swear on the relics*, L. Eth. 3, 2; Th. i. 292, 14: Th. Chart. 610, 31: Chr. 1131; Erl. 260, 10. Ðýlæs ǽnig unclǽnsod dorste on swâ micelne hâligdôm fôn ðære clænan ðegnenga ðæs sacerd hâdes *ne aut non purgatus adire quisque sacra ministeria audeat*, Past. 7, 1; Swt. 51, 1. Tô hâligdôm ðînre gesibsumnesse tô âsend *ad sacramentum tuæ reconciliationis admitte*, Lye. Þurh hâlgum hâligdôm Drihtnes lîchaman and blôdes *per sacrosanctum sacramentum Domini corporis ac sanguinis*, Lye. Hâligdôm and hâlige bêc handligan *reliquias et sacros libros manu tractare*, L. Ecg. P. 3, 4; Th. ii. 196, 27: 12; Th. ii. 200, 7. Hâligdôm and hâdas and gehâlgode Godes hûs man sceal weorþian georne *holy things and holy orders and the hallowed houses of God must be zealously honoured*, L. Eth. 7, 28; Th. i. 336, 1: 24; Th. i. 334, 23: L. E. B. 1; Th. ii. 240, 9. Wê lǽraþ ðæt ealle ða þingc ðe weofode neáh beón, and tô cirican gebyrian, beón swîðe clǽnelîce and wurþlîce behworfene, and ðǽr ǽnig þingc fûles neáh ne cume; ac gelogige man ðone hâligdôm swîðe ârwurþlîce *we enjoin, that all the things which are near the altar, and belong to the church, be very cleanly and worthily appointed, and where nothing foul may come near them; but let the holy things be very reverently arranged*, L. Edg. C. 42; Th. ii. 252, 23-6. Þurh ealne ðane hâligdôm ðe ic on Rôme for mê and for ealne þeódscype gesôhte *by all the relics that I sought out in Rome for myself and for all the nation*, Th. Chart. 117, 10. III. *a holy place, sanctuary*:—Ðînne hâligdôm *sanctuarium tuum*, Ps. Lamb. 73, 7. Hê getimbrade his hâligdôm *ædificavit sanctificium suum*, 77, 69. Tô ðæs hâligdômes dura *to the door of the sanctuary*, Ex. 21, 6. Tôweard ðam hâligdôme *toward the sanctuary*, Chr. 1083; Erl. 217, 20. Ân is mid ðæs kynges hâligdôme, ôðer is mid Leófrîce eorle and ðæt þridde is mid ðam bisceop *one* [*of the writings*] *is in the king's sanctuary, a second is with earl Leofric, and the third is with the bishop*, Th. Chart. 372, 29: 541, 25: 571, 20. [*Laym.* halidom *relic*: *Orm.* haliȝdom *holiness*; *pl. sacred things*: *Icel.* helgir dômar *relics*; helgidômr *a sanctuary*: *O. H. Ger.* heiligtuom *sacramentum, sanctuarium*: *Ger.* heiligthum *sacred thing, relic, sanctuary.*]

hâlig-ern, es; *n. A holy place, sanctuary*:—Hâligern *sanctuarium*, Blickl. Gl. Hâliern *sacellum*, Hpt. Gl. 482. On ðam hâlierne *in the holy place*, Ex. 29, 30.

hâlig-mônaþ, -mônþ, es; *m. Holy month, September*:—On ðæm nigoþan mônþe on geáre biþ xxx daga se mônaþ hâtte on lêden septembris and on ûre geþeóde hâligmônaþ for ðon ðe ûre yldran ðâ ðâ hî hǽðene wǽron on ðam mônþe hî guldon hiora deófolgeldum *in the ninth month in the year there are thirty days. The month is called in Latin September, and in our language holy month, because our ancestors, when they were heathen, sacrificed to their idols in that month*, Shrn. 124, 28-31: 136, 27. Hâligmônþ, Menol. Fox 325; Men. 164. [*Bede*, De temporum ratione, c. 13, gives *Halegmonath* as the native equivalent of September, v. Grmm. Gesch. D. S. 56 sqq.]

hâlig-nes, -ness, e; *f.* I. *holiness, sanctity*:—Hâlygnyss *sanctitas*, Ælfc. Gr. 5; Som. 5, 22. Hâlignys on hâlignysse hys *sanctimonia in sanctificatione ejus*, Ps. Spl. 95, 6. On rihtwîsnesse and on hâlignesse *in righteousness and in holiness*, Blickl. Homl. 31, 36: 155, 31. On hâlignesse *in sanctitate*, Lk. Skt. 1, 75: Ps. Th. 88, 32. II. *a holy thing, relic*:—Seó hâlignis *the relic*, St. And. 42, 7. Ic hâte ðê Veronix ðæt ðû âgif mê ða hâlignysse ðe ðû myd ðê hæfst. Veronix him ðâ swýðe wiðsôc and sǽde, ðæt heó nâne hâlignyssa myd hyre næfde *I command thee, Veronica, that thou give up to me the relic that thou hast with thee. Then Veronica vehemently refused and said that she had no relics with her*, 40, 31-4. III. *a holy place, sanctuary*:—Gecwǽdon ðæt hî hâlignesse Godes gesettan *dixerunt, possideamus sanctuarium Dei*, Ps. Th. 82, 9. Hâlignessa sindon tô griðleáse *sanctuaries are too unprotected*, Swt. A. S. Rdr. 106, 41. Inngongende and ûtgongende beforan Gode tô ðâm hâlignessum *quando ingreditur et egreditur sanctuarium in conspectu Domini*, Past. 15, 4; Swt. 93, 7. [*O. H. Ger.* heilagnissa *sanctificatio, sanctitas.*] Cf. hâlig-dôm.

hâlig-rift, -reft, -ryft, e; *f. A holy garment, veil*:—Hâligryft *theristrum*, Hpt. Gl. 525. Hió an hyre betsþ hâliryft *she gives her best veil*, Th. Chart. 538, 7. Heó ðǽr hâligryfte onfêng *accepto velamine sanctimonialis habitus*, Bd. 4, 19; S. 587, 42: Shrn. 94, 25: Lchdm. iii. 430, 26. Sca hylda wæs xxxiii geára on lǽwedum hâde and xxxiii geára under hâligryfte *St. Hilda was for thirty-three years in the world and for thirty-three years in the cloister*, Shrn. 149, 5. Effigenia is ðæs Heofenlîcan Cynges brýd and mid hâligrefte gehâlgod *Effigenia is the bride of the Heavenly King, and hallowed with the veil*, Homl. Th. ii. 476, 32. Mathêus lêde hâligreft ofer hire heáfod *Matthew placed a veil on her head*, 478, 5.

hâlig-wæcca, an; *m. One who observes vigils*:—Beón eáðmôde and ælmysfulle and hâligwæccan *ut humiles simus et eleemosynis largi et sanctarum vigiliarum studiosi*, L. Ecg. P. 4, 64; Th. ii. 224, 27.

hâlig-wæter, es; *n. Holy water*:—Sumne dǽl ðæs hâligwæteres *de aqua benedicta*, Bd. 5, 4; S. 617, 19: L. Ath. 4, 7; Th. i. 226, 24: L. M. 1, 64; Lchdm. ii. 138, 28. Mid hâligwætere *with holy water*, 62; Lchdm. ii. 136, 4. On hâligwætre *in holy water*, 45, 1; Lchdm. ii. 110, 14.

hâlig-waras, -ware; *pl. Holy people, saints*:—Þerh mûþe hâligwara *per os sanctorum*, Lk. Skt. Lind. 1, 70. Hâlgwara *sanctorum*, Rtl. 45, 1. [Cf. hâlga-waras.]

halm, hals. v. healm, heals.

hâlor *salvation*:—From hâlor âhwyrfan, oncyrran *to turn, seduce from salvation*, Exon. 70 b; Th. 262, 3; Jul. 327: 71 a; Th. 264, 6; Jul. 360: 72 a; Th. 268, 30; Jul. 440.

hâls, e; *f. Health, salvation*:—Ðæt hǽlubearn hâls eft forgeaf *that saviour-child gave salvation again*, Exon. 16 a; Th. 37, 3; Cri. 587. [*Icel.* heilsa *health.*] v. heáls-bôc.

hâlsere, es; *m. An exorcist*:—Hâlsere *exorcista*, L. Ecg. C. 41; Th. ii. 166, 21: Rtl. 194, 5. [*O. H. Ger.* heilisari *augur, aruspex.*] v. hâlsian.

hâlsian, heâlsian [Ettmüller connects this verb in the sense *obsecrare* with *hals*, and writes *halsian, healsian*; the forms in which *ea* occurs seem to favour this writing, while reference to cognate dialects seems to point to *â*] *To beseech, entreat, implore, adjure, conjure, exorcise*:—Ic hâlsige and bidde ðone gelǽredan ðæt hê ðæt ûs ne wîte *I beseech and beg the learned not to blame us for it*, Guthl. prol; Gdwin. 2, 10: Blickl. Homl. 57, 33. Ic hâlsige ðê þurh ðone lifiendan God *adjuro te per Deum vivum*, Mt. Kmbl. 26, 63: Exon. 72 a; Th. 269, 6; Jul. 446: Blickl. Homl. 151, 22. Ic eów hâlsige scucna englas ðæt gê leng ne beran *I adjure you, devils' angels, that ye bear him no longer*, 189, 7. Ic ðê hâlsige for ðînre þeówene Sancta Marian *I entreat thee for the sake of thy servant Saint Mary*, 89, 17: Exon. 73 b; Th. 274, 26; Jul. 539: Cd. 222; Th. 290, 28; Sat. 422. Ic ðê heâlsige *I beseech thee*, Bt. 22, 2; Fox 78, 10. Ic heâlsige *obsecro*, Past. 18, 6; Swt. 137, 17. Ic hâlsigo ðec *exorcizo te*, Rtl. 100, 27: 117, 34. Exorcista is on Englisc se ðe mid âþe hâlsaþ ða âwyrgedan gâstas ðe wyllaþ menn dreccan þurh ðæs Hǽlendes naman ðæt hý ða menn forlǽton *exorcista is in English he who with oath conjures the accursed spirits that will torment men, in the Saviour's name to leave those men*, L. Ælfc. C. 13; Th. ii. 348, 1. Hê ðone unlybban on Godes naman hâlsode *he exorcised the poison*, Homl. Th. i. 72, 24. For ðam ðe hê hâlsode Israhêla bearn *for he had strictly sworn the children of Israel*, Ex. 13, 19. Hê hie heâlsade *he entreated them*, Ors. 4, 6; Swt. 178, 14: Beo. Th. 4270; B. 2132. Fæder and môdor hâlsedon hî ðæt hî forlêtan ðone cristes geleáfan *father and mother implored them to forsake the faith of Christ*, Shrn. 92, 13. Heâlsa hine suâ suâ ðînne fæder *obsecra ut patrem*, Past. 25; Swt. 181, 2. On wigbedde tô hâlsienne *in altari ad augurandum*, Cot. 17, Lye. [*Laym. A. R.* halsien: *Chauc.* halse: *O. H. Ger.* heilison *augurari*: cf. *Icel.* heilsa *to salute, greet.*] v. gehalsian [*where read* ge-hâlsian] *and* hâlsung.

hâlsigend, es; *m. An exorcist*:—Exorcista is hâlsigend, L. Ælf. P. 34; Th. ii. 378, 6.

hâlsigendlîc, hâlsiendlîc; *adj. That may be entreated*:—Hâlsiendlîc *deprecabilis*, Ps. Spl. M. 89, 15.

hâlsigendlîce, hâlsiendlîce; *adv. Importune*, Greg. Dial. 1, 2, Lye.

hâlsung, heâlsung, e; *f. Supplication, beseeching, entreaty, adjuration, exorcising, exorcism, augury, greeting* [?]:—Micel is seó hâlsung and mǣre is seó hâlgung ðe deófla âfyrsaþ *great is the exorcising and greater is the hallowing that drives away devils*, L. C. E; Th. i. 360, 28. Hâlsung *exorcismus*, Mone Gl. 414. Mid wēpendre hâlsunga hine bǣdon *with weeping supplication prayed him*, Blickl. Homl. 87, 8. Hē breác ealdre heâlsunge *vetere usus augurio*, Bd. 1, 25; S. 486, 40. On hâlsunge *in auspicium*, 2, 9; S. 510, 13. Mid eárum onfôh mîne hâlsunge *auribus percipe obsecrationem meam*, Ps. Th. 142, 1. Hâlsunga dôþ *obsecrationes faciunt*, Lk. Skt. 5, 33. Se ðe hâlsunga behealdaþ *quicunque exorcismos observat*, L. Ecg. C. 29, note; Th. ii. 154, 29. Hie [*the rich*] hæfdon oforgedrync and dyslîce and unrǣdlîce hâlsunga *they had excessive drinking and foolish and thoughtless greetings* [?], Blickl. Homl. 99, 21. On hâlsungum *in obsecrationibus*, Lk. Skt. 2, 37. On hâlsungum *precibus*, L. Ecg. C. 2; Th. ii. 136, 19. [*A. R.* halsung *supplication*: *O. H. Ger.* heilisunga *omen, auspicium*: cf. [?] *Icel.* heilsan *greeting*.]

hâlsung-gebed, es; *n. Litany*, R. Ben. 9, Lye.

hâls-wurþung, e; *f. A celebration because of safety*, Cd. 171; Th. 215, 11; Exod. 581. v. hâls.

hâl-wenda, an; *m. A saviour*:—Mîne eágan habbaþ gesewen ðînne Hâlwendan. Se hâlwenda ðe hē embe spræc is ûre Hǣlend Crist se ðe com tō gehǣlenne ûre wunda ðæt sindon ûre synna *mine eyes have seen thy Saviour* [*viderunt oculi mei salutare tuum*]. *The Saviour that he spoke about is Jesus Christ who came to heal our wounds, that is, our sins*, Homl. Th. i. 142, 32: 136, 21. [Cf. Hǣlend.]

hâl-wende; *adj. Conducive to health, salutary, healing, wholesome*:—Ðes hâlwenda *hic saluber*, Ælfc. Gr. 9, 18; Som. 9, 64. Ðîn word is hâlwende *thy word is salutary*, Ps. Th. 118, 103. Hâlwoende ðîn *salutare tuum*, Lk. Skt. Lind. 2, 30. Se middangeard wæs mannum hâlwende *the earth was healthful for men*, Blickl. Homl. 115, 8: 209, 10. Ðisse sylfan wyrte sǣd on wîne gedruncen is hâlwende ongeán âttres drync *the seed of this same plant is wholesome against a draught of poison*, Herb. 142, 6; Lchdm. i. 264, 13: 157, 2; Lchdm. i. 284, 10. Hit is hâluwende bôte *it is a healing remedy*, 374, 24. Wē mâgon eów sellan hâlwende geþeahte hwæt gē dôn mâgon *possumus salubre vobis dare consilium quid agere valeatis*, Bd. 1, 1; S. 474, 14. Seó tunge ðe swâ monig hâlwende word gesette *illa lingua quæ tot salutaria verba composuerat*, 4, 24; S. 599, 11. Hâte baþu ðe wǣron hâlwende gecwedene âdligendum lîchaman *hot baths that were said to be salutary for diseased bodies*, Homl. Th. i. 86, 21. Ða hâlwendan men *the men who taught a saving faith, the disciples*, Blickl. Homl. 117, 8. Swâ se lǣcedôm yldra byþ swâ hē hâlwendra byþ *the older the medicine is the more healing it is*, Herb. 130, 3; Lchdm. i. 242, 5.

hâl-wendlîc; *adj. Salutary, healthful*:—Ðæs Hǣlendes tôcyme wæs hâlwendlîc ǣgðer ge mannum ge englum *the Saviour's advent was salutary for both men and angels*, Homl. Th. i. 214, 22: ii. 220, 20: 564, 7. Him se bisceop hâlwendlîce geþeaht forþbrohte *the bishop proposed to them salutary counsel*, Blickl. Homl. 205, 18.

hâl-wendlîce; *adv. Salutarily*:—Hâlwoendlîce *salubriter*, Rtl. 9, 29. Se ylca Hǣlend ðe nû hâlwendlîce clypaþ on his godspelle *the same Saviour that now cries out salutarily in his gospel*, Homl. Th. i. 94, 9.

hâl-wendnes, -ness, e; *f. Salubrity*:—Hibernia ge on brǣdo his stealles ge on hâlwendnesse ge on smyltnysse lyfta is betere mycle ðonne Breotone land *Hibernia et latitudine sui status et salubritate ac serenitate aerum multum Brittaniæ præstat*, Bd. 1, 1; S. 474, 29.

ham, hom, es; *m. A covering, garment, shirt*:—Ham *camisa*, Wrt. Voc. 288, 48. [*Icel.* hamr *a skin*.] v. hama. DER. byrn-, fyrd-, scîr-ham.

ham, hom, hamm, e; *f. The ham, the inner* or *hind part of the knee*:—Hamm *poples*, hamma *suffragines*, Ælfc. Gl. 75; Som. 71, 84, 83; Wrt. Voc. 44, 66, 65. Ham *poples*, 71, 50. Monegum men gescrincaþ his fēt tō his homme ... gebeðe ða hamma *with many a man the feet shrink up to the ham ... warm the hams*, L. M. 1, 26; Lchdm. ii. 68, 3–5. [*A. R.* mid hommen iuolden *with bent knees*: *Icel.* höm *the ham* or *haunch of a horse*: *O. H. Ger.* hamma *poples, suffrago*.]

ham, hom; *gen.* hammes; *m. A dwelling, fold,* or *enclosed possession.* 'It is so frequently coupled with words implying the presence of water as to render it probable that, like the *Friesic* hemmen, it denotes a piece of land surrounded with paling, wicker-work, etc., and so defended against the stream, which would otherwise wash it away.' Cod. Dipl. Kmbl. iii. xxvii, where see instances of the occurrence of the word in local names. It occurs as an independent word in the following passages:—Ðonne geúðe ic Ælfwine and Beortulfe ðes hammes be norþan ðære littlan dîc, iii. 421, 15. Of ðam beorg tō Cwichemhamme; of ðam hamme, v. 157, 24. Ðonne up on æscmēres hammas sûþewearde; of ðân hammum, 338, 32. Ða hammas ða ðēr mid rihte tōgebyriaþ, 383, 18.

hâm, es; *m. Home, house, abode, dwelling, residence, habitation, house with land, estate, property*; domus, domicilium, prædium, villa, mansio, possessio:—Se hâm is gefylled mid heofonlîcum gâstum *that abode* [*heaven*] *is filled with heavenly spirits*, Blickl. Homl. 25, 33: 9, 7. Ðes atola hâm *this horrid abode* [*hell*], Cd. 215; Th. 270, 26; Sat. 96. Tō cyniges hâme *ad mansionem regiam*, L. R. S. 1; Th. i. 432, 7: Shrn. 187, 7, 22. Ðâ gerâd Æþelwald ðone hâm æt Winburnan ... and sæt binnan ðæm hâm mid ðǣm monnum ðe him tō gebugon and hæfde ealle ða geatu forworht *then Ethelwald rode and occupied the residence at Winborne and sat within with those men that had joined him, and he had blockaded all the entrances*, Chr. 901; Erl. 96, 26–30. Mînre yldstan dēhter ðæne hâm æt Welewe and ðære gingestan ðone hâm æt Welig *to my eldest daughter the vill at Wellow, and to the youngest the vill at Welig*, Th. Chart. 488, 29–33. Gif cyning æt mannes hâm drincæþ *if the king drink at a man's house*, L. Eth. 3; Th. i. 4, 1: L. H. E. 15; Th. i. 32, 17: L. Alf. pol. 21; Th. i. 76, 1. Hǣlend com tō Lazares hâm *Jesus had come to the home of Lazarus*, Blickl. Homl. 69, 21. Ðâ Noe ongan hâm staðelian *then began Noah to establish his home*, Cd. 75; Th. 94, 4; Gen. 556. In hûs fadores mînes hâmas meniga sint *in domo patris mei mansiones multæ sunt*, Jn. Skt. Lind. 14, 2: 23. Nǣron ðâ welige hâmas *there were not then splendid mansions*, Bt. 15; Fox 48, 4. Wæs forðon hæbbend monigra hâmas *erat enim habens multas possessiones*, Mt. Kmbl. Lind. 19, 22. Hig cîptun ealle hire hâmas *vendebant omnia prædia sua*, Gen. 47, 20. On hira hâmon *in possessionibus suis*, 48, 6. Se cyng him wel gegifod hæfde on hâmon and on golde and seolfre and forbærndon Tegntûn and eác fela ôðra gôdra hâma ... and ðone hâm æt Peonhô ... and ðone hâm æt Wealthâm and ôðra cotlîfa fela *the king had given him many gifts of vills and of gold and silver. And they burned down Teignton and many other good vills too ..., and the vill at Penhoc ..., and the vill at Waltham, and many other hamlets*, Chr. 1001; Erl. 136, 16–32. Ðǣr hē râd betwih his hâmum oððe tûnum *equitantem inter civitates sive villas*, Bd. 2, 16; S. 520, 10. Abbud of Peortaneá ðam hâm *Abbas de Monasterio Peartanea*, S. 519, 28. Æt hâm *domi*, Mk. Skt. 9, 33: Lk. Skt. 9, 61. Ðû nēre æt hâm *you were not at home*, Cod. Dipl. Kmbl. iv. 26, 9. Hâm, *acc.* is *used adverbially after verbs of motion*:—Ðâ hē hâm com *cum venisset domum*, Mt. Kmbl. 9, 28. Hig cyrdon ealle hâm *reversi sunt unusquisque in domum suam*, Jn. Skt. 7, 53. Ðâ se cing lȳfde eallon Myrceon hâm *the king allowed all the Mercians to go home*, Chr. 1049; Erl. 172, 37: 1066; Erl. 200, 9. [*Goth.* haims; *f. a village*: *O. Sax.* hêm *a dwelling-place*: *Icel.* heimr *an abode, world, this world*: heim; *adv. home*: *O. H. Ger.* haim *domus, domicilium, patria*: haim; *adv*: *Ger.* heim.]

-hâm, es; *m.* 'The Latin word which appears most nearly to translate it is *vicus*, and it seems to be identical in form with the Greek κώμη. In this sense it is the general assemblage of the dwellings in each particular district, to which the arable land and pasture of the community were appurtenant, the *home* of all the settlers in a separate and well defined locality, the collection of the houses of the freemen. Whenever we can assure ourselves that the vowel is long, we may be certain that the name implies such a village or community,' Cod. Dipl. Kmbl. iii. xxviii–ix. The distinction between *-ham* and *-hâm* seems to have been lost before the Norman Conquest, as in the Chronicle one MS. has *tô Buccingahamme*, another *tô Buccingahâm*, 918; Th. i. 190, col. 1, 2, l. 21. [*Icel.* -heimr, e. g. Âlf-heimr *the abode of the elves*: *O. H. Ger.* -heim.]

hama, homa, an; *m. A covering.* [*Prompt. Parv.* hame thyn skynne *of an eye, or other like*: *K. Alis.* dragoun's hame (cf. *Icel.* hams *a snake's slough*): *O. Sax. O. H. Ger.* hamo *in compounds*: and cf. *O. H. Ger.* hemidi *camisa, vestimentum*.] v. ham. DER. byrn-, cild-, feðer-, flǣsc-, gold-, grǣg-, heort-, lîc-, wuldor-hama.

hâma, an; *m. A cricket*; cicada, Wrt. Voc. 281, 48. [*O. H. Ger.* heimo *cicada, grillus*: *Ger.* heime, heimchen *cricket*.] v. Grmm. D. M. 1222.

hamacgaþ [?]:—Se ðe gelîþ raðe hē hamacgaþ *he who takes to his bed will quickly be up again*, Lchm. iii. 184, 21.

hâm-bringan; *pp.* -broht *To bring a wife home, marry*:—Ne hî beóþ hâmbroht ne geǣwnode *neque nubentur*, Mone Gl. 357. [Cf. *O. H. Ger.* heimbringa, Grff. 3, 201.]

hâm-cûþ; *adj. Familiar*:—Ða hâmcûþa stôwa *familiaria loca*, Mt. Kmbl. p. 11, 1.

hâm-cyme, es; *m. A coming home, return*:—Æfter twegra geára ymbryne æfter ðæs wælhreówan hâmcyme *after two years had elapsed after the return of the cruel tyrant*, Homl. Th. i. 80, 31. [*Will.* homkome: *Icel.* heim-kvâma, -koma *return home*.]

hamele, hamule, an; *f. An oar-loop*, but the word occurs only in a phrase, which may be borrowed from the Scandinavian. *Icel.* hamla *an oar-loop*, is used in the phrase, til hömlu = *per man* [v. Cl. and Vig. Dict.], and apparently with the same meaning we get Chr. 1039; Erl. 167, 15, 21:—On his dagum man geald xvi scipan æt ǣlcere hamulan viii marc eall swâ man ǣr dyde on Cnutes cynges dagum ... Ðâ hî gerǣdden ðet man geald lxii scipon æt ǣlcere hamelan viii marc *in his days sixteen ships were paid, eight marks to each of the crew, just as before was done in king Cnut's days ... Then they decided that sixty-two ships should be paid, to each man eight marks.* William of Malmesbury says twenty marks were paid to the soldiers of each vessel, ii. 12. Florence of Worcester, Chr. 1040, says eight marks to each rower, and twelve to the steersman, 'octo marcas unicuique suæ classis remigi et xii unicuique gubernatori præcepit dependi.'

hamelian; *p.* ode; *pp.* od *To mutilate*:—Sume man hamelode *some were mutilated*, Chr. 1036; Erl. 164, 38. [*Chauc.* a foot is hameled of thi sorwe, Tr. and Cr. 2, 138: hamling *the operation of cutting the balls out of the feet of dogs*, Hall. Dict. *where see also* hamel: *Icel.* hamla *to mutilate*:—Sumir vōru hamlaðir at höndum eða fôtum *some had their hands or feet cut off*: *O. H. Ger.* bi-hamalon *mutilare*, pe-hamaloter *mutilatus*, Grff. iv. 945.]

hamer, homer, hamor, es; *m. A hammer*:—Hamor *porticulus*, Ælfc. Gr. 104; Som. 78, 13; Wrt. Voc. 56, 59. Cf. porticulus *a maylat*, 275, 1. 'Porticulus, malleus in manu portatus quo signum detur remigantibus,' Du Cange. Heoru hamere geþuren *the sword forged by the hammer*, Beo. Th. 2575; B. 1285. Carcernes dura hamera geweorc *the doors of the prison, the work of hammers*, Andr. Kmbl. 2155; An. 1079. Homra, Exon. 69 a; Th. 256, 25; Jul. 237. Homera lâfe *with the sword*, 102 b; Th. 388, 14; Rä. 6, 7: Chr. 937; Erl. 112, 6. [*O. Sax.* hamur: *Icel.* hamarr: *O. H. Ger.* hamar: *Ger.* hammer.] v. Grmm. D. M. 165. DER. scip-hamor.

hamer-secg, homor-, es; *m. Hammer-sedge*, L. M. i. 56, 2; Lchdm. ii. 126, 19.

hamer-wyrt, hamor-, e; *f. Black hellebore*, Lchdm. iii. 330, col. 1: ii. 390, col. 1.

hâmettan; *p.* te *To provide with a home, to house*:—Denewulf bisceop lŷfde Beornulfe his mêge ðæt hê môste ða inberðan menn hâmettan tô Ebblesburnan nû hebbe ic hî hâmet *bishop Denewulf allowed Beornulf his kinsman to house the inborn people at Ebblesburn. I have now housed them*, Th. Chart. 152, 3–7. v. ge-hâmettan.

hâm-færeld, es; *n. A going home*:—Ðâ Antigones ðæt ongeat ðâ forlêt hê ðæt setl; ac Ymenis him wênde fram Antigones hâmfæreld micelra untreówþa *when Antigonus heard that he abandoned the siege: but Eumenes anticipated for himself great treachery from Antigonus' going home*, Ors. 3, 11; Bos. 73, 21. [Cf. *Icel.* heim-ferð, -för *a going home*: *O. H. Ger.* heim-fart.]

hâm-fæst; *adj. Resident, dwelling at home*:—Hû mæg ðǽr ðonne ânes rîces monnes nama cuman ðonne ðǽr mon furðum ðære burge naman ne geheórþ ne ðære þeóde ðe hê on hâmfæst biþ *how can one great man's name come there, when the name of the town even and of the people among whom he dwells is not heard there*, Bt. 18, 2; Fox 64, 3: L. Ed. 1; Th. i. 158, 22. Gif mon becume on his gefân and hê hine ǽr hâmfæstne ne wite *si quis superveniat in hostem suum, et eum antea residentem nesciat*, L. Alf. pol. 42; Th. i. 90, 15. [Cf. hâm-sittende.]

hâm-faru, e; *f. Forcible entry into a man's house*; the same as hâm-sôcn, q. v. [*Trev.* hamfare:—'Hamsokene oðer Hamfare *a rese imade in house, a fray made in an howse*,' ii. 95: *Icel.* heim-för *an inroad*.]

hâm-hæn, -henn, e; *f. A domestic fowl*, L. M. 2, 37; Lchdm. ii. 244, 25.

hâm-leás; *adj. Homeless*:—Sceal hâmleás hweorfan *it must wander homeless*, Exon. 110 a; Th. 420, 25; Rä. 40, 9.

hâm-scir, e; *f. The office of an ædile*; ædilitas, officium ædile, Cot. 71, Lye.

ham-scyld [?], L. Eth. 32; Th. i. 12, 1, where see note. Leo in his work on Anglo-Saxon Names quotes a passage from Richthofen in which *skeld* occurs in the sense of fence; so that the crime referred to in the passage would be the breaking through the fence which surrounded the *ham*. v. the translation of Leo, p. 40, note 2.

hâm-sittende; *part. Sitting, dwelling at home, resident*:—Wê beódaþ se mon se ðe his gefân hâmsittendne wite ðæt hê ne feohte ǽrðam ðe hê him ryhtes bidde *we command that the man who knows his foe to be dwelling at his home fight not before he demand justice*, L. Alf. pol. 42; Th. i. 90, 2: Cd. 209; Th. 259, 6; Dan. 687: Andr. Kmbl. 1372; An. 686: Cd. 86; Th. 108, 33; Gen. 1815. [*O. Sax.* hêm-sittiandi.]

hâm-sôcn, e; *f. Attack on a man's house*; also *the fine paid for such a breach of the peace*. The following passage will illustrate the character of the offence:—'Hamsocna, quod domus invasionem Latine sonat, fit pluribus modis, extrinsecus vel et intrinsecus accidenciis. Hamsocna est, si quis alium in sua vel alterius domo cum haraido assaliaverit vel persequatur, ut portam vel domum sagittet vel lapidet vel colpum ostensibilem undecunque faciat. Hamsocna est, vel hamfare, si quis premeditate ad domum eat, ubi hostem suum esse scit, et ibi eum invadat, si die vel nocte hoc faciat; et qui aliquem in molinum vel ovile fugientem prosequitur, hamsocna judicatur. Si in curia vel domo, sedicione orta, bellum eciam subsequatur, et quivis alium fugientem in aliam domum infuget, si ibi duo tecta sint, hamsocna reputetur,' L. H. 80, 10, 11; Th. i. 587, 14–25. Other passages in the earlier laws and charters are:—Wê cwǽdon be hâmsôcnum seðe hit ofer ðis dô ðæt hê þolige ealles ðæs ðe âge and sî on cyninges dôme hwæðer hê lîf âge *we have ordained respecting 'ham-socns' that he who shall commit it after this forfeit all that he owns, and that it be in the king's judgment whether he have his life*, L. Edm. S. 6; Th. i. 250, 9: L. Eth. 4, 4; Th. i. 301, 18. Ðis syndon ða gerihta ðe se cyning âh ofer ealle men on Wesseaxan ðæt is hâmsôcne *these are the rights which the king has over all men in Wessex that is* [*the fines for*] '*ham-socn*,' L. C. S. 12; Th. i. 382, 13, see the note: 15; Th. i. 384, 6: Th. Chart. 333, 32: 359, 4: 369, 14. Gif hwâ hâmsôcne gewyrce gebête ðæt mid fîf pundan ðam cyningce *if any one commit 'ham-socn,' let him pay a fine of five pounds to the king*, 63; Th. i. 408, 27. [*Scot.* hame-sucken *the crime of beating* or *assaulting a person within his own house*: *Icel.* heim-sôkn *an inroad* or *attack on one's home*: *O. Frs.* ham-, hem-sekenge *attack on one's house*.] v. sêcan, in its sense of *to seek with a hostile intent*.

hâm-steall, es; *m. A homestead, residence*:—On his hâmstealle *at his homestead*, Cod. Dipl. Kmbl. iii. 255, 9. Ðane hâmstal ðet hê on set *the homestead at which he resides*, iv. 133, 8. [Homestall *a homestead*, Hall. Dict: *a mansion, seat in the country*, Bailey.]

hâm-stede, es; m. *A homestead*:—Tô hâmstede *to the homestead*, Cod. Dipl. Kmbl. iii. 77, 7. v. p. xxxviii s. v. stede for compounds in which the word occurs. [*O. Frs.* heem-steed *domicile*: cf. *Icel.* heim-stöð *a homestead*.]

Hâm-tûn [*or* Ham-tûn?] *Hampton*, a common local name, used for both the present Northampton, Chr. 917; Erl. 102, 12; and Southampton, Chr. 981; Erl. 129, 36: for other towns see the index to Cod. Dipl. Kmbl. vol. vi.

Hâmtûn-scir, e; *f. Hampshire*, Chr. 1001; Erl. 136, 5.

hamule. v. hamele.

hâm-weard; *adv. Homeward, in the direction of home*; domum versus, retro:—Ðâ heó hâmwerd wæs *when it was on its way home*, H. R. 103, 24. Ðâ hŷ hâmweard wǽron *when they were on the way home*, Ors. 4, 6; Bos. 85, 38, Êgeas wearþ gelǽht fram atelîcum deófle hâmwerd be wege ǽrðan hê tô hûse côme *Ægeas was seized by a horrible devil on the way home, before he came to his house*, Homl. Th. i. 598, 23. Æþelwulf ðâ him hâmweard fôr *Ethelwulf then journeyed homeward*, Chr. 855; Erl. 68, 29: 885; Erl. 82, 30. Se esne hig hâmweard lǽdde tô his hlâforde *the servant brought her home to his lord*, Gen. 24, 61.

hâm-weardes; *adv. Homewards*:—Sió ôðeru fierd wæs hâmweardes *the other force was returning home*, Chr. 894; Erl. 91, 1. [*O. H. Ger.* heimwartes *domum versus*: *Ger.* heimwärts.]

hâm-weorþung, e; *f. Honour* or *ornament to the house* or *home*:—Eofore forgeaf ângan dôhtor hâmweorþunge *he gave Eofor his only daughter, an ornament of his home*, Beo. Th. 5988; B. 2998.

hâm-weorud, es; *n. The body of people connected with a 'ham;'* vicani:—Ðâ com hê tô sumum hûse on ǽfentîd and eode on ðæt hûs ðǽr ðæt hâmweorud eall tô symble gesomnod wæs *pervenit ad vicum quendam vespere intravitque in domum in qua vicani cænantes epulabantur*, Bd. 3, 10; S. 534, 26.

hâm-wyrt, e; *f. Home-wort*; sempervivum tectorum, L. M. 3, 41; Lchdm. ii. 336, 4: 1, 1; Lchdm. ii. 18, 19: 1, 40; Lchdm. ii. 104, 14.

hana, an; *m. A cock*:—Se hana creów *gallus cantavit*, Mk. Skt. 14, 68, 30, 72. [*Goth.* hana: *O. Sax.* hano: *Icel.* hani: *O. H. Ger.* hano: *Ger.* hahn.]

han-crêd, -crǽd, hon-, es; *m. Cock-crowing, cock-crow, a division of the night*:—Hancrêd *conticinium* vel *gallicinium*, Ælfc. Gl. 94; Som. 75, 122; Wrt. Voc. 53, 4. Seó niht hæfþ seofan dǽlas . . . fîfta is gallicinium ðæt is hancrêd *the night has seven divisions . . . the fifth is gallicinium, that is, cock-crow*, Lchdm. iii. 244, 4. Hêr wæs se môna âþîstrod betwux hancrêd and dagunge *in this year the moon was eclipsed between cock-crow and dawn*, Chr. 795; Erl. 59, 25. On ǽfen ðe on midre nihte ðe on hancrêde ðe on morgen *sero, an media nocte, an galli cantu an mane*, Mk. Skt. 13, 35: Bd. 4, 23; S. 595, 27: Homl. Th. i. 74, 21. Honcrêd, Exon. 99 a; Th. 370, 32; Seel. 68. Ðone drenc on þreó þicge æt ðâm þrîm honcrêdum *let him take the drink at three times at the three cock-crowings*, L. M. 2, 65, 2; Lchdm. ii. 294, 5. Se cyning embe forman hancrêd ût gangende wæs *the king about the first cock-crowing was going out*, Lchdm. iii. 424, 34. Ðâ com se Hǽlend embe ðone feórþan hancrêd *quarta autem vigilia noctis venit Iesus*, Mt. Kmbl. 14, 25. [*O. Sax.* hano-krâd: *O. H. Ger.* hana-crât *gallicinium, galli cantus*.]

hand, hond, a; *f.* HAND, *side, power, control* [cf. mund]; used also of *the person from whom an action proceeds*:—Hand *manus*, Wrt. Voc. 64, 73. Middeweard hand *vola* vel *tenar* vel *ir*, Ælfc. Gl. 72; Som. 70, 130; Wrt. Voc. 43, 54. Ðîn seó swŷðre hand *dextera tua*, Ps. Th. 59, 5. Ðǽr unc hwîle wæs hand gemǽne *there for a time we two had a hand to hand struggle* [cf. *Ger.* handgemein werden *to fight hand to hand*], Beo. Th. 4281; B. 2137. Sette Ephraim on his swîðran hand ðæt wæs on Israhêles wynstran hand and Manasses on his winstran hand ðæt wæs on Israhêles swîðran healfe *he placed Ephraim on his right hand, that was on Israel's left hand, and Manasseh on his left hand, that was on Israel's right hand*, Gen. 48, 13. Seó hǽlo his ðære swŷðran handa *salus dextera ejus*, Ps. Th. 19, 6. Gif hê heáhre handa dyntes onfêhþ *if he receives a right* [?] *hand blow* [cf. *Icel.* hægri hönd *the right hand*, and see note on the passage for other translations. The analogy with the Icelandic, it may be observed, is not perfect, since the English does not (as in the case of swīdre) use the comparative; so that the phrase may perhaps refer to the hand being raised for defence; or the reference may be to the upraised hand of the striker], L. Eth. 58; Th. i. 18, 1. God ālȳsde hī lāđum of handa *quos redemit de manu inimici*, 106, 2. Tō onfōnne æt bisceopes handa *to receive at the hand of the bishop*, L. C. E. 22; Th. i. 374, 3: Chr. 942; Erl. 116, 22. Æt Seaxena handa forwurđan *to perish at the hand of the Saxons*, 605; Erl. 21, 29. Mid brādre hand slōgan *smote with open hand*, Blickl. Homl. 23, 32; Past. 41, 4; Swt. 303, 11. Mid đære ylcan hand *with the same hand*, Lchdm. iii. 68, 15. Đa witan đe đā nēh handa wǣron *the 'witan' that were near at hand*, Chr. 1100; Erl. 236, 19. Hand on handa *hand in hand*, Ap. Th. 19, 18. Đeóf đe æt hæbbendre handa gefangen sȳ *a thief who is taken with the stolen property upon him*, L. Ath. 1; Th. i. 198, 17. Siđđan ic hond and rond hebban mihte *since I could lift hand and shield*, Beo. Th. 1316: B. 656: Andr. Kmbl. 18; An. 9. Đǣr wæs micel wæl geslægen on gehwæđre hond *there was great slaughter made on either side*, Chr. 871; Erl. 74, 12: Byrht. Th. 135, 2; By. 112. On ǣgđera hand *on either hand*, L. Ath. 1, 23; Th. i. 212, 6. Wiđ ǣlce hand *on all sides, towards every one*, L. Ed. 10; Th. i. 164, 18. Ic wille đæt hit gange on đa nȳhstan hand mē *I will that it go to the next of kin to me*, Th. Chart. 491, 13: 481, 22. Đa witan gerehton đæt heó sceolde hire fæder hand geclǣnsian be swā miclan feó *the 'witan' decided that she should clear her father in respect to so much money;* sapientes decreverunt quod ego patrem meum purgare deberem, videlicet sacramento xxx librarum, easdem triginta libras patrem meum persolvisse, 202, 1. Būtan osterlandes bēc and hē đa bōc unnendre handa hire tō lēt *excepto libro de osterlande quem bona voluntate dimisit*, 37. Sī mē wuldres hyht hand ofer heáfod *may there be to me a hope of glory, hand over head*, i. e. *without difficulty* [hand-over-head *thoughtlessly extravagant; careless; at random; plenty*, Hall. Dict.], Lchdm. i. 390, 3, 5. Gif mon forstolenne man befō æt ōđrum and sīe sió hond ōđcwolen sió hine sealde đam men đe hine mon ætbefēng *if a stolen man be attached in another's possession, and the hand [person] be dead that sold him to the man in whose possession he is attached*, L. In. 53; Th. i. 134, 17: 136, 2: 75; Th. i. 150, 5: L. Eth. 2, 8; Th. i. 288, 18, 20. His feoh onfōn fremde handa *diripiant alieni omnes labores ejus*, Ps. Th. 108, 11. Handa đīne *manus tuæ*, 118, 73. Se đe ofer đis fals wyrce þolige đæra handa đe hē đæt fals mid worhte *he that after this makes counterfeit money, let him lose the hands with which he made the counterfeit*, L. C. S. 8; Th. i. 380, 17. Domicianus wearþ ācweald æt his witena handum *Domitian was killed by his senators*, Homl. Th. i. 60, 4. Gebindan handum and fōtum *to bind hand and foot*, 570, 10. Be heora handum gebundne *bound by the hands*, Blickl. Homl. 209, 36. Sȳ đeós gesetnys đus hēr geendod god helpe mīnum handum *so let this composition here end, God help my hands*, Lchdm. iii. 280, 16. Ealle forgielden đone wer gemǣnum hondum *let them all pay the wergild in common*, L. Alf. pol. 31; Th. i. 80, 17: L. E. G. 13; Th. i. 174, 21. Đā genam Sanctus Martinus hine be his handa *then St. Martin took him by the hand*, Blickl. Homl. 219, 19. Hit hyre on hand āgeaf *gave it into her hand*, Judth. 11; Thw. 23, 20; Jud. 130. Đȳlæs đe eów on hand become seó leáse gesetnys *lest the false account come into your hands*, Homl. Th. i. 436, 30. Him ealle on hand eodan đa hǣđnan leóde *then all the heathen people submitted to them*, Blickl. Homl. 203, 23: Chr. 882; Erl. 82, 13. Gif hig on hand gāþ *if they submit*, Deut. 20, 11. Ealle đa burgware ne mehton hiene ǣnne geniéddan đæt hē him an hand gān wolde *all the citizens could not force him, though a single man, to yield*, Ors. 3, 9; 134, 18. Đæs wīte on eówre handa geeode *on that account punishment came upon you*, Ps. 57, 2. Hē ealle gesceafta on his handa hafaþ *he hath all creatures in his hand*, Blickl. Homl. 121, 15. Se đe hie on handa hæfþ *who has it in his possession*, L. Eth. 2, 9; Th. i. 290, 17. Se hæfde his abbotrīce s' Iohs of Angeli on hande *he held his abbacy of St. John of Angeli*, Chr. 1127; Erl. 255, 27, 34: 256, 2. Ealle hē hī ođđe wiđ feó gesealde ođđe on his āgenre hand heóld *all of them he either sold for money or kept in his own hands*, 1100; Erl. 236, 6, 9. Mann sette Ælfgār đane eorldōm on handa đe Harold ǣr āhte *the earldom that Harold had before was put into Alfgar's hands*, 1048; Erl. 180, 29. Se đe ic hit nū on hand sette *he into whose hand I now put it*, L. O. 3; Th. i. 180, 3. Se đe unriht gestreón on his handa stōde *he in whose hands was the unjust gain*, L. Eth. 2, 9; Th. i. 290, 5: Th. Chart. 369, 7. Þridde gewrit ā mid đam đe đæt land on hande stande *the third copy always with him in whose possession the land is*, Cod. Dipl. Kmbl. iv. 235, 31. Gyf neód on handa stande *if there be present need*, L. Edg. H. 2; Th. i. 258, 6. Biþ mannes sunu geseald on synfulra hand *the Son of man shall be given into the hands of sinful men*, Blickl. Homl. 73, 1. On hand syllan *to give a pledge* or *promise:*—Hē sealde him on hand mid Cristes bēc đæt hē wolde đisne þeódscype swā wel haldan swā ǣnig kyngc ætforan him betst dyde *he promised him on the Gospels that he would rule this people as well as the king who before him had ruled best*, Chr. 1066; Erl. 202, 31: 1064; Erl. 196, 1. Slaga sceal his forspecan on hand syllan *the slayer shall give pledge to his advocate*, L. Edm. S. 7; Th. i. 250, 14: L. Eth. 2, 8; Th. i. 288, 16. Gif hwā his hand on hand sylle *if any one deliver himself up*, L. Ed. 9; Th. i. 164, 10. Cyricean hyrde tō cristes handa *shepherd of the Church for Christ*, Blickl. Homl. 171, 7. Đet land eall ābēgdon Willelme tō handa *brought all the land in subjection to William*, Chr. 1073; Erl. 212, 1. Him becōmon swā micele welan tō handa *so great wealth came into his hands*, Homl. Th. ii. 576, 30. Ic beóde đē đat đū berīde đās land đam hǣlge tō hande *I enjoin thee that thou perequitate these lands into the possession of the saint*, Th. Chart. 369, 22. Swā Ælfrīc hig mīnre mōder tō handa bewiste *as Alfric administered it on behalf of my mother* [cf. *Icel.* einum til handa], Cod. Dipl. Kmbl. iv. 222, 19: 226, 4. Sȳ đæt forworht đam cyningce tō handa *let it be forfeited to the king*, L. C. S. 13; Th. i. 382, 20. Tō Godes handa gefrætwod *equipped for God*, Homl. Th. i. 210, 32. Se cing lēt gerīdan ealle đa land đe his mōdor āhte him tō handa *the king had all the lands that his mother owned brought into his own power*, Chr. 1043; Erl. 168, 9: Cod. Dipl. Kmbl. iv. 222, 6. Drihten gewylt eów ealle þeóda tō handa *the Lord will reduce all nations to subjection to you*, Deut. 31, 3. Hī cwǣđon đæt hī him đet tō handa healdan scoldan *they said that they would hold it for him*, Chr. 887; Erl. 87, 3: 1036; Erl. 165, 6: L. I. P. 19; Th. ii. 326, 6. Drihten lēt hī tō handa đam hǣđenan leódscipe Madian *the Lord delivered them into the hand of Midian*, Jud. 6, 1: Chr. 1048; Erl. 180, 9. Hēr leót Ceolrēd Wulfrēde tō hande đet land of Sempigaham *in this year Ceolred let the land of Sempringham to Wulfred*, 852; Erl. 67, 33: 1091; Erl. 227, 7, 24: Anal. Th. 126, 14. Gif þeówwealh Engliscne monnan ofslihþ đonne sceal se đe hine āh weorpan hine tō honda hlāforde *if a British slave kill an Englishman, then shall he who owns him give him up to the lord*, L. In. 74; Th. i. 148, 15: 56; Th. i. 138, 12: L. Alf. pol. 21; Th. i. 76, 1: 24; Th. i. 78, 10. Gā bisceope under hand *arbitrio episcopi se dedat*, L. Ecg. P. 4, 52, note; Th. ii. 218, 33. Hī wǣron geseald under sweordes hand *tradentur in manus gladii*, Ps. Th. 62, 8. Alle þinge đe hī under honde habben *all things that they have in their possession*, Th. Chart. 582, 1, 19: Cod. Dipl. Kmbl. iv. 268, 32. [Cf. *Icel.* undir höndum einum *in one's power*.] Gelǣddon under hand hæleþ hǣđenum dēman *led the men in subjection to a heathen ruler*, Cd. 175; Th. 220, 14; Dan. 71. [*Goth.* handus: *O. Sax.* hand: *O. Frs.* hand, hond: *Icel.* hönd: *O. H. Ger.* hant: *Ger.* hand.] DER. mǣg-, wǣpned-, wīf-hand.

hand [=and (?)] *also:*—Ymbe midne dæg and nōntīde eode se hīrēdes ealdor ūt and dyde hand swā gelīce *exiit circa sextam, et nonam horam: et fecit similiter*, Anal. Th. 74, 4. Hī fērdon swā tō Sandwīc and dydon hand đæt sylfa *they went to Sandwich and did just the same*, Chr. 1052; Erl. 184, 5.

hand-bæftian, -beaftan, -beoftan; *p.* -bæftade, -beafte *To beat with the hands as an expression of grief* [?], *to lament:*—Đa đe gemǣndon and hondbæftadon *quæ plangebant et lamantabantur*, Lk. Skt. Lind. 23, 27. Wē hondbeafton *lamentavimus*, 7, 32. [Cf. apon þair brestes fast þai *beft*, Met. Homl. xviii.] v. beaftan.

hand-bana, -bona, an; *m. A murderer, homicide, one who slays with his own hand* [αὐτόχειρ], Beo. Th. 925; B. 460: 2665; B. 1330: 4997; B. 2502. [*O. Sax.* hand-bano: *Icel.* hand-bani *the actual slayer.*]

hand-bell, e; *f. A hand-bell:*—Đǣr nǣron ǣr būton vii upphangene bella and nū sind xiii upphangene and xii handbella *before there were but seven hung-up bells, and now there are thirteen hung-up bells and twelve hand-bells*, Th. Chart. 430, 6.

hand-bōc, e; *f. A hand-book, manual:*—Hand-bōc *manualis*, Wrt. Voc. 81, 46. Đa hālgan bēc saltere and pistolbōc . . . sangbōc and handbōc *the holy books: psalter and epistle-book . . . book of canticles and manual*, L. Ælf. C. 21; Th. ii. 350, 14. [*Ger.* hand-buch.]

hand-bona. v. hand-bana.

hand-brǣd, -brēd, e; *f. A hand's breadth:*—Handbrēd *vel* span *palmus*, Ælfc. Gl. 72; Som. 70, 127; Wrt. Voc. 43, 52. [*Chauc.* an hande brede, hondbrede: *Prompt. Parv.* hande brede *palmus:* cf. *Ger.* handbreit, *adj.*]

hand-bred, es; *n. The palm of the hand;* palma:—Đis handbred *hoc ir*, Ælfc. Gr. 8; Som. 7, 26. Handbred *palma*, Ælfc. Gl. 72; Som. 71, 2; Wrt. Voc. 43, 56. Hondbreodo *palmas*, Mt. Kmbl. Lind. 26, 67. Sleánde mid handbredum *striking with the palms of their hands*, Homl. Th. ii. 248, 13. [*O. Frs.* hond-brede *palma.*]

hand-clāþ, es; *n. A hand-cloth, towel:*—Ic geseó Godes engel standende ætforan đē mid handclāþe, and wīpaþ đīne swātigan limu *I see God's angel standing before thee with a handcloth, and he wipes thy sweaty limbs*, Homl. Th. i. 426, 30. [*Rel. Ant.* hand-clođ: *Icel.* hand-klæđi *a hand-towel.*]

hand-cops, es; *m. A handcuff, manacle:*—Handcops *manice*, Wrt. Voc. 86, 33. Tō gewrīdenne cyningas heora on fōtcopsum and æđele heora on handcopsum īsynum *ad alligandos reges eorum in compedibus et nobiles eorum in manicis ferreis*, Ps. Spl. C. 149, 8.

hand-cræft, es; *m. Skill* or *power of the hand, handicraft:*—Đes lama wædla būton handcræfte Godes beboda gefylde *this paralytic pauper without the use of his hands fulfilled God's commands*, Homl. Th. ii. 98, 17. Mid his handcræfte *with his manual skill* [*in tent-making*], i. 392, 16. Wē lǣraþ đæt preósta gehwilc tō-eácan lāre leornige handcræft georne *we enjoin that every priest besides book-learning diligently learn a handicraft*, L. Edg. C. 11; Th. ii. 246, 17. Eác him gerísaþ handcræftas gôde ðæt man on his hírêde cræftas begange *good handicrafts are also befitting him, that crafts may be practised in his household*, L. I. P. 8; Th. ii. 314, 23. [*O. Sax.* hand-kraft *strength, power of hand.*]

hand-cræftig; *adj. Mechanicus*, Lye.

hand-cweorn, -cwyrn, e; *f. A hand-mill:*—Hêton hine grindan æt hira handcwyrne *ordered him to grind at their mill*, Jud. 16, 21. [*Icel.* hand-kvern.]

hand-dǽd, e; *f. Handiwork*, Lye. [*O. H. Ger.* hant-tât *opus manuum.*]

hand-dǽda, an; *m. One who does a deed with his own hand:*—Ðonne wille ic ðæt eall seó mǽgþ sý unfâh bûtan ðam handdǽdan *then I will that all the kindred be free from the feud except the actual doer of the deed*, L. Edm. S. 1; Th. i. 248, 6, 12: L. Eth. 2, 5; Th. i. 286, 22. [Cf. hand-bana.]

hand-fæstan; *p.* -fæste *To pledge by giving the hand*, Lye. [*Orm.* hannd-fesst *betrothed*: *Scot.* hand-fast *to betroth by joining hands*: *Icel.* hand-festa *to strike a bargain by shaking hands, to pledge, betroth.*] v. next word.

hand-fæstung, -fæstnung, e; *f. A giving of the hand by way of pledge or assurance:*—Handfestnung *mandatum*, Ælfc. Gl. 13; Som. 57, 110; Wrt. Voc. 20, 48. [*Scot.* hand-fasting, -fastnyng *marriage with the encumbrance of some canonical impediment, not yet bought off*: *Icel.* hand-festa, -festning, -festr *striking a bargain, the joining hands.* 'In the early Dan. and Swed. laws the stipulation to be given by the king at his coronation was called haand-fæstning.' Cf. *O. H. Ger.* hant-feste *emunitas, cautio, testamentum, privilegium.*]

hand-full, e; *f. A handful*; manipulus:—Nimaþ handfulle axan of ðam ofene *tollite plenas manus cineris de camino*, Ex. 9, 8. Nime âne handfulle *tollet pugillum plenum*, Lev. 2, 2. Nim micle handfulle secges *take a great handful of sedge*, L. M. 3, 67; Lchdm. ii. 354, 26. Genim micle twâ handfulla *take two great handfuls*, 69; Lchdm. ii. 356, 12: Herb. 81, 5; Lchdm. i. 184, 19. Berende handfulla heora *portantes manipulos suos*, Ps. Lamb. 125, 6. [*Orm.* hanndfull: *A. R.* honful: *Icel.* hand-fyllr: *Ger.* hand-voll.]

hand-gang, -gong, es; *m. Laying on of hands:*—Handgang *manus impositio*, Ælfc. Gl. 112; Som. 79, 94; Wrt. Voc. 60, 3. [*Orm.* hanndganng *laying on of hands* (used in connection with the Apostles, and with bishops at confirmation).]

hand-gecliht. v. ge-cliht.

hand-gemǽne. v. hand.

hand-gemôt, es; *n. A hand-meeting, battle*, Beo. Th. 3056; B. 1526.

hand-gesceaft, e; *f. That which is formed by the hand, a creature*, Cd. 23; Th. 29, 24; Gen. 455.

hand-gesella, an; *m. A companion who is close to one's side, comrade*, Beo. Th. 2966; B. 1481.

hand-gestealla, an; *m. One whose place is close at one's hand, a comrade, an associate*, Beo. Th. 5186; B. 2596. [Cf. preceding word, *and* eaxl-gestealla.]

hand-geswing, es; *n. Stroke given by the hand:*—Ðǽr wæs heard handgeswing *there were hard blows dealt by the hand*, Elen. Kmbl. 229; El. 115.

hand-geweald, es; *n. Power:*—Hê hî on handgeweald hǽðenum sealde *tradidit eos in manus gentium*, Ps. Th. 105, 30.

hand-geweorc, es; *n. Work of the hand, handiwork:*—Ðæra hǽðenra anlícnyssa sind gyldene and sylfrene manna handgeweorc *the idols of the heathen are of gold and of silver, the work of men's hands*, Homl. Th. i. 366, 26: Deut. 4, 28. His handgeweorc *the work of his hands* [*Adam and Eve*], Cd. 13; Th. 16, 11; Gen. 241: Ps. Th. 18, 1. Gerece ûre handgeweorc *opus manuum nostrarum dirige*, 89, 19. On his handgeweorc byþ gefangen se synfulla *in operibus manuum suarum comprehensus est peccator*, 9, 15. [*Hom*: *Rel. Ant.* hond-iwerc: *O. Sax.* hand-giwerk.]

hand-gewinn, es; *n. Labour of the hands, struggle, strife, fighting:*—Ða munucas lifdon on hira âgenum handgewinne *the monks lived by the labour of their own hands*, Shrn. 37, 2. Be heora âgenum handgewinne lifigeaþ *proprio labore manuum vivant*, Bd. 4, 4; S. 571, 22: 4, 28; S. 606, note 2. Hefig hondgewinn *a heavy struggle*, Exon. 73 b; Th. 273, 34; Jul. 526. Hê sceal fore hǽðenra handgewinne gâst onsendan *he shall because of the heathens' warfare give up the ghost*, Andr. Kmbl. 372; An. 186.

hand-gewrit, es; *n. What is written by the hand, a deed, contract*; chirographum:—Handgewrit *cirographum*, Ælfc. Gl. 13; Som. 57, 113; Wrt. Voc. 20, 51. Hondgiwrit *chyrographum*, Rtl. 32, 39. Sum man wrât his handgewrit ðam âwyrgedan deófle *a certain man put his hand to a contract with the accursed devil*,

hand-gewriðen; *pp. Hand-twisted*, Beo. Th. 3878; B. 1937.

hand-gift, e; *f. A wedding-gift*, Hy. 10, 18; Hy. Grn. ii. 293, 18. [Cf. *O. Sax.* hand-geba.] v. gift.

hand-gripe, es; *m. Grasp*, Beo. Th. 1934; B. 965. [*O. H. Ger.* hant-grif *pugillus*: *Ger.* hand-griff.]

hand-griþ, es; *n. Peace, protection, security*, L. E. G. 1; Th. i. 166, 21: L. Eth. vi. 14; Th. i. 318, 24: vii. 2; Th. i. 330, 5; L. C. E. 2; Th. i. 358, 20. v. Stubbs' Const. Hist. i. 182.

hand-hæbbende; *part. Having* [*stolen property*] *in one's hand* [cf. under *hand* the phrase *æt hæbbendre handa*]:—Sit handhabenda, sit non handhabenda *whether the thief be taken with the stolen property upon him or not*, L. Eth. iii. 6; Th. i. 218, 32.

hand-hamer, es; *m. A hand-hammer*; malleus, Cot. 135.

hand-hefe, es; *m. A burden:*—Ne gehrînaþ ðǽm hondhæfum *non tangitis sarcinas*, Lk. Skt. Lind. 11, 46.

hand-hrægl, es; *n. A cloth for the hands, towel, napkin*; mantile, Ælfc. Gl. 30; Som. 61, 70; Wrt. Voc. 26, 67.

hand-hrine, es; *m. A touch with the hand:*—Þurh handhrine Hâliges Gâstes *through a touch with the hand of the Holy Ghost*, Andr. Kmbl. 1999: An. 1002.

hand-hwîl, e; *f. A moment:*—Nis nâ eów tô gewitenne ða tîd odðe ða handhwîle ðe mîn Fæder gesette þurh his mihte *it is not for you to know the hour or the moment that my Father hath appointed through his might*, Homl. Th. i. 294, 26. [*Orm.* inn an hanndhwile *in a moment of time*: *A. R.* hondhwule: *Piers P.* handwhile.]

hand-hwyrft, es; *m. A turning of the hand, the time occupied by such a turning, a moment*, Lye. [Cf. hand-hwîl.]

handle, es; *n. A handle.* Cf. sulh-handla *stiba*, Ælfc. Gl. 1; Som. 55, 8; Wrt. Voc. 15, 8. [*Prompt. Parv.* handyl *manutentum*: *Jul.* hondlen; *dat. pl.*]

hand-leán, es; *n. A reward, recompence given by the hand, retribution:*—Uton wê geþencean hwylc handleán wê him forþ tô berenne habban *let us consider what recompence we have to offer him*, Blickl. Homl. 91, 13: Cd. 143; Th. 178, 29; Exod. 19: Beo. Th. 3087; B. 1541: 4195; B. 2094. [*O. H. Ger.* hant-lôn *bravium.*]

handlian; *p.* ode; *pp.* od *To handle, feel:*—Gif mîn fæder mê handlaþ *si attrectaverit me pater meus*, Gen. 27, 12. Hý ða spǽce swâ lange handledon *they handled the suit so long*, Th. Chart. 302, 31. Hâlige bêc handligan *sacros libros manu tractare*, L. Ecg. P. iii. 4; Th. ii. 196, 28: 12; Th. ii. 200, 7: Lchdm. iii. 198, 23: 204, 2; 208, 24. [*Laym.* hondlien: *Orm.* hanndlenn: *Icel.* höndla: *O. H. Ger.* hantalôn *tractare*: *Ger.* handeln.]

hand-lîn, es; *n. A hand-cloth, napkin:*—Hand-lîn *manualis*, Ælfc. Gl. 27; Som. 60, 117; Wrt. Voc. 25, 57. iiii subdiâcones handlîn *four sub-deacon's handcloths*, Th. Chart. 429, 23. [Cf. *Icel.* hand-lín *sleeves.*]

handlinga; *adv. With the hands:*—Nis be him gerǽd ðæt hê handling ǽnigne man âcwealde *it is not read of him that he killed any man with his own hands*, Homl. Th. i. 386, 1.

hand-locen; *pp. Fastened, woven by the hand*, Beo. Th. 649; B. 322.

handlung, e; *f. Touching, handling:*—Ðone ðe se eádiga Benedictus nâ handlunge ac on beseónde fram his bendum âlýsde *whom the blessed Benedict not by touching him, but by looking on him, had released from his bonds*, Homl. Th. ii. 182, 4.

hand-mægen, es; *n. Might, power of hand*, Cd. 14; Th. 16, 22; Gen. 247: Andr. Kmbl. 1450: An. 725. [*O. Sax.* hand-magan, -megin: *Icel.* hand-megin, -megn.]

hand-mitta, an; *m. The sixth part of an ounce*; exagium, Lye.

hand-nægl, es; *m. A finger-nail:*—Ðonne beóþ him ða handnæglas wonne *then will his finger-nails be livid*, L. M. 3, 63; Lchdm. ii. 350, 22.

hand-plega, an; *m. Fighting:*—Heard handplega *hard fighting*, Cd. 160; Th. 198, 23; Exod. 327: 95; Th. 124, 3; Gen. 2057: Chr. 937; Erl. 112, 25. Hî nǽfre wyrsan handplegan on Angelcynne ne gemitton ðonne Ulfcytel him tôbrohte *they had never had more disastrous fighting in England than in their engagement with Ulfcytel*, Chr. 1004; Erl. 138, note 7. v. plega *for similar compounds.*

hand-preóst, es; *m. A chaplain*; sacellanus, Ælfc. Gl. 68; Som. 70, 13; Wrt. Voc. 42, 22. Stigand ðe was ðes cinges rǽdgifa and his handpreóst *Stigand who was the king's counsellor and chaplain*, Chr. 1051: Erl. 182, 20.

hand-rǽs, es; *m. Onset, attack*, Beo. Th. 4150; B. 2072.

hand-rôf; *adj. Distinguished for exploits accomplished by the hands* [*used of warriors*], Cd. 155; Th. 193, 15; Exod. 247.

hand-sceaft, e; *f. That which is formed by the hand, a creature*; creatura, Lye.

hand-sceát, es; *m. A napkin*; manutergium, sudarium, Lye.

hand-sció; *m. A glove*, Beo. Th. 4158; B. 2075. Grein considers this meaning to be inadmissible and translates *impetus manibus factus*; but cf. 4177; B. 2085.

hand-scôlu, -scâlu, e; *f. A retinue:*—Mid his hondscôle *with his retinue*, Beo. Th. 3931; B. 1963. Handscâle, 2638; B. 1317. [Cf. hand-gesella, geneát-scôlu.]

hand-scyldig; *adj. Liable to the penalty of losing the hand:*—Se ðe gewundaþ man binnan ciricwagum se biþ handscyldig *he that wounds* *a man within church walls shall be liable to lose his hand,* L. Eth. vii. 13; Th. i. 332, 9.

hand-seax, es; *n. A short sword, dagger:*—Hæfde hē twigecgede handseax *habebat sicam bicipitem,* Bd. 2, 9; S. 511, 15. Hæfdon handseax on heora handa *habentes in manibus vomeres,* 5, 13; S. 633, 16. Godes engel stōd mid handsexe *God's angel stood with a dagger,* Homl. Th. ii. 272, 17. Ān handsecs on hundeahtotigan mancysan goldes *a dagger worth eighty mancuses of gold,* Th. Chart. 501, 3: 502, 16. Handsex, 527, 8. [*Laym.* hond-sæx: *Icel.* hand-sax *a short sword, dirk.*]

hand-selen, e; *f. A giving into the hand of another;* mancipatio, Cot. 136, Lye. [Cf. *Icel.* hand-sal, -sala, -selja.]

hand-seten, e: *f. The setting of one's hand to a deed, etc., a signature, sign manual:*—Ðas trymeþ se forespecena kyng mid Cristes rōde tācne and his weotena hondsetena his geofa *thus the aforesaid king confirms his gifts with the sign of Christ's cross and the signature of his witan,* Cod. Dipl. Kmbl. ii. 304, 11: 14: 89, 11. Mē saldan heora hondsetene ðisse gerǣdnesse *they put their hands to this agreement,* 100, 29. Hēr is seó hondseten. Ego Ōswald archiepiscopus, etc. *here are the signatures. I Oswald archbishop, etc.,* iii. 260, 13. Ælfrēd cing Ōsulfe his hondsetene sealde *king Alfred gave his sign manual to Osulf,* ii. 133, 22.

hand-sliht, -slyht, es; *m. A slaying with the hand:*—Ne meahte hē ealdum eorle hondslyht giofan *he could not give a deadly blow to the old warrior,* Beo. Th. 5937: B. 2972: 5851; B. 2929. v. sliht *and its compounds.*

hand-smæll, es; *m. A slap with the hand:*—Sealdon him hondsmællas *dabant ei alapas,* Jn. Skt. Lind. Rush. 19, 3. v. smæll.

hand-spor, es; *n. A talon, claw,* Beo. Th. 1976; B. 986.

hand-stoc, es; *m. A handcuff, manacle;* manica, Hpt. Gl. 525, 526.

hand-þegen, es; *m. An attendant, one of a retinue, servant:*—Ðā hē ðā ðyder fērde ðā wǣron his handþegnas twegen *when he journeyed thither, two of his attendants were with him,* Guthl. 14; Gdwin. 62, 3. Willfriþ his preóst and his hond-þeng *Wilfrid his priest and attendant;* clericus illius, Bd. 5, 19; S. 638, 27: Cd. 224; Th. 295, 12; Sat. 485. [Cf. hand-gesella, -preóst.]

hand-þweál, es; *n. A washing of the hands:*—Hāndþweáles fæt *malluviæ,* Ælfc. Gl. 26; Som. 60, 87; Wrt. Voc. 25, 27.

hand-weorc, es; *n. Handiwork, work done by the hand:*—Handweorc Godes *the work of God's hand,* Cd. 167; Th. 209, 1; Exod. 492. Sinc hondweorc smiþa *treasure, the handiwork of artificers,* Exon. 105 b; Th. 401, 6; Rä. 21, 7. Þurh ðæt handweorc *by manual labour,* L. E. I. 3; Th. ii. 404, 19.

hand-worht; *adj. Hand-wrought, made with hands:*—Ic tōwurpe ðis handworhte tempel *ego dissoluam templum hoc manu factum,* Mk. Skt. 14, 58. [*Goth.* handu-waurhts.] DER. un-handworht.

hand-wundor, es; *n. A wondrous thing wrought by hand,* Beo. Th. 5530: B. 2768.

hand-wyrm, es; *m. An insect supposed to produce disease in the hand:*—Handwyrm *surio* vel *briensis* vel *sirineus,* Ælfc. Gl. 24; Som. 60, 25; Wrt. Voc. 24, 28. Handwyrm *ureius,* Wrt. Voc. 288, 4. Hondwyrm, Exon. 111 b; Th. 427, 24; Rä. 41, 96: 125 b; Th. 482, 15; Rä. 67, 2. Við hondwyrmum, L. M. 1, 50; Lchdm. ii. 122, 21.

hand-wyrst, -wrist, e; *f. The wrist:*—Fæðm betwux elboga and handwyrste *cubitum,* Ælfc. Gl. 72; Som. 70, 125; Wrt. Voc. 43, 51. [Halliwell gives *hand-wrists* as a Somersetshire word.]

hangian; *p.* ode; *pp.* od *To hang, be suspended, depend:*—Ic hongige *pendeo,* Ælfc. Gr. 26, 6; Som. 29, 11: Exon. 104 a; Th. 395, 21; Rä. 15, 11. Ðes hālga Hǣlend hangaþ unscyldig *this holy Jesus hangeth guiltless,* Homl. Th. ii. 256, 14: Beo. Th. 4886; B. 2447. Manega sind beboda mannum gesette ac hī ealle hangiaþ on ðisum twām wordum *many are the commandments appointed to men, but they all depend upon these two sentences,* Homl. Th. ii. 314. 21. Ðā ðā Crist hangode on rōde for ūre ālȳsednysse *when Christ hung on the cross for our redemption,* 240, 22: Lk. Skt. 23, 39. Wīde sceós hangodan on hira fōtum and bogan hangodan on hiora eaxlum *wide shoes hung on their feet and bows hung on their shoulders,* Shrn. 38, 8. His loccas hangodon tō ðām ancleowum *his locks hung down to his ancles,* Homl. Th. i. 466, 25. Swā hālig wer hangian ne sceolde *so holy a man ought not to be hung,* 596, 30. Hangigende, 594, 5. Hangiende, ii. 260, 25. [*Laym.* hongien; *p.* hongede: *A. R.* hongede: *Wick.* hangide: *O. Sax.* hangōn: *O. Frs.* hangia: *Icel.* hanga: *O. H. Ger.* hangen; *p.* hangeta.]

hangra, an; *m.* '*A meadow or grassplot, usually by the side of a road; the village green,*' Cod. Dipl. Kmbl. iii. xxix:—Of ðam hangran sūþ tō ðære strǣt *from the meadow south to the road,* 229, 27: V. 374, 29. Ealle ða hangran betweónan ðam wege and ðam ðe tō Stānleáge ligþ gebyriaþ ealle tō Fearnebeorgan *all the meadows between the road and that which goes to Stanley all belong to Farnborough,* iii. 409, 17. [*Anger in local names,* e. g. Shelfanger, Birchanger.]

hār; *adj. Hoar, hoary, grey, old;* canus:—Hār hǣþ *the grey heath,* Cd. 148; Th. 185, 5; Exod. 118. Se hāra wulf *the grey wolf,* Exon. 77 b; Th. 291, 15; Wand. 82. Hāres hyrste *the old warrior's arms,* Beo. Th. 5968; B. 2988: 3360; B. 1678: Cd. 164; Th. 193, 4; Exod. 241: 151; Th. 189, 7; Exod. 181. On ðone hāran hæsel *to the grey* [*with lichens?*] *hazel,* Cod. Dipl. Kmbl. iii. 279, 14. Æt ðære hāran apuldran *at the old apple-tree,* Chr. 1066; Erl. 202, 6. Of clife hārum *from the grey cliff,* Bt. Met. Fox 5, 25; Met. 5, 13. On brime hāran *on the grey sea,* Menol. Fox 423; Men. 213. Hē geseah sumne hārne stān *he saw a grey stone,* Blickl. Homl. 209, 32: Cod. Dipl. Kmbl. iii. 313, 26: Beo. Th. 1779; B. 887. Hārne middengeard *canescentem mundum,* Mt. Kmbl. p. i, 5. Hrīm and forst hāre hildstapan *rime and frost, hoary warriors,* Andr. Kmbl. 2517; An. 1260. Hāre byrnan *grey byrnies* [cf. grǣge syrcan, Beo. Th. 673; B. 334], Judth. 12; Thw. 26, 15; Jud. 328. [*Chauc.* hoor: *Piers P.* hore: *Ayenb.* hore vrostes: *Alis.* hore al so a wolf: *Icel.* hārr.]

hara, an; *m. A hare:*—Hara *lepus,* Ælfc. Gl. 19; Som. 59, 21; Wrt. Voc. 22, 62. Se hara mid ðysse wyrte hyne sylfne gelǣcnaþ *the hare doctors itself with this plant,* Herb. 114, 1; Lchdm. i. 226, 22: Med. ex Quadr. 4; Lchdm. i. 342, 14, 16, 18. Haran man mōt etan and hē biþ gōd wið lengtenādle and wið ūtsiht gesoden on wætere and his geallan man mæg wið pipor mengan wið mūþsāre *leporem licet comedere, et bonus est contra dysenteriam et diarrhœum, in aqua elixus; et fel ejus miscendum est cum pipere contra dolorem oris,* L. Ecg. C. 38; Th. ii. 162, 22. Genim haran wulle *take hare's fur,* L. M. 3, 65; Lchdm. ii. 354, 13. Ne onscūnode nān hara nǣnne hund *no hare was afraid of any hound,* Bt. 35, 6; Fox 168, 9. Ic gefeó hwīlon haran *capio aliquando lepores,* Coll. Monast. Th. 21, 33. Hē sætte be ðām haran ðæt hī mōsten freó faran *he decreed concerning hares, that they should go free,* Chr. 1086; Erl. 222, 30. [*Icel.* heri: *O. H. Ger.* haso: *Ger.* hase.]

haran hige *hare's foot;* trifolium arvense:—Genim ðās wyrte ðe man leporis pes and ōðrum naman haran hige nemneþ *take this plant which is called leporis pes and by another name hare's foot,* Herb. 62; Lchdm. 164, 17.

haran-specel, -sprecel *viper's bugloss;* echium vulgare, Lchdm. iii. 330.

haran-wyrt, hare- *harewort;* lepidium latifolium, Lchdm. iii. 330. Harewirta [MS. winta] *colocasia,* Ælfc. Gl. 42; Som. 64, 9; Wrt. Voc. 31, 20.

hār-hune [*and* hār hune], an; *f. Horehound;* marrubium vulgare:—Hārhune *marrubium* vel *prassium,* Ælfc. Gl. 43; Som. 64, 47; Wrt. Voc. 31, 67. Hārhune *marubium,* 79, 35. Rōmāne marubium nemnaþ and eác angle hāre hune *the Romans name it marrubium, the English also call it horehound,* Herb. 46; Lchdm. i. 148, 14. Genim ða hāran hunan *take horehound,* L. M. 1, 45; Lchdm. ii. 110, 24. Genim hwīte hare hunan *take white horehound,* Lchdm. i. 374, 18.

harian, horian; *p.* ode *To cry;* clamare:—Tō ðē ic horige *ad te clamabo,* Ps. Th. 27, 1, note. [*O. H. Ger.* haren *clamare,* Grff. iv. 978 sqq.]

hārian; *p.* ode *To grow grey:*—Ic hārige *caneo,* Ælfc. Gr. 26; Som. 28, 43. Ic sceolde wesan ceorl on hāriendum heáfde *I should have to be a husband when my head was growing grey,* Shrn. 39, 27.

Harold, Harald, es; *m.* I. *Harold, second son of Cnut:*—Hēr man geceás Harald ofer eall tō cinge and forsōc Harðacnut *in this year Harold was chosen everywhere king, and Hardacnut was renounced,* Chr. 1037; Erl. 166, 4. Hēr forþfērde Harold cyng on Oxnaforda *in this year king Harold died at Oxford,* 1039; Erl. 167, 12. II. *Harold, son of earl Godwin:*—Hēr forþfērde Eádward king and Harold eorl fēng tō ðam rīce and heóld hit xl wucena and ǣnne dæg *in this year departed king Edward and earl Harold came to the throne and held it forty weeks and one day,* 1066; Erl. 198, 1. Ðǣr wearþ ofslægen Harold kyng *there was king Harold slain,* 202, 10.

Harþacnut, Hardacnut, es; *m. Hardacnut, son of Cnut:*—On ðis ilcan geáre com Hardacnut cyng tō Sandwīc vii nihtum ǣr middan sumera. And hē wæs sōna underfangen ge fram Anglum ge fram Denum *in this same year king Hardacnut came to Sandwich seven days before midsummer. And he was at once received by both English and Danes,* Chr. 1039; Erl. 167, 17. Hēr forþferde Hardacnut cyng *in this year died king Hardacnut,* 1041; Erl. 167, 30.

hārung, e; *f. Greyness, hoariness, age:*—Ða meolchwītan hārunge *lacteam caniciem,* Ælfc. Gr. 50, 26; Som. 51, 64.

hārwelle; *adj. Hoary:*—Hārwelle *canescens,* Mt. Kmbl. p. 1, 5.

hār-wenge; *adj. Hoary, grey-haired:*—Hē wearþ fǣrlīce geþuht cnapa and eft hārwenge *he suddenly appeared a youth, and again grey-haired,* Homl. Th. i. 376, 13. Hē hæfþ sīde beardas hwōn hārwencge *he has a good deal of hair on his face, rather grey,* 456, 18.

hās; *adj. Hoarse:*—Hās *raucus,* Ælfc. Gr. 30; Som. 34, 38. Ic hæbbe sumne cnapan ðe nū hās ys *habeo quendam puerum qui modo raucus est,* Coll. Monast. Th. 19, 29. Mē syndan gōman hāse *raucæ factæ sunt fauces meæ,* Ps. Th. 68, 3. [*Piers P.* hos, hors: *Chauc.* hors: *O. and N.* hos: *Wick.* hoos, hors: *Icel.* hāss: *O. H. Ger.* heis: *Ger.* heiser.]

há-sæta, an; *m. A rower*:—And gerǽdde man ðá ðæt ða scipu gewendan eft ongeán tō Lundene and sceolde man setton ōðre eorlas and ōðre hásæton tō ðám scipum *it was decided that the ships should go back again to London, and other commanders and other rowers were to be appointed to the ships*, Chr. 1052; Erl. 183, 9. [*Icel.* há-seti (hár *a thole*) *a thole-sitter, an oarsman*, opposed to the captain or helmsman.]

hásian; *p.* ode; *pp.* od *To grow hoarse*:—Ic hásige *raucio*, Ælfc. Gr. 30; Som. 34, 38.

hás-ness, e; *f. Hoarseness*:—Hásnys *raucedo*, Ælfc. Gl. 10; Som. 57, 26; Wrt. Voc. 19, 32. Hásnyss *raucedo*, Ælfc. Gr. 9; Som. 8, 59. [*Prompt. Parv.* hoosnesse, hoorsnesse *raucitas, raucor.*]

hassuc, es; *m. Coarse grass, a place where such grass grows*:—On ðone hassuc, Cod. Dipl. Kmbl. iii. 223, 25. [v. *Prompt Parv.* p. 228, note 2, where a passage is quoted in which the phrase *usque ad tercium hassocum* occurs in the defining of a boundary. In Engl. Dial. Soc. No. 26, is the following:—'Hassock *or* Hassocks. A name sometimes assigned to *aira cæspitosa*, L. but more accurately regarded as a term indicating the large coarse tufts formed in meadows by this grass and some sedges, such as *Carex cæspitosa* and *C. paniculata*.' Cf. too No. 30:—'Hassocks. "Great tufts of rushes, etc., called in Suffolk *hassocks*."' No. 31. [Leicestershire]:—'*Hassock* a tuft of coarse rank grass; an ant-hill.']

hasu, heasu; *adj. Grey, ash-coloured, tawny;* cinereus, fulvo-cinereus:—Hē of earce forlēt haswe culufran *he let out of the ark a grey dove*, Cd. 72; Th. 87, 20; Gen. 1451. Hwílum ic onhyrge ðone haswan earn *sometimes I imitate the grey eagle*, Exon. 106 b; Th. 406, 21; Rä. 25, 4. Se haswa fugel, 57 b; Th. 206, 4; Ph. 121. Rēcas stígaþ haswe ofer hrōfum *grey smoke mounts o'er the roofs*, 101 a; Th. 381, 6; Rä. 2, 7. [*Icel.* höss *grey* (applied to the wolf and eagle as above): cf. Gen. and Ex. haswed, v. 1723. Grein quotes the following passage from Haupt's Zeitschrift, x. 346:—'*Hasu* wol ursprünglich wolfgrau, und adlergrau, jene gemischte Farbe von goldgelb und grau: bald überwiegt der Gedanke an das Goldgelbe (vgl. blond), bald das Grau der Mischung.']

hasu-fág; *adj. Grey-coloured*:—Hrægl is mín hasofág *my raiment is grey*, Exon. 103 b; Th. 392, 23; Rä. 12, 1.

hasu-páda, an; *m. One having a grey garment;* a term applied to the eagle, cf. hasu:—Ðane hasupádan, earn *the grey-coated one, the eagle*, Chr. 937; Erl. 115, 11, note.

haswig-feðera; *adj. Having grey plumage*, Exon. 58 a; Th. 208, 10; Ph. 153.

hát, es; *n. Heat*:—Hát biþ onæled *heat shall be kindled*, Exon. 116 a; Th. 445, 18; Dōm. 9: 116 b; Th. 447, 11; Dōm. 37. Hát and ceald *heat and cold*, Cd. 192; Th. 239, 29; Dan. 377; 216; Th. 273, 5; Sat. 132: Exon. 117 b; Th. 451, 20: Dōm. 106. Hát þrowian *to suffer heat*, Beo. Th. 5204; B. 2605. [*O. Sax.* hēt; *n.* cf. *O. H. Ger.* heiz, heizi; *f. fervor, æstus.*]

hát; *adj. Hot, fervent, fervid, fierce* [of pain, punishment, etc.]:—Wæs him seó Godes lufu tō ðæs hát and tō ðæs beorht on his heortan *the love of God was so fervent and bright in his heart*, Blickl. Homl. 225, 36. Hys gecynde is swíðe hát *its nature is very hot*, Herb. 158, 1; Lchdm. i. 284, 22: 124; Lchdm. i. 236, 11. Hungor se háta *fierce hunger*, Exon. 64 b; Th. 238, 32; Ph. 613. Wæs seó ádl hát *fierce was the disease*, 47 a; Th. 161, 1; Gū. 952: Homl. Th. i. 404, 6. Ðeós wyrt byþ cenned on hátum stōwum *this plant is produced in hot places*, Herb. 115, 1; Lchdm. i. 228, 6. Hē háte lēt teáras geótan *he let hot tears gush forth*, Exon. 48 a; Th. 165, 14; Gū. 1029. Swá háttra sumor swá mára þunor and líget on geáre *the hotter the summer the more thunder and lightning in the year*, Lchdm. iii. 280, 9. [*Orm.* hat: *Laym.* hat, hot: *A. R.* hot: *Chauc.* hot, hoot: *Prompt. Parv.* hoot: *O. Sax.* hēt: *Icel.* heitr: *O. H. Ger.* heiz: *Ger.* heiss: cf. *Goth.* heito; *f. a fever.*]

hát, es; *n. A promise, vow*:—Ic sendo hát fadores mínes *ego mitto promissum patris mei*, Lk. Skt. Lind. 24, 49. Hátes *promissionis*, Rtl. 14, 14. [*Orm.* hát: *Gen. and Ex.* hot: *Ps.* hates, hotes *vota*: *Icel.* heit; *n. a solemn promise, vow*: cf. *Goth.* haiti; *f. a command.*] v. ge-hát.

Hátabaðan *Bath*:—Æt Hátabaðum *at Bath*, Chr. 972; Erl. 125, 9. v. Baðan.

HÁTAN; ic háte, ðū hátest, hætsþ, hē háteþ, hát, hǽt, *pl.* hátaþ; *p.* hēht, hēt, *pl.* hēhton, hēton; *pp.* háten. I. *to bid, order, command*, (*a*) *with acc. and infin*:—Drihten hwæt hǽtst ðū mē dōn *Lord, what dost thou bid me do?* Past. 58; Swt. 443, 24. Drihten háteþ ða eorþan eft ágifan ðæt heó ǽr onfēng *the Lord shall bid the earth give up what it received before*, Blickl. Homl. 21, 30. Mid ðam gemete wē hátaþ ōðre men dōn sum þingc *with that mood* [*the imperative*] *we command other men to do something*, Ælfc. Gr. 21; Som. 23, 23. Hē hēht englas him tō cuman and hie cōman *he bade angels come to him and they came*, 181, 5: Andr. Kmbl. 729; An. 365. Ðá hēt hē mē on ðysne síþ faran *then he bade me go on this journey*, Cd. 25; Th. 32, 7; Gen. 499. Hie hine hēton ðæt áttor etan *they bade him eat the poison*, Blickl. Homl. 229, 17. Mid ðý ðe ðū mē háte of mínum líchoman gewítan *when thou shalt bid me depart from my body*, 139, 13. Hát mē cuman tō ðē *jube me venire ad te*, Mt. Kmbl. 14, 28. (*b*) *with infin. only*:—Ælfrēd kyning háteþ grētan Wærferþ biscep and ðē cýðan háte *king Alfred bids greet bishop Werferth; and I would that it should be known to you*, Past. Pref; Swt. 3, 1–2. Ic Elfrēd dux hátu wrítan and cýðan an ðissum gewrite Elfrēde regi *I alderman Alfred order to be written and made known in this writing to king Alfred*, Chart. Th. 480, 13. Ðonne háteþ Sanctus Micahel bláwan ða feówer bēman *then St. Michael will order the four trumpets to be blown*, Blickl. Homl. 95, 12. Hǽt [Cot. hát] fealdan ðæt segl *gives order to furl the sail*, Bt. 41, 3; Fox 250, 14. Ðá hēht hē Simon infeccan beforan hine *then he ordered that Simon should be brought in before him*, Blickl. Homl. 175, 1: Andr. Kmbl. 2459; An. 1231: Chart. Th. 137, 6. (*c*) *with a clause*:—Ic ðē háte ðæt ðū ðás gesyhþe secge mannum *I command thee to tell this vision to men*, Rood Kmbl. 187; Kr. 95. Hē hǽt hine ðæt hē hine fealde swá swá bōc *he shall bid it fold itself as a book*, Ps. Th. 49, 5. Ðē háteþ heofona cyning ðæt ðū onsende *Heaven's king bids thee send*, Andr. Kmbl. 3008; An. 1507. Hēht ðæt hē cuōme tō him *he commanded that he should come to him*, Chart. Th. 47, 11. Hēt ðæt ðū ǽte *he bade that thou shouldst eat*, Cd. 25; Th. 32, 8; Gen. 500. (*d*) *without an object, or with acc. only*:—Gif ðū hǽtst ðonne mæg ic *if thou biddest, then I can*, Homl. Th. ii. 390, 31. Wē dydon swá ðū ūs hēte *we have done as thou didst command us*, i. 394, 21. Ða mon sceal swá micle má hátan ðonne biddan *those are to be so much the more commanded than entreated*, Past. 26; Swt. 181, 21. (*e*) *with a verb of motion omitted*:—Hēht ōðre dæge hie ealle þrý in beforan hine *he commanded that next day they should all three come in before him*, Blickl. Homl. 175, 18. Ðá hēht hē him tō ealle his discipulos *he summoned to him all his disciples*, 225, 12: Cd. 127; Th. 161, 27; Gen. 2671: Elen. Kmbl. 305; El. 153. Hēt tōsomne síne leóde *summoned his people together*, Cd. 197; Th. 245, 26; Dan. 469. Maria hēht hý ōðre mid *Mary bade another accompany her*, Exon. 119 b; Th. 459, 35; Hö. 10. Ðá wæs tō ðam dōme Daniel háten *then was Daniel summoned to the judgment*, Cd. 201; Th. 249, 19; Dan. 532. II. *to promise, vow*:—Gif ðū hǽtsþ hǽðenfeoh *if thou dost vow heathen offerings*, Exon. 66 b; Th. 245, 31; Jul. 53. III. *to call, name, give a name to*:—Nolde hē nō ða rūmmōdnesse hátan mildheortnes ac ryhtwísnes *non hanc vocare misericordiam, sed justitiam maluit*, Past. 45, 1; Swt. 337, 2: Cd. 106; Th. 140, 13; Gen. 2327. Consul ðæt wē heretoha hátaþ *consul we call heretoha*, Bt. 1; Fox 2, 12. Ða deór hí hátaþ hránas *those deer they call rein-deer*, Ors. 1, 1; Bos. 20, 27: Cd. 80; Th. 99, 19; Gen. 1648. And tū hine hēte ðá flýman *and then you declared him a fugitive*, Chart. Th. 173, 6. God hēt ða fæstnisse heofenan *vocavit Deus firmamentum cælum*, Gen. 1, 8. Hē hēt his naman Adam *he called his name Adam*, 5, 2: Cd. 124; Th. 158, 7; Gen. 2613: Beo. Th. 5605; B. 2806. Rōmáne hý tictatōres hēton *the Romans gave them the name of dictators*, Ors. 2, 4; Bos. 42, 28. Sum consul Boetius wæs háten *a certain consul whose name was Boethius*, Bt. 1; Fox 2, 13: Cd. 79; Th. 99, 13; Gen. 1645. Is ðæt deór pandher bí noman háten *that beast is called by the name of panther*, Exon. 95 b; Th. 356, 17; Pa. 13. Hí nemnaþ ða eá archoboleta ðæt is háten ðæt miccle wæter *archoboleta vocant quæ est aqua magna*, Nar. 35, 21. [*Laym.* haten, heht. In Chaucer this verb and the next are confounded, thus *highte = hátte*; and *hight* is used for *háten*. *Goth.* haitan *to name, call, bid, command*: *O. Sax.* hētan: *Icel.* heita *to call, name, promise, vow*: *O. Frs.* hēta: *O. H. Ger.* heizan, heizzan *nominare, appellare, jubere, præcipere*: *Ger.* heissen.]

hátan; *pres.* and *p.* hátte, *pl.* hátton *To be called* or *named, have for a name*:—Cwæþ ðæt se hēhsta hátan sceolde Satan siððan *said that the highest should be called Satan afterwards*, Cd. 18; Th. 22, 22; Gen. 344. Án eá of ðám hátte Fison *one river of them is called Pison*, Gen. 2, 11. Saga hwæt ic hátte *say what I am called*, Exon. 106 b; Th. 406, 13; Rä. 24, 16. Hū ne hátte hys mōdor Maria *nonne mater ejus dicitur Maria?* Mt. Kmbl. 13, 55. Ðe swá hátte *that was thus called*, Cd. 180; Th. 226, 17: Dan. 172: Bt. Met. Fox 1, 105; Met. 1, 53. On ðǽm bōcum ðe hátton Apocalypsin *in the books called the Apocalypse*, Past. 58; Swt. 445, 35: Ors. 2, 4; Bos. 42, 34. [*Goth.* haitada *I am called*: *Icel.* heita, ek heiti: *O. H. Ger.* heizan, Grff. iv. 1077: *Ger.* heissen.]

háte; *adv. Hotly*:—Háte glōwende *hotly glowing*, Homl. Th. i. 424, 35: Cd. 19; Th. 24, 26; Gen. 383: 38; Th. 50, 18; Gen. 810: Judth. 10; Thw. 22, 36; Jud. 94. Swá hē hátost mǽge *as hot as possible*, L. M. 1, 2; Lchdm. i. 34, 10: Exon. 59 a; Th. 212, 13; Ph. 209.

háten [?] *heated*:—Mid hátene ísene *with heated iron*, L. M. 2, 25; Lchdm. ii. 218, 24.

hát-heort, es; *n. Fury, anger, wrath;* iracundia:—Nū is gefylled ðæt mycelle hátheort and ðæt mycelle yrre ðyses ealdermannes *now is completed the great fury and the great wrath of this ruler*, Blickl. Homl. 151, 10.

hât-heort; *adj. Furious, angry, irascible, passionate, ardent;* furiosus, iracundus, fervens:—Gif hwylc man tô đam hâtheort sig and strangmôd đæt hê tô nânum worldrihte and sybbe fôn nelle wiđ đæne đe wiđ hine âgylt *si homo quis adeo furiosus et duro corde sit, ut nullum sæculare jus et pacem admittere velit cum eo qui in eum deliquerit,* L. Ecg. P. ii. 28; Th. ii. 194, 5. Đes gerêfa is swîđe hâtheort and hê đê wile forleósan *this consul is very furious and will destroy thee,* Nar. 42, 4: Exon. 77 b; Th. 290, 16; Wand. 66. Đonne đa hâtheortan hie mid nâne foreþonce nyllaþ gestillan *cum iracundi nulla consideratione se mitigant,* Past. 40, 5; Swt. 297, 3. Timotheus hê ongeat hâtheortran đonne hê sceolde *ferventioris spiritus vidit esse Timotheum,* 3; Swt. 291, 22. Đâ wæs heora sum rêđra and hâtheortra đonne đa ôđre *then was one of them fiercer and more furious than the others,* Blickl. Homl. 223, 6.

hât-heorte, an; *f. Anger, fury, rage:*—Ic đê bletsige forđon đû mê ne forlête ût gangan mid mînre hâtheortan of đisse ceastre *I bless thee that thou didst not let me go out of this city in my anger,* Blickl. Homl. 249, 15.

hâtheort-lîce; *adv. Furiously, ardently, fervently:*—Đa đe hê ǽr hâtheortlîce lufode *which he before ardently loved,* Blickl. Homl. 59, 9: 17. Hie wǽron tô đon hâtheortlîce yrre đæt hie woldan đone câsere cwicenne forbærnan *they were so furiously angry that they wanted to burn the emperor alive,* 191, 11.

hâtheort-nes, -ness, e; *f. Wrath, anger, fury, rage, fervour, zeal:*—Đeós hâtheortnys *hic furor,* Ælfc. Gr. 9, 21; Som. 10, 26. Đis synt đa îdelnyssa đisse worlde . . . hâtheortnys . . . *hæ sunt vanitates hujus mundi . . . furor . . .,* L. Ecg. P. i. 8; Th. ii. 174, 33. Sió hâtheortness đæt môd gebringþ on đæm weorce đe hine ǽr nân willa tô ne spôn *mentem impellit furor, quo non trahit desiderium,* Past. 33, 1; Swt. 215, 8. Đonne wyrþ đæt môd beswungen mid đam welme đære hâtheortnesse *then is the mind scourged with the heat of anger,* Bt. 37, 1; Fox 186, 21. Hû gesceádwîs se reccere sceal bión on his hâtheortnesse *quæ esse debet rectoris discretio fervoris,* Past. 21; Swt. 151, 6. Fŷr ys onæled on mînre hâtheortnisse *a fire is kindled in mine anger,* Deut. 32, 22. Forlǽt yrre and hâtheortnesse *desine ab ira et derelinque furorem,* Ps. Th. 36, 8: Homl. Th. i. 360, 3.

hât-hirtan, -hiertan, -hyrtan; *p.* te *To make angry:*—Đonne is micel þearf đætte se, se đa hâtheortnesse ofercuman wille, đæt hê hiene ongeán ne hâthirte *necesse est, ut hi, qui furentes conantur reprimere, nequaquam se in furore erigant,* Past. 40, 5; Swt. 296, 6.

haþoliþa, an; *m. The elbow joint:*—Lǽt him blôd of đam hâlan haþoliþan *let him blood from the sound elbow,* L. M. 2, 51; Lchdm. ii. 264, 17. vide Glossary, s. v.

hât-hyge, es; *m. Anger, fury, wrath:*—Wê wǽron on đînum hâthige hearde gedrêfde *in furore tuo conturbati sumus,* Ps. Th. 89, 7. [Cf. hât-heort, -heorte.]

hatian, hatigean; *p.* ode, ede; *pp.* od, ed *To hate:*—Ne mæg middaneard eów hatian ac hê hataþ mê *non potest mundus odisse vos: me autem odit,* Jn. Bos. 7, 7. Đa đe đone rihtwîsan hatiaþ đa âgyltaþ *qui oderunt justum delinquent,* Ps. Th. 33, 21. Hie hatigaþ [hatigeaþ, Cot. MS.] hiera hiéramonna unþeáwas *they hate the vices of their subjects,* Past. 18; Swt. 137, 4. Dôþ đǽm wel đe eów ǽr hatedon *do well to those that formerly hated you,* 33; Swt. 222, 17. Hû ne hatige ic đa ealle, Dryhten, đa đe đê hatigaþ? Mid fulryhte hete ic hie hatode. Swa mon sceal Godes fiénd hatigean *do I not hate all those, O Lord, who hate thee? With a perfect hatred I hated them. So shall God's enemies be hated,* 46; Swt. 353, 5-8. Hê sceal rŷperas and reáferas hatian and hŷnan *he must hate and humiliate robbers and plunderers,* L. I. P. 2; Th. ii. 304, 19: Beo. Th. 4627; B. 2319. [*Goth.* hatan, hatjan: *O. Sax.* hatan, hatôn: *O. Frs.* hatia: *Icel.* hata: *O. H. Ger.* hazên, hazôn: *Ger.* hassen.]

hâtian; *p.* ode; *pp.* od *To become* or *get hot, to be hot:*—Hingrian þyrstan hâtian eall đæt is of untrumnysse đæs gecynnes *esurire, sitire, æstuare ex infirmitate naturæ est,* Bd. 1, 27; S. 494, 14. Nim ǽnne sticcan and gnîd tô sumum þinge hit hâtaþ đǽrrihte of đam fŷre đe him on lûtaþ *take a stick and rub it against something, it gets hot directly from the fire which lurks in it,* Lchdm. iii. 274, 4: Herb. 90, 13; Lchdm. ii. 198, 4. Hâtode heorte mîn *concaluit cor meum,* Ps. Spl. C. 38, 4. Ôþ đæt se clam hâtige *till the paste gets hot,* L. M. 3, 59; Lchdm. ii. 342, 19. Đonne byþ heó sôna hâtigende *it will at once be getting hot,* Herb. 90, 8; Lchdm. i. 196, 4. [*O. H. Ger.* heizên *fervere.*]

hatigend, es; *m. One who hates, an enemy:*—Hatigend ođđe feónd *osor,* Ælfc. Gr. 33; Som. 37, 1.

hatol. v. hetol.

hatte-fagol *a hedge-hog,* Ps. Spl. M. 103, 19.

hatung, e; *f. Hating, hate, hatred:*—Hatung Godes beboda *hate of God's commands,* Homl. Th. ii. 220, 6. Mid đære rêđan ehtnysse hatunge *with the hate of fierce persecution,* i. 84, 12. Đa unrihtwîsan ic hæfde on hatunge *iniquos odio habui,* Ælfc. Gr. 33; Som. 36, 61. Gê beóþ on hatunge eallum mannum *eritis odio omnibus,* Mt. Kmbl. 10, 22. On hatunga, Lk. Skt. 21, 17. Hê becom on hatunga his herges *he came to be hated by his army,* Blickl. Homl. 193, 2. Bânu sume handlian hatunge getâcnaþ *to handle bones betokens hate,* Lchdm. iii. 208, 24. [*O. H. Ger.* hazunga *æmulatio.*]

hâtung, e; *f. A growing hot, heating:*—Wiđ wunda hâtunge *against heating of wounds,* Herb. 2, 16; Lchdm. i. 84, 20, note.

hât-wende; *adj. Burning, hot, torrid:*—Hâtwendne lyft *the torrid air,* Cd. 146; Th. 182, 12; Exod. 74.

hâwere, es; *m. An observer, a spectator:*—Đŷlæs hie sîen tô ôđerra monna gefeohte holde hâweras, and dôn him selfe nâwuht *lest they be friendly spectators of other men's struggle, and themselves do nothing;* ne, si in hoc præsentis vitæ stadio ad certamen alienum devoti fautores, sed pigri spectatores assistant, Past. 34, 1; Swt. 229, 17. [*Laym.* hauwares, hæweres *spies.*]

hâwian; *p.* ode; *pp.* od *To view, look, observe, regard, survey, inspect:*—Ic hâwige bufan and đû beneoþan *ego supra aspicio, tu infra,* Ælfc. Gr. 47; Som. 47, 49. Drihten lôcaþ of heofenum and hâwaþ hwæđer hê geseó ǽnigne đæra đe hine sêce ođđe hine ongite *Dominus de cælo prospexit ut videat si est intelligens aut requirens Deum,* Ps. Th. 13, 3. Nŷtene gelîc đe hâwaþ symle tô đære eorþan *like a beast that ever looks to the ground,* Homl. Th. ii. 442, 8. Ǽlc man đara đe ǽagan heft ǽrest hâwaþ đæs đe hê geseón wolde ôþ đone first đe hê hyþ gegehâwaþ *every man who has eyes first looks towards what he wants to see, until he has got it under his observation,* Shrn. 178, 6. Þreó þinc sint neódbehæfe đâm eágan êlcere sâwle . . . ôđđer đæt heó hâwien đes đe heó geseón wolden þridde đæt hî mâgen geseón đæt đæt hî gehâwian *three things are necessary for the eyes of every soul . . . second that they look at what they want to see, third that they be able to see what they bring under their notice,* 179, 20. Gûþlâc eode sôna ût and hâwode and hercnode *Guthlac went out at once and looked and listened,* Guthl. 6; Gdwin. 42, 15. Sôna swâ hî wǽron swâ gehende đet ǽgđer on ôđer hâwede *as soon as they were so near as to be in sight of one another,* Chr. 1003; Erl. 139, 8. Hŷ mê hâwedon and mê beheóldon *ipsi consideraverunt et conspexerunt me,* Ps. Th. 21, 16. Drihten hâwa nû mildelîce on đâs earman eorþan *Lord, look now mercifully on this miserable earth,* Bt. 4; Fox 8, 20. Hâwa đæt se inra wind đê ne tôwende *look that the inward wind do not cast thee down,* Homl. Th. ii. 392, 32. Hâwa hwæđer his ceaflas sîn tôswollene *notice whether his jowls be swollen,* Lchdm. iii. 140, 8. Hâwiaþ be gehwilcum *take notice in the case of each one,* Homl. Th. i. 332, 15. Nân mon ne scyle dôn his hond tô đære sylg and hâwian underbæc *no man shall put his hand to the plough and look back,* Past. 51, 8; Swt. 403, 2. DER. be-, gehâwian.

hâwung, e; *f. Looking, observation:*—Ic eom gesceádwîsnes and ic eom ǽlcum manniscum môde on đam stale đe seó hâwung byþ đâm eágum *I am Reason, and in every human mind I hold the same place that observation does in the eyes,* Shrn. 178, 10: 21.

hê; *m:* heó; *f:* hit; *n. He, she, it:*—Đâ hê gefôr đâ fêng his sunu tô đam rîce *when he died his son came to the throne,* Chr. Erl. 2, 11. Him sprecendum hig cômon *eo loquente veniunt,* Mk. Skt. 5, 35. Hê hine miclum gewundode *he wounded him severely,* Chr. 755; Erl. 48, 34. Hê hiene him tô biscepsuna nam *he was godfather to him,* 853; Erl. 68, 14. Hê hire hand nam and heó sôna ârâs *he took her hand and she at once arose,* Mk. Skt. 5, 41-2. Hê him þearle bebeád đæt hî hyt nânum men ne sǽdon and hê hêt hire etan syllan *præcepit illis vehementer ut nemo id sciret et dixit dari illi manducare,* 43. Đâ cuǽdon hie đæt him nǽnig mæg leófra nǽre đonne hiera hlâford and hie nǽfre his banan folgian noldon *then said they that no kinsman was dearer to them than their lord, and they would never follow his murderer,* Chr. 755; Erl. 50, 18-20. Ealle đîne gebrôđru beóþ under his þeówdôme *all thy brethren shall be servants to him,* Gen. 27, 37. Tô tâcne đæt hê his gewald âhte *as a sign that he had had power over him,* Past. 28; Swt. 197, 22. Đa hǽđenan hæfdon heora geweald *the heathen had power over them,* Jud. pref. l. 8. Gedrinc his þreó full fulle *drink of it three cups full,* Herb. 1, 9; Lchdm. i. 74, 1. Hæbbe ic his on handa *I have some of it in my hand,* Cd. 32; Th. 42, 23; Gen. 678. Eorđe and ealle hire gefyllednys and eal ymbhwyrft and đa đe on đam wuniaþ ealle hit syndon Godes ǽhta *earth and all its fulness, and all the globe and those who dwell on it, all are God's possessions,* Homl. Th. i. 172, 10. Etaþ đisne hlâf hit is mîn lîchama *eat this bread, it is my body,* Homl. Th. ii. 266, 33. Ic hyt eom *ego sum,* Mt. Kmbl. 14, 27: 28. Hit ys âwriten, N. leofaþ se man be hlâfe ânum *scribtum est: Non in pane solo vivit homo,* 4, 4. Đâ rînde hit *then it rained,* 7, 27. Hit ǽfenlǽcþ *advesperascit,* Lk. Skt. 24, 29. Hit gelamp *it happened,* Homl. Th. i. 70, 23. Hit wæs winter *hiemps erat,* Jn. Skt. 10, 22. Hit lîcode Herode *it pleased Herod,* Mt. Kmbl. 14, 6. Đonne hit tôcymþ đæt hie hit sprecan sculon *when the time comes that they ought to speak,* Past. 46; Swt. 355, 10. Hit neálǽcþ đam ende; and đŷ hit is on worulde â swâ leng swa wyrse, and swâ hit sceal nŷde for folces synnum fram dæge tô dæge ǽr Antecristes tôcyme yfelian swîđe; and hûru hit wyrþ đonne egeslîc *it is drawing near the end; and therefore the longer it goes on the worse it is in the world, and so for the people's sins it needs must get very bad from day to day before*

Antichrist's coming; and especially then it will be awful, Swt. A. S. Rdr. 104, 1-5. Hwæt mâgon wê his nû dôn *what can we do now in the matter;* quid ergo faciemus, Past. 58; Swt. 443, 14. Sume hit ne gedýgdan mid ðam lîfe *some did not come out of it with life*, Chr. 978; Erl. 127, 12. Se arcebiscop âxode hýrsumnesse mid âþswerunge at him and hê hit forsôc *the archbishop required obedience with an oath of him, and he refused it*, 1070; Erl. 208, 16: 1039; Erl. 167, 19. Hî nâmon hit ðâ on twâ healfe Temese tô scipan weard *they took their way on both sides the Thames towards the ships*, 1009; Erl. 143, 11. Hû mæg ic hit on ðrîm dagum gefaran? ac mâ wên is ðæt ðû onsende ðînne engel, se hit mæg hrædlîcor gefaran . . . ic hit ne mæg hrædlîce gefaran *how can I do it in three days? it is better to send thy angel who can do it more quickly . . . I cannot do it quickly*, St. And. 4, 29-6, 2. Godes bearn nâmon him wîf *the sons of God took them wives*, Gen. 6, 2. Hie woldon ða men him tô mete dôn *they wanted to make the men food for themselves*, St. And. 4, 18. Sý ðæt ylfa ðe him sîe *be the elf what it may*, L. M. 2, 65; Lchdm. ii. 290, 29. Beó him æt hâm *let him be at home*, Deut. 24, 5: Chr. 1009; Erl. 143, 14. Abraham stôd him under ðam treówe *Abraham stood under the tree*, Gen. 18, 8. Heó sæt hire feorran *she sat her down a good way off*, 21, 16. Hî eodon heom *they went*, Chr. 1006; Erl. 140, 17: 21. Hî fleóþ him floccmælum *they fly in flocks*, Homl. Th. i. 142, 9. Ondrêd hê him *timuit*, Jn. Skt. 19, 8. Hæbbe hire ðæt heó hafaþ *let her have what she has*, Gen. 38, 23. Eác him wolde Eádrîc his ealdre gelǽstan *Eadric for his part would follow his chief*, Byrht. Th. 132, 4; By. 11. Ðâ bealh hê hine *indignatus est*, Lk. Skt. 15, 28. Ðâ beþohte hê hine *then he bethought himself*, 17. Reste ðæt folc hit on ðam seofoþan dæge *let the people rest on the seventh day*, Ex. 16, 30. Hie æt Tharse ðære byrig hie gemêtton *they met one another at the city of Tarsus*, Ors. 3, 9; Swt. 128, 2. Se eádiga Mathêus and se hâliga Andreas hie wǽron cyssende him betweónon *the blessed Matthew and the holy Andrew kissed one another*, St. And. 12, 19. Hî betwux him cwǽdon *inter se dicentes*, Mk. Skt. 1, 27. Hig grêtton hig gesybsumum wordum *they greeted each other with words of peace*, Ex. 18, 7. Hî ðâ hî gecyston *then they kissed each other*, Shrn. 89, 12. Hî micclum ege him ondrêdon and cwǽdon ǽlc tô ôðrum *timuerunt magno timore et dicebant ad alterutrum*, Mk. Skt. 4, 41: Bt. Met. Fox 25, 21; Met. 25, 11. Sume hî cômon feorran *quidam ex eis de longe venerunt*, Mk. 8, 3. Nû sceal hê sylf faran *now must he himself come*, Cd. 27; Th. 35, 18; Gen. 556. Hire selfre suna *her own sons*, Beo. Th. 2234; B. 1115. Pilatus hymsylf âwrât ealle ða þyng *Pilate himself wrote all the things*, Nicod. 34; Thw. 19, 33. On himselfum *in semetipso*, Past. 16, 2; Swt. 101, 1. Hû ne becýpaþ hig twegen spearwan tô peninge *are not two sparrows sold for a penny*, Mt. Kmbl. 10, 29: 5, 11. Hê dyde ðæt hî twelfe mid him wǽron *fecit ut essent duodecim cum illo*, Mk. Skt. 3, 14. Hî ealle þrý tôgædere grêtton ðone cyngc *all three of them together saluted the king*, Th. Ap. 19, 22: Homl. Th. ii. 384, 4. Gewiton hie feówer *they four departed*, Cd. 92; Th. 118, 12; Gen. 1964: 191; Th. 238, 28; Dan. 361. Heora begra ǽhte *the property of both of them*, 90; Th. 113, 27; Gen. 1893. Him bâm on breóstum *in the breasts of them both*, 10; Th. 12, 25; Gen. 190. Him eallum *to them all*, 156; Th. 194, 16; Exod. 261. Him twâm hê wæs ætýwed *duobus ex eis ostensus est*, Mk. Skt. 16, 12. Hê Ninus Soroastrem Bactriana cyning se cûðe manna ǽrest drýcræftas hê hine oferwann and ofslôh [*Ninus*] *Zoroastrem Bactrianorum regem, eundemque magicæ artis repertorem, pugna oppressum interfecit*, Ors. 1, 2; Swt. 30, 10: St. And. 4, 3, 6. Wæs hê se man in weoruldhâde geseted *in habitu sæculari constitutus*, Bd. 4, 24; S. 597, 3. Europa hió onginþ *Europa incipit*, Ors. 1, 1; Swt. 8, 14. Ða ðe his lîf ðæs eádigan weres cûðon *those who were acquainted with the life of the blessed man*, Guthl. prol: Gdwin. 4, 26. Wê gesâwon Enac his cynryn *we saw the children of Anak*, Num. 13, 29, 33: Deut. 1, 28. Nilus seó eá hire ǽwielme *the source of the river Nile*, Ors. 1, 1; Swt. 12, 19. Affrica and Asia hiera landgemircu onginnaþ of Alexandria *the boundaries of Africa and Asia begin from Alexandria*, 8, 28. Ðæt se hiera folgoþ hine ne ôðhebbe *istos ne locus superior extollat*, Past. 28; Swt. 189, 17. Ða ðe hiera mildheortlîce sellaþ *qui sua misericorditer tribuunt*, 44; Swt. 319, 16. Wê his syndon *we are his*, Ps. Th. 99, 2. Hyra ys heofonan rîce *ipsorum est regnum cælorum*, Mt. Kmbl. 5, 10. Hê biþ unscildig ðe hine slôh *then shall he that smote him be quit*, Ex. 21, 19. Dôþ sîðfæt ðæs sêftne and rihtne ðe hê sylfa âstâh ofer sunnan up *iter facite ei, qui ascendit super occasum*, Ps. Th. 67, 4. Se wer ðe his tôhopa byþ tô swylcum Drihtne *vir cujus nomen Domini spes ejus*, 39. 4: Elen. Kmbl. 324; El. 162. Mid mînum brôðer steffane ðe fiola gôddra dǽda siond be him âwritene *with my brother Stephen about whom many good deeds are written*, H. R. 13, 12: Ps. Th. 145, 4. Ðâm wîtgum ðe god self þurht hî spec *the prophets by whom God himself spoke*, Shrn. 107, 11. Ǽlc nýten biþ oððe hê oððe heó *every animal is either male or female*, Ælfc. Gr. 6; Som. 5, 35, 46. Woepen mon ł hee and hiuu ł wîfmon *masculum et feminam*, Mk. Skt. Lind. 10, 6. Hê ł woepenmon *masculinum*, Lk. Skt. Lind. 2, 23. [In later English the Northern dialect is first found adopting the forms which in Modern English have replaced the oldest, and the innovation gradually spread. Thus while the Northumbrian Metrical Psalter (before 1300) has *þai, þair, þam* in the plural, the declension in *Piers P.* is *hij* and *þei, here, hem*: and these forms with the exception of *hij*, are used by Wicklif and Chaucer. So with *she* for *heó*, which is still preserved in the Lancashire *hoo*. Amongst the cognate dialects the *O. Frs.* is that which agrees best with English. v. Hilfenstein, Comparative Grammar, p. 193.]

heá. v. heáh.

heaf, es; *n. Sea, water*, Beo. Th. 4947; B. 2477. [*Icel. Swed.* haf: *Dan.* hav *sea, ocean.*]

heáf, es; *m. Lamentation, mourning, weeping, wailing*:—Ðǽr is se ungeendoda heáf *there is the never-ending lamentation*, L. E. I; Th. ii. 394, 10: 400, 7. Wôp and heáf micel *ploratus et ululatus multus*, Mt. Kmbl. Rush. 2, 18. Ðǽr biþ heáf *illic erit fletus*, 24, 51. Nis hêr nǽnig wôp ne nǽnig heáf gehýred *there is no weeping nor wailing heard here*, Blickl. Homl. 85, 28: 115, 15: 219, 9: Exon. 48 a; Th. 164, 32; Gû. 1020: Ors. 4, 5; Bos. 81, 28. Ðû gehwyrfdest mînne heáf mê tô gefeán *convertisti planctum meum in gaudium mihi*, Ps. Th. 29, 11: Blickl. Homl. 195, 17. v. heóf.

heáfan; *p.* heóf, hôf *To mourn, wail, lament*:—Ðæt wîf hôf hreówigmôd *the woman mourned repentant*, Cd. 37; Th. 48, 5; Gen. 771. Heófon gehygd *they lamented their purpose*, 221; Th. 285, 28; Sat. 344. v. heófan.

heáfd. v. heáfod.

heáfian. v. heófian.

heáflîc; *adj. Mournful, lamentable, grievous*:—Ðæt heáflîce gewrit *that mournful sentence*, Blickl. Homl. 123, 6.

heafoc. v. hafoc.

heáfod; *gen.* heáfdes; *dat.* heáfde; *pl.* heáfdu [v. Ælfc. Gr. 15; Som. 18, 21-25] HEAD, *chief, source, 'the commencing point, or the highest point, of a stream, of a field, hill, etc.* In reference to running water, the head is exactly converse to the gemýðe or mouths. In the Saxon charters the word is of frequent occurrence, and, as it seems, generally to denote rising grounds. It is hardly distinguishable from the compound words and-heáfod, on-heáfod,' Cod. Dipl. Kmbl. iii. xxix:—Ðis forweard heáfod *hæc frons*, Ælfc. Gr. 9, 39; Som. 12, 60: Wrt. Voc. 70, 28: Homl. Th. ii. 266, 11. Ǽfteweard hæfod *occiput* vel *postea*: ofer healf heáfod *sinciput*, Ælfc. Gl. 69; Som. 70, 35, 36; Wrt. Voc. 42, 43, 44. Healf heáfod *hoc sinciput*, Ælfc. Gr. 9, 78; Som. 14, 24. Cûþ is ðæt se âwyrgda gâst is heáfod ealra unrihtwîsra dǽda, swylce unrihtwîse syndon deófles leomo *it is known that the accursed spirit is the source of all unrighteous deeds, as also unrighteous men are members of the devil*, Blickl. Homl. 33, 7. Hine ðe wæs ǽrur heáfod tô ðam unrǽde *the man that had before been the author of that mischief*, Chr. 1087; Erl. 225, 10. Heáfod ealra heáhgesceafta *the chief of all exalted creatures*, Cd. 1; Th. i. 7; Gen. 4: Hy. 7, 62; Hy. Grn. ii. 287, 62. Hê getimbrede ða burg Babylonie tô ðon ðæt heó wǽre heáfod ealra Asiria *Babyloniam urbem instauravit, caputque regni Assyrii ut esset instituit*, Ors. 2, 1; Swt. 60, 14. Stæfes heáfud *apicem*, Lk. Skt. Lind. 16, 17. Wið healfes heáfdes ece *for megrim*, L. M. 1, 1; Lchdm. ii. 20, 14, 17, 21. Þolige hê heáfdes *let him lose his head*, L. Edg. S. 11; Th. i. 276, 13. His heáfdes segl *his head's sun* [*the eye*], Andr. Kmbl. 100; An. 50. His eágan hâlge heáfdes gimmas *his eyes, his head's holy gems*, Exon. 51 b; Th. 180, 7; Gû. 1276. Hât mê heáfde beceorfan *order my head to be cut off*, Blickl. Homl. 183, 16. Wið tôbrocenum heáfde *for a broken head*, L. M. 1, 1; Lchdm. ii. 22, 10. On ðam heáfde foran *on the forehead*, 2, 64; Lchdm. ii. 288, 22: 65; Lchdm. ii. 290, 23. His heáfod forweard mid ðære hâlgan rôde tâcne gewǽpnige *let him arm his head in front with the sign of the holy rood*, L. E. I. 29; Th. ii. 426, 8. Wê sceolon fyligan ûrum Heáfde and faran fram deófle tô Criste *we ought to follow our Head, and pass from the devil to Christ*, Homl. Th. ii. 282, 20. Ic ðê gesette eallum Israhêlum tô heáfde *caput te constitui in tribubus Israel*, Past. 17, 4; Swt. 113, 10. Ðû settest ûs mænige men ofer heáfod *imposuisti homines super capita nostra*, Ps. Th. 65, 10. Hêr Offa hêt Æþelbryhte ðæt heáfod ofásleán *in this year Offa ordered Ethelbert's head to be struck off*, Chr. 792; Erl. 58, 2. Bûton hê healde iii niht hýde and heáfod *unless he keep the hide and head three nights*, L. Eth. iii. 9; Th. i. 296, 18. Fare seó buruhwaru sylf tô and begyte ða banan cuce oððe deáde heora nýhstan mâgas, heáfod wið heáfde *let the burghers themselves go and get the murderers, living or dead, or their nearest kinsmen, head for head*, ii. 6; Th. i. 286, 32. Æt ðam ôðran cyrre ne sý ðǽr nân ôðer bôt bûtan ðæt heáfod *the second time let there be no other reparation than the head*, i. 1, 2; Th. i. 282, 2, 23. Heáfdas feónda *capita inimicorum suorum*, Ps. Th. 67, 21. Hie heora heáfdu slôgan on ða wagas *they struck their heads against the walls*, Blickl. Homl. 151, 5. Hý habbaþ hunda heáfda *they have dogs' heads*, Nar. 34, 32. Ða heáfda wǽran ofácorfena *the heads were cut off*, Ors. 4, 1; Bos. 79, 7. Nim ðes leáces heáfda *take the heads of this leek*, Lchdm. i. 376, 3. Heáfdu, L. M. 2, 32; Lchdm. ii. 234, 20. Of Godes half and ealre hâdode heáfde *on behalf of God and of all persons in orders*, Chr. 675; Erl. 37, 25: 963; Erl. 123, 15. Swâ swâ heó on dæg dêþ bufan ûrum heáfdum *as by day it does above our heads*, Lchdm. iii. 234, 25. Ðone stân ðe æt his heáfdum læg *the stone that lay at his head*, Past. 16, 3; Swt. 101, 16. Ðá cómon ðyder tu wild deór and heóldan ðone líchoman óðer æt ðǽm heáfdum óðer æt ðǽm fótum *then came thither two wild beasts and guarded the body, one at the head, the other at the feet*, Shrn. 83, 25: Rood Kmbl. 126; Kr. 63. Heáfdan, Blickl. Homl. 145, 26. [*Laym.* heaved, hæfed: *Orm.* hæfedd: *A. R.* heaved: *Piers P. Chauc. Wick.* hed, heed. The cognate dialects seem to offer two forms, differing in the root vowel, each of which may be represented in the English. Thus heáfod may compare with *Goth.* haubiþ: *O. Sax.* hóbid: *O. H. Ger.* haupit, houbit; while hæfod, hafud may compare with *Icel.* höfuð; v. Cl. and Vig. Dict. s. v.]

heáfod-ǽdre, e; *f. The cephalick vein:*—Lǽt him blód on ðam winestran earme of ðære heáfodǽdre *let blood from the cephalick vein in his left arm*, L. M. 2, 42; Lchdm. ii. 254, 7.

heáfod-bán, es; *n. Head-bone, skull:*—Monnes heáfodbán bærn tó ahsan *burn a man's skull to ashes*, L. M. 1, 53; Lchdm. ii. 126, 2. Wulfes heáfodbán bærn swíðe *burn a wolf's skull thoroughly*, 61; Lchdm. ii. 132, 3. [*Laym.* hæfd-, heued-bon *skull*: *Icel.* höfuð-bein.]

heáfod-beáh; *gen.* -beáges; *m. A head-ring, crown:*—Heáfodbeáh gyldenne *a golden crown*, Bt. 37, 2; Fox 188, 8.

heáfod-beorh; *gen.* -beorge; *f. A head-shelter, helmet*, Beo. Th. 2065; B. 1030.

heáfod-beorht; *adj. Having a bright, splendid head*, Exon. 105 a; Th. 400, 2; Rä. 20, 2.

heáfod-biscop, es; *m. A head-bishop, high priest:*—Abiathar ðæra Iudéiscra heáfodbiscop *Abiathar high priest of the Jews*, Homl. Th. ii. 420, 31.

heáfod-bolla, an; *m. A skull:*—Heáfodbollan stówe *Golgotha*, Lye.

heáfod-bolster, es; *n. A pillow:*—Heáfdbolster *capitale*, Ælfc. Gl. 27; Som. 60, 104; Wrt. Voc. 25, 44. Under ðínum heáfodbolstre *under thy pillow*, L. M. 3, 58; Lchdm. ii. 342, 14.

heáfod-botl, es; *n. A chief dwelling, principal mansion:*—Dǽlon hí ðæt heáfodbotl him betweónan *let them share the chief dwelling between them*, Chart. Th. 529, 33: 542, 10: 597, 6. [*Icel.* höfuð-ból *a manor, domain.*]

heáfod-burh; *gen.* -burge; *f. Chief town, capital, metropolis:*—Forgeaf him wununge on Cantwarebyrig, seó wæs ealles his ríces heáfodburh *he gave him a dwelling in Canterbury, that was the chief town of all his kingdom*, Homl. Th. ii. 128, 31. Hí becómon æt néxtan tó ánre heáfodbyrig Suanir geháten *they arrived at last at a chief town called Suanir*, 494, 2. Cartaina heora heáfodburh *Carthage their principal city*, Ors. 4, 6; Bos. 84, 29. [*Orm.* ȝerrsalam wass hæfeddburrh off Issraeless riche: *Icel.* höfuð-borg *metropolis*: *O. H. Ger.* houpit-purch.]

heáfod-cláþ, es; *n. Head-cloth, head-dress:*—Heáfodcláþ *vel* cappa *capitulum* vel *capitularium*, Ælfc. Gl. 64; Som. 69, 14; Wrt. Voc. 40, 48. [*A. R.* hore heued-cloð sitte lowe, 424, 23.]

heáfod-cwide, es; *m.* I. *a saying of especial importance:*—Ða iiii heáfodcwidas in Actibus Apostolorum ðus bebeódaþ *quattuor dicta præcipua in Actibus Apostolorum sic præcipiunt*, L. Ecg. C. 38; Th. ii. 162, 33. II. *a chapter:*—Onginnaþ heáfudcuido *incipiunt capitulæ*, Rtl. 166, 17.

heáfod-cyrice, an; *f. A principal church, cathedral*, L. C. E. 3; Wilk. 127, 52. [*R. Glouc.* heued chirche of al Cristendom: *Icel.* höfuðkirkja *high-church, cathedral.*]

heáfod-ece, es; *m. Head-ache:*—Wið heáfodece *for head-ache*, Lchdm. i. 4, 15: Herb. 75, 6; Lchdm. i. 178, 15. [*A. R.* heavedeche.]

heáfodeht; *adj. Having a head* [of plants]:—Heáfdehtes porres *of a leek having a head to it*, L. M. 2, 30; Lchdm. ii. 230, 10.

heáfod-fæder; *m. A patriarch*, Lye.

heáfod-frætewnes, -ness, e; *f. A head-ornament*, Cot. 65, Lye.

heáfod-gemaca, -gemæcca, an; *m. An equal, a mate, fellow:*—Ða sylfan his heáfodgemacan hé forlét *his very fellows he forsook*, Guthl. 2; Gdwin. 16, 16. Ic mæg sleán míne heáfodgemæccan [heáfudgemæccean, Cot. MS.] *I may beat my fellow-servants*; cæperit percutere conservos suos, Past. 17, 8; Swt. 121, 12. Feówra sum his heáfodgemacene *with three of his equals*, L. Wih. 19, 21; Th. i. 40, 17, 21. Mid heora heáfodgemacum *cum suis similibus*, Bd. 4, 22; S. 591, 8. [Cf. heáfod-mǽg.]

heáfod-gerím, es; *n. The chief number, majority*; or *number of heads*, i. e. *of men* [cf. *the other compounds of* gerím], Judth. 12; Thw. 26, 4; Jud. 309. v. next word.

heáfod-getel, es; *n. A principal, cardinal number:*—*Cardinales numeros* ðæt synd ða heáfodgetel, Ælfc. Gr. 49; Som. 49, 64.

heáfod-gewǽde, es; *n. A head-dress, veil:*—Ðæt beó ðé tó heáfodgewǽdon *let it be to thee for a veil*, Gen. 20, 16.

heáfod-gim; *m. f.* [?] *Jewel of the head, the eye*, Exon. 27 a; Th. 81, 29; Cri. 1331: 89 b; Th. 336, 6; Gn. Ex. 44: Andr. Kmbl. 62; An. 31.

heáfod-gold, es; *n. A crown:*—Ðú him sylst heáfodgold tó mǽrþe *honore coronasti eum*, Ps. Th. 8, 6. [*Icel.* höfuð-gull *head-jewels.*]

heáfod-gylt, e; *f. A capital crime, deadly sin:*—Búton hine hwá mid heáfodgylte forwyrce ðæt hé weofudþénunge ðanonforþ wyrðe sí *unless any one by deadly sin render himself unworthy thenceforth of the altar-service*, L. N. P. L. 2; Th. ii. 290, 8.

heáfod-hǽr, es; *n. A hair of the head:*—Heáfod-hǽr *capilli*, Ælfc. Gl. 70; Som. 70, 55; Wrt. Voc. 42, 63.

heáfod-hriéfþo; *f. Head-roughness*; capitis scabies, L. M. 2, 30; Lchdm. ii 228, 13.

heáfod-land. v. hafud-land.

heáfod-leahter, es; *m. A capital offence, mortal sin:*—Ǽlc ðara manna ðe mid heáfodleahtre besmiten biþ *unusquisque eorum hominum, qui capitalibus criminibus polluti sunt*, L. M. I. P. 1; Th. ii. 266, 3. Se ðe ða heáfodleahtras wyrcþ and on ðám geendaþ hé mót forbyrnan on ðam écum fýre *he who commits the deadly sins and dies in them shall burn in the everlasting fire*, Homl. Th. ii. 590, 17.

heáfod-leás; *adj. Headless:*—Heáfodleás bodig *truncus*, Ælfc. Gl. 73; Som. 71, 30; Wrt. Voc. 44, 16: Exon. 104 a; Th. 395, 19; Rä. 15, 10.

heáfod-lencten-fæsten, es; *n. The chief Lent fast*, R. Concord.

heáfod-líc; *adj. Chief, capital:*—For heáfodlícum gyltum *pro capitalibus criminibus*, L. Ecg. C. 2; Th. ii. 134, 3. Ðæt wé ús healdan wið heáfodlícan leahtras *to keep ourselves from deadly sins*, Blickl. Homl. 37, 3.

heáfod-ling, es; *m. An equal, a fellow, mate:*—Heáfodlinges *coæquales*, Mt. Kmbl. Lind. 11, 16. Heáfudlinges *conservos*, 24, 49. [*Laym. has* hevedling *chief, captain, like Ger.* häuptling.]

heáfod-mǽg, es; *m. A near relation, a relation in the first degree*, Cd. 60; Th. 73, 6; Gen. 1200: 78; Th. 96, 36; Gen. 1605: Beo. Th. 1180; B. 588: 4308; B. 2151. v. next word; and cf. *Icel.* höfuð-niðjar, höfuðbarmsmenn *agnates*: v. also cneów-mǽgas, and see Grmm. R. A. pp. 468–70, for terms belonging to the body in their application to degrees of relationship.

heáfod-mága, an; *m. A near relation*, Andr. Kmbl. 1884; An. 944. v. preceding word.

heáfod-man, -mann, es; *m. A chief man, prince, captain, leader:*—Heáfodman *vel* þegn *primas*, Ælfc. Gl. 68; Som. 70, 5; Wrt. Voc. 42, 14: Homl. Th. ii. 514, 14. Þæt folc wearþ micclum ástyred, and ða heáfodmenn and ða bóceras *the people were much stirred up and the elders and the scribes*, i. 44, 30. Israhéla heáfodmen *heads of thousands in Israel*, Num. 1, 16: 13, 3: Jos. 23, 2. Þa heáfodmen *the lords* [*of the Philistines*], Jud. 16, 27: Chr. 1069; Erl. 207, 15: 1101; Erl. 237, 14, 25. Ðǽr on wǽron twægen heáfodmenn Cnut and Hácun eorl *in them were two leaders, Cnut and earl Hakon*, 1075; Erl. 214, 7. [*Laym.* hæfdmen, *pl*: *Orm.* hæfeddmann: *Icel.* höfuðs-maðr *a chief, leader*: *O. H. Ger.* haubitman *satrapa*: *Ger.* hauptmann *captain.*]

heáfod-mynster, es; *n. A chief minster, church*, L. Eth. ix. 5; Th. i. 340, 27: L. C. E. 3; Th. i. 360, 17.

heáfod-panne, an; *f. A skull:*—Heáfodpanne *calvaria*, Wrt. Voc. 64, 24: 282, 40. Forheáfod *vel* heáfodpanne *calvarium*, Ælfc. Gl. 69; Som. 70, 33; Wrt. Voc. 42, 41. Golgotha ðæt is heáfodpannan stów *Golgotha quod est calvariæ locus*, Mt. Kmbl. 27, 33: Jn. Skt. 19, 17. Heáfodpannena stów, Mk. Skt. 15, 22. Hundes heáfodpanne *a dog's skull*, L. M. ex Quad. 13, 3; Lchdm. i. 370, 3: L. M. 2, 55; Lchdm. ii. 342, 4.

heáfod-port, es; *m. A principal town*, Chr. 1086; Erl. 220, 21.

heáfod-ríce, es; *n. A chief kingdom, empire:*—Feówer heáfodrícu *quatuor regnorum principatus*, Ors. 2, 1; Swt. 58, 31.

heáfod-sár, es; *m. Pain in the head*, Herb. 4 7; Lchdm. i. 90, 28.

heáfod-sién, -sýn, e; *f. The eye:*—Ðǽr him hrefn nimeþ heáfodsýne *there* [*on the gallows*] *shall the raven take from him his eye*, Exon. 87 b; Th. 329, 19; Vy. 36. Heáfodsiéna, Cd. 114; Th. 150, 11; Gen. 2490.

heáfod-slæge, es; *n. Head of a pillar* [?]; capital, Cot. 50, Lye. [Cf. ofer-slege.]

heáfod-smæl *capitium*, Wrt. Voc. 288, 43.

heáfod-stede, es; *m. A chief place:*—Heora þeówas hie benóman heora heáfodstedes ðæt hie Capitoliam héton *servi invaserunt Capitolium*, Ors. 2, 6; Swt. 86, 30. Hwílum wǽran heáfodstedas and heálíce hádas micelre mǽðe wyrðe *formerly the chief places and high ranks were entitled to much honour*, L. Eth. vii. 3; Th. i. 330, 6. [*O. Sax.* hóbidstedi: *O. H. Ger.* houpit-stat *toparchia.*]

heáfod-stól, es; *m. A chief place, capital:*—Thébána fæsten ðætte ǽr wæs ealra Créca heáfodstól *the city of Thebes which before was the chief place of all Greece*, Ors. 3, 9; Swt. 124, 5: 3, 11; Swt. 144, 19. [*Icel.* höfuð-stóll *a chief seat.*]

heáfod-stów, e; *f. A place for the head:*—Seó heáfodstów cræftiglíce geworht ætýwde *locus capitis fabrefactus apparuit*, Bd. 4, 19; S. 590, 1.

heáfod-swíma, an; *m. Swimming in the head, dizziness*, Cd. 76; Th. 94, 28; Gen. 1568. [*Icel.* höfuð-svími *dizziness in the head.*]

heáfod-sýn. v. heáfod-sién.

heáfod-þweál, es; *n. A washing of the head*; capitilavium, Ælfc. Gl. 56; Som. 67, 26; Wrt. Voc. 37, 16. [*O. H. Ger.* houbit-twehela *caputlavium.*]

heáfod-wærc, es; *m. Pain in the head*, L. M. 1, 1; Lchdm. ii. 18,

5, 19. [*Prompt. Parv.* heedwerke, heedwarke *cephalia, cephalargia: Icel.* höfuð-verkr *head-ache.*]

heáfod-weard, es; *m. A chief guardian, chief officer:*—Cynnes heáfudwærd *tribunus*, Jn. Skt. Lind. 18, 12. Ðæs herefolces heáfodweardas *the leaders of the army*, Judth. 12; Thw. 25, 3; Jud. 239.

heáfod-weard, e; *f. A guarding of the* [*lord's*] *head, attendance as a guard upon the king.* The word occurs in an enumeration of the services required of the thane and the 'geneat,' Th. i. 432, 8, 17. So in Beowulf it is said of Wiglaf that he 'healdeþ heáfodwearde,' keeps guard over the dead king, Beo. Th. 5811; B. 2909. [Cf. *Icel.* höfuðvörðr *a body-guard.*]

heáfod-weard, e; *f. A chapter;* capitulum, Mt. Kmbl. p. 11, 17: 13, 13. [Cf. fore-weard.]

heáfod-wind, es; *m. A wind from one of the four chief points of the compass:*—Feówer heáfodwindas synd se fyrmesta is eásterne wind . . . se óðer heáfodwind is súðerne . . . se þridda heáfodwind hātte zephirus . . . se feórþe heáfodwind hātte septemtrio, Lchdm. iii. 274, 12–23. [*Icel.* höfuð-vindr.]

heáfod-wīsa, an; *m. A chief director, ruler*, Cd. 79; Th. 97, 28; Gen. 1619.

heáfod-wōþ, e; *f. The voice*, Exon. 103 a; Th. 390, 17; Rä. 9, 3.

heáfod-wund, e; *f. A wound in the head*, L. Alf. pol. 44; Th. i. 90, 13, 14. [*O. Sax.* hōbid-wunda.]

heáfod-wylm, es; *m. Burning* or *heat in the head*, L. M. 1, 1; Lchdm. ii. 26, 2.

heáfod-wyrhta, an; *m. A chief workman*, Homl. Th. ii. 530, 7.

heafola. v. hafela.

heáf-sang, es; *m. An elegy*, Cot. 118, Lye.

heág. v. heáh.

heáge; *adv. High:*—Heáge flīhþ se earn *sublime volat aquila*, Ælfc. Gr. 41, 16. Beheald ðās sunnan hū heáge heó āstīhþ *behold this sun how high it mounts*, Homl. Th. i. 286, 31.

heago-rūn, e; *f. A mystery in which magic is involved, necromancy:*—Hū mambres ontȳnde ða drȳlīcan bēc his brēðer iamnes and him geopenude ða heagorūne ðæs deófelgildes his brōður *aperuit mambres libros magicos fratris sui iamnis et fecit nicromantiam et eduxit ab inferis idolum fratris sui*, Nar. 50, 14. [Cockayne has the following note:—'Heag hic pro *veneficus, magicus* sumendus; nostrum HAG.']

heago-spind. v. hago-spind.

HEÁH, hēh; *adj.* HIGH, *tall, lofty, sublime, haughty:*—Heáh on bodige *statura sublimis*, Bd. 3, 14; S. 540, 7. Gyldenu onlīcnes twelf elna heáh *a golden image twelve ells high*, Shrn. 88, 23. Se beám geweóx heáh *the tree grew high*, Cd. 202; Th. 251, 15; Dan. 564. Hwæt elles getācnaþ se heá torr būton ðone heán foreþonc and ða gesceádwīsnesse ðara gōdena manna *what else does the high tower signify but the lofty forethought and the sagacity of good men*, Past. 56; Swt. 433, 24. Sió heá lār *lofty doctrine*, 63; Past. 459, 8. Seó heáge dūn *the high mountain*, Homl. Th. ii. 384, 29. Heáh heofoncyning *heaven's high king*, Cd. 23; Th. 30, 7; Gen. 463. Hē on hrōfe gestōd heán landes *he on the summit stood of the high land*, 140; Th. 175, 21; Gen. 2898. Hie be hliðe heáre dūne eorþscræf fundon *they found a cavern by the side of a lofty hill*, 122; Th. 156, 26; Gen. 2594. Se deófol gesette hine uppan ðam scylfe ðæs heágan temples *the devil placed him upon the summit of the lofty temple*, Homl. Th. i. 166, 18. Seó eádignes ðæs heán heáhengles tīd *the blessedness of the festival of the great archangel*, Blickl. Homl. 197, 4, 24. From stæþe heáum *from the high shore*, Exon. 106 a; Th. 405, 6; Rä. 23, 19. Uppan ānre swīðe heáhre dūne *upon a very high mountain*, Homl. Th. i. 166, 23. Unriht on heán hūse ācwǣdon *iniquitatem in excelso locuti sunt*, Ps. Th. 72, 6. On heágum *in excelso*, 9. Hōf ic mīne eágan tō ðam heán beorge *levavi oculos meos in montes*, 120, 1. Fram ðam heágan cederbeáme *from the tall cedar*, Homl. Th. ii. 578, 4. Hāt ðū mē ānne heáhne tor getimbrian *order a high tower to be built for me*, Blickl. Homl. 183, 3. Hē āsette mīne fēt on swīðe heánne stān, ðæt ys on swȳðe heáh setl *statuit super petram pedes meos*, Ps. Th. 39, 2. Ofer heáne hrōf heofones ðisses *beyond the lofty roof of the sky*, Bt. Met. Fox 24, 5; Met. 24, 3. Ðone heán heofoñ *high heaven*, Cd. 35; Th. 45, 33; Gen. 736. Se ðe gebīgde ðone heágan heofonlīcan bīgels *he who bowed the lofty vault of heaven*, Homl. Th. i. 170, 23: H. R. 103, 1. Ofer heáh wæter *over deep water*, Cd. 72; Th. 87, 19; Gen. 1451. Engel drihtnes lēt his hand cuman in ðæt heá seld *the angel of the Lord brought his hand into that lofty hall*, 210; Th. 261, 7; Dan. 722. Wǣron ōfras heá streámas stronge *the shores were high, the streams strong*, Exon. 106 a; Th. 404, 14; Rä. 23, 7. Wē ceorfaþ heáh treówu on holte *altum silvæ lignum succidimus*, Past. 58, 6; Swt. 443, 36. Wesan heā mihte handa ðīnre āhafen ofer hæleþas *may the excellent powers of thy hand be exalted over men*, Ps. Th. 88, 12. Heágum þrymmum *in excellent majesty*, Cd. 1; Th. 1, 16; Gen. 8. Hȳð heáum ceólum *a haven for the tall ships*, Bt. Met. Fox 21, 22; Met. 21, 11. On heán muntum heortas wuniaþ *montes excelsi domus cervis*, Ps. Th. 103, 17. Nā geþafian ðæt se heárra derige ðam heánran *not to permit the higher to hurt the lower*, L. I. P. 7; Th. ii. 314, 1. Stōl heáhran, heárran *a loftier throne*, Cd. 15; Th. 18, 16, 26; Gen. 274, 282. Hērra, Exon. 56 a; Th. 199, 20; Ph. 28. Tō hiéran hāde *to a higher rank*, Past. pref. Swt. 7, 15: Chr. 897; Erl. 95, 14. Se mægþhād is hīrra ðonne se gesinscipe *præeminere virginitatem conjugio*, Past. 52, 8; Swt. 409, 23. Wearþ him hȳrra hyge *he had a haughtier mind*, Cd. 198; Th. 247, 2; Dan. 491. Hȳrre ic eom heofone *higher am I than heaven*, Exon. 110 b; Th. 424, 12; Rä. 41, 38. Cwæþ ðæt his hergas hȳrran wǣron ðonne israēla ēce drihten *said that his gods were superior to the everlasting lord of Israel*, Cd. 210; Th. 262, 26; Dan. 715. Ðēh ðe hī selfe wilnien ðæs heáhstan *etsi summa appetunt*, Past. 16, 4; Swt. 103, 16: Ps. Th. 112, 4. Se geworden is hwommona heágost *hic factus est in caput anguli*, 117, 21. Ðæs hēhstan heofonrīces, 90, 1. Seó is ealra dūna mǣst and hīgest *mons maximus et altissimus*, Nar. 37, 32. Se hȳhsta ealra cyninga cyning *the most high king of all kings*, Exon. 32 b; Th. 103, 1; Cri. 1682. [*Goth.* hauhs: *O. Sax.* hōh: *O. Frs.* hāch, hāg: *Icel.* hār: *O. H. Ger.* hōh *altus, excelsus, celsus, excellens, sublimis: Ger.* hoch.]

heáh, heá; *adv. High:*—Bryne stīgeþ heáh tō heofonum *the burning mounts aloft to heaven*, Exon. 63 a; Th. 233, 7; Ph. 521: Cd. 166 Th. 207, 15; Exod. 467: Ps. Th. 138, 6. Heáor *altius*, Bd. 3, 8; S. 532, 16. On ðam gim āstīhþ on heofenas up hȳhst on geáre . . . *in it* [*June*] *the sun mounts highest in the year*, Menol. Fox 218; Men. 110. v. heáge.

heáh-beorg, es; *m. A high mountain:*—Hē ðās heáhbeorgas healdeþ swylce *et altitudines montium ipse conspicit*, Ps. Th. 94, 4. [*Icel.* hābjarg *a high rock;* hā-fjall *a high fell.*]

heáh-biscop, es; *m. An archbishop, chief bishop, pontiff:*—Birhtwald Bretone heáhbiscop *Birhtwald archbishop of Britain*, L. Wih. pref.; Th. i. 36, 8. Mid geþeahte Wulfhelmes mīnes hēhbisceopes *with the counsel of Wulfhelm my archbishop*, L. Ath. prm.; Th. i. 194, 13. Se heáhbiscop and se hālga Wilfriþ *Antistes eximius Vilfrid*, Bd. 5, 19; S. 636, 41. Heáhbiscop *pontifex*, 2, 3; S. 504, 44, note. Hēhbiscop *pontifex*, Rtl. 72, 8: *archiepiscopus*, 194, 27.

heáh-boda, an; *m. An archangel:*—Hēht sigores fruma his heáhbodan hider gefleógan *bade the triumphant Lord his archangel fly hither*, Exon. 12 a; Th. 19, 3; Cri. 295.

heáh-burh; *gen.* -burge; *f. A chief town, large town;* also *a town having an elevated situation:*—Ðǣr is Crēca heáhburg *there is the chief town of the Greeks*, Bt. 1; Fox 2, 21: Beo. Th. 2258; B. 1127. Tō ðære heáhbyrig *to the chief town* [*Babylon*], Cd. 209; Th. 259, 30; Dan. 699. Se kāsere geeode wel manega hēhburh *the emperor conquered a good many of the principal towns*, Chr. Erl. 5, 13. Ic wāt heáhburg hēr āne neáh lytle ceastre *I know that near here is a town placed on high, a little city*, Cd. 117; Th. 152, 8; Gen. 2517.

heáh-bytlere, es; *m. A chief-builder, architect*, Lye.

heáh-cleófa, an; *m. A principal chamber:*—His brȳdbūras and his heáhcleófan ealle wǣron eorcnanstānum unionibus and carbunculis ðǣm gimcynnum swīðast gefrætwode *talami cubiliaque margaritis unionibusque et carbunculis nitebant*, Nar. 5, 2.

heáh-clif, es; *n. A high, lofty cliff:*—Beorgas gemeltaþ and heáhcleofu *the hills shall melt and the lofty cliffs*, Exon. 22 a; Th. 61, 3; Cri. 979. [Cf. heáh-beorg.]

heáh-cræft, es; *m. Excellent art* or *skill*, Exon. 109 a; Th. 417, 13; Rä. 36, 4.

heáh-cyning, es; *m. A chief, great king, God:*—Mid heáhcyning *with God*, Exon. 62 b; Th. 231, 3; Ph. 483. On ða swȳðran healfe ðæs heáhcyninges *on the right hand of the great king* [*God*], Shrn. 118, 9: Cd. 6; Th. 8, 14; Gen. 124. Ðæt wæs hildesetl heáhcyninges *that was the war-seat* [*saddle*] *of the great king* [*Hrothgar*], Beo. Th. 2083; B. 1039.

heáh-deór, heá-, es; *n. A stag, deer:*—Swā swīðe hē lufode ða heádeór swilce hē wǣre heora fæder *he loved the stags as if he were their father*, Chr. 1086; Erl. 222, 29: Hexam. 9; Norm. 16, 3. [Cf. *Ger.* die hohe Jagd *the hunting of deer.*]

heáhdeór-hund, es; *m. A stag-hound, deer-hound, a dog for hunting great game:*—Twegen hafocas and ealle his heádōrhundas *two hawks and all his deer-hounds*, Chart. Th. 501, 7. Twegen and twegen fēdan ǣnne heádōrhund *duo et duo pascant unum molossum*, L. R. S. 4; Th. i. 434, 20.

heáhdeór-hunta, an; *m. A stag-huntsman:*—Mīnon heáhdeórhunton *to my stag-huntsman*, Chart. Th. 561, 24.

heáh-diácon, es; *m. An archdeacon:*—Næs nā ðām ānum ðe Gode sylfum underþeódde syndon mid myclum hādum, biscopas and cyningas and mæssepreóstas and heáhdiáconas *not to those alone who are subject to God himself in high positions, as bishops and kings and archdeacons*, Blickl. Homl. 109, 24: Shrn. 17, 11.

heáh-ealdor, es; *m. A chief ruler:*—Hī cōmon on ðæs heáhealdres hūs *veniunt in domum archi-synagogi*, Mk. Skt. 5, 38.

heáh-ealdorman; *gen.* -mannes; *m. A chief alderman, ruler, patrician:*—Ætius mǣre man se wæs iú ǣr heáhealdorman *Ætius vir inlustris qui et patricius fuit*, Bd. 1, 13; S. 481, 40. Ðe hǣlend cwæþ tō ðæm hēhaldurmenn *ihesus ait archesynagogo*, Mk. Skt. Rush. 5, 36. Hēhaldormenn *patricius*, Rtl. 193, 5.

heáh-engel, es; *m. An archangel*:—Heáhencgel *archangelus*, Ælfc. Gl. 67; Som. 69, 102; Wrt. Voc. 41, 52. Micahel se heáhengel se wæs ealra engla ealderman *Michael the archangel who was the chief of all angels*, Blickl. Homl. 147, 2. Englas and heáhenglas *angels and archangels*, 103, 32: Homl. Th. i. 10, 13. [*Orm.* heh-enngell.]

heáh-fæder; *m. A patriarch*; also *the great Father*, i. e. *God*:—Heáhfæder *patriarcha*, Ælfc. Gl. 68; Som. 69, 118; Wrt. Voc. 41, 68. Hēhfæder *patriarcha*, Rtl. 195, 10. Cuoeþ lā hēhfæder *dixit abba pater*, Mk. Skt. Lind. 14, 36. Seó stondeþ on ða swȳðran healfe ðæs heáhfæder *she stands on the right hand of the Father*, Shrn. 118, 9: Rood Kmbl. 266; Kr. 134. Ðeodosius se wæs ðære hǣðenre hēhfæder *Theodosius who was the patriarch of the heathens*, Nar. 40, 5. Be ðam heáhfædere Abrahame *concerning the patriarch Abraham*, Homl. Th. i. 46, 11. Jacob gestrȳnde twelf suna, ða sind gehātene twelf heáhfæderas *Jacob begat twelve sons, who are called the twelve patriarchs*, ii. 190, 25: i. 396, 9. [*Orm.* Godd heh-faderr *God the Father*: *O. H. Ger.* hōh-fater *patriarca*.]

heáh-fæst; *adj. Very fast, fixed*:—Hafaþ under heofonum heáhfæstne dōm *hath under heaven enduring glory*, Exon. 87 a; Th. 327, 8; Wid. 143.

heáh-fæsten, es; *n. A chief fortress, a city*:—Heáhfæsten *castrum*, Ælfc. Gl. 54; Som. 66, 109; Wrt. Voc. 36, 29. Hēhfæsten *polis* (πόλις), Rtl. 195, 14.

heáh-flōd, es; *m. High tide* [as opposed to *neap tide*], *deep water*:—Heáhflōd *malina*: nēpflōd *ledona*, Ælfc. Gl. 105; Som. 78, 30, 29; Wrt. Voc. 37, 12, 11. Lēt fleógan hrefn ofer heáhflōd *he let a raven fly over the deep water* [*of the deluge*], Cd. 71; Th. 87, 1; Gen. 1442. [Cf. *Icel.* hā-flæðr *a high flood-tide*.]

heáh-fore, e; *f. A heifer*:—Heáhfore *annicula* vel *vaccula*: fæt heáhfore *altilium*, Ælfc. Gl. 22; Som. 59, 85, 93; Wrt. Voc. 23, 44, 50. Heáhfru *altile*, Wrt. Voc. 287, 55. Eálond hwītre heáhfore *insula vitulæ albæ*, Bd. 4, 4; S. 570, 41. Gif hē hriðeru offrian wille bringe unwemme fear oððe heáfre *if he offer it of the herd, whether it be a male or female, he shall offer it without blemish*, Lev. 3, 1. Farra mīno and hēhfaro gislægno *tauri mei et altilia occisa*, Rtl. 107, 21. [hayfare *juvenca*, Wrt. Voc. 177, 7: *Prompt. Parv.* hekfere *juvenca*.]

heáh-freóls, es; *m. A high festival*, L. C. S. 48; Th. i. 404, 1.

heáhfreóls-dæg, es; *m. The day of a high festival*, L. Eth. vi. 25; Th. i. 320, 25.

heáhfreóls-tīd, e; *f. The time of a high festival*, L. Eth. vi. 22; Th. i. 320, 13.

heáh-gerēfa, an; *m. A high reeve, reeve of high rank.* Kemble, Saxons in England, ii. 156, observes of this word, 'It is a name of very indefinite signification, though not of very rare occurrence. It is obvious that it really denotes only a reeve of high rank, I believe always a royal officer; but it is impossible to say whether the rank is personal or official; whether there existed an office called *heáhgerēfscipe* having certain duties; or whether the circumstance of the shire or other reeve being a nobleman in the king's confidence gave to him this exceptional title. I am inclined to believe that they are exceptional, and perhaps in some degree similar to the Missi of the Franks, officers dispatched under occasional commissions to perform functions of supervision, hold courts of appeal, and discharge other duties, as the necessity of the case demanded; but that they are not established officers found in all the districts of the kingdom, and forming a settled part of the machinery of government.' See also Stubbs' Const. Hist. i. 125, 343. Hēhgerēfa *proconsul*, Ælfc. Gl. 106; Som. 78, 58; Wrt. Voc. 57, 38. Befora undercyningum ł hēhgeroefum *ante præsides*, Mk. Skt. Lind. 13, 9. Hēghgeroefa *comes*, Rtl. 193, 9. Cyninges heáhgerēfan gild iiii þūsend þrymsa *the 'wergild' of a king's high reeve four thousand 'thrymsas,'* L. Wg. 4; Th. i. 186, 8: Chr. 778; Erl. 55, 26: 779; Erl. 55, 36: 1001; Erl. 136, 6, 8, 23, 24: 1002; Erl. 137, 29.

heáh-gesamnung, e; *f. A chief assembly, synagogue*:—Ðā com sum of heáhgesamnungum *et venit quidam de archesynagogis*, Mk. Skt. 5, 22.

heáh-gesceaft, e; *f. An exalted creature*:—Hē is heáfod ealra heáhgesceafta *he is the head of all exalted creatures*, Cd. 1; Th. 1, 8; Gen. 4.

heáh-geþungen; *adj. Of high rank, distinguished*:—Ic lǣrde heáhgeþungene men ðæt hī ne āstigan on ofermēdu *I taught men of high rank not to be exalted in pride*, Blickl. Homl. 185, 13.

heáh-getimbrad; *adj. High-built*, Cd. 213; Th. 266, 29; Sat. 29. [*Icel.* hā-timbra *to build high.*]

heáh-getimbru, -getimbro; *pl. n. A lofty building, a place built on high*, Exon. 41 a; Th. 137, 9; Gū. 556: 22 a; Th. 60, 24; Cri. 974: 25 a; Th. 72, 34; Cri. 1182: Cd. 35; Th. 46, 5; Gen. 739. [*O. H. Ger.* hōh-gizimbri *pergama* (πέργαμα), *capitolia*.]

heáh-gnornung, e; *f. Deep grief, sorrow, mourning*:—Hē gehȳrde heáhgnornunge ðæra ðe gebundene bitere wǣron *ut audiret gemitum vinculatorum*, Ps. Th. 101, 18.

heáh-god, es; *m. High God, the most High*:—Ic cleopige tō heáhgode *clamabo ad Deum altissimum*, Ps. Th. 56, 2.

heáh-græft; *adj. Carved in bas-relief*:—Heáhgræfte *anaglypha*, Cot. 7, Lye.

heáh-hād, es; *m. A high order, religious order*:—Heáhhādes men *men in holy orders*, L. I. P. 22; Th. ii. 334, 6.

heáh-heort; *adj. High-hearted, haughty, proud*, Cd. 202; Th. 250, 1; Dan. 540. [*Goth.* hauh-hairts *proud*.]

heáh-hliþ, es; *n. A high hill*, Cd. 71; Th. 86, 31; Gen. 1439.

heáh-lǣce, es; *m. A physician of the greatest skill*:—Sc. cosmas and sc. damianus wǣron heáhlǣcas and hȳ lācnodon ǣghwylce untrumnesse monna *St. Cosmas and St. Damian were very excellent leeches, and cured every infirmity of men*, Shrn. 135, 13.

heáh-landrīca, an; *m. Irenarcha*; εἰρηνάρχης, Lye.

heáh-lāreów, es; *m. A chief teacher*; archimandrita, gymosophista, Lye.

heáh-līc, -līce. v. heá-līc, -līce.

heáh-lufe, an; *f. Deep love*, Beo. Th. 3912; B. 1954.

heáh-mæsse, an; *f. High mass*, L. E. I. 45; Th. ii. 440, 32, 34: 442, 3: Chr. 1125; Erl. 254, 2. [*Icel.* hā-messa: *Ger.* hoch-messe.]

heáh-miht, e; *f. Great, excellent power*:—On his heáhmihtum *in potestatibus ejus*, Ps. Th. 150, 2.

heáh-mōd; *adj. Of high, lofty mind, noble, proud, haughty*:—Siððan hine sylfne heáhmōd hefeþ on heánne beám *afterwards exultant raises itself on to a lofty tree*, Exon. 57 b; Th. 205, 13; Ph. 112. Se ðe hine sylfne āhefeþ heáhmōdne se sceal heán wesan *he who exalts his proud self shall be abased*, 84 a; Th. 316, 25; Mōd. 54. [*O. H. Ger.* hōh-mōti; Cf. *Ger.* hoch-müthig.]

heáh-mōdness, e; *f. Pride*:—Dryhten ongiet swīðe feorran ða heáhmōdnesse *Deus alta a longe cognoscit*, Past. 41, 1; Swt. 301, 1.

heáh-nama, an; *A great, exalted name*:—Swā is gehālgod ðīn heáhnama *thus is thy great name hallowed*, Hy. 7, 18; Hy. Grn. ii. 287, 18.

heáh-, heán-, heá-nes, -ness, e; *f. Highness, height, highest point, elevation, loftiness, sublimity, excellence*:—Ðæs heánes wǣre ōð monnes swyran *its height was up to a man's neck*, Shrn. 81, 13. Sió heánes ðara munta *altitudo montium*, Past. 51, 5; Swt. 397, 36. Hū micel sió heánes is and hū soðlīc *quam sit vera excellentia*, 41, 1; Swt. 299, 4. Mægnes heánnes *excellentia virtutis*, Bd. 3, 13; S. 538, 38. Heánnise hiordes *celsitudo pastoris*, Rtl. 32, 21. Heánnisse ðīnes mæht *sublimitatis tuæ potentia*, 97, 27. Þrittig fæðma on heáhnisse *thirty cubits in height*, Gen. 6, 15. Of eorþan heánesse ōð heofones heáhnesse *a summo terræ usque ad summum cœli*, Mk. Skt. 13, 27. On ðæs heáhnysse ufeweardre *on the very top of it* [*the stalk*], Herb. 173, 1; Lchdm. 302, 24. Wē ne māgon for ðære fyrlynan heáhnysse hī nǣfre geseón *we cannot ever see it* [*heaven*] *for its remote elevation*, Lchdm. iii. 232, 15. Hē hæfde swā mycele heánnesse on ðæt cynerīce *tantum in regno excellentiæ habuit*, Bd. 2, 16; S. 520, 8. For ðæs rīces heánesse him weóxon ofermetto *in tumorem superbiæ culmine potestatis excrevit*, Past. 17, 4; Swt. 113, 6, 20. Heó biþ āfeorrod swīðe feor from ðære sōðan heánesse *ab altitudine veræ celsitudinis elongatur*, 41, 2; Swt. 301, 20. On ðære heofonlīcan heánnesse *in heaven on high*, Shrn. 82, 20: Exon. 65 a; Th. 239, 34; Ph. 631: Elen. Kmbl. 2247; El. 1125. Gode sȳ wuldor on heáhnesse *gloria in altissimis deo*, Lk. Skt. 2, 14. Ðīn mægen is swā mǣre swā ðæt ǣnig ne wāt ðā deópnesse drihtnes mihta ne ða heáhnisse heofena kyninges *thy power is so excellent that none knows the depth of the might of the lord nor the height of heaven's king*, Hy. 3, 35; Hy. Grn. ii. 282, 35. Āstīgend on heáhnisse *ascendens in altum*, Rtl. 83, 3. Ōsanna on heáhnessum *osanna in excelsis*, Mk. Skt. 11, 10: Ps. Th. 92, 5: Exon. 13 b; Th. 25, 34; Cri. 410: 10 a; Th. 10, 35; Cri. 162. Of heánessum *de alto*, Ps. Th. 143, 8.

heáh-rodor, es; *m. The lofty sky*:—Under heáhrodore *under the lofty sky*, Cd. 8; Th. 10, 3; Gen. 151.

heáh-sacerd, es; *m. A chief priest*:—Ða heáhsacerdas and ða bōceras *summi sacerdotes et scribæ*, Mk. Skt. 14, 1: 11, 27: 8, 31.

heáh-sǣ; *f. High, deep sea*:—Wealdend heofones and eorþan and heáhsǣ *ruler of heaven and of earth and of deep sea*, Bt. Met. Fox 11, 6; Met. 11, 3.

heáh-sǣl, e; *f. Great happiness*:—Mīnes mūþes mē mōdes willa on heáhsǣlum hraþe gebringe *voluntaria oris mei beneplacita fac*, Ps. Th. 118, 108.

heáh-sǣ-þeóf, es; *m. A chief pirate*; archi-pirata, Cot. 9, 171.

heáh-samnung, e; *f. A chief synagogue*:—Of hēhsomnungum *de arche-synagogis*, Mk. Skt. Lind. 5. 22. v. heáh-gesamnung.

heáh-sangere, es; *m. A chief singer, arch-chanter*:—Se ārwurþa wer Johannes S. Petres cyricean ðæs apostoles heáhsangere *vir venerabilis Johannes archicantator ecclesiæ S. Apostoli Petri*, Bd. 4, 18; S. 586, 23.

heáh-sceáwere, es; *m. A chief overlooker, overseer*:—Hēhsceáware *pontifex*, Rtl. 21, 1.

heáh-sciremann, es; *m. A procurator*:—Hēhsciremenn *procuratores*, Rtl. 193, 11.

heáh-seld, es; *n. A throne*:—Ðonne wē tō hēhselde hnīgan þencaþ *when we intend to bend to the throne*, Cd. 217; Th. 277, 21; Sat. 208;

221; Th. 287, 25; Sat. 372. Ymb ðæt hālge heáhseld godes *around the holy throne of God*, Exon. 64 b; Th. 239, 11; Ph. 619. Hēhselda wyn *the joy of thrones*, Cd. 213; Th. 267, 25; Sat. 43.

heáh-sele; es; *m. A high hall*:—Tō ðæm heáhsele *to the high hall*, Beo. Th. 1298; B. 647. [*Icel.* hā-salr *a high hall.*]

heáh-setl, es; *n. A high seat, throne, seat of honour* [*at table*], *seat of justice*:—Ðīn heáhsetl *thronum*, Ps. Th. 88, 26. Forðon hēhseðil godes is *quia thronus Dei est*, Mt. Kmbl. Lind. 5, 34. Ðonne crist siteþ on his cynestōle on heáhsetle *when Christ sitteth on his royal seat, on his throne*, Exon. 25 b; Th. 75, 7; Cri. 1218: Lchdm. iii. 426, 6. Se rīca man ðe sitt on his heáhsetle hraðe geswīcþ hē his gebeórscipes gif ða þeówan geswīcaþ ðæra teolunga *the great man that sits on his high seat will soon discontinue his feast if the servants discontinue the attendance*, Homl. Th. i. 272, 35. Ðā hē ðā sett on hēhsettle *sedente autem illo pro tribunali*, Mt. Kmbl. Rush. 27, 19. Fore ðæm hēhsedle *pro tribunali*, Jn. Skt. Lind. 19, 13. Be ðām unrihtwīsum cyningum ða wē gesióþ sittan on ðām hēhstan heáhsetlum *concerning unjust kings whom we see sitting on the highest thrones*, Bt. 37, 1; Fox 186, 2. [*Laym.* hæh-setle *throne*: *O. H. Ger.* hōh-sedal *thronus, solium, triclinium*: cf. *Icel.* hā-sæti *a high seat* (*at table*).]

heáh-stede, es; *m. A high place*:—Ðenden ðǣr wunaþ on heáhstede hūsa sēlest *whilst there in its lofty place the best of houses continues*, Beo. Th. 575; B. 285. [*Icel.* hā-staðr *a high place.*]

heáh-stefn; *adj. Having a high stem* or *prow*:—Heáhstefn naca *the high-prowed boat*, Andr. Kmbl. 532; An. 266. Heáhstefn scipu *high-prowed ships*, Exon. 96 b; Th. 361, 2; Wal. 13.

heáh-strǣt, e; *f. High road*:—Swā in ða heáhstrǣt so *into the high road*, Cod. Dipl. Kmbl. iii. 167, 21. Tō ðære hǣhstrǣte *to the high road*, 246, 20.

hēh-sunn [?]; *adj. Very sinful*:—Openlīce synnige ɫ hēhsunne *publicani*, Mk. Skt. Rush. 2, 15.

heáh-synn, e; *f. Mortal sin, crime, wickedness*:—Hēhsynn *crimen*, Rtl. 187, 25. Būta hēhsynne sint *sine crimine sunt*, Mt. Kmbl. Lind. 12, 5. Bebeorh ðē wið ða eahta heáhsynna *cave tibi ab octo capitalibus criminibus*, L. Ecg. C. pref; Th. ii. 132, 5. Hēhsynna *scelera*, Rtl. 5, 16. Hēhsynno *facinora*, 42, 15.

heáh-þearf, e; *f. Great need*:—Æt heáhþearfe *at my greatest need*, Ps. Th. 117, 16, 20, 27.

heáh-þegen, es; *m. A great, high* or *chief minister* or *servant*:—On ðam wǣron gecorene twelf heáhþegenas *in that were chosen twelve chief ministers* [*the twelve apostles*], Homl. Th. ii. 520, 24.

heáh-þegnung, e; *f. High service*:—Heáhþegnunga hāliges gāstes *the high services of the holy Spirit*, Cd. 147; Th. 183, 23; Exod. 96.

heáh-þeód, e; *f. A great, chief people*:—Was sum æþela man on ðære hēhþeóde Myrcna rīce *there was a certain noble man in the great kingdom of Mercia*, Guthl. 1; Gdwin. 8, 2.

heáh-þrymness, e; *f. Great glory*, Hy. 7, 51; Grn. ii. 288, 51: 9, 43; Hy. Grn. ii. 292, 43.

heáhþu, hēhþo, hiéhþo; *generally indecl*; *f. Height, high place, glory*:—Hē his āras of heáhþu hider onsendeþ *he will send his messengers hither from above*, Exon. 19 a; Th. 47, 24; Cri. 760: 19 b; Th. 49, 21; Cri. 789: 69 b; Th. 258, 10; Jul. 263. On hēhþo *on high*, Andr. Kmbl. 1745; An. 875: 1995; An. 1000. Of hēhþo *from above*, 2289; An. 1146. Of hiéhþa, Elen. Kmbl. 2171; El. 1087. Heofona heáhþu gereccan *to tell the glory of the heavens*, Exon. 116 a; Th. 446, 33; Dōm. 31. Heofona heáhþu gestīgan *to mount to the heights of heaven*, 117 a; Th. 451, 2; Dōm. 97. Gesēgon hī on heáhþu hlāford stīgan of grundum *they saw the Lord ascend to heaven from earth*, 15 a; Th. 31, 19; Cri. 498. Heofonrīces hēhþe, Cd. 17; Th. 21, 8; Gen. 323. In heáhþum *on high*, Exon. 13 b; Th. 26, 8; Cri. 414: 44 a; Th. 149, 27; Gū. 768. Of heáhþum *from on high*, 46 b; Th. 158, 17; Gū. 910. [*Goth.* hauhiþa *height, loftiness, exaltation*: *O. H. Ger.* hōhida *altitudo, culmen.*]

heáh-þungen; *adj. Of high rank, distinguished, noble*:—Heáhþungen wer *the noble man* [*Moses*], Cd. 169: Th. 210, 18; Exod. 517. Hē befæste ðæt rīce heáhþungenum menn Harolde *he committed the kingdom to a noble man, to Harold*, Chr. 1065: Erl. 198, 11; Edw. 30. Ða kyningas and ða ōðre heáhþungene men *kings and other men of high rank*, Ors. 1, 1; Swt. 20, 22. Mōton wyt ðonne unc on heofonum heáhþungene beón *we two may then be exalted in heaven*, Soul Kmbl. 315; Seel. 161. v. heáh-geþungen.

heáh-tīd, e; *f. A high time, high day, festival, solemnity*:—Tō ǣghwilces apostoles heáhtīde fæste man and freólsige *at every apostle's festival let there be fasting and feasting*, L. Eth. v. 14; Th. i. 308, 15. Hēhtīde *solemnia*, Rtl. 8, 23: 9, 27. [*Icel.* hā-tīð *a high day, festival.*]

heáh-timber, es; *n. A lofty building*:—Heáhtimbra gehwæs *of every lofty building*, Exon. 79 a; Th. 296, 2; Crä. 45. v. heáh-getimbru.

heáh-torras; *pl. m. Alpes*, Hpt. Gl. 454.

heáh-treów, e; *f. An excellent, noble compact*, Cd. 162; Th. 202, 14; Exod. 388.

heáh-weofod, es; *n. The high altar*:—Gesceot bæftan ðæm heáhweofode *propitiatorium* vel *sanctum sanctorum*, vel *secretarium*, vel *pastoforum*, Ælfc. Gl. 109; Som. 79, 27; Wrt. Voc. 59, 1.

heáh-weorc, es; *n. Lofty work*:—Æfter heáhweorce heofenes ðīnes *secundum altitudinem cœli*, Ps. Th. 102, 11.

heáh-wita, an; *m. A chief councillor*:—Fērde se cyng him hām and ða ealdormenn and ða heáhwitan *the king went home and the aldermen and the chief 'witan,'* Chr. 1009; Erl. 142, 10. v. Kmbl. Saxons in England, ii. 209, 9.

heal, hal, es; *m. n.* [?] *A corner, an angle, a secret place* [?]:—Heal oððe hyrne *angulus*, Wrt. Voc. 80, 73. Ǣlc wag biþ gebiéged twiefeald on ðæm heale *duplex semper est in angulis paries*, Past. 35, 5; Swt. 245, 13. Ðā gemētte hē hine hleonian on ðam hale his cyrcan wið ðam weofode *he found him leaning in the corner of his church against the altar*, Guthl. 20; Gdwin. 82, 22. On halum *in abditis*, Ps. Spl. 16, 13. [Cf. we beth honted from hale to hurne, Pol. Songs Wrt. 150, 17. In one swiþe diȝele hale, O. and N. 2.]

heal. v. healh *and* heall.

heála, an; *m. Rupture, hydrocele*:—Gif hē hæfde heálan *si fuerit ponderosus*, Past. 11, 1; Swt. 65, 5. [Cf. *Icel.* haull; *m. hernia*: *O. H. Ger.* hola; *f.* [?] *hernia*, Grff. iv. 848.]

heal-ærn, es; *n. A house with a hall, palace*, Beo. Th. 156; B. 78.

heald, es; *n. Hold, guardianship, protection, rule*:—Hī gecuron Harold tō healdes ealles Engla landes *they chose Harold to rule over all England*, Chr. 1036; Erl. 164, 14. Wit synd ðisra landa hald and mund *we two will be a protection and a defence to these lands*, Cod. Dipl. Kmbl. iv. 73, 5. [*Orm.* hald *support*: *Icel.* hald; *n. upholding, support, custody, keeping.*] v. ge-heald.

heald; *adj. Bent, inclined*:—Ðeáh hī sīen āsigen tō yfele and ðider healde *though they are sunk to evil and thither inclined*, Bt. 24, 4; Fox 84, 29. Ealle bióþ of dūne healde wið ðære eorþan *all are bent down towards the earth*, 41, 6; Fox 254, 28. Ða men lāgon āþænede on ðære eorþan mid of dūne healdum ondwleotan *the men lay stretched out on the ground with faces turned downwards*, Shrn. 81, 26. [*Icel.* hallr *leaning, sloping*: *O. H. Ger.* hald *clivus, obliquus, pronus.*]

healdan, haldan; *p.* heóld; *pp.* healden. I. *to* HOLD, *keep, grasp, retain, restrain, confine, contain*:—Hēht Petrus and Paulus on bendum healdon *ordered Peter and Paul to be kept in bonds*, Blickl. Homl. 189 17: Bt. Met. Fox 1, 141; Met. 1, 71. Gif se hlāford wiste ðæt se oxa hnitol wǣre and hine healdan nolde *if the lord knew that the ox were wont to push with its horn, and would not keep it in*, L. Alf. 23; Th. i. 52, 12. Se wīsa hilt his sprǣce and bītt tīman *the wise man restrains his speech and bides his time*, Past. 33, 4; Swt. 220, 14. Afene streám healt ðone norþende *the river Avon bounds the north side*, Cod. Dipl. Kmbl. iii. 466, 21. Jacob heóld ðone yldran brōðer Esau be ðam fēt *Jacob held the elder brother Esau by the foot*, Homl. Th. i. 110, 22: Beo. Th. 1581; B. 788. Hē heóld his ǣhta him tō wlencum *he kept his possessions for his own glory*, Blickl. Homl. 53, 8. Judēi heóldon heora eáran *the Jews stopped their ears*, Homl. Th. i. 46, 33. Genim ðās ylcan wyrte and heald hȳ mid ðē *take this same plant and keep it with you*, Herb. 111, 3; Lchdm. i. 224, 22. Gif hē næbbe ǣhta ðonne healde hine man tō dōme *if he have no property, then let him be held to judgment*, L. Ed. 6; Th. i. 162, 21: L. C. S. 43; Th. i. 402, 1. Se ðe ofer ðæne dæg hit healde āgyfe ðam bisceope ðæne penig and ðǣrtō xxx penega *he that keeps it* [*Peter's pence*] *beyond that day, let him pay the penny to the bishop and thirty pence besides*, L. C. E. 9; Th. i. 366, 16. Healde ðonne on his mūþe of ðam ecede lange hwīle *let him hold some of the vinegar in his mouth a long while*, Herb. 181, 4; Lchdm. i. 318, 2. Hū nytt rehton wē nū and rīmdon ða cǣga būton wē eác feáwum wordum ætiéwen hwæt hie healden *of what use were it to describe and enumerate the keys, unless in a few words we shew what they lock up*, Past. 23; Swt. 178, 12. Wæterfatu healdende ǣnlīpige twȳfealde gemetu oððe þrȳfealde. Nis gecweden ðæt ða wæterfatu sume heóldon twȳfealde gemetu, sume þrȳfealde *waterpots holding singly two or three measures. It is not said that some of the waterpots held two, some three measures*, Homl. Th. ii 56, 21–5. II. *to hold, have, possess, occupy, inhabit*:—Hie leng ne māgon healdan heofonrīce *they may not longer occupy the heavenly kingdom*, Cd. 35; Th. 45, 25; Gen. 732: 26; Th. 33, 34; Gen. 530. Fundon on sande hlīnbed healdan ðone ðe him hringas geaf *they found him who had given them rings occupying a couch on the sand*, Beo. Th. 6060; B. 3034. Ðū ðe heofonhāmas healdest and wealdest *qui habitas in cœlo*, Ps. Th. 122, 1. Hēr Cynegils fēng tō rīce and heóld xxxi wintra *in this year Cynegils came to the throne and held it thirty-one years*, Chr. 611; Erl. 20, 34. Ðǣr heó ǣr mǣste heóld worolde wynne *in whom before she had had her chief joy in this life*, Beo. Th. 2163; B. 1078: 6079; B. 3043. Ūre ieldran ða ðe ðās stōwa ǣr hióldon *our forefathers who occupied these places before*, Past. pref; Swt. 5, 14: Beo. Th. 2432; B. 1214. III. *to rule, govern*:—Hie sealdon ānum unwīsum cyninges þegne Miercna rīce tō haldanne *they gave Mercia to a foolish king's thane to rule*, Chr. 874; Erl. 76, 28: Beo. Th. 3709; B. 1852. Gif hē hī rihtlīcor healdan wolde ðonne hē ǣr dyde *if he* [*Ethelred*] *would rule them more righteously than he had done before*, Chr. 1014; Erl. 150, 7: 1083; Erl. 217, 5. Ðū eorþbûende ealle healdest *gentes in terra dirigis*, Ps. Th. 66, 4. Heóld ðæt folc teala *he ruled that people well*, Cd. 62; Th. 74, 34; Gen. 1232: Beo. Th. 114; B. 57. Eác âh hlâforda gehwylc ðæs for mycle þearfe ðæt hê his men rihtlîce healde *also every lord has very great need to rule his men with justice*, L. C. E. 20; Th. i. 372, 13. IV. *to behave, conduct* [*one's self*]:—Hû se sacerd hine healdan sceal and se diácon *quomodo sacerdos et diaconus se gerere debeant*, L. Ecg. P. iii. pref. v; Th. ii. 194, 29. Nolde ða bêc âgifan ǽr heó wyste hû getrîwlîce hê hi [hine?] æt landum healdan wolde *she would not give up the charters before she knew with what faith he would conduct himself* [*or treat her?*] *as regarded the lands*, Chart. Th. 202, 27. Wê sceolan eall ûre lîf on eáðmôdnesse healdan *we should lead all our life in humility*, Blickl. Homl. 13, 1. Heó hit heóld ǽr tô fæste wið hine *she had before dealt too hardly with him*, Chr. 1043; Erl. 168, 10. Gif hê hine heólde swâ swâ hê sceolde *if he conducted himself as he ought*, L. R. 7; Th. i. 192, 15. Ic lǽrde weras ðæt hie be him ânum getreówlîce hie heóldan *I taught husbands to act faithfully, having to do with their wives only*, Blickl. Homl. 185, 24. V. *to guard, defend, keep, preserve, protect, maintain, sustain, regard, observe, take heed*:—Him behêton ðet hî woldon ðisne eard healdan *they promised him that they would defend this land*, Chr. 1012; Erl. 147, 10. Se ðe sceal healdan Israêla folc wið feóndum *qui custodit Israel*, Ps. Th. 120, 4. Ðâ hêht Neron healdan Simones lîc þrŷ dagas *Nero ordered Simon's body to be kept three days*, Blickl. Homl. 189, 20. Hî ǽfre woldon fryþ and freóndscype in tô ðisan lande haldan *they would ever maintain peace and friendship towards this land*, Chr. 1066; Erl. 201, 37. Uton healdan unc ðæt wit ne wênan swâ swâ ðis folc wênþ *let us guard ourselves from thinking as this people thinks*, Bt. 40, 2; Fox 236, 28. Healdan ðone hâlgan sunnan dæg *to keep the holy Sunday*, Lchdm. iii. 226, 2. Ðæt hê hŷ healdan wille swâ wær his wîf sceal *that he will keep her as a man shall his wife*, L Edm. B. 1; Th. i. 254, 6. Utan ǽnne cynehlâford holdlîce healdan *let us loyally support one royal lord*, L. Eth. v. 35; Th. i. 312, 21: vi. 1; Th. i. 314, 11. His mûþ hê sceal symble from yfelum wordum healdan *he shall ever keep his mouth from evil words*, L. E. I. 21; Th. ii. 416, 33. Clǽnnysse healdan *castitatem servare*, L. Ecg. P. iii. 5; Th. ii. 198, 2. Wê sceolan ða tên bebodu healdan *we ought to keep the ten commandments*, Blickl. Homl. 35, 11. Sceolde ic mînne brôðor healdon *am I my brother's keeper?* Gen. 4, 9. Ðære heorde ðe hî healdan sceoldan *to the flock that they should have kept*, Blickl. Homl. 45, 15. Hî ne dorstan nân gefeoht healdan wið Willelm cynge *they dared not have any battle with king William*, Chr. 1075; Erl. 214, 8. Oðer æt hâm beón heora land tô healdanne oðer ût faran tô winnanne *vicissim curam belli et domus custodiam sortiebantur*, Ors. 1, 10; Swt. 46, 17. Tô healdenne, Blickl. Homl. 11, 25. Se ðe hylt Israhêl *qui custodit Israel*, Homl. Th. ii. 230, 7. Swâ swâ sealt hylt ǽlcne mete wið forrotodnysse *as salt preserves every meat from corruption*, 536, 19. Healdeþ meotudes ǽ *keeps the law of the Lord*, Exon. 62 b; Th. 229, 19; Ph. 457. Wið ôðrum unþeáwum hî sylfe healdaþ *they keep themselves from other vices*, Homl. Th. ii. 550, 25. Ne ða Eástron swâ healdaþ swâ wê healdaþ *nec Pascha ita observant uti nos observamus*, L. Ecg. P. add. 5; Th. ii. 232, 18. Ðîne gebrôðru healdaþ scêp on Sichima *thy brethren are keeping sheep in Shechem*, Gen. 37, 13, 2. Ebrêi healdaþ heora geáres annginn on lenctenlîcre emnihte *the Hebrews keep the beginning of their year at the spring equinox*, Lchdm. iii. 246, 17. Ða gelǽredan hine healdaþ be ðisum foresǽdan gesceáde *the learned consider it in accordance with the aforesaid distinction*, 266, 11. Ðû heólde mîne lîchaman wið ǽlce besmittennysse *thou hast kept my body from every defilement*, Homl. Th. i. 74, 30. Hine swâ lange heóld ôð ðæt man hire gryþ salde *she held the castle until they made terms with her*, Chr. 1076; Erl. 214, 18. Se cyng heóld his hîrêd on Winceastre *the king held his court at Winchester*, 1085; Erl. 218, 39. Ðonne hî wǽron be eáston ðonne heóld man fyrde be westan *when the Danes were to the east then the 'fyrd' was assembled to the west*, 1009: Erl. 144, 5. Heó hyt swŷðe deórwyrþlîce heóld *she held it very dearly*, St. And. 38, 3. Ða weardas heóldon ðæs cweartennes duru *the keepers kept the door of the prison*, Homl. Th. ii. 382, 4. Wê nâðor ne heóldon ne lâre ne lage Godes ne manna swâ swâ wê scoldon *we have not kept as we should the doctrine or law of God or men*, Swt. A. S. Rdr. 107, 80. Ðâ heóldon ða Judêi on heálîcum gewunan *the Jews then held it as a solemn custom*, Homl. Th. ii. 252, 8. Heald ðonne georne ðæt se mete sî gemylt *observe then carefully that the meat be digested*, L. M. 2, 69; Lchdm. ii. 284, 2. Heald ðæt hie ne hrînan eorþan ne wætre *take care that they do not touch earth or water*, L. M. 3, 1; Lchdm. ii. 306, 7. Âsette gê ðone lîchoman tô ðære byrgenne and hine ðǽr healdaþ swâ ic eów bebeóde *put down the body in the tomb and keep it there as I shall bid you*, Blickl. Homl. 147, 32. Healden hie hie ðæt hie ne weorðen ealdormenn tô forlore hira hiéramonnum *caveat ne fiat subditis auctor ruinæ*, Past. 10, 2; Swt. 63, 16. Hit betere wǽre ðæt heora seht tôgædere wurde ðonne hŷ ǽnige sace hym betweónan heóldan *it would be better for them to come to an agreement than to maintain a suit between them*, Chart. Th. 377, 4: Blickl. Homl. 109, 16. VI. *to hold out, last, hold on, continue, hold with*:—Hê hêt ðæt werod healdan feste wið feóndum *he bade that band stand fast against the foes*, Byrht. Th. 134, 51; By. 102. Hê wel healdeþ stondeþ stîðlîce *it holds well, stoutly it stands*, Exon. 93 b; Th. 351, 27; Sch. 86. Feáwa ôðre ðe mid ðam eorle gyt heóldan *a few others that still continued with the earl*, Chr. 1106; Erl. 241, 7. Ðâ nolde seó burhwaru âbûgan ac heóldan mid fullan wîge ongeán *the citizens would not submit but held their ground against him by all warlike means*, Chr. 1013; Erl. 148, 12. Hig heóldon þurh ða brycge *they held on their way through the bridge*, 1052; Erl. 184, 23. Hî heóldon ofer sǽ tô Flandran *they took their way across the sea to Flanders*, 1075; Erl. 214, 9. [Cf. *halda* as a nautical term in Icelandic, Cl. & Vig. p. 233, col. 1.] [*Goth.* haldan *to hold, keep, keep sheep*: *O. Sax.* haldan: *O. Frs.* halda: *Icel.* halda: *O. H. Ger.* haltan *servare, custodire*: *Ger.* halten.] DER. an-, be-, for-, ge-, ofer-, tô-, ymb-healdan.

healdend, es; *m.* *One who holds, keeps, sustains, rules, a guardian, keeper, ruler*:—Hêr lîþ beheáfdod healdend ûre *here lies our ruler beheaded*, Judth. 12; Thw. 25, 32; Jud. 290. Ic ðæs folces beó hyrde and healdend *I will be the people's shepherd and keeper*, Cd. 106; Th. 139, 25; Gen. 2315. Se hâlga healdend and wealdend *the holy preserver and ruler*, Andr. Kmbl. 450; An. 225. Se healdend *the ruler*, Cd. 98; Th. 130, 17; Gen. 2161. From ðam healdende ðe mê hringas geaf *from the guardian who gave me rings*, Exon. 105 b; Th. 402, 1; Rä 21, 23. Mið haldendum *cum custodibus*, Mt. Kmbl. Lind. 27, 66. v. healdan.

heald-nes, -ness, e; *f.* *Holding, keeping, observance*:—Ealles mǽst ymb eástrena healdnyssa *maxime in Pascha observando*, Bd. 2, 4; S. 505, 7.

heálede; *adj.* *Ruptured, hydrocelous*:—Heálede *hirniosus*, Ælfc. Gl. 76; Som. 71, 126; Wrt. Voc. 45, 29. Heálede *ydropicus*, Wrt. Voc. 283, 62. Heálede *ponderosus*, Past. 11, 7; Swt. 73, 4, 9, 11: Herb. 78, 2; Lchdm. i. 182, 1: Lchdm. iii. 144, 26. [Cf. *Icel.* haula *ruptured*: *O. H. Ger.* holoht *ponderosus, cui humor viscerum in virilia labitur*.] v. heála.

healf, e; *f.* I. *a half*:—Healfe ðŷ swêtre *sweeter by half*, Bt. Met. Fox 12, 18; Met. 12, 9. II. *side, part*:—Mid ðæm worde biþ gecŷðed hwæþer healf hæfþ ðonne sige *with that phrase* [*asking permission to bury the dead*] *is declared which side has the victory*, Ors. 3, 1; Swt. 100, 9. Him be healfe stôd cniht *by his side stood a youth*, Byrht. Th. 136, 16; By. 152. Fram ðære uferran healfe *from the upper part*, L. M. 1, 27; Lchdm. ii. 68, 14. On ðâs healfe *hac*: on ða healfe *illac*: on ða swîðran healfe *dextrorsum*: on ða winstran healfe *sinistrorsum*, Ælfc. Gr. 38; Som. 40, 4, 6. Ðǽr stent lang leóma of hwîlum on âne healfe hwîlum on ǽlce healfe *there stands out from it a long light, sometimes on one side, sometimes on every side*, Chr. 891; Erl. 88, 20. On ǽgðere healfe *on either side*, 1014; Erl. 150, 15. Hî heregodon on heora healfe and Cnut on his healfe *they harried on their side and Cnut on his*, 1016; Erl. 154, 23: 1025; Erl. 163, 10. On twâ healfe ðære eás *on both sides of the river*, 896; Erl. 94, 11. Gif ðû fǽrst tô ðære winstran hælfe ic healde ða swîðran healfe gif ðû ðonne ða swîðran healfe gecîst ic fare tô ðære winstran healfe *if thou wilt take the left hand then I will go to the right hand; or if thou depart to the right hand then I will go to the left*, Gen. 13, 9: 48, 13. [*Goth.* halba: *O. Sax.* halba: *O. Frs.* halve: *Icel.* hâlfa: *O. H. Ger.* halb, halba, Grff. iv. 882–6: *Ger.* halbe.]

healf; *adj.* HALF:—Mê næs be healfan dǽle ðîn mǽrþ gecŷdd *thy greatness was not half told me*, Homl. Th. ii. 584, 23. Sîe be healfum ðæm ðonne sió bôt *let the fine then be half that*, L. Alf. pol 11; Th. i. 68, 18: 39; Th. i. 88, 2: L. M. 2, 65; Lchdm. ii. 292, 17. Gê ðǽr bûgiaþ on ðam fîftan dǽle healfum londes and unlondes *ye there dwell in the half of the fifth part* [*in the tenth part*, cf. l. 25] *of land and not-land*, Bt. 18, 1; Fox 62, 23. Heó mid ðæm healfan dǽle beforan ðæm cyninge farende wæs swelce heó fleónde wǽre *with half the army she was going before the king as if she were fleeing*, Ors. 2, 4; Swt. 76, 27. Healfne sealde ðæm þearfan and mid healfum hine sylfne besweóp *he gave half* [*his cloak*] *to the poor man and wrapped himself up with half of it*, Blickl. Homl. 215, 7. Ðeáh ðû wylle healf mîne rîce *licet demedium regni mei*, Mk. Skt. 6, 23: Lk. Skt. 19, 8. Habban hî ðone brŷce healfne and healfne ða munecas *let them have half the usufruct, and the monk's half*, Chart. Th. 547, 19. Heó healfne forcearf ðone sweoran him *she half cut through his neck*, Judth. 10; Thw. 23, 4; Jud. 105. Sele ðonne ðæt healf tô drincanne *then give half of it to drink*, L. M. 2, 2; Lchdm. ii. 180, 23. Hie wǽron simle healfe æt hâm healfe ûte *always half of them were at home and half out*, Chr. 894; Erl. 90, 17: Ors. 2, 6; Swt. 86, 25. Ic wille ðæt man frigæ hæalue mîne men *I desire that half my men should be freed*, Chart. Th. 522, 5. Æfter ôðer healf hund daga *after a hundred and fifty days*, Gen. 8, 3. Hê heóld ðæt rîce ôðrum healfum læs ðe xxx wintra *he reigned twenty-eight years and a half*, Chr. 901; Erl. 96, 24. Hit biþ ôðres healfes fôtes gemet bufan ðæm heáfde *it is a foot and a half above the head*, Shrn. 69, 2. Se bât wæs geworht of þriddan healfre hŷde *the boat was made of two and a half hides*, Chr. 891; Erl. 88, 9. Ic him sylle vii æcras feórþe hælfne on ânum stede and feórþe halfne an ôðrum stede *I give him seven acres, three and a half in one place and three and a half in another*, Cod. Dipl. Kmbl. iii. 263, 12–15. Nân rên ne com ofer eorþan feórþan healfan geáre *no rain came upon the earth for three years and a half*, Lchdm. iii. 276, 19. Ðæt wæs ehtoþe healf hīd *that was seven hides and a half*, Chart. Th. 550, 12. Seofon and twentigoþan healfes fōtes *twenty-six feet and a half long*, Lchdm. iii. 218, 4, 12, 16, 19. [*Goth.* halbs: *O. Sax.* half: *O. Frs.* half: *Icel.* hālfr: *O. H. Ger.* halb: *O. Frs. has the same use of* half *with the ordinals*, other, thredda, fiarda, etc., half; *so O. H. Ger. has* andar halb, dritde halp, Grff. iv. 890: *so Ger. In Icel. the ordinal is placed after* hālfr, hālfr annarr, etc.]

healf-clǣmed; *adj. Half finished* [*of house built with mud*]:—Mīn ðæt healfclǣmede hūs *my half-finished mud-hut*, Shrn. 39, 20.

healf-clypigende; *adj. Semi-vowel*:—Healfclypigende *semivocales*, Ælfc. Gr. 2; Som. 2, 55, 56.

healf-cwic; *adj. Half alive, half dead*:—Halfcwic *semivivus; half dead*, Lk. Skt. Lind. 10, 30. Helfcuicne, Past. 17; Swt. 125, 8. Funde hiene ǣnne be wege licgan healfcucne *invenit in itinere solum relictum et extrema vitæ efflantem*, Ors. 3, 9; Swt. 128, 14. Sume healfcwice flugon on fæsten *some half-dead fled to the fastness*, Elen. Kmbl. 266; El. 133: Blickl. Homl. 203, 19.

healf-deád; *adj. Half dead, palsied on one side*:—Wið ðære healfdeádan ādle *for the half-dead disease* [hemiplegia], L. M. 2, 59; Lchdm. ii. 280, 1: L. M. 1, 79; Lchdm. ii. 152, 2.

healf-eald; *adj. Half grown, of middle age*:—Halfeald swīn *half-grown swine*, L. M. 2, 37; Lchdm. ii. 246, 2.

healf-heáfod, es; *n. The fore part of the head*; sinciput, Ælfc. Gr. 9, 78; Som. 14, 24.

healf-hunding, es; *m. A creature having a dog's head*:—Healfhundingas *cenocephali*, Nar. 34, 30: 22, 15.

healf-hwīt; *adj. Half white, whitish*; subalbus, Ælfc. Gl. 79; Som. 72, 73; Wrt. Voc. 46, 30.

healf-mann, es; *m. Half man*:—Halfmann *semivir*, Ælfc. Gr. 8; Som. 7, 23.

healf-penig-wurþ, es; *n. A halfpennyworth*, L. C. E. 12; Th. i. 366, 32.

healf-reád; *adj. Reddish*:—Healfreáde peran *crustumie* vel *volemis* vel *insana* vel *melimendrum*, Ælfc. Gl. 60; Som. 68, 40; Wrt. Voc. 39, 25.

healf-slǣpende; *adj. Half asleep*:—Ætȳwde him gamalielus gāst healfslǣpendum *the spirit of Gamaliel appeared to him when half asleep*, Shrn. 113, 5.

healf-soden; *adj. Half cooked*:—On healfsodenum mete *in semicocto cibo*, L. Ecg. C. 40; Th. ii. 166, 2: Med. ex Quadr. 7, 2; Lchdm. i. 356, 18.

healf-trendel, es; *n. A hemisphere*:—Healftryndel, *emisperia*, Ælfc. Gl. 49; Som. 65, 71: Wrt. Voc. 34, 6.

healfunga; *adv. By halves, partially, imperfectly*:—Ðe shundredes ealdor geneálǣhte ðam Hǣlende nā healfunga ac fulfremedlīce *this centurion did not approach the Saviour by halves, but fully*, Homl. Th. i. 126, 23. Hit is nyttre ðæt hit mon healfunga sprece *it is better that it should be said in part only*, Past. 31; Swt. 207, 7: 32; Swt. 209, 22. Gif wē healfunga and be sumum dǣle heora gōdan weorc secgeaþ *si quædam illorum bona ex latere requiramus*, 211, 16.

healf-weard, es; *m. One who has a share of another's property or power*:—Hē sette hine on his hūse to halfwearde ealra him his ǣhta anweald betǣhte *constituit eum dominum domus suæ, et principem omnis possessionis suæ*, Ps. Th. 104, 17.

healf-wudu, a; *m. Field-balm*; calamintha nepeta, L. M. 1, 47; Lchdm. ii. 118, 1.

heal-gamen, es; *m. Hall-mirth, song*, Beo. Th. 2136; B. 1066.

healh, halh [*in the declension the final* h *seems to be omitted before an inflection*]; *m.* A word of doubtful meaning. Kemble, Cod. Dipl. iii. xxix. translates it *hall*, probably originally a *stone* building. Leo, A. S. Names, p. 52, takes it to be the same word as *ealh*. Somner gives *healh-stān* crusta, collyrida. In form it agrees with Latin *calx*. The following are some of the passages in which the word occurs:—Se westra eásthealh, Cod. Dipl. iii. 19, 6. On ðone west halh, 18, 25. Ōþ cyninges healh, i. 257, 33. On Scottes healh; of ðam heale, vi. 2, 2. In Streónes halh; of ðam hale, 214, 25. On Hengestes healh; of Hengestes heale, iii. 80, 20. In Titten halh, 52, 11. [The word seems to have the same force as *haga* in the same charter, as *æt Batenhale* and *æt Batanhagan* both occur.] Æt Wreodanhale, i. 166, 18. On Rischale; of Rischale, iii. 399, 18. On hwītan heal; of hwītan heale, iii. 444, 4-5. On ða halas, iii. 34, 13. On fearnhealas; of fearnhealan, iii. 81, 14-5. On cotan healas, v. 401, 34. Tō hǣþhalan; of hǣþhalan, iii. 77, 13. Streónes halh, Bd. 4, 23; S. 592, 37. On Streónes heale, Chr. 680; Erl. 40, 13. [Strenaeshalch quod interpretatur Sinus fari, Bd. 3, 25; S. 132, 7.]

healic, es; *m. A herring*; halec:—Healic ōðer sǣfisc *herring or seafish*, Cod. Dipl. Kmbl. iii. 250, 26.

heá-līc; *adj. High, elevated, lofty, sublime, proud, chief, very great, noble, distinguished, deep, profound*:—Nān gereord nis swā heálīc swā Ebreīsc *no language is so noble as Hebrew*, Homl. Th. ii. 86, 28. Abram ðæt is heálīc fæder *Abram, that is, great father*, i. 92, 13. Leóht swilce heálīc sunnbeám *a light like a splendid sunbeam*, Swt. A. S. Rdr. 100, 152. Swīðe heálīc nama *a name of great distinction*, Blickl. Homl. 167, 31: L. E. I. 40; Th. ii. 438, 11. Is ān ðæra eahta winda aquilo gehāten se blǣwþ heálīc and ceald *one of the eight winds is called aquilo; it blows high and cold*, Lchdm. iii. 276, 5. Heálīc on his weorcum *actione præcipuus*, Past. 12; Swt. 75, 8. Gebletsod ys Abram ðam heálīcan Gode . . . and gebletsod ys se heálīca God *blessed be Abram of the most high God . . . and blessed be the most high God*, Gen. 14, 19, 20. Nis nān leahter swā heálīc ðæt man ne mǣge gebētan *there is no crime so deep that it may not be expiated*, Homl. Th. ii. 602, 20. Hē næs ācweald þurh ðam heálīcan fylle *he was not killed by the fall from such a height*, 300, 20. Mid heálīcum gedwylde *through profound error*, 506, 27. On heálīcum gemōte *in a principal meeting*, Swt. A. S. Rdr. 67, 348. Ðæt lengtenfæsten mon sceal mid swīðe heálīcre gȳmene healdan *the fast of Lent ought to be kept with the very greatest care*, L. E. I. 37; Th. ii. 436, 5. Heálīc þingc ðū ðǣrmid ongitst *thereupon thou wilt observe a remarkable thing*, Herb. 57, 2; Lchdm. i. 160, 1. Swā heálīcne dem his āgnes hryres *alta ruinæ suæ damna*, Past. 58, 2; Swt. 441, 26. Hafaþ heálīce stefne *hath an excellent voice*, Exon. 79 b; Th. 298, 31; Crä. 93. Heálīce bodan *archangels*, Homl. Th. i. 342, 26: L. Eth. vii. 2; Th. i. 330, 6. Gif hie hwæt suā heálīcra yfela on him ongieten *if they perceive any very great evil in them*; si qua valde sunt eorum prava, Past. 28, 5; Swt. 197, 6. On heálīcum muntum *on lofty hills*, Homl. Th. ii. 160, 29. Wē lǣraþ ðæt man wið heálīce synna scylde swȳðe georne *we instruct people to guard very diligently against very great sins*, L. C. E. 23; Th. i. 374, 6. Heálīce gegaderunga *legitima conjugia*, L. Ecg. C. 28; Th. ii. 152, 35. Spræc heálig word wið drihten sīnne *spoke proud words against his lord*, Cd. 15; Th. 19, 21; Gen. 294. Ǣlc sāwul sȳ underþeód heálīcrum anwealdum *let every soul be subjected to the higher powers*, Homl. Th. ii. 362, 17. Se is heálīcost seðe ðone martyrdōm æfter Gode āstealde *he is most exalted who was the first martyr after God*, i. 50, 1. Ða recceras scoldon þencean ymb ðæt hēlīcuste and ða underþióddan scoldon dōn ðæt unweorðlīcre *a subditis inferiora gerenda sunt, a Rectoribus summa cogitanda*, Past. 18, 3; Swt. 131, 19.

hea-līce; *adv. Highly, on high, excellently*:—Is ðīn mildheort mōd āhafen heálīce *magnificatur misericordia tua*, Ps. Th. 107, 4: 137, 6. Heálīce ða Cyricean reccende *ecclesiam sublimiter regens*, Bd. 5, 19; S. 639, 12. Seó gōdnys is of ðam Scyppende se ðe is heálīce gōd *that goodness is from the Creator, who is supremely good*, Homl. Th. i. 238, 19. Se ðe on heofonum is heálīce sittende *who sitteth on high in heaven*, ii. 318, 3: 254, 27. Heálīce geweorþod *highly honoured*, Blickl. Homl. 125, 18. Ðus heálīce *in such a high degree*, 123, 2. Ðonne fremaþ hit heálīce *it will do very great good*, Herb. 4, 2; Lchdm. i. 90, 7. Hē wolde ðæt his lof ðē heálīcor weóxe *he desired that his praise should grow the greater*, Blickl. Homl. 33, 30. Heálīcost fremede *was beneficial in the highest degree*, Herb. 73, 3; Lchdm. i. 176, 10.

heá-līcness, e; *f. Loftiness, sublimity, greatness*:—Heálīcnyss *sublimitas*, Hymn Surt. 74, 26. Seó heofenlīce heálīcnyss wearþ geopenod *the greatness of heaven was revealed*, Homl. Th. i. 106, 31.

heall, e; *f. A hall, residence*:—Heall *aula*, Ælfc. Gl. 61, 107; Som. 78, 89; Wrt. Voc. 58, 4. Mycel and rūm heall *atrium*, 109; Som. 79, 21; Wrt. Voc. 58, 61. Seó heall ðæs Hālgan Gāstes *the residence of the Holy Ghost*, Blickl. Homl. 163, 13. Heal, Beo. Th. 2307; B. 1151. On his ðære hālgan healle *in aula sancta ejus*, Ps. Th. 95, 8. Hē dreám gehȳrde hlūdne in healle *loud merriment he heard in the hall*, Beo. Th. 178; B. 89: Cd. 210; Th. 261, 1; Dan. 719. Hie tō his healle ne tō his hīrēde eft wendan noldan *they would not return to his* [*Nero's*] *residence nor household*, Blickl. Homl. 173, 18. On cynges healle *in the king's hall*, L. Alf. pol. 7; Th. i. 66, 7, 8: L. R. 2; Th. i. 190, 17. Ða heofenlīcan healle innfērde *entered the heavenly hall*, Homl. Th. i. 52, 20. [*O. Sax.* halla: *Icel.* höll: *O. H. Ger.* halla *aula, palatium, templum*: *Ger.* halle.] DER. gif-, medo-heall.

heal-līc; *adj. Belonging to a hall* or *palace*; aulicus, palatinus, Cot. 194, Lye.

heall-reáf, es; *n. A piece of tapestry for a hall*:—Ælfwine ic geann ānes heallreáfes *I give to Alfwine a piece of tapestry*, Chart. Th. 530, 35.

heall-wahrift, es; *n. Tapestry for hanging on the wall of a hall*:—Ic geann mīnum suna ānes heallwahriftes, Chart. Th. 530, 33.

HEALM, es; *n.* I. HAULM, *straw, stem* or *stalk of grass, stalk of a plant*:—Healm *culmus*, Ælfc. Gl. 59; Som. 67, 127; Wrt. Voc. 38, 49. Healmes lāf *stipulæ*, Som. 67, 129; Wrt. Voc. 38, 51. Gān and gadrion him sylfe ðæt healm *let them go and gather straw for themselves*, Ex. 5, 7. Swā windes healm *sicut stipulam ante faciem venti*, Ps. Th. 82, 10. Genim rigen healm and beren *take rye and barley straw*, L. M. 1, 72; Lchdm. ii. 148, 11. II. *a roof of straw* [?]:—Ciricsceat mon sceal āgifan tō ðam healme and tō ðam heorþe ðe se mon on biþ tō middum wintra *ciricsceattum debet reddere homo a culmine et mansione, ubi residens erit in Natali*, L. In. 61; Th. i. 140, 13. [*Prompt. Parv.* halm *stipula*: *Icel.* hālmr; *m. straw*: *O. H. Ger.* halm; *m. culmus, calamus, stipula, festuca*: *Ger.* halm: *Grk.* κάλαμος *a reed*.]

healm-streaw, es; *n. Straw, stubble*:—Healmstreaw *stipulam*, Ps. Spl. 82, 12.

healoc, es; *m. n.* [?] *A hollow, corner, bending:* — Hēr sint tācn āheardodre lifre ge on ðām læppum and healocum and filmenum *here are symptoms of a hardened liver both on the lobes and hollows and membranes,* L. M. R. 21; Lchdm. ii. 204, 5. [Cf. (?) *Prompt. Parv.* halke *angulus, latibulum: Chauc.* halke, *corner.*] v. holc, hylca.

heal-reced, es; *n. A palace:*—Hē healreced hātan wolde medoærn micel men*gewyrcean *he would bid men make a palace, a great mead-house,* Beo. Th. 136; B. 68.

heals, hals, es; *m. The neck, the prow of a ship:*—Se hals *the neck,* Exon. 60 a; Th. 218, 22; Ph. 298. Gehæfted be ðam healse *fastened by the neck,* Cd. 19; Th. 24, 29; Gen. 385. Heals ealne ymbefēng *he clasped all the neck,* Beo. Th. 5376; B. 2691. Lēt his francan wadan þurh ðæs .hysses hals *he let his weapon pass through the man's neck,* Byrht. Th. 135, 60; By. 141. [*Orm.* halls: *Piers P. Chauc.* hals: *Prompt. Parv.* hals *collum, amplexatorium: Goth. O. Frs. O. Sax. O. H. Ger.* hals: *Icel.* hāls *neck, part of the bow of a ship.*]

heals-beág, es; *m. A ring for the neck, necklace;* monile, collare, Beo. Th. 4350; B. 2172. [*O. H. Ger.* hals-pouc *torques.*]

heals-beorh; *gen.* -beorge; *f. A protection for the neck, gorget, hauberk,* Hpt. Gl. 521, 423. [*Icel.* hāls-björg *a gorget: O. H. Ger.* hals-pirc, -perg *pectoria, lorica.*]

heáls-bōc, e; *f. A book which brings safety, an amulet, a phylactery,* Mt. Kmbl. 23, 5. [*Icel.* hāls-bōk *a book to swear upon.*] v. hāls.

healsed, healsod, healscod *a cloth for the head:*—Healsed *caputium,* Cot. 170, Lye. In halsado *in sudario,* Lk. Skt. Lind. 19, 20. Mið halsodo *sudario,* Jn. Skt. Rush. [halscode, Lind.] 11, 44. Halsodu *sudarium* [hascode, Lind.] 20, 7.

healseta, an; *m.* Se ealdormon rād þurh sumne wudu ðā rǣsde ān næddre of holum treowe æt ðam healsetan him on ðone bōsm and hyne tōslāt ðæt hē wæs sōna deád, Shrn. 144, 27.

heals-fæst; *adj. Stiff-necked. stubborn,* Cd. 102; Th. 135, 5; Gen. 2238.

heals-fang, es; *n.* A term occurring in the laws which Thorpe thus defines: 'The sum every man sentenced to the pillory would have had to pay to save him from that punishment had it been in use.' The word occurs in the following passages:—Gif ceorl būton wīfes wīsdōme deóflum gelde hē sīe ealra his ǣhtan scyldig and healsfange *if a married man without his wife's knowledge sacrifice to idols let him be liable in all his possessions and his 'heals-fang,'* L. Wih. 12, 11, 14; Th. i. 40, 5, 2, 10. Gylde man cxx scill. tō healsfange æt twelfhyndum were. Healsfang gebyreþ bearnum brōðrum and fæderan ne gebyreþ nānum mǣge ðæt feoh būte ðam ðe sȳ binnan cneówe. Of ðam dæge ðe ðæt healsfang āgolden sȳ . . . , L. E. G. 13; Th. i. 174, 23-7: L. Edm. S. 7; Th. i. 250, 20: L. Eth. vi. 51; Th. i. 328, 11: L. C. S. 37: Th. i. 398, 13: 45; Th. i. 402, 14: 61; Th. i. 408, 19: L. C. F. 14; Th. i. 428, 7: L. H. 11, 7, 10; Th. i. 521, 5, 10: 76, 6; Th. i. 582, 4. Schmid A. S. Gesetze, p. 609, suggests a different origin from that given by Thorpe, 'Es liegt nahe, an die Berechnung der Verwandtschaftsgrade nach den Gliedern des menschlichen Leiber zu denken, wo dann die nächsten Verwandten, die auf den Halsfang Anspruch haben, in den Hals zu stehen kommen könnten, und damit hängt vielleicht Zusammen, dass die Gradberechnungen nicht von dem gemeinschaftlichen Stammvater, sondern dessen Kindern beginnen, sodass die näherstehenden Verwandten als *binnan cneówe* befindlich bezeichnet werden konnten.' But while this explanation might suit the circumstances described in the passage given above, from Edmund's Laws, it would not be applicable in the earlier passage from Wihtræd's Laws. Schmid seems to refer the penalty, in its origin, too exclusively to cases of killing: 'Eine Geldbusse, die bei einer Tödtung in Verbindung mit dem Wergeld an die nächsten Verwandten des Getödteten gezahlt werden musste, die aber auch sonst zur Bestimmung der Grösse einer Busse genannt wird.' [Cf. *Icel.* hāls-fang; *n. embracing:* hāls-fengja *to embrace.*]

heals-gebedda, an; *f. A bedfellow, consort around whose neck the arms are thrown, one dearly loved,* Beo. Th. 126; B. 63. v. heals-mægeþ.

heals-gund, es; *m. A swelling in the neck;* struma, L. M. 1, 4; Lchdm. ii. 44, 10, 13, 15, etc.

heálsian. v. hālsian.

heal-sittende; *pl. People sitting in a hall,* Beo. Th. 4035; B. 2015: 5728; B. 2868.

heals-mægeþ, e; *f. A virgin embraced and beloved,* Cd. 98; Th. 130, 6; Gen. 2155. v. heals-gebedda.

heals-mene, -myne, es; *m. A necklace, chain for the neck:* — Hē dyde gyldene healsmyne ymbe his swuran *he put a gold chain about his neck,* Gen. 41, 42. [*O. Sax.* hals-meni; *n: Icel.* hāls-men; *n.*]

heals-ome, an; *f. A humour in the neck,* Lchdm. iii. 4, 26.

healsre-feðer, e; *f. The feathers of a pillow, down:*—Hnescre ic eom micle halsrefeðre *I am much softer than down,* Exon. 111 b; Th. 426, 28; Rä. 41, 80. [Cf. *O. H. Ger.* halsare *cervical.*]

heals-wiða, an; *m. A necklace:*—Me healswiðan hlāford sealde *my lord has given me a chain for my neck,* Exon. 102 b; Th. 387, 13; Rä. 5, 4.

heals-wyrt, e; *f.* In Lchdm. ii. Gloss. are given the following plant-names:—I. *Campanula trachelium, Dan.* halsurt: *Ger.* halswurz, halskraut: *Du.* halskrind. II. *Hare's ear;* bupleurum tenuissimum. III. *Scilla autumnalis.* IV. *Symphytum album.*

HEALT; *adj.* HALT, *lame, limping:*—Healt *claudus,* Wrt. Voc. 75, 35. Gif hē healt weorþ *if he become lame,* L. Ethb. 65; Th. i. 18, 14. Hæfdon him tō lādteówe ǣnne wīsne mon, þēh hē healt wǣre and him tō gielpworde hæfdon ðæt him leófre wǣre ðæt hie hæfdon healtne cyning ðonne healt rīce *they had as their leader a wise man though he was lame, and made it their boast that they had rather the king halted than the kingdom,* Ors. 3, 1; Swt. 96, 28-31: Mt. Kmbl. 18, 8. Him tō eodan blinde and healte *the blind and halt went to him,* Blickl. Homl. 71, 21: Nicod. 2; Thw. 1, 29: Elen. Kmbl. 2427; El. 1215: Andr. Kmbl. 1155; An. 578. [*Goth.* halts: *O. Sax. O. Frs.* halt: *Icel.* haltr: *O. H. Ger.* halz.]

heal-þegen, es; *m. A hall-thane, one who resides or is occupied in a hall,* Beo. Th. 287; B. 142: 1443; B. 719.

healtian; *p.* ode; *pp.* od *To halt, limp, be lame:* — Ic healtige *claudico,* Ælfc. Gr. 28; Som. 31, 27. Hī nū gyt heora ealdan gewunon healdaþ and fram rihtum stīgum healtiaþ *ipsi adhuc inveterati et claudicantes a semitis suis,* Bd. 5, 22; S. 644, 19. Hȳ healtodan on heora wegum *claudicaverunt a semitis suis,* Ps. Th. 17, 43. Ne healtigeaþ leng *ut non claudicans quis erret,* Past. 11, 1; Swt. 65, 18.

heal-wudu, a; *m. The woodwork of a hall,* Beo. Th. 2639; B. 1317.

heamol, hamol [?]; *adj. Frugal;* frugi, Cot. 86, Lye. [Cf. (?) *O. H. Ger.* hamal *mutilus.*]

heán; *adj. Low, mean, abject, poor, humbled, humble:*—Hiora heorte wæs heán on gewinnum *humiliatum est in laboribus cor eorum,* Ps. Th. 106, 11. Ic heán gewearþ hē mē hraðe lȳsde *humiliatus sum et liberavit me,* 114, 6. Nānig eft sīðade heán hyhta leás *none returned cast down and hopeless,* Exon. 46 a; Th. 157, 25; Gū. 897. Ðā ðū heán and earm ǣrest cwōme *when abject and poor thou first didst come,* 39 a; Th. 129, 23; Gū. 425. Dēmaþ ðam rīcan swā ðam heánan and ðam litlan swā ðam miclan *judge the high as the low, and the little as the great,* Deut. 1, 17: Homl. Th. i. 64, 30. Hū uncūþ biþ ǣghwylcum ānum men his līfes tīd ǣghweðer ge rīcum ge heánum ge geongum ge ealdum *how unknown to every single man is the period of his life, both to the rich man and to the poor, to the young and to the old,* Blickl. Homl. 125, 8. Habbaþ mē gehnǣged heánne tō eorþan *humiliavit in terra vitam meam,* Ps. Th. 142, 3. Ægðer ge welige ge heáne *simul in unum dives et pauper,* 48, 2. Swā rīce swā heáne *vel divites vel pauperes,* Bd. 3, 5; S. 526, 30. Se scearpa deáþ ðe ne forlēt ne rīce menn ne heáne se hine genam *stern death who spares neither rich men nor poor, that seized him,* Chr. 1086; Erl. 220, 35. Hī hī sylfe lēton ǣgðer ge for heáne ge for unwrǣste *ultima propemodum desperatione tabuerunt,* Ors. 3, 1; Swt. 98, 22. Hī taliaþ ðē wyrsan for heánan gebyrdan ða ðe heora yldran on worolde ne wurdan welige *they account the worse, for their humble birth, those whose forefathers were not rich in a worldly point of view,* L. Eth. vii. 21; Th. i. 334, 2. Ne wandige hē nā for rīcum ne for heánum *non vereri potentes neque humiles,* L. Ecg. P. i. 1; Th. ii. 172, 3. Heánra burhwered *vulgus* vel *plebs,* Ælfc. Gl. 8; Som. 56, 82; Wrt. Voc. 18, 37. Heánra man vel ceorlīc ǣhta *peculium,* 13; Som. 57, 122; Wrt. Voc. 22, 59. Se heánra hād *the weaker sex,* Exon. 9 a; Th. 7, 10; Cri. 99. Ne se heárra derige ðam heánran *nor let the higher injure the lower,* L. I. P. 7; Th. ii. 314, 1. Ðeáh hit se læsta wǣre and se heánosta *though it were the least and the lowest,* Blickl. Homl. 169, 23. [*Laym.* hæne, hene: *Goth.* hauns: *O. H. Ger.* hōn *humilis, infamis.*]

heán; *p.* heáde; *pp.* heád *To raise, heighten, exalt, advance:*—Mid singalum bysenum ārfæstre wyrcnysse hē ongan heán and miclian *continuis piæ operationis exemplis provehere curavit,* Bd. 2, 4; S. 505, 19. Heáþ and hebbaþ *exalt and raise,* Exon. 93 a; Th. 349, 6; Sch. 42. [*Goth.* hauhjan *to exalt: O. H. Ger.* hōhjan *exaltare: Ger.* erhöhen *exalt, raise.*]

heáne; *adv. Ignominiously, shamefully, abjectly:*—Ðū sylfa mē heáne gehnǣgdest *humiliasti me,* Ps. Th. 118, 71. Scyldigra scólu āscyred weorþeþ heáne from hālgum *the band of the guilty shall with shame be separated from the holy,* Exon. 31 b; Th. 98, 17; Cri. 1609: 75 b; Th. 283, 16; Jul. 681. Swā hē sȳn fram ðīnes handa heáne ādrifene *quidem ipsi de manu tua expulsi sunt,* Ps. Th. 87, 5. [In some of these passages the word may be a case of the adjective rather than an adverb.]

heá-nes. v. heáh-nes.

heán-līc; *adj. Ignominious, disgraceful, vile, poor:*—Tō heánlīc mē þinceþ ðæt gē mid ūrum sceattum tō scype gangon unbefohtene *too shameful methinks that ye with our treasures should go to your ships without a struggle,* Byrht. Th. 133, 25. Swīðe nearewe sent and swīðe heánlīce ða menniscan gesǣlþa *very scanty and very poor are human felicities;* anxia enim res est humanorum conditio bonorum, Bt. 11, 1; Fox 30, 26: Ors. 2, 5; Swt. 84, 12. [*O. H. Ger.* hōn-līh *infamis, fœdus, ridendus, dedecor, indecor.*]

heán-līce; *adj. Ignominiously, ingloriously, disgracefully, miserably,* *humbly*:—Fauius heánlíce hâmweard ōþfleáh *Fabius ignominiously fled homewards*, Ors. 3, 10; Swt. 140, 13. Ne lǣt swâ heánlíce đín handgeweorc forwurþan *let not thine handiwork so miserably perish*, Hy. 7, 111; Hy. Grn. ii. 289, 111: Exon. 8 a; Th. 3, 4; Cri. 31: 13 a; Th. 23, 21; Cri. 372.

heán-môd; *adj. Dejected, cast down, humiliated*:—Ic sceal sârigferþ heánmôd hweorfan *with sorrowing spirit and with dejected mind must I go*, Exon. 52 b; Th. 184, 32; Gû. 1353. Ic sceal feor đonan heánmôd hweorfan *I must go far thence with humiliated heart*, 71 a; Th. 265, 32; Jul. 390.

heán-spêdig; *adj. Scantily, poorly endowed*:—Đý læs hê forhycge heánspêdigran *lest he despise the more scantily endowed*, Exon. 78 b; Th. 295, 1; Crä. 26.

heáp, es; *m.* [*generally, but* đeós earme heáp *occurs*, Cd. 215; Th. 270, 9; Sat. 87.] *A* HEAP, *pile, great number, host, multitude, crowd, band, troop, body of people, assembly, company*:—Galađ đæt is gewitnesse heáp *Galand acervus testimonii interpretatur*, Past. 48, 2; Swt. 367, 5. Se hâlga heáp hêhfædera and wîtgena *the holy host of patriarchs and prophets*, Blickl. Homl. 81, 9. Fyrenfulra þreát heáp synnigra *peccatores*, Ps. Th. 91, 6. Þegna heáp *a troop of thanes*, Beo. Th. 805; B. 400. Be đam gesǣligan heápe đe mid đam Hǣlende on đisum lîfe drohtnode *of the blessed company that lived with the Saviour in this life*, Homl. Th. ii. 520, 22. Of đam yfelan heápe gehâdodra manna be đâm đe ûre Drihten cwæþ 'multi dicunt mihi, etc.' *of that evil band of men in orders about whom our Lord said, 'many will say to me, etc.'* L. Ælfc. P. 40; Th. ii. 380, 36: Apstls. Kmbl. 17; Ap. 9. Sum sceal on heápe hæleþum cwêman *one shall in company give pleasure to men*, Exon. 88 a; Th. 331, 32; Vy. 77. Gewîteþ mid đý wuldre mǣre tungol faran on heápe *the great star departs accompanied with that glory*, 93 b; Th. 350, 26; Sch. 69. Hwanon ferigeaþ gê herescefta heáp *whence bear ye a heap of war shafts*, Beo. Th. 675; B. 335. Hengestes heáp *Hengest's band*, 2186; B. 1091. His đone gecorenan heáp *electos suos*, Ps. Th. 104, 38: L. Ælfc. P. 21; Th. ii. 372, 3. Getalu *vel* heápas *vel* hundredu *centurias*, Ælfc. Gl. 96; Som. 76, 25; Wrt. Voc. 53, 34. Hine đâ đa heápas frugnon hwæt hie wyrcean mihton đæt hie Godes erre beflugon *when the multitudes asked him* [*John*] *what they could do to escape God's wrath*, Blickl. Homl. 169, 10: Cd. 161; Th. 202, 2; Exod. 382. Biscopan and gehâlgodan heápan *for bishops and consecrated bodies*, L. Eth. vii. 24; Th. i. 334, 23. Heápum *in troops*, Cd. 81; Th. 101, 36; Gen. 1693: 189; Th. 235, 6; Dan. 302: Exon. 15 b; Th. 34, 29; Cri. 549: Judth. 11; Thw. 23, 39; Jud. 163. [*O. Sax.* hôp: *O. Frs.* hâp: cf. *Icel.* hôpr *a troop, flock*: *O. H. Ger.* houf *strues, acervus*: *Ger.* haufe.] DER. gâr-, wîg-heáp.

heáp-mælum; *adv. In heaps, by troops, bands, companies, flocks*:—Telle đû and Aaron heápmǣlum *thou and Aaron shalt number them by their armies*, Num. 1, 3. Ne wæs đâ ylding tô đon đæt hî heápmǣlum côman mâran weorod of đâm þeódum đe wê ǣr gemynegodon *non mora ergo confluentibus certatim in insulam gentium memoratarum catervis*, Bd. 1, 15; S. 483, 31. Đa dumban niétenu hie hie gadriaþ heápmǣlum and hie ætsomne fêdaþ *gregatim animalia bruta pascuntur*, Past. 46, 4; Swt. 349, 23. Hý him heápmǣlum sylfe on hand eodon *they flocked to surrender to him*, Ors. 4, 5; Bos. 83, 8. [*O. H. Ger.* huufmâlum *catervatim.*]

heápung, e; *f. A heaping, heap*:—Onfôþ hine and on đa heápunge eówre niđerunge gelǣdaþ *accipite et in cumulum damnationis vestræ ducite*, Bd. 5, 13; S. 633, 14.

hearch. v. hearg.

HEARD, hard; *adj.* HARD, *harsh, austere, severe, rigorous, stern, stubborn, firm, hardy, brave*:—Hond and heard sweord *the hand and the hard blade*, Beo. Th. 5011; B. 2509. Ic wât đæt đû eart heard mann *scio quia homo durus es*, Mt. Kmbl. 25, 24. Heard is đeós sprǣc *this is an hard saying*; durus est hic sermo, Jn. Skt. 6, 60. Heó wæs ǣror đam cynge hire suna swîđe heard *she had been before very hard to the king her son*, Chr. 1043; Erl. 168, 36: Cd. 103; Th. 136, 20; Gen. 2261. Se mon se đe nû dêmeþ đǣm earmun bûton mildheortnesse, đonne biþ đam eft heard dôm geteód *the man who now judges the poor without mercy, on him shall a hard sentence be then passed in requital*, Blickl. Homl. 95, 36: Cd. 22; Th. 28, 7; Gen. 432. Him nǣnig gewin hêr on worlde tô lang ne tô heard þuhte *no labour here in the world seemed to him too long or too hard*, Blickl. Homl. 227, 3; Cd. 17; Th. 20, 30; Gen. 317. Hunger se hearda *severe famine*, 86; Th. 108, 32; Gen. 1815. Đǣr wæs heard plega wælgâra wrixl *there was hard fighting exchange of deadly darts*, 93; Th. 120, 5; Gen. 1989: Elen. Kmbl. 229; El. 115. Hê wæs ânrǣd heard and hygerôf *he was resolute, hardy and noble-minded*, Andr. Kmbl. 465; An. 233: Beo. Th. 689; B. 342. Đes hearda heáp *this stout band*, 868: B. 432. Wîges heard *bold in battle*, 1776; B. 886: Exon. 78 b; Th. 295, 27; Crä. 39; Byrht. Th. 135, 38; By. 130: Andr. Kmbl. 1677; An. 841. Hê wæs heardes cynnes *he was of a brave race*, Byrht. Th. 139, 39; By. 266. Đone deópan grund đæs hâtan lêges and đæs heardan lêges *the deep abyss of hot and cruel flame*, Blick. Homl. 103, 15. Hine đâ gegyrede mid hǣrenum hrægle swîđe heardum and unwinsumum *he clothed himself with raiment of hair very hard and unpleasant*, 221, 24. Ic hafu gecnâwen on heardum hyge đæt đû hǣlend eart middangeardes *I have acknowledged in my stubborn heart that thou art the saviour of the world*, Elen. Kmbl. 1614; El. 809. Beóþ đê hungor and þurst hearde gewinnan *hunger and thirst will be hard adversaries to thee*, Exon. 36 b; Th. 118, 28; Gû. 246. Đa heardan heortan *the hard hearts*, Past. 21, 3; Swt. 154, 2. Đa heardan þrowunga đe hê âdreág *the hard sufferings that he endured*, Blickl. Homl. 97, 15. Ic hine heardan clammum wrîđan þohte *I thought to bind him with hard bonds*, Beo. Th. 1931; B. 963. Mê þinceþ đæt đû wǣre đâm ungelǣredum mannum heardra đonne hit riht wǣre *videtur mihi quia durior justo indoctis auditoribus fuisti*, Bd. 3, 5; S. 527, 32. Hige sceal đê heardra đê ûre mægen lytlaþ *our courage shall be the stouter as our force lessens*, Byrht. Th. 140, 62; By. 312. Nô ic gefrægn heardran feohtan *I have never heard of a harder fight*, Beo. Th. 1157; B. 576. Nǣfre hê ǣr ne siđđan heardran hæle fand *never before or since did he find a stouter warrior*, 1442; B. 719. Se lîchoma đonne on đone heardestan stenc and on đone fûlostan biþ gecyrred *the body then shall be turned to the strongest and foulest stench*, Blickl. Homl. 59, 12. Đa đe gecwedene syndon đa heardestan men *who* [*the Scythians*] *are said to be very hardy men*, Ors. 1, 2; Swt. 30, 3. [*Goth.* hardus: *O. Sax.* hard: *O. Frs.* herd: *Icel.* harðr: *O. H. Ger.* hart, harti, hert, herti *durus, rigidus, asper, acer*: *Ger.* hart.]

heard-cwide, es; *m. Harsh language, reproach, abuse, contumely*:—Ic geþolade hosp and heardcwide *I suffered scorn and contumely*, Exon. 29 a; Th. 88, 22; Cri. 1444.

hearde; *adv. Severely, very much, greatly, sorely*:—Đâ cwæþ se Hǣlend đæt him hearde þyrste *then said Jesus that he was sore athirst*, Homl. Th. ii. 256, 31. Hearde ofsceamode *sorely ashamed*, 518, 31. Đæs đe wê wênaþ and hearde ondrǣdaþ *according to what we expect and very much fear*, L. Ælfc. P. 40; Ll. ii. 380, 35. Hine đæs heardost langode hwanne hê of đisse worlde môste *he very earnestly longed for the time when he might leave this world*, Blickl. Homl. 227, 1: Bt. 36, 2; Fox 174, 28.

heard-ecg; *adj. Hard of edge*:—Đâ wæs on healle heardecg togen sweord *then in the hall was drawn the sword hard of edge*, Beo. Th. 2581; B. 1288: 2984; B. 1490: Elen. Kmbl. 1513; El. 758: Exon. 102 b; Th. 388, 15; Rä. 6, 8. v. *other compounds with* ecg.

heard-fyrde; *adj. Difficult to carry*:—Đǣr oninnan bær eorl hardfyrdne dǣl goldes *there within bore the earl a weighty portion of gold*, Beo. Th. 4483; B. 2245.

heard-heáwa, an; *m. A chisel*; scalprum, Som.

heard-heort; *adj. Hard-hearted, stiff-necked*:—Heardheort biþ se mann đe nele þurh lufe ôđrum fremigan đǣr đǣr hê mæg *that man is hard of heart who will not from love benefit others when he can*, Homl. Th. i. 252, 19. Hwâ is swâ heardheort đæt ne mæg wêpan swylces ungelimpes *who is so hard of heart that he cannot weep at such misfortunes*, Chr. 1086; Erl. 219, 40. Đis folc is hardheort *thou art a stiff-necked people*, Ex. 33, 3, 5: Homl. Th. i. 108, 22: ii. 258, 22. Gê sind ealra folca ungeleáfulluste and heardheorteste *ye are of all nations the most unbelieving and most stiff-necked*, Deut. 9, 6.

heard-heortness, e; *f. Hard-heartedness*:—Hwæt is seó stǣnige eorþe bûton heardheortnyss *what is the stony ground but hard-heartedness*, Homl. Th. ii. 90, 35. Þurh đone wah seó heardheortnes đara hiéremonna *per parietem duritia subditorum*, Past. 21, 3; Swt. 153, 24. Ic can eówre heardheortnisse *I know thy stiff neck*, Deut. 31, 27.

heard-hicgende; *adj. Bold in purpose*, Beo. Th. 793; B. 394: 1602; B. 799.

heardian; *p.* ode *To be* or *become hard, to harden*:—Ic heardige *dureo* and *duro*, Ælfc. Gr. 35; Som. 38, 6: 37; Som. 39, 26: Herb. 1, 19; Lchdm. i. 76, 18: 2, 11; Lchdm. i. 84, 4. Đæt wyrmþ and heardaþ đone magan *it warms and hardens the stomach*, L. M. 2, 10; Lchdm. ii. 188, 18. Đonne onginþ sió heardian *then the liver begins to harden*, 19; Lchdm. ii. 200, 25.

hearding, es; *m. A brave man, warrior, hero*, Elen. Kmbl. 50; El. 25: 260; El. 130: Runic pm. Kmbl. 344, 1; Rûn. 22. [Cf. æđeling and v. Grmm. D. M. 316, 321.]

heard-lîc; *adj. Severe, fierce, hard, strict*:—Heardlîc eornost *severe seriousness*, L. I. P. 10; Th. ii. 318, 37: Andr. Kmbl. 3100; An. 1553: Exon. 116 b; Th. 447, 10; Dôm 37. Heardlîcu wîtu *severe punishments*, 69 b; Th. 258, 11; Jul. 263.

heard-lîce; *adv. Hardly, sorely, harshly, sternly, bravely, stoutly*:—Heardlîce *duriter*, Ælfc. Gr. 38; Som. 41, 41. Se Godes man ongan heardlîce and bitterlîce wêpan *the man of God began to weep sorely and bitterly*; solutus est in lacrymis, Bd. 4, 25; S. 600, 29. Hê heardlîce gewon wiđ Æþelbald cyning *he struggled hard with king Ethelbald*, Chr. 741; Erl. 46, 30. Đet landfolc hardlîce wiđstôdon *the people of the country withstood them stoutly*, 1046; Erl. 171, 4. Hê spræc heardlîcor wiđ hig đonne wiđ fremde men *he spoke more harshly to them than to strangers*, Gen. 42, 8. [*O. Sax.* hard-lîko.]

heard-lîcness, e; *f. Hardness, severity, strictness*:—Sume hî sǣdon ða heardlîcnysse his lîfes *some of them told the severity of his life*, Guthl. 17; Gdwin. 70, 15.

heard-mód; *adj. Of a hard, unyielding spirit, self-confident, stout-hearted, brave*:—Eádig biþ se man ðe symle biþ forhtigende and sôþlîce se heardmôda befylþ on yfel *blessed is the man that is ever fearing; and verily the self-confident man shall fall into evil*, Homl. Th. i. 408, 30. Hæleþas heardmôde *heroes stouthearted*, Cd. 15; Th. 19, 2; Gen. 285. [*O.H.Ger.* hart-muat *obstinatus*; hart-môti *constantia, obstinatio, duritia*. Cf. *O.Sax.* hard-môdig: *Icel.* harð-móðigr.]

heard-môdness, e; *f. Hardness of mind* or *heart*:—Stân is gesett ongeán ðone hlâf forðan ðe heardmôdnys is wiðerræ̂de sôþre lufe *a stone is put in opposition to bread, because hardness of mind is contrary to true love*, Homl. Th. i. 252, 18.

heard-neb, -nebb; *adj. Having a hard beak* [*epithet of the raven*]:—Ðâ cwæþ se hâlga tô ðâm heardnebbum *then said the saint to the ravens*, Homl. Th. ii. 144, 15. v. *other compounds of* neb.

heardness, e; *f. Hardness*:—For eówer heortan heardnesse *ad duritiam cordis vestri*, Mt. Kmbl. 19, 8: Mk. Skt. 10, 5: Ðû æteówdest ðînum folce heardnyssa *ostendisti populo tuo dura*, Ps. Lamb. 59, 5.

heardra, an; *m. The name of a fish*:—Heardra *mulus* vel *mugilis*, Ælfc. Gl. 102; Som. 77, 64; Wrt. Voc. 55, 68: *mullus*, Wrt. Voc. 77, 63.

heard-ræ̂d; *adj. Steadfast, firm*, Cd. 107; Th. 141, 21; Gen. 2348. [Cf. *Icel.* harð-ræði *hardiness*.]

heard-sæ̂lig; *adj. Having hard fortune, unfortunate, unhappy*:—Sum biþ wonspêdig heardsæ̂lig hæle *one is indigent, an unfortunate man*, Exon. 78 b; Th. 295, 12; Crä. 32: Bt. 31, 1; Fox 112, 20: Exon. 115 a; Th. 442, 27; Kl. 19.

heard-sæ̂lness, e; *f. Misfortune, calamity*:—Ðâ com eác seó ofermæ̂te heardsæ̂lnes *then came also the excessive calamity*, Ors. 3, 5; Swt. 104, 17.

heard-sæ̂lþ, e; *f. A hard fate, ill fortune, misfortune, unhappiness, wickedness, misconduct*:—Gong inn and geseoh ða heardsæ̂lþa and ða sconde ðe ðâs hêr dôþ *ingredere et vide abominationes pessimas quas isti faciunt hic*, Past. 21, 3; Swt. 155, 8. Ic wolde gewŷscan gif ic mihte ðæt hî næfdon ða heardsæ̂lþa ðæt hî mihton yfel dôn *uti hoc infortunio cito careant, patrandi sceleris possibilitate deserti, vehementer exopto*, Bt. 38, 2; Fox 198, 4. Hit gebyrede þurh ða heardsæ̂lþa ðara wrîtera ðæt hî for heora slæ̂wþe and for gîmelêste and for recceléste forlêton unwriten ðara monna dæ̂da ðe on hiora dagum foremæ̂roste wæ̂ron *quam multos clarissimos suis temporibus viros scriptorum inops delevit oblivio*, ᵀ8, 3; Fox 64, 33.

heard-wendlîce; *adv. Severely, strictly*:—Heardwendlîce [MS. B. heardlîce] *districtius*, Bd. 4, 25; S. 601, 40.

hearg-træf, es; *n. A heathen temple*, Beo. Th. 353; B. 175.

hearg-, herig-weard, es; *m. A guardian of a temple*, Andr. Kmbl. 2249; An. 1126.

hearh, hearch, herh, es; *m*: *pl.* hearga, *f. A temple, an idol*:—Se ylca hearh *quod fanum*, Bd. 2, 15; S. 518, 35. Sôna ðæs ðe hê gelîhte tô ðam hearge ðâ sceát hê mid his spere ðæt hit sticode fæste on ðam hearge *nec distulit ille, mox ut propiabat fanum, profanare illud, injecta in eo lancea quam tenebat*, 13; S. 517, 11. Siððan hê fôr tô ðæm hearge ðe Egypti sæ̂don ðæt hê wæ̂re Amones heora godes *inde ad templum Jovis Ammonis pergit*, Ors. 3, 9; Swt. 126, 23. Hê on ðam ylcan hearhge wigbed hæfde tô Cristes onsægdnyssa and ôðer tô deófla onsægdnysse *in eodem fano et altare haberet ad sacrificium Christi et arulam ad victimas dæmoniorum*, Bd. 2, 15; S. 518, 33. Hie onhnigon tô ðam herige *they bowed to the idol*, Cd. 181; Th. 227, 3; Dan. 181. Gif æ̂nig man gelŷfe on Moloches hearch *if any man believe on Moloch*, Lev. 20, 2. Hê hêt his gefêran tôworpon ealne hearh and ða getymbro and forbærnan *jussit sociis destruere ac succendere fanum cum omnibus septis suis*, Bd. 2, 13; S. 517, 14. Ealle ða hearga(s?) [cf. Swt. 157, 7] *universa idola*, Past. 21, 3; Swt. 153, 22. Cwæþ ðæt his hergas hŷrran wæ̂ron and mihtigran mannum tô friðe ðonne Israêla êce drihten *he said that his idols were greater and more mighty for the protection of men than the eternal Lord of the Israelites*, Cd. 210; Th. 260, 25; Dan. 715. On westhealfe Alexandres herga *aras Alexandri magni*, Ors. 1, 1; Swt. 8, 17. Ne ic ne clypige tô heora godum ne tô heargum ne gebidde mid mîne mûþe *nec memor ero nominum eorum per labra mea*, Ps. Th. 15, 4. Ða wuldriaþ in hergum heara *qui gloriantur in simulacris suis*, Ps. Stev. 96, 7. Ðâ ongunnon hî ða heargas edniwian *cæperunt fana restaurare*, Bd. 3, 30; S. 561, 42: 562, 15. Mid ðŷ hê sôhte hwâ ða wigbed and ða heargas ðara deófolgylda mid heora hegum ðe hî ymbsette wæ̂ron æ̂rest âîdlian and tôweorpan scolde *cum quæreret quis aras et fana idolorum cum septis quibus erant circumdata primus profanare deberet*, 2, 13; S. 516, 39. Heora hergas tôwearp *templa subvertit*, Ors. 3, 7; Swt. 114, 2: Exon. 14 b; Th. 30, 28; Cri. 485. And geeáþmêdaþ hira heargas *et adoraverint simulacra eorum*, Ex. 34, 15. Ne wirc gê eów hearga ne âgrafene godas . . . eówre hearga ic tôbrece *ye shall make you no idols nor graven image . . . I will cut down your images*, Lev. 26, 1, 30. [*Icel.* hörgr; *m.* '*a heathen place of worship, an altar of stone, erected on high places, or a sacrificial cairn, built in open air, and without images*,' Cl. and Vig. Dict: *O.H.Ger.* haruc, haruch, harug; *m. lucus, nemus, fanum, delubrum, ara*. The word perhaps occurs in the sense of *grove* in Exon. 54 b; Th. 192, 25; Az. 110. Grein so translates the word in this passage.]

HEARM, herm, es; *m.* HARM, *hurt, injury, evil, grief, affliction, pain, injurious speech, calumny, insult*:—Hŷnþ *vel* lyre *vel* hearm *dispendium* vel *damnum* vel *detrimentum*, Ælfc. Gl. 81; Som. 73, 24; Wrt. Voc. 47, 29. Eác is hearm gode môdsorg gemacod *pain also and heart-sorrow is caused to God*, Cd. 35; Th. 47, 2; Gen. 754. Nân hearm ne biþ ðeáh hit nô ne gewyrðe *there is no harm if it do not happen*, Bt. 41, 3; Fox 250, 4. Ic forhele ðæt mê hearmes swâ fela Adam gespræc eargra worda *I will conceal that Adam spoke so much calumny, so many evil words to me*, Cd. 27; Th. 36, 30; Gen. 579: 30; Th. 41, 24; Gen. 661: Exon. 10 a; Th. 11, 15; Cri. 171. Hê onfunde Godes ierre on ðam hearme ðe his bearne æfter his dagum becom *in damnationem secuturæ prolis ex eo iram judicis pertulit*, Past. 4, 1; Swt. 39, 4. Nô hê mid hearme gæst ne grêtte *not with insult did he greet the guest*, Beo. Th. 3788; B. 1892. Huscworde ongan herme hyspan *with words of contumely and insult began to revile him*, Andr. Kmbl. 1341; An. 671. Gif hwæs weorc forbyrnþ, hê hæfþ ðone hearm and biþ swâ ðeáh gehealden þurh fŷr *if any one's work is consumed he has the loss, and yet shall be saved by fire*, Homl. Th. ii. 588, 30. Hî gefeordon mâran hearm and yfel ðonne hî æ̂fre wêndon ðæt heom æ̂nig burhwaru gedôn sceolde *they got more damage and hurt than they ever expected any citizens would cause them*, Chr. 994; Erl. 133, 13. Æ̂r hî tô mycelne hearm gedydon *before they did too much harm*, 1004; Erl. 139, 20: Cd. 196; Th. 245, 6; Dan. 458. Ealle synt uncre hearmas gewrecene *all our injuries are avenged*, 35; Th. 47, 12; Gen. 759. Nyste ðæt hearma swâ fela fylgean sceolde monna cynne *knew not that so many ills to mankind must follow*, 33; Th. 44, 13; Gen. 708: Andr. Kmbl. 2889; An. 1447. Mê is ðæt hearma mæ̂st *that is greatest of griefs to me*, Byrht. Th. 138, 21; By. 233. [*O. Sax.* harm *pain, grief*: *Icel.* harmr *grief, sorrow, harm*: *O. H. Ger.* harm *calamitas, calumnia, contumelia, ærumna, injuria*: *Ger.* harm *grief, sorrow*.]

hearm = hreám [?] L. E. G. 6; Th. i. 170, 10, see note there and Schmid, p. 123.

hearm, herm; *adj. Causing harm* or *sorrow, grievous, injurious, evil, malicious*:—Herm bealowes gâst *the malicious spirit of evil*, Cd. 228; Th. 307, 19; Sat. 682. Hê mê âlŷsde of hearmum worde *ipse liberavit me a verbo aspero*, Ps. Th. 90, 3. Ða inwit and fâcen hycgeaþ on heortan þurh hearme geþoht *qui cogitaverunt malitias in corde*, 139, 2. Tugon longne sîð in hearmra hond *went a long journey into the power of evil ones*, Exon. 62 a; Th. 228, 20; Ph. 441. Ne hyld ðû mîne heortan ðæt ic hearme word þuruh inwitstæf ûtforlæ̂te *ut non declines cor meum in verbum malum*, Ps. Th. 140, 5.

hearma, an; *m. A shrew-mouse* [?]; nebila, Ælfc. Gl. 19; Som. 59, 6; Wrt. Voc. 22, 50. [*O. H. Ger.* harmo *mygale*.]

hearm-cwalu, e; *f. Grievous destruction*, Exon. 31 b; Th. 98, 18; Cri. 1609.

hearm-cwedelian; *p.* ode *To speak ill of, calumniate*:—Nâ hearmcwedelodon mê ofermôde *non calumnientur me superbi*, Ps. Spl. 118, 122.

hearm-cweðan; *p.* -cwæþ *To revile, speak ill of*:—Mid ðŷ menn iuih harmcueðaþ *cum homines vos exprobaverint*, Lk. Skt. Lind. 6, 22. Hearmcuæ̂don him *convitiabantur ei*, Mk. Skt. Lind. 15, 32.

hearm-cweðend, es; *m. A calumniator*:—Hê ða hermcweðend hŷneþ *humiliabit calumniatorem*, Ps. Th. 71, 5.

hearm-cwide, es; *m. Injurious, abusive speech, calumny, blasphemy, a sentence pronouncing harm* or *sorrow*:—Heora hearran hearmcwyde *their lord's sentence*, Cd. 29; Th. 39, 12; Gen. 625. Judêa cynn wið godes bearne âhôf hearmcwide *the race of the Jews against God's son blasphemed*, Andr. Kmbl. 1121; An. 561: 157; An 79. Âhrede mê hearmcwidum heánra manna *redime a calumniis hominum*, Ps. Th. 118, 134: Exon. 24 a; Th. 69, 15; Cri. 1121. [*O. Sax.* harm-quidi: *O. H. Ger.* harm-qhuiti *calumnia*.]

hearm-cwidian, -cwiddian; *p.* ode *To revile, calumniate, speak ill of*:—Ongan hine hyspan and hearmcwiddigan [-cwidian, Cott.] *he began to revile and speak ill of him*, Bt. 18, 4; Fox 66, 33.

hearm-cwidol; *adj. Given to speak evil, calumnious*:—Gebiddaþ for hearmcwidele *orate pro calumniantibus*, Mt. Kmbl. 5, 44. Ðâ wæ̂ron hî æfter æþelborennysse oferhŷdige and hearmcwydole *in consequence of noble birth they were haughty and given to speak contemptuously of others*, Homl. Th. ii. 174, 8.

hearm-edwît, es; *n. Grievous reproach*, Ps. Th. 68, 21.

hearm-fullîc; *adj. Harmful, hurtful*:—Swurdboran hine gewordene gesihþ hearmfullîc getâcnaþ *to see one's self become a gladiator betokens something hurtful*, Lchdm. iii. 204, 26.

hearm-heortness, e; *f. Murmuring, grieving*; murmuratio, Cot. 187, Lye.

hearmian; *p.* ode *To harm, hurt, injure*:—Gif preóst ôðerne unwarnode læ̂te ðæs ðe hê wite ðæt him hearmian wille *if a priest leave* *another unwarned of that which he knows will harm him*, L. N. P. L. 33; Th. ii. 294, 26: Lchdm. iii. 202, 33. Gif ðú hine forgitst hit hearmaþ ðē sylfum and nā Gode *if thou forgettest him it harms thyself and not God*, Homl. Th. i. 140, 31. Ðeáh ðe hit hearmige sumum *though it may do harm to some*, H. R. 105, 36. [*O. H. Ger.* harmēn *calumniari*: *Ger.* härmen *to afflict, grieve*: cf. *Icel.* hermask *to be annoyed.*]

hearm-leóþ, es; *n. A sorrowful song, lamentation*:—Hearmleóþ galan *to sing a song of grief*, Andr. Kmbl. 2256; An. 1129: 2684; An. 1344. Hearmleóþ āgōl earm and unlǣd *wretched and miserable sang a mournful song*, Exon. 74 b; Th. 279, 18; Jul. 615.

hearm-līc; *adj. Hurtful, injurious, painful, miserable, grievous*:—Hearmlīc him wǣre ðæt hē wurþe ðā ēce *it would have been hurtful for him to become eternal then*, Hexam. 18; Norm. 26, 17. Ðæt wæs hreówlīc and hearmlīc *that was sad and grievous*, Chr. 1057; Erl. 192, 21. [*O. Sax.* harm-līk.]

hearm-loca, an; *m. An enclosed place where hurt* or *affliction is suffered, a prison*:—Wræcstōwe under hearmlocan gefōran *they reached their place of exile in hell*, Cd. 5; Th. 6, 19; Gen. 91. Hē his magu-þegne under hearmlocan hǣlo ābeád *he announced safety to his servant in prison*, Andr. Kmbl. 189; An. 95: 2058; An. 1031: Elen. Kmbl. 1386; El. 695.

hearm-plega, an; *m. Strife*, Cd. 90; Th. 114, 2; Gen. 1898.

hearm-scearu, e; *f. What is imposed as a punishment or penalty* ['was zur pein und qual auferlegt wird,' Grmm. R. A. 681]:—Wyrþ him wīte gegearwod sum heard harmscearu *for them punishment will be prepared, some severe penalty*, Cd. 22; Th. 28, 7; Gen. 432: 37; Th. 48, 25; Gen. 781: 38; Th. 51, 19; Gen. 829. [*O. Sax.* harm-skara: *O. Frs.* herm-skere: *O. H. Ger.* harm-, haram-skara *plaga, percussio, afflictio, castigatio, contritio, dejectio, calamitas, supplicium, scantinea*, Grff. vi. 529.]

hearm-sceaða, an; *m. A grievous, pernicious spoiler*, Beo. Th. 1536; B. 766.

hearm-slege, es; *m. A grievous blow*, Exon. 28 b; Th. 88, 4; Cri. 1435.

hearm-sprǣc, e; *f. Slander; calumnia*, Som.

hearm-sprǣcol; *adj. Calumnious*, Som. v. hearm-cwidol.

hearm-sprǣcolness, e; *f. Slandering, traducing*, Som.

hearm-stæf, es; *m. Hurt, harm, sorrow, trouble, affliction*:—Wē nū gehȳraþ hwǣr ūs hearmstafas onwōcan *we now hear whence troubles arose for us*, Cd. 45; Th. 58, 1; Gen. 939. Ne mōstun hȳ Gūþlāces gæste sceððan ... ac hȳ āhōfun hearmstafas *they might not injure Guthlac's spirit ... but they raised up troubles*, Exon. 35 b; Th. 115, 35; Gū. 200. [Cf. *other compounds of* stæf.]

hearm-tān, es; *m. A twig of sorrow* or *evil*, Cd. 47; Th. 61, 4; Gen. 992.

hearpe, hærpe, an; *f. A harp*:—Hearpe *cithara*, Wrt. Voc. 73, 56: Ps. Th. 56, 10. Psalm æfter hærpan sang *canticum*: ǣr hærpan sang *psalmus*, Ælfc. Gl. 34; Som. 62, 57, 58; Wrt. Voc. 28, 37, 38. Ðǣr wæs hearpan swēg *there was the sound of the harp*, Beo. Th. 179; B. 89: 4908; B. 2458: 6039; B. 3023: 4517; B. 2262: 4221; B. 2107. Se hearpan ǣrest handum sīnum hlyn āwehte *he first awaked with his hands the sound of the harp*, Cd. 52; Th. 66, 5; Gen. 1079. Ðonne ðǣr wæs blisse intingan gedēmed ðæt hī ealle sceoldan þurh endebyrdnesse be hearpan singan ðonne hē geseah ða hearpan him neálǣcean ðonne ārās hē *cum esset lætitiæ causa ut omnes per ordinem cantare deberent ille ubi adpropinquare sibi citharam cernebat surgebat*, Bd. 4, 24; S. 597, 6. Ic ðē on sealmfatum singe be hearpan *psallam tibi in cithara*, Ps. Th. 70, 20: Exon. 86 b; Th. 325, 1; Vīd. 105. Ne biþ him tō hearpan hyge ... se ðe on lagu fundaþ *he has no mind to the harp ... who on the ocean puts forth*, 82 a; Th. 308, 23; Seef. 44. Sum sceal mid hearpan æt his hlāfordes fōtum sittan feoh þicgan *one shall at his lord's feet sit with the harp and receive treasure*, 88 a; Th. 332, 4; Vy. 80. Sum mid hondum mæg hearpan grētan *one with his hands can touch the harp*, 79 a; Th. 296, 11; Crä. 49: 91 b; Th. 344, 10; Gn. Ex. 171: 17 b; Th. 42, 8; Cri. 669. [*Icel.* harpa: *O. H. Ger.* harfa *plectrum, chelys, psalterium, cythara*: *Ger.* harfe.]

hearpe-, hearp-nægel, es; *m. An instrument for striking the strings of a harp*:—Hearpnægel *plectrum*, Ælfc. Gl. 71; Som. 70, 96; Wrt. Voc. 43, 27. Apollonius his hearpenægl genam *Apollonius took his harp-nail*, Ap. Th. 17, 7.

hearpene, an; *f. A nightingale*; aëdon, Cot. 19, Lye.

hearpere, es; *m. A harper*:—Hearpere *citharedus*, Ælfc. Gl. 114; Som. 80, 8; Wrt. Voc. 60, 44: *citharista*, 73, 55. Ān hearpere wæs on ðære þeóde ðe Thracia hātte ... ðæs nama wæs Orfeus *there was a harper in Thrace whose name was Orpheus*, Bt. 35, 6; Fox 166, 29: Past. 23; Swt. 175, 7. [*Icel.* harpari: *O. H. Ger.* harfere *citharedus.*]

hearpestre, an; *f. A female harper*:—Hearpestre *citharista*, Ælfc. Gl. 114; Som. 80, 9; Wrt. Voc. 60, 45.

hearpe-streng, es; *m. A harp-string*:—Hē ða hearpestrengas mid cræfte āstirian ongan *he began to move the strings of the harp skilfully*, Ap. Th. 17, 8. [*Icel.* hörpu-strengr.]

hearpian; *p.* ode *To play on the harp, to harp*:—Hē mihte hearpian ðæt se wudu wagode *he could play on the harp so that the wood moved*, Bt. 35, 6; Fox 166, 32: Ap. Th. 16, 16. Fægere hē hearpaþ *pulcre citharizat*, Ælfc. Gr. 38; Som. 41, 31. Ða hwīle ðe hē hearpode *whilst he played on the harp*, Bt. 35, 6; Fox 170, 5. Stefen swǣ hearpara hearpandra in hearpum sīnum *vocem sicut cytharedorum cytharizantium in cytharis suis*, Rtl. 47, 24.

hearp-sang, es; *m. A song to the harp, a psalm*:—Hearpsang *psalmus*, Ælfc. Gl. 34: Som. 62, 56; Wrt. Voc. 28, 36.

hearp-slege, es; *m. A striking, playing of the harp*:—On hearpan and on hearpslege and on stefne sealmcwides *in cithara, in cithara et voce psalmi*, Ps. Lamb. 97, 5. [*Icel.* hörpu-slagr *striking the harp.*]

hearp-swēg, es; *m. The sound of the harp*:—Sealmleóþ and hearpswēg *psalterium et cythara*, Blickl. Gloss.

hearpung, e; *f. Harping, playing on the harp*:—Hē hī hæfþ geearnod mid his hearpunga *he hath deserved her by his harping*, Bt. 35, 6; Fox 170, 8.

hearra, herra, hierra, an; *m. A lord.* The use of this word, which occurs only in poetry, is noticeable. It occurs twenty-three times in that part of the Genesis [vv. 235–851] for which Sievers claims an old Saxon origin, and only four times elsewhere, Cd. 192; Th. 240, 28; Dan. 393: Judth. 10; Thw. 22, 9; Jud. 56: Byrht. Th. 137, 51; By. 204: Chr. 1065; Erl. 198, 13. [In the Heliand *herro* occurs frequently. *Icel.* has *harri, herra*: *O. H. Ger.* *herro*: Grff. iv. 991.]

hearste-, hierste-panne, an; *f. A frying-pan*:—Hē him tǣhte ðæt hē him genāme āne īserne hearstepanna *tu sume tibi sartaginem ferream*, Past. 21, 5; Swt. 161, 7: 163, 22.

heart. v. heort.

hearwian *to cool*; refrigerare, Lye.

heaðorian, heaðerian; *p.* ode *To restrain*:—Se godcunda foreþonc heaðeraþ ealle gesceafta *the divine providence restrains all creatures*, Bt. 39, 5; Fox 218, 31. Mid þearfednesse ge mid heora ungelǣrednesse ðara lāreówa fōre heaðoradon *paupertate ac rusticitate sua doctorum arcebant accessum*, Bd. 4, 27; S. 604, 29. v. ge-heaðorian.

heaðu, heaðo *war*; a word occurring only in compounds. The word is found in proper names in Icelandic, e. g. Höð the name of a Valkyria, Höðbroddr, Höðr the slayer of Baldr; and in *O. H. Ger.* e. g. Hadu-praht, v. Grmm. D. M. 204: Cl. and Vig. Dict. höð. Cf. beadu, gūþ, hilde *and their compounds.*

heáðu [= heáhþu ?] *indecl. f. The deep, the sea*; altum:—Sceal hringnaca ofer heáðu bringan lāc and luftācen *over the deep shall the bark bring gift and love token*, Beo. Th. 3729; B. 1862.

heaðu-byrne, an; *f. A war-corslet*, Beo. Th. 3108; B. 1552.

heaðu-deór; *adj. Brave, stout in war*, Beo. Th. 1380; B. 688: 1548; B. 772.

heaðu-fremmende; *part. Doing battle, fighting*, Elen. Kmbl. 258; El. 130.

heaðu-fȳr, es; *n. Fierce, hostile fire*, Beo. Th. 5037; B. 2522: 5087; 2547.

heaðu-geong; *adj. Young and active in battle* (?) [*Hickes reads* hearo], Fins. Th. 3; Fin. 2.

heaðu-glemm, es; *m. A wound got in fight*, Exon. 114 a; Th. 438, 6; Rä. 57, 3. v. glemm.

heaðu-grim; *adj. Very fierce, cruel with the cruelty of war*:—Hungur heaðogrimne heardne *famne fierce and fell*, Ps. Th. 145, 6: Beo. Th. 1100; B. 548: 5375; B. 2691.

heaðu-helm, es; *m. A war-helm, casque*, Beo. Kmbl. 6304; B. 3156.

heaðu-lāc, es; *n. Battle*, Beo. Th. 1172; B. 584: 3952; B. 1974.

heaðu-lind, e; *f. A linden war-shield*, Chr. 937; Erl. 112, 6; Æðelst. 6.

heáðu-līðende; *part. Sea-faring*, Beo. Th. 3600; B. 1798: 5902; B. 2955: Andr. Kmbl. 851; An. 426.

heaðu-mǣre; *adj. Illustrious in war*, Beo. Th. 5596; B. 2802.

heaðu-rǣs, es; *m. A battle-rush, charge, onslaught*, Beo. Th. 1056; B. 526: 1119; B. 557: 2099; B. 1047.

heaðu-reáf, es; *n. War-dress, armour*, Beo. Th. 807; B. 401.

heaðu-rinc, es; *m. A warrior*, Judth. 11; Thw. 24, 9; Jud. 179: Thw. 24, 29; Jud. 212: Beo. Th. 745; B. 370: 4923; B. 2466: Cd. 154; Th. 193, 4; Exod. 241: Bt. Met. Fox 9, 89; Met. 9, 45.

heaðu-rōf; *adj. Famed for excellence in battle*, Beo. Th. 767; B. 381; 1732; B. 864: 4388; B. 2191: Exon. 59 a; Th. 213, 21; Ph. 228; Menol. Fox 27; Men. 14.

heaðu-sceared; *adj. In* Beo. Th. 5650; B. 2829; *according to Thorpe the reading of the MS. is* scearede, *other editors read* scearde. *In the former case may not the word be connected with* scear [q. v. *share in ploughshare*] *used here of the blade of a sword*, heaðo-scear *a war-share, blade? and* hearde heaðo-scearede = *with hard and deadly blades. If* scearde *is taken, the Icel.* skarð *may be compared, and the word = notched, hacked in battle.*

heaðu-seóc; *adj. Wounded in fight*, Beo. Th. 5501; B. 2754.

heáðu-sigel, es; *m. The sun* [the prefix seems to be used from seeing the sun rise or set over the sea], Exon. 126 b; Th. 486, 17; Rä. 72, 16. [Cf. merecandel.]

heaðu-steáp; *adj. Standing out prominently in battle* [an epithet of the helmet], Beo. Th. 2494; B. 1245: 4312; B. 2153.

heaðu-swât, es; *m. War-sweat, blood shed in battle*, Beo. Th. 2924; B. 1460: 3216; B. 1606: 3340; 1668.

heaðu-sweng, es; *m. A blow given in fight*, Beo. Th. 5155; B. 2581.

heaðu-torht; *adj. Clear-sounding and of warlike import*, Beo. Th. 5109: B. 2553.

heaðu-wǽd, e; *f. Warlike weeds, dress*, Beo. Th. 78; B. 39.

heaðu-wælm, -welm, -wylm, es; *m. Fierce, intense heat*, Cd. 17; Th. 21, 14; Gen. 324: 149; Th. 187, 8; Exod. 148: Beo. Th. 165; B. 82: 5630; B. 2819: Andr. Kmbl. 3082; An. 1544: Elen. Kmbl. 1154; El. 578: 2607; El. 1305.

heaðu-weorc, es; *n. A work of war, a fight*, Beo. Th. 5776; B. 2892.

heaðu-wêrig; *adj. Weary from fighting*, Vald. 2, 17.

HEÁWAN; *p.* heów, *pl.* heówon; *pp.* heáwen *To* HEW, *cut, strike, smite* [*with a sharp weapon*]:—Gif mon óðres wudu heáweþ unâliéfedne *if a man cut another's wood without leave*, L. Alf. pol. 12; Th. i. 70, 4. Mǽst ǽlc óðerne æftan heáweþ mid scandlícum onscytum *almost all men calumniate* [lit. *strike from behind*] *each other with shameful attacks*, Swt. A. S. Rdr. 107, 84. Se seðe unwærlíce ðone wuda hiéwþ *is qui incaute ligna percutit*, Past. 21, 7; Swt. 167, 16. Wê heáwaþ ðone wudu *ligna succidimus*, 167, 6. Hê heów ðð ðæt hê on hilde gecranc *he smote with his sword until in fight he fell*, Byrht. Th. 141, 18; By. 324. Heów ðæt hors mid ðam spuran *he struck the horse with the spurs* [cf. *Icel.* höggva hest sporum], Elf. T. 36, 25. Ðâ heówon hî ðone stân swâ swýðe swâ hî mihton *dolantes lapidem in quantum valebant*, Bd. 4, 11; S. 580, 5. Heówon hereflýman þearle mêcum mylenscearpum *they smote sorely the flying with falchions sharp ground*, Chr. 937; Erl. 112, 23; Æðelst. 23: Byrht. Th. 137, 4; By. 181. Linde heówon *they hewed the linden shields*, Judth. 12; Thw. 26, 1; Jud. 304: Chr. 937; Erl. 112. 6; Æðelst. 6: Mt. Kmbl. 21. 8. [*O.Sax.* hawan, hauwan: *O.Frs.* hawa, howa: *Icel.* höggva: *O.H.Ger.* houwan: *Ger.* hauen.]

HEBBAN, hæbban; *p.* hôf, *pl.* hôfon; *pp.* hafen, hæfen *To* HEAVE, *lift up, raise*:—Ic mîne handa tô ðê hebbe and þenige *expandi manus meas ad te*, Ps. Th. 87, 9. Tô ðê ic hæbbe mîn môd *ad te levavi animam meam*, 24, 1: Hine sylfne hefeþ on heáhne beám *raises itself into a lofty tree*, Exon. 57 b; Th. 205, 13; Ph. 112: Ps. Th. 148, 14. Forðon hiora heáfod hebbaþ *propterea exaltabit caput*, 109, 8. Tô ðê ic mîne eágan hôf *ad te levavi oculos meos*, 122, 1. Hôfon hlûde stefne *raised a loud voice*, Cd. 170; Th. 214, 24; Exod. 574: Exon. 45 b; Th. 156, 8; Gû. 871. Hefe ðû ðîne handa *leva manum tuam*, Ps. Th. 73, 4. Hebbaþ upp eówre eágan *levate oculos vestros*, Jn. Skt. 4, 35. God bebeád his englum be ðê ðæt hî ðê healdon and on heora handum hebban *God has given his angels charge concerning thee, that they may preserve thee and lift thee up in their hands*, Homl. Th. i. 516, 30. Siððan ic hond and rond hebban mihte *since I could lift hand and shield*, Beo. Th. 1317; B. 656. Hê wæs upp hafen engla fæðmum *he was lifted up in angels' bosoms*, Exon. 17 a; Th. 41, 5; Cri. 651: 756; Th. 284, 7; Jul. 693. Wæs wôp hæfen *then was a cry raised*, Andr. Kmbl. 2311; An. 1157: Beo. Th. 6038; B. 3023. [*Goth.* hafjan: *O. Sax.* hebbian: *O. Frs.* heva: *Icel.* hefja: *O. H. Ger.* heffan, heuen *levare, extollere*: *Ger.* heben.]

hebbendlíc; *adj. Exalted*; exaltatus, Rtl. 181, 27.

hebel, hebeld, heben. v. hefel, hefeld, heofon.

Hebrêisc; *adj. Hebrew*:—On Hebrêisc specan *to speak in Hebrew*, Nicod. 4; Thw. 2, 28. v. Ebrêisc.

HÉDAN; *p.* de *To* HEED, *take care, observe, attend, guard, take charge, take possession, receive*:—Lazarus ne môste ǽr on lîfe hêdan ðæra crumena his mýsan *before when alive Lazarus might not take the crumbs of his table*, Homl. Th. i. 330, 31. Wê hêdaþ ðæra crumena ðæs hlâfes and ða Judêiscan gnagaþ ða rinde *we take the crumbs of the bread and the Jews gnaw the crust*, ii. 114, 33. Ða Judêiscan ne hêdaþ nâ mâre bûton ðære stæflîcan gereccednesse *the Jews pay attention to nothing but the literal narrative*, 116, 4. Ne hêdde hê ðæs heafolan *he was not careful for his head*, Beo. Th. 5387; B. 2697. Bôte gesâwon hêddon hereréafes *they saw their compensation, took possession of the war spoils*, Cd. 171; Th. 215, 14; Exod. 583. Hêde seðe scire healde ðæt hê wite â hwæt eald landrǽden sý *videat qui scyrum tenet, ut semper sciat que sit antiqua terrarum institutio*, L. R. S. 4; Th. i. 434, 32. Ðonne him forþsîþ gebyrige hêde se hlâford ðæs hê lǽfe *when he dies let the lord take possession of what he leaves* [cf. 434, 27], 436, 9: L. In. 74; Th. i. 148, 19. Bisceopum gebyreþ ðæt hî hunda ne hafeca hêdan tô swýðe *it is befitting for bishops not to care too much for hounds or hawks*, L. I. P. 10; Th. ii. 316, 30. Gif ðâr nân man ne biþ ðe ðære heofonlîcan bodunge hêdan wille *if there be no man there that will heed the heavenly preaching*, Homl. Th. ii. 534, 16. [*O. Sax.* hôdian *to take care of, guard*: *O.H.Ger.* huoten *custodire, observare*: *Ger.* hüten.]

hed-clâþ, es; *m. A thick upper garment of coarse material, like a chasuble*, Med. ex Quadr. 4, 17; Lchdm. i. 346, 17. v. heden.

hêdd-, hýdd-ern, es; *n. A storehouse*:—Hýddern *cellarium*, Wrt. Voc. 83, 5. Hêddern *penu*, Ælfc. Gr. 11; Som. 15, 30: *poenum*, 13; Som. 16, 7. Besceáwiaþ ða hrefnas ðæt hig ne sâwaþ ne ne rîpaþ nabbaþ hig hêddern ne bern *considerate corbos quia non seminant neque metunt quibus non est cellarium neque horreum*, Lk. Skt. 12, 24. Swâ swâ mon hêddern ontýnde ðara swêtestena wyrta ðe on middangearde wǽron *quasi opobalsami cellaria esse viderentur aperta*, Bd. 3, 8; S. 532, 19. Drihten sent bletsunga ofer ðîne hêddernu *the Lord shall send blessings upon thy storehouses*, Deut. 28, 8.

heden, es; *m. A hood, chasuble*:—Heden *casla*, Cot. 32, Lye. Sacerd ðonne hê mæssan singe ne hæbbe hê on heden ne cæppan *sacerdos cum missam cantat ne portet cucullum nec cappam*, L. Ecg. C. 9; Th. ii. 140, 9. Swâ hwylc swâ wile lectiones rǽdan ne biþ hê nýded tô ðon ðæt hê him ofdô his oferhacelan oððe heden ac gyf hê euangelium rǽde wyrpe him of heden oððe cæppan on his gescyldro *quicunque lectiones legere velit, non necesse est ei cappam suam vel cucullum exuere; si autem evangelium legit, cucullum vel cappam super humeros dejiciat*, 20–24. Hæðen *mastruca*, Lye. [Cf. hede *dress*, Halliw. Dict: *Icel.* hêðinn, a *jacket of fur* or *skin*.]

hefe, es; *m. Weight*:—Hû mihte hê gefrêdan ǽniges hefes swǽrnysse ðâ ðâ hê ðone ferode ðe hine bær *how could he feel the heaviness of any weight when he carried one who bore him*, Homl. Th. i. 336, 26. Swilce hê bûton hefe wǽre *as if he were without weight*, ii. 164, 35. On gemete and on hefe and on getale *in mensura et pondere et numero*, 586, 32. Hê micelne hefe gefrêt æt hys heortan *he feels a great weight at his heart*, Lchdm. iii. 126, 10. Âwend hefas leahtra *evente moles criminum*, Hymn. Surt. 23, 7.

hefeld, hebeld, hefel, hebel, es; *m.* [?] *Thread for weaving*:—Hefeld *licium*, Ælfc. Gl. 110; Som. 79, 50; Wrt. Voc. 59, 21. [Hevel *fine twine*, Halliw. Dict: cf. *Icel.* hefill; *m. the clew-lines* and *bunt lines of a sail*.]

hefeld-gyrd, e; *f. A weaver's shuttle*; liciatorium, Cot. 120, Lye.

hefeldian, hefaldian *to fix the weft or woof*:—Ic hefaldige *ordior*, Ælfc. Gl. 111; Som. 79, 73; Wrt. Voc. 59, 42.

hefeld-, hefel-þrǽd, es; *m. A thread for weaving*; licium:—Gewrîð tô ânum hefel [MSS. H. B. hefeld] þrǽde *bind it to a yarn thread*, Herb. 183; Lchdm. i. 320, 6. Ðâ tôbræc hê ða râpas swâ swâ hefelþrǽdas *and he brake the withs as a thread of tow*, Jud. 16, 9. Hefelþrǽd *licium*, Cot. 193, Lye.

hefe-lîc, *adj. Weighty, heavy, grievous, serious, grave, tedious, wearisome*:—Ðǽr nân hefelîc gefeoht ne wearþ *no serious fighting took place there*, Chr. 868; Erl. 72, 28. Se cyng lêt beódan mycel gyld and hefelîc *the king had a great and grievous tax proclaimed*, 1083; Erl. 217, 34. Ðæs ilcan geáres wæs swîðe hefelîc geár *it was a very grievous year that same year*, 1085; Erl. 219, 18. For hefelîcum gyltum *pro gravibus peccatis*, L. Ecg. P. i. 6; Th. ii. 174, 17. Nû bidde ic ða ðe hit cunnon and ðis rǽdon ðæt hit him hefelîc ne beó *now I beg that my explanation may not be tedious to those who know the subject and read this*, Lchdm. iii. 280, 10.

hefe-lîce; *adv. Heavily, exceedingly, seriously, with difficulty*:—Hig hefelîce mid eárum gehýrdon *auribus graviter audierunt*, Mt. Kmbl. 13, 15. For ðære ilcan eádmôdnesse hê ofermôdgaþ innan micle ðý hefelîcor *de hac ipsa humilitate graviter interius superbitur*, Past. 43, 3; Swt. 313, 3: 46, 5; Swt. 351, 6.

hefe-tîme; *adj. Troublesome, displeasing, tedious*:—Hit þuhte Moise swîðe hefetîme *Moses was displeased*, Num. 11, 10. v. hefig-tîme.

HEFIG, hefeg; *adj.* HEAVY, *weighty, oppressive, grievous, difficult, serious, grieved, important*; gravis, molestus:—Wæs torn were hefig æt heortan *in the man's heart was grievous anger*, Cd. 47; Th. 60, 11; Gen. 980. Suîðe hefig is *quam difficile est*, Mk. Skt. Lind. 10, 24. Hit swîðe hefegu scyld is *it is a very grievous crime*, L. E. I. 27; Th. ii. 422, 36. Bûtan hefegum gefeohte *without heavy fighting*; sine ullo prælio, Bd. 1, 3; S. 475, 11. Âhôfon hine of ðam hefian wîte *they lifted him off that heavy punishment*, Rood Kmbl. 121; Kr. 61. Heó is hefegou swæce *it is of unpleasant smell*, Herb. 151, 1; Lchdm. i. 276, 9: 143, 1; Lchdm. i. 264, 20. Wermôd drincan sace hefige hit getâcnaþ *to drink wormwood betokens a serious dispute*, Lchdm. iii. 198, 24: Herb. 132, 7; Lchdm. i. 248, 11. Tô hwon syndon gê ðyses weorces swâ hefige *why are you so grieved at this work*, Blickl. Homl. 69, 15. Wurdon mê on yrre yfele and hefige *in ira molesti erant mihi*, Ps. Th. 54, 3. Hig bindaþ hefige byrðyna *alligant onera gravia*, Mt. Kmbl. 23, 4. Eorþe is hefige óðrum gesceaftum *earth is heavier than the other elements*, Bt. Met. Fox 20, 265; Met. 20, 133. Wê mâgon geþencean ðæt ðæt hefigre is ðæt man mid synnum him sylfum geearnige edwît *we may consider, what is more important, that with sins a man may get disgrace for himself*, Blickl. Homl. 101, 24. Ða þing ðe synt hefegran ðære ǽ *quæ graviora sunt legis*, Mt. Kmbl. 23, 23. Hî eów hefigran wîsan budon tô healdanne ðonne wê him budon *they commanded you to keep a harder rule than we commanded them*, L. Ælf. 49; Th. i. 56, 15. Wið fôtâdle deáh ðe heó hefegust sȳ *for gout, though it be very bad*, Herb. 132, 4; Lchdm. i. 246, 22. Mid đon gewunon đære heofogoston gewemmednesse synna *with the habit of the most grievous impurity of sins*, Blickl. Homl. 75, 6. [*O.Sax.* hebig: *O.H.Ger.* hebic, heuig *gravis, arduus, molestus.*]

hefige; *adv. Heavily, grievously, with difficulty, hardly*:—Đæs wīte eft on eówre handa hefige geeode *for that punishment came upon you heavily*, Ps. Th. 57, 2. Hefia *vix*, Lk. Skt. Lind. 9, 39. Forhwon āhēnge đū mec hefgor *why didst thou crucify me more painfully*, Exon. 29 b; Th. 91, 6; Gen. 1488. [*O.H.Ger.* heuigor *gravius.*]

hefigian; *p.* ode. I. *to make heavy, oppress, grieve, afflict, vex*:—Forđon sió byrđen đære sconde hine diógollīce hefegaþ *quia gravit hunc in abditis pondus turpe*, Past. 11, 7; Swt. 73, 15. Đone mete đe hine hefegaþ on his breóstum *cibum, qui pectus deprimebat*, 54, 1; Swt. 419, 29. Đa đe mē hefigiaþ *those who vex me*, Ps. Th. 37, 12. Wæs heó eft hefigod mid đām ǣrran sārum *erat prioribus aggravata doloribus*, Bd. 4, 19; S. 589, 5. Wolde mē hefigad beón mid sāre mīnes sweoran *me dolore colli voluit gravari*, 589, 28. II. *to become heavy, to be aggravated* or *increased, to be burdened* or *oppressed*:—Hū sió byrđen wiexþ and hefegaþ *molem crescentis tentationis*, Past. 21, 5; Swt. 163, 12. Seó untrumnys dæghwamlīce weóx and hefegode *languor per dies ingravescebat*, Bd. 4, 3; S. 568, 38. Monigum monnum đe heora eágan sārgedon and hefegodan *nonnulis oculos dolentibus*, 4, 19; S. 589, 35: Exon. 46 b; Th. 159, 20; Gū. 929: 47 b; Th. 163, 32; Gū. 1002. [*Laym.* heueȝe *to grow heavy, slumber*: *A. R.* heuegeþ *oppresses*: *Chauc.* hevieþ: *Prompt. Parv.* hevyyng *mestificio, gravo, aggravo, pondero.*]

hefig-līc; *adj. Grievous, troublesome*:—Ne sig đē hefilīc geþuht đæt đæt Sarra đē sǣde *let not that be grievous in thy sight which Sarah hath said*, Gen. 21, 12. Gif se līchoma hwǣr mid hefiglīcre hǣto sȳ gebysgod *if the body be anywhere troubled with inflammation*, Herb. 2, 6; Lchdm. i. 82, 8.

hefig-līce; *adv. Heavily, grievously*; graviter:—Abraham undernam hefiglīce đās word *the thing was very grievous in Abraham's sight*, Gen. 21, 11. Hefiglīce *graviter*, Mt. Kmbl. Lind. 13, 15. Hefilīce, Lk. Skt. 11, 53. Đa weras mon sceal hefiglecor and stīđlecor lǣran and đa wīf leóhtlecor *illis* [*viri*] *graviora, istis* [*feminæ*] *injungenda sunt leviora*, Past. 24; Swt. 179, 16.

hefig-mōd; *adj. Evil-minded, oppressive*:—Hefigmōde *molesti*, Ps. Spl. T. 54, 3.

hefig-ness, e; *f. Heaviness, slowness, weight, grief, affliction*:—Nān hæfignes đæs līchoman ne mæg eallunga ātión of his mōde đa rihtwīsnesse *no heaviness of the body can altogether take away rectitude from his mind*, Bt. 35, 1; Fox 154, 29: 156, 12. Ne geman heó đære hefinysse *non meminit pressuræ*, Jn. Skt. 16, 21. Yfelra ūserra hefignisse *malorum nostrorum pondere*, Rtl. 15, 30: Mt. Kmbl. Lind. 20, 12. Hefignise gebær *ægrotationes portavit*, 8, 17.

hefig-tīme, -tȳme; *adj. Grievous, wearisome, tedious, troublesome*:—Hefigtȳme leahter is ungefōh fyrwitnys *immoderate curiosity is a troublesome vice*, Homl. Th. ii. 374, 2. Gif hit is hefigtȳme on đyssere woruldè hit becymþ tō micelre mēde on đære tōweardan *if it is productive of trouble in this world, it attains to a great reward in that which is to come*, i. 56, 4: Ælfc. Gen. Thw. p. 1, 6. Ne þince đē tō hefitȳme tō gehȳrenne mīne sprǣce *do not let it seem too tedious to thee to hear my speech*, Basil admn. 7; Norm. 48, 12. Se hefigtīma cwide đe se wītega gecwæþ be sumum leódscipe *the grievous sentence that the prophet declared concerning a certain nation*, Swt. A. S. Rdr. 73, 543. Đa wudewan fram hefigtīmum heáfodece gehǣlde *healed the widow of a wearisome headache*, Homl. Th. i. 418, 22.

hefigtīmness, e; *f. Trouble, affliction, vexation*:—Đone hē tealde him tō frȳnd đe him sume hefigtȳmnysse on belǣdde *him he accounted his friend who brought some trouble upon him*, Homl. Th. ii. 546, 19. Hē is nū mid ylde ofsett, swylce mid gelomlǣcendum hefigtȳmnyssum tō deáþe geþreád *it is now oppressed with age, as if wearied to death with frequent troubles*, i. 614, 21.

hefung, e; *f. Heaving, lifting up*; elevatio, speculatio, Lye.

HEG, hig, es; *n. Hay, grass*; fœnum:—Heg [Rush. hoeg] londes *fœnum agri*, Mt. Kmbl. Lind. 6, 30. Đā bebeád se hǣlend đæt đæt folc sǣte ofer đæt grēne hig *præcipit illis ut accumbere facerent omnes super viride fœnum*, Mk. Skt. 6, 39. Heig [Rush. heg] *fœnum*, Jn. Skt. Lind. 6, 10. Đǣr nǣnig mann for wintres cȳle on sumera heg ne māweþ *nemo propter hiemem fœna secet æstate*, Bd. 1, 1; S. 474, 32. Dō hig on đīn beđ *put hay on your bed*, Lchdm. iii. 178, 6. Wē gesāwon oft in cyrcean ǣgđer ge corn ge hig beón gehealdene *we have often seen both corn and hay kept in the church*, L. E. I. 8; Th. ii. 406, 30. [*Laym.* hey, heie: *Chauc.* hei, hai: *Goth.* hawi: *Icel.* hey: *O.H.Ger.* hewi, howe, hou *fœnum*: *Ger.* heu.]

HEGE, es; *m. A* HEDGE, *fence*:—Hege *sepes*, Wrt. Voc. 84, 56: Ælfc. Gr. 9, 27; Som. 11, 24. Bebbanburh wæs ǣrost mid hegge betīned and đǣræfter mid wealle *Bamborough was first enclosed with a hedge and afterwards with a wall*, Chr. 547; Erl. 17, 9. Gā geond đās wegas and hegas *exi in vias et sepes*, Lk. Skt. 14, 23. Đū tōwurpe ealle hegas his *destruxisti omnes sepes ejus*, Ps. Spl. 88, 39. Gif hryđera hwelc sīe đe hegas brece *if there be any beast that breaks hedges*, L. In. 42; Th. i. 128, 12. Mid heora hegum đe hī ymbsette wǣron *cum septis quibus erant circumdata*, Bd. 2, 13; S. 516, 39: Homl. Th. ii. 448, 22. From hegum *a silvis*, Rtl. 118, 35. [Hay, hey *in provincial words*, e. g. heybote, hayboot = hedgeboot *the right of getting wood for mending fences*, Engl. Dial. Soc. vols. iii. vi. Haies, hays *ridges of lands as district boundaries*, vol. iv: *Prompt. Parv.* hedge, hegge.] v. hæg- *and* haga.

hege-clife, an; *f. Hedge clivers*; galium aparine, L. M. 1, 9; Lchdm. ii. 54, 8.

hegegian *to hedge, fence*, L. R. S. 2; Th. i. 432, 16.

hege-rǣwe, -rēwe, e; *f. A hedge-row*:—Đanon on đa hegerǣwe *thence to the hedge row*, Cod. Dipl. Kmbl. ii. 54, 11. Hegerēwe, iii. 48, 15.

hege-rife, an; *f. Heyriffe*; galium aparine, Lchdm. iii. Gloss. [*Prompt. Parv.* hayryf *rubea vel rubea minor, et major dicitur* madyr. v. note, p. 221. See English Plant-names, Engl. Dial. Soc. no. 26, p. 242 harif.]

heges-sugge *a hedge-sparrow*, Ælfc. Gl. 37; Som. 63, 5; Wrt. Voc. 29, 28. [*O. and N.* hei-sugge: *Flower and Leaf* hay-sogge; *Gloucestershire dialect* hay suck.]

heg-, hig-hūs, es; *n. A hay-house*; fœnile, Ælfc. Gl. 109; Som. 79, 20; Wrt. Voc. 58, 60.

heg-, hege-stōw, e; *f. A place enclosed by a hedge* [?], Cod. Dipl. Kmbl. iii. 77, 27: 213, 8, 9: 263, 23, 26.

hēh. v. heáh.

hel [?] *a pretext*:—Mid yfelan helan earme men beswīcaþ *with evil pretexts defraud poor men*, L. I. P. 12; Th. ii. 320, 18. [Cf. *O.H.Ger.* hal *tegmen*, Grff. iv. 844.]

HEL, hell, helle, e; *f.* HELL, *the place of souls after death, Hades, the infernal regions, the place of the wicked after death*:—Helle *infernus*, Ælfc. Gl. 54; Som. 63, 103; Wrt. Voc. 36, 24: Ælfc. Gr. 8; Som. 11, 34. Satanas đære helle ealdor cwæþ tō đære helle . . . Seó hell swīđe grymme andswarode *Satan the ruler of Hell said to Hell . . . Hell answered very fiercely*, Nicod. 26; Thw. 13, 32, 40. In đæt hāte hof đam is hel nama *into that hot abode whose name is hell*, Cd. 217; Th. 276, 24; Sat. 193. Đonne heofon and hel hæleþa bearnum fylde weorþeþ *when heaven and hell shall be filled with the children of men*, Exon. 31 a; Th. 97, 17; Cri. 1592. Hel nimeþ wǣrleásra weorud *hell shall take the host of the faithless*, 31 b; Th. 98, 26; Cri. 1613. Him hel onfēng *hell received him*, Beo. Th. 1709; B. 852. Helle gatu *portæ inferi*, Mt. Kmbl. 16, 18. Helle bearn *filium gehennæ*, 23, 15. Fȳr byrnþ ōđ helle endas *a fire shall burn unto the lowest hell*, Deut. 32, 22. Ōđ helle *in infernum*, Mt. Kmbl. 11, 23. For đam đa deádan đe on helle beóþ đīn ne gemunan ne đē andetaþ swā swā wē dōþ *quoniam non est in morte qui memor sit tui: in inferno quis confitebitur tibi*, Ps. Th. 6, 4. On đære sweartan helle *in the black hell*, Cd. 35; Th. 47, 16; Gen. 761. Hig intō helle cuce sīđodon *they went down alive into the pit*, Num. 16, 33. Ic fare tō mīnum sunu tō helle *I will go down into the grave unto my son*, Gen. 37, 35. Uton nū brūcan đisses undernmetes swā đa sculon đe hiora ǣfengife on helle gefeccean sculon *prandete tanquam apud inferos cænaturi*, Ors. 2, 5; Swt. 86, 2. Swā đæt fȳr on đære helle seó is on đam munte đe Ætne hātte *as the fire on the hell that is in mount Ætna*, Bt. 15; Fox 48, 20. Hire sāwle mon sceolde lǣdan tō helle *her soul was to be conducted to hell*, 35, 6; Fox 168, 5. [*Goth.* halja *Hades*: *O. Sax.* hel, hellia: *O. Frs.* hille: *Icel.* hel (*local and personal*): *O.H.Ger.* hella *gehenna, infernus, baratrum*: *Ger.* hölle.] v. Grm. D. M. 288–92: 760–7. See compounds with helle.

hel- v. hell-.

HĒLA, hǣla, an; *m. The* HEEL:—Hēla *calx*, Wrt. Voc. 283, 75. Hēl *calcaneum*, Jn. Skt. Lind. 13, 18. Genim haran hēlan [hǣlan MSS. H. B.] *take hare's heel* [lat. *talum*], Med. ex Quadr. 4, 17; Lchdm. i. 346 16. Heó gehȳden hǣlun mīne *ipsi calcaneum meum observabunt*, Ps. Th. 55, 6. Gif đæt wīf mid đām hēlum stæpeþ *if the woman steps with the heels*, Lchdm. iii. 144, 14. [*O. Frs.* hēla, heila: *Icel.* hǣll.]

helan; *p.* hæl, *pl.* hǣlon; *pp.* holen *To conceal, hide, cover*:—Gif đū mē hylest đīne heortan geþohtas *if thou dost conceal from me thy heart's thoughts*, Exon. 88 b; Th. 333, 12; Gn. Ex. 3. Đonne eówaþ hē hī nalles ne hilþ *then it shews them and does not conceal them*, Bt. 27, 1; Fox 94, 26. Swā hwā swā hilþ his gōdan weorc *si bona quæ agit occultat*, Past. 59, 4; Swt. 449, 29. Đa đe hira gōd helaþ đe hie dōþ *qui bona que faciunt abscondunt*, 23; Swt. 179, 9. Ic hæl mīne scylda *I concealed my sins*, Ps. Th. 31, 3: L. E. I. 30; Th. ii. 426, 21. Đū heora fyrene fæste hǣle *operuisti omnia peccata eorum*, Ps. Th. 84, 2. Hē hit hæl swīđe fæste wiđ his brōđor *he concealed it very carefully from his brother*, Ors. 6, 33; Swt. 288, 14. Hē đæt hæl ǣrest sc̄e petre *he at first concealed that from St. Peter*, Shrn. 74, 20. Ealle đa đe đone gylt mid him wiston and mid him hǣlon *all those who were cognisant of that crime and joined with them in concealing it*, Ors. 4, 4; Bos. 80, 24. Hī hǣlon đæt hī forhelan ne mihton *they hid what they could not keep hidden*, Lchdm. i. 392, 4. Đū him fæste hel sōþan sprǣce *hide carefully from them true speech*, Cd. 89; Th. 110, 11; Gen. 1836. Nān ōđrum his þearfe ne hele *let no one conceal from another what it is needful for him to know*, L. I.

P. 10; Th. ii. 316, 20: Andr. Kmbl. 2329; An. 1166. Ða ðe willaþ helan ðæt hī tō gōde dōþ *qui bona clam faciunt*, Past. 59; Swt. 447, 23. Nele hē ūs nānwiht helan se ðe ūs lǣt hyne sylfne cunnan *he will not conceal anything from us who lets us know himself*, Shrn. 202, 12. Ic ne mæg leng helan be ðam līfes treó *I cannot longer conceal concerning the tree of life*, Elen. Kmbl. 1408; El. 706. [*Chauc.* hele: *A.R.* i-holen, *part. p*: hele *to cover*, in the Surrey dialect: *O.Sax.* helan: *O.Frs.* hela: *O.H.Ger.* helan *celare, tegere*: *Ger.* hehlen.] DER. be-, for-helan.

held. v. hyld.

heldan. v. hyldan.

helde, an; *f. Allegiance, fealty*:—Hē ðǣr on ðæs cynges willelmes heldan tō cynge gesette *he placed Edgar there as king in allegiance to King William*, Chr. 1097; Erl. 234, 37. Heanrig ofer sǣ fōr on ðæs cynges heldan *Henry went over sea as liege man of the king*, 1095; Erl. 231, 9. [Cf. un-helde; hyld, hyldo.]

helde, an; *f. Tansy*; tanacetum vulgare:—Helde *tanicetum*, Wrt. Voc. 79, 24: *tanaceta*, Ælfc. Gl. 40; Som. 63, 87; Wrt. Voc. 30, 33. Genim heldan *take tansy*, L. M. 1, 36; Lchdm. ii. 86, 20.

hele-. v. helle-.

helerung, e; *f. The turning of a balance*; trutinæ inclinatio, Cot. 136, Lye. v. helur-bled, heolorian, heolra.

helfe, es; *m. n.* [?] *Helve, handle*:—Hæft and helfe *manubrium*, Ælfc. Gl. 52; Som. 66, 31; Wrt. Voc. 35, 20. Sió æcs āwient of ðæm hielfe *ferrum lapsum de manubrio*, Past. 21, 7; Swt. 167, 1. Gaderode me hylfa tō ǣlcum ðara tōla ðe ic mid wircan cūðe *I gathered me handles for each of the tools that I could work with*, Shrn. 163, 6. [*Orm.* hellfe: *Prompt. Parv.* helve *manubrium*: *Wick.* helve: *O.H.Ger.* halap, halp, halbe, helbe *manubrium*. *Helve* is a word given as still belonging to the dialects of East Anglia.]

helfling, es; *m. A halfpenny*:—Ne becȳpaþ hig fīf spearwan tō helflinge *are not five sparrows sold for two farthings*, Lk. Skt. 12, 6. [*O.H.Ger.* helbeling *obolus*.]

helian; *p.* ode, ede *To hide, conceal, cover*:—Mīn unriht ic nā ne helede wið ðē *injustitias meas non operui*, Ps. Th. 31, 5. Heó helode hire nebb ðæt hē hig ne mihte gecnāwan *she had covered her face that he might not know her*, Gen. 38, 15. Wē lǣraþ ðæt ǣnig gehādod man his sceare ne helige *we enjoin that no man in orders conceal his tonsure*, L. Edg. C. 47; Th. ii. 254, 13. [*A.R.* helien: *Piers P.* helien, hylien; *pp.* helid, hiled: *Laym.* helede, *p*: *Wick.* hilide: *O. Sax.* bi-helian: *O.H.Ger.* hellen: *Ger.* hehlen.]

hell. v. hel.

hell-bend; *m. f. A hell-bond*:—Hellbendum fæst *fast in the chains of hell*, Beo. Th. 6137; B. 3072.

hell-cræft, es; *m. Hellish art*, Andr. Kmbl. 2205; An. 1104.

hell-cwalu, e; *f. Hell-torment*, Exon. 25 a; Th. 73, 15; Cri. 1190.

hell-deóful, es; *m. n. Orcus, Pluto*, Cot. 145, Lye.

hell-dor, es; *n. The gate of hell*:—Tō helldore *in infernum*, Ps. Th. 87, 3. Æt heldore, Exon. 40 b; Th. 135, 29; Gū. 531: Cd. 19; Th. 24, 20; Gen. 380: 23; Th. 29, 8; Gen. 447. [*O.Sax.* hell-dor.]

helle-. *In the case of at least some of the following words which are given as compounds, they might be taken as independent words, the first of which is the genitive of* hel. *For the meaning of such combinations the second word may be referred to.*

helle-bealu; *gen.* wes; *n. Hell-bale, woe of hell*, Exon. 28 b; Th. 87, 18; Cri. 1427.

helle-brōga, an; *m. The terror of hell*:—On hellebrōgan gesette hī syndon *in inferno positi sunt*, Ps. Lamb. 48, 15. Of handa hellebrōgan *de manu inferi*, 48, 16.

helle-bryne, es; *m. Hell-fire*, Judth. 10; Th. 23, 11; Jud. 116.

helle-ceafl, es; *m. The jaws of hell*, Andr. Kmbl. 3403; An. 1705.

helle-cinn, es; *n. The race of hell*, Exon. 31 b; Th. 99, 5; Cri. 1620.

helle-clam, -clom, Cd. 19; Th. 24, 6; Gen. 373. v. clam.

helle-deóful, -dióful, Exon. 75 a; Th. 280, 15; Jul. 629: Elen. Kmbl. 1799; El. 901: Andr. Kmbl. 2598; An. 1300. [Cf. hell-deóful.]

helle-dor, Exon. 121 a; Th. 464, 14; Hö. 87. [Cf. hell-dor.]

helle-duru, Elen. Kmbl. 2457; El. 1230.

helle-flōr, Cd. 214; Th. 269, 9; Sat. 70.

helle-fȳr, Bt. Met. Fox 8, 101; Met. 8, 51; Exon. 26 b; Th. 78, 6; Cri. 1270. On helle fȳr *in gehennam ignis*, Mt. Kmbl. 18, 9. [*O.H.Ger.* hella-fiur *gehenna, tartarus*.]

helle-gāst, -gǣst, Exon. 72 a; Th. 269, 28; Jul. 457: 74 b; Th. 279, 17; Jul. 615: Beo. Th. 2552; B. 1274.

helle-geat, -gat, Homl. Th. i. 288, 1, 4.

helle-god, es; *n. A god of the infernal regions*:—Orfeus wolde gesēcan hellegodu and biddan ðæt hī him āgeáfan eft his wīf *Orfeus would visit the gods of the infernal regions and pray them to give him his wife again*, Bt. 35, 6; Fox 168, 13. [*O. H. Ger.* hella-got *pluto, dis*; *pl. eumenides, manes*.]

helle-grund, Exon. 11 b; Th. 17, 4; Cri. 265: 16 a; Th. 35, 23; Cri. 562: Elen. Kmbl. 2608; El. 1305. [*O.Sax.* helli-grund: *O.H.Ger.* hella-grunt *tartarus*.]

helle-grut *the abyss of hell*, Hpt. Gl. 422. v. grut.

helle-, hylle-gryre, Cd. 223; Th. 291, 20; Sat. 433.

helle-hæft, Cd. 227; Th. 304, 16; Sat. 631.

helle-hæfta, Beo. Th. 1580; B. 788.

helle-hæftling, Andr. Kmbl. 2683; An. 1344: Exon. 69 a; Th. 257, 12; Jul. 246: Salm. Kmbl. 253; Sal. 126.

helle-heáf, Cd. 2; Th. 3, 19; Gen. 38.

helle-hinca, an; *m. The hell-limper, -hobbler, the devil lamed by his fall from heaven*, Andr. Kmbl. 2343; An. 1173. Grimm [Deutsche Mythologie, 944–5] speaking of the devil observes 'Am ersten fällt sein lahmer fuss auf, daher der *hinkende teufel* [diable boiteux], *hinkebein*, vom sturz aus dem himmel in den abgrund der hölle scheint er gelähmt, wie der von Zeus herabgeschleuderte Hephäst.' [Cf. *Icel.* hinka: *O.H.Ger.* hinkan *claudicare*.]

helle-hund, es; *m. A hell-hound*:—Sȳ hē Judas geféra Cristes belǣwendes and sȳ hē toren of hellehundes tōþum on ðām egeslīcum hellewītum mid eallum deóflum būtan ǣlcum ende būtan hē hit ǣr his endedæge rihtlīce gebēte *may he be the companion of Judas the betrayer of Christ, and be torn by the teeth of a hell-hound in the awful torments of hell among all the devils without any end, unless he make due reparation before his last day*, Cod. Dipl. Kmbl. iii. 350, 18. [Cf. sceolde cuman ðære helle hund ongeán hine ðæs nama wæs Ceruerus *it was said that the hound of hell, whose name was Cerberus, came towards him*, Bt. 35, 6; Fox 168, 15.] v. Grimm. D. M. 948–9.

helle-hūs, Exon. 42 b; Th. 142, 24; Gū. 649.

helle-līc; *adj. Infernal*:—Helelīc deópnes *barathrum, vorago, profunda*, Ælfc. Gl. 54; Som. 66, 97; Wrt. Voc. 36, 20. [*O. H. Ger.* helle-līch *tartareus*.] v. hel-līc.

helle-mere, es; *m. The lake of hell, Styx*:—Hellemere *hæc styx*, Ælfc. Gr. 9; Som. 14, 13. Helemere *Styx*, Ælfc. Gl. 54; Som. 66, 99; Wrt. Voc. 36, 22.

helle-nīþ, Cd. 37; Th. 48, 13; Gen. 775.

helle-rūne, an; *f. One who is skilled in the mysteries of hell, the region of the dead, a sorceress, necromancer*:—Hellerūne *pythonissa*, Ælfc. Gl. 112; Som. 79, 102; Wrt. Voc. 60, 10. [*O.H.Ger.* hellirūna *necromantia*: v. Grm. D. M. 1175, 1178.] v. hell-rūna.

helle-scealc, Cd. 216; Th. 273, 8; Sat. 133.

helle-sceaþa, Elen. Kmbl. 1911; El. 957. v. hell-sceaþa.

helle-seáþ, es; *m. The pit of hell*:—Helleseáþ [Som. sceað] *erebum*, Ælfc. Gl. 54; Som. 66, 98; Wrt. Voc. 36, 21: Exon. 71 b; Th. 267, 29; Jul. 422.

helle-þegn, Exon. 48 a; Th. 166, 14; Gū. 1042.

helle-wīte, es; *n. Hell-torment, punishment, hell*:—Hellewīte *tartara* vel *gehenna*, Ælfc. Gl. 54; Som. 66, 100; Wrt. Voc. 36, 23. Se for ðam mēde onfēhþ ēcum tintregum hellewītes *æternas inferni pœnas pro mercede recipiet*, Bd. 1, 7; S. 477, 40: Hy. 6, 36; Hy. Grn. ii. 286, 36. Mid heardum hellewītum *with hard pains of hell*, Soul Kmbl. 94; Seel. 47: 64; Seel. 32: Andr. Kmbl. 2106; An. 1054. [*O. Sax.* helliwīti *hell-torment*: *Icel.* hel-vīti: *Dan.* helvede *hell*: *O. H. Ger.* hellawīzi *gehenna, tartara*.]

hell-firen, e; *f. A hellish crime*, Exon. 98 a; Th. 366, 3; Reb. 6.

hell-fūs; *adj. Bound for hell*, Andr. Kmbl. 99; An. 50: Exon. 24 a; Th. 69, 21; Cri. 1124.

hell-geþwing, es; *n. The restraint, constraint of hell*:—Se hellsceaða wiste ðæt hie sceoldon hellgeþwin[g] niéde onfōn *the devil knew that they must needs receive the restraint of hell*, Cd. 33; Th. 43, 20; Gen. 696. [*O. Sax.* helli-geþwing.]

hell-heóþo; *indecl*; *f. Hell*, Cd. 228; Th. 308, 29; Sat. 700. v. heóþu.

hel-līc; *adj. Hellish, infernal*:—Ðeós hellīce sūsl *hic tartarus*, Ælfc. Gr. 13; Som. 16, 29; Homl. Th. ii. 78, 20. Seó fæstnung ðære hellīcan clȳsinge ne geþafaþ ðæt hī ǣfre ūtābrecon *the fastening of the enclosure of hell does not permit them ever to break out*, i. 332, 20: ii. 80, 6. Wē wǣron mid eallum ūrum fæderum on ðære hellīcan deópnysse *we were with all our fathers in the deep of hell*, Nicod. 24; Thw. 12, 19. Ða hellīcan fȳnd *the fiends of hell*, Homl. Th. i. 380, 27.

hell-rūna, an; *m. One skilled in the mysteries of hell, a sorcerer, necromancer*, Beo. Th. 328; B. 163. v. helle-rūne.

hell-sceaða, an; *m. A hell-harmer, fiend, devil*, Cd. 33; Th. 43, 22; Gen. 694: Exon. 13 a; Th. 23, 5; Cri. 364: Byrht. Th. 137, 2; By. 180.

hell-træf, es; *m. A hellish, infernal building*, Andr. Kmbl. 3379; An. 1693.

hell-trega, an; *m. Hell-torment*, Cd. 4; Th. 5, 18; Gen. 73.

hell-waran; *pl. The inhabitants of hell*:—Ðās hellwaran *hi manes*, Ælfc. Gr. 13; Som. 16, 14. Him urnon ealle hellwaran ongeán *all the inhabitants of hell ran to meet him*, Bt. 35, 6; Fox 168, 29. Hlōgan helwaran *the dwellers in hell laughed*, Exon. 120 a; Th. 460, 22; Hö. 21. Ðū mīne sāwle ālȳsdest of helwarena hinderþeóstrum *eripuisti animam meam ex inferno inferiori*, Ps. Th. 85, 12: 140, 9. Helwarena stefn wæs gehȳred *the voice of hell's people was heard*, Blickl. Homl.

87, 3. Cýðnise hellwarana *testamentum inferorum*, Rtl. 11, 9. Tō hellwarum *ad inferos*, 101, 16. Ne forlǣt ðū mīne sāwle mid hellwarum *leave not my soul in hell*, Blickl. Homl. 87, 33. v. hell-ware, -waru.

hell-ware, -wara; *pl. The inhabitants of hell*:—Ealle gesceafta heofonwara eorþwara helwara onbūgaþ Criste *all creatures, those in heaven, those on earth, those in hell, bow to Christ*, Homl. Th. ii. 362, 1: i. 36, 26. Ealle hellwara *all the inmates of hell*, Exon. 121 b; Th. 466, 18; Hö. 123. Wuldorweorudes and helwara *of the glorious host and of the dwellers in hell*, Exon. 12 a; Th. 18, 20; Cri. 286: 114 a; Th. 437, 12; Rä. 56, 6. v. hell-waru.

hell-waru, e; *f. The body of inhabitants in hell*:—On ðam mycelan dōme ðǣr heofonwaru and eorþwaru and helwaru beóþ ealle gesomnode *in magno judicio ubi cælicolæ et terricolæ et inferi omnes congregabuntur*, L. Ecg. C. pref; Th. ii. 132, 22: Hy. 7, 95; Grn. ii. 289, 95. Tō ðare helware [or ðara helwara (?)] stīðe pīnnesse *to the severe torment of the people of hell*, Chart. Th. 369, 34. [Cf. burh-ware, -waru, -wara.]

HELM, es; *m.* I. *a* HELM, *helmet*:—Leðer helm *galea*: īren helm *cassis*, Ælfc. Gl. 51; Som. 66, 13, 14; Wrt. Voc. 35, 3, 4. Helmes camb *crista*: helmes býge *conus*, 53; Som. 66, 76, 77; Wrt. Voc. 36, 2, 3. Se hwīta, hearda helm, Beo. Th. 2900, 4502; B. 1448, 2255. II. *a crown, the top, overshadowing foliage of trees*:—Helm *corona*, Wrt. Voc. 64, 39. Mid þyrnenum helme his heáfod befēngon *encircled his head with a crown of thorns*, Homl. Th. ii. 252, 26; Mk. Skt. 15, 17. Ful oft unc holt wrugon wudubeáma helm *full oft the wood covered us the shady top of the forest trees*, Exon. 129 a; Th. 496, 2; Rä. 85, 8. Ðæt se stemn and se helm mōte ðý fæstor and ðý leng standon *that the stem and top may stand the faster and longer*, Bt. 34, 10; Fox 148, 33: Fox 150, 3. Hire hyrdeman sume āc āstāh and his orf læswode mid treowenum helme *her herdsman had ascended an oak and was feeding his cattle with its woody crown*, Homl. Th. ii. 150, 31. Forðæm se þorn ðære gītsunga ne wyrþ forsearod on ðæm helme gif se wyrttruma ne biþ færcorfen oððe forbærned æt ðæm stemne *si enim radix culpæ in ipsa effusione non exuritur, numquam per ramos exuberans avaritiæ spina siccatur*, Past. 45, 3; Swt. 341, 10: Runic pm. 18; Kmbl. 342, 31; Hick. Thes. i. 135. III. *a covering* [in this sense the word is preserved in some dialects. Thus in Yorkshire and Lincolnshire Glossaries, English Dial. Soc. vols. ii. v. vi, *helm*, a hovel, an open shed for cattle, a shed built on posts]:—Wǣges helm [holm ?] *the covering made by the wave, the sea*, Elen. Kmbl. 459; El. 230. Under lyfte helm *under the air's covering*, Exon. 102 a; Th. 386, 19; Rä. 4, 64. Helme gedýgled *concealed with a covering*, 1226; Th. 470, 10; Hy. 11, 33. IV. *in poetry the word is applied to persons, thus God and Christ are spoken of as* æþelinga, hæleþa, hāligra, duguþa, dryhtfolca, engla, gāsta, heofona, heofonrīces, wuldres helm *and* helm wera, ælwihta. *Similar phrases occur in speaking of earthly rulers*, æþelinga, heriga, lidmanna, wedra, weoruda helm and helm Scyldinga, Scylfinga. [*Goth.* hilms *a helmet*: *O. Sax.* helm: *Icel.* hjālmr: *O. H. Ger.* helm, *galea, cassis*: *Ger.* helm.] DER. bān-, grīm-, gūþ-, hæleþ-, heaþu-, heoloþ-, lyft-, mist-, niht-, sceadu-, sund-, wæter-helm.

Helma, an; *m. A* HELM, *rudder*:—Helma *clavus*, Ælfc. Gl. 104; Som. 77, 124; Wrt. Voc. 56, 42. Be ðæm is swīðe sweotol ðætte God ǣghwæs wealt mid ðæm helman his gōdnesse *Deus omnia bonitatis clavo gubernare jure credatur*, Bt. 35, 4; Fox 160, 14. [*Icel.* hjālm; *f.*]

helm-berend, es; *m. One who wears a helmet*:—Ne rōhte hē helmberendra *he recked not of helmeted warriors*, Exon. 120 a; Th. 461, 18; Hö. 37. Gegrētte hwate helmberend *he greeted the bold warriors*, Beo. Th. 5027; B. 2517: 5277; B. 2642. [*O. Sax.* helm-berand: *and cf. the epithet* Hjālm-beri *helmbearer, given to Odin.*]

helmian; *p.* ode *To cover*:—Niht helmade beorgas steápe *night covered the high hills*, Andr. Kmbl. 2612; An. 1307.

helmiht; *adj. Full of leaves* or *boughs*; frondosus, Cot. 75, 198, Lye. v. helm II.

HELP, e; *f*: *also* es; *m.* HELP, *aid, succour*:—On ðǣm burgum wæs getācnad ðæt Crist is eáðmōdegra help *probans se esse conservatorem humilium*, Ors. 3, 2; Swt. 100, 25. Ðǣr is help gearu æt mǣrum manna gehwylcum *there is help ready at the hand of the mighty one for every man*, Andr. Kmbl. 1814; An. 909. Gionn helpe *præsta subsidium*, Rtl. 71, 37. Ða ðe hine helpe biddaþ *who ask him for help*, Ps. Th. 118, 2: Andr. Kmbl. 2061; An. 1033. Gehýr helpys bēnan *exaudi me*, Ps. Th. 101, 2. Uton helpan aa ðam raðost ðe helpes betst behōfaþ *let us ever help him first who has most need of help*, L. C. S. 69; Th. i. 412, 3. Helpes bedǣled *deprived of help*, MS. Cott. Nero A. i. fol. 73. Helpes biddende *asking for help*: sumes helpes biddende *asking for some help*, Lchdm. iii. 365, col. 2. Hwā him tō hǣle and tō helpe on ðās world āstāg *who came down to this world as their salvation and help*, Blickl. Homl. 105, 32. Ðām burgwarum com māra fultum tō ūtan tō helpe *more aid came from without to the citizens to help them*, Chr. 921; Erl. 107, 19. Rūmlīcum helpe *benigno favore*, Rtl. 17, 35. Þurh ða gebedu gē māgon on swīðe mycelan hylpe beón ge libbendum ge forþfarenum *by prayers you may be of very great help both to the living and the departed*, L. E. I. 3; Th. ii. 404, 18: 21; Th. ii. 414, 36. Nǣnige helpe ðam byrnendan hūse gedōn mihton *nil ardenti domui prodesse valentes*, Bd. 3, 10; S. 534, 34. Ðā nǣnig him ǣnige helpe findan mihte *cum nil salutis furenti superesse videretur*, 3, 11; S. 536, 25. Helpe ūserne *adjutorium nostrum*, Rtl. 172, 23. Ðǣr mē wið lāþum līcsyrce mīn helpe gefremede *there against the foes my coat of mail afforded me help*, Beo. Th. 1107; B. 550. Gehýr mē and mē help freme *exaudi me*, Ps. Th. 68, 17: Cd. 184; Th. 230, 20; Dan. 236. Dǣleþ help and hǣlo hæleþa bearnum *distributes help and salvation to the children of men*, 226; Th. 301, 15; Sat. 586 [*O. Sax.* helpa; *f*: *O. Frs.* helfe; *f*: *Icel.* hjālp; *f*: *O. H. Ger.* helfa; *f. auxilium, adjutorium, subsidium, solatium*: *Ger.* hülfe.] v. helpe.

helpan; *p.* healp, *pl.* hulpon; *pp.* holpen; *v. trans. followed by gen. or dat. To help, aid, assist, succour*:—Ðū monegum helpst *thou helpest many*, Hy. 7, 44; Hy. Grn. ii. 288, 44. Wið fefre hylpþ marubis tō drincanne *for fever it helps to drink marrubium*, L. M. 1, 62; Lchdm. ii. 134, 27. Hē helpeþ þearfan *parcet pauperi*, Ps. Th. 71, 13. Ðonne helpe gē wel ðām ðe gē lǣraþ gif hī eówre lārum fyligean willaþ *then do ye well help those whom ye teach, if they will follow your teaching*, L. I. P. 21; Th. ii. 332, 21. Hē nyle helpan ðæs folces mid ðam ðe God his healp *ex muneribus quæ perceperit prodesse aliis non curat*, Past. 5, 2; Swt. 45, 5. Ðonne ðu hulpe mīn *when thou didst help me*, Ps. Th. 70, 20. Ða steortas hulpan ealle ðæs heáfdes *all the tails helped the head*, Shrn. 162, 16: Exon. 27 b; Th. 83, 10; Cri. 1354. Help mīn *help me*, Ps. Th. 60, 1. God ūre helpe. Amen *may God help us. Amen*, Swt. A. S. Rdr. 112, 225. Wē on ðisum līfe māgon helpan ðām forþfarenum ðe on wītnunge beóþ *we in this life may help the departed that are being punished*, Homl. Th. ii. 356, 11. Wē sceolon earmra manna helpan *we ought to help poor people*, 442, 14. Helpa *fovere*, Rtl. 122, 37. [*Chauc. Piers. P. p.* halp, help, *pl.* holpen; *pp.* holpen: *the pp.* holpen *occurs in the authorized version of the Bible*: *Goth.* hilpan: *O. Sax.* helpan: *O. Frs.* helpa: *Icel.* hjālpa: *O. H. Ger.* helfan: *Ger.* helfen.] DER. ā-, ge-helpan.

helpe, an; *f. Help*:—Gif ðās fultumas ne sýn helpe *if these remedies are no help*, L. M. 2, 48; Lchdm. ii. 262, 15. [*Or should this be placed under* help?] Hē him helpan ne mæg ǣnige gefremman *he can give him no help*, Beo. Th. 4888; B. 2448.

helpend, es; *m. A helper*:—Helpend *adjutor*, Rtl. 45, 18. Ealles middangeardes hǣlend and ealra sāula helpend *the saviour of all the earth and the helper of all souls*, Blickl. Homl. 105, 190. Helpend and hǣlend wið hellsceaðum *a helper and saviour against the harmers of hell*, Exon. 68 a; Th. 252, 2; Jul. 157. Helpend ne hafo ic *I have no helper*, Jn. Skt. Lind. 5, 7. Syððan hē ne hæbbe helpend ǣnne *quia non est qui eripiat eum*, Ps. Th. 70, 10. Helpendra leás *without helpers*, Exon. 28 b; Th. 86, 27; Cri. 1414.

helpend-bǣre; *adj. Helpful, assistant*; opifer, Cot. 148, Lye.

helpend-līc; *adj. Auxiliary.*

hēl-spure, an; *f. A heel*:—Unrehtwīsnis hēlspuran [hellspuran, Ps. Spl. 48, 5] mīnre *iniquitas calcanei mei*, Ps. Stev. 48, 6. Hēlspuran [hellspuran, Ps. Spl. 55, 6] mīne *calcaneum meum*, 55, 7.

helto; *f. Haltness, lameness*:—Āfyrr ðū drihten from ðære stōwe blindnesse and helto and dumbnesse *remove O Lord from the place blindness and lameness and dumbness*, Shrn. 101, 35.

helur-bledu, e; *f. The scale of a balance*; lanx, Cot. 26, Lye. v. bledu.

hem; *m. A hem, border*:—Hem *limbus*, Ælfc. Gl. 28; Som. 61, 7; Wrt. Voc. 26, 6. [*Laym.* þane hem: *Prompt. Parv.* hemme *fimbria, limbus.*] Cf. ham *an enclosure.*

hemlīc, hymlīc, es; *m*: hymlīce, an; *f. Hemlock*:—Hemlīc *cicuta*, Ælfc. Gl. 43; Som. 64, 47; Wrt. Voc. 31, 57. Hemlīc hātte wyrt *a plant called hemlock*, L. M. 1, 77; Lchdm. ii. 150, 15. Wyrc hie of hemlīc *make the salve of hemlock*, 58; Lchdm. ii. 128, 7. Nim hemlīc *take hemlock*, 31; Lchdm. ii. 74, 6. Wyll nyoðerweardne hymlīc *boil the lower part of hemlock*, Lchdm. iii. 50, 17. Hymlīce *cicuta*, p. 331, col. 1. Dō tō hymlīcan *put hemlock to it*, L. M. 1, 1; Lchdm. ii. 18, 27.

hemming, es; *m. A kind of shoe*; pero, Cot. 155, Lye.

hen. v. hæn.

hēnan. v. hýnan.

-hende. v. an-, ān-, ge-, of-, on-, spær-hende.

henge-clif, es; *n. A steep, precipitous cliff*; prærūptum, Ælfc. Gl. 101; Som. 77, 38; Wrt. Voc. 55, 43.

hengen, e; *f.* I. *hanging*:—Eode and hī sylfe āheng . . . Se deóful hī tō hire āgenre hengene gelǣrde *she went and hung herself . . . The devil persuaded her to her own hanging* [*to hang herself*], Homl. Th. ii. 30, 24. Hēt hine hōn and mid hengene þrāwan tō langere hwīle *bade hang him and for a long time torture him with hanging*, 308, 31. II. *that on which any one is hung, a gibbet, gallows, cross*:—Crist ðone ðe hī on hengene fæstnodon *Christ whom they fastened on a cross*, Homl. Th. ii. 256, 22: 308, 30. Laurentius āstreht on ðære hengene þancode his Drihtne . . . Hē hēt ālýsan ðone diácon of ðære hengene *Lawrence stretched on the cross thanked his Lord . . . He ordered the deacon to be released from the cross*, i. 426, 32, 35. III. *prison, confinement, durance.* Schmid, p. 609, suggests a connection between this meaning and that given under I. in the following remark: 'Die grammatische Bedeutung des Wortes fürht darauf, dass ursprünglich darunter das Anhängen an einen Block oder das Einspannen in den Stock, als die Art der Sicherung eines Gefangenen, der man sich bediente, wenn Gefängnisse fehlten, verstanden worden sei.' Accordingly he translates the following passage, L. Alf. pol. 35; Th. i. 84, 4:—Gif hē hine on hengenne [MS. B. hengene] ālecgge 'wenn er ihn in den Stock legt,' which Thorpe renders *if he lay him in prison.* In the latter sense it is found L. C. S. 35; Th. i. 396, 27:—Gif freóndleás man swā geswenced weorþe ðæt hē borh næbbe ðonne gebūge hē hengenne [MS. B. hengene] and ðǣr gebīde ǒþ ðæt hē gā tō Godes ordāle *if a friendless man be so distressed that he have no surety, then let him submit to prison, and there abide, until he go to God's ordeal.* Cf. L. H. 65, 5; Th. i. 568, 14, ponatur in *hengen.* [Cf. *O. Sax.* hie (Krist) welda thesa werold alla mid is henginnia alōsian, Hel. Heyne 5435: thuo sprak therō mannō ōðer (the penitent thief) an thero henginna thār hie geheftid stuod, 5591.]

hengen-wītnung, e; *f. The punishment of imprisonment:*—Gif forworht man friþstōl gesēce and þurh ðæt feorh geyrne ðonne sȳ þreóra ān for his fēore būte man bet geárian wille wergild ēce þeówet hengenwītnung *if a man who has forfeited his life gain a sanctuary, and thereby secure his life, let there be one of three things instead of his life, unless he obtain remission more favourably, wergild, perpetual thraldom, imprisonment,* L. Eth. vii. 16; Th. i. 332, 18.]

hengest, es; *m. A gelding, horse, steed:*—Hengst *canterius*, Ælfc. Gl. 20; Som. 59, 46; Wrt. Voc. 23, 8. Ān hundred wildra horsa and xvi tame hencgestas *a hundred wild horses and sixteen tame steeds,* Chart. Th. 548, 11. [*Laym.* hængest: *O. Frs.* hengst: *Icel.* hestr *a stallion, horse*: *O. H. Ger.* hengist *eunuchus, spado, cantarius, equus castratus*: *Ger.* hengst *a stallion.*] DER. brim-, faroþ-, fæt-, frīd-, mere-, sǣ-, sund-, wǣg-hengest.

Hengest, es; *m. Hengest*, Bd. 1, 15; S. 483, 28: Chr. 449; Erl. 13, 1-21: 455; Erl. 13, 22-25: 457; Erl. 12, 17-20: 465; Erl. 12, 21: 473; Erl. 12, 25: 488; Erl. 14, 3-4.

heng-wīte, es; *n. A fine to be paid for not keeping a criminal in custody so that he may be brought before the proper tribunal:*—Si quis latronem vel furem, sine clamore et insecutione ejus, cui dampnum factum est, ceperit, et captum ultra duxerit dabit x solid. de henwite [hengwite, French text], L. Will. I. 4; Th. i. 469, 27.

henna, an; *m. A fowl:*—Gif swȳn oððe henna ete of mannes līchaman *si porcus vel gallina de corpore hominis ederit*, L. Ecg. P. iv. 57; Th. ii. 220, 13. v. hæn.

henne-belle. v. hænne-belle.

hentan; *p.* te *To pursue, follow after, seize* [?]:—Gif hē man tō deáþe gefylle beó hē ðonne ūtlah and his hente mid hearme ǣlc ðara ðe riht wille *if he fell a man to death, let him then be an outlaw, and let every one that desires right pursue him with hue and cry* [?], L. E. G. 6; Th. i. 170, 10: L. C. S. 49; Th. i. 404, 11. Nime ðonne leáfe ðæt hē mōte hentan æfter his āgenan *let him then take leave to follow after his own,* 19; Th. i. 386, 17. [*Chauc. Piers P.* hente *to seize, take, get*: *Prompt. Parv.* hentin *rapere.*] v. ge-hentan.

hēnþ, hēnþu. v. hȳnþ, hȳnþu.

heó. v. hē.

heó-dæg; *adv. To-day;* hodie, Cd. 30; Th. 41, 23; Gen. 661. [*O. Sax.* hiudu: *O. Frs.* hiudega, hiude: *O. H. Ger.* hiutu: *Ger.* heute: cf. *Goth.* himma daga.]

heóf, es; *m. Lamentation, grief, sorrow:*—Maximus mid micelum heófe gedrēfed him tō com *Maximus troubled with great grief came to him,* Homl. Th. i. 414, 17. Sǣde ðæt hie hæfden bet gewyrht ðæt him mon mid heáfe [heófe MS. C.] ongeán cōme ðonne mid triumphan *Fabius oblatum sibi a senatu triumphum suscipere recusaret, quia luctus potius debebatur,* Ors. 2, 4; Swt. 70, 20. Heóf mīnne *planctum meum,* Ps. Spl. 29, 13 [heáf, Ps. Th. 29, 11].

heófan; *p.* de *To lament, grieve, wail, mourn:*—Hungre heófeþ *laments for hunger,* Exon. 91 b; Th. 342, 30: Gn. Ex. 150. Heófaþ mid handum [Ps. Th. wēpaþ and heówaþ] *plaudite manibus,* Ps. Spl. T. 46, 1: 97, 8. Wē heófdon and gē ne weópon *lamentavimus et non plorastis,* Lk. Skt. 7, 32. Gif hē mid inweardre heortan heófe *if he heartily grieve,* L. Pen. 8; Th. ii. 280, 10. Heófende spræc *lamenting he spoke,* Andr. Kmbl. 3113; An. 1559. Ālegdon ðā tō middes mǣrne þeóden hæleþ hiófende hlāford leófne *warriors lamenting laid down in their midst the great prince, the lord beloved,* Beo. Th. 6275; B. 3142. [*Goth.* hiufan; *p.* hauf, v. Lk. 7, 32: *O. Sax.* heobandi, hiobandi, *part. pres*: *O. H. Ger.* hiufit *luget;* hiufanti *luctuosus.*] v. heófian, heáfan.

heófe-līce; *adj. Lamentable, grievous;* funebris, Som.

heofen. v. heofon.

heófian; *p.* ode *To lament, mourn, wail, bewail:*—Ic heófige *lugeo,* Ælfc. Gr. 26; Som. 28, 63. Gē heófiaþ and wēpaþ *plorabitis et flebitis vos,* Jn. Skt. 16, 20. Hieremias heófode miclum ðæs folces synna swā swā his bōc ūs segþ *Jeremiah lamented greatly the people's sins, as his book tells us,* Swt. A. S. Rdr. 70, 440. Ðā weópon hig ealle and heófodon hī *flebant autem omnes et plangebant illam,* Lk. Skt. 8, 52. Hī heófodon folces synna *they bewailed people's sins,* Homl. Th. i. 540, 30. Wā eów ðe nū hlihgaþ gē sceolon heófian and wēpan *woe to you that laugh now, ye shall mourn and weep,* 180, 15. Ðā ongann Ypolitus sārlīce heófian *then Hippolytus began sorely to lament,* 428, 12: 408, 9: L. E. I. prm; Th. ii. 398, 36. Heófigende *lugens,* Ps. Spl. 34, 17. Heófiende *flebilis,* Bt. 2; Fox 4, 8. Of heófigendre menigu *from a mourning multitude,* Homl. Th. i. 86, 33. Mid heófigendum stemnum *with lamenting voices,* ii. 420, 16. v. heófan.

HEOFON, heofen, heofun, hefon, heben. hiofon, es; *m.* HEAVEN; cælum:—Heofon and heofuna heofun and eorþe and ealle ða þing ðe sind on him sind Drihtnes *the heaven and the heaven of heavens is the Lord's, the earth with all that therein is,* Deut. 10, 14. Heofen and eorþe sīde sǣflōdas *cæli et terra, mare,* Ps. Th. 68, 35. Heofon and hel *heaven and hell,* Exon. 31 a; Th. 97, 17; Cri. 1592. Heben til hrōfe *heaven for a roof,* Swt. A. S. Rdr. 195, 13. Heofonas god *the god of heaven,* Hy. 3, 58; Hy. Grn. ii. 282, 58: Andr. Kmbl. 3000; An. 1503. Hiofones leóhtes beorhto *the brightness of the light of heaven,* Bt. Met. Fox 21, 77; Met. 21, 39. Of hefene *from heaven,* Beo. Th. 3146; B. 1571. Mid his worde synt getrymede heofonas *verbo Domini cæli firmati sunt,* Ps. Th. 32, 5. Ðā wǣron fullfremode heofenas and eorþe *the heavens and the earth were finished,* Gen. 2, 1. Heofona rīce *regnum cælorum,* Mt. Kmbl. 13, 24. Of heofonum ðe of mannum *e cælo an ex hominibus,* 21, 25. Gif ic on heofenas up āstīge *si ascendero in cælum,* Ps. Th. 138, 6. [*O. Sax.* heban *and* himil: *Icel.* hifinn *and* himinn: *Goth.* himins: *O. Frs.* himul, himel: *O. H. Ger.* himil *cælum, lacunar*: *Ger.* himmel.] v. Grmm. D. M. 661.

heofon, heófon [?]:—Hergas on helle heofon ðider becom druron deófolgyld, Cd. 145; Th. 180, 17; Exod. 47. Grein translates *heofon* lamentation and *druron* mourned; but may not *hergas* be from hearg q. v. and parallel to *deófolgyld,* and the passage be translated *the idols and false gods fell to hell and heaven came there?*

heofon-beácen, es; *n. A heavenly beacon* or *sign* [*the fiery pillar*], Cd. 148; Th. 184, 15; Exod. 107.

heofon-beohrt; *adj. Heaven-bright, bright with the light of heaven,* Cd. 190; Th. 237, 21; Dan. 341: Exon. 23 a: Th. 63, 13; Cri. 1019.

heofon-bȳme, an; *f. A heavenly trumpet,* Exon. 21 b; Th. 59, 8; Cri. 949.

heofon-candel, -condel, e; *f. A heavenly candle* or *light* [*the sun*], Andr. Kmbl. 486; An. 243: [*the fiery pillar*] Cd. 148; Th. 184, 31; Exod. 115: [*sun and moon*] Exon. 16 b; Th. 38, 17; Cri. 608: [*the stars*] 93 a; Th. 349, 30; Sch. 54.

heofon-col, es; *n. The coal of the heavens:*—Brūne hātum heofoncolum *brown with the sun's heat* [*the Ethiopians*], Cd. 146; Th. 182, 5; Exod. 71.

heofon-cund; *adj. Heavenly, celestial:*—Heofuncund mett *manna,* Jn. Skt. Lind. 6, 31. Seó heofencunde weorþung *the heavenly honour,* Blickl. Homl. 165, 26. Heáh and hālig heofuncund þrȳnes *O! high and holy heavenly Trinity,* Exon. 13 a; Th. 24, 4; Cri. 379. Hȳ ðæs heofoncundan boldes bīdaþ *they wait for the heavenly dwelling,* 33 b; Th. 107, 6; Gū. 54: 35 a; Th. 112, 11; Gū. 142. Ða beóþ ðære heofencundan Jerusalem burgware *who are citizens of the heavenly Jerusalem,* Bt. 5, 1; Fox 10, 7. [Cf. *Goth.* himina-kunds *cælestis.*]

heofon-cyning, es; *m. The king of heaven, heavenly king:*—God heáh heofoncyning *God high king of heaven,* Cd. 23; Th. 30, 7; Gen. 463. Ic eom heáhengel heofoncyninges *I am an archangel of the king of heaven,* Blickl. Homl. 201, 5: Cd. 23; Th. 30, 28; Gen. 474: Andr. Kmbl. 184; An. 92. Heofoncining on heora heortum beran *to bear the king of heaven in their hearts,* Blickl. Homl. 79, 32. Heofoncyning hȳhst *most exalted of heavenly kings,* Exon. 117 b; Th. 451, 23; Dōm. 108. [*O. Sax.* heban-, himil-kuning: *O. H. Ger.* himel-chuning *superum regem* (*jovem*).]

heofon-dēma, an; *m. A heavenly judge,* Cd. 228; Th. 306, 4; Sat. 658.

heofon-dreám, es; *m. Heavenly joy, joy of heaven,* Ps. Th. 113, 11: Soul Kmbl. 206; Seel. 104: Exon. 54 a; Th. 190, 27; Az. 79.

heofon-duguþ, e; *f. A heavenly host,* Exon. 32 a; Th. 101, 7; Cri. 1655.

heofone, an; *f. Heaven:*—Heofone næs nā ǣr ǣrðan ðe se ælmihtiga wyrhta hī geworhte on anginne *heaven was not before the almighty workman wrought it in the beginning,* Hexam. 1; Norm. 4. Heofenan rīce *the kingdom of heaven,* Homl. Th. i. 68, 2: 58, 4. God gesette hig on ðære heofenan ðæt hie scinon ofer eorþan *God set them in the firmament of heaven to give light upon the earth,* Gen. 1, 17, 14. On anginne gesceóp God heofenan and eorþan *in the beginning God created the heaven and the earth,* 1, 1.

heofon-engel, es; *m. An angel of heaven,* Exon. 15 a; Th. 31, 8; Cri. 492: 21 b; Th. 57, 34; Cri. 928: 75 a; Th. 281, 7; Jul. 642: Hy. 7, 13; Hy. Grn. ii. 287, 13.

heofon-feld, es; *m. A Northumbrian local name:*—Is seó stōw on Englisc nemned Heofenfeld wæs heó geára swā nemned for tācnunge ðæra tōweardra wundra forðon ðe ðǣr ðæt heofonlīce sigebeácen ārǣred beón sceolde and ðǣr heofonlīc sige ðam cyninge seald wæs *vocatur locus ille* *lingua Anglorum Hefenfelth, quod dici potest Latine cælestis campus, quod certo utique præsagio futurorum antiquitus nomen accepit significans nimirum quod ibidem cæleste erigendum trophæum, cælestis inchoanda victoria*, Bd. 3, 2; S. 524, 33. Seó stōw is gehāten Heofonfeld on Englisc wið ðone langan weall ðe ða Rōmāniscan worhton *the place is called in English Heavenfield, by the long wall that the Romans made*, Swt. A. S. Rdr. 96, 33.

heofon-fugol, es; *m. A bird of the air, fowl of heaven:*—Heofonfugelas healdaþ eardas *volucres cæli habitabunt*, Ps. Th. 103, 11: Cd. 192; Th. 240, 16; Dan. 387: 74; Th. 91, 21; Gen. 1515: 10; Th. 13, 11; Gen. 201.

heofon-hæbbende *arcitenens, sagittarius*, Lye.

heofon-hālig; *adj. Heaven-holy, of celestial holiness*, Andr. Kmbl. 1455; An. 728.

heofon-hām, es; *m. A heavenly home, heaven:*—On heofonhāme *in cælo*, Ps. Th. 102, 18: 137, 6: 148, 4: Exon. 12 a; Th. 18, 33; Cri. 293. Ðū ðe heofonhāmas healdest and wealdest *qui habitas in cælo*, Ps. Th. 122, 1.

heofon-heáh; *adj. Heaven-high, reaching to heaven:*—Heofonheánne beám *a tree the height whereof reached unto heaven* [Dan. 4, 11], Cd. 202; Th. 250, 29; Dan. 554.

heofon-heall, e; *f. A heavenly hall:*—Ne hī swā fūle ne mōton intō his fægeran heofonhealle *nor may they so foul enter into his fair heavenly hall*, L. Ælfc. P. 41; Th. ii. 382, 10.

heofon-hlāf, es; *m. Heavenly bread, bread from heaven, manna:*—Hī heofonhlāfe hālige gefylde *pani cæli saturavit eos*, Ps. Th. 104, 35. [Cf. *O. H. Ger.* himel-brot.]

heofon-hrōf, es; *m.* I. *the roof of heaven, heaven:*—Under heofunhrōfe *under the roof of heaven*, Exon. 58 a; Th. 209, 19; Ph. 173. II. *a roof, ceiling:*—Heofenhrōf *lacunar*, Cot. 119, Lye. [Cf. *O. H. Ger.* himil *laqueare, lacunar, camera:* himilizi *lacunar, laquear.*]

heofon-hwealf, e; *f. The vault of heaven*, Andr. Kmbl. 1089; An. 545: 2803; An. 1404.

heofonisc; *adj. Heavenly:*—Hū ðæt heofenisce fȳr forbærnde ðæt lond on ðæm wǣron ða twā byrig on getimbred Sodome and Gomorre *how fire from heaven consumed the land in which were built the two cities Sodom and Gomorrah*, Ors. tit. 3; Swt. 1, 6. [Cf. *O. Sax. O. H. Ger.* himilisk: *O. Frs.* himelesk: *Icel.* hifneskr, himneskr.]

heofon-leóht, es; *n. Heavenly light*, Andr. Kmbl. 1948; An. 976. [Cf. *O. H. Ger.* himel-lieht.]

heofon-leóma, an; *m. A heavenly radiance, light*, Andr. Kmbl. 1675; An. 840. [Cf. *Icel.* himin-ljōmi.]

heofon-līc; *adj. Heavenly:*—Mīn se heofenlīca Fæder *Pater meus cælestis*, Mt. Kmbl. 18, 35: Ps. Th. 67, 14. Ðīn rihtwīsnes is swā heáh swā ða heofonlīcan muntas *justitia tua sicut montes Dei*, 35, 6. Heofonlīcæ þing *cælestia*, Jn. Skt. 3, 12. [Cf. *O. H. Ger.* himil-līh *cælestis.*]

heofon-līce; *adv. From heaven, heavenly;* celitus, Ælfc. Gr. 38; Som. 42, 3.

heofon-ligende [lifigende?] *cælebs, virgo, quod vitam cælestem agat*, Som.

heofon-mægen, es; *n. Heavenly might:*—Bibodu hālgan heofonmægnes *the commands of the holy heavenly power* [*God*], Exon. 118 a; Th. 454, 19; Hy. 4, 35. Heofonmægna God *God of the heavenly powers*, 256; Th. 75, 8: Cri. 1218.

heofon-rīce, es; *n. The kingdom of heaven:*—Biþ him heofonrīce āgiefen *to them shall be given the kingdom of heaven*, Exon. 26 a; Th. 77, 22; Cri. 1260. Heofenrīces duru *the door of the kingdom of heaven*, Blickl. Homl. 9, 1. Heofonrīces weard *auctorem regni cælestis*, Bd. 4, 24; S. 597, 20: Cd. 69; Th. 82, 17; Gen. 1363. [*O. Sax* heban-rīki: cf. *O. Sax.* himil-rīki: *O. Frs.* himel-rīk: *Icel.* himin-rīki: *Dan.* himme-rige: *O. H. Ger.* himil-rīchi: *Ger.* himmel-reich.]

heofon-steorra, an; *m. A star of heaven:*—Seó mænigeo mǣre wǣre swā heofonsteorran *the multitude should be great as the stars of heaven*, Cd. 190; Th. 236, 15; Dan. 321: 192; Th. 239, 17; Dan. 371. Hreósaþ heofonsteorran *the stars of heaven shall fall*, Exon. 23 a; Th. 64, 27; Cri. 1044.

heofon-stōl, es; *m. A heavenly throne*, Cd. 1; Th. 1, 15; Gen. 8.

heofon-þreát, es; *m. A heavenly band*, Cd. 218; Th. 278, 15; Sat. 222.

heofon-þrym, -mes; *m. Heavenly glory* or *majesty*, Andr. Kmbl. 962; An. 481: 3436; An. 1722.

heofon-timber, es; *n. A heavenly structure*, Cd. 8; Th. 9, 23; Gen. 146.

heofon-torht; *adj. Heaven-bright*, Exon. 93 b; Th. 351, 1; Sch. 73: Cd. 146; Th. 182, 19; Exod. 78: Andr. Kmbl. 2035; An. 1020: 2539; An. 1270: Bt. Met. Fox 23, 6; Met. 23, 3.

heofon-tungol, es; *n. A heavenly body:*—Hādor heofontungol *the sun*, Bt. Met. Fox 22, 47; Met. 22, 24. Hǣdre heofontungol *bright heavenly bodies*, Exon. 18 a; Th. 43, 23; Cri. 693; 56 a; Th. 199, 28; Ph. 32: Cd. 199; Th. 247, 23; Dan. 501. [Cf. *O. Sax.* himil-tungal: *Icel.* himin-tungl: *O. H. Ger.* himil-zungal *sidus.*]

heofon-ware; *pl. The inhabitants of heaven:*—Ealle gesceafta ge heofonware ge eorþware *all creatures, both those in heaven and those on earth*, Blickl. Homl. 11, 4. Ða hālgan heofenware *the holy dwellers in heaven*, 135, 17. v. next word.

heofon-waru, e; *f. The inhabitants of heaven:*—Hē dyde ðæt eal heofonwaru wundrode *he caused all the inhabitants of heaven to wonder*, Homl. Th. i. 442, 35: Hy. 7, 95; Hy. Grn. ii. 289, 95. Ealle heofonwara and eorþwara on his andwerdnysse beóþ onstyred *all those in heaven and on earth shall be moved in his presence*, Chart. Th. 390, 10: Homl. Th. ii. 360, 32. Bearn heofonwara *children of heaven-dwellers*, Salm. Kmbl. 930; Sal. 464. Ætforan heofonwarum and eorþwarum and helwarum *before the inhabitants of heaven and of earth and of hell*, Homl. Th. ii. 604, 5. Cristes ācennednys gegladode heofenwara and eorþwara and helwara, i. 36, 25.

heofon-weard, es; *m. The guardian of heaven, God*, Cd. 6; Th. 8, 6; Gen. 120: 86; Th. 107, 28; Gen. 1796. [*O. Sax.* heban-ward *an angel.*]

heofon-wolcen, es; *n. A cloud of heaven, of the sky:*—Of heofonwolcnum *from the clouds of heaven*, Ps. Th. 147, 6. Ðǣr mec fēddon hruse and heofonwolcn [? MS. wlonc] *where earth and rain from heaven fed me*, Exon. 126 b; Th. 485, 23; Rä. 72, 2. [Cf. *O. Sax.* himil-wolcan: *O. H. Ger.* himil-wolchen *nubes cæli.*]

heofon-wōma, an; *m. A heavenly sound, the sound heard at the day of judgment*, Exon. 20 a; Th. 52, 18; Cri. 835: 22 b; Th. 62, 10; Cri. 999.

heofon-wuldor, es; *n. Heavenly glory*, Hy. 6, 12; Hy. Grn. ii. 286, 12.

heóf-sang, es; *m. An elegy*, Lye.

heófung, e; *f. Mourning, lamentation, grieving:*—Ðonne beóþ heora siblingas tō heófunge geneádode *then will their relations be forced to mourn*, Homl. Th. i. 88, 1. Mid micelre heófunge *with great lamentation*, ii. 516, 19. Biddende forgifennysse mid wōpe and heófunge *asking forgiveness with weeping and lamentation*, H. R. 107, 27. On ðære wǣron āwritene heófunga *scriptæ erant in eo lamentationes*, Ælfc. Gr. 48; Som. 49, 8, 9. Ǣr hē tō heófungum sōðre behreówsunge gecyrran mæge *before he can turn to the lamentations of true repentance*, Homl. Th. ii. 124, 15.

heófung-dæg, es; *m. A day of mourning:*—Ða heófungdagas wǣron ðā gefyllede *completi sunt dies planctus*, Deut. 34, 8.

heófung-tīd, e; *f. A time of mourning:*—Fram ðisum dæge ōþ eástron is ūre heófungtīd *from this day until Easter is our time of mourning*, Homl. Th. ii. 86, 25.

heolca, an; *m.* [?] *Hoar-frost, rime:*—Swā swā bytte on heolcan *sicut uter in pruina*, Ps. Lamb. 118, 83.

heolfor, es; *n. Blood from a wound, gore;* cruor:—Blōd ūt ne com heolfor of hreþre ðeáh mec bite stīðecg stȳle *there came not out blood or gore from my breast though the steel with stiff edge bit me*, Exon. 130 a; Th. 499, 9; Rä. 88, 13. Heolfres þurstge *thirsty for gore*, 99 b; Th. 373, 24; Seel. 114. Flōd blōde weól hātan heolfre *blood and hot gore bubbled up in the water*, Beo. Th. 2850; B. 1423: 1702; B. 849: 2609; B. 1302: Andr. Kmbl. 2483; An. 1243: 2555; An. 1279: Cd. 166; Th. 206, 9; Exod. 449: Th. 208, 1; Exod. 476.

heolfrig; *adj. Gory, bloody:*—Heolfrig herereáf *gory armour*, Judth. 12; Thw. 26, 8; Jud. 317: 11; Thw. 23, 20; Jud. 130.

heoloran, holrian; *p.* ede *To weigh in a balance, to consider:*—Hē holrede *pensavit, cogitavit*, Mone B. 1604. Heolorende *librantes*, Cot. 123: 180, Lye.

heoloþ-cynn, es; *n. A race living in a place of concealment* [?], *the devils in hell*, Exon. 30 b; Th. 94, 19; Cri. 1542. v. *next word; and* cf. heolstor.

heoloþ-helm, es; *m. A helm which conceals* or *makes invisible the wearer*, Exon. 97 a; Th. 362, 31; Wal. 45. [*Icel.* huliðs-hjālmr.] v. hæleþ-helm.

heolra, heolora, an; *m. The scale of a balance, a balance* [?]:—Twīfeald heolra *bilanx*, Lye. v. helur-blæd, heoloran.

heolstor, es; *n. That which covers* or *conceals, darkness, a veil, covering, place of concealment:*—Siððan geāra goldwine mīnne hrusan heolstre biwrāh *since long ago the veil of earth enwrapped my bounteous patron*, Exon. 76 b; Th. 287, 32; Wand. 23. Nāgan wē ðæs heolstres ðæt wē ūs gehȳdan māgon *we have not the place of concealment to hide ourselves in*, Cd. 215; Th. 271, 5; Sat. 101. Gewitan him ðā gangan under beámsceade hȳddon hie on heolstre ðā hie hālig word drihtnes gehȳrdon *they retired then under the trees' shade, hid themselves in the darkness when they heard the holy word of the Lord*, 40; Th. 53, 12; Gen. 860. Ðā com beácna beorhtost of heolstre *then came the sun out of darkness*, Andr. Kmbl. 485; An. 243: Elen. Kmbl. 2223; El. 1113. Heolstre gehȳded helme gedȳgled þȳstre oferfæðmed *with a veil hidden, with a covering concealed, with darkness enwrapped*, Exon. 122 b; Th. 470, 9; Hy. 11, 13: 61 b; Th. 227, 4; Ph. 418: 69 a; Th. 257, 2; Jul. 241: Elen. Kmbl. 2161; El. 1082. Sume wuniaþ on wēstennum gesittaþ hāmas on heolstrum *some dwell in deserts, occupy homes in hidden* *places*, Exon. 33 b; Th. 107, 5; Gū. 54. [*Goth.* hulistr; *n. a veil*: cf. *Icel.* hulstr; *m. a sheath, case*: *Dut.* holster *holster. In Romaunt of Rose* hulstred *occurs* = *hidden* 'I wol herborow me There I hope best to hulstred be,' 6146.]

heolstor; *adj. Dark*:—Ðǣr wunian sceal in ðam heolstran hām hyht-wynna leás *there shall dwell in that dark abode reft of the joys of hope*, Judth. 10; Thw. 23, 14; Jud. 121.

heolstor-cōfa, an; *m. A dark, concealed chamber, grave*:—Deáþræced hæleþa heolstercōfan onhliden weorþaþ *the death houses, the graves of men shall be uncovered*, Exon. 56 b; Th. 200, 31; Ph. 49.

heolstor-hof, es; *n. A dark dwelling, hell*, Elen. Kmbl. 1524; El. 764.

heolstor-loca, an; *m. A dark enclosure, prison*, Andr. Kmbl. 288; An. 144: 2010; An. 1007.

heolstor-sceado; *f. A shadow that hides*, Cd. 5; Th. 7, 9; Gen. 103.

heolstor-scūwa, an; *m. Dark shadow, darkness*, Andr. Kmbl. 2508; An. 1255.

heolstrig; *adj. Latebrosus*, Cot. 169, Lye.

heona. v. heonan.

heonan, heonon, heonun, hionan; *adv. of place and time. Hence, from here*:—Heonon *abhinc*, Ælfc. Gr. 16; Som. 20, 4. Feor heonan *far from here*, Exon. 55 b; Th. 197, 19; Ph. 1. Ic mæg heonon geseón *I can see from here*, Cd. 32; Th. 41, 34; Gen. 666. Ǣr ðū heonan mōte *ere thou mayest go hence*, Exon. 72 a; Th. 269, 29; Jul. 457. Ðis is mīn āgen cȳþ ic wæs ǣr hionan cumen *this is my own country, from here did I formerly come*, Bt. Met. Fox 24, 100; Met. 24, 50. Gāþ heonun *recedite*, Mt. Kmbl. 9, 24. Āsend ðē heonun nyþer *mitte te hinc deorsum*, Lk. Skt. 4, 9. Ge heonon ge ðanon *from here and there, from any quarter*, L. C. S. 19; Th. i. 386, 16. Ic forþ heonun ðīne gewitnesse wel geheólde *I should henceforth keep thy testimony well*, Ps. Th. 118, 31, 24: Exon. 16 a; Th. 36, 27; Cri. 582. Heonon forþ and ōþ on woruld *ex hoc nunc et usque in sæculum*, Blickl. Gloss: Gen. 8, 21. Gif hit sceal heonan forþ gōdiende weorþan *if things from this time forward are to be improving*, Swt. A. S. Rdr. 105, 19. Mīn feorh heonan on ðisse eahteþan ende gesēceþ *my life shall reach its end on the eighth day from this time*, Exon. 47 b; Th. 164, 10; Gū. 1009. [*Laym.* heonne, hinnes: *Piers P.* hennes: *O. Sax.* hinan: *O. H. Ger.* hinan, hinnan *hinc*: *Ger.* hennen.]

heonane, heonone; *adv. Hence*:—Far heonone *transi hinc*, Mt. Kmbl. 17, 20. Ðū miht heonane gehȳran *thou mayest hear from this place*, Cd. 37; Th. 49, 18; Gen. 794: 39; Th. 51, 24; Gen. 831. [*O. Sax.* hinana: *O. H. Ger.* hinana *hinc*.]

heonan-sīþ, es; *m. Departure, death*, Exon. 117 a; Th. 450, 12; Dōm. 86.

heonon-weard; *adj. Going hence, passing away*:—Ðeós world is heononweard *this world is passing away*, Blickl. Homl. 115, 20: Cd. 71; Th. 86, 15; Gen. 1431.

heonu, heono, henu, hona; *interj. Lo, behold*:—Heonu [henu, Rush.] *ecce*, Mt. Kmbl. Lind. 11, 8. Heono, Jn. Skt. Lind. 1, 29. Hona lā mīn hlāford *ecce dominus meus*, Shrn. 60, 14.

heópa, an; *m. A briar, bramble*:—Ætt ðæm heápe [heópe, Rush.] *secum rubum*, Lk. Skt. Lind. 20, 37. (*Or should this be placed under* heópe?) [*O. Sax.* hiopo: *O. H. Ger.* hiufo; *m. tribulus*.]

heóp-bremel, es; *m. A dog-rose, wild rose, bramble, briar*:—Heóp-brymel *rubus*, Ælfc. Gl. 47; Som. 65, 22; Wrt. Voc. 33, 22. Heóp-bremles leáf *leaves of the dog-rose*, L. M. 2, 51; Lchdm. ii. 266, 8.

heópe, an; *f. A hip, seed-vessel of the dog-rose*; also *the plant on which the hip grows* [?]:—Heópe *butunus* [i.e. button, *Fr.* bouton, *knob*], Ælfc. Gl. 40; Som. 63, 90; Wrt. Voc. 30, 36. Genim brēr ðe hiópan on weaxaþ *take briar on which hips grow*, L. M. 1, 38; Lchdm. ii. 96, 15. [*Chauc.* hepe.] v. heópa.

heorcnian, hercnian; *p.* ode *To hearken, listen*:—Gūþlāc eode sōna ūt and hāwode and hercnode *Guthlac went out directly and looked and listened*, Guthl. 6; Gdwin. 42, 15. Ypolitus mid geþylde heora wordum heorcnode *Hippolytus listened to their words with patience*, Homl. Th. i. 442, 2. Maria gesæt æt Godes fōtum his word heorcnigende *Mary sat at the feet of God hearkening to his words*, ii. 440, 16. Ðæt hit tō hefigtȳme ne þince ðām heorcnigendum *that it may not seem too tedious to the listeners*, 72, 23. [*Orm.* herrcnenn: *A. R.* hercnen: *Laym.* hercnede; *p*: *Chauc.* herkneth.]

heorcnung, hearcnung, e; *f. Hearkening, listening, hearing, power of hearing*:—Wē sceolon ūre eáran fram yfelre heorcnunge āwendan *we must turn away our ears from evil listening*, Homl. Th. i. 96, 23: ii. 564, 4: Ælfc. Gr. 1; Som. 2, 29. Hē forgeaf deáfum heorcnunge *he gave to the deaf hearing*, Homl. Th. i. 26, 13: ii. 16, 13. Hearcnunge, H. R. 7, 14. Drihten ic gehȳrde heorcnunge ðīne *Domine audivi auditionem tuam*, Cant. Abac. Lamb. fol. 189, 2.

HEORD, e; *f. A* HERD, *flock*:—Hiord *arimentum*, Wrt. Voc. 287, 53. Ðǣr wæs ān swȳna heord *erat grex porcorum*, Mt. Kmbl. 8, 30. Ic hæbbe ōðre sceáp ða ne synt of ðisse heorde *alias oves habeo quæ non sunt ex hoc ovili*, Jn. Skt. 10, 16. Hē drāf his heorde tō inneweardum ðam wēstene *he led the flock to the backside of the desert*, Ex. 3, 1: L. R. S. 4; Th. i. 434, 21. Rihtwīs hyrde ofer cristene heorde *a righteous shepherd over a christian flock*, L. I. P. 2; Th. ii. 304, 10. Of eówrum heordum *de gregibus tuis*, Ps. Th. 49, 10. Heora heorda wīslīce healdan *to keep their flocks wisely*, L. Eth. vi. 2; Th. i. 314, 14. Godcunde heorda *spiritual flocks*, L. C. E. 26; Th. i. 374, 34. [*Goth.* hairda: *Icel.* hjörð: *O. H. Ger.* herta *grex*: *Ger.* heerde.] v. hrīðer-heord.

heordan '*hards of flax*; lini fila utiliora. Stuppa, Gl. C. 58 b. Naptarum heordena, Gl. Cleop. 65 c.' Lchdm. iii. 331, col. 1. [*Prompt. Parv.* hyrdys or herdys of flax, or hempe *stuppa, napta*. See note, p. 241. Hards, hurds *tow*, East Norfolk Gloss: Engl. Dial. Soc. vol. ii.]

heorde; *f. Care, guarding, custody*:—Hē ūt wæs gongende tō neáta scȳpene ðara heorde him wæs ðære nihte beboden *egressus esset ad stabula jumentorum quorum ei custodia nocte illa erat delegata*, Bd. 4, 24; S. 597, 9. Forhwon beóþ ǣfre swǣ þrīste ða ungelǣredan ðæt hī underfōn ða heorde ðæs lāreówdōmes *ab imperitis ergo pastorale magisterium qua temeritate suscipitur*, Past. 1; Swt. 25, 17. Monige underfōþ heorde *nonnulli gregis curam suscipiunt*, 18, 5; Swt. 135, 25. [Cf. (?) *Icel.* hirð *a king's body-guard*: hirði- a prefix, *tending, keeping*.]

heorde. v. hirde.

heord-, hyrd-rǣden, e; *f. Guard, guardianship, care, keeping*:—Him is sinderlīce betǣht hyrdrǣden ofer eallum cristenum monnum *to him is especially committed the guardianship over all christian men*, Homl. Th. ii. 290, 26. Geþyld is wyrtruma and hyrdrǣden ealra hāligra mægna *patience is the root and guard of all holy virtues*, 544, 5. Hī geswencaþ heora hlāford þurh ymbhīdignysse heordrǣdene *they distress their possessor through solicitude of guarding*, 92, 18. Gehwilc hæbbe him betǣhtne engel tō hyrdrǣdene *each has an angel assigned to him as guard*, i. 516, 32. Se stæf getācnaþ gȳmene and hyrdrǣdene *the staff indicates care and guardianship*, ii. 280, 35. Tō heordrædene *ad custodiam*, Hymn. Surt. 11, 27. Ðā gesette God æt ðam infære engla hyrdrǣdene *then God set a guard of angels at the entrance*, Gen. 3, 24: Boutr. Scrd. 20, 32. Gē habbaþ heordrǣdenne *habetis custodiam*, Mt. Kmbl. 27, 65. Heordrēdena se ðe gesihþ swicunge hit getācnaþ *to see pickets betokens deception*, Lchdm. iii. 202, 13.

heóre, hȳre; *adj. Gentle, mild, pleasant*:—Nis ðæt heóru stōw *it is a savage place*, Beo. Th. 2749; B. 1372. Culufre fōtum stōp on beám hȳre *the dove with her feet stepped on to the tree, gentle*, Cd. 72; Th. 88, 20; Gen. 1468. Ðǣr se hȳra gæst þīhþ an þeáwum *where the gentle spirit thrives in morals*, Exon. 38 a; Th. 126, 9; Gū. 368. [*Icel.* hȳrr *sweet, smiling, mild*.] v. un-heóre.

heoro. v. heoru.

heorot, heort, es; *m. A hart, stag, male deer*:—Nān heort ne onscūnode nǣnne león *no hart shunned any lion*, Bt. 35, 6; Fox 168, 9. Heorot hornum trum *the hart firm of horns*, Beo. Th. 2742; B. 1369. Heorut *cervus*, Ps. Stev. 41, 1. Swā hwā swā slōge heort oððe hinde hine man sceolde blendian *whoever killed hart or hind should be blinded*, Chr. 1086; Erl. 222, 27, 28. Mid heortes horne and mid ylpenbāne *with hart's horn and with ivory*, Herb. 131, 2; Lchdm. i. 244, 8: Med. ex Quadr. 2, 1, 2, 3; Lchdm. i. 334, 2, 5, 9. Heortas and hinda *harts and hinds*, Bt. Met. Fox 19, 33; Met. 19, 17. Heortas *cervos*, Coll. Monast. Th. 21, 31. [*Icel.* hjörtr: *O. H. Ger.* hiruz *cervus*: *Ger.* hirsch.]

heorot-berge, an; *f. Berry of the buckthorn*, Lchdm. iii. 331, col. 1. [hart-berries *vaccinium myrtillus*, Engl. Dial. Soc. No. 26.]

heorot-brembel, es; *m. Buckthorn*; rhamnus, Lchdm. ii. 391–2.

heorot-brēr, e; *f. v.* [?] heorot-brembel:—Heortbrēre *moro*, Lk. Skt. Rush. 17, 6.

heorot-, heort-clæfre, an; *f. Hart-clover*; medicago maculata, Lchdm. ii. 392.

heorot-crop *a bunch of the flowers of hartwort*, Lchdm. ii. 392.

Heorot-, Heort-ford, es; *m. Hertford*:—Æt Heorotforda [Heortforda MS. D.] *at Hertford*, Chr. 913; Erl. 102, 1: 673; Erl. 36, 2; 37, 2.

heorr, hior; *m. f. A hinge, cardinal point*; cardo:—Ðeós heorr *hic cardo*, Ælfc. Gr. 9, 3; Som. 8, 61. Seó hior ðe eall gōd on hwearfaþ *the hinge on which all good turns*, Bt. 34, 7; Fox 142, 35. Wæs ðæt beorhte bold tōbrocen swīðe heorras tōhlidene *the splendid dwelling was sorely shattered, hinges were broken*, Beo. Th. 2002; B. 999. Heorras *serras*, Blickl. Gloss. Ðis gesceád ys æfter ðām feówor heorren *this distinction is according to the four cardinal points*, Lchdm. iii. 84, 11. [*Chauc.* 'no dore that he nolde heve of *harre*;' *Prompt. Parv.* herre of a lock *cardo*. v. note, p. 237: *Icel.* hjarri *a hinge*.]

heorra, an; *m.* [?] *A bar, hinge* [?]:—Hē gestrangode heorran geata ðīnra *confortavit seras portarum tuarum*, Ps. Lamb. 147, 2. v. heorr.

heort. v. heorot.

-heort. v. blīð-, ceald-, earm-, gram-, grim-, hāt-, heáh-, heard-, mild-, riht-, rūm-, sam-, stearc-, wulf-heort. [*Goth.* -hairts: *O. Sax.* -hert.]

heort-cōðu, es; *f. A disease of the heart*, L. M. 2, 1; Lchdm. ii. 176, 13.

HEORTE, an; *f. The* HEART:—Gif ðīn heorte ace *if thy heart ache*, Lchdm. iii. 42, 1. Ōþ ðæt him heortan blōd foldan gesēceþ *until his heart's blood seek the earth*, Salm. Kmbl. 314; Sal. 156 Wyxþ wind on ðære heortan *wind waxeth in the heart*, L. M. 1, 17; Lchdm. ii. 60, 7. Of ðære heortan cumaþ yfle geþancas *de corde exeunt cogitationes malæ*, Mt. Kmbl. 15, 19. Lustum heortena *desideriis cordum*, Ps. Th. 80, 12. [*Laym. A. R.* heorte: *Orm.* heorrte, herrte: *Chauc. Wick.* herte: *Goth.* hairto: *O.Sax.* herta: *O.Frs.* hirte: *Icel.* hjarta: *O.H.Ger.* herza: *Ger.* herz: *Lat.* cord-: *Grk.* καρδία.]

heort-ece, es; *m. Pain at the heart*:—Heó wið heortece well fremaþ *it is very beneficial for heartache*, Herb. 18, 3; Lchdm. i. 110, 19: *ad cardiacos*, 89, 3; Lchdm. i. 192, 16.

heorten; *adj. Of a hart*:— Healfes pundes gewihte beran smeruwes and heortenes *of bear's grease and of hart's, by weight of half a pound*, Herb. 101, 3; Lchdm. i. 216, 15.

heort-gesída; *pl. The entrails*; enta, Lev. 3, 3.

HEORÞ, es; *m. A* HEARTH, *fire-place;* and taking the name of the whole from that of a part, *a house*:—Heorþ *foculare*, Ælfc. Gl. 30; Som. 61, 73; Wrt. Voc. 27, 2: *arula*, Wrt. Voc. 63, 76. Hí ofslógon hine binnan his ágenan heorþæ *they slew him in his own house*, Chr. 1048; Erl. 177, 40. Hé sceolde bebeódan ðæt hí náman æt ǽlcum heorþe ánes geáres lamb *he was to command them to take a yearling lamb for every house*, Homl. Th. ii. 262, 27: Chart. Th. 609, 7, 11, 30. Of ǽlcum heorþe, 27. Be ǽlcum frigan heorþe, L. Edg. I. 2; Th. i. 262, 17: L. C. E. 11; Th. i. 366, 29: L. In. 61; Th. i. 140, 14. Beþe hwílum ða säran stöwe æt heorþe *warm the sore place at times at the hearth*, L. M. 2, 59; Lchdm. ii. 280, 26. Genim ðæt séleste hunig dó ofer heorþ *take the best honey, put it over the fire*, 2, 28; Lchdm. ii. 224, 17. Be heorþe, Lchdm. iii. 122, 21. Hweorfaþ æfter heorþe *they pass along the hearth* [*the floor of the fiery furnace*], Exon. 55 b; Th. 196, 18; Az. 176. [*Prompt. Parv.* herthe, where fyre ys made *ignearium, focarium*: *O.Frs.* herth, hirth, herd: *O. H. Ger.* hert *arula*: *Ger.* herd.]

heorþa, herþa, an; *m. A deer-skin*:—Heorþa *nebris*, Wrt. Voc. 86, 39.

heort-hama, an; *m. A covering of the heart*:—Heorthama *bucleamen*, Ælfc. Gl. 75; Som. 71, 102; Wrt. Voc. 45, 9. Ðú nymst ðone heart-haman *thou shalt take the fat that covers the inwards*, Ex. 29, 22. [*O. Frs.* hert-hamo *præcordia*.]

heorþ-bacen; *adj. Baked on the hearth*:—Heorþbacen hláf *subcinericius* vel *focarius*, Ælfc. Gl. 66; Som. 69, 64; Wrt. Voc. 41, 20. Mid heorþbacenum hláfe *with a loaf baked on the hearth*, Herb. 45, 2: Lchdm. i. 148, 8. Abraham nam ðæt flǽsc mid ðám heorþbacenum hláfum, Gen. 18, 8. Hí worhton þeorfe heorþbacene hláfas *they baked unleavened cakes*, Ex. 12, 39.

heorþ-cniht, es; *m. A domestic, servant, attendant*:—Hió dyde sciella tó bisene his heorþcneohtum and ðus cwæþ *sub squamarum specie de ejus satellitibus perhibetur*, Past. 47, 3; Swt. 361, 18.

heorþ-fæst; *adj. Having a house of one's own*:—Sý hé heorþfæst sý hé folgere *whether he have a house of his own or be the follower of another man*, L. C. S. 20; Th. i. 386, 23.

heorþ-geneát, es; *m. A hearth-comrade, a follower who shares the hearth of his lord*:—Wé synt Hygeláces heorþgeneátas, Beo. Th. 528; B. 261: 3165; B. 1580: 4365; B. 2180: 6341; B. 3180; Byrht. Th. 137, 50; By. 204.

heort-hogu, e; *f. Heart-care*:— Ðis mæg tó heorthoge ǽghwylcum bisceope *this may be care of heart for every bishop*, L. I. P. 5; Th. ii. 308, 27. v. hogu.

heorþ-pening, -peneg, es; *m. A tax of a penny to be paid by every house* [e.g. *Peter's pence*]:— Be ðon heorþpeninge. Sý ǽlc heorþpenig ágifen be Petres mæsse dæge: and seðe hine tó ðam ándagan gelǽst næbbe, lǽde hine tó Róme, and ðǽr tó eácan xxx pænega and bringe ðonne swutelunge ðæt hé ðǽr swá micel betǽht hæbbe. And ðonne hé hám cume gylde ðam cynge hundtwelftig scillinga *of the hearth-penny. Let every hearth-penny be paid up by St. Peter's mass day: and he who shall not have paid by that time, let him be led to Rome, and in addition thereto pay xxx pence, and then bring a certificate that he has there paid so much. And when he comes home let him pay the king a hundred and twenty shillings*, L. Edg. I. 4; Th. i. 264, 6-12. Sylle his heorþpænig on hálgan þunresdæg *let him pay his hearth-penny on holy Thursday*, L. R. S. 3; Th. i. 432, 26: 4; Th. i. 434, 19. Heorþpenegas, Chart. Th. 432, 24.

heorþ-swǽpe, an; *f. A bridesmaid;* pronuba, Som. [Cf. hád-swápe.]

heorþ-werod, es; *n. A band of household retainers, those who share the same hearth, a family*:—Ðá wearþ Jafeðe áféded heorþwerod suna and dóhtra *then for Japhet was reared a family of sons and daughters*, Cd. 78; Th. 96, 35; Gen. 1605. Se hálga héht his heorþwerod wǽpna onfón *the holy man bade his retainers take their weapons*, 94; Th. 123, 4; Gen. 2039: 95; Th. 125, 8; Gen. 2076: Byrht. Th. 132, 30; By. 24.

heort-lufe, an; *f. Love which comes from the heart*, Hy. 9, 29; Hy. Grn. ii. 292, 29.

heort-seóc; *adj. Heart-sick;* cardiacus, Cot. 209, Lye.

heort-seócnes *cardialgia*, Lye.

heort-wærc, es; *m. Pain in the heart*:—Wið heortwærce *for pain in the heart*, L. M. 1, 17; Lchdm. ii. 60, 4.

heoru, heoro, hioro; *m. A sword*, Beo. Th. 2574; B. 1285: Exon. 92 a; Th. 346, 10; Gn. Ex. 202. The word is a poetical one both in English and Icelandic, and in these dialects, as in Old Saxon, is mostly used in compounds. [*Goth.* hairus: *O. Sax.* heru (in compounds only): *Icel.* hjörr.]

heoru-cumbul, es; *n. A warlike ensign*, Elen. Kmbl. 213; El. 107.

heoru-dolg, es; *n. A sword-wound, deadly wound*, Andr. Kmbl. 1883; An. 944.

heoru-dreór, es; *m. Blood coming from wounds made by the sword, gore*, Beo. Th. 978; B. 487: 1703; B. 849.

heoru-dreórig; *adj.* I. *bloody with sword-wounds, gory*, Beo. Th. 1875; B. 935: 3564; B. 1780: 5434; B. 2720: Andr. Kmbl. 1991; An. 998: 2167; An. 1085: Elen. Kmbl. 2427; El. 1215. [*O. Sax.* heru-drórag.] II. *very sad, sad unto death*, Exon. 59 a; Th. 212, 28; Ph. 217.

heoru-drync, es; *m. The sword's drink, blood flowing from a wound*, Beo. Th. 4706; B. 2358. [Cf. *Icel.* hjör-lögr (lögr *any liquid*) *blood*.]

heoru-fæðm, es; *m. A deadly, hostile grasp*:—Wolde heoru [huru MS.] fæðmum hilde gesceádan *meant with deadly grasps to decide the conflict*, Cd. 167; Th. 209, 24; Exod. 504. [Cf. wælfæðmum, Th. 208, 9; Exod. 480.]

heoru-gífre; *adj. Greedy, eager to destroy*, Exon. 22 a; Th. 60, 29; Cri. 977: 23 b; Th. 65, 25; Cri. 1060: 74 a; Th. 276, 16; Jul. 567: Th. 277, 25; Jul. 586: Beo. Th. 3000; B. 1498.

heoru-grǽdig; *adj. Greedy to destroy, bloodthirsty, savagely greedy*, Andr. Kmbl. 75; An. 38: 158; An. 79.

heoru-grim; *adj. Very fierce* or *cruel, savage*, Exon. 30 a; Th. 93, 10; Cri. 1524: 31 b; Th. 98, 25; Cri. 1613: 47 a; Th. 161, 1; Gú. 952: 53 a; Th. 186, 29; Az. 27: 111 a; Th. 425, 12: Rä. 41, 55: Beo. Th. 3132; B. 1564: 3698; B. 1847: Elen. Kmbl. 237; El. 119: Andr. Kmbl. 61; An. 31: Cd. 189; Th. 235, 16; Dan. 307.

heoru-hóciht; *adj. Furnished with sharp hooks, barbed*, Beo. Th. 2880; B. 1438.

heoru-scearp; *adj. Terribly sharp*, Exon. 102 b; Th. 388, 15; Rä. 6, 8.

heoru-sceorp, es; *n. Warlike dress*, Exon. 120 b; Th. 463, 20; Hö. 73.

heoru-serce, an; *f. A war-shirt, coat of mail*, Beo. Th. 5072; B. 2539.

heoru-swealwe, an; *f. A hawk*, Exon. 88 b; Th. 332, 17; Vy. 86.

heoru-sweng, es; *m. A blow with a sword*, Beo. Th. 3184; B. 1539: Andr. Kmbl. 1903; An. 954.

heoru-wǽpen, es; *n. A weapon of war, a sword*, Judth. 12; Thw. 25, 16; Jud. 263.

heoru-weallende; *part. pres. Boiling fiercely*, Beo. Th. 5556; B. 2781.

heoru-wearh; *gen.* -wearges; *m. A savage, bloody wolf*, Beo. Th. 2538; B. 1267.

heoru-word, es; *n. A hostile, fierce word*, Exon. 81 a; Th. 305, 7; Fä. 84.

heoru-wulf, es; *m. A fierce wolf, a warrior*, Cd. 151; Th. 189, 7; Exod. 181. [Cf. here-wulf.]

heóþu, e; *f. A room, hall*:—Hé on heóþe gestód *he in the hall halted*, Beo. Th. 813; B. 404. [Dietrich in Haupt. x. 366 compares the word with κύτος: Heyne suggests a derivation from the root from which comes *heáh*, and translates as do Kemble and Thorpe *dais*, at the same time he gives the other etymology as a possible one.] v. hell-heóþo.

heow. v. hiw.

heowaþ, Ps. Th. 46, 1. v. heófan.

HÉR; *adv.* HERE, *in this world, at this time*:—Hér *hic*, Ælfc. Gr. 38; Som. 40, 1. Ðá ic hér ǽrest com *when I first came here*, Cd. 129; Th. 164, 8; Gen. 2711. Hér gehýrþ Drihten ða ðe hine biddaþ and him sylleþ heora synna forgyfnesse. Hér is his mildheortnes ofer ús ac ðér is se éca dóm *in this world the Lord heareth those that ask him and giveth them forgiveness of their sins. In this world his mercy is upon us, but in the next is the eternal judgement*, L. E. I. prm: Th. ii. 394, 4-16. Hér *in this year*, Chr. *passim*. [*Goth.* hér: *O. Sax.* hér, hier: *O. Frs.* hír; *Icel.* hér: *O.H.Ger.* hiar, hier: *Ger.* hier.]

hér *hair*. v. hǽr.

hér; *adj. Noble, excellent, honourable, holy, sublime*:—Gehýr ðis hére spel [herrespel, Thorpe], *hear this noble lay*, Exon. 93 a; Th. 348, 32; Sch. 37. [*O. Sax.* hér: *O.H.Ger.* hér, hére *almus, sanctus, magnificus*: *Ger.* hehr.]

héra, an; *m. One who obeys another, a servant, follower*:—Héra ɫ embehtmonn *minister*, Mk. Skt. Lind. 10, 43. Héra ɫ þegn *minister*, Jn. Skt. Lind. 12, 26. Héro *ministros*, Rtl. 11, 35. Æþelinga hleó beorna beággifa hérna hildfruma *the shelter of princes, ring-giver of warriors, warlike chief of his followers*, Elen. Kmbl. 201; El. 101. v. ambeht-héra *and* hýran.

hér-æfter; *adv. Hereafter*:— Swá swá wé eft héræfter secgaþ *as we shall again hereafter say*, Bd. 3, 30; S. 562, 5.

héran. v. hýran.

hēr-būende; *pl. People living in this world*, Cd. 52; Th. 66, 4; Gen. 1079: Judth. 10; Thw. 22, 38; Jud. 96: Bt. Met. Fox 29, 124; Met. 9, 62.

hēr-bufan; *adv. Here above*:—Swā swā wē ǽr hērbiufan sǽdon on đisse ilcan bēc *as we said before above in this same book*; sicut in priori hujus voluminis parte jam diximus, Past. 50, 4; Swt. 393, 2.

hēr-cyme, es; *m. A coming here, coming to this world, advent*:—Þurh đīnne hērcyme *through thy advent*, Exon. 11 b; Th. 16, 8; Cri. 250.

herd. v. heord.

herdan. v. hyrdan.

herde. v. hirde.

HERE; *gen.* heres, heriges, herges; *m. An army, a host, multitude, a large predatory band* [it is the word which in the Chronicle is always used of the Danish force in England, while the English troops are always the *fyrd*], hence the word is used for *devastation* and *robbery*:—Ne dohte hit nū lange inne nē ūte ac wæs here and hunger bryne and blōdgyte *it is now long since matters were thriving at home or abroad, but there has been ravaging and famine, burning and bloodshed*, Swt. A. S. Rdr. 106, 68. Micel here *turba multa*, Mt. Kmbl. Lind. 14, 14. Here *legio*, Lk. Skt. Lind. 8, 30: *exercitus*, 23, 11. Þeófas wē hātaþ ōđ vii men from vii. hlōþ ōđ xxxv siđđan biþ here *up to seven men we call thieves, from seven to thirty-five a gang, after that it is an army*, L. In. 13; Th. i. 110, 14. [Cf. L. In. 15; Th. i. 112, 1, be herige; and L. Alf. 28; Th. i. 52, 2.] Hē gearo wǽre tō đæs heres þearfe *he would be ready to supply the needs of the Danes*, Chr. 874; Erl. 76, 32: 878; Erl. 80, 3. Đæs heriges hām eft ne com ǽnig tō lāfe *of that host came no remnant back home*, Cd. 167; Th. 209, 30; Exod. 507: Elen. Kmbl. 410; El. 205. Herges, 285; El. 143. On East-Englum wurdon monige men ofslægene from đam herige *in East Anglia many men were slain by the Danes*, Chr. 838; Erl. 66, 15: Andr. Kmbl. 2397; An. 1200. Herge, Cd. 4; Th. 4, 9; Gen. 51: Beo. Th. 2500; B. 1248. Se đæm here waldeþ *who rules that host*, Bt. Met. Fox 25, 30; Met. 25, 15. Sió fierd đone here gefliémde *the English force put the Danish to flight*, Chr. 894; Erl. 90, 26. Swā oft swā đa ōđre hergas mid ealle herige ūt fōron đonne fōron hie *as often as the other armies marched out in full force then they marched*, Erl. 90, 5. Tuelf hergas *duodecim legiones*, Mt. Kmbl. Lind. 26, 53. Hergia[s] *agmina*, Rtl. 115, 10. Đȳ læs ǽfre cweđan ōđre þeóda hǽđene herigeas *nequando dicant in gentibus*, Ps. Th. 78, 10: Andr. Kmbl. 1304; An. 652. Herigea mǽste *with the greatest of hosts*, 3001; An. 1503. Herega, Cd. 209; Th. 259, 29; Dan. 699. Heriga, Elen. Kmbl. 295; El. 148. Herga, 230; El. 115. Betwuh đǽm twām hergum *between the two armies*, Chr. 894; Erl. 90, 9: Elen. Kmbl. 219; El. 110. Herigum, 811; El. 406. [*Laym. Orm.* here: *Goth.* harjis: *O. Sax.* heri: *O. Frs.* hiri, here: *Icel.* herr: *O. H. Ger.* hari, heri *exercitus, agmen*: *Ger.* heer.] DER. æsc-, ēgor-, flot-, forþ-, gūþ-, inn-, īsern-, sin-, scip-, þeód-, ūt-, wæl-here.

hēre, e; *f. Dignity, majesty, greatness*:—Hwæt hiora hēre būton se hlīsa ān *what is their greatness but report alone*, Bt. Met. Fox 10, 107; Met. 10, 54. The prose, Fox 70, 10, has 'Hwæt is heora nū tō lāfe būtan se lytla hlīsa and se nama mid feáum stafum āwriten *signat superstes fama tenuis pauculis inane nomen litteris*.' [*O. H. Ger.* hēre: *f. dignitas, majestas, magnitudo*: cf. *O. H. Ger.* hēr-tōm *dignitas, auctoritas, principatus*, Grff. iv. 994: *O. Sax.* hēr-dōm.]

here-beácen; -beácn, es; *n. A military ensign, standard*; also *a beacon, lighthouse*:—Herebeácn *farus*: upstandende herebeácn *pira*, Ælfc. Gl. 67; Som. 69, 93, 90; Wrt. Voc. 41, 45, 43. Herebeácen and segnas beforan mē lǽddon *cum signis et vexillis*, Nar. 7, 16. [*O. H. Ger.* heri-pouhan *vexillum, signum*.]

here-bleáþ; *adj. Fearful in fight, timorous*:—Flugon forhtigende woldon herebleáþe hāmas findan *fearful they fled and shunning the battle would find their homes*, Cd. 166; Th. 206, 17; Exod. 453.

here-brōga, an; *m. The terror produced by an army* or *by war*, Beo. Th. 928; B. 462.

here-bȳme, an; *f. A war-trumpet*, Cd. 147; Th. 183, 29; Exod. 99. [Cf. *Icel.* her-horn, her-luðr *a trumpet*: *O.H.Ger.* heri-, her-horn *classicum, tuba*.]

here-byrne, an; *f. A war-corslet*, Beo. Th. 2890; B. 1443. [*Laym.* here-burne.]

here-cirm, es; *m. A war-shout, shout raised by a host*, Exon. 45 b; Th. 156, 9; Gū. 872.

here-cumbol, -combol, es; *m. A military signal*:—Wordum and bordum hōfon herecombol *with shouts and shields they raised the war-signal*, Elen. Kmbl. 49; El. 25. Cf. [?] Tacitus, Germania c. 3: 'As their line shouts, they inspire or feel alarm. It is not so much an articulate sound, as a general cry of valour. They aim chiefly at a harsh note and a confused roar, putting their shields to their mouths, so that, by reverberation, it may swell into a fuller and deeper sound.' [*Icel.* her-kuml *a war-token, arms on shields* or *helmets*.]

here-cyst, -cist, e; *f. A warlike troop*, Cd. 151; Th. 188, 32; Exod. 177: 156; Th. 194, 7; Exod. 257: 158; Th. 197, 3; Exod. 301.

here-draca, an; *A war-drake, an arrow*:—Herdracan, Hickes' Thes. p. 192. [Cf. hilde-nædre.]

here-feld, es; *m. A field, battle-field*, Elen. Kmbl. 537; El. 269: 251; El. 126: Andr. Kmbl. 19; An. 10: 35; An. 18.

here-feoh; *gen.* -feós; *n. Booty*:—Eal đæt herefeoh forlēton *prædam amiserunt*, Ors. 3, 7; Swt. 118, 5.

here-fēđa, an; *m. A martial band*, Exon. 22 b; Th. 63, 1; Cri. 1013.

here-flēma, an; *m. One who flees from battle*, Chr. 937; Erl. 112, 23; Æđelst. 23.

here-folc, es; *n. People forming an army*, Judth. 11; Thw. 24, 40; Jud. 234. [*O. Frs.* hiri-folk: *Icel.* her-fōlk *men of war*.]

here-fong, es; *m. An osprey*; ossifragus, Wrt. Voc. 280, 6.

Here-ford, es; *m. Hereford*:—Đa men of Herefordа *the men from Hereford*, Chr. 918; Erl. 102, 31.

here-fugol, es; *m. A bird which attends an army, eagle, vulture, raven*, Cd. 150; Th. 188, 2; Exod. 161. v. earn, hrefn.

here-gang, es; *m. An irruption, attack by an army*:—Tō widscūfanne swā rēþum heregange *ad repellendas tam feras inruptiones*, Bd. 1, 14; S. 482, 37, MS. B. [*Laym.* hire-ȝeong: *Gen. and Ex.* heregong *military expedition*: *O. Frs.* hiri-, heri-gong *an attack*: cf. *Icel.* her-ganga; *f. a march*.]

heregeat-land, es; *n. Heriot-land*, Chart. Th. 546, 37.

here-geatu; *gen.* -geatwe; *f.* I. *military equipment*:—Hī willaþ eów tō gafole gāras syllan ǽttrynne ord and ealde swurd đa heregeatu đe eów æt hilde ne deáh *they will give you as tribute spears, the poisoned point and the swords they inherit, equipment for war that will not profit you in battle*, Byrht. Th. 133, 10; By. 48. Heregeatewa, MS. A: heregeatowe, B. wægeþ *it bears arms*, Salm. Kmbl. 106; Sal. 52. Đa beóþ mid gyldenum hyltsweordum and mid manigfealdum heregeatwum gehyrste *septos tristibus armis*, Bt. 37, 1; Fox 186, 6: Bt. Met. Fox 25, 17; Met. 25, 9. II. as a technical term, *heriot*. The amount of the heriot for various ranks is given L. C. S. 72; Th. i. 414, 4–20; further mention is also made in L. C. S. 71; Th. i. 412, 26–414, 2: 74; Th. i. 416, 3–18: 79; Th. i. 420, 13–17. The word also occurs in the following passages in wills, Chart. Th. 499, 29: 512, 16: 540, 5; 550, 28: 573, 3. For the origin and nature of the heriot see Stubbs' Const. Hist. s. v. Kemble's Saxons in England, ii. 98. [Cf. Grmm. R. A. 372–3.]

heregend-līc. v. herigend-līc.

here-gild, es; *n. A war-tax, the Danegild, tax to support an army*:—Hēr wæs đet heregeold gelǽst đæt wǽron xxi þūsend punda and xcix punda *in this year the Danegild was paid, it was twenty-one thousand and ninety-nine pounds*, Chr. 1040; Erl. 167, 23. Swā fela sȳđe swa menn gyldaþ heregyld ođđe tō scipgylde *quotiens populus universus persolvit censum Danis, vel ad naves seu ad arma*, Chart. Th. 307, 23. Scotfrē fram heregeld *free from payment of the war-tax*, Cod. Dipl. Kmbl. iv. 224, 20.

here-grīma, an; *m. A helmet*, Beo. Th. 797; B. 396: 4104; B. 2049: 5203; B. 2605.

heregung. v. hergung.

here-hand, a; *f. A hostile hand* or *power*:—Swā đæt ne cyricum ne mynstrum seó herehand ne sparode ne ārode *ita ut ne ecclesiis quidem, aut monasteriis manus parceret hostilis*, Bd. 4, 26; S. 602, 8.

here-hlōþ, e; *f. A hostile troop*, Exon. 48 a; Th. 166, 13; Gū. 1042.

here-hȳþ, -hūþe, e; *f. Spoil, booty, plunder*:—Hēr wæs mycel herehūþe [herehȳþe, MS. C.] đǽr genumen *in this year much spoil was taken at Bamborough*, Chr. 993; Erl. 133, 2. Hē his đone feórþan dǽl and đære herehȳþe for Gode gesealde *quartam partem ejus et prædæ Domino daret*, Bd. 4, 16; S. 584, 10. Hiera heres đone mǽstan dǽl hām sendon mid hiora herehȳþe *præcipuam exercitus sui partem onustam præda domum revocant*, Ors. 1, 10; Swt. 46, 21. Mid đære herehȳþe [herehūþe, MS. E.], Chr. 885; Erl. 82, 30. Đa mycele herehūþe tō scipon brohton *they brought the great booty to the ships*, 1001; Erl. 137, 15. Đa herehȳhþ đe on helle genumen hæfde *the spoil that he had taken in hell*, Blickl. Homl. 89, 33. Genimon myccle herehȳþ *to take great spoil*, 95, 2. Ymbe đa herehūþe hlemmeþ tōgædre grimme gōman *on the prey he snaps together his fierce jaws*, Exon. 97 b; Th. 363, 29; Wal. 61. Đone here gefliémde and đa herehȳþ āhreddon *put the Danes to flight and rescued the spoils*, Chr. 894; Erl. 90, 26. [*O. H. Ger.* heri-hunda, -hunta *preda*.]

here-lāf, e; *f. The remnant of an army* or *people, what is left of an army after a battle, what is left after a battle, spoil*:—Se Chaldēa cyning com tō his earde mid đære hūþe and đære herelāfe on đære wæs Daniel se wītega and đa þrī cnihtas *the king of Chaldea came to his country with the spoil and the remnant of the people, among which was the prophet Daniel and the three children*, Swt. A. S. Rdr. 68, 380, 392. Gūþrum se hǽđene king twelf dages hēr on lande wunede and syđđan gewende mid his herelāfe tō his āgenen earde *Guthrum the heathen king stopped twelve days in this land and afterwards returned with what remained of his army to his own country*, Shrn. 17, 8. Þurh gītsunge wearþ beswicen Sawl se cyning đā đā him leófran wǽron đa forbodenan herelāfa đonne Godes willa *through avarice was king Saul betrayed when he preferred* the forbidden spoils of the host [of the Amalekites, v. 1 Sam. xv. 9] to the will of God, Basil. admn. 9; Norm. 54, 8. Costontinus ne Ánláf mid heora herelâfum hlehhan ne þorftun *not Constantine nor Anlaf, with the remnants of their forces, had cause for laughing*, Chr. 937; Erl. 114, 13; Æđelst. 47.

here-líc; *adj. Warlike, military:* — Đa herelícan *res militares*, Cot. 47, Lye.

here-lof, es; *n. Praise gained in war, fame, glory;* also *a trophy;* rumor, fama, Hpt. Gl. 406, 511, 512: 447.

here-mæcg, es; *m. A man of war, warrior, man* [*used of the men of Sodom when attacking Lot*], Cd. 114; Th. 149, 31; Gen. 2483. [Cf. *Icel.* her-megir *warriors.*]

here-mægen, es; *n. A warlike force, an army, a host, multitude*, Exon. 116 b; Th. 447, 10; Dóm. 37: Andr. Kmbl. 1172; An. 586: 1456; An. 728: 2597; An. 1300: 3299; An. 1652: Elen. Kmbl. 339; El. 170.

here-man, -mann, es; *m. A soldier:* — Heremenn *milites*, Lk. Skt. Lind. 7, 8. [*Icel.* her-maðr.] v. Grmm. R. A. 292.

hére-man. v. híre-man.

here-medel, es; *n. A warlike assembly;* concio, Elen. Kmbl. 1096; El. 550.

here-nes, -nis, -ness, e; *f. Praise:* — Herenes mín *laudatio mea*, Ps. Th. 103, 32: 110, 8: 117, 14. Herenis *laus*, Rtl. 30, 23: 174, 31. In herenesse Godes *in laudem Dei*, Bd. 4, 24; S. 597, 17: 599, 12; Ps. 55, 10. Hê geearnode đæt hê đa hâlgan hærenesse gehýrde *laudes beatas meruit audire*, Bd. 3, 19; S. 547, 35. v. here-word.

here-net, -nett, es; *n. A war-net, coat of mail, corslet*, Beo. Th. 3110; B. 1553.

here-níþ, es; *m. Hostility, enmity which is felt by those at war with one another*, Beo. Th. 4938; B. 2474.

here-nitig [?] *expeditio*, Cot. 73, Lye.

here-pád, e; *f. A coat of mail*, Beo. Th. 4508; B. 2258.

here-, her-paþ, es; *m. A road for an army, military road, road large enough to march soldiers upon* [occurs not unfrequently in charters]:— Ondlong herpoþes, Cod. Dipl. Kmbl. ii. 172, 18. Up tô herpaþe and fram đam herpaþe súþrihte, 205, 20. On đone brâdan herpaþ, iii. 23, 35. Wísde herepoþ tô đære heán byrig *shewed a road for his army to the lofty city*, Cd. 174; Th. 218, 12; Dan. 38. Hí swyrdum herpaþ worhton þurh lâđra gemong *they with their swords wrought a road through the press of their foes*, Judth. 12; Thw. 26, 1; Jud. 303. DER. þeód-herpaþ.

here-ræ̂swa, an; *m. A chieftain*, Elen. Kmbl. 1987; El. 995.

here-reáf, es; *n. Spoil, plunder, booty:*—Herereáf *spolia* vel *manubie* vel *prede*, Ælfc. Gl. 52; Som. 66, 52; Wrt. Voc. 35, 38: *manubiæ, spolia*, Ælfc. Gr. 13; Som. 16, 16, 23. Achan behýdde of đam herereáfe *Achan concealed some of the spoil*, Jos. 7, 1, 11. Đú ús mycel herereáf gehête *thou didst promise us much spoil*, Blickl. Homl. 85, 19. Hengest and Æsc gefuhton wiđ Walas and genâmon unârímedlîco herereáf *Hengest and Æsc fought with the Britons and took countless spoils*, Chr. 473; Erl. 12, 26: 584; Erl. 18, 25. Hê tôdæ̂lþ his herereáf *spolia ejus distribuit*, Lk. Skt. 11, 22. Ic geseah betwux đam herereáfum sumne gildene dalc *I saw among the spoils a wedge of gold*, Jos. 7, 21.

here-rinc, es; *m. A warrior*, Bt. Met. Fox 1, 141; Met. 1, 71: [here-ric, MS.] Beo. Th. 2356; B. 1176. [*O. Sax.* heri-rink.]

here-sceaft, es; *m. A war-shaft, spear*, Beo. Th. 675; B. 335.

here-sceorp, es; *n. War-dress*, Fins. Th. 90; Fin. 45.

here-serce, -syrce, an; *f. A coat of mail*, Beo. Th. 3027; B. 1511.

here-síþ, es; *m. The journey of an army, a military expedition, march*, Elen. Kmbl. 265; El. 133: Exon. 108 a; Th. 411, 24; Rä. 30, 4: 84 a; Th. 317, 3; Mód. 60.

here-spêd, e; *f. Success in war*, Beo. Th. 129; B. 64.

here-spel. v. hêr.

here-stræl, es; *m. An arrow*, Beo. Th. 2874; B. 1435.

here-stræ̂t, e; *f. A military road, one allowing the passage of an army, highway, high road:*—Lêton đone hâlgan be herestræ̂te swefan on sibbe *they left the saint sleeping in peace by the highway*, Andr. Kmbl. 1662; An. 833. Đanan on herestræ̂t *thence to the high road*, Cod. Dipl. Kmbl. ii. 265, 30. [Cf. ođ đa wýdestræ̂te, 32.] Wegas syndon drýge herestræ̂ta *the ways* [*through the Red Sea*] *are dry, the roads for the host*, Cd. 157; Th. 195, 29; Exod. 284. Ne mê herestræ̂ta ofer cald wæter cûþe sindon *nor are the highways over the cold water known to me*, Andr. Kmbl. 400; An. 200. Gegier đæt đíne willas iernan bî herestræ̂tum *in plateis aquas divide*, Past. 48, 6; Swt. 373, 6. Æfter cyninga herestræ̂tum *along king's highways*, 373, 18. Ic hí âdilgode swâ swâ wind dêþ dust on herestræ̂tum *ut lutum platearum delebo eos*, Ps. Th. 17, 40. Omnes herestrete omnino regis sunt, L. H. 10, 2; Th. i. 519, 11. [*O. Frs.* hiri-strete: *O. H. Ger.* heri-strâza *via publica.*] Cf. here-paþ, -weg.

here-swêg, es; *m. A martial sound*, Exon. 124 a; Th. 477, 12; Ruin. 23.

here-teám, es; *m.* I. *plundering, spoiling, devastation, taking part in a* 'here,' i. e. *a predatory band of more than thirty-five members* [v. here]:—Se đe hereteáme betogen sý *he who is accused of taking part in a* 'here,' L. In. 15; Th. i. 112, 2, MS. H. Heardlíc hereteám *fierce devastation*, Andr. Kmbl. 3100; An. 1553. II. *what is got by an army, plunder, booty, spoil:*—Đæs hereteámes ealles teóþan sceat *a tithe of all the spoil*, Cd. 97; Th. 128, 4; Gen. 2121. Gewât hâm síþian mid đý hereteáme đe him se hâlga forgeaf *departed home with the spoil that the holy man gave him*, 98; Th. 130, 19; Gen. 2162.

here-têma, -týma, an; *m. A leader of an army, of a people, a ruler, general:* — Se heretêma cyning selfa *the leader, the king himself* [*Theodoric*], Bt. Met. Fox 1, 62; Met. 1, 31. Se heretýma, caldêa cyning, Cd. 205; Th. 253, 30; Dan. 603. Đâ cwæþ hê hwæs sunu is hit đâ cwæþ se bisceop mínes heretêman *then said he 'whose son is it?' Then said the bishop 'my prince's'* [?], Shrn. 130, 9. Hê wearþ tô heretêman *he became general*, Elen. Kmbl. 20; El. 10.

here-þreát, es; *m. A troop, band of soldiers*, Cd. 170; Th. 214, 24; Exod. 574: *cohortes*, Cot. 51, Lye.

here-þrym *a cohort*, Cot. 84, Lye.

here-toga, -toha, an; *m. The leader of an army* or *of a people, a general;* dux, consul: — Heretoga *vel* heorl *dux*, Ælfc. Gl. 68; Som. 70, 2; Wrt. Voc. 42, 11. Heretoga *comes*, Rtl. 193, 9. Of đê forþgæ̂þ se heretoga seđe recþ mín folc *ex te exiet dux, qui reget populum meum*, Mt. Kmbl. 2, 6. Consul đæt wê heretoha hâtaþ *consul which we call 'heretoha,'* Bt. 1; Fox 2, 12: 21; Fox 76, 4. Sum biþ heretoga fyrdwísa from *one is a leader, a good guide of the host*, Exon. 79 b; Th. 297, 31; Crä. 76. Se heretoga Moyses *the leader Moses*, Homl. Th. i. 92, 25. Moises se mæ̂ra heretoga *Moses the great leader*, Num. 13, 1: Jud. 1, 1: Swt. A. S. Rdr. 60, 107. Uton ús gesettan heretogan *let us make a captain*, Num. 14, 4. Heora heretogan twegen gebrođra Hengest and Horsa *duces eorum duo fratres Hengest and Horsa*, Bd. 1, 15; S. 483, 28. Heora heretogena sum ofslægen wearþ *one of their leaders was slain*, Chr. 794; Erl. 59, 21. Twelf heretogan hê gestrînþ *twelve princes shall he beget*, Gen. 17, 20. De heretochiis, L. Ed. C; Th. i. 456, note a. [*Laym.* here-toȝe: *O. Sax.* heri-togo: *Icel.* her-togi: *O. H. Ger.* heri-zoho, -zogo *dux, imperator: Ger.* herzog.] v. Stubbs' Const. Hist. s. v.

here-togen [?]; *pp. Captive:* — Seó herelâf wunode đæs heretogan [heretogenan?] folces on Chaldêiscum earde *the remnant of the captive people dwelt in the land of Chaldea*, Swt. A. S. Rdr. 69, 393. [Cf. *Icel.* her-numinn, -tekinn *captive.*]

here-wæ̂d, e; *f. War-weed, armour*, Beo. Th. 3798; B. 1897. [*Icel.* her-vâðir *armour.*] v. Grmm. R. A. 566-7.

here-wæ̂pen, es; *n. A weapon of war*, Ps. Ben. 34, 3; Ps. Grn. ii. 149, 3.

here-wæsmun:—Nô ic mê an herewæsmun hnâgran talige gûþgeweorca đonne Grendel hine, Beo. Th. 1358; B. 677. *Thorpe reads* wæstmum [*see the use of* wæstm *in the plural*] *and translates 'in martial vigour.' Grein translates by* vis bellica *and refers the word to a nominative* wæ̂sma, *comparing O. H. Ger.* wahsamo, wasmo, wasma *vigor, fructus, fertilitas*, Grff. i. 689. *Leo and Heyne connect with a root meaning rage, fury*, v. Leo. 494. *Taking either of the first the passage might be translated 'I do not account myself worse in the warlike fruits of martial deeds than Grendel himself;'* or an herewæsmum *and* gûþgeweorca *might be taken as both dependent upon* hnâgran.

here-wæ̂da, an; *m. A war-hunter, a hunter whose game is the enemy*, Judth. 11; Thw. 23, 17; Jud. 126: Thw. 24, 5; Jud. 173. v. Grmm. Geschicht. D. S. 12 sqq.

here-weg, es; *m. A highway, high road:*—Ealles hereweg *publica via*, Ælfc. Gl. 57; Som. 67, 52; Wrt. Voc. 37, 39. [*O. Frs.* heer-wei: cf. *Icel.* her-vegir *war-paths.*] v. here-paþ, -stræ̂t.

here-weorc, es; *n. A warlike deed* or *work*, Elen. Kmbl. 1308; El. 656.

herewian; *p.* ode *To despise:* — Tô swîđe wê herewiaþ ús selfe *we despise ourselves too much*, Bt. 13; Fox 40, 12. Leófsunu herewade đæs arcebiscopes gewitnesse *Leofsunu incepit vituperare archiepiscopum et testimonium ejus irritum facere*, Chart. Th. 273, 2. v. herwan.

here-wíc, es; *n. An encampment, camp, dwelling:* — Míne welan đe ic hæfde syndon ealle gewitene and míne herewíc syndon gebrosnode *my riches that I had are all departed and my dwellings are decayed*, Blickl. Homl. 113, 26. Him mon sægde đæt đæ̂r mon cymen wæs of Alexandres herewícum *he was told that a man was come from Alexander's camp*, Nar. 18, 9: Cd. 95; Th. 123, 26; Gen. 2051.

here-wísa, an; *m. The director, guide of an army, a leader, general*, Cd. 160; Th. 198, 15; Exod. 323.

here-wóp, es; *m. The shout raised by an army*, Cd. 166; Th. 207, 2; Exod. 460. [*Icel.* her-óp *war-whoop, war-cry.*]

here-word, es; *n. Praise, applause:* — Đâ wolde Brihtríc geearnian him hereword *tunc cogitavit Brihtricus adquirere sibi laudem*, Chr. 1009; Erl 142, note 8. [*Laym.* hære-, here-word: A. R. 'a windes puf of worldes hereword, of mannes heriunge,' 148, 3.] v. here-nes, herian *to praise.*

here-wósa, an; *m. One who is fierce in fight, a warrior* [?]: — Herewōsan hige *a warrior's soul*, Cd. 206; Th. 255, 24; Dan. 629. Siđđan herewōsan heofon ofgǣfon *since those who fiercely fought gave up heaven*, 5; Th. 6, 7; Gen. 85. [Cf. ealo-wōsa, wudu-wāsa.]

here-wulf, es; *m. A war-wolf, warrior*, Cd. 94; Th. 121, 25; Gen. 2015.

herfest. v. hærfest.

hergan. v. herian.

hergaþ, hergoþ, es; *m. Harrying, plundering, making war*:—Hē wæs đā ūtāfaren on hergaþ *he was then gone out a harrying*, Chr. 894; Erl. 91, 20: 911; Erl. 100, 25: 918; Erl. 102, 30. Faran on hergoþ *to wage war*, Thw. 162, 37.

heregend-līc. v. herigendlīc.

hergere, es; *m. One who praises; laudator*, Rtl. 124, 17.

hergian; *p.* ode; *pp.* od *To harry, pillage, plunder, ravage, waste, devastate, make an incursion* or *a raid, make war*:—Đa Cwēnas hergiaþ hwīlum on đa Norþmen ofer đone mōr hwīlum đa Norþmen on hȳ *sometimes the Fins made incursions across the mountains on the Norwegians, sometimes the Norwegians on them*, Ors. 1, 1; Swt. 19, 3. Se here hergade on Peohtas *the Danes made raids upon the Picts*, Chr. 875; Erl. 78, 1. Fōr Willelm cyng into France mid fyrde and hergode uppan his āgenne hlāforde Philippe *king William marched with an army into France and made war upon his own lord Philip*, 1086; Erl. 220, 25: Homl. Th. ii. 58, 5. Wera hof hergode *laid waste the dwellings of men*, Cd. 69; Th. 83, 15; Gen. 1380. Đa hǣđenan on Norþhymbrum hergodon *the heathens ravaged in Northumbria*, Chr. 794; Erl. 59, 20. Hie hergodon ofer Mercna land ōþ hie cōmon tō Creccagelāde *they carried on their ravages across Mercia until they came to Cricklade*, 905; Erl. 98, 14. Mycel sciphere hider com and hergedon swīđe be Sefærn *a great fleet came to this country and committed great depredations along the Severn*, 910; Erl. 101, 7. Gif ǣnig sciphere on Engla lande hergie *if any fleet commit ravages in England*, L. Eth. ii. 1; Th. i. 284, 15, 18. Sǣdon đæt hī woldan him sylfe niman and hergian đǣr hī hit findan mihton *protestantur se cuncta insulæ loca vastaturos*, Bd. 1, 15; S. 483, 38. Hī sceoldan ealle ætgædere faran and hergian *they should go all together and harry*, Chr. 1014; Erl. 151, 3. Hē wæs heriende and feohtende fīftig wintra *arma foras extulit, cruentamque vitam quinquaginta annis bellis egit*, Ors. 1, 2; Swt. 28, 28. [*Laym.* hærȝien: *Chauc.* haried, harwed: *Icel.* herja *to harry;* herjask ā *to wage war on one another*: *O. H. Ger.* harion, herion *populare, vastare*: cf. *Ger.* verheeren.] DER. ge-, ofer-, on-hergian.

hergung, heregung, e; *f. Harrying, harrowing, plundering, devastation, waging war, an irruption, incursion, invasion, a raid, plunder*:—Seó hergung wæs þurh Alaricum Gotena cyning geworden *inruptio quæ per Alaricum regem Gothorum facta est*, Bd. 1, 11; S. 480, 11. Hēđenra manna hergung ādiligode Godes cyrican in Lindisfarena ee þurh reáflāc and mansleht *the harrying of heathen men destroyed God's church at Lindisfarne by plundering and slaughter*, Chr. 793; Erl. 59, 11. Đæt mǣste yfel đe ǣfre ǣnig here dōn mihte on bærnette and hergunge and on manslihtum *the greatest evil that any army could do in the way of burning and plundering and manslayings*, 994; Erl. 133, 18. On ānre heregunge *in a single invasion*, Jos. 10, 40. Be his ǣriste and be his hergunga on helle *concerning his resurrection and his harrowing of hell*, Blickl. Homl. 83, 29. Hell oncneów Crist đā đā heó forlēt hyre hæftlingas ūt þurh đæs Hǣlendes hergunge *Hell acknowledged Christ when it let out its captives through the harrowing of Jesus*, Homl. Th. i. 228, 17. Hī hergodon and brohton tō đam castele đa hergunge *they plundered and brought the plunder to the castle*, Chr. 1087; Erl. 224, 19. Đā forlēt hē his hergunga *then he left off his harryings*, 1016; Erl. 154, 10.

herian, hærian, hergan; *p.* ode, ede; *imper.* hera *and* here; *pp.* ed *To praise*:—Đē ic herige swā swā wīsne man *te laudo ut sapientem*, Ælfc. Gr. 15; Som. 17, 64: Ps. Th. 55, 4, 9. Ic herge, Exon. 41 b; Th. 138, 28; Gū. 583. Đæt đæt mon hereþ *hoc ipsum quod laudatur*, Past. 48, 5; Swt. 373, 2. Leofaþ sāwl mīn and đē hereþ *vivet anima mea et laudabit te*, Ps. Th. 118, 175. Heraþ, 101, 16. Weleras đē mīne heriaþ *labia mea laudabunt te*, 62, 3. Wē đē hæriaþ *we praise thee*, Hy. 7, 116; Hy. Grn. ii. 289, 116. Herigaþ, Cd. 214; Th. 267, 33; Swt. 47. Ic nāt for hwȳ gē đa tīda swelcra brōca swā wel hergeaþ *I know not why ye praise so highly the times of such miseries*, Ors. 3, 7; Swt. 120, 4: Blickl. Homl. 89, 31. Hergaþ, Cd. 192; Th. 239, 24; Dan. 375. Heó Drihten herede *she praised the Lord*, Blickl. Homl. 13, 4: Lk. Skt. 16, 8. Đæs cininges ealdormenn heredon hig beforan him *the princes of Pharaoh commended her before Pharaoh*, Gen. 12, 15. Hit is āwriten ne hera đū nǣnne man on his līfe *it is written 'Praise no man during his life,'* Homl. Th. ii. 560, 13. Đē silfne ne hera *do not praise thyself*, Salm. Kmbl. 262, 21. Here đū, Sion, swylce đīnne sōþne God *lauda Deum tuum, Sion*, Ps. Th. 147, 1. Mīn hearpe herige Drihten *let my harp praise the Lord*, 56, 10. Herge, Beo. Th. 6333; B. 3177. Đeáh hira hīeremenn hie mid ryhte heregen *though their subjects with justice praise them*, Past. 19; Swt. 145, 22. Herian, Ps. Th. 65, 1. Hergen, Exon. 54 b; Th. 191, 27: Az. 94. Hie heofona helm herian ne cūđon *they did not know how to praise the heaven's protector*, Beo. Th. 367; B. 182. Hergan, Exon. 8 b; Th. 4, 8; Cri. 49. Herigean, Bd. 4, 24; S. 597, 20. Heó is ūs tō herianne *she is to be praised by us*, Blickl. Homl. 11, 11. Tō herigenne, 63, 21. Tō hergenne, 223, 27. Se hālga wer hergende wæs metodes miltse *the holy man was praising the Lord's mercy*, Cd. 190; Th. 237, 8; Dan. 334. Herigende, Andr. Kmbl. 1314; An. 657. Đū byst hered *perfecisti laudem*, Ps. Th. 8, 2; Blickl. Homl. 67, 4. [*Laym.* herien, hærien: *A. R.* herede; *p*: *Chauc. Wick.* herie: *Spens.* herry, hery: *Goth.* hazjan *to praise.*]

herian [=herewian; cf. gearwian, gerian] *to despise*:—Agar ongan āgendfreán herian *Hagar despised her mistress* [cf. Gen. 16, 4 'her mistress was despised in her eyes'], Cd. 102; Th. 135, 5; Gen. 2238.

herigend-, hergend-līc; *adj. Praiseworthy, laudable*:—Ne biþ nān angiun herigendlīc būtan gōdre geendunge *no beginning is praiseworthy without a good ending*, Homl. Th. i. 56, 26; 212, 29. Hergendlīc in worlda world *laudabile in secula seculorum*, Blickl. Homl. 139, 11. Hergiendlīc *laudabilis*, Rtl. 181, 27. Đa giftu beóþ herigendlīce *that marriage is praiseworthy*, Homl. Th. ii. 54, 10.

herigend-, hergend-līce; *adv. Praiseworthily*:—Hē sylf herigendlīce leofode *he himself lived praiseworthily*, Homl. Th. ii. 118, 14. Hergiendlīce *laudabiliter*, Rtl. 105, 3. Hergeondlīce, Past. 7; Swt. 49, 193.

hēr-inne; *adv. Herein*, Homl. Th. ii. 312, 4.

hēr-, hǣr-līc; *adj. Noble, excellent*:—Næs đæt hērlīc dǣd *that was no noble deed*, Bt. Met. Fox 9, 36; Met. 9, 18. Hǣrlīc, 1, 86; Met. 1, 43. [*O. H. Ger.* hēr-līh *insignis.*] v. hēr; *adj.*

hēr-nis, herstan, hērsum. v. hȳr-nis, hyrstan, hȳrsum.

hēr-ongemong; *adv. Here-among, amongst the rest, meanwhile*:—Gif wē Æfneres dǣda sume hērongemong secgaþ *si Abner factum ad medium deducamus*, Past. 40, 5; Swt. 295, 13. Gif wē Salamones cuida sumne hērongemong eówiaþ *si Salamonis ad medium verba proferantur*, 49, 5; Swt. 385, 33.

herra. v. hearra.

herþan; *pl. Testiculi*, Wrt. Voc. 65, 31. Wiđ hærþena sāre, L. Med. ex. Quadr. 8, 2; Lchdm. i. 358, 4: Lchdm. iii. 116, 15; L. Alf. pol. 65; Th. i. 96, 25.

herþ-belig, -bylig, es; *m. Viscus, scrotum*:—Herþbelig, herþbylig *viscus*, Wrt. Voc. 283, 35: 65, 13. Wiđ herþbylges sāre, L. Med. ex. Quadr. 5, 10; Lchdm. i. 350, 6.

herung, hering, e; *f. Praising, praise*:—Herung *laudatio*, Ps. Spl. 110, 10. For manna herunge *for the praise of men*, Homl. Th. i. 60, 33: 38, 10: 180, 20. On đære heringe đæs eádgan weres *in praise of the blessed man*, Past. 56, 7; Swt. 435, 18: Bt. 27, 3; Fox 100, 4: 30, 1; Fox 108, 22.

herwan. v. hyrwan.

HETE, es; *m.* HATE, *hatred, enmity, malignity, malice, spite*:—Hete *nequitia*, Mt. Kmbl. Rush. 22, 18. Ūs hōl and hete derede swīđe þearle *slander and hate have injured us very sorely*, Swt. A. S. Rdr. 106, 70. Wæs his hete grim *fierce was its hate*, Exon. 109 a; Th. 416, 1; Rä. 34, 5: Beo. Th. 5101; B. 2554: 286; B. 142. Hē forseah and on hete hæfde *odio habebat et despiciebat*, Bd. 3, 21; S. 551; 25. Se wæs on hete heofoncyninges *he was hateful to the king of heaven*, Cd. 30; Th. 40, 32; Gen. 648. Đa Iudēiscan bōceras mid hete đæt tǣldon *the Jewish scribes blamed that with malice*, Homl. Th. i. 338, 20. Đū scealt hine ālȳsan of lāþra hete *thou shalt release him from the hate of foes*, Andr. Kmbl. 1888; An. 946. Đone mǣstan hete hē sent on eów *he shall pour upon you his fiercest hate*, Deut. 28, 59. Hete *malitiam*, Ps. Stev. 35, 5. Ic flȳma wæs đæt ic mē his hete berh and wearnode *qui vagabundus, hostium vitabam insidias*, Bd. 2, 12; S. 513, 28. Đa tō Sione hete hæfdon *qui oderunt Sion*, Ps. Th. 128, 3. Hete hæfde hē æt his hearran gewunnen *he had gained hate from his lord*, Cd. 16; Th. 19, 34; Gen. 301: 37; Th. 47, 29; Gen. 768: 103; Th. 137, 13; Gen. 2273. Mid fulryhte hete ic hie hatode *perfecto odio oderam illos*, Past. 46, 5; Swt. 353, 6. Mid inlīce hete *domestico odio*, Bd. 5, 23; S. 646, 38. Hetas *malitias*, Ps. Stev. 93, 23. [*Laym.* hete: *Orm.* hēte: *Prompt. Parv.* hate: *Goth.* hatis: *O. Sax.* heti: *Icel.* hatr: *O. H. Ger.* haz *odium*: *Ger.* hass.] DER. bil-, cumbol-, ecg-, leód-, mōd-, morþor-, nīþ-, scyld-, teón-, wǣpen-, wīg-hete.

hete-grim; *adj. Of malignant cruelty* or *fierceness*, Andr. Kmbl. 2789; An. 1397: 3122; An. 1564. [*O. Sax.* heti-grim.]

hete-līc; *adj. Inspired by hate, hostile, malicious, evil*:—Heorowearh hetelīc *a wolf hostile and malignant*, Beo. Th. 2538; B. 1267. Mid hetelīcum geþance *with evil intent*, H. R. 99. 4. Atregeas and Thigesþres hū hī heora fæderas ofslōgan and ymb hiora hetelīcan forlignessa ic hit eall forlǣte *Atrei et Thyestis odia, stupra et parricidia dissimulo*, Ors. 1, 8; Swt. 42, 20. [*O. Sax.* heti-līk: *O. H. Ger.* haz-līh *invidus*: *Ger.* hässlich *ugly, wicked.*]

hete-līce; *adv. Fiercely, violently, vehemently*:—Hetelīce *mordicus*, Ælfc. Gr. 38; Som. 42, 5. Hine hetelīce swung [cf. Bd. 2, 6; S. 508, 13 mid grimmum swingum swong] *scourged him vehemently*, Chr. 616; Erl. 23, 3. Ūs Godes yrre hetelīce on sitt *God's anger presses on us fiercely*, Swt. A. S. Rdr. 108, 109. Hit sāh hetelīce swīđe *it sank with great violence*, Homl. Th. ii. 508, 34. Hē hine hetelīce þīdde *he stabbed him violently*, Jud. 3, 21: Homl. Th. i. 452, 14: H. R 107, 7. Hig hetelīce slōh and nān þing ne belǽfde lybbende on him *smote them fiercely and left no thing living among them*, Jos. 11, 8. Ā hetelīce stȳre đam đe þwyres willan *ever to punish those severely that desire perverseness*, L. I. P. 2; Th. ii. 304, 17.

hetend. v. hettend.

hete-nīþ, es; *m. Enmity, hostility, malice, wickedness*:—Hī sprǽcon heteniþ *locuti sunt nequitiam*, Ps. Spl. T. 72, 8. Geheald đū mē wiđ hetenīþas and wiđ firenfulles folman *custodi me de manu peccatoris*, Ps. Th. 139, 4: Exon. 94 a; Th. 352, 22; Sch. 101. Grendel hetenīþas wæg *Grendel bore enmity*, Beo. Th. 307; B. 152.

hete-rōf; *adj. Active in hate* or *hostility, hostile*, Andr. Kmbl. 2839; An. 1422.

hete-rūn, e; *f. A charm causing hate* or *evil*, Exon. 109 a; Th. 416, 6; Rä. 34, 7.

hete-sprǽc, e; *f. Hostile* or *malicious speech*, Cd. 14; Th. 17, 22; Gen. 263.

hete-sweng, es; *m. A hostile blow*, Beo. Th. 4453; B. 2225.

hete-þanc, es; *m. A hostile thought*, Beo. Th. 955; B. 475: Exon. 70 a; Th. 261, 14; Jul. 315.

hete-þancol; *adj. Having hostile* or *evil designs*, Judth. 10; Thw. 23, 4; Jud. 105.

hetlen; *adj. Bearing hate, hostile, malignant*, Exon. 13 a; Th. 23, 5; Cri. 364.

hetol, hetel; *adj. Full of hate, hostile, malignant, evil*:—Se heáhengel đe nū is hetol deófol *the archangel that now is a devil full of malice*, Boutr. Scrd. 17, 22. Maxentius đa burh geheóld mid hetelum geþance *Maxentius held the town with hostile intent*, Homl. Th. ii. 304, 21. Hī habbaþ nū đone hetolan deófol him tō hlāforde *they have now the malignant devil as their lord*, 254, 1: Swt. A. S. Rdr. 66, 327. Hēr sind on earde cyrichatan hetole *here in the land are foes of the church full of malice*, 109, 154. [*A. R.* hetel: *O. H. Ger.* hazzal *malitiosus*.]

hettan; cf. hatian, *and see next word.*

hettend, hetend, es; *m. An enemy*:—Hettend lǽddon ūt mid ǽhtum abrahames mæg *the enemy led forth Abraham's kinsman with his possessions*, Cd. 94; Th. 121, 17; Gen. 2011: 154; Th. 191, 4; Exod. 209: Chr. 937; Erl. 112, 10; Æđelst. 10: Andr. Kmbl. 61; An. 31. Hetend, Elen. Kmbl. 237; El. 119. Hettende, Exon. 62 a; Th. 228, 21; Ph. 441. Hetende, Beo. Th. 3660; B. 1828. Hettendra, Cd. 97; Th. 127, 13; Gen. 2110: Exon. 75 b; Th. 282, 14; Jul. 663. Hettendum, Beo. Th. 6000; B. 3004. Hetendum, Elen. Kmbl. 35; El. 18. [*O. Sax.* hettend, hetteand, hetand.] DER. eald-hettend.

hice-māse, an; *f. The blue titmouse*:—Hicemāse *vel* wrenna *parrax*, Ælfc. Gl. 38; Som. 63, 38; Wrt. Voc. 29, 56. [Cornish dialect, hickmal, hekky-mal *the blue titmouse.*] Cf. col-māse.

hicgan. v. hycgan.

hīd, e; *f. A hide of land.* The form *hīged*, which occurs Cod. Dipl. Kmbl. ii. 5, 25, seems to shew that the word is connected with *hīwan, hīgan*, and this etymology is supported by the use of *familia* and *hīd* in the Latin and English versions respectively of Bede's Ecclesiastical History. The original meaning of the word would thus be 'as much land as will support one family.' v. Bd. 1, 25; S. 486, 19: 2, 9; S. 87, 32 [Latin]: 3, 4; S. 106, 33 [Latin]: 4, 16; S. 584, 14. Further, in the charters, *hīwisc* [q. v.] is used as equivalent to *hīd*. The Latin words used as equivalent are *mansus, mansa, mansio, manens, cassatus, terra tributarii, familia*, Cod. Dipl. Kmbl. iii. xxx. See for further discussion of the word Kemble's Saxons in England, i. 4: Stubbs' Const. Hist. s. v: Schmid. A. S. Gesetze, p. 610.

hīdan. v. hȳdan.

hider; *adv. Hither*:—Hider *huc*, Ælfc. Gr. 38; Som. 39, 65. Hideror *citerius*, Som. 41, 3. Sittaþ hēr ōþ đæt ic gā hider geond *sedete hic donec vadam illuc*, Mt. Kmbl. 26, 36. Hider and geond *huc illucque*, Bd. 5, 12; S. 629, 3. Hider and đider *huc illucque*, Past. 9; Swt. 59, 5. Ne mæg hió hider ne đider sīgan đē swīđor đe hió symle dyde *it cannot decline to one side or the other more than it ever did*, Bt. Met. Fox 20, 328; Met. 20, 164. Sume hyder sume đyder *some on one side, some on the other*, Elen. Kmbl. 1093; El. 548. [*Chauc. Piers P.* hider: *Wick.* hidir: *Goth.* hidre: *Icel.* hēđra.] v. hidres.

hider-cyme, es; *m. A coming hither, to this world, advent*:—Đīn hidercyme *thy advent*, Exon. 13 a; Th. 23, 12; Cri. 367. Fram Cristes hidercyme *ab incarnatione Domini*, Bd, 1, 3; S. 475, 16: 1, 4; S. 475, 26. On his hidercyme *in his coming hither* [*to Hell*], Blickl. Homl. 87, 2, 11. Hidercyme đinne on wrāþra geweald *thy coming hither into the power of enemies*, Andr. Kmbl. 2634; An. 1318: Exon. 10 a; Th. 9, 29; Cri. 142: 62 a; Th. 227, 10; Ph. 421: 16 a; Th. 37, 2; Cri. 587.

hider-weard; *adj. Hitherward, in this direction*:—Hie ǽr fætte wǽron and beóþ hiderwearde *they were before fat and are still disposed this way*, L. M. 2, 36; Lchdm. ii. 242, 5.

hider-weard; *adv. Hitherward*:—On đisum geáre menn sǽdon đæt Cnut cyng fundade hiderward *in this year men said that king Cnut was making for this country*, Chr. 1085; Erl. 217, 40. [*Laym.* hider-ward, -wardes: *Piers P.* hiderward.]

hīd-gild, es; *n. A land tax, tax paid on every hide*:—Đis mycel is gegolden of đære cyricean W. cyninge syđđan hē đis land āhte wiđūtan đam hīdgelde đe nān man wiđūtan Gode ānum ātellan ne mæg *this much has been paid from the church* [*of Worcester*] *to king William since he owned this country, besides the hide-tax, which no one but God alone can reckon*, Chart. Th. 439, 22. [Cf. Chr. 1083; Erl. 217, 33-5, Se cyng lēt beódan mycel gyld and hefelīc ofer eall Engla land đæt wæs æt ǽlcere hȳde twā and hundseofenti peanega.]

hīd-mǽlum; *adv. By hides*:—Đæt līþ hīdmǽlum and æcermǽlum *it lies by hides and by acres*, Cod. Dipl. Kmbl. vi. 98, 4.

hidres; *adv. In the phrase* hidres đidres *hither and thither*:—Ic ondrǽde đæt ic đē lǽde hidres đidres on đa paþas of đīnum wege đæt đū ne mǽge eft đīnne weg āredian *verendum est, ne deviis fatigatus, ad emetiendum rectum iter sufficere non possis*, Bt. 40, 5; Fox 240, 21: Past. 22; Swt. 168, 13.

hie. v. hē.

hiénþo. v. hȳnþ.

hiéran, etc. v. hȳran, etc.

hierde. v. hirde.

hierstan. v. hyrstan.

hiertan. v. hyrtan.

hiéwe-stān, es; *m. A hewn stone*:—Ǽlcne hiéwestān tōbeátan *to beat to pieces every hewn stone*, Ors. 4, 13; Bos. 100, 10.

hīf. v. hȳf.

hig *hay.* v. heg.

hig *they.* v. hē.

hīgan. v. hīwan.

hige. v. hyge.

hī-gedryht, e; *A band of household retainers*, Exon. 94 b; Th. 353, 32; Reim. 21.

higera, higora, an; *m*: higere, an; *f. A magpie* or *a woodpecker*; see Exon. 106 b; Th. 406, 14; Rä. 25 where the name of a bird that can imitate various sounds is given by the runes G, A, R, O, H, I. Higera *picus*, Wrt. Voc. 62, 34. Higere *picus*, 281, 5: *gaia* vel *catanus*, Ælfc. Gl. 37; Som. 63, 14; Wrt. Voc. 29, 37: *cicuanus*, Cot. 34, Lye. [*O. H. Ger.* hehara, hehera *picus, attacus, orin.*] v. Grein, ii. 72.

higian; *p.* ode *To hie, hasten, strive*:—Đonne hē higaþ tō đǽm godcundum þingum ānum *cum ad sola, quæ interiora sunt, nititur*, Past. 14, 3; Swt. 83, 14. Se đonne se đe suā higaþ tō andweardnesse his scippendes *qui igitur sic ad auctoris speciem anhelat*, 14, 6; Swt. 87, 10. Se đe æfter đæm higaþ đæt hē eádig sīe on đisse worulde *qui festinat ditari*, Past. 44, 9; Swt. 331, 14. Higaþ ealle mægne đæt hē wolde . . . *strives with all his might to* . . ., Bt. 30, 1; Fox 110, 4: Bt. Met. Fox 13, 130; Met. 13, 65. Gehiéren đa reáferas đa đe higiaþ wiđ đæs đæt hie willaþ ōđre men bereáfian hwæt be him gecweden is *cum aliena rapere intendunt, audiant, quod scriptum est*, Past. 44, 8; Swt. 329, 16. Đætte suā hwelc suā inweard higige tō gangenne on đa duru đæs ēcean līfes *ut, quisquis intrare æternitatis januam nititur*, 16, 5; Swt. 105, 14: Bt. 22, 2; Fox 78, 18: 37, 2; Fox 118, 16. Đa đe hē gesyhþ tō Gode higian *those that he sees striving towards God*, Blickl. Homl. 29, 22. Hē sceal simle higian đæt hē weorþe geedniwad *he must ever strive to be renewed*, Past. 22, 1; Swt. 169, 10. [*Orm.* hiȝhenn: *Laym.* hiȝeden, *p. pl*: *A. R.* hien: *Piers P.* hyed, hiȝed, *p*: *Wick.* hiȝed, *pp.*]

higre [cf. higera] *or* hīgre [cf. hīwan] *verna*, Cot. 23, Lye: Gl. Epin. 663.

hīg-scipe. v. hīw-scipe.

hiht, hihtan. v. hyht, hyhtan.

hilc. v. hylc.

hild *grace.* v. hyld.

hild, e; *f.* [a poetical word] *War, battle*; pugna, prælium:—In the Scandinavian mythology Hildr is the name of one of the Valkyrias, and Grimm considers that the word occurs, denoting a person, in the Anglo-Saxon poetry, e. g. gif mec hild nime, Beo. Th. 909; B. 452: 2967; B. 1481. v. Grmm. D. M. 392 sqq. Hild sweđrode *war ceased*, Beo. Th. 1807; B. 901: 3180; B. 1585: 3698; B. 1847: Andr. Kmbl. 2840; An. 1422: Elen. Kmbl. 36; El. 18: 298; El. 149. Hyne Hetware hilde gehnǽgdon *him the Hetwaras conquered in battle*, Beo. Th. 5825; B. 2916: 4159; B. 2076: 4586; B. 2298: Exon. 100 a; Th. 378, 10; Deór. 14: Menol. Fox 493; Gn. C. 17: Apstls. Kmbl. 41; Ap. 21: Cd. 150; Th. 188, 3; Exod. 162. Nǽfre hit æt hilde ne swāc manna ǽngum *never had it failed in fight any man*, Beo. Th. 2925; B 1460: 3322; B. 1659: 5143; B. 2575: 5361; B. 2684: Cd. 98; Th. 129, 25; Gen. 2149: Byrht. Th. 133, 24; By. 55: 135, 24; By. 123: 138, 20; By. 223: 140, 14; By. 324: 131, 15; By. 8: Wald. 6; Vald. 1, 4: Andr. Kmbl. 823; An. 412: Salm. Kmbl. 320; Sal. 159: Fins. Th. 75; Fin. 37: Wald. 55; Vald. 1, 30: Exon. 79 a; Th. 297, 5; Crā. 63: 104 a; Th. 395, 7; Rä. 15, 4: 120 a; Th. 461, 17; Hö. 37: Cd. 95; Th. 124, 11; Gen. 2061: 155; Th. 193, 5; Exod. 241: Elen. Kmbl. 63; El. 32: 97; El. 49: 103; El. 52: 129; El. 65. Ongenþeów hæfde Higelāces hilde gefrunen *Ongentheow had heard of Higelac's fighting*, Beo. Th. 5897; B. 2952: 1299; B. 647: 3984; B. 1990;

Wald. 87; Vald. 2, 15: Exon. 16 a; Th. 35, 31; Cri. 566: Cd. 151; Th. 189, 3; Exod. 181: 167; Th. 209, 25; Exod. 504: Judth. 12; Thw. 25, 9; Jud. 251. Heardre hilde *with hard fighting*, Elen. Kmbl. 165; El. 83: Judth. 12; Thw. 25, 36; Jud. 294. Fela ic gebād heardra hilda *many hard battles have I experienced,* Fins. Th. 52; Fin. 26: Andr. Kmbl. 2980; An. 1493. [*O. Sax.* hild: *Icel.* hildr: *O. H. Ger.* hilt.] v. Grff. iv. 912.]

hild-bedd, es; *n. Deathbed,* Andr. Kmbl. 2186; An. 1094.

hilde-bil, -bill, es; *n. Battle-blade, sword,* Beo. Th. 3337; B. 1666: 1118; B. 557: 3044; B. 1520: 5351; B. 2679.

hilde-bord, es; *n. A war-shield,* Beo. Th. 799; B. 397: 6270; B. 3139.

hilde-calla, an; *m. A war-herald,* Cd. 156; Th. 193, 26; Exod. 252.

hilde-corðor, es; *n. A warlike troop,* Apstls. Kmbl. 82; Ap. 41.

hilde-cyst, e; *f. Excellence in war, valour*:—Hildecystum *valorously,* Beo. Th. 5189; B. 2598.

hilde-deóful, es; *n. A devil, demon*:—Sindon ealle hǣðene godu hildedeóful *omnes dei gentium dæmonia,* Ps. Th. 95, 5.

hilde-deór; *adj. Stout in war, brave,* Beo. Th. 629; B. 312: 1672; B. 834: 4220; B. 2107: 4372; B. 2183. Hæle hildedeór *a warrior brave,* 3296; B. 1646: 3636; B. 1816: 6213; B. 3111: Andr. Kmbl. 2003; An. 1004: Elen. Kmbl. 1868; El. 936. Hildedeóre *brave men,* Beo. Th. 6320; B. 3170. [Thorpe and Kemble take *deór* to be a noun.]

hilde-freca. v. hild-freca.

hilde-frōfor, e; *f. War-help, a weapon, sword* [?], *shield* [?]:—Hæfde him on handa hildefrōfre [MS. frore] *had in his hand help for battle,* Vald. 2, 12.

hilde-gæst, -giest, es; *m. An enemy,* Exon. 113 b; Th. 436, 5; Rä. 54, 9.

hilde-geatwe; *pl. f. War equipments,* Beo. Th. 1353; B. 674: 4713; B. 2362.

hild-egesa, an; *m. Terror of battle,* Elen. Kmbl. 226; El. 113.

hilde-gicel, es; *m. A drop of blood,* Beo. Th. 3217; B. 1606.

hilde-grǣdig; *adj. Eager for battle,* Cd. 150; Th. 188, 3; Exod. 162.

hilde-grāp, e; *f. Hostile grasp,* Beo. Th. 2896; B. 1446: 5007; B. 2507. In the latter passage Thorpe and Kemble take *grāp* to be a verb.

hilde-hlem, -hlæm, mes; *m. Crash of battle,* Beo. Th. 4691; B. 2351: 5081; B. 2544: 4408; B. 2201.

hilde-leóma, an; *m. A hostile, warlike ray,* Beo. Th. 2291; B. 1143 [*a sword*]: 5159; B. 2583.

hilde-leóþ, es; *n. A battle-song, war-song,* Judth. 11; Thw. 24, 28; Jud. 211.

hilde-mæcg, es; *m. A warrior,* Beo. Th. 1603; B. 799.

hilde-mēce, es; *m. A war-falchion,* Beo. Th. 4411; B. 2202.

hilde-nædre, an; *f. A war-adder, an arrow, dart, warlike missile,* Elen. Kmbl. 238; El. 119: 281; El. 141: Judth. 11; Thw. 24, 34; Jud. 222.

hilde-pīl, es; *m. A dart, bolt, javelin,* Exon. 105 a; Th. 399, 5; Rä. 18, 6: 104 b; Th. 397, 33; Rä. 16, 28.

hilde-rǣs, es; *m. A warlike onset,* Beo. Th. 605; B. 300.

hilde-rand, es; *m. A shield,* Beo. Th. 2489; B. 1242.

hilde-rinc, es; *m. A warrior,* Beo. Th. 2618; B. 1307: 2994; B. 1495: 3156; B. 1576: 6239; B. 3124: Byrht. Th. 136, 50; By. 169: Chr. 937; Erl. 114, 5; Æðelst. 39: Elen. Kmbl. 525; El. 263: Rood Kmbl. 122; Kr. 61: 143; Kr. 72.

hilde-sæd; *adj. Wearied with battle,* Beo. Th. 5439; B. 2723.

hilde-sceorp, es; *n. War-clothing,* Beo. Th. 4316; B. 2155.

hilde-scūr, es; *m. War-shower, flight of missiles,* Exon. 49 b; Th. 170, 24; Gū. 1116.

hilde-serce, an; *f. A war-shirt, corslet,* Elen. Kmbl. 468; El. 234.

hilde-setl, es; *m. A war-seat, saddle of a war-horse,* Beo. Th. 2082; B. 1039.

hilde-spell, es; *n. A warlike speech,* Cd. 170; Th. 214, 22; Exod. 573.

hilde-strengo; *f. Warlike strength,* Beo. Th. 4232; B. 2113.

hilde-swāt, es; *m. Hostile vapour* or *steam,* Beo. Th. 5109; B. 2558.

hilde-swég, es; *m. Sound of battle,* Cd. 93; Th. 120, 7; Gen. 1991.

hilde-þremma, an; *m. A warrior,* Exon. 66 b; Th. 246, 19; Jul. 64.

hilde-þrym, mes; *m. Warlike prowess,* Andr. Kmbl. 2064; An. 1034.

hilde-þryþ, e; *f. Strength in war,* Exon. 105 a; Th. 400, 6; Rä. 20, 4.

hilde-torht; *adj. Having warlike splendour,* Bt. Met. Fox 25, 18; Met. 25, 9.

hilde-tusc, -tux, es; *m. A battle-tusk, a tusk* or *tooth that serves as a weapon,* Beo. Th. 3026; B. 1511. [Cf. *Icel.* hildi-tannr.]

hilde-wǣpen, es; *m. A weapon of war,* Beo. Th. 77; B. 39.

hilde-wīsa, an; *m. A military leader, general,* Beo. Th. 2133; B. 1064.

hilde-wōma, an; *m. The crash and rush of battle,* Andr. Kmbl. 436; An. 218: Exon. 75 b; Th. 282, 15; Jul. 663: 67 b; Th. 250, 32; Jul. 136. v. Grmm. And. u. El. xxx.

hilde-wrǣsen, e; *f. A chain used to secure those taken in war* [?], Salm. Kmbl. 586; Sal. 292.

hilde-wulf, es; *m. A war-wolf, warrior,* Cd. 95; Th. 123, 25; Gen. 2051.

hild-freca, hilde-, an; *m. A warrior,* Beo. Th. 4721; B. 2366: 4416; B. 2205: Andr. Kmbl. 251; An. 126: 2141; An. 1072. v. freca.

hild-from; *adj. Stout* or *bold in war,* Andr. Kmbl. 2405; An. 1204.

hild-fruma, an; *m. A military chief* or *prince,* Elen. Kmbl. 19; El. 10: 201; El. 101: Exon. 65 b; Th. 243, 7; Jul. 7: Beo. Th. 3360; B. 1678: 5291; B. 2649: 5662; B. 2835.

hild-lata, an; *m. One sluggish in war, slow to fight, a coward,* Andr. Kmbl. 466; An. 233: Beo. Th. 5684; B. 2846.

hild-stapa, an; *m. One who steps to war, a warrior,* Andr. Kmbl. 2517; An. 1260.

hild-þracu; *gen.* -þræce; *f. Power, force in war,* Cd. 98; Th. 130, 9; Gen. 2157.

hil-hāma. v. hylle-hāma.

hill. v. hyll.

hilt, es; *m. n. Hilt, handle* [the plural, as in much later times, e. g. Shakspere's, is used of a single weapon]:—Ðā wæs gylden hilt gamelum rince on hand gyfen *then was the golden hilt given into the old man's hand,* Beo. Th. 3358; B. 1677. Ðæs swurdes mid ðam sylfrenan hylte *the sword with the silver hilt,* Chart. Th. 558, 11. Ic ðæt hilt ðanon ætferede *I bore the hilt away from there,* 3341; B. 1668. Hylt, 3379; B. 1687. Blīcaþ ða hiltas *the hilt shines,* Salm. Kmbl. 446; Sal. 223. Ða hilt since fāge *the hilt many-coloured with treasure,* Beo. Th. 3233; B. 1614. Be hiltum *by the hilt,* 3152; B. 1574. [*Icel.* hjalt; *n. the boss* or *knob at the end of a sword's hilt;* also *the guard between the hilt and blade.* For some account of the hilts of old swords see Worsaae's Primeval Antiquities, pp. 29, 49.] DER. fealo-, fetel-, hroðen-, wreoðen-hilt. v. next word.

hilte, an; *f. A hilt, handle*:—Hilte *capulus, capulum* [?], Ælfc. Gl. 52; Som. 66, 47, 26; Wrt. Voc. 35, 34, 14. Hiltan *capulum,* Wrt. Voc. 84, 21. Swā ðæt ða hiltan eodon intō ðam innoþe *the haft went in after the blade,* Jud. 3, 22. Ōþ ða hiltan *capulotenus,* Mone Gl. 432. [*O. H. Ger.* helza *capulus.*]

hilte-cumbor, es; *n. An ensign having a hilt,* Beo. Th. 2048; B. 1022.

hilted; *part. p. Provided with a hilt,* Beo. Th. 5966; B. 2987.

hilt-leás; *adj. Without a hilt*:—Hiltleás sweord *ensis,* Ælfc. Gl. 52; Som. 66, 46; Wrt. Voc. 35, 33.

hīna. v. hīne, hīwan.

hinan. v. heonan.

hinca. v. helle-hinca.

hind. v. hynd.

hind, e; *f. A hind, the female of the hart*:—Hind *cerva,* Ælfc. Gl. 19; Som. 59, 23; Wrt. Voc. 22, 64. Hynd *cerva,* Wrt. Voc. 78, 27. Ðā geseah se godes þeów wilde hinde melce *then the servant of God saw a wild hind in milk,* Shrn. 130, 3. Hē lægde laga ðæt swā hwā swā slōge heort oððe hinde ðæt hine man sceolde blendian *he made laws that whoever should kill hart or hind should be blinded,* Chr. 1086; Erl. 222, 27. Sēcan heorotas and hinda *to hunt harts and hinds,* Bt. Met. Fox 19, 33; Met. 19, 17. [*Icel. Dan.* hind: *O. H. Ger.* hinta, hinda *cerva*: *Ger.* hinde, hindinn.]

hindan; *adv. From behind, at the back, in the rear, behind*:—Ðā hēt hē gewrīðan ðone pāpan and ðone ōðerne preóst tō his hricge hindan *then he ordered the pope to be bound, and the other priest behind to his back,* Homl. Th. ii. 310, 31. Hindan þyrel *pierced from behind,* Exon. 129 b; Th. 497, 24; Rä. 87, 5. Is him ðæt heáfod hindan grēne *its head is green at the back,* 60 a; Th. 218, 12; Ph. 293. Hie hindan ofrīdan ne meahte *could not overtake them,* Chr. 877; Erl. 78, 21: 894; Erl. 92, 22: Erl. 93, 7: 911; Erl. 100, 26: Ors. 6, 36; Bos. 131, 25. Heówan hereflēman hindan þearle *smote sorely the fugitives, pressing on their rear,* Chr. 937; Erl. 112, 23; Æðelst. 23. Se cyng fērde him æt hindan and offērde hī *the king marched in their rear* [*pursued them*] *and overtook them,* 1016; Erl. 158, 1. Pharao fērde him æt hindan *Pharao pursued after them,* Swt. A. S. Rdr. 63, 226. [*Goth.* hindana *beyond*: *O. Sax.* bi-hindan: *O. H. Ger.* hintana: *Ger.* hinten.]

hindan-weard; *adv. At the further end, hindwards*:—Sindon ða fiðru hwīt hindanweard *the wings are white at the tips,* Exon. 60 a; Th. 218, 21; Ph. 298.

hind-berige, -berie, -berge, an; *f. A raspberry*:—Hyndberige *acimus, erimigio,* Wrt. Voc. 66, 59: 67, 62. Genim hindbergean *take raspberries,* L. M. 2, 51; Lchdm. ii. 266, 8. Hindberge *ermigio,* Lchdm. iii. 302, col. 1. [hind-berry, hine-berry, v. English Plant Names, E. D. S. No. 26: *O. H. Ger.* hind-beri: *Ger.* him-beere.]

hind-brēr, es; *m. A raspberry plant;* rubus idæus, Lchdm. iii. 22, 31.

hind-cealf, es; *m. n. A fawn*:—Hindcealf *hinnulus,* Ælfc. Gl. 19; Som. 59, 26; Wrt. Voc. 22, 67: 78, 29. [*Halliw. Dict.* hind-calf, *a hind of the first year*: *O. H. Ger.* hint-kalb *hinnulus, damma, dammula.*]

hindema; *adj. Last:*—Hindeman síðe *for the last time*, Beo. Th. 4105; B. 2049: 5023; B. 2517. [Cf. *Goth.* hindumists.] Cf. next word.

hinder; *adv. Back, on the further side, behind, down:*—Morðor món sceal under eorþan befeolan hinder under hrusan *murder must be buried under earth, down under ground*, Exon. 91 a; Th. 340, 24; Gn. Ex. 116. Hí mē āsetton on seáð hinder *posuerunt me in lacu inferiori*, Ps. Th. 87, 6. Gengde on hinder *conversus est retrorsum*, 113, 3. On hinder hē eode *he [the devil] went behind*, Homl. Th. i. 172, 35. Hē on hinder gǣþ *he shall go back*, Salm. Kmbl. 254; Sal. 126. On hinder in helle hūs *down into hell*, Exon. 42 b; Th. 142, 23; Gū. 648. [*Goth.* hindar *beyond: O. H. Ger.* hintar, hindar *retro, post: Ger.* hinter.]

hinder-geap, -gep; *adj. Crafty, cunning, guileful, deceitful:*—Hindergeap *versutus*, Ælfc. Gl. 84; Som. 73, 104; Wrt. Voc. 49, 11. Hindergepe *versuti*, Coll. Monast. Th. 32, 29. [*Orm.* þatt mann iss fox and hinnderrȝæp and full off ille wiless, 6646. Cf. *Goth.* hindar-weis *deceitful:* hindar-weisei *guile.* Cf. *also* Carrais hine biðohte of ane hindere cræfte [hiþer crafte, 2nd MS.]: *Laym.* 10489: þe grune of hindre þat is of bipeching, *O. E. Homl.* ii. 213, 23: hinder-word, 59, 18: hinderfulle rede *consilium impiorum*, 23.] v. geap.

hinder-hōc, es; *m. A stratagem, artifice, snare*, Exon. 83 b; Th. 315, 20; Mōd. 34. [Cf. hinder-geap, hinder-scipe.]

hinderling, es; *m. A mean, base, contemptible person:*—Occidentales Saxonici, scilicet execastre, habent in proverbio summi despectus, quod summa ira commotus, unus vocat alterum hinderling, i. ab omni honestate dejectum, L. Ed. C. 35; Th. i. 459, 36. [*Orm.* halde þe forr hinnderrling and forr well swiþe unnwresste, 4860. Halliwell in his Dictionary says under *hilding* 'the word is still in use in Devon, pronounced *hilderling* or *hinderling*.']

hinder-scipe, es; *m. Wickedness;* nequitia, Hpt. Gl. 415.

hinder-þeóstru; *pl. Darkness in a remote* or *low place:*—Of helwarena hinderþeóstrum *ex inferno inferiori*, Ps. Th. 85, 12. v. hinder.

hinder-weard; *adj. Backward, slow:*—Nis hē hinderweard swā̄r ne swongor swā sume fuglas ða ðe late þurh lyft lācaþ fiþrum *non tamen est tarda, ut volucres quæ corpore magno incessus pigros per grave pondus habent*, Exon. 60 a; Th. 220, 2; Ph. 314.

hinde-weard, -werd; *adj. Hindward:*—Mid hindewerdum ðam sceafte *aversa hasta*, Past. 40, 5; Swt. 297, 10 13: 295, 17: L. Alf. pol. 36; Th. i. 84, 17: Exon. 106 a; Th. 403, 29; Rā. 22, 15.

hind-fald, es [*or* -falda, an]; *m. A hind-fold*, Cod. Dipl. Kmbl. vi. 112, 33.

hind-hælеþe, -heolaþ, -heoloþe, -hioloþe, an; *f. Water agrimony:*—Hyndhæleþe *ambrosia*, Wrt. Voc. 66, 60. Hindheolaþ, 79, 51. Genim hindhæleþan, Lchdm. iii. 74, 4. Hindheoloþan, L. M. 2, 51; Lchdm. ii. 266, 7; 1, 15; Lchdm. ii. 56, 21. Hindhioloþan, L. M. 1, 66; Lchdm. ii. 142, 3: 1, 70; Lchdm. ii. 144, 22. v. Lchdm. iii. 331, col. 2.

hindrian; *p.* ede *To hinder, obstruct, keep back, repress:*—Ā hē sceal hǣðendōm hindrian *he must always repress heathenism*, L. I. P. 2; Th. ii. 306, 7. [*Icel.* hindra: *O. H. Ger.* hintarian, Grff. iv. 704: *Ger.* hindern.] v. ge-hindred.

hind-síð. v. hin-síð.

hine [=(?) hīnan *as* gehūse = gehūsan, hiwæ = hīwan *in the same verse*] *domesticos*, Mt. Kmbl. Rush. 10, 25. Is this the word which gives later English *hine*, Mod. E. *hind*, or are these taken from the gen. pl. of *híwan*, *hína*, which occurs most frequently in phrases *hina fæder*, etc., and which may have come to be looked upon as an uninflected word used in such cases as the first part of a compound? In v. 36 *domestici* is glossed *hígu* ł *hine* ł *híwen*, and 24, 34 *pater-familas* = *hine-fæder* [but this may be for *hínafæder*]. [*Laym.* children and hinen, 368: *O. E. Homl.* ðin owune hine, i. 197, 112: *Chauc. Piers P.* hine.] v. hīwan.

hin-fūs; *adj. Ready to go away* or *depart*, Beo. Th. 1514; B. 755: Andr. Kmbl. 1223; An. 612.

hin-gang, -gong, es; *m. A going hence, departure, death*, Exon. 28 b; Th. 86, 24; Cri. 1413: 30 b; Th. 95, 10; Cri. 1555: 44 b; Th. 150, 24; Gū. 783. [*O. H. Ger.* hina-gang *secessus.*]

hingrian. v. hyngrian.

hin-síð, hinn-, hind-, es; *m. A journey hence, away, from this world, departure, death*, Exon. 119 b; Th. 459, 29; Hō. 7: 87 a; Th. 328, 7; Vy. 13: 97 b; Th. 364, 9; Wal. 68: 52 b; Th. 183, 22; Gū. 1331: Cd. 33; Th. 44, 32; Gen. 718: Th. 45, 3; Gen. 74: Judth. 10; Thw. 23, 11; Jud. 117. Hindsíð, Blickl. Homl. 123, 6. [Cf. *O. Sax.* hin-fard: *O. H. Ger.* hine-fart *exitus, obitus.*]

hinsíð-gryre, es; *m. Terror connected with death*, Cd. 223; Th. 293, 17; Sat. 456.

hió. v. hē.

hiofon. v. heofon.

hioful *the face:*—Ondwlita ł hioful *facies*, Mt. Kmbl. p. 9, 11.

hion, e; *f. A bone of the head* [?]:—Gif sió ūterre hion gebrocen weorþeþ, L. Ethb. 36; Th. i. 12, 6, v. note, and cf. L. H. 93, 2; Th. i. 605, 12 si exterius os percussum sit.

hióp. v. heóp.

hior. v. heorr.

hiord. v. heord.

hioro. v. heoru.

hír. v. hȳr.

híran. v. hȳran.

hird *retinue, court:*—Hē fērde tō Wudestoke and his biscopes and his hird eal mid him *he [Henry] went to Woodstock, and his bishops and his court all with him*, Chr. 1123; Erl. 249, 30. Dis geár heáld se kyng Heanri his hird on Windlesoure *this year king Henry held his court at Windsor*, 1127; Erl. 255, 1. This form as it occurs in late specimens may be merely a contraction of *híréd* [q. v.], or it may be a form influenced by the Danish *hirð*. In the former case it should be written *hírd.*

hírd-clerc. v. hírd-preóst.

hirde, hierde, heorde, hiorde, hyrde, es; *m. A herd, shepherd, pastor, guardian, guard, keeper:*—Hierde *arimentarius*, Wrt. Voc. 287, 52. Crist ðū gōda hyrde *Christ, thou good shepherd*, Blickl. Homl. 191, 24. Ic eom ðære stōwe hyrde *I am the guardian of the place*, 201, 9. Hire āgenes hūses hirde *the keeper of her own house*, Bt. Met. Fox 13, 61; Met. 13, 31. Rīces hirde *the guardian of a kingdom, a prince, king*, 26, 16; Met. 26, 8. Cilda hyrde *vel* lāreów *pædagogus*, Ælfc. Gl. 80; Som. 72, 103; Wrt. Voc. 46, 60. Ic ðæs folces beó hyrde and healdend *I will be the people's keeper and preserver*, Cd. 106; Th. 139, 25; Gen. 2315. Ne ic hyrde wæs brōðer mīnes *I was not my brother's keeper*, 48; Th. 62, 1; Gen. 1007. Heorde, Exon. 43 b; Th. 146, 33; Gū. 719. Hiorde, Ps. Grn. ii. 279, 101. Rihtwīs hyrde ofer cristene heorde *a righteous shepherd over a christian flock*, L. I. P. 2; Th. ii. 304, 9. Hie settan him hyrdas *to they set guards over him*, Blickl. Homl. 177, 26: 237, 18: Andr. Kmbl. 1986; An. 995. Ūre ealdan fæderas wǣron ceápes hierdas *antiqui patres nostri pastores*, Past. 17, 2; Swt. 109, 5. Hyrdas *pastores ovium*, Gen. 46, 32. Hē hæfþ geset his englas ūs tō hyrdum *he hath appointed his angels as our guardians*, Homl. Th. i. 170, 10. [*Goth.* hairdeis: *O. Sax.* hirdi: *Icel.* hirðir: *O. H. Ger.* hirti *pastor, custos: Ger.* hirte.] DER. beór-, cū-, feorh-, gāt-, grund-, hors-, hriðer-, neát-, sceáp-, swīn-hirde.

hirde-belg, -belig, es; *m. A shepherd's bag:*—Ðā nam hē fīf stānas on his herdebelig *then he took five stones in his shepherd's bag*, Blickl. Homl. 31, 17.

hirde-bōc, hierde-, e; *f. Liber Pastoralis*, Past. Pref. Swt. 7, 19.

hirde-leás; *adj. Without a shepherd:*—Ne beóþ hī hyrdeleáse ðonne hī ðē habbaþ *having thee they will not be without a shepherd*, Homl. Th. i. 382, 23. Scēp heordeleáse *oves non habentes pastorem*, Mt. Kmbl. Rush. 9, 36.

hirde-líc; *adj. Pastoral:*—Ða byrðenne ðære hirdelecan giémenne *pastoralis curæ pondera*, Past; Swt. 23, 11.

hirde-wyrt, e; *f.* I. the greater, *chlora perfoliata.* II. the lesser, *erythæa centaureum*, Lchdm. iii. 332, col. 1.

hird-ness, hyrd-, e; *f. Guard, keeping, custody:*—Hē betǣhte hig ða þrī dagas tō hirdnysse *tradidit ergo illos custodiæ tribus diebus*, Gen. 42, 17. Gif hwā befæst his feoh tō hyrdnysse *si quis commendaverit pecuniam in custodiam*, Ex. 22, 7. Swā hī on niht hyrdnesse begangaþ *sicut custodia in nocte*, Ps. Th. 89, 5. On hyrdnyssa *in custodias*, Lk. Skt. 21, 12.

hírd [=híréd] **-preóst**, es; *m. A domestic chaplain:*—Æilrīc mīn hīrdprēst, Cod. Dipl. Kmbl. iv. 269, 8: Chart. Th. 574, 10, 11.

hí-réd, hírd, es; *m. A household, house, family, the body of domestic retainers of a great man* or *king, a court, the members of a religious house, a company, band of associates:*—Hīrēd *vel* hīwrǣden *familia*, Wrt. Voc. 72, 28. Se hālga hȳrēd wæs wunigende ānmōdlīce on gebedum *the holy company continued with one accord in prayers*, Homl. Th. i. 314, 4: Cd. 226; Th. 302, 1; Sat. 592: 221; Th. 288, 5; Sat. 376. Se hīrd on Seynt Eádmundsbiri *the brotherhood at Bury St. Edmunds*, Chart. Th. 574, 28, 33. Mīn ōwen hīrd *my own family*, 575, 21. Hīrēdes fæder *paterfamilias*, Mt. Kmbl. 10, 25. Hīrēdes ealdor, 20, 1. Hȳrēdes hlāford, Wrt. Voc. 73, 20. Hīrēdes mōder *materfamilias*, 73, 21. An gewitnesse ðes hīrēdes æt Cristes cirican *with the witness of the brotherhood at Christchurch*, Cod. Dipl. Kmbl. ii. 3, 36. Gif hē stalie on gewitnesse ealles his hīrēdes gongen hie ealle on þeówot *if he steal with the knowledge of all his household let them all go into slavery*, L. In. 7; Th. i. 106, 17. Of Davides hūse and hīrēde *de domo et familia David*, Lk. Skt. 2, 4. Tō dæg is ðisum hīrēde hǣl gefremmed *hodie salus domui huic facta est*, Homl. Th. i. 582, 5. Cwæþ ðæt hē mid ðam Hǣlende on hȳrēde wǣre *said that he was in company with Jesus*, ii. 248, 31. Hit ne biþ nā hūs būton hit beó mid hīrēde āfylled *it is no house unless it be filled with a household*, 582, 13. Ic wille ðat alle mīne men bēn frē on hīrde and on tūne *I desire that all my men be free both in my household and vill*, Cod. Dipl. Kmbl. iv. 269, 12. Ðam hīrēde intō ealdan mynstre *to the brotherhood at the old monastery*, Chart. Th. 499, 14. Lucinius bebeád ðæt nān cristen mon ne cōme on his hierēde *Licinius omnes Christianos e palatio suo jussit expelli*, Ors. 6, 30; Swt. 282, 28. On sumes cyninges hīrēde *in tanti patris familias dispositissima domo*, Bt. 36, 1; Fox 172, 18: 29, 2; Fox 104, 29: L. Edm. S. 4; Th. i. 248, 23: L. C. S. 60; Th. i. 408, 14: L. R. 3; Th. i. 190, 20. Ðā oferhogode herodes hine mid hys hîrêde *sprevit autem illum erodes cum exercitu suo,* Lk. Skt. 23, 11: Cd. 222; Th. 290, 30; Sat. 423. God geswang Farao and ealne his hîrêd *flagellavit Dominus Pharaonem et domum ejus,* Gen. 12, 17. Ðone geset hys hlâfurd ofer his hîrêd *quem constituit dominus suus supra familiam suam,* Mt. Kmbl. 24, 45: Cd. 106; Th. 139, 16; Gen. 2310. Gif hê beó tô ðam gewelegod ðæt hê hŷrêd and êht âge *if he be so enriched as to have a household and property,* L. Wg. 7; Th. i. 186, 23 [cf. 13 hîwisc landes]. Frióne hierêd *a free monastery,* L. Alf. pol. 2; Th. i. 62, 1, v. note. Se cyng heóld ðǣr his hîrêd v dagas *the king held his court there five days,* Chr. 1085; Erl. 218, 18, 39. [*O. E. Hom.* hired: *Orm.* hird, hirrd: *Laym.* hiredes, *gen;* hirde, *dat: A. R.* hird: *O. H. Ger.* hî-rât *connubium: Ger.* heirath.] DER. in-hîrêd. v. hîwan.

hîrêd-cniht, es; *m. A man belonging to a 'hîrêd,' a domestic:*—Þurh Paules bodunge gelŷfdon ðæs câseres þegnas and hîrêdcnihtas *through Paul's preaching the members of the emperor's household believed,* Homl. Th. i. 374, 34. [*Laym.* hird-cniht.]

hîrêd-lîc; *adj. Familiaris,* Hpt. Gl. 463, 504.

hîrêd-mann, hîrd-man, es; *m. A member of a 'hîrêd:'*—Pharaones yldestan hîrêdmen *senes domus Pharaonis,* Gen. 50, 7. His hîrêdmen fêrdon ût mid feáwe mannan of ðam castele and geslôgen and gelǣhton fîf hundred manna *the members of his household sallied out with few men from the castle, and slew and captured five hundred men,* Chr. 1087; Erl. 224, 29. Ongunnon ða hîrêdmen heardlîce feohtan *the [earl's] household retainers began to fight stoutly,* Byrht. Th. 139, 28; By. 261. Hæbbe ǣlc hlâford his hîrêdmen [hîrdmen (MS. A.)] on his âgenum borge *let every lord have the members of his household in his own 'borg,'* L. C. S. 31; Th. i. 394, 27: L. Eth. i. 1; Th. i. 282, 9. [*Laym.* hired-, heredman (priveman, 2nd MS.)].

hîrêd-wîfmann, es; *m. A female member of a household:*—Ic geann eallum mînum hîrêdwîfmannum *I give to all the women of my household,* Chart. Th. 531, 6.

hîrêd-wist, e; *f. Familiaritas,* Lye.

hîre-man. v. hŷre-man.

hirstan. v. hyrstan.

hîrsum. v. hŷrsum.

hiscan. v. hyscan.

hise. v. hyse.

hispan. v. hyspan.

hittan; *p.* hitte *To hit upon, meet with:*—Ðâ com Harold ûre cyng on unwær on ða Normenn and hytte hî begeondan Eoforwîc æt Stemford brygge *then our king Harold came upon the Northmen unexpectedly and met with them beyond York at Stamford bridge,* Chr. 1066; Erl. 201, 26. [Borrowed from [?] *Icel.* hitta *to hit upon, meet with.*]

hiw, hiow, e; *f. Fortune:*—Swâ hit oft gesǣleþ on ðǣm sêlran þingum and on ðǣm gesundrum ðæt seó wyrd and sió hiow hie oft oncyrreþ *ut aliquid plerumque in secundis rebus fortuna obstrepit,* Nar. 7, 27.

hiw, heow, hiow, heó, es; *n. Shape, make, form, fashion, species, kind, appearance, symbol, hue, colour, beauty:*—Hiw *species,* Ælfc. Gl. 70; Som. 70, 45; Wrt. Voc. 42, 53. Hiw *figura, scema, specimen, forma, species,* Ælfc. Gr. 2: 9: 14; Som. 2, 45, 46: 8, 22: 9, 31: 17, 19, 20. Hiw *figmentum,* Blickl. Gl. Ðeós gerŷnu is wedd and hiw *this mystery is a pledge and a symbol,* Homl. Th. ii. 272, 60. Sǣde hwylc ðæs biscopes hiw wǣre *effigiem ejusdem Paulini referre esset solitus,* Bd. 2, 16; S. 519, 32: Andr. Kmbl. 1449; An. 725. Heó is on onsŷne ûtan yfeles heowes *outside it is in appearance of a very poor kind,* Blickl. Homl. 197, 11. Seó is brûnes heowes *it is of a brown colour,* 73, 22. Ânes hiwes *uniformis,* Ælfc. Gr. 49; Som. 59, 42. Hwælan hiwes *of a whale's shape,* Salm. Kmbl. 527; Sal. 263. Æt ânes heowes cŷ *from a cow all of one colour,* Lchdm. iii. 24, 13. Hiwes binotene *bereft of their [angelic] form,* Exon. 45 b; Th. 156, 10; Gû. 872. On ôðrum hiwe *in alia effigie,* Mk. Skt. 16, 12. Hî ealle wurdon âwende of ðam fægeran hiwe ðe hî on gesceapene wǣron tô lâðlîcum deóflum *they were all changed from the fair form in which they were created to loathly devils,* Homl. Th. i. 10, 30. On næddran hiwe *in the form of a serpent,* 16, 32: 104, 23. On fŷres hiwe *like as of fire,* 232, 15. On cuman hiwe *as a guest,* ii. 96, 35. Heowe, Blickl. Homl. 235, 29. Æfter his hiwe *secundum speciem suam,* Gen. 1, 12. Ðû eart wlitig on hiwe *pulchra sis mulier,* 12, 11. Siððan heó wunode mid fǣmnum on hira hiwe *afterwards she lived with women as a woman,* Shrn. 31, 16: 52, 24. Se sunu onfêng mennisc hiw *the son took the form of a man,* Nar. 39, 23: Exon. 18 b; Th. 45, 19; Cri. 721: 46 a; Th. 156, 28; Gû. 881. Heó, Elen. Kmbl. 12; El. 6. Tôcnâwan heofones hiw *faciem cœli dijudicare,* Mt. Kmbl 16, 3. Scînende hiow and gewǣdu *shining face and garments,* Homl. Th. ii. 350, 18. Nû berþ Petrus ðæt hiw oððe getâcnunge ðære hâlgan gelaþunge *Peter is now the figure or symbol of the holy church,* 390, 14: 406, 11. Weorþeþ sunne on blôdes hiw *the sun shall become the colour of blood,* Exon. 21 b; Th. 58, 15; Cri. 936. Hiw *decorem,* Ps. Spl. C. 44, 13. Gimmas hwîte and reáde and hiwa gehwæs *gems, white and red and of every hue,* Bt. Met. Fox 19, 46; Met. 19, 23: Exon. 95 b; Th. 356, 31; Pa. 20. Behealdaþ eów wið leásum wîtegum ðe tô eów cumaþ on sceápa hiwum *take heed of false prophets that come to you as sheep,* Homl. Th. ii. 404, 4. On mistlîcum and mænigfealdum hiwum *of divers and manifold forms,* Lchdm. iii. 234, 13. [*Goth.* hiwi *form.*] v. feala-, scîn-hiw.

hîwan, hîgan; *pl. Members of a household, of a religious house, a family:*—Heora hîwan *their household,* Cd. 133; Th. 168, 10; Gen. 2780. Hine ofslôgon his hîwan [cf. hîrêd] *the members of his household slew him,* Chr. 757; Erl. 53, 8. Hîwan *members of a religious house,* L. Alf. pol. 5; Th. i. 64, 14. Ðenewulf bisceop and ða hîwan in Wintanceastre *bishop Denewulf and the brethren at Winchester,* Chart. Th. 151, 5. Hîgen, Chart. Th. 47, 33: 70, 33: 461, 18, 33. Ða hîwan ðe on ðam mynstre wǣron *qui erant in monasterio,* Bd. 3, 11; S. 535, 18. Hîgo *familia,* Lk. Skt. Lind. 2, 4: 12, 42. Hîgo ða ðe gihaldaþ *familia quæ abstinet,* Rtl. 16, 11: 14, 30. Hîgu *domestici,* Mt. Kmbl. Rush. 10, 36. Faderes hîgna *patris familias,* Mt. Kmbl. Lind. 13, 27; Lk. Skt. Lind. 13, 25: Chart. Th. 460, 9. Fæder hîna, Mt. Kmbl. Rush. 20, 1: 21, 33. Gehwilcne ðe his hîna wæs wǣpned cynnes *every one that of his family was of the male sex,* Cd. 107; Th. 142, 34; Gen. 2371. Ðâ hrŷmde heó tô hire hîwun *vocavit ad se homines domus suæ,* Gen. 39, 14. Mid hira hîwun *cum domibus suis,* Ex. 1, 1. Gâ tô ðînum hûse tô ðînum hîwum *vade in domum tuam ad tuos,* Mk. Skt. 5, 19. Bûton Noe and his seofan hîwon *except Noah and the seven members of his family,* Homl. Th. ii. 58, 34: i. 20, 34. On middum hire hîwum *in medio eorum [the members of the monastery],* Bd. 4, 19; S. 588, 20: Chart. Th. 468, 19: L. Alf. pol. 2; Th. i. 62, 5. Gilêf hîgum ðînum *concede famulis tuis,* Rtl. 30, 17. Ût of earce hîwan lǣd ðû *lead thy family out of the ark,* Cd. 73; Th. 90, 3; Gen. 1489. Hîwan [MS. A. munecas], Chr. 716; Erl. 45, 17. Hîwæ *domesticos,* Mt. Kmbl. Rush. 10, 25. [*Ayenb. Chauc. Piers P.* hewe *a servant: Orm.* hiwenn *a family:* cf. *Goth.* heiwa-frauja οἰκοδεσπότης: *O. Sax.* hîwa *a wife: Icel.* hjú, hjún, hjón *man and wife, family, household: O. H. Ger.* hîwo *a married man;* hîwa *a married woman.*] DER. gesam-, gesin-, in-, sam-, sin-hîwan.

hiw-beorht, hiow-; *adj. Bright of hue, beautiful in form or colour,* Elen. Kmbl. 145; El. 73: Cd. 14; Th. 17, 27; Gen. 265.

hîw-cûþ, heow-; *adj. Familiar, well known:*—Hîwcûþ *familiaris,* Ælfc. Gl. 115; Som. 80, 62; Wrt. Voc. 61, 36. Ic ne eom him suâ hîwcûþ *familiaritatis ejus notitiam non habemus,* Past. 10, 2; Swt. 63, 5: Herb. 67, 1; Lchdm. i. 170, 13. Se ðe hine selfne hîwcûþne ne ongiet Gode *qui familiarem se ejus gratiæ esse nescit,* Past. 10, 2; Swt. 63, 8. Ða syndon heowcûþe ðe wê geseón ne mâgon *those things are familiar that we cannot see,* Blickl. Homl. 97, 23. Hîwcûþe, Bt. Met. Fox 10, 122; Met. 10, 61.

hîw-cûþlîce, hiew-; *adv. Familiarly:*—Ða ðe hine hîwcûþlîce cûþan *qui eum familiariter noverunt,* Bd. 5, 2; S. 614, 27. Hê biþ hiewcûþlîce þeów ðæm Godes feónde *hosti Dei familiarius servit,* Past. 47, 2; Swt. 361, 1. Hine God hiewcûþlîcor on eallum þingum innan lǣrde ðonne ôðre menn mid his gelômlîcre tôsprǣce *quem de cunctis interius per conversationem cum Deo sedulam locutio familiaris instruebat,* 41, 5; Swt. 304, 18.

hîwcûþ-rǣdness, e; *f. Familiarity, intimacy;* familiaritas, Ælfc. Gl. 116; Som. 80, 66; Wrt. Voc. 61, 40.

hiwe; *adj. Beautiful in form or colour,* Exon. 60 a; Th. 218, 8; Ph. 291: Th. 219, 4; Ph. 302. [Cf. twî-hiwe: *or is* hiwe *dative of* hiw?]

hîwen, es; *n. A family, household:*—Ða þing ðe eówre hîwenu beþurfon *cibaria domibus vestris necessaria,* Gen. 42, 33. Tô mete eówrum hîwenum *in cibum familiis,* 47, 24. Hîwen *domestici,* Mt. Kmbl. Rush. 10, 36. [*Orm.* hiwenn *a family.*] v. hîwan.

hiwene [?] *discoloration,* Lchdm. iii. 126, 8.

hiwere, es; *m. One who pretends, a hypocrite:*—Hiwere *simulator,* Ælfc. Gr. 85; Som. 73, 105; Wrt. Voc. 49, 12. Wâ eów hiwerum *woe to you hypocrites,* Homl. Th. ii. 404, 17.

hîw-gedâl, es; *n. A separation of man and wife, divorce:*—Hê sylle hyre hyra hîwgedâles bôc *det illi libellum repudii,* Mt. Bos. 5, 31: 19, 7; Mk. Skt. 10, 4. [Cf. *Icel.* hjóna-skilnaðr *a divorce.*]

hiwian; *p.* ode; *pp.* od. *To form, fashion, shape, colour, feign, pretend:*—Hiwian *colorare,* Ælfc. Gl. 99; Som. 76, 112; Wrt. Voc. 54, 54. Ic hiwige *fingo,* Ælfc. Gr. 28; Som. 31, 61. Ðû hiwast swilce ðû ðînum cildum hit sparige *you make as if you are saving it for your children,* Homl. Th. ii. 104, 8. Ealle ðe hiwiaþ hî widûtan mid eáwfæstum þeáwum and widinnan sind geǣttrode mid ârleásnysse *all that fashion themselves outwardly with pious manners, but inwardly are poisoned with impiety,* 404, 13. Sum fǣmne hî hiwode sârlîce seóce *some woman feigned herself very ill,* 506, 5. Herodes hiwode hine sylfne unrôtne *Herod pretended to be troubled,* i. 484, 26. Ðû hiwodest *formasti,* Blickl. Gl: Ps. Spl. C. 138, 4: 93, 9. Hiwgende lang gebed *simulantes longam orationem,* Lk. Skt. 20, 47. v. ge-hiwian.

hîwian; *p.* ode; *To marry:*—Hie forbiódaþ mannum ðæt hie hîwien *prohibentium nubere,* Past. 43, 9; Swt. 318, 1.

hiwing. v. hiwung.

hîwisc, hîgwisc, es; *n. A family, household, house;* also *a hide of land* [v. hîd]:—Fæder hiogwuisc, hiowisc, hiuwisc *paterfamilias,* Lk. Skt. Lind. Rush. 12, 39: 13, 25: 14, 21. Gif hê hæbbe hîwisc landes *if he have a hide of land,* L. Wg. 7; Th. i. 186, 13 [cf. l. 23]. On Cotenesfelde ân hŷwysce and þôðer dêl of Branok hyalf hîwisce *in Cotensfield one hide, and the other part of Branok half a hide*, Chart. Th. 107, 26-8. Hîwisc, 428, 17. God bebeád Moyse ðæt hê and eall Israhêla folc sceoldon offrian æt ǽlcum hîwisce Gode ân lamb ânes geáres *God commanded Moses that he and all the people of Israel should offer a lamb of the first year to God from every family* [*a lamb for an house*, Ex. 12, 3], L. In. 44; Th. i. 130, 5.

hiw-leás; *adj. Wanting in form* or *in colour*:—Hiwleás *deformis*, Wrt. Voc. 72, 16. Hû hiwleáse hie beóþ *how colourless the patients are*, L. M. 2, 36; Lchdm. ii. 242, 2.

hiwleás-ness *want of form*; deformitas, Som.

hiw-lîc; *adj. Having good form* or *colour, shapely*; formosus:—Ansîne hiwlîce hine habban fultum getâcnaþ *to see one's self with a handsome face betokens support*, Lchdm. iii. 204, 8. Reáf hiwlîc habban blisse getâcnaþ *to have a handsome robe betokens bliss*, 212, 6. Hiwlîc *figuratus*, Hpt. Gl. 432.

hîw-lîc *matronalis*, Cot. 129, Lye.

hîw-rǽden, e; *f. A family, household, house, a religious house*:—Hŷwrǽden *domus*, Ælfc. Gl. 106; Som. 78, 66; Wrt. Voc. 57, 45. Godes wîngeard is Israhêla hîwrǽden *God's vineyard is the house of Israel*, Homl. Th. ii. 72, 31: Mt. Kmbl. 10, 6. Gang in tô ðam arce and eall ðîn hîwrǽden *ingredere tu et omnis domus tua in arcam*, Gen. 7, 1: 50, 8. For bênum abbodes and ðære heórǽdene æt Bercleá *for the prayers of the abbot and of the brethren at Berkeley*, Chart. Th. 129, 30: 168, 24. Sib sî disse hîwrǽddenne *pax huic domui*, Lk. Skt. 9, 5: 19, 9: Gen. 28, 2: Ex. 2, 1. Hîwrǽdene underfêhþ *familiam susceperit*, L. Ecg. P. ii. 16; Th. ii. 188, 2.

hîw-scipe, hîg-, es; *m. A family, household, house*:—Hîwscype *domus*, Ps. Lamb. 113, 17. Wæs sum hîwscipes fæder and hîna ealdor *erat paterfamilias*, Bd. 5, 12; S. 627, 9. Ðâ onfêng heó ǽnes hîwscipes stôwe *accepit locum unius familiæ*, 4, 23; S. 593, 18. Ealle hîwscipas þeóda *universæ familiæ gentium*, Ps. Lamb. 21, 28. [*O. E. Hom.* of elchan hiwscipe, i. 87, 8. v. Ex. 12, 3.] DER. sin-hîwscipe.

hiwung, hiwing, e; *f. Forming, shaping, form, figure, pretence, feigning, hypocrisy, dissimulation*:—Hê ne biþ ðonne geleáfa ac biþ hiwung *it is not then belief but hypocrisy*, Homl. Th. i. 250, 21. Hywung, ii. 220, 32. Gê sind wiðinnan âfyllede mid hiwunge and unrihtwîsnysse *within ye are filled with hypocrisy and unrighteousness*, 404, 21. Ða leásan lîcceteras ðe mid hiwunge God sêcaþ *the false hypocrites that seek God with outward show*, i. 120, 2. Hê com mid hiwunge *he came with dissimulation*, Chr. 1049; Erl. 172, 32. Mid ðære hiwunga ðe hió lîcet ðæt hió sîe gôd *mendacium specie bonorum*, Bt. 29; Fox 72, 1. Hî on fruman tô Godes hîwunga gesceapene wǽron *in the beginning they were created in the image of God*, Blickl. Homl. 61, 7. Þurh hiwwinge *per figuras*, Num. 12, 8. Ðæt hluttre môd ðe Gode gelîcaþ forsihþ ða hiwunga and healt sôðfæstnysse *the pure mind that pleases God despises pretences and holds the truth*, Basil admn. 5; Norm. 46, 8. Þurh deófles hiwunga *per diaboli figmenta*, L. Ecg. C. iii. 14; Th. ii. 202, 5. v. hiwian.

hîwung, e; *f. Marriage*:—Mid his hîwunge and his gefêrena *with the marriage of himself and of his companions*, Ors. 2, 2; Swt. 64, 24. v. hîwian.

hladan; *p.* hlôd; *pp.* hladen. I. *to heap, pile up, build, place, lade, load, freight*:—Ic mê hrycg hlade ðæt ic habban sceal *I load my back with what I am to have*, Exon. 102 a; Th. 386, 21; Rä. 4, 65. Wyrd wôp wecceþ weán hladeþ *fate awakens grief, heaps up misery*, Salm. Kmbl. 874; Sal. 436. Wê gelîce sceolon leánum hleótan swâ wê weorcum hlôdun *we shall obtain rewards according as we built with our deeds* [cf. 1 Cor. 3, 12-14], Exon. 19 a; Th. 49, 12; Cri. 784. Hlôdan *they loaded*, 106 a; Th. 404, 19; Rä. 23, 10. Ongan ðâ âd hladan *began then to build the pile*, Cd. 140; Th. 175, 25; Gen. 2901. Hŷ ne môston on bǽl hladan leófne mannan *they might not place the beloved man on the pile*, Beo. Th. 4259; B. 2126. Him on bearm hladan bunan and discas *to heap up in his bosom cups and dishes*, 5543; B. 2775. Naca hladen herewǽdum *the bark laden with war weeds*, 3798; B. 1897. Wæs wunden gold on wǽn hladen *twisted gold was laden on the wain*, 6260; B. 3134. Hærfest wæstmum hladen *autumn laden with fruits*, Menol. Fox 281; Men. 142. II. *to lade, draw* [*water*]; haurire:—Ic hlade *haurio*, Ælfc. Gr. 30; Som. 34, 40. Swâ hwæt swâ ðû hlætst of ðam flôde *quidquid hauseris de fluvio*, Ex 4, 9. Hê hlôd wæter mid ûs *hausit aquam nobiscum*, 2, 19. Ðâ mid âne helme hlôd hit, Nar. 8, 3: Homl. Th. ii. 118, 21. Ða þênas ðe ðæt wæter hlôdon *ministri qui haurierant aquam*, Jn. Skt. 2, 9. Hladaþ *haurite*, 8. Hlade ðonne mid ðære ylcan hand ðæs wæteres mûþ fulne *let him then take up with the same hand a mouthful of the water*, Lchdm. iii. 68, 15; 74, 16. Wæter tô hladanne *ad hauriendam aquam*, Ex. 2, 16. Ne ðû næfst nân þing mid tô hladenne *neque in quo haurias habes*, Jn. Skt. MS. A. 4, 11. Gemêtte ǽnne ealdne munuc wæter hladende *found an old monk drawing water*, Homl. Th. ii. 180, 7. [*Orm.* lodenn. *p. pl*; lădenn, *pp. to draw* (*water*): *Ayenb.* lhade: *Prompt. Parv.* ladyn̄ i. *onero, sarcino*; ii. *vatilo*: *Goth.* hlaþan *to load*: *O. Sax.* hladan (*like A. Sax.*): *O. Frs.* hlada *to lade*: *Icel.* hlaða *to lade, pile up, build*: *O. H. Ger.* hladan *onerare, ponere*: *Ger.* laden.] DER. â-, ge-, tô-hladan.

hladung, e; *f. A drawing*, haustus, Som.

hlæd, es; *n. A heap, pile, mound*:—Beraþ hiere hlæd tô *comportabis aggerem*, Past. 21, 5; Swt. 161, 5: 163, 10, 11. [*Icel.* hlað; *n*: hlaði; *m. a pile, stack.*] v. hladan.

hlædder. v. hlæder.

hlæd-disc, es; *m. A dish on which many things are heaped up* [?]; satura [MS. satira], Ælfc. Gl. 30; Som. 61, 69; Wrt. Voc. 26, 66. v. hlæd.

hlædel, es; *m. An instrument for drawing water, a ladle*; antlia, Hpt. Gl. 418. [*Chauc. Piers P.* ladel.] v. hladan.

hlæden *a vessel for drawing water, a bucket*; hauritorium, Ælfc. Gl. 25; Som. 60, 54; Wrt. Voc. 24, 50.

hlæder, hlædder, e; *f*: hlæddre, an [?]; *f. A ladder, flight of steps*; scala:—Ðâ geseah hê on swefne standan âne hlædre and godes englas up stîgende and nyðer stîgende on ðære hlædre *viditque in somnis scalam stantem, angelos quoque dei ascendentes et descendentes per eam*, Gen. 28, 12, 13: Past. pref; Swt. 23, 17: Exon. 114 a; Th. 437, 11; Rä. 56, 6. On lǽddran sittan, Lchdm. iii. 210, 23. Tô heofnum up hlædræ rǽrdon *they raised ladders up to the heavens*, Cd. 80; Th. 101, 1; Gen. 1675. Hie æfter hlæddrum âstigon *they mounted by steps*, Blickl. Homl. 209, 7. [*Ayenb.* lheddre: *Piers P.* laddre: *O. Frs.* hladder, hleder: *O. H. Ger.* hleitar, leitara: *Ger.* leiter.]

hlæder-wyrt, hlædder-, e; *f. Ladder-wort, ladder to heaven, Jacob's ladder*; polemonium cæruleum *or* polygonatum multiflorum [v. E. D. S. No. 26, 'ladder to heaven'], Lchdm. iii. 8, 25.

hlæd-hweól, -weogl, -wiogl, es; *n. A wheel used in drawing water*; antlia, Cot. 9, 101, Lye.

hlæd-trendel, es; *m. A wheel used in drawing water*; rota hauritoria, Hpt. Gl. 418.

hlǽfdige, hlǽfdie, an; *f. A lady, mistress of a house*; after Bertric's time it is the title given to the wife of the West-Saxon king. v. William of Malm. bk. ii. c. 2:—Hlǽfdige, *domina*, Wrt. Voc. 72, 79. Hîrêdes hlǽfdige *materfamilias*, 73, 21. Gif hwylc wîf hire wîfman swingþ and heó þurh ða swingle wyrþ deád and heó unscyldig biþ fæste seó hlǽfdige vii geár *si mulier aliqua ancillam suam flagellis verberaverit et ex illa verberatione moriatur, et innocens sit, domina vii annos jejunet*, L. Pen. ii. 4; Th. ii. 184, 2. Cristes þegnas cweþaþ ðæt ðû sîe hlǽfdige wuldorweorudes *Christ's servants say that thou* [*the Virgin Mary*] *art the queen of the glorious host*, Exon. 12 a; Th. 18, 15; Cri. 284. Hlǽfdige mîn *O lady mine!* Elen. Kmbl. 1309; El. 656. Ðâ com seó hlǽfdige hider tô lande *then came the lady* [*Ethelred's wife*] *to this country*, Chr. 1002; Erl. 137, 30: 1013; Erl. 149, 29. Æþelflæd Myrcena hlǽfdige, 918; Erl. 103, 1 [cf. Henry of Hunt. 'Hæc igitur domina tantæ potentiæ fertur fuisse, ut a quibusdam, non solum domina vel regina sed etiam rex vocaretur']. On þŷs ilcan geáre forþfêrde seó ealde hlǽfdige Eádwerdes cinges môder *in this same year departed the old lady, the mother of king Edward*, 1051; Erl. 176, 19. Cnut cyncg and Ælfgifu seó hlǽfdige, Chart. Th. 328, 20. Swâ eágan gâþ earmre þeówenan ðonne heó on hire hlǽfdigean handa lôcaþ *sicut oculi ancillæ, in manibus dominæ suæ*, Ps. Th. 122, 3: Cd. 103; Th. 137, 13; Gen. 2273. Agar forseah hire hlǽfdian *Agar despexit dominam suam*, Gen. 16, 4. Ðâ forlêt se cyng ða hlǽfdian seó wæs gehâlgod him tô cwêne [*of Eward putting away his wife, Godwin's daughter*], Chr. 1048; Erl. 180, 20. Him tô wîfum dydon ða ðe ǽr wǽron heora hlǽfdian *those who before had been their mistresses, they made their wives*, Ors. 4, 3; Bos. 80, 6. [*Laym.* lafdi, leafdi: *Orm.* laffdiȝ: *Ayenb.* lhevedi: *Chauc. Piers P.* lady, ladi.] v. hlâford.

hlǽnan; *p.* de *To cause to lean, to incline*:—Siððan hŷ tôgædere gâras hlǽndon *after they had inclined their spears together*, Exon. 66 b; Th. 246, 18; Jul. 63. DER. â-, bi-hlǽnan.

hlǽne; *adj. Lean, meagre*; macer:—Hlǽne *macer*, Ælfc. Gl. 89; Som. 74, 102; Wrt. Voc. 51, 15. Oxan fûle and swîðe hlǽne *boves fœdæ confectæque macie*, Gen. 41, 3. Nû wê sind hlǽne *anima nostra arida est*, Num. 11, 6: Ors. 4, 13; Bos. 100, 25. [*Laym. Piers P. Chauc.* lene.]

hlǽnian; *p.* ode *To make lean* or *to become lean*:—Ðæt hê his lîchoman hlǽnige *ut caro maceretur*, Past. 14, 6; Swt, 87, 17. Ðonne ðæt flǽsc hlǽnaþ *dum carnem macerant*, 43, 6; Swt. 313, 20. [*Prompt. Parv.* lenyn̄ *or* make lene *macero*.]

hlǽnnes, -ness, e; *f. Leanness*:—Hlǽnnes *macies* vel *tabitudo*, Ælfc. Gl. 89; Som. 74, 104; Wrt. Voc. 51, 17. Môdes hlǽnnys *leanness of the mind*, Homl. Th. i. 522, 31.

hlǽnsian; *p.* ode *To make lean*; macerare, castigare, Hpt. Gl. 433. [Cf. *O. E. Hom.* '*Carnis maceratio* fleises lensing. Mon lenseþ his fleis hwenne he him ȝefeð lutel to etene,' i. 147.]

hlæst, es; *n. Burden, freight, lading*:—Eów is holmes hlæst and heofonfuglas and wildu deór on geweald geseald *into your power is given the ocean's freight* [*fishes*] *and the fowls of the air and wild beasts*, Cd. 74; Th. 91, 20; Gen. 1515. Hwâ ðæm hlæste onfêng *who received that freight*, Beo. Th. 104; B. 52; Cd. 71; Th. 85, 29; Gen. 1422.

Hlæst beran *to bear a burden*, Exon. 101 a; Th. 381, 23; Rä. 2, 15. Ic āstīge mīn scyp mid hlæstum mīnum *ego ascendo navem cum mercibus meis*, Coll. Monast. Th. 26, 31. [*Chauc.* last: *Prompt. Parv.* leste, nowmbyr, as heryngys, and other lyke *legio*: *O.Frs.* hlest: *Icel.* hlass *a cart-load*: *Ger.* last *onus.*] v. hladan, brim-hlæst.

hlæstan. v. ge-hlæstan.

hlǣw, hlāw, hlāu, hlēw, es; *m.* **I.** *a low* or *law* [*occurring in names of places*], *a rising ground, an artificial as well as a natural mound, a funeral mound;* tumulus:—Wæs đǣr on đam eálande sum hlāw mycel ofer eorþan geworht, đone ylcan men for feós wilnunga gedulfon and brǣcon *there was on the island a great mound made upon the earth, which same from the desire of treasure men had dug into and broken up*, Guthl. 4; Gdwin. 26, 5, 7: Beo. Th. 2244; B. 1120. Đā hȳ ofer đone hlǣw ridan *when they rode over the hill*, Lchdm. iii. 52, 14. Hātaþ hlǣw gewyrcean se sceal tō gemyndum mīnum leódum heáh hlifian on Hrones næsse, đæt hit sǣlīđend syđđan hātan Biówulfes biorh *bid them make a mound; it shall as a memorial to my people tower high on Hronesness, so that hereafter may seafarers call it Beowulf's mount*, Beo. Th. 5597; B. 2802: 6295; B. 3158: 6319; B. 3170. Geworpene on wīdne hlǣw *projecti in monumentis*, Ps. Th. 87, 5. On hwelcum hlǣwa hrusan þeccen bān Wēlandes *in what tomb do Weland's bones cover the ground?* Bt. Met. Fox 10, 85; Met. 10, 43. Beorgas đǣr ne muntas steápe ne stondeþ, ne stānclifu heáh hlifiaþ ne dene ne dalu ne dūnscrafu hlǣwas ne hlincas *nec tumulus crescit, nec cava vallis hiat*, Exon. 56 a; Th. 199, 13; Ph. 25. The word is found in local names, e.g. Cwicchelmes hlǣw, Chr. 1006; Erl. 140, 21 [for other examples see Cod. Dipl. Kmbl. iii. xxxi], and exists still in the forms *-low*, as Ludlow, Hounslow; and *-law*, frequently applied to hills in Scotland. [Cf. *Icel.* haugr *a mound, funeral mound; how* in local names.] **II.** *the interior of a mound, a cave*:—Draca sceal on hlǣwe *a serpent shall dwell in a cave*, Menol. Fox 512; Gn. C. 26: Beo. Th. 5539; B. 2773. Eorþsele hlǣw under hrusan *an earth-hall, a cave under ground*, 4813; B. 2411. [*Orm.* illc an lawe & illc an hill: *Havel.* lowe: *Goth.* hlaiw *a grave, tomb;* hlaiwasna *grave, sepulchre*: *O. Sax.* hlēwe (*dat.*) *grave*: *O. H. Ger.* hlaeo *mausoleum*; laeo *acervus*; hlēo *agger*; lēuua *aggeres.*]

HLĀF, es; *m. Bread, food, a loaf*:—Gehafen hlāf *fermentacius panis*: ceorlisc hlāf *cibarius*: geseórid hlāf *acrizimus panis*: hwǣten hlāf *siligeneus* vel *triticeus*: heorþbacen hlāf *subcinericius* vel *focarius*: ofenbacen hlāf *clibanius*: gehyrst hlāf *frixius panis*, Ælfc. Gl. 66; Som. 69, 59–69; Wrt. Voc. 41, 15–23. Litel hlāf *pastillus*: ofenbacen hlāf *fermentum*, 31; Som. 61, 84, 94; Wrt. Voc. 27, 14, 24. Him hylpþ eác ofenbacen hlāf, L. M. 2, 27; Lchdm. ii. 222, 17. Smæl hlāf *artolaganus*, Cot. 21, Lye. Tū hund greátes hlāfes and þridde smales *two hundred* [*loaves?*] *of coarse bread, and a third of fine*, Chart. Th. 158, 25. Hwītes hlāfes cruman *crumbs of white bread*, L. M. 1, 2; Lchdm. ii. 34, 21. Ne sȳ neáta cwyld ne ādl ne hlāfes hungor *let there not be murrain among cattle, or disease, or lack of food*, Shrn. 104, 27. Sing đis on ānum berenan hlāfe and syle đan horse etan *sing this over a barley loaf and give it the horse to eat*, Lchdm. iii. 68, 31: Blickl. Homl. 179, 31: Jn. Skt. 6, 9. Man sceolde dōn dǣdbōte on hlāfe and on wætere *pœnitentia sit agenda in pane et aqua*, L. Ecg. C. 2; Th. ii. 134, 4. Ūrne dæghwamlīcan hlāf syle ūs tōdæg *give us to-day our daily bread*, Mt. Kmbl. 6, 11. Mid Grēcum diáconas ne mōton brecan gehālgodne hlāf *apud Græcos diaconis non licet frangere panem sanctum*, L. Ecg. C. 35; Th. ii. 160, 9: L. M. 3, 41; Lchdm. ii. 334, 22: L. Edg. C. 43; Th. ii. 254, 1. For hwon ne rǣcst đū ūs đone hwītan hlāf đone đū sealdest Saban *quare non nobis porrigis panem nitidum quem Saba dabas*, Bd. 2, 5; S. 507, 14. Cyse and drygne hlāf *cheese and dry bread*, L. M. 2, 26; Lchdm. ii. 278, 21. Hlāf wexenne *a wax plaster*, Lchdm. iii. 210, 1, 2. Gesufelne hlāf, L. Ath. V. 8, 6; Th. i. 236, 36. Đeorfe hlāfas *unleavened loaves*, Homl. Th. ii. 264, 3. cxx. hwǣtenra hlāfa and xxx. clǣnra *one hundred and twenty wheaten loaves and thirty made without bran*, 460, 16. cxx gesuflra hlāfa, 32: 469, 3. On xii mōnþum đū scealt sillan đīnum þeówan men vii hund hlāfa and xx hlāfa būton morgenmetum and nōnmetum *in twelve months thou shalt give thy slave-man seven hundred and twenty loaves, besides meals at morn and noon*, Salm. Kmbl. 192, 18. Cweþ đæt đa stānas tō hlāfum geweorþan *tell the stones to become loaves*, Blickl. Homl. 27, 7. [*Orm.* laf: *Laym.* laves, *pl*: *Ayenb.* lhove: *Goth.* hlaibs: *Icel.* hleifr: *O. H. Ger.* hlaiba, leib *panis, tortella*: *Ger.* laib.] DER. heofon-, offrung-hlāf.]

hlāf-ǣta, an; *m. A loaf-eater, domestic, servant*:—Ceorles hlāfǣta *a 'ceorl's' servant*, L. Ethb. 25; Th. i. 8, 10. [Cf. hlāford, *and v.* (?) *under* hlāf *the passage from* Salm. Kmbl. 192, 18.

hlāf-gang, es; *m. The procession with the host*, L. Eth. vii. 27; Th. i. 334, 34.

hlāf-gebrece, es; *n. A fragment of bread*:—Swā hlāfgebrece *sicut frustum panis*, Ps. Th. 147, 6.

hlāf-gebroc, es; *n. A fragment of bread*:—Đara hlāfgebroca wæs tō lāfe twelf binna fulle *of the fragments there remained twelve baskets full*, Shrn. 48, 31.

hlāf-hwǣte, es; *m. Wheat for making bread*, Chart. Th. 144, 34.

hlāf-leást, e; *f. Lack of bread*:—For đære hlāfleáste đa eorþan ǣton *for lack of bread they ate the earth*, St. And. 34, 20.

hlāf-mæsse, -messe, an; *f. Lammas, a name for the first of August*:—Đæt wæs on đære tīde calendas Agustus and on đæm dæge đe wē hātaþ hlāfmæsse *it was on the first of August, on the day that we call Lammas*, Ors. 5, 13; Swt. 246, 17. On đære nihte đe gē hātaþ Hlāfmesse *on the day that you call Lammas*, Homl. Th. ii. 384, 11. Bringeþ Agustus Hlāfmæssan dæg *August brings Lammas-day*, Menol. Fox 277; Men. 140. Betwix hlāfmæssan and middum sumera *between Lammas and midsummer*, Chr. 921; Erl. 106, 5. Tōforan Hlāfmæssan, 1101; Erl. 237, 24. Æfter hlāmmessan, 1009; Erl. 142, 16. Tō Lāmmæssan, 1085; Erl. 219, 3. [*Piers P.* lammasse: *Prompt. Parv.* lammasse *festum agnorum* vel *Festum ad vincula Sancti Petri.*] v. next word, and hlāf-sēnung.

hlāfmæsse-dæg, es; *m. Lammas-day, the first of August*:—Of đam gehālgedan hlāfe đe man hālige on hlāfmæssedæg *from the hallowed bread which is hallowed on Lammas-day*, Lchdm. iii. 290, 27. Ǣr hlāfmæsse [dǣge?], L. M. 1, 72; Lchdm. ii. 146, 9. Æfter hlāmmǣssedæge, Chr. 1100; Erl. 235, 33.

hlāford, es; *m. A* LORD; dominus, herus:—Hlāford *heros*, Ælfc. Gl. 87; Som. 74, 46; Wrt. Voc. 50, 28. Scipes hlāford *nauclerus*, 83; Som. 73, 66; Wrt. Voc. 48, 4. Hie cwǣdon đæt him nǣnig mǣg leófra nǣre đonne hiera hlāford *they said that no kinsman was dearer to them than their lord*, Chr. 755; Erl. 50, 20. Cwǣdon đæt him nān leófre hlāford nǣre đonne heora gecynde hlāford, 1014; Erl. 150, 6. Hē wæs ǣgđer mīn mǣg and mīn hlāford *he was both my kinsman and my lord*, Byrht. Th. 138, 23; By. 224. Đæs þegenes lof is đæs hlāfordes wurþmynt. Sȳ lof đam Hlāforde đe leofaþ on ēcnysse *the servant's praise is the Lord's honour. Praise be to the Lord that liveth for ever*, Homl. Th. ii. 562, 6. Sum sceal mid hearpan æt his hlāfordes fōtum sittan feoh þicgan *one shall sit with the harp at the feet of his lord, receive money*, Exon. 88 a; Th. 332, 5; Vy. 80. Hine gecēs tō hlāforde Scotta cyning, *the king of Scots chose him as his lord*, Chr. 924; Erl. 110, 14. Tō hlāforde geceósan *to elect king*, Ors. 3, 11; Bos. 74, 39. Ōhthere sǣde his hlāforde Ælfrēde cyninge *Ohthere said to his lord, king Alfred*, 1, 1; Bos. 19, 25. Ic geann mīnum hlāforde syxti mancusa goldes *I give to my lord sixty mancuses of gold*, Chart. Th. 516, 32. Ūrum hlāforde holde *loyal to our lord*, L. C. E. 20; Th. i. 372, 8. Ic mē be healfe mīnum hlāforde be swā leófan men licgan þence *beside my lord, by one so loved, I mean to lie*, Byrht. Th. 141, 7; By. 318: Judth. 12; Thw. 25, 9; Jud. 251: Andr. Kmbl. 823; An. 412. Heora hlāford gewrecan *to avenge their lord*, Ors. 3, 9; Swt. 134, 30. Hē bebeád đone hlāford lufian swā hine selfne *he commanded to love the lord as himself*, L. Alf. 49; Th. i. 58, 13. Āhte ic fela wintra folgaþ tilne holdne hlāford *I had for many years a good service, a gracious lord*, Exon. 100 b; Th. 379, 26; Deór. 39. Ālegdon đā tōmiddes mǣrne þeóden hlāford leófne *they laid down in their midst the great prince, their beloved lord*, Beo. Th. 6276; B. 3142. Đa menn đa đǣr hlāfordas wǣron *the men that were lords there*, Chart. Th. 459, 16. Hlāforda wīn *honorarium vinum*, Ælfc. Gl. 32; Som. 62, 1; Wrt. Voc. 27, 67. Heó [*Hagar*] gewāt hire hlāfordum [*Abram and Sara*], Cd. 104; Th. 138, 21; Gen. 2295. [*Laym.* laverd: *Orm.* laferrd: *A. R.* loverd: *Proclam. H. III.* lhoaverd: *Ayenb.* lhord: *Piers P. Chauc.* lord.] DER. cyne-, eald-, hūs-, worold-hlāford.

hlāford-dōm, es; *m. Dominion, lordship*:—For Godes ege under đæm geoke his hlāforddōmes þurhwunigen and hine for Godes ege weorþigen, suā mon hlāford sceal *divino timore constricti ferre sub eis jugum reverentiæ non recusent*, Past. 28, 5; Swt. 197, 8. Se đe on lāreówes onlīcnesse đa þenenga đæs ealdordōmes gecierþ tō hlāforddōme *qui ex simulatione disciplinæ ministerium regiminis vertit in usum dominationis*, 17, 9; Swt. 121, 24. [*Orm.* laferrd-dom.]

hlāford-gift *principatus*, Hpt. Gl. 412. [Cf. [?] Hlafordes gifu, L. Eth. iii. 3; Th. i. 292, 16, and see the Glossary.]

hlāford-hyldo; *f.* -hyld, -held [?] *m; or* -hyldu, e; *f. Fidelity to a lord, loyalty*:—Ac hī gecȳđdon rađe đæs hwylce hlāford-hyldo hī þohton tō gecȳđanne on heora ealdhlāfordes bearnum *but soon after they shewed what kind of loyalty they intended to shew to the children of their late lord*, Ors. 6, 37; Bos. 132, 23. Eall đæt wē ǣfre for riht-hlāfordhelde dōþ *all that we ever do from true loyalty*, L. C. E. 20; Th. i 372, 10.

hlāford-leás; *adj. Lordless, not having a lord*:—Ætwītan mē đæt ic hlāfordleás hām sīđie *to taunt me that I return home without my lord*, Byrht. Th. 139, 8; By. 251: Exon. 105 b; Th. 401, 35; Rä. 21, 22: Beo. Th. 5863; B. 2935: Andr. Kmbl. 810; An. 405. Be hlāfordleásum mannum *concerning men who have no lord*, L. Ath. 1, 2; Th. i. 200, 4.

hlāford-scipe, es; *m. Lordship, rule;* dominatio:—Hlāfordscipe đīn *dominatio tua*, Ps. Spl. 144, 13. Hwī wæs Adame ān treów forboden đā đā hē wæs ealles ōđres hlāford? Tō đan đæt hē hine ne onhōfe on swā micclum hlāfordscipe *why was one tree forbidden to Adam, when he was lord of every other? To the end that he might not exalt himself with so great lordship*, Boutr. Scrd. 17, 28. Đū winsþ wiđ đam hlāfordscipe đe đū self gecure *you strive against the rule you have yourself chosen*, Bt. 7,

2; Fox 18, 30. Đonne wē āgyltaþ wiđ đa hlāfordas, đonne āgylte wē wiđ đone God đe hlāfordscipe gescōp *cum præpositis delinquimus, ejus ordinationi, qui eos nobis prætulit, obviamus*, Past. 28, 6; Swt. 201, 3: 29; Swt. 201, 22. Dominationes sind hlāfordscypas gecwedene, Homl. Th. i. 342, 32.

hlāford-searu; *f. n. Plotting against the life of a king* or *lord*:—Būton æt hlāfordsearwe đam hie nāne mildheortnesse ne dorston gecwæđan *except in cases of treason against a lord; to that they dared not assign any mercy*, L. Alf. 49; Th. i. 58, 9. Be hlāfordsearwe. Gif hwā ymb cyninges feorh sierwie, sīe hē his feores scyldig and ealles đæs đe hē āge *of plotting against a lord. If any one plot against the king's life, let him forfeit his life and all that he owns*, L. Alf. pol. 4; Th. i. 62, 14: 1; Th. 60, 4: L. Ath. i. 4; Th. i. 202, 1: L. Edg. ii. 7; Th. i. 268, 23: L. C. S. 26; Th. i. 392, 1. [Cf. L. Eth. v. 5; Th. i. 312, 5: vi. 37; Th. i. 324, 16: L. C. S. 58; Th. i. 408, 1.]

hlāford-sōcn, e; *f. The 'seeking' a lord for the purpose of being in his service, and under his protection* [cf. hlāford sēcan, L. Alf. pol. 37; Th. i. 86, 3: L. Ath. iv; Th. i. 220, 24]:—Ne dominus libero homini hlafordsoknam interdicat si eum recte custodierit, L. Ath. ii. 4; Th. i. 216, 25: iii. 5; Th. i. 218, 25.

hlāford-swica, an; *m. A betrayer of his lord, a traitor to his lord*:—Se man đe đis gefæst ne þearf hē him nā ondrǣdan hellewītan būtan hē beó hlāfordswica *the man that keeps this fast need not fear the pains of hell, unless he be a traitor to his lord*, Lchdm. iii. 228, 24. Hēr sind on earde on mistlīce wīsan hlāfordswican manige *here in the land are in divers manners many traitors*, Swt. A. S. Rdr. 107, 88: 110, 176. [*Laym.* lauerd-, louerd-swike *traitor*.]

hlāford-swice, es; *m. Treachery to a lord, treason*:—Ealra mǣst hlāfordswice se biþ on worulde đæt man his hlāfordes sāwle beswīce and full mycel hlāfordswice eác biþ đæt man his hlāford of līfe forrǣde ođđe of lande lifigendne drīfe *the greatest treachery in the world against one's lord is to betray his soul, and very great treachery also is it to deprive him of life, or to drive him from the country alive*, Swt. A. S. Rdr. 107, 88. v. hlāford-searu.

hlāf-sēnung, e; *f. Blessing of bread, which took place on August first* or *Lammas-day*:—On đam ylcan dæge [Aug. 1] æt hlāfsēnunga, Shrn. 112, 8. v. hlāf-mæsse.

hlagol; *adj. Apt to laugh*, Lye.

hlām-mæsse. v. hlāf-mæsse.

hlanc; *adj. Lank, lean, gaunt*:—Đæs se hlanca gefeah wulf in walde *at that rejoiced the gaunt wolf in the wood*, Judth. 11; Thw. 24, 25; Jud. 205. Swā đū on hrīme setest hlance cylle *sicut uter in pruina*, Ps. Th. 118, 83.

hland, hlond, es; *n. Urine*, Lchdm. i. 362, 18: ii. 40, 20: 156, 14. [*Icel.* hland.]

hlāw. v. hlǣw.

hleahtor, hlehter, es; *m. Laughter*:—Hleahter *risus*, Wrt. Voc. 83, 35. Đa gesīđas wōp and hleahtor *the comrades weeping and laughter*, Salm. Kmbl. 695; Sal. 347: Beo. Th. 1226; B. 611. Hie habbaþ suā micle mēde ōđerra monna gōdra weorca suā wē habbaþ đæs hleahtres đonne wē hliehaþ gligmonna unnyttes cræftes *sic eis virtutum sanctitas, sicut stultis spectatoribus ludicrarum artium vanitas placet*, Past. 34, 2; Swt. 231, 6. Đū ūs gesettest tō hleahtre and tō forsewennesse eallum đǣm đe ūs ymbsittaþ *posuisti nos derisu et contemptu his qui in circuitu nostro sunt*, Ps. Th. 43, 15. Hē wæs heáfde becorfen for scondfulles gebeórscypes hleahtre *he* [*John the Baptist*] *had his head cut off for the amusement of a shameful feast*, Shrn. 123, 8. Be hleahtre đe of milte cymþ *of laughter that cometh from the spleen*, L. M. 2, 36; Lchdm. ii. 142, 21. Hē ne sceal sprecan ȳdelu word đa đe unnytte hleahtor up āhebben ne hē eác sceal lufigean micelne and ungemetlīcne cancettende hleahtor, L. E. I. 21; Th. ii. 416, 35. Se herewīsa hleahtor ālegde *the host's leader hath put away laughter* [*is dead*], Beo. Th. 6033; B. 3020. Hleahtor ālegdon đā hī swīđra oferstāg weard *they put away laughter when a stronger guard had overcome them*, Exon. 35 b; Th. 116, 1; Gū. 200. God mē worhte hlehter *risum fecit mihi deus*, Gen. 21, 6. Hwǣr beóþ đa ungemetlīcan hleahtras *where are the immoderate laughings*, Blickl. Homl. 59, 18: 195, 15. [*Laym.* lehtre: *A. R.* leihtres, *pl*: *Icel.* hlātr: *O. H. Ger.* hlahter *risus*.]

hleahtor-bǣre; *adj. Given to laughter*, Lye.

hleahtor-full; *adj. Scornful, derisive*:—Geþence ǣlc đara tǣlendra and hleahterfulra *let every one that blames and derides reflect*, Guthl. prol.; Gdwin. 2, 14.

hleahtor-līc; *adj. Ridiculous*:—Gif hē hēr hwylc hleahterlīc word onfinde *if he here find any ridiculous word*, Guthl. prol.; Gdwin. 2, 12.

hleahtor-smiþ, es; *m. One who causes laughter, mirth, joy*:—Wōp wæs wīde worulddreáma lyt wǣron hleahtorsmiþum handa belocne *widespread was the wailing and little of this world's joys, the hands of those who wrought laughter were closed*, Cd. 144; Th. 180, 10; Exod. 43.

hleápan; *p.* hleóp, *pl.* hleópon *and* hlupon [cf. *Icel.* hlupu]; *pp.* hleápen *To* LEAP, *jump, dance, run*:—Ic hleápe *salio*, Ælfc. Gr. 30; Som. 34, 45. Đonne hleápþ se healta swā swā heort *the lame shall leap as a hart*, Homl. Th. ii. 16, 18. Se đe hleápeþ *he who* ... 88 b; Th. 332, 11; Vy. 83. Hē hleóp on đæs cyninges stē ... *emissarium regis*, Bd. 2, 13; S. 517, 9: 3, 9; S. 534, 3. ... of heom se hleóp intō đam castele æt Norþwīc *Roger was* ... *one of them, he threw himself into the castle at Norwich*, Chr. 1... 224, 34. Hēr Eádwine eorl and Morkere eorl hlupon ūt and ... fērdon on wuda and feldon *in this year earl Edwin and earl Morc*... *away and went different ways through wood and open country*, ... Erl. 210, 26. Đæt hie ne hliépen unwillende on đæt scorene clif unþe... *per multa, quæ non appetunt, iniquitatum abrupta rapiuntur*, Past. 33, ... Swt. 214, 7. Lege on đa wunde gyf heó tōsomne hleápan wolde *lay* ... *the wound if it be ready to close up* [cf. *Icel.* sárið var hlaupit í sundr], Herb. 90, 13; Lchdm. i. 198, 2. Hwīlum hleápan lēton on geflit faran fealwe mearas *at times they made their fallow steeds run, contend on the course*, Beo. Th. 1733; B. 864. Hē ā wæs gangende and hleápende *ambulans et exsiliens*, Bd. 5, 2; S. 615, 23. Heó him beforan hleápende wæs *the hind kept running before them*, Lchdm. iii. 426, 32. Herodes swōr đæt hē wolde đære hleápendan dēhter forgyfan swā hwæt swā heó bǣde *Herod swore that he would give the dancing daughter whatever she asked*, Homl. Th. i. 452, 34. [*Laym.* lepen; *p. pl.* leopen, lupen: *Orm.* læpen; *subj. p.* lupe: *Ayenb.* lheape; *p.* lhip: *Piers P.* lepen; *p. pl.* lope: *Chauc.* lepe; *p.* lep, leep: *Goth.* us-hlaupan *to leap up*: *O. Sax.* a-hlōpan: *O. Frs.* hlāpa: *Icel.* hlaupa *to leap; also to run*: *O. H. Ger.* hlaufan *currere*: *Ger.* laufen.] DER. ā-, æt-, be-, ge-, ofer-hleápan.

hleápere, es; *m. A leaper, dancer, runner, courier*:—Hleápere *saltator*, Wrt. Voc. 73, 70. Tuegen hleáperas Ælfrēd cyning sende mid gewritum *king Alfred sent two couriers with letters*, Chr. 889; Erl. 86, 23. [*Prompt. Parv.* lepare *or* rennare *cursor*: *Scot.* land-louper: *Icel.* hlaupari *a courser, charger*: *O. H. Ger.* loufari *circumcellio, cursor*: *Ger.* laufer.]

hleápestre, an; *f. A dancer*; saltatrix, Wrt. Voc. 73, 71.

hleápe-wince, an; *f. The lap-wing*:—Hleápewince *cucurata*, Wrt. Voc. 62, 22: *cucu*, 280, 27. [*Ayenb.* lhap-wynche: *Gower.* lappewinke: *Prompt. Parv.* lappe-wynge, lap-wynke *upipa*: *Wick.* lap-, leep-winke.]

hleáppettan; *p.* te *To leap up*:—Hē ongunne hleápettan *exsiliens*, Bd. 5, 2; S. 615, 22.

hleápung, e; *f. Leaping, dancing*:—Herodias swā mǣres mannes deáþ tō gife hire dēhter hleápunge underfēng *Herodias received as a gift for her daughter's dancing the death of so illustrious a man*, Homl. Th. i. 488, 3: 480, 35.

hlec; *adj. Having cracks* or *rents*:—Hlec, *rimosus, scissurosus*, Hpt. Gl. 529. Swīđe lytlum sīceraþ đæt wæter and swīđe dēgellīce on đæt hlece scip, and đeáh hit wilnaþ đæs ilcan đe sió hlūde ȳþ dēþ on đære hreón sǣ būton hit mon ǣr ūtāweorpe *hoc agit sentina latenter excrescens, quod patenter procella sæviens*, Past. 57, 1; Swt. 437, 15.

hlecan; *p.* hlæc [?] *To join, unite, cohere*:—Swā eác his folgeras swā hie unwiđerweardran and gemōdran beóþ swā hie swīđur hlecaþ tōsomne and eác fæstor tōsomne beóþ gefēgde tō gōdra manna hiénþe *sequaces quippe illius, quo nulla inter se discordiæ adversitate divisi sunt, eo in bonorum gravius nece glomerantur*, Past. 47, 3; Swt. 361, 20.

hlēda, hlēde; *m. A seat*:—Đes hlēda, hlēde *sedile*, Ælfc. Gr. 9, 2; Som. 8, 26.

hleglende [= hlegiende, cf. (?) hlehhan *or* hlēgiende, cf. (?) hlōwan] *sonans*, Cot. 24, Lye.

hlehhan, hlæhan, hlihhan, hlichan, hlihan, hlihgan; *p.* hlōh; *pl.* hlōgan *To* LAUGH [*with gladness* or *contempt*], *to deride*:—Ic hliche *rideo*, Ælfc. Gr. 26, 3; Som. 28, 53: 47; Som. 47, 15. Hē gedēþ đæt wē hlihhaþ on morgen *ad matutinum lætitia*, Ps. Th. 29, 5. Eádgo đa đe nū gie woepeþ forđon gie hlæheþ *beati qui nunc fletis quia ridebitis*, Lk. Skt. Lind. 6, 21. Wǣ iúh đa đe hlǣhas forđon gie woepaþ *væ vobis qui ridetis nunc quia lugebitis*, 25. Hlihgaþ, Homl. Th. i. 180, 14. Hlihaþ, Blickl. Homl. 25, 23. Hliehaþ, Past. 27; Swt. 187, 19. Đonne wē hliehaþ gligmonna unnyttes cræftes *when we laugh at the useless art of gleemen*, 34, 1; Swt. 231, 7. Ne hlōh ic nā . . . . ac đū hlōge *non risi . . . . sed risisti*, Gen. 18, 15. Đū hlōge and ic weóp *thou didst laugh and I wept*, L. E. I. pref; Th. ii. 398, 15. Se eorl wæs đē blīđra hlōh đā, Byrht. Th. 136, 6; By. 147: Judth. 10; Thw. 21, 17; Jud. 23: Cd. 33: Th. 45, 10; Gen. 724. Hlōgun ł tēldon hine *deridebant eum*, Lk. Skt. Lind. 8, 53. Đa apostoli hlōgon đæra deófla leásunga and se ealdorman cwæþ mē stent ege đysse andsware and gē hlihaþ *the apostles laughed at the devils' lying words, and the general said 'Fear comes upon me at this answer, and you laugh,'* Homl. Th. ii. 482, 25. Ealle geseónde mē hlōgon on bysmor *omnes videntes me deriserunt me*, Ps. Lamb. 21, 8: Exon. 120 a; Th. 160, 22; Hō. 21. Đeáh đē mon hwylces hlihge and đū đē unscyldigne wite ne rēhst đū hwæt hȳ rǣdon hȳ teóþ đē đæs đe hȳ sylfe habbaþ *though you are derided* [or *blamed?*] *for anything, and know yourself to be innocent, you shall not care what they say; they accuse you of what they have themselves*, Prov. Kmbl. 12. Hē sǣde đæt hē gesāwe crist selfne and đæt hē him hlōge tō *he said that he saw Christ himself, and that he smiled upon him*, Shrn. 70, 9. Hlehhan ne þorftun *they had no* *need to laugh*, Chr. 937; Erl. 114, 13; Æðelst. 47. Ne þorfton hlûde hlihhan, Cd. 4; Th. 5, 17; Gen. 73. Hwæt sceal ic ðonne bûton hliehchan [Cot. MS. hliehhan] ðæs ðonne gê tô lose weorþaþ *what shall I do but laugh at it, when you come to ruin*; ego quoque in interitu vestro ridebo, Past. 36, 1; Swt. 249, 1. Forðon hî hlyhhan mægen *for this reason they can laugh*, L. M. 2, 36; Lchdm. ii. 242, 24. Ða deóflu sægdon hlûde hlihhende *the devils said, laughing loudly*, Homl. Th. ii. 350, 30: i. 376, 5: Herb. 9; Lchdm. i. 98, 27. Hlichende, Ælfc. Gr. 48; Som. 49, 18. Mid hlihendum mûþe *with a smile on his lips*, Homl. Th. i. 428, 34: Elen. Kmbl. 1986; El. 995. Ðæm hlæhendum *ridentibus*, Lk. Skt. p. 5, 7. [*Orm.* lahhȝhenn: *Laym.* lehȝen, lihȝen; *p.* loh, *pl.* loȝen: *A. R.* lauhwen: *Ayenb.* lheȝȝe: *Piers P. Chauc.* laughen: *Wick.* laȝhen, leiȝe; *p.* leiȝede: *Goth.* hlahjan; *p.* hlôh: *O. Sax.* hlahan; *p.* hlôg; *pp.* hlagan: *O. Frs.* hlaka; *p.* hlackade: *Icel.* hlæja; *p.* hlô, *pl.* hlôgu; *pp.* hleginn: *O. H. Ger.* hlahan; *p.* hlôc: *Ger.* lachen.] DER. â-, be-, bi-hlehhan.

hlehter. v. hleahtor.

hlem, mes; *m. A sound, noise, crash*:—Nân monn ne gehiérde ne æxe hlem ne biétles swêg *absque mallei sonitu*, Past. 36, 5; Swt. 253, 17. [Cf. *Icel.* hlam; *n. a dull, heavy sound; hlamman crash, din.*] DER. hilde-, inwit-, uht-, wæl-hlem.

hlemman; *p.* de *To cause to sound, to clash*:—Hê ymbe ða herehûþe hlemmeþ tôgædre grimme gôman *about the prey he clashes his fierce jaws together*, Exon. 97 b; Th. 363, 30; Wal. 61. [*O. Sax.* hlamon: *Icel.* hlamma: *O. H. Ger.* hlamon *crepitare.*] v. hlimman.

hlenca or hlence, an; *m. or f. A link, a chain of links, a coat of mail formed with links or rings* [cf. hringlocen serce *and other compounds of* hring]:—Moyses bebeád frecan ârîsan habban heora hlencan beran beorht searo *Moses bade the warriors arise, take their coats of mail, bear their bright arms*, Cd. 153; Th. 191, 21; Exod. 218. Cf. L. M. 3, 55; Lchdm. ii. 342, 4; gif men sió heáfodpanne beó gehlenced *if a man's skull seem to be iron-bound*. [*Icel.* hlekkr; *m. a link, a chain of links*: *Dan.* lænke.] v. wæl-hlenca.

hlenor-teár, es; *m. Hyssop*:—Hlenorteáre *hyssopo*, Ps. Lamb. 508.

hleó. v. hleów.

hleomoc, hleomoce, an; *f. Brook-lime*, Lchdm. Gloss. ii. iii.

hleón. v. hleówan.

hleonaþ, hleonian, hleonung. v. hlinaþ, hlinian, hlinung.

hleór, es; *n. A cheek, face*:—Hleór *malæ*, Ælfc. Gl. 71; Som. 70, 79; Wrt. Voc. 43, 12. Hleór *maxilla*, Wrt. Voc. 70, 38: *facies*, 282, 37: Exon. 90 a; Th. 337, 18; Gn. Ex. 66: 29 a; Th. 88, 5; Cri. 1435. On ðâm nôsum oððe on ðam hleóre *on the nose or on the cheek*, Herb. 2, 18; Lchdm. i. 86, 2: L. Ethb. 46; Th. i. 14, 11. Dô his hleór xxx sîðum tô eorþan *vultum suum xxx vicibus ad terram inclinet*, L. Ecg. C. 5; Th. ii. 138, 8: Exon. 37 b; Th. 122, 13; Gû. 305: Elen. Kmbl. 2195; El. 1099: Cd. 107; Th. 140, 33; Gen. 2337. [*Laym.* leores, *pl*: *A. R.* leor: *Piers P.* lere: *O. Sax.* hlior, hlier, hlear, hleor: *Icel.* hlýr *cheek.*]

-hleór; *suffix in adjectives* blâc-, dreórig-, fæted-, swâtig-, teárig-hleór.

hleór-bân, es; *n. Cheek-bone, temple*:—Þunwængum ɫ hleórbânum *temporibus*, Ps. Lamb. 131, 5.

hleór-beran:—Eofor lic scionon [o]fer hleor beran gehroden golde fat [and] fyr heard ferh wearde heold, Beo. Th. 612-6; B. 303-5. Grein and Heyne take *hleor beran* as a compound, the former explaining '*was auf dem Gesicht getragen wird, Helmvisier?* [oder *faciei munimentum?*]' the latter rendering it *cheek*. Thorpe reads *bæron*, Kemble *beran*, an infinitive after *scionon* = they seemed [?]. But may not the verb on which *beran* depends be *gewiton*, v. 607, vv. 608-11 be parenthetical, and *scionon* an adverb, the passage then being translated thus, *they went bearing above their faces the boar's shape, fairly* [scionon] *adorned with gold?*

hleór-bolster, es; *m. A cushion for the cheek, pillow*, Beo. Th. 1381; B. 688. [Cf. heáfod-bolster.]

hleór-dropa, an; *m. A tear*, Exon. 52 a; Th. 182, 24; Gû. 1315. [Cf. *Icel.* hlýra skúrir *tears.*]

hleór-sceamu, e; *f. Shame* or *confusion of face*, Ps. Th. 68, 8.

hleór-slæge, -slege, es; *m. A blow on the cheek* or *face*:—Hleórslægeas hê underfêng *alapas accepit*, Past. 36, 9; Swt. 261, 6.

hleótan; *p.* hleát, *pl.* hluton. I. *to cast lots*:—Ic hleóte *sortior*, Ælfc. Gr. 31; Som. 35, 55. Ðâ hluton ða consulas hwelc hiera ǽrest ðæt gewinn underfênge. Ðâ gehleát hit Quintus Flaminius *then the consuls cast lots which of them should first undertake that war. Then the lot fell to Quintus Flaminius*, Ors. 4, 11; Swt. 202, 33. Ðonne seó tîd gewinnes and gefeohtes com ðonne hluton hî mid tânum tô ðâm ealdormannum and swâ hwylc heora swâ him se tân ætýwde ðonne gecuron hî ðone him tô heretogan *Satrapæ, ingruente belli articulo mittunt æqualiter sortes, et quemcumque sors ostenderit hunc tempore belli ducem omnes sequuntur*, Bd. 5, 10; S. 624, 24. Lêton tân wîsian hluton hell-cræftum, Andr. Kmbl. 2205; An. 1104. Uton hleótan *sortiamur*, Jn. Skt. 19, 24. II. *to obtain by lot, get a share, share in, participate, obtain*:—Ðæs ðû gife hleótest hâligne hyht gif . . . *for that shalt thou obtain grace and holy hope, if . . .*, Andr. Kmbl. 960; An. 480. Hê feorhwunde hleát *he got a mortal wound*, Beo. Th. 4760; B. 2385. Hî dôm hlutan eádigne upwæg *they obtained glory, a blessed ascension*, Menol. Fox 382; Men. 192. Ða Godes þeówas on Israhêla þeóde nâne landâre hleótan ne môston *to the servants of God among the people of Israel might not be allotted any landed possessions*, Homl. Th. ii. 224, 5. Hê sceolde þurh deáþes cyme dômes hleótan *he was to gain glory through the coming of death*, Exon. 47 a; Th. 160, 18; Gû. 945: 48 a; Th. 164, 20; Gû. 1014: 74 b; Th. 280, 1; Jul. 622: Runic pm. 1; Kmbl. 339, 6. Leánum hleótan *to obtain rewards*, Exon. 19 a; Th. 49, 10; Cri. 783. [*O. Sax.* hliotan: *Icel.* hljóta *to get*: *O. H. Ger.* hliozan *sortiri.*] DER. ge-hleótan.

hleoðo, hleoðu. v. hlið.

hleóðor, es; *n.* I. *hearing*:—Ontýn eárna hleóðor ðæt gehêrnes hehtful weorðe on gefeán blîðse forþweard tô ðê *auditui meo dabis gaudium et lætitiam*, Ps. C. 50, 77; Ps. Grn. ii. 278, 77. [Cf. *Icel.* hljóð, *e. g.* gefa hljóð, biðja hljóðs *to give, ask for, a hearing*: *Goth.* hliuþ.] II. *what is heard, sound, noise, voice, speech, song*:—Ðâ hleóðor cwom býman stefne ofer burhware *when the sound came of the voice of the trumpet over the city-dwellers*, Cd. 181; Th. 226, 29; Dan. 178: Exon. 86 b; Th. 325, 2; Vîd. 105: 94 b; Th. 353, 46; Reim. 28: Andr. Kmbl. 3101; An. 1553. Heofonlîce hleóðor gehýred wæs *a heavenly voice was heard*, Exon. 52 a; Th. 181, 22; Gû. 1297: Cd. 162; Th. 204, 6; Exod. 417: Andr. Kmbl. 1478; An. 740. Hleóðor hâligra *the voice of saints*, Exon. 65 b; Th. 241, 14; Ph. 656: 108 b; Th. 414, 9; Rä. 32, 17. Biþ ðæs hleóðres swêg eallum songcræftum swêtra *the sound of its voice is sweeter than all singing*, 57 b; Th. 206, 24; Ph. 131: 52 a; Th. 181, 15; Gû. 1293. Heriaþ hine on hleóðre bêman *laudate eum in sono tubæ*, Ps. Th. 150, 3: 107, 2: Exon. 104 a; Th. 395, 8; Rä. 15, 4. Him brego sægde æt hleóðre hwæt hê freman wolde *in speech with him the Lord told him what he meant to do*, Cd. 64; Th. 78, 8; Gen. 1290. Ic onhyrge gûþfugles hleóðor *I imitate the war bird's* [*eagle's*] *voice*, 106 b; Th. 406, 22; Rä. 25, 5: 81 b; Th. 307, 8; Seef. 20: 49 b; Th. 171, 19; Gû. 1129: 42 b; Th. 143, 7; Gû. 657. Hleóðra wyn *the delightful sound of the voices heard in heaven*, 56 a; Th. 198, 18; Ph. 12. Stefnum herigaþ hâlgum hleóðrum heofoncyninges þrym *with voices and holy songs they praise the glory of heaven's king*, Andr. Kmbl. 1445; An. 723: Bt. Met. Fox 13, 94; Met. 13, 47: Exon. 46 a; Th. 156, 22; Gû. 878: Cd. 81; Th. 102, 1; Gen. 1693. [*O. H. Ger.* hlioda *sonitus*: cf. *also Icel.* hljóð *sound*; hljóðan *a sound, tune*: *Dan.* lyd: *Swed.* ljud.] DER. efen-, ofer-, swêg-, word-hleóðor.]

hleóðor-cwide, -cwyde, es; *m. A saying, vocal utterance, words, speech, discourse*:—Ic ðæt gehýre þurh ðînne hleóðorcwide ðæt . . . *I learn from thy words that . . .*, Exon 72 b; Th. 270, 7; Jul. 461: Beo. Th. 3962; B. 1979. Êces word hâlges hleóðorcwide, Exon. 61 b; Th. 226, 1; Ph. 399: Andr. Kmbl. 1786; An. 895. Bodan þurh hleóðor-cwide hyrdum cýðdon *messengers made known to the shepherds by speech*, Exon. 14 a; Th. 28, 21; Cri. 450. Hleóðorcwyde, Cd. 179; Th. 225, 16; Dan. 155: 190; Th. 236, 5; Dan. 316: 109; Th. 143, 20; Gen. 2382. Þurh hleóðorcwidas, Exon. 53 b; Th. 187, 18; Az. 32. Hleóðor-cwydas, Cd. 107; Th. 141, 1; Gen. 2338. Wuton wuldrian weorada Dryhten hâlgan hlióðorcwidum *let us glorify the Lord of hosts with holy songs*, Hy. 8, 2; Hy. Grn. ii. 290, 2. Andreas herede hleóðorcwidum hâliges lâre *Andrew praised with his words the doctrine of the holy one*, Andr. Kmbl. 1637; An. 820. Æfter hleóðorcwidum *according to the words*, 3240; An. 1623. [Cf. meðel-cwide.]

hleóðor-cyme, es; *m. A coming that is attended with sound* [*of trumpets*; cf. hleóðor cwom býman stefne, v. hleóðor], *the coming of an army*:—Hie iudéa blǽd forbrǽcon billa ecgum and þurh hleóðorcyme herige genâmon beorhte frætwe ðâ hie tempel strudon *they destroyed the glory of the Jews with the edge of the sword, and by their coming took with their host the bright ornaments, when they spoiled the temple*, Cd. 210; Th. 260. 15; Dan. 710. [Cf. þrym-cyme *a glorious coming.*] Thorpe and Bouterwek translate *oraculum, prophetia*; Grein takes *cyme* as a separate word, and as an adjective.]

hleóðor-stede, es; *m. A place where words have been spoken*, Cd. 109; Th, 145, 1; Gen. 2399. [Cf. meðel-stede.]

hleóðrian; *p.* ode *To sound, make a sound* [*with the voice*], *to speak, sing, cry, exclaim, resound*:—Drihten hleóðraþ of heofonum and se hýhsta syleþ his stefne *intonuit de cælo Dominus et altissimus dedit vocem suam*, Bd. 4, 3; S. 569, 19: Ps. Spl. 17, 15. Ðonne hleóðriaþ hâlge gǽstas sâwla sôþfæste song âhebbaþ *when holy spirits shall lift up their voices, just souls raise a song*, Exon. 63 b; Th. 234, 12; Ph. 539. Ðâ hleóðrade hlûdan stefne *then cried with a loud voice*, Andr. Kmbl. 2719; An. 1362: 1073; An. 537. Hleódrode, 921; An. 461. Geornlîce on gebede hleóðrede *obnixius orationi incumberet*, Bd. 4, 3; S. 569, 11. Azarias hleóðrade drihten herede and ðâ word âcwæþ *Azarias cried out, praised the Lord, and these words then spake*, Cd. 188; Th. 233, 25; Dan. 281: Fins. Th. 2; Fin. 2. Ðæt lond hleóðrade for ðara wyrma hwistlunge *sibilabat tota regio*, Nar. 13, 21. Him þuhte ðæt hit eall betweox heofone and eorþan hleóðrode ðâm egeslîcum stefnum *it seemed to him that all between heaven and earth it resounded with those awful voices.*

Guthl. 5; Gdwin. 36, 4. Ic gehýrde ðæt hit hleóðrode *I heard that it* [*the cross*] *uttered a sound*, Rood Kmbl. 52: Kr. 26. Hit hleóðrode ðá swíðe tóward Haraldes *the general voice was very much in favour of Harold*, Chr. 1036; Erl. 164, 28. Hyre stefn oncwæþ word hleóðrade *her a voice addressed, a word was heard*, Exon. 69 b; Th. 259, 17; Jul. 283: Andr. Kmbl. 2860; An. 1432. Hé wæs ðæra worda wel gemyndig ðe hé hleóðrade tó Abrahame *memor fuit verbi quod locutus est ad Abraham*, Ps. Th. 104, 37. Fýnd ðíne hleóðrodon *inimici tui sonuerunt*, Ps. Spl. C. 82, 2. Hí ealle samod mid gedrémum sange Godes wuldor hleóðrodon *they all together with melodious song sounded the glory of God*, Homl. Th. i. 38, 7. Swá hleóðrodon *so spake*, Andr. Kmbl. 1383; An. 691. Eáran habbaþ ne hí áwiht mágon holdes gehýran ðeáh ðe him hleóðrige *aures habent et non audient*, Ps. Th. 134, 17. Hé sæde ðæt hé openlíce hí gehýrde betwyh óðer leóþ monig hleóðrian and singan *referre erat solitus, quod aperte eos inter alia resonare audiret*, Bd. 3, 19; S. 547, 37. Ongan ðá hleóðrian helle deófol hwæt is ðis lá manna *then exclaimed the devil of hell: Lo! what man is this*, Elen. Kmbl. 1798; El. 901. Múþ habbaþ and ne mágon wiht hleóðrian *os habent, et non loquentur*, Ps. Th. 113, 13. Hleóðrian *increpare, redarguere*, Cot. 51: 105, Lye. Mid hleóðrigende dreáme *consona vocis harmonia*, Hpt. Gl. 467. Hleóðriyndum *sonantibus*, Ps. Spl. C. 150, 5. [Cf. *Icel.* hljóða *to sound, cry out.*]

hleóðrung, e; *f. Speaking, reproving, reproof:*—Ná hæbbende on múþe his hleóðrunga *non habens in ore suo redargutiones*, Ps. Spl. 37, 15.

hleów, hleó, es; *n. A shelter, protection, covering, refuge; often applied to persons:*—Dægscealdes hleó *the sun's* [cf. *Icel.* himin-targa = *the sun*] *covering*, i. e. *the pillar of cloud*, Cd. 146; Th. 182, 22; Exod. 79. God hleó þarfendra *deus, refugium pauperum*, Rtl. 40, 25. Constantínus æðelinga hleó, Elen. Kmbl. 198; El. 99. Beorna hleó éce ælmihtig, Exon. 69 b; Th. 258, 28; Jul. 272. Duguþa hleó [*Guthlac*], 48 a; Th. 165, 26; Gú. 1034. Wes earmra hleó *be a refuge for the poor*, Cd. 203; Th. 252, 32; Dan. 587. Eorla hleó [*Beowulf*], Beo. Th. 1586; B. 791: *Hrothgar*, 2074; B. 1035: 3736; B. 1866: Exon. 100 b; Th. 379, 30: Deór. 41. Tó ðam bisceope reordode: Ðú eorla hleó, Elen. Kmbl. 2145; El. 1074. Freónda hleó [*Guthlac*], Exon. 47 b; Th. 162, 33; Gú. 985. Sóþne god gǽsta hleó, 66 b; Th. 245, 23; Jul. 49. Hæleþa hleó [*Byrhtnoth*], Byrht. Th. 133, 62; By. 74. Heriga helm wígena hleó [*Constantine*], Elen. Kmbl. 300; El. 150. Wígendra hleó [*Hrothgar*], Beo. Th. 863; B. 429: [*Sigemund*], 1803; B. 899: [*Beowulf*], 3949; B. 1972: Andr. Kmbl. 1011; An. 506: [*Andrew*], 1792; An. 898. Ðú eart weoroda god wígendra hleó, Exon. 13 b; Th. 25, 31; Cri. 409. Wíggendra hleó Eádmund cyning, Chr. 942; Erl. 116, 18; Edm. 12. Ðonne hí tó his húse hleówes wilniaþ *when they desire shelter at his house*, Ps. Th. 108, 10. Under hleó *under shelter*, Cd. 209; Th. 259, 13; Dan. 691: Exon. 16 b; Th. 38, 13; Cri. 606: 61 a; Th. 224, 11; Ph. 374: Andr. Kmbl. 1664; An. 834: Elen. Kmbl. 1011; El. 507. Ðe hé of hleó sende *whom he sent from the shelter* [*of heaven*], Cd. 5; Th. 7, 7; Gen. 102. Eallum tó hleó *as a refuge for all*, Exon. 25 a; Th. 73, 29; Cri. 1197: Andr. Kmbl. 221; An. 111: 1133; An. 567. Uton gán on ðisne weald innan on ðisses holtes hleó *let us go into this wood, into the shelter of this grove*, Cd. 39; Th. 52, 7; Gen. 840: Exon. 62 a; Th. 227, 26; Ph. 429. Hé him beád his recedes hleów *he offered them the shelter of his house*, Cd. 112; Th. 147, 18; Gen. 2441. Ðæt hé ðonne stán nime wið hungres hleó hláfes ne gýme *that he should take a stone then as a protection against hunger, and care not for the bread*, Elen. Kmbl. 1228; El. 616. [*O. Sax.* hleo *in* waldes hleo: *O. Frs.* hlí: *Icel.* hlé; *n. lee (a sea-term).* Cf. also *Icel.* hlý *warmth*; hlýr *warm*; hlýja *to shelter*: *Goth.* hlija *a tent.*] DER. hús-, turf-hleów.

hleówan, hleón, hlýwan; *p.* de. I. *to make warm, cherish, protect, shelter:*—Ðære sunnan hǽto ðe ðás eorðan hlýweþ *the heat of the sun which warms this earth*, Blickl. Homl. 51, 21. Wudubearwas eorþwelan hleóþ [cf. holtes hleó; *or is* rén *the subject of the verb?*] *the groves protect the earth's wealth*, Exon 54 a; Th. 191, 8; Az. 85. Se king ðǽr sæt hleówwinde hine beo ðan fýre *the king sat there warming himself by the fire*, Shrn. 16, 16. [*Icel.* hlýja *to cover, shelter, make warm.*] II. *to become warm:*—Gif hit wæter sý hǽte man hit óþ hit hleówe tó wylme *if it be water let it be heated until it become so warm as to boil*, L. Ath. iv. 7; Th. i. 226, 14. v. hleów, hleówe, gehlýwan.

hleów-bord, es; *n. A board which serves for covering or protection* [*the binding of a book*], Exon 107 a; Th. 408, 14; Rä. 27, 12.

hleów-burh; *gen.* -burge; *f. A city which affords shelter, protection*, Beo. Th. 1828; B. 912: 3467; B. 1731.

hleów-dryhten, es; *m. A lord who protects, a patron*, Exon. 86 a; Th. 324, 13; Wíd. 94.

hleówe; *adj. Warm, sheltered:*—Gefere ðæne mannan on swíðe fæstne cleofan and wearmne gereste him swíðe wel hleówe ðǽr and wearme glēda bere man gelóme inn *carry the man into a room very fast shut and warm, let him rest himself there quite warm and snug, and let warm coals be often carried in*, L. M. 2, 59; Lchdm. ii. 280, 12. [Cf. *Icel.* hlúa að einum *to make one warm and snug*: hlýr, hlær, *warm, mild*: *Wick.* lew *lukewarm.*] DER. ge-, un-hleówe.

hleów-fæst; *adj. Sheltering, protecting:*—Heáh gǽst hleófæst *exalted and sheltering spirit*, Exon. 13 a; Th. 22, 27; Cri. 358.

hleów-feðer, e; *f. A sheltering wing:*—Gefór hleówfeðrum þeaht *journeyed covered by* [*his creator's*] *sheltering wings*, Cd. 131; Th. 165, 31; Gen. 2740.

hleów-hræscnes?:—Miclode ofor mé hleóhræscnesse ł forcæncednysse *magnificavit super me supplantationem*, Ps. Lamb. 40, 10.

hleów-leás; *adj. Not having or not affording shelter, protection, comfort, cheerless:*—Ða ðe hleóleásan wíc wunedon *those who had occupied a cheerless dwelling*, Andr. Kmbl. 261; An. 131. Ne mótun hí on eorþan eardes brúcan ac hý hleóleáse háma þoliaþ *they may not enjoy a home on earth but shelterless lose their dwellings*, Exon. 35 b; Th. 115, 21; Gú. 193.

hleów-lora weorþan *to become unprotected*, Cd. 92; Th. 117, 14; Gen. 1953.

hleów-mǽg, es; *m. A near relation, one who is bound to offer shelter or help* [?], Cd. 48; Th. 61, 34; Gen. 1007: 75; Th. 94, 3; Gen. 1556: 78; Th. 96, 16; Gen. 1596: 76; Th. 95, 21; Gen. 1582: Exon. 81 b; Th. 307, 18; Seef. 25.

hleów-sceorp, es; *n. A protecting garment*, Exon. 103 a; Th. 391, 15; Rä. 10, 5.

hleów-stede, es; *m. A sheltered, warm place:*—Hleówstede *apricus locus*, Wrt. Voc. 86, 24.

hleów-stól, es; *m. A place of protection, one's native city:*—Síðedon fǽmnan and wuduwan freóndum beslægene from hleówstóle *damsels and widows bereft of friends journeyed from their sheltering home* [*of the people of Sodom driven from their city*], Cd. 94; Th. 121, 16; Gen. 2011.

hleówþ, hleóþ, hlíwþ, hlýwþ, e; *f. Shelter, protection, warmth:*—Hleówþ *apricitas*, Wrt. Voc. 86, 25. Ðonne him cælþ hé cépþ him hlýwðe *when he gets cold he looks out for warmth*, Hexam. 20; Norm. 28, 23. Tó neste bǽron heora briddum tó hleówþe *bore it to their nest to shelter their young*, Homl. Th. ii. 144, 23. Foresceáwian bigleofan and hleówþe *to provide food and shelter*, 462, 18. Hlýwþe, Basil admn. 9; Norm. 52, 23. Cold bæþ ongeán ða hlíwþe *a cold bath to atone for the warmth*, L. Pen. 16; Th. ii. 284, 5. Ða hlýwþe gódra weorca *the shelter of good works*, L. E. I. 32; Th. ii. 430, 24. Gé hyra hulpon and him hleóþ géfon *ye helped them* [*the poor*] *and gave them shelter*, Exon. 27 b; Th. 83, 11; Cri. 1354. [*Laym.* leoð *protection.*]

hleówung, hlýwing, e; *f. Shelter, refuge:*—Hlýwing *refugium*, R. Conc. 11, Lye.

hlét, hliét, es; *m. A lot; sors:*—Missenlíce hléte *varia sorte*, Bd. 2, 20; S. 521, 10. Be hléte *sorte*, Hpt. Gl. 426. Hé hí hæfþ oferstigene mid ðam hliéte his anwaldes *quos sorte potestatis excesserit*, Past. 17, 3; Swt. 111, 16. [*Goth.* hlauts; *m. a lot*: *O. Sax.* hlót; *m*: *O. H. Ger.* hlóz; *m. n.*] v. hlot, hlyt.

hlichan. v. hlehhan.

hlid, es; *n. A lid, cover, the opening which is closed by the cover:*—Hlidd *opertorium*, Ps. Spl. 101, 28. Ðá lédon ða þegenas ðone Hǽlend ðǽron and mid hlide belucon úre ealra Álýsend *then the thanes laid Jesus therein, and closed up with a cover the Redeemer of us all*, Homl. Th. ii. 262, 4. Se engel áwylte ðæt hlid of ðære þryh *the angel rolled away the cover from the tomb*, i. 222, 8. Hé tóáwylte mycelne stán tó hlide ðære byrgene *advolvit saxum magnum ad ostium monumenti*, Mt. Kmbl. 27, 60. [*Icel.* hlið *gate, gateway*: *O. H. Ger.* hlit *operculum.*] DER. ge-hlid.

hlídan. v. be-, of-, on-, to-hlídan.

hlid-fæst; *adj. Having a lid:*—Hió becwyþ Eádmǽre áne hlidfæsþe cuppan *she bequeaths to Eadmer a cup with a lid*, Chart. Th. 536, 4.

hlid-geat, es; *n. A swing-gate, folding-door:*—On ðonæ stocc ðæ ðæt hlidgeat on hangodæ *to the post that the swing-gate hung on*, Cod. Dipl. Kmbl. iii. 176, 13. Of ðam hlidgeate, 236, 25. Hlidgata *valva*, Ælfc. Gl. 29; Som. 61, 36; Wrt. Voc. 26, 35.

hliépa. v. hlýpa.

hliét. v. hlét.

hlifendre *minium*, Lye.

hlifian; *p.* ode *To stand out prominently, tower up, to be raised high:*—Ic hlifige under heofenum *I am high raised under the heavens*, Rood Kmbl. 167; Kr. 85. Se beorhta beág eádigra gehwam hlifaþ ofer heáfde *the bright crown rises o'er the head of each blessed one*, Exon. 64 b; Th. 238, 14; Ph. 604. Beorgas ne muntas steápe ne stondaþ ne stánclifu heáh hlifiaþ *nec tumulus crescit*, 56 a; Th. 199, 9, 27; Ph. 23, 32. Hlifiaþ eáran ofer eágum *ears stand up above my eyes*, 104 b; Th. 396, 14; Rä. 16, 4. Wudubeám hlifode tó heofontunglum *the tree towered up to the stars of heaven*, Cd. 199; Th. 247, 22; Dan. 501. Hlifade, Beo. Th. 163, 3801; B. 81, 1898. Hlifodon, Andr. Kmbl. 1681; An. 843. Hlifedon, Cd. 146; Th. 183, 9; Exod. 89. Gesáwon salo hlifian *saw the halls towering up*, 109; Th. 145, 10; Gen. 2403: Exon. 113 b; Th. 435, 16; Rä. 54, 1. Heáh hlifian, Beo. Th. 5602; B. 2805. Hlifigan, Cd. 139; Th. 174, 12; Gen. 2877: 205; Th. 253, 29; Dan. 603. Hlifigean, 66; Th. 79, 35; Gen. 1321. Mid ðý ðe hé wæs hlifigende ofer sǣs brim *whilst he was standing high up above the sea*, Blickl. Homl. 143, 5. DER. ofer-hlifian.

hlīgan or hligan? *To allow one a reputation for anything, to give one glory*:—Ne forlēt ðū ūsic ēce drihten for ðām miltsum ðe ðec men hlīgaþ *forsake us not, eternal Lord, because of those mercies for which men account thee glorious*, Cd. 190; Th. 235, 25; Dan. 311. Willaþ mid ðȳ gedōn ðæt hie mon hlīge wīsdōmes *they desire thereby to make men allow them a reputation for wisdom*; doctrinæ sibi opinionem faciunt, Past. 48, 2; Swt. 367, 19. v. hlīsa.

hligiung, e; *f. Laughing*, L. M. 2, 46; Lchdm. ii. 258, 20.

hligsa. v. hlīsa.

hlihan, hlihhan. v. hlehhan.

hlimman; *p.* hlamm; *pl.* hlummon *To sound, roar* [*as the sea*], *clang, clash*:—Gārsecg hlymmeþ *the ocean roars*, Andr. Kmbl. 784; An. 392. Hlimmeþ, Exon. 101 a; Th. 382, 2; Rä. 3, 5. Ðrǣd mē ne hlimmeþ *the thread makes no sound to me*, 109 a; Th. 417, 18; Rä. 36, 6. Scildas hlūde hlummon *loud clanged the shields*, Judth. 11; Thw. 24, 24; Jud. 205. Ic ne gehȳrde būtan sǣ hlimman *I heard nought but the sea roaring*, Exon. 81 b; Th. 307, 4; Seef. 18. v. hlemman.

hlimme, an; *f. A torrent*:—Dō him swā ðū dydest Madiane and Sisare swylce Jabin ealle ða nāmon Ændorwylle and Cisone clǣne hlimme *fac illis sicut Madian et Sisaræ; sicut Jabin in torrente Cisson; disperierunt in Endor*, Ps. Th. 82, 8. Ða ðe on wege weorðaþ wætres æt hlimman deópes ondrincaþ *de torrente in via bibet*, 109, 8. Oft ūre sāwl swȳðe frēcne hlimman gedēgde hlūdes wæteres *torrentem pertransivit anima nostra*, 123, 4: 125, 4. v. hlimman; *and* cf. hlyn.

hlin. v. hlyn.

hlinaþ, hleonaþ, es; *m. A place to lie down in*:—Ic getimbre hūs and hleonaþ, Exon. 36 a; Th. 117, 10; Gū. 222.

hlin-bedd, es; *n. A couch*:—Fundon on sande sāwulleásne hlin- [MS. hlim-] bed healdan *they found him without life occupying his couch*, Beo. Th. 6060; B. 3034. [Cf. *O. H. Ger.* hlīna *recubitus, accubitus, reclinatorium.*]

hlinc, es; *m.* I. *a link, linch, rising ground*; 'agger limitaneus, parœchias, etc. dividens,' Junius. The word occurs in the charters, e. g:—Of ðere dīc on þornhlinch; ðanone on dynes hlinch; of ðam hlince, Cod. Dipl. Kmbl. iii. 223, 29. Ðanon on ðone miclan hlinc, Chart. Th. 160, 24. Fearnhlinc, landsore hlinc, sweord hlincas, wotan hlinc are other instances of its occurrence. In later times the word is given with a similar sense in provincial glossaries, e. g. in Suffolk some woods are called *links*: *linchets* grass partitions in arable fields, Lisle: *linch* a bawke or little strip of land, to bound the fields in open countries, Pegge's Kenticisms. v. E. D. S. Publications, and Halliwell's Dict. II. *a hill, rising ground*:—Beorgas ne muntas steápe ne stondaþ ne stānclifu heáh hlifiaþ ne dene ne dalu ne dūnscrafu hlǣwas ne hlincas *nec tumulus crescit nec cava vallis hiat*, Exon. 56 a; Th. 199, 13; Ph. 25. Heá hlincas, 101 b; Th. 384, 7; Rä. 4, 24.

hlīn-duru, a; *f. A door formed of lattice-work, a grated door*:—Helle hlīnduru [cf. *Icel.* Hel-grindr], Exon. 97 b; Th. 364, 29; Wal. 78. Geseh hē fore hlīndura hyrdas standan *he saw guards standing before the grated door* [*of his prison*], Andr. Kmbl. 1985; An. 995. [Cf. *O. H. Ger.* hlīnun, *pl. cancelli*, Grff. iv. 1096.]

hlinian, hleonian; *p.* ode *To lean, bend, lie down, recline, rest*:—Ic hlinige *cubo*, Ælfc. Gr. 24; Som. 25, 55. Ne ðǣr hleonaþ unsmēðes wiht *nor does aught unsmooth rest there*, Exod. 56 a; Th. 199, 14; Ph. 25. Ða ðe him godes egsa hleonaþ ofer heáfdum *those on whose heads rests the fear of God*, 33 b; Th. 106, 20; Gū. 44. Monige hleonigaþ mid Abraham *multi recumbent cum Abraham*, Mt. Kmbl. Rush. 8, 11. Hlionigaþ [hlinigaþ, Lind.] ł restaþ *accumbent*, Lk. Skt. Rush. 13, 29. Hlionede hē in hūse *discumbente eo in domo*, Mt. Kmbl. Rush, 9, 10. Hleonede [hlionade, Lind.], 26, 20. Ān ðæra leorning cnihta hlinode on ðæs hǣlendes bearme *erat recumbens unus ex discipulis ejus in sinu iesu*, Jn. Skt. 13, 23. Æt ðæm uferran ende Drihten hlinode *Domino desuper innitente*, Past. 16, 3; Swt. 101, 20. Ānra gehwylc hleonade wið handa *each one leaned on his hand*, Cd. 222; Th. 291, 19; Sat. 433. Ne hlina [hliona, Rush.] ðū *non discumbas*, Lk. Skt. Lind. 14, 8. Hī sēcaþ ðæt hie fyrmest hlynigen æt ǣfengieflum *primos in cœnis recubitus quærunt*, Past. 1, 2; Swt. 27, 7. Hē fyrgenbeámas ofer hārne stān hleonian funde *he found the mountain trees resting on the grey rock*, Beo. Th. 2835; B. 1415. Ofer ða se hālga bisceop hlyniende forþfērde *cui incumbens obiit*, Bd. 3, 17; S. 544, 18. Heó wæs hleonigende ofer hire ræste *she was lying on her bed*, Blickl. Homl. 145, 26. Fond hlingendne freán *found his master lying in his bed*, Exon. 49 b; Th. 171, 2; Gū. 1120. [*Laym.* leonede, *p*: *A. R.* leonie, *subj*: *O. Sax.* hlinon: *O. H. Ger.* hlinen *obcumbere, incumbere, recumbere, inniti.*] DER. ge-, on-hlinian: v. hlǣnan.

hlīn-ræced, es; *n. A place with grated doors, a prison*, Andr. Kmbl. 2924; An. 1465: Exon. 69 a; Th. 257, 6; Jul. 243. [Cf. hlīn-duru.]

hlīn-scūa, -scūwa, an; *m. The darkness of a prison*, Andr. Kmbl. 2143; An. 1073: Exon. 73 b; Th. 275, 2; Jul. 544. v. preceding word.

hlinung, e; *f. Leaning, resting, a couch*:—Hlinunge wiðersæc *unfavourable to leaning*, L. M. 2, 46; Lchdm. ii. 258, 20. Ða forman hlininga *primos discubitos*, Lk. Skt. 20, 46.

hlīsa, hligsa, hliosa, an; *m. Sound, rumour, report, reputation, renown, fame, glory*:—Hlīsa *fama*, Wrt. Voc. 76, 1. Ðā fērde hys hlīsa intō ealle Syriam *abiit opinio ejus in totam Syriam*, Mt. Kmbl. 4, 24. Ðes hlīsa wearþ cūþ ðæra leóda cynegum ðe begeondan Iordane eardiende wǣron *this report became known to the kings of the nations that were dwelling beyond Jordan*, Jos. 9, 1. Hwæt is heora nū tō lāfe būtan se lytla hlīsa and se nama mid feáum stafum āwriten *signat superstes fama tenuis pauculis inane nomen litteris*, Bt. 19; Fox 70, 10: 68, 21, 4. Hī wilnodon ðæs hlīsan æfter heora deáþe, 18, 4; Fox 68, 9. Sume hī gebycgaþ weorþlīcne hlīsan ðisses andweardan līfes mid heora āgnum deáþe forþam hī wēnaþ ðæt hī næbben nān oðer fioh ðæs hlīsan [hliosan, Bod.] wyrðe būtan hiora āgnum fiore *nonnulli venerandum sæculi nomen, gloriosæ pretio mortis, emerunt*, Bt. 39, 11; Fox 228, 27. Ðeáh ðē monig mon herige ne gelȳf ðū him tō wel: ac ðæs hlīsan þenc ðē silf hwæt ðæs sōþes sȳ *though many men praise thee, do not believe them too much; but thyself consider how much of this reputation is true*, Prov. Kmbl. 69. Gif wē mid hlȳsan gōdra weorca ūrne Drihten sēcaþ *if we come to our Lord with the fame of good works*, Homl. Th. i. 222, 4: Exon. 34 b; Th. 111, 17; Gū. 128: 33 a; Th. 105, 31; Gū. 31. Ðæt is ðonne ðæt mon his mearce brǣde ðæt mon his hligsan [hlīsan, Hatt MS.] and his noman mǣrsige *terminum vero suum dilatare est opinionis suæ nomen extendere*, Past. 48, 2; Swt. 366, 13. Ðā gehȳrde heó Salomones hlīsan *she heard of Solomon's fame*, Homl. Th. ii. 584, 8: Exon. 54 a; Th. 191, 9; Az. 85. Gē gehȳraþ gefeoht and gefeohta hlīsan *audituri estis prælia et opiniones præliorum*, Mt. Kmbl. 24, 6. v. hlīgan.

hlīs-bǣre; *adj. Famous, glorious*, Som.

hlīs-eádig; *adj. Successful in acquiring fame, famous, renowned*:—Biþ hlīseádigra se ðe hit selþ ðonne se ðe hit gaderaþ: eác ða welan beóþ hlīseádigran ðonne ðonne hie mon selþ ðonne hie beón ðonne hī mon gaderaþ. Seó gītsung gedēþ heore gītseras lāðe and ða cysta gedōþ ða hlīseádige *hæc effundendo magis quam coacervando melius nitent: avaritia odiosos, claros largitas facit*, Bt. 13; Fox 38, 11–17. Gif hē nǣre hlīseádig *egere claritudine*, 33, 1; Fox 120, 35.

hlīseádig-ness, e; *f. Renown, celebrity*; claritudo, Bt. 33, 1; Fox 122, 3.

hlīs-ful; *adj. Famous, of good repute, renown*:—Hlīsful *famosus* vel *opinosus*, Ælfc. Gl. 82; Som. 73, 35; Wrt. Voc. 47, 39: *famosus*, Wrt. Voc. 75, 71. Ðȳ læs ðe hē wurde tō hlīsful on worulde and ðæs heofenlīcan lofes fremde wǣre *lest he should become too famous in this world and be a stranger to the praise of heaven*, Homl. Th. ii. 142, 26. Cumlīðnys is swīðe hlīsful þing *hospitality is a thing of very good repute*, 286, 16. Hlīsfulle weras *men of renown*, Gen. 6, 4.

hlīsful-līce; *adv. Gloriously*:—Ōswold cyning his cynedōm geheóld hlīsfullīce *king Oswald maintained his kingdom gloriously*, Swt. A. S. Rdr. 99, 119.

hliþ, es; *n. A slope, declivity, hill-side, hill*:—Of hliþes nōsan *from the promontory*, Beo. Th. 3789; B. 1892: Exon. 123 b; Th. 473, 28; Bo. 22. Beneoþan ðæm hliþe *under the hill*, Cod. Dipl. Kmbl. iii. 52, 15. Swā tō ðam westhliþe, 123, 5. Hie be hliþe heáre dūne eorþscræf fundon *they found a cavern on the slope of a lofty hill*, Cd. 122; Th. 156, 25; Gen. 2594. Weallsteápan hleoþu *hills steep as walls*, 86; Th. 108, 8; Gen. 1803. Hleoþo, 72; Th. 88, 3; Gen. 1459. Hleoþa, Exon. 101 a; Th. 382, 6; Rä. 3, 7. Hliþo, 130 a; Th. 498, 17; Rä. 88, 3. Beorgas steápe hleoþum hlifedon *steep hills rose high with their slopes*, Andr. Kmbl. 1681; An. 843. [*Icel.* hlíð *a slope, mountain side*: *O. H. Ger.* hlīta *clivus*: *Ger.* leite in cpds. Grff. iv. 1096.] DER. beorg-, burh-, fen-, heáh-, mist-, næs-, sand-, stān-, wulf-hliþ.

hlīwþ. v. hleówþ.

hlodd. v. hlot.

hlond. v. hland.

hlosnere, es; *m. A listener*; auscultator, Hpt. Gl. 461.

hlosnian; *p.* ode *To listen, be silent in expectation of hearing, listen for the coming of a person, watch, await, be on the look out*:—Ðā on sumere nihte hlosnode sum ōðer munuc his færeldes and mid sleaccre stalcunge his fōtswaðum filigde *then one night another monk was on the watch for his going, and with stealthy tread followed his footsteps*, Homl. Th. ii. 138, 5. Eoda ðā tō mæssan and hlosnode georne be ðære līflīcan onsægednesse *he went then to mass and waited eagerly for the living sacrifice*, Homl. Swt. 3, 157. Æfter ðissum wordum weorud hlosnode swīgodon ealle *after these words the multitude listened* [*astonished* or *expectant*], *all were silent*, Andr. Kmbl. 1522; An. 762. Ðæt folc hlosnende wæs gehērde hine *populus suspensus erat audiens illum*, Lk. Skt. Lind. 19, 48. Hlosniend *attonitus*, Cot. 3, Lye. [Cf. *O. H. Ger.* hlosen *audire, attendere, obedire, auscultari*: hlosenti *adtonitus*.]

hlot, es; *n. A lot, portion, share*:—Ðis hlot *hæc sors*, Ælfc. Gr. 9, 44; Som. 13, 3. Hig wurpon hlot ðǣr ofer *sortem mittentes*, Mt. Kmbl. 27, 35. Hlott, Mk. Skt. Lind. 15, 24. Hlott ł tān, Jn. Skt. Lind. 19, 24. Æfter gewunan ðæs sacerdhādes hlotes *secundum consuetudinem sacerdoti* sorte, Lk. Skt. 1, 9. Sel mē dǣl ł hlodd [hlott, Rush.] striónes *da mihi portionem substantiæ*, Lind. 15, 12. Hie sendon hlot him betweónum *they cast lots among them*, Blickl. Homl. 229, 5. Hlotu wurpon *mittentes sortem*, Mk. Skt. 15, 24: Lk. Skt. 23, 34. v. hlēt, hlyt.

hlōþ, e; *f.* I. *spoil, booty*:—Hē yteþ hlōþe *comedet prædam*, Bd. 1, 34; S. 499, 27. Mycle hlōþe þurh his lāre and fulluhte ðam ealdan feónde āfyrde *magnas antiquo hosti prædas docendo et baptizando eripuit*, 2, 20; S. 522, 22. II. *a band, troop, company, gang, crew, body of robbers*:—Þeófas wē hātaþ ōþ vii men from vii hlōþ ōþ xxxv siððan biþ here, L. In. 13; Th. i. 110, 13. Ðȳ geáre gegadrode ōn hlōþ wīcenga *in that year a gang of vikings collected*, Chr. 879; Erl. 80, 28. Com ðā hǣðenra hlōþ hāliges neósan *then came a band of heathens visiting the saint*, Andr. Kmbl. 2777; An. 1391: 3085; An. 1545. Feónda hlōþ *a fiendish crew*, Exon. 46 a; Th. 157, 5; Gū. 887. Gif mon twȳhyndne mon unsynnigne mid hlōþe ofsleá gielde se ðæs sleges andetta sīe wer and wīte and ǣghwelc mon ðe on sīþe wǣre geselle xxx scill. tō hlōþbōte *if any one in company with others slay an unoffending 'twyhynde' man let him who acknowledges the blow pay 'wer' and 'wite;' and let every one who was engaged in the matter pay thirty shillings as fine*, L. Alf. pol. 29; Th. i. 80, 6-9. Ne cōman hig nā tō fiohtanne ac ðæt hig woldan mid hlōþe geniman *they did not come to fight, but with the intention of robbing*, Shrn. 38, 10. Geseh hē hǣðenra hlōþ, Andr. Kmbl. 1984; An. 994: 84; An. 42. Heó ðæt weorud āgeaf hlōþe of ðam hātan hreþre *she gave up that multitude, troops from her hot bosom*, Exon. 24 b; Th. 71, 29; Cr. 1163: 75 b; Th. 283, 6; Jnl. 676. Hē ðā his here on tū tōdǣlde sum ymb ða burg sætt and hē mid sumum hlōþum fōr and monega byrg bereáfode on Cheranisse *inde propter agendam prædam et curandam obsidionem divisit exercitum. Ipse autem cum fortissimis profectus, multas Cheronesi urbes cepit: profligatisque populis opes abstulit*, Ors. 3, 7; Swt. 116, 17: 3, 1; Swt. 100, 2. Fōran hie hlōþum *they went in bands*, Chr. 894; Erl. 90, 12: Exon. 45 b; Th. 156, 1; Gū. 868: 99 b; Th. 373, 23; Seel. 114. III. *the crime of taking part in the action of a* hlōþ:—Be hlōþe. Seðe hlōþe betygen sīe geswicne se hine be cxx hīda oððe swā bēte, L. In. 14; Th. i. 110, 15. DER. here-hlōþ.

hlōþ-bōt, e; *f. Compensation* or *fine to be paid by a member of a 'hlōþ' for the wrong committed by any one of them*, L. Alf. pol. 29; Th. i. 80, 9. v. hlōþ.

hlōþere, es; *m. A robber, spoiler*; prædator, Cot. 170, Lye.

hlōþ-gecrod, es; *n. A press of troops* or *bands*:—Biersteþ hlūde heáh hlōþgecrod *with loud noise breaks the press of [cloud-] troops on high*, Exon. 102 a; Th. 386, 17; Rä. 4, 63.

hlōþian; *p.* ede *To take booty, rob, spoil*:—Ða ðe ǣlce geáre ofer ðone sǣ hlōþedon and hergedon *qui anniversarias prædas trans maria cogere solebant*, Bd. 1, 12; S. 481, 2. Ða ðe monige geár ǣr hī onhergedon and hlōþedon *qui per multos annos prædas in terra agebant*, 1, 14; S. 482, 19.

hlōþ-sliht, es; *m. Slaying by a member of a 'hlōþ,'* L. Alf. pol. 29; Th. i. 80, 5. v. hlōþ.

hlōwan; *p.* hleów *To low, bellow, make a loud noise*:—Oxa hlēwþ *bos mugit*, Ælfc. Gr. 22; Som. 24, 9. Hleówon hornboran *the trumpeters sounded*, Elen. Kmbl. 107; El. 54. Hlōwendra fearras flǣsc *the flesh of lowing oxen*, Homl. Th. i. 590, 15. [*Icel.* hlōa *to roar (of streams)*: *O. H. Ger.* hlōon *mugire, rudere.*]

hlōwung, e; *f. Lowing, noise*:—Hlōweng *bombus*, Cot. 27, Lye. [*O. H. Ger.* hlōhunga *mugitus.*]

HLŪD; *adj.* LOUD, *sonorous*:—Heora stefn wæs swīðe hlūd *their voice was very loud*, Blickl. Homl. 149, 27: Cd. 148; Th. 184, 14; Exod. 107. Hlimman hlūdes wæteres *torrentem*, Ps. Th. 123, 4. Hlūdre stefne *with a loud voice*, Blickl. Homl. 181, 18. Hlūddre stefne, 15, 19: Cd. 227; Th. 302, 18. Hlūdan stefne, Andr. Kmbl. 2720; An. 1362. Hlūde wǣran hȳ ðā hȳ ofer ðone hlǣw ridan *loud were they when they rode over the hill*, Lchdm. iii. 52, 13. Francan wǣron hlūde *loud was the sound of the javelins*, Cd. 93; Th. 119, 20; Gen. 1982. Hlūddra sang *chorea*, Ælfc. Gl. 34; Som. 62, 47; Wrt. Voc. 28, 28. Ðæt ār ðonne hit mon slihþ hit biþ hlūdre ðonne ǣnig ōðer ondweorc *aes dum percutitur amplius metallis ceteris sonitum reddit*, Past. 37, 3; Swt. 267, 24. Hlūdast, Menol. Fox 467; Gn. C. 4. [*O. Sax. O. Frs.* hlūd: *O. H. Ger.* hlūt: *Ger.* laut.]

hlūd-clipol; *adj. Calling aloud*, R. Ben. interl. 7.

hlūde; *adv. Loudly*:—Folc ðe hlūde singeþ *a people that sings loudly*, Blickl. Homl. 149, 30: 217, 33. Ðæs cocces þeáw is ðæt hē micle hlūdor singþ on uhtan ðonne on dægrēd *gallus profundioribus horis noctis altos edere cantus solet*, Past. 63; Swt. 461, 2.

hlūd-stefn, -stemn; *adj. Loud-voiced*, Cot. 105, Lye.

hlūd-swēge; *adv. With a loud voice*:—Se hana sōna hlūdswēge sang *the cock straightway crowed with a loud voice*, Homl. Th. ii. 248, 33. Marcus swā swā leó hlūdswēge clipode, Ælfc. T. p. 25; Grn. 13, 8.

hlutor, hluttor; *adj. Clear, pure, bright, sincere*:—Hluttor wæter *limpha*, Ælfc. Gl. 97; Som. 76, 69; Wrt. Voc. 54, 13. Swīðe wynsum and hluttor wǣta *a very pleasant and pure stream*, Blickl. Homl. 209, 2. Hlutor, Bt. Met. Fox 5, 26; Met. 5, 13. Wæs hē hluttor and clǣne on his līfe *he was pure and clean in his life*, Blickl. Homl. 217, 9: Ps. Th. 72, 17. Ōþ ðæt byþ āhafen hluttor mōna *donec extollatur luna*, 71, 7: Exon. 58 b; Th. 210, 9; Ph. 183. Gif ðīn eáge biþ hluttor *si oculus tuus fuerit simplex*, Lk. Skt. 11, 34. xxx ambra hluttres ealoþ, L. In. 70; Th. i. 146, 17. Hlutres aloþ, Chr. 852; Erl. 67, 38. Ðæt hig drincon hluttor wīn *'thou didst drink the pure blood of the grape,'* Deut. 32, 14. Genim ða ylcan sealfe hluttre *take the same salve clear*, L. Med. ex Quadr. 3, 3; Lchdm. i. 340, 2. Ōþ hlutturne dæg *usque ad ortum diei*, Bd. 4, 19; S. 588, 13. Þurh hlutterne dæg *during the daylight*, Exon. 105 b; Th. 401, 5; Rä. 21, 7. Hluttor pic *resin*, L. M. 1, 4; Lchdm. ii. 44, 24: 1, 31; Lchdm. ii. 72, 25. Dō on hluttor æg *add the white of an egg*, 2, 64; Lchdm. ii. 288, 9. Lǣt standan ōþ hit sȳ hluttor nim ðonne ðæt hluttre *let it stand till it be clear, then take the clear part*, Lchdm. iii. 4, 3. Weder hluttor gesihþ ceápes ferþrunge hit getācnaþ *if he sees clear weather, it betokens furthering of traffic*, 198, 17. Hluttre mōde and bylehwite *simplici et pura mente*, Bd. 4, 24; S. 599, 8: Exon. 12 a; Th. 18, 34; Cri. 293. Mid hluttrum sāwlum *with pure souls*, Cd. 21; Th. 25, 21; Gen. 397. Mid hlutrum eágum *with clear eyes*, Bt. Met. Fox 21, 74; Met. 21, 37. Ðone hlutrestan streám *the stream most pure*, 23, 5; Met. 23, 3. [*Orm.* lutter: *Goth.* hlutrs *pure*: *O. Sax.* hluttar: *O. Frs.* hlutter: *O. H. Ger.* hlutar *clarus, lotus, purus, mundus*: *Ger.* lauter.] DER. glæs-hlutor.

hlutor-, hluttor-līce; *adv. Clearly, plainly*:—Hlutorlīce tōcnāwaþ *clearly distinguish*, Lchdm. iii. 440, 29. Gif hē him ðæt hluttorlīce gecȳðan wolde hwæt hē wǣre *si simpliciter sibi quis fuisset proderet*, Bd. 4, 22; S. 591, 37: 5, 13; S. 634, 2.

hlutor-, hluttor-ness, e; *f. Clearness, purity*:—Hū heora gecynd būtan ǣlcre besmitennysse on ēcere hluttornysse þurhwunaþ *how their nature continues without any pollution in eternal purity*, Homl. Th. i. 538, 29. Tō hluttornisse geleáfan *ad simplicitatem fidei*, Bd. 2, 5; S. 507, 42. On hluttornesse and on clǣnnesse *in sinceritate*, 4, 9; S. 576, 21: 2, 15; S. 518, 30.

hlutre, hluttre; *adv. Clearly, brightly*:—Heofon hluttre ongeat *heaven clearly perceived*, Exon. 24 b; Th. 71, 3: Cri. 1150. Ðonne heofontungol hlutrost scīneþ *when the sun shines brightest*, Bt. Met. Fox 22, 48; Met. 22, 24. DER. dæg-hluttre.

hluttran [?] *to grow* or *make pure, clean, bright*, Exon. 54 a; Th. 191, 8; Az. 85. v. next word.

hluttrian; *p.* ode. I. *to become clear*:—Hit wile hluttrian *it will become clear*, Lchdm. iii. 76, 7. II. *to make clear, purify* [v. āhluttrian]:—Morgenrēn hluttraþ [*or is the verb in the plural?*] *the morning rain purifies*, Exon. 54 a; Th. 191, 8; Az. 85.

hlȳd, es; *n. A sound*:—Losaþ gemynd heora mid hlȳde [MS. hlydne] *periit memoria eorum cum sonitu*, Ps. Spl. T. 9, 7. [*Laym.* mid lude.] v. ge-hlȳd.

hlȳda, an; *m. The month noisy with wind and storm, March*:—Hagolscūrum færþ geond middangeard Martius rēðe Hlȳda *with hail-showers passes through the earth rude March [which we call] Hlyda*, Menol. Fox 74; Men. 37. Mōnaþ Martius ðe menn hātaþ hlȳda, Lchdm. iii. 152, 30. Ðæs mōnþes ðe wē hātaþ Martius ðone gē hātaþ Hlȳda, Homl. Th. i. 100, 5. On Martio ðæt is on hlȳdan mōnþe, Lchdm. iii. 152, 9; 250, 5. Se ǣresta frigedæg ðe man sceal fæsten is on hlȳdan *the first Friday to fast on is in March*, 228, 21. [*Lide* as a name for March is given in the E. D. S. East Cornwall Glossary.]

hlȳdan; *p.* de *To sound, make a loud noise, to clamour, vociferate*:—Ic hlȳde *strepo*, Ælfc. Gr. 28; Som. 30, 63. Ic hlȳde *garrulo*, 36; Som. 38, 29. Se tympano biþ geworht of drygum felle and ðæt fell hlȳt ðonne hit mon sliehþ *in tympano sicca et percussa pellis resonat*, Past. 46, 2; Swt. 347, 5. Ðīne fȳnd hlȳdaþ *inimici tui sonaverunt*, Jud. 5; Thw. 156, 1: Exon. 20 b; Th. 55, 14; Cri. 883. Se uncer hlāford hlȳdde ðǣr ūte *that master of ours was vociferating without*, Shrn. 43, 14. Hlōh and hlȳdde *he laughed and clamoured*, Judth. 10; Thw. 21, 18; Jud. 23. Ðā hī hlȳddon hig and cwǣdon *at illi invaliscebant dicentes*, Lk. Skt. 23, 5. Ðā hē geseah hwistleras and hlȳdende menigeo *cum vidisset tibicines et turbam tumultuantem*, Mt. Kmbl. 9, 23. Hlȳdende *clamando*, Past. 15, 2; Swt. 91, 22, 23. Hlȳdende swīðust innan *sounding chiefly from within*, L. M. 2, 46; Lchdm. ii. 258, 19. Se ðe wylle drincan and dwæslīce hlȳdan drince him æt hām nā on Drihtnes hūse *he who wants to drink and make a foolish noise let him drink at home, not in the Lord's house*, L. Ælfc. C. 35; Th. ii. 357, 40. Hēt hī mid handum sleán on ðæt hleór ðæt heó hlȳdan ne sceolde *he bade strike her with their hands on the face that she should not declaim*, Homl. Swt. 8, 70. [*O. Sax.* a-hlūdian: *O. H. Ger.* hlūtian *sonare, clamare, concrepare*: *Ger.* lauten.]

hlȳden. v. hlȳd.

hlȳdend *garrulus*, Cot. 170, Lye. v. hlȳdan.

hlȳdig *garrulus*, Hpt. Gl. 439. [Cf. *O. H. Ger.* -hlūtig *-sonus*, Grff. iv. 1098.]

hlȳd-mōnaþ. v. hlȳda.

hlyn, hlin, es; *m.* [?] *The name of a tree, maple* [?], Exon. 114 a; Th. 437, 17; Rä. 56, 9. [*Icel.* hlynr *maple.*]

hlyn, hlynn, hlin, es; *m. A sound, noise, clamour, din*:—Tō ðon đonne hit hât wǣre and mon đa earman men oninnan dōn wolde hū se hlynn mǣst wǣre đonne hie đæt sūsl đǣron þrowiende wǣron *ut cum inclusus ibidem subjectis ignibus torreretur, sonum vocis extortæ capacitas concavi aeris augeret*, Ors. 1, 12; Swt. 54, 25. Hlynn wearþ on ceastrum *a great cry arose in the cities*, Cd. 119; Th. 153, 30; Gen. 2546. Hlyn scylda and sceafta *the din of shields and shafts*, 95; Th. 124, 12; Gen. 2061. Hlin, Exon. 101 a; Th. 381, 7; Rä. 2, 7. Hearpan hlyn *the sound of the harp*, 57 b; Th. 207, 1; Ph. 135: Cd. 52; Th. 66, 7; Gen. 1081: Beo. Th. 1227; B. 6, 11. DER. ge-hlynn.

hlynian; *p.* ode *To make a noise, roar*:—Wælfȳra mǣst hlynode *the greatest of funeral fires roared*, Beo. Th. 2244; B. 1120.

hlynn, e; *f. A torrent*:—Ofer þah hlynne *trans torrentem*, Jn. Skt. Rush. 18, 1. [*Scott.* lin, lyn, lynn *a cataract*.] v. *previous and following words, and* cf. hlimme *and* hlimman.

hlynnan; *p.* ede *To sound, make a noise, shout*:—Gūþwudu hlynneþ scyld scefte oncwyþ *the war-wood resounds, shield replies to shaft*, Fns. Th. 11; Fin. 6. Gārsecg hlynede *the ocean roared*, Andr. Kmbl. 476; An. 238. Hlynede and dynede *raised shout and din*, Judth. 10; Thw. 21, 18; Jud. 23. Stefn in becom hlynnan under hārne stān *the voice got in and sounded under the grey stone*, Beo. Th. 5099; B. 2553. Hlynnende hlūde streámas, *torrentes*, Ps. Th. 73, 15.

hlynsian, hlinsian; *p.* ode *To sound, resound*:—Reced hlynsode *the mansion resounded*, Beo. Th. 1545; B. 770. Hlinsade, Exon. 108 b; Th. 415, 26; Rä. 34, 3. Hōfan and hlynsadan hlūdan reorde *elevaverunt flumina voces suas*, Ps. Th. 92, 4. Hlynsodon, Andr. Kmbl. 3089; An. 1547.

hlȳp, es; *m. A leap, jump*:—Hlȳp *saltus*, Ælfc. Gl. 61; Som. 68, 49; Wrt. Voc. 39, 33: Ælfc. Gr. 11; Som. 15, 14. Se dæg is gehāten saltus lunæ đæt is đæs mōnan hlȳp *the day is called saltus lunæ, that is, the moon's leap*, Lchdm. iii. 264, 24: Exon. 18 b; Th. 45, 16, 29; 46, 1, 13; Cri. 720, 726, 730, 736. Hlȳpum *by leaps*, Th. 46, 31; Cri. 747. Heorta hlȳpum *leaping like the hart*, Cd. 203; Th. 252, 5; Dan. 574. [*Laym.* lupe, leope: *A. R.* lupes, *pl*: *Icel.* hlaup; *n*: *O. H. Ger.* louf *cursus*: *Ger.* lauf.]

hlȳp, e; *f.* [?]:—Dis sind đa landgemǣra ... of đære ealdan hæcce into Presta hlȳpe ... of đam æsce tō đære ældan hlȳpe of đare hlȳpe, Chart. Th. 394, 16: 395, 9, 34, 35.

hlȳpa, hliépa, an; *m. That which helps in leaping, in leaping on* or *mounting a horse, a horse-block*:—Siđđan hē wæs đæm cyninge tō đon geset ōþ his līfes ende, đæt hē sceolde swā oft stūpian swā hē tō his horse wolde, and hē đonne se cyning hæfde his hrycg him tō hliépan *hoc infamis officii continua donec vixit damnatione sortitus, ut ipse acclinis humi, regem super adscensurum in equo dorso adtolleret*, Ors. 6, 24; Swt. 274, 25. Æt hinde hlȳpan, Cod. Dipl. Kmbl. ii. 249, 35. [v. Halliwell's Dict. 'leaping-block *a horse-block*: leaping *the operation of lowering tall hedges for the deer to leap over*.']

hlȳp-geat, es; *n.* [?]:—Ondlang geardes on đæt hlȳpgeat, Cod. Dipl. Kmbl. iii. 180, 28.

hlȳrian *to puff out the cheeks as in blowing a trumpet, to blow* [*a trumpet*]:—Bȳmaþ ł hlȳriaþ mid bȳman *buccinate tuba*, Ps. Lamb. 80, 4. v. hleór.

hlȳsa. v. hlīsa.

hlyst, es; *m*: e; *f. The sense of hearing, hearing, listening*:—Hlyst *auditus*, Ælfc. Gr. 11; Som. 15, 15. Đa fīf andgitu ... hlyst ... *the five senses ... hearing ...*, Homl. Th. ii. 550, 11: i. 138, 27. Gif se hlyst ōþstande đæt hē ne mǣge gehiéran *if the hearing be stopped so that he cannot hear*, L. Alf. pol. 46; Th. i. 92, 23. Đā wearþ hæleþa hlyst *then was there listening of men*, Cd. 181; Th. 226, 28; Dan. 178: Exon. 55 b; Th. 196, 5; Az. 169. On đæs folces hlyste *in aures plebis*, Lk. Skt. 7, 1. On hlyste *auditione*, Ps. Th. 111, 6: Ælfc. Gr. 1; Som. 2, 29. Lǣcedōmas wiđ yfelre hlyste *leechdoms against bad hearing*, L. M. 1; Lchdm. ii. 2, 14. Gif[mon] yfelne hlyst hæbbe *if a man have bad hearing*, i. 3; Lchdm. ii. 40, 26. [*Laym.* lust: *O. Sax.* hlust *hearing*: *Icel.* hlust *the ear*.] DER. ge-hlyst.

hlystan; *p.* te *To list, listen to, hear, hearken*:—Hī gefeallaþ on đa heortan đe hiera hlyst *they fall on the heart that listens to them*, Past. 15, 6; Swt. 97, 1. Mid đam đe hē hlyste đæs heofonlīcan sanges *whilst he was listening to the heavenly song*, Homl. Th. ii. 98, 5. Ne hlyst đū nā ungesceádwīses monnes worda *do not listen to the words of an indiscreet man*, Prov. Kmbl. 47: Nicod. 3; Thw. 2, 5. Hlyst hider *hearken*, Past. 49, 2; Swt. 381, 14. Sunu mīn hlyste mīnre lāre *fili mi acquiesce consiliis meis*, Gen. 27, 8. Ne hliste đū his worda *non audies verba illius*, Deut. 13, 3. Hlystaþ hwæt ic secge *hear what I say*, L. I. P. 5; Th. ii. 310, 8. Hlyste hē gōdes rǣdes *let him hearken to good counsel*, Homl. Th. i. 54, 16. Wē biddaþ đē leóf đæt đū hlyste ūre sprǣce *oramus, domine, ut audias nos*, Gen. 43, 20. Man lāreówum hlyste *let teachers be listened to*, L. Eth. vii. 19; Th. i. 332, 26. Hig hlyston him *audiant illos*, Lk. Skt. 16, 29. Hē sceal bōclārum hlystan swȳđe georne *he must pay diligent attention to the teaching of books*, L. I. P. 2; Th. ii. 306, 8. Hig fundon hine hlystende *they found him listening*, Lk. Skt. 2, 46: Past. 49, 5; Swt. 385, 23. [*Laym.* lusten: *Orm.* lisstenn: *Ayenb.* lheste: *Icel.* hlusta.]

hlystend, es; *m. A hearer, listener*:—On mōde đære hlystendra *in the mind of the hearers*, Homl. Th. i. 362, 18.

hlystere, es; *m. A hearer, listener*:—Đæt āþweahþ his hlysteras from synna horewum *that washes its hearers from the foulnesses of sins*, Homl. Th. ii. 56, 7.

hlyt [*or* hlȳt?], es; *m. A lot, portion*:—Hlyt *sors*, Ælfc. Gr. 9, 44; Som. 13, 3. Đū gedydest đæt wē mǣtan ūre land mid rāpum and mīn hlyt gefeóll ofer đæt betste *funes ceciderunt mihi in præclaris*, Ps. Th. 15, 6. On handum đīnum hlyt mīn *in manibus tuis sortes meæ*, Ps. Spl. 30, 18. Hlyt wīsode đǣr hie dryhtnes ǣ dēman sceoldon *the lot appointed where they should judge the Lord's law*, Apstls. Kmbl. 18; Ap. 9. On hlyte *sorti*, Ælfc. Gr. 38; Som. 41, 18. Đū hit tōdǣlst mid hlyte *tu eam sorte divides*, Deut. 31, 7. Mid hāligra hlyte wunigan *to dwell with the saints*, Elen. Kmbl. 1639; El. 821. Hī sendon hlyt *miserunt sortem*, Ps. Spl. 21, 17. Swā him dryhten sylf hlyt getǣhte *as God himself assigned a lot to them*, Andr. Kmbl. 12; An. 6: 28; An. 14. Ne sēc đū þurh hlytas hū đē geweorþan scyle *do not seek by casting of lots what thy fate is to be*, Prov. Kmbl. 32. Gif hwā hlytas begā *si quis sortilegia exerceat*, L. Ecg. P. iv. 19; Th. ii. 210, 11. [*The Pastoral has the form* hliet (v. hlēt), *which seems to correspond with the Gothic* hlauts *and would suggest* ȳ *not* y *in* hlyt. *But compare Icel.* hlutr, hlaut, Cl. and Vig. Dict.] v. hlot.

hlyta, hlytta, an; *m. A diviner, one who divines by casting lots*:—Flaminius forseah đa sægene đe đa hlyttan him sǣdon đæt hē æt đæm gefeohte ne cōme wiđ Gallie *Flaminius contemtis auspiciis quibus pugnare prohibebatur adversum Gallos*, Ors. 4, 7; Swt. 184, 26. Tānhlyta *sortilegus*, Ælfc. Gl. 112; Som. 79, 106; Wrt. Voc. 60, 13. v. efen-hlytta; hlyt.

hlytere. v. tān-hlytere.

hlyþran, Gen. 41, 27. v. lyþer.

hlytm *a parting* or *deciding by lot, an arranging of shares*:—Næs đā on hlytme hwā đæt hord strude *the part of each in despoiling the hoard was not carefully allotted* [*each took what he could*], Beo. Th. 6243; B. 3126.

hlyttrian *to purify*:—Ic hlyttrige *liquo*, Ælfc. Gr. 37; Som. 39, 41.

hlyttrung, e; *f. A purifying, refining*; defecatio *vel* purgatio, Ælfc. Gl. 100; Som. 77, 23; Wrt. Voc. 55, 27.

hlȳwing. v. hleówung.

hlȳwþ. v. hleówþ.

hnǣcan. v. nǣcan.

hnǣgan; *p.* de *To neigh*:—Ic hnǣge *hinnio*, Ælfc. Gr. 30, 5; Som. 34, 58. Hors hnǣgþ *equus hinnit*, 22; Som. 24, 9. [*Wick.* neȝen: *Prompt. Parv.* neyyñ *hinnio*: *Icel.* gneggja, hneggja.]

hnǣgan; *p.* de *To cause to bow, bring low, humble, humiliate*:—Ic bebeóde bearnum mīnum đæt hie đē hnǣgon æt gūþe *I command my sons to humble thee in battle*, Andr. Kmbl. 2660; An. 1331. [*Goth.* hnaiwjan *to abase*: *Icel.* hneigja *to bow*: *O. H. Ger.* hneigjan *subjicere, inclinare*: *Ger.* neigen.] v. ge-hnǣgan, hnāh, hnīgan.

hnǣgan, Beo. Th. 2641; B. 1320. v. nǣgan.

hnǣgung, e; *f. Neighing*:—Horsa hnǣgung *neighing of horses*, Ælfc. Gr. 1; Som. 2, 35.

hnæpf, hnæpp, hnæp, es; *m. A cup, bowl*:—Hnæp *ciatus, anthlia*, Ælfc. Gl. 25; Som. 60, 50, 51; Wrt. Voc. 24, 46, 47. Hnæp *anaphus*, Wrt. Voc. 82, 43. Hnæpp *patera*, 290, 74. Of đam hnæpfe *from the bowl*, Chart. Th. 439, 31. ii gebonede hnæppas *two polished bowls*, 429, 30. [*Laym.* nap *a cup*: *A. R.* nep: *Du.* nap, *a cup, basin*: *O. H. Ger.* hnapf *cratera, patera*, Grff. iv. 1130: *O. French* hanap: *Low Lat.* hanapus, v. Skt. Dict. *hamper*.]

hnæppan *to strike* [?]:—Swā swā sió nafu simle biþ swā gesund hnæppen đa felga on đæt đe hī hnæppen *if the nave is always quite safe the fellies may strike against what they will*, Bt. 39, 7; Fox 222, 26. [Cf. (?) nap *to strike the head sharply with a stick*, E. D. S. Mid-Yorkshire Glossary; knap *to strike*; nap *a stroke*, Halliwell Dict.]

hnæppian, hnæppung. v. hnappian, hnappung.

hnæsce. v. hnesce.

hnāh; *adj. Bent down, low, lowly, humble, abject, mean, poor*:—And hē hnāh tō eorþan āleát wiđ đæs engles *adoravitque eum pronus in terram*, Num. 22, 31. Næs hió hnāh ne tō gnēþ gifa *she was not mean nor too sparing of gifts*, Beo. Th. 3863; B. 1929. Iudas cwæþ đæt hē wēnde him trage [Kmbl. þrage] hnāgre *Judas said that he expected for himself humiliating pain*, Elen. Kmbl. 1333; El. 668. Wēndon hie wera cwealmes þrænge hnāgran *they expected the death of men, a still worse time*, Andr. Kmbl. 3195; An. 1600. Nō ic mē hnāgran talige đonne Grendel hine *I think myself no worse man than does Grendel himself*, Beo. Th. 1359; B. 677. Ful oft ic leán teohhode hnāhran rince sǣmran æt sæcce *full oft have I appointed reward to a warrior inferior and of less worth in battle*, 1909; B. 952. [*Goth.* hnaiws *lowly, humble*.]

hnappian, hnæppian; *p.* ode *To slumber, sleep, doze*:—Ne slǣpþ ne ne hnappaþ se đe hylt Israhēl *non dormitabit neque dormiet qui custodit Israel*, Homl. Th. ii. 230, 6. Hnæppaþ, Ps. Spl. 120, 4. Se đe hnæppaþ *qui dormit*, 40, 9. Đa mǣdenu hnappiaþ *the maidens slumber*, Homl. Th. ii. 566, 26. Ne slǣpþ se nō fæsđe ac hnappaþ *non autem dormire ed dormitare est*, Past. 28, 4; Swt. 195, 8. Ac đonne hnæppiaþ ūre brǽwas *palpebræ vero dormitant*, 195, 2. Gif hē hwōn hnappode ðǽrrihte hine drehton nihtlīce gedwimor *if he dozed a little, straightway nightly phantoms tormented him*, Homl. Th. i. 86, 18. Ic hnæppode *ego dormivi*, Ps. Spl. 3, 5. Ðā hnappedon hig ealle and slēpon *dormitaverunt omnes et dormierunt*, Mt. Kmbl. [MS. A.] 25, 5. Ne ne hnæppie se ðe healde ðē *neque dormitet qui custodit te*, Ps. Spl. 120, 3. Ne ne hnappigen ðīne brǽwas *ne dormitent palpebræ tuæ*, Past. 28, 4; Swt. 193, 24, 19. Hnappiende *dormiens*, Ps. Spl. 77, 71. [*A.R.* nappen: *Chauc. Wick. Piers P.* nappe: *Prompt. Parv.* nappyñ *or* slomeryñ *dormito*: cf. *O.H. Ger.* nafizan, Grff. ii. 1053.]

hnappung, hnæppung, e; *f. Slumbering, dozing, drowsiness*:—Ǽresð mon hnappaþ gif hē ðonne ðære hnappunge ne swīcþ ðonne hnappaþ hē ōþ ðæt hē o wierþ on fæstum slǽpe *dormitando vero oculus ad plenissimum somnum ducitur*, Past. 28, 4; Swt. 195, 11. Wið hnappunge *against drowsiness*, L. Med. ex Quadr. 8, 10; Lchdm. i. 358, 24. Hnæppunge *dormitationem*, Ps. Spl. 131, 4: hnappunga, Ps. Th. *and* Lamb. [*Wick.* napping: *Prompt. Parv.* nappynge *or* slomerynge *dormitacio*: *O.H. Ger.* naffezung *dormitatio*.]

hnātan; *p.* hneót *To strike together, clash*, Andr. Kmbl. 8; An. 4. v. hnītan.

hneáw; *adj. Stingy, near, niggardly*:—Ðȳ læs se hneáwa and se gītsigenda fægnige ðæs ðætte menn wēnen ðæt hē sīe gehealdsum on ðæm ðe hē healdan scyle oððe dǽlan *ne aut cor tenacia occupet, et parcum se videri in dispensationibus exultet*, Past. 20; Swt. 149, 17. Ic ðē hneáw ne wæs landes and lissa *I was no niggard to thee of land and favours*, Cd. 136; Th. 171, 5; Gen. 2823. [*Icel.* hnöggr *niggardly, stingy*: *Ger.* ge-nau.] DER. un-hneáw.

hneáw-līce; *adv. Sparingly, stingily*:—Him ðæs leán āgeaf nalles hneáwlīce *to him for that the Lord gave reward with no sparing hand*, Cd. 86; Th. 108, 20; Gen. 1809.

hneáw-ness, e; *f. Stinginess, parsimony, niggardliness*:—Monig mon dēþ micel fæsten, and hæfþ ðone hlīsan ðæt hē hit dō for forhæfdnesse and dēþ hit ðeáh for hneáwnesse and for feohgītsunge *many a man fasts much, and has the reputation of doing it for abstinence, and yet does it for stinginess and avarice*; sæpe sub parsimoniæ nomine se tenacia palliat, Past. 20; Swt. 149, 6. Swā ða rūmmōdan fæsthafolnessee lǽren, swā hī ða uncystegan on yfelre hneáwnesse ne gebrengen *sic prodigis prædicetur parcitas, ut tamen tenacibus periturarum rerum custodia non augeatur*, 60; Swt. 453, 29.

HNECCA, an; *m. A* NECK, *nape of the neck, back of the head*:—Hnecca *cervix* vel *jugulum*, Ælfc. Gl. 72; Som. 70, 116; Wrt. Voc. 43, 44: Wrt. Voc. 70, 26. Wā ðǽm ðe willaþ lecggean bolster under ǽlcne hneccan menn mid tō gefōnne . . . Ðonne biþ se hnecca underlēd mid bolstre *væ his qui faciunt cervicalia sub capite universæ ætatis ad capiendas animas . . . Quasi cervicalibus caput jacentis excipitur*, Past. 19, 1; Swt. 143, 14. Gnīd ðone hneccan mid ðȳ *rub the back of the neck with it*, L. M. 1, 1; Lchdm. ii. 20, 25. Ðæt ðū næbbe nān þing hāles fram ðām fōtwolmum ōþ ðone hneccan *sanari non possis a planta pedis usque ad verticem tuum*, Deut. 28, 35. [*Laym.* necke: *Chauc. Piers P. Prompt. Parv.* nekke *collum*: *O. Frs.* hnecka: *Icel.* hnakki *the nape of the neck, back of the head*: *O.H. Ger.* hnach *testa capitis, occiput, cacumen*: *Ger.* nacken.]

hnesce, hnæsce, hnysce; *adj. Nesh, soft, delicate, tender, effeminate*:—Hnysce hwītel *linna*, Ælfc. Gl. 63; Som. 68, 113; Wrt. Voc. 40, 23. Hnesce on mōde tō flǽsclīcum lustum *yielding easily to the lusts of the flesh*, Homl. Th. ii. 220, 4. Gefrēdan hwæt biþ heard hwæt hnesce *to feel what is hard, what soft*, 372, 32: Elen. Kmbl. 1226; El. 615. Heó is hnesce on æthrine *it is soft to the touch*, Herb. 15, 1; Lchdm. i. 108, 1. Sīe ðǽr eác lufu næs ðeáh tō hnesce *sit itaque amor, sed non emolliens*, Past. 17, 11; Swt. 127, 2. Hwæt getācnaþ ðonne ðæt flǽsc būton unfæsð weorc and hnesce *quid enim per carnes nisi infirma quædam ac tenera*, 34, 6; Swt. 235, 15. Ðonne hys twig byþ hnesce *cum ramus ejus tener fuerit*, Mt. Kmbl. 24, 32. Ǽghwæt hnesces oððe heardes, L. de Cf. 9; Th. ii. 264, 6: Salm. Kmbl. 574; Sal. 286. Ðonne geþafaþ him mon on ðære hnescean ōlecunge *eique mollities favoris adhibetur*, Past. 19, 1; Swt. 143, 21. Swā hē ðone hnescan þafettere on rēcelēste ne gebrenge *ut remissis ac lenibus non crescat negligentia*, 60; Swt. 453, 25. Ne gedafenaþ ūs ðæt wē symle hnesce beón on ūrum geleáfan *it befits us not to be ever delicate in our belief*, Homl. Th. i. 602, 12. Mann hnescum gyrlum gescrȳdne *hominem mollibus vestitum*, Mt. Kmbl. 11, 8; Lk. Skt. 7, 25. Heó biþ hnesceum leáfum *it is a plant with soft leaves*, Herb. 6, 1; Lchdm. i. 96, 14. Ic hæbbe hnesce litlingas *parvulos habeam teneros*, Gen. 33, 13. Syle him etan hnesce ægere *give him lightly boiled* (?) *eggs to eat*, Lchdm. iii. 134, 22. Ǽlc wuht biþ innanweard hnescost *every creature is softest inside*, Bt. 34, 10; Fox 150, 6. Drihten nǽfre ne forsyhþ ða eáþmōdan heortan ne ða hnescestan *the Lord never despises the humble heart nor the weakest*, Blickl. Homl. 99, 5. [*A. R.* nesche: *Orm.* nesshe: *Chauc.* nesh: *Goth*, hnaskwus *soft*.]

hnescian, hnexian; *p.* ode *To make*, or *to become, soft, to soften*:—Ic hnexige *mollio*, Ælfc. Gr. 30; Som. 34, 53. Lege ðonne on ðǽr hit heardige hnescaþ hyt sōna *apply where it is hard, it will at once soften*, Herb. 2, 11; Lchdm. i. 84, 4. Ðonne hnescaþ se swile sōna *then the swelling will soften at once*, L. M. 2, 19; Lchdm. ii. 202, 10. Se hearda stān aðamans hnescaþ ongeán ðæt līðe buccan blōd *durus adamas leni hircorum sanguine mollescit*, Past. 37, 4; Swt. 271, 4. Hī hnescodon sprǽca his *molliti sunt sermones ejus*, Ps. Spl. 54, 24. Ongunnon ða godes cempan hnexian *God's warriors began to yield*, Homl. Skt. 5, 48, 51: 8, 29. [*Orm.* nesshenn: *Ayenb.* nhesseþ, *pres*: *Prompt. Parv.* neschyñ *or* make nesche *mollifico*.] DER. ā-hnescian.

hnesc-līc; *adj. Effeminate*:—Hē wæs swīðe hnesclīc man *he* [*Sardanapalus*] *was a very effeminate man*, Ors. 1, 12; Bos. 35, 15. Hī beóþ hneslīce swā forlegene *hi sunt delicati ita fornicantes*, L. Ecg. P. iv. 68, 6; Th. ii. 228, 18.

hnesc-līce; *adv. Gently, softly, tenderly*:—Hē his hiéremonna yfelu tō hnesclīce forberan ne sceal *subditorum mala tolerari leniter non debent*, Past. 21, 5; Swt. 159, 25. Ðonne hē his wambe suā hnesclīce ōlecþ *dum ventri molliter serviunt*, 43, 5; Swt. 313, 12.

hnesc-ness, e; *f. Softness, delicacy, gentleness, weakness*:—Hnescnyss *mollities*, Ælfc. Gr. 12; Som. 15, 56. Ðære hnescnesse ūres flǽsces wē beóþ underþiédde *corruptionis nostræ infirmitatibus subjacemus*, Past. 21, 4; Swt. 159, 5. Genim ðyses wæstmes hnescnysse innewearde *take the inward soft part of this fruit*, Herb. 185, 2; Lchdm. i. 324, 9. Gif hwā for his hnescnysse ðæt fæsten āberan ne mæg *si quis præ mollitie sua jejunium perferre nequeat*, L. Ecg. P. iv. 60; Th. ii. 220, 24. Gif þurh his hnescnysse seó heord forwurþ *if through his want of vigour the flock perish*, L. I. P. 19; Th. ii. 326, 22.

hnifol, es; *m. The forehead*:—Hnifol *frons*, Wrt. Voc. 282, 46. Smire mid ða þunwangan and ðone hnifol and ufan ðæt heáfod *smear therewith the temples and the forehead and the top of the head*, L. M. 3, 1; Lchdm. ii. 306, 6.

hnifol-crumb; *adj. Cernuus*, Cot. 45, 56, Lye.

hnīgan; *p.* hnāh; *pp.* hnigen *To bend, bow down, incline, descend, decline, sink*:—Ðonne hnīge eft under lyfte helm londe neár *then I bend again under the airy cover nearer the land*, Exon. 102 a; Th. 386, 18; Rä. 4, 63. Loth ðām giestum hnāh *Lot bowed to the guests*, Cd. 112; Th. 147, 15; Gen. 2440. Hnāg ic ðām secgum tō handa *I bowed down within the reach of the men*, Rood Kmbl. 118; Kr. 59. Hnigon ðā mid heáfdum heofoncyninge tōgeánes *bent then their heads before heaven's king*, Cd. 13; Th. 16, 1; Gen. 237: 218; Th. 279, 18; Sat. 240: 225; Th. 298, 15; Sat. 533. Wit noldon hnīgan mid heáfdum hālgum Drihtne *we would not bend our heads to the holy Lord*, 35; Th. 46, 10; Gen. 742: 217; Th. 277, 22; Sat. 208. Ðā hē tō helle hnīgan sceolde *when he must sink to hell*, 221; Th. 288, 4; Sat. 375. [*Goth.* hneiwan *to bend downwards, decline*: *O. Sax.* hnīgan: *Icel.* hnīga *to bow down, sink, fall gently*: *O. H. Ger.* hnīgan *obstipare, adorare*.] DER. ge-, on-, under-hnīgan; *and see* hnǽgan.

hnigian; *p.* ode *To bend down* [*the head*]:—Ðonne uplang āsitte hnigie *let him sit up and bend his head downwards*, L. M. 1, 1; Lchdm. ii. 18, 16.

hnipend *humilis*, Hpt. Gl. 436. v. next word.

hnipian; *p.* ode *To bow the head*:—Biþ wuhta gehwilc onhnigen tō hrusan hnipaþ of dūne on weoruld wlītaþ wilnaþ tō eorþan [cf. *in the prose version*, Fox 254, 28, ealle bióþ of dūne healde wið ðære eorðan] *prona tamen facies hebetes valet ingravare sensus*, Bt. Met. Fox 31, 26; Met. 31, 13. Ðā wearþ Cain suīðe hrædlīce irre and hnipode of dūne *iratusque est Cain vehementer, et concidit vultus ejus*, Past. 34, 5; Swt. 235, 6. [Þa nipeden hyo ealle *dormitaverunt omnes*, Mt. Kmbl. 25, 5, col. 2: *Laym.* þa sunne gon to nipen: cf. *Icel.* hnípa *to be downcast, droop*: hnipna *to droop, despond*: *M.H. Ger.* nipfen: *Ger.* nippen *to nod*.]

hnītan; *p.* hnāt, *pl.* hniton; *pp.* hniten *To strike, thrust, push, come against with a shock*:—Ðonne hniton fēðan *in the shock of meeting hosts*, Beo. Th. 2659; B. 1327: 5082; B. 2544. Gif oxa hnite wer oððe wīf *si bos percusserit virum aut mulierem*, Ex. 21, 28. Ðonne ic hnītan sceal hearde wið heardum *when I shall batter hard on the hard*, Exon. 129 b; Th. 497, 21; Rä. 87, 4. [*Icel.* hníta *to strike, clash*.] DER. of-hnītan.

hnitol; *adj. Given to striking, thrusting, pushing, having the head bent* [*as an animal when it butts* (?)]:—Hnitol *vel* eádmōd *cernuus, pronus* vel *inclinatus*, Ælfc. Gl. 9; Som. 56, 116; Wrt. Voc. 19, 1. Gif se oxa hnitol wǽre *si bos cornupeta fuerit*, Ex. 21, 29, 36: L. Alf. 21; Th. i. 48, 29.

hnitu, e; *f. A nit*:—Hnitu *lens* vel *lendix*, Ælfc. Gl. 23; Som. 60, 8; Wrt. Voc. 24, 12. Hnite and wyrmas on weg tō dōnne ðe on cildum beóþ *to remove nits and worms that are on children*, L. Med. ex Quadr. 9, 15; Lchdm. i. 364, 6. [*Prompt. Parv.* nyte, wyrme *lens*: *Icel.* gnit; *f*: *O. H. Ger.* niz: *Ger.* niss.]

hnoc *mutinus*, Ælfc. Gl. 22; Som. 59, 83; Wrt. Voc. 23, 49. v. [?] hnot.

hnol, hnoll, es; *m. The top, crown of the head*:—Hnol *vertex*, Ælfc. Gl. 69; Som. 70, 32; Wrt. Voc. 42, 40: 64, 22. Eástdǽl his hnol heóld *the crown of his head held the east*, Homl. Th. ii. 256, 2. Fram ðam hnolle ufan ōþ his fōtwylmas neoðan *from the crown of his head down to the soles of his feet*, 480, 12: 452, 26: 524, 2. On hnol his *in verticem ejus*, Ps. Spl. 7, 17: 67, 23. [*Wick.* nol *cervix*: *O. H. Ger.* hnol *culmen, cacumen, vertex, sinciput.*]

hnoppa, an; *m. Nap of cloth;* villus, Som. [*Prompt. Parv.* noppe of a clothe *villus, tomentum*, see note.]

hnossian; *p.* ode *To beat, strike*:—Mec hnossiaþ homera lâfe *swords shall strike me*, Exon. 102 b; Th. 388, 13; Rä. 6, 7. [Cf. *Icel.* hnoss *an ornament.*]

hnot; *adj. Bald, shaven, close-cut*:—Calu oððe hnot *glabrio*, Ælfc. Gr. 9, 3; Som. 8, 37. Hnot *mutilum, mutilatum*, Cot. 131, Lye. Tô đon hnottan seale *to the pollard-willow*, Cod. Dipl. Kmbl. v. 193, 35. On đa hnottan dîc of đære hnottan dîc *the dike without turf* (?), iii. 211, 24. [*Chauc.* not-heed, Prol. 109: *Dep. Rich.* not of his nolle, 3, 46: *Halliwell Dict.* not *smooth, without horns; to shear, poll*: see *Nares' Gloss.* nott, nott-pated, -headed.]

hnut-beám, es; *m. A nut tree;* corylus avellana:—Hnutbeám *nux* vel *nucarius*, Ælfc. Gl. 47; Som. 65, 38; Wrt. Voc. 33, 35. Hnutbeámes rind, L. M. i. 3, 6; Lchdm. ii. 42, 3; 52, 1. Hnutbeámes leáf, Lchdm. iii. 6, 15. [*O. H. Ger.* hnuz-boum *amygdalus, nux, nucus, corylus*: *Ger.* nuss-baum.]

hnut-cyrnel, es; *m. n. A nut kernel*:—Genim hnutcyrnla, L. M. 1, 2; Lchdm. ii. 34, 19.

hnutu, e; *f. A nut*:—Hnutu *juglantis* vel *nux*, Ælfc. Gl. 45; Som. 64, 97; Wrt. Voc. 32, 32. For æppla and hnuta ǽte *from eating of apples and nuts*, L. M. 2, 39; Lchdm. ii. 246, 21. Hnute hula *culliole*, Ælfc. Gl. 31; Som. 61, 105; Wrt. Voc. 27, 34. Ôðera hnutena cyrnlu *kernels of other nuts*, iii. 134, 23. Of frencissen hnutu[m] *made of French nuts*, 122, 28. Cyrnlu of pîntrȳwenum hnutum *kernels out of pine tree nuts*, Herb. 134, 2; Lchdm. i. 250, 9. Gif heó gelôme eteþ hnyte *if she is often eating nuts*, iii. 144, 20. Hnyte somnian, gaderian *to gather nuts*, 174, 5: 208, 18. On đam ôðrum dæge wæs Aarones gyrd gemêtt grôwende and berende hnyte *on the next day Aaron's rod was found growing and bearing nuts*, Homl. Th. ii. 8, 16, 18. Bringaþ đam men lâc sumne dǽl tyrwan and hunig and hnite *deferte viro munera, modicum resinæ et mellis et amygdalarum*, Gen. 43, 11. [*Ayenb.* nhote: *Prompt. Parv.* note *nux, nucleus*: *Icel.* hnot; *f. pl.* hnetr: *O. H. Ger.* hnuz, nuz *nux, migdola*: *Ger.* nuss.] DER. hæsel-, pîn-hnutu.

hnygela [or hnigela ?], hnygele, an; *m. f. A shred, clipping*:—Hnygela *tomentum*; seolce hnygele *platum* [= placium, Som.] Ælfc. Gl. 64; Som. 69, 3, 4; Wrt. Voc. 40, 37, 38. Hnyglan *putamina*, Cot. 152, Lye. [Cf. (?) nig *the clippings of money*: niggling *clipping*: niggler *a clipper*, Grose's Slang Dict: see also *Halliw. Dict.* niggle, niggling.]

hnȳlung, e; *f. A kneeling, reclining;* accubitus, Ælfc. Gl. 65; Som. 69, 52; Wrt. Voc. 41, 9.

hnyte. v. hnutu.

hô. v. hôh.

hô-banca, an; *m. A couch, sofa;* sponda, Wrt. Voc. 290, 13. v. hôh.

hoc; *gen.* hocces *Hock, mallow*:—Hocces leáf, L. M. 3, 37; Lchdm. ii. 330, 3. Hocces moran, 41; Lchdm. ii. 334, 27. Hoc, Lchdm. iii. 22, 2. [In E. D. S. Plant Names 'hock *althæa rosea, malva sylvestris, malva rotundifloria.*' Skeat, Etymol. Dict. supposes the word was borrowed from Celtic: Welsh *hocys* mallows.]

HÔC, es; *m. A* HOOK:—Hooc *arpago* vel *palum*, Ælfc. Gl. 3; Som. 55, 71; Wrt. Voc. 16, 43. Ic eom swâ swâ fisc on hôce *I am as the fish on the hook*, Nar. 40, 33. Đonne biþ hê geteald tô đære fȳrenan eá and tô đam îsenan hôce *then shall he be assigned to the fiery river and the iron hook*, Blickl. Homl. 43, 25, 27. Wîngearda hôcas đe hî mid bindaþ đæt him nêhst biþ *capreoli* vel *cincinni* vel *uncinuli*, Ælfc. Gl. 59; Som. 68, 9; Wrt. Voc. 38, 59. Đâ sôhtan heora gewinnan him sarwe and worhtan him hôcas *at contra non cessant uncinata hostium tela*, Bd. 1, 12; S. 481, 21: Homl. Th. i. 362, 27. v. hinder-hôc.

hôced; *adj. Shaped like a hook, curved*:—Ôþ đat hit cymþ tô đan hôkedan gâran *until it comes to the curved strip of land*, Cod. Dipl. Kmbl. iii. 434, 10.

hôcer. v. hôcor.

hociht; *adj. Full of mallows*:—Ǽrest onlong Foss on đa hocihtan dîc of đere hocihtan dîc on đone brâdan þorn *to the mallowy ditch*, Cod. Dipl. Kmbl. ii. 365, 25. [So Cockayne, Lchdm. iii. 332, col. 1, translates the word; or should the word be written *hôciht* = with many bends? Cf. hôced.]

hôciht. v. heoru-hôciht.

hoc-leáf, es; *n. Mallow*:—Hocleáf *malva*, Wrt. Voc 79, 11. Hocleáf. Đeós wyrt đe man *maluæ erraticæ* and ôðrum naman hocleáf nemneþ byþ cenned ǽghwǽr on begânum stôwum *this plant, which is called malva erratica, and by another name hockleaf, is produced everywhere in cultivated places*, Herb. 41, 1; Lchdm. i. 142, 4: L. M. 3, 8; Lchdm. ii. 312, 17. Hoclǽf, Lchdm. iii. 48, 18.

hôcor, es; *m.* [?] *Mockery, scorn, insult, derision*:—Tô oft man mid hôcere gôddǽda hyrweþ *too often good deeds are depreciated with derision*, Swt. A. S. Rdr. 110, 162. [*O. E. Hom.* to lusten hoker: *Laym.* hoker and scarn: *Chauc.* hoker and bissemare.]

hôcor-wyrde; *adj. Using scornful, mocking language*:—Hêr sind on earde hôcorwyrde ǽghwǽr *there are in the land here everywhere men of scornful speech*, Swt. A. S. Rdr. 109, 156. [Cf. *Laym.* Sexisce men mine unhæle me atwiten mid heore hokerworden.]

hôd, es; *m. A hood;* cucullus, caputium, Cot. 31, Lye. [*Laym. A. R.* hod: *O. H. Ger.* huot, hôt; *m. mitra, tiara, cidaris*: *Ger.* hut.]

hoeg. v. heg.

hoelan = hêlan *to speak evil of, calumniate*:—Hoelende *calumniantes*, Mt. Kmbl. Rush. 5, 44. [*Icel.* hæla *to praise, flatter, boast.*] v. hôl, hôlian.

hof, es; *n. A house, hall, dwelling, building;* ædes, domus:—Lytel hof *ædicula*, Ælfc. Gl. 107; Som. 78, 84; Wrt. Voc. 57, 60. Cinges hof *basilica*, Som. 78, 86; Wrt. Voc. 58, 1. Hof sêleste *dwelling most excellent* [*the ark*], Cd. 69; Th. 84, 6; Gen. 1393: 66; Th. 79, 25; Gen. 1316: 67; Th. 81, 15; Gen. 1345: 73; Th. 90, 2; Gen. 1489. Gif hwâ hwylce hefige yfelnysse on his hofe geseó genime mandragoran on middan đam hûse swâ mycel swâ hê đonne hæbbe ealle yfelu hê ût ânȳdeþ *if any one see some grievous evil in his home, let him take mandragora into the middle of the house, as much as he has at the time, he will drive out all evils*, Herb. 132, 7; Lchdm. i. 248, 11: Cd. 76; Th. 94, 29; Gen. 1569: 112; Th. 148, 13; Gen. 2456. Hê gewât from his âgenum hofe isaac lǽdan *he departed from his own house leading Isaac*, 1-39; Th. 173, 32; Gen. 2870. Him Hrôđgâr gewât tô hofe sînum rîce tô reste *Hrothgar had gone to his sleeping-chamber*, Beo. Th. 2477; B. 1236. Tô hofe sînum *to her dwelling*, 3019; B. 1507: 3953; B. 1974. Se hâlga wæs tô hofe lǽded in đæt dimme ræced *the saint was led to the building* [*prison*] *into that dark house*, Andr. Kmbl. 2616; An. 1309. Of đam engan hofe, Exon. 73 b; Th. 274, 12; Jul. 532: Elen. Kmbl. 1420; El. 712. Tô hofe *to the* [*queen's*] *house*, 1111; El. 557. In đam reónian hofe *underground*, 1664; El. 835. Him hof tǽhte *pointed out to them the dwelling* [*of Hrothgar*], Beo. Th. 630; B. 312. Đæt rǽdleáse hof *hell*, Cd. 2; Th. 3, 32; Gen. 44: 217; Th. 276, 23; Sat. 193. Hofa *ædes*, Ælfc. Gl. 107; Som. 78, 83; Wrt. Voc. 57, 59. Hê đa hofa gehealdeþ and begȳmeþ *qui illa oppida maritima observat*, Nar. 37, 26. Hofu, Andr. Kmbl. 1676; An. 840: Exon. 124 a; Th. 477, 26; Ruin. 30. On Faraones hofun *in domos Pharaonis*, Ex. 8, 24. Hofum, Beo. Th. 3677; B. 1836. [*O. Sax. O. Frs.* hof: *Icel.* hof *a temple*: *O. H. Ger.* hof *curtis, curta, atrium, aula, domus*: *Ger.* hof.] DER. ceaster-, gæst-, gnorn-, grorn-, heolstor-, mearc-, morþor-, sand-, stân-, sûsl-, ȳþ-hof.

HÔF, es; *m. A* HOOF:—Hôf *ungula*, Ælfc. Gl. 72; Som. 71, 6; Wrt. Voc. 43, 59: Wrt. Voc. 71, 76. Hors hôfum wlanc *the horse proud of hoofs*, Runic pm. Kmbl. 343, 5; Rûn. 19. [*Icel.* hôfr: *O. H. Ger.* huof *ungula*: *Ger.* huf.]

hofding, es; *m. A chief, captain, principal, ringleader*:—Rawulf eorl and Rogcer eorl wǽron hofdingas [cf. yldast tô đam unreode, l. 13] æt đisan unrǽde *earl Ralph and earl Roger were ringleaders in this evil counsel*, Chr. 1076; Erl. 213, 31. [Borrowed from *Icel.* hôfðingi *a chief, leader, ringleader.*]

hofe. v. dim-hofe.

hôfe, an; *f. Hove, alehoof* [v. English Plant Names, E. D. S.]; glechoma hederacea:—Hôfe *viola*, Ælfc. Gl. 41; Som. 63, 132; Wrt. Voc. 31, 13. Genim hôfan *take hove*, L. M. 1. 1; Lchdm. ii. 20, 5. Brûne hôfe, Lchdm. iii. 292, 9. Genim đa reádan hôfan, L. M. 1, 2; Lchdm. ii. 34, 14. Mersc-hôfe, 1, 38; Lchdm. ii. 94, 10. Tûnhôfe, 3, 60; Lchdm. iii. 344, 2.

hofer, es; *m.* [?] *A hump, swelling*:—Hofer *gibbus* vel *struma*, Wrt. Voc. 86, 71. [*O. H. Ger.* houar, houer *gibbus.*]

hoferede; *adj. Humpbacked*:—Hoferede *gybberosus* vel *strumosus*, Wrt. Voc. 86, 70: 49, 7. Đæt cild biþ hoforode *the child is humpbacked*, Lchdm. iii. 144, 26. Hoferede *gibbus*, Past. 11, 1, 3; Swt. 65, 4; 66, 12. [*O. H. Ger.* houaradi *gibbus*; hofaroht *gibberosus.*]

hoffing, es; *m. A circle;* orbis:—Hoffingas *orbes*, Lye. [Leo, 40, 20; 197, 12, gives a gloss hôf-ring, hôf-hring *orbis*, explaining the word as a *horse-shoe.*]

hôf-rec, -ræc, es; *n. Hoof-track*:—Sing on đæt hôfrec *sing over the hoof-track*, Lchdm. i. 392, 9. Dryp on đæt hôfræc đæt wex *drop the wax into the hoof-track*, iii. 286, 4.

hof-rede; *adj. Confined to the house;* clinicus, Ælfc. Gl. 77; Som. 72, 30; Wrt. Voc. 45, 62.

hof-þela *tesqua*, Lye.

hof-weard, es; *m. An ædile;* ædilis, Ælfc. Gl. 8; Som. 56, 105; Wrt. Voc. 18, 54.

hog-. v. hoh-.

hoga; *adj. Careful, thoughtful, prudent*:—Hoga *prudens*, Rtl. 105, 1. Geleáffull þegn and hoga *fidelis servus et prudens*, Mt. Kmbl. Lind. 24, 25. Wosas gê hogo *estote prudentes*, 10, 16. Hogum *prudentibus*, 11, 25. Gearnfulle ł hogo wosa *solliciti esse*, Lk. Skt. Lind. 12, 11.

hoga, an; *m. Care*, R. Ben, 53, Lye. v. ymb-hoga.

hoga-fæst; *adj. Careful, prudent*:—Hogofæste, *prudentes*, Mt. Kmbl. Lind. 25, 2, 4. v. hoh-fæst.

hoga-scipe, es; *m. Prudence, carefulness, thoughtfulness, wisdom*:—

Hogascip *prudentia*, Rtl. 81, 14. Hogescip *prudentia*, Lk. Skt. Lind. 2, 47. Tō hogascipe *ad prudentiam*, 1, 17.

hogde. v. hycgan.

hogian; *p.* ode *To employ the mind, to think, mind, consider, know, understand, care, be solicitous* or *anxious, to purpose, strive, intend, be intent on, resolve*:—Ymbe mīne māgas ic hogige *erga propinquos curo*, Ælfc. Gr. 47; Som. 47, 29. Ðū hogast embe ðīne neóde *thou art busied about thy needs*, Homl. Th. i. 488, 23. Ne hogaþ hē be ðam heofenlīcan lǣcedōme *he is not anxious about the heavenly medicine*, ii. 470, 16. Hē hogaþ tō ðære betran wynne *he directs his mind to the better joy*, Exon. 95 a; Th. 355, 23; Reim. 81. Hogaþ *satagit*, Mone Gl. 356. Hogiaþ *satagunt*, 435. Hia hogaþ *sapiant*, Mt. Kmbl. p. 2, 5. For ðām mannum ðe mid māran gewilnunge ðæs āteorigendlīcan līfes hogiaþ ðonne ðæs ēcan *for those men whose minds are busied with a greater desire of the life that perishes than of the life eternal*, Homl. Th. ii. 368, 4: 342, 28. Ymbe ðīne handgeweorc ic hogode georne *in factis manuum tuarum meditabar*, Ps. Th. 142, 5. Mið ðȳ ic wæs lytel ic hogade swǣ lytel *cum essem parvulus sapiebam ut parvulus*, Rtl. 6, 17. Ic ðæt hogode ðæt ic eówra leóda willan geworhte *I purposed to work your people's will*, Beo. Th. 1268; B. 632. Hwæt hogodest ðū hidercyme ðīnne on wrāðra geweald *why didst thou resolve to come hither into the power of hostile men*, Andr. Kmbl. 2633; An. 1318. Ic on ðīnre hǣlu hogode *I thought on thy salvation*, Ps. Th. 118, 81. Ðū ne hogodest *thou didst not consider*, Soul Kmbl. 83; Seel. 42. Hē on heortan hogode georne hū hē mid searuwe swylce ācwealde *he diligently considered in his heart how with cunning he might kill such*, Ps. Th. 108, 16: Swt. A. S. Rdr. 98, 92. Hē lythwōn hogode ymbe his sāwle þearfe *he thought little about the needs of his soul*, 101, 201; Homl. Th. ii. 118, 15. Se feónd hogode on ðæt micle morþ men forweorpan *the foe intended to cast men into that great perdition*, Cd. 32; Th. 43, 14; Gen. 690. Hē tō friþe hogode *his purpose was to protect*, Andr. Kmbl. 1244; An. 622. Ealle ðe mē yfel hogedon *qui cogitant mihi mala*, Ps. Th. 69, 3: 57, 2. Hī hine lufedan leáse mūþe ne ðæs on heortan hogedan āwiht *dilexerunt eum in ore suo, et lingua sua mentiti sunt ei*, 77, 35. Ðæt hī ðȳ læs ymb fleám hogodan *minus posse fugam meditari*, Bd. 3, 18; S. 546, 26. Hogedon āninga *their only purpose was*, Judth. 12; Thw. 25, 9, 22; Jud. 250, 273. Hogodon georne hwā ðǣr mid orde ǣrost mihte on fǣgean men feorh gewinnan *they eagerly strove who there first with the sword's point might of the fey man win the life*, Byrht. Th. 135, 25; By. 123. Ne hoga ðū embe ðæt *be not anxious about that*, Homl. Swt. 3, 416. Hogiaþ *consider*, Homl. Th. ii. 124, 14. Hogiaþ *sapite*, Ps. Spl. C. 93, 8. Hogaþ gie *sapite*, Rtl. 13, 21: 25, 5. Hogige se yfela ðæt hē āstande *let the evil man be intent upon standing*, Homl. Th. i. 56, 23. Wē sceolon hogian embe ða bōte *we must busy ourselves about the reparation*, 274, 11. Wē sceolon carfullīce hogian ðæt wē ðone māran gylt forfleón *we ought anxiously to endeavour to flee from the greater guilt*, 484, 5. Wē sceolon hogian hū wē hī begyton *we must consider how we may obtain it*, ii. 316, 25. Ne þurfon gē nō hogian on ðam anwealde ne him æfter þringan *ye need not aim at power nor press after it*, Bt. 16, 1; Fox 50, 29. Ne beó gē nā hogiende ymb ða morgenlīcan neóde *nolite esse solliciti in crastinum*, Mt. Kmbl. 6, 34. Hogiende *cogitantes*, Mone Gl. 390. Hogiendum *nitentibus*, 420. [*Laym.* hoȝede, *p*: *Icel.* huga; *pp.* hugat: *O. H. Ger.* hugeta, hogeta, *p.*] DER. be-, for-, ge-, ofer-, wið-, ymb-hogian. v. hycgan.

hogo-. v. hoga-.

hogu, e; *f. Care, anxiety, solicitude*:—Habbon hī hoge ðæt hī sȳn swilce ðæt hī wurþfullīce herigan māgon *let them have a care that they be such that they may worthily praise*, Homl. Th. i. 446, 32. Hē næfþ nān andgit ne hoga embe Godes beboda *he hath no understanding nor cares about God's commandments*, 132, 13. [*O. and N.* hoȝe: *R. Glouc.* howe.] v. heort-hogu, hoga.

hogung, e; *f. Caring, care*; cura, Lye.

hōh, hō; *gen.* hōs; *m. A heel, hough*:—Hōh niþeweard *calx*, Wrt. Voc. 283, 75. Hō *calx*, Ælfc. Gr. 9, 72; Som. 14, 17. Hwæt is ðæs wīfes hō? . . . Ðæs wīfes hō getācnode . . . *what is the woman's heel?* . . . *The woman's heel signified* . . ., Boutr. Scrd. 20, 13, 19. Hōs mīnes *calcanei mei*, Ps. Spl. 48, 5. Dō on ðīnne winstran scō under ðīnum hō *put it into thy left shoe under thy heel*, Lchdm. i. 396, 2. Āhefþ hys hō ongeán mē *levabit contra me calcaneum suum*, Jn. Skt. 13, 18: Gen. 3, 15. Him on hōh beleác heofonrīces weard merehūses mūþ *God closed the door of the ark behind him*, Cd. 69; Th. 82, 16; Gen. 1363. Mīnra hōa *calcanei mei*, Ps. Th. 48, 5. Pharao him filigde æt ðām hōu *Pharaoh followed at their heels*, Homl. Th. ii. 194, 22. Hōs mīne *calcaneum meum*, Ps. Spl. 55, 6. [Cf. *Icel.* hā-sin.]

hōh, hōgh, hō, hoo a form occurring in local names whose meaning is thus given by Kemble: 'Originally a point of land, formed like a heel, or boot, and stretching into the plain, perhaps even into the sea,' Cod. Dipl. iii. xxvi, where see the references to the various forms. Kemble's supposition is borne out by the following passage, in which the word occurs independently:—Wē ðā fōron forþ be ðæm sǣ and ðǣr ða heán hōs and dene and gārsecg ðone æthiopia wē gesāwon *promuntoria ad oceanum in ethiopia vidimus*, Nar. 24, 9. [Cf. (?) over hil and hogh, Cursor Mundi 15826.]

hoh-, hog-fæst; *adj. Firm of mind, prudent, wise*:—Hogfæstum *prudentibus*, Mt. Kmbl. Lind. 11, 25. v. hoga-fæst.

hōh-fōt, es; *m. The heel*:—Hō ł hōhfōt *calcaneum*, Ps. Lamb. 55, 7.

hoh-, hog-ful; *adj. Mindful, careful, anxious, wise, prudent*:—Ic nū on sibbe gesitte on mīnne cynestōl hohful embe ðæt hū ic his lof ārǣre *quiete pace perfruens, studiosus sollicite de laudibus Creatoris omnium occupor addendis*, Chart. Th. 240, 8. Ðā wearþ ðæt mǣden mycclum hohful hū heó ǣfre wæras wissian sceolde *then became the maiden very anxious how she was ever to direct men*, Homl. Skt. 2, 121. Ðām ðe lufiaþ swīðor ða heálīcan clǣnnysse ðonne ða hohfullan gālnysse *to those that love exalted chastity more than the wantonness which is full of care*, Homl. Th. ii. 324, 5. Hogfullum *prudentibus*, Mt. Kmbl. Lind. 11, 25. [*Laym.* hoh-fulle, *pl*: *Orm.* hoȝhe-full.]

hohful-ness, e; *f. Anxiety, care, trouble*:—Sǣde ic mīnum witun mīnes mōdes hohfulnysse *I told the anxiety of my mind to my 'witan,'* Cod. Dipl. Kmbl. iii. 349, 11.

hōh-hwyrfing, e; *f. A turning on the heel so as to describe a circle* [?]; orbis, Som.

hohinge-rōd, e; *f. A cross, gibbet*, W. Cat. p. 294.

hoh-, hog-līce; *adv. Prudently, thoughtfully*:—Hoglīce, *prudenter*, Lk. Skt. Lind. 16, 8.

hoh-mōd; *adj. Having an anxious mind, anxious*, Lye.

hohmōd-ness, e; *f. Anxiety, trouble, care*, Som.

hōh-scanca, an; *m. The shank*; crus:—Sceápes hōhscancan, L. M. 1, 2; Lchdm, ii. 38, 8.

hōh-sinu, we; *f. Hough-sinew, ham-string, heel-sinew*:—Gif hōhsino forad sīe *if a heel-sinew be broken*, L. M. 1, 71; Lchdm. ii. 146, 3. Heora horsa hōhsina ðū ofcirfst *equos eorum subnervabis*, Jos. 11, 6. [*Wick.* houȝ-senu: *Icel.* hā-sin: *Dan.* hase: cf. *O. H. Ger.* hahsanon *subnervare*, Grff. iv. 800.]

hōh-spor, es; *n. The heel*; calx, Ælfc. Gl. 75; Som. 71, 97: Wrt. Voc. 45, 5.

HOL, es; *n. A* HOLE, *hollow, cavern, den*:—Tō ðam ealdan hole; of ðam hole, Cod. Dipl. Kmbl. iii. 423, 22. Swā swā leó dēþ of his hole *quasi leo in cubile suo*, Ps. Th. 9, 29. Mec hæleþ ūt tȳhþ of hole hātne *a man draws me out hot from a hole*, Exon. 125 a; Th. 480, 6; Rä. 63, 7. On ðis dimme hol *into this dark den* [*prison*], Bt. Met. Fox 2, 21; Met. 2, 11. Ðæt cūðe hol, Exon. 112 b; Th. 431, 10; Rä. 45, 5. Wild deóra holl and denn *lustra*, Ælfc. Gl. 110; Som. 79, 38; Wrt. Voc. 59, 10. Hwelpas leóna on heora holum beóþ gelogode *catuli leonum in cubilibus suis collocabuntur*, Ps. Lamb. 103, 22. Foxas habbaþ holu *vulpes foveas habent*, Mt. Kmbl. 8, 20: Lk. Skt. 9, 58. Hola, Homl. Th. i. 160, 33. [*Laym.* hol: *Chauc.* hole: *Prompt. Parv.* hoole or pyt in an hylle *caverna*: *O. Frs. O. Dut. Icel. O. H. Ger.* hol *concavum, caverna spelunca, antrum*: cf. *Goth.* hulundi *spelunca.*] v. hola.

hol, es; *n. A covering* [?]:—Ān hol stæfes *apex*, Mt. Kmbl. Rush. 5, 18.

hol; *adj. Hollow*:—On middan hol *hollow in the middle*, Herb. 174, 1; Lchdm. i. 306, 9. Gif se weobud ufan hol nǣre *si in altari fossa non esset*, Past. 33, 2; Swt. 217, 21. Hol stān *fornix*, Cot. 93, Lye. Sca maria hine ācende on ðære nihte on ānum holum stānscræfe *St. Mary gave birth to him in a hollow cave*, Shrn. 29, 28. Ðæt wæter dranc of his holre hand *drank the water out of the hollow of his hand*, 50, 11. On ānne ealdne holne weg *to an old hollow way*, Chart. Th. 495, 8. Hole dene *convallem*, Ps. Spl. 59, 6. Hȳ beóþ innan hole *they are hollow within*, Herb. 180, 1; Lchdm. i. 316, 2. Gif heó hæfþ hole eágan *if she be hollow-eyed*, Lchdm. iii. 144, 7. [*Prompt. Parv.* hol *cavus, concavus*: *York-dialect* holl: *O. Frs.* hol: *Icel.* holr: *O. H. Ger.* hol *cavus, concavus*: *Ger.* hohl.] v. holh.

hol; *adj. Having a covering* or *crust* [?]:—Holne hlāf *tortam panis unius crustulam*, Ex. 29, 33. [Cf. hal-, heal-, healh-stān *crusta, crustulum*, Cot. 191, Lye.] v. also heal, healh; hol.

hól, es; *n. Vain speech, evil speaking without cause, calumny, slander*:—Hōl and hete and rȳpera reáflāc ūs derede *slander and hatred and the rapine of robbers hath harmed us*, Swt. A. S. Rdr. 106, 70. Hōl *calumnia*, Off. Episc. 8, Lye. Ne teó ic N. ne for hete ne for hōle [MS. H. hēle] ne for unrihtre feohgyrnesse *I do not accuse N. from hate or with the intention of slandering him or from an unjust desire for money*, L. O. 4; Th. i. 180, 11. Ðæs deópne āþ Drihten āswōr and ðone mid sōðe swylce gefrymede ðæt hē hine for hōle ǣr ne āswōre gehēt Dauide swā hē him dyde syððan *juravit Dominus David veritatem, et non frustrabitur eam*, Ps. Th. 131, 11; cf. Grff. iv. 849, huolian. [*Icel.* hōl *flattery, boasting.*] v. hōlunga, hoelan, hōlian.

hola, an; *m. A hole*:—Of ðam oterholan *from the otter hole*, Cod. Dipl. Kmbl. iii. 23, 30. [*Prompt. Parv.* hole *foramen*: *Icel.* hola; *f. a hole*: *O. H. Ger.* holi: *Ger.* höhle.]

holc, es; *n.* [?] *A hollow, cavity*:—Weaxcþ ðæt yfele blōd on ðām holcum ðæs līchoman *the evil blood increases in the hollow parts of the* body, L. M. I, 72; Lchdm. ii. 148, 7. On ðám holcum ðære lifre *in the hollows of the liver*, Lchdm. ii. 160, 26. [Cf. snikeð in ed te breoste holke, O. E. Homl. i. 251, 19: *Halliwell Dict.* holke, holket *hollow*: or is the meaning similar to that of *hylca*, q. v?]

hold, es; *m. A title which seems to have been introduced by the Danes. It occurs several times in the Chronicle*, e. g. Ysopa hold and Óscytel hold, 905; Erl. 98, 34. Þurcytel eorl and ða holdas ealle, 918; Erl. 104, 22. Þurferþ eorl and ða holdas, 921; Erl. 107, 28. *It is the Norse* höldr *which is thus defined* 'sá er höldr er hann hefir óðöl at erfðum tekit bæði eptir föður ok móður, þau et hans forellrar hafa átt áðr fyrir þeim,' see Cl. and Vig. Dict. höldr. *The importance of the hold in England is marked in the following passage*:—Holdes and cyninges heáhgeréfan wergild iiii þúsend þrymsa, L. Wg. 4; Th. i. 186, 8.

hold, es; *n. A carcase, body*:—Swá hwǽr swá hold byþ *ubicunque fuerit corpus*, Mt. Kmbl. 24, 28. Ðá woldon óðre fugelas fleón tó ðam holde *descenderunt volucres super cadavera*, Gen. 15, 11. Swá swá grǽdigeræmmas ðar ðar hí hold geseóþ *like greedy ravens, where they see a carcase*, L. Ælfc. P. 49; Th. ii. 386, 3: L. I. P. 19; Th. ii. 328, 5. Tódǽlon ðæs deádan hold him betwýnan *cadaver mortui inter se dispertient*, Ex. 21, 35. [Þu fule hold *olidum cadaver*, O. E. Homl. ii. 183, 15: *Icel.* hold *flesh.*]

hold; *adj. Kind, friendly, pleasant, favourable, gracious* [*of a prince to his subject*], *faithful, loyal, devoted, liege* [*of a subject to his prince*]:—Drihten gedyde ðæt ðæs cwearternes ealdor him wærþ swíðe hold *dominus dedit ei gratiam in conspectu principis carceris*, Gen. 39, 21. Hé wearþ cristnum monnum swíðe hold *benignus erga Christianos*, Ors. 6, 12; Swt. 266, 22. Swá hold is God mancynne ðæt hé hæfþ geset his englas ús tó hyrdum *God is so gracious to mankind that he hath appointed angels as our guardians*, Homl. Th. i. 170, 9: Cd. 60; Th. 73, 10; Gen. 1202: 107; Th. 142, 26; Gen. 2367. Ðam byþ God hold ðe biþ his hláforde rihtlíce hold *God will be gracious to him who is rightly faithful to his lord*, L. C. E. 20; Th. i. 372, 12. Hé cwæþ ðæt hé heom hold hláford beón wolde, Chr. 1014: Erl. 150, 10. Ðonne biþ se holda þeówa geset ofer manegum gódum *then will the faithful servant be set over many goods*, Homl. Th. ii. 552, 23. Ic wille beón N. hold and getríwe *I will be faithful and true to N.*, L. O. 1; Th. i. 178, 4: Cd. 196; Th. 244, 4; Dan. 443: Beo. Th. 2463; B. 1229. Ic eom ðín hold scealc *tuus sum ego*, Ps. Th. 118, 94. Fram sóðum martirdóme ðæs hálgan weres his holdan pápan *from the true martyrdom of the holy man, his gracious pope*, Homl. Th. ii. 310, 29. Hé horn hefeþ holdes folces *exaltavit cornu populi sui*, Ps. Th. 148 14. Heriaþ hine on hleóðre holdre béman *laudate eum in sono tubæ*, 150, 3. Eáran habbaþ ne hí áwiht mágon holdes gehýran *ears have they but nought pleasing can they hear*, 134, 17. Holdum Gode ic sealmas singe *psallum Deo meo*, 145, 1. Ic gebócie sumne dǽl landes mínum holdan and getriówan þegne, Cod. Dipl. Kmbl. iii. 256, 8. Hé hí on hihte holdre lǽdde *deduxit eos in spe*, Ps. Th. 77, 53. Áhte ic holdne hláford *I had a gracious lord*, Exon. 100 b; Th. 379, 26; Deór. 39: Ps. Th. 150, 1: Cd. 106; Th. 139, 22; Gen. 2313. Ic geornlíce gode þegnode þurh holdne hyge *I diligently served God with loyal mind*, 28; Th. 37, 7; Gen. 586. Heó dyde hit deáh þurh holdne hyge *yet did she it with purpose kind*, 33; Th. 44, 12; Gen. 708: Beo. Th. 539; B. 267. Áhyld mé ðín eáre tó holde móde *graciously incline thine ear to me*, Ps. Th. 70, 2: 85, 6. Nele mé Israhél behealdan holde móde *Israel will not regard me with loyalty*, 80, 11; 118, 112. Ealle Rómáne wurdon cristnum monnum swá holde ðæt hie on monegum templum áwriten ðæt ǽlc cristen mon hæfde friþ *all the Romans shewed so much favour to the Christians that they wrote up in many temples that every Christian man should have protection*, Ors. 6, 13; Swt. 268, 19: Exon. 36 b; Th. 119, 7; Gú. 251. Holde frýnd mé sǽdon *faithful friends told me*, Homl. Th. 414, 7. Uton beón á úrum hláforde holde and getrýwe *let us ever be to our lord loyal and true*, L. C. E. 20; Th. i. 372, 8: Homl. Th. ii. 68, 9. Hí woldon him beón holde and gehýrsume *they* [*the monks*] *would be loyal and obedient to him* [*the abbot*], Chr. 1083; Erl. 217, 6. Alle míne þegnes and míne holde freónd on Hertfordesire *all my thanes and faithful friends in Hertfordshire*, Cod. Dipl. Kmbl. iv. 217, 5. Frýnd synd hie míne georne holde on hyra hygesceaftum ic mæg hyra hearra wesan, Cd. 15; Th. 19, 8; Gen. 288. Wé witon ðæt ǽghwylcum men biþ leófre swá hé hæbbe holdra freónda má *we know that the more faithful friends a man has the better he likes it*, Blickl. Homl. 123, 1: Beo. Th. 979; B. 487. Is sáwl mín symble on ðínum holdum handum *anima mea in manibus tuis semper*, Ps. Th. 118, 109. Holdost *most faithful*, Byrht. Th. 132, 31; By. 24. [*Laym.* þin holde mon: *Orm.* þin laferrd birrþ þe beon hold and trigg: *O. E. Homl.* mid holde mode: *O. Sax. O. Frs.* hold: *Icel.* hollr *gracious, faithful, wholesome*: *O. H. Ger.* hold *propitius, fidelis, devotus*: *Ger.* hold.] v. un-hold.

hold-áþ, es; *m. An oath of fealty*:—Hí wéron his menn and him holdáþas swóron ðæt hí woldon ongeán ealle óðre menn him holde beón *they did homage to him and swore oaths of fealty to him that they would be loyal to him against all other men*, Chr. 1085; Erl. 219, 7. Hé dyde ðæt ealle ða heáfodmæn on Normandig dydon manrǽden and holdáþas his sunu Willelme, 1115; Erl. 245, 12. [*R. Glouc. Havel.* holde-, holdoþ.]

holde; *adv. Graciously, with devotion*, Ps. Th. 71, 2: 142, 6. v. hold.

holdigean *eviscerare*, Gl. Prud. 337.

hold-líce; *adv. Graciously, with kindness* or *friendliness, with devotion* or *attachment, faithfully, loyally*:—Holdlíce *affectuose* vel *devote*, Ælfc. Gl. 115; Som. 80, 50; Wrt. Woc. 61, 28. Hé cwæþ swíðe holdlíce be ús 'Fæder mín ic wille ðæt ða ðe ðú mé forgeáfe beón mid mé ðǽr ic beó' *he said very graciously concerning us 'My Father, I will that those whom thou hast given me be with me where I am*,' Homl. Th. ii. 368, 10: Cd. 220; Th. 283, 27; Sat. 311: Ps. Th. 54, 1: 58, 3. Holdlíce *kindly*, Exon. 27 b; Th. 83, 18; Cri. 1358. Hé mé holdlíce þegnade *he served me faithfully*, Ps. Th. 100, 6. Hwá ðás ælmesse holdlíce healde healde hine God, Chart. Th. 369, 29. Cwǽdon holdlíce hýran woldon *said they would listen devoutly*, Andr. Kmbl. 3276; An. 1641. Eádwearde hýrdon holdlíce *loyally obeyed Edward*, Chr. 1065; Erl. 196, 33; Edw. 14: Exon. 41 b; Th. 138, 14; Gú. 576. Ðæt Drihtne ful holdlíce hýran *ut serviant Domino*, Ps. Th. 101, 20.

hold-rǽden, e; *f. Faithfulness, loyalty, faithful discharge of duty to a superior*:—Hire hyrdeman þurh holdrǽdene sume ác ástáh *her herdsman in the discharge of his duty had ascended an oak*, Homl. Th. ii. 150, 30.

hold-scipe, es; *m. Loyalty, fealty, allegiance*:—Eallra ðæra manna land hí fordydon ðe wǽron innan ðæs cynges holdscipe *they destroyed the lands of all those men that were in allegiance to the king*, Chr. 1087; Erl. 224, 15. Sægdon ðæt hí hit dyden for ðes mynstres holdscipe *said that they did it on account of the loyalty of the monastery*, 1070; Erl. 209, 15.

holen, holegn, es; *m. Holly*:—Holen *acrifolius*, Ælfc. Gl. 47; Som. 65, 23; Wrt. Voc. 33, 23: *ulcia*, Wrt. Voc. 80, 12: *acrivolus*, 285, 37. Holegn *acrifolius*, Gl. Amplon. 131: Gl. Mett. 34 [Leo]. Holenrinde *holly-bark*, L. M. 1, 32; Lchdm. ii. 78, 12. Holenleáfa *holly leaves*, 3, 69; Lchdm. ii. 356, 11. Holen sceal in æled *holly shall to the fire*, Exon. 90 a; Th. 338, 17; Gn. Ex. 80. Se fealwa holen *the sere holly*, Exon. 114 a; Th. 437, 19; Rä. 56, 10. [*A. R.* holin, holie. For the form *hollen* (*hollin, holyn*) see E. D. S. Plant Names, p. 263.] v. cneówholen.

holenga. v. holunga.

holh, holg, es; *n. A hollow, cavity, hole*:—Hwæt tácnaþ ðæt holh on ðæm weobude búton gódra monna geþyld? Forðam ðonne mon his mód geeáðmódgeþ ðæt hé wiðerweardnesse and scande forbere ðonne geeácnaþ hé sum holh on his móde swá swá ðæt weobud hæfþ on him uppan. Holh wæs beboden ðæt sceolde beón on ðæm weobude uppan ... wel hit wæs gecueden ðæt ðæt holh sceolde beón on ðæm weobude ánre elne brád and ánre elne long *quod est altaris fossa, nisi bonorum patientia quæ, dum mentem ad adversa toleranda humiliat, quasi more foveæ hanc in imo positam demonstrat? Fossa ergo in altari fiat ... Bene autem hæc eadem fossa unius cubiti esse monstratur*, Past. 33, 3; Swt. 219, 1–10. Ðǽr ðǽr se iil hæfde his holh *ibi habuit foveam ericius*, 35, 3; Swt. 241, 7. In ðæm wæs ðæt holg ðæs nearwan scræfes, Lchdm. iii. 365, col. 1. [*Laym.* holȝes, *pl. and* holh; *adj*: *R. Glouc.* holu, *sing. adj*; holwe, *pl*: *Chauc.* holwe *pl. adj.*]

holian; *p.* ode *To hollow out, make hollow, dig, make a hole*; cavare:—Hí ðá hwæthwega holodon and ðǽrrihte ðæt wæter swá genihtsumlíce út fleów ðæt hit arn streámrynes of ðam munte *they then hollowed out* [*the rock*] *a little, and straightway the water flowed out so abundantly that it ran streaming from the mountain*, Homl. Th. ii. 162, 7. [*A. R.* ne holieþ nout aduneward ase doþ þe uoxes: *Prompt. Parv.* holyn̄ *cavo, perforo, terebro*: *Goth.* us-hulon *to excavate*: *Icel.* hola *to make hollow*: *O. H. Ger.* holian, holon *fodere, perforarare, excavare*: *Ger.* höhlen.] DER. á-holian.

hólian *to speak evil of, slander, calumniate*:—Ne sele ðú mé hóliendum mé *non tradas me calumniantibus me*, Ps. Lamb. 118, 121. [*Orm.* holen o þe laȝhe leod, 9319, *with which compare Goth.* holon *in Lk.* 3, 14: cf. *O. H. Ger.* huolian, Grff. iv. 849.] v. hól, hólunga.

hólinga. v. hólunga.

holl. v. hol.

holm, es; *m. A mound, hill, rising ground;* but in this sense, which belongs to the word in the Old Saxon, it is not found in English. **I.** Its most common use in the latter, in the poetry, is in reference to water with the meaning *wave, ocean, water, sea*:—Freá engla héht wesan wæter gemǽne ðá stód hraðe holm under heofonum síd ætsomne *the lord of angels bade the waters be together, then quickly stood ocean under heaven far-stretching continuously*, Cd. 8; Th. 10, 23; Gen. 161. Holm *the* [*Red*] *sea*, 157; Th. 195, 30; Exod. 284: 166; Th. 206, 9; Exod. 449. Holm *the water of the deluge*, 71; Th. 86, 15; Gen. 1431. Holm storme weól, Beo. Th. 2267; B. 1131. Holm heolfre weóll [*of the lake where Grendel dwelt*], 4282; B. 2137: 3189; B. 1592. Wíde rád ofer holmes hrincg hof séleste [*of the ark*], Cd. 69; Th. 84, 5; Gen. 1393. Eów is holmes hlæst and heofonfuglas and wildu deór on geweald geseald *the fishes of the sea, the fowls of the air, and the beasts of the earth are* *delivered into your hand*, 74; Th. 91, 20; Gen. 1515. Wið holme foldan sceldun *guarded land against sea*, Exon. 22 a; Th. 61, 4; Cri. 979. On holme, 97 a; Th. 363, 9; Wal. 51: Beo. Th. 1090; B. 543: 2875; B. 1435. Æt holme *by the sea*, 3832; B. 1914. Sealt wæter hreóh mē holme besencte *tempestas demersit me*, Ps. Th. 68, 2. Ðā wæs heofonweardes gāst ofer holm boren *the spirit of God moved upon the face of the waters*, Cd. 6; Th. 8, 7; Gen. 121. Lēton holm beran *they let the sea bear him*, Beo. Th. 96; B. 48. Ofer wīdne holm, Exon. 79 a; Th. 296, 23; Crä. 55. Ofer heánne holm, Elen. Kmbl. 1962; El. 983: Cd. 213; Th. 266, 4; Sat. 17: Exon. 77 b; Th. 291, 14; Wand. 82. Ðā ic on holm gestāh *when I embarked*, Beo. Th. 1269; B. 632: Andr. Kmbl. 858; An. 429. Heá holmas *deep waters*, Exon. 54 b; Th. 193, 17; Az. 123. Holmas dǣlde waldend ūre *God divided the waters*, Cd. 8; Th. 9, 24; Gen. 146: Exon. 93 a; Th. 349, 31; Sch. 54. Hider ofer holmas *hither over the waves*, Beo. Th. 485; B. 240. Windge holmas *stormy seas*, Exon. 20 a; Th. 53, 26; Cri. 856. Holma begang *the way across the waters*, Ps. Th. 138, 18: Andr. Kmbl. 390; An. 195: Bt. Met. Fox 11, 69; Met. 11, 30. Holma geþring, Beo. Th. 4271; B. 2132. Holma gelagu, Exon. 82 a; Th. 309, 28; Seef. 64. II. From the Scandinavian *hólmr* an islet especially in a bay, creek, lake, or river, it is used in English with the meaning *land rising from the water, an island in a river, etc., holm* [*in local names*]:—Ðȳ ilcan geáre wæs ðæt gefeoht æt ðam Holme Cantwara and ðara Deniscra, Chr. 902; Th. 180, col. 2. Hēr fōr Cnut Cyng tō Denmearcon mid scipon tō ðam holme æt eá ðære hālgan, 1025; Erl. 163, 7. [*Laym.* holm: *Prompt. Parv.* holm, place besydone a water *hulmus*; of a sonde yn the see *bitalassum* vel *hulmus*. v. p. 243, note 2, and 244, note 2.] DER. sǣ-, wǣg-holm.

holm-ærn, es; *n. A sea-house, vessel, ship*:—Holmærna mǣst earc Noes, Cd. 71; Th. 85, 30; Gen. 1422.

holm-clif, es; *n. A sea-cliff, cliff by the water-side*:—On, fram ðam holmclife [*the* holm *is the lake where Grendel dwelt*], Beo. Th. 2846, 3274; B. 1421, 1635. Se ðe holmclifu healdan scolde *he who had to guard the sea-cliffs*, 465; B. 230. [*O. Sax.* holm-klif *a hill*.]

holmeg; *adj. Oceanic*:—Holmegum wederum *with storms such as blow at sea*, Cd. 148; Th. 185, 6; Exod. 118.

holm-mægen, es; *n. The might of the ocean, the ocean*, Exon. 101 a; Th. 382, 10; Rä. 3, 9.

holm-þracu; *g.* -þræce; *f. The violence of the sea, the tossing of the waves, the ocean*, Andr. Kmbl. 933; An. 467. Ðū geworhtest heofon and eorþan and holmþræce *thou didst make heaven and earth and the sea with its tossing waves*, Elen. Kmbl. 1453; El. 728: Exon. 17 b; Th. 42, 25; Cri. 678: 57 b; Th. 205, 19; Ph. 115.

holm-weall, es; *m. A wall formed by the sea*, Cd. 166; Th. 207, 16; Exod. 467.

holm-weard, es; *m. One who keeps guard at sea, a sea-warder*, Andr. Kmbl. 718; An. 359.

holm-weg, es; *m. A way over the sea*, Andr. Kmbl. 764; An. 382.

holm-wylm, es; *m. The surge of the sea*, Beo. Th. 4814; B. 2411.

holor, holrian. v. heolora, heoloran.

HOLT, es; *m. n.* I. *a* HOLT, *wood, grove, copse*:—Holt *lucus*, Ælfc. Gr. 8; Som. 7, 30: *nemus*, 9, 32; Som. 12, 17: *saltus*, Ælfc. Gl. 45; Som. 64, 104; Wrt. Voc. 32, 39: *nemus* vel *saltus*, Wrt. Voc. 80, 34. Wildeóra holt, Salm. Kmbl. 116; Sal. 82. Holtes frætwe *fruit*, Exon. 57 a; Th. 202, 22; Ph. 73. Hē lēt him ðā of handon fleógan hafoc wið ðæs holtes *he let the hawk fly from his hands towards the wood*, Byrht. Th. 131, 14; By. 8: Rood Kmbl. 58; Kr. 29. Uton gān innan on ðisses holtes hleó *let us go within the shelter of this grove*, Cd. 39; Th. 52, 7; Gen. 840; Exon. 62 a; Th. 227, 26; Ph. 429. Wulf holtes gehlēða, Elen. Kmbl. 225; El. 113. Sum sceal on holte of heáhbeáme feallan, Exon. 87 b; Th. 328, 21; Vy. 21: Bt. Met. Fox 13, 103, 73; Met. 13, 52, 37. Gewiton āweg tō holte *they went away to the wood*, Homl. Th. ii. 516, 12. Holt ofgeáfon *they left the wood*, Beo. Th. 5685; B. 2846: 5190; B. 2598. Abraham ðā plantode ǣnne holt *Abraham vero plantavit nemus*, Gen. 21, 33. Ful oft unc holt wrugon wudubeáma helm, Exon. 129 a; Th. 496, 1; Rä. 85, 7. Ðū geond holt wunast *thou shalt dwell among the woods*, Cd. 203; Th. 252, 6; Dan. 574. II. *wood*; lignum:—Ic geseah holt hweorfende *I saw wood moving*, Exon. 114 a; Th. 438, 5; Rä. 57, 3. Holte bi[h]lǣnan *to pile wood round*, 74 a; Th. 277, 7; Jul. 577. [*Laym. Chauc.* holt: *Prompt. Parv.* holt, lytylle wode *lucus, virgultum*, p. 244, v. note: *O. Frs.* holt *wood, stick*: *Icel.* holt *wood, coppice* (nearly obsolete); *a rough stony hill*: *O. H. Ger.* holz *nemus, silva, saltus, arbor, lignum*: *Ger.* holz.] DER. æsc-, firgen-, ofer-, wudu-holt.

holt-hana, an; *m. A wood-cock*; acegia, Gl. Mett. 41: Gl. Amplon. 138.

hōl-tihte, an; *f. Calumny, slander*:—Hōltihte *vel* teóne *calumnia*, Ælfc. Gl. 15; Som. 58, 36; Wrt. Voc. 21, 29.

holt-wudu, a; *m.* I. *a wood*; silva, nemus, Beo. Th. 2743; B. 1369: Exon. 58 a; Th. 209, 16; Ph. 171. II. *wood from a holt, forest-wood*; lignum, Beo. Th. 4669; B. 2340: Rood Kmbl. 179; Kr. 91.

hōlunga; *adv. In vain, to no purpose, without cause, without intent*:—Hōlunga *sine causa*, Mt. Kmbl. Lind. 15, 9. Nales hōlunge *not without cause*, Cd. 48; Th. 61, 14; Gen. 997. Nalles hōlinga, Beo. Th. 2156; B. 1076. Wæs his fæder gelǣred in ða gerȳno Cristes geleáfan ac hōlinga *pater ejus sacramentis Christianæ fidei imbutus est, sed frustra*, Bd. 2, 15; S. 518, 29. Gif hē hit hōlinga dō fæste i geár *si casu fecerit, i annum jejunet*, L. Ecg. P. iv. 68, 22; Th. ii. 230, 27. Ðære tīde wæs ðæt mǣste wæll geworden on Norþanhymbra þeóde and cyrican. Ne wæs ðæt hōlenga forðon ōðer ðæra heretogena wæs hǣðen ōðer wæs ðam hǣðenan grimra *quo tempore maxima est facta strages in ecclesia vel gente Nordanhymbrorum, maxime quod unus ex ducibus paganus, alter erat pagano sævior*, Bd. 2, 20; S. 521, 19. Mid ðȳ wē wið ðam winde and wið ðam sǣ holonga campodan *cumque cum vento pelagoque frustra certantes*, 5, 1; S. 613, 27.

hom, hōme, homer. v. ham, ōme, hamer.

homela, homola, an; *m.* A word of uncertain meaning occurring in the following passage:—Gif hē hine on bismor tō homolan bescire mid x scill. gebēte. Gif hē hine tō preóste bescire mid xxx scill. gebēte, L. Alf. pol. 35; Th. i. 84, 5. See the note there; see also on cutting the hair as a mark of disgrace, Grimm's Deutsche Rechtsalterthümer, pp. 702–3. v. hamelian, and cf. [?] *Scot.* hummel, homyll *having no horns*.

hōn; *p.* hēng; *pp.* hangen *To hang, suspend, crucify*:—Gē hig hōþ *crucifigetis*, Mt. Kmbl. 23, 34. Hine man hēng *ille suspensus est in cruce*, Gen. 41, 13. Hig hine hēngon *crucifixerunt eum*, Lk. Skt. 23, 33. Ðone hēngon on heáne beám fæderas ūsse, Elen. Kmbl. 847; El. 424. Hōh hine *crucifige eum*, Mk. Skt. 15, 13. Hōh hyne hōh hyne; Ðā cwæþ pilatus tō him Nime gē hine and hōþ, Jn. Skt. 19, 6. Hōh on earm *hang it on to the arm*, Med. ex Quadr. 9, 12; Lchdm. i. 362, 27. Ðone ōðerne hē hēt hōn on gealgan *alterum suspendit in crucem*, Gen. 40, 22. Hēt se wælhreówa hine hōn on heardre hengene, Homl. Th. ii. 308, 29. Ðǣr wǣron gelǣdde twegen sceaþan for heora synnum tō hōnne *there were brought two thieves to be crucified for their sins*, 254, 22. Tō hōanne *ad crucifigendum*, Mt. Kmbl. Lind. 20, 19. Ic hæbbe mihte ðē tō hōnne, Jn. Skt. 19, 10. Ðǣm hōendum *crucifigentibus*, Lk. Skt. 11, 7. Frignan ongan on hwylcum ðara beáma bearn wealdendes hangen wǣre, Elen. Kmbl. 1701; El. 851. [*Laym.* hon; *p.* heng: *Orm. Chauc. Piers P.* heng, *p*: *Goth.* hahan; *p.* haihah: *Icel.* hanga; *p.* hēkk *pendere*: *O. Frs.* hua; *p.* heng; *pp.* huen: *O. H. Ger.* hahan; *p.* hieng *figere, crucifigere, suspendere*.] DER. a-, be-, bi-, ge-hōn.

hōn *tendrils of a vine* [?]:—Ðā geseah ic gyldenne wīngeard trumlīcne and fæstlīcne and ða twīgo his hongodon geond ða columnan. ða wundrode ic ðæs swīðe. wǣron in ðǣm wīngearde gyldenu leáf and his hōn and his wæstmas wǣron cristallum and smaragdus eác ðæt gimcyn mid ðǣm cristallum ingemong hongode *vineamque solidam auro argentoque inter columnas pendentem miratus sum. in qua folia aurea racemique cristallini ligis erant interpositi, distinguentibus smaragdis*, Nar. 4, 31.

hona, hon-, hond, hongian. v. hana, heonu, han-, hand, hangian.

hōp. v. fen-, mōr-hōp.

HOPA, an; *m.* HOPE:—Geleáffullum mannum mæg beón micel hopa tō ðam menniscum Gode Criste *believing men may have great hope on the human God, Christ*, Homl. Th. i. 350, 24. Ne bepǣce Ezechias eów mid leásum hopan *let not Hezekiah deceive you with false hope*, 568, 8. [*Laym. Orm. A. R.* hope: *Du.* hoop: *Dan.* haab: *M. H. Ger.* hoffe.] DER. tō-hopa.

hōp-gehnāst, es; *n. The dashing together of waves in a bay* [?]:—Bīdaþ stille stealc stānhleoþu streámgewinnes hōpgehnāstes ðonne heáh geþring on cleofu crȳdeþ *the steep rocks await quietly the strife of the sea, the dash of the waves, when the press of waters towering up crowds on to the cliffs*, Exon. 101 b; Th. 384, 13; Rä. 4, 27. [Cf. *Icel.* hóp *a small landlocked bay* or *inlet*: *Scot.* hope *a haven*.]

hopian; *p.* ode, ede *To hope, have hope* or *confidence* [*in a person*], *expect, watch for* [*with gen.*]:—Ic hopige tō him swā gōdan and swā mildheortan ðæt hē hit nylle sylf dōn *I have confidence in him, so good and merciful, that he himself will not do it*, Chart. Th. 548, 20. Ðū dysegost manna ðū hopast ðæt ðū hæbbe þoftrǣdene tō ðam āwyrigedan deófle *thou most foolish of men, thou trustest that thou hast fellowship with the accursed devil*, Homl. Th. ii. 416, 14. Swā eác ūre hiht ne becom nā tō ðam ðe hē hopaþ *so also our hope has not arrived at that for which it hopes*, i. 250, 25. Ðonne hē eall forsihþ eorþlīcu gōd and hopaþ tō ðām ēcum, Bt. Met. Fox 7, 87; Met. 7, 44. Se synfulla hopaþ symle ðæs rihtwīsan *considerat peccator justum*, Ps. Th. 36, 32. Ðæt ðæt Maria dyde tō ðam wē hopiaþ *that which Mary did, for that we hope*, Homl. Th. ii. 442, 33. Landfranc gewāt of ðissum līfe ac wē hopiaþ ðæt hē fērde tō ðæt heofanlīce rīce, Chr. 1089; Erl. 226, 15. Ic tō ðē hopode *in e speravi*, Ps. Th. 30, 17. Hē hopode ðæt hē gesāwe sum tācen *sperabat signum aliquod videre*, Lk. Skt. 23, 8. Hæbbende ðæs ðe wē ǣr hopedon, Homl. Th. i. 250, 35. Wē tō ðīnum hidercyme hopodan and hyhtan, Blickl. Homl. 87, 11. Hopedon *sperabamus*, Lk. Skt. 24, 21. Ðā fīf cyningas hopodon tō līfe *the five kings hoped to save their lives*, Jos.

10, 16. Ne hopige nān man tō ðyssere leásunge, Homl. Th. ii. 572, 21. Hit nys nō unnyt ðæt wē hopien tō Gode forðæm hē ne went swā swā wē dōþ *it is not vain for us to have hope in God; for he does not change as we do*, Bt. 42; Fox 258, 20. Ðæt hī swā hopigen tō ðære forgiefnesse *ut sic de spe fiduciam habeant*, Past. 53, 5; Swt. 415, 19. Bebeódaþ ðæt hī ne hopian on heora ungewissum welan *bid them not to put their trust in their uncertain riches*, Homl. Th. i. 256, 25. Ne þearf hē hopian nō ðæt hē ðonan mōte *he has no ground for hoping that he may go thence*, Judth. 10; Thw. 23, 12; Jud. 117. Ða hopiendan on ðē *sperantes in te*, Ps. Spl. 16, 8. [*M. H. Ger.* hoffen.] DER. tō-hopian.

hōpig; *adj. In hills and hollows [applied to the sea in reference to the deep depressions between high waves;* cf. *Scot.* hope *a sloping hollow between two hills, or the hollow that is formed between two ridges on one hill*]:—Com ic on sǣs hricg ðǣr mē sealt wæter hreóh and hōpig holme besencte *veni in altitudinem maris; et tempestas demersit me*, Ps. Th. 68, 2.

hoppa. v. gærs-hoppa.

hōp-pāda, an; *m. An upper tunic, cope*:—Hōppāda *ependeton* [= ἐπενδύτης], Ælfc. Gl. 112; Som. 79, 83; Wrt. Voc. 59, 52.

hoppe, an; *f. An ornament suspended from the neck, a bell* [?] *hung from a dog's neck*:—Hryðeres belle and hundes hoppe ǣlc biþ ānes scitt. weorþ and ǣlc is melda geteald *an ox's bell and that on a dog's collar, each is worth a shilling and each is reckoned an informer*, L. Edg. H. 8; Th. i. 260, 16. Hie eall him gesealdon ðæt hie ðā hæfdon būton ðæt ǣlc wīfmon hæfde āne yndsan goldes and ān pund seolfres and ǣlc wǣpnedmon ǣnne hring and āne hoppan *ita ut nihil præter annulos singulos, bullasque sibi ac filiis, et deinde per filias uxoresque suas singulas tantum auri uncias, et argenti non amplius quam singulas libras relinquerent*, Ors. 4, 10; Swt. 196, 21.

hoppere, es; *m. A dancer;* saltator, Som.

hoppestre, an; *f. A female dancer*:—Ðæs mǣran wītegan deáþ ðære lyðran hoppystran tō mēde forgeaf *rewarded that vile dancer with the death of the illustrious prophet*, Homl. Th. i. 484, 3. [*Chauc.* hoppestre.]

hoppetan; *p.* te *To jump about* [*for joy*], *leap, rejoice, to throb* [*of a wound*]:—Swā benne ne burnon ne burston ne hoppetan *so that the wounds should neither burn nor burst nor throb*, L. M. 3, 63; Lchdm. ii. 352, 1. Ðæne ðe mēder on rife hoppetende beclȳsed Johannes undergeat *quem matris alvo gestiens clausus Johannes senserat*, Hymn. Surt. 51, 1. v. next word.

hoppian; *p.* ode *To hop, leap, dance*:—Ðā blissode mīn cild on mīnum innoþe and hoppode ongeán his Drihten *then rejoiced my child in my womb, and leaped towards his Lord*, Homl. Th. i. 202, 18. [*Chauc. Piers P.* hoppe *to dance, jump*: *Icel.* hoppa *to skip, bound*: *M. H. Ger.* hoppen: *Ger.* hüpfen.]

hopp-scȳte, an; *f. A coverlet* [?]:—Ic geann ānes beddreáfes mid wahhryfte and mid hoppscȳtan, Chart. Th. 529, 12.

hopu *lygustra*, Lchdm. iii. 332, col. 2.

horas. v. horh.

hora-seáþ, Bt. 37, 2; Fox 188, 1. v. horu-seáþ.

hōr-cwene, an; *f. An adulteress, whore*:—Hōrcwenan, L. E. G. 11; Th. i. 172, 21: L. Eth. vi. 7; Th. i. 316, 21: L. C. S. 4; Th. i. 378, 7. [*Icel.* hōr-kona *an adulteress*.]

HORD, es; *n. m.* HOARD, *treasure*:—Hord *thesaurus*, Wrt. Voc. 86, 47. Ðā wæs ōþboren beága hord *then was borne off the hoard of rings*, Beo. Th. 4557; B. 2284: 6015; B. 3011. Hyrde ðæs hordes *keeper of the hoard*, Exon. 130 a; Th. 498, 7; Rä. 87, 9: Beo. Th. 1778; B. 887. Ðæs ðe heáh hlioþo horde onfēngon *after the lofty hills had received the treasure* [*the ark*], Cd. 71; Th. 86, 32; Gen. 1439. Hǣðnum horde, Beo. Th. 4438; B. 2216. Hord eald enta geweorc, 5540; B. 2773. Ðæt hord, 6244; B. 3126. Hord under hrusan [*the nails of the cross*], Elen. Kmbl. 2181; El. 1092. Hī ealgodon hord and hāmas *they defended treasures and homes*, Chr. 937; Erl. 112, 10; Æðelst. 10. Hē ðæt fācen hafaþ in his heortan, hord unclǣne *he hath that deceit in his heart, a hoard unclean*, Frag. Recd. 11; Leás 6. Hord, heortan geþohtas, Exon. 23 a; Th. 65, 1; Cri. 1048: 23 b; Th. 65, 17; Cri. 1056. Breósta hord, Th. 66, 17; Cri. 1074. Breósta hord, gāst *the breast's treasure, the spirit*, Cd. 79; Th. 97, 6; Gen. 1608. His synna hord ontēnde *he confessed his sins*, Ps. C. 50, 28; Grn. ii. 277, 28: 151, 155; Grn. ii. 280, 151, 155. Sāwle hord, Beo. Th. 4835; B. 2422. Hordas, gerȳne *arcana*, Mone B. 4216 (v. gold-hord). [*Laym. Orm. A. R. Chauc.* hord: *Goth.* huzd; *n*: *O. Sax.* hord; *n*: *Icel.* hodd; *n.* (*but a late form* hoddar; *pl. occurs*) in poetry only *hoard, treasure*: *O. H. Ger.* hort; *n. thesaurus*.] DER. beáh-, bōc-, brand-, breóst-, feorh-, flǣsc-, gold-, greót-, līc-, māðm-, mōd-, sāwl-, wamb-, word-, wyrm-hord.

hord-burh, -burg, e; *f. A city containing treasure*, Cd. 93; Th. 121, 9; Gen. 2007: Beo. Th. 938; B. 467.

hord-cleófa, -clȳfa, an; *m. A treasure-chamber, treasury, store-room, closet*:—Hī gāþ in tō ðīnum hūse and tō ðīnum bedde and tō ðīnum hordclȳfan *ingredientur cubiculum lectuli tui et super stratum tuum*, Exod. 8, 3. Ic hæbbe on mīnum hordcleófan ān wundorlīc weorc *I have in my treasury a wondrous work*, Homl. Skt. 5, 260. Hī sōhton ðone behīddan mete on heora hordcleófan *they sought the hidden food in their closets*, Ælfc. T. 42, 14; Grn. 21, 13. v. next word.

hord-cōfa, an; *m. A place for treasure, a retired chamber, closet, a place where the thoughts are stored* [v. hord], *the breast, heart*:—Ðā æfter ðon ðā cēgde seó hālige Mariæ tō eallum apostolum on hire hordcōfan *post hec vocavit Sancta Maria omnes apostolos in cubiculo suo*, Blickl. Homl. 143, 34. Ðæt hē his ferþlocan fæste binde healde [MS. healdne] his hordcōfan *that he close fast his mind's coffer and preserve the treasury of his thoughts*, Exon. 76 b; Th. 287, 14 [cf. 22]; Wand. 14. Hine mid ealle innancundum heortum hordcōfan helpe biddaþ *in toto corde exquirunt eum*, Ps. Th. 118, 2.

hordere, es; *m. A treasurer, steward, chamberlain* [v. Kemble's Saxons in England ii. 106]:—Hordere *cellerarius*, Wrt. Voc. 83, 6. Ðā hēt hē his hordere ðæt glæsene fæt syllan ðam biddendan subdiácone. Se hordere cwæþ him tō andsware gif hē ðam biddendum sealde ðæt hē nān þing næfde his gebrōðrum tō syllenne *then he bade his steward give the glass vessel to the requesting subdeacon. The steward said in answer, that if he gave it he should have nothing to give to his brethren*, Homl. Th. ii. 178, 22: Chr. 1131; Erl. 260, 12. Ðis forward wæs makid wid ordrīc hordere, Chart. Th. 438, 3, 7. Cynges hordera odde ūra gerēfena swilc, L. Ath. 1, 3; Th. i. 200, 23, see note. Nān man ne hwyrfe nānes yrfes būtan ðæs gerēfan gewitnesse ... odde ðæs horderes, 9; Th. i. 204, 19. [*Ayenb.* hordier *treasurer*.]

hord-ern, -ærn, es; *n. A store-house, store-room, treasury*:—Hordern *cellarium*, Ælfc. Gl. 108; Som. 78, 100; Wrt. Voc. 58, 15: Lk. Skt. Lind. 12, 24. *Cellaria uini id est* hordern *promptuaria*, Blickl. Gl. 259, 5: Ps. Surt. 143, 13. Būton hit under ðæs wīfes cǣglocan gebroht wǣre ðæt is hire hordern and hire cyste *unless it has been put into the places which the wife locks up, that is, her storeroom and her chest*, L. C. S. 77; Th. i. 418, 21. Hordærne neáh *near to the treasure-house*, Beo. Th. 5655; B. 2831. Hē is gōd hordern on tō scǣwiene *it is a good day for examining a storeroom*, Lchdm. iii. 180, 6. Heora hordernu wǣron mid monigfealdum wlencum gefylde *their storehouses were filled with manifold riches*, Blickl. Homl. 99, 16. Hordærna sum, Beo. Th. 4548; B. 2279.

horder-wice, an; *f. The office of a treasurer* or *steward*, Chr. 1137; Erl. 263, 14.

hord-fæt, es; *n. A vessel for holding treasure*:—Se Hālga Gāst wunode on ðam æþelan innoþe and on ðam gecorenan hordfæte [*of the Virgin Mary*], Blickl. Homl. 105, 15: Hy. 11, 18; Hy. Grn. ii. 294, 18. Hī geopenodon heora hordfatu [cf. Mt. 2, 11 *apertis thesauris suis*] and him lāc geoffrodon, Homl. Th. i. 78, 27: 116, 3. On heora hordfatum behīddon *absconderunt inter vasa sua*, Jos. 7, 11.

hord-geat, -gat, es; *n. A door through which a treasure is reached*:—Hwylc ðæs hordgates cǣgan cræfte ða clamme onleác *which, by the key's art, unlocked the fastenings of the door to the treasure*, Exon. 112 a; Th. 429, 28; Rä. 43, 11.

hord-gestreón, es; *n. Hoarded, accumulated wealth, that which has been acquired and now forms a 'hord'*:—Sum wæs ǣhtwelig in commedia heóld hordgestreón *there was one of large possessions, he kept in Nicomedia his stored-up wealth*, Exon. 66 a; Th. 244, 3; Jul. 22. Ne mōt hē hionane lǣdan of ðisse worulde wuhte ðon māre hordgestreóna ðonne hē hider brohte, Bt. Met. Fox 14, 21; Met. 14, 11: Beo. Th. 6175; B. 3092. Mæst hlifade ofer Hroþgāres hordgestreónum *the mast towered above the riches that had come from Hrothgar's hoard*, 3803; B. 1899. Næs him hyht tō hordgestreónum *no hope had they in hoarded wealth*, Andr. Kmbl. 2229; An. 1116.

hordian; *p.* ode *To* HOARD, *lay up* [*treasure*], *store*:—Ðæt hē for gȳtsunge uncyste nānum ōðrum syllan ne mæg ðæt hē hordaþ and nāt hwam swā swā se wītega cwæþ 'on īdel biþ ǣlc man gedrēfed se ðe hordaþ and nāt hwam hē hit gegaderaþ' *what he from the vice of avarice can give to no other he hoards, and knows not for whom, as the prophet says 'In vain is every man troubled who hoards, and knows not for whom he gathers it,'* Homl. Th. i. 66, 3. Hordiaþ eówerne gold hord on heofenum *lay up your treasure in heaven*, ii. 104, 31. DER. ge-hordian.

hord-loca, an; *m. A treasure-chest, coffer*, metaph. *the mind* [v. hord]:—Ðeáh ðe hē feohgestreón under hordlocæn ǣhte *though he had wealth in his coffer*, Exon. 66 b; Th. 245, 11; Jul. 43. Heald hordlocan hyge fæste bind *keep thy thought's treasury, fast bind thy mind*, 122 a; Th. 469, 16; Hy. 11, 3: Andr. Kmbl. 1342; An. 671.

hord-mādmum, es; *m. A valuable present, jewel*:—Healsbeága mǣst, hordmādmum, Beo. Th. 2400; B. 1198.

hord-mægen, es; *n. Abundance of wealth, riches*, Cd. 209; Th. 258, 13; Dan. 675.

hord-weard, es; *m. A guard of a hoard* or *treasure*:—Hordweard *the dragon which watched over the treasure*, Beo. Th. 4576; B. 2293: 4594; B. 2302: 5102; B. 2554: 5179; B. 2593. Hordweard hæleþa *the Danish king*, 2098; B. 1047: 3708; B. 1852. Hordwearda hryre [*of the death of the first-born in Egypt*], Cd. 144; Th. 179, 27; Exod. 35: [*of the destruction of the Egyptians in the Red Sea*], 169; Th. 210,

6; Exod. 511. Hordwearda gestreón *the wealth of the princes of Israel,* 174; Th. 220, 3; Dan. 65.

hord-wela, an; *m. Hoarded, stored-up wealth*:—Ðeáh ðe hordwelan heólde lange, Beo. Th. 4677; B. 2344.

hord-weorþung, e; *f. The honouring a person by bestowal of treasure,* Beo. Th. 1908; B. 952.

hord-wynn, e; *f. The delightful object that consists in hoarded treasure [applied to the treasure guarded by the dragon],* Beo. Th. 4533; B. 2270.

hōre, an; *f. A whore, harlot;* meretrix, Hpt. Gl. 475, 484. [*Laym. A. R.* hore: *Icel.* hóra: *O. H. Ger.* huora: *Ger.* hure.]

horeht. v. horheht.

horh, horg, es; *m. n. A clammy humour, phlegm, rheum*:—Hrog [= horg] *phlegma,* Wrt. Voc. 64, 51. Horg *flegma,* 282, 67. Sió gífernes ārist of ðæs hores wǣtan *the voracity arises from the humour of the phlegm,* L. M. 2, 16; Lchdm. ii. 196, 3. Wið langum sāre ðara tōþa þurh horh, 1, 1; Lchdm. ii. 24, 4. Gif him ofstondeþ on innan ǣnigu ceald wǣte ðonne spīwaþ hie ðæt horh . . . ðæt ofstandene þicce horh, 2, 16; Lchdm. ii. 194, 15–21. Ðonne spīwaþ hie sōna ðone þiccan horh, 2, 28; Lchdm. ii. 224, 15. Horas *pituita,* i. e. *minuta saliva,* Ælfc. Gl. 78; Som. 72, 55; Wrt. Voc. 46, 15. v. horu.

horheht; *adj. Full of phlegm, phlegmatic*:—Mid yfelre wǣtan horhehtre, L. M. 2, 28; Lchdm. ii. 224, 9: 2, 27; Lchdm. ii. 222, 26. v. horweht.

horian, Ps. Th. 27, 1, note. v. harian.

horig, horhig; *adj. Foul, dirty, defiled*:—Swā hit gedafenlīc is ðæt his reáf ne beó horig *so is it proper that his vestment be not foul,* L. Ælfc. C. 22: Th. i. 350, 21. Næs his reáf horig, Homl. Th. i. 456, 20. Mid horium reáfe, 528, 24. Mid horhgum scicelse, Th. Ap. 13, 26. [*O. E. Homl.* þat brinþ hori to clene: *Wick.* hoori *unclean*: *Chauc.* horowe; *pl*: *O. H. Ger.* horig *lutulentus, cenosus.*]

hōring, es; *m. An adulterer, fornicator*:—Hēr sindon miltestran and bearnmyrðran and fūle forlegene hōringas, Swt. A. S. Rdr. 110, 181. [Cf. *Goth.* hōrs: *Icel.* hōrr.]

HORN, es; *m.* A HORN, *a drinking-horn, a cupping-horn, a trumpet, the horn-shaped projection on the gable-end of a house* [v. Dasent's translation of Njála, plate 3, p. cvii], *a pinnacle*:—Oxan horn biþ x pæninga weorþ *an ox's horn shall be worth ten pence,* L. In. 58; Th. i. 138, 21. Se horn mīnre hǣlo *cornu salutis meæ,* Ps. Th. 17, 3. Horn stundum song *sometimes the horn sounded,* Beo. Th. 2851; B. 1423. Hwīlum teóh mid glæse odðe mid horne *draw at times with a cupping-glass or horn,* L. M. 2, 18; Lchdm. ii. 200, 13. Sete horn on ða openan scearpan *put a cupping-horn on the open scarifications,* 1, 56; Lchdm. ii. 126, 21. Gif feorrancumen man odðe fræmde būton wege gange and hē ðonne nāwþer ne hrȳme ne hē horn ne blāwe for þeóf hē biþ tō prōfianne *if a man come from a distance, or a stranger, go out of the highway, and he then neither shout nor blow a horn, he is to be tried as a thief,* L. Wih. 28; Th. i. 42, 24. Syððan hie Hygelāces horn and bȳman galan ongeáton, Beo. Th. 5879; B. 2943. ii hnæppas and iiii hornas *two bowls and four drinking-horns,* Chart. Th. 429, 31. Ne bȳman ne hornas, Exon. 57 b; Th. 206, 30; Ph. 134. Ne hēr ðisse healle hornas [horn næs, Th.] ne byrnaþ *nor here do this hall's gables burn,* Fins. Th. 7; Fin. 4. Ic wiht geseah wundorlīce horna ābitweónum hūþe lǣdan *I saw a creature [the moon] wondrously bringing spoil between its horns,* Exon. 107 b; Th. 411, 19; Rä. 30, 2. Heorot hornum trum *the hart firm-antlered,* Beo. Th. 2742; B. 1369. Óþ wigbedes hornas *usque ad cornu altaris,* Ps. Th. 117, 25. [*Goth.* haurn; *n. a horn, drinking-horn, trumpet, husk*: *O. Sax.* horn-[seli]: *O. Frs.* horn; *n. cornu, tuba*: *Icel.* horn; *n. a horn, drinking-horn, trumpet; a corner*: *O. H. Ger.* horn; *n. cornu, tuba, promontorium*: *Ger.* horn; *n.*] DER. blǣd-, drenc-, fyhte-, gūþ-horn. v. ān-horn.

horn [horh?]-ādl, e; *f. A disease of foul humours in the stomach,* L. M. 2, 27; Lchdm. ii. 222, 31.

horn-bǣre; *adj. Horned, having horns;* corniger, Ælfc. Gr. 8; Som. 7, 20.

horn-blāwere, es; *m. A horn-blower, trumpeter*: — Hornblāwere *cornicen,* Wrt. Voc. 73, 63: Ælfc. Gr. 9; Som. 9, 24. Ðǣr mihte wel bēn ābūton twenti ōðer þritte hornblaweres, Chr. 1127; Erl. 256, 36. [Cf. *Goth.* haurnja: *O. H. Ger.* horn-blāso *tubicen, cornicen.*]

horn-boga, an; *m. A bow with the ends curved like a horn* or *a bow made of horn* [?], [cf. *Icel.* horn-bogi *a horn-bow,* Cl. and Vig. Dict.]:—Lēton forþ fleógan hildenædran of hornbogan, Judth. 11; Thw. 24, 34; Jud. 222: Beo. Th. 4866: B. 2437. Ðǣr hē hornbogan [horn bogan?] hearde gebendeþ *ibi confregit cornua arcuum,* Ps. Th. 75, 3.

horn-bora, an; *m. A horn-bearer, trumpeter,* Elen. Kmbl. 107; El. 54.

horn-fisc, es; *m. A garfish, a kind of pike*: — Hornfisc plegode glād geond gārsecg, Andr. Kmbl. 740; An. 370. [*Icel.* horn-fiskr: *Dan.* hornfisk *garfish,* esox belone.]

horn-geáp; *adj. Having a wide extent between the 'horns'* [v. horn], an epithet of a building:—Tempel dryhtnes heáh and horngeáp, Andr. Kmbl. 1335; An. 668: Beo. Th. 164; B. 82. [Cf. under geápne hrōf, 1677; B. 836.]

horn-gestreón, es; *n. An abundance of pinnacles,* Exon. 124 a; Th. 477, 11; Ruin. 23.

horn-pīc, es; *n.* [?] *A pinnacle*:—Sette hine ofer hornpīc temples *statuit eum supra pinnam templi,* Lk. Skt. Lind. 4, 9.

horn-reced, es; *n. A house having 'horns'* [v. horn] or *pinnacles,* Beo. Th. 1412; B. 704.

horn-sæl, es; *n. A hall having 'horns' in its roof*:—Hornsalu, Andr. Kmbl. 2318; An. 1160: Exon. 101 b; Th. 383, 10; Rä. 4, 8. v. horn-reced, -sele.

horn-sceaða, an; *m. A pinnacle*: — Ofer hornsceaðe temples *supra pinnaculum templi,* Mt. Kmbl. Lind. 4, 5. v. sceaða.

horn-scip, es; *n. A ship having a beak* [rostrum], *a ship with a horn-like projection in the bow,* Andr. Kmbl. 547; An. 274.

horn-sele, es; *m. A building having pinnacles,* Cd. 86; Th. 109, 11; Gen. 1821. [*O. Sax.* horn-seli.] v. horn-sæl.

hornung-sunu, a; *m. A bastard,* Cot. 142. [*O. Frs.* horning *spurius, nothus*: *Icel.* hornungr *a bastard son.*] v. Grmm. R. A. 476, note.

horo-. v. horu-.

hor-pyt, -pytt, es; *m. A dirt-pit, slough* [?]:—Tō ðæm horpytte, Cod. Dipl. Kmbl. iii. 37, 21: 162, 9. v. horu.

HORS, es; *n.* A HORSE:—Geþracan hors *mannus* vel *brunnicus*: hors of stēden *vel* of asrenne *burdo,* Ælfc. Gl. 5; Som. 56, 18, 19; Wrt. Voc. 17, 23, 24. Hors hōfum wlanc, Runic pm. Kmbl. 343, 5; Rūn. 19. Ne beó gē nā swylce hors *nolite fieri sicut equus,* Ps. Th. 31, 10. Ðā wæs Hrōðgāre hors gebæted wicg wundenfeax *then for Hrothgar was a horse bitted, a steed with plaited mane,* Beo. Th. 2803; B. 1399. Ne hē on horses hrycge cuman wolde ac hē his fōtum geeode *non equorum dorso sed pedum incessu vectus,* Bd. 3, 5; S. 526, 28. Nis horses flǣsc forboden *caro equina non est prohibita,* L. Ecg. C. 38; Th. ii. 162, 16. Wið horses hreófle . . . dō on ðæt hors swā hit hātost mǣge *for a horse's leprosy . . . apply it to the horse as hot as possible,* L. M. 1, 88; Lchdm. ii. 152, 10. Gelīcnes horses and monnes, Exon. 109 b; Th. 418, 26; Rä. 37, 11. Ðī byþ swīðe dysig se ðe getrūwaþ on his horses swiftnesse *falsus equus ad salutem,* Ps. Th. 32, 15. Cwæþ mid hospe horse mete is bere *said contemptuously 'Barley is food for a horse,'* Homl. Skt. 3, 216. Man his hors under him ofsceát *his horse was shot under him,* Ors. 5, 2; Bos. 101, 42. Ic seah sroh [*the word is written in runes*] hygewloncne, Exon. 105 a; Th. 400, 1; Rä. 20, 1. Horsa steal *carceres,* Ælfc. Gl. 61; Som. 68, 54; Wrt. Voc. 39, 37. Horsa hnǣgung *neighing of horses,* Ælfc. Gl. 1; Som. 2, 38. Hē wæs mid ðǣm fyrstum mannum on ðæm lande næfde hē ðeáh mā ðonne twentig hrȳðera and twentig sceápa and twentig swȳna; ond ðæt lytle ðæt hē erede hē erede mid horsan *he [Ohthere] was among the first men of the country; and yet he had not more than twenty oxen and twenty sheep and twenty swine; and the little that he ploughed, he ploughed with horses,* Ors. 1, 1; Swt. 18, 12–15. Ða hors ōþbær *it bore away the horses,* Exon. 106 a; Th. 404, 20; Rä. 23, 10. [*O. Sax.* hros; *n*: *O. Frs.* hars, hers, hors, ros; *n*: *Icel.* hross; *m*: *O. H. Ger.* hros; *n*: *Ger.* ross.] v. cræte-hors.

Horsa, an; *m. Horsa*:—On hiera dagum Hengest and Horsa gesōhte Bretene, Chr. 449; Erl. 12, 1. Hēr Hengest and Horsa fuhton wið Wyrtgeorne ðam cyninge in ðære stōwe ðe is gecueden Agælesþrep and his brōður Horsan man ofslōg, 455; Erl. 12, 13.

hors-bǣr, e; *f. A horse-bier;* feretrum caballarium, Bd. 4, 6; S. 574, 5. [*Laym. R. Glouc.* horse-bere: *Prompt. Parv.* hors-bere *lectica,* p. 247, see the note.]

horsc; *adj. Quick, ready, active, valiant,* applied generally to mental activity [cf. snel *active*: *Icel.* snjallr *eloquent*], *wise, sagacious, sharp, quick-witted*:—Horsc *prudens,* Cot. 191, Lye. Hwylc is hæleþa ðæs horsc and ðæs hygecræftig ðæt ðæt mǣge āsecgan *who amongst men is so quick and cunning of mind as to be able to declare that,* Exon. 101 a; Th. 380, 36; Rä. 2, 1. Nis ǣnig ðæs horsc ne ðæs hygecræftig ðe ðīn frumcyn mǣge fira bearnum sweotule gesēðan, 11 a; Th. 15, 24; Cri. 241. Horsc and hreðergleáw herges wīsa *a guide of the host, prompt and prudent,* Cd. 143; Th. 178, 17; Exod. 13. On horscum wyllan *by the quick-flowing* [?] *spring,* Cod. Dipl. Kmbl. iii. 456, 15. Þurh horscne hād *through wisdom,* Exon. 8 b; Th. 4, 7; Cri. 49. Mōdum horsce *sagacious of mind,* 54 a; Th. 190, 12; Az. 72. Horsce mē heredon hilde generedon feóndon biweredon *the valiant praised me, from battle saved me, from foes defended me,* 94 a; Th. 353, 27; Reim. 19. [*O. Sax.* horsk (hugiskaft): *Icel.* horskr *wise*: *O. H. Ger.* horsc *alacer, celer, præproperus, volucer, promtus, sagax,* v. Grff. iv. 1039–42.]

hors-camb, es; *m. A horse-comb, curry-comb;* strigilis, Wrt. Voc. 83, 34.

horsc-līce; *adv. Readily, promptly, with activity [bodily or mental], wisely, prudently*:—Biþ seó tunge tōtogen forðon heó ne mæg horsclīce [MS. horslīce] wordum wrixlan wið ðone wergan gǣst *the tongue shall be rent asunder, therefore it will not be able to converse readily with the accursed spirit,* Exon. 99 b; Th. 373, 28; Seel. 116. [Hors[c]līce *prudenter,* Cot. 138, Lye. [*O. H. Ger.* horsc-līcho *naviter, strenue, agiliter.*]

hors-cræt, es; *n. A chariot;* biga, Lye.

hors-elene, -helene, an; *Elecampane;* inula helenium, Lchdm. iii. 333, col. 1. Horshelene *helena*, Ælfc. Gl. 44; Som. 64, 68; Wrt. Voc. 32, 4. Horselene, Wrt. Voc. 79, 42. See horshele, E. D. S. Plant Names.

hors-ern, es; *n. A horse-house, stable:* — Horsern *æquiale*, Ælfc. Gl. 2; Som. 55, 33; Wrt. Voc. 16, 7.

hors-gærstūn, es; *m. A meadow for the pasturing of horses:*—Onbūtan ðone horsgærstūn, Cod. Dipl. Kmbl. iii. 414, 25.

hors-here, es; *m. A mounted force;* exercitus equestris, Lye. v. here.

hors-hirde, -hyrde, es; *m. A horse-keeper, groom:*—Horshyrde *pabulator*, Ælfc. Gl. 9; Som. 56, 123; Wrt. Voc. 19, 6. Horshyrde *agaso*, Ælfc. Gr. 9; Som. 8, 37.

hors-hwæl, es; *m. A walrus:* — Swīðost hē fōr ðider tōeácan ðæs landes sceáwunge for ðǣm horschwælum for ðæm hie habbaþ swīðe æðele bān on heora tōþum *his principal object in going there, in addition to the observation of the country, was to get the walruses, for they have very excellent ivory in their tusks*, Ors. 1, 1; Swt. 17, 36. [*Icel.* hross-hwalr: *Ger.* wall-ross.]

horsian; *p.* ode *To horse, provide with horses:*—West Seaxe horsodon ðone here *the people of Wessex provided the Danes with horses*, Chr. 1015; Erl. 153, 1. Hē beád ðæt man sceolde his here metian and horsian, 1013; Erl. 148, 3: 1014; Erl. 151, 2. DER. be-, ge-horsian.

hors-minte, an; *f. Wild mint;* menthastrum, Lye. v. E. D. S. Plant Names, horse mint.

hors-syðða, an; *m:* v. hors-bǣr.

hors-þegn, es; *m.* I. *a groom:* — Horsþēn *agaso*, Ælfc. Gl. 20; Som. 59, 42; Wrt. Voc. 23, 5: *mulio*, Hpt. Gl. 438: Gl. Mett. 516. II. *the title of an officer of the royal household* [cf. marescalcus *among the Franks*]:—Ecgulf cynges horsþegn, Wulfrīc cynges horsþegn, Chr. 897; Erl. 95, 5: 96, 16. v. Kemble's Saxons in England ii. 107–8.

hors-wægn, -wǣn, es; *m. A chariot:*—Horswǣn *carpentum, currus*, Ælfc. Gl. 48; Som. 65, 68; Wrt. Voc. 34, 3.

hors-wealh, es; *m. A servant that attends to horses* [*Thorpe takes* wealh *to mean one of British origin*, v. Glossary]:—Be cyninges horsweale. Cyninges horswealh se ðe him mǣge geǣrendian ðæs wergield biþ cc scill., L. In. 33; Th. i. 122, 12.

hors-weard, e; *f. A taking care of horses:*—Horswearde healdan, L. R. S. 2; Th. i. 432, 17.

hors-weg, es; *m. A horse-road:* — Tō horsweges heale, Cod. Dipl. Kmbl. iii. 219, 2.

horu; *gen.* -wes; *m. Dirt, filth, foulness:* — Fæormaþ gyf ðǣr hwæt horwes on biþ *cleanse if there be any foulness in it*, Herb. 9, 2; Lchdm. i. 100, 4. Horewes, Mone B. 3561. Gē mid horu speówdon on ðæs andwlitan *ye foully spat on his face*, Elen. Kmbl. 594; El. 297. Mīn flǣsc is ymscrȳd mid dustes horwum *my flesh is clothed with the filth of dust*, Homl. Th. ii. 456, 10. On his blōde āþwogen fram synna horwum *washed in his blood from the impurities of sins*, Homl. Swt. 11, 297. Horewum, Homl. Th. ii. 56, 8. [*O. E. Homl.* horie, hore (of þe hore þat is cleped hordom): *O. Sax.* horu *dirt:* *O. Frs.* hore: *O. H. Ger.* horo; *gen.* horawes; *dat.* horowe, horewe, horwe, hore *limus, cenum, lutum, palustre.*] v. horh.

horu-seáþ, es; *m. A foul pit, sink:*—Gesihst ðū nū on hū miclum and on hū diópum and on hū þióstrum horaseáþe [MS. Cott. horoseáþa] ðara unþeáwa ða yfelwillendan sticiaþ *videsne igitur quanto in cœno probra volvantur*, Bt. 37, 2; Fox 188, 1.

horu-weg, es; *m. A dirty road, a lane* [?]:—Ðar horoweg ūtt sceát, Cod. Dipl. Kmbl. v. 173, 17. Horwegstige *devia semita*, Cot. 61, Lye.

horweht; *adj. Foul, filthy, dirty:*—Hine ðā lǣddon on ðone sweartan fenn and hine ðā on ða horwehtan wæter bewurpon *they led him then to the black fen and flung him into the foul water*, Guthl. 5; Gdwin. 36, 9. v. horheht.

hōs, e; *f. A bramble, thorn:* — Hōs *butrus*, Wrt. Voc. 285, 27: *rhamnus, vimen; butrus*, Cot. 25, 165, Lye. Twīgu ł hōsa *rhamnum*, Ps. Spl. C. 57, 9.

hōs, e; *f. A company, band:*—Mid mægþa hōse *with a band of maidens*, Beo. Th. 1853; B. 924. [*Goth.* hansa *multitudo:* *O. H. Ger.* hansa *cohors:* cf. Hanse *applied to an association of towns.*]

hosa, an; *m.* [or hose; *f.* (?) v. next word, and cf. other dialects]. I. *a covering for the leg*, HOSE:—Hosa *caliga* vel *ocrea*, Wrt. Voc. 81, 48. [*Prompt. Parv.* hose *caliga*, p. 248, see note: *Laym.* hose, v. 15216: *R. Glouc.* (*in the corresponding passage*) hose: *A. R.* hosen; *pl:* *Chauc.* hosen: *Icel.* hosa; *f. a covering for the leg between the knee and the ankle, serving as a kind of legging or gaiter:* *O. H. Ger.* hose; *f. caliga:* *Ger.* hose; *f. breeches, hose.*] II. *a husk, a covering for a grain* or *seed* [or is this a different word?]:—Wilnade gefylle womb his of beánbælgum ł pīsum hōsum *cupiebat implere ventrem suum de siliquis*, Lk. Skt. Lind. 15, 16. v. Jamieson's Dict. hose *the seed-leaves of grain:* *vagina, the* hose *of corn.* See also E. D. S. Reprinted Glossaries, No. 5.

hose-bend, es; *m. A hose-band, garter:* — Hosebendas *periscelides*, Lye: Hpt. Gl. 517. [Cf. *Icel.* hosna-reim.]

hosp, es; *m. Reproach, opprobrium, contempt, contumely, insult, blasphemy:*—Hosp *opprobrium*, Ps. Spl. 14, 4: 21, 5. Ða ðe forþgewēteþ of welerum mīnum nā ic dō hosp *quæ procedunt de labiis meis, non faciam irrita*, 88, 34. Hē geseah mīnne hosp āfyrran *respexit auferre opprobrium meum*, Lk. Skt. 1, 25. Nū tō dæg ic ādyde ðæra Egiptiscra hosp fram eówrum cynne *this day have I rolled away the reproach of Egypt from off you*, Jos. 5, 9. Hǣðenra hosp, Judth. 11; Thw. 24, 30; Jud. 215: Exon. 10 b; Th. 11, 16; Cri. 171: 29 a; Th. 88, 22; Cri. 1444. Hī mid hospe his lāre forsāwon *they with contumely despised his teaching*, Homl. Th. ii. 110, 5. Cwæþ mid hospe *said contemptuously*, Homl. Swt. 3, 216. Ðā hrȳmde Julianus mid hospe and earmlīce gewāt *then cried out Julian blaspheming and miserably died*, 275. Swā hwilcne swā hī tō hospe habban woldon hī cwǣdon be ðam ðæt hē wǣre Samaritanisc *whomsoever they wished to hold up to contempt, they said of him that he was a Samaritan*, Homl. Th. ii. 228, 32. Ðonne wurdon hī tō hospe gedōne *then were they made a reproach*, Ælfc. T. 12; Grn. 6, 22. Unrihtwīse habbaþ on hospe ða ðe him sindon rihtes wīsran *the unrighteous hold in contempt those that are better skilled in right than themselves*, Bt. Met. Fox 4, 87; Met. 4, 44. Hospe gereccan *to reproach opprobriously*, Exon. 70 a; Th. 260, 21; Jul. 300: 90 a; Th. 337, 17; Gn. Ex. 66. Menigfealde earfoþnyssa and hospas wolde gehwā eáðelīce forberan wið ðan ðæt hē mōste sumum rīcan men tō bearne geteald beón *anybody would put up with all kinds of hardships and affronts on condition that he might be accounted the son of some great man*, Homl. Th. i. 56, 11.

hosp-cwide, es; *m. Contemptuous, opprobrious, insulting language*, Elen. Kmbl. 1044; El. 523.

hosp-sprǣc, e; *f. Contemptuous, insulting language:* — Se eádmōda biscop ðe wē ymbe sprecaþ wæs swīðe geþyldig wið þwyrum mannum and him ne eglede heora hospsprǣc ac forbær blīðelīce ðeáh ðe him man bysmor cwǣde *the lowly-minded bishop that we are talking about was very patient with perverse people, and their contemptuous language did not vex him, but he cheerfully bore with it, though he was reviled*, Homl. Th. ii. 514, 11.

hosp-word, es; *n. A word expressing contempt, contumely, reproach, abuse:*—Ān ðæra hospworda hē forbær suwigende *one of their reproaches he bore with in silence*, Homl. Th. ii. 230, 8. Ðā hēt martianus mid his hospwordum ðæt hē sǣde his sīþ him eallum *then Martianus bade him with expressions of contempt tell his journey to them all*, Homl. Swt. 4, 283: Exon. 68 b; Th. 253, 33; Jul. 189. Ongan tō ðam hālgan hospword sprecan *began to speak words of contempt to the saint*, Andr. Kmbl. 2632; An. 1317.

hoðma, an; *m. A covering* [?], *cloud* [?], *darkness:*—Ðǣr wīsna fela wearþ inlīhted ðe ǣr under hoðman biholen lǣgon *there many things were illumined that before lay concealed in darkness*, Exon. 8 b; Th. 3, 32; Cri. 45. Rīdend swefaþ hæleþ in hoðman *knights and warriors sleep in the darkness* [*of death*], Beo. Th. 4907; B. 2458. [Cf. heóðu.]

hrā. v. hrǣw.

hrāca, an; *m. Expectoration, spittle, matter brought up when clearing the throat:*—Ðæs seócan mannes hrāca biþ maniges hiwes *the sick man's expectoration is many-coloured*, L. M. 2, 46; Lchdm. ii. 260, 13. Hyt gelīðigaþ ðone hrācan, Herb. 55, 2; Lchdm. i. 158, 10. Wið swīðlīcne hrācan, 146, 2; Lchdm. i. 270, 2. Mycelne hrācan, 158, 1; Lchdm. i. 284, 23. [*Icel.* hráki *spittle.*] v. hrǣcan.

hracca [hnacca?] *the back part of the head;* occiput, Som. [Cf. a *rack* of mutton, *dorsum ovile*, E. D. S. vol. 3, B. 18.]

hrace, an; *f:* hraca, an; *m. The throat:*—Hrace *gula*, Wrt. Voc. 283, 4: hracu, 64, 64. Ðǣr gȳnude on ðare hracan swylce ðǣr hwylc seáþ wǣre *there yawned in the throat as if there had been a pit*, Lchdm. ii. 364, col. 1. Ne hī on hracan āwiht hlūde ne cleopiaþ *non clamabunt in gutture suo*, Ps. Th. 134, 19. Ne him gāst on hracan eardaþ *neque est spiritus in ore eorum*, 113, 16. Swille ða hracan *let him swill the throat*, L. M. 1, 1; Lchdm. ii. 24, 27. Stinge him on ða hracan ðæt hē māge spīwan, 1, 18; Lchdm. ii. 62, 12. Hire man bestang sweord on ða hracan, Shrn. 56, 14. Fȳrene tungan and gyldenne hracan *a fiery tongue and a golden throat*, Salm. Kmbl. 148, 32. Hracan [bracan, Som.] *fauces*, Ælfc. Gl. 72; Som. 70, 109; Wrt. Voc. 43, 37. [*O. H. Ger.* racho *sublinguium:* *Ger.* rachen *throat, jaws.*]

hracing, e; *f. A holding back, stopping, stay;* detentio, Rtl. 65, 27. [Cf. (?) *Icel.* hrakning *bad treatment, insult.*]

hracod *laceratus*, Som. [Cf. *Icel.* hrekja *to worry, vex.*]

hradian; *p.* ode *To quicken, hasten, accelerate, forward:*—Hreaða *accelera*, Ps. Stev. 30, 3. Hreaðedon *acceleraverunt*, 15, 4. DER. for-, ge-hradian.

hradung, e; *f. A hastening;* festinatio, acceleratio, Lye.

hrǣc. v. hreác.

hrǣcan; *p.* hrǣhte *To clear the throat, hawk, spit:*—Ic hrǣce oððe ic spǣte *screo*, Ælfc. Gr. 26, 6; Som. 29, 17. Hrǣce hió him on ðæt nebb foran *huic in faciem mulier expuat*, Past. 5, 2; Swt. 43, 15. Gif hwā blōd swīðe hrǣce *if any one spit much blood*, Herb. 40, 2; Lchdm. i.

142, 1. Wið ðæt man hefelíce hrǽce *for difficulty in clearing the throat in cases of cold*, 46, 1; Lchdm. i. 148, 12, 15. [*Icel.* hrækja *to hawk, spit*: cf. *O. H. Ger.* rachison *screare.*] v. hrâca.

hrǽcea, an; *m. Clearing the throat, hawking*:— Þurh spâtl and hrǽcean *by spittle and clearing the throat*, L. M. 1, 1; Lchdm. ii. 24, 8.

hrǽcetung, e; *f. Retching, eructation*:—Wið bitere hrǽcetunge, L. M. 2, 8; Lchdm. ii. 186, 26.

hrǽc-gebræc, es; *n. A cold in the chest, hoarseness*:— Hrǽc-gebræc *branchos* [=βράγχος], Ælfc. Gl. 10; Som. 57, 23; Wrt. Voc. 19, 29. v. bræc, gebræceo.

hrǽctan; *p.* te *To eructate, retch*:—Biþ sió wamb âþened and hrǽctaþ gelôme *the stomach is extended and they eructate frequently*, L. M. 2, 28; Lchdm. ii. 224, 12.

hræc-tunge, an; *f. The uvula*:— Biþ reád ymb ða hræctunga[n?], L. M. 1, 4; Lchdm. ii. 46, 10.

hrǽcung, e; *f. A clearing of the throat, hawking*:—Gelome spǽtunga oððe hrǽcunga *frequent spittings or hawkings*, L. M. 2, 1; Lchdm. ii. 174, 21. DER. blod-, wyrs-hrǽcung.

hræd, hræð, hreð; *adj. Quick, swift, speedy, sudden, alert, rapid, prompt, active*:—Hræd oððe glæd *agilis*: hrædre *agilior*: ealra hrædost *agillimus*, Ælfc. Gr. 5; Som. 5, 6. Hræd oððe glæd *alacer*, 9, 18; Som. 9, 66. Tô hræd ierre *præceps ira*, Past. 13, 2; Swt. 79, 14, 11. Worda tô hræd, Exon. 88 a; Th. 330, 13; Vy. 50. Sum biþ hræd tæfle *one is quick at games of chance*, 79 a; Th. 297, 25; Crä. 73. Ðæt wæs hræd ǽrendraca se tylode tô secganne hys ǽrndunge ǽr ðon ðe hê lyfde *that was a quick messenger, who strove to tell his message before he lived*, Shrn. 95, 20. Se gâst is hræd *spiritus promptus est*, Mt. Kmbl. 26, 41. Níþ godes hreð [hrêð?] of heofonum *God's anger swift from heaven*, Cd. 206; Th. 255, 6; Dan. 620. Hræd and unlæt, Exon. 113 b; Th. 436, 9; Rä. 54, 11. Ðú ðe on hrædum færelde ðone heofon ymbhweorfest *qui rapido cælum turbine versas*, Bt. 4; Fox 6, 31. On hræde sprǽce *in prosam*, Bd. 5, 23; S. 648, 22. Hræde weámetta *sudden sadnesses*, L. I. P. 10; Th. ii. 318, 32. Hrade [MS. T. hræþe; Ps. Th. hraðe] fôt heora tô âgeótenne blôd *veloces pedes eorum ad effundendum sanguinem*, Ps. Spl. 13, 6. Ða hradan ðonne sint tô manianne *præcipites admonendi sunt*, Past. 39, 1; Swt. 281, 20. Mê is fenýce fôre hreðre is ðæs gores sunu gonge hrædra *more swift than I is the fen-frog in its course, the son of dirt* [*beetle*] *is more rapid in its walk*, Exon. 111 a; Th. 426, 9–12; Rä. 41, 71–2. [*Icel.* hraðr *swift, fleet*: *O. H. Ger.* hrat, hrad *velox.*]

hræd-, hræð-bíta, an; *m. An insect which eats away clothes*, etc; blata, Wrt. Voc. 281, 44.

hrædding. v. hredding.

hræd-fērness, e; *f. Quickness, rapidity*:—Behealdaþ ða hrædfērnesse ðisses heofenes *respicite cæli celeritatem*, Bt. 32, 2; Fox 116, 6.

hræd-hýdigness, e; *f. Precipitancy, hastiness*:—Ðý læs hie unnytlíce forweorpen ðæt ðæt hie sellen for hira hrædhýdignesse *ne præcipitatione hoc quod tribuunt inutiliter spargant*, Past. 44, 2; Swt. 321, 18. Ðonne oncann hê hiene selfne for ðære hrædhýdignesse ðe hê ǽr tô fela sealde *occasionem contra se impatientiæ exquirit*, 4; Swt. 325, 16. For hrædhýdignesse *præcipiti festinatione*, 49, 1; Swt. 375, 16.

hræding, e; *f. Hurry, haste*:—Be ðisum þeófum ðe man on hrædinge fûle geâxian ne mæg and man eft geâxaþ ðe hê fûl biþ *concerning the thieves that are not at once found out to be guilty, and afterwards it is found on enquiry that he is guilty*, L. Æðelst. v. 9; Th. i. 238, 29. Hí burigdon swâ swâ heó líhtlucost mihten on swylce [h]rædinge *they buried him as best they could in such a hurry*, Th. An. 123, 22.

hræd-líc; *adj. Quick, hasty, sudden, speedy, precipitate*:—Hit wǽre tô hrædlíc gif hê ðâ on cildcradole âcweald wurde *it had been precipitate, had he been slain then in the cradle*, Homl. Th. i. 82, 28. Æfter hrædlíce tíde *after a short time*, Ors. 1, 10; Swt. 44, 28. Hê wæs mid hrædlíce deáþe forgripen *morte immatura præreptus est*, Bd. 4, 23; S. 594, 36. Ðǽr forþfērde Sideman bisceop on hrædlícan deáþe *died suddenly*, Chr. 977; Erl. 127, 36.

hræd-líce; *adv. Quickly, hastily, speedily, immediately, at once, forthwith*:— Hrædlíce *actutum*, Ælfc. Gr. 38; Som. 41, 64. Hrædlíce hê âstâh of ðam wætere *confestim ascendit de aqua*, Mt. Kmbl. 3, 16: *continuo*, 13, 5, 20. Gif ðû wille mildheortnesse ûs dôn sæge ûs ðæt hrædlíce *if thou wilt do us kindness, tell us so at once*, Blickl. Homl. 233, 19. Him ðâ âþas swôron ðæt hie hrædlíce of his ríce fôren *they swore oaths to him that they would speedily march out of his kingdom*, Chr. 876; Erl. 78, 11. Hê wæs æfter ðam swíðe hrædlíce gehâlgod tô cyninge *very soon after that he was consecrated king*, 979; Erl. 129, 30. Hrædlícor *ocius*; hrædlícost *ocissime*, Ælfc. Gr. 38; Som. 42, 9. Se hit mæg hrædlícor geférran *he can perform the journey more quickly*, Blickl. Homl. 231, 24: Bd. 3, 14; S. 540, 19.

hræd-líciness, e; *f. Quickness, suddenness, rapidity, haste*:—Ða micclan welan ðe hig ǽrhwîlon âhton hê geseh on hrædlícnysse ealle gewîtan *the great riches that they formerly owned he saw all quickly pass away*, Guthl. 2; Gdwin. 14, 23.

hræd-ness, e; *f. Quickness, rapidity*:—Wundorlícre hrædnysse *with wonderful quickness*, Herb. 18, 4; Lchdm. i. 112, 1. Ond wê ðâ mid wunderlícre hreðnysse porrum ðone cyning ofercwomon *mira celeritate poro rege devicto*, Nar. 4, 4. Se on hrædnesse swâ mycele menigo heora fornom *quæ in brevi tantam ejus multitudinem stravit*, Bd. 1, 14; S. 482, 30.

hræd-sprǽce. v. un-hrædsprǽce.

hræd-wægn, -wǽn, es; *m. A swift chariot*:—Se stiórþ ðam hrædwǽne eallra gesceafta *volucrem currum regit*, Bt. 36, 2; Fox 174, 20: Bt. Met. Fox 24, 81; Met. 24, 41.

hræd-wilness, e; *f. Precipitancy, haste*:— Sió hâtheortness and sió hrædwilnes ðæt môd gebringþ on ðæm weorce ðe hine ǽr nân willa tô ne spôn *mentem impellit furor, quo non trahit desiderium*, Past. 33, 1; Swt. 215, 9. Ðeáh for hrædwilnesse tô fôþ *tamen præcipitatio impellit*, 23, 2; Swt. 177, 15: 49, 1; Swt. 375, 20. [Cf. hræd-hýdigness.]

hræd-wyrde; *adj. Quick, hasty of speech*:—Ne sceal nô tô hâtheort ne tô hrædwyrde *he must not be too passionate nor too hasty of speech*, Exon. 77 b; Th. 290, 17; Wand. 66.

hræfn, es; *m. A raven*:—Hrefn *corvus*, Wrt. Voc. 280, 33. Hræmn, Ælfc. Gr. 8; Som. 7, 35. Blac hræm *niger corvus*, 6; Som. 4, 21; Wrt. Voc. 77, 13. Noe âsende ût ǽnne hremn se hremn fleáh ðâ ût and nolde eft ongeán cirran *Noe dimisit corvum, qui egrediebatur et non revertebatur*, Gen. 8, 7. Ðâ wæs sum wild hrem . . . hê ðâ wearp ðam hremme ðone geǽttrodan hlâf *there was a wild raven . . . he threw the poisoned bread to the raven*, Homl. Th. ii. 162, 21, 23. Se wanna hrefn wælgífre fugel, Judth. 11; Thw. 24, 25; Jud. 206: Beo. Th. 6041; B. 3024. Hrefn blaca, 3606; B. 1801. Se swearta hrefn, Soul Kmbl. 108; Seel. 54. Ðǽr him hrefn nimeþ heáfodsýne slíteþ salwigpâd sâwelleásne *there shall the raven, dark-coated, pluck from him his eyes, shall tear him lifeless*, Exon. 87 b; Th. 329, 18; Vy. 36. Hræfen wan, Elen. Kmbl. 104; El. 52: Fins. Th. 69; Fins. 34. Ðǽr wæs se gûðfana genumen ðê hî ræfen hêton *there was the banner taken which they* [*the Danes*] *called the Raven* [see Asser's life of Alfred under the year 878 for an account of this banner; and see further references in Cl. and Vig. Icel. Dict. under *hrafn*], Chr. 878; Erl. 81, 3. Hrefnes briddum *pullis corvorum*, Ps. Th. 146, 10. His sunu hangaþ hrefne tô hrôðre *his son hangs a solace for the raven*, Beo. Th. 4887; B. 2448. Saluwigpâdan ðone sweartan hræfn hyrnednebban *the black raven, dusky-coated, hard-beaked*, Chr. 937; Erl. 115, 10; Æðelst. 61. Hí læccaþ eallswâ gýfre hremnas of holde dôþ *they seize just as greedy ravens do from a corpse*, L. I. P. 19; Th. ii. 328, 5. Swâ swâ grǽdige ræmmas, L. Ælfc. P. 49; Th. ii. 386, 3. Besceáwiaþ ða hrefnas *considerate corvos*, Lk. Skt. 12, 24. [*Laym.* rem: *Icel.* hrafn, hramn: *O. H. Ger.* hraban, hram *corvus, corax*: *Ger.* rabe.] DER. niht-hræfn.

hræfn, es; *m. A crab*:— Se hrefn ðe sume menn hâtaþ crabba *the 'hrefn' that some people call a crab*, Shrn. 162, 21. Hrefnes geallan and leaxes *a crab's gall and a salmon's*, L. M. 3, 2; Lchdm. ii. 308, 6, see note. Hræfnes geallan, Lchdm. iii. 2, 21. Genim cucune hrefn âdô ða eágan of and eft cucune gebring on wætre *take a live crab, put its eyes out, and put it back in the water alive*, L. M. 3, 2; Lchdm. ii. 306, 20. v. hæfern.

hræfn-cynn, es; *n. The raven-kind*:—Nân þing hrefncynnes, Lev. 11, 17.

hræfnes fôt *ravensfoot*; ranunculus gramineus, see Lchdm. iii. 333, col. 1.

hræfnes leác *orchis*, see Lchdm. iii. 333, col. 1. v. Grmm. D. M. 1144.

hrægel, hrægl, es; *n. A garment, dress, robe, rail* [in *night-rail*] *clothing*:—Gerǽwen hrægel *segmentata vestis*: þicce gewefen hrægel *pavidensis*: þenne gewefen hrægel *levidensis*: purpuren hrægel *clavus* vel *purpura*: feala hiwes hrægel *polymita*: wôgum bewerod hrægel *ralla* vel *rasilis*: geedniwod eald hrægel *interpola vestis*: geclûtad hrægel *panucla*: gediht hrægel *acupicta*: þrýlen hrægel *trilicis*, Ælfc. Gl. 63; Som. 68, 99–109; Wrt. Voc. 40, 10–19. Hrægl and hringas *robe and rings*, Beo. Th. 2394; B. 1195. Sæt ðǽr sum þearfa nacod bæd hrægles and ælmessan *a beggar sat there naked asked for a garment and an alms*, Blickl. Homl. 213, 33. Hrægles þearfa ic mê leáfum þecce *lacking raiment I cover me with leaves*, Cd. 40; Th. 53, 25; Gen. 866. Ðisses hrægles neót *use this robe*, Beo. Th. 2439; B. 1217. Wíf môton under brûnun hrægle tô hûsle gân *mulieribus licet sub nigro velamine eucharistiam accipere*, L. Ecg. C. 37; Th. ii. 162, 7. Wese hê hrægle gelíc *fiat ei sicut vestimentum*, Ps. Th. 108, 19. Mid mete and mid hrægle *with food and clothing*, Blickl. Homl. 41, 29. Se ðe mid ðon ânum hrægle wæs gegyrwed *who was dressed in that one garment*, 169, 1. On medmyclum hrægle gehealdene *moderate in dress*, 185, 17. Man hine forbærneþ mid his wǽpnum and hrægle *he is burnt with his arms and clothing*, Ors. 1, 1; Swt. 21, 8. Ðæt hrægl ðe hê ǽr ðæm þearfan sealde *the cloak that he had given to the beggar*, Blickl. Homl. 215, 18: 223, 8. Ongan his hrægl teran *began to rend his robe*, Judth. 12; Thw. 25, 28; Jud. 283. Ða hwîtan hrægl ðara engla *the white robes of the angels*, Blickl. Homl. 121, 24. Sylle earmum mannum his ealde hrægl *let him give his old clothes to the poor*, 53, 13. Hie hæfdon manige glengas deórwyrþra hrægla *they had many ornaments of costly garments*, 99, 19. Beaduscrûda betst hrægla sêlest, Beo. Th. 912; B. 454. Ân cild hreglum [hræglum, MS. C.] bewunden *infantem pannis involutum*, Lk. Skt. 2, 12. Mid godwebbenum hræglum *with purple raiment*, Blickl. Homl. 95, 20.

Hrægl *spolia*, Ps. Spl. 67, 13. [*O. Frs.* hreil, reil: *O. H. Ger.* hregil *indumentum, coturnus; pl. trophæa, spolia.*] DER. beadu-, beód-, brēc-, frum-, fyrd-, hrycg-, mere-, set-, setl-, wīte-hrægel.

hrægel-cist, e; *f. A clothes-chest, trunk*:—Ān hræglcysđ *one clothes-chest*, Chart. Th. 538, 20.

hrægel-gefrætwodness, e; *f. Elegance* or *adornment of dress*:—Hwǣr is nū heora gold and heora hrægelgefrætwodnes? L. E. I. prm; Th. ii. 396, 27.

hrægel-gewǣde, es; *n. Dress, clothes*, Cot. 118, Lye.

hrægel-hūs, es; *n. A vestry*; vestiarium, C. R. Ben. 67, Lye. [Railhus *vestiarium*, Wrt. Voc. 93, 56.]

hrægel-talu, e; *f. A fund for providing vestments*:—Ic đās land ǣcelīce sælle into sanctæ trinitatan đām hīwum tō hira beódlandæ and tō hregltalæ *ego has terras dono æternaliter familiæ æcclesiæ sanctæ trinitatis ad refectorium fratribus et ad vestimenta*, Cod. Dipl. Kmbl. v. 218, 20.

hrægel-þegn, -þēn, es; *m. An officer of the royal household* or *of a monastery*:—Ic Leófrīc hrægelþēn, Cod. Dipl. Kmbl. iii. 351, 16. Ælfrīc wæs đā hrǣlþēn, Chart. Th. 170, 10. Hē scolde setten đǣr prior of Clunni and circeweard and hordere and reilþein, Chr. 1131; Erl. 260, 12. Hræglþegn *vestiarius*, C. R. Ben. 55, Lye. [See Kemble's Saxons in England, ii. 106.]

hrægel-weard, es; *m. One who has charge of vestments*:—Hræglweard *vestiarius*, Wrt. Voc. 289, 69.

hrægl. v. hrægel.

hræglung, e; *f. Clothing*; vestitus, Ælfc. Gl. 62; Som. 68, 85; Wrt. Voc. 39, 68.

hrægn-loca = [?] brægn-loca *that which encloses the brain, the skull*, Exon. 126 b; Th. 487, 1; Rä. 72, 21.

hræm, hræmn. v. hræfn.

hrǣn *capreolus*, Som. v. hrān.

hrǣron. v. hreran.

hrætele, hrætel-wyrt *rattlewort*, Lchdm. iii. 333, col. 2.

hræđ. v. hræd.

hrǣđa. v. hrēđa.

hræđe. v. hrađe.

hrǣw, hrāw, hreáw, hrā, es; *n. m. The body of a man living or dead, a corpse, carcase, trunk, carrion*:—Līc vel hreáw *funus*, Ælfc. Gl. 85; Som. 74, 1; Wrt. Voc. 45, 25. Đū earma nū đū byst geworden đæt fūleste hreáw and wyrma mete *thou miserable thing, now art thou become a very foul corpse and food for worms*, L. E. I. prm; Th. ii. 398, 16. Hrā wundum wērig *the body weary with wounds*, Andr. Kmbl. 2556; An. 1279: 2062; An. 1033: Exon. 36 b; Th. 119, 14; Gū. 254. Hē đæt hrā gescōp *he created the body*, 8 a; Th. 2, 5; Cri. 14. Hrā biþ ācōlad *the corpse is cooled*, 59 a; Th. 213, 22; Ph. 228: Elen. Kmbl. 1767; El. 885. Hrā wide sprong *far away sprang the trunk* [*as the head was severed from it*], Beo. Th. 3181; B. 1588. Đonne flǣsc onginneþ hrāw cōlian *when the flesh, the body begins to grow cold*, Runic pm. 29; Kmbl. 345, 14. Wealdendes hrǣw *the ruler's* [*Christ*] *body*, Rood Kmbl. 106; Kr. 53: 144; Kr. 72. Đā lōcade hē on his āgenne līchoman swā swā on uncūþne hreáw *he gazed on his own body as on an unknown corpse*, Shrn. 52, 4. Đa sticca Simones hreáwes *the pieces of Simon's carcase*, Homl. Th. i. 380, 34. Sang se wanna fugel hrǣs on wēnan *the dusky fowl sang hoping for carrion*, Cd. 93; Th. 119, 25; Gen. 1985. Furseus đā beseah tō his līchaman swilce tō uncūþum hreáwe, Homl. Th. ii. 346, 7. Đa līchoman heáhfædera hrā *the bodies, the patriarchs' corpses*, Andr. Kmbl. 1581; An. 792. Heora fædera hreáw *cadavera patrum*, Num. 14, 33. Hrǣ, hrǣw [other MSS. hrāw, hrā] *corpses*, Chron. 937; Erl. 115, 9; Æđelst. 60. Reócende hrǣw *reeking carcases*, Judth. 12; Thw. 26, 7; Jud. 314. Hrǣwas ł đa deáþlīcan đīnra þeówana *morticina servorum tuorum*, Ps. Lamb. 78, 2. Deádra hrǣwum *over the corpses of the dead*, Cd. 144; Th. 180, 6; Exod. 41. [*O. Sax.* hrēo: *O. Frs.* hrē: *Icel.* hræ *a corpse, carrion*: *O. H. Ger.* hrēo *cadaver, funus*: cf. *Goth.* hraiwa-dubo.]

hrǣw *raw*. v. hreáw.

hrā-fyl, -fyll, es; *m. Slaughter*, Beo. Th. 559; B. 277.

hragan. v. ofer-hragan.

hrā-gīfre; *adj. Greedy for corpses, deadly*:—Hrāgyfra *funestus*, Cot. 90, Lye. [Cf. wæl-gīfre.]

hrāgra, an; *m. A heron*:—Hrāgra *ardea*, Ælfc. Gl. 36; Som. 62, 111; Wrt. Voc. 29, 9: 63, 13. Hrāgra *larum*, Shrn. 29, 18. [*O. H. Ger.* raiger, regera *ardea*: *Ger.* reiher *a heron*.]

hrā-līc; *adj. Deadly* [?], *funereal* [?]; funebris, Cot. 88, Lye. [*O. H. Ger.* rē-līh *funestus, funebris*.]

hramma, an; *m. Cramp, spasm*:—Hramma *spasmos*, Ælfc. Gl. 10; Som. 57, 12; Wrt. Voc. 19, 21. Gif hwylcum men hramma derige *if cramp annoy any man*, Herb. 94, 11; Lchdm. i. 206, 21. Wiđ hramman, 153, 5; Lchdm. i. 280, 5. [Cf. *Icel.* hrammr *that with which one clutches, a bear's paw*.] v. hremman.

hramsan; *pl. Ramsons, broad-leaved garlic*; allium ursinum, Lchdm. iii. 333, col. 2. [See Skeat, Etymol. Dict.]

hran, hron, es; *m. A whale, a mussel* [?]:—Hran *ballena*, Wrt. Voc. 65, 62. Hron *ballena* vel *pilina*, 281, 55. Hran *musculus*, Ælfc. Gl. 102; Som. 77, 78; Wrt. Voc. 56, 1. On huntunge hranes *in venationem balenæ*, Coll. Monast. Th. 24, 25. Hēr beóþ oft fangene seolas and hronas and mereswȳn *capiuntur sæpissime et vituli marini, et delphines necnon et ballenæ*, Bd. 1, 1; L. 473, 16. Hronesnæs, Beo. Th. 5603, 6264; B. 2805, 3136.

hrān, es; *m. A reindeer*:—Se byrdesta sceall gyldan fīf hrānes fell *a man of the highest rank has to pay five reindeer skins*, Ors. 1, 1; Swt. 18, 20. Đa deór hī hātaþ hrānas; đara wǣron syx stælhrānas: đa beóþ swȳđe dȳre mid Finnum, forđæm hȳ fōþ đa wildan hrānas mid *those deer they call 'rein;' six of them* [*Ohthere's*] *were decoys: those are very precious among the Fins, for they catch the wild reindeer with them*, 10–12. [*Icel.* hreinn, see Cl. and Vig. Dict.]

hrand-spearwa, an; *m. A sparrow*:—Hrondsparwas ł staras *passeres*, Mt. Kmbl. Lind. 10, 29.

hran-fisc, es; *m. A whale*:—Hronfixas, Beo. Th. 1085; B. 540.

hran-mere, es; *m. The whale-mere, the sea*:—Hronmere, Bt. Met. Fox 5, 19; Met. 5, 10.

hran-rād, e; *f. The whale-road, the sea*:—Ūs bær on hranrāde heáhstefn naca *us the high-stemmed bark bore on the sea*, Andr. Kmbl. 531; An. 266: 1267; An. 634. Geond hronrāde *throughout the ocean*, Cd. 10; Th. 13, 19; Gen. 205: Beo. Th. 19; B. 10: Andr. Kmbl. 1641; An. 822.

hrađe, hræđe, hređe; *adv. Quickly, immediately, at once, soon, forthwith, straightway*:—Gā hrađe on đa strǣta *exi cito in plateas*, Lk. Skt. 14, 21: 16, 6. Cūþ is đætte hrađe Drihten đæs đe hē of đam fulwihtes bæþe eode đā fæstte hē sōna *it is known that the Lord directly after he came from baptism at once fasted*, Blickl. Homl. 27, 23. Đā wæs hrađe geworden đæt hē gelȳfde *then immediately it came to pass that he believed*, 153, 13. Gif heó hrađe gǣþ *if she walks quickly*, Lchdm. iii. 144, 8. Hrađe æfter *directly after*, Ps. Th. 59, 3. Mē hrađe syđđan gefultuma *ad adjuvandum me festina*, 69, 1. Tō hrađe *too soon*, Bt. 3, 1; Fox 4, 23. Hē wæs Godes bearn swā hrađe swā hē mannes bearn wearþ *he was the Son of God so soon as he became the Son of man*, Homl. Th. ii. 526, 1. Swīđe hræđe *repente*, Past. 21, 7; Swt. 166, 14. Hēton ūt hræđe æþeling lǣdan *they bade quickly lead out the noble one*, Andr. Kmbl. 2545; An. 1274: 3039; An. 1522. Đū ealne hræđe hefon ymbhwearfest *rapido cælum turbine versas*, Bt. Met. Fox 4, 6; Met. 4, 3. Đā wæs hāten hređe *then was bidden straightway*, Beo. Th. 1986; B. 991. Hređe siđđan *directly after*, Bt. Met. Fox 25, 94; Met. 25, 47. Ne scule gē hit nō đȳ hrađor þurhteón *none the sooner shall ye accomplish it*, Ps. Th. 4, 5: Cd. 212; Th. 263, 2; Dan. 756. Nō hē fleótan meahte hrađor on holme *not more swiftly than I could he float on the ocean*, Beo. Th. 1090; B. 543. Hī hogedon hū hī unriht hrađost ācwǣdon *they considered how soonest they might utter iniquity*, Ps. Th. 72, 6. Swā hwilc swā gearo wearþ hrađost *whosoever was soonest ready*, Chr. 755; Erl. 51, 3. Hē ārās swā hē hrađost meahte *he arose as quickly as ever he could*, Exon. 49 a; Th. 168, 24; Gū. 1082. And hrađost is tō cweđenne *in short*, Swt. A. S. Rdr. 106, 60. Đæt is nū hrađost tō secganne, Bt. 7; Fox 60, 14. [Cf. *Icel.* ok er þat skjótast af honum at segja.] [*Laym. Orm. A. R. Piers P. Chauc.* raþe; *compar.* raþer: *Icel.* hratt *quickly*; *superl.* (sem) hrađast: *O. H. Ger.* hrado *celeriter, protinus, continuo*; *compar.* hrador; *superl.* hradost *contissime*.]

hrađer. v. hređer.

hrađian. v. hradian.

hrāw. v. hrǣw.

hrā-wērig; *adj. Wearied in body*, or *grievously wearied, wearied to death* [cf. hrā-līc]:—Ic hæle hrāwērig gewīte on longne sīþ *I, a man sore wearied, shall depart on a long journey*, Exon. 63 b; Th. 235, 8; Ph. 554.

hreác, es; *m. A heap, stack, rick, reek* [in dialects, v. E. D. S. Old Country and Farming Words, ii, iii, and Halliwell's Dict.]:—Hreác *acervus*, Wrt. Voc. 89, 44. Healfne æcer gauolmǣde on hiora āgienre hwīle and đæt on hreáce gebringan [*to mow*] *half an acre of 'gafol-meadow' in their own time and to bring the hay together in a reek*, Chart. Th. 145, 4. Hreácas *acervi*, Cot. 18, Lye. [*Prompt. Parv.* hreek *acervus*: *Chauc. Wick.* rekes; *pl*: *Icel.* hraukr *in* torf-hraukr *a peat-stack*.] v. hrycce.

hreác-copp, hreác-mete *food given to the labourers on completing a rick*, L. R. S. 21; Th. i. 440, 28, 27. The Latin version has *macoli summitas, caput macholi* for the former, and *firma ad macholum faciendum* for the latter. Thorpe in explanation of the passage quotes the following from Spelman 'Habetur macholum pro ipsa frugum seu garborum strue, quam hodie dicimus *a reack or stack of corn*. Hujus olim ad constructionem epulari solebant agricolæ et messores.'

hreám, es; *m. A cry, outcry, hue and cry, crying, tumult, uproar*:—Đæra Sodomitiscra hreám ys gemenigfyld *clamor Sodomorum multiplicatus est*, Gen. 18, 20: Past. 55; Swt. 427, 33: Cd. 229; Th. 309, 28; Sat. 717. Đam hālgan were wæs geþuht đæt đæs gefeohtes hreám mihte beón gehȳred geond ealle eorþan *it seemed to the holy man that the uproar of the conflict could be heard over all the earth*, Homl. Th. ii. 336, 17: Cd.

166; Th. 206, 10; Exod. 449: Beo. Th. 2608; B. 1302. Hreám and wōp *crying and weeping*, Blickl. Homl. 61, 36: 115, 15. Of đam leahtre cymþ hreám dyslīc dyrstignys and mansliht *from that sin comes uproar, foolhardiness and manslaughter*, Homl. Th. ii. 220, 14. Hās ys for hreáme *raucus est præ clamatione*, Th. An. 19, 31. Julianus mid anþræcum hreáme forswealt *Julian with a horrible cry died*, Homl. Th. i. 452, 16. Đa heorde mid hreáme bewerian *to defend the flock with outcry*, L. I. P. 19; Th. ii. 326, 10. Gif hwā þeóf gemēte and hine his þances āweg lǽte būton hreáme . . . and gif hwā hreám gehȳre and hine forsitte *if any one find a thief and voluntarily let him escape without hue and cry . . . and if any one hear hue and cry and disregard it*, L. C. S. 29; Th. i. 392, 14-17: 170, 10 [MS. hearme]. [*Laym.* ræm, ream: *Orm.* ræm: *A. R.* ream: cf. *Icel.* hreimr (= hreymr?) *a scream, cry*: hraumi *a noisy fellow.*] v. hrēman.

hreámig. v. hrēmig.

hreán:—Wiđ hreán *for indigestion* [?], L. M. 2, 41; Lchdm. ii. 252, 16. Somner gives *phthisis*, but see hreáw, and cf. *Icel.* hrāi *crudeness.*

hreáđe-mūs, e; *f. A mouse ornamented, furnished with wings* [cf. hreóđan?], *a bat*:—Tōsnidenre hreáđemūse blōd *the blood of a bat cut up*, L. M. 2, 33; Lchdm. ii. 236, 17. Swilce eác cwōman hreáđemȳs . . . hæfdon hie eác đa hreáđemȳs tēþ in monna gelīcnesse *sed et vespertilionum vis ingens . . . habentes dentes in morem hominum*, Nar. 15, 5-8. [Cf. hrēre-mūs.]

hreáw *a body*. v. hrǽw.

HREÁW, hrǽw [*also written* hreów]; *adj.* RAW, *uncooked*:—Ne ne eton gē of đam nān þing hreówes *non comedetis ex eo crudum quid*, Ex. 12, 9. Ne ete gē of đam lambe nān þing hreáw, Homl. Th. ii. 264, 5. Syle etan ođđe gesodene ođđe hrǽwe *give* [*the plant*] *to eat either sodden or raw*, Herb. 136, 2; Lchdm. i. 254, 5. Ete đara hundteóntig hreáwra *eat a hundred of them* [*lentils*] *raw*, L. M. 2, 13; Lchdm. ii. 190, 17. Meng wiđ hreáw ægru *mix with raw eggs*, 1, 39; Lchdm. ii. 102, 7. Gif hī mon hreáwe swylgeþ *if they are swallowed raw*, L. Med. ex Quadr. 4, 10; Lchdm. i. 344, 16. Flǽscmettas hreáwe *carnes crudas*, Coll. Monast. Th. 29, 13. [*Icel.* hrár *raw*: *Dan.* raa: *Swed.* rå: *Du.* raauw: *O. H. Ger.* rou *crudus*: *Ger.* roh.]

hreá-wīc, es; *n. A place of the dead, a place where people lie slain*, Beo. Th. 2432; B. 1214. [Cf. wæl-stōw.]

HREDDAN; *p.* de *To* RID, *take away, save, liberate*:—God hī hredde wiđ heora fȳnd *God rid them of*, or *saved them from, their enemies*, Homl. Th. i. 312, 9. Hrede ł nere *eripe*, Blickl. Gl. Ps. 58, 2. Būtan đū ūsic æt đam leódsceaþan hreddan wille *unless thou wilt save us from the destroyer*, Exon. 11 b; Th. 17, 23; Cri. 274. Hwīlum ic wrāđđum sceal stefne mīnre forstolen hreddan *sometimes with my voice I shall save the stolen from enemies*, 104 a; Th. 396, 4; Rä. 15, 18. Ōþ đæt him god wolde þurh hryre hreddan heá rīce *until god would take from him by death his exalted power*, Cd. 208; Th. 258, 5; Dan. 671. [*Orm.* redden: *O. Frs.* hredda, reda: *O. H. Ger.* rettan, Grff. 2, 471; *Ger.* retten.] DER. ā-hreddan.

hredding, e; *f. Saving, salvation, liberation*:—Ūs becom deáþ and forwyrd þurh wīf and ūs becom līf and hredding þurh wimman *death and destruction came upon us by a woman, and by a woman came life and salvation*, Homl. Th. i. 194, 33. His āgen līf syllan for đæs folces hreddinge *to give his own life for the redemption of the people*, 240, 14. Ongunnon for his hreddinge biddan *began to pray for his liberation*, 534, 27. Heó mid hreáme hyre hræddinge ofclypode *the result of her outcry was to save her*, Homl. Swt. 2, 219.

hrēd-mōnaþ. v. hrēđ-mōnaþ.

hrēfan; *p.* de *To roof*:—Hē lǽt it rēfen *he had it roofed*, Chr. 1137; Erl. 263, 8. v. ge-hrēfan.

hrefl, Wrt. Voc. 66, 12. v. hrisil.

hrefn. v. hræfn.

hrēh. v. hreóh.

hrem. v. hræfn.

hrēman. v. hrȳman. [*From the meaning the word would seem to correspond to O. Sax.* hrōmian: *O. H. Ger.* hrōmian, hruomian *gloriari, jactare; but the adjective* hreámig, hrēmig, *though especially in the compound* sige-hrēmig *it agrees in meaning with the O. Sax.* hrōmag: *O. H. Ger.* hrōmag, hruomag *gloriosus*: siguhrōmlīh *triumphalis, points to a connection with the noun* hreám: *the verb is therefore given under* hrȳman, *the most usual form under which the verb connected with* hreám *in form and meaning occurs.*]

hrēmig, hreámig; *adj. Clamorous* [*from joy* or *grief*], *exultant, lamenting, boasting, vaunting*:—Blissum hrēmig *exultant*, Andr. Kmbl. 3394; An. 1701: Elen. Kmbl. 2273; El. 1138: Exon. 48 b; Th. 168, 18; Gū. 1079: 57 b; Th. 206, 14; Ph. 126: 64 b; Th. 237, 19; Ph. 592. Gehþum hrēmig *lamenting*, 98 a; Th. 367, 18; Seel. 9. Hūþe hrēmig *exulting in spoil*, Beo. Th. 248; B. 124: 3768; B. 1882: 4114; B. 2054: Elen. Kmbl. 297; El. 149: Andr. Kmbl. 1728; An. 866. Wuldrum hrēmge *gloriously exulting*, Exon. 8 b; Th. 4, 17; Cri. 54. Wīges hreámige [*the* e *is written above the line*] *boasting of battle*, Chr. 937; Erl. 115, 8; Æđelst. 59. Hrēmge [*so the* MS.], Beo. Th. 4715; B. 2363. DER. sige-hrēmig. v. hrēman.

hremman; *p.* de *To hinder, obstruct, cumber*:—Forceorf hit tō hwī hremþ hit đisne stede *cut it down; why cumbereth it this place?* Homl. Th. ii. 408, 4. Ūre unlustas and leahtras đe ūs hremaþ *our evil desires and vices that hinder us*, i. 156, 12. Đī læs đe seó smeáung đæra ǽhta hī æt đære lāre hremde *lest the contemplation of the possessions should be a hindrance to them in learning*, 60, 30: 394, 14. Ne hremmaþ mīnne martyrdōm *hinder not my martyrdom*, 592, 7. [Cf. *Icel.* hremma *to clutch.*]

hremming, e; *f. A hindering, hindrance, obstruction, obstacle, impediment*:—Nū is đære eorþan sinewealtnys and đære sunnan ymgang hremming đæt se dæg ne byþ on ǽlcum earde gelīce lang *now the roundness of the earth and the course of the sun is an obstacle to the day being equally long in every country*, Lchdm. iii. 258, 11. Mycele swȳđor sceal se sōþa Godes cempa būton ǽlcere hremminge hræđe gehȳrsumian Cristes sylfes bebodum *much more shall the true soldier of God, without any hindrance, at once obey the commands of Christ himself*, Basil admn. 2; Norm. 34, 23.

hremn. v. hræfn.

hrenian *redolere*, Scint. 28, Lye.

hreoce *rubellio, rutilus*, Lye. v. reohhe.

HREÓD, es; *n. A* REED:—Hwī fērde gē on wēstene geseón đæt hreód đe byþ mid winde āstyred *quid existis in desertum videre harundinem vento moveri*, Lk. Skt. 7, 24: Mt. Kmbl. 11, 7. For cynegyrde him hreód forgeáfon *gave him a reed for a sceptre*, Homl. Th. ii. 252, 27. Hreódes spīr *a spike of a reed*, L. M. 2, 51; Lchdm. ii. 266, 10. Grōwnys hreódes and ricsa *viror calami et junci*, Bd. 3, 23; S. 554, 23. Synd đǽr manige eáland and hreód *there are there many islands and reeds*, Guthl. 3; Gdwin. 20, 6. [*O. Dutch* ried: *O. H. Ger.* reod, ried, riet *carectum, carex.*]

hreód-bedd, es; *n. A reed-bed*:—Đā wæs đǽr on middan đam mere sum hreódbed *there was in the middle of the mere a reed-bed*, Guthl. 9; Gdwin. 50, 15. Heó āsette hyne on ānum hreódbedde be đæs flōdes ōfre *exposuit eum in carecto ripæ fluminis*, Ex. 2, 3. Đeós wyrt biþ cenned on dīcon and on hreódbeddon *this plant* [*lion-foot*] *is produced in dikes and reed-beds*, Herb. 8, 1; Lchdm. i. 98, 13.

hreódeum [= hreódegum? cf. hreódiht] *reedy, covered with rough grass* [?]:—In heágum mōrum and in hreódeum [other MS. hrēþum] *in arduis asperisque montibus*, Bd. 4, 27; S. 604, 27.

Hreód-ford *Redbridge, Hants*, Bd. 4, 16; S. 584, 29.

hreódiht; *adj. Reedy*:—On đone hreódihtan mōr, Cod. Dipl. Kmbl. iii. 121, 20.

hreód-wæter, es; *n. Fenny land where reeds are growing*:—Đā wæs đæt land eall swā wē gefērdon ādrigad and fien and hreádwæteru *palus erat sicca et ceno habundans*, Nar. 20, 23.

hreód-writ, es; *n. A reed for writing, pen*; calamus scribæ, Ps. Spl. C. 44, 2.

hreóf; *adj. Rough, rugged, scabby, leprous*:—Hreóf *leprosus*, Mt. Kmbl. Rush. 8, 2. Đonne biþ se līchoma hreóf đonne se bryne đe on đæm innoþe biþ ūtāslihþ tō đære hȳde *fervor intimus usque ad cutis scabiem prorumpit*, Past. 11, 5; Swt. 71, 5. In hūse simonis đæs hreófan *in domo Simonis leprosi*, Mt. Kmbl. Rush. 26, 6. Symones hreáfes, Mk. Skt. Lind. 14, 3. Lǽcedōm wiđ hreófum līce *a recipe for a scabby body*, L. M. 1, 32; Lchdm. ii. 78, 1. Is đæs hiw gelīc hreófum stāne *it looks like a rough stone*, Exon. 96 b; Th. 360, 20; Wal. 8. Monige hreófe [hreáfo, Lind.] *multi leprosi*, Lk. Skt. Rush. 4, 27: 17, 12: Elen. Kmbl. 2428; El. 1215: Blickl. Homl. 177, 15, Hreófum, Andr. Kmbl. 1155; An. 578. [*Icel.* hrjúfr *rough, scabby*: *O. H. Ger.* riob *leprosus.*]

hreófl, hreófol, e; *f. Roughness of the skin, scabbiness, leprosy*:—Đonne bī đam sceabbe suīđe ryhte sió hreófl getācnaþ đæt wōhhǽmed *in scabie fervor viscerum ad cutem trahitur, per quam recte luxuria designatur*, Past. 11, 5; Swt. 71, 4. Hreóful [Lind. hriófol] *lepra*, Mt. Kmbl. Rush. 8, 3. Hriófal [Lind. riófol], Mk. Skt. Rush. 1, 42: Lk. Skt. Lind. 5, 13. Wer full hrióflе *vir plenus lepra*, 12. Wiđ horses hreófle . . . gif sió hreófol sīe micel, L. M. 1, 88; Lchdm. ii. 156, 10, 13. Wiđ hreóf[l]e, L. Med. ex Quadr. 6, 10; Lchdm. i. 352, 18. Seđe ete his līchaman hreófel *qui corporis sui scabiem edit*, L. Ecg. P. iv. 52; Th. ii. 218, 30.

hreófl; *adj. Leprous*:—Đā brohte hē hig [his hand] forþ hreófle swā hwīt swā snāw *quam protulit leprosam instar nivis*, Ex. 4, 6. v. next word.

hreófla, an; *m. A leper*:—Đā geneálǽhte ān hreófla tō him *ecce leprosus veniens*, Mt. Kmbl. 8, 2. On simones hūse ānes hreóflan, Mk. Skt. 14, 3. Đæs hreóflan, Mt. Kmbl. 26, 6. Moyses ǽ forbeád tō hrepenne ǽnigne hreóflan *the law of Moses forbade to touch any leper*, Homl. Th. i. 122, 5. Hreóflan synt gehǽlede *leprosi mundantur*, Lk. Skt. 7, 22.

hreófla, an; *m. Leprosy, scabbiness*:—Se hreófla him fram fērde *lepra discessit ab illo*, Lk. Skt. 5, 13: Mt. Kmbl. 8, 3: Homl. Th. i. 120, 15. Swā mycel hreófla *tanta scabies*, Bd. 5, 2; S. 614, 44. Geseah đæt hire lîchama wæs âfylled mid hreóflan *eam vidisset perfusam lepra*, Num. 12, 10. Wiđ sceápa hreóflan *against scab in sheep*, Lchdm. iii. 56, 19.

hreóflia. v. hreóf-lig.

hreóf-lîc; *adj. Having elephantiasis*; elephantinus, Hpt. Gl. 519. v. next word.

hreóf-lig; *adj. Leprous*:—Đâ com sum hreóflig *there came a certain leprous man*, Homl. Th. i. 120, 11. Se hreoflia *the leper*, 122, 10. Getâcnode đes hreóflia man eal mancyn đe wæs âtelîce hreóflig . . . Lâđlîc biþ đæs hreóflian lîc *this leper betokened all mankind that was foully leprous . . . Loathsome is the body of the leper*, 16–21: 33. Wacode ealle đa niht mid đam wædlian hreóflian, Homl. Swt. 3, 486. Reóflium menn gelîc *like a leper*, Homl. Th. ii. 178, 13. Martinus getâcnode ǽnne hreóflinne mannan, 512, 5.

hreóf-ness, e; *f. Leprosy*:—Hreófnis swâ snâw *lepra quasi nix*, Num. 12, 10.

hreóh, hrēh; *n. Roughness of weather, storm, tempest*:—Flôd ł hrēh miđđȳ âwarþ *inundatione facta*, Lk. Skt. Lind. 6, 48. Sumne sceal hungor âhîđan sumne sceal hreóh fordrîfan *famine shall waste one man, a storm drive another to destruction*, Exon. 87 a; Th. 328, 10; Vy. 15. Ic bîde đæs beornes đe mē bôte eft mindôm and mægenes hreóh *expectabam eum, qui me salvum faceret a pusillo animo et tempestate*, Ps. Th. 54, 7. v. hreóh-full, and next word.

HREÓH; *adj.* ROUGH, *fierce, savage, rough* [*of the weather, the sea, etc.*], *stormy, tempestuous, disturbed* [*of the mind*]:—Hreóh weder *tempestas*, Mt. Kmbl. 16, 3. Heom on becom swîđe hreóh weder, Chr. 1075; Erl. 212, 23. Hit wæs hreóh sǽ *mare exsurgebat*, Jn. Skt. 6, 18. Flôd hreóh under heofonum, Cd. 69; Th. 83, 29; Gen. 1387: Andr. Kmbl. 933; An. 466: 3083; An. 1544. Hreóh wæter, Ps. Th. 68, 1. Ne wedra gebregd hreóh under heofonum *non ibi tempestas nec vis furit horrida venti*, Exon. 56 b; Th. 201, 18: Ph. 58. Brond hreóh onetteþ *the flame hurries fierce*, 59 a; Th. 212, 19; Ph. 217. Hrióh biþ đonne seó đe ǽr gladu onsiéne wæs *rough then is the sea that before was smooth*, Bt. Met. Fox 5, 20; Met. 5, 10. Ân wiht is hreóh and rēđe *there is a creature fierce and fell*, Exon. 127 b; Th. 491, 20; Rä. 81, 2. Yrre gebolgen hreóh and hygeblind *angry, cruel and blind of mind*, 66 b; Th. 246, 13; Jul. 61: 74 b; Th. 278, 9; Jul. 595. Hreóh and heorogrim, Beo. Th. 3132; B. 1564. Wæs him hreóh sefa ege from đam eorle *troubled was his mind, he was in fear of the man*, Bt. Met. Fox 1, 142; Met. 1, 71. Ne mæg wērig môd wyrde wiđstondan ne se hreó hyge helpe gefremman *a weary heart cannot withstand fate nor the troubled mind afford help*, Exon. 76 b; Th. 287, 18; Wand. 16: 94 b; Th. 354, 9; Reim. 43. Đâ wæs beorges weard on hreóum môde *then became the hill-ward of fierce mood*, Beo. Th. 5156; B. 2581. On đære hreón sǽ *turbato mari*, Past. 9; Swt. 59, 2. On hreón môde *troubled*, Beo. Th. 2619; B. 1307. Wē geliden hæfdon ofer hreóne hrycg *we had sailed over a troubled sea*, Exon. 20 b; Th. 53, 31; Cri. 859. Hreó hæglfare *a hailstorm*, 78 a; Th. 292, 26; Wand. 105. Hreó wǽron ȳđa *rough were the billows*, Beo. Th. 1101; B. 548: Andr. Kmbl. 1496; An. 749: Exon. 55 a; Th. 194, 19; Az. 141. Hreóra wǽga, 56 b; Th. 200, 24; Ph. 45. Đonne seó sǽ hreóhost byþ đonne wôt hē gewiss smelte wedere tôwæard *when the sea is roughest then he knows certainly that fair weather is to come*, Shrn. 179, 18. [*Laym.* reh, ræh: *O. Sax.* hrē.] v. hreów.

hreohehe = **reohhe**, q. v.

hreóh-full; *adj. Stormy*:—Hreóhfull geár *a stormy year*, Lye. v. hreóh.

hreóh-môd; *adj. Savage, fierce of mind, ferocious, troubled in mind*:—Hât and hreóhmôd *angry and savage*, Beo. Th. 4581; B. 2296. Hreóhmôd wæs se hǽđena þeóden *fierce of heart was the heathen prince*, Cd. 186; Th. 231, 4; Dan. 242. Se þeóden hreóhmôd *the prince with troubled heart*, Beo. Th. 4270; B. 2132. v. hreóh.

hreóhmôd-ness, e; *f. Ferocity*, Som.

hreóh-, hreó-ness, e; *f. Roughness of the weather, of the sea, storm, tempest*:—Ofer eów cymeþ mycel storm and hreóhnes *tempestas vobis superveniet*, Bd. 3, 15; S. 541, 33. Hreánis *tempestas*, Mt. Kmbl. Rush. 16, 3. On ymbhwyrfte his hreóhnys strang *in circuitu ejus tempestas valida*, Ps. Spl. 49, 4: Homl. Th. ii. 18, 5. Micel hreóhnys on đære sǽ, 378, 14. Seó hreóhnys wearþ gestilled *the tempest was stilled*, i. 246, 10, 1. Ic geseó đæt đâs brôđor synd geswencede of đisse sǽwe hreónesse *I see that these brethren are wearied from the roughness of the sea*, Blickl. Homl. 233, 26. On đissere cealdan hreóhnysse *in this cold storm*, Homl. Swt. 11, 187. Gif hwâ hreóhnysse on rēwytte þolige . . . seó hreóhnys byþ forboden *if any one suffer stormy weather in rowing . . . the rough weather will be stopped*, Herb. 171, 3; Lchdm. i. 302, 5. Wiđ hagol and hreóhnysse . . . heó âwendeþ hagoles hreóhnysse, 176; Lchdm. i. 308, 10, 14, 16, 23. Hē dyde swîđe hreónesse đære sǽwe *he made the sea very rough*, Blickl. Homl. 235, 5. On đissere woruldе hreóhnyssum *in the storms of this world*, Homl. Th. ii. 384, 26.

hreól *a reel*; alibrum, Ælfc. Gr. 111; Som. 79, 55; Wrt. Voc. 59, 26. [*Prompt. Parv.* reel, womannys instrument *alabrum*.]

Hreopa-, Hreope-, Hrypa-dûn, e; *f. Repton*, Chr. 755; Erl. 52, 1: 874; Erl. 76, 21: 875; Erl. 76, 33. Gûþlâc fērde tô mynstre đe ys gecweden Hrypadûn and đǽr đa gerȳnelîcan sceare onfēng Sce Petres *Guthlac went to a monastery that is called Repton and there received the mystical tonsure of St. Peter*, Guthl. 23; Gdwin. 16, 20.

hreórig; *adj. Ruinous*:—Hrôfas sind gehrorene hreórge torras *the roofs are fallen, the towers ruinous*, Exon. 124 a; Th. 476, 6; Ruin. 3.

hreósan; *p.* hreás; *pl.* hruron; *pp.* hroren *To fall* [*rapidly, headlong*], *fall down, go to ruin*; ruere, corruere:—Ic hreóse *ruo*; tô hreósenne *ruiturus*, Ælfc. Gr. 28; Som. 30, 54. His weorc hrȳst tô micclum lyre *his work falls to great perdition*, Homl. Th. i. 368, 25. Đâ hrȳsþ se stôl nyđer *then the throne falls down*, L. I. P. 4; Th. ii. 308, 2. On hærfest hrēst and fealuwaþ *in autumn it falls and fades*, Bt. Met. Fox 11, 116; Met. 11, 58. Twegen unþeáwas hreósaþ on ǽnne man *duorum vitiorum languor irruit*, Past. 62, 1; Swt. 457, 9. Wongas hreósaþ *the plains shall sink away*, Exon. 19 b; Th. 51, 5; Cri. 811. Hreósaþ tôbrocene burgweallas, 22 a; Th. 60, 30; Cri. 977. Hreósaþ heofonsteorran *the stars of heaven shall fall*, 23 a; Th. 64, 27; Cri. 1044. Đǽr ne hægl ne hrîm hreósaþ tô foldan, 56 b; Th. 201, 23; Ph. 60. Heofon and eorþe hreósaþ tôgadore *heaven and earth shall rush together*, Andr. Kmbl. 2875; An. 1440. Ne hreósaþ hî tô hrusan hearde gebîged *non est ruina maceriæ*, Ps. Th. 143, 8. Swâ đæt hē hreás and feóll on eorþan *ita ut corruens in terram*, Bd. 4, 31; S. 610, 13. Gomela Scylfing hreás blâc *the aged Scylfing fell down pale*, Beo. Th. 4969; B. 2488: 5654; B. 2831. Hie hrûron gâre wunde *they fell wounded by the spear*, 2153; B. 1074. Hruron him teáras *tears fell from him*, 3749; B. 1872. Hie onweg hruron *they plunged away* [*of the creatures on the top of the water which sank to the bottom on the appearance of Beowulf and his companions*], 2865; B. 1430: Andr. Kmbl. 3199; An. 1602. Đæt se swâ stronglîce hrure on đa circan *that it* [*the wind*] *beat so strongly on the church*, Shrn. 81, 22. Hreósan under heolstorhofu, Elen. Kmbl. 1525; El. 764: Exon. 28 b; Th. 86, 25; Cri. 1413. Gesihþ hreósan hrîm and snâw, 77 a; Th. 289, 14; Wand. 48. Hit hreósan wile sîgan sond æfter rēne, Bt. Met. Fox 7, 44; Met. 7, 22. Hió is mâ hreósende for ealddôme đonne of ǽniges cyninges niéde *magis imbecillitate propriæ senectutis quam alienis concussæ viribus contremiscunt*, Ors. 2, 4; Swt. 76, 2. Đȳ læs cild sȳ hreósende đæt is fylleseóc *lest a child be falling, that is, be ill of the falling sickness* [*epilepsy*], L. Med. ex Quadr. 5, 12; Lchdm. i. 350, 12. Hrîđ hreósende *the storm rushing*, Exon. 78 a; Th. 292, 20; Wand. 102. Ongeán đam hreósendum treówe *towards the falling tree*, Homl. Th. ii. 508, 35. Synt swîđe hreósende đâs gesǽlþa *these goods are very perishable*, Bt. 11, 2; Fox 34, 22. [*Laym.* reosen; *p.* rees; *pl.* ruren: *Icel.* hrjósa *to shudder*.] DER. â-, be-, ge-, of-, ofer-, on-, tô-hreósan.

hreóse. v. wind-hreóse.

hreósende. v. hreósan.

hreósend-lîc; *adj. Frail, perishable, ready to fall*:—Gē sēcaþ đære heán gecynde gesǽlþa and heore weorþscipe tô đâm niđerlîcum and tô đâm hreósendlîcum þingum *ab rebus infimis excellentis naturæ ornamenta captatis*, Bt. 14, 2; Fox 44, 30. Hreósendlîc *cassabundus, corruendus*, Hpt. Gl. 422, 459.

hreóđa. v. bord-, scild-hreóđa.

hreóđan. v. hroden.

hreóung, hrîung, e; *f. Shortness of breath, hardness of breathing*:—Hrîung *suspirium*, Ælfc. Gl. 10; Som. 57, 28; Wrt. Voc. 19, 34. Hreóung hlȳdende swîđust innan *hard breathing sounding chiefly from within*, L. M. 2, 46; Lchdm. ii. 258, 19.

hreów *raw.* v. hreáw.

hreów, e; *f. Sorrow, regret, penitence, penance, repentance*:—Bûton him seó sôþe hreów gefultmige *unless true penitence help them*, Blickl. Homl. 101, 7: Bt. Met. Fox 18, 21; Met. 18, 11. Ân hreów ys wydewan and fǽmnan *viduæ et puellæ una est pœnitentia*, L. Ecg. P. iv. 68, 9; Th. ii. 228, 30. Ic đec lǽdan sceal tô đam hâlgan hâm đǽr nǽfre hreów cymeþ *I shall lead thee to that holy home where sorrow never comes*, Exon. 32 b; Th. 102, 20; Cri. 1675: Beo. Th. 4645; B. 2328. Hû langæ đû on hreówe ǽwunian sceole *quamdiu pœnitentiæ insistere*, Bd. 4, 25; S. 600, 11. On gôdre hreówe *in vera pœnitentia*, L. Ecg. C. 2; Th. ii. 136, 24. Mid synna hreówe *with repentance for sins*, L. Wih. 3; Th. i. 36, 18: 5; Th. i. 38, 8. From đære incundan hreówe *ab intentione pœnitentiæ*, Past. 53, 5; Swt. 415, 36. Bûtan hreówe *without regret*, 44, 5; Swt. 324, 18. Dôn wē ûrum Drihtne sôþe hreówe and bôte, Blickl. Homl. 35, 36. Hreówe and dǽdbôte, 79, 5. Ne hē wihte hafaþ hreówe on môde đæt him hâlig gǽst losige *he hath not regret for the loss of his holy spirit*, Exon. 30 b; Th. 95, 16; Cri. 1558. Hreówa tornost *most grievous of sorrows*, Beo. Th. 4265; B. 2129. Hreówum gedreahte *afflicted with regrets*, Exon. 22 b; Th. 61, 34; Cri. 994. [*O. and N.* reowe: *O. H. Ger.* hriuwa, hriuwi *pœnitentia, pœnitudo, dolor*: *Ger.* reue.]

hreów; *adj.* In Andr. Kmbl. 2233; An. 1118 the alliteration seems to require *reów*. In the compounds blôd-, wæl-hreów the second syllable seems to be *hreóh* [or is it *reów*, or may *hreów* be a confusion of the two forms?], as the form *hreóh* does not occur independently in the sense of *fierce.* Grein separates *hreóh* [*hreów*] under two heads with the meanings *sævus, mæstus*, but this seems unnecessary, as the idea of mental disturbance may be derived from that of physical disturbance in *hreóh*, q. v. see also *hreówe*. However, as Ettmüller, p. 504, observes, perhaps the three forms *hreóh, hreów, hreáw* are sometimes confounded.

hreówan; *p.* hreáw *To rue, make sorry, grieve; often impers*:—Him nān yfel ne hrīwþ *quam mala nulla contristant*, Past. 53, 5; Swt. 417, 1. Hī hēr syngiaþ and hit him nō ne hreówþ *they sin in this world and are not sorry for it*, 55, 2; Swt. 429, 17. Hreóweþ, Exon. 44 b; Th. 150, 23; Gū. 783: Cd. 22; Th. 27, 31; Gen. 426. Đonne hreóweþ hire ðæt heó hire gehāt ne gefylde *pœnitentia mota quod votum suum non impleverit*, L. Ecg. C. 33; Th. ii. 158, 7. Hreáw him *pœnituit eum*, Ps. Spl. 105, 42. Hreáw hine, Ps. Th. 105, 34: Cd. 64; Th. 77, 17; Gen. 1276. Gif ðū ongite ðæt him his synna hreówen *if you see that his sins cause him sorrow*, L. de Cf. 2; Th. ii. 260, 19. Swā swā hī læsse ongietad on him selfum ðæs ðe him hreówan þyrfe *cum minus se respiciunt habere quod defleant*, Past. 52, 9; Swt. 411, 5. For ðæm ðe hie ne māgon ealneg ealla on āne tīd emnsāre hreówan *neque enim uno eodemque tempore æque mens de omnibus dolet*, 53, 3; Swt. 413, 29. Ne hit him ne lǣt hreówan *does not let it trouble him*, Bt. 39, 12; Fox 232, 2: Cd. 38; Th. 50, 29, 36; Gen. 816, 819: Exon. 28 b; Th. 86, 28; Cri. 1415: 100 a; Th. 376, 5; Seel. 150. [*Laym.* reouwen: *Orm.* reoweþþ, *prs; ræw, p: Chauc.* reweþ: *Prompt. Parv.* ruwyn *peniteo, penitet; compatior: O. Sax.* hrewan: *Icel.* hryggja, hryggwa *to distress, grieve: O. H. Ger.* [h]riuwan; *Ger.* reuen.] DER. ge-, of-hreówan.

hreów-cearig; *adj. Troubled, anxious, sorrowful*:—Hreðer innan swearc hyge hreówcearig *his soul grew dark within, his mind distressed*, Exon. 48 a; Th. 165, 9; Gū. 1026: 73 b; Th. 274, 21; Jul. 536: Rood Kmbl. 49; Kr. 25. Hreówcearigum help *help to the troubled*, Exon. 13 a; Th. 23, 11; Cri. 367.

hreówe; *adj. Sad, grieved, sorrowful, penitent*:—Hreówum teárum *lacrymis pœnitentiæ*, Bd. 4, 25; S. 600, 15. [*O. Sax.* hriwi: *Icel.* hryggr *afflicted, grieved.*] v. hreów, *and for the form of the word* cf. treówe.

hreówian *to repent*:—Hreówigas *pœnitemini*, Mk. Skt. Lind. 1, 15. [*O. Sax.* hriwōn: *O. H. Ger.* hriuwōn.]

hreówig; *adj. Sad, mournful*:—Nū wit hreówige māgon sorgian for his sīþe *now may we mournful sorrow for his journey*, Cd. 38; Th. 49, 29; Gen. 799. [*O. Sax.* hriwig: *O. H. Ger.* [h]riuwag *pœnitens, compunctus corde.*]

hreówig-mōd; *adj. Sad at heart*:—Wīf hreówigmōd [*Eve*] Cd. 37; Th. 48, 5; Gen. 771. Hī hreówigmōde wurpon hyra wǣpen of dūne *they disconsolate flung down their weapons*, Judth. 12; Thw. 25, 33; Jud. 290. [*O. Sax.* hriwig-mōd.]

hreów-, hrīw-līc; *adj. Grievous, miserable, pitiful, sad*:—Hreówlīc *calamitosus*, Hpt. Gl. 518. His wīf wyrþe wydewe hreówlīc *fiat uxor ejus vidua*, Ps. Th. 108, 9. Wālā ðǣt wæs hreówlīc sīþ *alas! that was a miserable thing*, 1057; Erl. 192, 20. Wē geseóþ ðæt wē elles hrȳwlīcum deáþe forwurþan sceolon *we see that otherwise we shall perish by a miserable death*, St. And. 36, 7. [*Laym.* reowlich: *R. Glouc.* rewlich.]

hreów-līce; *adv. Miserably, cruelly, grievously*:—Đa ðe swā hreówlīce ācwealde wǣron *crudeliter interemptos*, Bd. 1, 15; S. 484, 3: Chr. 1036; Erl. 164, 35. Blǣdran swīðe hreówlīce berstende *blisters bursting very painfully*, Ors. 1, 7; Swt. 38, 7. Māgon hie swā hreówlīce wēpan swā gē māgon ðara ōðra blīþelīce hlihhan, 3, 7; Swt. 120, 6. Earme menn sindon hreówlīce besyrwde *poor men are grievously ensnared*, Swt. A. S. Rdr. 106, 47. Hreówlīce gefærþ seðe hine sylfne ðus forþ forscyldigaþ and gesǣlig biþ hē ðeáh . . . *miserably does he fare who thus continues to incur guilt; and yet he will be happy* . . . , L. Pen. 12; Th. ii. 280, 28: Chr. 1096; Erl. 233, 22.

hreów-ness, e; *f. Penitence, repentance, sorrow, contrition*:—Æfter his dǣdbōte hreównysse *post pœnitentiæ contritionem*, L. Ecg. P. Th. ii. 170, 13. Hreównisse [hrēunisse, Rush.] *pœnitentiam*, Mt. Kmbl. Lind. 11, 21. Hreónisse, 3, 8. Hreáwnise, 21, 29: Mk. Skt. Lind. 6, 12. Hreóunisse *pœnitentia*, Rtl. 8, 33.

hreów-ness. v. wæl-hreówness, *and* hreów.

hreówsian, hrȳwsian; *p.* ode *To be sorry, grieve, repent, do penance*:—Đæt hē ǣfre ne beþence ymbe ða hreówsunge ðe hē ǣr hreówsade *deque pœnitentia qua antea pœnituit nunquam cogitare*, L. Ecg. P. i. 7; Th. ii. 174, 26. Hire sint forgifena swīðe manega synna forðæmðe hīō swīðe hreówsade, Past. 52, 9; Swt. 411, 12. Hrȳwsode *pœnituit*, Ps. Spl. C. 105, 42. Hreówsiaþ *pœnitemini*, Mk. Skt. Rush. 1, 15. Sume wyllaþ ðæt hē hreówsige *nonnulli volunt ut pœniteat*, L. Ecg. C. 24; Th. ii. 150, 9. Đæt se rihtwīsa man hreówsige hine sylfne swylce hē wið God forwyrht sig *ut justus homo pœnitentiam agat eorum, quæ erga Deum deliquerit*, L. Ecg. P. i. 5; Th. ii. 174, 6. Heora synna hreówsian and dǣdbōte dōn, Ors. 6, 2; Swt. 256, 13. Đā ongann hē hreówsian *pœnitentia ductus*, Mt. Kmbl. 27, 3. Mīnum hreówsiendan geþohte *to my sorrowing thought*, Bt. 3; Fox 4, 26. For hreówsigendne man *pro pœnitenti*, L. Ecg. C. 36; Th. ii. 160, 20. Fore hreósendum *pro pœnitentibus*, Rtl. 177, 7. [*Laym.* reousien: *O. H. Ger.* [h]riuwisōn.] DER. be-hreówsian.

hreówsung, e; *f. Sorrowing, sorrow, penitence, repentance*:—Hreówsung *pœnitudo*, Hpt. Gl. 510. Se apostol bebeád ðæt hī þrītig daga be hreówsunge dǣdbētende Gode geoffrodon *the apostle ordered that they for thirty days with penitence should offer to God doing penance*, Homl. Th. i. 68, 17. Gif hī hwæt gesyngodon hī hit eft mid hreówsunge gebēton *if they sinned in aught they should make amends therein with repentance*, Bt. 41, 3; Fox 248, 14. Hig hreówsunge dydon *pœniterent*, Lk. Skt. 10, 13. Đæt hē þurh ða hreówsunga gemēte forgiefnesse beforan ðære sōþfæsðnesse *ut per lamenta veniam in conspectu veritatis obtineat*, Past. 21, 7; Swt. 165, 22. Forlǣtaþ eówre hreówsunga *cease your lamentations*; capita vestra nolite nudare et vestimenta nolite scindere, Lev. 10, 6. Be his sylfes heortan hreówsungum *according to the penitence of his own heart*, L. Pen. 3; Th. ii. 278, 11. [*Orm.* reowwsunnge.] v. be-hreówsung.

hrepian, hreopian; *p.* ode *To touch, treat*:—Se ðe eów hrepaþ hit mē biþ swā egle swylce hē hreppe ða seó mīnes eágan *he that touches you, it will be as painful to me as if he touches the apple of my eye*, Homl. Th. i. 392, 15: 516, 22. Seó hrepaþ swȳðost ymbe Cristes godcundnysse *it* [*the gospel of St. John*] *treats chiefly of Christ's divinity*, 70, 1. Swā hraðe swā his sceadu hī hreopode *as soon as his shadow touched them*, 316, 16: 492, 25. Hrepede, 176, 6. Gif ic his reáfes gefnædu hreppe . . . heó hrepode his reáfes fnædu . . . Hwā hreopode mē . . . ðū āxast hwā dē hreopode . . . ðæt wīf hine hrepode, ii. 394, 10–18. Wē ne hrepodon ðone traht *we did not treat the exposition*, i. 104, 6. Ne hrepa ðū ðæs treówes wæstm *touch not the fruit of the tree*, 14, 1: Homl. Swt. 5, 302. Gōd bebeád ūs ðæt wē ðæt treów ne hrepodon *præcepit nobis deus ne tangeremus illud* [*lignum*], Gen. 3, 3. v. gehrepod, *and next word.*

hreppan *to touch, treat*:—Ic hreppe *tango*, Ælfc. Gr. 28; Som. 32, 56. Ic hreppe Pharao mid ānum wīte *una plaga tangam Pharaonem*, Ex. 11, 1. Se ðe wudu hrepeþ *he who touches the wood*, Exon. 127 b; Th. 490, 7; Rä. 79, 7. Đa wē ne hreppaþ *those* [*nouns*] *we shall not treat of*, Ælfc. Gr. 9; Som. 12, 30. Đeáh hī hwā hreppe heó hit ne gefrēt *though any one touch it* [*the soul*] *it does not feel it*, Homl. Swt. 1, 220. Đa rēðe deór ne dorston hī reppan *the fierce beasts durst not touch them*, 4, 405. Hire on beseón oððe hī hreppan *to look upon her or touch her*, 7, 151. Hwā dearr hī hreppan, Homl. Th. i. 458, 17. His eágan hreppan mid ðam seáwe *to touch his eyes with the juice*, Herb. 31; Lchdm. i. 128, 12. Moyses ǣ forbeád tō hrepenne ǣnigne hreóflan *the law of Moses forbade to touch any leper*, Homl. Th. i. 122, 5. v. preceding word, and for such pairs of verbs see March's Anglo-Saxon Grammar, § 222. [*Icel.* hreppa *to reach, catch, obtain.*]

hrepsung, e; *f. The evening*:—Æfen oððe hrepsung *vesper*, Som.

hrepung, e; *f. Touch, touching*:—Hrepung *tactus*, Ælfc. Gr. 11; Som. 15, 15. Đa andgitu sint gehātene ðus . . . tactus hrepung on eallum limum *the senses are named thus* . . . tactus *touch, in all the limbs*, Homl. Swt. 1, 199: Homl. Th. ii. 372, 26. Hē mihte mid his worde hine gehǣlan būton hrepunge ac hē geswutelode ðæt his hrepung is swīðe hālwende geleáfullum *he could have healed him with his word without touching; but he shewed that his touch is very salutary to believers*, Homl. Th. i. 122, 9. Drihten gehǣlde ða untruman þurh his reáfes hrepunge *the Lord healed the sick by the touch of his garment*, ii. 394, 5.

hrēr; *adj. Rear* [provincial], *not thoroughly cooked, lightly boiled* [*of eggs*]:—Nim hrēr henne æg *take a hen's egg lightly boiled*, L. M. 2, 52; Lchdm. ii. 272, 16. [*Prompt. Parv.* rere, or nesche, as eggys *mollis*; see the note p. 430.] v. hrēren-brǣden.

hreran [?] *to fall*:—Đæt ic hryre ł gefealle [=? hrure ł gefeólle] *ut caderem*, MS. T: hī hrǣron, Ps. Spl. 117, 13.

hrēran; *p.* de *To move, shake, stir*:—Ic wudu hrēre *I move the wood*, Exon. 101 a; Th. 381, 9; Rä. 2, 8. Hrēra, 101 b; Th. 383, 9; Rä. 4, 8. Forhwī drēfe gē eówru mōd mid unrihte fióunge swā swā ȳða for winde ða sǣ hrēraþ *quid tantos juvat excitare motus*, Bt. 39, 1; Fox 210, 25: Bt. Met. Fox 27, 5; Met. 27, 3. Hig wegdan hrērdan heora heáfod *moverunt capita sua*, Ps. Th. 108, 25. Hrēr swīðe *stir thoroughly*, L. M. 1, 38; Lchdm. ii. 94, 9, 21. Hrēr mid sticcan, 3, 26; Lchdm. ii. 322, 28. Hrēre ðonne swīðe *let it be thoroughly shaken*, 1, 36; Lchdm. ii. 88, 1: 38; Lchdm. 92, 4: 94, 13. Hē ne lǣtaþ mīne fēt lāðe hrēran *non dedit commoveri pedes meos*, Ps. Th. 65, 8. Hrēran mid hondum hrīmcalde sǣ *to row on the ice-cold sea*, Exon. 76 b; Th. 286, 21; Wand. 4. Sum mæg fromlīce ofer sealtne sǣ sundwudu drīfan hrēran holmþræce, 17 b; Th. 42, 25; Cri. 678. [*O. Sax.* hrōrian: *Icel.* hræra *to move, stir*: *O. H. Ger.* hruorian *movere, agitare, tangere*: *Ger.* rühren.] v. on-hrēran. hrōr.

hrēred-ness, e; *f. Agitation, haste, precipitation*:—Ealle word hrȳrednesse *omnia verba præcipitationis*, Ps. Lamb. 51, 6.

hrēre-mūs, e; *f. A rear-, rere-mouse, bat*:—Hrēre-mūs *vespertilio*, Wrt. Voc. 77, 40. [See Nare's Gloss. *rear-*; *rere-mouse*, and cf. *Ger.* fleder-maus.] v. hreáðe-mūs: hrōr.

hrēren-brǣden; *adj. Not thoroughly cooked*:—On ān hrērenbrǣden æg *over an egg lightly cooked*, Lchdm. iii. 294, 8. v. hrēr.

hrēr-ness, e; *f. Motion, disturbance, agitation, commotion, storm*:—Hroernis michelo geworden wæs in sǣ *motus magnus factus est in mari*, Mt. Kmbl. Lind. 8, 24. Gāst hrȳrenesse ł stormes *spiritus procellæ*, Ps.

Lamb. 106, 25. Eorþ hroernisse *terræ motu*, 27, 54. Swā đū hī on yrre ehtest and drēfest đæt hī on hrērnesse hrađe forweorþaþ *ita persequeris illos in tempestate tua; et in ira tua conturbabis eos*, Ps. Th. 82, 11. v. eorþ-hrērness.

hresigende. v. hrisian.

hrēst = hrȳst, Bt. Met. Fox 11, 116; Met. 11. 58. v. hreósan.

hrētan. v. hrȳtan.

hreþ. v. hræd.

hrēđ, es; *m.* [?] *Glory, fame, triumph, honour*:—Siđđan him gesǣlde sigorworca hrēđ đæt hē ealdordōm āgan sceolde ofer cynerīcu *afterwards fell to him the glory of victorious deeds, that he should have dominion over kingdoms*, Cd. 158; Th. 198, 2; Exod. 316. Him wyrd ne gescrāf hrēđ æt hilde *fate ordained not for him triumph in battle*, Beo. Th. 5143; B. 2575. [*O. H. Ger.* hruodi (*in proper names*), Grff. iv. 1153: cf. *Icel.* hróðr *praise, fame.*] v. gūþ-, sige-hrēđ; hrēđig, hrōđor.

hrēđa, an; *m. A garment made of goat's skin*; melotes, Cot. 133, Lye. v. bord-, scild-hreóđa [-hrēđa].

hrēđan; *p.* de *To glory, triumph*:— Hrēđdon hildespelle *they triumphed with the song of* [*victorious*] *battle*, Cd. 170; Th. 214, 22; Exod. 573.

hrēđe; *adj. Fierce, cruel, savage, rough*:—Wearþ hire wrāþ on mōde heard and hrēđe *was wroth with her, harsh and cruel*, Cd. 103; Th. 136, 20; Gen. 2261. Deáþ neálǣcte strong and hrēđe, Exon. 49 b; Th. 170, 18; Gū. 1113. Hroeđo suīđe *sævi nimis*, Mt. Kmbl. Lind. 8, 28. In heágum mōrum and hrēđum *in arduis asperisque montibus*, Bd. 4, 27; S. 604, 27. Đām hrēđestum feóndum *sævissimis hostibus*, Mone Gl. 346. v. rēđe.

hrēđ-eádig; *adj. Glorious, noble, triumphant*:—Biþ đǣr his þegna eác hrēđeádig heáp *there too shall be a triumphant band of his servants*, Exon. 21 b; Th. 58, 33; Cri. 945. Sum biþ on huntoþe hrēđeádigra deóra drǣfend *one is more famous in hunting, a chaser of wild beasts*, 78 b; Th. 295, 23; Crā. 37. [*Thorpe and Grein take* hrēđeádigra *as gen., but see* Th. 298, 1; Crā. 78 *for another comparative.*] Hærfest biþ hrēđeádegost hæleþum bringeþ gēres wæstmas đa đe him god sendeþ *autumn is most glorious, it brings to man the fruits of the year which God sends them*, Menol. Fox 475; Gn. C. 8. [Cf. *Icel.* hróðr-auðigr *famous.*]

hrēđe-mōnaþ. v. hrēđ-mōnaþ.

hređer, hræđer, hrađer, es; *m.* [?] *Breast, bosom*:—Hređor innan wæs wynnum āwelled *the breast within was joyously agitated*, Andr. Kmbl. 2036; An. 1020. Hređer [hreder, MS.] innan weóll beorn breóstsefa, Exon. 15 b; Th. 34, 9; Cri. 539: 46 b; Th. 158, 15; Gū. 910: Beo. Th. 4233; B. 2113. Hređer innan swearc hyge hreówcearig *dark within grew his breast, troubled with care his mind*, Exon. 48 a; Th. 165, 8; Gū. 1025. Hređer ædme weóll *his breast heaved with breathing*, Beo. Th. 5780; B. 2593. Is mē ænige gāst innan hređres *anxiatus est in me spiritus meus*, Ps. Th. 142, 4. On breóston inne on hrađre, Bt. Met. Fox 25, 91; Met. 25, 46. Him of hræđre [hwæđre, MS.] gewāt sāwol *from his bosom departed the soul*, Beo. Th. 5631; B. 2819. Him on hređre heáfodswīma heortan clypte *in his bosom stupor clasped his heart*, Cd. 76; Th. 94, 27; Gen. 1568. Đe dryhtnes bebod heóldon on hređre *who kept the lord's command in their breast*, Exon. 24 b; Th. 71, 23; Cri. 1160. Him wæs hreów on hređre hygesorga mǣst, Beo. Th. 4645; B. 2328. Hē mē in hređre bileác wīsdōmes giefe, Exon. 51 a; Th. 176, 33; Gū. 1219: Andr. Kmbl. 138; An. 69: Cd. 161; Th. 201, 2; Exod. 366: Beo. Th. 2306; B. 1151. Ys mē on hređre heorte gedrēfed *cor meum conturbatum est in me*, Ps. Th. 54, 4: 70, 8. Biþ on hređre drepen biteran strǣle *is smitten in the breast with the bitter shaft*, Beo. Th. 3494; B. 1745. Æt helle duru dracan eardigaþ hāte on hređre *at hell's door dwell dragons that send fire from within* [*firedrakes*], Cd. 215; Th. 271, 1; Sat. 99. Bađu hāt on hređre *hot baths*, Exon. 124 b; Th. 478, 16; Ruin. 42: Beo. Th. 6287; B. 3148. Blōd ūt ne com of hređre *blood came not from my breast*, Exon. 130 a; Th. 499, 9; Rā. 88, 13. Mē on hređre heáfod sticade *in her bosom she stuck my head*, 124 b; Th. 479, 9; Rā. 62, 5. Hālig heofonlīce gāst hređer weardode æđelne innoþ *the holy heavenly spirit guarded her breast, her noble womb*, Elen. Kmbl. 2288; El. 1145: Exon. 49 a; Th. 169, 20; Gū. 1102. Him hildegrāp hređre ne mihte aldre gesceđđan *the hostile grasp could not harm his breast, his life*, Beo. Th. 2897; B. 1446. Hređra gehygd *counsel*, 4096; B. 2045: Exon. 77 b; Th. 290, 28; Wand. 72. v. mid-hriđre.

hređer-bealo; *n. Breast-bale, hurt to the mind, care, grief*, Beo. Th. 2690; B. 1343.

hređer-cōfa, an; *m. The breast*, Exon. 27 a; Th. 81, 25; Cri. 1329.

hređer-gleáw; *adj. Prudent of mind*, Cd. 143; Th. 178, 17; Exod. 13.

hređer-loca, an; *m. The breast*, Exon. 51 a; Th. 178, 1; Gū. 1237: 82 a; Th. 309, 17; Seef. 58: 23 b; Th. 65, 17; Cri. 1056: Elen. Kmbl. 172; El. 86.

hrēđig; *adj. Triumphant, exultant.* [*Goth.* hrōþeigs *victorious, triumphant*: *Icel.* hróðugr *triumphant, glorious*; mod. *boasting.*] DER. eád-, eáđ-, sige-, will-hrēđig.

hrēđ-leás; *adj. Inglorious, joyless, without the joy of victory*, Exon. 46 a; Th. 156, 21; Gū. 878.

hrēđ-, hrēđ-mōnaþ, es; *m. March*:—On đæm þriddan mōnþe on geáre biþ ān and þrittig daga and se mōnþ is nemned on lǣden martius and on ūre geþeóde hrēđmōnaþ *in the third month in the year are one and thirty days, and the month is called in latin* martius, *and in our language* hrēđmōnaþ, Shrn. 59, 9. Đonne se hrēđmōnaþ biþ āgān đonne biþ seó niht twelf tīda lang and se dæg đæt ilce *when March is past then the night is twelve hours long and the day the same*, 69, 7. Bede in his work 'De temporum ratione' c. 13 says 'Rhedmonath a dea illorum Rheda, cui in illo sacrificabant, nominatur.' Grimm quotes similar forms from other German sources, *Retmonat, Redimonet*, as names of March or February; and supposes an *O. H. Ger. Hruod, Hruoda* to correspond to the English *Hrêd, Hrêde*, which would be connected with *hruod* [v. hrēđ] fame, glory. See D. M. 267.

hrēđ-ness, e; *f. Fierceness, roughness* [*of weather*], *cruelty*:—Hroeđnise *sævitiam*, Rtl. 122, 14. Hroeđnise *tempestatem*, Lk. Skt. Lind. 8, 24. [Cf. hreóh-ness.]

hređor. v. hređer.

hrēđ-sigor, es; *m. Glorious victory*, Beo. Th. 5160; B. 2583.

hric, hricg. v. hrycg.

hricsc [= ? hrisc *or* hrics] *a rick, crick, a wrench accompanied with a small sound*:—Of fylle ođđe of slege ođđe of hricsca hwilcum *from a fall or from a blow or from any crick*, L. M. 1, 31; Lchdm. ii. 72, 23. [Cf. hriscan.]

hriddel, es; *n.* [?] *A riddle, sieve*, Som. [*Prompt. Parv.* rydyl *cribrum.*] v. hriđian, hridder.

hridder, es; *n. A sieve, instrument for winnowing corn*:—Hridder *capisterium, taratantara*, Ælfc. Gl. 50; Som. 65, 116, 117; Wrt. Voc. 34, 45, 46. Đā ābæd his fōstormōder ān hridder . . . Benedictus genam đa sticcu đæs tōclofenan hriddores . . . hī đæt hridder up āhēngon æt heora cyrcan geate, Homl. Th. ii. 154, 16-24. [*O. H. Ger.* ritra *cribrum, cribellum.*] v. hriddel.

hridrian; *p.* ode *To sift, winnow*:—Satanas gyrnde đæt hē eów hridrude swā swā hwǣte *Satanas expetivit vos ut cribraret sicut triticum*, Lk. Skt. 22, 31. [*O. H. Ger.* ritaron *cribrare*; *Ger.* reitern *to sift.*]

hrif, rif, es; *n. The womb, belly*; uterus, venter:—Đīn đæt fædmlīce hrif *thine enfolding womb*, Blickl. Homl. 7, 29. Hrif *uterus*, Mt. Kmbl. Lind. 1, 8: 19. 12: Rtl. 51, 27. Đæt uferre hrif, L. M. 2, 28; Lchdm. ii. 224, 8. Rif *vel* seó inre wamb *alvus*, Ælfc. Gl. 74; Som. 71, 55; Wrt. Voc. 44, 38. Wiđ hrifes āþundennesse *for puffing of the visceral cavity*, Lchdm. iii. 70, 24. Of mōdur hrife mīnre *de utero matris meæ*, Ps. Th. 138, 11: 70, 5. Of hryfe *ex utero*, Ps. Spl. 21, 8. On hrife đære ā clǣnan fǣmnan, Blickl. Homl. 33, 15. Bān biþ funden on heortes heortan hwīlum on hrife *a bone is found in a hart's heart, sometimes in its belly*, L. Med. ex Quadr. 2, 17; Lchdm. i. 338, 6. Ācsedon hwider hie fleón woldon đæt hie ōđer gener næfden būton hie on heóra wīfa hrif gewiton *quærentes, num in uteros uxorum vellent refugere*, Ors. 1, 12; Swt. 54, 4. Lācnung on đæt hrif tō sendanne *to send medicine into the belly*, L. M. 2, 32; Lchdm. ii. 234, 19. Þurh mīnre mōdor hrif, Exon. 111 a; Th. 424, 27; Rā. 41, 44: 14 a; Th. 27, 4; Cri. 425. [*O. Frs.* rif, ref: *O. H. Ger.* href, ref *uterus.*] v. mid-hrif.

hrīfþo, hriéfþo; *f. Roughness of the skin, scurf*:—Heáfdes hrīfþo, L. M. 2, 35; Lchdm. ii. 240, 20. v. hreóf.

hrif-wirc, -wærc, es; *m. A pain in the belly*; yleos, Ælfc. Gl. 10; Som. 57, 16; Wrt. Voc. 19, 24.

hrif-wund; *adj. Wounded in the belly*:— Gif [hē] hrifwund [hrif wund, Thorpe] weorþeþ xii scill. gebēte. Gif hē þurhþirel weorþeþ xx scill. gebēte *if he be wounded in the belly let twelve shillings be paid. If he be run through let twenty shillings be paid* [cf. the passage given in the note from Alamannic Laws, 'si in interiora membra transpunctus fuerit, quod *hrefwunt* dicunt, cum xii sol. componat. Si transpunctus fuerit cum xxiv sol. componat.' See, too, Graff. i. 897-8], L. Ethb. 61; Th. i. 18, 6.

hrig. v. hrycg.

hrilæcung [?] *ratiocinatio*, Som.

HRĪM, es; *m.* RIME, *hoar-frost*:—Hrīm *pruina*, Ælfc. Gl. 94; Som. 75, 102; Wrt. Voc. 52, 52. Hrīm and forst hāre hildstapan, Andr. Kmbl. 2516; An. 1259. Se hearda forst hrīm heorugrimma, Exon. 111 a; Th. 425, 12; Rā. 41, 55. Hægel se hearda and hrīm, 127 b; Th. 490, 11; Rā. 79, 9. Đǣr ne hægl ne hrīm hreósaþ tō foldan *nec gelido terram rore pruina tegit*, 56 b; Th. 201, 22; Ph. 60. Hrīm hrusan bond hægl feól on eorþan *frost bound the land, hail fell on earth*, 81 b; Th. 307, 31; Seef. 32. Ne hægles hryre ne hrīmes dryre, 56 a; Th. 198, 27; Ph. 16. Mid herige hrīmes and snāwes *with the legions of frost and snow*, Menol. Fox 406; Men. 204. On hrīme *in pruina*, Ps. Th. 118, 83. Hrīme gehyrsted *adorned with hoar-frost*, Menol. Fox 70; Men. 35: Exon. 77 b; Th. 291, 4; Wand. 77. Wineleás guma gesihþ him beforan bađian brimfuglas brǣdan feđra hreósan hrīm and snāw hagle gemenged *the friendless man sees before him the sea-birds bathe, and spread their wings, sees rime and snow fall mingled with hail*, 77 a; Th. 289, 14; Wand. 48. Nǣnig mōste heora hrōrra hrīm æpla gedīgean *occidit moros* *eorum in pruina*, Ps. Th. 77, 47. [*Icel.* hrím; *n.* hrími; *m*: *O. H. Ger.* rime *gelu*, Grff. ii. 506.]

hrîman. v. hrȳman.

hrîm-ceald; *adj. Icy cold*:—Hrīmcalde sǽ, Exon. 76 b; Th. 286, 22; Wand. 4. [*Icel.* hrím-kaldr.]

hrîm-gicel, es; *m. An icicle*;—Bihongen hrīmgicelum, Exon. 81 b; Th. 307, 1; Seef. 17.

hrîmig; *adj. Rimy, covered with hoar-frost*:—Swīđe hrīmige bearwas *woods thickly covered with hoar-frost*, Blickl. Homl. 209, 32: 207, 27 [?]. Winter biþ cealdost lencten hrīmigost *black frosts in winter, white frosts in spring*, Menol. Fox 411; Gn. C. 6.

hrîmig-heard; *adj. Hard with frost, hard frozen*, Exon. 130 a; Th. 498, 25; Rä. 88, 7.

hrînan; *p.* hrān; *pp.* hrinen *To touch, reach, strike.* I. *with gen*:—Đū his hrīnan meaht *thou mayest touch it*, Cd. 29; Th. 38, 34; Gen. 616. II. *with dat*:—Grundum ic hrīne *the depths I touch*, Exon. 125 b; Th. 482, 22; Rä. 67, 5: 102 b; Th. 389, 8; Rä. 7, 4: 104 b; Th. 397, 31; Rä. 16, 28. Gif ic hrīno wēde his *if I touch his garment*, Mt. Kmbl. Lind. 9, 21. Se hǽlend and hrān [*or* andhrān? cf. *O. Sax.* ant-hrīnan] ēgum heora *Iesus tetigit oculos eorum*, Rush. 20, 34. Se hǽlend hrān him *tangens eum*, Mk. Skt. Rush. 1, 41: Exon. 110 a; Th. 421, 18; Rä. 40, 30. Hrinon hearmtānas drihta bearnum, Cd. 47; Th. 61, 4; Gen. 992. Đeáh đe him wund hrine *though the wound had touched him*, Beo. Th. 5945; B. 2976. Ele synfulra ǽfre ne mōte heáfde mīnum hrīnan *oleum peccatorum non impinguet caput meum*, Ps. 140, 7. Nǽnig wæter him hrīnan ne mihte *no water might reach him*, Beo. Th. 3035; B. 1515: 1981; B. 988: Cd. 69; Th. 84, 11; Gen. 1396. Đæt hȳ him mid hondum hrīnan mōsten, Exon. 38 b; Th. 127, 5; Gū. 381: 73 a; Th. 273, 7; Jul. 512. Đē hondum hrīnan, 36 b; Th. 119, 13; Gū. 254. Hrīnande him *tangens eum*, Mk. Skt. Lind. 1, 41. III. *with acc*:—Ic hrīno đone hiorde *percutiam pastorem*, 14, 27. Gif hē mid his mihte muntas hrīneþ *qui tangit montes*, Ps. Th. 103, 30: Exon. 106 b; Th. 406, 4; Rä. 24, 12. Hrīn đa gōman mid *touch the fauces with it*, L. Med. ex Quadr. 5, 3; Lchdm. i. 348, 10. Ne sceolon mīne đa hālgan hrīnan *nolite tangere christos meos*, Ps. Th. 104, 13. Wāt ic Matheus þurh mǽnra hand hrīnan heorudolgum, Andr. Kmbl. 1883; An. 944. IV. *with object omitted*:—Đæt hē mā wolde afrum onfengum earme gǽstas hrīnan lēton *that he would further let the wretched spirits with their dire attacks touch him* [*Guthlac*], Exon. 40 a; Th. 133, 17; Gū. 491. Swā hit him on innan com hrān æt heortan *so it came within him, touched him at his heart*, Cd. 33; Th. 45, 9; Gen. 724. Ōþ đæt deáþes folm hrān æt heortan *until the hand of death touched him at his heart*, Beo. Th. 4532; B. 2270. [*A. R.* rineđ, *prs*: *Orm.* ran, *p*: *O. Sax.* hrīnan: *Icel.* hrína *to cleave, to hurt*: *O. H. Ger.* hrīnan *tangere, obtrectare.*] DER. æt-, and-, ge-, on-hrīnan.

hrind. A word of doubtful meaning occurring in the following passage, 'Nis đæt feor heonon đæt se mere standeþ ofer đæm hongiaþ hrinde bearwas wudu wyrtum fæst wæter oferhelmaþ,' Beo. Th. 2731; B. 1363. Thorpe translates *barky*, Kemble *rinded*, but in this case there should be no initial *h*. In Ælfc. Gl. 59; Som. 68, 5, 6; Wrt. Voc. 38, 56, 57 *hrind* translates *caudex* vel *codex*, and *liber* is translated *seó inre hrind*, but perhaps the better reading for the former would be *rind = cortex*. Otherwise *hrinde bearwas* might be [?] 'groves with [large-] stemmed trees.' Grein compares the word with forms given by Halliwell *rind* frozen to death, *rinde* to destroy, and suggests *dead*; Heyne takes *hrinde* = *hrīnende* and compares with *Icel.* hrína *sonare*. Might *hrinde* = *hringde* in the sense 'placed in a ring or circle,' so that *hrinde bearwas* would be the trees placed round or encircling the mere?

hrindan; *p.* hrand, *pl.* hrundon *To push, thrust*:—Hē hrand [MS. rand], Exon. 113 b; Th. 436, 21; Rä. 55, 4. [*Icel.* hrinda *to thrust.*]

hrine, es; *m. Touch*:—Hrine *tactus*, Wrt. Voc. 282, 32. Drihten đū đe wē ne māgon ongytan mid hrine *Lord thou whom we cannot perceive with the touch*, Shrn. 166, 21. v. æt-hrine.

hrine-ness, e; *f. Touching, contact*:—Fram werelīce hrinenesse *a viri contactu*, Bd. 4, 19; S. 587, 37. Mid đa ylcan hrinenesse *eodem tactu*, 31; S. 610, 34. v. ge-hrineness.

HRING, hrincg, es; *m. A* RING, *circle, circuit, cycle, orb, globe, festoon*:—Āgymmed hrincg *ungulus*: geheáfdod hringce *samothracius*: lytel hring *anelus*, Ælfc. Gl. 65; Som. 69, 30, 31, 49; Wrt. Voc. 40, 59, 60; 41, 6. Hringc *ansa*, Wrt. Voc. 66, 34: 284, 7. Hring *fibula, legula, sertum*, Cot. 85, 186, 190, Lye. Ān fȳren hring *globus ignis*, Ors. 5, 10; Swt. 234, 3. Mon geseah ymbe đa sunnan swelce ān gylden hring *circulus ad speciem cœlestis arcus orbem solis ambiit*, 14; Swt. 248, 9. Đæs seó hringc *circulus* [*pupillæ*], Ælfc. Gl. 70; Som. 70, 64; Wrt. Voc. 42, 72. Se hring ealles geáres *totius anni circulus*, Bd. 4, 18; S. 586, 40. Hring ūtan ymbbearh *the ring* [*armour formed of rings*] *protected him without*, Beo. Th. 3011; B. 1503: 4513; B. 2260. Sunnan hring beága beorhtast *the rainbow* [?], Exon. 60 a; Th. 219, 11; Ph. 305. Đone hālgan hringe beteldaþ flyhte on lyfte *contrahit in cœtum sese genus omne volantum*, 60 b; Th. 221, 24; Ph. 339. Đonne đæt gecnāwaþ feónd đætte fira gehwylc on his hringe biþ fæste gefēged *when the devil knows that any man is fast fixed in his ring* [*fetters, chain* or *circle over which his power extends*?], 97 a; Th. 362, 22; Wal. 40. Gim sceal on hringe standan *the gem must stand in the ring*, Menol. Fox 594; Gn. C. 22. Syllaþ him hring on his hand *date anulum in manum ejus*, Lk. Skt. 15, 22. Seđe his geleáfan hring mē lēt tō wedde, Homl. Swt. 7, 30. Dyde him of healse hring gyldenne *doff'd from his neck a golden ring*, Beo. Th. 5611; B. 2809. Gewyrc ānne hring ymb đone slite *make a ring round the incision*, L. M. 1, 45; Lchdm. i. 112, 1. Đū geáres hring mid gyfe bletsast *benedices coronæ anni benignitatis tuæ*, Ps. Th. 64, 12. Ǽr sunne twelf mōnþa hringc ūtan ymbgān hæbbe, Guthl. 21; Gdwin. 96, 5. Ofer holmes hrincg *over the ocean's circuit*, Cd. 69; Th. 84, 5; Gen. 1393. Hrincg đæs heán landes, 137; Th. 172, 34; Gen. 2854. Wīngearda hringa[s] *corimbi*, Ælfc. Gl. 59; Som. 68, 11; Wrt. Voc. 38, 60. Hrægl and hringas *raiment and rings*, Beo. Th. 2394; B. 1195. Hringa hyrde, 4482; B. 2245: 3018; B. 1507: 4680; B. 2345. Heortan unhneáweste hringa gedāles *the heart least niggardly in the giving of rings*, Exon. 85 b; Th. 323, 4; Vīd. 73. Hæft mid hringa gesponne *bound with the linked chain*, Cd. 35; Th. 47, 17; Gen. 762: 19; Th. 24, 14; Gen. 377. Hringum gehrodene *adorned with rings*, Judth. 10; Thw. 21, 27; Jud. 37: Beo. Th. 2187; B. 1091. Hringum gyrded, Exon. 129 b; Th. 497, 22; Rä. 87, 4. Hringan, 102 b; Th. 387, 8; Rä. 5, 2. Hē wolde đæs beornes beágas gefecgan reáf and hringas, Byrht. Th. 136, 34; By. 161. Hringas dǽlan, Beo. Th. 3944; B. 1970: 6061; B. 3034. Đa nigontȳnlīcan hringas rihtra Eástrana and hēt fordilgian đa gedwolan hringas feówer and hundeahtatig geára *circuli Paschæ decennovenales oblitteratis erroneis octoginta et quatuor annorum circulis*, Bd. 5, 21; S. 643, 26. [*Icel.* hringr *a ring, ring of a coat of mail, circle*: *O. H. Ger.* hring *circulus, orbis, spira, sphæra, bulla, corona, sertum, torques, vinculum, laqueus*: *Ger.* ring.] DER. bān-, bridels-, eág-, eáh-, eár-hring. v. beág.

hring, *in the phrase* wōpes hring *occurs four times, in poems by the same author*:—Đā cwom wōpes hring þurh đæs beornes breóst blāt ūt faran weóll wađuman streám, Andr. Kmbl. 2558; An. 1281. Đā wæs wōpes hring hāt heáfodwylm ofer hleór goten nalles for torne teáras feóllon, Elen. Kmbl. 2262; El. 1132. Đǽr wæs wōpes hring torne bitolden wæs seó treówlufu hāt æt heortan hređer innan weóll, Exon. 15 b; Th. 34, 5; Cri. 537. Him đæs wōpes hring torne gemonade teagor ȳđum weól hāte hleórdropan, 52 a; Th. 182, 21; Gū. 1313. *The meaning given by Grein*, sonus [cf. hringan], *does not seem to suit the context very well, which, as in the second passage, where the phrase appears equivalent to* hāt heáfodwylm, *points to shedding tears as the idea to be conveyed. Grimm explains* fletus intensissimus, quasi circulatim erumpens, And. u. El. p. 130, *and this seems to give the meaning though the connection with* hring *is not very evident.*

hringan; *p.* de; v. *trans. and intrans. To ring*:—His searo hringeþ *his armour rings*, Salm. Kmbl. 534; Sal. 266. Byrnan hringdon *their byrnies rang*, Beo. Th. 660; B. 327. Hī ringden đa belle *they rang the bells*, Chr. 1131; Erl. 259, 37. Hringe tācn *sonet signum*, Lye. Yc gef leáua đām munche tō hringinde hyre tȳde *I give leave to the monks to ring their hours*, Chart. Th. 437, 13. [*Laym.* ringe; *p.* ringeden: 2nd MS. rongen: *R. Glouc. Chauc. Piers P.* ringe; *p.* rong: *Icel.* hringja.]

hring-bân, es; *n. A circular bone, bone in the shape of a ring*:—Hringbān đæs eágan *teuco*, Ælfc. Gl. 70; Som. 70, 73; Wrt. Voc. 43, 6.

hring-boga, an; *m. A serpent* [*from its being bent into coils* (hring)], Beo. Th. 5115; B. 2561. [Cf. *Icel.* hring-laginn *coiled up*; hringa sik *to coil* (*of a serpent*).]

hringed; *adj. Furnished with rings, formed of rings*;—Hringedu byrne *lorica*, Cot. 121, Lye: Beo. Th. 2495; B. 1245: 5224; B. 2615. [*Icel.* hringa *to furnish with a ring*; *and cf.* hringa-brynja *a coat of ring-mail*: *O. H. Ger.* gi-ringotero *hamata* (*lorica*).]

hringed-stefna, an; *m. A ship having its stern adorned with spiral* or *ring-shaped ornaments* [?], or *furnished with a ring* or *hook*; or *having a curved stern*, Beo. Th. 64; B. 32: 3799; B. 1898: 2266; B. 1132. [Cf. wunden-stefna; hring-naca; *and Icel.* hring-horni *the mythol. ship of the Edda.*]

hring-fâh; *adj. Of many colours, diversified with circular spots of colour* [?]:—Hringfēgh *polimita* vel *oculata*, Ælfc. Gl. 29; Som. 61, 29; Wrt. Voc. 26, 28. Hēt wircean him hringfāge tunecan *fecit ei tunicam polymitam*, Gen. 37, 3. v. hring-wīse.

hring-finger, es; *m. The ring-finger, the third finger*:—Hringfinger *anularis*, Wrt. Voc. 283, 23. Mid þuman and mid hringfingre, L. Med. ex Quadr. 1, 5; Lchdm. i. 330, 21. v. Halliwell Dict. ring-finger.

hringian *to surround, encircle.* [*Icel.* hringja: cf. *O. H. Ger.* ga-hringjan *congyrare.*] v. ymb-hringian.

hring-îren, es; *n. The iron rings of a coat of mail*:—Gūþbyrne scān heard hand-locen hringīren scīr song in searwum *the corslet shone, hard, hand-wrought, the bright iron rings rang in their armour*, Beo. Th. 650; B. 222.

hring-loca, an; *m. A coat of mail formed with rings*, Byrht. Th. 136, 2; By. 145.

hring-mǽl; *adj. Ornamented with inlaid rings* [*of a sword*], Beo. Th.

3133; B. 1564. [Cf. *Icel.* mál *used of inlaid ornaments*, e.g. mála-sax *an inlaid sword;* and for ring ornaments see Worsaae's Primeval Antiquities, p. 40.]

hring-mǣled; *adj. Ornamented with inlaid rings:*—Hringmǣled sweord, Cd. 93; Th. 120, 10; Gen. 1992. v. preceding word.

hring-mere, es; *n. A round pool, a bath,* Exon. 124 b; Th. 478, 21; Ruin. 45.

hring-naca, an; *m. See* hringed-stefna, Beo. Th. 2728; B. 1862.

hring-nett, es; *n. A net-work of rings, a coat of mail formed of rings:*—Hringnet bǣron locene leoþosyrcan, Beo. Th. 3783; B. 1889. [Cf. *Icel.* hring-kofl, -serkr, -skyrta *a coat of mail;* hring-ofinn *woven of rings*, an epithet applied to such a coat.]

hring-sele; *m. A hall in which rings are distributed* or *stored up*, Beo. Th. 4024; B. 2010 [*Hrothgar's palace*]: 6008; B. 3053 [*the cavern where the dragon guarded the treasure*]: 5672; B. 2840. v. beág-sel, -sele.

hring-seta *circenses ludi*, Cot. 43, Lye.

hring-sete *circus*, Cot. 183, Lye.

hring-sittend *circumsedens, spectans*, Hpt. Gl. 407.

hring-stede *circulare stadium*, Lye.

hring-þegu, e; *f. Acceptance of rings, of gifts given by a lord:*—Ne biþ him tō hearpan hyge ne tō hringþege, Exon. 82 a; Th. 308, 24; Seef. 44. v. beág-þegu.

hring-weorþung, e; *f. Honouring by the gift of a ring:*—Ne mægþ habban on healse hringweorþunge *no maiden's neck shall be graced with a ring*, Beo. Th. 6027; B. 3017. v. hord-weorþung.

hring-windel *sphæra*, Lye.

hring-wīse, an; *f. In the phrase* on hringwīsan *ring-wise, in rings:*—Hwītes hiowes and eác missenlīces wæs hió on hringwīsan fāg *candido versicolore in modum ranarum*, Nar. 16, 1. v. hring-fāh.

hrīnung, e; *f. Touch;* tactus:—In hrīning hlāfes *intincti panis*, Jn. Skt. p. 7, 3. Mið rīning ł miððȳ gehrān *tactu*, 8, 7.

hrīs, es; *n. A twig, branch,* RISE:—Hrīs *frondes*, Cot. 93, Lye. [*Laym. O. and N. Chauc.* ris: v. *Halliwell Dict.* rise: *Icel.* hrís; *n. shrubs, brushwood: O. H. Ger.* hrīs *ramus, frondes, ramusculus: Ger.* reis *a twig, rod.*]

hriscan. v. hryscan.

hrīseht; *adj. Bushy, bristly;* setosus, Cot. 186, Lye.

hrisel, hresl, es; *m.* [?] *A shuttle;* radius:—Hrisl *radiolum*, Ælfc. Gl. 110; Som. 79, 54; Wrt. Voc. 59, 25: *radium*, Wrt. Voc. 281, 75. Hresl [hrefl, Wrt.] *radius*, 66, 12. Hrisil, Exon. 109 a; Th. 417, 20; Rä. 36, 7. v. hrisian, *and* cf. scytel.

hrisian; *p.* ede *To shake:*—Syrcan hrysedon *shook their coats of mail*, Beo. Th. 458; B. 226. Hrisedon heáfud *moverunt capita*, Ps. Surt. 21, 8: 108, 24. [Cf. Hresigende *febricitans*, Mk. Skt. 1, 30 (later MS.).] Stefn drihtnes hrysiendis wēsten *vox Domini concutientis desertum*, Ps. Spl. T. 28, 7. [*Laym.* rusien: *Ayenb.* resie: *Chauc.* rese: *Goth.* hrisian: *O. Sax.* hrisian *to shake, tremble:* cf. *Icel.* hrista *to shake.*] v. ā-hrisian.

hristenda [hriscenda?] *astridulus, stridulus*, Lye. v. hryscan, *or next word* [?].

hristlan *to rustle:*—Hristlend[e] *crepens*, Lye.

hristlung, e; *f. A rustling;* crepitus, strepitus, Lye.

hristung, e; *f. A quivering, spasmodic action:*—Ceolan hristung and hreóung hlȳdende swīðust innan [*or should* hristlung (v. *preceding word*) *be read?*], L. M. 2, 46; Lchdm. ii. 258, 18. *Cockayne, who explains as above, compares with Icel.* hrista *to shake. See also* hristenda.

hrīð, e; *f. A storm, tempest:*—Hrīð hreósende *the driving storm*, Exon. 78 a; Th. 292, 20; Wand. 102. [*Icel.* hríð; *f. a storm, snow-storm.*]

hrīð, es; *m. Fever;*—Fefer ðæt is micel hǣto and hrīð [MS. hruð], L. M. 2, 24; Lchdm. ii. 214, 7. [*O. H. Ger.* rito; *m. febris.*]

hrīð-ādl, e; *f. A fever:*—Gif him hrīðādl getenge biþ *if fever be upon him*, L. M. 2, 24; Lchdm. ii. 214, 16.

hrīðer, hrȳðer, es; *n. Horned cattle, ox, cow, heifer:*—Jung hrȳðer *juniculus* [*anniculus?*], Ælfc. Gl. 22; Som. 59, 86; Wrt. Voc. 23, 45. Geong hrȳðer L. M. 2, 16; Lchdm. ii. 196, 24. Se hlāford geāhsode ðæt ðæt hrȳðer [cf. fear, 7] geond ðæt wēsten fērde *the master learned that the bull was going through the desert*, Blickl. Homl. 199, 9, 11, 14, 19, 26. Ðǣr wǣron gecȳpe hrȳðeru and scēp *there were for sale oxen and sheep*, Homl. Th. i. 406, 18. Hwīlum hȳ him rāredon on swā hrȳðro *sometimes they bellowed at him like oxen*, Shrn. 141, 10. Gif hrȳðera steorfan *if cattle are dying*, Lchdm. iii. 54, 31. Ðǣron næs orfcynnes nān māre būton vii hruðeru, Cod. Dipl. Kmbl. iv. 275, 7: Ex. 34, 19. Bige mid ðam ylcan feó swā hwæt swā ðē līcige hrȳðera and sceáp *emes ex eadem pecunia quidquid tibi placuerit sive ex armentis sive ex ovibus*, Deut. 14, 26. Hrȳðera and scēp, Jos. 6, 21. Næfde hē mā ðonne twentig hrȳðera and twentig sceápa and twentig swȳna, Ors. 1, 1; Swt. 18, 14. Hrȳðera gehlōw *the lowing of oxen*, Ælfc. Gr. 1; Som. 2, 35. Hine oftorfodon mid bānum and mid hrȳðera [hrȳðeres, MS. F: neáta, MS. D.] heáfdum *they stoned him to death with bones and heads of cattle*, Chr. 1012; Erl. 146, 18. Hrȳðra fald *bucetum*, Ælfc. Gl. 1; Som. 55, 23; Wrt. Voc. 15, 22. Of hrīðerum *de armento*, Lev. 1, 3. Of nȳtenum ðæt ys of hrīðerum and of sceápum *de pecoribus id est de bobus et ovibus*, 2. [*A. R.* reoðer: *Laym.* ruðeren, roðere; *pl; R. Glouc.* roþeren: *O. Frs.* hrither, rither, reder: cf. *O. H. Ger.* hrind *armentum, bos: Ger.* rind.] v. eald-hrīðer.

hrīðeren; *adj. Of cattle;* bovinus:—Genim hrȳðeren flǣsc *take ox-flesh*, L. M. 2, 7; Lchdm. ii. 186, 18. [Cf. *O. H. Ger.* rinderin *bovinus, bubula (caro).*]

hrīðer-freóls *taurilia*, Hpt. Gl. 515.

hrīðer-heáwere, es; *m. A butcher:*—Hrȳðerheáwere *bucida, qui boves mactat*, Ælfc. Gl. 33; Som. 62, 33; Wrt. Voc. 28, 16.

hrīðer-heord, e; *f. A herd of cattle:*—Eówre sceáp and eówer hrȳðerheorda *oves tuæ et armenta tua*, Gen. 45, 10.

hrīðer-hirde, es; *m. A neat-herd, herdsman:*—Amos hātte sum hrȳðerhyrde *Amos was the name of a certain herdsman*, Homl. Th. i. 322, 35. [Cf. *O. E. Hom.* Amos het a reoðer heorde.]

hriðian; *p.* ode *To shake, quake, have a fever:*—Sió wamb hryt *the stomach is fevered*, L. M. 2, 25; Lchdm. ii. 216, 20. Hie hriðiaþ *they are feverish*, 26; Lchdm. ii. 220, 5. Hē hriðode *he was sick with a fever*, Homl. Th. i. 86, 7. Hriðgende [cf. Lind. cuacende ł bifigende] *febricitantem*, Mt. Kmbl. 8, 14. Hriðigende, Mk. Skt. 1, 30. Hē biþ hriðende *he is feverish*, L. M. 2, 17; Lchdm. ii. 198, 21. [Cf. *O. H. Ger.* ridan *febricitare.*] v. hrisian.

hriðing, e; *f. Fever, feverishness:*—Mid hriðingum swīðe strangum *with very violent fevers*, L. M. 2, 46; Lchdm. ii. 258, 2.

hrið-suht [?], e; *f. Fever:*—Hāl of ridesohte *the fever left her*, Mk. Skt. Rush. 1, 31. Perhaps the word is borrowed; cf. *Icel.* riðu-sótt *fever, ague.*

HRŌC, es; *m. A* ROOK, *a raven, a jackdaw:*—Hrōc *gracculus* vel *garrulus*, Ælfc. Gl. 38; Som. 63, 27; Wrt. Voc. 29, 47: 77, 44. Hrōc *gralus, grallus*, 62, 31: 281, 1: *garrula*, Shrn. 29, 1. Se selþ nȳtenum mete and briddum hrōca cīgendum hine *qui dat jumentis escam ipsorum, et pullis corvorum invocantibus eum*, Ps. Spl. 146, 10. [*O. and N.* rok: *Prompt. Parv.* rook *frugella, graculus: O. Du.* rouca *garula: Icel.* hrókr: *O. H. Ger.* hruoh *graculus.*]

hroden; *pp. of* hreóðan *Laden, laden with ornaments, ornamented, adorned:*—Brȳd beága hroden *a bride adorned with rings*, Exon. 12 a; Th. 18, 31; Cri. 292. Ðā wæs heal hroden feónda feorum *then was the hall burdened with the lives of his foes* [*filled with the slain*], Beo. Th. 2307; B. 1151. Hroden ealowæge *the ornamented ale-cup*, 995; B. 495: 2048; 1022. [Cf. *Icel.* hroðian *in* hroðit sigli.] v. beág-, ge-, gold-, sinc-hroden; on-hreóðan.

HRŌF, es; *m. A* ROOF, *the top, summit, highest part* [cf. Tennyson's 'Why should we only toil the *roof* and crown of things?'] :—Gōma *vel* hrōf ðæs mūþes *palatum* vel *uranon*, Ælfc. Gl. 71; Som. 70, 106; Wrt. Voc. 43, 35. Hrōf *camara*, 290, 2. Se hrōf hæfde mislīce heáhnysse *the roof was not all of one height*, Homl. Th. i. 508, 18. Ðæt hēhste gōd is hrōf eallra ōðra gōda *the chief good is the roof and crown of all other goods*, Bt. 34, 7; Fox 142, 35. Wið ðæs heán hrōfes ðæs hēhstan andgites *in summæ intelligentiæ cacumen*, 41, 5; Fox 254, 16. Under fæstenne folca hrōfes *under the firmament*, Cd. 8; Th. 10, 8; Gen. 153. Mec feredon under hrōfes hleó *bore me under the shelter of the sky*, Exon. 107 b; Th. 409, 22; Rä. 28, 5. Martinus āstāh on ðam sticelan hrōfe, Homl. Th. ii. 510, 7. Ðe ne beóþ tō ðam hrōfe ðonne git cumen fulfremedra mægena *nondum ad extremam manum virtutum perfectione perductas*, Bt. 18, 1; Fox 60, 22. From hrōf eardes *a summo terræ*, Mk. Skt. Lind. 13, 27. On hrōfe gestōd heán landes *he stopped on the summit of the mount*, Cd. 140; Th. 175, 20; Gen. 2898. Of hē[um] heofnes hrōfe *ex summa cæli arce*, Rtl. 101, 24. Hē gescōp eorþan bearnum heofon tō [h]rōfe *qui filiis hominum cælum pro culmine tecti creavit*, Bd. 4, 24; S. 597, 22. Ðenden hē on ðysse worulde wunode under wolcna hrōfe, Judth. 10; Thw. 22, 19; Jud. 67: Elen. Kmbl. 178; El. 89: Cd. 158; Th. 196, 28; Exod. 298. Ðæt wē tō ðam hȳhstan hrōfe gestīgan *that we may mount to heaven*, Exon. 18 b; Th. 47, 3; Cri. 749. Ðe ðæs hūses hrōf staðeliaþ *qui ædificant domum*, Ps. Th. 126, 1. Gif hwylc wīf seteþ hire bearn ofer hrōf *si mulier aliqua infantem suam super tectum posuerit*, L. Ecg. C. 33; Th. ii. 156, 45. Ofer ðeánne hrōf, Beo. Th. 1970; B. 983: 1857; B. 926: 1677; B. 836. Under beorges hrōf *in the cave*, 5504; B. 2755. Ðā gewāt se engel up on heánne hrōf heofona rīces, Cd. 196; Th. 244, 2; Dan. 442. Fiðru mid ðǣm ic fleógan mæg ofer heáne hrōf heofones ðisses *pennæ quæ celsa conscendant poli*, Bt. Met. Fox 24, 5; Met. 24, 3: Cd. 46; Th. 58, 34; Gen. 956. Ofer wealles hrōf *super muros*, Ps. Th. 54, 9: Exon. 108 a; Th. 412, 1; Rä. 30, 7. Hylles hrōf, 104 b; Th. 397, 30; Rä. 16, 27. Helmes hrōf, Beo. Th. 2064; B. 1030. Under wætera hrōfas [*of passing through the Red Sea*], Cd. 170; Th. 214, 18; Exod. 571. Bodiaþ uppan hrōfum *prædicate super tecta*, Mt. Kmbl. 10, 27. [*Laym.* rōf: *Orm.* rhof: *O. Frs.* hrōf: *Icel.* hróf *a shed under which ships are built* or *kept.*] DER. heofon-, inwit-hrōf.

Hrofes-, Hrofe-ceaster, e; *f. Rochester*, Chr. 741; Erl. 46, 31: 885; Erl. 82, 20. Tō Hrofeceastre *in civitate quam gens Anglorum a pri-*

mario quondam illius qui dicebatur Hrof, Hrofæs cæstræ cognominat, Bd. 2, 3; S. 504, 25.

hróf-fæst; *adj. Having the roof firmly fixed*:—Healle hróffæste, Bt. Met. Fox 7, 11; Met. 7, 6.

hróf-sele, es; *m. A hall having a roof*:—Nǽnig wæter him for hrófsele hrínan ne mihte *no water could touch him for the roofed hall*, Beo. Th. 3034; B. 1515.

hróf-stán, es; *m. A roof-stone, stone forming part of a roof*:—Of ðam hrófstáne, Homl. Th. i. 508, 33. [Cf. hróf-tigel: *Mod. E.* roof-tree.]

hróf-tigel, e; *f. A tile for roofing*:—Hróftigla *tegulæ, imbrices, lateres* vel *laterculi*, Ælfc. Gl. 58; Som. 67, 92; Wrt. Voc. 38, 18.

hróf-timber, es; *n. Material for roofing*, imbrex, Hpt. Gl. 459.

hróf-wyrhta, an; *m. A workman who works at roofs, a builder*:—Hrófwyrhta *sarcitector* vel *tignarius*, Ælfc. Gl. 9; Som. 56, 125; Wrt. Voc. 19, 8.

hromese *acitula*, Cot. 206. v. hramsan.

hron, hrond-. v. hran, hrand-.

hrop. v. rop.

hróp, es; *m. Crying, clamour, outcry*:—Ðǽr biþ á wóp and hróp *there shall be ever weeping and wailing*, Blickl. Homl. 185, 7. [*Laym.* rop: *Scot.* roup *an outcry, a sale by auction*; cf. *Goth.* hrópei *clamor*; *Icel.* hróp; *n. scurrility, crying*: *O. H. Ger.* hruof; *m. clamor*: *Ger.* ruf.]

hrópan; *p.* hreóp *To cry out, clamour, make a noise, shout, scream*:—Hreópon friccan *the heralds shouted*, Andr. Kmbl. 2314; An. 1158: Elen. Kmbl. 108: 1097; El. 550. Hreópon mearcweardas *the warders of the border* [*the wolves*] *clamoured*, Cd. 151; Th. 188, 14; Exod. 168. On hwǽl hreopon [MS. hwreopon] herefugolas *the birds of war wheeled about screaming*, 150; Th. 188, 1; Exod. 161. Wóp áhófun hreópun hwílum wédende swá wilde deór, Exon. 46 a; Th. 156, 21; Gú. 878. Hrefnes briddum ðonne heó hrópende him cígeaþ tó *pullis corvorum invocantibus eum*, Ps. Th. 146, 10. [*A. R.* roped, *prs*; *Scot.* roup *to cry, shout*; *to sell by auction*: *Goth.* hrópjan; *p.* hrópida *to cry out*; *O. Sax.* hrópan; *p.* hreóp: *O. Frs.* hrópa; *p.* róp *and* rópte: *Icel.* hrópa; *p.* hrópaði *to slander*; *to call aloud*: *O. H. Ger.* hruofan; *p.* hriof: hruofian; *p.* hruofta (Grff. iv. 1135) *clamare*; *Ger.* rufen; *p.* rief.]

hrór; *adj. Stirring, active, agile, nimble, vigorous, stout, strong*:—Hrór hægstealdmon *a stout fellow*, Exon. 113 b; Th. 436, 18; Rä. 55, 3. Sǽde ðæt his byrne ábrocen wǽre heresceorpum hrór [heresceorp unhrór, Th.] *said that his byrnie was broken, strong* [*though it was*] *as armour*, Fins. Th. 90; Fin. 45. Ðá Israélas ǽhte gesǽtan hróres folces *et habitavit in tabernaculis eorum tribus Israel*, Ps. Th. 77, 56. Swá seó strǽle byþ strangum and mihtigum hrórum on handa *sicut sagittæ in manu potentis*, 126, 5. Ðá wæs of ðæm hróran [*Beowulf*] helm and byrne lungre álýsde, Beo. Th. 3262; B. 1629. Drihten his heáhsetl hrór timbrade *Dominus paravit sedem suam*, Ps. Th. 102, 18: 88, 26. Geseoh hróre meaht hysse ðínum *da potestatem tuam puero tuo*, 85, 15. Hróre stence *with strong perfume*, 132, 2. Ðæt hé folc gesceóp fægere Drihten heraþ holdlíce hróre geþance *populus qui creabitur laudabit Dominum*, 101, 16. Nǽnig móste heora hrórra hrím æpla gedígean *occidit moros eorum in pruina*, 77, 47. Hrórum neátum oððe unhrórum *mobilibus belluis aut immobilibus animantibus*, Bt. 41, 5; Fox 254, 14. [*O. Sax.* hrór: cf. *O. H. Ger.* ga-hrórig *viridis, floridus, florens*: *Ger.* rührig: cf. *also Prompt. Parv.* rooryn or ruffelyn amonge dyuerse thyngys *manumitto*; *and the epithet* roaring *as applied in the Elizabethan times to bullies*, v. Nares' Gloss. s. v.] v. fela-, un-hrór; *and* hréran.

hroren-líc; *adj. Ready to fall*; ruiturus, Som.

hróst, es; *m. A wooden framework* [*of a roof*], *a* ROOST:—Hróst *petaurum*; henna hróst *gallinarium*, Lye. [*Scot.* roost *the inner roof of a cottage, composed of spars reaching from the one wall to the other*: cf. *O. Sax.* he (*Christ*) ina kuman gisah thurh thes huses hrost (*of the man who was let down through the roof*): *O. Du.* roest *craticula, gallinarium*; *Ger.* rost '*craticula focaria, clathrum, fundamentum ædificii in cratis modum positum, clathrum galeæ*,' Grein: v. Grff. ii. 552, róst; *m. craticula, arula, sartago, catasta*.]

hróst-beág [?] *the woodwork of a circular roof*:—Tigelum sceádeþ hróstbeáges hróf [MS. hrost beages rof] *the woodwork of the roof parts from the tiles, the tiles fall off leaving the woodwork of the roof bare*, Exon. 124 a; Th. 477, 29; Ruin. 32.

hrot, es; *n. Thick fluid, scum, mucus*:—Gewyrc ðé lǽcedóm ðus of ecede and of hunige, genim ðæt séleste hunig dó ofer heorþ áseóþ ðæt weax and ðæt hrot of *make yourself a medicine thus of vinegar and honey; take the best honey, put it over the fire, seethe* [*strain?*] *off the wax and the scum*, L. M. 2, 28; Lchdm. ii. 224, 17. [*O. H. Ger.* hroz, roz *mucca, mucus, vomen, phlegma, reuma*; *Ger.* rotz.]

Hróð- *in proper names*, e. g. Hróð-gár, -mund, -wulf. [Cf. hréð, hréðig.]

hroð [or roð?]-**hund**, es; *m. Inutilis canis*, Ælfc. Gl. 21; Som. 59, 77; Wrt. Voc. 23, 36. v. roð-hund.

hróðor, es; *m. Solace, comfort, benefit, pleasure*:—Ic ðé Andreas onsende tó hleó and tó hróðre *I will send Andrew to you to protect and comfort you*, Andr. Kmbl. 221; An. 111: 1133; An. 567. His sunu hangaþ hrefne tó hróðre *his son hangs a solace for the raven*, Beo. Th. 4887; B. 2448: Apstls. Kmbl. 190; Ap. 95. Ðú ðe cwóme heánum tó hróðre *thou* (*Christ*) *who hast come for a comfort to the humble*, Exon. 13 b; Th. 26, 7; Cri. 414. Feóndum tó hróðor *to the delight of thy foes*, 17 a; Th. 39, 16; Cri. 623. Hungrum tó hróðor [cf. Soul Kmbl. 224, hungregum tó frófre], 99 b; Th. 373, 27; Seel. 116: 71 b; Th. 267, 17; Jul. 416. Tó hleó and tó hróðer, 25 a; Th. 73, 29; Cri. 1197: Elen. Kmbl. 32; El. 16: 2317; El. 1160. Forðon ðé hróðra oftíhþ gréne folde *therefore shall the green earth withdraw from thee her delights* [*fruits*], Cd. 48; Th. 62, 21; Gen. 1017. Gehwæðer óðrum hróðra gemyndig *each to other was mindful of benefits*, Beo. Th. 4349; B. 2171. Wérigmód heán hróðra leás *wearied, humbled, comfortless*, Andr. Kmbl. 2733; An. 1369. Heánmód hróðra bidǽled, Exon. 71 a; Th. 265, 33; Jul. 390. v. hréð.

hrúm, es; *m. Soot*:—Hrúm *cacobatus*, Wrt. Voc. 291, 24. Micelne sigelhearwan ðæm wæs seó onsýn sweartre ðonne hrúm *a great Ethiopian with a face blacker than soot*, Shrn. 120, 24. v. cetel-hrúm; hrýme.

hrúmig; *adj. Sooty*; fuliginosus, Cot. 31, Lye. v. be-hrúmig.

hrung, e; *f. A rung, staff, rod, beam, pole*:—Ongunnon stígan on wægn weras and hyra wicg somod hlódan under hrunge ðá ða hors óðbær wægn tó lande *the men mounted the wain and their steeds with them, they stowed them under the rung* [*the pole that supported the covering?*]; *then the wain bore the horses to land*, Exon. 106 a; Th. 404, 19; Rä. 23, 10. [*Chauc. Piers P.* rong (*of a ladder*): *Goth.* hrugga *a staff*: cf. *Icel.* Hrungnir *name of a giant*, v. Grmm. D. M. 494: *Ger.* runge *a pin, bolt*.] v. scil-hrung.

hruse, an; *f. The earth, ground*:—Beofaþ middangeard hruse under hæleþum *the world shall tremble, the earth under men*, Exon. 20 b; Th. 55, 13; Cri. 883: Beo. Th. 5110; B. 2558. Ðǽr mé siteþ hruse on hrycge *there the earth presses on my back*, Exon. 101 b; Th. 383, 5; Rä. 4, 6. Ic goldwine mínne hrusan heolstre biwráh *I buried my lord*, 76 b; Th. 287, 32; Wand. 23. Ligeþ him behindan hefig hrusan dǽl *there remains behind the heavy earthy part*, Bt. Met. Fox 29, 107; Met. 29, 53. Ne gelýfdon ðætte líffruma in monnes hiw from hrusan áhafen wurde *did not believe that the author of life had been raised from the ground in the form of a man*, Exon. 17 b; Th. 41, 19; Cri. 658. Ne hreósaþ hí tó hrusan *non est ruina maceriæ*, Ps. Th. 143, 18. Under hrusan *under ground*, Beo. Th. 4813; B. 2411: Elen. Kmbl. 435; El. 218. Wæs hungor ofer hrusan *there was a famine upon the earth*, Chr. 975; Erl. 126, 29; Edg. 55. Hreás on hrusan nalles æfter lyfte lácende hwearf, Beo. Th. 5654; B. 2831. Heofonas ðú wealdest hrusan swylce *tui sunt cæli et tua est terra*, Ps. Th. 88, 10: 120, 2: 133, 4. Under eorþan befeolan hinder under hrusan, Exon. 91 a; Th. 340, 24; Gn. Ex. 116. For ansýne écean Drihtnes heofonas droppetaþ hrusan forhtiaþ *terra mota est; etenim cæli distillaverunt a facie Dei*, Ps. Th. 67, 9. Heofenas blissiaþ hrusan swylce gefeóþ *lætentur cæli et exultet terra*, 95, 11. Hyllas and hrusan and heá beorgas ðec wurðiaþ, Cd. 192; Th. 240, 7; Dan. 383. [Grimm D. M. p. 230 says 'mit *crusta* wird das ags. hruse genau verwandt sein.']

hrut or hrút *balidus*, Cot. 28, Lye. *Ettmüller suggests* balidus = balans animal, *and compares Icel.* hrútr *a ram*: *Ducange has the following* 'balidus fortasse pro validus, ad coitum aptus.' *See* hryte.

hrútan; *p.* hreát, *pl.* hruton *To make a noise, to snore*; stridere, stertere:—Ic hrúte *sterto*, Ælfc. Gr. 28, 3; Som. 30, 64. Ne æt mé hrútende hrisil scríðeþ *nor does the shuttle come whizzing at me*, Exon. 109 a; Th. 417, 19; Rä. 36, 7. [*Prompt. Parv.* rowtyn, yn slepe *sterto*: *Chauc.* route *to snore, roar*, 'the wynde so loude kan to *route*:' *Wick.* routeþ *stertit*: *Piers P.* rutte *snored*: *E. D. S. Reprint. Gloss.* B. 15, rute *to cry fiercely*; rowt, rawt *to low like an ox or cow*: *Icel.* hrjóta (*older* rjóta) *to snore*: *O. H. Ger.* riuzan; *p.* róz, *pl.* ruzun *flere, plangere, stridere*: cf. *also* ruzian, ruzon *stertere*; ruzonti *stridulus, stridens*, Grff. ii. 562.] v. reótan.

hruð, hruðer. v. hrið, hríðer.

hruxl *a noise*; strepitus, Som. v. hryscan, ge-hruxl.

hryc. v. hrycg.

hrycce. v. corn-hrycce.

hrycg, es; *m.* I. *a back of a man* or *animal*; dorsum, spina:—Hricg *dorsum*, Ælfc. Gl. 74; Som. 71, 47; Wrt. Voc. 44, 30. Hricc, Blickl. Gl. Bæc ł hricc, Ps. Spl. 17, 42. Swylce mé wǽre se hrycg forbrocen *dum configitur* [*confringitur*, Ps. Surt.] *spina*, Ps. Th. 31, 4. Hiora hrygc simle gebiéged . . . se hrygc ðæt sint ða hiéremenn . . . se hrycg færþ æfter ǽlcre wuhte *dorsum illorum semper incurva . . . qui subsequenter inhærent dorsa nominantur*, Past. 1, 4; Swt. 29, 9–14. Hét gewríðan ðone pápan and ðone óðerne preóst tó his hricge hindan, Homl. Th. ii. 310, 31: 416, 10. Pricaþ innan ðán sculdru[m] and on ðan hrigge swilce ðár þornas on sý *there are prickings in the shoulders and back as if there were thorns in*, Lchdm. iii. 120, 10. Ne hé on horses hrycge cuman wolde *non equorum dorso vectus*, Bd. 3, 5; S. 526, 28. Se cyning hæfde his hrycg him tó hliépan *ut ipse acclinis humi regem* *super adscensurum in equum dorso ad'olleret*, Ors. 6, 24; Swt. 274, 24. Đonne went hē his hrycg tō him *jam terga in ejus faciem mittit*, Past. 52, 4; Swt. 407, 8: Lchdm. iii. 242, 13. Of hry[g]um *de spinis*, Mt. Kmbl. Lind. 7, 16. Hrygas *spinæ*, 13, 7. II. *a ridge, rigg* [*of barley*, etc; *see* Halliw. Dict. *rig*], *high line of continuous hills, an elevated surface*:—Anlang hrycges tō đære eorþburh *along the ridge to the earthen fort*, Cod. Dipl. Kmbl. iii. 411, 21. Eal būtan ānan hrycge, 19, 4. West đonan on đone hrycg, 416, 17. Ofer đæs temples hricg *supra pinnam templi*, Lk. Skt. 4, 9. Com ic on sǣs hricg *veni in altitudinem maris*, Ps. Th. 68, 2. Ofer sǣs hrygc, Lchdm. iii. 34, 16. Sende ic ofer wæteres hrycg ealde mādmas *I sent across the water old treasures*, Beo. Th. 947; B. 471. On wæteres hricg, Salm. Kmbl. 38; Sal. 19. Ǣr đon wē tō londe geliden hæfdon ofer breóne hrycg *ere to land we came across the rough sea*, Exon. 20 b; Th. 53, 31; Cri. 859. Rīdan ȳđa hrycgum *to ride on the crests of the waves*, 101 b; Th. 384, 25; Rä. 4, 33. [*Laym.* rugge: *A. R.* rug: *Ayenb.* reg: *Havel.* rig: *Piers P.* rugge: *Prompt. Parv.* rygge, of a lond *porca*: *Icel.* hryggr *back, spine; a ridge*: *Dan.* rug: *O. H. Ger.* hrucki *dorsum, tergum*: *Ger.* rücken.] v. stān-, sund-hrycg. The word under the forms *rig, ridge* may be found in many compounds among various dialects. See E. D. S. Reprinted Glossaries, Halliwell's Dictionary, and Jamieson's Scottish Dictionary.

hrycg-bān, es; *n. Back-bone, spine*:—Hrygcbān *spina*, Ps. Lamb. 31, 4. [Rygboon, v. Halliw. Dict. under *rig*: *Prompt. Parv.* ryggebone of bakke (rigbone *or* bakbone) *spina, spondile*: *Dan.* ryg-ben *backbone, spine*: *O. H. Ger.* hrucki-beini *spina*.]

hrycg-brædan [-brǣdan?]; *pl. The parts of the back which stand out on the right and left side*:—Smyre ābūtan đane swyran and ābūtan đa hrigbræde *smear the neck and on either side of the spine*, Lchdm. iii. 118, 24. [Cf. lenden-brædena (*gen. pl.*) *and O. H. Ger.* ruggi-bratun *palæ, sunt dorsi leva dextraque eminentia membra*. v. Grff. iii. 284–5, *where see the remark under* brat *as to the vowel*.]

hrycg-hǣr, es; *n. Hair on the back of an animal*:—Gif đū hafast mid đē wulfes hrycghǣr and tæglhǣr đa ȳtemestan on sīđfæte būtan fyrhtu đū đone sīđ gefremest ac se wulf sorgaþ ymbe his sīđ *if you have with you on a journey hairs from a wolf's back and from the tip of its tail, without fear you will perform the journey; but the wolf will have trouble about his journey*, L. Med. ex Quadr. 9, 3; Lchdm. i. 360, 20.

hrycg-hrægel, es; *n. A dorsal, mantle*:—Ic geann ānes hricghrægles đæs sēlestan đe ic hæbbe *I give one dorsal the best that I have*, Chart. Th. 529, 10, where Thorpe appends this note in explanation of the word, '"manteau très riche d'ornemens, qui n'étoit porté que par les gens de haute condition." Roquefort, *voce* Dossal. A dorsal is also a wall-hanging of tapestry, used chiefly in the church at the back of the stalls.' vii setlhrægel and iii ricghrægel and ii wahræft, 429, 28.

hrycg-mearh *the spinal marrow*. [*Dan.* ryg-marv *spinal marrow*.] v. next word.

hrycgmearh-liþ, es; *n. The spine*:—Hrygmerglịþ *spina*, Wrt. Voc. 283, 46.

hrycg-ribb, es; *n. A rib*:—Hricgrib *spondilia*, Wrt. Voc. 65, 22. Hrycrib, 283, 49.

hrycg-rible, -riple *the parts of the back which stand out on the right and left side*:—Ricgrible *pale*, Wrt. Voc. 65, 20. Hrycriple *palæ*, 283, 45. v. hrycg-brædan.

hrycg-teúng, e; *f. A spasm in the lower part of the back*:—Hrigteúng *vel* hrifwirc *yleos*, Ælfc. Gr. 10; Som. 57, 16; Wrt. Voc. 19, 24.

hrycg-weg, es; *m. A road running along a ridge* or *elevated piece of ground*:—On đone beorh tō đem ricgwege đonne eást andlang hricgweges *on to the hill to the road that runs along it, and then east along the road*, Cod. Dipl. Kmbl. iii. 427, 33.

hrycigan *to plough into ridges*; resulcare, Gl. Prud. 716.

hryding, e; *f. A clearing, a patch of cleared land*:—Hryding *subcisiva*, Ælfc. Gl. 57; Som. 67, 71; Wrt. Voc. 37, 57. [Cf. *O. E. Homl.* þe schal ruden þine wei *qui præparabit viam tuam*: *E. D. S. Cumberland Gloss.* rid, rud *to uproot trees or hedges*. 'The frequent names of Ridding and Rudding applied to houses and fields have doubtless originated from this:' *Icel.* [h]ryđja *to clear land, a road*, etc.]

hrȳfing, e; *f. Roughness, scab, crust of a healing wound*:—Smire mid hunige đæt đȳ đē raþor sió hrȳfing of fealle, L. M. 1, 35; Lchdm. ii. 86, 4.

hrygile-būc, es; *m.* [?] Of đam æscene đe is ōđre namon hrygilebūc gecleopad, Chart. Th. 439, 26. [Cf. ridgil-back *a back having a rise* or *ridge in the middle*, Halliwell's Dict. According to this the word might mean 'having a prominent belly' and refer to the shape of the vessel.]

hrȳman, hrēman; *p.* de *To call, cry out, to cry out* [*with exultation* or *in lamentation, complaint*], *boast, exult, lament, murmur*:—Ne hē ne hrȳmþ *neque clamabit*, Mt. Kmbl. 12, 19. Wē biddaþ ł wē hrēmaþ *imploramus*, Rtl. 121, 1. Forhuon gie hrēmas *quid ploratis*, Mk. Skt. Lind. 5, 39. Đa hrȳmaþ tō hyra efengelīcon *clamantes coæqualibus*, Mt. Kmbl. 11, 16. Hig hrȳmaþ tō mē and ic gehīre hira hreám *vociferabuntur ad me et ego audiam clamorem eorum*, Ex. 22, 23. Đā hrȳmde heó tō hire hīwun ... đā hē gehīrde đæt ic hrīmde *vocavit mulier ad se homines domus suæ ... cum ego succlamassem et audisset vocem meam*, Gen. 39, 14, 15. Đā hrȳmde sum wōd man and cwæþ, Homl. Th. i. 458, 2. Se cǣsere wēdde and hrȳmde dæges and nihtes *the emperor raved day and night*, Shrn. 139, 6. Ne đȳ hrađor hrēmde *nor the more vaunted*, Cd. 212; Th. 263, 2; Dan. 756. Israhēla bearn hrīmdon and ongeán Moisen micclum ceorodon *the children of Israel murmured against Moses*, Num. 13, 31. Gaas đætte hrēme *vadit ut ploret*, Jn. Skt. Lind. 11, 31. Gif feorrancumen man ođđe fræmde būton wege gange and hē đonne nāwđer ne hrȳme ne hē horn ne blāwe *if a man from a distance or a stranger go off the high road and then neither call out nor blow a horn*, L. Wih. 28; Th. i. 42, 24. Đā ongunnon đa hrȳman đe þurh đæs dracan blǣde ālēfode wǣron, Homl. Th. ii. 294, 30. Wē sceolon hrȳman swīđor and swīđor tō đam Hǣlende, i. 156, 22. Đā begann hē tō hrȳmenne and cwæþ, 152, 15. Mid fleáme com on his cyþþe Constontinus hrēman ne þorfte *by flight Constantine got home, had little cause to boast*, Chr. 937; Erl. 114, 5; Æđelst. 39. Hrēmende *ululatus*, Mt. Kmbl. Lind. 2, 18: *plorantem*, Jn. Skt. Lind. 11, 33. Mid micelre stemne hrȳmende *crying with a loud voice*, Homl. Th. i. 46, 33. [*Laym. A. R.* remen: *Halliw. Dict.* reem, reme.] v. hreám, hrēmig.

hrȳme *soot*; fuligo, Cot. 83, Lye. v. hrūm.

hrympelle. v. rimpel.

hryre, es; *m. Fall, downfall, ruin, destruction, perdition, decay, decline, death*:—Hryre *casus*, Ælfc. Gr. 11; Som. 15, 10: *ruina*, Ps. Spl. 105, 28. His hryre wæs micel *fuit ruina ejus magna*, Mt. Kmbl. 7, 27. Hægles hryre *fall of hail*, Exon. 56 a; Th. 198, 26; Ph. 16. Đæt đæs folces sceolde micel hryre beón *that there should be a great destruction among the Romans*, Ors. 4, 1; Bos. 77, 45. Līces hryre *the fall of the body* [*death*], Exon. 48 b; Th. 167, 26; Gū. 1066: 65 a; Th. 240, 27; Ph. 645: Andr. Kmbl. 457; An. 229. Đǣr him næs ne līfes lyre ne līces hryre *there was for him* [*Adam*] *no loss of life, no bodily decay*, Exon. 44 b; Th. 151, 27; Gū. 801. Yfle preóstas bióþ folces hryre *laqueus ruinæ populi mei sacerdotes mali*, Past. 2, 1; Swt. 31, 9. Đætte hie đone spild đæs hryres him ondrǣden *ut præcipitem ruinam metuant*, 52, 5; Swt. 407, 21. Gif wē æfter đæm hryre ūrre scylda tō him gecierdon *nobis post lapsum redeuntibus*, 52, 3; Swt. 405, 16. Betwux đæra stāna hryre betǣhte hē his fȳnd Gode *whilst the stones were falling he commended his foes to God*, Homl. Th. i. 50, 23. Đis cild is gesett manegum mannum tō hryre *positus est in ruinam multorum*, 144, 18: Bt. Met. Fox 9, 8; Met. 9, 4. Đa twā forman gesceapennyssa feóllon on hryre and seó þridde wæs on hryre ācenned, Homl. Th. ii. 8, 31. Ne fægnode ic on mīnes feóndes hryre, 448, 22. On myclum hryre seó heord wearþ on sǣ besceofen *magno impetu grex præcipitatus est in mare*, Mk. Skt. 5, 13. Đone hryre đe se feallenda deófol on engla werode gewanode *the loss which the falling devil had caused in the host of angels*, Homl. Th. i. 32, 23, 28. Hordwearda hryre, Cd. 169; Th. 210, 6; Exod. 511: Exon. 76 b; Th. 287, 1; Wand. 7. Ne timbreþ hē nō healle ac hryre *non habitaculum sed ruina fabricatur*, Past. 49, 3; Swt. 383, 33. Mid gelōmlǣcendum hryrum *by frequent destructions*, Homl. Th. i. 578, 34. Hē gefylde hryras *implebit ruinas*, Ps. Spl. 109, 7. Hwilce hryras *quantas ruinas*, Bt. 16, 4; Fox 58, 1. v. leód-, līc-, wīg-hryre; *and* cf. dryre.

hryre; *adj.* [?] *Falling, decaying, perishing*:—Sōđlīce mid đisum wordum is geswutelod đæt đises middangeardes wæstm is hryre. Tō đam hē wext đæt hē fealle *verily by these words is manifested that the fruit of this world is decaying* [*or a ruin* (?) *v. preceding word*]. *It grows that it may fall*, Homl. Th. i. 614, 8. [Cf. *for a similar relation in form between adj. and verb O. Sax.* luggi; *adj.* and liogan.]

hrȳred-ness, hrȳre-mūs, hrȳre-ness. v. hrēred-ness, hrēre-mus, hrēr-ness.

hrysc, hrysca *irruptio*, Som.

hryscan *to make a noise*:—Hriscan *stridere*, Hpt. Gl. 494. Hristenda [hriscende?] *astridulus, stridulus*, Lye. v. hruxl.

hrysian. v. hrisian.

hrystan. v. hyrstan.

hrȳtan; *p.* te *To scatter*:—Se đe hrēt *qui sternit*, Prov. 10, Lye. [*Icel.* hreyta *to spread, scatter*.]

hryte or hrȳte; *adj. Balidinus*, Ælfc. Gl. 79; Som. 72, 94; Wrt. Voc. 46, 41. *The word occurs in a list of names of colours, but the meaning is uncertain. Ducange has* '*balidinus* forte legendum *badius* vel *balius* nostris *bay, bayard*.' v. hrut.

hrȳđer. v. hrīđer.

hryđig; *adj. Dismantled?* [cf. *Icel.* hrjóđa *to strip, clear*] or *tottering?* [cf. hriđian], Exon. 77 b; Th. 291, 5; Wand. 77.

hryđđa. v. ryđđa.

hrȳw-līc, hrȳwsian. v. hreów-līc, hreówsian.

HŪ; *adv. How*. I. *in direct questions*:—Hū mæg man ingān on stranges hūs *quomodo potest quisquam intrare in domum fortis?* Mt. Kmbl. 12, 29: 34. Hū ne synt gē sēlran đonne hig *nonne vos magis plures estis illis?* 6, 26: 25. Hū sculon wit nū libban *how are we to live?* Cd. 38; Th. 50, 7; Gen. 805. II. *in exclamations* [*see also* I]:—Hū la! ne gewearþ unc tō ānum peninge *how now! was not our agreement for a penny?* Th. An. 74, 20. Hū gōd is ēce God *quam bonus*

Deus, Ps. Th. 72, 1. Eálā gǣsta god hū ðū mid noman ryhte nemned wǣre emmanuhel *oh! God of spirits, how rightly wast thou named by the name of Emmanuel!* Exon. 9 b; Th. 9, 6; Cri. 130: 11 a; Th. 14, 8; Cri. 216. Eálā on hū grimmum and on hū grundleásum seáðe swinceþ ðæt sweorcende mōd, Bt. Met. Fox 3, 1, 2; Met. 3, 1. III. *in dependent clauses with indic. or subjunct:* — Nū wundraþ gehwā hū se deófol dorste geneálǣcan tō ðam Hǣlende *now every one will wonder how the devil durst come near Jesus*, Homl. Th. i. 166, 32. Wē gehīrdon hū gē ofslōgon twegen cynegas Seon and Og *audivimus quod interfecistis Sehon et Og*, Jos. 2, 10. Hī gehȳrdon hū seó hālige spræc, Judth. 11; Thw. 23, 37; Jud. 160. Wē gesāwon hū hē wæs on heofenas āstīgende, Nicod. 18; Thw. 8, 39. Ūs secgaþ bēc hū āstāg in middangeard bearn godes, Exon. 19 a; Th. 49, 15; Cri. 786. Ðā angan Thomas his spǣce hū hē com tō Cantuuarebyri and hū se arcebiscop āxode hȳrsumnesse at him *then Thomas began his speech, how he had come to Canterbury, and how the archbishop had demanded obedience from him*, Chr. 1070; Erl. 208, 14. Ðā āxode se cāsere ðone ǣnne preóst hū his nama wǣre oððe hū gefyrn hē gelȳfde, Homl. Th. ii. 310, 15. Ðā wearþ ðæt mǣden hohful hū heó ǣfre wæras wissian sceolde, Blickl. Swt. 2, 122. Gefada embe hū ðū wylle *dispose of it how thou wilt*, 3, 285. Hycgaþ his ealle hū gē hī beswīcen *consider of it all, how ye may entrap them*, Cd. 22; Th. 28, 9; Gen. 433. Ābīdan sceal miclan dōmes hū him metod scrīfan wille *must abide the great doom, how the Lord will adjudge to him*, Beo. Th. 1962; B. 979. IV. *with a comparative* [cf. þȳ, swā]: — Lufade hine lenge hū geornor, Exon. 34 b; Th. 110, 18; Gū. 109. V. *qualifying, or in combination with, other words:*— Hū mycel scealt ðū *quantum debes?* Lk. Skt. 16, 5. Hū mycel gōd is on gehȳrsumnesse and hū mycel yfel on ungehȳrsumnysse, Boutr. Scrd. 19, 26. On ðyssere dǣde is geswutelod hū micclum fremige ðære sōðan lufe gebed, Homl. Th. i. 50, 35. Hū micele swīðor *how much more?* 68, 24. On hū manegum wīsum is Godes weorc? Boutr. Scrd. 18, 14. Hū fela se hǣlend him dyde *quanta sibi fecisset ihesus*, Mk. Skt. 5, 20. Hū fela sagena hig ongēn ðē secgeaþ *quanta adversum te dicant testimonia*, Mt. Kmbl. 27, 13. Hū lange forbere ic eów *usque quo patiar vos?* 17, 17. Hū long tīd *quantum temporis*, Mk. Skt. 9, 21. Be gebrōðrum hū gesibbe wīf hig habban mōton *de fratribus quam prope cognatas uxores habere possint*, L. Ecg. C; Th. ii. 130, 8: 13. Hū hēh and deóp hell seó, Cd. 228; Th. 309, 9; Sat. 707. Witan hū ðū æðele eart, Hy. 3, 14; Hy. Grn. ii. 281, 14. Mē com swīðe oft on gemynd hū gesǣliglīce tīda wǣron giond Angelcynn *it has often come into my mind what happy times there were in England*, Past. Pref. Swt. 3, 4. Ðæt se lāreów ðe him tela tǣce him sylf elles hū dō *that the teacher who teaches him well, himself act otherwise*, L. E. I. 21; Th. ii. 418, 4. Ne meg nū hū ælles beón *it cannot be otherwise*, Shrn. 195, 7. Hū geáres *according to the time of year*, L. M. 2, 34; Lchdm. ii. 238, 22. Swā hū swā hit gewurde *however it may have happened*, Homl. Th. i. 588, 29. Hī habbaþ æt Gode swā hū swā hī geearniaþ *they will have from God, in accordance with whatever they merit*, ii. 326, 30. [*Laym. Orm.* hu: *A. R.* hwu, hu: *Ayenb.* hou: *Goth.* hwē: *O. Frs.* hu, ho: *O. Sax.* hwō: *O. H. Ger.* hweó, v. Grff. iv. 1193: *Ger.* wie.] v. ge-hū; hū-meta, -hwega.

hu-. v. hw-.

hucs. v. husc.

hūdenian *in the following passage:*—Hūdenige ǣrest hine selfne, ōþ hē wacige and āhrisige siððan ōðre tō geornfulnesse gōdra weorca *prius se per sublimia facta excutiant, et tunc ad bene vivendum alios sollicitos reddant*, Past. 64; Swt. 461, 16. [Sweet, in the note on this passage, suggests that the word may be from the same root as *quatio*, adding that Prof. Skeat compares the Scotch *houd* to shake. May not the word however be used from a misconception of the Latin word, by which *excutere* is considered as connected with *cutis* = *hȳd?*]

hūf, es; *m. Part of the mouth* or *upper part of the throat, a tumour affecting that part:* — Hūf *sublinguium*, Ælfc. Gl. 71; Som. 70, 98; Wrt. Voc. 43, 28. Ad ufam. Ðes lǣcecræft deáh wyð ðone hūf *ad uvam. This medicine is good for tumour on the epiglottis*, Lchdm. iii. 106, 6. Of ðan ūve droppaþ uppan ða tunga, 138, 28.

hūf, es; *m. A horned owl;* bubo, Wrt. Voc. 63, 19. [The word occurs both in English and *O. H. Ger.* with and without initial *h*, hūf, ūf; hūvo, ūvo *bubo*.] v. ūf.

hūfe, an; *f. A covering for the head:*—Hūfe *cidaris* vel *mitra*, Ælfc. Gl. 64; Som. 69, 11; Wrt. Voc. 40, 45. Biscopes hūf *flammeolum* vel *flammeum*, 112; Som. 79, 88; Wrt. Voc. 59, 55. Hūfan hættes *mitræ*, Lye. [*Chauc. Piers P.* houve: *Prompt. Parv.* howe, heed hyllynge *tena, capedulum, sidaris;* and see the note, p. 249: *Scot.* how *a coif, hood*: *Icel.* húfa *a hood, cap, bonnet*: *O. H. Ger.* hūba *mitra, thyara*: *Ger.* haube.]

hūfian; *p.* ode *To put on a* hufe:—Hē his suna hūfode swā drihten bebeád *he put bonnets upon them, as the Lord commanded;* imposuit mitras ut jusserat dominus, Lev. 8, 13.

Hugas; *n. pl. The name of a people in the neighbourhood of West Friesland*, Beo. Th. 4998; B. 2502: 5820; B. 2914.

hugu. v. hwega.

hū-hwega, -hugu; *adv. About, somewhere about:*—Hūhugu ymb ða teóþan tīd dæges *hora circiter decima diei*, Bd. 3, 27; S. 558, 12. Hūhugu syx hund hīda *familiarum circiter sexcentarum*, 4, 19; S. 590, 3. Hūhwega ymb iii niht *somewhere about three days*, L. M. 2, 59; Lchdm. ii. 280, 16. Hūhwego fīf hund manna, Blickl. Homl. 201, 14.

hū-ilpa, an; *m. The name of a bird so called from its note* [cf. *Ger.* uhu *owl*]? — Dyde ic mē tō gomene ganetes hleóþor and huilpan swēg, Exon. 81 b; Th. 307, 9; Seef. 21.

hulc, es; *m.* [?] *A light ship, a hulk* [*but in later times the word is applied to a heavy ship of clumsy make*]; liburna, Ælfc. Gl. 103; Som. 77, 102; Wrt. Voc. 56, 23. Si adveniat ceol *vel* hulcus, L. Eth. iv. 2; Th. i. 300, 9. [*Prompt. Parv.* hulke, shyppe *hulcus*, and see the note, p. 252: *O. Du.* hulke *navis oneraria*: *O. H. Ger.* holcho *actuaria navis*.]

hulc, es; *m. A hut, hovel, cabin:*—Hulc *tugurium*, Ælfc. Gr. 8; Som. 7, 62: Ælfc. Gl. 108; Som. 78, 116; Wrt. Voc. 58, 30: 85, 74. Gyf hē his scip uppe getogen hæbbe oððon hulc geworhtne oððon geteld geslagen ðæt hē ðǣr friþ hæbbe and ealle his ǣhta *if he have drawn his ship ashore or have built a hut or pitched a tent, let him and all his property be unmolested*, L. Eth. i. 3; Th. i. 286, 9. Hē wolde geneálǣcan his hulce *he* [*the leper*] *wanted to reach his hut*, Homl. Th. i. 336, 10. On wāclīcum screafum oððe hulcum lūtigende *lurking in miserable dens or hovels*, 544, 30. [*Wick.* hulke, Is. 1, 8.]

hulfestre, an; *f. A plover;* pluvialis [the word occurs in a list of names of birds], Ælfc. Gl. 38; Som. 63, 24; Wrt. Voc. 29, 44.

hulfstan *ciupella*, Wrt. Voc. 63, 24.

hū-līc; *pron. Of what sort;* qualis:—Hē āhsode hwæt alexander se cyning dyde and hūlīc mon hē wǣre and in hwylcere yldo *he asked what king Alexander was doing, and what sort of man he was, and of what age*, Nar. 18, 12. Nū ic wille secgan hūlucu heó wæs *I will tell you what it* [*Carthage*] *was like*, Ors. 4, 13; Bos. 99, 57. Hūlīc is ðes *qualis est hic?* Mt. Kmbl. Rush. 8, 27. Hūlīc is se organ tō begonganne, Salm. Kmbl. 107; Sal. 53. Hūlig, Lk. Skt. Lind. 1, 29. Gisih hūlīce [hūlco, Lind.] stānas and hūlīc [huulig, Lind.] timber *aspice quales lapides et quales structuræ*, Mk. Skt. Rush. 13, 1. v. hwilc.

hulu, e; *f. A hull, husk:*—Hnute hula *culliole*, Ælfc. Gl. 31; Som. 61, 105; Wrt. Voc. 27, 34: Gl. Prud. 156: Hpt. Gl. 439. [*Prompt. Parv.* hoole or huske *siliqua;* hoole of pesyn or benys or oder coddyd frute *techa;* see note, p. 242: *Scot.* hule *a husk*: cf. *O. H. Ger.* hulsa *siliqua*: *Ger.* hülse.]

Humbre, an; or *indecl. f. The Humber:* — Ōþ gemǣro Humbre [streámes] *ad confinium usque Humbræ fluminis*, Bd. 1, 25; S. 486, 17. Ōþ Humbre streám *Humbræ fluvio*, 2, 5; S. 506, 11. Behionan Humbre . . . begiondan Humbre, Past. Pref; Swt. 3, 14, 16. Be sūþan Humbre, Chr. 827; Erl. 62, 33. Ofer Humbre mūþan, 867; Erl. 72, 6. Humbra [MS. B. Humbran] eá, 942; Erl. 116, 10. Tō Humbran mūþan, 993; Erl. 132, 12. Com Tostig eorl intō Humbran mid lx scipum, 1066; Erl. 201, 6.

hū-meta; *adv. How, in what manner;* quomodo:—Hūmeta eodest ðū in *quomodo intrasti?* Mt. Kmbl. 22, 12. Hūmeta bitst ðū æt mē drincan *quomodo bibere a me poscis?* Jn. Skt. 4, 9. Hūmeta bodaþ hē [*Paul*] Cristes geleáfan? Homl. Th. i. 388, 2. Nū is tō besceáwigenne hūmeta se ælmihtiga God geþafaþ ðæt . . . *now it is to be considered how it is that the almighty God permits that . . .*, 486, 17. Ðū sǣdest ðæt ðū ne mihte witan hūmeta hē his weólde oððe hū hē his weólde *you said that you could not see in what manner or by what means he governed it* [*the world*]; quibus gubernaculis mundus regatur, Bt. 35, 2; Fox 156, 25.

hun [hūn?], e; *f. Impurity* [?]; tabes, Cot. 192. v. hunel.

Hūnas *and* Hūne; *pl. The Huns:*—Hūne *Hunni*, Bd. 5, 9; S. 622, 15. Hūnas, Elen. Kmbl. 42; El. 21. Hūna cyning, 64; El. 32: Chr. 443; Erl. 10, 22. Ætla weóld Hūnum, Exon. 85 a; Th. 319, 26; Vid. 18: 85 b; Th. 322, 2; Vīd. 57. [*Icel.* Húnar: *M. H. Ger.* Hiune.] v. Grmm. D. M. 489–91.

HUND, es; *m. A* HOUND, *dog; applied to persons as a term of abuse in English and in other dialects:*—Ðā hē ðider com ðā sceolde cuman ðære helle hund ongeán hine ðæs nama wæs Ceruerus *when he came thither, it is said, that then the dog of hell, whose name was Cerberus, came towards him*, Bt. 35, 6; Fox 168, 15. Wið hundes slite *for the bite of a dog*, Herb. 177, 2; Lchdm. i. 310, 8. Of ðæs hundes handa *de manu canis*, Ps. Th. 21, 18. Ðone hǣðenan hund *the heathen dog* [*Holofernes*], Judth. 10; Thw. 23, 7; Jud. 110. Swā hundas *ut canes*, Ps. Th. 58, 6. Dumbe hundas *canes muti*, Past. 5, 1; Swt. 89, 17. Hunda gebeorc *barking of dogs*, Ælfc. Gr. 1; Som. 2, 35. Nys hit nā gōd ðæt man nime bearna hlāf and hundum worpe *non est bonum sumere panem filiorum et mittere canibus*, Mt. Kmbl. 15, 26. [*Goth.* hunds: *O. Sax. O. Frs.* hund: *Icel.* hundr: *O. H. Ger.* hunt: *Ger.* hund.] DER. heáhdeór-, helle-, hroð-, wēde-hund.

hundes beó *a dog-fly*, Cot. 54, Lye.

hundes cwelcan *berries of the wayfaring tree;* baccæ de viburno opulo, colocinthidæ, Lchdm. iii. 333, col. 2.

hundes fleóge *a dog-fly:* — Hundes fleóge *cinomia*, Ælfc. Gl. 21;

Som. 59, 119; Wrt. Voc, 23, 37. Hundes fleógan *muscam caninam*, Ps. Th. 77, 45: Ors. 1, 7; Swt. 38, 1. [*Wick.* hound-fleȝe: *O. H. Ger.* hunt-, huntes-fliuge *cynomia, musca canina.*]

hundes heáfod *snapdragon*, Lchdm. ii. 395, col. 2.

hundes lús *a dog-fly*; cinomia, Wrt. Voc. 77, 54. [Cf. *Ger.* hundslaus.]

hundes micge *cynoglossum officinale*, Lchdm. ii. 333, col. 2.

hundes tunge *hound's tongue*; cynoglossum officinale, Lchdm. ii. 333, col. 2. [*O. H. Ger.* huntes-zunga *cynoglossa.*] v. E. D. S. Plant Names, hounds-tongue.

hundes wyrm *a dog-worm*; ricinus, Ælfc. Gl. 24; Som. 60, 33; Wrt. Voc. 24, 33.

HUND; *n. A* HUNDRED; centum:—Gyf hwylc mann hæfþ hund sceápa *si fuerint alicui centum oves*, Mt. Kmbl. 18, 12. Hund sestra . . . hund mittena hwǽtes, Lk. Skt. 16, 6, 7. Senatum ðæt wæs án hund manna ðéh heora æfter fyrste wǽre þreó hund, Ors. 2, 4; Swt. 70, 36. Mid án hund scipa, Bt. Met. Fox 26, 30; Met. 26, 15. Sum hund scipa *some hundred ships*, Chr. 894; Erl. 91, 5. Ðæt flód stód ðá swá án hund daga and fíftig daga *obtinuerunt aquæ terram centum quinquaginta diebus*, Gen. 7, 24. Æfter óðer healf hund daga *post centum quinquaginta dies*, 8, 3. Mid penningum twǽm hundum *denariis ducentis*, Mk. Skt. Lind. 6, 37. Ðǽr wǽron twá hund and eahta and feówertig wera, Blickl. Homl. 239, 14. Mid ccl hunde [þridde healf hund, MS. E.] scipa, Chr. 893; Erl. 88, 25. Ðá geceás Gedeon þreó hund manna, Jud. 7, 6. Þreó hund manna and eahtatýne men, Gen. 14, 14. Geseald tó þrím hunde penega *sold for three hundred pence*, Blickl. Homl. 69, 8: 75, 22. Þriim hundum peninga, Jn. Skt. Lind. 12, 5. Feówer hund geára, Gen. 15, 13. Ðá ðá hé wæs fíf hund geára, 5, 32. Nigon hund wintra and lxxi, Blickl. Homl. 119, 2. Hira monig hund ofslógon *slew many hundreds of them*, Chr. 895; Erl. 93, 28. Hund síðon on dæge *a hundred times a day*, Homl. Th. i. 456, 21. [*Goth.* hund: *O. Sax.* hund: *O. H. Ger.* hunt. This word is the representative of a fuller form which is seen in Gothic as *taihun-têhund*, *-taihund* [Lk. 15, 4: 16, 6], and which points to a primitive *dakan-dakanta* = ten-tenth = hundred. The Latin *centum* shews a similar modification.] v. next word.

hund- as a prefix to numerals from 70 to 120 is a shortened form of the word which appears in Gothic as *têhund, taihund* [v. preceding word], and may be explained *decade. O. Sax.* prefixes *ant* [= *hund?*], in *O. Frs.* the prefix is *t*, and a trace of such forms is yet left in the Modern Dutch *t-achtig* = 80. On these numerals March remarks 'Gothic has *sibuntêhund*. The Anglo-Saxon form was once *hund-seofonta* [decade seventh], like *O. Sax. ant-sibunta*. The *-ta* changed to *-tig* through conformation with the smaller numbers, and *hund-*, whose meaning had faded, was retained as a sign of the second half of the great hundred.' Grammar, p. 75. See also Helfenstein's Comparative Grammar, p. 229. For the great huudred [120] cf. *Icel. tólfrætt hundrað* as distinguished from *tírætt hundrað*. See Cl. and Vig. Dict. *hundrað*.

hund-eahtatig; *num. Eighty*:—Hundeahtatig *octoginta*, Ælfc. Gr. 49; Som. 49, 44. Heó wæs wudewe óþ feówer and hundeahtatig geára *hæc vidua usque annos octoginta quatuor*, Lk. Skt. 2, 37. Mid hundehtatigum scipum, Chr. Erl. 5, 2. Ǽr ðæm ðe Rómeburg getimbred wǽre iiii hunde wintrum and hundeahtatigum *anno ante urbem conditam* cccclxxx, Ors. 1, 10; Swt. 44, 4.

hundeahtatig-wintre; *adj. Eighty years old*:—Hundeahtatigwintre and sixwintre wæs Abram ðá ðá Ager ácende Ysmael, Gen. 16, 16.

hunden; *adj. Of a dog, canine*:—Hundene *caninam*, Blickl. Gloss. [*O. H. Ger.* huntin *caninus.*]

hund-endlefontig; *num. One hundred and ten*:—Feówer and hundændlæftig ealdra swína *one hundred and fourteen old swine*, Chart. Th. 163, 3.

hund-endleftigoða; *num. One hundred and tenth*:—On ðæm eahta and hundælleftiogoðan psalme *in the hundred and eighteenth psalm*, Past. 65, 5; Swt. 465, 23.

hundes beó, etc. *See above after* hund.

hund-feald; *adj. Hundredfold*:—Hundfeald getel is fulfremed *the number a hundred is perfect*, Homl. Th. i. 338, 27. Swá hwæt swá wé be ánfealdan Godes þearfum syllaþ hé hit ús forgylt be hundfealdum, ii. 106, 2. Mid hundfealdum, i. 180, 26. Sealdon wæstm sum hundfealdne *dabant fructum aliud centesimum*, Mt. Kmbl. MS. A. 13, 8.

hund-líc; *adj. Doglike, canine*:—Hundlíce [téþ] *canini*, Wrt. Voc. 282, 74. Nú sende hé hundas tó mé forðan ðe hé næfþ godcundlíce englas, ac hæfþ hundlíce *now has he sent dogs to me, for he has not divine angels, but he has doglike ones*, Homl. Th. i. 378, 3.

hund-nigontig; *num. Ninety*:—Hundnigontig *nonaginta*, Ælfc. Gr. 49; Som. 49, 44. Se sumor hafaþ hundnygontig daga . . . Se winter hæfaþ tú and hundnigontig daga, Shrn. 83, 33; 146, 7. Hundteóntig geára wæs Abraham and his gebedda hundnigontig *Abraham was a hundred years old and his consort ninety*, Homl. Th. i. 92, 21. Nigon and hundnigontig *nonaginta novem*, Lk. Skt. 15, 4. Mid þrím and hundnigentigon scipum, Chr. 993; Erl. 132, 2. Feówer hund geára and hundnigontig geára, Swt. A. S. Rdr. 71, 459.

hundnigontig-wintre; *adj. Ninety years old*, Gen. 17, 17.

hundred; *pl.* u; *n. A hundred*:—Getalu *vel* heápas *vel* hundredu *centurias*, Ælfc. Gl. 96; Som. 76, 25; Wrt. Voc. 53, 34. Ðeáh ðe heora hundred seó *though there be a hundred of them*, Ps. Th. 89, 10. On lxv and þreó hundræd hí beóþ tódǽlede *they are divided into three hundred and sixty-five*, Nar. 49, 25. Seox hundred wintra and iii and hundseofenti wintra, Chr. 656; Erl. 33, 34. Hundrað scillinga *centum denarios*, Mt. Kmbl. Lind. 18, 28. On twegera hundred penega wurþe, Jn. Skt. 6, 7. Wið þrím hundred penegon, 12, 5. Mid twám hundred penegon, Mk. Skt. 6, 40. Hí ðá sǽton hundredon and fíftigon *discubuerunt per centenos et per quinquagenos*, 37. [*O. Frs.* hundred, hunderd: *Icel.* hundrað: *O. H. Ger.* hundert: *Ger.* hundert. Two etymologies are suggested for the word; according to one *hunder-* corresponds to *Lat. centur-ia*; according to the other *-red* (*Icel.* rað) is a suffix akin to the *-ræðr* which is found in *Icel.* átt-rædr, etc. v. Grmm. Gesch. D. S. 175-6.]

hundred, es; *n. A hundred, a territorial division, the assembly of the men in such a division*:—Hú mon ðæt hundred haldan sceal. Ǽrest ðæt hí heó gegaderian á ymb feówer wucan and wyrce ǽlc man óðrum riht *how the* [*assembly of the*] *hundred is to be held. First, they* [*the men of the hundred*] *are to assemble themselves every four weeks; and each man is to do justice to other*, L. Edg. H; Th. i. 258, 2-4, and see the whole section. Fó se hláford tó healfan and tó healfan ðæt hundred *let the lord take half, and the hundred half*, L. Edg. 2, 7; Th. i. 268, 20. Gewitnys sý geset tó ǽlcere byrig and tó ǽlcum hundrode, L. Edg. S. 3; Th. i. 274, 8, 10. Twegen þegenas innan ðam hundrede, L. Eth. i. 1; Th. i. 280, 11: L. C. S. 17; Th. i. 384, 30: 19; Th. i. 386, 12. [Various explanations of the word have been given. 'It has been regarded as denoting simply a division of a hundred hides of land; as the district which furnished a hundred warriors to the host; as representing the original settlement of the hundred warriors; or as composed of a hundred hides, each of which furnished a single warrior,' Stubbs' Const. Hist. 1, 97; see also following pages and pp. 71-3: Grmm. R. A. 532 sqq: Kemble's Saxons in England, c. ix: Schmid A. S. Gesetz. p. 613-4.]

hundredes ealdor, es; *m.* I. *a centurion*:—Ðá geneáhlǽhte hym án hundredes ealdor *accessit ad eum Centurio*, Mt. Kmbl. 8, 5. II. *the presiding officer of the court of the hundred*:—Gif se hundrodes ealdor ðæt geáscoþ, L. Edg. S. 10; Th. i. 276, 8. Cýðan hit ðæs túnes men ðam hundredes ealdre, 8; Th. i. 274, 28.

hundredes man *apparently the same as preceding word*, II:—Cýðe hit man ðam hundredes men, L. Edg. H. 2; Th. i. 258, 7. v. hundredmann.

hundred-gemót, hundredes gemót, es; *n. The assembly of the hundred* [v. hundred]:—Séce man hundredgemót swá hit ǽr geset wæs and ðǽr beó on scirebisceop and se ealdorman *let the hundredmoot be attended as was before appointed; and let the bishop of the shire and the alderman be there present*, L. Edg. ii. 5; Th. i. 268, 2-5. Séce man hundredes gemót be wíte *let the hundredmoot be attended under penalty of a fine*, L. C. S. 17; Th. i. 386, 1.

hundred-mann, es; *m. The chief of a hundred men, a centurion*:—Ðá clypode hé ðæne hundredman *accersito centurione*, Mk. Skt. 15, 44. Sette hig tó ealdrum and tó hundredmannum and tó fíftigesmannum and tó teóðingmannum *constitui eos principes, tribunos et centuriones et quinquagenarios et decanos*, Deut. 1, 15. Þúsendmen and hundrydmen and fíftiesmen and teóðingmen *tribunos et quinquagenarios et decanos*, Ex. 18, 21. [Cf. *O. H. Ger.* hunteri *centurio.*]

hundred-penig, es; *m.* '*A collection made for the support of his office by the sheriff or lord of the hundred*:'—Hundredpenegas, Chart. Th. 432, 25: 433, 29. v. Glossary.

hund-seofontig; *num. Seventy*:—Hundseofontig *septuaginta*, Ælfc. Gr. 49; Som. 49, 43. Ealles hundseofontig manna *seventy men in all*, Homl. Th. ii. 190, 30. His suna gestríndon twá and hundseofontig suna *his sons begot seventy-two sons*, Swt. A. S. Rdr. 61, 154. Ne secge ic ðé óþ seofon síðas ac óþ seofon hundseofontigon síðon *non dico tibi usque septies, sed usque septuagies septies*, Mt. Kmbl. 18, 22.

hundseofontig-feald; *adj. Seventy-fold*:—Septuagesima is hundseofontigfeald getel, Homl. Th. ii. 84, 28: 86, 2.

hundseofontig-wintre; *adj. Seventy years old*:—Ðá hé wæs seofonhundwintre and seofon hundseofontigwintre, Gen. 5, 31.

hund-teóntig; *num. A hundred*:—Hundteóntig *centum*, Ælfc. Gr. 49; Som. 49, 44. Hundteóntig geára wæs Abraham *Abraham was a hundred years old*, Homl. Th. i. 92, 20. Joseph leofode hundteóntig geára and tín tó eácan *Joseph lived a hundred and ten years*, Swt. A. S. Rdr. 63, 208. Hundteóntig and twentig *a hundred and twenty*, Shr. 85, 12. Hundteóntig and þreó and fíftig, Jn. Skt. 21, 11. Fæder Abrahames wintra hæfde twá hundteóntig and fífe eác *and the days of Terah were two hundred and five years*, Cd. 83; Th. 104, 26; Gen. 1741.

hundteóntig-feald; *adj. Hundredfold*:—Tó hundteóntigfealdre méde, Blickl. Homl. 41, 19.

hundteóntigfeald-líc; *adj. Hundredfold*:—Ðæt hé on ðyssum lífe hundteóntigfealdlíce méde onféngе *ut in hac vita centuplum acciperet*, Bd. 5, 19; S. 636, 36.

hundteóntig-geáre; *adj. Aged a hundred*:—Adam leofode hundteóntigeáre and þrittegeáre, Gen. 5, 3.

hund-twelftig; *num. A hundred and twenty*:—Hundtwelftig geára wæs Moses ðá ðá hē gewāt *Moyses centum et viginti annorum erat, quando mortuus est*, Deut. 34, 7: Cd. 64; Th. 76, 26; Gen. 1263. Se wudu is eástlang and westlang hundtwelftiges míla lang oððe lengra *from east to west the wood is a hundred and twenty miles long, or longer*, Chr. 893: Erl. 88, 28.

hund-twentig; *num. A hundred and twenty*:—Mid ðam ðe hē wæs on ylde hundtwentig wintra *when he was a hundred and twenty years of age*, Ælfc. T. Grn. 6, 1. Hē gean ðæra hundtwæntiga hída æt Wyrðæ *he gives the hundred and twenty hides at Worth*, Chart. Th. 526, 32.

hundtwentig-wintre; *adj. A hundred and twenty years old*:—Ic eom tō-dæg hundtwentigwintre *centum viginti annorum sum hodie*, Deut. 31, 2.

hund-wealh, es; *m. A servant to attend to dogs*:—Hundwælh *canum servitor*, Ælfc. Gl. 8; Som. 56, 110; Wrt. Voc. 18, 58.

hund-wintre; *adj. A hundred years old*:—Hē sylf wæs ðá hundwintre *cum centum esset annorum*, Gen. 21, 5. Wēnst ðū lā ðæt sunu beó ācenned of hundwintrum men *putasne centenario nascetur filius?* 17, 17.

hune, an; *f. Horehound*; marrubium vulgare:—Hunan seáw *juice of horehound*, L. M. 1, 3; Lchdm. ii. 42, 19. Nim hunan *take horehound*, 31; Lchdm. ii. 74, 8. Wyll ða hāran hunan *boil the horehound*, Lchdm. iii. 48, 14. v. hār-hune.

Hūne. v. Hūnas.

hunel; *adj. Foul, wanton, impudent*; procax, protervus, immodestus, impudicus, Lye. v. hun.

HUNGOR, es; *m.* HUNGER, *famine*:—Nis ðǽr hungor ne þurst slǽp ne swār leger ne sunnan bryne *there is there neither hunger nor thirst, sleep nor grievous sickness, nor burning heat of the sun*, Exon. 32 a; Th. 101, 20; Cri. 1661. Beóþ ðē hungor and þurst hearde gewinnan, 36 b; Th. 118, 27; Gū. 246. Hæfde hī hungor and þurst *esurientes et sitientes*, Ps. Th. 106, 4. Hēr wæs se micla hungor on Angelcynne *in this year was the great famine in England*, Chr. 976; Erl. 127, 34. Hēr on ðyssum geáre wæs se mycla hungor geond Angelcynn swilce nān man ǽr ne gemunde swā grimme, 1005; Erl. 139, 36. Hungor se hāta ne se hearda þurst, Exon. 64 b; Th. 238, 32; Ph. 613. Se grimma hungor ne se hāta þurst, 112 a; Th. 430, 5; Rä. 44, 3. Hunger se hearda hāmsittendum wælgrim werum, Cd. 86; Th. 108, 32; Gen. 1815. Hungres on wēnum blātes beódgæstes *in expectation of hunger, pallid guest at the board*, Andr. Kmbl. 2176; An. 1089. Hungre wǽron þearle geþreátod swā se þeódsceaða hreów rícsode, 2230; An. 1116. Lǽtaþ cuelan hungre Cristes þearfan *cum fame crucientur Christi pauperes*, Past. 44, 6; Swt. 327, 6. Ic on hungre forwurðe *fame pereo*, Lk. 15, 17. Hungre ācwelan *to die of hunger*, Chr. 894; Erl. 92, 28: 918; Erl. 104, 13. Hungre heófeþ wulf se grǽga *the grey wolf howls for hunger*, Exon. 91 b; Th. 342, 30; Gn. Ex. 150. Hungur heaðugrimne heardne, Ps. Th. 145, 6. Manncwealmas and hungras *pestilentiæ et fames*, Mt. Kmbl. 24, 7. [*Goth.* huhrus: *O. Sax.* hungor: *O. Frs.* hunger, honger: *Icel.* hungr: *O. H. Ger.* hungar *fames*: *Ger.* hunger.]

hungor-biten; *adj. Hunger-bitten, suffering from hunger*:—Ac ðes folces ðe be Hungire fōr fela þūsenda ðǽr and be wæge earmlíce forfōran and fela hreówlice and hungerbitene ongeán winter hām tugon *but of the people that went by Hungary many thousands perished miserably there and by the way, and many came home towards winter in pitiful plight and suffering from hunger*, Chr. 1096; Erl. 233, 22.

hungor-geár, es; *n. A year of famine*:—Ðā hæfde se hālga wer gedǽled ðæs mynstres þing hafenleásum mannum for ðam hungergeáre *the saint had distributed the provisions of the monastery to indigent men on account of the year of famine*, Homl. Th. ii. 178, 20.

hungor-lǽwe; *adj. Hungry, famished*:—Ða hungerlǽwan gefylde synt *famelici saturati sunt*, Ps. Lamb. Cantic. Annæ, 5.

hungrig; *adj. Hungry, famished*:—Gewāt se wilda fugol hungri, Cd. 72; Th. 88, 10; Gen. 1463. Ðæm hungrige *esurienti*, Rtl. 5, 22. Gif ðū ðissere hungrige ceasterwaran gehelpest *if thou helpest this starving town*, Th. Ap. 9, 18. Hungrig *esuriens*, Mt. Kmbl. Lind. 25, 37. Hȳ him hungrige ymb hond flugon, Exon. 43 a; Th. 146, 13; Gū. 709. Ða hungrian, Ps. Th. 106, 8. Hungrium, 35: 131, 16. Hungregum tō frōfre, Soul Kmbl. 224; Seel. 116. [*Orm.* hunngriȝ: *O. H. Ger.* hungarag *impastus, esuriens, famelicus*: *Ger.* hungerig, hungrig.]

hunig, es; *n. Honey*:—Ðǽr [Estland] biþ swȳðe mycel hunig and fisc[n]aþ and se cyning and ða rícostan men drincaþ myran meolc and ða unspēdigan and ða þeówan medo *in that country there is very much honey and fishing; and the king and the principal men drink mare's milk, and the poor and the slaves mead*, Ors. 1, 1; Swt. 20, 15. Doran hunig *dumbledore's honey*, L. M. 1, 2; Lchdm. ii. 28, 20. [Cf. *O. H. Ger.* humbel-honag.] Englisces huniges *of English honey*, 2, 65; Lchdm. ii. 292, 23: 3, 71; Lchdm. ii. 358, 10. Þynceþ þegna gehwelcum huniges bíbreád healfe ðȳ swētre gif hē hwēne ǽr huniges teáre bitres onbyrgeþ *dulcior est apium mage labor, si malus ora prius sapor edat*, Bt. Met. Fox 12, 17; Met. 12, 9. Swā þicce swā huniges teár *as thick as honey that drops from the comb*, L. M. 1, 31; Lchdm. ii. 74, 4: 2; Lchdm. ii. 28, 4. Tō ðam lande ðe eall flēwþ on riðum meolce and hunies . . . of ðam lande ðe weóll meolce and hunie *in terram, quæ fluit rivis lactis et mellis . . . de terra, quæ lacte et melle manabat*, Num. 16, 14, 13. Beón gif hī man ācwellaþ cwelle hig man raðe ǽr hī tō ðam hunige cumon, L. Ecg. C. 39; Th. ii. 164, 2. [*Orm.* huniȝ: *A. R.* huni: *Ayenb.* honi: *O. Frs.* hunig: *Icel.* hunang: *O. H. Ger.* honag, honig: *Ger.* honig.] v. wudu-hunig.

hunig-æppel, es; *m. Pastillus*, Cot. 155, Lye.

hunig-bǽre; *adj. Mellifluus*, Hpt. Gl. 408, 457.

hunig-camb, e; *f. Honey-comb*:—Hunigcamb teáres *favum nectaris*, Lchdm. ii. 396, col. 1.

hunig-flōwende; *adj. Flowing with honey, dropping honey, mellifluous*:—Wyrta geblōwene hunigflōwende, Exon. 51 a; Th. 178, 26; Gū. 1250. [Cf. *Icel.* hunangs-fljótandi *flowing with honey*.]

hunig-gafol, es; *n. Rent paid in honey*:—Syllan huniggafol *to pay rent in honey*, L. R. S. 4; Th. i. 434, 31. [Cf. mid ūs is gerǽd ðæt hē (beó-ceorl) sylle v. sustras huniges tō gafole, 5; Th. i. 436, 1.]

hunig-smæc; *gen.* -smæcces; *m. Taste* or *flavour of honey*:—Hafaþ on gehātum hunigsmæccas *use honeyed words in their promises*, Frag. Kmbl. 53; Leás. 28.

hunig-sūce, -sūge, an; *f. Privet, a plant from which honey may be sucked*:—Hunisūge *ligustrum*, Ælfc. Gl. 47; Som. 65, 31; Wrt. Voc. 33, 30. Hunisūce, Wrt. Voc. 68, 3.

hunig-swǽs; *adj. Like honey*; melleus, Hpt. Gl. 481.

hunig-swēte; *adj. Sweet as honey, mellifluous*:—Hē hlōd ðā mid þurstigum breóste ða flōwendan lāre ðe hē eft æfter fyrste mid hunigswētre þrotan bealcette, Th. An. 45, 4.

hunig-teár, es; *m.* '*Distillation from the comb, without squeezing, virgin honey*; mel purissimum, e favo sponte quod effluxit, mell stillativum,' Lchdm. ii. 396, col. 1:—Hunigteár *nectar*, Hpt. Gl. 468. Hunigteáres *nectaris*, Mone Gl. p. 384. Sȳ gemenged tōgædre hunigteár and wīn *let virgin honey and wine be mixed together*, Lchdm. iii. 292, 16. Besmyra mid hunigteáre, 11. [Cf. *O. E. Hom.* swete al swā ān hunitīar felle upe ȝīure hīerte, i. 217, 27.]

hunig-teáren; *adj. Sweet as honey* or *nectar*:—Hunigteárenne *nectareum*, Gl. Prud. p. 140.

hunigteár-líc; *adj. Like nectar*; nectareus, Cot. 138, Lye.

hūn-spuran '*dolones*; great spars or staves with small heads of iron, and swords within,' Som. Lye gives *hun-spera, -spura* dolo, Cot. 62. v. hūn-þyrel.

hunt, e; *Hunting*:—Of hunte *de venatione*, Rtl. 117, 4. [*Or is* hunte *for* huntunge?].

hunta, an; *m. A hunter*:—Hunta *venator*, Ælfc. Gr. 36; Som. 38, 43; Wrt. Voc. 73, 43. Ǣnne cræft ic cann. Hunta ic eom *unam artem scio. Venator sum*, Coll. Monast. Th. 21, 1-6: 22, 27. Wē lǽraþ ðæt preóst ne beó hunta ne hafecere *we enjoin that a priest be not a hunter nor a hawker* [cf. Chaucer's Monk: 'He ȝaf nat of that text a pulled hen, That seith, that hunters been noon holy men'], L. Edg. C. 64; Th. ii. 258, 7. Eal wēste būton ðǽr huntan gewícodon oððe fisceras, Ors. 1, 1; Swt. 17, 29. Wēste land būtan fiscerum and fugelerum and huntum, Swt. 17, 26. Bethsaida is gereht *domus venatorum* ðæt is huntena hūs, Shrn. 78, 9. [Ðā sōn ðǽræfter ða sǽgon and hērdon fela men feole huntes hunten. Ða huntes wǽron swarte and micele and lādlíce, Chr. 1127; Erl. 256, 28. *Laym.* hunte; *pl.* hunten: *Orm.* hunnte: *Chauc.* hunte.] v. hwæl-hunta.

hunta, an; *m. A hunting spider*; salticus scenicus *or* aranea tarantula [?]:—Wið ðon gif hunta gebīte mannan ðæt is swíðra *in case a hunting spider bite a man, that is the stronger*, L. M. 1, 68; Lchdm. ii. 142, 18 [see the note]: 14, 19. Wið huntan bite, 144, 2, 5.

Huntan-dūn, e; *f. Huntingdon*:—Fōr se here of Huntandūne and of Eástenglum and worhton ðæt geweorc æt Tæmese forda and forlēton ðæt ōðer æt Huntandūne . . . And ðā se firdstemn fōr hām ðā fōr ōðer ūt and gefōr ða burg æt Huntandūne and hie gebētte and geedneowade ðǽr heó ǽr tōbrocen wæs be Eádweardes cyninges hǽse, Chr. 921; Erl. 106, 16: 107, 31. Tōward Huntendūne porte, 656; Erl. 31, 19.

Huntandūn-scir, e; *f. Huntingdonshire*:—Tō Huntandūnscire, Chr. 1016; Erl. 154, 7.

huntaþ, huntoþ, es; *m. Hunting, game*; venatio:—On feáwum stōwum wíciaþ Finnas, on huntoþe on wintra and on sumera on fiscaþe be ðære sǽ, Ors. 1, 1; Swt. 17, 5. On huntoþe, Exon. 78 b; Th. 295, 22; Cri. 37. Tō huntaðe [*a prayer*] *for hunting*, Rtl. 117, 1. On ðæt gerād ðet ðenne ðæs neód biþ his men beón gearuwe tō huntoþe *on the condition that, when there shall be need for it, his men may be ready for hunting*, Chart. Th. 148, 3. Isaac lufode Esau for his huntoþe *Isaac amabat Esau, eo quod de venationibus illius vesceretur*, Gen. 25, 28. Bring mē of ðínum huntoþe *affer mihi de venatione tua*, 27, 7: Homl. Th. ii. 576, 34. Huntaþ dōn gestreón getācnaþ *to hunt betokens gain*, Lchdm. iii. 212, 2. Mōna se fíf and twentigoþa huntoþas begān nytlíc *the five and twentieth moon is good for all sorts of hunting*, 196, 1. [*R. Glouc.* Edgar an honteþ ywend was.] v. hwæl-huntaþ.

huntaþ-faru, e; *f. A hunting expedition, hunting:* — Cýpinga and folcgemóta and huntaþfara and woroldlícra weorca on ðam hálgan dæge geswíce man georne *let people diligently abstain from marketings and folk-moots and hunting expeditions and secular employments on the holy day* [*Sunday*], L. Eth. vi. 22; Th. i. 322, 12: L. C. E. 15; Th. i. 368, 18. [Cf. the Icelandic law 'Maþr a at fiskja drottins dag eþa messu dag eþa veiþa annat ef hann vill. Hann scal hafa messu um morgininn aþr oc lata eigi veiþina standa fyrir tiþa socninni.']

hún-þyrel, es; *n. The hole in the mast-head through which the halyard went:*—Húnþyrlu *carchesia*, Wrt. Voc. 63, 49. [*Icel.* húnn *a knob at the end of a staff, at the top of a mast;* hún-bora *the hole in the mast-head through which the halyard went.*]

huntian; *p.* ode *To hunt:*—Ic ásende míne fisceras and hí gefixiaþ hí míne huntan and hí huntiaþ hí of ǽlcere dúne and of ǽlcere hylle *I will send for many fishers and they shall fish them; and after will I send for many hunters and they shall hunt them from every mountain and from every hill* [A. V. Jer. 16, 16], Homl. Th. i. 576, 28. Gif him þince ðæt hé huntige beorge him georne wið his fýnd *if he fancies that he is hunting, let him guard himself well against his foes,* Lchdm. iii. 172, 19. Ne canst ðú huntian búton nettum *nescis venari nisi cum retibus,* Coll. Monast. Th. 21, 21. Ic fare huntian *venatum pergo,* Ælfc. Gr. 24; Som. 25, 10. Huntigendra *venantium,* Ps. Spl. 90, 3: 123, 6.

huntigestre, an; *f. A huntress:*—Huntigystran *venatrices,* Nar. 38, 3.

huntig-spere, es; *n. A hunting-spear, boar-spear:* — Bárspere *vel* huntigspere *venabulum,* Ælfc. Gl. 51; Som. 66, 23; Wrt. Voc. 35, 12.

huntnaþ, huntnoþ, es; *m. Hunting:*—Be huntnaþe. Ic wylle ðæt ǽlc man sý his huntnoþes wyrðe on wuda and on felda on his ágenan. And forgá ǽlc man mínne huntnoþ hwǽr ic hit gefriþod wille habban *Of hunting. I will that every man have the right to hunt in wood and in open country on his own property. And let every man leave my hunting alone where I wish to have it preserved,* L. C. S. 81; Th. i. 420, 23-6. Wǽre ðú tó-dæg on huntnoþe *fuisti hodie in venatione?* Coll. Monast. Th. 21, 35. Hé of huntnoþe com *venerat de venatu,* Bd. 3, 14; S. 540, 33. On fiscnoþum and on huntnoþum and on fugelnoþum *piscationibus, venationibus, aucupationibus,* Cod. Dipl. Kmbl. iii. 350, 9.

huntung, e; *f. Hunting:*—Mǽre on huntunge heorta and rána *cervorum caprearumque insignis,* Bd. 1, 1; S. 474, 41. Gyrstandæg ic wæs on huntunge *heri fui in venatione,* Coll. Monast. Th. 22, 3. Hwæt ðést ðú be ðínre huntunge? Ic sylle cync swá hwæt swá ic gefó *quid facis de tua venatione? Ego do regi quicquid capio,* 25-7. Of huntungum *de venationibus,* Rtl. 118, 39.

hup-bán, -seax. v. hype-bán, -seax.

húru; *adv. At least, at all events, at any rate, in any case, however, even, yet, only, indeed, certainly, especially:*—Húru gif ic hæfde ǽnne penig *saltim si haberem unum denarium,* Ælfc. Gr. 44; Som. 46, 35. Húru nú hæfþ mín heáfod uppáhafen ofer míne fýnd *nunc autem exaltavit caput meum super inimicos meos,* Ps. 26, 7. Ðæt ic húru underfó sum fóstercild of hyre *si forte saltem ex illa suscipiam filios,* Gen. 16, 2. Beó ðú húru gehyrt *tu tantum confortare,* Jos. 1, 18, 17. Húru ðæt hig ofer niht ðǽron ne wunigon *ita saltem ut non per noctem ibi restent,* L. Ecg. C. 39; Th. ii. 164, 2. Óðre lytle fugelas sind læssan ðonne heó sý and hwæðere hí ofsleáþ sum þing húru ðás fleógan *other little birds are less than it* [*the dove*] *is, and yet they kill something, at any rate these flies,* Homl. Th. ii. 46, 17. Woldon hine habban húru swá deádne *they would have him when he was dead at any rate,* 518. 23. Húru fífténe míla brád *at least fifteen miles broad,* Ors. 1, 1; Swt. 20, 8. Ðæt hé húru þreó þing ðananforþ healdan wille, L. Eth. v. 6; Th. i. 306, 8: L. C. E. 19; Th. i. 370, 33. Be emnihte oððe húru be ealra hálgena mæssan *by the equinox or in any case by Allhallows' mass,* L. Eth. ix. 9; Th. i. 342, 22. Eallum cristenum gebyreþ ðæt hí riht lufian and húru [*certainly*] gehádode men scylon á riht rǽran, L. I. P. 7; Th. ii. 312, 34. Húru hit wyrþ ðonne egeslíc, Swt. A. S. Rdr. 104, 5. Gif hit on ǽnegum men ǽnige hwíle fæstlíce wunaþ se deáþ hit húru áfirreþ, Bt. 8; Fox 26, 4. Ðæt deáh tó ǽlcum and húru tó deópun dolgum *it is good for all, and especially for deep wounds,* L. M. 1, 45; Lchdm. ii. 114, 1. Ðæt man cristene men and unforworhte of earde ne sylle ne húru on hǽðene leóde *certainly not to a heathen nation,* L. Eth. v. 2; Th. i. 304, 15. Heora eáþmetto ne mihton náuht forstandan ne húru heora ofermetta *their humility could not avail aught, and certainly not their pride,* Bt. 29, 2; Fox 104, 34. [*A. R.* hure.]

húru-þinga; *adv. Especially, at least, at any rate:*—Húruþinga *presertim,* Ælfc. Gr. 38; Som. 41, 65. Hú ne scolde hine húruþinga sceamian seofon dagas *nonne debuerat saltem septem diebus rubore suffundi?* Num. 12, 14. Hyne bǽdon ðæt hig húruþinga his reáfes fnæd æthrinon *rogabant eum ut vel fimbriam vestimenti ejus tangerent,* Mt. Kmbl. 14, 36. Lǽtaþ mé fyrst óþ tómerigen húruþinga fyrst óþ tómerigen *allow me respite until to-morrow, only until to-morrow,* Homl. Th. i. 414, 23. Swilce hé swutellíce cwǽde 'Gif gé noldon Gode lybban on cildháde, ne on geógoþe, gecyrraþ nú húruþinga on ylde to lífes wege,' ii. 78, 13.

HÚS es; *n. A* HOUSE, *a family:*—*Hic lar* þis fýr on ánfealdum getele, and hit getácnaþ hús on mænigfealdum getele, *hi lares* ðás hús; ðanon is gecweden *lardum* spic, forðan hit on húsum hangaþ lange, Ælfc. Gr. 9; Som. 9, 48. Baðiendra manna hús ðǽr hí hí unscrédaþ inne *apodyterium,* i. e. *domus qua vestimenta balneantium ponuntur,* Ælfc. Gl. 55: Som. 67, 9; Wrt. Voc. 37, 6. Lytle hús of bredan *tabernæ* vel *gurgustia,* Wrt. Voc. 37, 8. Byþ gelíc ðam wísan were se hys hús ofer stán getimbrode *assimilabitur viro sapienti qui ædificavit domum suam supra petram,* Mt. Kmbl. 7, 24. Gewát neósian heán húses *went and visited the lofty house,* Beo. Th. 233; B. 116. Maria húse gesætt *Maria domi sedebat,* Jn. Skt. Lind, 11, 20. Lét fleógan hrefn of húse út [*out of the ark*], Cd. 71; Th. 87, 2; Gen. 1442. Se wilda fugel ofer heánne beám hús getimbreþ, Exon. 58 b; Th. 211, 24; Ph. 202. Ðæt fǽge hús *the corpse,* Elen. Kmbl. 1759; El. 881. Israhéla hús *domus Israel,* Ps. Th. 113, 18, 1, 19: 134, 21. Nis nán wítega búton wurþscipe búton on his éðele and on his mægþe and on his húse *non est propheta sine honore nisi in patria sua et in cognatione sua et in domo sua,* Mk. Skt. 6, 4. [*Goth. O. Sax. O. Frs. Icel. O.H. Ger.* hús: *Ger.* haus.] DER. ambiht-, bán-, bed-, dóm-, eorþ-, feld-, feoh-, feorh-, friþ-, gæst-, geofon-, gift-, græf-, helle-, mán-, mere-, morðor-, nicor-, sáwel-, wíg-, wíte-hús.

húsa, an; *m. A member of a household:* — Fióndes menn húsa his *inimici hominis domestici ejus,* Mt. Kmbl. Lind. 10, 36. v. ge-húsa.

hús-bonda, -bunda, an; *m. The master of a house:*—Án his manna wolde wícian æt ánes bundan húse his unþances and gewundode ðone húsbundon and se húsbunda ofslóh ðone óðerne. Ðá wearþ Eustatius uppon his horse and his gefeoran uppon heora and férdon tó ðam húsbundon and ofslógon hine binnan his ágenan heorþa *one of his men wanted to stop at a man's house against his will, and wounded the man of the house, and the man of the house slew the other. Then Eustace got on his horse and his companions on theirs, and went to the man of the house and slew him in his own home,* Chr. 1048; Erl. 177, 35-40. [*O. E. Homl.* þe husbonde þat is wit warneþ his hus þus, i. 247, 19: *Laym.* of æverelche huse þat husbonde wunede, 31958: *Prompt. Parv.* hose-, hus-bonde *paterfamilias;* also *maritus: Icel.* [*from which the word seems borrowed*] hus-bóndi [=-búandi] *a house-master; a husband.* Cf. *Chauc. Wick.* husbond-, housbonde-man *a householder.*]

hús-bonde, an; *f. The mistress of a house:*—Ða Israéliscan wíf biddaþ æt ðám Egiptiscean wífon æt hira néhgebúron and æt hira húsbondum sylfrene fatu *postulabit mulier a vicina sua et ab hospita sua vasa argentea,* Ex. 3, 22.

hús-brice, es; *m. Housebreaking, burglary:*—Húsbrice [-brec, MS. A.] and bærnet æfter woruldlage is bótleás *housebreaking and arson are according to the secular law inexpiable,* L. C. S. 65; Th. i. 410, 5. Cf. quedam non possunt emendari, que sunt husbreche, et bernet, L. H. 12, 1; Th. i. 522, 27: 47; Th. i. 546, 10. [*O. Frs.* hús-breke: cf. *Icel.* hús-brot *housebreaking, burglary: and O.H. Ger.* hús-prehho *prædator.*] v. brecan, á-brecan.

hús-bryne, es; *m. The burning of a house, a fire:*—Æt húsbryne ǽlc mon ánne pening *at the burning of a house let every man contribute one penny,* Chart. Th. 614, 13. [*Icel.* hús-bruni: cf. *O. Frs.* hús-brand.]

husc, hucs, hux, es; *m.* [cf. hosp.] *Insult, scorn, scoffing, mockery:*—Abraham mid hucse bewand ða hleóðorcwidas on hige sínum [cf. *Sarah laughed within herself,* Gen. 18, 12], Cd. 107; Th. 140, 34; Gen. 2337: 109; Th. 143, 21; Gen. 2382. Þurh hucx *per ironiam,* Cot. 186, Lye. [*Laym.* hux and hoker: *O. L. Ger.* hosc *subsannatio: O. H. Ger.* hosc *sugillatio.*] v. hux-líc.

hús-carl, es; *m.* [*A word apparently taken from the Scandinavians, as the English form would be* hús-ceorl.] *A member of the king's body-guard:* — Ðurstán mín húskarll *præfectus meus palatinus Ðurstanus,* Cod. Dipl. Kmbl. iv. 202, 4. Urk mín húskarl, 221, 6. On gewitnesse eallra ðæs kynges húscarlan [-carla?], 291, 15. Ða Densca húscarles, Chr. 1070; Erl. 207, 25. Man gerǽdde ðæt Ælfgifu Hardacnutes módor sǽte on Winceastre mid ðæs cynges húscarlum hyra suna, 1036; Erl. 165, 5. [*O. Frs.* hús-kerl: *Icel.* hús-karl I. *a man-servant,* opposed to húsbóndi *a master;* II. *a member of the king's body-guard.* See Cl. and Vig. Dict.] v. Kemble's Saxons in England, ii. 118 sqq: Stubbs' Const. Hist. i. 150.

husc-word, es; *n. An insulting, scornful word* or *speech:*—Huscworde ongan ealdorsacerd hyspan, Andr. Kmbl. 1338; An. 669. [*Laym.* hux-word.]

HÚSEL, húsul, húsl, es; *n. The* HOUSEL, *consecrated bread and wine, the Eucharist:*—Ðæs hláfes wé onbyriaþ ðonne wé mid geleáfan tó húsle gáþ forðan ðe ðæt hálige húsel is gástlíce Cristes líchama *that bread we taste when we believingly go to the Lord's supper, for the consecrated bread is spiritually Christ's body,* Homl. Th. i. 34, 18. Hwí is ðæt hálige húsel gecweden Cristes líchama oððe his blód, gif hit nis sóþlíce ðæt ðæt hit gehâten is? Sóþlíce se hláf and ðæt wín ðe beóþ þurh sacerda mæssan gehálgode óðer þing hí æteówiaþ menniscum andgitum wiðútan and óðer þing hí clypiaþ wiðinnan geleáffullum módum. Wiðútan hí beóþ gesewene hláf and wín ǽgðer ge on hiwe and on swæcce, ac hí beóþ sóþlíce æfter ðære hálgunge Cristes líchama and his blód þurh gástlícere gerýnu, ii. 268, 21-9. Ðæt húsel is Cristes líchama ná líchamlíce ac gástlíce ná se líchama ðe hé on þrowode ac se líchama ðe hé embe spræc ðá ðá hé bletsode hláf and wīn tō hūsle . . . and cwæþ be đam gebletsodan hlāfe Đis is mīn līchama and be đam gehālgodan wīne Đis is mīn blōd . . . Understandaþ đæt se Drihten dæghwamlīce bletsaþ þurh sacerda handa hlāf and wīn tō his gāstlīcan līchama and blōde *the housel is Christ's body, not bodily but spiritually; not the body that he suffered in, but the body that he spoke about when he blessed bread and wine for housel . . . and said of the bread he had blessed: 'This is my body,' and of the hallowed wine: 'This is my blood' . . . Understand that the Lord daily blesses, by the priest's hands, bread and wine so that they become his spiritual body and blood,* L. Ælfc. C. 36; Th. ii. 360, 15–24. Đæm folce hūsl syllan *Eucharistiam populo dare,* Bd. 2, 5; S. 507, 13. Hē frægn hwæđer hī ǣnig hūsel đǣrinne hæfdon. Đā andswaredon hī hwylc þearf is đē hūsles . . . Cwæþ hē Beraþ mē hwæđere hūsel tō *interrogavit, si Eucharistiam intus haberent. Respondebant, 'Quid opus est Eucharistia?' 'Et tamen' ait 'afferte mihi Eucharistiam,'* 4, 24; S. 598, 35–9: L. Ælfc. C. 36; Th. ii. 358, 16–38, 360, 5–15, 24–29. Tō hūsle gān *to go to the sacrament,* Blickl. Homl. 207, 5: 209, 6. Hūsle gereorded đȳ æþelan gyfle *having been fed with the Eucharist, that noble meal,* Exon. 51 b; Th. 180, 4; Gū. 1274. [*The older meaning of the word is seen from the Gothic* hunsl *sacrifice;* hunslian *to offer;* hunsla-staþs *an altar,* see Grmm. D. M. 35. The word is found in *Icel.* húsl: *Swed.* husl: *Orm. A. R. O. E. Hom.* husel: *R. Glouc.* hosel: *Piers P. Chauc.* housel: and for later use see Nares' Gloss.]

hūsel-bearn, es; *n. A person who may partake of the Eucharist:*—Hālig hūsulbearn [*Guthlac*], Exon. 40 b; Th. 135, 28; Gū. 531.

hūsel-disc, es; *m. Housel-dish, the plate for the consecrated bread, the paten:*—Hūseldisc *patena,* Ælfc. Gl. 26; Som. 60, 91; Wrt. Voc. 25, 31: *patina,* Wrt. Voc. 81, 2. Đis mon sceal wrītan on hūsldisce and on đone drenc mid hāligwætere þweán and singan on *this is to be written on a paten and washed into the drink and sung over,* L. M. 1, 62; Lchdm. ii. 136, 3.

hūsel-fæt, es; *n. A sacrificial vessel,* [*in Christian times*] *a sacramental vessel:*—Hūselfatu *vasa sacra,* Bd. 1, 29; S. 498, 9. Subdiaconus is underdiácon se đe đa fatu byrþ forþ tō đam diácone and þēnaþ under đam diácone æt đam hālgan weófode mid đām huselfatum, L. Ælfc. C. 15; Th. ii. 348, 11. Hūslfatu hālegu *the vessels of the temple,* Cd. 209; Th. 260, 5; Dan. 705: 212; Th. 262, 24; Dan. 749.

hūsel-gang, es; *m. Attendance upon* or *partaking of the sacrament:*—Fulluht and synna forgyfenys hūselgang sind eallum gemǣne earmum and eádigum *baptism and forgiveness of sins, attendance at the sacrament, are common to all, to poor and rich,* Homl. Th. i. 64, 32: ii. 48, 29. Se đe hit singþ æt his endedæge đonne forstent hit him hūselgang *he who sings it at his last day, for him it shall stand instead of receiving the Eucharist,* Lchdm. iii. 288, 16. Gearwige tō hūslgange oft and gelōme gehwā hine sylfne, L. Eth. v. 22; Th. i. 310, 7. Gearwige hine tō hūselgange hūru þrīwa on geáre, vi. 27; Th. i. 322, 7: L. C. E. 19; Th. i. 370, 32. v. next word.

hūsel-genga, gengea, an; *m. One who goes to the Lord's supper, a communicant:*—Gif hē hūslgengea sīe, L. Wih. 23; Th. i. 42, 7: L. In. 19; Th. i. 114, 11. Be hūslgengum, 15; Th. i. 112, 4.

hūsel-hālgung, e; *f. The sanctifying that comes from receiving the Eucharist, attendance at the Eucharist:*—Đreó heálīce þing gesette God mannum tō clǣnsunge ān is fulluht ōđer is hūselhālgung þridde is dǣdbōt . . . Se hūselgang ūs gehālgaþ, Homl. Th. ii. 48, 27. Ūre gāstlīcan lāc sind ūre gebedu and lofsang and hūselhālgung *our spiritual gifts are our prayers and praise and attendance at the Eucharist,* i. 54, 27.

hūsel-lāf, e; *f. What is left of the housel:*—Man ne mōt hālgian hūsel on Langa Frigedæg . . . Gange se preóst tō đam weofode mid đære hūsellāfe đe hē hālgode on Đunresdæg *housel must not be hallowed on Good Friday . . . Let the priest go to the altar with what remains of the housel that he hallowed on Thursday,* L. Ælfc. C. 36; Th. ii. 358, 22.

hūsel-portic, es; *m. Sacristy:*—His līchoma wæs bebyriged beforan đam hūselportice *sepultus est corpore ante secretarium,* Bd. 2, 1; S. 500, 15.

hūsel-þegn, es; *m. An acolyte:*—*Acolitus* đæt is hūslþēn, L. Ecg. C. 41; Th. i. 166, 20.

hūsel-wer, es; *m. One who may take the sacrament, a communicant:*—Hūsulweras, Exon. 44 a; Th. 149, 28; Gū. 768.

hūs-fæst; *adj. Having a house, being a householder:*—Ǣlc man hūsfæst on his ōwe land *every man having a house on his own land,* Chart. Th. 438, 5.

hūs-heofon, es; *m. A ceiling:*—Hūshefen *lacunar,* Cot. 119, Lye.

hūs-hlāford, es; *m. The master of a house:*—Secgeaþ đam hūshlāforde *dicetis patrifamilias,* Lk. Skt. 22, 11.

hūs-hleów, es; *n. Shelter afforded by a house:*—Gif[e] his hūshleów and mete and munde đam đe đæs beþurfe *let him give the shelter of his house and food and protection to him that needs it,* L. Pen. 15; Th. ii. 282, 25.

hūsian; *p.* ode *To house, give shelter in a house:*—Fēde þearfan and scrȳde and hūsige *let him feed the needy and clothe and house them,* L. Pen. 14; Th. ii. 282, 15. [*Icel.* húsa *to shelter;* hýsa *to house.*]

hūs-incel, es; *n. A small house, a habitation;* domicilium, tabernaculum:—Husincil *tabernaculum,* Rtl. 181, 5, 15. In hūsincle *in domicilio,* Ps. Surt: hūsincyle, Ps. Spl. C. 101, 7. [Cf. *O. H. Ger.* hūsili *domiclium, domuncula.*]

hūsl. v. hūsel.

hūslian; *p.* ode *To housel, to administer the sacrament:*—Hȳ mihton wel habban wīf on đām dagum forđan đe hȳ nǣfre ne mæssodon ne menn ne hūslodon *they might well have wives in those days for they never celebrated mass nor administered the Eucharist to men,* L. Ælfc. C. 7; Th. ii. 346, 8. Wē lǣraþ đæt ǣlc preósta seóce men hūslige đonne heom þearf sī, L. Edg. C. 65; Th. ii. 258, 10. Diaconus mōt đæt folc hūsligan, L. Ælfc. C. 16; Th. ii. 348, 14. [Cf. Diaconus mōt hlāf sillan, L. Ælfc. P. 34; Th. ii. 378, 12.] Gif man biþ tō hūsligenne, 29; Th. ii. 352, 31. [*Orm.* huslenn: *Prompt. Parv.* howselyn wythe the sacrament *communico,* see note, p. 250: *Piers P. Chauc.* houseled; *pp:* cf. *Shaks.* un-houseled: *Goth.* hunslian *to offer: Icel.* húsla *to give the Corpus Domini to a sick person.*]

hūslung, e; *f. The administration of the sacrament:*—Ǣfter đære hūslunge gewāt tō đam līfigendan gode, Homl. Swt. 3, 622: Homl. Th. ii. 548, 9.

hūs-rǣden, e; *f. A house, family:*—Hūsrǣden israhēles *domus israel,* Ps. Lamb. 113 [2nd], 9. Hūsrǣdenne hire *domus ejus,* 47, 14.

hūs-stede, es; *m. The site of a building:*—Đeós wyrt byþ cenned on ealdum hūsstedum, Herb. 52, 1; Lchdm. i. 154, 25: 85, 1; Lchdm. i. 188, 12. [*O. Sax.* hūs-stedi: *O. Frs.* hūs-stede: *Icel.* húsa-staðr: *O. H. Ger.* hūs-stat.]

hūs-ting, es; *n. A word taken from the Scandinavians* [*Icel.* hús-þing *a council* or *meeting* to which a king, earl or captain summoned his people or guardsmen], *a meeting, court, tribunal,* apparently so called from its being held within a building when other courts were held in the open air. The word occurs in the following passages [Latin]:—Debet eciam in Londoñ, que caput est regni et legum, semper curia domini regis singulis septimanis die Lune hustingis sedere et teneri, L. Th. i. 457, 36. Ad folkemoth vel ad husteng, 463, 11. Non on hustenge neque in folkesmote, 503, 3. Ad pondus Hustingie Londonensis, Chart. Th. 533, 10. It is found also in English:—Mid hundeahtigum marcan hwītes seolfres be hūstinges gewihte, 329, 22. Hī [the Danes] leaddon đone biscop tō heora hūstinga, Chr. 1012; Erl. 146, 17.

hūs-wist, e; *f. A house, household:*—Ic ingange on đīnum hūswiste ł intō đīnum hūse *introibo in domum tuam,* Ps. Lamb. 5, 8.

hūđe [v. herehūđe], e; *f. Prey, spoil, booty:*—Hūđe hrēmig *exulting in spoil,* Elen. Kmbl. 297; El. 149: Beo. Th. 248; B. 124. Cōmon tō Moyse mid micelre hūđe *adduxerunt prædam ad Moysen,* Num. 31, 12. Se Chaldēa cining com đā tō his earde mid đære hūđe, Ælfc. T. Grn. 8, 23: Cd. 174; Th. 220, 2; Dan. 65. Habbaþ nū đa hūđe and đæt orf eów gemǣne *prædam vero et omnia animantia diripiens vobis,* Jos. 8, 2: Cd. 97; Th. 127, 19; Gen. 2113: 98; Th. 129, 24; Gen. 2149. Hūđa mǣste *greatest of spoils,* Exon. 16 a; Th. 35, 35; Cri. 568. [Cf. *Goth.* hunths *captivity: O. H. Ger.* heri-hunda *præda.*] v. here-hȳđ.

hūđe, tō *in portum,* Ps. Lamb. 106, 30. v. hȳđ.

hux-, husc-līc; *adj. Ignominious, involving shame, scorn, insult:*—Huxlīc *dedecor,* Ælfc. Gr. 9, 21; Som. 10, 34. Đā þuhte him tō huxlīc đæt hē hīran sceolde ǣnigum hlāforde *it seemed to him too ignominious to obey any lord,* Ælfc. T. Grn. 2, 36. Đā þuhte đam heáhgerēfan huxlīc đæt heó ōđerne tealde tōforan his gebyrdum, Homl. Swt. 7, 24. v. husc.

hux-līce; *adv. Ignominiously, disgracefully, unbecomingly:*—Đone seó eorþlīce ārleásnyss huxlīce tealde *whom earthly impiety had disgracefully calumniated,* Homl. Th. i. 48, 23. Đa đe hī huxlīce hēr on līfe gedrehton *those who shamefully afflicted them in this life,* Jud. 5; Thw. 156, 10. Gelǣdde đone kining mid him swīđe huxlīce *carried the king with him very ignominiously,* Ælfc. T. Grn. 8, 20.

hwā; *m. f.;* hwæt; *n. Who; what.* I. *in direct questions* [*with indic. or subj.*]:—*Quis* hwā is werlīc hād *que* hwilc is wīflīc, *cujus* hwæs, *cui* hwam *a quo* fram hwam . . . Gif ic cweđe *quis hoc fecit* hwā dyde đis đonne biþ se *quis interrogativum* đæt is āxigendlīc, Ælfc. Gr. 18; Som. 21, 12–27. Hwā hwylc mann swā Drihten ondrǣt *quis est homo qui timeat Dominum?* Ps. Th. 24, 10. Hwā is moncynnes đæt ne wundrie *what man is there that does not admire?* Bt. Met. Fox 28, 10; Met. 28, 5. Hwā þegna, 86; Met. 28, 43. Hwæt is se gewuldroda cyning *quis est iste rex gloriæ?* Ps. Th. 32, 10. Hwæt hātte Noes wīf *what was Noe's wife called?* Salm. Kmbl. 184, 28. Hwæt wēnst đū hwæt is đes *quis putas est iste?* Mk. Skt. 4, 41: Lk. Skt. 5, 21. Hwæt ys đes mannes sunu? Jn. Skt. 12, 34. Hwæt sind đās būton þrymsetl heora Scyppendes *what are these but thrones of their Creator?* Homl. Th. i. 346, 11. Hwæt sind đa strangan? Đa beóþ strange and trume đe þurh geleáfan wel þeónde beóþ, ii. 390, 22. Đā cwæþ Isaac: Hwæt eart đu? Hē andwirde: Ic eom Esau. Đā cwæþ Isaac: Hwæt wæs se đe mē ǣr brohte of huntoþe? Gen. 27, 32–3. Hwæt is se đe đē slōh *quis est qui te percussit?* Mt. Kmbl. 26, 68. Hwæt eom ic manna đæt ic mihte god forbeódan *what manner of man am I, that I could forbid God,* Homl. Swt.

10, 191: Elen. Kmbl. 1802; El. 903: Beo. Th. 479; B. 237. Hwæt is þinga đe bitere síe *what thing is there that is bitterer?* Past. 21; Swt. 164, 1. Hwæt næddercynna sí on eorþan *how many kinds of snakes are there on the earth?* Salm. Kmbl. 204, 7. Hwæt suna hæfde Adam *what sons had Adam?* 184, 31. Hwæt synt đînum esne ealra dagena *quot sunt dies servi tui?* Ps. Th. 118, 84. Hwæt gôdes dô ic *quid boni faciam?* Mt. Kmbl. 19. 16. Hwæt þincþ eów be Criste hwæs sunu ys hê *quid vobis videtur de Christo? cujus est filius?* 22, 42. Hunta ic eom. Hwæs? *venator sum. Cujus?* Coll. Monast. Th. 21, 7. Hwæs wênaþ se đe nyle gemunan *what does he expect that will not remember?* Exon. 25 b; Th. 74, 1; Cri. 1200. Tô hwam gâ wê *ad quem ibimus?* Jn. Skt. 6, 68. Bí hwon scealt đû lifgan *by what art thou to live?* Exon. 36 b; Th. 118, 23; Gû. 244. For hwan nǽron eorþwelan gedǽled gelîce *why have not earth's treasures been equally divided?* Salm. Kmbl. 685, 693, 703; Sal. 342, 346, 351. For hwan gǽst đû swâ bûton wæstme đînes gewinnes? St. And. 24, 15: Ps. Th. 73, 11: 113, 5. For hwon sêcest đû sceade? Cd. 42; Th. 54, 7, 12; Gen. 873, 876. On hwam mæg man geseón mannes deáþ *by what can one foresee a man's death?* Salm. Kmbl. 206, 10. On hwan *in quo?* Ps. Th. 118, 9. Tô hwæm willaþ gê þider faran *why will ye go thither?* St. And. 6, 18. Tô hwam, Salm. Kmbl. 894; Sal. 446. Tô hwan, Soul Kmbl. 39; Seel. 17. Hwæne sêce gê *quem quæritis?* Jn. Skt. 18, 7. For hwî *quare?* Ps. Th. 113, 5: Coll. Monast. Th. 24, 19. For hwî swâ *cur sic?* 27. Tô hwî stande gê îdele *why stand ye idle,* Homl. Th. ii. 74, 35. Hwý biþ his anwald âuhte đý mâra gif hê nâh his selfes geweald *in what way will his power be at all the greater if he has not command over himself?* Bt. Met. Fox 16, 39; Met. 16, 20. **II.** *in dependent clauses*:—Gif ic cweþe *nescio quis hoc fecit* nât ic hwâ đis dyde đon biþ se *quis infinitivum* đæt is ungeendigendlîc. Gif ic cweþe *tu scis quis hoc fecit* đû wâst hwâ đys dyde đon biþ se *quis relativum* đæt is edlesendlîc, Ælfc. Gr. 18; Som. 21, 27–30. Hogodon georne hwâ ǽrost mihte on fǽgean men feorh gewinnan *strove eagerly who might first obtain the life of a 'fey' man,* Byrht. Th. 135, 26; By. 124. Men ne cunnon secgan hwâ đæm hlæste onfêng, Beo. Th. 104; B. 52: Andr. Kmbl. 761; An. 381. Ic nû scortlîce secgan scyle hwâ đæs ordfruman wǽron *I will now shortly tell who its authors were,* Ors. 5, 9; Swt. 232, 18. Næfdon hwæt hî ǽton *nec haberent quod manducarent,* Mk. Skt. 8, 1. Ne rǽdde gê đæt hwæt dauid dyde đâ hine hingrede *nec hoc legistis quod fecit dauid cum esurisset,* Lk. Skt. 6, 3. Đonne sceal gehwâ him æteówian hwæt hê mid đam punde geteolod hæfþ, Homl. Th. ii. 558, 10. Gehiéren hwæt âwriten is, Past. 44; Swt. 323, 7: 45; Swt. 341, 12: 52; Swt. 405, 29. Geþince gê hwæt gê síen and hwelce gê síen *pensa quod es,* Past. 21, 4; Swt. 159, 14: 1, 3; Swt. 27, 23. Hê sǽde hyre hwæt heó man ne wæs *he told her how she was not a man,* Homl. Swt. 2, 78. Seó eorþe is tô wundrienne hwæt heó ǽrest ođđe gôdra þinga cenne *mirandum est terra quantum aut bonarum rerum pariat,* Nar. 2, 12. Mê wæs uncûþ hwæt đæs đâm lîcian wolde đe æfter ûs wǽren *I did not know how much of it would please those that should be after us,* L. Alf. 49; Th. i. 58, 22. Hit næs nâ gesǽd hwæt Pirruses folces gefeallen wǽre, Ors. 4, 1; Bos. 77, 30. [Đæt is ungeliéfedlîc tô gesecganne] hwæt đæs ealles wæs *what there was of it all,* 5, 12; Swt. 240, 16: Chr. 1046; Erl. 171, 3. Hê nyste hwæt đæs sôđes wæs *he did not know how much truth there was in it,* Ors. 1, 1; Swt. 17, 33. Hý ne âhsedan hwæt đæra gefarenra wǽre, ac hwæt heora đonne tô lâfe wǽre *they did not ask how many were dead, but how many of them were then left,* 4, 4; Bos. 80, 12. Đâ befran se sceađa hwæt hê manna wǽre, Homl. Th. ii. 502, 27: Cd. 64; Th. 77, 6; Gen. 1271. Saga hwæt ic hâtte *say what I am called,* Exon. 102 b; Th. 387, 1; Rä. 4, 72. Đæt hie geþencen hwæs folgeras hie sindon *ut cujus sint sequaces agnoscant,* Past. 47, 1; Swt. 357, 16. Wê cwǽdon hwæs se wyrđe wǽre đe ôđrum ryhtes wyrnde, L. Ed. 2; Th. i. 160, 10. Ic cýđe hwæs ic gean intô ealdan mynstre, Chart. Th. 333, 10: Andr. Kmbl. 290; An. 145. Swâ wæs gemearcod hwam đæt sweord geworht ǽrest wǽre *so was marked for whom that sword was first wrought,* Beo. Th. 3397; B. 1696. Ic ne can for hwam se streám ne môt stillan nihtes *I know not why the stream cannot rest at night,* Salm. Kmbl. 795; Sal. 397. Lyt đû gemundest tô hwan đînre sâwle þing siđđan wurde *little didst thou mind to what thy soul's condition would come,* Soul Kmbl. 39; Seel. 20: Beo. Th. 4149; B. 2071. Sió hâlige gesomnung þurh gesceádwísnesse gesiehþ of huan ǽlc costung cymeþ *sancta ecclesia, quæ ex causis singulis tentamenta prodeant, per discretionem conspicit,* Past. 11, 2; Swt. 65, 24. Ac đû findst wiđ hwone đû meaht flîtan *sed contra quos valeatis vos extendere, semper invenitis,* 44, 8; Swt. 331, 5. Be hwý *according to what principle,* Chart. Th. 171, 7. Ic wundrige for hwý se gôda God lǽte ǽnig yfel beón *I wonder for what reason the good God allows any evil to exist,* Bt. 36, 1; Fox 172, 4. For hwig, St. And. 32, 13. Frægn hî mid hwî hî gescildan heora hûs *he asked them what they protected their house with,* Shrn. 90, 7. **III.** [an indefinite pronoun] *any one, some one; anything, something*:—Gif hwâ on cirican hwæt þeófige *if any one steal anything in a church,* L. Alf. pol. 6; Th. i. 66, 2. Gyf hwâ eów ǽnig þingc tôcwyþ *si quis vobis aliquid dixerit,* Mt. Kmbl. 21, 3. Nellaþ hî gelýfan đeáh hwâ of deáþe ârise *they will not believe, though one rose from death,* Homl. Th. i. 334, 21: Bt. Met. Fox 10, 53; Met. 10, 27. Đeáh ânra hwâ ealles wealde đæs îglandes *though any one rule all that island,* 16, 31; Met. 16, 16. Hwæt hwâ ôđrum tô wô gedô *what any one does wrongfully to another,* L. E. I. 35; Th. ii. 432, 26. Bûton hwâ þurh flânes flyht fyl genâme, Byrht. Th. 133, 56; By. 71. Gif hê næbbe hwæt hê selle *if he have not anything to give,* L. Alf. 24; Th. i. 50, 16. Ne furþum ne giémaþ hwæt hie dôn ođđe hwonne hie hwæt dôn *qui nequaquam, quæ quando agant, inspiciunt,* Past. 39, 3; Swt. 287, 7. Ânes hwæt tô singanne *to sing something,* 46, 2; Swt. 347, 6: Beo. Th. 6013; B. 3010. Tô đæm gleáw đæt hê swelces hwæt tôcnâwan cunne so *skilled that he can distinguish in a matter of such a kind,* Past. 52, 10; Swt. 411, 26. Blæc ođđe won ođđe swilces hwæt *pale or livid or something of that kind,* L. M. 1, 35; Lchdm. ii. 82, 13: Beo. Th. 1764: B. 880. Gif hwæt yfles on biþ, L. M. 2, 24; Lchdm. ii. 214, 13. Lytles hwæt, Ors. 3, 7; Swt. 120, 4: 3, 9; Swt. 136, 18. Gif friþgeard sî on hwæs lande *if a 'friþgeard' be on any one's land,* L. N. P. L. 54; Th. ii. 298, 16. Gif hwæs brôđor deád biþ *si cujus frater mortuus fuerit,* Mk. Skt. 12, 19. Đonne đæt môd hwæs wilnode tô witanne đæs đe hit ǽr for sweotole ongytan ne meahte, Shr. 164, 19. Đeáh hwæm swâ ne þince *though to any one it seem not so,* Bt. 20; Fox 70, 32. Rinca hwæm, Bt. Met. Fox 22, 56; Met. 22, 28. Oft hwæm gebyreþ đæt hê hwæt mǽrlîces and wundorlîces gedêþ, Past. 4, 1; Swt. 39, 6: 40, 5; Swt. 297, 4. Hit biþ on ânes hwæm đê unfæstre *impar quisque invenitur ad singula,* 4, 1; Swt. 37, 15. Sôna swâ sacerda hwylc hwone on wôh gesyhþ *directly any priest sees any one in error,* L. E. I. 28; Th. ii. 424, 26. Đeáh mon hwone gôdra mid rihte herige, Bt. 30, 1; Fox 108, 8: Bt. Met. Fox 10, 1; Met. 10, 1: Beo. Th. 312; B. 155. **IV.** *in combination with* swâ, *whosoever, whatsoever, whatever*:—Swâ hwâ *quicunque,* Ælfc. Gr. 18; Som. 21, 37: swâ hwâ *quisquis,* 34. Swâ hwâ swâ đê genýt þûsend stapa *quicunque te angariaberit mille passus,* Mt. Kmbl. 5, 41: Cd. 22; Th. 28, 20; Gen. 438: 24; Th. 31, 10; Gen. 483. Swâ hwæt swâ hig woldon *quæcumque voluerunt,* Mt. Kmbl. 17, 12: Cd. 35; Th. 47, 4; Gen. 755. [Hî môsten cêsen of clerchâdes man swâ hwam (*acc.*) swâ hî wolden, Chr. 1123; Erl. 250, 11. **V.** *taking the place of the earlier* se:—Hê wiđ đone cyng geworhte for hwan hine se cyng ealles benǽmde *he acted against the king; on which account the king deprived him of everything,* 1104; Erl. 239, 31: 1110; Erl. 243, 15: 1117; Erl. 246, 21.] [*Laym.* wha; whæt, what, wat: *Orm.* wha; whatt: *A. R.* hwo; hwat: *O. and N.* hwo, wo; hwat, what, wat: *R. Glouc.* wo; wat: *Ayenb.* huo; huet: *Chauc. Piers P.* who; what: *Goth.* hwas, *m*: hwô; *f*: hwa; *n*: *O. Sax.* hwe; hwat: *O. Frs.* hwa; hwet: *Icel.* hvar; hvat: *O. H. Ger.* hwer; hwaz: *Ger.* wer; was: *Lat.* quis; quid.] v. hwæt, hwý; ge-whâ.

hwæcca *a chest, hutch*: — Corn-hwæcca *arca frumentaria,* Lye. [*Piers P.* (A.) Til perneles porfyl be put in heore *whucche,* iv. 102: *Allit. Poems* Alle woned in the *whichche* (*ark*) þe wylde & þe tame, 49, 362: *Jos. of Arith.* Make a luytel *whucche,* 2, 39: *Prompt. Parv.* whyche or hoche, hutche *cista, archa,* pp. 242, 255, see note on latter page.]

hwæder, hweder; *adv. Whither*: — Hwæder gâ ic *ego quo ibo,* Gen. 37, 30. Ic gesette him hwæder hê bûgan sceal *constituam tibi locum, in quem fugere debeat,* Ex. 21, 13. Gif hê eów âxie hweder gê willon *si interrogaverit 'quo vadis?'* Gen. 32, 17. [*Goth.* hwadre *whither.*] v. hwider.

hwæg, hwæig, hweg, es; *n.* [?] *Whey*:—Hwæg *serum,* Wrt. Voc. 290, 36. Đeówan wîfmen hwæig on sumera *to a servant maid shall be given whey in summer,* L. R. S. 9; Th. i. 436, 32. Sceáphyrdes riht is đæt hê hæbbe ... blede fulle hweges ođđe syringe eahe sumor, 14; Th. i. 438, 25. DER. cýse-, wring-hwæg.

hwæl, es; *m. A whale*: — Hwæl *balena* vel *cete* vel *cetus* vel *pistrix,* Ælfc. Gl. 101; Som. 77, 54; Wrt. Voc. 55, 57. Hwæl *cætus,* Ælfc. Gr. 8; Som. 7, 31. Se hwæl biþ micle læssa đonne ôđre hwalas *the walrus is much less than other whales,* Ors. 1, 1; Swt. 18, 3. On đæs hwæles innoþe *in ventre ceti,* Mt. Kmbl. 12, 40. Hwæles êđel *the sea,* Andr. Kmbl. 548; An. 274: Exon. 82 a; Th. 309, 20; Seef. 60: Chr. 975; Erl. 126, 22; Edg. 48. Bî đam miclan hwale *concerning the great whale,* Exon. 96 b; Th. 360, 10; Wal. 3. God đâ gegearcode ǽnne hwæl and hê forswealh đone wîtegan, Homl. Th. i. 246, 12. Wilt đû fôn sumne hwæl? Nic. For hwî? Forđam plyhtlîc þingc hit ys gefôn hwæl *vis capere aliquem cetum? Nolo. Quare? Quia periculosa res est capere cetum,* Coll. Monast. Th. 24, 15–22. Hê gesceóp đa micclan hwalas, Lchdm. iii. 234, 12. [*Icel.* hvalr: *O. H. Ger.* wal *balæna, cetus,* Grff. i. 839.] v. hors-hwæl.

hwǽl:—On hwǽl hreópon [hwreopon, MS.] herefugolas *the birds of war screamed as they wheeled round,* Cd. 150; Th. 188, 1; Exod. 161. [Cf. *Icel.* hvel.] v. hwêl *in* hweogul.

hwæla, an; *m. A whale*:—Hê is on middon hwælan hiwes *he is of a whale's shape in the middle,* Salm. Kmbl. 527; Sal. 263.

hwæl-hunta, an; *m. A whale-hunter, whale-fisher, whaler*:—Hwælhunta *cetarius,* Ælfc. Gl. 101; Som. 77, 55; Wrt. Voc. 55, 59. Đâ wæs hē swā feor norþ swā ða hwælhuntan firrest faraþ *was as far north as the whalers ever go*, Ors. 1, 1; Swt. 17, 12.

hwæl-huntaþ, es; *m. Whale-fishing, whaling*:—On his āgnum lande is se betsta hwælhuntaþ, Ors. 1, 1; Swt. 18, 5.

hwæl-mere, es; *m. The sea*, Exon. 101 a; Th. 382, 2; Rä. 3, 5: Andr. Kmbl. 739; An. 370.

hwæm *a corner*. v. hwem.

hwǣne. v. hwēne.

hwænne. v. hwanne.

hwǣr [or hwær?], hwar; *adv. Where*. I. *in direct questions*:—Gyf ic cweþe *ubi posuisti meum librum*, hwǣr lēdest ðū mīne bōc ðonne is se *ubi interrogativum* ðæt is āxigendlīc, Ælfc. Gr. 38; Som. 40, 60. Hwǣr ys se Judēa cyning ðe ācenned ys *ubi est qui natus est rex Judæorum?* Mt. Kmbl. 2, 2. Hwǣr cwom mearg hwǣr cwom mago hwǣr cwom māððumgyfa *where is the steed gone, where the rider, where the giver of treasure?* Exon. 77 b; Th. 291, 34; Wand. 92: Cd. 213; Th. 267, 11; Sat. 36. II. *in dependent clauses*:—Gif ic cweþe *tu scis ubi liber tuus est* ðonne biþ *ubi relativum*. Gif ic cweðe *nescio ubi inveniam meum librum*, nāt ic hwǣr ic finde mīne bōc, ðonne biþ se *ubi infinitivum*, Ælfc. Gr. 38; Som. 40, 61. Ic næbbe hwǣr ic mǣge ealle mīne wæstmas gegaderian *I have not where I may gather together all my fruits*, Homl. Th. ii. 104, 16: Mt. Kmbl. 8, 20. Hī gesāwon hwǣr hē ða deádan tō līfe ārǣrde, Homl. Th. ii. 414, 8: Cd. 32; Th. 41, 35; Gen. 667. Hwǣr mon unsōfte getilaþ on forewearde ða ādle *where the treatment is severe in the early stage of the disease*, L. M. 2, 46; Lchdm. ii. 260, 15. Lōca hwǣr ðæt blōd ūtwealle *see where the blood wells out*, Lchdm. iii. 142, 15: 226, 13. Ðā frægn wuldres aldor cain hwǣr abel eorþan wǣre *the Prince of glory asked Cain where on earth Abel was*, Cd. 48; Th. 61, 26; Gen. 1003. Ic sēce mīne gebrōðru hwar hig healdon hyra heorda, Gen. 37, 16. III. *indefinite, anywhere, somewhere*:—Gyf hȳ hwǣr hit tōbræcaþ *if they violate it anywhere*, L. Ælfc. C. 34; Th. ii. 356, 16: Homl. Th. i. 170, 18: 482, 26. Gif se līchoma hwǣr mid hefiglīcre hǣto sȳ gebysgod, Herb. 2, 6; Lchdm. i. 82, 8. Swǣ gelǣrede biscepas swǣ swǣ nū wel hwǣr [*or* welhwǣr] siendon *bishops so learned as now are nearly everywhere*, Past. pref. Swt. 9, 5: Chr. 897; Erl. 95, 19. Elles hwǣr *elsewhere*, Beo. Th. 277; B. 138. Hȳ writon hwǣr ānne dōm hwǣr ōðerne *they wrote at one place one doom, at another another*, L. Alf. 49; Th. i. 58, 16. IV. *combined with* swā, *wheresoever, wherever*:—Swā hwǣr swā hold biþ *ubicunque fuerit corpus*, Mt. Kmbl. 24, 28. Swā hwǣr swā hē on wīc oððe on tūnas eode *quocunque introibat in vicos vel in villas*, Mk. Skt. 6, 56. Swā hwǣr swā *ubicunque*, 14, 9. [*A. R.* hwar; *O. and N.* hwar, war: *Orm.* whær: *Laym.* whær, wher: *Chauc. Wick. Piers P.* wher: *Ayenb.* huer: *Goth.* hwar: *O. Sax.* hwār: *O. Frs.* hwēr: *Icel.* hvar: *O. H. Ger.* hwār.] DER. ā-, ǣ-, ǣg-, ge-, gewel-, nā-, nāt-, ō-, wel-hwǣr.

hwær *a vessel*. v. hwer.

hwæs; *adj. Sharp, keen*:—Hī hwæsne beág ymb mīn heáfod heardne gebȳgdon *they encircled my head with a crown sharp and hard* [*the crown of thorns*], Exon. 29 a; Th. 88, 23; Cri. 1444. [*Goth.* hwass-aba *sharply*: *Icel.* hvass *sharp*.] Cf. hwæt.

hwǣstrian, hwǣstrung. v. hwāstrian, hwāstrung.

hwæt; *neut.* of hwā, *used as an adv.* or *interj. Why, what! ah!*—Be ðæs folces heringe ic nāt hwæt ðæs fægniaþ *as regards popular applause, I know not why we rejoice at it*, Bt. 30, 1; Fox 108, 22. Hwæt befealdest ðū folmum ðīnum brōðor ðīnne *why hast thou felled thy brother with thy hands?* Cd. 48; Th. 62, 6; Gen. 1010: Andr. Kmbl. 1257; An. 629. Hwæt ðū leóda feala forleólce and forlǣrdest *how many people hast thou deceived and seduced!* 2726; An. 1365: Beo. Th. 1064; B. 530. Hwæt iudas hēt ðā settan ðæt līc *ah! then Judas bade them put down the body*, H. R. 13, 26. Hwæt mē ðīn hand ðyder lǣdeþ *etenim illuc manus tua deducet me*, Ps. Th. 138, 8. Hwæt ðā Sem and Jafeth dydon ānne hwītel on hira sculdra *at vero Sem et Japheth pallium imposuerunt humeris suis*, Gen. 9, 23. Hwæt ðū ēce God *O! thou eternal God*, Bt. Met. Fox 20, 7; Met. 20, 4: 20, 92; Met. 20, 46. Hwæt ðū eart se sylfa God ðe ūs ādrife fram dōme *nonne tu Deus qui repulisti nos?* Ps. Th. 107, 10. Hwæt wē nū gehȳraþ *ah! now we learn*, Cd. 45; Th. 57, 36; Gen. 939. Hwæt wē gefrunon twelfe tīreádige hæleþ *lo! we have heard of twelve glorious heroes*, Andr. Kmbl. 1; An. 1: Beo. Th. 1; B. 1: Cd. 143; Th. 177, 27; Exod. 1: Rood Kmbl. 1; Kr. 1. Eá lā hwæt! Bt. Met. 4, 49; Met. 4, 25. [*So O. Sax.* hwat: *Icel.* hvat: *O. H. Ger.* waz *cur, quid, quare*.] v. hwā, hū.

hwæt; *adj. Quick, active, vigorous, stout, bold, brave*:—Sum biþ tō horse hwæt *one is a bold rider*, Exon. 79 b; Th. 298, 7; Crā. 81. Nis mon ofer eorþan tō ðæs hwæt ðæt hē ā his sǣfōre sorge næbbe *there is no man on earth so bold as never to have anxiety for his journey on the sea*, 82 a; Th. 308, 16; Seef. 40. Ne scyle se hwata esne ymb ðæt gnornian hū oft hē feohtan scule *virum fortem non decet indignari, quoties increpuit bellicus tumultus*, Bt. 40, 3; Fox 238, 10: Beo. Th. 6048; B. 3028. Hwatum Heorowearde, 4328; B. 2161. Hwate Scyldingas, 3206; B. 1601: 4111; B. 2052. Hȳ beóþ heortum þȳ hwætran *they will be the stouter of heart*, Exon. 107 a; Th. 408, 30; Rä. 27, 20. Ðēh ðe Sciþþie hæfdon māran monmenie and self hwætran wǣron *cum Scythæ et numero et virtute præstarent*, Ors. 3, 7; Swt. 116, 25. Ðone cræftgestan dǣl and ða hwatestan men ealles ðises middangeardes *fortissimas mundi partes*, 1, 10; Swt. 48, 6. Of ðǣm hwatestan monnum Germanie *from the bravest men of Germany*, Swt. 48, 14. [*O. E. Homl.* hwat, wat: *Laym.* whæt, wat: *Ayenb.* huet: *O. Sax.* hwat: *Icel.* hvatr.] DER. ār-, bearhtm-, blēd-, dǣd-, dōm-, flyht-, fyrd-, gold-, gūþ-, leód-, mōd-, sund-, swīð-hwæt; *and see* hwæs, hwettan.

HWǢTE, es; *m.* WHEAT:—Hwǣte *triticum*, Wrt. Voc. 287, 17. Grǣg hwǣte *far*, Ælfc. Gr. 9, 17; Som. 9, 52. Þurh ða gemetgunge hwǣtes *per mensuram tritici*, Past. 63; Swt. 459, 13. Fyrsas ða ðe willaþ derian clǣnum hwǣte, Bt. Met. Fox 12, 9; Met. 12, 5. Hē hī fēdde mid hwǣte, Ps. 80, 15. Tō ðæm ðæt hē him tō tīde gemetlīce gedǣle ðone hwǣte *ut det illis in tempore tritici mensuram*, Past. 63; Swt. 459, 13. Fullne hwǣte on ðam eare *plenum frumentum in spica*, Mk. Skt. 4, 28. Hwǣtas *frumenta*, Ælfc. Gr. 13; Som. 16, 10. On hwǣtum *frumento*, Ps. Th. 64, 14. [*Orm.* whæte: *Ayenb.* huete: *Piers P.* whete: *Goth.* hwaiteis: *O. L. Ger.* huēte: *Icel.* hveiti; *n*: *Dan.* hvede: *O. H. Ger.* hwaizi *triticum, frumentum*: *Ger.* weizen.] DER. hlāf-hwǣte.

hwæt-eádig; *adj. Successful in war* [cf. *other compounds of* eádig]:—Biþ se hwæteádig wīggeweorþod se ðe ðæt wicg byrþ *he shall be successful and honoured in war whom that steed bears*, Elen. Kmbl. 2388; El. 1195.

hwǣte-corn, es; *n. A grain of wheat*:—Genim hnutcyrnla and hwǣtecorn *take nut-kernels and grains of wheat*, L. M. 1, 2; Lchdm. ii. 34, 19. [*O. E. Homl.* hwete-corn: *Icel.* hveiti-korn.]

hwǣte-cynn, es; *n. Wheat-kind*:—Hē ðē gesadade mid ðȳ sēlestan hwǣtecynnes holde lynde *adipe frumenti satiat te*, Ps. Th. 147, 3.

hwǣte-god *Ceres*, Lye.

hwǣte-gryttan; *pl. Coarse wheaten meal*:—Hwǣtegryttan *apludes* vel *cantalna* [= *cantabra*], Ælfc. Gl. 50; Som. 65, 124; Wrt. Voc. 34, 53.

hwæte-healm, es; *m. The straw* or *stalk of wheat*:—Genim hwǣtehealm and gebærn tō duste, L. M. 1, 60; Lchdm. ii. 130, 14.

hwǣte-land, es; *m. Wheat-land, land for growing wheat upon*:—Ðæt hæft se arcebisceop genumen tō hwǣtelande, Cod. Dipl. Kmbl. iii. 159, 23.

hwǣte-melu, wes; *n. Wheaten meal* or *flour*:—Mid hwǣtemelwe, L. M. 3, 65; Lchdm. ii. 354, 12. [*Icel.* hveiti-mjöl.]

hwǣten; *adj. Wheaten*:—Hwǣten hlāf *siligeneus* vel *triticeus panis*, Ælfc. Gl. 66; Som. 69, 63; Wrt. Voc. 41, 19. Ic secge eów ðæt hwǣtene corn wunaþ āna būton hyt fealle on eorþan and sȳ deád *dico vobis nisi granum frumenti cadens in terram mortuum fuerit ipsum solum manet*, Jn. Skt. 12, 24. Mid hwǣtenan meluwe, Herb. 184, 4; Lchdm. i. 322, 13. Of hwǣtenum mealte geworht, iii. 74, 3. Hwǣtenne hlāf, L. M. 1, 53; Lchdm. ii. 126, 1: Ps. Th. 77, 25. On hwǣtene wyrte *in wheaten wort*, L. M. 2, 57; Lchdm. ii. 268, 12. Nim hwǣten corn, L. M. 1, 75; Lchdm. ii. 150, 8. cxx hwǣtenra hlāfa, Chart. Th. 460, 15.

hwǣte-smedeme, an; *f. Fine wheaten flour*:—Hunig and hwǣtesmedman, Lchdm. iii. 18, 5.

hwǣte-wæstm, es; *m.* [?] *Corn*; frumentatio, Ps. Vos. 77, 29, Lye.

hwæðer; *pron.* I. *which of two*:—Hwæðer ðara twegra dyde ðæs fæder willan *whether of them twain did the will of his father?* Mt. Kmbl. 21, 31. Hwæðer ys māre ðe ðæt gold ðe ðæt templ ðe ðæt gold gehālgaþ *whether is greater, the gold or the temple that sanctifieth the gold?* 23, 17, 19. Hwæðer wǣre twegra strengra wyrd ðe warnung? Salm. Kmbl. 853; Sal. 426. Gebīde gē hwæðer sēl mǣge wunde gedȳgan uncer twega, Beo. Th. 5054; B. 2530. Hwæðres ðonne ðara yfelra is betre ǣr tō tilianne būton swæðres swæðer frēcenlīcre is *quæ igitur pestis ardentius insequenda est, nisi quæ periculosius premit?* Past. 62, 1; Swt. 457, 21. Hwæðres biþ hira folgoþ betra? Salm. Kmbl. 740; Sal. 369. Hwæðerne wylle gē ðæt ic forgyfe eów of ðīsum twām *whether of the twain will ye that I release unto you?* Mt. Kmbl. 27, 21. Ðā befran Pilatus hwæðerne hī gecuron Hǣlend oððe Barraban? Homl. Th. ii. 252, 12. Nāst ðū hwæðer beóþ ðæs rīcan mannes bān hwæðer ðæs þearfan *thou knowest not which are the rich man's bones, which the poor one's*, Homl. Th. i. 256, 16. II. *one or other of two, either*:—Hie hit gesund begen āgifan swā hit hwæðer hiora ǣr onfēnge būton hiora hwæðer þingode ðæt ... *let them both return it sound as either of them may have before received it, unless either of them made a condition that* ..., L. Alf. pol. 19; Th. i. 74, 11: Bt. Met. Fox 5, 81; Met. 5, 41. Gif hwā tō hwæðrum ðissa genied sīe *if any one be forced to either of these*, L. Alf. pol. 1; Th. i. 60, 3. Tō manigenne sint ða gesomhīwan ðeáh hira hwæðrum hwæthwugu hwīlum mislīcige on ōðrum ðæt hie ðæt geþyldelīce forberen *admonendi sunt conjuges, ut ea, in quibus sibi aliquando displicent, patientes invicem tolerent*, Past. 51, 3; Swt. 395, 32. III. *each of two, both*:—Hwæðer hāt and ceald hwīlum mencgaþ *both heat and cold at times mingle*, Cd. 216; Th. 273, 5; Sat. 132. IV. *in combination with* swā, *whichever of two*:—Heora eáþmetto ne mihton nāuht forstanden ne hūru heora ofermetta dydon swā hwæþer swā hȳ dydon *their humility availed naught nor indeed did their pride, whichever course they followed*, Bt. 29, 2; Fox 106, 1. Bī swā hwaðerre efes swā hit ðonne fierdleás wæs *on whichever border there was then no force*, Chr. 894; Erl. 90, 13. On swâ hwæðere hond *on whichever hand*, Beo. Th. 1376; B. 686. Drihtenes âre oððe deófles þeówet swâ hwæðer wê geearniaþ hêr on life, Hy. Grn. ii. 289, 99; Hy. 7, 99. [*Laym.* whaðer: *O. and N.* hweþer: *Chauc.* whether: *Goth.* hwaþar: *O. Sax.* hwedar: *O. Frs.* hweder: *Icel.* hvárr: *O. H. Ger.* hwedar.] DER. â-, ǽg-, nâ-, nô-hwæðer; *and see* swæðer.

hwæðer, hweðer; *conj. Whether.* I. *in direct questions*:—Hwæðer ic môte lybban ôþ ðæt ic hine geseó *may I live till I see him?* Homl. Th. i. 136, 30. Hwæðer gê willen on wuda sêcan gold ðæt reáde? Bt. Met. Fox 19, 9, 29; Met. 19, 5, 15. Hwæðer ðe ðîn eáge mânful ys forðam ðe ic gôd eom *an oculus tuus nequam est, quia ego bonus sum?* Mt. Kmbl. 20, 15. Hwæðer cweþe wê ðe ûre ðe ðæra engla *shall we say ours or the angels?* Homl. Th. i. 220, 20. Cwyst ðû hwæðer ic hyt sî *numquid ego sum?* Mt. Kmbl. 26, 25. II. *in dependent clauses*:—Lǽtaþ ðæt wê geseón hwæðer elias cume *sinite videamus si veniat helias*, Mk. Skt. 15, 36. Gregorius befran hwæðer ðæs landes folc cristen wǽre ðe hǽðen, Homl. Th. ii. 120, 23. Hî nysten hwæðer hê on Godes mihte ða þing worhte ðe þurh deófles cræft, Guthl. 17; Gdwin. 70, 17. Swîðe hræðe æfter ðon hê gecýðde hwæðer hê mǽnde ðe ðæs môdes fôster ðe ðæs lîchoman *qui hoc in loco pastionem cordis an corporis suaderet, aperuit*, Past. 18, 6; Swt. 137, 18. Hwæðer hit sig ðe sôþ ðe leás *utrum vera an falsa sint*, Gen. 42, 16. Josep âxode hig hwæðer hira fæder wǽre hâl oððe hwæðer hê lyfode *ille interrogavit eos dicens: Salvusne est pater vester? adhuc vivit?* 43, 27. Sceáwiaþ ðæt land hwæðer hit wæstmbǽre sî . . . and hwæðer ðæt landfolc sî tô gefeohte stranglîc oððe untrumlîc, feáwa on getele hwæðer ðe fela, Num. 13, 19–20. [*O. Sax.* hweðar: *O. Frs.* hweder: *Icel.* hvárt: *O. H. Ger.* hwedar.] v. preceding word.

hwæðere, hwæðre, hwæððre, hweðre; *adv. Yet, however, nevertheless*:—Ac nǽnig hwæðere him gelîce dôn ne mihte *but none however could do like him*, Bd. 4, 24; S. 596, 39. Hwæðere ðû meaht mê singan *attamen mihi cantare habes*, 597, 15. Hwæðere for fremsumnysse *tamen pro benignitate*, 1, 27; S. 493, 7. Hwæðere *verumtamen*, Ps. Th. 61, 5, 9: 67, 21. Ðeáh ðe . . . hwæðere *although . . . yet*, Beo. Th. 3441; B. 1718. Ne ðû hweðere on môde milde weorþest eallum *non miseraris omnibus*, Ps. Th. 58, 5. Nô hweðere reste fand *did not find rest however*, Cd. 72; Th. 87, 30; Gen. 1456. Hwæþre hê getrymede heora geleáfan mid ðon heofonlîcon weorce ðeáh hie ðæt word ðæs heofonlîcan gerýnes ne ongeáton, Blickl. Homl. 17, 7. Hwæðre ðeáh *however*, Bt. Met. Fox 20, 108; Met. 20, 54. Hwæðre swâ ðeáh, Beo. Th. 4876; B. 2442. Hwæððre, Past. 56, 2; Swt. 431, 26. Hweðre, Blickl. Homl. 125, 31: 207, 34. v. ðeáh-hwæðere.

hwæðere, hwæðre [=hwæðer]; *conj. Whether*, Exon. 37 b; Th. 123, 15; Gû. 323: Beo. Th. 2632; B. 1314.

hwæt-hwega, -hwigu, -hugu; *pron.* and *adv.* [cf. *use of* something *in Shakspere.*] *Something, somewhat, a little*:—Sing mê hwæthwegu *canta mihi aliquid*, Bd. 4, 24; S. 597, 12. Hwæthugu wundurlîcre hâlignesse *aliquid miræ sanctitatis*, 3, 9; S. 534, 1. Hwæthwegu seldcûþes *something strange*, Bt. 34, 4; Fox 138, 28. Hwæthwygo *aliquid*, Nar. 1, 18. Ic hwæthwugo on bôcum geleornode, 39, 19. Huodhuoegu *aliquid*, Jn. Skt. Lind. 7, 4. Hwæthwega *paulisper, parumper*, Ælfc. Gr. 38; Som. 41, 65. Hê hwæthwego fram ðam wage ða limu âhôf, Guthl. 20; Gdwin. 82, 27: Homl. Th. ii. 90, 29. Hwæthwega ufor gân, 32, 22. Hwæthwegu tôdǽled *somewhat separated*, Bt. 34, 6; Fox 142, 14. Hwæthwiga *aliquantulum*, Ps. Th. 89, 15. Hwæthwygu, 93, 8. Hwæthwugu, Bt. Met. Fox 221; Met. 20, 111.

hwæt-hweganunges, -hwugununges, -huguningas; *adv. Somewhat*:—Hwæthweganunges [MS. Cot. -hwugunungés] *aliquantum*, Bt. 11, 1; Fox 30, 27. Hwæthwegnunges, 11, tit; Fox xii. 10. Ða niétenu ðonne beóþ hwæthuguningas [MS. Cott. -hwugununges] from eorþan âhæfen *in animalibus vero jam quidem cogitationes aliquantulum a terra suspensæ*, Past. 21, 3; Swt. 155, 15.

hwæt-hwoegno; *pron. Anything, something*; aliquid, Jn. Skt. Rush. 7, 4. v. hwæt-hwega.

hwæt-lîce; *adv. Quickly, speedily*:—Gehýr mê hwætlîce *exaudi me*, Ps. Th. 137, 4. Hwætlîcor *citius*, Coll. Monast. Th. 31, 23. [*Icel.* hvat-liga *quickly.*]

hwæt-môd; *adj. Stout-hearted, bold*:—Hæleþ hwætmôde *men stout of heart*, Elen. Kmbl. 2009; El. 1006: Exon. 55 b; Th. 197, 3; Az. 184.

hwæt-ness, e; *f. Quickness, agility*:—Seó fægernes and seó hwætnes ðæs lîchoman geblissaþ ðone mon *pulcritudo atque velocitas videntur præstare celebritatem*, Bt. 24, 3; Fox 84, 8.

hwæt-rǽd; *adj.* [?] *Strong of purpose* or *counsel*:—Hwætrêd, hygerôf, Exon. 124 a; Th. 477, 5; Ruin. 20.

hwæt-scipe, es; *m. Quickness, boldness, bravery, valour*:—Oft mon biþ swîðe rempende and rǽsþ suîðe dollîce on ǽlc weorc and hrædlîce and ðeáh wênaþ þ men ðæt hit sîe for arodscipe and hwætscipe *sæpe præcipitata actio velocitatis efficacia putatur*, Past. 20, 1; Swt. 149, 13. For hiora cræftum and for hiora hwætscipe iówra selfra anwald[es] eóweres unþonces habban mehton *by their strength and valour might have had dominion over you against your will*; armis vindicare potuissent, Ors. 1, 10; Swt. 48, 21. Sinope tôeácan hiere hwætscipe and hiere monigfealdum duguþum hiere lîf geendade on mægþhâde *Sinope singularem virtutis gloriam perpetua virginitate cumulavit*, Swt. 46, 24.

hwalf. v. hwealf.

hwall; *adj. Procax*, Cot. 171, Lye. [*O. H. Ger.* hwell *procax*; hwelli *pertinacia.*]

hwalwa [=hwalfa?] *devexus*, Cot. 67, Lye. v. hwealf.

hwamm, hwomm, es; *m. A corner*:—Heáfod hwommys *caput anguli*, Ps. Spl. C. 117, 21. Huommes, Mk. Skt. Lind. 12, 10: Lk. Skt. Lind. 20, 17. Ðâ eode ût of ðæs karcernes hwomme swîðe egeslîc draca *then came a very horrible dragon out of a corner of the prison*, Nar. 43, 13. Hwommona heágost *caput anguli*, Ps. Th. 117, 21. On ðînes hûses hwommum *in lateribus domus tuæ*, 127, 2. In hwommum worþana *in angulis platearum*, Mt. Kmbl. Rush. 6, 5. Ofer ealle heá hwommas *super omnes angulos excelsos*, Past. 35, 5; Swt. 245, 7. v. hwemm.

hwam-stân, es; *m. A corner-stone*:—In heáfut huomstânes *in caput anguli*, Mt. Kmbl. Lind. 21, 42.

hwanan, hwanon, hwonan, hwanone; *adv. Whence.* I. *in direct questions*:—*Interrogativa* synd âxigendlîce, *unde* hwanan, Ælfc. Gr. 38; Som. 41, 58. Hwanon hæfde hê coccel *unde habet zizania?* Mt. Kmbl. 13, 27. Hwanun wât ic þis *unde hoc sciam?* Lk. Skt. 1, 18. Hwanone sceoldest ðû specan on Hebrêisc *how should you speak in Hebrew?* Nicod. 4; Thw. 2. 27. II. *in dependent clauses*:—Hî spyredan hwæt and hwonan hê wæs *investigantes unde vel quis esset*, Bd. 1, 33; S. 499, 12. Ic ne wât hwonon his cyme sindon *I know not whence is his coming*, Exon. 50 b; Th. 175, 18; Gû. 1196. Hwanan, Beo. Th. 4798; B. 2403. Ðâ næfde hê hwanon hê his wer âgulde *he had not means to pay his 'wer,'* Chart. Th. 207, 36. [*Laym.* whanene: *O. and N.* wanene, hwenene, hwenne: *Ayenb.* huannes: *Chauc.* whennes: *O. Sax.* hwanan: *O. H. Ger.* hwanan, hwanana: *Ger.* wannen.] DER. ǽg-, ge-, nâ-, ô-hwanon.

hwanne, hwænne, hwonne; *adv. When.* I. *in direct questions*:—*Quando venisti* hwænne côm ðû? is *interrogativum*, Ælfc. Gr. 38; Som. 40, 64. Hwonne ǽr beó deád oððe hwænne his nama âspringe *quando morietur, et peribit nomen ejus?* Ps. Th. 40, 5. II. *in dependent clauses*:—*Quando ero doctus* hwænne beó ic gelǽred, is *infinitivum*, Som. 40, 65. Sege ûs hwænne ðâs þing gewurdon *dic nobis quando ista fient*, Mk. Skt. 13, 4: Mt. Kmbl. 2, 7. Þincþ him tô lang hwænne hê beó genumen of ðyses lîfes earfoþnyssum *it seems to him too long [to the time] when he shall be taken from the troubles of this life*, Homl. Th. i. 140, 9. Lǽt gebîdan beornas ðîne hwænne ðû eft cyme *let thy men await the time of thy return*, Andr. Kmbl. 800; An. 400. Ðâ wæs ðæt hê sorgiende bâd hwonne seó âdl tô him côme *qui cum sollicitus horam accessionis exspectaret*, Bd. 3, 12; S. 537, 6. Hit biþ long hwonne se hlâford cume *moram facit Dominus meus venire*, Past. 17, 8; Swt. 121, 12. Hit earfoþe is ǽnegum menn tô witanne hwonne hê geclǽnsod sîe *it is difficult for any man to know when he is cleansed*, 7, 2; Swt. 51, 5. Sǽles bîdeþ hwonne ǽr heó cræft hyre cýðan môte *it waits for the time for displaying its art* [cf. *O. Sax.* that werod bêd hwan êr the frôdo man gifrumid habdi waldandes willeon], Exon. 108 b; Th. 413, 29; Rä. 32, 13. III. *indefinite, at some time*:—Se ilca ûs wile nû hwonne eft mid eallum egesan gesêcan *the same will visit us again at some time with all terror*, Blickl. Homl. 123, 32. [*Laym.* whenne, wonne: *Orm.* whanne: *O. and N.* hwanne, wonne: *A. R.* hwonne, hwon: *Wick.* whanne: *Chauc.* whan: *Goth. O. Sax.* hwan: *O. H. Ger.* hwanne, hwenne *quando, aliquando*: *Ger.* wann.]

hwar. v. hwǽr.

hwarne, Mt. Kmbl. Lind. 8, 30. v. hwergen.

hwast, es; *or* [?] hwasta, an; *m. An effeminate person* [?], *a eunuch*:—Hwastas *molles*, Som. Huastana *eunuchorum*, Mt. Kmbl. p. 18, 9.

hwâstrian, hwǽstrian; *p.* ede *To whisper, murmur, mutter*:—Âgên mê hwǽstredun ealle fýnd mîne *adversum me susurrabant omnes inimici mei*, Ps. Lamb. 40, 8. Huǽstredon *murmurabant*, Mt. Kmbl. Lind. 20, 11: Lk. Skt. Lind. 19, 7: Jn. Skt. Lind. 6, 41, 61. Huǽstria *murmurari*, 6, 43. Huǽstrende *murmurantem*, 7, 32. [Cf. hwisprian, hwistlian; and *Icel.* hvískra, hvísla *to whisper.*]

hwâstrung, hwǽstrung, e; *f. A whispering, murmuring, muttering*:—Þurh hwâstrunge *per susurrationem*, Confess. Peccat. Huǽstrung micel *murmur multus*, Jn. Skt. Lind. 7, 12. [Cf. *Icel.* hvískran *a whispering.*]

hwat, es; *n. Augury, divination*:—Ne gîmon hwata ne swefna *non augurabimini nec observabitis somnia*, Lev. 19, 26. Wê lǽraþ ðæt preósta gehwilc forbeóde hwata and galdra *we enjoin that every priest forbid auguries and incantations*, L. Edg. C. 16; Th. ii. 248, 3. v. hwatung.

hwata; *adj.* v. hwæt.

hwata, an; *m. An augur, diviner*:—Warna ðê ðæt ðû ne gîme drýcræfta ne swefena ne hwatena *nec inveniatur in te, qui ariolos sciscitetur et observet somnia et auguria*, Deut. 18, 10. v. fugel-hwata.

hwatend *iris illyrica*, Lchdm. iii. 334, col. 1.

hwatung, e; *f. Divination*:—Âlýfed nys îdele hwatunga tô begânne *permissum non est vanas divinationes exercere*, L. Ecg. P. ii. 23, title; Th. ii. 180, 36. Nis nā sōðlīce ālȳfed nānum cristenum men ðæt hē īdele hwatunga begā swā hǣðene men dōþ ðæt is ðæt hig gelȳfon on sunnan and on mōnan and on steorrena ryne and sēcon tīda hwatunga hyra þing tō begynnanne *homini christiano certe non est permissum vana auguria facere, uti gentiles faciunt, id est, quod credant in solem et lunam, et in cursum stellarum; et auguria temporum exquirant, ad negotia sua incipienda*, 23; Th. ii. 190, 30–3. Gif hwā hwatunga begā *si quis divinātiones exerceat*, iv. 19; Th. ii. 210, 11. v. hwat.

hwealf, e; *f. An arched* or *vaulted covering:*—Under heofenes hwealf *under the vault of heaven*, Beo. Th. 1156; B. 576: 4034; B. 2015. Behealde hē hū wīdgille ðæs heofenes hwealfa bīþ *late patentes ætheris cernat plagas*, Bt. 19; Fox 68, 22. Hū wīdgil sint heofones hwealfe, Bt. Met. Fox 10, 13; Met. 10, 7. Hwalf *clima*, Cot. 56, Lye. [*Icel.* hválf; *n. a vault; the concavity of a shield.*] v. heofon-hwealf.

hwealf; *adj. Arched, vaulted, concave* [*of a shield*]:—Hwealfum lindum, Judth. 11; Thw. 24, 29; Jud. 214. v. preceding word.

hwealfian *to arch, vault*, Som. [*Icel.* hwelfa *to arch, vault.*]

hwearf, es; *m. A crowd, troop, band of people:*—Hwearfum þringan *to press in crowds*, Judth. 12; Thw. 25, 8; Jud. 249: Exon. 36 a; Th. 118, 3; Gū. 234. [*O. Sax.* hwarf *a crowd*. Cf. hweorfan; *and* gang *a number of people* (*in its connection with the verb* gangan).]

hwearf, hwerf, es; *m. A turn, space, change, exchange, that which is exchanged:*—Be hwearfe. Nān man ne hwyrfe nānes yrfes būtan ðæs gerēfan gewitnesse . . . Gif hit hwā dō fō se landhlāford tō ðam hwearfe *Of exchange. Let no man exchange any property without the witness of the reeve . . . If any one do so let the lord take possession of the property exchanged*, L. Ath. i. 10; Th. i. 204, 16–21. In huarf *in spatio*, Lk. Skt. Lind. 24, 13. Huelc seles monn hwerf fore sāuel his *quam dabit homo commutationem pro anima sua*, Mt. Kmbl. 16, 26. Huoerf, Mk. Skt. Lind. 8, 37. Gif huerf gie sellas *si mutuum dederitis*, Lk. Skt. Lind. 6, 34. Huoerf, 35. Ðæt wharfe and ðæt foreward *pactionem et commutationem*, Cod. Dipl. Kmbl. iv. 241, 37. [Cf. *O. Frs.* hwarf, werf (*with numerals*) achte werf *octies: O. H. Ger.* sibun warb *septies*; hwarba *motus, vicis*, Grff. iv. 1235. Cf. *the use of* sīþ *in A. S. and the corresponding forms in other dialects, and the use of* gang *in Danish and Swedish, with numerals.*] v. ge-hwearf, hwearf-līce.

hwearf, es; *m. A wharf, bank, shore:*—Ðā gyrnde ðæt hē mōste macian foran gēn Mildryþe æker ǣnne hwerf wið ðon wōdan tō werianne *then he desired that he might make a bank opposite Mildred's field for protection against floods* [?], Chart. Th. 341, 7. v. mere-hwearf.

hwearf; *adj. Turning about, shifting, veering, changeable:*—Norþan wind heaþogrim and hwearf *a wind from the north deadly fierce and whirling in eddies*, Beo. Th. 1100; B. 548. Thorpe, Kemble, Heyne read *andhwearf* = came against [us]; Grein takes *and hwearf*, and compares *Icel.* hverfr *shifty*. The word may describe a strong wind often shifting its direction and whirling round with violent gusts. Cf. ge-hweorf; hwerf-līc.

hwearfan. v. hwerfan.

hwearfian; *p.* ode *To turn, change, roll about, revolve, wander, move, toss about:*—Ic nū giet hwearfige mē self on ðǣm ȳðum mīnra scylda *adhuc in delictorum fluctibus versor*, Past. 65, 7; Swt. 467, 22. Ælc gesceaft hwearfaþ on hire selfre swā swā hweól and tō ðam heó swā hwearfaþ ðæt heó eft cume ðǣr heó ǣr wæs *every creature turns on itself as a wheel, and it so turns to the end that it may come again where it was before:* repetunt proprios quæque recursus, redituque suo singula gaudent, Bt. 25; Fox 88, 32: Bt. Met. Fox 13, 150; Met. 13, 75. Hē biþ fremede freán ælmihtigum englum ungelīc āna hwearfaþ *he shall be a stranger to the almighty Lord, unlike angels, alone shall he wander*, Salm. Kmbl. 70; Sal. 35. Drihtnes stīge hwearfaþ aa wīsra gewyrdum *Ascension-day ever changes according to the rules of the learned*, Menol. Fox 131; Men. 65. Wē hwearfiaþ heánlīce *we wander abjectly*, Exon. 13 a; Th. 23, 21; Cri. 372. Hālige englas ðǣrābūtan hwearfiaþ *holy angels hover round about the place*, L. C. E. 4; Th. i. 360, 34. Ðū wāst hū ða woruldsǣlþa hwearfiaþ . . . hwī ne hwearfost ðū mid him *thou knowest how worldly blessings change . . . why dost thou not change with them?* Bt. 7, 2; Fox 18, 6. Swā swā on wǣnes eaxe hwearfiaþ ða hweól *as the wheels turn on the axle of a waggon*, 39, 7; Fox 220, 32. Gūþ hwearfode *the battle rolled on* [or could *gūþ* here be taken as a person, one of the Valkyrias, and *hwearfode* = hover about, as in the passage above, L. C. E. 4 ?], Cd. 149; Th. 187, 29; Exod. 159. Fana hwearfode on sceafte *the banner waved on its staff*, Bt. Met. Fox 1, 20; Met. 1, 10. Hwæt is ðē ðæt ðū ðǣrmid ne ne hwearfige *why shouldest thou not change with them?* Bt. 7, 3; Fox 22, 22. Nis ǣnegu gesceaft ðe ne hwearfige swā swā hweól dēþ, Met. Fox 13, 147; Met. 13, 74. Hwearfode, 20, 411; Met. 20, 206. Hwearfian, Bt. 33, 4; Fox 132, 11. Heán hwearfian *to wander abject*, Andr. Kmbl. 1781; An. 893. Fōran hwearfigende [hwearfiende, MS. Cott.] geond ðæt wēsten *they went wandering through the desert;* per vasta deserti evagatur, Ors. 6, 31; Swt. 286, 19. [*Goth.* hwarbôn *to go about: O. Sax.* hwarbōn: *Icel.* hvarfa *to wander about: O. H. Ger.* hwarbōn *versari.*]

hwearf-līce; *adv. In turn:*—Huoerflīce *vicissim*, Lk. Skt. p. 10, 6.

hwearflung. v. hwerflung.

hwearft, es; *m. A circuit, circle, revolution:*—Hwæt bīdaþ gē on hwearfte *why do ye stand round waiting?* Exon. 15 a; Th. 32, 12; Cri. 511. Under heofones hwearfte *under heaven's circuit*, 110 b; Th. 424, 3; Rä. 41, 33. Brādne hwearft *the broad expanse* [*of the sky*], 53 b; Th. 187, 29; Az. 38. Ymb wintra hwearft *after years have rolled on*, Th. 188, 5; Az. 41. v. ymb-hwearft, hwyrft.

hwearftlian; *p.* ode *To turn round, roll round, revolve, move about, rove:*—Ic hwearftlige *verso*, Ælfc. Gr. 37; Som. 39, 15. Ða eágan ðe nū þurh unālȳfedlīce gewilnunga hwearftliaþ *the eyes that now rove through unallowed desires*, Homl. Th. i. 530, 31. Se cwyrnstān ðe tyrnþ singallīce and nǣnne færeld ne þurhtīhþ getācnaþ woruldlufe ðe on gedwyldum hwyrftlaþ and nǣnne stæpe on Godes wege gefæstnaþ *the millstone that is continually turning and makes no progress, betokens worldly love, that goes round and round in errors and takes no firm step in the way of God*, 514, 21. Micel trūwa hwearftlode on Petres heortan *great trust was revolving in Peter's heart*, 392, 34.

hwearfung, e; *f. A turning, revolution, change, exchange, barter:*—Ðē wæs ðeós hwearfung betere forðam ðe ðissa woruldsǣlþa tō wel ne lyste *this change was more tolerable to thee, because thou didst not take too much pleasure in temporal blessings*, Bt. 7, 3; Fox 22, 23. On midre ðisse hwearfunga, Fox 22, 19. Ðæt tācnaþ ceápunge and hwearfunge *that betokens chaffer and barter*, Lchdm. iii. 156, 6. Ne miht ðū ðara woruldsǣlþa hwearfunga onwendan *nor canst thou avert the revolutions of worldly happiness*, Bt. 7, 2; Fox 18, 37. v. hwerfung.

hweg. v. hwæg.

hwega. v. hū-, hwæt-, hwilc-hwega.

hwelan, hwylan; *p.* hwæl *To roar, bellow:*—Streámwelm hwileþ *the surf roars*, Andr. Kmbl. 990; An. 495. [Cf. *Icel.* hvellr *a shrill sound;* hwellr *shrill.*] v. on-hwelan; hwelung.

hwelc. v. hwilc.

hwele *putrefaction*, Som. [*Prompt. Parv.* whele or whelke [whelle] *pustula.*] v. next word.

hwelian; *p.* ode, ede *To turn to matter;* in pus converti:—Ðanon se andiga hwelaþ *inde invidus contabescit*, Lchdm. iii. 365, col. 1. Gif ðæt līc heard sī ūtan lege on ðane lǣcedom ðe ðæt heard forðī hwelige and ðæt yfel ūt teó *if the body be hard on the outside apply such leechdom as the hard part may turn to matter thereby, and may draw out the mischief*, L. M. 2, 59; Lchdm. ii. 282, 23. [*Prompt. Parv.* whelyn̄, as soorys *pustulo.*] v. ge-hweled; hwele.

HWELP, es; *m. A* WHELP, *a young dog, the young of other animals;* catulus:—Hund *canis*, hwylp *catulus*, Wrt. Voc. 78, 53. Hwelp *catulus* [*leonis*], Ps. Th. 16, 11. Ða hwelpas etaþ of ðām crumum ðe of hyra hlāforda beódum feallaþ *catelli edunt de micis quæ cadunt de mensa dominorum suorum*, Mt. Kmbl. 15, 27: Mk. Skt. 7, 28. [*Laym.* whelp: *Orm.* (leness) whellp: *A. R.* hweolp: *Prompt. Parv.* whelp, lytyl hownde *catellus, catulus: O. Sax.* hwelp: *Icel.* hvelpr: *Dan.* hvalp: *O. H. Ger.* hwelf *the young of animals* (*lion, tiger, ape*).] DER. león-, wæl-hwelp.

hwelung, e; *f. Sound, noise:*—Hwelung *clangor tubæ*, Cot. 109, Lye. v. hwelan.

hwem, hwemm, es; *m. A corner, angle:*—Hwæt fremaþ ðære burhware ðeáh ðe ðæt port beó trumlīce on ǣlce healfe getimbrod gif ðǣr biþ ān hwem open forlǣten ðæt se onwinnenda here þurh ðam infær hæbbe *what does it avail the citizens, though the town be firmly built on every side, if a corner be left open, so that the assailing host may have entrance through it?* Homl. Th. ii. 432, 4. Hwæm *angulus*, Ps. Spl. T. 117, 21. Ða feówer hwemmas ealles middangeardes *the four corners of the whole world*, Homl. Th. i. 130, 21: ii. 252, 3. v. hwamm.

hwem-dragen; *adj. Sloping, not perpendicular:*—Wæs ðæt ilce hūs hwemdragen nalas æfter gewunan mennisces weorces ðæt ða wagas wǣron rihte ac git swīðor on scræfes onlīcnesse ðæt wæs æteówed *that same house had sloping walls, not at all after the custom of men's work so that the walls should be perpendicular, but it appeared much more like a cave*, Blickl. Homl. 207, 17. v. next word.

hwemman; *p.* de *To slope, incline:*—Hī hwemdon ðā mid ðām scypon wið ðæs norþlandes *they inclined then with the ships towards the north shore*, Chr. 1052; Erl. 184, 25.

hwēne, hwǣne [= hwoene]; *adv. A little, somewhat:*—Hwēne ǣr *a little before*, Bt. 23; Fox 78, 27. Hwēne ǣror, Homl. Th. i. 358, 24. Hwēne wīddre ðonne bydenfæt *somewhat wider than a bushel measure*, Blickl. Homl. 127, 6. Hwēne rūmedlīcor *paulo latius*, Past. 12; Swt. 75, 17. Nioþor hwēne *somewhat lower*, Beo. Th. 5392; B. 2699. Hwǣne heardor and strangor *paulo districtius*, Bd. 1, 27; S. 490, 12. Hwǣne ǣr, Shrn. 50, 13. Hwǣne gangende *progressus pusillum*, Mt. Kmbl. Rush. 26, 39. Hwoene læssan *paulo minus*, Ps. Stev. 8, 6. [*In Cumberland Dialect* wheen, whun *a few: Scot.* quheyne *few;* quhene *a small number;* wheen *a number.*] v. hwōn.

hweogul, hweowol, hweohl, hweól, es; *n. A wheel:*—Se firmamentum went on ðām twām steorrum swā swā hweogel [hweogul, MS. L; hweowul,

MSS. R. P.] tyrnþ on eaxe *the firmament turns on those two stars just as a wheel turns on an axle*, Lchdm. iii. 270, 22. Swá swá hweowol *ut rotam*, Ps. Spl. 82, 12. Wǽnes hweowol *a waggon-wheel*, Shrn. 32, 12. Swá swá yrnende hweowol, Hexam. 5; Norm. 8, 29. Ðære sunnan hweogul *solis rota*, Hymn. Surt. 22, 25. Hweól *rota*, Ælfc. Gl. 2; Som. 55, 48; Wrt. Voc. 16, 20. Ðæt hweól hwerfþ ymbútan, Bt. 39, 7; Fox 220, 29. Ðæt unstille hweól ðe Ixion wæs tó gebunden ðæt óþstód, 35, 6; Fox 168, 31. Ðæs hweohles [hweoles, MS. Cott.] felga, 39, 7; Fox 222, 19. On hweohle *in rota*, Ps. Spl. 76, 17. Hwēl in hwēlum *rota in rota*, Mt. Kmbl. p. 9, 20. [*A.R.* hweol: *Ayenb.* hueȝel: *Orm.* wheol, whel: *Icel.* hvel, hjól: *Dan. Swed.* hjul. Zacher in his 'Das Gothische Alphabet,' pp. 114–5, compares the two forms *hweol*, *hweogel* with the Greek κίρκος, κύκλος (= κύκυλος) respectively, and so does not write hweól. See also Grmm. D. M. p. 664, where *hweol* is taken as corresponding to a Gothic *hwil*.]

hweóled; *adj. Provided with wheels*:—Héhhwiólad wǽn *a waggon having high wheels*, Lye.

hweól-fág; *adj. Circular and ornamented* [*applied to a dress*]:—Hwiólfág *cyclas*, Cot. 49, Lye,

hweop *a whip*; flagellum, Som.

hweorf. v. hwearf.

hweorfa, an; *m. Something which turns, a joint, a whorl* [*of a spindle*]:—Hweorfa *vertuba*, Wrt. Voc. 65, 16. Hwerfa *vertigo*, Ælfc. Gl. 74; Som. 71, 49; Wrt. Voc. 44, 32 [*in both cases the words occur among names of parts of the body—the two following are found among words connected with spinning*]. Hweorfa *verticillum*, Wrt. Voc. 66, 16: *vertelum*, 281, 72. Nim ðone hweorfan ðe wíf mid spinnaþ bind on his sweoran *take the whorl that women spin with, bind it on his neck*, L. M. 3, 6; Lchdm. ii. 310, 21. [Halliwell quotes Kennett's description of a *whorle*, 'the piece of wood put upon the iron spindle to receive the thread.' Cf. *O. H. Ger.* hwerbo *vortex, vorago*.] v. þeóh-hweorfa.

hweorfan, hworfan, hwurfan *To turn, change, go, return, depart, go about, wander, roam, hover about*:—Nǽfre ic from hweorfe ac ic mid wunige áwa tó ealdre *I will never go from you, but I will dwell with you for ever*, Exon. 14 b; Th. 30, 8; Cri. 476. Ðú hweorfest of hēnþum in gehyld godes *thou shalt pass from humiliations into the favour of God*, Andr. Kmbl. 233; An. 117. Mín folc hider hweorfeþ *revertetur huc populus meus*, Ps. Th. 72, 8: Exon. 76 a; Th. 284, 27; Jul. 703. Siððan heó ofer brim hweorfeþ *after it* [*the sun*] *goes beyond the ocean*, 93 b; Th. 351, 17; Sch. 81: 110 a; Th. 422, 13; Rä. 41, 5. Gé tó mé on hyge hweorfaþ *ye turn to me in thought*, 98 a; Th. 366, 2; Reb. 6. On hinderling hweorfaþ míne feóndas *convertentur inimici mei retrorsum*, Ps. Th. 55, 8: 69, 3. On heora ágen dust æfter hweorfaþ *in pulverem suum revertentur*, 103, 27. Hí tówrecene wíde hweorfaþ *ipsi dispergentur*, 58, 15. Hweorfaþ æfter heorþe *they walk along the floor of the furnace*, Exon. 55 b; Th. 196, 18; Az. 176. Swá hweorfaþ gleómen *so gleemen roam about*, 87 a; Th. 326, 28; Víd. 135. Ðá seó scyld ðá tó his heortan hwearf *ad cor suum rediit*, Bd. 4, 25; S. 599, 35. Ierre hé hwearf ðonan tó his ágnum, Chr. 584; Erl. 18, 25. Hé ána hwearf mondreámum from *he went alone from human joys* [i. e. *died*], Beo. Th. 3433; B. 1714. Hwearf geond ðæt healreced Hæreðes dóhtor, 3965; B. 1981. Hé hwearf æfter wegum *he went along the roads*, Blickl. Homl. 199, 13: Beo. Th. 5657; B. 2832. Hwearf ðǽr Hróðgár sæt, 717; B. 356. Fæder ellor hwearf, 110; B. 55: Judth. 10; Thw. 23, 9; Jud. 112. Hwærf him ðá tó heofenum hálig drihten *the holy Lord returned to heaven*, Cd. 13; Th. 16, 7; Gen. 240. Hwearf eft tó his ágnum biscopdóme, Chr. 813; Erl. 60, 22. Hé hwearf be wealle *he went along the wall*, Beo. Th. 3150; B. 1573: 2380; B. 1188. Hengest hwearf him on láste *Hengest went after them*, Fins. Th. 35; Fin. 17. Gástas hwurfon sóhton engla éþel *spirits went and sought the angels' country*, Andr. Kmbl. 1280; An. 640. Hyssas hále hwurfon in ðam hátan ofne *the men walked unharmed in that hot furnace*, Cd. 188; Th. 233, 5; Dan. 271. Bláce hworfon sceaþan hwearfdon, 214; Th. 269, 11; Sat. 71. Ǽr hí on tú hweorfon *before they separated*, Andr. Kmbl. 2102; An. 1052. Hweorfon ða hǽðenan hæftas fram ðám hálgan cnihton *the heathen slaves went from the holy youths*, Cd. 187; Th. 232, 28; Dan. 267. Hweorfaþ eft tó mé *return to me*, Blickl. Homl. 235, 16. Him his gebed hweorfe tó fyrenun *oratio ejus fiat in peccatum*, Ps. 108, 6. Ðý læs hé for wlence of gemete hweorfe and forhycge heánspēdigran *lest from pride he depart from moderation and despise the more scantily endowed*, Exon. 78 b; Th. 294, 35; Crä. 25. Ǽr hé on weg hwurfe gamol of geardum, Beo. Th. 534; B. 264. Hogedon georne ðæt ǽ godes ealle gelǽste and ne áwácodon wereda drihtne ne ðan má gên [(?) þan mægen, Th: heánmægen, Grein: mægenhwyrfe, Btwk.] hwyrfe in hǽðendóm *they strove earnestly to perform all God's law, and not to be apostate from the Lord of hosts any more than to turn to heathendom*, Cd. 183; Th. 229. 22; Dan. 221. Hwonne se dæg cume ðæt hé sceolde ðæs ealles ídel hweorfan *when the day comes that he must depart having nothing of it at all*, Blickl. Homl. 97, 26. Ðæt ic meahte hweorfan ymbe ðínne ðone hálgan alter *circumdabo altare tuum*, Ps. Th. 25, 6: Cd. 32; Th. 42, 5; Gen. 669. Ðam þegne ongan his hige hweorfan *the man's mind began to change*, 33; Th. 44, 8; Gen. 706. Hweorfan fram helltrafum tó fægeran gefeán, Andr. Kmbl. 3378; An. 1693. Hé lǽteþ hworfan monnes módgeþonc *he lets the mind of man roam*, Beo. Th. 3461; B. 1728. Hweorfan, Exon. 77 b; Th. 290, 29; Wand. 72. Hámleás hweorfan *to wander homeless*, 110 a; Th. 420, 25; Rä. 40, 9. Ic seah searo hweorfan giellende faran, 108 b; Th. 414, 29; Rä. 33, 3: Cd. 219; Th. 281, 11; Sat. 270: 215; Th. 272, 16; Sat. 120. On wræc hweorfan, 43; Th. 57, 15; Gen. 928: 48; Th. 62, 15; Gen. 1014. Of gesyhþe ðínre hweorfan *to go from thy presence*, 50; Th. 63, 21; Gen. 1035. Ðæt hé in ðone grimman gryre gongan sceolde hweorfan gehýned, Exon. 41 a; Th. 136, 20; Gú. 544. Com on sefan hwurfan swefnes wóma, Cd. 177; Th. 222, 25; Dan. 110. Hie wǽron eft hám hweorfende *they were returning home*, Blickl. Homl. 67, 10. Ðá wæs Maria eft hweorfende tó hire húse, 139, 3. Hie ymb ðæt fuhton on hweorfendum sigum *Samniticum bellum ancipiti statu gestum*, Ors. 3, 5; Swt. 106, 3. In the following passage the verb is transitive:—Fulwiaþ folc hweorfaþ tó heofonum *baptize people and turn them to heaven*, Exon. 14 b; Th. 30, 25; Cri. 485. [*Goth.* hwairban *to walk*: *O. Sax.* hwerƀan *to go, wander*: *O. Frs.* hwerva: *Icel.* hverfa: *O. H. Ger.* hwerban *redire, reverti, remeare, ambulare*.] DER. á-, æt-, be-, ge-, geond-, on-, tó-, ymbe-hweorfan; v. hwerfan. [Cf. *Mod. E.* walk, went.]

hweorf-, hwyrf-, hwer-bán, es; *n. A joint* [*of the back*], *vertebra*, [*of the knee*], *the knee-cap*:—Hwyrfbán *vertibulum*, Ælfc. Gl. 11; Som. 57, 43; Wrt. Voc. 19, 46. Hwerbán *vertibulum* vel *vertebra*, 74; Som. 71, 50; Wrt. Voc. 44, 33. Hweorbán *vertibula*, Wrt. Voc. 283, 38. Hwiorfbán, Lchdm. ii. 396, col. 1. [Cf. *Prompt. Parv.* whyrle-bone, or hole of a joynt *anca, vertebrum, vertibulum*, and see note, p. 524: *Scot.* whorle-bane *hip-joint*: *Ger.* wirbel-bein *vertebra*.]

hweoða. v. hwiða.

hweoðerian, hwoðerian; *p.* ode *To roar, be tempestuous*:—Se brym hwoðerode under his fótswaðum *the sea roared under his footsteps*, Homl. Th. ii. 388, 19. v. hwiða.

hweoðerung, e; *f. Murmuring*; murmuratio, Lye.

hweowol. v. hweogul.

hwer, es; *m. A kettle, pot, basin, caldron, cooking-vessel*:—Hwer *lebes*; cyperen hwer *cucuma*, Ælfc. Gl. 26; Som. 60, 84, 83; Wrt. Voc. 25, 24, 23. Moab mínes hyhtes hwer *Moab olla spei meæ*, Ps. Th. 59, 7. Ðá hēt se cásere meltan on hwere leád and pic and hé hēt ðone cniht on ðæs hweres welm ásetton *the emperor ordered lead and pitch to be melted in a caldron, and ordered the young man to be put into the boiling of the caldron*, Shrn. 91, 7. Áwyl ða wyrte on hwere *boil the plants in a pot*, L. M. 1, 32; Lchdm. ii. 76, 18. Ǽnne sylfrene hwer· on v pundon *a silver basin of five pounds*, Chart. Th. 558, 35. Ðǽr wǽron inne geseted hweras and pannan and hé clypte ða hweras and cyste ða pannan ðæt hé wæs eall sweart and behrúmig *pots and pans had been put in there, and he embraced the pots and kissed the pans, so that he was all black and sooty*, Shrn. 69, 27, 30. [*Icel.* hverr *a caldron, boiler*; hverna *a pan, basin*.]

hwer-bán. v. hweorf-bán.

hwerf, hwerfa. v. hwearf, hweorfa.

hwerfan, hwierfan, hwirfan, hwyrfan; *p.* de; *pp.* ed. I. *to turn, revolve, move about, go, return, depart*:—Óþ ðæt ðú eft hwyrfest tó him *until thou shalt return to him*, Blickl. Homl. 233, 29. Mannes sáwl hweóle gelícost hwærfeþ ymbe hý selfe *man's soul, just like a wheel, revolves about itself*, Bt. Met. Fox 20, 422; Met. 20, 211. Hwærfþ, 434; Met. 20, 217. Hwerfeþ, 28, 30; Met. 28, 15. Hwyrfeþ, Exon. 103 b; Th. 394, 3; Rä. 13, 12. Hægl hwyrft of heofones lyfte *hail whirls down from the sky*, Runic pm. 9; Kmbl. 341, 5. Hí hám hwyrfaþ *domum redeunt*, L. Ecg. P. i. 14; Th. ii. 178, 6. Cynna gehwylcum ðara ðe cwice hwyrfaþ *for every race that living moves*, Beo. Th. 197; B. 98. Hig eft syððan tógædere hwyrfdon *postea iterum se conjunxerint*, L. Ecg. P. iv. 8; Th. ii. 206, 8. Hie eft hwirfdon tó hiora ealdormannum *they returned to their rulers*, Blickl. Homl. 239, 29. Hwearfdon geond ðæt atole scref *roamed through that horrid den*, Cd. 214; Th. 269, 13; Sat. 72. Gehwá hám hwyrfe *let every one return home*, L. E. I. 24; Th. ii. 422, 1. On gemynd hwyrfe unrihtwísnys fædera his *in memoriam redeat iniquitas patrum ejus*, Ps. Spl. 108, 13. Hwyrf eft on ða ceastre *go again to the city*, Blickl. Homl. 249, 8. Wæs eft hwyrfende *was returning*, 199, 6: 207, 30: 249, 12. Ðæt hwerfende hweól *the revolving wheel*, Bt. 7, 2; Fox 18, 35. II. *to turn, change* [*trans.* and *intrans.*]:—Hé hwierfde his stemne nales his mód *vocem, non mentem mutavit*, Past. 36, 7; Swt. 257, 18. Adame his hyge hwyrfde and his heorte ongann wendan tó hire willan *Adam's mind changed, and his heart began to turn to her desire*, Cd. 33; Th. 44, 28; Gen. 716. Ðeáh ðe his leóht gelómlíce hwyrfe *though its light change frequently*, Lchdm. iii. 242, 16. Hwærfe hia *convertantur*, Mt. Kmbl. Lind. 13, 15. Hiora heortan hé ongan hwyrfan *convertit cor eorum*, Ps. Th. 104, 21. Hwý ðú woldest ðæt seó wyrd swá hwyrfan sceolde *cur tantas lubricā versat fortuna vices?* Bt. 4; Fox 8, 12. III. *to exchange, barter* [*with gen.*]:—Aðelwold bisceop and Wulfstán Uccea hwyrfdon landa on Eádgáres cyninges gewytnesse *bishop Athelwold and Wulfstan Uccea exchanged lands with the witness of king Edgar*, Chart. Th. 230, 1. Nán man ne hwyrfe nānes yrfes būtan ðæs gerēfan gewitnesse *let no man exchange any property without the witness of the reeve*, L. Ath. i. 10; Th. i. 204, 17. Nān man ne bycge ne hwyrfe [hwirfe, MS. H.] būton hē gewitnesse hæbbe *let no man either buy or barter unless he have a witness*, L. Eth. 1, 3; Th. i. 282, 26. Huerfa *mutuari*, Mt. Kmbl. Lind. 5, 42. [*Laym.* whærven; *p.* whærfde: *Orm.* wherrfedd *perverse*: *O. Sax.* gi-hwerðian *to turn, change*: *Icel.* hverfa; *p.* hverfði *to turn*: *O. H. Ger.* hwarbian; *p.* hwarpta *versare, rotare, redire, convertere, revertere*, Grff. iv. 1233.] DER. ā-, be-, for-, ge-, on-, ymb-hwerfan; *and see* hweorfan, hwearfian.

hwerfel. v. sin-hwerfel. [*O. H. Ger.* sin-hwerbal *rotundus, teres.*]

hwerfere, es; *m. A changer, trader.* [*O. H. Ger.* werbare *negotiator.*] v. pening-hwerfere.

hwerf-lic; *adj. Changeable, shifting, not enduring*:—Hū hwerflīce ðās woruldsǽlþa sint *quam sit mortalium rerum misera beatitudo*, Bt. 11, 1; Fox 32, 37. [*O. H. Ger.* hwarb-, hwerb-līh *versatilis, volubilis*: cf. *Icel.* hwerfull *shifty, changeable.*] v. hwearf; *adj.*

hwerflung, e; *f. Wandering, error*:—Hwærflung *error*, Mt. Kmbl. Lind. 24, 24. [Cf *Icel.* hvarfla *to wander.*] v. hwurf.

hwerfung, e; *f. Change, mutation, vicissitude*:—Hwæt singaþ ða leóþwyrhtan ōðres be ðisse woruld būton mislīca hwerfunga ðisse worulde *quid tragœdiarum clamor aliud deflet, nisi indiscreto ictu fortunam felicia regna vertentem?* Bt. 7, 3; Fox 22, 21. v. hwearfung.

hwergen; *adj. Somewhere*:—Elles hwergen *elsewhere, somewhere else*, Beo. Th. 5173; B. 2590. [*O. Sax. O. H. Ger.* hwergin *usquam, alicubi*: cf. *Icel.* hwargi *wheresoever.*]

hwer-hwette, an; *f. A cucumber*:—Hwerhwette *cucumer*, Ælfc. Gl. 40; Som. 63, 99; Wrt. Voc. 30, 47. Hwerwette, L. M. 1, 23; Lchdm. ii. 66, 9. Hwerhwettan gesihþ on swefnum untrumnysse getācnaþ *if a man sees in dreams a cucumber it betokens illness*, Lchdm. iii. 200, 16.

hwerwe *a plant name*, perhaps *colchicum autumnale*:—Ða greátan wyrt hwerwe hātte, L. M. 2, 52; Lchdm. ii. 268, 22. [Cf. Ðeós wyrt ðe man hieribulbum and ōðrum naman greáte wyrt nemneþ, Herb. 22, 1; Lchdm. i. 118, 13. v. Lchdm. ii. 396, col. 1.]

hwēsan; *p.* hweós *To wheeze, make a noise in breathing, to breathe hard*:—Gif hē mid earfoþnysse hwēst *if he breathes with difficulty*, Lchdm. iii. 122, 3. Hē hwēst swȳðe hefelīce, 126, 9. Hē egeslīce hweós *he wheezed terribly*, Homl. Th. i. 86, 1. [*Icel.* hvæsa *to hiss.*]

hwet-stān, es; *m. A whetstone*:—Hwetstān *cos*, Ælfc. Gl. 58; Som. 67, 100; Wrt. Voc. 38, 25: Ors. 4, 13; Bos. 100, 30. Nim ðonne hwetstān brādne *then take a broad whetstone*, Lchdm. iii. 16, 21. [*O. H. Ger.* wezi-stein, *cos*: *Ger.* wetz-stein.]

hwettan; *p.* te *To* WHET, *sharpen, instigate, urge, incite, excite*:—Ic hwette *acuo*, Ælfc. Gr. 28; Som. 30, 48: Exon. 103 b; Th. 393, 1; Rä. 12, 3. Se lǽce his seax hwæt *the physician sharpens his knife*, Past. 26, 3; Swt. 187, 5. Ūsic lust hwæteþ *desire urges us*, Andr. Kmbl. 571; An. 286. Ðurh ðæt his mōd hweteþ *by that means excites his mind*, Salm. Kmbl. 988; Sal. 495: Exon. 82 a; Th. 309, 26; Seef. 63: 83 b; Th. 314, 23; Mōd. 18. Hwettaþ hyra blōdigan tēþ *they whet their bloody teeth*, L. E. I. prm; Th. ii. 396, 6. Ic hig hwette tō fleánne *I instigated her to fly*, Shrn. 41, 25. Swā ðīn sefa hwette, Beo. Th. 985; B. 490. Hwetton higerōfne, 413; B. 204. Hȳ hwetton *exacuerunt*, Blickl. Gloss. [*Laym.* whætte; *p*: *Icel.* hvetja *to whet, incite*: *O. H. Ger.* wezzen *acuere, exacuere, provocare*: *Ger.* wetzen.] DER. ā-, ge-hwettan.

hwī. v. hwȳ.

Hwiccas, Hwicceas, *and* Hwiccan [?] *or* [?] Hwicce [cf. Seaxe]; *pl. The people of a small state which extended over Gloucestershire, Worcestershire, and part of Warwickshire*:—Ðæt is geseted in Huicca mægþe in ðære stōwe ðe mon hāteþ Weogernaceaster *it is situated in the province of the Hwiccas, in the place that is called Worcester*, Chart. Th. 28, 31. Fērde ðā in Hwicca mægþe ðǽr wæs ðā Ōsrīc cyning *divertit ad provinciam Huicciorum cui tunc rex Osric præfuit*, Bd. 4, 23; S. 594, 22. Wilfrid is Hwicna biscop *provinciæ Huicciorum Vilfrid episcopus*, 5, 23; S. 646, 22. Ðȳ ilcan dæge rād Æþelmund aldorman of Hwiccium [Hwiccum MS. E.] ofer æt Cynemǽres forda. Ðā mētte hine Weoxtan aldorman mid Wilsǽtum, Chr. 800; Erl. 60, 5. Seó cwēn ðære nama wæs Æbbe on hire mægþe ðæt is on Hwyccum wæs gefullad *regina nomine Eabæ in sua, id est, Huicciorum provincia fuerat baptizata*, Bd. 4, 13; S. 582, 16.

hwider; *adv. Whither* [*in direct interrogation, or in dependent clauses*]:—Hwider wylt ðū *quo vadis?* Gen. 16, 8: Deut. 1, 28. Hwyder gǽst ðū *quo vadis?* Jn. Skt. 13, 36. Ðū nāst hwanon hē cymþ ne hwyder hē gǽþ *non scis unde veniat et quo vadat*, 3, 8: 12, 35. [*O. and N.* hwider, wider: *Ayenb.* huider: *Laym.* whuder, woder: *Gen. and Ex.* quider: *Wick.* whidir.] v. hwæder.

hwig. v. hwȳ.

HWĪL, e; *f. A* WHILE, *space of time*:—Wæs seó hwīl micel *it was a great while*, Beo. Th. 295; B. 146. Ðā wæs hwīl dæges ǽr hē ðone grundwong ongytan mihte *it was a day's space ere he might feel the bottom*, 2995; B. 1495. Ǽr dæges hwīle *before day-time*, 4630; B. 2320. On dæges hwīle *in the day-time*, Cd. 191; Th. 238, 4; Dan. 349. Crist on ðære hwīle tō helle gewende *Christ during that time* [*while in the tomb*] *went to hell*, Homl. Th. i. 26, 35. In hwīle tīde *in momento temporis*, Lk. Skt. Lind. 4, 5. Tō hwīle lǽn *momentum*, Ælfc. Gl. 15; Som. 58, 47; Wrt. Voc. 21, 36. Bētan tō hwīle *to make better for a time*, L. M. 3, 62; Lchdm. ii. 348, 21. Tō langre hwīle *for a long while*, Cd. 24; Th. 31, 22; Gen. 489. Tō litelre hwīle, Homl. Th. i. 64, 14. Tō suīðe scortre hwīle, Past. 36, 6; Swt. 255, 11. Ða hwīle his līfes *vivendi spatia*, 2; Swt. 249, 25. Ða hwīle ðisses andweardan līfes *the time of this present life*, Bt. 18, 3; Fox 66, 4. Ða hwīle ðe his līf [tīma, l. 20] wæs, Chr. 1016; Erl. 155, 18. Sume hwīle *some time*, 1055; Erl. 190, 12. Gōde hwīle ðone here gefliémde *put the Danes to flight for a good while*, 837; Erl. 66, 8. Nū is ðīnes mægnes blǽd āne hwīle *for a while*, Beo. Th. 3528; B. 1762. Ǽnige hwīle, 5090; B. 2548. Ealle hwīle *all the while*, Byrht. Th. 140, 47; By. 304. Nū hwīle *just now*, Blickl. Homl. 109, 6. Grendel wan hwīle wið Hrōðgār *Grendel strove for a time with Hrothgar*, Beo. Th. 306; B. 152: 211; B. 105. Ða ðe on carcerne hwīle wunedon, Andr. Kmbl. 262; An. 131. Man gīslade ða hwīle *hostages were given the while*, Chron. 994; Erl. 133, 29. Ða hwīle ðe ðū eart on wege mid him *dum es in via cum eo*, Mt. Kmbl. 5, 25. Ðā besæt sió fierd hie ðǽr ūtan ða hwīle ðe hie ðǽr lengest mete hæfdon *the English force besieged the Danes there as long as ever they had provisions there*, Chr. 894; Erl. 90, 29. Hwīle mid weorce hwīle mid worde hwīle mid geþohte *at one time with deed, at another with word, at another with thought*, Hy. 3, 44–5; Hy. Grn. ii. 282, 44–5. Ðæs ungeendodan līfes hwīla *æternitatis infinita spatia*, Bt. 18, 3; Fox 66, 5. [*O. and N.* hwile: *A. R.* hwule: *Orm.* while: *Laym.* while, wile: *Goth.* hweila: *O. Sax.* hwīla: *O. Frs.* hwīle: *O. H. Ger.* hwīla *hora, momentum*: *Ger.* weile: cf. *Icel.* hvíla *a bed*; hvíla *rest.*] DER. bearhtm-, dæg-, earfoþ-, gesceap-, gryre-, hand-, langung-, orleg-, rōt-, sige-, þræc-, wræc-hwīl. v. hwīlum.

hwilc, hwylc, hwelc; *pron.* I. *which, who, of what kind,* [*in direct questions*]:—*Quis* hwā is werlīc hād, *que*, hwilc is wīflīc, *quod*, hwilc nis nāðres cynnes; *cujus* hwilces; *cui* hwilcum; *quem virum laudas* hwilcne wer herast ðū; *a quo* fram hwilcum. *Pluraliter qui* hwilce; *quorum* hwilcera; *quibus* hwilcum; *quos laudas* hwilce herast ðū; *a quibus* fram hwilcum . . . *Qualis* hwilc getācnaþ þreó þingc *interrogationem* and *infinitionem* and *relationem*. Gif ic cweðe *qualis est rex* hwilc is se cingc, ðon biþ hē *interrogativum* . . . Ðū cwyþst *qualis est ille* hwilc is hē, ic cweðe *talis est* swilc hē is, Ælfc. Gr. 18; Som. 21, 12–18, 57–63. Hwylc man is of eów *quis est ex vobis homo?* Mt. Kmbl. 7, 12. Hwylc þearf is ðē hūsles *quid opus est Eucharistia?* Bd. 4, 24; S. 598, 37. Hwā is ūre Fæder? Se Ælmihtiga God. And hwilcera manna Fæder is he? Swutelīce hit is gesǽd, yfelra manna. And hwilc is se Fæder? *who is our Father? The Almighty God. And of what sort of men is he Father? It is plainly said, of evil men. And of what kind is the Father?* Homl. Th. i. 254, 5–8. Hwylc is mihtig God būtan ūre se mǽra God *quis Deus magnus sicut Deus noster*, Ps. Th. 76, 11. Hwylc is wīsra ðe ðās mid gehygde healdan cunne *quis sapiens et custodiet hæc?* 106, 42. Hwylces ðæra sufona byþ ðæt wīf *cujus erit de septem uxor?* Mt. Kmbl. 22, 28. Hwylcum bigspelle wiðmete wē hit *cui parabolæ cumparabimus illud?* Mk. 4, 30. II. [*in dependent clauses*]:—Gif ic cweðe *nescio qualis est rex* nāt ic hwilc se cyngc is, ðon is se *qualis infinitivum*. Gif ic cweðe *tu scis bene qualis est* ðū wāst wel hwilc hē is, ðon biþ hit *relativum*, Ælfc. Gr. 18; Som. 21, 59–61. Geseó hē hwylc se man sig oððe ðæt neát *videat qualis homo sit vel pecus*, L. Ecg. C. 14; Th. ii. 142, 19. Gē habbaþ gehȳred hwilc ðes god is ðe gē wēndon ðæt eów gehǽlde, Homl. Th. i. 464, 10. Hwelc se bión sceal ðe tō reccenddōme cuman sceal *qualis quisque ad regimen venire debeat*, Past. 10; Swt. 61, 5. Bæd ðæt hē him geswutelode hwylc basilius wǽre on wurðscype mid him *prayed that he would reveal to him what manner of man Basil was in honour as compared with himself*, Homl. Swt. 3, 498. Sege ūs hwilc tācn sī ðīnes tōcymys *dic nobis quod signum adventus tui*, Mt. Kmbl. 24, 3. Hēt sēcan hwilc ðære geógoþe gleáwost wǽre *bade seek which of the youth was most skilled*, Cd. 176; Th. 220, 34; Dan. 81: Andr. Kmbl. 821; An. 411. Cwēn frignan ongan on hwylcum ðara beáma bearn wealdendes hangen wǽre, Elen. Kmbl. 1698; El. 851. Dō mē wegas wīse ðæt ic wite on hwylcne ic gange *notam mihi fac viam, in qua ambulem*, Ps. Th. 142, 9. Geþence gē hwæt gē sīen and hwelce gē sīen *pensa quod es*, Past. 21, 4; Swt. 159, 14. Ðā onfunde se mōdiga, hwilce his mihta wēron *then the proud spirit found out what his powers were*, Ælfc. T. Grn. 2, 47. III. *indef. pron. any one, any, of any kind, some*:—Oððe gif hwylc cyningc wyle faran *aut quis rex iturus*, Lk. Skt. 14, 31. Hwæt wēnstū nū, gif hwelc forworht monn cymþ and bitt ūrne hwelcne ðæt wē hine lǽden tō sumum rīcum menn and him geþingien *si enim fortasse quis veniat, ut pro se ad intercedendum nos apud potentem quempiam virum ducat*, Past. 10, 2; Swt. 63, 1. Ne hig ne gelȳfaþ ðeáh hwylc of deáþe ārise *neque si quis ex mortuis surrexerit credent*, Lk. Skt. 16, 31. Swelc ic wǽre hwelc folclīc mon and mē wǽre mete and wīnes þearf *ut vini et carnis quidam emptor*, Nar. 18, 4. Wēn is ðæt hwilc wundor ineode on ðæt carcern, St. And. 14, 28. Manslyht oððe elles hwilc ðara heáfodlīcra leahtra *manslaughter or any other of the capital crimes*, L. E. I. 26; Th. ii. 422, 5. Sōna swā sacerda hwylc hwone on wōh gesyhþ *as soon as any priest sees any one in error*, 28; Th. ii.

424, 25. Gif mīnra þegna hwilc, Cd. 22; Th. 27, 7; Gen. 414. Ānra hwilc *each one*, Bt. Met. Fox 20, 129; Met. 20, 65. Gif him þince ðæt hē on hwylcere fægerre stōwe sī *if it seems to him that he is in some fair place*, Lchdm. iii. 174, 26. Æt mǣstra hwelcre misdǣde *for almost every misdeed*, L. Alf. 49; Th. i. 58, 6. Gyf hwylce ðǣr beóþ ðara ðe hwæt ǣbylhþa wið ōðre habbaþ *if there are any there who have any grudges against others*, L. E. I. 36; Th. ii. 434, 7. Wē gesāwon oft in cyrcean ǣgðer ge corn ge hig ge hwylce woroldlīcu þing beón gehealdene *we have often seen in churches corn and hay, and any kind of secular things kept*, 8; Th. ii. 406, 31. Gif hwā biþ mid hwelcum welum geweorþod and mid hwelcum deórwyrþum ǣhtum gegyrewod, Bt. 14, 3; Fox 46, 11. IV. *combined with* swā:—*Quisquis* swā hwā, *quæque* swā hwilc, *quodquod* swā hwilc; *quicunque* swā hwā, *quæcunque* swā hwilc, Ælfc. Gr. 18; Som. 21, 35, 37. Ðæs cyninges þegnas ðider urnon swā hwelc swā ðonne gearo wearþ *the king's thanes ran thither, whichever of them was ready*, Chr. 755; Erl. 50, 3. Swā hwylc swā sylþ ānne drinc *quicumque potum dederit*, Mt. Kmbl. 10, 42. Swā hwylcum manna swā him gemet þuhte, Beo. Th. 6106; B. 3057: 1890; B. 943. Swā hwylce daga *in quacumque die*, Ps. Th. 137, 4. Ðæt git ne lǣstan wel hwilc ǣrende swā hē sendeþ *that ye will not perform what business soever he sends*, Cd. 26; Th. 35, 15; Gen. 555. V. *correlative of* swilc [v. I]:—Hit is scondlīc ymb swelc tō sprecanne hwelc hit ðā wæs *it is shameful to talk about such a state of things as it then was*, Ors. 1, 10; Swt. 48, 4. [*O. E. Homl.* hwilche: *A. R.* hwuch: *Laym.* whilc, whulc: *Orm.* whillc: *R. Glouc.* wuch: *Piers P. Chauc.* which: *Goth.* hwēleiks, hwileiks: *O. Sax.* hwilīk: *O. Frs.* hwelīk, hwelk, hulk, hwek: *Icel.* hvílíkr: *O. H. Ger.* hwelīh: *Ger.* welcher.] DER. ǣg-, ge-, wel-hwilc.]

hwilc-hwega, -hwugu, -hugu [*in the Northern Gospels the whole form is declined, elsewhere only* hwilc]; *pron. Some, any, some one*:—Gehrān mec huoelchuoege *tetigit me aliquis*, Lk. Skt. Lind. 8, 46. Hwilc-æthwega yfel wǣte *some evil humour*, L. M. 2, 59; Lchdm. ii. 284, 27. Brōðer huoelchuoeges *frater alicujus*, Lk. Skt. Lind. 20, 28. Swā hē sīe mid hwilcre-hwega byrþenne gehefegod *as if he is weighted with some burden*, L. M. 2, 23; Lchdm. ii. 212, 11. Gif man forleóse gehālgodne mete hwylcne-hwugu dǣl *si quis perdiderit cibi consecrati aliquantulum*, L. Ecg. P. iv. 52, note; Th. ii. 218, 23. Hwelcne-hugu dǣl, Ors. 3, 7; Swt. 110, 13. Hwelce-hwugu gerisenlīce leáfe dyde *he gave some suitable leave*, Past. 51, 4; Swt. 397, 25. Heó geþingode tō gode sumre hǣðenre fǣmnan gǣste hwylce-hwegu ræste in ðære ēcan worulde, Shrn. 133, 16. Ðe hwilce-hwega gefēlnesse hæbbe, L. M. 1, 35; Lchdm. ii. 82, 30. Hafaþ ðæt mōd hwylce-hugu scyldo *habet animus aliquem reatum*, Bd. 1, 27; S. 496, 42. Hwylce-hugu tīd *aliquanto tempore*, 4, 22; S. 591, 31. Huælchuoego *quid*, Mk. Skt. Lind. 13, 15. Huoelchuoegu *aliquid*, Rtl. 146, 23. [Cf. hwæt-, hū-hwega; and next word.]

hwilc-hwēne, -hwōne; *pron. indef. Some, some one*:—Bēcon hwelchuoene *signum aliquid*, Lk. Skt. Lind. 23, 8. Wið huelchuōne *adversus aliquem*, Mk. Skt. Lind. 11, 25.

hwilc-ness, e; *f. Quality*:—Sume synd *qualitatis* ðe getācniaþ hwilcnysse, Ælfc. Gr. 38; Som. 40, 31. [Cf. *O. H. Ger.* hweolīhi, hweolīhnissi *qualitas*.] v. ge-hwilcness.

hwīlen; *adj. Lasting only for a time, transitory, brief*:—Uton sibbe tō him on ðās hwīlnan tīd hǣlu sēcan *let us seek in this brief season* [*the present life*] *peace and salvation from him*, Exon. 97 b; Th. 365. 10; Wal. 87. [*O. H. Ger.* hwīlin *temporalis*.] v. un-hwīlen.

hwīlend-līc; *adj. Lasting only for a time, of time, temporal, temporary, transitory*:—Þrió þing sindon on ðīs middanearde. Ān is hwīlendlīc ... Ōðer þing is ēce ... Þridde þing is ēce *three things there are in this world. One is of time ... the second ... and the third are of eternity*, Bt. 42; Fox 256, 15. Ðā se cyning wæs ceasterwara gefremed ðæs ēcan rīces and wolde eft ðæt ēþel sēcan his hwīlendlīcan rīces *rex æterni regni jam civis effectus, temporalis sui regni sedem repetiit*, Bd. 3, 22; S. 552, 33. Mid ðȳs hwīlendlīcan onwalde *temporali potentia*, Past. 17, 4; Swt. 113, 11. Mid ðissum hwīlendlīcum þingum *temporali sollicitudine*, 18, 7; Swt. 139, 7. Ðū næfst ða hwīlendlīcan ārwyrþnessa ðe ðū ǣr hæfdest *thou hast not those temporary dignities that thou hadst before*, Bt. 8; Fox 24, 31. v. hwīlwendlīc.

hwīl-fæc *a space of time*, Lye.

hwīlon. v. hwīlum.

hwīl-stycce, es; *n. A fragment* or *short portion of time*:—Ǣghwæ ðæs ðe hie on ǣnegum hiora hwīlsticcum gearnian mǣgen *all that they can earn in any of their fragments of time*, L. Alf. pol. 43; Th. i. 92, 12.

hwīl-tīdum; *dat. pl. as adv. At times, sometimes*:—Hwīltīdum oððe nū ðā *modo*, Ælfc. Gr. 38; Som. 41, 37: *aliquando*, Past. 57, 1; Swt. 437, 3: Lchm. iii. 240, 23: 242, 18. Eác hē sceal hwīltīdum geara beón on manegum weorcum tō hlāfordes willan *also at certain times he must be prepared for many kinds of work at the lord's pleasure*, L. R. S. 5; Th. i. 436, 3. Ðeós woruld ðeáh ðe heó myrige hwīltīdum geþuht sȳ *this world though sometimes it appear joyous*, Homl. Th. i. 154, 17. Seó sǣ is hwīltīdum smylte and myrige on tō rōwene, hwīlon eác swīðe hreóh and egeful on tō beónne, 182, 32. [Cf. *O. H. Ger.* stunt-hwīla *momentum*, Grff. iv. 1226]

hwīlum, hwīlon; *dat. pl. as adv. At times, for a time, sometimes, whilome*:—Hwīlon ic dyde swā *aliquando feci sic* ... *Dudum* gefyrn, *quandam* hwīlon, and *olim* getācniaþ þreó tīda, forþgewitene and andwerde and tōwerde, Ælfc. Gr. 38; Som. 39, 62-4. Ic wiste ðæt ðū hwīlon lufodest God *scivi te aliquando amasse Deum*, 24; Som. 25, 9. Ða ðe on horsum hwīlon wǣron *qui ascenderunt equos*, Ps. Th. 75, 5. Hwīlum tō gebede feóllon *sometimes they fell to praying*, Cd. 37; Th. 48, 18; Gen. 777: 38; Th. 50, 17; Gen. 810. Hī hwīlum gelȳfaþ *qui ad tempus credunt*, Lk. Skt. 8, 13. Hwīlon ǣr wē wǣron hēr and bohton ūs hwǣte *jam ante descendimus, ut emeremus escas*, Gen. 43, 20. Ic secge ðæt ic hwīlon ǣr forsūwode *I say what I sometime before passed over in silence*, Boutr. Scrd. 18, 27. Hwīlan ǣr, Bt. Met. Fox 29, 106; Met. 29, 53. Hwīlum on āne healfe hwīlum on ǣlce healfe *now on one side, now on every side*, Chr. 891; Erl. 88, 20. Ða hālgan lāreówas hwīlon sprecaþ be ðam Ælmihtigan Fæder and his Sunu, hwīlon swutollīce embe ðære Hālgan Ðrynnesse, Homl. Th. ii. 56, 26: Cd. 216; Th. 273, 7-12; Sat. 132-5. [*O. Sax.* hwīlun: *O. H. Ger.* hwīlon *paulatim, nunc*; hwīlom ... hwīlom *modo* ... *modo*: *M. H. Ger.* wīlont, Grff. iv. 1225: *Ger.* weiland *formerly*.]

hwīl-wende; *adj. Temporary, lasting for a time, not eternal*:—Him fremede tō ēcere hǣlþe seó hwīlwende ehtnys *the persecution that lasted but for a time, helped him to the salvation which lasts for ever*, Homl. Th. ii. 528, 7. Hē hī mǣrsaþ on ðære ēcan worulde for heora hwīlwendum geswince ðises sceortan līfes, 562, 5. Ðæt hī gelȳfon tō geágenne ða ēcan welan, ða ðe for his naman ða hwīlwendan spēda forhogiaþ, i. 64, 20. [Cf. *Goth.* hweila-hwairbs *lasting only for a time*.]

hwīlwend-līc; *adj. Temporary, lasting only for a time, not eternal*:—Hit is hwīlwendlīc *est temporalis*, Mt. Kmbl. 13, 21. Þreó þing synd on middanearde ān is hwīlwendlīc ... ōðer þing is ēce ... þridde þing is ēce, Homl. Swt. 1, 25. Manna freóndscipe biþ swīðe hwīlwendlīc *the friendship of men lasts but a very short time*, Blickl. Homl. 195, 26. Se ælmihtiga se ðe is ēce leóht ǣrest ðæt hwīlwendlīc leóht geworhte, Boutr. Scrd. 19, 5. Hwīlwendlīc līf ... ēce līf *the life of time ... the life of eternity*, Homl. Th. ii. 240, 15-20. Nalæs ðæt ān ðæt hē hī fram yrmþum ēcre niðerunge ac swylce eác fram ðam mānfullan wæle hwīlwendlīcre forwyrde generede *non solum eam ab ærumna perpetuæ damnationis, verum et a clade infanda temporalis interitus eripuit*, Bd. 4, 13; S. 582, 27. Hē swanc for heofonan rīce swīðor ðonne hē hogode hū hē geheólde on worulde ða hwīlwendlīcan geþincþu, Swt. A. S. Rdr. 98, 93. Ðæt wē ða heofonlīcan þinga mid ðām eorþlīcum and ða ēcelīc mid ðām hwīlwendlīcum geearniaþ, L. Ath. i. prm; Th. i. 196, 27. [*Orm.* hwilwendlic: cf. *O. H. Ger.* wīlwendige *fortuna*, Grff. i. 763.] v. hwīlend-līc.

hwīlwend-līce; *adv. Temporarily, for a time only*:—Beóþ blōwende and welige hwīlwendlīce ðæt gē ēcelīce wædlion *be flourishing and wealthy for time that ye may be beggars for eternity*, Homl. Th. i. 64, 15: 162, 15: ii. 384, 26.

hwīnan; *p.* hwān; *pl.* hwinon *To make a whistling, whizzing sound* [*as an arrow, etc. in its flight*]:—Ful oft of ðam heápe hwīnende fleág giellende gār *full oft from that band flew whistling the shrieking javelin*, Exon. 86 b; Th. 326, 12; Vīd. 127. [*Prompt. Parv.* whynyn̄, as howndys or oþer beestys *ululo, gannio*: *Chauc.* for as an hors I coude bite and whine: *Icel.* hvína; *p.* hvein *to give a whizzing sound* [*as an arrow*], e. g. örvarnar flugu hvínandi yfir höfuð þeim: *Dan.* hvine *to whistle* (*of the wind*); hvin *a piercing shriek*.]

hwióð. v. hweóð.

hwioð. v. hwið.

hwirfan. v. hwerfan.

hwirfel, es; *m. A whirl-pool* [?]:—On ðone hwyrfel, Cod. Dipl. Kmbl. iii. 412, 8. [Cf. *Icel.* hvirfill *a ring*; *the crown of the head*; *a top, summit*: *Dan.* hvirvel *a whirl-pool*; *the top of the head*: *O. H. Ger.* hwirvil *turbo*: *Ger.* wirbel.]

hwirf-pōl, es; *m. A whirl-pool*:—Hwyrfepōle *vorago, syrtis*, Cot. 59, Lye.

hwisprian; *p.* ode, ede *To mutter, murmur*, WHISPER:—Alle hwispredon *omnes murmurabant*, Lk. Skt. Rush. 19, 7. Hwispradun, Jn. Skt. Rush. 6, 41: *murmurarent*, 61. Nallaþ gē hwispriga *nolite murmurari*, 43. [*Prompt. Parv.* whysperyn̄ *mussito*: *O. Du.* wisperen: *O. H. Ger.* hwispalōn *sibilare*: *Ger.* wispern.] v. following words.

hwisprung, e; *f. A muttering, murmuring*, WHISPERING:—Hwisprung *murmur*, Jn. Skt. Rush. 7, 12.

hwistle, an; *f. A pipe, flute*, WHISTLE;—Hwistle oððe pīpe *musa*; hwistle *fistula*, Wrt. Voc. 73, 60, 65. Mid hwistlum *tibiis*, Lk. Skt. Lind. 7, 32. [*Chauc.* so was hire joly whistle wel ywette.]

hwistlere, es; *m. A piper, player on a flute*:—Pīpere oððe hwistlere *tibicen*, Ælfc. Gr. 9; Som. 9, 25. Ðā hē geseah hwistleras *cum vidisset tibicines*, Mt. Kmbl. 9, 23.

hwistlian; *p.* ode *To make a hissing sound, to hiss, whistle*:—Hē hwystlode stranglīc[e] stemne *he* [*the devil*] *made a great hissing*, Nar. 43, 17. [*Wick.* whistlen *hiss* (A. V.): *Piers P.* whistlen (*to birds*).]

hwistlung, e; *f. A hissing*, WHISTLING, *piping, music*:—Ðeós hwistlung *hic sibilus*, ðás hwystlunga *hæc sibila*, Ælfc. Gr. 13; Som. 16, 28. Hwistlung *sibilatio*, Ælfc. Gl. 79; Som. 72, 67; Wrt. Voc. 46, 24. Huislung *simphonia*, Lk. Skt. Lind. 15, 25. Ic beswíce fugelas mid hwistlunge *decipio aves sibilo*, Coll. Monast. Th. 25, 15. Suā suā mid líðre wisðlunga mon hors gestilleþ suā eác mid ðære illcan wistlunga mon mæg hund āstyrigean *lenis sibilus equos mitigat, catulos instigat*, Past. 23; Swt. 173, 21.

HWÎT; *adj.* WHITE, *bright, clear, fair, splendid*:—Hwít *albus*; *amineus* vel *albus*, Ælfc. Gl. 79; Som. 72, 71-2; Wrt. Voc. 46, 28-9. His reáf hwít scínende *vestitus ejus albus refulgens*, Lk. Skt. 9, 29. Wlitescȳne hwít and hiwbeorht hæleþa nāthwylc *some man beauteous, shining and bright of hue*, Elen. Kmbl. 145; El. 73. Hwít heard stān *creta* vel *cimolia*, Ælfc. Gl. 56; Som. 67, 40; Wrt. Voc. 37, 29. Se hwíta stān mæg wið stice *the white stone is effective against stitch*, L. M. 2, 64; Lchdm. ii. 290, 9. Se hwíta helm *the shining helm*, Beo. Th. 2900; B. 1448. Ðū ne miht ǣnne locc gedōn hwítne oððe blacne *non potes unum capillum album facere aut nigrum*, Mt. Kmbl. 5, 36. Hæfde hē hine swā hwítne geworhtne gelíc wæs hē ðām leóhtum steorrum *so splendid had he formed him he was like the bright stars*, Cd. 14; Th. 17, 4; Gen. 254. Leóht hwít *clear light*, 29; Th. 38, 33; Gen. 616. Ðone hwítan hlāf *panem nitidum*, Bd. 2, 5; S. 507, 14. Fæst ǣlce dæge and forgang hwít *jejuna quotidie et abstine te ab albo*, L. Ecg. C. prm; Th. ii. 132, 5. Gedō æges hwít tō *add white of egg*, L. M. 3, 59; Lchdm. ii. 342, 18. Dō æges ðæt hwíte tō, 1, 13; Lchdm. ii. 56, 6: 25; Lchdm. ii. 66, 21: Homl. Th. i. 40, 27. His reáf wǣron swā hwíte swā snāw *vestimenta ejus facta sunt alba sicut nix*, Mt. Kmbl. 17, 2. Ða scíran dagas hwítan *the clear bright days*, L. M. 2, 41; Lchdm. ii. 252, 10. Hwíte metas *lacticinia* [cf. *Icel.* hvítr matr *milk, curds, etc. opposed to flesh*], Lye. Wǣron on ðyssum felda unrīme gesomnunge hwíttra manna and fægera *erant in hoc campo innumera hominum albatorum conventicula*, Bd. 5, 12; S. 629, 25. Engla and deófla, beorhtra and blacra, hwítra and sweartra, Exon. 21 a; Th. 56, 9; Cri. 898. Hire þuhte hwítre heofon and eorþe *heaven and earth seemed brighter to her*, Cd. 29; Th. 38, 7; Gen. 603. Engla scȳnost and hwíttost *most beautiful and most splendid of angels*, 18; Th. 22, 11; Gen. 339. [*Goth.* hweits: *O. Sax. O. Frs.* hwít: *Icel.* hvítr: *O. H. Ger.* hwīz *albus, candidus, lacteus*: *Ger.* weiss.] v. eall-, geolu-, healf-, snāw-hwít.

hwíta. v. sweord-hwíta.

hwítan *to make white, to polish*, Exon. 95 a Th. 354, 48; Reim. 62. v. hwítian.

Hwít-cirice, an; *f. A local name*, WHITCHURCH:—Æt Hwíticiricean, Chr. 1001; Erl. 136, 7.

hwít cwidu, cudu, es; *n.* v. cwudu.

hwítel, es; *m. A* WHITTLE, *a cloak, mantle, blanket*:—Hwítel *sagum*, Ælfc. Gl. 27; Som. 60, 111; Wrt. Voc. 25, 51. Hnysce hwítel *linna*, 63; Som. 68, 112; Wrt. Voc. 40, 23. Seó wimman mid hire hwítle bewreáh hine *she covered him with a mantle*; opertus ab ea pallio, Jud. 4, 18: L. M. 1, 32; Lchdm. ii. 76, 23. Ðā hēt Benedictus beran ða tōcwysedan lima on ānum hwítle intō his gebedhūse, Homl. Th. ii. 166, 21. Sem and Jafeth dydon ānne hwítel on hira sculdra *Sem et Japheth pallium imposuerunt humeris suis*, Gen. 9, 23. Ðā eode ðes brōðor sume dæge ðæt hē wolde his reówan and hwítlas ða ðe hē on cumena būre brūcende wæs on sǣ wacsan and feormian *hic cum quadam die lenas sive saga quibus in hospitale utebatur in mari lavasset*, Bd. 4, 31; S. 610, 10. [*A. R.* (MSS. C. T.) hwitel (other MS. kurtel): *Piers P.* for when he streyneþ hym to strecche þe straw is hus whitel, C-text 17, 76: *Halliwell Dict.* whittle '*a blanket. Kennett says "a coarse shagged mantle." The whittle, which was worn about* 1700, *was a fringed mantle, almost invariably worn by country women out of doors*': *Icel.* hvítill *a white bed cover.*] v. gafol-hwítel.

Hwít-ern, es; *n. Whitherne in Galloway*:—His mynster is æt Hwíterne, Chr. 565; Erl. 19, 7. [Cf. Bd. 3, 4:—Qui locus ad provinciam Berniciorum pertinens, vulgo vocatur *Ad candidam casam*, eo quod ibi ecclesiam de lapide, insolito Brittonibus more fecerit. See also 5, 23:—On ðære stōwe ðe is gecīged æt Hwítan earne *quæ candida casa vocatur*, S. 646, 31.]

hwít-fōt; *adj. Having white feet*:—Hwítfōt *albipedius*, Wrt. Voc. ii. 6, 48. Huítfoot, 99, 71.

hwiða, hweoða, an; *m*: hweoðu, e; *f. A breeze*:—Hwiða oððe weder *aura*, Wrt. Voc. 76, 43: Ælfc. Gl. 94; Som. 75, 109; Wrt. Voc. 52, 59. Hwioðan oððe oreþe *aura*, ii. 6, 56. Ǣlc hwiða windes *every breath of wind*, Past. 42. 1; Swt. 306, 6. Hē ȳste mæg eáðe oncyrran ðæt hī windes hweoðu weorþeþ smylte *statuit procellam in auram*, Ps. Th. 106, 29. On lyftu ɫ tō hwiðan ɫ tō wedere *in auram*, Ps. Lamb. 106, 28. On lyfte [MS. C. wedyre ɫ hweoðan], Ps. Spl. 106, 29. [*Icel.* hviða *a squall of wind.*]

hwítian; *p.* ode *To be* or *become white, to whiten*:—Ic hwítige *albeo, albesco*, Ælfc. Gr. 35; Som. 38, 6: *albo, albico*, 36; Som. 38, 29-30. Ðæt ðæt fel hwítige *that the skin may become white*, L. M. 1, 38; Lchdm. ii. 96, 6. [*A. R.* hwiteþ *prs. becomes white*: *Piers P.* whitten *to make white*: *Prompt. Parv.* whytoñ or make whyte *dealbo, candido*: *Goth.* ga-hweitjan *to make white*: *O. H. Ger.* hwīzēn *to become white*; gahwīzit *albatus*: *Ger.* weissen *to whiten.*]

hwíting, e; *f. Whiting, chalk and size*:—Of hwítingmelwe, L. M. 3, 39; Lchdm. ii. 332, 20.

hwíting-treów, es; *n. Whitten tree*; pirus aria:—Hwítingtreów *variculus*, Ælfc. Gl. 47; Som. 65, 25; Wrt. Voc. 33, 25. v. Lchdm. iii. 334. col. 1.

hwít-leác, es; *n. Onion*; allium cæpe:—Hwítleác *poletis*, Ælfc. Gl. 41; Som. 63, 118; Wrt. Voc. 30, 61.

hwít-loc; *adj. Having white* or *bright, shining hair*:—Exon. 112 a; Th. 429, 12; Rä. 48, 3. v. next word.

hwít-locced; *adj. Fair-haired, having bright hair*, Exon. 127 a; Th. 489, 7; Rä. 78, 4.

hwít-ness, e; *f. Whiteness*:—Seó reádnes ðære rōsan and seó hwítnes ðære lilian, Blickl. Homl. 7, 30: Homl. Th. i. 444, 14. His gewǣda scinon on snāwes hwítnysse *his raiment shone with the whiteness of snow*, ii. 242, 7.

Hwít-sand *Wissant near Calais*, Chr. 1095; Erl. 231, 5.

hwít-stōw *is the translation of Libanus*, Ps. Spl. 71, 16.

hwom. v. hwamm.

hwōn; *adj. Little, few* [but the word occurs for the most part only in the neuter acc. with a substantive or adverbial force = *a little*]:—Dō huniges hwōn tō *put a little honey to it*, L. M. 1, 2; Lchdm. ii. 32, 15. Hwōn buteran, 8; Lchdm. ii. 54, 3. Hwōn buteran and pipores hwōn and hwōn sealtes, 2, 52; Lchdm. ii. 268, 25-6. Swā hwæt swā hē læs and hwōn hæfde gearnunge *si quid minus haberet meriti*, Bd. 4, 29; S. 608, 1. Bealosīþa hwōn, Exon. 81 b; Th. 307, 24; Seef. 28. Dō hwōn on ðíne tungan *put a little on to your tongue*, L. M. 2, 52; Lchdm. ii. 272, 18: 1, 59; Lchdm. ii. 130, 7. Genim hwōn sealt *take a little salt*, 2; Lchdm. ii. 32, 3. Ācrind and hwōn wermōd gecnua *pound oak rind and a little wormwood*, 52; Lchdm. ii. 124, 22. Huōn aron ða ðe onfindes ða ilco *pauci sunt qui inveniunt eam*, Mt. Kmbl. Lind. 7, 14. Ofer lytla ɫ huōn *super pauca*, 25, 21. Huōn ɫ unmonige *paucos*, p. 15, 7. Būta hwōn untrymigo gehǣlde *nisi paucos infirmos curavit*, Mk. Skt. Lind. 6, 5. Huōnum *paucis*, Lk. Skt. p. 7, 19. Ðanon hwōn āgān *progressus inde pusillum*, Mk. Skt. 1, 19. Uton ūs hwōn restan *requiescite pusillum*, 6, 31. Huōn *paululum*, Lind. 14, 35. Hine hwōn fram ðām cnihtum gewænde, Ap. Th. 21, 27. Gif huidir huōn ic sægde *quominus dixissem*, Jn. Skt. Lind. 14, 2. Gif hē hwōn hnappode *if he dozed a little*, Homl. Th. i. 86, 18. Ðā hwōn onslēp, Shrn. 60, 17. Hwōnn, Bd. 3, 9; S. 534, 11. Ðām mannum ðe māgon hwōn gehȳran *for those people who can hear but little*, L. Med. ex Quadr: Lchdm. i. 362, 20. Mōt ic nū cunnian hwōn ðínne fæstrǣdnesse *pauculis rogationibus*, Bt. 5, 3; Fox 10, 34. Hē wæs hwōn giernende ðissa woroldþinga and micelra onwalda *vir tranquillissimus*, Ors. 6, 30; Swt. 280, 28. Hē ðǣr bād westanwindes and hwōn norþan *he there waited for a wind rather from the north of west*, 1, 1; Swt. 17, 15. Hwōn lange *rather long*, Herb. 152, 1; Lchdm. i. 276, 24. Hwōn weredre swæce *of a rather sweet taste*, 151, 1; Lchdm. i. 276, 9. Tō hwōn God andrǣdeþ *fear God too little*; minime, Past. 17, 2; Swt. 109, 15: 63, 7; Swt. 417, 35. [*O. E. Hom.* wan: *Laym.* whon.] v. lyt-hwōn; hwōn-líc, -líce; hwēne.

hwonan. v. hwanan.

hwōn-líc; *adj. Little, slight, small*:—Gif wē eów ða gāstlícan sǣd sāwaþ hwōnlíc biþ ðæt wē eówere flǣslícan þing rīpon *if we sow the spiritual seeds for you, it is a slight matter that we reap your fleshly goods*, Homl. Th. ii. 534, 26. Ic wearþ belocen on ānre lytlan byrig mid hwōnlícum fultume *I was shut up in a little town with an inconsiderable force*, Homl. Swt. 7, 347.

hwōn-líce; *adv. Little, slightly*:—Ða hwílwendlícan geþincþu ðe hē hwōnlíce lufode *the temporal dignities that he loved but little*, Swt. A. S. Rdr. 98, 94. Nū gē habbaþ hwōnlíce tō geswincenne, Homl. Th. ii. 78, 14. Hē byþ hwōnlíce biter on byrgincge *it is a little bitter of taste*, Herb. 140, 1; Lchdm. i. 260, 9. Hwōnlíce þyrnihte, 161, 1; Lchdm. i. 288, 16. Heó hwōnlíce undergǣþ ðære eorþan geendunge *it goes a little below the horizon*, Lchdm. iii. 260, 6: 134, 3. Him hwōnlíce speów *he had but little success*, Homl. Skt. 7, 94. Mid ðære sceall seó sāwul ealle þing gemætegian ðæt hit tō swíðe ne sȳ ne tō hwōnlíce *therewith shall the soul moderate all things, that there be not error by excess or by defect*, 1, 162. Hwōnlícor *minus*, Ælfc. Gr. 38; Som. 40, 47. On ðām māran ðe swȳðor syngaþ, on ðām læssan ðe hwōnlícor syngaþ, Homl. Th. i. 460, 27. Hwōnlícost *minime*, Ælfc. Gr. 38; Som. 40, 49.

hwōn-lotum; *adv. A little while*:—Huōnlotum *parumper*, Wrt. Voc. ii. 116, 46.

hwonne, hwonon. v. hwanne, hwanon.

hwōpan; *p.* hweóp *To threaten*:—Ne ondrǣd ðū ðē deáh ðe elþeódige egesan hwōpan heardre hilde *fear not though strangers threaten terror and cruel war*, Elen. Kmbl. 164; El. 82. Bǣlegsan [bell egsan, MS.] hweóp hātan līge ðæt hē on wēstenne werod forbærnde nymðe hie moyses hȳrde *with terror of fire, with hot flame it* [*the pillar of fire*] *threatened that it would consume the host in the wilderness, unless they hearkened to Moses*, Cd. 148; Th. 185, 12; Exod. 121. Geofon deáþe hweóp *the ocean threatened death*, 166; Th. 206, 6; Exod. 447: Th. 208, 3; Exod. 477. Ongan ðā þurh swefn sprecan tō ðam æþelinge and him yrre hweóp *then did God speak in a dream to the prince and in anger threatened him*, 125; Th. 159, 18; Gen. 2636. Ðonne hȳ him yrre hweópan frēcne fȳres wylme, Exon. 35 a; Th. 113, 22; Gū. 161. Ðǣr ǣnig ne mæg lǣþþum hwōpan *there cannot any threaten injuries*, 64 a; Th. 236, 31; Ph. 582. [*Goth.* hwōpan *to boast.*]

hworfan. v. hweorfan.

hwôsan. v. hwêsan.

hwôsta, an; *m. A cough:*—Hwôsta *tussis*, Wrt. Voc. 289, 5: Ælfc. Gr. 9; Som. 14, 33. Hwôsta and nearones breósta, L. M. 2, 21; Lchdm. ii. 204, 26. Hine dreceþ þyrre hwôstan and him on ðam hwôstan hwîlum losaþ sió stemn *he is troubled with a dry cough and at times during the cough he loses his voice*, 51; Lchdm. ii. 264, 13. Wið hwôstan hû hê missenlîce on mon becume and hû his mon tilian scyle *for cough, in what different ways it comes on a man and how it must be treated*, 1, 15; Lchdm. ii. 56, 13. [*Prompt. Parv.* hosse, host, hoost *tussis*: *Scott.* host, hoast, hoist *a cough*: *Icel.* hósti: *O. H. Ger.* huosto *tussis*: *Ger.* husten.]

hwôstan; *p.* te *To cough:*—Hwôstaþ [hwosaþ, MS.] gelôme *they cough frequently*, L. M. 2, 46; Lchdm. ii. 258, 7. [*Prompt. Parv.* hostyñ, *or* rowhyñ, *or* cowghyñ *tussio, tussito*: *Scott.* host, hoist *to cough*: *Icel.* hósta: *Dan.* hoste: *O. H. Ger.* huostôn: *Ger.* husten.]

hwoðerian. v. hweoðerian.

hwu. v. hû.

hwugu. v. hwega.

hwurf *a going about, wandering, error:*—Huurf *error*, Mt. Kmbl. Lind. 27, 64.

hwurfan. v. hweorfan.

hwurf-bân, Lchdm. iii. 98, 16. v. hweorf-bân.

hwurf-lîc; *adj. Changeable;* mutabilis, Hpt. Gl. 470, 62. v. hwerf-lîc.

hwurfling, es; *m. That which turns:*—Hwurflinces *orbis*, Hpt. Gl. 453.

hwurful; *adj. Changeable, fickle:*—Hwæt getâcniaþ ða truman ceastra bûtan hwurfulu môd *what do the strong cities betoken but fickle minds;* quid per civitates munitas nisi suspectæ mentes, Past. 35, 5; Swt. 245, 7.

hwurful-ness, e; *f. Changeableness, mutability:*—Ða twigu ðære hwurfulnesse *genimina mutabilitatis*, Past. 42, 3; Swt. 308, 1. Hió hit gecŷþ self mid hire hwurffulnesse ðæt hió biþ swîðe wancol *se instabilem mutatione demonstrat*, Bt. 20; Fox 70, 34.

HWŶ, hwî; *inst. of* hwæt. WHY. I. *in direct questions:*—*Interrogativa* synd âxigendlîce *cur* hwî, Ælfc. Gr. 38; Som. 40, 58. Hwî didest ðû ðæt *quare hoc fecisti?* Gen. 3, 13: Mt. Kmbl. 9, 11. Hwŷ sceal ic æfter his hyldo þeówian? Cd. 15; Th. 18, 33; Gen. 282. II. *in dependent clauses:*—Se wîsa Augustinus smeáde hwî se hâlga cŷðere cwǽde ... *the wise Augustine inquired why the holy martyr said ...*, Homl. Th. i. 48, 10. Eall ðæra Iudêiscra teóna ârâs þurh ðæt hwî Drihten Crist seðe æfter flǽsce sôðlîce is mannes sunu eác swilce wǽre gecweden Godes sunu *all the quarrel of the Jews had its origin from this, why Christ, who according to the flesh is truly the son of man, should also be called the son of God*, 16. Ðâ âscade hê Æðelm hwŷ hit him ryht ne þuhte ðæt wê him gereaht hæfden *then he asked Æthelm why that did not seem right to him which we had arranged for him*, Chart. Th. 171, 12. Ða ôðre ða ðe ðǽr nǽron þurh gewrite atîwdon hwî hî ðǽr beón ne mihton *the others who were not there shewed by letter why they could not be there*, Chr. 1070; Erl. 206, 6. v. hwâ.

Hwyccas, hwyder, hwylc. v. Hwiccas, hwider, hwilc.

hwylca, an; *m. A swollen vein;* varix, Ælfc. Gl. 76; Som. 71, 129; Wrt. Voc. 45, 32.

hwyrfan, hwyrf-bân, hwyrfel, hwyrfere, hwyrfolung, hwyrf-pôl. v. hwerfan, hweorf-bân, hwerfel, hwerfere, hwerflung, hwirf-pôl.

hwyrf-ness, e; *f. Giddiness:*—Wið brægenes hwyrfnesse, Lchdm. iii. 70, 20.

hwyrft, es; *m. A turn, revolution, going, course, orbit, circuit, orb, circle:*—Ða ðe ofercumaþ allum hwyrfte *quæ superveniunt universo orbi*, Lk. Skt. Rush. 21, 26. Hwâ ne wundraþ ðætte sume tunglu habbaþ scyrtran hwyrft ðonne sume habban *who does not wonder that some stars have a less orbit than others?* Bt. 39, 3; Fox 214, 18. Heofonsteorran bebûgaþ brâdne hwyrft *the stars of heaven encompass a spacious circle* [*the earth*], Cd. 190; Th. 236, 16; Dan. 322. Geþancmeta on hwilce healfe ðû wille hwyrft dôn cyrran mid ceápe *consider on which side thou wilt bend thy course, turn with thy cattle*, 91; Th. 115, 12; Gen. 1918. Gif ic on helle gedó hwyrft ǽnigne *si descendero in infernum*, Ps. Th. 138, 6. Helle hlinduru nâgon hwyrft ne ûtsîþ ǽfre *never is there return or passage out through the grated doors of hell*, Exon. 97 b; Th. 364, 30; Wal. 78. Nâhton mâran hwyrft *they could go no further*, Cd. 154; Th. 191, 6; Exod. 210. Nâh ic hwyrft weges [*Grein reads* hwyrftweges] *I cannot return*, Exon. 101 b; Th. 383, 6; Rä. 4, 6. Sôna æfter ðǽm wordum helle hæftas hwyrftum scrîðaþ þûsendmǽlum *straightway after those words shall the captives of hell by thousands bend thither their steps*, Cd. 227; Th. 304, 17; Sat. 631: Beo. Th. 329; B. 163. Ðâ wæs âgangen geára hwyrftum *then had passed in course of years*, Elen. Kmbl. 2; El. 1. DER. ed-, ymb-hwyrft. v. hwearft.

hwyrftlian. v. hwearftlian.

hŷ. v. hê.

hycgan, hycgean; *p.* hogde. I. *to employ the mind, take thought, be mindful, think, consider, meditate:*—Bêc bodiaþ ðam ðe wiht hycgeþ *books tell to him that thinks at all*, Salm. Kmbl. 476; Sal. 238. Hycgeþ ymbe se ðe wile *he shall think about it who will*, Bt. Met. Fox 19, 2; Met. 19, 1. Ðâm ðe mid heortan hycgeaþ rihte *his qui recto sunt corde*, Ps. Th. 72, 1. Ða inwit and fâcen hycgeaþ on heortan *qui cogitaverunt malitias in corde*, 139, 2, 8. Gif gê teala hycgaþ, Andr. Kmbl. 3223; An. 1614. Hwæt hê on hyge hogde heortan geþoncum *what he meditated in his mind with the thoughts of his heart*, Exon. 51 a; Th. 177, 14; Gû. 1227. Ðû wið Criste wunne hogdes wið hâlgum *thou didst strive with Christ, didst plot against the saints*, 71 b; Th. 267, 28; Jul. 422. Hycgaþ his ealle hû gê hî beswîcen *all think of this, how ye may deceive them*, Cd. 22; Th. 28, 8; Gen. 432. Hicgeaþ on ellen *let your thoughts be of valour*, Fins. Th. 21; Fin. 11. Ðæt seó forlǽtene cyrice ne hycgge ymb ða ðe on hire neáwiste lifgeaþ *that the forsaken church will take no thought for those that live in her neighbourhood*, Blickl. Homl. 43, 1. Hû ðû ymb môdlufan mînes freán on hyge hycge *how thou mayest think in thy mind of the love of my lord*, Exon. 123 a; Th. 473, 5; Bo. 10. Hû gôd biþ ðætte brôður on ân hicgen *how good it is that brothers should be unanimous*, Ps. 132, 1. Wærwyrde sceal wîsfæst hæle breóstum hycgan *a man cautious of words and wise must keep his thoughts to himself*, Exon. 80 b; Th. 303, 24; Fä. 58. Uton wê hycgan hwǽr wê hâm âgen and ðonne geþencan hû wê ðider cumen *let us consider where we may have a home, and then devise how we may come thither*, 83 a; Th. 312, 30; Seef. 117. Â sceal snotor hycgean ymbe ðisse worulde gewinn *ever must the prudent man meditate about the struggle of this world*, Menol. Fox 570; Gn. C. 54. Iç mid heortan ongann hycggean *meditatus sum cum corde meo*, Ps. Th. 76, 6. Hycgan on ellen, Cd. 154; Th. 191, 22; Exod. 218. Micel is tô hycganne wîsfæstum menn hwæt seó wiht sŷ *to a sagacious man it is a great subject for thought what the creature may be*, Exon. 107 b; Th. 411, 14; Rä. 29, 13. Hycgenne, 108 b; Th. 414, 21; Rä. 32, 23. Hycgende mon *a man who thinks*, 92 b; Th. 347, 10; Sch. 10. Wê sculon â hycgende hǽlo rǽdes gemunan sigora waldend *mindful of saving counsel must we ever remember the disposer of victories*, 84 b; Th. 318, 13; Môd. 82. Gemune ûs on môdsefan forþ hycgende folces ðînes *remember us, being continually mindful of thy people;* memento nostri in beneplacito populi tui, Ps. Th. 105, 4. II. *to direct the mind* [*to an object*], *to be intent upon, to intend, purpose, determine, endeavour, strive:*—Ic hicge *molior*, Ælfc. Gr. 31; Som. 35, 51: *nitor*, 36; Som. 38, 53. Ic mid ealre mînre heortan hige hycge swîðe ðæt ic ðîn bebod âtredde *ego in toto corde meo scrutabor mandata tua*, Ps. Th. 118, 69. Ic hycge ðæt ic sôðne dôm symble healde *statui custodire judicia justitiæ tuæ*, 106: 146. Hió hogde georne ðæt hire mægþhâd clǽne geheólde *she earnestly determined to keep her maidenhood pure*, Exon. 66 a; Th. 244, 18; Jul. 29. Freóndrǽdenne heó from hogde *her mind revolted from relationship with him* [i.e. *she determined not to marry*], Th. 244, 28; Jul. 34. Hicg þegenlîce *viriliter age*, Jos. 1, 18. Hycge swâ hê wille ne mæg wêrigmôd wyrde wiðstondan *strive as he will the weary-hearted cannot withstand fate*, Exon. 76 b; Th. 287, 15; Wand. 14. Ne hycge tô slǽpe se ðe heoldeþ ðê *neque obdormiet qui custodit te*, Ps. 120, 3. Hêt ðâ hyssa hwæne hicgan tô handum *he bade then each of his men look to the arms in their hands*, Byrht. Th. 131, 6; By. 4. Ongunnon ðæt ðæs monnes mâgas hycgan þurh dyrne geþoht ðæt hŷ tôdǽlden unc *this did the man's kinsmen through dark design endeavour, to part us two*, Exon. 115 a; Th. 442, 12; Kl. 11. Wê ðæs sculon hycgan georne ðæt ... *we must therefore earnestly endeavour to ...*, Cd. 19; Th. 25, 22; Gen. 397: 226; Th. 302, 6; Sat. 594. III. *to direct the mind with a feeling of confidence, to hope:*—Ic on ðê geare hycge *sperabo in eum*, Ps. Th. 90, 2. Ic hycge tô ðê *in te speravi*, 142, 8. Hycge him hâlig folc hǽlu tô Drihtne *sperate in eum, omnis conventus plebis*, 61, 8. Wê cunnon hycgan and hyhtan ðæt ... *we can hope that ...*, Frag. Kmbl. 83; Leas. 44. [*Goth.* hugjan: *O. Sax.* huggian: *Icel.* hyggja *to think, intend, purpose*: *O. H. Ger.* huggen *meditari, sperare*, Grff. iv. 786.] DER. â-, be-, for-, ge-, ofer-, on-, wið-hycgan; *and see* hogian.

-hycgende. v. bealu-, deóp-, gleáw-, gram-, heard-, morðor-, nîþ-, rǽd-, stîð-, swîð-, þanc-, þrîst-, wîs-, wiðer-hycgende.

HŶD, e; *f.* HIDE, *skin:*—Hŷd *cutis* vel *pellis; corium* vel *tergus*, Ælfc. Gl. 73; Som. 71, 31, 32; Wrt. Voc. 44, 17, 18. Getannede hŷd *subacta coria* vel *medicata* vel *confecta*, 17; Som. 58, 103; Wrt. Voc. 22, 19. Hiora hŷd biþ swîðe gôd tô sciprâpum *their* [*walruses'*] *hide is very good for ship-ropes*, Ors. 1, 1; Swt. 18, 2. Him seó hŷd âheardod wæs on ðǽm cneówum swâ olfendan cneó beóþ *the skin on his knees had got as hard as a camel's knees are*, Shrn. 93, 10. Þurh ðære hŷde wunda âdwæscte his môdes wunda *through the wounds of his skin extinguished the wounds of his mind*, Homl. Th. ii. 156, 31. Twegen sciprâpas ôðer of hwæles hŷde geworht ôðer of sioles, Ors. 1, 1; Swt. 18, 22. Se bât wæs geworht of þriddan healfre hŷde *the boat was made of two hides and a half*, Chr. 891; Erl. 88, 9. Þincþ him [*cattle*] genôg on ðam ðe hî binnan heora ǽgenre hŷde habbaþ tôeácan ðam fôdre ðe him gecyndelîc biþ, Bt. 14, 2; Fox, 44, 23. Gif mon ôðrum rib forsleá binnan gehâlre hŷde geselle x scill. tô bôte gif sió hŷd sîe tôbrocen ... *if a man fracture another's rib without breaking the skin let him pay ten shillings in compensation; if the skin be broken ...*, L. Alf. pol. 70; Th. i. 98, 11–13. Ðâ heó [*the snake*] gefylled wæs hê hêt hŷ behyldan and ða hŷde tô

Rôme bringan . . . heó wæs hundtwelftiges fôta lang, Ors. 4, 6; Bos. 85, 1. Hē healde iii niht hȳde [*of an ox*] and heáfod and sceápes eallswā. And gif hē đa hȳde āweg sylle gilde xx ōran, L. Eth. iii. 9; Th. i. 296, 18. Hwæt sind gescȳ būton deádra nȳtena hȳda? Homl. Th. ii. 280, 30. Ic bicge hȳda and fell *ego emo cutes et pelles*, Coll. Monast. Th. 27, 29. Horses hȳda hī habbaþ him tō hrægle *pelliculas equorum ad vestimentum habentes*, Nar. 38, 2. In the Laws the word is used in technical phrases relating to flogging [cf. colloquial 'to give one a *hiding*']:—Wealh gafolgelda cxx scill. . . . . weales hȳd twelfum *the 'wer' of a tenant of British race is one hundred and twenty shillings . . . the 'hide-gild' of a man of British race is twelve shillings* [the 'hide-gild' of a *þeów* (v. infra), whose *wer* was half that of a *wealh*, was six shillings; if the same proportion was kept, the *weales hȳd* would be, as here, twelve shillings], L. In. 23; Th. i. 118, 4. Þeówman þolie his hȳde odđe hȳdgyldes *let a slave be flogged or pay the 'hide-gild,'* L. E. G. 7, 8; Th. i. 172, 1, 7: L. C. S. 45: 47; Th. i. 402, 16, 26. Đara hyrda ǣlc þolige đære hȳde, L. Edg. S. 9; Th. i. 276, 3. Gif þeów deóflum geldaþ vi scill. gebēte odđe his hȳd *if a slave offer to devils let him pay six shillings or be flogged*, L. Wih. 13: 15: 10; Th. i. 40, 8, 11: 38, 22. Gif hwā his hȳde forwyrce and cirican geierne sīe him sió swingelle forgifen *if any one be liable to flogging* [lit. *forfeit his hide*] *and escape into a church, let the scourging be forgiven him*, L. In. 5; Th. i. 104, 15. Se đe ǣnig đissa dō, gilde wīte, frīman xii. ōr, þeówman đa hȳde, L. N. P. L. 56; Th. ii. 298, 25. v. Grm. R. A. 703. [*Laym. A. R. O. and N.* hude: *O. Frs.* hūd, hēd: *Icel.* húð *a hide*: also a law term as above, e. g. fyrirgöra húð sinni *to forfeit one's hide*; leysa húð sína *to redeem one's hide*; cf. hȳða *to flog*: *O. H. Ger.* hūt *cutis, corium, pellis, tergus, birsa*: *Ger.* haut.]

-hȳd = -hygd, q. v.

HȲDAN; *p.* de *To* HIDE, *conceal*:—Ic mē wiđ heora hete hȳde *absconderem me ab eo*, Ps. Th. 54, 12. Se lǣce hȳd his īsern wiđ đone monn đe hē snīđan wile *the surgeon hides his knife from the man that he means to cut*, Past. 26, 3; Swt. 185, 25. Hȳt *abscondit*, Swt. 187, 9. Se đe his hwǣte hȳtt *qui abscondit frumenta*, 49, 1; Swt. 377, 13. Hȳdeþ, Exon. 82 b; Th. 311, 34; Seef. 102. Hī on holum hȳdaþ hī *in cubilibus suis se collocabunt*, Ps. Th. 103, 21. Fleóþ đonne tō muntum and hié hȳdaþ for đara engla onsȳne, Blickl. Homl. 93, 26: Past. 15, 1; Swt. 89, 15. Ic on mīnre heortan hȳdde *in corde meo abscondi*, Ps. Th. 118, 11: Bt. Met. Fox 29, 109; Met. 29, 55. Đe hǣlend hine hȳdde *Iesus abscondit se*, Jn. Skt. Rush. 8, 59. Hȳddon hié *they hid themselves*, Cd. 40; Th. 53, 12; Gen. 860. Hȳde se đe wylle *hide who will*, Beo. Th. 5526; B. 2766. Ne sylþ hē hit ūs tō đon đæt wē hit hȳdon, Blickl. Homl. 53, 17. Crist hēt hine hȳdan đæt hearde īsen [*put up his sword*], Homl. Th. ii. 246, 24. Nō đū mīnne þearft hafelan hȳdan [*bury*], Beo. Th. 896; B. 446. Hwǣr se wuldres beám under hrusan hȳded wǣre *where the tree of glory* [*the cross*] *under ground was hidden*, Elen. Kmbl. 436; El. 218. Đǣr đa æđelestan hȳdde wǣron, 2214; El. 1108. [*Orm.* hidenn; *Laym. A. R. O. and N.* huden: *Ayenb.* hede: *Chauc.* hide.] DER. ā-, be-, bi-, for-, ge-hȳdan.

hȳdd-ern. v. hēdd-ern.

hȳdels, es; *m. A place of concealment, hiding-place, cavern*:—Hȳdels þeáfana *spelunca latronum*, Mk. Skt. Rush. 11, 17. Gif hit on hȳdelse funden sȳ *if it be found in a place of concealment*, L. Ath. iv. 6; Th. i. 226, 4. [*Laym.* an hudlese wuneden *lived in caverns*: *A. R.* inȩ hudles *in secret*: *Trev.* break out of his hydels (hudels, huydels) *de latibulo suo erumpens*): *Wick.* in hidils (hudlis) *in abscondito*.]

hȳd-gild, es; *n. A payment made to escape the punishment of flogging.* v. hȳd.

hȳdig; *adj. Made of hide, leathern*:—Hȳdig fæt *bulga*, Ælfc. Gl. 29; Som. 61, 28; Wrt. Voc. 26, 28. [Cf. leđer-coddas *bulgæ*, 16; Som. 58, 58; Wrt. Voc. 21, 45.]

hȳdig = hygdig, q. v.

HȲF, e; *f. A* HIVE:—Hȳf *canistrum* vel *alvearium*, Ælfc. Gl. 25; Som. 60, 60; Wrt. Voc. 25, 2. Hȳf *alvearia*, Wrt. Voc. 284, 40. Hȳfe *alvearii*, ii. 4, 64. Hȳfi *alvearia*, 100, 1. Wiđ đæt beón æt ne fleón genim đās ylcan wyrte đe wē veneriam nemdon and gehōh tō đære hȳfe đonne beóþ hȳ wungynde *that bees may not fly away, take this same plant that we called veneria and hang it to the hive, then will they be stationary*, Herb. 7, 2; Lchdm. i. 98, 1. Mæderecīþ on đīnre hȳfe đonne ne āsponþ nān man đīne beón ne hī man ne mæg forstelan đa hwīle đe se cīþ on đære hȳfe biþ [*put*] *a plant of madder in your hive; then nobody will lure away your bees, nor can they be stolen while the plant is in the hive*, Lchdm. i. 397, 2-4. [Hē wunede eall riht swā drāne dōþ on hīue *he lived exactly as drones do in the hive*, Chr. 1127; Erl. 256, 20. *Rel. Ant.* huive: *M. L. Ger.* huve.]

-hygd. v. ge-, ofer-, wan-hygd, -hȳd.

hygdig, hȳdig; *adj. Disposed, minded, careful, considerate, chaste, modest*:—Þancolmōd wer þeáwum hȳdig *a man of thoughtful mind, virtuously disposed*, Cd. 82; Th. 102, 25; Gen. 1705. Hygdig *casta*, Rtl. 68, 12. Hygdigo friódōm *casta libertas*, 105, 1. Hygdego, 109, 35. [*O. Sax.* hugdig, hūdig (*in compounds*).] DER. ān-, bealu-, deóp-, fæst-, gleáw-, gram-, læt-, lytel-, nīþ-, ofer-,ređe-, stīđ-, þrīst-, un-, wan-, wīs-, wiđer-hygdig, -hȳdig.

hygdig-līce; *adv. Chastely*:—Hia seolfa hia hygdiglige beheóldon *seipsos castraverunt*, Mt. Kmbl. Lind. 19, 12.

hygdig-ness, e; *f. Chastity, modesty*:—Hygdignisse *castitatis*, Rtl. 77, 33: 103, 40. Hygdignisse *pudore*, 110, 5.

hyge *the upper part of the throat, fauces*:—Hyge *faus* [*faux* or *fauces*?] Wrt. Voc. 282, 78: ii. 36, 46.

hyge, es; *m. Mind, heart, soul*:—Cwæþ đæt hine his hige speóne đæt hē wyrcean ongunne getimbro *he said that his heart lured him to attempt making buildings*, Cd. 15; Th. 18, 17; Gen. 274. Ōþ hine his hyge forspeón and his ofermetta ealra swīđost *until his heart seduced him, and his pride most of all*, 18; Th. 22, 34; Gen. 350. Hyge Euan wīfes wāc geþoht *the mind of Eve, weak thought of woman*, 30; Th. 40, 34; Gen. 648. Đam þegne ongan his hige hweorfan *the man's mind began to change*, 33; Th. 44, 8; Gen. 706. Næs him blīđe hige *no cheerful mind was his*, 178; Th. 223, 10; Dan. 117. Wearþ him hȳrra hyge đonne gemet wǣre *haughtier grew his soul than was meet*, 198; Th. 247, 2; Dan. 491. Him wæs geómor sefa hyge murnende *mournful was their mind, sorrowing their soul*, Exon. 15 a; Th. 31, 24; Cri. 500. Forđon is mīn hyge geómor, 115 a; Th. 442, 24; Kl. 17. Se hreó hyge, 76 b; Th. 287, 18; Wand. 16. Ys mīnre heortan hige hluttor and clǣne *quia delectatum est cor meum*, Ps. Th. 72, 17. Hyge wearþ mongum blissad *the heart of many was made glad*, Exon. 24 b; Th. 71, 30; Cri. 1163. Hlihende hyge *a gladsome mind*, Elen. Kmbl. 1986; El. 995. Hyge wæs him hinfūs *he was minded to flee away*, Beo. Th. 1514; B 755. Ne biþ him tō hearpan hyge *no mind hath he for the harp*, Exon. 82 a; Th. 308, 23; Seef. 44. Ne wæs him bleáþ hyge *no coward heart had he* [cf. *Icel.* hug-blauðr *timid*; hug-bleyði *cowardice*], Andr. Kmbl. 462; An. 231. Đā wæs hyge onhyrded *then was his heart confirmed*, Elen. Kmbl. 1678; El. 841. Se hearda hyge wunade *the stout heart continued*, Exon. 40 b; Th. 134, 31; Gū. 517. Hyge sceal heardum men *a bold man must have courage*, 92 a; Th. 346, 15; Gn. Ex. 205. Hige sceal đē heardra heorte đē cēnre đē ūre mægen lytlaþ *the firmer must courage be, braver the heart, the more our force dwindles*, Byrht. Th. 140, 62; By. 312. Hyge weallende *a mind agitated by violent emotions*, Andr. Kmbl. 3415; An. 1711. Weóll him on innan hyge ymb his heortan, Cd. 18; Th. 23, 5; Gen. 354. Mīn hyge dreóseþ bysig æfter bōcum: hwīlum hyge heortan neáh hearde wealleþ, Salm. Kmbl. 122-6; Sal. 60-2. Đū wāst đæt ic eom unwīs hyges *tu scis insipientiam meam*, Ps. Th. 68, 6. Ic mīn gehāt mid hyge gylde đæt mīne weleras ǣr wīse gedǣldan *reddam vota mea, quæ distinxerunt labia mea*, 65, 12: 102, 19. Ic andette đē mid hyge ealle heortan mīnre *confitebor tibi in toto corde meo*, 110, 1: 118, 69: 94, 10. Wesan đīne eáran gehȳrende mid hige on eall gebedd esnes đīnes *fiant aures tuæ intendentes in orationem servi tui*, 129, 2. Mid hyge þencan *to think with the mind*, Exon. 82 b; Th. 311, 23; Seef. 96. Wese heorte mīn on hige clǣne *fiat cor meum immaculatum*, Ps. Th. 118, 80. On mīnum hyge hreóweþ *I am grieved to think*, Cd. 22; Th. 27, 31; Gen. 426. Ne meahte hē æt his hige findan đæt hē wolde þeódne þeówian *he could not find it in his heart to serve his prince*, 14; Th. 18, 1; Gen. 266. Hālig on hige *holy of thought*, 133; Th. 168, 9; Gen. 2780: Exon. 73 b; Th. 274, 14; Jul. 533. On heardum hyge *in my hard heart*, Elen. Kmbl. 1614; El. 809. Hēt hicgan tō hige gōdum *bade them see to it that they were of good courage*, Byrht. Th. 131, 7; By. 4. Hī on heofon setton hyge hyra mūþes *posuerunt in cœlum os suum*, Ps. Th. 72, 7. Hæfde hyge strangne *he had a strong heart*, Cd. 23; Th. 29, 9; Gen. 447. Heardrǣdne hyge, 107; Th. 141, 21; Gen. 2348. Ic geornlīce gode þegnode þurh holdne hyge *diligently I served God with loyal heart*, 28; Th. 37, 7; Gen. 586: Beo. Th. 539; B. 267. Þurh yrne hyge *in anger*, Exon. 16 b; Th. 39, 10; Cri. 620: Andr. Kmbl. 1941; An. 973. Đīnne hyge gefæstna *strengthen thine heart*, Exon. 93 a; Th. 348, 33; Sch. 37: Andr. Kmbl. 2427; An. 1215. Dōþ eówre heortan hige hāle and clǣne *effundite coram illo corda vestra*, Ps. Th. 61, 8. Nyllan gē eów on heortan đa hige stađelian *nolite cor apponere*, 11. [*Laym.* huȝe: *Orm.* hiȝ: *Goth.* hugs: *O. Sax.* hugi: *O. Frs.* hei: *Icel.* hugi, hugr: *O. H. Ger.* hugu, hugi *animus, sensus, affectus*.] DER. hāt-hyge.

hyge-bend, es; *m*: e; *f. A tie or bond which is furnished by the mind*:—Hygebendum fæst *fixed firm by the mind's chains*, Beo. Th. 3761; B. 1878.

hyge-blind; *adj. Having the mind blinded*, Exon. 66 b; Th. 246, 13; Jul. 61.

hyge-blīđe; *adj. Glad at heart*, Andr. Kmbl. 3378; An. 1693: Exon. 107 a; Th. 408, 31; Rā. 27, 20.

hyge-clǣne; *adj. Pure in mind*, Ps. Th. 104, 3.

hyge-cræft, es; *m. Mental power, intellect, wisdom*:—Ealle þeóde ēcne Drihten mid hygecræfte herigan *let all nations praise the Lord with the powers of their minds*, Ps. Th. 116, 1: 118, 61, 73. Gif đū mē đīnne hygecræft hylest and đīne heortan geþohtas *if thou dost conceal from me thy wisdom and thy heart's thoughts*, Exon. 88 b; Th. 333, 12; Gn. Ex. 3. Wīsdōm higecræft heáne, Cd. 176; Th. 222, 1; Dan. 98. Hygecræftum, Hy. 6. 3; Hy. Grn. ii. 286, 3.

hyge-cræftig; *adj. Having mental power, wise, sagacious*, Exon.

11 a; Th. 15, 25; Cri. 241: 92 b; Th. 348, 8; Sch. 25: 101 a; Th. 380, 37; Rä. 2, 1.

hý-gedriht. v. hí-gedryht.

hyge-fæst; *adj. Firm of mind, prudent, wise,* Exon. 112 a; Th. 429, 33; Rä. 43, 14. [*Icel.* hug-fastr *steadfast.*] Cf. hoga-fæst.

hyge-frōd; *adj. Wise of mind, prudent,* Cd. 92; Th. 117, 13; Gen. 1953.

hyge-frōfor, e; *f. Comfort for the mind* or *heart,* Elen. Kmbl. 709; El. 355: Hy. 9, 13; Hy. Grn. ii. 291, 13.

hyge-gǣlsa; *adj. Slow, sluggish*:—Nis hē hinderweard ne hygegǣlsa swār ne swongor swā sume fuglas đa đe late þurh lyft lācaþ fiþrum *non tamen est tarda, ut volucres quæ corpore magno incessus pigros per grave pondus habent,* Exon. 60 b; Th. 220, 3; Ph. 314. v. gǣlan.

hyge-gāl; *adj. Light-minded, wanton,* Exon. 103 b; Th. 394, 2; Rä. 13, 12. v. gāl.

hyge-gār, es; *m. A dart of the mind, a wile, device,* Exon. 83 b; Th. 315, 21; Mōd. 34.

hyge-geómor, -giómor; *adj. Sad in mind, mournful, sorrowful,* Cd. 42; Th. 54, 18; Gen. 879: Andr. Kmbl. 2175; An. 1089: 3112; An. 1559: Exon. 49 b; Th. 171, 20; Gū. 1129: Beo. Th. 4807; B. 2408: Exon. 21 a; Th. 55, 29; Cri. 891. Hygegeómorne, 115 a; Th. 442, 28; Kl. 19. Hygegeómre, 10 a; Th. 10, 17; Cri. 154: 22 b; Th. 61, 33; Cri. 994: 70 b; Th. 262, 4; Jul. 327: 45 b; Th. 155, 8; Gū. 857: 46 a; Th. 157, 31; Gū. 900: Elen. Kmbl. 2429; El. 1216.

hyge-gleáw; *adj. Wise, prudent, having clear mental vision,* Exon. 25 a; Th. 73, 23; Cri. 1194: Chr. 975; Erl. 126, 25; Edg. 51: Elen. Kmbl. 665; El. 333.

hyge-grim; *adj. Cruel of mind, fierce, savage,* Exon. 74 b; Th. 278, 9; Jul. 595.

hyge-leás; *adj. Thoughtless, careless, foolish*:—Ne gerīseþ biscopum ne æt hām ne on sīđe tō higeleás [iuncglīc, MS. G] wīse ac wīsdōm and weorþscipe gedafenaþ heora hāde *a too thoughtless manner is not seemly for bishops, neither at home nor when travelling, but wisdom and dignity are becoming to their rank,* L. I. P. 10, note; Th. ii. 318, 41. Higeleás plega *senseless play,* Homl. Th. ii. 220, 6. Hygeleáse *lacking wisdom* [*the rebellious angels*], Cd. 3; Th. 4, 10; Gen. 51. Leahtra hegeleásra *of sins committed thoughtlessly,* Ps. C. 50, 144; Ps. Grn. ii. 280, 144. [*Icel.* hug-lauss *fainthearted.*]

hyge-leást, e; *f. Thoughtlessness, foolishness, folly, want of wisdom, heedlessness*:—Eálā gē cildra gāþ ūt būtan hygeleáste tō claustre ođđe tō leorninge *O vos pueri egredimini sine scurrilitate in claustrum vel in gymnasium,* Coll. Monast. Th. 36, 9. Ne ūs ne gedafenaþ đæt wē ūrne līchaman đe Gode is gehālgod mid unþæslīcum plegan and higleáste gescyndan *it doth not beseem us to put our body, that is sanctified to God, to shame with indecent play and folly,* Homl. Th. i. 482, 12. Wē sceolon blissian on ūrum Drihtne nā on higleáste *we ought to rejoice in our Lord, not in folly,* ii. 292, 32. Englas wǣron befeallene on đa hātan hell þurh hygeleáste and þurh ofermētto *angels had fallen into the hot hell through folly and through pride,* Cd. 18; Th. 21, 29; Gen. 331. Biscopum gebiraþ wīsdōm ... ne gerīsaþ heom micele ofermētta ne ǣnige higelīste, L. I. P. 10, note; Th. ii. 318, 32. [Cf. *Icel.* hug-leysa *timidity.*]

hyge-mǣđ, e; *f. Honour that is shewn with the heart* or *mind, reverence;* or *fitness that is determined by the mind* [?]:—Wīglāf healdeþ higemǣđum [hige mēđum, Th.] heáfodwearde *Wiglaf keeps guard reverently* [or *duly*], Beo. Th. 5810; B. 2909. v. mǣđ.

hyge-mēđe; *adj. Wearying the heart* or *mind,* Beo. Th. 4875; B. 2442.

hyge-rōf; *adj. Stout, strong of mind* or *heart, magnanimous,* Exon. 124 a; Th. 477, 6; Ruin. 20: 46 b; Th. 159, 13; Gū. 926: Andr. Kmbl. 465; An. 233: 2009; An. 1007: Beo. Th. 413; B. 204: Cd. 82; Th. 102, 32; Gen. 1709: 75; Th. 93, 22; Gen. 1550: Exon. 15 b; Th. 33, 31; Cri. 534: Judth. 12; Thw. 26, 1; Jud. 303.

hyge-rūn, e; *f. A secret of the mind* or *heart*:—Cyriacus hygerūne ne māþ gāstes mihtum tō Gode cleopode *Cyriacus did not conceal the secret of his heart, but with the powers of the spirit cried to God,* Elen. Kmbl. 2196; El. 1099. v. Grmm. A. u. E. 139. [*Icel.* hug-rúnar *magical runes with a power of wisdom.*]

hyge-sceaft, e; *f. Mental constitution, mind, disposition, heart*:—Frȳnd synd hié mīne georne holde on hyra hygesceaftum *they are my zealous friends, loyal in their hearts,* Cd. 15; Th. 19, 8; Gen. 288. [*O. Sax.* hugi-skafti; *pl.*]

hyge-snottor; *adj. Wise of mind, prudent, sagacious,* Exon. 49 a; Th. 168, 23; Gū. 1082: 71 a; Th. 265, 24; Jul. 386: Bt. Met. Fox 10, 14; Met. 10, 7.

hyge-sorh, -sorg, e; *f. Mental care, anxiety,* Cd. 94; Th. 122, 31; Gen. 2035: Exon. 10 b; Th. 11, 21; Cri. 174: 47 b; Th. 162, 28; Gū. 982: 50 a; Th. 174, 15; Gū. 1178: 51 a; Th. 176, 32; Gū. 1219: Cd. 37; Th. 48, 16; Gen. 776: Beo. Th. 4646; B. 2328.

hyge-teóna, an; *m. Deliberate injury* or *offence*:—Ic him hygeteónan hwītan seolfre bēte *with white silver will I make reparation to him for injury,* Cd. 130; Th. 165, 13; Gen. 2731: 69; Th. 83, 16; Gen. 1380. Higeteónan spræc on fǣmnan *from her heart spoke injuriously against the woman,* Cd. 103; Th. 136, 21; Gen. 2261.

hyge-þanc, es; *m. Thought,* Andr. Kmbl. 1634; An. 818: Exon. 27 a; Th. 81, 30; Cri. 1331: 109 a; Th. 417, 14; Rä. 36, 4: Elen. Kmbl. 311; El. 156: Ps. Th. 74, 5.

hyge-þancol; *adj. Thoughtful,* Andr. Kmbl. 681; An. 341: Cd. 176; Th. 221, 26; Dan. 94: Judth. 11; Thw. 23, 20; Jud. 131.

hyge-þrymm, es; *m. Strength of heart* or *mind,* Beo. Th. 683; B. 339.

hyge-þrȳþ, e; *f. Pride of heart* or *mind, insolence*:—Higeþrȳþe wæg *was insolent,* Cd. 102: Th. 135, 6; Gen. 2238.

hyge-þyhtig; *adj. Doughty of heart,* Beo. Th. 1497; B. 746.

hyge-treów, e; *f. Faith deliberately pledged,* Cd. 107; Th. 142, 25; Gen. 2367.

hyge-wælm, es; *m. Agitation of the mind, violent emotion,* e. g. *anger,* Cd. 47; Th. 60, 12; Gen. 980.

hyge-wlanc; *adj. Proud, elated in mind,* Exon. 105 a; Th. 400, 1: Rä. 20, 2: 112 b; Th. 431, 21; Rä. 46, 4.

hyht, es; *m.* [*f.* Ps. Th. 77, 53.] *Hope, joyous expectation, joy*:—Hiht on Gode *hope in God,* Homl. Th. ii. 602, 11. Đære gāstlīcan strenge mycel hyht *the great hope of spiritual strength,* Blickl. Homl. 135, 28. Mē is hālig hyht on hine *spes mea in Deo est,* Ps. Th. 61, 7: 70, 4. Đū eart hyht ealra đe on đysse eorþan ūtan syndon *spes omnium finium terræ,* 64, 6. Hwīlum hié gehēton æt heargtrafum wigweorþunga bǣdon đæt him gāstbona geóce gefremede. Swylc wæs þeáw hyra hǣđenra hyht *sometimes they vowed in their temples idolatrous honours, prayed that the destroyer of souls would afford them help. Such was their custom, such the hope of the heathens,* Beo. Th. 360; B. 179. Đū eart mīn se sōđa hiht *tu es spes mea,* Ps. Th. 141, 5. Ǣlc hyht līfes *omnis spes vitæ,* Rtl. 3, 28. Đū cēgst his noman Iohannes and đē biþ đonne hyht and gefeá *vocabis nomen suum Johannem et erit gaudium tibi et exultatio,* Blickl. Homl. 165, 10. Līfes hyht and ealles leóhtes gefeá, Exon. 16 a; Th. 36, 32; Cri. 585: 42 a; Th. 141, 23; Gū. 631. Đǣr is hyht and blis *there is joy and bliss,* Exon. 18 b; Th. 47, 5; Cri. 750: 15 b; Th. 33, 22; Cri. 529: 46 b; Th. 159, 14; Gū. 926. Ne biþ him tō hearpan hyge ne tō wīfe wyn ne tō worulde hyht *he hath no mind for the harp, nor delight in woman, nor joy in life,* 82 a; Th. 308, 26; Seef. 45. Næs him tō māđme wyn hyht tō hordgestreónum, Andr. Kmbl. 2229; An. 1116. Sigbēg hyhtes *corona spei,* Rtl. 1, 15. Hygtes, 3, 26. Is mē Moab mīnes hyhtes hwer *Moab olla spei meæ,* Ps. Th. 59, 7. Đære hǣlo đe hē ūs tō hyhte forgeaf *for the salvation which he hath given us to hope for,* Exon. 16 b; Th. 38, 28; Cri. 613. Hæbbe ic mē tō hyhte heofonrīces weard *I have the guardian of the kingdom of heaven as my hope,* 68 b; Th. 255, 10; Jul. 212. Hæfdon hym tō hyhte helle flōras beornende bealo *they had the bottom of hell and burning torments to look forward to,* Cd. 214; Th. 269, 8; Sat. 70. Nabbaþ wē tō hyhte nymþe weán and wītu *we have nothing to expect but woe and punishments,* 220; Th. 285, 9; Sat 335. Se beorn wæs on hyhte *the man was in good hopes* [*of performing his journey*], Andr. Kmbl. 478; An. 239: 1274; An. 637. Ic eom wunderlīcu wiht wīfum on hyhte *I am a wondrous creature giving joy to women,* Exon. 106 b; Th. 407, 7; Rä. 26, 1: Runic pm. Kmbl. 342, 16; Rūn. 16. Hē hī on hihte holdre lǣdde *deduxit eos in spe,* Ps. Th. 77, 53. Ic hāligne gāst hyhte belūce emne swā ēcne *I believe the Holy Ghost to be just as eternal,* Hy. 10, 41; Hy. Grn. ii. 293, 41. Hē him forgeaf ēces līfes hyht, Blickl. Homl. 137, 7. Hī on God ǣnne heora hyht gesetton *they placed their hope on God only,* 185, 15: Ps. Th. 113, 20. Beón đa ófdrǣdde đa đe sint ofsette mid flǣsclīcum lustum, and nabbaþ nǣnne hiht tō engla werode *let those be afraid that are oppressed with fleshly lusts and have nothing to hope for from the angelic host,* Homl. Th. i. 222, 29. Đæt hī gleáwne hiht tō Gode hæfdan *ut ponant in Deo spem suam,* Ps. Th. 77, 9. Ic hiht on đon hæbbe georne *exultabo,* 62, 7. Hyhta leáse helle sōhton *hopeless they sought hell,* Exon. 75 b; Th. 283, 18; Jul. 682. Hyhtum tō wuldre *with hopes of glory,* 116 b; Th. 448, 3; Dōm. 48. [*O. E. Homl.* huht, hiht: *Orm.* hihht: *O. and N.* hihte, hiȝte.] DER. tō-, woruld-hyht.

hyhtan; *p.* te *To hope, trust, look forward to with hope* or *joy, rejoice*:—Ic under fiđrum hihte *sub pennis ejus sperabis,* Ps. Th. 90, 4. Ic đē hihte tō *sperantem in te,* 85, 2. Hihte ic tō đīnra handa hālgum dǣdum *in operibus manuum tuarum exultabo,* 91, 3. Heorte mīn and flǣsc hyhtaþ georne on đone lifgendan Drihten *cor meum et caro mea exultaverunt in Dominum vivum,* 83, 2. Hē hyhte tō mē *in me speravit,* 91, 14. Đām [đe] longe his hyhtan hidercyme *to those who had long hoped for his advent,* Exon. 10 a; Th. 9, 29; Cri. 142. Sione bearn symble hihtan *filii Sion exultant,* Ps. Th. 149, 2. Se þeóda lāreów lǣrde đa rīcan đæt hī heora hiht ne besetton on đām swicelum welum, ac hihton on God đæra gōda syllend *the teacher of the gentiles taught the rich that they should not set their hope on deceitful riches, but should hope in God, the giver of good things,* Homl. Th. ii. 328, 1. Wē cunnon hyhtan đæt wē heofones leóht āgan mōton *we can hope that we may possess the light of heaven,* Fragm. Kmbl. 84; Leás. 44. Ic ellen wylle habban and hlyhhan and mē hyhtan tō *I will have courage, and laugh and look forward with hope,* Exon. 119 a; Th. 456, 22; Hy. 4, 70: 12 b; Th. 21, 26; Cri. 340. Gōd ys on Dryhten tō hyhtanne *bonum est confidere in Domino,* Ps. Th. 117, 9. [*O. and N.* hihte.] v. ge-hyhtan.

hyht-ful; *adj. Full of hope* or *joy, joyous, exultant, glad, pleasant*:—Ic þurh Judas ǽr hyhtful gewearþ and nú gehýned eom þurh Judas eft *through Judas formerly I became exultant, and now again through Judas am I humiliated*, Elen. Kmbl. 1842; El. 923. Ontýn eárna hleóðor ðæt mín gehẽrnes hehtful weorþe *auditui meo dabis gaudium*, Ps. C. 50, 78; Ps. Grn. ii. 278, 78. Him on lãste beleác hihtfulne hãm hãlig engel *a holy angel closed behind them the pleasant abode* [*paradise*], Cd. 45; Th. 58, 14; Gen. 946. Wẽ hyhtfulle hǽlo gelýfaþ *we, filled with hope, trust the salvation* [*or* hyhtfulle *may agree with* hǽlo], Exon. 9 b; Th. 8, 17; Cri. 119.

hyht-gifa, an; *m. One who gives hope* or *joy* [*an epithet of Christ*], Elen. Kmbl. 1700; El. 852.

hyht-gifu, e; *f. A gift which causes hope* or *joy*, Exon. 94 b; Th. 353, 31; Reim. 21.

hyhting, e; *f. Exultation, joy*:—Hihting *exultatio, lætitia*, Wrt. Voc. ii. 146, 30.

hyht-leás; *adj. Without hope* [*of that which is promised*], *joyless*:—Āhóf brýd Abrahames hihtleásne hleahtor *Abraham's wife laughed incredulously* [*without hope that the promise of a son would be fulfilled*], Cd. 109; Th. 144, 9; Gen. 2387. v. hyht-ful.

hyht-líc; *adj. Giving*, or *having, cause for hope* or *joy, hopeful, pleasant, joyous, exultant*:—Hyhtlíc heorþwerod *a hopeful family*, Cd. 78; Th. 96, 35; Gen. 1605. Beóþ ðonne eádge ðe ðǽr in wuniaþ hyhtlíc is ðæt heorþwerud *happy are they that dwell therein, joyous is that band*, Exon. 93 b; Th. 352, 1; Sch. 91: Cd. 95; Th. 125, 8; Gen. 2076. Hyhtlíc heofontimber *the pleasant frame of heaven*, 8; Th. 9, 23; Gen. 146: Exon. 116 a; Th. 446, 18; Dóm. 24. Hyhtlícra hãm, Cd. 218; Th. 278, 3; Sat. 216: 216; Th. 273, 17; Sat. 138. Ðonne biþ hyhtlícre . . . biþ ðæt ǽrende eádiglícre, Soul Kmbl. 250; Seel. 129. Hãma hyhtlícost, Andr. Kmbl. 207; An. 104. [*O. E. Hom.* hihtliche bure *a pleasant chamber*: cf. *Laym.* un-huhtlic.]

hyht-plega, an; *m. Joyous play, sport*, Exon. 18 b; Th. 46, 14; Cri. 737: 105 b; Th. 402, 12; Rä. 21, 28.

hyht-willa, an; *m. Desire accompanied by hope* or *joy*:—Hyhtwillan leás *without hope of attaining any good*, Cd. 216; Th. 274, 25; Sat. 159.

hyht-wynn, e; *f. Joy of hope*:—Ne þearf hẽ hopian nõ ðæt hẽ ðonan mõte ac ðǽr wunian sceal hyhtwynna leás *no need has he to hope that he may go thence, but there shall he dwell hopeless and joyless*, Judth. 10; Thw. 23, 14; Jud. 121.

hylc, es; *m. A bend, turn, winding*:—Ābrocen land *vel* hilces *anfractus*, Ælfc. Gl. 100; Som. 77, 9; Wrt. Voc. 55, 12. Wõge hylcas *anfractus, reflectus*, Hpt. Gl. 448. Hylcas *anfractus*, 486. Hylcum *anfractibus*, 493.

hyld, held, es; *m. Favour, protection, grace* [*of a superior to an inferior*], *loyalty, allegiance* [*of the inferior to the superior*]:—Ic hãlsige eów for ðæs cãseres helda ðæt gẽ mẽ secgon *I adjure you by your allegiance to the emperor that you tell me*, Nicod. 8; Thw. 4, 7. Gecýþe ðæt on Godes helde and on hlãfordes *let him declare that on his faith towards God and the lord*, L. C. S. 23; Th. i. 388, 23. On gesyhþe ðara hãligra ðe ðínne held curan *in the sight of the saints that chose thine allegiance* [*chose thee as their lord*]; ante conspectum sanctorum tuorum, Ps. Th. 51, 8. Ðe his hyld curon, Cd. 198; Th. 246, 19; Dan. 481. Gẽ ðe úres ðæs hãlgan Godes held begangeþ *ye who practise loyalty towards our holy God*, Ps. Th. 133, 2. Ðeáh ðe ic on mínes húses hyld gegange *si introiero in tabernaculum domus meæ*, 131, 3. Hyld hæfde his ferlorene *he had lost the favour of his chief*, Cd. 16; Th. 20, 1; Gen. 301. Hæfde wuldres beám werud gelǽded on hild godes *the pillar of glory had conducted the host into the favour of God*, 170; Th. 214, 13; Exod. 568. On gãstes hyld, 195; Th. 243, 23; Dan. 440. Hylda leáse *without favours*, Exon. 53 a; Th. 186, 20; Az. 21. Ðẽ ǽfre on fullum hyldum hold and on fulre lufe *faithful to thee with full faith and with full love*, Chart. Th. 598, 31. For eówrum hyldum ðe gẽ mẽ symble cýddon *for your fidelity that you have ever shewn me*, L. Edg. 5, 12; Th. i. 276, 19. v. helde, hyldu, gehyld, hold; Grmm. R. A. 252.

hyldan, heldan; *p.* de; *trans.* and *intrans. To bend, incline, heel, tilt*:—Ðú gestaþoladest eorþan swíðe fæstlíce ðæt heó ne helt on nãne healfe *thou hast fixed earth very firmly, so that it does not incline to any side*, Bt. 33, 4; Fox 130, 36. Heldeþ, Bt. Met. Fox 20, 327; Met. 20, 164. Hylde hine hleór bolster onfẽng *he bent himself* [*to the couch*] *and the pillow received his cheek*, Beo. Th. 1380; B. 688. Ðã hig hyra andwlitan on eorþan hyldan *cum declinarent vultum in terram*, Lk. Skt. 24, 5. Hié tõ gebede hyldon *they bent down to pray*, Andr. Kmbl. 2054; An. 1029. Ne hyld ðú míne heortan *ut non declines cor meum*, Ps. Th. 140, 5. Ic hyldan mẽ ne dorste *I dare not bow myself* [*the Ruthwell cross has* hælda ik ni darstæ], Rood Kmbl. 90; Kr. 45. Is mín feorh tõ helldore hylded geneahhe *vita mea in infernum appropinquavit*, Ps. Th. 87, 3. [*Laym.* scipen gunnen helden: *A. R.* helden wiṅ ine wunden: *Prompt. Parv.* heldyn̄ *or* bowyn̄ *inclino, flecto, deflecto*, p. 234, see note: *Wick. Piers P.* helde *fundere*: *O. Sax.* af-heldian: *Icel.* halla *to lean* or *turn sideways*; hella *to pour out*: *Dan.* hælde *to incline*: *Swed.* hälla: *O. H. Ger.* halden *vergere, recubare*; haldian, heldian *inclinare, declinare*.] DER. ã-, on-hyldan.

hyldan; *p.* de *To flay, take off the skin*:—Hyldeþ *discoriat*, Wrt. Voc. ii. 140, 78. And hyldon ða offrunge *detractaque pelle hostiæ* Lev. 1, 6. [*Laym. Wick.* hilde: *Icel.* hylda *to slash*.] v. be-, on-hyldan; hold *and* hyldere.

hyld-āþ, es; *m. An oath of fealty* or *fidelity*:—Ðus man sceal swerigean hyldãþas *in this manner are oaths of fealty to be sworn*, L. O. 1; Th. i. 178, 2: see 252, 5. v hold-āþ.

hylde, an; *f. The slope of a hill*:—Ōþ ðæs clifas norþ hyldan *to the north side of the cliff*, Cod. Dipl. Kmbl. iii. 418, 24. [*Icel.* hallr; *m. a slope, hill*: *O. H. Ger.* halda; *f. clivus*.] v. hyldan, held.

-hylde. v. earfoþ-, on-hylde *and* heald.

hylde-mǽg, es; *m. A near and dear kinsman*, Cd. 52; Th. 67, 1; Gen. 1094: 94; Th. 122, 25; Gen. 2032.

hyldere, es; *m. A flayer, butcher*:—Hyldere oððe cwellere oððe flǽsctawere *lanio* vel *lanista* vel *carnifex* vel *macellarius*, Ælfc. Gl. 113; Som. 79, 121; Wrt. Voc. 60, 27. From hylderum *a lanionibus*, Wrt. Voc. ii. 10, 2. v. hyldan, hold.

hylding, e; *f. A bending, inclination*; curvatura, Wrt. Voc. ii. 23, 66.

hyld-rǽden, e; *f. Fidelity*:—Ǽlc óðrum ãþ on hãligdóme sealde sóðre heldrǽdenne *each should give to other on the relics an oath of true fidelity*, Chart. Th. 610, 32. v. hold-rǽden.

hyldu, e; hyldo; *indecl. f. Kindness, favour, affection, friendship, grace, fidelity, loyalty* [v. hold.]:—Ys mẽ heortan gehygd hyldu Drihtnes *Deus cordis mei*, Ps. Th. 72, 21. His hyldo is unc betere tõ gewinnanne ðonne his wiðermẽdo *his favour is better for us to gain than his hostility*, Cd. 30; Th. 41, 20; Gen. 659. Ðẽ wæs leófra his sibb and hyldo ðonne ðín sylfes bearn *his* [*God's*] *peace and grace were dearer to thee than thine own child*, 141; Th. 176, 33; Gen. 2921. Unc is his hyldo þearf *we need his favour*, 32; Th. 41, 30; Gen. 664: Judth. 9; Thw. 21, 3; Jud. 4. Hyldo tõ wedde *as a pledge of favour*, Beo. Th. 5989; B. 2998. For ealdre hyldo *from old friendship*; amicitia vetus, Ors. 3, 9; Swt. 130, 28. Eallum monnum nãnuht swã gõd ne þuhte swã hié tõ his hyldo becõme *to all men nothing seemed so good as to obtain his favour*, 5, 15; Swt. 250, 18. Ācwæþ hine fram his hyldo, Cd. 16; Th. 20, 6; Gen. 304. Hyldo *affectum*, Wrt. Voc. ii. 1, 12. Swã ic ãge Pharaones helde *so may I possess the favour of Pharaoh*; per salutem Pharaonis, Gen. 42, 15. Wẽ hraðe begytan hyldo ðíne *cito anticipet nos misericordia tua*, Ps. Th. 78, 8. Wutun úrum Hǽlende hyldo gebeódan *jubilemus Deo salutari nostro*, 94, 1. Ic hyldo sóhte *I sought grace*, 118, 123. Englas ðe ǽr godes hyldo gelǽston *angels who were loyal to God*, Cd. 17; Th. 21, 9; Gen. 321: Ps. Th. 55, 10: 84, 8. [*O. Sax.* huldi *grace, favour, devotion*: *O. Frs.* helde, hulde: *Icel.* hylli *favour, grace*: *O. H. Ger.* huldi *gratia, favor, devotio, fides*: *Ger.* huld.] DER. hlãford-, un-hyldu; *and see* helde, hyld.

hyll. v. hel.

hyll, es; *m*: e; *f. A hill*:—Hyll *collis*, Ælfc. Gl. 97; Som. 76, 62; Wrt. Voc. 54, 6. Þurh hylles hrõf *through the top of the hill*, Exon. 104 b; Th. 397, 29; Rä. 16, 27. Stondende on lytlum hylle, Shrn. 70, 14. Hí huntiaþ hí of ǽlcere hylle *they shall hunt them from every hill*, Homl. Th. i. 576, 28. Hyllas *montes*, Ps. Spl. C. 71, 3. Hyllas and heá beorgas, Cd. 192; Th. 240, 7; Dan. 383. Hyllas and cnollas, Exon. 18 a; Th. 45, 11; Cri. 717. Gebígde synt hylla middaneardes *incurvati sunt colles mundi*, Cant. Abac. 6. Dũna and hylla *montes et colles*, Hymn. T. P. 75. Ðonne hie cweþaþ tõ ðǽm dúnum and tõ ðǽm hyllum *tunc incipient dicere montibus et collibus*, Blickl. Homl. 93, 33: Lk. Skt. Lind. 23, 30. [*Laym. A. R.* hul: *Orm.* hill: *Ayenb.* hell: *Prompt. Parv.* hylle.] v. sand-hyll.

hyll-hãma, an; *m. A cricket*:—Hilhãma *cicada*, Ælfc. Gl. 37; Som. 63, 7; Wrt. Voc. 29, 29. Hyllehãma oððe gærstapa *cicada*, ii. 21, 54. v. hãma.

hyll-wyrt, e; *f. Hill-wort*:—Hylwurt *samum*, Ælfc. Gl. 40; Som. 63, 82; Wrt. Voc. 30, 34. Hylwyrt *pollegia*, 44; Som. 64, 83; Wrt. Voc. 32, 19. v. Lchdm. ii. 392, col. 2. In E. D. S. Plant Names hill-wort is given as [1] *mentha pulegium*; [2] *thymus serpyllum*.

hyl-song *a timbrel*:—On hylsongæ *in tympano*, Ps. Spl. T. 150, 4.

hylsten. v. hilstan (*Appendix*).

hylte, es; *m. A wood, shrubbery*:—Scoom hylti *frutices*, Wrt. Voc. ii. 39, 60.

hymblícae *cicuta*, Ep. Gl. 7 d, 8. v. hemlíc.

Hymbre. v. Norþan-, Norþ-, Súþ-hymbre.

hymele, an; *f. The hop plant*; humulus lupulus, Lchdm. ii. 392, col. 2. [*Icel.* humall: *Dan.* humle *hop-plant*.]

hymen, es; *m. A hymn*:—Be ðam hymene ðe wẽ be hire geworhton *of the hymn that we composed about her*, Bd. 4, 19; S. 587, 16.

hýnan, hẽnan; *p.* de *To abuse, humiliate, rebuke, correct, treat with insult* or *contumely, despise, oppress, afflict, ill-treat, bring* or *lay low, subject*:—Ðãm ilcan monnum ðe hẽ ðǽr þreátaþ and hẽnþ *ipsis fratribus qui corriguntur*, Past. 17, 7; Swt. 117, 16. Ða ðe hẽ ðǽr hínþ *those whom he subjects there*, 33, 2; Swt. 218, 19. Hẽ hermcweðend hýneþ *humiliabit calumniatorem*, Ps. Th. 71, 5. Seðe iuih gehẽneþ mec hẽnes seðe wutedlíce mec hẽnes gehẽneþ ðone seðe mec sende *qui vos spernit me spernit, qui autem me spernit spernit eum qui me misit*, Lk. Skt. Lind. 10, 16. Ðæt se bealofulla hýneþ heardlíce *the baleful one cruelly afflicts it*, Exon. 11 b; Th. 16, 27; Cri. 260. Hí hýnaþ ða heorde ðe hí sceoldan healdan *they ill-treat the flock that they ought to keep*, L. I. P. 12;

Th. ii. 320, 17: Swt. A. S. Rdr. 109, 135. Ic hiora fȳnd fylde and hȳnde *ad nihilum inimicos eorum humiliassem*, Ps. Th. 80, 13. Hē Godes hālgan hȳnde mid wītum *he oppressed God's saints with torments*, Homl. Th. ii. 310, 25. Hē bebeád ðæt hié mon on ǣlce healfe hiénde *he ordered that they should be treated with insult on every side*, Ors. 6, 3; Swt. 258, 6. Se gūþsceaþa Geáta leóde hatode and hȳnde, Beo. Th. 4627; B. 2319. Hē heów and hȳnde *he smote and felled*, Byrht. Th. 141, 18; By. 324. Hī Godes cyrican hȳndan and bærndon *they evilly entreated and burned the churches of God*, Chr. 684; Erl. 41, 22. Hȳ ða slōgon and hȳndon ðe ealle Rōmāne friþian woldon, Ors. 4, 1; Bos. 79, 4. Hefe ðū ðīne handa and hȳn hiora oferhygd *raise thine hand and humble their pride*; leva manum tuam in superbiam eorum in finem, Ps. Th. 73, 4. Ne hēn ðū *ne despicias*, Rtl. 43, 13. Hergian and hȳnan *to ravage and ill-use*, Ors. 4, 1; Bos. 79, 1. Of ðæs handum ðe hine hȳnan wolde *from the hands of him that would have laid him low*, Homl. Th. ii. 510, 23. Hē sceal rȳperas and reáferas hatian and hȳnan *robbers and plunderers he must hate and humble*, L. I. P. 2; Th. ii. 304, 20. Ic wolde helpan ðæs ðe unscyldig wǣre and hēnan ðone ðe hine yfelode, Bt. 38, 6; Fox 208, 17. Hēnan ða yflan and fyrþrian ða gōdan *to bring the evil low and to promote the good*, 39, 2; Fox 212, 22. Ic eom frymdi tō ðē ðæt hī helsceaþan hȳnan ne mōton *I am suppliant to thee that fiends of hell may not evil entreat it* [*the soul*], Byrht. Th. 137, 3; By. 180. [*O. E. Hom.* stala and steorfa swiðe eow scal hene: *Laym.* hænen and hatien; *Goth.* haunjan *to humiliate*: *O. Frs.* hēna: *O. H. Ger.* hōnjan *debilitare, illudere*: *Ger.* höhnen.] DER. ā-, for-, ge-hȳnan; *and see* heán.

-hynde. v. six-, twelf-, twȳ-hynde.

hynden, e; *f. A legal association of one hundred men. It will appear from the following passage that the* hynden *was an association of ten tithings*:—Ðæt wē tellan ā x. menn tōgædere and se yldesta bewiste ða nigene tō ǣlcum ðara gelāste ðara ðe wē ealle gecwǣdon and syððan ða hyndena heora tōgædere and ǣnne hyndenman ðe ða x. mynige tō ūre ealre gemǣne þearfe and hig xi. healdan ðære hyndene feoh [*resolved:*] *that we always count ten men together, and that the chief one should direct the nine in each of those duties that we have all agreed upon; and then groups of ten tithings and* [*in each such group*] *one chief man* [hyndenman] *who may admonish the ten* [*chiefs of tithings*] *to the common benefit of us all; and let these eleven keep the money of the* hynden *to which they belong*, L. Æðelst. v. 3; Th. i. 230, 22–232, 3. On ðære hyndenne, L. In. 54; Th. i. 136, 11. v. next word; and see for a discussion of the term Kemble's Saxons in England, i. 242, sqq.

hynden-mann, es; *m. The head man of a* hynden:—Ðæt wē ūs gegaderian a emban ǣnne mōnaþ gif wē māgon and æmtan habban ða hyndenmenn and ða ðe ða teóþunge bewitan ... and habban ða xii [xi?] menn heora metscype tōgædere [*resolved:*] *that we gather to us once every month, if we can and have leisure, the* hyndenmen *and those who direct the tithings* ... *and let these eleven* [*the* hyndenman *and one from each tithing in the* hynden *of which he was the head*] *have their refection together*, L. Æðelst. v. 8; Th. i. 236, 1–6. v. preceding word; and cf. hundred-mann.

hyngrian, hyngran; *p.* ode, ede *To hunger*. I. *with nom. of person*:—Eádige synd gē ðe hingriaþ nū *beati qui nunc esuritis*, Lk. Skt. 6, 21. Eádige ða ðe rihtwīsnesse hingriaþ *beati qui esuriunt justitiam*, Mt. Kmbl. 5, 6. Hingrian is of untrumnysse ðæs gecynnes *esurire ex infirmitate naturæ est*, Bd. 1, 27; S. 494, 14. Hwænne gesāwe wē ðē hingrigendne *quando te vidimus esurientem*, Mt. Kmbl. 25, 37. Ðane hingriendan *famelicum*, Wrt. Voc. ii. 34, 27. Gē gēfon hingrendum hlāf, Exon. 27 b; Th. 83, 12; Cri. 1355. God gefylþ ða hingrigendan mid his gōdum, Homl. Th. i. 202, 35. II. *with dat. or acc. of person*:—Siððan him hingrode *afterwards he hungered*, 166, 12. Him nān þing ne hingrode, 168, 19. Hine hingrede *esuriit*, Lk. Skt. 4, 2. Mē hingrode *esurivi*, Mt. Kmbl. 25, 35. Ðā ongan hyne syððan hingrian *postea esuriit*, 4, 2. [*Piers P.* þe hungreþ: *Goth.* huggrjan *impers. with acc.*: *O. Sax.* gihungrian: *O. Frs.* hungera: *Icel.* hungra: *O. H. Ger.* hungarian *pers. and impers. with acc. esurire*: *Ger.* hungern.] v. ge-hyngran.

hyngrig; *adj. Hungry*:—Ic wæs hingcgrig *esurivi*, Mt. Kmbl. Lind. 25, 35. v. hungrig.

hȳn-ness, e; *f. Humiliation, abasement, proscription*:—Unsceaþþiendra hȳnnysse *proscriptionibus innocentum*, Bd. 1, 6; S. 476, 25, note. v. heán, hȳnan.

hynni-laec *ascolonium*, Ep. Gl. 2 d, 6. v. enne-leác.

hȳnþ, e; hȳnþu [-o]; *indecl. f. Humiliation, abasement, disgrace, contempt, injury, harm, loss*:—Hȳnþ *vel* lyre *vel* hearm *dispendium* vel *damnum* vel *detrimentum*, Ælfc. Gl. 81; Som. 73, 24; Wrt. Voc. 47, 29. Mycel hȳnþ and sceamu hyt ys men nelle wesan ðæt ðæt hē ys and ðæt ðe hē wesan sceal *magnum damnum et verecundia est homini nolle esse quod est, et quod esse debet*, Coll. Monast. Th. 32, 3. Hēnþa *detrimentum, damnum*, Wrt. Voc. ii. 140, 69. Sorh is mē tō secganne hwæt mē Grendel hafaþ hȳnþo gefremed *a grief it is to me to say what harm Grendel hath done me*, Beo. Th. 954; B. 475: 1190; B. 593. Undōm dēman earmum tō hȳnþe *to judge unjust judgment to the injury of the poor*, L. I. P. 11; Th. ii. 318, 24. Hī willaþ geinnian ða æftran hīnþe mid ðām uferan gestreónum *they desire to supply the consequent loss with the heavenly gains*, Homl. Th. i. 340, 33. Hȳnþu and hrāfyl *injury and slaughter*, Beo. Th. 559; B. 277. Wē hēnþo geþoliaþ *we shall suffer humiliation*, Cd. 222; Th. 289, 18; Sat. 399. Helle hiénþu heofones mǣrþu *the disgrace of hell, the glory of heaven*, Exon. 16 b; Th. 37, 10; Cri. 591. Hȳnþu unrim *ills unnumbered*, Cd. 37; Th. 48, 15; Gen. 776. Fela heardra hȳnþa *many cruel injuries*, Beo. Th. 334; B. 166. Hēnþa, Bt. Met. Fox 12, 41; Met. 12, 21. Nā beóþ ða eádige ðe for hȳnþum oððe lirum hwīlwendlīcra hyðða heófiaþ *they are not blessed, who mourn for losses of temporal comforts*, Homl. Th. i. 550, 28. Eall gē ðæt mē dydon tō hȳnþum *ye did all that against me*, Exon. 30 a; Th. 92, 24; Cri. 1514. Hié in hȳnþum sculon wergþu dreógan *in abject state shall they undergo damnation*, Elen. Kmbl. 420; El. 210. Ðū hweorfest of hēnþum in gehyld godes *thou shalt go from humiliations into the grace of God*, Andr. Kmbl. 233; An. 117. Ðæt wē on ðam tōweardan līfe hȳnþa forbūgan māgon *that in the life to come we may escape disgrace*, H. R. 17, 29. Hēnþa, Dōm. L. 6, 88. Ic heóld nū nigon geár wið ealle hȳnþa ðīnes fæder gestreón *I have kept now nine years thy father's wealth from all losses*, Homl. Skt. 9, 42. [*O. E. Hom.* henð: *O. H. Ger.* hōnida *contumelia, ignominia, calumnia, dedecor, crimen, humilitas.*] v. heán, hȳnan.

HYPE, es; *m. The* HIP, *haunch, upper part of the thigh*:—Hype *clunis*, Wrt. Voc. 71, 49: *ilia*, ii. 110, 54. Ānra gehwylc hæfde sweord ofer his hype for nihtlīcum ege *every man had his sword upon his thigh because of fear in the night* [Song of Sol. 3, 8], Blickl. Homl. 11, 18. Dō his sweord tō his hype *ponat vir gladium super femur suum*, Past. 49, 2; Swt. 383, 2. Hypas *clunes*, Ælfc. Gl. 74; Som. 71, 70; Wrt. Voc. 44, 52. [*A. R. R. Glouc.* hupe: *Wick. Chauc.* hipe, hippe: *Goth.* hups; *m*: *Icel.* huppr: *m*: *O. H. Ger.* huf; *f. femur, coxa, clunis*: *Ger.* hüfte.]

hȳpe, an; *f. A heap*:—Hȳpe *acervus*, Wrt. Voc. 74, 70. Hī beóþ gegaderode tō micelre hȳpan gif wē hī weaxan lǣtaþ *they will be gathered together into a great heap, if we let them grow*, Homl. Th. ii. 466, 7. Goldes and seolfres ungerīme hȳpan, i. 450, 21. [Cf. *O. H. Ger.* hūfo; *m. strues, acervus, tumulus, congeries.*] v. mold-hȳpe, heáp.

hype-bān, es; *n. The hip-bone*, Ælfc. Gl. 74; Som. 71, 54; Wrt. Voc. 44, 37. Hupbān *catacrinis*, ii. 22, 63. Hupbānan *lumbi*, 54, 11.

hȳpel, es; *m. A heap*:—On hȳpel *in cumulum, in augmentationem*, Hpt. Gl. 465. Hypplas *congeries*, 499. On reáde hȳplas *in rubicundas congeries*, 449. Cf. scald-hȳflas *vel* sond-hyllas *alga*, Wrt. Voc. ii. 99, 73. [Hupel *acervus*, Wrt. Voc. 89, 44: *Wick.* hipil: *Trev.* huples; *pl.* Cf. also *Wick.* hipilmelum *acervatim.*]

hype-, hup-seax, es; *n. A knife hanging at the hip, a dagger, short sword*:—Lytel sweord *vel* hypesex *pugio* vel *clunabulum*, Ælfc. Gl. 52; Som. 66, 50; Wrt. Voc. 35, 37. Helm oððe hupseax, Exon. 79 a; Th. 297, 6; Crā. 64. Helmas and hupseax, Judth. 12; Th. 26, 15; Jud. 328.

hype-werc, es; *m. Pain in the hip, sciatica*:—Hipwerc *sciascis*, Ælfc. Gl. 11; Som. 57, 42; Wrt. Voc. 19, 45.

HȲR, e; *f.* HIRE, *payment for service done* or *money lent, interest*:—Ne nim ðū nā māre æt him tō hȳre ðonne ðū sealdest. Ne syle ðū ðīn feoh tō hȳre *computabuntur fructus ex tempore, quo vendidit, et quod reliquum est, reddet emptori. Pecuniam tuam non dabis ad usuram*, Lev. 25, 27, 37. Tō hīre *ad usuram*, Deut. 23, 19. Hwī ne sealdest ðū mīn feoh tō hȳre *quare non dedisti pecuniam meam ad mensam*, Lk. Skt. 19, 23. Ðe hyra feoh lǣnaþ tō hȳre *qui pecuniam suam mutuam dant fœnore*, L. Ecg. P. iii. proem; Th. ii. 194, 31. [*Laym.* hure: *A. R.* hure, huire: *Piers P.* hyre: *Wick.* hire: *Du.* huur *wages*: *Dan.* hyre *hire*: *O. Frs.* hēre *a lease.*]

hȳra, an; *m. A hired servant, hireling*:—Se hȳra se ðe nis hyrde *mercenarius qui non est pastor*, Jn. Skt. 10, 12, 13: Homl. Th. i. 238, 14: 240, 15. Hȳrena þeáwe gē fleóþ ... swā se hȳra ðonne hē ðone wulf gesyhþ *ye flee after the manner of hirelings* ... *as the hireling does when he sees the wolf*, Past. 15, 1; Swt. 38, 14.

hȳra, an; *m. One who is subject to another*:—Æþelbryhtes hȳra *sub potestate positus Ædilbercti*, Bd. 2, 3; S. 504, 21.

HȲRAN, hēran, hiéran; *p.* de [*with acc., with infin., and with acc. and infin.*] I. *to* HEAR, *hear of*:—Morgensteorran ðe wē ōðre naman ǣfensteorra nemnan hēraþ *the morning star which we hear called evening star by another name*, Bt. Met. Fox 4, 29; Met. 4, 15. Nǣnigne ic sēlran hȳrde hordmādmum *no better treasure did I ever hear of*, Beo. Th. 2399; B. 1197. Ǣfre ic ne hȳrde ðon cymlīcor ceól gehladenne heáhgestreónum *never have I heard of a bark any fairer laden with treasures*, Andr. Kmbl. 720; An. 360. Wundorlīcor ðonne ǣfre byre monnes hȳrde *more wonderfully than ever child of man heard*, Exon. 57 b; Th. 206, 19; Ph. 129. Ic londbūend secgan hȳrde *I have heard the people of the country say*, Beo. Th. 2697; B. 1346. Ne hȳrde ic idese lǣdan mægen fægerre *I have not heard of a queen leading a fairer force*, Elen. Kmbl. 480; El. 240. Hȳrde ic ðæt hē ðone healsbeáh Hygde gesealde *I have heard that he gave the collar to Hygd*, Beo. Th. 4350; B. 2172. II. *to listen to, follow, serve, obey, be subject to, belong to*:—Ic hēro *servio*, Lk. Skt. Lind. 15, 29. Se port hȳrþ in on Dene *the port belongs to the Danes*, Ors. 1, 1; Swt. 19, 24. Ic gean ðæs landes æt Holungaburnan and ðæs ðe ðǣrtō hȳrþ *I grant the land at*

Hollingbourn and what belongs thereto, Chart. Th. 558, 27. Se haga æt Wiltūne ðe hȳrþ intō Wilig, Cod. Dipl. Kmbl. iii. 415, 4. Hē mīnum lǣrum hȳreþ [MS. hyraþ] *he listens to my teachings*, Exon. 71 a; Th. 264, 29; Jul. 371. Ða men ðe hīraþ intō heora mynstre *the men that belong to their minster*, L. Ælfc. P. 49; Th. ii. 384, 4. Ða īgland ðe in Denemearce hȳraþ, Ors. 1, 1; Swt. 19, 31. Ðās land eall hȳraþ tō Denemearcan, 36; 20, 4. Inc hȳraþ eall *all shall be subject to you two*, Cd. 10; Th. 13, 20; Gen. 205. Gif gē hȳraþ mē *if ye obey me*, 106; Th. 139, 26; Gen. 2315. Ðū tunglu genēdest ðæt hie ðē tō hēraþ *legem pati sidera cogis*, Bt. Met. Fox 4, 10; Met. 4, 5. Hȳrde on ðam ða bysene ðæs ǣrestan hyrdes Godes cyricean *in quo exemplum sequebatur primi pastoris ecclesiæ*, Bd. 2, 4; S. 505, 11. Hié cwǣdan ðæt se ān wǣre sōþ God se ðe Martinus hȳrde *they said that he alone was true God whom Martin followed*, Blickl. Homl. 231. 1. Englas hērdon him *angeli ministrabant illi*, Mk. Skt. Rush. 1, 13. Ðæt Israhēlisce folc hȳrdon gode and Moise his þeówe *populus crediderunt domino et Moysi servo ejus*, Ex. 14, 31. Tō ðǣm landum eallum ðe ðǣrtō hiérdon *to all the lands that thereto belonged*, Chr. 912; Erl. 100, 32. Filgan hī ðam lāfordscipe ðe ðæt land tō hȳre *let them follow the lordship that the land belongs to*, Chart. Th. 549, 33. Eal ðæt folc ðe ðē hīran sceal *omnis populus qui subjectus est tibi*, Ex. 11, 8. Ne mæg nān mon twām hlāfordum hiéran *nemo potest duobus dominis servire*, Past. 18, 2; Swt. 129, 24. Hēra, Mt. Kmbl. Lind. 6, 24. Gif hē Gode wile rihtlīce hȳran, L. Edg. C. 60, note; Th. ii. 256, 36. Him ǣghwilc hȳran scolde gomban gyldan *him each one had to obey, to him pay tribute*, Beo. Th. 20; B. 10. Hēran, Bt. Met. Fox 1, 61; Met. 1, 31. Holdlīce hȳran woldon *were ready loyally to obey*, Andr. Kmbl. 3277; An. 1641. Hǣðengild hȳran wig weorþian *to follow false Gods, to worship idols*, Apstls. Kmbl. 94; Ap. 47. [*Goth.* hausjan: *O. Sax.* hōrian *to hear, obey*: *O. Frs.* hēra: *Icel.* heyra *to hear, hearken; belong to*: *Dan.* höre: *O. H. Ger.* hōrian *audire, auscultare, obedire, pertinere*: *Ger.* hören.] DER. ge-, mis-, ofer-hȳran.

hȳran *to hire.* v. hȳrian.

hyrcnian *to hearken*, Andr. Kmbl. 1307; An. 654: Exon. 47 b; Th. 162, 21; Gū. 979. v. heorcnian.

hyrdan, herdan, hierdan; *p.* de *To make hard, strong* or *bold, to embolden, encourage, brace*:—Sōna æfter ðon suīðe līðelīçe hierde [hirde, Cott. MS.] ða ðe hē unfæsðrāde wisse *caute monendo postmodum, quæ infirma sunt, roborat*, Past. 32, 2; Swt. 213, 8. Tō ðam wāge gesāg heafelan onhylde hyrde ðā gēna ellen on innan *to the wall he sank, bowed his head, yet within did he brace up his strength*, Exon. 51 a; Th. 178, 15; Gū. 1244. Hyrde hine georne *diligently encouraged him*, Wald. 1; Vald. 1, 1. Herd hyge ðinne heortan staðola *make thy soul strong, firm fix thine heart*, Andr. Kmbl. 2427; An. 1215. [*Goth.* ga-hardjan *to harden*: *O. Sax.* gi-herdian *to make strong, firm*: *O. Frs.* herda: *Icel.* herða *to harden, temper* [*iron*]; *to exhort, cheer*: *O. H. Ger.* hartian *confortare.*] DER. ā-, for-, ge-, on-hyrdan. v. heardian.

hyrde. v. hirde.

hyrdel, es; *m. A hurdle, a frame of intertwined twigs* or *bars*:—Hyrdel *cleta, cratis*, Ælfc. Gl. 29; Som. 61, 44; Wrt. Voc. 26, 43: *cratis* i. *flecta*, 49; Som. 65, 88; Wrt. Voc. 34, 20. Ðā forlēt se cāsere ðone hālgan līchaman uppon ðam īsenan hyrdle *then the emperor left the holy body* [*of St. Lawrence*] *on the iron hurdle*, Homl. Th. i. 430, 23. Hyrþil *cratem, flecta*, Wrt. Voc. ii. 105, 45. Hyrdlas *crates*, 80, 22. [*Prompt. Parv.* hyrdel *plecta, flecta, cratis*: *R. Glouc.* an chyrche of herdles and of ȝerden: cf. *Goth.* haurds *a door*: *Icel.* hurð *a door, a hurdle*: *O. H. Ger.* hurt *crates, craticula*: *Ger.* hürde *a hurdle.*]

hyrd-ness. v. hird-ness.

hyrd-rǣden. v. heord-rǣden.

hyrdung, e; *f. Strengthening, restoring*:—Hyrdung *constructio* vel *instructio*: ealdere timbrunga bōte *instructio*: niwe timbrung *constructio*, Ælfc. Gl. 62; Som. 68, 74–6; Wrt. Voc. 39, 57–9. v. hyrdan, ā-hyrding.

hȳre *hire.* v. hȳr.

hȳre-borg, es; *m. Interest, usury*:—Hiéreborg (*or*? hiére, borg) *fenus*, Wrt. Voc. ii. 88, 18.

hȳ-rēd. v. hī-rēd.

hȳred-ness *fame, report*; fama, Lye.

hȳre-gilda, an; *m. One who receives* (?) *pay for service, a mercenary*:—Hȳregildan *mercedarii*, Ælfc. Gl. 8; Som. 56, 96; Wrt. Voc. 18, 46.

hyrel [?]:—Andlang ðære fyrh ðæt hit cymþ tō hyrel; ðonne þwyres ofer hyrel on ða furh ofer clǣnan dūne, Cod. Dipl. Kmbl. iii. 435, 9.

hȳre-, hiére-, hȳr-mann, es; *m. One who obeys*, or *is subject to, another, a subject, follower, servant, subordinate*, [*as an ecclesiastical term*] *a parishioner, a hearer*:—Forðon oft for ðæs lāreówes unwīsdōme misfaraþ ða hiéremenn and oft for ðæs lāreówes wīsdōme unwīsum hiéremonnum biþ geborgen *for often from the ignorance of the teacher the followers go astray, and often from the wisdom of the teacher the followers are preserved*; per pastorum ignorantiam hi, qui sequuntur, offendant, Past. 1, 4; Swt. 29, 5. Se hrygc ðæt sint ða hiéremenn *hi, qui subsequenter inhærent, dorsa nominantur*, Swt. 29, 12. On ōðre wīsan sint tō monianne ða ealdormen on oðre wīsan ða hiéremenn *quomodo admonendi subditi et prælati*, 28; Swt. 189, 13. Bist ðū ūre cyning oððe beóþ wē ðīne hȳrmen *rex noster eris aut subjiciemur ditioni tuæ?* Gen. 37, 8. Wē beódaþ eác ūrum hīremannum *we also command our subjects*, L. Æðelst. v. 8, 7; Th. i. 238, 1. Æt his hȳremannum *from his subordinates*, 11; Th. i. 240, 16. Eówrum hȳremonnum cȳðon *to make known to your parishioners*, L. E. I. 26; Th. ii. 422, 20. His hiéremonnum *auditores suos*, Past. 8; Swt. 53, 17. His hȳrmen, L. Ælfc. P. 46; Th. ii. 384, 22. Is gehwylcum mæssepreóst micel þearf ðæt hē his hȳremen geoine lǣre, L. E. I. 25; Th. ii. 422, 6; 28; Th. ii. 424, 33. v. hȳran.

hȳr-geoht, es; *n. A hired yoke of oxen*:—Be hȳrgeohte, L. In. 60; Th. i. 140, 7.

hȳrian; *p.* ode: hȳran; *p.* de; *pp.* ed *To hire*:—Ūs nān man ne hȳrode *nemo nos conduxit*, Mt. Kmbl. 20, 7. Nān man ūs ne hȳrde, Homl. Th. ii. 76, 5. Seðe wolde hȳrian wyrhtan, 72, 19. [*A. R.* huren: *Prompt. Parv.* hyryn̄ *conduco*: *Laym.* hureden, *p. pl*: *Piers P.* huyred, *pp*: *O. Frs.* hēra: *O. Dut.* hueren: *M. L. Ger.* huren.] v. ā-hȳrian, ge-hȳran.

hyrian; *p.* ede *To imitate*:—Hió hyrigaþ monnum *they imitate men*, Bt. 41, 5; Fox 252, 26. v. æfter-, on-hyrian.

hȳrig-mann, es; *m. A subject, follower, parishioner*:—Hȳrigmonnum, L. E. I. 26; Th. ii. 422, 27. Hȳrigmen, 28; Th. ii. 424, 16. v. hȳre-mann.

hȳrig-mann, es; *m. A person hired to work*:—Ðā gewearþ ðam hlāforde and ðām hȳrigmannum wið ānum peninge *an agreement to work for a penny was made between the lord and the workmen he had hired*, Th. An. 73, 30.

hȳrling, es; *m. A hireling, one who works for hire*:—Hī heora fæder on scipe forlēton mid hȳrlingum *relicto patre suo in navi cum mercenariis*, Mk. Skt. 1, 20.

hȳr-mann, es; *m. One who works for hire*:—Hȳrman *mercenarius*, Wrt. Voc. 86, 40. Mid ðǣm hȳremonnum *cum mercenariis*, Mk. Skt. Rush. 1, 20. [Hurmon, Wrt. Voc. 95, 51.]

hȳr-mann. v. hȳre-mann.

hyrnan; *p.* de *To project in the shape of a horn* or *wedge*:—Andlang ðæs streámes on ðone mǣdham ðe hyrnþ into Scylftūne and fram Scylftūne andlang streámes ðæt it cymþ tō ðam mylewere ðe hyrnþ intō duceling dūne *along the stream to the meadow-enclosure that projects wedge-shaped into Scylfton; and from Scylfton along stream until it comes to the mill-weir that juts out into Ducklingdown*, Cod. Dipl. Kmbl. iv. 92, 29. [Cf. '*Herne*, a nook of land, projecting into another district, parish, or field,' Forby.] v. hyrne.

hyrne, an; *f. A horn, corner, angle*:—Hyrne *angulus*, Wrt. Voc. 80, 73. Ðæt wæter ðe man ða bān mid āþwōh binnan ðære cyrcan wearþ āgoten on ānre hyrnan *the water that the bones were washed with in the church was poured away in a corner*, Swt. A. S. Rdr. 100, 162. Tō ðæs hegges hyrnan *to the corner of the hedge*, Cod. Dipl. Kmbl. iii. 423, 18. Tō mōrmǣde norþ hyrnan, 449, 19. On strǣta hyrnum *in angulis platearum*, Mt. Kmbl. 5, 6. On ðæs weofodes hyrnan *super cornua altaris*, Ex. 29, 12: Lev. 4, 18: 8, 15. On ða feówer hyrnan ðære earce *per quatuor arcæ angulos*, Past. 22, 1; Swt. 169, 21. [*A. R.* hurne: *R. Glouc.* hurne: *Prompt. Parv.* hyrne *angulus*, see note, p. 241: *Chauc.* herne: *Piers P.* huirne, hirne, hyrne: *O. Frs.* herne: *Icel.* hyrna *one of the horns* or *points of an axe-head; a mountain peak.*] v. horn.

-hyrne. v. ān-, þreó-hyrne.

hyrned; *adj. Provided with a horn* or *beak* [*of a ship*], *having angles* or *corners*:—Ða hyrnedan næddran *the horned snakes*, Homl. Th. i. 102, 7. Hyrnde ciólas *ships having horn-shaped prows*, Bt. Met. Fox 26, 46; Met. 26, 23. v. ān-, eahta-, ofer-, six-hyrned.

hyrned-nebba; *adj. Horny-* or *hard-beaked* [*epithet of raven and eagle*], Judth. 11; Thw. 24, 28; Jud. 212: Chr. 937; Erl. 115, 11; Æðelst. 62.

hyrnen; *adj. Made of horn*:—On stefne bēmen hyrnenre [Ps. Spl. bȳman hyrnendre; Ps. Stev. hornes hyrnes; *Wick.* þe hornene trumpe] *voce tubæ corneæ*, Ps. Lamb. 97, 6. [*O. H. Ger.* hurnin *corneus.*]

hȳr-ness, e; *f. Obedience, subjection, a district in subjection to secular* or *ecclesiastical authority*:—His mōd biþ āfēdd mid ðære smeáunga ðære wilnunga ōðerra monna hiérnesse *in occulta meditatione cogitationis ceterorum subjectione pascitur*, Past. 8, 2; Swt. 55, 6. Hē underþeódde and him tō hērenysse geteáh *subjecit*, Bd. 3, 24; S. 557, 33. Wæs hē ǣrest arcebiscopa ðæt him eall Angelcynn hȳrnysse geþafode *is primus erat in archiepiscopis, cui omnis Anglorum ecclesia manus dare consentiret*, 4, 2; S. 565, 22. Underþeódde on hērnysse *subjecti*, 30; S. 561, 36. Ne spane nān mæssepreóst nǣnne mon of ōðre cyrcean hȳrnysse tō his cyrcan ne of ōðre preóstscyre lǣre ðæt mon his cyrcan geséce *let no priest entice any man from the parish of another church to his church, nor persuade any one to come from another district to attend his church*, L. E. I. 14; Th. ii. 410, 31. Eall Beorcleá hȳrnesse hī āwǣston, Chr. 1087; Erl. 224, 21. From hwǣm ondfōaþ gæfle oððe hērnisse *a quibus accipiunt tributum vel censum?* Mt. Kmbl. Rush. 17, 25. v. mis-hȳrness; hȳran, hȳre-mann.

hyrnetu, hyrnet, e; *f. A hornet*:—Hyrnet *crabro*, Ælfc. Gl. 22; Som. 59, 107; Wrt. Voc. 23, 63. Hyrnetu *crabro*, ii. 16, 25. Hurnitu, 105, 46. Ic āsende hyrnytta *mittam crabrones*, Ex. 23, 28. [*O. H. Ger.* hornuz *crabro, scabro*: *Ger.* horniss.]

hyrn-ful; *adj. Full of corners*; angulosus, Hpt. Gl. 409.

hyrn-stān, es; *m. A corner-stone*:—Hē is se hyrnstān ðe gefēgþ ða twegen weallas tōgædere *he is the corner-stone that joins together the two* *walls*, Homl. Th. i. 106, 12, 23. [*Orm.* he wass himm sellf þatt hirnestan þatt band ta twe33enn wa3hess.]

hýr-oxa, an; *m. A hired ox*, L. In. 60; Th. i. 140, 7, note.

hyrst, e, *f. An ornament, a decoration, jewel, anything of value, trapping, equipment, armour, implement*:—Hyrsta *falerarum*, Wrt. Voc. ii. 36, 74. Hryste *farelas*, 108, 34. Hyrsta scýne bord and bräd swyrd brúne helmas *beautiful equipments, shield and broad sword, brown helms*, Judth. 12; Thw. 26, 9; Jud. 317: Fins. Th. 41; Fin. 20. Bēg and siglu eall swylce hyrsta swylce on horde ǽr men genumen hæfdon *ring[s] and jewels, just such ornaments as before men had taken in the hoard*, Beo. Th. 6309; B. 3165. Íren byrnan heard swyrd hilted and his helm hāres hyrste *the iron byrnie, the hard and hilted sword, and his helm, the hoary one's equipments*, 5968; B. 2988. Hyrste [hyrsta, Soul Kmbl. 114] ða reádan ne gold ne seolfor [*not*] *the red ornaments, nor gold nor silver*, Exon. 99 a; Th. 370, 15; Seel. 57. Hwílum mec āhebbaþ hyrste míne *sometimes my trappings* [*wings*] *raise me up*, 103 a; Th. 390, 1; Rä. 8, 4: 103 b; Th. 392, 16; Rä. 11, 8: Th. 392, 24; Rä. 12, 1. Hyrste gerīm rodores tungel *number* [*heaven's*] *ornaments, the stars of the firmament*, Cd. 100; Th. 132, 7; Gen. 2189. Ðeáh ðe hyrsta unrīm ǽhte *though he owned jewels unnumbered*, Exon. 66 b; Th. 245, 12; Jul. 43. Ne mōt hē ðara hyrsta hionane lǽdan wuhte ðon māre hordgestreóna ðonne hē hider brohte *defunctum leves non comitantur opes*, Bt. Met. Fox 14, 17–22; Met. 14, 9–11. Fyrnmanna fatu hyrstum behrorene *vessels of men of old, deprived of their ornaments*, Beo. Th. 5517; B. 2762. Hilderincas hyrstum gewerede, Elen. Kmbl. 526; El. 263. Hyrstum frætwed wlitig on wāge, Exon. 104 a; Th. 395, 22; Rä. 15, 11: 108 b; Th. 413, 15; Rä. 32, 20: 113 b; Th. 436, 1; Rä. 54, 7: 129 a; Th. 495, 22; Rä. 85, 7. [*O. H. Ger.* hrusti, Grff. ii. 546.] DER. ge-, wīg-hyrst.

hyrst, es; *m. A hurst, copse, wood.* The word occurs most frequently in compounds, e. g. *hnut-hyrst, æsc-hyrst*, etc., and is still found as *hurst* in names of places. See Cod. Dipl. Kmbl. iii. xxxii, and Leo's Anglo-Saxon Names, p. 107:—In hyrst sciofingden, Cod. Dipl. Kmbl. i. 273, 6. Wermōd hēr on hyrstum heasewe standeþ *wormwood stands dusky here in the woods* [Grein takes *hyrstum* under the previous word], Exon. 111 a; Th. 425, 24; Rä. 41, 61. v. horst, hurst, Grff. iv. 1042.

hyrstan, hrystan; *p.* te; *pp.* ed *To ornament, decorate, deck*:—Beón hyrst *comi*, Wrt. Voc. ii. 23, 43. Hyrsted sweord, Beo. Th. 1349; B. 672. Helm hyrsted golde, 4503; B. 2255. Hyrsted gold *gold fairly wrought*, Cd. 98; Th. 130, 5; Gen. 2155. Hyrstedne hrōf hālgum tunglum *the* [*heavenly*] *canopy adorned with holy stars*, 46; Th. 58, 34; Gen. 956. Beorc byþ on helme hyrsted [hrysted, MS.] fægere *the birch at its top is fairly adorned*, Runic pm. Kmbl. 342, 32; Rūn. 18. [*O. H. Ger.* hrusten *ornare*, Grf. ii. 546.] v. ge-hyrstan; īsen-hyrst.

hyrstan, hierstan; *p.* te; *pp.* ed *To fry, roast*:—Ic herste *frigo*, Ælfc. Gr. 28; Som. 31, 64. Hwæt is þinga ðe bietere sīe on ðæs lāreówes mōde oððe hit suīður hierste *quid vero acrius doctoris mentem frigit?* Past. 21, 6; Swt. 165, 2. Nim āne clǽne panne and hyrste hȳ mid ele *take a clean pan and fry them with oil*, Lchdm. iii. 136, 4. Hē hine hēt āþenian on īrenum bedde and hine cwicne hirstan and brǽdan and swā hine mon mā hirste swā wæs hē fægera on ondwlitan *he ordered him to be stretched on an iron bed and roasted alive; and the more he was roasted the fairer was his face*, Shrn. 116, 3–5. v. ge-hyrstan.

hyrste *a little gridiron*; craticula, Wrt. Voc. ii. 136, 53.

hyrste-panne. v. hearste-panne.

hyrst-geard, es; *m. An enclosed wood* [?]:—In ðone hyrstgeard, Cod. Dipl. Kmbl. iii. 19, 1.

hyrsting, hiersting, e; *f. Frying, burning, a frying-pan* [?]:—Hyrstincg *cremium*, Ps. Lamb. 101, 4. Hyrstyngc[-panne?] *frixorium*, Wrt. Voc. 82, 69. Hyrstung *frixorium*, Ælfc. Gr. 28; Som. 31, 65. Hyrsting *frixura*, Wrt. Voc. ii. 150, 84. Mid ðisse pannan hierstinge wæs Paulus onbærned *Paulus hujus sartaginis urebatur frixura*, Past. 21, 6; Swt. 165, 3. [Cf. *O. H. Ger.* harsta *frixura.*]

hyrsting-hlāf, es; *m. Crust*:—Herstinghlāfum *crustis*, Wrt. Voc. ii. 18, 51.

hyrsting-panne, an; *f. A frying-pan*:—Hyrsting [dyrsting, MS.] panne *sartago* vel *frixorium*, Ælfc. Gl. 25; Som. 60, 59; Wrt. Voc. 25, 1.

hyrsudon [?], Bd. 3, 14; S. 540, 11, note.

hȳr-, heár-sum; *adj. Obedient, compliant*:—Se ðe him hȳrsum beón wolde hē gehēt *qui sibi obtemperantibus promitteret*, Bd. 1, 25; S. 486, 26. Him hȳrsum beón *ei obtemperare*, 2, 12; S. 574, 16. Hit biþ his lāreówum hȳrsum *it is obedient to its teachers*, Salm. Kmbl. 798; Sal. 398. Wē beóþ hīrsume *erimus obedientes*, Ex. 24, 7. Nemne ic gode sylle hȳrsumne hige *unless I give to God an obedient mind*, Exon. 37 b; Th. 124, 13; Gū. 340. Heársume, 42 b; Th. 144, 13; Gū. 677: 43 a; Th. 145, 19; Gū. 697. [*O. E. Homl.* her-sum: *Orm.* herr-summ: *Laym.* hær-sum: *O. H. Ger.* hōr-sam.] v. ge-hȳrsum.

hȳrsumian; *p.* ode, ede *To be obedient, obey, serve*:—Windas and sǽ him hȳrsumiaþ *venti et mare obediunt ei*, Mt. Kmbl. 8, 27; Homl. Th. ii. 368, 28. Hȳrsumiaþ *ancillantur*, Ælfc. Gl. 100; Som. 77, 6; Wrt. Voc. 55, 9. Wē ðē on ðissum ne hērsumiaþ *we shall not obey thee in this*, Blickl. Homl. 243, 19. Ða hālgan heofonware him hȳrsumedon, 135, 17. Hē ðǽm bebodum heársumede, Bd. 2, 6; S. 508, 41. [*O. E. Homl.* hersumian: *O. H. Ger.* hōrsamōn *obedire.*] v. ge-hȳrsumian.

hȳrsum-ness, e; *f. Obedience, subjection*:—Myrcna cyninge on hȳrsumnesse underþeódded syndon *Merciorum regi subjectæ sunt*, Bd. 5, 23; S. 646, 27. Þurh ða hȳrsumnysse ðe wē heom hȳrsomiaþ *through the obedience with which we obey them*, L. Edg. S. 1; Th. i. 272, 21. [*O. E. Homl.* hersamnisse: *Laym.* hersumnesse.] v. ge-hȳrsumnys.

hyrtan, hiertan; *p.* te *To* HEARTEN, *encourage, animate*:—To heora āgenre þearfe hyrteþ *ad propriam eorum necessitatem animat*, L. M. I. P. 13; Th. ii. 266, 8. Hyrt *cohortat*, Wrt. Voc. ii. 136, 5. Mid ōðrum worde hē hierte mid ōðrum hē brēgde *favet ergo ex desiderio, et terret ex præcepto*, Past. 8, 1; Swt. 53, 11. Hyrte hyne hordweard *the hoard-ward* [*dragon*] *took courage*, Beo. Th. 5179; B. 2593. [*Laym.* hirten: *Prompt. Parv.* hertyn *animo.*] v. ge-hyrtan.

hyrwan, hyrwian; *p.* de, ede *To speak ill* or *contemptuously of any one, blaspheme, despise, condemn, treat ill, oppress, vex, harass*:—Óðerne herweþ *alterum contemnet*, Mt. Kmbl. Rush. 6, 24. Ða earman ðe nū Godes bebodu hyrwiaþ beóþ cwylmede *the miserable men that now despise God's commandments shall be tormented*, L. E. I; Th. ii. 396, 36. Ðū heruwdest Godes bebodu, Blickl. Homl. 49, 36. Hē hyrwde godes naman and wirigde hine *cum blasphemasset nomen et maledixisset ei*, Lev. 24, 11. Ðā hyrwdon hī ealle hine *omnes condemnaverunt eum*, Mk. Skt. 14, 64. Hié hyrwdon ðē *they despised thee*, Elen. Kmbl. 710; El. 355. Gē gewritu herwdon *ye despised the scriptures*, 774: El. 387. Ne hyrw ðū ūre godas *blaspheme not our gods*, Homl. Th. i. 424, 13. Ne hyrwe gē ūtancymenne man *non exprobretis advenæ*, Lev. 19, 33. Sceal wīs cyning cristendōm miclian and mǽrsian and ā hē sceal hǽðendōm hindrian and hyrwan *a wise king must extend and magnify christianity, and ever must he hinder and harass heathendom*, L. I. P. 2; Th. ii. 306, 7. [*O. H. Ger.* harwian *exasperare*, Grff. iv. 1043.] v. ge-hyrwan.

hyrwe *name of a tree*; torriculum, Wrt. Voc. 285, 50.

hyrwend, es; *m. A blasphemer*:—Lēd ūt ðone hirwend *educ blasphemum*, Lev. 24, 14.

hyrwend-līc; *adj. Contemptible, despicable*:—Heruuendlīcae *contemptum*, Ep. Gl. 7 d, 9. Heuuendlīce, Wrt. Voc. ii. 104, 31. Ða hirwendlīcan *contemtibiliora*, 15, 62.

hyrw-ness, e; *f. Contempt, reproach*:—Hirwnessæ *contemptus*, Ps. Spl. T. 118, 141. Gefylled wē synd hirwnesseum *repleti sumus despectione*, 122, 4.

hyscan; *p.* te *To mock, deride, taunt, reproach*:—Hē hiscþ geþeahtas ealdra *reprobat consilia principum*, Ps. Lamb. 32, 10. Seðe eardaþ on heofonum hyseþ [hyscþ?] hȳ *qui habitat in cælis irridebit eos*, Ps. Spl. T. 2, 4. Ðonne hyscte hē on ða godcundan lāreówas, Wulfst. 235, 25. Hyhsan *conviciari*, Gl. Prud. 696. Hihsendes *subsannantis*, Hpt. Gl. 524. v. husc, ge-, in-hyscan.

hyse, es; *m. A young man, warrior*:—Hyse cwom gangan *there came a young man*, Exon. 113 b; Th. 436, 14; Rä. 55, 1. Him be healfe stōd hyse unweaxen cniht on gecampe *by his side stood a youth not yet grown up, a boy in battle*, Byrht. Th. 136, 17; By. 152. Hyse [*Beowulf*], Beo. Th. 2438; B. 1217: Andr. Kmbl. 1190; An. 595: 1622; An. 812: Elen. Kmbl. 1043; El. 523. Hē lēt his francan wadan þurh ðæs hysses hals *he pierced the man's neck with his javelin*, Byrht. Th. 135, 60; By. 141. Hysse ðīnum *puero tuo*, Ps. Th. 85, 15. Tō Abrahame his āgenum hysse *ad Abraham puerum suum*, 104, 37. Ðissum hysse hold *gracious to this man*, Andr. Kmbl. 1099; An. 550. Hysas, Byrht. Th. 135, 24; By. 123. Beornas feóllon, hyssas lāgon, 135, 2; By. 112. Noldon ða hyssas hȳran lārum hǽðnum *the youths would not listen to heathen lore*, Cd. 183; Th. 229, 14; Dan. 217: 184; Th. 230, 11; Dan. 231. Hēt hyssa hwæne *bade each man*, Byrht. Th. 131, 2; By. 2: 135, 34; By. 128: Fins. Th. 96; Fin. 48. v. þegn-hyse.

hyse-beorþor, -berþor, -borþor, es; *n. The bearing of male offspring, the offspring itself, a young man*:—Hyseberþor *puerperium*, Mone B. 3894. Hyseborþor, 4975. Hysebeorþ[or], Wrt. Voc. ii. 94, 42. Woldon on ðam hysebeorþre [cf. 2253, se geonga] heafolan gescēnan *they would hurt the head of the man*, Andr. Kmbl. 2285; An. 1144. v. beorþor.

hyse-berþling, es; *m. The bearing of a male child, a male child* [?]; *puerperium*, Ælfc. Gl. 5; Som. 56, 8; Wrt. Voc. 17, 16.

hyse-cild, es; *n. A male child*:—Ǽlc hysecild betwux eów beó ymbsniden *circumcidetur ex vobis omne masculinum*, Gen. 17, 10. Gif hit hysecild byþ *si masculus fuerit*, Ex. 1, 16. Hyscild *mas*, Ælfc. Gl. 86; Som. 74, 22; Wrt. Voc. 50, 6. Beó hit hysecild beó hit mǽdencild *sit masculus infans, sit femina*, L. Ecg. P. ii. 21; Th. ii. 190, 21: L. M. cont. 2, 60; Lchdm. ii. 172, 17. Ðā fēddon hié ða mǽdencild and slōgon ða hysecild *mares enecant, feminas nutriunt*, Ors. 1, 10; Swt. 46, 11: Homl. Th. i. 30, 15.

hyseþ, Ps. Spl. T. 2, 4. v. hyscan.

hyse-wīse, an; *f. The manner of young men*:—Hysewīse *hircitallo*, Wrt. Voc. ii. 43, 26. This gloss is sufficiently explained by the following quotation from Paulus' epitome of Festus, ed. Müller, p. 101:—*Hirquitalli* pueri primum ad virilitatem accedentes, a libidine scilicet hircorum dicti. Further, in the notes to this word is added, *hirquitalli βούπαιδες*; *irquitalus νηπιώτατος*.

hyspan; *p.* te *To mock, scorn, taunt, revile, insult, reproach*:—Drihten hispeþ hý *Dominus subsannabit eos*, Ps. Spl. 2, 4. Hú lange hyspeþ feónd *usque quo improperabit inimicus?* 73, 11. Se ðe hespþ *qui calumniatur*, Kent. Gl. 497. Hý mē hyspaþ *exprobraverunt me*, Ps. Th. 41, 12. Tōgeánes mē hyspton ealle fýnd míne *adversum me susurrabant omnes inimici mei*, Ps. Spl. C. 40, 8. Hyne hyspdun *improperabant ei*, Mt. Kmbl. 27, 44. Ðone hyspton *quod exprobraverunt*, Blickl. Gl. Hié Cristes bebod hyspton and hit forsāwon *they scorned Christ's commandment and despised it*, Ors. 6, 3; Swt. 256, 25. Hysptun hearmcwidum *mocked opprobriously*, Exon. 24 a; Th. 69, 15; Cri. 1121. Ðæt nā hyspen *ut non insultent*, Blickl. Gl. Hyspan *exprobrare*, Mt. Kmbl. 11, 20. Ongan hine hyspan and hearmcwiddigan, Bt. 18, 4; Fox 66, 33: Andr. Kmbl. 1341; An. 671. Fram stemne hyspendes *a voce exprobrantis*, Ps. Spl. 43, 18. Hyspendra *exprobrantium*, Blickl. Gl. v. hosp, ge-hyspan.

hyspend. v. hyspan.

hysping, e; *f. Reproach, reviling, contumely*:—Siððan hē his hyspinge gehēred hæfde *acceptaque contumelia*, Bt. 18, 4; Fox 66, 35.

hysp-ness, e; *f. Reproach, opprobrium*:—Ðū settest ūs hyspnesse neáhgebūrum ūrum *posuisti nos opprobrium vicinis nostris*, Ps. Spl. T. 43, 15.

HÝÐ, e; *f.* '*A* HITHE, or *place that receives the ship, etc., on its landing; a low shore, fit to be a landing place for boats, etc.,' a port, haven*:—Hýð *angiportus, i. refrigerium navium*, Ælfc. Gl. 5; Som. 56, 32; Wrt. Voc. 17, 36: *confugium*, i. *statium, portus*, ii. 131, 51. Hýð *portus*, Ælfc. Gr. 11; Som. 15, 8. Seó ān hýð byþ simle smyltu æfter eallum ðām ýstum ūrra geswinca *hic portus placida manens quiete*, Bt. 34, 8; Fox 144, 27: Bt. Met. Fox 21, 21, 25; Met. 21, 11, 13. Ðæt hie wilnigen ðære hýðe ðæs gesinscipes *ut conjugii portum petant*, Past. 51, 8; Swt. 401, 33. Martha swanc ðā swilce on rēwette and Maria sæt stille swilce æt ðære hýðe, Homl. Th. ii. 440, 32. Hera ðone steórman ac nā ǣrðan ðe hē become gesundful tō ðære hýðe, 560, 22. Cōmon ðǣr þrý men tō ðære hýðe *three men came to the landing-place*, Guthl. 11; Gdwin. 54, 24. Ðǣr æt hýðe stōd æðelinges fær, Beo. Th. 63; B. 32: Elen. Kmbl. 495; El. 248: Exon. 52 a; Th. 182, 8; Gū. 1307. Hē hí on hǣlo hýðe gelǣdde *eduxit eos in portum*, Ps. Th. 106, 29; Exon. 20 b; Th. 53, 34; Cri. 860: Salm. Kmbl. 489; Sal. 245. [*Prompt. Parv.* hyþe, where bootys ryve to londe, or stonde *stacio.* 'Hithe occurs in the names of seaports, and also landing-places on rivers, far from the coast,' p. 242, note 1. Kemble, Cod. Dipl. iii. xxxii, notes 'Rotherhithe (hrýðra hýð) the place where oxen were landed; Clayhithe, near Cambridge; Erith, in Kent and Cambridge, Eárhýð; Cwēnhýð, Queenhithe.']

hyð; *gen.* hyðde; *f. Advantage, gain, profit, benefit*:—Hyð *vel* freme *commodum, questus*, Ælfc. Gl. 81; Som. 73, 25; Wrt. Voc. 47, 30. Gif feohbōt ārīseþ ðæt gebyreþ rihtlīce tō þearfena hyðde *if a money-fine arises, it is properly applied for the benefit of the needy*, L. Eth. vi. 51; Th. i. 328, 6. Uton dōn þearfum sume hyðde ūre gōda *let us do some good to the needy with our wealth*, Homl. Th. ii. 100, 35. Ða ðe for lirum hwīlwendlīcra hyðda heófiaþ *those who mourn for losses of temporary advantages*, i. 550, 29. On earmra manna hyððum *for the advantage of poor men*, L. I. P. 19; Th. ii. 328, 11. Se hýra smeáþ embe ða woruldlīcan hyðða and lǣt tō gýmeleáste ðæra sceápa lyre *the hireling inquires after worldly advantages, and leaves to neglect the loss of the sheep*, Homl. Th. i. 240, 29.

hýðan; *p.* de *To despoil, plunder, lay waste, pillage, ravage*:—Hīðeþ and tō hām týhþ *it plunders and brings home*, Exon. 109 a; Th. 416, 25; Rä. 35, 4. Hýðaþ wíde gīfre glēde *widely shall the greedy flames lay waste*, 23 a; Th. 64, 28; Cri. 1044. Hit feor and wíde hýðde and hergode *longe lateque devastans*, Bd. 3, 16; S. 542, 17. Cwæþ ðæt hē mid his gesīðum wolde hýðan eal heofona rīce *said that with his comrades he would ravage all the kingdom of heaven*, Salm. Kmbl. 909; Sal. 454. Hīðende lēg *the wasting flame*, Exon. 22 a; Th. 60, 23; Cri. 974: 130 b; Th. 499, 28; Rä. 88, 22: 109 a; Th. 416, 5; Rä. 34, 7. Hīðendum *grassantibus*, Wrt. Voc. ii. 41, 49. [Cf. *O. H. Ger.* far-hundit *captivus*, Grff. iv. 965.] v. hūð, ā-hýðan.

hyðegung, e; *f. Profit, advantage*; commodum, Lye. v. ge-hyðegod.

hyðe-lic; *adj. Convenient, advantageous*:—Ðæt wæs hyðelīc *that was convenient*, Exon. 124 b; Th. 478, 17; Ruin. 42. v. hyð, ge-hyðelīc, be-hyðelīce.

hýð-gild, es; *n. A port-due* [?]:—Hýðgilda *portunalia*, Hpt. Gl. 515.

hýð-lic; *adj. Relating to a port*:—Ða hýðlīcan *portunalia*, Wrt. Voc. ii. 67, 19.

hýð-scip, es; *n. A pirate-ship*:—Hīðscip *myoparo*, Ælfc. Gl. 103; Som. 77, 100; Wrt. Voc. 56, 21. Hýdscip *mioparo*, ii. 59, 26. v. hýðan.

hýð-weard, es; *m. One who guards a hithe*, Beo. Th. 3833; B. 1914.

hyw. v. hiw.

hýwyt *hewn, cut*; dolatum, i. incisum, planum, Wrt. Voc. ii. 141, 63.

I

THE Runic character ᛁ for this vowel was named *ís*:—Īs byþ oferceald ungemetum slidor; glisnaþ glæshluttur gimmum gelícust, Runic pm. Kmbl. p. 341.

The short *i* generally corresponds to Gothic *i*, e. g. *in*, Goth. *in*, *biddan*, Goth. *bidjan*; the long *i*, which is sometimes written *ii*, é. g. *riiknæ* on the Ruthwell Cross, to Gothic *ei*, e. g. *ísern*, Goth. *eisarn*, *bídan*, Gothic *beidan*. In early West Saxon MSS., however, *i*, *í* are found arising from other sources. Thus the mutation of the breaking *ea* is written *i*, e. g. *ildu*, *irmþu* from *eald*, *earm*; and the mutations of *eó*, *eá* are written *í*, e. g. *onlíhtan*, *híran*. In such cases, however, instead of *i* the diphthong *ie* is very often found; and not only in such, but also in those where the root-vowel is *i* or *í*, e. g. *ongietan*, *wietan* [= *wítan*]; even in the place of *ý*, e. g. *iedegende*. In the later MSS. instead of *i* or *ie*, *y* is found very commonly; indeed even in the earlier MSS. *y* has in some instances already made its way into the place of *i*, thus *ryht* is the form regularly used in Alfred's translation of Gregory's Pastoral Care. In the case of *niht* in the earliest times, in that of *miht* and its compounds in later, *i* takes the place of original *a*.

Initial *i* before *a*, *o*, *u* is found where most generally *ge* is used; for examples see below.

iā; *adv. Yea*:—Ǣt ðū tōdæg? Iā ic dyde *manducasti hodie? Etiam feci*, Ælfc. Gr. 31; Som. 40, 17. Eart ðū Esau mīn sunu? And hē cwæþ: Iā leóf ic hit eom *tu es filius meus Esau? Respondit: Ego sum*, Gen. 27, 23. Se kyng befealh georne hire brēðer ōþ ðæt hē cwæþ jā wið *the king pressed her brother eagerly until he said yes in reply*, Chr. 1067; Erl. 204, 23. v. geá.

iáces sūre, Wrt. Voc. 286, 21. v. geác.

iacinð, es; *m. Jacinth*:—Iacinðe [iacinte, Cot. MS.] *ex hyacintho*, Past. 14, 4; Swt. 87, 3.

Ianuarius; *m. January*:—Forma mōnaþ folc mycel Ianuarius hēton *the Romans called the first month January*, Menol. Fox 19; Men. 10.

IC; *pron. of* 1*st pers. s. I*:—Ic Æðelstān cyningc cýðe *I, king Athelstan, proclaim*, L. Ath. 1, prm; Th. i. 194, 2. Ic hyt eom *it is I*; ego sum, Mt. Kmbl. 14, 27. Ic sylf hit eom *ipse ego sum*, Lk. Skt. 24, 39. Ic eom Gabriel ic ðe stande beforan gode *ego sum gabrihel qui adsto ante deum*, 1, 19. For Wulfgāres sāwle ðe ic hit selle *for Wulfgar's soul* [*I*] *who give it*, Chart. Th. 496, 24. [*Laym. O. and N.* ic, ich, ihc: *Orm.* icc, I: *Chauc.* ich, I: *Goth. O. Frs. O. Sax.* ik: *Icel.* ek: *Dan.* jeg: *Swed.* jag: *O. H. Ger.* ih: *Ger.* ich: *Lat.* ego; *Gk.* ἐγώ.] For other forms in the declension of the pronoun of the first person, see the several words.

īcan, iécan, īcean, ýcan; *p.* īhte, īcte *To* EKE, *increase, add to, augment*:—Ðū ýcest ðīne yrmþo *thou dost increase thy misery*, Andr. Kmbl. 2381; An. 1192. Hwæt is ðis manna ðe īceþ ealdne nīð *what man is this that adds to ancient hate?* Elen. Kmbl. 1806; El. 905. Ýceþ, Exon. 89 a; Th. 335, 9; Gn. Ex. 31. Sunne and mōna iécaþ eorþwelan *sun and moon increase the wealth of earth*, 16 b; Th. 38, 23; Cri. 611. Ýcaþ, 119 a; Th. 457, 32; Hy. 4, 93. Ðā īhte hē eft his synna *auxit peccatum*, Ex. 9, 34. Ðǣr eác ýcte tō *also he added thereto*, Bd. 4, 16; S. 584, 15. Iécte, Cd. 55; Th. 68, 25; Gen. 1122: 108; Th. 143, 9; Gen. 2376. Īcte, 59; Th. 72, 22; Gen. 1190. Siððan wōcan ða īcton mǣgburh Caines *afterwards were born those who increased the kindred of Cain*, 52; Th. 65, 13; Gen. 1065. In eallum hī ðissum īhtan synne *in omnibus his peccaverunt adhuc*, Ps. Th. 77, 31. Ac ða hwīle ðe hē giernþ ðæt hē his welan iéce hē āgiémeleásaþ ðæt hē forbūge his synna *profecto enim, qui augere opes ambit, vitare peccatum negligit*, Past. 44, 9; Swt. 331, 16. Hwylc eówer mæg þencende īcan āne elne tō his anlīcnesse *quis vestrum cogitando potest adjicere ad staturam suam cubitum unum?* Lk. Skt. 12, 25. Ðū gehēte ðæt ðū hýra frumcyn īcan wolde *thou didst promise that thou wouldest increase their race*, Cd. 190; Th. 236, 8; Dan. 318. Hī sculon ǣlce dæg eácan [Cott. MS. ýcan] ðæt mon ǣlce dæg wanaþ, Bt. 26, 2; Fox 94, 1. Ýcan, Judth. 11; Thw. 24, 11; Jud. 183: Exon. 108 a; Th. 413, 3; Rä. 31, 9. Ýcean *augmentare*, Bd. 2, 4; S. 505, 16. Ýced *increased*, Exon. 53 b; Th. 187, 25; Az. 36. [*Laym.* æchen, eche: *Orm.* ekenn: *R. Glouc. Chauc.* eche: *O. Sax.* ōkian: *O. H. Ger.* auhhōn *augere, adjicere.*] v. eác, ēcan, eácan.

ice. v. yce.

īcend, es; *m. One who increases* or *augments*:—Ðon hē cymþ of ðam worde *augeo* ic geīce and hē getācnaþ geeácnunge ðon macaþ hē *hic auctor* ðes īcend and *hæc auctrix* ðeós īcestre *when it comes from the word* augeo *I increase, and indicates augmentation, then it makes* hic auctor *this augmenter, and* hæc auctrix *this augmentress*, Ælfc. Gr. 9, 21; Som. 10, 42–4.

īcestre, an; *f.* v. preceding word.

icge gold, Beo. Th. 2219; B. 1107. The translation of this phrase is difficult. Thorpe has 'moreover,' Kemble 'heaped up;' Heyne suggests comparison with *Sskr.* iç *dominare, imperare*, and gives 'Schatzgold, reiches gold;' Grein's note is as follows: 'Sollte vielleicht zu *icg* das Altn. *yggr* [terror] zu halten sein, da das Gold Altn. auch *ógnar ljómi* [splendor terroris] heisst? oder sollte sich etwa der Begriff Sühngold herausbringen lassen?' Grundtvig suggests the reading *éce-gold*, i.e. gold given in addition on the occasion of a solemn reconciliation.

Iclingas; *pl. The name of a Mercian family to which St. Guthlac belonged*:—Hē was ðæs yldestan and ðæs æðelstan cynnes ðe Iclingas wǣron genemnede *he* [*Guthlac's father*] *was of that chiefest and noblest race that were called Iclings*, Guthl. 1; Gdwin. 8, 4. [Icelingtūn (*Ickleton in Cambridgeshire?*) occurs Cod. Dipl. Kmbl. iv. 300, 24; *and there is* Icklingham *in Suffolk.*]

ī-dæges; *adv. On the same day*:—Se đe sleá his āgenne þeówne esne and hē ne sȳ īdæges deád *he who smites his own slave, and he die not on the same day*, L. Alf. 17; Th. i. 48, 13. Hī ne mōston metes þicgan gif hī igdæges tō mynstre gecyrran mihton *they were not allowed to partake of food if they could return to the monastery on the same day*, Homl. Th. ii. 166, 32. Swā hraþe swā hē him tō com ȳdæges swā gewāt hē of đisum andwerdum līfe *as soon as he came to him, on the same day, he departed from this present life*, 176, 3. [Cf. ī-sīđes.]

ĪDEL; *adj.* I. *empty*:—Tō hwan mæg đis eorþlīce hūs gif hit ȳdel stent? Hit ne biþ nā hūs būton hit beó mid hīrēde āfylled *what purpose can this earthly house serve, if it stand empty? It is not a house unless it be filled with a household*, Homl. Th. ii. 502, 12. Is nū forđī gehwilcum men tō hogienne đæt hē ȳdel ne cume his Drihtne tōgeánes on đam gemǣnelīcum ǣriste *now is it therefore for every man to take care that he come not empty-handed to meet his Lord at the general resurrection*, 558, 18. Đonne se geohsa of đære īdlan wambe cymþ *when the hiccup comes from the empty stomach*, L. M. 1, 18; Lchdm. ii. 60, 28. Īdelne hine forlēton *dimiserunt eum inanem*, Lk. Skt. 20, 10, 11. Sāwle īdle *animam inanem*, Ps. Th. 106, 8. Hē forlēt đa rīcan īdele, Homl. Th. i. 204, 6. II. *not possessing, destitute, void, devoid* [*with gen.*]:—Londrihtes mōt monna ǣghwilc īdel hweorfan *every man must wander destitute of land-right*, Beo. Th. 5768; B. 2888. Se deófol on sumum uncystum gebringþ đone đe hē gemēt īdelne ǣlces gōdes weorces *the devil brings into some vices him whom he finds devoid of every good work*, L. E. I. 3; Th. ii. 404, 13. Đa đe īdle beóþ swelcra giefa *those who are devoid of such gifts*, Past. 9; Swt. 59. 17. III. *vain, useless, idle, to no purpose*:—Seó eorþe wæs ȳdel and æmtig *terra erat inanis et vacua*, Gen. 1, 2. Īdel sangere *temelici*, Ælfc. Gl. 61; Som. 68, 57; Wrt. Voc. 39, 40. Eall eówer geswinc biþ īdel *consumetur incassum labor vester*, Lev. 26, 20. Ȳdel biþ se lǣcedom đe ne mæg đone untruman gehǣlan; swā biþ eác ȳdel seó lār đe ne gehǣlþ đære sāwle leahtras *vain is the medicine that cannot heal the sick; so also is the doctrine vain that does not heal the sins of the soul*, Homl. Th. i. 60, 11. Wese wīc heora wēste and īdel *fiat habitatio eorum deserta*, Ps. Th. 68, 26. Unnyt ođđe ȳdel *supervacuus*, Ælfc. Gr. 47; Som. 48, 46. Oft biþ swīđe īdel and unnyt đara yfelena manna hreówsung *plerumque mali inutiliter compunguntur*, Past. 54, 4; Swt. 431, 1. Đes wīda grund stōd īdel and unnyt, Cd. 5; Th. 7, 14; Gen. 106: Beo. Th. 830; B. 413: 293; B. 145. Man byþ merwe gesceaft mihtum īdel *homo vanitati similis factum est*, Ps. Th. 143, 5. Īdel gelp him on ne rīcsode *vanæ gloriæ contemptorem*, Bd. 3, 17; S. 545, 9. Īdel gylp *vanitas*, Ps. Th. 51, 6. Īdel searu, 138, 17. Īdel gielp *inanis gloria*, Past. 62, 1; Swt. 457, 20. Īdel wuldor *vainglory*, Exon. 33 a; Th. 107, 12; Gū. 57. Hē nǣfre nōht leásunga ne īdeles leóþes wyrcean ne mihte *nihil unquam frivoli et supervacui poematis facere potuit*, Bd. 4, 14; S. 596, 42. Đa bodan đæs īdlan fætes *the messengers of the useless vessel*, Past. 47, 3; Swt. 361, 16. Hig đā æfter ridon īdelum færelde *they rode after, but their journey was to no purpose*, Jos. 2, 7. Guman geþancas īdle synt *cogitationes hominum vanæ sunt*, Ps. Th. 93, 11. Đǣr đæt heáfod biþ unhāl eall đa limu bióþ īdelu *languente capite membra incassum vigent*, Past. 18, 2; Swt. 129, 8. Ȳdele spellunga *fabulæ*, Ælfc. Gr. 50, 29; Som. 52, 2. Ne hī đǣr ǣnig unnit ne geþafian ne īdele spǣce ne īdele dǣde, L. Edg. C. 26; Th. ii. 250, 6: Hy. 7, 108; Hy. Grn. ii. 289, 108. Īdel word *idle words*, Exon. 37 a; Th. 120, 30; Gū. 279. On īdel *in vain*; nequiquam, Ælfc. Gr. 38; Som. 41, 55. On īdel gē swincaþ and eówre fȳnd his brūcaþ *frustra seretis sementem, quæ ab hostibus devorabitur*, Lev. 26, 16. Ne nemne gē drihtnes naman on īdel, Deut. 5, 11. Ne sint hig eów on īdel beboden *non incassum præcepta sunt vobis*, 32, 47. On īdel hī mē wurđiaþ *in vanum me colunt*, Mk. Skt. 7, 7: Ps. Th. 62, 8. IV. *idle, unemployed*:—Hē geseah ōđre on strǣte īdele standan *vidit alios stantes in foro otiosos*, Mt. Kmbl 20, 3. Hwī stande gē hēr eallne dæg īdele, 6: Exon 92 a; Th. 345, 6; Gn. Ex. 184. [*Orm. Piers P. Chauc.* on idel *in vain*: *O. Sax.* īdal: *O. Frs.* īdel: *O. H. Ger.* ītal *vanus, inanis*: *Ger.* eitel.] v. mān-īdel.

īdel, es; *n. Idleness, vanity, futility, frivolity*:—Đæt ȳdel fēt unþeáwas *idleness nourishes bad habits*, Prov. Kmbl. 1. Ǣlc ȳdel fēt unhǣlo, 61. Wē lǣraþ đæt preóstas đǣr ne geþafian ne īdele spǣce ne īdele dǣde ne ǣnig īdel *we enjoin that priests do not permit there* [*in the church*] *idle talk or action or any frivolity*, L. Edg. C. 26; Th. ii. 250, 27. Gif đū gesihst manega gēt ȳdel getācnaþ *if thou seest many goats it betokens frivolity*, Lchdm. iii. 214, 1. Nys eác mid īdele tō forlǣtenne đæt wundor đæt þurh wītedōmes cræft hē wiste *nor is the miracle, that he knew things by prophetic power, to be lightly dismissed*, Guthl. 17; Gdwin. 70, 2 [cf. 76, 10]. Đa īdlo *vanitates*, Rtl. 162, 32. v. preceding word.

īdel-georn; *adj. Fond of idleness, lazy, inert*:—Ne beó đū tō slǣpor ne tō īdelgeorn forđan đe slēp and đæt ȳdel fēt unþeáwas and unhǣlo đæs līchoman *be not too fond of sleep or idleness, for sleep and idleness nourish bad habits and bad health in the body*, Prov. Kmbl. 1. Eálā gē eargan and īdelgeornan *ah! ye sluggish and lazy ones*; inertes, Bt. 40, 4; Fox 238, 30.

īdel-gild, es; *n. False worship, idolatry*:—Hig mē tirigdon mid hira īdelgildum *ipsi me provocaverunt in eo qui non erat deus et irritaverunt in vanitatibus suis*, Deut. 32, 21. v. īdelness.

īdelgild-offrung, e; *f. An offering to an idol*:—Īdelgildoffrung *idolothytum*, Ælfc. Gl. 18; Som. 58, 109; Wrt. Voc. 22, 25.

īdel-hende; *adj. Empty-handed, empty*:—Ne cum đū tō mīnum hūse īdelhende *nec apparebis in conspectu meo vacuus*; none shall appear before me empty, Ex. 34, 20. Gif hē cume īdelhende tō *si vacuus appropinquat*, Past. 49, 2; Swt. 379, 21. Hē biþ ealra his ǣhta īdelhende *he shall be destitute of all his possessions*, Blickl. Homl. 49, 26. Nō īdelhende bona of đam goldsele gongan wolde, Beo. Th. 4169; B. 2081. Ne lǣt đū hine gān īdelhende fram đē *nequaquam vacuum abire patieris*, Deut. 15, 13. Forleórton hine īdelhende *dimiserunt eum inanem*, Lk. Skt. Lind. 20, 10, 11. Đonne gē ūt faraþ ne fare gē īdelhende *cum egrediemini, non exibitis vacui*, Ex. 3, 21. [Cf. *Ayenb.* idel-honded.]

īdel-ness, e; *f. Idleness, vanity, frivolity, uselessness, futility, emptiness, falseness*:—Seó ȳdelnes is đære sāwle feónd *idleness is an enemy of the soul*, L. E. I. 3; Th. ii. 404, 11. Ǣlces libbendes mannes mægen and anwald is īdelnes *universa vanitas omnis homo vivens*, Ps. Th. 38, 6. Đonne hī mid fulle gesceáde ongietaþ đæt đæt wæs leás and īdelnes đæt hī ǣr heóldon *cum certo judicio deprehenderint falsa se vacue tenuisse*, Past. 58, 1; Swt. 441, 19. Sebastianus cwæþ đis is swutol gedwyld and leás ȳdelnyss, Homl. Skt. 5, 274. Sanctus Paulus cwæþ đæt sió gītsung wǣre hearga and īdelnesse gefēra *avaritia quæ est idolorum servitus*, Past. 21, 3; Swt. 157, 6. On īdelnisse gē fæstniaþ eówer mōd on him *incassum cor figitis*, 51, 2; Swt. 395, 29. Ne mīnne noman ne cīg đū on īdelnesse, L. Alf. 2; Th. i. 44, 7. Hierusalem winþ for rihtwīsnysse and Babilonia winþ ongeán for unrihtwīsnysse seó ōđer for sōđfæstnysse ōđer for ȳdelnysse *Jerusalem fights for righteousness, and Babylon fights in opposition for unrighteousness: the one for truth, the other for falsehood*, Homl. Th. ii. 66, 31. Đa gīmeleásan men đe heora līf ādrugon on ealre īdelnisse *the careless men who passed their lives quite idly*, Ælfc. T. Grn. 1, 13. Nys eác mid īdelnysse tō forelǣtenne đæt wundor đe đes hālga wer foresǣde *nor is the wonder which this holy man foretold to be lightly dismissed*, Guthl. 19; Gdwin. 77, 10 [cf. 70, 2]. Ne đū manna bearn tō īdelnesse geworhtest *non vane constituisti filios hominum*, Ps. Th. 88, 40: Bd. 4, 3; S. 567, 27. Forhwan gē mid īdelnesse ealle ārīseþ ǣrđon leóht cume *in vanum est vobis ante lucem surgere*, Ps. Th. 126, 3. Hwī lufige gē īdelnessa and sēcaþ leásuncga *quid diligitis vanitatem, et quæritis mendacium?* 4, 3. Hē forlēt đa īdelnesse deófolgylda *relictis idolorum superstitionibus*, Bd. 2, 15; S. 518, 26. Đis synt đa īdelnyssa đisse worlde *hæ sunt vanitates hujus mundi*, L. Ecg. P. 1, 8; Th. ii. 174, 32. On īdelnyssum heora *with their vanities*, Cant. Moys. ad fil. 21. [*O. Frs.* tō ȳdelnisse *in vain*: *O. H. Ger.* ītalnissa *desolatio*.]

īdel-sprǣce; *adj. Talking idly, vainly*:—Đa felaīdelsprǣcan *multiloquio vacantes*, Past. 23; Swt. 175, 25.

ides, e; *f. A woman* [it is a word little used except in poetry, and it is supposed by Grimm to have been applied, in the earliest times, like the Greek νύμφη, to superhuman beings, occupying a position between goddesses and mere women, v. D. M. 372]:—Ides *virgo*, Kent. Gl. 1196. Freólecu mæg ides ǣwiscmōd [*Eve*], Cd. 42; Th. 55, 18; Gen. 896. Freólecu mæg ides eaforan fēdde [*Cain's wife*], 50; Th. 64, 22; Gen. 1054. Wlitebeorht ides [*Sarah*], 82; Th. 103, 34; Gen. 1728. Monig blāchleór ides [*the women of Sodom and Gomorrah*], 92; Th. 118, 24; Gen. 1970. Freólecu mæg ides egyptisc [*Hagar*], 101; Th. 134, 19; Gen. 2227. Ides ælfscīnu [*Judith*], Judth. 9; Thw. 21, 11; Jud. 14. Ides Helminga beághroden cwēn [*Wealtheow, Hrothgar's queen*], Beo. Th. 1245; B. 620. Ides Scyldinga, 2341; B. 1168. Idese onlīcnes *a woman's form*, 2706; B. 1351. Him brȳda twā idesa eaforan fēddon [*Lamech's wives*], Cd. 52; Th. 65, 34; Gen. 1076. Weras and idesa, Exon. 50 b; Th. 176, 7; Gū. 1205. Eorlas and hira idesa mid, Andr. Kmbl. 3275; An. 1640. A weak form occurs in Hpt. Gl. 456, 76:—Tō, on ydesan *in juvenculam*. [*O. Sax.* idis: *O.H. Ger.* itis *matrona*; itis-līh *matronalis*, Grff. i. 159. Grimm D. M. 373 takes the Icel. *dís* to be the same word, and compares the phrase from the Edda *dís skjöldunga* with the similar phrase given above from Beowulf.]

idig [?]; *adj. Busy, active*:—Tōþas idge *busy teeth* [*referring to the eating of the forbidden fruit by Adam and Eve*], Exon. 61 b; Th. 226, 18; Ph. 407. [Cf. *Icel.* iðja *activity*: iðinn *assiduous, diligent*; iðja *to be active, busy*. The passage is somewhat uncertain, as the MS. has *to þas*, and Thorpe prints as if there were a gap between *þas* and *idge*.]

īdisc, ȳddisc, es; *pl.* e; *m. n* [?]. *Property, household stuff*:—Ȳddisc *supellex*, Ælfc. Gl. 27; Som. 80, 98; Wrt. Voc. 25, 38. Ȳddisce *supplex*, Wrt. Voc. 83, 28. Ne forlǣte gē nān þing of eówrum ȳddisce *nec dimittatis quidquam de supellectili vestra*, Gen. 45, 20. Āgif đises ceorles ȳddysce [cf. ǣhta l. 1, þing, l. 23] *give up this fellow's property*, Homl. Th. ii. 180, 27. DER. in-īdisc. v. eád, ēdisc.

īdlian; *p.* ode *To become vain* or *idle, come to nought, to make vain* or *empty*:—Him hyge brosnaþ īdlaþ þeódscype *their mind corrupts, discipline comes to nought*, Exon. 81 a; Th. 304, 13; Fä 69. Īdlodon on īdelnyssum heora *irritaverunt in vanitatibus suis*, Cant. Moys. ad. fil. 21. Wæs īdlod *cassaretur*, Hpt. Gl. 515. Īdelude *exinanita*, Ps. Spl. T. 74, 8. [Cf. *O. H. Ger.* ki-ītallent *adnullabunt*: *Ger.* ver-eiteln.] DER. ā-, ge-īdlian.

ídol, es; *n. An idol*:—Hǽðenscype biþ ðæt man ídola [idol, MS. 13; deófolgyld, MS. G.] weorðige *it is heathendom, to worship idols*, L. C. S. 5; Th. i. 378, 18. Ídola wurðing *worship of idols*, L. N. P. L. 48; Th. ii. 298, 1.

ié *gen. dat.* of eá, Ors. 1, 1; Swt. 8, 10, 11, 14.

ie, ié. *For words beginning with these combinations look under* i, í, *and see the preliminary remarks under the letter* I.

IFIG, ifegn, es; *n. Ivy*:—Ifig *eder*, Wrt. Voc. 286, 2. Ifegn *eder*, ii. 106, 78. Yfig. Ðeós wyrt ðe man hederam crysocantes and óðrum naman ifig nemneþ is gecweden crysocantes forðý ðe heó byrþ corn golde gelíce *Ivy. This plant, which is named hedera crysocantes, and by another name ivy, is called crysocantes, because it bears berries like gold*, Herb. 121; Lchdm. i. 234, 1-4. Nim ðæt ifig ðe on stáne weaxe *take the ivy, which grows on stone*, L. M. 3, 30; Lchdm. ii. 326, 3. Ifies seáw *juice of ivy*, 1, 3; Lchdm. ii. 40, 26. Weal se is mid ifige bewrigen *a wall that is covered with ivy*, Shrn. 139, 27. [*O. and N.* ivi: *Prompt. Parv.* ivy *edera*: *O. H. Ger.* ebah *hedera*, Grff. i. 91.] DER. eorþ-ifig.

ifig-crop, -cropp, es; *m. A cluster of ivy berries*:—Ifigcrop *corymbus*, Wrt. Voc. 68, 2.

ifig-croppa, an; *m. A cluster of ivy berries*:—Ifigcroppena fíf and xx *five and twenty bunches of ivy berries*, L. M. 2, 24; Lchdm. ii. 214, 18.

ifig-leáf, es; *n. An ivy leaf*:—Nim ifigleáf ðe on eorþan wixþ *take leaves of ivy that grows on the ground*, L. M. 3, 31; Lchdm. ii. 326, 11.

ifig-tearo; *n*: -tara, an; *m. Ivy tar, gum that comes from ivy when it is cut*:—Nim scipteаro and ifigtearo, L. M. 1, 76; Lchdm. ii. 150, 12. Dó clǽne ifigtaran ðǽr ón gif ðú hæbbe [cf. dó gódne sciptaran tó, 326, 14], 3, 26; Lchdm. ii. 322, 27.

ifiht; *adj. Covered with ivy*:—On ðonæ ifihtan stoc *to the ivy-covered post*, Cod. Dipl. Kmbl. iii. 176. 8. In ða ifihtan ác, 379, 29. On ðone ibihttan alr; of ðam ibihtan alre, v, 124, 27.

-ig *a suffix connoting possession of an object denoted by the stem, used in the formation of adjectives, and represented in modern English by* y. *Early English and cognate forms may be seen in the following examples*: *Orm.* modiȝ: *Laym.* modi: *A. S.* módig: *Goth.* módags: *O. Sax.* módag, módig: *Icel.* móðugr, móðigr: *O. H. Ger.* muotig, muotich, muodic: *Ger.* müthig: *Orm.* mahhtiȝ: *Laym.* mæhti: *A. S.* meahtig: *Goth.* mahteigs: *O. Sax.* mahtig: *O. Frs.* machtich: *Icel.* máttugr, máttigr: *O. H. Ger.* mahtig: *Ger.* mächtig: *A. S.* hálig: *Icel.* heilagr: *Goth.* handugs.

íg, e; *f. An island*:—Wulf is on iége ic on óðerre fæst is ðæt églond fenne biworpen sindon wælreówe weras ðǽr on íge *the wolf is on one island, I on another; closely is that island surrounded with fen, fierce men are there on the island*, Exon. 100b; Th. 380, 6-11; Rä. 1, 4-6. *The word occurs in names of places*:—Án ígland ðæt is Meresíg háten, Chr. 895; Erl. 93, 24. Hér hǽðne men on Sceápíge sǽtun, 855; Erl. 68, 23. Æt Æðelinga íge, [eigge, MS. A.], 878; Erl. 81, 5. Of Ceortesíge, 964; Erl. 124, 3. On Beardanigge, 716; Erl. 44, 14. [*Icel.* ey *frequent in local names*, e. g. Fær-eyjar *the Faroe islands*, Orkneyjar *the Orkneys*: *Dan.* öe: *Swed.* ö.]

íg-búend, es; *m. A dweller in an island, an islander*:—Hí ígbúend óðre worde Baðan nemnaþ *island-dwellers by another name call it Bath*, Chr. 973; Erl. 124, 12. Ðis ǽrendgewrit Agustinus ofer sealtne sǽ súðan brohte iégbúendum *this letter Augustine brought across the salt sea from the south to the islanders*, Past. Pref; Swt. 9, 8. [Cf. *Icel.* ey-búi *an islander.*] v. ég-búend *and next word.*

íg-búende; *part. Dwelling in an island*:—Swá hine cígaþ ígbúende Engle and Seaxe weras mid wífum *so call it the island-dwellers, Angles and Saxons, men and women*, Menol. Fox 367; Men. 185. v. *preceding word.*

ig-dæges. v. í-dæges.

-íge *-eyed.* v. -eáge.

ígeoþ, ígoþ, iggaþ, iggoþ, es; *m. An eyot, ait, islet, small island*:—Ðá ásende hé hine on wræcsíþ tó ánum ígeoþe ðe is Paðmas gecíged *then he sent him away into exile to an island that is called Patmos*, Homl. Th. i. 58, 31. Binnan ánum ígoþe Pathmos gehâten, Ælfc. T. Grn. 16, 23. Binnan iggoþe, Cod. Dipl. Kmbl. iii. 61, 7. Hié flugon up be Colne on ánne iggaþ *they fled up along the Colne on to an island*, Chr. 894; Erl. 90, 28. Ðus feale synden ðere ýgetta ðe liggeþ intó Chertesége *so many are the islets that belong to Chertsey*, Cod. Dipl. Kmbl. v. 17, 30.

igil, íl, es; *m. A hedgehog, porcupine, an urchin*:—Se mára igil *istrix* [= ὕστριξ], Ælfc. Gl. 24; Som. 60, 29; Wrt. Voc. 24, 30. Íl *yricius* vel *equinacius*, Wrt. Voc. 78, 21. Se læssa íl *iricius*; se mára íl *istrix*, ii. 49, 52, 53. Hé wæs ðara [strǽla] swá full swá igl biþ byrsta *he* [*St. Sebastian*] *was as full of arrows as a hedgehog is of bristles*, Shrn. 55, 9. Se iil ǽrðæm hé gefangen weorðe mon mæg gesión ǽgðer ge his fét ge his heáfod ac sóna swá hiene mon geféhþ swá gewint hé tó ánum cliewene and tíhþ his fét swá hé inmest mæg and gehýt his heáfod *ericius cum apprehenditur, ejus et caput cernitur, et pedes videntur; sed mox ut apprehensus fuerit, semetipsum in sphæram colligit, pedes introrsus subtrahit, caput abscondit*, Past. 35, 3; Swt. 241, 9-12. Íl, Swt. 243, 6. Ðonne biþ ðæs íles heáfud gesewen *caput enim ericii cernitur*, 241, 16. Hé [Eádmund] all wæs biset mid heoræ scotungum swylce ýles burstæ swá swá Sebastianus wæs, Th. An. 122, 17. Íles byrsta, Homl. Skt. 5, 428. Stán is gener iglum [Blickl. Gl. ílum] *petra est refugium erinaceis*, Ps. Lamb. 103, 18. [*A. R.* ylespilles felles *hedgehogs' skins*: *Trev.* iles piles *ericii*: *Icel.* ígull *a sea-urchin*; ígul-köttr *a hedgehog*: *O. H. Ger.* igil *erinacius*: *Ger.* igel *hedgehog, urchin.*]

íg-land, es; *n. An island*:—Brittene ígland is ehta hund míla lang and twá hund bråd. And hér sind on ðís íglande fíf geþeóde *the island of Britain is eight hundred miles long and two hundred broad. And at present there are five languages in this island*, Chr. pref; Erl. 3, 1. Heora cyng him gesealde ðæt ígland ðe man Ii nemnaþ, 565; Erl. 18, 1. Sió wunode on ðam íglande, Bt. 38, 1; Fox 194, 21. Hié cómon on án ígland ðæt is úte on ðære sǽ ðæt is Meresíg háten, Chr. 895; Erl. 93, 24: Bt. 38, 1; Fox 184, 11. Ðæt íland ðe wé hátaþ Thyle, 29, 3; Fox 106, 23. [*Laym.* i-lond: *Icel.* ey-land.] v. eá-, ég-, eig-land.

ígoþ. v. ígeoþ.

-iht *an adjective suffix having much the same meaning as* -ig, *or as the Latin* -osus, e. g. stǽniht: *O. H. Ger.* steinaht: *Ger.* steinicht *petrosus. Icel. has a suffix* -óttr.

íht, e; *f. Increase*:—Ic sóhte hwylc wǽre elnes oððe iéhte eorlscipes se Pater Noster *I sought what in respect of power or increase of valour the Pater Noster might be*, Salm. Kmbl. 22; Sal. 11. v. ícan.

Ii, Hii, *Iona*:—Heora cyng him gesealde ðæt ígland ðe man Ii nemnaþ . . . Nu sceal beón ǽfre on Ii abbod and ná biscop and ðan sculon beón underþeódde ealle Scotta biscopas forðan ðe Columban was abbod ná biscop *their king gave him* [*Columba*] *the island that is called Iona . . . Now there must always be in Iona an abbot and not a bishop, and to him all the bishops of the Scots must be subject, for Columba was abbot, not bishop*, Chr. 565; Erl. 18, 1-8. Wæs hé sended of ðám eálande and of ðam mynstre ðe Hii is nemned *de insula quæ vocatur Hii*, Bd. 3, 3; S. 526, 11.

iil, íl. v. igil.

ilca; *pron.* [*occurs in the weak declension only*]. *The same*:—Hé sylf oððe se ylca *ipse*; heó sylf oððe seó ylce *ipsa*; hí sylfe oððe ða ylcan *ipsi*, Ælfc. Gr. 15; Som. 18, 53-4. Ðú byst se ilca se ðú ǽr wǽre *tu idem ipse es*, Ps. Th. 101, 24. Se ilca hét ácwellan ða rícostan witan *the same man* [*Nero*] *ordered the greatest senators to be killed*, Bt. Met. Fox 9, 47; Met. 9, 24. Hæfþ se ilca god eorþan and wætere mearce gesette *the same God hath appointed a limit to earth and water*, 11, 127; Met. 11, 64. Ðis is se ilca ealwalda god ðone on fyrndagum fæderas cúðon, Andr. Kmbl. 1501; An. 752. Seó ylce bóc *idem libellus*, Bd. 4, 10; S. 578, 16. Hé weorþan sceolde eft ðæt ilce ðæt hé ǽrðon wæs *it should become again the same, that it was before*, Exon. 61 a; Th. 224, 21; Ph. 379. Hié cwǽdon ðæt tæt ilce hiera geférum geboden wǽre *they said that the same offer had been made to their comrades*, Chr. 755; Erl. 50, 22. On ðisse ylcan tíde *hac ipsa hora*, Ex. 9, 18. On ðære ylcan tíde *eadem hora*; Wick. *in the same hour*, Lk. Skt. 24, 33. Hí smeágaþ unriht and on ðam ilcan forweorþaþ *scrutati sunt iniquitatem; defecerunt scrutantes scrutinio*, Ps. Th. 63, 5. Gelíce ðisse ilcan ðe wé ymb sprecaþ *like the very one we are talking about*, Bt. Met. Fox 26. 5; Met. 26, 3. Ðisne ilcan þreát *this same band*, Exon. 16 a; Th. 36, 2; Cri. 570. Ðyssum ylcum tídum *his temporibus*, Bd. 5, 7; S. 621, 14. Swá ðám ilcum byþ ðe nellaþ ðínre ǽ bebod healdan *so shall it be with those, who will not keep thy law*, Ps. Th. 118, 36. [*Ilk* is used as late as the time of Chaucer, and remains yet in the phrase 'of that ilk,' but its place was gradually occupied by *same* (the Icelandic *sami*) which occurs once in the Ormulum.]

ilce; *adv. In the same way*:—Hú ne eom ic monn suá ilce suá ðú *am I not a man the same as you are?* Past. 17, 6; Swt. 115, 12. Eft swá ilce *again in the same way*, Bt. 16, 1; Fox 50, 10. [Cf. swilce.]

ild, e; *f.* I. *an age, period of time*; ævum, sæculum:—Yld *ævum*, Ælfc. Gl. 94; Som. 75, 118; Wrt. Voc. 52, 68. Hér wæs seó forme yld ðissere worulde and seó óðer yld wæs óþ Abrahames tíman . . . Seó þridde yld wæs ðá wuniende óþ David *at this time was the first age of this world, and the second age was till Abraham's time . . . The third age was lasting then till David*, Ælfc. T. Grn. 4, 5, 34. Hé com on ðære syxtan ylde, Blickl. Homl. 71, 26. Se eahtoþa dæg getácnode ða eahtoþan ylde ðyssere worulde, Homl. Th. i. 98, 8. Be ðám syx yldum, Bd. 5, 24; S. 648, 15. II. *age, time of life, years*; ætas:—Eádig is heora yld seó ðe ðá gyt ne mihte Crist andettan and móste for Criste þrowian *blessed is their* [*the children of Bethlehem*] *age, which as yet could not confess Christ, and might suffer for Christ*, Homl. Th. i. 84, 3. Ealle wé cumaþ tó ánre ylde on ðam gemǽnelícum ǽriste ðeáh ðe wé nú on myslícere ylde of ðyssere worulde gewíton *we shall all come at one age at the general resurrection, though now we depart from this world at different ages*, 23-5. Deóplícor mid ús ðú smeágast ðonne yld úre anfón mǽge *profundius nobiscum disputas quam ætas nostra capere possit*, Th. An. 33, 11. Hé wæs ðá sixhund geára on ylde *he was six hundred years of age*, Gen. 7, 6. Ðá was ágán his ielde xxiii wintra *he was then twenty-three years of age*, Chr. prm; Erl. 4, 19. Hé leng ne leofaþ ðonn on midre ilde *he will not live beyond middle age*, Lchdm. iii. 162, 21. Ǽrðæmðe hé self wǽre fulfremedre ielde *nisi perfecta ætate*, Past. 49, 5; Swt. 335, 19. Hundehtatig ylda *octoginta anni*, Ps. Th. 89, 11. III. *mature* or *old age, eld*; senectus, vetustas:—Yld *senectus*, Ælfc. Gr. 9; Som. 12, 28. Seó nóntíd biþ ūre yld forðan ðe on nōntīde āsīhþ seó sunne and ðæs ealdigendan mannes mægen biþ wanigende *the ninth hour is our old age, for at the ninth hour the sun sinks, and the force of the man that grows old is diminishing*, Homl. Th. ii. 76, 20. Geswenced yld *wearied age*, Dōm. L. 16, 255. Ðonne mē ylde tīd on gesīge *in tempore senectutis*, Ps. Th. 70, 8. On hyre ylde ācende sunu *peperit filium in senectute sua*, Gen. 21, 2. Cild ðæt ðe heó Abrahame on his ylde ācende *filium quem peperit ei* [*Abraham*] *jam seni*, 7: Beo. Th. 43; B. 22. Sume beóþ gelǣdde on cildhāde tō rihtum līfe, sume on cnihthāde, sume on geþungenum wæstme, sume on ylde, sume on forwerodre ealdnysse, Homl. Th. ii. 76, 26. Ðǣr is geógoþ būton ylde *there is youth without age*, Blickl. Homl. 65, 17: Exon. 32 a; Th. 101, 6; Cri. 1654. Gōd sceal wyð yfele geógoþ sceal wið ylde sacan, Menol. Fox 562; Gn. C. 50. Nǣron eówre gescī mid ylde fornumene *nec calceamenta pedum vestrorum vetustate consumpta sunt*, Deut. 29, 5. Gesceádlīce tōsceádan ylde and geóguþe *to distinguish discreetly between age and youth*, L. de Cf. 4; Th. ii. 262, 5. **IV.** *age, old people, chief people* [v. eald]:—Seó yld hī gebæd and seó iúguþ wrāt *age prayed and youth wrote*, Homl. Th. ii. 506, 21. Ðǣr wærþ Eást-Engla folces seó yld ofslagen *there the principal men of the East Angles were slain*, Chr. 1004; Erl. 139, 33. [*Goth.* alds, alþs *an age, generation*: *O. Sax. O. L. Ger.* eldi [*old*] *age*; *antiquitas, senectus*: *O. Frs.* elde: *Icel.* elli *old age*: *O. H. Ger.* alti, elti *ætas, ævum, senium, senectus, vetustas.*] v. eld, æfter-yld; ildu.

ilda. v. ildu.

ildan; *p.* de *To delay, tarry, defer, put off, postpone, procrastinate. delay the notice of anything, connive at, dissimulate*:—Tō hwon yldestū middangeard tō onlȳhtenne *why dost thou delay to enlighten the world?* Blickl. Homl. 7, 33. Tō hwon yldest ðū ðæt ðū raðost dō ðæt man ðās menn wītnige and cwelle *why dost thou delay at once to cause these men to be punished and killed*, 183, 1. Seó hālige cyrice sum þing þurh sceáwunge yldeþ and swā ābireþ and ældeþ ðæt oft ðæt wiðerwearde yfel āberende and yldende beweraþ *sancta ecclesia quædam per considerationem dissimulat, atque ita portat et dissimulat, ut sæpe malum quod adversatur portando et dissimulando compescat*, Bd. 1, 27; S. 491, 29-32. Ðā se brȳdguma ylde *moram faciente sponso*, Mt. Kmbl. 25, 5. Hē ilde [Cott. MS. ielde] and þafode ða scylda *dissimulavit culpas*, Past. 21, 1; Swt. 151, 22. Hē ða gewilnunge nāht lange ne ylde *he did not long delay that desire*, Th. Ap. 1, 17. Ne ylde hē hit ðā leng *nec exinde distulit*, Bd. 2, 12; S. 512, 34. Hē ylde ðā gyt *distulit*, Ps. Th. 77, 23. Ne yld ðæt ðū mē ārie *ne tardaveris*, 39, 21. Ðeáh ðe ic hit læng ylde *though I should longer delay to notice the matter*, Chr. 1100; Erl. 236, 11. Ne ðæt se aglǣca yldan þohte *nor did the wretch mean to delay that*, Beo. Th. 1483; B. 739: 4471; 2239. Yldan *dissimulare*, Wrt. Voc. ii. 27, 37. Yldende tō andettenne *differentes confiteri*, Bd. 5, 12; S. 630, 5. Ðonne se lāreów ieldende sēcþ ðone tīman ðe hē his hiéremenn sidelīce on þreátigean mǣge *cum tempus subditis ad correptionem quæritur*, Past. 21, 2; Swt. 153, 5. [*O. H. Ger.* altian *differre*; altōn *dissimulare*; altinōn *differre, dissimulare, elongare.*] v. ældan, ildcian, ildian; for-ildan.

ildcian; *p.* ode *To delay*:—Se dysega ungeþyldega all his ingeþonc hē geypt ac se wīsa hit ieldcaþ and bītt tīman *totum spiritum suum profert stultus, sapiens autem differt et reservat in posterum*, Past. 33, 4; Swt. 220, 10. v. elcian, eldcung.

ilde; *pl. m. Men* [a poetical term]:—Hātaþ ylde eorþbūende fison *men, earth-dwellers, call it Pison*, Cd. 12; Th. 14, 19; Gen. 221. Yldo ofer eorþan, 163; Th. 205, 15; Exod. 436. Nædran ða aspide ylde nemnaþ, Ps. Th. 57, 4. Ylda ǣghwilc *every man*, Cd. 24; Th. 31, 4; Gen. 480. Ylda gehwilc, Ps. Th. 77, 4. Earmlīc ylda cwealm *miserable slaughter of men*, Andr. Kmbl. 363; An. 182: 3108; An. 1557. Ylda Waldend *God*, Beo. Th. 3327; B. 1661. Ilda cyn *the race of men*, Elen. Kmbl. 1040; El. 521, Ylda bearn *the children of men*, Cd. 113; Th. 149, 6; Gen. 2470: 177; Th. 222, 17; Dan. 106. Sceal mid yldum wesan ismahel hāten *shall be called among men Ishmael*, 104; Th. 138, 3; Gen. 2286: Beo. Th. 154; B. 77. Ðæt wæs yldum cūþ, 1415; B. 705: Ps. Th. 144, 9. Niht becwom ōðer tō yldum, Beo. Th. 4240; B. 2117: Menol. Fox 174; Men. 88: Elen. Kmbl. 1581; El. 792. [*O. Sax.* eldī; *pl. men*; eldeō barn *children of men*: *Icel.* öld; aldir; *pl.* [*in poetry*] *men*; alda börn *children of men.*]

ildend, es; *m. One who delays*:—Næs ðā nǣnig yldend [ylding?] tō ðam ðæt syððan hī on ðæt hūs cōmon hī ðā sōna ðone hālgan wer gebundon *there was no one, after they had got into the house, who delayed at once to bind the holy man*, Guthl. 5; Gdwin. 36, 5. *See note, where the other reading* ylding *is given.*

ildend-līc; *adj. Tardy, dilatory*:—Eldendlīce *morosa*, Wrt. Voc. ii. 54, 58.

ildest; *superl. of* eald. **I.** *eldest, oldest*:—Ūre ieldesta mǣg *parens primus* [*Adam*], Past. 43, 5; Swt. 313, 15. Hē sōhte fram ðam yldestan ōþ ðone gingestan *quos scrutatus, incipiens a majore usque ad minimum*, Gen. 44, 12. Ða yldestan *senes*, Ps. Th. 104, 18. Ða yldestan chus and cham hātene wǣron *the eldest were named Cush and Ham*, Cd. 79; Th. 97, 22; Gen. 1616. **II.** As the *oldest* might be supposed best fitted to fill the highest positions the word gets the meaning *principal, chief, greatest*:—Se yldesta *cardinarius, i. primarius*, Ælfc. Gl. 48; Som. 65, 66; Wrt. Voc. 34, 1. Yldest byrla *magister calicum*, 113: Som. 79, 130; Wrt. Voc. 60, 34. Hē wæs ieldesð [*summus*] ofer ða hālgan cirican, Past. 17, 6; Swt. 115, 16. Hwylc hyra yldest wǣre *quis eorum major esset*, Lk. Skt. 9, 46, 22, 24. Ieldesta bisceop *pontifex maximus*, Ors. 5, 4; Swt. 224, 2. Tyrus hēt him tō clypian ðone ðe on ðam scype yldost wǣre *Tyrus bade call to him the principal man on the ship*, St. And. 28, 6. Hē clipode him tō his yldestan gerēfan *dixit ad servum seniorem*, Gen. 24, 2. Aaron and ða yldestan men *tam Aaron quam principes synagogæ*, Ex. 34, 31. Ða ieldestan men ðe tō Bedanforda hiérdon, Chr. 918; Erl. 104, 23. Ða yldestan witan gehādode and leáwede Angelcynnes, 1012; Erl. 146, 7: 978; Erl. 127, 9. Ða yldestan þægenas, 1015; Erl. 151, 19. Ealle ða yldestan menn on West-Seaxon *all the principal men of Wessex*, 1036; Erl. 165, 1. Ða ðe ieldeste wǣron *equites*, Ors. 6, 4; Swt. 260, 24. Ða yldstan setl on gesamnungum *the highest seats in the synagogues*; primas cathedras in synagogis, Lk. Skt. 20, 46. Ic hit rehte ðām yldostan Egiptan witum *I told it to the chief wise men of Egypt*, Gen. 41, 24. [*Laym.* ældeste: *Ayenb.* eldeste: *Icel.* ellztr: *O. H. Ger.* altist, altost *primus, primogenitus*; thie altoston thes folkes *seniores*. For the use similar to that given under **II.** of a word denoting in the first instance age, cf. *Goth.* þai sinistans (lit. *eldest*) manageins *by which Ulfilas translates* οἱ πρεσβύτεροι τοῦ λαοῦ; *and the passage in Ammianus Marcellinus* 'sacerdos omnium maximus apud Burgundios vocatur *sinistus*.'] v. ildra.

ildian; *p.* ode *To delay, defer, put off*:—Nis forðī nānum synfullum tō yldigenne āgenre gecyrrednysse ðȳlæs ðe hē mid sleacnysse forleóse ða tīd Godes fyrstes *it is not, therefore, for any sinner to delay his own conversion, lest by remissness he lose the time of God's respite*, Homl. Th. i. 350, 14. v. ildan.

ilding, e; *f. Delay, putting off, deferring, prolonging, delaying to notice anything, connivance*:—Ylding *tricatio*, Wrt. Voc. ii. 88, 19. Ne wæs ðā ylding tō ðon ðæt hī heápmǣlum cōman *non mora ergo confluentibus catervis*, Bd. 1, 15; S. 483, 31. Ne wæs ðā ylding ðæt monige gelȳfdon *quid mora? crediderunt nonnulli*, 1, 26; S. 487, 39: 3, 9; S. 533, 38. Ðā hit mycel ylding wæs *cum mora multa fieret*, Mk. Skt. 6, 35. Hwæt is ðæt līf elles ðysses middangeardes būton lytelu ylding ðæs deáþes *what else is the life of this world but a little deferring of death?* Blickl. Homl. 59, 27. Hit biþ deáþes ylding swīðor ðonne līfes *it is rather the deferring of death, than the prolonging of life*, 32. Beó ðū on tīd gearu ne mæg ðæs ǣrendes ylding wyrðan *be thou at the time ready, the errand may not brook delay*, Andr. Kmbl. 430; An. 215. Ðā bæd hē hine yldinge and fyrstes *petens inducias*, Bd. 4, 1; S. 564, 7. Būtan ǣnigre yldinge *sine ulla dilatione*, 1, 27; S. 493, 30. Būton yldinge, Homl. Th. i. 84, 34. Būton ǣlcere yldinge, Blickl. Homl. 87, 4. Be ðære ildinge [MS. Cott. ieldinge] suīðe wel Drihten þreáde Iudēas *qua dissimulatione bene Iudæam Dominus corripit*, Past. 21, 1; Swt. 151, 19. Ðæt ic yldinge onfō tō lifianne *ut inducias vivendi accipiam*, Bd. 3, 13; S. 538, 34. Ieldinga *morarum*, Wrt. Voc. ii. 54, 57. v. ildan, eldung.

ildo. v. ildu.

ildra; *m.* ildre; *f. n. comp. of* eald. **I.** *elder, older, grand* [in *grand-father*, cf. eald-fæder, -mōder]:—Ældra *senior*, Wrt. Voc. ii. 120, 48. Seó yldre hātte Lia and seó gingre Rachel *nomen majoris Lia, minor vero appellabatur Rachel*, Gen. 29, 16. Hys yldra sunu wæs on æcere *erat filius ejus senior in agro*, Lk. Skt. 15, 25. Mīn yldra mǣg *my elder brother*, Beo. Th. 940; B. 468. Yldra brōðor, 2653; B. 1324. Ōþ ðæt hē yldra wearþ *until he got older*, 4746; B. 2378. Ic eom micle yldra *I am much older*, Exon. 111 a; Th. 424, 20; Rā. 41, 42. Ældra fæder *avus*, Wrt. Voc. ii. 101, 22. Yldra fæder *avita*, 78, 3. Geornful tō witanne ðætte ǣr wæs ǣr ðū ācenned wēre oððe furðum ðīn yldra fæder geboren wēre *desirous to know what was before you were begotten, or even before your grandfather was born*, Shrn. 198, 29: Elen. Kmbl. 872; El. 436. For mīne sāwle and for mīnes fæder and for mīnes ieldran fæder *for my soul, and for my father's, and for my grandfather's*, Chart. Th. 496, 21: 497, 15. Þurh heora yldran mōdor lāre hī gelȳfdon gode *through their grandmother's teaching they believed on God*, Shrn. 53, 10, 16, 21. Ða gingran ārīsaþ wið ðām yldrum *the younger shall arise against the elder*, Blickl. Homl. 171, 23. Swelce snytro swylce manegum ōðrum ieldran gewittum oftogen is *such wisdom as is withheld from many older minds*, Bt. 8; Fox 24, 28. **II.** *greater, superior* [v. yldest **II.**]:—Hwæðer ys yldra ðe se ðe þēnaþ ðe se ðe sitt *quis major est qui recumbit an qui ministrat?* Lk. Skt. 22, 27. Gewurþe hē swā swā gingra seðe yldra ys betwux eów *qui major est in vobis fiat sicut junior*, 26. Ða ðe synt yldran habbaþ anweald on him *qui majores sunt, potestatem exercent in eos*, Mt. Kmbl. 20, 25. [*Orm.* elldre: *Laym.* ældre, eldere: *O. Sax.* aldiro (*as a noun*): *Icel.* ellri: *O. H. Ger.* altero.] v. next word.

ildra, an [*but the singular rarely occurs*]; *m. A parent, ancestor, father, forefather, predecessor, elder*:—Ðā mē yldra mīn āgeaf andsware fæder reordode *then my father answered me and spake* [cf. 872; El. 436: 891; El. 447: 906; El. 454], Elen. Kmbl. 921; El. 462. Hī forgeten hæfdon ðara wundra heora yldran on lōcadan *obliti sunt mirabilium quæ ostendit coram patribus eorum*, Ps. Th. 77, 13. Ūre ieldran ða ðe ðās stōwa ǣr hióldon hié lufodon wīsdōm *our forefathers, who formerly held these places, loved wisdom*, Past. Pref.; Swt. 5, 14: Exon.

47 a; Th. 160, 20; Gū. 946. Ūre yldran swultan and swīðe oft ūs from wendan *our parents have died and very often gone from us*, Blickl. Homl. 195, 26. Wǣron his yldran fæder and mōdor hǣðne *his parents, father and mother, were heathens*, 211, 19: 213, 2. Ūre yldrena lage *traditionem seniorum*, Mt. Kmbl. 15, 2. Twegen gebrōðru ðe hæfdon behwyrfed eall heora yldrena gestreón on deórwyrþum gymstānum *two brothers who had converted all their parents' wealth into precious stones*, Homl. Th. i. 60, 23. Bebirge mē mid mīnum yldrum *condas me in sepulchro majorum meorum*, Gen. 47, 30. Eafora æfter yldrum *the son after the parents*, Cd. 56; Th. 69, 1; Gen. 1129. Suna ic lǣrde ðæt hié hȳrdon heora yldrum *I taught sons to obey their parents*, Blickl. Homl. 185, 20. Nolde hē him geceósan welige yldran *he [Christ] would not choose wealthy parents for himself*, 23, 25. [*Laym.* aldren, ældere, eldre *forefathers*: *R. Glouc.* eldren: *Piers P. Chauc.* eldres: *O. Sax.* aldiro *a forefather; pl. parents;* eldiron, *pl. parents*: *O. Frs.* alder, elder, aldera, ieldera *father, parent*: *O. H. Ger.* altiron, eldiron *parentes*: *Ger.* ältern, eltern *parents.*] v. eldran.

ildu; *indecl. f.* I. *an age;* ævum:—Nis ðæt tō geortrȳwianne ðæt on ūre yldo ðæt beón mihte ðæt forþgongendre yldo oft geworden getreówe spell secgaþ *nec diffidendum est nostra etiam ætate fieri potuisse, quod ævo præcedente aliquoties factum fideles historiæ narrant*, Bd. 4, 19; S. 587, 32: 3, 27; S. 558, 31. II. *age, time of life;* ætas:—Ōþ nigon and fīftig wintra mīnre yldo *usque ad annum ætatis meæ quinquagesimum nonum*, 5, 24; S. 647, 32. On ðære ǣrestan yldo his līfes *in prima ætate*, 5, 13; S. 633, 32. Mid ðī ðe heó bicom tō giftelīcre yldo *when she arrived at a marriageable age*, Th. Ap. 1, 10. Ða ðe nabbaþ nāwþer ne ildo ne wīsdōm *quos vel imperfectio vel ætas prohibet*, Past. 49, 3; Swt. 383, 21. III. *age, old age;* senectus:—Seó yldo and se ende ðæs heora līfes *their old age and the end of their life*, Blickl. Homl. 163, 5. Heora ylda gelīffæsted wæs, 18. Him æfter ðȳ yldo ne derede *after that age should not harm him*, Cd. 23; Th. 30, 24; Gen. 471. Nis ðǣr on ðam londe yldu ne yrmþu *there is not in that land old age nor misery*, Exon. 56 b; Th. 201, 6; Ph. 52. On geóguþe . . . on yldo, 88 a; Th. 330, 32, Vy. 60. Geógoþ būton yldo, Blickl. Homl. 103, 35. Heó hire on ylda ðā wǣre *she was in her old age*, 163, 10. Nū gyt syndan manige manna swylce ðe hiom yldo gebīdan ǣr tō genihte *adhuc multiplicabuntur in senecta uberi*, Ps. Th. 91, 13. Ða yldu wendan tō līfe *to turn old age to life*, Exon. 58 b; Th. 210, 23; Ph. 190. Mīne yldo beóþ ǣghwǣr genihtsum *senectus mea in misericordia uberi*, Ps. Th. 91, 9. [*Orm. A. R. R. Glouc. Ayenb. Piers P. Chauc. Wick.* elde *age, old age, eld*: *Icel.* öld *an age.* v. ild *for other related words.*] v. æfter-, ǣr-, frum-yldo; ældo, eldo, ild.

ile, es; *m.* I. *the sole of the foot:*—Ile [? cf. 283, 75 hela *calx, occurring in a very similar list*] *calx*, Wrt. Voc. 65, 47. Ilas, wearras *calces*, ii. 127, 45. From his hnolle ufewerdan ōþ his ilas neoþewerde *from the crown of his head to the soles of his feet*, Homl. Th. ii. 452, 27. Mid īsenum pīlum heora ilas gefæstnode *fastened the soles of their feet with iron nails*, Homl. Skt. 5, 388. II. *hard skin [such as comes on the sole of the foot?], callosity:*—Ile *callus*, Ælfc. Gl. 78; Som. 72, 51; Wrt. Voc. 46, 11. Weorras *vel* ill *callos*, ii. 103, 16. Him weóxon ylas on olfendes gelīcnysse on his cneówum *callosities grew on his knees, just as on a camel's*, Homl. Th. ii. 298, 26. [To þe yle of hire helen, Marh. 10, 19: *O. Frs.* ili, ile, il *hard skin*: *Icel.* il; *gen.* iljar; *f. the sole of the foot.*]

ilf, e; *f. An elf:*—Ðanon untydras ealle onwōcon eotenas and ylfe *thence sprang all monstrous things, giants and elves*, Beo. Th. 224; B. 112. Gif hit wǣre ēsa gescot oððe hit wǣre ylfa gescot oððe hit wǣre hægtessan gescot *if it were Æsir's shot, or elves' shot, or witches' shot*, Lchdm. iii. 54, 10. [Cf. *Scot.* elf-shot; elf-arrow, *Halliw. Dict;* Grmm. D. M. 429: *Prompt. Parv.* elfe *lamia*, 138, see note: *M. H. Ger.* elbe; *f.* see Grmm. D. M. 411.] v. ælf, -elfen.

ilfette, an: ilfetu, e; *f. A swan:*—Aelbitu *olor, cicnus*, Wrt. Voc. ii. 115, 47: *tantalus*, 98, 30. Ilfatu *alvor*, 6, 55. Ilfetu *olor*, 63, 40. Ylfete *cignus*, Ælfc. Gl. 36; Som. 62, 105; Wrt. Voc. 29, 3. Elfetu, Wrt. Voc. 62, 5. Ylfette *olor* vel *cingnus*, 77, 25. Ylfete song *the song of the swan*, Exon. 81 b; Th. 307, 6; Seef. 19. Sume fugelas beóþ langsweorede swā swā ylfettan *some birds are long-necked, such as swans*, Hexam. 8; Norm. 14, 17. [*Icel.* álpt, álft 'the common Icel. word for *swan;* svan is only poët:' *O. H. Ger.* albiz, alpiz, elpiz *olor*, Grff. i. 243.]

ilfig; *adj. Affected by elves [?], mad, frantic:*—*Fanaticus*, i. *minister templi, futura præcinens, vel* ylfig, Wrt. Voc. ii. 147, 40. Ylfie *vel* mōnaþseóce *comitiales*, i. e. *garritores*, 132, 26. *Comitiales, lunaticos* wanseóce i. *garritores*, ylfie, Hpt. Gl. 519, 44.

illeracu, e; *f. A surfeit;* crapula, Wrt. Voc. ii. 21, 62. v. ge-illerocaþ.

ilnetu *ciciris* [? v. DuCange 'cicurris *domesticus sus*'], Wrt. Voc. ii. 16, 15.

im-byrdling. v. in-byrdling.

impe [?], an; *f. An imp, scion, graft, shoot:*—Ðæt is sió hālige gesomnung Godes folces ðæt eardaþ on æppeltūnum ðonne hie wel begāþ hira plantan and hiera impan ōþ hié fulweaxne beóþ *ecclesia quippe in hortis habitat, quæ ad viriditatem intimam exculta plantaria virtutum servat*, Past. 49, 2; Swt. 381, 17. [Gunge *impen* me bigurt mid þornes, *A. R.* 378, 24: Yzet mid guode *ympen.* Þe ilke *ympen* byeþ þe virtues, *Ayenb.* 94, 34: I was the coventes gardyner, for to graffe *ympes*, *Piers P.* 5, 137: *Prompt. Parv.* impe or graffe *surculus*: cf. *O. H. Ger.* impitunga *insertio;* ga-impitōn *inserere*, Grff. i. 262: and see Skeat's Etym. Dict. *imp.*]

IN; *prep. cum dat. inst. acc.* '*In* is not found in Alfred's Metres, in the Runic poem, or in Byrhtnoþ; it occurs twice in the metrical Psalms, three times in Cædmon's Genesis; elsewhere in the poetry *in* and *on* freely interchange; but *in* prevails in the North, *on* in the South. The distinctive *on* has a vertical element [*up* or *down*], which easily runs to *against* or *near*,' March, p. 163. I. *with dat. inst. In, on:*—Wē sceolan on ðisse sceortan tīde geearnian ēce ræste ðonne mōtan wē in ðære engellīcan blisse gefeón mid ūrum Drihtne *we must in this short time earn eternal rest, then may we in angelic bliss rejoice with our Lord*, Blickl. Homl. 83, 2. On sumre stōwe hē wæs ðæt man mid his handa neálīce gerǣcean mihte in sumre eáðelīce mid heáfde gehrīnan *in one place the roof was so that it could hardly be reached with the hand, in another it could easily be touched with the head*, 207, 22. Hē wæs on Pannania ðære mǣgðe ǣrest on woruld cumen, in Arrea ðæm tūne. Wæs hē hweðre in Italia āfēded, in Ticinan ðære byrig, 211, 16–18. Ðara monna ðe in ðam here weorþuste wǣron *of the men that were most distinguished in the army*, Chr. 878; Erl. 80, 21. In woruldhāde *in sæculari habitu*, Bd. 4, 23; S. 592, 42: 4, 7; S. 574, 34. In regollīces līfes lāre swȳðe geornful *regularis vitæ institutioni multum intenta*, 4, 23; S. 593, 33. Eall ða hē in gehērnesse geleornian mihte *cuncta quæ audiendo discere poterat*, 4, 24; S. 598, 5. Hafaþ in hondum heofon and eorþan, Exon. 42 a; Th. 140, 32; Gū. 619. Wē sculon ā gemunan in mōde ðone sigora waldend *we must ever keep in mind the disposer of victories*, 84 b; Th. 318, 15; Mōd. 83. Lifgan fracoþ in folcum *to live vile among nations*, 10 b; Th. 12, 33; Cri. 195. Ðū ðe in dryhtnes noman cwōme *thou who didst come in the name of the Lord*, 13 b; Th. 26, 5; Cri. 413. In hwītum hrægl<?>um gewerede *clad in white raiment*, 14 a; Th. 28, 15; Cri. 447: Cd. 154; Th. 191, 10; Exod. 212. Wuniaþ in wynnum *they dwell in delights*, 224; Th. 296, 26; Sat. 508. Þafaþ in geþylde *allows in patience*, Exon. 79 a; Th. 297, 20; Crā. 71. Ic on unrihtum eác ðan in synnum geeácnod wæs *I was conceived in iniquity and in sin*, Ps. C. 50, 60; Ps. Grn. ii. 278, 60: Bd. 2, 12; S. 574, 9. In campe *in battle*, Beo. Th. 5003; B. 2505. In Caines cynne ðone cwealm gewræc ēce Drihten *the eternal Lord avenged that death among the race of Cain*, 214; B. 107. Ne mōste Efe ðā gyt wlītan in wuldre *Eve might not as yet look on glory*, Cd. 222; Th. 290, 2; Sat. 409. Ne hafu ic in heáfde hwīte loccas *I have not white hairs on my head*, Exon. 111 b; Th. 427, 28; Rā. 41, 98. Ābīdan sceolan in sinnihte *they shall abide in eternal night*, 31 b; Th. 99, 29; Cri. 1632. In grimmum sǣlum *in rough seasons*, 89 b; Th. 336, 20; Gn. Ex. 52. In līfdagum *in lifetime*, Cd. 163; Th. 204, 22; Exod. 423. In geárdagum *in days of yore*, Beo. Th. 2; B. 1. [Cf. On fyrndagum, Andr. Kmbl. 2; An. 1.] On stōwe seó is gecīged in Hripum, Bd. 5, 19; S. 638, 38. In ðȳs ginnan grunde *in this wide world*, Judth. 9; Thw. 21, 1; Jud. 2. II. *with acc. into, in, to:*—Ǣr ðon ðe hē in heofenas āstige *before he ascended into heaven*, Blickl. Homl. 125, 16. Genāman his līc and in ða stōwe āsetton ðe Vaticanus hātte *they took his body and put it into the place called the Vatican*, 191, 33. Ðā eode hē in ða cetan *then he went into the cell*, 219, 14. Gūþlāc sette hyht in heofenas, Exon. 39 a; Th. 128, 18; Gū. 406. Heó hine in ðæt mynster onfēng . . . Hē eall in ðæt swēteste leóþ gehwyrfde *susceptum in monasterium . . . Ipse cuncta in carmen dulcissimum convertebat*, Bd. 4, 24; S. 598, 3–7. Ðā gewāt heó in Eást-Engla mǣgþe *secessit ad provinciam Orientalium Anglorum*, 4, 23; S. 593, 8: Exon. 96 b; Th. 361, 7; Wal. 16. Ne inlǣd ūsih in [West Sax. on] costunge *ne inducas nos in temtationem*, Mt. Kmbl. Lind. 6, 13: Hy. 6, 28; Hy. Grn. ii. 286, 28. Beraþ forþ scīre helmas in sceaþena gemong *bear forth your bright helms into the press of the foes*, Judth. 11; Thw. 24, 17; Jud. 193. Hēton æðeling lǣdan in wrāðra geweald, Andr. Kmbl. 2547; An. 1275. Ðā wæs eft geseted in aldordōm babilone weard *the king of Babylon was restored to sovereignty*, Cd. 208; Th. 256, 16; Dan. 641. Ðā hié ðā in ðone heofon lōcodan æfter him *as they looked after him unto heaven*, Blickl. Homl. 121, 21. Se āgend upārǣrde reáde streámas in randgebeorh *the Lord hath raised up the waters of the Red Sea as a protection*, Cd. 156; Th. 196, 24; Exod. 296. Gelǣred in ða gerȳno Cristes geleáfan, Bd. 2, 15; S. 518, 28. In ða tīd bād ðone ēcan sige *ipso tempore coronam exspectabat æternam*, Bd. 4, 23; S. 593, 14: 2, 3; S. 504, 20. In āne tīd *in one hour*, Andr. Kmbl. 2183; An. 1093. Ðīn dōm wunaþ in ǣlce tīd *thy glory lasteth to all time*, Exon. 13 b; Th. 25, 26; Cri. 406. In ealle tīd, Exon. 83 a; Th. 313, 15; Seef. 124: 95 b; Th. 356, 25; Pa. 17. In woruld weorulda *in sæcula sæculorum*, Elen. Kmbl. 901; El. 452. III. In *sometimes follows its case:*—Ðǣr se eádga mōt eardes neótan, wyllestreáma wuduholtum in, wunian in wonge, Exon. 61 a; Th. 223, 20; Ph. 362. Blǣd wīde sprang Scyldes eaferan Scedelandum in, Beo. Th. 38; B. 19. [*Goth. O. Frs. O. H. Ger. Ger.* in: *Icel.* í: *Lat.* in: *Grk.* ἐν.]

in [*adv. and noun*]. v. inn.

in-, inn-. In the case of some of the verbs where *in* is given as a prefix perhaps it should be separated; the passages may then be taken as illustrating the adverb *inn.*

in-âberan; *p.* -bær *To bring in*:—Be ðam hunde ðe his hand eft innâbær *of the dog that brought his hand in again*, Homl. Th. ii. 520, 14.

in-âdl, e; *f. An internal disease*:—Sâra inâdle, L. M. 2, 1; Lchdm. ii. 174, 28. Wið eallum inâdlum, 2, 41; Lchdm. ii. 252, 6.

in-ǽlan; *p.* de *To kindle*:—Eów wæs âd inǽled *for you a pile was kindled*, Exon. 42 a; Th. 142, 6; Gû. 640. v. on-ǽlan.

in-âsendan; *p.* de *To send in*:—Hî inâsendan ðæt bed *summiserunt grabatum*, Mk. Skt. 2, 4.

in-âwritting, e; *f. An inscription*:—Innâwritting *inscribtio*, Lk. Skt. Lind. 20, 24.

in-bærniss, e; *f. Incense, frankincense*:—Inbærnis *tus*, Wrt. Voc. 289, 54. Inbernisse *incensum*, Ps. Surt. 140, 2. v. an-, on-bærniss; and cf. in-rêcels.

in-belǽdan; *p.* de *To lead in, introduce*:—Ðû inbelǽdst hig *introduces eos*, Cantic. Moys, 17.

in-belgan; *p.* -bealg; *pp.* -bolgen *To exasperate*:— Ða inbolgeno *aspirando*, Rtl. 15, 40. v. â-belgan.

in-belûcan; *p.* -leác *To shut*:—Ðâ ða duru inbeleác æfter him *then he shut the door after them*, Blickl. Homl. 217, 26.

in-bend; *m. f. An internal bond*:—Wæs se bâncofa âdle onǽled inbendum fæst *his body was inflamed with disease, fast with the fetters within*, Exon. 46 b; Th. 159, 18; Gû. 928.

in-beódan; *p.* -beád; *pp.* -boden *To announce, declare, proclaim*:— Inboden fæsten *indicto jejunio*, Mt. Kmbl. p. 9. 5. v. on-beódan.

in-beornan; *p.* -bearn *To burn, be on fire*:—Inbiorne wê *inardescamus*, Rtl. 95, 27.

in-beran; *p.* -bær *To bring in*, Beo. Th. 4310; B. 2152.

in-berdling. v. in-byrdling.

in-berþ. v. in-byrd.

in-bestingan; *p.* -stang *To pierce, penetrate, make a thrust which enters but does not go quite through*:—Gif hê þurhstinþ .vi. scill. gebête. Gif man inbestinþ .vi. scill. gebête, L. Ethb. 64; Th. i. 18, 12.

in-bewindan; *p.* -wand *To wrap up, enwrap*:—Innbewand *involvit*, Lk. Skt. Lind. 23, 53. Innbewunden *involutum*, 2, 12.

in-bewreón; *pp.* -wrigen *To cover up*:—Heora andwlitan inbewrigenum *with their faces covered up*, Cd. 77; Th. 95, 28; Gen. 1585.

in-bindan; *p.* -band *To unbind*:—Ân sceal inbindan forstes fetre *one shall unbind the fetters of frost*, Exon. 90 a; Th. 338, 8; Gn. Ex. 75. v. an-, on-bindan.

in-birding. v. in-byrding.

in-birigan; *p.* de *To taste*:—Inberigde *gustavit*, Jn. Skt. Rush. 2, 9. v. on-birian.

in-blâwan; *p.* -bleów *To inspire, breathe upon*:—Inbleów on hine *insuflavit*, Jn. Skt. Rush. 20, 22. Ðec inblâwende *te inspirante*, Rtl. 103, 32.

in-borh; *gen.* -borges; *m. A security required in cases where property had been stolen, bail*:—Gif hwâ þîfþe betogen sý . . . ðonne niman ða ðe hit tôgebyreþ on his ǽhtan inborh *if any one be accused of theft . . . then let those to whom it appertains take security from his property*, L. Ed. 6; Th. i. 162, 20. Ðonne sette mon inborh *let security be given* [the property in dispute is *þeófstolen*, v. l. 12], L. O. D. 8; Th. i. 356, 10. [Cf. L. H. 1; Th. i. 589, 19, de suo aliquid pro *inborgo* retineatur. Heore godfaderes scullen beo *inborȝes* for hem, O. E. Homl. i. 73, 32. Inboreges, ii. 17, 20.]

in-brengan; *p.* -brohte *To bring in or to, present*:—Hû micele hefigra biþ se wênenda deáþ ðonne se inbrohta *how much more grievous is death when it is expected than when it is presented to us*, Shrn. 42, 31. v. next word.

in-bringan *to bring in, present*:—Ðâ hî ne mihton hine inbringan *cum non possent offerre eum illi*, Mk. Skt. 2, 4.

in-bryne, es; *m. A fire, burning*:—Inbyrno *incendia*, Rtl. 64, 12.

in-bryrdan; *p.* de *To stimulate, instigate, incite, animate, inspire*:— Inbryrdendre Godes gefe *God's grace instigating me*, Chart. Th. 129, 25. Breóstum inbryrded *animated in spirit*, Exon. 73 b; Th. 274, 18; Jul. 535. Breóstum inbryrded tô ðam betran hâm, 42 a; Th. 141, 12; Gû. 626. Ðâ wæs, þurh ðæt hâlige treó, imbryrded breóstsefa, Elen. Kmbl. 1680; El. 842. Inbryrded breóstsefa, 2089; El. 1046. v. on-bryrdan.

in-bryrdniss, e; *f. Inspiration, animation, compunction, feeling*:—Mid ða mǽstan swêtnesse and inbryrdnisse [inbrydnisse, MS.] *maxima suavitate et compunctione*, Bd. 4, 24; S. 596, 34: 3, 19; S. 549, 21. Tô inbryrdnesse [inbyrdnesse, MS.] and tô gemynde ðære æfterfyligendra *ad instructionem memoriamque sequentium*, 17; S. 585, 16, note. v. on-bryrdniss.

in-bûan *to inhabit*:—Seðe inbýeþ in ðæm *qui inhabitat in ipso*, Mt. Kmbl. Lind. 23, 21.

in-bûend, es; *m. An inhabitant, native*:—Inbûend *colonus, incola, inquilinus*, Wrt. Voc. ii. 134, 25.

in-burh; *gen.* -burge; *f. A hall, vestibule*:—Inburh *atrium*, Wrt. Voc. 84, 35.

inburh-fæst; *adj. Stationed in a hall*; atriensis; scil. atrii janitor, seneschallus, lictor, Lye.

in-byrde; adj. *Born in a master's house*:—Dunne wæs inbyrde tô Hǽdfelda *Dunne belonged by birth to Hatfield*, Chart. Th. 650, 28. Wifûs and Dunne and Seoloce syndan inbyrde tô Hǽdfelda, 649, 33. Ða inberðan menn tô Eblesburnan, 152, 8. See next two words, and Kemble's Saxons in England, i. 203 sqq. [Cf. *Icel.* inn-borinn *native*: *O. H. Ger.* in-burto *oriundus*; in-burtig *indigena*: *O. L. Ger.* in-burdig *indigena*.]

in-byrding, es; *m. A slave born in a master's house*:—Inbirding *vernaculus*, Ælfc. Gl. 8; Som. 56, 103; Wrt. Voc. 18, 52. v. next word.

in-byrdling, es; *m. A slave born in a master's house*:—Inberdling *vel* fôstorling *verna* vel *vernaculus*, Ælfc. Gl. 86; Som. 74, 34; Wrt. Voc. 50, 17. Inbyrdlingc *vernaculus*, Wrt. Voc. 72, 82. Sicul inberdli[n]c, sicilisc inhyrdlincg (= -byrdling) *siculus indigena*, Hpt. Gl. 499. Mîn inbyrdling biþ mîn yrfenuma *vernaculus meus heres meus erit*, Gen. 15, 3. Ǽlc werhâdes man on eówrum mǽgðum and inbyrdlingum and geboht þeówa *omne masculinum in generationibus vestris, tam vernaculus quam emptitius*, 17, 12. Ealle werhâdes men his inhîrêdes ǽgðer ge imbyrdlingas ge gebohte þeówan *omnes viri domus illius, tam vernaculi quam emptitii*, 27.

inc; *dat*: inc, incit; *ac*: incer; *gen. of dual of pronoun of 2nd person*:—Inc âgênyrnþ sum man *occurrit vobis homo*, Mk. Skt. 14, 13. Nys mê inc tô syllanne *non est meum dare vobis*, Mt. Kmbl. 20, 23. Hwî gewearþ inc swâ ðæt gyt dorston fandian Godes *why have ye* [*Ananias and Sapphira*] *agreed to tempt God?* Homl. Th. i. 316, 33. Bǽm inc *to you both*, Exon. 13 a; Th. 22, 26; Cri. 357. Inc bâm twâm, Cd. 27; Th. 35, 30; Gen. 562. Neótaþ inc ðæs ôðres ealles wariaþ inc wið ðone wæstm ne wyrþ inc wilna gǽd, 13; Th. 15, 18-21; Gen. 235-6. Incit, 130; Th. 165, 16; Gen. 2732: 139; Th. 174, 19; Gen. 2880. Incer twega *of you two*, Exon. 123 b; Th. 475, 14; Bo. 47. Yncer ǽgðer ofslyhþ ôðerne and hundas licciaþ eówre blôd and fugelas fretaþ incer flǽsc and yncer wîf beóþ on ânum dæge wudewan, Shrn. 148, 1-4. Gehwæðer incer *either of you two*, Beo. Th. 1173; B. 584. [*Laym.* 1st MS. inc selven; 2nd MS. ȝou seolve: *Marh.* inc baðen: *Orm.* ȝunnc baþe; gunkerr baþre.] v. git, incer.

inca, an; *m. Doubt, question, cause of complaint, offence, ill-will* or *fear*:— Inca *apporia*, Wrt. Voc. ii. 10, 8: *occasio*, R. Ben. 38, Lye. Ðâ ongan hê mê âcsian hwæðere ic wiste hwæðer ic on riht bûtan incan gefullad wǽre *cœpit me interrogare, an me esse baptizatum absque scrupulo nossem*, Bd. 5, 6; S. 619, 45. Ðâ frægn hê hwæðer hî ealle smylte môd and bûtan eallum incan blîðe tô him hæfdon. Ðâ andswaredon hî ealle ðæt hî nǽnigne incan tô him wiston *then he asked them, whether they all were peaceably and kindly disposed to him without any cause of complaint. Then they all answered that they knew no cause of complaint against him*; interrogavit, si omnes placidum erga se animum, et sine querela controversiæ ac rancoris haberent. Respondebant omnes, se mentem ad illum ab omni ira remotam habere, 4, 24; S. 598, 39-41. Ðû mê scealt edwîtt mîn of âwyrpan ðæt mê tô incan âhwǽr gangeþ *thou shalt cast from me my reproach, which everywhere goes as a cause of fear to me*; amputa opprobrium meum, quod suspicatus sum, Ps. Th. 118, 39. Ðeáh ðe ic nô [MS. on] ingcan wiste hû ic mîne heortan heólde mid sôðe *though I did not know any cause of complaint, as to the manner in which I had kept my heart truly*; ergo sine causa justificavi cor meum, 72, 11. Ne ic culpan in ðê incan ǽnigne ǽfre onfunde womma geworhtra *I found not fault in thee, nor cause of complaint for sins committed*, Exon. 10 b; Th. 11, 29; Cri. 178. Incan *scrupulum*, Wrt. Voc. ii. 85, 7. Incan *causas*, 130, 13.

-incel *a diminutive suffix*, e. g. râp-incel, scip-incel, hûs-incel.

in-cempa, an; *m. A member of a household capable of bearing arms*:— Incempa, gescota *commanipularius, collega, miles*, Wrt. Voc. ii. 132, 48. v. in-hirdman, in-hîrêd, in-cniht.

incer; *adj. pron. 2nd person dual. Of* or *belonging to you two*:—Ic nû ðâs þing wrîte tô ðê gemǽnelîce and tô mînre mêder and mînum geswustrum forðon incer lufu sceal beón somod gemǽne *nunc tibi et matri meæ sororibusque meis de singulis regni mei commodis scribebam, que tibi et illis communia esse arbitror*, Nar. 3, 6-9. Sý inc æftyr incrun [MS. A eowrum] geleáfan *secundum fidem vestram fiat vobis*, Mt. Kmbl. 9, 29. Ðý læs gyt lâð gode incrum [*Adam and Eve*] waldende weorðan þyrfen, Cd. 27; Th. 36, 25; Gen. 577. Tô incre andsware, Th. 35, 19; Gen. 557. Biddaþ incerne [*Moses and Aaron*] god, Ex. 10, 17. Dǽlan somwist incre [*Hagar and Sarah*], Cd. 104; Th. 137, 27; Gen. 2280. Fyllaþ eorþan incre [*Adam and Eve*] cynne, 10; Th. 13, 4; Gen. 197. [*Laym.* 1st MS. incker moder inc hateþ; 2nd MS. ȝoure moder ȝou hoteþ: *Gen. a. Ex.* gunker: *Goth.* iggkwar.] v. git, inc.

incge, *in the phrase* incge lâfe [*a sword*], Beo. Th. 5747; 13, 2577, *appears to be a proper name.* Ing *occurs in stanza 22 of the Runic poem, and* Ing-winas *is a name of the Danes in Beowulf.*

in-cîgan; *p.* de *To invoke*:—Ic incêgo *invoco*, Rtl. 119, 5.

in-cîgung, e; *f. Invocation*:—Innceigungum *invocationibus*, Rtl. 121, 26. Innceiginge *invocationem*, 122, 22. Inceigence, 172, 8.

incit. v. inc.

in-cleofa, an; *m. An inner chamber, closet, bed-chamber, den, cave*:—Incleofa *cellarium*, Wrt. Voc. ii. 130, 56: *camera*, 127, 79. Incleofe *spelunca*, Ps. Spl. T. 9, 10. Forþ of hire inclifan *out of her closet*, Chart. Th. 230, 17. On inclifum [bedcliofum, MS. T.] eówrum *in cubilibus vestris*, Ps. Spl. 4, 5. On incleofum [bedcliofum, MS. T.] his *in cubili suo*, 35, 4. On incleofum [bedclyfum, MS. T.] heora *in cubilibus suis*, 149, 5: Blickl. Gl. Âcende eorþe heora froggan on inclyfum heora cyninga *edidit terra eorum ranas in penetralibus regum ipsorum*, Ps. Lamb. 104, 30. Hwelpas leóna on incleofum heora hí gesomniaþ *catuli leonum in cubilibus suis collocabuntur*, Ps. Spl. 103, 23.

in-cnapa, an; *m. A domestic servant*, Lye. v. next word.

in-cniht, es; *m. A servant in a house, household* or *domestic servant*:—Incniht *cliens* vel *clientulus*, Wrt. Voc. 72, 80. Incniht *parasitus, cliens, domesticus*, Hpt. Gl. 427, 483, 514. Se hláford gegaderode micele menigu his incnihta *the master gathered together a great many of his household servants*, Homl. Th. i. 502, 13. [*O. L. Ger.* in-kneht *apparitor*: *O. H. Ger.* in-kneht *vernaculus, servus* vel *domigena, verna, inquilinus, apparitor*.]

in-cofa, an; *m. An inner chamber*, [*metaph.*] *the breast, heart*:—On his incofan ł on his clyfan *in cubili suo*, Ps. Lamb. 35, 5. On díglum ł on incofan ł on eówrum clyfum *in cubilibus vestris*, 4, 5. Eal ðæt hé hæfde on his incofan *all that he had in his breast*, Bt. Met. Fox 22, 35; Met. 22, 18. v. breóst-cofa.

in-coðu, e; *and* an; *f. An internal disease*:—Wið incoðe, L. M. 2, 55; Lchdm. i. 276, 6. Fela incoða hé gehǽlde untrumra sáwla mislícra manna *many diseases of sick souls of diverse men he healed*, Homl. Th. ii. 560, 33. Incoða *infirmitates*; incoðe *fibras* [=*febris*?], Hpt. Gl. 453. Incoðan *melancholias*, 478. [Cf. in-ádl.]

in-cuman; *p.* -com *To come in, enter*:—Ðonne gé incumaþ on ðæt lond ðe ic eów sille *cum ingressi fueritis terram, quam ego dabo vobis*, Lev. 23, 10. On swá hwilcum húse swá gé incumaþ *whatever house you enter*, Homl. Th. ii. 534, 8. Gá hé út mid swilcum reáfe swilce hé incom *cum quali veste intraverit, cum tali exeat*, Ex. 21, 3. Ðá hié tósamne incóman *when they entered together*, Blickl. Homl. 173. 5. Ðǽr nǽfre nǽnig dǽl regnes incuman ne mæg *never can any rain enter there*, 125, 33. Incuma *introire*, Mk. Skt. Lind. 1, 45.

in-cund; *adj. Internal, inward, intimate*:—Ða óðre werod brúcaþ ðære incundan embwlátunge his godcundnysse swá ðæt hí náteshwón fram his andweardnysse ásende ne gewítaþ *the other hosts enjoy the closest contemplation of his divinity, so that on no account do they depart on any mission from his presence*, Homl. Th. i. 348, 7. Ðære þeóde sáwla þurh ða ýttran wundra beóþ getogene tó ðære incundan gife *the souls of that people are drawn by those outward miracles to the inward grace*, ii. 132, 3. Ðonne hé ða úterran þing dón sculon, ðæt hié ne síen ðæm incundum ingeþance áfirrede . . . hié lǽtaþ ácólian ða incundan lufan *ne, dum cura ab eis exterior agitur, ab interna intentione mergantur . . . ab intimo amore frigescunt*, Past. 18, 7; Swt. 138, 5-9. Wið ǽghwylcum incundum earfoþnyssum *for all internal difficulties*, Herb. 90, 11; Lchdm. i. 196, 21. Tó incundum *ad intima*, Kent. Gl. 999. v. innan-, inne-cund.

in-cúð; *adj. Strange, not friendly, grievous*:—Hé wolde eác swylce þurh ðone regul oncnáwan ða wíslícan gefadunge ðe snotorlíce geset is be incúðra þinga endebyrdnesse *he wished also to know by means of the Rule* [*of Benedict*] *the wise arrangement, that is prudently appointed concerning the disposition of strange matters*, Lchdm. iii. 440, 26. Hé hálegra cyricena land incúðum reáferum tódǽlde *he* [*Edwy*] *distributed the lands of holy churches to strangers and robbers*, 436, 1. v. next word.

in-cúðlíce; *adv. Grievously, sorely*:—Ðá begann se ealda incúðlíce siccetan and mid wópe wearþ ofergoten *then the old man began to sigh grievously and became suffused with tears*, Ælfc. T. Grn. 18, 1.

in-dǽlan; *p.* de *To impart, infuse*:—Ðæt léht scínende indǽl heartum úsum *illud lumen splendidum infunde cordibus nostris*, Rtl. 2, 13. Indǽlde *infudit*, 47, 1.

Indea, India *India*:—Ðæt sint India gemǽro *in his finibus India est*, Ors. 1, 1; Swt. 10, 15. Hé fór on Indie *Indiam petit*, 3, 9; Swt. 132, 4. Ðá wilnode ic Indeum innwearde tó geseónne *interiorem indiam perspicere cupiens*, Nar. 5, 17. On Indea *to India*, Chr. 883; Erl. 83, 17.

Indéas; *pl. Indians*:—Ðæm strengstan Indéa cyninge *fortissimo Indorum rege*, Ors. 3, 9; Swt. 132, 17. Tó Indéum, Apstls. Kmbl. 85; Ap. 43: Bt. 29, 3; Fox 106, 22. Óþ Indéas, Bt. Met. Fox 16, 35; Met. 16, 18.

in-dípan; *p.* te *To dip in, immerse*:—Ðætte indépe útaweard fingeres in wætre *ut intinguat extremum digiti in aquam*, Lk. Skt. Lind. 16, 24. [Cf. *Goth.* daupjan.]

Indisc; *adj. Indian*:—Ðone gársecg mon hǽt Indisc *e qua oceanus Indicus vocari incipit*, Ors. 1, 1; Swt. 10, 8. On indisc sprecende *indice loquentes*, Nar. 25, 16. Indisce mýs *mures indici*, 16, 5. Indiscum wordum *indico sermone*, 29, 8.

in-drencan; *p.* te *To soak, saturate, inebriate*:—Hí ðá sylfe betweónum indrencton mid ðám cerenum ðære gódspellícan swétnysse *they mutually saturated each other with the wines of evangelic sweetness*, Guthl. 17; Gdwin. 72, 7. [Cf. *Ger.* ein-tränken *to soak, impregnate.*] v. indrincan.

in-drífan; *p.* -dráf *To impel, send forth, utter*:—Hé in wítum word indráf *in torments he spoke impetuously*, Cd. 214; Th. 269, 29; Sat. 80.

in-drincan; *p.* -dranc *To imbibe, drink*:—Indranc *inbibit*, Mt. Kmbl. p. 1, 7. Indrungno [*Rush.* indruncne] *inebriati*, Jn. Skt. Lind. 2, 10.

in-dryhten; *adj. Noble, courtly, befitting one who belongs to a king's body-guard* [cf. *Icel.* inn-drótt *a king's body-guard*]:—Ðæt biþ in eorle indryhten þeáw ðæt hé his ferþlocan fæste binde *it is a noble habit in a man, to bind fast his mind's casket*, Exon. 76 b; Th. 287, 11; Wand. 12. Ic eom indryhten and eorlum cúð *I am noble and known to men*, 130 b; Th. 500, 3; Rä. 89, 1. Ic wát indryhtne giest, 112 a; Th. 430, 1; Rä. 44, 1. *Does* indryhten wicg *ippus* (=? ἵππος), Wrt. Voc. ii. 48, 37 *belong here?*

in-dryhto; *f. Nobleness, honour, glory*:—Blǽd is gehnǽged eorþan indryhto ealdaþ and searaþ *glory is laid low, earth's honour grows old and withers*, Exon. 82 b; Th. 311, 8; Seef. 89. Gehwone wyrta wynsumra ðe wuldercyning ofer eorþan gescóp tó indryhtum ælda cynne *every pleasant plant that the king of glory created on earth as honours for the race of men*, 58 b; Th. 211, 15; Ph. 198.

Ine, es; *m. Ine, king of the West Saxons from* A. D. 688 *to* 726:—Hér Ine féng tó Wesseaxna ríce and heóld xxxvii wint., Chr. 688; Erl. 42, 4. Hér Ine férde tó Róme and ðǽr his feorh gesealde, 728 [726, MS E]; Erl. 44, 33. Ine wæs Cénréding. pref; Erl. 4, 10. The laws of Ine are given in Thorpe's Ancient Laws and Institutes of England, vol. i. pp. 102-150.

in-éddisc. v. in-ídisc.

in-elfe. v. in-ylfe.

in-erfe. v. in-irfe.

in-fær, es; *n. An entrance, ingress*:—Ðá gesette God æt ðam infære engla hyrdrǽdene *then God set a guard of angels at the entrance*, Gen. 3, 24. Mid ðam innfære mid ðam ðe hé inn áfaren wæs *by the entrance at which he had entered*, Homl. Th. i. 178, 2. Hé hæfþ gerýmed rihtwísum mannum infær tó his ríce *he hath opened to righteous men an entrance to his kingdom*, 28, 13. Geopenige úre sárnys ús infær sóðre gecyrrednysse *let our affliction open to us an entrance to true conversion*, ii. 124, 7. Of inferum *ex aditis*, i. *ex ingressibus*, Wrt. Voc. ii. 144, 49. v. in-faru.

in-færeld, es; *n. An entrance*:—Úre gást forhtode tó eówrum infærelde *elanguit cor nostrum ad introitum vestrum*, Jos. 2, 11. Infæreld *introitus*: infærelda *vestibula, introitus*, Hpt. Gl. 498.

infangeneþeóf '*the right to judge one's own thief when taken within the jurisdiction, and the privilege consequent upon that jurisdiction, viz. the receiving of the mulct, or money-payment for the crime*,' Cod. Dipl. Kmbl. i. xlv. The word, which does not occur in the earlier laws, is thus defined in those of Edward the Confessor:—De infangeneþef. Justicia cognoscentis latronis sua est de homine suo, si captus fuerit super terram suam, L. Ed. C. 22; Th. i. 452, 4. In the preceding chapter, 'descripcio libertatum diversarum,' it is said the lords 'haberent eos [*their men who had committed crime*] ad rectum in curia sua, si haberent sacham et socham, tol et theam, et infangene thef.' Other passages in which the word is found are L. Wil. I. 2; Th. i. 467, 27, Si quis eorum, qui habent soche et sache et tol et them et infangene theof, implacitetur in comitatu; and L. H. xx. c; Th. i. 528, 9, Archiepiscopi, episcopi, comites, et alie potestates in terris proprie potestatis sue sacam et socnam habent tol et theam et infongentheaf. The word also occurs in the following charters of Edward the Confessor:—Concedo eis in omnibus terris suis prænominatis, consuetudines hic Anglice scriptas, scilicet, infangene þeóf, etc. Chart. Th. 359, 3. A similar enumeration occurs in 384, 25 and in 411, 32. In 369, 13 the word occurs in an Anglo-Saxon charter. See also Cod. Dipl. Kmbl. iv. 227, 9, where is the form 'mid infangenum þeófe.'

in-faran; *p.* -fór *To go into, enter*:—Ic infare on húse ðínum *introibo in domum tuam*, Ps. Spl. 5, 8. Innfæreþ *ingredietur*, Jn. Skt. Lind. 10, 9. Infór se cingc on ða sǽ *ingressus est pharao in mare*, Cantic. Moys. 19. Ðis synd Israhéla naman ðe infóron on Egipta land *hæc sunt nomina filiorum Israel, qui ingressi sunt in Ægyptum*, Gen. 46, 8. Infaraþ tó his cafertúnum *introite in atria ejus*, Ps. Lamb. 95, 8. Ne mæg hé infaran on godes ríce *non potest introire in regnum dei*, Jn. Skt. 3, 5. Ðæt hé ælmessan underféncge æt ðám infarendum *that he might receive alms from those entering*, Homl. Skt. 10, 27.

in-faru, e; *f. Invasion, march into a country, inroad*:—Se cyng bæd hine faran intó Cent . . . ac se eorl nolde ná geþwǽrian ðære infare *the king bade him* [*Godwin*] *march into Kent . . . but the earl would not assent to the invasion*, Chr. 1048; Erl. 178, 11.

in-feccan *to fetch in*:—Ðá héht hé ðone drý infeccan beforan hine *he ordered the sorcerer to be fetched into his presence*, Blickl. Homl. 175, 1.

in-féran; *p.* de *To enter*:—Infoerden *ingrediuntur*, Mk. Skt. Lind. 1, 21. Gé in giwinne hiora infoerdun *vos in laborem eorum introistis*, Jn. Skt. Rush. 4, 38.

in-fiht, -feoht, es; *n. An attack made upon a person by one inhabiting the same dwelling; it was a breach of the peace for which a fine had to be paid to the head of the house if he were competent to exercise jurisdiction*:—Infiht [infitht, MS.] *vel insocna est quod ab ipsis qui in domo sunt contubernales agitur; hoc eciam wita emendabitur patrifamilias, si questionem habent querentem vel quesitam*, L. H. 80, 12; Th. i. 587, 25.

in-findan; *p.* -fand *To find, discover*:—Soecaþ gé and gé infindes *quærite et invenietis*, Mt. Kmbl. Lind. 7, 7. Infund restende *invenit vacantem*, 12, 44. Ic ne infand in him intinga *ego non invenio in eo causam*, Jn. Skt. Rush. 19, 6. Infunden wæs *inventa est*, Mt. Kmbl. Lind. 1, 18. v. on-findan.

in-flǽscness, e; *f. Incarnation*, Lye.

in-fléde; *adj. Full of water* [*of a stream*]:—Tigris eá infléde *Tigris, stream of abundant flood*, Cd. 12; Th. 15, 12; Gen. 232. Lǽt nú streámas weallan, eá infléde, Andr. Kmbl. 3006; An. 1506. v. fléde.

in-fôster, es; *n. Rearing, breeding:*—Hit mîn âgen ǽht is and mîn infôster *it is my own property and my rearing*, L. O. 3; Th. i. 180, 7.

in-frôd; *adj. Very old* or *very wise:*—Hê him helpe ne mæg eald and infrôd ǽnige gefremman *old and stricken in years he can afford him no help*, Beo. Th. 4889; B. 2449. Him wæs wên ealdum infrôdum, 3752; B. 1874.

-ing *a suffix of feminine nouns denoting action.*

-ing. I. *a patronymic suffix:*—Sume naman syndon patronymica, ðæt synd fæderlîce naman, æfter Grêciscum þeáwe, ac seó Lêdensprǽc næfþ ða naman; hî sind swâ ðeáh on Engliscre sprǽce, Penda, and of ðam Pending, Ælfc. Gr. 5; Som. 4, 52-4. Ælfred Æþelwulfing *Alfred the son of Ethelwulf*, Chr. 871; Erl. 76, 3. The use of this suffix is well shown by the genealogies in the Chronicle, e. g. pref; Erl. pp. 2, 4: 855; Erl. 68, 69, with which may be compared similar lists in Icelandic where *-son* is used. See also Lk. Skt. Lind. 3, 23-38 where the suffix is used with the foreign names, e. g. *Seth Adaming* Seth son of Adam. In a rather extended sense the suffix is found in the names of families or peoples, who are regarded as descendants of a common ancestor, and traces of this use remain in many place-names in England. 'The Wælsings, in Old Norse Völsungar, reappear at Walsingham in Norfolk, Wolsingham in Northumberland, and Woolsingham in Durham. The Billings at Billing, Billingham, Billinghoe, etc. Such local names are for the most part irregular compositions, of which the former part is the patronymic *-ing*, declined in the genitive plural. The second portion is a mere definition of the locality, as -geat, -hyrst, -hâm, -wîc, -tûn, -stede, and the like. In a few cases the patronymic stands alone in the nominative plural, as Tôtingas, Tooting, Surrey; Wôcingas, Woking, Surrey; Meallingas, Malling, Kent. . . . In dealing, however, with these names, some amount of caution is necessary: it is by no means enough that a name should end in *-ing*, to convert it into a genuine patronymic. On the contrary it is a power of that termination to denote the genitive or possessive, which is also the generative case: and in some local names we do find it so used: thus Æðelwulfing lond [Cod. Dipl. No. 179, a. 801] is exactly equivalent to Æðelwulfes lond, the estate of a duke Æðelwulf, not of a family called Æðelwulfings. So again, ðæt Folcwining lond [Cod. Dipl. No. 195, a. 811], ðæt Wynhearding lond [Cod. Dipl. No. 195, a. 811], imply the land of Folcwine, of Wynheard, not of marks or families called Folcwinings, and Wynheardings. [Cf. Câsering ꝉ caseres gafel *didrachma*, Mt. Kmbl. Lind. 17, 24.] Woolbedington, Wool Lavington, Barlavington, are respectively Wulfbæding tûn, Wulflâfing tûn, Beórlâfing tûn, the tûn or dwelling of Wulflâf, Wulfbæd, and Beórlâf. Between such words and genuine patronymics the line must be carefully drawn, a task which requires both skill and experience; the best security is, where we find the patronymic in the genitive plural. . . . Changes for the sake of euphony must also be guarded against, as sources of error: thus Abingdon in Berks would impel us strongly to assume a family of Abingas; the Saxon name Æbban dûn convinces us that it was named from an Æbba [*m.*] or Æbbe [*f.*]. Dunnington is not Duning tûn, but Dunnan tûn.' Kemble's Saxons in England, i. 59, nn; see also the text in the following pages, and Taylor's Names and Places, pp. 82-3, 89. As was seen above in *Adaming*, the native suffix could be applied in the case of individuals to foreign names: it was so also in the case of peoples. Thus in the Rushworth Gloss, Mt. 8, 28, 'in lond geransinga' translates *in regionem Gerasenorum*; in 10, 15 'eorðe sodominga and gomorringa' is the rendering of *terra Sodomorum et Gomorræorum*, and above in v. 5 of the same chapter we have 'cæstra samaringa' for *civitates samaritanorum*. These may be compared with the forms in the Chronicle, West Kentingas, 999; Erl. 134, 28; Eást Centingas, 1009; Erl. 142, 19; Centingas, 1011; Erl. 144, 27. II. The suffix is also found in nouns formed from adjectives with a force which may be seen in the following examples:—æðeling *a prince:* earming *a wretch.*

ing *the name of the nasal guttural* ᛝ ng, *in the Runic alphabet. In the Gothic the name seems to have been* iggws, see Zacher, Das Gothische Alphabet, p. 3. *In the Runic poem* 22; Kmbl. 343, 27 *it is taken as the name of a prince of the East Danes:*—Ing wæs ǽrest mid Eást Denum gesewen secgum; ôþ hê siððan eft ofer wǽg gewât. Ðus heardingas ðone hæle nemdon. This name [cf. Gothic form] may be the same as that found in a genealogy in the Chronicle a. 547:—Esa wæs Inguing Ingui Angenwitting, Erl. 16, 11. As a proper name or as part of a proper name Ingi occurs in Icelandic, e. g. Ingi-björg, Ing-veldr, Ingi-mundr, Ingólfr: 'many more compounds are found in the Swedish-Runic stones as this name was national among the ancient Swedes; cf. also Yngvi and Ynglingar.' Cl. and Vig. Ingi. For the Rune see Zacher, pp. 30, 56-7: Taylor's Greeks and Goths, pp. 31, 82: and for the name Grmm. D. M. pp. 320-1.

ing, e; *f. A meadow, an ing* [in dialects of north and east, see E.D.S. Reprinted Glossaries, Nos. 2, 15, 16, 17]. The word occurs in local names, e. g. Ing-ham, Ing-thorpe, Ink-set, Ink-pen; see Cod. Dipl. Kmbl. vi. 306. [*Icel.* eng; *f. a meadow;* engi; *n. meadowland, a meadow: Dan.* eng: *Swed.* äng.]

in-gân; *p.* -eode *To go in, enter:*—On swâ hwylce burh swâ gê ingâþ . . . Ðonne gê ingân on ðæt hûs *in quamcumque civitatem intraveritis . . . Intrantes in domum*, Mt. Kmbl. 10, 11, 12. Ðâ hê ineode *ingresso*, Gen. 48, 3. Hê on ðæs gesíðes hûs ineode, Bd. 5, 4; S. 617, 16. Hû mæg man ingân on stranges hûs *quomodo potest quisquam intrare in domum fortis*, Mt. Kmbl. 12, 29: Lk. Skt. 8, 51. Hê nolde ingân *nolebat introire*, 15, 28.

in-gang, es; *m. Entrance, entry, ingress, entrance-fee:*—Þurh ðê sceal beón se ingang eft geopenod *through thee* [*the Virgin Mary*] *shall the entrance* [*to heaven*] *be again opened*, Blickl. Homl. 9, 8. Hundteóntiga swîna ingang *right of entry into a pasture for a hundred swine*, Cod. Dipl. Kmbl. iii. 283, 12. Ingong and ûtgong *ingress and egress*, Chart. Th. 578, 26. Ðæt beó gelǽst binnan twâm dagum be ðæs inganges wîte *let that be done within two days, under penalty of forfeiting the entrance-fee*, 606, 10, 20. Gebête hê be his ingange, 25. Gylde his ingang, 35. Be ûtgonge Israhêla folces of Ægypta lande and be ingonge ðæs gehâtlondes *de egressu Israel ex Ægypto et ingressu in terram repromissionis*, Bd. 4, 24; S. 598, 11. Him ôðres lîfes ingang gegearwode *vitæ alterius ingressui paravit*, S. 599, 2. Ingang ðîn and ûtgang ðîn *thy going out and thy coming in*, Ps. Spl. 120, 8. Inngang, Ps. Th. 117, 19. [*O. E. Homl. A. R.* in-ȝong: *Laym.* in-ȝeong: *Piers P.* in-gong, -gang *entrance: O. Frs.* in-gong, -gung: *Icel.* inn-ganga, -gangr *entrance, entering: O. H. Ger.* in-gang *introitus, aditus, vestibulum, janua: Ger.* ein-gang.]

in-gangan; *p.* -gêng *To enter, go in:*—Ic ingange *ingredior*, Ælfc. Gr. 29; Som. 33, 47. Ic on unscyldignyssa mînre ic ingange *ego in innocentia mea ingressus sum*, Ps. Spl. 25, 1. Ingangeþ cyningc wuldres *introibit Rex gloriæ*, 23, 7. Ôþ ðæt ic ingange on hâligra godes *donec intrem sanctuarium Dei*, 72, 17. Gê nû þyder ingongaþ *do ye now enter in*, Blickl. Homl. 207, 2. Cyricean duru ingangan *ecclesiæ januam ingredi*, Bd. 5, 14; S. 634, 19. Wæs ingangende on ðære hâlgan Marian hûs *entered the house of the Holy Mary*, Blickl. Homl. 147, 1. Ingongende, 4. Ðæt deófol genam mid him ôðre seofon deóflo and ingangende on ðæt carcern, 243, 5. Ðonne is ôðer ingangendum ðam mônþe ðe wê agustus hâtaþ se ǽresta mônan dæg *the second day is at the beginning of the month that we call August, the first Monday*, Lchdm. iii. 76, 16. Ðæt ða ingangendan leóht geseón *ut intrantes videant lumen*, Lk. Skt. 8, 16.

in-geat [?] *cubiculum*, Lye.

in-gebed, es; *n. Hearty, earnest prayer:*—Gange mîn ingebed [*or* gebed in?] on ðîn gleáwe gesihþ *intret oratio mea in conspectu tuo*, Ps. Th. 87, 2. [From the Latin *intret* the *in* might be expected to belong to the verb; if so it should occupy some other place.]

in-gebyrigan; *p.* de *To taste:*—Ingeberigde *gustavit*, Jn. Skt. Lind. 2, 9.

in-gedôn *to put in:*—Hê on ðæt gemynegade mynster ingedôn wæs *monasterio supra memorato inditus*, Bd. 5, 12; S. 631, 9.

in-gefeoht, es; *n. Intestine* or *civil war:*—Ðætte Bryttas sume tîd gestildon fram ûtgefeohte and hie sylfe þræston on ingefeohtum *ut Brittones quiescentibus ad tempus exteris, civilibus sese bellis contriverint*, Bd. 1, 22; S. 485, 12. [Cf. in-gewinn.]

in-gefolc, es; *n. A native race*, Cd. 149; Th. 186, 22; Exod. 142. [Cf. in-geþeóde.]

in-gehrif, es; *n. The womb:*—Of ingerife *ex utero*, Ps. Spl. T. 21, 8. v. hrif.

in-gehygd, -hýd, e; *f:* es; *n. Thought, mind, intent, sense, knowledge, understanding, conscience, intention, purpose:*—Hwæt fremaþ ðê ðæt ðîn cyst stande ful mid gôdum and ðîn ingehýd beó æmtig ǽlces gôdes *what doth it profit thee that thy chest stand full of good things, and thy mind be empty of every good thing?* Homl. Th. ii. 410, 11. Ðæs mannes wîsdôm is ârfæstnys and sôð ingehýd ðæt heó yfel forbûge *the fear of the Lord, that is wisdom; and to depart from evil is understanding*, Homl. Skt. 1, 237. Ǽfæstre ingehýde *religiosæ intentionis*, Bd. 4, 28; S. 605, 10. Treów ingehýdes gôdes and yfeles *lignum scientiæ boni et mali*, Gen. 2, 9. Gê ætbrudun ðæs ingehýdes cǽge *tulistis clavem scientiæ*, Lk. Skt. 11, 52. Cherubin is gecweden gefyllednys ingehýdes oððe gewittes, Homl. Th. i. 344, 3. Ûre wuldor is seó gecýðnys ûres ingehýdes *our glory is the testimony of our conscience*, ii. 564, 32. Mid ealle inngehygde heortan mînre *in toto corde meo*, Ps. Th. 118, 145. Ðâ onwende heó hine fram ðære yfelan ingehygde his môdes *revocavit eum illa ab intentione*, Bd. 2, 12; S. 574, 37. Wæs se ylca munuc mid hluttre ingehýde ðæs upplîcan edleánes *erat idem monachus pura intentione supernæ retributionis*, 4, 3; S. 567, 18. Ðâ andwyrde eugenia and cwæþ mid ðisum ingehýde ðæt ða gewylnunga ðissere andweardan worulde synt swîðe swicole *then answered Eugenia and spoke to this effect, that the desires of this present world are very deceitful*, Homl. Skt. 2, 163. Mid ingehygde *conscientia*, Ps. Stev. ii. 203, 11. Se Hâlga Gâst him forgeaf ingehýd ealra gereorda *the Holy Ghost gave them knowledge of all languages*, Homl. Th. i. 318, 13. Sumum men hê forgifþ wîsdom sumum gôd ingehýd *to one man he gives wisdom, to another good knowledge* [cf. 1 Cor. xii. 8], 322, 26. Wæter getâcnaþ on ðyssere stôwe mennisc ingehýd, ii. 280, 2. Ða [*the seven gifts of the Holy Spirit*] sind wîsdôm and andgit, rǽd and strengþ, ingehýd and ǽrfæstnys; Godes ege is se seofoða, 292, 23. Hê heóld his þeáwas swâ swâ heálîc biscop and his munelîce ingehýd swâ þeáh betwux mannum *he behaved as an exalted bishop, and yet to all intents and purposes was a monk among men*, 506, 13. Hî hæfdon ðæt gôde ingehýd on heora heortan ðæt hî woldon Gode ânum gecwêman and nâ cêpan dysegra manna herunge *they had the good sense in their hearts, to wish to please God only, and not to care for the* *praise of foolish men*, 564, 29. Seó geladung geopenaþ Criste hire ingehýd and ða dígelan geþohtas on sóðre andetnysse *the church opens her mind and secret thoughts to Christ in true confession*, 586, 20. Ðus áfandaþ God his gecorenan, ná swilce hé nyte heora ingehýd, Boutr. Scrd. 23, 7. Ðæt gold getácnode úrne geleáfan and úre góde ingehíd ðe wé Gode offrian sceolon, Gen. pref. Thw. 3, 33. On ðam is godcundnesse wén ðe manna ingehygd wát and can, Blickl. Homl. 179, 26. Ða eorþlícan sorga hie forléton and ða ingehýd heora heortan ful fæstlíce on ðone heofonlícan hyht gestaþelodon *they dismissed earthly cares, and fixed full firmly the intents of their heart on the heavenly hope*, 135, 29. Ingehýd *conscientias*, Hymn. Surt. 127, 8. Ic ingehygd eal geondwlíte *I survey all his mind*, Exon. 71 b; Th. 266, 16; Jul. 399. Sió swíðe gedræfþ sefan ingehygd monna gehwelces *sorely does it trouble the thought of every man's mind*, Bt. Met. Fox 25, 84; Met. 25, 42. God ingehýda drihten is *Deus scientiarum dominus est*, Cantic. An. 3. [Cf. in-geþanc.]

in-gehygdness, e; *f. Intention, purpose:*—Ic ontýne on sealmlofe ingehygdnessa ł foresetnysse *aperiam in psalterio propositionem*, Ps. Lamb. 48, 5.

in-gelǽdan; *p.* de *To lead* or *bring in, introduce:*—Ingelédde ofer hie Drihten weter séwe *the Lord brought upon them the water of the sea*, Cantic. Moys. 23; Thw. notæ, p. 30. Óþ ðæt ic ðé ingelǽde on mínes Fæder hús *until I bring thee into my father's house*, Blickl. Homl. 191, 19. Ingelǽded *introducta*, Bd. 4, 9; S. 576, 37.

in-geladian; *p.* ode *To invite:*—Se ðe ðé ingeladode *is qui te vocavit*, Lk. Skt. 14, 9, 10. Ðá sǽde hé sum bigspel be ðám ingeladudan *dicebat ad invitatos parabolam*, 7.

in-gemynd, es; *n:* e; *f. Memory, mind, remembrance:*—Ic ðæs wuldres treówes oft hæfde ingemynd *oft had I remembrance of the tree of glory*, Elen. Kmbl. 2504; El. 1253. Húlíc is se organ ingemyndum tó begonganne ðam ðe his gást wile ásceádan of scyldum *of what nature is the Pater Noster for use by the mind, in the case of him who will separate his spirit from guilt*, Salm. Kmbl. 108; Sal. 53. v. in-gehygd.

in-gemynde; *adj. Recollected, remembered, in mind, in memory:*—Ðá wæs ðam folce on ferhþsefan ingemynde swá him á scyle wundor ða ðe worhte weoroda dryhten *then did the people remember in mind, as is ever their duty, the miracles which the Lord of Hosts wrought*, Elen. Kmbl. 1788; El. 896.

in-genga, an; *m. An aggressor, invader:*—Seoððan Grendel wearþ ingenga mín *since Grendel became my aggressor*, Beo. Th. 3557; B. 1776.

in-geótan; *p.* -geát *To pour in:*—Hí on ǽlce healfe inguton *they poured in on every side*, Guthl, 5; Gdwin. 34, 18.

in-geóting, e; *f. A pouring in, purification:*—Yngeóting *lustramentum*, Hpt. Gl. 483.

in-gerec, es; *n. A tumult:*—Hé ðá eác on ðam ingerece óðerne cyninges þeng mid ðý mánfullan wǽpne ácwealde *in ipso tumultu etiam alium de militibus sica nefanda peremit*, Bd. 2, 9; S. 511, 26. v. ungerec, gerec.

in-gerif. v. in-gehrif.

in-gesteald, es; *n. Household goods:*—Tó scypum feredon eal ingesteald swylce hie æt Finnes hám findan meahton sigla searogimma, Beo. Th. 2314; B. 1155.

in-geswell, es; *n. An internal swelling;* empus [= ἔμπυος], Ælfc. Gl. 10; Som. 57, 30; Wrt. Voc. 19, 36.

in-geþanc, es; *m. n. Thought, thinking, cogitation, intent, mind, heart, conscience:*—Seaxes ord and seó swíðre hond eorles ingeþonc and ord somod *the knife's point and the right hand, the mind of man and the point combined*, Exon. 123 a; Th. 472, 8; Rä. 61, 13. Ðæt ingeþonc ǽlces monnes ðone líchoman lít [lǽt?] ðider hit wile *the mind of every man bends [leads?] the body whither it will*, Bt. Met. Fox 26, 235; Met. 26, 118. Gif hé his ingeþances anweald næfþ *if he has not power over his mind*, Bt. 29, 3; Fox 106, 26. Eft sint tó manigenne ða geþyldegan ðætte ðæt hie mid hiera wordum and dǽdum forgiefaþ ðæt hie ðæt eác on hiera ingeþonce forgifen ðý læs hé mid ðý níðe yfles ingeþonces tóweorpe ða mægenu ðæs gódan weorces ðe hé Gode útan anwealglíce forgeaf *contra admonendi sunt patientes, ne in eo, quod exterius portant, interius doleant: ne tantæ virtutis sacrificium, quod integrum foras immolant, intus malitiæ peste corrumpant*, Past. 33, 5; Swt. 220, 19. Mid eáðmóde ingeþonce ðú mé cíddesð *me humili intentione reprehendis*, prm; Swt. 22, 10. Suelcum ingeþonce gerist *cujus intentioni bene congruens*, 10, 1; Swt. 61, 9. Se Déma se ðe ðæt inngeþonc eall wát hé eác ðæm inngeþonce démþ *intus quippe est qui judicat, intus, quod judicatur*, 4, 2; Swt. 39, 11. Geleornigen eác ða bearn ðæt hí suá hiéren hira ieldrum suá suá hie selfe wieten on hira inngeþonce beforan ðæs díeglan Déman eágum ðæt hí hit for Gode dón *illi discant, quomodo ante occulti arbitri oculos sua interiora componant*, 28, 1; Swt. 191, 2. Of úrum ágnum ingeþonce *a nobismet ipsis*, 49, 4; Swt. 385, 9. Mid ealles módes geornfullan ingeþance higie *with diligent thought of the whole mind strive*, Bt. 22, 2; Fox 78, 18. Agustinus worhte twá béc be his eágnum ingeþance *Augustine composed two books about his own mind*, Shrn. 164, 16. Ðú ongitst ðín ágen ingeþanc ðæt hit biþ micele beorhtre ðonne seó sunne, Bt. 35, 1; Fox 154, 28. God besceáwaþ ǽlces mannes inngeþanc *Deus intuetur cujuslibet hominis cogitationem*, L. Ecg. P. i. 2; Th. ii. 172, 13. Hyra ingeþanc hig forleósaþ on hyra wege *they lose their conscience on their way*, L. E. I. 35; Th. ii. 432, 22. Nú ic wilnige ðæt ðeós sprǽc stigge on ðæt ingeþonc ðæs leorneres *ut ad lectoris sui animum gradiatur*, Past. prm; Swt. 23, 16. Se dysega ungeþyldega all his ingeþonc hé geypt *totum spiritum suum profert stultus*, 33, 4; Swt. 220, 10. Drync se onwende gewit wera ingeþanc *a drink that perverted the wit, the mind of men*, Andr. Kmbl. 70; An. 35. Næfdon hí máre monnum gelíces ðonne ingeþonc; hæfde ánra gehwylc his ágen mód, Bt. Met. Fox 26, 188; Met. 26, 94. Hie forgytaþ ðæt hie hwéne ǽr ymbhygdigum eárum and ingeþancum gehýrdon reccean *they forget what they a little before with anxious ears and minds have heard related*, Blickl. Homl. 55, 27. Ðá azarias ingeþancum hleóðrade *then did Azariah sing full thoughtfully*, Cd. 188; Th. 233, 24; Dan. 280. Ingeþoncum beofiaþ *they tremble at heart*, Exon. 22 b; Th. 63, 4; Cri. 1014. Hiorte geclǽnsod and geeádmédedd ingeþancum, Ps. C. 50, 128; Ps. Grn. ii. 279, 128. Óþ ðæt hé ongeat ðæs módes ingeþancas *until he understood the mind's thoughts*, Bt. 7, 1; Fox 16, 5. Hie behealdaþ ealle ða ingeþoncas hiora módes *tota illud mentis intentione custodiunt*, Past. 21, 5; Swt. 161, 14. Unclǽne ingeþoncas *impure thoughts*, Exon. 27 a; Th. 80, 34; Cri. 1316. Uton word and weorc rihtlíce fadian and úre inngeþanc clǽnsian georne *let us order our words and works aright, and purify our thoughts diligently*, Swt. A. S. Rdr. 111, 218. Gesamnige swá hé swíðost mǽge ealle tó ðæm ánum his ingeþonc *let him collect, as far as possible, all his thoughts to that one object*, Bt. Met. Fox 22, 24; Met. 22, 12.

in-geþeóde; *pl. Peoples, nations:*—Dryhten is ofer ealle ingeþeóde [? MS. inca þeode.] se heáhsta *excelsus super omnes gentes Dominus*, Ps. Th. 112, 4: Cd. 163; Th. 205, 30; Exod. 443.

in-gewinn, es; *n. An intestine struggle:*—Scortlíce ic hæbbe nú gesǽd hiora ingewinn *I have now shortly related their intestine struggles*, Ors. 2, 6; Swt. 88, 29. [Cf. in-gefeoht.]

in-gewitness, e; *f. Knowledge, knowing, consciousness, conscience:*—Besmitene syndon ge heora mód ge heora ingewitnys *coinquinata sunt et mens eorum et conscientia*, Bd. 1, 17; S. 494, 42. Ða wyrstan ingewitnesse mé ic geseó *pessimam mihi scientiam præ oculis habeo*, 5, 13; S. 632, 32.

Ingwine; *pl. A name of the Danes*, Beo. Th. 2092; B. 1044: 2642; B. 1319. v. Grmm. D. M. 320–1; *and see* Ing.

in-heald *interrasilis*, Wrt. Voc. ii. 46, 24.

in-hebban *to raise, remove*, Exon. 12 a; Th. 20, 6; Cri. 313.

in-heord, e; *f. A herd belonging to the lord and kept on his estate:*—Ǽhteswáne ðe inheorde healt gebyreþ . . . *servo porcario, qui dominicum gregem curie custodit, pertinet . . .*, L. R. S. 7; Th. i. 436, 22.

in-here, es; *m. A native army, the army of a country, home-force:*—Se here férde swá hé sylf wolde and se fyrdinge dyde ðære landleóde ǽlcne hearm ðet him náðor ne dohte ne innhere ne úthere *the Danes went as they liked, and the English levy did every kind of harm to the people of the country, so that neither the native nor the foreign army did them any good*, Chr. 1006; Erl. 140, 13.

in-hirdmann, es; *m. A member of a retinue* or *body-guard:*—Þegnas ł innheardmenn *milites*, Mt. Kmbl. Lind. 8, 9. v. hird.

in-híréd, es; *m. Household, family, house:*—Tirus wæs on Cryst gelýfende hé sylf and eall hys ynhýréd *Tyrus believed on Christ, he himself and all his household*, St. And. 30, 15. Inhýrédes *clientelæ*, Hpt. Gl. 523. Ealle werhádes men his inhírédes ǽgðer ge inbyrdlingas ge gebohte þeówan *omnes viri domus illius, tam vernaculi quam emptitii*, Gen. 17, 27. Ðá wearþ gefullod fæder and sunu mid heora innhýréde *then was baptized the father and son with their household*, Homl. Skt. 5, 308. v. in-híwan.

in-hírness, e; *f. A belonging to any one:*—Ðe Ǽðelréd cyning geúðe God elmihtigum and his hálgan apostolan Petre and Paule on éce inhýrnesse *which king Ethelred granted to Almighty God and to his holy apostles Peter and Paul to belong to them for ever*, Cod. Dipl. Kmbl. vi. 136, 14.

in-híwan, -hígan; *pl. Members of a household, of a convent, domestics:*—Gif gesíþcund mon þingaþ wið cyning for his inhíwum *if a 'gesithcund' man make terms with the king for his household*, L. In. 50; Th. i. 134, 3. Ǽlce gǽre áne dægfeorme inhiowum *every year one day's provision for the members of the convent*, Chart. Th. 509, 14. Gie aron inhígo godes *estis domestici Dei*, Rtl. 82, 33. [Cf. Al mi nestfalde cun beoð me meast feondes and mine *inhinen* alre meast hearmen, Jul. 33, 5.] v. híwan.

in-hoh; *adj. Evidens, manifestus*, Hpt. Gl. 523.

in-hold; *adj. Thoroughly loyal, loyal from the heart:*—Abbodissum wé tǽcaþ ðæt hí inholde sín and ðæs hálgan regoles gebodum eallum móde þeówigen *we teach abbesses to be heartily loyal, and to be subservient to the commands of the holy rule with all their mind*, Lchdm. iii. 442, 28.

in-ídisc, es; *m. n.* [?] *Household furniture:*—Ineddisc *vel* inorf *entheca* g. *suppellex*, Ælfc. Gl. 58; Som. 67, 90; Wrt. Voc. 38, 16.

in-ilve. v. in-ylfe.

in-irfe, es; *n. Household stuff* or *goods:*—Se ðe micel inerfa [MS.

Cott. innierfe] and mislîc âgan wile hê beþearf eác micles fultumes *pluribus adminiculis opus est ad tuendam pretiosæ supellectilis varietatem*, Bt. 14, 2; Fox 44, 10. v. in-orf; *and cf. O.Frs.* in-bold, in-gôd *household furniture.*

in-lâd, e; *f. A way in, bringing in, introduction, entrance-fee* [? v. in-gang]:—Æhtu ôra seulfres tô inlâde *eight oras of silver as entrance-fee*, Jn. Skt. p. 188, 9. Mid inlâde and ûtlâde *cum inductione et eductione*, Cod. Dipl. Kmbl. iv. 209, 5. v. lâd.

in-lǽdan; *p.* de *To lead* or *bring in, introduce*:—Ne inlǽd ûsih in costunge *ne inducas nos in temtationem*, Mt. Kmbl. Lind. 6, 13. Se đe mâ manna inlǽde đonne hê sceole *he who introduces more men than he ought*, Chart. Th. 606, 32. Miđ đý inlǽddon đone cnæht aldro his *cum inducerent puerum parentes ejus*, Lk. Skt. Lind. 2, 27.

in-lænde, -lændisc. v. in-lende, -lendisc.

in-lagian; *p.* ode *To restore an outlaw to the protection of the law*:—Ǽrest đæt hê his âgenne wer gesylle đam cyninge and Criste and mid đam hine sylfne inlagige *first, that he* [*a man who has committed manslaughter in a church*] *pay his own 'wer' to the king and to Christ, and therewith inlaw himself*, L. Eth. ix. 2; Th. i. 340, 13. Inlagie, L. C. E. 2; Th. i. 360, 3. Cf. Si rex paciatur ut qui in ecclesia fecerit homicidium ad emendacionem veniat, primo episcopo et regi precium nativitatis sue reddat, et ita se *inlegiat*, L. H. 11, 1; Th. i. 520, 11. v. ge-inlagian.

in-land, es; *n.* '*Demesne land, that part of a domain which the lord retained in his own hands, in contradistinction to* ût-land *terra tenementalis, signifying land granted out for services;* terra dominicalis, pars manerii dominica':—Wulfêge đæt inland and ælfêge đæt ûtland, Chart. Th. 502, 13. Sex æceras innlondes ǽgđer ge mǽdlondes ge eyrþlondes, Cod. Dipl. Kmbl. ii. 95, 16. xxx hîda .ix inlandes and xxi. hîda gesettes landes . . . is sum inland sum hit is tô gafole gesett *thirty hides, nine of 'inland' and twenty-one hides of let land . . . some is 'inland,' some of it is let*, iii. 450, 11-18. Ǽgđer ge of þegnes inlande ge of geneátlande, L. Edg. i. 1; Th. i. 262, 8. Đat inlond đe Leófrîc hædde for his eádmôdre hêrsumnesse, Cod. Dipl. Kmbl iii. 256, 11. His hlâfordes inland, L. R. S. 3; Th. i. 432, 27.

in-lađian; *p.* ode *To invite*:—Đâ cwæþ hê tô đam đe hine inlađode *dicebat ei qui se invitaverat*, Lk. Skt. 14, 12. Ic wæs cuma and gê mê inlađodon *hospes eram, et collegistis me*, Mt. Kmbl. 25, 35.

in-lenda, an; *m. A native*:—Inlenda *indigena*, Ælfc. Gl. 8; Som. 56, 102; Wrt. Voc. 18, 51: ii. 49, 47. Inle[n]da *accola, habitator*, Hpt. Gl. 490, 52. Inlendan *accolas*, Hymn. Surt. 57, 10. v. next word.

in-lende; *adj. Native, indigenous*:—Inlænde ic eam on eorþan *incola ego sum in terra*, Ps. Lamb. 118, 19. Đǽr on fyrd hyra fǽrspell becwom ôht inlende *there to their host came tidings sudden and terrible, fear of the men of the land* [*the Israelites hearing of the pursuit by the Egyptians*], Cd. 148; Th. 186, 9; Exod. 136. David mǽnde tô Drihtne be his feóndum ǽgđer ge inlendum ge ûtlendum *David complained to the Lord about his enemies, both of his own land and of other lands*, Ps. Th. 2, Arg. [*Icel.* inn-lendr *native*: cf. *O. Frs.* in-lendes: *O. H. Ger.* in-lenti *patria*, Grff. ii. 238.]

in-lendisc; *adj. Native, indigenous*:—Inlendisc *indigena* vel *incola*, Wrt. Voc. 74, 63. Sî hê gemang eów swâ inlendisc *sit inter vos quasi indigena*, Lev. 19, 34. Đǽr ûtlendisc man inlendiscan derie *where a foreigner injures a native*, L. O. D. 6; Th. i. 354, 29. Se forsǽda bisceop angan tô befrînenne sume inlendisce ymbe đæs îglondes gewunan *the aforesaid bishop began to ask some of the natives about the customs of the island*, Lchdm. iii. 432, 28. Hæbben for đî đa ungelǽredan inlendisce đæs hâlgan regules cýđđe þurh âgenes gereordes anwrigennesse *the unlearned natives therefore may have knowledge of the holy Rule, through an explanation in their own language*, 442, 8. [*Icel.* inn-lenzkr *indigenous*: *Ger.* in-ländisch.]

in-lendiscness, e; *f. Incolatus, peregrinatio*, Lye.

in-lîc; *adj. Inner, internal, inward*:—Inlîca *intimus*, Hymn. Surt. 66, 13. Se inlîca dêma *internus arbiter*, Bd. 3, 15; S. 541, 19. Mid đone inlîcan gewitan *apud internum testem*, 5, 6; S. 618, 32. Mid inlîce hete *domestico odio*, 5, 24; S. 646, 38. Fram đâm inlîcum bendum đara synna *internis peccatorum vinculis*, 4, 25; S. 600, 2. [*O. Frs.* in-lêk, -lîk: *O. H. Ger.* in-lîh *internus.*]

in-lîce; *adv. Inwardly, internally, thoroughly, heartily*:—Hê hine bæd and hêt đæt hê inlîce đam biscope freónd wǽre *amicum episcopo fieri petiit et impetravit*, Bd. 5, 19; S. 641, 8. Đû miht openlîce ongiton đæt đæt is for inlîce gôd þing đæt . . . *you can plainly perceive that that is a very thoroughly good thing that* . . ., Bt. 34, 12; Fox 152, 32. [*Piers P.* in-liche: *O. H. Ger.* in-lîho *medullitus.*]

in-lîchamung, e; *f. Incarnation*:—Inlîchomung *incarnatio*, Rtl. 44, 40: 66, 27.

in-lîhtan; *p.* te *To illumine, enlighten*:—Đû tîda gehwane inlîhtes *thou dost enlighten every season*, Exon. 9 b; Th. 7, 29; Cri. 108. Inlêhteþ đec *inluminabit te*, Lk. Skt. Rush. 11, 36. Inlîhteþ *inluminat*, Jn. Skt. Lind. 1, 9. Hine inlýhte *he enlightened him*, Exon. 34 a; Th. 108, 9; Gû. 70. Đæt đû inleóhte *that thou illumine*, 9 b; Th. 8, 9; Cri. 115. Inlîhte *inluminare*, Lk. Skt. Lind. 1, 79. Inlîhted, Exon. 8 b; Th. 3, 29; Cri. 43. Inlýhted, 42 a; Th. 141, 14; Gû. 817. v. on-lîhtan.

in-lîhtend, es; *m. One who enlightens*:—Inlîhtend *inluminator*, Rtl. 2, 11.

in-lîhtian; *p.* ode *To illumine, enlighten*:—Inlêhtaþ đec *inluminabit te*, Lk. Skt. Lind. 11, 36. Inlîchtade *inluminasset*: inlîchtet *inluminatus*, Jn. Skt. p. 6, 1, 2.

in-liþewâc; *adj. Inflexible, intractable*; intractabilis, Wrt. Voc. ii. 48, 72. v. un-liþewác.

in-lîxan, -lîxian *to shine, grow light*:—Sunnadæg inlîxade [wæs inlîxende, Rush.] *sabbatum inlucescebat*, Lk. Skt. Lind. 23, 54.

in-merca *inscribtio*, Mk. Skt. Lind. 12, 16.

INN, es; *n. A dwelling, house, chamber, lodging*:—Næs Beówulf đǽr ac wæs ôđer in ǽr geteohhod *Beowulf was not there, but other lodging had before been assigned to him*, Beo. Th. 2604; B. 1300. Đâ eode hê tô his inne đǽr hê hine restan wolde *intravit cubiculum, quo dormire disponebat*, Bd. 2, 12; S. 513, 18: Cd. 76; Th. 94, 25; Gen. 1567: Judth. 10; Thw. 22, 21; Jud. 70. Hê com tô his inne *venit in domum*, Mt. Kmbl. 13, 36. Sôna swâ hî ût of đam inne eodon *directly they went out of the house*, Guthl. 11; Gdwin. 54, 16. Đâ lǽdde heó hine on đa cyrcan . . . and on đam ylcan inne hê oncneów hwæt đǽr inne wæs *then she led him into the church . . . and in the same house he recognized what was therein*, 22; Gdwin. 96, 23-98, 5. Đâ hê tô his inne com hê hine ǽnne đǽr inne beleác and hine sylfne ofslôh *when he came to his house, he shut himself in alone, and slew himself*, Ors. 4, 5; Bos. 81, 39: Homl. Th. ii. 490, 10. Se steorra him đæs cildes inn gebîcnode *the star pointed out to them* [*the Magi*] *the child's lodging*, Homl. Th. i. 110, 16. Đǽr Petrus inn hæfde *where Peter lodged*, 372, 34. [*Laym.* he hafde an *in* iȝarked toȝeines him: *Orm.* þær he wass at *inne*: *A. R.* in: *Piers. P.* where dowel was at *inne*: *Icel.* inni; *n. abode, home.*]

inn-. v. in-.

inn, in; *adv. In, within*:—Ic wæs cuma and gê mê ne in ne gelađodun *I was a stranger, and ye did not invite me in*, Mt. Kmbl. 25, 43. Waciaþ and gebiddaþ eów đæt gê in ne gân on costunge *vigilate et orate ut non intretis in temtationem*, 26, 41. Gangaþ inn þurh đæt nearwe geat *intrate per angustam portam*, 7, 13: Ps. Th. 117, 19. Đæne se geatweard lǽt in *whom the porter lets in*, Jn. Skt. 10, 3. Hê âwearp đa scyllingas in on đæt templ *he cast the money into the temple*, Mt. Kmbl. 27, 5. Ǽt hâm gebring and nǽfre in on đone mon *bring it home and never into the man's presence*, L. M. 2, 65; Lchdm. ii. 292, 26. Đæt land beág đǽr sûþryhte ođđe seó sǽ in on đæt land, Ors. 1, 1; Swt. 17, 18. Hêht ôđre dæge hie ealle þrý in beforan hine *next day he ordered them all three in before him*, Blickl. Homl. 175, 18. Đǽr gedydon twâ weofedu in *they put two altars in there*, 205, 15. Duru đæt mannes heáfod ge đa sculdro mâgan in *a door so that a man's head and shoulders may get in*, 127, 9. Đâ heó đâ in tô đære hâlgan Elizabethe eode *when she went in to the holy Elizabeth*, 165, 28. Đâ eode Simon in tô Nerone, 175, 10. Đâ eodan hî in tô swǽsendum, Bd. 3. 14; S. 540, 31. Hreóh wæter tô mînum feore inn flôweþ and gangeþ *introierunt aquæ usque ad animam meam*, Ps. Th. 68, 1. Đâ mê gerýmed wæs sîđ inn under eorþweall *when a road was cleared for me in under the earthwall*, Beo. Th. 6171; B. 3090. [*Goth.* inn: *O. Sax. O. Frs.* in: *Icel.* inn: *O. H. Ger.* in, Grff. i. 287: *Ger.* ein.]

inna [?], an; *m. The womb*:—In inna *in utero*, Lk. Skt. Lind. 1, 15, 31, 41: 2, 21. Inna *vulvam*, 2, 23.

innan; *adv. and prep. gen. dat. acc. In, into, within, from within.* I.—Gê synt innan fulle reáflâces *intus estis pleni rapina*, Mt. Kmbl. 23, 25. Hig synt innan fulle deádra bâna *intus plena sunt ossibus mortuorum*, 23, 27. Heorot innan wæs freóndum âfylled, Beo. Th. 2039; B. 1017. Breóst innan weóll þeóstrum geþoncum *his breast was agitated within by dark thoughts*, 4652; B. 2331. Smire mid đa eágan innan *smear the eyes therewith inside*, L. M. 3, 2; Lchdm. ii. 308, 5. Innan of manna heortan yfele geþancas cumaþ *abintus de corde hominum malæ cogitationes procedunt*, Mk. Skt. 7, 21. Innan and ûtan, Cd. 66; Th. 80, 1; Gen. 1322: Exon. 22 b; Th. 62, 21; Cri. 1005: 60 a; Th. 219, 2; Ph. 301. II. *with gen*:—Is mê ænige gâst innan hređres *anxiatus est in me spiritus meus*, Ps. Th. 142, 4. Hie hiora onweald innanbordes [cf. *Icel.* innan-borđs] gehióldon *they maintained their power at home*, Past. pref; Swt. 3, 7. Innabordes *intus*, Rtl. 2, 21. III. *with dat*:—Đâ hê sæt innan hûse *discumbente eo in domo*, Mt. Kmbl. 9, 10. Hê âdrâf ût ealle đa đe ceápodun innan đam temple *ejiciebat omnes vendentes et ementes in templo*, 21, 12. Gif hê ǽr on đæs ofermôdan engles wîsan innan his geþance of Godes gesiehþe ne âfeólle *nisi more superbientis angeli a conspectu conditoris prius intus aversione mentis caderet*, Past. 47, 1; Swt. 359, 1. Hê wæs bebyrged innan đære cyrican *he was buried inside the church*, Chr. 789; Erl. 57, 32. Rôdetâcn wearþ æteówed innan đære dagenge *a cross appeared at dawn*, 806; Erl. 60, 24. IV. *with acc*:—Feall innan đa sǽ *jacta te in mare*, Mt. Kmbl. 21, 21. Ne gâ gê innan samaritana ceastre *in civitates Samaritanorum ne intraveritis*, 10, 5: Andr. Kmbl. 2350; An. 1176. Innan đâs týd Gifemund forþférde and Brihtwald gehâlgode Tobian on his steall *at this time* [or *meanwhile*] *Gifemund died and Brihtwald consecrated Tobias in his place*, Chr. 693;

Erl. 43, 17. Hēr fōr se here innan Mierce *in this year the Danes marched into Mercia*, 868; Erl. 72, 21. V. *in combination with* in, on [cf. *O. Sax.* an innan], geond, be:—Ðā hēt ic feá strǣla sendan in ða burh innan *paucas in civitatem dejici sagittas imperavi*, Nar. 10, 22. In ðone ofn innan, Cd. 184; Th. 230, 24; Dan. 238: Exon. 58 b; Th. 211, 19; Ph. 200. On ðæt morþer innan, Cd. 18; Th. 22, 18; Gen. 342. Burgum in innan, Beo. Th. 3941; B. 1969. In innan *intrinsecus*, Mt. Kmbl. Rush. 7, 15. Eardode ic in innan, Exon. 98 a; Th. 368, 31; Seel. 33. Ne wæs mē feorh ðā gēn, ealdor in innan, 103 a; Th. 391, 10; Rä. 10, 3. Innan on ðisses holtes hleó, Cd. 39; Th. 52, 7; Gen. 840. On innan ðē *in te*, Ps. Th. 147, 2. Geond woruld innan, Exon. 14 b; Th. 29, 28; Cri. 469: 95 b; Th. 355, 43; Pa. 4. Geond Bryten innan, 45 b; Th. 155, 5; Gū. 855. Be innan ðam carcerne, Bt. 1; Fox 4, 2. [*Laym.* inne: *A. R.* inne, ine: *Ayenb.* ine: *Goth.* innana; *adv. and prep. with gen: O. Sax.* innan *adv. and prep. with dat. acc: O. Frs.* inna, ina; *id: Icel.* innan; *adv. and prep. with gen: O. H. Ger.* innan, innana; *adv. and prep. gen. dat. acc.* Grff. i. 296: *Ger.* innen.] v. innane.

innan-bordes. v. innan, II.

innan-burhware; *pl. Those living within a town*—Ða geferscipas innanburhwara and ūtanburhwara *the fellowships of the in-townsmen and of the out-townsmen*, Chart. Th. 510, 31.

innan-cund; *adj. Inward, internal, not superficial, thorough, earnest, genuine, sincere*:—Ðonne deáh hit wiđ ǣghwylcre innancundre unhǣlo *then it does for every internal complaint*, Herb. 2, 22; Lchdm. i. 86, 18: Lchdm. iii. 44, 27. Ic ðē mid ealre innancundre heortan sēce *in toto corde meo exquisivi te*, Ps. Th. 118, 10, 2. v. in-, inne-cund.

innane; *adv. Within*:—Hig beóþ innane reáfigende wulfas *intrinsecus sunt lupi rapaces*, Mt. Kmbl. 7, 15. v. innan.

innan-onfeall. v. onfeall.

innan-weard; *adj. Inward, internal, interior*:—Ǣlc wuht cwices biþ innanweard hnescost *mollissimum quodque, sicuti medulla est, interiore semper sede reconditur*, Bt. 34, 10; Fox 150, 6. Flet innanweard *the interior of the hall*, Beo. Th. 3957; B. 1976: 1987; B. 991. Breóst innanweard *the breast within*, Andr. Kmbl. 1294; An. 647: Exon. 71 b; Th. 266, 19; Jul. 400. Eal innanweard wæs wynsumra ðonne hit in worulde mǣge stefn āreccan *all the interior of the dwelling was more delightful than any voice in the world can declare*, 52 a; Th. 181, 16; Gū. 1294. Mec īsern innanweardne bennade *iron wounded me within*, 130 a; Th. 499, 6; Rä. 88, 11. [*Icel.* innan-verðr.] v. inne-weard.

inne; *adv. In, within, inside, in-doors*:—Ðonne ðǣr biþ man deád hē līþ inne unforbærned mid his freóndum ... and ealle ða hwīle ðe ðæt līc biþ inne ðǣr sceal beón gedrync and plega *when there is a man dead, he lies unburnt in the house among his friends ... and all the while that the body lies inside, there has to be drinking and playing*, Ors. 1, 1; Swt. 20, 20-6: Bd. 5, 4; S. 617, 7. Gif man inne feoh genimeþ se man iii geldė gebēte *if a man take property within* [i. e. *in a house*] *let that man pay a threefold compensation*, L. Ethb. 28; Th. i. 10, 1 [cf. *Icel.* brenna inni *to be burnt to death in a house*]. Hwæðer ðe ūte ðe inne *utrum intus an foris*, Bd. 2, 12; S. 513, 39. Ne mæg ðē deófol sceþþan inne ne ūte *the devil cannot harm thee in-doors nor out*, L. M. 3, 58; Lchdm. 342, 15. Sīe se drenc ðǣr inne ðǣr se seóca man inne sīe *let the drink be in the same place that the sick man is in*, 3, 64; Lchdm. ii. 352, 15. On ðām scyran ðe ordrīc abbud hæfþ land inne *in those shires that abbot Ordric has land in*, Cod. Dipl. Kmbl. iv. 228, 5. Alle ða ðe ðǣr inne eardedon *all who dwelt therein*, Chr. 491; Erl. 14, 6. Hie sume inne wurdon *some of them got inside* [*York*], 867; Erl. 72, 14. Ðone here mētton ðǣr on ðam geweorce and hine inne besetton *they found the Danes there in the fort, and besieged them inside*, 868; Erl. 73, 25. Ðǣr wǣron fīf wucan inne *they were in there five weeks*, 910; Erl. 100, 15. Seó ān inne āwunode, Bd. 5, 12; S. 627, 16. Bēte swā seó dōmbōc sæcge gif hit sȳ hēr inne. Gif hit sȳ eást inne gif hit sȳ norþ inne bēte be ðam ðe ða friþgewritu sæcgan *let him make* 'bōt' *as the law says, if it be in this part of the country. If it be in the east or north let him make* 'bōt' *according to what the treaties say*, L. Ed. 8; Th. i. 164, 7. Inne on ðære þeóde, Bt. 18, 3; Fox 64. 31. On breóstum inne *within their breasts*, Bt. Met. Fox 25, 90; Met. 25, 45. Hēr inne *herein*, Cd. 22; Th. 28, 16; Gen. 436. Hié ðǣr inne fulgon *they got in*, Chr. 755; Erl. 50, 27: Beo. Th. 2567; B. 1281. [*Goth*, inna: *O. Sax. O. Frs.* inne: *Icel.* inni *in-doors: O. H. Ger.* inna, inni, inne *adv. and prep. intus, intra.*] v. innor, innemest.

inne-cund; *adj. Internal, inward*:—Is geornlīce tō behealdenne ðonne hie ða ūterran þing dōn sculon ðæt hie ne sīen ðæm innecundan ingeþonce āfierrede ... hī ðonne lǣtaþ ācōlian ða innecundan lufan *est vigilanter intuendum, ne, dum cura ab eis exterior agitur, ab interna intentione mergantur ... ab intimo amore frigescunt*, Past. 18, 7; Swt. 139, 5-8. v. in-, innan-cund.

inne-fare, an; *f. The intestines*:—Wiđ wambe cōðe and wiđ inneforan sāre *for dysentery*, L. M. 2, 30; Lchdm. ii. 228, 22. Sió filmen biþ þeccende ða wambe and ða innefaran *the film covers the stomach and the inwards*, 2, 36; Lchdm. ii. 242, 17.

innemest; *adv. A superlative form from* inne:—Innemest *intime*, Ælfc. Gr. 38; Som. 42, 13.

innemest; *adj. Inmost*:—Ealle ða innemestan geþohtas *all the inmost thoughts*; omnia cogitationum interiora, Past. 21, 3; Swt. 155, 7.

innera, innra; *adj. Inner, interior*:—Seó inre hrind *liber*, Ælfc. Gl. 59; Som. 68, 6; Wrt. Voc. 38, 57. Se innra man ðæt is seó sāwl *interior homo, id est anima*, L. Ecg. P. iv. 63; Th. ii. 224, 6. Se inra wind, Homl. Th. ii. 392, 32. Þurh ða twā pund wæs getācnod ǣgðer ge ðæt ȳttre andgit ge ðæt inre *by the two pounds was signified both the external and the internal sense*, 554, 34. Se leó gewāt on ðæt inre wēsten *the lion departed into the interior of the desert*, Glostr. Frag. 110, 22. Eall mīn inneran *omnia interiora mea*, Ps. Th. 102, 1. Ealle mīne ða inneran, Blickl. Homl. 89, 2. Ðeáh hē mē ðara ūterrena gewinna gefreóde ðeáh winnaþ wiđ mē ða inran unrihtlustas *though he has freed me from outward struggles, yet the inner lusts strive with me*, Ps. Th. 15, 7. On ðām inneran gōdum ge on ðām ūttran *interioribus bonis et exterioribus*, Bd. 4, 13; S. 582, 39. [*O. Frs.* inra: *Icel.* inri, iðri: *O. H. Ger.* innero, Grff. i. 297.]

inne-weard; *adj. Inward, internal, interior*; the word may generally be rendered by the phrase *the inner part of* [the noun with which it agrees]. In the neut. sing. and pl. it is used as a noun, *intestines, viscera, the inward part*:—Inneweard þeoh *femen*, Ælfc. Gl. 75; Som. 71, 78; Wrt. Voc. 44, 60. Ðes windiga sele eall inneweard *all the interior of this windy hall*, Cd. 216; Th. 273, 15; Sat. 137. Hū hēh and deóp hell inneweard seó, 228; Th. 309, 10; Sat. 707: Beo. Th. 2000; B. 998. Tō inneweardum ðam wēstene *ad interiora deserti*, Ex. 3, 1. Ðā com of inneweardre ðære byrigenne swā mycel swētnysse stencg *tantæ fragrantia suavitatis ab imis ebullivit*, Bd. 3, 8; S. 532, 17. Of inneweardre heortan *intimo ex corde*, 2, 1; S. 501, 14: 3, 27; S. 559, 4. Mid inneweardum mōde *with all my mind*, Bt. 22, 1; Fox 76, 7, 24. Inneweard *intestina*, Ælfc. Gl. 74; Som. 71, 62; Wrt. Voc. 44, 44. Innoþes inneweardė *viscera*, 75; Som. 71, 99; Wrt. Voc. 45, 7. Ðā gewand him ūt eall his inneweardė *all his intestines came out*, Homl. Th. i. 290, 19. Etaþ ðæt heáfod and ða fēt and ðæt inneweardė, ii. 264, 6: 280, 7. Etaþ his heáfod and his fēt and innewærde *caput cum pedibus ejus et intestinis vorabitis*, Ex. 12, 9. Innewerde, 29, 17. v. innan-, in-weard.

innian; *p.* ode *To get within, put in, bring in, put up, lodge*:—Hē werodaþ syððan hē innaþ *interius recepta dulcescant*, Bt. 22, 1; Fox 76, 31. Ðā hī ðider cōmon ðā woldon hī innian hī ðǣr heom sylfan gelīcode *when they came thither then they wanted to put themselves up, where it pleased themselves*, Chr. 1048; Erl. 177, 35. [Me nuste wære hem inny *people did not not know where to lodge them*, R. Glouc. 336, 14. Þe kyng lette lede hem to a feir old court and *innes* hem þere, Jos. 174 Theseus *ynned* hem, everich at his degre, Chauc. Kn. T. 1334. *O. Frs.* innia *to harbour, lodge: O. H. Ger.* innōn *recipere, suscipere, adjungere, afferre*, Grff. i. 298.] v. inne, ge-innian.

innihte; *adv. Within certain limits*:—Innihte beborene *municipales*, Wrt. Voc. ii. 59, 16.

in-niwian; *p.* ode *To renew*:—Inniwa *innova*, Rtl. 168, 23.

innon. v. innan.

innor; *adv. cpve of* inne:—Innor *interius*, Ælfc. Gr. 38; Som. 42, 13. [*O. H. Ger.* innor *interius.*]

INNOÞ, innaþ, es; *m. f.* [?] *The inner part of the body, the inside, stomach, womb, bowels, the breast, heart*:—Innoþ *alvus*; wīfes innoþ *uterus*, Ælfc. Gr. 8; Som. 7, 52, 30: *viscus*, 9; Som. 12, 12. Wīfmannes innoþ *matrix, uterus*, Ælfc. Gl. 74; Som. 71, 56; Wrt. Voc. 44, 39. Eádig is se innoþ ðe ðē bær *beatus venter qui te portavit*, Lk. Skt. 11, 27. His innoþ tōfleów *his bowels gushed out*, Homl. Th. ii. 250, 26. Ðætte hira mōdes innaþ yfele and hefiglīce mid gefylled wæs *quæ mentis intima deprimebat*, Past. 54, 1; Swt. 419, 32. Sió his innaþ wan wætere gelīc *intravit sicut aqua in interiora ejus*, Ps. Th. 108, 18. Wiđ innoþes sār *for sore of inwards*, Herb. 11, 2; Lchdm. i. 102, 11. Wiđ innoþes fæstnysse *for costiveness*, 62; Lchdm. i. 164, 16. Wæstm ðe of his innaþe āgenum cwōme *de fructu ventris tui*, Ps. Th. 131, 12. Ða litlingas fuhton on hire innoþe *collidebantur in utero ejus parvuli*, Gen. 25, 22. Hē biþ swīđe līþe on ðam innoþe *it is very mild in the stomach*, Bt. 22, 1; Fox 76, 31. Ealle ðās yfelu of ðam innoþe cumaþ *omnia hæc mala ab intus procedunt*, Mk. Skt. 7, 23. Ðē ic andette mid mūþe and mid mīnre heortan and mid eallum innoþe ic ðē gewilnige *with my mouth and with my heart I confess thee, and with all that is within me I desire thee*, Homl. Skt. 7, 237. Hālig gāst hreðer weardode æðelne innoþ, Elen. Kmbl. 2289; El. 1146. Mæg hē eft cuman on his mōdor innoþ *numquid potest in ventrem matris suæ iterato introire?* Jn. Skt. 3, 4. Inneþas *viscera*, Wrt. Voc. 283, 76. Eádige synt ða innoþas ðe ne cendun *beati ventres qui non genuerunt*, Lk. Skt. 23, 29. Wiđ innoþa wræc *for pain of intestines*, L. Med. ex Quadr. 2, 18; Lchdm. i. 338, 9. Wiþ tōbrocenum innoþum *for ruptured bowels*, L. M. 2, 33; Lchdm. ii. 236, 23. On innoþas his *in interiora ejus*, Ps. Spl. M. 108, 17. Ðæt sār hwyrfde on hire innoþas *converso ad interanea dolore*, Bd. 4, 23; S. 595, 26. Innaþo *viscera*, Rtl. 13, 33. [*O. E. Homl.* inneþ: *O. L. Ger.* innethron *viscera: O. H. Ger.* innod *uterus, viscera*; innodili *viscera.*]

innoþ-tyderness, e; *f. A weakness of the intestines*:—Wiđ eallum innoþtydernessum, L. M. 2, 64; Lchdm. ii. 288, 24.

innoþ-wund, e; *f. A wound of the intestines*:—Wiđ innoþwundum, L. M. 2, 33; Lchdm. ii. 236, 18, 21.

innung, e; *f. A putting* or *getting in, what is put* or *got in*:—Se heofon is betera and fægera đonne eall his innung būton monnum ānum *the heaven is better and fairer than all it includes, except men only*, Bt. 32, 2; Fox 116, 10. Đes tūnes cȳping and seó innung [*the getting in*, or *revenue?*] đara portgerihta gange intō đere hālgan stōwe *villæ mercimonium censusque omnis civilis sanctæ æcclesiæ deserviat*, Cod. Dipl. Kmbl. iii. 138, 10.

in-orf, es; *n. Household goods*:—Inēddisc *vel* inorf *entheca*, g. *suppellex* Ælfc. Gl. 58; Som. 67, 90; Wrt. Voc. 38, 16. Gif hit sȳ innorf *if it be goods from a house* [*that are taken*], Lchdm. iii. 286, 5. For hwilcum gylta fērdest đū đus æfter mē and tōwurpe eall mīn inorf *quam ob culpam meam sic exarsisti post me et scrutatus es omnem supellectilem meam?* Gen. 31, 36. v. in-irfe.

inra. v. innera.

in-rǣsan; *p.* de *To rush upon*:—Inrǣsdon *inruerunt*, Mt. Kmbl. Lind. 7, 25. Inrǣsan *inrumpere*, Wrt. Voc. ii. 44, 84.

in-rēcels, es; *n. Incense*:—Inrēcels, *incensum*, Lk. Skt. Rush. 1, 9.

in-sǣte; *adj. Belonging to one who is 'settled in' the household of the lord, one who lives close to the lord's mansion* [?]:—Insǣte hūs *vel* lytel hūs *casa* vel *casula*, Ælfc. Gl. 108; Som. 78, 113; Wrt. Voc. 58, 28. v. -sǣta, -sǣte.

in-sceáwere, es; *m. An inspector*:—Ofer-insceáweras *super-inspectores*, Rtl. 194. 25, 29.

in-sceáwung, e; *f. Inspection*, Mt. Kmbl. p. 4, 6.

in-segel, es; *n. A seal, signet*:—Insegel *sigillum* vel *bulla*, Ælfc. Gl. 29; Som. 61, 31; Wrt. Voc. 26, 30. Insegl *sigillum*, Wrt. Voc. 83, 4. Geþenc nū gyf đīnes hlāfordes ǣrendgewrit and his insegel tō đē cymþ hwæđer đū mǣge cweþan đæt đū hys willan đǣr on gecnāwan ne mǣge *consider now, if your lord's letter and his seal come to you, whether you can say that you cannot recognise his pleasure in them*, Shrn. 176, 10. Insegle *signaculo*, Hpt. Gl. 504, 37. Đā com Sparhafoc tō him mid đæs cynges gewrite and insegle, Chr. 1048; Erl. 177, 20. Swā hwæđer swā heó beó fūl swā clǣne binnan đam insegle *whether it* [*the hand*] *be foul or clean within the seal*, L. Æđelst iv. 7; Th. i. 226, 32. Đā sende se cyning his insegel tō đam gemōte, Chart. Th. 288, 22. [Þet inseil þe þe deofel ne mei nefre tobreocan, O. E. Homl. i. 127, 33. He haueđ his merke on me iseilet wiđ his inseil, Marh 5, 16. Bisett wiþþ seffne inseȝȝless, Orm. *O. Frs.* in-sigel, -sigil *a seal*: *Icel.* inn-sigli *a seal, a seal-ring;* also *the wax* affixed to a deed: *O. H. Ger.* in-sigili *sigillum, signaculum, lunula, annulus, moneta*: *Ger.* in-siegel.] v. insigle.

in-seglian; *p.* ode *To seal, place a seal upon*:—Hig innseglodon đone stān *signantes lapidem*, Mt. Kmbl. 27, 66. Inseglige man đa hand *let a seal be put upon the hand*, L. Æđelst. iv. 7; Th. i. 226, 30. [*Icel.* inn-sigla *to seal*: *O. H. Ger.* in-siglian *signare*.] v. ge-inseglian.

in-seglung, e; *f. A sealing, seal*:—Ic bidde đē for godes lufan đæt đū mē unlȳse đa insæglunge *I pray thee for the love of God that thou unloose for me the seal*, Homl. Skt. 3, 537. [*Icel.* inn-siglan *sealing*.]

in-sendan; *p.* de *To send in*:—Insendes *inmittit*, Mt. Kmbl. Lind. 9, 16. Insende engel dryhten *inmittit angelum Dominus*, Ps. Surt. 33, 8: 39, 4.

in-setness, e; *f. A rule, regulation, institute*:—Insetnissum *institutis*, Rtl. 34, 14. Insætnissum, 18, 21.

in-settan; *p.* te *To appoint, institute*:—Insette *instituit*, Bd. 4, 23; S. 593, 38.

in-sigle, es; *n. A seal, signet*:—Hē brohte insigle tō mē ... Đā āgeaf ic đæt insigle đē *he brought a signet to me ... Then I gave the signet to thee*, Chart. Th. 173, 8, 11. Wyrđe arđ onfōa bōc and untȳne insigloe his *dignus es accipere librum et aperire signaculum ejus*, Rtl. 29, 19. v. in-segel.

in-siht, e: *f. An account, narrative, argument*:—Onginneþ insiht æfter iohannem *incipit argumentum secundum Johannem*, Jn. Skt. p. 1, 1. [*Goth.* in-sahts *narrative*.]

in-sittende; *part. Sitting within*:—Ealra wǣron fīfe eorla and idesa insittendra, Exon. 112 b; Th. 432, 3; Rä. 47, 7.

in-smoh; *gen.* -smōs [?]; *m. A slough*:—Hē āgeaf đone clǣnan gāst and đæs līchaman insmoh [*exuvias*] forlēt monnum tō mundbyrde *he gave up the clean spirit, and left the slough of the body as a protection for men*, Shrn. 126, 2. v. smūgan; and cf. *O. Frs.* in-smuge *a creeping in*.

in-spinn, es; *n. An instrument for spinning, a spindle*:—Inspinn *netorium*, Ælfc. Gl. 110; Som. 79, 46; Wrt. Voc. 59, 17. Inspin, Wrt. Voc. 66, 15. [Netorium *fusus* quo netur: *fusum, fusile*, Du Cange.]

in-stæppan; *p.* te *To step in, enter*:—Ic ne instæppe ođđe ingā ođđe ic ne fare *non introibo*, Ps. Lamb. 25, 4. Insteppaþ ođđe ingāþ on gesihþe his *introite in conspectu ejus*, 99, 2. On unscyldignysse mīnre instæppende ic eom *in innocentia mea ingressus sum*, 25, 11. Hī sume gesāwon englas instæppende *some of them saw angels entering*, Homl. Th. ii. 546, 23.

in-stæpe, es; *m. Entrance*:—Hī gemētton đæt ēce līf on instæpe đæs andweardan līfes *they found the life eternal at the entrance of the present life*, Homl. Th. i. 84, 7. [*O. Frs.* in-stap, in-steppi *entrance*.] v. next two words.

in-stæpe, -stepe; *adv. At the outset, at once, directly, immediately*:—Instæpe *confestim*, Bd. 2, 12; S. 514, 21: *extemplo*, 4, 25; S. 601, 30. Ārās hē instæpe *surrexit continuo*, 5, 5; S. 618, 14. Hī instæpe fram mīnre gesihþe gewiton *statim disparuerunt*, 5, 13; S. 633, 15. Đonne wǣre mīn blōd instæpe āgoten *then had my blood been at once shed*, Shrn. 39, 17. Seó strǣl instepe wearþ eft gecyrred, Blickl. Homl. 199, 21. v. next word.

in-stæpes, -stepes; *adv. At once, immediately*:—Se mon se đe ōđerne ācwelþ and instæpes hine sylfne ongyteþ đæt hē mycel mān gedōn hæbbe *the man who kills another, and at once perceives himself to have done a great wrong*, Blickl. Homl. 65, 5. Hē đā sōna instæpes geseh *he then immediately saw*, 15, 27. Đēh gē sōna instæpes đǣre mēde ne ne onfōn, 41, 13. Instepes, 33, 19. Đæt fæsten wæs ongunnen instepes đæs đe ... *the fast was begun directly after ...*, 35, 5. Hī flugon instæpes *they fled forthwith*, Elen. Kmbl. 254; El. 127.

in-standan; *p.* -stōd *To be near* or *present*; instare:—Ēce instondaþ wuldur *perennis instat gloria*, Rtl. 165, 7. Instond[end]um *instantibus*, 69, 11.

in-standendlīc; *adj. Present, of to-day*:—Hlāf ūre instondendlīce sel ūs tō dæge *give us to-day our daily bread*, Mt. Kmbl. Rush. 6, 11.

in-stede, -styde [or in stede; cf. *Icel.* í-stađ *on the spot, at once*]; *adv. On the spot, at once, immediately*:—Instyde *continuo*, Mt. Kmbl. Rush. 27, 48. Instyde *statim*, Mk. Skt. Rush. 1, 28: 2, 12.

in-stice, es; *m. An inward stitch, a pricking sensation within*:—Wiđ instice, L. M. 2, 54; Lchdm. ii. 274, 27.

in-stihtian; *p.* ode *To arrange, regulate, dispose*:—Instihtade ł dihtade *instigante*, Lk. Skt. p. 2, 6. v. stihtian.

in-sting, es; *m. Authority*:—Nān đere biscope ne habbe nān insting on đæt mynster *let no bishop have any authority in that monastery*, Chart. Th. 348, 12. v. on-sting.

in-swān, es; *m. The herd who had charge of the lord's swine*:—Ǣlc gebūr sylle .vi. hlāfas đam inswāne đonne hē his heorde tō mæstene drīfe *omnis geburus det vi. panes porcario curie quando gregem suum minabit in pastinagium*, L. R. S. 4; Th. i. 434, 21.

in-swāpen. v. swāpan.

in-swōgenness, e; *f. A rushing in with a loud sound, violent entrance*:—Hē mid đæs unclǣnan gāstes inswōgennisse þrycced wæs *spiritus inmundi invasione premebatur*, Bd. 2, 5; S. 507, 4. v. swōgan.

inđer; *adv. Apart*; seorsum, Mt. Kmbl. Rush. 17, 1.

in-þicce; *adj. Gross, thick*:—Inþicce is hearta folces đisses *incrassatum est cor populi hujus*, Mt. Kmbl. Lind. 13, 15.

in-þīnen, e; *f. A female domestic servant*; incola, Germ. 401, 125.

in-timbrian; *p.* ede, ode *To instruct*:—Hē hī intimbrade and gelǣrde *he instructed and taught them*, Bd. 4, 16; S. 584, 34. Intimbrede, 4, 27; S. 603, 45. In cyriclīcum þeódscipum and in mynsterlīcum heálīce intimbred *ecclesiasticis ac monasterialibus disciplinis summe instructus*, Bd. 5, 8; S. 621, 35: S. 622, 2. v. on-timbrian.

in-tinga, an; *m. A cause, sake, plea, case, occasion, matter, affair, business*:—Intinga *pragma*, Ælfc. Gl. 12; Som. 57, 93; Wrt. Voc. 20, 34: *negotium*, 81; Som. 73, 17; Wrt. Voc. 47, 24: *causa* vel *negotium*, 90; Som. 74, 115; Wrt. Voc. 51, 28: *causa*, Wrt. Voc. 83, 62. Đysse þeóde wæs se ǣresta intinga tō onfōnne Cristes geleáfan đæt ... *huic genti occasio fuit percipiendæ fidei, quod ...*, Bd. 2, 9; S. 510, 18. His intinga wæs geondsōhte beforan Agaþone *causa ejus ventilata est præsente Agathone*, 5, 19; S. 639, 28. Se forma intinga mennisces forwyrdes wæs đā đā se deófol āsende ōđerne deófol tō Evan *the first cause of man's perdition was when the devil sent another devil to Eve*, Homl. Th. i. 194, 30. Đæt mīn sāwul lybbe for đīnum intingan *ut vivat anima mea ob gratiam tui*, Gen. 12, 13. For hwilcum intingan *quam ob causam*, 19. Tō đisum is genumen se grēcisca y for intingan grēciscra namena *to these* [*the vowels*] *is added the Greek y for the sake of Greek names*, Ælfc. Gr. 2; Som. 2, 51. For his intingan hē hit dēþ *sui causa facit*, 17; Som. 20, 50: Homl. Th. i. 84, 2. Ic ongann be đam intingan hwæthwega geornlīcor smeágan *I began to inquire somewhat more diligently about the matter*, ii. 32, 23. Gif hió of cealdum intingan cymþ đonne sceal mon mid hātum lǣcedōmum lācnian *if it* [*the disease*] *comes from a cold cause then it is to be cured with hot medicines*, L. M. 1, 1; Lchdm. ii. 22, 5. Būton intingan *sine causa*, Ps. Spl. 3, 7. Būtan intingan hig mē wurđiaþ *sine causa colunt me*, Mt. Kmbl. 15, 9. Đā hī đā heora intingan him wēpende sǣdon đā wæs hē sōna mid mildheortnysse gefylled *when with tears they had told him their business, he was at once filled with pity*, Guthl. 12; Gdwin. 58, 25. Tōsceáđ intingan mīnne *discerne causam meam*, Ps. Spl. 42, 1. Dēm intingan đīnne *judica causam tuam*, 73, 23. Ne finde ic nānne intingan on đysum men *nihil invenio causæ in hoc homine*, Lk. Skt. 23, 4, 14. Hē nolde syllan intingan đām Iudēiscum đæt hē hī forsāwe đe Godes ǣ heóldon and đæt hǣđene folc him tō getuge *he would not give the Jews cause to complain, that he despised those who kept God's law, and drew to him the heathen people*, Homl. Th. ii. 112, 5. Forđon misenlīce intingan gelimpeþ *quia diversæ causæ impediunt*, Bd. 4, 5; S. 573, 7.

in-tō; *prep. Into.* I. *with dat*:—Đū gǣst intō đam arce ... and twegen gemacan đū lǣtst intō đam arce *ingredieris arcam ... et bina induces in arcam*, Gen. 6, 18, 19. Noe eode intō đam arce *ingressus est Noe in arcam*, 7, 7. Ic gange intō đǣre byrig *in urbem vado*. Ic gange intō ðīnum huse *introibo in domum tuam.* Intō ðære ceastre rād se kyning *in civitatem equitavit rex,* Ælfc. Gr. 47; Som. 48, 15-7. Ðā se hǣlend com intō ðæs ealdres healle *cum venisset Iesus in domum principis,* Mt. Kmbl. 9, 23. Sume urnon intō cyrcean and belucan ða duran intō heom *some ran into the church and shut the doors upon them,* Chr. 1082; Erl. 217, 13. II. *with acc*:—Fērde his hlīsa intō ealle Syriam *abiit opinio ejus in totam Syriam,* Mt. Kmbl. 4, 24. Wið feó sealdon wīde intō leódscipas *they sold them far and wide into various nations,* Blickl. Homl. 79, 23. III. *with inst*:—Ðā ongeáton hie ðæt se eádiga Michael him sylfa ðæt tācn ðæs siges gecȳðde intō ðȳ swīðan slǣpe *then they perceived that the blessed Michael had himself made known that token of victory in the deep sleep,* 205, 4.

in-trahtnung, e; *f. Explanation, interpretation*: — Sōþ intrahtnung *vera interpretatio,* Mt. Kmbl. p. 2, 6.

in-trifelung, e; *f. Intritura,* Cot. 109, Lye.

in-wǣte, an; *f. An inward humour*:—Gif hit biþ cumen of yfelre inwǣtan *if it is come of an evil inward humour,* L. M. 2, 46; Lchdm. ii. 258, 27.

in-weard; *adj. Inward, inner, internal*: — Gif gē hine mid inweardre heortan sēceaþ *si toto corde quæsieris,* Deut. 4, 29. Biddaþ mid inweardre heortan ðysne Godes apostol, Homl. Th. i. 68, 8. Ðā wilnode ic indeum innewearde tō geseónne *interiorem indiam perspicere cupiens,* Nar. 5, 17. v. innan-, inne-weard.

in-weard; *adv. Within*: — Ðætte inweard is *quod intus est,* Lk. Skt. Lind. 11, 39. Ðā hig inweard fōron ðā gemytton hig twegen ealde weras *when they went in, they met two old men,* Nicod. 31; Thw. 18, 3. [Let þene lust gon inward, A. R. 272, 8. Inwardes, 92, 6.]

inweard-līc; *adj. Inward, internal*:—Innweardlīc *interius,* Rtl. 4, 20. On heora inweardlīcum stōwum *in their inward parts,* L. Med. ex Quadr. 3, 1; Lchdm. i. 338, 19, MS. H.

inweard-līce; *adv. Inwardly, thoroughly, heartily, earnestly*: — Heroðes innweardlīce gelearnade from him *Herodes diligenter didicit ab eis,* Mt. Kmbl. Lind. 2, 7, 8. Innweardlīce cliopaþ hine *invocate eum,* Rtl. 10, 26. Is ðæt for inweardlīce riht racu *that is a very thoroughly right explanation,* Bt. 40, 1; Fox 236, 9. Se ðe æfter rihte mid gerece wille inweardlīce æfterspyrian swā deóplīce ðæt hit tōdrīfan ne mæg monna ǣnig *quisquis profunda mente vestigat verum, cupitque nullis ille deviis falli,* Bt. Met. Fox 22, 3; Met. 22, 2. Wearþ ðā him inweardlīce gelufod *he was heartily loved by him,* Homl. Th. i. 58, 18. Ða ðe tō geleáfan cyrden hē ða inweardlȳcor lufade *credentes arctiori dilectione amplecteretur,* Bd. 1, 26; S. 488, 16.

in-weorud, es; *n. A band of domestics* or *courtiers, a household*:— Ðæt wæs innweorud Earmanrīces, Exon. 86 b; Th. 325, 13; Vīd. 111. [Cf. in-hīrēd.]

inwid, inwit, es; *n. Fraud, guile, deceit, evil, wickedness*:—Inwid *dolus,* Ps. Spl. T. 14, 3. Ne beó nǣnig man hēr on worldrīce bregda tō full ne inwit tō leóf *let no man in this world be too full of wiles, nor let guile be too dear to him,* Blickl. Homl. 109, 29. Ne wæs ǣfre fācen ne inwid on his heortan *nor was ever deceit nor guile in his heart,* 223, 31. Gramlīc inwit *nequitia,* Ps. Th. 54, 15. Mān and inwit, 9. Forðan mē inwit næs on tungan *quia non est dolus in lingua mea,* 138, 2. Mān inwides *dolus,* 54, 10. For inwite *propter dolos,* 72, 14. Mið inwite [mit fācne, A. S.] *dolo,* Mt. Kmbl. Lind. 26, 4. Gē on heortan hogedon inwit *in corde iniquitates operamini,* Ps. Th. 57, 2. Hió ðā inwit feala ȳwdan on tungan *locuti sunt adversum me lingua dolosa,* 108, 2. His esnum inwit fremedan *dolum facerent in servos ejus,* 104, 21. Ða inwit and fācen hycgeaþ on heortan *qui cogitaverunt malitias in corde,* 139, 2. Hie sprecaþ fācen and inwit, Cd. 109; Th. 145, 31; Gen. 2414. Inwit syredon *they plotted evil,* Andr. Kmbl. 1220; An. 610. Hwǣr āhangen wæs waldend þurh inwit, Elen. Kmbl. 413; El. 207. [*O. Sax.* inwid: cf. *Goth.* inwindiþa *injustice.*]

inwid-. v. inwit-.

inwidda, inwit; *adj. Guileful, deceitful, evil, wicked, malicious*:— Gelpan ne þorfte eald inwidda [inwitta, MSS. B. C. inwuda MS. D.], *no cause to boast had he, old and crafty,* Chr. 937; Erl. 114, 12; Æðelst. 46. Swā se inwidda ofer ealne dæg dryhtguman sīne drencte mid wīne *so the evil one* [*Holofernes*] *all through the day his men drenched with wine,* Judth. 10; Thw. 21, 20; Jud. 28. Ealle weleras inwiddæn *universa labia dolosa,* Ps. Spl. T. 11, 3. Wordum inwitum *with guileful words,* Cd. 229; Th. 310, 22; Sat. 731. [Cf. *Goth.* inwinds *unjust, perverse.*]

in-wise, an; *f. A condiment*:—Ðæt hit sīe on ða onlīcnesse geworht ðe senop biþ getemprod tō inwisan *that it may be made like mustard when it is mixed for a condiment,* L. M. 2, 6; Lchdm. ii. 184, 22.

inwit. v. inwid, inwidda.

inwit-feng, es; *m. A wily* or *malicious grasp,* Beo. Th. 2898; B. 1447.

inwit-flān, es; *m. A treacherous shaft,* Exon. 83 b; Th. 315, 27; Mōd. 37.

inwit-full; *adj. Deceitful, guileful, malicious, evil*:—Inwitfull *dolosus, insidiosus, fraudulentus, callidus,* Wrt. Voc. ii. 141, 66. Ne mæg ðǣr inwitfull ǣnig geferan womscyldig mon *there may none guileful come, none guilty of sin,* Cd. 45; Th. 58, 18; Gen. 498. From ðære inwitfullan yflan tungan *a lingua dolosa,* Ps. Th. 119, 3. Hē āfylleþ ða inwitfullan word of his tungan *he causes deceitful words to fall away from his tongue* [cf. Ps. Th. 14, 3, non egit dolum in lingua sua], Blickl. Homl. 55, 16. Ðā geseah sigora waldend hwæt wæs monna mānes and ðæt hī wǣron inwitfulle *then saw the Lord of victories what the wickedness of men was, and that they were full of deceit,* Cd. 64; Th. 77, 10; Gen. 1273. Synfulra and inwitfulra mūþas *os peccatoris et dolosi,* Ps. Th. 108, 1.

inwit-gæst, es; *m. A guileful, evil guest,* Beo. Th. 5333; B. 2670.

inwit-gecynd, es; *n. A malicious, evil nature,* Salm. Kmbl. 660; Sal. 329.

inwit-gyren, e; *f. A treacherous snare*:—Forhȳddon mē oferhȳdge inwitgyrene *absconderunt superbi laqueos mihi,* Ps. Th. 139, 5.

inwit-hlemm, es; *m. A stroke treacherously* or *maliciously given,* Rood Kmbl. 93; Kr. 47.

inwit-hrōf, es; *m. A deceitful, evil roof* [*the fire-drake's den*], Beo. Th. 6238; B. 3123.

inwit-net, es; *n. A net of treachery* or *malice,* Beo. Th. 4340; B. 2167.

inwit-nīþ, es; *m. Malicious, treacherous enmity,* Beo. Th. 3720; B. 1858: 3898; B. 1947: Hy. 3, 46; Hy. Grn. ii. 282, 46. [*O. Sax.* inwid-nīð.]

inwit-rūn, e; *f. Malicious, guileful counsel,* Exon. 74 b; Th. 279, 7; Jul. 610.

inwit-scear, es; *m. Slaughter effected by craft,* Beo. Th. 4949; B. 2478. [Cf. gūþ-scear.]

inwit-searo; *n. Malicious* or *treacherous artifice,* Beo. Th. 2206; B. 1101.

inwit-sorh; *gen.* -sorge; *f. Sorrow brought about by malice* or *guile,* Beo. Th. 1666; B. 831: 3477; B. 1736.

inwit-spell, es; *n. A tale of evil,* Cd. 94; Th. 122, 9; Gen. 2024.

inwit-stæf, es; *m. Evil, wickedness, malice*; nequitia, Ps. Th. 54, 15: 140, 5.

inwit-þanc, es; *m. Evil, malicious, deceitful thought* or *purpose,* Andr. Kmbl. 1339; An. 670: 1118; An. 559: Elen. Kmbl. 616; El. 308: Bt. Met. Fox 9, 16; Met. 9, 8: 27, 46; Met. 27, 23: Beo. Th. 1502; B. 749.

inwit-wrāsen, e; *f. A chain of guile* or *malice,* Andr. Kmbl. 126; An. 63: 1892; An. 948.

in-wreón; *p.* -wrāh; *pl.* -wrigon *To uncover, reveal*:—Ðū mē inwrige wyrda gerȳno *thou hast revealed to me the mysteries of fate,* Elen. Kmbl. 1621; El. 813. v. on-wreón.

in-writting, e; *f. An inscription*; inscriptio, Mt. Kmbl. p. 4, 5.

in-wund, e; *f. An inward wound*:—Wið inwunde magan *for an inward wound of the stomach,* L. M. 2, 9; Lchdm. ii. 188, 11. [Cf. *O. Frs.* in-werdene *internal injury.*]

in-wuneness, e; *f. Persistence, perseverance*; instantia, Wrt. Voc. ii. 47, 41.

in-wunung, e; *f. Habitation, dwelling,* Lye.

in-ylfe, es; *n. A gut, bowel*: — Inelfe *intestinum,* Wrt. Voc. 65, 55. Inilve, 284, 2. Inelve *interamen,* 286, 60. Ðȳ læs ðæt innelfe ūtsīge *lest the matrix prolapse,* L. M. 3, 37; Lchdm. ii. 328, 25. Gif men sīe innelfe ūte . . . gedō ðæt innelfe on ðone man *if a man's bowel protrude . . . put the bowel into the man,* 3, 73; Lchdm. ii. 358, 23-5. Inelfe *viscera,* Wrt. Voc. 65, 32. Inilve, 285, 58. Sume nimaþ hwelpes innylfe *some take a whelp's intestines,* L. Med. ex Quadr. 9, 5; Lchdm. i. 362, 7. [*Icel.* inn-yfli, -ylfi; *n. pl. entrails, bowels*: *O. H. Ger.* inn-uveli, -oveli *viscera.*]

Iob, es; *m. Job*:—Sum wer wæs geseten on ðam lande ðe is gehāten Hus, his nama wæs Iob, Homl. Th. ii. 446, 10. Iobes dōhtra, 458, 32. Tō mīnum þeówan Iobe, 456, 30. Be ðan eádigan were Iob, 446, 4.

Iob, es; *m. Jove, Jupiter*:—Job Saturnes sunu, Bt. 35, 4; Fox, 162, 5. Ercules Iobes sunu, 16, 2; Fox 52, 34. Iobes templ, Nar. 37, 23. v. Iofes.

ioc. v. iuc, geoc.

Iofes, es; *m. Jove*:—Ðanc hafa ðū, Iofes, Ors. 4, 1; Bos. 77, 37. Hyra hēhstan godes hūs Iofeses, 4, 2; Bos. 79, 11. v. Iob.

Iól *Yule,* Chart. Th. 423, 5. v. Geól.

iór, es; *m. The name of the rune* ⋇; also of a fish, perhaps *the eel*:— ⋇ byþ eáfixa [sum] and ðeáh ā brūceþ fōdres on faldan *eel is a river-fish, and yet ever eats food on the ground,* Runic pm. 28; Kmbl. 345, 4. See Zacher's Das Gothische Alphabet, p. 26; Taylor's Greeks and Goths, pp. 97-8.

Iotas, Iutan; *pl. The Jutes*:—Ðā cōmon ða men of þrīm mēgðum Germanie of Ald-Seaxum of Anglum of Iotum. Of Iotum cōmon Cantwara and Wihtwara ðæt is seó mēgð ðe nū eardaþ on Wiht and ðæt cyn on West Sexum ðe man nū git hǣt Iutna cyn *then came the men from three tribes of Germany, from old Saxons, from Angles, from Jutes. From the Jutes came the people of Kent and Wight, that is, the tribe that now lives in Wight and the race among the West Saxons that is to the present time called the Jutes' race,* Chr. 449; Erl. 13, 10-14. The Anglo-Saxon version of Bede, i. 15, has *Geat* for *Iot,* but in 4, 16 *Iutorum provincia* is rendered *Eota land.* See Grmm. Gesch. D. S. 511 sqq. [*Icel.* Iótas *Jutes.*]

íów, íówian, íówih. v. eów, eówian, eówic.

ir; *adj. Angry*:—Yr on móde, Cd. 4; Th. 4, 33; Gen. 63. v. irre, ir-scipe.

Íra-land, es; *n. Land of the Irish, Ireland*:—Gewitan him ðá Norþmenn Dyflen sécean eft Íraland [Yraland, hira land], Chr. 937; Th. 206, col. 2, l. 15; Æðelst. 56. In Ors. 1, 1; Swt. 19, 15, 16 Íraland *is doubtful*. In the Anglo-Saxon version of Bede's History *Hibernia* generally is rendered by *Hibernia Scotta eáland*. v. Ír-land.

Íras; *pl. The Irish* [v. Íra-land]:—Férde twelf geár bodiende betwux Yrum and Scottum and siððan ofer eal Angelcyn *he went twelve years preaching among the Irish and Scotch, and afterwards over all England*, Homl. Th. ii. 346, 35. *But the people of Ireland are often spoken of as* Scottas, e. g:—Pyhtas cóman ǽrost on norþ Ybernian up and ðǽr bǽdon Scottas ðæt hí ðǽr móston wunian, Chr. Erl. 3, 9. Scotta sum dǽl gewát of Ybernian on Brittene, 18. Þrie Scottas cuómon tó Ælfréde of Hibernia, 891; Erl. 88, 5. *So in Alfred's Orosius it is said* Igbernia ðæt wé Scotland hátaþ, 1, 1; Swt. 24, 16. [*Icel.* Írar.]

íren, es; *n. Iron, an iron weapon* [cf. use of *steel* in modern English], *a sword, blade*:—Ðæt swurd, drihtlic íren, Beo. Th. 1788; B. 892. Gif ðæt gegangeþ ðæt ádl oððe íren nimeþ ealdor ðínne *if it come to pass, that disease or sword take off thy prince*, 3700; B. 1848. Mé sceal wǽpen niman, ord and íren, Byrht. Th. 139, 12. Áres and írenes *æris et ferri*, Bd. 1, 1; S. 473, 23, note. Heardes írenes grindlas *gratings of hard iron*, Cd. 19; Th. 24, 25; Gen. 383. Ðeáh hé wǽre mid írne ymbfangen, 224; Th. 297, 15; Sat. 513. Hét his sweord niman, leóflíc íren, Beo. Th. 3622; B. 1809. His sweord, írena cyst, 1350; B. 673: 1609; B. 802. Bite írena, 4511; B. 2259. Íren ecgheard, Andr. Kmbl. 2363; An. 1183. [*Icel.* járn: *Dan.* jern: *Swed.* järn.] v. hring-íren; ísen, ísern.

íren; *adj. Of iron, iron*:—Ecg wæs íren *the edge was of iron*, Beo. Th. 2922; B. 1459: 5549; B. 2778. Hé hine hét áþenian on írenum bedde and hine cwicne hırstan *he bade stretch him on an iron bed, and roast him alive*, Shrn. 116, 2. Mid írenum gyrdum *with iron rods*, 115, 24: Salm. Kmbl. 55; Sal. 28: 942; Sal. 470. Scyttelas ýrenne hé forbræc *vectes ferreos confregit*, Ps. Spl. 106, 16. v. eal-íren, *the following compounds, and* ísen, ísern.

íren-bend, es; *m. An iron bond* or *band*:—Licgaþ mé ymbe írenbendas, Cd. 19; Th. 24, 2; Gen. 371. Írenbendum fæst, Beo. Th. 2001; B. 998. [Cf. *Goth.* eisarna-bandi.]

íren-byrne, an; *f. An iron byrnie*:—Námon írenbyrnan, heard swyrd hilted, and his helm, Beo. Th. 5965; B. 2986.

íren-gelóma, an; *m. An iron implement*:—Ða írengelóman *ferramenta*, Nar. 9, 19. v. gelóman.

íren-heard; *adj. Iron-hard*, Beo. Th. 2227; B. 1112.

íren-helm, es; *m. An iron helmet*:—Írenhelm [*or* íren helm; *but cf. preceding compounds*] *cassis*, Ælfc. Gl. 51; Som. 66, 14; Wrt. Voc. 35, 4. [Cf. *Icel.* járn-hattr a kind of *helmet*.]

íren-þreát, es; *m. A band having iron armour*, Beo. Th. 666; B. 330.

ire-þweorh; *adj. Having the mind perverted by rage*, Exon. 67 a; Th. 248, 3; Jul. 90.

irfan; *p.* de *To inherit*:—Yrfan hí swá hí wyrðe witan *let the land devolve upon such as they know to be worthy* or *entitled* [v. wyrðe], Chart. Th. 578, 9. v. [?] Cod. Dipl. Kmbl. i. xxxiii–v on the leases of church lands for lives, in which such phrases as the following occur:—His dæg forgeaf, and æfter his dæg twám *yrfeweardum*. Such lives were sometimes named in the instrument setting forth the grant. [*O. Frs.* ervia *to inherit*: *O. L. Ger.* gi-ervan *hereditare*: *Icel.* erfa *to honour with a funeral feast*; mod. *to inherit*: *O. H. Ger.* erbet *hæreditabit*: *Ger.* erben.]

irfe, ierfe, yrfe, es; *n. Inheritance, property*:—Gewriten yrfe *legatum*, Ælfc. Gl. 13; Som. 57, 96; Wrt. Voc. 20, 37. Ungewriten yrfe *intestata hereditas*, Som. 57, 101; Wrt. Voc. 20, 41. Yrfe drihtnes *hereditas Domini*, Ps. Spl. 126, 4. Yrfe sceal gedǽled deádes monnes *a dead man's property must be divided*, Exon. 90 a; Th. 338, 18; Gen. Ex. 80. Ne wilna ðú ðínes néhstan ierfes mid unrihte *covet thou not thy neighbour's goods*, L. Alf. 9; Th. i. 44, 21. Þolige his wǽpna and his ierfes *let him forfeit his weapons and his property*, L. Alf. pol. 1; Th. i. 60, 14. Gif hwá gefeohte on cyninges húse síe hé scyldig ealles his ierfes, L. In. 6; Th. i. 106, 3. Ðonne is riht ðæt heó sý healfes yrfes wyrðe and ealles gif hý cild gemǽne hæbban *then is it right that she be entitled to half the property, and to all if they have children together*, L. Edm. B. 4; Th. i. 254, 15. Ðú ðínes yrfes æðele gyrde álýsdest *liberasti virgam hæreditatis tuæ*, Ps. Th. 73, 3. Malalehel wæs æfter iarede yrfes hyrde fæder on láste *Mahalaleel was after Irad the guardian of the heritage, in succession to his father*, Cd. 52; Th. 65, 17; Gen. 1067. Nelle ic from mínum hláforde ne from mínum wífe ne from mínum bearne ne from mínum ierfe *I will not go from my lord, nor from my wife, nor from my child, nor from my goods*, L. Alf. 11; Th. i. 46, 9. Ne sylle gé ðæt land on éce yrfe *terra non vendetur in perpetuum*, Lev. 25, 23. His yrfe forhogode *hæreditatem suam sprevit*, Ps. Th. 77, 62. Gif hé wite hwá ðæs deádan ierfe hæbbe tiéme ðonne tó ðam ierfe and bidde ða hond ðe ðæt ierfe hafaþ ðæt hé him gedó ðone ceáp unbeceásne oððe gecýðe ðæt se deáda nǽfre ðæt ierfe áhte *if he know who has the property of the dead, let him then vouch the property to warranty, and demand of the hand which has that property, that he make the chattel uncontestable to him; or prove that the dead man never owned that property*, L. In. 53; Th. i. 136, 4–8. Him on láste heóld land and yrfe malalehel, Cd. 58; Th. 71, 8; Gen. 1167. [Under the single form *yrfe* two words seem to be comprised; the one just given, also written *ærfe, erfe*, and another, which would correspond with a Gothic *aurbi*, connected with *orf*, with the meaning *cattle*. With the former may be compared *Goth.* arbi; *n. heritage, inheritance*: *O. Sax.* erbi; *n*: *O. L. Ger.* ervi; *n. hæreditas*: *O. Frs.* erve; *n*: *O. H. Ger.* arbi, erbi, arpi; *n. possessio*: *Ger.* erbe; *n*: *Icel.* arfr; *m. inheritance*; erfð; *f. inheritance*. *See* yrfe, orf]. v. sundor-irfe; and Grmm. R. A. pp. 466–7; 565.

irfe-béc; *pl. f. A will, testament*:—Uncwedene yrfebéc *ruptum testamentum*: forswíged yrfebéc *suppressum testamentum*: underne yrfebéc *nuncupatio*: samhíwna yrfebéc *jus liberorum*, Ælfc. Gl. 13; Som. 57, 102–8; Wrt. Voc. 20, 42–6: ii. 49, 14. Áwǽgune yrfebéc *inritum testamentum*: unárlíce yrfebéc *inofficiosum testamentum*, 49, 15–18.

irfe-first, es; *m. A delay before entering upon an inheritance*; cretio, Ælfc. Gl. 13; Som. 57, 106; Wrt. Voc. 20, 44.

irfe-gedál, es; *n. A division of an inheritance* or *property*:—Yrfegedál *familiæ erciscundæ*, Ælfc. Gl. 13; Som. 57, 109; Wrt. Voc. 20, 47. Yrfegedál *familia erciscundæ, quia æerciscunda enim apud veteres divisio nuncupabatur*, ii. 39, 26.

irfe-geflit, es; *n. A dispute about inheritance*:—Ðá gehýrde wé manegu yrfegeflitu *then did we hear of many disputes about the inheritance*, Chart. Th. 486, 12.

irfe-gewrit, es; *n. Writing concerning an inheritance, a will, testament*:—Ac hit gelamp ðæt Æðelréd cingc gefór ðá ne cýðde mé nán mann nán yrfegewrit ne náne gewitnesse ðæt hit ǽnig óðer wǽre bútan swá wit on gewitnesse ǽr gecwǽdon *but it happened that king Ethelred died; then no man made known to me any testament or any witness that it was any other than as we two before with witness agreed*, Chart Th. 486, 7. On ðam yrfegewrite *in the testament*, 32.

irfe-hand, a; *f. One who manages the estate of a deceased person, an administrator* [?]:—Se mann se tó londe fóe ágefe hire erfehonda xiii pund pendingæ and heó forgifeþ xv pund for ðý ðe mon ðás feorme ðý soel gelǽste *let the man who succeeds to the land give to her administrator thirteen pounds of pennies; and he will give fifteen pounds, in order that this refection may be the better provided*, Chart. Th. 474, 9. v. hand.

irfe-láf, e; *f. An hereditary relic, heirloom, what is left of an inheritance, inheritance, heir*:—Hé fédeþ folc Iacobes and Israhéla yrfeláfe *pascere Jacob servum suum, et Israel hæreditatem suam*, Ps. Th. 77, 70. Ǽghwylcum máððum gesealde yrfeláfe *to each he gave a gift, an heirloom*, Beo. Th. 2110; B. 1053. Hé bátwearde swurd gesealde, ðæt hé syððan wæs mádme ðý weordra, yrfeláfe, 3810; B. 1903. Wolde líge gesyllan his swǽsne sunu ángan ofer eorþan yrfeláfe *he* [*Abraham*] *was ready to give to the flame his dear son, the only heir that was left him on earth*, Cd. 162; Th. 203, 14; Exod. 403.

irfe-land, es; *n. Land that passes as an inheritance, heritable land*:—Ic cýðo hú mín willa is ðet mín ærfelond fére ðe ic gebohte on ǽce ærfe *I declare how my will is that my heritable land shall go, that I bought in perpetual inheritance*, Chart. Th. 476, 12. Hie dydon mín land him selfum tó ierfelonde *dederunt terram meam sibi in hereditatem*, Past. 50, 2; Swt. 387, 30. Gebletsa ðín yrfeland *benedic hæreditati tuæ*, Ps. Th. 27, 10. Sealde heora eorþan on yrfeland *dedit terram eorum hæreditatem*, 135, 22.

irfe-numa, an; *m. One who takes an inheritance, an heir*:—Ðes and ðeós yrfenuma *hic et hæc heres*, Ælfc. Gr. 6; Som. 5, 33. Mín inbyrdling biþ mín yrfenuma . . . Ne byþ ðes ðín yrfenuma ac ðone ðú hæfst tó yrfenuman ðe of ðé sylfum cymþ *vernaculus meus heres meus erit . . . Non erit hic heres tuus, sed qui egredietur de utero tuo, ipsum habebis heredem*, Gen. 15, 3–4: 21, 10. Ðes ys yrfenuma *hic est heres*, Mt. Kmbl. 21, 38: Mk. Skt. 12, 7. Hit wǽre geþuht ðæs ðé máre gemynd ðæs fæder, ðá ðá se sunu, his yrfenuma, wæs gecíged ðæs fæder naman, Homl. Th. i. 478, 11. Fæderas and móddru bestandaþ heora bearna líc and heora yrfenuman him sylfum tó forwyrde forestæppaþ *fathers and mothers stand about the corpses of their children, and their heirs precede them to destruction*, ii. 124, 18. Se ðe sitte uncwydd and uncrafod on his áre on lífe ðæt nán man on his yrfenuman ne spece æfter his dæge *he who sits without contest or claim on his property during life, that no one bring an action against his heir after his day*, L. Eth. iii. 14; Th. i. 298, 10. Gif hwá tó deádan týme, búton hé yruenoman hæbbe ðe hit clǽnsie, ii. 9; Th. i. 290, 9. Gif se bónda ǽr hé deád wǽre beclypod wǽre ðonne andwyrdan ða yrfenuman swá hé sylf sceolde ðeáh hé líf hæfde *if the man of the house before his death were cited; then let the heirs answer as he himself would have had to do if he had lived*, L. C. S 73; Th. i. 416, 1. Se man ðe on fyrdunge ætforan his hláforde fealle, beón ða heregeata forgyfene, and fón ða yrfenuman tó lande and tó ǽhtan, 78; Th. i. 420, 16. [*Goth.* arbi-numja *an heir*: *O. H. Ger.* arpi-, erpi-nomo *hæres*: *Ger.* erb-nehmer: cf. *Icel.* arf-takari, arf-taki, arf-tökumaðr *an heir*.]

irfe-stōl, es; *m. An hereditary seat:*—Se burgstede, eádges yrfestōl, Exon. 52 a; Th. 181, 14; Gū. 1293. Eafora chuses yrfestōle weóld, Cd. 79; Th. 98, 13; Gen. 1629. Ne þearf ic yrfestōl eaforan bytlian ǽnegum mīnra . . . ne sealdest đū mē sunu *I need not build an hereditary seat for any descendant of mine . . . thou hast not given me a son*, 99; Th. 131, 14; Gen. 2176.

irfe-weard, es; *m. The guardian of an inheritance, an heir, possessor of a property:*—Hēr ys se yrfeweard [erfuard, Lind: erfeword, Rush.] *hic est heres*, Lk. Skt. 20, 14. Đǽr mē gifeđe ǽnig yrfeweard æfter wurde *if any heir to follow me had been granted me*, Beo. Th. 5455; B. 2731: Cd. 83; Th. 103, 33; Gen. 1727. Óđres ne gȳmeþ tō gebīdanne yrfeweardas *cares not to await another heir*, Beo. Th. 4897; B. 2453. Wæs swā mycel mancwealm đæt manige land binnan đære byrig wǽran būtan ǽlcum yrfewearde *there was so great a pestilence that many lands within the city were without any to inherit them*, Ors. 5, 2; Bos. 102, 13. Ús is swīđe uncūþ hwæt ūre yrfeweardas and lāstweardas dōn willon æfter ūrum līfe *we are very ignorant of what our heirs and successors will do after our life*, Blickl. Homl. 51, 35. Đa đe God bletsiaþ beóþ eorþan yrfeweardas *benedicentes eum possidebunt terram*, Ps. Th. 36, 21. Gerēfa mīn mynteþ đæt mē æfter sīe eaforan sīne yrfeweardas *my steward supposes that after me his children shall be heirs*, Cd. 100; Th. 131, 29; Gen. 2183. Hwæđer freá wille ǽnigne đē yrfewearda on woruld lǽtan, 101; Th. 134, 26; Gen. 2230. Đa sylfan wilniaþ him tō yrfeweardum tō habbanne *ipsos habere heredes quærunt*, Bd. 1, 27; S. 490, 18. Ic landes sumne dǽl sumum wīfe hiere dæg forgeaf and æfter hiere dæge twām yrfeweardum *I granted a certain portion of land to a certain woman for her life, and after her death to be held for two other lives*, Cod. Dipl. Kmbl. iii. 5, 10. See i. xxxiv. Forlēt hē đæs hwīlenlecan rīces yrfeweardas his suna þrȳ *tres suos filios regni temporalis heredes reliquit*, Bd. 2, 5; S. 507, 8. [*Gen. and Ex.* er(f)ward: *O. Sax.* erƀi-ward: *Icel.* (poët.) arf-vörðr *an heir.*]

irfe-, irf-weardness, e; *f. An inheritance:*—Yrfeweardnes *hereditas*, Ælfc. Gl. 13; Som. 57, 95; Wrt. Voc. 20, 36. Drihtnes dǽl wæs his folc and Iacob his yrfeweardnis *pars domini populus ejus, Jacob funiculus hereditatis ejus*, Deut. 32, 9. God cwæþ đæt hē sylf wǽre heora yrfweardnyss, Homl. Th. ii. 224, 7. Đonne biþ ūre seó yrfeweardnes *nostra erit hereditas*, Mk. Skt. 12, 7.

irfe-, irf-weardian; *p.* ode *To inherit, possess an inheritance:*—Đū yrfweardast on eallum þeódum *tu hæreditabis in omnibus gentibus*, Ps. Spl. 81, 7. Hī yrfweardiaþ eorþan *hæreditabunt terram*, 36, 11. Đæt đū yrfweardige eorþan, 36. DER. be-irfeweardian.

irfeweard-wrītere, es; *m. One who specifies his heir in writing, a testator:*—Yrfeweardwrītere *legatarius*, Ælfc. Gl. 13; Som. 57, 99; Wrt. Voc. 20, 39.

irfe-wrītend, es; *m. One who writes concerning the disposition of his property, one who makes a will:*—Yrfewrītend *testator*, Ælfc. Gl. 13; Som. 57, 100; Wrt. Voc. 20, 40.

irf-. v. irfe-.

irgþ, e: irgþu, irgþo; *indecl; f. Sluggishness, cowardice, timorousness, pusillanimity:*—Wē witon georne đæt hie for iergþe nāđer ne durran ne swā feor friþ gesēcan ne furþon hie selfe æt hām hie werian *we know well that they from cowardice dare neither seek peace at such a distance, nor even defend themselves at home*, Ors. 3, 9; Swt. 136, 28. For eówre forhtnysse and yrhþe đe eów eglaþ *propter cordis tui formidinem, qua terreberis*, Deut. 28, 67. Se man đe ætfleó fram his hlāforde ođđe fram his gefēran for his yrhþe sȳ hit on scipfyrde sȳ hit on landfyrde þolige ealles đæs đe hē āgē and his āgenes feores *the man that flies from his lord, or from his comrade, from cowardice, be it on an expedition by sea or by land, let him lose all that he owns and his own life*, L. C. S. 78; Th. i. 420, 8. Đā hēton hī secgan đysses landes wæstmbǽrnysse and Brytta yrgþo *nunciatum est simul et insulæ fertilitas, ac segnitia Brittonum*, Bd. 1, 15; S. 483, 15. Þurh lyđre yrhþe Godes bydela đe clumedon mid ceaflum đǽr hī scoldon clipian *through the vile sluggishness of God's messengers, who mumbled with their mouths when they should have cried aloud*, Swt. A. S. Rdr. 111, 202. [*Laym.* Arđur, ærhđe bideled, 23546: *O. and N.* he for arehþe hit ne forlete, 404: *O. H. Ger.* argida *hebitudo, ignavia.*] v. earg.

irhþ. v. irgþ.

Iringes weg *via secta*, Wrt. Voc. ii. 123, 50. v. Grmm. D. M. 332.

Īr-land, es; *n. Ireland:*—Đrie Scottas cuōmon tō Ælfrēde cyninge of Ȳrlande, Chr. 891; Erl. 88, 6, note. Tō Īrlande, 918; Erl. 104, 15: 1051; Erl. 176, 18. Se preóst cwæþ đæt ān wer wǽre on Īrlande gelǽred, Swt. A. S. Rdr. 101, 200. Hē fērde geond eal Yrrland, Homl. Th. ii. 346, 28. v. Īra-land.

ir-līc; *adj. Angry:*—Hē swīđe irlīcum andwlitan beseah tō đam iungan cnyhte *he looked at the young man with a very angry countenance*, Th. Ap. 4, 6: 5, 3.

irman; *p.* de *To make miserable* or *wretched, to afflict, vex:*—Đā ongunnan twā þeóda Pyhtas norþan and Scottas westan hī onwinnan and heora ǽhta niman and hergian and hī fela geára yrmdon and hȳndon *then began two peoples, the Picts from the north, the Scots from the west, to attack them, and to take their possessions, and to harry, and afflicted and vexed them many years; Brittania denique subito duabus gentibus transmarinis vehementer sævis, Scottorum a circio, Pictorum ab aquilone, multos stupet gemitque per annos*, Bd. 1, 12; S. 480, 24. Hē hæfde him tō gamene hū hē eorþcyningas yrmde and cwelmde *he* [*Nero*] *made it his sport, how he could vex and torment the kings of this earth*, Bt. Met. Fox 9, 94; Met. 9, 47. Ic mæg sleán and ierman mīne heáfodgemæccan *I can beat and vex my companions*, Past. 17, 8; Swt. 121, 12. [Cf. *O. H. Ger.* ki-ermit uuerdemes *aporiamur*, Grff. i. 423.] v. for-, ge-yrman.

irmen, yrmen; *adj.* A word occurring mostly as a prefix with the idea of *greatness, universality.* In the following passages it occurs independently:—Faraþ geond ealne yrmenne grund *go through the whole earth*, Exon. 14 b; Th. 30, 18; Cri. 481. Ofer ealne yrmenne grund, 66 a; Th. 213, 14; Jul. 10. [*O. Sax.* irmin-: *Icel.* jörmun-, e. g. jörmungrund *the earth*. See Grmm. D. M. 104–7: 325, sqq.] v. eormen-.

irmen-þeóde; *pl. The peoples of the earth:*—Bringeþ Agustus yrmenþeódum hlāfmæssan dæg *August brings Lammas day to all the nations of earth*, Menol. Fox 276; Men. 139. [Cf. *O. Sax.* ik allun skal irminthiodun dōmōs adēlian *I shall judge all the nations of the world*, Hel. 3316.]

irming, es; *m. A poor, mean, wretched, miserable person, a wretch:*—Ic eom āna forlǽten yrming *unicus et pauper sum ego*, Ps. Th. 24, 14. Ic eom yrming and þearfa *ego egenus et pauper sum*, 39, 20. Đū eart đē godes yrming *as to thee, thou art God's pauper*, Exon. 36 b; Th. 118, 22; Gū. 243. Betere is đē đæt đē sceamige nū hēr beforan mē ānum yrmingce đonne eft beforan Gode on đam mycelan dōme *melius est tibi nunc hic coram me solo misero pudefieri, quam posthac coram Deo in magno judicio*, L. Ecg. C. prm; Th. ii. 132, 20. Đā đa iermingas đe đǽr tō lāfe wurdon ūt of đǽm holan crupon đe heó on lutedan *when the wretched people that remained crept out of the holes that they had lurked in*, Ors. 2, 8; Swt. 92, 29. Se đe ǽnigne đissa iermingu besuīcþ *qui scandalizaverit unum de pusillis istis*, Past. 2, 2; Swt. 30, 17. Đæt is sió friþstōw and sió frōfor ān eallra yrminga æfter đissum weoruldgeswincum *that alone is the asylum and the comfort of all the wretched after these labours in the world*, Bt. Met. Fox 21, 33; Met. 21, 17. [Makede him *erming* þer he was er king, O. E. Homl. 2, 62: Þu *erming* þu wrecche gost, O. and N. 1111: Agag þe king, þu ært an *ærming*, Laym. 16690: *Icel.* armingi *a poor fellow, a wretch: O. H. Ger.* arming *pauper.*] v. earming, erming.

irmþ, e; irmþu, irmþo; *indecl. f. Poverty, penury, misery, wretchedness, calamity, distress, disorder:*—Yrmþ *miseria*, Ælfc. Gr. 33; Som. 37, 24. Nis đǽr on đam londe yldu ne yrmþu *in that land there is not age or misery*, Exon. 56 b; Th. 201, 6; Ph. 52: 64 b; Th. 238, 34; Ph. 614. Him gewearþ yrmþu tō ealdre *upon them* [*Adam and Eve*] *came misery for ever*, 73 a; Th. 272, 24; Jul. 504: 119 a; Th. 457, 15; Hy. 4, 84. Ne biþ him hyra yrmþu ān tō wīte ac đara ōđerra eád tō sorgum *nor alone shall their own misery be torment, but the bliss of the others shall be a grief*, 26 b; Th. 79, 19; Cri. 1293. For yrmþe unspēdig[ra] *propter miseriam inopum*, Ps. Spl. 11, 5. Đeós of hyre yrmþe eall đæt heó hæfde sealde *hæc de pœnuria sua omnia quæ habuit misit*, Mk. Skt. 12, 44. Đonne sende hē him fultum þurh sumne dēman đe hī ālīsde of heora yrmþe *then he sent them help by some judge, who released them from their misery*, Ælfc. T. Grn. 6, 26. Wiđ đæs migđan yrmþe *for disorder of the urine*, Herb. 163, 3; Lchdm. i. 292, 7. Ic ādreáh feala yrmþa ofer eorþan *I suffered many miseries on earth*, Andr. Kmbl. 1939; An. 972: Exon. 26 b; Th. 78, 5; Cri. 1269. Ic eom gefylled mid iermþum *saturatus sum miseria*, Past. 36, 5; Swt. 253, 8. Seđe hine fram swā monigum yrmþum and teónum generede *qui se tot ac tantis calamitatibus ereptum*, Bd. 2, 12; S. 514, 19. Đæt hī đām yrmþum ā ne wiđstanden *in miseriis non subsistent*, Ps. Th. 139, 10. Gif hē đære tīde yrmþo beswicode *si temporis illius ærumnis exemptus*, Bd. 2, 12; S. 512, 36. Đus hī heora yrmþo ārehton *ita suas calamitates explicant*, 1, 13; S. 481, 43. Đisse worlde yrmþa *the miseries of this world*, Blickl. Homl. 61, 3. Yrmþo, 203, 20. Dreógan yrmþu būtan ende *to suffer endless misery*, Elen. Kmbl. 1902; El. 953. Đū scealt ēcan đīne yrmþu, Andr. Kmbl. 2767; An. 1386. Yrmþo, 2381; An. 1192. Ides yrmþe gemunde *the woman remembered her misery*, Beo. Th. 2523; B. 1259. Hē đa yrmþu oncyrde đe wē ǽr drugon *he averted the miseries that before we suffered*, Exon. 16 b; Th. 38, 29; Cri. 614. [*O. E. Homl.* ermđe *poverty: Laym.* ærmđe *misery: O. H. Ger.* armida *paupertas, inopia, penuria.*] v. ermþu, earmþu, eormþu, weoruld-irmþu.

irnan; *p.* arn, *pl.* urnon; *pp.* urnen *To run:*—Ic yrne *cucurri*, Ps. Spl. T. 118, 32. Seó eá Danai irnþ đonan sūþryhte *the river Don runs thence due south*, Ors. 1, 1; Swt. 8, 17. Ǽspringe irneþ wiđ his eardes, Bt. Met. Fox 5, 29; Met. 5, 15. Hē arn him sylf tō his hrȳđera falde *ipse ad armentum cucurrit*, Gen. 18, 7. Đonne orn hē eft inn tō đæm temple *ad templum recurrit*, Past. 16, 3; Swt. 103, 4. Đū urne mid him *simul currebas cum eo*, Ps. Th. 49, 19. Đā urnon him tōgēnes twegen đe hæfdon deófolseócnesse *occurrerunt ei duo habentes dæmonia*, Mt. Kmbl. 8, 28. Gangende đyder urnon, Mk. Skt. 6, 33: Jn. Skt. 20, 4. Tō đam ylcan ryne đe hié ǽr urnon, Bt. 21; Fox 74, 12. Đæt hī mǽgen iernan and fleón tō đæs lāreówes mōde *ut ad pastoris mentem recurrant*, Past.

16. 4; Swt. 103, 22. Hē sceal yrnan forþ *he must run forth*, Exon. 128 b; Th. 494, 9; Rä. 82, 5. Seó [eá] is irnende of norþdǽle, Ors. 1, 1; Swt. 8, 15. Ac hī forweorþan wætere gelīcost đonne hit yrnende eorþe forswelgeþ *ad nihilum devenient, velut aqua decurrens*, Ps. Th. 57, 6. Óþ đæt wintra biþ þūsend urnen *until a thousand years are passed*, Exon. 61 a; Th. 223, 23; Ph. 364. DER. ā-, be-, ge-, geond-, ofer-, on-, ōþ-, tō-, þurh-, under-, up-, ymb-irnan. v. rinnan.

irnere. v. fore-irnere.

irre, es; *n. Anger, wrath, ire, rage:*—Đonne tyht hie đæt ierre [Cott. MS. irre] đæt hie wealwiaþ on đa wēdenheortnesse . . . Đonne đæt ierre æfþ anwald đæs monnes hē self nāt hwæt hē on đæt irre dēþ *impellente ira in mentis vesaniam devolvuntur . . . Quos cum furor agit in præceps, ignorant quidquid irati faciunt*, Past. 40, 1; Swt. 289, 5–10. Godes yrre ys ofer hig *egressa est ira a domino*, Num. 18, 46. Nū is gefylled đæt mycelle hātheort and đæt mycelle yrre đyses ealdermannes *now is completed the great rage and anger of this ruler*, Blickl. Homl. 151, 11. Sīe ǽlc monn lætt tō iorre iorra fordon weres sōþfæst godes ne giwyrcaþ *sit omnis homo tardus ad iram; ira enim viri justitiam Dei non operatur*, Rtl. 28, 21: 40, 35: 41, 3. Seó gesceádwīsnes sceal wealdan ǽgđer ge đære wilnunga ge đæs yrres *reason must rule both desire and anger*, Bt. 33, 4; Fox 132, 9. Hē him weg worhte wrāđan yrres *viam fecit semitæ iræ suæ*, Ps. Th. 77, 50. Ic bidde đē, hlāford, đæt ic mōte būtan yrre wiđ đē sprecan *oro, domine mi, loquatur servus tuus verbum in auribus tuis et ne irascaris*, Gen. 44, 18. Wurdon mē on yrre yfele and hefige *in ira molesti erant mihi*, Ps. Th. 54, 3. Đæt gē fleón fram đam tōwerdan yrre *fugite a ventura ira*, Lk. Skt. 3, 7. Đā cwæþ se hlāford mid yrre *tunc iratus paterfamilias dixit*, 14, 21. Mid miclum wylme and yrre onstyred *nimio furore commotus*, Bd. 1, 7; S. 477, 41. Đā wæs hē mid yrre swīđlīce onstyred, Blickl. Homl. 199, 16. Ic ondrēd his graman and his yrre *timui indignationem et iram illius*, Deut. 9, 19. Āgeót ofer hī đīn đæt grame yrre *effunde super eos iram tuam*, Ps. Th. 68, 25. Đa hine on yrre gebringaþ *qui in ira provocant*, 65, 6. Đē læs gē habban godes yrre *ne super omnem coetum oriatur indignatio*, Lev. 10, 6. Hē gearwe wiste đæt hie godes yrre habban sceoldon, Cd. 33; Th. 43, 24; Gen. 695: Exon. 61 b; Th. 226, 20; Ph. 408. Godes yrre bær *the wrath of God was upon him*, Beo. Th. 1427; B. 711. [Godess irre iss upponn himm, Orm. 18000: *O. E. Homl. A. R.* eorre: *Reliq. Antiq.* urre.] v. eorre, *and next word.*

irre, yrre; *adj.* I. *Gone astray, wandering, confused, perverse, depraved:*—Đæt wæs earfoþcynn yrre and rēđe *genus pravum et peramarum*, Ps. Th. 77, 10. Óþ đæt his eáge biþ æfþancum ful yrre geworden *until his eye is filled with evil thoughts and gone astray*, Salm. Kmbl. 994; Sal. 498. Sumum mēces ecg yrrum ealowōsan ealdor ōþþringeþ *the edge of the sword crushes the life out of one, confused* [or *angry?*] *and mad with drink*, Exon. 87 b; Th. 330, 10; Vy. 49. Ealle synt yrre đa đe unwīse heora heortan hige healdaþ mid dysige *turbati sunt omnes insipientes corde*, Ps. Th. 75, 4. II. *angry, enraged, wrathful, indignant:*—And ierre hē hwearf đonan *and he went away in a rage*, Chr. 584; Erl. 18, 25. Iorra *iratus*, Rtl. 179, 36. Hwī eart đū yrre *quare iratus es?* Gen. 4, 6. Se cyning wæs yrre wiđ mē, 41, 10. Hē wæs mē yrre, Deut. 1, 37. Đā wearþ yrre god and đam werode wrāþ, Cd. 2; Th. 3, 12; Gen. 34. Ne hine nǽnig man yrne ne grammōdne ne funde *nor did any man find him angry or cruel*, Blickl. Homl. 223, 33. Þurh yrne hyge *with cr[uel] purpose*, Exon. 16 b; Th. 36, 10; Cri. 620. Hē hine on yrre mōd gebrohtan *exacerbaverunt eum*, Ps. Th. 77, 40. Đa irran [Cott. MS. ierran] nyton hwæt hie on him selfum habbaþ and eác đætte wierse is đætte hie ful oft wēnaþ đætte hiera hierre [Cott. MS. ierre] sīe ryhtwīslīc anda *ignorant quidquid a semetipsis patiuntur irati; nonnunquam vero, quod est gravius, iræ suæ stimulum justitiæ zelum putant*, Past. 40, 1; Swt. 289, 10. Hie wǽron tō đon hātheortlīce yrre đæt hie woldan đone cāsere cwicenne forbærnan *they were so furiously enraged, that they wanted to burn the emperor alive*, Blickl. Homl. 191, 11. Yrre wǽron begen rēđe *angry were both and fierce*, Beo. Th. 1543; B. 769. [Ford wende þe eorl ire [2nd MS. yr] on his mode, Laym. 18597: Þe eorre Demare *iratus Judex*, A. R. 304, 24: *Goth.* airzis wisan *or* wairþan *to go astray, err*; airzei, airziþa *error*; airzjan *to lead astray*: *O. Sax.* irri *angry*; irrian *to disturb, confuse*: *O. L. Ger.* irrōn *errare, commovere*: *O. H. Ger.* irri *vagus, lascivus*; irre sīn *errare*; irra-heit *error*; irrado *impedimentum*: irran *impedire, confundere*; irrōn *errare, apostatare*: *Ger.* irre *confused, wandering*; irren *to err, go astray*. Cf. irsian, *and see* Diefenbach i. 21: Grff. i. 449 sqq.] v. eorre.

irre-mōd; *adj. Of angry mood, angry-minded:*—Eode yrremōd, him of eágum stōd līge gelīcost leóht unfæger, Beo. Th. 1456; B. 726.

irre-weorc, es; *n. A work undertaken in anger:*—Engla drihten wile uppe heonan sāwla lǽdan and wē seođđan ā đæs yrreweorces hēnþo geþoliaþ *the Lord of angels will up from hence lead souls, and we ever after shall suffer the humiliation of that angry feat* [*the harrowing of Hell*], Cd. 222; Th. 289, 17; Sat. 399.

irringa, irrenga; *adv. Angrily, in anger:*—Be đæm ilcan hē cwæþ eft ierrenga *hinc iterum iratus dicit*, Past. 56, 7; Swt. 435, 11. Đā tō evan god yrringa spræc, Cd. 43; Th. 56, 27; Gen. 918. Seó beó sceal losian đonne heó hwæt yrringa stingþ *the bee shall perish when she stings anything in anger*, Bt. 31, 2; Fox 112, 26: Bt. Met. Fox 18, 13; Met. 18, 7. Yrrenga, 26, 167; Met. 26, 84. Se brǽda sǽ of clomme bræc up yrringa on eorþan fæđm *the broad sea from durance broke up angrily on to earth's bosom*, Exon. 24 b; Th. 70, 31; Cri. 1147. Gē mec yrringa up gelǽddon đæt ic of lyfte londa getimbru geseón meahte, 39 b; Th. 131, 13; Gū. 455. Hē yrringa slōh *he angrily smote*, Beo. Th. 3135; B. 1565: 5921; B. 2964. v. eorringa.

ir-scipe, es; *m. Anger:*—Ǽfter mycelnes[se] his irscipes *secundum multitudinem iræ suæ*, Ps. Lamb. second 9, 4.

irsian; *p.* ode. I. *to be angry, to rage:*—Hū lange yrsast đū on đīnes esnes gebed *quousque irasceris in orationem servi tui*, Ps. Th. 79, 5. Synfull yrsaþ *peccator irascetur*, 111, 9. Đonne ūs đara manna mōd yrsade and ūs wiđerwearde wǽron *cum irasceretur animus eorum adversum nos*, 123, 3. Swā him yrsade se for ealle spræc feónda mengu *so did he, who spake for all the multitude of fiends, rage against him* [*Guthlac*], Exon. 35 a; Th. 114, 11; Gū. 171. Moises đā yrsode and āxode *iratusque Moyses ait*, Num. 31, 14. His gebrōđru yrsodon swīđe wiđ hine *invidebant ei fratres sui*, Gen. 37, 11. Ne yrsa đū wiđ mē, Nar. 43, 7. Yrsiaþ *irascimini*, Ps. Lamb. 4, 5. Ic bidde đæt đū ne yrsie *obsecro ne irascaris*, Gen. 18, 32. Yrre is đære sāwle forgifen tō đȳ đæt heó yrsige ongeán leahtres *anger is given to the soul that it may be angry against vice*, Homl. Skt. 1, 104. Đæt đe hió mid ryhte irsian sceall *that with which rightly it must be angry*, Past. 40, 4; Swt. 293, 13. Đǽr đǽr đū neóde irsian scyle gemetiga đæt đeáh *in case you needs must be angry, still be moderate*, Prov. Kmbl. 24. Ūþwitan secgaþ đæt sió sāwul hæbbe þrió gecynd ān is đæt heó biþ wilnigende ōđer đæt hió biþ irsiende þridde đæt hió biþ gesceádwīs *philosophers say that the soul hath three natures, one is that it desires, the second that it is angry, the third that it is rational*, Bt. 33, 4; Fox 132, 4. Đæt irsigende mōd hē gegremeþ and wierse ierre [Cott. MS. irre] hē āstyreþ *irati animus ad deteriora provocatur*, Past. 10, 3; Swt. 63, 13. Hwæthwugu biþ betweoh đǽm irsiendan and đǽm ungeþyldgan . . . đa iersigendan him tō getióþ đæt đætte hie eáþe būtan bión meahton *in hoc ab impatientibus iracundi differunt . . . isti, quæ tolerentur, important*, 40, 4; Swt. 293, 15. Đa Iudēiscan yrsigende cwǽdon tō Criste *the Jews being angry said to Christ*, Homl. Th. ii. 236, 4. II. *to make angry, to anger, provoke:*—Hī yrsodon moyses *irritaverunt Moysen*, Ps. Spl. 105, 16.

irsigend-līc; *adj. Capable of anger:*—Ūþwytan secgaþ đæt đære sāwle gecynd is þrȳfeald. Ān dǽl is on hire gewylnigendlīc ōđer yrsigendlīc þrydde gesceádwīslīc *philosophers say that the nature of the soul is threefold. There is one part in her capable of desire, a second capable of anger, a third is rational* [cf. Bt. 33, 4; Fox 132, 4], Homl. Skt. 1, 97.

irsung, e; *f. Anger, readiness to anger, irascibility:*—Twā đara gecyndu habbaþ nētenu swā same swā men ōđer đara is wilnung ōđer is irsung *two of those natures beasts have the same as men, one of them is desire, the other is anger*, Bt. 33, 4; Fox 132, 6. Yrsung, Bt. Met. Fox 20, 371; Met. 20, 185. Oft ungemetlīcu irsung biþ gelīcet đæt menn wēnaþ đæt hit sīe ryhtwīslīc anda *sæpe effrenata ira spiritalis zeli virtus æstimatur*, Past. 20, 1; Swt. 149, 11. Sió gesceádwīsnes sceal on gehwelcum waldan semle irsunge [cf. wealdan đæs yrres, Fox 132, 10], Bt. Met. Fox 20, 397; Met. 20, 199. Of irsunge wyxt seófung and of đære geþwǽrnesse lufu *from anger grows sighing, and from gentleness love*, Prov. Kmbl. 23. Gē yldran ne sceolan gē eówru bearn tō yrsunge geciegean *ye parents, ye shall not provoke your children to anger*, L. E. I. 33; Th. ii. 430, 39. Hē hyne sceal forhabban wyđ yrsunga *he shall restrain himself from anger*, Lchdm. iii. 140, 27. Ac đa irsunga [Cott. MS. iersunga] sindun swīđe ungelīca ōđer biþ swelce hit sīe irres anlīcnes . . . ōđer biþ đæt ierre đæt mon sīe gedrēfed on his mōde būtan ǽlcre ryhtwīsnesse ōđer đara irsunga biþ tō ungemetlīce ātyht on đæt đe hió mid ryhte irsian sceall ōđer on đæt hió ne sceal biþ ealneg tō swīđe onbærned *sed longe alia est ira, quæ sub æmulationis specie subripit, alia, quæ turbatum cor et sine justitia prætexta confundit. Illa enim in hoc, quod debet, inordinate extenditur; hæc autem semper in his, quæ non debet, inflammatur*, Past. 40, 4; Swt. 293, 9–14.

irþ, e; *f.* I. *ploughing, tilling:*—For yrþe *for ploughing*; ad arandum, L. R. S. 21; Th. i. 440, 27. II. *the produce of arable land, a crop:*—Đæt đæs wæstmes yrþ đǽr mā upyrnende wǽre. Đā him đā đæt sǽd broht wæs ofer ealle tīd tō sāwenne and ofer eallne hiht wæstm tō beranne đe hē on đam ylcan land seów đā georn đǽr sōna upp genihtsumlīc yrþ and wæstm *ut illius frugis ibi potius seges oriretur. Quod dum sibi adlatum, ultra omne tempus serendi, ultra omnem spem fructificandi, eodem in agro sereret; mox copiosa seges exorta est*, Bd. 4, 28; S. 605, 38–602, 1. Ic sello đās land mid cwice erfe and mid earþe and mid eallum þingum đe tō londum belimpaþ *I give these lands with the live stock, and crops and all things that belong to the lands*, Chart. Th. 481, 3. Rīpe yrþe *maturam segetem*, Bd. 1, 12; S. 480, 35, note. III. *ploughed land:*—Cf. on đa foryrþe eāstewerde, Cod. Dipl. Kmbl. iii. 449, 32 *where Kemble translates* foryrþ '*the land which is first ploughed,*' xlii. [On erthes *aracionibus*, Pall. 4, 68: *Scott.* earth *the act of earing or ploughing.*] v. gærs-, gafol-, lencten-yrþ; *and* erian.

irþ-land, es; *n. Arable land:*—Ierþland *arva*, Wrt. Voc. 285, 6. Yrþland arva, 289, 77. Ðanon up andlang yrþlandes, Cod. Dip. Kmbl. iii. 23, 31. Ic âwêste ðinne buruh and gewyrce tô yrþlande *I will lay waste thy city and make it into ploughed land*, Homl. Skt. 3, 224. Ðonne is ðes londes ðe ic hîgum selle xvi gioc ærþelandes and mêdwe *now of the land that I give to the convent there are sixteen acres of arable land and meadow*, Chart. Th. 477, 26.

irþling, es; *m.* I. *a husbandman, farmer, ploughman*:—Yrþlingc *arator*, Wrt. Voc. 73, 34: Ælfc. Gr. 41; Som. 44, 8. Noe ðâ yrþling began tô wircenne ðæt land *coepitque Noe vir agricola exercere terram*, Gen. 9, 20. Môna se twentigoþa cild âcenned yrþlincg *a child born on the twentieth day of the moon will be a husbandman*, Lchdm. iii. 194, 6. Hwæt sægest ðû Yrþlingc *quid dicis tu, Arator?* Coll. Monast. Th. 19, 11. Hwilce ðê geþuht betwux woroldcræftas heoldan ealdordôm? Eorþtilþ forðam se yrþling ûs ealle fêtt *qualis tibi videtur inter seculares artes retinere primatum? Agricultura, quia arator nos omnes pascit*, 30, 23–8. Sume synt yrþlincgas sume scêphyrdas sume oxanhyrdas *alii sunt aratores, alii opiliones, quidam bubulci*, 19, 3. *Laboratores* sind yrþlingas and ǣhtemen, tô ðam ânum betǣhte, ðe hig ûs bigleofan tiliaþ, Ælfc. T. Grn. 20, 19. II. *the name of a bird, a cuckoo* [?]:—Irþling *cucuzata*, Wrt. Voc. 281, 14: *birbicariolus*, 281, 22. Ærþling *tanticus*, 29, 63. Geác *cuculus*, eorþling *birbicaliolus*, 63, 3–4. Yrþling *berbigarulus* vel *tanticus*, Wrt. Voc. ii. 12, 60. Erdling *bitorius*, 102, 1. Erþling *enistrius*, 143, 57. In connection with the cuckoo it may be noticed that *cucusare* is given in DuCange as the verb properly used of the note of the cuckoo; and see Grmm. D. M. 640, sqq. on the cuckoo as associated with a particular season of the year. However, in Wrt. Voc. 62, 22 the *lapwing* is glossed by *cucurata*.

is *is*. v. eom.

ÎS, es; *n.* I. ICE:—Îs *glacies*, Ælfc. Gl. 94; Som. 75, 103; Wrt. Voc. 52, 53. Hwî ne wundriaþ hî hwî ðæt îs weorþe *why do not they wonder why ice comes?* Bt. 39, 3; Fox 214, 35. Ofer eástreámas îs brycgade *the ice formed a bridge over the streams*, Andr. Kmbl. 2524; An. 1268: Exon. 90 a; Th. 338, 4; Gn. Ex. 73. Îses gicel *stiria, stillicidia*, Ælfc. Gl. 16; Som. 58, 68; Wrt. Voc. 21, 55. Hit eal gemealt îse gelîcost *it all melted just like ice*, Beo. Th. 3221; B. 1608. Ðâ eode hê sumre nihte on îse unwærlîce *dum incautius forte noctu in glacie incederet*, Bd. 3, 2; S. 525, 1. Styccum healfbrocenra îsa *semifractarum crustis glacierum*, 5, 12; S. 631, 26. II. *the name of the Rune* ᛁ = i:—ᛁ byþ oferceald ungemetum slidor *ice is exceedingly cold and excessively slippery*, Runic pm. 11; Kmbl. 341, 14. [*O. Frs. O. H. Ger.* îs; *n*: *Icel.* íss; *m*: *Ger.* eis; *n.*]

-isc, *modern -ish, a suffix of adjectives, connoting the quality of the object denoted by the stem*, e. g. ceorl-isc *churl-ish*, cild-isc *child-ish*; *also connotes origin from a place or stock*, e. g. Engl-isc, Grêc-isc, Iudê-isc. The suffix may be seen in the cognate dialects in the following words, *Goth.* þiud-isk-o *after the manner of the Gentiles*; Iudaiw-isk-s: *O. Sax.* menn-isk *human*: *O. Frs.* mann-isk: *Icel.* bern-sk-r *childish*; En-sk-r *English*: *Dan.* Engel-sk *English*: *O. H. Ger.* diut-isc: *Ger.* deut-sch.

îs-ceald; *adj. Ice-cold*:—Îsceald sǣ, Exon. 81 b; Th. 306, 28; Seef. 14: 307, 5; Seef. 19: Bt. Met. Fox 27, 6; Met. 27, 3.

isen, iesen, iesend. v. Lchdm. iii. 361, col. 2; *and* gesen *in the appendix.*

ÎSEN, es; *n. Iron, steel, an implement made of iron*:—Îsen *ferrum*, Wrt. Voc. 85, 13: Ælfc. Gr. 5; Som. 4, 58. Ðis ŷsen *hic calibs*, 9; Som. 13, 18. Eorþe swilce îsen *terra ferrea*, Deut. 28, 23. Ðâ wæs se ofen onhǣted îsen eall þurhglêded *then was the furnace heated, the iron made red hot*, Cd. 186; Th. 231, 8; Dan. 244. Îsenes scearpnyss *acumen*, Ælfc. Gr. 9; Som. 9, 31. Gemeng tôgædere mid glôwende îsene *mix together with a glowing iron*, L. M. 2, 24; Lchdm. ii. 216, 1. Ne delfe nân man ða moran mid îsene *let no man dig up the roots with iron*, Lchdm. iii. 30, 24. Bûtan ǣlcan îsene genumen *gathered without using any iron implement*, Lchdm. iii. 4, 29 [cf. Grmm. D. M. 1148, sqq. as to the use of iron in getting plants]. *The two following passages refer to the ordeal* [v. îsen-ordâl] *by hot iron*:—Gif hê hine lâdian wille ðonne gâ hê tô ðam hâtum îsene and lâdige ða hand mid ðe man tŷhþ *if he be willing to clear himself, then let him go to the hot iron, and clear the hand therewith that is accused*, L. Ath. i. 14; Th. 206, 23. Ǣlc tiónd âge geweald swâ hwæðer hê wille swâ wæter swâ îsen, L. Eth. iii. 6; Th. i. 296, 4. Âcêle ðû wealhât îsen ðonne hit furþum sîe of fŷre âtogen *cool very hot iron when it is just drawn from the fire*, L. M. 2, 45; Lchdm. ii. 256, 15. [*Ayenb.* izen (*but the general form in middle English is that with* r): *O. H. Ger.* îsen: *Ger.* eisen.] v. îren, îsern; brand-, delf-, gâd-, ordâl-îsen.

îsen; *adj. Iron, made of iron*:—Îsen *ferreus*, Ælfc. Gr. 5; Som. 4, 58. Seó gyrd wæs eal îsen *the rod was all iron*, Homl. Th. ii. 312, 17. Hig hyne on ânum ŷsenum scrŷne gebrohton on ðære byrig Damascus *they brought him in an iron chest to the city of Damascus*, St. And. 38, 8. Drihten sett îsen geoc on eówerne swuran *dominus ponet jugum ferreum super cervicem tuam*, Deut. 28, 48. Îsene bendas *vincula ferrea*, Ps. Th. 149, 8. Âdrîfan îsene næglas þurh ða handa, Homl. Th. i. 146, 11. Ðâ wurdon hrædlîce forþ âborene îsene clûtas and îsene clawa and îsen bedd . . . Decius cwæþ 'Lecgaþ ða îsenan clûtas hâte glôwende tô his sîdan,' 424, 18–35. v. îren, îsern.

îsen-grǣg; *adj. Iron-grey*:—Îsengrǣg *ferrugo*, i. *color purpuræ subnigræ*: îsengrǣgum blôstme *ferrugineo flore* vel *purpureo*, Wrt. Voc. ii. 147, 63–67. Ða îsengrǣgan *ferrugineas*, 38, 44. [*Icel.* járn-grár: *Ger.* eisen-grau.]

îsen-hearde, an; *f. Ironhard*; centaurea nigra, Lchdm. iii. 4, 28: 22, 31: 334, col. 2. See Plant Names in E. D. S. Pub. iren-harde, iron-heads, iron-weed.

îsen-hyrst; *adj. Fitted with iron*:—Ǣrest of îsenhyrste gate . . . eft in on îsenhyrsten geat *first, from the gate fitted up with iron . . . back to the same gate*, Cod. Dipl. Kmbl. iii. 130, 27 . . . 131, 19. [Cf. *Icel.* járnsleginn *mounted with iron.*]

îsenian; *p.* ode. *To furnish* or *cover with iron* (*armour*): Ða îsnodan truman *ferratas acies*, Wrt. Voc. ii. 147, 52.

îsen-ordâl, es; *n. The ordeal by hot iron*, in which the accused who wished to clear himself had to bear, on the naked hand, a piece of red hot iron. The passages from which the following extracts are taken will illustrate this mode of trial:—Gif hit sŷ ŷsenordâl beón þreó niht ǣr man ða hand undô *if it be the ordeal by hot iron, let it be three days before the hand be undone*, L. Ath. i. 23; Th. i. 212, 3. Wê cwǣdon . . . ðæt man . . . myclade ðæt ordâlŷsen ðæt hit gewege þrŷ pund . . . and hæbbe se teónd cyre swâ wæterordâl swâ ŷsenordâl swâ hwæðer him leófre sŷ *we have ordained that the ordeal-iron be increased so that it weigh three pounds . . . and let the accuser have the choice of ordeal by water or by iron, whichever he prefer*, iv. 6; Th. i. 224, 12–16. *See too*, Dôm be hâtan îsene, 7; Th. i. 226, 7, sqq; *and* Schmid A. S. Gesetz. p. 419. [Cf. *Icel.* bera járn, járn-burðr *in* Cl. and Vig. Dict. *and see* Grmm. R. A. 915, sqq.] v. ordâl.

îsen-panna, -panne, an; *m. f. A frying-pan*:—Îsenpanna *sartago*, Wrt. Voc. 82, 68. Îsenpanne, Ælfc. Gl. 26; Som. 60, 94; Wrt. Voc. 25, 34. *See other compounds of* îren, îsen, îsern.

îsen-smiþ, es; *m. An iron-smith, worker in iron, blacksmith*:—Tubalcain wæs êgðer ge goldsmiþ ge îsensmiþ *Tubalcain fuit malleator et faber in cuncta opera æris et ferri*, Gen. 4, 22. Ic hæbbe smiþas îsen[e]smiþas goldsmiþ seolforsmiþ ârsmiþ *habeo fabros, ferrarios, aurificem, argentarium, ærarium*, Coll. Monast. Th. 29, 35. [Cf. *Wick.* iren-smiþ: *Icel.* járn-smiðr *a blacksmith*: *O. H. Ger.* îsarn-smid *faber ferrarius*: *Ger.* eisenschmied.] v. îsen-, îsern-wyrhta.

îsen-swât, es; *m.* [?]:—Smît on îsenswât, L. M. 2, 65; Lchdm. ii. 296, 18. *See* iii. 366, col. 1.

îsen-tanga, an; *m. A pair of snuffers*:—Candel *candela*; îsentanga *munctorium*, Wrt. Voc. 81, 34–5. v. tang, tange.

îsen-wyrhta, an; *m. A worker in iron, blacksmith*:—Îsenwyrhta *ferrarius*, Wrt. Voc. 73, 28. v. îsen-smiþ, îsern-wyrhta.

îsern, es; *n. Iron, an instrument* or *weapon made of iron*:—Sweord sceal on bearme drihtlîc îsern *the sword shall lie in the lap, the noble steel*, Menol. Fox 511; Gn. C. 26. Oft mec îsern scôd sâre on sîdan *oft has iron harmed me sorely in the side*, Exon. 126 a; Th. 485, 14; Rä. 71, 13: 130 a; Th. 499, 5; Rä. 88, 11. Âres and îsernes *æris, ferri*, Bd. 1, 1; S. 473, 23: Cd. 52; Th. 66, 23; Gen. 1088. Îsernes dǣl, Exon. 114 b; Th. 439, 25; Rä. 59, 9. Wið slege îsernes oððe stenges *for a blow from iron* [*sword*] *or stick*, Herb. 32, 8; Lchdm. i. 132, 4. Wið wunda som hŷ sŷn of îserne som hŷ sŷn of stenge, 63, 3; Lchdm. i. 166, 9. Achilles mid ðysse sylfan wyrte (*yarrow*) gehǣlde ða ðe mid îserne geslegene and gewundude wǣran, 90, 1; Lchdm. i. 194, 8. Ðû swyltst nalles mid îserne âcweald swâ ðû wênst ac mid âtre *morieris, non ferro quod suspicaris, sed veneno*, Nar. 31, 27. Gebundene on îserne *ligatos in ferro*, Ps. Th. 106, 9. Îserne wund, Exon. 102 b; Th. 388, 2; Rä. 6, 1. Þurh ðæt îsern ðæt mægen ðara þreátunga is getâcnod *per ferrum increpationis fortitudo signatur*, Past. 21, 6; Swt. 163, 24. Se lǣce hŷd his îsern wið ðone monn ðe hê snîðan wile *the surgeon hides his knife from the man he wants to cut*, 26, 3; Swt. 185, 25. [*Goth.* eisarn *iron, an iron fetter*: *O. Sax.* îsarn: *O. L. Ger.* îsarn *chalybs*: *O. Frs.* îsern: *Icel.* ísarn (*occurs five times in old poetry; the usual form is* jârn): *O. H. Ger.* îsarn.] v. îren, îsen; hôc-, leóht-, mearc-, stemping-îsern.

îsern; *adj. Iron, made of iron*:—Hê him tǣhte ðæt hê him genâme âne îserne hearstepannan and sette betweoh hine and ða burg for îserne weall *et tu sume tibi sartaginem ferream, et pones eum murum ferreum inter te et inter civitatem*, Past. 21, 5; Swt. 161, 7: Cd. 186; Th. 231, 16; Dan. 248. Îserne steng *vectes ferreos*, Ps. Th. 106, 15. Hêt gebindan beám ðone miclan ǣrenum clammum and îsernum *he bade bind that great tree with brazen bands and with iron*, Cd. 200; Th. 248, 29; Dan. 520. [*Goth.* eisarneins: *O. L. Ger. O. H. Ger.* îsarnin: *Ger.* eisern.] v. îren, îsen.

îsern-byrne, an; *f. An iron byrnie* or *corslet*:—Hê him of dyde îsernbyrnan, Beo. Th. 1347; B. 671. v. îren-byrne.

îsern-gelôman. v. gelôman.

îsern-here, es; *m. An iron-clad host*:—Îsernhergum ân wîsode, Cd. 160; Th. 199, 33; Exod. 348.

îsern-wyrhta, an; *m. A worker in iron, a blacksmith*; ferrarius, Ælfc. Gl. 2; Som. 55, 46; Wrt. Voc. 16, 18. v. îsen-wyrhta.

îs-gebind, es; *n. A bond of ice*:—Winter ŷðe beleác îsgebinde *winter locked up the wave with icy bond*, Beo. Th. 2270; B. 1133.

îs-geblǣd, es; *m.* [?] *A blister that is produced by ice*:—Wið ŷsgeblæd Lchdm. iii. 36, 22.

ís-gicel. v. gicel.
ísig; *adj. Icy, covered with ice*:—Đǽr stōd hringedstefna ísig and útfūs, Beo. Th. 65; B. 33. v. eall-ísig.
ísig-feðera; *adj. Having ice on the wings*:—Stearn ísigfeðera, Exon. 81 b; Th. 307, 15; Seef. 24.
í-síðes; *adv. At that time, at once, directly*:—Man ísíðes sōna ðǽræfter swytelaþ *it is immediately thereafter manifested*, L. I. P. 24; Th. ii. 338, 11. [Cf. í-dæges.]
Ismahēli; *pl. m. Ishmaelites, Bedouins*:—Đā þiccodan ðider semninga ða ismahēli on horsum and on olfendum *then crowded thither on a sudden the Bedouins, on horses and camels*, Shrn. 38, 4.
Ismahēlitas; *pl. m. Ishmaelites*:—Ismæhélita, *Ismahelitum*, Ps. Th. 82, 6. Ysmahélitum *Ismaelitis*, Gen. 37, 28.
Ismahēlitisc; *adj. Ishmaelite*:—Æt ðām Ismahēlitiscum mannum *de manu Ismaelitarum*, Gen. 39, 1.
ís-mere, es; *m. A mere covered with ice*:—Scíneþ sunne sōna ísmere weorþeþ tō wætre *the sun shines, at once the icy lake turns to water*, Bt. Met. Fox 28, 123; Met. 28, 62.
Ispania *Spain*; Hispania, Ors. 1, 1; Swt. 24, 1, 7, 9.
-isse. *This suffix, Lat.* -issa, *which in later English became the common suffix to mark the feminine gender, is found before the Norman Conquest in the word* abbud-isse *abbess*. [Cf. -estre.]
Ístas; *pl. m. The Esthonians*:—Ic wæs mid Ístum, Exon. 86 a; Th. 323, 31; Víd. 87. [*Icel.* Eistir.] v. Éste; *and see* Grmm. Gesch. D. S. 499, sqq.
istoria *history*:—Istoriam Indēa rīces, Salm. Kmbl. 7; Sal. 4.
-istre. v. -estre.
Italie, a; *pl. The Italians* or *Italy*:—Pencentes Italia folc, Ors. 4, 2; Swt. 160, 27. Pirrus fōr of Italium (*ab Italia*), 4, 1; Swt. 158, 30: 154, 32.
íð, íeð, ýð; *adv. compve. More easily*:—Đæt hie hiera godum ðe íeð blōtan mehten *that they might the more easily sacrifice to their gods*, Ors. 2, 2; Swt. 64, 29. Hwā meahte íeð monnum rǽdan būtan scylde ðonne se ðe hí gescōp *quis principari hominibus tam sine culpa, quam is, qui hos nimirum regeret, quos ipse creaverat?* Past. 3. 1; Swt. 33, 16. Đý ýþ, Exon. 120 b; Th. 463, 6; Hö. 66. v. eáðe, ēð.
íðan; *p.* de *To lay waste, desolate, destroy*:—Ic ýðde eotena cyn and on ýðum slōg niceras nihtes, Beo. Th. 846; B. 421. Ýðde ðisne eardgeard ælda scyppend *the creator of men laid waste this world*, Exon. 77 b; Th. 291, 20; Wand. 85. Ýðan, 126 a; Th. 484, 13; Rä. 70, 7. Íðende *depopulis*, Wrt. Voc. ii. 27, 27. [*Icel.* eyða *to lay waste, destroy, waste desolate*: *O. H. Ger.* ōdian *desolare*, Grff. i. 150: *Ger.* ver-öden.] v. ā-íðan.
íðast, íðost; *adv. superl. Most easily*:—Ýðast meahtan frōfre findan *might find comfort most easily*, Exon. 19 b; Th. 50, 15; Cri. 800. Ýðæst, 26 b; Th. 79, 1; Cri. 1284. Ýðost, Hy. 7, 3; Hy Grn. 287, 3. v. íð.
íð-belig; *adj. Easily made angry*:—Ne wē tō ýðbelige [eáðbylige, MS. D.] ne sýn, ne tō langsum yrre hæbben, Wulfst. 253, 11.
íð-dǽde; *adj. Easy to do*:—Hit wæs Gode ýðdǽde, ðā hē hit swā gedōn habban wolde, Wulfst. 15, 18. v. eáð-dǽde.
íðe; *adj. Easy, pleasant*:—Nō ðæt ýðe byþ tō befleónne *that is not easy to flee from*, Beo. Th. 2009; B. 1002: 4822; B. 2415. On his heortan hē Gode þancie ealles ðæs ðe hē him forgeaf ǽgðer ge ýðran ge unýðran *in his heart let him thank God for all that he has given him, both pleasant and unpleasant*, L. E. I. 29; Th. ii. 426, 11. Ús ðis se æðeling ýðre gefremede *this the prince has made easier for us*, Exon. 17 a; Th. 39, 25; Cri. 627. v. eáðe, ēðe, un-íðe.
íðe-líce; *adv. Easily*:—Iéðelíce and scortlíce ic hæbbe nū gesǽd hiora ingewinn *without making the account difficult or long I have now related their intestine struggle*, Ors. 2, 6; Swt. 88, 28. Iéðelíce forneáh būton ǽlcon gewinne *easily, almost without any struggle*, 3, 7; Swt. 112, 28. Ýðelíce, Beo. Th. 3116; B. 1556. Forðæm se lytega feónd swā micle iéðelícor ðæt mōd gewundaþ swā hē hit ongiet nacodre ðare byrnan wærscipes *quia hostis callidus tanto liberius pectus percutit, quanto nudum a providentiæ lorica deprehendit*, Past. 56, 1; Swt. 431, 10. v. eáðe, ēðelíce, un-íðelíce.
íð-fynde; *adj. Easy to find*:—Ýðfynde, Andr. Kmbl. 3092; An. 1549. v. eáð-, ēð-fynde.
íð-gesýne; *adj. Easy to see*:—Ýðgesýne, Beo. Th. 2493; B. 1244. v. ēð-gesýne.
íð-ness, e; *f. Easiness, freedom, ease, satisfaction, delight*:—Hwelce íðnesse hæfþ God æt ūrum wītum *neque Deus nostris cruciatibus pascitur*, Past. 54, 5; Swt. 425, 11. v. un-íðness, ēðness.
iú. v. geó.
iuc, ioc *a yoke*; jugum, Wrt. Voc. 284, 54: ii. 46, 37: *juger*, 38. Ioc *jugum*, Ælfc. Gl. 3; Som. 55, 58; Wrt. Voc. 16, 30: Ps. Spl. C. 2, 3: Mt. Kmbl. Rush. 11, 29, 30: Rtl. 108, 21. [*These examples should be given under* geoc.] v. geoc.
iuc-boga, an; *m. The bow* or *curved part of a yoke*:—Iucboga *jujula* [among things connected with vehicles], Wrt. Voc. 284, 50: *jugula*, ii. 46, 36.
iucian; *p.* ode *To join, yoke*:—Ic iucige *jungo*, Ælfc. Gr. 28; Som. 31, 53. v. ge-iukod.
iuc-sticca, an; *m. The bar of a yoke*:—Ioc-sticca *obicula*, Ælfc. Gl. 3; Som. 55, 61; Wrt. Voc. 16, 33. (Cf. *O. H. Ger.* iuh-rota *pertica*, Grff. ii. 491.]
iuc-tēma, an; *m. An animal yoked with another*:—Ioctēma *jugalis*, Ælfc. Gl. 3; Som. 55, 59; Wrt. Voc. 16, 31. [cf. ge-týme.]
Iudan burh *Jedburgh*, Chr. 952; Erl. 118, 26.
iú-dǽd, e; *f. A deed done of old* or *formerly*:—Gū-dǽda, Exon. 64 a; Th. 235, 12; Ph. 556. Iúdǽdum, 76 a; Th. 284, 26; Jul. 703: Cd. 217; Th. 276, 10; Sat. 186.
Iudēa *Judea*:—Fram Iudēa *de Judæa*, Mt. Kmbl. 4, 25. On ðam wēstene Judēæ *in deserto Judææ*, 3, 1.
Iudēas; *gen.* a; *pl. m. The Jews*; Judæi, Jn. Skt. 2, 20. Eal Iudēa þeód *omnis Iudæa* Mt. Kmbl. 3. 5. Betwux ðām Iudēum, Jn. Skt. 10, 19.
Iudēisc; *adj. Jewish*:—Đā stōd ān Iudēisc wer, ðæs nama wæs Nichodemus, Nicod. 11; Thw. 5, 38: Jn. Skt. 18, 35. Crist cwæþ be ðām ungeleáffullum Iudēiscum wā eów *Christ said of the unbelieving Jews 'Woe to you,'* Ælfc. Gr. 48; Som. 49, 5.
iú-geára; *adv. Formerly*:—Breoton wæs iúgeára Albion hāten *Brittania cui quondam Albion nomen fuit*, Bd. 1, 1; S. 473, 8. v. geó-geára.
iugian *to join, yoke*:—Ic iugie hí tō syl *jungo eos ad aratrum*, Coll. Monast. Th. 19, 15. v. iucian.
iúgoþ *youth, young people*, Jos. 5, 5: Homl. ii. 506, 21: Homl. Skt. 6, 2. v. geógoþ.
Iúla, an; *m. December* or *January*:—Mōnaþ Decembris, ǽrra Iūla, Menol. Fox 439; Men. 221. v. Geóla.
iú-leán, es; *n. A reward for something done long ago*:—Iúleán ðæs ðe hine of nearwum Widia ūt forlēt *a reward, because in time past Widia released him from straits*, Wald. 2, 7.
iú-mann, es; *m. A man of old, of a former time*:—Iúmonna gold, Beo. Th. 6096; B. 3052. v. gió-mann.
iú-meówle, an; *f. One who was a maiden long ago, an old woman*:—Ió-meówlan, Beo. Th. 5854; B. 2931.
iung; *adj. Young*:—Sum iung man, Th. Ap. 3, 23: 4, 7: Bd. 2, 12; S. 514, 27: Ælfc. Gl. 45; Som. 64, 106; Wrt. Voc. 32, 41: 64, 93; Wrt. Voc. 32, 28. v. geong.
iung-líc; *adj. Youthful*:—Iunglícre ylde, Ælfc. T. Grn. 16, 40. v. geong-líc.
iung-ling, es; *m. A youth*:—Iunglingc *juvenis*, Wrt. Voc. 73, 19: Gen. 4, 23. Sum iungling him fyligde *adulescens quidam sequebatur eum*, Mk. Skt. 14, 51: Homl. Th. ii. 312, 16. v. geong-ling.
Iútan, Iútas. v. Iótas.
iú-wine, es; *m. A friend of old* or *former times*:—Wāt his iúwine eorþan forgiefene *knows that his friends of old are committed to earth*, Exon. 82 b; Th. 311, 15; Seef. 92.
ÍW, es; *m. Yew*:—Íw *taxus*, Ælfc. Gl. 46; Som. 64, 131; Wrt. Voc. 32, 65: Wrt. Voc. 79. 74: 285, 49. Se hearda íw, Exon. 114 a; Th. 437, 18; Rä. 56, 9. On ðone ealde íw ðonan of ðon íwe *to the old yew; thence from the yew*, Cod. Dipl. Kmbl. iii. 218, 35. *In proper names*, vi. 306, col. 2; 307, col. 1. [*Chauc.* ew: *Icel.* ýr *a yew, a bow*: *O. H. Ger.* íwa *taxus*: *Ger.* eibe.] v. eow.
íwan; *p.* de *To show, bring before the eyes, display, reveal*:—Ýweþ and yppeþ *shews and reveals*, Salm. Kmbl. 985; Sal. 494. Đā ýwde hē ðǽr synne wisan *culpam esse demonstravit*, Bd. 1, 27; S. 496, 2. Đā ýwde ic him sōna ða ylcan bōc ðara reogola *quibus statim protuli eundem librum canonum*, 4, 5; S. 572, 25. Mid his sylfes dǽde ýwde and cýdde *propria actione præmonstraret*, 4, 27; S. 604, 40. Ýwaþ mē ānne peninc *ostendite mihi denarium*, Lk. Skt. 20, 24. Wēnþ gif hē hit him íewe ðæt hē him nylle geþafigean ðæt hē hine snīðe *he expects, if he show it* [*the knife*] *to him, that he will not allow him to cut him*, Past. 26, 3; Swt. 185, 25. Đíne miltse ýwe *show thy mercy*, Exon. 11 b; Th. 15, 32; Cri. 245. Đæt land ðe ic ðē ýwan wille *the land that I will show thee*, Cd. 83; Th. 105, 11; Gen. 1751. Ord and ende ðæs ðe him ýwed wæs *the beginning and end of what was revealed to him*, 180; Th. 225, 31; Dan. 162. DER. æt-, ge-, ōþ-íwan [-ýwan]; *and see* eáwan, eówan.

K.

THE letter *k* appears to have had no distinct duty to perform in the oldest English, but to have been a mere variant of *c*. In the MSS. (more particularly the Cotton) of Alfred's translation of Gregory's Pastoral Care, where in the words *kyning*, *kynn* &c. it occurs not unfrequently, this writing is not uniform. Thus in Sweet's edition *Angelkynn* is found p. 2, ll. 3, 13, but *Angelcynn* l. 4; whilst in each case the Hatton MS. has *c*. So in the following page in l. 10, *kynn*, in l. 20, *cynn*. On pp. 2, 3, l. 1 *kyning* is the writing of both MSS. while pp. 34, 35, l. 14 it is *cyning*: p. 32, 20–1 we find *kyning*, *kynehad*, the Hatton MS. in the same passage has *c*: p. 38, ll. 13, 18 *kyning*, *kynestol*, where the Hatton MS. has *cyning*, *kynestol*: pp. 6, 7, l. 18 both have *kynerice*: p. 84, ll. 10, 12, 13 *kynelic* occurs four times, in the Hatton MS. it is twice written with *c*, twice with *k*. On p. 212, l. 15 is found *Crist*, while the Hatton writes *Krist*; on p. 152, line 5 the Cotton MS. has *kræft*, the Hatton MS. *cræft*. On p. 459, ll. 29, 31, 32 (Hatton MS.) occur the forms *kokka*, *kokkum*, *kok*. So in the Chronicle, Erl. p. 8, l. 15 *kyning*, but

p. 6, l. 23 *cyning*: p. 24, l. 1, *kyning*; 26, 1, *cyning*. The later use with regard to the letter may be, to some extent, illustrated from the concluding years. For many years previous to 1111 the form is *cyng*, in that year we have *Kyng* Henri; again until 1122 the opening line of each annual contains the phrase *Cyng* Henri, then until the end the spelling is *k*.

Words beginning with *k* are to be looked for under *c*.

L

In the later specimens of the West Saxon dialect those words in which the vowel *a* immediately preceded a combination of consonants beginning with *l* are generally found to have undergone a change which was represented by writing *ea* instead of *a*. This change does not occur to the same extent in the earlier specimens, and seems not to occur at all in the Northumbrian dialect, or in the kindred languages. Thus in the translation of Gregory's Pastoral Care and in the Parker MS. of the Chronicle *alle*, *onwald* are found as well as *ealle*, *onweald*, while in Ælfric's Homilies they are regularly written in the latter form. So the West Saxon forms, *healdan*, *sealt*, *healf*, are found in the Northumbrian Gospels as *halda*, *salt*, *half*, and in Gothic, O. Sax., Icel., O. H. Ger. the vowel also is *a*.

In the Runic alphabet the character, which in name and form agrees with the Scandinavian rune ᛚ, *lögr*, was ᛚ, *lagu*. The same name seems to have been given to the corresponding letter in the Gothic alphabet, though it occurs only in a corrupt form *laar* = *lagus*. The meaning of this word may be seen from the verses in the Runic poem that are devoted to the letter:

Lagu byþ leódum	*water to wanderers*
langsum geþuht	*wearisome seemeth*
gif hī sculun nēþan	*if they must venture*
on nacan tealtum	*on vessel unsteady*
and hī sǣȳþa	*and them the sea-waves*
swȳđe brēgaþ	*sorely affright*
and se brimhengest	*and the sea-horse*
bridles ne gȳmþ	*steering despiseth.*

Runic pm. 21; Kmbl. 343, 19–26.

lā. I. *interj. Lo! Oh! Ah!*:—Lā næddrena cyn *Oh! generation of vipers*, Mt. Kmbl. 3, 7: 12, 34. Lā đū līccetere, 7, 5. Lā freónd *amice*, 22, 12. Lā Drihten *Domine*, Ps. Th. 21, 17: 118, 176. Lā hū oft hī gremedon hine *quotiens exacerbaverunt eum!* Ps. Spl. 77, 45. Āfæst lā and hī lā hī and wel lā well and đyllīce ōđre syndon englisc interjectiones, Ælfc. Gr. 48; Som. 49, 28. Weg lā weg lā *euge, euge*, Ps. Th. 69, 4. Wā lā se tōwyrpþ đæt tempel *ua qui destruit templum*, Mk. Skt. 15, 29. Wā lā āhte ic mīnra handa geweald *alas! had I power over my hands*, Cd. 19; Th. 23, 32; Gen. 368. Wā lā wā *heu, proh dolor!* Bd. 2, 1; 8. 501, 14. Wei lā wei, [cf. Chauc. *weilawey*: Shakspere *welladay*] Bt. 35, 6; Fox 170, 12, Cott. MS. Wel lā men wel *oh! men*, 34, 8; Fox 144, 23. Wel lā, Bt. Met. Fox 21, 1; Met. 21, 1. II. *Enclitic particle used to emphasise interrogation, exclamation, entreaty, affirmation, negation*:—Understenst đū lā *sentisne*, wylt đū lā *visne*, Ælfc. Gr. 44; Som. 45, 47. Is đǣr genoh lā *satisne est*, Som. 46, 40. Hū lā ne wurpe wē þrȳ cnihtas intō đam fȳre *why, did not we cast three youths into the fire?* Homl. Th. ii. 20, 12. Wēnst đū lā đæt đū beó ālȳsed fram đisum tintregum *do you suppose then that you will be released from these torments?* Homl. Th. i. 424, 29. Đā cwæþ ic hwæt is đæt lā *then said I 'what then is that?'* Bt. 34, 5; Fox 140, 14, Hwæt is đæt lā þinga? 38, 3; Fox 200, 2. Hwæt is đis lā manna? Elen. Kmbl. 1802; El. 903. Hwæt biþ hit lā elles būton flǣsc seođđan se ēcea dǣl of biþ hwæt biþ lā elles seó lāf būton wyrma mete *why, what else is it but flesh when the eternal part is away? what else then is the remnant but worms' food?* Blickl. Homl. 111, 31. Hwǣr biþ lā đonne se īdla lust? hwǣr beóþ đonne đa symbelnessa? 58, 16. Is đis lā wundorlīc and winsum spell *this is indeed a wonderful and delightful speech*, Bt. 34, 5; Fox 140, 10. Đæt lā mæg secgan se đe sōđ and riht fremeþ *that indeed may he say who does truth and right*, Beo. Th. 3404; B. 1700: 5720; B. 2864. Đæt lā wæs fæger, Cd. 223; Th. 293, 18; Sat. 457. Uton lā geþencan *let us then determine*, 227; Th. 305, 9; Sat. 644. Ac feor đæt lā sī đæt ... *sed absit ut* ... Bd. 1, 27; S. 490, 24. Ic đæs lā wīsce đæt wegas mīne on đīnum willan weorđan gereahte *I do indeed wish that my ways may be directed according to thy will*; utinam dirigantur viæ meæ, Ps. Th. 118, 5. Bidde ic đē lā gif ... *precorque si* ... Bd. 3, 13; S. 538, 40: 4, 3; S. 568, 27: Dōm. L. 6, 65. Nese lā nese, Bt. 27, 2; Fox 96, 27. v. eálā.

lāc; *generally neuter, but occasionally feminine* [v. Shrn. pp. 3–4], *or masculine, as in the compound* lyb-lāc q. v. The idea which lies at the root of the various meanings of this and of the next word seems to be that of motion. Thus *lācan* and Icel. *leika* are used to describe the motion of a vessel riding on the waves, the flight of a bird as it rises and falls in the air, the flickering, wavering motion of flame, and the like; while Gothic *laikan* renders σκιρτᾶν in Luke i. 41, 44: vi. 23. From this idea of activity we pass to that of *games, playing, dancing* &c.; and so Gothic *laiks* = χορός in Luke xv. 25; in Icel., where the meaning *play, sport* is the prevailing one (see also compounds in which *leik-* occurs), *leikr* is used of *dancing, athletics, various games, music*, as in *strengleikr*, *leika* = to play, to *lake* in the dialect of the North of England. In O. H. Ger. the application is generally to music, *leih*, *leich* = modus, modulus, carmen versus, but in *rang-leih* = wrestling the meaning is similar to the Icelandic (see Grff. ii. 152–3.) And just as *plega* is used, by itself or in its compounds, of war and battle, so in the Icelandic poetry we have *Hildar leikr*, *sverða leikr* = battle (see Cl. and Vig. Dict. p. 382, col. 2), and in English *lác* could be applied in the same way. But in the latter language the more frequent meanings are those of *offering, gift*, and to connect these with the preceding ones Grimm notes the association of dancing and playing with offerings and sacrifices. From this special meaning of *offering* the more general one of *gift, present* might easily come. To quote his words 'Das wort (*lác*) scheint einer wurzel mit dem goth. *laiks* (saltatio) ahd. *leih* (ludus, modus) altn. *leikr*, ursprünglich also tanz und spiel, die das opfer begleiteten, allmählich die gabe selbst zu bezeichnen,' D. M. 35. The passages which follow will shew the English use of the word. I. *battle, struggle*:—Wīga unlæt lāces *a warrior not slow to fight* (*referring to death which was approaching Guthlac*), Exon. 47 b; Th. 164, 5; Gū. 1007. II. *an offering, sacrifice, oblation*:—Gode onsægdnesse tō beranne đæs hālgan lāces *ad offerendas Domino victimas sacræ oblationis*, Bd. 4, 22; S. 592, 26. Hī him sculon lāces lof lustum bringan *sacrificent sacrificium laudis*, Ps. Th. 106, 21. Ic đē lāces lof lustum secge *tibi sacrificabo hostiam laudis*, 115, 7. Ic đē lustum lāce cwēme *voluntarie sacrificabo tibi*, 53, 6. And bærnon uppan đam weofode drihtne tō lāce *adolebuntque super altare in oblationem domino*, Lev. 3, 5. Offrian tō lāce *to offer as a sacrifice*, Ælfc. T. Grn. 4, 27. Hie drihtne lāc begen brohton *they both brought an offering to the Lord*, Cd. 47; Th. 60, 2; Gen. 975. Se rinc Gode lāc onsægde, 85; Th. 107, 21; Gen. 1792. Onbleót đæt lāc Gode, 142; Th. 177, 21; Gen. 2933. Đū scealt blōtan sunu, and leófes līc forbærnan, and mē lāc bebeódan, 138; Th. 173, 9; Gen. 2858. Đū dīnne lāc offrige, Homl. Skt. 7, 119. Þurh lāc đære hālwendan onsægdnesse *per oblationem hostiæ salutaris*, Bd. 4, 22; S. 592, 22. Māra is allum cwicum lācum and sægdnissum *majus est holocaustomatibus et sacrificiis*, Mk. Skt. Rush 12, 33. Ǣnig đæra þinga đe gedwolgodum tō lācum betǣht biþ *any thing that is appointed to false gods for sacrifices*, Swt. A. S. Rdr. 105, 30. Nemne hē lufige mid lācum đone đe gescōp heofon and eorþan *unless by offerings he shew his love to him that created heaven and earth*, Exon. 67 a; Th. 249, 13; Jul. 111. Mid hāligra lofsanga lācum cōman *with offerings of holy hymns they came*, Blickl. Homl. 207, 9. Gode lāc onsægdon, 201, 13: Guthl. 20; Gdwin 32, 13. On đām lācum geleáfsumra *fidelium oblationibus*, Bd. 1, 27; S. 488, 38. Geoffrode lāc *obtulit holocausta*, Gen. 8, 20. Genimaþ eów lāc and ingangaþ on his wīctūnas *tollite hostias et introite in atria ejus*, Ps. Th. 95, 8. Seó cwēn Sabæ geseah đa lāc đe man Gode offrode *the queen of Sheba saw the offerings that were made to God*, Homl. Th. ii. 584, 16. Hē fræt fīftȳne men and ōđer swylc ūt offerede lāđlīcu lāc *he* (*Grendel*) *devoured fifteen men and as many bore away, horrid sacrifices*, Beo. Th. 3172; B. 1584. III. *a gift, present, grace, favour, service; a present* or *offering of words, a message*:—Lāc *munus*, Ælfc. Gr. 9, 22; Som. 12, 14. Lāc *munus* vel *zenia*, Ælfc. Gl. 35; Som. 62, 77; Wrt. Voc. 28, 55. Lāc *elogia*, i. e. *munus*, Wrt. Voc. ii. 143, 19: 29, 24: *xenium, donum*, Hpt. Gl. 496: *munificentia*, 414. Gūþlāc se nama ys on rōmānisc *belli munus*, Guthl. 2; Gdwin 10, 23. Leóht wē geseóþ lāce *lumen videmus muneris*, Hymn. Surt. 43, 17. Behātenre fæderes lāce *promisso Patris munere*, 95, 27. Lāce *eulogiæ, benedictionis*, Hpt. Gl. 496. Tōforan đære cynelīcan lāce đe hē hire geaf, Homl. Th. ii. 584, 31. Sende tō lāce *sent it as a present*, Elen. Kmbl. 2398; El. 1200. Hē đære mægeþ sceolde lāce (*acc. fem.?*) gelǣdan lāþspel tō sōþ *he to the maiden must bring the message, the grievous tale too true*, Exon. 52 a; Th. 182, 28; Gū. 1317. Tīd is đæt đū fēre and đa ǣrendu eal biþence ōfestum lǣde swā ic đē ǣr bibeád lāc tō leófre *time is that thou go and think about those errands* [cf. Th. 173, 24 sqq. where Guthlac speaks of his burial], *with speed bring, as I before bid thee* [cf. Th. 172, 31 sqq], *the message to my dear sister*, 51 b; Th. 179, 35; Gū. 1272. Heó lāc weorđade đe hire brungen wæs *she honoured the gift* [*the nails of the cross*] *that was brought her*, Elen. Kmbl. 2272; El. 1137. Cwæþ hē his sylfes suna syllan wolde ... Hie đa lāc hrađe þēgon tō þance *he said he would give his own son ... They that gift soon accepted thankfully*, Andr. Kmbl. 2224; An. 1113. Đa hālgan þrȳnesse georne biddan đæt heó đæt lāc đæt hie þurh đone hālgan heáhengel ǣrest æteówde mannum wundorlīc tācn đæt hie đæt mannum tō fylgenne oncȳđde *earnestly to entreat the holy Trinity that the grace of shewing by the holy archangel a wondrous token to men, that that it would make known to men for their guidance*, Blickl. Homl. 205, 30. Đonne onfōþ hī from Gode māran mēde đonne hī from ǣnigum ōđrum lācum dōn *then shall they receive from God greater reward than they do from any other gifts*, 45, 34. Him lācum cwēmaþ *dona adducent*, Ps. Th. 71, 10. Lācum, þeódgestreónum, Beo. Th. 86; B. 43. Him eorla hleó gesealde māþmas xii, hēt hine mid ðǣm lācum leóde sēcean, 3740; B. 1868. Culufre gewāt fleógan eft mid lācum hire (*the olive branch*), Cd. 72; Th. 88, 28; Gen. 1472. Hī geopenodon heora hordfatu and him lāc geoffrodon gold and rēcels and myrram *they opened their treasures, and presented unto him gifts; gold, and frankincense, and myrrh* [Mt. 2, 11], Homl. Th i. 78, 27. Lāc gifan, Exon. 100 b; Th. 380, 2; Rä. 1, 1. Bringan lāc and luftācen *to bring gifts and love-tokens*, Beo. Th. 3730; B. 1863. Lǣc *munera*, Ps. Spl. T. 14, 6. IV. *medicine*:—Heofendlīcere lāc [=heofenlīcere lāce] *cœlestis medicinæ*, Hpt. Gl. 415, 36. Lāc *medicamine*, 507, 77. Lāc *medicamenti*, 527, 18. [*Laym.* 1st MS. lac, 2nd MS. lock *gift*: *Orm.* lac *a sacrifice, offering*: *Gen. a. Ex.* loac; *Piers P.* laik *a game.*] v. ag-, ǣfen-, beadu-, berne-, brȳd-, cwic-, feoht-, freó-, ge-, hǣmed-, headu-, lyb-, mæsse-, reáf-, sǣ-, scīn-, wed-, wīf-, wīte-lāc. *It also occurs in proper names*, e. g. Gūþ-lāc, Hyge-lāc.

lācan; *p.* leólc, lēc; pp. lācen. I. *to swing, wave about, move as a ship does on the waves, as a bird does in its flight, as flames do*:—Ic lāce mid winde *I wave about with the wind*, Exon. 108 a; Th. 412, 17; Rä. 31, 1. Sum lāceþ on lyfte *one swings in the air* [*of the man who is hung on a tree*], 87 b; Th. 328, 25; Vy. 23. Is ðæt frēcne streám ȳða ofermǣta ðe wē hēr on lācaþ *perilous is the stream, huge the waves, on which here we toss*, 20 a; Th. 53, 24; Cri. 855. Hie ofer feorne weg ceólum lācaþ, Andr. Kmbl. 506; An. 253. Fuglas ða ðe late þurh lyft lācaþ fiðrum *birds which slowly through the air move with their pinions*, Exon. 60 b; Th. 220, 7; Ph. 316. Brondas lācaþ on ðam deópan dæge *fires shall flame up on that solemn day* [cf. *to play* applied to flame, and *Icel.* logi lēk um þā v. Cl. and Vig. Dict. leika II. 2], 116 b; Th. 448, 23; Dōm. 58. Ða ðe lācaþ ymb eaxe ende *those stars that revolve about the pole*, Bt. Met. Fox 28, 44; Met. 28, 22. Leólc on lyfte *he took his flight through the air* [*of the lost angel who was to tempt Adam*], Cd. 23; Th. 29, 10; Gen. 448: Exon. 114 a; Th. 438, 15; Rä. 57, 8. Hē leólc ofer laguflód *he bounded o'er the water*, 75 b; Th. 283, 2; Jul. 674. Fugel uppe sceal lācan on lyfte *up in the air must the bird wing its flight*, Menol. Fox 537; Gn. C. 39. Hwylc hyra [*the seraphim*] nēhst mǣge nergende flihte lācan, Exon. 13 b; Th. 25, 11; Cri. 399. Ðū meahtes ofer rodorum feðerum lācan, feor up ofer wolcnu windan, Bt. Met. Fox 24, 17; Met. 28, 9. Heofonfuglas ða ðe lācende geond lyft faraþ, Exon 55 a; Th. 194, 24; Az. 144: Beo. Th. 5657; B. 2832: Elen. Kmbl. 1797; El. 900. Lagu lācende *the tossing waves*, Andr. Kmbl. 873; An. 437. Lācende līg *the leaping flame*, Cd. 197; Th. 246, 8; Dan. 476: Exon. 31 a; Th. 97, 23; Cri. 1595: Elen. Kmbl. 1156; El. 580: 2219; El. 1111. II. *to play* [as in 2. Sam. 2, 14 'Let the young men play before us ... And every one thrust his sword in his fellow's side,' cf. æsc-plega], *make use of a weapon, fight*: Ða ne dorston ǣr dareðum lācan on hyra mandrȳhtnes miclan þearfe *who before had not dared at their lord's dire need to join in the javelin-play*, Beo. 5689; B. 2848. III. *to play* [*a musical instrument*]:—Hió dumb wunaþ hwæðre hyre is on fōte fæger hleóþor; wrætlīc mē þinceþ hū seó wiht mǣge wordum lācan þurh fót neoþan *dumb does it dwell, yet in its foot hath a fair voice; wondrous it seems to me how the wight can play with words by its foot from below*, Exon. 108 b; Th. 414, 13; Rä. 32, 19. [*Orm.* to þeowwtenn Godd and lakenn [*sacrifice*], 973; þa þre kingess lakedenn [*presented*] Crist wiþþ þrinne kinne lakess, 7430: *Havel.* leike; *p.* leikede *to play*: *Piers P.* laike *to play*: *Goth.* laikan; *p.* lailak: *Icel.* leika; *p.* lēk: *M. H. Ger.* leichen.] DER. be-, for-, geond-lācan: daroþ-, faroþ-, lyft-lācende. v. lǣcan, ellen-lǣca, and preceding word.

lāc-dǣd, e; *f.* *Munificence*; munificentia, Hpt. Gl. 496.

lāc-gifa, an; *m.* *One who gives gifts*:—Drihten is lācgeofa manna bearnum *dominus dedit dona hominibus*, Ps. Th. 67, 18.

lacing (?):—Ðis sint ða landgemǣra. ǣrest of cealcforda on ealdan lacing ... ðoñ tō smalan wege and on lacing, Cod. Dip. Kmbl. ii. 317, 22-26. [Cf. (?) lacu.]

lāc-līc; *adj.* *Sacrificial, having the nature of a sacrifice* or *offering*:—Swā oft swā hī offrodon ða lāclīcan lāc ðe ðā gewunelīce wǣron *as often as they offered the sacrificial offerings that were then customary*, L. Ælfc. P. 39; Th. ii. 380, 18.

lācnian; *p.* ode *To heal, cure, tend, take care of, treat, dress* (*a wound*):—Ic lācnige *medeor*, Ælfc. Gr. 33; Som. 36, 47. Se lǣce ðonne hē on untīman lācnaþ wunde hió wyrmseþ *secta immature vulnera deterius infervescunt*, Past. 21, 2; Swt. 153, 3. Ðæt lācnaþ ðone milte *that heals the milt*, L. M. 2, 38; Lchdm. ii. 246, 11. Hē mid ælmessan sāwla lācnaþ, Exon. 122 a; Th. 467, 30; Alm. 9. Betwyh ðon ðe hine mon lācnode *inter medendum*, Bd. 4, 26; S. 603, 15. Lācnode *fomentat*, Wrt. Voc. ii. 37, 17. Lǣcnode, 91, 39. Hē hine lācnude *curam ejus egit*, Lk. Skt. 10, 34. Lēcnade monigo *curavit multos*, Mk. Skt. Lind, 1, 34. Ne ða wanhālan gē ne lācnedon *neque ægras sanavistis*, L. Ecg. P. iii. 16; Th. ii. 202, 26. Ðonne ðæt dolh open sȳ genim ða ylcan wyrte unsodene ... lācna ða wunde ðǣrmid ðonne byþ heó sōna hāl *when the incision* (*made by a snake*) *is open, take the same plant unsodden ... dress the wounds therewith; it will soon be well*, Herb. 90, 16; Lchdm. i. 198, 16. Lācna mid ðȳ, L. M. 1, 30; Lchdm. ii. 70, 19. Lā lēce lēcna ðec solfne *medice cura te ipsum*, Lk. Skt. Rush. 4, 23. Cymeþ and lēcnigaþ *venite et curamini*, 13, 14. Ðonne sceal man mid cealdum lǣcedōmum lācnian *it must be cured with cold medicines*, L. M. 1, 1; Lchdm. ii. 22, 4. Ðan scealt ðū hine ðus lācnigean, Lchdm. iii. 126, 12. Freónd ðe his gȳmenne dyde and his wunda lācnian wolde *amicos qui sui curam agerent*, Bd. 4, 22; S. 591, 2. Ðis is þearf ðæt se se ðe wunde lācnian (Hatt. MS. lācnigean) wille géote wīn on *necesse est, ut, quisquis sanandis vulneribus praeest, in vino morsum doloris adhibeat*, Past. 17, 10; Swt. 124, 11. Se lācnigenda *the physician*, 21, 2; Swt. 153, 4. Lācnod wæs fram his wundum *curabatur a vulneribus*, Bd. 4, 16; S. 584, 30. [*O. E. Homl.* lechinen: *Laym.* lechinien (2nd MS. lechnie), lacnien (2nd MS. lechni): *A. R.* lecnen: *Piers P.* lechnede (*other* MS. lechede), *p.*: *Goth.* lēkinon, leikinon *to cure, heal*: *O. L. Ger.* lācnōn *mederi*: *Icel.* lækna: *O. H. Ger.* láhinon *mederi, fomentare, temperare.*] v. ge-lācnian, lǣcnan; lǣce.

lācnigend-līc; *adj.* *Medical, surgical*:—Lācnigendlīc tōl *a surgical instrument*, Hpt. Gl. 478.

lācnung, lǣcnung (v. sealf-lǣcnung), e; *f.* *Healing, cure, remedy, medicine*:—Lācnung *medicamen*, R. Ben: *medicamentum*, Hpt. Gl. 478. On gōdan lǣce biþ gelang seóces mannes lācnung *the sick man's cure depends on a good doctor*, L. Pen, 1; Th. ii. 278, 4. Ða hē gehǣlde ðe lācnunga beþorftun *eos qui cura indigebant sanabat*, Lk. Skt. 9, 11. Gebēte wið hine ða wunde and begyte him ða lācnunge *compenset ei vulnus, et sanationem ei comparet*, L. Ecg. P. iv. 22; Th. ii. 210, 25 [*O. E. Homl.* hit (*Christ's blood*) beo mi *lechnunge*, i. 202, 16: *Jul.* ne mahte he wið ute þe *lechnunge* of hire luue libben, 7, 4: *Icel.* lækning *a cure, medicine; the art of healing*: *Dan.* lægning *healing*: *O. H. Ger.* lāchenunga *medicine.*]

lacra, Fins. Th. 68; Fin. 34. v. læc.

lāc-sang, es; *m.* *A song made when offering* (?):—Lācsang (MS. lane sang) *offertorium*, Ælfc. Gl. 34; Som. 62, 62; Wrt. Voc. 28, 42.

lactuca, an; *f.* This word seems to retain its Latin form in the nominative, but otherwise conforms to English usage, and is generally treated as a weak noun. The form *lactucas*, however, occurs in the Leechdoms, which, though it looks like a strong plural masc., seems to be singular:—Lactuca hātte seó wyrt ðe hī etan sceoldon mid ðām þeorfum hlāfum heó is biter on þigene *lettuce was the name of the herb that they were to eat with the unleavened loaves; it is bitter in the eating*, Homl. Th. ii. 278, 26. Nim lactucan āne hand fulle *take a hand full of lettuce*, Lchdm. iii. 114, 13. Eton þeorfe hlāfas mid ðære lactucan ðe on felda wixþ *edent azymos panes cum lactucis agrestibus*, Ex. 12, 8. Etan þeorfe hlāfas mid feldlīcere lactucan, Homl. Th. ii. 264, 3. Lācnian innan mid lactucan *to cure by the internal application of lettuce*, L. M. 2, 37; Lchdm. ii. 244, 16. Mid feldlīcum lactucum, Homl. Th. ii. 278, 19. Him is tō sellanne lactucas *lettuce is to be given him*, L. M. 2, 33; Lchdm. ii. 212, 7. Him is nyt ðæt hē hlāf þicge and lactucas ðæt is leahtric *it is beneficial for him to eat bread, and* lactucas, *that is, lettuce*, 16; Lchdm. ii. 194, 6. [*O. H. Ger.* ladducha, latoch, lattouch *lactuca*, Grff. ii. 202.]

lacu, e; *f.* *A pool, pond, piece of water, lake*:—Ōþ ðæt seó lacu ūt scȳt—ðæt norþ andlang lace *to the point where the water runs out of the lake ... then along the lake*, Cod. Dip. Kmbl. ii. 250, 26. Ðonne of exa[n] on ða smala[n] lace of ðære lace eft on exan *then from the Exe to the small pool, from the pool again to the Exe*, ii. 205, 10. Tō æscwylles lace heáfdon, 24. Tō æscwylles lace, 20. On Suttūninga lace, iii. 211, 23. Andlang foslace, 25, 19. On ða ealdan lace; andlang lace on ða norþeá, vi. i. 20. Laca *lacos*, Wrt. Voc. ii. 51, 52. [Meres and laces, Chr. 656; Erl. 31, 19: *Laym.* ouer þen lac (2nd MS. þe lake) of Siluius and ouer þen lac (2nd MS. þan lake) of Philisteus: *Prompt. Parv.* lake *lacus*. It might be supposed that *lacu* was taken from Latin *lacus*, and the fact that the gender of the Latin is not that of the English word does not disprove the supposition; for feminine *porticus* gives masculine *portic*, and masculine *versus* gives neuter *fers*. And in the specimens of later English just quoted (in *Laym.* it will be observed the gender is no longer feminine) it may have been to Latin that the English word is due; but there may have been at an earlier time a native word: cf. leccan to water, and O. H. Ger. *lacha*; *f.* palus, botinus, Grff. ii. 100.]

lād, e; *f.* I. *a course, way*:—Micel is lād ofer lagustreám *great is the way across the water*, Andr. Kmbl. 845; An. 423: Exon. 94 a; Th. 353, 17; Reim. 14. Brimwudu lāde fūs *the ship swift in its course*, 52 a; Th. 182, 6; Gū. 1306. Ne lǣt ðū ðec sīðes getwǣfan lāde gelettan lifgende monn *do not thou let living man divert thee from thy journey, hinder thee from thy way*, 123 b; Th. 474, 3; Bo. 24: Beo. Th. 1142; B. 569. Hū lomp eów on lāde ðā ðū gehogodest sæcce sēcean ofer sealt water, 3978; B. 1987. Ic freónda beþearf on lāde ðonne ic sceal langne hām āna gesēcan *I need friends on my way, when alone I must seek my long home*, Apstls. Kmbl. 183; Ap. 92: Andr. Kmbl. 551; An. 276. Noe tealde ðæt hē (*the raven*) hine, gif hē on ðære lāde land ne funde, sēcan wolde, Cd. 72; Th. 87, 5: Gen. 1444. Se ūs ðās lāde sceóp *who shaped this course for us*, 89: Th. 110, 21; Gen. 1841. II. *a lode, watercourse* (*as a component in local names*):—Mariscem quam circumfluit Iaegnlaad, Cod. Dip. Kmbl. i. 190, 6. Ad aquæ ripam Iaenlāde, 163, 16. Cappelād, Wodelād are other instances occurring in the Charters. III. *carrying, carriage, bringing* (*see* lǣdan):—Sunnandæges cȳpinge wē forbeódaþ and ǣlc weorc and ǣlce lāde ǣgðer ge on wǣne ge on horse ge on byrdene *we forbid Sunday traffic and all work and all carrying (of goods, &c.) both by waggon and by horse and by the man himself*, L. N. P. L. 55; Th. ii. 298, 22. [The word *lád* in this passage can hardly be translated 'journeying;' for, in the first place, such a meaning does not well suit the phrase *on byrdene*, and, next, some journeying was allowed. Thus, L. E. I. 24; Th. ii. 420, 21–, it is said no secular work was to be done 'bútan hwam gebyrige ðæt hé nýde faran scyle; ðonne mót hé swá rídan swá rówan swá swilce færelde faran swylce tó his wege gebyrige.' The threefold division of the means of carriage seems to be that found in the Icelandic law where, dealing with the observance of Sunday, it is said of the amount that might be carried in journeying on that day 'er rétt at bera á sjálfum ser (= on byrdene) eþa fara á skipi eþa bera á hrossi.'] On sumon hé sceal láde lǽdan *on some lands the 'geneát' has to furnish means of carriage*, L. R. S. 2; Th. I. 432, 14. Cf. 436, 5-6:—Hé sceal beón gehorsad ðæt hé mǽge tó hláfordes seáme ðæt syllan oððe sylf lǽdan. The word used in both cases in the Latin translation is *summagium*, in reference to which, and to the English words which it translates, may be quoted Thorpe's explanation in his glossary: 'Lád, seám, summagium. A service, which consisted in supplying the lord with beasts of burthen, or, as defined by Roquefort (*voce* somey): "Service qu'un vassal devoit à son seigneur, et qui consistoit à faire faire quelques voyages par ses bêtes de somme." *See* Spelman *sub voce, and* Du Cange voce Sagma.' The phrase *láde lǽdan* occurs in a similar passage, dealing with the duties of the 'geneát,' in Cod. Dip. Kmbl. iii. 450, 31–:—Se geneát [at *Dyddanham*] sceal wyrcan swá on lande, swá of lande, hweðer swá man být and rídan, and auerian, and láde lǽdan, dráfe drífan, and fela óðra þinga dón. The later English *lode* seems to keep this meaning. Thus *Prompt. Parv.* 310, loode or caryage *vectura*; lodysmanne *vector, lator, vehicularius*: the verb *lead* is found with the sense of *carry*, e. g. p. 62 cartyn or *lede* wythe a carte; and in the note, and again in a note on p. 293, we have the phrases 'to *lede* dong,' 'to *lede* wheet,' &c. See also scip-lád. IV. *Sustenance, provision, means of subsistence*:—Ne sceal se dryhtnes þeów in his módsefan máre gelufian eorþan ǽhtwelan ðonne his ánes gemet ðæt hé his líchoman láde hæbbe *nor shall the servant of the Lord love more of earth's possessions, than a sufficiency for himself, that he may have sustenance for his body*, Exon. 38 a; Th. 125, 27; Gú. 360. With this use of *lád* may be compared the later English *lif-lode* which, besides the meaning *conduct*, has that of *sustenance*:—Heo tilede here lyflode . . . heo fonden hem sustynance ynow, R. Glouc. 41, 22: *Prompt. Parv.* lyvelode *victus*; lyflode or warysone *donativum*. So *O. H. Ger.* líb-leita *victus, annona, alimonium*. [In further illustration of *lád* the following native and foreign words are given. *Orm.* Þe steoressmann aȝȝ lokeþþ till an steorrne þatt stannt aȝȝ still . . . forr þatt he wile follȝhenn aȝȝ þatt illke steorrness *lade* (*guidance*); o lade *on the way*: *A. R.* lode *burthen* (v. III): *Mod. E.* lode-star: *Icel.* leið. I. *a way, course, road*. II. *a levy*: *O. H. Ger.* leita, *funus, ducatus; pl. exequiæ; see also compounds of* leiti, Grff. ii. 187]. DER. brim-, eá-, ge-, in-, lagu-, líf-, mere-, sǽ-, scip-, út-, ýð-lád.

lád, e; *f.* I. *excuse, defence against a charge*:—Nú hí nabbaþ náne láde be hyra synne *nunc excusationem non habent de peccato suo*, Jn. Skt. 15, 22. Ðætte hé náne láde ne mǽge findan ac síe súa mid his ágnum wordum gebunden *et in nulla sui defensione se exerceat, quam sententia proprii oris ligat*, Past. 26, 3; Swt. 185, 16. Ða nǽnige láde gedón ne mágon on dómes dæge ah sceolon mid deóflum in éce wíte gefeallan *those will not be able to make any defence at the day of judgment, but will have to fall with devils into everlasting punishment*, Blickl. Homl. 57, 20. II. as a technical term in the laws, *purgation, exculpation, the clearing one's self from a charge or accusation*. The accused might clear himself by his own oath, supported by the oaths of a certain number of compurgators, or he might undergo some form of ordeal. The *lád* varied with the character of the deed with the commission of which the accused was charged. In the *ánfeald lád*, if the purgation were by oath, the oaths of the accused, and two others were necessary, in the *þrýfeald lád*, the accused was to bring five compurgators; if the ordeal was used, in the former case the iron weighed one pound, in the latter, three. Other passages than those cited below, which may illustrate the terms *ánfeald, þrýfeald*, are the following:—Wé cwǽdon be ðám morþslyhtum ðæt man dýpte ðone áþ be þrýfealdum and myclade ðæt ordálísen ðæt hit gewege þrý pund, L. Ath. iv. 6; Th. i. 224, 12–14. Gange hé tó ðam þrýfealdan ordále; and ofgá man ðæt þrýfealde ordál ðus: nime fífe and beó hine sylfa syxta, L. C. S. 30; Th. i. 394, 3–5: 44; Th. i. 402, 7. The term 'lád,' it will be seen from the following passages, does not, as Schmid observes, occur in the laws before Ethelred's time, *canne* and *andsæc* being used previously:—Gyf mon ðone hláford teó . . . nime him fíf þegnas tó and beó him sylf syxta and ládie hine ðæs. And gif seó lád forþcume beó hé ðæs weres wyrðe *if the lord be accused . . . let him take to himself five thanes, and be himself the sixth, and clear himself of the charge. And if he be successful in clearing himself, let him be entitled to the 'wer*,' L. Eth. i. 1; Th. i. 282, 7: L. C. S. 30; Th. i. 394, 22. Gif him seó lád byrste *if the attempt to clear himself fail*, L. Eth. i. 1; Th. i. 282, 14: L. C. S. 8; Th. i. 380, 21: 31; Th. i. 396, 5. Gif lád forberste, 54; Th. i. 406, 10. Ðeáh lád teorie, L. O. D. 4; Th. i. 354, 14: 6; Th. i. 354, 31. Ne stent nán óðer lád æt tihtlan búte ordál betweox Wealan and Englan búte man þafian wille *no other method of clearing a man upon accusation is valid between Welsh and English but the ordeal, unless it be permitted*, 2; Th. i. 354, 1. Láde wyrðe beón *to be entitled to clear one's self (by oath or by ordeal)*, L. C. S. 20; Th. i. 386, 21. Sý ǽlc getrýwa man ðe tihtbysig nǽre and náðor ne burste ne áþ ne ordál ánfealdre láde wyrðe *let every true man that has not previously been accused, and in whose case neither oath nor ordeal has failed, be entitled to single purgation*, 22; Th. i. 388, 11. Dúnstán gedémde ðæt se mæssepreóst nǽre, gif hé wíf hæfde, ǽnigre óðre láde wyrðe, bútan eallswá lǽwede sceolde ðe efenboren wǽre, gif man mid tihtlan ðæne beléde, L. Edg. C. 60, note; Th. ii. 256, 38. Gebyreþ ðæt mon óðrum riht wyrce ge at láde ge æt ǽlcre sprǽce ðe him betweox biþ *it is proper for men to do right to one another both as regards clearing themselves of charges and as regards any suits that there are between them*, L. O. D. 2; Th. i. 352, 17. Gif æt láde mistíde déme se bisceop *if the attempt to clear himself miscarry, let the bishop pass sentence*, L. C. S. 57; Th. i. 406, 27. Geládige hine mid fulre láde, 42; Th. i. 400, 25. Geládige swá mid þrýfealdre swá mid ánfealdre láde be ðam ðe seó dǽd sí, L. C. E. 5; Th. i. 364, 2: L. Eth. ix. 27; Th. i. 346, 15. Ládige hine mid þrýfealdre láde, L. C. S. 8; Th. i. 380, 20: 48; Th. i. 404, 3. Ofgá man ánfealde láde mid ánfealdan foráþe and þrýfealde láde mid þrýfealdan foráþe [*the Latin version has the following in explanation*:—Qui autem conquirere debet simplicem purgationem, simplici sacramento hoc faciat, hoc est, accipiat duos et sit ipse tertius, et sic jurando conquirat. Triplex vero juramentum sic conquiratur; accipiat quinque et ipse sit sextus, et sic jurando acquirat triplex judicium aut triplex juramentum'], 22; Th. i. 388, 14. Se geréfa namige ða láde *let the reeve name the compurgators*, L. Eth. iii. 13; Th. i. 298, 1. Se ðe ofer ðæt láde geþafie oððe se ðe hý sylle gilde vi healfmarc *he that admits, or he that offers, purgation after that, shall pay six half-marks*, Th. i. 298, 7. Hér swutelaþ an (ðissum gewrite) ðæt Godwine hæfþ gelǽd fulle láde æt ðan unrihtwífe ðe Leófgár bisceop hine tihte and ðæt wæs lǽd æt Licitfelda *in this writing is declared that Godwine has fully cleared himself of the charge in the matter of the woman about whom bishop Leofgar accused him: and he cleared himself at Lichfield*, Chart. Th. 373, 31. *See* wer-lád, cor-snæd, ordál, ládian; Stubb's Const. Hist. i. 609–; Grmm. R. A. 856, 859–; Du Cange *sub voce* lada; Richthofen's Altfries. Wört. léde, láde.

ládian, *p.* ode. I. *to excuse, clear [one's self of a charge], exculpate, defend*:—Ðe hit symle lytiglíce ládaþ *sese callide defendentis*, Past. 35, 3; Swt. 244, 9. For ðan ðú tówyrpest ðíne fýnd and ealle ða ðe unrihtwísnesse ládiaþ and scyldaþ *ut destruas inimicum et defensorem*, Ps. Th. 8, 3. Ðære leóhtmódnesse sanctus Paulus hine ládode ðá hé cwæþ . . . *a mentis levitate se alienum Paulus fuisse perhibuit, cum dicit* . . . Past. 42, 3; Swt. 308, 7. Ðá ládode hé hine *ille se excusans*, Bd. 3, 7; S. 530, 26. Ðá cwæþ Petrus wǽre ðú mid ðínum fæder ðá hé mé swá ládode ðæt hie mé ne gegripon *then said Peter 'Wast thou with thy father when he made such excuse for me that they did not seize me?'* Blickl. Homl. 151, 26. Him Rómáne his forwierndon and hit under ðæt lǽdedon for ðon ðe hé ǽr æt ðæm óðrum cirre sige næfde *the Romans refused it [the triumph] to him, and excused [the refusal] under the pretext that before on the other occasion he had not gained the victory*, Ors. 5, 2; Swt. 216, 31. Ic bidde ðé ðæt ðú mé ládige *I pray thee to excuse me*, Homl. Th. ii. 374, 10. Ðæt synfulle mód ðe hit simle wile ládian *peccantem animam excusantemque se*, Past. 35, 3; Swt. 241, 7. Hú mæg ic ládigan láðan sprǽce oððe andsware ǽnige findan wráðum tówiðere *how can I clear myself of the hateful charge, or find any answer in reply to my foes?* Exon. 10 b; Th. 12, 9; Cri. 183. II. as a technical legal term [lád, II.] *to clear from an accusation*. [Amongst instances in which suspicion of crime is removed by the oath of the suspected party and the oaths of compurgators, may be taken that of King Alfonso who, when suspicion rested on him of complicity in the murder of his brother Sancho, cleared himself by the oaths of himself and twelve of his vassals. See the account in the Cronica del Cid. cc. 76–79.]:—Gif se húshláford hit nát ládie hine [*shall clear himself by oath*] *si latet fur, dominus domus . . . jurabit, quod non extenderet manum in rem proximi sui*, Ex. 22, 8. Gif hé hine ládian wille gá hé tó ðam hátum ísene and ládige ða hand mid ðe man týhþ ðæt hé ðæt fácen mid worhte *if he be willing to clear himself, then let him undergo the ordeal by hot iron, and therewith clear the hand with which he is accused of committing the fraud*, L. Ath. i. 14; Th. i. 206, 22–4. Gyf mon ðone hláford teó, nime him fíf þegnas tó, and beó him sylf syxta, and ládie hine ðæs [*by his own oath and the oaths of five compurgators clear himself of that charge*], L. Eth. i. 1; Th. i. 282, 4–6, 13. Hé hine twelfa sum ládige ðæt hé ða sócne nyste *let him clear himself by his own oath, supported by the oaths of eleven others, from the charge of having known that the slain man had sought sanctuary*, L. Ath. iv. 4; Th. I. 224, 2. Gif man hwilcne man teó ðæt hé ðone man féde ðe úres hláfordes griþ tóbrocen habbe ládige hine mid þrinna xii (cf. *Icel.* þrennar tylftir), L. Eth. iii. 13; Th. i. 296, 29. Mæssepreóst ládige hine on ðam húsle . . . Diacon nime six his gehádan and ládige mid ðám . . . &c. L

Eth. ix. 19-27; Th. i. 344, 346: L. C. E. 5; Th. i. 362, 364. Bûtan hê hine lâdian mæge ðæt hê him nân fácn on nyste *unless he can clear himself from the charge of having known of any fraud in the man*, L. Ath. iv. 4; Th. i. 224, 6. Bûtan hê hine lâdian durre be ðæs flýman were [*the degree* of lâd *to be determined by the status of the fugitive*) ðæt hê hine flýman nyste, i. 20; Th. i. 210, 13. Lâdian be ðæs cynges wergilde oððe mid þrýfealdan ordâle, L. Eth. v. 30; Th. i. 312, 6. Lâdian be ðam deópestan âþe oððe mid þrîfealdan ordâle, vi. 37; Th. i. 324, 18. Gif mon cyninges þegn beteô manslihtes, gif hê hine lâdian dyrre, dô hê ðæt mid xii cyninges þegnum, L. A. G. 3; Th. i. 154, 6. Gif se hlâford hine lâdian wylle mid twâm gôdum þegenum, L. Eth. iii. 4; Th. i. 294, 12. DER. â-, be-, ge-lâdian; *see previous word.*

lâdigend-lîc; *adj. Excusable*:—Lâdiendlîce *excussabile*, Wrt. Voc. ii. 146, 19.

lâd-mann, es; *m. A leader, guide*:—Ðû canst wegas geond ðæt wêsten beó ûre lâdmann *thou knowest the ways through the desert; be our guide;* eris ductor noster, Num. 10, 31. Abram fêrde of Egipta lande and Farao him funde lâdmen *præcepit Pharao super Abram viris et deduxerunt eum*, Gen. 12, 20. [Cf. *Laym.* ȝe scullen habben lædesmen and forð ȝe scullen liðen (2nd MS. lodesmen forþ ȝou to lede): *Ayenb.* þe ssipmen yhyerþ þane smite of þe lodesmanne: *Prompt. Parv.* p. 311, n. lodesman *pilot.*]

lâd-rinc, es; *m. A word of uncertain meaning occurring in the following passage*:—Gif cyninges ambihtsmiþ oððe laadrinc mannan ofslehþ meduman leódgelde forgelde *if the king's smith or 'lâdrinc' kill a man, let him pay for it with a half fine* [cf. § 21; Th. i. 8, 3), L. Ethb. 7; Th. i. 4, 8. The word, as Schmid observes, might have the same meaning as *lâd-mann* q. v. just as Layamon uses the compound *lod-cniht*, 'biforen rad heore *lod-cniht*' 25730; or taking *lád* in the sense of journey the reference may be to a messenger of the king, cf. L. In. 33; Th. i. 122, 13 where it speaks of 'Cyninges horswealh se ðe him mæge geǽrendian.' But there is another use of lâd [v. lâd, III) which perhaps is that in the passage; then the *lád-rinc* would be the king's carrier, one who did for the king similar service to that which the *geneát* does for his lord. In the Prompt. Parv. *lodysmanne* is rendered by *vector, lator, vehicularius.*

ladsar *laserwort*; laserpitium:—Nim ladsar, Lchdm. iii. 88, 20.

lâd-scipe, es; *m. Leadership, command;* ducatus, Wrt. Voc. ii. 72, 70.

lâd-teáh, lât-têh; *gen.* -teáge, -têge: *f. A leading-rein*:—Lâttêh *ducale*, Ælfc. Gl. 21; Som. 59, 64; Wrt. Voc. 23, 24.

lâd-teów, es; *m. A leader, guide, conductor, a leader in war, general*:—Ǽnne of þâm þrîm englum ða ðe him on ǽghwæðere gesihþe lâdteów wæs *unum de tribus angelis, qui sibi in tota utraque visione ductores adfuerunt*, Bd. 3, 19; S. 548, 31. Ðæt hê his lâdteów beón sceolde on Breotone *ut ipse eum perduceret Brittaniam*, 4, 1; S. 564, 15. Hengest se ðe wæs ǽrest lâdteów and heretoga Angelcynnes on Breotene *Hengist qui Brittaniam primus intravit*, 2, 5; S. 506, 34. Hê sende fyrd ðære wæs Beorht lâdteów and heretoga *misso cum exercitu duce Bercto*, 4, 26; S. 602, 5. Lâdteáw, Bt. tit. 36; Fox xviii. 4. Lâteáu, Kent. Gl. 131. Lâdtow *dux*, Ps. Surt. 30, 4: 54, 14. Mîn lâdþeów *dux mihi*, Ps. Th. 30, 4: Ps. Spl. C. 54, 14. Ðû eart ǽgðer ge weg ge lâdþeów *tu semita, dux*, Bt. 33, 4; Fox 132, 37. Lâtteów *dux*, Ælfc. Gr. 33; Som. 37, 49. Heretoga and lâtteów *dux*, Bd. 1, 16; S. 484, 18. Lâtteów wæs ðara leóda *duces eorum*, Ps. Th. 67, 25. Ic eom ealdor and lâtteów drihtnes heres *sum princeps exercitus domini*, Jos. 5. 14. Wilferþ bæd ðæt hê him ðæs siiþfætes lâtteów wǽre *Vilfridum ducem sibi itineris fieri rogaret*, Bd. 4, 5; S. 571, 35: 2, 20; S. 521, 41. Lâtteów ðæs weges, Ælfc. T. Grn. 18, 11. God, lîfes lâtteów, Elen. Kmbl. 1037; El. 520: 1794; El. 899. Lîfes lâtþeów, Cd. 147; Th. 184, 8; Exod. 104. Wæs ðæt se mîn lâtþeów se ðe mê ǽr lǽdde *ille erat ipse qui me ante ducebat*, Bd. 5, 12: S. 629, 8. Lâtþeów *ductor*, S. 629, 40. Lâtþeów *dux*, Ps. Spl. 54, 14. Lîfes lâððeów *the guide of life*, Dôm. L. 52, 9. Ðes and ðeós lâteów oððe heretoga *hic et hæc dux*, Ælfc. Gr. 9; Som. 14, 9: Wrt. Voc. 72, 60. Drihten ðe eówer lâteów ys *dominus qui ductor est vester*, Deut. 31, 8. Ðæt hê ðæs lâtteówes lârum hýre *that he listen to the guide's instructions*, Exon. 37 b; Th. 124, 5; Gû. 335: Elen. Kmbl. 2417; El. 1210. Hê sôhte hine him tô lâtðeówe on ðæm wege *ducem requirebat in via*, Past. 41, 5; Swt. 305, 5. Seó leó gif heó blôdes onbirigþ âbît ǽrest hire lâdteów *the lioness, if she tastes blood, will first rend her keeper;* primusque lacer dente cruento domitor rabidas imbuit iras, Bt. 25; Fox 38, 14. Þurh sume ða Wyliscean ðe him tô wǽron cumen and his lǽdteówas wǽron *by means of some of the Welsh who had come to him and were his guides*, Chr. 1097; Erl. 233, 39. Hig synt blinde and blindra lâtteówas (Lind. lâtuas) *cæci sunt, duces cæcorum*, Mt. Kmbl. 15, 14. Wǽron heora lâtteówas and heretogan twegen gebrôðra Hengest and Horsa, Bd. 1, 15; S. 483, 27. Ic mê ðâ mid genom .cc. lâdþeówa and eác .l. ðe ða gênran wegas cûðan ðara sîðfato *acceptis .cl. ducibus qui brevitates itinerum noverant*, Nar. 6, 7. Gê preóstas synd gesette tô lâdþeówum and tô lâreówum ofer Godes folc. L. Ælfc. P. 5; Th. ii. 366, 4. Him ðâ Rômâne æfter ðæm lâdteówas gesetton, ðe hie consulas hêton, Ors. 2, 2; Swt. 68, 2. Ealle mîne lâdþeówas ðe mec on swelc earfeðo gelǽddon *locorum demonstratores qui nos in insidias deducebant*, Nar. 16, 25. In Mt. Kmbl. Lind. 2, 6: Rtl. 38, 15: 193, 15, the form *látwa* with pl. *látuas*, Mt. 15, 14, occurs; also *látwu*, Rtl. 193, 17, 19; and in 2, 5 *látuan* glosses *ducere.* [*O. E. Homl.* latteu *a guide*: *Jul.* lauerd, liues lattow: *cf. Icel.* leið-togi *a guide.*] v. under-lâdteów.

lâdteów-dôm, es; *m. Leadership, guidance, conduct*:—Mid engla lâdþeówdôme *ducentibus angelis*, Bd. 4, 3; S. 568, 41. Ðýlæs hî underfô ðone lâdteówdôm (Hat. MS. lâtteówdôm) ðæs forlores *ne ducatum suscipiat perditionis*, Past. 3, 1; Swt. 32, 9 Ðone lâdteówdôm (Hat. MS. lâttiówdôm) ðæs folces *plebium ducatum*, 7, 2; Swt. 50, 18. Lâdteówdôm (Hat. MS. lâtteówdôm) geearwian *ducatum præbere*, 18, 7; Swt. 138, 16. Lâdteówdôm *magisterium, pædagogium*, Hpt. Gl. 477.

lâdung, e; *f.* I. *An excusing, a clearing of* or *defending against a charge, an apology, excuse, a defence, exculpation*:—Lâdung *apologia*, Ælfc. Gl. 106; Som. 78, 64; Wrt. Voc. 57, 43: *excussatio*, Wrt. Voc. ii. 146, 15. God lǽt him fyrst ðæt hê his mândǽda geswîce gif hê wile: gif hê nele ðæt hê beó bûtan ǽlcere lâdunge swîðe rihtlîce tô deófles handa âsceofen *God allows the wicked man time, that he may, if he will, cease from his wicked deeds: that, if he will not, he may, having nothing to plead in his defence, very justly be thrust into the hands of the devil*, Homl. Th. i. 270, 1. Môd ymbtrymedu mid lytelîcre lâdunge *mentes fallaci defensione circumdatæ*, Past. 35, 5; Swt. 245, 8. Hî simle sêceaþ endeleáse lâdunga *semper improbas defensiones quærunt*, 35, 2; Swt. 239, 8. II. as a legal term, *purgation, the clearing himself on the part of an accused person, by oath or by some form of ordeal, of the charge made against him*:—And stande betwux burgum ân lagu æt lâdunge, L. C. S. 34; Th. i. 396, 22. Bisceop sceall æt tihtlan lâdunge gedihtan ðæt ǽnig man ôðrum ǽnig wôh beódan ne mǽge âðor oððe on âþe oððe on ordâle *when accusation is made, the bishop shall so order the proceedings by which the accused is to clear himself, that no man may be able to offer wrong to another in the matter of taking oath or of undergoing the ordeal*, L. I. P. 7; Th. ii. 312, 15. v. lâd, lâdian, be-lâdung.

lǽ *hair*:—Lǽ wîffex *cæsaries*, Wrt. Voc. ii. 16, 46. [*Icel.* lá *hair*: cf. lô, lôð *shagginess; also a flock of wool.*] Perhaps we may compare here *lee* of threde, Prompt. Parv. 291, where the following note is given. 'Forty threads of hemp-yarn are termed in Norfolk a lea. The "lea" by which linen yarn was estimated at Kidderminster, contained 200 threads.' Halliwell gives as a northern word '*lea* the seventh part of a hank or skein of worsted.'

lǽc *a gift.* v. lâc.

læc; *adj.* The word, if this be the true form of it, occurs only once, in the following passage:—Gârulf gecrang ealra ǽrest ... ymb hyne gôdra fela hwearf lacra hrǽr hræfn wandrode sweart and sealobrûn, Fins. Th. 64-70; Fin. 33-5. All the editors for *hrær*, which Hickes gives, read *hréw*, but in the MSS. *r* (ꞃ) and *s* (ꞅ) are so nearly alike that perhaps *hrǽs*, the genitive of *hrá*, was the original word. With regard to *lacra* various explanations have been given. Kemble and Conybeare print *hwearflacra*, Ettmüller reads *hwearflicra*, Thorpe *hwearf láðra*, Grein *hwearf lacra.* Taking the word to be independent, and retaining the reading of Hickes, we may compare it with *Icel. lakr* lacking, defective, and render it by *weak, failing (from wounds), wounded.* Another form that attracts comparison is given by Graff ii. 100, *lah*, which has reference to cutting, and this suggests the rendering *wounded.* With the reading *hrǽs* for *hrær* the passage might be translated '*first of all sank down Garulf ... around him moved many a stout man weak or wounded in body: the raven wheeled round swart and dusky.*' Ettmüller p. xxiv, giving a meaning to *wandrian* which it will hardly bear, translates the doubtful part of the passage '*volubilium (=mortuorum) cadavera corvus conculcavit.*' Similarly, as regards the first part, Conybeare has '*circa illum fortes multi caduci moriebantur.*'

lǽca, an; *m. A leech, doctor, physician*:—Se lǽca ðe sceal sâre wunda wel gehǽlan hê môt habban gôde sealfe ðǽrtô *the doctor who has to make a good cure of painful wounds, must have good salve for the purpose*, L. Pen. 4; Th. ii. 278, 15: 5; Th. ii. 278, 20. v. lǽce.

-lǽca. v. ag-, ellen-, lyb-, scîn- lǽca.

lǽcan; *p.* lǽhte, lǽcte *To move quickly, spring, leap [as flame]*:—Hwîlum se wonna lêg lǽhte wið ðes lâþan *at times the lurid flame leaped towards the fiend*, Cd. 229; Th. 309, 25; Sal. 716. DER. Ǽfen-, dyrst-, ed-, efen-, geân-, gedyrst-, geneâ-, geriht-, geþrîst-, lof-, neâ-, riht-, sumor-, þrîst-, winter- lǽcan; *and see* lâcan.

læccan, læccean; *p.* læhte; *pp.* læht *To take, grasp, seize, catch, apprehend, capture*:—Lǽdeþ hine and læceþ and hine geond land spaneþ *leadeth and taketh him, and through the land lures him*, Salm. Kmbl. 989; Sal. 496. Hî læccaþ of manna begeatum hwæt hî gefôn mâgon eallswâ gýfre hremnas of holde dôþ *they seize of men's gettings what they can grasp, just as greedy ravens do from a corpse*, L. I. P. 19; Th. ii. 328, 4. Hî gærs ǽton georne and ǽlc læhte of ôðrum gif hê hwæt litles hæfde *they eagerly ate grass, and each seized from the other, if he had any little bit*, Ælfc. T. Grn. 21, 10. Heora ǽgðer uppon ôðerne tûnas bærnde and eác menne læhte *in their struggle they burned one another's towns and captured one another's men*, Chr. 1094; Erl. 230, 13. Ðætte ðióstro iuih ne læcga *ut non tenebræ vos comprœhendant*, Jn. Skt. Lind. 12, 35. Allswǽ tô þeáfe gié foerdon mið suordum and stengum tô læccanne mec *tam-*

quam ad latronem existis cum gladiis et lignis comprehendere me, Mk. Skt. Lind. 14, 48. Ðæt wíf wearþ ðá læht and gelǽd tó ðam cininge *sublata est mulier in domum Pharaonis*, Gen. 12, 15. [*Orm.* to lacchenn þurrh trapp; bikahht and lahht (*pp.*): *A.R.* lecche; *p.* lahte: *O. and N.* grine þe for to lacche: *Piers P.* to lacche foules; *p.* lauȝte: *Gen. and Ex.* lagt *pp.*] v. ge-læccan.

LǢCE, es; *m.* I. A LEECH, [Shakspere uses the word once, and even now it has not quite died out, but perhaps, in prose at least, its meaning is usually that given by Bailey in his Dictionary 'a Farrier or Horse-Doctor,' a doctor rather for animals than men], *doctor, physician*:—Lǽce *medicus*, Wrt. Voc. 74, 4. Eálá lǽce gehǽl ðé sylfne [lǽ lēce lēcne ðec seolfne, Lind.] *medice cura te ipsum*, Lk. Skt. 4, 23. Cyneferþ lǽce se æt hire wæs ðá heó forþférde *medicus Cynifrid, qui morienti illi adfuit*, Bd. 4, 19; S. 588, 41. Hálig lǽce [*the Deity*] Hy, 7, 62; Hy. Grn. ii. 288, 62. Hé [*the Pater Noster*] is lamena lǽce, Salm. Kmbl. 155; Sal. 77. Lǽteþ flint brecan his sconcan ne biþ him lǽce gód *he shall cause the stones to break his legs, no doctor shall avail him*, 206; Sal. 102. Nys hálum lǽces nán þearf *non est opus valentibus medico*, Mt. Kmbl. 9, 12: Lk. 5, 31: Exon. 89 b; Th. 336, 8; Gn. Ex. 45. Hé hine gelǽdde on his lǽcehús and hine lácnude and brohte óðrum dæge twegen penegas and sealde ðam lǽce *duxit illum in stabulum et curam ejus egit, et altera die protulit duos denarios et dedit stabulario*, Lk. Skt. 10, 34–5. Oððe hí lǽceas (Ps. Spl. lǽcas) weccean *aut medici suscitabunt*, Ps. Th. 87, 10. Ðeáh ða woroldlecon lǽceas [Hat. MS. lǽcas] scomaþ ðæt hí onginnem ða wunda lácnian ðe hí gesión ne mágon .... hwílon ne scomaþ ða ðe ðæs módes lǽceas bión sceoldon ðeáh ðe hí náne wuht ongitan ne cunnon ðara gǽstlecena beboda ðæt hí him onteóþ ðæt hí sín heortan lǽceas *tamen sæpe qui nequaquam spiritalia præcepta cognoverunt, cordis se medicos profiteri non metuunt: dum qui pigmentorum vim nesciunt, videri medici carnis erubescunt*, Past. 1, 1; Swt. 24, 19–26, 2. Witodlíce ne mágon lǽceas [MS. B. lǽcas] náht mycel hǽlan bútan ðisse wyrte *certainly, doctors cannot heal much without this plant*, Herb. 20, 4; Lchdm. i. 114, 22. Lǽcas lǽraþ ðisne lǽcedóm, L. M. 2, cont. 18, 20; Lchdm. ii. 160, 17, 22. Lǽceas secgaþ, 19; Lchdm. ii. 160, 19. Seó códu ðe lǽcas hátaþ paralisin, Homl. Th. ii. 546, 29. Gelácna ðú hý forðan ðú ēdest miht ealra lǽca, Hy. 1, 6; Hy. Grn. ii. 280, 6. Fram manegum lǽcum *a compluribus medicis*, Mk. Skt. 5, 26. Is seó geoluwe swá ðeáh swíðost lǽceon [MS. B. lǽcon] gecwēme *the yellow is however most suitable for doctors*, Herb. 165, 1; Lchdm. i. 294, 11. Josep beád his þeówan lǽcon *Joseph præcepit servis suis medicis*, Gen. 50, 1. Seó fordǽlde on lǽcas eall ðæt heó áhte *in medicos erogaverat omnem substantiam suam*, Lk. Skt. 8, 43. Lēceas, Ep. Gl. 18 b, 21. [*O. E. Homl.* lache, leche: *Orm.* læche: *A. R.* leche: *Chauc. Piers P.* leche: *Prompt. Parv.* leche *aliptes, empiricus, medicus, cirurgicus*, a surgion; p. 291 note, q. v.: *Goth.* lēkeis, leikeis: *O. Frs.* leza, letza, leischa: *O. H. Ger.* láhhi, láche *medicus*: *Dan.* læge: cf. *Icel.* laknari, læknir.] v. heáh-lǽce. II. *a leech* (species of worm):—Lǽce *sanguisuga* vel *hirudo*, Ælfc. 23; Som. 60, 5; Wrt. Voc. 24, 9: *sanguisuga*, Wrt. Voc. ii. 71, 17. Lýces *sanguissuge*, Kent. Gl. 1085. [*Prompt. Parv.* leche.] **-lǽcea.** v. ag-lǽcea.

lǽce-bóc, e; *f. A book on medicine, book of recipes*:—Ðonne sceal him mon blód lǽtan on ðás wísan ðe ðeós lǽcebóc segþ *then shall he be let blood in these ways that this book on medicine sayeth*, L. M. cont. 2, 42; Lchdm. ii. 168, 12. [*Dan.* læge-bog *a medical book.*]

lǽce-cræft, es; *m. The art of medicine, a particular instance of the application of this art, a remedy, recipe, medicine*:—Swá gedéþ se lǽcecræft ðæt se mon biþ lǽce *medicina medicos facit*, Bt. 16, 3; Fox 54, 31. Ic ðé wille nú secgan hwelc se lǽcecræft is mínre láre hé is swíðe biter on múþe *I will now tell thee of what kind the medicine of my teaching is. It is very bitter in the mouth*, Bt. 22, 1; Fox 76, 28. Ðes lǽcecræft ys áfandud *this remedy is a proved one*, Herb. 183, 1; Lchdm. i. 320, 9. Brúce ðysses lǽcecræft[es] *use this remedy*, Lchdm. iii. 126, 20. Ðis sceal ðan manna tó lǽcecræfte *this shall be a remedy for the men*, 22. Wé habbaþ hwæðere ða bysne on hálgum bócum ðæt mót se ðe wile mid sóðum lǽcecræfte his líchaman getemprian *we have however the examples in holy books that he who will may cure his body with true leechcraft* [cf. wiccecræft l. 22], Homl. Th. i. 474, 34. Lǽcecræftas and dolgsealfa and drencas wið eallum wundum *medicines and unguents and potions for all wounds*, L. M. cont. 1, 38; Lchdm. ii. 8, 26. Lǽcecræftas be lifre ádlum *recipes for diseases of the liver*, L. M. cont. 2, 17; Lchdm. ii. 160, 10. Be wylddeóra lǽcecræftum *of medicines obtained from wild animals*, Lchdm. i. 326, 9. On ðissum ǽrestan lǽcecræftum gewritene sint lǽcedómas wið eallum heáfdes untrymnessum *in these first recipes are written remedies for all infirmities of the head*, L. M. 1, 1; Lchdm. ii. 18, 1. [Ne þurh nenne lǽchecræft ne mihte he lif habben, Laym. 7616: Þurrh Crissteenndomess læchecrafft, Orm. 1869: he ne secheð nout leche ne lechecraft, A. R. 178, 13: þe kyng lette do under lechecraft hem þat ywonded were, R. Glouc. 141, 6: lered lechecraft his lyf for to save, Piers P. 16, 104: *Dan.* læge-kraft *healing power.*] cf. lǽce-dóm.

lǽce-cræftig; *adj. Skilled in medicine*:—Arestolobius wæs háten án cing hé wæs wís and lǽcecræftig hé ðá gesette forðon gódne morgendrænc wið eallum untrumnessum ðe mannes líchoman iond styriaþ *there was a king named Arestolobius, he was wise and skilled in medicine, for which reason he composed a good-morning drink for all infirmities that stir throughout man's body*, Lchdm. iii. 70, 16.

lǽce-cynn, es; *n. The race of physicians* or *surgeons*:—Nǽfre [ic] lǽcecynn on folcstede findan meahte ðara ðe mid wyrtum, wunde gehǽlde *never could I find on the battlefield the leeches, those who with herbs my wounds would heal*, Exon. 102 b; Th. 388, 20; Rä. 6, 10.

lǽce-dóm, es; *m. Medicine, a medicine, remedy, cure*:—Lǽcedóm *medecina*, Wrt. Voc. 74, 5: Lchdm. ii. 16, 9–27. Lēcedom, Kent. Gl. 148. Lǽcedóm *malagma*, Wrt. Voc. ii. 75, 59: *cura*, 92, 61. In untrymnisse wæs ðú lēcedóme *in infirmitate sis medecina*, Rtl. 105, 13. On ðare smyrunge biþ lǽcedóm and sinna forgifnes and ne biþ ná hádung *unction is medicinal, and in it there is forgiveness of sins, but there is no ordination*, L. Ælfc. P. 48; Th. ii. 384, 32. Ýdel biþ se lǽcedóm ðe ne mæg ðone untruman gehǽlan *vain is the medicine that cannot heal the sick*, Homl. Th. i. 60, 34. Búton hé ðone tíman árēdige ðæs lǽcedómes ðonne biþ hit swutol ðæt se lácnigenda forliésþ ðone cræft his lǽcedómes *nisi cum tempore medicamenta conveniant, constat procul dubio, quod medendi officium amittant*, Past. 21, 2; Swt. 153, 3–5. Hwí ne bidst ðú ðé lífes lǽcedómes æt lífes freán, Dóm. L. 6, 81. Mycel wund behófaþ mycles lǽcedómes *grande vulnus grandioris curam medelæ desiderat*, Bd. 4, 25; S. 599, 40. Tó lǽcedóme and tó hǽle untrumra manna *ad medelam infirmantium*, 3, 10; S. 534, 24. For hwylcum lǽcedóme *pro aliquo remedio*, L. Ecg. C. 21; Th. ii. 156, 14. Becuman tó ðam sóþan lǽcedóme *pervenire ad veram medelam*, L. Ecg. P. i. 4; Th. ii. 174, 4: Blickl. Homl. 107, 15. Ne hogaþ hé be ðam heofenlícan lǽcedóme, Homl. Th. ii. 470, 16. Wið untrumnysse lǽcedóm sǽcan *medicamentum contra ægritudines explorare*, Bd. 1, 27; S. 494, 18. Him lǽcedom bǽron *illis solent adferre medelam*, 4, 6; S. 574, 10. Ðá sóhte Colemannus ðysse unsibbe lǽcedóm *quæsivit Colmanus huic dissensioni remedium*, 4, 4; S. 571, 6. Ic wolde ymbe ðone lǽcedóm ðara ðínra lára hwéne máre gehýran *remedia audiendi avidus vehementer efflagito*, Bt. 22, 1; Fox 76, 17. Ús is nédþearf ðæt wé sēcan ðone lǽcedóm úre sáuwle, Blickl. Homl. 97, 31. Þurh his lǽcedóm *by means of the remedy he has provided*, Cd. 226; Th. 301, 30; Sat. 589. Lǽcedóm findan, Exon. 31 a; Th. 96, 13; Cri. 1573. Lǽcedómas, see Lchdm. ii. pp. 2–16: pp. 158–174. Hí tó ðám dweoligendum lǽcedómum deófolgylde ēfeston *ad erratica idolatriæ medicamina concurrebant*, Bd. 4, 27; S. 604, 7. Tó lēcedómum ēcum *ad remedia æterna*, Rtl. 23, 20. Untrymnessa lǽcedómas onfēngon *languorum remedia conquisiere*, Bd. 3, 17; S. 544, 47. Lege on lǽcedómas ða ðe út teón ða yfelan wǽtan *apply remedies that may draw out the evil humour*, L. M. 1, 4; Lchdm. ii. 46, 26. [*O. E. Homl.* ȝif he lechedom con, i. 111, 2: *Orm.* Drihhtiness læchedom and sawless eȝhe sallfe, 1851: *O. H. Ger.* láh-tuom *medicina, medicamentum, fomentum*: cf. *Icel.* læknis-dómr *medicine*: *Dan.* læge-dom *medicine, healing power, cure.*]

lǽcedóm-ness, e; *f. A plaster*:—Lǽcedómnessa oððe sealfe *cataplasma*, Wrt. Voc. ii. 18, 30.

lǽce-feoh; *g.* -feós; *n. A physician's fee, money paid to a doctor*:—Swá hwylc man swá óðrum womwlite ongewyrce forgylde him ðone womwlite and his weorc wyrce óþ ðæt seó wund hál sig and ðæt lǽcefeoh ðam lǽce gylde, *quicunque homo alio vulnus in faciem inflixerit, emendet ei vulnus, et opus ejus operetur, donec vulnus sanetur, et mercedem medico solvat*, L. Ecg. C. 22; Th. ii. 148, 19. [Cf. Si vulneraverit quis alium, et satisfacere debeat, in primis reddat ei *lich-fe* quantum scilicet in curam vulneris impendit, L. W. I. 1, 10; Th. i. 471, 25. Cf. *Icel.* læknis-fé.]

lǽce-finger, es; *m. The leech-finger, the fourth finger* [though in one gloss it seems to be the *little-finger*]:—Þuma *pollex*, scytelfinger *index*, middelfinger *medius*, lǽcefinger *medicus*, eárefinger *auricularius*, Wrt. Voc. 71, 30–34. At p. 44, 7–8 the names are different:—Goldfinger *medicus* vel *annularis*, lǽcefinger *auricularis*, Ælfc. Gl. 73; Som. 71, 22. Sing on ðíne lǽce-finger paternoster, Lchdm. i. 394, 2. [In later times it was the fourth finger e. g. Halliwell in his Dictionary quotes from a MS. of the 15th cent.

Ilke a fyngir has a name, als men thaire fyngers calle,
The lest fyngir hat *lityl man*, for hit is lest of alle;
The next fynger hat *leche man*, for qwen a leche dos oȝt,
With that fynger he tastes all thyng. howe that hit is wroȝt.

In Prompt. Parv. p. 291 note the reason for the name is given differently. 'The fourth finger was called the leech finger, from the pulsation therein found, and supposed to be in more direct communication with the heart, as in the tract attributed to Joh. de Garlandiâ . . . it is said '*Stat medius* [medylle fyngure] *medio, medicus* [leche fyngure] *jam convenit* [accordyt] *egro*."' See too in the same writer's *Dictionarius*, Wrt. Voc. p. 121, 35 '*medicus* dicitur digitus eo quod illo medici imponunt medicinam.' Cf. *Icel.* læknis-fingr.]

lǽce-hús, es; *n. A hospital, a house where the sick are tended by a leech*:—Hé hine gelǽdde on his lǽcehús [Lind. lēcehús] and hine lácnude And brohte óðrum dæge twegen penegas and sealde ðam lǽce and ðus cwæþ Begým hys *illum duxit in stabulum et curam ejus egit. Et altera* *die protulit duos denarios et dedit stabulario et ait curam illius habe*, Lk. Skt. 10, 34-5. [The translator seems not to have kept close to the text, but to have rendered the passage in accordance with the part played by the Good Samaritan. A more literal translation is given Past. 17, 10; Swt. 125 where *in stabulum* is rendered *tó ðæm giesðhúse*.] [*Prompt. Parv.* a leche house *laniena, quia infirmi ibi laniantur*, p. 291, note 4.]

lǽce-sealf, e; *f. A medicinal salve* or *ointment, a plaster*; malagma, Wrt. Voc. ii. 87, 77.

lǽce-seax, es; *n. A surgeon's knife*:—Se lǽce hȳt đonne his lǽceseax under his clāđum *medicus abscondit igitur ferrum medicinale sub veste*, Past. 26, 3; Swt. 187, 9.

lǽce-wyrt, e; f. I. *a herb having medicinal virtue*:—Se wīsa Augustinus cwæþ đæt unpleólīc sȳ đeáh hwā lǽcewyrte þicge ac đæt hē tælþ tō unālȳfedlīcere wiglunge gif hwā đa wyrta on him becnitte būton hē hī tō đam dolge gelecge *the learned Augustine said, that it is not dangerous, though any one eat a medicinal herb; but he considers it as unlawful sorcery, if any one bind the herbs on himself, unless he lay them to the wound*, Homl. Th. 1. 476, 4. II. *the name of a particular plant*:—Lǽcewyrt *quinquenerina* [*quinquenervia*], Wrt. Voc. 286, 39. Lēciwyrt *quinquenervia*, Wrt. Voc. ii. 118, 57. Lǽcewyrt. Đeós wyrt đe man lichanis stefanice and ōđrum naman lǽcewyrt nemneþ *this plant which is named λύχνις στεφανική and by another name leechwort* [Cockayne Lchdm. ii. 396, col. 2 suggests *campions* or *ragged robin* or one of that kindred as the plant here meant], Herb. 133, 1; Lchdm. i. 248, 15-7. Lǽcewyrt *plantago lanceolata*, L. M. 1, 32; Lchdm. ii. 78, 7: 1, 38; Lchdm. ii. 96, 14. See Cockayne as above where he gives lakeblad *plantago major*, in West Gothland. [*Dan.* læge-urt *medicinal plant*: cf. *Icel.* læknis-gras *a healing herb*.]

lǽcing, e; *f. Blame, reproof*; redargutio, Somner. [Cf. *Chauc. Piers P.* to lakke *to blame, dispraise, speak ill of*; *Prompt. Parv.* lakkyn *vitupero, culpo*; lacke *or* blame *vituperium*, p. 285, note 3, where this line from Lydgate, besides other instances, is given 'with lawde or *lack* liche as they have deserved': *O. Frs.* laking *impugnatio*; lakia *impugnare*.]

lǽcnan *to tend*:—Lǽcnende *procurans*, Wrt. Voc. ii. 90, 72. v. lācnian.

lǽcnung. v. lācnung.

lǽcung, e; *f. Healing, remedy*. [*O. E. Homl.* hit beo mi lechunge hit beo mi bote, i. 187, 35: *O. H. Ger.* lāhunka *remedium*.] v. sealf-lǽcung, *and* cf. lācnung.

lǽd, Chart. Th. 166, 21. v. lǽwed.

lǽd. v. un-lǽd.

LǢDAN; *p.* de; *pp.* lǽded, lǽd TO LEAD, *conduct, take, carry, bring, bring forth, produce* [the word translates the Latin verbs *ducere, ferre* with many of their compounds]:—Ic naman Drihtnes herige and hine mid lofsange lǽde swylce *laudabo nomen Dei mei cum cantico, et magnificabo eum in laude*, Ps. Th. 68, 31. Twegen gemacan đū lǽtst in tō đam arce *bina induces in arcam*, Gen. 6, 19. Se wīsa mon eall his līf lǽt on gefeán [cf. orsorg līf lǽdaþ woruldmen wīse, Bt. Met. Fox 7, 80; Met. 7, 40] *duces serenus ævum*, Bt. 12; Fox. 36, 24. Se blinda gyf hē blindne lǽt *cæcus si cæco ducatum præstet*, Mt. Kmbl. 15, 14. Lēt, Dōm. L. 18, 294. Se đe nimeþ ł lǽdeþ synne middangeardes *qui tollit peccatum mundi*, Jn. Skt. Lind. 1, 29. Gē cunnon hwæt se hlāford is se đisne here lǽdeþ, Exon. 16 a; Th. 36, 11; Cri. 574. Man đa moldan nimeþ and men wīde geond eorþan lǽdaþ tō reliquium *the earth is taken, and men carry it far and wide over the world as relics*, Blickl. Homl. 127, 16. Hī hergiaþ and tō scipe lǽdaþ *they harry and carry off the plunder to their ships*, Swt. A. S. Rdr. 109, 137. Hī Crist heriaþ and him lof lǽdaþ *Crist they laud and to him bring praise*, Hy. 7, 25; Hy. Grn. ii. 287, 25. Ic wille ācwellan cynna gehwylc đara đe lyft and flōd lǽdaþ and fēdaþ *I will destroy every kind that air and water produce and nourish*, Cd. 65; Th. 78, 25; Gen. 1298. Wæstme tydraþ ealle đa on Libanes lǽdaþ [MS. lǽdeþ] on beorge cwice cederbeámas đa đū sylfa gesettest *cedri Libani quas plantasti*, Ps. Th. 103, 16. Đa men mon lǽdde tō Winteceastre tō đæm cynge *the men were brought to Winchester to the king*, Chr. 897; Erl. 96, 10. Se deófol hine genam and lǽdde hine on swīđe heáhne munt *assumpsit eum diabolus in montem excelsum valde*, Mt. Kmbl. 4, 8: Blickl. Homl. 27, 16. Đā cwæþ hē tō đam engle đe hine lǽdde *then said he to the angel that conducted him*, 43, 32. Eal đæt folc hine lǽdde mid gefeán, 249, 21. Ecgbryht lǽdde fierd wiđ Norþanhymbre *Egbert led a force against the Northumbrians*, Chr. 827; Erl. 64, 7: Hē wæs ofslegen mid ealle đȳ weorude đe hē lǽdde, Bd. 1, 34; S. 499, 34. Hē onbeád đæt hē of Rōme cōme and đæt betste ǽrende lǽdde *mandavit se venisse de Roma ac nuncium ferre optimum*, 1, 25; S. 486, 26. Hē ancorlīf lǽdde *vitam solitariam duxerat*, 4, 27; S. 603, 28. Hē lǽdde *eduxit*, Blickl. Gl. Hē hine lǽdde forþ tō đon cafortūne đæs hūses. Blickl. Homl. 219, 20. Lǽde mon hider tō ūs sumne untrumne mon. Đā lǽdde mon forþ sumne blindne mon of Angelcynne. Wæs hē ǽrest lǽded tō Brytta biscopum *adducatur aliquis æger . . . Allatus est quidam de genere Anglorum, oculorum luce privatus; qui oblatus Brittonum sacerdotibus*, Bd. 2, 2; S. 502, 21-5. Đā Abraham ǽhte lǽdde of Egypta ēđelmearce, Cd. 90; Th. 112, 20; Gen. 1873. Hē hēt smiđian āne lytle rōde đa hē lǽdde on his swīđran *he ordered a little cross to be forged, that he laid upon his right hand*, Homl. Th. ii. 304, 16. His đegnas lǽddon him tō đone eosol *his disciples brought the ass to him*, Blickl. Homl. 71, 6. On hæftnēd lǽddon *led into captivity*, 79, 22. Đa fīf cyningas mit hūđe lǽddan (*predati sunt*) Loth gebundenne, Prud. 2 a. Mē lǽddon *me deduxerunt*, Ps. Spl. 42, 3. Đa ilcan đe ǽr landgemǽre lǽddon *the same that before had marked the boundaries of the land*, Chart. Th. 376, 19. Hettend lǽddon ūt mid ǽhtum abrahames mǽg of Sodoma byrig, Cd. 94; Th. 121, 17; Gen. 2011. Ne lǽd đū ūs in cōstunge *lead us not into temptation*, Hy. 6. 27; Hy. Grn. ii. 286, 27. Lǽd ūt mid đē *educ tecum*, Gen. 8, 17. Đā cwæþ hē tō his gerēfan lǽde in đās menn and gearwa ūre þēnunga *præcepit dispensatori domus suæ dicens*: *Introduc viros domum, et instrue convivium*, 43, 16. Đā cwæþ hē lǽde hig tō mē *adduc, inquit, eos ad me*, 48, 9. Lǽdaþ hig forþ and forbearnaþ hig *producite eam ut comburatur*, 38, 24. Fare gē tō eówrum hūse and lǽde eówerne gingstan brōđor tō mē *vos abite in domos vestras et fratrem vestrum minimum ad me adducite*, 42, 20. Gāþ and lǽdaþ ūt đæt wīf *producite eam*, Jos. 6, 22. Lǽde seó eorþe forþ cuce nītenu *producat terra animam viventem*, Gen. 1, 24. Lǽdæ þrounc *tollat crucem*, Mk. Skt. Lind. 8, 34. Hē his đa menniscan gecynd on heofenas lǽdon wolde *he would take his human nature into heaven*, Blickl. Homl. 127, 24. Hē hēt his līchoman up ādōn and lǽdon tō Wintonceastre *translatus in Ventam civitatem*, Bd. 3, 7; S. 529, 24: Blickl. Homl. 193, 10. Hē forđon cōme đæt hē sceolde mete lǽdan *propter victum adferendum*, Bd. 4, 22; S. 591, 8. Hī hæfdon ǽrend đe hī him lǽdan sceolden *haberent aliquid legationis quod deberent ad illum perferre*, 5, 10; S. 624, 22. Ne dorste siđđan nān Scotta cininga lǽdan here on đās þeóda, Chr. 603; Erl. 21, 16. Sceal ic lǽdan đīnne sunu eft tō đam lande đe đū of fērdest? Beó wær æt đam đæt đū nǽfre mīnne sunu đyder ne lǽde *numquid reducere debeo filium tuum ad locum, de quo egressus es? Cave, ne quando reducas filium meum illuc*, Gen. 24, 4-5. Wīf lǽdan *to take a wife*, Lchdm. iii. 190, 5: 212, 8. Þuhte mē đæt ic gesāwe treów on lyft lǽdan *methought that I saw a tree borne aloft*, Rood Kmbl. 9; Kr. 5. Wudu mōt him weaxan tānum lǽdan *wood may grow, be productive of twigs*, Exon. 119 b; Th. 458, 23; Hy. Grn. ii. 285, 105. Ecbyrht munuclīf wæs lǽdende on Hibernia, Bd. 3, 27 tit.; S. 558, 8. Hē wæs eft swā ǽr lof lǽdende *he was again as before bringing forth praise*, Andr. Kmbl. 2952; An. 1479. Se āna ealra beáma up lǽdendra *it alone of all trees that bear on high their branches*, Exon. 58 b; Th. 209, 30; Ph. 178. Sagaþ Matheus đætte se Hǽlend wǽre lǽded on wēsten, Blickl. Homl. 27, 4. Đā wæs geond đa werþeóde wīde lǽded mǽre morgenspel *then was a mighty report carried far and wide among the people*, Elen. Kmbl. 1935; El. 969. Feorran lǽded *brought from far*, Exon. 107 b; Th. 411, 2; Rā 29, 6. Đæt wæs lǽd æt Licitfelda *that* [*the exculpation from the charge*] *was produced at Lichfield*, Chart. Th. 373, 34. Tō đam ēcan setle đæs heofonlīcan rīces lǽded wæs *ad æternam regni cælestis sedem translatus est*, Bd. 2, 1; S. 500, 11. Forđon of Breotone nædran on scipum lǽdde wǽron *nam de Brittania adlati serpentes*, Bd. 1, 1; S. 474, 34. [*Laym.* læden *to lead, take*: *Orm.* ledenn ȝuw *to conduct yourselves*: *A. R.* lede lif: *Gen. and Ex.* leden song *to sing*: *O. Sax.* lēdian *to lead, bring, bear*: *O. L. Ger.* lēdian, leidan *ducere, deducere*: *O. Frs.* lēda *to lead, conduct*: *Icel.* leiđa: *O. H. Ger.* leitan: *Ger.* leiten.] v. lād, III. ā-, an-, for-, ge-, in-. on-, ōþ-, ūt-, wiđ-lǽdan.

lǽdan, *to excuse*. v. lǽdend.

Lǽden, es; *n.* I. *Latin, the Latin tongue*:—Is đæt Lēden on smeáunge gewrita eallum đām ōđrum gemǽne *quæ* [i. e. *lingua Latinorum*] *meditatione scripturarum cæteris omnibus est facta communis*, Bd. 1, 1; S. 474, 4. Swā gelǽred đæt hē Grēcisc gereord of miclum dǽle cūþe and Lēden him wæs swā cūþ swā swā Englisc *in tantum institutus, ut Græcam linguam non parva ex parte, Latinam non minus quam Anglorum noverit*, 5, 20; S. 641, 34. Wē ne durron nā māre āwrītan on Englisc đonne đæt Līden hæfþ, ne đa endebirdnisse āwendan būton đam ānum đæt đæt Lēden and đæt Englisc nabbaþ nā āne wīsan on đære sprǽce fadunge [fandunge, Thw.]. Ǽfre se đe āwent of Lēdene on Englisc, ǽfre hē sceal gefadian hit swā đæt đæt Englisc hæbbe his āgene wīsan, elles hit biþ swīđe gedwolsum tō rǽdenne đam đe đæs Lēdenes wīsan ne can, Ælfc. Gen. Thw. 4, 5-11. Hē Grēcisc geleornode mid Lēdene *Græcam cum Latina didicit linguam*, Bd. 5, 23; S. 645, 16. Of Lǽdene on Englisc āreccean *to translate from Latin into English*, Past. pref; Swt. 3, 15. Of Lǽdene tō Engliscum spelle gewendan, Bt. pref; Fox viii, 9. *Glossa* is đonne man glēsþ đa earfoþan word mid eáđran lēdene *faustus* is on ōđrum lēdene *beatus* đæt is eádig *fatuus* is on ōđrum lēdene *stultus* đæt is stunt *a gloss is when the difficult words are explained with easier Latin*; *another Latin word for* faustus *is* beatus i. e. *happy*; *another Latin word for* fatuus *is* stultus i. e. *foolish*, Ælfc. Gr. 50; Som. 51, 43-4. Đa bōc đe is genemned on Lǽden Pastoralis, and on Englisc Hierdebōc, Past. pref.; Swt. 7, 19. Hēr is geleáfa lǽwedum mannum đe đæt lēden ne cunnon, Homl. Th. ii. 596, 2. Gitrahtad on lǽden [Lind. in Latin] *interprætatum*, Mk. Skt. Rush. 5, 41. On lǽden [Lind. lǽddin] *latine*, Jn. Skt. Rush. 19, 20. Didymus, geminus in lætin, Lind. 20, 24, margin. Hī beóþ oft ōðres cynnes on lēden, and ōðres cynnes on englisc; wē cweþaþ on lēden *hic liber*, and on englisc ðeós bōc, Ælfc. Gr. 6; Som. 5, 37-40. On lēden *latine* and *latialiter*, 38; Som. 41, 32. Gelǣrede on lēden and on grēcisc, Homl. Skt. 2, 44: Bd. 4, 1; S. 564, 11. Sum mæssepreóst cūðe be dǣle Lȳden understandan *a certain mass-priest could understand Latin partially*, Ælfc. Gen. Thw. p. 1, 20. [Cf. *Icel.* Lātīna; *f.*] II. *any tongue, speech, language*:—Spasmus ðæt ys on ūre leódene hneccan sār σπασμός, *that is in our language, a pain at the back of the neck*, Lchdm. iii. 110, 1. Mara ðæt ys on ūre lȳden biternys, Ex. 15, 23. Ealle hig sprecaþ ān lȳden *est unum labium omnibus*, Gen. 11, 6. [*Laym. cerno* an Englisc leoden, ich iseo, 29677: *Marh.* þe moneþ ðat on ure ledene is ald englisch esterlið inempnet, 23, 6: *A.R.* on ebreuwische ledene, 136, 24; on englische leodene, 170, 9: *Piers P.* I leve his ledne be in owre lordes ere lyke a pyes chiteryng, 12, 253: *Chauc.* every thing that any foul may in his ledene seyn, F. 435 [see Skeat's note in the Clarendon Press edition]. For the extended use of forms in Romance from *latinus* cf. the passage, given in that note, of Dante's Canzone beginning 'Fresca rosa novella,' 'Cantino gli augelli ciascuno in suo *latino*;' Parad. iii. 63 si che 'l raffigurar m'è piu latino [*clear*]; Convito bk. 2, c. 3 a piu *latinamente* veder la sentenza. In Old Spanish *ladino* is explained 'el que sabe otra lengua o lenguas ademas de la suya.' Is it possible that in the case of English the forms *geþeóde*, *þeód* may have had some influence in giving currency to *lȳden* in the general sense of *language*, by suggesting a connection of this latter form with *leód*?]

Lǣden; *adj. Latin*:—Lēden *latinus*, Ælfc. Gr. 38; Som. 41, 32. Ealle naman lēdenre sprǣce [lēdensprǣce, MS. O.] ðe on a geendiaþ *all latin nouns that end in a*, 7; Som. 6, 55. Ða gemetu gebyriaþ tō lēdenum leóðcræfte *metres belong to latin poetry*, 50; Som. 51, 66. On lēdenum gereorde, Homl. Skt. 6, 367. Lēdene lāreówas maciaþ on sumum namum accusativum on *im*, Ælfc. Gr. 9; Som. 14, 32. Stafum crēciscum and lǣdenum [latinum, Lind.] *litteris græcis et latinis*, Lk. Skt. Rush. 23, 38. See the compounds of which *Lǣden* forms the first part.

Lǣden-bōc; *f. A Latin book*:—Nān man næfþ lēdenbōca angit be fullon būton hē ðone cræft cunne *no man perfectly understands Latin books, unless he know that art* [*grammar*], Ælfc. Gr. 50; Som. 50, 65. Āwriten on lēdenbōcum *written down in Latin books*, Homl. Skt. p. 4, 48. Ða ealdan lǣces gesetton on lēdonbōcum, Lchdm. iii. 152, 1.

lǣdend, es; *m. One who leads* or *brings*:—Se wæs ǣ bringend, lāra lǣdend, Exon. 10a; Th. 9, 27; Cri. 141.

lǣdend, es; *m. One who excuses*:—Ne hyld ðū mīne heortan ðæt ic lǣdend wese lāðra firena *ut non declines cor meum ad excusandas excusationes in peccatis*, Ps. Th. 140, 5. Cf. lādian.

Lǣden-gereord, -gereorde, es; *n. Latin, the Latin language*:—Of lǣdengereorde on englisc, Lchdm. iii. 440, 27.

Lǣden-geþeóde, es; *n. The Latin language*:—Lǣre mon furður on Lǣdengeþiode ða ðe mon furðor lǣran wille ... Ðā ic ðā gemunde hū sió lār Lǣdengeþiódes āfeallen wæs giond Angelcynn *let those to whom it is desired to give further instruction, be instructed in Latin ... When I remembered how the teaching of Latin was decayed throughout England*, Past. Pref; Swt. 7, 13-17.

Lǣdenisc; *adj. Latin*:—On Lēdenisc gereorde ge on Grēcisc, Bd. 4, 1; S. 563, 33. On Lēdennisc, 4, 2; S. 565, 28: 5, 8; S. 622, 1. On lǣddin ɫ lǣdinisc *latine*, Jn. Skt. Kmbl. 19, 20. [Cf. *O. H. Ger.* in latinisgon *latine*.]

Lǣden-nama, an; *m. A Latin noun*:—Gif ðū nāst sumne lēdennaman [lǣden- MS. H] hwylces cynnes hē sȳ *if you do not know some Latin noun, of what gender it is*, Ælfc. Gr. 50; Som. 51, 35.

Lǣden-sprǣc, e; *f. The Latin speech* or *language*:—Ealle naman lēdensprǣce [*also* lēdenre sprǣce] *all Latin nouns*, Ælfc. Gr. 7; Som. 6, 55. On lēdensprǣce, 2; Som. 2, 47. Hālige lāreówas hit āwriton on lēdensprǣce, Homl. Skt. p. 6, 51. Se cræft geopenaþ lēdensprǣce [MS. H. lǣden-] Ælfc. Gr. 50; Som. 50, 65.

Lǣden-stæf, es; *m. A Latin letter*:—Hit wæs āwriten grēcisceon and lēdenstafon *erat scribtum græce et latine*, Jn. Skt. 19, 20. [Cf. *Icel.* Lātīnu-stafr.]

Lǣden-ware; *pl. The Latins, the Romans*:—Lǣdenware wendon hié ealla on hiora āgen geþeóde *the Romans turned them all into their own language*, Past. Pref; Swt. 6, 3. On Lēdenwara gereorde *lingua Latinorum*, Bd. 1, 1; S. 474, 4. *Sui* næfþ nǣnne nominativum nāðer ne mid Grǣcum ne mid Lēdenwarum, Ælfc. Gr. 15; Som. 18, 5. Firgilius wæs mid Lǣdenwarum sēlest *amongst the Romans Virgil was best*, Bt. 41, 1; Fox 244, 5.

Lǣden-word, es; *n. A Latin word*:—Ðās word ne beóþ nā lēdenword gif se *r* byþ āweg gedōn, Ælfc. Gr. 19; Som. 22, 54.

lǣdere, es; *m. A leader, guide*, Cant. Moys. [?], Lye. [Piers P. leder: *O. Frs.* folk-lēdera: *O. H. Ger.* leitari *dux*.]

lǣd-ness, e; *f. A bringing forth, production*:—On ðæs tuddres lǣdnysse *in prolis prolatione*, Bd. 1, 27; S. 493, 21 note. v. forþ-lǣdness.

lǣd-teów. v. lād-teów.

lǣf. v. lāf, leáf.

lǣfan; *p.* de. I. *to leave*:—Ic lǣfe eów sibbe *pacem relinquo vobis*, Jn. Skt. 14, 27. Ic lēfe *lego*, Wrt. Voc. ii. 49, 66. Gif hwæs brōðor deád biþ and lǣfþ his wīf *si cujus frater mortuus fuerit et dimiserit uxorem*, Mk. Skt. 12, 19. Hig ne lǣfaþ on ðē stān ofer stāne *non relinquent in te lapidem super lapidem*, Lk. Skt. 19, 44. Se forma lǣfde his brōðer his wīf *primus reliquit uxorem suam fratri suo*, Mt Kmbl. 22, 25. Ða men ðe hē beæftan him lǣfde ǣr *those men that before he had left behind him*, Chr. 755; Erl. 50, 13. Hié begeáton welan and ūs lǣfdon *they got wealth and left it us*, Past. pref; Swt. 5, 15. Swā hit his yldran begeáton and lētan and lǣfdon ðam tō gewealde ðe hȳ wel ūðan, L. O. 14; Th. i. 184, 3. Ðīnum māgum lǣf folc and rīce *leave to thy kinsmen people and power*, Beo. Th. 2361; B. 1178. Ðonne him forþsīð gebyrige gȳme his hlāford ðæs hē lǣfe *when his death happens, let his lord take charge of what he leaves*, L. R. S. 4; Th. i. 434, 28: 5; Th. i. 436, 9. Ne biþ lǣfed stān uppan stāne, Mt. Kmbl. 24, 2. Ān byþ genumen and ōðer byþ lǣfed, 24, 41. Heora landāre ðe him lǣfed wæs *their landed property that was left them*, Homl. Skt. 4, 82. Nā lǣfedum sǣde *non relicto semine*, Mk. Skt. 12, 20. Ðæt ða bān āne beón lǣfed *so that the bones only are left*, L. Med. ex Quad. 3, 11; Lchdm. i. 340, 26. II. *to remain, be left remaining*:—Gif hwæt lǣfde *if anything remained*, Homl. Th. ii. 40, 14. Hia lǣfdun *superaverunt*, Jn. Skt. Rush. 6, 12. [*Goth.* bi-laibjan *to remain*: *O Sax.* farlēbian *to remain*; lēbōn *to be left*: *O. Frs.* lēva *to leave*: *Icel.* leifa *to leave*: *O. H. Ger.* leibjan *relinquere*: leibēn *to remain.*] DER. be-, ge-, ofer-lǣfan.

lǣfan *to allow*. v. līfan.

læfel, es; *m. A cup, vessel, bowl*:—Læfel *sciffus*, Wrt. Voc. 85, 66. Lævel, 25, 18. Lævil *manile*, 290, 69. Læuel *aquemanile*, Wrt. Voc. ii. 7, 14. Label *aquemale*, 100, 60. Lebil *manile*, 113, 43. Lebl *triplia*, 122, 62. Se læfyl ðe gē forstǣlon wæs mīnum hlāforde swīðe dȳre *scyphus, quem furati estis, ipse est, in quo bibit dominus meus*, Gen. 44, 5. Ǣren fæt, læfel oððe cēc, Lchdm. iii. 292, 9. Of ðæm hlæfle, Chart. Th. 439, 30. Ðonne gesealde Aðelwold biscop his cynehlāforde ānne sylfrenne lefel on fīf pundum *dedit autem Athelwoldus episcopus regi quoddam vas argenteum quinque libras appendens*, 236, 11. Nym mīnne sylfrenan læfyl *scyphum meum argenteum*, Gen. 44, 2. viii læflas *eight cups*, Chart. Th. 429, 36. [*Laym.* water me brohte mid guldene læflen: *O. L. Ger.* lavil *pelvis*: *O. H. Ger.* label, lapel *labium, concha, pelvis*, Grff. ii. 78-9.]

lǣfend, es; *m. One who misleads* [*a traitor*, = lǣwend?]; seductor, Ælfc. Gl. 85; Som. 73, 110; Wrt. Voc. 49, 17.

læfer, e; *f.* I. *a rush*:—Læfer *pirus* [l. *papyrus*], *gladiolus*, Ælfc. Gl. 47; Som. 65, 15; Wrt. Voc. 33, 15: *scirpio*, Wrt. Voc. 69, 9: *scirpia*, 289, 44. Lebr *scirpea*, Wrt. Voc. ii. 119, 81. Eórisc, leber *scirpea*, 120, 17. Genim læfre neoðowearde *take the lower part of a bulrush*, Lchdm. i. 382, 21. II. *a thin plate of metal*:—Gylden læfr *bractea*, Ælfc. Gl. 58; Som. 67, 111; Wrt. Voc. 38, 34. Xerxes beworhte ða bīgelsas mid gyldenum læfrum *Xerxes wrought over the arches of the roof with golden plates*, Homl. Th. ii. 498, 3. Mid læfrum *liscis*, Wrt. Voc. ii. 51, 9. [See E. D. S. Plant Names s. v. *levers*: Grff. ii. 80 leber *scirpus, herba rotunda*.]

læfer-bedd, es; *n. A bed of rushes*:—Læferbed *pirorium* [v. læfer], Ælfc. Gl. 47; Som. 65, 14; Wrt. Voc. 33, 14. [Cf. *liver-ground* the place where the plant grows, E. D. S. Plant Names s. v. levers.]

-læg. v. or-læg.

lǣl, lēl, e; *f.* I. *a pliant twig, withe, whip, switch*:—Lǣl *vimen*, Ælfc. Gl. 46; Som. 65, 13; Wrt. Voc. 33, 12: *vibex*, Wrt. Voc. ii. 88, 4: 96, 35. Lǣla *mastigias* [mastigia *flagrum, flagellum, virga*, Ducange], 55, 25. Lēlan *vibice*, 123, 68. II. *a weal, mark left on the flesh by a stroke from a rod, stripe, mark, bruise, swelling*:—Sylle wunde wið wunde lǣl wið lǣle *reddat vulnus pro vulnere, livorem pro livore*, Ex. 21, 25: L. Ælfc. 19; Th. i. 48, 22. Ne sȳ him blōdig wund līces lǣla ac gē hine gesundne āsettaþ ðǣr gē hine genōman *let there be no bloody wound on him, no stripes on his body, but do you put him down sound, where you took him*, Exon. 42b; Th. 143, 34; Gū. 671. Lēla *livor*, Kent. Gl. 763. Lǣla *nevorum*, Wrt. Voc. ii. 59, 50. Wið lāðum lǣlum and wommum *ad perniones*, L. Med. ex Quad. 2, 20; Lchdm. i. 338, 15. Wið ðæt man lǣla and ōðre sār of līchaman gedō *in order that weals and other sores may be removed from the body*, Herb. 102, 2; Lchdm. i. 216, 21. Wið yfele lǣla οἰδήματα, 153, 4; Lchdm. i. 280, 1. Ðā eode se mæssepreóst tō ðam bysceope and hym eówde ða lǣla ðæra swyngellan ðe hē from dryhtne onfēng *then the priest went to the bishop and shewed him the marks of the scourging that he had received from the Lord*, Shrn. 98, 18. [(?) *Scot.* leill *a single stitch in marking on a sampler.*] v. lǣlan, lǣlian; *and cf.* [*for the double use*] walu.

lǣlan *to become black and blue with blows, to be bruised*:—Geseoh nū seolfes swæðe ðīn swāt āgeát blōdige stīge līc lǣlan *see now thy track, where thy blood hath poured forth, a bloody path, see thy body bruised*, Andr. Kmbl. 2884; An. 1445. *Kemble and Grimm read* līclǣlan *spots* [*of blood*] *on the body, but cf.* lǣlian.

lǣlian *to become black and blue*; livescere, Wrt. Voc. ii. 50, 41.

laembis lieg. v. lendis lieg.

lǽmen; *adj. Made of clay, earthen:*—Lǽmen fæt *lagena*, Ælfc. Gl. 26; Som. 60, 93; Wrt. Voc. 25, 33. Lēmen fet *vas fictile*, Kent. Gl. 1001. Lǽmen crocca *testa*, Ps. Th. 21, 13. Lǽmen fæt *a vessel of earth*, Exon. 74 a; Th. 277, 2; Jul. 574: L. Ath. iv. 7; Th. i. 226, 15. Lǽmene fatu *fictilia* vel *samia*; reádde lǽmene fatu *aretina* [MS. *alsierina*], Ælfc. Gl. 66; Som. 69, 94, 95; Wrt. Voc. 41, 46, 47. Lǽmene fatu beóþ on ofne āfandode, Homl. Th. i. 554, 33. Leomo lǽmena *limbs of clay*, Exon. 8 a; Th. 2, 6; Cri. 15. Lǽmina *fictilia*, Wrt. Voc. ii. 36, 35. [*O. H. Ger.* leimin *fictilis, luteus.*]

lǽn, lān [*v. under* lǽn-land], e; *f.* I. *a loan, grant, gift:*—Lǽn *commodum*, Ælfc. Gl. 14; Som. 58, 5; Wrt. Voc. 21, 1. Lǽn *commodum, lucrum*, Wrt. Voc. ii. 132, 1: *depositum* i. e. *commendatum*, 139, 1. Borg *vel* lǽn *fenus* i. e. *lucrum, usura*, 148, 24. Tō hwīle lǽn *momentum*, Ælfc. Gl. 15; Som. 58, 47; Wrt. Voc. 21, 36. Ðæt hridder tōbærst on ðære lǽne. Seó fōstormōdor weóp for ðære āwyrdan lǽne *the sieve broke in two during the loan. The foster-mother wept for the injured loan*, Homl. Th. ii. 154, 16. Sum man sceolde āgyldan healf pund and wæs ðearle geswenct for ðære lǽne *a certain man had to pay back half a pound, and was exceedingly harassed on account of the loan*, 176, 35. Hē tō ðære lǽne fācn ne wiste *he knew of no ill-design in the loan* [*of arms*], L. Alf. pol. 19; Th. i. 74, 7. Se ðe æt his nēhstan hwæt tō lǽne ābit *qui a proximo suo quidquid mutuo postulaverit*, Ex. 22, 14. Ðē biddaþ manega þeóda ðīnes þinges tō lǽne and ðū ne bitst nānne *fœnerabis multis gentibus, et ipse a nullo fœnus accipiens*, Deut. 28, 12. Tō lǽne syllan *mutuum dare*, 15, 8. Tō lǽne beón *to be lent*, Past. pref; Swt. 9, 7. Lǽne syllaþ *mutuum date*, Lk. Skt. 6, 35. Ðā meahte heó wīde geseón þurh ðæs lāðan lǽn *then could she widely see through the fiend's gift*, Cd. 29; Th. 38, 3; Gen. 601. Lǽn Godes, ælmihtiges gife, 32; Th. 43, 18; Gen. 692. Ðeáh hē him nānra ōðerra lǽna [*but* Cott. MS. leana] ne wēne *though he expect no other benefits*, Bt. 24, 3; Fox 84, 1. II. [*in connection with land*] *a grant that may be recalled, lease, fee, fief:*—Landes lǽn *precarium*, Ælfc. Gl. 14; Som. 58, 6; Wrt. Voc. 21, 2. Mon gerehte ðæt yrfe cinge forðon hē wæs cinges mon and Ordlāf fēng tō his londe forðon hit wæs his lǽn ðæt hē onsǽte hē ne meahte nā his forwyrcan *the property went to the king because he* [*Helmstan*] *was the king's man; and Ordlaf took the land, for the land that he* [*Helmstan*] *occupied was held in fee from Ordlaf, so he* [*Helmstan*] *could not forfeit it*, Chart. Th. 173, 4. v. Cod. Dip. Kmbl. i. lix. Ðā oferbād Ælfēh his brōðor and fēng tō his lǽne [cf. geūðe hē him &c. 9-12] *then Ælfeh survived his brother, and resumed the lands he had granted to him;* mortuo Ælfrico Ælfegus statim omnia præstita sua, quæ fratri suo viventi præstiterat [resumpsit], 272, 13, 21. Ǽlcne man lyst siððan hē ǽnig cotlȳf on his hlāfordes lǽne getimbred hæfþ ðæt hē hine mōte hwīlum ðar on gerestan and his on gehwilce wīsan tō ðære lǽnan [*is this a form* lǽne, an; *f.* = lǽn, *or can it be the adj.* lǽne *transitory, as the opposite of which* ǽce *occurs afterwards, with the noun that it qualifies omitted?*] tilian ōþ ðone fyrst ðe hē bōcland and ǽce yrfe geearnige *every man, after he has built any cottage on land granted him by his lord, desires that he may rest himself therein at times, and in some fashion provide for himself from the grant* [*?*], *until the time that he has gained a freehold and a perpetual possession*, Shrn. 164, 2-8. Æþelwald and Alhmund his sunu hit woldon habban on his lǽne and hīna *Ethelwald and his son Alhmund would hold it* [*certain land*] *of him* [*the bishop*] *and of the convent in fee*, Chart. Th. 140, 32. Denewulf bisceop and ða hȳwan on Wintanceastre ænlǽnaþ Ælfrēde his deg xl hīda landes æt Alresforda æfter ðære lǽna ðe Tūnbryht bisceop ǽr ālēnde his yldran *bishop Denewulf and the convent at Winchester lease to Alfred for his life xl hides of land at Alresford, according to the lease that Tunbryht granted before to his parents*, 147, 29. [*O. E. Hom.* se riche *lane* as beoð þeos sustren, i. 257, 22: *A. R. Ayenb.* lone *what is lent: Piers P.* lone, loone, lene. The double form of the word in later English may be partly owing to Scandinavian influence. Icelandic has both lēn; *n. a fief, fee, grant*, and lān; *n.* (though an older feminine is indicated) *a loan, fief. O. Frs.* lēn; *n. a grant, fee, fief: O. H. Ger.* lēhan; *n. fœnus, beneficium, usura, præstatio: Ger.* lehen; *n. fief, fee.*] v. Kemble's Saxons in England, i. 310.

lǽnan; *p.* de *To lend, grant, lease:*—Lǽnþ *commodat*, Ps. Spl. 36, 27: 111, 5: Blickl. Gl. Lēnþ *fenerator*, Kent. Gl. 699. Gif gē lǽnaþ ðām ðe gē eft æt onfōþ hwilc þanc is eów sōþlīce synfulle synfullum lǽnaþ *si mutuum dederitis his a quibus speratis accipere quæ gratia est vobis? nam et peccatores peccatoribus fœnerantur*, Lk. Skt. 6, 34. Hig lǽnaþ eów and gē ne lǽnaþ him *ipse fœnerabit tibi et tu non fœnerabis ei*, Deut. 28, 44. Ðæt hē hæbbe ðæt land æt Ludintūne iii. geár for ðām þreóm pundum ðe hē lǽnde, Chart. Th. 434, 33. Lǽn mē þrȳ hlāfas *commoda mihi tres panes*, Lk. Skt. 11, 5. Lǽne mē ða bōc tō rǽdenne *commoda mihi librum ad legendum*, Ælfc. Gr. 24; Som. 25, 20. Ne lǽne ðīnum brēðer nān þing tō hīre *non fœnerabis fratri tuo ad usuram pecuniam*, Deut. 23, 19. Ys forboden ðæt hē his feoh tō nānum unrihtum gafole ne lǽne *prohibitum est, pecuniam suam ullo injusto fœnore mutuam dare*, L. Ecg. P. ii. 30; Th. ii. 194, 16. Ymb ðæt land ðæ ðū mǽ firmdig tō wǽræ ðæt ic dǽ ēndæ *de terra illa, de qua egisti apud me, ut ego eam tibi commodarem*, Chart. Th. 162, 15. Him drihten mihte spēde lǽnan *the Lord could grant him success*, Cd. 95; Th. 124. 8; Gen. 2059. Hlǽnan *mutuare*, Wrt. Voc. ii. 56, 10. [*Laym.* lenen *to grant:*—þis lond he hire lende, 228: *Orm.* lenen: *Chauc.* lene: *Prompt. Parv.* leendyn *presto, fenero: O. Fris.* lēna *to lend. grant: Icel.* lēna *to grant;* lāna *to lend: O. H. Ger.* lēhanon *mutuari: Ger.* lehnen.] DER. ā-, be-, ge-, on-lǽnan.

lǽn-dagas; *pl. m. The days granted to a man in which to live, the time during which a man lives:*—Sceolde lǽndaga [MS. þend daga] æþeling ende gebīdan worulde līfes *the end of the days that had been granted, of life in this world, was to come upon the prince*, Beo. Th. 4672; B. 2341. Swā sceal ǽghwylc mon ālǽtan lǽndagas, 5175; B. 2591. Cf. lǽne.

lænding. v. lending.

lǽne, an; *f.* = [?] lǽn, Shrn. 164, 6. v. lǽn II.

lǽne; *adj. Granted as a* lǽn [q. v.], *granted for a time only, not permanent, transitory, temporary, frail* [generally used as an epithet of things of this world when they are contrasted with those of the next]:—Ac ic wolde witan hweðer ðē þuhte be ðam ðe ðū hæfst hweðer hyt wēre ðe lǽne ðe ǽce *but I would know whether you thought of what you have, that it was temporary or eternal*, Shrn. 176, 29. Hēr biþ feoh lǽne hēr biþ freónd lǽne hēr biþ mon lǽne *in this world shall not wealth endure, or friend, or man*, Exon. 78 a; Th. 292, 32; Wand. 108: Elen. Kmbl. 2539; El. 1271. Ðis lǽne līf ðe wē lifiaþ on *this transitory life in which we live*, Ps. Th. 62, 3. Ðis deáde līf, lǽne on londe, Exon. 82 a; Th. 309, 32; Seef. 66. Ðeós lǽne gesceaft [*the world*], 20 a; Th. 52, 34; Cri. 843. Ðis is lǽne dreám [*the present life*], Cd. 169; Th. 211, 25; Exod. 531. Lǽnes landes bryce *fructus*, Wrt. Voc. ii. 39, 31. Lǽnan līfes leahtras, Exon. 62 b; Th. 229, 16; Ph. 456: Cd. 156; Th. 194, 29; Exod. 268. Ende him on becom ðisses lǽnan līfes *there came upon him an end of this life which is but for a moment*, Blickl. Homl. 113, 8. Ne biddan wē ūrne Drihten ðyses lǽnan welan, ne ðyssa eorþlīcra geofa ðe hrædlīce from monnum gewītaþ, 20, 11. Se dæg wæs fruma ðyses lǽnan leóhtes, and hē biþ fruma ðæs ēcan æfterfylgendan, 133, 10. Mā dereþ monna gehwylcum mōdes unþeáw ðonne mettrymnes lǽnes līchoman, Bt. Met. Fox 26, 225; Met. 26, 119. Eádgār ðis wāce forlēt līf ðis lǽne, Chr. 975; Erl. 124, 32. Suelce hē cwǽde ic eów onlǽne ðās gewītendan and ic eów geselle ða þurwuniendan. Gif ðonne ðæs monnes mōd and his lufu biþ behleápen eallunga on ða lǽnan sibbe ðonne ne mæg hē nǽfre becuman tō ðære ðe him geseald is *relinquo scilicet transitoriam, do mansuram. Si ergo in ea cor, quæ relicta est, figitur, nunquam ad illam quæ danda est, pervenitur*, Past. 46, 5; Swt. 350, 12-16. Monnes līfdagas lǽne syndan, Ps. Th. 102, 14. Ǽghwilc þing ðe on ðīs andweardan līfe līcaþ lǽnu sindon eorþlīcu þing ā fleóndu *everything that pleases in this present life, transient are they, earthly things ever fleeting*, Bt. Met. Fox 21, 58; Met. 21, 29. Sceoldon sēcan dreám æfter deáþe, and ðās lǽnan gestreón, īdle ǽhtwelan forhogodon, Apstls. Kmbl. 166; Ap. 83. Gylt gefremmaþ þurh līchaman lēne geþohtas, Ps. C. 50, 15; Ps. Grn. ii. 277, 15. [*O. E. Homl.* ȝif we forleosað þas lenan worldþing, i. 105, 30: *O. Sax.* lēhni (fehu, werold).] DER. un-lǽne.

lǽne-, lǽn-lic; *adj. Transitory, transient, not enduring:*—Cwæþ se godspellere Martha and Maria getācniaþ ðis lǽnelīce līf and ðis gewītendlīce, Blickl. Homl. 73. 9. Hēr is seó lǽnlīc winsumnes ac ðǽr is seó syngale nearones *in this world is the delight that endures not, but in the next is the anxiety that continues for ever*, L. E. I. pref; Th. ii. 394, 7.

lǽnend, es; *m. A creditor, lender:*—Lǽnend *fenerator* vel *commodator* vel *creditor, redditor*, Wrt. Voc. ii. 148, 26. Twegen gafolgyldon wǽron sumum lǽnende *duo debitores erant cuidam feneratori*, Lk. Skt. 7, 41.

lǽnend-līc; *adj. Transitory, transient:*—Uton geþencan hū lǽnendlīc ðeós woruld ys, Wulfst. 136, 27. v. lǽne-līc.

lǽnere, es; *m. A creditor, lender:*—Lǽnere *creditor*, Ælfc. Gl. 113; Som. 79, 124; Wrt. Voc. 60, 29. [*Ayenb.* lenere: *Wick.* leenere: *Prompt. Parv.* lendare *fenerator, creditor: O. Frs.* lēner: *O. H. Ger.* int-lēhenari *fœnerator.*]

lǽnian, Gen. 50, 15. v. leánian.

lǽn-land, es; *n. Land let on lease, which was never out of the possession of the lessor:*—Ðonne is ðæs landes iii hīda ðe Ōswald arcebisceop bōcaþ Eádrīce his þegne swā swā hē hit ǽr hæfde tō lānlande *there are three hides of land that archbishop Oswald conveys by charter to the possession of Eadric his thane, such as before he held by lease*, Cod. Dip. Kmbl. iii. 165, 5. Fīf hīda ðe Ōswald bōcaþ Eádrīce swā swā hē hit ǽr hæfde tō lǽnlande, 217, 20. Wē wrītaþ ðæt hē hæbbe hit swā rūm tō bōclande swā hē ǽr hæfde tō lǽnlonde, 258, 29. Eall ðæt yrfe ðæ ic hæbbe on lǽnelendum, v. 333, 21. v. lǽn; and see Cod. Dip. Kmbl. i. lxii: Kemble's Saxons in England, i. c. xi.

lǽnung. v. feoh-lǽnung.

læpeldre *a dish, platter:*—Læpeldre fæt *paropsis* vel *catinus*, Ælfc. Gl. 26; Som. 60, 89; Wrt. Voc. 25, 29. Se ðe bedypþ on disce mid mē his hlāf on læpeldre *qui intingit mecum manum in parapside* [Mt. 26, 23], Homl. Th. ii. 244, 4.

-læpped *having laps* or *lobes:*—Fīf-læppedu, Lchdm. ii. 160, 12.

læppa, an; *m. A skirt* [*of a garment*], *lappet, lobe* [*of the ear* &c.],

lap [in dew-*lap*; cf. also *lop*-eared], *a detached portion, a district*:—Læppa oððe ende *ora*, Ælfc. Gr. 50; Som. 51, 30. Hȳ mōstan ðam læppan friþ gebicgean ðe hȳ under cyngces hand oferhæfdon *they might purchase peace for that district which, subject to the king, they ruled over*, L. Eth. ii. 1; Th. i. 284, 13. On læppan his hrægles *in oram vestimenti ejus*, Ps. Spl. C. 132, 3. Hē genam his loðan ǣnne læppan tō tācne ðæt hē his geweald āhte, Past. 3, 2; Swt. 36, 6. Hē forcearf his mentles ǣnne læppan *oram chlamydis ejus abscidit*, 28, 6; Swt. 197, 21: 199, 11, 17. Læppan *vel* fnado *fimbria*, Ælfc. Gl. 64; Som. 68, 128; Wrt. Voc. 40, 33. Lappan *lacinia*, Wrt. Voc. ii. 51, 51. Lifre læppan *vel* þearmas *fibræ*, 76; Som. 71, 110; Wrt. Voc. 45, 16. Hēr sint tācn āheardodre lifre ge on ðām læppum and filmenum *here are symptoms of a hardened liver both on the lobes and the membranes*, L. M. 2, 21; Lchdm. ii. 204, 4. Sió lifer hæfþ fīf læppan, 2, 17; Lchdm. ii. 198, 1. [*P. L. S.* þe lappe of oure loverdes cloþ, 21, 29: *Laym.* leyde uppe his lappe [1st MS. bærm], 30261: *Chauc.* lappe: *Piers P.* he shal lese for hir loue a lappe of caritatis, 2, 35: *Prompt. Parv.* lappe, skyrte *gremium*, p. 287 where see note: *O. Frs.* lappa: *Dut.* lap *a remnant, patch*: *Dan.* lap *a patch*: *O. H. Ger.* lappa *lacinia*: *Ger.* lapp.] DER. eár-, fræt-, lifer- læppa.

lǣr. v. lār.

lǣran; *p.* de *To teach, instruct, educate, to give religious teaching, to preach, to teach a particular tenet* or *dogma, to enjoin a rule, to exhort, admonish, advise, persuade, suggest*:—Ic lǣre *instruo*, Ælfc. Gr. 29; Som. 32, 4: *erudio*, 30; Som. 34, 60. Ic tȳ oððe lǣre *imbuo*, 28, 3; Som. 32, 46. Ic eów lǣre Godes ege *timorem Domini docebo vos*, Ps. Th. 33, 11. Ānra manna gehwylcne ic myngie and lǣre ðæt ānra gehwylc hine sylfne ongyte *I admonish and exhort every man to understand himself*, Blickl. Homl. 107, 11. Ic lǣre *persuadeo*, Ælfc. Gl. 99; Som. 76, 107; Wrt. Voc. 54, 50. For ðon ic lǣre ðæt ðæt tempel wē on fȳre forbærnon *unde suggero ut templa igni contradamus*, Bd. 2, 13; S. 516, 33. Ne mæg ic ðæt dōn ðæt ðū mē lǣrest *non hoc facere possum quod suggeris*, 2, 12; S. 513, 24. Ðū lǣrst ūs *tu doces nos*, Jn. Skt. 9, 34. Paulus ðæt ilce lǣreþ, Blickl. Homl. 175, 13. Lērþ *erudit*, Kent. Gl. 470. Wē lǣraþ ðæt . . . *we enjoin that*, L. Edg. C; Th. ii. 244–258. Gyf se dēma ðiss geāxaþ wē lǣraþ hyne and gedōþ eów sorhleáse *si hoc auditum fuerit a præside, nos suadebimus ei et securos vos faciemus*, Mt. Kmbl. 28, 14. Ic lǣrde sibbe ymb manige þeóda; ǣrest ic lǣrde ðæt men lufodan hié him betweónan . . . Fæderas ic lǣrde ðæt hié heora bearnum ðone þeódscipe lǣrdon Drihtnes egsan, Blickl. Homl. 185, 10–20. Se Hālga Gāst hié ǣghwylc gōd lǣrde, 131, 30. Lǣrde Paulinus Godes word *prædicabat Paulinus verbum*, Bd. 2, 16; S. 519, 18. Ðæt Agustinus Brytta biscopas lǣrde and monade *ut Augustinus Brittonum episcopos monuerit*, 2, 2; S. 502, 2. Lǣrde hine and manede *ammonens*, 2, 12; S. 514, 37: Blickl. Homl. 19, 36: Chr. 1042; Erl. 169, 16. Ðā lǣrde se cāsere hine ðæt hē forlēte Cristes geleáfan *the emperor advised him to leave the faith of Christ*, Shrn. 83, 14. Ðā gewunode se cyning ðæt hē hine trymede and lǣrde *solebat eum hortari*, Bd. 3. 22; S. 552, 10. Hī lǣrde tō healdenne reogollīces līfes þeódscipe *disciplinam vitæ regularis custodire docuit*, S. 553, 10. Hē ful baldlīce beornas lǣrde *full boldly he exhorted the warriors*, Byrht. Th. 140, 61; By. 311. Se wiðermēda wordum lǣrde folc tō gefeohte, Andr. Kmbl. 2392; An. 1198. Leóde lǣrde on līfes weg *he brought people by his teaching into the way of life*, 339; An. 170. Hē lǣrde men geornlīce tō Godes geleáfan *he urged men in his teaching to a belief in God*, Shrn. 125, 8. Se bisceop hié lǣrede ðæt hié sendon tō ðæm pāpan *the bishop advised them to send to the pope*, Blickl. Homl. 205, 18. Scottas lǣrdon geonge and ealde on reogollīcne þeódscipe *imbuebantur præceptoribus Scottis parvuli Anglorum, una cum majoribus, studiis et observatione disciplinæ regularis*, Bd, 3, 3; S. 526, 9. Hī hī on metercræfte and on tungolcræfte and on gramatisccræfte tȳdan and lǣrdon, 4, 2; S. 565, 26. Hī him līfes weg bodedon and lǣrdon *verbum ei vitæ prædicarent*, 1, 25; S. 487, 8. Ða ðe bododan and lǣrdon *qui dogmatizabant*, 5, 19; S. 639, 34. Hī hī trymedon and lǣrdon ðæt hī fæsten worhtan, 1, 12; S. 480, 31. Ðā cleopedon his þegnas him tō and hine bǣdon and geornlīce lǣrdon ðæt hē hine ofslōge *cum eum viri sui ad feriendum Saul accenderent*, Past. 28, 6; Swt. 197, 18. Mē bǣdon and lǣrdon Rōmāne ðæt ic gewāt heonon onweg, Blickl. Homl. 191, 13. Hine hys yldran tō woruldfolgaþe tyhton and lǣrdon, 211, 28. Sume lǣrdon ðæt hine mon onweg ācurfe *quidam abscidendum esse dicebant*, Bd. 4, 32; S. 611, 20. Lǣr ūs *doce nos*, Lk. Skt. 11, 1: Ps. Th. 118, 12. Ðū ðē lǣr be ðon, Beo. Th. 3449; B. 1722. Lǣraþ ðæt hig healdon ealle ða þing ðe ic eów bebeád, Mt. Kmbl. 28, 20. Lǣre Pharao *ut suggeras Pharaoni*, Gen. 40, 14. Ða men ðe bearn habban lǣran hié ðām rihtne þeódscipe, Blickl. Homl. 109, 17. Heora scrifbēc tǣcan and lǣran, 43, 8. Se mæg hine sylfne be ðare bysene lǣran *he may teach himself by this example*, 101, 6. Hē ongan lǣran tō healdenne ða þing, Bd. 4, 5; S. 571, 41. Lange sceal leornian se ðe lǣran sceal *long must he learn who is to teach*, L. Ælfc. P. 46; Th. ii. 384, 15: L. I. P. 14; Th. ii. 322, 8. Mid brōðorlīce lufan hī manigean and lǣran *eis fraterna admonitione suadere*, Bd. 2, 2; S. 502, 8. Wæs ic seald tō fēdanne and tō lǣranne *datus sum educandus*, Bd. 5, 24; S. 647, 22. Cyningas and rīce men sendon heora dōhtor ðider [*France*] tō lǣranne *filias suas erudiendas mittebant*, 3, 8; S. 531, 18. Ðæt willsume weorc ðām þeódum godspell tō lǣranne *desideratum evangelizandi gentibus opus*, 5, 11; S. 625, 33. Godcunde lāre tō lǣranne on Angelþeóde, 2, 2; S. 502, 10. Tō lǣrenne, Blickl. Homl. 233, 17. Lǣrende and strangende hira heortan, 249, 17. Lǣrendum Athamnano *instante Adamnano*, Bd. 5, 15; S. 635, 10. Cneohtas and geonge men tȳdde and lǣrde wǣron *pueri erudirentur*, 3, 18; S. 546, 1: Elen. Kmbl. 345: El. 173. [*Orm. Laym.* læren: *A. R.* leaven, leren: *Gen. and Ex.* leren *to learn*: *R. Glouc.* lere *to learn*: *Piers P.* lere: *Chauc.* lere *to learn*: *Prompt. Parv.* lerȳn *or* techȳn another *doceo*; lerȳn *or* receyue lore of anothere *addisco*: *Goth.* laisjan *to teach*: *O. Sax.*, *O. L. Ger.* lērian: *O. Frs.* lēra: *Icel.* læra *to teach*; but in modern usage *to learn*: *Dan.* lære *to teach, learn*: *O. H. Ger.* lēran *docere, instruere, monere, redarguere*: *Ger.* lehren.] DER. ā-, for-, ge-lǣran.

-lǣred. v. ge-, sam-, þurh-, un-lǣred.

lærest, *least*:—Æt ðam lærestan wlitewamme iii scillingas and at ðam māran vi scill. *for the smallest disfigurement of the face iii shillings, for the greater vi shillings*, L. Ethb. 56; Th. i. 16, 15. As this seems to be the only instance in which this form occurs, Schmid suggests that *r* is wrongly written for *s*, but the O. Frs. *lerest* may justify the presence of the *r*. v. læssa.

lǣrestre, an; *f. A female teacher, an instructress, preceptress*:—Lǣrestre *doctrix*, Ælfc. Gr. 9, 64; Zup. 71, 8. Siððan clypode heó hire tō ða ylcan lǣrestran, Homl. Th. ii. 543, 8. [Cf. *Wick.* lerere: *Prompt. Parv.* lerare *doctor, instructor*: *Goth.* laisareis: *O. H. Ger.* lērari: *Ger.* lehrer; *but the form to which these point, and which would be a masculine corresponding to* lǣrestre, *seems not to occur, the usual word being* lāreów.]

lǣr-gedēfe:—Leorna lāre lǣr gedēfe wene ðec in wīsdōm. Exon. 806; Th. 303, 31; Fä. 61. *In this passage Ettmüller and Grein take* lǣrgedēfe *as an adj. but* lǣr *may well be, as Thorpe takes it, the imperat. of* lǣran, *which verb naturally accompanies* leornian.

lǣrig. A word of doubtful meaning occurring only twice:—Bærst bordes lǣrig, Byrht, Th. 140, 6; By. 284. Ne him bealubenne gebiden hæfdon ofer linde lǣrig, Cd. 154; Th. 192, 29; Exod. 239. Grein suggests comparison with λαισήϊον *a buckler, target*, and that the word like *rand* may mean *the rim of the shield* and also *the body of the shield*. Either rendering is admissible so far as the sense is concerned.

lǣring, e; *f. Instruction, teaching* [see next two words and *Icel.* læring *teaching, learning*: *O. H. Ger.* lērunga *institutio, doctrina*.]

lǣring-mǣden, es; *n. A girl who is receiving instruction, a female pupil*:—Nim nū lāreów and bryng ðīnum lǣrincgmǣdene *take now, master, and bring them to thy pupil*, Th. Ap. 20, 13. [Cf. *Icel.* læri-mær *a female disciple*.]

lǣring-mann, es; *m. A disciple*; discipulus, R. Ben. 5, Lye. [Cf. *Icel.* læri-sveinn *a disciple*.]

lǣre; *adj. Empty* [see next word.] [*O. and N.* lere house: *R. Glouc.* was þis lond of Romaynes almest lere, 81, 1: *O. Sax.* lāri: *O. H. Ger.* lāri *inanis*: *Ger.* leer.] v. ge-lǣr.

lǣr-ness, e: *f. Emptiness*:—Se cymþ of tō micelre lǣrnesse *it* [*hiccup*] *comes of too much emptiness*, L. M. 1, 18; Lchdm. ii. 60, 20.

lǣs, we, e; *f. A pasture, leasow* [still found in local names]:—Lǣs *pascua*; gemǣne lǣs *compascuus ager*, Ælfc. Gl. 96; Som. 76, 44, 47; Wrt. Voc. 53, 51, 54. Se wudu and seó lǣs is gemǣne tō ðām ān and twentigum hīdum, Cod. Dip. Kmbl. v. 319, 28. Sceáp lǣswe ðīnre *oves pascuæ tuæ*, Ps. Spl. 73, 1: 78, 14: 94, 7: 99, 4: 22, 1. Hit is gescræpe on lǣswe sceápa and neáta *alendis apta pecoribus ac jumentis*, Bd. 1, 1; S. 473, 14. Ic wylle hī healdan on genihtsumere lǣse *I will keep them in an abundant pasture*, Homl. Th. i. 242, 15. On gemǣnre lǣse, L. Edg. 5, 8; Th. i. 274, 26: 9; Th. i. 276, 1: L. R. S. 12; Th. i. 438, 14. Ic drīfe sceáp mīne tō heora leáse *mino oves meas ad pascua* . . . Ic lǣde hig tō lǣse *ego duco eos* [boves] *ad pascua*, Coll. Monast. Th. 20, 13, 27. Ne land ne lǣsse [lǣswe? MS. H. lǣse], L. O. 14; Th. i. 184, 7. Fint lǣse [lēsua, Lind: lēswe, Rush.] *pascua inveniet*, Jn. Skt. 10, 9. Waldon ða swāngerēfan ða lǣswe forður gedrīfan, Chart. Th. 70, 20. Lǣswe *pascua*, Wrt. Voc. 80, 49. Lǣsa *pascua*, Ælfc. Gr. 13; Som. 16, 24. Mid heora fæder heordum on lǣsum *in pascendis gregibus patris*, Gen. 37, 12. [*O. E. Homl.* leswe; *acc*: *Laym.* leswa [2nd MS. lesewes]; *pl*: *A. R.* leswe: *Wick.* leswe, lesewe: *R. Glouc.* lese. Tusser uses *lease = pasture*.] v. eten-lǣs.

lǣs, e; *f. A letting* [*of blood*]:—Blōdes lǣs *bloodletting*, L. M. 3, 47, cont.; Lchdm. ii. 302, 23. Cf. Þurh ða blōdlǣse geclǣnsad, 2, 23; Lchdm. ii. 210, 18; and v. blōd-læswu, lǣtan: cf. ǣs *and* etan.

LÆS; *adv. also used in conjunctional phrases and as a noun. Less, lest*:—Hió mē lytle læs lāðe woldan ðisses eorþweges ende gescrīfan *paulominus consummaverunt me in terra*, Ps. Th. 118, 87. Nōht ðon læs *nihilominus*, Bd. 2, 14; S. 516, 6. Nōhte ðon læs, 3, 6; S. 528, 10. Nōhte ðȳ læs unārǣfnendlīc *non minus intolerabile*, 5, 12; S. 627, 38. Cȳð ðis folc ðæt hig ne gān ofer ða gemǣro ðē læs hig swelton *contestare populum ne forte velit transcendere terminos et pereat*, Ex. 19, 21, 24: Ps. Th. 68, 14. Ðē les *ne*, Kent. Gl. 161. Wē hine mid swā micle māran unryhte oferhycgeaþ swā hē læs forhogaþ ðæt hē ūs tō him spane, Past. 52, 4; Swt. 407, 18. Ðȳ læs ðe, Homl. Th. i. 88, 32: Gen. 32, 11. Ān læs twentig *undeviginti*, twâm læs twentig *duodeviginti*, Ælfc. Gr. 49; Som. 50, 41. Hé rîxode twâ læs xxx geára, Chr. 641; Erl. 27, 16. Óðrum healfum læs ðe xxx wintra, 901; Erl. 96, 24. Ðý ilcan sumera forwearþ nó læs ðonne xx scipa *that same summer no less than twenty ships were lost*, 897; Erl. 96, 14. Ðâ wæs âgangen fîf þûsend geára and âne geáre læs ðonne twâ hund, Shrn. 29, 34. Gif læs manna beó *sin minor est numerus*, Ex. 12, 4. Swâ man mâre sprycþ swâ him læs manna gelýfeþ *the more a man speaks, the fewer men believe him*, Prov. Kmbl. 38. Swâ mid læs worda swâ mid mâ *whether with fewer words or with more*, Bt. 35, 5; Fox 166, 12. Forðon hit næs þeáw on ðæm tîdum ðæt mon ǽnig wæl on ða healfe rîmde ðe ðonne wieldre wæs bûton ðǽr ðý læs ofslagen wǽre *quia scriptorum veterum mos est, ex ea parte quæ vicerit occisorum non commemorare numerum: nisi forte cum adeo pauci cadunt*, Ors. 4, 1; Swt. 156, 22. Ðes dæg is geweorþod mid manegum godcundum geofum næs ðara gifena læs ðonne Drihtnes ǽrist and eác ðonne seó gifu ðæs Hâlgan Gâstes *this day is distinguished by many divine gifts, no less gifts than the Lord's resurrection, and also than the gift of the Holy Ghost*, Blickl. Homl. 133, 3. Âhte ic holdra ðý læs, Beo. Th. 929; B. 487: 3897; B. 1946: Exon. 103 a; Th. 391, 27; Rä. 10, 11. Ða ðe læs âgun 33 b; Th. 106, 33; Gû. 50. Læsast brûcan, 37 b; Th. 122, 22; Gû. 309. Licgende beám læsest grôweþ, 91 b; Th. 343, 19; Gn. Ex. 159. Ðonne hî læst wênaþ *when they least expect*, Ps. Th. 13, 9: 10, 2: Homl. Th. ii. 104, 12: Bd. 4, 25; S. 601, 30. Hû gê fullecost mâgon Gode þiówian ðæt eów læst þing mierþ *quod facultatem præbeat sine impedimento Domino observiendi*, Past. 51, 7; Swt. 401, 17. [*O. Sax.* les.]

læsast, læsest. v. læs, læssa.

læs-boren; *adj. Of inferior birth*:—Wê lǽraþ ðæt ǽnig forþboren preóst ne forseó ðone læsborenan *we enjoin that any highborn priest do not despise the one of inferior birth*, L. Edg. C. 13; Th. ii. 246, 21.

lǽs-hosum = [?] lǽst-hosan; *pl. Some species of covering for the foot, socks without soles*:—Fôt-leáste [= -lǽste], lǽshosum [= lǽsthosan] *cernui* ['*cernui* socci sunt sine solea,' Ducange], Ælfc Gl. 28; Som. 61, 17; Wrt. Voc. 26, 16. v. lǽst, lǽst-wyrhta.

lǽsian. v. lǽswian.

læssa; *adj. cpve. Less*:—Se ðe læssa ys ys on heofena rîce him mâre *qui autem minor est in regno cælorum, major est illo*, Mt. Kmbl. 11, 11. Hwæðere hê ðâm ðe on sceare mâran wǽron on ðâm mægnum eáþmôdnesse and hýrsumnesse nôhte ðon læssa wæs *verum eis quæ tonsura majores sunt virtutibus humilitatis et obedientiæ non mediocriter insignitus*, Bd. 5, 19; S. 637, 18. Ðæt mâre leóht and ðæt læsse leóht *luminare majus et luminare minus*, Gen. 1, 16. Gaderodon sum mâre sum læsse *collegerunt, alius plus, alius minus*, Ex. 16, 17. Ne eart ðû læst [læsæst, Rush.] *nequaquam minima es*, Mt. Kmbl. 2, 6. Nis ðæt læsast, Exon. 43 b; Th. 148, 7; Gû. 741. Ðara ânum ðeáh hit se læsta wǽre and se heánosta *to one of them, though it were the least and the humblest*, Blickl. Homl. 169, 22. Ðæt læste fæc *parvissimum spatium*, Bd. 2, 13; S. 516, 20. Ðone læstan dǽl þunges *the least bit of aconite*, L. M. 2, 52; Lchdm. ii. 268, 31. Ðara læstena worda hreówsian *se de tenuissima verbi laceratione reprehendunt*, Past. 28, 6; Swt. 199, 15. Se ðe tôwyrpþ ân of ðysum læstum [leasestum, Lind: læsest, Rush.] bebodum... se biþ læst [leasest, Lind: se læsesta, Rush.] genemned on heofonan rîce *qui solverit unum de mandatis istis minimis, ... minimus vocabitur in regno cælorum*, Mt. Kmbl. 5, 19. Æt læstan l scypa *at least 50 ships*, Chr. 1049; Erl. 173, 15. [*O. Frs.* lessa.] v. lærest.

læst. v. læssa, læs.

lǽst *a track*. v. lâst.

lǽst, e; *f. A covering for the foot, a boot*:—Lǽste *ocreæ*, Ælfc. Gl. 29; Som. 61, 25; Wrt. Voc. 26, 24. v. lǽs-hosum, lǽst-wyrhta, lâst, *and Icel.* leistr; *m. a short sock*: *O. H. Ger.* leist *calopodium, forma*: *Ger.* leisten.

lǽst *act, performance* (?):—Nalles hige gehyrdon hâliges lâre siððan leófes leóþ lǽste neár swêg swiðrode *they did not neglect the holy one's [Moses] teaching, after the loved one's lay, when the time drew nearer for action [crossing the Red Sea], and his voice died away*, Cd. 158; Th. 197, 17; Exod. 308. v. Bouterwek's Cædmon i. 321; *and* cf. ful-lǽst, ge-lâst.

lǽstan; *p.* te. I. *to follow, attend, accompany, do suit and service*:—Sôna ða beótunge dǽdum lǽstan *neque segnius minas effectibus prosequuntur*, Bd. 1, 15; S. 483, 39, MS. C. Allum ðâm ðe him lǽstan woldon *with all those who would follow him*, Chr. 874; Erl. 76, 31. Gif hî leódfruman lǽstan dorsten, Bt. Met. Fox 1, 54; Met. 1, 27. Him se lîchoma lǽstan nolde *the body would not do him service [of Grendel powerless in the grasp of Beowulf]*, Beo. Th. 1629; B. 812. II. *to do, perform, observe, carry out, execute, discharge [a debt* or *duty]*:—Ic lufan symle lǽste wið eówic *I will ever love you*, Exon. 14 b; Th. 30, 10; Cri. 471. Gif hê lǽst mîna lâra *if he does my teachings*, Cd. 29; Th. 39, 3; Gen. 619. Ðenden ðû mîne lâre lǽstest, 99; Th. 130, 32; Gen. 2169. Lǽstes, 27; Th. 36, 15; Gen. 572. Forðon hê ða godspellîcan bebode heóld and lǽste *quod evangelica præcepta servaret*, Bd. 3, 22; S. 553, 23: 4, 25; S. 600, 20. Ðæt hî ða ungeweirgadre geornfullnysse fylidon and lǽston *ut instituta indefessa instantia sequerentur*, 4, 3; S. 568, 15. Ðæt mid dǽdum lǽston ða ðe hî ongitan mihton *ut ea quæ intelligere poterant, operando sequerentur*, 4, 27; S. 604, 18. Wê sôðfæstes swaðe folgodon, lǽston lârcwide, Andr. Kmbl. 1347; An. 674. Lǽstun, Exon. 25 b; Th. 75, 21; Cri. 1225. Bibeád ic eów . . . earge gê ðæt lǽstun *my command was . . . ill have ye performed it*, 30 a; Th. 92, 3; Cri. 1503. Leófa Beówulf lǽst eall tela, Beo. Th. 5320; B. 2662: Cd. 106; Th. 139, 4; Gen. 2304. Lǽste ðû georne his ambyhto *do diligently his messages*, 25; Th. 33, 9; Gen. 517. Ðû lǽstan scealt ðæt his bodan bringaþ, Th. 32, 26; Gen. 509. Geongordôm lǽstan, 30; Th. 41, 26; Gen. 663. Gif ðû wilt his wordum hýran and his bebodu lǽstan *if thou wilt hear his words, and do his commands*, Blickl. Homl. 185, 1: Exon. 45 a; Th. 152, 28; Gû. 815. [Ic an six marc silures and ðat schal Godrîc mîne brôðer lêsten (*pay*), Chart. Th. 566, 23, 31.] III. *to continue, last*:—Ðonne him dagas lǽstun *in their life-time*, Exon. 26 b; Th. 79, 12; Cri. 1289. [Ðæt fîr læste swa lange ꝥ hit wæs liht ofer eall, Chr. 1122; Erl. 249, 25. ð lastede þa xix wintre wile Stephne was king, 1137; Erl. 262, 19.] [*Gen. and Ex.* lesten *to perform*: *Orm.* lasstenn *to last*: *Laym.* læsteþ *lasts*: *O.E. Homl.* lasteþ: *A.R.* lesteþ: *Marh.* leasteþ: *Mand.* laste *to perform*: *Goth.* laistjan *to follow*: *O. Sax.* lêstian *to do, perform*: *O. Frs.* lâsta, lêsta, *to do, perform, pay*: *O. H. Ger.* leistan *reddere*: *Ger.* leisten.]

lǽste, es; *m* [?]. *A shoemaker's last*:—Læste *musticula* ['*mustricola* machina ad stringendos pedes, hoc est, ad calceum suendum qui pedes tegit et stringit: forma in qua calceus suitur,' Ducange]. Ælfc. Gl. 29; Som. 61, 25; Wrt. Voc. 26, 24. Lǽste *vordalium* [?], Wrt. Voc. 287, 37. [lest *formipedia*, Wrt. Voc. 181, 13: *Prompt. Parv.* leste, sowtarys forme *formula, calopodia*: *Dan.* læst *a last*: *O.H.Ger.* leist *calopodium, forma*: *Ger.* leisten.] v. lǽst.

lǽstend, es; *m. One who performs* or *executes*:—Ðara þinga ðe hê ôðre lǽrde tô dônne hê sylfa wæs se wylsumesta fyllend and lǽstend *eorum quæ agenda docebat erat executor devotissimus*, Bd. 5, 22; S. 644, 4. Fylgend and lǽstend, 4, 3; S. 568, 15, note.

Læsting, Læstinga eá *Lastingham in Yorkshire*:—Fram ðâm brôðrum ðæs mynstres ðe Læstinga eá is nemned, Bd. pref: S. 472, 17. Getimbrede ðǽr mynster ðæt is nû gecýged Læstinga eá, 3, 23; S. 555, 3. Hê gewât tô his mynsterscire ðæt is on Læstinga eá, 5, 19; S. 639, 14. On Læstinge, 4, 3; S. 566, 28.

lǽst-wyrhta, an; *m. A shoemaker*:—Lǽstweorhta *caligarius*, Ælfc. Gl. 28; Som. 61, 23; Wrt. Voc. 26, 22. Lǽstwyrhta, Wrt. Voc. ii. 127, 66. v. lǽst.

lǽswian, lǽsian: *p.* ode, ede, *trans. and intrans. To pasture, feed, graze*:—Ic lǽswige *pasco*, Ælfc. Gr. 35; Som. 38, 13. Ic lǽsewige, lǽswige, 28: Som. 30, 33. Ic hî lǽswige on dôme and on rihtwîsnysse *I will feed them in judgement and righteousness*, Homl. Th. i. 242, 18. Hig man lǽswode on môrium lande *pascebantur in locis palustribus*, Gen. 41, 2. Ðâ lǽswede heó hire fêstermôdor sceápum *then she fed her foster-mother's sheep*, Shrn. 101, 14. Ðâ lǽswede hê mid his fæder sceápum, 108, 31. Ða assan wið hî lǽswodon *the asses were grazing by them*, Homl. Th. ii. 450, 6. Lǽswa mîne scêp *feed my sheep*, 290, 30. Oxanhyrde môt lǽswian ii. oxan oððe mâ on gemǽnre lǽse *bubulco licet adherbare duos boves, et alicubi plus, in communibus pascuis*, L. R. S. 12; Th. i. 438, 13. Heord lǽswiende *grex pascens*, Mt. Kmbl. 8, 30. Lǽsgende, Mk. Skt. 5, 11. Hwylc eówer hæfþ þeów scêp lǽsgende [lêsuande, Lind.] *quis vestrum habens servum pascentem*, Lk. Skt. 17, 7. Heord swýna lǽsiendra [lêsuuandra, Lind.] *grex porcorum pascentium*, 8, 32. On lǽswigendum eówdum *in pascendis gregibus*, Ælfc. Gr. 26; Som. 28, 20. [*O. E. Homl.* lesweþ, *prs.* 3: *A. R.* leswe, *imper*: *Wick.* leseweden, *p.* 3.]

læt, es; *m. One of a class that was inferior to that of the ceorl but above that of the slave*. The word occurs only in the following passage:—Gif [man] læt ofslæhþ ðone sêlestan lxxx scill. forgelde gif ðane ôðerne ofslæhþ lx scillingum forgelde ðane þriddan xl scillingum forgelden *if any one slay a 'læt' of the highest class, let him pay eighty shillings; if he slay one of the second, let him pay sixty shillings; let them pay for one of the third with forty shillings*, L. Ethb. 26; Th. i. 8, 12–14. See Stubbs' Const. Hist. s. v: Grmm. R. A. 305–309: Grff. ii. 190: Thorpe's Glossary: Kemble's Saxons in England, i. c. 8: Lappenberg's Hist. ii. 321.

læt; *adj. Late, slow, sluggish, tardy*:—Wundrodon ðæt hê on ðam temple læt wæs *mirabantur quod tardaret ipse in templo*, Lk. Skt. 1, 21. Hræd tô gehiéranne and læt tô sprecenne *velox ad audiendum, tardus ad loquendum*, Past. 38, 8; Swt. 281, 6. Hlæt, Rtl. 28, 19. Nalas elnes læt *not slow of courage*, Beo. Th. 3063; B. 1529. Ne sceal se tô sǽne beón, ðissa lârna tô læt, seðe him wile lifgan mid Gode, Exon. 117 a; Th. 450, 17; Dôm. 89: Apstls. Kmbl. 66; Ap. 33. Se mæssepreóst se ðe biþ tô læt ðæt hê ðæt deófol of men âdrîfe *the priest who is too slow in driving the devil from a man*, Blickl. Homl. 43, 22: Exon. 74 a; Th. 276, 29; Jul. 573: 76 a; Th. 285, 11; Jul. 712. Heora behreówsung wæs tô lætt *their repentance was too late*, Homl. Th. ii. 572, 15. Nis seó stund latu dæt . . . *the time does not tarry, when* . . . Andr. Kmbl. 2422; An. 1212: Exon. 46 a; Th. 156, 16; Gû. 875. Nis seó tîd latu, 51 a; Th. 178, 4; Gû. 1239. Be latre meltunge *of sluggish digestion*, L. M. 2, 33; Lchdm. ii. 238, 6. Wið latre meltunge, 2, 34;

Lchdm. i. 238, 27. Late gange *gradu lento*, Wrt. Voc. ii. 41, 76. Læte *dissides*, i. *tardi*, 141, 6. Ne beóþ ǽfre tō late *numquam sunt sera*, 62, 18. Swæfna gewisse synt oft late *dreams are certain, but often late of fulfilment*, Lchdm. iii. 186, 27. Ðæt hī ne beón ne wordes ne weorces, ne ealles tō hræde ne tō swīðe læte, L. I. P. 10; Th. ii. 318, 36. Nalæs late wǽron eorre æscberend tō ðam orlege, Andr. Kmbl. 92; An. 46. On heortan læte [hlatto, Lind.] tō gelȳfenne *tardi corde ad credendum*, Lk. Skt. 24, 25. Ðæt hē ðȳ lætra biþ tō uncystum *that it* [*the body*] *be the less ready to vices*, L. E. I. 3; Th. ii. 404, 20. And ā swā hit forþwerdre beón sceolde swā wæs hit lætre *and ever as things ought to have been more forward, did they go on more slowly*, Chr. 999; Erl. 134, 33. Siððan ðū sprǽce tō ðīnum þeówe ic hæfde ðē lætran tungan *ex quo locutus es ad servum tuum, impeditioris et tardioris linguæ sum*, Ex. 4, 10. [*Goth.* lats *slothful*: *O. Sax.* lat: *O. Frs.* let: *Icel.* latr: *O. H. Ger.* laz *piger, segnis, stupidus, tardus*: *Ger.* lass.] v. unlæt, lata; lætemest, lætest. **-lǽta.** v. freó-, frig-, scyld-lǽta.

LǼTAN, *p.* lēt, leórt; *pp.* lǽten. The ellipsis of a verb in the infinitive, the meaning of which may be inferred from the context, not unfrequently takes place after *lǽtan*; and the connection of many of the meanings which follow with the simple one seems explainable in this way. **I.** *to* LET, *allow, permit, suffer*:—God lǽt him fyrst ðæt hē his māndǽda geswīce *God allows him time that he may cease from his crimes*, Homl. Th. i. 268, 32. Ðonne ne lǽteþ hē ūs nō costian ofer gemet *then he will not let us be tempted beyond measure*, Blickl. Homl. 13, 8. Gif Drihten ðē lǽteþ ðone teóþan dǽl ānne habban *if the Lord lets thee have only the tenth part*, 51, 3. God lēt hī habban āgenne cyre, Homl. Th. i. 10, 19. Ne leórt ǽnigne monno tō fylgenne hine *non admisit quemquam sequi se*, Mk. Skt. Lind. 5, 37. Ðā onlȳsde hē hine and lēt hine fēran æfter ðam biscope *absolvit eum, et post Theodorum ire permisit*, Bd. 4, 1; S. 565, 3. Se dēma lēt ða mōdor tō ðam suna on synderlīcre clȳsingce *the judge allowed the mother to come to the son in a chamber apart*, Homl. Skt. 4, 342. Se ēca Drihten hine sylfne lēt lǽdon on ða heán dūne *the Lord eternal allowed himself to be led on to the high mountain*, Blickl. Homl. 33, 10. Drihten ealle ða gefylde ða ðe hié on eorþan lēton hingrian and þyrstan for his naman *the Lord had filled all those who let themselves*, or *were content to, hunger and thirst for his name's sake* [cf. in Icel. *láta* with a reflex. infin.], 159, 17. Lǽt beón ealne dæg *let it be all day*, L. M. 2, 22; Lchdm. ii. 206, 25. Lǽtaþ ǽgðer weaxan *sinite utraque crescere*, Mt. Kmbl. 13, 30. Lēte *pateretur*, Wrt. Voc. ii. 67, 4. Hē lifde būton synnum ðeáh ðe hē hine lēte costian, Blickl. Homl. 33, 17. Lǽtan nānne lybban *to let none live*, Ex. 14, 5. Se ðe mȳn blōd nolde lǽtan āgeótan *he that would not suffer my blood to be shed*, Nicod. 20; Thw. 10, 17. Lēton, Exon. 46 b; Th. 152, 3; Gū. 921. Gif ðū ðē wilt dōn manegra beteran ðonne scealt ðū ðē lǽtan ānes wyrsan *if thou wilt make thyself the superior of many, thou must allow thyself to be the inferior of one*, Bt. 32, 1; Fox 114, 14. **II.** *to let* [*alone*], *let go, give up, dismiss, leave, forsake, let* [*blood*]:—Ne recce ic hwæt hī dēman. Ic lǽte tō ðīnum dōme mā ðonne tō hiora *I care not what judgements they make. I give myself up*, or *trust, to your judgement more than to theirs*, Bt. 38, 5; Fox 206, 14. Hwȳ nelt ðū gēman ðæt mīn sweostor mē lǽt āne þegnian *why dost thou not heed that my sister leaves me to serve alone?* Blickl. Homl. 67, 31. Hē lǽt his hlāfordes gebod tō giémeliéste *he leaves to neglect* [*neglects*] *his lord's command*, Past. 17, 8; Swt. 121, 14. Lǽtt ðonne ān ðæt gefeoht sume hwīle *he lets the battle alone then for some time*, 33, 7; Swt. 227, 10. Hē cwæþ tō him lǽtaþ ðæt nett on ða swīðran healfe ðæs rēwettes . . . hig lēton *dixit eis mittite in dexteram navigii rete . . . miserunt*, Jn. Skt. 21, 6. Ðæt ic sylf ongeat ne lēt ic ðæt unwriten *what I myself knew, I did not leave unwritten*, Bd. pref; S. 472, 26. God hine lēt frigne *God left him free*, Homl. Th. i. 18, 29. Ic lēt mīne wylne tō ðē *ego dedi ancillam meam in sinum tuum*, Gen. 16, 5. Se arcebiscop lēt hit eall tō heora ǽgene rǽde *the archbishop left it all to their own discretion*, Chart. Th. 341, 11. God hī hǽðenum leódum lēt tō anwealde *God left them to the power of heathen nations*, Jud. 1, 8. Hē lēt hī tō handa Madian *tradidit illos in manu Madian*, 6, 1. Ðā gyrnde se cyng ealra ðæra þegna ðe ða eorlas ǽr hæfdon, and hī lēton hī ealle him tō handa, Chr. 1048; Erl. 180, 9. Gē forsāwon eall mīn geþeaht and lēton eów tō giémelēste ðonne ic eów cīdde *despexistis omne consilium meum et increpationes meas neglexistis*, Past. 36, 1; Swt. 247, 22. Swā swā hit his yldran lētan and lǽfdan ðam tō gewealde *as his parents left and bequeathed it to be at his disposal*, L. O. 14; Th. i. 184, 3; Lchdm. iii. 286, 15. Hine eft ðǽm mannum hālne and gesundne āgeaf ðām ðe hine ǽr deádne lēton *gave him back safe and sound to the men who before had left him dead*, Blickl. Homl. 219, 22. Lǽt ðīne lāc beforan ðam altare *relinque munus tuum ad altare*, Mt. Kmbl. 5, 24. Lǽt ðū him blōd on ǽdre *let blood for him from a vein*, L. M. 1, 4; Lchdm. ii. 46, 22. Beó ðū be ðīnum and lǽt mē be mīnum *be thou with thine, and leave me with mine*, Lchdm. iii. 288, 8. Gif hē tōþ of āsleá lǽt hig frige *dentem si excusserit, dimittet eos liberos*, Ex. 21, 27. Lǽte hig frige, 26. Wē lǽraþ ðæt man ǽnig ne lǽte unbiscpod tō lange, Wulfst. 120, 15. Lǽte [ðæt feoh] ān and fō se āgend tō *let him give up* [*the property*], *and let the owner take it*, L. H. E. 7; Th. i. 30, 9: 12; Th. i. 34, 12. Hwilce hwīle hine wille Drihten hēr on worlde lǽtan *how long the Lord will leave him in this world*, Blickl. Homl. 125, 9. Hē sceal lǽtan his unnyttan geþancas of his mōde *he must dismiss his idle thoughts from his mind*, Wulfst. 234, 26. Ðonne hē hī nyle lǽtan tō hiera āgnum wilnungum *quos in sua desideria non relaxat*, Past. 50, 4; Swt. 391, 22. Hē nō be ðæm ānum lǽtan wolde ac ofer ðone gārsecg ðone ylecan leóman ðæs fullan geleáfan āspringan lēt *he would not leave off when that* [*the spreading of the gospel over part of the world*] *only was done, but caused the same beam of the perfect faith to spring forth across the ocean* [*to England*], Lchdm. iii. 432, 16. Wið poccum swīðe sceal mon blōd lǽtan, L. M. 1, 40; Lchdm. ii. 106, 3. Nis him blōd tō lǽtanne, 35; Lchdm. ii. 82, 16. **III.** *to let, cause, make, get, have, cause to be, place*:—Ic hine symble gehȳre and mīne mildse ofer ðone lǽte *I will ever hear him, and my mercy shall be upon that man*, Wulfst. 264, 11. Swā hī hiora lufe neár Gode lǽtaþ swā hī bióþ orsorgru *the nearer to God they place their love, the more free are they from care*, Bt. 39, 7; Fox 222, 24: 40, 7; Fox 242, 26–28. Hē lēt betwux him and mīnum feóndum ðæt hē nǽfre gesewen [wæs] fram him *posuit tenebras latibulum suum*, Ps. Th. 17, 11. Ðā fōr hē norþryhte be ðæm lande lēt him ealne weg ðæt wēste land on ðæt steórbord *then he sailed due north along the coast: he had the waste land all the way on his starboard*, Ors. 1, 1; Swt. 17, 10. Ða hē lēt standan beforan ymbeūtan ða eardungstōwe *quos stare fecit circa tabernaculm*, Num. 11, 24. Hē sette scole and on ðære hē lēt cnihtas lǽran *he set up a school, and had boys taught in it*; instituit scholam in qua pueri literis erudirentur, Bd. 3, 18; S. 545, 45. Se cing lēt gerīdan ealle ða land ðe his mōdor āhte him tō handa, Chr. 1042; Erl. 169, 19: 1023; Erl. 162, 35: 1035; Erl. 164, 22. Wit ðæt ðā lētan and uneþelīce þurhtugan ðæt hē ðæs geþafa wolde beón *with difficulty we got him to assent to it*, Bd. 5, 4; S. 617, 17. Hī lēton hig hādian tō bisceopum *they got themselves ordained bishops*, 1053; Erl. 188, 14. **IV.** *to make a thing appear* [*so and so*], *make as if, make out, profess, pretend, estimate, consider, suppose, think*:—Ic lēto *existimabo*, Lk. Skt. Lind. 13, 18. Hē lēttes *arbitretur*, Jn. Skt. Lind. 16, 2. Ne lǽtaþ wē *non dissimulamus*, Wrt. Voc. ii. 62, 22. Ealle wē lǽtaþ efendȳrne Engliscne and Deniscne *we estimate all at the same amount, Englishman and Dane*, L. A. G. 2; Th. i. 152, 12. [Cf. *Icel.* manngjöld skyldi jöfn látin ok spora-höggit.] Ðonne wē ðisses middangeardes welan foresettaþ and ūs leófran lǽtaþ ðonne ða lufan ðara heofonlīcra eádignessa *cum mundi divitias amori cælestium præponimus*, Bd. 3, 19; S. 548, 16. Fela is ðæra ðe embe bletsunga oððe unbletsunga leóhtlīce lǽtaþ *many are there that esteem lightly of blessings or cursings* [cf. *Piers P.* iv. 160–161 moste peple . . . *leten* mekenesse a maistre and Mede a mansed schrewe. Loue *lete* of hir liȝte and lewte ȝit lasse: *Orm.* 7523– uss birrþ *lætenn* unnornliȝ and litell off uss sellfenn and *lætenn wel* off oþre menn], L. I. P. 6; Th. ii. 310, 36. Gē beótlīce lǽtaþ *ye boast*, Wulfst. 46, 15. Hȳ þencaþ and lǽtaþ ðæt tō warscype, ðæt hȳ ōðre māgan pǽcan, 55, 2. Hē lēt ðæt hyt Dryhtnes sylfes andwlyta wǽre *he supposed that it was the face of the Lord himself*, St. Andr. 42, 9. Ðā sendun hig mid searwum ða ðe rihtwīse lēton *observantes miserunt insidiatores qui se justos simularent*, Lk. Skt. 20, 20. Ðā lēton hȳ sume ðæt ðæt mycel unrǽd wǽre *some of them considered it a very bad plan*, Chr. 1052; Erl. 179, 32. Manige lēton ðæt hit cometa wǽre *many supposed that it was a comet*, 1097; Erl. 234, 13. Ðæs ðe men lēton *as men supposed*, Erl. 234, 17. Hī hī selfe lēton ǽgðer ge for heáne ge for unwrǽste *they considered themselves as abject and undone*; ultima propemodum desperatione tabuerunt [cf. *Piers P.* xv. 5 somme *leten* me for a lorel], Ors. 3, 1; Swt. 98, 22. Lēton ðā gedwealde men, swylce Simon Godes sylfes sunu wǽre, Wulfst. 99, 7. Ðæt man þurh ðæt lǽte ðæt hē sī ðæs legeres wyrðe so *that for that reason it be considered that he is worthy of such burial*, L. Edg. C. 29; Th. ii. 250, 17. Ðæt hē ða ðe him underþiédde sīen lǽte him gelīce *æqualem se subditis deputet*, Past. 17, 1; Swt. 107, 15. Ðæt cild ðe læg on cradele ða gȳtseras lǽton efenscyldig and hit gewittig wǽre, L. C. S. 77; Th. i. 420, 2. Ic wælle lēta *æstimabo*, Lk. Skt. Lind. 13, 20. Se ealdormonn sceal lǽtan hine selfne gelīcne his hiéremonnum, Past. 17, 1; Swt. 107, 8. **V.** *to behave towards, treat*:—Ðam elþeódigan and ūtancumenan ne lǽt ðū nō uncūþlīce wið hine *as regards the alien and foreigner do not behave unkindly towards him* [cf. *Icel.* björn lætr allblītt við hana], L. Alf. 47; Th. i. 54, 20. **VI.** *to let* [*land, &c.*]:—Eádward cyning and ða hīwan in Wintanceastre lǽtaþ tō Dænewulfe bisceope twentig hīda landes, Chart. Th. 158, 7. Ðā com sum ōðer and beád māre ðonne ðe ōðer ǽr sealde and se cyng hit lētt ðam menn ðe him māre beád *then some other man came and offered more than the other had before given, and the king let it to the man that offered more*, Chr. 1086; Erl. 220, 10. Ðā hȳ lētan him tō ðæt land æt Eádburge byrig, Cod. Dip. Kmbl. iv. 76, 5: Chart. Th. 151, 6. **VII.** *with adverbs*:—Ðās ōðre lǽtaþ ðone n āweg on sopinum *these others let the n fall away in the supine*, Ælfc. Gr. 28; Som. 31, 60. Ælmǽr abbod hī lǽtan āweg *they let abbot Aylmer go away*, Chr. 1011; Erl. 145, 13. Ðā cwǽdon ða witan ðæt betere wǽre ðæt man ðene āþ āweg lēte ðonne hine man sealde . . . Ðá lēt hē ðone āþ āweg *then the witan said that it would be better that the oath should be dispensed with than that it should be taken . . . Then he omitted the oath*, Chart. Th. 289, 24–30. Æt ealre ðære hergunge and æt eallum ðām hearmum ðe ǽr ðam gedōn wǽre ǽr ðæt friþ geset wǽre man eall onweig lǽte and nān man ðæt ne wræce ne bōte ne bidde *as regards all the harrying and all the injuries that were done before the peace was made, let it all be dismissed, and let no man avenge it or ask for compensation*, L. Eth. ii. 6; Th. i. 288, 3. Petrus cnucode ōþ ðæt hī hine inn lēton *Peter knocked until they let him in*, Homl. Th. i. 382, 23. Hē lǽt him eáþelíce ymbe ðæt *he takes it easily*, Wulfst. 298, 30: Homl. Skt. 4, 342. [*Goth.* lētan: *O. Sax.* lātan: *O. Fries.* lēta: *Icel.* lāta: *O. H. Ger.* lāzan.] DER. ā-, for-, ge-, of-, on-, tō- lǽtan.

læt-byrd, e; *f. A late* or *slow birth*:—Se wīfman se hire cild āfēdan ne mæg gange tō gewitenes mannes birgenne . . . and cweþe ðās word ðis mē tō bōte ðære lāþan lætbyrde *let the woman who cannot nourish her* [*unborn*] *child go to the grave of a dead man . . . and say these words: 'May this help me with the troublesome late birth*,' Lchdm. iii. 66, 21.

-lǽte. v. ā-lǽte.

lætemest; *a double superlative of* læt. *Last*:—In ðǽm lætemestan dæge *in novissimo die*, Jn. Skt. Rush. 6, 44: 39, 40. Stōwe ða lætemestu *novissimum locum*, Lk. Skt. Rush. 14, 9, 10. Monige wutudlīce bióþun ǽrist ða foerþmestu and ða lætemestu foerþmest *multi autem erunt primi novissimi et novissimi primi*, Mk. Skt. Rush. 14, 31. Ða endo ł lætmesta *novissima*, Mt. Kmbl. Lind. 12, 45.

lætemest; *adv. Lastly, at last, finally*:—Lætemest (lætmest, Lind.) *novissime*, Mk. Skt. Rush. 16, 14.

lǽtere. v. blōd-lǽtere.

lætest; *superl.* of læt. *Last*:—Ðe lætest [ða lætmesta, Lind.] *the last*, Mt. Kmbl. Rush. 22, 27. [*O. Eng. Homl.* latest: *Orm.* latst: *A. R. Laym.* last.]

lǽð, es; *n. Land*:—Dō swā ic lǽre beó ðē [Lchdm. ðū] be ðīnum and lǽt mē be mīnum ne gyrne ic ðīnes ne lǽðes ne landes ne sace ne sōcne ne ðū mīnes ne þearft *do as I advise; be thou with thine and leave me to mine; I desire nothing of thine, neither lea nor land, neither 'sac' nor 'socn'; nor needest thou mine*, L. O. 14; Th. i. 184, 15; Lchdm. iii. 288, 8. The Icelandic has the same alliterative phrase, e. g. 'deyr fē; deyja frændr; eyðisk land ok lāð.'

lǽð *a lathe* [e. g. Kent is divided into six *lathes*], *a district containing several hundreds*, v. Stubbs' Const. Hist. i. 100. The word occurs in the Latin laws of Edward the Confessor:—In quibusdam vero provinciis Anglice vocabatur *lēð*, quod isti dicunt tithinge [*or* trihinge], Th. i. 455, n. 3. In L. Hen. I. viii. 2 occurs amongst the names of other officials *leidegrevei* = *lǽðgerēfan*, Th. i. 514, note 1. Cf. *Icel.* leið, leiðangr *a levy*: *Dan.* leding. Skeat, Etymol. Dict. under *lathe*, suggests that lǽð = lægð, in which case perhaps it may be compared with *Dan.* lægd *a levying district*.

lǽðan; *p.* de *To speak ill of, accuse, abuse, execrate, detest, hate*:—Man eall hyrweþ ðæt man scolde herian and lāðeþ [lǽðeþ?] ðæt man scolde lufian *people scorn what they ought to praise, and hate what they ought to love*, Swt. A. S. Rdr. 110, 167. Gif hwelc cymiþ tō mē and ne lǽdes [lǽðues, Lind] fæder his *si quis venit ad me et non odit patrem suum*, Lk. Skt. Rush. 14, 26. Miððȳ iuih lǽðeþ menn *cum vos oderint homines*, Lind. 6, 22. Ða ðe lǽðes ł lǽðedon *qui oderunt*, Mt. Kmbl. Lind. 5, 44. Ða ðe lǽðdon, Lk. Skt. Lind. i, 71. Hȳ wǽron ealle ānsprǽce ðonne hȳ mē leahtrodon and lǽðdon *loquebantur simul*, Ps. Th. 40, 7. [Cf. *Icel.* leiða *to make a person loathe a thing*: *O. Sax.* a-lēðian *to disgust*: *O. H. Ger.* leidan *accusare, detestari*; leidēn *execrari, odiosum facere*.] v. be-lǽðan, lāðian.

lǽðð[u], e; lǽððo; *indecl.*; *f. An injury, offence, hatred, enmity, malice*:—Lǽððe *livoris*, Wt. Voc. ii. 50, 16. Mið lǽðo hæfe ðū fiónd ðīnne *odio habebis inimicum tuum*, Mt. Kmbl. Lind. 5, 43. Lǽððo *odio*, 24, 10. Seðe unlage rǽre oððe undōm gedēme heononforþ for lǽððe oððe for feohfange *he that from this time forth shall set up unjust law, or judge unjust judgement on account of malice or of bribery*, L. C. S. 15; Th. i. 384, 9. Þurh Pendan lǽððe hyra cyninges, Bd. 3, 18; S. 546, 14. Ðæt is ðonne ðæt ǽrest ðæt man tō ōðrum lǽððe hæbbe *now first it is murder, that a man hate another*, Blickl. Homl. 63, 36. Ne dōm ic ðē laæðo *non facio tibi injuriam*, Mt. Kimbl. Lind. 20, 13. Ðæt hié ongieten ðæt ðæt sindon ða forman lǽððo ðe hié Gode gedoon mægen *ut noverint, quod hanc primam injuriam faciunt Deo*, Past. 45, 2; Swt. 339, 7. Ðara lǽðða ðe gē lange drugon *for the injuries that ye have suffered long*, Judth. 11; Thw. 23, 36; Jud. 158. Hē mid lǽððum ūs eglan mōste, Thw. 24, 12; Jud. 185. Ðone Jacobum Judǽa leorneras otslōgan for Cristes lǽððum *that James the disciples of the Jews slew from hatred to Christ*, Shrn. 93, 12. Lǽððum hwōpan *to threaten injuries*, Exon. 64 a; Th. 236, 31; Ph. 582. [Cf. *Icel.* leiða; *f. irksomeness*: *O. H. Ger.* leida; *f. accusatio*.]

læt-hȳdig; *adj. Slow-minded, slow of thought, dull*:—Nis mon on moldan . . . ðæs lǽthȳdig ðæt hine se ārgifa ealles biscyrge mōdes cræfta *no man is there on earth so dull, that the bounteous giver hath quite cut him off from powers of mind*, Exon. 78 b; Th. 294, 5; Crā. 10.

læt-līce; *adv. Slowly*:—Ðā andswarode hē him lætlīce *then he answered him slowly*, Guthl. 20; Gdwin, 80, 12. Lætlīcor *more slowly* Exon. 118 a; Th. 454, 16; Hy. 4, 33.

lætmest. v. lætemest.

læt-rǽde; *adj. Slow of counsel, deliberate*:—Oft mon biþ suīðe wandigendre æt ǽlcum weorce and suīðe lætrǽde and wēnaþ menn ðæt hit sīe for suārmōdnesse and for unarodscipe and biþ ðeáh for wisdōme and for wærscipe *often a man will be very hesitating in every action, and very deliberate, and men suppose that it is from stupidity and from cowardice, and yet it is from wisdom and caution*; the Latin however has 'sæpe agendi tarditas gravitatis consilium putatur,' Past. 20, 1; Swt. 149, 14.

lætsum; *adj. Slow, late*:—Wæs swīðe lætsum geár on corne and on ǽlces cynnes wæstmum *it was a very late year for corn and crops of every kind*, Chr. 1089; Erl. 226, 18.

lætt, e; *f. A lath*:—Lætta *asseres*, Ælfc. Gl. 29; Som. 61, 42; Wrt. Voc. 26, 41. Latta *vel* reafteres *asseres*, 108; Som. 78, 123; Wrt. Voc. 58, 35. [*Hic asser* a lath, Wrt. Voc. 235, 37: *Prompt. Parv.* lathe latthe, laththe *tignus, tignum, tigillum*: *O. H. Ger.* latta, lata *tignum, asser, tegula*: *Ger.* latte *a lath*.]

læuw. v. leów.

lǽwa, an; *m. A betrayer, traitor*:—Lǽwa *proditor* vel *traditor*, Wrt. Voc. 85, 43. Judam scarioð se wæs lǽwa [hlēga, Lind] *iudam scarioth qui fuit proditor*, Lk. Skt. 6, 16. His lǽwa him tācen sealde *dederat traditor ejus signum eis*, Mk. Skt. 14, 44: Homl. Th. ii. 246, 10. Mid Judan ðe Cristes lēwa wæs, Cod. Dip. Kmbl. iii. 138, 21. Hēr is ðæs lǽwan hand *ecce manus tradentis me*, Lk. Skt. 22, 21.

lǽwan; *p.* de *To betray*:—Ðonne lǽweþ brōðer ōðerne hǽðnum on deáþ and sunu se lǽweþ his fæder *then one brother shall betray another to the heathen to death, and a son he shall betray his father*, Blickl. Homl. 171, 21. [*Goth.* lēwjan, *to betray*: *O. H. G.* gi-lāti; *p.* (*he*) *betrayed*.] v. be-lǽwan.

lǽwed, lēud, es; *m. A layman*:—Gif man lēud ofsleá an þeófþe licge būtan wyrgelde *if a layman be slain while thieving, let no wergild be paid for the slaying*. L. Wih. 25; Th. i. 42, 13. v. next word.

lǽwede; *adj. Lay, laic, not learned, not of the church*; by gradual change of meaning it has become the later *lewd*:—Lǽwede man *laicus*, Wt. Voc. 72, 8. Ðara manna sum wæs bescoren preóst sum wæs lǽwede sum wæs wīfmon *e quibus hominibus quidam erat adtonsus ut clericus, quidam laicus, quædam femina*, Bd. 5, 12; S. 628, 35. Hī underfēngon ða dīgelnyssa ðære lāre ðe ðæt lǽwede folc undergitan ne mihte *they* [*the apostles*] *received the mysteries of the doctrine that the unlearned people could not understand*, Homl. Th. i. 190, 13. Būton ða lāreówas screádian symle ða leahtras þurh heora lāre āweg ne biþ ðæt lǽwede folc wæstmbǽre on gōdum weorcum, ii. 74, 17. Hē munuclīce leofode betwux ðam lǽwedan folce *he lived as a monk among laymen*, 97, 67. Sum wer wæs on lǽwedum hāde *fuit vir in laico habitu*, Bd. 5, 13; S. 632, 7. Ðeáh ðe hē ðā gyt on lǽwedum hāde beón sceolde . . . hē munuclīfe gyta swīðor lifde ðonne ðonne lǽwedes mannes, Blickl. Homl. 213, 9–11. Ðæt hit nǽfre on lǽdu hand ne wende *that it should never pass to a lay hand*, Chart. Th. 166, 21. Ealle ge bescorene ge lǽwede, Bd. 3, 5; S. 526, 36: 5, 7; S. 621, 14. Ða ðe mid him wǽron swīðust lǽwde *qui cum ipso erant, maxime laici*, 5, 6; S. 618, 42. Ða witan ealle ge hādode ge lǽwede *all the witan both churchmen and laymen*, Chr. 1014; Erl. 150, 4. Ne ūre nǽnig his līf ne fadode swā swā hē scolde, ne gehādode regollīce ne lǽwede lahlīce, Swt. A. S. Rdr. 107, 78. Þurh gelǽredra regolbryce and þurh lǽwedra lahbryce *through breach of* [*monastic*] *rule by the learned and breach of law by the unlearned*, Swt. A. S. Rdr. 111, 199. [In the later English the *lewed* are contrasted with the *lered*, e. g. *Orm.* ȝa læwedd follc, ȝa læredd; and Robert Manning writes 'not for þe lerid bot for the *lewed*:' *Prompt. Parv.* lewde *illitteratus, inscius, ignarus, laicus*.]

lǽwend, es; *m. One who betrays, a traitor*:—Lǽwend *proditor*, Ælfc. Gl. 85; Som. 73, 125; Wrt. Voc. 49, 18: Wrt. Voc. ii. 68, 75. Lēwend, Kent. Gl. 1156.

lǽwerce. v. lāwerce.

Læwes, Læwe *Lewes in Sussex*:—Tō Læwe [other MS. Læwes] *at Lewes*, L. Ath. i. 14; Th. i. 208, 1. Æt Hamme wið Læwe, Cod. Dip. Kmbl. ii. 388, 18. Hamme juxta Læwes, vi. 46, 11.

lāf, e; *f.* I. *what is left, remnant, remains, relic, remainder, rest, lave* [in northern dialects]:—Lāf *superstes*, Ælfc. Gr. 9; Som. 11, 7. Healmes lāf *stipulæ*, Ælfc. Gl. 59; Som. 67, 131; Wt. Voc. 38, 51. Ðǽr wæs ungemetlīc wæl geslægen and sió lāf wið ðone here friþ nam *there was immense slaughter, and those who were left made peace with the Danes*, Chr. 867; Erl. 72, 17: 894; Erl. 93, 1. Seó wǽpna lāf *the weapons' leavings, the survivors of a battle*, Cd. 93; Th. 121, 5; Gen. 2005. Secg gāra lāf se ða gūþe genæs, 94; Th. 121, 32; Gen. 2019. Ða Norþmen dreórig daraþa lāf, Chr. 937; Erl. 115, 3; Æðelst. 54. Seoððan se ēcea dǽl of biþ ðæt is seó sāwl hwæt biþ elles seó lāf būton wyrma mete *when the eternal part, that is the soul, is gone, what else is the rest but food for worms?* Blickl. Homl. iii. 32. Ic beó tō lāfe *resto*, Ælfc. Gr. 24; Som. 25, 62. Ne wearþ ðǽr forþon ān Bret tō lāfe *there* [*at Anderida*] *was not even one Briton left*, Chr. 491; Erl. 14, 7. Ðæs folces ðe ðǽr tō lâfe wæs, Blickl. Homl. 79, 20. Betǽcan eów on hǽđenra hand heries lâfe *to deliver you into the hands of the heathen, all that is left of* or *by a host*, Wulfst. 295, 20. Sumes þinges lâfe *reliquiæ*, Ælfc. Gr. 13; Som. 16, 19. Lâfa ârleásra forwurþaþ *reliquiæ impiorum interibunt*, Ps. Spl. 36, 40. Wætra lâfe *the survivors of the flood*, Cd. 75; Th. 93, 21; Gen. 1549. Hî nâmon đa lâfa *tulerunt reliquias*, Mt. Kmbl. 14, 20. **II.** *used in poetry of weapons with the gen. of the implement employed in making them*:—Ic eom wrâđra lâf fýres and feóle *I am the leaving of foes, of fire and of file* [a sword, forged in the fire and sharpened by the file], Exon. 126 a; Th. 484, 6; Rä. 70, 3. Homera lâfa *swords*, Beo. Th. 5651; B. 2829: Exon. 102 b; Th. 388, 14; Rä. 6, 7: Chr. 937; Erl. 112, 6; Æđelst. 6. **III.** *what is left as an inheritance, legacy, heirloom* [of armour or weapons: 'das schwert ist des mannes grösztes kleinod, das nur auf seinen nächsten männlichen erben übergeht' Grmm. Gesch. D. S. p. 12]:—Beaduscrûda betst đæt mîne breóst wereþ; đæt is Hrædlan lâf, Welandes geweorc, Beo. Th. 913; B. 454. Gomel swyrd Eánmundes lâf *an ancient sword, an heirloom from Eanmund*, 5216; B 2611: 5250; B. 2628. Đǽr brægd eorl Beówulfes ealde lâfe, 1595; B. 795: 2981; B. 1488. Hêt in gefetian Hrêđles lâfe; næs sincmâđđum sêlra on sweordes hâd, 4389; B. 2191. **IV.** *a relict, widow*:—Lâf *vel* forlǽten wîf *derelicta*, Ælfc. Gl. 88; Som. 74, 65; Wrt. Voc. 50, 46. Ne nime đæs forþfarenan lâf nânne ôđerne man bûton his brôđur *uxor defuncti non nubet alteri, sed accipiet eam frater ejus*, Deut. 25, 5. And ǽfre ne geweorþe đæt Cristen man gewîfige on đæs lâfe đe swâ neáh wǽre on woroldcundre sibbe *and never let it happen that a Christian man marry the relict of him who was so near* [*within the prohibited degrees*] *in worldly relationship*, L. Eth. vi. 12; Th. i. 318, 15: L. C. E. 7; Th. i. 364, 23. Se forlêt his fulluht and lifode on hêđenum þeáwe swâ đæt hê heafde his feder lâfe tô wîfe, Chr. 616; Erl. 21, 40. Paulinus genam Æđelburge Eádwines lâfe and gewât on scipe tô Cent, 633; Erl. 25, 21. Đâ gewât Eádrîc . . . Đâ hæfde Eádrîc lâfe and nân bearn *then Eadric died . . . Eadric left a widow but no child*, Chart. Th. 272, 22. [*Goth.* laiba *a remnant*: *O. Frs.* lâva: *O. Sax*, lêba: *Icel.* leif: *O. H. Ger.* leiba.] DER. ege-, ende-, eormen-, here-, hûsel-, met-, sǽ-, un-, weá-, ýđ-, yrfe-lâf.

lafian; *p.* ode *To lave, bathe, pour water on*:—Nim đone wǽtan and wyrm and lafa đîn heáfod mid *take the liquor and warm it and lave thy head with it*, Lchdm. iii. 48, 7. Wyrc đæt bæþ of đâm ilcum wyrtum on cealdum wyllewætre gecnuwa đa wyrta swîđe wel lege on đæt wæter lafa on đone swile *make the bath of the same herbs in cold spring-water, pound the herbs very thoroughly, lay on, pour the water on to the swelling*, L. M., 1, 31; Lchdm. ii. 74, 29. Genim beren eár beseng lege on swâ hât and hât wæter lafa on *take a barley ear, singe it, apply it as hot as possible, and pour hot water on*, 1, 51; Lchdm. ii. 124, 18. [*O. H. Ger.* labian, labên, labôn *reficere, refocillare*: *Ger.* laben.] v. ge-lafian.

lafor, es; *m. A leopard* [so Cockayne, but ought not the word in the following passage to be *eoforas*?]:—Swelce eác laforas đǽr cwôman unmǽtlîcre micelnisse and monig ôđer wildeór and eác tigris *nec minus apri ingentis forme mixti maculosis lincibus tygribusque*, Nar. 15, 1.

-lafte. v. twî-lafte.

lag-. v. lah-.

laga, an; *m. Law*:—Stande ân laga, L. C. S. 34; Th. i. 396, 22, MS. B. Rǽde gê forþ lagan fyrþor ic wolde gif mê tô anhagode *proceed further in determining laws; I would, if it were convenient for me*, Wulfst. 275, 11. v. riht-, woruld-laga.

-laga. v. ân-, ût-laga.

lagian; *p.* ode *To make a law, ordain*:—Lagiaþ gôde woruldlagan and lecgaþ đǽrtôeácan đæt ûre cristendôm stande *ordain good secular laws, and add thereto the establishment of our christianity*, Wulfst. 274, 7. [*Kath.* lahede *ordained*.] v. ge-in-, in-, ût-lagian.

lago-. v. lagu-.

lagu, e; *f. Law, statute, decree, regulation, rule, fixed custom*:—Lagu *jus*, Ælfc. Gr. 9; Som. 12, 22. God him sette ǽ đæt ys open lagu đam folce tô steóre *God appointed them law, that is a plain rule, for the guidance of the people*, Ælfc. T. Grn. 5, 36. *Deuteronomium* đæt ys ôđer lagu, 39. Gif hê hine lâdian wille dô đæt be đam deópestan âđe on Engla lage and on Dena lage be đam đe heora lagu sî *if he will clear himself, let him do it by the most solemn oath in the district under English law; in that under Danish, by what their law may be*, L. Eth. vi. 37; Th. i. 324, 20. Manna gehwilc ôđrum beóde đæt riht đæt hê wille đæt man him beóde and đæt is swýđe riht lagu *let every man offer that justice to another that he wishes to be offered to himself, and that is a very just rule*, 49; Th. i. 326, 32. Nû is seó ealde lagu geendod æfter Cristes tôcyme and men ne ceósaþ nû on đissere cristenan lage of nânum biscopcynne ôđerne biscop ac of ǽlcum cynne *now the old law is ended after Christ's advent, and men do not now under the Christian law choose a bishop from an episcopal race, but from any race*, L. Ælfc. P. 40; Th. ii. 380, 24. Hig gesceótaþ tô Aarones dǽle and his suna êcre lage *cedent in partem Aaron et filiorum ejus jure perpetuo*, Ex. 29, 28. Hwî forgýmaþ đîne leorningcnihtas ûre yldrena lage? . . . Gê for nâht dydon Godes bebod for eówre lage *quare discipuli tui transgrediuntur traditionem seniorum? . . . Irritum fecistis mandatum Dei propter traditionem vestram*, Mt. Kmbl. 15, 2, 6. Đǽr hæfþ âne lage earm and se welega *there poor and rich shall have one law*, Dôm. L. 12, 163. Godes lage healdan, Swt. A. S. Rdr. 105, 36, 23. Hê niwade đǽr Cnutes lage, Chr. 1064; Erl. 196, 2. Đǽr þegen âge twegen costas lufe ođđe lage *where a thane has two alternatives love or law* [i. e. where a case may be arranged amicably or by appeal to law], L. Eth. iii. 13; Th. i. 298, 6. Đis synd đa bebodu and dômas and laga đe drihten gesette *hæc sunt judicia atque præcepta et leges quas dedit dominus*, Lev. 26, 46. Đis ys seó ǽ đe Moises foresette and laga and dômas *ista est lex quam proposuit Moyses, et hæc testimonia et ceremoniæ atque judicia*, Deut. 4, 44-45. Ic wille đæt hig beón swâ gôdera lagana wurđe swâ hig betst wǽran on ǽniges cynges dæge *I will that they be entitled to as good laws as there ever have been in any king's day*, Chart. Th. 416, 24. And ic wille đæt woruldgerihta mid Denum standan be swâ gôdum lagum swâ hý betst geceósen mǽgen, L. Edg. S. 2; Th. i. 272, 30. Hwilc ôđer þeód is swâ mǽre đæt hæbbe laga and rihte dômas and ealle ǽ *quæ est alia gens sic inclyta, ut habeat ceremonias justaque judicia et universam legem*, Deut. 4, 8. Hê lægde laga đæt swâ hwâ swâ slôge heort ođđe hinde đæt hine man sceolde blendian, Chr. 1086; Erl. 222, 26. Ic wylle đæt man rihte laga upp ârǽre and ǽghwilce unlage georne âfylle, L. C. S. 1; Th. i. 376, 7. In the phrases *on Engla, Dena*, &c. *lage*, which may be compared with the *Icel. í þrænda lögum*, *lagu* is nearly equivalent to 'district in which certain [English, Danish, &c.] laws prevail,' and in Cl. & V. Dict. [v. lög ii.] *lög* is rendered 'law community, communion, also a law district.' So in L. E. G. 7; Th. i. 172, 3 it is said:—Gif hlâford his þeówan freólsdæge nýde tô weorce gylde lahslitte inne on Deone lage and wîte mid Englum. These laws are the first in which *lagu* or *lah-* occurs, afterwards these forms are not unfrequent, and are continued in the Laws of William the Conqueror 'en Dene lahe, en Merchene lahe, en West Sexene lahe,' Th. i. 466, and in L. H. I. 'in Denelaga,' 566. From the time of the appearance of the word it would seem that its use was due to Scandinavian influence. v. Steenstrup's Normannerne, iv. 15 sqq. In Icelandic the word is used in the sense of law only in *pl.* lög: *Dan.* lov. v. land-, mǽg-, riht-, þegen-, un-, woruld- lagu; laga *and* lah.

lagu, lago; *m.* **I.** *sea, water*:—Đæt gelimpan sceal đætte lagu flôweþ ofer foldan *it shall come to pass that the sea shall flow over the earth* [*at the last day*], Exon. 115 b; Th. 445, 1; Dôm. 1. Lagu, wæter under wolcnum, Beo. Th. 3265; B. 1630. Lagu lâcende *the tossing water*, Andr. Kmbl. 873; An. 437. Lyft and lagu [cf. *Icel.* lopt ok lögr] land ymbclyppaþ gârsecg embegyrt gumena rîce *air and sea embrace earth, ocean girds round the kingdom of men*, Bt. Mt. Fox 9, 72; Met. 9, 40. Stille þynceþ lyft ofer londe and lagu swîge, Exon. 101 b; Th. 383, 16; Rä. 4, 11. Lagu land gefeól lyft wæs onhrêred *sea fell to earth, air was stirred* [*of the destruction of the Egyptians in the Red Sea*], Cd. 167; Th. 208, 12; Exod. 482. Đâ gesundrod wæs lago wiđ lande, 8; Th. 10, 27; Gen. 163. Lago yrnende, 12; Th. 13, 32; Gen. 211. Willflôd ongan lytligan eft, lago ebbade [*of the subsiding deluge*], 71; Th. 85, 12; Gen. 1413. Mid lande and mid loge mid wude and mid felde *cum terra et cum aqua, cum sylva et cum agro*, Cd. Dip. Kmbl. iv. 202, 1. Under lyft ofer lagu, Exon. 57 a; Th. 204, 21; Ph. 101. Â hafaþ longunge seđe on lagu fundaþ, 82 a; Th. 308, 30; Seef. 47. Ne lagu drêfde ne of [on?] lyfte fleág *it troubled not water, nor flew it in air*, 106 a; Th. 404, 31; Rä. 23, 16. Ic ymb sîþ spræce and on lagu þence, 119 a; Th. 458, 9; Hy. 4, 97. **II.** *the name of the Rune* ᛚ:—Lagu byþ leódum langsum geþuht gif hî sculun nêđan on nacan tealtum *water to men wearisome seemeth, if they must venture on vessel unsteady*, Runic pm. Kmbl 343, 19; Rûn. 21. Swâ ᛚ tôglîdeþ, Elen. Kmbl. 2536; El. 1269. [*Goth.* (see the name of Gothic *l*) lagus: *O. Sax*, lagu (in cpds.): *Icel.* lögr; *m. sea, water, liquid*; also *name of Rune* ᛚ: *O. H. Ger.* lagu *name of Runic letter*.]

lagu-cræftig; *adj. Skilled in matters connected with the sea*:—Lagucræftig mon, Beo. Th. 423; B. 209.

lagu-fæđm, es; *m. A watery embrace*:—Ýđ sió brûne lagufæđme beleólc *the dark wave played round me with its watery embrace*, Exon. 122 b; Th. 471, 26; Rä. 61, 7.

lagu-fæsten, es; *n. A water-fastness, sea, ocean*:—Ofer lagufæsten, Andr. Kmbl. 796; An. 398: 1650; An. 826: Elen. Kmbl. 2031; El. 1017. Lagofæsten, 497; El. 249.

lagu-flôd, es; *m. Sea, ocean, stream, wave, water*:—Laguflôd *unda*, Wrt. Voc. ii. 130, 33. Lyfthelm and laguflôd *air and sea*, Menol. Fox 553; Gn. C. 46. Swâ wê on laguflôde ofer ceald wæter ceólum lîđan geond sîdne sǽ, Exon. 20 a; Th. 53, 16; Cri. 851. Heliseus leólc ofer laguflôd on swonrâde, 75 b; Th. 283, 2; Jul. 674. Fereþ oft lagoflôd on lyfte *oft bears water aloft*, 114 b; Th. 440, 3; Rä. 59, 12. Ǽr gescôp êce dryhten laguflôda bigong *before had the Lord eternal created the course of the waters*, 54 b; Th. 193, 29; Az. 129: Bt. Met. Fox 20, 345; Met. 20, 173. Twelf sîþum đæt tîrfæste lond geondlâce laguflôda wynn *fons duodecies undis irrigat omne nemus*, Exon. 56 b; Th. 202, 16; Ph. 70. Lageflôdum þodenum *ceruleis turbinibus*, Wrt. Voc. ii. 133, 38. ᛚ flôdum bilocen, Exon. 19 b; Th. 50, 26; Cri. 807. Ofer lagoflôdas, Andr. Kmbl. 487; An. 244.

lagu-lád, e; *f. A way across water*, Exon. 76 b; Th. 286, 19; Wand. 3: Andr. Kmbl. 627; An. 314. [Cf. *O. Sax.* lagu-līđandi *a seafarer.*]

lagu-mearh, -mearg; *m. A sea-steed, ship*, Exon. 52 a; Th. 182, 7; Gú. 1306. [Cf. *Icel.* lög-dýr, -fákr *a ship.*]

lagu-síþ, es; *m. A sea-journey:*—Ðære láfe lagosíþa *for those who are left after sea-journeyings* [*those who were saved in the ark*], Cd. 67; Th. 81, 11; Gen. 1343. Lagosíþa rest *rest from sea-journeyings* [*on coming out of the ark*], 73; Th. 89, 26; Gen. 1486.

lagu-strǽt, e; *f. A sea-road, the sea:*—Ofer lagustrǽte, Beo. Th. 483; B. 239.

lagu-streám, es; *m. Sea, stream, river, water:*—Folde and lagu-streám *earth and sea*, Bt. Met. Fox 11, 86; Met. 11, 43. On lago-streáme [*the Danube*], Elen. Kmbl. 273; El. 137. Lyft wiđ lagustreám *air with water*, Exon. 93 b; Th. 351, 22; Sch. 84. Lád ofer lagustreám, Andr. Kmbl. 845; An. 423: Bt. Met. Fox 26, 31; Met. 26, 16. Ðǽr lagustreámas wyllan onspringaþ *fons in medio est*, Exon. 56 b; Th. 201, 27; Ph. 62. Lagustreáma full *full of water*, 102 a; Th. 385, 1; Rä. 4, 38. Álýs mé and genere wiđ lagustreámum manegum wæterum *eripe me, et libera me de aquis multis*, Ps. Th. 143, 8: Cd. 91; Th. 115, 21; Gen. 1923. Ofer lagustreámas [*the waters of the deluge*], 161; Th. 201, 5; Exod. 367. Ofer lagustreámas *across the sea*, Beo. Th. 599; B. 297. [*O. Sax.* lagu-strōm.]

lagu-swimmend, es; *m. A creature that swims, a fish:*—Lagu-swimmendra, Salm. Kmbl. 580; Sal. 289.

lah; *n.*(?) *Law:*—Ǽlc mynetere đe betihtlad sí bicge him lah mid xii óran [cf. bicge him lage, Th. i. 294, 8] *let every minter that is accused buy himself law with xii ores* [v. lah-ceáp], L. Eth. iii. 8; Th. i. 296, 16. [*Icel.* lög, is neuter.] v. lagu; lah-ceáp.

lah-breca, an; *m. A law-breaker*, Scint. 2, Lye.

lah-bryce, es; *m. A breach of the law:*—Ðæt wæs geworden đæs đe hé sǽde ꝥurh gelǽredra regolbryce and þurh lǽwedra lahbryce *that happened, according to him* [*Gildas*], *through the violation of their rule by ecclesiastics, and through the breaking of the law by laymen*, Swt. A. S. Rdr. 111, 199. Deóflíce dǽda on mistlícan lahbrycan [MS. D. lag-brycan] on hádbrycan and on ǽwbrycan *devilish deeds in the shape of diverse violations of law, of holy orders and of marriage*, L. Eth. v. 25; Th. i. 310, 18: vi. 28; Th. i. 322, 18. Wearþ đes þeódscipe swíđe forsyngod þurh lahbrycas and þurh ǽswicas þurh hádbrycas and þurh ǽwbrycas, Swt. A. S. Rdr. 109, 147.

lah-ceáp, -cóp, es; *m. Payment made for re-entry into legal rights which have been lost;* redemptio privilegiorum quæ per utlagationem fuerint amissa:—Lahceáp, L. N. P. L. 67; Th. ii. 302, 5. Lahcóp, L. Eth. iii. 3; Th. i. 294, 1. In the note on the latter passage an illustration is quoted from old Danish Law, where 'bylagh' [*town law*] being lost under certain conditions after an absence of a year and a day, a man 'bör at *köbe* sigh thet igen a ny.' The term is found in Old Sleswick Law:—'Rex habet quoddam speciale debitum in Slæswick, quod dicitur *Læghköp*, quo redimitur ibi hereditas [quorundam] morientium.' In the same passage occurs the phrase 'emere lagh.' v. lah.

lah-líc; *adj. Lawful*, Scint. 9, Lye. v. next word.

lah-líce; *adv. Lawfully, according to law;*—Ne úre nǽnig his líf ne fadode swá swá hé scolde ne gehádode regollíce ne lǽwede lahlíce *nor hath any one of us ordered his life as he should, neither those ordained according to their rules nor the laymen according to the law*, Swt. A. S. Rdr. 107, 78. Ðæt hí lǽran đæt gehádode menn regollíce libban and lǽwede lahlíce heora líf fadian, L. I. P. 18; Th. ii. 324, 27.

lah-mann, es; *m. A man acquainted with, and whose duty it was to declare, the law:*—xii lahmenn scylon riht tǽcean Wealan and Ǽnglan vi Engliscne and vi Wylisce. Þolien ealles đæs hý ágon gif hí wóh tǽcen oþþe geládian hí đæt hí bet ne cúþon *xii lawmen shall declare the law to Welsh and English, vi English and vi Welsh. Let them forfeit all they own if they declare wrong; or clear themselves* [*on the ground*] *that they knew no better*, L. O. D. 3; Th. i. 354, 9. In L. Ed. C. 38; Th. i. 461, 21 the latinized form of the word occurs:—Postea inquirat justicia per *lagemannos*, et per meliores homines de burgo vel hundredo vel villa. See Cl. & Vig. Dict. *sub voce* lögmađr.

lah-riht, es; *n. Legal right:*—Ǽghwylc lahriht ge burhriht ge landriht *every legal right, both of town and country*, L. I. P. 7; Th. ii. 312, 19. Gif hwá openne wiđercwyde ongeán lahriht Cristes oþþe cyninges gewyrce *if any one act in open contradiction to the legal right of Crist or of the king*, L. Eth. v. 31; Th. i. 312, 9.

lah-slit; *n*[?]; -sliht, -slite, es; *m*; -slitt, e: *f.* According to its component parts the word means *a breach or violation of the law;* in the Laws however it is applied to *the fine payable for the breach*, and is used only with reference to the Danes, the corresponding term among the English being *wite:*—Beó se wiđ đone cyningc hundtwelftig scill. scyldig on Engla lage . . . and on Dena lage lahslites scyldig, L. C. S. 15; Th. i. 384, 15. Gebéte đæt be đæm đe seó dǽd sý swá be wíte swá be lahslitte [lahslite, MS. B.] *let him make 'bot' for that according to what the deed is, either by 'wite'* [*if English*] *or by 'lahslit'* [*if Danish*], L. E. G. 3; Th. i. 168, 6. Gif preóst fulluhtes forwyrne đam đe đæs þearf sý, gylde wíte mid Englum and mid Denum lahslit, đæt is twelf óran, 10–13. Gylde swá wíte swá lahslitte [lahslite, MS. B], 2; Th. i. 168, 3. Gylde lahslitte inne on Deone lage and wíte mid Englum, 7; Th. i. 172, 3. Lahslite, 8; Th. i. 172, 7. Lahslit, 9; Th. i. 172, 11. Ðonne gilde hé lahsliht, L. N. P. L. 51: 52: 53; Th. ii. 298, 9: 12: 15. The word is continued in the Laws of William the Conqueror:—In Danelahe erit in forisfactura de suo *laslite* [*laxlite* in French], Th. i. 483, 24. In Th. i. 168, note a, a passage is quoted from old Swedish law in which 'lagsliht' occurs. See also Grmm. R. A. 623: Steenstrup's Normannerne, iv. 264 sqq.

lah-wita, an; *m. One who has a knowledge of law, a lawyer:*—Cyningan and bisceopan eorlan and heretogan geréfan and déman lárwitan and lahwitan gedafenaþ mid rihte đæt hí Godes riht lufian *it rightly befits kings and bishops, nobles and generals, sheriffs and judges, those who have learning and those who know law, to love God's justice*, L. I. P. 5; Th. ii. 308, 14.

lám, es; *n. Clay, mud, mire, earth:*—Laam *argilla*, Ælfc. Gl. 56; Som. 67, 35; Wrt. Voc. 37, 25: Wrt. Voc. ii. 100, 66. Lám *a*[*r*]*gella*, Wrt. Voc. 285, 7: *limus*, Ælfc. Gr. 13; Som. 16, 4: Wrt. Voc. ii. 112, 81. Lámes gelícnes *the body* [*after death*], Exon. 98 a; Th. 368, 9; Seel. 19. God gesceóp man of đære eorþan láme *formavit dominus deus hominem de limo terræ*, Gen. 2, 7: Homl. Th. i. 12, 29: 236, 15. Áfæstnod ic eom on láme grundes *I sink in deep mire;* infixus sum in limo profundi, Ps. Spl. 68, 2. Genera mé of láme *deliver me out of the mire;* eripe me de luto, C. 68, 18. Láme bitolden *covered with earth* [*buried*], Exon. 64 a; Th. 235, 11; Ph. 555: 50 a; Th. 173, 27; Gú. 1167: 117 b; Th. 451, 5; Dóm. 99. Ic áworpe đa myht fram mé đe mé fram đé geháten ys swá đæt lám đe ic myd mýnum fótum ontrede *I cast away from me the power that is promised me by thee, as the dirt that I tread upon with my feet*, Shrn. 151, 22. [*O. L. Ger.* lémo, leimo *limus: O. H. Ger.* leim *argilla, limus, lutum: Ger.* lehm.]

lama, loma, lame; *adj. Lame, disabled in the limbs, maimed, crippled, weak, paralysed, palsied, paralytic:*—On sídan lama *pleuriticus*, Ælfc. Gl. 10; Som. 57, 25; Wrt. Voc. 19, 31. Lame *debilis* vel *enervatus*, 77; Som. 72, 22; Wrt. Voc. 45, 55. *Conclamatus* i. *commotus, convocatus, desperatus, vel* loma, Wrt. Voc. ii. 136, 28: *conclamatus*, 105, 20. Áune man se wæs lama *hominem qui erat paraliticus*, Lk. Skt. 5, 18. Ic eom lama þearfa *egenus et pauper sum*, Ps. Th. 108, 22. Đá læg đǽr sum creópere lama fram cildháde *then lay there a cripple lame from his childhood*, Homl. Skt. 10, 25. Ánne bædrydan for eahte geárum lama *a bedridden man paralysed for eight years*, 42. Man ne mót nán þing gehǽlan on restedagum þéh hyt lama beó nú hǽlþ hé ǽgđer ge healte ge blynde ge deáfe ge dumbe ge gebýgede laman and deófolseóce, Nicod. 2; Thw. 1, 29. Án mǽden seó wæs lama *puella paralytica*, Bd. 3, 9; S. 533, 5. Hé wæs lama and eallra his lima þénunge benumen *deficiente penitus omni membrorum officio*, 5, 5; S. 617, 37. Mid langre ádle laman legeres swíđe gehefigod *longo paralysis morbo gravatam*, 3, 9; S. 534, 5. Oft him feorran tó laman liomseóce cwómon healte hreófe and blinde *oft to him from far came the lame, the crippled, the halt, the leprous, and the blind*, Elen. Kmbl. 2425; El. 1214. Lamena [lamana, MS. B.] hé is lǽce *of the lame it is the leech*, Salm. Kmbl. 155; Sal. 77. Iii hit oftræd and hié tó loman gerénode đæt hié mec ǽnigre note nytte beón ne meahton *duos et l. calcatos inutiles fecit*, Nar. 15, 26. Laman *paralyticos*, Mt. Kmbl. 4, 24. [*O. Sax.* lamo: *O. Frs.* lam, lom: *Icel.* lami, lama: *Dan.* lam *lame, palsied, paralytic: O. H. Ger.* lam *claudus, mancus, debilis, paralyticus.*] v. ád-, lim- lama.

lamb, es; *and* lamber; *n. A lamb:*—Ðæt lamb sceal beón ánwintre *erit agnus anniculus*, Ex. 12, 5. Hér is Godes lamb *ecce agnus dei*, Jn. Skt. 1, 29. Swá plegende lamp *quasi agnus lasciviens*, Kent. Gl. 214. Hé gefullode đone wulf and geworhte tó lambe *he baptized the wolf and made it a lamb*, Homl. Th. i. 390, 26. Godes lomber folgian, Exon. 48 a; Th. 164, 22; Gú. 1015. Nyme ǽlc mann án lamb *tollat unusquisque agnum*, Ex. 12, 3. Swá swá lamb *sicut agni*, Ps. Spl. 113, 4. Swá sceóne lambru, Ps. Th. 113, 4, 6. Lambra, Ps. Spl. 113, 6. Mid lamba rysle *cum adipe agnorum*, Deut. 32, 14. Abram gesette seofon lamb on sundron *statuit Abram septem agnas seorsum*, Gen. 21, 28. Ic eów sende swá swá lamb [lombro, Lind: lombor, Rush.] betwux wulfas *ego mitto vos sicut agnos inter lupos*, Lk. Skt. 10, 3. Heald míne lamb [lombor, lomboro, Lind: lombor, Rush.] *pasce agnos meos*, Jn. Skt. 21, 15, 16. [*Orm.* lammbre; *pl*: *Ayenb. Piers P.* lambren: *Goth. O. Sax. Icel. O. H. Ger.* lamb; in *O. H. Ger.* lember, lembir *as well as* lamb *are found in pl.* v. Grff. ii. 214.]

lambes cerse, an; *f. Lamb's cress;* cardamine hirsuta;—Cersan sǽdes sume men hátaþ lambes cersan, L. M. 1, 1; Lchdm. i. 24, 16. v. E. D. S. Plant names.

Lamb-, Lambe-hýþ, e; *f. Lambeth in Surrey:*—Hér forþferde Hardacnut æt Lambhýþe, Chr. 1041; Erl. 167, 30. Ðis synd đa landgemǽre intó Lambehýþe, Cod. Dip. Kmbl. iv. 158, 4. v. hýþ.

lam-byrd, e; *f. A lame, weak, imperfect birth*, Lchdm. iii. 66. 22. v. læt-byrd.

lám-fæt, es; *n. A vessel of clay, the body*, Exon. 74 a; Th. 277, 9, Jul. 578: 100 a; Th. 375, 4; Seel. 133.

lamprede, an; *f. A lamprey* [Low Latin *lampreda.*]:—Hwilce fixas geféhst ðú? Lampredan *quales pisces capis? murænas*, Coll. Monast. Th. 23, 35. [*O. H. Ger.* lampreda, lantprida *murenula*, Grff. ii. 241.]

lâm-pytt, es; *m. A clay-pit:*—Swâ andlang mearce on lâmpyttas, Cod. Dip. Kmbl. iii. 252, 24.

lâm-seáðe [?], an; *f. A clay-* [*or mud-*] *pit:*—Of sceadwellan in lâmseáðan; of lâmseáðan in ledene, Cod. Dip. Kmbl. iii. 80, 14.

lâm-wyrhta, an; *m. A worker in clay, a potter:*—Lâmwyrhte [-wrihta, Lind.] *figuli*, Mt. Kmbl. Rush. 27, 7. Lâmwyrhtæ [-wrihtæs, Lind.], 10.

LAND, es; *n.* I. LAND as opposed to water or air, *earth:*—Wê ðec in lyft gelǽddun oftugon ðê landes wynna *we led thee aloft, earth's pleasures withdrew from thee*, Exon. 39 b; Th. 130, 15; Gû. 438. Ðâ siððan tôfêrdon ða apostolas wîde landes geond ealle ðâs world *then afterwards the apostles separated and went far and wide on earth, throughout all this world*, L. Ælfc. P. 21; Th. ii. 372, 6: Wulfst. 105, 6. Monigra folca ceápstôw of lande and of sǽ cumendra *multorum emporium populorum terra marique venientium*, Bd. 2, 3; S. 504, 19. Úsic æt lande gebrohte, 5, 1; S. 614, 10. Hig tugon hyra scypo tô lande *subductis ad terram navibus*, Lk. Skt. 5, 11. Ðâ cômon hié tô londe on Cornwalum, Chr. 891; Erl. 88, 11. Wǽron ða menn uppe on londe of âgâne, 897; Erl. 95, 24. Ân scip flotigende swâ nêh ðan lande swâ hit nýxt mǽge, 1031; Erl. 162, 7. Ðâ gesundrod wæs lago wið lande, Cd. 8; Th. 10, 27; Gen. 163. Com ðâ tô lande swîðmôd swymman, Beo. Th. 3250; B. 1623. Stille þynceþ lyft ofer londe, Exon. 101 b; Th. 383, 15; Rä. 4, 11. Lifigende ða ðe land tredaþ *living creatures that walk the earth*, Cd. 10; Th. 13, 16; Gen. 203. II. *a land, country, region, district, province:*—Ðæs landes gold ys golda sêlost *aurum terræ illius optimum est*, Gen. 2, 12. Is seó cirice on Campania ðæs landes gemǽro *the church is on the borders of the land of Campania*, Blickl. Homl. 197, 19. Úres landes mann *nostras:* eówres landes mann *vestras*, Ælfc. Gr. 15; Zup. 94, 8: 102, 21. Ne nim ðú nâne sibbe wið ðæs landes menn *ne ineas pactum cum hominibus illarum regionum*, Ex. 34, 15. Twegen landes menn and ân ælþeódig, Homl. Th. ii. 26, 20. Twegen sacerdas ðe ǽr on lîfe wǽron his landes menn *two priests who before, when living, had been his countrymen*, 342, 3. Ðâ cômon ða landes menn [*the Northumbrians*] tôgeánes him and hine ofslôgon, Chr. 1068; Erl. 205, 2. Hî wǽron of Galilêam ðæm lande, Blickl. Homl. 123, 21. Hê leng on ðam lande gewunian ne mihte *he could not live longer in that country*, 113, 11. On Lindesse lande *in provincia Lindissi*, Bd. 3, 27; S. 558, 34. Andreas sette his hand ofer ðara wera eágan ðe ðǽr on lande wǽron *Andrew placed his hand upon the eyes of the men who were there in that country*, Blickl. Homl. 239, 3. Ceólwulf and Eádbald of ðæm londe âfôron *Ceolwulf and Eadbald left the country*, Chr. 794; Erl. 58, 6. Ælþeódige mæn of lande mid heora ǽhtum and mid synnum gewîten *let foreigners depart from the country with their goods and with their sins*, L. Wih. 4; Th. i. 38, 2. Þerh ôðer woeg eft gecerrdon in lond hiera *per aliam viam reversi sunt in regionem suam*, Mt. Kmbl, Lind. 2, 12. Mid ðý hî ðider côman on land *cum illo advenissent*, Bd. 5, 10; S. 624, 1. Ðæt wǽron ða ǽrestan scipu Deniscra monna ðe Angelcynnes lond gesôhton, Chr. 787; Erl. 56, 16. Ǽlc ðæra landa ðe ǽnigne friþige ðæra ðe Ængla land hergie *every land that affords protection to any of those that harry England*, L. Eth. ii. 1; Th. i. 284, 17. Ðâ lǽdde hê mê on fyrran lænd *cum me in ulteriora produceret*, Bd. 5, 12; S. 628, 9. In ða nêsta gemǽro and londo [lond, Rush.] *in proximas villas et vicos*. Mk. Skt. Lind. 6, 36. III. *land, landed property, estate, cultivated land, country* [as opposed to *town*]:—Gesâwen æcer *vel* land *seges*, Ælfc. Gl. 97; Som. 76, 48; Wrt. Voc. 53, 55. Land *solum* vel *tellus* vel *terra*, vel *arvum*, 98; Som. 76, 98; Wrt. Voc. 54, 42. Ðis land *hoc rus*, Ælf. Gr. 9; Som. 12, 21. Land *agellum*, Bd. 4, 12; S. 581, 5. Se ârfæsta bigenga ðæs gâstlîcan landes *pius agri spiritalis cultor*, Bd. 2, 15; S. 519, 8. xii hîda gesettes landes *xii hides of cultivated land*, L. In. 64: 65; Th. i. 144, 6: 9. Be gyrde londes *of a yard of land*, 67; Th. i. 146, 1. Þolige landes and lîfes *let him lose land and life*, L. C. E. 2; Th. i. 358, 21. On lande *ruri*, Ælfc. Gr. 38; Som. 41, 18. Sý hit binnan byrig sý hit upp on lande, L. C. S. 24; Th. i. 390, 5. Ge on lande ge on ôðrum þingum ge on ôðrum gestreónum *consisting of land and of other things and of other acquisitions*, Blickl. Homl. 51, 7. Noe began tô wircenne ðæt land *cœpit Noe exercere terram*, Gen. 9, 20. Bûton earmre wudewan ðe næfde nân land *except a poor widow that had no land*, L. Ath. v. 2; Th. i. 230, 20. Færende on lond *euntes in villam*, Mk. Skt. Lind. 16, 12. Heora wlenca wǽron swîðe monigfealde on landum and on wîngeardum, Blickl. Homl. 99, 15. Hêr geswutelaþ on ðissum gewrite ðæt Leófrîc eorl and his gebedda habbaþ geunnen twâ land *hac inscriptione manifestatur Leofricum comitem et Godgivam comitissam duas villas concessisse*, Cod. Dip. Kmbl. iv. 72, 20. Ǽlc ðe forlǽt land [londo, Lind.] *omnis qui reliquit agros*, Mt. Kmbl. 19, 29: Bd. 5, 19; S. 636, 35. Feówer land hê forgeaf ælþeódigum tô andfencge and tô ælmesdǽdum *he gave four estates for the reception of strangers and for deeds of charity*, Homl. Skt. 7, 386. Byrig and land þurhféran *oppida et rura peragrare*, Bd. 3, 28; S. 560, 32: 3, 30; S. 562, 13. [The word occurs in all the Teutonic languages.] DER. burg-, eá-, eard-, eást-, êg-, el-, ele-, êðel-, feld-, feor-, folc-, gehlot-, heáfod-, heáh-, îg-, in-, irfe-, irþ-, lîn-, mearc-, môr-, omer-, sand-, sîd-, sundor-, sundorgeref-, tûn-, þeód-, un-, ût-, wea[lh]-, wîd-, wyn-, wyrðe-land.

-landa. v. ge-landa.

land-âdl, e; *f. Nostalgia* [so Cockayne, but cf. lond-iuil *epilepsy*, Prompt. Parv.]:—Wið londâdle, L. M. 2, 65; Lchdm. ii. 296, 13.

land-ælf, e; *f. A land-elf:*—Landælfe *ruricolas musas*, Wrt. Voc. ii. 88, 83.

land-âgend, es; *m. A land-owner, one of those to whom a country belongs, a native:*—Hî wǽron on myclum ege ðâm sylfan landâgendum ðe hî ǽr hider laþedon *ipsis qui eos advocaverant indigenis essent terrori*, Bd. 1, 15; S. 483, 34 note. [Cf. *Icel.* land-eigandi *a land-owner*.]

land-âgende; *adj. Owning land:*—Gif gesîþcund mon landâgende forsitte fyrde, geselle cxx scill. and þolie his landes, L. In. 51; Th. i. 134, 8. Landâgende man, L. N. P. L. 49: 52; Th. ii. 298, 4: 10. Landâgende men ic lǽrde ðæt hié heora gafol mid gehygdum âguldon, Blickl. Homl. 185, 21. DER. un-landâgende.

land-âr, e; *f. Property in land, landed estate:*—Of Seint Petres landâre *in territorio Sancti Petri*, Cod. Dip. Kmbl. iv. 242, 16. Hê him ða landâre forgeaf ðe hê ðæt mynster on getimbrade *quo concedente et possessionem terræ largiente, ipsum monasterium fecerat*, Bd. 4, 18; S. 586, 35. Wilniende ðætte heó him funden swylce londâre swylce hê mid ârum on beón mehte *desiring that they should provide him such an estate as he might reside on with dignity*, Chart. Th. 47, 21. Ðæt land æt Boccinge intô Cristes cyrcean, and his ôðre landâre intô ôðran hâlgan stôwan, 540, 26. Nimaþ ðis gold and bicgaþ eów landâre, Homl. Th. i. 64, 12. Ða ðe landâre hæfdon hî hit beceápodon, 316, 10: ii. 224, 5. Ic wille ðæt se cyng beó hlâford ðæs mynstres ðe ic getimbrede, and ðære landâra ðe ic ðyderinn becweden hæbbe, Chart. Th. 547, 31.

land-begenga, an; *m.* I. *a cultivator of land, husbandman, farmer:*—Se mǽra landbegenga [londbegengea, MS. Cott.] *magnus colonus*, Past. 40, 3; Swt. 293, 2. Gif hit on Wôdnes dæig þunrige ðæt tâcnaþ landbigencgena cwealm and cræftigra *if it thunder on Wednesday, that betokens death of husbandmen and craftsmen*, Lchdm. iii. 180, 14. Âgæf ða ðǽm londbigencgum [-bigengum, Rush.] *locavit eam agricolis*, Mk. Skt. Lind. 12, 1. II. *an inhabitant of a country, a native:*—Ðâ sægdon mê ða londbigengan *mihi locorum incole affirmabant*, Nar. 20, 16. Ðâm sylfan landbigengum *ipsis indigenis*, Bd. 1, 15; S. 483, 34. Ealle ða landbigengan ûtamǽran *omnes indigenas exterminare*, 4, 16; S. 584, 6. [*O. H. Ger.* lant-pikengeo *accola, indigena*.]

land-begang, es; *m. Cultivation of land*, or *habitation in a land:*—Londbigonges mînes *incolatus mei*, Ps. Surt. 118, 54. v. preceding word.

land-bôc; *f. A charter in which land is granted:*—Ðis is ðara xxv hîda landbôc ðe Eádgâr cyng gebôcede Gode and Sca. Marian intô Abbandûne, Cod. Dip. Kmbl. iii. 29, 10. Ic wylle ðæt man âgyfe ðâm hîwum æt Domrahamme hyra landbêc, ii. 116, 35. Landbêc *donatio*, Wrt. Voc. ii. 141, 77.

land-brǽce, es; *m. Breaking up* or *ploughing of* [*fallow*] *land:*—Landbrǽce *proscissio*, Ælfc. Gl. 1; *Som.* 55, 20; Wrt. Voc. 15, 20. [Cf. *O.H. Ger.* brâhha *aratio prima;* brâhhôn *proscindere*, Grff. iii. 268: *Ger.* brachen *to plough a field after it has been lying fallow*.]

land-bûend, es; *m.* I. *a cultivator of the land, husbandman:*—Fæder mîn londbûend [-býend, Rush.] is *pater meus agricola est*, Jn. Skt. Lind. 15, 1. Ða landbûendo *agricolæ*, Mt. Kmbl. Lind. 21, 38. Ðǽm londbûendum *agricolis*, 33: 40: Mk. Skt. Lind. Rush. 12, 2. Ðǽm scipmannum is beboden gelîce and ðǽm landbûendum ðæt ealles ðæs ðe him on heora ceápe geweaxe hig Gode ðone teóþan dǽl âgyfen *it is commanded to those who trade with ships, just as to those who cultivate land, that they give to God the tenth part of all their increase*, L. E. I. 35; Th. ii. 432, 28. Sende ða londbûend *misit agricolas*, Mt. Kmbl. Lind. 21, 34. II. *an inhabitant of a country, a native, a dweller on earth:*—Hæleþ wǽron irre landbûende *the men were angry, the inhabitants of the land*, Judth. 11; Thw. 24, 36; Jud. 226. Ælda bearn, londbûendra, Exon. 130 b; Th. 500, 23; Rä. 89, 11. Gesette sunnan and mônan leóman tô leóhte landbûendum, Beo. Th. 191; B. 95. Londbûendum, Exon. 78 b; Th. 295, 7; Crä. 29: 87 a; Th. 326, 22; Vîd. 132. Londbûendum [*the Jews*], Judth. 12; Thw. 26, 7; Jud. 315. Ic ðæt londbûend leóde mîne secgan hýrde *I heard the land's inhabitants, my people, say*, Beo. Th. 2694; B. 1345. v. next two words.

land-bûend, e; *f. A settlement, colony:*—Seó landbûend *colonia*, Nar. 33, 8. v. note p. 78.

land-bûende; *adj. Inhabiting a country, living on the earth:*—Hwâ ðæs leóhtes londbûende brûcan môte *who that lives on land may enjoy that light*, Exon. 93 b; Th. 351, 15; Sch. 80.

land-bûness, e; *f. A settlement, colony:*—Seó landbûness is swîðost cýpemonnum geseted *hæc colonia est maxime negotiatorum*, Nar. 33, 15. Londbûnes *colonia*, 35, 18.

land-ceáp-, côp, es; *m. A fine* or *tax paid when land was purchased:*—Landceáp, L. Eth. iii. 3; Th. i. 292, 16. Landceáp, L. N. P. L. 67; Th. ii. 302, 5. Ego Berchtwulf cyning sile Forðrêde mînum þegne nigen hîgida lond . . . hê salde tô londceápe xxx mancessan and nigen hund scill. wið ðæm londe *I, King Berchtwulf, sell my thane Forthred nine hides of land . . . he gave xxx mancusses as fine at the purchase, and nine hundred shillings for the land,* Cod. Dip. Kmbl. ii. 5, 24-31. [Cf. *Icel.* land-kaup; *n. the purchase of land;* in Norse, *a fine to be paid to the king* by one exiled or banished: *O. Frs.* land-kāp.] v. lah-ceáp.

land-cofa, an; *m.* A translation of *Sicima* [Shechem], Ps. Lamb. 59, 8.

landes mann. v. land.

land-fæsten, es; *n. A land-fastness, a strong military position on land, a pass:*—Leoniða on ānum nearwan londfæstenne him wiðstōd *Leonida in angustiis Thermopylarum obstitit,* Ors. 2, 5; Swt. 80, 14.

land-feoh; *gen.* -feós; *n. 'A recognitory rent for land,'* Cod. Dip. Kmbl. v. 143, 22. v. Kemble's Saxons in England ii. 328-9.

land-fird, e; *f. An expedition, journey by land, a land-force:*—Ne him tō ne dorste sciphere on sǣ ne landfyrd *the fleet durst not approach them at sea nor the land force* [*on land*], Chr. 1001; Erl. 137, 18. Man sceolde mid scypfyrde and eác mid landfyrde hym ongeán faran, 999; Erl. 134, 30. Se man ðe ætfleó fram his hlāforde sȳ hit on scypfyrde sȳ hit on landfyrde þolige ealles ðæs ðe hē āge and his āgenes feores, L. C. S. 78; Th. 1. 420, 9. Ðæt is fyrdfara sig hit on scipfyrde sig hit on landfyrde *scilicet expeditio, sive sit in navali collectione, sive in pedestri,* Chart. Th. 333, 20. Ðā gestihtade hē ðæt hē wolde landfyrde ðider gelǣdan *terrestri itinere illo venire disponebat,* Bd. 3, 15; S. 541, 26.

land-folc, es; *n. The people of a land* or *country:*—Hwæðer ðæt landfolc sī tō gefeohte stranglīc oððe untrumlīc *populum, utrum fortis sit an infirmus,* Num. 13, 20. Ðet landfolc hardlīce wiðstōd *the people resisted stoutly,* Chr. 1046; Erl. 171, 4: 1070; Erl. 207, 22. On sumere tīde com micel hungor on ðam lande and gehwǣr ðæt landfolc micclum geangsumode *at one time a great famine came on the land and very much afflicted the people everywhere,* Homl. Th. ii. 170, 32: 164, 19.

land-fruma, an; *m. A prince of a country:*—Leóf landfruma, Beo. Th. 61; B. 31.

land-gafol, es; *n. Rent for land:*—Hē sceal landgafol syllan *he must pay rent,* L. R. S. 2; Th. i. 432, 13. Hē sceal . . . his lāforde wyrcan . . . ne þearf hē landgafol syllan *he must work for his lord, then he need not pay rent,* 3; Th. i. 432, 23. v. gafol-land.

land-gehwearf, es; *n. An exchange of land;* commutatio terræ:—Ðis is seó gerǣdnes ðe Byrhtelm biscop and Aþelwold abbod hæfdon ymbe hira landgehwerf . . . Se biscop gesealde ða hīda æt Cenintūne and se abbud gesealde ðæt seofontȳne hȳda æt Crydanbricge, Chart. Th. 191, 6.

land-gemaca, an; *m. A neighbour:*—*Vicinum* landgemacena, (*in margin*) *affinium* landgemaca, Hpt. Gl. 480, 18-20.

land-gemǣre, es; *n. A boundary, confine:*—Ligeþ ðæt londgemǣre [*of Asia and Africa*] sūþ ðonan ofer Nilus ða eá, Ors. 1, 1; Swt. 8, 29. Cirus fōr ofer ðæt londgemǣre ofer ða eá ðe hātte Araxis *Cyrus passed the boundary, the river that was called Araxis,* 2, 4; Swt. 76, 6. Ðis syndon ðara twegra hīda landgemǣru *these are the boundaries of the two hides,* Cod. Dip. Kmbl. iii. 206, 25. Landgemǣro, 207, 34. The word is of frequent occurrence in the Charters. Sī se man āwirged, ðe forhwyrfe his freóndes landgemǣro *maledictus, qui transfert terminos proximi sui,* Deut. 27, 17. Ofer landgemǣru *extra terminum,* Ælfc. Gr. 47; Som. 47, 29. Ðā cōman hī mid sciphere on heora landgemǣro *advecti navibus inrumpunt terminos,* Bd. 1, 12; S. 480, 34: Ps. Th. 45, 8.

land-gemirce, es; *n. A boundary:*—Se westsūþende Europe landgemirce is in Ispania westeweardum et ðæm gārsecge *Europæ in Hispania occidentalis oceanus terminus est,* Ors. 1, 1; Swt. 8, 23. Ðǣr Asia and Europe hiera landgemircu tōgædre licgaþ, 10. Affrica and Asia hiera landgemircu onginnaþ of Alexandria, 28. Landgemyrcu, Beo. Th. 424; B. 209.

land-gesceaft, es; *n. The earthly creation, created things on earth:*—Bǣdon bletsian eall landgesceaft ēcne drihten *they called upon all created things on earth to bless the Lord eternal,* Cd. 191; Th. 238, 25; Dan. 360.

land-geweorc, es; *n. The principal stronghold of a country, one which it has been the work of the country to build* [cf. Beo. Th. 135-152; B. 67-76], Beo. Th. 1880; B. 938.

land-gewyrpe, es; *n. A heap of earth thrown up* [?]:—Andlang ðare landgewirpa, Cod. Dip. Kmbl. iii. 453, 30. On ða landgewyrpu . . . andlang ðara landgewyrpa, 434, 2-4.

land-hæbbende; *adj.* I. *owning land:*—Monnes landhæbbendes, L. In. 45; Th. i. 130, 10. Cf. landāgende. II. *holding a country as a ruler:*—Landhæbbende ł his cynnes lātwa *tribunus,* Rtl. 193, 15.

land-hæfen, e; *f. Property in land:*—Be Wilisces monnes londhæfene. Gif Wylisc mon hæbbe hīde londes, his wer biþ cxx scill., L. In. 32; Th. i. 122, 8.

land-here, es; *m. A military force which acts on land* [opposed to *sciphere*], or *which belongs to the land* [opposed to a foreign force]:—Æfter ðam gegadorode micel here hine of EástEnglum ǣgðer ge ðæs landheres ge ðara wīcinga ðe hié him tō fultume āspanen hæfdon *after that a great force collected from East Anglia, both of the native force and of the vikings that they had allured to their assistance,* Chr. 921; Erl. 107, 15. Hēr fōr Æþelstān in on Scotland ǣgðer ge mid landhere ge mid scyphere, 933; Erl. 110, 27. [*Icel.* land-herr *people of the land.*]

land-hlāford, es; *m.* I. *a land-lord, an owner of land, lord of the manor:*—Tōdǣle man ða eahta dǣlas on twā and fō se landhlāford tō healfum tō healfum se bisceop sȳ hit cynges man sȳ hit þegnes [cf. H. I. 11; Th. i. 520, 18-20 reliquum in duas partes dividant, dimidium habeat dominus, dimidium habeat episcopus, sit homo regis vel alterius], L. Edg. i. 3; Th. i. 264, 3: L. Eth. ix. 8; Th. i. 342, 19: L. C. E. 8; Th. i. 366, 9. Healde se landhlāford ðæt forstolene orf ōþ ðæt se āgenfrigea ðæt geācsige *let the lord keep the stolen cattle until the owner get to hear of it,* L. Edg. S. 11; Th. i. 276, 14: L. Eth. i. 3; Th. i. 282, 27. And nān man ne hwyrfe nānes yrfes būtan ðæs gerēfan gewitnesse oððe ðæs mæssepreóstes oððe ðæs landhlāfordes, L. Ath. i. 10; Th. i. 204, 18. II. *the lord of a country:*—Hū stīðe se landhlāford spræc wið hig, and hig cwǣdon se landhlāford wēnde ðæt wē wǣron sceáweras *locutus est nobis dominus terræ dure et putavit nos exploratores esse,* Gen. 42, 30.

land-lagu, e; *f. Law* or *regulation prevailing in a district:*—Ðeós landlagu stænt on suman lande *hæc consuetudo stat in quibusdam locis,* L. R. S. 4; Th. i. 434, 29. Landlaga sȳn mistlīce swā ic ǣr sǣde *leges et consuetudines terrarum sunt multiplices et varie, sicut prelibavimus,* 21; Th. i. 440, 19.

land-leás; *adj. Landless, not having land:*—Be landleásum mannum. Gif hwylc landleás man folgode on ōðre scire, L. Ath. i. 8; Th. i. 204, 4.

land-leód, es; *pl.* e, an [cf. Seaxe, Seaxan]; *m. An inhabitant of a country:*—Landleód *accola,* Wrt. Voc. ii. 3, 76: [*in*]*digena,* 28, 59. Eft hē frægn hwæðer ða ylcan landleóde Cristene wǣron *rursus interrogavit, utrum iidem insulani Christiani essent,* Bd. 2, 1; S. 501, 12: 4, 26; S. 602, 8. Ac hii ða londlēóde tiolode mā ūssa feónda willan tō gefremmanne ðonne ūrne *sed illi* [*periti regionum*] *majorem hosti quam mihi favorem accommodantes,* Nar. 6, 19. Ðā wurdon ða landleóde his ware and him wið gefuhton, Chr. 917; Erl. 102, 16. Ðæt folc eal ðæt ðǣr tō lāfe wæs ðara landleóda beág tō Eádwearde cyninge *the people, all that remained of the inhabitants of the district, submitted to king Edward,* 921; Erl. 108, 1. Hē wæs ðæs cynges swica and ealra landleóda, 1055; Erl. 189, 4. Hié from ðām londleódum þurh seara ofslægene wurdon *conspiratione finitimorum per insidias trucidantur,* Ors. 1, 10; Swt. 44, 28. Hē betealde hine wið Eádward cyng his hlāford and wið ealle landleódan *he cleared himself to his lord king Edward and to all the people,* Chr. 1052; Erl. 187, 20.

land-leód, es; *m.* [?]: e; *f. The people of a country:*—Se wer gebiraþ māgum and seó cynebōt ðām leódum; *other reading:*—Ðam were habbaþ ða mǣgas and ðam cynebōt se [seó?] landleód, L. Wg; Th. i. 190, 9, and note 14. Schmid p. 396 gives the further reading:—Ðæt cynebōt tō ðam landleód. [These passages seem corrupt, so that much reliance perhaps cannot be placed upon them for determining the gender, but it may be noticed that *O. H. Ger. lant-liut* is masc. v. Grff. ii. 195.] Se fyrdinge dyde ðære landleóde ǣlcne hearm *the levy did the people of the country every kind of harm,* Chr. 1006; Erl. 140, 12. Ealle ðās landleóda belicgaþ ūs *all these people will surround us,* Jos. 7, 9.

land-lyre, es; *m. Loss of land:*—For his landlyre hēr on lande *on account of his loss of land in this country,* Chr. 1105; Erl. 240, 11.

land-mann, es; *m. A native of a country:*—Nāh nāðer tō farenne ne Wylisc man on Ænglisc land ne Ænglisc on Wylisc ðē mā būtan gesettan landmen se hine sceal æt stæðe underfōn and eft ðǣr būtan fācne gebringan. Gyf se landman ǣniges fācnes gewita sȳ ðonne sȳ hē wītes scyldig, L. O. D. 6; Th. i. 354, 23-7. Landmanna cyme *the coming of the men of the country,* Cd. 151; Th. 189, 4; Exod. 179. v. landes mann *under* land. [*O. H. Ger.* lant-man *patriota.*]

land-mearc, e; *f. Boundary of an estate* or *of a country:*—Seó landmearce līþ of Terstān upp be Hohtūninga mearce, Cod. Dip. Kmbl. iii. 189, 5. Londmearce neáh *near to the land's boundary,* Exon. 75 a; Th. 280, 27; Jul. 635. [*O. H. Ger.* lant-marcha *funiculum.*] Cf. landgemǣre, -gemirce.

land-mearc; *adj. Belonging to the boundaries of a country:*—Mīn is se landmearca and mīn is mannaseisca landsplot *meus est galaad* (= heap of witness) *et meus est mannases,* Ps. Lamb. 59, 9.

land-openung, e; *f. Breaking up of land;* proscissio, Ælfc. Gl. 57; Som. 67, 68; Wrt. Voc. 37, 54.

land-rǣden, ne; *f. Institution, disposition, ordinance of a district* or *country:*—Hēde se ðe scīre healde ðæt hē wite ā hwæt eald landrǣden sȳ and hwæt þeóde þeáw *videat qui scyram tenet, ut semper sciat que sit antiqua terrarum institutio, vel populi consuetudo,* L. R. S. 4; Th. i. 434, 33.

land-rest, e; *f. A land-couch, grave:*—Lǣtan landreste *to leave the grave,* Andr. Kmbl. 1561; An. 782.

land-rīca, an; *m. A powerful man in a district, a landed proprietor, a land-lord;* the term seems equivalent to *land-hlāford,* q. v.:—Heáh landrīca *ierarchon,* Wrt. Voc. ii. 48, 29. Fō se landrīca tō healfan, and tō healfan ðæt hundred, L. Edg. S. 8; Th. i. 274, 30. Gif cyninges þegn oððe ǣnig landrīca hit forhæbbe, gilde x. healf-mearc, healf Criste healf cynge, L. N. P. L. 58, 59; Th. ii. 300, 3: 6, 7. Fare ðæs cinges gerēfa tō, and ðæs bisceopes, and ðæs landrīcan [cf. landhlāford, 11], L. C. E. 8; Th. i. 366, 8: L. Eth. ix. 8; Th. i. 342, 16. Healf landrīcan, healf wǣpentake, L. Eth. iii. 3; Th. i. 294, 8, 9. Hē ðeáh gange ðam landrīcan tō ordāle, 4; Th. i. 294, 20. Healf landrīcan, healf cinges gerēfan binnan port, 7; Th. i. 296, 8. Gylde ðam cyninge oððe landrīcan, L. C. S. 37; Th. i. 348, 13. Healf Criste and healf landrīcan, L. N. P. L. 49; Th. i. 298, 5. Gif hwā borhleás orf hæbbe, and landrīcan hit befōn, āgife ðæt orf and gilde xx ōran, L. Eth. iii. 5; Th. i. 296, 1.

land-rīce, es; *n. A territory, region, estate*:—Bōcland *vel* landrīce *fundos*, Wrt. Voc. ii. 152, 18. Hē ðāgiet lytel landrīce hæfde būton ðære byrig ānre *he had as yet little territory except the town only*, Ors. 2, 2; Swt. 66, 14. Ic hæbbe gesǣd ymb ða þrié dǣlas ealles ðises middangeardes ac ic wille nū ðara þreóra landrīca gemǣre gereccan *tripartiti orbis divisiones dedi, ipsarum quoque partium regiones significare curabo*, 1, 1; Swt. 10, 5.

land-riht, es; *n.* I. *the law of the land, the rights and privileges belonging to the inhabitant of a country* or *to the owner of land* [?]:—Londrihtes mōt ðære mǣgburge monna ǣghwilc īdel hweorfan *shall each man of the family wander lacking the rights of those who live in the land*, Beo. Th. 5765; B. 2886. Grimm, R. A. 731 q. v. quotes in illustration from Saxo the order of Frotho: 'Si quis in acie primus fugam capesseret, *a communi jure alienus* existeret.' See also pp. 39–42. Mid rihtum landrihte swā hit on lande stonde *in accordance with the regular law of the land, as it stands in the land*, Cod. Dip. Kmbl. iii. 435, 35. Unc mōdige ymb mearce sittaþ . . ne willaþ rūmor unc landriht heora *round our border sit bold ones, who will not more largely allow us their landright*, i. e. *will not allow us to possess more land in their country*, Cd. 91; Th. 114, 28; Gen. 1911. Hē landriht geþah *he received landright, he was settled in the country with the right of a native*, 161; Th. 200, 10; Exod. 354. Āhte ic fela wintra folgaþ tilne holdne hlāford óððæt Heorrenda nū leóðcræftig mon londryht geþah ðæt mē eorla hleó ǣr gesealde *good service had I for many a winter, a kind lord; until now Heorrenda, a man skilled in song, has received land right; the prince had before given me that*, i. e. *H. was now admitted, as Deór had been before, to the rights of a native, and had succeeded in attracting to himself the favour before shown to Deór*, Exon. 100 b; Th. 379, 29; Deór. 40. II. *that which is due from land or estates*:—Ðegenes lagu is ðæt hē þreó þinc of his lande dō . . . Eác of manegum landum māre landriht ārīst tō cynges gebanne *the law as regards the thane is that he do three things for his land. Also for many lands* or *estates, more extensive dues arise upon decree of the king*, L. R. S. 1; Th. i. 432, 6. [*O. Sax.* land-reht *law of the land* e. g. irō aldironō ēo, therō liudiō landreht: *O. Frs.* land-riucht: *O. H. Ger.* lant-reht *jus, lex*: *Ger.* land-recht *common law.*]

land-sǣta, an; *m. One settled in a country, a colonist*:—Ōðres eardes landsēta *colonus*, Ælfc. Gl. 8; Som. 56, 100; Wrt. Voc. 18, 49. [*O. L. Ger.* land-sētio: *Ger.* land-sass.]

land-sceap, es; *n. A district, tract of country, land*:—Swā hē on landsceape stille stande ðǣr hine storm ne mæg wind āwecgan *as if it* [*the vessel*] *stand still on land, where storm or wind cannot move it*, Andr. Kmbl. 1002; An. 501. v. land-scipe.

land-scearu, e; *f.* I. *a share, division,* or *portion of land, land, country*:—Sume hine lǣtaþ ofer landscare rīdum tōrinnan. Nis ðæt rǣdlīc þing gif swā hlutor wæter tōflōweþ æfter feldum ōð hit tō fenne werþ *some let it* [*spring of water*] *run away over their land in rills. It is not a wise thing if water so pure disperses itself along the fields, until it becomes a marsh*, Past. 65; Swt. 469, 5. Hēton lǣdan ofer landsceare . . . drōgon æfter dūnscræfum ymb stānhleoðo efne swā wīde swā wegas tōlǣgon innan burgum strǣte stānfāge *they bade lead him over the country . . . they dragged him by mountain caves, across rocky slopes, far as the roads stretched, within the towns, the streets with many-coloured stones*, Andr. Kmbl. 2460; An. 1231. II. *a boundary of land* [cf. *Icel.* skör *a rim, edge*]. With this meaning the word occurs in charters which Kemble [Cod. Dip. iii. xii.] notices as being of comparatively late date and belonging to the extreme south of England:—Ðis his ðara fīf hīda landscaru tō westtūne [*then follow the boundaries*: cf. landgemǣra *in such phrases*], Cod. Dip. Kmbl. iii. 338, 4. Of ðam hlince tō ðam beorge tō Ælfrēdes landscare; ðonne is hit ðǣr feówer furlanga brād būtan feówer gyrdan; ðonne gǣþ hit ðǣr niðer be ðara wyrhtena landscare, 420, 25–7. Ðonne eást andlang hricgweges tō Brytfordinga landsceare, 302, 16. *The word also occurs in compounds* landscar-hlinc [*also* landscare hlinc], landscar-āc. [Halliwell in his Dictionary gives *land-share* as a Devonshire word, meaning 'headland of a field': he also gives the word *land-score*.]

land-scipe, es; *m. A tract of land, region*:—Ic ā ne geseah lāðran landscipe *never saw I a more hateful region*, Cd. 19; Th. 24, 11; Gen. 376. [*O. Sax.* land-skepi: *Icel.* land-skapr *a region*: *O. H. Ger.* lant-scaf *regio, provincia, patria.*]

land-seten, e; *f.* I. *Land in possession* or *occupation, an estate*:—Ðis his sió landseten æt Stāntūne ðe Cēnwold hæfde [then follow the boundaries], Cod. Dip. Kmbl. iii. 403, 24. [cf. ii. 143 where it is said 'Æþelwulf suo fideli ministro nomine Cenwold jure hereditario possidendam condonavit terram in loco ubi a ruricolis Stantun nominatur.' And 144, 'Territoria istius agelli his terminibus circumdata esse videntur.' II. *occupation of land*:—Gebyreþ ðæt him man tō landsetene sylle ii oxan and i cū and vi sceáp *moris est ut ad terram assidendam dentur ei ii boves, et i vacca, et vi oves*, L. R. S. 4; Th. i. 434, 23.

land-setla, an; *m. An occupier of land, a tenant*:—Ic an mīne landsedlen here toftes tō ōwen āchte *I give to my tenants their tofts into their own possession*, Cod. Dip. Kmbl. iv. 282, 29. [*O. H. Ger.* land-sidilo *accola, colonus, indigena*, Grff. vi. 310: also *a tenant*. v. Grmm. R. A. 317: cf. *Icel.* land-seti *a tenant.*]

land-sidu, a; *m. Custom of a country*:—Gemacaþ ðæt his ege wierþ tō gewunan and tō landsida *he causes the fear of him to become a habit and custom of the country*, Past. 17, 9; Swt. 121, 25. Be landside *according to the usage of the district*, L. R. S. 8; Th. i. 436, 27. Ealle landsida ne sȳn gelīce *omnium terrarum instituta non sunt equalia*, 4; Th. i. 434, 30. [*O. Sax.* land-sidu.]

land-sittende; *adj. Occupying land*:—Hē lētt gewrītan hū mycel ǣlc man hæfde ðe landsittende wæs innan Englalande on lande oððe on orfe and hū mycel feós hit wǣre wurþ *he* [*William I.*] *caused to be written how much every man that was in the occupation of land in England, had in land or in cattle, and how much money it was worth*, Chr. 1085; Erl. 218, 32.

land-sōcn, e; *f. Search for land* or *country*:—Tōfaran on landsōcne *to separate in search of land* [*of the dispersion at the tower of Babel*], Cd. 80; Th. 100, 17; Gen. 1665: 81; Th. 102, 12; Gen. 1699.

land-spēd, e; *f. Property in land*:—Ða munecas tō biscopan gewurdan ðære cyrcean landspēde [*substantiam aecclesiae*], Cod. Dip. Kmbl. iii. 349, 24.

land-spēdig; *adj. Rich in landed property, having large estates*:—Landspēdig *locuples*, Ælf. Gl. 88; Som. 74, 72; Wrt. Voc. 50, 52. Ðes and ðeós landspēdiga *hic et hæc locuples*, Ælfc. Gr. 9, 27; Som. 11, 22.

land-splott, es; *m. A small portion,* or *plot, of ground*:—Mín is mannaseisca landsplot *meus est mannases*, Ps. Lamb. 59, 9. Ðisne landsplot becwæþ Æþelwine intō Abbendūne [it is spoken of before as *parva ruris particula, ruris particula*], Cod. Dip. Kmbl. iv. 39, 12.

land-stede, es; *m. Land, country*, Exon. 115 a; Th. 442, 22; Kl. 16.

land-stycce, es; *n. A small portion of land*:—Him gebyreþ sum landstycce for his geswince *convenit, ut aliquam terre portiunculam habeat pro labore suo*, L. R. S. 18; Th. i. 440, 8. Him man hwilces landsticces geann, 19; Th. i. 440, 14.

land-waru, e; *f. The people of a country, country*, Beo. Th. 4631; B. 2321. [Cf. burh-, ceaster-waru.]

land-weard, es; *m. The guard of a country, prince, ruler*, Beo. Th. 3785; B. 1890.

land-wela, an; *m. The wealth of this earth*, Exon. 63 a; Th. 232, 11; Ph. 505.

lane, an; *f. A lane, a narrow and bounded path, a street in a town*:—Hit cymeþ on ægles ionan; ondlang ðære lonan ðæt hit cymeþ eft in ða burnan, Cod. Dip. Kmbl. iii. 33, 7. On ða ealdan lanan, 456, 3. Ðīnne līchoman geond ðisse ceastre lanan hié tōstenceaþ *thy body shall they scatter through the streets of this city*, Blickl. Homl. 237, 5: 241, 21, 25. [*O. Frs.* lona, lana.] v. norþ-lane.

lane-sang. v. lāc-sang.

lang *length of time*. v. leng.

LANG; *adj.* LONG, *tall*:—Hē sǣde ðæt ðæt land síe swīðe lang norþ ðonan *he said that the land stretches thence far to the north*, Ors. 1, 1; Swt. 17, 4. Se wudu is eástlang and westlang hundtwelftiges mīla lang oððe lengra *the wood, measuring from east to west, is a hundred and twenty miles long, or longer*, Chr. 893; Erl. 88, 28. Ðæt is þrittiges mīla lang eást and west *habet ab oriente in occasum triginta circiter milia passuum*, Bd. 1, 3; S. 475, 19. Ðæt hē wǣre lang on bodige *quod esset vir longæ staturæ*, 2, 16; S. 519, 33. Ðæt is nū ðæs līchoman gōd ðæt mon síe fæger and lang and brād, Bt. 34, 6; Fox 140, 32. Eádweard se langa, Byrht, Th. 139, 53; By. 273. Se biþ lang līfes and welig *he shall be long-lived and wealthy*, Lchdm. iii. 156, 18. Næs lang tō ðȳ ðæt his brōðor ðyses lǣnan līfes tīman geendode *it was not long before his brother died*, 434, 24. Nis hit lang tō ðon, Bd. 4, 24; S. 599, 5. Hié tealdon ðætte Israhēla rīce sceolde beón hēr on eorþan mycel and lang *they reckoned that the kingdom of Israel should be great and lasting here on earth*, Blickl. Homl. 117, 18. Tō langum gemynde *as a lasting memorial*, Homl. Skt. pref. 51. Langere tīde *tanto tempore*, Bd. 1, 25; S. 487, 11. Mid langre ādle *longo morbo*, 3, 9; S. 534, 5. Ofer swā langne weg sǣs and landes *per tam prolixa terrarum et maris spatia*, 2, 18; S. 520, 36. Ealle ðās naman habbaþ langne .o. on eallum casum *all these nouns have long o in all cases*, Ælfc. Gr. 9; Som. 8, 52. Ðā andswarode hē ymbe long *then answered he after long*, Bt. 39, 2; Fox 214, 8. Lange tīde *multis temporibus*, Lk. Skt. 8, 27, 29. Hiwgende lang gebed *simulantes longam orationem*, 20, 47. Ða beóþ eahta and feówertiges elna lange and ða mǣstan fīftiges elna lange. Ors. 1, 1; Swt. 18, 6. Ða ðe tō lang tō secgenne syndon *which are too long to narrate*, Bd. 3, 8; S. 532, 12. Wæs se līchoma sponne lengra ðære þrȳh *corpus mensura palmi longius erat* *sarcofago*, 4, 11; S. 580, 5. Ne biþ hē lengra đonne syfan elna lang, Ors. 1, 1; Swt. 18, 4. Đis eálond hafaþ mycele lengran dagas on sumera đonne đa sūþdǣlas middangeardes, Bd. 1, 1; S. 473, 32. Đā bebeád hē đæt him mon lengran cwidas beforan cwǣde *præcepit eum sententias longiores dicere*, 5, 2; S. 615, 14. Đa onfōþ lengestne dōm *hi accipient prolixius judicium*, Mk. 12, 40. [The word occurs in all the Teutonic dialects.] DER. and-, dæg-, ealdor-, ge-, morgen-, niht-, sumor- lang; *it also is found in combination with the words denoting the points of the compass*, eást-lang, &c.

Langa-Frige-dæg *Good-Friday*:—Đes passio gebyreþ on Langa-Frigadæg, Jn. Skt. 18, 1, rubric. Man ne mōt hālgian hūsel on Langa-Frigedæg forđan đe Crist þrowode on đone dæg for ūs *the eucharist must not be consecrated on Good Friday, for Christ suffered for us on that day*, L. Ælfc. C. 36; Th. ii. 358, 16. [On langfridæi him on rode hengen, Chr. 1137; Erl. 263, 25.] [*Icel.* Langi-frjádagr: *Da.* Lang-fredag. In the E. D. S. Holderness Glossary *Lang-Friday* is given as the first Friday in Lent.]

Langa-land, es; *n. Langeland* an island in the Baltic belonging to Denmark:—On bæcbord him wæs Langaland . . . and đās land eall hȳraþ tō Denemearcan, Ors. 1, 1: Swt. 19, 35. [*Icel.* Langa-land.]

langaþ. v. langoþ.

Lang-beardas, -beardan; *m. pl. The Lombards*:—Đa Gallie đe mon nū hǣt Longbeardas, Ors. 4, 7; Swt. 180, 25. Tō Longbeardna londe, Chr. 887; Erl. 86, 9. Longbeardum, Exon. 85 a; Th. 320, 21; Vīd. 32: 86 a; Th. 323, 18; Vīd. 80. [*Icel.* Lang-barðar.] v. Grmm. Gesch. D. S. c. xxv; cf. Heađo-beardan.

lange; *adv. Long, a long time, far*:—Lange *diu*; leng *diutius*; ealra lengst *diutissime*, Ælfc. Gr. 38; Som. 42, 10. Longe *procul*, Wrt. Voc. ii. 66, 71: *penitus*, 72. Đā hē đā lange and lange hearpode *when then he had harped a long, long time*, Bt. 35, 6; Fox 170, 5. Hū longe *how long*, Past. pref; Swt. 9, 4. Hū langæ, Bd. 4, 25; S. 600, 10. Nōht longe æfter đon *not long after that*, Shrn, 105, 9. Swā lange swā gē dydon ānum of đysum mīnum læstum gebrōđorum swā lange gē hyt dydon mē *quamdiu fecistis uni de his fratribus meis minimis, mihi fecistis*, Mt. Kmbl. 25, 40: Blickl. Homl. 169, 21. Genōh lange *long enough*, Deut. 1, 6. Hwæt mæg ic leng dōn *ultra quid faciam?* Gen. 27, 37. Hwider mæg ic nū leng fleón *quo enim nunc fugiam?* Bd. 2, 12; S. 513, 27. Swađer uncer leng wǣre [lifede, 38] *which of us two lived the longer*, Chart. Th. 485, 29. Đænne đū lengc ne mōst līfes brūcan, Dōm. L. 32, 61. Lencg, Lk. Skt. 16, 2. Leng swā swīđor, Cd. 47; Th. 60, 30; Gen. 989. Swā leng swā swīđor, Exod. 19, 19. Nā leng heó ne gebād đonne hit dæg wās *she waited only till it was day*, Apol. Th. 19, 2. Đone aldormon đe him lengest wunode *the alderman that stopped with him longest*, Chr. 755; Erl. 48, 21.

lang-fǣre; *adj. Lasting, enduring, old*:—Nānwuht nis langfǣres on đīs andweardan līfe *there is nothing lasting in this present life*, Bt. 38, 2; Fox 198, 6. On langfǣre ylde bet hē dēþ *at an advanced age he will do better*, Lchdm. iii. 188, 26. Eác đa treówa đe beóþ āheáwene on fullum mōnan beóþ heardran wiđ wyrmǣtan and lengfǣrran [lang-ferran, MS. L.], 268, 10. Swā eác treówa gif hī beóþ on fullum mōnan geheáwene hī beóþ heardran and langfǣrran tō getimbrunge *so too trees, if they are cut down at the full moon, are harder and more lasting for building*, Homl. Th. i. 102, 23. [*O. H. Ger.* lanc-fāri *longævus*, Grff. 3, 574.]

lang-first, es; *m. A long space of time*:—Nolde fæder engla in đisse līfe longfyrst ofer đæt wunian lēton *the father of angels would not let him remain in this life a long space after that*, Exon. 46 b; Th. 159, 2; Gū. 920.

langian; *p.* ode *To grow long*:—Đonne se dæg langaþ đonne gǣþ seó sunne norþweard ōþ đæt heó becymþ tō đam tācne đe is gehāten Cancer, Lchdm. iii. 250, 9. Se langienda dæg, 252, 6, 9. Eft on langiendum dagum hē ofergǣþ đone sūđran sunnstede, 14.

langian; *p.* ode: *v. impers. with acc. of pers. To cause longing, desire, discontent,* or *pain in a person*:—Langaþ đē āwuht *dost thou desire aught?* Cd. 25: Th. 32, 1; Gen. 496. Hæleþ langode hwonne hié of nearwe stæppan mōsten *the men longed for the time when they might step from durance*, 71; Th. 86, 16; Gen. 1431. Hine đæs heardost langode hwanne hē of đisse worlde mōste, Blickl. Homl. 227, 1. Mec longade *I was ill at ease*, Exon. 115 a; Th. 442, 18; Kl. 14. Longiga *tædere*, Mk. Skt. Lind. 14, 13. Đæt ūs nū æfter swelcum longian mǣge swelce đā wǣron *that we should now long for such times as then were*, Ors. 2, 5; Swt. 84, 27. Đā ongan hine eft langian on his cȳđđe *then he began to long again for his native land*, Blickl. Homl. 113, 15. [*O. Sax.* langōn (*with acc. of pers.*): *Icel.* langa (*pers. and impers.*): *O. H. Ger.* langēn, langōn (mih langet *desidero*.)]

langian; *p.* ode *To summon, call*:—Godes æncgel cwæþ đæt hē sceolde đē him tō langian [MS. U. gelangian] *God's angel said that he was to summon thee to him*, Homl. Skt. 10, 122. v. ge-langian.

langian; *p.* ode *To belong, pertain*:—Alle đa land đe longen intō đare hālagen stówe *all the lands that belong to the holy place*, Cod. Dip. Kmbl. iv. 215, 4. [*O. H. Ger.* ge-langōn *pertingere*.] v. lengan *to belong*.

lang-līce; *adv. Long, at length, for a long time*:—Langlīce *tractim*, Ælfc. Gr. 38; Som. 41, 12. Hēt đone diácon langlīce swingan, Homl. Th. i. 426, 13: ii. 490, 5. Langlīce on gebedum læg, 160, 35: 510, 25. Langlīce bæd, i. 66, 23. [Cf. *O. H. Ger.* lang-līh *long* (of time): *Icel.* lang-liga *for a long time past*.]

lang-līfe -līf; *adj. Long-lived*:—Langlīfe *longævus*, Ælfc. Gl. 35: Som. 62, 95; Wrt. Voc. 28, 72. Langlīf [MS. C. langlīfe, Zup. 320, 1] *longaevus*, Wrt. Voc. 85, 59. Đæt đū sī langlīfe *ut longo vivas tempore*, Deut. 5, 16: 4, 1. Longlīfe and gileáffull suǣ Sarra *longeva et fidelis ut Sarra*, Rtl. 109, 39. Langlīfe hē biþ *he shall live long*, Lchdm. iii. 184, 4. [*Icel.* lang-lífr: *O. H. Ger.* lanc-līp *longaevus*, Grff. 2, 46.]

lang-mōd; *adj. Patient, long-suffering*:—Longmōd *longanimis*, Ps. Stev. 7, 12. [*Ps.* 102, 8 lang-mode: *O. H. Ger.* lanc-mōt *longanimis*: cf. *Ger.* lang-müthig *patient, long-suffering*.]

lang-ness, e; *f. Length*:—Brādnyss langnyss heáhnyss and deópnyss *breadth, length, height and depth*, Homl. Th. ii. 408, 21. Langnysse dagena ic gefylle hine *longitudine dierum replebo eum*, Ps. Spl. 90, 16. Đonne sceal man đysne wyrttruman gedrīgean and đa langnysse tōceorfan on pysena gelīcnysse *this plant is to be dried, and its length cut up into pieces about the size of peas*, Herb. 140, 1; Lchdm. i. 260, 15. Ealle ōđre dagas on twelf mōnþum habbaþ mislīce langnisse *all other days in the twelve months have various lengths*, Lchdm. iii. 258, 2.

langoþ, es; *m. Longing, desire, discontent,* or *weariness that arises from unsatisfied desire*:—Æfter men dyrne langaþ born *a secret longing for the man burned within him*, Beo. Th. 3763; B. 1879. Hine ne meahte longaþ gelettan, Exon. 37 b; Th. 123, 29; Gū. 330. Ic ǣfre ne mæg đære mōdceare mīnre gerestan ne ealles đæs longaþes đe mec on đissum līfe begeat *never can I be at rest from my grief of mind, nor from all the weariness that in this life hath laid hold on me*, 115 b; Th. 444, 2; Kl. 41. Wā biþ đam đe sceal of [on?] langoþe leófes ābīdan *woe to him that must wait, with unsatisfied longing, for one that he loves*, Th. 444, 26: Kl. 53. Hæfde him tō gesīþþe sorge and longaþ *he had for company sorrow and discontent*, 100 a; Th. 377, 14; Deór. 3. Forđon mec longeþas lyt gegrētaþ *therefore longings visit me little*, 37 a; Th. 121, 11; Gū. 287. Forlēt longeþas lǣnra dreáma *he gave up desires for transitory delights*, Th. 122, 5; Gū. 301.

lang-sceaft; *adj. Having a long shaft*:—Mid longsceaftum sperum *longas habebamus hastas*, Nar. 13, 24. Mid longsceaftum sperum *venabulis*, 15, 28. [Cf. *Icel.* lang-skeptr.]

lang-scip, es; *n. A long-ship, a large war-ship*:—Đā hēt Alfrēd cyng timbran langscipu [*other* MSS. lange scipu] ongēn đa æscas, Chr. 897; Erl. 95, 11. [*Icel.* lang-skip.]

lang-strang *glosses* longanimis *in* Ps. Lamb. 102, 8.

lang-sum; *adj. Long, taking a long time, prolix, lasting a long time, long-enduring, long-suffering*:—Nis mē đæs þearf tō secgenne forđon hit longsum is and eác monegum cūþ *nec per ordinem nunc retexere nostrum est, quia et operi longum et omnibus notum videtur*, Ors. 1, 11; Swt. 50, 16. Đa tō talanna longsum is *quos enumerare longissimum est*, Mt. Kmbl. p. 7, 7: Andr. Kmbl. 2962; An. 1484. Hū langsum wæs him se hlīsa *how lasting was that fame for him?* Bt. 18, 4; Fox 68, 5: Beo. Th. 3076; B. 1536. Hwæt gif ic bīde merigenes se ebrēisca cwæþ ne biþ hit swā langsum '*What if I last till morning?*' *The Jew said* '*It will not be so long*,' Homl. Skt. 3, 585. Đonne seó āheardung đære lifre tō langsum wyrþ *when the hardening of the liver lasts too long*, L. M. 2, 22; Lchdm. ii. 210, 4: Beo. Th. 268; B. 134: Homl. Skt. 4, 128. On đam tīman wæs swīđe langsum līf on mancynne *at that time life lasted long among men*, Homl. Th. ii. 460, 3. Lufu langsumu *lasting love*, Cd. 91; Th. 114, 18; Gen. 1906. Langsum *longanimis*, Ps. Spl. 102, 8. Mid heora langsuman gebede *sub obtentu prolixæ orationis*, Mk. Skt. 12, 40: Hpt. Gl. 500, 25. Đam þeódscype tō langsuman rǣde *to the lasting advantage of the nation*, L. I. P. 4; Th. ii. 308, 5: Cd. 219; Th. 280, 4; Sat. 250. Gehǣlede fram heora langsumum brōce *healed from their long sickness*, H. R. 105, 2. Him and his gebeddan tō langsumum gemynde *as a lasting memorial for him and his consort*, Chart. Th. 605, 12. His sāwle tō gescyldnesse on langsuman sȳđe *as a protection to his soul on its long journey*, Chr. 959; Erl. 121, 7. Đa þrȳ cyningas hæfdon langsume sprǣce wiđ đone gedrehtan Job, Homl. Th. ii. 456, 24. Langsume *longanimem*, Wrt. Voc. ii. 53, 52. Tō langsumum wȳtum, Homl. Skt. 4, 120. Him ēce geceás langsumre līf *he chose for himself a more enduring, an eternal life*, Apstls. Kmbl. 39; Ap. 20. Ūs selfum betst word and longsumast æt ūrum ende gewyrcan *to gain for ourselves the best and most enduring fame at our death*, Ors. 2, 5; Swt. 82, 2. [*O. Sax.*, *O. H. Ger.* langsam *longus, diuturnus, prolixus*: *Ger.* langsam *slow*.]

langsum-ness, e; *f. Length*:—Langsumnysse daga *longitudinem dierum*, Ps. Spl. 20, 4. Swā đæt hī ne beón þurh đa deópnysse ǣmōde ne þurh đa langsumnysse ǣþrytte *so that they be not discouraged by the deepness, nor wearied by the length*, Homl. Th. ii. 446, 8. Ealle ōđre dagas on twelf mōnþum habbaþ mislīce langsumnysse, Lchdm. iii. 258, 2 note. Đa brādsumnessa and đa langsumnessa, Wulfst. 244, 27.

lang-sweored, -swyred; *adj. Having a long neck, long-necked*:—Sume fugelas beóþ langsweorede swā swā swanas *some birds are long-*

necked, such as swans, Hexam. 8; Norm. 14, 16. Ða beóþ langswyrede ðe lybbaþ be gærse swā swā olfend and assa, 9; Norm. 16, 2.

lang-twidig; *adj. Granted for a long time*:—Ðū scealt tō frōfre weorþan eal langtwidig leódum ðīnum *thou, granted for long to them, shalt prove a comfort to thy people*, Beo. Th. 3420; B. 1708.

langung, e; *f. Longing, desire, weariness* or *grief* that comes from unsatisfied desire:—Hié langung beswāc eorþan dreámas ēces rǣdes *the longing for the joys of earth cheated them of eternal good*, Cd. 173; Th. 217, 28; Dan. 29. Hē for ðære langunga and for ðære geómrunga ðæs ōðres deáþes leng on ðam lande gewunian ne mihte ... him nǣfre seó langung ne geteorode *for grief and sorrow at the other's death he could not live in that land any longer ... his grief never wore itself out*, Blickl. Homl. 113, 10–14. Ðā wæs him micel langung and sorh on heora heortan ðā hié ðæt ongeáton ðæt hē leng mid him līchomlīce wunian nolde, 135, 21. Ða myclan byrþenne āberan ðære mycclan langunga heora ðæs leófes Hlāfordes *to bear the great burden of the great longing after their dear [departed] Lord*, 135, 8. Tō frōfre for ðære miclan langunga Drihtnes framfundunga *as a comfort for the great grief at the Lord's departure*, 131, 14. For longunge *præ tædio*, Ps. Spl. C. 118, 28. Longunge fūs *longingly eager*, Exon. 119 a; Th. 458, 8; Hy. 4, 97. Ā hafaþ longunge se ðe on lagu fundaþ *ever hath he weariness whose way is on the water*, Exon. 82 a; Th. 308, 29; Seef. 47. Langunga habban æfter ðām freóndum *to think with grief of dead friends*, Blickl. Homl. 131, 26.

langung, e; *f. Lengthening, prolonging, delay*:—Longunga *prolixae*, Mk. Skt. Lind. 12, 40; *prolixa* [in both cases = *prolixe*], Jn. Skt. p. 7, 18. On ǣlcre longunge geþyldige *patient in every delay*, Past. 5, 1; Swt. 41, 16.

langung-hwīl, e; *f. A time of longing* or *weariness*:—Feala[ic] ealra gebād langunghwīla, Andr. Kmbl. 249; An. 125.

lann, lonn, e; *f. A bond, fetter*:—Licgeþ lonnum fæst *lies fast in fetters*, Salm. Kmbl. 531; Sal. 265. Fæste gebindan, lonnum belūcan, 557; Sal. 278. [Grein refers to Grff. 2, 217 'Lanna *lamina* (among words referring to weaving.)']

lapian; *p.* ode *To lap, lick*:—Ic lapige *lambo*, Ælfc. Gr. 28; Som. 32, 25. Gedō ðonne on glæsfæt and ðonne mid hlāfe oððe mid swā hwilcum mete swā ðū wille lapa on *then put it into a glass vessel, and then, with bread or with whatever food you will, lap it up*, L. M. 2, 6; Lchdm. ii. 184, 24. Lapien on hunig *let them lap up honey*, 16. [Cf. *Icel.* lepja *to lap* as a dog: *O. H. Ger.* laffan; *p.* luof *lambere*.]

lappa. v. læppa.

LÁR, e; *f.* I. LORE, *teaching, instruction, learning, knowledge, cunning, science, preaching, doctrine, dogma, precept*:—Lār *disciplina: doctrina*, Ælfc. Gl. 80; Som. 72, 100, 101; Wrt. Voc. 46, 57, 58. Folclīc lār *omilia*, 35; Som. 62, 75; Wrt. Voc. 28, 53. Lār *dogma*, Ælfc. Gr. 9; Som. 8, 24. On ðam wæs āwriten Lār and Sōðfæstnys *in quo erat Doctrina et Veritas*, Lev. 8, 8. Seó hālige lār *sancta prædicatio*, Bd. 1, 27; S. 495, 40. Seó rihtgelȳfde lār wæs dæghwamlīce weaxende *crescente per dies institutione catholica*, 3, 28; S. 560, 39. Bisceopes dægweorc biþ ... lār oððon leornung *a bishop's daily work .. is ... teaching or learning*, L. I. P. 8; Th. ii. 314, 19. Him tō fultume godcundre lāre *sibi adjutorem evangelizandi*, Bd. 2, 4; S. 505, 14. Mynster tō timbrianne ðām monnum ða ðe Scotta lāre fyligdon *ad construendum monasterium his qui Scottos sequebantur*, 5, 19; S. 638, 39. Lāre *gravitate*, Wrt. Voc. ii. 40, 34. Ic mē gūþbordes sweng lāre gebearh *I warded off the blow from me by cunning*, Cd. 128; Th. 163, 7; Gen. 2693. Hē sceal habban lāre ðæt hē māge Godes folc mid wīsdōme lǣran *he must have learning, that he may be able to instruct God's people with wisdom*, Homl. Th. i. 206, 26. Hū giorne ða godcundan hādas wǣron ǣgðer ge ymbe lāre ge ymbe liornunga ... and hū man ūtanbordes wīsdōm and lāre hieder on lond sōhte *how diligent the clergy were about teaching and learning ... and how wisdom and instruction were sought here by foreigners*, Past. pref; Swt. 3, 9–12. Ne sceolan ða lāreówas āgīmeleásian ða lāre, Blickl. Homl. 47, 29: 7, 11. Tō bodigenne godcunde lāre *ad prædicandum*, Bd. 2, 3; S. 504, 16. Þurh his lāre *docendo*, 2, 20; S. 522, 22. Hē godspellīce lāre lǣrde *opus evangelizandi exsequens*, 3. 19; S. 547, 9. Hāliges lāre [cf. langsum leornung, 2962] *the story of the saint*, Andr. Kmbl. 2955; An. 1480. Lǣre *disciplinam*, Ps. Spl. 118, 66. Bodigende his lāre *prædicans præceptum ejus*, Ps. Lamb. 2, 6. Hālige lāra *dogmatum*, Wrt. Voc. ii. 27, 58. Ic wolde ymbe ðone lǣcedōm ðara ðīnra lāra hwēne māre gehȳran *I would hear a little more of the medicine of those instructions of thine*, Bt. 22, 1; Fox 76, 17. Lārna, Exon. 117 a; Th. 450, 17; Dōm. 89: Andr. Kmbl. 964; An. 482. Gif wē ōðre men teala lǣraþ, and hié be ūrum lārum rihtlīce for Gode libbaþ, ðonne bringe wē Drihtne swētne stenc on ūrum dǣdum and lārum, Blickl. Homl. 75, 14. Hig lǣraþ manna lāra *docentes doctrinas hominum*, Mt. Kmbl. 15, 9. Betwih ōðre lāre tō lifigeanne *inter alia vivendi documenta*, Bd. 3, 5; S. 526, 20. Wið Arreum and his lāre *contra Arium et ejusdem dogmata*, 4, 17; S. 585, 44: 586, 1. Wē sceolan healdan ða lāra ðara feówer godspellera *we must keep the precepts of the four evangelists*, Blickl. Homl. 35, 11. II. *exhortation, admonition, counsel, suggestion, instigation, persuasion*:—Mid his getrymnesse and lāre *ejus hortatu*, Bd. 1, 33; S. 498, 35. Mid his dæghwamlīcre lāre *quotidiana exhortatione*, 2 9; S. 510, 37. Lāre *hortamentis*, Wrt. Voc. ii. 42, 55. Ealle ða men Julius hēt ofsleán ðe æt ðære lāre wǣron ðæt mon Pompeius ofslōg *Julius ordered all the men to be killed who advised that Pompey should be slain*, Ors. 5, 12; Swt. 242, 23. Hē wið his hlāford wan for ōðra manna lāre *he fought against his lord at the instigation of other men*, 6, 35; Bos. 131, 11. Hlyste mīnre lāre *acquiesce consiliis meis*, Gen. 27, 8. Þurh Wulfheres lāre *suggerente rege Wulfhere*, Bd. 4, 13; S. 582, 7. Wes ðū ūs lārena gōd *be liberal to us of thy counsels*, Beo. Th. 544; B. 269. Lārum *hortamentis*, Bd. 2, 2; S. 502, 14. Hié swȳðor fylgaþ deófles lārum *they rather follow the suggestions of the devil*, Blickl. Homl. 25, 10: 61, 13. Ðīn rīce for his lārum gefealleþ *thy kingdom will fall because of his counsels*, 181, 34. [*O. Sax.* lēra: *O. Frs.* lāre: *O. H. Ger.* lēra *doctrina, dogma, sermo, præceptum, exhortatio, consultum*: *Ger.* lehre.] DER. bōc-, folc-, freónd-, mis-, un- lār.

lār-bōc; *f. A book which conveys instruction*: Swā swā Beda āwrāt, Engla þeóde lāreów, on his lārbōcum, Chart. Th. 241, 20.

lār-bysn, e; *f. An example, proof, specimen*:—Lārbysn *documentum* vel *specimen*, Ælfc. Gl. 80; Som. 72, 104; Wrt. Voc. 46, 61.

lār-cræft, es; *m. Knowledge, science*:—Ic īglanda eallra hæbbe lārcræftas onlocen. Salm. Kmbl. 5; Sal. 3.

lār-cwide, es; *m. Precept, doctrine*:—Wē sōðfæstes lǣston lārcwide, Andr. Kmbl. 1347; An. 674.

lāreów, es; *m. A teacher, master, preacher*:—Lāreów *doctor* vel *imbutor*, vel *eruditor*: *dogmatista*, Ælfc. Gl. 80; Som. 73, 98, 102; Wrt. Voc. 46, 55, 59. Cilda lāreów *pædogogus*, Som. 73, 103; Wrt. Voc. 46, 60. Lāreów *dogmatista*, Wrt. Voc. ii. 28, 50. Wē cildra biddaþ ðē eálā Lāreów ðæt ðū tǣce ūs sprecan *nos pueri rogamus te, Magister, ut doceas nos loqui*, Coll. Monast. Th. 18, 1. Ne gyrne gē ðæt eów man Lāreówas nemne ān ys eówer Lāreów *nolite vocari Rabbi: unus enim est Magister vester*, Mt. Kmbl. 23, 8. Hē is ordfruma and lāreów ealre clǣnnesse *he is the origin and teacher of all purity*, Blickl. Homl. 13, 21. Heó æfter ðon wæs magister and lāreów ðæs mynstres *deinde magistra exstitit*, Bd. 3, 24; S. 557, 5. On ðære heó mihte Gode willsumra wīfmonna lāreów and fēstermōdur gestandan *in quo ipsa Deo devotarum mater ac nutrix possit existere feminarum*, 4, 6; S. 574, 17. Wæs se Columba se ǣresta lāreów ðæs cristenan geleáfan *erat Columba primus doctor fidei christianæ*, 5, 9; S. 622, 40. Be ðære lāre mīnes lāreówes, Blickl. Homl. 185, 8: Exon. 14 b; Th. 29, 6; Cri. 458. Hī sendon Aidan ðone biscop Angelþeóde tō lāreówe *ad prædicationem gentis Anglorum Aidanum miserant antistitem*, Bd. 5, 22; S. 644, 25: 3, 5; S. 527, 29. Hē ða hālgan lāreówas hider onsende *alios prædicatores mittens*, 2, 1; S. 501, 36. [*Orm.* lārew: cf. *O. Sax.* lēreo.] DER. heáh-lāreów.

lāreów-dōm, es; *m. The office of a teacher, mastership, governance, teaching*:—Forðonðe nān cræft nis tō lǣranne ðæm ðe hine ǣr geornlīce ne leornode forhwon beóþ ǣfre suǣ þrīste ða ungelǣredan ðæt hī underfōn ða heorde ðæs lāriówdōmes ðonne se cræft ðæs lāreówdōmes biþ cræft ealra cræfta *nulla ars doceri præsumitur, nisi intenta prius meditatione discatur. Ab imperitis ergo pastorale magisterium qua temeritate suscipitur, quando ars est artium regimen animarum*, Past. 1, 1; Swt. 25, 15–19. Ne hī scoldon ne underfōn ða āre ðæs lāreówdōmes *ne locum regiminis subeant*, 2, arg; Swt. 29, 19. Ðæt biþ ðæs recceres ryht ðæt hē þurh ða stemne his lāriówdōmes ætiéwe ðæt wuldor ðæs uplīcan ēðles *debitum rectoris est supernæ patriæ gloriam per vocem prædicationis ostendere*, 21, 5; Swt. 159, 22. Tō Criste hē Angle gehwyrfde mid ārfæstnysse lāreówdōmes *ad Christum Anglos convertit pietate magistra*, Bd. 2, 1; S. 500, 28. Mid ealdorlīcnesse lāreówdōmes *auctoritati magistri*, 4, 27; S. 603, 44. Wæs on his lāreówdōme āfēded *erat in magisterio illius educatus*, 4, 3; S. 569, 6: 5, 19; S. 638, 15: L. Ælfc. P. 10; Th. ii. 368, 3. Ðætte unlǣrde ne dyrren underfōn lāreówdōm *ne venire imperiti ad magisterium audeant*, Past. 1, arg; Swt. 25, 14: Homl. Th. ii. 320, 12.

lāreów-līc; *adj. After the manner of a teacher*:—Lēreówlīc *exhortatorium*, Hpt. Gl. 512, 45. Lāreówlīcum cræftum *gymnicis* (gl. *magisterialis*) *artibus*, 405, 8.

lāreów-setl, es; *n. The seat of a teacher* or *doctor*:—Ofer Moyses lāreówsetl *super cathedram Mosi*, Mt. Kmbl. 23, 2.

lār-hlystend, es; *m. One who listens to instruction, a catechumen*, Mone B. 2802.

lār-hūs, es; *n. A house for instruction, a school*; gymnasium, Hpt. Gl. 405, 11.

lār-leást, -lȳst, e; *f. Lack of learning* or *instruction*:—Þurh lārleáste hī ne cunnon ne lǣdan ne lǣran hī *through want of knowledge they cannot guide or teach them*, L. I. P. 19; Th. ii. 326, 28. Wē sceolon bodigan ðām lǣwedum ðȳ læs ðe hȳ for lārlȳste losian sceoldan *we must preach to the laymen, lest for lack of instruction they should perish*, L. Ælfc. C. 23; Th. ii. 352, 1: Wulfst. 79, 19.

lār-līc; *adj. Instructive*:—Sume Godes þeówan mid lārlīcre sprǣce ōðre getrymmaþ *some servants of God confirm others with instructive discourse*, Homl. Th. i. 346, 22. Hit is swīðe gedafenlīc ðæt gē sume lārlīce word æt eówerum lāreówum gehȳron, ii. 282, 31.

lár-smiþ, es; *m. A wise man, a counsellor*:—Lārsmiþas, Elen. Kmbl. 406; El. 203. Lārsmeoþas, Andr. Kmbl. 2441; An. 1221.

lár-spell, es; *n. A discourse, sermon, homily, treatise*:—God cwæþ be lāreówum on his lārspelle *God said of teachers in his sermon*, Homl. Th. ii. 320, 25. Se bisceop ðam folce sǣde lārspell, Homl. Skt. 3, 141. Ic gesett hæbbe wel feówertig lārspella *I have composed quite forty homilies*, Ælfc. T. Grn. 13, 45. Swā swā wē āwriton ǣror on ōðrum lārspellum, 4, 15. Ða apostoli gesetton eác swilce lārspell [*the epistles*] tō ðām leódscipum ðe tō geleáfan bugon, 14, 3. [*Laym. Orm.* lar-spell *a sermon.*]

lár-swic, es; *m. n.* [?] *Deception, seduction, delusion, treachery*:—Mycel is nȳdþearf manna gehwylcum, ðæt hē wið deófles lārswice warnige symle, Wulfst. 309, 14.

lár-wita, an; *m. A learned man*:—Lārwitan and lahwitan, L. I. P. 5; Th. ii. 308, 14.

laser, es; *m. n.* [?]. *A tare, cockle*:—Laser, *zizania*, Ælfc. Gl. 101; Som. 77, 29; Wrt. Voc. 55, 34. Lasur *lolium*, Wrt. Voc. ii. 54, 15. Ǣtan ł lasor *zizania*, 72, 61.

lást, lǣst, leást, es; *m. A step, footstep, sole of the foot, track, trace*:—Lǣst *solum*, Ælfc. Gl. 75; Som. 71, 98; Wrt. Voc. 45, 6. Ðū ðās werþeóde wræccan lāste feorran gesōhtest *from far with the foot of an exile this people hast thou sought*, Cd. 114; Th. 149, 22; Gen. 2478. Sarran brȳde lāste beddreste gestāh, 129; Th. 164, 15; Gen. 2715. Of lāste *e vestigio, statim*, Wrt. Voc. ii. 144, 33. On lāste *e vestigio*, 107, 41. Him on lāste setl wīde stōdan *behind them heaven stood spacious*, Cd. 5; Th. 6, 10; Gen. 86. Malalehel wæs ǣfter Jarede yrfes hyrde fæder on lāste *Mahalaleel was after Jared the guardian of the heritage in succession to his father*, 52; Th. 65, 18; Gen. 1068. Him on lāste fōr sweót Ebrēa *on their track marched the band of Hebrews*, Judth. 12; Thw. 25, 38; Jud. 298. Yldran ūsse ān forlēton ðone wlitigan wong on lāste *our parents left that beauteous plain behind*, Exon. 62 a; Th. 228, 18; Ph. 440. Frætwe lēton licgan on lāste, 104 a; Th. 394, 30; Rā. 14, 11. Ðā wearþ forht ferþ manig folces on lāste *then was the mind of many a man of that folk left in fear*, Andr. Kmbl. 3191; An. 1598. Hié ðæs lāðan lāst sceáwedon *they marked the track of the foe*, Beo. Th. 265; B. 132. Lāst weardian [cf. lāst-weard] *to guard the track of one gone before, to remain behind*; also *to follow in the steps of another*. Cyning ūre gewāt þurh ðæs temples hrōf ðǣr hȳ tō sēgun ða ðe leófes lāst weardedun [*of the disciples watching the ascension of Christ*], Exon. 15 a; Th. 31, 16; Cri. 496. Se ðe his mondryhten līfe bilidene lāst weardian wiste *who knew his lord, of life bereft, remained behind*, 52 a; Th. 182, 19; Gū. 1312. Sceal se līchoma leást weardigan eft on eorþan *the body shall again be left in the ground*, Bt. Met. Fox 20, 482; Met. 241. Hē his folme forlēt lāst weardian, Beo. Th. 1947; B. 971. Hȳrde ic ðæt ðām frætwum feówer mearas lāst weardode *I heard that four steeds followed those trappings*, 4335; B. 2164. Him arn on lāst þȳstre genip *dark cloud succeeded it*, Cd. 8; Th. 9, 8; Gen. 138. Him fleáh on lāst earn ǣtes georn, Judth. 11; Thw. 24, 27; Jud. 209. Geseoh nū seolfes swæðe . . . Ðā on lāst beseah leóflīc cempa '*see now thine own track.*' . . . *Then the good warrior looked behind*, Andr. Kmbl. 2880–90; An. 1443–48. On lāst faran *to return*. Beo. Th. 5883; B. 2945. Wesseaxe on lāst legdun lāþum þeódum *the West Saxons hung on the rear of the foe*, Chr. 937; Erl. 112, 22; Ædelst. 22. On lāst [cf. *Icel.* ā lesti] *at last*. Ðū sārgige on lāsð *gemas in novissimis*, Past. 36, 2; Swt. 249, 13. Hit on lāst of his tungan ūtābirst tō openum bismere *ad extremum usque ad apertas lingua contumelias erumpat*, 38, 7; Swt. 279, 8. Ðæt mōd him ǣrest nā ne ondrǣt ða lytlan scylda, ne ðonne on lāst ða miclan, 57, 2; Swt. 437, 28: Bt. 7, 20; Fox, 16, 11; Fox 72, 7. Lāstas wǣron wīde gesȳne, gang ofer grundas, Beo. Th. 2809; B. 1402. Ic sume in bryne sende ðæt him lāsta wearþ sīðast gesȳne *some have I sent into the fire, so that no trace of them was left*, Exon. 72 b; Th. 270, 33; Jul. 474. Blōdgum lāstum, 36 b; Th. 119, 25; Gū. 260. Ðonne is ðǣr geworht emb ða lāstas . . . ðæt man mæg tō ðǣm lāstum onhnīgan and mænige men ða moldan neomaþ on ðǣm lāstum *the footsteps are built about, yet so that people can stoop down to the footsteps, and many men take the earth from the footsteps*, Blickl. Homl. 127, 5–11, 15, 19. Ðæt nǣnig man ða lǣstas sylfe ufan oferwyrcean ne mihte ne mid golde ne mid seolfre *so that no man might overlay the footsteps themselves, neither with gold nor with silver*, 125, 35. Sceáwian lāðes lāstas, Beo. Th. 1686; B. 841. Lāstas lecgan [cf. colloquial *to make tracks*] *to journey, travel*. Ic lāstas sceal wīde lecgan *wide must I wander*, Cd. 49; Th. 63, 3; Gen. 1026. Gewīt ðū fēran, lāstas lecgan, 137; Th. 172, 26; Gen. 2850: 118; Th. 153, 9; Gen. 2536: 109; Th. 145, 3; Gen. 2400. [*Goth.* laists *a footstep.*] DER. æf-, feorh-, fēt-, fēðe-, fōt-, sweart-, ūrig-, wīd-, wræc-lāst. v. lǣst.

lást. v. ge-lāst.

lástian. v. wræc-lāstian.

lást-weard, es; *m. One who keeps in the steps of another, a successor, pursuer*:—Ðone lāstweard, his swǣsne sunu [*Isaac*], Cd. 162; Th. 203, 7; Exod. 400. Wræcmon gebād lāðne lāstweard *the fugitive awaited the foe that followed*, 148; Th. 186, 13; Exod. 138. Ūs is swīðe uncūþ hwæt ūre yrfeweardas and lāstweardas getreówlīces dōn willon efter ūrum līfe *it is quite unknown to us how faithfully our heirs and successors will act after our death*, Blickl. Homl 51, 36. Ic ne mīne lāstweardas *neither I nor my successors*, Chart. Th. 29, 12.

lást-word, es, *n. Report, reputation*:—Eorla gehwam lāstworda betst *the best reputation for every man*, Exon. 82 b; Th. 310, 12; Seef. 73.

lata, an; *m. One who is late* or *slow*:—Ðeáh heó ðæs bearnes lata wǣre *though she were late in bearing the child*, Blickl. Homl. 163, 8. [*Icel.* lati *the lazy one.*] v. hild-lata.

late; *adv. Slowly, late, at length, at last*:—Alexander late unweorðlīcne sige gerǣhte [*anceps*] *pugna tandem tristem pene victoriam Macedonibus dedit*, Ors. 3, 9; Swt. 134, 8. Hū ne cymþ se deáþ ðeáh ðe hē late cume and ādēþ eów of ðisse worulde *sera vobis rapiet hoc etiam dies*, Bt. 19; Fox, 70, 16. Gif wit ðæt ealle sculon dsomeágan ðonne cume wit late tō ende ðisse bēc oððe nǣfre, 42; Fox, 256, 22. Hū late hī on ðysne middangeard ācennede wurdon and hū raþe hī him eft of gewītan sceolan, Blickl. Homl. 59, 23. Late on geáre *late in the year*, Chr. 867; Erl. 72, 11. Late mylt gǣten flǣsc *goat's flesh digests slowly*, L. M. 2, 16; Lchdm. ii. 196, 16. Gif heó gǣþ late . . gif heó hraþe gǣþ, Lchdm. iii. 144, 7: Exon. 49 b; Th. 172, 2; Gū. 1137. Ic ðæt gecneów tō late *too late I perceived it*, 72 a; Th. 269, 2; Jul. 444: Elen. Kmbl. 1412; El. 708. Sīð and late *at last*, Judth. 12; Thw. 25, 24; Jud. 275. Ǣr oððe lator *prius aut posterius*, Athan. 25. Lator *tardius*, Bd. 4, 9; S. 577, 10. Ðæt ðæt lator biþ, ðæt hæfþ anginn, Homl. Th. i. 284, 7. Onbūtan Martines mæssan and gyt lator, Chr. 1089; Erl. 226, 20. Ðæt hit hraþost weaxan mæg, and latost wealowigan, Bt. 34, 10; Fox 148, 22. Sȳ āgifen be emnihte oððe latest be ealra hālgena mæssan *let it be paid by the equinox, or at latest by All-Hallows' Mass*, Wulfst. 208, 5.

lateów. v. lād-teów.

láð, es; *n. What is hateful* or *harmful, harm, evil, injury, hurt, trouble, grief, pain, annoyance, enmity*:—Ðætte monnum hēh is laaþ [*adj.*?] is mið Gode *quod hominibus altum est, abominatio est apud deum*, Lk. Skt. Lind. 16, 15. Hit sōna nǣnig lāð ne biþ *it* [*the pain*] *will soon be no annoyance*, Herb. 1, 11; Lchdm. i. 74, 10. Hē mē nōwiht lāðes ætȳwde *ille mihi nil inimicitiarum intulerit*, Bd. 2, 12; S. 513, 25. Ðæt hē ðē nānwiht lāðes ne dō *ut nec ipse tibi aliquid mali faciat*, 514, 3. Ðæt him mon nōht lāðes gedōn dorste *ne qui prædicantibus quicquam molestiæ inferret*, 5, 10; S. 624, 6. Ic eom mid ðæs lāðes sāre swīðe ofþrycced *I am sorely oppressed with the pain of this trouble*; insitus animum mœror praegravat, Bt. 8; Fox 24, 14. Ða ungeþyldegan ne māgon āberan nānwuht ðæs lāðes ðe him mon on legþ oððe mid wordum oððe mid dǣdum *the impatient cannot bear any annoyance that is put upon them either by word or deed*; impatientes ab aliis illata non tolerant, Past. 40, 4; Swt. 293, 16. Ðeáh hié nān mann mid lāðe ne grēte hié sēceaþ ða ðe hié fleóþ *though no man attacks them, they seek those that flee from them*; iracundi se declinantes insequuntur, 293, 19. Hié hit tō nānum fācne ne tō nānum lāðe næfdon ðætte ða earman wīfmen hié swā tintredon *nec tamen miseriæ hominum pressura temporum deputata est*, Ors. 1, 10; Swt. 48, 13. Wið ðæm ðe hié of ðæm londe mōsten būton lāðe *ut tutum et incolumem exercitum a locorum periculo liberaret*, 6, 32; Swt. 286, 28. Mid lufe ge mid lāðe *with what is pleasant and what is unpleasant*, Blickl. Homl. 45, 8. Nis hit gōd ðæt hié sīen on ðam lāðe *it is not good that they be in that durance* [*the fiery furnace*], Cd. 193; Th. 243, 2; Dan. 430. Ne dō ic him nā lāð *I will not harm them*, Gen. 18, 30: Nar. 16, 22. Eálā hwæt ðū mē mycel yfel and lāð dēst mid ðīnre ærninge *O quam magnum væ facis mihi sic equitando*, Bd. 5, 6; S. 619, 14: Cd. 21; Th. 25, 11; Gen. 392. Wið eal ðæt lāð ðe intō land fare *against all the harm that comes into the land*, Lchdm. i. 388, 14. Ðonne hié lāð gedōþ hié sculon lufe wyrcean *when they do evil, they must act so as to regain love*, Cd. 29; Th. 39, 11; Gen. 624. Ðū mīne sāwle of deáþes lāðum wiðlǣddest *eripuisti animam meam de morte*, Ps. Th. 55, 11. [*O. Sax. O. Frs.* lēð: *O. H. Ger.* leid *dolor, moeror, injuria, malum, execratio*: *Ger.* leid.]

láð; *adj.* I. *Causing hate, evil, injury, annoyance; hateful, hated, loathed, loth, displeasing, injurious, grievous*:—Lāth *ingratus*, Ep. Gl. 12 b, 16. Laath *invisus*, 12 f, 5. Ðā wæs ic swīðe onscūniende and mē lāð wæs *multum detestatus sum*, Bd. 5, 12; S. 630, 32. Ðeáh hit lāð wǣre, Chr. 1006; Erl. 141, 7. Him wæs lāð tō āmyrrene his āgenne folgaþ, 1048; Erl. 178, 11. Fram allum mannum hē biþ lāð *he shall be hated of all men*, Lchdm. iii. 162, 19. Se wæs lāð Gode, on hete heofoncyninges, Cd. 30; Th. 40, 31; Gen. 647. Swā lāð wæs Pēna folc Scipian *so hateful were the Carthaginians to Scipio*, Ors. 4, 10; Swt. 198, 15. Mānswara lāð leóda gehwam, Exon. 10 b; Th. 12, 31; Cri. 194. Leófest on līfe lāð biþ ðænne *what is dearest in this life, shall then be hateful*, Dōm. L. 16, 243. Lāð biþ ǣghwǣr wineleás hæle *he is everywhere unloved, a friendless man*, Exon. 87 b; Th. 329, 9; Vy. 31. Wæs ðæt gewinn tō lāð and longsum *that strife was too grievous and long*, Beo. Th. 268; B. 134. Hē mē ālȳsde of lāðum grine huntum unholdum *ipse liberavit me de laqueo venantium*, Ps. 90, 3. Lǣdan on lāðne sīþ *to lead to hell*, Exon. 118 b; Th. 455, 20; Hy. 4, 52. Ðec gelegdon on lāðne bend *they put thee into grievous captivity*, Cd. 225; Th. 298, 27; Sat. 539. Ða fuglas ūs nǣnige lāðe ne yfle ne wæron *aves non nobis perniciem ferentes*, Nar. 16, 18. Ða rihtwísan sint láðe and forþrycte *the righteous are hated and oppressed*, Bt. 3, 4; Fox 6, 23. Hē hæfde fela ǽhta ðe him wǽron láðe tō forlǽtenne *he had many possessions that he was loth to leave*, Basil admn. 9; Norm. 56, 7. Gē habbaþ ús gedōn láðe Pharaone, Ex. 5, 21. Láð gewidru *grievous storms*, Beo. Th. 2754; B. 1375. Næs ic him láðra ōwihte ðonne his bearna hwylc *I was not a whit less dear to him than any of his children*, 4856; B. 2432. Ic ā ne geseah láðran landscipe *never saw I scene more hateful*, Cd. 19; Th. 24. 11; Gen. 376. Sege ðínum leódum miccle láðre spell *tell to thy people a tale that will please much less*, Byrht. Th. 133, 15; By. 50. Gnornsorga mǽst wyrda láðost *greatest of griefs, most grievous of fates*, Elen. Kmbl. 1953; El. 978. Ðǽr ðē láðast biþ, Exon. 41 a; Th. 137, 17; Gū. 560. Āne ða mǽstan synne and Gode þa láðustan *one of the greatest sins and most displeasing to God*, Ex. 32, 21. II. *bearing hate to another, hostile, malign, inimical*:—Ne leóf ne láð *nor friend nor foe*, Beo. Th. 1026; B. 511. Láð wið láðum *foe with foe*, 884; B. 440. Láðe cyrmdon *the foes shouted*, Cd. 166; Th. 207, 3; Exod. 461. Wið láðra lygesearwum *against false wiles of foes*, Exon. 19 a; Th. 48, 23; Cri. 776: Judth. 12; Thw. 25, 38; Jud. 304. Ðæt on land Dena láðra nǽnig sceððan meahte, Beo. Th. 490; B. 242. Láðan fingrum *with hostile fingers*, 3015; B. 1505. Láðum eágan, Cd. 151; Th. 189, 3; Exod. 179. Láðum wordum, Exon. 28 a; Th. 84, 17; Cri. 1376. Ālȳs mē fram láðum *libera me a persequentibus me*, Ps. Th. 141, 7. Ðæt hē ðē ne forlǽte láðum tō handa, Dōm. L. 30, 29. Hē ne lǽteþ míne fēt láðe hrēran, Ps. Th. 65, 8. [*O. Sax. O. Frs.* lēð: *Icel.* leiðr: *O. H. Ger.* leid *exosus, odiosus, invisus, tristis, malignus, ingratus*: *Ger.* leid.] v. þurh-láð.

láð-bite, es; *m. A wound*:—Blōd ætsprang láðbite līces, Beo. Th. 2248; B. 1122.

láðe; *adv. With hatred* or *enmity, in detestation*:—Hió mē lytle læs láðe woldon ðisses eorþweges ende gescrīfan *paulominus consummaverunt me in terra*, Ps. Th. 118, 87. Ðis ungesǽlige geár gyt tō-dæg láðe wunaþ *this miserable year still continues in detestation to-day*, Bd. 3, 1; S. 523, 33. [*O. H. Ger.* leido *invise, odiose.*]

láðettan; *p.* te *To be odious or hateful, be hated, be hostile, to abominate, hate*:—Láðetteþ *detestantur*, Wrt. Voc. ii. 26, 8. Man láðette tō swȳðe ðæt man scolde lufian *people hated too much what they ought to love*, Wulfst. 168, 13. Uncer láðette ǽgðer ōðer ðeáh ðe hē hīt ōðrum ne sǽde *each of us hated the other, though he did not say so to the other*, Shrn. 39, 22. Ðās gyltas ne mǽgon ūre sāwla ofsleán ac hī māgon hī āwlǽtan and Gode láðettan *these sins cannot destroy our souls, but they can pollute them and be hateful to God*, Homl. Th. ii. 590, 29. Hundas beorcynde gesihþ oððe him láðhetan *if a man sees dogs barking, or be hostile to him*, Lchdm. iii. 200, 26. Olfendas geseón and fram him gesihþ láðhetan *to see camels and if he sees himself to be hated by them*, 31. [*O. H. Ger.* leidezan, leidezzan *detestari, abominari, aversari, inhorrescere*, Grff. 2, 177.] v. láðian.

láð-geníðla, an; *m. A foe, enemy*, Exon. 56 b; Th. 201, 3; Ph. 50: 69 a; Th. 256, 15; Jul. 232.

láð-geteóna, an; *m. One who does evil, an enemy*, Beo. Th. 1953; B. 974: 1123; B. 559.

láð-gewinna, an; *m. A hated opponent, an enemy*, Exon. 104 b; Th. 397, 33; Rä. 16, 29.

laðian; *p.* ode *To invite, call, call upon*:—Hwīlum ic rincas laðige tō wīne *at times I invite men to wine*, Exon. 104 a; Th. 395, 32; Rä. 15, 16. Ðyder ðe unc laðaþ and cēgþ uncer Drihten *whither our Lord invites and calls us*, Blickl. Homl. 187, 26: Cd. 226; Th. 301, 29; Sat. 589 Loth hig laðode geornlīce *Lot compulit illos oppido*, Gen. 19, 3. Hē hī laðede ðæt hī onfēngon ðam gerȳno Cristes geleáfan *ad fidei suscipiendæ sacramentum invitaret*, Bd. 3, 5; S. 526, 31. Mē of weorulde cīgde and laðode *me de sæculo evocare dignatus est*, 4, 3; S. 568, 18. Heora ða leásan godas hié him laðodan on fultum *they called upon their false gods to help them*, Blickl. Homl. 201, 31. Hē hēht hām laðian Mellitum and Iustum *revocavit Mellitum et Justum*, Bd. 2, 6; S. 508, 33. Ðā hēt hē Willfriþ tō ðam sinoþe laðian *vocari jussit Vilfridum*, 5, 19; S. 639, 35. Hē sende his þeówan tō laðigenne mancynn tō ðære ēcan feorme, Homl. Th. ii. 372, 5. [*Goth.* laþōn: *O. Sax.* lathian: *O. Frs.* lathia: *Icel.* laða: *O. H. Ger.* ladōn: *Ger.* laden.]

láðian; *p.* ode *To be hateful* or *loathed*:—Heora fela wǽron mid olfendes hǽrum tō līce gescrȳdde and ðǽr láðode sōftnys *many of them were clad with camel's hair next to the body, and there softness was hateful*, Homl. Th. ii. 506, 24. Hió ðæm folce láðade *she was hateful to the people*, Ors. 3, 11; Swt. 148, 15. [Þe schal laðin his luue, Jul, 16, 6: þat te schal laði þi lif, H. M. 9, 2: him loðie, A. R. 324, 27: us lotheth þe lyf, Piers P. prol. 155: *O. Sax.* lēðōn: *O. H. Ger.* leidōn.] v. lǽðan, láðettan.

láð-leás; *adj. Innocent, harmless, free from harm* or *annoyance*:—Gif hē láðleás [MS. H. ladleas] beó sēce swylcne hlāford swylcne hē wille forðȳ ðe ic an ðæt ǽlc ðara ðe láðleás [MS. H. ladleas] beó folgie swylcum hlāforde swylcum hē wille, L. Ath. iv. 1; Th. 1, 220, 24–222, 1. Láðleáse *immunes*, Wrt. Voc. ii. 43, 68.

láð-líc; *adj. Hateful, loathsome, disgusting, unpleasant, detestable, abominable, horrible*:—Láðlīc *detestabile*, Wrt. Voc. ii. 26, 5. Láðlīc biþ ðæs hreóflian līc mid menigfealdum springum *the leper's body is loathsome with manifold ulcers*, Homl. Th. i. 122, 21. Ðæt is láðlīc līf ðæt hī swā maciaþ *it is an abominable life that they do so*, L. I. P. 14; Th. ii. 322, 26: Exon. 266; Th. 78, 19; Gri. 1276. Þincþ his neáwist láðlīco and unfæger *his* [*the dead man's*] *nearness seems disgusting and displeasing*, Blickl. Homl. 111, 30. Nis ðǽr ne se láðlīca cyle ne láðlīc storm, Dōm. L. 16, 259, 262: Soul Kmbl. 306; Seel. 157. Hine mon ðǽr láðlīce deáþe ācwealde *eum detestanda omnibus morte interfecit*, Bd. 3, 14; S. 539, 46: 541, 10. Láðlīc wīte, Elen. Kmbl. 1038; El. 520. Hēr æfter sint lungenādla láðlīcu tācn *here follow the unpleasant symptoms of lung disease*, L. M. 2, 51; Lchdm. ii. 264, 9. Ða láðlecan *obscena*, Wrt. Voc. ii. 63, 12. [*Prompt. Parv.* lothli *abominabilis*; *O. Sax.* lēð-līc: *Icel.* leiði-ligr: *O. H. Ger.* leid-līh *detestabilis, execrabilis, exosus, horrendus.*]

láð-líce; *adv. Hatefully, detestably, horribly, unpleasantly*:—Ongunnon láðlīce rȳnan *they began to roar horribly*, Bt. Met. Fox 26, 166; Met. 26, 83. Wit gewīdost lifdon láðlīcost *we should live as far apart as possible, and in most grievous sort*, Exon. 115 a; Th. 442, 17; Kl. 14.

láð-scipe, es; *m. A painful condition, calamity*:—Abram wolde Loth ālynnan of láðscipe [*when Lot was carried off captive*], Cd. 95; Th. 123, 20; Gen. 2048.

láð-searu *a fell device*, Cd. 195; Th. 243, 14; Dan. 436.

láð-síþ *a painful journey*, Cd. 144; Th. 180, 12; Exod. 44.

láð-spell, es; *n. A painful, grievous story*:—Hié ealle ðǽr ofslōgon būton ānum se ðæt láðspel æt hām gebodade *omnes ibidem trucidati sunt; uno tantum ad enunciandam cladem reservato*, Ors. 2, 4; Swt. 72, 19: Andr. Kmbl. 2160; An. 1080: Exon. 52 b; Th. 182, 29; Gū. 1317.

láð-treów *a fell, harmful tree* [*the tree of knowledge*], Cd. 30; Th. 40, 25; Gen. 644.

laðu. v. freónd-, neód-, word-laðu.

laðung, e; *f. A calling, invitation*; vocatio, Past. 52, 4; Swt. 405, 23. [*O. H. Ger.* ladunga *vocatio, evocatio, ecclesia.*] v. ge-laðung.

láð-wende; *adj. Evilly disposed, evil, hostile, malignant*:—Wæs láðwendo ongan wið Sarran winnan *Hagar was evilly disposed and began to strive with Sarah*, Cd. 102; Th. 135, 7; Gen. 2239. Gyf mon mēte ðæt hē gǽt geseó ðonne mæg hē wēnan ðæs láðwendan feóndes him on neáwyste *if a man dream that he sees goats then may he expect the devil in his neighbourhood*, Lchdm. iii. 176, 3. Láðwende here [*the fallen angels*], Cd. 4; Th. 5, 7; Gen. 68. Ludon láðwende rēðe wæstme *fruits evil and dire sprang forth*, 47; Th. 60, 29; Gen. 989. Láðwende men *evil men*, Exon. 31 a; Th. 97, 24; Cri. 1595. [Cf. *O. H. Ger.* leid-wentige *calamitas*, Grff. 1, 763.]

láðwende-mōd; *adj. Evilly* or *hostilely disposed*, Cd. 23; Th. 29, 11; Gen. 448.

láð-weorc, es; *n. An evil work, work that is hateful to another*:—Leornedan láðweorc Gode, Ps. Th. 105, 26. [*O. Sax.* lēð-werk: and cf. *O. H. Ger.* leid-tāt *supplicium.*]

latian; *p.* ode *To be slow, to linger, loiter, delay*:—Ic latige on sumere stōwe *moror*, Ælfc. Gr. 25; Som. 27, 14. Hwī latast ðū swā lange ðæt ðū ðē lǽce ne cȳðst *why dost thou delay so long to show thyself to the leech?* Dōm. L. 6, 66. Lataþ *tardat*, Wrt. Voc. ii. 138, 48. Deáþ ne lattaþ *mors non tardat*, Rtl. 11, 7. Eall līchoma hefegaþ and latiaþ ða fēt *all the body grows heavy, and the feet are sluggish*, L. M. 2, 25; Lchdm. ii. 216, 23. Ic latode *distuli*, Cant. M. ad f. 27. Ðeáh ðe hē ðā get latode on ðissum līchomlīcum gebyrde *though his birth was still deferred*, Blickl. Homl. 167, 7. Hit is swytol ðæt man ðæs latode ealles tō lange, Wulfst. 168, 2. Ne lata ðū *ne cuncteris*, Wrt. Voc. ii. 60, 34. Ne yld ðū ł ne lata ðū *non tardaveris*, Ps. Spl. 39, 24: Ps. Th. 69, 7: Exon. 13 a; Th. 23, 23; Cri. 373. Smeáge hūru georne gehwā hine sylfne and ðæs nā ne latige tō lange *at any rate let every one examine himself, and not delay in that too long*, Swt. A. S. Rdr. 111, 192. Nō latiendum *non cunctante*, Wrt. Voc. ii. 61, 22. [*Icel.* lata *to be slow*: *O. H. Ger.* lazōn *tardare.*]

latta. v. lætt.

lát-tēh, -teów. v. lád-teáh, -teów.

latu. v. word-latu.

látwa. v. lád-teów.

laur, lawer, es; *m. Laurel, bay*:—Laures croppan, seáw, blēda, leáf, Lchdm. ii. 20, 17: 226, 2: 228, 25: 230, 3. Mid lawere gebeágod *crowned with laurel*, Blickl. Homl. 187, 27.

laur-beám, es; *m. Laurel*:—Laurbeám *daphnis* vel *laurus*, Ælfc. Gl. 45; Som. 64, 110; Wrt. Voc. 32, 45. Lauwer [lawer] beám *laurus*, Wrt. Voc. 79, 78. Laurbeáme gelīce *similes lauro*, Nar. 36, 30.

laur-berige, an; *f. A berry of the laurel*:—Lauberigan, Lchdm. iii. 122, 22: 6, 16. Laurberigie, 106, 1. Lauwinberigean, 136, 28. Lauwerberian, i. 376, 6.

laur-treów, es, *n. Laurel*:—Laurtreówes leáf, Lchdm. iii. 88, 10. Of lawertreówe, i. 174, 11.

lawer, laber *laver* [a plant. v. E. D. S. Plant Names], Lchdm. i. 254, 1, 2.

láwerce, an; *f. A lark, laverock*:—Lāuerce *alauda*, Ælfc. Gl. 37;

Som. 62, 127; Wrt. Voc. 29, 22. Lāwerce *tilaris*, Wrt. Voc. 62, 42: *laude*, Wrt. Voc. ii. 50, 49. Lǣwerce *caradrion*, 13, 46. Lāuricae *allauda*, 100, 9. Lāurice *laudæ*, 112, 26. Lāfercan beorh *occurs several times in charters.* v. Cod. Dip. Kmbl. vi. 307. Cf. *O. H. Ger.* Lērichanvelt. [*Icel.* lævirki: *O. H. Ger.* lērahha *caradrius, caradrion, aloda, laudula*: *M. H. Ger.* lērche: *Ger.* lerche.]

leác, lǣc, lēc, es; *n.* Generally, *a garden herb* [as in leác-tūn, &c.], *an alliaceous plant* [v. compounds], *a leek*:—Ðis lēc *hoc cepe*: ðis leác *hoc porrum*, Ælfc. Gr. 13; Som. 16, 32, 35. Leác *ambila*, Wrt. Voc. 284, 24: Wrt. Voc. ii. 8, 49. Láec, Ep. Gl. 2 d, 8. Leáces heáfod *cartilago*, 17, 40. Ðæt greáta crāuleác; nim ðes leáces heáfda, Lchdm. i. 376, 3. On ðære mycele ðe leáces, Herb. 49; Lchdm. i. 152, 16. Leáces sǣd, Lchdm. i. 104, 26. Gebeát ðæt leác [*garlic*]. L. M. 2, 32; Lchdm. ii. 234, 21. Leác, 1, 32; Lchdm. ii. 78, 7: iii. 16, 10. Nim forcorfen leác and cnuca hyt, 102, 13. v. brāde-, crāw-, crop-, enne- [ynne-], gār-, hol-, hwīte-, por-, secg-leác. [*Icel.* laukr; *m.*: *O. H. Ger.* louch *cepa, porrum.*]

leác-cærse, an: *f.* '*A cress with an onion-like smell*, alliaria officinalis' E. D. S. Plant Names. Cockayne says 'erysimum alliaria,' Lchdm. ii. 318, 7: 320, 3. In Wrt. Voc. ii. 60, 40, leáccærse *id est* tūncærse glosses *nasturcium.*

leác-, leáh- tric, es; *m. A lettuce*:—Leáhtric *lactuca*, Wrt. Voc. 67, 47: ii. 50, 57. *Lactucas* ðæt is leáhtric, L. M. 2, 16; Lchdm. ii. 194, 6: 3, 8; Lchdm. ii. 312, 20. Ðā geseah heó ǣnne leáhtric ðā lyste hī ðæs and hine genam and forgeat ðæt heó hine mid Cristes rōdetācne gebletsode *then she saw a lettuce and had a longing for it, and took it and forgot to bless it with the sign of the cross*, iii. 336, col. 1. Wudu-lēctric *lactuca silvatica*, Herb. 31; Lchdm. i. 128, 6, 8.

leác-trog, -troc, es; *m. A bunch of berries*:—Leáctrogas *corimbos*, Wrt. Voc. ii. 14, 78: 104, 70. Leáctrocas *corimbus*, Ep. Gl. 8 f, 34. Cockayne, Lchdm. iii. 336, col. 1, puts this with the preceding word.

leác-, leáh-, lēh- tūn, es; *m. A garden of herbs, a kitchen-garden*:—Leáhtūn *ortus olerum*, Wrt. Voc. 285, 76: ii. 64, 9 Ðēr wæs lēhtūn *ubi erat hortus*, Jn. Skt. Lind. 18, 1: 19, 41. Nān man on ðysne dæg wyrte in lēhtūne ne fatige, Wulfst. 227, 8: 231, 18. Monn sende in lēhtūne his *homo misit in hortum suum*, Lk. Skt. Lind. 13, 19. [*Misc.* leyhtun *a garden.*] Cf. wyrt-tūn.

leáctūn-weard, es; *m. A gardener*:—Lēctūnweard *olitor*, Ælfc. Gl. 31; Som. 61, 82; Wrt. Voc. 27, 12. [*Misc.* leyhtunward *a gardener.*]

leác-weard, es; *m. A gardener*:—Leácweard *holitor*, Wrt. Voc. ii. 42, 57. Lēcueard *hortulanus*, Jn. Skt. Lind. 20, 15. Lēcword, p. 8, 4. Cf. wyrt-weard.

LEÁD, es; *n. Lead*:—Leád *plumbum*, Wrt. Voc. 85, 11. Ðæt leád is hefigre ðonne ǣnig ōðer andweorc *plumbum ceteris metallis est gravius*, Past. 37, 3; Swt. 269, 7. Īrenes and leádes ða men on ðǣm londum wædliaþ and goldes genihtsumiaþ *ferro et plumbo egent, auro habundant*, Nar. 31, 4: Bd. 1, 1; S. 473, 23. Beworhte mid leáde, Homl. Skt. 3, 532. Ðū herast ðone mancgere ðe begytt gold mid leáde, Homl. Th. i. 254, 26.

leáden; *adj. Leaden*:—Leáden *plumbeus*, Ælfc. Gr. 5; Som. 4, 60. Sī ðæt ālfæt īsen oððe ǣren leáden oððe lǣmen, L. Ath. iv. 7; Th. i. 226, 15: Nar. 46, 3. Mid leádenum swipum swingan, Homl. Th. i. 426, 13.

leád-gedelf, es; *n. A lead-mine*:—Eft in leádgedelf; of leádgedelfe, Cod. Dip. Kmbl. iii. 401, 7.

leád-stæf, es; *m. A scourge* [cf. *last entry under* leáden]:—Leádstafum *mastigiis*, Wrt. Voc. ii. 54, 75.

LEÁF, es; *n. A* LEAF *of a tree, of a book, a shoot*:—Leáf hys ne fylþ *folium ejus non defluet*, Ps. Spl.; his leáf and his blǣda ne fealwiaþ ne ne seariaþ *folium ejus non decidet*, Ps. Th. 1, 4. Leáf *antes*, Wrt. Voc. ii. 9, 16. Leáf *folia*, Mt. Kmbl. 21, 19: 24, 32: Mk. Skt. 13, 28: Bt. Met. Fox 11, 114; Met. 11, 57. Man scōf ðara bōca leáf ðe of Hibernia cōman and ða sceafþan dyde on wæter *rasa folia codicum qui de Hibernia fuerant, et ipsam rasuram aquæ immissam*, Bd. 1, 1; S. 474, 37. Mid grēnum leáfum *virentibus foliis*, Gen. 8, 11. [*Goth.* laufs; *m.*: *O. Sax.* lōf: *O. Frs.* lāf: *Icel.* lauf: *O. H. Ger.* laub *folium, frons*: *Ger.* laub.] DER gold-leáf.

LEÁF, e; *f.* LEAVE, *permission, license*:—Leáf *licentia*, Ælfc. Gr. 33; Som. 37, 17. Lōciaþ dæt ðiós eówru leáf ne weorðe ōðrum monnum tō biswice *videte, ne forte hæc licentia vestra offendiculum fiat infirmis*, Past. 59, 6; Swt. 451, 32. Gif him līf seald wǣre, Bd. 1, 23; S. 486, 8, note. Ða seofan cnihtas ðe be ðīnre leáfa lyfedan būton ehtnisse *the seven youths that by your leave lived without persecution*, Homl. Skt. 4, 255. Se Englisca be fulre leáfe hine werige *Anglicus plena licentia defendat se*, L. Wil. ii. 2; Th. i. 489, 13. Hē sæt on ðam biscoprīce ðe se cyng him ǣr geunnan hæfde be his fulre leáfe, Chr. 1048; Erl. 177, 27. Be ðæs cynges lǣfe and rǣda, 1043; Erl. 169, 25. Būtan ðæs cyninges leáfe and his witena, 901; Erl. 96, 28. Būton ðæs bisceopes leāfe *absque permissu episcopi*, Bd. 4, 5; S. 573, 4. Ða ðe willaþ grīpan on swelcne folgaþ for hiera gītsunge hié dōþ him tō leáfe ðone cwide ðe sanctus Paulus cwæþ *qui præesse concupiscunt, ad usum suæ libidinis instrumentum apostolici sermonis arripiunt, quo ait*, Past. 8, 1; Swt. 53, 7. Hē begeat ðā leáfe ðæt hē of ðam lande mōste *he got leave to go out of the country*, Homl. Skt. 5, 328. Hī habbaþ leáf [Cott. MS. leáfe) yfel tō dōnne *they have leave to do evil*, Bt. 38, 4; Fox 204. 13. Hæbbe hē fulle leáfe swā tō dōnne, L. Wil. ii. 1; Th. i. 489, 8. Ðā ðā Aulixes leáfe hæfde ðæt hē ðonan mōste, Bt. Met. Fox 26, 42; Met. 26, 21. Mē ða leáfe forgyf tō geopenienne ðone ingang ðīnre hālgan cyrcan, Glostr. Frag. 106, 13. Leāfe syllan *to give leave*, Gen. 50, 5: Lchdm. iii. 424, 27. Hī bǣdon lǣfa æt mē *they asked leave of me*, Guthl. 14; Gdwin 62, 13. [Cf. *Icel.* leyfi, *leave*: *O. Sax.* or-lōf: *Icel.* or-lof: *O. H. Ger.* urlaup *licentia, permissus.*]

leáfa, an; *m. Belief, faith*:—Hū mæg se leáfa [other MS. geleáfa] beón forþgenge gif seó lār and ða lāreówas āteoriaþ *how can belief be prosperous if teaching and teachers fail*, Ælfc. Gr. pref; Som. 1, 37. Leáfa *fides*, Mt. Kmbl. Lind. 8, 10: 15, 28. Leáfo, 21, 21. [*O. H. Ger.* laubo.] v. ge-leáfa.

leáfa [?], an; *m. Leave*:—Be his leáfan ārǣrde mynster *with his leave raised a monastery*, Homl. Skt. 6, 145.

leáf-full; *adj. Believing, faithful*:—Leāffull *fidelis*, Mt. Kmbl. Lind. 25, 21: Jn. Skt. Lind. 20, 27. Ic cȳðe on ðissan gewrite eallum leáffullum mannum hwet ic gerēdd habbe wið mīne arcebiscōpes, Chart. Th. 347, 26. God cwæþ tō Moysen ðæt hē wolde cuman and hine ætforan ðam folce gesprecan ðæt hī ðȳ leáffulran wǣron *God said to Moses that he would come and talk with him before the people, that they might be the more believing* [v. Exod. 19, 9], Homl. Th. ii. 196, 18.

leáf-helmig; *adj. Having a leafy top*; frondicoma Germ. 390.

leáf-hlystend, es; *m. A catechumen*:—[Ge?] leáfhlestend *catechumenus*, Hpt. Gl. 457, 12. v. geleáfhlystend.

leáf-, lēf-, lȳf-ness; e; *f. Leave, permission, licence*:—Gif him lēfnys seald wǣre *if leave had been given him*, Bd. 1, 23; S. 486, 8. Lȳfnes *licentia*, 4, 18; S. 586, 34: 2, 1; S. 501, 32: 5, 19; S. 640, 10. Būtan heora leóda geþafunge and leáfnysse *absque suorum consensu ac licentia*, 2, 2; S. 502, 35. Būtan kyninges lēfnesse [MSS. B. H. leáfe], L. Alf. pol. 8; Th. i. 66, 16. Mid his lēfnysse *accepta ab eo licentia*, Bd. 1, 25; S. 486, 11. Mid Ebrinum lȳfnysse, 4, 1; S. 564, 44. Heó his leáfnysse hæfde ðæt . . . *she would have his permission to* . . . 1, 25; S. 486, 34. Nymðe þurh leáfnysse his āgenes abbudes *nisi per demissionem proprii abbatis*, 4, 5; S. 572, 38. Hī māran lēfnysse onfēngon tō lǣranne *majorem prædicandi licentiam acciperent*, 1, 26; S. 488, 5. Lȳfnesse, 5, 11; S. 625, 30. Lȳfnesse sealde ðæt . . . *gave leave to* . . ., 1, 25; S. 487, 20. Him lȳfnesse sealde tō farene, 4, 1; S. 564, 34. Heó freó lēfnesse sealdon, 2, 5; S. 507, 10. Forgeaf him lȳfnesse, 4, 22; S. 592, 9. v. leáf.

leáf-scead, es; *n. A place made shady by leaves* or *foliage*, Exon. 58 b; Th. 212, 4; Ph. 205.

leáf-wyrm, es; *m. A canker, caterpillar*:—Hē sealde leáfwyrme (MS. C. treowyrme) wæstm heora *he gave their increase unto the caterpillar* (A.V.), Ps. Spl. 77, 51.

leágung, e; *f. Lying*:—Ðȳ læs on mē mǣge īdel spellung oððe scondlīc leágung [leásung?] beón gestǣled *ne aut fabulæ aut turpi mendacio dignus efficiar*, Nar. 2, 21.

leáh; *g.* leás; *m. A lea, meadow, open space, untilled land*:—Ðanne is ðēr se leáh ðe man ðæt lond mid friþe haldan scæl an eásthealfe sió ealdæ strǣt &c. *now there is the open space* (?) *by which the land is protected; on the east side the old road &c.*, Cod. Dip. Kmbl. ii. 71, 20. Ðonne geūðe ic Ælfwine and Beorhtulfe ðæs leás and ðæs hammes be norþan ðære lytlan dīc *I granted Alfwine and Beorhtulf the meadow and the enclosure to the north of the little dike*, 249, 33. Æt ðam leá ufeweardan, 36. Tō ðam leá . . . on eásteweardan ðam leá . . . tō fealuwes leá ðæt on fealuwes leá . . . fram fealuwes leá, 250, 2, 16, 29, 32. Æt Eardulfes leá . . . tō Aþelwoldes leá, Chart. Th. 291, 19, 22. Ðæt intō Eardulfes leá; of ðan leá, ðæt eft tō ðære greátan dīc, 292, 4. Þurh ðone leá tō ðam miclan hæslwride, Cod. Dip. Kmbl. 250, 34. Betweox ða twegen leás, 21. Lytle leás *amarcas*, Wrt. Voc. ii. 10, 14. v. next word.

leáh; *g.* leáge; *f. A lea*, as a termination of local names *-leigh, -ley, -ly*; it occurs frequently in the charters:—Hrīðra leáh *campus armentorum*, Cod. Dip. Kmbl. i. 232, 21. Ðis syndon ða landgemǣro tō madanleáge (cf. 120, 28 madan lieg) ǣrest on witena leáge, iii. 121, 13-4. On mapodorleáge; be eáston ðære leáge . . . eft on Heortleáge westeweardre, 407, 7, 8, 13. On hemlēclēge, 437, 4. Ðonne on ðæt (ða?) lēge . . . ðonon on gerihte on riscleáge, 10, 24-5. Of ðam clyfe on heán leage: ðæt on lungan leáge . . ðonne on Swonleáge, 48, 6, 7. On Wytleáhe; of Wytleáge, 14, 6. Oð ða lēge, 406, 27. [*Piers P.* bad hym eryen his leyes, 7, 5: *Promp. Parv.* lay, londe not telyd, see note 2, p. 285; cf. *Pol. Songs Wrt.* mi lond leye liþ and leorneþ to slepe, 152, 10: ley lond *tere freche*, Wrt. Voc. 153, 4. *O. H. Ger.* v. Grmm D. M. 1202, *has* lōh; *m. lucus*, which occurs also in local names, e. g. Hohenlohe, Grff. 2, 127-8: the same suffix is found in Water-*loo.*] v. preceding word.

leáh; *g.* leáge; *f. Lye, a mixture of ashes and water*:—Lāeg *lœxiva*, Wrt. Voc. ii. 112, 28. Leáh *lexiva* 50, 50: *lixa*, 52, 13. On bitere lēge, L. Med. Ex. Quad. 9, 14; Lchdm. i. 364, 5. Ofergeót ða ascen mide, mac swā tō lēga, 378, 11. Wyrc him leáge of ellenahsan, L. M. 3, 47; Lchdm. ii. 338, 25. [*Ayenb.* we byeþ alle ywesse of onelepi leȝe, 145, 22: *Prompt. Parv.* ley for waschynge *lixivium*, 294, see note: *O. H. Ger.* louga *lixivia*.]

leahan. v. leán.

leáh-hrycg, es; *m. The ridge of a lea*:—Tō ðæm ealdan lǣghrycge, Cod. Dip. Kmbl. iii. 437, 17.

leáh-mealt-wurt *some kind of wort*:—Lēhmealtwurt *lexinum* (? *lixivum*, cf. *lixivum mustum* the wine that runs out of the grapes before they are pressed), Ælfc. Gl. 33; Som. 62, 23; Wrt. Voc. 34, 6.

leahter, es; *m.* **I.** *a moral defect, a crime, fault, offence, sin, vice, disgraceful* or *shameful act, reproach, opprobrium, blame, disgrace*:—Leahter *crimen*, Ælfc. Gr. 9; Som. 9, 29. Hosp, lehter *probrum*, Wrt. Voc. ii. 67, 35. Ǣghwilc mennisc leahter on ðǣm eádigan Sancte Johanne cennendum gestilled wæs *every human vice was stilled in the blessed St. John's parents*, Blickl. Homl. 163, 15, 1. Būtan leahtre *sine crimine*, Ælfc. Gr. 47; Som. 48, 3: Mt. Kmbl. 12, 5. Hié eodan on eallum Drihtnes bebodum būtan leahtre *they walked in all the commandments of the Lord blameless*, Blickl. Homl. 161, 31. Būtan ǣlcon womme and swā clǣne fram ǣlcon leahtre *stainless and pure from every vice*, Nicod. 28; Thw. 16, 31. *Vitia* ðæt synd lehtras on lēdensprǣce, Ælfc. Gr. 50; Som. 51, 53. Swā sceal wīsdōmes bodung healdan manna heortan wið brosnunge fūlra leahtra, Homl. Th. ii. 536, 21. Ic mē synnum and leahtrum þeódde *vitiorum implicamentis solebam servire*, Bd. 3, 13; S. 538, 30. Hē unscyldig and būtan leahtrum wæs clǣne gemēted *absque crimine inventus est*, 5, 19; S. 639, 30. Bysmrian leahtrum belecgan *to revile and load with opprobrium*, Andr. Kmbl. 2591; An. 1297. Hē begann tō lufienne leahtras tō swīðe *he began to love vices too much*, Ælfc. T. Grn. 17, 13. Leahtras *noxas* (cf. gylt *noxam*, 50), Wrt. Voc. ii. 61, 41. Ȳdel byþ seó lār ðe ne gehǣlþ ðære sāwle leahtras (v. II.) and unþeáwas, Homl. Th. i. 60, 35. Wið ða heáfodlīcan leahtras *against the deadly sins*, Blickl. Homl. 37, 3. **II.** *a bodily defect, disease, disorder, hurt, malady*:—Hyt āfeormaþ ðone leahtor ðe grēcas hostopyturas hātaþ, ðæt ys, scurf ðæs heáfdes, Herb. 184, 4; Lchdm. i. 322, 15. Hyt ealne ðone leahtor genimeþ *it takes away all the malady*, 13, 3; Lchdm. i. 106, 2. Heó ðone leahtor [*cancer*] gehǣlan mæg, 32, 3; Lchdm. i. 130, 14. Leahtras *noxas* [cf. dare *noxam*, 64], Wrt. Voc. ii. 61, 41. Wið leahtras ðæs mūþes *for blotches of the mouth*, Herb. 145, 3; Lchdm. i. 268, 13. Wið misenlīce leahtras ðæs bæcþearmas, 165, 3; Lchdm. i. 294, 15. DER. syn-leahter.

leahter-cwide, es; *m. Opprobrious, insulting, injurious speech, blasphemy*:—Æfter leahtorcwidum, Exon. 68 b; Th. 254, 18; Jul. 199.

leahter-full; *adj. Vicious, seductive*:—Leahterfulle þeáwas *vitiosos mores*, Bd. 3, 13: S. 538, 32. Leahte[r]fulle *decipulosa* i. *inlecibrosa*, Wrt. Voc. ii. 138, 1.

leahter-leás; *adj. Faultless, free from defect, free from sin, innocent*:—Forðon nis nān man leahtorleás *quoniam nemo vitiorum expers est*, L. Ecg. P. i. 9; Th. ii. 176, 16. Ðonne ðū ōðerne man tǣle, ðonne geþenc ðū ðæt nān man ne byþ leahterleás, Prov. Kmbl. 3. Ic ða meorde wāt leahtorleáse *I know the reward to be faultless*, Exon. 48 b; Th. 167, 14; Gū. 1060. Hié freóndrǣdenne fæste gelǣston leahtorleáse *firmly should they friendship maintain, free from offence*, Elen. Kmbl. 2415; El. 1209.

leahter-līce; *adv. Viciously, noisomely*:— Ðæt deáde flǣsc rotaþ leahtorlīce ðonne se deádlīca līchama þeówaþ gālnysse *the dead flesh rots noisomely when the mortal body is a slave to lust*, Homl. Th. i. 118, 13.

leahter-wyrþe. v. un-leahterwyrþe.

leahtrian; *p.* ode. **I.** *to charge with crime, impeach, accuse, blame, revile, reproach*:—Ic leahtrige *criminor*; ic leahtrode *criminatus sum*, Ælfc. Gr. 25; Som. 26, 61. Man godfyrhte lehtreþ ealles tō swīðe *godfearing men are reviled far too much*, Swt. A. S. Rdr. 110, 163. Ða ðe ða tīda ūres cristendōmes leahtriaþ *hi qui de temporibus Christianis murmurant*, Ors. 2, 1; Swt. 62, 33. Ðā herede hē and nānuht ne leahtrade *laudavit*, 6, 1; Swt. 254, 14. Hȳ wǣran ealle ānsprǣce ðonne hȳ mē leahtrodon and lǣþdon *loquebantur simul*, Ps. Th. 40, 7. Ðæt hié ðās tīda leahtrien, Ors. 3, 9; Swt. 136, 31. Gif se midwinter byþ on Seternes deag ða clēnan beóþ leahtrode *if midwinter be on a Saturday the guiltless will be accused*, Lchdm. iii. 164, 12. Leahtrian *insimulare*, Hpt. Gl. 506, 3. **II.** *to corrupt, vitiate*:—Lehtriende *inficians*, Wrt. Voc. ii. 48, 7. v. ge-leahtrian.

leáh-tric. v. leác-tric.

leahtrung, e; *f. Accusation, blame, detraction*:—Lehtrung *derogatio*, Ælfc. Gl. 61; Som. 68, 44; Wrt. Voc. 39, 28.

leáh-tūn. v. leác-tūn.

leán, es; *n. Reward, recompense, remuneration, requital, retribution*:— Leán *meritum laboris*, Wrt. Voc. ii. 143, 40. Se ðe ðæt gelǣsteþ him biþ leán gearo, Cd. 22; Th. 28, 14; Gen. 435. Him ðæs grim leán becom *terrible retribution befel them for that*, 2; Th. 3, 36; Gen. 46. Gif hē eal wel gefriðaþ [ðe] hē wealdan sceal ðonne biþ hē gōdes leánes ful wel weorðe *if he protects well all that he has to keep, then is he quite entitled to good pay*, L. R. S. 20; Th. i. 440, 18. Ic ðē tō leánes ðinne noman mǣrsige *in recompense I will magnify thy name*, Lchdm. iii. 436, 28. Hwæt dēst ðū ūs ðæs tō leáne *what recompense will you give us for that?* Homl. Th. i. 392, 33: Cd. 135; Th. 170, 27; Gen. 2819. Sigores tō leáne *as a reward of victory*, Beo. Th. 2047; B. 1021. Be hundfealdon hē onfēhþ leán *centuplum accipiet*, Mt. Kmbl. 19, 29. Wē sceolan habban ānfald leán ðæs ðe wē on līfe ǣr geworhtan, L. C. E. 18; Th. i. 370, 21. Gebyreþ ðæt man his geswinces leán gecnāweþ *it is proper that the reward of his labour be acknowledged* [i. e. *he be rewarded for his labour*], L. R. S. 20; Th. i. 440, 12. Ðǣr leán cumaþ werum bī gewyrhtum *there rewards come to men according to their deserts*, Exon. 27 b; Th. 84, 2; Cri. 1367. Sægde leána þanc and ealra ðara ðe him sīð and ǣr gifena drihten forgifen hæfde, Cd. 142; Th. 177, 22; Gen. 2933. Gē eów ondrǣdaþ ðæt gē onfōn tō lytlum leánum *you are afraid of receiving too little reward*, Blickl. Homl. 41, 21. Leánum mīne gife gyldan *to requite my gift*, Cd. 22; Th. 27, 4; Gen. 412. Nealles ic ðām leánum forloren hæfde, mægnes mēde, Beo. Th. 4296; B. 2145. Ðonne forliést gōd man his leánum ðonne hē his gōd forlǣt *tum suo praemio carebit, cum probus esse desierit*, Bt. 37, 2; Fox 189, 26. Ðæt edleán is ofer ealle ōðre leán tō lufienne, Fox 190, 1. [*Goth.* laun: *O. Sax.* lōn: *O. Frs.* lān: *Icel.* laun; pl.: *O. H. Ger.* lōn *praemium, merces, stipendium, remuneratio*: *Ger.* lohn.] DER. æfter-, and-, dǣd-, drinç-, ed-, eft-, ende-, feorh-, fōstor-, hand-, iú-, morþor-, sige-, sigor-, wiðer-, word-, wuldor-leán.

leán; *p.* lōg [*a weak form also occurs* (cf. *Icel.*):—Se ðe wolde leógan oftost on his wordon, ealle hine *leádan*, ða ðe God lufedan, Wulfst. 168, 17.] *To blame, reproach, find fault with, disapprove, scorn*:—Ne leá ic ðē nā ðæt ðū ǣgðer lufige *I blame thee not for loving either*, Shrn. 197, 2. Hȳ nǣfre man lyhþ se ðe secgan wile sōð æfter rihte *a man that will rightly tell the truth will never blame them*, Beo. Th. 2101; B. 1048. Ða ðe ðæt unliéfde leáþ and swā ðeáh dōþ *qui accusant prava, nec tamen devitant*, Past. 55, 1; Swt. 427, 12. Paulus ðæt yfel ðære forlegnesse swā manegum āwiergdum leahtrum lōh *Paulus fornicationis vitium tot criminibus execrandis inseruit*, 51, 8; Swt. 401, 26. Hē him lōh ðæt hē hæfde his brōðor wīf him tō cifese *he reproached him with having his brother's wife as his concubine*, Shrn. 123, 1. Nales wordum lōg mēces ecge *he brought no word of blame against the blade's edge*, Beo. Th. 3627; B. 1811. Ðara monna ðe mē ðæt lōgon ðæt ic ðǣm wegum fērde *hominum qui dixerant mihi ne festinarem*, Nar. 6, 27. Ðone sīðfæt him snotere ceorlas lythwōn lōgon *prudent men a little blamed him for that journey*, Beo. Th. 408; B. 203. Ne hié winedrihten wiht ne lōgon, 1729; B. 862. Ne ðē silfne ne hera ne ðē silfne ne leah *neither praise thyself, nor blame thyself*, Prov. Kmbl. 36. Herigaþ oft suā suīðe suā hié hit leán scoldon *plerumque laudant etiam, quod reprobare debuerant*, Past. 17, 3; Swt. 111, 6. Ða dēman beóþ swīðor tō herigenne ðonne tō leánne, Blickl. 63, 21. Eal swilc is tō leánne nǣfre tō lufianne, L. Eth. vi. 29; Th. i. 322, 22. Bōclāre leánde and unriht lufiende *scorning booklearning and loving wrong*, Wulfst. 82, 2. [*Goth.* laian; *p.* lailō *to revile*; *O. Sax.* lahan; *p.* lōg: *Icel.* lā; *p.* lāði *to blame*: *O. H. Ger.* lahan; *p.* luog *vituperare*.] v. be-leán.

leán-gifa, an; *m. One who gives recompense* or *reward*:—Swylce se rihtwīsa leángyfa nō mid wordum ac mid dǣdum ðus cwǣde *as if the righteous Recompenser had said not with words but with deeds*, Lchdm. iii. 436, 23.

leánian; *p.* ode *To reward, recompense, requite, pay*:—Ic ðē ða fǣhþe leánige ealdgestreónum *I will recompense thee for the strife with ancient treasures*, Beo. Th. 2765; B. 1380. Ðū ūs leánest unfreóndlīce *thou dost requite us unkindly*, Cd. 127; Th. 162, 29; Gen. 2688. God mǣrlīce leánaþ ǣghwylcum ðara ðe him gōd behēt and ðæt eft fullīce gelǣst, Lchdm. iii. 436, 16: Exon. 20 a; Th. 52, 4; Cri. 828: 113 a; Th. 434, 12; Rä. 51, 9. Gūþlāce God leánode ellen mid ārum, 39 a; Th. 129, 13; Gū. 420. Mē ðone wælrǣs wine Scyldinga leánode manegum māðmum, Beo. Th. 4211; B. 2102. Lofe leánige, Exon. 54 b; Th. 193, 13; Az. 121. Ðæt hió him leánige ðæt hē ǣr tela dyde *that it may reward him for having done well*, Bt. 40, 1; Fox. 236, 4. Ðām gōdum leánian hiora gōd *to reward the good for their goodness*, 39, 12; Fox 230, 25. Nū ic wolde ðē ðone unþanc mid yfele leánian *valet manus mea reddere tibi malum*, Gen. 31, 29. Ðā cwæþ heó ðæt heó ne dorste him swā leánian swā hē hire tō geearnud hæfde *then said she, that she dared not requite him as he had deserved of her*, Chart. Th. 202, 21. Ǣghwylcum ānum men gyldan and leánigean æfter his sylfes weorcum, Blickl. Homl. 123, 34. [*O. Sax.* lōnōn: *O. Frs.* lānia: *Icel.* launa: *O. H. Ger.* lōnōn *retribuere, munerare, reddere*: *Ger.* lohnen.] v. ge-leánian.

leánung, e; *f. Reward, recompense*:—Leánung [? leasung. Wrt.] *hostimen*, Wrt. Voc. ii. 43, 20. v. ed-leánung.

leáp, es; *m.* **I.** *a basket, a basket containing a certain amount*, [two-thirds of a bushel? '*Lepe* quod est tertia pars duorum bussellorum;' in Sussex, time of Ed. I.] *a weel for catching fish*:—Leáp *corbis*, Wrt. Voc. ii. 23, 6: *calatus*, 127, 73. Leóht leáp *imbilium*, Wrt. Voc. 287, 27: ii. 46, 40. Leáp *vel* wilige *cophinus*, Ælfc. Gl. 101; Som. 77, 32; Wrt. Voc. 55. 37. Leáp *vel* bogenet *nassa*, 84; Som. 73, 90; Wrt. Voc. 48, 28. Sǣdere gebyreþ ðæt hē hæbbe ǣlces sǣdcynnes ǣnne leáp fulne, L. R. S. 11; Th. i. 438, 9. Leápas *corbes*, Wrt. Voc. ii. 20, 52. Ðā bær man up of ðan ðe hī lǣfdon twelf leápas fulle, Wulfst. 293, 32. **II.** *trunk* [*of the body*], Judth. 10; Thw. 23, 8; Jud. 111. [The word is to be found among English dialects, see the note in Prompt. Parv. p. 296; also the following reference in E. D. S. Publications '*Leap* a large deep basket; a chaff basket, B. 2. *Leap* or *lib* half a bushel [in Sussex], B. 16, 18. *Lep* a large wicker basket, Gloss. of old farming words, vi. *Leap* a wicker basket for catching eels, Lincoln. *Icel.* laupr *a basket of lattice work.*] v. sǽd-leáp.

leás; *adj.* I. *loose, free from, destitute* or *void of, without*:—Hē wæs ealra fyrena leás *he was free from all sins*, Blickl. Homl. 135, 2: Exon. 9 b; Th. 8, 25; Cri. 123. Wer womma leás *a man spotless*, Cd. 188; Th. 233, 29; Dan. 283. Land leóhtes leás and līges full *a land without light and full of flame*, 18; Th. 21, 32; Gen. 333. Rīces leás *powerless*, 19; Th. 24, 4; Gen. 372. Būendra leás *without inhabitants*, 5; Th. 6, 16; Gen. 89. Alles leás ēcan dreámes *void of all eternal joy*, 217; Th. 276, 1; Sat. 182: Beo. Th. 1705; B. 850. Nāge wē nāne þearfe ðæt wē ðyses weorþan leáse ac utan dōn swā ūs þearf is gelǽstan hit georne *we have no need to fail in this; but let us do, as there is need for us, diligently perform it*, Wulfst. 38, 13. II. *vain, false, lying, deceitful, deceptive, faulty*:—Leás *pellax*, Wrt. Voc. ii. 95, 60. *Solocismus* biþ sum leás word on ðam verse, Ælfc. Gr. 50; Som. 51, 51. Ðonne sægde Petrus ðæt hē wǽre leás drȳ *then said Peter that he was a false sorcerer*, Blickl. Homl. 175, 7. Hit is swīðe leás tōhopa *falsus equus ad salutem*, Ps. Th. 32, 15. Hwæðer hit sig ðe sōð ðe leás ðe gē secgaþ *utrum vera an falsa sint, quæ dixistis*, Gen. 42, 16. Se leása gewita *the false witness*, Deut. 19, 19. Se leása gylp *vainglory*, Blickl. Homl. 59, 18. Mid leásre gecȳðnesse *with false witness*, 173, 35. Ne beó ðū on liésre gewitnysse ongēn ðīnne nēhstan *non loqueres contra proximum tuum falsum testimonium*, Exod. 20, 16: Wulfst. 40, 11. Leáse mūðe *with lying mouth*, Ps. Th. 77, 35. Sume sǽdon leáse cȳðnesse āgēn hine *quidam falsum testimonium ferebant adversus eum*, Mk. Skt. 14, 57. Leáse sybbe ne sceal mon syllan *feigned friendship must not be formed*, Glostr. Frag. 112, 14. Ðonne cumaþ leáse Cristas and leáse wītegan *surgent enim pseudo-cristi et pseudo-prophetæ*, Mt. Kmbl. 24, 24. Ðās leásan spell *hæc fabula*, Bt. 35, 6; Fox 170, 15. Fram leásum wītegum *a falsis prophetis*, Mt. Kmbl. 7, 15. Wiðsacaþ ðām leásum welum *renounce the deceitful riches*, Blickl. Homl. 53, 23. Ða leásan godas *false gods*, 201, 30. Fiscere ðone leásostan *a fisherman most false*, 179, 14. [*R. Glouc.* les: *Prompt. Parv. Chauc.* lees: *Goth.* laus *empty, vain*: *O. Sax.* lōs *free from; false*: *O. Frs.* lās: *Icel.* lauss *loose, free, void*: *O. H. Ger.* lōs *levis, turpis*: *Ger.* los.]

leás es; *n.* *Falsehood, falseness*:—Hī ongietaþ ðæt ðæt wæs leás and īdelness ðæt hī ǽr heóldon *they perceive that that was falsehood and vanity that they formerly held*; deprehenderint falsa se vacue tenuisse, Past. 58, 1; Swt. 441, 18. Ðæt leás, Elen. Kmbl. 1157; El. 580. Gif gē ðisum leáse leng gefylgaþ *if longer ye follow this falsehood*, 1148; El. 576. Būtan leáse *truly*, Bt. 41, 1; Fox 244, 12: Bt. Met. Fox 30, 36; Met. 30, 18. [*A. R.* leas *falsehood*, 82, 16: *Laym.* buten lese.]

-leás a frequently occurring suffix used to form adjectives, having the force of *without* [v. leas I.], modern *-less*. It is found in the cognate dialects. v. leás.

leás-bregd, -brēd; *adj.* *False, deceitful, cheating*:—Ðū leásbrēda feónd and fācnes ordfruma, Homl. Skt. 6, 314.

leás-bregd, -brēd, es; *m.* *Deceit, fraud, a trick, cheat, wile*:—Hē hiwode þurh drȳcræft fela leásbregda *he performed many tricks by magic*, Wulfst. 99, 16. Swicol on dǽdum and on leásbregdum, 107, 2. Þurh his leásbregdas, 252, 19. Mid leásbregdum earmum mannum derian *to harm poor men with tricks*, L. I. P. 12; Th. ii. 320, 25.

leás-bregdende, -brēdende; *adj.* *Wily, deceitful*:—Hund sīðon līhþ se leásbrēdenda *centies mentitur versipellis*, Ælfc. Gr. 49; Som. 50, 31.

leás-bregdness, -brēdness e; *f.* *Deception, falsehood*, Leo. 220, 22.

leás-cræft, es; *m.* *A false art, deception*:—Hē hié getȳhþ tō eallum uncystum and tō ðære lufan ðisse worlde mid his leáscræftum *he draws them to all vices and to the love of this world with his false arts*, Blickl. Homl. 25, 12.

leásere, es; *m.* I. *a false person, hypocrite*:—Leáseras ł lēgeras *falsos*, Mt. Kmbl. p. 15, 8. II. *one who feigns* or *acts, a buffoon, jester*:—Se wæs ǽrest sumes kāseres mima, ðæt is leásere and sang beforan him scandlīcu leóþ *first he was some emperor's mima, that is, jester, and sang obscene songs before him*, Shrn. 121, 9. Ðā gesealde hē ða fǽmnan his leáserum, 154, 23. Ðā hēt hē his leáseres hine lǽdan tō ðæm wuda, 83, 18. [*O. H. Ger.* lōsare *dolosus*.]

leásettan; *p.* te *To feign, pretend*:—Leásetende ðæt hī woldon hine eft tō līfe ārǽran *pretending that they would raise him to life again*, Homl. Th. ii. 474, 10.

leás-ferhþness, e; *f.* *Inconstancy, falseness, folly*:—Hū micel leóhtmōdnes and leásferþnes *quanta mentis levitas*, Past. 43, 5; Swt. 313, 10. v. leás-līc.

leás-fyrhte (=(?) leás-ferhþ), *false*:—Leásfyrhte is unrihtwīsnys him *mentita est iniquitas sibi*, Ps. Spl. 26, 18.

leás-gewitness, e; *f.* *False witness*:—Leásgewitnyssa, Homl. Th. ii. 592, 5.

leás-gilp, es; *m.* *Vain-glory*:—Ðæt hié ne wilnigen leásgielpes *ne inanem gloriam quaerant*, Past. 48, 2; Swt. 367, 24.

leásian; *p.* ode *To lie*:—Leásiaþ ðē fȳnd ðīne *mentientur tibi inimici tui*, Ps. Spl. C. 65, 2.

leásing, es; *m.* *A false person* [cf. earming]:—Nǽfre ðū gelǽrest ðæt ic leásingum dumbum and deáfum deófolgieldum gaful onhāte *never shalt thou persuade me to promise tribute to false creatures, to dumb and deaf idols* [or is leásingum = *with lies, falsely*. v. leásung], Exon. 68 a; Th. 251, 23; Jul. 149.

leás-līc; *adj.* *False, vain, frivolous*:—Wēnþ ðæt hit hæbbe sum heálīc gōd gestrȳned . . . ond mē þincþ ðæt hit hæbbe geboht sume swīðe leáslīce mǽrþe *it supposes that it has gained some exalted good . . . and methinks it has purchased a very false greatness*, Bt. 24, 3; Fox 82, 24. Leáslīce cristene *false christians*, Wulfst. 93, 8. Leóhtlīcu weorc and leáslīcu *levitas operis*, Past. 43, 1; Swt. 309, 1. Mid leáslīcum wordum hī hine beswīcaþ *with false words they deceive him*; blandientes sermone ut decipiant eos, Nar. 37, 5. Ða leáslīcan ceápas binnan ðam Godes hūse geþafedon *they allowed false bargains within God's house*, Homl. Th. i. 406, 15.

leás-līce; *adv.* *Falsely, deceptively*:—Leáslīce *falso*, Ælfc. Gr. 38; Som. 41, 35. Leáslīce geclypode oððe āwritene *pronounced or written wrongly*, 50; Som. 51, 52. Hit biþ swīðe leáslīce on siolufres hiewe [*stannum*] *argenti speciem mentitur*, Past. 37, 3; Swt. 269, 3: Bd. 2, 9; S. 511, 20 note.

leás-līcettan; *p.* te *To dissemble, feign*:—Leáslīccettan *dissimulari*, Wrt. Voc. ii. 27, 38.

leás-līcettung, e; *f.* *Dissimulation, pretence*:—Næs hē begangende leáslīcetunge *he did not practise dissimulation*, Guthl. 2; Gdwin 12, 18.

leásmōd-ness, e; *f.* *Inconstancy, want of stability*:—Ðære leóhtmōdnesse and ðære leásmōdnesse sanctus Paulus hine lādode *a quibus* [*mentis levitas, cogitationum inconstantia*] *se alienum Paulus fuisse perhibuit*, Past. 42, 3; Swt. 308, 6.

leás-ness, e; *f.* *Levity, fickleness; falseness, lying*:—Þurh leásnesse *per mendacium*, Confess. Peccat. Ðæt ic swā wǽre ālȳsed from ðære scylde ðære swȳðe īdlan leásnesse *ut sic absolvar reatu supervacuæ levitatis*, Bd. 4, 19; S. 589, 30.

leás-ōlecung, e; *f.* *Flattery, cajolery*:—Leásōlecung *lenocinia*, Wrt. Voc. ii. 49, 68.

leás-sagol; *adj.* *Saying what is false, mendacious*:—Se ðe wǽre leássagol weorðe se sōðsagol *he that told lies, let him tell the truth*, Wulfst. 72, 16.

leás-spanung, e; *f.* *Seduction, allurement, enticement*:—Leássponunge *nec lenonum* [*lenocinium?*], Wrt. Voc. ii. 59, 71.

leás-spell, es; *n.* *A false story, fiction, fable*:—Leásspel *figmenta*, Wrt. Voc. ii. 34, 43. Be swylcum menn leásspell secgaþ *de qualibus fabulæ ferunt*, Bd. 4, 22; S. 591, 26.

leás-spellung, e; *f.* *Idle, vain*, or *false talking*:—Leásspellunga *fabulationum*, Bd. 4, 25; S. 601, 14. Leásspellunga *nenias*, Wrt. Voc. ii. 59, 74. Sōna swā hit forlǽt sōðcwidas swā folgaþ hit leásspellunga *ut quoties abjecerint veras, falsis opinionibus induantur*, Bt. 5, 3; Fox 14, 16.

leást. v. lǽst.

-leást, -liést, -lēst, -lȳst *a termination of nouns formed from adjectives in* -leás.

leás-tyhtan; *p.* te *To wheedle, flatter*:—Leástyhtendum *lenocinantibus*, Wrt. Voc. ii. 50, 15.

leás-tyhtung, e; *f.* *Wheedling, flattery, cajolery*:—Leástihtinge *lenocinia*, Wrt. Voc. ii. 49, 68.

leásung, e; *f.* *Leasing, lying, vain* or *frivolous speech, fiction, false witness, falsehood, falseness, hypocrisy, deception, deceitfulness, artifice*:—Leásung *vel* faam *famfaluca* (*Ital.* fanfaluca, *a whim, trifle*, and see Ducange, s. v.), Ep. Gl. 9 d, 12. Leásung ðissa woruldwelena *fallacia divitiarum*, Mt. Kmbl. 13, 22. Leásung *falsitas*, Rtl. 37, 31. Heóra leásung wæs gecyrred tō heom sylfum *mentita est iniquitas sibi*, Ps. Th. 26, 14. Ðæs forwyrd and leásung and forleornung swīðe raþe cymþ tō him ðe hē hine sylfne dēþ tō ðon ðe hē nis *for this reason destruction and lying and error come quickly to him, that he makes himself out what he is not*, Blickl. Homl. 183, 34. Sōðfæstnysse feóung and seó lufu līges and leásunge *odium veritatis amorque mendacii*, Bd. 1, 14; S. 482, 24. *Nebulonis* heowunga; *fallacis* scūan ł leásunge, Hpt. Gl. 459, 14. Hē nǽfre nōht leásunga ne īdeles leóþes wyrcean ne mihte *nihil unquam frivoli et supervacui poematis facere potuit*, 4, 24; S. 596, 52. Fulle mid leásunge *pleni hypocrisi*, Mt. Kmbl. Lind. 23, 28. Ne beó ðū leás gewita. Ðis bebod wiðcweþ leásunge '*Thou shalt not be a false witness.*' *This commandment forbids leasing-making* [cf. *Scott.* '*leasing-making* the crime of uttering falsehood against the king to the people or *vice versa*], Homl. Th. ii. 208, 27. Ða Judēiscan noldon gehȳran Cristes sōðfæstnysse, forðan ðe hī wǽron āfyllede mid heora fæder leásunge, 226, 24. Ðonne glād ðæt deófol ūt mid his leásunge swā swā smȳc æt his eágdura *then the devil by his artifice stepped out at his eye in the form of smoke*, Shrn. 52, 33. Wrec ðē gemetlīce ðȳ læs ðe men [man?] leásunga teó ðæt ðū ðīne cysta cȳðe *revenge thyself in moderation, lest the charge be falsely made, that thou display thy virtues*, Prov. Kmbl. 46. Leásunga *frivola*, Wrt. Voc. ii. 34, 55. Leásunga *factiones*, Hpt. Gl. 472, 3. Leásunga *lenonum*, 500, 55. On leásungum *in mendaciis*, Coll. Monast. Th. 32, 29. Se hlīsa ðe hē ǽr mid leásungum wilnode *the reputation* (*of philosopher*) *that he had before desired under false pretences*, Bt. 18, 4; Fox 68, 5. Nelle wē eác mid leásungum þyllīc līccetan, Homl. Skt. pref. 49. Leásingum beswicen ðæt hē wēneþ furþon ðæt hē man ne sȳ [so] *deceived by false notions that he thinks even that he is not man*, Blickl. Homl. 179, 5: Elen. Kmbl. 2243; El. 1123. For ðīnum leásungum *on account of thy falsehoods*, Cd. 214; Th. 268, 28; Sat. 62. Ðū fordēst ða ðe symle leásinga specaþ *thou shalt destroy them that speak leasing* [A. V.], Ps. Th. 5, 5. Onscūna ðū ā leásunga, L. Ælf. 44; Th. i. 54, 14: Homl. Th. ii. 482, 25. Fācen and leásunga from ūrum heortum ādoon *to remove deceit and falseness from our hearts*, Blickl. Homl. 95, 27. Þurh āðbrycas and þurh weddbrycas and þurh mistlīce leásunga, Swt. A. S. Rdr. 109, 151. Būton ðū forlǣte ða leásinga, weohweorðinga, Exon. 68 a; Th. 253, 13; Jul. 179: Elen. Kmbl. 1375; El. 689. Ðyllīce leásunga hī worhton and mihton eáþe secgan sōþsped gif him ða leásunga nǣron swētran, Bt. 35, 4; Fox 162, 14: 38, 1; Fox 196, 8. [*Prompt. Parv.* leesynge *mendacium;* lesynge *nuga: Icel.* lausung *lying, falsehood.*]

leásung-spell, es; *n. A false* or *foolish story, a fable:*—Ðā hæfdon monige unwīse menn him tō worde and tō leásungspelle ðæt sió hǣte nǣre for hiora synnum ac sǣdon ðæt hió wǣre for Fetontis forscapunge *ex quo quidam, dum non concedunt Deo potentiam, suas inanes ratiunculas conquirentes, ridiculum Phaetontis fabulam texuerunt*, Ors. 1, 7; Swt. 40, 8.

leáþor, es; *n* [?]. *A kind of nitre used for soap, lather:*—Leáþor *nitrum*, Wrt. Voc. ii. 62, 3. Of leáþre *nitria*, 61, 27. Gnīd swīðe ðæt heó sȳ eall gelēþred þweah mid ðȳ leáþre ðæt heáfod gelōme *rub strongly so that it may be all lathered, wash the head frequently with the lather*, Lchdm. iii. 2, 4. [*Icel.* lauðr; *n. froth* or *foam* of the sea water; a kind of *nitre* or *soap.*]

leáþor-wyrt, e; *f. Lather-wort, soap-wort;* saponaria officinalis:—Leáþorwyrt, *borith, erba fullonum*, Wrt. Voc. ii. 12, 47: 38, 43: L. M. 1, 3; Lchdm. ii. 42, 22.

leáw-finger, es; *m. The forefinger:*—Leáwfinger *index*, Ps. Th. 72, 11. [Cf. [?] O. H. Ger. gi-lou *versutus, sollers, gnarus*, Grff. 2, 35.]

leax, læx, lex, es; *m. A salmon, lax* [Scott.]:—Lex *salmo* vel *esocius*, Ælfc. Gl. 102; Som. 77, 65; Wrt. Voc. 55, 70. Leax *ysox*, 65, 66: *esox*, Wrt. Voc. ii. 30, 48. Laex *isic*, 112, 8. Leax sceal on wǣle mid sceóte scrīðan *swiftly shall the salmon in the stream's eddy move*, Menol. Fox 538; Gn. C. 39. Leaxes geallan, L. M. 3, 2; Lchdm. ii. 308, 6. Hwȳ gē nū ne settan on sume dūne fiscnet eówru, ðonne eów fōn lysteþ leax? Bt. Met. Fox 19, 23; Met. 19, 12. Hwæt fēhst ðū on sǣ? Hæringcas and leaxas *quid capis in mari? Aleces et isicios*, Coll. Monast. Th. 24, 9. Ðis is seó gerǣdnes . . . gesyllan ǣlce geare xv. leaxas *this is the agreement . . . that they give xv salmon every year*, Cod. Dip. Kmbl. iii. 295, 34: L. In. 70; Th. i. 146, 19. [*Icel.* lax *a salmon: O. H. Ger.* lahs *salmo, esox: Ger.* lachs.]

leax-heáfod, es; *n.*?:—Lex heáfod *capital*, Wrt. Voc. ii. 128. 43.

leber, lebr. v. læfer.

lec *rimosus*, Germ. 400. v. hlec.

lec (?), *sweet:*—Lec *dulcia*, Hpt. Gl. 411, 47.

lēc. v. leác.

lēc, es; *m. Look, sight:*—Wē sceolon āwendan ūrne lēc fram yfelre gesihþe, urne hlyst fram yfelre sprǣce, Homl. Th. ii. 374, 3. v. on-lēc.

leccan; *p.* lehte, leohte *To moisten, wet:*—Ic lecce *rigabo*, Ps. Spl. 6, 6. Hæglas and snāwas and se oftrǣda rēn leccaþ ða eorþan on wintra *hiemem defluus irrigat imber*, Bt. 39, 13; Fox 234, 16: Met. Fox 29, 128; Met. 29, 64: Exon. 56 b; Th. 202, 4; Ph. 64. Sumu twigu hē lehte mid wætere *some twigs he watered*, Past. 40, 3; Swt. 293, 7. His eágospind mid teárum leohte *wetted his cheeks with tears*, Guthl. 20; Gdwin 82, 4. Leohte ðæt līðe land lago yrnende, Cd. 12; Th. 13, 30; Gen. 210. Seó wæs wætrum weaht and wæstmum þeaht lagostreámum leoht *it was refreshed by the waters, covered with various growths, irrigated by running streams*, 91; Th. 115, 21; Gen. 1923. Leccende *rigans*, Ps. Surt. 103, 13. [*O. H. Ger.* lekjan; *p.* lacta *rigare, irrigare: Ger.* lecken: cf. *Icel.* leka; *p.* lak *to drip.*] DER. ge-, geond-leccan.

leccing, e; *f. Watering, moistening:*—Leccinc *inrigatio*, Kent. Gl. 33.

lēce. v. lǣce.

lecg, e; *f. Some part of a weapon, the cross bar in the hilt* [?]:—Ān handsex and [an?] ðæræ lecge is hundeahtati mancussa goldæs, Chart. Th. 527, 9. Leo takes *lecg* = gift, legacy, and then a dish of three pounds and a cup of equal amount would go to make up the amount of eighty mancusses. As regards the value of a *handseax*, Chart. Th. 501, 5 may be quoted, where one worth eighty mancusses is mentioned. [Cf. *ledge*, a bar E. D. S. Publ. B. 20: *ledge* the horizontal bar of a gate, Lincolnshire. In *Prompt. Parv.* legge, ouer twarte byndynge *ligatorium*, occurs: other words that suggest themselves by their form for comparison are *M. H. Ger.* lecke *leiste, saum: O. H. Ger.* legge *tornaturus, intransversum ligna tornata: Icel.* lögg the *ledge* or *rim at the bottom of a cask.*]

LECGAN; *p.* legde, lægde, lēde *To cause to lie.* I. *to lay, place, put, lay* [*a dead body in the grave.*]:—Syððan hē ðanne grundweall legþ *postea quam posuerit fundamentum*, Lk. Skt. 14, 29. Ða ungeþyldegan ne māgon āberan nānwuht ðæs lāðes ðe him mon on legþ *impatientes ab aliis illata non tolerant*, Past. 40, 4; Swt. 293, 17. Wā ðǣm ðe willaþ under ǣlcne elnbogan lecggean pyle . . . Se legeþ pyle under ǣlces monnes elnbogan seðe . . . *væ his qui consuunt pulvillos sub omni cubito manus . . . Pulvillos sub omni cubito manus ponere, est* . . . 19, 1; Swt. 143, 14. Cwēn mec hwīlum hond on legeþ, Exon. 127 a; Th. 489, 8; Rä. 78, 4. Ða land ðe hig ðiderin lecgeaþ beón ða ðām gebrōðran ðe ðǣr binnan beóþ tō fōdnoþe and tō scrūde *let the lands, that they assign thereto, be for the feeding and clothing of the brethren there*, Chart. Th. 370, 25. Sege mē hwar ðū hine lēdest *dicito mihi ubi posuisti eum*, Jn. Skt. 20, 15. Se cyng lægde hī wið Eádward kyng hire hlāforde *the king laid* [*buried*] *her by King Edward her lord*, Chr. 1075; Erl. 214, 12. Lēde him ætforan *posuit coram eis*, Gen. 18, 8. Hē nam stānas and lēde under his heáfod, 28, 11. Hine betellan æt ǣlc ðæra þinga ðe him man on lēde *to clear himself from every thing that was laid to his charge*, Chr. 1048; Erl. 180, 12. Abraham legde hleór on eorþan, Cd. 107; Th. 140, 32; Gen. 2336. Se mec wrǣde on æt frumsceafte legde *who at the beginning binding laid on me*, Exon. 101 b; Th. 383, 22; Rä. 4, 14. Wē on bearm lægdon *we put them into our laps*, Salm. Kmbl. 864; Sal. 431. Gē on his wergengan wīte legdon *ye imposed pain upon his pilgrim*, 43 a; Th. 144, 29; Gū. 685. Ðæt folc geald heom swā mycel swā hī heom on legden *the people paid as much as they imposed*, Chr. 1052; Erl. 183, 15. Hig lægdon ǣrende on hine tō ðam cynge *they commissioned him to the king*, 1064; Erl. 194, 24. Ðā lægdon hī fȳr on *they set fire to it*, 1083; Erl. 209, 1. Lege hit hēr beforan ðīnum freóndum *pone hic coram fratribus tuis*, Gen. 31, 37. Lecgaþ ðǣrtōeácan *add thereto*, Wulfst. 274, 7. Sleá mon hine and on fūl lecge *let him be slain and buried in unconsecrated ground*, L. Eth. i. 4; Th. 284, 2: vi. 21; Th. i. 320, 6: L. C. S. 33; Th. i. 396, 17. Hwā wolde gelȳfan ðæt Sarra sceolde lecgan cild tō hyre breóste tō gesoce *quis crederet, quod Sara lactaret filium*, Gen. 21, 7. Josue hēt lecgan him on uppan ormǣte weorcstānas *præcepit, ut ponerent super os ejus saxa ingentia*, Jos. 10, 27. Lecgan ðone mæst *to lower the mast*, Bt. 41, 3; Fox 250, 15. Ægru lecgan *to lay eggs*, Lchdm. iii. 204, 30. Lāstas lecgan *to go, journey*, Cd. 109; Th. 145, 3; Gen. 2400: 118; Th. 153, 9; Gen. 2536: Exon. 82 a; Th. 309, 14; Seef. 57. II. *to cause to lie* [*dead.* v. licgan], *to slay:*—Hine lecge for þeóf seðe him tō cume *let him that comes at him slay him for a thief*, L. Ath. i. 2; Th. i. 200, 10. Gif hine hwā lecge, L. Eth. iv. 4; Th. i. 222, 9. Se ðe mid þeófe stande and mid feohte, lecge hine man mid ðam þeófe. v. 1, 3; Th. i. 228, 23. Ðæt hine man lecgan ne mōste, Th. i. 230, 6. [*Goth.* lagjan: *O. Sax.* leggian: *O. Frs.* leia: *Icel.* leggja: *O. H. Ger.* legjan: *Ger.* legen.] DER. a-, be-, ge-, of-, tō-, under-, wið-lecgan.

lecþ, e; *f.*?:—Lecþ [=? legþ] *peana*, Wrt. Voc. 287, 29. Ducange gives '*peanius* lignum tectis conficiendis aptum;' Spanish has *peana* a pedestal, a frame put at the foot of an altar to tread upon.

lecþa, an; *m. The lowest part of a ship, in which bilge water collects:*—*Sentina* lectha *ubi multae aque colliguntur in navem*, Ep. Gl. 23 d, 15. Lectha *sentina*, Wrt. Voc. ii. 120, 27. Cf. (?) lec, hlec.

Lēden. v. Lǣden.

lēf [*or* lef?]; *adj. Weak, injured, infirm:*—Lēf *debilis*, Germ. 389. On fȳre hī ne lyst lōcian gif se æppel lēf biþ *men do not like to look at fire if the apple of the eye be injured*, Bt. 38, 5; Fox 204, 29. Lēf mon lǣces behōfaþ *a sick man needs a doctor*, Exon. 89 b; Th. 336, 8; Gn. Ex. 45. On fēðe līf seonobennum seóc *weak for walking, sick with sinew-wounds*, 87 b; Th. 328, 16; Vy. 18. Oft him feorran tō laman liomseóce lēfe cwōmon *oft from far to him the paralytic, the cripple, the infirm came*, Elen. Kmbl. 2426; El. 1214. See note to Grmm. A. u. E. p. 166. [*O. Sax. O. Frs.* lēf: *Dut.* loof.] v. ā-, ge-lēfan; lēf; *n*; lēfung.

lēf, es; *n. Hurt, damage, injury:*—Ðeore feórþan niht gif wind byþ lēf byþ litel *if there is wind on the fourth night, the damage will be little*, Lchdm. iii. 164, 17.

lēfan *to permit.* v. līfan.

lefel. v. læfel.

lēf-ness. v. leáf-ness.

lēft, e; *f. A vow;* votum, Ps. Spl. T. 64, 1: 65, 12. [Cf. (?) *Icel.* leyfð *praise.*]

lēfung, e; *f. Weakening, laming, lameness, paralysis:*—Ðī læs ðe hī ðās lēfunge on heora limum gebrohton *lest they should bring this paralysis* [*want of power to speak, walk and see*] *upon their limbs*, Homl. Th. ii. 486, 18.

lēg. v. līg.

leger, es; *n.* I. *a lying:*—Hys spēda hȳ forspendaþ mid ðan langan legere ðæs deádan mannes inne *they squander his wealth with the long lying of the dead man in the house*, Ors. 1, 1; Swt. 21, 9. II. *a lying sick* or *dead, sickness, death:*—Nis ðǣr hungor ne þurst ne slǣp ne swār leger *there is neither hunger nor thirst nor sleep nor grievous sickness*, Exon. 32 a; Th. 101, 21; Cri. 1662: 56 b; Th. 201, 15; Ph. 56. On ðam sixtan dæge his legeres *on the sixth day of his illness*, Homl. Th. ii. 186, 28. Mid langre ādle laman legeres swīðe gehefigod *longo paralysis morbo gravatam*, Bd. 3, 9; S. 534, 6. Moyses and Aaron geendodon heora līf swāðeáh būton legere *Moses and Aaron ended their lives, yet without sickness*, Homl. Th. ii. 212, 13. Se preóst sceal smyrigan ða seócan symble on legere *the priest must always anoint the sick in ill-*

ness, L. Ælfc. C. 32; Th. ii. 354, 14. Tó hæbbenne and tó syllanne for lífe and for legere *to have and to give during life and at death*, Chart. Th. 208, 3. Ðá cwæþ se cyng ðæt mihte beón geboden him wið clǽnum legere *then the king said, the offer might have been made to him, if the death had been by fair means* [it was by drowning], 31. III. *a place to lie in, a couch, a lair, a place where the dead lie, a grave*:—Hálig leger [legerstów (?)] *cimiterium*, Ælfc. Gl. 49; Som. 65, 74; Wrt. Voc. 34, 9. Þolige hé clǽnes legeres and Godes mildse *let him forfeit a hallowed grave and God's mercy*, L. N. P. L. 62, 63; Th. ii. 300, 19, 22: Wulfst. 39. 19. Wé lǽraþ ðæt man innan circan ǽnigne man ne birige búton ... hé sí ðæs legeres wyrðe *we enjoin that no man be buried within a church, unless he be worthy of such a place of burial*, L. Edg. C. 29; Th. ii. 250, 17. On gehálgodan legere licgan *to be buried in consecrated ground*, 22; Th. ii. 248, 20. Ge on lífe ge on legere *both alive and in the grave*, L. Eth. v. 9; Th. i. 306, 22: vi. 5; Th. i. 316, 14: ix. 28; Th. i. 346, 19. Unsac hé wæs on lífe beó on legere swá swá hé móte, i. 184, 13; Lchdm. iii. 288, 6. Líchoman, se ðe on legre sceal weorþan wyrme tó hróðor, Exon. 71 b; Th. 267, 15; Jul. 415. Be ðære róde ðe ǽr in legere wæs lange bedyrned [*of the cross that had been buried*], Elen. Kmbl. 1200; El. 602: 1442; El. 723. Líc legere fæst, 1762; El. 883. Se wæs fíftiges fótgemearces lang on legere *he was fifty feet long in the place where he lay*, Beo. Th. 6078; B. 3043. Leger ðis *lectum istum*, Rtl. 111, 24. On legir *in lectum*, 181, 7. Frýnd leger weardiaþ ðonne ic on úhtan ána gonge *my friends rest in their couches, when ere the dawn I go solitary*, Exon 115 b; Th. 443, 23; Kl. 34. [*O. E. Homl.* (to) leire *couch*: *O. Sax.* legar: *O. Frs.* legor: *O. H. Ger.* legar *cubile, lustrum, accubitus, concubitus*: *Ger.* lager: *Goth.* ligrs; *m. a couch.*]

leger-bǽre; *adj. Suffering from sickness*:—Bútun hé on hláfordes neóde beó oððe legerbǽre *unless he be on his lord's necessary business, or suffering from sickness*, Chart. Th. 611, 20.

leger-bedd, es; *n. A sick-bed, bed of death, grave*:—Sum mǽden hé gehǽlde ðæt ðe langlíce læg on legerbedde seóc *a maiden he healed that had long been confined to her bed by sickness*, Homl. Th. ii. 510, 25. Árís nú and ber hám ðín legerbed, i. 472, 25. Ðæt ðú ðus láðlíc legerbed cure *that thou shouldst choose so loathly a couch* [*the grave*], Soul Kmbl. 307; Seel. 157: Wulfst. 187, 12. Sceal ðis sáwelhús legerbedde fæst wunian wælræste, Exon. 47 b; Th. 164, 2; Gú. 1005: Beo. Th. 2019; B. 1007. [*O. Sax.* legar-bed.]

-legere. v. for-legere.

leger-fæst; *adj. Sick, ill*, R. Ben. 39, Lye. [*O. Sax.* legar-fast.]

legerian; *p.* ode *To be ill, afflicted with sickness.* v. ge-legerian.

leger-stów, e; *f. A burial-place, cemetery*:—Hálig leger [legerstów ?] *cimeterium, poliandrium*, Ælfc. Gl. 49; Som. 65, 74; Wrt. Voc. 34, 9. Cyricean ðe legerstów on sý *a church at which there is a burial-place*, L. Edg. i. 2; Th. i. 262, 12: L. C. E. 11; Th. i. 366, 24: 3; Th. i. 360, 23. Ðæt hí þolian woroldǽhta and gehálgodre legerstówe *that they forfeit worldly possessions and a consecrated burial-place*, L. Edm. E. 1; Th. i. 244, 14: 4; Th. i. 246, 6. Ypolitus bebyrigde ðone hálgan líchaman on ðære wudewan legerstówe *Hippolytus buried the holy body in the burial-place of the widow*, Homl. Th. i. 430, 26. [*Laym.* leir-stow.]

leger-teám, es; *m. Matrimony, sexual intercourse* [*lawful or unlawful*]:—Matheus him sægde ðæt hé wǽre swá synnig wið God gif hé ða gehálgodan fǽmnan tó legerteáme onfénge swá se þeów wǽre se ðe fénge on kyninges quéne tó unryhtum hǽmde *Matthew said to him, that he would be as guilty against God, if he received the consecrated virgin as his wife, as the slave would be who took a king's queen to commit adultery with her*, Shrn. 132, 4. Legerteám *flagitium*, Wrt. Voc. ii. 39, 34.

leger-wíte, es; *n. A fine for lying with a woman*, L. H. 23; Th. i. 529, 23: 81; Th. i. 589, 3. [*Trev.* leir-wite *fine for lying with a bond-woman.*]

légetu *lightning*. v. lígetu.

Legra ceaster. v. Ligora ceaster.

léh *lye*. v. leáh.

léhtan *to alleviate*. v. líhtan.

lehter *disgrace*. v. leahter.

léh-tric, -tún. v. leác-tric, -tún.

lél. v. lǽl.

leloþre [*error for* geloþre *according to Cockayne*. v. gelod-wyrt], *A kind of dock*:—Lelodrae *lapatium* (= λάπαθον; cf. uude docce *lapatium*, Lchdm. iii. 303, col. 2), Ep. Gl. 13 f, 31. Lelothras *radinape*, 22 b, 32. Leloþre *lapadium*, Wrt. Voc. 69, 14: ii. 54, 24. Lelodrae *lapatium*, 112, 35. Lelothrae *rodinope*, 119, 24.

lemian; *p.* ede *To lame, cripple, enfeeble, strike* [?]:—Swá wildu hors ðonne wé hié ǽresð gefangnu habbaþ wé hié stráciaþ mid brádre handa and lemiaþ *equos indomitos blanda prius manu tangimus*, Past. 41, 4; Swt. 303, 11. Hine sorhwylmas lemedon [MS. lemede] tó lange *the waves of care had crippled him too long*, Beo. Th. 1814; B. 905. [*Icel.* lemja *to beat so as to lame* or *disable, to suppress*: *O. H. Ger.* lemian *debilitare*: *Ger.* lähmen.]

lempedu, e; *f. A lamprey*:—Lempedu *lemprida*, Wrt. Voc. ii. 53, 42.

lemp-healt, laempi-halt; *adj.* The word occurs in Wrt. Voc. ii. 51, 20, and in Ep. Gl. 13 f, 4 as the gloss of *lurdus* which Ducange explains as *foul*, cf. Ital. *lordo*, or *stupid*, cf. Fr. *lourde, lourdand*. Lye quotes without reference *lempe* lenitas; *Icel.* has *lempiligr* pliant, could the word mean 'unable to bend, stiff, awkward?'

lencg; *adv. Longer.* v. lange.

lencten, lengten, lenten, es; *m. Spring, Lent*:—Lencten *ver*: foreweard lencten *vel* middewærd lencten *ver novum*: æfterwærd lencten *ver adultum*, Ælfc. Gl. 95; Som. 76, 7, 12–14; Wrt. Voc. 53, 21, 26, 27. Swá nú lencten and hærfest; on lencten hit grēwþ, and on hærfest hit fealwiaþ, Bt. 21; Fox 74, 22. Gif middes wintres messedeg biþ on sunnandeg, ðonne biþ gód winter and lengten windi, Lchdm. iii. 162, 26. Winter biþ ceald-ost, lencten hrímigost, Menol. Fox 471; Gn. C. 6. Wæs ðá lencten ágán bútan vi. nihtum ǽr sumeres cyme on Maias Kl., Elen. Kmbl. 2452; El. 1227. Ðæs sylfan lentenes hé fór tó Róme *in the course of the same spring he went to Rome*, Chr. 1048; Erl. 177, 13. Ðá com Æðelréd cyning innan ðam lenctene hám tó his ágenre þeóde, 1014; Erl. 150, 17. Sunnan glǽm on lenctenne lífes tácen weceþ *the sun's gleam in spring wakes signs of life*, Exon. 59 b; Th. 215, 16; Ph. 254. Ðé má ðe man mót on lenctene flǽsces brúcan *any more than flesh may be eaten in Lent*, Wulfst. 305, 25. Sumor ðú and lencten swylce geworhtest *æstatem et ver tu plasmasti ea*, Ps. Th. 73, 16. Ðone lencten wǽron him on Cent *during the spring they were in Kent*, Chr. 1009; Erl. 143, 14. Nis nán blódlǽstíd swá gód swá on foreweardne lencten *there is no time for letting blood so good as in the early spring*, L. M. 1, 72; Lchdm. ii. 148, 3: 2, 30; Lchdm. ii. 228, 8. Gif mon in lencten hálig ryht in folce bútan leáfe álecgge gebéte mid cxx. scill *if any one in Lent suppress holy law among the people without leave, let him make amends with cxx shillings*, L. Alf. pol. 40; Th. i. 88, 13. Ðú dydes sumer and lenten, Ps. Surt. 73, 17. [*Piers P.* lenten: *Prompt. Parv.* lente: cf. *O. H. Ger.* lengiz *and* lenzo *ver*: *Ger.* lenz. v. Grmm. D. M. 715.]

lencten-ádl, e; *f. A fever, typhus fever, tertian fever*:—Lengtenádl *tipus*, Ælfc. Gl. 10; Som. 57, 24; Wrt. Voc. 19, 30. Lenctenádl *tertiana*, 289, 58. Lenctinádl *tertiana*, ii. 122, 20. Án lytel cniht fram lengtenádle wæs gelácnod ... sum cniht on langre lengtenádle wæs hefiglíce geswenced *puerulus e febre curatus sit* ... *puerulus quidam longo febrium incommodo graviter vexatus fuit*, Bd. 3, 12; S. 537, 2–5. Ða ðe on lengtenádle wǽron *febricitantes*, 4, 6; S. 574, 6. Wið lenctenádle, L. M. 1, 62; Lchdm. ii. 134, 28: 3, 1; Lchdm. ii. 306, 12.

lencten-bryce, es; *m. A breach of the Lenten fast*:—Gif hwá openlíce lengctenbryce gewyrce, L. C. S. 48; Th. i. 402, 29.

lencten-dæg, es; *m. A day in Lent*:—Lengctendagum, L. C. E. 17; Th. i. 370, 3: Wulfst. 117, 15.

lencten-eorþe, an; *f. Land ploughed in the spring*; veractum. Ducange gives '*veractum* champ reonné' and refers to *warectum* 'terra novalis, seu requieta, quia alternis requiescit, sic dicta, inquit Edw. Cokus quasi vere novo victum, vel subactum.'], Ælfc. Gl. 1; Som. 55, 16; Wrt. Voc. 15, 16.

lencten-fæsten, es; *n. The fast of Lent*, L. Alf. pol. 5; Th. i. 64, 25: 40; Th. i. 88, 12: L. C. E. 16; Th. i. 368, 22: Wulfst. 117, 9.

lencten-líc; *adj. Vernal, lenten*:—Lengtenlíc dæg *dies vernalis*, Ælfc. Gl. 95; Som. 76, 11; Wrt. Voc. 53, 25. Manegra manna cwyddung is ðæt seó lenctenlíce emniht gebyrige rehtlíce on Marian mæssedæge, Lchdm. iii. 256, 4. Ða clǽnan tíd lenctenlíces fæstenes *the pure time of the Lenten fast*, Homl. Th. ii. 98, 24. Ðæs lænctenlíces emnihtes dæg *the day of the vernal equinox*, Lchdm. iii. 238, 17. Ebréi healdaþ heora geáres anginn on lenctenlícre emnihte, 246, 17. On lenctenlícre tíde *in spring time*, Hexam. 4; Norm. 8, 3. Nú is ús álýfed ðæt wé dæghwomlíce on ðyssere lenctenlícan tíde úre líchaman gereordigan mid forhæfednysse and clǽnnysse. Stuntlíce fæst se lenctenlíc fæsten, se ðe on ðisum clǽnum tíman hine sylfne mid gálnysse befýlþ, Homl. Th. ii. 100, 13–17.

lencten-sufel, es; *n. Food for the spring* or *for Lent*:—Syster beána tó længtensufle *i. sester fabe ad quadrigesimalem convictum*, L. R. S. 9; Th. i. 436, 31.

lencten-tíd, e; *f. Spring-time, spring, Lent*:—*Ver* is lenctentíd, Lchdm. iii. 250, 9. Hit wæs lenctentíd *erat vernum tempus*, Gen. 48, 7. On lengtentíde mónþes tíde *mense verni temporis*, Ex. 34, 18. Nǽfre on lenctentíde *never in Lent*, Wulfst. 305, 24. Hé on lenctentíd gesceóp ðone forman dæg ðyssere worulde ðæt is xv cl. Aprilis *he in spring created the first day of this world, that is the 18th of March*, Hexam. 4; Norm. 8, 4: Bt. Met. Fox 29, 135; Met. 29, 68.

lencten-tíme; *adj. Vernal*:—Lenctentíme *vernali* (s. *tempore*) Hpt. Gl. 496, 44.

lencten-wicu, an; *f. A week in Lent*:—Ðys sceal on Þursdæg on ðære óðre lenctenwucan *this shall be read on Thursday in the second week in Lent*, Rubc. Jn. Skt. 5, 30.

-lenda, -lende. v. in-, ut-lenda, -lende.

lendan; *p.* de *To arrive, come to land*:—Man hine lǽdde tó Eligbyrig ... sóna swá hé lende on scype man hine blende *he was brought to Ely ... as soon as he arrived he was blinded on board ship*, Chr. 1036; Erl. 165, 27; Ælf. Tod. 14. [*Icel.* lenda *to come to land, get to*: *O. H. Ger.* lantian *applicare.*] v. ge-lendan.

lenden-bán, es; *n. The loin-bone*:—Lendenbán neoþeweard *sacra spina*, Ælfc. Gl. 74; Som. 71, 52; Wrt. Voc. 44, 35. [Cf. *Misc.* 12, 360, leigeð his skinbon on oðres *lendbon.*]

lenden-, lende-brǽd, e, *f*: -brǽda, an; *m*. *A loin*:—Lendebrǽde *lumbulos*, Wrt. Voc. ii. 51, 31. Lendebrēde, 113, 35. Wið lendenbrǽdena sāre *against lumbago* [?], Herb. 1, 10; Lchdm. i, 74, 3. Sió helt ða lendenbrǽdan *it* [*the liver*] *has a hold on the false ribs*, L. M. 2, 17; Lchdm. ii. 198, 1. [Cf. *O. H. Ger*. lenti-prāto; *m*. *ren, renunculus, lumbulus, lumbus*, Grff. 3, 285: *Ger*. lenden-braten *loin, sirloin: and see* hrycg-brǽdan.]

lenden-reáf, es; *n*. *A covering for the loins, an apron*:—Lenden-, sīd-reáf *lumbare* vel *renale*, Ælfc. Gl. 63; Som. 68, 112; Wrt. Voc. 40, 22.

lendenu; *pl*. *The loins, reins*:—Lendenu *renes* vel *lumbi*, Ælfc. Gl. 74; Som. 71, 53; Wrt. Voc. 44, 36. Lændenu *lumbi*, 65, 26. Lendena *renes*, 71, 41. Laendino *rien*, Wrt. Voc. ii. 119, 17. Lendene *renes*, Ps. Spl. T. 15, 7. Beón eówer lendena ymbgyrde . . . On ðām ymbgyrdum lendenum is se mægþhād tō understandenne *let your loins be girded . . . By the girded loins virginity is to be understood*, Homl. Th. ii. 564, 25. Beóþ eówre lændenæ ymbgirde . . . on ðām lændenum is getācnad swā swā wē leorniaþ on bōcum seó fūle gālnes, L. Ælfc. P. 13–14; Th. ii. 368, 32–35. Begyrdaþ eówer lendenu *renes vestros accingetis*, Ex. 12, 11: Homl. Th. ii. 264, 8. Se Johannes hæfde fellenne gyrdel embe hys lendenu *ipse Joannes habebat zonam pelliciam circa lumbos ejus*, Mt. Kmbl. 3, 4. [Cf. *O. L. Ger*. lenda; *f*. *ren*: *Icel*. lend; *f*: *O. H. Ger*. lenti: *f*: *Ger*. lende; *f*.]

lenden-wærc, es; *m*. *A disease of the kidneys*; nefresis [nefritis?], Ælfc. Gl. 10; Som. 57, 39; Wrt. Voc. 19, 42.

lending, e; *f*. *Landing, landing-place*:—Ic ann ealle ða lændinge and ða gerihte of ðam ilkan wætere *concedo omnes exitus ejusdem acquæ*, Chart. Th. 317, 22. [*Icel*. lending *landing, landing-place*.]

lendis lieg *bofor*, Wrt. Voc. ii. 102, 12. Laembis lieg, 11, 28.

-lendisc. v. dūn-, eówer-, in-, up-, ūre-, ūt-lendisc.

leng; *adv*. *Longer*. v. lange.

leng, e; *f*. *Length* [of time or space], *height, stature*:—Mannes leng *statura*, Ælfc. Gr. 43; Som. 45, 4. Nǽfre ne sȳ se hālga eásterdæg gemǽrsod ǽr ðan ðe ðæs dæges lenge [lencge MS. P; længe, MS. L.] ofer-stīge ða niht *never let the holy Easter-day be celebrated, before the length of the day exceed the night*, Lchdm. iii. 256, 13. Swā micel swā seó sǽ heó mǽst wiðteóhþ and git ānes mannes lenge ðe healt ānne spreót on his hand and strecþ hine swā feor swā hē mæg ārǽcan intō ðere sǽ *quantum mare plus se retraxerit, et adhuc statura unius hominis tenentis lignum quod Angle nominant* spreót, *et tendentis ante se quantum potest*, Chart. Th. 318, 10. Lenge *proceritatis*, Wrt. Voc. ii. 66, 8. Hū lang wæs Adam on lenge gesceapen *how tall was Adam created?* Salm. Kmbl. 180, 19. Hwilc eówer mæg geīcan āne elne to his lenge? Homl. Th. ii. 464, 2. Forneán on lenge ungeendod *almost infinite in length*, 350, 7. Þreóhund fæðma biþ se arc on lenge, Gen. 6, 15. Far geond ðis land on lenge and on brǽde *perambula terram in longitudine et in latitudine sua*, 13, 17: Nar. 33, 22. Leáf on fingeres længe *leaves of the length of a finger*, Herb. 147, 1; Lchdm. i. 270, 22. On fingres lencge, 150, 1; Lchdm. i. 274, 14. Seó sunne stōd stille ānes dæges lencge [længce, MS. M.] *the sun stood still for the length of one day*, Lchdm. iii. 262, 9. Dō ðus ða lange ðe hit beþurfe *do thus for the length of time that is necessary*, 114, 18. Tele ða lenge ðære hwīle . . . *compare the length of time* . . . Bt. 18, 3; Fox 66, 6. On ðīnum handum synd ða lenge mīnra tīda *in manibus tuis tempora mea*, Ps. Th. 30, 17. [*O. H. Ger*. lengi: *Ger*. länge.] v. lengu.

lengan; *p*. de *To make or to become long, protract, delay, extend, lengthen*:—Lengeþ, Exon. 107 b: Th. 411, 6; Rä. 29, 8. Ðā lengde hit man swā lange *it was so long delayed*, Chr. 1052; Erl. 183, 10. Ne lengde ðā leóda aldor wītegena wordcwyde ac hē wīde beád metodes mihte *the prince was not slow to heed the prophet's words, but widely proclaimed the might of the Lord*, Cd. 208; Th. 256, 25; Dan. 646. Hyre lof lengde geond londa fela *her praise extended through many lands*, Exon. 86 a; Th. 324, 23; Vīd. 99. Giestas lisse lengdon *the guests prolonged their pleasure*, 94 a; Th. 353, 13; Reim. 12. Hī lengdon (*prolongaverunt*) unrihtwīsnyssa heora, Ps. Spl. 128, 3. [*Havel*. lenge *to prolong*: *Ayenb*. lenge *to delay*: *Piers P*. lenge *to delay, tarry*: *Icel*. lengja *to lengthen, prolong*: *O. H. Ger*. lengjan *protrahere, differre*.] DER. gelengan.

lengan; *p*. de *To pertain, belong*:—Ðonne heó byþ ii and xx niht eald ðæt ðū gesihst hit lengeþ tō gōde and gefeán *when the moon is twenty-two nights old, what thou seest belongs to good and to joy*, Lchdm. iii. 160, 9. v. lenge, langian, ge-lang.

lenge; *adj*. *Belonging, related*:—Him biþ lenge hūsel *to them belongs the housel*, Exon. 32 b; Th. 103, 9; Cri. 1685. Gōd biþ wið God lenge *good hath affinity with God*, 91 a; Th. 341, 5; Gn. Ex. 121. v. *preceding word, and* ge-lenge.

lengian; *p*. ode *v. impers*. *To long*:—Lengaþ hine hearde *sorely doth he long*, Salm. Kmbl. 542; Sal. 270. [Cf. *Icel*. lengjask mjök *to long exceedingly*.]

lengeo, lengo. v. lengu.

leng-fǽrra. v. lang-fǽre.

lengten. v. lencten.

lengþ, e; *f*. *Length*:—On lengþe mid him hē begeat ealle ða eástlond *at length with them he gained all the east country*, Ors. 3, 11; Swt. 144, 1. [Hit weáx on lengþe *it grew in length*, Chr. 1122; Erl. 249, 22.] [*Icel*. lengd *length*.]

lengu; *indecl*. *f*. *Length*:—Gerisenlīcre lengo tō gemete ðæs līchoman *congruæ longitudinis ad mensuram corporis*, Bd. 4, 11; S. 580, 14. Seó wæs ungeendodre lengo *infinitæ longitudinis*, 5, 12; S. 627, 36. Hī tōætȳcton lengeo ðære þrȳh twegra fingra gemet *addiderunt longitudini sarcofagi quasi duorum mensuram digitorum*, 4, 11; S. 580, 6. Ðæs lengo ne his heánesse ǽnig ende gesewen wæs *cujus neque longitudini neque altitudini ullus esse terminus videretur*, 5, 12; S. 629, 13. Tō lengo his *ad staturam suam*, Mt. Kmbl. Lind. Rush. 6, 27. Lengu dæga *longitudine dierum*, Ps. Surt. 90, 16. Lengu, Lk. Skt. Rush. 12, 25. Se ðe līfa gehwæs lengu wealdeþ *he who determines the length of every life*, Exon. 40 a; Th. 133, 2; Gū. 483. Tele nū ða lengu ðære hwīle, Bt. 18, 3; Fox 66, 6 note. v. leng.

lent, e; *f*. *A lentil*:—Lent *legumen* (cf. lentis, legumen, Ep. Gl. 13 e, f, 8), Germ. 390. [Cf. *O. H. Ger*. linsi; *f*. *lens*: *M. H. Ger*. linse.]

leó, *g*. león; [*a dat*. leóne *and acc*. *f*. leó *are found as well as regular forms* león: *the dat*. *pl*. leónum *is put under* leóna q. v.] *m*. *f*. *A lion, lioness*:—Leó *leo*, Wrt. Voc. 77, 78. Leó *leo, leena*, Wrt. Voc. ii. 53, 47, 49. Ðæt nǽfre mīne fȳnd ne grīpen mīne sāwle swā swā leó *nequando rapiat ut leo animam meam*, Ps. Th. 7, 2: 21, 11. Ðā ongan seó leó fægnian . . . Seó leó mid hire earmum scræf geworhte, Glostr. Frag. 110, 7, 15. Ðonne seó leó bringþ his hungregum hwelpum hwæt tō etanne, Ors. 3, 11; Swt. 142, 24. Seó leó ðeáh hió wel tam sē and hire magister swīðe lufige, Bt. 25; Fox 88, 9. Etan león flǽsc . . . Nim león gelynde *to eat lion's flesh . . . take lion's suet*, L. Med. ex Quad. 10, 12; Lchdm. i. 364, 22, 24. Gefriða mē of ðæs león mūðe *libera me de ore leonis*, Ps. Th. 21, 19. Of león hwelpum, 56, 4: 103, 20. León hwelpas *leunculi*, Wrt. Voc. ii. 51, 42. *Griffus* fiðerfōte fugel, leóne gelīc on wæstme, Wrt. Voc. 78, 2. Hió sceolde forsceoppan tō león and ðonne seó sceolde sprecan ðonne rȳnde hió *she turned into a lioness, and when it ought to have spoken, then she roared*, Bt. 38, 1; Fox 194, 33. Nān heort ne onscūnode nǽnne león, 35, 6; Fox 168, 9. Hē gelǽhte āne león be wege, Jud. 14, 5. Ða wildan leó hē gewylde *the wild lion he subdued*, Ælfc. T. Grn. 7, 16. Ðū miht tredan león and dracan *conculcabis leonem et draconem*, Ps. Th. 90, 13: Glostr. Frag. 110, 3. Ūs symle león and beran ūre ehtan *incursantibus leonibus ursisque*, Nar. 12, 3. Ða ðe león wǽron ongunnon rȳnan, Bt. Met. Fox 26, 165; Met. 26, 68. Tōlȳseþ leóna mægen *molas leonum confringet*, Ps. Th. 57, 5. Hwelpas leóna *catuli leonum*, Ps. Spl. 103, 22. Hȳ mon sende in wildra deóra menigo, in leóna and in berena, Shrn. 133, 10: Wulfst. 200, 23. Hwænne āhredst [ðū] mīne āngan sāwle æt ðǽm leóum (leóm, Ps. Surt.) *restitue a leonibus unicam meam*, Ps. Th. 34, 17. Hē hēt gelǽdan león and beran, manega and mycele, Homl. Skt. 4, 403. [In *Orm*. and *Laym*. leo *occurs as well as* leon. *Icel*. leó; *m*: *O. H. Ger*. lio, leuuo; *g*. leuuen, Grff. 2, 31.]

leód, es; *pl*. [which is more frequent] leóde; *m*. *A man*, poet. *a prince* [cf. *Icel*. ālfa ljóði]; in *pl*. *men, people, people of a country, country* [cf. *the use of proper names*, e. g. hē gewāt intō Galwalum *he departed into Gaul*, Chr. Erl. 5, 14]:—Leód Ebréa [*Abraham*], Cd. 136; Th. 171, 28; Gen. 2835. Ebrēa leód, 98; Th. 130, 21; Gen. 2163. Wedera leód [*Beowulf*], Beo. Th. 687; B. 341: 702; B. 348: 1254; B. 625. Gif hwā his āgenne geleód [MS. H. leód] bebycgge *if any one sell his own countryman*, L. In. 11; Th. i. 110, 3. Ðā hatedon hine his leóde *cives autem ejus oderant eum*, Lk. Skt. 19, 14. Ða leóde ðā flugon ðā hié ðone here tōweardne wiston *the people fled when they knew the army was coming*, Blickl. Homl. 79, 12. Ðā flugon ða hǽðnan leóde, 203, 16. Lifigende leóde, Cd. 205; Th. 255, 3; Dan. 618. Leóde ne cūðan mōdblinde men meotud oncnāwan *people, men mind-darkened, could not their maker recognize*, Exon. 25 a; Th. 73, 10; Cri. 1187. Wedera leóde, Beo. Th. 455; B. 225. Wē synt gumcynnes Geáta leóde *by race are we men of the Gauts*, 526; B. 260. Hē ealle ða landbigengan wolde ūtāmǽran and his āgenra leōda mannum gesettan *omnes indigenas exterminare, ac suæ provinciæ homines pro his substituere contendit*, Bd. 4, 16; S. 584, 7. Hit nā geweorþan sceolde ðæt se wǽre leóda cyning se ðe ǽr wæs folce þeów *it ought not to be, that he that had been a servant to a people, should be a king of men*, Ors. 4, 6; Swt. 178, 21. Leóda līfgedāl Lothes gehȳrde brȳd *Lot's wife heard the death of men*, Cd. 119; Th. 154, 25; Gen. 2561. Leóda ǽnigum nytte *of use to any man*, Beo. Th. 1591; B. 793. Lāþ leóda gehwam, Exon. 10 b; Th. 12, 31; Cri. 194. Hæleþa ēðel, leóda gesetu, Andr. Kmbl. 2519; An. 1261. Wē ðissa leóda land gesōhton, 535; An. 268. Ðǽr wæs þreó þūsend ðæra leóda *there was three thousand of the people*, Elen. Kmbl. 570; El. 285. Leóda bearn [cf. *O. Sax*. liudi-barn] *the children of men*, Exon. 24 a; Th. 69, 11; Cri. 1119: Chr. 975; Erl. 124, 32; Edg. 24. Leóda [MS. leode] þeódum, Ps. Th. 80, 12. Geáta leóda cempan *warriors of the men of the Gauts*, Beo. Th. 416; B. 205. Ic eówra leóda willan geworhte, 1273; B. 634. Næs ðǽr mā sīnra leóda nemne elleffne orettmæcgas, Andr. Kmbl. 1326; An. 663. Wæs hē eallum his leōdum leóf *ipse* [*Oswin*] *amabilis omnibus præfuit*, Bd. 3, 14; S. 539, 33. Bæd hē Theodor ðæt hē him and his leódum bisceop funde [*sibi suisque*], 4, 3; S. 566, 25. Tō nytnysse his leódum *utilitati suæ gentis*, 2, 16; S. 520, 3. Ðæt Sūþseaxna mǽgþ sceolde habban ágenne bisceop on heora leódum *ut provincia Australium Saxonum ipsa proprium haberet episcopum*, 5, 18; S. 636, 14. Æþelwulf tó his leódum cuom, Chr. 855; Erl. 68, 31. Ælþeódige men . . . swǽse men in leódum *aliens . . . natives of the country*, L. Wih. 4; Th. i. 38, 3. [Cf. below, Beo. Th. 3741.] Ðǽm Cristenum leódum com Godes engel on fultum *God's angel had come to the Christians as a help*, Blickl. Homl. 203, 25, 20: Cd. 24; Th. 31, 22; Gen. 489: 157; Th. 195, 16; Exod. 277. Hié wíf tó Denum feredon lǽddon tó leódum *they bore her to Denmark*, Beo. Th. 2322; B. 1159. Wǽron æþelingas eft tó leódum fúse tó farenne *the nobles were eager to go back to their people*, 3613; B. 1804. Gif cyning his leóde tó him gehâteþ and heom mon ðǽr yfel gedó *if a king summon his people to him and evil is done to them there*, L. Ethb. 2; Th. i. 2, 8. Ceadwealla slóh ða Norþhymbran leóde æfter heora hláfordes fylle, Swt. A. S. Rdr. 95, 9. Leóda, 96, 40. Leóde hogode on ðæt micle morþ, men forweorþan, Cd. 32; Th. 43, 14; Gen. 690: Andr. Kmbl. 339; An. 170. Leóde, Judéa cyn, Elen. Kmbl. 416; El. 208. Hét hine leóde swǽse sécean *bade him seek his own people*, Beo. Th. 3741; B. 1868: 2677; B. 1336. Land and leóde, Andr. Kmbl. 2643; An. 1323: Chr. 1065; Erl. 198, 6; Edw. 25. Gif ðú ðæt gerǽdest ðæt ðú ðíne leóda lýsan wille *if you decide to save thy men*, Byrht. Th. 132, 56; By. 37. [*O. L. Ger.* liud; *m*; *pl.* liudí: *O. Sax.* liudí: *O. Frs.* liode, liude: *Icel.* lýðir; *pl.* [e. g. af lýðum sínum *by his people*]: *O. H. Ger.* liuti *homines*: *Ger.* leute.] v. burh-, eást-, ge-, land- leód; *and next word.*

leód, e; *f. A people, nation, race, district occupied by a people* [v. *preceding word, and* cf. mǽgþ], *country*:—Hit wæs hwílum on Engla lagum ðæt leód and lagu fór be geþincþum *at one time it was in the laws of the English, that the people and the law went according to ranks*, L. R. 1; Th. i. 190, 11. Ðæt leód and lagu trumlíce stande, Wulfst. 74, 8. Feówer folccyningas, leóde rǽswan, Cd. 95; Th. 125, 6; Gen. 2075. Ða fǽhþe eówer leóde *the hostility of your people*, Beo. Th. 1197; B. 596. Tó fela Deniga leóde, 1396; B. 696: 1202; B. 599. Se wæs Cantwara leóde *oriundus de gente Cantuariorum*, Bd. 3, 14; S. 539, 27. Moyses leóde *from the Israelites*, Cd. 149; Th. 187, 16; Exod. 152. Wæs his gewuna ðæt hé his ágene leóde Norþanhymbra mǽgþe sóhte *solebat suam, id est, Nordanhymbrorum provinciam revisere*, Bd. 3, 23; S. 554, 6. Hé wæs ealle ða land and leóde þurhfærende *omnia pervagatus*, 3, 30; S. 562, 13. Úres hláfordes gerǽdnes is ðæt man cristene menn of earde ne sylle ne húru on hǽðene leóde *our lord's ordinance is, that Christian men be not sold out of the land, certainly not into a heathen country* [*or* leóde = *men*, preceding word], L. Eth. v. 2; Th. i. 304, 16: Beo. Th. 387; B. 192. Ðone Denisca leóda lufiaþ swýðost *him* [*Thor*] *the Scandinavian peoples love most*, Wulfst. 106, 23. Beneuentius and Sepontanus hâtton ða twá leóde *Benevento and Sepontus were the two places called*, Blickl. Homl. 201, 22. Ealle him leóda lácum cwemaþ *all nations shall make offerings to please him*, Ps. Th. 71, 10. [*O. Sax.* liud-: *O. Frs.* liod: *Icel.* ljóð-; lýðr; *m. people, common people*: *O. H. Ger.* liut; *m. n.* populus, plebs.] v. land-leód, *and preceding word.*

leód, es; *m. Fine for slaying a man* [cf. leudus, id est weregildus; *and see other passages in* Grmm. R. A. 652]:—In xl nihta ealne leód forgelde *let him pay the whole fine within forty days*, L. Ethb. 22; Th. i. 8, 6. Healfne leód, 23; Th. i. 8, 7. v. leód-geld, wer-geld.

leóda, an; *m. A man, one of a people* or *country*:—Gif hwá his ágenne geleód [MS. B. leódan] bebycgge *if any one sell a man of his own people*, L. In. 11; Th. i. 110, 3. Be leódan bygene *concerning the sale of a man of one's own country*, Th. i. 110, 1 note.

leódan; *p.* leád; *pl.* ludon *To spring, grow*:—Swá Libanes beorh líðeþ and gróweþ *sicut cedrus Libani multiplicabitur*, Ps. Th. 91, 11. Of ðam twige ludon réðe wæstme *from that branch sprang dire fruits*, Cd. 47; Th. 60, 29; Gen. 989. [*Goth.* liudan: *O. Sax.* liodan: *O. H. Ger.* ar-, fram-liutan.] DER. á-, ge-leódan.

leód-bealu, wes; *n. Harm* or *bale which affects a people*, Beo. Th. 3448; B. 1722: 3896; B. 1946.

leód-biscop, es; *m. A bishop of a district, province*, or *diocese, a bishop subordinate to an archbishop, a suffragan. The* leódbiscop *ranks with the* ealdorman, *the* arcebiscop *with the* æþeling. In Rtl. 194, 34–40 occurs the following 'Chore episcopi; Grece core, Latine vicari, episcopi: hii in vicis et villis constituti habentes licentiam constituere gradum minorem, non presbiterum neque diaconum, propter scientiam episcopi in cujus regione est.' The Greek form is here glossed by *liódbiscop*, the Latin by *scírebiscop*. Ercebisceop *archiepiscopus*; leódbisceop, *episcopus*, Wrt. Voc. 71, 70, 71. Se hálga Cúðbertus Lindisfarnensiscere gelaþunge leódbiscop [cf. hé wæs tó biscope gecoren ðære cyricean æt Lindisfarena eá, Bd. 4, 28; S. 606, 7], Homl. Th. ii. 148, 22. Gif hwá arcebisceopes oððe æþelinges borh abrece . . . Gif hwá leódbisceopes oððe ealdormannes, L. C. S. 69; Th. i. 408, 8–10. Ðæt Turonisce folc hine geceás him tó leódbiscope *the people of Tours chose him as their bishop*, Homl. Th. ii. 506, 3: Chr. 971; Erl. 125, 34. Bútan hit beforan cyninge oððe leódbisceope oððe ealdormen beó, Chart. Th. 612, 13. Séce man tó ðam leódbiscope; and gif man furþor scule tó ðam arcebiscope; and syððan tó ðam pápan, Wulfst. 275, 6. Gif hé sóhte leódbiscop oððe ealdorman ðonne áhte hé vii nihta griþ, L. Eth. vii. 5; Th. i. 330, 14. Ðá bǽdon ealle ða leódbisceopas ðone hálgan apostol ðæt hé ða feórþan bóc gesette *then all the provincial bishops asked the apostle to compose the fourth gospel*, Homl. Th. i. 70, 6. Hé létt gewrítan hú mycel landes his arcebiscopas hæfdon and his leódbiscopas and his abbodas and his eorlas, Chr. 1085; Erl. 218, 30. [Mid arcebiscopes and leódbiscopes and abbotes, 1125; Erl. 254, 8. Ealle ða leódbiscopes ða ðá wǽron on Englalande, 1129; Erl. 258, 10.] [*Icel. adopts from English* ljóð-, lýð-biskup *a suffragan bishop.*] Cf. scír-biscop.

leód-burh; *f. A people's town, a town of a country, town occupied by a people*:—Of ðysse leódbyrig [*Sodom*], Cd. 116; Th. 150, 33; Gen. 2501. Hé eaferum lǽfde lond and leódbyrig *he to his children left his land and its towns*, Beo. Th. 4933; Th. 2471.

leód-cyning, es; *m. The king of a people*:—Beówulf Scyldinga leóf leódcyning, Beo. Th. 107; B. 54. [*Laym.* lead-king.]

leóde; *pl. people.* v. leód.

leód-fruma, an; *m. The first in time of a people, the founder of a people, a patriarch; the first in rank among a people, a prince, chieftain, king*:—Him wæs án fæder leóf leódfruma *one father had they, founder beloved*, Cd. 161; Th. 200, 9; Exod. 354. Leódfruma [*St. Andrew*], Andr. Kmbl. 3318; An. 1662: [*Constantine*], Elen. Kmbl. 382; El. 191. Mín leódfruma *my lord*, Exon. 115 a; Th. 442, 5; Kl. 8. Sethes cynn, leófes leódfruman, Cd. 63; Th. 75, 26; Gen. 1246. Of ðam leódfruman brád folc cumaþ *from that patriarch* [*Isaac*] *shall come nations wide-spreading*, 106; Th. 140, 24; Gen. 2332. Gif hí leódfruman lǽstan dorsten *if they durst follow their chief*, Bt. Met. Fox 1, 53; Met. 1, 27. Cyning, leófne leódfruman, Exon. 60 b; Th. 222, 7; Ph. 345: [*Hrothgar*], Beo. Th. 4266; B. 2130: [*St. Andrew*], Andr. Kmbl. 1977; An. 991.

leód-geard, es; *m. The dwelling of a people, country*:—Sunu æfter heóld leódgeard, Cd. 62; Th. 74, 20; Gen. 1225. Ethiopia land and leódgeard, 12; Th. 15, 6; Gen. 229: 85; Th. 106, 18; Gen. 1773. [Cf. *Icel.* ljóð-heimar *the people's abode, the world.*]

leód-gebyrga, an; *m. The protector of a people, a prince, chief man*:—Se æþeling, leódgebyrga [*Constantine*], Elen. Kmbl. 405; El. 203. Hláford ðínne, leódgebyrgean [*Hrothgar*], Beo. Th. 543; B. 269. Leódgebyrgean *the chief men of the city* [cf. ceastre weardas *applied to the same persons in* v. 767], Elen. Kmbl. 1108; El. 556.

leód-geld, es; *n. The fine paid for slaying a man*, L. Ethb. 21; Th. i. 8, 4: 7; Th. i. 4, 9. v. Grmm. R. A. 653, *and* leód.

leód-geþyncþ, es; *f. Rank existing amongst a people*:—Be leódgeþincþum, L. R.; Th. i. 190, 10.

leód-gewinn, es; *n. Strife*:—Lǽt sace restan, láð leódgewin, Exon. 68 b; Th. 254, 22; Jul. 20.

leód-gryre, es; *m. Terror affecting a people*, Salm. Kmbl. 558; Sal. 278.

leód-hata, an; *m. A tyrant*:—Nalæs swá swá sigefæst cyning ac swá swá leódhata *non ut rex victor sed quasi tyrannus*, Bd. 3, 1; S. 523, 29. Bana, láð leódhata [*the angel that destroyed the first-born in Egypt*], Cd. 144; Th. 180, 4; Exod. 40. For wédenheortnesse ðæs leódhatan Brytta cyninges *propter vesanam Brittonici regis tyrannidem*, Bd. 3, 1; S. 524, 2: Bt. 16, 2; Fox 52, 30. Láðne leódhatan [*Holofernes*], Judth. 10; Thw. 22, 22; Jud. 72. Hér sind on earde leódhatan grimme ealles tó manege *here in the land are fierce tyrants all too many*, Swt. A. S. Rdr. 109, 155. Áwyrgede womsceaðan, leáse leódhatan, Elen. Kmbl. 2597; El. 1300. Cyningas ða habbaþ under him mænigfealde leódhatan *reges sub se multos habentes tyrannos*, Nar. 38, 19.

leód-hete, es; *m. Hate* or *enmity felt by a people*, Andr. Kmbl. 2278; An. 1140: 224; An. 112: 2300; An. 1151.

leód-hryre, es; *m. Fall* or *destruction of a people*, Beo. Th. 4771; B. 2391: 4064; B. 2030.

leód-hwæt; *adj. Very brave* [cf. leud *a prince*?]:—Se leódhwate lindgeborga, Elen. Kmbl. 21; El. 11. [*Grein suggests* lindhwata leódgeborga; cf. leód-gebyrga.]

leód-mǽg, es; *m. A kinsman as being one of the same race, tribe* or *people, a man of the same nation with one's self*:—Hí fundon fíf hund leódmǽga *they found five hundred of their race*, Elen. Kmbl. 759; El. 380. Leódmágum feor *far from my kinsmen* [*Abraham in Egypt*], Cd. 128; Th. 163, 6; Gen. 2694.

leód-mægen, es; *n. The might of a people, its fighting men*:—Ðæt leódmægen, gúþrófe hæleþ, eorlas æscrófe, Elen. Kmbl. 544; El. 272. Lofige hine eall his leódmægen *laudate eum omnes virtutes ejus*, Ps. Th. 148, 2. Leódmægnes worn *a host of warriors*, Cd. 151; Th. 190, 7; Exod. 195: Th. 188, 13; Exod. 167.

leód-mearc, e; *f. A people's territory, a country*, Andr. Kmbl. 572; An. 286: 1554; An. 778.

leód-riht, es; *n. Public law, common law, the law which affects a whole people, law of the land*; jus publicum:—Mid rihtum landrihte and leódrihte swá hit on lande stonde *in accordance with the common law of the land*, Cod. Dip. Kmbl. iii. 435, 35. Bútan leódrihte, Andr. Kmbl. 1357; An. 679. v. folc-, land-riht.

leód-rúne, an; *f. A witch, wise woman* [cf. burh-rúne *furia*; helle-rūne *pythonissa*: Grmm. D. M. 375 *on the forms of feminine names in* -rūn, -rūna]:—Wiđ ǣlcre yfelre leódrūnan ... eft ōđer dust and drenc wiđ leódrūnan, L. M. 1, 64; Lchdm. ii. 138, 23, 26. Cockayne translates the word 'heathen charm.' Cf. *Laym.* 9121 seolcuđe leodronen [tocke, 2nd. MS.]: leoten weorpen & fondien leodrunen [*incantations*], 15499, 15511: leodrunen [deorne rouning, 2nd MS.], 14553.

leód-scearu, e.; *f. A people, nation,* Cd. 160; Th. 199, 12; Exod. 337. Cf. folc-scearu.

leód-sceađa, an; *m. A harmer of men, a public enemy*:—Lāđ leódsceađa [*the serpent*], Cd. 43; Th. 56, 24; Gen. 917. Æt đam leódsceađan hreddan *to save from the devil,* Exon, 11 b; Th. 17, 20; Cri. 273. Ic đam leódscađan [*Grendel*] hondleán forgeald, Beo. Th. 4193; B. 2093. Hearmcwide lāđra leódsceađena [*the Mermedonians who abused St. Matthew*], Andr. Kmbl. 159; An. 80. [*O. Sax.* liud-skađo (*the devil*).] cf. folc-sceađa.

leód-scipe, es; *m. A people, nation, country occupied by a people*:—Đe đes leódscype longe bieode *whom this people have long worshipped,* Exon. 68 b; Th. 255, 2; Jul. 208. Of đam leódscipe đe is Siria gehāten *from the country that is called Syria,* Homl. Th. i. 400, 7: Exon. 64 a; Th. 236, 30; Ph. 582. Eallum his leódscipe tō þearfe *for the behoof of all his people,* L. Edg. pref; Th. i. 262, 4: L. Eth. ii. 1; Th. i. 284, 10. Woruldrihta ic wille đæt standan on ǣlcum leódscipe [*English and Danish and British, see the rest of the section*], L. Edg. S. 2; Th. i. 272, 23: Beo. Th. 4400; B. 2197. On đam leódscipe [*the Greeks*], Bt. Met. Fox 30, 3; Met. 30, 2. Hwæt tō bōte mihte æt đæm fǣrcwealme đe his leódscipe swȳđe drehte, L. Edg. S. 1; Th. i. 270, 10: Chr. 1014; Erl. 150, 9: Beo. Th. 5495; B. 2751: Bt. Met. Fox 1, 135; Met. 1, 68. Đrȳ leódscipas sind gehātene India, Homl. Th. i. 454, 11. Hī cyning habban woldon swā swā ōđre leódscipas hæfdon *they wanted to have a king, as other nations had,* Ælfc. T. Grn. 6, 45. Tō đām leódscipum đe tō geleáfan bugon, 14, 3. Đa cynegas đe eardodon on đām leódscipum *reges Amorrhæorum et Chanaan,* Jos. 5, 1. Bodigende geleáfan đām leódscipum đe sind gecwedene Galatia, Cappadocia, Bithinia, Asia, Italia, Homl. Th. i. 370, 26: L. I. P. 23; Th. ii. 334, 28. Hē wiđ feó sealdon wīde intō leódscipas *sold them into distant countries,* Blickl. Homl. 79, 23. [*O. Sax.* liud-skepi *a people*: *O. H. Ger.* liut-scaf.] Cf. þeód-scipe.

leód-stefn, es; *m. A race, family, people,* Ps. Th. 82, 7. [*O. H. Ger.* liut-stam: cf. *O. Sax.* liud-stemni; *adj. belonging to a people.*]

leód-þeáw, es; *m. Custom of a people* or *country*:—Đā hē tō mē cwom đā grētte hē mē sōna and [h]ālette his leódþeáwe *cum me more rituque salutaret,* Nar. 27, 3. Ne wolde đām leódþeáwum Loth onfōn *Lot would not adopt those customs of the country,* Cd. 92; Th. 116, 18; Gen. 1938.

leód-weard, e; *f. The guard* or *government of a people* or *country,* Cd. 59; Th. 72, 1; Gen. 1180: 60; Th. 72, 3; Gen. 1196: 145; Th. 181, 6; Exod. 57.

leód-wer, es; *m. A man of a nation*:—Leódweras [*the Egyptians*], Cd. 89; Th. 110, 5; Gen. 1833. Ofer leódwerum [*the Israelites*], 148; Th. 184, 20; Exod. 110.

leód-werod, es; *n. The host formed by a people*:—Wolcen lǣdde leódwerod [*the Israelites*], Cd. 146; Th. 182, 17; Exod. 77.

leód-wita, an; *m. A man of intelligence in a people*:—Đā wǣron þeódwitan [leódwitan, MS. H.] weorþscipes wyrþe, eorl and ceorl, þegen and þeóden, L. R. 1; Th. i. 190, 12. v. Grmm. R. A. 267.

leód-wynn, e; *f. Joy that comes from being among one's own people*:—Leódwynna leás, wineleás wræcca, Exon. 119 a; Th. 457, 25; Hy. 4, 89.

leóf, *used as a form of address to one* or *to many,* cf. *modern 'dear sir'*:—Wē biddaþ đē leóf đæt đū hlyste ūre sprǣce *oramus, domine, ut audias nos,* Gen. 43, 20: 3, 10: Ælfc. Gen. Thw. 1, 5, 14. Đā cwæþ đæt wīf tō him leóf đæs mē þingþ đū eart wītega *dicit ei mulier domine video quia propheta es tu,* Jn. Skt. 4, 19. Hī cwǣdon, leóf, wē wyllaþ geseón đone hǣlend, 12, 21. Seó gegaderung his leorningcnihta cwæþ Drihten leóf wilt đū nū gesettan ende đysre worulde *the assembly of his disciples said, Lord, wilt thou now put an end to this world,* Homl. Th. i. 294, 24. Ic bidde eów leóf đæt gē gecirron tō mīnum hūse *obsecro, domini, declinate in domum pueri vestri,* Gen. 19, 2. Gefyrn ic hine cūđe leóf... La leóf nele hē gelȳfan mīnum wordum *long ago I knew him, Sir ... Ah! Sir, he will not believe my words,* Glostr. Frag. 2, 10, 19. Lā leóf *O Lord,* Gen. 18, 23, 25, 28, 30, 31. Hī cwǣdon tō đām apostolon lā leóf hwæt is ūs tō dōnne *they said to the apostles, Sirs, what shall we do?* Homl. Th. i. 314, 33. v. next word.

LEÓF; *adj.* LIEF, *desirable, pleasant, acceptable, loved, beloved, dear*; used substantively, *one who is dear, a friend, loved one*:—Se đe gōd onginneþ and đonne āblinneþ ne biþ hē Godes leóf on đæm nēhstan dæge *he who begins good and then ceases, will not be God's friend at the last day,* Blickl. Homl. 21, 35. Wæs hē eallum his gefērum leóf *he was dear to all his companions,* 213, 12: Cd. 4; Th. 5, 30; Gen. 79. Hē wæs leóf Gode, 130; Th. 165, 26; Gen. 2737. Ealre his þeóde leóf heora rīce tō habbanne and tō healdenne *totæ suæ genti ad tenenda servandaque regni sceptra exoptatissimus,* Bd. 5, 19; S. 636, 33. Ne ǣnig mon ne leóf ne lāđ *no man, neither friend nor foe,* Beo. Th. 1026; B. 511. Gode is swīđe leóf đæt gē earmum mannum syllon *it is very acceptable to God, that you give to poor men,* Blickl. Homl. 53, 28. On đa tīd wæs mannum leóf ofor eorþan and hālwende *at that time it was pleasant for men upon earth, and healthful,* 115, 8. Đā cwæþ Petrus and Andreas tō Johanne đū leófa drihten gecȳđe ūs hwylce gemete đū cōme tōdæg tō ūs *then said Peter and Andrew to John, 'Dear Sir, tell us how thou camest to us to-day,'* 141, 20. Brūc đisses beáges, Beówulf leófa, mid hǣle, Beo. Th. 2437; B. 1216. Eálā leóf hlāford, *O, mi domine,* Coll. Monast. Th. 19, 13. Hēr is mīn leófa sunu *hic est filius meus dilectus,* Mt. Kmbl. 17, 5. Matheus mīn se leófa, beheald on mē, Blickl. Homl. 229, 30. Forþfērde Gode se leófa fæder Agustinus *defunctus est Deo dilectus pater Augustinus,* Bd. 2, 3; S. 504, 30. Se leófa cuma and se lufigendlīca *hospes ille amabilis,* 4, 3; S. 568, 16. Mē sealde sunu on leófes stæl đæs đe Cain ofslōh *he gave me a son in place of the loved one, him whom Cain slew,* Cd. 55; Th. 68, 7; Gen. 1113. Leófes and lāđes *of friend and foe,* Beo. Th. 5813; B. 2910. Fela sceal gebīdan leófes and lāđes *he shall experience much pleasure and pain,* 2126; B. 1061. Ic đē wolde leófum lofsang cweþan, Ps. Th. 118, 164. Ālēdon leófne þeóden on bearm scipes, Beo. Th. 68; B. 34. Hlāford leófne, 6276; B. 3142. Leófe đīne *dilecti tui,* Ps. Th. 59, 4. Mīne brōđru leófon *my dear brethren,* Bd. 4, 24; S. 598, 43. Đǣr ne biþ leófra gedāl ne lāđra gesamnung *there shall not be parting of friends there, or meeting of foes,* Blickl. Homl. 65, 20. Đā cwǣdon hié đæt him nǣnig mǣg leófra nǣre đonne hiera hlāford *then they said that no kinsman was dearer to them than their lord,* Chr. 755; Erl. 50, 19. Hī cwǣdon đæt him nān hlāford leófra nǣre đonne hiora gecynda hlāford, 1014; Erl. 150, 25. Leófre mē ys đæt ic hig sylle đē đonne ōđrum men *melius est, ut tibi eam dem, quam alteri viro,* Gen. 29, 19. Ic wylle and mē leófre sig gif đū māge *volo et multum delector, si potes,* Bd. 5, 3; S. 616, 31. Ǣghwilcum men biþ leófre swā hē hæbbe holdra freónda mā *the more true friends he has, the better every man likes it,* Blickl. Homl. 121, 36. Ūs biþ đonne leófre đonne eal eorþan wela gif hē ūs miltsian wile *if he will shew us mercy, shall we not prefer that to all the wealth of earth?* 51, 29. Ǣnne tīman đonne ūs wǣre leófre đonne eall đæt on middanearde is, đæt wē āworhtan georne Godes willan, L. C. E. 18; Th. i. 370, 18. Ne dēm đū ōđerne dōm đam liófran and ōđerne đam lāđran, L. Alf. 43; Th. 1, 54, 12. Him wǣron ǣr his ǣhta leófran tō hæbbenne đonne Godes lufu *he would rather have his possessions than God's love,* Blickl. Homl. 195, 9. Eall forlǣteþ đæt him wæs leófost tō āgenne and tō hæbbenne, 111, 26. For oft hit wyrþ rađost forloren đonne hit wǣre leófost gehealden *too often it is most quickly lost, when keeping it would be most pleasant* [or leófost *adv.*?], Wulfst. 109, 4. Đes is mīn leófesta sunu *hic est filius meus carissimus,* Mk. Skt. 9, 7. Đū leófesta [Hat. MS. leófusta] brōđur *frater carissime,* Past; Swt. 22, 9. Ic sende gerētan đone leófastan cyning Ceólwulf, Bd. ded; S. 471, 8. Mīne gebrōđra đa leófostan *my dearest brethren,* Homl. Th. ii. 4, 19. Men đa leófostan, 188, 25: Blickl. Homl. 165, 33. Leófestan, 9, 13. Đa word đe hē wēnþ đæt him leófoste sȳn tō gehȳrenne *the words that he thinks will be most pleasant for him to hear,* 55, 20. [*Goth.* liubs: *O. Sax.* liof: *O. Frs.* liaf, lief: *Icel.* ljúfr: *O. H. Ger.* liub, liob, lieb *gratus, desiderabilis, carus, optatus, amicus*: *Ger.* lieb.] DER. fela-, mōd-, ofer-, un-leóf. The word occurs forming part of proper names, e.g. Leóf-rīc, Leóf-sunu, Leóf-wine; so in other dialects.

leófan; *p.* leáf; *pl.* lufon. Grein suggests that this verb is found in the following passage:—Ēđelweardas lufan līfwelan đenden hié lēt metod, Cd. 174; Th. 219, 17; Dan. 56. Is it possible however that a verb such as *hæfdon* should be supplied, and that *lufan* is the accusative after it?

leofen. v. lifen.

leofian. v. lifian.

leófian, *p.* ode *To be dear* or *pleasant, to delight*:—Him leófedan londes wynne bold on beorhge *the pleasures of the country were dear to him, the house on the hill,* Exon. 34 b; Th. 110, 19; Gū. 110. [Cf. *O. L. Ger.* ge-lievan *delectari, delectare*: *O. H. Ger.* liubjan *diligere, affectare, commendare.*]

leóf-lic; *adj. Lovely, beautiful, delightful, pleasant, lovable, dear*:—Wīglāf leóflīc lindwīga *Wiglaf, warrior dear,* Beo. Th. 5199; B. 2603. Leóflīc cempa, Andr. Kmbl. 2891; An. 1448. Leóflīc wīf, Elen. Kmbl. 572; El. 286. Eafora leóflīc on līfe, Cd. 82; Th. 103, 4; Gen. 1713. Leóflīc geþwǣrnes *fair concord,* Dōm. L. 18, 270. Đone wlitigan wong and wuldres setl leóflīc *the beauteous plain and the pleasant seat of glory,* Exon. 62 a; Th. 228. 18; Ph. 440. Hié Sarran wlite heredon ōđ đæt hē lǣdan hēht leóflīc wīf tō his selfes sele, Cd. 89; Th. iii. 16; Gen. 1856. His sweord leóflīc īren *his sword, weapon of price,* Beo. Th. 3622; B. 1809. Lofiaþ leóflīcne *they laud the beloved* (*God*), Exon. 13 b; Th. 25, 13; Cri. 400. [*Goth.* liuba-leikr *lovely* (Phil. 4, 8): *O. Sax.* liof-līk: *O. Frs.* liaf-līk: *O. H. Ger.* liub-līh *amoenus, venustus, pulcher, gratus, elegans, splendidus*: *Ger.* lieb-lich.]

leóf-līce; *adv. Kindly, graciously, gladly, lovingly*:—Đeáh đe ic scyle ealle wucan fæstan ic đæt leóflīce dō *though I have to fast all the week, I will do it gladly,* Bd. 4, 25; S. 600, 7. Hē leóflīce līfes ceápode moncynne *graciously he purchased life for mankind,* Exon. 24 a; Th. 67,

29; Cri. 1096. Fore onsȳne ēces dēman lǣddon leóflīce *before the face of the eternal judge they led him lovingly,* 44 a; Th. 149. 3; Gū. 756. [*O. H. Ger.* liub-lîho *gratifice, perfloride, evitaliter.*]

leóf-spell, es; *n. A pleasant message*:—Leófspell manig, Elen. Kmbl. 2032; El. 1017.

leóf-tǽle, -tǣl; *adj. Loving, dear, desirable, estimable, grateful, pleasant, gracious*:—Hē biþ freónd and leóftǣl lufsum and līðe *he (Christ) shall be friendly and gracious, kind and gentle,* Exon. 21 a; Th. 57, 4; Cri. 913. Hē is monþwǣre, lufsum and leóftǣl, 96 a; Th. 357, 21; Pa. 32. Ōðer biþ unlǣde on eorþan ōðer biþ eádig swīðe leóftǣle mid leóda duguþum *one will be miserable on earth, the other fortunate, high in favour with the best of men,* Salm. Kmbl. 733; Sal. 366. Nān cræft nis Gode deórwyrðra ðonne sió lufu ne eft ðam deófle nān cræft leóftǣlra ðonne hié mon slīte *nil pretiosius est Deo virtute dilectionis, nil est desiderabilius diabolo extinctione caritatis,* Past. 47, 2; Swt. 359, 24. Ða welan beóþ hlīseádigran and leóftǣlran ðonne ðonne hié mon selþ ðonne hié beón ðonne hī mon gadraþ. Seó gītsung gedēþ heore gītseras lāðe ǣgðer ge Gode ge monnum and ða cysta gedōþ ða simle leóftǣle and hlīseádige *divitiæ effundendo magis quam coacervando melius nitent: siquidem avaritia semper odiosos, claros largitas facit,* Bt. 13; Fox. 38, 13–17.

leóf-wende; *adj. Pleasing, gracious, acceptable, amiable, estimable*:—Nō liófwende *non gratus,* Wrt. Voc. ii. 61, 62. Sum biþ leófwende hafaþ mōd and word monnum geþwǣre *one man is amiable, he hath mind and speech in accord with men,* Exon. 79 b; Th. 298. 13; Crä. 84. Ne beó ðū nō tō tǣlende ac beó leófwende *be not too ready to blame, but be amiable,* 81 a; Th. 305, 22; Fä. 92. Ðæt ic meotud ðīnum lārum leófwendum lyt geswīce *that I, O Lord, little desert thy pleasant precepts,* Andr. Kmbl. 2581; An. 1292. Wuton wuldrian weorada dryhten lufian liófwendum līfes āgend *let us glorify the Lord of hosts, gratefully love the disposer of life,* Hy. 8, 3; Hy. Grn. ii. 290, 3: Exon. 14 b; Th. 29, 31; Cri. 471. Ðeáh hit gōd seó and deóre ðeáh biþ hlīseádigra and leófwendra se ðe hit selþ ðonne se ðe hit gaderaþ and on ōðrum reáfaþ *though it (gold) be good and precious, yet will he be of better repute and esteem who gives it, than he who collects it and robs it from another,* Bt. 13; Fox 38, 12.

LEÓGAN; *p.* leáh; *pl.* lugon *To lie, tell a lie, say falsely, break one's word, play false, deceive, feign*:—Ic leóge *mentior,* Ælfc. Gr. 31; Som. 35, 53. Eal hit is swā, ne leóge ic, Blickl. Homl. 179. 3. Ðū līhst ðæt ðū God sȳ *thou sayest falsely that thou art God,* Homl. Th. i. 378, 7. Seó orsorge wyrd simle līhþ and līcet *prospera fortuna semper mentitur,* Bt. 20; Fox 70, 30: Ælfc. Gr. 49; Som. 50, 30. Hē līhþ him sylfum, Wulfst 66, 3. Se ðe lȳhþ oððe ðæs sōðes ansaceþ, Salm. Kmbl. 364; Sal. 181. Mā sceamigan ðonne fagnian ðonne hí geheóraþ ðæt him man on līhþ *qui falso prædicantur, suis ipsi necesse est laudibus erubescant,* Bt. 30, 1; Fox 108, 8. Ic geseó tō sōðe nales mē sefa (MS. selfa) leógeþ *I do indeed see, my mind deceives me not,* Cd. 193; Th. 242, 9; Dan. 416. Ðīne feóndas ðē fǣcne leógaþ (lēgaþ, Ps. Surt.) *mentientur tibi inimici tui,* Ps. Th. 65, 2: 80, 14. Nū cwǣdon gedwolmen ðæt deófol gesceópe sume gesceafta, ac hī leógaþ, Homl. Th. i. 16, 20. Oft ða unþeáwas leógaþ and līcettaþ ðæt hī sién gōde þeáwas *plerumque vitia virtutes se esse mentiuntur,* Past. 20; Swt. 149, 2. Ðā ðā hē leág *fefellisset,* Wrt. Voc. ii. 34, 26: Exon. 84 b; Th. 318, 12; Mōd. 81. Hēr begann se deófol tō reccanne hālige gewrita and hē leáh mid ðære race *here the devil began to expound holy writ, and he spake falsely in his exposition,* Homl. Th. i. 170, 4. Ðā swōran hié swīðe ðæt hié sōð sægdon and nōht lugon ðara þinga *quibus jurantibus se nichil falsi commiscere,* Nar. 25, 28. Sǣdon ðæt hī wǣran on Criste gelȳfede, ac hī lugon swā ðeáh, Homl. Skt. 2, 303. Hig hym fæla ongeán lugon *they brought many false charges against him,* Nicod. 34; Thw. 19, 39. Gē tō dæge wǣron Somnitum þeówe gif gē him ne ālugen (other MS. lugon) iówra wedd *hodie Romani Samnio servirent, si fidem fœderis ipsi Samnitibus servavissent,* Ors. 3, 8; Swt. 122, 13. Ne leóh ðū leng *noli ultra fallere,* Ex. 8, 29. Ne leóh ðū *non mentiemini,* Lev. 19, 11. Swā wēnaþ manige men, ðæt ðes diáccon leóge be ðam fȳre, Wulfst. 206, 13. Ðone ilcan geþang ic ðē ǣr sǣde, ǣr hē leóge, ðæt hē ðē leógan ne durre, Blickl. Homl. 179, 29. Būton Priscianus luge *unless Priscian have made a mistake,* Ælfc. Gr. 17; Som. 20, 49. Se ðe wolde leógan on his wordon, Wulfst. 168, 17. Ðonne onginþ him leógan se tōhopa ðære wræce *then the hope of revenge begins to deceive them,* Bt. 37; Fox 186, 23: Bt. Met. Fox 25, 100: Met. 25, 50: Exon. 90 a; Th. 337, 27; Gn. Ex. 71. Ðæne nǣnig mæg leógan *quem nemo potest fallere,* Hymn. Surt. 33, 15. Ðū leógende sagast, Blickl. Homl. 179, 22. Ðonne hī secgeaþ ǣlc yfel ongēn eów leógende *cum dixerint omne malum adversum vos mentientes,* Mt. Kembl. 5, 11. Gē sind leógende *mentita es,* Past. 21, 1; Swt. 151, 21. [*Goth.* liugan: *O. Sax.* liogan: *O. Frs.* liaga: *Icel.* ljúga: *O. H. Ger.* liugan *mentiri, fallere, fingere*: *Ger.* lügen.] Der. ā-, for-, ge-, of- leógan.

leógere, es; *m. A liar, one who speaks or acts falsely, a false witness*:—Up ārīsaþ leáse leógeras, Wulfst. 79, 4. Leógeras, L. C. S. 5; Th. i. 380, 5. Ðā cōmon twegen ðæra leógera *venerunt duo falsi testes,* Mt. Kmbl. 26, 60. [*Icel.* ljúgari *a liar*: *O. H. Ger.* liugari *fictor.*]

LEÓHT, līht, es; *n.* light, *a light*:—Geweorþe leóht and leóht wearþ geworht *fiat lux, et facta est lux,* Gen. 1, 3. Tweóne leóht *crepusculum*: tweónul leóht *maligna lux* vel *dubia,* Ælfc. Gl. 94; Som. 75, 122, 125; Wrt. Voc. 53, 3, 6. Ðæt leóht ðe wē dægrēd hātaþ *the light that we call dawn,* Lchdm. iii. 234, 28. Ic geseó ðis hūs mid swā mycele leóhte gefylled ðætte ðæt eówer blācern and leóht mē is eallinga þȳstre gesewen *domum hanc tanta luce impletam esse perspicio, ut vestra illa lucerna mihi omnimodis esse videatur obscura,* Bd. 4, 8; S. 576, 3. Ðære sunnan beorhtnys and ðæs mōnan leóht and ealra tungla, Homl. i. 64, 29: Blickl. Homl. 91, 23. Ðenden him leóht and gǣst somod fæst seón *whilst he lives,* Exon. 31 a; Th. 96, 27; Cri. 1580. Ðū eart dōhtor mīn mīnra eágna leóht *thou art my daughter, the light of mine eyes,* 67 a; Th. 248, 14; Jul. 95. Leóhtes leóhting *lucubrum,* Ælfc. Gl. 67; Som. 69, 89; Wrt. 41, 42. Se blinda bæd his eágena leóhtes *the blind man asked for his eye-sight,* Blickl. Homl. 21, 6: Elen. Kmbl. 596; El. 298. Se dæg wæs fruma ðyses lǣnan leóhtes *the day was the beginning of this transitory light,* Blickl. Homl. 133, 10. Godes cyrcan mid leóhte and lācum gelōme gegrētan *to visit God's church frequently with candles and offerings,* Wulfst. 308, 28. Of ðissum leóhte ālǣded *de hac vita subtractus,* Bd. 3, 20; S. 550, 23. Ða ðe hī of ðissum leóhte foreode *qui eas ex hac luce præcesserant,* 4, 7; S. 575, 4. Se sacerd forbærnþ ða drihtne tō leóhte and tō wynsumum stence *adolebit ea sacerdos in holocaustum et suavem odorem domino,* Lev. 1, 9. On lifgendra leóhte *in lumine viventium,* Ps. Th. 55, 11. Ic tō ðē æt leóhte gehwam wacie *ad te de luce vigilo,* 62, 1. Be dæges leóhte *by daylight,* Exon. 107 b; Th. 410, 17; Rä. 28, 17. Hē hié lǣdeþ tō līhte ðǣr hī līf āgon ā tō aldre, Cd. 221; Th. 287, 2; Sat. 361. Geearnian leóht ðæs ēcan līfes, Blickl. Homl. 17, 21. Ðæt þridde ne geseah ðære sunnan leóht nǣfre, Glostr. Frag. 8, 27. Hē Godes leóht geceás *he died,* Beo. Th. 4930; B. 2469: Exon. 52 b; Th. 184, 13; Gū. 1343. Eádgār ceás him ōðer leóht, Chr. 975; Erl. 124, 30; Edg. 22. Drihten nam in ōðer leóht Agustinus, Menol. Fox 191; Men. 97. Beó nū leóht on ðære heofenan fæstnysse *fiant luminaria in firmamento cœli,* Gen. 1, 14. Gesceóp God twā miccle leóht *God created two great lights,* Lchdm. iii. 234, 7. Wē sceolon on ðisum dæge beran ūre leóht tō cyrcan and lǣtan hī ðǣr bletsian *we must on this day carry our lights to church and have them blessed there,* Homl. Th. 1, 150, 27. [*Goth.* liuhaþ: *O. Sax.* lioht: *O. Frs.* liacht: *Icel.* ljós: *O. H. Ger.* lioht, lieht *lux, candela, lucerna, lumen*: *Ger.* licht.] Der. ǣfen-, fȳr-, heofon-, morgen-leóht.

leóht, lēht, līht; *adj. Light, bright, cheerful* (perhaps the passages in which the word has the meaning of *cheerful* should be put under the next word v. leóht-mōd), *shining, clear*:—Cwæþ ðæt his līc wǣre leóht and scēne *he said that his body was bright and beautiful,* Cd. 14; Th. i. 26; Gen. 265. Lēht (līht, Rush.) biþ all līchoma ðīn *lucidum erit totum corpus tuum,* Mt. Kmbl. Lind. 6, 23. Bebod drihtnes leóht *præceptum dominum purum,* Ps. Spl. C. 18, 9. Him wæs leóht sefa . . . blīðheort wunode *his soul was unclouded by sorrow . . . blithe of heart he continued,* Andr. Kmbl. 2504; An. 1253. Him wæs leóht sefa, ferhþ gefeónde, Elen. Kmbl. 346; El. 173. Swā leóhtes andwlitan men *tam lucidi vultus homines,* Bd. 2, 1; S. 501, 15. Ðam ðe ic ofonn leóhtes geleáfan *to whom I grudge clear belief,* Exon. 71 a; Th. 265, 8; Jul. 378: Apstls. Kmbl. 131; Ap. 66. Leóhte gesihþe *lucidus aspectu,* Bd. 5, 12; S. 627, 32. Æt leóhtum fȳre *at a bright fire,* L. M. 1, 2; Lchdm. ii. 30, 7. Se ðe reáfaþ man leóhtan dæge *he who robs a man in daylight,* L. Eth. iii. 15; Th. i. 298, 11. Ða þióstro ðīnre heortan willaþ mīnre leóhtan lāre wiðstondan, Bt. Met. Fox 5, 43; Met. 5, 22. Mid leóhtum andgite *with clear understanding,* Blickl. Homl. 105, 31: Wulfst. 252, 5. Gē syttaþ ealle niht and drincaþ ōð leóhtne dæg, and swā āwendaþ dæg tō nihte and niht tō dæge, 297, 28. Be leóhtne dæg *in matutino,* Ps. Th. 72, 11. Dō ðīne ansȳne esne ðīnum leóhte *faciem tuam illumina super servum tuum,* 118, 135. Ðonne wurþaþ ðīn eágan swā leóht *then shall thine eyes become so clear,* Cd. 27; Th. 35, 34; Gen. 564. Gelīc wæs hē (*Lucifer*) ðām leóhtum steorrum, 14; Th. 17, 7; Gen. 256. Ðæt wē māgon oft leóhtum dagum geseón *quam sæpe lucidioribus diebus aspicere solemus,* Bd. 1, 1; S. 474, 15. Leóhte nihte on sumera hafaþ *lucidas æstate noctes habet,* S. 473, 29. Se heofen mōt brengon leóhte dagas, Bt. 7, 3; Fox 20, 21. Wurde ðīn līchoman leóhtra micle, Cd. 25; Th. 32, 13; Gen. 502. Eác wǣre ðam earman leóhtre on mōde gif hē ðæs rīcan mannes welan ne gesāwe *also the poor man would have been more cheerful, if he had not seen the rich man's wealth,* Homl. Th. i. 330, 11. Benedictus ðe ūs bōc āwrāt leóhtre be dǣle ðonne Basilius *Benedict who wrote us a book clearer in some respects than Basil did,* Basil prm; Norm. 32, 9. Ingeþonc leóhtre and beorhtre ðonne se leóma sunnan on sumera, Bt. Met. Fox 22, 43; Met. 22, 22: Ors. 5, 14; Swt. 248, 11. Lēga leóhtost *brightest of flames,* 9, 33; Met. 9, 17. [*O. Sax.* lioht: *O. Frs.* liacht: *Icel.* ljóss: *O. H. Ger.* lioht, lieht *lucidus*: *Ger.* licht.]

leóht, lēht, līht [*from comparison with other dialects the proper spelling would seem to be* līht, *but* leóht (*or* leoht?), *in West-Saxon at least, is the regular form*]; *adj. Light, not heavy, inconsiderable; not slow, quick, ready, nimble, fickle, easy*:—Mīn byrðyn ys leóht (Lind. lēht; Rush. līht) *onus meum leve est,* Mt. Kmbl. 11, 30. Leóht and leoþuwāc *nimble and supple,* Exon. 79 b; Th. 298, 12; Crä. 84. Hē is snel and swift and leóht *levis et velox est,* 60 b; Th. 220, 9; Ph. 317: 52 a; Th. 182, 6;

Gú. 1306. Mē leóht slǣp oferarn *levis mihi somnus obrepsisset*, Bd. 5, 9; S. 622, 33. Leóht drenc *a light drink*, L. M. 2, 51; Lchdm. ii. 264, 26. Leóht wȳn, Lchdm. iii. 122, 1. Hwīlum ða leóhtan scylda beóþ beteran tō forlǣtenne *aliquando leviora vitia relinquenda sunt*, Past. 62; Swt. 457, 7. Hȳ habbaþ swȳðe lytle scypa and swīðe leóhte *they have very little ships and very light ones*, Ors. 1, 1; Swt. 19, 8. Ðæt sió wamb ðȳ ðē leóhtre sīe *by it the stomach may be relieved*, L. M. 2, 25; Lchdm. ii. 218, 1. Wið mōdes (? innoþes, MS.) hefignesse . . . sōna biþ ðæt mōd leóhtre, Lchdm. iii. 50, 23. Leóhtre ic eom micle ðonne ðes lytla wyrm *I am much lighter than this little worm*, Exon. 111 b; Th. 426, 19; Rä. 41, 76. Līhtre *tolerabilius*, Mt. Kmbl. Lind. 10, 15. Wē underfōþ scortne ryne ðæs leóhtran gewinnes *we have a short course of the easier conflict*, Homl. Th. i. 418, 10. Mid nānum leóhtran þinge gebēte ðonne him mon āceorfe ða tungan of, L. Alf. pol. 32; Th. i. 80, 21. Hȳ habbaþ ðæs ðē leóhtran gang *they shall walk the easier for it*, L. Med. ex Quad. 3, 15; Lchdm. i. 342, 12. Se hæfde moncynnes leóhteste hond *he had of all men the readiest hand*, Exon. 85 b; Th. 323, 1; Wīd. 72. [*Goth.* leihts: *O. Sax.* līht(-līc): *O. Frs.* lìcht: *Icel.* lēttr: *O. H. Ger.* līhti *levis, facilis*: *Ger.* leicht.]

leóhtan; *p.* te *To give light, to illumine, make light, cause to shine*:—Ðǣr leóhtes ne leóht lytel sperca earmum ǣnig *there doth not any little spark give light to the miserable ones*, Dōm. L. 14, 218. Hē lofe leóhteþ leófe ða hālgan *hymnus omnibus sanctis ejus*, Ps. Th. 148, 14. Ðīne līgetta leóhteþ and beorhteþ, 143, 7. Beorhte leóhte ðīnne andwlitan *illuminet vultum suum*, 66, 1. v. līhtan.

leóht-bǣre; *adj. Luminous, brilliant, splendid*:—Hyra leóhtbǣran ryne *their* (*the stars*) *luminous course*, Lchdm. iii. 272, 10. Ā ðæs dōm āge leóhtbǣre lof se ūs ðis līf giefeþ *ever therefore may he have glory, splendid praise, who giveth us this life*, Exon. 80 a; Th. 299, 34; Crä. 112.

leóht-beámed; *adj. Having bright beams* or *rays*:—Sind sume steorran leóhtbeámede, fǣrlīce ārīsende and hrædlīce gewītende, Homl. Th. i. 610, 2.

leóht-berend, es; *m. Lucifer*:—Leóhtberend *Lucifer*, Ælfc. Gr. 8; Som. 7, 19. Ðā wæs ðæs teóþan werodes ealdor swīðe fæger and wlitig gesceapen swā ðæt hē wæs gehāten Leóhtberend, Homl. Th. i. 10, 22. Se hātte Lucifer, ðæt ys Leóhtberend, Ælfc. T. Grn. 2, 35.

leóht-berende; *adj. Light-bearing, Lucifer, luminous*:—Lucifer hāten, leóht-berende, Cd. 221; Th. 287, 15; Sat. 367. Swylce ān ofen eall smōciende and leóhtberende fȳr fērde ofer ða lāc *apparuit clibanus fumans et lampas ignis inter divisiones illas*, Gen. 15, 17.

leóht-brǣdness, e; *f. Illumination*:—Leóhtbrǣdnesse *facibus*, Hpt. Gl. 515, 11.

leóhte; *adv. Brightly, clearly*:—Leóhte and beorhte scīnaþ *clearly and brightly they shine*, Blickl. Homl. 127, 35: Exon. 116 a; Th. 446, 10; Dōm. 20: 26 a; Th. 76, 14; Cri. 1239: Elen. Kmbl. 2229; El. 1116: Bt. Met. Fox 9, 25; Met. 9, 13. Leóhte oncnāwan *clearly recognise*, Exon. 24 a; Th. 69, 12; Cri. 1119: Elen. Kmbl. 1929; El. 966. Wæs se blāca beám bōcstafum āwriten beorhte and leóhte, 183; El. 92. Wearþ mē on hige leóhte *my mind was enlightened*, Cd. 32; Th. 42, 20; Gen. 676. Scȳnan leóhtor *to shine more brightly*, Exon. 21 a; Th. 56, 18; Cri. 902.

leóhte; *adv. Lightly, easily, gently*:—Līhte *lento*, Wrt. Voc. ii. 49, 62. Ðā wæs heó gesewen þurh twegen dagas ðæt hire leóhtor wǣre *videbatur illa per biduum aliquanto levius habere*, Bd. 4, 19; S. 589, 3. [*O. Sax.* liohto: *O. H. Ger.* līhto *leviter, leniter*.]

leohte; *p.* leoht; *pp.* v. leccan.

leóht-fæt, es; *n. A lamp, light, lantern*:—Leóhtfæt *lucernarium*, Ælfc. Gl. 30; Som. 61, 55; Wrt. Voc. 26, 54. Ðīnes līchaman leóhtfæt is ðīn eáge *lucerna corporis est oculus*, Mt. Kmbl. 6, 22. Leóhtfatu *lampades*, 25, 1. Judas com mid leóhtfatum *Judas venit cum lanternis*, Jn. Skt. 18, 3: Homl. Th. ii. 246, 9. Hē leóhtfatu (lehtfeatu, Ps. Surt.) micel geworhte *fecit luminaria magna*, Ps. Th. 135, 7: Hymn. Surt. 126, 12. [*O. Sax.* lioht-fat: *O. H. Ger.* lioht-faz *lucerna, lampas, luminarium* (cœli), *lanterna*.]

leóht-fruma, an; *m. The author* or *origin of light* (cf. lucis auctor, Exon. 65 b; Th. 242, 3; Ph. 667):—Līfes leóhtfruma *God*, Cd. 9; Th. 11, 14; Gen. 175: 43; Th. 57, 10; Gen. 926: Exon. 41 a; Th. 137, 26; Gū. 565: 41 b; Th. 138, 24; Gū. 581: Ps. C. 50; Ps. Grn. ii. 277, 46: Bt. Met. Fox 11, 143; Met. 11, 72.

leóht-gesceot, -gescot, es; *n. Contribution made to furnish the church with lights.* The various regulations respecting it may be seen in the following passages:—Gif hwā leóhtgesceot ne gelǣste, gylde lahslit mid Denum, wīte mid Englum, L. E. G. 6; Th. i. 170, 4. Gelǣste man leóhtgescot þrīwa on geáre, L. Eth. V. 11; Th. i. 308, 2: vi. 19; Th. i. 320, 3. Leóhtgescot gelǣste man tō Candelmæssan; dō oftor se ðe wile, ix. 12; Th. i. 342, 31. Leóhtgesceot þrīwa on geáre: ǣrest on Eásterǣfen, healfpenigwurþ wexes ǣt ǣlcre hīde; and eft on Ealra Hālgena mæssan eall swā mycel; and eft tō ðǣm Sanctam Mariam clǣnsunge eal swā, L. C. E. 12; Th. i. 366, 31. Leóhtgescot þreówa on geáre: ǣrest healfpeningwurþ wexes tō Candelmæssan, and eft on Eásterǣfen and þriddan sīþe tō Ealra Hālgena mæssan. Wulfst. 116, 6. Leóhtgescota, 113, 11. Leóhtgescot gelǣste man be wīte tō Cristes mæssan and tō Candelmæssan and tō Eástron; dō oftor se ðe wylle, 311, 9. [Cf. *Icel.* ljóstollr *fee to a church for lighting*.]

leóhtian; *p.* ode *To give light*:—Leóma leóhtade leóda mǣgþum *a ray gave light to the tribes of men*, Exon. 11 a; Th. 15, 10; Cri. 234. v. līhtan.

leóhtian, *p.* ode *To grow light, become less heavy*, or *easy, be relieved*:—Ðonne leóhtaþ him se līchoma *his body will be relieved of the pain*, Herb. 1, 16; Lchdm. i. 76, 2. v. līhtan *to ease*.

leóhting, e; *f. Lighting*:—Leóhtes leóhting *lucubrum*, Ælfc. Gl. 67; Som. 69, 89; Wrt. Voc. 41, 42. v. līhting.

leóht-īsern, es; *n. A candlestick*:—Lēhtīsern *candelabrum*, Mt. Kmbl. Lind. 5, 15: Mk. Skt. Lind. 4, 21: Lk. Skt. Lind. 8, 16.

leóht-leás; *adj. Without light*:—Hē sǣde ðæt hē wǣre gelǣd tō leóhtleásre stōwe *he said that he was conducted to a place without light*, Homl. Th. ii. 504, 29.

leóht-līc; *adj. Light, bright, shining*:—Lyftfæt leóhtlīc [*the moon*], Exon. 108 a; Th. 411, 21; Rä. 30, 3.

leóht-līc; *adj. Light, of little weight* or *value*:—Leóhtlīcu weorc *levitas operis*, Past. 43, 1; Swt. 309, 1. [*O. Sax.* līht-līk: *Icel.* lētt-ligr: *O. H. Ger.* līht-līh *levis, infimus, humilissimus*.] v. next word.

leóht-līce; *adv. Lightly, slightly, gently, without trouble* or *effort, easily, quickly*:—Swā swā leóhtlīce gebylged *quasi leviter indignata*, Bd. 4, 9; S. 577, 24. Swā swā hē leóhtlīce onslǣpte *quasi leviter obdormiens*, 4, 11; S. 580, 2. Geswēt swīðe leóhtlīce mid hunige *sweeten very slightly with honey*, L. M. 1, 2; Lchdm. ii. 36, 3: 1, 19; Lchdm. ii. 62, 20. Hī forlēton ða scipo ðus leóhtlīce . . . and lēton ealles þeódscipes geswincg ðus leóhtlīce forwurþan *they abandoned the ships thus lightly . . . and let all the nation's labour thus lightly come to nought*, Chr. 1009; Erl. 142, 10–13. Ða weras mon sceal hefiglecor lǣran and ða wīf leóhtlecor *illis* [men] *graviora, istis* [women] *injungenda sunt leviora*, Past. 24; Swt. 179. 16. [Swā swā heó līhtlucost mihten *as quickly as they could*, Th. An. 123, 21.] [*Icel.* lētt-liga *lightly, easily, readily*: *O. H. Ger.* līht-līhho *leniter, levius*: *Ger.* leicht-lich.]

leóht-mōd; *adj. Of light* or *cheerful mind, light-hearted, easy-tempered; light-minded* (v. next word), *inconstant, fickle*, Exon. 90 a; Th. 338, 30; Gn. Ex. 86. [Cf. *Icel.* lētt-lātr *cheerful*; lētt-lyndr *easy-tempered*; lētt-ūð *light-heartedness*; mod. *levity, frivolity*: *O. H. Ger.* līht-mōtig *levis*.]

leóhtmōd-ness, e; *f. Lightness of mind, want of gravity* or *steadiness, levity, frivolity, inconstancy*:—Gif ǣresð se wyrtruma biþ forcorfen ðæt is sió leóhtmōdnes . . . Mon hine bewarige wið ða leóhtmōdnesse . . . Paulus cwæþ 'Wēne gē nū ðæt ic ǣnigre leóhtmōdnesse brūce' . . . hē ðære leóhtmōdnesse unþeáwes nānwuht næfde *cum prius radicem levitatis abscidunt . . . Mentis levitas caveatur . . . Paulus dicit 'Numquid levitate usus sum?' . . . levitatis vitio non succumbo*, Past. 42, 3; Swt. 308, 2–11: 32, 2; Swt. 215, 2: 33, 6; Swt. 225, 12. For hira leóhtmōdnesse *levitate cogitationum*, 42, 1; Swt. 305, 17. [Cf. *O. H. Ger.* līht-mōti *levitas*.]

leóht-sceáwigend *light-seeing*; lucivida, Wrt. Voc. ii. 51, 56.

leóht-sceot. v. leóht-gesceot.

leólc. v. lācan.

leóma, an; *m. Light, radiance, sheen, splendour, lightning, ray* or *beam of light*:—Ðes leóma *hoc jubar*, Ælfc. Gr. 9; Som. 9, 43. Candeles leóma *lampas*, Ælfc. Gl. 67; Som. 69, 88; Wrt. Voc. 41, 41. Leóma *globus*; leómum *globis*, Wrt. Voc. ii. 40, 74, 75: 109, 73: *globis, luminibus*, Hpt. Gl. 472, 27. Fȳres leóma *illuminatio ignis*, Ps. Th. 77, 16. Sunnan leóma *the light of the sun*, Exon. 21 a; Th. 56, 16; Cri. 901. Swegles leóma *the radiance of the sky*, 57 a; Th. 204, 26; Ph. 103. Berhtre ðonne se leóma sunnan on sumera *brighter than sun-light in summer*, Bt. Met. Fox 22, 46; Met. 22, 23. Stōd se leóma him of swylce fȳren þecele ongeán norþdǣle middangeardes *the brightness* [*tail of a comet*] *proceeded from them*[*two comets*] *as a fiery torch towards the north*, Bd. 5, 23; S. 645, 29: Beo. Th. 5532; B. 2769. God eástan sende leóhtne leóman *God from the east sent bright radiance*, Judth. 11; Thw. 24, 16; Jud. 191: Cd. 223; Th. 294, 11; Sat. 469. Ðæt nānes mannes gesihþ ðæs leóhtes leóman sceáwian ne mihte, Homl. Th. i. 76, 11. Fȳrleóht geseah blācne leóman beorhte scīnan *he saw the firelight, a pale gleam, shine brightly*, Beo. Th. 3038; B. 1517. Seó sunne byþ swā feorr sūþ āgān ðæt hyre leóman ne māgon tō ðam lande gerǣcan *the sun is gone so far south, that its rays cannot reach that land*, Lchdm. iii. 260, 10: Cd. 148; Th. 184, 25; Exod. 112. Leóman *fulgura*, Hymn. T. P. 73: Ps. Lamb. 134, 7. Leómena leás *blind*, Exon. 87 a; Th. 328, 13; Vy. 17. Leómum inlȳhted *illumined with his rays*, 42 a; Th. 141, 14; Gū. 627. Seó sunne behȳdde hire hātan leóman *the sun hid its hot beams*, Homl. Th. ii. 256, 34. [*O. Sax.* liomo: *Icel.* ljómi *radiance, a ray*.] DER. æled-, beadu-, bryne-, fȳr-, ge-, heofon-, hilde-, sweord- leóma.

leomu *limbs*. v. lim.

león. v. leó.

león; *p.* lāh. *To lend, grant for a time*:—Mīn lond ðe ic hæbbe, and mē God lāh, Chart. Th. 469, 25: Beo. Th. 2916; B. 1456. Līh mē þreó hlāfas *commoda mihi tres panes*, Lk. Skt. Lind. 11, 5. [*Goth.*

leihwan: *O.Sax.* far-lîhan: *O.L.Ger.* lîan: *O.Frs.* lîa: *Icel.* ljá: *O.H.Ger.* lîhan *commodare, fenerare, mutuare: Ger.* leihen.] v. on-lēon.

león-fōt, es; *m. Lion's foot* [plant name]; alchemilla vulgaris:—Leónfōt *leontopodium*, Wrt. Voc. 67, 50: Herb. 8, 1; Lchdm. i. 98, 12. Liónfōt *leontopedium*, Wrt. Voc. ii. 53, 48. [*Icel.* ljóns-fōtr *alchemilla.*]

leóna, an; *m. A lion* or *lioness:*—Zosimus tō đam leónan cwæþ: Éálā đū mǣsta(e) wildeór [cf. l. 15 seó leó mid hire earmum], Glostr. Frag. 110, 9. Oft hālige men wunedon on wēstene betwux wulfum and leónum, Homl. Th. i. 102, 5: 488, 4: 572, 13: ii. 192, 24. Fram leónum *a leonibus*, Ps. Spl. 34, 20. [*Icel.* leóna *a lioness:* león, ljón; *gen.* ljóns: *m. n. a lion.*] v. leó.

leonian. v. linian.

leópard, es; *m. A leopard:*—Fore hundum tigros and leópardos hī fēdaþ *pro canibus tigres et leopardos nutriunt*, Nar. 38, 4. [*Icel.* leóparðr, hlébarðr: *O. H. Ger.* lēbarto, lēbard, leóparto.]

leóran; *p.* de *To go, depart, pass, pass away:*—Ic ne leóru *non emigrabo*, Ps. Surt. 61, 7. Leoreþ *transeat*, 56, 2. Wid đa hwīle liōres [geleóreþ, Rush.] heofon and eorþo *donec transeat cælum et terra*, Mt. Kmbl. Lind. 5, 18. Hē leórde đonan *transiit inde*, 11, 1: Andr. Kmbl. 247; An. 124. Hē tō drihtne mid sibbe leórde *he departed in peace to the Lord*, Glostr. Frag. 110, 30. Hē leórde tō heófonum *migravit ad cælos*, Bd. 2, 7; S. 509, 36. Of đissum leóhte leórde, 3, 20; S. 550, 26. Leórde *transivit*, 4, 23; S. 592, 39. Đe of weorulde leórdan *qui de sæculo migraverant*, 4, 22; S. 592, 27. Đā leórdon đa gāstas tō ēcum gefeán, Shrn. 134, 7. Lungre leórdon, nalas leng bidon, Andr. Kmbl. 2085; An. 1044. Leór ɫ gewīt heonan *transi hinc*, Mt. Kmbl. Rush. 17, 20. Đē gedafenaþ đæt đū leóre on đīne bǣre, Blickl. Homl. 149, 11. Leóre from mē đes calic *transeat calix iste*, Mt. Kmbl. Rush. 26, 39. Đætte munecas ne leóran of stōwe tō ōđre *ut monachi non migrent de loco ad locum*, Bd. 4, 5; S. 572, 37. Leóran *transire*, Mt. Kmbl. Rush. 26, 42. Leórendum dagum *in the transitory days* [*of this life*], Exon. 118 a; Th. 454, 9; Hy. 4, 30. DER. ā-, forþ-, be-, fore-, ge-, ofer-, þurh-leóran.

leóred-ness, e; *f. Migration, departure, extasy, vision:*—Liórednesse *visione spiritali*, Hpt. Gl. 486, 30. v. ge-leóredness.

leornere, es; *m. A learner, disciple scholar, learned person, reader:*—Be đam wrāt Beda se leornere *of him the scholar Bede wrote*, Shrn. 155, 25. Gif leornere geþēh þurh lāre đǣt hē hād hæfde and þēnode Criste *if a scholar succeeded by learning so that he had holy orders and served Christ*, L. R. 7; Th. i. 192, 12. Brȳde beág bēc leornere *a ring for a bride, books for a scholar*, Exon. 91 a; Th. 341, 25; Gn. Ex. 131. Đone leornere ic nū bidde *lectorem obsecro*, Bd. pref; S. 472, 31. Swā leorneras secgaþ *as scholars say*, Shrn. 63, 10: Exon. 62 a; Th. 227, 17; Ph. 424. Se Hǣlend tōbræc đa hlāfas and sealde his leornerum, Homl. Th. ii. 400, 21: Blickl. Homl. 131, 20. Johannes gesende twægen leorneras his *Joannes mittens duos de discipulis suis*. Mt. Kembl. Rush. 11. 2, 1: 10, 1. Ealle đa gelǣredestan men and đa leorneras *multis doctioribus viris*, Bd. 4, 24; S. 597, 30. v. stæf-leornere.

leór-ness, e; *f. Going, departure, withdrawal:*—Dægas leórnisse his *dies assumptionis ejus*, Lk. Skt. Rush. 9, 51. Leornisse *transmigrationis*, Ps. Surt. ii. 191, 3. In leórnisse *in secessu* [cf. gang II.], Mt. Kmbl. Rush. 15, 17. v. ge-, ofer-leórness.

leornesse [?] Bd. 6, 5; S. 527, 16, *other MSS. have* geornesse.

leornian; *p.* ode *To learn, study, read:*—Swā swā in đære bēc his līfes gemēteþ swā hwylc swā hī rǣdeþ and leornaþ *sicut in volumine vitæ ejus quisque legerit inveniet*, Bd. 4, 31; S. 611, 7. Ǣlc đe gehȳrde æt fæder and leornode *omnes qui audivit a patre et didicit*, Jn. Skt. 6, 45. Fram đām hē đæt gemet leornode regollīces þeódscipes *a quibus normam disciplinæ regularis didicerat*, Bd. 3, 23; S. 554, 35. Hē hālige gewritu leornade and smeáde *scripturis legendis operam daret*, S. 555, 29. Đa đe hē on gewritum leornode tō dōnne *ea quæ in scripturis agenda didicerat*, 3, 28; S. 560, 16. Gē ne leornodan *non legistis*, 4, 3; S. 569, 17. Leorna đæt đū ondrǣde drihten *ut discas timere dominum*, Deut. 14, 23. Leorneaþ æt mē *discite a me*, Mt. Kmbl. 11, 29. Leornigeaþ bigspell be đam fictreówe *ab arbore fici discite parabolam*, 24, 32. Syle andgit đæt ic đīne gewitnesse wel leornige *da mihi intellectum ut sciam testimonia tua*, Ps. Th. 118, 125. Ic hit for đære hǣlo đe hit leornige ođđe gehȳre āwrāt *ob salutem legentium, sive audientium narrandam esse putavi*, Bd. 5, 13; S. 634, 2. Lange sceal leornian se đe lǣran sceal *long must he learn who has to teach*, L. Ælfc. P. 46; Th. ii. 384, 15: L. I. P. 14; Th. ii. 322, 8. Bēc on tō leornianne *libros ad legendum*, Bd. 3, 27; S. 558, 27. Đa hūs đa đe on tō gebiddenne and tō leornigenne geworhte wǣron *domunculæ quæ ad orandum vel legendum factæ erant*, 4, 25; S. 601, 12. Ealswā David dyde leornigendum mōde [*with docile mind*], Wulfst. 172, 22. [*O. Frs.* ge-lerna, -lirna: *O. H. Ger.* lernēn, lirnēn *discere, meditari: Ger.* lernen. *Goth.* has leisan, *and* ga-laisjan sik: *O. Sax.* linōn: *mod. Scandinavian dialects use forms corresponding to* lǣran.] v. ge-leornian.

leornung, e; *f. Learning, study, meditation, reading:*—Lār ođđe leornung *teaching or learning*, L. I. P. 8; Th. ii. 314, 20: Past. pref; Swt. 3, 10. Micel is tō secganne langsum leornung đæt hē in līfe ādreág *much is it to tell, lengthy the reading, what he in life underwent*, Andr. Kmbl. 2962; An. 1484. Geleoso đære godcundan leornunge *studia divinæ lectionis*, Bd. 3, 13; S. 538, 29. On smeáwunge and on leornnnge hāligra gewrita . . . đonne hī on heora leornunge wǣron and heora bēc rǣddon and beeodan *meditationi scripturarum . . . cum illi intus lectioni vacabant*, 4, 3; S. 567, 29-34. On leornunge ūra stafa *nostrarum lectione litterarum*, 5, 14; S. 635, 8. On leornunge *in discendo*, Coll. Monast. Th. 18, 18. Gāþ ūt tō claustre ođđe tō leorninge *egredimini in claustrum vel in gymnasium*, 36, 9. Hī hiene niéddon tō leornunga đēh hē gewintred wǣre *they compelled him to go to school, though he was an old man*, Ors. 6, 31; Swt. 284, 21. Tō liornunga ōđfæste, Past. pref; Swt. 7, 12. Đū hatodest leornunga *tu odisti disciplinam*, Ps. Th. 49, 18. Mid đa leornunga đissa bōca *hujus* [*libri*] *lectione*, Bd. 5, 18; S. 636, 4. Tō begangenne his leornunge *lectioni operam dare*, 5, 2; S. 614, 35. Hē micle gȳminge hæfde hāligra leorninga *curam non modicam lectionibus sacris exhibebat*, 3, 19; S. 547, 27. On hālgum leornungum, 4, 2; S. 565, 33. [*O. H. Ger.* lirnunga, lernunga *disciplina, industria, doctrina, lectio.*]

leornung-cild, es; *n. A scholar, pupil, disciple:*—Benedictus bemǣnde đæt his leorningcild Maurus đæs ōđres deáþes fægnian sceolde, Homl. Th. ii. 164, 10.

leornung-cniht, es; *m. A youth engaged in study, scholar, disciple:*—Leorningcniht *discipulus* vel *mathites*, Ælfc. Gl. 80; Som. 72, 99; Wrt. Voc. 46, 56. Nys se leorningcniht ofer his lāreów *non est discipulus super magistrum*, Mt. Kmbl. 10, 24. Sī đū his leorningcniht, wē synt Moyses leorningcnihtas, Jn. Skt. 9, 28. [The word occurs frequently in the Gospels, as it regularly translates *discipulus.*] Monige đeáh đe hī nǣfre leorningcnihtas nǣren wilniaþ đeáh lāreówas tō beónne *plerique qui, quæ non didicerint, docere concupiscunt*, Past. proem; Swt. 25, 8. Đā undergeat se preóst đæt hē ne mihte đone hālgan wer līchamlīce ācwellan, and wolde đā his leorningcnihta sāwla fordōn, Homl. Th. ii. 162, 30.

leornung-cræft, es; *m. Learning, erudition:*—Đa đe leornungcræft hæfdon *scholars*, Elen. Kmbl. 760; El. 380.

leornung-hūs, es; *n. A house for study, a school:*—Leorninghūs *gymnasium*, Ælfc. Gl. 107; Som. 78, 76; Wrt. Voc. 57, 54; Wrt. Voc. ii. 46, 56.

leornung-mann, es; *m. A learner, pupil, scholar, student, disciple:*—Sum leorningman well gelǣred on gewritum *scholasticus quidam doctus studio literarum*, Bd. 3, 13; S. 538, 18. Ǣrest discipula and leorningmon reogollīces līfes *primo discipula regularis vitæ*, 3, 24; S. 557, 4. Ic wylle tō him gecyrran and biddan đæt ic mōte heononforþ his leorningman beón, Homl. Th. ii. 414, 15. Hī [*Martha and Mary*] wǣron đæs Hǣlendes leorningmen, 438, 18. Mæssepreóstas sceolon symble æt heora hūsum leorningmonna sceole habban, and gif hwylc gōdra wile his lytlingas hiom tō lāre befæstan, hig sceolon swīđe lustlīce hig onfōn and him ēstlīce tǣcan, L. E. I. 20; Th. ii. 414, 7-10.

leórt. v. lǣtan.

leósan. v. be-, for-leósan.

LEÓÞ, es; *n. A song, poem, ode, lay, verses:*—Đis leóþ *hoc carmen*, Ælfc. Gr. 9; Som. 9, 28. Leóþ *poema*, Ælfc. Gl. 112; Som. 79, 98; Wrt. Voc. 60, 6. Sārlīc leóþ *tragœdia*, Wrt. Voc. ii. 82, 37. Leóþ wæs āsungen *the song was recited*, Beo. Th. 2323; B. 1159. Leóþ Gode ūrum *carmen Deo nostro*, Ps. Spl. 39, 4. Hē for đon nǣfre nōht leásunga ne īdeles leóþes wyrceanne mihte *unde nihil unquam frivoli et supervacui poematis facere potuit*, Bd. 4, 24; S. 596, 42. Đȳ betstan leóþe geglenged *optimo carmine compositum*, S. 597, 37. Đæt leóþ singan *dicere carmen*, 597, 31. Đis leóþ him andswaraþ for gewitnysse and đæt leóþ ne ādiligaþ nān man of đīnes ofspringes mūþe *respondebit ei canticum istud pro testimonio, quod nulla delebit oblivio ex ore seminis tui*, Deut. 31, 21. Ic geworhte hī eft tō leóþe *I made a poetical version of it*, Bt. proem; Fox viii, 10. Đā ic đis leóþ āsungen hæfde *when I had recited these verses*, 3, 1; Fox 4, 16. Leóþ *odai*, Wrt. Voc. ii. 64, 63. Leóþa gleáw *skilled in songs*, Exon. 79 a; Th. 296, 16; Crā. 52. Omerus wæs mid Crēcum leóþa cræftgast, Bt. Met. Fox 30, 4; Met. 30, 2. Ic lióþa fela sang, 2, 1; Met. 2, 1: Exon. 91 b; Th. 344, 8; Gn. Ex. 170. Leóþum and spellum leódum reahte *in songs and stories he related to men*, Bt. Met. Fox 30, 15; Met. 30, 8. Đa lióþ đe ic geó lustbǣrlīce song *carmina qui quondam studio florente peregi*, Bt. 2; Fox 4, 6. Hē gewunode gerisenlīce leóþ wyrcean đa đe tō ǣfæstnesse and tō ārfæstnesse belumpon *carmina religioni et pietati apta facere solebat*, Bd. 4, 24; S. 596, 31. Ne wēne ǣnig ælda cynnes đæt ic lygewordum leóþ somnige wrīte wōđcræfte *let none imagine of the race of men that with lying words my lays I compose, writing in verse*, Exon. 63 b; Th. 234, 29; Ph. 547. [*Goth.* awi-liuþ: *Icel.* ljóð: *O. H. Ger.* leod, lied *carmen: Ger.* lied.] DER. ǣfen-, bismer-, brȳd-, byrgen-, byrig-, dæg-, dryht-, fūs-, fyrd-, galdor-, gift-, gryre-, gūþ-, hearm-, hilde-, līc-, sǣ-, sige-, sorg-, wīg-, wōp-leóþ.

leóþ-cræft, es; *m. The art of poetry, poetry, verse, a poem:*—Đes leóþcræft *hoc poema:* đās leóþcræftas *hæc poemata* [all the other cases are also given], Ælfc. Gr. 9; Som. 8, 16-21. Hē biþ swā đeáh on leóþcræfte ǣgđer ge lang ge sceort *it* [*i of the genitive in certain words*] *is however in poetry both long and short*, 18; Som. 21, 51. Đa gemetu gebyriaþ tō lēdenum leóþcræfte *metres pertain to Latin poetry*, 50; Som. 51, 66. Sixfealdum leóþcræfte *exametro heroico*, Wrt. Voc. ii. 144, 47. Hē đone leóþcræft geleornode *canendi artem didicit*, Bd. 4, 24; S. 596, 40.

leóþ-cræftig; *adj. Skilled in poetry:*—Leóþcræftig mon, Exon. 100 b; Th. 379, 28; Deór. 40.

leóþ-cwide, es; *m. A poem:*—Ic nât for hwî eów sindon ða ǽrran gewin swâ lustsumlîce on leóþcwidum tô gehiéranne *I do not know why the earlier contests are so pleasant for you to hear in poems*, Ors. 3, 7; Swt. 120, 2.

leóþ-gidding, e; *f. A poem, song*, Andr. Kmbl. 2956; An. 1481.

leoþian. v. â-leoþian, liþian.

leóþian; *p.* ode *To sing, sound:*—Wôð ôðer ne lythwôn leóþode ðonne in lyft âstâg ceargesta cirm *a second cry sounded, nor weakly, when to the heavens rose the wail of the troubled spirits*, Exon. 38 a; Th. 125, 32; Gû. 363. Folcum ic leóþode *to peoples I sang*, 94 b; Th. 354, 4; Reim. 40. [*Goth.* liuþôn *to sing*: *O. H. Ger.* liudôn *canere, jubilare.*]

leóþ-lîc; *adj. Poetical:*—Beda ðises hâlgan lîf ǽgðer ge æfter ânfealdre gereccednysse ge æfter leóþlîcere gyddunge âwrât *Bede wrote this saint's life both in prose and in verse*, Homl. Th. ii. 134, 1.

leoba. v. leoþu.

leóþ-sang, es; *m. A song, poem:*—In swinsunge leóþsanges *in modulationem carminis*, Bd. 4, 24; S. 597, 35. For his leóþsongum *cujus carminibus*, S. 596, 36.

leoþu. v. liþ.

leoþu [?]:—Wæs on lagustreáme lâd ðǽr mê leoþu ne biglâd [cf. (?) *Icel.* lið *a host, people*, or lið *a ship*], Exon. 94 a; Th. 353, 18; Reim. 14.

leoþu-bend; *m. f. A fetter, bond:*—Ic ðê âlýse of ðyssum leoþubendum *I will release thee from these bonds*, Andr. Kmbl. 200; An. 100: 2746; An. 1375: 327; An. 164. Of leoþobendum, 2066; An. 1035: 3127; An. 1566. Lioþobendum, Cd. 19; Th. 24, 23; Gen. 382. [*O. Sax.* lido-bend.]

leoþu-bîge, -bîg; *adj. Flexible at the joints, humble, meek:*—Ðâ wearþ ðæt hâlige lîc hâl on eorþan gemêt liþebîge on limum *the holy body was found in the earth sound, and with the limbs not yet stiff*, Homl. Th. ii. 152, 33. Ic gesette eów sôðe gebysnunge, ðæt eówer ǽlc sceole ôðres fêt âþweán, swâ swâ ic lâreów eów liþebîg [*humble*] âþwôh, 242, 28.

leoþu-cǽge, an; *f. A limb-key, key which consists of limbs:*—Ðê [*the Virgin Mary*] æfter him engla þeóden eft unmǽle lioþucǽgan bileác, Exon. 12 b; Th. 21, 13; Cri. 334.

leoþu-cræft, es; *m. Bodily skill, skill in the use of the limbs:*—Se gedǽleþ missenlîce leoþucræftas londbûendum, Exon. 78 b; Th. 295, 6; Crä. 29. Segn eallgylden hondwundra mǽst gelocen leoþocræftum [*skilfully; or* leóþocræftum, (cf. leóþcræft *and next word*) *with charms, magically*; cf. the Danish banner, the Raven, supposed to be woven by the daughters of Ragnar, and to which extraordinary qualities were attributed. See also Burnt Njal, c. 156.]

leóþu-cræft, es; *m. Poetic art* or *skill*, Elen. Kmbl. 2499; El. 1251. v. preceding word.

leoþu-cræftig; *adj. Skilful with the limbs*, Exon. 59 b; Th. 216, 14; Ph. 268.

leoþu-fæst; *adj. Firm of limb, strong, able:*—Sum biþ bôca gleáw, lârum leoþufæst, Exon. 79 b; Th. 298, 34; Crä. 95.

leoþu-geþynd. v. leoþu-sâr.

leoþu-lîc; *adj. Belonging to the limbs, bodily:*—Leoþolîc and gâstlîc, Andr. Kmbl. 3254; An. 1630. [*O. H. Ger.* lido-lîh.]

leóþu-rûn, e; *f. Counsel conveyed in verse*, Elen. Kmbl. 1042; El. 522.

leoþu-sâr, es; *n. A pain of the limbs* or *joints:*—Leoþusár *vel* geþind *condolomata articula*, Wrt. Voc. ii. 135, 67.

leoþu-sirce, an; *f. A coat of mail:*—Locene leoþosyrcan, Beo. Th. 3014; B. 1505: 3784; B. 1890.

leoþu-wâc; *adj. With pliant joints, flexible, pliant, supple:*—Liþowâc *habile*, Wrt. Voc. ii. 42, 67. Leoþuwâc, 110, 25. Leóht and leoþuwâc *nimble and supple*, Exon. 79 b; Th. 298, 12; Crä. 84. Swilce liðewâcum *velut lentescente*, Hpt. Gl. 520, 36. Liðewâcum tagum [? tânum] *lentis viminibus*, 514, 69. [*O. H. Ger.* lido-weih *flexible*; lentus.] v. un-leoþuwâc.

leoþuwâc-ness. v. un-leoþuwâcness.

leoþu-wâcung, e; *f.* In Ps. Spl. T. 78, 11 *compeditorum* is glossed by *liþewâcunga.*

leoþuwǽcan, liþewǽcan; *p.* -wǽhte *To become* or *to make soft*, or *pliant, to grow calm, to assuage, soften:*—Liþewǽcaþ brymmas sǽs *the surges of the sea become still*, Hymn. Lye. Liþewǽhte *lentesceret*, Hpt. Gl. 479, 30. Liþewǽhtan *mollescerent, delenirent*, 481, 13. Leoþewǽce *mitigare, pacificare*, 495, 22. v. ge-liþewǽcan.

leóþ-weorc, es; *n. Song-making, poetry*; poesis, Ælfc. Gl. 112; Som. 79, 99; Wrt. Voc. 60, 7.

leóþ-wîse, an; *f. A poetical manner, verse:*—Mycel Englisc bôc on leóþwîsan geworht *a large English book composed in poetry*, Chart. Th. 430, 24. Âwend of Lêdene on Englisc on leóþwîson, Homl. Th. ii. 520, 10.

leóþ-word, es; *n. A word in a poem*, Andr. Kmbl. 2975; An. 1490.

leóþ-wyrhta, an; *m. A poet:*—Leóþwyrhta *poeta* vel *vates*, Ælfc. Gl. 112; Som. 79, 100; Wrt. Voc. 60, 8: 73, 68. Hleot [= leóþ] wyrhta *melopius*, 291, 26. Leódwyrhta *melopius*, Wrt. Voc. ii. 56, 50. Ælfrêd cyning Westsexna leóþwyrhta, Bt. Met. Fox introduc. 5; Met. Einl. 3.

leów, es; *pl.* (?) leówer, leówera; *n. A thigh, ham:*—Ân hrîðres læuw *a ham of beef*, Cod. Dipl. Kmbl. ii. 355, 7. Leówer *pernas*, Lchdm. i. lxix, 13. Léwera, lxxiii, 31. [*Or is* leower *a different word.* Cf. *Icel.* lær *thigh*, and see Lchdm. iii. 366, col. 1.]

leówe, an; *f. A league, a mile:*—Leóuue *miliarium*, Ælfc. Gl. 57; Som. 67, 81; Wrt. Voc. 38, 7. ['*Lat.* leuca, leuga *a Gallic mile of* 1500 *Roman paces*; a word of Celtic origin.' Skt. Etym. Dict. under *league.*]

lepeþ:—Sum sceal wildne fugel âtemian ... fêdeþ on feterum ... lepeþ lyftswiftne lytlum gieflum ôþ ðæt se wælisca his ǽtgiefan eáþmôd weorþeþ, Exon. 88 b; Th. 332, 14–27; Vy. 85–91. Grein compares with *M. H. Ger.* erlaffen *languefacere*, the passage would then mean that the hawk's fierceness and wildness were subdued by giving it little to eat. Might we however for *lepeþ* read *léfeþ* [cf. *léf*] or *lêweþ* [cf. *ge-léwan*] = weakens, which would give very much the same meaning?

les. v. ge-les.

lesan; *p.* læs; *pl.* lǽson; *pp.* lesen *To lease* [= *glean* dialect.], *gather, collect:*—Se eorþlîca anweald nǽfre ne sǽwþ cræftas ac lisþ and gadraþ unþeáwas *earthly power never sows virtues, but collects and gathers vices*, Bt. 27, 1; Fox 94, 25. Gif gê lesaþ wyrte on Sunnandæg *if ye gather herbs on Sunday*, Wulfst. 231, 18. Ic læs *I collected*, Elen. Kmbl. 2474; El. 1238. Hî lǽson ǽfre forþ mid heom ealle ða butsecarlas ðe heó gemêtton *they kept on all the while collecting and joining to themselves all the sailors they found*, Chr. 1052; Erl. 184, 15. Ne gê ne gaderion ða eár ðe bæftan eów beóþ ac lǽtaþ þearfan and ûtâcymene hig lesan *nec remanentes spicas colligetis, sed pauperibus et peregrinis dimittetis eas*, Lev. 23, 22. [*Piers P. Wick.* lese *to glean*: *Goth.* lisan: *O. Sax.* lesan: *O. L. Ger.* lesan *to read*: *O. Frs.* lesa: *Icel.* lesa: *O. H. Ger.* lesan *legere, colligere*: *Ger.* lesen.] DER. â-lesan.

lêsan *to loose.* v. lîsan.

lesu; *indecl. f. Numen:*—Leso *numine*, Wrt. Voc. ii. 62, 19.

lesu; *adj.* v. lysu.

letanîa, an; also with *pl.* -as; *m. A litany:*—Ðæt hê ðysne letanîan sungan *quia hanc litaniam modularentur*, Bd. 1, 25; S. 487, 24. Mid reliquium and mid letanîan, Wulfst. 170, 18. Cristes folc mǽrsiaþ letanîas, Shrn. 79, 28.

leter. v. eald-leter.

LEÐER, es; *n. Hide, skin, leather.* [The word is found chiefly, if not exclusively, in compounds. So in Icelandic, though frequent in modern usage, it is not found in old writers except in compounds. *O. H. Ger.* leder *corium.*] v. geweald-, heals-, weald-leðer.

leðer-codd, es; *m. A leather bag:*—Leðercoddas *bulgæ*, Ælfc. Gl. 16; Som. 58, 58; Wrt. Voc. 21, 45.

leðeren, liðeren, leðern, leðren; *adj. Leathern, of leather:*—Leðern *scorteus*, Ælfc. Gl. 99; Som. 76, 126; Wrt. Voc. 54, 66. Leðren fæt *scortia*, 16; Som. 60, 75; Wrt. Voc. 25, 15. Liðerene trymsas *asses corteas*, Wrt. Voc. ii. 7, 18. Lidrinae *scorteas*, Ep. Gl. 2 b, 10. [*O. H. Ger.* lidirin *pellicea*: *Ger.* ledern.]

leðer-helm, es; *m. A leather helmet*; galea, Ælfc. Gl. 51; Som. 66, 13; Wrt. Voc. 35, 3.

leðer-hose [-hosu?]; *f. A leather covering for the leg, gaiter:*—Leðerhosa [-hosan?] *caligas*, Coll. Monast. Th. 27, 33. [*Icel.* leðrhosa; *f. a gaiter*: *O. H. Ger.* leder-hosa; *f. ocrea, cenarga.*] v. hosa.

leðer-wyrhta, an; *m. A tanner, currier*; byrseus, byrsarius, Wrt. Voc. ii. 11, 49: 102, 38: 127, 31. Lediruuyrcta, Ep. Gl. 6 d, 13.

lêðran. v. lîðran.

letig. v. lytig.

lettan; *p.* te *To cause to be slow* [læt], *to let, hinder, impede, delay:*—Ne leteþ *non tricaverit*, Wrt. Voc. ii. 60, 75. Ðæs andweardan wela âmerþ and læt [MS. Cot. let] ða men ðe beóþ âtihte tô ðâm sôþum gesǽlþum, Bt. 32, 1; Fox 114, 3. Ðæt flǽsc oft lett [MS. Hat. lætt] ða geornfulnesse and ðone willan ðæs þeóndan môdes hêr on worulde. Swǽ swǽ mon oft lett fundiende monnan and his færelt gǽlþ, swâ gǽlþ se lîchoma ðæt môd, Past. 36, 7; Swt. 256, 4–6. Ôþ oreldo hî hine hwîlum lettaþ *they sometimes defer it* (*death*) *until extreme old age*, Bt. 41, 2; Fox 246, 10. Ðæt syððan nâ brimlîþende lâde ne letton *so that afterwards they did not hinder seafarers from their course*, Beo. Th. 1142; B. 569. Ac ic ðê hâlsige ðæt ðû mê nô leng ne lette *tu modo quem excitaveris ne moreris*, Bt. 36, 3; Fox 174, 32. Gyf ðonne ðissa þreóra þinga ǽnig hwylcne man lette, ðæt hine tô ðam fæstene ne onhagie *if any of these three things hinder any man, so that the fast be inconvenient to him*, Wulfst. 285, 4. Hwî wille gê lettan ûre sîþfæt *why will ye hinder our journey?* Homl. Th. ii. 336, 11. Wê ðê ðæs nû nellaþ lettan ðæs ðû ǽr geþoht hæfdest *we will not hinder thee from that which thou didst before purpose*, Guthl. 5; Gdwin. 30, 24. [*O. Sax.* lettian: *O. Frs.* letta: *Icel.* letja: *O. H. Ger.* lezjan *retardare.*] v. ge-lettan, latian.

letting, e; *f. Letting, hindering, obstruction, delay, retarding:*—Ðeós yl[d]fulle letting *hæc morosa tricatio*, Hpt. Gl. 529, 6. Lettinge *obstaculo*, 523, 16. Lettincge *offendiculo*, 429, 35. On ðære lettinge his færeltes *in ejus itineris retardatione*, Past, 36, 7; Swt. 254, 20. [Se cyng scipa ût on sǽ sende his brôðer tô ðære and tô lættinge, Chr. 1101; Erl. 237, 19.] Blindne se ðe hine gesihþ lettincge getâcnaþ *if a man* [in a dream] *sees himself blind, it betokens hindrance*, Lchdm. iii. 200, 14: 202, 3: 204, 2.

leu, leuw. v. leów.

lēwsa, an; *m. Weakness, infirmity, misery:*—Eágan mīne sārgodon for lēwsan *oculi mei languerunt præ inopia*, Ps. Spl. T. 87, 9. v. lēf, ge-lēwan.

lib-. v. lyb-.

LIBBAN; *p.* lifde To live:—For đam ic lybbe and gē lybbaþ *quia ego vivo et vos vivetis*, Jn. Skt. 14, 19. Ne lybbe ic, ac Crist leofaþ, Blickl. Homl. 165, 23. Wē lybbaþ mislīce on twelf mōnþum; nū sceole wē lybban Gode, wē đe ōđrum tīman ūs sylfum leofodon, Homl. Th. i. 180, 17. Godes þeōwas đe be gōdra manna ælmessan libbaþ *God's servants who live by the alms of good men*, Wulfst. 120, 4. Hié be ūrum lārum libbaþ *they live according to our instructions*, Blickl. Homl. 75, 15. Eal his līf hē lifde būton synnum, 33, 16. Hē on wynsumnesse lifde, 113, 7: Bd. 3, 27; S. 559, 27. Hē on ællþeódignesse lifde *exulabat*, S. 559, 30. Hē hēr on eorþan engelīce līfe lifde, Blickl. Homl. 167, 33: 213, 11. Se þeódcyning þeáwum lyfde *the king lived virtuously*, Beo. Th. 4295; B. 2144. Wynnum lifde *lived joyously*, Exon. 111 b; Th. 428, 13; Rä. 41, 107. Wē ealne đysne geár lifdon mid ūres līchoman willan *we have lived all this year as it was pleasing to our body*, Blickl. Homl. 35, 27. Æfter đon đe hī lǣrdon hī sylfe þurh eall lifdon *secundum ea quæ docebant ipsi per omnia vivendo*, Bd. 1, 26; S. 487, 37. Hī đāgyt on hǣđennysse gedwolum lifdan *paganis adhuc erroribus essent implicati*, 2, 1; S. 501, 13. Đā nāmon hī him wintersetl on Temesan and lifdon [lifedon, MS. E.] him of Eást Seaxum *they took up their winter quarters on the Thames and got their provisions out of Essex*, Chr. 1009; Erl. 143, 4 note. Swā đā drihtguman dreámum lifdon, Beo. Th. 199; B. 99. Swā swā diácon đe regollīf libbe, L. Eth. ix. 21; Th. i. 344, 21. Swīnes scearn đæs đe on dūnlande and wyrtum libbe, L. M. 1, 20; Lchdm. ii. 62, 28. Ne hié selfe đȳ beteran ne taligen đe đa ōđre đeáh đa ōđre be him libben *ne se meliores æstiment, quia contineri per se ceteros vident*, Past. 44, 1; Swt. 319, 19. Đa niétenu onlūtaþ tō đære eorþan forđon hié sculon be đære libban, 21, 3; Swt. 154, 17. *Laboratores* syndon weorcmen, đe tilian sceolon đæs đe eal þeódscipe big sceal lybban, Wulfst. 267, 15. Uton libban đam līfe đe scrift ūs wīsige, 112, 18: 150, 13. Līfe swilcum libban *vitam talem vivere*, Hymn. Surt. 90, 13. Hē sǣde đæt hē wolde ōđer ođđe đǣr libban ođđe đǣr lecgan *he said that he would either live [conquer] there or die there*, Chr. 901; Erl. 96, 33: Ors. 3, 10; Swt. 158, 32. Hē hié ealle geniédde đæt hié āþas swōran, đæt hié ealle ætgædere wolden ođđe on heora earde licggean, ođđe on heora earde libban, 4, 9; Swt. 190, 27. Hē cwæþ 'Đū eart đæs lifigendan Godes sunu.' Se is lybbende God đe hæfþ līf þurh hine sylfne, Homl. Th. i. 366, 33. Eall đæt ic hæbbe on libbandan and on licgendan *all the live and dead stock that I have*, Chart. Th. 548, 12. Nān man nān þing ne bycge ofer feówer peninga weorþ ne libbende ne licgende, L. C. S. 24; Th. i. 390, 3. Hȳ hit be đān libbendan habban *let them have it during their lifetime*, Chart. Th. 491, 25. [*Goth.* liban: *O. Sax.* libbian: *O. Frs.* libba: *Icel.* lifa: *O. H. Ger.* lebēn.] v. lifian.

libn. v. lifen.

līc, es; *n. A body [living or dead]* generally the latter; the word remains in *lich*-gate, *lyke*-wake:—Līc ođđe līchama *corpus*, Ælfc. Gr. 9, 32; Som. 12, 16. Līc ǣgđer ge cuces ge deáđes *corpus;* līc ođđe hreáw *funus;* līc ođđe hold *cadaver*, Wrt. Voc. 85, 51-54: 49, 25. Næs nān hūs on eallum Egipta lande đe līc inne ne lǣge *neque erat domus, in qua non jaceret mortuus*, Ex. 12, 30. Ealle đa hwīle đe đæt līc biþ inne, đǣr sceal beón gedrync and plega, Ors. 1, 1; Swt. 20, 25. Đǣr đæs hǣlendes līc ālēd wæs *ubi positum fuerat corpus iesu*, Jn. Skt. 20, 12. Cwæþ đæt his līc wǣre leóht and scēne, Cd. 14; Th. 17, 25; Gen. 265. Đendan bu somod līc and sāwle lifgan mōte *whilst both soul and body may live together*, Exon. 27 a; Th. 81, 21; Cri. 1327. Līc and gǣst, 46 b; Th. 160, 8; Gū. 940: 50 a; Th. 172, 25; Gū. 1149. Næs fȳre gemǣled ne līc ne leoþu *neither body nor limbs were marked by the fire*, 74 a; Th. 278, 3; Jul. 592. Līc sāre gebrocen, bānhūs blōdfāg, Andr. Kmbl. 2808; An. 1406. Đē is gedāl wītod līces and sāwle, Cd. 43; Th. 57, 20; Gen. 931. Sweostor mīn līces mǣge *my sister, kinswoman according to the flesh*, 89; Th. 110, 4; Gen. 1833. Līces lustas *lusts of the flesh*, Exon. 71 b; Th. 267, 2; Jul. 409: 26 b; Th. 79, 28; Cri. 1297. Gang tō ciricean tō đæs hālgan Ōswaldes līce and site đǣr *ingredere ecclesiam, et accedens ad sepulcrum Osualdi, ibi reside*, Bd. 3, 12; S. 537, 9. Stōd se biscop æt đam līce, 4, 11; S. 580, 13: L. Edg. c. 65; Th. ii. 258, 13. Bæþ wiđ đam miclan līce *a bath for elephantiasis*, L. M. 1, 32; Lchdm. ii. 78, 18. Mynte đæt hē gedǣlde ānra gehwylces līf wiđ līce *meant to part the life of each one from the body*, Beo. Th. 1470; B. 733. Hē đæt andweorc of Adames līce āleoþode, Cd. 9; Th. 11, 18; Gen. 177. Hē sceáf reáf of līce, 76; Th. 94, 21; Gen. 1565. Forþ gewāt Cham of līce *Ham died*, 79; Th. 97, 35; Gen. 1623. Hī his līc nāmon and hine on byrgene lēdon, Mk. Skt. 6, 29: Beo. Th. 4261; B. 2127: L. Eth. v. 12; Th. i. 308, 5: vi. 21; Th. i. 320, 6. Đæs mynstres brōđra đydon scē. Cūþberhtes līc of eorþan, and hī đæt gemētton swā gesund swā hē đāgyt lifde, Shrn. 82, 14. Se ūs līf forgeaf, leomu, līc and gǣst, Exon. 19 a; Th. 48, 25; Cri. 777. His [*the Phœnix*] līc, 59 b; Th. 216, 14; Ph. 268. Hē wearp hine đā on wyrmes līc, Cd. 25; Th. 31, 26; Gen. 491. Eowre līc sceolon sweltan on đisum wēstene *vestra cadavera jacebunt in solitudine*, Num. 14, 32. Đǣr đara arcebisceopa līc bebyrigde syndon *ubi archiepiscopi Cantiæ sepeliri solent*, Bd. 4, 1; S. 565, 5. Forleósan līca gehwilc đara đe līfes gāst fæđmum þeahte, Cd. 64; Th. 77, 26; Gen. 1281. Līcu *cadavera*, Hymn. Surt. 52, 27. [*Goth.* leik: *O. Sax. O. Frs.* līk: *Icel.* līk: *Dan.* lig: *Swed.* lik: *O. H. Ger.* līh: *Ger.* leiche.] der. eofor-, wyrm-līc.

-līc. v. ge-līc, *and the numerous adjectives of which* -līc [*modern* -ly] *forms the last part.*

-līca. v. efen-, ge-, man-, swīn-līca.

līcan *to please:*—Ne līcaþ him đeāh his earfoþu *his troubles do not please him*, Ps. Th. 40, 1. Wel līcaþ Drihtne đa đe hine him ondrǣdaþ *beneplacitum est Domino super timentes eum*, 146, 12. [*Goth.* leikan: *O. H. Ger.* līchēn.] v. līcend-līc; līcian.

līc-beorg [beorg; *m. a hill, funeral mound;* or beorg; *f. protection;* or beorg *connected with* beorgan *to taste, eat, a literal reproduction of* sarcophagus?] *a sarcophagus:*—Līcbeorg *sarcofago*, Wrt. Voc. ii. 119, 50

līc-bysig; *adj. Of active body, active with the body:*—Ic eom līcbysig lāce mid winde *active am I of body, move hither and thither with the wind*, Exon. 122 b; Th. 470, 22; Rä. 31, 1.

liccettan. v. līcettan.

liccian; *p.* ode To lick:—Ic liccige *linguo*, Ælfc. Gr. 28; Som. 31, 57: *lambo*, 32, 25. Seó lyft liccaþ and ātȳhþ đone wǣtan of ealre eorþan and of đære sǣ, and gegaderaþ tō scūrum, Lchdm. iii. 276, 12. Fȳnd his eorþan licciaþ [liccigeaþ, Th.] *inimici ejus terram lingent*, Ps. Spl. 71, 9. Đa rēđan deór heora liþa liccodon mid līđran tungan, Homl. Skt. 4, 407: Lk. Skt. 16, 21. Liccedon *linxerunt;* liccigan *lincxere*, Wrt. Voc. ii. 51, 54, 55. His fētlāstas licciende. Glostr. Frag. 110, 3. [*O. Sax.* likkōn: *O. H. Ger.* lechōn *lambere, lingere: Ger.* lecken.] v. ge-liccian.

liccung, e; *f. Licking:*—Hundes liccung gehǣlþ wunda *a dog's licking heals wounds*, Homl. Th. i. 330, 23.

-līce *a frequent adverbial termination, modern -ly.*

līcend-līc; *adj. Pleasing, pleasant:*—Forđon on his folce is fægere Drihtne wel līcendlīc *quia beneplacitum est Domino in populo suo*, Ps. Th. 149, 4. v. līciend-līc.

līcend-līce; *adv. Pleasingly:*—Forđon mīn gebed nū gyt bēcnum standeþ đæt him on wīsum is wel lȳcendlīce *quoniam adhuc est oratio mea in beneplacitis eorum*, Ps. Th. 140, 8.

Licetfeld, a; *m. Lichfield in Staffordshire:*—Hæfde hē bisceopsetl on đære stōwe đe gecȳd is Licitfeld, Bd. 4, 3; S. 566, 44. Liccetfelda bisceop, 5, 24; S. 646, 14. Æt Licettfelda, Shrn. 59, 20. On Licetfelda, Chr. 716; Erl. 45, 14. Æt Licetfelda, Chart. Th. 373, 34.

līcettan; *p.* te *To feign, pretend, profess falsely, simulate:*—Forđam seó orsorge wyrd simle līhþ and līcet đæt mon scyle wēnan đæt heó is sió sōþe gesǣlþ *illa* [*prospera fortuna*] *enim specie felicitatis, cum videtur blanda, mentitur*, Bt. 20; Fox 70, 30. Oft đa unþeáwas leógaþ and līcettaþ đæt hī sīen gōde þeáwas *plerumque vitia virtutes se esse mentiuntur*, Past. 20; Swt. 149, 2. Hē līcette hine selfne đæt hē wǣre ungeleáfful *in se personam infidelium transfigurans*, 16, 2; Swt. 101, 8. Job līcette đæt hē sceolde bión se hēhsta god *Jove feigned to be the supreme god*, Bt. 28, 1; Fox 194, 13. Līcetton *scemmatizarunt*, Wrt. Voc. ii. 84, 49. Đā līcettan hī fleám beforan him *simulantibus fugam hostibus*, Bd. 4, 26; S. 602, 19. Đæt is wīsdōm đæt wīs man līcette dysig *it is wisdom for a wise man to feign folly*, Prov. Kmbl. 37. Đeáh hē līccete untrymnesse, Ps. Th. 40, 9. Nelle wē mid leásungum đyllīc līccetan *we will not feign such things with falsehoods*, Homl. Skt. pref. 49. Monige sint đe mon sceal wærlīce līcettan *nonnulla prudenter dissimulanda sunt*, Past. 21, 1; Swt. 151, 13. Biþ gōd tō līcettanne suelce hē hit nyte *it is good to make as if he did not know it*, 151, 9. Līccettende *scemmatizans*, Wrt. Voc. ii. 94, 70. Đus mid wordum līccetende *offering the following pretext*, Homl. Th. i. 400, 18. [*O. H. Ger.* līhizan *simulare, fingere*]. v. ge-, leás-līcettan.

līcettere, es; *m. One who feigns, a hypocrite:*—Līccetere *ypochrita*, Wrt. Voc. 85, 39: *fictor* vel *hipocrita*, 49, 13. Swylce leáse līceteras [līcetteras, Rush.] *sicut hypocritæ*, Mt. Kmbl. 6, 16. Wā eów līcceteras *væ vobis, hypocritæ*, 23, 13. Līccetteras, 23, 15. Līceteras and leógeras Godes graman habban būton hig geswīcan *may those who are false in deed and in word have the wrath of God, unless they desist*, L. C. S. 7; Th. i. 380, 5. Wel wītegod Isaias be eów līcceterum *bene prophetavit Esaias de vobis hypocritis*, Mk. Skt. 7, 6. [*O. H. Ger.* līhizari *hypocrita.*] der. riht-, þeód-līcettere.

līcettung, e; *f. Feigning, pretence, false representation, simulation, hypocrisy:*—Līcetung *hypocrisis*, Lk. Skt. 12, 1. Hwǣr com seó manigfealde līcetung heora freónda *what is become of the manifold flattery of their friends?* Blickl. Homl. 99, 33. Innan gē synt fulle līccettunge [MSS. A. B. līcetunge] *intus pleni estis hypocrisi*, Mt. Kmbl. 23, 28. Būtan līcetunge *sine hypocrisi*, Coll. Monast. Th. 33, 7. Đæt his gesacan on miclum dǣle līcettunge and leáse wiđ hine syredon and onsægdon *accusatores ejus nonnulla in parte falsas contra eum machinasse calumnias*, Bd. 5, 19; S. 640, 14. Þurh līcetunge *per simulationem*, Confess. Peccat. [*O. H. Ger.* līhizunga *dissimulatio.*] v. leás-līcettung.

līc-fæt, es; *n. The body*, Exon. 48 b; Th. 167, 20; Gū. 1063.

LICGAN; *p.* læg: *pl.* lǣgon; *pp.* legen. I. To lie, *be at rest*, *be in bed, lie dead, lie low, fail* :—Árís nú hwí líst ðú neowel on eorþan *surge! cur jaces pronus in terra?* Jos. 7, 10. Hwæt ligst ðú on horwe? Dóm. L. 6, 77. Mín cnapa líþ on mínum húse lama *puer meus jacet in domo paralyticus*, Mt. Kmbl. 8, 6. Gif hine on iii nihte ealdne mónan gestandeþ se líþ fæste and swylt *if sickness attack him when the moon is three days old he will be confined to his bed and will die*, Lchdm. iii. 182, 8. Ðonne ðín flǽsc ligeþ *when thou art dead*, Cd. 100; Th. 132, 5; Gen. 2188. Nú se wyrm ligeþ *the serpent is dead*, Beo. Th. 5484; B. 2745. Ðonne wind ligeþ weder biþ fæger *when the wind is at rest the weather is fair*, Exon. 58 b; Th. 210, 7; Ph. 182. Swá ðín blǽd líþ *so shall thy glory lie low*, Cd. 202; Th. 251 13; Dan. 563. Ða creópendan licgeaþ mid ealle líchoman on eorþan *creeping things lie on the earth with all the body*, Past. 21, 3; Swt. 155, 17. Heora líchoman licggaþ on eorþan and beóþ tó duste gewordne, Blickl. Homl. 101, 2. Á ðǽr hé læg [*in his bed*] hé hæfde his handa upweardes, 227, 16. Hé læig æt forþsíðe *he lay at the point of death*, Homl. Th. i. 128, 7: Homl. Skt. 3, 301. Nǽfre on óre læg [*failed*] wídcúþes wíg, Beo. Th. 2088; B. 1041. Ðǽr se cyning ofslægen læg, Chr. 755; Erl. 50, 14. Hié simle feohtende wǽron óð hié alle lǽgon *they kept on fighting until they all lay dead*, 50, 7. On carcernum lǽgon *they lay in prison*, Ors. 5, 1; Swt. 214, 18. Hí eallne ðone geár an monncwealme lǽgan *all that year they suffered from a pestilence*, 3, 5; Swt. 106, 10. Lige on ða sídan *lie on the side*, L. M. 1, 47; Lchdm. ii. 118, 10. Licge bútan wyrgelde *let him lie* [*dead*] *without wergeld*, L. Wih. 25; Th. i. 42, 13. Gif hine mon ofsleá licgge hé orgilde, L. Alf. pol. 1; Th. i. 60, 15. Hine wulfas ábiton ðǽr hé ástifod lǽge, Blickl. Homl. 193, 8. Hié gemétton ða seofon hyrdas deáde licgan, 239, 25. Tó tácne ðæt hié óðer woldon oððe ealle libban oððe ealle licgan *parato animo, ni vincant, mori*, Ors. 3, 10; Swt. 138, 32: Chr. 901: Erl. 96, 28. Gif hé nylle hit geþafian léton hine licgan *if he will not allow it, they shall kill him*, L. Ath. i. 20; Th. i. 210, 9. Ðǽr ða scipu sceoldan licgan *the ships were to lie there*, Chr. 1009; Erl. 141, 24. Hwæt hé gefélde cealdes æt his sídan licgean, Bd. 3, 2; S. 525, 15. Hé má gewunode on his smiþþan dæges and nihtes sittan and licgean *magis in officina sua die noctuque residere consuerat*, 5, 14; S. 634, 16. Licggean, Ors. 4, 9; Swt. 190, 27. Ðæt mægn ðæs licgendan *the virtue of the dead man*, Glostr. Frag. 110, 7. Hana ða licgenda[n] áwecþ *gallus jacentes excitat*, Hymn. Surt. 6, 36. Licgende feoh *dead* [*as opposed to live*] *stock, other property than cattle, ready money*: — Heó beceápode ða scínendan gymmas and eác hire landáre wið licgendum feó *she sold the shining gems and her landed property too, for ready money*, Homl. Skt. 9, 54. Eall ðæt ic hæbbe on libbandan and on licgendan *all the live and dead stock that I have*, Chart. Th. 548, 13. Ðǽr wæs xx M horsa gefangen ðéh hié ðǽr nán licgende feoh ne métten *pecorum magna copia abducta, auri atque argenti nihil repertum*, Ors. 3, 7; Swt. 116, 32. And nán man nán þing ne bycge ofer feówer peninga weorþ ne libbende ne licgende, L. C. S. 24; Th. i. 390, 3. See Grmm. R. A. pp. 491 sqq. II. *to lie, be situated* [*of a place*], *go* or *run* [*of a road or stream*]: — On ðam wege ðe líþ tó Euphrate *in via, quæ ducit Euphratam*, Gen. 35, 19. Swá swá se weg líþ, wé faraþ, Num. 21, 22. Tó ðam wege ðǽr eást ligþ . . . on ðone wege ðe líþ tó Stánleáge . . . ðam wege ðe tó Stanleáge ligþ, Cod. Dip. Kmbl. iii. 409, 2-17. Sió stów ðe se weg tó ligþ, Bt. 33, 4; Fox 132, 37. Seó Wisle líþ út of Weonodlande and líþ in Estmere . . . and ligeþ of ðæm mere west and norþ on sǽ, Ors. 1, 1; Swt. 20, 7-12. On Swalewan streáme se ligþ be Ceterehttúne *in fluvio Sualua, qui vicum Cataractam præterfluit*, Bd. 2, 14; S. 518, 15. Lindesse ligeþ út on sǽ *Lindissi, pertingens usque ad mare*, 2, 16; S. 519, 19: 1, 25; S. 486, 21. On his gehlotland ðe líþ on Ephraim dúne *in finibus possessionis suæ, quæ est sita in monte Ephraim*, Jos. 24, 30. Saulus ríce swá hit súþ licgeþ ymbe Gealboe, Salm. Kmbl. 382; Sal. 190. Seó forme India líþ tó ðæra Silhearwena ríce seó óðer líþ tó Medas, seó þridde tó ðam micclum gársecge *the first India extends to the kingdom of Ethiopia, the second to Media, the third to the great ocean*, Homl. Th. i. 454, 12. On ðam wege ðe læg tó Thamnaþa *in bivio itineris, quod ducit in Thamnam*, Gen. 38, 14. Ðá læg ðǽr án micel eá up in on ðæt land, Ors. 1, 1; Swt. 17, 20. Hé wolde fundian hú longe ðæt land norþryhte lǽge *he wanted to try how far the land extended due north*, Swt. 17, 8. III. *with prep.* or *adv.*:— Se hláford ðe ryhtes wyrne and for his yfelan man licge *the lord who refuses justice, and makes his wrong doing man's cause his own*, L. Ath. i. 3; Th. i. 200, 15. Godwine eorl and ealle ða yldestan menn on West Seaxon lágon ongeán swá hí lengost mihton *earl Godwin and all the chief men in Wessex opposed as long as ever they could*, Chr. 1036; Erl. 165, 2. xiiii æceras and ða mǽde ðe ðǽr tó líþ *xiiii fields and the meadow belonging thereto*, Cod. Dip. Kmbl. ii. 3, 34. Mid eallon ðám þingon ðe ðǽr tó læg forðam ðe his witan him sǽdon ðæt hit hwílon ǽr læg ðiderin *with everything that belonged thereto; for his witan told him that in former times it had belonged to that place*, vi. 190, 20. Ǽlc ðæra landa ðe on mínes fæder dæge læg intó Cristes cyrcean, iv. 232, 10. [Ic wille ðæt ðæt ligge intó sainte Petre 219, 26: 220, 19.] [*Goth.* ligan: *O. Sax.* liggian: *O. Frs.* liga: *Icel.* liggja: *O. H. Ger.* ligan, liggan: *Ger.* liegen.] DER. á-, æt-, be-, dyrn-, for-, ge-, tó-licgan.

líc-hama, an; *m. The body* [*generally of a living person*], *the corporeal, in contrast to the spiritual, part of man*: — Se líchoma biþ líchoma ða hwile ðe hé his lima ealle hæfþ, Bt. 34, 9; Fox 148, 6. Is ðæs monnes líchoma betera ðonne ealle his ǽhta . . . seó sáwl betere ðonne se líchoma, 32, 2; Fox 116, 11-13: Mt. Kmbl. 6, 25. Hire líchama wæs áfylled mid hreófian, Num. 12, 10. Ðæt ðín líchama sí eallum fugelum tó mete *sit cadaver tuum in escam cunctis volatilibus cœli*, Deut. 28, 26. Ðis is mín líchaman [líchama, MS. A.] *hoc est corpus meum*, Mt. Kmbl. 26, 26. Án líchama mid his fæder wæs *una caro cum patre fuit*, Bd. 1, 27; S. 491, 15. Cépecnihtas hwítes líchoman and fægeres andwlitan *pueros venales candidi corporis, ac venusti vultus*, 2, 1; S. 501, 7. Ðínes líchaman leóhtfæt is ðín eáge, Mt. 6, 22. Hé wearþ ðá mann gesceapen on sáwle and on líchaman *he became then man formed of soul and body*, Homl. Th. i. 12, 30. Ðonne betǽcþ Crist ða mánfullan mid líchaman and mid sáwle intó hellewíte *then will Christ deliver the wicked, body and soul, into hell*, ii. 608, 7. Hí tú beóþ in ánum líchoman *erant duo in carne una*, Bd. i, 27; S. 491, 14. Hé wæs álǽded of líchaman *raptus est e corpore*, 3, 19; S. 547, 33: 4, 3; S. 569, 46. Ne beó gé brégyde fram ðám ðe ðone líchaman ofsleáþ and nabbaþ syððan hwæt hig má dón, Lk. Skt. 12, 4. In ðam ealra ærcebiscopa líchoman syndon bebyrged bútan twegra, heora líchaman sindon on ðære cyricean sylfre gesette, Bd. 2, 3; S. 504, 36. Wé nán ðing nabbaþ búton land and líchaman, Gen. 47, 18. Hé healdeþ ða deádan líchoman ungemolsnode *he keeps the dead bodies undecayed*, Shrn. 82, 21. [*O. Sax.* lík-hamo: *O. Frs.* líkkoma, lícma: *Icel.* líkami, líkamr: *O. H. Ger.* líchamo.]

lícham-leás; *adj. Without a body, incorporeal*:—Englas líchamleáse, Ælfc. T. Grn. 2, 25.

lícham-, lícum-líc [cf. *cognates under* líc-hama]; *adj. Bodily, corporeal, material, carnal, not spiritual*: — Seó [heofene] is geháten firmamentum seó is gesewenlíc and líchamlíc *it* [*heaven*] *is called the firmament; it is visible and material*, Lchdm. iii. 232, 14. Hyre líchomlíce dóhtor *filia ipsius carnalis*, Bd. 5, 3; S. 616, 3. His lícumlíce untrumness *corporea infirmitas*, 4, 1; S. 564, 5. Óswald hæfde lícumlícre yldo xxxvii wintra *anno ætatis suæ trigesimo octavo*, 3, 9; S. 533, 13. Hí wilnodon ðæs líchomlícan deáþes . . . wið ðan écan lífe, Bt. 11, 2; Fox 36, 3; Blickl. Homl. 103, 10. Se hálega gást ástáh líchamlícre ansýne *corporali specie*, Lk. Skt. 3, 22. Wæs hé líchomlícre gebyrdo æþeles cynnes *erat carnis origine nobilis*, Bd. 2, 7; S. 509, 15. Lícumlícre gegaderunga *copulæ carnalis*, 2, 9; S. 511, 1. Ealle ða líchamlícan gód biþ forcúþran ðonne ðære sáwle cræftas, Bt. 24, 3; Fox 84, 5. Ne geseó wit unc ofer ðæt líchomlícum eágum *we shall never see one another after that with our bodily eyes*, Bd. 4, 29; S. 607, 21: Blickl. Homl. 21, 20. [*Icel.* líkamligr: *O. H. Ger.* líhham-líh *corporalis, carnalis*.] DER. un-líchamlíc.

lícham-, lícum-líce; *adv. Bodily, in the body*:—Ðeáh ðe hé líchamlíce on heora slege andwerd nǽre *though he was not present in the body at their slaughter*, Homl. Th. i. 82, 33. Líchamlíce *corporaliter*, Ælfc. Gr. 38; Som. 41, 6. Seó stów ðe Drihten líchomlíce néhst on stód on middangearde, Blickl. Homl. 125, 15. Hié hine líchomlíce gesáwon *they saw him with their bodily eyes*, 135, 19. Ðeáh ðe hé lícumlíce æfward wære *quamvis corporaliter absens*, Bd. 3, 15; S. 542, 6.

líc-hord, es; *n; The inner parts of the body*, Exon. 46 b; Th. 159, 19; Gú. 929: 47 b; Th. 163, 31; Gú. 1002.

líc-hrægel, es; *n. Winding-sheet*:— Hí dydon scē Cúþberhtes liic of eorþan . . . ðá bǽron hí ðæs líchrægles dǽl tó Eádberhte ðæm biscope, Shrn. 82, 16.

líc-hryre, es; *m. Fall of the body, death*, Cd. 52; Th. 67, 11; Gen. 1099.

lícian; *p.* ode *To please*:—Ic lícige *placebo*, Ps. Spl, T. 114, 9. Ne mæg nán man hine sylfne tó cynge gedón ac ðæt folc hæfþ cyre tó ceósenne ðone tó cyninge ðe him sylfum lícaþ *no man can make himself king, but the people have the option of choosing him as king who pleases them*, Homl. Th. i. 212, 8. Hé mé wel lícaþ, ii. 40, 5. Ðé lícaþ se almihtiga God bet ðonne Þeodisius, Shrn. 196, 35. Ealle ða þing ðe hér lícíaþ sint eorþlíce, Bt. 34, 8; Fox 144, 35. Hit lícode Herode, Mt. Kmbl. 14, 6: Mk. Skt. 6, 22. Swá heó wiste ðæt his fæder lícode, Gen. 27, 14. Ac mé swá ðeáh nó ne lícade on him ðæt hé ða weorþunge Eástrena on riht ne heóld *however I did not like in him his not keeping Easter rightly*, Bd. 3, 17; S. 545, 2. For ðí sceolde ǽlc mon beón on ðam wel gehealden ðæt hé on his ágenum earde lícode *erit igitur pervagata inter suos gloria quisque contentus*, Bt. 18, 3; Fox 64, 28. Hí cwǽdon ðæt him ealle ða wel lícedon, 4, 5; S. 572, 24. Ðé is sélost ðæt ðú Gode lície, Blickl. Homl. 64, 34. Ac lícige swá hit lícige *but please as it may*, Wulfst. 191, 21. Ǽghwylc man þurh góde dǽda Gode lícian sceal, Blickl. Homl. 129. 34. Hé ðam cyninge wæs líciende, Bd. 5, 13; S. 632, 9. Him silfan lícigende, Lchdm. iii. 190, 24. [*O. Sax.* líkón: *O. Frs.* likia: *Icel.* líka.] DER. ge-, mis-lícian; v. lícan.

líciend-líc; *adj. Pleasing, pleasant*:—Se is Gode wel líciendlíc *beneplacitum est Deo*, Ps. Th. 67. 16. Teala líciendlíc, 68. 13. v. lícend-líc.

líc-lǽlan. v. lǽlan.

líc-leóþ, es; *n. A funeral song, dirge*; epicedion, Wrt. Voc. ii. 31, 2.

líc-mann, es; *m. A person having to do with a corpse*:—Ealle ða lícmenn wurdon áfyllede mid ðam wynsumum stence, Homl. Th. ii. 98, 8: 334, 31. His líc læg ealle ða niht inne beset, ac hé árás of deáþe. Ða lícmenn ðá ealle flugon áweg, 348, 20: 548, 15. Ðá bær sum wuduwe hire suna líc tó bebyrgenne . . . Seó dreórige módor mid ðám lícmannum hí ástrehte æt ðæs hálgan apostoles fótum . . . Johannes ofhreów ðære méder and ðæra lícmanna dreórignysse, i. 66, 15-21. [*Icel.* lík-maðr.]

líc-ness, e; *f. Likeness, form, image, stature*:—Lícnessa *imaginis*, Mt. Kmbl. p. 19, 5. Tó lícnesse *ad staturam*, 6, 27. an-, ge-, un-ge-lícness.

líc-pytt, es; *m. A grave*:—Lícpytt [MS. ic pytt] *scrobs*, Ælfc. Gr. 9, 51; Som. 13, 17.

líc-rest, e; *f. A place of rest for a dead body, tomb, sepulchre*:—Hé hæfde ðæt land syððan him sylfon tó lícreste *he had the land afterwards for his own burial place*, Gen. 23, 20. On líchryste *in cœmeterio*, Hpt. Gl. 507, 67. Man slóh án geteld ofer ða hálgan bán binnan ðære lícreste, Swt. A. S. Rdr. 100, 150. Heó hyre lícreste geceás on élig byrig *she chose her burial place in Ely*, Lchdm. iii. 430, 17. [*Laym.* þu hit scalt leden to ðere *lichraste* . . . þer þine wines liggeþ.]

lícsan. v. líxan.

líc-sang, es; *m. A funeral song, dirge*:—Wópleóþ ł birisang ł lícsang *tragœdiam, miseriam, luctum*, Hpt. Gl. 488, 56. [*Icel.* líksöngr.]

líc-sár, es; *n. A body-wound, a mortal wound* [?], Beo. Th. 1635; B. 815: Exon. 28 b; Th. 87, 25; Cri. 1430.

líc-sirce, an; *f. A coat of mail*, Beo. Th. 1105; B. 550.

líc-þegnung, -þénung, e; *f. Last offices done to the dead, funeral, exequies*:—Ic mæg habban árwurþfulle lícþénunge of heófigendre menigu *I may have honourable service done to my corpse by a mourning multitude*, Homl. Th. i. 86, 33. Ðá ðá his frýnd ða lícþénunge gearcodon *when his friends were performing the last offices for the dead*, ii. 28, 3. Ða fǽmnan dedan hire liicþénunge and lǽddon hí tó byrgenne, Shrn. 87, 27. Lícþénunga *exsequiæ*, Ælfc. Gr. 13; Som. 16, 17.

líc-þeóte, an; *f. A pore*:—Lícþeótan *pori* i. *spiramenta unde sudor emanat*, Ælfc. Gl. 73; Som. 71, 41; Wrt. Voc. 44, 25.

líc-þrowere, es; *m. A leper, one suffering from ulcers on the body*:—Lícþrowere *leprosus*, Ælfc. Gl. 78; Som. 72, 32; Wrt. 45, 64. Lazarus wæs lícþrowere [*ulceribus plenus*], Homl. Th. i. 328, 15: Homl. Skt. 3, 480. On Simones húse ðæs lícþroweres *in the house of Simon the leper*, Blickl. Homl. 73, 2. Manega lícþroweras *multi leprosi*, Lk. Skt. 4, 27: H. R. 105, 2. [Cf. *Icel.* lík-þrá *leprosy*.]

líc-tún, es; *m. An enclosure in which to bury people, a grave-yard, cemetery*:—Hí woldon ðæt heora líctún wǽre geseted *cimeterium fieri vellent*, Bd. 4, 7; S. 574, 37: Glostr. Frag. 8, 20. On ðæra bróðra líctune wæs bebyriged *in cœmeterio fratrum sepultum est*, Bd. 3, 17; S. 543, 46: 4, 10; S. 578, 2, 17, 28: Chart. Th. 157, 23. Hé nǽfre binnan nánum gehálgodum líctúne ne licge *let him never lie in a consecrated graveyard*, L. Ath. i. 25; Th. i. 212, 20: L. C. E. 22; Th. i. 372, 35.

lícum-líc. v. lícham-líc.

lícung, e; *f. Pleasing, pleasure, gratification*:—Ðætte hié for ðære lícunga ðære heringe ðe hié lufigeaþ eác geþafigen ða tælinge *ut dura admittunt favores, quos diligunt, etiam correptiones recipiant*, Past. 41, 4; Swt. 303, 19. Wel gedafonaþ ðætte ða gódan recceras wilnigen ðæt hié monnum lícigen, forðæm ðætte þurh ða lícunga hí mǽgen gedón ðætte hiera Dryhten lícige ðæm folce, 19, 3; Swt. 147, 7. Ne sylþ Gode lícungæ his *non dabit Deo placationem suam*, Ps. Spl. T. 48, 7. Lícongum *libitos*, Wrt. Voc. ii. 52, 34.

líc-wiglung, e; *f. Necromancy*, L. Edg. C. 16; Th. ii. 248, 3.

líc-wund, e; *f. A wound*, Cd. 154; Th. 193, 1; Exod. 239. [*O. Sax.* lík-wunda.]

líc-wyrþe; *adj. Fit to please, pleasant, well-pleasing, acceptable, agreeable, estimable, sterling* [*of money*]:—Ne mæg heó nán ðæra þinga gedón ðe Gode lícwyrþe beó *nequit quidquid eorum facere quæ Deo grata sunt*, L. Ecg. P. ii. 16; Th. ii. 188, 5: Wulfst. 279, 17. Lícworþe, Shrn. 170, 31. On ðære lícwyrþe is Gode eardian *in quo beneplacitum est Deo habitare*, Ps. Lamb. 67, 17. Swǽ wæs lícewyrþe before ðec *sic fuit placitum ante te*, Mt. Kmbl. Lind. 11, 26. Ðé micle má lícwerþe se gehnysta gást *much more pleasing to thee is the contrite spirit*, Ps. C. 50, 126; Ps. Grn. ii. 279, 126. Ne lǽt ðú unlofod ðæt ðú swutele ongite ðæt lícwyrþe sý *leave not unpraised what you clearly see is estimable*, Prov. Kmbl. 62. Hwæt biþ ðǽr ðonne lícwyrþes búton his gód and his weorþscipe ðæs gódan cyninges *quid in eis aliud, quam probitas utentium, placet?* Bt. 16, 1; Fox 50, 16. iiii pund lícwyrþes feós *four pounds of sterling money*, Cod. Dip. Kmbl. iii. 254, 15. For his lícweorþan feó, 255, 11. Ðinre ðære lícwurþan mundbyrdnesse *to thine acceptable protection*, Glostr. Frag. 108, 16. Him swá gecwéme and lícwyrþe folc, Lchdm. iii. 434, 5. Hié Gode swíðe lícwyrþe forhæfdnesse brengaþ *placentem Deo abstinentiam offerunt*, Past. 43, 8; Swt. 314, 21.

lícwyrþ-ness, e; *f. Good pleasure*:—On ðíure lícwyrþnysse *in beneplacito tuo*, Ps. Lamb. 88, 18.

lid, es; *n. A vessel, ship*:—On lides [*the ark*] bósme, Cd. 67; Th. 80, 21; Gen. 1332: 71; Th. 85, 6; Gen. 1410: Chr. 937; Erl. 112, 27; Aðelst. 27. Tó lides stefne, Erl. 112, 34; Aðelst. 34: Andr. Kmbl. 806; An. 403: 3411; An. 1709. Seó [*the dove*] eft ne com tó lide [*the ark*] fleógan, Cd. 72; Th. 89, 11; Gen. 1479. Lǽt nú geferian flotan úserne, lid tó lande, Andr. Kmbl. 795; An. 398. [*Icel.* lið; *n. a ship* (almost exclusively in poetry.)] v. liþ.

lida, an; *m. A sailor, traveller*:—Lida biþ longe on síþe, Exon. 90 b; Th. 339, 34; Gn. Ex. 104. [*Icel.* liði *a sailor, traveller.*] v. sǽ-, sumor-, ýð-lida; *and* líðan.

lȳdeþ, Ps. Th. 91, 11. v. leódan.

lid-mann, es; *m. A sailor, seaman*:—Wícinga werod . . . lidmen, Byrht. Th. 134, 44; By. 99. Lidmanna sum, 136, 41; By. 164. Lidmanna helm (*Beowulf*), Beo. Th. 3251; B. 1623. Liðmonna freá [*Ulysses*], Bt. Met. Fox 26, 126; Met. 26, 63. [Cf. *Icel.* liðs-maðr.]

lid-weard, es; *m. One who guards a ship*:—Lidweardas on merebáte, Andr. Kmbl. 487; An. 244.

lid-wérig; *adj. Weary of being on shipboard*, Andr. Kmbl. 963; An. 482.

Lid-wiccas, Lid-wícingas; *pl.* The people of Brittany [or using the name of the people for the country] *Brittany*:—Carl féng tó eallum ðam westríce . . . bútan Lidwiccium *Charles took all the western kingdom . . . except Brittany*, Chr. 885; Erl. 84, 13. Two other MSS. have Lidwícingum, Th. 154, 155, and this form occurs in the Scop's Tale:—Ic wæs mid Lidwícingum, Exon. 86 a; Th. 323, 17; Víd. 80. Micel sciphere com súþan of Lidwicum, Chr. 910; Erl. 101, 32. Lidwiccum, 918; Erl. 102, 22. The word seems to contain the British name for Armorica, *Llydaw*. v. notes to the passages from the Cod. Exon. and from the Chron. 918.

LÍF, es; *n.* LIFE [the opposite of death], *mode of life, period during which a man lives*:—Hwæt is ðæt líf elles ðysses middangeardes búton lytelu ylding deáþes, Blickl. Homl. 59, 27. Twá líf sind sóðlíce . . . ðæt án líf is deádlíc, ðæt óðer undeádlíc, Homl. Th. i. 224, 14-16. Ðis andwarde líf manna on eorþan, Bd. 2, 13; S. 516, 14. Lífes treów *lignum vitæ*, Gen. 2, 9. Lífes wæter *aqua viva*, Jn. Skt. 4, 10. Lífes weg, Blickl. Homl. 17, 19. Lífes bæþ, Bd. 2, 5; S. 507, 19. For heora lífes geearnunge geþungon ðæt hí wǽron abbudissan *on account of the merit of their lives succeeded in becoming abbesses*; præ merito virtutum, 3, 8; S. 531, 23. Seó þearlwísnes ðæs heardan lífes *districtio vitæ arctioris*, 4, 25; S. 599, 32. Reogollíces lífes þeódscipe, 3, 22; S. 553, 10. On ðære béc Cúþberhtes lífes, 4, 30; S. 609, 32. Ealle hig wǽron háliges lífes menn, Wulfst. 270, 15. Hé geendode his dagas æfter mycclum geswince his lífes, Chr. 1016; Erl. 155, 3. On ðam ýtemestan dæge his lífes, Bd. 3, 17; S. 543, 19, col. 1. Lífes *alive*:—Ætýwde ðæt hé lífes wæs *quia viveret demonstrans*, 5, 19; S. 640, 24. Geáxlan hwæðer hé lífes wǽre, Homl. Th. ii. 186, 1: L. Eth. ii. 9; Th. i. 290, 14: Chart. Th. 471, 34: Cod. Dipl. Kmbl. i. 234, 28. 32. Ðǽr belifon swáðeáh lífes on ðam mynstre feówer and twentig muneca, Homl. Skt. 6, 351. Gif hé biþ vi nihta eald and hine ádl gestandeþ se biþ lífes [*he will survive*], Lchdm. iii. 182, 12. [*Icel.* lífes *alive.*] Sume hit ne gedýgdan mid ðam lífe *some did not get off with their lives*, Chr. 978; Erl. 127, 13. Heó of deáþe férde tó lífe *she went from death unto life*, Bd. 4, 23; S. 595, 32. Hé forþférde of ðyssum lífe and férde tó ðam sóðan lífe, 2, 1; S. 500, 13. On ðís lífe, Dóm. L. 32, 80. Hé nǽre ná man geþuht, gif hé mannes lífe ne lyfode, Homl. Th. i. 150, 8: Blickl. 167, 33. Se hálga Augustinus be his hálan líue hine hádode tó biscope [*while alive and in health*], Chr. 616; Erl. 22, 27. Ðearfendum lífe wunedon *pauperem vitam agebant*, Bd. 1, 15; S. 484, 8. Be muneca lífe *de vita monachorum*, 2, 4; S. 505, 33. On munuclícum lífe geseted, 4, 27; S. 603, 24: 5, 1; S. 613, 6. Seó bóc þe is áwriten be his lífe, 3, 19; S. 547, 32. Seó freólsbóc ealra ðare landa ðe in tó ðæm mynechina lífe [*nunnery*, v. munuc-líf] æt Wiltúne forgifene sint, Cod. Dip. Kmbl. iii. 117, 25. On, tó lífe [*Icel.* á lífi *alive*] *alive, living*:—Ðá hé on lífe wæs *adhuc vivens*, Mt. Kmbl. 27, 63. Hé wæs on lífe eorþlíc cing, hé is nú æfter deáþe heofonlíc sanct, Chr. 979; Erl. 129, 9. Ða hwíle ðe hig on lífe beón *quamdiu in vivis erunt*, L. Ecg. P. ii. 19; Th. ii. 188, 28. Hwí hig heóldon ða wífmenn tó lífe *why they kept the women alive*, Num. 31, 15. Hé lǽfde uneáðe ǽnne tó lífe, Wulfst. 106, 8. Se deáþ cymeþ ðæt hé ðæt líf áfyrre, Bt. 8; Fox 26, 7. Sylle líf wið lífe *reddat animam pro anima*, Ex. 21, 23. Ðeáh hé líf hæfde *if he had been alive*, L. C. S. 73; Th. i. 416, 1. Wé ús nyton witod líf æt ǽfen, Wulfst. 151, 17. Líf and land werian, 274, 17. Preóstas and nunnan heora líf rehtan *let priests and nuns order their lives*, 269, 15. Liif, Bd. 3, 18; S. 545, 42, col. 2. Nis mé tíd mín líf tó onwendenne *there is no time for me to change my life*, 5, 14; S. 634, 32: Past. 17, 4; Swt. 111, 23. Seó Cúþburh ðæt lýf [*monastery*] æt Winburnan árǽrde, Chr. 718; Erl. 45, 19. [*O. Sax. O. Frs. Icel.* líf: *O. H. Ger.* líp *vita, conversatio, habitus.* In Icelandic the word has also the meanings *body* [e. g. líf ok sála] *person*, and the latter use is found in Piers. P. e. g. no *lyf* elles. In *O. H. Ger.*, v. Grff. ii. 44, it is seldom, if ever, used with the meaning of the modern *leib.* DER. ancor-, edwít-, ende-, feorh-, munuc-, mynster-, regol-, sundor-, woruld-líf.

líf, *permission.* v. leáf.

líf; *adj.* v. léf.

lifat [?], Lchdm. iii. 82, 13.

lífan, léfan, lýfan; *p.* de *To give leave, allow, permit*:—Ða feówer ic eów lýfe tó sǽde and tó mete *quatuor reliquas permitto vobis in sementem* *et in cibum*, Gen. 47, 24. Ic ðē selfes dōm līfe *I allow you to decide*, Cd. 91; Th. 115, 7; Gen. 1916. Moyses lȳfde eów eówer wīf tō forlǣtenne *Moses permisit vobis dimittere uxores vestras*, Mt. Kmbl. 19, 8. God lȳfde Adame, ðæt hē mōste brūcan ealra wæstma, Wulfst. 9, 6: Blickl. Homl. 189, 22. Ðā bǣdon hȳ ðæt hē lȳfde him on ða gān. Þā lȳfde hē him, Lk. Skt. 8, 32. Ðā se cing lȳfde eallon Myrceon hām and hig swā dydon *then the king gave leave to all the Mercians to go home, and they did so*, Chr. 1049; Erl. 172, 37. Wē hit ne selfe ne lufedon ne eác ōðrum monnum ne līfdon [lēfdon, Hat. MS] *we did not love it ourselves nor allow it to other men*, Past. pref; Swt. 4, 6. Ic bidde ðæt ðū mē lȳfe ofer ðīn land tō fērenne *obsecro, ut transire mihi liceat per terram tuam*, Num. 21, 22. Tō ðam dyrstig, ðæt hē ǣfre līfe ǣnigan men ðis fæsten tō ābrecenne, Wulfst. 174, 60. Gif priόst lǣfe unrihthǣmed, L. Wih. 6; Th. i. 38, 9. Gif eów Crist lȳfan wylle, ðæt . . . Exon. 41 a; Th. 137, 27; Gū. 565. [*Icel.* leyfa *to permit*] v. ā-, ge-līfan.

līfan, lēfan, lȳfan; *p.* de *To believe*:—Ðā lȳfde Simplicus and fulwihte onfēng, Shrn. 146, 18. Ða dysegan men ðe ðysum drȳcræftum lȳfdon, Bt. Met. Fox 26, 197; Met. 26, 99. Swā is tō lȳfenne ðæt . . . Blickl. Homl. 11, 12. [*Goth.* laubjan.] v. ge-līfan.

līfan *to remain*. v. be-līfan.

līf-brycgung, e; *f. Life, intercourse;* conversatio, Rtl. 7, 29.

līf-bysig; *adj. Busy about saving life, struggling for life, anxious about life;*—Ðæt hē for mundgripe mīnum scolde licgean līfbysig būtan his līce swice *that for my handgrip he should lie struggling for life, unless his body should escape*, Beo. Th. 1936; B. 966.

līf-cearu, e; *f. Care* or *anxiety about life*, Andr. Kmbl. 2856; An. 1430: Cd. 42; Th. 54, 17; Gen. 878.

līf-dæg, es; *m. A day of life, any portion of the time that a person lives*:—Ðīn geleáfa in līfdæge ūrum mōde þurhwunige *may belief in thee while we live continue in our hearts*, Hy. 6, 8; Hy. Grn. ii. 286, 8. Swā his līfdagas lǣne syndon, Ps. Th. 102, 14. Ic on līfdagum healde ðīnra worda waru *vivam et custodiam sermones tuos*, 118, 17: 139, 8: Cd. 162; Th. 203, 25; Exod. 409: Elen. Kmbl. 880; El. 441. On hyra līfdagum *in the days of their life*, Exon. 25 b; Th. 75, 22; Cri. 1225: 97 b; Th. 364, 23; Wal. 75: Bt. Met. Fox 15, 11; Met. 15, 6. Ic him līfdagas lange sylle *longitudine dierum replebo eum*, Ps. Th. 90, 16: Chart. Th. 372, 18. Gyf God ne gescyrte ðæs þeódscaþan līfdagas, Wulfst. 86, 17. Sumon dægbōte and sumon mā daga and sumon ealle his līfdagas, L. Pen. 3; Th. ii. 278, 14: Cd. 43; Th. 56, 10; Gen. 910. Hē him līfdagas leófran ne wisse ðonne hē hȳrde heofoncyninge *no pleasanter time in his life did he know, than when he obeyed heaven's king*, 162; Th. 203, 25; Exod. 409. Oflēt līfdagas *died*, Beo. Th. 3248; B. 1622. [*Icel.* līf-dagar.]

lifen, leofen, e; *f. That by which one lives, support, sustenance*:—Libn *vicatum* [=*victum*], Wrt. Voc. ii. 123, 51; Ep. Gl. 28 b, 17. Līfes tō leofne *for the support of life*, Andr. Kmbl. 2247; An. 1125. [Cf. *Goth.* libains *life*.] v. and-lifen.

LIFER, e; *f.* The LIVER:—Lifer *jecur*, Wrt. Voc. 65, 50: 71, 6. Lifre læppan *fibræ*, Ælfc. Gl. 76; Som. 71, 110; Wrt. Voc. 45, 16. Ðære lifre nett *reticulum jecoris*, Ex. 29, 13. Ealle ða þing ðe tō ðære lifre clifiaþ *cuncta, quæ adhærent jecori*, Lev. 1, 8. Se vultor sceolde forlǣtan ðæt hē ne slāt ða lifre Tyties ðæs cyninges, Bt. 35, 6; Fox, 170, 3. [*Icel.* lifr: *O. H. Ger.* libara: *Ger.* leber.]

lifer *a level surface* [?]; libramentum, Wrt. Voc. ii. 50, 78. v. [?] læfer.

lifer-ādl, e; *f. Disease of the liver*, L. M. Cont. 2, 23; Lchdm. ii. 162, 2.

lifer-bȳl, e; *f. A prominence on the liver*, L. M. 2, 21; Lchdm. ii. 204, 20. v. next word.

lifer-hol, es; *n. A hollow in the liver*:—Hwæðer on ðām liferbȳlum ðe on ðām liferholum, L. M. 2, 21; Lchdm. ii. 204, 20.

lifer-læppa, an; *m. A lobe of the liver*:—Liferlæppa *fibra* i. *vena*, Wrt. Voc. ii. 148, 55. Librlæppan *fibræ*, 108, 54.

lifer-wærc, es; *m. Pain in the liver*:—Wið eallum liferwærcum, L. M. Cont. 2, 24; Lchdm. ii. 162, 5.

lifesne, Bd. 4, 27; S. 604, 9. v. lybesn.

līf-fadung, e; *f. The ordering* or *regulating of one's life*:—Be gehādodra manna līffadunge *of the ordering of the life of men in orders*, L. Wilk. 82, 22.

līf-fæc, es; *n. The time during which life lasts, life*:—On lǣnan līffæce, L. Eth. vii. 21; Th. i. 334, 4. Æfter heora līffæce, Wulfst. 4, 6: 5, 5.

līf-fæst, *adj. Living, having life, quickened*:—Ðæt hē onfōn wolde ðam gerȳne ðære līffæstan rōde Cristes *ad suscipiendum mysterium vivificæ crucis*, Bd. 2, 12; S. 512, 29: Glostr. Frag. 108, 4. Ic mid ða līffæstan ȳðe þurgoten wæs *vitali unda perfusus sum*, Bd. 5, 6; S. 620, 17. Ða līffæstan leoþu, Exon. 37 a; Th. 327, 19; Vy. 6. v. next word.

līf-fæstan; *p.* te *To give life, quicken, vivify*:—Ðonne hine God līffæsteþ *when God shall quicken him;* Deo vivificante, Bd. 2, 1; S. 500, 20. Gāst is se ðe līffæsteþ *spiritus est qui vivificat*, Jn. Skt. Rush. 6, 63. Hē is se līffæstenda God, Homl. Th. i. 280, 23: ii. 598, 7. v. ge-līffæstan.

liffettan. v. lyffettan.

līf-freá, an; *m. The Lord of life* [epithet of God], Exon. 8 a; Th. 2, 7, 30; Cri. 15, 27: Beo. Th. 32; B. 16: Cd. 40; Th. 53, 28; Gen. 868: 1; Th. 2, 9; Gen. 16: 86; Th. 108, 18; Gen. 1808: 156; Th. 195, 3; Exod. 271: 192; Th. 240, 33; Dan. 396.

līf-fruma, an; *m. The author of life*, [*Christ*], Exon. 17 b; Th. 41, 16; Cri. 656: [*God*], 23 a; Th. 64, 25; Cri. 1043: Andr. Kmbl. 2570; An. 1286: [*Christ*] 1124; An. 562: Elen. Kmbl. 670; El. 335: Exon. 15 a; Th. 31, 31; Cri. 504: 42 a; Th. 140, 13; Gū. 609: [*God*], Cd. 208; Th. 256, 20; Dan. 643.

līf-gedāl, es; *n. Parting with life, separation from life, death*, Beo. Th. 1687; B. 841: Exon. 87 b; Th. 330, 2; Vy. 45: 48 a; Th. 164, 29; Gū. 1019: Cd. 119; Th. 154, 25; Gen. 2561.

līf-gesceaft, e; *f. A condition of life as ordered by fate*, Beo. Th. 3910; B. 1953: 6120; B. 3064.

līf-getwinnan; *pl. m. Twins*, Salm. Kmbl. 284; Sal. 141.

LIFIAN, leofian; *p.* ode To LIVE:—Ne swelte ic ac ic lifige *non moriar, sed vivam*, Ps. Th. 117, 17: 118, 93. Ðū eádig leófast, 127, 2. Ðenden ðū hēr leofast, Cd. 43; Th. 57, 29; Gen. 935. Ðǣr hit lifaþ swā unnyt swā hit wæs *where it continues as useless as it was before*, Beo. Th. 6316; B. 3168. Lyfaþ *vivet*, Ps. Th. 71, 15. Þurh Godes fultum, ðe lyfaþ and rīxaþ ā būtan ende, Blickl. Homl. 131, 6. Leofaþ, 13, 29. Ða gāstlīcan lāre, ðe ūre sāul big leofaþ, 57, 9. On gewinne and on swāte hē leofaþ, 59, 36. Se ðe him sylfum leofaþ *he who lives to himself*, Homl. Th. ii. 78, 4. Be heora āgenum handgewinne lifigeaþ *proprio labore manuum vivant*, Bd. 4, 4; S. 571, 22: 4, 28; S. 605, 16. Be ðæm balzamum ða men in ðæm londe lifgeaþ *opobalsamo vescuntur*, Nar. 31, 6. Godes is ðæt yrfe ðe wē big leofiaþ, Blickl. Homl. 51, 18. Ðǣm mannum ðe be his lārum lifiaþ, 61, 13. On hwylcum geswince hié lifiaþ, 59, 25. Gif wē ða dagas fulfremedlīce for Gode lifgeaþ, 35, 25. Ða hwīle ðe wē lifgaþ hēr on worlde, 35, 35. Se cyning Eglippus leofode his līf on eáwfæstre drohtnunge, 476, 16. Se hālga swā leofode swā hē tǣhte, Homl. Th. ii. 186, 19. Se æþeling lyfode [other MS. leofode] ðā gyt, Chr. 1036; Erl. 165, 21. Hē ðǣr sum fæc on forhæbbendum līfe lifede *aliquandiu continentissimam gestit vitam*, Bd. 5, 11; S. 626, 16. Hī for heofonan rīces lufan on ellþeódignesse lifedon *pro æterna patria exulaverant*, 5, 10; S. 624, 12. Ðū leofa būtan mē gif ðū mǣge *live without me, if you can*, Wulfst. 259, 5. Ic beó lāreów georn ðæt hē monþeáwum mīnum lifge *I am diligent in teaching him to live according to my customs*, Exon. 71 b; Th. 267, 5; Jul. 410. Ðone geleáfan ðȳ Cristenan þeáwe lifigean and ðone wel healdan *fidem more christiano servare*, Bd. 2, 9; S. 510, 31. Hū hī mid heora gefērum drohtian and lifigean scylon *qualiter cum suis clericis conversentur*, 1, 27; S. 488, 37. Leofigean, S. 489, 21. Hē wolde his līf on ælþeódignysse lyfian *peregrinus vivere vellet*, 3, 27; S. 559, 9. Se līchoma būtan mete and drence leofian ne mæg, Blickl. Homl. 57, 10. On forhæfdnesse lifgean, 35, 21. Hē ongan lifgean ongeán Gode ǣrðon ðe hē him sylfum lifgean mihte, 165, 22. Gif seó upplīce ārfæstnys mē ǣnig fæc tō lifianne forgifan wylle, Bd. 3, 13; S. 538. 31. Ic symle tilode tō lifigenne tō ðīnes mūþes bebode, 4, 29; S. 607, 28. On dwolan lifigende, 2, 15; S. 518, 42. Be Diocletiane lyfgendum *vivente Diocletiano*, 1, 8; S. 479, 28: Chart. Th. 485, 33. Sume forlǣtaþ ða hig ǣr hæfdon and be lifiendre cwenan eft ōðre nimaþ *some leave the wives they had before, and while the wife is still living, take another*, Wulfst. 269, 23. Sum ðēh hē forlǣte ða hē ǣr hæfde, hē be lifiendre ðære eft ōðere nimþ, L. Eth. vi. 5; Th. i. 316, 10. Hine þurh ðone lifigendan Drihten hālsedon, Bd. 4, 28; S. 606, 14. [*O. Frs.* livia.] v. ā-, ge-lifian; cwic-, un-lifigende; libban.

līf-lād, e; *f. Conduct of life, way of life, life*, R. Ben. 1, Lye [cf. hwa so eauer boc writ of mi *liflade*, Marh. 20, 16: heo god mid gode *liflode* touward þe riche of heouene, A.R. 350, 4. It is also used to mean that by which life is supported, *livelihood*:—Heo tilede here *lyflode*, R. Glouc. 41, 22: lyvelode *or* lyfhode *victus*, Prompt. Parv. 308. So *O. H. Ger.* līb-leita *victus, annona, alimonium, alimentum.*]

līf-leás; *adj. Lifeless, without life*:—Ðū bist deád and ða ðe ðē tō lōciaþ beóþ līfleáse eác *morte morieris tu et omnia quæ tua sunt*, Gen. 20, 7. Fela templa ārǣrdon and mid andgitleásum and līfleásum anlīcnyssum āfyldon *erected many temples, and filled them with images that were without sense and without life*, Homl. Th. ii. 574, 28.

līf-leást, -lǣst, e; *f. Loss of life, death*:—On ǣlcum ðara daga gif man ǣnige ǣddran geopenaþ on ðara tīde ðæt hit biþ līfleást oððe langsum sār *on each of those days, if a vein be opened at that hour, it is death or long disease*, Lchdm. iii. 152, 5. Bendas oððe dyntas hwīlum līflǣsta *bonds or blows, at times death*, L. Pen. 3; Th. ii. 278, 27.

līf-līc; *adj. Pertaining to life, living, causing life, vital*:—Līflīc *vitalis*, Ælfc. Gr. 9, 28; Som. 11, 36. Līflīc ys blód lǣtan *to let blood* [*at this time*] *is as much as a man's life is worth*, Lchdm. iii. 190, 28. Is hwæðere swā tō lǣtanne swā ðæt līflīce mægen ne āspringe *blood however is to be let so that vital power be not dissipated*, L. M. 2, 42; Lchdm. ii. 254, 12. Wyll līflīc *fons vivus*, Hymn. Surt. 92, 15. Ic eom se līflīca hlāf ðe of heofenum āstāh *I am the living bread, that came down from heaven*, Homl. Th. ii. 202, 5. Ðæra næddrena geslit wæs deádlīc Cristes deáþ wæs līflīc *the bite of the serpents brought death; Christ's death brought* *life*, 238, 31. Líflíc onsægednys *a living sacrifice*, i. 358, 18: 482, 12. Ádylegode of ðære liflícan béc *blotted from the book of life*, 68, 11. Líflícum blóde *vivido sanguine*, Hymn. Surt. 80, 21. God ábleów on his ansýne líflícne blǽd, Hexam. 11; Norm. 18, 26.

líf-líce; *adv. Vitally, so as to infuse life*:—Hé genam ðá hláf and hine liflíce hálgode, Homl. Th. ii. 244, 10.

líf-lyre, es; *m. Loss of life*:—Gif líflyre wurþe *if loss of life occur*, L. E. B. 2; Th. ii. 240, 11.

líf-neru, e; *f. Support of life, food*:—Tó lífnere Andr. Kmbl. 2180; An. 1091. [*O. Sax. O. L. Ger.* líf-nara *sustenance*: *O. H. Ger.* líb-nara *victus, alimonia.*]

lifnes, Bd. 4, 27; S. 604, 9 note. v. lyfesn.

lifrig; *adj. Connected with the liver*:—Ðæt þiccæ and lifrige blód, L. M. 2, 40; Lchdm. ii. 250, 10.

lift *the air*. v. lyft.

líft, lýft *a grant, allowance*:—Ús bóceras beteran secgaþ lengran lýft wynna *learned men tell us of a better and longer grant of joys*, Cd. 169; Th. 211, 24; Exod. 531. Cf. lífan. [*Bouterwek suggests* lyst (= lust) wynna, Grmm. Gr. ii. 466 *would read* lyftwynn *recreatio in aere*; *Thorpe suggests* líf *for* lyft.]

líf-weard, es; *m. A guardian of life* [*Christ*], Elen. Kmbl. 2069; El. 1036.

líf-weg, es; *m. A way which leads to life, way of life, one's path in life*:—Lífweg [*the road followed by the Israelites under the guidance of the pillar of cloud*], Cd. 147; Th. 184, 9; Exod. 104. Uton nú ealle úre lífwegas geornlíce rihtan *let us diligently amend our ways*, Wulfst. 75, 22. Líðe lifwegas, Exon. 43 b; Th. 148, 5; Gú. 740.

líf-wela, an; *m. Riches that confer or possess life, heavenly riches, wealth belonging to this, or to the next, life*:—Him wæs wuldres dreám, lífwela leófra ðonne ðás leásan godu, Apstls. Kmbl. 97; Ap. 49. Ða lífwelan, swáse swegldreámas, Exon. 27 b; Th. 82, 33; Cri. 1348. Lífwelan *the wealth of this world*, Cd. 174; Th. 219, 17; Dan. 56.

líf-welle; *adj. From a living spring*:—Lífwelle wæter [wæter cwicwelle, Rush.] *aquam vivam*, Jn. Skt. Lind. 4, 10.

líf-wraðu, e; *f. A support of life*, Beo. Th. 1946; B. 971: 5746; B. 2877.

líf-wynn, e; *f. A pleasure or joy of life*:—Hé lytle hwíle lífwynna breác *a little while he enjoyed the pleasures of life*, Beo. Th. 4201; B. 2097: Exon. 19 b; Th. 50, 27; Cri. 807: Elen. Kmbl. 2535; El. 1269.

líg, lég, es; *generally masc. but* ðæt lég *occurs. Flame, lightning*:—Líg *flamma*, Wrt. Voc. 76, 49: 82, 52. Lég, 284, 12. Ðæt fýr and ðæt lég [se líg MS. C.] swíðe weóx ... Ðá fór se wallenda lég ... ðǽr se lég mǽst wæs, Bd. 2, 7; S. 509, 19–24. Se lég ongan sleán ongeán ðone wind, Blickl. Homl. 221, 12. Wonna lég *the pale flame*, Beo. Th. 6221; B. 3115. Hlemmeþ háta lég, Exon. 21 b; Th. 58, 9; Cri. 933. Reáda lég, 19 b; Th. 51, 2; Cri. 810. Sweart líg, Cd. 110; Th. 145, 33; Gen. 2415. Ne biþ ðǽr [*heaven*] nánes líges gebrasl, Dóm. L. 16, 259: Beo. Th. 166; B. 83. Wylm ðæs wæfran líges *the heat of the flickering flame*, Cd. 185; Th. 231, 2; Dan. 241. Ligges leóma, 190; Th. 237, 25; Dan. 343. Ðone deópan grund ðæs hátan léges and ðæs heardan léges [*hell*], Blickl. Homl. 103, 15. For ðæs léges [*lightning*] bryne, 203, 11. Léges blæstas, Andr. Kmbl. 3103; An. 1554. Biscopas mid folcum mid íserne and líge fornumene wǽron *presules cum populis ferro et flammis absumebantur*, Bd. 1, 15; S. 484, 2. Fýres líge wæs fornumen, 4, 25; S. 599, 20. On fíres líge *in flamma ignis*, Ex. 3, 2. On brádum ligge, Wulfst. 188, 3. Ligge gelícost, Beo. Th. 1458; B. 727. For dracan lége *for the flame that was sent forth by the dragon*, 5092; B. 2549. Blácan lýge, Andr. Kmbl. 3081; An. 1543. Úre synna líg, Wulfst. 287, 9. Hí wǽron on ǽnne unmǽtne lég gesomnade *in immensum adunati sunt flammam*, Bd. 3, 19; S. 548, 21. Ðǽr [*hell*] hé hæfþ weallendene lég, and hwílum cýle ðone grimmestan, Blickl. Homl. 61, 35. On ðæt líg tó ðé hweorfan, Cd. 35; Th. 46, 33; Gen. 753. Líga *fulminum*, Hpt. Gl. 509, 30. On fýrenra léga onlícnesse *in the form of flames of fire*, Blickl. Homl. 133, 20. Légea, 135, 3. Monige heápas sweartra lígea *crebri flammarum tetrarum globi*, Bd. 5, 12; S. 628, 16, 22. Léga leóhtost, Bt. Met. Fox 9, 33; Met. 9, 17. Wununga áfyllede mid brastligendum lígum, Homl. Th. i. 68, 5: Bd. 2, 7; S. 509, 34. Brand and bráde lígas, Cd. 18; Th. 21, 16; Gen. 325: 36; Th. 47, 20; Gen. 763. Mellitus ða lígeas his byrnendre ceastre gebiddende ádwæscte *Mellitus flammas ardentes suæ civitatis orando restinxerit*, Bd. 2, 7; S. 509, 2. Lígeas gemonigfealdaþ and hí gedréfeþ *fulgura multiplicavit et conturbavit eos*, 4, 3; S. 569, 20. Lías *flammas*, Hymn. Surt. 10, 29. [*O. E. Homl.* leies; *pl.*: *Piers P.* leye: *A. R.* leie: *Jul.* ley: *Icel.* leygr *a flame* [poet.]: *O. H. Ger.* louch, loug *flamma*: cf. *O. Sax.* lógna: *Icel.* log, logi *a flame, lowe.*]

líg-bǽre; *adj. Flame-bearing, flaming, fiery*:—Lígbǽrum *flammifera*, Hpt. Gl. 433, 71. Ligbǽrum scridum *flammigeris quadrigis*, Wrt. Voc. ii. 149, 13.

líg-berend; *adj. Flame-bearing, fiery*:—Lígberend *flammiger*, Wrt. Voc. ii. 149, 9. Légberend, 36, 52.

líg-bryne, es; *m. Burning of flame, fire*:—Æfter lígbryne, Exon. 64 a; Th. 236, 20; Ph. 577. Légbryne, 22 b; Th. 62, 15; Cri. 1002.

líg-cwalu, e; *f. Torment, or death by fire*, Elen. Kmbl. 591; El. 296.

líg-draca, an; *m. A fire-drake, dragon vomiting flames*, Beo. Th. 4655; B. 2333. Légdraca, 6073; B. 3040.

Lige *the river Lea*. v. Lyge.

lige, ligen, *a lie*. v. lyge, lygen.

líg-egesa, an; *m. Fear caused by fire*, Beo. Th. 5554; B. 2780.

lígen; *adj. Flaming, fiery*:—Lígen *flammaticus*, Wrt. Voc. ii. 149, 5. Ðǽr wæs lígen swurd gelogod æt ðam ingange *there was placed a flaming sword at the entrance*, Hexam. 19; Norm. 28, 1. Légene sweorde, Elen. Kmbl. 1511; El. 757. Heofen lígenne gesihþ *if he sees the heavens fiery*, Lchdm. iii. 200, 14. Lígen ðære sunnan hweogul *flammeam solis rotam*, Hymn. Surt. 22, 23. Se ealda deófol hine æteówode mid byrnendum múþe and lígenum eágum, Homl. Th. ii. 164, 23. [*O. H. Ger.* laugin *flammeus.*]

líget, es; *m. n.*: lígetu, e; *f. Lightning, a flash of lightning*:—Lígit *fulgor* vel *fulmen*, Wrt. Voc. 52, 46. Hys ansýn wæs swylce lígyt, Mt. Kmbl. 28, 3: 24, 27. Ðǽr begann tó brastlígenne micel þunor and líget sceótan, Homl. Th. ii. 196, 23. Swá hättra sumor swá mára þunor and líget, Lchdm. iii. 280, 10. [Swá stor þunring and lǽgt wes, swá ðæt hit ácwealde manige men, Chr. 1085: Erl. 219, 22.] Æfter ðæm wolcne cymeþ légetu and þunor, Blickl. Homl. 91, 33. Légitu, Ps. Surt. ii. 196, 19. Légite *fulgoris*, 190, 15. Men sweltaþ for ðæs þunres ege ánum and ðære lígette, Wulfst. 207, 26. Ðæt fýr ábyrst út þurh lígett [lígette, MS. R. P.], Lchdm. iii. 280, 7. Hé lǽdeþ wind and líget, Ps. Th. 134, 7. Gif lígette and þunorráde eorþan and lyfte brégdon *si corusci ac tonitrua terras et aera terrerent*, Bd. 4, 3; S. 569, 12. Lígette *coruscationes*, Ps. Th. 76, 15. Lígetta, 143, 7: *fulgura*, Ex. 19, 16: Exon. 54 b; Th. 192, 15; Az. 102. Ðá flugon ða légetu swylce fýrene strǽlas, Blickl. Homl. 203, 9. Lígetu, Ps. Th. 17, 12: Cd. 192; Th. 240, 2; Dan. 380. Lígetas, Bd. 4, 3; S. 569, 22. Lígettas *fulgura*, Ps. Lamb. 17, 15. Lígetta [lýgyttu, MS. C.] *fulgura*, Ps. Spl. 134, 7. Hé gemanigfealdode his lígeta *fulgura multiplicavit*, Ps. Th. 17, 14. Légite, Ps. Surt. ii. 197, 34. [Cf. *Goth.* lauhatjan *to lighten*: *O. H. Ger.* laugazan: lóhazan *rutilare, micare, coruscare.*]

líget-ræsc, es; *m. Lightning*:—Ic geseah Satanan swá swá lígetræsct of heofone feallende, Lk. Skt. 10, 18, MS. A. v. líg-ræsc.

líget-sliht, e; *f. A flash of lightning*:—Ðá com þunerrád and léget-sleht and ofslóh ðone mǽstan dǽl ðæs hǽðnan folces, Shrn. 57, 35. Léged-slæht *fulgor*, Lk. Skt. Lind. 10, 18.

líg-fǽmende, -fámbláwende, -fýrberende [-ferbærnde, MS.] *vomiting flame*; flammivomus [the words are those used by the several MSS. in] Bd. 5, 12; S. 630, 12.

líg-fýr, es; *n. Flaming fire*, Cd. 146; Th. 182, 18; Exod. 77.

líg-hrægel [?]:—Lígrægel *orbiculata* [*vestis*], Ælfc. Gl. 29; Som. 61, 30; Wrt. Voc. 26, 29. Cf. Ducange 'duo *orbicularia* de opere ad acum' *under* orbiculare.

líg-locc; *adj. Having flaming locks*:—Lígloccum *flammicomis*, Wrt. Voc. ii. 149, 12.

líg-loccod; *adj. Furnished with fiery locks*:—Lígloccode [-liccode, Wrt.] *flammicomos*, Wrt. Voc. ii. 149, 10.

lígnian; *p.* ede *To deny*:—Ðú lígnest nú ðæt síe lifgende se ofer deóflum dugeþum wealdeþ, Cd. 212; Th. 263, 18; Dan. 764. Hú hine [*Christ*] lýgnedon leáse on geþoncum, Exon. 24 a: Th. 69, 13; Cri. 1120. [*Goth.* laugnjan: *O. Sax.* lógnian *to deny*: *O. H. Ger.* laugaunan *negare, diffiteri, inficiari*: *Ger.* laugnen.]

líg-ræsc, es; *m. Lightning, a flash of lightning, bright light*:—Lígræsc *coruscatio i. fulgor*, Wrt. Voc. ii. 136, 2. His ansýn wæs swylce lígræsc, Nicod. 15; Thw. 7, 20. Ic geseah Satanan swá swá lígræsc of heofone feallende *videbam Satanan sicut fulgor de cælo cadentem*, Lk. Skt. 10, 18: 17, 24. Ðæt leóhtfæt ðæs lígræsces *lucerna fulgoris*, 11, 36. For lígræsce *præ fulgore*, Ps. Spl. 17, 14. Lígrascas *coruscationes*, 76, 18. Lígræscas *fulgura*, 96, 4. Légræscas, 17, 16: *coruscationes*, Blickl. Gl. Ðæt ðú áwende hagolas and lígræsceas [-ræceas, MS. O.] *that thou avert hail and lightning*, Herb. 176; Lchdm. i. 308, 23. Lígræsceas gesihþ orsorhnesse hit getácnaþ, Lchdm. iii. 202, 17. Líghræscas, Ps. Lamb. 134, 7.

líg-ræscetung, e; *f. Lightning*:—Lígrescetunga *fulgura*, Ps. Lamb. 17, 15.

líg-spiwol; *adj. Vomiting flame*:—Ðǽr beóþ ða welras gefylde lígspiwelum bryne, Dóm. L. 14, 209: Wulfst. 139, 9.

líg-þracu; *gen.* -þræce; *f. Violence or tumultuous movement of flames*:—Æfter lígþræce *after the fire has spent its force*, Exon. 59 a; Th. 213, 15; Ph. 225.

líg-ýþ, e; *f. A wave of flame*, Beo. Th. 5338; B. 2672.

líht. v. leóht.

líhtan; *p.* te *To shine, lighten, give light*:—Hit líht *fulminat*, Ælfc. Gr. 22; Som. 24, 7. Ðæt leóht lýht on þýstrum *lux in tenebris lucet*, Jn. Skt. 1, 5. Se móna líht on niht, Bt. 21; Fox. 74, 25. Swá swá ðæt leóhtfæt liéht on nieht úrum eágum, ðætte ða gewritu on dæg liéhten úrum móde, Past. 48, 1; Swt. 365, 15. Líhteþ *luceat*, Ps. Surt. ii. 202, 11: Exon. 64 a; Th. 237, 9; Ph. 587. Wedercondel (*the sun*) wearm weorodum lýhteþ, 58 b; Th. 210, 18; Ph. 187. Ne hér dæg lýhteþ *day shines not here*,

Cd. 215; Th. 271, 14; Sat. 105. Lîhte *aurorescerent*, Wrt. Voc. ii. 88, 54. Đã dæg lȳhte *at dawn*, 180; Th. 225, 23; Dan. 158: Andr. Kmbl. 2794; An. 1399: Exon. 21 b; Th. 58, 21; Cri. 939. Swã se lîgræsc lȳhtende scînþ *sicut fulgor coruscans fulget*, Lk. Skt. 17, 24. Hē wæs byrnende leóhtfæt and lȳhtende *ille erat lucerna ardens et lucens*, Jn. Skt. 5, 35. Sumre niwre gyfe lîhtendre *nova quadam relucente gratia*, Bd. 5, 22; S. 644, 26. [*Goth.* liuhtjan: *O. Sax.* lióhtian: *Icel.* lȳsa: *O. H. Ger.* liuhtjan: *Ger.* leuchten.] DER. ā-, geond-, in-, on- lîhtan; *and see* leóhtan.

lîhtan; *p.* te. I. *to make light* or *easy, to alleviate, relieve, assuage*:—Lîht đæt đone swencendan magan *that relieves the labouring stomach*, L. M. 2, 7; Lchdm. ii. 186, 20: 2, 44; Lchdm. ii. 256, 13. Gif đǣr hwylc wîteþeówman sȳ būtan đyson hió gelȳfþ tō hyre bearnon đæt hî hine willon lȳhtan for hyre sâulle *if there be any penal slave besides these, she trusts to her children that they will relieve* (*release*, v. lîhting) *him for her soul's sake*, Chart. Th. 535, 38. Đā wolde ic mînne þurst lēhtan *sitim levare cupiens*, Nar. 8, 28. II. *to relieve of a burden, to light, alight*:—Hē lȳhte of his horse *he alighted from his horse*, Bd. 3. 22; S. 553, 32. Đā lîhte se eorodman, 3, 9; S. 533, 33: H. R. 103, 17: Byrht. Th. 132, 28; By. 23. [*Icel.* lēhta *to lighten, ease, leave off what is laborious; O. H. Ger.* ga-lîhtjan *lenire, levare, relevare.*] DER. ā-, ge-lîhtan; *and see* leóhtian *to grow light.*

lîhte. v. leóhte.

lîhting, e; *f. Lighting, shining, illumination, giving light*:—On lîhtinge fȳres *in illuminatione ignis*, Ps. Spl. 77, 17. God geworhte đæt māre leóht tō đæs dæges lîhtinge, Gen. 1, 16. Đa steorran sint tō nihtlîcere lîhtinge gesceapene, Homl. Th. i. 110, 15. Mid sōđre sunnan lîhtincge ūre heortan âlîhte, Btwk. 196, 17. Nū is ǣlc dæg of đære sunnan lȳhtinge, Lchdm. iii. 234, 18. Hî (*the stars*) nabbaþ nāne lȳhtinge for đære sunnan andwerdnysse, 236, 1. Se mōna næfþ nāne lîhtincge *the moon shall not give her light*, Wulfst. 137, 12. Đæt swearte fȳr him nāne lîhtinge ne dēþ '*from those flames no light*,' Homl. Th. i. 132, 17. Healde man ǣlces sunnandæges freólsunga fram nōntîde đæs Sæternes dæges ōþ đæs mōnandæges lîhtinge, L. Edg. i. 5; Th. i. 264, 20: Wulfst. 117, 4: 207, 12. Đæt đa gesceaftu gesewenlîce wurdon þurh đæs dæges lîhtinge, Hexam. 4; Norm. 8, 3. Lîhtunge *coruscationes*, Ps. Spl. T. 76, 18. DER. ā-, on-lîhting. v. leóhting.

lîhting, e; *f. Lightening, alleviation, relief, mitigation, release*:—Đis is seó lîhtinge đe ic wylle eallon folce gebeorgan đe hig ǣr đyson mid gedrehte wǣron ealles tō swȳđe *this is the relief that I will secure to all folk in regard to matters with which they were ere this all too much harassed*, L. C. S. 70; Th. i. 412, 18. Đonne biþ him geseald his synna lîhtingc *then shall a release from his sins be given him*, L. Pen. 18; Th. ii. 286, 3. Gif đæt riht tō hefig sȳ sēce siđđan đa lîhtinge tō đam cynge, L. Edg. ii. 2; Th. i. 266, 12.

lîhting-ness, e; *f. Lightness of taxation*; levitas tributi, L. I. P. 3; Th. ii. 306, 22.

lîht-lîce. v. leóht-lîce.

lîht-ness, e; *f. Lightness, brightness*:—Se sunnandæg is wuldorlîc dæg and lîhtnesse dæg, Wulfst. 230, 12. [*O. H. Ger.* liuht-nissa *illuminatio.*] DER. ā-lîhtness.

lilie, lilige, an; *f. A lily*:—Lilie *lilium*, Ælfc. Gl. 39; Som. 63, 60; Wrt. Voc. 30, 10. Liliæ. Đās wyrt man lilie and ōđrum naman *lilium* nemneþ, Herb. 109; Lchdm. i. 222, 5. Lilige, Lchdm. iii. 24, 9. Genim đa twā wyrta, đæt is, lilie and rōse; ber tō bearneácenum wîfe . . . gif heó nimþ lilian, heó cenþ cnyht; gif heó nimþ rōsan, heó cænþ mǣden, 144, 10–13. Đeáh đe lilie sȳ beorht on blōstman ic eom betre đonne heó, Exon. 110b; Th. 423, 24; Rä. 41, 27. Drince hē lilian wyrttruman āwylledne on wîne, L. M. 1, 37; Lchdm. ii. 90, 13. Genim neoþeweardelilian, Lchdm. i. 374, 6. Godes gelaþung hæfþ on sibbe lilian, đæt is clǣne drohtnung; on đam gewinne, rōsan, đæt is martyrdōm, Homl. Th. ii. 546, 2. Besceáwiaþ æcyres lilian, Mt. Kmbl. 6, 28: Lk. Skt. 12, 27. [*O. Sax.* lilli: *Icel.* lilja: *O. H. Ger.* lilia; *f.*; lilio; *m*: *Ger.* lilie.]

LIM, es; *n.* (but it also occurs with adj. fem. :). *A limb, joint, member of a body, branch of a tree*:—Ān lim *membrum*; mā lima *membra*, Wrt. Voc. 70, 20, 21. Gif men cîne hwylc lim, genim regen mela, dō on đæt lim, L. M. 1, 73; Lchdm. ii. 148, 22. Be đæs limes (*the finger*) micelnysse, Homl. Th. ii. 204, 6. Limes dǣl *commata* (*commota*, Wrt.) Wrt. Voc. ii. 20, 25. On ǣlcre lime, L. M. 2, 64; Lchdm. ii. 288, 22. Wid foredum lime *for a broken limb*, 1, 25; Lchdm. ii. 66, 22, 26. Ne biþ nān tō đæs lytel liþ on lime āweaxen, Soul Kmbl. 192; Seel. 96. Ic nān lim onstyrian ne mihte *I could not stir a limb*, Bd. 5, 6; S. 619, 26. Hafa đînne niéxtan swā swā đîn āgen lim, Basil Admn. 5; Norm. 44, 24. Monegu limu beóþ on ānum men, and weorþaþ đeáh ealle tō ānum lîchoman, Bt. 34, 6; Fox 140, 25. Gif wē tō lange sittaþ, slapaþ đa lima, Homl. Th. i. 490, 1. Gē sindon Cristes lîchama and leomu (cf. *Icel.* Guđs, fjándans limir), ii. 276, 19. Unrihtwîse syndon deófles leomo, Blickl. Homl. 33, 8. Đæs biscopes leoma on đysse byrigenne syndon betȳned, Bd. 2, 1; S. 500, 22. Leomu gnornian *the* (*leafless*) *branches* (*shall*) *mourn*, Exon. 89a; Th. 334, 35; Gn. Ex. 26. Ān đînra lima *unum membrorum tuorum*, Mt. Kmbl. 5, 29: Bd. 4. 9; S. 577, 17. Hē biþ Cristes lima ān, Wulfst. 37, 5. Þurh deófles ođđe his lima lāre, Cod. Dip. Kmbl. iii. 138, 16. Leoma, Blickl. Homl. 147, 15. Leomena, Salm. Kmbl. 205; Sal. 102. Fram ārleásum deófles limum, Homl. Th. i. 556, 8: Wulfst. 37, 7: Ps. Th. 21, 15. Ic geseó ōđre ǣ on mînum leomum . . . synne ǣ seó is on mînum limum, Bd. 1, 27; S. 497, 35–37. Leomum, Blickl. Homl. 33, 11: 167, 2. Leomum and leáfum *with branches and leaves*, Beo. Th. 194; B. 97. Hē ongan his limu þræstan, Bd. 3, 11; S. 536, 15. Hē his lima gesette and hine gerestan wolde, 4, 11; S. 579, 32. Limo 4, 24; S. 597, 10. Leomu, 2, 6; S. 508, 11. Âdyde đa leomu and đæt heáfod on weg đæs sceápes, Blickl. Homl. 183, 24. Leomo lǣmena, Exon. 8 a; Th. 2, 6; Cri. 15. [*Icel.* limr; *m. a limb, a joint* (*of an animal*): lim; *n. a branch*; limar; *pl. f. branches of a tree.*] DER. gecynd-, sceam- lim.

LÎM, es; *m.* LIME, *material which causes adhesion, cement, mortar, glue, gluten, bird lime, thick substance made of curds, paste*:—Ânes cynnes lîm *bitumen*, Ælfc. Gl. 56; Som. 67, 43; Wrt. Voc. 37, 31. Lîm tō fugele *gluten*; eglîm *glara*, Ælfc. Gl. 80, 81; Som. 72, 118, 119; Wrt. Voc. 47, 1, 2. Gebærnd lîm *calcis viva*, Wrt. Voc. ii. 127, 49. Lîm *cementum*, i. *cesura lapidis*, 130, 62: *bitumen*, 11, 8: *cola*, 20, 24: *gluten*, 40, 25: *glus*, 40, 72. Liim, caluuer *galmilla*, 109, 55. Lîm, molecgn *galmilla*, 40, 62. Liim, molegn, Ep. Gl. 10 f, 32. Lîm *calmilla*, Wrt. Voc. 290, 35: *gluten*, Ælfc. Gr. 9, 12; Som. 9, 30. Swā lîm gefæstnaþ fell tō sumum brede *as glue fastens a skin to a board*, 44; Som. 45, 25. Lîmes *calcis*, Wrt. Voc. ii. 19, 52. Âfæstnod ic eom on lîme grundes *infixus sum in limo profundi*, Ps. Spl. 68, 2. Ic beswîce fugelas mid lîme *decipio aves glutino*, Coll. Monast. Th. 25, 13. Eorþan lîme . . . đæt is syndrig cynn, symle biþ đȳ heardra đē hit swearte sǣstreámas swîđor beátaþ, Cd. 66; Th. 80, 2–10; Gen. 1322–1326. Þurh lîm *per cola*, Hpt. Gl. 411, 7. [*Icel.* lîm; *n. lime, glue, paste*: *O. H. Ger.* lîm *bitumen, gluten, viscus*: *Ger.* leim; *m.*] DER. æg-, fugel-, stān-lîm; and see ge-lîman, -lîmian.

limb-stefning, e; *f. An awning, curtain*; peripetasma, Ælfc. Gl. 116; Som. 80, 69; Wrt. Voc. 61, 46.

lim-gelecg, es; *n. The disposition* or *arrangement of the limbs, form, shape*:—Limgelecg *liniamento*, Wrt. Voc. ii. 52, 31.

lim-hâl; *adj. Sound of limb*, Exon. 42 b; Th. 143, 14; Gū. 661.

lîmian. v. ge-lîmian (*Appendix*).

lîming, e; *f. Daubing, plastering, cementing*:—Lîming *liture*, Wrt. Voc. ii. 52, 43. Lîminge *lituræ*, Hpt. Gl. 509, 54. [*A. R.* limung *joining*: *Icel.* lîming *glutinatio.*]

lim-lǣw, e; *f. Injury to the limbs, mutilation*:—Bendas ođđe dyntas . . . hwîlum lim-lǣwa and hwîlum lîflǣsta *bonds and blows . . . at times mutilations of the limbs, and at times deprivation of life*, L. Pen. 3, note; Th. ii. 278, 27. v. next word.

lim-lǣweo; *adj. Maimed* or *injured in the limbs*:—Gif limlǣweo (other MS. -læpeo) lama đe forworht wǣre weorþe forlǣten and hē æfter đam þreó niht âlibbe siđđan man mōt hylpan *if a criminal that has been mutilated be left, and he live after that three days, then he may be helped*, L. E. G. 10; Th. i. 172, 16. v. lēf, ge-lēfan, lēwsa *and preceding word.*

lim-lama; *adj. Lame in the limbs, crippled*:—Manege đǣr wurdan hāle, đe ǣr wǣran limmlaman, Wulfst. 4, 12.

lim-leás; *adj. Without limbs*:—His (*Christ's*) gāstlîca lîchama, đe wē hūsel hātaþ, is of manegum cornum gegaderod, būton blōde and bāne, limleás and sāwulleás, Homl. Th. ii. 270, 22.

lim-mǣlum; *adv. Limb-meal* (used by Shakspere in Cymbeline), *limb by limb, a limb at a time*:—Limmǣlum *membratim*, Wrt. Voc. ii. 54, 55: *membratim, particulatim*, Hpt. Gl. 443, 3: *membratim, per singula membra*, 486, 44. [*Laym.* he hine limmele todroh.]

lim-nacod; *adj. With uncovered limbs, naked*:—Se eádega wer [*Noah*] him selfa sceáf reáf of lîce; læg đā limnacod, Cd. 76; Th. 94, 23; Gen. 1566.

-limp. v. ge-, mis-limp.

limpan; *p.* lamp, *pl.* lumpon *To befall, happen, fall* (*to one's share*), *pertain, belong, affect, concern*:—Đa yfelan habbaþ gesǣlþa, and him gelimpþ (Cott. MS. limpþ) oft æfter heora āgnum willan, Bt. 39, 2; Fox 214, 5. Đa unrihtwîsan ne beóþ nā swylce ne him eác swā ne limpþ *non sic impii, non sic*, Ps. Th. 1, 5. Eádig biþ đæt folc đe him swā on foldan fægre limpeþ *beatum populum, cui hæc sunt*, 143, 19: Exon. 81 b; Th. 306, 26; Seef. 13. Hwæt limpeþ đæs tō đē of hwylcum wyrtruman ic âcenned sî *quid ad te pertinet qua sim stirpe genitus?* Bd. 1, 7; S. 477, 27. Sorgaþ ymb ōđerra monna wîsan đe him nāuht tō ne limpþ *is busied about other men's affairs, that do not all concern it*, Past. 53, 5; Swt. 415, 21. Đis sind đa landgemǣra đæs londes đe lympþ tō Stūre *these are the boundaries of the land that belongs to Stour*, Cod. Dip. Kmbl. iii. 81, 34. Hū lomp eów on lāde *what hap was yours by the way?* Beo. Th. 3978; B. 1987. Twegra sceopa đǣrtō đe limpende beóþ *of two ships that are thereto pertaining*, Chart. Th. 28, 26. [*O. H. Ger.* limphan, limfan *convenire.*] DER. ā-, be-, ge-limpan.

limp-lîce; *adv. Fitly, opportunely, conveniently*:—God swîđe limplîce geset đæt gewrixle eallum his gesceaftum, Bt. 21; Fox 74, 21.

lim-rǣden, e; *f. A cloak (?).* In Hpt. Gl. 465, 72 *limrǣdenne* is given as a marginal reading against *chlamide.*

lim-seóc; *adj. Having diseased limbs,* Andr. Kmbl. 1157; An. 579: Elen. Kmbl. 2425; El. 1214.

lim-wǣd, e; *f. A garment:*—Swâ limwǣdum *sicut vestimento,* Ps. Th. 103, 2.

lim-wæstm, es; *m. Limb-growth, stature, size of body:*—Ic eom limwæstmum ðæt ic gelutian ne mæg *so large am I of limb, that lie hid I cannot,* Cd. 216; Th. 273, 2; Sat. 130.

lim-wêrig; *adj. Having the limbs wearied:*—Âlêdon hié ðǣr limwêrigne, Rood Kmbl. 125; Kr. 63.

lîn, es; *n. Flax, linen, something made of linen:*—Flæx ɫ lîn *linum,* Mt. Kmbl. Rush. 12, 20. Lîn *manitergium,* Wrt. Voc. ii. 113, 44. Besweópun hine mid lîne *ligaverunt eum linteis,* Jn. Skt. Rush. 19, 40. Mid ðý onfêng ðæt lîn *cum accepisset linteum,* 13, 4. Bohte lîn and hine biwand in lîne *mercatus sindonem eum involvit sindone,* Mk. Skt. Rush. 15, 46: Lk. Skt. Rush. 23, 53. Gisæh ða lîn gisetedo *vidit linteamina posita,* Jn. Skt. Rush. 20, 6. [*Goth.* lein *linen*: *O. Sax.* lîn: *Icel.* lîn *flax, linen*: *O. H. Ger.* lîn *linum*: *Ger.* lein.] DER. biscop-, heáfod-, breóst-, hand-, swât- lîn.

lind, e; *and* linde, an; *f.* I. *the linden* or *lime-tree:*—Lind *seno* vel *tilia,* Ælfc. Gl. 45; Som. 64, 111; Wrt. Voc. 32, 46. Linde *tilie,* Wrt. Voc. ii. 75, 29. In ða greátan lindan; of ðære lindan, Cod. Dip. Kmbl. iii. 79, 24. On ða gemearcodan lindan; of ðære gemearcodan lindan, vi. 182, 2. Ðonon in âne linde, iii. 392, 1. II. *what is made of the wood of the tree, a shield* (in poetry):—Wisse hê gearwe, ðæt him holtwudu helpan ne meahte, lind wið lîge, Beo. Th. 4671; B. 2341. Ofer linde lǣrig, Cd. 154; Th. 192, 29; Exod. 239. Under linde *protected by the shield,* Andr. Kmbl. 91; An. 46. Leófsunu his linde âhôf, Byrht. Th. 138, 63; By. 244. Rond, geolwe linde, Beo. Th. 5213; B. 2610. On fyrd wegan fealwe linde, Cd. 94; Th. 123, 14; Gen. 2044. Under lindum, 154; Th. 192, 7; Exod. 228: 155; Th. 193, 23; Exod. 251. Bordum beþeahte, hwealfum lindum, Judth. 11; Thw. 24, 30; Jud. 214. Beraþ linde forþ, Thw. 24, 16; Jud. 191. Scyldas wêgon, linde bǣron, Byrht. Th. 134, 45; By. 99: Beo. Th. 4719; B. 2365. Hwîte linde, Cd. 158; Th. 107, 4; Exod. 301. [*Icel.* lind *a lime-tree; poet. a shield, a spear*: *O. H. Ger.* linta *tilia*: *Ger.* linde.] DER. heaðu-lind; *and see* linden.

lind-croda, an; *m. Shield-press, battle,* Cd. 93; Th. 120, 21; Gen. 1998.

linden; *adj. Made of the lime-tree:*—Scyld, leóht linden bord, Exon. 90 b; Th. 339, 16; Gn. Ex. 95.

Lindisfaran; *pl. Name of people settled in part of Northumbria* (the word occurs generally with *eá* or *eá-land*):—Ôswald Aidanum on Lindesfarona eálonde biscopsetl forgeaf (*in insula Lindisfarnensi*): on Lindesfearona eá, Bd. 3, 3; S. 525, 20, 35. Lǣdde mon his lîchoman tô Lindisfarena eá, 3, 17; S. 543, 37, col. 2. Mid ðâm brôðrum ðære cyricean æt Lindisfarena *a fratribus ecclesiæ Lindesfarnensis,* pref; S. 472, 29. Is Cynebyrht Lindisfarena biscop *provinciæ Lindisfarorum Cyneberct episcopus præest,* 5, 24; S. 646, 22. Hêr forþferde Higbald Lindisfarna biscop, Chr. 803; Erl. 61, 22. Hê wæs on ðam munuclîfe ðe is Lindisfarneá gehâten, Homl. Th. ii. 142, 6.

Lindisfarnensisc; *adj. Of Lindisfarne:*—Se hâlga Cûþberhtus, Lindisfarnensiscere gelaþunge leódbiscop, Homl. Th. ii. 148, 22.

Lindesse, Lindisse, Lindesîge *Lindsey, the northern part of Lincolnshire* [Lat. Lindi colonia]:—Lǣrde Scs. Paulinus Godes word on Lindesse: seó mǣgþ is seó nýhste on sûþhalfe Humbre streámes, ligeþ ût on sǣ, Bd. 2, 16; S. 519, 18. On Lindesêge mǣgþe, 519, 16. On Lindese, 3, 11; S. 535, 14. On Lindesse and on Eást-Englum, Chr. 838; Erl. 66, 13: 873; Erl. 76, 19: 874; Erl. 76, 21. Lindisse, 627; Erl. 25, 5. On Lindesîge ge on Norþhymbran, 993; Erl. 133, 4: 1013; Erl. 147, 20: 1014; Erl. 151, 2. His lýchama resteþ on Lyndesse mǣgþe Shrn. 155, 24.

Lindis-ware; *pl. The people of Lindsey:*—Man gehâlgode Lindiswarum tô biscope Eádhêd; se wæs on Lindissi ǣrost biscopa, Chr. 678; Erl. 41, 8.

lind-geborga, an; *m. A protector bearing a shield, a warlike protector* [?]. v. leód-hwæt.

lind-gecrod, es; *n. A shield-bearing crowd,* Andr. Kmbl. 2442; An. 1222.

lind-gelâc, es; *n. A shield-conflict, battle,* Apstls. Kmbl. 151; Ap. 76.

lind-gestealla, an; *m. A companion in arms,* Beo. Th. 3950; B. 1973.

lind-hæbbende; *part. as noun. Shield-bearer, warrior,* Beo. Th. 495; B. 245: 2808; B. 1402.

lind-hôh; *gen.* -hôs; *m. A* hôh [q. v.] *where lime-trees are growing* [?]:—On lindhôh; of lindhô, Cod. Dip. Kmbl. iii. 76, 33.

lind-hrycg, es; *m. A ridge on which lime-trees are growing* [?]:—On lindrycg; of lindrycge, Cod. Dip. Kmbl. iii. 79, 20.

lind-plega, an; *m. Shield-play, battle,* Beo. Th. 4085; B. 2039: [MS. hild-] 2151; B. 1073.

lind-weorud, es; *n. A band armed with shields,* Elen. Kmbl. 283; El. 142.

lind-wîga, an; *m. A warrior armed with a shield,* Beo. Th. 5199; B. 2603.

lind-wîgend, -wiggend, es; *m. A warrior armed with a shield,* Bt. Met. Fox 1, 25; Met. 1, 13: Judth. 10; Thw. 22, 1; Jud. 42: Elen. Kmbl. 539; El. 270.

lîne, an; *f.* I. *a line, rope, a coil of rope:*—Langre lînan *with a long line,* Salm. Kmbl. 589; Sal. 294. Lînan *spiræ,* Ælfc. Gl. 104; Som. 78, 14; Wrt. Voc. 56, 60. II. *a line, row, line for guidance, rule, canon:*—Þurh ðæs cantices cwide, Cristes lînan [*the rule laid down by Christ in the Lord's Prayer*], Salm. Kmbl. 34; Sal. 17. Ðǣr sceal wesan se torhta æsc ân an lînan âcas twegen hægelas swâ some 'æ' *must occur once,* 'a' *and* 'h' *twice* [*in forming the words* hæn, hana], Exon. 112 a; Th. 429, 25; Rä. 43, 10. [*Icel.* lîna *a line* (*cord*), *line* (mathem.): *O. H. Ger.* linna *linea.*] DER. sceát-, steding-, sund-, toh-lîne.

lînen; *adj. Made of flax, linen:*—Lînen *lineum*: lînen wearp *linostema,* Ælfc. Gl. 62, 63; Som. 68, 97, 98; Wrt. Voc. 40, 6, 8. Lînnin rýhae *villa,* Ep. Gl. 28 d, 19. Lînen *byssina,* Hpt. Gl. 526, 31. Hig bewundon hine mid lînenum clâþe [lînninum hræglum, Lind.] *ligaverunt eum linteis,* Jn. Skt. 19, 40. Mid lînenum reáfe *subucula linea,* Lev. 8, 7: Past. 14, 4; Swt. 83, 23. Lînen hrægel *linteum,* Jn. Skt. 13, 4. Hió becwiþ lînnenne cyrtel oððe lînnen web *she bequeathes a linen kirtle or a piece of linen,* Chart. Th. 537, 24. Ne hê wyllenra hrægla breác ac lînenra ealra, Shrn. 93, 8. [*O. H. Ger.* lînin *lineus*: *Ger.* leinen.]

lînen-werd; *adj. Dressed in linen:*—Hê wæs lînenwerd and his lændena wǣron ymbgirde *he was clothed in linen, and his loins were girded,* L. Ælfc. P. 17; Th. ii. 370, 11. [Cf. wolleward *dressed in woollen garments,* Piers P. B. 18, 1.]

lînete, an; *f. A linnet* [*for connection with* lîn cf. *Ger.* hanf *hemp,* hänfling *linnet*]:—Lînete *cardella,* Wrt. Voc. 62, 46.

lîne-twige, -twigle, an; *f. A linnet:*—Lînetwige *carduelis,* Wrt. Voc. ii. 13, 43: 103, 13: *fronulus,* 36, 3. Lînetuigle *fronulus,* 109, 14. Cf. þisteltuige *cardella,* 102, 76. [Cf. *Scot.* lyntquhit *a linnet.*]

-ling. v. deór-, eorþ-, geong-, hæft-, hýr-, nîd-ling.

-ling, -linga, -lunga. v. bæc-, ears-, hinder-ling; bæc-, grund-, hand-linga.

lîn-hǣwen; *adj. Flax-coloured* [?]:—Þurh lînhǣwenne clâþ, Lchdm. iii. 2, 23: 4, 22.

linian, leonian *to leave* [?]:—Ic leonige ôðrum eorþcyningum tô bysne ðæt hié witen ðý gearwor ðæt mîn þrym and mîn weorþmynd mâran wǣron ðonne ealra ôðra kyninga ðe in middangearde ǣfre wǣron *I leave it* [*an account of my exploits*] *as an example to other kings, that they may the better know that my glory and honour were greater than all other kings that ever were in the world,* Nar. 33, 2. v. â-linian.

lîn-land, es; *n. Land where flax grows:*—Ðæt lytle lînland, Cod. Dip. Kmbl. iii. 19, 4. [Cf. *Icel.* lîn-akr.]

linnan; *p.* lann, *pl.* lunnon *To cease, leave off, desist, part from, lose:*—Blǣd his blinniþ blisse linniþ [-aþ MS.] listum [lissum?] linneþ *his glory comes to an end, he ceases from joy, desists from delights,* Exon. 95 a; Th. 354, 30; Reim. 53. Lunnon sâwlum *they parted from their souls* i. e. *they died,* Cd. 167; Th. 209, 9; Exod. 496. Ealdre linnan *to die,* Exon. 88 a; Th. 330, 21; Vy. 54: An. 2277; An. 1139: Beo. Th. 2960; B. 1478. Ealdres linnan, 4878; B. 2443. [*Goth.* af-linnan: *Icel.* linna: *O. H. Ger.* bi-linnan.] DER. â-linnan, blinnan [= be-linnan], â-, ge-blinnan.

lîn-sǣd, es; *n. Linseed:*—Lînsǣd *elimos* vel *lini semen,* Wrt. Voc. 69, 32. Mid lînsǣde, Herb. 39, 3; Lchdm. i. 140, 13.

lîn-wǣd, e; *f. A linen garment, linen cloth:*—Hê drîgde hig mid ðære lînwǣde ðe hê wæs mid begyrd *coepit extergere linteo quo erat praecinctus,* Jn. Skt. 13, 5. Hê geseah ða lînwǣda licgan *videt posita linteamina,* 20, 5: Lk. Skt. 24, 12. [*O. H. Ger.* lîn-wât *linteamen.*]

lîn-wyrt, e; *f. Flax,* L. M. 1, 25; Lchdm. ii. 66, 17: 3, 65; Lchdm. ii. 354, 10.

lippa, an; *m. A lip:*—Ufeweard lippa *labium*: niðera lippe *labrum*: foreweard feng ðære lippena, tôgædere *rostrum,* Ælfc. Gl. 71; Som. 70, 93–95; Wrt. Voc. 43, 24–26. Lippan *labia,* Hpt. Gl. 481, 24. Âwergode beón heora tungan and lippan, Wanl. Catal. 137, 51. Wið lippe sâr. Eft sôna ðes lǣcedôm sceal ðan manne ða hyra lippa beóþ sâre oððe hyra tunga . . . smire mid ða lippa, Lchdm. iii. 100, 15–21. [*O. Frs.* lippa; *m*: cf. *O. L. Ger.* lepor: *O. H. Ger.* leffur *labium*: lefs *labium.*]

lira, an; *m. Fleshy part of the body without fat or bone, brawn:*—Lira *pulpa* vel *viscum,* Ælfc. Gl. 73; Som. 71, 37; Wrt. Voc. 44, 21. Lira *pulpa,* Wrt. Voc. 65, 12: 290, 48: ii. 76, 10. Sâr þeóh and lira *the thigh and the fleshy parts are sore,* L. M. 2, 51; Lchdm. ii. 264, 11. Ða liran ðara lendena sâriaþ *the fleshy parts of the loins get sore,* 2, 25; Lchdm. ii. 216, 24. [Toleac lið ba and lire *broke both joints and flesh,* Jul. 59, 10. Lire *the flesh of an animal* or *rather the increasing substance as it grows bulky,* E. D. S. Whitby Glossary. See also Halliw. Dict. *Scot.* lire *flesh or muscles, as distinguished from the bones.*] DER. ears-, spear-lira.

lireht; *adj. Brawny, fleshy:*—Hî habbaþ lirehte fêt, L. M. 2, 36; Lchdm. ii. 242, 14.

lísan, lýsan; *p.* de *To loosen, release, redeem, deliver*:—Mín sáwl ða ðú sylf lýsdest *anima mea, quam redemisti*, Ps. Th. 70, 21. Se sylfa cyning mid síne líchoman lýsde of firenum, Exon. 25 b; Th. 74, 22; Cri. 1210. Gif hé ða hand lésan [álýsan, MS. H; lýsan, MS. B.] wille . . . gelde swá tó his were belimpe, L. Alf. pol. 6; Th. i. 66, 5: Byrht. Th. 132, 57; By. 37: Elen. Kmbl. 592; El. 296: Rood Kmbl. 82; Kr. 41. [*Goth.* lausjan: *O. Sax.* lósian: *O. Frs.* lésa: *Icel.* leysa: *O. H. Ger.* lósen: *Ger.* lösen.] v. á-, ge-, on-, tó-lísan; untólísende.

lísian *to release, redeem*:—Gif hé on hand gán wille dó hine man on carcern swá hit æt Greátanleá gecweden wæs and hine be ðam ylcan lýsige *if he is ready to submit, let him be put in prison, as it was determined at Greatanlea* [v. Th. i. 198], *and according to the same let him be redeemed*, L. Æthelst. v. 12; Th. i. 240, 33.

lísing, es; *m. A freedman*:—Lísingas and þeówe, Chart. Th. 592, 1. Búton ðam ceorle ðe on gafollande sit, and heora [*the Danes*] liésingum [lýsingum]; ða syndan efendýre, ǽgðer tó cc. scill., L. A. G. 2; Th. i. 154, 3. [*Icel.* leysingi, leysingr *a freedman.*]

lísing, e; *f. A loosing, releasing, redemption*:—Lésing *redemtio*, Lk. Skt. Lind. 2, 38. v. á-, crism-lísing.

lisne, Ps. Th. 52, 6. v. [?] lyswen.

lís-ness, e; *f. Redemption, release, deliverance*; redemtio, Mk. Skt. Lind. Rush. 10, 45: Lk. Skt. Lind. Rush. 1, 68: 2, 38. DER. á-, tó-lísness.

lisnian. v. be-lisnian.

liss, e; *f. Mildness, lenity, mercy, kindness, favour, grace, delight, joy*:—Hé bæd ðæt Lazarus móste his tungan drýpan ac him næs getíðod ðære lytlan lisse *he prayed that Lazarus might put a drop of water on his tongue; but that little favour was not granted to him*, Homl. Th. i. 330, 30. Ic ðé biddan wile lífes and lisse *I will ask thee for life and favour*, Ps. C. 50, 69; Ps. Grn. ii. 278, 69. Hé þancode lífes leóhtfruman lisse and ára, Cd. 90; Th. 113, 19; Gen. 1889. Hé him ðære lisse leán forgildeþ *he will requite him for that grace* [*honouring God*], Exon. 14 a; Th. 27, 21; Cri. 434. Ða eádigan ceasterwaran gefeóþ and wynsumiaþ on lisse and on blisse and on écum gefeán, Wulfst. 265, 12. Lifgan in lisse lucis et pacis *to live in the delight of light and peace*, Exon. 656; Th. 242, 12; Ph. 672. Hé onfón sceal blisse mínre lufan and lisse *he shall receive my joy, my love and my favour*, Cd. 106; Th. 140, 23; Gen. 2332: 190; Th. 237, 19; Dan. 340. Forgif mé tó lisse bitre bealodǽde *in mercy to me forgive my evil deeds*, Exon. 118 a; Th. 453, 21; Hy. 4, 18. Lífes tó lisse *to save life*, Andr. Kmbl. 2223; An. 1113. Lisse ic gelýfe leahtra gehwylces *I believe in the forgiveness of sins*, Hy. Grn. ii. 294, 54. Se rinc on líchoman lisse sóhte *Enoch while yet in the body sought* [*heaven's*] *joy*, Cd. 60; Th. 73, 14; Gen. 1204. Ðé is ǽðelstól gerýmed, lisse on lande, 73; Th. 89, 25; Gen. 1486. Ic ðé lissa lifigendum giet lǽte brúcan, 126; Th. 161, 10; Gen. 2663: 136; Th. 171, 6; Gen. 2824: Exon. 13 a; Th. 23, 24; Cri. 373: Beo. Th. 4306; B. 2150. Wilna biscirede, lufena and lissa, Exon. 48 b; Th. 166, 27; Gú. 1049. Lufum and lissum, Cd. 130; Th. 165, 25; Gen. 2737. Wé ðé getǽhton land tó lissum ðú ús leánest nú unfreóndlíce *we assigned thee land for thy delight, now dost thou repay us in fashion unfriendly*, 127; Th. 162, 28; Gen. 2688. Lissum *kindly, graciously*, Andr. Kmbl. 1735; An. 870. v. líðs

lissan *to soften, weaken, tame, subdue*:—Yldo beoþ on eorþan ǽghwæs cræftig . . . lisseþ eal ðæt heó wile beám heó ábreóteþ . . . friteþ wildne fugol . . . heó oferwígeþ wulf *on earth age has power over everything . . . she subdues all that she will; the tree she destroys . . . the wild bird she devours . . . the wolf she conquers*, Salm. Kmbl. 590; Sal. 294. [Cf. I trowe my peyne shalle never *lisse*, Chauc. R. R. 4128: it shulde *lisse* me, Gow. iii. 82, 19: hire care to *lisse*, Will. 631. Jamieson gives the verb in his Scottish Dict. lis *to ease, assuage*; liss *to cease, stop.*] v. liss.

list, es; *m*: list, e; *f. Art, skill, craft, cunning, artifice*:—Lot sceal mid lyswe list mid gedéfum *cunning goes with evil, skill with things proper*, i. e. lot *and* list *are the names for a corresponding vice and virtue*, Exon. 92 a; Th. 345, 17; Gn. Ex. 189. Ðú miht león and dracan liste gebýgean *conculcabis leonem et draconem*, Ps. Th. 90. 13. List *art* (*of poetry*), Bt. Met. Fox Introd. 5; Met. Einl. 3: Exon. 79 a; Th. 296, 13; Crä. 50. Þurh ealle list, 27 a; Th. 81, 5; Cri. 1319. Ðæs líchoman listas and cræftas of ðæm móde cumaþ *the arts and powers of the body come from the mind*; intus est hominum vigor arce conditus abdita, Bt. Met. Fox 26, 216; Met. 26, 108. Hé fela onginþ leornian lista *many arts doth he learn*, 28, 153; Met. 28, 77: Cd. 13; Th. 16, 5; Gen. 239. Mid listum speón idese on ðæt unriht *with wiles he lured the woman to that wrong*, 28; Th. 37, 12; Gen. 588: 32; Th. 43, 8; Gen. 687. Listum *skilfully, craftily, cunningly*:—Him listum áteáh rib of sídan *skilfully drew a rib from his side*, 9; Th. 11, 19; Gen. 177: 77; Th. 95; 29; Gen. 1586; Judth. 10; Thw. 23, 2; Jud. 101: Bt. Met. Fox 13, 84; Met. 13, 42: 1, 118; Met. 1, 59: Beo. Th. 1566; B. 781: Ps. Th. 87, 10. Wyl tógædere listum *boil them skilfully together*, L. M. 1, 1; Lchdm. ii. 24, 11: 1, 2; Lchdm. ii. 26, 8. Hé ðé hét listas lǽran *he bade teach thee arts*, Cd. 25; Th. 33, 8; Gen. 517. [*Goth.* lists: *O. Sax.* list: *O. Frs.* lest: *Icel.* list; *f*: *O. H. Ger.* list; *m. f. ars, ingenium, astutia, peritia*: *Ger.* list; *f.*]

líste, an; *f. A list, hem, border, selvage*:—Líste *lembus*, Wrt. Voc. ii. 113, 1: 50, 68. Lístan *lembum*, 112, 54. Lístum, *lembus*, 50, 69. [*Icel.* lista; *f*: listi; *m. list, border*: *O. H. Ger.* lísta; *f. limbus, fimbria*: *Ger.* leiste.]

list-hendig; *adj. Having skilful hands*:—Sum biþ listhendig tó áwrítanne wordgerýnu, Exon. 79 b; Th. 299, 1; Crä. 95.

listig-, liste-líce; *adv. Skilfully*: Seóð æt leóhtum fýre listelíce, L. M. 1, 2; Lchdm. ii. 30, 7.

list-wrenc, es; *m. Wile, artifice*, Lye. v. lot-wrenc.

lítan [*from* lútan, *as* bígan *from* búgan] *to cause to bow, to bend, incline*:—Ðæt ingeþonc ǽlces monnes ðone líchoman lít ðider hit wile *the mind of every man inclines the body whither it will*, Bt. Met. Fox 26, 237; Met. 26, 119.

lite-líce. v. lytig-líce.

liþ, es; *m. n. A joint, lith* [Scott. e. g. the Laird of Auchinleck to Johnson, Cromwell 'gart kings ken they had a *lith* in their necks'], *member of the body, limb*:—Liþ *artus*: lytel liþ *articulus*, Wrt. Voc. 283, 16, 17: Soul Kmbl. 191; Seel. 96. Ðætte sum man fram deáþes liþe wæs gehǽled *ut sit quidam a mortis articulo revocatus*, Bd. 3, 13; S. 538, 3. Ðæt hé dyppe his fingres liþ on wætere *that he may dip the tip of his finger in water*, Lk. Skt. 16, 24. On ðone liþ ðæra eaxla, L. M. 2, 36; Lchdm. ii. 242, 12. On ðæt liþ, 1, 61; Lchdm. ii. 132, 6. Liþu *artus*, Wrt. Voc. 64, 77. Ða máran liþa *artus*, Ælfc. Gl. 72; Som. 71, 4; Wrt. Voc. 43, 58. Gif men his leoþu acen, Herb. 3, 1; Lchdm i. 86, 21. Foxes leoþu, L. Med. ex Quad. 3, 1; Lchdm. i. 338, 20: Exon. 87 a; Th. 327, 18; Vy. 6: 74 a; Th. 278, 3; Jul. 592. Sint mé leoþ tólocen líc sáre gebrocen, Andr. Kmbl. 2807; An. 1406. Býgendlíc on ðám geþeódnessum his liþa *flexilibus artuum compagibus*, Bd. 4, 30; S. 608, 38. Betwyh liþum *inter femora*, L. Ecg. P. iv. 68, 6; Th. ii. 228, 24. Hé ðé worhte of liþum mínum, Cd. 38; Th. 50, 33; Gen. 818. Leoþum onfón, Exon. 23 a; Th. 64, 3; Cri. 1032. Liþa *articulos*, Hpt. Gl. 443, 61. Bígdon heora heáfda tó ðære hálgena fótum and heora liþa liccodon, Homl. Skt. 4, 407. Of láme ic ðé leoþe gesette, Exon. 28 a; Th. 84, 31; Cri. 1382. Leoþo, Andr. Kmbl. 1562; An. 782. Leomena liþ, Salm. Kmbl. 205; Sal. 102. [*Goth.* liþus; *m. a limb, member*: *O. Sax.* lið; *m*: *O. Frs.* lith; *n*: *Icel.* liðr; *m. a joint, limb*: *O. H. Ger.* lid; *m. n. artus, articulus, membrum*: *Ger.* g-lied.] v. hrycgmearh-liþ, leoþu-.

líþ, es; *n. Strong drink*:—Ðá him ðæt líþ gescired wæs *digesto vino*, Past. 40, 4; Swt. 295, 6. Ðam men ðe hine ne lyst his metes ne líþes *for the man that does not care for his meat or drink*, L. M. 1, 19; Lchdm. ii. 62, 16. Of mistlícum dryncum ðæs líþes *from various strong drinks*, Bt. 37, 1; Fox 186, 17. Se ðe ús oferdrencþ mid ðæs écan lífes líþe *aeterna nos dulcedine inebrians*, Past. 36, 9; Swt. 261, 15. Ðá bær unc mon líþ forþ *oblato poculo*, Bd. 5, 3; S. 616, 31. [*Goth.* leiþus οἶκερα: *O. Sax.* líð: *O. Frs.* líth: *Icel.* líð *cider*: *O. H. Ger.* líd, líth *potus, liquor, poculum, fiala, sicera*: *it remains in some provincial German words*, e. g. leit-haus *an ale-house*; leit-geber *keeper of an ale-house.*]

liþ, es; *n.* [*The Scandinavian form of* lid q. v.] *a fleet*:—Ðæs sumeres com ðet liþ of Humbran *in the course of the summer the fleet came from the Humber*, Chr. 1070; Erl. 210, 4: 1052; Erl. 183, 12: 1069; Erl. 207, 12. [*Icel.* lið *a host* by land or sea.]

líð; *adj.* v. líðe.

Líða, an; *m. Name of the months June and July*:—Se mónaþ is nemned on lǽden Iunius, and on úre geþeóde se ǽrra Líða, for ðon seó lyft biþ ðonne smylte and ða windas. Ond monnum biþ ðonne gewunelíc ðæt hí líðaþ ðonne on sǽs bryme, Shrn. 87, 34. Se ǽrra Lýða, 99, 11. Ǽrra Líða, Junius, Menol. Fox 213; Men. 108. Mónaþ ðone wé nemnaþ on lýden Iulius . . . ðone mónaþ wé nemnaþ on úre geþeóde se æftera Lýða, Shrn. 99, 26: 110, 24. [iþe moneþ ꝥ on ure ledene is ald englisch efterlið inempnet iulius o latin, Marh. 23, 6.] v. Grmm. Gesch. D. S. 56 sqq.

liþ-ádl, e; *f. Gout*:—Liþádl *artericus* vel *artriticus*, Ælfc. Gl. 11; Som. 57, 44; Wrt. Voc. 19, 47. Wið liþádle, L. Med. ex Quad. 3, 11; Lchdm. 1, 340, 25.

líðan; *p.* láð *To go* [generally by sea], *sail*:—Ic tólíðe, ic líðe *applicabo*, Wrt. Voc. ii. 4, 54. Monnum biþ gewunelíc ðæt hí líðaþ ðonne [ǽrra Líða, *June*] on sǽs bryme, Shrn. 88, 1. Ða ðe sǽ sécеaþ mid scipe líðaþ *qui descendunt mare in navibus*, Ps. Th. 106, 22. Hé ofer sǽ láð in Gallia ríce *navigavit Galliam*, Bd. 3, 19; S. 550, 1: Shrn. 60, 5. Se cyning sylfa and se hálga bisceop liðan on ðæt ealond *rex ipse cum sanctissimo antistite insulam navigavit*, Bd. 4, 28; S. 606, 12. Nú is ðon gelícost swá wé on laguflóde ofer cald wæter ceólum líðan, Exon. 20 a; Th. 53, 18; Cri. 852. Líðan cymeþ *comes sailing*, Exon. 90 b; Th. 340, 11; Gn. Ex. 109: 108 b; Th. 415, 23; Rä. 34, 1: Andr. Kmbl. 512; An. 256: Bt. Met. Fox 26, 119; Met. 26, 60. Liðendum wuda *a ship*, Exon. 103 b; Th. 392, 9; Rä. 11, 5. Ða líðende land gesáwon *those sailing saw land*, Beo. Th. 447; B. 221. Ðá wæs sund liden *then was the sea passed* [cf. *Icel.* líða *as a transitive verb*], Beo. Th. 452; B. 223. Dóhtor mín eácen up liden *my daughter, great and grown up* [?], Exon. 109 a; Th. 416, 13; Rä. 34, 11. [*Goth.* ga-leiþan: *O. Sax.* líðan: *Icel.* líða: *O. H. Ger.* ga-lídan *peregrinari, cedere, evanescere.*] DER. be-, for-, ge-, ofer-, tó-, ymb-líðan; brim-, eá-, heaðu-, mere-, sǽ-, scip-, wǽg-líðende.

līðan *to suffer loss* [?]:—Beám sceal leáfum līðan *a tree must lose its leaves*, Exon. 89 a; Th. 334, 34; Gn.Ex. 26. [Cf. (?) *O. H. Ger.* lîdan *to suffer.*]

līðan *to assuage, mitigate, soften*:—Ðæt se hié līðe and hǣle *foveantur sananda*, Past. 17, 10; Swt. 124, 12. v. līðian.

līðe, līð; *adj. Lithe, soft, gentle, meek, mild, serene, benign, gracious, pleasant, sweet*:—Swā fæder þenceþ his bearnum milde weorþan swā ūs God ðām ðe hine lufiaþ līðe weorþeþ *sicut miseretur pater filiis, ita misertus est Dominus timentibus se*, Ps. Th. 102, 13. Leorniaþ æt mē ðæt ic eom līðe and swīðe eádmōd *discite a me, quia mitis sum et humilis corde*, Homl. Th. i. 210, 18. Hē biþ ðām gōdum lufsum and līðe, Exon. 21 a; Th. 57, 5; Cri. 914. Ōðer [wæstm] wæs swā wynlīc wlitig and scēne līð *the other [fruit] was so delightful, beauteous and fair, delicate*, Cd. 23; Th. 30, 17; Gen. 468. Hwæðer him cume ðe rēþu wyrd ðe līðu *whether fortune foul or fair come to him*, Bt. 40, 3; Fox 238, 9. Līðe ł smilte *serenum*, Hymn. Surt. 24, 15. Hē forlēt eall ðæt ðǣr līðes wæs and swētes *vino epulisque deseruit*, Ors. 2, 4; Swt. 76, 14. Cumb fulne līðes aloþ *a coomb full of mid ale*, Cod. Dip. Kmbl. i. 203, 8: Chart. Th. 105, 12. Dreám līðes līfes *the joy of the serene life [of heaven]*, Exon. 32 a; Th. 100, 7; Cri. 1638. Mid līðre *mulsa*, Hpt. Gl. 481, 14. Mid līðra tungan *with lithe tongue*, Homl. Skt. 4, 407. Mid līðran gesceafte [*water*], Boutr. Scrd. 22, 30. Andwlitan mid līðan *vultu sereno*, Hymn. Surt. 22, 11: 143, 2. Mid līðere sprǣce *with gentle speech*, Ap. Th. 2, 25. Mid līðre wisðlunga mon hors gestilleþ *lenis sibilus equos mitigat*, Past. 23; Swt. 173, 21. On līðum wīne, Herb. 57, 1; Lchdm. i. 160, 1: 80, 2; Lchdm. i. 182, 19. Līðne (*lenis*) drenc, Bt. 39, 9; Fox 226, 12. Ðæt līðe land *the pleasant land*, Cd. 12; Th. 13, 31; Gen. 211. Eádige beóþ ða līðan ... Ða synd līðe and gedēfe, ða ðe ne wiðstandaþ yfelum, ac oferswȳðaþ mid heora goodnesse ðone yfelan, Homl. Th. i. 550, 19: Mt. Kmbl. 5, 5. Līðe æppla *mitia poma*, Ælfc. Gr. 47; Som. 48, 26. Nū ic freónda beþearf līðra on lāde *now need I gracious friends on my course*, Apstls. Kmbl. 183; Ap. 92. Hearda wunda beóþ mid līðum beðengum gehnescode *dura vulnera per lenia fomenta mollescunt*, Past. 26, 2; Swt. 183, 20. Swīðe līðum wordum *with very gentle words*; humanitatis lege eos mulcens, Nar. 25, 10: Exon. 37 b; Th. 124, 3; Gū. 334. Mid līðum styrungum *with gentle gestures*, Glostr. Frag. 110, 8. Lagu lācende sceal līðra wyrðan *the tossing wave shall become calmer*, Andr. Kmbl. 874; An. 437. Oft byþ ðæt brocc līðre *the disease is often less severe*, Wulfst. 12, 5. Ðǣr syndon lȳðran wedera ðonne on Brettania *coeli solique temperie magis utilis*, Ors. 1, 1; Swt. 24, 19. Se sceortigenda dæg hæfþ līðran gewederu ðonne se langienda dæg, Lchdm. iii. 252, 9. Līðesta *mittissime*, Hymn. Surt. 65, 11: 126, 2. Manna mildust, leódum līðost, Beo. Th. 6346; B. 3183. [*O. Sax.* līði: *Icel.* linr: *O. H. Ger.* linde lind *lenis, mollis*: *Ger.* ge-lind, -linde.] DER. cum-, gæst-, uncum-, un- līðe; v. līðig.

liþe-bīge. v. leoþu-bīge.

liðeg. v. līðig.

līðe-līc; *adj. Gentle, mild, soft*:—Līðelīce stefne *lena voce*, Nar. 36, 21. Mid līðelīcum wordum *with gentle words*, Past. 30, 2; Swt. 205, 8.

līðe-līce; *adv. Gently, mildly, softly, kindly, graciously*:—Līðelīce, fæg-ere *pedetemtim*, Wrt. Voc. ii. 64, 49. Hē hié līðelīce hǣlan wolde *graciously he would heal them*, Blickl. Homl. 105, 26. Līðelīce hē ādlaþ *he will have a mild attack of illness*, Lchdm. iii. 186, 15. Hwīlum līðelīce tō þreát-ianne hwīlum suīðlīce and stræclīce tō þrafianne *aliquando leniter arguenda, aliquando vehementer increpanda*, Past. 21, 1; Swt. 151, 11. Ðū scealt līðelīce monian *suadendo, blandiendo*, Bd. 1, 27; S. 492, 22. Sume þearflīcor sume līðelīcor synd gerihte *quidam districtius, quidam levius corrigantur*, S. 490, 11: L. C. S. 69; Th. i. 412, 5.

līðend, es; *m. A traveller, sailor*:—Līðend brohte elebeámes twig ān tō handa *the traveller (the dove) brought home an olive-branch* [Bouterwek takes *līðend* to be a dative; if it is, the word refers to Noah], Cd. 72; Th. 88, 29; Gen. 1472. v. sǣ-līðend, līðan.

līðercian; *p.* ode *To soften, charm, flatter*:—Līðercaþ, ōleccaþ *adulatur*, Wrt. Voc. ii. 127, 7. Līðercade *promulserit*, 117, 72. Līðircadae, Ep. Gl. 17 f, 30.

liðere, an; *f*: liðera, an; *m. A sling*:—Liðere *funda*, Wrt. Voc. 84, 34. Lydre, 35, 30. Liðre, Wrt. Voc. ii. 109, 41. Leðera *funda*: liðer-an *fundibulæ*, 36, 23, 24. Swā mycelre brǣdo swā mon mæg mid liðeran geworpan *amplitudinis quasi jactus fundæ*, Bd. 4, 13; S. 583, 11. Mid his liðeran ofwearp ðone geleáfleásan ent, Ælfc. T. Grn. 7, 18. Of blacere liðran, Salm. Kmbl. 54; Sal. 27. v. stæf-liðere.

liðeren. v. leðeren.

liðer-līc; *adj. Of a sling*:—Liðerlīcum swēge *fundali stridore*, Wrt. Voc. ii. 152, 16.

liþe-wāc, liþewǣcan. v. leoþu-wāc, leoþuwǣcan.

liþ-geat. v. hlid-geat.

līðian; *p.* ode *To be, become*, or *make* līðe [q. v.]:—Miltsige man for Godes ege and līðige man georne *let mercy be shewn for fear of God, and let kindness be diligently shewn*, L. Eth. vi. 53; Th. i. 328, 28. Swā hwæt swā gē gebindaþ hēr ofer eorþan eall hit wyrþ on heofenan mid Godes yrre gebunden būtan gē līðian *whatsoever ye bind on earth shall all be bound in heaven with God's anger, unless ye be gracious*, Wulfst. 178, 4. Biþ ðæs innoþes sār līðigende ðæt hit sōna nǣnig lāð ne biþ *the disease of the stomach will grow easier, so that soon it will be no annoyance*, Herb. 1, 11; Lchdm. i. 74, 10. [*Icel.* lina *to soften, alleviate, abate*: *O. H. Ger.* lindian *mollire, blandiri.*] DER. ge-, on-līðian; v. līðigian, līðan.

līðig; *adj. Lithe, pliant, supple, flexible, soft, yielding*:—Heó biþ līðig swā clāþ ongeán deófles lāre *it* [*a man's heart*] *is pliant as cloth to the devil's teaching*, Wulfst. 234, 22. Ðā gelǣhte Petrus hire līðian [līðigan, MSS. U. B.] hand *then Peter took her supple hand*, Homl. Skt. 10, 73. On his līðegum cneówum, Homl. Th. ii. 298, 27. His līðegan fingeras, 512, 1.

līðigian, līðegian; *p.* ode *To make*, or *be soft* or *yielding, to assuage, calm*:—Gewylc ȳða his ðū līðegast *motum fluctuum ejus tu mitigas*, Ps. Spl. 88, 10. Se ðe on ðam ǣrran tōcyme līðegode se dēmþ stīðne dōm æt ðam æfteran tōcyme *he that was mild at the first advent shall judge stern judgement at the second*, Homl. Th. i. 320, 17. Ðæt ðū līðegie *ut mitiges*, Ps. Spl. 93, 13. Uton līðegian ūre mōde *leniamus animum nostrum*, L. Ecg. P. iv. 66; Th. ii. 226, 26. v. ge-līðian.

liþ-incel, es; *n. A little joint*; articulus, Wrt. Voc. 283, 17: ii. 8, 3.

liþ-līc. v. riht-liþlīc.

lið-mann. v. lid-mann.

līð-ness, e; *f. Softness, gentleness, mildness, lenity, kindness*:—Hī sind gesewene mid līðnysse ac heora līðnys is sōðlīce āsolcennys *they appear with gentleness, but their gentleness is really sluggishness*, Homl. Th. ii. 46, 11. On līgette is ōga and on snāwe līðnyss ðære beorhtnysse *in lightning is the terror of brightness, in snow its mildness*, i. 222, 32. Hē forbær manna yfelnysse þurh his līðnysse *he endured the evil of men by reason of his gentleness*, 320, 16. Swā is tō mengenne ða līðnesse wið ða rēðnesse *miscenda ergo est lenitas cum severitate*, Past. 17, 11; Swt. 124, 13. DER. cum-, gæst-līðness.

līþrian, *p.* ede *To lather, smear*:—Lēðrede *unxit*, Jn. Skt. Lind. 11, 2. Lȳþre mid sāpan, L. M. 1, 50; Lchdm. ii. 124, 5. [*Icel.* leyðra *to wash.*]

līðs, e; *f. Gentleness, calm, ease, pleasure*:—Līðsa and wynna hām *a home of pleasures and of joys* [*Eden*], Cd. 45; Th. 58, 13; Gen. 945. Līðsum gewunedon *they lived at ease*, 80; Th. 100, 28; Gen. 1671. v. liss.

liþ-seáw, es; *n. The oily matter between the joints, synovia*:—Gif mon biþ on eaxle wund ðæt ðæt liþseáw ūt flōwe gebēte mid xxx scill., L. Alf. pol. 53; Th. i. 94, 22. Manegum men liþseáu sȳhþ ... wið liþseáwe, L. M. 1. 61; Lchdm. ii. 132, 10-13.

liðs-, lits-mann *a sailor*:—Ða liðsmenn [*the Danes*], Chr. 1036; Erl. 164, 14. Litsmanna, 1047; Erl. 175, 11. [*Icel.* liðs-maðr.] v. lid-mann.

liþule [= liþ-ele, Cockayne, Lchdm. ii. 398, col. 1] *synovia*:—Gif liþule ūt yrne, L. M. 1, 61; Lchdm. ii. 134, 3, 8. v. liþ-seáw.

līðung, e; *f. Relieving, alleviation, relief*:—Hē ongit ðæs innoþes līðunge *he will find relief for the stomach*, Herb. 18, 4; Lchdm. i. 112, 2.

liþ-wærc, es; *m. Pain in the joints*:—Wið liþwærce, L. M. 1, 61; Lchdm. ii. 132, 2, 4.

līþ-wǣge, es; *A drinking-cup, wine-cup*, Beo. Th. 3969; B. 1982.

līð-wyrt, e; *f. Dwarf elder*:—Lȳðwyrt. Ðeós wyrt ðe man ostriage and ōðrum naman lȳðwyrt nemneþ, Herb. 29, 1; Lchdm. i. 124, 13. Līð-wyrt, L. M. 1, 61; Lchdm. ii. 132, 13. Līðwyrt *ostriago*, Wrt. Voc. 69, 26: *eripheon*, 68. 12: *ostriago*, ii. 65, 48. v. Gloss. to Lchdms. ii. iii.

litel, litig. v. lytel, lytig.

līxan, līcsan; *p.* te *To shine, glitter, gleam*:—Seó reádnes ðære rōsan līxeþ on ðē, and seó hwītnes ðære lilian scīneþ on ðē, Blickl. Homl. 7, 30. Mōna līxeþ, Exon. 18 a; Th. 44, 6; Cri. 698. Ðæt nebb līxeþ swā glæs oððe gim *the beak glitters like glass or gem*, 60 a; Th. 218, 24; Ph. 299. Sōðfæste scīnes ł līxeþ swǣ sunna *justi fulgebunt sicut sol*, Mt. Kmbl. Lind. 13, 43. Līxaþ, 64 b; Th. 238, 15; Ph. 604. Līxte *fulminavit*, Wrt. Voc. ii. 37, 18: Exon. 15 a; Th. 31, 34; Cri. 505: Beo. Th. 627; B. 311. Ðonne dæg līxte, 975; B. 485. Sumum scinan ða scilla and līxtan swylce hié wǣron gyldene *auri fulgori similes*, Nar. 13, 19: Elen. Kmbl. 46; El. 23: 180; El. 90: 2229; El. 1116: Cd. 148; Th. 185, 20; Exod. 125. Hié gesāwon eóred līxan *they saw the host glitter*, 149; Th. 187, 28; Exod. 157: Exon. 57 a; Th. 204, 8; Ph. 94. Ðonne līgette līxan cwōman *illuxerunt coruscationes tuæ*, Ps. Th. 76, 15: Bt. Met. Fox 9, 25; Met. 9, 13. Līxende *fulgens*, Lk. Skt. Lind. 24, 4: *lucens*, Jn. Skt. Lind. 5, 35. Līcxændum *coruscantibus*, Rtl. 3, 1. Liéx-ende līgetta, Exon. 54 b; Th. 192, 14; Az. 106. Līxende lof *brilliant praise*, 93 a; Th. 349, 20; Sch. 49. v. in-līxan.

līxende; *adv. Splendidly*:—Fegerlīce ł līcsendo *splendide*, Lk. Skt. Lind. 16, 19.

līxung, līcsung, e; *f. Splendour, brightness*:—Līxung *splendor*, Mt. Kmbl. p. 14, 11: Rtl. 3, 13. Līcsung, 38, 29.

lobbe, an; *f. A spider*:—Ūre gēr swā swā lobbe oððe rynge beóþ āsmeáde *anni nostri sicut aranea meditabuntur* [cf. Ps. Th. 89, 10, anlīcast geongewefran ðonne hió geornast biþ ðæt heó āfǣre fleógan on nette], Ps. Lamb. 89, 9. Mistlīce þreála gebyriaþ for synnum bendas oððe dyntas carcernþȳstra lobban *various punishments are proper for sins, bonds or blows, prison darkness, spiders*, L. Pen. 3; Th. ii. 278, 26. Cf. (?) *Icel.* lubbi *a shaggy longhaired dog.*]

loc, es; *n.* I. *A lock, bolt, bar, that by which anything is closed, an enclosed place, enclosure, fold:*—Loc *clausura*, Wrt. Voc. 81, 17. Locc *mandra* vel *ovile*, 23, 55. Loc *caula*, 85, 73. Gāta loc *titula*, 288, 20. Loce ł fæstene *clustello*, Hpt. Gl. 527, 72. In scīpa locc *in ovile ovium*, Jn. Skt. Lind. 10, 1: p. 6, 2. Ic scitte sum loc oððe hæpsige *sero*, Ælfc. Gr. 37; Som. 39, 21. Uton belūcan ðās circan and ðæt loc insegliain, Homl. Skt. 3, 329. Sceápa locu *caule*, Ælfc. Gl. 2; Som. 55, 21; Wrt. Voc. 16, 6. Ða locu feóllan, clūstor of ðām ceastrum, Exon. 120 a; Th. 461, 22; Hö. 39. Ealle ða īsenan scyttelas helle loca wurdan tōbrocene, Blickl. Homl. 87, 5. Hwylc manna is ðæt his āgene sāwle fram helle locum generige *quis eruet animam suam de manu inferi*, Ps. Th. 88, 41. Tō helle locum gelǽded beón sceolde *ad inferni claustra raperetur*, Bd. 3, 13; S. 538, 22: 5, 13; S. 633, 20. Mid ðām trumestum locum getimbrade *seris instructa firmissimis*, 1, 1; S. 473, 27. Ðonne wē sittaþ innan ceastre ðonne wē ūs betȳnaþ binnan ðǽm locum ūres mōdes *in civitate quippe considemus, si intra mentium nostrarum nos claustra constringimus*, Past. 49, 4; Swt. 385, 6: L. E. I. 45; Th. ii. 442, 13. Heó hēht ða rōde in seolfren fæt locum belūcan, Elen. Kmbl. 2051; El. 1027. Locu *mandras, caulas*, Hpt. Gl. 476, 30. Loca *caulas*, Coll. Monast. Th. 20, 17. Godes engel undyde ða locu ðæs cweartернes, Homl. Th. i. 572, 27: Exon. 12 b; Th. 20, 21; Cri. 321. II. *A close, conclusion, settlement:*—Loces *syllogismi, conclusionis*, Hpt. Gl. 481, 65. And ðises loces ǽrendracan wǽran... Ðonne is hēr seó gewitnes ðe æt ðisum loce wæs *and of this settlement the commissioners were... Here are the witnesses that were at this settlement*, Chart. Th. 303, 12–19. Mid ðām ilcan mannan ðe ǽr ðæt loc makedon *with the same men that had before made the settlement*, Chr. 1094, Erl. 230, 3. [*Icel.* lok *a conclusion*; loka *a lock, latch.*] DER. ār-, clūster-, word-loc; v. loca.

lōc, lōca *look, see, look you*; the word often occurs in connection with a pronominal form, and seems equivalent to a suffixed *-ever*, loca hū *however*, &c.:—Efne oððe lōca nū hēr hit is *en*, Ælfc. Gr. 38; Som. 40, 56: Homl. Th. i. 358, 9. Hig cwǽdon Lōca nū hū hrædlīce þæt fictreów forscranc *dicentes: quomodo continuo aruit ficulnea*, Mt. Kmbl. 21, 20. Lōca nū hū hē hyne lufode *ecce quomodo amabat eum*, Jn. Skt. 11, 36. Þreá hig lōca hū ðū wylle *punish her, look you, as you will*, Gen. 16, 6. Ðū hæfst ðæt feoh mid ðē, gefada embe, lōca, hū ðū wylle, Homl. Skt. 3, 285: 4, 262. Hī fērdon lōc [MSS. C.D. lōca] hū hī wolden *they went however they liked*, Chr. 1009; Erl. 142, 26. Lōca, hwā ūt gange, licge hē ofslagen, Jos. 2, 19. Lōca, hwā ðære mihte āge, hē mōt gehæftne man ālȳsan [*whoever has the power*], Wulfst. 294, 32. Lōca hwylc cristen man sȳ ungesibsum, 295, 4. Hlystan lōca hwæt ða lāreówas tǽcan, 294, 26. Dōn lōc hwæt wē māgon, 141, 28: 150, 11. Lōc hwæt eald sī *hic et hæc et hoc vetus*, Ælfc. Gr. 9, 32; Som. 12, 9. Lōc hwæt hæbbe tȳn fēt *decempes*, 49; Som. 50. 49. Bide mē lōce hwæs ðū wille *ask me for whatever you will*, Homl. Th. ii. 576, 10. Lōc hwǽr ic hit gefriþod wille habban *wherever I will have it protected*, L. C. S. 81; Th. i. 420, 26. Lōca hwonne *whenever*, Wulfst. 199, 16. Swā ðæt lōc hwenne ðæt flōd byþ ealra hēhst, Chr. 1031; Erl. 162, 5. Lōc hweðer ðæra gebrōðra ōðerne oferbide wǽre yrfeweard ealles Englalandes *whichever of the two brothers should survive the other, should inherit all England*, 1101; Erl. 237, 31: Chart. Th. 605, 27. v. lōcian.

loca, an; *m. That which closes or shuts, a bar, bolt, lock, an enclosed place, locker:*—Hepse ł loca *clustella, serra*, Hpt. Gl. 500. Ālȳsde leóda bearn of locan deóflа [*hell*], Elen. Kmbl. 362; El. 181. Under helle cinn under līges locan, Exon. 31 b; Th. 99, 7; Cri. 1621: 72 b; Th. 270, 32; Jul. 19. Se ðe healdeþ locan *who guards the lock*, 8 a; Th. 2, 14; Cri. 19: Salm. Kmbl. 371; Sal. 185. DER. bān-, brægn-, breóst-, burg-, feorh-, ferhþ-, ferþ-, fȳr-, fyrhþ-, gewit-, hearm-, heolstor-, hord-, hreðer-, hring-, nīþ-, þeóster-, word-loca; v. loc.

loca, an; *m. A lock of wool:*—Loca *floccus*, Wrt. Voc. ii. 35, 71, cf. locc.

loc-bore, an; *f. One wearing long hair, a free woman:*—Frī wīf locbore, L. Ethb. 73; Th. 1. 20, 7. See the note there, and Grmm. R. A. 286, 239.

locc, es; *m. The hair of the head, a hair, a lock of hair, a curl, ringlet:*—*Comatus* se ðe hæfþ loccas, *coma* is locc, Ælfc. Gr. 43; Som. 45, 9. Locc unscoren *coma* vel *cirrus*, Wrt. Voc. 42, 45. Locc *uncinus*, 42, 48. Loc *coma*, 70, 33: *cicinnus* i. *vinnus*, ii. 131, 12: *cirrus, crinus*, 24. Ne ān loc of eówrum heáfde forwyrþ *not a hair of your head shall perish*, Blickl. Homl. 243, 33: Andr. Kmbl. 2845; An. 1425. Locces *cincinni*, Hpt. Gl. 526, 44. Se deófol lǽdde hine ūt of ðære cyrican be ðam locce, Wulfst. 236, 10. Ðū ne miht ǽnne locc gedōn hwītne oððe blacne *non potes unum capillum album facere aut nigrum*, Mt. Kmbl. 5, 36. Se scīnenda līg his locc up ātéah *the shining flame drew up his hair*, Homl. Th. ii. 514, 3. Wīfmannes loccas *crines*: loccas *vel* unscoren hǽr *comæ*, Wrt. Voc. 42, 49, 64. Loccas *capilli*, 64, 27. Loccas oððe feaxeácan *antiæ frontis*, Wrt. Voc. ii. 3, 66. Winde loccas *cincinni*, 20, 43: 14, 23. Locca *crinicolorum*, Hpt. Gl. 435, 27. Cyrpsum loccum *crispantibus*, 435, 11. Loccum *cirris*, Wrt. Voc. ii. 18, 70. Hī ne scoldon hira loccas lǽtan weaxan *non comam nutrient*, Past. 18, 7; Swt. 139, 13. Teóh him ða loccas and wringe ða eáran and ðone wangbeard twiccige, L. M. 2, 16; Lchdm. ii. 196, 13. Hē hæfde crispe loccas *capillis crispis*, Bd. 5, 2; S. 615, 30. Fȳrene loccas, Cd. 148; Th. 185, 10; Exod. 120. Wundne loccas *curled locks*, Exon. 111 b; Th. 428, 7; Rä. 41, 98. [*Icel.* lokkr: *O. H. Ger.* loc, locc *cincinnus, capillus, crinis*: *Ger.* locke.] DER. eár-, hǽr-locc.

-locc, -locced, *-locked*. v. hwīt-, līg-, wunden-locc, hwīt-, līg-locced.

loccian. v. ge-loccian.

locen, *an enclosed place* (?), Cd. 220; Th. 283, 6; Sat. 300.

locer *a carpenter's tool, a plane:*—Locor *runcina*, Wrt. Voc. 287, 12. Locer, sceaba, ii. 119, 32. Locaer *vel* scraba, Ep. Gl. 22 b, 23.

loc-feax, es; *n. Hair:*—Ðæs wonges locfeax *cæsaries*, Wrt. Voc. ii. 22, 57.

loc-gewind, es; *n. Hair:*—Locgewind *vel* fexnes *capillatura*, Wrt. Voc. ii. 128, 38.

LÓCIAN; *p.* ode *To* LOOK, *see, gaze, observe, regard, take heed, look* (*to*), *belong, pertain:*—Gif ic on ealle ðīne bebodu lōcie *dum respicio in omnia mandata tua*, Ps. Th. 118, 6. Ðū eádmōdra lōcast *humilia respicit Dominus*, 137, 6. Ðās sǽlāc ðe ðū tō lōcast *these offerings from the sea that thou dost look at*, Beo. Th. 3313; B. 1654. Hē on ðās eorþan ealle lōcaþ *qui respicit terram*, Ps. Th. 103, 30. Lōcaþ unhióre *looks fiercely*, Salm. Kmbl. 532; Sal. 265. Ealles ðæs ðe mē ðǽr tō lōcaþ *all that there belongs to me*, Chart. Th. 542, 11. Ðās ii bēc lōciaþ intō Ryppel, Cod. Dip. Kmbl. iii. 19, 22: 256, 31. Būton Raab āna libbe and ða ðe lōciaþ tō hire *sola Rahab vivat cum universis, qui cum ea in domo sunt*, Jos. 6, 17: 8, 1. Hié simle lōcigeaþ tō ðære eorþan *they* (*animals*) *always look to the earth*; ad terram semper inclinentur, Past. 21, 3; Swt. 155, 20. Hwæt stondaþ gē hēr and up on ðysne heofon lōciaþ? Blickl. Homl. 123, 22. Ðā lōcode Petrus tō Paule, 187, 34. Lōcode ðā up wið Simones, 189, 6. Hē forþ lōcade of his ðam heán hālgan setle *prospexit de excelso sancto suo*, Ps. Th. 101, 17. Hē on heofon lōcode *intuens in cælum*, Mk. Skt. 6, 41. Ōþ hē on ðone æþeling lōcude *until his eyes fell on the atheling*, Chr. 755; Erl. 48, 34. Hié lōcodan æfter him, Blickl. Homl. 121, 22. Blinde men gehǽlde ðæt hié lōcodan *healed blind men so that they saw*, 173, 28: Wulfst. 5, 1. Ðǽr men tō lōcedon *where men were looking on*, 98, 21. Lōcæ feónd mīnne *respice inimicos meos*, Ps. Spl. T. 24, 20. Lōca nū *receive thy sight*, Blickl. Homl. 15, 26. 'Lōca hider;' ðā lōcade hē ðider, Wulfst. 236, 20. Lōciaþ brāde and nān þing gecnāwaþ *look far and wide, and understand nothing*, 47, 13. Gāþ and lōciaþ *ite et videte*, Mk. Skt. 6, 38. Lōciaþ nū ðæt ðiós eówru leáf ne weorðe ōðrum monnum tō biswice *videte, ne forte hæc licentia vestra offendiculum fiat infirmis*, Past. 59, 6; Swt. 451, 32. Fore cyningum ðǽr hig eágum on lōcian *in conspectu regum*, Ps. Th. 118, 46. Ic rǽhte mīne hond tō eów nolde iówer nān tō lōcian *extendi manum meam, et non fuit qui aspiceret*, Past. 36, 1; Swt. 247. 22. God hēt hyne lōcian tō heofonum *suspice cælum*, Gen. 15, 5. Hié ongeán lōcian ne mihton for ðæs lēges bryne, Blickl. Homl. 203, 11. Swīðe fæger an tō lōcianne, Ors. 2, 4; Swt. 74, 13. Matheus ðā lōciende geseah Drihten Crist, Blickl. Homl. 229, 30. Forðam ðe lōciende hig ne geseóþ *quia videntes non vident*, Mt. Kmbl. 13, 13. v. lōc.

locor. v. locer.

loddere, es; *m. A beggar, poor person:*—Se rīca besihþ on his pællenum gyrlum and cwyþ 'Nis se loddere mid his tættecon mīn gelīca *but the rich man looks at his purple robes and says* '*the beggar with his rags is not my fellow*,' Homl. Th. i. 256, 8. [*Icel.* loddari *a tramp, juggler*: cf. *O. H. Ger.* lotar *cassus, vanus, inanis*.] v. lodrung.

lodrung, e; *f. Nonsense, triviality:*—Lodrung *nenias*, Wrt. Voc. ii. 71, 51. [cf. *O. H. Ger.* loter unde unreht *iniquitas*; lotarum sprācha *nenias*, Grff. ii. 204.] v. loddere.

lof, es; *n. m. Praise, glory, a song of praise, hymn:*—Ðam Dryhtne sȳ lof and wuldor *to the Lord be praise and glory*, Blickl. Homl. 53, 32. Sȳ ðē þanc and lof ðīnre mildse, Hy. 7, 58; Hy. Grn. ii. 288, 58. Ðǽr biþ gehȳred ðīn hālige lof, 7, 32; Hy. Grn. ii. 287, 32. Ðis lof *hic pean*, Ælfc. Gr. 9, 11; Som. 9, 21. Be ðam Fortunatus on fǽmnena lofe cwæþ *de quo Fortunatus in Laude Virginum ait*, Bd. 1, 7; S. 476, 32. Be ðam is gecweden on ðære brȳde lofe, Past. 11, 2; Swt. 65, 22. Gecwedenum lofe *hymno dicto*, Mk. Skt. 14, 26. Wē cweþaþ lof ymb hié, Blickl. Homl. 149, 32. Drihtnes lof singende, 231, 9. Lof secgean, Ps. Th. 106, 31. Eall folc Gode lof sealde, Lk. Skt. 18, 43. Wē herigaþ hira cræftas and ðeáh nyllaþ hī habban forðæm wē hiera nabbaþ nān lof *we praise their arts, and yet do not wish to have them, for we get no credit from them*, Past. 34, 2; Swt. 231, 8. Ic eów sylle mīne sibbe þurh mīn ðæt hēhste lof (*the Holy Ghost*), Blickl. Homl. 157, 30. Gegān longsumne lof *to earn lasting praise*, Beo. Th. 3076; B. 1536. Lofa ic cwæþe ðē *laudem dixi tibi*, Ps. Spl. 118, 164. Lofu ł herunga *præconia, laudes, favores*, Hpt. Gl. 500, 2: *melos*, Hymn. Surt. 5, 31. [*O. Sax., O. L. Ger., O. Frs., Icel.* lof: *O. H. Ger.* lob *laus, favor, hymnus*: *Ger.* lob.] DER. here-lof.

lōf, es; *m.?*—Hæfde sigora weard on ðam wangstede wǽre betolden leófne leódfruman mid lōfe sīnum, Andr. Kmbl. 1978; An. 991. Grimm A. u. E. 989 would translate 'lōf' *hand*, comparing *Goth.* lōfa: *Icel.* lófi (*Scott.* loof) *the palm of the hand.* In Hpt. Gl. 525, 8 *redimicula* is glossed 'wrǽdas odde cynewiddan, lofas;' would this be the same word as that in the above passage?

lof-bǽre; *adj. Laudatory, giving praise:*—Lofbǽrum werodum *hymniferis choris*, Hymn. Surt. 57, 12.

lof-dǽd, e; *f. A deed deserving praise*, Beo. Th. 48; B. 24.

lof-georn; *adj. Desirous of praise:*—Se đe wǽre lofgeorn for ídelan weorþscype weorþe se carfull hú hé swýđast mǽge gecwéman his drihtne *he that was eager for praise on account of empty honour, let that man be careful how best he may please his Lord*, Wulfst. 72, 10. Manna lofgeornost *of all men most desirous to deserve praise* (*Beowulf*), Beo. Th. 6347; B. 3183. [*Jactancia* þet is idelȝelp on englisc, đenne mon biþ lofȝeorn and deþ for ȝelpe mare þenne for godes luue, O. E. Homl. i. 103, 29. *Icel.* lof-gjarn: cf. *O. H. Ger.* lob-gerni *jactantia*.]

lof-herung, e; *f. Praising, commendation:*—Ic ágylde lofherunga đé *reddam laudationes tibi*, Ps. Lamb. 55, 12.

lofiah; *p.* ode *To praise, value, put a price upon:*—Míne weleras gefeóþ wynnum lofiaþ đonne ic đé singe *gaudebunt labia mea dum cantavero tibi*, Ps. Th. 70, 21. Wé đé hæriaþ and lofiaþ *we laud and praise thee*, Dóm. L. 48, 116: Cd. 192; Th. 240, 33; Dan. 396: Elen. Kmbl. 904; El. 453: Exon. 13 b; Th. 25, 13; Cri. 400. Job herede helm wera, hǽlend lofede, 17 a; Th. 40, 6; Cri. 634. Song áhófun, lofedun líffruman, 15 a; Th. 31, 31; Cri. 504. Hé gehýrde hú hí God lofodon and heredon, Bd. 3, 19; S. 547, 36. Lofa *lauda*, Ps. Lamb. 147, 1. Đec mihtig God gástas lofige, Cd. 192; Th. 239, 21; Dan. 373. Lofigen, Exon. 54 b; Th. 192, 2; Az. 100. Ic gehýrde hine đíne dǽd and word lofian, Cd. 25; Th. 32, 24; Gen. 508. [*O. Sax.* lofón: *Icel.* lofa: *O. H. Ger.* lobôn *hymnizare, glorificare, commendare, magnificare*: *Ger.* loben.] v. ge-lofian; lofung.

lof-lác, es; *n. An offering made to do honour:*—Đa hǽđenan him brohton oft mistlíce lofláс *the heathens often brought him offerings of divers kinds to do him honour*, Wulfst. 107, 6.

lof-lǽcan; *p.* -lǽhte *To praise:*—Sáwle mín lóflǽceþ [MS. -aþ] ł heraþ đé *anima mea laudabit te*, Ps. Lamb. 118, 175.

lof-líc; *adj. Praiseworthy, laudable, honorable:*—Of lofflícere *laudabili, honorabili*, Hpt. Gl. 498, 45. [*Icel.* lof-ligr: *O. H. Ger.* lobe-líh *laudabilis*: *Ger.* löb-lich.]

lof-líce; *adv. Honorably, gloriously:*—Uton wé gehýran hú swíđe loflíce Sanctus Johannes wæs mid đæs Hálgan Gástes mægenum gefylled, Blickl. Homl. 165, 16. [*Icel.* lof-liga *gloriously*.]

lof-mægen, es; *n. Abundance* or *greatness of praise:*—Hwylc mæg spédlíce eall Drihtnes lofmægen leóde gehýran *quis auditas faciet omnes laudes Domini*, Ps. Th. 105, 2.

lof-sang, es; *m. A song of praise, hymn, psalm*, as an ecclesiastical term *lauds:*—Lofsang *ymnus*, Ælfc. Gl. 34; Som. 62, 45; Wrt. Voc. 28, 26. Fram đære tíde đæs úhtlícan lofsanges *a tempore matutinæ laudis*, Bd. 3, 12; S. 537, 23. Đá se sealmsang gefylled wæs đæs úhtlícan lofsanges *expletis matutinæ laudis psalmodiis*, 4, 7; S. 575, 3. Mid lofsange *cum cantico*, Ps. Th. 68, 31: Ex. 15, 21. Mid þysum lofsange *with this psalm* (v. Ps. Th. 53, 1), Homl. Skt. 11, 89. Moises sang Gode lofsang *cecinit Moyses carmen hoc Domino*, Ex. 15, 1. Đá hig hæfdon heora lofsang gesungenne *hymno dicto*, Mt. Kmbl. 26, 30. Lofsang cweþan *laudem dicere*, Ps. Th. 118, 164. Æfter đa hálgan lofsangas and mæssan gefyllede wǽron *after the holy psalms and masses were completed*, Blickl. Homl. 207, 29. God heriaþ mid gástlícum lofsangum, Ælfc. Gr. 48; Som. 49, 11. Him lofsangum cwémdan *cantaverunt laudes ejus*, Ps. Th. 105, 11. 'Gloria in excelsis Deo' sungon englas . . . Nú forlǽte wé đás lofsangas, Homl. Th. ii. 88, 3. Ic sang úhtsang æfter đá wé sungon dægrédlíce lofsangas *cantavi nocturnam, deinde cantavimus matutinales laudes*, Coll. Monast. Th. 33, 27; Bd. 4, 7; S. 575, 5. [*O. Sax.* lof-sang: *Icel.* lof-söngr: *O. H. Ger.* lob-, lobe-sang *hymnus*.]

lof-singende *hymning, hymn-singing:*—Lofsingende *hymnizantes*, Hpt. Gl. 519, 9.

lof-sum; *adj. Deserving praise, excellent, noble:*—Wæstm wæs lofsum, Cd. 23; Th. 30. 17; Gen. 468. [*O. Sax.* lof-sam; *O. H. Ger.* lob-sam *probabilis, meritus*: *Ger.* lobe-sam.]

loft *air:*—Heó ne líþ on nánum þinge ac on lofte heó stynt *it* (*the earth*) *does not rest on anything, but stands in the air*, Hexam. 6; Norm. 10, 20. v. lyft.

lofung, e; *f. Praising, appraising:*—Næfþ Godes ríce nánes wurþes lofunge ac biþ gelofod be đæs mannes hæfene. Heofenan ríce wæs álǽten đisum gebróđrum for heora nette and scipe and đam rícan Zacheo tó healfum dǽle his ǽhta and sumere wudewan tó ánum feorþlinge and sumum menn tó ánum wæteres drenc *God's kingdom hath no fixed price, but a price is put upon it according to a man's property. The kingdom of heaven was allowed to these brothers for their net and ship, and to the rich Zacheus for half his possessions, and to a certain widow for a farthing, and to a certain man for a drink of water*, Homl. Th. i. 580, 21–26. Lofunga ł herunga *laudationes*, Ps. Lamb, 9, 15.

-loga. v. ád-, treów-, wǽr-, wed-, word-loga.

lógian (v. lóh); *p.* ode *To lodge, place, put in order, arrange, frame:*—Tó þreágenne gé lógiaþ eówere sprǽce *ye frame your speech to reprove*, Homl. Th. ii. 454, 25. Hí on heora scype heora nett lógodon *in navi componentes retia*, Mk. Skt. 1, 19. Wé lǽraþ đæt man intó circan ǽnig þinga ne lógige đæs đe đartó ungedafenlíc sí *we enjoin that nothing be lodged in the church that is unsuitable for the place*, L. Edg. c. 27; Th. ii. 250, 11. [Ne neuer se stede ne uurþe lóged mid óđere hódes manne đanne mid moneke, Cod. Dip. Kmbl. iv. 231, 9.] v. ge-logian.

logđor, logeđer *plotting mischief, wily, crafty:*—Logđor *cacomicanus*, Wrt. Voc. ii. 102, 77: 127, 35. Logđer, 13, 31. Logeđer *marsius* (cf. (?) '*Marsi* homines, quibus naturalem vim contra serpentes inesse olim creditum, incantatores,' Ducange, v. wyrm-galere), 55, 58.

lóh; *gen.* lóges; *n. A place, stead:*—Gehádode Tobias on his lóh (on his steall, two other MSS.), Chr. 693; Thorpe 67, 9 col. 3. [*O. Frs.* lóch; *dat.* lóge *a place*; *O. H. Ger.* luog *specus, cubile*: *M. H. Ger.* luoc *locus*. v. Grmm. R. A. 955.]

lóh-sceaft, es; *m. A bolt, bar* (?):—Gaderode mé kigelas and stuþan sceaftas and lóhsceaftas, Shrn. 163, 6.

Loidis *Leeds:*—Đa æftran cyningas him botl worhton on đam lande đe Loidis[is] háten *reges posteriores fecere sibi villam in regione quæ vocatur Loidis*, Bd. 2, 14; S. 518, 21: 3, 24; S. 557, 12.

lóma *a tool*. v. and-, andge-, ge-lóman.

lomb, lond, long. v. lamb, land, lang.

lóm-lǽcan; *p.* -lǽhte *To use often, repeat, frequent:*—Lómlǽhtan *frequentabant*, Hpt. Gl. 457, 44. v. ge-lómlǽcan.

loppe, an; *f. A flea* (?), *a spider* (?); also *a silk-worm:*—Furþum đeós lytle loppe hine hwílum deádne gedéþ *even this little flea sometimes kills him*, Bt. 16, 2; Fox 52, 13. Seolucwyrm odđe sídwyrm odđe loppe *bombix*, Wrt. Voc. ii. 12, 23 (or is this a different word, corresponding to another meaning of *bombix*, 'silk or fine wool;' cf. *Icel.* lyppa *wool drawn into a long hank before being spun*? In Ps. Lamb. 38, 12 *sicut araneam* is glossed 'swá swá ǽtterloppan'; if this is not a mistake for 'áttercoppan,' by which the word is rendered in Ps. Spl. 38, 15, 'loppe' would be rather a *spider* than a *flea*, and the same word might be used for the silk worm, as both insects are spinners. And in Wrt. Voc. 24, 1 *loppe* (apparently however intended to be a Latin word) is given as the equivalent of 'fleónde næddre *vel* áttorcoppe.') [Lop *a flea*, in some dialects, v. E. D. S. Reprinted Gloss. B. 15, 22; C. 1; and gloss. of Mid-Yorkshire and Holderness: *Dan.* loppe.]

lopystre, an; *f. A lobster, a locust:*—Loppestre *polypus*, Ælfc. Gl. 102; Som. 77, 77; Wrt. Voc. 56, 2: 77, 69. Lopust *locusta*, ii. 113, 11. Hwæt fêhst đú on sǽ? Crabban and lopystran *quid capis in mari? Cancros et polypodes*, Coll. Monast. Th. 24, 13. Lopestro (loppestra, Rush.) *lucustas*, Mk. Skt. Lind. 1, 6.

lor, es; *n.* (v. đæt forlor, Past. Swt. 403, 13). *Loss, destruction:*—Đæt tó lore weorþe án đíne lioma *ut pereat unum membrorum tuorum*, Mt. Kmbl. Rush. 5, 29: 9, 17: 10, 6. Đæt nǽniges mannes feorh tó lore weard for đam ofslægenan cyninges bréđer *ut nullius anima hominis pro interfecto regis fratre daretur*, Bd. 4, 21; S. 590, 23. Đás heán mihta hér on worulde áfeallaþ and tó lore wurþaþ *these lofty powers here on earth decay and perish*, Wulfst. 149, 4: 262, 17. Édel đe nǽfre tó lore ne weorþeþ *nunquam amittenda hæreditas*, Past. 36, 6; Swt. 255, 4. Đonne hié him ǽr tíde tó tióþ đæt hí ne mágon, đonne is him tó ondrǽdenne đæt him weorþe tó lore đæt hié tó ryhtre tíde gefolgian meahton, đæt is se wisdóm, đe hié ǽr tíde wilniaþ and eówiaþ, ac hé him wyrþ đonne swíđe ryhtlíce tó lore *admonendi ne, cum arripiunt intempestive, quod non valent, perdant etiam quod implere quandoque tempestive potuissent: atque scientiam, quia incongrue conantur ostendere, juste ostendantur amisisse*, 49, 3; Swt. 383, 25–28. Đonne đín líchoma beó tó lore gedón and đín flǽsc gebrosnod *quando consumseris carnes et corpus tuum*, 36, 2; Swt. 249, 13. Tó hwon sceolde đeós smyrenes đus beón tó lore gedón *why should this ointment be thus wasted?* Blickl. Homl. 69, 7. DER. for-lor; *and see* los.

lorh, lorg, e; *f. A pole, a weaver's beam:*—Lorh *vel* webbeám *liciatorium* [lignum in quo licium involvitur, et laqueus qui de filo solet fieri, Ducange], Ælfc. Gl. 110; Som. 79, 48; Wrt. Voc. 59, 19. Lorg *amitis* [*amis* lignum bifurcatum, per quod venatores expandunt retia, ad capiendas feras, Ducange], 285, 17: ii. 8, 38. Loerge *amites*, Ep. Gl. 1 b, 3.

lorian. v. losian.

los, es; *n. Loss, destruction:*—Đa þing tó lose wurdon đe on đam scipe wǽron *perditis his quæ in navi erant rebus*, Bd. 5, 9; S. 623, 20. Đonne gé tó lose [Cott. MSS. lore] weorþaþ *in interitu vestro*, Past. 36, 1; Swt. 249, 1. Weg điú lǽdas tó lose *via quæ ducit ad perditionem*, Mt. Kmbl. Lind. 7, 13. Đæt tó lose weorþe *ut pereat*, Rush. 18, 14: 5, 30. Hú hine mæhtes tó lose gedóa *quomodo eum perderent*, Lind. 12, 14. [*Icel.* los *looseness, breaking up*.] v. lor.

los-, lose-wist, e; *f*: es, *m*. [?] *Hurt, loss, destruction, waste:*—Tó huon losuist điós smirinisse áworden wæs *quid perditio ista ungenti facta est*, Mk. Skt. Lind. 14, 4. Loswist [losewest, Rush.] walana *deceptio divitiarum*, 4, 19. Suna losuistes [loswest, Rush.] *filius perditionis*, Jn. Skt. Lind. 17, 12. Of losuist *de interitu*, Rtl. 169, 33. Sáules loswist geþolas *animæ detrimentum patiatur*, Mt. Kmbl. Lind. 16, 26. Losuist [losewest] gedóe, Mk. Skt. Lind. 8, 36: Lk. Skt. Lind. Rush. 9, 25.

lose [?] *frutectum, locus ubi ponunt*, Wrt. Voc. ii. 109, 23.

losian; *p.* ode *To perish, be lost, stray, escape*:—'Drihten ic losige.' Cweþ 'ic losige' ðý læs ðe ðú losige '*Lord, I perish.*' *Say* '*I perish,*' *lest thou perish*, Homl. Th. ii. 394, 1–2. Hwílum losaþ sió stemn *sometimes the voice is lost*, L. M. 2, 51; Lchdm. ii. 264, 14. Hwæt losaþ ǽfre ðam ælmihtigan Gode *what is ever lost to the Almighty God?* Homl. Skt. 11, 278. Gif hwylc mann hæfþ hund sceápa and him losaþ ân of ðám . . . ða nigon and hundnigontig ðe ná ne losedon *si fuerint alicui centum oves et erraverit una ex eis . . . nonaginta novem, quæ non erraverunt*, Mt. Kmbl. 18, 12, 13: Homl. Th. i. 338, 27. Nó hé on helm losaþ *she shall not escape into shelter*, Beo. Th. 2789; B. 1392. Ealra ðæra sáwla ðe þurh ðæt losiaþ *all the souls that perish through that*, L. I. P. 19; Th. ii. 328, 37. Ðæt sǽd ðe feóll be ðam wege mid twýfealdre dare losode [*perished*], Homl. Th. ii. 90, 14. Ðá losade hió him sóna *she was at once lost to him*, Bt. 35, 6; Fox 170, 15. Hé onweg losade *he escaped*, Beo. Th. 4199; B. 2096. Fíftig þurh fleám onweg losedon *quinquaginta fuga lapsos esse*, Bd. 2, 2; S. 504, 6. Ðý læs ðe ðú losige *ne tu pereas*, Gen. 19, 15. Gif hé losige and hine mon eft gefó *if he escape and be caught a second time*, L. Alf. pol. 7; Th. i. 66, 11: 1; Th. i. 60, 17. Gif hit [feoh] him losige, 20; Th. i. 74, 17. Gaderiaþ ða láfe and hí ne losion *gather the remnants, and let them not be lost*, Homl. Th. i. 182, 21. Ne sceal hé for ðám læssan losian *he shall not be lost for the lesser sins*, ii. 336, 22. Swá swá seó beó sceal losian, ðonne heó hwæt yrringa stingþ, Bt. 31, 2; Fox 112, 26. Ðætte nú foraldod is ðæt is forneáh losad *quod enim antiquatur, prope interitum est*, Past. 30; Swt. 205, 9. Ðonne ðé mon ǽrest secge ðæt ðín ceáp sý losod, Lchdm. iii. 60, 9: L. Eth. ii. 8; Th. i. 288, 15. Mé syndon losode fóta gangas *effusi sunt gressus mei*, Ps. Th. 72, 1. v. ge-losian.

losigend-líc; *adj. Ready to perish, in danger of destruction*:—Ða tóweardan frecednyssa ðises losigendlícan middangeardes, Homl. Th. ii. 538, 7. Se ðe ða losigendlícan buruhware [*people of Jerusalem*] bemǽnde, i. 408, 6.

losing, e; *f. Loss, perdition*: Tó lose ł losing *ad perditionem*, Mt. Kmbl. Lind. 7, 13.

lot, es; *n. Deceit, guile, fraud, craft, cunning*:—Náuht ne deregaþ monnum máne áþas ne ðæt leáse lot ðe beoþ mid ðám wrencum bewrigen *nil perjuria, nil nocet ipsis fraus, mendaci compta colore*, Bt. 4; Fox 8, 17: Exon. 92 a; Th. 345, 16; Gn. Ex. 189 [v. list]. Mid his lote bewunden *encompassed with his deceit*, Past. 35, 3; Swt. 243, 1: 46, 3; Swt. 347, 19. Þurh ðara scuccena lot *daemonum solertia*, Bt. 36, 6; Fox 220, 14 note. v. lytig.

lotendra? *madendum*, Wrt. Voc. ii. 57, 46.

loða, an; *m. A cloak, upper garment*:—Loða *lodix*, Wrt. Voc. ii. 52, 58: *lacerna*, 53, 65: *sandalium*, 119, 55: *sagulum*, 119, 58: *colobium, dictum quia longum est, et sine manicis*, 134, 37. Hé genom his loðan ǽnne læppan *he took a skirt of his robe*, Past. 3, 2; Swt. 37, 5. Loðan *clamidem*, Wrt. Voc. ii. 21, 31. Hloðan, gegirelan *liniamento*, 50, 4. Heora andwlitan bewrigenum under loðum *their faces wrapped under their cloaks*, Cd. 77; Th. 95, 29; Gen. 1586. [*Icel.* loði *a fur cloak*; cf. loðinn *shaggy*: *O. H. Ger.* ludo, lodo *birrus, penula, lodix, genus vestimenti*.]

lot-wrenc, es; *m. Deceit, deception, cunning, fraud, device, wile, craft*:—Lotwrænc *deceptio, fraus*, Wrt. Voc. ii. 138, 13. Mid hwelcum lotwrence hit deófla dydon *with what deception devils did it*, Ors. 3, 3; Swt. 102, 18. Philippus mid his lotwrence áliéfde ðæt heora anwaldas móston standan swá hié ǽr dydon *Philip, with his craftiness, allowed their powers to stand as they did before*, 3, 7; Swt. 118, 9. Gif hwá mid his lotwrencum óðres mannes folgere fram him ápǽce *si quis versutiis suis alius hominis pedisequam ab eo allexerit*, L. Ecg. P. ii. 14; Th. ii. 186, 22. Ðá wearþ se mann mid deófles lotwrencum bepǽht, Homl. Th. i. 192, 11: 376, 9: Wulfst. 84, 19. For his lotwrencium, Past. 30, 1; Swt. 203, 19. Þurh ðara scuccena mislíce lotwrencas *daemonum varia solertia*, Bt. 36, 6; Fox 220, 14. Hé heora lotwrencas [-wrenc-ceas, MS. B.] wiste *sciens versutiam eorum*, Mk. Skt. 12, 15. Ða ðe ðisse worulde lotwrenceas cunnon *sapientes hujus seculi*, Past. 30, 1; Swt. 203, 5: Swt. 205, 17.

lotwrenc-ceást, e; *f. Wiliness, cunning*:—Hé heora lotwrencceáste *sciens versutiam eorum*, Mk. Skt. 12, 15.

lox, es; *m. A lynx*:—Lox *linx*, Ælfc. Gl. 19; Som. 59, 14; Wrt. Voc. 22, 55. Aristoteles sǽde ðæt deór wǽre ðæt mihte ǽlc wuht þurhseón ge treówa ge furþum stánas; ðæt deór wé hátaþ lox, Bt. 32, 2; Fox 116, 22. [*O. H. Ger.* luchs, lohs *lynx, pardus, panthera*: *Ger.* luchs.]

loxe *in* loxanwudu, Cod. Dip. Kmbl. v. 345, 5. Cf. [?] Grff. ii. 163 luhsa, *Linsa* [*sylvestris, Gottheit*]'; *or* loxan wudu = *lynx-wood*.'

lúcan; *p.* leác, *pl.* lucon; *pp.* locen *To close, conclude, fasten, lock*:—Ðæt hé leác on hálre tungon *qui statim conclusit et omnino confirmavit totum quod pater suus in vita sua fecerat*, Chart. Th. 272, 5. On ðæt geræ̂d ðe ðæt stande ðe wit beforan ðam ealdormen lucan *on the condition that that arrangement stand which we concluded before the alderman*, 597, 32. Hrím and forst lucon leóda gesetu *rime and frost shut up men's dwellings*, Andr. Kmbl. 2519; An. 1261. Ðǽr com flówende flód æfter ebban lucon lagustreámas *there came flowing flood after ebb, the streams intertwined* or *closed up* [*the surface of the water shewing a network of lines from the varying currents, as the tide flowed up the river*], Byrht. Th. 133, 46; By. 66. Siððan ða ýslan eft onginnaþ lúcan tógædere geclungne tó cleowenne *afterwards the ashes begin to close up again, pressed to a ball*; in massam cineres coactos, Exon. 59 a; Th. 213, 16; Ph. 225. Lúcan eorþan cíðas (*frost shall*) *lock up the germs of earth*, 90a; Th. 338, 6: Gn. Ex. 74. Lúcan [onlúcan?], Cd. 220; Th. 283, 5; Sat. 300. Sincgim locen *the jewel fastened in its setting*, Elen. Kmbl. 528; El. 264. Locen *is applied to coats of mail, which were formed of* [*interlacing*] *rings fastened on to some material to which they might be sewn, see* hring *with its compounds, and* cf. brogden byrne; *also Icel.* hring-ofin:—Locene leoþosyrcan, Beo. Th. 3014; B. 1505: 3784: 1890. Locen beág *a closed ring* [*not a spiral* wunden beág], 5982; B. 2995: Andr. Kmbl. 605; An. 303. [*O. Sax.* ant-, bi-lúkan: *O. Frs. Icel.* lúka: *O. H. Ger.* lûhhan.] DER. á-, be-, ge-, on-, tó-, un-lúcan.

lúcan; *p.* leác *To pull up*:—Swá swá londes ceorl of his æcere lýcþ yfel weód monig, Bt. Met. Fox 12, 55; Met. 12, 28 [*E. D. S. Mid-York. Gloss.* louk, look *to weed*: *Holderness Gloss.* lookers *weeders in a corn-field*; look *to hoe weeds in a field of young corn*: lowker *runcinator*, Wrt. Voc. 218, col. 2: *O. H. Ger.* ar-, úz-liuhhan *evellere*, Grff. ii. 138.] v. á-lúcan.

lud-geat, es; *n. A back door, postern*:—Þurh ludget *per seudoterum* [ψευδοθυρον], Wrt. Voc. ii. 67, 72. Þorh ludgæt, 116, 70: Ep. Gl. 18 b, 16.

lufe. v. lufu.

lufe-líc. v. luf-líc.

lufen, e; *f. Hope* [?]:—Sceal eall éðelwyn eówrum cynne lufen álicgean [lufena licgean, MS.] *all delight in their country and hope shall fail your kin*, Beo. Th. 5764; B. 2886. [Grein who emends thus compares *lufen* with Gothic *lubains*; Grimm takes *lufen* = *leofen* victus, R. A. 731.]

lufestice, es, *also*, an; *m. Lovage*:—Lufestice *lubestica*, Ælfc. Gl. 39; Som. 63, 79; Wrt. Voc. 30, 27: 69, 23. Lubestica *conixe*, 67, 40. Lufestice *libestica*, 79, 2. Genim lubastican wyrttruman, Herb. 146, 3; Lchdm. i. 270, 7. Lufestices sǽd, L. M. 3, 12; Lchdm. ii. 314, 20: iii. 128, 22. Genim lufestice, 4, 10.

lufestre, an; *f. A sweetheart*:—Lufestran *amatricis*, Hpt. Gl. 509, 70.

lufian; *p.* ode *To love, feel affection for, shew love to*:—Simon lufast ðú mé . . . hé cwæþ tó him ðú wást ðæt ic ðé lufige *Simon diligis me . . . dicit ei tu scis quia amo te*, Jn. Skt. 21, 15. Se ðe lufaþ his sáwle forspilþ hig *qui amat animam suam perdet eam*. 12, 25. Lufiaþ mid lácum ða ðe læs águn *shew their love with gifts to those that have less*, Exon. 33 b; Th. 106, 32; Gú. 50. Hé ágsode hý, hwá wolde on ðære geférrǽdenne beón ðe hé wǽre, and ðæt lufian ðæt hé lufode, L. Edg. 4; Th. i. 162, 6. Hé mé mid syndrige lufan lufode, Bd. 5, 6; S. 619, 33. Hú ús wuldres weard wordum and dǽdum lufode in lífe, Andr. Kmbl. 1193; An. 597. Ðú mé on ðínum weorcum lufadest *delectasti me in factura tua*, Ps. Th. 91, 3. Hí hine lufedan leáse múðe *dilexerunt eum in ore suo*, 77, 35. Lufigean his néhstan swá hine sylfne, Mk. Skt. 12, 33. Ðæt is tó lufigenne on ðysse wyrte ðæt heó hafaþ gehwǽdne wyrttruman *it is an excellent property of this plant, that it has a small root*, Herb. 140, 1; Lchdm. i. 260, 5. Ðes lufigenda wer *hic amans vir*; ðis lufigende wíf *hæc amans fœmina*, Ælfc. Gr. 5; Som. 3, 49. Hé wæs fram eallum mannum lufad, Bd. 3, 14; S. 540, 11: 5, 19; S. 637, 19. v. ge-lufian.

lufiend, lufigend, es; *m. A lover*:—*Amans Deum*, lufigende God, is participium, and *amans Dei* is nama, ðæt is, *amator Dei*, Godes lufigend, Ælfc. Gr. 43; Som. 44, 61. Swá swíðe se cyning wæs geworden lufiend ðæs heofonlícan ríces, Bd. 3, 18; S. 546, 5 col. 2. Ic hæbbe óðerne lufiend *I have another lover*, Homl. Skt. 7, 27. Se wísdóm gedéþ his lufiendas wíse, Bt. 27, 2; Fox 98, 1. Lufigendas, Homl. Th. ii. 392, 27.

lufiend-, lufigend-líc; *adj. Lovely, lovable, amiable*:—Lufigendlíc *amabilis*, Ælfc. Gr. 9, 28; Som. 11, 40. Lufigendlíc miht *amanda virtus*, 26; Som. 28, 19. Luffendlíc stede *amenus locus*, Ælfc. Gl. 48; Som. 65, 63; Wrt. Voc. 33, 59. Swíðe lufigendlíc and leóf ǽghwæðere þeóde *utrique provinciæ multum amabilis*, Bd. 4, 21; S. 590, 16: 4, 3; S. 568, 16. Swíðe lufiendlíce sind geteld ðín *quam amabilia sunt tabernacula tua*, Ps. Surt. 83, 2.

luf-líc; *adj. Lovely, lovable, worthy of love, amiable, dear*:—Luflíc *amabilis*, Hymn. Surt. 38, 5. Cild ácenned gód luflíc *a child born at this time will be good and amiable*, Lchdm. iii. 190, 5. Hú luflíce geteld ðín *how amiable are thy tabernacles*; quam dilecta tabernacula tua, Ps. Spl. 83, 1.

luf-líce; *adv. Amiably, kindly, dearly, with good will* or *love, willingly*:—Luflíce *affabiliter*, Wrt. Voc. ii. 5, 11. Hé luflíce him hýrde *libenter eum audiebat*, Mk. Skt. 6, 20. Ðæt hé luflíce swá gedyde *libentissime se facturum*, Bd. 4, 11; S. 579, 31: Blickl. Homl. 203, 33. Ælfréd cyning háteþ grétan Wærferþ biscep his wordum luflíce and freóndlíce *with love and friendship*, Past. Swt. 3, 1: Blickl. Homl. 199, 36. Hú luflíce hé ús gesóht hider on middangeard *with how great love he visited us here on earth*, 129, 11: Wulfst. 204, 16. Ic wylle cýpan luflícor ðonne ic gebicge *volo vendere carius quam emi*, Coll. Monast. Th. 27, 19.

luf-rǽdenn, e; *f. Love*:—Hig gesetton hatunge for lufrǽddenne mínre *posuerunt odium pro dilectione mea*, Ps. Lamb. 108, 5.

luf-sum; *adj. Amiable, pleasant, lovable*:—Lufsum swǽ Rahel *amabilis ut Rachel*, Rtl. 109, 37. Lufsum and líðe leófum monnum *amiable and kind to the men that are dear to him*, Exon. 21 a; Th. 57, 5; Cri. 914: 96 a; Th. 357, 21; Pa. 32.

lufsum-líce; *adv. Kindly, graciously*:—Ðá sende Vitalianus se pápa cyninge lufsumlíce ǽrendgewrit, Bd. 3, 29; S. 561, 18.

lufsum-ness, e; *f. Amiability, pleasantness, love, kindness*:—Lufsumness *delectatio*, Wrt. Voc. ii. 138, 56. Lufsumnisse *dilectionis*, Rtl. 3, 24: 13, 21. Lufsumnisse *jocunditatem*, 45, 33.

luf-tácen, es; *n. A token of love*, Beo. Th. 3730; B. 1863.

luf-tíme; *adj. Giving rise to love, pleasant, grateful*:—Gregorius ðæt luftýme weorc gefremode *Gregory performed that grateful work* [*the conversion of the English*], Homl. Th. ii. 126, 26.

LUFU, e *and* an [v. Anglia vi. 176]; *f.* LOVE:—*Te amo* ðé ic lufige, ðon befylþ mín lufu on ðé and ðú miht cweþan *amor a te* ic eom gelufod fram ðé, Ælfc. Gr. 19; Som. 22, 36. Gif ðonne ðæs monnes mód and his lufu biþ behleápen on ða lǽnan sibbe *si ergo in ea* [*pace*] *cor quæ relicta est figitur*, Past. 46, 5; Swt. 351, 14. Swá mycel lufu tó godcundre láre *tantus amor persuadendi*, Bd. 4, 27; S. 604, 20. Sǽde hire ðá his lust and his willan ðæt his lufu wǽre ðæt hé ða stówe neósode ðara eádigra apostola *indicavit ei desiderium sibi inesse beatorum apostolorum limina visitandi* 5, 19; S. 637, 30. On ðæm welme ðære sóþan lufan, Blickl. Homl. 29, 10: Exon. 107 a; Th. 409, 7; Rä. 27, 25. Mid bróðorlíce lufan hí lǽran ðæt hí rihte sibbe and lufan betwih him hæfdon, Bd. 2, 2; S. 502, 8. For Godes lufon *pro Domino*, 3, 19; S. 547, 16. For úre lufan *for love of us*, Blickl. Homl. 23, 35. Mid lufe ge mid láðe, 45, 8. For hylde and lufe *affectu*, Wrt. Voc. ii. 3, 65. Gif hé secge ðæt hé hæbbe hire freóndscipe ðæt ys be lufe *si dicat se amicitiam ejus habere, id est, amatorie*, L. Ecg. P. iv. 68, 17; Th. ii. 230, 17. Hié sceolan lǽran Godes lufan and manna, Blickl. Homl. 77, 20. Godes ege and his lufe fæstlíce on úrum heortum healdan, 131, 3. And ðar þegen áge twegen costas lufe oððe lage and hé ðonne lufe geceóse *and where a thane has a choice of two courses, love or law* [*an amicable settlement or appeal to law*] *and he choose the former*, L. Eth. iii. 13; Th. i. 298, 5. Ðeós woruld nǽre wyrðe ðæt man tó hire lufe hæfde ealles tó swíðe *this world does not deserve to be loved too much*, Wulfst. 273, 14. For Godes ege and for his lufu, 302, 27. Ðǽr wé sib and lufu samod gemétaþ, Hy. 7, 30; Hy. Grn. ii. 287, 30. Lufena tó leáne, Exon. 119 b; Th. 459, 11; Hy. 4, 115. Ðeáh monn good onginne for sumes wítes ege, hit mon sceal ðeáh geendigean for sumes gódes lufum, Past. 37, 1; Swt. 265, 7. For ðǽm lufum ðe hí tó him habbaþ *per caritatem*, 52, 7; Swt. 409, 13. Ðone mon lufaþ for lufum, Bt. 24, 3; Fox 82, 34. For ðínum lufum, 22, 2; Fox 78, 12. Hé onféng ða ilcan gecynde for úrum lufon *he received the same nature for our sakes*, Blickl. Homl. 23, 24. For mínum lufan, Wulfst. 231, 17. Lufum *voluntariis*, Hpt. Gl. 435, 64. DER. bearn-, brýd-, eád-, eard-, feoh-, freónd-, fyrhþ-, gást-, heáh-, heort-, mǽg-, man-, mód-, ofer-, sib-, sorg-, treów-, wíf-lufu.

luf-wende; *adj. Beloved, amiable, pleasant*:—Cild ácenned lufwende *a child born* [*at that time will be*] *amiable*, Lchdm. iii. 186, 24. Mid lufwendum módes willan *cum benevolo animi affectu*, Lye. Ða lufwende eardas *dilecta rura*, Wrt. Voc. ii. 140, 42.

lufwend-líc; *adj. Amiable*; amabilis, Lye.

luh (a borrowed word apparently, Welsh *llwch*; cf. *pól* and Welsh *pwll*]; *n. A loch, lough*:—Ofer ðæt luh *trans fretum*, Mt. Kmbl. Lind. 14, 34: Mk. Skt. Lind. 8, 13: Lk. Skt. Lind. 8, 22. Ofer luh ł lytel sǽ, Mt. Kmbl. Lind. 14, 22: Mk. Skt. Lind. Rush. 5, 1.

Lunden *London*:—Hé bebohte hine on Lundenne *he sold him in London*, Bd. 4, 22; S. 592, 3: Chr. 839; Erl. 66. 16: 898; Erl. 96, 20. Of Eástenglum and of Lunden, 992; Erl. 131, 33.

Lunden-burh; *f. London*:—Ðes geáres forbarn Lundenburh, Chr. 1077; Erl. 215, 12. Ða Bryttas forlēton Kentland and myclum ege flugon tó Lundenbyrig, Chr. 456; Erl. 13, 29: 872; Erl. 76, 15. Ðý ilcan geáre gesette Ælfréd cyning Lundenburg, 886; Erl. 84, 26.

Lunden-ceaster, e; *f. London*:—Is heora [*East Saxons*] ealdorburh nemmed Lunden-ceaster on ofre geseted ðæs foresprecenan streámes [*the Thames*] . . . Ðá hét Æþelbyrht on Lundenceastre cyricean getimbrian and ða gehálgian Sce. Paule, Bd. 2, 3; S. 504, 17-23. Se wæs Lundenceastre biscop, 2, 7; S. 509, 8. Eác swylce Eást-Seaxum hé gesette Ercenwold biscop in Lundenceastre, 4, 6; S. 573, 43.

Lundenisc; *adj. Belonging to London*:—Lundenisc *Lundoniensis*, Ælfc. Gr. 5; Som. 4, 28.

Lunden-waran, -ware; *pl. The people of London*:—Mellitum ðone biscop Lundenwaran onfón ne woldon *Mellitum Lundonienses episcopum recipere noluerunt*, Bd. 2, 6; S. 508, 37. Ðá wurdon Lundenware hédene, Chr. 616; Erl. 23, 10.

Lunden-wíc, es; *n. London*:—Æþelbyrht gesealde Mellite biscopsetle on Lundenwíc, Chr. 604; Erl. 21, 22.

lund-laga, an; *m. Rein, kidney*:—Ðes lundlaga *hic rigen* oððe *ren*, Ælfc. Gr. 9, 13; Som. 9, 34. Lundlaga *lien*, Wrt. Voc. 45, 14: *renunculus*, ii. 118, 72. Lundlagan *renunculi*, Wrt. Voc. 44, 67: *renunculæ*, 65, 58. Ðú nymst twegen lundlagan *sumes duos renes*, Ex. 29, 13: Lev. 8, 25. [Cf. *Icel.* lundir; *pl. f. the flesh along the back*: *O. H. Ger.* lunda *arvina*; *and see* gelynd, gelyndu.]

lungen, e; *f. A lung*:—Lungen *pulmo*, Wrt. Voc. 45, 11: *pulmon*, 65, 51. Lungena *pulmones*, 71, 5. Ðone man ðe biþ lungenne wund, L. M. 1, 38; Lchdm. ii. 92, 21. [*Icel.* lungu; *pl. n. the lungs*; *O. H. Ger.* lunga, lungina; *f. pulmo*: *Ger.* lunge.]

lungen-ádl, e; *f. Disease of the lungs*, Lchdm. iii. 20, 24: 22, 8.

lungen-sealf, e, *f. A salve for the lungs*:—Ðás wyrte sculon tó lungensealfe, Lchdm. iii. 16, 6.

lungen-wyrt, e; *f. Lung-wort*, Lchdm. ii. 398, col. 1: iii. 337, col. 1.

lungre; *adv. Quickly, soon, at once, straightway, speedily*:—Loth eode lungre út *Lot went out straightway*, Cd. 113; Th. 148, 24; Gen. 2461: Beo. Th. 5480; B. 2743. Cyning álýsde hine lungre, Ps. Th. 104, 16. Wén is ðæt hí ús lifigende lungre wyllen, snióme forsweolgan, 123, 2. Ðǽr him lífgedál lungre weorþeþ *there the parting with life shall happen to him suddenly*, Exon. 87 b; Th. 330, 3; Vy. 45: 10 a; Th. 11, 8; Cri. 167. Hié lungre ǽr feorh áléton *just before they had lost their lives*, Andr. Kmbl. 3255; An. 1630. Næs him gewemmed wlite ne wlóh of hrægle lungre álýsed *his beauty was not spoiled nor a fringe of his garment even loosened* [Grimm would translate *lungre* here *acriter, fortiter*], 2942; An. 1474. [Cf. *O. Sax.* lungar *strong*: *O. H. Ger.* lungar *strenuus*.]

lús; *f. A louse*:—Lús *pediculus* vel *sexpes*, Wrt. Voc. 24, 11. Swínes lús *usia*, 24, 34. Luus *peducla*, ii. 117, 8. Hine byton lýs, Hexam. 17; Norm. 24, 30. Hé áfylde eal heora land mid froggon, and siððan mid gnættum, eft mid hundes lúsum, Homl. Th. ii. 192, 21. [*Icel.* lús: *f*; *pl.* lýss: *O. H. Ger.* lús *pediculus*: *Ger.* laus.]

LUST, es; *m.* LUST, *desire, pleasure, voluptuousness*:—Epicurus sǽde ðæt se lust wǽre ðæt héhste gód *Epicurus summum bonum voluptatem esse constituit*, Bt. 24, 3; Fox 84, 23. Swá mycel hǽto and lust Cristes geleáfan *tantus fervor fidei et desiderium*, Bd. 2, 14; S. 518, 4. Him wæs metes micel lust *he had a craving for food*, Homl. Th. i. 86, 6. Lust oððe gǽlsa *luxus*, Ælfc. Gr. 11; Som. 15, 11. Hwǽr beóþ ðonne se ídla lust and seó swétnes ðæs hǽmedþinges ðe hé ǽr hátheortlíce lufode, Blickl. Homl. 59, 16. Lustes *veneris*, Wrt. Voc. ii. 92, 79. Luste *oblectamento*, Hpt. Gl. 525, 68. Mid ungeswencedlíce luste heofonlícra góda *infatigabili cælestium bonorum desiderio*, Bd. 5, 12; S. 631, 35. Nú is ðín folc on luste *now is thy people desirous*, Andr. Kmbl. 2046; An. 1025: Elen. Kmbl. 276; El. 138. Wedres on luste *glad on account of fair weather* or [?] *desirous of fair weather*, Exon. 97 a; Th. 361, 28; Wal. 26. Of luste flǽsces *ex voluntate carnis*, Jn. Skt. Rush. 1, 13. In lust *in luxum*, Wrt. Voc. ii. 47, 3: Hpt. Gl. 514, 5. Him sǽde his willan and his lust *ei indicasset desiderium suum*, Bd. 2, 15; S. 519, 7. Ofer lust mínne *a desiderio meo*, Ps. Th. 139, 8. Ðonne hafaþ hé micelne lust *ita ingentem libidinem haberet*, L. Med. ex Quad. 8, 8; Lchdm. i. 358, 20. Plegan, lustas *ludrica*, Wrt. Voc. ii. 52, 64. Him swedraden synna lustas *sinful lusts were stilled in him*, Exon. 34 a; Th. 109, 3; Gú. 84. Se man hine forhabban sceal on manegum þingum his lífes lusta *homini a multis vitæ suæ libidinibus abstinendum sit*, L. Ecg. P. 1, 5, arg; Th. ii. 170, 10. Hé hine ætbrǽd ðám flǽsclícum lustum, Homl. Th. i. 58, 19. Hé fulgǽþ his lustum and his plegan *he follows his desires and his pleasure*, 66, 12. Tó ðám upplícan lustum *ad superna desideria*, Bd. 4, 29; S. 607, 15. Of lustum ðiss lífes *voluptatibus vitæ*, Lk. Skt. 8, 14. Lustum *joyfully, gladly, voluntarily*, Cd. 1; Th. 2, 8; Gen. 16. Ic ðé lustum láce cwéme *voluntarie sacrificabo tibi*, Ps. Th. 53, 6. Néde oððe lustum, Bt. Met. Fox 9, 88; Met. 9, 44. Mid lustum, Dóm. L. 6, 70. Wesan on lustum *to live joyously*, Cd. 23; Th. 30, 26; Gen. 473. Here wæs on lustum *joyous were the people*, Judth. 11; Thw. 23, 38; Jud. 162. Ne heora lustas ne heora willan gefyllan *nec desideria vel vota complere*, Bd. 1, 7; S. 477, 38. Líces lustas, Exon. 71 b; Th. 267, 2; Jul. 409. [*Goth.* lustus: *O. Sax. O. Frs. O. H. Ger.* lust *luxus, appetitus, venus, delectatio, concupiscentia*: *Ger.* lust.] DER. firen-, syn-, un-lust.

lust; *adj.* (?) *Pleased, glad, desirous*:—Ðæt ðú ne gehýre lustum móde ðæra twýsprǽcena word *that thou be not glad* or *desirous to hear the words of the double-tongued* [or does *lustum* belong to the preceding word?], Wulfst. 246, 10.

lust-bǽre; *adj. Producing* or *having desire* or *pleasure, desirous, desirable, pleasant, agreeable*:—Lustbǽre *libens*, Ælfc. Gr. 33; Som. 37, 18: 44; Som. 46, 32. Lustbǽre on gesihþe *aspectu delectabile*, Gen. 3, 6. Ic wæs swíðe lustbǽre hine tó gehýranne *me audiendi avidum*, Bt. 22, 1; Fox 76, 7. Sió hǽlu hine gedéþ lustbǽrne *salubritas videtur praestare voluptatem*, 24, 3; Fox 84, 9. Wǽron lustbǽre for ðone leófan drihten wíta tó þrowienne, Homl. Skt. 4, 116. Ðás word sind lustbǽre tó gehýrenne *these words are pleasant to hear*, Homl. Th. i. 130, 16.

lustbǽr-líc; *adj. Desirable, pleasant*:—Eálá hú lustbǽrlíce tída on ðam dagum wǽron *O tempora desiderio dignissima!* Ors. 2, 5; Swt. 84, 25.

lustbǽr-líce; *adv. With delight, pleasure, eagerness, pleasantly*:—Ða leóþ ðe ic geó lustbǽrlíce song *carmina qui quondam studio florente peregi*, Bt. 2; Fox 4, 7. Ðá se wísdóm ðis leóþ lustbǽrlíce ásungen hæfde *hæc cum philosophia leniter suaviterque cecinisset*, 36, 1; Fox 170, 25.

lustbǽr-ness, e; *f. Desire, pleasure, pleasantness*:—Lustbǽrnes *delectatio*, Wrt. Voc. ii. 138, 56. Ða bereáfodon ǽlcere lustbǽrnesse *they robbed me of every pleasure*, Bt. 2; Fox 4, 11. Wē ðonne ne beóþ onǽlde mid ðære lustbǽrnesse ūres mōdes ðonne bistilþ sió slǽwþ on ūs ōþ ðæt heó ūs āwyrtwalaþ from ǽlcere lustbǽrnesse gōdra weorca *ipsa quippe mentis desidia, dum congruo fervore non accenditur, a bonorum desiderio funditus convalescente furtim torpore mactatur*, Past. 39, 1; Swt. 283, 3. Hit biþ onstyred mid ðære lustbǽrnesse *ex delectatione pulsatur*, 53, 6; Swt. 417, 13. Þurh Evan lustbǽrnesse oferswīðed *delectatione superatus*, 53, 7; Swt. 417, 28. Hī nāne lustbǽrnisse nabbaþ hī tō sēcanne *they have no desire to seek them*, Bt. 32, 3; Fox 118, 23. Lustbǽrnesse nimþ *cupidinem contrahat*, L. Ecg. P. iii. 14; Th. ii. 202, 4: Wrt. Voc. ii. 23, 72.

lust-full; *adj. Desirous*:—Gif his hwā sīe lustfull māre tō witanne sēce him ðonne self ðæt *if any one be desirous to know more of it, let him seek it himself*, Ors, 3, 2; Swt. 100, 27.

lustfullian; *p.* ode *To rejoice, be glad, take pleasure* [*in*]:—Swā ic lustfullige on ðisum lāðum wītum, swā swā se ðe gesihþ ðone ðe hē gewilnode, Homl. Skt. 8, 116. Heó lustfullode on hire fōstormōder hūse, Nar. 40, 12. Se cyning ongan lustfullian ðæt clǽneste līf hāligra and heora ðām swētestan gehātum [*rex*] *ipse delectatus vita mundissima sanctorum, et promissis eorum suavissimis*, Bd. 1, 26; S. 488, 8. Mid ðȳ se līchoma ongynneþ lustfullian *cum caro delectari cœperit*, 1, 27; S. 497, 22. Wē witan ðæt se līchoma ne mæg lustfullian būtan ðam mōde *cum caro delectare sine animo nequeat*, 497, 28. Ðā ongan hē lustfullian ðæs biscopes wordum, 2, 9; S. 511, 34. Ðā ongan se biscop lustfullian his wīslīcra worda, 5, 19; S. 637, 46. Evan swā swā līchoma wæs lustfulliende *Eva velut caro delectata est*, 1, 27; S. 497, 15: 5, 12; S. 630, 32. Lustfulligende, 4, 25; S. 600, 22. DER. ge-lustfullian.

lustful-līce; *adv. With joy* or *pleasure, joyfully, gladly*:—Lustfullīce *libenter*, Bd. 4, 27; S. 604, 30. Se mildheorta Drihten onfēhþ swīðe lustfullīce eallum ðǽm gōdum ðe ǽnig man gedēþ his ðæm nēhstan, Blickl. Homl. 37, 25.

lustful-ness, e; *f. Pleasure, delight, desire*:—Lustfulnes *oblectamenta*, Wrt. Voc. ii. 62, 49. Seó lustfulnys biþ þurh līchoman *delectatio fit per carnem*, Bd. 1, 27; S. 497, 13, 10, 18, 12, 30: Past. 53, 6; Swt. 417, 7, 8, 21, 24, 25. Drihten eallum geleáffulum monnum heora gong gestaþelade tō līfes wege ðæt hié māgon þurh ða lustfulnesse heora mōdes mid gōdum dǽdum geearnian leóht ðæs ēcan līfes *the Lord established for all believers their passage to the way of life, that they may through the ardent desire of their mind earn with good deeds the light of everlasting life*, Blickl. Homl. 17, 20.

lustfullung, e; *f. Pleasure, delight*:—Of ȳdelum gylpe biþ ācenned lustfullung leásre herunge *from vainglory is born a delight in false praise*, Homl. Th. ii. 220, 33. Lustfullunge *oblectamento*, Hpt. Gl. 525, 68.

lustgeorn-ness, e; *f. Desire, concupiscence*:—Lustgeornnisse *fornicationis*, Mt. Kmbl. p. 14, 16. Lustgiornisses *concupiscentiæ*, Mk. Skt. Lind. 4, 19.

lust-grin, e; *f. Snare set by pleasure*, Soul Kmbl. 46; Seel. 23. [The MS. has *lustgryrum* for which Grein proposes to read *lustgrynum*.]

lūs-þorn, es; *m. The spindle tree*; euonymus Europæus:—On lūsþorn; of lūsþorne, Cod. Dip. Kmbl. iii. 77, 19. [v. *E. D. S. Plant Names* louse-berry tree: *Dutch* luizen-boom.]

lust-līce; *adv. With pleasure, gladly, willingly*:—Lustlīce *libenter*, Ælfc. Gr. 44; Som. 46, 32. Lustlīce onfōn *libenter excipere*, Bd. 3, 11; S. 535, 18: 3, 3; S. 525, 30. For ðē wē wolden lustlīce sweltan *for thee we would gladly die*, Ap. Th. 26, 6. Ðe nū lustlīce sibbsumes friþes æt eów biddende sindon *who now are willing to ask a friendly peace from you*, Ors. 1, 11; Swt. 48, 22. Ða godcundan lāre lustlīce gehȳran, Blickl. Homl. 47, 28: 49, 32. v. for-lustlīce.

lustmoce, an; *f. Lady's smock*; Cardamine pratensis:—Lustmoce croppan, L. M. 1, 38; Lchdm. ii. 92, 23. Lustmocan crop, Lchdm. ii. 92, 8. Genime lustmocan, 1, 30; Lchdm. ii. 70, 17.

lustsum-līc; *adj. Pleasant, delectable*:—Ic nāt for hwī eów sindon ða ǽrran gewin swā lustsumlīce on leóþcwidum tō gehiéranne, Ors. 3, 7; Swt. 120, 2. [Cf. *O. H. Ger.* lustsam *amoenus, dulcis, delectabilis.*]

LŪTAN; *p.* leát; *pl.* luton; *pp.* loten *To lout, bow, bend forward, stoop, fall down before one*:—Hē lūteþ æfter *he boweth after it*, Salm. Kmbl. 806; Sal. 402. Leótt [hleát, Lind.] tō fōtum his *procidit ad pedes ejus*, Mk. Skt. Rush, 5, 22. Hē ārās and ðā tō eorþan leát *he rose up, and then bowed to the ground*, Guthl. 17; Gdwin. 74, 7. Hē leát tō ðæs cāseres eáre *he bent down to the emperor's ear*, Homl. Th. i. 376, 28. Ðæt heofonlīce wolcn leát wið his and hine genam *the cloud from heaven stooped towards him, and received him*, 296, 2. Hē forþ leát on his andwlitan *procideret in faciem*, Bd. 4, 3; S. 569, 11. Hē leát forþ ðæt him man āslōh ðæt heáfod of *he bent forward so that his head was struck off*, Ors. 6, 34; Bos. 130, 16. Hē leát forþ tō ðæm men ðe hine sleán mynte, Blickl. Homl. 223, 7. Gāsta unclǽnra lutun tō him *spiritus inmundi procidebant ei*, Mk. Skt. Rush. 3, 11. Loð and Josue luton wið heora (*the angels they saw*), Homl. Th. i. 38. 21. Ðeáh heó onsīge and lūte tō ðære eorþan *though she* [*the sun*] *sink and stoop to the earth*, Bt. 25; Fox 88, 25. Forþ lūten wē *procidamus*, Ps. Surt. 94, 6. [*R. Glouc. Chauc.* Piers P. loute: *Icel.* lūta *to bow down.*] DER. ā-, ge-, on-, under-lūtan.

luðer-. v. lyðer-.

lutian; *p.* ode *To lie hid, be concealed, lurk, skulk, be latent*:—Sum gedwyld lutaþ ðǽr *aliquis latet error*, Ælfc. Gr. 44; Som. 45, 46. Of ðam fȳre ðe him on lutaþ *from the fire that is latent in it*, Lchdm. iii. 274, 4. Hū moniga dīgla costunga ðæs ealdan feóndes lutigeaþ on ðȳs andweardan līfe *quanta in hujus vitae itinere tentamenta antiqui hostis lateant*, Past. 21, 5; Swt. 159, 24. Ðū lutodest ōþ ðis on ðam lāðum cristendōme *thou hast skulked until now in that detestable Christianity*, Homl. Skt. 5, 413. Ða iermingas ūt of ðæm holan crupon ðe heó on lutedan *the wretched creatures crept out of the holes that they had lurked in*, Ors. 2, 8; Swt. 92, 30. Ða ōðre ðe lutedon on ðære dīgelnisse *insidiæ, quæ latebant*, Jos. 8, 19. Lutiaþ ðǽr þrȳ dagas *ibi latitate tribus diebus*, 2, 16. Eal ðæt gehȳddes lutige *omne, quod clausum latet*, Past. 21, 3; Swt. 153, 15. Nys hyt swā stearc winter ðæt ic durre lutian æt hām for ege hlāfordes mīnes *non est tam aspera hyems ut audeam latere domi prae timore domini mei*, Coll. Monast. Th. 19, 17. Fērde ðā lutigende geond heges and weges geond wudes and feldes swā ðæt hē [*king Alfred*] gesund becom tō Æþelingēge, Shrn. 16, 11. Dīgelne leahter on menniscre heortan lutigende *secret sin lurking in the human heart*, Homl. Th. i. 496, 18. Cwæþ ðæt hē god wǽre on mannes hiwe lutiende *said that he was a god concealed in the form of a man*, ii. 474, 22. [*Laym. Trev. Piers P. Chauc.* lotie *to lie hid*: *O. H. Ger.* luzēn *latere*, Grff. ii. 322.] Cf. lot, lytig.

lybb, es; *n. Medicine, drug, simple*, in a bad sense *poison*; the word often implies the use of witchcraft, see the compounds; as Grimm says 'aus der bedeutung des erlaubten φάρμακον gieng hernach die des schädlichen, zauberhaften hervor,' D. M. 1103:—Lyb *obligamentum*, Wrt. Voc. ii. 65, 31. Lybb, Ep. Gl. 17 b, 13. Ðæt biþ lyb wið eágena dimnesse *that is a medicine for dimness of eyes*, L. M. 1, 2; Lchdm. ii. 30, 14. Oxna lyb *green or black hellebore*, Lchdm. ii. 34, 28. Ðis ðē lib be cyrneles *this may be a medicine for thee for churnel*, iii. 62, 21. [*O. L. Ger.* lubbe; *dat. suco*: cf. lubbian *medicare*: *Icel.* lyf; *f.* also *n. a herb, simple*, esp. with the notion of healing, witchcraft, or supernatural power; cf. ū-lyfjan *poison*; lyfja *to heal*: *O. H. Ger.* luppi; *n. maleficium, succus lethiferus*; luppōn *medicare*: cf. *Goth.* lubja-leisei φαρμακεία.] v. cȳs-lybb, un-lybbe, lybesn.

lybbestre, an; *f. A witch, sorcerer*:—Lybbestran *carios*, Wrt. Voc. ii. 129, 12. v. lybb, lyb-lǽca; *and* cf. *O. H. Ger.* luppari *veneficus, maleficus.*

lyb-corn, es; *n.* '*A grain of purgative effect*, especially the seeds of various *euforbias*, probably also of some of the gourds, as *momordica elaterium, cucumis colocynthis*,' Cockayne Lchdm. ii. 397, col 2:—Libbcorn *catharticum*, Wrt. Voc. 67, 8. Libcorn *lacyride*, 67, 73: *tytymalosca*, 68, 55. Lybcorn *cartomo*, ii. 14, 14; *lattyride*, 54, 23: *cartam*, 103, 53; *chartamo*, 76: *catarticum, potus*, 129, 43. Wyrc ūtyrnendne drænc genim fīf and hundeahtatig lybcorna *make a purgative drink thus; take eighty-five purgative seeds*, Lchdm. iii. 18, 12: 20, 1. Wyrc ōðerne [spīwdrænc] of beóre and of feówertig lybcorna, 20, 10.

lyb-cræft, es; *m. Magic, witchcraft, skill in the use of* lybb:—Hió him sealdon āttor drincan ðæt mid myclen lybcræfte wæs geblanden, Blickl. Homl. 229, 12.

lybesn, lyfesn, lybsen, e; *f. A charm, an amulet*:—Lyb, lybsn *obligamentum*, Wrt. Voc. ii. 115, 23. Lyb, lyfesn, 63, 23. Lybsin *lustramenta*, 82, 10. Lyfesna *filacteria*, 36, 72: 73, 16. Lybesne *strenas*, 121, 36. Swā swā hī ðæt sende wīte fram Gode scyppende þurh heora galdor oððe lifesne oððe ōðre dīgolnesse deófolcræftes bewerian mihte *quasi missam a Deo conditore plagam per incantationes, vel fylacteria, vel alia dæmonicæ artus arcana cohibere valerent*, Bd. 4, 27; S. 604, 9.

lyb-lāc, es; *n. m. Sorcery, witchcraft, the art of using drugs* or *potions for the purpose of poisoning*, or *for magical purposes*:—Ðis synt ða īdelnyssa ðisse worulde ... lyblāc ... scīncræft *hæ sunt vanitates hujus mundi ... maleficium ... ars magica* [cf. Gal. 5, 20 *where Gothic has* lubjaleisei = φαρμακεία, A. V. witchcraft], L. Ecg. P. i. 8; Th. ii. 174, 34. Hēr ys seó bōt hū ðū meaht ðīne æceras bētan gif ðǽr hwilc ungedēfe þing on gedōn biþ on drȳ oððe on lyblāce, Lchdm. 1, 398, 3. Gif hī hwilc man niman wile oððe hyra æthrīneþ ðonne forbærnaþ hī sona eall his līc ðæt syndon ungefrægelīcu lyblāc *if any man wants to catch them* [*certain fowls*] *or touches them, then at once they consume all his body: those are most extraordinary cases of witchcraft*, Nar. 34, 3. Wið ealra bealwa gehwylc ðara lyblāca *against every harm from sorceries*, Lchdm. i. 402, 11. Wē cwǽdon be ðǽm wiccecræftum and be liblācum gif ðǽr man ācweald wǽre ... *we have ordained concerning witchcrafts and sorceries, if in such cases any one were killed ...*, L. Ath. i. 6; Th. i. 202, 10. Be liblācum. Ða ðe lyblāc wyrcaþ sȳn hī ā fram ǽlcum Godes dǽle āworpene, būton hī tō rihtre dǽdbōte gecyrran, L. Edm. E. 6; Th. i. 246, 13–16. Bebeorh ðē wið lyblācas and āttorcræftas *cave tibi a maleficiis et veneficiis* [cf. ne unrihtlyblācas ne ongynne wē, Wulfst. 253, 11, MS. D.], L. Ecg. C. prm; Th. ii. 132 9. DER. unriht-lyblāc. v. next word.

lyb-lǽca, an; *m. A sorcerer*:—Lyblǽcan *caragios* [*caragius sortilegus, præstigiator qui characteribus magicis utitur*, Ducange], Wrt. Voc. ii. 13, 53. v. fugel-hwata.
lyb-wyrhta. v. unlyb-wyrhta.
lȳcþ, Bt. Met. 12, 55; Met. 12, 28. v. lūcan.
lȳden. v. lǽden.
lȳfan. v. līfan.
lyfesn. v. lybesn.
lyffetere, es; *m. A flatterer*:—Lyffetere *adulator*, Wrt. Voc. 85, 40. Liffetere, 49, 14. Đonne ādumbiaþ đa ȳdelan lyffeteras *then shall the vain flatterers be dumb*, Homl. Th. ii. 570, 35. Faraþ tō đām lyffeterum đe eów ǽr leáslīce ōlæhton *go to the flatterers that before fawned on you falsely*, 570, 23: i. 494, 10.
lyffettan; *p.* te *To flatter, pay court to*:—Ic lyffytte *adulor*, Ælfc. Gr. 25; Som. 26, 63. Đa byrþeras đe hine tō byrgenne feredon synd ōlæcunga lyffetyndra geférena *the bearers who carried him to the grave are the blandishments of flattering companions*, Homl. Th. i. 492, 28. Lyffetyndra tungan gewrīđaþ manna sāwla on synnum *the tongues of flatterers bind the souls of men in sins*, 494, 6.
lyffetung, e; *f. Flattery, adulation, paying court to*:—Lyffetung *adulatio*, Wrt. Voc. 85, 41. Liffetung, 49, 15. Herige hine nā on đisum līfe, ac æfter his geendunge, đonne ne deraþ nān lyffetung đām herigendum, and nān upāhefednys ne costnaþ đone geheredan, Homl. Th. ii. 560, 19. Ne hlyste gē heora geswǽsan lyffetunge, 404, 29. Heora nān ne gedyrstlǽce đæt heó Godes landāre woroldrīcum sellen for lyffetunge *let none of them dare to give God's lands to the powerful of the earth as a means of paying court to them*, Lchdm. iii. 442, 32. Đæt mǽden ne mihte beón bepǽht þurh ǽnige lyffetunge fram hire leófan drihtne, Homl. Skt. 7, 86. Hwǽr beóþ đa līđan lyffetunga đe hine forlǽddon ǽror *where are the fair flatteries that formerly seduced him?* Basil admn. 8; Norm. 50, 27. Đa smēđan lyffetunga, Homl. Th. ii. 572, 1. Lyffetungum befangen, i. 492, 32.
lȳf-ness. v. leáf-ness.
lyft, es, e; *m. f. n. Air, atmosphere, breeze, sky, heavens, cloud*:—Lyft *aer*, Wrt. Voc. 52, 55. Lybt *sudum*, ii. 121, 66. Stemn is geslagen lyft ... ǽlc stemn biþ geworden of đæs mūþes clypunge and of đære lyfte cnyssunge; se mūþ drȳfþ ūt đa clypunge and seó lyft biþ geslagen mid đære clypunge, Ælfc. Gr. 1; Som. 2, 31–35. Ān đæra [*the elements*] is eorþe, ōđer wæter, þridde lyft, feówrþe fȳr, Bt. 33, 4; Fox 128, 30. Đeós lyft đe wē on libbaþ is ān đæra feówer gesceafta ... Lyft is swȳđe þynne, seó ofergǽþ ealne middangeard, and up āstīhþ forneán ōþ đone mōnan, on đam fleóþ fugelas ... Ne mihte heora nān fleón nǽre seó [đæt MS. R.] lyft đe hī byrþ. Ne nān man nǽfþ nāne orþunge būton þurh đa lyfte [đæt lyft MS. M.], Lchdm. iii. 272, 12–22. Seó lyft đonne heó āstyred is byþ wind, 274, 10. Se storm and seó stronge lyft *the storm and the strong blast*, Exon. 22 b; Th. 61, 28; Cri. 991. Seó hǽwene lyft *the azure air*, Cd. 166; Th. 207, 33; Exod. 476. Đeós lyft scīnþ unwederlīce *rutilat triste cælum*, Mt. Kmbl. 16, 3. Lyft *nubes, aer*, Hpt. Gl. 493, 52. Seó lyft hī ofersceadewude and stefn com of đære lyfte *facta est nubis obumbrans eos et venit vox de nube*, Mk. Skt. 9, 7. Đære lyfte fugelas, Gen. 1, 28. Laguflōda gelāc lyfte and tungla *the movement of waters, of air and of stars*, Bt. Met. Fox 20, 346; Met. 20, 173. Under lyfte helm, Exon. 102 a; Th. 386, 19; Rä. 4, 64. Līxeþ lyftes mægen, 116 b; Th. 448, 16; Dōm. 55. On genipum lyftes *in nubibus aeris*, Ps. Spl. 17, 13. Se giem jacintus, se is lyfte onlīcusđ on hiwe, Past. 14; Swt. 85, 5. Beorc byþ lyfte getenge *the birch towers to the sky*, Runic pm. Kmbl. 343, 2; Rūn. 18. Hægl hwyrft of heofones lyfte, 341, 5; Rūn. 9: Exon. 116 a; Th. 446, 10; Dōm. 20. Nān wolcn næs on đære lyfte gesewen *no cloud was seen in the sky*, Homl. Th. ii. 182, 35. Leólc on lyfte *sported in air*, Cd. 23; Th. 29, 10; Gen. 448. On lyfte cumende *venientem in nube*, Lk. Skt. 21, 27. On lofte heó stynt *it* [*the earth*] *rests in the air*, Hexam. 6; Norm. 10, 20. Under lyfte *sub divo*, Wrt. Voc. ii. 83, 34: Andr. Kmbl. 839; An. 420. Nalles æfter lyfte lācende hwearf *he went not sporting through the air*, Beo. Th. 5656; B. 2832. Hē gesette storm his on lyfte *statuit procellam ejus in auram*, Ps. Spl. 106, 29. Hē gesceóp đæt upplīce lyft, Hexam. 4; Norm. 6, 24. Đæt lyft hē gesceóp, Norm. 8, 17. Sōna swā hī [*snakes*] đæs landes [*Ireland*] lyft gestuncan, swā swulton hī, Bd. 1, 1; S. 474, 35. Đonne līgette and þunorrāde eorþan and lyfte brēgdon, 4, 3; S. 569, 13. Swā oft swā hē lyft onstyrige, 569, 29. Hī fleóþ geond đās lyft, Homl. Th. ii. 90, 21: Elen. Kmbl. 1464; El. 734. On lyft āstāh *rose into the air*, 1796; El. 900. Đū þurh lyft lǽtest leódum tō freme mildne morgenrēn *for the benefit of men thou dost let the gentle morning rain fall through the air*, Exon. 54 a; Th. 190, 30; Az. 81. Fugel under lyft ofer lagu lōcaþ georne, 57 a; Th. 204, 21; Ph. 101. Āhafen on đa heán lyft *raised aloft*, Cd. 69; Th. 84, 22; Gen. 1401. Hātwendne lyft *the torrid air*, 146; Th. 182, 12; Exod. 74. Đonne gē geseóþ đa lyfte cumende on westdǽle *cum videritis nubem orientem ab occasu*, Lk. Skt. 12, 54. Hibernia on smyltnysse lyfta is betere mycle đonne Breotone land *Hibernia serenitate aerum multum Brittaniæ præstat*, Bd. 1, 1; S. 474, 30. Geleht lyftum *moistened by the clouds*, Bt. Met. Fox 20, 195; Met. 20, 98. Lyftu *æthera, aera*, Hpt. Gl. 457, 48. Geond lyftu *per aera*, Hymn. Surt. 66, 5. Đās lyfta and windas hē āstyraþ, Wulfst. 196, 6. [*Goth.* luftus; *m*: *O. Sax.* luft; *m. f*: *Icel.* lopt; *n*; *O. H. Ger.* luft; *f. n.*: *Ger.* luft; *f.*]
lȳft. v. līft.
lyft-ādl, e; *f. Palsy, paralysis*:—Mid đa ādle đe Grēcas nemnaþ *paralysis*, wē cweþaþ lyftādl, Bd. 4, 31; S. 610, 17. Fram lyftādle gehǽled *a paralysi sanatus*, 610, 2. Wiđ lyftādle, L. M. 1, 59; Lchdm. ii. 130, 1.
lyft-edor, es; *m. An enclosure formed by clouds* [? v. lyft]:—Sīđboda lyftedoras bræc *the pillar of fire broke through the clouds*, Cd. 155; Th. 193, 24; Exod. 251.
lyften; *adj. Aërial, airy*:—Hwī is đæt tācn on đære lyftenan heofonan gesewen *why is that sign* [*the rainbow*] *seen in the aërial heaven?* Boutr. Scrd. 21, 23. Hī sind genumene tō lyftenre heofenan nā tō rodorlīcre *they* [*Enoch and Elijah*] *are taken to the aërial heaven, not to the etherial heaven*, Homl. Th. i. 308, 3. Lyftene gnættas *the gnats of the air*, Hexam. 17; Norm. 24, 30. [*O. H. Ger.* luftin *aëreus.*]
lyft-fæt, es; *n. An aërial vessel* [*the moon*], Exon. 108 a; Th. 411, 21; Rä. 30, 3.
lyft-fleógend, es; *m. That which flies in the air, a bird*:—Lyftfleógendra, Salm. Kmbl. 579; Sal. 289.
lyft-floga, an; *m. A flier in the air* [*a dragon*], Beo. Th. 4619; B. 2315.
lyft-gelāc, es; *n. Motion in* or *of the air*:—þurh lyftgelāc on land becwom [*he was borne through the air*], Andr. Kmbl. 1653; An. 828. þurh lyftgelāc lēges blæstas weallas ymbwurpon [*the winds blew the flames*], 3102; An. 1554.
lyft-geswenced; *adj. Weather-beaten*:—Ceól lyftgeswenced on lande stōd, Beo. Th. 3830; B. 1913.
lyft-helm, es; *m. The air, atmosphere, cloud*:—Lyfthelm and laguflōd *air* [or *cloud?*] *and water*, Menol. Fox 553; Gn. C. 46. Wǽron land heora lyfthelme beþeaht *their lands were covered with cloud*, Cd. 145; Th. 181, 13; Exod. 60.
lyft-lācende *sporting* or *playing in the air, moving hither and thither in the air*:—Ic bidde đæt đū mē gecȳđe hwæt đes þegn sȳ lyftlācende, Exon. 69 b; Th. 259, 12; Jul. 281. Forlǽt rēc āstīgan lyftlācende, Elen. Kmbl. 1588; El. 796. Sīđ tugon lyftlācende *took their way in flight through the air* [*of evil spirits*], Exon. 34 b; Th. 110, 31; Gū. 117. Hefonfugelas lyftlācende, Cd. 192; Th. 240, 17; Dan. 388.
lyft-sceaþa, an; *m. The robber of the air* [*the raven*], Exon. 87 b; Th. 329, 24; Vy. 39.
lyft-wundor, es; *n. A wonder of the air* [*the pillar that conducted the Israelites*], Cd. 146; Th. 183, 11; Exod. 90.
lyft-wynn, e; *f. The pleasantness of the air*:—Lyftwynne heóld *enjoyed himself* [*the dragon*] *by flying through the air*, Beo. Th. 6079; B. 3043.
Lyge, an; *f. The river Lea*:—Ūre landgemǽra up on Temese and đonne up on Ligan [Ligean, 2nd text] and andlang Ligan [Ligean] ōþ hire ǽwylm *our* [*English and Danes*] *boundaries: up on the Thames, then up on the Lea, up to its source*, L. A. G. 1; Th. i. 152, 9. Đa Deniscan tugon hira scipu up on Temese, and đā up on Lygan, Chr. 895; Erl. 93, 32. Se foresprecena here worhte geweorc be Lygan, 896; Erl. 93, 35. Lygean, 913; Erl. 102, 2.
lyge, es; *m. A lie, lig* [provincial], *falsehood*:—Ic eów tō sōþe secgan wille and đæs in līfe lyge ne wyrþeþ *in truth I will tell you, and never shall it prove false*, Elen. Kmbl. 1147; El. 575. Sōþfæstnysse feóung and seó lufu liges and leásunge *odium veritatis amorque mendacii*, Bd. 1, 14; S. 482, 24. Liges fȳr *mendacii ignis*, 3, 19; S. 548, 13. Būta lyg *verumtamen*, Mt. Kmbl. Lind. 11, 24. Hī on lige lange feredon *de mendacio compellantur*, Ps. Th. 58, 12. Mengan lyge wiđ sōđe, Elen. Kmbl. 613; El. 307. Đū ǽr sægdest sōþlīce and nū on lyge cyrrest, 1329; El. 666. Đū ūs gelǽrdæst þurh đīnne lyge *thou didst persuade us through thy falsehood*, Cd. 214; Th. 268, 11; Sat. 53. Hwæđer him mon sōþ đe lyge sagaþ, Exon. 27 a; Th. 80, 16; Cri. 1307. Ic đe tō sōþe secgan wille, nelle ic lyge fremman, 67 b; Th. 250, 27; Jul. 133. Mān on mōde, in mūþe lyge, 80 b; Th. 302, 13; Fä. 35. [*Icel.* lygi; *f. a lie*: *O. H. Ger.* lugi; *f. mendum, falsum, figmentum, fabula*: *Ger.* lüge.]
lyge, lycce; *adj. Lying, mendacious, false*:—Sōhtun lyge gewitnisse wiđ đone hǽlend ... đonne monige lyge [leáse ɫ lycce, Lind.] gewitu cwōmun ætnǽhste đā cwōman twægen lyge [leáso ɫ liycce, Lind.] gewitu *quærebant falsum testimonium contra Jesum ... cum multi falsi testes accessissent novissime autem venerunt duo falsi testes*, Mt. Kmbl. Rush. 26, 59–60. Monige lyge ɫ leáse wītga *multi pseudoprophetæ*, 24, 11: 24, 44. Behaldeþ eów wiđ lyge ɫ leáse wītgu *attendite a falsis prophetis*, 7, 15. [*O. Sax. O. L. Ger.* luggi: *O. H. Ger.* luggi, lucki *mendax, falsus.*] *See also the compounds of which* lyge *is the first part.*
lyge *a plant name*, sicalia, Wrt. Voc. 68, 72.
Lygean-burh, *Lenborough, near Buckingham*:—Hēr Cūþwulf genom Lygeanburg, Chr. 571; Erl. 18, 13. See Green's Making of England, pp. 118 sqq.
Lyge-tūn, Lyg-tūn *Leighton, in Bedfordshire*:—Đæt rād ūt wiđ Lygtūnes, Chr. 917; Erl. 102, 16. Æt Lygetūne, Cod. Dip. Kmbl. i. 196, 3.

lygen, e; *f. A lie, falsehood*:—Ðǽr lyt gehâta biþ ðǽr biþ lyt lygena *where there are few promises, there are few lies*, Prov. Kmbl. 7. Mid ligenum *with lies*, Cd. 25; Th. 31, 36; Gen. 496: 26; Th. 34, 2; Gen. 531: 28; Th. 37, 11; Gen. 588. Lygenum, Th. 37, 31; Gen. 598. [*O. Sax.* lugina: *O. H. Ger.* lugina *mendacium.*]

lygen-word, es; *n. A lying word, lie, falsehood*:—Mid ligenwordum, Cd. 33; Th. 43, 32; Gen. 699. Cf. lyge-word.

lyge-searu, wes; *n. A false trick, artifice, wile, snare, lying art*:—Hý ligesearwum âhôfun hearmstafas *with lying arts they stirred up mischiefs*, Exon. 35 b; Th. 115, 34; Gú. 199: Elen. Kmbl. 415; El. 208. Lygesearwum, Exon. 19 a; Th. 48, 23; Cri. 776.

lyge-spell, es; *n. A false speech*:—Mid ligespelle *me[n]dosa mandata*, Wrt. Voc. ii. 58, 32. [Cf. *Icel.* lygi-saga *a lying story, false report.*]

lyge-synnig; *adj. Guilty of lying, false*:—Lygesynnig feónd, Elen. Kmbl. 1795; El. 899.

lyge-torn, es; *n. Feigned anger* or *grief* [?]:—Ne biþ cwênlîc þeáw ðætte freoþuwebbe feores onsæce æfter ligetorne leófne mannan *it is no womanly fashion that a peaceweaver [woman] attack a loved man's life, having only a pretended cause for anger against him* [? *Thorpe reads* lîgtorn *burning anger*], Beo. Th. 3890; B. 1943.

lyge-word, es; *n. A lying word, lie, falsehood*:—Lygeword spǽcon *locuti sunt falsa*, Ps. Th. 57, 3: Cd. 210; Th. 261, 3; Dan. 720. Ne wêne ǽnig ðæt ic lygewordum leóþ somnige, Exon. 63 b; Th. 234, 28; Ph. 547. [*Icel.* lygi-orð.]

lyge-wyrhta, an; *m. A liar, a forger of lies*:—Mid ðâm ligewyrhtum *with the forgers of lies*, Fragm. Kmbl. 19; Leás. 11.

lyg-ness, e; *f. Deceitfulness, falseness*:—Lygnisse weolan *fallacia divitiarum*, Mt. Kmbl. Rush. 13, 22.

lýgnian. v. lîgnian.

lýhtan. v. lîhtan.

lynd, e; *f. Grease, fat, fatness*:—Lind *arvina*, Wrt. Voc. 65, 14. Lynde *[a]rvina*, 284, 6. Hê hî fêdde mid fætre lynde hwǽte *cibavit eos ex adipe frumenti*, Ps. Th. 80, 15: 147, 3. [*O. H. Ger.* lunda *arvina.*]

lyni-bôr [v. Wrt. Voc. ii. 98, 7 boor *dasile*] *a gimlet, auger*:—Lynibôr *terebellus*, Wrt. Voc. ii. 287, 14. v. next word.

lynis, es; *m. An axletree*:—Spâcan *radii*: felg *canti*: lynis *axedo*: eax *axis*, Wrt. Voc. 284, 47-51. Lynis *axsedo*: lynisas *axsedones*, ii. 7, 52, 51. [*Wm. of Shoreham* linses *axles*: cf. *O. H. Ger.* lun *obex*: *Du.* luns: *Ger.* lünse *a linch-pin*: *Dan.* lun-stikke *a linch-pin.* Linch-, lin-pin *is earlier spelt* lins-pin.]

lypen-wyrhta, an; *m. A tanner, currier*:—Lypenwyrhta *byrseus*, Wrt. Voc. 288, 14. Leðerwyrhta oððe lypenwyrhta *byrseus*, ii. 11, 49.

lyre, es; *m. Loss, damage, destruction, detriment*:—Lyre *jactura*, Wrt. Voc. 74, 51. Hýnþ *vel* lyre *vel* hearm *dispendium* vel *damnum* vel *detrimentum*, 47, 29. Hire lima lyre [*of a person paralysed*], Homl. Th. ii. 546, 31. 'Ic wille ofgân æt ðê his blôd' ðæt is his lyre '*I will require at thy hands his blood*;' *that is, his destruction*, i. 6, 27. Lîfes lyre *death*, Exon. 44 b; Th. 151, 26; Gú. 801. Ne se enga deáþ, ne lîfes lyre, 56 b; Th. 201, 8; Ph. 53. Ne biþ ðǽr wædl ne lyre ne deáþes gryre, Dôm. L. 16, 265: Wulfst. 139, 32. Hê macode heora lîf tô lyre *he destroyed them*, 106, 6. Hwîlum forlidenesse ic þolie mid lyre ealra þinga mînra *aliquando naufragium patior, cum jactura omnium rerum mearum*, Coll. Monast. Th. 27, 1. On lyre *in perditione*, Ps. Lamb. 87, 12. Lyre *jacturam, damnum*, Hpt. Gl. 480, 43. Nâ beóþ ða eádige ðe for hýnþum oððe lirum hwîlwendlîcra hyðða heófiaþ, Homl. Th. i. 550, 28. DER. feorh-, land-, lîf-lyre; *and see* lor.

lýsan, lýsing. v. lîsan, lîsing.

lyssen. v. lyswen.

LYSTAN; *p.* te *To* LIST, *cause pleasure* or *desire* [with dat. or acc. of person in whom the feeling is caused, and gen. of the thing, or infin.]:—Mê ne lyst *piget*, Ælfc. Gr. 33; Som. 37, 23. Mê lyst rǽdan *lecturio*, 34; Som. 37, 56. Hine ne lyst his willan wyrcean, Blickl. Homl. 51, 16. Hú ne biþ ǽlc mon genôg earm ðæs ðe hê næfþ ðonne hit hine lyst habban *is not every man poor enough as regards that which he has not, when he desires to have it?* Bt. 26, 1; Fox 92, 2. Ne him nǽfre genôg ne þincþ ǽr hê hæbbe eall ðæt hine lyst, 33, 2; Fox 124, 7. Wel mê lîcode ðæt ðú ǽr sǽdest and ðises mê lyst nú get bet *I liked well what you said before, and am still better pleased with this*, 35, 4; Fox 162, 3; 34, 6; Fox 142, 12. Ðam men ðe hine ne lyst his metes *for the man who has no appetite for his food*, L. M. 1, 19; Lchdm. ii. 62, 15. Ðonne hine ǽtes lysteþ, Exon. 97 a; Th. 363, 12; Wal. 52: Bt. Met. Fox 10, 27; Met. 10, 14. Se leahtor dêþ ðæt ðam men ne lyst nân þing tô gôde gedôn *that sin causes a man to have no desire to do anything to good purpose*, Homl. Th. ii. 220, 22. Him lyste ðǽr on dîgolnysse his gebedu begangan, Bd. 3, 16; S. 542, 33. Hine lyste mid him etan and drincan *ipse delectaretur manducare et bibere cum eis*, 5, 5; S. 618, 16: Beo. Th. 3591; B. 1793. Hine nânes þinges ne lyste on ðisse worulde *he cared for nothing in this world*, Bt. 35, 6; Fox 168, 12: Bt. Met. Fox 26, 142; Met. 26, 71. Se gesceádwîslîca willa ðæt hine ðara twega lyste *the rational will which delights in them both*, Bt. 14, 2; Fox 44, 26: Bt. Met. Fox 10, 2; Met. 10, 1. Hê sceal syllan his gôd on ða tîd ðe hine sylfne sêlest lyste his brûcan, Blickl. Homl. 101, 20. [Cf. *Goth.* lustôn (*with gen.*) *to desire*: *O. Sax.* lustean (*acc. of pers., gen. of thing*): *Icel.* lysta (*acc. of pers.*): *O. H. Ger.* lustjan (*acc. of pers., gen. of thing,* or *infin.*); cf. *also* lustôn *to desire*: *Ger.* lüsten (*impers.*)] DER. ge-, of-lystan.

lystere (=? hlystere):—Lysteres *fautoris*, Hpt. Gl. 571, 40.

lysu; *adj. Depraved, corrupt, evil, dishonourable, shameful, profligate*:—Lyswe lârsmeoþas *corrupt counsellors*, Andr. Kmbl. 2441; An. 1222. Cf. lyswen.

lysu, wes; *n. What is depraved* [v. preceding word]:—Gif cyning æt mannes hâm drincæþ and ðǽr man lyswæs hwæt gedô ii bôte gebête *if the king be entertained at a man's house, and any evil be done there, let a double fine be paid*, L. Ethb. 3; Th. i. 4, 2. Gif frî wîf leswæs hwæt gedêþ xxx scill. gebête, 73; Th. i. 20, 7. Lot sceal mid lyswe, list mid gedêfum [v. list], Exon. 92 a; Th. 345, 16; Gn. Ex. 189.

lyswen, lyssen; *adj. Full of matter, corrupt, purulent; depraved* [?]:—Ðonne se swile tôbyrst ðonne biþ seó micge lyswen swilce worms, L. M. 2, 17; Lchdm. ii. 198, 26. [In Ps. Th. 52, 6 the word *lisne* occurs; can this be the adverb from this adjective, taken in the sense given to *lysu*:—Manna bân mihtig Drihten lisne tôsceádeþ *scatters with shame* or *dishonour?*] v. lysu *and next word.*

lyswen, lyssen *matter, purulence*:—On ðære þrotan biþ swyle and lyssen, L. M. 1, 4; Lchdm. ii. 46, 14.

lyt; *indecl. used as subst. adj. and adv. Few, little*:—Ðæra is nú tô lyt ðe wile wel tǽcan *there are now too few of those that will teach well*, Homl. Th. i. 6, 22. Ðæra biþ ealles tô lyt, ðe hê ne beswîce, Wulfst. 97, 7. Is swîðe lyt monna ðæt ne sý mid ðǽm sumum besmiten *there are very few men that are not defiled with some of them*, L. E. I. 31; Th. ii. 428, 4. Wôp wæs wîde, worulddreáma lyt, Cd. 144; Th. 180, 9; Exod. 42. Ðê eádes tô lyt þuhte, Exon. 28 a; Th. 86, 1; Cri. 1401. Wergendra tô lyt þrong ymbe þeóden, Beo. Th. 5758; B. 2882. Ðæt lyt manna þâh *it succeeded with few*, 5665; B. 2836. Hê on folce lyt freónda hæfde, Cd. 124; Th. 158, 32; Gen. 2626. Cyning hæfde wîgena tô lyt, Elen. Kmbl. 126; El. 63. Hê mid lyt wordum ac geleáffullum his hǽle begeat *he obtained his salvation with words few but full of faith*, Dôm. L. 6, 61. Ne sceal hê tô lyt þancian heora ælmessan *he shall not be too sparing of thanks for their alms*, Blickl. Homl. 43, 13. Forðon hê lyt genihtsumede on smeáwunge and on leornunge hâligra gewrita hê ðý mâ mid his handum wonn and worhte *nam quo minus sufficiebat meditationi scripturarum, eo amplius operi manuum studium impendebat*, Bd. 4, 3; S. 567, 29. Hê lyt ongeat ðæt him swâ earme gelamp. Cd. 76; Th. 94, 24; Gen. 1566. Ðæt eów swâ lyt gespeów, Andr. Kmbl. 2688; An. 1346. [*O. Sax.* lut (werodes).]

lyteg. v. lytig.

LYTEL; *adj.* LITTLE:—Nú gyt is ân lytel fyrst *adhuc modicum*, Jn. Skt. 14, 19. Hwæt is ðæt lîf elles bûton lytelu ylding ðæs deáþes, Blickl. Homl. 59, 27. Lytulu sprǽc, Exon. 116 a; Th. 445, 16; Dôm. 8. Se lytla finger, L. Alf. pol. 60; Th. i. 96, 7. Lâ lytle heord *pusillus grex*, Lk. Skt. 12, 32. On swâ lytlum fæce *in such a little space*, Elen. Kmbl. 1917; El. 960. Ælfrêd cyning gefeaht wið alne ðone here lytle werede, Chr. 871; Erl. 76, 5. Lytle læs *paulo minus*, Ps. Th. 118, 87. Lytle ǽr, Elen. 1325; El. 664. Lytle lengre ðonne seofon fôta, Lchdm. iii. 220, 4. Lytle mâre ðonne feówer, 220, 12. Ðæt lytle ðæt hê erede, hê erede mid horsan, Ors. 1, 1; Swt. 18, 15. Lytle hwîle sceolde hê his lîfes niótan, Cd. 24; Th. 31, 16; Gen. 486. Se lîcette litlum and miclum, gumena gehwylcum, Bt. Met. Fox 26, 72; Met. 26, 36. On ǽlcum þingum ðe ðǽr unbecweden biþ, on bôcum and on swylcum lytlum, Chart. Th. 536. 26. On swîðe lytlon hiera hæfþ seó gecynd genôg *paucis minimisque natura contenta est*, Bt. 14, 1; Fox 42, 10. Ða lytlan *parvulos*, Ps. Th. 114, 6. Lytlum *by little, by degrees, in little pieces, a little at a time*:—Lytlum *paulatim*, Ælfc. Gr. 38; Som. 40, 30. Tôlrec hig lytlum *divides eos minutatim*, Lev. 2, 6. Sele ðæt lytlum sûpan, L. M. 2, 52; Lchdm. ii. 270, 1. Hê gewýt swâ lytlum and lytlum fram Gode *so little by little he departs from God*, Ælfc. Gr. pref; Som. 1, 35: Past. 39, 1; Swt. 283, 9. Ic geseah weaxende blôsman litlum and litlum *videbam crescere paulatim in gemmas*, Gen. 40, 10. [*Goth.* leitils; *O. Sax.* luttil: *Icel.* lîtill: *O. H. Ger.* luzil, luzzil.]

lytel; *neut. of adj. used as subst.* or *adv. A little*:—Dô lytel sealtes tô *put a small quantity of salt to it*, Herb. 2, 19; Lchdm. i. 86, 7. Hwerhwette niþewearde ân lytel *the lower part of cucumber, a little*, L. M. 3, 41; Lchdm. ii. 336, 4. Mycel *multum*, lytel *parum*, Ælfc. Gr. 38; Som. 40, 34. Ymbe lytel *post pusillum*, Mk. Skt. 14, 70. Ymbe ân lytel gê mê ne geseóþ and eft ymbe lytel gê mê geseóþ *modicum non videbitis me et iterum modicum et videbitis me*, Jn. Skt. 16, 16.

lytel-fôta; *adj. Having small feet*:—Litelfôta *petilus*, Ælfc. Gl. 76; Som. 71, 132; Wrt. Voc. 45, 35.

lytel-hygdig-, **hýdig**; *adj. Small-minded, pusillanimous*:—Mon ðæs lytelhýdig ne ðæs læthýdig *no man of mind so small and so sluggish*, Exon. 78 b; Th. 294, 4; Crä. 10.

lyte-lîc. v. lytig-lîc.

lytel-môd; *adj. Of little courage, faint-hearted, pusillanimous*:—Se mec hālne dyde from lytelmōdum *qui me salvum faceret a pusillanimo,* Ps. Surt. 54, 9. Ða lytelmōdan and ða unþrīstan ðonne hié ongietaþ hiera unbældo and hiera unmiehte hié weorþaþ oft ormōde *pusillanimes dum nimis infirmitatis suæ sunt conscii, plerumque in desperationem cadunt,* Past. 32, 1; Swt. 209, 7.

lytel-ne; *adv. All but, almost, nearly:*—Hē lytelne [lytesne?] Breotona rīce forlēt *Brittaniam pene amisit,* Bd. 1, 3; S. 475, 22.

lytel-ness, e; *f. Littleness:*—Sume [*adverbs*] syndon *quantitatis;* ða getācniaþ mycelnysse oððe lytelnysse, Ælfc. Gr. 38; Som. 40, 34.

lytes-nā, lytes-ne, lytest-ne; *adv. Almost, nearly, within a little:*—Lytesnā *concedam,* Wrt. Voc. ii. 104, 49. Lytisnā, 14, 65: Ep. Gl. 7 d, 31. Wæs his rīce brād wīd ofer werþeóde lytesnā ofer ealne yrmenne grund *his realm was broad, wide over mankind, almost over all the world,* Exon. 66 a; Th. 243, 13; Jul. 10. Lytestne eall his weorod ofslegen wæs *omnis pene ejus est cæsus exercitus,* Bd. 1, 34; S. 499, 32: 3, 24; S. 556, 30. Lytesne [*pene*] of ealre Lindesse stōwum, 3, 11; S. 535, 25. Lytesne of eallum *de cunctis prope,* 3, 14; S. 540, 11. Bōc lytestne unāberendlīcre byrþenne *codicem ponderis pene importabilis,* 5, 13; S. 633, 6.

lyðer-, luðer- full; *adj. Base, vile, dissolute, depraved:*—Leófan men ne beón gē nāðor ne leáse ne luðer- [lyðer- MS. B] fulle, ne fūle ne fracode, ne on ǣnige wīsan tō lehterfulle, Wulfst. 40, 5.

lyðer-lic; *adj. Sordid, mean, vile:*—Se cyning self mid swīðe lyðerlīcum gegierelan *ipse imperator sordida servilique tunica discinctus,* Ors. 4, 5; Swt. 166, 16. [The word comes to mean *lazy* in later times. Cf. Tusser 'some *litherly* lubber leaveth undone that another will do.']

lyðer-līce; *adv. Wickedly, vilely:*—Luðerlīce *pessime,* Ælfc. Gl. 99; Som. 76, 101; Wrt. Voc. 54, 45. [Leiden swa *luðerliche* on hire lichðæt hit brec oueral, Marh. 5, 21: A. R. 290, 8. A clerk hath *litherly* byset his while Bot if he cowde a carpenter bygyle, Chauc. Miller's Tale, 113.]

lyðre; *adj. Evil, wicked, base, mean, poor, sordid, vile, lewd, depraved:*—Ðæt Godes feoh ne ætlicge and hē beó lyðre þeówa gehāten *that God's money be not idle, and he be called a wicked servant,* Ælfc. Gr. pref; Som. 1, 30. Lytel is se fyrst ðyses līfes and lyðre is *few and evil are the days of this life,* Wulfst. 109, 2. Hū lǣne and hū lyðre ðis līf is on tō getrūwianne, 189, 3. Eálā ðū lyðra þeówa *serve nequam,* Mt. Kmbl. 18, 32: Lk. Skt. 19, 22: Homl. Th. ii. 552, 6. Ic eom se lytla for ðē and se lyðra man, se syngige swīðe genehhe, Hy. 3, 41; Hy. Grn. ii. 282, 41. Eówre lyðre mōd *incircumcisa mens,* Lev. 26, 41. Gif hwylc wīf for hwylcum lyðrum andan hire wīfman swingþ *si mulier aliqua, ex prava aliqua invidia, ancillam suam flagellis verberaverit,* L. Ecg. P. ii. 4; Th. ii. 182, 32: L. M. I. P. 12; Th. ii. 268, 11. Se ðe Crist belǣwde for lyðrum sceatte *who betrayed Christ for filthy lucre,* Homl. Th. ii. 244, 26: Wulfst. 297, 26. Ðæs mǣran wītegan deáþ ðære lyðran hoppestran [*the daughter of Herodias*] tō mēde forgeaf, Homl. Th. i. 484, 3. Lyðerne earhscype *base cowardice,* Wulfst. 53, 12. Þurh lyðre wrhþe, 166, 26. Ða seofon hlyðran ear *septem spicæ tenues,* Gen. 41, 27. Oðre lyðre cynn *cetera adulterina genera,* Ælfc. Gl. 101; Som. 77, 31; Wrt. Voc. 55, 36. Lyðra bearn *filii excussorum,* Ps. Th. 126, 5. Se Hǣlend geþafode lyðrum mannum ðæt hī hine ofslōgon, Homl. Th. i. 168, 6. Se ealdorman hī betǣhte liðrum mannum tō behealdenne *the aldorman entrusted it to base* [cf. ða wǣron yfele and earge l. 27] *men to hold,* Ors. 6, 36; Bos. 131, 23. Eár lyðre and forscruncene *spicæ tenues et percussæ uredine,* Gen. 41, 6. Þurh līchaman leðre geþohtas *through the wicked thoughts of the body,* Ps. C. 50, 41; Ps. Grn. ii. 277, 41. [*A. R. Laym.* luðer: *Piers P.* luþer, liþer: *Prompt. Parv.* lyder or wyly *cautus* [see note for *lither* = lazy in later English]: cf. *Ger.* lüder-, lieder-lich.]

lyðre; *adv. Badly, vilely:*—Habbaþ wē alle for ðīnum leásungum lyðre geférēd *we have all fared miserably for thy falsehoods,* Cd. 214; Th. 268, 29; Sat. 62.

lyt-hwōn; *subst.* and *adv. A little* [*space, time, quantity*]:—Meng lythwōn wið hunig *mix a little with honey,* L. M. 1, 1; Lchdm. ii. 22, 20. Lythwōn becom cwicera tō cȳððe *few living reached their country,* Judth. 12; Thw. 26, 5; Jud. 311: Elen. Kmbl. 284; El. 142. Ðā hē wæs lythwōn ðanon āgān *progressus pusillum,* Mt. Kmbl. 26, 39: Mk. Skt. 14, 35. Hē his eágan lythwōn fram ðære eorþan up āhōf, Glostr. Frag. 104, 13. Ðara ðe lythwōn rēccaþ embe bōca beboda, L. I. P. 6; Th. ii. 310, 34: Swt. A. S. Rdr. 101, 200: Beo. Th. 408; B. 203. Ne lythwōn *not a little,* Exon. 38 a; Th. 125, 32; Gū. 363. Ðā geswīgode heó lythwōn *parumper reticuit,* Bd. 4, 9; S. 577, 22. v. lyt.

lytig, lyteg; *adj. Cunning, astute, sly, artful, crafty, wily:*—Litig *procax,* Wrt. Voc. ii. 67, 48. Se lytega sǣtere *seductor callidus,* Past. 65, 2; Swt. 463, 11. Hū manega costunga ðæs lytegan feóndes *quanta hostis callidi tentamenta,* 21, 5; Swt. 161, 18. Forðæm him [*a simple person*] is micle iéðre tō gestīganne on ðone ryhtan wīsdōm, ðonne ðæm lytegan sīe tō anbūganne, for ðæm ðe hē biþ ǣr upāhæfen for his lotwrencium, 30, 1; Swt. 203, 18. Marius ðone consul ā swā lytigne swā hē wæs *Marii consulis, qui non minore pene quam ipse præditus erat astutia,* Ors. 5, 7; Swt. 228, 32. Ðone leásan lytegan ðū scealt hātan fox *insidiator occultis surripuisse fraudibus gaudet? vulpeculis exaequetur,* Bt. 37, 4; Fox 192, 17. On leásungum lytige *in mendaciis vafri,* Coll. Monast. Th. 32, 29. Ða lytegan *sapientes hujus seculi,* Past. 30, 1; Swt. 203, 6, 24: 205, 3.

lytigian; *p.* ode *To act cunningly:*—Ongunnon lytegian ðā lāðe gystas *began then to act guilefully the hateful guests,* Byrht. Th. 134, 18; By. 86. v. be-lytigian.

lytig-, lyte-līc; *adj. Deceitful, false:*—Ymbtrymedu mid lytelīcre lādunge *fallaci defensione circumdatæ,* Past. 35, 5; Swt. 245, 8.

lytig-, lyte-līce; *adv. Cunningly, artfully, craftily:*—Ðe hit symle lytiglīce lādaþ *sese callide defendentis,* Past. 35, 3; Swt. 241, 8. Litelīce *callide,* Ex. 32, 12. Ða woruldsǣlþa mid swīðe manigre swētnesse swīðe lytelīce ōleccaþ ðǣm mōdum, Bt. 7, 1; Fox 16, 10. Hū lytelīce hȳ ðonne deófol bepǣhte, Wulfst. 11, 9, 16. Ne weorþeþ on worulde lytelīce swicolra ðonne hē wyrþeþ *none in the world is more craftily deceitful than he,* 54, 22. Se ðe litelīcost cūðe leáslīce hiwian unsōþ tō sōþe *he that most cunningly could make untruth appear truth,* 128, 9.

lytig-ness, e; *f. Cunningness, craftiness, astuteness:*—Ðære nædran lytignes *astutia serpentis,* Past. 35, 1; Swt. 237, 22.

lytlian; *p.* ode *To make* or *to become little, to lessen, diminish:*—Gidæfnaþ ðæt ih lytlige *oportet me minui,* Jn. Skt. Rush. 3, 30. Ðonne lytlaþ him se tōhopa ðe hē hæfde ðā hē synful wæs *spem, quæ esse potuit de peccatore, subtraxit,* Past. 58, 10; Swt. 447, 14. Heorte sceal ðē cēnre mōd ðē māre ðē ūre mægen lytlaþ *heart shall the hardier be, courage the more, the fewer our forces,* Byrht. Th. 140, 65. Lytlaþ ðæt his anweald and ēcþ his ermþa *it lessens his power, and increases his miseries,* Bt. 29, 1; Fox 102, 19. Drenc ðe lytlaþ ða yfelan wǣtan, L. M. 2, 59; Lchdm. ii. 282, 10. Ðonne lyttlaþ hē ðæt fæsten *tunc breviabit jejunium,* L. Ecg. P. Add. 19; Th. ii. 234, 18. Cristes lage wanedon and cyninges lage lytledon *Christ's laws waned, and the king's laws were weakened,* L. Eth. ix. 37; Th. i. 348, 19. Lytligen ða grambǣran hiera gedrēfednesse *damnent iracundi perturbationem,* Past. 40, 2; Swt. 291, 2. Willflōd ongan lytligan, Cd. 71; Th. 85, 11; Gen. 1413. Hȳ mon sceal lytlian *they shall be lessened,* L. M. 2, 1; Lchdm. ii. 178, 12. Se ðe hit þence tō litlianne, gelitlige hine God elmihtig hēr on worulde, Cod. Dipl. Kmbl. iv. 171, 21. Biþ se ece litliende [litligende, MS. B], Herb. 3, 3, 4; Lchdm. i. 88, 2, 7.

lytling, es; *m. A little one, a young person, child:*—Se ðe underféhþ ǣnne lytling on mīnum naman *he that receives one little one in my name,* Homl. Th. ii. 286, 30. Lyttlingas, i. 512, 21. Furþon litlincgas nellaþ forbīgean mē *nec parvuli nolunt præterire me* [*the baker*], Coll. Monast. Th. 29, 1. Ða litlingas fuhton on hire innoþe, Gen. 25, 22. Ǣnne of ðyssum lytlingum *unum de pusillis istis,* Mt. Kmbl. 18, 6: Homl. Th. i. 84, 11. His efenealdan lytlingas [*the children killed in Bethlehem*], 88, 12. Ic hæbbe hnesce litlingas *parvulos habeam teneros,* Gen. 34, 13: 50, 21. Gif hwylc gōdra wile his lytlingas hiom [*priests*] tō lāre befæstan, hig sceolon swīðe lustlīce hig onfōn, and him tǣcan, L. E. I. 20; Th. ii. 414, 8.

lytluc[c], es; *m. A bittock, small piece:*—Lytluccas (MS. lyttuccas) *segmenta, particulas,* Germ. 400, 531.

lytlum. v lytel.

M

Original *m*, generally speaking, is preserved in Anglo-Saxon, and is found corresponding to *m* in the Gothic and other cognate dialects, e. g. *mē, manna, dōm;* Goth. *mik, manna, dōms.* When, however, *m* is not initial, the correspondence is not always maintained; thus, A.S. *fīf,* but Goth. *fimf;* A.S. *sōfte,* O.H.Ger. *samfto.* Also for earlier *fn* is found *mn,* as in *emn* along with *efn,* Goth. *ibn;* *stemn* and *stefn,* Goth. *stibna.* In some inflexions *m* is no longer found; so in the 1st pers. sing. pres. indic. *eom* is the only instance in which the old person-ending has maintained itself; though *beón, dōn,* and *gān* offer occasional instances of its retention in the Northern Gospels; while the *m* which is found in the plural of the Gothic and O. H. Ger. conjugations has left no trace. In declensions *n* in the later times began to take the place of *m* in the dative, so *ðan* for *ðam.*

The form of the Runic letter, whose name was *man,* was ᛗ, but from the similarity to the *d*-rune (*dæg*) ᛞ, the two seem to be sometimes confounded. In each case the symbol was sometimes employed, after the runes had been generally supplanted by the Latin letters, to express the word which was its name; thus in the Durham Ritual *quis* is glossed *ǣnig* ᛞ, *nemo, ne ǣnig* ᛞ: the same symbol being also used to gloss *dies.* The form of the rune accompanying the Runic poem is ᛗ, Kmbl. plate 16, fig. 11, and the verse attached to it the following:—

Man byþ on myrgþe	Men will be cheerful,
his māgan leóf	dear to their friends,
sceal ðeáh ānra gehwylc	shall yet each one
ōðrum swīcan	depart from other,
forðam dryhten wile	for the Lord will
dōme sīnum	by his doom
ðæt earme flǣsc	the 'vile body'
eorþan betǣcan.	commit to earth.

Kmbl. 343, 11–18.

mā; *indecl. cpve. used as subst. and adj. More.* I. *as subst.*:—Sume naman sind *omonima*; ða getācniaþ mā þinga mid ānre clypunge, Ælfc. Gr. 5; Som. 4, 13. Seó þridde declinatio hefþ eahta and hundseofontig geendunga oððe mā, 9; Som. 8, 15: Elen. Kmbl. 1264; El. 634. Hē hæfþ weána mā ðonne ǣniges mannes gemet sȳ ðæt hié ārīman mǣge, Blickl. Homl. 61, 36: 213, 28. Ǣghwylcum men biþ leófre swā hē hæbbe holdra freónda mā, 123, 1. Mid ðȳ eówer mā is *cum sitis numero plures*, Bd. 2, 2; S. 503, 13. Ne gehērde ða ondsware mā manna ðonne ða mīne getreówestan freónd, Nar. 32, 15. Mā ðæra Iudēiscra ealdra embe Cristes cwale smeádon, Homl. Th. i. 88, 28. Næfde hē mā ðonne twentig swȳna, Ors. 1, 1; Swt. 18, 14. Nō ðē lāðes mā gedōn mōton *no worse may they do thee*, Andr. Kmbl. 2885; An. 1446. Ða habbaþ twegen mislīce casus and nā mā on gewunan ... nis ðǣr nā mā mislīcra casa *they have two different cases, and no more generally* ... *there are no more different cases*, Ælfc. Gr. 14; Som. 17, 3-7: 15; Som. 17, 38: Blickl. Homl. 35, 24. Donatus tēþ gyt mā tō ðysum .. Gyt synd mā ðyssera æfter Priscianus, Ælfc. Gr. 44; Som. 46, 6-10. Gyt mā wæs ðe ðæt dōn ne wolde *there were yet more who would not do that*, Bd. 1, 14; S. 482, 17. Swā ðǣr mā beáh tō ðam sōðan geleáfan, Homl. Th. ii. 540, 27. Ðā geneálǣhton mā hine meldigende, 248, 32. Nabbaþ syððan hwæt hig mā dōn *non habent amplius quod faciant*, Lk. Skt. 12, 4. Hwæt sceal ic ðonne mā secgean fram Sancte Johanne, Blickl. Homl. 169, 24: Bd. 3, 27; S. 559, 22: Ps. Th. 125, 2. Gif hē mā wille, drince hē hāt wæter, L. M. 2, 59; Lchdm. ii. 284, 5. Be ðam man mæg gecnāwan and be mā þinga, Wulfst. 5, 4. Swā mid læs worda, swā mid mā, Bt. 35, 5; Fox 166, 12. Hē ne ūðe ðæt ǣnig ōðer man ǣfre mǣrða ðon mā gehēdde ðonne hē sylfa *he would not allow that any other man should have any more distinctions than he himself had*, Beo. Th. 1012; B. 504. Wāt ic sorga ðȳ mā, Cd. 42; Th. 54, 33; Gen. 886. Mǣ wundra *plura signa*, Jn. Skt. Lind. 7. 31. II. *as adj.*:—Seó sāwul ys mā ðonne se līchama and se līchama mā ðonne ðæt reáf *anima plus est quam esca, et corpus quam vestimentum*, Lk. Skt. 12, 23. Mā wēn is ðæt ðū onsende ðīnne engel *there is more hope if you send your angel*, Blickl. Homl. 231, 23. Mā wæter of ðīnum mūþ ðū ne send, 247, 7. Ic nelle nān word mā of ðīnum mūþe gehȳran, Nar. 45, 23. Ic wæs sixtȳne sīðum on sǣbāte ... is þys āne mā *I have been sixteen times in a sea boat...this is once more*, Andr. Kmbl. 984; An. 492. Ðæt wæs mā cræft ðonne hit eorþbūend ealle cūþan [cf. use of *mikil* in *O. Sax.* kūðean kraft mikil], Exon. 13b; Th. 26, 24; Cri. 421. Ne synd nā mā namanspeligende būtan ðās fīftēne *there are no more pronouns than these fifteen*, Ælfc. Gr. 15; Som. 17, 46. v. *next word, and* mǣst.

mā, mǣ; *adv. More, rather, further*:—Mǣ *amplius*, Ps. Surt. 50, 4. Gāþ mā tō ðām sceápum *potius ite ad oves*, Mt. Kmbl. 10, 6: 28. Ǣlces monnes æþelo bióþ mā on ðam mōde ðonne on ðam flǣsce, Bt. 30, 1; Fox, 110, 2: Past. 17, 9; Swt. 121, 22. Nis him blōd tō lǣtanne ac mā hira man sceal tilian mid wyrtdrencum *he is not to be let blood, but rather the symptoms are to be treated with drinks made from herbs*, L. M. 1, 35; Lchdm. ii. 82, 16. Hē ðone nā eft ne wyrge, ac hine mā bletsige, L. E. I. 21; Th. ii. 416, 12. Forðon ðe Godes willa is ðæt tō Columban mynstre hē mā fære and lǣre *Dei enim voluntatis est ut ad Columbæ monasteria magis pergat docenda*, Bd. 5, 9; S. 622, 39. Hē mā geceás ðæt hē wæs eft hām hweorfende *he preferred to return home*, 5, 2; S. 615, 33. Him wīslīcre and gehyldre wǣre ðæt hī mā hām cyrdan ðonne hī ða eallreordan þeóde gesēcan sceoldan, 1, 23; S. 485, 32. Ðæt hié mā mehten heora weras wrecan *that they might better avenge their husbands*, Ors. 1, 10; Swt. 46, 4. Gyt mā oððe gyt swīðor *immo*, Ælfc. Gr. 38; Som. 42, 18: Bt. 32, 1; Fox, 114, 17. Ne ðonne mā *nor further*, 16, 3; Fox, 54, 29. Ongunnon hī Moyses mā bysmrian, Ps. Th. 105, 14. Se mā eallum Angelcyningum Brytta þeóde fornom *qui plus omnibus Anglorum primatibus gentem vastavit Brittonum*, Bd. 1, 34; S. 499, 19. Wēnestū recce hē hire ǣfre mā *numquid revertetur ad eam ultra*, Past. 52, 3; Swt. 405, 12: Cd. 216; Th. 273, 21; Sat. 140. Ne synga ðū nǣfre mā, Jn. Skt. 8, 11. Ðæt ðū mā ne sīe mīnra gylta gemyndig, Elen. Kmbl. 1630; El. 817. Mā of heora mūþe hit ne eode *it (water) no longer came out of its mouth*, Blickl. Homl. 247, 9. Sægdon ðæt hī nō mā ne mihton swencte beón *they said that they could not be troubled any more*, Bd. 1, 12; S. 481, 3. Ðam mycle mā hē scrȳt eów *quanto magis vos vestit*, Mt. Kmbl. 6, 30. Mycle mā, 7, 11. Swā mycele mā, Lk. Skt. 12, 28. Hwæt is ðæt ðe mā ðæt ǣnig man mǣge ōðrum dōn ðæt hē ne mǣge him dōn ðæt ilce *quid autem est, quod in alium facere quisquam potest, quod sustinere ab alio ipse non potest*, Bt. 16, 2; Fox 52, 27. Ðā clypodon hig ðæs ðē mā [*so much the more*, cf. *O. H. Ger.* des diu mēr: *Ger.* desto mehr], Mt. Kmbl. 20, 31: Mk. Skt. 6, 51: 10, 48. Hit ðǣr ne weaxt ðē mā ðe gimmas weaxaþ on wīngeardum *it does not grow there any more than jewels grow in vineyards*, Bt. 32, 3; Fox 118, 10: 34, 1: Fox 134, 15. Ðæra māðma ne rōhte ðē mā ðe reócendes meoxes, Homl. Skt. 7, 20: L. Edg. C. 7; Th. ii. 280, 6. Gelpan ne þorfte Costontinus ne Anlāf ðȳ mā *no need had Constantine to boast, no more had Anlaf*, Chr. 937; Erl. 114, 12; Æðelst. 46. Næs him se swēg tō sorge ðon mā ðe sunnan scīma *the noise (of the flames) was not troublesome to them any more than sunshine*, Cd. 187; Th. 232, 23; Dan. 264. Hié ðæs ne onmunden ðon mā ðe eówre gefēran, Chr. 755; Erl. 50, 25. Ðā ne wolde se pāpa ðæt geþafigean ne ða burhware ðon mā *then the pope would not permit it, no more would the citizens*; et si pontifex concedere illi quod petierat voluit, non tamen cives potuere permittere, Bd. 2, 1; S. 501, 33: Ps. Th. 93, 13: Salm. Kmbl. 436; Sal. 218. Mā and mā *magis magisque*, Bd. 4, 29; S. 607, 15. Weaxan ā mā and mā, Past. 37, 1; Swt. 263, 18. Se wela ðe [hī] him dæghwamlīce gesamnodan mā and mā, Blickl. Homl. 99, 29. [*Mo, moe* remains down to Shakspere's time. *O. Frs.* mā; *adv. and subst.*; other dialects have forms which contain the comparative suffix: *Goth.* mais: *adv.*; ni þana mais *no more*; *O. Sax.* mēr; *subst. and adv.*; þan mēr *any more*: *Icel.* meir: *adv.*; *O.H.Ger.* mēr; *adv.*]

maca, an; *m. A make, mate, match*:—Fadores æc gimaca ðæm maca *patrisque compar unice* (the glosser seems to have misunderstood *unice*), Rtl. 165, 11. [*Make* is used by Ben Jonson. *Icel.* maki *a match, mate*: *Dan.* mage.] v. ge-maca, ge-mæc.

maca-, macca-līc; *adj. Fit, suitable, convenient*:—Mið ðȳ dæg maccalīc [macalīc, Rush.] gecuom *cum dies opportunus accidisset*, Mk. Skt. Lind. 6, 21 [*Scot.* makly *seemly*: *Icel.* mak-ligr *meet, becoming, fitting.*] v. ge-mæc, *and preceding word.*

MACIAN; *p.* ode *To* MAKE, *do, act*:—Ic macige ðē mycelre mǣgþe *faciam te in gentem magnam*, Gen. 12, 2. Seó forme declinatio macaþ hire genitivum on *ae*, Ælfc. Gr. 7; Som. 6, 4: 24; Som. 24, 24. Ðæt is ðæt hēhste gōd ðæt hit eall swā mehtiglīce macaþ *that is the highest good, which does everything so mightily*, Bt. 35, 4; Fox 162, 1. Ne swincaþ ā ymbe ǣnige þearfe ac maciaþ eall be luste and be ēþnesse... Ðæt is lāþlīc līf ðæt hī swā maciaþ *they never labour at any necessary matter, but do all for pleasure and ease .. It is a detestable life, that they act so*, L. I. P. 14; Th. ii. 322, 23-26. Sweriaþ mē ðæt gē dōn wið mē swilce mildheortnisse, swā ic macode wið eów, Jos. 2, 12. Ðā befrān heó ðæt cild hū hit macode on eallum ðam fyrste *then she asked the child what it had been doing in all the time*, Homl. Th. i. 566, 20. Swā hē hit macode on his līfe *such was his practice in his life*, ii. 354, 24. Jubal wæs fæder ðæra ðe organan macodun, Gen. 4, 21. Forðan hī macodon mǣst ðet unseht betweónan Godwine eorle and ðam cynge, Chr. 1052; Erl. 187, 27. Ðæt ic macige mete ðīnum fæder ðǣr of, Gen. 27, 9. Ðæt ða cristenan hine tō martyre ne macion *that the Christians may not make a martyr of him*, Homl. Skt. 5, 460. Hē (*Lucifer*) wolde hine macian tō gode, Ælfc. T. Grn. 2, 43. Bǣdon sume ðæt Samson mōste him macian sum gamen *some asked, that Samson should make sport for them*, Jud. 16, 25. Riht is ðæt mynecena mynsterlīce macian *it is right that nuns that should practise the rules of their monasteries*, L. I. P. 15; Th. ii. 322, 32. Gestihtode hū men sceoldon ðǣrinne hit macian *qualiter debeant conversari dispensat*, Past. 16, 1; Swt. 98, 11. Se wīsdōm sǣde him hū hē hit macian sceolde gif hē heora þegen beón sceolde, Bt. tit. 7; Fox x, 16. [*O. Sax.* makōn: *O. Frs.* makia: *O. H. Ger.* machōn: *Ger.* machen.] v. ge-macian.

mā-cræftig; *adj. Very* (?) *skilled* or *powerful*:—Hwanon cōmen gē ceólum līðan mācræftige menn, Andr. Kmbl. 513; An. 257. Nǣfre ic sǣlidan sēlran mētte, mācræftigran, 943; An. 472. [Grimm in a note on the former passage suggests that *mā* in this compound may be a substantive from the same root and with the same meaning as *mere*.]

macung, e; *f. Making, doing, action*:—Þurh ðes macunge mǣst se eorl Rotbert ðises geáres ðis land mid unfriþe gesōhte *it was mostly his doing that Earl Robert attacked this country in the course of this year*, Chr. 1101; Erl. 238, 1.

mād (v. ge-maad *vecors*, Wrt. Voc. ii. 123, 36); *adj. Unreasoning, foolish, mad*:—Þrinteþ him on innan ungemēde mād mōd *within him (one guilty of* oferhygd) *swells a mind displeasing by its folly*, Exon. 83b; Th. 315, 2; Mōd. 25. v. ge-mǣd.

mādm. v. māðm.

mǣ, *more.* v. mā.

mæc; *adj. Well-matched, equal, agreeable* (?):—Hār hildering hrēman ne þorfte mæcan (*other MSS.* mecca, meca, mecga) gemǣnan *the grey-haired warrior had no need to boast of well-matched intercourse*, i. e. *would not boast of being a match for those against whom he fought, and by whom he had been defeated*, Chr. 937; Erl. 114, 6; Æðelst. 40. [*Prompt. Parv.* make *or* fyte *and* mete; mak, fyt, esy *aptus, conveniens*: *Icel.* makr *suitable, easy to deal with.*] v. ge-mæc.

mæced [= mā-ēced? cf. mā-geēct] *glosses* mactus, Wrt. Voc. ii. 79, 53.

Mæcedonie; *pl. The Macedonians*:—Philippus Mæcedonia cyning, Ors. 4, 11; Swt. 204, 5. Gewin wið Mæcedonie, Swt. 202, 33.

Mæcedonisc; *adj. Macedonian*:—Ðæt Mæcedonisce gewin, Ors. 4, 11; Swt. 208, 5.

mǣce-fisc. v. mēce-fisc.

mæcg, mecg, es; *m. A man*:—Ic meþelcwide mæcges (*the angel that visited Guthlac*) ongeat, Exon. [illegible]b; Th. 175, 9; Gū. 1192. Mægþ and mæcgas, 45a; Th. 153, 29: Gū. 833: 113a; Th. 434, 7; Rä. 51, 7. Frēfra ðīne mæcgas (*the disciples of St. Andrew*), Andr. Kmbl. 843; An. 422. Mæcga misgehȳd *men's evil intent*, 1543; An. 773. Mæcgea (mecga, MS. C.) mundbora (*Edmund*), Chr. 942; Erl. 116, 8.

Mecga (*those in hell*) gnornunge, Cd. 220; Th. 285, 8; Sat. 334. Mæcgum (*the children in the fiery furnace*), 187; Th. 232, 24; Dan. 265. Adam iécte siddan mægþum and mæcgum mǣgburg sîne *Adam afterwards increased his family with daughters and sons*, 55; Th. 68, 26; Gen. 1123. DER. ambeht-, earfoþ-, eóred-, Geát-, gigant-, here-, hilde-, oret-, wræc-mæcg.

mæcga, an; *m. A man*, Exon. 88 a; Th. 330, 16; Vy. 52. v. gûþ-, ofer-, wræc-mæcga.

mæcige, Lchdm. iii. 126, 19. v. mecgan.

mæctor. v. mǣte.

MǢD, e *and* we; mǣdwe, an; *f. also* (?) mǣdwa, an; *m. A* MEAD, *meadow*:—Mǣd *pratum*, Ælfc. Gl. 57; Som. 67, 75; Wrt. Voc. 38, 1: 96; Som. 76, 45; Wrt. Voc. 53, 52. XII æcras an westhealfe dære strǣte and ān mēdwa beneoþan dæm hliþe *xii acres on the west side of the road, and one meadow beneath the hill*, Cod. Dipl. Kmbl. iii. 52, 15. vi æcras mǣde on da gerēfmǣde, 53, 2. xvi gioc ærþelandes and mēdwe, i. 316, 26. On Wîferþes mǣduan hege *to the hedge of Wiferth's meadow*, iii. 78, 21. Andlang heges on Eomeres mǣduan (cf. on Eomeres mēdwa, 405, 24); of dam mǣduan . . . andlang burnan on Hereferþes mǣduan, 78, 6-9. Tô wudumǣdwan; of dæm mǣdwan, 246, 22. (In the last two passages perhaps the forms are plural as in) Tô dǣm mǣdwum wid sūdan da mǣdwa, 169, 2-3. [Mid lǣswe and mid mǣdwe, Chr. 777; Erl. 55, 12.] Gelîce and mon mǣd māwe *just as one mows a meadow*, Ors. 2, 8; Swt. 92, 15. XIIII æceras and da mǣde de dār tô līþ Dūnstān gebohte æt Uhtlufe *xiiii acres and the meadow pertaining thereto Dunstan bought of Uhtlufu*, Cod. Dipl. Kmbl. ii. 3, 34. Norþrihte on mǣre mǣde westewearde, iii. 416, 18. Of dere ealdan dîc dæt on wylihte mǣdwan; of wylihte mǣdwan, 235, 16. On rȳdmǣdwan ufewarde, 378, 14. Eahta æceras mǣdwa . . . xii æceras mǣdwa, 4, 12-13. Mǣda *prata*, Hpt. Gl. 409, 38. Deós wyrt biþ cenned on mǣdum *this plant is produced in meadows*, Herb. 1, 1; Lchdm. i. 70, 2. [Cf. *Ger.* mähde *a meadow*.] v. gafol-, gerēf-, mōr-mǣd; mǣþ.

mǣd, mǣdan. v. ge-mǣd, ge-mǣdan.

mǣden. v. mægden.

mæder (?), *a measure*:—Ofgeót mid. iii. mædrum ealoþ, Lchdm. iii. 28, 16.

mædere, an; *f. Madder*:—Mæddre *vermiculi, rubia*, Ælfc. Gl. 42; Som. 64, 13, 19; Wrt. Voc. 31, 24, 29. Mædere *anchorum*, 67, 38: *veneria*, 68, 38: *sandix* (*herba*), Hpt. Gl. 524, 41. Deós wyrt de man *gryas* and ōdrum naman mædere nemneþ, Herb. 51, 1; Lchdm. i. 154, 12: L. M. 2, 51; Lchdm. ii. 268, 15. [*Icel.* madra.] v. feld-mædere.

mædere-cîþ, es; *m. A sprig of madder*, Lchdm. i. 397, 2.

mǣd-land, es; *m. Meadow-land, grass-land which is mown*:—Ǣgder ge mǣdlondes ge eyrþlondes *both of land for mowing and of arable land*, Cod. Dipl. Kmbl. ii. 95, 16. Mēdlandes, vi. 219, 4. v. mǣdwe-land.

mǣd-mǣwect, *the mowing of a meadow*:—Eác hē sceal hwîltîdum geara beón on manegum weorcum tô hlāfordes willan tōeácan . . . mǣdmǣwecte *also he shall at times be ready for labour of many kinds at his lord's pleasure, besides . . . mowing his meadows*, L. R. S. 5; Th. i. 436, 3-5.

mǣd-rǣdenn, e; *f. A mowing, grass mown on a piece of land*:—Seó mǣdrǣden beniþan dîc betweónan cealdan lace and cullig, Cod. Dipl. Kmbl. vi. 153, 10. Cf. wudu-rǣdenn.

mǣd-splott, es; *m. A plot of meadow-land*:—Ǣnne mǣdsplot, Cod. Dip. Kmbl. iv. 72, 7.

mǣdwa. v. mǣd.

mǣdwe-land, es; *n. Meadow-land, land where grass that is to be mown grows*:—Hió sellaþ him dæt mēdweland bî westan Sæferne . . Ēc twelf æceras gōdes mǣdwelandes, Cod. Dipl. Kmbl. ii. 150, 10-18: vi. 219, 3. v. mǣd-land.

MǢG, es; *m. A relative, kinsman*:—Mǣg *propinquus*, Wrt. Voc. 72, 45: Ælfc. Gr. 5; Som. 4, 51. Hwylc þyncþ dē dæt sȳ dæs mǣg de on da sceadan befeóll *quis videtur tibi proximus fuisse illi qui incidet in latrones?* Lk. Skt. 10, 36. Meig *contribulius*, Wrt. Voc. ii. 104, 26. Meeg, Ep. Gl. 6 f, 17. Se wæs his mǣg and his freónd and hæfde his sweoster tō wîfe *qui erat cognatus et amicus ejus, habens sororem ipsius conjugem*, Bd. 3, 21; S. 551, 6: Blickl. Homl. 113, 22. Him cȳþdon dæt hiera mǣgas him mid wǣron . . And dā cuǣdon hié dæt him nǣnig mǣg leófra nǣre donne hiera hlāford . . and dā budon hié hiera mǣgum dæt hié gesunde from eodon, Chr. 755; Erl. 50, 17-21. Hēr Æþelherd cining forþfērde and fēng Cūdrēd his mǣg tō West-Seaxna rîce, 740; Erl. 47, 33: 754; Erl. 49, 18: 962; Erl. 120, 2. Abrahames mǣg (*Lot*), Cd. 94; Th. 121, 19; Gen. 2012. Higelāces mǣg (*Beowulf*), Beo. Th. 820; B. 408. Ūre ieldesta mǣg *our first parent*, Past. 43, 5; Swt. 313, 15. Ne hǣme nān man wid his mǣges (*fratris*) wîf, Lev. 18, 16. Mǣges *filii*, Cd. 140; Th. 176, 5; Gen. 2907. Moises heóld his mǣges (*soceri*) sceáp, Ex. 3, 1. Moises gecirde tō his mǣge, 4, 18. Abrahame, mǣge Lothes, Cd. 141; Th. 177, 2; Gen. 2923. Cēnwalh gesalde Cūþrēde his mǣge (*fratrueli*), Chr. 648; Erl. 26, 15. Ne bysmra dū dînne mǣg *non facies calumniam proximo tuo*, Lev. 19, 13. Gif man gehādodne man odde ælþeódigne forrǣde donne sceal him cyningc beón for mǣg and for mundboran, L. C. S. 40; Th. i. 400, 6. Ne his māgas (*fratres*) ne gelȳfdon on hyne, Jn. Skt. 7, 5. His eorþlîcan māgas *his kinsmen according to the flesh*, Chr. 979; Erl. 129, 12. His māgas and his frȳnd *cognati atque amici*, L. Ecg. C. 36; Th. ii. 160, 22. Gif bana of lande gewîteþ his māgas healfne leód forgelden, L. Ethb. 23; Th. i. 8, 7. Bōcland him his mǣgas (MS. B. his yldran) leáfden, L. Alf. pol. 41; Th. i. 88, 16. Hine mōton his mǣgas (MS. B. māgas) unsyngian *his kindred may exculpate him*, L. In. 21; Th. i. 116, 8. Sunu odde mǣgas (MS. B. māgas), 23; Th. i. 116, 15. Māga *affinium*, Hpt. Gl. 480, 18. Ǣnig dînra māga odde yldrena *aliquis de tuis parentibus aut cognatis*, Bd. 2, 12; S. 514, 15. Mid gȳmenne mînra māga *cura propinquorum*, 5, 24; S. 647, 22. Se wæs ædelboren of ǣwfæstum māgum *he was nobly born of pious parents*, Homl. Skt. 4, 3. Suna ic lǣrde dæt hié hȳrdon heora yldrum and heora māgum, Blickl. Homl. 185, 21. Sūþ-Seaxe and Eást-Seaxe from his mǣgum (*ancestors*) ǣr mid unryhte ānîdde wǣrun, Chr. 823; Erl. 62, 23. Gē beóþ gesealde fram māgum and gebrōdrum and cūdum and freóndum *trademini a parentibus et fratribus et cognatis et amicis*, Lk. Skt. 21, 16. Lǣraþ eówre suna and eówre māgas *docebis filios ac nepotes tuos*, Deut. 4, 9. Māgos *propinquos*, Kent. Gl. 368. Bearn ārîsaþ ongēn māgas *insurgent filii in parentes*, Mt. Kmbl. 10, 21. Ymbe mîne māgas ic hogige *erga propinquos curo*, Ælfc. Gr. 47; Som. 47, 29. Dîne leófostan frȳnd fæder and mōdor and dîne māgas *patrem tuum et matrem et omnem cognationem tuam*, Jos. 2, 18: Ps. Th. 73, 8. Ealle wyrd forsweóp mîne māgas, Beo. Th. 5622; B. 2815: Blickl. Homl. 139, 16. [*Laym.* mæi *a cousin*: *Goth.* mēgs *a son-in-law*: *O. Sax.* māg *a relation*: *O. Frs* mēch: *Icel.* māgr *a father-in-law*: *O. H. Ger.* māg *cognatus, affinis*.] v. cneó-, fæderen-, freó-, fride-, heáfod-, hleó-, hylde-, leód-, mēdren-, neáh-, wine-, woruld-mǣg; un-mǣg; ge-māgas.

mǣg, e; *f. A woman, kinswoman*:—Freólecu mǣg (*Eve*), Cd. 42; Th. 55, 17; Gen. 895: (*Cain's wife*), 50; Th. 64, 21; Gen. 1053: (*Hagar*), 101; Th. 134, 18; Gen. 2226. Drihtlîcu mǣg (*Sara*), 89; Th. 111, 2; Gen. 1850: 133; Th. 168, 12; Gen. 2781. Mǣg ælfsciéno (*Sara*), 86; Th. 109, 23; Gen. 1827: 130; Th. 165, 11; Gen. 2730. Seó eádge mǣg, sancta Maria, Exon. 9 a; Th. 6, 21; Cri. 87. Seó æþele mǣg (*Juliana*), 68 a; Th. 253, 4; Jul. 175. Seó wuldres mǣg, 74 b; Th. 278, 20; Jul. 600. Cāseres mǣg (*Elene*), Elen. Kmbl. 660; El. 330: 1335; El. 669. [*Laym.* may: *Orm.* maȝȝ: *Chauc.* mai.] v. eád-, wyn-mǣg.

mæg *may*. v. magan.

mǣg-bana, an; *m. A destroyer of one's kinsmen*:—Hit (*surfeiting*) biþ mǣgbana, and hit ne murneþ for nānum men, ne for fæder ne for mēder ne for brōder ne for swuster ne for nānum gesibban men, Wulfst. 242, 5.

mǣg-bōt, e; *f. The 'bōt' paid to the kinsman of a slain man for the slaying of the latter.* It seems to be used only in the case of the spiritual relationship of godfather and godchild:—Gif hwā ōdres godsunu sleá odde his godfæder sîe sió mǣgbōt and sió manbōt gelîc. Weaxe sió bōt be dam were swā ilce swā sió manbōt dēþ de dam hlāforde sceal . . . Gif hē on done geonbyrde de hine slōg donne ætfealle sió bōt dæm godfæder swā ilce swā dæt wîte dam hlāforde dēþ *if any one slay another's godson or his godfather, let the compensation to the godfather or godson and that to the lord of the dead man be alike. Let them both increase in proportion to the 'wer' . . . If he (the slain man) strove against him that slew him, then let there be no 'bōt' to the godfather just as there is no 'wîte' to the lord*, L. In. 76; Th. i. 150, 13-20. Ǣgder ge mǣgbōte ge manbōte fullîce gebēte, L. C. E. 2; Th. i. 360, 7.

mǣg-burh; *gen.* -burge; *f. Kindred, family, relatives, tribe*:—Mǣgburg *cognatio*, Wrt. Voc. ii. 15, 70. Weóx under wolcnum mǣgburh Semes, Cd. 82; Th. 102, 20; Gen. 1703: 100; Th. 132, 14; Gen. 2193: 81; Th. 102, 4; Gen. 1695. Ne weorþeþ sió mǣgburg gemicledu eaforan mînum, Exon. 105 b; Th. 401, 31; Rä. 21, 20. Heó ongan his mǣgburge men geîcean sunum and dōhtrum, Cd. 56; Th. 69, 7; Gen. 1132: 101; Th. 134, 5; Gen. 2220: Beo. Th. 5766; B. 2887. Hē hit ne mōste sellan of his mǣgburge *he might not sell it* (bōcland) *out of the family*, L. Alf. pol. 41; Th. i. 88, 18. Wes mǣgburge mînre ārfæst *be kind to my kindred*, Cd. 136; Th. 171, 8; Gen. 2825: Exon. 88 a; Th. 331, 3; Vy. 62. Gielden siddan his mǣgas done wer gif hē mǣgburg (-borh, MS. B.: -burh, MS. H.) hæbbe freó *let his kinsmen afterwards pay the wergild, if he have free kindred*, L. In. 74; Th. i. 148, 19. Mǣgburge mîne *my children*, Exon. 104 b; Th. 397, 15; Rä. 16, 20. Iécte mǣgburg sîne, Cd. 55; Th. 68, 27; Gen. 1123. Mǣgburh, 52; Th. 65, 14; Gen. 1066. Cūde ǣghwilc mǣgburga riht *each one knew the rights of the tribes*, 161; Th. 200, 5; Exod. 352. Da de mǣgburge mǣst gefrunon frumcyn feora fæderæþelo gehwæs *those who were best informed as to families, as to the origin of men, and the ancestry of each*, Th. 200, 21; Exod. 360.

mǣg-cild, es; *n. A young kinsman*:—Hine āhsode hwǣr hē his mǣgcildum cumen hæfde de hē him forstolen hæfde *asked him what he had done with his young kinsmen* (*cousins*) *whom he had stolen away from him*, Lchdm. iii. 424, 37. Dȳ læs ǣnig man cwede dæt ic mîne mǣgcild mid wō fordēmde *lest any man say that I wrongfully decided against my kinsmen* (*nephews*), Chart. Th. 486, 27.

mǣg-cūd; *adj. Related*:—Mǣgcūdre sibbe *cognate propinquitatis*, Wrt. Voc. ii. 133, 34.

mǣg-cwealm, es; *m. Murder of a father* or *kinsman*:—Mēgcualm *parricidio*, Wrt. Voc. ii. 116, 53.

mǽg-cynren, es; *n. Race, family*:—Macynnere [=(?) mægcynrene] *prosapia*, Hpt. Gl. 437, 11.

mægden, mǽden, es; *n. A maiden, girl, virgin*:—Mǽden oððe geong wífman *puella*, Wrt. Voc. 73, 5. Nis ðis mǽden ná deád ac heó slǽpþ... Hē nam ðæs mǽdenes mōdor, Mk. Skt. 5, 39–40. Ðū nū sceáwa ðínes mæg(d)enes (*the Virgin Mary*) eáþmōdnesse, Blickl. Homl. 159, 4. Ðā wearþ ðæs mægdnes mōd miclum geblissad, Exon. 74 b; Th. 279, 3; Jul. 608. Hit sealde ðam mǽdene (*the daughter of Herodias*), and ðæt mǽden hit sealde hire mēder, Mk. Skt. 6, 28. Gif hwā mǽden nȳdnǽme *si quis violenter virginem opprimat*, L. C. S. 53; Th. i. 406, 3. Ne nȳde man nāðer ne wíf ne mǽden tō ðam ðe hyre sylfre mislícige *let no woman, whether she have been married before or not, be forced to a marriage which she dislikes*, 75; Th. i. 416, 20: L. Edm. B. 1; Th. i. 254, 2. Mǽdenu *virgines*, Ps. Th. 44. 15. Tō abbudissan gehādod ofer mā ðonne twām hund mǽdenum, Homl. Th. ii. 476, 20. Mǽdenu niman on þeáwe gōdne tíman getācnaþ, Lchdm. iii. 208, 28. [*O. H. Ger.* magatín: *M. H. Ger.* magetín.]

mægden-ǽw, e; *f. Marriage with a virgin*:—Ðæt biþ rihtlíc líf ðæt cniht þurhwunige on his cnihthāde ōþ ðæt hē on rihtre mǽdenǽwe gewífige and hæbbe ða syððan and nǽnige ōðre ða hwíle ðe seó libbe *that is right life, that a young man remain a bachelor until in lawful matrimony he take a maiden to wife, and let him have her afterwards and no other while she lives*, L. I. P. 22; Th. i. 332, 29.

mægden-cild, es; *n. A female child, girl*:—Gif hit hysecild byþ ofsleáþ ðæt gif hit sí mǽdencild healdaþ ðæt *si masculus fuerit, interficite eum, si femina reservate*, Ex. 1, 16. Ðonne ða wíf heora bearn cendon, ðonne fēddon hié ða mǽdencild and slōgon ða hysecild, and ðǽm mǽdencildum hié fortendun ðæt swíðre breóst foran, Ors. 1, 10; Swt. 46, 10–12. Tǽcende ðām mǽdencildum *docendo puellas*, Ælfc. Gr. 26; Som. 28, 16.

mægden-hād, es; *m. Maidenhood, virginity*:—Ðeáh wæs hyre (*the Virgin Mary*) mægdenhād ǽghwæs onwalg, Exon. 28 b; Th. 87, 5; Cri. 1420. Gif ǽnig wer oððe wíf gehāte ðæt hē wylle mǽdenhād gehealdan *si quis vir aut mulier voverit virginitatem servare*, L. Ecg. C. 19; Th. ii. 146, 1. v. mægþ-hād.

mægden-, mǽden-heáp, es; *m. A virgin band, troop of maidens*, Dōm. L. 18, 288.

mægden-líc; *adj. Maidenly, girlish, virgin, virginal*:—Mǽdenlíc *puellaris, virginalis*, Ælfc. Gr. 5; Som. 5, 23. Seó mǽdenlíce clǽnnys *virginalis castitas*, Hymn. Surt. 118, 21. Mǽdenlícere *virginalis*, Hpt. Gl. 506, 38. Godes sunu þurh mǽdenlícne innoþ ācenned wearþ, Homl. Th. i. 458, 33.

mægden-mann, es; *m. A maid, virgin*:—Mǽdenman *virgo*, Wrt. Voc. 73, 6. Gā ān mǽdenman tō, and hō hit on his sweoran, Lchdm. iii. 42, 9. Gif hwylc mǽdenman on geferrǽdene mid gehādodum wunaþ *si puella aliqua in societate cum ordinatis habitet*, L. Ecg. P. ii. 17; Th. ii. 188, 9. Gif man wið cyninges mægdenman geligeþ, L. Ethb. 10; Th. i. 6, 4. For ðon Mesiane noldon ðæt Læcedemonia mægdenmenn mid heora ofreden and heora godum onsægden *propter spretas virgines suas in solemni Messeniorum sacrificio*, Ors. 1, 14; Swt. 56, 16. [*Orm.* Sannte Marȝe wass æfre *maȝȝdennmann.*] v. mægþ-mann.

mǽge, an; *f. A kinswoman*:—Elizabeth ðín mǽge (MSS. A. B. mage.) *Elisabeth cognata tua*, Lk. Skt. 1, 36. Hēr sit Leóflǽd mín mǽge, Ðurcilles wíf, Chart. Th. 337, 30. Cwæð ðæt heó wǽre gramena mǽge, Deáðes dōhtor, Homl. Skt. 2. 173. Saga ðæt ðū síe sweostor mín, líces mǽge, Cd. 89; Th. 110, 4; Gen. 1833: 127; Th. 162, 18; Gen. 2683. In Dauides dȳrre mǽgan (*the Virgin Mary*), Exon. 9 a; Th. 7, 5; Cri. 96. v. māge, mǽg.

Mægelan, Mægelang, *Milan*:—Tō Mægelan [Mægolange, MS. C.] *apud Mediolanum*, Ors. 6, 36; Swt. 294, 30.

MÆGEN, es; *n.* I. MAIN, *might, strength, force, power, vigour, efficacy, virtue, faculty, ability*:—Ūrum líchoman cymþ eall his mægen of ðam mete ðe wē þicgaþ *all its strength comes to our body from the food that we take*, Bt. 34, 11; Fox 150, 34. Ðæt mycle mægen mínra handa *the mighty power of my hands*, Ps. Th. 80, 13. Micel drihten ūre and micel mægen his *Magnus Dominus noster, et magna virtus ejus*, Ps. Spl. 146, 5. Ðǽm monnum ðe him mægen and cræft wiexþ eác hwílum eákiaþ æfter ðæm mægenum ða costunga *crescente virtute plerumque bella tentationis augentur*, Past. 21, 5; Swt. 163, 8. Se wæs moncynnes mægenes strengest *he was mightiest among men*, Beo. Th. 395; B. 196. Nānne man ðæs ne tweóþ ðæt se seó strong on his mægene ðe mon gesihþ ðæt stronglíc weorc wyrcþ *nemo dubitat esse fortem, cui fortitudinem inesse conspexerit*, Bt. 16, 3; Fox 54, 28. Ǽr hí geseón Godes ríce on mægne cuman *donec videant regnum dei veniens in virtute*, Mk. Skt. 9, 1. Hē sealde ǽghwylcum be hys āgenum mægene *dedit unicuique secundum propriam virtutem*, Mt. Kmbl. 25, 15. Lufa ðínne drihten mid eallum mægne *diliges dominum tuum ex tota fortitudine tua*, Deut. 6, 5. Of eallum ðínum mihtum and of eallum ðínum mægene *ex omnibus viribus tuis et ex omni mente tua*, Lk. Skt. 10, 27. Eallon mægene tilian, Bt. 24, 2; Fox 82, 6. Wiðstandan ealle mægene, Past. 15, 1; Swt. 91, 1: Beo. Th. 5328; B. 2667. Ðū ne wēnst ðæt heó mǽge swā mycel mægen habban *you will not expect that the plant can have so great efficacy*, Herb. 12, 4; Lchdm. i. 104, 12. Hē moncynnes mǽste hæfde mægen and strengo, Cd. 79; Th. 98, 19; Gen. 1632. Ða ðe snyttro mægn and mōdcræft mǽste hæbben *those who in the greatest degree have wisdom, ability and mental power*, Elen. Kmbl. 815; El. 408. Ðonne hí ðæt mægen ðære unmǽtan hǽto ārǽfnan ne mihton *cum vim fervoris immensi tolerare non possent*, Bd. 5, 12; S. 627, 41. Mægyn and mihta (*angeli*) *potentes virtute*, Ps. Th. 102, 19. Eall his bearna mægen *omnes virtutes ejus*, 20. Seó sȳfernes and ōðre mægnu *sobrietas et alie virtutes*, Prud. 54 a: 64 a. Ðā sōðan welan ðæt sind hālige mægnu *the true riches, they are holy virtues*, Homl. Th. ii. 88, 310. Mægenu, Basil admn. 2; Norm. 38, 9. Mægno and cræftas, Bt. 32, 1; Fox 116, 1. Wísdōm mōdur eallra mægena *virtutum omnium nutrix*, 10; Fox 26, 24. Mycelre mægna fǽmne *magnarum virgo virtutum*, Bd. 3, 8; S. 531, 12. Geleáfa is ealra mægena fyrmest, Homl. Th. 1. 134, 2. Geþyld is wyrtruma ealra hāligra mægna, and ungeþyld is ealra mægna tōstencednys, ii. 544, 6. Þurh ðínra mægna spēd *through the abundance of thy powers*, Bt. Met. Fox 20, 516; Met. 20, 258: Cd. 1; Th. 1, 6; Gen. 3. Eallum hire mihtum and mægenum, L. M. 3, 63; Lchdm. ii. 352, 5. Ða ðe faraþ fram leahtrum tō mægnum *those who pass from vices to virtues*, Homl. Th. ii. 54, 26. Mægnum, Prud. 28 a. Ðā ongunnon hí mōd and mægen niman . . . Mōd and mægen Bryttas onfēngon *ceperunt illi vires animosque resumere . . . vires capessunt Brittones*, Bd. 1, 16; S. 484, 15–19. Ðeáh ðe ic nū gyt ða ǽrran mægen ne hæbbe *etsi necdum vires pristinas recepi*, 5, 3; S. 616, 34: 5, 4; S. 617, 25. Heó hæfþ ðās mægnu *it* (*henbane*) *has these virtues*, Herb. 5, 1; Lchdm. i. 94, 10. Megene *vires*, Kent. Gl. 930. II. *an exercise of power, effort, a mighty work, miracle*:—Mægene *conamine*, Wrt. Voc. ii. 24, 57. Hē ne mihte ǽnig mægen wyrcan *non poterat virtutem ullam facere*, Mk. Skt. 6, 5. Ān mægen and ān wundor of monegum āsecgan *unum e pluribus virtutis miraculum enarrare*, Bd. 3, 2; S. 524, 38. Monige mægen and hǽlotācen gefremede wǽron *innumeræ virtutes sanitatum noscuntur esse patratæ*, S. 524, 28. On him synd mægenu geworht, Mk. Skt. 6, 14. Ða burga on ðām wǽrun gedōne manega hys mægena, Mt. Kembl. 11, 20. III. *a force, military force*:—Gif ðet full mægen ðǽre wǽre ne eodan hí nǽfre eft tō scipon *if the full force had been there, they would never have got back to the ships*, Chr. 1004; Erl. 139, 34. Ūre mægen lytlaþ *our force lessens*. Byrht. Th. 140, 65; By. 313. Mægen, folc Ebrēa, Judth. 12; Thw. 25, 15, 10; Jud. 261, 253. Werod, mōdigra mægen, Cd. 147; Th. 184, 2; Exod. 101: 158; Th. 197, 1; Exod. 300. Mægen forþ gewāt, 160; Th. 199, 30; Exod. 346. Mægen (*the Egyptian army*) wæs ādrenced, 166; Th. 206, 28; Exod. 458. Seó sibgedriht bād māran mægenes *the Israelites awaited the greater force of the Egyptians*, 154; Th. 191, 15; Exod. 215. Mægenes wísa (*Belshazzar*), 209; Th. 260, 2; Dan. 703. Se wæs mid his dǽdum snelra ðonne hē mæ[ge]nes hæfde *he was quicker in his actions than in proportion to the force he had*; celeritate magis quam virtute fretus, Ors. 2, 5; Swt. 78, 27. Hē self fōr ðǽrtō mid eallum ðæm mægene ðe hē ðǽrtō gelǽdan mehte *he himself marched thither with all the troops that he could lead there*, Swt. 80, 24. Martyra mægen unlytel *no small host of martyrs*, Andr. Kmbl. 1752; An. 878: Beo. Th. 894; B. 445. Mægen unríme *hosts innumerable*, Elen. Kmbl. 121; El. 61. [*O. Sax.* megin: *Icel.* magn *and* megin: *O. H. Ger.* magan, megin, *robur, vigor, vis, virtus, fortitudo.*] DER. beadu-, deáþ-, eal-(æl-), eorþ-, eorl-, folc-, gæst-, gesíþ-, hand-, here-, heáh-, heofon-, holm-, hord-, leód-, lof-, ofer-, rǽd-, tōþ-, þeód-mægen.

mægen-āgende; *adj. Possessing strength, mighty*, Beo. Th. 5666; B. 2837.

mægen-byrðenn, e; *f. A mighty burden*, Beo. Th. 3254; B. 1625: 6174; B. 3091.

mægen-corþer, es; *n. A powerful band*, Cd. 93; Th. 119, 27; Gen. 1986.

mægen-cræft, es; *m. Main force, great power* or *might, mighty power*:—Mægencræft ðe him meotud engla forgiefen hæfde *the power which the Lord of angels had given him*, Exon. 49 a; Th. 170, 1; Gū. 1105. Is ðæt mægencræft micel mōda gehwylces ofer líchoman (cf. hit is micel cræft ðæs mōdes for ðone líchoman, Bt. 38, 1; Fox 196, 10), Bt. Met. Fox 26, 209; Met. 26, 105. Ðæt hē þrittiges manna mægencræft on his mundgripe hæbbe, Beo. Th. 765; B. 380. Mircne mægencræft, Exon. 26 b; Th. 78, 26; Cri. 1280. [*O. Sax.* megin-kraft: *O. L. Ger.* megin-craft *majestas*: *O. H. Ger.* magan-kraft *majestas.*]

mægen-cyning, es; *m. A chief, mighty* or *powerful king*:—Mægencyning (*God*), Elen. Kmbl. 2493; El. 1248: Exon. 116 b; Th. 448, 21; Dōm. 57: (*Christ*), 21 a; Th. 57, 11; Cri. 917. Mægencyninga meotod *the Lord of mighty kings*, 21 b; Th. 58, 29; Cri. 943: 116 a; Th. 445, 12; Dōm. 6. [Cf. *Icel.* megin-drōttning (*the Virgin Mary*): megin-skjöldungr (*Christ*).]

mægen-dǽd, e; *f. A mighty deed, an action requiring strength*, Exon. 78 b; Th. 294, 9; Crā. 12.

mægen-eáca, an; *m. An increase of strength, succour*:—Monnum tō mægeneácan *a succour for men*, Exon. 55 a; Th. 194, 14; Az. 138.

mægen-eácen; *adj. Endowed with strength, powerful*:—Mōde mægeneácen, Exon. 79 b; Th. 299, 7; Crä. 98. Mægeneácen folc (*the victorious Hebrews*), Judth. 12; Thw. 25, 35; Jud. 293.

mægen-earfeþe, es; *n. A great labour* or *hardship*:—Nales fore lytlum geómre, ac fore ðám mǽstum mægenearfeþum, Exon. 22 a; Th. 60, 4; Cri. 964. Mægenearfeþu, sār and swār gewin and sweartne deáþ, 28 b; Th. 86, 20; Cri. 1411.

mægen-ellen, es; *n. Mighty valour*, Beo. Th. 1323; B. 659.

mægen-fæst; *adj. Strong, vigorous, firm*:—Sealde him snyttru mægenfæste gemynd *he gave him wisdom, vigorous thought*, Exon. 39 b; Th. 130, 28; Gū. 445. Ǽlc līchamlīce gesceaft ðe eorþe ācenþ is fulre and mægenfæstre on fullum mōnan ðonne on gewanedum *every bodily creature that earth produces is more complete and more vigorous at the full moon than when the moon has waned*, Homl. Th. i. 102, 21. [Cf. mægen-leás.]

mægen-folc, es; *n. A mighty people*:—Mægenfolc micel (cf. *O. Sax.* meginfolk mikil *the multitude that flocked about Christ*) *a people mighty and vast* (*the good at the day of judgment*), Exon. 20 b; Th. 55, 1; Cri. 877.

mægen-fultum, es; *m. A powerful help*:—Næs ðæt mǽtost mægenfultuma (*the sword lent to Beowulf by Hunferth*), Beo. Th. 2915; B. 1455.

mægen-heáp, es; *m. A powerful band*:—Mægenheápum, Cd. 151; Th. 190, 11; Exod. 197.

mægen-heard; *adj. Very strong, powerful*:—Ðam ðe sitteþ on ufan meare mægenheardum, Runic pm. 5; Kmbl. 340, 5.

mægenian, mægnian; *p.* ode *To gain strength*:—Mōd mægnode *mind gained might*, Exon. 94 b; Th. 353, 55; Reim. 33. v. ge-mægened.

mægen-leás; *adj. Without strength, powerless, weak, feeble*:—Mægenleás *enervis*, Wrt. Voc. i. 46, 6: *elumbis*, Germ. 396, 216. Seó sāwul, gif heó næfþ ða hālgan lāre, heó biþ ðonne weornigende and mægenleás, Homl. Th. i. 168, 33. [*Icel.* megin-lauss.]

mægenleas-līce; *adv. Feebly, impotently*:—Mægenleaslīce *eviscerando*, Germ. 398, 122.

mægen-leást, e; *f. Weakness, feebleness, impotence*:—Ðā ofhreów ðam munece ðæs hreóflian mægenleást (*inability to walk*), Homl. Th. i. 336, 11. Mōdes mægenleást *weakness of mind*, ii. 220, 5. Hī ne mihton for heora mægenleáste ða meniu bewerian (*of the Jews reduced by famine during the siege of Jerusalem*), Ælfc. T. Grn. 21, 8.

mægen-rǽs, es; *m. A mighty* or *violent attack*:—Mægenrǽs forgeaf hilde bille (*Beowulf attacking Grendel's mother*), Beo. Th. 3043; B. 1519.

mægen-rōf; *adj. Of great power*:—Mōdig and mægenrōf mid ðære miclan hand (*applied to God*), Cd. 156; Th. 195, 11; Exod. 275. Þegn, mægenrōfa man, Exon. 109 b; Th. 419, 9; Rä. 38, 3.

mægen-scipe, es; *m. Power, might*:—Metodes mægenscipe, Cd. 173; Th. 217, 9; Dan. 20.

mægen-spēd, e; *f. Abundance of strength, strength* (cf. on ðīnes mægenes miclum spēdum *in virtute tua*, Ps. Th. 73, 13), *power, virtue*:—Ic ðē sceal meotudes mægenspēd gesecgan *to thee am I to tell the Maker's abundant might*, Exon. 92 b; Th. 348, 6; Sch. 24. Hē mec for miltsum and mægenspēdum nǽfre wille ān forlǽtan *on account of his mercy and his might he will never forsake me*, 42 a; Th. 140, 17; Gū. 611: Andr. Kmbl. 2572; An. 1287. Mīn mūþ sægeþ ðīne mægenspēde *os meum pronuntiabit justitiam tuam*, Ps. Th. 70, 14.

mægen-stān, es; *m. A mighty stone* or *rock*:—Him on innan felþ muntes mægenstān (cf. þǽr micel stān wealwiende of ðam heáhan munte on innan fealþ, Bt. 6; Fox 14, 28), Bt. Met. Fox 5, 31; Met. 5, 16. Ðis synd ðæra xx hīda gemǽro . . andlang wægæs ōþ ðonæ mægenstān, Cod. Dip. Kmbl. v. 112, 18.

mægen-strang; *adj. Strong in power*:—Hū ðū mǽre eart mihtig and mægenstrang *how great thou* (*Christ*) *art, how mighty and strong in power*, Hy. 3, 21; Hy. Grn. ii. 282, 21. Ðū eart se miccla and se mægenstranga, 3, 38; Hy. Grn. ii. 282, 38. Mægenstrong, Exon. 129 a; Th. 495, 5; Rä. 84, 3.

mægen-strengo; *indecl. f. Main strength, great force*:—Gūþcyning (*Beowulf*) mægenstrengo slōh hilde bille *with mighty force the warrior-king smote with his battle-blade*, Beo. Th. 5350; B. 2678. Sum biþ gleáw mōdes cræfta sum mægenstrengo onfēhþ *one is skilled in the arts of the mind, another receives great bodily strength*, Exon. 78 b; Th. 295, 15; Crä. 33.

mægen-strengþu; *indecl.*: **-strengþ**, e; *f. Great strength, power*:—Hī ðīne mægenstrengþu mǽrsien wīde *magnitudinem tuam narrabunt*, Ps. Th. 144, 6. Ic siges mihte and mægenstrengþe swā micele eów sille ðæt gē eów tō gamene feónda āfillaþ swā fela swā gē reccaþ *I will give you so great victorious might and power, that it shall be sport to you to slay as many foes as you can count*, Wulfst. 132, 19.

mægen-þegen, es; *m. A mighty minister* (an angel), Exon. 49 a; Th. 169, 23; Gū. 1099.

mægen-þreát, es; *m. A mighty band*, Cd. 174; Th. 218, 26; Dan. 45: 169; Th. 210, 8; Exod. 512.

mægen-þrymm, es; *m.* (The word is used almost exclusively in reference to the Deity). **I.** *Majesty, greatness, glory*:—Se myccla mægenþrym *the great majesty* (*of Christ*), Blickl. Homl. 179, 8. Mægenþrymmes God *Deus majestatis*, Ps. Th. 28, 3. Mægenþrymmes ðīnes *majestatis tuæ*, 144, 5. His mægenþrymmes *magnitudinis ejus*, 150, 2. His rīces ongin, ne his mihte, ne his mægenþrymmes nǽfre gewonad ne weorþeþ, Blickl. Homl. 9, 17. Hē (*Christ*) hine ungyrede ðæs godcundan mægenþrymmes, and gegyrede hine þeówlīce, 105, 3. Ðonne se heofenlīca dēma cymþ on egeslīcum mægenþrymme, Homl. Th. ii. 558, 9: Lk. Skt. 9, 26, 31, 32. Mid ðȳ mǽstan mægenþrymme, Exon. 22 b; Th. 62, 30: Cri. 1009. Johannes on Godes mægenþrymme hī gebletsode, Homl. Th. i. 64, 4. Wē gesāwon Godes mægenþrim and his micelnisse (*majestatem et magnitudinem suam*), Deut. 5, 24. **II.** (*using the attribute for the person*), *Christ*:—Mægenþrym ārās, sigefæst and snottor, Exon. 120 a; Th. 420, 25; Hö. 22. **III.** *great power, might*:—Gē geseóþ mannes Bearn sittende on ða swȳðran healfe Godes mægenþrymmes *videbitis filium hominis sedentem a dextris virtutis Dei*, Mt. Kmbl. 26, 64. Ic sōhte hwylc wǽre mægenþrymmes oððe elnes se Pater Noster, Salm. Kmbl. 20; Sal. 10. In ðam mægenþrymme mid ðam sȳ āhefed heofon and eorþe *in that mighty power with which is uplifted heaven and earth*, Exon. 93 b; Th. 351, 31; Sch. 88. Hē hine of sāwle deáþe āwehte þurh ðone mægenþrym *he raised him from the death of the soul through divine power*, Blickl. Homl. 77, 10. Mægenþrymmum mǽst *mightiest*, Cd. 160; Th. 199, 35; Exod. 349. **IV.** *an instance in which the divine glory or power is displayed*:—Eftwyrd cymþ, mægenþrymma mǽst, dæg dǽdum fāh (*doom's day*), Cd. 169; Th. 212, 16; Exod. 540. **V.** *the glory of heaven, heaven, the angels who inhabit heaven*:—Wuldres ealdor middangeardes and mægenþrymmes *the prince of glory, of earth and of heaven*, Exon. 68 a; Th. 251, 33; Jul. 154. Hē is cyning middangeardes and mægenþrymmes, wuldre biwunden, 65 b; Th. 241, 33; Ph. 665: 16 a; Th. 35, 13; Cri. 557. Ufan of roderum, of his mægenþrymme, 98 a; Th. 368, 24; Seel. 29. Hēht sigores fruma his heáhbodan hider (*to earth*) gefleógan of his mægenþrymme, 12 a; Th. 19, 5; Cri. 296. Næs ǽnig ðā giet engel geworden ne ðæs miclan mægenþrymmes nān *was not any angel then created, nor any of that great and glorious band*, 12 b; Th. 22, 16; Cri. 352.

mægenþrym-ness, e; *f. Majesty, magnificence, glory*:—His mægenþrymnes (-þrymmes, MS.) micellīc standeþ *magnificentia opus ejus*, Ps. Th. 110, 2. Mæg[en]þrymnysse *majestatis*, Hpt. Gl. 486, 18. Ælmihtig God, ānes gecyndes, and ānre mægenþrymnisse on ānre godcundnysse, Hexam. 2; Norm. 4, 23. Ðonne sit hē on dōmsetle his mægenþrymnysse, Wulfst. 287, 31. Mæg[n]þrumnysse *majestati*, Hpt. Gl. 416, 52. God sylf se ðe ǽfre þurhwunode on his miclan wuldre and on his mægenþrimnisse, Ælfc. T. Grn. 2, 4. Ða ðe gesāwon mīne mægenþrimnisse *qui viderunt majestatem meam*, Num. 14, 22.

mægen-þyse, an; *f. Violence, force*:—Sōna ðæt onfindeþ se ðe mec fēhþ ongeán and wið mægenþisan mīnre genǽsteþ ðæt hē hrycge sceal hrusan sēcan *soon doth he find that fights against me, and with my force comes into conflict, that with his back he must visit the earth*, Exon. 107 b; Th. 410, 2; Rä. 28, 10. [Cf. *Icel.* þysja *to rush.*]

mægen-weorc, es; *n. A mighty work*:—Hū micle synt ðīne mægenweorc *quam magnificata sunt opera tua*, Ps. Th. 91, 4. [*Icel.* megin-verk; *pl. mighty works.*]

mægen-wīsa, an; *m. The leader of a force* or *army*, Cd. 170; Th. 213, 17; Exod. 553.

mægen-wudu, a; *m. A mighty spear-shaft*:—Þegn Hrōðgāres cwehte mægenwudu mundum *Hrothgar's thane shook his mighty shaft with his hands*, Beo. Th. 477; B. 236.

mægen-wundor, es; *n. A very great wonder* (of the circumstances attending the day of judgement), Exon. 21 b; Th. 57, 31; Cri. 927.

mæger; *adj. Meagre, lean*:—Ða men beóþ mægre and blāce on onsȳne ðeáh ðe hié ǽr fætte wǽron *the men will be lean and pale of aspect, though before they were fat*, L. M. 2, 36; Lchdm. ii. 242, 3. [*Icel.* magr: *Dan., Swed., Du.* mager: *O. H. Ger.* magar *macilentus*: *Ger.* mager.]

mægerian; *p.* ode *To macerate, emaciate, make lean*:—Mægeregan *macerare*, Wrt. Voc. ii. 57, 16: 96, 34. [*Icel.* megra *to emaciate*: *O. H. Ger.* magarian *macerare, macrescere*; cf. magar fleiski *pulpa*: *Ger.* magern.]

mægeþ, mǽgeþ. v. mægþ, mǽgþ.

mægeþe *name of a plant*. v. mageþe.

mǽg-gemōt, es; *n. A meeting of kinsmen*:—Hē bebeád ofer ealne middangeard ðæt ǽlc mǽgþ tōgædere cōme, ðæt ǽlc man ðȳ gearor wiste hwǽr hē gesibbe hæfde. Ðæt tācnode ðæt on his dagum sceolde beón geboren se se ðe ūs ealle tō ānum mǽggemōte gelaþaþ, Ors. 5, 14; Swt. 248, 18.

mǽg-gewrit, es; *n. A writing containing a list of kinsmen, a genealogical table, pedigree*, Cot. 213, Lye.

mǽg-gildan (?) *to pay part of the wergild for a homicide committed by a kinsman*:—Ne þearf se frigea mid ðam þeówan mǽggieldan (*or should this be* mǽge gieldan? cf. *MS. B. which has* mid ðam þeówan men gyldan. But the word is supported by L. H. i. 70, 5:—Non cogitur liber cum servo *meggildare*), L. In. 74; Th. i. 150, 1.

mǽg-hǽmed, es; *n. Incest*:—Nǽnig mǽghǽmed ne unclǽne fremme *nullus incestum faciat*, Bd. 4, 5; S. 573, 15.

mǽg-hand, a; *f. A relation, kinsman*:—Nis Eðelmōde ǽnig mǽghond neór ðes cynnes ðanne Eádwald *there is no nearer relative to Ethelmod in the family than Eadwald*, Chart. Th. 466, 1. Wes hit becueden his brōðar suna and siððan nēniggra mēihanda mā ðes cynnes, 465, 20. Cf. ða nȳhstan hand mē, 491, 13.

mægister. v. magister.

mǽg-lagu, e; *f. Law regulating the duties and responsibilities of kinsmen* (mǽgas), e. g. in the matter of paying or receiving certain parts of the wergild if one of their number slew or was slain :—Hē (mynster-munuc) gǽþ of his mǽglage ðonne hē gebȳhþ tō regollage, L. Eth. ix. 25; Th. i. 346, 2. v. mǽgþ-lagu *and* lagu.

mǽg-leás; *adj. Without kinsmen* :—Gif hē sī mǽgleás *if he have no kinsmen*, L. Eth. ix. 24; Th. i. 344, 28: L. In. 23; Th. i. 116, 16: L. C. E. 5; Th. i. 362, 24. Fædrenmǽga mǽgleás mon *a man having no kinsmen on the father's side*, L. Alf. pol. 27; Th. i. 78, 20.

mǽg-līc; *adj. Belonging to kinsmen* :—Hē hine lufode nā swā micclum for ðære mǽglīcan sibbe *he loved him, not so much because they were relations*, Homl. Th. i. 58, 4. Næfde hē ðæt andgit þurh mǽglīce lāre *he did not have that intelligence through the teaching of his parents*, 368, 10.

mǽg-lufu, an; *f. Love* :—Heó sagaþ ðæt heó mǽglufan mīnre ne gȳme *she* (*Juliana*) *says that she cares not for my* (*Heliseus'*, *who wished to marry Juliana*) *love*, Exon. 66 b; Th. 246, 31; Jul. 70.

mǽg-morðor, es; *n. Murder of a kinsman* :—Mǽgmorðor *parricidium*, Hpt. Gl. 519, 74. Mǽgmorðres wītnung *parricidii actio*, Ælfc. Gl. 14; Som. 58, 15; Wrt. Voc. 21, 10. [Cf. *O. H. Ger.* māg-mord *parricidium*.]

mǽg-myrðra, an; *m. One who murders a kinsman, a parricide* :—Mǽgmyrðra *parricida*, Wrt. Voc. ii. 67, 15: Hpt. Gl. 509, 72.

mægn. v. mægen.

mǽg-racu, e; *f. The account of a family, a genealogy* :—Ðis is seó bōc Adames mǽgrace *hic est liber generationis Adam*, Gen. 5, 1. Gif ðū telst ða mǽgrace fram Judan ðonne findst ðū fīf mǽgþa *if you reckon the genealogy from Judah, then you will find five generations*, Boutr. Scrd. 22, 19.

mǽg-rǽdenn, e; *f. Kinship, relationship* :—Gesibbere mǽgrǽdene *consanguinitatis*, Hpt. Gl. 472, 20. Hē (*Julius Cæsar*) hiene (*Octavianus*) for mǽgrǽdenne gelǽrde, Ors. 5, 13; Swt. 244, 24. Nǽfre ic ðæs þeódnes þafian wille mǽgrǽdenne *I will never consent to marry the prince*, Exon. 67 a; Th. 249, 9; Jul. 109.

mǽg-rǽs, es; *m. An attack by men upon their kinsmen* :—Wearþ ðes þeódscype swȳðe forsyngod þurh morðdǽda and þurh māndǽda . . þurh mǽgrǽsas and þurh manslihtas *this nation is sunk in sin through deeds fell and foul . . through attacks of kinsmen upon kinsmen and through manslaughters*, Wulfst. 164, 4.

mǽg-scīr, e; *f. A division of a people, containing the kinsmen of a particular family* :—Teá monna lātwu ofer tēno oððe of mēgscīre is *decanus super x. vel decurio* (the glosser seems to have taken *de* as a separate word) *est*, Rtl. 193, 19.

mǽg-sibb, e; *f.* I. *kinship, relationship* :—Eva hine hālsode for scā Marian mǽgsibbe ðæt hē hire miltsade. Heó cwæþ tō him gemyne mīn drihten ðæt heó wæs bān of mīnum bānum and flǽsc of mīnum flǽsce *Eve conjured him* (*Christ*) *on account of her kinship to St. Mary to pity her. She said to him 'Remember, my Lord, that she was bone of my bone and flesh of my flesh*,' Shrn. 68, 15. Hē (*Christ*) hym (*men*) his mildse onwreáh and his mǽgsibbe gecȳdde. Ǽr ðam wē wǽron steópcild gewordene, Wulfst. 252, 9: Blickl. Homl. 107, 2. Wel is tō warnianne ðæt man wite ðæt hȳ (*the man and woman about to be married*) þurh mǽgsibbe tō gelænge ne beón (i. e. *are not within the prohibited* (*seven*) *degrees*), L. Edm. B. 9; Th. i. 256, 9. Seó hālige ǽ forbeódeþ ða sceondlīcnysse onwreón mǽgsibba (ðære mǽgsibbea, MS. B.) *sacra lex prohibet cognationis turpitudinem revelare*, Bd. 1, 27; S. 491, 7. II. *Love between kinsmen, affection* :—Mēgsibbe *affectui* vel *dilectione*, Wrt. Voc. ii. 99, 52. Mēgsibbi, Ep. Gl. 3 b, 9.

mǽgsib-līc; *adj. Of kin, related* :—Mǽgsiblīcum *contribulibus*, Wrt. Voc. ii. 20, 18.

mǽg-slaga, an; *m. The slayer of a kinsman* :—Mǽgslaga *parricida*, Ælfc. Gl. 85; Som. 73, 114; Wrt. Voc. 49, 21: Ælfc. Gr. 7; Som. 6, 46. Se mǽgslaga Cain *the fratricide Cain*, Homl. Th. ii. 58, 28. Hēr syndan mannslagan and mǽgslagan, Wulfst. 165, 27: 266, 26.

mǽg-sliht, es; *m. The slaughter of a kinsman* :—Wearþ ðes þeódscipe swīðe forsingod þurh manslihtas and þurh mǽgslihtas, Wulfst. 130, 2. [*O. H. Ger.* māg-slaht; *f. parricidium*.]

mægþ, mægeþ; *without inflection in the sing. and in the n. ac. pl., f. A maid, virgin, girl, maiden, woman* (almost confined to poetry) :—Gif man mægþ gebigeþ ceápe geceápod sȳ gif hit unfācne is *if a man make terms for his marriage with* (lit. *buys with a price*, cf. *Icel.* kona mundi keypt) *a woman, let the bargain stand, if it be without fraud*, L. Ethb. 77; Th. i. 22, 1. Wæs seó fǽmne geong, mægþ mānes leás (*the Virgin Mary*), Exon. 8 a; Th. 3, 14; Cri. 36. On fǽmnan, mægeþ unmǽle, 18 b; Th. 45, 18; Cri. 721: 122 b; Th. 470, 14; Hy. 11, 16. Þa torhtan mægþ (*Judith*), Judth. 10; Thw. 22, 1; Jud. 35. Mægþ scȳne *maiden fair*, Beo. Th. 6025; B. 3016. Ofer mægþ giunge, Bt. Met. Fox 26, 134; Met. 26, 67. Þurh Judithe lāre, mægþ mōdigre, Judth. 12; Thw. 26, 18; Jud. 335. Mægeþ, brȳde ðīnre (*Sarah*), Cd. 134; Th. 169, 10; Gen. 2797. Hē ðære mægeþ (*Guthlac's sister*) sceolde lāce gelǽdan lāð spel, Exon. 52 a; Th. 182, 27; Gū. 1316. Mægþ and mæcgas, 45 a; Th. 153, 29; Gū. 833. Mægeþ and mæcgas, 113 a; Th. 434, 7; Rä. 51, 7. Him tō nimaþ mægeþ tō gemæccum *take to themselves maidens as mates*, Cd. 64; Th. 76, 18; Gen. 1259. Mægþa sīð *the maidens' coming*, 123; Th. 157, 11; Gen. 2604: Beo. 1853; B. 924. Swā hwylc mægþa swā ðone magan cende, 1890; B. 943. Mægþa cynnes *of womankind*, Exon. 73 b; Th. 275, 16; Jul. 551. Mægþum and mæcgum, Cd. 55; Th. 68, 26; Gen. 1123. [*Goth.* magaþs *a maid, virgin*: *O. Sax.* magað: *O. Frs.* megith: *O. H. Ger.* magad *virgo*: *M. H. Ger.* maget: *Ger.* magd.] v. heals-mægeþ.

mǽgþ, e; *f. Importunate desire, ambition* :—Ðæt mōd sǽde ðæt him nǽfre seó mǽgþ and seó gītsung forwel ne līcode, Bt. tit. 17; Fox xii, 24. Cf. Ðū wāst ðæt mē nǽfre seó gītsung and seó gemǽgþ ðisses eorþlīcan anwealdes forwel ne līcode *scis ipsa minimum nobis ambitionem mortalium rerum fuisse dominatum*, 17; Fox 58, 23. v. māh, ge-mǽhþ (*with which* ge-mǽgþ *in the above passage should be put*).

mǽgþ, mǽgeþ, e; *f. A collection of* mǽgas. I. with a more limited extent, *a family, stock, race* :—Mǽgþ oððe styb *styrps*, Ælfc. Gr. 3; Som. 3, 17. Mǽgþ *progenies*, Wrt. Voc. 72, 48: *cognatio*, Ps. Spl. 73, 9. Mȳgþ *propinquus*, Kent. Gl. 876. Ðā wæs ān mǽgþ ðe nǽfre ne ābeáh tō nānum deófolgylde . . Seó mǽgþ āsprang of Noes eltstan suna . . And ðyssere mǽgþe God sealde ǽ . . forðan ðe hē wolde of ðyssere mǽgþe him mōdor geceósan, Homl. Th. i. 24, 5-20. Woldon ofsleán Claudius for Gaiuses þingum ðæs ǽrran cēsares and ealle ða de ðære mǽgþe wǽron *evertenda penitus Caesarum universa familia decrevissent*, Ors. 6, 4; Swt. 258, 25. Rīm miclade monna mǽgþe, Cd. 63; Th. 75, 22; Gen. 1244. Mǽgþe ðīnre (*Abraham's*), 84; Th. 105, 34; Gen. 1763. Nis nān wītega būton wurþscipe būton on his ēðele and on his mǽgþe (*cognatione*) and on his hūse, Mk. Skt. 6, 4. Ða hwīle ðe ǽnig man wǽre on hira mǽgþe ðe godcundes hādes beón walde *as long as there was any man of their stock that was willing to take orders*, Chart. Th. 166, 16. II. as a technical term in the laws, *relatives, kindred, the* mǽgas *who were living at the same time, and to whom the* mǽg-lagu *applied* :—Gā seó mǽgþ him on borh *let the family go bail for him* (*the thief*), L. Ath. i. 1; Th. i. 198, 24. Gif ðonne ðæt gebyrige ðæt ǽnig mǽgþ tō ðan strang sȳ . . ðæt ðonne þeóf foran forstande, V. 8, 2; Th. i. 236, 9: 12, 2; Th. i. 242, 3: L. Edm. S. 1; Th. i. 248, 5. Bēte ðam cyninge swā ilce swā ðære mǽgþe *let amends be made to the king in the same way as to the kindred*, L. In. 76; Th. i. 150, 17: L. Ath. i. 2; Th. i. 200, 7. Ealle of ǽgðere mǽgþe, L. E. G. 13; Th. i. 174, 21. Se slaga wile bētan wið mǽgþe, L. Edm. S. 7; Th. i. 250, 15. Gebēte wið ða mǽgþe, L. C. S. 39; Th. i. 398, 27: L. Edm. S. 4; Th. i. 248, 25. III. in a wider sense, *descendants of a common ancestor living at the same time, a generation* :—Ðē ic geseah sōðlīce rihtwīsne ætforan mē on ðissere mǽgþe *te enim vidi justum coram me in generatione hac*, Gen. 7, 1. On ealræ mǽgþe *in omni generatione*, Ps. Spl. 44, 19. Hwī is āwriten on ðære bēc Genesis ðæt Abrahames cynn sceolde gecyrran ongeán fram Aegypta lande on ðære feórþan mǽgþe and seó ōðer bōc Exodus sægþ ðæt hī fērdon of Aegyptan lande on ðære fiftan mǽgþe? . . Gif ðū telst ða mǽgrace fram Iudan ðonne findst ðū ðǽr fīf mǽgþa, and gif ðū telst fram Leui ðonne findst ðū ðǽr feówer mægþa, Boutr. Scrd. 22, 16-20: Homl. Th. ii. 458, 34. Noe wæs rihtwīs wer on his mǽgþum *Noe vir justus fuit in generationibus suis*, Gen. 6, 9: 9, 12. IV. with wider limits than those implied by *family*, (*a*) *a tribe, subdivision of a people* :—Mǽgþ *tribus*, Wrt. Voc. 72, 48: Ælfc. Gr. 11; Som. 15, 23. Gegaderiaþ eów tō mǽgþum [and gange] ðæt gehlot fram mǽgþe tō mǽgþe and be manna hīwrǽdenum *accedetis singuli per tribus vestras, et quamcumque tribum sors invenerit, accedit per cognationes suas*, Jos. 7, 14. Of Asseres mǽgþe *de tribu Asser*, Lk. Skt. 2, 36. Leóda mǽgþe *the tribes of men*, Cd. 80; Th. 100, 16; Gen. 1665. Ðæra mǽgþa ealdras *principes tribuum*, Num. 1, 4. Of ðām twelf mǽgþum, 13, 3: Blickl. Homl. 155, 30. (*b*) *a people, nation* :—Ðære mǽgþe monwīsan *the manners of the people* (*of Sodom*), Cd. 92; Th. 116, 20; Gen. 1939. Nā dyde hē swylc ǽlcre mǽgþe *non fecit taliter omni nationi*, Ps. Spl. 147, 9: 49, 7. Gebannan manigre mǽgþe geond ðisne middangeard, Beo. Th. 150; B. 75. Ðonne hē ys tōweard on micelre mǽgþe and ða strengstan mǽgþe nū ealra eorþan mǽgþ beóþ on him gebletsode *cum futurus sit in gentem magnam ac robustissimam et benedicendæ sint in illo omnes nationes terræ*, Gen. 18, 18. Fremde þeóde, ōðre mǽgþe, Ps. Th. 88, 43. Hæfdon ða mǽgþa ǽlcne for ēcne god *the nations held each to be god eternal*, Bt. Met. Fox 26, 98; Met. 26, 49. Mǽgþa tīda *tempora nationum*, Lk. Skt. 21, 24: Cd. 124; Th. 158, 12; Gen. 2616: Beo. Th. 49; B. 25: 9; B. 5. (*c*) as in the case of proper names the word for the people is used for their country, so *province, country* :—Seó mǽgþ West-Seaxna *provincia occidentalium Saxonum*, Bd. 3. 7; S. 529, 2. Seó ylce mǽgeþ ǽrest ðysne biscop āgenne onfēng *hunc primum eadem provincia proprium accepit praesulem*, 4. 12; S. 581,

24. Willferþ bisceop Súþ-Seaxna mǽgþe (*provinciæ*), 4, 13; S. 581, 37. From Armoricano ðære mǽgeþe, 1, 1; S. 474, 7. Mid his mǽgþe Eást-Englum, 2, 15; S. 518, 27. On Beornicia mǽgþe, 2, 14; S. 518, 14. Hé férde geond ealle Angelcynnes mǽgþe *perlustrans universa*, 4, 2; S. 566, 1. Him twá mǽgþe (*duas provincias*) forgeaf, 4, 13; S. 582, 10. Ða mǽgþe ðe mon hátеþ Gallia Belgica, 1, 1; S. 473, 12. On Palestina ðære mǽgþe, Shrn. 100, 26. On Tiro ðære mǽgþe, Th. Ap. 3, 24: Blickl. Homl. 211, 16: Andr. Kmbl. 528; An. 264. [*Orm.* off Asæress maȝȝþe.] v. fæderen-, folc-, ge-, médren-, súþ-, wer-mǽgþ.

mægþa, an; *m. Maithen, may-weed;* anthemis cotula:—Mægþa *herba putida*, Ælfc. Gl. 42; Som. 64, 11; Wrt. Voc. 31, 22: *caluna* (= *calmia*, v. Lchdm. ii. 398, col. 2); 39; Som. 63, 71; Wrt. Voc. 30, 19. Him mon mægþan tó mete gegyrede, Lchdm. iii. 34, 11. v. mageþe.

Mægþa land *the Polish province of Mazovia* (?):—Be norþan Horiti is Mægþa land; and be norþan Mægþa londe Sermende óþ ða beorgas Riffen, Ors. 1, 1; Swt. 16, 21.

mægþ-, mægeþ-blæd, es; *n. Pudendum muliebre:*—Mægeþblǽdd *virginal*, Germ. 400, 8. Leo 508, 9 says on this word 'Dieselbe Bedeutung hat Blatt noch in der deutschen Jägersprache: das Blatt einer Ricke, einer Hinde.'

mægþ-bót, e; *f. The fine to be paid by an unmarried woman:*—Mægþbót sí swá friges mannes *let the fine to be paid by an unmarried woman be the same as that by a free man* (*for the same offence*), L. Ethb. 74; Th. i. 20, 9. This regulation follows one that settles the fine to be paid by 'frí wíf locbore.'

mægþ-, mægeþ-hád, es; *m.* I. *maidenhood, virginity, celibacy, chastity:*—Ðú cennest cyning ealra clǽnnessa and ðínne mægþhád nó ne gewemmest, Blickl. Homl. 7, 36: Exon. 12 a; Th. 18, 25; Cri. 289: 9 a; Th. 6, 16; Cri. 85: Homl. Th. i. 460, 4. Mægþhád is ǽgðer ge on wǽpmannum ge on wífmannum. Ða habbaþ rihtne mægþhád ða ðe fram cildháde wuniaþ on clǽnnesse, 148, 13. Mæigþhád, 7. Ðæt sindan ða ða ðe mid wífum ne beóþ besmitene, and hira mægeþhád habbaþ gehealdenne, Past. 52, 7; Swt. 409, 7. Mæ[g]þhádes *virginitatis, puritatis*, Hpt. Gl. 411, 32: *castitatis*, 441, 69: *celibatus, pubertatis*, 453, 56. Hé sceal foresceáwian ðam mǽdene hire mægþhádes wurþ (*pretium pudicitiæ*), Ex. 21, 10: L. Alf. 12; Th. i. 46, 18. Án man ðe sý mægþhádes man, cnapa oððe mægden, Herb. 104, 2; Lchdm. i. 218, 21. Hire meiþhádes *pupertatis sue*, Kent. Gl. 26. Ic bidde ðé for Scam. Marian mægþháde, Bt. Fox 260, 3. II. *a body of young persons:*—Mægeþháde *pedagogio*, Wrt. Voc. ii. 77, 30. [*Marh.* meiðhad: *Orm.* maȝȝþhadd: *O. H. Ger.* magad-heit *virginitas, pubertas, coelibatus*.] v. mægden-hád.

mǽgþ-hád, es; *m. Kinship, relationship:*—'Se ðe his bróðor ne lufaþ hé wunaþ on deáþe.' Ealle wé sind gebróðra ðe on God gelýfaþ and wé ealle cweþaþ 'Úre Fæder ðe eart on heofonum.' Ne gedyrstlǽce nán man be mǽgþháde bútan sóðre lufe '*he who loveth not his brother continueth in death*' . . . *All we are brethren that believe on God, and we all say 'our Father that art in heaven.' Let no man presume on kinship without true love*, Homl. Th. i. 54, 6–11.

mægþhád-líc; *adj. Virgin, virginal:*—Mæg[þ]hádlícre sidefulnysse *pudicitiæ virginalis*, Hpt. Gl. 440, 65.

mǽgþ-lagu = **mǽg-lagu** q.v., L. C. E. V; Th. i. 362, 28.

mǽgþ-leás; *adj. Belonging to no family, not of distinguished family;* ignobilis, Wrt. Voc. ii. 138, 73.

mægþ-mann, es; *m. A maiden, virgin:*—Gif man mægþman néde genimeþ *if a maiden be carried off by force* (*to be married*), L. Ethb. 82; Th. i. 24, 3. v. mægden-mann.

mǽgþ-sibb, e; *f. Kindred:*—Mǽgþsybbe *parentelæ*, Hpt. Gl. 523, 10. v. mǽg-sibb.

mǽg-tudor, es; *n. That which is produced from the same stock:*—Mǽgtudre *cognatæ*, Hpt. Gl. 469, 52. Cf. magu-tudor.

mǽg-wine, es; *m. A kinsman and friend:*—Mon mænig be his mǽgwine *many a man standing by his kinsman* (of the people at the tower of Babel), Cd. 80; Th. 100, 9; Gen. 1661. Mǽgwinas míne, Beo. Th. 4951; B. 2479. Mǽgwinum, Cd. 149; Th. 187, 4; Exod. 146: 158; Th. 197, 28; Exod. 314: Salm. Kmbl. 719; Sal. 359. [*O. Sax.* mág-wini.]

mǽg-, még-wlite, es; *m. Appearance, form, species;* species, forma, aspectus:—Mégwlit *aspectus*, Mt. Kmbl. Lind. 28, 3. Mǽgwlit (mégwlitt, Rush) onsióne his *species vultus ejus*, Lk. Skt. Lind. 9, 29. Tó mǽgwlite andgytes *ad formam sensus*, Bd. 5, 24; S. 647, 34. Ðæt ðú meahte mínum weorþan mǽgwlite gelíc, Exon. 28 b; Th. 87, 30; Cri. 1433. Gedyde ic ðæt ðú onsýn hæfdest, mǽgwlite mé gelícne, 28 a; Th. 84, 35; Cri. 1384: Andr. Kmbl. 1711; An. 858. Ne mégulit (mégwlit, Rush.) his geségon *neque speciem ejus vidistis*, Jn. Skt. Lind. 5, 37. Mégwlite, Rtl. 2, 7. Mégewlit Godes *majestatem Dei*, 1, 19. Mon ne mǽge ða lástas on óðerne mǽgwlite oncyrran; ah hié á beóþ on ðære ilcan onsýne *the footsteps cannot be changed into another form; but they always appear the same*, Blickl. Homl. 127, 19. Ǽlc hafaþ mǽgwlite metodes and engla, Cd. 75; Th. 92, 17; Gen. 1530. Monge mǽgwlitas *many species*, Exon. 43 a; Th. 146, 7; Gú. 706: Bt. Met. Fox 31, 9; Met. 31, 5. Woroldgife monige on misenlícum mǽgwlitan *dona in diversis speciebus perplura*, Bd. 1, 32; S. 498, 21.

mǽgwlitian *to form, shape:*—Oferhiuad ł [ofer] mégwlitgad *transfiguratus*, Mt. Kmbl. Lind. 17, 2.

mǽgwlit-líce; *adv. Figuratively:*—Mégwlitlíce *figuraliter*, Mk. Skt. p. 4, 10.

mæhe (*for* mæhte?) *dicione*, Wrt. Voc. ii. 27, 75.

mæht, mæhtig. v. meaht, meahtig.

mǽl, mál, mél, es; *n. m.* (?) I. *a measure:*—Dó wínes þrié mél on *pour three measures of wine on*, L. M. 1, 45; Lchdm. ii. 110, 26. v. cucler-mǽl, dæg-mǽl, fot-mǽl, mǽl-tange; *and cf. Icel.* mál *a measure: Dan.* maal. II. *a mark, sign, cross, crucifix:*—Hér óþiéwde reád Cristes mǽl on hefenum *in this year a red cross appeared in the sky*, Chr. 773; Erl. 52, 23. Mid ðám wæs sum mycel gylden Cristes mǽl *in quibus crucem magnam auream*, Bd. 2, 20; S. 522, 9. Hé ðæt Cristes mǽl hræde weorce geworhte . . and ðæt Cristes mǽl genam and on ðone seáþ sette, 3, 2; S. 524, 16–18. Bǽron Cristes róde tácen sylfrene Cristes mǽl *crucem pro vexillo ferentes argenteam*, 1, 25; S. 487, 3. Ǽnne sylfrene mǽle on V. pundon *a silver crucifix of five pounds*, Chart. Th. 558, 33. Ðon on ealdan Cristes mǽle; of ðam Cristes mǽle, Cod. Dip. Kmbl. vi. 66, 34. Ealle hit writen mid Cristes mǽl *all signed it with a cross*, Chr. 963; Erl. 123, 25. v. fýr-mǽl, ge-mǽl, grǽg-mǽl: *O. Sax.* hobid-mǽl *head on a coin* and cf. *Icel.* mál *applied to the inlaid ornamenting of weapons: and English* hring-, wunden-mǽl. *The word is also used for the sword itself* brogden mǽl, Beo. Th. 3236; B. 1616: 3338; B. 1667: Elen. Kmbl. 1574; El. 759. v. mál-sweord. III. *fixed, suitable, appointed time, season, occasion:*—Mǽl is mé tó féran *it is time for me to go*, Beo. Th. 637; 316. Ðá wæs sǽl and mǽl ðæt tó healle gang Healfdenes sunu, 2021; B. 1008. Ðá ðæs mǽles wæs mearc agongen *then was the appointed time past*, Cd. 83; Th. 103, 16; Gen. 1719: 224; Th. 296, 12; Sat. 501. Ic ðæt mǽl geman ðonne wé gehéton ússum hláforde *I remember the time when we promised our lord*, Beo. Th. 5259; B. 2633. Ǽlce mǽle *on each occasion*, Exon. 119 a; Th. 457, 30; Hy. 4, 92. Se geweald hafaþ sǽla and mǽla *he hath power over times and seasons*, Beo. Th. 3226; 1611. Efne swylce mǽla swylce . . . *just at such times as . . .*, 2502; B. 1249. Mǽla gehwylce *on every occasion*, 4121; B. 2057: Ps. Th. 118, 62. Ðú him mete sylest mǽla gehwylce and ðæs tídlíce tíd gemearcast *tu das escam illis in tempore opportuno*, 144, 16: 21. Ðæt ǽr feala mǽla behýded wæs *which long before was hidden*, Elen. Kmbl. 1971; El. 987. Ǽrran mǽlum *on former occasions*, Beo. Th. 1819; B. 907: 4466; B. 2237: 6062; B. 3035. IV. *the time for eating, a meal:*—Ðás hálgan lenctenlíce tíde gehealdan mid clǽnum fæstene ǽlce dæge tó ánes mǽles (*having only one meal a-day*, cf. *Icel.* fasta einmælt), Wulfst. 285, 2. Hé gereordade æt ánum mǽle fíf þúsend manna *he fed at one* (*meal*) *time five thousand men*, 293, 27. Yfel biþ ðæt man rihtfæstentíde ǽr mǽle ete, L. C. S. 47; Th. i. 402, 24: Homl. Th. ii. 590, 25. Gífernys biþ ðæt se man ǽr tíman hine gereordige oððe æt his mǽle tó micel þicge *it is greediness when a man eats before the time or takes too much at his meal*, 218, 30. Ne fæsþ se nó Gode ac him selfum se ðe ðæt nyle þearfum sellan ðæt hé ðonne on mǽle lǽfþ ac wile hit healdan eft tó óðrum mǽle *non Deo, sed sibi quisque jejunat, si ea quæ ventri ad tempus subtrahit, non egenis tribuit sed . . custodit*, Past. 43, 8; Swt. 317, 4. Múþa gehwylc mete þearf mǽl sceolon tídum gongan *every mouth needs meat; meals must there be at times*, Exon. 91 a; Th. 341, 13; Gn. Ex. 125. [Laym. Orm. mæl: *O. E. Homl. A. R.* mel: *Chauc.* mel, meel *a meal: Prompt. Parv.* meel *pastus: Goth.* mél *a time: Icel.* mál *time, meal-time, season: O. H. Ger.* mál *time, occasion: M. H. Ger.* mál: *Ger.* ein-mal, etc.: *M. H. Ger.* mál *time for eating, meal: Ger.* mahl.] v. -mǽlum.

mǽl, e; *f. A speech, talk, conversation:*—Gemuna ða mǽla ðe wé oft æt meodo sprǽcon *think of the talks that we oft had at table*, Byrht. Th. 137, 66; By. 212. [*Icel.* mál; *n. speech, colloquy, talk.*] v. mǽlan.

mǽl, es; *n. A cause, suit, action* (?):—Ðú symle furðor feohtan sóhtest mǽl ofer mearce *thou didst ever press on to fight, didst pursue thy cause* (i. e. *carry on war*) *over the border*, Wald. 1, 33; Vald. 1, 19. Cf. *Icel.* mál *a suit, cause;* sækja mál *to prosecute* (as a law term). Stephens takes *mǽl* here = *mark, goal:* Rieger (quoted by Grein) takes it = *gemót, concio*, so figuratively battle. v. mál.

mǽlan; *p.* de *To speak:*—Se stán mǽlde for mannum *the stone spake before men*, Andr. Kmbl. 1533; An. 768. Wícinga ár wordum mǽlde, Byrht. Th. 132, 35; By. 26: 133, 1; By. 43: 137, 63; By. 210. Hyre se feónd oncwæþ, wordum mǽlde, Exon. 70 b; Th. 263, 18; Jul. 351. Be eów Essaias for weorodum wordum mǽlde, Elen. Kmbl. 702; El. 351. Him ðá tó wuldorgást wordum mǽlde, Cd. 141; Th. 176, 16; Gen. 2913. Him Andreas wið, wine þearfende, wordum mǽlde, Andr. Kmbl. 600; An. 300. Him ðá tógénes ða gleáwestan wordum mǽldon, Elen. Kmbl. 1072; El. 537. Hwæt mé God on mínum módsefan mǽlan wille *quid loquatur in me dominus*, Ps. Th. 84, 7. [*Orm.* mælenn: *Havel.* mele: *Icel.* mæla *to speak.*] v. ge-, on-mǽlan.

mǽlan *to mark.* [*Goth.* méljan *to write: O. Sax.* málon *to mark* (of a wound made by a sword): *O. H. Ger.* mālōn, mālēn *pingere: Ger.* malen *to paint.*] v. hring-, scīr-mǣled; mǣl II.

mǣlan *to spot, blemish.* v. ge-mǣlan, māl, un-mǣle.

mǣl-cearu, e; *f. Care* or *trouble belonging to a particular time:*—Swā ða mǣlceare maga Healfdenes singala seáþ *so did Healfdene's son ever brood over the trouble of that time,* Beo. Th. 380; B. 189.

mǣl-dæg, es; *m. A day, season, an appointed time:*—Hē ðæs mǣldæges self ne wēnde ðæt him Sarra bringan meahte on woruld sunu *he himself never hoped for the day when Sarah could bring him a son into the world,* Cd. 107; Th. 141, 4; Gen. 2339. Hē moncynnes mǣste hæfde on ðǣm mǣldagum mægen and strengo, 79; Th. 98, 18; Gen. 1632.

mǣl-dropa, an; *m. Phlegm:*—Mǣldropa *flegma.* i. *saliva,* Wrt. Voc. ii. 149, 39.

mǣl-dropiende *phlegmatic;* flegmaticus, Ælfc. Gl. 77; Som. 72, 13; Wrt. 45, 47.

Mældūn Maldon *in Essex,* Chr. 913; Erl. 102, 5: 920; Erl. 104, 32: 993; Erl. 132, 5.

mǣle *spotted.* v. un-mǣle.

mǣl-gesceaft, e; *f. That which happens at its appointed time in accordance with the decrees of fate:*—Ic bād mǣlgesceafta *I waited for that which in due time fate would assign me,* Beo. Th. 5467; B. 2737.

mǣl-mete, es; *m. Food to eat:*—Ne biþ ðec mǣlmete nymþe mōres græs *no food shall there be for thee but the grass of the moor,* Cd. 203; Th. 252, 7; Dan. 575. [*Grein, quoting Dietrich, would read* mǣl mēte (=*obvius*), v. Hpt. Zeitsch. x. 358.]

mǣl-sceafa, an; *m. A canker:*—Mǣlscæafa *eruca,* Ælfc. Gl. 23; Som. 60, 3; Wrt. 24, 7. Mǣlsceafa *caniglata,* Wrt. Voc. ii. 128, 19. Mǣlsceafa *eruca,* Wrt. Voc. 78, 66; Zup. 310, 5. In the last reference one MS. (v. Wrt. Voc. 91, 23) has *mæslesceafe;* in Wrt. Voc. 161, 23 *maseles* translates *rugeroles* (see also Skeat's Dict. s.v. *measles*), so *mǣl,* in this word, would mean a *spot.*

mǣl-tange, an; *f.* -tang, es; *m.* (?) *A pair of compasses:*—Mǣltange *circinum,* Ælfc. Gl. 49; Som. 65, 70; Wrt. Voc. 34, 5: 62; Som. 68, 78; Wrt. Voc. 39, 61. Mǣltanges prica *centrum,* 39, 62.

-mǣlum *-meal* (in piece-*meal*). v. æcer-, bit-, dǣl-, drop-, flocc-, folc-, fōt-, heáp-, hīd-, lim-, nam-, sceáf-, stæp-, stund-, stycce-, þrag-, þreát-, þūsend-, worn (wearn)-, wræd-mǣlum.

mǣnan; *p.* de *To mean.* I. of persons (*a*) *to intend to convey a certain sense:*—Gif hē of wege ǣnigne gebrohte .. ðæt is ðæt ic mǣne gif hē ǣnigne man on synne bespeóne *if he have brought any man out of the way . . ., what I mean, is, if he have lured any man to sin,* L. Pen. 16; Th. ii. 284, 12. Hwet mǣnde Crist ðā cwæþ: 'Ða unrihtwīsan faraþ on ēce wītu,' Shrn. 197, 18. God ðā geopenude Abrahame hwæt hē mid ðære sprǣce mǣnde, Gen. 18, 20. (*b*) *to intend to indicate a certain person* or *thing without direct statement:*—Cweþan swā hē tō ānum sprece and hwæðre ealle mǣneþ *to say, as if he speaks to one and yet means all,* Exon. 28 a; Th. 84, 24; Cri. 1378. Hē gecȳðde ðæt hē ne mǣnde (*indicaret*) ðis andwearde līf, Past. 50, 2; Swt. 389, 22. Hwylc beren mǣnde hē ðonne elles būton heofona rīce, Blickl. Homl. 39, 27. Crist mǣnde ðone ēcan deáþ . . . ða Iudēiscan mǣndon ðisne andweardan deáþ, Homl. Th. ii. 232, 20. Ne mǣnde ūre Drihten mid ðisum wordum ða treówa ðe on appeltūne wexaþ, 406, 9. (*c*) *to mean, purpose, have as an object to which the mind is directed, intend:*—Gif hē ðara nān ne dēþ ðonne nāt hē hwæt hē mēnþ (Cott. MS. mænþ) *if he does none of these, then he does not know what he means,* Bt. 38, 2; Fox 198, 28. Ðā ongon hē sprecan swīðe feorran ymbūtan swilce hē nā ða sprǣce ne mǣnde, 39, 5; Fox 218, 12. Hwæt ðū ðonne mǣne mid ðære gītsunge ðæs feós *what do you mean by the greed of money?* 32, 1; Fox 114, 7. II. (of things) *to signify, have a certain signification* or *purpose:*—Saga hwæt ic mǣne, Salm. Kmbl. 472; Sal. 236: Exon. 124 b; Th. 479, 18; Rä. 62, 9. Oft gehwā gesihþ fægre stafas and nāt hwæt hī mǣnaþ, Homl. Th. i. 186, 3. Hwæt mǣnde ðæt syxtig wera strongera? Blickl. Homl. 11, 22: Homl. Th. ii. 234, 31. Faraþ and leorniaþ hwæt ðæt mǣne: 'Ic wylle mildheortnysse, and nā offrunge,' 470, 18. Geleornian hwæt fulluht mǣne, Wulfst. 123, 4. Understandan hwæt ða twā word mǣnan, *abrenuntio* and *credo,* 38, 8. [*O. Sax.* mēnian: *O. Frs.* mēna: *O. H. Ger.* meinian: *Ger.* meinen.] v. ge-mǣnan.

mǣnan; *p.* de *To tell of, relate, declare:*—Ne wyrneþ word lofes, wīsan mǣneþ mīne for mengo (cf. *O. Sax.* thū fora thesaro thiod telis, mahtig mēnis), Exon. 105 b; Th. 401, 14; Rä. 21, 11. Hæleþ hȳ hospe mǣnaþ *men speak of her contemptuously,* 90 a; Th. 337, 17; Gn. Ex. 66. Secgas nemnaþ, mǣnaþ mid mūþe meodugāles gedrinc, 88 a; Th. 330, 26; Vy. 57. Ðȳ læs ðæt weras gieddum mǣndan be mē lifgendum *lest men should tell of it in songs during my lifetime,* 50 b; Th. 176, 9; Gū. 1206. Ic mæg singan and secgan, spell mǣnan, hū mē cynegōde cystum dohten, 85 b; Th. 321, 32; Wīd. 55: Beo. Th. 2139; B. 1067. Ðǣr wæs Beówulfes mǣrþo mǣned *there was told Beowulf's greatness,* 1718; B. 857. [*O. Sax.* mēnian, gi-mēnian *to make known: O. H. Ger.* meinian *dicere:* ga-meinian *dicere, dicare,* Grff. ii. 785, 788.]

mǣnan; *p.* de *To lament, mourn, complain.* I. *intrans.:*—Ðū simle mid wōpe and mid unrōtnesse mǣnst gif ðē ǣnies willan wana biþ (*tu*) *qui abesse aliquid tuae beatitudini tam luctuosus atque anxius conqueraris,* Bt. 11, 1; Fox 30, 22. Ðā hē gehiérde ðæt ðæt folc mǣnde tō him Arone ymb hiera earfeðo *Moyses cum contra se et Aaron conqueri populum cognovisset,* Past. 28, 6; Swt. 201, 4. Eallē wordum mǣndon, Cd. 222: Th. 288, 24; Sat. 386. II. *followed by a clause:*—Ða welan ðe dū mǣndest ðæt ðū forlure *the wealth which you complain of having lost,* Bt. 7, 3; Fox 20, 18. Bonan mǣndon ðæt hȳ monnes bearn oferþunge, Exon. 38 b; Th. 128, 8; Gū. 401. III. *with acc.:*—Hū Boetius his earfoðu tō Gode mǣnde, Bt. tit. cap. 4. His tungan hē mǣnde swīðost *he complained most of his tongue,* Homl. Th. i. 330, 31. Basilius mēnde ðæt unriht, Homl. Skt. 3, 322. Hē misbeád his munecan and ða munecas hit mǣndon lufelīce, Chr. 1083; Erl. 217, 4. Hī mǣndon mondryhtnes cwealm *they mourned their lord's death,* Beo. Th. 6289; B. 3149. Ic wundrige hwæt ðē seó oððe hwæt ðū mǣne *admiror cur aegrotes,* Bt. 5, 3; Fox 12, 11. Hū miht ðū mǣnan ðæt wyrse nū ðū ðæt leófre hæfst gehealden *poterisne, meliora quæque retinens, de infortunio jure caussari?* 10; Fox 28, 10. Cyning mǣnan *to mourn their king,* Beo. Th. 6324; B. 3172. Ic gehēre gnorniende cynn grundas mǣnan (*the devils in hell*), Cd. 216; Th. 273, 10; Sat. 134. Ðæt ic sceal teárum mǣnan *that I must mourn with tears,* Exon. 76 a; Th. 285, 10; Jul. 712. v. bemǣnan.

mǣne; *adj.* I. *mean, wicked, false, evil:*—Synna lustas mǣne mōdlufan *the pleasures of sin, vicious love,* Exon. 71 a; Th. 364, 26; Jul. 370. Hygeleáse mǣne *mad and false* (*the rebel angels*), Cd. 4; Th. 4, 11; Gen. 52. Þurh mǣnra hand searonettum beseted, Andr. Kmbl. 1882; An. 943. II. the word however occurs most often in reference to oaths:—Se ðe his þances mǣnne āþ swerige and hē wite ðæt hē mǣne biþ æfter ðam *qui sua sponte perjuraverit et postea scit quod perjurus est,* L. Ecg. C. 34; Th. ii. 158, 20, 14, 16. Gif hwā swereþ and se āþ beó mǣne . . se ðe mǣne āþas begā *si quis juraverit et perjurium sit . . . Qui perjuria commiserit,* L. Ecg. P. iv. 68; Th. ii. 228, 7–9: L. Edg. C. 8; Th. ii. 262, 31. Gif mæssepreóst stande on leásre gewitnesse oððe on mǣnan āþe *if a masspriest be concerned in false witness or perjury,* L. Eth. ix. 27; Th. i. 346, 9: L. C. E. 5; Th. i. 362, 30. Se ðe mānāþ (*other MS.* mǣnne āþ) swerige, L. Ath. i. 25; Th. i. 212, 18. Be mǣnan āþe. Gif hwā mǣne āþ swerige, L. C. S. 36; Th. i. 398, 3–4. Gebēte ðone mǣnan āþ, L. In 35; Th. i. 124, 13. Swerian mǣnne āþ þurh swā miclan mægenþrymme, Wulfst. 214, 15. Eall yfel forlǣtan ge on manslihte ge on mǣnum āþum, 228, 21. v. un-mǣne; mān.

mǣne; *adj. Common:*—Mǣna lǣse *common pasturage,* Cod. Dip. Kmbl. iv. 284, 8. v. ge-mǣne.

mængan, Mæn-īg, mænig, mænigeo, mænnisc. v. mengan, mon-īg, manig, menigu, mennisc.

maenoe. v. mene.

mǣnsumian; *p.* ode. I. *to have the companionship of a person, to marry:*—Ne hiá mǣnsumiaþ (mǣnsumigaþ, Rush.) ne hiá biþon gemǣnsumad (*i.* ne ceorl hæfis wīfes gemāna ne wīf hæfis ceorles) *neque nubent neque nubentur,* Mk. Skt. Lind. 12, 25. II. *to share with another, to communicate:*—Mēnsumede *participavit, communicavit,* Hpt. Gl. 467, 2.

mǣnsumung, e; *f.* I. *communion, admission to fellowship with others* (opp. of excommunication):—Benedictus cwæþ ðæt hī unāmānsumode wǣron . . . Hī underfēngon ða hālgan mǣnsumunge æt Gode þurh his þeówan Benedicte, Homl. Th. ii. 174, 31. II. *participation:*—Hē ūs forgeáfe dǣl on his rīce, and mǣnsumunge on his godcundnysse, i. 140, 11.

mæntel. v. mentel.

mær. v. wudu-mær.

mæra, mera, an; *m. An incubus:*—Mera ł satyrus *incuba,* Ep. Gl. 12 f, 14. v. mære.

mǣr-āc, e; *f. An oak which serves as part of a boundary* (?):—Of ðære āc in ða mǣrāc, Cod. Dip. Kmbl. iii. 379, 31. v. mǣr-brōc, mearc-bēce.

mǣran, māran; *p.* de *To make known, celebrate, declare, proclaim:*—Mīn mūþ sægeþ ðīne mægenspēde and ðīn sōþfæst weorc mǣreþ *os meum pronuntiabit justitiam tuam,* Ps. Th. 70, 14. Songe lofiaþ mǣraþ mōdigne meaglum reordum *they praise with song and with powerful voices celebrate the noble bird,* Exon. 60 b; Th. 221, 21; Ph. 338. For cyning mǣraþ leófne leódfruman *they proclaim the loved chief as king,* Th. 222, 6; Ph. 344. Swylce mīn tunge tīdum mǣrde ðīn sōþfæst weorc *sed et lingua mea tota die meditabitur justitiam tuam,* Ps. Th. 70, 22. Ðæt hī heora bearnum budun and sægdun and cinn ōðrum cȳðden and mǣrden *ut notam faceret eam filiis suis; ut cognoscat generatio altera,* 77, 7. Gē scyldigra synne secgaþ, sōþfæstra nō mōd and monþeáw mǣran willaþ, Exon. 40 a; Th. 132, 26; Gū. 478. Hit nǣnig mon ūt cȳðan ne mōste, ðȳ læs ða elreordigan kyningas on ðæt fǣgon, ðæt ic swā lytle hwīle lifgean mōste. Ne hit ǣnig mon ðære ferde ðon mā ūt māran mōste, ðȳ læs hié for ðon ormōde wǣron, Nar. 32, 22. [*Goth.* mērjan *to proclaim, announce: O. Sax.* mārian; *Icel.* mæra *to praise: O. H. Ger.* mārian *diffamare, declarare, clarificare, praedicare.*] v. ge-mǣran.

mǣr-apeldre, an; *f. An apple-tree which serves as a boundary:*—Hit cymeþ tō mǣrapeldran, Cod. Dip. Kmbl. iii. 390, 5.

mǣr-brōc, es; *m. A brook which forms a boundary*, cf. mearc-brōc:—Tō mǣrbrōce; of mǣrbrōce, Cod. Dip. Kmbl. iii. 79, 5: 438, 27: v. 284, 29 (*where* mēr-brōc *is the same as* merc-brōc *of* l. 13). v. mere *and* mǣre *a boundary.*

mærc. v. mearc, mearh.

mǣr-dīc, e; *f. A boundary dike*:—On ða mǣrdīc, Cod. Dip. Kmbl. iii. 378, 24. On ða ealdan mǣrdīc, 449, 10.

mære *a mere.* v. mere.

mære, mare, mere, an; *f. A night-mare, a monster oppressing men during sleep* (cf. passage quoted in Cl. and Vig. under *mara*: 'En er hann hafði lītt sofnat, kallaði hann ok sagði at mara trað hann. Menn hans fōru til, ok vildu hjálpa honum; en er þeir tōku uppi til höfuðsins, þā trað hōn fōtleggina swā at nær brotnuðu. Þā tōku þeir til fōtanna, þā kafði hōn höfuðit, svā at þar dō hann'):—Mære *faecce*, Wrt. Voc. ii. 108, 44: *incuba*, 111, 46. Mere *fecce*, 35, 26. Gif mon mare rīde, L. M. 1, 64; Lchdm. ii. 140, 9. Hī beóþ gōde wið nihtgengan and maran, 3, 1; Lchdm. ii. 306, 12. [*Prompt. Parv.* mare or nyȝhte mare *epialtes*; mare or wyche *magus, maga, sagana*, and see note, p. 326: *Icel.* mara: *M.H.Ger.* mare: *Ger.* mahr: cf. *French* cauchemar.] v. mær, mæra.

mǣre, es; *n. A boundary, limit, confine, border*:—Ondlong ðæs mǣres (meres?) heges, Cod. Dip. Kmbl. iii. 32, 30: ii. 250, 7 (?). In mǣre Judēana *in fines Judæa*, Mt. Kmbl. Rush. 19, 1. In mǣrum *in villas*, Mk. Skt. Lind. 6, 56. In mǣrum (mǣro, Rush.) *in vicos*, Lk. Skt. Lind. 14, 21. [Cf. *Icel.* mærr *a border-land.*] v. ge-mǣre; mǣr-āc, -apeldre, -brōc, -dīc, -heg, -stān, -þorn, -weg.

mǣre; *adj. Great, excellent, distinguished, illustrious, sublime, splendid, celebrated, famous, widely known* (of persons or things):—Mǣre *clarus, insignis, nobilis, perspicuus*, Wrt. Voc. ii. 131, 66: *inclytus*, 46, 10, 11. Mēre weard *percrebuit*, Ep. Gl. 18 b, 10. Mǣre *celeber*, Ælfc. Gr. 9, 18; Zup. 44, 10. Mǣrne *celebre*, Hpt. Gl. 525, 45. Beorht ł mǣre *præclara, splendida*, 436, 43. Mǣr[re] *illustrius*, 460, 25. I. (*of persons and* (a) *in a good sense*):—Dryhten ys mǣre God and mihtig *Dominus est deus magnus et potens*, Deut. 10, 17. Ðū eart mǣre God, and Jacobes God se mǣra, Ps. Th. 83, 8: 103, 23. God mǣre (*excelsus*) ālȳsend heora is, Ps. Spl. 77, 39. Freá ælmihtig, mǣre þeóden, Cd. 40; Th. 52, 34; Gen. 853. Se mǣra Fæder (*God*), L. Ælfc. C. 3; Th. ii. 344, 4. Hē byþ mǣre beforan Drihtne *erit magnus coram domino*, Lk. Skt. 1, 15: 32. Ðeáh hē on ðam lande seó mǣre ðonne biþ hē on ōðrum unmǣre *though he be famous in one country, he is not in another*, Bt. 30, 1; Fox 108, 15. Wæs hē (*St. Martin*) swīðe mǣre geond middangeard, Blickl. Homl. 221, 1. Mǣru cwēn *the illustrious queen* (*Wealhtheow*), Beo. Th. 4037; B. 2016. Sunu se ðe biþ gōde mǣre *a son* (*Isaac*) *who shall be great in goodness*, Cd. 100; Th. 132, 24; Gen. 2198: Beo. Th. 3909; B. 1952. Mihtum mǣre *great in power*, Elen. Kmbl. 679; El. 340. Marian mǣrre meówlan *of Mary, maiden illustrious*, Exon. 14 a; Th. 28, 13; Cri. 446. Smeágende cwidas and dǣda ðara mǣrena (*illustrium*) wera ūre þeóde, Bd. pref.; S. 471, 13. Ðes ys mǣrra (*major*) ðonne ðæt templ, Mt. Kmbl. 12, 6. Nis betwux wīfa bearnum nān mǣrra wītega ðonne Johannes, Lk. Skt. 7, 28. Nān man ne biþ for ōðres gōde nō ðȳ mǣrra ne nō ðȳ geheredra *splendidum te aliena claritudo non efficit*, Bt. 30, 1; Fox 108, 27. David wæs hearpera mǣrost, Ps. C. 50; Ps. Grn. ii. 276, 4. Ðās mānfullan men wǣron getealde for ða mǣrostan godas, Wulfst. 106, 17. (*b*) in a bad sense, *notorious, distinguished by evil deeds*; insignis:—Hæfdum ǣnne gebundenne mǣrne (mērne, Lind.) monn se wæs hāten Barrabas (cf. *O. Sax.* māri meginthiof) *habebat vinctum insignem qui dicebatur Barabbas*, Mt. Kmbl. Rush. 27, 16. Grendel, mǣre mearcstapa, Beo. Th. 206; B. 103: 1528; B. 762 (?). II. (*of things*):—Sum deófolgild ðe mid ðǣm hǣðenum mannum swīðe weorþ and mǣre wæs *a certain idol that was held in high honour and esteem among the heathens*, Blickl. Homl. 221, 7. Swīðe mǣre burh se is hāten Sepontus *a very famous town which is called Sepontus*, 197, 20. On ðam mǣran (*inlustri*) tūne, se is nemned æt Walle, Bd. 3, 21; S. 551, 11: Cd. 205; Th. 254, 10; Dan. 609. Tō ðære mǣran byrig (*the heavenly Jerusalem*), 227; Th. 304, 4; Sat. 624. Tempel heáhst and hāligost, hæleþum gefrǣgost, mǣst and mǣrost (*Solomon's temple*), 162; Th. 202, 28; Exod. 395. Ðæt wæs ðæt mǣreste hūs ðe on eorþan geworht wurde *that* (*the temple*) *was the most splendid house that was built in the world*, Wulfst. 278, 1. Mǣre wurdon his wundra geweorc wīde and sīde *far and wide spread the fame of the wonders he wrought*, Exon. 45 b; Th. 155, 1; Gū. 853. Eall ðeós mǣre gesceaft *the universe*, Rood Kmbl. 24; Kr. 12. Mǣre wundur *mirabilia*, Ps. Th. 106, 30: 110, 3. Sunne mǣre tungol *the sun, resplendent star*, Chr. 937; Erl. 112, 14; Æðelst. 14. Mǣrost tungla, Exon. 57 b; Th. 205, 28; Ph. 119. In dege mērum *in die insigni*, Ps. Surt. 80, 4. Ðone mǣron symbeldæg Drihtnes upstige, Blickl. Homl. 131, 10: Cd. 8; Th. 10, 11; Gen. 155. Seó mǣre tiid (*Easter*), Menol. Fox 114; Men. 57. Se mǣra dæg *the great and terrible day of the Lord*, Exon. 23 b; Th. 65, 16; Cri. 1055. Ðæt is mǣre spell *no common tale is that*, Cd. 119; Th. 155, 2; Gen. 2566: Elen. Kmbl. 1936; El. 970. Æfter ðisse dǣde his noma wæs weorþ and mǣre geworden *after this deed his name became honoured and famous*, Blickl. Homl. 219, 4: Exon. 107 a; Th. 409, 11; Rä. 27, 27. Is wuldur ðīn wīde and sīde ofer ðās eorþan ealle mǣre *in omnem terram gloria tua*, Ps. Th. 56, 6. Se mǣresta hlīsa *fama celeberrima*, Bd. 3, 13; S. 538, 37. Ðæt is mǣro wyrd *that is a tremendous event* (*the deluge*), Cd. 69; Th. 84, 18; Gen. 1399. Ðīn mægen is swā mǣre, swā ðæt ǣnig ne wāt eorþbūende ða deópnesse Drihtnes mihta, Hy. 3, 31; Hy. Grn. ii. 282, 31. (*In a bad sense*) Caudenes Furcules seó stōw gewearþ swīðe mǣre for Rōmāna bismere *Caudinas furculas satis celebres et famosas Romanorum fecit infamia*, Ors. 3, 8; Swt. 120, 21. [Cf. *Goth.* waila-mērs *of good report*; wailamēreins *good report*: *O. Sax.* māri: *Icel.* mærr: *O. H. Ger.* māri *memorabilis, famosus, illustris, insignis, clarus.*] v. efen-, folc-, fore-, forþ-, freá-, frǣ-, heaðo-, un-, wīd-mǣre.

mǣre *pure, in the phrase* mǣre peningas = *Lat. meri denarii* i.e. coins made of pure silver, v. Ducange s.v. *merus*, quoted by Schmid. The passage in which the word is found occurs in L. Alf. pol. 3; Th. i. 62, 10:—Mid V. pundum mǣrra pæninga. With this may be compared the following passage:—For his līcweorðan feó, ðæt is ii pund mērehwītes seolfres, Cod. Dip. Kmbl. iii. 255, 12.

mǣrels, mārels, es; *m. and* **mǣrels-rāp**, es; *m. A rope for mooring a ship*; pronesium [v. Ducange: '*pronexium* funis quo navis religatur ad palum']:—Mǣrelsrāp *pronesium*, Ælfc. Gl. 105; Som. 78, 21; Wrt. Voc. 57, 3. Mārels *prosnesium*, 63, 62. [Both words occur in lists giving the names of ships, and their various parts. Cf. *Du.* marlijn, *also* marl-reep = mar-reep *a marline, a small cord used for binding large ropes, to protect them*: *O. Du.* maren *to tie knots*, which occurs in English in the phrase to *moor* a ship. *Also* cf. marlyñ *illaqueo*, marlyd *illaqueatus*, Prompt. Parv. 327, and note.] v. scip-mǣrels.

mǣre-torht. v. mere-torht.

mærh. v. mearh.

mǣr-heg, es; *m. A boundary* (?) *hedge*:—Ondlong ðære burnan ōþ hit cymeþ tō ðæm mǣrhege; ondlong ðæs mǣres heges ðæt hit cymeþ up on ða dūne, Cod. Dip. Kmbl. iii. 32, 29. Cf. gemǣr-haga.

mǣr-hlīsa, an; *m. Great fame, celebrity*:—Mid mǣrhlīsan *cœlebri*, Wrt. Voc. ii. 23, 74.

mǣrian; *p.* ode *To become great, be distinguished*:—Swā mǣregend[iend]um cȳðere *tanto prestanti martiri*, Hymn. Surt. 46, 3.

mæring *a plant name*:—Hwīt mæringc (Cockayne suggests *sweet basil*), Lchdm. iii. 2, 21.

mǣr-līc; *adj. Great, magnificent, glorious, splendid, illustrious* (of persons or things):—Mǣrlīce *magnificas*, Gl. Wülck. 254, 11. I. (*of persons*):—Mǣrlīc (*God*) on hālignysse *magnificus in sanctitate*, Cant. Moys. 11. Ðæt wæter feóll ofer Pharaones mǣrlīcum riddum *the water fell upon Pharaoh's splendid knights*, Ælfc. T. Grn. 5, 31. II. (*of things*):—Mȳrlīc cynehelm *corona inclita*, Kent. Gl. 67. Gabrihel bodade Zacharian his mǣrlīcan drohtnunge *Gabriel announced to Zacharias his* (*John's*) *glorious life*, Homl. Th. i. 352, 26. Ðā hæfde ðæt cild swīðe mǣrlīce stemne *the boy had a magnificent voice*, Wulfst. 152, 11. Hwæðer mā mǣrlecra dǣda gefremed hæfde ðe Philipus ðe Alexander *which had performed more splendid deeds, Philip or Alexander*, Ors. 3, 9; Swt. 130, 27. Hwæðer ðē ðonne þynce unweorþ and unmǣrlīc seó gegaderung ðara þreóra þinga . . oððe hwæðer hit ðē þince eallra þinga weorþlīcost and mǣrlīcost *obscurumne hoc, atque ignobile censes esse, an omni celebritate clarissimum?* Bt. 33, 1; Fox 120, 31. [*O. Sax.* mār-līk: *O. H. Ger.* māri-līh.] v. fore-, un-mǣrlīc.

mǣrlīce; *adv. Magnificently, excellently, nobly, splendidly, with distinction*:—Mǣrlīce *insigniter*, Wrt. Voc. ii. 85, 81: Hpt. Gl. 512, 47. Ðam sȳ mǣrlīce mægen and wurðment būtan ænde *cui sit magnifice virtus et honor sine fine*, Hymn. Surt. 47, 32: Hy. 7, 19; Hy. Grn. ii. 287, 19. Hē mǣrlīce weorhte *magnifice fecit* (he hath done excellent things, A. V.), Cant. Es. 5. Sum welig man . . dæghwamlīce mǣrlīce (*splendide*) leofode, Homl. Th. i. 328, 13. Joseph leofode on ðam lande (*Egypt*) mǣrlīce, Ælfc. T. Grn. 5, 8. Hwæt is ðes mihtiga ðe ðus mǣrlīce fēreþ (*Christ entering Jerusalem*), Blickl. Homl. 71, 14. Mǣrlīce ðæt līc behwurfon mid miclum wōpe *celebrantes exequias planctu magno*, Gen. 50, 10. Healdaþ ðisne dæg on eówerum gemynde and freólsiaþ hine mǣrlīce, Homl. Th. ii. 264, 15. Swā hē ūs mǣrlīcor gifeþ swā wē him mǣrlīcor þancian scylon *the more excellent his gifts are, the more excellent ought our thanks to be*, Wulfst. 261, 20. [*O. Sax.* mār-līko.]

mǣr-ness, e; *f. Greatness, distinction, celebrity*:—Mycelnesse ł mǣrnesse *magnitudinis*, Ps. Lamb. 144, 3. Mǣrnesse *insignia*, Wrt. Voc. ii. 45, 12. Mǣrnessa *preconia*, 66, 39. v. fore-mǣrness.

mǣr-pytt, es; *m. A pit that forms part of a boundary* (?):—On ðone mǣrpyt; of ðam pytte, Cod. Dip. Kmbl. iii. 439, 1. Eást tō mǣrpytte, ii. 250, 5.

mǣrsere, es; *m. One who proclaims* or *makes widely known, a herald*:—Mērseris *preconis*, Rtl. 56, 35.

mǣrsian; *p.* ode. I. *to make great, extend*:—Hig tōbrǣdaþ hyra heálsbǣc and mǣrsiaþ heora reáfa fnadu *dilatant philacteria sua, et magnificant fimbrias*, Mt. Kmbl. 23, 5. II. *to make known, spread the knowledge of anything, declare, proclaim, announce, celebrate*:—Ic mǣrsige *insignio*, Ælfc. Gr. 30; Som. 34, 60. Mǣrsaþ tunge mîn spǽce ðîne *pronuntiabit lingua mea eloquium tuum*, Ps. Lamb. 118, 122. Wē mērsiaþ *prædicamus*, Rtl. 71, 25: 6, 11. Ðîne mægenstrengþu mǽrsien wîde *magnitudinem tuam narrabunt*, Ps. Th. 144, 6. Ðǽr gǽsta gedryht Hǽlend hergaþ, and heofoncyninges meahte mǽrsiaþ, singaþ Metude lof, Exon. 64 b; Th. 239, 6; Ph. 617. Sceal manna gehwylc weorc Godes wîde mǽrsian (*annuntiaverunt*), Ps. Th. 63, 8. Wuldur ðîn wîde mǽrsian (*cantare*), 70, 7. Mērsiga ðæt word *diffamare sermonem*, Mk. Skt. Lind. 1, 45. Ðætte hiá ne mērsades hine *ne manifestarent eum*, 3, 12. Ðæt is ðæt mon his mearce brǽde ðæt mon his hlîsan and his naman mǽrsige *terminum suum dilatare, est opinionis suæ nomen extendere*, Past. 48, 2; Swt. 367, 14. Mǽrsedon *celebrabant*, Hpt. Gl. 514, 21. Mǽrsud [wearþ] *crebruit*, Wrt. Voc. ii. 23, 71. Ðǽr hǽlo untrumra manna and neáta mǽrsode syndon *sanitates infirmorum et hominum et pecorum celebrari non desinunt*, Bd. 3, 9; S. 533, 19. III. *to celebrate (a particular event, season, &c.)*:—His symbeldæg wē mērsiaþ *ejus natalitia celebramus*, Rtl. 44, 30. Be ðisse hâlgan tîde (*birthday of John the Baptist*) weorþunga ðe wē nū tódæg mǽrsian sceolan . . . swîðe ūs is ðes dæg tō mǽrsienne . . nǽniges Godes hâligra gebyrd ciricean ne mǽrsiaþ, nemþe Cristes sylfes and ðyses Johannes, Blickl. Homl. 161, 4–11: Bd. 5, 10; S. 625, 19: Homl. Th. i. 324, 8. Wē ðe his ǽriste mǽrsiaþ, Blickl. Homl. 91, 8. Swēg mǽrsiendes *the voice of one celebrating a festival*; sonus epulantis, Ps. Lamb. 41, 5. IV. *to celebrate, perform a rite, ceremony, &c. with due solemnity*:—Ða hâlgan gerȳne mǽrsian *sacra mysteria celebrare*, Bd. 1, 27; S. 496, 23. Ða symbelnysse tō mǽrsianne massæsanges *missarum sollemnia celebrandi*, S. 497, 1: 2, 5; S. 507, 12. V. *to magnify, exalt, praise, glorify*:—Clypa mē on dæge ðînre gedrēfednysse and ic ðē âhredde and ðū mǽrsast mē *invoca me in die tribulationis; eripiam te, et magnificabis me*, Homl. Th. ii. 126, 8. Mǽrsa ðînne Sunu ðæt ðîn Sunu ðē mǽrsige *clarifica filium tuum ut filius tuus clarificet te*, 360, 8. Mîn sâwl mǽrsaþ Drihten *magnificat anima mea dominum*, Lk. Skt. 1, 46. Ic onginne ðē tō mǽrsigenne *incipiam exaltare te*, Jos. 3, 7. Ðǽr Sicilia sǽstreámum in ēþel mǽrsaþ *where Sicily, the sea streams among, her land makes illustrious*, Bt. Met. Fox 1, 32; Met. 1, 16. [*O. L. Ger.* ge-mārsōn *mirificare*.] v. ge-, wîd-mǽrsian; mǽran.

mǽr-stân, es; *m. A boundary-stone*:—Ðis syndon ða landgemǽro . . . On mǽrstân; of mǽrstâne on ðone ealdan gâran, Cod. Dip. Kmbl. iii. 438, 28.

mǽrsung, e; *f.* I. *a making known, report, rumour*:—Spranc mērsung ðiús (*fama hæc*) in alle eorþo, Mt. Kmbl. Lind. 9, 26. Gefehto and mērsungo (*opiniones*) ðara gefehto, Mk. Skt. Lind. 13, 7. II. *fame, renown, celebrity*:—Gesprang mērsung his in alle Syria *abiit opinio ejus in totam Syriam*, Mt. Kmbl. Lind. 4, 24. Herodes gehērde mērsung (*famam*) Hǽlendes, 14, 1. Gesprang mērsung (*rumor*) his in all lond, Mk. Skt. Lind. 1, 28. III. *celebration (of a rite, festival, &c.)*:—Gibedes ðisses gērlîcre mērsunge *observationis hujus annua celebritate*, Rtl. 9, 21. Mǽrsung his gebyrdtîde *the celebration of his birthday*, Homl. Th. i. 480, 34. Ðâs fiftig daga sind ealle gehâlgode tō ânre mǽrsunge, 312, 23. On ðære Eástrena mǽrsunge *in celebratione Paschæ*, Bd. 3, 17; S. 545, 21. Mid ða mǽrsunga ðara heofonlîcra gerȳna, 2, 9; S. 510, 37; 4, 22; S. 591, 21. IV. *a making great, magnifying, glorification*:—Se Fæder hine sette tō his swîðran on heofenan rîce . . Ðeós is Cristes mǽrsung æfter ðære menniscnysse, Homl. Th. ii. 360, 28. Mid ealre þoncunga and mǽrsunga hine herian *to praise him with giving thanks and glory to him*, Blickl. Homl. 31, 21. V. *Greatness, magnificence, excellency, honour, favour*:—Syllaþ mǽrsunge Gode ūrum *date magnificentiam deo nostro*; ascribe ye greatness to our God (A. V.), Cant. M. ad f. 4. Mērsunge *favore*, Rtl. 8, 40. Ofer gesamnunge is his mǽrsung *his excellency* (magnificentia) *is over Israel*, Ps. Lamb. 67, 35: Ps. Spl. 110, 3: 70, 23. Ðæt ic synge ealne dæg mǽrsunga (*magnitudinem*) ðîne, 70, 9. Stefn Drihtnes on mǽrsungum *the voice of the Lord is full of majesty*, 28, 4. v. cyric-, ge-mǽrsung.

mǽrsung-tîma, an; *m. A time of celebration* or *glorification*:—Ðā wæs his mǽrsungtîma, ðæt se Fæder hine mǽrsode swā ðæt hē hine sette tō his swîðran on heofenan rîce, and him forgeaf andweald on heofenan and on eorþan, and eác ofer hellwarum, Homl. Th. ii. 360, 25.

mærþ *a weasel*. v. mearþ.

mǽr-þorn, es; *m. A hawthorn tree which serves as a boundary*:—Of ðæm pytte on ðone dîc, ðæt on mǽrþorne; of ðæm þorne norþ on ðone hwîtan stân, Cod. Dip. Kmbl. iii. 168, 33.

mǽrþu, mǽrþo; *indecl.*: mǽrþ, e; *f.* I. *greatness, honour, glory, fame*:—Gesprang mērþu his in all lond Galileæ *processit rumor ejus in omnem regionem Galilaeae*, Mk. Skt. Lind. 1, 28. Lof wîde sprang, miht and mǽrþo, ofer middangeard, þeodnes þegna, Apstls. Kmbl. 13; Ap. 7. Ðǽr wæs Beówulfes mǽrþo mǽned *there was celebrated Beowulf's glory*, Beo. Th. 1718; B. 857: 1322; B. 659. Mǽrþo fremman *to achieve glory*, 4274; B. 2134. Ðæt hié him tō mǽrþe burh geworhte *that they should build a city in their own honour*, Cd. 80; Th. 100, 12; Gen. 1663. Ðū ongunne ætȳwan ðîne mǽrþe (*magnitudinem*), Deut. 3, 24: Ps. Lamb. 150, 2. Sillaþ mǽrþe (*magnificentiam*) ūrum Gode, Deut. 32, 3. Dryhtne ðe hyre weorþmynde geaf mǽrþe *to the Lord that gave her honour and glory*, Judth. 12; Thw. 26, 25; Jud. 344. Geceósan swā helle hiénþu swā heofones mǽrþu, Exon. 16 b; Th. 37, 11; Cri. 591. Mē þincþ ðæt hit hæbbe geboht sume swîðe leáslîce mǽrþe, Bt. 24, 3; Fox 82, 24. Ic ongite ðæt . . ða mǽstan mǽrþa ne sint on ðysse woruldgylþe *video . . nec celebritatem gloria posse contingere*, 33, 1; Fox 120, 4. Mǽrþa gesǽligost *most blessed of glories*, Salm. Kmbl. 136; Sal. 67. Mǽrþa ðîne hig tellaþ *magnitudinem tuam narrabunt*, Ps. Lamb. 144, 6. Eálā mîn drihten . . mǽrþum gefrǽge, Bt. Met. Fox 20, 4; Met. 20, 2. Hine God trymede mǽrþum and mihtum *him God confirmed with glory and with might*, Elen. Kmbl. 29; El. 15. II. *a great, honourable, glorious action, a wonderful thing, mighty work*:—Hē hēt ða hȳde tō Rôme bringan and hié ðǽr tō mǽrþe âþenian for ðon heó wæs hundtwelftiges fōta lang *corium (serpentis) Romam devectum (quod fuisse centum viginti pedum spatio ferunt) cunctis miraculo fuit*, Ors. 4, 6; Swt. 174, 16. Sceoldon hiera senatus ða menn beforan him drîfan gebundene ðe ðǽr gefongene wǽron, ðæt heora mǽrþa sceoldon ðȳ þrymlîcran beón, 2, 4; Swt. 70, 30. Ðǽr syndon ða micclan mǽrþa ðæt syndon ða geweorc ðe Alexander hēt gewyrcean *ibi sunt illa magna insignia que Alexander operari jusserat*, Nar. 33, 20. Mǽrþa georne *eager to do great things*, Cd. 80; Th. 101, 5; Gen. 1677. Hæbbe ic mǽrþa fela ongunnen, Beo. Th. 821; B. 408: 5284; B. 2645: Exon. 82 b; Th. 310, 34; Seef. 84. Ðū hit worhtes eall . . ðeáh ðē nǽnegu nēdþearf wǽre ealra ðara mǽrþa *thou didst make it all . . though thou didst not need all those mighty works*, Bt. Met. Fox 20, 51; Met. 20, 26. Mǽrþa fruma *God*, Chr. 975; Erl. 126, 15; Edg. 41. Standaþ and geseóþ Drihtnes mǽrþa (*magnalia*), Ex. 14, 13: Hy. Surt. 96, 36. Mârþa, Ps. Spl. 105, 21. Ic wylle fǽhþe sēcan, mǽrþum (*gloriously, nobly*) fremman, Beo. Th. 5021; B. 2514. Hǽfdon neowne gefeán mǽrþum (*wondrously, miraculously*) gemēted, Elen. Kmbl. 1738; El. 871. [*Goth.* mēritha *fame, report*: *O. Sax.* māriða: *O. H. Ger.* mārida *fama, opinio, rumor, praeconium, claritudo*.] v. ellen-mǽrþu.

mǽr-weg, es; *m. A boundary* (?) *road*:—On ðone mǽrweg; ondlong ðæs mǽrweges, Cod. Dip. Kmbl. iii. 32, 33. Ondlong ðæs lytlan weges ðæt hit cymeþ on ðone norþran mǽrweg; ondlong ðæs mǽrweges, 33, 5: 77, 26. [Cf. mearc-weg, 202, 5; *but also* on piddes meres weg, 77, 14.]

mǽr-weorc, es; *n. A great, splendid work*, Ps. Th. 110, 4.

Mǽs, e; *f. The Maes* or *Meuse*; Mosa:—Hēr fōr se here up onlong Mǽse feor on Fronclond, Chr. 882; Erl. 82, 7. [*O. H. Ger.* Masa: *Ger.* Maas.]

mæscre, an; *f. A mesh of a net*:—Mæscre *macula*, Wrt. Voc. ii. 59, 5. v. masc.

mæsen [*for* (?) mæseren]; *adj. Of maple*:—Vi mæse[r]ne sceala *vi vessels of maple*, Chart. Th. 429, 29. [Cf. *Icel.* mösur-skâl *a vessel of maple*; 'such bowls are frequently mentioned in inventories of churches; cp. mid. H. G., where *maser* is even used of *a chalice, a maple-wood cup*.' Cl. and Vig. Dict. See also *Prompt. Parv.* masere *murrus*, p. 328 and note there. The noun perhaps occurs in Maser-feld, Chron. 641; Erl. 27, 8.]

mæslen, mæsling v. mæstling.

mæsle-sceafe. v. mǽl-sceafa.

mæsse, messe, an; *f.* I. *a service of the church, mass*:—Mæsse *missa*, Wrt. Voc. ii. 59, 8. Ǽne þrowade Crist, ac swâðeáh dæghwomlîce biþ his þrowung geednîwod þurh gerȳnu ðæs hâlgan hūsles æt ðære hâlgan mæssan; forðî fremaþ seó hâlige mæsse miclum ge ðâm lybbendum ge ðâm forþfarenum, Homl. Th. ii. 376, 10–13. Nū is seó mæsse gemynd Drihtnes þrowunge, L. Ælfc. P. 31; Th. 6, 13. Mæssan singan *to celebrate mass*, Bd. 1, 27; S. 496, 23: 4, 22; S. 592. 8. Mæssan dōn, 4, 22; S. 591, 29 note. Se biscop and se mæssepreóst sceolan hūru embe seofon niht mæssan gesingan for eal cristen folc ðe ǽfre âcenned wæs, Blickl. Homl. 45, 31. Æfter ðon ðe ðǽr wǽron ða hâlgan lofsangas and mæssan gefyllede, 207, 59. II. *a festival day when a solemn mass was celebrated, -mas in Christmas, Michaelmas, &c.*:—Temples mæssa *scenopegia*, Jn. Skt. Lind. 7, 2. Æfter Andrēas mæssan, Ælfc. Gr. 9, 18; Som. 9, 56. Tō sanctae Michaheles mæssan, Blickl. Homl. 197, 2. Tō sancte Martines mæssan, 211, 11. Ǽr ealra hâligra mæssan, Chr. 901; Erl. 96, 22. Tō Cristes mæssan, 1104; Erl. 239, 13. Wē Marian mæssan healdaþ, Menol. Fox 40; Men. 20: L. Alf. pol. 43; Th. i. 92, 7. [From Low Latin *missa* v. Skeat's Dict. s. v. *mass*, for the meaning. *Icel.* messa: *O. H. Ger.* messa, missa: *M. H. Ger.* messe: *Ger.* messe.] v. candel-, capitol-, hlâf-mæsse; mæsse-dæg.

mæsse-ǽfen, es; *m. The eve of a festival*, e. g. *Christmas Eve*:—On sc̄e Michaeles mæsseǽfan, Chr. 1014; Erl. 151, 13. Fæstaþ ðæra hâligra martyra mæsseǽfenas, Wulfst. 136, 19.

mæsse-bóc; *gen.* -bēc; *f. A mass-book, missal*:—Saltere and pistolbōc, godspellbōc and mæssebōc, sangbōc and handbōc, gerîm and pastoralem, penitentialem and rǽdingbōc, ðâs bēc sceal mæssepreóst nēde habban, L. Ælfc. C. 21; Th. ii. 350, 13; Chart. Th. 430, 7. On ðǽm ealdan sacramentorium, ðæt is on ðǽm ealdan mæssebōcum, Shrn. 88, 5. [*Orm.* Havel. messe-bok: *O. H. Ger.* missi-puoh *missalis*: *Icel.* messu-bōk.]

mæsse-créda, an; *m. The creed used in the service of the mass, the Nicene creed*:—On ðam sinoþe (on ðære ceastre Nicēa) wǽron gesette ða hālgan cyricþēnunga, and se mæssecrēda, L. Ælfc. C. 4; Th. ii. 344, 9. *The* mæssecrēda *is given in* Homl. Th. ii. 596, 24–598, 14.

mæsse-dæg, es; *m. A festival* (v. mæsse, II.):—Uton sēcan ūre cyrcean Sunnandagum and mæssedagum *frequentemus ecclesias nostras diebus Dominicis, et diebus festis,* L. Ecg. P. iv. 66; Th. ii. 226, 29: Blickl. Homl. 47, 27. Be mæssedaga freólse, L. Alf. pol. 43; Th. i. 92, 1. November onginþ on ealra hālgena mæssedæg, Ælfc. Gr. 9, 18; Som. 9, 56. Uppon sc̄e Laurent mæssedæg, Chr. 1103; Erl. 239, 5. [*Orm.* messedaȝȝ to freollsenn: *Ayenb.* messedaȝes *holidays.*]

mæsse-gierela, an; *m. Vestment used at the celebration of the mass,* Past. 14, 6; Swt. 87, 19.

mæsse-hacele, an; *f. A cope:*—Mæssehacele *casula,* Wrt. Voc. 81, 42. [Ic ān þeódrēd mīn wīte massehakele ðe ic on Pauie bouhte, Chart. Th. 515, 16: 512, 30. Messehacel, Chr. 963; Erl. 123, 16. Mæssehakeles, 1070; Erl. 207, 35: 1122; Erl. 249, 8.] [*Icel.* messuhökul *a cope: O. H. Ger.* missa-hachul *casula.*]

mæsse-hrægel, es; *n. A surplice:*—Se sacerd scolde beón fæste bewǣfed on bǣm sculdrum mid ðæm mæssehrægle *in utroque humero sacerdos velamine superhumeralis adstringitur,* Past. 14, 3; Swt. 83, 9. Ðes pāpa gesette ðæt mæssepreóstas ne sceoldon brūcan gehālgodra mæssehrægla būton on cyrcean ānre, Shrn. 112, 19.

mæssian; *p.* ode *To say mass:*—Be ðam sacerde ðonne hē mæssaþ hwæt hē on him hæbbe *de iis quibus indutus esse debet sacerdos, cum missam celebrat,* L. Edg. C. tit. ix.; Th. ii. 128, 19. Mæssode se apostol ðam folce, Homl. Th. ii. 478, 14. For mē gelōmlīce mæssaþ *pro me missas crebras facit,* Bd. 4, 22; S. 591, 29. For hreówsigendne man man mōt mæssian ymb. xxx nihta, L. Ecg. C. 36; Th. ii. 160, 21. Hȳ mihton wel habban wīf on ðām dagum forðan ðe hȳ nǣfre ne mæssodon, L. Ælfc. C. 7; Th. ii. 346, 8. Wē lǣraþ ðæt preóst on ǣnigum hūse ne mæssige, būton on gehālgodre cirican, L. E. B. 30; Th. ii. 250, 18. (*For other regulations see* §§ 31–33, 35, 37; and L. N. P. L. 13, 14, 16, 18; Th. ii. 292, 16–24.) Benedictus āsende āne ofeletan, and hēt mid ðære mæssian, Homl. Th. ii. 174, 27. Ymbe underntīd ðā ðā se brōðor wæs gewunod tō mæssigenne, 358, 21. [*Icel.* messa.]

mæsse-lác, es; *n. The mass-offering, the host:*—Mæsselāc *fertum,* Wrt. Voc. ii. 39, 41: 147, 76. Messelāc, Ælfc. Gl. 34; Som. 62, 61; Wrt. Voc. 28, 41. [v. Ducange: '*fertum* genus panis, in Glossis MSS. Isidoro et Papiæ dicitur oblatio, quæ ad altare fertur et sacrificatur a Pontificibus, a quo offertorium nominatur. In Festus; *fertum* genus libi dictum, quod crebrius ad sacra ferebatur altero genere libi.']

mæsse-niht, e; *f. The night which precedes a festival* (mæsse-dæg):—Ðis sceal on mydde-wyntres mæssenyht (i.e. *on Christmas morning*) tō ðære forman mæssan, Lk. 2, 1 (rubric). Nāgan lǣwede men wīfes gemānan mæssenihtum, Wulfst. 305, 23.

mæsse-preóst, es; *m.* I. *A priest not of the Christian church:*—Melchisedec wæs cyningc and mæssepreóst, Prud. 5 a. Ðā cwǣdon ða ealdras and ða mæssepreóstas tō Pilate, Nicod. 10; Thw. 5, 22: 11; Thw. 6, 2. II. *a priest of the Christian church, who had attained the last of the seven appointed orders, and might celebrate the mass. His orders were the same as those of the bishop, but the latter alone could ordain priests, confirm children, and consecrate churches. He might be a regular or not. There is the* mæssepreóst ðe regollīce libbe *or the* folcisc mæssepreóst ðe regollīf næbbe, L. Eth. ix. 19, 21; Th. i. 344, 11, 21; *but he was forbidden to marry. As compared with the laity his oath was equal to that of a thane, and he was worthy of thane-right.* [v. mæsse-þegen.] *His presence was necessary at a wedding, and he was one of those who were proper witnesses when property was exchanged. For manslaughter and other crimes he might be deprived of his orders.* See the passages below taken from the Laws. Mæssepreóst *presbiter,* Wrt. Voc. 42, 21: 71, 75. Swā hwæðer ðū sȳ swā mæssepreóst swā munuc, Coll. Monast. Th. 31, 35. Ǣlc mæssepreóst sceal beón swā hē gehāten is *sacerdos,* ðæt is on Lēden *sacrum dans* . . Hē sceal syllan hālignysse ðam folce ðe hē tō lāreówe biþ geset, L. Ecg. P. iii. 16; Th. ii. 202, 16. *Presbiter* is mæssepreóst oððe ealdwita; nā ðæt ǣlc eald sȳ, ac ðæt hē eald sȳ on wīsdōm. Se hālgaþ Godes hūsel, L. Ælfc. C. 17; Th. ii. 348, 20. Beggen sind on ānum hāde, se biscop and se mæssepreóst, ðæt is on ðam seofoþan cirichāde, L. Ælfc. P. 35; Th. ii. 378, 14. Nis nā māre betwyx mæssepreóste and bisceop būton se bisceop biþ gesett tō hādigenne preóstas, and tō bisceopgenne cild, and tō hālgyenne cyrcan, and tō gȳmenne Godes gerihta, L. Ælfc. C. 17; Th. ii. 348, 25. Mæssepreóstes āþ and woruldþegenes is on Engla lage geteald efendȳre; and for ðām seofon cirichādan ðe se mæssepreóst geþeáh ðæt hē hæfde, hē biþ þegenrihtes wyrðe, L. O. 12; Th. i. 182, 14. *For the books necessary for the* mæssepreóst *and for rules to be observed by him in celebrating mass see passages given under* mæsse-bōc, mæssian *respectively.* Æt ðām giftan sceal mæssepreóst beón mid rihte, L. Edm. B. 8; Th. i. 256, 6. Nān man ne hwyrfe nānes yrfes būtan ðæs gerēfan gewitnesse, oððe ðæs mæssepreóstes, oððe ðæs landhlāfordes oððe ðæs horderes, oððe ōðres ungelygenes mannes, L. Ath. i. 10; Th. i. 204, 18. Gif hwā ðonne ða teóþunge gelǣstan nelle, fare ðæs cynges gerēfa and ðæs bisceopes, and ðæs mynstres mæssepreóst, L. Edg. i. 3 Th. i. 262, 25. Mæssepreóstum and diáconum is eallunge forboden ǣlc hǣmed. Þreó hund biscopa and eahtatȳne gesetton canon, ðæt nān mæssepreóst oððe diácon on his wununge wīfhādes mann næbbe, būton hit sȳ his mōder, oððe sweoster, oððe faðu, oððe mōdrie; and gif hē ðearnunge oððe eáwunge wīfes brūce, ðæt hē his hādes þolige, Homl. Th. ii. 94, 27–33: L. Ecg. P. iii. 1; Th. ii. 196, 12: iii. 6; Th. ii. 198, 7. *But the rule is still stricter in* L. E. I. 12; Th. ii. 410, 7. Nis hyt ryht ðæt ǣnig wīfmon mid mæssepreóste on hūsum wunige. *Other regulations which concern the* mæssepreóst *follow q.v.* Gif mæssepreóst manslaga wurðe oððe elles mānweorc tō swīðe gewurce, ðonne þolige hē ǣgðres ge hādes ge eardes, L. Eth. ix. 26; Th. i. 346, 4: L. Ecg. P. iii. 3; Th. ii. 196, 23: iv. 2; Th. ii. 204, 10. For other crimes and their punishment see L. Eth. ix. 27; Th. i. 346, 8–16: L. Ecg. P. iv. 7; Th. ii. 206, 1. Ic Ælfrīc munuc and mæssepreóst, Homl. Th. i. 2, 12. Arrius se mæssepreóst *Arius presbyter,* Ors. 6, 30; Swt. 282, 33. Mammēa sende æfter Origenise ðæm gelǣredestan mæssepreóste, 6, 18; Swt. 270, 27. [*Icel.* messu-prestr.] v. efen-mæssepreóst.

mæssepreóst-hād, es; *m. The orders of a mass-priest:*—Of ðære tīde ðæs ðe ic mæssepreósthāde onfeng *ex quo tempore accepti presbyteratus,* Bd. 5, 24; S. 647, 32: 5, 1; S. 613, 12.

mæssepreóst-scīr, e; *f. The district attached to the church at which a masspriest officiated:*—Gif man hwylc metrum cild tō mæssepreóste bringe, sȳ of swylcre mæssepreóstscȳre swylce hyt sȳ, L. E. I. 17; Th. ii. 412, 21. Cf. Ne spane nān mæssepreóst nānne mon of ōðre cyrcean hȳrnysse tō his cyrcan, ne of ōðre preóstscȳre lǣre ðæt mon his cyrcan gesēce, and him heora teóþinge syllan, and ða geryhtu ðe hig ðam ōðrum syllan sceoldan, 14; Th. ii. 410, 30–33.

mæsser-bana, an; *m. One who slays a priest:*—Mæsserbanan (MS. C. sacerdbanan), Wulfst. 165, 28.

mæssere, es; *m. One who says mass, a mass-priest:*—Mæssere *presbyter,* L. Ecg. C. 7; Th. ii. 140, 1: Exon. 55 a; Th. 194, 34; Az. 149.

mæsse-reáf, es; *n. Vestment used when celebrating mass:*—Wē lǣraþ ðæt ǣlc preóst hæbbe corporalem ðonne hē mæssige, and subuculam under his alban and eal mæssereáf wurðlīce behworfen, L. Edg. C. 33; Th. ii. 250, 28: L. Ælfc. C. 22; Th. ii. 350, 19. Ic geann ānes mæssereáfes mid eallum ðam ðe ðǣrtō gebyreþ, Chart. Th. 529, 8.

mæsse-sang, es; *m. The service of the mass:*—Ða symbelnysse tō mǣrsianne mæssæsanges *missarum sollemnia celebrandi,* Bd. 1, 27; S. 497, 1. Mæssesong dōn *missas facere,* 1, 26; S. 488, 4. Gewuna mæssesonga *consuetudo missarum,* 1, 27; S. 489, 33. On mæssesangum and on sealmsangum, L. Edg. C. 14; Th. ii. 282, 17.

mæsse-þegen, es; *m. A mass-priest:*—Mæsseþegnes and woruldþegnes wergild ii þūsend þrymsa, L. Wg. 5; Th. i. 186, 10. v. mæsse-preóst.

mæsse-tíd, e; *f. A time at which mass was said:*—Æt mæssetīdum *tempore missæ,* L. Ecg. C. 9; Th. ii. 140, 20.

mæsse-wín, es; *n. Wine used in the service of the mass:*—Messewīn *infertum vinum,* Ælfc. Gl. 32; Som. 61, 126; Wrt. Voc. 27, 52. [*Icel.* messu-vīn.]

mæst, es; *m. A pole to support a sail, a mast:*—Mæst *malus* vel *artemo: artemon* vel *malus,* Ælfc. Gl. 83, 104; Som. 73, 81: 77, 126; Wrt. Voc. 48, 19: 56, 43. Mest *malus,* 63, 47. Mæstum *malis,* Wrt. Voc. ii. 57, 15. Mæst (?) *columbarium,* 134, 61 (cf. ār-locu *columbaria,* Wrt. Voc. 63, 41). Segelgyrdena, mæsta *antennarum,* Hpt. Gl. 529, 20: Menol. Fox 508; Gn. C. 24: Beo. Th. 71; B. 36: 3801; B. 1898: 3814; B. 1905: Andr. Kmbl. 929; An. 465. Hē hēt fealdan ðæt segl, and eác hwīlum lecgan ðone mæst, Bt. 41, 3; Fox 250, 15; Ors. 4, 6; Swt. 172, 5. [*O. H. Ger.* mast *malus.*]

mæst, es; *m. Mast, fruit of forest trees* e.g. *oak, beech, used for feeding swine:*—Ðrīm hunde swīna mæst, ond se biscop and ða hīgen āhten twǣde ðæs wuda ond ðæs mæstes, Cod. Dip. Kmbl. i. 279, 3. Mid wude and mid felde mid mæste *cum sylva et cum agro, cum porcorum esca,* iv. 202, 2. Micle beámas ða ðe mæst and wæstm mannum bringaþ *ligna fructifera,* Ps. Th. 148, 9. [*O. H. Ger.* mast *sagina.*] v. mæsten, mæstan.

mǣst. v. micel.

mǣst; *adv.* I. *most, chiefly, especially:*—Se westsūþende Europe landgemirce is in Ispania westeweardum and mǣst (*maixme*) æt ðæm īglande ðætte Gaðes hātte, Ors. 1, 1; Swt. 8, 24. Ðara nȳtena meolc ðe hȳ mǣst bī libbaþ, 1, 2; Swt. 30, 10. Geond ealle world, and ðeáh mǣst in Thasalia, 1, 6; Swt. 36, 8. Swā hié mǣst mehten *as much as ever they could,* 6, 5; Swt. 260, 32: Past. 28; Swt. 190, 9. Ealles mǣst *maxime,* Bd. 2, 4; S. 505, 7. Preóst oftor ne mæssige ðonne þrīwa mǣst ðara þinga (*at the utmost*), L. Edg. C. 37; Th. ii. 252, 4. II. *with the adj.* eall, *almost, nearly:*—Hit is eal mǣst mid hāligra manna naman geset *it is almost all occupied with holy men's names,* Homl. Th. ii. 466, 22. Ðæt him sealde mǣst eal his sunu *almost all of which his son gave him,* Chart. Th. 271, 33. Wīgheard and mǣst ealle (*omnes pene*) his gefēran, Bd. 4, 1; S. 563, 25. Hié mǣst ealle ofslægene wurdon, Ors. 2, 5; Swt. 80, 22. Swā swā ealle mǣst ðyssere declinunge, Ælfc. Gr. 9, 7; Som. 9, 9. Ða ōðre ealle mǣst *almost all the others,* 9, 4; Som. 10, 24. Ealle mǣst ðās word, 30; Som. 38, 35. v. mā, *and* micel.

mæstan; *p*. mæste; *pp*. mæsted, mæst *To fatten*:—Maestun *saginabant*, Wrt. Voc. ii. 119, 61: Ep. Gl. 24 b, 27. Ic wylle ðæt man mæste mînum wîfe twâ hund swîna, Chart. Th. 596, 21. Is mæst *saginatur, nutritur*, Hpt. Gl. 489, 43. Weorþaþ mæsted *pinguescent*, Ps. Th. 64, 13. [*Prompt. Parv*. Mastyñ beestys *sagino, impinguo*; mast-hog, mastid swyne *maialis*: *O. H. Ger*. mastian *to feed*; ge-mestet, ge-mast *fattened*, v. Grff. ii. 882: *Ger*. mästen.] v. â-, ge-mæstan.

mæst-cist, e; *f*. *The hole in which the mast is fixed*:—Mest *malus*: mastcyst *modius*, Wrt. Voc. 63, 48, 49. Mæstcyst *modius*, ii. 59, 27. ['dicitur *modius* cavum illud in navi cui arbor instititʼ, Forcellini.]

mæstel-bearh; *gen*. -bearges; *m*. *A fattened barrow pig*:—*Ante porcos*, before bergum; ðæt sindon ða mæstelbergas; ðæt aron ða gehâdade menn, and ða gôde menn, and ða wlonce menn forhogas Godes bebod and godspelles, Mt. Kmbl. Lind. 6, 6 note.

mæsten [n], es; *m*. *Mast-pasture, pasture for swine, consisting of the fruit of forest trees*:—Man mæste mînum wîfe twâ hund swîna, ðænne ðǽr mæsten sŷ, Chart. Th. 596, 23: Cod. Dip. Kmbl. iv. 20, 5. Be unâliéfedes mæstennes onfenge. Gif mon on his mæstene unâliéfed swîn gemête, L. M. 49; Th. i. 132, 11. Ðonne hê [se inswân] his heorde tô mæstene drîfe, L. R. S. 4; Th. i. 434, 21. [Ðis geár wæs gǽsne on mæstene, Chr. 1116; Erl. 245, 36.] v. mæsten-rǽden.

mæsten-treów, es; *n*. *A tree producing mast*:—Mæstentriów *suberies* (*suberes*?) Ælfc. Gl. 45; Som. 64, 102; Wrt. Voc. 32, 37.

mæsten-rǽden [n], e; *f*. *The right to feed swine in places where there was mast*:—[Hæbbe] mæstenrǽdene ðonne mæsten beó, Cod. Dip. Kmbl. iii. 451, 10. v. mæst-rǽden.

mæst-land, es; *n*. *Land on which mast is produced*:—Eall ðæt wudulond ðæt Æþelbald gesealde tô mæstlonde, Chart. Th. 140, 2.

mæstling, mæsling, mæslen [n], es; *n*. I. *A kind of brass*. The word is used to gloss *aes, aurichalcum*, and *electrum*:—Mæstlingc ǽr and tin *aurichalcum, aes et stannum*, Coll. Monast. Th. 27, 11. Mæstlinc, grêne âr *auricalcos*, Wrt. Voc. 286, 66. Cwicseolfer *vel* mæstling *electrum* i. *sucus arboris*, ii. 142, 78. Mæslen *aes*, Mk. Skt. Lind. Rush. 6, 8. Ðæt mæslenn (mæslen, Rush.), 12, 41. Mæslen, Jn. Skt. Lind. Rush. 2, 15. II. *a vessel made of the metal* (? v. *Halliw. Dict*. 'Plater, disse, cop and *maseline*ʼ):—Calicea frymþa and ceáca and ârfata and mæstlinga *baptismata calicum et urceorum et eramentorum et lectorum*, Mk. Skt. 7, 4. Gedôn on cyperen fæt oððe mæstling [-fæt?] oððe bræsen, Lchdm. iii. 292, 17. [*A. R*. copper, *mestling*, breas: al is icleopet or: *Halliw. Dict*. bras, *maslyn*, yren and stel; where also *mastelyn* panne: *R. Glouc*. mastling: cf. also *Icel*. mersing, messing *brass*: *M. H. Ger*. messinc: *Ger*. messing.] v. gold-mæstling.

mæstling-, mæsling-smiþ, es; *m*. *A worker in brass*:—Mæstlincsmiþ *aerarius*, Ælfc. Gl. 81; Som. 73, 7; Wrt. Voc. 47, 14. Mæslingcsmiþ, 73, 32.

mæst-lôn (?) *pulleys at the top of the mast over which the ropes are drawn*:—*Carceria*, mæstlôn, *sunt in cacumine arboris trocliae, quasi flicteria, per quas funes trahuntur*, Wrt. Voc. ii. 128, 59.

mæst-rǽden [n], e; *f*. *The right of feeding swine in places where mast is produced*:—Hê nǽfre hine bereáfian wolde ðære mæstrǽddene ðe hê him âlêfed hæfde on Longan hrycge, Chart. Th. 140, 35. v. mæsten-rǽden.

mæst-râp, es; *m*. *A rope fastening a sail to a mast*, Cd. 146; Th. 182, 27; Exod. 82.

mæst-twist, es; *m*. *A rope to support a mast, a stay*:—Mæsttwist *parastates*, Ælfc. Gl. 104; Som. 77, 127; Wrt. Voc. 56, 44. Mæstwist, 63, 48.

mæt = mete, q.v.

mǽtan; *p*. te *To dream* (with dat. or acc. of person; cf. *Icel. dreyma* which takes acc. of dreamer and of dream):—On ânre nihte ealdne mônan, swâ hwæt swâ ðê mǽteþ ðæt cymþ tô gefeán, Lchdm. iii. 154, 15. Gyf mon (*acc*. cf. l. 27) mêteþ ðæt hê geseó . . . , 168, 8. Gyf man mǽte ðæt hê hæbbe . . , 176, 2. Ongitan swelce eów mǽte, Bt. 26, 1; Fox 90, 4: tit. 26; Fox xiv, 16. Hit gelamp ðæt hine mǽtte, Gen. 37, 5. Mîn swefen ðe mê mǽtte, 37, 6. Ôðer swefen hine mǽtte, 37, 9: 41, 5, 11: 42, 9. Gif hê secge ðæt him mǽtte swefen, Deut. 13, 1. Ðære Perpetuan mǽtte ðæt heó wǽre on weres hiwe, Shrn. 60, 28. [*Chauc*. meten.] v. ge-mǽtan.

mǽte; *adj*. *Moderate, mean* (*between two extremes*), *small, poor, bad*; in the cpve. *inferior*, applied to persons, *of a middle* or *lower class*:—Reste hê ðǽr mǽte weorode (*alone*), Rood. Kmbl. 138; Kr. 69. *So again* Ic âna wæs mǽte werede, 245; Kr. 124. Unrîm ealra cwycra, mycelra and mǽtra (*pusilla et magna*), Ps. Th. 103, 24: 113, 21: Exon. 33 a; Th. 105, 16; Gû. 24. Ic ðê feáwe dagas mînra mǽttra môde secge *I will tell thee the fewness of my days poor and evil*; paucitatem dierum meorum enuntia mihi, Ps. Th. 101, 21. Ðe mǽtu sprecaþ ofer mê *qui maligna loquuntur super me*, Ps. Spl. T. 34, 30. Biþ seó sîþre tîd sǽda gehwylces mǽtræ in mægne (*inferior in virtue*), Exon. 33 a; Th. 105, 2; Gû. 17. Gif hió biþ gôd drenc, biþ on peninge; gif mǽtra, biþ on ôðrum healfum oððe on twâm; and gif ifel þrîm, ac ne mǽ, L. M. 2, 52; Lchdm. ii. 272, 24. Hors tô healfan punde gif hit swâ gôd sŷ; and gif hit mǽtre sŷ, gilde be his wlites wyrþe, L. Ath. V. 6; Th. i. 232, 25. Nalæs ðæt ân ðætte ða mǽttran (mǽteran, MS. B.) . . ac eác swylce cyningas and ealdormen *non solum mediocres* . . *sed etiam reges et principes*, Bd. 4, 23; S. 593, 43 note. Eall ðâs getimbro ge ða mâran ge ða mǽttran *cuncta hæc ædificia publica vel privata*, 4, 25; S. 600, 33. Micle and mǽttran (MS. and micle mǽttan), Chart. Th. 510, 32. Mǽtran, Bt. 39, 7; Fox 222, 11 note. Næs ðæt mǽtost mægenfultuma *not poorest of aids was that*, Beo. Th. 2914; B. 1455. Mêtestum *pessimi*[*s*?], Kent. Gl. 711. v. ge-, ofer-, or-, un-, unge-mǽte.

mǽþ, e; *f*. (*but* ofer ðînne mǽð, Prov. Kmbl. 27.) I. *measure, degree, proportion*:—Gilde be ðære giftan mǽþe *reddet pecuniam juxta modum dotis*, Ex. 22, 17: L. Ecg. P. i. 11; Th. ii. 176, 28. Be ðære synne mǽþe *secundum peccati gradum*, tit. i; Th. ii. 170, 5: Ors. 1, 12; Swt. 56, 4. Be dǽde mǽþe, L. C. E. 5; Th. i. 364, 1. Beó seó ǽht gescyft swiðe rihte wîfe and cildan and nêhmâgon ǽlcum be ðære mǽþe ðe him tô gebyrige *let the property be shared among the wife and children and near relatives with strict justice, to each according to the proportion that is proper for him*, L. C. S. 71; Th. i. 414, 2. II. *the measure* or *extent of power, ability, capacity, efficacy*:—Nis nâ eówer mǽþ tô witenne ðone tîman *it is not for you to know the time* (Acts 1, 7), Homl. Th. i. 298, 12. Ûre mǽþ nis ðæt wê ealle Godes gecorenan eów gereccan, ii. 72, 1: 188, 28. Nis ǽfre ǽniges mannes mǽþ ðæt hê cunne God swâ forþ geherian swâ hê wyrþe is *it is never within any man's power to praise God to the extent he deserves*, Btwk. 194, 15. Ðeáh hit ûre mǽþ ne sîe ðæt wê witan hwæt hê sîe, wê sculon ðeáh be ðæs andgites mǽþe ðe hê ûs gifþ fundigan, Bt. 42; Fox 256, 2. Ælc winþ be his andgites mǽþe *each strives according to the measure of his understanding*, 41, 4; Fox 250, 26: Homl. Th. i. 344, 22. Crist dǽlþ his gyfe his limum be gehwylces mannes mǽþe *according to each man's ability*, ii. 526, 8. Gif ðû oncnǽwst ðînne Drihten mid ðînum ǽhtum be ðînre mǽþe, i. 140, 30. Gôdne dǽl ǽlces be ðære mǽþe (*efficacy* of the ingredient), Lchdm. iii. 12, 20. Dô ðǽrtô be ðæs huniges mǽþe, 76, 9. Gôde sind ðâs þing (*bread, fish, &c*.) be heora mǽþe *these things are good as far as they go*, Homl. Th. i. 252, 26. Ofer mǽþe ûre ðû forþtŷhst sprǽce *ultra ætatem nostram protrahis sermonem*, Coll. Monast. Th. 32, 11. Ðeáh wê nû ofer ûre mǽþ þencen *sive mente excedimus*, Past. 16, 2; Swt. 101, 11. Ðæt môd ðe ofer his mǽþ biþ upâhæfen *animus qui extra se in elationem ducitur*, 36, 7; Swt. 255, 18. Ðû scealt gelŷfan on ðone lifigendan God and nâ ofer ðîne mǽþe môtian be him, Hexam. 3; Norm. 6, 17. Ðû bǽde ofer mîne mǽþe *thou hast asked beyond my power*, Homl. Skt. 3, 515. Ne wilna ðû ofer ðînne mǽd tô witanne ymbe ða heofonlîcan þing, Prov. Kmbl. 27. Manna gehwylc mæg be his mǽþe, mid ðâm lâcum ðe hê hæfþ, Gode eáðe gecwêman, forðam ne gewilnaþ hê nâ mâran ðonne ðæs mannes mǽþa beóþ, Wulfst. 280, 27. III. *degree, rank, status, condition*:—'Ne onwreáh ðê flǽsc ne blôd ðisne geleáfan.ʼ Flǽsc and blôd is gecweden his flǽsclîce mǽiþ '*flesh and blood did not reveal this belief to thee*.ʼ *His fleshly condition is called flesh and blood*, Homl. Th. i. 368, 9. Ðâ wǽron þeódwitan weorþscipes wyrþe, ǽlc be his mǽþe, eorl and ceorl, þegen and þeóden, L. R. 1; Th. i. 190, 13. Eallum cristenum mannum gebyraþ ðæt hî hâda gehwylcne weorþian be mǽþe, L. C. E. 4; Th. i. 360, 28: L. Eth. vii. 3; Th. i. 330, 8. IV. *due measure, right*:—Hê þeáh swâ hit mǽþ wæs fægere forþwerd *he made good progress, as was right and fit*, Wulfst. 17, 8. Manna gehwilc ôðrum beóde ðæt riht ðæt hê wille ðæt man him beóde, be ðam ðe hit mǽþ sî, L. Eth. vi. 49; Th. i. 326, 31. Manna mâ ðonne hit ǽnig mǽþ wǽre *more men than was at all right*, Byrht. Th. 137, 33. Ofer mǽþe *justo amplius*, Ger. 395, 58. V. *due measure in regard to others, honour, respect* (v. mǽþ-full):—Hwîlum wǽron heáfodstedas and heálîce hâdas micelre mǽþe and munde wyrþe, and griþian mihton ða ðe ðæs beþorftan and ðǽrtô sôhtan aa be ðære mǽþe ðe ðǽrtô gebyrede *formerly chief places and high orders were entitled to much respect, and to the right of giving protection, and they could afford sanctuary to those that needed it, and repaired thereto, ever according to the dignity that thereto belonged*, L. Eth. vii. 3; Th. i. 330, 7. Se wæs ðonne mǽþe and munde swâ micelre wurþe, swâ ðonne ðam hâde gebirede, L. R. 7; Th. i. 192, 13. Ðæt Godes circan beón beteran mǽþe and munde wyrþe, Wulfst. 266, 9. Godes þeówas syndan mǽþe and munde gewelhwar bedǽlde, 157, 19. Man sceal mǽþe on hâde gecnâwan *people must feel respect for the clergy*, L. C. E. 4; Th. i. 362, 4: L. I. P. 19; Th. ii. 328, 26. Ælc cristen man âh mycele þearfe ðæt hê on ðam griþe mycle mǽþe wite (*shew great respect to*), 25; Th. ii. 338, 38: Wulfst. 161, 2. Se hæfþ ârfæstnysse ðe mǽþe cann on ôðrum mannum . . and nele forseón ôðerne, 51, 30. Deófol sendeþ ârleásnesse ðæt ungesǽlig man mǽðe ne geseó on his underþeóddum ne on his efenlîcan *shews no respect for his subordinates or equals*, 53, 24. [*Orm*. mett and mæþ i claþess: *Allit. Pms*. in mesure and meþe.]

mǽþ, es; *n*. (?) *Math* in after-*math, mowing, hay-harvest*:—Freóh ǽlces weoruldcundes þeówetes bûton þreom þingum ân is circsceat and ðæt hê mid eallum cræfte twuga on geáre [wyrce?] ǽne tô mǽþe and ôðre sîþe tô rîpe *free from every secular service except three things; one is church scot, and* (*the other two*) *that he* [*work*] *with all his might twice a-year, once at hay-harvest, the other time at corn-harvest*, Cod. Dip. Kmbl. ii. 400, 30. [*O. H. Ger*. mâd: *M. H. Ger*. mât; *gen*. mâdes; *n*: also *f*: *Ger*. mahd; *f*.] v. mǽðere.

Mǣðas, Mǣðe, Mēðas, Mēdas *the Medes*:—Siððan hæfdon Mǣðe onwald: ofer Mēðas ðæt lond: Asiria anwald gehwearf on Mēðas: Mǣða rīce, onwald: on ðara Mēða anwalde: Mēða ealdorman: betuh Mǣðum: Mǣðum gafol guldon: cyning in Mēðen, Ors. 1, 12; 2, 1; Swt. pp. 52, 54, 60. Mēda māððumselas, Salm. Kmbl. 379; Sal. 189: Cd. 209; Th. 259, 7; Dan. 688. Mēdum, Th. 258, 26; Dan. 681. v. Mǣðisc.

mæðel, meðel, medel, es; *n.* I. *an assembly, a deliberative* or *judicial meeting, council*:—In maeðle *in curia*, Wrt. Voc. ii. 111, 45: Ep. Gl. 12 d, 35. An medle oððe an þinge, L. H. E. 8; Th. i. 30, 12. Sum in mæðle mæg mōdsnottera folcrǣdenne forþ gehycgan, ðǣr witena biþ worn ætsomne, Exon. 79 a; Th. 295, 30; Crä. 41: 128 b; Th. 494, 16; Rä. 83, 2. On meðle, Elen. Kmbl. 1088; El. 546: 1182; El. 593. Se þeóden ongan geþinges wyrcan . . and ðā on ðam meðle bebeád, Cd. 197; Th. 245, 28; Dan. 470. Upp āstōdon manige on meðle *many stood up in the assembly*, Andr. Kmbl. 3250; An. 1628. Æt meðle on ðam miclan dæge *at the assembly on that great day* (*of judgment*), 2870; An. 1438: Exon. 63 b; Th. 234, 10; Ph. 538. Mæðel hēgan *to hold a meeting, take counsel, consult, address* (cf. *Icel.* heyja þing):—Ðā mōdigan mid him mæðel gehēdon (*took counsel together*), Andr. Kmbl. 2100; An. 1051. Hē wið ǣnne ðæra (*pillars*) mæðel gehēde (*addressed*), 2991; An. 1498. II. *speech, address, harangue, conversation*:—Ðū gehȳrdest ðone hālgan wer Moyses on meðle (cf. *Icel.* vera ā māli *to converse*) *thou didst hear the holy man Moses when conversing with him*, Elen. Kmbl. 1568; El. 78 b. Mōdiges meðel monige gehȳrdon *many heard the proud one's harangue* (*of Moses addressing the Israelites when pursued by Pharaoh*), Cd. 156; Th. 194, 3; Exod. 255. [*Goth.* maþl ἀγορά: *O. H. Ger.* madal *in cpds.* v. Grff. ii. 706: cf. *O. Sax. O. H. Ger.* mahal *concio.*] v. mæðlan, maðelian, here-meðel.

mæðel-ærn, -ern, es; *n. A house of meeting for speaking or for consulting*:—In mæðelern *in preterium* (l. *pretorium*), Wrt. Voc. ii. 46, 52: 74, 23.

mæðel-cwide, es; *m. Discourse, converse*:—Ic ðæs þeódnes word meðelcwide ongeat gæstes sprǣce *I the words of the prince, his discourse, have heard, the guest's speech*, Exon. 50 b; Th. 175, 9; Gū. 1192. Hyrcnigan hālges lāra mildes meðelcwida *to listen to the instructions of the holy man, the discourses of the kind one*, 47 b; Th. 162, 23; Gū. 980. Meaht ðū meðelcwidum worda gewealdan *are words at thy command for discourse*, Th. 163, 4; Gū. 988. Ðonne wē on geflitum sǣton meðelcwidas mengdon *when we sat in discussion, and now one, now another spoke*, Salm. Kmbl. 865; Sal. 432.

mæðel-hēgende; *part. pres. Attending, holding* or *addressing an assembly* or *council, consulting, conversing* (cf. Icel. *þing-heyjandi* 'the law term for any person who visits a *þing*, on a summons to perform any public duty,' Cl. and Vig.):—Biscopas and bōceras and ealdormen mæðelhēgende (*in council*), Andr. Kmbl. 1217; An. 609. Beornas cōmon mæðelhēgende . . Ðā wæs tō ðam þingstede þeód gesamnod *men came who had to attend the meeting . . Then was the people collected at the meeting-place*, 2194; An. 1098. Hwæt se manna wæs meðelhēgendra *who of men that speak was he*, 524; An. 262. Hēht gebeódan meðelhēgende on gemōt cuman, ða ðe deóplīcost Dryhtnes gerȳno reccan cūðon, Elen. Kmbl. 557; El. 279. v. mæðel.

mæðel-hergende; *past. pres. Speech-praising, esteeming conversation highly*:—Monige beóþ mæðelhergendra, sittaþ æt symble, wordum wrixlaþ, Exon. 83 b; Th. 314, 13; Mōd. 13.

Mæð-hild, e; *f. A woman's name, Matilda*:—Wē ðæt Mæðhilde gefrugnon, Exon. 100 a; Th. 378, 10; Deór. 14. *Grein would read* mǣð hilde, *comparing* mǣð *with Icel.* meiða *to injure, spoil.*

mæðel-stede, es; *m.* I. *A place of assembly, place where a meeting is held* (cf. þing-stede):—Tō ðam meðelstede manige cōmon snottere selerǣdend, Andr. Kmbl. 1315; An. 658: 1393; An. 697. Swā him Offa ǣr āsǣde on ðam meðelstede ðā hē gemōt hæfde, Byrht. Th. 137, 40; By. 199. Is eów rǣdes þearf on meðelstede (*in the queen's palace*), mōdes snyttro, Elen. Kmbl. 1104; El. 554: Cd. 179; Th. 224, 33; Dan. 145. Tō ðam meðelstede (*Mount Moriah*), 162; Th. 203, 1; Exod. 397. On ðam meðelstede (*the place of the last judgment*), 169; Th. 212, 20; Exod. 542. II. *a place of hostile meeting, a battle-place*:—Hē ne meahte on ðæm meðelstede wið Hengeste wiht gefeohtan, Beo. Th. 2169; B. 1082. [Cf. *O. H. Ger.* mahal-stat *curia.*]

mæðel-word, es; *n. A word used in a formal address*:—Þegn Hrōðgāres meðelwordum frægn (*of the question put by the coast-guard to Beowulf on his landing*), Beo. Th. 478; B. 236.

mǣðere, es; *m. A mower*:—Sīþberend *vel* mǣðre *falcarius*, i. *falciferens* vel *falcifera*, Wrt. Voc. ii. 146, 80. Mǣðeras *fenisece*, 148, 21. [*O. H. Ger.* mādari *feniseca, messor.*]

mǣþ-full; *adj. Shewing respect to others, courteous, humane* (v. mǣþ, V.):—Mǣðfull *humanus*, Ælfc. Gr. 45; Som. 41, 42. v. mǣþ-līc, mǣþian.

mǣþian; *p.* ode *To regard, respect*:—Hē sylþ ārleásnysse ðæt hē ne ārige ne eác ne mǣþige his underþeóddum ne his gelīcum *the devil gives pitilessness, so that the man neither spares nor regards his subordinates or his equals*, Wulfst. 59, 17. v. mǣþ, V; ge-mǣðian.

Mǣðisc, Mēdisc; *adj. Of the Medes*:—Mycel fyrd Mēdiscra monna, Nar. 17, 8. v. Mǣðas.

mæðlan, meðlan, a word occurring only in poetry, *to speak*:—Ðǣr (*at the day of judgment*) hē (*Christ*) tō ðām eádgestum ǣrest mæðleþ, Exon. 27 b; Th. 82, 14; Cri. 1338. Gehȳreþ cyning mæðlan, sprecan rēðe word, 19 b; Th. 50, 9; Cri. 797. Ic God mæðlan gehȳrde, Cd. 26; Th. 33, 23; Gen. 524. Ongan wordum mæðlan, 101; Th. 134, 2; Gen. 2218: Exon. 27 b; Th. 83, 30; Cri. 1364: 50 a; Th. 174, 10; Gū. 1175. Meðlan, Andr. Kmbl. 2879; An. 1442. v. maðelian.

mǣþ-leás; *adj. Without moderation, greedy*:—'Ðās fugelas habbaþ feónda gelīcnysse, ðe menn grǣdelīce grīpaþ tō grimre helle.' Ðā hēt Martinus ða mǣþleásan fugelas ðæs fixnoþes geswīcan, Homl. Th. ii. 516, 11.

mǣþ-līc; *adj. Moderate, in accordance with due measure, proper to a person's degree, having regard to others* (v. mǣþ-līce):—Beón ða heregeata swā hit mǣþlīc sȳ *let the heriots be as is proper to the several degrees* (*earl's, king's thane, &c.*), L. C. S. 72; Th. i. 414, 4. Gif hwilc forwyrht man hiówan gesǣce, bió se þingad swā hit mēdlīc sió be ðæs geltes mēðe *if any criminal betake himself to the convent, let terms be made for him, as may be fit and proper according to the measure of the crime*, Chart. Th. 509, 23. v. mǣþ, un-mǣþlīc.

mǣþ-līce; *adv. With due regard to others, courteously*:—Mǣþlīce *humaniter*, Ælfc. Gr. 45; Som. 41, 43: 42, 6.

mǣþrian; *p.* ode *To shew respect to, honour*:—Būton hē hwæne furþor gemǣþrian (mǣðrian, MS. A. gemǣðian, MS. B.), and hē him ðæs weorþscipes geunne, L. C. S. 12; Th. i. 382, 15.

mǣting, e; *f. A dream*:—On xxii nihta seó mǣtinga biþ eall costunge full; ne biþ ðæt nā gōd swefen, Lchdm. iii. 156, 7. Gē mǣtinge mīne ne cunnon, Cd. 179; Th. 224, 24; Dan. 141.

mǣt-līc. v. ofer-, un-ge-mǣtlīc.

mǣt-ness. v. or-, un-mǣtness.

mǣw, meáu, mēu, es; *m. A sea-mew, gull*:—Mǣw *alcedo* vel *alcion*, Ælfc. Gl. 37; Som. 63, 1; Wrt. Voc. 29, 24: 62, 13: *alacid*, Wrt. Voc. ii. 7, 62: *alcido*, 10, 31. Meáu *alcido*, 100, 2: *gabea*, 109, 56: *larus*, 112, 35. Mēu *larus*, 50, 59. Mēu *vel* mēg *larum*, Shrn. 29, 2. Se grǣga mǣw, Andr. Kmbl. 742; An. 371. Mǣw singende, Exon. 81 b; Th. 307, 11; Seef. 22. Mǣwes song, 106 b; Th. 404, 25; Rä. 25, 6. Mere, mǣwes ēðel, 123 b; Th. 474, 6; Bo. 25. [*Icel.* mār: *Dan.* maage: *Du.* meeuw: *O. H. Ger.* mēh: *Ger.* möwe.]

maffa, an; *m. A caul*; omentum, Wrt. Voc. ii. 63, 43: Ep. Gl. 17 d, 23.

maga, an; *m. The* MAW, *stomach*:—Maga *stomachus*, Ælfc. Gl. 76; Som. 71, 114; Wrt. Voc. 45, 19: 65, 54: Wrt. Voc. ii. 121, 40. *Fleumon*, magan untrymness, 39, 12. Magan *masdi*, 56, 9. Gif se maga āþened sīe, L. M. 2, 2; Lchdm. ii. 158, 4. Be geswelle ðæs magan, 158, 6. Hū ðone cealdan magan ungelīclīce mettas lyste, 2, 16; Lchdm. ii. 160, 7. Hit ðone magan ealne āfeormaþ, Herb. 70; Lchdm. i. 162, 19. Lege ofer ðone magan, L. M. 2, 15; Lchdm. ii. 192, 20. [*H. M.* mahe: *A. R. Chauc. Piers. P.* mawe: *Icel.* magi: *Dan.* mave: *O. H. Ger.* mago: *Ger.* magen.] v. mage.

maga; *adj. used as subst. Powerful, strong, a powerful person*:—Ic lǣre ǣlcne ðara ðe maga sī *I advise every one that is powerful*, Shrn. 163, 12. Ne derige se maga ðam unmagan *let not the strong injure the weak*, L. I. P. 7; Th. ii. 314, 1. Se maga and se unmaga ne māgon nā gelīce byrdene āhebban, L. Edg. C. 4; Th. ii. 262, 2: L. Eth. vi. 52; Th. i. 328, 160. Ne mæg se unmaga ðam magan gelīce byrðene āhebban, L. C. S. 69; Th. i. 412, 7. v. dirn-, un-maga.

māga, an; *m.* (cf. nið *for similar division of meanings*) I. *a relative*, v. heáfod-, nīd-māga; māge. II. *a son*:—Māga Healfdenes (*Hrothgar*), Beo. Th. 381; B. 189: 2953; B. 1474: 4293; B. 2143. Māga Ecgþeówes (*Beowulf*), 5168; B. 2587. Ic (*Christ*) sylf gestāg māga in mōdor, Exon. 28 b; Th. 87, 4; Cri. 1420. Fæder eft lǣrde māgan, 80 a; Th. 301, 32; Fä. 28. Ðonne mōdor māgan cenneþ, Salm. Kmbl. 742; Sal. 370. On māgan, ðīn āgen bearn, Cd. 109; Th. 144, 26; Gen. 2395. Māgan (*Isaac*) gelǣdde Abraham, 162; Th. 203, 2; Exod. 397. Se eorl wolde sleán eaferan sīnne, māgan, Th. 204, 2; Exod. 413. III. *a man*:—Se māga geonga (*Wiglaf*), Beo. Th. 5343; B. 2675. On ðære mǣgþe māga wæs hāten Tubal Cain, Cd. 52; Th. 66, 11; Gen. 1082. Māga cystum eald *a man old in virtues*, Exon. 80 a; Th. 300, 7; Fä. 2. Se māga (*Christ*), Andr. Kmbl. 1278; An. 639: 1630; An. 816: (*St. Andrew*), 1967; An. 986: 1249; An. 625. Māga māne fāh (*Grendel*), Beo. Th. 1960; B. 978. v. gūþ-, wuldor-māga.

MAGAN (*the infin. does not occur in* W. S. *but* mæge *glosses* posse, Mk. Skt. p. 3, 1; *and* **magende** (cf. *Icel.* megandi) = *quiens*, Ælfc. Gr. 41; Som. 44, 21. Megende *valens*, Kent. Gl. 189: *the later English forms seem to point to* mugan, *Gen. and Ex.* mugen: *Orm.* muȝhenn: *Chauc.* mowen: *Wick.* mowe: *Prompt. Parv.* mown. *Icel.* has mega: *O. H. Ger.* magan *and* mugan: *M. H. Ger.* mugen, mügen: *Ger.* mögen); *prs.* ic, hē mæg ðū meaht, mæht, meht, miht; *pl.* māgon, māhan, mægon (*or* magon?): *Goth.* keeps *a* throughout: *Icel.* megum: *O. Sax. O. Frs.* mugan: *O. H. Ger.* (sie) magun, mugun (*later* mugen); *p.* meahte, mæhte, mehte, mihte (*Goth.* mahta: *O. Sax.* mahta, mohta; *O. Frs.* machte: *Icel.* mátti: *O. H. Ger.* mahta, mohta: *M. H. Ger.* mohte: *Ger.* mochte); *subj. prs.* mǽge, mâge, mêge, meige (*or* mæge? *Icel.* megi: *O. Sax.* mugi: *O. H. Ger.* megi, mugi) I. *to be strong, efficacious, to avail, prevail, be sufficient*:—Gif đú meht *si vales*, Kent. Gl. 52. Wel mæg đæm dæg wêrignise his *sufficit diei malitia sua*, Mt. Kmbl. Lind. 6, 34; Mk. Skt. Lind. Rush. 14, 41. Ne meg mon *non praevaleat homo*, Ps. Surt. 9, 20. Ne mâgon úre woruldfrýnd ús đonne ǽnigum gôde *our friends will avail us nothing then*, Wulfst. 151, 12. Helle gatu ne mâgon ongên đa *portæ inferi non prævalebunt adversum eam*, Mt. Kmbl. 16, 18. Magan tô *to serve a purpose, be good for, have an effect, be the cause of*:—Ne mæg tô nâhte *ad nihilum valet*, 5, 13. Biþ men ful lytle đý bet đeáh đe hê gôdne fæder hæbbe, gif hê self tô nâuhte ne mæg, Bt. 30, 1; Fox 108, 30. Tô hwan mæg đis eorþlîce hûs, gif hit ýdel stent, Homl. Th. ii. 582, 12: 432, 15: Past. Swt. 7, 12. Him mæg tô sorge đæt hê nât hwæt him tôweard biþ *it causes him anxiety that he knows not what will happen to him*, Bt. 11, 1; Fox 32, 12. Wæs geworden đætte seó ylce eorþe mihte tô hǽle *factum est ut ipsa terra gratiæ salutaris haberet effectum*, Bd. 3, 11; S. 535, 34: Exon. 21 b; Th. 57, 21; Cri. 922: 100 a; Th. 374, 17; Seel. 127: 82 b; Th. 311, 30; Seef. 100. Magan wiđ (cf. *Icel.* mega viđ) *to prevail with or against, to be efficacious against* (of a medicine) *to be good for* (*a disease*):—Gif ic swâ wel wiđ đê mæg *if I am so influential with thee*, Homl. Skt. 3, 176. Wiđ ǽlcum âttre mâgon *contra venenum valent*, Bd. 1, 1; S. 474, 36. Đeós wyrt mæg wiđ manega untrumnyssa, Herb. 171, 1; Lchdm. i. 300, 24: L. Med. ex Quad. 5, 3; Lchdm. i. 348, 9: L. M. 2, 64; Lchdm. ii. 290, 10. Đis mæg horse wiđ đon đe him biþ corn on đa fêt, Lchdm. iii. 62, 24. Migtigra wîte wealdeþ đonne hê him wiđ mǽge *one too mighty for him to withstand is the disposer of punishment*, Cd. 200; Th. 249, 1; Dan. 523. II. *to be strong, be in good health* (so *Icel.* mega vel, &c.):—'Hú mæg hê?' Hig cwǽdon đæt hê wel mihte '*sanusne est?*' '*Valet,*' *inquiunt*, Gen. 29, 6. Đâ sǽde se cnapa đæt hê swîđe wel mihte, Homl. Skt. 3, 435. Đonne đú mê getrymedest, đæt ic teala mihte, Ps. Th. 70, 20. III. *to be able, may* (because a thing is possible):—Ic mæg *queo*; magende *quiens*, Ælfc. Gr. 41; Som. 44, 21. Ic mæg *queo*, đú miht *quis*, hê mæg *quit*; ic mihte *quivi*, 30; Som. 35, 5. (1) *With infin.*:—Ic mid handum ne mæg heofon gerǽcan, Cd. 216; Th. 275, 9; Sat. 169. Hêr ys seó bôt hú đú meaht đîne æceras bêtan, Lchdm. i. 398, 1: Cd. 27; Th. 36, 1; Gen. 565. Đú . . đe ǽghwylc miht wundor gewyrcean, Ps. Th. 76, 11. Hú mæg đæt yfel beón đætte ǽlces monnes ingeþanc wênþ đætte gôd sîe, Bt. 24, 4; Fox 86, 12. Đæt mæg engel đín eáþ geféran, 387; An. 194. Eall đis mâgon him sylfe geseón . . . mâgun leóda bearn oncnâwan, Exon. 24 a; Th. 69, 5-12; Cri. 1115. Hí ne mâgon đone earman gefyllan, Bt. 11, 1; Fox 34, 1. Him đa stormas derian ne mâhan (mǽgon, Cott. MS.), 7, 3; Fox 22, 6. Wê đæt sôþ mǽgon secgan, Cd. 94; Th. 121, 21; Gen. 2013. [Beo đan wê mugen understanden, Shrn. 17, 26.] Đæt hê âna mǽge gerîman, Cd. 163; Th. 205, 21; Exod. 439. Ic mæege, Mt. Kmbl. Lind. 26, 61. Ic mêge *possim*, Ps. Surt. 70, 8. Đú meige *possis*, Kent. Gl. 958. Đæt ic mâge geseón, Homl. Th. i. 152, 22. Cunnige mâge man of eágum teáras gerǽcan *try whether tears can be drawn from their eyes*, L. P. M. 3; Th. ii. 288, 4. Gif wê hit mǽgen âþencan, Cd. 21; Th. 26, 2; Gen. 400: 226; Th. 302, 11; Sat. 597. Uê mǽgi, Rtl. 45, 3. Mǽgi hiá, 95, 16. Wîddra đonne befæđman mǽge foldan sceattas, 163; Th. 204, 32; Exod. 428. [Đæt heó þurh đa mugen tô lîfes wege becumen . . đæt đa đe đǽr ingâþ mugen đone leóme geseón, Shrn. 12, 10-13.] Ne meahte hê æt his hige findan, Cd. 14; Th. 18, 1; Gen. 266: Beo. Th. 3322; B. 1659. Mehte, 2168; B. 1082. Eáþe heó mehte beón geseald, Blickl. Homl. 69, 7. Swâ swâ mihte beón fîf þúsend wera, Homl. Th. i. 182, 16. Đú meahtes geseón ǽgđer ge fêt ge heáfod, Past. 35; Swt. 241, 14: St. And. 10, 22: Exon. 39 b; Th. 130, 19; Gú. 440. Mihtest, Blickl. Homl. 175, 28. Đa ne meahton âsecgan, 145, 13: Cd. 115; Th. 150, 14; Gen. 2491. Wê đæt deór gewundigan ne meahte, Nar. 21, 4. Maehtun, Ps. Surt. 20, 12. Mehton, Blickl. Homl. 15, 13. Mihton, 79, 16. Đæt lâđra nǽnig sceđđan ne meahte, Beo. Th. 492; B. 243. Ôþ đæt đú meahte . . forsión, meahtes . . lâcan, Bt. Met. Fox 24, 11-17; Met. 24, 6-9. Mihte, Blickl. Homl. 45, 27. Swâ hit men fægrost geþencean meahton, 125, 23: Elen. Kmbl. 648; El. 324. Meahten, Exon. 64 a; Th. 236, 13; Ph. 573. Meahte, 39 a; Th. 128, 14; Gú. 404. Mehten, Ors. 3, 1; Swt. 98, 3. Mihtan, Blickl. Homl. 45, 14: 137, 1. Mihten, Cd. 224; Th. 298, 11; Sat. 500 Mihton, Blickl. Homl. 49, 10. Mihte, Ps. Th. 77, 1. (2) *followed, by a clause*:—Hwâ mæg đæt hê ne wundrige, Bt. 34, 10; Fox 150, 9. (3) *with ellipsis of the infin.* (*a*) *of a verb which occurs elsewhere in the sentence*:—Gêlácna đú hý forđan đú êđest miht (gelâcnian), Hy. 1, 6; Hy. Grn. ii. 280, 6. Nelle ic aldre beneótan, đeáh ic eáđe mǽge, Beo. Th. 1365; B. 680. Đæs ofereode, đisses swâ mæg, Exon. 100 a; Th. 377, 22; Deór. 7. Telle đâs steorran, gif đú mâge, Gen. 15, 5: Bd. 5, 3; S. 616, 31. Forlǽte swâ hê oftost mǽge, Bt. Met. Fox 22, 18; Met. 22, 9: 27, 58, 66; Met. 27, 29, 33. Ârás swâ hê hrađost meahte, Exon. 49 a; Th. 168, 24; Gú. 1080. Wolde ic freóndscipe đînne, gif ic mihte, begitan, Andr. Kmbl. 958; An. 479. (*b*) *of a verb whose place is taken by* swâ:—Wolde freádrihtnes feorh ealgian, đǽr hié meahton swâ, Beo. Th. 1599; B. 797. Cwǽdon đæt heó rîce âgan woldon, and swâ eáđe meahtan, Cd. 3; Th. 4, 4; Gen. 48. Wyllen forsweolgan, gif hî swâ mâgon, Ps. Th. 123, 2. (*c*) *of a verb to be inferred from the context* (i) *verbs of motion*:—Nô đý ǽr fram meahte (*might escape*), Beo. Th. 1513; B. 754. Ic ne mæg of đissum lioþobendum, Cd. 19; Th. 24, 22; Gen. 381. Ne mæg hê on đæt *non intrabit in illud*, Mk. Skt. 10, 15. On đone forecwedenan portic mâ ne mihte *prædicta porticus plura capere nequivit*, Bd. 2, 3; S. 504, 38. Đæt ic up heonon mǽge, Cd. 222; Th. 291, 3; Sat. 425. (ii) *other verbs* (see also I):—Wel đæt swâ mæg *that may well be so*, Bd. 2, 1; S. 501, 18. Þuhte heom đæt hit mihte swâ, đæt hié wêron seolfe swegles brytan, Cd. 213; Th. 266, 15; Sat. 22: Andr. Kmbl. 2786; An. 1395. Wolde hyre búr âtimbrian, gif hit swâ meahte, Exon. 108 a; Th. 411, 28; Rä. 30, 6. Wîsdôm sǽde đæt men mihton (*could understand*) be Gode swelce hî mǽte, Bt. tit. 26; Fox xiv. 16. Ne mâgon đam breahtme býman ne hornas (*cannot equal*), Exon. 57 b; Th. 206, 29; Ph. 134. IV. *may* (*because a thing is permissible or lawful, because there is sufficient cause*):—Đú miht đæs habban þanc, đæt đú mînra gifa wel bruce. Ne miht đú nô gereccan đæt đú đines âuht forlure, Bt. 7, 3; Fox 20, 12. Hú miht (mæht, Lind.) đú secgan đînum brêđer, Lk. Skt. 6, 42. Đú meaht đê forþ faran, Cd. 26; Th. 34, 25; Gen. 543. Hié leng ne mâgon healdan heofonrîce, 35; Th. 45, 24; Gen. 731. Nú wit mâgon sorgian for his sîđe *we have good cause to rue his journey*, 38; Th. 49, 29; Gen. 799; Exon. 9 b: Th. 8, 34; Cri. 127. Hwæđer sêl mǽge wunde gedýgan, Beo. Th. 5054; B. 2530. Hit ne meahte swâ *that was not allowed*, Exon. 41 a; Th. 136, 29; Gú. 548. V. *in the Northumbrian Gospels the verb is used as an auxiliary in the translation of the Latin subjunctive, or fut. indic.*:—Synngiga mæge *peccabit*, Mt. Kmbl. Lind. 18, 21. Wê habbas ł mâgon habba *habebimus*, 21, 38. (*Also the W. S. version in* Mt. Kmbl. 26, 54, *has* hú mâgon beón gefyllede *quomodo implebuntur*.) Hú hine mæhtes tô lose gedôa *quomodo eum perderent*, 12, 14. Đatte hiá êton ł mæhton eata *quod manducarent*, Mk. Skt. Lind. 8, 1. Huu hine hiá âcuoella mæhton (mæhtun, Rush.) *perderent*, 11, 18. Mæghton (mæhtun, Rush.), Lk. Skt. Lind. 22, 2.

magdala-treów, es; *n. An almond-tree*; amigdala *vel* nutida, Ælfc. Gl. 47; Som. 65, 36; Wrt. Voc. 33, 34.

mage, an; *f. The belly*; ventriculus, Ælfc. Gl. 74; Som. 71, 43; Wrt. Voc. 44, 26. v. maga.

mâge, an; *f. A kinswoman*:—Elizabeþ đîn mǽge (mâge, MSS. A. B.) *cognata tua*, Lk. Skt. 1, 36. Seó cwên his mâge *regina propinqua illius*, Bd. 3, 24; S. 557, 24. Đa landes đe hire mâge hire geúþe, Chart. Th. 338, 14: 337, 27. From bearme ânre mâgan, Exon. 112 b; Th. 430, 25; Rä. 44, 14. Grendles mâgan (*mother*) gang, Beo. Th. 2786; B. 1391. Be hire mâgan (*propinqua*), Bd. 3, 8; S. 531, 3. Ne hǽme nân man wiđ his mâgan ne wiđ his mǽges wîf, Lev. 18, 16. Se wolde niman his mâgan (*cousin*) tô wîfe, Homl. Th. ii. 476, 19. Menn hæfdon on frymþe heora mâgan tô wîfe, Homl. Skt. 10, 215. v. mǽge, mâga.

mâ-geêct (mâ = *magis*, ge-êcan = *augere*), *mactus* (= *magis auctus*):—Đa mâgeêctan *macta*, Wrt. Voc. ii. 55, 3. Cf. 54, 71. Mâgeêcte *morota* (*macta?*), 57, 24.

Mage-sǽte, -sǽtan; *pl. The people of Herefordshire*, Chr. 1016; Erl. 158, 4.

mageþe, an; *f.* A plant-name, *maythe, chamomile, ox-eye*:—Mageþe *beneolentem* [*camemelon*], Wrt. Voc. i. 67, 27: *obtalmon*, 68, 50. Magoþe *optalmon*, ii. 65, 52. Đâs wyrte đe man *camemelon*, and ôđrum naman mageþe nemneþ, Herb. 24; Lchdm. i. 120, 14. Wildre magþan wyrttruman (*matricaria chamomilla*) L. M. 2, 22; Lchdm. ii. 206, 15. Magođe, L. M. 1, 64; Lchdm. ii. 140, 7. Đa reádan magoþan (*anthemis tinctoria*), 140, 4. [Maiþe *camomilla*, Wrt. Voc. i. 140, 27. Mathen (maythe) *ameroke*, 162, 20. Maythe *embroca*, 190, 51. See Lchdm. ii. 398, col. 2, iii. 337, col. 1, and E. D. S. Plant-names under *mathes* and *May-weed*.] v. mægþa.

magister, mægister, es; *m. A master*:—Se magister, Past. 61; Swt. 455, 20. Byrla magister (cf. byrla ealdor, v. 20), Gen. 40, 21. Mægister, Wrt. Voc. i. 75, 6. Mîn mægister Euripides, Bt. 31, 1; Fox 112, 20. For his magistre, Bd. 1, 7; S. 477, 10. Đeáh hió hire magister lufige, Bt. 25; Fox 88, 10. His âgenne mægistre, 29, 2; Fox 104, 19. Magistra betst, Bt. Met. Fox 30, 8; Met. 30, 4. Hî hæfdan magistras, Bd. 4, 2; S. 565, 34. Mægestras, Ex. 1, 11.

magu, a; *m.* I. *A child, son*:—Đâ wearþ eafora fêded, mago Caines, Malalahel, Cd. 58; Th. 70, 28; Gen. 1160. Mago Ecglâfes (cf. Ecglâfes bearn, 1003), Beo. Th. 2935; B. 1465. Mago Healfdenes (cf. sunu Healfdenes, 541), 3738; B. 1867: 4027; B. 2011. Eald fæder ongon his mago monian, Exon. 80 b; Th. 303, 28; Fä. 60. Đînum magum (mâgum?) lǽf folc and rîce, Beo. Th. 2361; B. 1178. II. *a young person, a servant* (cf. cniht, cnapa, geongra):—Ongan his magu frignan (cf. ombehtþegn, l. 9), Exon. 47 b; Th. 162, 30; Gū. 983. III. *a young, strong man, a man* (cf. cniht):—Hwǣr cwom mearg hwǣr cwom mago *where is the steed gone? where his rider?* 77 b; Th. 291, 34; Wand. 92. Mago Ebrēa (*Abraham*), Cd. 100; Th. 132, 34; Gen. 2203: 109; Th. 145, 25; Gen. 2411: 127; Th. 161, 32; Gen. 2674. Maga gemēdu, Beo. Th. 499; B. 247. [*Goth.* magus παῖς (*puer, servus*): *O. Sax.* magu *child*: *Icel.* mögr *a son, a man.*]

magu-dryht, e; *f. A band of young men*:—Ōþ ðæt seó geóguþ geweóx, magodriht micel, Beo. Th. 134; B. 67.

magu-geóguþ, e; *f. Youth*, Exon. 28 b; Th. 87, 23; Cri. 1429. [Cf. *O. Sax.* magu-jung *young*].

magu-rǣdend, es; *m. One who advises men*:—Woldon cræfta gehygd magorǣdendes (*St. Andrew*) mōd oncyrran, Andr. Kmbl. 2920; An. 1463.

magu-rǣswa, an; *m. A leader of men, a chief*:—Se magorǣswa mǣgþe sīnre dōmas sægde, Cd. 79; Th. 98, 2; Gen. 1624. Se ðe lǣdde, mōdig magorǣswa (MS. -ræwa), 145; Th. 181, 2; Exod. 55: 143; Th. 178, 25; Exod. 17.

magu-rinc, es; *m. A child, young man, a man, warrior*:—Se magorinc sceal wesan Ismahel hāten, Cd. 104; Th. 138, 2; Gen. 2285: (*Isaac*), 106; Th. 140, 15; Gen. 2328. Ða magorincas (*youths*), Abraham and Loth, 82; Th. 103, 6; Gen. 1714: (*Cato and Brutus*), Bt. Met. Fox 10, 111; Met. 10, 56. Cwom LX monna . . ne meahton magorincas ofer mere feolan, Exon. 106 a; Th. 404, 9; Rā. 23, 5. Magorinca heáp (*the men in Hrothgar's hall*), Beo. Th. 1464; B. 730. Magorinca mōd, Bt. Met. Fox 1, 51; Met. 1, 26.

magu-þegn, *m. A thane, vassal, follower, retainer, warrior, servant*:—Ic eom Higelāces mǣg and magoþegn, Beo. Th. 820; B. 408: (*Beowulf's follower, Wiglaf*), 5507; B. 2757. Mǣrum maguþegne (*a retainer of Hrothgar*), 4164; B. 2079: (*God's servant, Matthew*), Andr. Kmbl. 188; An. 94: (*St. Andrew*), 2416; An. 1209. His engel, mǣrne maguþegn, 731; An. 366. Ic maguþegnas (*servants*) mīne hāte flotan eówerne healdan, Beo. Th. 591; B. 293. Mōdige maguþegnas (*the Mermedonians*), Andr. Kmbl. 2281; An. 1142: 3028; An. 1517: Exon. 77 a; Th. 290, 8; Wand. 62: Judth. 12; Thw. 25, 1; Jud. 236. Magoþegna ðone sēlestan (*Æschere* s. vv. 2654 sqq.), Beo. Th. 2815; B. 1405.

magu-timber, es; *n.* I. *A child*:—Ðā heó wæs magotimbre eácen worden *when she was with child*, Cd. 101; Th. 134, 36; Gen. 2235. Mē sealde sunu sigora waldend, and mē cearsorge mid ðȳs magotimbre of mōde āsceáf, 55; Th. 68, 10; Gen. 1115. [Cf. *Icel.* manns-efni (efni *material, stuff*) *a promising young man.*] II. *progeny, all those who are born*:—Ne sȳ ðæs magutimbres gemet ofer eorþan gif hī ne wanige se ðās worulde teóde *there would be no bounds upon earth to those who are born, if they waned not through him that created the world*, Exon. 89 a; Th. 335, 13; Gn. Ex. 33.

magu-tudor, es; *n. Offspring*:—Ǣr ðȳ magotudre mōdor wǣre eácen be eorle, Cd. 132; Th. 167, 13; Gen. 2765. Ūs ðis se æþeling gefremede . . monnes magutudre *for us, the human race, the prince* (*Christ*) *did this*, Exon. 17 a; Th. 39, 28; Cri. 629. Cf. magu-timber.

māh; *adj. Wicked, wanton*, Exon. 95 a; Th. 354, 47; Reim. 62. v. ge-māh.

māl, es; *n. A mole, spot, mark*:—Fūll maal on [h]rægel *stigmentum*, Ælfc. Gl. 28; Som. 61, 13; Wrt. Voc. 26, 12. Māl *maculam*, Wrt. Voc. ii. 57, 9: 92, 19. [*Goth.* mail *spot, blemish*: *O. H. Ger.* meil.]

māl, es; *n.* I. *an action, suit, cause*:—Māl *clasma* (cf. *clasma* clam oððe wed oððe wæra. 'This barbarous word meant in medieval Latin, an action at law, for a bond or other obligation,' 21, 2), Wrt. Voc. ii. 83, 42: Hpt. Gl. 496, 4. [*Icel.* māl *an action*: *O. H. Ger.* mahal *concio, pactio, fœdus.*] II. occurring late in the chronicle and borrowed from Icelandic (?):—Ðǣr bær Godwine up his māl (*case*) (cf. *Icel.* bera upp māl), Chr. 1052; Erl. 187, 19. Eádwerd scylode ix scypa of māle (= *Icel.* skilja af māli) *put an end to the agreement with, paid off, nine ships*, 1049; Erl. 174, 38. Hē sette ealle ða litsmen of māle, 1050; Erl. 176, 13. Se cyng sealde his lande swā deóre tō māle swā heó deórost mihte *made as hard terms as ever he could*, 1086; Erl. 220, 8. [*Icel.* māl *a case; terms, agreement.*] v. mǣl *and next word.*

māl-dæg, es; *m. An agreement, covenant, settlement* (?) (*Icel.* māldagi) *or a day on which terms are fixed* (?) (*O. H. Ger.* mahal-tag *dies sponsionis*) *a day when the dowry was settled*:—Ic an mīne wife al þe þing þe ic haue on Norfolke so ic hire gaf tō mund and to māldage, Chart. Th. 574, 1. v. mǣl-dæg.

māletung, e; *f. Verbosity*:—Hlȳdig gewyrd, malelung (maletung?) *garrula verbositas*, Hpt. Gl. 439, 60.

malscra. v. next word.

malscrung, e; *f. Bewitching, fascination*:—Malscrung *fascinatus*, i. *laudatis stultæ*, Wrt. Voc. ii. 35, 7: *fescinatio*, 108, 23. Wið malscrunge, Lchdm. iii. 36, 13. Wið feóndes costunga and nihtgengan and maran and malscra (malscrunga?), L. M. 3, 1; Lchdm. ii. 306, 13. [*O. H. Ger.* mascrunc *fascinatio, laus stulta*: cf. *Goth.* untila-malsks προπετής: *O. Sax.* malsk *proud*: *Allit. pms.* Þe mon malskred (*fascinated, spell-bound*) in drede; þat malscrande mere: *Will.* hou he hade . . malskrid (*wandered as under the influence of a charm, mazed*) aboute.]

māl-sweord, es; *n. A sword with inlaid ornament*:—Ic geann ðæs mālswurdes, Chart. Th. 560, 33. [Cf. *Icel.* māla-sax *an inlaid sword.*]

malt, malu. v. mealt, mealu.

Mame-ceaster, e; *f. Manchester*:—Mameceaster on Norþhymbrum, Chr. 923; Erl. 110, 4.

mamme, an; *f. A teat, breast* (*Lat.* mamma):—An mamman *in papillas*, Germ. 401, 77.

mamor, es; *m. Deep sleep, unconsciousness*:—Mamor *soporem*, Kent. Gl. 695. Momna (= mamor?) *sopor*, Wrt. Voc. ii. 120, 82. v. next word.

mamorian, mamrian *to be deep in thought about anything* (?):—Hī mamriaþ mān and unriht *they are plunged in thought of crime and wrong*; scrutantes scrutinio, Ps. Th. 63, 5. [*Somner gives* mamerung *dormitio, dormitatio*: cf. *later English* mammering:—He sits now in a *mammering*, As one that minds it not. Halliw. Dict. q. v. See also Nare's Glossary.]

man, mon; *indef. pron.* (*originally nom. of noun* mann q. v.; cf. *French* on *from* homo). *One, anyone, they, people*; it is often used with the active voice where modern English would take the passive:—Man brohte his heáfod on ānum disce and sealde ðam mǣdene *allatum est caput ejus in disco, et datum est puellæ*, Mt. Kmbl. 14, 11. Tō middyre nihte man hrȳmde *media nocte clamor factus est*, 25, 6. His brōþur Horsa man ofslōg, Chr. 455; Erl. 12, 15. Man gehālgode ii. biscopas on his stal, 678; Erl. 41, 7. Hine man hēng . . Hyne man dyde up and hine man efosode and scrȳdde hine and brohte hine tō ðam cynge *ille suspensus est in cruce. Eductum de carcere Joseph totonderunt, ac veste mutata obtulerunt regi*, Gen. 41, 13, 14. Ne ete man his flǣsc *non comedentur carnes ejus*, Ex. 21, 28. Gif hē næbbe hwæt hē wið ðære stale sylle sylle man hine wið feó. Gif man cucu finde ðæt hē stæl *si non habuerit, quod pro furto reddat, ipse venundabitur. Si inventum fuerit apud eum, quod furatus est, vivens*, 22, 3, 4. Hū mæg man (*quisquam*) ingān on stranges hūs, būton hē gebinde ǣrest ðone strangan, Mt. Kmbl. 12, 29. Worhte man hit him tō wīte, Cd. 17; Th. 21, 2; Gen. 318. Hit gedēfe biþ ðæt mon his winedryhten herge, Beo. Th. 6332; B. 3176. [*Later English* me: *Du.* men: *Ger.* man.]

mān, es; *n. A bad, shameful action, a crime, crime, guilt, wickedness*:—Maan *facinus*, Ælfc. Gl. 84; Som. 73, 98; Wrt. Voc. 49, 5. Mān, Wrt. Voc. ii. 34, 54: *piaculum*, 68, 68. Mān and inwit *guilt and guile*, Ps. Th. 54, 9. Mān and unriht *iniquitas*, 118, 69. Mān, yfel endeleás, Andr. Kmbl. 1388; An. 694. Mān and morðor (cf. *O. Sax.* mēn endi morðwerk), misdǣda worn (v. Fox 58, 2, hwilc mān hē weorhte), Bt. Met. Fox 9, 13; Met. 9, 7. Mānes *fraudis*, Wrt. Voc. ii. 33, 44. Mānes wyrhtan *peccatores*, Ps. Th. 100, 8. Māne *piaculo*, Hpt. Gl. 432, 50: Lev. 19, 29. Mid manegum māne *with many a crime* (cf. eác ðam wæs unrīm ōðres mānes, Met. 1, 44), Bt. Fox 1, 10. Gē mid māne men ongunnon *irruitis in homines*, Ps. Th. 61, 3: Cd. 16; Th. 19, 30; Gen. 299. For þȳ māne (*the murder of Abel*), Beo. Th. 220; B. 110. Māne fāh *stained with crime*, 1960; B. 978. Mān *nequitiam*, Ps. Spl. 72, 8: Ps. Th. 140, 4. Tō ðam ilcan men (*Achan*) ðe ðæt mān (*taking of the forbidden spoil*) gefremode, Jos. 7, 17: Cd. 10; Th. 12, 22; Gen. 189. Ne swera ðū mān (cf. *O. Sax.* ni thū mēnes ni sweri) *non perjurabis*, Lev. 19, 12. Se man ðe swereþ mān, 5, 4. For ǣghwæðerum ðyssa māna *utroque scelere*, Bd. 2, 5; S. 506, 40. Hī geclǣnsian ðæra ǣrrena māna *a pristina flagitiorum sorde purgare*, 3, 23; S. 554, 28. On manegum mānum (*flagitias*) hī sylfe besencton, 1, 22; S. 485, 12. Ealle ða mān (*scelera*) ðe ic ǣfre gefremede, 5, 13; S. 633, 8. [*Orm.* man inn aþess and i wittness: *O. Sax.* mēn: *O. H. Ger.* mein *nefas, inlicitum*: *Icel.* mein *hurt, harm.*] v. next word.

mān; *adj. Wicked, false, base*:—Mān inwitstæf *nequitia*, Ps. Th. 54, 15. Heora mænige māne swultan *many a wicked one of them died*, 77, 30. Nāuht ne deregaþ monnum māne āþas *nil perjuria nocet ipsis*, Bt. 4; Fox 8, 16. Mānum treówum woldon hié ðæt feorhleán, fācne gyldan, Cd. 149; Th. 187, 11; Exod. 149. [*Icel.* meinn *mean, base*: *O. Frs.* mēn *false* (*oath*): *O. H. Ger.* mein.] v. mǣne *and preceding word.*

man-. v. mann-.

mān-āþ, es; *m. A false oath, perjury*:—Se ðe mānāþ [*other reading* mǣnne āþ] swerige *he who commits perjury*, L. Ath. i. 25; Th. 212, 18. [*Orm.* þatt tu ne swere nan manaþ: *O. E. Homl.* man-að: *O. Sax. O. L. Ger. O. Frs.* mēn-ēð: *Icel.* mein-eiðr: *Da.* meen-ed: *O. M. Mod. H. Ger.* mein-eid.] v. mān; *adj.*, mǣne.

mān-bealu, wes; *n. Wicked injury*, Cd. 174; Th. 218, 27; Dan. 45.

mān-bryne. v. mann-bryne.

mancus, es; *m. A mancus, the eighth of a pound, the sum of thirty pence*:—Fīf penegas gemacigaþ ǣnne scillingc and xxx penega ǣnne mancus (*other MSS.* manccus, mancs), Ælfc. Gr. 50; Som. 52, 8. *In Cnut's laws the heriot of an earl included* twā hund mancus goldes (*which is rendered in a Latin version by* quinquaginta marcas auri, v. Schmid. p. 309, *so that the* mancus *is the fourth of a* marc), L. C. S. 72; Th. i. 414, 8. Cf. *for an instance of the manner in which this might be* *paid the will of an* ealdorman *where the heriot included* feówer beágas twegen on hundtwelftigum mancosum and twegen on hundeahtatigum, Chart. Th. 500, 3. *The value of the* mancus *is also seen from* L. Ath. v. 6, 2; Th. i. 234, 1:—Oxan tō mancuse *compared with* Th. i. 232, 7 *where an ox is rated at thirty pence,* be xxx pænega ođđe be ānum hrȳđere. The word occurs not unfrequently in the charters. Gedǣle hē ǣlcum mæssepreóste binnan Cent mancus goldes, Chart. Th. 471, 19. Āgyfe man mīnra (*king Alfred*) ealdormanna ǣlcum ān hund mangcusa . . . and Æđerēde ealdormenn ān sweord on hundteóntigum mancusum, 489, 29–33. Ic geann ǣlcum bisceope v. mancessa goldes, 544, 8. Ān hund mancosa, 596, 9. Mancussa, 530, 13. Ǣnne beáh on þrittigan mancysan, 501, 9. Ānes beáges on sextigum mancussum goldes, 529, 4: 531, 4. Mid xvi. mancussum reádes goldes, 536, 21. Tȳn mancusas goldes, v. mancusas goldes, 544, 11–14. [*O. H. Ger.* mancusa, manchusa, manchussa (*nummos*) *aureos, philippos, solidos,* Grff. ii. 808: *O. L. Ger.* mancusi *aureos.*]

mand, mond, e; *f. A basket, mand, maund* (archaic or dialectic v. E. D. S. Pub. Gloss. B. 1: 15: 16: Mid-Yorkshire and Lincolnshire Gloss. *Prompt. Parv.* mawnd, skype *sportula,* p. 300, see the note for other examples):—Mand *corvis,* Wrt. Voc. i. 291, 20: *cophinus,* ii. 74, 47: 104, 62: *qualus,* 118, 47: *corben,* 104, 42. Manda *coffinos,* 17, 47: 72, 68. Twælf monde fulle *duodecim cophinos plenos,* Mt. Kmbl. Rush. 14, 20: 16, 9. Hū monig monda *quot sportas,* Lind. 16, 10. Mondo, Mk. Skt. Lind. 8, 8. Huu monig mondo (monde, Rush.) *quot cophinos,* 19.

mān-dǣd, e; *f. An evil deed, crime, sin*:—Māndǣd *crimen, peccatum,* Wrt. Voc. ii. 137, 3. Māndǣda *scelera,* 149, 29. Hē sume māndǣde (*aliquid sceleris*) gefremede, Bd. 4, 25; S. 599, 34. Māndǣda forlǣtan *intermissis facinoribus,* S. 601, 27. His synne and māndǣde *scelera sua,* 5, 13; S. 632, 12: Exon. 62 b; Th. 229, 18; Ph. 457. Māndǣda *facinorum, peccatorum,* Hpt. Gl. 415, 14: 469, 9: *flagitiorum,* 529, 73: Ors. 1, 8; Swt. 42, 17. Đā đā hē đa mōdigan preóstas for heora māndǣdon đanan ūt ādrēfde and đērinne munecas gelógode, Chart. Th. 227, 21. Wolde mid māndǣdum menn beswīcan, Cd. 23; Th. 29, 16; Gen. 451. [*O. E. Homl.* man-dede: *O. Sax.* mēn-dād: *O. H. Ger.* mein-tāt *scelus, flagitium, facinus, piaculum*: cf. *Icel.* mein-görđ *offence.*]

mān-dǣde; *adj. Doing evil, wicked, flagitious*:—Hē sceal māndǣde men þreágean þearle *he must sharply rebuke evil-doers,* Wulfst. 266, 24: L. I. P. 2; Th. ii. 304, 18. Ealles tō īdele ǣlcere gōddǣde and tō māndǣde *far too deficient in every good deed and too ready to do evil,* 14; Th. ii. 322, 14. [Cf. *O. Sax.* mēn-dādig: *O. H. Ger.* mein-tātig *flagitiosus, sacrilegus.*]

mān-deorf; *adj. Labouring to do evil, wicked*:—Ne mæg se yfela preóst mid his yfelnysse, đeáh hē māndeorf sȳ and mānful on dǣdum, ne mæg hē nǣfre Godes þēnunge gefilan, nāđer ne đæt fulluht, ne đa mæssan, L. Ælfc. P. 41; Th. ii. 382, 12. v. deorfan.

mān-drinc, es; *m. An evil, poisonous drink*:—Đone māndrinc (*the poison from an arrow,* cf. ǣttren l. 7), Exon. 106 b; Th. 406, 6; Rä. 24, 13.

manetian (?), *to admonish, reprove*:—Gē monetigaþ Godes ēce bearn (cf. vv. 1331 sqq. *for the speech of the* ealdorsacerd), Andr. Kmbl. 1492; An. 747. Cf. manian.

mān-fǣhþu; *f. Guilt, wickedness* (cf. māne fā, morþorscyldige, Andr. Kmbl. 3196; An. 1601: *also* Beo. Th. 1960; B. 978):—Mānfǣhþu bearn (*those who were drowned by the deluge*), Cd. 69; Th. 83, 11; Gen. 1378.

mān-feld, es; *m. The field of crime*:—Mon hǣtt đæt lond Mānfeld đǣr hié mon byrgde *obruta est in campo, qui nunc Sceleratus vocatur,* Ors. 3, 6; Swt. 108, 20.

mān-folm, e; *f. A hand that does evil*:—Alȳs mē and genere wiđ mānfolmum fremdra beorna, Ps. Th. 143, 8.

mān-fordǣdla, an; *m. One who wickedly destroys*:—Mānfordǣdlan (*the sea monsters that attacked Beowulf*), Beo. Th. 1130; B. 563.

mān-forwyrht, es; *n. Sin, crime*:—Fore moncynnes mānforwyrhtum, Exon. 24 a; Th. 67, 28; Cri. 1095.

mān-freá, an; *m. The prince of evil, the devil*:—Morđres mānfreá, Andr. Kmbl. 2627; An. 1315: Elen. Kmbl. 1880; El. 942: Exon. 73 b; Th. 275, 6; Jul. 546.

mān-fremmende; *part. Doing evil, working wickedness*:—Mid mannum mānfremmendum *cum hominibus operantibus iniquitatem,* Ps. Th. 140, 6: Exon. 67 b; Th. 250, 34; Jul. 137: 29 a; Th. 88, 9; Cri. 1437: Elen. Kmbl. 1810; El. 907.

mān-full; *adj. Evil, wicked, flagitious, producing an evil effect, dire*:—Mānful *profanus,* Ælfc. Gl. 84; Som. 73, 101; Wrt. Voc. 49, 8: *infandum,* Wrt. Voc. ii. 111, 2: *flagitiosus, criminosus,* 149, 27. Mānfull *nequam,* Ælfc. Gr. 9, 78; Som. 14, 30: Mt. Kmbl. 6, 23. Mānful, 20, 15. Ān sundorhālga ođer mānfull (*publicanus*), Lk. Skt. 18, 10, 11, 13. Đæt mānfulle wuht *the devil,* Blickl. Homl. 31, 7. Mānfulles *fanaticae,* Hpt. Gl. 467, 61. Mānfulles scīnlāces *fanaticæ superstitionis, nefandæ vanitatis,* 488, 40: 509, 38. Becom đæt tō eáran đæs mānfullan (*nefandi*) ealdormannes, Bd. 1, 7; S. 477, 6. Đone mānfullan *flagitiosum,* Wrt. Voc. ii. 33, 52. Mānfulle and synfulle *publicani et peccatores,* Mt. Kmbl. 9, 10, 11: Mk. Skt. 2, 15, 16. Đonne ūs mānfulle menn onginnaþ *cum insurgerent homines in nos,* Ps. Th. 123, 2; Andr. Kmbl. 359; An. 180. Mānfulre wurte *dirorum* (*nefandorum*) *graminum,* Hpt. Gl. 450, 9. Sodoman and Gomorran đæra mānfulra þeóda, Gen. 14, 10: Andr. Kmbl. 84; An. 82: Salm. Kmbl. 298; Sal. 148. Đa mānfullan *infandas,* Wrt. Voc. ii. 47, 69. Eác mycle mānnfullran (*sceleratiora*) fremedon, Bd. 4, 25; S. 601, 29. [*O. Sax.* mēn-ful: *O. H. Ger.* mein-fol *profanus, flagitiosus, nefarius, funestus.*]

mānful-līc; *adj. Evil, wicked*:—Hē sǣwþ mānfullīce geþohtas intō đæs mannes heortan, Boutr. Scrd. 20, 17.

mānful-līce; *adv. Wickedly,* Scint. 4.

mānful-ness, e; *f. Wickedness*:—Git Martianus for his mānfulnysse nolde on God gelȳfan, Homl. Skt. 4, 389. Hē leornode ǣfre māran and māran on his mānfulnysse and ne lēt nānne his gelīcan on yfele, Ælfc. T. Grn. 17, 28.

mān-genga, an; *m. One conversant with* or *practising evil, a sacrilegious person*:—Đone māngengan and đone wiđfeohtend *rebellem ac sacrilegum,* Bd. 1, 7; S. 477, 18.

mān-genīþla, an; *m. A wicked, evil persecutor*:—Đæt ne mōton māngenīþlan, grame grynsmiþas, gāste gesceđđan, Andr. Kmbl. 1832; An. 918.

mangere, es; *m. A monger* (in iron-*monger,* cheese-*monger,* &c.), *merchant, trader, dealer*:—Mangere *mercator* vel *negotiator,* Wrt. Voc. i. 73, 72. Hwæt sægst đu, mancgere (*mercator*)? Coll. Monast. Th. 26, 23. Ne preóst ne beó mangere *a priest shall not be a merchant* (cf. *Icel.* prestar skulu eigi fara međ mangi nē okri), L. Ælfc. C. 30; Th. ii. 354, 1. Wē lǣraþ đæt preósta gehwilc tilige him rihtlīce and ne beó ǣnig mangere mid unrihte, L. Edg. C. 14; Th. ii. 246, 24. Heofena rīce is gelīc đam mangere (*negotiatori*), Mt. Kmbl. 13, 45. Đū herast đone mancgere đe begytt gold mid leáde, Homl. Th. i. 254, 25. [*Icel.* mangari: *O. H. Ger.* mangari, mengari; *Graff quotes an O. L. Ger.* fleiscmengere.] v. flǣsc-mangere.

mān-gewyrhta, an; *m. A worker of wickedness,* Ps. Th. 77, 38.

mangian; *p.* ode *To trade, traffic, act as a monger*:—Ic mangige *mercor,* Ælfc. Gr. 25; Som. 27, 12. Mid sceápum hē mangaþ *he traffics with sheep,* Homl. Th. i. 412, 6. Gif man mid cirican mangie, bēte be lahslite, L. N. P. L. 20; Th. ii. 292, 28. Hwæt forstent ǣnigum menn đæt đeáh hē mangige đæt hē ealne đisne middangeard āge gif hē his sāule forspildt *what does it benefit any man, though he come to own all this world by his trading, if he destroys his soul,* Past. 44, 10; Swt. 333, 9. [*A. R.* mangen: *O. Sax.* mangōn: *Icel.* manga *to trade*: cf. *Du.* mangelen *to barter.*] v. ge-mangian.

mangung, e; *f. Trade, traffic, business, commerce, dealing;* also *merchandise*:—Mangung *mercimonium,* gestreón i. *commercium,* Hpt. Gl. 500, 44. Mid mangunge ł gestreóne *commercio,* 478, 31. Fram mangunge *a negotio,* Ps. Lamb. 90, 6. Hig fērdun, sum tō his tūne, sum tō his manggunge (*negotiationem*), Mt. Kmbl. 22, 5. Se færþ embe his mangunge (cf. sume tō heora ceápe, l. 9), Homl. Th. i. 524, 12. [Cf. *Icel.* mang *traffic.*]

mangung-hūs, es; *n. A house for traffic*:—Ne wyrce gē mīnes feder hūs tō mangunghūse (*domum negotiationis*), Jn. Skt. 2, 16.

mān-hūs, es; *n. A house of wickedness, hell*:—Mānhūs fæst under foldan, đǣr biþ fȳr and wyrm, open scræf yfela gehwylces, Cd. 169; Th. 212, 7; Exod. 535.

manian, manigean, monian; *p.* ode. I. *to bring to mind what ought to be done, to urge upon one what ought to be done, to admonish, exhort, instigate*:—Đonne manige ic đæt gē eów ālēsan of eówrum synnum, Blickl. Homl. 51, 32. Ic myngige and manige manna gehwylcne đæt hē his āgene dǣda georne smeáge, 109, 11. Manaþ *cohortatur, ammonet,* Hpt. Gl. 451, 52. Uton forhradian Godes ansȳne on andetnysse, swā swā se wītega ūs manaþ, Homl. Th. ii. 124, 24. Monaþ mōdes lust tō fēran, Exon. 82 a; Th. 308, 7; Seef. 36. Ealle đa gemoniaþ mōdes fūsne fēran tō sīþe . . . swylce geác monaþ, Th. 309, 6; Seef. 53. Menede *instigavit, monuit,* Hpt. Gl. 511, 30. Hē manode hig georne đæt hig Moyses ǣ heóldon, Jos. 23, 6. Manade, Bd. 5, 13; S. 632, 11. Agustinus Brytta biscopas for rihtgeleáffulra sibbe lǣrde and monade (*monuerit*), 2, 2; S. 502, 3. Hine mid đisum wordum manode, Homl. Th. ii. 130, 33. Hī hī manedon and lǣrdon đæt hī him wǣpno worhton, Bd. 1, 12; S. 481, 5. Ongan hī manigean and lǣran đæt hī sibbe hæfdon, 2, 2; S. 502, 8. Manian, Byrht. Th. 138, 31; By. 228. Maniende *instigantes, incitantes, cohortantes,* Hpt. Gl. 416, 23. II. *to bring to mind what should not be forgotten, to admonish, remind, suggest, prompt*:—Forþon ic eów manige ealle đæt *therefore I remind you all of it,* Blickl. Homl. 143, 7. Hēr ūs manaþ and myngaþ be (*we are here reminded of*) đisse hālgan tīde weorþunga, 161, 3. Manaþ swā and myndgaþ sārum wordum Beo. Th. 4120; B. 2057. Mec đæs þearf monaþ, micel mōdes sorg, Exon. 76 a; Th. 285, 21; Jul. 717. III. *to tell what ought to be done, to teach, instruct, advise*:—Hē hié mid đissum wordum lǣrde and manode *he taught them what they should do in these words,* Blickl. Homl. 169, 12. Hē ūs lǣrde and monade, hū wē ūs gebiddan sceoldan, 19, 36. Hē dyde swā swā hē manede, Homl. Th. i, 238, 23. God bebeád Moyse đæt hē manode ðæt folc, ðæt swâ hwâ swâ âbiten wǽre, besâwe up tô ðære ǽrenan næddran, ii. 238, 17. Heó lǽrde hine and manede, ðæt ðæt ne gedafenade, ðæt hē sceolde his freónd on gold bebycgean, Bd. 2, 12; S. 514, 37. Fæder ongon his mago monian (cf. l. 13 lǽrde), Exon. 80 b; Th. 303, 28; Fä. 60. IV. *to claim of a person* (acc.) *what is due* (gen); in jus vocare (cf. *the Frankish* ad mallum mannire, *and the use of* monere *in the laws.* v. Grmm. R. A. 842; *Mod. Ger.* mahnen *to ask payment of a debt*: *Icel.* mana *to provoke, challenge*):—Hwane manaþ God mâran gafoles ðonne ðone biscop *of whom will God demand more tribute, than of the bishop?* Blickl. Homl. 45, 16. Drihten manaþ ǽghwylcne man ðæs ðe hē him hēr syleþ, 49, 31. Ðam ðe Drihten micel syleþ, mycles hē hine eft manaþ, Wulfst. 261, 22: 148, 18. Forgield mē ðīn līf...ðæs līfes ic manige, Exon. 29 b; Th. 90, 24; Cri. 1479. Lâþ se ðe londes monaþ, leóf se ðe mâre beódeþ, 89 b; Th. 337, 5; Gn. Ex. 60. Ðā cwæþ se ðe ðæs feós manode, Shrn. 127, 30. Mana ðone ðæs ângyldes, L. In. 22; Th. i. 116, 11. [*O. Sax.* manôn: *O. Frs.* monia *to admonish; to claim* (with gen.): *O. H. Ger.* manôn, manēn *monere, suggerere* with acc. of person (and gen. of thing)]. v. â-, fore-, ge-manian; maniend, manung.

mân-îdel; *adj. Wicked and vain*:—Ðara mūþas sprecaþ mânīdel word *quorum os locutum est vanitatem*, Ps. Th. 143, 9, 13.

maniend, es; *m. One who claims* (*debts* &c.):—Se wæs ǽrest theloniarius ðæt is gafoles moniend *he* (*St. Matthew*) *was first theloniarius, that is a tax-gatherer*, Shrn. 131, 24.

MANIG, maneg, monig, mænig; *adj.* I. with a noun or adjective, MANY, (with sing. noun) *many a*:—Ðǽr biþ swȳðe manig burh, Ors. 1, 1; Swt. 20, 14. Ðā wæs ymb ða gifhealle gūþrinc monig, Beo. Th. 1681; B. 838. Manig man cwyþ *multi dicunt*, Ps. Th. 4, 7. Geong manig, Beo. Th. 1712; B. 857. Monig, 345; B. 171. With a plural verb:—Wlanc manig on stæþe stōdon, Elen. Kmbl. 461; El. 231. Maniges þinges hē wilniaþ, Bt. 34, 7; Fox 142, 32. Ðises hī wundriaþ and manies þyllīces, 39, 3; Fox 214, 31. Mid manegum mâne, 1; Fox 2, 10. Manegum men þuhte, 11, 1; Fox 32, 24. Swīðe manigne hlâford and swīðe manigne mundboran, Shrn. 35, 32. Mid monige wīte, 101, 23. Ðē biddaþ manega þeóda, Deut. 28, 12. Hū ða monegan yflan wundor wurdon on Rōme, Ors. 4, 2, tit; Swt. 3, 25. Ic sceal ðara monegena gewinna geswīgian, 5, 2; Swt. 218, 20. Ðū bist manegra þeóda fæder, Gen. 17, 4. Hē sende Agustinum and ōðre monige munecas, Bd. 1, 23; S. 485, 27. II. used absolutely:—On manig dǽlan, Bt. 33, 1; Fox 120, 11. Ðū tōsyndrodest hig on manega, Hy. 7, 65; Hy. Grn. ii. 288, 65. Mænego, 9, 21; Hy. Grn. ii. 291, 21. Ðyllīcu þing and ōðre manega, Shrn. 35, 28. Mænige gefōþ hwælas, Coll. Monast. Th. 25, 1. Hwī ārīsaþ swâ mænige wið mē, Ps. Th. 3, 1. Ðǽr mōdlīce manega sprǽcon, Byrht. Th. 137, 43; By. 200. Hié witon ðæt ðæt ilce yfel ofereode, swâ ða monegan ǽr dydan, Ors. 5, 2; Swt. 218, 3. Manigra sumne *one of many*, Beo. Th. 4188; B. 2091. III. with a genitive:—Moniges breác wintra, Cd. 62; Th. 74, 31; Gen. 1230. Heáfod hē gebreceþ hæleþa mæniges, Ps. Th. 109, 7. Heora manigne ofslōg, Bt. 35, 4; Fox 162, 25. Monige sint cwucera gesceafta unstyriende, 41, 5; Fox 252, 20. Monige ðara brōðra sǽdon, Bd. 3, 8; S. 532, 4. Geseah hē rinca manige, Beo. Th. 1461; B. 728. [*Goth.* managa: *O. Sax.*, *O. H. Ger.* manag: *O. Frs.* monich: *Ger.* manch.] v. un-manig.

manig-brǽde (?); *adj. Consisting of many things*:—Mænibrǽde dōm *satura lex* (*lanx*?), Ælfc. Gl. 13; Som. 57, 111; Wrt. Voc. 20, 49. Cf. (?) brǽdan *to roast*.

manig-feald; *adj.* I. *Manifold, multifarious, of many kinds, various, consisting of many parts, complex*:—Mænigfeald *multiplex*, Ps. Th. 67, 17. Ys mænigfeald *multiplicata est*, 118, 69. Ðes pistol is swīðe menigfeald ūs tō gereccenne *this epistle is very complex for us to expound*, Homl. Th. i. 448, 7. Ūs þincþ tō manigfeald ðæt wē swīðor ymbe ðis sprecon, Lchdm. iii, 276, 8. Manigfealde *multifariam*, Wrt. Voc. ii. 57, 51. Manigfealdne *multimodam*, 58, 20: Exon. 17 b; Th. 41, 27; Cri. 662. On swâ manigfeald gedǽled, Bt. 34, 9; Fox 146, 17. Wē swâ monigfeald witon, alra tâcna gehwylc, Elen. Kmbl. 1284; El. 644. Ða manigfealdan mīne geþohtas, Exon. 18 a; Th. 453, 1; Hy. 4, 8. Þurh monigfealdra mǽgna gerȳno, 16 b; Th. 38, 7; Cri. 603: 42 a; Th. 140, 26; Gū. 616. For ðǽm mistlīcum and manigfealdum weoruldbisgum, Bt. prooem; Fox viii, 5. Hit sceal heonanforþ mænigfealdre weorþan, Wulfst. 83, 19. Monigfealdran, Exon. 51 a; Th. 177, 2; Gū. 1221. Wæs ðǽr seó monigfealdeste wōl, mid moncwealme, ge eác ðætte ne wīf ne niéten ne mehton nānuht libbendes geberan, Ors. 4, 1; Swt. 158, 17. II. *Manifold, numerous, abundant*; as a grammatical term, *plural*:—Menifeld *augmentatus*, Hpt. Gl. 440, 51. *Numerus* is getel, *singularis* anfeald, and *pluralis* menigfeald, Ælfc. Gr. 13; Som. 15, 59. Sume naman maciaþ heora mænigfealdan dativum on *-bus*, 7; Som. 6, 64. On hyra menigfealdan spǽce *in multiloquio suo*, Mt. 6, 7. Manifealde *copiosa*, Hpt. Gl. 468, 5. Mid mænifealdre *crebra*, 512, 34. Heora ǽhta wǽron menifælde, Gen. 13, 6. Hī cōmon swâ mænigfealde swâ swâ sandceosol, Jos. 11, 4. Mænigfealdum þénungum *exequiis pluribus*, Wrt. Voc. ii. 144, 78. [*Goth.* manag-falþs: *O. Sax.*, *O. H. Ger.* manag-fald *multiplex, frequens, varius.*]

manigfeald-lîc; *adj. Manifold, having many parts, of many kinds, various*:—Ðeáh hit ūs manigfealdlīc þince, sum gōd, sum yfel, hit is ðeáh him ānfeald gōd, Bt. 39, 6; Fox 220, 8. Forðon wǽron swâ manigfealdlīce sorga Cristes þegnum *therefore Christ's servants had such manifold sorrows*, Blickl. Homl. 135, 18. Sangeras and mæssepreóstas and manigfealdlīce ciricean þegnas *Church ministers of many kinds*, 207, 32.

manigfeald-lîce; *adv. Manifoldly, in many ways*; as a grammatical term, *in the plural*:—Monīgfaldlīce *multipliciter*, Ps. Surt. 62, 2. Wē mihton be eallum ðām ōðrum stafum mænigfealdlīce sprecan *we might speak of all the other letters under various heads*, Ælfc. Gr. 2; Som. 3, 10. Mænigfealdlīce *pluraliter*, 5; Som. 3, 42: 13; Som. 16, 9, 12. Se ealda mænegfealdlīce bæd *the old man made many prayers*, Glostr. Frag. 110, 18. Mænifealdlīce, Menol. Fox 185; Men. 94. [*O. H. Ger.* managfalt-lîho *multifariam.*]

manigfeald-ness, e; *f. Multiplicity, complexity; abundance, great number*:—Manifealdnes *perplexitas*, Wrt. Voc. ii. 68, 20. Of monigfaldnise *ex habundantia*, Lk. Skt. Lind. 6, 45. On mænigfealdnysse *in multitudine*, Ps. Spl. 65, 2: 68, 20: Cant. Moys. 7. [Cf. *O. H. Ger.* managfaltî *multitudo, affluentia.*]

manigfildan; *p.* de *To multiply*:—Ic mænigfylde *multiplico*, Ælfc. Gr. 24; Som. 25, 55. [Cf. *O. H. Ger.* managfaltôn *multiplicare.*] v. ge-mænigfyldan.

manig-sîðes; *adv. Many times, often*:—Manisīðes swutelaþ ðæt man wile on ǽnne God gelȳfan, Wulfst. 144, 11.

manig-teáw, -tîwe; *adj. Skilful, dexterous*:—Mænigtīwe *sollers*, Wrt. Voc. 73, 49. [Menituwe, 88, 48.] Mænigtȳwe, Ælfc. Gr. 9, 43; Som. 12, 67. Mænigteáwum *sollerti*, Hpt. Gl. 512, 29. Ðære mæniteáwestan *sollertissimæ*, 407, 65. v. æl-teáw.

manigteáw-ness, e; *f. Skill, dexterity*:—Mæniteáwnys *sollertia*, Hpt. Gl. 428, 3. Meniteáwnysse *sollertiam*, 407, 7.

MANN, man, monn, es; *m.* I. MAN, *a human being of either sex*:—*Hic et hæc homo* ǽgþer is mann ge wer ge wīf, Ælfc. Gr. 9; Som. 8, 54. Ðes mann *iste homo*, ðises mannes *istius hominis*, *dat.* ðisum menn, *acc.* ðysne mann, *abl.* fram ðisum menn; *pl. n. acc.* ðās menn, *gen.* ðyssera manna, *dat.* ðisum mannum, 15; Som. 18, 25–28. Uton wircean man (*hominem*) tō ūre andlīcnisse . . God gesceóp man tō his andlīcnisse, Gen. 1, 26, 27. Se man (*homo*) wæs geworht on libbendre sâwle, 2, 7. Wâst ðū hwæt mon sīe. Ðā cwæþ ic: Ic wât ðæt hit is sâwl and līchoma. Ðā cwæþ hē: Hwæt ðū wâst ðæt hit biþ mon ða hwīle ðe seó sâwl and se līchoma undǽlde beóþ; ne biþ hit nân mon siððan hī tōdǽlde bióþ, Bt. 34, 9; Fox 148, 3–6. Hū Hanna ân mon wæs onwaldes giernende, Ors. 4, 5 tit; Swt. 3, 32. Hiene ofslōg Othon ân mon, 6, 6; Swt. 262, 9. Hē geceás him tō fultume Traianus ðone mon, 6, 10; Swt. 264, 18. Hē ofslōg Albīnus ðone mon, 6, 15; Swt. 270, 10: 6, 26; Swt. 276, 23: 6, 31; Swt. 284, 20. Gif hund mon tōslīte, L. Alf. pol. 23; Th. i. 78, 2. Gif mon swâ gerâdne mon ofsleá, 28; Th. i. 80, 2. Syxhynde mon, 30; Th. i. 80, 11. Gif mon cierliscne mon gebinde, 35; Th. i. 84, 2. Hwæne secgeaþ menn ðæt sȳ mannes sunu *quem dicunt homines esse filium hominis?* Mt. Kmbl. 16, 13. Hwæt eom ic manna ðæt ic mihte God forbeódan '*what was I, that I could withstand God?*' Homl. Skt. 10, 191. Ðā ðū ǽrest tō monnum becōme *cum te matris ex utero natura produxit*, Bt. 7, 3; Fox 20, 10. Englas hē worhte, ða sind gâstas, and nabbaþ nǽnne līchaman. Menn hē gesceóp mid gâste and mid līchaman. Nȳtenu hē gesceóp on flǽsce būtan sâwle. Mannum hē gesealde uprihtne gang, ða nȳtenu hē lēt gân âlotene, Homl. Th. i. 276, 1–5. *Used of a male*:—Ðeós biþ gecīged fǽmne, for ðam ðe heó ys of were genumen. For ðam forlǽt se man fæder and mōdor and geþeót hine tō his wīfe, Gen. 2, 23–24. Gelīc ðam dysigan men (*viro*, cf. wīsan were, 24), Mt. Bos. 7, 26. Hē sǽde hyre hwæt heó man ne wæs *he told her that she* (*Eugenia*) *was no man* (cf. vv. 48–53 from which it is seen that Eugenia was dressed as a man), Homl. Skt. 2, 78. *Used of a female*, cf. wīf-man:—Ðæt se mon (*woman*) swǽte swīðe, L. M. 3, 38; Lchdm. ii. 332, 1. Ercongota hâli fēmne and wundorlīc man, Chr. 639; Erl. 27, 5. Agathes clypode: 'Mīn drihten ðe mē tō menn gesceópe,' Homl. Skt. 8, 185. His mōdor wæs cristen, swīðe gelȳfed mann, Homl. Th. ii. 306, 4. *Used of both*:—Twegen men, wer and wīf (*Adam and Eve*), 206, 21: Hexam. 17; Norm. 24, 24: Cd. 33; Th. 45, 18; Gen. 728. II. *a man who is under the authority of another* (cf. mann-rǽden), *a servant, vassal, liege-man*; as an ecclesiastical term, *a parishioner*:—Se cyng Melcolm griðede wið ðone cyng Willelm and his man wæs, Chr. 1072; Erl. 211, 6. Sȳ hit cynges man, sȳ hit þegnes, L. Edg. i. 3; Th. i. 264, 4. Sȳ ðæs mannes man ðe hē sȳ, L. C. S. 13; Th. i. 382, 20. Nân man his men fram him ne tǽce, ǽr hē clǽne sȳ ǽlcere sprǽce, 28; Th. i. 392, 11. Ne underfō nân man ōðres mannes man būtan ðæs leáfe ðe hē ǽr fyligde, L. Ed. 10; Th. i. 164, 16: L. Ath. i. 22; Th. i. 210, 20. Ealle ða landsittende men ofer eall Englaland, wǽron ðæs mannes men ðe hī wǽron. And ealle hī bugon tō him and wǽron his menn, Chr. 1086; Erl. 219, 4–6. Se ðe hȳ feormige oððe hyra manna ǽnigne, L. Ath. iv. pref.; Th. i. 220, 12. Eác is mæssepreóstum micel þearf ðæt hig hyra mannum cȳðen, L. E. I. 27; Th. ii. 422, 34. III. *the name of the Rune* for M, which is sometimes used instead of writing the word *man*, e.g. ǽnig ᛗ *quis*, Rtl. 11, 41. Ne ǽnig ᛗ *nemo*, 13, 25, 29. ᛗ byþ on myrgþe, Runic pm. Kmbl. 343, 11; Rún. 20. *So the compound* mann-dreám *is written with the rune in*, Exon. 124 a; Th. 477, 14; Ruin. 24. The word forms the second part of very many compounds. [Cognate forms are found in all the Teutonic dialects, but in Gothic a nominative occurs only in the weak form, and in *Icel.* the nom. takes the form *maðr.*] v. man, manna.

manna, monna, an; *m. Man, a man:*—Hwæt is se manna *quid est homo?* Ps. Th. 143, 4. On mannan mód, 117, 8. For ðissum earfoþnessum ðe wē ðissum mannan dydon, Blickl. Homl. 247, 18. Ic ádilige ðone mannan *delebo hominem*, Gen. 6, 7. God geworhte ǽnne mannan of láme, Homl. Th. i. 12, 29. Ðá wolde God wyrcan mannan, Hexam. 11; Norm. 18, 9. Gif man frigne mannan ofsleahþ, L. Ethb. 6; Th. i. 4, 6. Eorlcundne mannan, L. H. E. 1; Th. i. 26, 8. Gif frigman mannan forstele, 5; Th. i. 28, 10. Abraham, leófne mannan, Cd. 121; Th. 156, 11; Gen. 2587. Geongne monnan, Exon. 89 b; Th. 336, 9; Gn. Ex. 45. Fremde monnan, 90 b; Th. 339, 32; Gn. Ex. 103. [*Goth.* manna: *Icel.* manni.] v. mann.

manna, monna; *indecl. Manna:*—Nemdon ðone mete manna, Ex. 16, 31: Ps. Spl. T. 77, 28: Num. 11, 9. Monna, Past. 17, 11; Swt. 125, 19.

mann-bǽre; *adj. Productive of men:*—Ic tō̆wurpe ðás burh and tó yrþlande áwende, swá ðæt heó biþ cornbǽre swíðor ðonne mannbǽre, Homl. Th. i. 450, 12.

mann-bōt, e; *f. A fine to be paid to the lord of a man slain.* Its amount was regulated by that of the 'wer':—Síe sió mǽgbōt and sió manbōt gelíc. Weaxe sió [mǽg]bōt be ðam were swá ilce swá sió manbōt dēþ ðe ðam hláforde sceal, L. In. 76; Th. i. 150, 14–16. Æt twýhyndum were mon sceal sellan tō monbōte xxx. scill, æt vi. hyndum LXXX. scill, æt twelfhyndum cxx., 70; Th. i. 146, 13–15: L. Edm. S. 7; Th. i. 250, 21: L. E. G. 13; Th. i. 174, 27: L. C. E. 2; Th. i. 360, 7; L. W. I. 7; Th. i. 471, 11: L. H. I. 43; Th. i. 543, 27. [*Icel.* mannbætr; *pl.*]

mann-bryne, es; *m. A fire in which men lose their lives* (?):—Ðá wæs swíðe micel mancwealm, and se micela manbryne wæs on Lundene, and Paules mynster forbarn, Chr. 962; Erl. 120, 6. [Thorpe with previous translators renders the word by *fever;* Earle would read *mánbryne* = destructive fire. If *mánbryne* be taken perhaps an *incendiary fire* is meant.]

mann-cwealm, es; *m. Death of men, pestilence, mortality, slaughter:*—Mancwealm *pestilentia*, Bd. 1, 14, tit; S. 482, 14. On ðǽm dagum wæs se mǽsta mancwealm (*pestes plurimas dirosque morbos*), Ors. 1, 6; Swt. 36, 15. Se micla moncwealm *ingens pestilentia*, 3, 3; Swt. 102, 4. Ðý ilcan geáre wæs micel mancwealm, Chr. 664; Erl. 34, 21. Wæs swíðe micel mancwealm (cf. se fǽrcwealm ðe his (*Edgar*) leódscipe swýðe drehte and wanode, L. Edg. 5; Th. i. 270. 9), 962; Erl. 120, 5. On ða tíd ðæs mancwealmes *tempore mortalitatis*, Bd. 3, 30, tit; S. 561, 31. Mec ongan hreówan ðæt moncynnes tuddor sceolde mancwealm seón, Exon. 28 b; Th. 86, 33; Cri. 1417. Hú monege missenlíce moncwealmas gewurdon *quantae clades gentium fuere*, Ors. 1, 12; Swt. 52, 11. Manncwealmas (*pestilentiæ*) beóþ, Mt. Kmbl. 24, 7.

mann-cwealmness, e; *f. Man-slaying, homicide:*—Monncualmniss *homicidium*, Mk. Skt. Lind. (moncwælmnisse, Rush.) 15, 7.

mann-cwild, e; *f. Mortality, pestilence:*—On ða tíd ðæs miclan wōles and moncwylde *tempore mortalitatis*, Bd. 3, 13; S. 538, 15.

mann-cynn, es; *n.* I. *mankind, men, the human race:*—Engla hláf ǽton mancynn *panem angelorum manducavit homo*, Ps. Th. 77, 25. Sende se Fæder his áncennedan sunu tō cwale for mancynnes álýsednysse, Homl. Th. ii. 6, 17. For ealles mancynnes hǽle, Blickl. Homl. 129, 14. Ord moncynnes (*Adam*), Cd. 55; Th. 68, 2; Gen. 1111. Drihten of deáþe árás mancynne tō bysene, Blickl. Homl. 83, 21. Hié sceoldan geond ðysne middangeard mancynne bodian, 121, 4. Hine on woruld tō moncynne mōdor brohte, Cd. 132; Th. 167, 23; Gen. 2770. Hine feor forwræc Metod mancynne fram *the Lord drove him away far from men*, Beo. Th. 221; B. 110. Hē wolde mancyn lýsan, Rood Kmbl. 82; Kr. 41: Blickl. Homl. 71, 26. Hē ealle eádmōdnysse wið mancynn gecýðde, 123, 31. II. *a race of men, a people, men* (a limited number):—Ðonne is sum eáland on ðære Reádan Sǽ ðǽr is moncynn (*hominum genus*) ðæt is mid ús Donestre genemned, Nar. 37, 1. Æfter ðam ðe Iosue ðæt mankyn (*the Israelites*) gebrohte tō ðam behátenan earde, Jud. pref. 3. Hē ða burg gewann and eall ðæt moncynn ácwealde *he took the town and slew all the inhabitants*, Ors. 3, 7; Swt. 112, 16. Micel ðæs moncynnes sum ácwealde sum on Mæcedonie lǽdde *magnam Romanorum praesidiorum multitudinem partim occidit, partim in Macedoniam duxit*, 4, 11; Swt. 208, 15. [*Laym.* mon-kun: *Orm.* mann-kinn: *Ayenb.* man-kende: *O. Sax.* man-kunni: *Icel.* mann-kyn: *O. H. Ger.* man-chunni *humanum genus, generatio.*]

mann-dreám, es; *m. Human joy, joyous life among men, joyous noise:*—Ðú ne gemyndgast æfter mandreáme, ne wást bútan wildeóra þeáw *thy mind shall not be according to human life, nor shalt thou* (*Nebuchadnezzar*) *know aught but the habit of wild beasts*, Cd. 203; Th. 251, 30; Dan. 37: Andr. Kmbl. 74; An. 37. Cain fág gewát mandreám fleón, Beo. Th. 2533; B. 1264. Lifde and lissa breác Malalehel mondreáma hēr, Cd. 59; Th. 71, 26; Gen. 1176. Meodo heall moni g ᛗ dreáma full, Exon. 124 a; Th. 477, 14; Ruin. 24. Hē ána hwearf mondreámum from, Beo. Th. 3435; B. 1715. [*Laym.* þa aras þe *mondrem* þat þe uolde dunede aȝen.]

mann-dryhten, es; *m. A lord of men, liege lord* (cf. mann, II.):—Mandryhten, Beo. Th. 3961; B. 1978. Úre mandryhten (*Beowulf*), 5287; B. 2647. Mondryhten, 5722; B. 2865. Mondrihten, 876; B. 436. Æfter mandrihtne, æfter ðam æðelinge (*Nebuchadnezzar*), Cd. 207; Th. 256, 8; Dan. 637. Ðá ic ðæt wíf (*Sarah*) gefrægn wordum cýðan hire mandrihtne (*Abraham*), 102; Th. 135, 15; Gen. 2243. Hē fore his mondryhtne mōdsorge wæg (*of Guthlac and his disciple*), Exon. 48 a; Th. 165, 5; Gú. 1024: (cf. onbehtþegn, Th. 170, 29) 49 b; Th. 171, 10; Gú. 1124. [*O. Sax.* Mattheus warð im úses drohtines man, kōs . . milderan medgebon than ēr is mandrohtin wāri an thesero weroldi, 1200.]

mann-eáca, an; *m. An increase of human beings:*—Ðæt hié wǽron ortriéwe hwæðer him ǽnig moneáca cuman sceolde *ut defectura successio crederetur* (*on account of pestilence no children were born alive*), Ors. 4, 1; Swt. 158, 20.

mann-faru, e; *f. A going of men* or *a moving band of men*, v. faru:—Wē ðás wíc māgun fōtum áfyllan, meara þreátum and monfarum, Exon. 36 b; Th. 119, 20; Gú. 257. [Cf. *Laym.* al mi mon-uerde (2nd MS. alle mine cnihtes), 16453: he sende after man-ferde (1st MS. monweored), 10747.]

mann-fultum, es; *m. Military force, troops:*—Hié ǽr tweóde hwæðer hiene mon mid ǽnige monfultume geflíéman mehte *they before doubted whether he* (*Hannibal*) *could be routed by any troops*, Ors. 4, 9; Swt. 192, 16: 5, 7; Swt. 230, 9. Hié gegaderodon máran monfultum ðonne Philippus hæfde *they got together a greater force than Philip had*, 3, 7; Swt. 118, 16.

mannian; *p.* ode *To supply with men, to garrison:*—Heora ǽlc fērde tō his castele and ðone mannoden and metsoden swá hig betst mihton *every one of them went to his castle and garrisoned and provisioned it as well as ever they could*, Chr. 1087; Erl. 224, 16. v. ge-mannian, full-mannod.

mann-leás; *adj. Without men, uninhabited, deserted:*—Rōfleáse and monleáse ealde weallas *parietinæ*, Ælfc. Gl. 110; Som. 79, 35; Wrt. Voc. 59, 8. [*Icel.* mann-lauss.]

mann-líca, an; *m. A human form, image of a man, statue:*—Ǽfre siððan se monlíca (*the pillar of salt into which Lot's wife was turned*) stille wunode, Cd. 119; Th. 155, 1; Gen. 2566. Eall Adames cynn ðe mōdor gebær tō manlícan *all the race of Adam that mother gave the form of man to at birth*, Wulfst. 137, 26: Dōm. L. 131. Ǽnne manlícan (*the golden image which Nebuchadnezzar set up*), gyld of golde árǽrde, Cd. 180; Th. 226, 20; Dan. 174. Hē þurh dreócræft worhte stǽnene manlícan and ǽrene, and hié hié styredan, Blickl. Homl. 173, 23. Twegen manlícan (*images in the sick man's eyes of the observer*) beóþ on mannes eágum; gif ðú ða ne gesihst, ðonne swilt se man, and biþ gewiten ǽr þrím dagum, Salm. Kmbl. p. 206, 11. v. Grmm. D. M. 1133. [*Goth.* man-leika *imago: O. H. Ger.* man-líha *statua, imago, figura, effigies: Icel.* mann-líkan *a human image, idol, being in human shape.*]

mann-líce; *adv. Manfully, in a manner becoming to a man, nobly:*—Swá manlíce mǽre þeóden heaðorǽsas geald mearum and mádmum, Beo. Th. 2096; B. 1046. [*Icel.* mann-liga: cf. *O. H. Ger.* man-líh *virilis.*]

mann-lufu, an; *f. Love of men:*—Woldun ðæt him tō mōde fore monlufan sorg gesōhte, ðæt hē síþ tuge eft tō ēþle *they desired that for love of men care would visit his mind, that he might take his journey back to his country* (*and not remain as a hermit*), Exon. 37 b; Th. 123, 18; Gú. 324.

mann-mægen, es; *n. A force of men, a troop of men, cohort:*—Ðæt monnmægen ł þegna uorud *cohortem*, Jn. Skt. Lind. 18, 3. [Cf. *O. Sax.* man-kraft *a host of people.*]

mann-menigu; *f. A multitude of people;*—Manmenio (*the tribe of Reuben*), Cd. 160; Th. 199, 5; Exod. 334. [*Grein reads* mán menio *but there seems no reason to apply such an epithet to the* menio *in question.*] Ðēh ðe Sciþþie hæfdon máran monmenie *cum Scythae numero praestarent*, Ors. 3, 7; Swt. 116, 24.

mann-mirring, es; *f. Destruction of men:*—Ac man þǽr ne gespǽdde bútan manmyrringe *they did not succeed without loss of men*, Chr. 1096; Erl. 233, 29.

mann-rǽdenn, -rǽden, e; *f.* I. *homage, the condition of being another's man* (v. mann, II.):—Ðá cwǽdon úre frínd ðæt wē cōmon tō eówre manrǽdene *then our friends said that we should come and make submission to you*, Jos. 9, 11. Ealle hig bugon tō Israēla manrǽdene, 13, 1. 5: Th. An. 120, 27. Sum man deófle mannrǽdene befæste *a certain man sold himself to the devil*, Homl. Th. i. 448, 15. [Hē dyde ðæt ealle ða heáfodmæn on Normandig dydon manrǽden his sunu Willelme, Chr. 1115; Erl. 245, 12. Cf. Hí hadden him manréd maked, 1137; Erl. 261, 32. *Laym.* he heora monredne onfeng.] II. *service* or *dues paid by the tenant to the owner*:—Ðæt is ǽrest of ðam lande æt Nigon hídon seó mannrǽdden intó Tantún, cirhsceattas . . ., Chart. Th. 432, 22.

mann-rím, es; *n. A number of men*:—Ðínre mǽgþe monrím, Cd. 84; Th. 105, 35; Gen. 1763. Monrím mægeþ (mægþa?) *a number of women* (*the Egyptian women spoken of before as* freó and þeówe), 131; Th. 166, 15; Gen. 2748. Hwæt ðǽr eallra wæs on manríme . . . deádra gefeallen, Elen. Kmbl. 1296; El. 650.

mann-scipe, es; *m. Humanity, kindness, civility*:—Manscipes weldǽdum underþeódde *humanitatis offitiis deditos*, Cod. Dip. Birch 154, 38. Manscipe gyfan beþearfendum and ælþeódigum *humanitatem peregrinis et egentibus impendere*, 155, 5.

mann-silen, e; *f. The wrongful selling of men into slavery*:—Þurh mannsylena, Wulfst. 164, 1. Mansilena, 130, 1. Leódhatan ðe þurh mansylene bariaþ ðás þeóde, 310, 5. Cf. earme men wǽron út of ðisan earde gesealde swýðe unforworhte fremdum tó gewealde, 158, 13. *And see* L. Eth. v. 2; Th. i. 304, 14.

mann-slaga, an; *m. A homicide, man-slayer*:—Manslaga *homicida*, Wrt. Voc. i. 85, 44: L. Edm. E. 4; Th. i. 246, 7. Ne beó ðú manslaga *non occides*, Deut. 5, 17: L. Eth. ix. 1; Th. i. 340, 8: L. C. S. 41; Th. i. 400, 13. Gé sind manslagan *ye are murderers*, Homl. Th. i. 46, 24. Ðyder sculan mannslagan, Wulfst. 26, 14. [*O.H.Ger.* man-slago.]

mann-slege, es; *m. Man-slaying, homicide*:—Gif þeóf brece mannes hús nihtes and hé weorðe ðǽr ofslegen, ne síe hé (*the slayer*) ná mansleges scyldig. Gif hé æfter sunnan upgonge ðis déþ, hé biþ mansleges scyldig, and hé ðonne self swelte, L. Alf. 25; Th. i. 50, 18–21: Blickl. Homl. 189, 34. Be manslege. Gif Ǽnglisc man Deniscne ofsleá gylde hine mid xxx pundum, oððon mon ðone handdǽdan ágyfe, L. Eth. i. 5; Th. i. 286, 20.

mann-sliht, -slieht, -slæht, sleht, es; *m. Manslaughter, homicide, murder*:—Ða heáfodleahtras sind, mansliht . . ., Homl. Th. ii. 592, 4. Ðonne mæg hé beón orsorg ðæs monnslihtes (monnsliehtes, Hatt. MS.) *reus perpetrati homicidii non tenetur*, Past. 21, 7; Swt. 166, 20. Manslehtes beteón, L. A. G. 3; Th. i. 154, 5. Be monslihte (monnslyhte, MS. H.), L. In. 34; Th. i. 122, 15: L. Edm. E. 3; Th. i. 246, 1: L. Edm. S. 1; Th. i. 248, 1. Be ðám monnum ðe heora wǽpna tó monslyhte lǽnaþ. Gif hwá his wǽpnes óðrum onlǽne ðæt hé mon mid ofsleá, L. Alf. pol. 19; Th. i. 74, 1–4. Manslyht gewyrcan *to commit murder*, Mk. Skt. 15, 7. Hǽðenra manna hergung ádiligode Godes cyrican þurh reáflác and mansleht, Chr. 793; Erl. 59, 12. Manslæht, Confess. Peccat. Ðis synt ða ídelnyssa ðisse worlde . . manslehtas (*homicidia*), L. Ecg. P. i. 8; Th. ii. 174, 34: Wulfst. 164, 4. Ðǽr wǽron swá micle monslihtas on ǽgðere healfe ðæt hié mon bebyrgan ne mehte *inhumatas strages reliquit*, Ors. 4, 6; Swt. 176, 30. Ungetíma ǽgder ge on monslehtum ge on hungre, 1, 11; Swt. 50, 19: Chr. 994; Erl. 133, 18. [*Laym.* monslæht: *A.R.* mon-sleiht: *Gen. and Ex.* manslagt: *O.Sax.* man-slahta: *O.Frs.* mon-slachta: *O.H.Ger.* man-slaht.]

mann- (mán-?) **swica**, an; *m. A traitor*:—Ðyder (*to hell*) sculan mannslagan and ðider sculan manswican, Wulfst. 26, 15.

mann-þeáw, es; *m. A manner, custom, practice*:—Gé scyldigra synne secgaþ sóþfæstra nó monþeáw mǽran willaþ *ye rehearse the sin of the guilty, the practice of the just ye will not celebrate*, Exon. 40 a; Th. 132, 25; Gú. 478. Ðæt hé monþeáwum mínum lifge *that he live according to my customs*, 71 b; Th. 267, 4; Jul. 410. Hé forlǽteþ láre ðíne, and manþeáwum mínum folgaþ, Elen. Kmbl. 1856; El. 930. In monþeáwas, Exon. 55 b; Th. 197, 15; Az. 190. [Cf. þe hwile hit (*a child*) is lutel ler him *monþewes*, Morris Spec. i. 152, 432.] Cf. mann-wíse.

mann-þeóf, es; *m. A man-stealer*:—Manigu wítu [wǽron] máran ðonne óðru; nú sint ealle gelíce bútan manþeófe, cxx scill, L. Alf. pol. 9; Th. i. 68, 7. Cf. Gif mon *forstolenne* man befó æt óðrum, L. In. 53; Th. i. 134, 16. Gif þeówne man man *forstǽle*, L. Æðelst. v. 6; Th. i. 234, 4. Man-stealing is dealt with in Theodore's Liber Penitentialis: 'si quis servum alterius, vel quemcunque hominem, furtu quolibet in captivitatem duxerit aut transmiserit, vii annos pæniteat, ii in pane et aqua,' xxiii. 13. See also xlii. 5.

mann-þwǽre; *adj. Gentle, mild, meek, not harsh, courteous*:—Manþwǽre *cicur*, i. *mansuetus*, *placidus*, Wrt. Voc. ii, 131, 35; *cicur*, 17, 12; i. 288, 46. Cyningc ðín cymeþ ðé monnþwǽre (*mansuetus*), Mt. Kmbl. Rush. 21, 5. Milde and monþwǽre, Blickl. Homl. 71, 4. Earmum mannum milde and manþwǽre *pauperibus benignus et mitis*, L. Ecg. C. pref.; Th. ii. 132, 14. Manþwǽre (*propitius*) heora fyrendǽdum, Ps. Th. 77, 37. Mildheort and manþwǽre *misericors et miserator*, 144, 8: Bt. 42; Fox 258, 9. On þeáwum monþwǽre *moribus civilis*, Bd. 3, 14; S. 540, 8. On óðre wísan sint tó manienne ða monþwǽran on óðre ða grambǽran *quomodo admonendi mansueti et iracundi*, Past. 40; Swt. 287, 20: Ps. Th. 33, 2: 149, 4. God geriht ða manþwǽran (*mites*) on dómum, 24, 7. Manna mildust and monþwǽrost *most gentle and courteous of men*, Beo. Th. 6345; B. 3182.

mann-þwǽrness, e; *f. Gentleness, meekness, courtesy*:—Forðam oft gebyreþ ðæm monþwǽran ðonne hé wierþ riéce ofer óðre menn ðæt hé for his monnþwǽrnesse ásláwaþ and wierþ tó unbeald forðæm sió unbieldo and sió monnþwǽrnes bióþ swíðe anlíce *nonnunquam enim mansueti, cum praesunt, vicinum et quasi juxta positum torporem desidiae patiuntur*, Past. 40, 1; Swt. 287, 24. Manþwǽrnes *mansuetudo*, Ps. Th. 89, 12: 131, 1. Mycelre monþwǽrnysse (*mansuetudinis*) mon, Bd. 3, 3; S. 525, 31. On his hátheortnesse (*fervor*) and on his monþwǽrnesse (*mansuetudo*), Past. 21, tit; Swt. 151, 6. Scearpnyssa beóþ áwende tó smeðum wegum, ðonne ða yrsigendan mód, and unlíþe gecyrraþ tó manþwǽrnysse, Homl. Th, i. 362, 30: ii. 226, 9: Blickl. Homl. 33, 29.

mann-werod, es; *m. A band of people, an assembly*:—Ðá Philippuse gebyrede ðæt hé for ðæm plegan út of ðæm monweorode árád, Ors. 3, 7; Swt. 118, 33. Gemun ðín mannweorod *memento congregationis tuæ*, Ps. Th. 73, 2. [*Laym.* mon-weored: *O. Sax.* man-werod.]

mann-weorþ, es; *n. The value* or *price of a man*;—Gif mannes esne eorlcundne mannan ofslæhþ . . se ágend ágefe ðone banan, and dó ðǽr þrió manwyrþ tó. Gif se bana óþbyrste feórþe manwyrþ hé tó gedó, L. H. E. 1–2; Th. i. 26, 8–28, 1: 3–4; Th. i. 28, 4–8.

mann-weorþung, e; *f. The worshipping human beings*:—Wé lǽraþ ðæt preósta gehwilc forbeóde wilweorþunga . . and manweorþunga, L. Edg. C. 16; Th. ii. 248, 3.

mann-wíse, an; *f. Custom, fashion, usage, manner of men*:—Æfter monwísan *after the manner of men*, Exon. 9 a; Th. 5, 30; Cri. 77. Hé ðære mǽgþe monwísan fleáh *he shunned the customs of that country*, Cd. 92; Th. 116, 21; Gen. 1939.

mán-sceaða, -scaða, an; *m.* I. *A wicked and harmful person*:—Se mánsceaða (*the firedrake*), Beo. Th. 5022; B. 2514. Se mánscaða (*Grendel*), 1428; B. 712: 1479; B. 737: (*Grendel's mother*), 2682; B. 1339. Míne myrðran and mánsceaðan (*evil spirits*), Exon. 42 a; Th. 141, 5; Gú. 622: 46 a; Th. 156, 27; Gú. 881: (*the giants before the flood*), Cd. 64; Th. 77, 2; Gen. 1269: (*the Egyptians who oppressed the Israelites*), 144; Th. 179, 31; Exod. 37. II. *a sinner, one who wickedly does wrong*:—Ðonne mánsceaða fore Meotude forht on ðam dóme standeþ, Exon. 30 b; Th. 95, 20; Cri. 1560. Ðǽr fýr maansceaðan ða synfullan forbærnde *flamma combussit peccatores*, Ps. Th. 105, 16. [*O. Sax.* mēn-skaðo *applied to the devil and to the Jews.*]

mán-sceatt, es; *m. Usury, unjust gain*:—Of mánsceatte and of máne *ex usuris et iniquitate*, Ps. Th. 71, 14.

mán-scyld, e; *f. Guilt, sin*:—Ðú eart ðæt hálige lamb ðe mánscilde middangeardes tówurpe, Hy. 8, 23; Hy. Grn. ii. 290, 23. [*O Sax.* alāt ūs managorō mēnskuldio *forgive us our trespasses.*]

mán-scyldig; *adj. Guilty of crime*:—Mé mánscyldigne (*Cain*), Cd. 49; Th. 63, 7; Gen. 1028: 50; Th. 64, 11; Gen. 1048.

mán-slagu, e; *f. A wicked blow*:—Ne móton hié ðínne líchoman lehtrum scyldige deáþe gedǽlan, ðeáh ðú drype þolige, myrce mánslaga (*or* manslagan *in apposition to* scyldige?), Andr. Kmbl. 2437; An. 1220.

mánsumian. v. á-mánsumian.

mánsumung, e; *f. Anathema*:—Nellaþ ða apostoli nǽnne rihtwísne mid heora mánsumunge [ámánsumunge?] gebindan, Homl. Th. i. 370, 10. v. á-mánsumung.

mán-swara, -swora, an; *m. A perjurer, one who swears falsely*:—Gif man mannan mánswara háteþ, L. H. E. 11; Th. i. 32, 4: Exon. 10 b; Th. 12, 30; Cri. 193. Mánswaran, Blickl. Homl. 61, 13: 63, 13. Mánsworan, Wulfst. 26, 16: Exon. 31 b; Th. 98, 23; Cri. 1612: L. Ed. 3; Th. i. 160, 18, 19: L. E. G. 11; Th. i. 172, 19, 20. [*Icel.* mein-svari: *O.H.Ger.* mein-swero *perjurus.*]

mán-swaru, e; *f. Perjury*:—Mánswara *perjuria*, Wrt. Voc. ii. 96, 70: L. Eth. v. 25; Th. i. 310, 15: vi. 28; Th. i. 322, 15. [*Laym.* monsware: cf. *Icel.* mein-særi; *n.*]

mán-swerian; *p.* swór; *pp.* -sworen *To swear falsely, commit perjury, forswear*:—Gif man wát ðæt óðer mánsweraþ (*or* mán sweraþ, cf. se man ðe swereþ mán, v. 2), Lev. 5, 1. Be mánsworum. Ða ðe mánsweriaþ, L. Edm. S. 6; Th. i. 246, 14. Ne swerige hé ðýlæs hé mánswerige, L. E. I. 21; Th. ii. 416, 8. Ða mánsweriendan *perjurantes*, Hpt. Gl. 472, 8. [*Laym.* ꝥ he weore touward his lauerd manswore: *Scott.* to mansweir *to perjure*; manswearing *perjury*: Mid. York. Gl. main-swear *to forswear.*]

manung, e; *f.* I. *monition, admonition, advice*:—Seó monung ðære godcundan árfæstnesse *admonitio divinæ pietatis*, Bd. 4, 25; S. 599, 24. Ðá sealdon hí strange manunge *dant fortia monita*, 1, 12; S. 481, 13. Tó onfónne and tó ongitanne ða monunge ðære hálwendan láre *ad suscipienda et intelligenda doctrinæ monita salutaris*, 2, 12; S. 512, 26. II. *a claiming* or *exaction of debt, tribute, &c.*:—Gafules manung *exactio*, Wrt. Voc. ii. 30, 10. Ic beóde ðæt hý nán man ne brocie mid feós manunge, Chart. Th. 472, 10. III. *the place where toll is demanded, the district in which a power of summoning or exacting is exercised*:—Monno sittende æt gæflæs monunge *hominem sedentem in teloneo*, Mt. Kmbl. Rush. 9, 9. Nemne man on ǽlces geréfan manunge swá fela manna swá man wite ðæt ungelygne sýn, L. Ath. iv. 1; Th. i. 222, 9. Ðæt wé rídan be eallum tó mid ðam geréfan ðe hit on his monunge sý, v. 8, 2; Th. i. 236, 13. IV. *the people residing in such a district, and bound to answer his summons*:—Fó se geréfa tó mid his monunge, and ádríſe ðæt spor út of his scíre, v. 8, 4; Th. i. 236, 22. v. manian.

mán-wamm, es; *m. A blot caused by sin*:—Mánwomma gehwone geseón on ðám sáwlum *to see every guilty stain in the souls*, Exon. 26 b; Th. 78, 27; Cri. 1280.

mán-weorc, es; *n. A wicked work, crime*:—Gif mæssepreóst mánweorc tó swíðe gewurce, L. Eth. ix. 26; Th. i. 346, 4: L. C. S. 41; Th. i. 400, 14. Ðæt hý móstun mánweorca tóme lifgan, Exon. 25 b; Th. 74, 25; Cri. 1211; 72 b; Th. 270, 2; Jul. 459. Ðæt ic in mánweorcum mód oncyrre, 72 a; Th. 268, 28; Jul. 439. Ǽr man áweódige ða unriht and ða mánweorc ðe man wíde sǽwþ, Wulfst. 243, 19. [*O. Sax.* mén-werk.] Cf. mán-dǽd.

mán-weorc; *adj. Doing evil, wicked*:—Ðæt ðú mé swá mánweorcum inwrige wyrda gerýno, Elen. Kmbl. 1621; El. 812. v. mán-wyrhta.

mán-word, es; *n. A wicked word*:—Ys hyra múðes scyld mánworda feala ða hí mid welerum ásprǽcan *delicta ores eorum sermo labiorum ipsorum*, Ps. Th. 58, 12.

mán-wyrhta, an; *m. A worker of wickedness, a sinner*:—Mánwyrhtan *peccatores*, Ps. Th. 93, 3: *qui operantur iniquitatem*, 118, 3.

mapulder (-dur, -dor); *m.* (?) *f.* (?) *A maple tree*:—Mapuldur *acerabulus*, Ep. Gl. 26, 14: Wrt. Voc. ii. 99, 1. Mapuldor, 4, 26: L. M. 1, 36; Lchdm. ii. 86, 6. Mapulder *acer*, Ælfc. Gl. 46; Som. 65, 1; Wrt. Voc. 33, 1. Mabuldor *acerabulos*, 285, 35. On ðære (ðæne?) ealdan mapolder, Chart. Th. 146, 26. Tó ðon reádleáfan mapuldre; of ðam mapuldre, Cod. Dip. Kmbl. v. 298, 16. The word is found in several place-names in the Charters v. Cod. Dip. vi. 313, and still occurs, e. g. Mappledurwell in Hampshire, Mapplederham in Oxfordshire. v. mapul-treów, *and* cf. apulder.

mapulderen; *adj. Made of maple*:—Mapuldern *acernum*, Ælfc. Gl. 46; Som. 65, 1; Wrt. Voc. 33, 1. On mapoldren geat, Cod. Dip. Kmbl. iii. 81, 18.

mapul-treów (*it is made masc. in the following*):—In ðonne mapultré . . from ðam mapoltré, Cod. Dip. Kmbl. iii. 381, 1-2. v. mapulder.

mára, *more*. v. micel.

máran. v. mǽran.

marc, es; *n. A mark, half a pound* (in the laws only the half-mark occurs):—Swíðe strang gyld, ðæt wæs viii. marc, Chr. 1040; Erl. 166, 21. Six marc silures . . áne marc goldes, Chart. Th. 566, 21-29. ii marc gold, 567, 33. Tó marc goldes tó ðe kynges heregete and half-marc goldes ðe erl Harold and half-marc goldes Stígand bisscop, 573, 10-14. Wið x marcun goldes, Wanl. Cat. 150, 11. Gilde x healfmarc, L. N. P. L. 48; Th. ii. 298, 2. (See also several of the following paragraphs.) Tó viii. healfmarcum ásodenes goldes, L. A. G. 2; Th. i. 154, 1. [*O. Frs.* merk, mark; *f*: *Icel.* mörk; *f*: *M. Lat.* marca.]

mare, márels. v. mære, mǽrels.

mare, an; *f. Silverweed*, L. M. 1, 37; Lchdm. ii. 74, 9. [*Icel.* mara. v. Lchdm. ii. 399, col. i.]

margen. v. morgen.

marian. v. á-marian *and* mirran.

market, es; *n. Market*:—Ðat market æt Dúnhám *mercatum de Dunham*, Chart. Th. 422, 20 (a charter of Edward the Confessor). [Market and toll. Ic wille ðat markete beó in þe selue tún, Chr. 963; Erl. 122, 5-18.] [*O. Frs.* merked, market: *Icel.* markaðr: *O. H. Ger.* markat *mercatus, forum*; all from Latin *mercatus*.] v. geár-market.

marma, an; *m. Marble*:—Heó hæfþ hwítes marman (marbran, MS. H.) bleoh *it has the colour of white marble*, Herb. 51, 1; Lchdm. i. 154, 14. [Cf. *Icel.* marmari: *O. H. Ger.* marmul.] v. marman-stán.

marman-stán, es; *m. Marble, a piece of marble*:—Gehér ðú marmanstán, Andr. Kmbl. 2994; An. 1500. Þrúh of marmanstáne, Homl. Th. i. 564, 20. On ðam marmanstáne, 506, 11: Blickl. Homl. 203, 35: 207, 13. [Cf. *Icel.* marmara-steinar *slabs of marble*.]

marm-stán, es; *m. Marble, a piece of marble*:—Ðes marmstán *hoc marmor*, Ælfc. Gr. 9, 21; Som. 10, 31: Wrt. Voc. i. 85, 19. Of marmstáne geworht, Chart. Th. 241, 12. On mearmstáne, Exon. 60 b; Th. 221, 12; Ph. 333. Of fiðerscítum marmstánum geworht *made of squared blocks of marble*, Homl. Th. ii. 496, 35. [*Laym.* mearm-stán, marbre-ston: *R. Glouc.* marbre-ston: *O. E. Homl.* marbel-ston: cf. *O. H. Ger.* marmulstein *marmor*.]

marmstán-gedelf, es; *n. Marble-quarrying*:—Má ðonne twá þúsend cristenra manna ðe tó marmstángedelfe gesette wǽron, Homl. Th. i. 560, 32.

Maroara; *The people of Moravia*:—Hié Maroara habbaþ bewestan him Þyringas . . . Be eástan Maroara londe is Wisle lond, Ors. 1, 1; Swt. 16, 10-17.

martyr, martyre, es: *m. A martyr*:—Se strengesta martyr *martyr fortissimus*, Bd. 1, 7; S. 478, 33. Wæs se martyre from moncynnes synnum ásundrad, Exon. 40 a; Th. 133, 5; Gú. 485. Hé wilnade ðæt hé mid ðone martyr þrowian móste, Bd. 1, 7; S. 478, 18. Hí cóman tó ðæs martyres húse, S. 477, 9. Ðǽr martiras meotode cwémaþ, Cd. 228; Th. 305, 30; Sat. 655. Hé gemynegode ðara eádigra martyra, Bd. 1. 7; S. 476, 33: Andr. Kmbl. 1751; An. 878. Martira gemynd, Menol. Fox 137; Men. 69. Æfter gerisenre áre martyrum, Bd. 5, 10; S. 625, 17. [*O. L. Ger.* martir: *O. Frs.* martir, martil: *O. H. Ger.* martyr.]

martyr-dóm, es; *m. Martyrdom*:—Mid sige martyrdómes, Homl. Th. i. 374, 24. Hé (*Stephen*) is fyrmest on martyrdóme, ii. 34, 22. His martyrdóme wyrþe *ejus martyrio condigna*, Bd. 1, 7; S. 479, 7. Hé gearcodon heora mód tó ðam martyrdóme, Homl. Skt. 5, 150. Martyrdóm (*martirium*) þrowiende, Bd. 5, 10; S. 623, 36: Menol. Fox 249; Men. 126: 287; Men. 145. [*O. H. Ger.* martar-toam *martyrium*.]

martyr-hád, es; *m. Martyrdom*:—Se ðe rǽdeþ bóc mínes martirhádes, Nar. 47, 11. Hé martyrhád gelufade, Exon. 39 b; Th. 130, 24; Gú. 443. Ne heora martyrháda wona wǽron heofonlícu wundru *nec martyrio eorum cœlestia defuere miracula*, Bd. 5, 10; S. 625, 4.

martyrian. v. ge-martyrian.

martyrung, e; *f. Suffering as a martyr*:—Ymbe his martyrunga *de passione Christi*, Ors. 6, 2; Swt. 254, 24. [*O. H. Ger.* martirunga *passio*.]

masc, max, es; *n. A mesh, a net, toil*:—Ic wyrpe max míne on eá *pono retia mea in amne*, Coll. Monast, Th. 23, 9: 21, 13. On ðám maxum *in retibus*, 21, 19. [*Prompt. Parv.* maske of a nette *macula*: *Scott.* mask *a crib for catching fish*; to mask *to catch in a net*: cf. *Icel.* möskvi *a mesh*: *O. L. Ger. O. H. Ger.* masca *a mesh*; mascun; *pl. retia, plagæ, maculæ*.] v. mæscre.

mǽsc-, máx-wyrt, e; *f.* '*Mash-wort, the wort in the mash-tub.* On the malt boiling water is poured and allowed to stand three quarters of an hour; the liquid is wort, or mash-wort,' Lchdm. ii. 399, col. i:—Máxwyrte amber fulne, L. M. 1, 41; Lchdm. ii. 106, 16. Wylle swíðe on máxwyrte, 1, 36; Lchdm. ii. 86, 14. Dó picce máxwyrt on gemang, 1, 38; Lchdm. ii. 96, 18. [Cf. *Prompt. Parv.* maschyn yn brewynge *misceo*, maschynge *mixtura*: *Scott.* to mask *to infuse*; mask-fat *a vat for brewing*: *Dan.* mask *grains*: *Swed.* mäsk: *Ger.* meisch *mash*; meisch-fass *mash-tub*.]

máse, an; *f.* (*Mouse* in) *tit-mouse*:—Másae *parrula*, Ep. Gl. 20 b, 13. Máse *parula*, Wrt. Voc. ii. 67, 62: 116, 36. [*O. and N.* mose: *O. H. Ger.* meisa *parus, parix*: *Ger.* meise: *Du.* mees: *Icel.* meisingr.] v. col-, cum-, fræc-, hice-, spic-máse.

masian. v. á-masian.

massere, es; *m. A merchant*:—Gif massere geþeáh ðæt hé férde þrige ofer wídsǽ be his ágenum cræfte, se wæs ðonne syððan þegenrihtes weorþe, L. R. 6; Th. i. 192, 9. Ne beó ǽnig mangere mid unrihte, ne gítsigende massere, L. Edg. C. 14; Th. ii. 246, 24: L. Ælfc. C. 30; Th. ii. 354, 1.

maða, an; *m. A grub, worm, maggot*:—Maþa *tomus* (= *tarmus*), Ælfc. Gl. 23; Som. 60, 12; Wrt. Voc. 24, 16. Maða (maðu?) *cimex*, Wrt. Voc. ii. 131, 44. His gesceapu maðan weóllon, Homl. Th. i. 86, 10. Cf. Eorþ-mata (-maða?) *vermis*, Wrt. Voc. ii. 123, 44. [York. Gl. mad *an earthworm*: *Prompt. Parv.* make, maþe, wyrm yn þe fleshe *tarmus*: *O. E. Homl.* meaðen i forrotet flesch, i. 251, 19: *Goth.* maþa *a worm*: *O. L. Ger.* matho *lignorum et lardi vermis*: *O. H. Ger.* mado *tarmus, tarmes*: *Ger.* made: cf. *Icel.* maðkr *grub, worm*.] v. maðu.

maðelian; *p.* ode *To speak, harangue, make a speech, declaim*:—Maðelaþ *concionatur*, i. *conclamat, loquitur, contestatur in populo*, Wrt. Voc. ii. 135, 34. Maðalade *contionatur, declamat*, Wülck. Gl. 15, 36. Satan maðelode, sorgiende spræc, Cd. 18; Th. 22, 27; Gen. 347. Abraham maðelode . . ongan his brýd wordum lǽran, 86; Th. 109, 9; Gen. 1820: Beo. Th. 701; B. 348: 747; B. 371. Byrhtnoþ maðelode, wordum mǽlde, Byrht. Th. 132, 66; By. 42. Byrhtwold maðelode, hé ful baldlíce beornas lǽrde, 140, 60. Elene maðelade, and fore eorlum spræc, Elen. Kmbl. 807; El. 404. Wídsíþ maðolade, wordhord onleác, Exon. 84 b; Th. 318, 19: Víd. 1. Maðeliendra *concionatorum, rhetorum*, Hpt. Gl. 460, 76. v. mæðlan.

maðelere, es; *m. One who speaks* or *harangues*:—Maðelere *contionator*, Wrt. Voc. ii. 24, 72. Mótere *vel* maðelere *concionator*, i. *locutor*, 135, 32.

maðelig; *adj. Tumultuous, inciting to tumult* as in the case of one who harangues people (?):—Maðeli *tumultuosa*, Kent. Gl. 725.

maðelung, e; *f. Loquacity, garrulity*:—Maðelunge *garrulitatis, verbositatis, loquacitatis*, Hpt. Gl. 475, 42.

máðm. v. máðum.

maðu, e; *f. A bug, maggot* (?):—Maðu *cimex*, Ælfc. Gl. 23; Som. 60, 9; Wrt. Voc. 24, 13: 78, 69. [*Prompt. Parv.* mathe *cimex, tarmus*.] v. flǽsc-maðu, maða.

máðum, máðm, mádm, máððum, es; *m. A precious* or *valuable thing* (often refers to gifts), *a treasure, jewel, ornament*:—Gylden mádm, sylofren sincstán, searogimma nán, middangeardes wela módes eágan ne onlýhtaþ, Bt. Met. Fox 21, 40; Met. 21, 20. Máððum óðres weorþ gold mon sceal gifan *treasure shall change hands, gold must be given*, Exon. 91 b; Th. 343, 11; Gn. Ex. 155. Næs him tó máðme wynn, hyht tó hordgestreónum, Andr. Kmbl. 2228; An. 1115. Deórum mádme (*a sword*), Beo. Th. 3060; B. 1528. Ǽghwylcum eorla drihten máððum gesealde *to each the lord of earls* (*Hrothgar*) *gave a rich present*, 2109; B. 1052. Hē ðone māððum byreþ ðone ðe ðū mid rihte rǣdan sceoldest *he the jewel bears, that of right should be thine*, 4117; B. 2055. Māðm, goldhilted sweord, Exon. 114 a; Th. 437, 26; Rä. 56, 13. Ðis synd ða mādmas ðe Æðelwold sealde intō ðam mynstre . . ōn Cristes bōc mid sylure berēnod, and iii. rōde eác mid sylure berēnode, ii. sylure candelsticcan and ii. ouergylde, Cod. Dip. Kmbl. vi. 101, 21–26. Fato ꝉ māðmas *vasa*, Mt. Kmbl. Lind. 12, 29. Hió hyre ða betstan mādmas tō Cantwaran cyricean brohte, Lchdm. iii. 422, 14. Heora dȳre gold ne biþ nāhte wurþ wið ða foresǣdan mādmas (*St. Swiðhun's bones*), Glostr. Frag. 2, 30. Hī be hyra gate tō sǣ eodon, and mādmas ofer L mīla fram sǣ fættan, Chr. 1006; Erl. 140, 27. Ic (*Hrothgar*) ðæm gōdan (*Beowulf*) sceal mādmas beódan, Beo. Th. 776; B. 385. Māðmas, 3739; B. 1867. Ealde mādmas (*the spoil of the Egyptians drowned in the Red Sea*), Cd. 171; Th. 215, 19; Exod. 585. Welan þicgan, māðmas and meoduful, Exon. 88 a; Th. 331, 2; Vy. 62. Gehēt unrīm māðma and cynelīcra gyfena *promisit se ei innumera ornamenta regia vel donaria largiturum*, Bd. 3, 24; S. 556, 8. Ða ciricean giond eall Angelcynn stōdon māðma and bōca gefyldæ, Past. pref.; Swt. 5, 10. Unc sceal worn fela māðma gemǣnra *many a precious thing will we share*, Beo. Th. 3572; B. 1784: 5590; B. 2799. Ðǣr wæs māðma fela, frætwa gelǣded, 72; B. 36. Mādma, 81; B. 41. Dȳrwurþre eallum māðmum *omnibus ornamentis pretiosior*, Bd. 2, 12; S. 514, 41. Ðæt se fēnge ǣgðer ge tō lande ge tō mādmum and tō eallum his ǣhtum *that he should succeed to the land and to the valuables and to all his possessions*, Chart. Th. 486, 1. On circlīcum mādmum (*then follows a list of crucifixes, chalices and other valuables connected with a church*), 429, 11. [Se cyng sende his dōhter mid mænigfealdan mādman ofer sǣ, Chr. 1110; Erl. 242, 33.] Rūmheort beón mearum and māðmum, Exon. 90 a; Th. 339, 2; Gn. Ex. 88: Beo. Th. 3800; B. 1898: 2100; B. 1048. Wine Scyldinga fættan golde fela leánode, manegum māðmum, 4212; B. 2103. [*Laym.* maðmes; *pl.* (2nd MS. godes): *Orm.* maddmess; *pl.* (*the gifts brought by the Magi*): *Goth.* maiþms δῶρον: *O. Sax.* mēðmōs; *pl. gifts, precious things*: *Icel.* meiðmar; *pl. gifts, presents*.] v. dryht-, gold-, hord-, ofer-, sinc-, þeóden, wundor-māðum.

māðum-ǽht, e; *f. A costly possession, valuable, treasure*:—Ne nom hē māðmǣhta mā, ðeáh hē monige geseah, būton ðone hafelan and ða hilt somod since fāge *more things of price he took not, though many he saw, than the head and the hilt gay with gold*, Beo. Th. 3230; B. 1613. Draca māðmǣhta wlonc *the dragon proud of his treasures*, 5659; B. 2833.

māðum-cist, e; *f. A treasure-chest, treasury*:—Nys hyt nā ālȳfed ðæt wē āsendon hyt on ūre māðmcyste (*in corbanan*, cf. *Goth.* kaurban, þatei ist maiþms, Mk. 7, 11), Mt. Kmbl. 27, 6.

māðum-fæt, es; *n. A costly vessel*:—Māððumfæt mǣre, Beo. Th. 4801; B. 2405. Ðā genam hē ða māðmfatu, gyldene and sylfrene, binnon Godes temple, Homl. Th. ii. 432, 25. Ða mādmfatu ðæs temples ungerīme, gyldene and sylfrene, mid ōðrum goldhordum, 66, 7. [Ðā Ælfrēd king forlēt his mādmes and mādmfaten, Shrn, 16, 10.]

māðum-gesteald, es; *n. Treasure, riches*:—Eall ðæt māððumgesteald ðe in ðæs æðelinges ǣhtum wunade, Exon. 66 a; Th. 244, 32; Jul. 36.

māðum-gestreón, es; *n. Treasure*:—Næs heó tō gneáð gifa Geáta leódum, māðmgestreóna, Beo. Th. 3866; B. 1931.

māðum-gifa, an; *m. A giver of costly gifts, a liberal prince*:—Hwǣr cwom māððumgyfa? Exon. 77 b; Th. 292, 1; Wand. 92. [*O. Sax.* mēðom-gibo (*Christ*).]

māðum-gifu, e; *f. A costly gift*:—Æfter māððumgife, Beo. Th. 2606; B. 1301.

māðum-hirde, es; *m. A treasurer*:—Ða māðmhyrdas ðe ðæt feoh heóldon ðe mon ðām ferdmonnum on geáre sellan sceolde, Bt. 27, 4; Fox 100, 13.

māðum-hord, es; *n. Treasure*:—Māðmhorda mǣst (*the Ark with its contents*), Cd. 161; Th. 201, 6; Exod. 368. [*O. Sax.* mēðom-hord.]

māðum-hūs, es; *n. A treasure-house, treasury*:—Mādmhūs *gazophilacium*, Ælfc. Gl. 81; Som. 73, 11; Wrt. Voc. 47, 18. Māðmhūs, 86, 48: *erarium*, Wrt. Voc. ii. 30, 42. On ðæs cynges māðmhūse *in ærarium regis*, Gen. 47, 14: Ors. 6, 3; Swt. 258, 13. Gesæt se Hǣlend binnan ðam temple ætforan ðam māðmhūse, Homl. Th. i. 582, 12. Hē lǣdde ða ællþeódgan ǣrendracan on his māðmhūs and him geiéwde his goldhord, Past. 4, 1; Swt. 39, 3. Ðā fōr Julius and ābræc hiera māðmhūs (*ærarium*), Ors. 5, 12; Swt. 240, 15.

māðum-sele, es; *m. A hall in which a prince gives costly gifts*, or *a hall containing costly things* (cf. gold-sele):—Mēda māððumselas, Salm. Kmbl. 379; Sal. 189.

māðum-sigle, es; *n. A costly jewel*:—Geseah māððumsigla fela, Beo. Th. 5508; B. 2757.

māðum-sweord, es; *n. A costly sword*:—Mǣre māððumsweord, Beo. Th. 2050; B. 1023.

māðum-wela, an; *m. Wealth consisting of costly things*:—Æfter māððumwelan (*the contents of the fire-drake's cave*), Beo. Th. 5493; B. 2750.

matt, meatt, e; meatte, an; *f. A mat*:—Matte *spiato* (=*psiato*), Wrt. Voc. ii. 121, 7. Meatte *matta*, i. 82, 20. Meatta *storia* vel *psiata*, i. 41, 30. [*Prompt. Parv.* matte *matta*, *storium*: *O. H. Ger.* matta, madda *psiatum*, *matta*.]

mattuc, mattoc, mettoc, meottic, es; *m. A mattock, kind of pickaxe*:—Mattuc *ligonem*; mattucas *lagones*, Wrt. Voc. ii. 51, 35, 36. Mettac *tridens*, i. 289, 59. Mettocas *ligones*, *rastros*, Ep. Gl. 22 d, 29: *lagones*, 13 b, 20: *ligones*, 13 f, 1: Wrt. Voc. ii, 50, 77: *rastros*, 118, 68. Meottoc *tridens*, 122, 64. Meotticas *ligones*, 112, 66. Ðonne hēt hē hiene (*the rock*) mid fȳre onhǣtan and siððan mid mattucum heáwan *rupes igni ferroque rescindit*, Ors. 4, 8; Swt. 186, 19. [Mattok *bidens*, Wrt. Voc. 234, 10: *Prompt. Parv.* mattok, pykeye or twybyl *ligo*, *marra*. Welsh matog, *a hoe*.]

māwan; *p.* meów [cf. *Laym.* medewen heo *meowen* (2nd MS. *mewen*)]; *pp.* māwen *to mow*:—Ðǣr nǣnig mann heg ne māweþ, Bd. 1, 1; S. 474, 32. Gelīce ond mon mǣd māwe, Ors. 2, 8; Swt. 92, 15: Ps. Th. 128, 5. Rīpan and māwan, L. R. S. 2; Th. i. 432, 15. Māwenum hege, Ps. Th. 102, 14. [*O. H. Ger.* mājan: *Ger.* mähen.]

max, māx-wyrt. v. masc, māsc-wyrt.

mē; *dat.*: mē, mec, meh, mech; *acc. of pronoun of first person. Me*:—Ealle þing mē synt gesealde *omnia mihi tradita sunt*, Mt. Kmbl. 11, 27. Ælcne ðe mē (Lind. meh; Rush. mec) cȳð *omnis qui confitetur me*, Mt. Kmbl. 10, 32. Ða ðe swencaþ mec *qui tribulant me*, Ps. Surt. 3, 2, 5, 6. Hālne mē dōa *salvum me fac*, 3, 7; 4, 2. Se ðe gelēfes on mech (mec, Rush.) *qui credit in me*, Jn. Skt. Lind. 6, 35. Ne hæfes ðū dǣl mech (mec, Rush.) mið *non habes partem mecum*, 13, 8. Hē mē habban wile dreóres fāhne, gif mec deáþ nimeþ, Beo. Th. 897, 899; B. 446, 447. [*Goth.* mis; *dat.*; mik; *acc.*; *O. Sax.* mi; mi, mik: *O. Frs.* me; mi: *Icel.* mēr; mik: *O. H. Ger.* mir; mih.]

meagol, megol; *adj. Earnest, strenuous, firm*:—Ðæt ic Gode and Sancta Marian meaglum mōde on ēce yrfe geseald hæbbe *what I, with mind immovable, have given as a perpetual inheritance to God and St. Mary* (cf. the form 'Ego donationem *indeclinabiliter* consensi,' 322, 6), Cod. Dip. Kmbl. v. 331, 5. Mandryhten holdne gegrētte meaglum wordum *the lord* (*Hygelac*) *greeted his liege* (*Beowulf, on his return*) *with earnest words, gave him a hearty greeting*, Beo. Th. 3964; B. 1980: Exon. 43 a; Th. 146, 8; Gū. 706. Fugla cyn hine weorþedon meaglum stefnum, 46 a; Th. 157, 13; Gū. 891: 60 b; Th. 221, 22; Ph. 338. v. un-meagol *and following words*.

meagol-līce; *adv. Earnestly, strenuously*:—Hié ðone lifgendan God and ðone hālgan heáhengel Michael meagollīce (cf. Homl. Th. i. 504, 7 *where in the same narrative* geornlīce bǣdon *occurs*) gebǣdon *they earnestly prayed to the living God and the holy archangel Michael*, Blickl. Homl. 201, 13. Hē hafaþ wīslīcu word, wile meagollīce mōdum tǣcan, Cd. 169; Th. 211, 16; Exod. 527.

meagol-mōd; *adj. Of earnest mind, earnest, strenuous*:—Ic synful bydde ðæt ðū onsende in mē (mē in?) heortan meagolmōd gemynd and gedēfe hreówe and sōðe ondetnesse ealra mīnna synna *I, sinful, pray that thou send into my heart an earnest mind, and suitable penitence, and the true confession of all my sins*, Wanley Cat. 246, 9.

meagolmōd-ness, e; *f. Earnestness, diligence*:—Hē sang ǣghwylce dæge mæssan Gode tō lofe myd swȳðe mycelre meagolmōdnysse and myd wēpendum teárum *every day he sang mass to the praise of God with very great earnestness, and with tears*, Shrn. 98, 3. Ðæs wē sceolan mid ealre heortan meagolmōdnesse ūrum Drihtne þanc secgan, Blickl. Homl. 123, 16. v. next word.

meagol-ness, e; *f. Earnestness*:—Lufian wē hine mid eallre ūre heortan megolnesse *let us love him in all earnestness of heart*, Blickl. Homl. 65, 23. v. preceding word.

meaht, maht, mæht, meht, mieht, miht, e; *f.* (*but* mihtes, Ps. Th. 70, 18). I. *Might, power, virtue, ability*:—Meaht eorþlīces rīces *potestas terreni imperii*, Bd. 2, 9; S. 510, 13. Seó godcunde meht, Blickl. Homl. 19, 20. Gif hǣto oððe meht ne wyrne lǣt him blōd *if heat, or his ability to bear it do not forbid, let him blood*, L. M. 2, 42; Lchdm. ii. 254, 4. Miht is Drihtnes *potestas Dei est*, Ps. Th. 61, 12. Meahte *opis*, Wrt. Voc. ii. 65, 26: *potentatus*, 77, 78. Mihte lufigend *amans virtutis*, Ælfc. Gr. 43; Zup. 255, 10. His rīces ongin, ne his mehte, ne his mægenþrymmes nǣfre gewonad ne weorþeþ, Blickl. Homl. 9, 17. Ðīnes mihtes þrym *potentiam tuam*, Ps. Th. 70, 18. Meahte *nutu*, Wrt. Voc. ii. 60, 78: 91, 31. Ungelǣredne fiscere, nāwðer ne on worde ne on gebyrdum mid nǣnigre mihte (*ability*) gewelgode, Blickl. Homl. 179, 15. Hē on mihte (mæhte, Lind.) and on mægene unclǣnum gāstum bebȳt (*in potestate et virtute*), Lk. Skt. 4, 36. Būtan ðīnre miht *abs te*, Ps. Th. 138, 10. Maht *potentiam*, Ps. Surt. 144, 4. Meahte *numen*, Wrt. Voc. ii. 61, 25. Ðīn wuldor ūs gecȳð, cræft and meaht, Exon. 53 b; Th. 188, 11; Az. 44. Swā swā mæht hæbbende *sicut potestatem habens*, Mt. Kmbl. Rush. 7, 29. Ða mæhte (ðæt mæht, Lind.) seðe eode from him *virtutem quæ exierat de eo*, Mk. Skt. Rush. 5, 29. Hē nǣnige mehte wið ūs nafaþ, Blickl. Homl. 31, 33. Þurh his godcunde meht, 121, 15. Ðīn mægen is āterod and ða mihte ðū næfst, Homl. Skt. 3, 611. Se weard hafaþ miht and strengþo, Cd. 45; Th. 58, 22; Gen. 950. *Virtutes* sind geewedene mihta, þurh ða wyrcþ God fela wundra, Homl. Th. i. 342, 27. His meahte synt *powers are his*, Ps. Th. 98, 10. Þurh ðīnra mehta spēd *through the abundance of thy powers*, Bt. Met. Fox 4, 64; Met. 4, 32. His mihta name *nomen majestatis ejus*, Ps. Th. 71, 19. Ðū sǽs wealdest mihtum *tu dominaris potestati maris*, 88, 8. Gāstes miehtum, Hy. 8, 12; Hy. Grn. ii. 290, 12. Eallum hire mihtum and mægenum *with all her might and main*, L. M. 3, 63; Lchdm. ii. 352, 5. Eallum mihtum, L. C. E. 20; Th. i. 372, 9. Mid eallum mægene and eallum mihtum *ex omni virtute, et omnibus viribus*, L. Ecg. C. pref.; Th. ii. 132, 13. On hyre yldrena mihtum *in potestate parentum suorum*, 27; Th. ii. 152, 15. Ðæt geþyld oferswīðdum leahtrum sprecþ tō ðām mihton (mægnum, 28 a) *patientia devictis vitiis ad virtutes loquitur*, Prud. 28 b. On dīne ða myclan mihte *in potentias Domini*, Ps. Th. 70, 15. Mihta strange, 102, 6. II. *an exercise of power, mighty work*:—Swilce mihta (mæhto, Lind.: mæhte, Rush.) ðe þurh his handa gewordene synd *virtutes tales quæ per manus ejus efficiuntur*, Mk. Skt. 6, 2. Ne dyde mæhto ł mægno monigo *non fecit virtutes multas*, Mt. Kmbl. Lind. 13, 58: 14, 2. [*O. E. Homl.* maht: *Laym.* mæht, miht: *Orm.* mahht, mihht: *Ayenb.* miȝt: *Goth.* mahts: *O. Sax.* maht: *O. Frs.* macht, meht: *Icel.* māttr: *O. M. H. Ger.* maht: *Ger.* macht: *Du.* magt.] v. eall-, heáh-, un-meaht.

meaht; *adj.* I. *mighty, powerful*:—Se meahta moncynnes fruma, Exon. 61 a; Th. 224, 17; Ph. 377. Se micla dæg meahtan Dryhtnes, 20 b; Th. 54, 16; Cri. 869. Ealle dīnes mūðes meahte dōmas, Ps. Th. 118, 13. II. *possible*:—Alle mæhte sindun mið God *omnia possibilia sunt apud Deum*, Mk. Skt. Rush. 10, 27. [*Goth.* mahts *possible.*] v. æl-miht.

meahte-, meaht-līc; *adj. Possible*:—Gode synt mihtelīce ða ðing ðe mannum synt unmihtelīce *quæ impossibilia sunt apud homines possibilia sunt apud Deum*, Lk. Skt. 18, 27. Ealle þing synd gelȳfedum mihtlīce (MS. A. myhtelīce), Mk. Skt. 9, 23. [Cf. *Icel.* māttu-ligr *mighty; possible*: *O. H. Ger.* maht-līh *possibilis.*] v. un-mihtelīc.

meahte-, meaht-līce; *adv. Mightily, powerfully, with power, in power*:—Mihtelīce *potenter*, Hy. Surt. 26, 4. Myhtylīce *potentialiter*, 29, 11. Mihtlȳce *potenter*, 49, 19. Sǽ oncneów ðā Cristofer hyre ȳða mihtelīce eode *the sea acknowledged him, when Christ in his might walked over the waves*, Homl. Th. i. 108, 17. Mid ðām hē ðȳ mihtlīcor wiðscūfan mihte *quibus potentius confutare posset*, Bd. 5, 21; S. 642, 39. Meahtelīcor, Exon. 111 a; Th. 425, 27; Rä. 41, 62. [Cf. *Icel.* māttu-liga *mightily.*] v. meahtig-līce.

meahtig, mæhtig, mehtig, mihtig; *adj.* I. *mighty, powerful, able*:—Meahtig God, Ps. Th. 98, 9: Exon. 44 a; Th. 149, 12; Gū. 760: Hy. 4, 108; Hy. Grn. ii. 285, 108. Dryhten strong and maehtig (*potens*), Ps. Surt. 23, 8: 71, 12: Mk. Skt. Lind. 9, 29. Mæhtih, Lk. Skt. Lind. 24, 19. Meahtig God, Ps. C. 50; Ps. Grn. ii. 278, 89. Cyning rīce and mihtig *rex potentissimus*, Bd. 1, 25; S. 486, 16. Wyrta mōdor, innan mihtigu, Lchdm. iii. 32, 8. Heó was swā mihtegu wið God ðæt heó sealde blindum gesihþe, Shrn. 31, 12. Meotud biþ meahtigra ðonne ǣnges monnes gehygd, Exon. 83 a; Th. 312, 28; Seef. 116. Migtigra, Cd. 200; Th. 248, 33; Dan. 522. Allra mæhtigust is snytro *omnium potentior est sapientia*, Rtl. 81, 9. On ðysum eahta dǽlum (*parts of speech*) synd ða mǽstan and ða mihtigostan *nomen* and *verbum*, Ælfc. Gr. 5; Som. 4, 5. II. *possible*:—Mæhtiga *possibilia*, Mk. Skt. Lind. 9, 23: Lk. Skt. Lind. 18, 27. Cf. meaht; *adj.* and meahte-līc, meahtelīce. [*Goth.* mahteigs: *O. Sax. O. L. Ger. O. H. Ger.* mahtig: *Ger.* mächtig: *O. Frs.* machtich: *Icel.* māttigr.] v. eal-, efen-, fela-, fore-, ofer-, swīð-, tīr-, un-meahtig.

meahtig-līce; *adv. Mightily, powerfully, with might*:—Ðæt is ðæt hēhste gōd ðæt hit eall swā mihtiglīce macaþ, Bt. 35, 4; Fox 160, 32. Mihtiglīce hē mihte mid his worde hine gehǽlan būton hrepunge *by an exercise of power he could have healed him with his word, without touching*, Homl. Th. i. 122, 8. Ðās seofonfealdan gifa wunodon on Criste æfter ðære menniscnysse swīðe mihtiglīce, Wulfst. 57, 9. [*O. Sax.* mahtiglīk *mighty.*] v. meahte-līce.

meaht-leás; *adj. Powerless*:—Ðonne (*at the day of judgement*) stent ealra hergea mǽst heortleás and earh, mihtleás and āfǣred, Wulfst. 137, 23. [*Icel.* mātt-lauss *weak.*]

meaht-mōd, es; *n. Strong feeling, passion*:—Wǣron heaðowylmas heortan getenge mihtmōd wera *fierce rage pressed on the heart, and the mighty passions of men*, Cd. 149; Th. 187, 10; Exod. 149.

meala. v. melu.

Mealdumes burh *Malmsbury*:—Aldhelme abbode æt Mealdumesbyrig, Cod. Dip. Birch 154. 6. Æt Meldum, ðæt is ōðrum naman Maldumes buruh geclypud, 24, Binnon Mealdelmes byrig, Chr. 1015; Erl. 152, 3: Cod. Dip. Kmbl. vi. 312, col. 2.

meale-hūs. v. melu-hūs.

mealm, es; *m. Sand, chalk*(?) (see next two words). [*Goth.* malma; *m.* ἄμμος: *O. Sax. O. H. Ger.* melm; *m. pulvis*: *Icel.* mālmr; *m. sand* (in names of places).]

mealmiht; *adj. Sandy, chalky*(?):—Tō mealmehtan leáhe (*the land lay in Surrey*), Cod. Dip. Kmbl. iii. 394, 13. [E. D. S. Ellis' Farming Words, 'The chalk and mould were so mixed together, that in Hertfordshire we call it a *maumy* (*malmey*) earth.' 'A chalk or a *maume*.' 'Chalk, *maume*, or loam.']

mealm-stān, es; *m. Maum-stone.* 'In agro Oxoniensi lapidem invenies friabilem, quem *maum* vocant indiginæ.' E. D. S. Gloss. B. 15. A correspondent of Dr. Bosworth's writes: 'The *Maumstone* is to be found, more or less, all over Wiltshire, especially towards Stonehenge. It is used for the foundation of walls, and the poor people use it for whitening, in keeping their hearth-stones clean. It is not so white as chalk, and is much more brittle.'—Mon heardlīce gnīde ðone hnescestan mealmstān, Ors. 4, 13; Swt. 212, 28.

mealt; *adj. Cooked, boiled*(?):—On gewylledre mealtre meolce (mealtre = gewylledre? Cockayne says the word should be struck out), Lchdm. iii. 6, 17. v. miltan.

mealt, malt, es; *n. Malt*:—Malt *bratium*, Ep. Gl. 6 b, 2: Wrt. Voc. ii. 102, 18. Mealt, 11, 44: 127, 15: *macetum*, 58, 13. [*Icel.* malt; *n. O. H. Ger.* malz *brasium.*] v. alo-malt.

mealt-gescot, es; *n. A contribution of malt*:—Sceóte man swā hwæt swā witan gerǽdan, hwīlum weaxgescot, hwīlum mealtgescot, Wulfst. 171, 2.

mealt-hūs, es; *n. A malt-house*; brationarium, Ælfc. Gl. 108; Som. 78, 127; Wrt. Voc. 58, 38. [Cf. *Icel.* malt-hlaða.]

mealt-wyrt, -wurt, e; *f. Malt-wort*:—Maltwyrt *acinum*, Wrt. Voc. ii. 10, 37, 54. Mealtwurt, i. 28, 7. v. leáh-mealtwurt.

mealwe, an; *f. Mallow*:—Malwe *malva*, Ælfc. Gl. 42; Som. 64, 31; Wrt. Voc. 31, 41. Mealewe, 67, 56. Wildre mealwan seáw, L. M. 2, 24; Lchdm. ii. 214, 14. Hē hlāf þicge and mealwan, 16; Lchdm. ii. 194, 6: 33; Lchdm. ii. 238, 14. [From *Lat.* malva.] v. mersc-mealwe.

mearc, e; *f.* I. *a mark, sign* made upon a thing:—Tācon ł merca *titulus*, Mk. Skt. Lind. 15, 26. Cf. onmerca *inscribtio*, 12, 16. Merce ł stæfes heafud *apicem*, Lk. Skt. Lind. 16, 17. Mearce *caracteres*, Wrt. Voc. ii. 23, 81. II. *a mark, ensign*:—Hē nam ðone stān and ārǽrde hine tō mearce (*in titulum*; for a pillar, A. V.), Gen. 28, 18. Moyses getimbrode twelf mearca (*titulos*; pillars, A. V.), Ex. 24, 4. Nimaþ ða sigefæstan mearca *victricia tollite signa*, Ælfc. Gr. 9, 64; Som. 13, 66. [*O. Frs.* merke; *f. a mark*; macula: *Icel.* mark; *n. a mark, sign*; merki; *n. a mark, landmark; standard*: *O. H. Ger.* marcha, marca *titulus*: *M. H. Ger.* marc; *n. a sign.*]

mearc, e; *f.* I. *a limit, bound, term* (of time):—Ðā ðæs mǽles wæs mearc agongen *then was the limit of the time passed*, Cd. 83; Th. 103, 17; Gen. 1719: 224; Th. 296, 13; Sat. 501. Him ðæt tō mearce wearþ hē ðǽr feorhwunde hleát *that proved his life's limit; there his death-wound he got*, Beo. Th. 4758; B. 2384. II. *a limit, boundary* (of place), (a):—Beó ðǽr gemeten nygon fēt of ðam stacan tō ðære mearce (*the limit up to which the hot iron had to be carried*; cf. Grmm. R. A. 918), L. Ath. iv. 7; Th. i. 226, 13. Hē hæfþ heora mearce swā gesette ðæt hié ne mōt heore mearce gebrǽdan ofer ða stillan corþan *ut fluctus avidum mare certo fine coerceat, ne terris liceat vagis latos tendere terminos*, Bt. 21; Fox 74, 27: Bt. Met. Fox 11, 129, 139, 146; Met. 11, 65, 70, 73: 20, 177; Met. 20, 89. Swā ðæt heora nān ōðres mearce ne ofereode, Bt. 33, 4; Fox 128, 32. (b) *a boundary* (= gemǣre) *of a particular estate*:—Ðis is eástmærc tō stānmere . . . swā tō Rithmærce, Cod. Dip. B. 280, 18, 12. Swā be mearce . . . ðonon sūð andlang mearce, 148, 31–37. His metis rus hoc gyratur . . . forþ on ða mearce . . . andlang mearce . . . ðonon tō Æðelbirhtes mearce . . . ðonan forþ on ða mearce tō Beonetlēgæ gæmǣre . . . ðonan west on ða mearce ðǽr Ælfstān līþ on hǽðenan byrgels . . . ðonan Wulfstanes mearce, Cod. Dip. Kmbl. iii. 130, 26–131, 13. Be rihtre mearce (cf. be gerihtum gemǣre, l. 22) tō ðǣm gemǣrþornan; ðæt tō ðære reádan rōde; swā forþ be ealdormonnes mearce; ā be mearce ðæt hit cymþ on Icenan, 404, 31–405, 2. Heallingwara mearc, 400, 24. (c) *a boundary, confine of a district, border*:—Sī swā hwǽr swā hit sȳ, swā be norþan mearce, swā be sūþan, ā of scīre on ōðre, L. Ath. v. 8, 4; Th. i. 236, 26: 4; Th. i. 232, 19. Cēpeman oððe ōðerne ðe sió ofer mearce cuman, L. H. E. 15; Th. i. 32, 17: L. Wih. 8; Th. i. 38, 17. (Thorpe in the last two examples would take mearc to be the limit of an estate.) Ðū symle furðor feohtan sōhtest mǽl ofer mearce, Wald. 1, 33; Vald. 1, 19. Ðæt is ðonne ðæt mon his mearce brǽde . . . hira mearce mid tō rȳmanne *terminum suum dilatare est . . . ad dilatandum terminum suum* (cf. getryman hira landgemǣru, 4), Past. 48, 2; Swt. 367, 13–15: Cd. 136; Th. 171, 19; Gen. 2830. Unc mōdige ymb mearce sittaþ (*sit on our borders*), 91; Th. 114, 21; Gen. 1907. Merce gemǣrde wið Myrgingum, Exon. 85 a; Th. 321, 6; Vīd. 42. Hē sume on wræcsīð forsende sume on ōðra mearca gesette *alios avulsos a sedibus suis, alios in extremis regni terminis statuit*, Ors. 3, 7; Swt. 114, 34. III. *the territory within the boundaries*; fines:—Hit wæs geond ealle Rōmāna mearce ðæt *it was the custom throughout all the Roman territories* (cf. *O. Sax.* thero marka giwald ēgan *to succeed to the throne*), Bt. 37, 4; Fox 100, 13. Hwīlum wycg byreþ mec ofer mearce, hwīlum merehengest fereþ ofer flōdas, Exon. 104 a; Th. 395, 11; Rä. 15, 6. Mearce healdan (*or* II. c), Cd. 98; Th. 128, 32; Gen. 2135. Nǣfre on his weorþige weá āspringe mearce mā scȳte man inwides *non defecit de plateis ejus usura, et dolus*, Ps. Th. 54, 10. [*Goth.* markōs; *pl. borders* (of a country): *O. Sax.* marka *border, district: O. L. Ger.* marka *district: O. Frs.* merke *limit, district: Icel.* mörk *a forest;* in compounds, *a border-land, district: O. H. Ger.* marcha, marka *limes, confinium, terminus, fines: Lat.* margo.] v. ēđel-, first-, land-, leód-, tæl-, þeód-, Weder-mearc; ge-mearc, ge-mirce, *and the following compounds with* mearc-; *and cf. these with compounds of* mǣr-. On the *mark* see Stubbs' Const. Hist. i. 49–52, and Kemble's Saxons in England, vol. i.

mearc-bēce, an; *f. A beech-tree which forms part of a boundary:*—Đis synd đæra viii. hīda landgemēra . . . tō đære mearcbēcean; of đære bēcean, Cod. Dip. B. i. 295, 9. On đa ealdan mearce bēcan, 296, 26.

mearc-beorh; *gen.* -beorges; *m. A hill which forms part of a boundary:*—Prædicta tellus his terminis circumcincta. Ǣrest on æscwoldes hlāw: đonne on gemōtbiorh . . . đonne on mearcbiorh, Cod. Dip. Kmbl. ii. 195, 14. Ǣt đæne mearcbeorh, iii. 175, 35. Cf. gemǣr-beorh, iii. 403, 27. [Kemble says 'the *mearcbeorh* appears to denote the hill or mound which was the site of the *mearc-mōt*.' Saxons in England, i. 56.]

mearc-brōc, es; *m. A brook which serves as a boundary:*—Andlang Ecclesburnon tō đam mearcbrōce, Cod. Dip. Kmbl. v. 193, 31. Đis synd đa landgemǣra. Ǣrest đǣr mercbrōc scȳt on Seolesburnan; of mearcbrōce . . . swā andlang burnan eft on mērbrōce, 284, 12–30.

mearc-denu, e; *f. A valley which serves as a boundary:*—Tō mearcdene, Cod. Dip. Kmbl. iii. 404, 23.

mearc-dīc, e; *f. A ditch which serves as a boundary:*—On đa caldan mercdīc, Cod. Dip. B. i. 295, 7.

mearcere, es; *m. A notary, writer:*—Mærcerum, wrī[terum] *notariis*, Hpt. Gl. 528, 67.

mearc-hof, es; *n. A dwelling in a mark* or *country*, Cd. 145; Th. 181, 14; Exod. 61.

mearcian; *p.* ode (mearc *a mark*). I. *to make a mark on anything:*—Hē byreþ blōdig wæl . . . mearcaþ (*marks with blood*) mōrhopu, Beo. Th. 904; B. 450. Mearciaþ on marmstāne hwonne se dæg and seó tīd geeáwe *in marmore signant titulo remque diemque*, Exon. 60 b; Th. 221, 11; Ph. 333. Mearcode *sulcaret* ł *scriberet* ł *labararet*, Hpt. Gl. 465, 6. Hē mearcode đa stōwe, Homl. ii. 160, 35. Mearca đē sylfne mid tācne đære hālgan rōde, i. 534, 22. Mearcie (*brand*) man hine (þeówman) æt đam forman cyrre, L. C. S. 32; Th. i. 396, 9. Mercande *signantes*, Mt. Kmbl. Lind. 27, 66. II. *to mark out, design:*—Ǣlc cræftega þencþ and mearcaþ his weorc on his mōde ǣr hē it wyrce *every artificer considers and marks out his work in his mind before he does it*, Bt. 39, 6; Fox 220, 4. Him tō gingran metot mearcode *the Lord marked them out for his servants*, Cd. 23; Th. 29, 33; Gen. 459. [*O. Sax.* markōn *to mark out: O. Frs.* merkia: *Icel.* marka *to mark; mark out, design;* merkja *to mark: O. H. Ger.* marchōn *significare, notare;* markjan, markēn *notare, designare.*] v. ge-, tō-mearcian; foremearcod.

mearcian; *p.* ode (mearc *a limit*) *To fix the bounds* or *limits of a place:*—Se mearcode đa stōwa đe gē eówre geteld on sleán sceoldon *metatus est locum, in quo tentoria figere deberetis*, Deut. 1, 33. [*O. H. Ger.* marchōn *definire, collimitare.*]

mearc-īsen, es; *n. A branding-iron:*—Mearcīsen *cauterium*, Wrt. Voc. ii. 13, 18. Mearcīsene *cauterio*, Hpt. Gl. 453, 22. Hē sǣde đæt hē gesēge đæt ic wǣre gemearcod mid deófles mearcīsene, Shrn. 37, 13. v. next word.

mearc-īsern, es; *n. A branding-iron:*—Mearcīsern *cauterium*, Ep. Gl. 8 d, 35: Wrt. Voc. ii. 129, 76: *ferrum quo note pecudibus inuruntur*, 3. Mercīseren, 102, 58.

mearc-land, es; *n.* I. *a border-land, waste land lying outside the cultivated:*—Se mylenhām and se myln and đæs mearclandes swā mycel swā tō þrīm hīdon gebyraþ, Cod. Dip. Kmbl. iii. 189, 11. v. Kemble's Saxons in England, i. 50. Mearclonde (*the sea coast*) neáh, Exon. 101 b; Th. 384, 6; Rä. 4, 23. Him đe feára sum mearclond gesæt (*of Guthlac when he retired to his hermitage.* Cf. *what is said before of his dwelling place:*—Wæs seó londes stōw bimiđen fore monnum, ōđđæt meotud onwrāh beorg on bearwe, 34 b; Th. 110, 32–35), Exon. 35 a; Th. 112, 17; Gū. 145. Hēht ymbwīcigean Æthanes byrig mearclandum on *bade them encamp about Etham's town, in its borders*, Cd. 146; Th. 181, 27; Exod. 67. II. *a district, country, territory:*—Đæt mearcland, folcstede gumena, hæleþa ēđel, Andr. Kmbl. 37; An. 19. Geweoton đa wītigan mearcland tredan, 1603; An. 803. v. Kemble's Saxons in England, i. 46 sqq. [*Icel.* mark-land *forest-, border-land.*]

mearc-mōt, es; *n. The place where the assembly* (mōt) *of a district* (mearc) *was held:*—Đis syndon đa landgemǣra . . . tō mercemōt; fram mercemōte, Cod. Dip. Kmbl. iii. 71, 31. v. Saxons in England, i. 55.

mearc-pæđ, es; *m. n.*(?) *A path leading through a country:*—Be mearcpađe, strǣte neáh, Andr. Kmbl. 2124; An. 1063. Ic sīđade wīddor mearcpađas (*paths across the marches?*) træd, mōras pæđde, Exon. 126 a; Th. 485, 7; Rä. 71, 10. Gewāt hē đā fēran ofer mearcpađu (-pađum? -wađu, Grimm, Kemble), đæt hē on Membre becom, Andr. Kmbl. 1575; An. 789. v. mearc-wæd.

mearc-stapa, an; *m. One who wanders about the desolate mark* or *border-land:*—Grendel, mǣre mearcstapa, Beo. Th. 206; B. 103. Hiē gesāwon swylce twegen micle mearcstapan mōras healdan; ōđer wæs idese onlīcnes ōđer on weres wæstmum wræclāstas træd . . . Hié dȳgel lond warigeaþ, wulfhleoþu, windige næssas, frēcne fengelād, 2698–2722; B. 1347–1359. v. Kemble's Saxons in England, i. 48.

mearc-stede, es; *m. Desolate, border-land:*—Saga mē from đam lande đǣr nǣnig fira ne mæg fōtum gestæppan . . . Hē on đam felde geslōg xxv dracena, . . forđan đās foldan ne mæg fira ǣnig, đone mearcstede, mon gesēcan, fugol gefleógan, ne đon mā foldan neát, Salm. Kmbl. 418–436; Sal. 209–218. v. preceding word.

mearc-þreát, es; *m. A band of men occupying the frontier of a country:*—Manna þengel mearcþreáte rād (cf. Th. 187, 33: 188, 14), Cd. 151; Th. 188, 25; Exod. 173.

mearc-treów, es; *n. A tree serving as a boundary:*—Đonne tō mearctreówe, Cod. Dip. Kembl. iii. 434, 18. Cf. gemǣr-treów.

mearcung, e; *f.* I. *a marking, mark:*—*Nota* đæt is mearcung Đæra mearcunga sind manega, Ælfc. Gr. 50; Som. 51, 19. Mærcunge *characteres*, Hpt. Gl. 473, 13. II. *a marking out, description, arrangement, disposition:*—Mercung *descriptio*, Lk. Skt. Rush. 2, 2. Mearcung *capitulatio*, Wrt. Voc. ii. 128, 40. Mearcunge *constellationem, constellationes*, Hpt. Gl. 468, 1, 3. [*O. H. Ger.* marchunga *propositum, institutio.*] v. fore-, ge-, on-mearcung.

mearc-wæd, es; *n. Boundary-water, the water by the shore:*—Wlanc monig on stæþe stōdon stundum wrǣcon ofer mearcwađu and đā gehlōdon hildesercum wǣghengestas *many a proud one stood on the shore; now and again they pressed over the border-floods, and then laded the wave-steeds with their war-shirts* (but cf. mearc-pæđ), Elen. Kmbl. 465; El. 233.

mearc-weard, es; *m. A mark-warden, a wolf*, Cd. 151; Th. 188, 14; Exod. 168.

mearc-weg, es; *m. A road that forms part of a boundary:*—Andlang mearcweges, Cod. Dip. Kmbl. v. 40, 3. On mearcwei, iii. 202, 5. Cf. mǣr-, gemǣr-weg.

meard. v. meord.

mear-gealla, an; *m. A kind of gentian:*—Mergelle, Lchdm. iii. 24, 1. Wyl mergeallan on meolcum, L. M. 2, 65; Lchdm. ii. 296, 18. v. mersc-meargealla.

mearh, mærh, es; *n. m. Marrow, pith;* also *a sausage.* Cf. mearh-gehæcc:—Mearh *medulla*, Wrt. Voc. i. 65, 23. Mearg, 283, 48. Mærh, 70, 47. Merg, ii. 114, 3. Mearh *lucanica* (*lucanica* genus farciminis ex porcinis carnibus concisis a Lucanis populis, a quibus Romani milites primum didicerunt, Forcellini), 51, 55: *amilarius* (?), 6, 59: 100, 19. Mærh, 113, 22. Meargh, Wrt. Voc. i. 286, 53 (given amongst words *de suibus*). Mearh *medulla* vel *lucanica*, 44, 42. Mid mearche *cum medulla*, Cant. M. ad fil. 14. Wuduþistles đone grēnan mearh đe biþ on đam heáfde, L. M. 3, 70; Lchdm. ii. 358, 1. Gedō đæt mearh on đa eágan, 1, 2; Lchdm. ii. 38, 9. Heortes smeoruw ođđe đæt mearh, Herb. 96, 3; Lchdm. i. 208, 22. Nim foxes smero and rāhdeóres mearh, Lchdm. iii. 2, 25. Wulfes mearh, L. Med. ex Quad. 9, 6; Lchdm. i. 362, 9. Heortes mearg, 10, 4; Lchdm. i. 366, 4. Nim mærc, sāpan (MS. mærcsāpan) and hinde meolc, Lchdm. iii. 4, 1. Mearga *medullas*, Germ. 397, 493. [*O. L. Ger.* marg: *O. Frs.* merg: *Icel.* mergr; *m.: O. H. Ger.* marag, marg, mark: *Ger.* mark; *n.*]

mearh; *g.* meares; *m. A horse, steed:*—Mearh moldan træd, Elen. Kmbl. 109; El. 55. Cyninges mearh, 2383; El. 1193. Se swifta mearh burhstede beáteþ, Beo. Th. 4521; B. 2264. Hwǣr cwom mearg, hwǣr cwom mago, Exon. 77 b; Th. 291, 34; Wand. 92. Sum biþ meares gleáw *one is skilful in the management of a steed*, 79 a; Th. 297, 17; Crä. 69. Tomes meares, 91 a; Th. 342, 13; Gn. Ex. 142. Đā hē on meare rād, on wlancan đam wicge, Byrht. Th. 138, 54: Elen. Kmbl. 2349; El. 1176. Đe him mænigne mear gesealde, Byrht. Th. 137, 19; By. 188. Eahta mearas, Beo. Th. 2075; B. 1035. Fealwe mearas, 1735; B. 865. Mearas æppelfealuwe, 4333. Meara and māđma, 4338; B. 2166. Mearum and māđmum, 3800; B. 1898. Beornas cōmon wiggum gengan on mearum mōdige, Andr. Kmbl. 2193; An. 1098. [*Icel.* marr *a steed* (in poetry; used in compounds, e. g. vāg-marr *wave-steed*, of ships: *O. H. Ger.* marah, march *equus.*] v. lagu-, sǣ-, ȳđ-mearh.

mearh-cofa, an; *m. A marrow-chamber, a bone:*—Mearhcofan *ossa*, Ps. Th. 101, 3.

mearh-gehæcc, es; *n. A kind of pudding, a sausage:*—Mearhgehæc *isica* (*insicia* genus farciminis, seu obsonii ex carne concisa, Forcellini), Wrt. Voc. ii. 48, 35. Mærhgehæc (-hæt, Wrt.) *isicia*, i. 27, 22. [Halliwell gives '*hack* the lights, liver, and heart of a boar or swine: *hackin* a pudding made in the maw of a sheep or hog: *hack-pudding* a mess made of sheep's heart, chopped with suet and sweet fruits: *hatcher* a dish of minced meat.] v. *next word and* haccian.

mearh-hæccel, es; *n. A sausage, hog's-pudding:*—Gehæcca ođđe mearhhæccel *farcimen* (*farcimen* intestinum varie ac minutim concisa carne refertum, Forcellini), Wrt. Voc. ii. 39, 77. v. preceding word.

mearh-, mearg-līc; *adj. Marrowy, fat:*—Onsegdnisse merglīce ic offriu *holocausta medullata offeram*, Ps. Surt. 65, 15. [Cf. *O. H. Ger.* marag-haft (*in same passage*).]

mearrian; *p.* ode *To err, go astray*:—Ne þyncþ ðeáh ðám monnum ðæt hí áuht mearrigen ðe ðæs wilniaþ tó begitanne ðæt hí máran ne þu.fon tilian *num enim videntur errare hi, qui nihilo indigere nituntur?*, Bt. 24, 4; Fox 86, 1. v. ge-mearr, mirran.

mearþ, es; *m. A marten, a kind of weasel*:—Mearth *furuncus*, Ep. Gl. 9 d, 11. Mearþ, Wrt. Voc. ii. 36, 21: *furo, idem deminutive furunculus*, 39, 58: *ferunca* vel *ferunculus*, i. 22, 51. Mærþ *feruncus*, 78, 17: *rumusculus*, ii. 76, 36. Merþ *ferunca*, 40, 12. Se byrdesta sceall gyldan xv mearþes fell (cf. *Icel.* marð-skinn.), Ors. 1, 1; Swt. 18, 20. Ofer mearþes hrycg (*in an enumeration of boundaries*), Cod. Dip. Kmbl. iii. 391, 20. [*Icel.* mörðr.]

mearu, mæru, meru, myru; *adj. Tender, soft, delicate*:—Ðonne his twig biþ mearu (*tener*), Mk. Skt. 13, 28. Merwe, Mt. Kmbl. Rush. 24, 32. Mearuwe *delicatus i. tenerus*, Wrt. Voc. ii. 138, 40. Gyf se líchoma mearu (MS. B. mearuw) sý *if the body be tender* (*with sores*), Herb. 102, 2; Lchdm. i. 216, 24. Hwæðer sió gecynd ðæs líchoman síe heard ðe hnesce and mearwe, L. M. 1, 35; Lchdm. ii. 84, 14. Man byþ merwe gesceaft, Ps. Th. 143, 5. Myra *tenellus*, Kent. Gl. 62. Se myrwa *mactus*, Wrt. Voc. ii. 54, 71. Ðære mærwan cyrican weaxnesse *tenellis ecclesiæ crementis*, Bd. 2, 5; S. 506, 37. Blód fleów of hire ðæm merwan líchoman, Shrn. 101, 22. Genim ðás wyrte swá mearwe *take this plant as young and tender as possible*, Herb. 89, 1; Lchdm. i. 192, 8, 12. Mearawa *tenera, gracilia*, Hpt. Gl. 457, 42. Ne gedafenaþ ús ðæt wé symle hnesce beón on úrum geleáfan swá swá ðás merwan cild, Homl. Th. i. 602, 13. Þurh ða myrwan *per tenera*, Wrt. Voc. ii. 66, 23. Hí (*the leaves*) beóþ mearwran (MS. H. mearuwran), Herb. 153, 1; Lchdm. i. 278, 15. Ða hwítan líchoman beóþ mearuwran and tedran ðonne ða blacan, L. M. 1, 35; Lchdm. ii. 84, 21. Mærwost, 2, 14; Lchdm. ii. 190, 21. On mearwis[tum?] *in tenerrima, gracillima*, Hpt. Gl. 444, 69. Merewistan *gracillima*, 521, 29. [*A. R.* meruwe (*of young trees*): *O. H. Ger.* marawi, maro *tener, delicatus*; *there is besides* muruwi, murwi *with same meaning*: *M. H. Ger.* mürwe: *Ger.* mürbe.]

mearuw-ness, e; *f. Tenderness, delicacy*:—Hira módes mearuwnesse (Cott. MSS. meruwenesse) *eorum teneritudinem*, Past. 32, 2; Swt. 211, 18. Marenysse *teneritudine*, Hpt. Gl. 441, 35.

meatt. v. matt.

meáu. v. mǽw.

mec. v. mé.

méce, es; *m. A sword, falchion, blade*:—Méce *machera*, Hpt. Gl. 470, 44: 424, 30: Wrt. Voc. ii. 54, 47: *mucro*, 114, 35. Mécha *aciem gladii, vim gladii*, 98, 36. Méche *frameam*, Ps. Spl. T. 16, 14. Méces ecge, Beo. Th. 3628; B. 1812. Mid áwendenlícum méce *romphæa versatili vel volubili ancipiti, utraque parte acutus*, Hpt. Gl. 433, 70. Slóh fágum méce, Judth. 10; Thw. 23, 4; Jud. 104. Scírne méce *a bright blade*, Exon. 79 a; Th. 297, 8; Crä. 65. Heardne méce, Byrht. Th. 136, 47; By. 167. Mécea gemánan, Chr. 937; Erl. 114, 6; Æðelst. 40. Mécum mylenscearpan, Erl. 112, 24; Æðelst. 24. [*Laym.* mæche: *Goth.* mêki (*acc.*): *O. Sax.* máki: *Icel.* mækir.]

méce-fisc, es; *m. A mullet*:—Méce-(mǽce-)fisc *mugil*, Ælfc. Gl. Zup, 308, 5. Cf. gár-fisc.

mecg. v. mæcg.

mecgan; *p.* mægde (?) *To stir, mix*:—Cnuca eall ðás tógadere and magce tógadere *pound all these together, and stir together*, Lchdm. iii. 134, 8. Níme ðat dust and mæcige mid ðan æge *take the dust and stir it up with the egg*, 126, 19. Streám sceal mecgan mereflóde *the river shall stir up* (*as it pours in*) or *mix with, the ocean*, Menol. Fox 507; Gn. C. 24.

mechanisc; *adj. Mechanical*:—Án wurþlíc weorc on mechanisc geweorc, Homl. Skt. 5, 251.

méd, e; *f. Meed, reward*:—Méd *merces*, Ælfc. Gr. 9, 27; Som. 11, 25: Wrt. Voc. i. 61, 45: *merx*, ii. 58, 41. Ðín méd byþ swíðe micel, Gen. 15, 1: Lk. Skt. 6, 35. Hwæt byþ ús tó méde, Mt. Kmbl. 19, 27: Judth. 12; Thw. 26, 19; Jud. 335. Elles næbbe gé méde mid eówrum fæder ðe on heofenum ys, Mt. Kmbl. 6, 1. Méde onfón, 6, 5. Hé mé méde gehét, Beo. Th. 4275; B. 2134. Ðé sind gehealdene ðíne méda gewisse, Homl. Th. ii. 516, 24: Cd. 19; Th. 130, 29; Gen. 2167. Ðú médum scealt onfón, 141; Th. 176, 24; Gen. 2916: Bd. 4, 3; S. 568, 34. [*O. Sax. O. L. Ger.* méda, miéda: *O. Frs.* méde, meide, míde: *O. H. Ger.* mieta, miata: *Ger.* miete.] v. meord.

médan. v. on-médan.

Médas, Médisc. v. Mǽðas, Mǽðisc.

médder, méddern. v. módor, médren.

med-drosna; *pl. f. Dregs of mead*, L. M. 1, 56; Lchdm. ii. 126, 15.

-méde; *subst.* and *adj.* v. eáþ-, ge-, ofer-, unblíðe-, unge-, wiðer-méde (-médu).

medel. v. mæðel.

medeme. v. medume.

méderce. v. mýdrece.

méderen. v. médren.

meder-wyrhta. v. meter-wyrhta.

Medeshámstede, es; *m. Peterborough*:—Abbud ðæs mynstres ðe. gecweden is Medeshámstyde on Gyrwan lande, Bd. 4, 6; S. 573, 41. Nama hit gáuen Medeshámstede, forðan ðet ðǽr is án wæl ðe is geháten Medeswæl, Chr. 654; Erl. 29, 9. Hé geaf hit ðá tó nama Burch ðe ǽr hét Medeshámstede, 963; Erl. 123, 34. See also Cod. Dip. Kembl. vi. 312.

méd-gilda, an; *m. One who receives pay, a needy person*:—Wædla ł médgylda *mendicus*, Ps. Lamb. 39, 18. Se hýra oððe se médgylda *the hireling or the mercenary*, Homl. Th. i. 242, 5. Swá swá médgildan (*hireling's*) dagas, ii. 454, 27. Nafa ðú ðínne néhstan for weal and for médgildan *non fratrem tuum opprimes servitute famulorum*, Lev. 25, 39.

-medla. v. an-, on-, ofer-medla.

medlen. v. midlen.

méd-líc. v. mǽþ-líc.

med-micel; *adj.* I. *not great, moderate, small* (of time, space, quantity):—Se medmicla fyrst *modica illa intercapedo*, Bd. 5, 1; S. 614, 14: Blickl. Homl. 111, 24. Is on westan medmycel duru, 127, 8. Se yfela déma onféhþ medmycclum feó, 61, 30. Ðá féng hé tó medmycclan bigleofan, ðæt wæs tó ðam berenan hláfe, Guthl. 5; Gdwin. 34, 5. Hæfde hé medmycel (*permodicum*) mynster, Bd. 4, 13; S. 582, 21. Cærenes gódne bollan fulne, and ecedes medmicelne, L. M. 1, 1; Lchdm. ii. 24, 20. Midmycle (*other MS.* medmycle), Bd. 2, 16; S. 519, 34. Medmiclu and miclu *pusilla et magna*, Blickl. Gl. *Used as a noun*:—Dó medmicel on ða eágan *put a little into the eyes*, 1, 2; Lchdm. ii. 36, 8. Medmicel pipores, 2, 44; Lchdm. ii. 256, 5. Medmicel hláfes, Bd. 3, 27; S. 559, 35. Ðæs medmásta (*or* medmasta? *from* medume. v. *also under* II, III) geleáfe *minime fidei*, Mt. Kmbl. Rush. 10, 30. II. *not great, trifling, venial, not important*:—Gif man medmycles (*exigui*) hwæthwega deófium onsægþ, fæste i. geár; gif hé mycles hwæt onsecge, fæste x winter, L. Ecg. C. 32; Th. ii. 156, 15. Medmycel ǽrende wé ðyder habbaþ, Blickl. Homl. 233, 11. Ða gód ðe ic ǽfre dyde wǽron swíðe feáwe and medmicle (*nimium pauca et modica*), Bd. 5, 13; S. 632, 38. Ne mágon wé búton ðǽm medmyclum synnum beón, Blickl. Homl. 37, 10. On mycclum gyltum oððe on medmycclum, 107, 14. Micclum þingum and medmiclum, Cod. Dip. Kmbl. ii. 304, 12. Ðæt ic on ðam medemǽstan (medemæstan?) geþohte gesyngode *quæ tenuissima cogitatione peccavi*, Bd. 5, 13; S. 633, 10. III. *not great, lowly, mean, poor*:—On medmyclum hrægle gehealdene *content with mean apparel*, Blickl. Homl. 185, 17. On ðone medmycclan innoþ ðære á clǽnan fǽmnan *into the lowly womb of the ever clean virgin*, 5, 18, 33: 23, 23. Æt ánum of ðissum medmǽstan *unum de pusillis istis*, L. Ecg. P. Add. 23; Th. ii. 236, 10.

medmicel-ness, e; *f. Smallness*:—Medmicelnysse gástæs *pusillanimitate spiritus*, Ps. Spl. 54, 8.

medmicle; *adv. Humbly, meanly*:—Oft wíc beóþ on manegum stówum medmyccle gesette; seó ceaster ðonne wæs héh and aldorlíc, Blickl. Homl. 77, 24.

medo. v. medu.

médren, médern, méddern; *adj. Maternal*, (of lineage) *on the mother's side*:—Eádweard his bróðor on médren (cf. *Icel.* móðerni *the mother's side*), Chr. 1041; Erl. 166, 28. Þurh médderne *per maternam*, Hpt. Gl. 404, 70. Of médernum hrífe *de vulva*; médernum *maternis*, 441, 41, 25. Of méddernum geeácnungum *partubus*, 480, 9. v. *following words and* ge-médred.

médren-cynn, es; *n. Maternal kin, kin by the mother's side*:—Ælfrédes reht meódrencynn *Alfred's direct maternal kin*, Chart. Th. 483, 5. Ðæt wé ðín médrencynn mótan cunnan, nú wé áreccan ne mágon ðæt fædrencynn, Exon. 11 b; Th. 15, 34; Cri. 246.

médren-gecynd, es; *n. Nature derived from the mother*:—Hé wæs sóð man þurh his médrengecynd (méddrengecynd) *he was very man in the nature derived from his mother*, Wulfst. 17, 7.

médren-mǽg, es; *m. A kinsman by the mother's side, maternal kinsman*:—Méddernmágas *cognati*, Wrt. Voc. i. 51, 80. Ðara médrenmǽga (méddrenmága, MS. H.) dǽl, L. Alf. pol. 8; Th. i. 66, 21. Gif hé médrenmǽgas náge, 27; Th. i. 78, 21.

médren-mǽgþ, e; *f. Kindred by the mother's side*:—Gebyriaþ twelf men tó werborge, viii fæðerenmǽgþe, and iii. médrenmǽgþe, L. E. G. 12; Th. i. 174, 19.

med-ríce; *adj. Of little power, not powerful, of the lower as opposed to the higher classes*:—Medríca gesetnyssa *plebisscita*; ríccra gesetnes *senatus consultum*, Wrt. Voc. i. 20, 65–66.

med-sǽlþ, e; *f. Bad fortune, ill success*:—Ðæt hié mósten gefandian hweðer hié heora medsélþa oferswíðan mehte, Ors. 4, 4; Swt. 164, 28.

méd-sceatt, es; *m.* I. *payment in reward of service done, a reward, wages, fee*:—Ne onféng hé ðæt tó médsceatte *he did not accept it as a fee*, Shrn. 135, 24. Hé ne sealde Gode nánne métsceat for his sáule . . . Ðæt is ðonne se médsceat wið his sáule ðæt hé him gielde gód weorc *non dabit Deo pretium redemtionis animæ suæ. . . Pretium namque redemtionis dare, est opus bonum reddere*, Past. 45, 2; Swt. 339, 9–11. Swelce hié ða métsceattas ríman ðe hié Gode sellen . . . Ac hié sceoldon gehiéran ðone cwide ðe áwriten is: 'Se ðe mēdsceattas gaderaþ hē legeþ hié on þyrelne pohchan.' An þyrelne pohchan se legþ ðæt hē tō mētsceatte sellan þencþ *quasi mercedem numerant . . . Audiant, quod scriptum es: 'Qui mercedes congregavit, misit eas in sacculum pertusum.' In sacculo pertuso videtur, quando pecunia mittitur,* 45, 4; Swt. 343, 16-21. II. *payment for service or favour expected* (generally in a bad sense), *a gift, present, a bribe:*—Sī se āwirged ðe unscildigne man belǽwe wið mēdscette *maledictus, qui accepit munera, ut percutiat animam sanguinis innocentis,* Deut. 27, 25. Ǽlc wōh for lyðran mēdsceatte gelǽtaþ tō rihte, Wulfst. 297, 26. Se man ðe bringþ mēdsceat ðam gerēfan, se geǽrendaþ bet ðonne se ðe nǽnne ne bringþ, 238, 8. Gif hwā æt þeófe mēdsceatt nime, L. Ath. i. 17; Th. i. 208, 14. Swylc gerēfa swylc mēdsceat nime, and ōðres ryht þurh ðæt ālecge, iv. 1; Th. i. 222, 5: L. E. I. 16; Th. ii. 412, 12. Mēdsceattas *munera propriæ,* Wrt. Voc. ii. 59, 9. Mēdsceattas āblendaþ wīsra manna geþancas, Deut. 16, 19. Swȳðre heora gefylled is of mēdsceattum (*muneribus*), Ps. Spl. 25, 10: L. Alf. 46; Th. i. 54, 17: L. Ed. 7; Th. i. 162, 25.

med-spēdig; *adj. Unprosperous, poorly provided:*—Ne biþ ǽnig ðæs earfoþsǽlig mon on moldan, ne ðæs medspēdig ðæt hine se ārgifa ealles biscyrge mōdes cræfta *no man upon earth is there of such hard fortune or so meanly endowed, that the gracious giver quite cuts him off from powers of mind,* Exon. 78 b; Th. 294, 3; Crä. 9.

med-strang; *adj. Of moderate means, of middle rank:*—Ic lǽrde wlance men and heáhgeþungene . . . Ic lǽrde eác ða medstrangan men (cf. Homl. Th. i. 370, 20, *see under* medume) . . . and þearfum ic lǽrde, Blickl. Homl. 187, 13-17.

med-, met-trum; *adj.* I. *not strong in health, infirm, weak, ill:*—Hwā biþ medtrum ðæt ic ne sīe for his þingum seóc *quis infirmatur, et ego non infirmor?* Past. 21, 6; Swt. 165, 4. Se mettruma līchoma *debile corpus,* 61, 2; Swt. 455, 27. Sint tō manianne ða mettruman (*ægri*), 36, 4; Swt. 251, 20. Manega wurdon mettrume gehǽlede, Homl. Th. ii. 512, 7. Mettrumra *ægrotorum,* Hpt. Gl. 415, 20. II. *of inferior position* (?):—Nalæs ðæt ān ðætte ða metruman (MSS. O. T. mǽttran: MS. B. mǽteran) men ymb heora nēdþearfnesse wǽron ac eác cyningas and ealdormen from hire geþeaht sōhton *non solum mediocres in necessitatibus suis, sed etiam reges ac principes ab ea quærerent consilium,* Bd. 4, 23; S. 593, 43. Cf. med-strang.

med-, met-trum-, -trym-ness, e; *f. Infirmity, ill-health, sickness, illness:*—Seó lange mettrumnes ðæs seócan mannes, ðonne hine God forlǽtan nele ēþelīce lifian, ne hē swyltan ne mōte, Blickl. Homl. 59, 28. Hwīlum ofþrycþ ðone līchoman ungemetlīcu mettrymnes (*languor*). Ongeán swelce metrymnesse mon beþorfte strónges lǽcedōmes . . . swā hē mǽge ða mettrymnesse (*morbum*) mid geflíeman, Past. 61, 2; Swt. 455, 26-30. Se ðe biscephād underfēhþ hē underfēhþ ðæs folces mettrymnesse *quasi ad ægrum medicus accedit,* 9; Swt. 59, 23. Hē gefōr on ðære mettrymnesse, Ors. 6, 30; Swt. 282, 21. Ðā gehǽldon hié sum wīf of micelre medtrumnesse, Shrn. 135, 16. Mettrumnesse, Ps. Th. 5, arg: 6, arg: 15, arg: Guthl. 20; Gdwin. 82, 13. Ða lǽcas cunnon heora medtrumnesse ongitan, Bt. 39, 9; Fox 226, 16. Mettrymnysse *infirmitates,* Ps. Spl. C. 15, 3. Metrymnisse *ægrotationes,* Mt. Kmbl. Rush. 8, 17. Wīf sceolon gemunan hyra mettrumnessa and hyra hādes tyddernessa *women must remember their infirmities and the weaknesses of their sex,* L. E. I. 6; Th. ii. 406, 12.

medu, meodu, a; *m.*: wes; *n. Mead, a drink made from honey:*—Medu *medo* vel *medus,* Wrt. Voc. i. 27, 41. Meodu *medo,* 82, 30. Medo *mulsum,* 290, 60. Medo, geswēt *vel* weall *defrutum,* i. *vinum,* ii. 138, 24. Meodu, Andr. Kmbl. 3051, An. 1528. Medewes *defruti,* Hpt. Gl. 480, 74. Ða mǽla ðe wē oft æt meodo sprǽcon, Byrht. Th. 137, 66; By. 212. Tō medo, Beo. Th. 1212; B. 604. Ðā wē medu þēgon, 5260; B. 2633. Ða þeówan drincaþ medo, Ors. 1, 1; Swt. 20, 17. Wylle swā swȳðre medo, L. M. 2, 52; Lchdm. ii. 270, 7. Gedō on ðone drenc swīðe gōd medo, 2, 53; Lchdm. ii. 274, 15. Hwītne medu, Fins. Th. 78; Fin. 39. Ðǽr hȳ meodu drincaþ, Exon. 105 b; Th. 401, 16; Rä. 21, 12. Medewa, wīn *defruta, decocta vina,* Hpt. Gl. 468, 38. [*Icel.* mjöðr; *m: O. H. Ger.* meto, mito *mulsum, medum: Ger.* meth: *Lithuan.* middus: *Gk.* μέθυ.]

medu-ærn, es; *n. A house in which mead is drunk, a banqueting-house:*—Medoærn micel, Beo. Th. 138; B. 69.

medu-benc, e; *f. A bench in a banqueting-hall:*—Medubenc monig, Beo. Th. 1556; B. 776. On ðære medubence, 2108; B. 1052. Medobence, 4376; B. 2185. Meodobence, 3808; B. 1902. Meodubence, Exon. 87 b; Th. 330, 9; Vy. 48.

medu-burh; *f. A city in which mead is drunk, one in which mead-drinking warriors live:*—On ðære medobyrig, Judth. 11; Thw. 24, 2; Jud. 167. On meoduburgum, Exon. 123 a; Th. 473, 18; Bo. 16.

medu-dreám, es; *m. Joy attending mead-drinking, festivity:*—Ne seah ic medudreám māran, Beo. Th. 4036; B. 2016. Meododreáma, Exon. 123 b; Th. 475, 8; Bo. 44.

medu-drenc, es; *m. Mead:*—Ðonne biþ heom heora meodudrenc wīn and beór eall tō ēcum þurste āwend *then shall their mead and wine and beer all be turned for them to eternal thirst,* Wulfst. 245, 4.

medu-drinc, es; *m. Mead-drinking:*—Fore medodrince *instead of mead-drinking,* Exon. 81 b; Th. 307, 12; Seef. 22.

medu-full, es; *n. A mead-cup:*—Meoduful, Exon. 88 a; Th. 331, 2; Vy. 66. Medoful, Beo. 1253; B. 624: 2034; B. 1015.

medu-gāl; *adj. 'Flown with wine,' excited with mead:*—Holofernus mōdig and medugāl, Judth. 10; Thw. 21, 19; Jud. 26: Cd. 209; Th. 260, 1; Dan. 703. Meodugāl, Exon. 88 a; Th. 330, 16; Vy. 52. Meodugāles gedrinc, 330, 27; Vy. 57.

medu-heall, e; *f. A mead-hall, banqueting-hall:*—Ðeós (*Hrothgar's*) medoheal, Beo. Th. 972; B. 484. Meodoheall, Exon. 124 a; Th. 477, 13; Ruin. 24. In meoduhealle, 76 b; Th. 288, 6; Wand. 27: 79 a; Th. 297, 16; Crä. 69: 85 b; Th. 321, 33; Vīd. 55. In medohealle, Elen. Kmbl. 2515; El. 1259.

meduma, meoduma, an; *m. A weaver's beam:*—Meoduma *insubula,* Wrt. Voc. i. 66, 33: 282, 18. (Cf. Webbeámas *insubulæ,* 59, 43.) Meodoma, ii. 46, 33.

medume, medeme, meodume; *adj.* I. *middling, moderate, common:*—Medeme *mediocer,* Ælfc. Gr. 9, 18; Som. 9, 67. Gif hwylc man forstele deórwurþe þing . . . Gif hwylc man medeme þing (*rem mediocrem*) stele, L. Ecg. P. ii. 25; Th. ii. 192, 17-20. II. *occupying the middle* or *mean position as regards* (*a*) *size, amount,* etc.:—Medume leódgeld *a half fine* (cf. *medietas leudis,* and other examples, Grmm. R. A. 653), L. Ethb. 7; Th. i. 4, 9: 21; Th. i. 8, 3. Hē hæfþ medemne wæstm *he is of middle height,* Homl. Th. i. 456, 18. Heáfdu medumra manna *heads of average, ordinary men,* Salm. Kmbl. 525; Sal. 262. Gehwar gebūrrihta sȳn hefige, gehwar medeme (*moderate*), L. R. S. 4; Th. i. 434, 5. Se mǽsta segl *acateon;* se medemesta segl *epidromas;* se lesta *dalum,* Wrt. Voc. i. 56, 51-53. (*b*) *place, rank, means:*—Medemra þegna heregeata *the medial thanes' heriots,* L. C. S. 72; Th. i. 414, 12. Ic tǽhte ðām rīcan . . . ic tǽhte ðām medeman mannum . . . Ic bebeád þearfum, Homl. Th. i. 378, 20. Heáfodmynstres griþbryce . . . medemran mynstres . . and ðonne gīt lǽssan, L. Eth. ix. 5; Th. i. 342, 1: L. C. E. 3; Th. i. 360, 21. Ðæs medemestan līfes (*the life mid-way between the best and worst,* cf. mon forlǽt ðæt wyrreste līf and ne mæg gīt cuman tō ðæm betstan, 10), Past. 51, 6; Swt. 399, 15. (*c*) *age:*—Mīnre yldstan dēhter . . . ðære medemestan . . . ðære gingstan, Chart. Th. 488, 28-32: 489, 23-25. III. *observing the just mean, perfect, meet, fit, worthy:*—Hē wæs þurh eall meodum (MS. B. medeme: MS. O. medum) *erat dignus per omnia,* Bd. 4, 3; S. 567, 19. Meoduma, Mt. Kmbl. Rush. 10, 37. Hwelc se beón scolde ðe medome (*dignus*) hierde bión sceolde, Past. 11, 7; Swt. 73, 20. Medeme, Blickl. Homl. 129, 35. Hē wyrþ ǽlces cræftes medeme (*fit for, capable of*) . . . ǽlces þinges swā medeme swā hē ǽfre medemast (medomist, MS. Cott.), Bt. 38, 5; Fox 206, 25-29. Hwylc ðæt medeme gōd wæs hwylc ðæt unmedeme *quæ sit imperfecti, quæ perfecti boni forma,* 35, 1; Fox 134, 4. Medeme fæsten *a proper fast,* L. E. I. 39; Th. ii. 436, 35. Medeme lāc, Blickl. Homl. 37, 32. Ful medomne wæstm, 55, 5. Drihtne tō geearnienne medome folc ('*a prepared people,*' Lk. 1, 17), 165, 15. Ne gedēþ se anweald gōdne ne meodumne (MS. Cott. medomne) *power makes him neither good nor worthy,* Bt. 16, 3; Fox 56, 20. Gōde and medeme, Blickl. Homl. 129, 23, 32. Mid medemum wæstmum hreówe *dignis pænitentia fructibus,* Bd. 4, 27; S. 604, 24: Mt. Kmbl. 3, 8. Medeme þinc *res dignas,* Kent. Gl. 396. Drihten ðū ðe eall medemu geworhtest and nāht unmedemes, Shrn. 165, 31. Ne māgon wē nānwuht findan betere (MS. Cott. medemre) ðonne God, Bt. 34, 4; Fox 138, 26. Nis meodumre ne māra ðonne *it is not too good nor too great for,* Exon. 38 a; Th. 125, 16; Gū. 355. Ðæt medemæste *the best,* Bt. 24, 4; Fox 86, 10. Ða medumestan ealdras *exspectabiles senatores,* Wrt. Voc. ii. 145, 51. [*O. H. Ger.* metam, metem.] v. un-medume.

medumian, medemian, medmian; *p.* ode. I. *to fix the measure of anything:*—Dōm æfter dǽde medemige man be mǽðe *according to the deed let the measure of doom be fixed in proportion,* L. Eth. vi. 10; Th. i. 318, 6: vi. 53; Th. i. 328, 17. Man sceal medmian and gescādlīce tōscādan ylde and geógoþe *youth and age must have their proper place assigned them, and be discreetly distinguished,* vii. 52; Th. i. 328, 18. Medmian (medemian), L. C. S. 69; Th. i. 412, 8. II. *to deem worthy* (v. medume, III.), *respect, esteem:*—Ic gemedemige (*other* MSS. medemige) ðē tō ðam þinge *dignor te illa re,* and medemigende ðē tō ðam þinge *dignans te illa re,* Ælfc. Gr. 41; Zup. 250, 9-10. Weofodþēna mǽðe medemige man, L. Eth. ix. 18; Th. i. 344, 9. [*O. H. Ger.* metamēn *temperare, moderare, dimidiare.*] v. ge-medemian.

medum-līc; *adj.* I. *middling, moderate, small:*—Gehwǽdum ł medemlīcum *mediocri,* Hpt. Gl. 505, 55. Hē hæfþ medemlīce nosu (cf. medmicle neosu þynne *naso pertenui,* Bd. 2, 16; S. 519, 34) *he has a slender nose,* Homl. Th. i. 456, 18. II. *worthy, honourable:*—Medomlīcan *dignitosam,* Wrt. Voc. ii. 28, 64. Medomlīce *dignitosa,* 106, 55: 140, 27.

medum-līce; *adv.* I. *moderately, in a small degree, imperfectly:*—Medomlīce *mediocriter,* Wrt. Voc. ii. 140, 27. Wē cunnon ðære leóde gereord, nā medemlīce ac fulfremedlīce, Homl. Th. ii. 474, 3. II. *worthily, fitly, kindly* (cf. mǽþ-līce, medum-ness):—Hī ne mâgon medomlîce (Cott. MSS. medumlîce) þênian *ministrare digne nequeunt*, Past. 1, 2; Swt. 27, 10. Suîðe medomlîce Iacobus his stîrde *hinc pie Iacobus prohibet*, 3, 1; Swt. 33, 9. Medomlîce *benigniter*, Wrt. Voc. ii. 11, 3. Meodomlîce *digne*, Rtl. 2, 41.

medumlîc-ness, e; *f. Smallness*:—Gehwǽdnys ł medemidlîcnys (medemlîcnys?) *mediocritas, parvitas*, Hpt. Gl. 467, 14.

medum-ness, e: *f.* I. *worth, dignity*:—Medumnes (Cott. MSS. medomnes) *dignitas*, Bt. 16, 3; Fox 56, 25. Nân man for his rîce ne cymþ tô cræftum and tô medemnesse ac for his cræftum and for his medumnesse hê cymþ tô rice *non virtutibus ex dignitate, sed ex virtute dignitatibus honor accedat*, 16, 1; Fox 50, 20-22. Gê underþiódaþ eówre héhstan medemnesse under ða eallra nyðemestan gesceafta *vos dignitatem vestram infra infima quæque detruditis*, 14, 2; Fox 44, 34. Ðæt gê nǽfre swâ heálîce medumnesse (*the priestly office*) ne forwyrcen, L. E. I. 1; Th. i. 402, 27. Ealdordômes medomnysse, Shrn. 151, 19. II. *kindness, condescension, appreciation of worth in others* (cf. mǽþ, V):—Medemnysse ðînre *benignitatis tuæ*, Blickl. Gl.: Ps. Spl. 64, 12. Medumnysse *benignitatem*, 51, 3: Blickl. Homl. 145, 33. Cf. medumlîce, II.

medumung, e; *f.* I. *the fixing of the measure of anything*:—Â sceal dôm æfter dǽde and medemung be mǽðe *ever shall doom be according to deed, and fine be fixed with fair measure*, L. Eth. ix. 5; Th. i. 342, 5: L. E. B. 10; Th. ii. 242, 11. II.?:—Ðonon â be ecge on ða medemuncga (medemunga); of ðære medemuncge (mædemunge) on ðone ealdan wiðig, Cod. Dip. Kmbl. iii. 25, 21-23: v. 286, 31-33. [*O. H. Ger.* metemunga *temperies, temperamentum.*] v. medumian.

medu-rǽden[n], e; *f. Strong drinks, cellar* (in the sense of the liquors contained in it):—Rûmheort beón meodorǽdenne *liberal with liquors*, Exon. 90 a; Th. 339, 3; Gn. Ex. 88.

medu-scenc, es; *m. A draught* or *cup of mead*:—Meoduscencum hwearf geond ðæt healreced (cf. Ymbeode ides Helminga ôððæt heó Beówulfe medoful æt bær, 1244-), Beo. Th. 3965; B. 1980.

medu-seld, es; *n. Mead-house, house in which feasting takes place*, Beo. Th. 6123; B. 3065.

medu-setl, es; *n. A mead-seat, a seat in a banqueting-hall*, Beo. Th. 10; B. 5.

medu-stîg, e; *f. Path to the mead-hall*:—Cyning of brýdbûre treddode ... and his cwên mid him medostîg gemæt ... Hrôðgâr tô healle geóng, Beo. Th. 1845-1855; B. 920-925.

medu-wæge, an: -wæg, e; *f. The Medway*:—Sint ðæs londes gemǽra: an westhealfæ Scipfliót, an norþhalfe Meodowæge, Cod. Dip. Kmbl. ii. 71, 25. Miodowæge, iii. 400, 26. Partem fluminis Meduwaeian, i. 135, 34. Andlang Medwæge, 283, 4. Andlang Medwægan, Chr. 999; Erl. 134, 24. In tô Medewæge, 1016; Erl. 157, 4. Ôþ mediwægan sindan ða gemǽra. Fram Miadawegan, Cod. Dip. Kmbl. ii. 86, 24. Ôþ Miodowegan, 17. In flumen Medewiæge, iii. 386, 26. Ôþ ða eá Medewegan, 400, 31.

medu-wang, es; *m. A mead-plain, the ground surrounding the house where mead is drunk*:—Tô sele comon feówertýne Geáta gongan, môdig (*Beowulf*) on gemonge meodowongas træd. Ðâ com ingân ealdor þegna, Beo. Th. 3291; B. 1643.

medu-wêrig; *adj. Sated with feasting*, Judth. 11; Thw. 24, 38; Jud. 229: 12; Thw. 25, 6; Jud. 245.

medu-wyrt, e; *f. Meadow-sweet*, also *mead-sweet*:—Meodowyrt *melleuna*, Wrt. Voc. ii. 59, 43: L. M. 1, 38; Lchdm. ii. 94, 14. Medowyrt, Lchdm. ii. 96, 17: 1, 44; Lchdm. ii. 108, 11. Medewyrt *malletina* (?), Wrt. Voc. i. 31, 1: Lchdm. iii. 6, 12: 16, 9. Meodeuyrt *mellauna, papamo*, 304, 1, 35. [*Scott.* med-uart: *Dan.* mjöd-urt.]

med-wîs; *adj. Not wise, dull, foolish*:—Ða medwîsan *hebetes*, Past. 30, 1; Swt. 203, 6, 15, 21; 205, 2, 4, 17. Sume wîsran sume medwîsran *quosdam sapientes, quosdam tardiores*, 30, 2; Swt. 205, 7. Medwîsum men, Exon. 102 b; Th. 387, 24; Rä. 5, 10.

még, megen, megende. v. mǽg, mǽw, mægen, magan.

meh, meht. v. mê, meaht.

mêi, meig. v. mǽg.

mela. v. melu.

melc, meolc; *adj. Giving milk, milch*:—Melc *foetus*, Wrt. Voc. i. 287, 57: *fetus*, ii. 36, 33. Melce and tydrende *foetus*, 36, 32. Hê geseah wilde hinde melce and se geþyrsta mon meolcode ða hinde, Shrn. 130, 3. Wið tittia sâr wîfa ðe beóþ melce, Herb. 19, 4; Lchdm. i. 112, 16. Meolce breóst *ubera*, Wrt. Voc. i. 44, 14. [*Icel.* mjólkr *giving milk*: *O. H. Ger.* melch *foetus*: *Ger.* melk.]

melcan; *p.* mealc, *pl.* mulcon; *pp.* molcen *To milk*:—Ic melce *mulgeo*, Ælfc. Gr. 26, 3; Som. 28, 55. Melke, Coll. Monast. Th. 20, 17. Se ðe melcþ *qui emulget*, Kent. Gl. 1121. Milciþ *morgit* (?), Ep. Gl. 14 f, 16. Mîlcet, Wrt. Voc. ii. 55, 73. Milcit, 114, 17: *mulgit*, Wülck. 33, 26. Hê êwa melce, Shrn. 61, 19. Ðæt fæt ðe ðû wille on melcan, L. M. 1, 67; Lchdm. ii. 142, 9. Nîge molcen, 2, 27; Lchdm. ii. 222, 13: 2, 25; Lchdm. ii. 218, 22. [*O. H. Ger.* melchan.] v. meolcian.

melcing-fæt, es; *n. A milk-pail*:—Melcingfata *mulctra*, Germ. 390, 66. v. meolc-fæt.

meld, e; *f.* [*O. H. Ger.* melda; *f. delatura, delatio, proditio*] *Declaration, proclamation*:—Hê wîde beád Metodes mihte ðǽr hê meld âhte *he declared the Lord's power widely, where he could proclaim it*, Cd. 208; Th. 256, 30; Dan. 648.

melda, an; *m.* I. *a narrator, an informer, announcer*:—Ðæs ðe ic ǽfre on ealdre ǽngum ne wolde monna ofer moldan melda weorþan *what I would never relate to any man upon earth*, Exon. 50 b; Th. 176, 3; Gû. 1203: 73 b; Th. 275, 28; Jul. 557. Sió æsc biþ melda, nalles þeóf *the axe is an informer, not a thief* (i. e. the noise made by hewing with an axe would attract the attention, which a thief would certainly shun, v. Grmm. R. A. 47), L. In. 43; Th. i. 128, 23: L. Edg. H. 8; Th. i. 260, 17. Þurh ðæs meldan hond; se sceolde wong wîsian, Beo. Th. 4802; B. 2405. Ic tô meldan wearþ *I turned informer* (cf. Th. 259, 28 sqq., 270, 10 for the narrative forced from the devil by Juliana: cf. also Jul. pp. 39 sqq.), Exon. 74 b; Th. 279, 30; Jul. 621. Ðæt wê ðæs morþres meldan ne weorþen *that we be not informers of the crime*, Elen. Kmbl. 856; El. 428. II. *a betrayer*:—Gê sind meldan and manslagan (*betrayers and murderers*, Acts vii. 52), Homl. Th. i. 46, 24. [Cf. *O. L. Ger.* meldari *sponsor*: *O. H. Ger.* meldari *delator, proditor.*]

meldan; *p.* ede *To announce, declare*:—Ûs frunon fǽcnum wordum meldedan *they questioned us, with crafty words declared*, Ps. Th. 136, 3. Ic ne mæg word sprecan, mældan for monnum, Exon. 105 a; Th. 399, 18; Rä. 19, 2. Meldan, 109 b; Th. 411, 13; Rä. 29, 12. v. tô-meldan, meldian.

melde, an; *f. Orach*, a plant-name:—Melde, Lchdm. iii. 6, 11. Nim meldon ða wyrt, 54, 23. [*Dan.* meld: *O. H. Ger.* malta *beta*; melda *atriplex*: *Ger.* melde.] v. tûn-melde.

meld-feoh, *gen.* -feós; *n. Fee paid for giving information*:—Se ðe hit (forstolen flǽsc) ofspyraþ, hê âh ðæt meldfeoh, L. In. 17; Th. i. 114, 4. v. Grmm. R. A. 656.

meldian; *p.* ode, ede. I. *to declare, announce, tell*:—Mûþ habbaþ and ne meldiaþ wiht os *habent, et non loquentur*, Ps. Th. 134, 16. Hî sprecaþ unnyt sæcgeaþ and wôh meldiaþ *pronuntiabunt et loquentur iniquitatem*, 93, 4. Ælfrêd cræft meldode *Alfred displayed his art*, Bt. Met. Fox Introd. 4; Met. Einl. 2. Ic sceal môd meldian swâ ðû mê beódest *I must tell all my mind, as thou dost bid me*, Exon. 72 b; Th. 270, 10; Jul. 463. Ongan meldigan ðone hâlgan wer *the devil began to tell who the holy man was*, Andr. Kmbl. 2341; An. 1172. Ðâ geneálǽhton mâ hine meldigende (*declaring that Peter was with Jesus*), Homl. Th. ii. 248, 32. II. *to inform against, accuse*:—Oft mec îsern scôd sâre on sîdan, ic swîgade, nǽfre meldade monna ǽngum (*never accused any man* (?) or *told no man*), Exon. 126 a; Th. 485, 17; Rä. 71, 15. Meldadun *vel* wroegdun *defferuntur*, Wrt. Voc. ii. 106, 17. Meldedun, 25, 26. *Desequunt vel* meldadan i. *accusabant*, 139, 15. Hê nolde meldian on his geféran ðe mid him sieredon *he would not inform against his companions who had plotted with him*, Bt. 16, 2; Fox 52, 20. [*O. Sax.* meldôn *to declare, betray, proclaim*: *O. H. Ger.* meldên, meldôn *prodere, deferre, producere*: *Ger.* melden.] v. ge-meldian, meldan.

meldung, e; *f. Information* (against a person), *betrayal*:—Hê swýðe mânfullîce âcweald wæs þurh meldunga his âgenes wîfes *multum nefarie peremptus est proditione conjugis suæ*, Bd. 3, 24; S. 557, 39. [*O. H. Ger.* meldunga *proditio, delatura*: *Ger.* meldung.]

mêle, mǽle, es; *m. A cup, bowl, basin*:—Meeli *aluium*, Ep. Gl. 26, 38: Wrt. Voc. ii. 99, 72. Mêli *avum* (= *alvium*?), 101, 31. Mêle *albium*, 8, 27: i. 285, 9: *patera*, 24, 39. Mêlas *karchesia*, 24, 42: *ciatos*, ii. 22, 44. Dô mêle fulne buteran on, L. M. 1, 36; Lchdm. ii. 86, 17. [Halliw. Dict. meles and payles.] v. wæter-mêle (-mǽle).

mele-, mil-deáw, es; *n. m. Honey-dew, nectar*:—Hunig[deáw] oððe mildeáw *nectar*, Wrt. Voc. ii. 61, 38. Nô hê fôddor þigeþ mete on moldan nemne meledeáwes dǽl gebyrge se dreóreþ oft æt midðre nihte *non illi cibus est nostro concessus in orbe, ambrosios libat cælesti nectare rores, stellifero teneri qui cecidere polo*, Exon. 59 b; Th 215, 29; Ph. 260. [Swetter is munegunge of þe þen mildeu o muðe, O. E. Homl. i. 269, 5. In *Prompt. Parv.* and *Wick.* the word has the modern sense *blight, uredo, aurugo*; so *O. H. Ger.* mili-tou: *M. H. Ger.* mili-tou: *Ger.* mehl-thau. The first part of the word seems to mean *honey*, cf. milisc and *Goth.* miliþ *honey*. Grmm. D. M. p. 607, gives another etymology, connecting it with *Icel.* mêl *bit* (*of a bridle*), the dew being the foam which fell from the bit of the horse Hrîmfaxi.]

melsc. v. milisc.

meltan; *p.* mealt, *pl.* multon; *pp.* molten. I. *to melt, become liquid, be consumed, dissolved*:—Ic mylte *liqueo*, Ælfc. Gr. 35; Som. 38, 7. Mylt *dissolvitur*, Wrt. Voc. ii. 147, 25. Swâ weax melteþ, Ps. Th. 57, 7. Mylteþ, 67, 2. His sylfes hâm brynewylmum mealt (*was consumed*), Beo. Th. 4642; B. 2326. Multon meretorras (*when the waters of the Red Sea fell upon the Egyptians*), Cd. 167; Th. 208, 16; Exod. 484. Ðonne mê mægen mylte *dum defecerit virtus mea*, Ps. Th. 70, 8. Ne sceal âne hwæt meltan (*be consumed on the pile*), Beo. Th. 6014; B. 3011. Weax miltende *cera liquescens*, Ps. Spl. 21, 13. Myltende *liquidas*, Hpt. Gl. 470, 73. II. of food, *to digest*:—Late mylt gǽten flǽsc *goat's flesh digests slowly*, L. M. 2, 16; Lchdm. ii. 196, 16, 25. Ða scearpan þing unýþelîce meltaþ, 2, 23; Lchdm. ii.

212, 2. Wiđ đon đe men mete untela melte, 2, 29; Lchm. ii. 226, 5. Đa đe on đære uferan wambe gewuniaþ and ne mâgon meltan, 1, 2; Lchdm. ii. 26, 17. Myltan, 2, 27; Lchdm. ii. 222, 18. Wel meltende mettas, 2, 16; Lchdm. ii. 196, 21. v. for-, ge-meltan; miltan.

meltung, e; *f. Melting* (of food), *digestion*:—Đara metta meltung, L. M. 2, 17; Lchdm. ii. 198, 3. Hió næfþ gôde meltunge *it* (*the stomach of a watery nature*) *hath not good digestion*, 2, 27; Lchdm. ii. 220, 27. v. un-meltung.

melu, melo, mela, meolu, mealu, wes; *n. Meal, flour*:—Melu odđe offrung *ador*, Ælfc. Gr. 9, 21; Som. 10, 32: *farina*, Wrt. Voc. i. 83, 17: ii. 38, 70. Swâ swâ mon melo (Cott. MS. meolo) sift, đæt melo (meolo) þurhcrýpþ ǽlc þyrel, Bt. 34, 11; Fox 152, 2. Đæt mela biþ gôd, L. M. 1, 38; Lchdm. ii. 94, 2. Genim hwǽtenes meluwes smedman, L. M. 1, 61; Lchdm. ii. 134, 4. Melwes (Lind. mælo) *farinæ*, Mt. Kmbl. 13, 33. Melues *similæ*, Lev. 6, 20. Melewes smedma *simila*, 83, 65. Melewes *polline*, mealewes *farinæ*, Hpt. Gl. 497, 36, 37. Đrittig mittan clǽnes melowes (*fine flour*) and sixtig mittan ôđres melowes, Homl. Th. ii. 576, 32. Meolwes, Chart. Th. 40, 10. *Pollis* smedma, *pollinis* of melowe, Ælfc. Gr. 9, 28; Som. 11, 48. Windlas mid meluwe *canistra farinæ*, Gen. 40, 16. Of rigenum melwe, L. M. 2, 32; Lchdm. ii. 236, 9. Genim beren mela gôd, L. M. 1, 5; Lchdm. ii. 50, 3. Beren meala, Lchdm. iii. 8, 15. [*Icel.* mjöl: *O. H. Ger.* melo *farina, polenta, pulvis*: *Ger.* mehl.] v. ed-melu.

melu-gescot, es; *n. A contribution* or *payment made in meal*:—Hwîlum weaxgescot, hwîlum mealtgescot, hwîlum melagescot, Wulfst. 171, 2 note. [Cf. *Icel.* mjöl-skuld *rent to be paid in meal*.]

melu-hûs, es; *n. A house in which to keep meal*:—Mealehûs *farinale*, Wrt. Voc. i. 58, 41.

men *in* nim sealtes, þrý men *take of salt three parts*, L. M. 1, 50; Lchdm. ii. 124, 4. [*Cockayne compares the word with Swedish* mån *apart*.]

mend-lîc (?); *adj. Moderate, small*:—Tô medmyclum (MS. C. mendlîcum) fæce *ad modicum*, Bd. 2, 13; S. 516, 21.

mene, myne, es; *m. A necklace, an ornament*:—Maenoe *crepundia*, Wrt. Voc. ii. 105, 44. Mene *lunules*, 71, 1. Myne *crepundium* i. *monile gutturis*, 136, 68. Myne *vel* sweorbêh *monile* vel *serpentinum*, i. 40, 50: 74, 58. Đes myne *hoc monile*, Ælfc. Gr. 9, 2; Som. 8, 28. Brôsinga mene, Beo. Th. 2403; B. 1199. (v. Grmm. D. M. 283.) Menas *monilia*, Wrt. Voc. i. 16, 60: *crepundia, ornamenta, monilia*, Hpt. Gl. 419, 30: 517, 29. Mynas, 481, 43: *lunulas*, 458, 30. Menum *monilibus*, 434, 71. Mynum *lunulis*, Wrt. Voc. ii. 49, 71. [*O. Sax.* hals-meni: *Icel.* men; *n. a necklace*: *O. H. Ger.* menni; *pl. monilia*.] v. heals-mene.

menen, mennen, minnen, es; *n. A female servant, bondwoman, handmaid*:—Ân menen ł þeówæ *ancilla*, Mt. Kmbl. Rush. 26, 69: *vernacula*, Wrt. Voc. ii. 123, 37. Mennen *ancilla*, 2, 39. Sunu menenes đînes *filius ancillæ tuæ*, Ps. Surt. 115, 16: 122, 2. Minenes, p. 200, 6. Be ceorles mennenes niédhǽmede. Gif mon ceorles mennen tô nédhǽmde geþreáteþ, L. Alf. pol. 25; Th. i. 78. 11–12: Cd. 103; Th. 136, 14; Gen. 2258: 97; Th. 128, 13; Gen. 2126. Đeáh hwâ bebycgge his dôhtor on þeówenne ne sîe hió ealles swâ þeówu swâ ôđru mennen is, L. Alf. 12; Th. i. 46, 13. CCL đara monna, esna and mennena (*servos et ancillas*), Bd. 4, 13; S. 583, 20. [Cf. *Icel.* man; *n. a bondman* or *bondwoman*: *O. H. Ger.* mana-houpit = *a servant*; v. Grmm. R. A. 301.] v. drunc-, mere-, þeów-menen (-mennen).

menen-lîc (= ?), myniend-lîc *hortandus, ammonendus*, Hpt. Gl. 485, 64.

mene-scilling, es; *m. A coin worn as an ornament*:—Menescillingas *lunules*, Ep. Gl. 13 b, 37: Wrt. Voc. ii. 113, 15. Mynescillingas, 49, 72.

mengan, mængan, mencgan; *p.* de. I. *to mix, mingle, combine*:—Ic menge *mango* (?), Wrt. Voc. ii. 58, 42. Mengio, 113, 59: Epl. Gl. 156, 36. Mænge *margo* (*mango*?), Wrt. Voc. ii. 58, 48. Menget *confundit*, 105, 11. Ic mînne drinc mengde wiđ teárum *potum meum cum fletu temperabam*, Ps. Th. 101, 7. Đû wiđ fýre foldan mengdest, Bt. Met. Fox 20, 223; Met. 20, 112. Đara blôd Pilatus mengde (*miscuit*) mid hyra offrungum, Lk. Skt. 13, 1. Đonne wê medelcwidas mengdon *when we conversed*, Salm. Kmbl. 865; Sal. 432. Hî hî wiđ mânfullum megndan þeóde *commisti sunt inter gentes*, Ps. Th. 105, 26. Hî mînne mete mengde wiđ geallan, 68, 22. Meng đa blisse wiđ đa unrôtnesse, Prov. Kmbl. 71. Fîfleáfon seáw mencg (mængc, MS. B) tô wîne, Herb. 3, 6; Lchdm. i. 88, 12. Menge mon wiđ âseowen hunig, L. M. 2, 26; Lchdm. ii. 220, 10. Nânne wǽtan hî ne cûþon wiđ hunige mengan, Bt. 15; Fox 48, 10. Mængan, Bt. Met. Fox 8, 48; Met. 8, 22. Mengan lyge wiđ sôđe, Elen. Kmbl. 612; El. 306. *Of sexual intercourse*:—Is eác bewered đæt mon hine menge wiđ his brôđor wîfe *cum cognata misceat prohibitum est*, Bd. 1, 27; S. 491, 16, 10. II. *intrans*:—Hât and ceald hwîlum mencgaþ, Cd. 216; Th. 273, 6; Sat. 132. III. *to mingle together, stir up, disturb*:—Mengan merestreámas, Exon. 123 b; Th. 475, 3; Bo. 42. Meregrundas mengan, Beo. Th. 2903; B. 1449. [Cf. his mod him gon mengen, Laym. 3407; wraþþe meinþ þe heorte blod, O. and N. 945. *Prompt. Parv.* mengyn *misceo*: *O. Sax. O. L. Ger.* mengian: *O. Frs.* mengia: *O. H. Ger.* chi-menghid; *pp.*: *Ger.* mengen.] v. ge-, geond-mengan.

mengung, mencgung, e; *f. Mixture, preparation, composition*:—Mencingc *confectio*, Hpt. Gl. 250, 30. [*Prompt. Parv.* mengynge *mixtura, commixtio*.] v. ge-mengung.

menian, menig. v. mynian, manig.

menigdu; *f. A multitude, a body of people*:—Menigdu *manum*, Wrt. Voc. ii. 58, 26. [*O. H. Ger.* managoti; *f. manus*.]

menigu, **mengu**, menigeo; *indecl.*: also *gen.* e; *f. A many, multitude, crowd, great number*:—Seó menigu đara freónda, Bt. 29, 2; Fox 106, 6. Menigo, Andr. Kmbl. 898; An. 449. Menego, Cd. 214; Th. 270, 1; Sat. 83. Menigeo (MS. A. mænigeo) *turba*, Mk. Skt. 2, 13. Mænigeo (MS. A. mænio), Mt. Kmbl. 9, 8. Mænegeo, Cd. 121; Th. 156, 14; Gen. 2588. Mengu, Elen. Kmbl. 450; El. 225. Mengeo, Cd. 80; Th. 100, 13; Gen. 1663. Mengio, Bt. 14, 1; Fox 42, 20. Menio, Cd. 223; Th. 294, 25; Sat. 476. Mænieo, 173; Th. 216, 12; Dan. 5. Đære menigo þeáw, Andr. Kmbl. 354; An. 177. Menego, Cd. 220; Th. 284, 14; Sat. 321. On menigeo *in multitudine*, Ps. Th. 65, 2. Mænigeo, 68, 13. Mid manigeo, Rood Kmbl. 300; Kr. 151. From mengu *a multitudine*, Ps. Surt. 63, 3: Exon. 66 b; Th. 245, 16; Jul. 45. Mid mengo, Elen. Kmbl. 754; El. 377. For đære meniu, Gen. 16, 10. For đære miclan menige, Ors. 3, 9; Swt. 124, 36. Of menge wetra *de multitudine aquarum*, Ps. Surt. 17, 17. For đære mænige, Rood Kmbl. 221; Kr. 112: Bt. Met. Fox 26, 121; Met. 26, 61. Ic âlýse ealle đa menigo, Andr. Kmbl. 201; An. 101. Menigeo (MS. A. mænio) *turbam*, Mt. Kmbl. 9, 25. Mænegu (Rush. mengu), 15, 33. Mænego, Cd. 91; Th. 116, 7; Gen. 1932. Manegu, Hy. 10, 8; Hy. Grn. ii. 293, 8. Mengu *multitudinem*, Ps. Surt. 9, 25. Mengo, Exon. 128 b; Th. 493, 12; Rä. 81, 29. Mengeo, Cd. 83; Th. 103, 30; Gen. 1726. Meniu *exercitum*, Wrt. Voc. ii. 106, 46. God đa miclan Pharones menge gelytlode, Ors. 1, 7; Swt. 38, 27: Cd. 56; Th. 69, 8; Gen. 1132. Cômon menigu (MS. A. mænigu: Lind. menigo) *conveniunt turbæ*, Mk. Skt. 10, 1. Đa menigeo (MS. A. mænio: B. mænigeo: Rush. menigu: Lind. menigo) *turbæ*, Mt. Kmbl. 12, 23. Forlǽt đâs mænegeo (MS. A. mænygeo: B. mænegu: Rush. mengu) *demitte turbas*, 14, 15. Đa eargan mengo *fugaces turmas*, Wrt. Voc. ii. 151, 48. [*Goth.* managei: *O. Sax. O. L. Ger.* menegî, menigî: *O. Frs.* menî: *O. H. Ger.* managî, manegî, menigî *multitudo, turba, legio, caterva*: *Ger.* menge.] v. mann-menigu.

menisc, men-lufigende, mennen. v. mennisc, menn-lufigende, menen.

mennisc; *adj. Human*:—Nân mennisc man *no human being*, Bt. 33, 2; Fox 122, 15. Ne gegrîpe eów nǽfre nân costung bûton menniscu *tentatio vos non apprehendat, nisi humana*, Past. 11, 5; Swt. 71, 12. Đus mǽrsode se mennisca Crist his heofenlîcan Fæder, Homl. Th. ii. 362, 11. Đâ getreówde hê in godcundre fultom đǽr se mennesca wan wæs, Bd. 2, 7; S. 509, 23. Anginn menniscre âlýsednysse . . . intinga mennisces forwyrdes, Homl. Th. i. 194, 27–30. Mennisce handa hit ne mihton tôwurpan, Homl. Th. ii. 510, 13. Hæleþa forlor, menniscra morþ, Cd. 33; Th. 45, 5; Gen. 722. [*Goth.* mannisks: *O. Sax.* mennisk, mannisk: *O. Frs.* mannisk: *Icel.* mennskr: *O. H. Ger.* mennisc.]

mennisc, es; *n. Men, people*:—Đis is đæt mennisc đe ealle mîne dǽda mid heora wordum onwendan, Blickl. Homl. 175, 24. Đonne eówre wærgaþ mennisc *when men curse you*, Mt. Kmbl. Rush. 5, 11. Gif đǽr ôđer mennisc borh sîe *if other people be surety*, L. Alf. pol. 1; Th. i. 60, 19. Đâ wearþ micel mennisc geweaxen *then men began to multiply*, Homl. Th. i. 20, 21. Đǽr wæs mycel mennisc tôweard *there was a great multitude of people coming*, 182, 5. Đeáh eal mennisc wǽre gegaderod *though all men were gathered together*, 26, 26. Đære þeóde mennisc swâ wlitig wǽre *the men of that nation were so beautiful*, ii. 120, 22. Đæt đû ne nyme wîf mînum suna of đisum menisce (*de filiabus Chananæorum*), Gen. 24, 3. Josue ofslôh eall đæt mennisc đe on muntum wunode (*omnem terram montanam*), Jos. 10, 40: Thw. 161, 37. Âcwealde đæt earme mennisc, Homl. Th. ii. 474, 7. [Cf. *O. H. Ger.* mannisco, mennisco *homo*: *Ger.* mensch.]

mennisc-lîc; *adj. Human*:—Mennisclîc *humanus*, Ælfc. Gr. 38; Som. 41, 42. Menniscl̂ic (*humanum*) is đæt mon on his môde costunga þrowige, Past. 11, 5; Swt. 71, 13. [*O. H. Ger.* manisc-, menisc-, mennisc-lîh *humanus*: *Ger.* mensch-lich.]

mennisc-lîce; *adv. Humanly, after the manner of men*; humaniter, humanitus, Ælfc. Gr. 38; Som. 41, 43: 42, 6.

mennisc-ness, e: *f.* I. *humanity, human nature* (generally in reference to Christ), *incarnation*:—Crist becom on hire innoþ and þurh hî on menniscnysse wearþ âcenned (*was born a man*), Homl. Th. i. 194, 8. Ne wearþ se Fæder mid menniscnysse befangen, 284, 23. Wê wurþiaþ ûres Hǽlendes âcennednysse æfter đære menniscnysse. Hê wæs âcenned mid lîchaman and mid sâwle, se đe wæs ǽfre mid đam Fæder wunigende on đære godcundnysse, ii. 4, 20. Ûre Hǽlend Crist underfêng menniscnysse, 600, 6. Fram Drihtnes menniscnysse *ab incarnatione Domini*, Bd. 1, 5; S. 476, 5. Æfter đære drihtenlîcan menniscnysse, 1, 6; S. 476, 16. II. *humaneness, humane behaviour*:—Hî syndon fremfulle (*benigni*) menn, and gyf hwylc mann tô him cymeþ đonne gyfaþ hî him wîf ǽr hî hine on weg lǽtan. Se Macedonisca Alexander đâ đâ hê him tô com đâ wæs hê wundriende hyra menniscnysse (*miratus* *est eorum humanitatem*), Nar. 38, 25. [*O. H. Ger.* mannisc-nissa; *and* cf. mennisg-heit *humanitas, incarnatio.*]

menniscu, e; *f. Humanity, state of man*:—Hē forleás his mennisce *ut homo esse perderet*, Past. 4, 2; Swt. 39, 24. [*Mid. E.* menske *honour*: *O. Sax.* menniskī *humanitas*: *Icel.* menska: *O. H. Ger.* mennisgī.]

mentel, es; *m. A mantle, cloak*:—Mentel *colobium*, Wrt. Voc. ii. 134, 38. Hē forcearf his mentles ǣnne læppan *oram chlamydis ejus abscidit*, Past. 28, 6; Swt. 197, 21. Mid twyfealdum mentle *diploide*, Ps. Spl. 108, 28. Hyre beteran mentel, Chart. Th. 537, 32. [*Lat.* mantellum: *Icel.* möttull: *O. H. Ger.* mantel, mandal *chlamys, pallium.*]

mentel-preón, es; *m. A mantle-pin, brooch*:—Hió becwiþ hyre mentelpreón, Charl. Th. 533, 33.

meó; *gen.* meón *A shoe* or *sock covering the foot*:—Meó *pedula*, Wrt. Voc. i. 26, 2. Meón *pedulos* (cf. Wülck. 601, 19–21 '*pedules*, pars caligarum que pedem capit, *a vampey*: *pedulus* a pynson, or a sok'), 82, 1: *calsus* (cf. *Fr.* chausser: *Span.* calzar *to put on shoes*), ii. 127, 71.

meodu-, meocs, meohs, meolc; *adj.* v. medu-, meox, melc.

meolc, meoluc, milc, e; *f. Milk*:—Ðeós meolc *hoc lac*, Ælfc. Gr. 9, 76; Som. 14, 21: Wrt. Voc. i. 283, 31. Sūr meolc *oxygala, acidum lac*: þicce meolc *colustrum*, 28, 2–3. Āwilled meolc *juta*, 290, 45. Hē (*the Pater Noster*) biþ sāwle hunig and mōdes meolc, Salm. Kmbl. 135; Sal. 67. Meoluc, Wrt. Voc. i. 65, 9: Ps. Th. 118, 70. Of ðam lande ðe weóll meolce and hunie . . . ðe flēwþ on riðum meolce and hunies, Num. 16, 13–14. Mid þynre meolce *with skim milk*, Bd. 3, 27; S. 559, 35. Mid lytle meolc (MS. B. meoloce) wætere gemengedre *cum parvo lacte aqua mixto*, 3, 23; S. 554, 33. Ðe flēwþ meolece and hunie, Ex. 3, 8. Abraham nam meoloc, Gen. 18, 8. Meoluc, Deut. 32, 14. Dō on þeorfe meoluc *put into skim milk*, L. M. 2, 52; Lchdm. ii. 272, 1. Ða rīcostan men drincaþ myran meolc, Ors. 1, 1; Swt. 20, 17. Is ðæt eálond welig on meolcum *dives lactis insula* (*Hibernia*), Bd. 1, 1; S. 474, 40. Wyl on meolcum *boil in milk*, L. M. 2, 65; Lchdm. ii. 296, 19. Mid cū. meolcum, 2, 25; Lchdm. ii. 218, 22. From milcum ādōen *ablactatus*, Blickl. Gl. [*Goth.* miluks: *O. Frs.* melok: *Icel.* mjólkr: *O. H. Ger.* miluh.] v. frum-meolc.

meolc-fæt, es; *n. A vessel for holding milk, a milk-pail*:—Meolcfæt *mulctrale* vel *sinum* vel *mulctrum*, Wrt. Voc. i. 25, 13. [*O. H. Ger.* melich-faz *multra.*] v. melcing-fæt.

meolc-hwīt; *adj. Milk-white*:—Of meolchwȳttre *lacteo*, Germ. 389, 70. Meolchwītum *lacteis*, 397, 32.

meolcian; *p.* ode. I. *to milk, take milk from an animal*:—Se geþyrsta mon meolcode ða hinde and dranc ða meolc, Shrn. 130, 4. Nān wīf hire yrfe ne meolcige, būtan heó ða meolc for Godes lufan syllan, Wulfst. 227, 10. Hyt biþ gōd ceáp tō milcian, Lchdm. iii. 178, 30. II. *to give milk, to suckle* (v. ge-milcian):—Ða breóst ða ðe nǣfre meolcgende nǣron, Blickl. Homl. 93, 32. [*Icel.* mjólka *to milk*; also *to give milk.*] v. melcan.

meolc-sūcend, es; *m. A suckling*:—Meolocsūcendra *lactantium*, Wrt. Voc. ii. 51, 71. Meolcsucgendra, 73, 9.

meolc-teónd, es; *m. A suckling*:—Of mūðe cilda and milcdeóndra *ex ore infantium et lactentium*, Ps. Surt. 8, 3.

meolu, meoluc. v. melu, meolc.

meord, meorð, meard, e; *f. Reward, pay*:—Byþ ðē meorð wið God, Andr. Kmbl. 550; An. 275. Meard *premium*, Rtl. 165, 5. Leán ł meard (mearða, *pl.* Lind.) *merces*, Mt. Kmbl. Rush. 5, 12. Leán ł mearde *mercedem*, 6, 2; (meard, Lind.), 10, 41. Geld him meard *redde illis mercedem*, Lind. 20, 8. Meorde (mearda, Lind.) onfōeþ *mercedem accipit*, Jn. Skt. Rush. 4, 36: Exon. 48 b; Th. 167, 13; Gū. 1059: 62 b; Th. 230, 15; Ph. 472: 76 a; Th. 286, 9; Jul. 729. Meorda hleótan, gingra geafena, 48 a; Th. 164, 20; Gū. 1014. Ðē sīe þonc meorda and miltsa *to thee be thanks for rewards and mercies*, 118 b; Th. 456, 15; Hy. 4, 67. Morða, 95 a; Th. 355, 24; Reim. 82. [*Goth.* mizdo: *Gk.* μισθός.]

meoring, e; *f. Obstacle, impediment, hindrance*:—Moyses ofer ða fela meoringa fyrde gelǣdde *Moses with many hindrances led the army across them*, Cd. 145; Th. 181, 16; Exod. 62. [Cf. *O. H. Ger.* marunga *impedimentum.*] v. mirran.

meornan; *p.* mearn, *pl.* murnon; *pp.* mornen *To care, feel anxiety, trouble one's self about anything, reck*:—Nalles for ealdre mearn *he recked not of life*, Beo. Th. 2889; B. 1442. Nalas for fǣhþe mearn *for fear of the feud was not troubled*, 3079; B. 1537. Nō mearn fore fyrene *he cared not for the crime he committed*, 273; B. 136. Lyt ǣnig mearn ðæt hié ūt geferedon dȳre māðmas *little anxiety did any feel about bringing out the precious treasures*, 6250; B. 3129. Wōdon wælwulfas for wætere ne murnon (*cared nought for water*), Byrht. Th. 134, 39; By. 96. v. be-meornan *and* murnan.

meós, es; *m. n.* (?) *Moss*:—Treówes meós *muscus*, Wrt. Voc. ii. 57, 72. Ragu and meós fornymþ eówres landes wæstmas *omnes fruges terræ tuæ rubigo consumet*, Deut. 28, 42. Sumne dǣl ealdes meóses ðe on ðam hālgan treówe geweaxen wæs (*aliquid de veteri musco*), Bd. 3, 2; S. 525, 10: Swt. A. S. Rdr. 96, 30. Meóse *muscum*, Wrt. Voc. ii. 59, 38. Cf. meós mōr, Cod. Dip. Kmbl. iii. 81, 29. [*O. H. Ger.* mios: *M. H. Ger.* mies; *m. n.*] v. mos *and next word.*

meós; *adj. Mossy*:—Innon meóson mōre; of meóson mōre, Cod. Dip. Kmbl. iii. 384, 23.

meóse, meotud, meottuc. v. mēse, metod, mattuc.

meoto *thought* (?) *in*:—Site nū tō symle and onsǣl meoto secgum swā ðīn sefa hwette *sit now at the feast, let loose thy thoughts to men, as thy mind prompts thee*, Beo. Th. 983; B. 489.

meówle, an; *f. A maid, damsel, virgin, woman*:—Ǣnlīcoste meówle *juvencula pulcherrima*, Hpt. Gl. 456, 39. Seó hālige meówle (*Judith*), Judth. 10; Thw. 22, 10; Jud. 56. Him brȳd sunu, meówle (*Mahalaleel's wife*) tō monnum brohte, Cd. 58; Th. 71, 17; Gen. 1172. Afrisc meówle, 171; Th. 215, 7; Exod. 579. Meówle, seó hyre bearn gesihþ brondas þeccan, Exon. 87 b; Th. 330, 5; Vy. 46. Secg oððe meówle *man or maid*, 102 b; Th. 387, 15; Rä. 5, 5. Ceorles dōhtor, mōdwlonc meówle, 107 a; Th. 407, 18; Rä. 26, 7. Freólīcu meówle *a damsel fair*, 124 b; Th. 479, 2; Rä. 62, 1. Marian, mǣrre meówlan, 14 a; Th. 28, 13; Cri. 446. In wīfes lufan, fremdre meówlan, 80 b; Th. 302, 20; Fä. 39. Wið ða hālgan mægþ, Metodes meówlan (*Judith*), Judth. 12; Thw. 25, 15; Jud. 261. [*Goth.* mawilo *a damsel, girl.*] v. iū-meówle.

meox, mix, myx, es; *n. Muck, dung, ordure, dirt*:—Meox *stercus*, Ælfc. Gr. 9, 32; Som. 12, 17: *coenum*, 13; Som. 16, 6: *rudera* vel *ruina*, Wrt. Voc. i. 22, 12. Fugeles meox *avium stercus*, L. Ecg. P. add. 10; Th. ii. 232, 32. Ðæt treów biþ bedolfen and mid meoxe beworpen . . . ðæt meox is ðæt gemynd his fūlan dǣda . . . Hwæt is fūlre ðonne meox? Homl. Th. ii. 408, 29–33: Lk. Skt. 13, 8. Licgaþ forsewene swā swā meox (Cott. MS. miox) under feltūne, Bt. 36, 1; Fox 172, 11: Homl. Skt. 2, 241. Heó eall forseah on meoxes gelīcnysse, 8, 38. Ða nȳtenu forrotedon on heora meoxe, Homl. Th. i. 118, 15. Būton hē ǣrest ārīse of ðam reócendum meoxe, ii. 320, 23. Ðone hlāf ðe biþ tō meoxe āwend, i. 258, 2. Tō meohxe, Ps. Th. 82, 8. Meoxe (meoxene?) *sterquilinio*, Hpt. Gl. 488, 21. Mixe, horwe *ceno*, i. *luto*, Wrt. Voc. ii. 130, 70. Of myxe dustes *de fece pulveris*, Hy. Surt. 136, 1. Meoxa *stercorum*, 484, 22. [*Mid. E.* mix, mex: *Frs.* miux: cf. *Goth.* maihstus: *O. H. Ger.* mist.]

meox-bearwe, an; *f. A dung-barrow, basket for carrying dung*:—Wylige oððe meoxbearwe *corbis* vel *cofinus*, Wrt. Voc. i. 86, 2. v. meox-wilige.

meoxen. v. mixen.

meox-force, an; *f. A fork used for removing dirt*:—Myxforce *rotabulum* (*rotabulum* furca vel illud lignum cum quo ignis movetur in fornace causa coquendi: et dicitur sic, quia rotat et proruit ignem furni gratia coquendi vel *stercora* purgandi), Wrt. Voc. i. 16, 34.

meox-wilige, an; *f. A basket for carrying dung*:—On meocswilian *in cophino*, Ps. Lamb. 80, 7. v. meox-bearwe.

merc, Merce, Mercisc, merce, mercels. v. mearc, Mirce, Mircisc, merece, mircels.

mere, mære, es; *m. f* (?). I. *the sea* (*mer* in *mer*-maid):—Mere swīðe grāp on fǣge folc (*of the waters of the deluge*), Cd. 69; Th. 83, 18; Gen. 138. Mere (*the Red Sea*) stille bād, 158; Th. 197, 2; Exod. 300: 166; Th. 206, 27; Exod. 458. Mere sweoðerade, ȳða ongin eft oncyrde, Andr. Kmbl. 930; An. 465. Æt meres ende *on the shore*, 442; An. 221. Ofer wīdne mere, 566; An. 283. Ofer sealtne mere, Menol. Fox 203; Men. 103. Mere sēcan, mǣwes ēþel, Exon. 123 b; Th. 474, 5; Bo. 25. II. *a mere, lake*:—Meri *stagnum*, Ep. Gl. 25 b, 16. Mere *stagnum*, Wrt. Voc. i. 54, 15: ii. 121, 28. Nis ðæt feor heonon ðæt se mere standeþ, Beo. Th. 2729; B. 1362. In eálonde ðæs myclan meres (*stagni*), Bd. 4, 29; S. 607, 10. Seó menigeo ðe stōd begeondan ðam mere, Jn. Skt. 6, 22. On culfran mere; of ðæm mere . . . On weorces mere; of ðære mere, Cod. Dip. Kmbl. iii. 76, 37–77, 3. Wið ðone mere *secus stagnum*, Lk. Skt. 5, 1, 2: 8, 22. Ðæt wē fundon sumne swīðe micelne mere in ðæm wǣre fersc wæter, Nar. 11, 26. On mære *in stagnum*, Blickl. Gl. Be norþan hodes mære . . . ðonon up on ðone mære, Cod. Dip. Kmbl. iii. 10, 19–26. Ofer burnan ge ofer meras and ofer ealle wæterpyttas *super rivos ac paludes et omnes lacus aquarum*, Ex. 7, 19. III, *an artificial pool, cistern*:—On Syloes mere *in natatoria Siloae*, Jn. 9, 7, 11. Drinc ðæt wæter of ðīnum āgenum mere *bibe aquam de cisterna tua*, Past. 48, 5; Swt. 373, 4, 8. [*Goth.* marei; *f.*: *O. Sax. O. L. Ger.* meri; *f.*: *Icel.* marr; *m.*: *O. H. Ger.* mari, meri; *m. n.*: *Ger.* meer; *n.*: *Lat.* mare.] v. fisc-, hran-, hring-, hwæl-, īs-, sund-, wīn-, ȳð-mere.

mere, myre, an; *f. A mare*:—Mere *equa*, Wrt. Voc. i. 23, 7. Mire, 287, 78. Myre, ii. 30, 42: Ælfc. Gr. 7; Som. 7, 2. Myran meolc, Ors. 1, 1; Swt. 20, 16. Ðære myran sunu, Bd. 3, 14; S. 540, 30. On myran rīdan, 2, 13; S. 517, 7. [*Icel.* merr: *O. H. Ger.* meriha, marha: *Ger.* mähre.] v. ass-, stōd-mere.

mēre. v. mǣre.

mere-bāt, es; *m. A sea-boat*, Andr. Kmbl. 492; An. 246.

mere-candel, e; *f. The sea-candle, the sun which rises from*, or *sets in the sea*, Bt. Met. Fox 13, 114; Met. 13, 57. Cf. heáðu-sigel.

merece, merce, es; *m. Marche* (a plant), *smallage*; apium graveolens:—Merici *apio*, Ep. Gl. 1 f, 4. Merice, Wrt. Voc. ii. 100, 46. Merce, 8, 44:

i. 286, 5: *apium*, 30, 37: 66, 69. Swînes mearce *apiaster*, ii. 7, 7. Merce *mercurialis*, 59, 45: *apiaster*, Ælfc. Gr. 8; Som. 7, 16. Merces sǽd, Herb. 97, 1; Lchdm. i. 210, 8. Grênes merces leáf, L. M. 1, 39; Lchdm. ii. 98, 23. Genim merce niođoweardne, 1, 61; Lchdm. ii. 134, 3. Merece (meric, Lind.) *mentam*, Lk. Skt. Rush. 11, 42. [*Dan.* mærke *smallage, water-parsley.*] v. stân-, wudu-merece (-merce).

mere-cist, e; *f. A sea-chest:*—Noe ongan wyrcan micle merecieste (*the ark*), Cd. 66; Th. 79, 26; Gen. 1317.

mere-deáþ, es; *m. Death in the sea, death by drowning*, Cd. 169; Th. 210, 9; Exod. 512. Meredeáþa mǽst (*the destruction of the Egyptians in the Red Sea*), 166; Th. 207, 9; Exod. 464.

mere-deór, es; *n. A sea-beast*, Beo. Th. 1120; B. 558. [*O. L. Ger.* meri-dier *a water-fowl: O. H. Ger.* meri-tier.]

mere-fara, an; *m. A sea-farer*, Beo. Th. 1008; B. 502.

mere-faroþ, es; *m. Sea-waves:*—On merefaroþe *on the waves*, Andr. Kmbl. 577; An. 289: 701; An. 351: Exon. 122 b; Th. 471, 16; Rä. 61, 2.

mere-fisc, es; *m. A sea-fish:*—Wæs merefixa mód onhrêred, Beo. Th. 1102; B. 549. [*O. H. Ger.* mere-uisc *piscis maris.*]

mere-flód, es; *m.* I. *a flood of water, deluge:*—Mereflód *diluvium*, Exon. 56 b; Th. 200, 18; Ph. 42: Cd. 67; Th. 81, 7; Gen. 1341. Streám fleów ofer foldan . . . miclade mereflód, Andr. Kmbl. 3050; An. 1528. II. *a body of water, flood, ocean:*—Mereflódes ýþa, Bt. Met. Fox 27, 4; Met. 27, 2: Cd. 167; Th. 209, 23; Exod. 503. On mereflóde middum *in the midst of the waters*, 8; Th. 9, 21; Gen. 145. Bisencte on mereflóde *drowned in ocean*, Exon. 72 b; Th. 271, 10; Jul. 480: 82 a; Th. 309, 19; Seef. 59.

mere-grot, es; *n. A pebble or stone of the sea, a pearl:*—Ne forlǽte ic đê nǽfre, mîn meregrot! Blickl. Homl. 149, 2. Is heofena rîce gelîc đam mangere đe sôhte đæt gôde meregrot. Đá hê funde đæt ân deórwyrđe meregrot đá bohte hê đæt meregrot, Mt. Kmbl. 13, 45–46. Bergean swylce meregrota (*margaritæ*), Nar. 37, 29. Gefrætwod swá swá mid meregrotum, Homl. Th. i. 596, 8. [Cf. *O. H. Ger.* meri-grioz *margarita, unio.*] v. next word.

mere-grota, an; *m. A pearl:*—Meregrota *margarita*, Wrt. Voc. i. 85, 24. On đám beóþ oft gemêtte đa betstan meregrotan *quibus inclusam sæpe margaritam optimam inveniunt*, Bd. 1, 1; S. 473, 18. [Cf. *O. Sax.* meri-grita, -griota.]

mere-grund, es; *m. The bottom of a sea or lake*, Beo. Th. 2902; B. 1449: 4207; B. 2100.

mere-hengest, es; *m. A sea-steed, a ship*, Exon. 104 a; Th. 395, 12; Rä. 15, 6: Bt. Met. Fox 26, 49; Met. 26, 25.

mere-hrægel, es; *n. A sea-garment, a sail:*—Merehrægla sum, segl sâle fæst, Beo. Th. 3815; B. 1905.

mere-hûs, es; *n. A sea-house* (*Noah's ark*), Cd. 65; Th. 78, 34; Gen. 1303: 69; Th. 82, 18; Gen. 1364.

mere-hwearf, es; *m. A sea-wharf, sea-shore*, Cd. 169; Th. 210, 16; Exod. 516.

mêre-hwît. v. mǽre *pure.*

mere-lâd, e; *f. A sea-way, the road which the sea furnishes*, Exon. 123 b; Th. 474, 9; Bo. 27.

mere-lîđende *sea-faring, a sea-faring person*, Cd. 71; Th. 84, 34; Gen. 1407: Beo. Th. 515; B. 255: Andr. Kmbl. 705; An. 353. [Cf. *Icel.* mar-lîđendr; *pl. sea-farers.*]

mere-men[n], e; *f. A siren:*—Meremen *sirena*, Wrt. Voc. i. 289, 6. Meremenna *sirenarum*, Hpt. Gl. 498, 65. [Brutus iherde siggen þurh his sæmonnen of þan ufele ginnen þe cuđen þa *mereminnen*, Laym. 1337: *O. H. Ger.* mer-min *siren;* meri-meni, -menni *scylla.*] v. next word and Grmm. D. M. 404–407.

mere-menen, -mennen, e; *f. A siren:*—Meremenin *sirina*, Wülck. 47, 7. Meremennena *sirenarum*, Wrt. Voc. i. 84, 12. [Cf. *Icel.* mar-mennill; *m. a sea-goblin.*] Cf. mere-wîf.

mere-næddra, an; *m.* -nædre, an; *f. A sea-adder, a lamprey:*—Merenæddra *murena* vel *murina* vel *lampreda*, Wrt. Voc. i. 55, 65. Myrenæddra, 77, 72. Merenædre, ii. 59, 23.

mere-smylte; *adj. Having the sea calm:*—Meresmylta wîc, Bt. Met. Fox 21, 24; Met. 21, 12.

mere-strǽt, e; *f. The road which the sea furnishes*, Elen. Kmbl. 483; El. 242: Beo. Th. 1032; B. 514.

mere-streám, es; *m. A sea-stream, the sea, water of the sea*, Cd. 39; Th. 51, 27; Gen. 833: 154; Th. 191, 5; Exod. 210: 166; Th. 207, 17; Exod. 468. Merestreám ne dear ofer eorþan sceát eard gebrǽdan (cf. sǽ, Bt. Fox 74, 26), Bt. Met. Fox 11, 130; Met. 11, 65: 20, 228; Met. 20, 114. Óþ merestreámas *unto the waters of the sea*, Cd. 199; Th. 247, 27; Dan. 503: Bt. Met. Fox 28, 65; Met. 28, 33. Manegum merestreámum *de aquis multis*, Ps. Th. 143, 12. [*O. Sax.* meri-strôm.]

mere-strengu; *f. Strength in the sea, strength for swimming:*—Ic merestrengo mâran âhte, earfeþo on ýđum, đonne ǽnig óđer man, Beo. Th. 1070; B. 533.

mere-swîn, es; *n. A sea-pig, porpoise, dolphin:*—Đes mereswîn *hic delfin*, Ælfc. Gr. 9, 14; Som. 9, 37: Wrt. Voc. ii. 26, 15: i. 281, 56. Mereswîn *bacharus*, 281, 57: 65, 61: *delphin* vel *bocharius* vel *simones*, 55, 60. Mereswýn *bacharus*, 21, 46. Meresuîn *bacarius*, ii. 102, 11. Ælc seldfyndefisc đe weordlîc byþ, styria and mereswýn, Cod. Dip. Kmbl. iii. 450, 28. Nim mereswînes fel, L. M. 3, 40; Lchdm. ii. 334, 1. Mereswýn and stirian *delphinos et sturias*, Coll. Monast. Th. 24, 9: Bd. 1, 1; S. 473, 17. [*Icel.* mar-swîn: *O. H. Ger.* meri-suîn: *Ger.* meerschwein *dolphin, porpoise.*]

mere-þyssa, an; *m. A sea-rusher, a ship:*—On mereþyssan, Andr. Kmbl. 892; An. 446. On mereþissan, 514; An. 257. [Cf. *Icel.* þysja *to rush;* þyss *uproar.*]

mere-torht; *adj. Bright from bathing in the sea* (epithet of morning):—Sió sunne brencþ eorþwarum morgen meretorhtne *the sun rising from the sea brings bright morn to men*, Bt. Met. Fox 13, 121; Met. 13, 61. Becwom ofer gârsecges [begong] morgen mæretorht [*or* mǽretorht *splendidly bright*, cf. *O. H. Ger.* mâri-mihil], Cd. 160; Th. 199, 29; Exod. 346. Cf. mere-candel.

mere-torr, es; *m. A tower formed by the sea* (*the walls formed by the waters of the Red Sea*), Cd. 167; Th. 208, 16; Exod. 484.

mere-weard, es; *m. A sea-ward, one who keeps guard in the sea:*—Se mereweard (*the whale*), Exon. 97 a; Th. 363, 13; Wal. 53.

mere-wêrig; *adj. Weary of journeying on the sea:*—Merewêrges mód *the mind of the sea-weary man*, Exon. 81 b; Th. 306, 23; Seef. 12.

mere-wîf, es; *n. A water-witch, woman living in a lake* (*Grendel's mother*), Beo. Th. 3042; B. 1519. [*O. H. Ger.* meri-wîb *sirena.*]

mergen. v. merigen.

merian; *p.* ede; *pp.* ed *To purify, refine:*—Đam đe his gâst wile mergan (MS. B. merian) of sorge âsceádan of scyldum *for him who will purify his spirit from the dross of care, separate it from guilt*, Salm. Kmbl. 112; Sal. 55. v. â-merian.

merig. v. mirig.

merigen, merien, mergen, es; *m.* I. *morning:*—Ûres andgites merigen is ûre cildhâd, Homl. Th. ii. 76, 14. Đá se mergen geworden wæs *when it was morning*, St. And. 10, 3. Mergen þridda, Cd. 8; Th. 10, 11; Gen. 155: Beo. Th. 4213; B. 2103: 4255; B. 2124. Merien *mane*, Wrt. Voc. i. 76, 53. On mergenne *mane*, Ps. Spl. 91, 2: Ps. Th. 54, 17: 89, 16: Beo. Th. 1134; B. 565. In merne *mane*, Mt. Kmbl. Lind. 20, 1: 21, 18. Tó merne, 16, 3. On đam dæge worhte God merigen and ǽfen, Homl. Th. i. 100, 5. On mergen *mane*, Ps. Spl. 89, 6. II. *the morning of the next day, morrow:*—Đû đe nâst hwæđer đû merigenes gebîde *thou that knowest not whether thou wilt live to see the morrow*, Homl. Th. ii. 104, 26. Hwæt gif ic bîde merigenes, Homl. Skt. 3, 585. In merne *in crastinum*, Mt. Kmbl. Lind. 6, 34. On merne, Jn. Skt. Lind. 1, 43: 12, 12. Tó merne *cras*, Lk. Skt. Lind. 13, 32. On mergen *in crastinum*, Jn. Skt. 1, 43: 12, 12. On merien, Homl. Th. ii. 502, 16. Wê nyton hwæt tó merigen biþ tóweard, 82, 17: i. 374, 21: 462, 3. Tó merigen *cras*, Ælfc. Gr. 38; Som. 39, 59. v. ǽr-, ǽrne-mergen, *and* morgen.

merigen-, mergen-dæg, es; *m. Morrow:*—Hê đæs mergendæges gebîdan môste, Blickl. Homl. 213, 25. v. morgen-dæg.

merigen-, mergen-lîc; *adj.* I. *belonging to the morning:*—Se merigenlîca tilia *the labourer who came to work in the morning*, Homl. Th. ii. 74, 29. Se mergenlîca steorra *the morning star*, Blickl. Homl. 137, 32. II. *belonging to the morrow:*—Đam ne fyligþ merigenlîc dæg, forđan đe him ne forstóp se gysternlîca, Homl. Th. i. 490, 19. Đýs mergenlîcan dæge, Blickl. Homl. 143, 21: 147, 29. v. morgen-lîc.

merigen-, mergen-tîd, e; *f. Morning-time, morning:*—Fram đære mǽran mergentîde óþ đæt ǽfen cume *a custodia matutina usque ad noctem*, Ps. Th. 129, 6. v. morgen-tîd.

merisc. v. mersc.

merne. v. merigen.

merra, merran, merring. v. mirra, mirran, mirring.

mersc, es; *m. A marsh:*—Mersc *calmetum*, Wrt. Voc. ii. 13, 42: 103, 10: 127, 55. Tó mærsce, Cod. Dip. Kmbl. iii. 175, 32. Đat lond at Þorpe mid mêdwe and mid merisce, iv. 295, 7. On sealtum mersce, Ps. Spl. 106, 34. Hê đa weaxendan wende eorþan on sealtne mersc (*in salsuginem*), Ps. Th. 106, 33: Blickl. Gl.: Cd. 160; Th. 199, 4; Exod. 333. Ne fersc ne mersc, Lchdm. iii. 286, 21. Sumra wyrta eard biþ on merscum *alias herbas ferunt paludes*, Bt. 34, 10; Fox 148, 23. On feldum and on mǽdum and on sealtum merscum, Cod. Dip. Kmbl. iii. 350, 8. Mersc *Romney Marsh*, Chr. 796; Erl. 58, 11.

mersc-land, es; *n. Marsh-land:*—Forneáh ǽlc tilþ on mersclande forfêrde, Chr. 1098; Erl. 235, 12.

mersc-mealwe, an; *f. Marsh-mallow:*—Merscmealewe *althea*, Wrt. Voc. i. 67, 20. Merscmealwe *hibiscum*, ii. 43, 3. Merscmealuwe. Þeós wyrt đe man *hibiscum* and óđrum naman merscmealwe (mealuwe, MS. B.) nemnaþ, Herb. 39; Lchdm. i. 140, 3–5. Merscmealwan crop, L. M. 3, 63; Lchdm. ii. 350, 24. Nim merscmealwan, 3, 8; Lchdm. ii. 312, 12.

mersc-mear-gealla, an; *m. A kind of gentian;* gentiana pneumonanthe:—Nim merscmeargeallan, L. M. 1, 39; Lchdm. ii. 100, 5: 1, 50; Lchdm. ii. 124, 1.

Mersc-ware; *pl. The inhabitants of marshy land:*—Myrcena cining oferhergode Cantware and Merscware (*men of Romney Marsh*), Chr. 796;

Erl. 59, 40. Monige on Merscwarum *many of the men of the fens*, 838; Erl. 66, 12.

mertze (?):—Mertze *merx*, Wrt. Voc. ii. 113, 82. [Cf. *O. H. Ger.* merzi *merx*, Grff. ii. 861.]

mes (?) *dung*:—Gesomna cūe mesa *collect cow-dung*, L. M. 1, 38; Lchdm. ii. 98, 5. ['Mes *stercus, fimus* (Kilian),' Cockayne.]

mēsan *to feed, eat*:—Ic mēsan mæg meahtelīcor ealdum þyrse *I can eat mightier meals than an old giant*, Exon. 111 a; Th. 425, 26; Rä. 41, 62. v. mōs.

mēse, meóse, mīse, mȳse, an; *f. A table;* also *what is on a table*:—Mīse (MS. T. mēse) *mensa*, Ps. Spl. 68, 27. Meóse *mensorium* (*mensorium* quod est in mensa, ut mantile, et vas escarium), Wrt. Voc. i. 26, 61. Mȳse ł beód *mensa*, 82, 21. Đa hwelpas etaþ of đām crumon đe feallaþ of heora hlāfordes mȳsan ... Seó mȳse is bōclīce lār ... Be đære mȳsan cwæþ se wītega: Drihten đū gegearcodest mȳsan on mīnre gesihþe, Homl. Th. ii. 114, 24–28: i. 330, 31, 34: Ps. Spl. 127, 4: Mk. Skt. 7, 28: Lk. Skt. 12, 21, 30. [*Goth.* mēs: *O. H. Ger.* mias, meas *mensa.*]

met. v. ge-, tæl-met.

metan; *p.* mæt, *pl.* mǣton; *pp.* meten. I. *to mete, measure*:—Ic mete *metior*, Ælfc. Gr. 31; Som. 35, 32. Ic meotu *metibor*, Ps. Surt. 59, 8: 107, 8. Ǣlc đæra þinga đe man met on fate *everything that is measured in a vessel*, Ælfc. Gr. 13; Som. 16, 8. On đam ylcan gemete đe gē metaþ eów byþ gemeten *qua mensura mensi fueritis, remetietur vobis*, Mt. Kmbl. 7, 2. Hwīlum mid folmum [hē] mæt weán and wītu, Cd. 229; Th. 309, 22; Sat. 714. II. *to measure out, mark off, assign the bounds of a place*:—Se geleáfa and seó lufu mǣton đone stede hwǣr hió drihtnes tempel rǣran woldan, Prud. 80. Đū gedydest đæt wē mǣtan ūre land mid rāpum, Ps. Th. 15, 6. Wīcsteal metan *castra metari*, Cd. 146; Th. 183, 16; Exod. 92. III. *to measure by paces, to traverse, pass over*:—Him eoh fore mīlpađas mæt, Elen. Kmbl. 2523; El. 1263. Fērdon forþ đanon, fēđelāstum foldweg mǣton, Beo. Th. 3271; B. 1633: 1032; B. 514: 1838; B. 917. Forþ gesāwon līfes lātþeów līfweg (liftweg?) metan, Cd. 147; Th. 184, 9; Exod. 104. IV. *to measure one thing by* or *with another, to compare*:—Se swēg wæs be winde meten *the sound was compared to the wind*, Blickl. Homl. 133, 31. Hē mæt đone welan tō đære winestran handa *he compared wealth to the left hand*, Past. 50, 2; Swt. 389, 18. Ne sint hī nō wiþ eów tō metanne *they are not to be compared with you*, Bt. 13; Fox 40, 10: 39, 8; Fox 224, 5: Bt. Met. Fox 21, 83; Met. 21, 42. Tō metenne wiđ đæt mōd, Bt. 16, 2; Fox 52, 6: 32, 2; Fox 116, 7. Tō mettanne, 18, 1; Fox 62, 4. [*Goth.* mitan: *O. L. Ger.* metan: *O. Frs. Icel.* meta: *O. H. Ger.* mezan: *Ger.* messen.] v. ā-, be-, ge-, wiđ-, wiđer-metan.

mētan; *p.* te *To paint*:—Ic mēte *pingo*, Ælfc. Gr. 28, 5; Som. 31, 60. Swā mēteras mētaþ on anlīcnyssan *as painters paint in likenesses*, Wrt. Voc. i. 41, 5. Seó đe mētan sceall *pictura*, Ælfc. Gr. 43; Som. 45, 3. Mētton ofergeweorke *depicto mausoleo*, Coll. Monast. Th. 32, 35. [Þe33 haffdenn liccness metedd, Orm. 1047. Cf. *Goth.* maitan *to cut*: *Icel.* meita *to cut*; meitill *a chisel*: *O. H. Ger.* meizan *to cut*; meizil *a chisel.*] v. ā-, ge-mētan, *and* mēting.

mētan; *p.* te *To meet with, come upon, come across, find*:—Ealle đe hē mildheorte mēteþ and findeþ, Ps. Th. 75, 6. For đȳ hī hit ne gemētaþ (MS. Cott. mētaþ) đe hī hit on riht ne sēcaþ, Bt. 36, 3; Fox 178, 4. Gē unæþelne ǣnigne [ne] mētaþ (gē nānne ne māgon mētan unæþelne, Bt. 30, 2; Fox 110, 16), Bt. Met. Fox 17, 34; Met. 17, 17. Moette *offendit*, Wrt. Voc. ii. 115, 41. Mētte, 63, 35. Đā eode hē furþor ōþ hē gemētte (MS. Cott. mētte) đa Parcas *then he went on until he came upon the Fates*, Bt. 35, 6; Fox 168, 24. Đā mētte hē đane man forþfēredne *he found the man departed*, Blickl. Homl. 217, 17. Hē ne mētte mundgripe māran, Beo. Th. 1506; B. 751: Andr. Kmbl. 942; An. 471: 1106; An. 553. Hē þreó mētte rōda ætsomne *he came upon three crosses together*, Elen. Kmbl. 1663; El. 833. Hī mētton *invenerunt*, Ps. Spl. 106, 4. Nime se đe hit on his æcere mēte, L. In. 42; Th. i. 128, 14. Swā ǣr swā hē hādes wyrþne mon mētan mihte *as soon as he could meet with a man worthy of the* (*episcopal*) *rank*, Bd. 3, 29; S. 561, 26. Đǣr byþ sōþ symble mēted *truth is ever found there*, Ps. Th. 118, 160. Đæt sigorbeácen mēted wǣre, funden in foldan, Elen. Kmbl. 1969; El. 986. [*Goth.* ga-mōtjan: *O. Sax.* mōtian: *O. Frs.* mēta: *Icel.* mœta.] v. ge-mētan.

met-cund (? meter-cund, q. v.); *adj. Metrical*:—Đȳ metcundan (dymetcunda, Wrt.), Wrt. Voc. ii. 75, 30. v. next word.

metcund-līc; *adj. Metrical*:—Metcundlīcere getincnesse *metrica facundia*, Hpt. Gl. 409, 17. v. preceding word.

METE, mæte, es; *m.* MEAT, *food*:—Mete *cibus*, Wrt. Voc. ii. 22, 80. Mīn mete (mett, Lind. Rush.) is đæt ic wyrce đæs willan đe mē sende, Jn. Skt. 4, 34. Gesoden mæt on wætere *elixus cibus*, Wrt. Voc. i. 27, 17. Swēte mete *dapis*, ii. 28, 29. Đū scealt mid earfoþnyssum đē metes tilian *thou shalt with hardships get thyself food*, Homl. i. 18, 15. Đæt hig beón eów tō mete *ut sint vobis in escam*, Gen. 1, 29: Cd. 38; Th. 50, 25; Gen. 814. Gā hyt eft in tō đam hālegan mynstre mid mete and mid mannum *let it revert to the holy monastery with meat and with men*, Chart. Th. 379, 21. Wyt ǣton swētne mete (*dulces cibos*), Ps. Th. 54, 13. Đæt ic macige mete đīnum fæder *ut faciam escas patri tuo*, Gen. 27, 9. Gif hȳ him syđđan ne dōþ mete ne munde *if they afterwards give him neither food nor favour*, L. Edm. S. 1; Th. i. 248, 7. Đǣr mæte þygde, Bd. 5, 4; S. 617, 11. Mettas *cibaria*, Wrt. Voc. ii. 15, 71: *dapes*, 28, 1: *fercula*, Hpt. Gl. 492, 75. Đa mettas (*cibos*) đe God self gesceóp, Past. 43, 9; Swt. 319, 1. Mīnum þeówum ic sylle mettas, Ælfc. Gr. 15; Som. 18, 65. Se đe mettas (*escas*) hæfþ, Lk. Skt. 3, 11. Earmra hungur hē oferswȳþde mid mettum, Bd. 2, 1; S. 500, 24. Mid cynelīcum mettum (*regalibus epulis*) gefylled, 2, 6; S. 528, 14. Fram swēttrum mettum *a cibis luculentioribus*, Wrt. Voc. ii. 6, 25. [*Goth.* mats: *O. Sax.* meti: *O. Frs.* mete: *Icel.* matr: *O. H. Ger.* maz; *n. esca.*] v. ǣfen-, cōcor-, dæg-, ēst-, flǣsc-, hreác-, mǣl-, morgen-, nōn-, pan-, undern-, wyrt-mete.

mete-ærn, es; *n. A room for taking meals in*:—Gemǣne metern *cœnaculum*, Wrt. Voc. i. 58, 50.

mete-āfliúng, e; *f. Atrophy;* atrophia, Wrt. Voc. i. 19, 44.

mete-bælg, es; *m. A bag for food, wallet*:—Būta metbælge (metbælig, Lind.) *sine pera*, Lk. Skt. Rush. 22, 35.

mete-corn, es; *n. Corn for food*:—Ilk habbe his metecū and his metecorn, Chart. Th. 580, 7. v. next word.

mete-cū, e; *f. A cow that is to furnish food*:—Ānan esne gebyreþ tō metsunge xii pund gōdes cornes and i gōd metecū, L. R. S. 8; Th. i. 436, 27. v. preceding word.

mete-fæt, es; *n. A dish*:—Micel and rūm metfæt *graves et ampla parabsis*, Germ. 403, 18.

mete-fætels, es; *m. A wallet*:—Metefætels *sitarchia*, Wrt. Voc. i. 16, 39.

mete-fisc, es; *m. An edible fish*:—Đes metefisc *hic mugil*, Ælfc. Gr. 9, 8; Som. 9, 10.

mete-gafol, es; *n. Tax* or *rent paid in food*:—On sumen lande gebūr sceal syllan huniggafol, on suman metegafol, on suman ealugafol, L. R. S. 4; Th. i. 434, 32.

mete-gearwa; *pl. f. Preparations of food*:—Ōđre hwǣtene (MS. wætan) metegearwa sint tō forbeódanne *other preparations of wheaten food are to be forbidden*, L. M. 2, 23; Lchdm. ii. 210, 26.

mete-gird. v. met-gird.

metegian, metegung. v. metgian, metgung.

mete-lāf, e; *f. A remnant of food*:—Dǣlon ealle đa metelāfe *let them distribute all the remnants of food*, L. Ǣđelst. v. 8, 1; Th. i. 236, 7. On đīne metelāfa *in reliquias ciborum tuorum*, Ex. 8, 3. Đa metlāfo *reliquias*, Mt. Kmbl. Lind. 14, 20.

mete-leás; *adj. Without food, lacking food*:—On sumere tīde wæs micel menigu mid đam Hǣlende on ānum wēstene meteleás (*nec haberent, quod manducarent*), Homl. Th. ii. 396, 1: Elen. Kmbl. 1220; El. 612: 1392; El. 698. Heó wunode seofon niht meteleás *she remained seven days without food*, Homl. Skt. 10, 283. [*Icel.* mat-lauss.]

mete-leást, -liést, -lǣst, -lēst, -līst, e; *f. Want of food*:—Him ofhreów đæs folces meteleást, Homl. Th. ii. 396, 19. Đā wǣron hié mid meteliéste gewǣgde *they were reduced by want of food*, Chr. 894; Erl. 92, 27. For meteliéste heora līf ālǣtan, Ors. 3, 8; Swt. 120, 30. Metelǣste *inedia*, Hpt. Gl. 480, 34. Metelēste, 497, 31. Meteleáste *cibi inopia*, 517, 66. Murnende mōd nales metelīste, Exon. 101 a; Th. 380, 29; Rä. 1, 15. For meteleáste mēđe, Andr. Kmbl. 77; An. 39: 2315; An. 1159. [Cf. *O. Sax.* meti-lōsi: *Icel.* mat-leysa *lack of food.*]

metend, es; *m. One who measures* or *metes*:—Him leán āgeaf metend (*God*), Cd. 86; Th. 108, 21; Gen. 1809. Middangeardes metend *ex Ormista* (the A. S. gloss seems to be intended as a translation of the title commonly given to Orosius' History, [H]Ormesta Mundi, and is *the measurer* or *describer of the world*, i. e. a general history of the world), Wrt. Voc. ii. 30, 18. Cf. metod, metten.

metend-līce, meten-ness. v. ā-metendlīce, wiđ-metenness.

meter, es; *n. Metre*:—Missenlīce metre *diverso metro*: eroico metre *heroico metro*, Bd. 5, 24; S. 648, 36, 37. [*O. H. Ger.* meter; *n.*]

meter-cræft, es; *m. The art of versification;* ars metrica, Bd. 4, 2; S. 565, 25.

meter-cund; *adj. Relating to metre*:—Metercund *catalecticus, ubi in pede versus una sillaba deest*, Wrt. Voc. ii. 129, 41. Đȳ metercundum *catalectico*, 17, 67.

mētere, es; *m. A painter*:—Mētere *pictor*, Wrt. Voc. i. 46, 72: 75, 18. Sīd reáf swylce mētere[s] wyrceþ on anlīcnysse *toga;* scrūd swā mēteras mētaþ on anlīcnyssan *cinctus gabinus*, 41, 3, 5. Ælfnōþ đe mētere, Cod. Dip. Kmbl. iv. 261, 20. v. mētan, mēting.

meter-fers, es; *n. Hexameter verse*:—Be his līfe wē āwriton ge meterfers ge gerǣdre sprǣce *de vita illius et versibus heroicis et simplici oratione conscripsimus*, Bd. 4, 28; S. 605, 13. Meterfersum *versibus hexametris*, 5, 18; S. 636, 6.

meter-geweorc, es; *n. Verse*:—Paulinus bēc of metergeweorce on gerāde sprǣce ic gehwyrfde *I turned Paulinus' books from verse into prose*, Bd. 5, 23; S. 648, 21.

meter-līc; *adj. Metrical, poetical*:—Mid meterlīcum fōtum *pedibus poeticis*, Hpt. Gl. 411, 3. [*O. H. Ger.* meter-līh.]

met-ern. v. mete-ærn.

meter-wyrhta, an; *m. A verse-maker, poet*:—Mederwyrhta *metricus*, Wrt. Voc. ii. 114, 7. Meterwyrhta, 55, 64. [Cf. *O. H. Ger.* meter-wurcha *poetica musa*.]

mete-, met-[?]sacca, an; *m. A kind of measure*:—Metesacca *legula* (*ligula* mensuræ genus quod alio nomine cochlea dicitur et est octava pars cyathi) vel *coclea*, Wrt. Voc. i. 26, 62.

mete-seax, es; *n. A meat-knife, knife used in cutting food, dagger*:—Hiene mid heora metseacsum ofsticedon, Ors. 5, 12; Swt. 244, 18. [*O. H. Ger.* maz-sahs *cultellum*.]

mete-sōcn, e; *f. Desire for food, appetite*:—Of ðæs magan ādle cumaþ ungemetlīca metesōcna, L. M. 2, 1; Lchdm. ii. 174, 27.

mete-swamm, es; *m. An edible mushroom*:—Metteswam *fungus* vel *tuber*, Wrt. Voc. i. 31, 52.

mete-þearfende; *part. Wanting food*:—Hié ǽghwylcne ellþeódigra dydon him tō mōse meteþearfendum *they made every foreigner food for themselves in want of meat*, Andr. Kmbl. 54; An. 27: 272; An. 136.

mete-þegn, es; *m. An officer whose duty it is to see after food, a sewer*, Cd. 148; Th. 185, 31; Exod. 131. [Cf. disc-þegn.]

mete-ūtsiht, e; *f. A disease which causes food to pass the bowels without digestion*:—Meteūtsiht *lienteria* (λειεντερία), Wrt. Voc. i. 19, 54. Meteūtsihþ, ii. 53, 75.

met-fæt. v. mete-fæt *and* gemet-fæt.

metgian, metegian, metian; *p.* ode. I. *to assign due measure* (with dat.):—Ðonan metgaþ ǽlcum be his gewyrhtum *thence assigns to each due measure according to his deserts*; quid unicuique conveniat, agnoscit, et, quod convenire novit, accomodat, Bt. 39, 9; Fox 226, 23. II. *to moderate, regulate* (with acc.):—Se ilca God se ðæt eall metgaþ *the same God who regulates all that*, Bt. Met. Fox 11, 188; Met. 11, 88. III. *to measure in the mind, consider, meditate upon* (cf. *Goth.* mitōn *to consider*):—Ic ðīne gewitnysse on mōde metegie georne *testimonia tua meditatio mea est*, Ps. Th. 118, 24. Ðæt ic ǽ ðīne metige *lex tua meditatio mea est*, 118, 174. Ic ǽ ðīne on mōde metegade, 118, 97, 143: 142, 5. Ic on ðīnre sōðfæstnesse symble meteode (*meditabor*), 118, 16. Ic metegian ongan mænigra weorca *meditatus sum in omnibus operibus tuis*, 76, 10. v. ge-metgian.

met-gird, -geard, -gyrd, e; *f. A rod for measuring, a rod, perch*:—Metgeard *pertica*, Wrt. Voc. i. 38, 5. Riht is ðæt ne beó ǽnig metegyrd lengre ðonne ōðer, L. I. P. 7; Th. ii. 314, 6. Ðonne is ðæs imbganges ealles þrió furlanges and þreó metgeurda, Chart. Th. 157, 27. Twegræ metgyrda brād, 252, 17.

metgung, metegung, e; *f.* I. *moderation, temperance*:—Wīsdōm is se hēhsta cræft, and se hæfþ on him feówer ōðre cræftas, ðara is ān wærscipe, ōðer metgung, þridde is ellen, feórþe rihtwīsnes, Bt. 27, 2; Fox 96, 34. II. *meditation*:—Mē is metegung hū ic ǽ ðīne efnast healde *lex tua meditatio mea est*, Ps. Th. 118, 77. v. ge-metgung.

Mēðas, meðel. v. Mǽðas, mæðel.

mēðe; *adj.* I. *weary, exhausted* (with labour, hunger, disease, etc.):—Hē hine ðǽr hwīle reste, mēðe æfter ðam miclan gewinne, Rood Kmbl. 129; Kr. 65. Mēðe and meteleás, Elen. Kmbl. 1220; El. 612: 1392; El. 698: Exon. 90 b; Th. 340, 15; Gn. Ex. 111. Mēðe for ðām miclan bysgum *exhausted by disease*, 49 a; Th. 168, 25; Gū. 1083. Mē swā mēðum (*exhausted from want of food*), Elen. Kmbl. 1620; El. 812. Mēðne *fessum*, Wrt. Voc. ii. 38, 26: Exon. 47 b; Th. 163, 3; Gū. 988: 49 b; Th. 171, 23; Gū. 1131. Mēðe stōdon, hungre gehæfte, Andr. Kmbl. 2316; An. 1159: 78; An. 39. Hié slǽp ofereode mēðe be mæste, 929; An. 465. II. *weary in mind, troubled, sad*:—Ðē unrōtne, mēðne, mōdseócne, Exon. 51 a; Th. 177, 30; Gū. 1235. Hyge geómurne, mēðne mōdsefan, 52 a; Th. 182, 16; Gū. 1311. Ongunnon sorhleóþ galan, ðā hié woldon sīðian mēðe fram ðam mǽran þeódne, Rood Kmbl. 137; Kr. 69. Mēðra frēfrend *comforter of the weary-hearted*, Exon. 62 a; Th. 227, 13; Ph. 422. III. *troublesome, causing weariness*:—Nelle ðū mē moeðe ł hefig wosa *noli mihi molestus esse*, Lk. Skt. Rush. 11, 7. [*O. Sax.* mōði: *Icel.* mōðr *weary, exhausted*: *O. H. Ger.* muodi *fessus, fatigatus, lassus*: *Ger.* müde.]

meðema = (?) meduma:—Meðema persa (wersa, Wrt.) *tramarium*, Wrt. Voc. i. 59, 27.

mēðian *to grow weary*:—Wið miclum gonge ofer land . . . mucgwyrt nime him on hand oððe dō on his scō ðȳ læs hē mēðige *for much walking over the country* . . . *let him take mugwort into his hand, or put it into his shoe, lest he grow weary*, L. M. 1, 86; Lchdm. ii. 154, 10. [*O. H. Ger.* muoden *fatiscere, lassari*: cf. *Icel.* mœða *to weary, trouble.*] Cf. ge-mēðgian.

mēðig; *adj. Weary, exhausted*:—Hié hiene mēðigne on cneówum sittende mētten, Ors. 3, 9; Swt. 134, 31. Ða ðe tō lāfe beón mōston wǽron tō ðæm mēðie ðæt hié ne mehton ða gefarenan tō eorþan bringan *the survivors* (*of the pestilence*) *were exhausted to such a degree, that they could not inter the dead*, 2, 6; Swt. 86, 28. v. mēðe.

metian *to supply with food*:—Ðā beád hē ðæt man sceolde his here metian (MS. C. mettian) and horsian *he ordered that his army should be supplied with food and with horses*, Chr. 1013; Erl. 148, 3. v. metsian.

mēting, e; *f. A painting, picture*:—Mētincg *pictura*, Ælfc. Gr. 28, 5; Som. 31, 61. Mētingc, Wrt. Voc. i. 46, 73: 75, 19. Swā swā on mētinge biþ forsewen seó blace anlīcnys, ðæt seó hwīte sȳ beorhtre gesewen, Homl. Th. i. 334, 12. On ōðre wīsan wē sceáwiaþ mētinge, and on ōðre wīsan stafas. Ne gǽþ nā māre tō mētinge būton ðæt ðū hit geseó and herige, 186, 5-7. v. mētan.

met-līc. v. un-metlīc.

metod, metud, meotud, meotod, es; *m.* A word found only in poetry (the phrase *se metoda drihten* occurs twice in Ælfric's Homilies, but in alliterative passages). The earlier meaning of the word in heathen times may have been *fate, destiny, death* (cf. metan), by which Grein would translate *metod* in Wald. 1, 34; Val. 1, 19:—Ðȳ ic ðē metod ondrēd ðæt ðū tō fyrenlīce feohtan sōhtest (Stephens here takes *metod* as vocative with the meaning of prince); in this sense it seems to be used in its compounds, and in the Icelandic *mjötuðr* weird, bane, death (Cl. and Vig. mjötuðr, II). Could this be the meaning in the phrase *se metoda drihten* used of Christ in the following passages?—Ne dorston ða deóflu, ðā ðā hī ādrǽfde wǽron, intō ðām swȳnum, gif hē him ne sealde leáfe, ne intō nānum men forðan se metoda drihten ūre gecynd hæfde on him sylfum genumen, Homl. Th. ii. 380, 4-7. Gemyndig on mōde hū se metoda drihten cwæþ on his godspelle be his godcundan tōcyme, 512, 27. But the word, which occurs frequently, is generally an epithet of the Deity as the O. Sax. *metod*; so too Icel. *mjötuðr* (Cl. and Vig. mjötuðr, I) is applied to heathen gods:—Metod engla, līfes brytta, Cd. 6; Th. 8, 9; Gen. 136. Blīðheort cyning, metod alwihta monna cynnes, 10; Th. 12, 29; Gen. 193. Hine forwræc metod mancynne fram, Beo. Th. 220; B. 110. Metud *O Lord!* Elen. Kmbl. 1634; El. 819. Middangeardes meotud, Exon. 116 b; Th. 449, 2; Dōm. 65. Cyninga wuldor, meotud mancynnes, Andr. Kmbl. 343; An. 172. Sōðfæst meotud, 772; An. 386. Meotod hæfde miht ðā hē gefestnade foldan sceátas, Cd. 213; Th. 265, 3; Sat. 2. Meotod mancynnes, 223; Th. 293, 22; Sat. 459. Meotod alwihta, 228; Th. 308, 24; Sat. 697. Mægencyninga meotod, Exon. 21 b; Th. 58, 29; Cri. 943. Cf. metend, metten.

metod-gesceaft, e; *f. Decree of fate, death*:—Sum sceal seonobennum seóc sār cwānian, murnan meotudgesceaft (*approaching death*), Exon. 87 b; Th. 328, 19; Vy. 20. [*O. Sax.* hie iro mundoda wiðer metodigiskeftie (*the death of her son*).] v. next word.

metod-sceaft, e; *f. Decree of fate, doom, fate after death*:—Ealle Wyrd forsweóp mīne māgas tō metodsceafte (*to their doom*), Beo. Th. 5623; B. 2815. Gāst onsende Matheus his tō metodsceafte (*to the fate appointed to it*), in ēcne gefeán, Menol. Fox 342; Men. 172. Weccaþ of deáþe dryhtgumena bearn tō meotudsceafte *the children of men shall awake from death to doom*, Exon. 21 a; Th. 55, 24; Cri. 888. Hē forþ gewāt metodsceaft seón *he died*, Cd. 83; Th. 104, 31; Gen. 1743: Beo. Th. 2364; B. 1180. Heó metodsceaft (*the death of her kinsmen*) bemearn, 2158; B. 1077.

metod-wang, es; *m. The plain where the decrees of fate are executed, a battlefield*:—Ðonne rond and hand on herefelda helm ealgodon, on meotudwange, Andr. Kmbl. 21; An. 11.

met-rāp, es; *m. A line for sounding the depth of water*:—Sundgyrd on scipe *vel* metrāp *bolidis* (βολὶς), Wrt. Voc. ii. 126, 46: 11, 17.

met-seax. v. mete-seax.

met-scipe, es; *m. Food, refection*:—Habban ða xii heora metscype tōgædere, and fēdan hig swā swā hig sylfe wyrðe munon, and dǽlon ealle ða metelāfe, L. Æðelst. v. 8, 1; Th. i. 236, 6. [*Icel.* mat-skapr *victuals, food.*]

metsian; *p.* ode. I. *to feed*:—Ðū metsast ūs *cibabis nos*, Ps. Spl. 79, 6. Hē metsode hī *cibavit illos*, 80, 15: *nutriebat*, Hpt. Gl. 466, 28: *saginaverit*, 493, 9. Ðū ūs geþafodest him tō metsianne swā swā sceáp, Ps. Th. 43, 13. II. *to furnish with provisions*:—Heora ǽlc fērde tō his castele and ðone mannoden and metsoden swā hig betst mihton *each of them went to his castle and manned and provisioned it as well as ever they could*, Chr. 1087; Erl. 224, 16. Him man metsod *they were furnished with provisions*, 1006; Erl. 141, 11. v. ge-metsian.

metsung, e; *f. Provision, food*:—Be manna metsunge. Ānan esne gebyreþ tō metsunge xii pund gōdes cornes, L. R. S. 8; Th. i. 436, 25. Hí tō metsunge fēngon and tō gafle *they accepted provisions and tribute*, Chr. 1002; Erl. 137, 26. Ðā gerǽdde se cyng ðæt man him gafol behēte and metsunge, 994; Erl. 133, 23: 1006; Erl. 141, 10. Beád ðā Swegen full gild and metsunga tō his here, 1013; Erl. 149, 3. Heom man geaf gīslas and metsunga, 1052; Erl. 184, 6.

mettoc. v. mattoc.

metten, e; *f. One of the Fates*:—Ða graman gydena (MS. Cott. mettena) ðe folcisce men hātaþ Parcas, Bt. 35, 6; Fox 168, 24. Cf. metend, metod.

mētto, met-trum, metud, mēu. v. eáþ-, ofer-mētto, med-trum, metod, mǽw.

micel; *adj. Mickle, great.* I. of size; magnus:—Mycel *magnus*, Wrt. Voc. i. 83, 54, 67. Mycel belle *campana*, 81, 39. Þurhslegene mid ðare ādle ðæs myclan līces (*elephantiasis*), Lchdm. ii. 399, col. 2. Micel *grandem*, Wrt. Voc. ii. 41, 70. Ða miclan tān *alloces*, 5, 18.

God geworhte twā micele leóht, ðæt māre leóht tō ðæs dæges līhtinge, and ðæt læsse leóht tō ðære nihte līhtinge, Gen. 1, 16. Se læssa īl *iricius;* se māra īl *istrix*, Wrt. Voc. ii. 49, 52, 53. Ic tōwurpe mīne bernu and ic wyrce māran (*majora*), Lk. Skt. 12, 18. Hit is ealra wyrta mǣst *majus est omnibus holeribus*, Mt. Kmbl. 13, 32. Feldhūsa mǣst, Cd. 146; Th. 183, 3; Exod. 85. Of mǣstan dǣle *maxima ex parte*, Bd. 5, 13; S. 633, 2: Ors. 1, 1; Swt. 21, 2. Ðā geseah ic beforan unc ðone mǣstan weal, 5, 12; S. 629, 13. Ða tēþ of ādō ða ðe hē mǣste hæbbe *remove the biggest teeth it has*, L. Med. ex. Quad. 1; Lchdm. i. 326, 13. **II.** of quantity, *much, many;* multus:—Mycel *multum*, Wrt. Voc. i. 83, 67. Þā com micel wynsum stenc, Shrn. 91, 28. Gē sāwaþ micel sǣd and rīpaþ litel *sementem multam jacies in terram et modicum congregabis*, Deut. 28, 38. Him fyligdon mycele menigu (*turbæ multæ*), Mt. Kmbl. 4, 25. Eálā sāwel ðū hæfst mycele gōd (*multa bona*), Lk. Skt. 12, 19. Ðes man wyrcþ mycele tācna (*multa signa*), Jn. Skt. 11, 47. Him mon sōhte mǣstra daga ǣlce *they were attacked most days*, Chr. 894; Erl. 90, 15. His fultum mihte mǣstra (MS. C. mǣstne) ǣlcne heora flāna on heora feóndum āfæstnian, Ors. 6, 36; Bos. 132, 10. **III.** *great* in a metaphorical sense:—God, ðū eart se miccla kyning, Hy. 3, 38; Hy. Grn. ii. 282, 38. Ic ne eom swā micel swelgere *I am not so great a glutton;* non sum tam vorax, Coll. Monast. Th. 34, 35. Ðā wæs geworden mycel (*loud*) stefn of heofonum, Blickl. Homl. 145, 14: Mt. Kmbl. 27, 46. Micel sido mid Rōmwarum wæs ðæt ðǣr nāne ōðre on ne sǣton būton ða weorþestan (*a custom carefully observed*), Bt. 27, 1; Fox 96, 1. Micel is ðæt and wundorlīc ðæt ðū gehǣtst *magna promittis*, 36, 3; Fox 174, 30. Micel ōga him becom, Gen. 15, 12. Biþ ðǣr seó miccle milts āfyrred, Exon. 28 a; Th. 84, 9; Cri. 1371. On ðam miclan dæge (*the day of judgment*), 23 a; Th. 65, 7; Cri. 1051. On hyra mandryhtnes miclan þearfe, Beo. Th. 5691; B. 2849. Mǣre ł miclu weorc drihtnes *magna opera domini*, Ps. Lamb. 110, 2. Se līcette litlum and miclum, gumena gehwylcum, Bt. Met. Fox 26, 72; Met. 26, 36. Ne ārās betwyx wīfa bearnum māra Johanne Fulwihtere, Mt. Kmbl. 11, 11. Ðes is māra ðonne Saolmon, 12, 42. Nys ōðer māre bebod, Mk. Skt. 12, 31. Ne þorfte hē nā māran fultumes ðonne his selfes, Bt. 26, 2; Fox 92, 23: 33, 1; Fox 120, 13. Se hæfþ māran synne se ðe mē sealde, Jn. Skt. 19, 11. Ǽgðer ge on ðǣm māran (*main*) landum ge on ðǣm īglandum, Ors. 1, 1; Swt. 16, 25. Ðonne ðæt gefeoht mǣst wǣre *when the fight was hottest*, 4, 11; Swt. 206, 18. Se mǣsta *precipuus*, Wrt. Voc. ii. 81, 66. Drihten is on Sion dēma se mǣsta, Ps. Th. 98, 2. Manege tellaþ ðæt tō mǣstum gōde and tō mǣstere gesǣlþe ðæt mon sīe simle blīðe, Bt. 24, 2; Fox 82, 12. On ðæm mǣstan dæge (*the day of judgment*), Exon. 115 b; Th. 445, 11; Dōm. 6. Pirrusan ðone mǣstan feónd Rōmānum, Ors. 3, 5; Swt. 106, 4. On ðām wǣron ða ǣrestan and ða mǣstan (*primi et præcipui*), Bd. 1, 29; S. 498, 7. **IV.** *neuter used substantively* (a) *with gen.:*—Ic nāt nāht gewislīce hwæðer ðæs feós swā micel is, ne ic nāt ðeáh his māre sȳ, Chart. Th. 490, 15. Heora heriges wæs mycel ofslægen, Bd. 3, 18; S. 546, 35. Hē wæs wilniende ðæt hē ðæs gewinnes mehte māre gefremman *he was desirous to carry on the struggle*, Ors. 2, 5; Swt. 82, 8. Hit māre ðæs landes forbærnde ðonne hit ǣfre ǣr dyde, 5, 2; Swt. 220, 16. Ðæt hī þurh ðæt mǣge mǣst bearna begitan, Bt. 24, 3; Fox 82, 25. Ðǣr manna wese mǣst ætgædere, Ps. Th. 78, 10. Se ðissum herige mǣst hearma gefremede, Andr. Kmbl. 2397; An. 1200. (b) *without gen.:*—On swā miclum heó hæfþ genōg swā wē ǣr sprǣcon. Gif ðū heore māre selest . . ., Bt. 14, 1; Fox 42, 11. Ðæt hē mid swā lytle weorode swā micel anginnan dorste, Ors. 3, 9; Swt. 124, 16. Hū mycel scealt ðū *quantum debes?* Lk. Skt. 16, 5. Hū mycel hē dyde mīnre sāwle, Ps. Th. 65, 14. Ðæt hē genōg hæbbe and nō māran ne þurfe, Bt. 26, 1; Fox 92, 10. Ðǣm ðe ǣnigre wuhte māre habbaþ . . . swā hē māre hæfþ swā hē mā monna ōleccan sceal, 26, 2; Fox 92, 29–33: 26, 3; Fox 94, 16. Ic scealerian fulne æcer oððe māre . . . Hwæt māre dēst ðū? Gewyslīce māre ic dō, Coll. Monast. Th. 19, 23–35. Ðonne hī mǣst tō yfele gedōn hæfdon, ðonne nam man grið and frið wið hī, Chr. 1011; Erl. 145, 2. **V.** *oblique cases used adverbially:*—Se lǣce biþ micles tō beald (*much too bold*), Past. 9; Swt. 61, 2. Ðara micles tō feala winþ wiþ gecynde, Bt. Met. Fox 13, 32; Met. 13, 16. Micles on æþelum wīde is geweorðod hāligra tīd, Menol. Fox 236; Men. 119. Hié God wolde onmunan swā micles, Andr. Kmbl. 1789; An. 897. Micclum *nimium*, Ǽlfc. Gr. 38; Som. 40, 46. Ne cweþe ic nā ðæt ðeós bōc māge micclum tō lāre fremian, pref.; Som. 1, 43: Herb. 17, 2; Lchdm. i. 110, 10. Ealle micclum ðæs wundrodon, Homl. Th. i. 42, 16, 21: Ps. Th. 103, 14. Ne him mycelum ondrǣdeþ, 111, 6. Swā man æt mēder biþ miclum fēded, 130, 4: Andr. Kmbl. 244; An. 122: Bt. Met. Fox 13, 40; Met. 13, 20. Micel ic gedeorfe *multum laboro*, Coll. Monast. Th. 20, 25. Oftor micle *much oftener*, Bt. Met. Fox 19, 37; Met. 19, 19. Hē wæs micle ðē blīðra, 9, 63; Met. 9, 32. Swīðe micle scyrtran ymbhwearft, 28, 14; Met. 28, 7. Nōht micle ǣr, Bd. 4, 23; S. 593, 21. Ðam mycle mā (*quanto magis*) hē scrȳt eów, Mt. Kmbl. 6, 30. Ic þegnum ðīnum dyrnde and sylfum ðē swīðost micle *I concealed it from thy servants, and from thee much the most*, Cd. 129; Th. 164, 12; Gen. 2713. [*Laym. O. E. Homl. A. R. Chauc. Ayenb.* muchel, mochel: *Orm. Havel.* mikel; *Gen. a. Ex.* mikel, michel: *Goth.* mikils: *O. Sax. O. L. Ger.* mikil: *Icel.* mikill: *O. H. Ger.* michil.] v. efen-, frǣ-, mis-, ofer-, wuldor-micel, *and* mā.

micel-ǣte; *adj. Eating much, gluttonous:*—Ic geseó dæighwamlīce ðæt ðū mycelǣte eart, Shrn. 16, 20. Cf. ofer-ǣte.

micel-dōend; *adj. Doing great things;* magnificus, Rtl. 45, 14.

micel-heáfded; *adj. Having a great head:*—Mycelheáfdode *capitosus*, Wrt. Voc. i. 45, 34. Micelheáfdede, ii. 22, 69.

micelian, miclian, micclian; *p.* ode. **I.** *to become great, to increase in size* or *in quantity:*—Micelaþ *grandescit, crescit*, Wrt. Voc. ii. 42, 42. Rīm miclade, Cd. 63; Th. 75, 21; Gen. 1243: Andr. Kmbl. 3050; An. 1528. Wæter micladon *the waters waxed*, 3105; An. 1555. Ðæt folc ongan weaxan and myclian (*grandescere*), Bd. 1, 15; S. 483, 33. On ðǣm dagum wæs ðæt norþmeste (rīce) micliende, Ors. 6, 1; Swt. 252, 12. **II.** *to make great, to increase the size* or *quantity* of a thing:—Man myclade ðæt ordālȳsen *the ordeal-iron should be increased in weight*, L. Æðelst. iv. 6; Th. i. 224, 13. Ðæt ic mǣgburge mōste ðīnre rīm miclian, Cd. 101; Th. 134, 7; Gen. 2221. **III.** metaphorically, *to extol, magnify:*—Miclaþ sāwel mīn drihten *magnificat anima mea dominum*, Lk. Skt. Rush. 1, 46. Mycclaþ, Blickl. Homl. 7, 2. Ic micliu *magnificabo*, Ps. Surt. 68, 31. Wē micliaþ *magnificabimus*, 11, 5. Eal ðæt folc his noman myccledon, Blickl. Homl. 15, 29. Mycclian wē his noman, 13, 7. [*Jul.* muchelin, mucli: *A. R.* muchelen: *Ps.* mikel: *Goth.* mikiljan: *Icel.* mikla: *O. H. Ger.* michilēn.] v. ge-miclian.

micel-līc; *adj. Great, grand, magnificent, splendid, illustrious:*—Micellīc *magnificum*, Wrt. Voc. ii. 54, 64. Wæs se wer for Gode and for mannum micellīc (*magnificus*), Bd. 5, 20; S. 641, 38. Hū his mægenþrymmes mycellīc standeþ, Ps. Th. 110, 2. Hwæt ðæt sīe mǣrlīces and micellīces ðæt git mec gehātaþ *quid sit illud quod mihi tam illustre et tam magnificum pollicemini*, Nar. 25, 12: Bt. 18, 1; Fox 62, 21. Hū micellīce (*magnificata*) sind werc ðīn, Ps. Surt. 91, 6. [*Icel.* mikilligr: *O. H. Ger.* michil-līh *illustris, magnificus.*]

micel-līce; *adv.* **I.** *greatly, grandly, splendidly:*—Singaþ dryhtne forðon micellīce (*magnifice*) dyde, Ps. Surt. p. 184, 15. **II.** *greatly, exceedingly:*—Micellīce intimbred *multipliciter instructus*, Bd. 5, 8; S. 622, 2. Micellīce gelǣred *doctissimus*, 5, 23; S. 645, 13. [*Icel.* mikilliga: *O. H. Ger.* michil-līho *magnifice, magnopere, exaggerative.*]

micel-mōd; *adj. Having a great mind, magnanimous:*—Nis his micelmōdes mægenes ende *magnitudinis ejus non est finis*, Ps. Th. 144, 3. [*O. H. Ger.* michil-muot *magnanimus, animosus.*]

micel-ness, e; *f.* **I.** *greatness, bigness, size:*—Stānas on pysna mycelnysse *stones the size of peas*, Herb. 180, 1; Lchdm. i. 314, 22: Blickl. Homl. 181, 21. Se clāð wæs swīðe gemǣte hire micelnysse *the garment was exactly adapted to her size*, Homl. Skt. 7, 157. His micelnesse ne mæg nān man āmetan, Bt. 42; Fox 258, 12. **II.** *greatness* (of quantity), *multitude, abundance:*—Ðā wæs geworden mid ðam engle mycelnes (*multitudo*) heofonlīces werydes, Lk. Skt. 2, 13. Ne meahton āsecgan for ðæs leóhtes mycelnesse, Blickl. Homl. 145, 14. Ǽfter micelnisse ðīnre mildheortnisse, Num. 14, 19. **III.** *greatness, magnificence:*—Micylnys *magnificentia*, Ps. Spl. C. 8, 2. In micelnisse *in magnificentia;* in mikelnes, Ps. Surt. 28, 4. On mycelnysse earmes ðīnes *in magnitudine brachii tui*, Cant. Moys. 16: Ps. Spl. 78, 12. Ūs weorþ þuruh ðīne mycelnesse milde and blīðe, Ps. Th. 66, 1. Sancte Johannes mycelnesse se Hǣlend sylfa tācn sægde, Blickl. Homl. 167, 17. [*Wick.* michelnes: *O. H. Ger.* michil-nessi *majestas.*]

micel-sprecende; *adj. Talking big, boasting:*—Tungan micelsprecende *linguam magniloquam*, Ps. Lamb. 11, 4.

micelu, e; *f. Size:*—On ðære mycele ðe leáces *of the size of a leek*, Herb. 49, 1; Lchdm. i. 152, 16. [*Goth.* mikilei *greatness: O. H. Ger.* michilī *magnitudo, quantitas.*]

micelung, miclung, e; *f. A doing of great things;* magnificentia:—Miclung ł mǣrsung weorc his *magnificentia opus ejus*, Ps. Lamb. 110, 3. v. ge-miclung.

micga, an; *m. Urine:*—Hlond *vel* micga *lotium*, Wrt. Voc. i. 21, 63: *urina*, 46, 8. Drince buccan micgan . . . sēlost ys se micga ðæt hē sȳ oftost mid fēded, L. Med. ex Quad. 6, 16; Lchdm. i. 354, 12, 15. Fūles hlondes, miggan *foetentis lotii*, Hpt. Gl. 483, 19. Stingendum miggan *putenti lotio* (*urina*), 487, 65. [*A. R.* migge.] v. micge.

micge, an; *f. Urine:*—Gesceáwa ǣlce dæge ðæt ðīn ūtgong and micge sīe gesundlīc. Gif sió micge sīe lytelu . . ., L. M. 2, 30; Lchdm. ii. 226, 20. Ðonne onginþ ðære hǣto welm wanian þurh ða micgean, 2, 23; Lchdm. ii. 212, 7: 1, 37; Lchdm. ii. 88, 20.

micgern. v. mycgern.

micgþa. v. migþa.

micgung, e; *f. Making water:*—Miggung *minctio*, Wrt. Voc. i. 46, 9.

micle, micles, miclum; miclung. v. micel; micelung.

MID, (in Gloss. Ep. and Lindisfarne Gospels) mið; *prep. with dat. acc. inst. With;* at the root of the various meanings lies the idea of association, of being together. **I.** having very nearly the same force as *and*, (a) *with dat.* or *inst.:*—Hig lǣddon hī of ðære byrig mid eallum hire māgum (*Rahab et cunctum cognationem illius*), Jos. 6, 23. Wē sungon seofon seolmas mid letanian, Coll. Monast. Th. 33, 29. Se feónd mid his gefērum eallum feóllon of heofnum, Cd. 16; Th. 20, 10; Gen. 306. Ðū scealt friþ habban mid sunum ðīnum *thou and thy sons shall be protected*, 65; Th. 78, 28; Gen. 1300. Æðelinga bearn, weras mid wīfum, 83; Th. 104, 20; Gen. 1738. (b) *with acc.*:—Wes ðū hāl mid ðās willgedryht, Andr. Kmbl. 1828; An. 916. II. with the idea of joint action or companionship, *in conjunction with, in company with, along with,* (a) *with dat.* or *inst.*:—Ic sang ūhtsang mid gebrōðrum *cantavi nocturnam cum fratribus*, Coll. Monast. Th. 33, 25. Mittan wītegan clypige, R. Ben. 29, 6. Mit ðam wītegan cweðan, 31, 16. Ðā fērde se Hǣlend mid him, Lk. Skt. 7, 6. Mycel menegu wæs mid hyre, 7, 12. Ðā bebeád se fæder ðæm consule ðæt hē mid his fierde angeán fōre, and hē beæftan gebād mid sumum ðæm fultume, Ors. 3, 10; Swt. 140, 19. Gefeaht Æþelhelm wið Deniscne here mid Dornsǣtum, Chr. 837; Erl. 66, 8. Se winterlīca wind wan mid (*in league with*) ðam forste, Homl. Skt. 11, 144. Ic fleáh mid fuglum, Exon. 126 b; Th. 487, 16; Rä. 73, 3. Hē fulluhtes gerȳno onfēng mid his þegnum ðe mid hine wǣron, Bd. 3, 3; S. 525, 27. Ða eágan ... ætgædere mid ðæs martyres heáfde on eorþan feóllan, 1, 7; S. 478, 38. (b) *with acc.*:—Ðē dǣlnimende gedēþ mid hine, 2, 12; S. 515, 29. Hē bæd ðæt hē mid ðone martyr þrowian mōste, 1, 7; S. 478, 18: 1, 23; S. 485, 27. Nemþe hē Cristes geleáfan onfēnge mid ða þeóde ðe hē ofer cyning wæs, 3, 21; S. 551, 1. Hē gewāt mid cyning engla, Cd. 60; Th. 73, 26; Gen. 1210: Beo. Th. 1329; B. 662. Ðæt mīnne līchaman mid mīnne goldgyfan glēd fæðmie, 5297; B. 2652. Ic mid mec gelǣdde mīne frȳnd, Nar. 29, 26. Mid dryhten rūne besǣton, Andr. Kmbl. 1252; An. 626. (c) *with inst.*:—Eode hē in mid āne his preósta, Bd. 3, 5; S. 527, 4. His hand mid ðȳ earme ðe of his līchoman āslegen wæs hē hēt tō āhōn, 3, 12; S. 537, 34. Mid medmycele werede hē fērde, 3, 24; S. 556, 20. III. with the idea of reciprocal action:—Hē wolde mid his freóndum sprǣce and geþæht habban, Bd. 2, 13; S. 515, 36. IV. expressing the relation between animate and inanimate things, (a) *with dat.* or *inst.*:—Ðā ða wīfmen urnon mid stānum wið ðara wealla *cum matronae currerent, et convehere in muros saxa gestirent*, Ors. 4, 10; Swt. 194, 11. Twelf stānas hī hæfdon forþ mid him, Jos. 4, 8. Faran tō eá mid scype mīnum, Coll. Monast. Th. 24, 23. Ic āstīge mīn scyp mid hlæstum mīnum, 26, 31: Beo. Th. 250; B. 125. Hǣlend cymeþ mid wolcnum, Cd. 227; Th. 303, 5; Sat. 608. Hī fērdon mid ðȳ hālgan Cristes mǣle, Bd. 1, 25; S. 487, 22. (b) *with acc.*:—Ða (*these things*) mid hine brohte, 2, 4; S. 505, 38. Mid ða nōþe niðer gewīteþ, Exon. 97 a; Th. 361, 31; Wal. 28. V. with the idea of an association which affords protection or help:—For ðan ðe ic beó mid ðē on eallum ðām ðe ðū tō færst, Jos. 1, 9; Mt. Kmbl. 28, 20. Theodosius hæfde ðone wind mid him, ðæt his fultum mehte mǣstra ǣlcne heora flāna on hiora feóndum āfæstnian, Ors. 6, 36; Swt. 294, 26. VI. with the idea of permanent association, (residing) *with, at,* (when the relation expressed is that of one to many) *among;* apud, penes, (a) *with dat.*:—Elles næbbe gē mēde mid eówrum Fæder (*apud patrem vestrum*), Mt. Kmbl. 6, 1. Bæd æt Gode ðæt hē him geswutelode hwylc Basilius wǣre on wurðscype mid him (*in what estimation he was with God*), Homl. Skt. 3, 498. Eallum ūs leófre ys wīkian mid (*apud*) ðam yrþlinge ðonne mid (*apud*) ðē, Coll. Monast. Th. 31, 1. Ys seó mildheortnes mid (*apud*) ðē, Ps. Th. 129, 4. Albanus hæfde ðone andettere mid (*penes*) him, Bd. 1, 7; S. 477, 7. Mid mannum ic eom *apud homines sum*, mid ðam biscope hē wunaþ *apud episcopum manet*.. mid eów hē is *penes vos est*, mid dēmum *penes judices*, Ælfc. Gr. 47; Som. 47, 23–47. Ic wæs mid Englum, Exon. 85 b; Th. 322, 10; Vīd. 61 (and often). Ic hæfde ðē mid ðām fyrmestan ðe mīnum hȳrēde folgodon *I held thee among the first who followed my court*, Homl. Skt. 5, 412: Ors. 1, 1; Swt. 18, 13. Gefrugnen mid folcum *known among nations*, Exon. 11 a; Th. 14, 26; Cri. 225. (b) *with acc.*:—Is mīn hyht mid God, 37 a; Th. 121, 16; Gū. 289: 39 a; Th. 128, 27; Gū. 410. Sibb sȳ mid eówic, 75 b; Th. 282, 25; Jul. 668. Wuna mid ūsic, Cd. 130; Th. 164, 29; Gen. 2722. VI a. *between*:—Dēma mid unc twih *a judge between us two*, 102; Th. 136, 5; Gen. 2253. VII. expressing an accompanying circumstance, the phrase being often equivalent to an adverb of manner, (a) *with dat.*:—Mid gōdum willan fæstan, Blickl. Homl. 37, 27: 35, 27. Mid his sylfes willan, willum *ultro*, Bd. 1, 7; S. 477, 22, 15. Mid mycelre willsumnysse bodian *magna devotione predicare*, 3, 3; S. 526, 4. Hē hæfde hī mid mycelre āre mid him, 4, 1; S. 564, 33. Wæs sió fǣmne mid hyre fæder willan beweddad, Exon. 66 a; Th. 244, 24; Jul. 32. Brūc ðisses beáges mid hǣle, Beo. Th. 2438; B. 1217. Ic eów mid gefeán ferian wille, Andr. Kmbl. 693; An. 347. Winnan mid māne (*criminally*), Cd. 16; Th. 19, 30; Gen. 299. Mid swāte and mid sorgum libban, 24; Th. 31, 8; Gen. 482. Wīf ðonne heó mid cylde biþ *mulier gravida*, L. Ecg. C. 28, tit; Th. ii. 130, 14. Heó wæs mid bearne (cf. *Icel.* ganga með barni), Shrn. 60, 33. Ðā heó mid ðam bearne wæs, 149, 1. Swā mid ðam cilde wearþ, Homl. Th. i. 460, 7. (b) *with acc.*:—Ðæt hē mid ða mǣstan swētnesse (*maxima suavitate*) geglencde, Bd. 4, 24; S. 596, 34.

(c) *with inst.*:—Ðā ongan hē mid gleáwe mōde þencean, 3, 10; S. 534, 20: Past. 9, 1; Swt. 55, 20. VIII. expressing the idea of instrumentality, *by, through,* (a) *with inst.* or *dat.*:—Hié wǣron gebrocede... mid ðæm ðæt manige ðara sēlestena cynges þēna forþfērdon *they suffered from the death of many of the best king's thanes*, Chr. 897; Erl. 94, 32. Ne canst ðū huntian būton mid nettum?...Mid swiftum hundum ic betǣce wildeór, Coll. Monast. Th. 21, 21–27. Ðū ðæt land tōdǣlst mid hlyte (*sorte*), Deut. 31, 7. Mid ðissum woruldgesǣlþum and mid ðīs andweardan welan mon wyrcþ oftor feónd ðonne freónd, Bt. 24, 3; Fox 84, 2–4. Mid his handum gesceóp, Cd. 14; Th. 16, 30; Gen. 251. Hié heora līchoman leáfum beþeahton, weredon mid ðȳ wealde, 40; Th. 52, 19; Gen. 846. Stōd bewrigen folde mid flōde, 8; Th. 10, 15; Gen. 157. Ofgeót mid scīre wīne ealde, L. M. 2, 11; Lchdm. ii. 188, 20. Mid monige wīte þreágan, Shrn. 101, 23. Mid ðȳ blōde gewurþad, Bd. 1, 7; S. 478, 24. Mid deáþe fornumen, forgripen, 1, 27; S. 492, 30: 3, 8; S. 532, 27. Mid his lāre *by means of his teaching*, 3, 28; S. 560, 38. Mid gȳmenne mīnra māga *by the care of my kinsmen*, 5, 24; S. 647, 22. Dǣle hē swā mycel feoh for hyne swā hē ǣr mid him nam (*as much as he got with him*, i. e. *by selling him*), L. Ecg. P. iv. 26; Th. ii. 212, 12. Eom ic leóhte geleáfan and mid lufan gefylled, Exon. 42 a; Th. 141, 9; Gū. 624. Hē frægn hī mid hwī hī gesceldan heora hūs wið ðæs fȳres frēcennysse, Shrn. 90, 7. Gewiton mid ðȳ wǣge in forwyrd sceacan *carried by the wave they hurried to destruction*, Andr. Kmbl. 3186; An. 1596: Cd. 12; Th. 14, 5; Gen. 214. (b) *with acc.* (*and inst.*):—Hē mid hī fēran sceolde tō ðon ðæt hē ða fǣmnan ǣghwæðer ge mid ða (ðære, MS. B.) mǣrsunge heofonlīcra gerȳna ge mid his dæghwamlīcre lāre trymede, Bd. 2, 9; S. 510, 37. Hē monige ... mid ða leornunga ðissa bōca gelǣdde, 5, 18; S. 636, 4: Cd. 100; Th. 133, 9; Gen. 2208. Se mihtiga slōh mid hālige hand, 167; Th. 208, 18; Exod. 485. IX. having reference to time, *with, at*:—On ūhtan mid ǣrdæge, Beo. Th. 253; B. 126: Andr. Kmbl. 2776; An. 1390: 3048; An. 1527: Cd. 121; Th. 155, 19; Gen. 2575. X. *giving direction*:—Onlong brōces mid streáme *along the brook in the direction in which it runs*, Cod. Dip. Kmbl. vi. 226, 20. XI. in adverbial or conjunctional phrases, (a) *with* eallum, ealle:—Hyne myd scrȳne myd eallum on feastum cwearterne beclȳsdon *they shut him up cage and all in prison*, St. And. 38, 9. Mid ealle *penitus*, Ælfc. Gr. 38; Som. 40, 46. Mid stybbe mid ealle *stirpitus*; mid wyrttruman mid ealle *radicitus*, Som. 42, 3–4. Hié āsettan hī on ǣnne sīþ ofer mid horsum mid ealle, Chr. 893; Erl. 88, 24 (cf. *Icel.* með öllu). (b) *with dat. or inst. case of the demonstrative*, denoting that the two actions expressed by the verbs in the connected clauses are in close association, being either simultaneous, or the one following upon, and being regarded, more or less, as the result of the other, *when, since, seeing that;* cum:—Mid ðam ðe se apostol stōp intō ðære byrig, ðā bær man him tōgeánes ānre wydewan līc, Homl. Th. i. 60, 11. Mid ðam ðe hē hig geseah ðā ēfste hē *quos cum vidisset, cucurrit*, Gen. 18, 2. Hū yfele mē dōþ manege woruldmenn, mid ðam ðæt ic ne mōt wealdan mīnra āgenra þeówa *how ill do many men act towards me, when I may not rule my own servants*, Bt. 7, 3; Fox 20, 19. Mid ðȳ ðe heó gehȳrde...ðā cwæþ heó, Blickl. Homl. 7, 19: 15, 6. Mid ðī ðe hié cōmon...hié gemētton seofon hyrdas standan, 237, 17. Mid ðȳ ðe (*dum*) hē hine geseah on singalum gebedum ... ðā wæs hē semninga mid ðam godcundan gyfe gemildsad, Bd. 1, 7; S. 476, 37. Mittē *dum*, Ps. Surt. 67, 8. Mid ðȳ (*cum*) Peohtas wīf næfdon, bǣdon him fram Scottum, Bd. 1, 1; S. 474, 19. Gif hē eów ne wyllan ārīsan tōgeánes, mid ðȳ eówer mā is (*cum sitis numero plures*), 2, 2; S. 503, 13: 1, 27; S. 493, 42. Mid ðī hē ðis cwæþ, hē āstāh on heofenas, Blickl. Homl. 237, 15. XII. *used after its case* or *as an adverb*:—On ðam clifian ðe him gōd mid worhte *cleave to him who did good with them*, Bt. 16, 3; Fox 56, 10, 12. Ða him mid scoldon *which were to go with him*, Beo. Th. 82; B. 41. Ðara ðe hē him mid hæfde, 3255; B. 1625: 1783; B. 889: Homl. Th. ii. 490, 24. Manega ōðre ðe him mid (*simul cum eo*) fērdon, Mk. Skt. 15, 41. Mid fērdan *comeant, simul pergebant*, Wrt. Voc. ii. 132, 45. Hē his heres þriddan dǣl gehȳdde and him self mid wæs, Ors. 3, 7; Swt. 116, 27. Hine mid wunode ān ombehtþegn, Exon. 47 a; Th. 162, 8; Gū. 972. Biddan ðone ele ðæt ðū Adam myd smyrian mōte *to ask for the oil, to anoint Adam with*, Nicod. Thw. 13, 23. Smyre ðone man mid, Herb. 54, 3; Lchdm. i. 158, 2. Ðā sceolde hē sendan lȳgetu and windas, and tōwyrpan eall hira geweorc mid, Bt. 35, 4; Fox 162, 14. Ic wilnode andweorces ðone anweald mid tō gereccenne, 17; Fox 60, 8: 20; Fox 72, 24. Se forma hād and se ōðer hād beóþ ǣfre ætgedere ... se þridda hād is hwīlon mid, hwīlon on ōðre stōwe, Ælfc. Gr. 15; Som. 17, 39. Ðonne se mon nō his āgenne gielp mid ne sēcþ, Past. 59; Swt. 451, 15. Gif hē nōht geseón ne mǣge mid, L. Alf. pol. 47; Th. i. 94, 6. Hē hæfde mildheortnysse ða þearfan mid tō frēfrigenne, Bd. 3, 17; S. 545, 13. Geond ðone ofen eodon and se engel mid, Cd. 191; Th. 238, 14; Dan. 354. Ðæt wæs Satane and his gesīðum mid, Exon. 30 a; Th. 93, 7; Cri. 1522. Ǣlc ðara ðe mid stande *every one that stands by* (*assists*) *him*, L. Ath. i. 1; Th. i. 200, 3. [*Mid* occurs in Piers P., and still remains in *mid*-wife: *Goth.* miþ, mid;

O. Sax. midi, mid: *O. Frs.* mith, mit, mei: *O. L. Ger.* mid, mit, met: *Icel.* međ: *Swed. Dan.* med: *O. H. Ger.* miti, mit: *Ger.* mit: *Du.* met.]

midd; *adj. with superl.* midemest, midmest *Mid, middle.* I. of place:—Seó burh wæs on midre đære eá (*in medio amne*), Nar. 10, 11. Đā wē wǣron on middre đære sǣ (*in medio mari*), Bd. 5, 1; S. 613, 23. Is on middre đære cyricean, 2, 3; S. 504, 39. Hire (*the axis*) midore ymbe (cf. ymb đa eaxe middewearde, Bt. 39, 3; Fox 214, 23), Bt. Met. Fox. 28, 46; Met. 28, 23. On middum đīnum temple *in medio templi tui*, Ps. Th. 47, 8. On mereflōde middum, Cd. 8; Th. 9, 22; Gen. 145. Gāþ from geate tō geate þurh midde đa ceastre (*per medium castrorum*), Past. 49, 2; Swt. 383, 3: St. And. 14, 17. On middum đǣm ūrum wīcum *in media castrorum parte*, Nar. 12, 24. Đa gesettan scēp in middum wulfum (*in medio luporum*), Bd. 2, 6; S. 508, 16. Hē mē lǣdde betweoh midde đa þreátas *inter choros medios*, 5, 12; S. 629, 26. Hālettend midemest finger *salutarius*; ǣwiscberend midmesta finger *impudicus*, Wrt. Voc. i. 283, 21–22. Gif hī đone midmestan weg āredian willaþ, Bt. 40, 3; Fox 238, 23. Đa sēlestan men . . . đa midmestan . . . swā bióþ đa midmestan men, 39, 7; Fox 222, 1–10, 15. II. of time:—Tō middes dæges Crist wæs on rōde āþened, Btwk. 216, 14. On middes wintres mæsseniht, Chr. 827; Erl. 62, 30. Swā hē in swoloþan middes sumeres wǣre *quasi in mediae aestatis caumate*, Bd. 3, 19; S. 549, 30. Sunnon upgong æt middan sumere *ortum solis solstitialem*, 5, 12; S. 627, 35. Fæste ān lengten foran tō middan wintra (*ante Natale Christi*) . . . fæste ii lengtenu, ān tōforan middan sumera (*ante mediam æstatem*), ōđer foran tō middan wintra, L. Ecg. P. iv. 22, 23; Th. ii. 210, 25–28. Tō middan (middum, MS. B.) wintre, L. Ath. iv. pref.; Th. i. 226, 5. Tō middyre (MS. A. myddre) nihte *media nocte*, Mt. Kmbl. 25, 6. Æt midre niht, Ps. Th. 118, 62. Æt middre nihte, Exon. 59 b; Th. 216, 2; Ph. 262. Æt middere niht, Cd. 144; Th. 179, 32; Exod. 37. Hē leng ne leofaþ đonn on midre ilde *he will not live beyond middle age*, Lchdm. iii. 162, 21: Ps. Th. 54, 24. On midne dæg *meridie*, Ælfc. Gr. 38; Som. 41, 47. Seó seofoþe tīd dæges, đæt is ān tīd ofer midne dæg, Bd. 5, 6; S. 619, 27. On midne winter, Chr. 878; Erl. 78, 28. Ofer đone midne sumor *after midsummer*, 1006; Erl. 140, 5. Ofer midne sumor, Lchdm. iii. 74, 11. On midde niht, Bd. 4, 8; S. 575, 40. [*Goth.* midjis: *O. Sax.* middi: *O. Frs.* midde: *Icel.* miđr: *O. H. Ger.* mitti.] v. on-middan, tō-middes.

mid-dæg, es; *m. Mid-day*:—Middæg *sexta*, Wrt. Voc. i. 53, 12: Coll. Monast. Th. 33, 33: Jn. Skt. 4, 6. Middæg *meridies*, Ælfc. Gr. 12; Som. 15, 46: Hymn. Surt. 16, 29. Đæs middæges gereord, R. Ben. 65, 20. Tō middæges, 65, 18. Tō middæge *at midday*, Lchdm. iii. 218, 4, 6, 9, etc. On đæm sumerlīcan sunnstede on middæge (MS. R. middan dæge), 258, 15. [*O. Frs.* mid-dei: *Icel.* miđ-dagr: *O. H. Ger.* mittitag: *Ger.* mit-tag.] v. middel-, midne-dæg.

middæg-līc; *adj. Midday, meridian*:—Đære middæglīcan sunnan scīman beorhtre *solis meridiani radiis præclarior*, Bd. 5, 12; S. 629, 23. Fram deófle middæglīcum *ab daemonio meridiano*, Ps. Spl. C. 90, 6. [*O. H. Ger.* mittitaga-līh.]

middæg-sang, es; *m. The midday service*:—Ūhtsang and prīmsang, undernsang and middægsang, nōnsang and ǣfensang, and nihtsang, L. Ælfc. C. 19; Th. ii. 350, 7. *De officio sextae horae.* Middægsang. On midne dæg wē sculon God herian, Btwk. 216, 13: R. Ben. 39, 19: 40, 7.

middæg-tīd, e; *f. The midday hour, noon*; meridies, Wrt. Voc. ii. 58, 66.

middandæg-līc, *adj. Midday, meridian*:—Fram middendægīīcum deófle *ab daemonio meridiano*, Ps. Lamb. 90, 6.

middan-eard, es; *m. The middle dwelling, the abode of men, the earth, the world* (in a physical sense):—*De mundo.* Middaneard is gehāten eall đæt binnan đam firmamentum is . . . Seó heofen and sǣ and eorþe synd gehātene middaneard, Lchdm. iii. 254, 6–9. Hē sǣde, đæt eal đes middaneard nǣre đē māre drīges landes ofer đone mycelan gārsecg, đonne man ǣnne prican āpricie on ānum brādum brede. And ys đes middaneard būton swylce se seofoþa dǣl ofer đone mycelan gārsecg, se đe mid his ormǣtnysse ealle đās eorþan ūtan emblīþ, Wulfst. 46, 19–24. Middaneardes gewissast đū đe getimbrunge *mundi regis ui fabricum*, Hymn. Surt. 91, 21. Đone eard Asiam, se đe is geteald ō healfan dǣle middaneardes, Homl. Th. i. 68, 35. Eálā middaneard! Eálā dæg leóhta! eálā upheofon! Cd. 216; Th. 275, 2; Sat. 165. ıme sceolon hweorfan geond hæleþa land . . . geond middaneard, 219; h. 281, 16; Sat. 272. Geond eorþan . . . ofer middaneard, Ps. Th. 137, : 144, 12. Đū miht on ānre hand befealdan ealne middaneard, Hy. 7, ıo; Hy. Grn. ii. 290, 120. II. *the world, mankind*:—Ealle đē riaþ . . . eall middaneard, 9, 38; Hy. Grn. ii. 292, 38. Middaneardes ǣlynd *salvator mundi*, Jn. Skt. 4, 42. Ic eom middaneardes leóht đa ıīle đe ic on middanearde eom, 9, 5: 8, 12. [*Laym.* midden-erd; cf. ıym. *Orm. Gen. and Ex. Havel.* middel-erd, -ærd.] v. middan-geard d *next word.*

ıiddaneard-līc; *adj. Earthly.* I. in a physical sense:—Đæt ō mid hyre hǣtan middaneardes (other MSS. middaneardlīce) wæstmas ne forbærne, Lchdm. iii. 250, 17. II. as distinguished from spiritual or heavenly, *worldly, mundane, earthly*:—Godes sunu becom tō đissum middanearde tō đī đæt hē mid his hālgan lāre middaneardlīc gedwyld (*human error*) ādwǣscte, Homl. Th. ii. 90, 13: 366, 9. On middaneardlīcum lustum *in worldly pleasures*, 368, 3. Ealle middaneardlīce þing forhogiende *despising all the things of this world*, 130, 1. Middaneardlīce genipu *mundana nubila*, Hymn. Surt. 74, 3: 91, 23: Homl. Skt. 2, 241.

middan-geard, es; *m.* I. *the middle dwelling* (*between heaven and hell*), *the earth, world*:—Middangeard *chosmos*, Wrt. Voc. ii. 16, 36. Se læssa middangeard *microchosmos*, 56, 22. On Godes onwealde is eal đes middangeard, and đās windas and đās regnas syndon ealle his, and ealle gesceafta syndon his, Blickl. Homl. 51, 19. Đes middangeard wæs tō đon fæger, đæt hē teáh men tō him þurh his wlite, 115, 10. Đes middangeard daga gehwylce fealleþ and tō ende ēfsteþ, 59, 26: Exon. 77 a; Th. 290; Wand. 62. Cwealmdreóre swealh middangeard *earth drank gore*, Cd. 47; Th. 60, 23; Gen. 986. Gefylled wearþ eall đes middangeard monna bearnum, 75; Th. 93, 30; Gen. 1554. Beofaþ middangeard, hrūse under hæleþum, Exon. 20 b; Th. 55, 12; Cri. 882. Ealne đisne ymbhwyrft đises middangeardes swā swā Oceanus ūtan ymbligeþ *orbem totius terrae, Oceani limbo circumseptum*, Ors. 1, 1; Swt. 8, 1. Middangeardes, eorþan sceátta, Beo. Th. 1507; B. 751. Rīce middangeardes đǣr nō men būgaþ *hunc orbem, mors ubi regna tenet*, Exon. 58 a; Th. 208, 17; Ph. 157. Rīcsian on điosan middangearde, Ors. 1, 2, tit.; Swt. 1, 4. Seó rōd biþ ārǣred on đæt gewrixle đara tungla, seó nū on middangearde āwergede gāstas flēmeþ, Blickl. Homl. 91, 24. Đæt nǣre nǣfre nǣnig tō đæs hālig mon on đissum middangearde, ne furþum nǣnig on heofenum, 117, 26. Swā hwǣr swā đys godspel byþ gebodud on eallum myddangearde (*in toto mundo*), Mt. Kmbl. A. 26, 13. Geond ealne middangeard, Blickl. Homl. 69, 19. Đā ic wīde gefrægn weorc gebannan manigre mǣgþe geond đisne middangeard, Beo. Th. 151; B. 75: Exon. 33 a; Th. 104, 1; Gū. 1: 95 b; Th. 355, 37; Pa. 1. God đysne middangeard tōcleófeþ, Blickl. Homl. 109, 35: Andr. Kmbl. 322; An. 161. II. *the world and they that dwell therein, mankind*:—Se middangeard ūs wæs lange underþeóded, and ūs deáþ mycel gafol geald, Blickl. Homl. 85, 11. Him æteówde eal eorþan rīce and īdel wuldor đisses middangeardes, 27, 17: 65, 15. Līf đysses middangeardes *this present life*, 59, 27. Gē synt middanearde (-geardes, MS. A.) leóht *vos estis lux mundi*, Mt. Kmbl. 5, 14. Đa hwatestan men ealles đises middangeardes, Ors. 1, 10; Swt. 48, 6. Hū gesǣlig seó forme eld wæs đises middangeardes, Bt. 15; Fox 48, 3. Heofones waldend, ealles waldend middangeardes, Exon. 16 a; Th. 35, 12; Cri. 557: 65 b; Th. 241, 32; Ph. 665: Andr. Kmbl. 453; An. 227. Middangeardes weard (*Nebuchadnezzar*), Cd. 205; Th. 253, 17; Dan. 597. Gecȳþ nū middangearde blisse, Blickl. Homl. 87, 24. Hē getācnaþ đysne middangeard, se wæs synna and māna full, 75, 5. Hē com on đære syxtan ylde on đysne middangeard mancyn tō ālȳsenne, 71, 26: Homl. Th. i. 62, 11. [*Goth.* midjun-gards οἰκουμένη: *O. H. Ger.* mittan-, mittin-gart: cf. myddellyard *the world*, Chest. Plays 1, 67: *O. Sax.* middel-gard: *O. H. Ger.* mittil-gart *orbis*: *Icel.* miđ-garđr. 'The Icel. Edda has preserved the true mythical bearing of the word.—The earth (miđgarđ), the abode of men, is seated in the middle of the universe, bordered by mountains and surrounded by the great sea (ūthaf); on the other side of this sea is the Ūt-garđ, the abode of giants; the Miđgarđ is defended by the Ās-garđ (*the burgh of the gods*), lying in the middle (the heaven being conceived as rising above the earth). Thus the earth and mankind are represented as a stronghold besieged by the powers of evil from without, defended by the gods from above and from within.'—Cl. and Vig. Dict. s. v. See also Grmm. D. M. 754.] v. middan-eard.

middangeard-līc; *adj. Terrestrial, physical as opposed to spiritual*:—Forđon hē oft stormas đara werigra gāsta fram his sylfes sceþenisse and his gefērena mid bedum widsceáf, wæs đæt đæs wyrþe đæt hē wiđ đam middangeardlīcum windum and līgum swīđian mihte (*ventus flammisque mundialibus*), Bd. 2, 7; S. 509, 34. v. middaneard-līc.

middan-sumor, -winter. v. *under* midd, II, *where perhaps in the instances in which* middan *occurs that word is to be taken as the first part of a compound.* Cf. midde-sumor, -winter, and middandæg-līc.

midde, an; *f. The middle* (*only in the phrase* on middan):—Se fugel hafaþ iiii heáfdu . . . and hē is on middan hwǣlan hiwes *the bird hath four heads . . . and in the middle it is of a whale's shape*, Salm. Kmbl. 526; Sal. 262. Forwrāt hē wyrm on middan, Beo. Th. 5404; B. 2705. Mūđ wæs on middan, Exon. 108 b; Th. 415, 10; Rä. 33, 9. On æge biþ gioleca on middan, Bt. Met. Fox 20, 339; Met. 20, 170. [*O. Sax.* middea (an middean): *Icel.* miđja (ī miđju): cf. *O. H. Ger.* mittī (in mittī): *Ger.* mitte.] v. on-middan.

middel, es; middela (?), an; *m. The middle, centre*:—In midle *in centro*, Wrt. Voc. ii. 92, 13. On middele (Ps. Lamb. midle) innoþes mīn *in medio ventris mei*, Ps. Spl. 21, 13, 21. Hē ānne cnapan gesette on hyra middele (*in medio eorum*), Mk. 9, 36. Se đe ālǣdde Israhel of middele heora . . . þurh middele his, Ps. Spl. 135, 11, 14. Of midle *ex centro*, Wrt. Voc. ii. 31, 47. Of đæs wuda midle, Exon. 56 b; Th. 202,

6; Ph. 65. Hió is gesceapen on ðam midle, betwux ðære drȳgan and ðære cealdan eorþan and ðam hātan fȳre, Bt. 33, 4; Fox 128, 37. Hió is on midle fȳres and eorþan, Bt. Met. Fox 20, 163; Met. 20, 82. On midle mīnra dagena, Ps. Th. 101, 21. Is ðis eálond geseted ongeán midle Sūþ-Seaxna (*contra medium Australium Saxonum*), Bd. 4, 16; S. 585, 1. Intō ðam middelan (intō middan, other MS.) ðere strēte, Cod. Dip. Kmbl. iii. 385, 9. On middel ðæs unmǣtan cyles, Bd. 5, 12; S. 627, 42: 628, 1. On ðone middel ðære mǣran byrig, Elen. Kmbl. 1724; El. 864. Hié gegripan on hire middel *laid hold of her waist* (cf. Laym. 28069, þa leo iueng me bi þan midle: Piers. P. 5, 358, B. text), Blickl. Homl. 141, 29. [Cf. *Icel.* ā, ī meðal *among*; ā, ī milli (*from* miðli) *between*: *M. H. Ger.* mittel.] v. next word.

middel; *superl.* midlest; *adj. Middle*:—Be midelen streáme *in mid stream*, Cod. Dip. Kmbl. iii. 385, 15. Se midlesta finger *the middle finger*, L. Alf. pol. 58; Th. i. 96, 3. Be ðam midlæstan (*the third in a list of five names*) is nū tō secgenne, Bd. 4, 23; S. 594, 15. Swā biþ ðām midlestan monnum *so it is with men of an intermediate class* (*between the best and the great majority of mankind*), Bt. 39, 7; Fox 222, 4 (v. midd). [*O. Sax.* middil-gard: *O. Frs.* middel; *superl.* midlest, -ost, -ast: *Icel.* meðal-, *in cpds.*: *O. H. Ger.* mittil: *Laym. Gen. and Ex. A. R. Ayenb. have superl.* midlest.] *Middel* is found as the first part of many names of places, e.g. *Middel-tūn* Middleton, *Middel-hām* Middleham, etc., Cod. Dip. Kmbl. vi. 315; see also following words.

middel-dæg, es; *m. Mid-day*:—Syle drincan middeldagum, Lchdm. iii. 74, 6: L. M. 1, 15; Lchdm. ii. 56, 22. Hē ðonne on middeldagum inne gewunode, 1, 72; Lchdm. ii. 146, 13. [Cf. *O. H. Ger.* mittila-tagun *meridianus* (*ventus*).] Cf. middel-niht.

middel-dǣl, es; *m. The middle*:—Ongēn ðæm middeldǣle (other MS. middele) on ðæm eástende *ad mediam frontem orientis*, Ors. 1, 1; Swt. 10, 6.

Middel-Engle, a; *pl. The Middle Angles, the Angles of Leicestershire* (v. Green's Making of England, pp. 74-80):—Of Engle cōman Eást-Engle and Middel-Engle and Myrce and eall Norþhembra cynn *de Anglis Orientales Angli, Mediterranei Angli, Merci, tota Nordanhymbrorum progenies . . sunt orti*, Bd. 1, 15; S. 483, 25. Midel-Angle, Chr. 449; Erl. 12, 12. Middel-Engla mǣgþ . . . wæs cristen geworden. Ðissum tīdum Middel-Engle Cristes geleáfan onfēngon, Bd. 3, 21; S. 550, 36-39. Ðā wæs Dēma biscop geworden Middel-Engla and eác Myrcna samod . . . hē forþfērde on Middel-Englum on ðam þeódlande ðe is nemned on Feppingum, S. 551, 32-36: 3, 24; S. 557, 17. [When the Middle Angles had a bishop of their own the see was at Leicester.] Færpinga þreó hund hȳda is in Middel-Englum, Cod. Dip. B. i. 414, 27. Ðone Ceaddan se ercebiscop ǣsænde Myrceon tō biscope and Middel-Englum and Lindesfarum, Shrn. 59, 14.

middel-finger, es; *m. The middle finger*:—Middelfinger *medius* vel *impudicus*, Wrt. Voc. i. 44, 6: 71, 32: ii. 58, 5. Gif man middelfinger of āslæhþ iv. scill. gebēte, L. Ethb. 54; Th. i. 16, 11.

middel-flēra, an; *m.* -flēre, an; *f. A partition* (?; it occurs as an alternative with words meaning) *the gristle of the nose, bridge of the nose*:—Middelflēra *interpinnium*, Wrt. Voc. ii. 49, 48. Nose grystle *vel* middelflēre *internasus* vel *interfinium* vel *interpinium*, i. 43, 20. [v. interfinium *the grystell of the nose*, Wülck. 590, 15: *bryg of the nese*, 634, 9: 675, 25.]

middel-fōt, es; *m. The middle of the foot, the instep*:—Middelfōt *subtel*, Wrt. Voc. i. 45, 3.

middel-gemǣru; *pl. n. A middle* or *central district*:—On Filistina middelgemǣrum *in the centre of the land of the Philistines*, Salm. Kmbl. 509; Sal. 255.

middel-gesculdru, -gescyldru; *pl. n. The part between the shoulders*:—Middelgesculdru *interscapilium*, Wrt. Voc. i. 44, 29. Middelgescyldru *interscapulum*, ii. 49, 49. [Cf. *Icel.* mið-herðar *mid-shoulders*.]

middel-niht, e; *f. Mid-night*:—Nalles æfter lyfte lācende hwearf middelnihtum, Beo. Th. 5658; B. 2833: 5557; B. 2782: Bt. Met. Fox 28, 93; Met. 28, 47: Exon. 129 b; Th. 498, 4; Rä. 87, 7. Cf. middel-dæg *and* mid-niht.

Middel-Seaxe, -Seaxan; *pl. The Middle-Saxons*, Saxons who settled in the district west of London, and whose name is preserved in the present Middlesex: they appear to have been an offshoot of the East Saxons. v. Green's Making of England, p. 111, note:—Hēr Middel-Seaxe (*but* MS. E. Middal-Engla, *v. under* Middel-Engle) onfēngon ryhtne geleáfan, Chr. 653; Erl. 26, 24. Hī hæfdon ðā ofergān i. Eást-Engle, and ii. Eást-Sexe, and iii. Middel-Sexe, 1011; Erl. 144, 33. In provincia quæ nuncupatur Middel-Seaxan, Cod. Dip. Kmbl. i. 59, 20 (the charter is of a king of Essex). In Middil-Saexum, 142, 7.

middes. v. tō-middes.

midde-sumor, es; *m. Mid-summer*:—Ðis godspel gebyraþ on middesumeres mæsseǣfen, Lk. Skt. 1, 1, rubric. On middesumeres dæg, Herb. 4, 5; Lchdm. i. 90, 17. [*Icel.* mið-sumar.] v. middewinter, mid-sumor.

midde-weard; *adj. Mid-ward, middle of* (the noun with which the word agrees):—Middeweard hand *vola* vel *tenar* vel *ir*, Wrt. Voc. i. 43, 54. Middewærd lencten *vel* foreweard lencten *ver novum*, 53, 26. Middeweard hit mæg bión þrītig mīla brād oððe brādre *Norway may be thirty miles or more across the middle*, Ors. 1, 1; Swt. 18, 31. Andlangæs brōces middesweardes *along the middle of the brook*, Cod. Dip. B. i. 295, 31. On middeweardum (-an, MSS. R. L.) hyre ryne, Lchdm. iii. 250, 26. On middeweardre sǣ *in medio mari*, Cant. Moys. 8. Ymb ða eaxe middewearde hwearfaþ *they revolve about the middle of the axis*, Bt. 39, 3; Fox 214, 23. Seó eá is irnende þurh middewearde Babylonia burg *mediam Babyloniam interfluentem*, Ors. 2, 4; Swt. 74, 3: 1, 3; Swt. 32, 6. *As a noun*:—On middeweardan innoþes mīnes *in medio ventris mei*, Ps. Lamb. 21, 15.

midde-winter, es; *m. Mid-winter, Christmas*:—Ðis sceal on Sunnandæg betweox myddewintres mæssedæge and twelftan dæge, Lk. Skt. 2, 33, rubric. Ne miht ðū wīn wringan on midne winter (meddewinter, MS. Bod.), Bt. 5, 2; Fox 10, 32. v. midde-sumor, mid-winter.

mid-eard, es; *m. The world*:—Mideardes ordfruman *mundi originem*, Hymn. Surt. 13, 30. Seó sunne ðe onlīht ealne mideard, Homl. Skt. 1, 72. v. middan-eard.

mid-fæsten, es; *n. Mid-Lent*:—Wæs mycel gemōt tō midfestene, Chr. 1047; Erl. 175, 11. [Cf. *Icel.* mið-fasta *mid-Lent*.]

mid-feorh, *gen.* -feores; *m. n. The period of middle age*:—Midferh *juventus*, Wrt. Voc. ii. 112, 17. Oft biþ on hālgum gewrietum genemned midfeorh (MS. mid feorwe) tō giúguþhāde *aliquando adolescentia juventus vocatur*, Past. 49, 5; Swt. 385, 31. [Cf. Ps. Th. 54, 24 on middum feore: *O. Sax.* (man) mid-firi: *O. H. Ger.* mitti-uerha *dimidio* (*dierum meorum*).] v. next two words.

mid-ferhþ, es; *m. n. Middle life* or *age*:—On cnihthāde . . . swā forþ eallne giógoþhād . . . and ðonne lytle ǣr his midferhþe, Bt. 38, 5; Fox 206, 25.

mid-ferhtness, e; *f. Middle age*:—Seó heora iúgoþ and seó midfyrhtnes būtan ǣgwylcum leahtre gestanden, hwylc talge wē ðæt seó yldo and se ende ðæs heora līfes wǣre? Blickl. Homl. 163, 3-6.

mid-help, es; *m*: e; *f. Help, assistance*:—Tō miðhelpe *adjuvando*, Rtl. 29, 36.

mid-hrif, es; *n. m.* [mid *middle*, hrif *ventus*] *The mid-riff, the diaphragm, separating the heart from the stomach, etc.*; also *the entrails*:—Midrif *disseptum*, Wrt. Voc. i. 44, 51: *exta*, 44, 49. Wið ðæt mannes midrif ace, Herb. cont. 3, 6; Lchdm. i. 6, 21. Midrife, Lchdm. i. 88, 11. On ðam uferan hrife oððe on ðam midhrife, L. M. 2, 46; Lchdm. ii. 260, 20. Of ðam midhrife, se is betweox ðære wambe and ðære lifre, 2, 56; Lchdm. ii. 278, 10. [*O. Frs.* mid-ref.] v. *next word, and see* hrif.

mid-hriðere, -hridir, es; *n. The membrane enclosing the entrails*:—Midhridir, nioþanweard hype *ilia*, Wrt. Voc. ii. 110, 54. Midhriðre *omentum*, i. 65, 56. Midhryðre, 284, 3. Midhryðere, ii. 64, 4. [*O. Frs.* midrithere *membrana qua jecor et splen pendent*; cf. *also* mid-rede, -rith *the mid-riff*: mydrede *diafragma*, Wrt. Voc. i. 208, 31.]

midl, es; *n.* I. *a bit, curb* (*of a bridle*):—Midl *frenum* vel *lupatum*: brīdles midl *chamus*, Wrt. Voc. i. 23, 21, 22. Midlum *lupatis* (*repagulis*), Hpt. Gl. 406, 27. Of īsenum midlum ł brīdlum *ferratis salivaribus* (*repagulis*), 458, 3: Homl. Th. i. 360, 19: Elen. Kmbl. 2349; El. 1176: 2384; El. 1193. Miðlum, Wrt. Voc. ii. 119, 49. II. *the thong which bound the oar to the pin*:—Midla *strupiar*, Wrt. Voc. i. 57, 6. Midlu, 63, 65. [Cf. *in the same list of words connected with ships* ār-wiððe *struppus*, 56, 37.]

midlen, es; *n. The middle, midst, centre*:—Of midlene *ex centro* i. *ex medio*, Wrt. Voc. ii. 145, 66. On medlene *in meditullio* i. *in medio*, Hpt. Gl. 405, 37. Ic eom on eówrum midlene, Lk. Skt. 22, 27. On fȳres midlene *de medio ignis*, Deut. 4, 15: 5, 24. Hē eardode in hǣðenra midlene . . . on þorna midlynæ, Shrn. 125, 7-8. Ða englas āsyndriaþ ða yfelan of ðæra gōdra midlene, Mt. Kmbl. 13, 49. Ic eom on hyra midlene, 18, 20. On midline *in dimidio*, Blick. Gl. Se Hǣlend gesette ǣnne lytling on hyra midlen, 18, 2. Ðā fērde hē þurh hyra midlen, Lk. Skt. 4, 30.

mid-lencten, es; *n. m. Mid-Lent*:—On mydlenctenes Sunnandæg, Jn. Skt. 6, 1, rubric. Tō midlængtene, Chart. Th. 349, 28.

midlest. v. middel.

midl-hring, es; *m. The ring of a bit*:—Midlhringas *armillae*, Wrt. Voc. ii. 10, 18.

midlian; *p.* ode *To bridle, curb, restrain*:—Forðæm is sió tunge gemetlīce tō midliganne (midlianne, Cot. MSS.) *lingua itaque discrete frenanda est*, Past. 38, 5; Swt. 275, 11. v. ge-midlian; ā-, un-, unge-midled.

midlian; *p.* ode *To mediate.* [*Icel.* miðla *to mediate*.] v. midligend *and* ge-midlian.

mid-liflend, es; *m. One co-existent with another*:—Uppstige ðæs midlifiendes [ðæs lifigendan, MS. Ca.], Bd. 3, 17; S. 545, 24, note. v. next word.

midligend, es; *m. A mediator*:—Uppstige ðæs midligendes Godes *ascensionem mediatoris, Dei*, Bd. 3, 17; S. 545, 24, note.

midlung, e; *f. The middle, midst*:—Of midlunge hwelpa *de medio catulorum*, Ps. Lamb. 56, 5. Of midlunge ðīnum bōsme *de medio sinu* *tuo*, 73, 11. On midlunge sceaduwe dǽþes *in medio umbrae mortis*, Ps. Spl. 22, 4: Cant. Moys. 19: Cant. Abac. 2: Ps. Lamb. 73, 12. On midlunga, 81, 1. v. next word.

midlunga; *adv. To a moderate* or *middling degree, intermediate between much and little*:—Sam hē hine miclum lufige, sam hē hine lytlum lufige, sam hē hine mydlinga lufige, Shrn. 194, 14. v. preceding word.

midmest. v. midd.

midne-dæg, es; *m. Mid-day*:—Se rehta geleáfa swē swē midnedæg *fides velut meridies*, Ps. Surt. ii. 201, 25. Cf. ǽrne-mergen *in another version of the same hymn*:—Clǽnnyss sȳ swā swā ǽrnemergen, geleáfa swā swā middæg, Hymn. Surt. 16, 27.

mid-ness, e; *f. Middle, midst*:—In midnesse ðæs mynstres . . . wit wǽron on midnesse miccles eges; ðā genāmon wit on midnysse ðæs eówdes twegen buccan, Shrn. 41, 20–27.

mid-niht, e; *f. Mid-night*:—Seó niht hæfþ seofan dǽlas . . . feórþa is *intempestum*, ðæt is midniht, Lchdm. iii. 244, 3: Wrt. Voc. ii. 49, 32. Midniht *intempestum* vel *intempesta nox*, i. 53, 5. On middre nihte wearþ clypung gehȳred . . . Hwæt getācnaþ seó midniht būton seó deópe nytennys, Homl. Th. ii. 568, 4. [Cf. *Icel.* mið-nætti: *O. H. Ger.* mitti-naht: *Ger.* mitter-nacht.] v. middel-niht; midd, **II.**

mid-rād, e; *f. A riding with another*:—Ðæt ǽlc man wǽre ōðrum gelāstfull ge æt spore ge æt midrāde (*in accompanying the other in following the trace of the lost property*), L. Æðelst. v. 4; Th. i. 232, 12. [*Icel.* með-reið.]

mīdrece. v. mȳdrece.

mid-rif. v. mid-hrif.

mid-singend, es; *m. One who sings with another*; concentor, Wrt. Voc. i. 28, 23.

mid-sīðian; *p.* ode *To accompany*:—Hū ne midsīðgadest ðū *comitarisne tū?* Midsīðige *comitatur, sequitur*, Wrt. Voc. ii. 132, 34–38. Midsīðudu *comitata*, 23, 39. v. ge-midsīðian.

mid-spreca, an; *m. One who speaks on behalf of another*:—Paulus wæs midspreca and bewerigend ðære ealdan ǽ *Paul was an advocate and defender of the old law*, Homl. Th. i. 388, 32. [Cf. *Icel.* með-mæli *the speaking a good word for one.*]

mid-sumor, es; *m. Mid-summer*:—Ǽr midsumeres mæsseǽfen, Chr. 1052; Erl. 182, 5. v. midde-sumor.

[**midsumor-dæg**, es; *m. Midsummer-day*:—Tō midsumer dæi, Chr. 1131; Erl. 259, 34.]

mid-weg, es; *m. Mid-way*:—Segor stōd on midwege betweox ðǽm muntum and ðǽm merscum, Past. 51, 5; Swt. 399, 13.

mid-winter, es; *m. Mid-winter, Christmas*:—Gif se (seo, MS.) midwinter biþ on Wōdnesdæg, ðonne biþ heard winter and grim . . . Gif heó byoþ on Ðunresdæg, ðonne byoþ gōd winter . . . Gif se midwinter byþ on Frigendæge, ðonne byþ onwendædlīc winter . . . Gif se midwinter byþ on Seternesdæg, ðonne byþ winter gedrēfedlīc, Lchdm. iii. 164, 1–10. On ðære hālgan midwintres tīde, L. C. E. pref.; Th. i. 358, 7. [*O. Frs.* mid-winter.] v. mid-sumor, midde-winter.

mid-wist, e; *f. The being with others, presence, society*:—Þurh fonthālgunge gewyrþ sōna Godes midwist *by the hallowing of the font God becomes at once present*, Wulfst. 36, 2. Ǽlc ðe gewita oððe gewyrhta sī ðǽr ūtlendisc man inlendiscan derie gelādie ðære midwiste *let every one that is cognisant or co-operating, where a stranger injures a native, clear himself of the participation*, L. O. D. 6; Th. i. 354, 29. Snottre men lufiaþ midwist mīne, Exon. 130 b; Th. 500, 17; Rä. 89, 8. [*O. H. Ger.* mite-wist *consortium, participatio.*]

mid-wunung, e; *f. Dwelling with others*:—Þūsend þūsenda þēnodon wealdende, and tēn þūsend sīðan hundfealde þūsenda him mid wunodon. Ōðer is þēnung, ōðer is midwunung, Homl. Th. i. 348, 5. Ēce līf and midwununcg mid Gode, R. Ben. 133, 18. Ðæt wē on ðam tōweardan līfe diófla midwununga forbūgan māgon, H. R. 17, 29.

mid-wyrhta, an; *m. One who works with others, a co-operator*:—On ðæt gerād ðæt hē wǽre his midwyrhta ǽgðer ge on sǽ ge on lande *on the condition that he would co-operate with him by sea and by land*, Chr. 945; Erl. 116, 31: Past. 38, 8; Swt. 279, 25. Hyt āwriten hys, ðæt ǽlcum welwyrcendum God myd beó mydwyrhta, Shrn. 179, 29.

mīgan; *p.* māh, *pl.* migon *To make water*:—Ic mīge *mingo*, Ælfc. Gr. 28, 5; Som. 31, 63. Ic mīge *meio*; mīge gē *meite*; mīgan *meire*, 33; Som. 37, 44–45. Ðæt hē mȳhþ (*mingit*), byþ sweart, Lchdm. iii. 140, 22. Ðām ðe under hȳ mīgaþ, L. Med. ex Quad. 8, 12; Lchdm. i. 360, 8. [*Laym.* mæh, meh; *p.*: *Icel.* mīga: *M. L. Ger.* mīgen.] v. ge-mīgan.

miggung. v. micgung.

mīging, e; *f. A making water*; minctio, Wrt. Voc. ii. 58, 10.

migol; *adj. Diuretic*:—Ðām monnum synd tō sellanne migole drincan, L. M. 2, 22; Lchdm. ii. 206, 27: 208, 7. Mid wyrtdrencum ūtyrnendum oððe migolum, 1, 35; Lchdm. ii. 206, 17.

migoþa, migþa, micgþa, an; *m. Urine*:—Gif se micgþa ætstanden sȳ, Herb. 7, 3; Lchdm. i. 98, 5. Heó earfoþlīcnysse ðæs migþan āstyreþ, 143, 1; Lchdm. i. 266, 3. Mid his selfes migoþan, ii. 42, 1. Swā hwæt swā ðæne migþan gelet, 4, 6; Lchdm. i. 90, 26: 7, 3; Lchdm. i. 98, 8: 152, 1; Lchdm. i. 278, 4. v. micga, micgung, cū-migoþa.

miht. v. meaht.

mīl, es; *n. Millet*:—Miil *milium*, Wrt. Voc. ii. 114, 9. Mīl, 55, 68.

mīl, e; mīle (?), an; *f. A mile*:—Ālecgaþ hit on ānre mīle ðone mǽstan dǽl fram ðæm tūne, ðonne ōðerne . . . ōð ðe hyt eall ālēd biþ on ðære ānre mīle, Ors. 1, 1; Swt. 20, 30–32: Blickl. Homl. 129, 4. Leóuue, mīle *milliarium*, Wrt. Voc. i. 38, 7. Twelf mīla, Blickl. Homl. 197, 23. Of ðære burnan tō mīla stāne, Cod. Dip. Kmbl. iii. 382, 22. Hund þūsenda mīla, Cd. 229; Th, 310, 9; Sat. 724. Ehta hund mīla lang, Bd. 1, 1; S. 473, 11. On nygan mīlum, 4, 27; S. 603, 30. [*Icel.* mīla: *O. H. Ger.* mīla, mīlla.]

milc. v. meolc.

milcen; *adj. Of milk*:—Mylcen mete *food made of milk*, L. M. 1, 67; Lchdm. ii. 142, 14.

milcian. v. meolcian, melcan.

mild-beorht; *adj. Mildly bright, serene*:—Miltbeorhtum leóhte *luce serena*, Hpt. Gl. 484, 29.

MILDE; *adj.* I. MILD, *gentle, meek, benign, liberal* (?):—Se wæs milde wer and monþwǽre *vir omnium mansuetissimus ac simplicissimus*, Bd. 4, 27; S. 603, 35. Heora cining cymeþ milde and monþwǽre (*mansuetus*, cf. Mt. 21, 5), Blickl. Homl. 71, 4. Ic eom milde and eáþmōdre heortan *mitis sum et humilis corde*, Bd. 2, 2; S. 503, 4. Ðæt milde mōd (*Guthlac*), Exon. 43 b; Th. 146, 17; Gū. 711. Of ārfæstre heortan and mildre, Blickl. Homl. 37, 27. Milde *mitia*, Wrt. Voc. ii. 57, 43. Spræc mildum wordum, Beo. Th. 2348; B. 1172. Mildre *indulgentior*, Ælfc. Gr. 43; Som. 44, 49. Manna mildost (*Moses*), Cd. 170; Th. 213, 8; Exod. 549. Cwǽdon ðæt hē wǽre manna mildust and monþwǽrost *they said that he was kindest and most courteous of men*, Beo. Th. 6344; B. 3182. Se leó gewāt swā swā ðæt mildoste lamb, Glostr. Frag. 110, 22. II. of the more towards the less powerful, *merciful, clement, propitious*:—Biddende ðæt Drihten him ārfæst and milde wǽre *Dominum sibi propitium fieri precabatur*, Bd. 4, 31; S. 610, 31. God beó ðū milde (*propitius*) mē synfullum, Lk. Skt. 18, 13: Ps. Lamb. 98, 8: Blickl. Homl. 47, 32. Mē milde weorþ *miserere mei*, Ps. Th. 56, 1. His milde gehigd *misericordia sua*, 56, 4. Cyning cystum gōd, clǽne and milde (*clement*), Chr. 1065; Erl. 199, 6. Ðam mildestan cyninge Wihtrǽde rīxigendum *in the reign of the most clement king Wihtræd*, L. Wih. pref.; Th. i. 36, 4. [*Goth.* milds: *O. Sax.* mildi: *O. Frs.* milde: *Icel.* mildr *mild*; also *munificent*: *O. H. Ger.* milti *mansuetus, largus, munificus.*] v. un-milde.

milde; *adv. Mercifully, graciously*:—Ūs milde æteów ðīnne andwlitan, Ps. Grn. 79, 18: Ps. C. 50, 72; Ps. Grn. ii. 278, 72: Hy. 6, 35; Hy. Grn. ii. 286, 35: Exon. 11 b; Th. 16, 7; Cri. 249. [*O. Sax.* mildo.]

mil-deáw. v. mele-deáw.

milde-līc; *adj. Merciful, clement, propitious*:—Mildelīc *propitius*, Rtl. 37, 19. [*Icel.* mild-ligr *gentle.*]

milde-līce; *adv. Graciously, kindly, mercifully*:—His se cyning mildelīce onfēng *the king received him kindly*, Ors. 1, 8; Swt. 40, 18. Swā mildelīce wæs Rōmeburg on fruman gehālgod mid brōðor blōde, 2, 2; Swt. 66, 4. Hāwa mildelīce on ðās earman eorþan, Bt. 4; Fox 8, 20. Mildelīce *propitiatus*, Rtl. 120, 9. [*O. H. Ger.* milt-līhho *largiter*: *Icel.* mild-liga *gently.*]

mild-heort; *adj.* I. *kind-hearted, of gentle disposition, meek*:—Leorniaþ æt mē forðon ðe ic eom mildheort and eáþmōd (*mitis et humilis corde*, Mt. 11, 29), Blickl. Homl. 13, 19. Uton beón eáþmōde and mildheorte and ælmesgeorne, 95, 26. Ðā weóp hē eác sylf . . . swā hē wæs manna mildheortost, 225, 23. II. *merciful, compassionate, gracious, clement*:—Ðū God mildheort (*misericors*), Ps. Spl. 85, 14: *miserator*, 102, 8. Beóþ mildheorte swā eówer fæder is mildheort, Lk. Skt. 6, 36: Blickl. Homl. 97, 32. Ðīn mildheort mōd *misericordia tua*, Ps. Th. 107, 4. Mid mildheortum weorcum *with works of mercy*, Blickl. Homl. 37, 19. Cyng ðū mildheortesta *rex clementissime* (*Christ*), Hymn. Surt. 86, 29: Ors. 6, 30; Bos. 126, 39 note. Hē wæs eallra monna mildheortast *he was most compassionate of all men*, 5, 12; Swt. 242, 20. [*O. H. Ger.* milt-herzi *misericors.*]

mildheort-līce; *adv. Kindly, compassionately, mercifully*:—Mildheortlīce *misericorditer*, L. Ecg. P. i. 9; Th. ii. 176, 15: ii. 2; Th. ii. 182, 27: Past. 44, 1; Swt. 319, 12, 14: Blickl. Homl. 101, 36. Mildheortlīcor *clementius*, Hymn. Surt. 138, 1.

mildheort-ness, e; *f. Mercy, compassion, pity, clemency*:—Hys mildheortnes *misericordia ejus*, Lk. Skt. 1, 50. Drihtnes mildheortnes, Blickl. Homl. 49, 24. Ūre sāula smerian mid mildheortnesse ele, 73, 24. Þurh mildheortnesse weorc, 97, 2. Mid ānre mildheortnyssa *sola clementia*, Hymn. Surt. 115, 27: Bd. 3, 17; S. 545, 13. Mildheort God . . . ðū ðe gehilst mildheortnysse *Deus misericors . . . qui custodis misericordiam*, Ex. 34, 6. Hī nāne mildheortnesse ne gearnodon, Bt. 38, 4; Fox 202, 28. Godes mōdor hire mildheortnisse ðære burhware gecȳðde, Chr. 994; Erl. 133, 15. Ðǽr beóþ gegearwode Godes mildheortnessa,

Blickl. Homl. 193, 20: 103, 18. Hē him lytle mildheortnesse gedyde, Ors. 3, 9; Swt. 128, 15.

mild-hleahtor, es; *m. Gentle laughter*:—Bysmrodon mē mildleahtre (or mid hleahtre?) *subsannaverunt me subsannatione*, Ps. Spl. 34, 19.

mildian; *p.* ode *To become mild*:—Mildode *mansuescit*, Germ. 399, 435. v. ge-mildian.

milds, mildsian, mildsiend, mildsung. v. milts, miltsian, miltsiend, miltsung.

milescian. v. miliscian.

mīl-gemearc, es; *n. Space of a mile* or *distance measured by miles*:—Nis ðæt feor heonon mīlgemearces ðæt se mere standeþ *it is not far hence, measuring by miles, that the mere lies*, Beo. Th. 2728; B. 1362. Cf. fōt-, geár-gemearc, *and* mīl-getæl.

mīl-gemet, es; *n. A mile-measure, a mile-stone*:—On ðæt mīlgemæt, Cod. Dip. Kmbl. iii. 252, 21.

mīl-getæl, es; *n. The number of paces in a mile, a mile*:—On rīme ðæs læssan mīlgetæles ðe *stadia* hātte fīf hund and ðæs miclan mīlgetæles ðe *leuua* hātte þreó hund and eahta and syxtig *reckoning according to the smaller mile, which is called* stadia, *it is five hundred miles, and according to the great mile, which is called* leuua (*league*), *it is* 368, Nar. 33, 9–11.

milisc; *adj. Honeyed, sweet, mellow*, (of drink) *mulled*:—Milisc apuldor *melarium*: milisc æppel *metianum*, Wrt. Voc. i. 285, 54, 55. (Melarium, *pomarium melis* (μῆλοις), *hoc est malis, consitum*, Du Cange: the Anglo-Saxon glosser seems to connect the word with *mel*?.) Milisc æppel *nicalalbum*, 289, 74: ii. 60, 42. Ðære miliscan *mulsæ*, 32, 66: 54, 35. Myliscre, Hpt. Gl. 520, 39. Drince mylsce drincan, sió gebēt ða biternesse ðæs geallan, L. M. 1, 42; Lchdm. ii. 108, 2. Milscra (milscre, Wrt.) treówa blōsman *qui[n]tinas*, g. *caducas* (Du Cange quotes Isidore: 'Flores malorum (*punicorum*) a Græcis appellati sunt quintinæ. Latini caducum vocant'), Wrt. Voc. i. 22, 16. Melsc appla *nicolaos* (cf. *nicolaus* = *dactulus*, Wrt. Voc. ii. 75, 79; *nicolatis* palmæpla, 60, 67), Hpt. Gl. 496, 65. Genim milsce æppla (*dates*?), L. M. 2, 4; Lchdm. ii. 182, 19. Mylsce æppla, 2, 16; Lchdm. ii. 194, 9. [Cf. *Icel.* milska *a honeyed beverage*; milska *to mix* (a beverage): *Goth.* miliþ *honey*.] v. next word.

miliscian *to become sweet* or *mellow*:—Milescian *mitescere*, Wrt. Voc. ii. 55, 8.

mīl-pæþ, es; *m. A road along which miles are reckoned*:—Wlance þegnas mǣton mīlpaþas meara bōgum *proud thanes traversed the roads on their steeds*, Cd. 151; Th. 188, 20; Exod. 171: Elen. Kmbl. 2523; El. 1263: Runic pm. Kmbl. 340, 16; Rūn. 5.

miltan, mieltan, meltan; *p.* te. I. *trans.* (a) *To melt*:—Nim heortes mearg mylt *take heart's marrow, melt it*, L. Med. ex Quad. 10, 4; Lchdm. i. 366, 4. Mylt buteran, Lchdm. iii. 6, 22. Beó ǣlc calic geworht of myldendum antimbre (*of fusible material*), gilden oððe seolfren, glæsen oððe tinen; ne beó nā hyrnen, ne hūru treówen, L. Ælfc. P. 45; Th. ii. 384, 6. (b) *to digest*:—Sió wamb seó ðe biþ hātre gecyndo melt mete wel . . . Seó ðe biþ wæterigre gecyndo næfþ gōde meltunge, swīðost on ðām mettum ðe uneáþe melte beóþ, L. M. 2, 27; Lchdm. ii. 220, 22–28. (c) *to refine by melting*:—Ðæm ðe his gāst wile meltan (MS. B. miltan) wið morðre āsceádan of scyldum *by him who will refine his spirit from the dross of crime, separate it from sins*, Salm. Kmbl. 111; Sal. 55. II. *intrans.* (= meltan) *To melt, become liquid*:—Ic mylte *liqueo*, Ælfc. Gr. 35; Som. 38, 8. Ðonne mē mægen and mōd mylte *dum defeceret virtus mea*, Ps. Th. 70, 8. Weax miltende *cera liquescens*, Ps. Spl. 21, 13. Myltende *madens*, Wrt. Voc. ii. 57, 56. Myltende[s] *liquidas*, Hpt. Gl. 470, 73. [*Icel.* melta *to digest*.] v. ge-miltan, meltan.

milt-coðu, e *and* an; *f. Disease of the spleen*; lienosis, Wrt. Voc. ii. 53, 74.

MILTE, es; *m.*: an; *f. The* MILT, *spleen*:—Milti, Ep. Gl. 256, 24. Milte *lien*, Wrt. Voc. ii. 53, 67: 112, 71: *splen*, i. 45, 12: *splena*, 65, 52. Se milte biþ emlang ðære wambe, L. M. 2, 36; Lchdm. ii. 242, 15, 22, 28. Þeós milte *hic splen*, Ælfc. Gr. 9, 13; Som. 9, 34. Hyt gelamp hwīlon ðæt man þearmas mid ðære miltan uppan ðās wyrte gescearp, ðā geclyfude seó milte tō ðysse wyrte and heó hrædlīce ða miltan fornam . . hȳ beón būtan miltan gemētte, Herb. 57, 1; Lchdm. i. 160, 3–10. Wið miltan sāre . . . heó ðæt sǣr fornimþ ðære miltan, 32, 6; Lchdm. i. 130, 22: L. Med. ex Quad. 2, 8; Lchdm. i. 334, 23. Wið ðam wǣtan yfle ðæs miltes . . . ðæt lācnaþ ðone milte, L. M. 2, 38; Lchdm. ii. 246, 9–11, 18. Of milte, Lchdm. ii. 248, 1. Wið āswollenum milte, 2, 45; Lchdm. ii. 256, 16. [*O. Frs.* milte; *f.*: *Icel.* milti; *n.*: *O. H. Ger.* milzi; *n.*: *Ger.* milz; *f.*]

milte-seóc; *adj. Splenetic*:—Milteseóc *lienosus*, Wrt. Voc. i. 19, 41. Wið milteseócum men, him mon sceal sellan eced, L. M. 2, 39; Lchdm. ii. 248, 9: 2, 41; Lchdm. ii. 252, 5.

milte-wærc, milt-wræc, es; *m. Pain in the spleen*:—Be miltewærce, L. M. 2, 36; Lchdm. ii. 242, 1: 3, 16; Lchdm. ii. 318. 9. Wið miltwræce, L. Med. ex Quad. 9, 5; Lchdm. i. 362, 5.

miltestre, an; *f. A harlot*:—Myltestre *meretrix* vel *scorta*, Wrt. Voc. i. 86, 72: Gen. 38, 15. Ne lǣt ðū ðīne dohtor beón myltestre *ne prostituas filiam tuam*, Lev. 19, 29. Beclypte seó myltestre ðæt clǣne mǣden, Homl. Skt. 2, 169: 7, 178. Cōmon tō ānre miltistran hūse *ingressi sunt domum mulieris meretricis*, Jos. 2, 1. Melt[r]estran hūs *lupanar*, Hpt. Gl. 500, 61. Myltistryna hūs, Ælfc. Gr. 9, 16; Som. 9, 45: Homl. Skt. 7, 148. Oððe ðū mid mǣdenum ðīnne lāc geoffrige, oððe ðū lāðum myltestrum scealt beón geférlǣht, 7, 119. Mānfulle and myltystran *publicani et meretrices*, Mt. Kmbl. 21, 31, 32.

miltestre-hūs, es; *n. A brothel*:—Myltestrehūs *lupanar*, Wrt. Voc. i. 58, 53.

milts, milds, e; *f.* I. *mildness, kindness, favour, mercy* (most commonly with reference to the Deity):—Mid ðec milds is *apud te propitiatio est*, Ps. Surt. 129, 4. Ðonne wurþe ūs eallum Godes milts ðē gearuwre, L. C. E. 19; Th. i. 372, 5: L. C. S. 85; Th. i. 424, 23: Past. 44; Swt. 325, 13. Biþ ðǣr seó miccle milts āfyrred . . . ðæs Ælmihtigan, Exon. 28 a; Th. 84, 10; Cri. 1371. Ūs wæs ā syððan Merewioingas milts ungyfeþe, Beo. Th. 5835; B. 2919. Þolige hē clǣnes legeres and Godes mildse, L. N. P. L. 62; Th. ii. 300, 19. Ðū mid mildse mīnre fērest *thou shalt depart with my favour*, Andr. Kmbl. 3344; An. 1676. Hē Drihtnes mildheortnysse gecȳgde and ða mildse bæd monna cynne *misericordiam Domini invocaret, et eam generi humano propitiari rogaret*, Bd. 4, 3; S. 569, 9. Miltse gecȳdan, onwreón, Blickl. Homl. 39, 23: 107, 2. Hæbbe hē Godes miltse (mildse), L. Eth. v. 9; Th. i. 306, 20: L. N. P. L. 64; Th. ii. 300, 24. Gemyne mildsa ðīnra *reminiscere miserationum tuarum*, Ps. Surt. 24, 6: 68, 17. Secggan wē him þanc ealra his miltsa, Blickl. Homl. 103, 26: 109, 10. Āsecggan ða miltsa ðe hē wið ðis mennisce cynn gecȳðde, 103, 19. For his miltsum *by his mercies*, Exon. 88 b; Th. 333, 6; Vy. 98: 42 a; Th. 140, 16; Gū. 611. II. *meekness, humility* (?), *joy* (?), (cf. *O. H. Ger.* milti *hilaritas*):—Ðec Ananias and Azarias and Misahel miltsum [*humbly* (?), *joyously* (?)] hergaþ, Exon. 55 a; Th. 195, 11; Az. 154: Th. 194, 29; Az. 146: 54 b; Th. 193, 8; Az. 118.

miltsian, mildsian; *p.* ode *To have* or *take pity upon a person, shew mercy, be merciful, pity.* I. *not followed by an object*:—Ic miltsige *indulgeo*, Ælfc. Gr. 26, 3; Som. 28, 54: *ignosco*, 28, 1; Som. 30, 31. Miltsige (mildsige, MS. B.) man for Godes ege *for fear of God let mercy be shewn*, L. C. S. 68; Th. i. 410, 22: L. Eth. vi. 53; Th. i. 328, 28. Cum and mildsa, Hy. 7, 27; Hy. Grn. ii. 287, 27. II. *with dative*:—Ic miltsige ðē *misereor tui* . . . miltsa ūs Drihten *miserere nostri Domine*, Ælfc. Gr. 41; Som. 43, 63–64. Ðū eallum miltsast ðǣm ðe on ðē gelȳfaþ, Blickl. Homl. 145, 19. Hē bæd ðæt Hǣlend him miltsade, 19, 13. Hē ðīnum māndǣdum miltsade eallum *qui propitiatur omnibus iniquitatibus tuis*, Ps. Th. 102, 3. Mon mildsige ðām yfelum, Bt. 39, 1; Fox 212, 7: 38, 7; Fox 210, 18. Gebrōðru, miltsige eów God, Homl. Th. ii. 158, 24. Eálā! ðū man, miltsa ðē, L. E. I. pref.; Th. ii. 394, 30. Miltsa mē *miserere mei*, Mk. Skt. 10, 48. Miltsa eallum ðīnum wiðerwinnum, and āgyld gōd for yfele, Homl. Th. ii. 344, 2. Mildsa monna cynne, Hy. 8, 32; Hy. Grn. ii. 290, 32. Him wile git God miltsian, Blickl. Homl. 47, 7. Gif hē ūs ārian and miltsian wile, 51, 30. Biþ hē sōna ūs efenþrowiende and hraðe miltsiende, 19, 30. Hǣlend wæs miltsigende Adame, 87, 35. III. *with genitive*:—Hē þearfendra miltsude, Ps. Th. 106, 40. Miltsa mīn *miserere mei*, 56, 1. Tīd tō mildsiende his *tempus miserendi ejus*, Ps. Surt. 101, 14. Miltsigende ðīn *miserens tui*, miltsigende his *miserens illius*, Ælfc. Gr. 41; Som. 43, 63. IV. *with a preposition*, v. miltsiend. v. ge-miltsian.

miltsiend, mildsiend, es; *m. One who takes pity*:—Ðū nǣre miltsiend ofer heora cild, Blickl. Homl. 249, 6. Mildheort and mildsiend *miserator et misericors*, Ps. Spl. 102, 8. Mildsiend *miserator*, Ps. Lamb. 85, 15. Milsend, Rtl. 69, 7: 170, 9. v. ge-mildsiend.

miltsigend-līc; *adj. To be pardoned, venial*:—Miltsigendlīc *propitiabilis*, Germ. 401, 130. Hwī wæs ðæs heáhengles syn unmiltsigendlīc and ðæs mannes miltsigendlīc? Boutr. Scrd. 17, 21.

miltsung, mildsung, e; *f. Mercy, pity, compassion, a shewing mercy, pardon, indulgence*:—Hit is rihtre ðæt him mon mildsige ðæt is ðonne hiora mildsung ðæt mon wrece hiora unþeáwas *it is more fitting that mercy be shewn them. Now this it is to shew them mercy, to punish their vices*, Bt. 38, 7; Fox 210, 18. Ealle for miltsunge stefne uton sellan *omnes pro indulgentia vocem demus*, Hymn. Surt. 37, 22. Swā micclum swā ðæs mannes gecynd unmihtigre wæs swā hit wæs leóhtre tō miltsunge *the weaker was man's nature, the easier was it to pardon*, Boutr. Scrd. 17, 24. Būtan forgifenysse ł miltsunge (milsunge) *sine respectu*, Hpt. Gl. 487, 53. Hē ūs mid his miltsunge (*sua miseratione*) gescylde, Bd. 3, 2; S. 524, 24. Petrus tīhþ ða geleáffullan þurh þingrǣdene þurh miltsung him forgyfenre mihte *Peter draws the faithful by intercession, by the merciful exercise of the power given to him*, Homl. Th. ii. 292, 2. Crist mæg ðīne nytennysse þurh his miltsunge onlīhtan, Homl. Skt. 5, 200. Gemune miltsunga ðīnra (*miserationum tuarum*), Ps. Spl. 24, 8: 50, 2. v. un-miltsung.

milt-wræc. v. milte-wærc.

mimor. v. ge-mimor *and next word.*

mimorian; *p.* ode *To keep in the memory, remember*:—Pater noster and crēdan mymerian (mynegian, MS. C.) ða yldran and tǽcan heora gingran, Wulfst. 74, 15.

min; *adj.* I. *small*:—Ne ðē sunne on dæge ne gebærne ne ðē mōna on niht min ne geweorþe *may the sun not burn thee by day, nor the moon withhold her light from thee by night*, Ps. Th. 120, 6. II. *mean, vile*:—Hwīlum cyrdon eft minne mānsceaþan on mennisc hiw *at times the vile criminals turned into human form*, Exon. 46 a; Th. 156, 27; Gū. 881. [The positive does not occur in the other Teutonic dialects, but comparative and superlative forms are found in Gothic, O. Frs., O. Sax., Icel. and O. H. Ger. Cf. also Lat. *minor, minimus*.] v. minsian, min-dōm.

mīn; *pron. gen.* of ic *Of me*:—Beó ðū mīn gemyndig, Ps. Th. 24, 6. Miltsa mīn, 56, 1. Ne æthrīn ðū mīn, Jn. Skt. 20, 17. Ic sprece *ego loquor*, mīn sprǽc *mei locutio*, Ælfc. Gr. 15; Som. 17, 56. Ǽr ðū ða miclan meaht mīn oferswīðdest, Exon. 73 a; Th. 273, 25; Jul. 521. Ne wāt ic hygeþoncum mīn, 109 a; Th. 417, 14; Rä. 36, 4. Hē wæs mīn on ða swīðran, Elen. Kmbl. 694; El. 347. Mīn sylfes gāst wæs ōrmod worden, Ps. Th. 76, 4. Mīn sylfes weorc hī gesāwon, 94, 9. (Cf. next word, V.) [*Goth.* meina: *O. Sax. O. Frs. Icel. O. H. Ger.* mīn.]

mīn; *adj. pron. Mine, my.* I. *with a noun*:—Mīn cnapa līþ on mīnum hūse lama ... Ne eom ic wyrðe ðæt ðū ingange under mīne þecene ... Ic cweþe tō mīnum þeówe, Mt. Kmbl. 8, 6–9. Hwylc is mīn mōdor and hwylce synt mīne gebrōðra, 12, 48. Fæder mīn! 26, 39. Ðis is mīnes fæder willa, Jn. Skt. 6, 40. Mīnre faðan yldre mōder, Wrt. Voc. i. 52, 19. On mīnre gesihþe, Ps. Th. 88, 31. Ne cunne gē mē ne mīnne fæder, Jn. Skt. 8, 19. Nimaþ mīn geoc ofer eów, Mt. Kmbl. 11, 29. Mīne fearras and mīne fuglas synt ofslegene, and ealle mīne þing synt gearwe, 22, 4. Mid lyre ealra þinga mīnra, Coll. Monast. Th. 27, 1. Hū gelȳfe gē mīnum wordum, Jn. Skt. 5, 47. II. *as predicate*:—Eall eorþe ys mīn, Ex. 19, 5. Ealle ða þing synd mīne, Gen. 31, 43. Ðīne twegen suna beóþ mīne, 48, 5. III. *used substantively*:—Wlwine habbe ðat lond ðe hē mīnes hafde, Chart. Th. 580, 24. Ic heóld mīn tela, Beo. Th. 5468; B. 2737. Gif ic mōt mīne wealdan, Cd. 102; Th. 136, 1; Gen. 2251. Ealle mīne synt ðīne, and ðīne synt mīne, Jn. Skt. 17, 10. Ðū mundbora wǽre mīnum, Exon. 120 b; Th. 463, 25; Hö. 75. Ða mīnan, Cd. 224; Th. 296, 19; Sat. 504. IV. *with a pronoun*:—Hēr is mīn se gecorena sunu *hic est filius meus dilectus*, Mt. Kmbl. 3, 17. Ðes mīn sunu, Lk. Skt. 15, 24. Se mīn wine, Exon. 115 b; Th. 444, 21; Kl. 50. Mīn se ēca dǽl in gefeán fareþ, 38 a; Th. 125, 11; Gū. 352. Mīn se swētesta sunnan scīma, 68 a; Th. 252, 20; Jul. 166. Bi ðam bitran deáþe mīnum, 29 b; Th. 90, 18; Cri. 1476. Ic mid mec gelǽdde mīne þrié ða getreówestan frȳnd, Nar. 29, 27. Mīne ða hālgan, Ps. Th. 104, 13: 121, 8. Ða manigfealdan mīne geþohtas, Exon. 118 a; Th. 453, 1; Hy. 4, 8. V. *with* self (a) *agreeing with the noun* (see also preceding word):—On mīnne sylfes dōm, Beo. Th. 4301; B. 2147. (b) *agreeing with* self:—Mīnes sylfes mūþ *os meum*, Ps. Th. 77, 2. Mīnes sylfes gebed *oratio mea*, 140, 2. Mīnre sylfre sīþ, Exon. 115 a; Th. 441, 20; Kl. 2. VI. *with* āgen:—Ic ne mōt wealdan mīnra āgenra þeówa, Bt. 7, 3; Fox 20, 20. [*Goth.* meins: *O. Sax. O. Frs. O. H. Ger.* mīn: *Icel.* mīnn.]

min-dōm, es; *m. Smallness, abjectness, pusillanimity*:—Ic bīde ðæs beornes ðe mē bōte (? bēte) eft mindōm *expectabam eum qui me salvum faceret a pusillo animo*, Ps. Th. 54, 7. v. min, minsian.

mine, es; *m. A minnow*:—Myne *vel* ǽlepūte *capito*, Wrt. Voc. i. 55, 75. Mynas and ǽlepūtan *menas et capitones*, Coll. Monast. Th. 23, 33.

mīn-līce; *adv. In my way, in my manner*:—Mīnlīce *meatim* (= *meo more*, Wülck. 32, 20), Wrt. Voc. ii. 58, 46.

minna (?) *a sheaf*:—Ða minnan gaderaþ *qui manipulos colliget*, Ps. Spl. T. 128, 6.

minsian; *p.* ode *To lessen, diminish, become small*:—Wlite minsode, Cd. 187; Th. 232, 30; Dan. 268. Minsade, Exon. 94 a; Th. 353, 48; Reim. 29. Cf. Ne mæg ǽnig man Godes mihta ne his mǽrþa geminsian, Wulfst. 35, 3. [*O. Sax. O. L. Ger.* minsōn *to make less*: cf. *Icel.* minnka *to make less*.] v. next word.

minsung, e; *f. Parsimony*:—Forhæuednys *parsimonia*; minsong *abstinentia*, Hpt. Gl. 494, 41.

minte, an; *f. Mint*:—Minte *menta*, Wrt. Voc. i. 31, 11: ii. 98, 18: *mentha*, i. 67, 65. Eal mintan cyn *mentastrum*, ii. 56, 34. Gē ðe teóðiaþ mintan, Lk. Skt. 11, 42: Mt. Kmbl. 23, 23. v. brōc-, feld-, fen-, hors-, sǽ-, tūn-minte.

mirc-apuldor *a dark apple-tree*:—Mircapuldur *melarium* (as if from μέλας?), Wrt. Voc. ii. 113, 78. v. milisc.

Mircan. v. next word.

Mirce, Mierce, Myrce; *pl. The Mercians*, (and as the name of the people is used where modern English uses the name of their country) *Mercia* [see Green's The Making of England, p. 85]:—Hēr Mierce wurdon Cristne, Chron. 655; Erl. 28, 1. Ðā nāmon Mierce (Myrce, MS. E.) friþ wið ðone here, 872; Erl. 76, 16. Of Engle cōman Eást-Engle and Middel-Engle and Myrce (*Merci*) and eall Norþhembra cynn, Bd. 1, 15; S. 483, 25. Miercna cyning, land, rīce, Chr. 853; Erl. 68, 7: 877; Erl. 78, 26: 794; Erl. 58, 7. Mircena cining, 704; Erl. 43, 30. Mercna land, rīce, cyningcynn, 905; Erl. 98, 14: 655; Erl. 28, 4: Bd. 2, 20; S. 521, 8. Myrcna cynn, mǽgþ, þeód, 3, 21; S. 551, 23: 4, 3; S. 566, 24: 2, 12; S, 515, 7. Myrcna landes is þrittig þūsend hȳda ðǽr mon ǽrest Myrcna hǽt, Cod. Dip. B. i. 414, 15. Myrcena cining, land, Chr. 792; Erl. 59, 1: 796; Erl. 59, 39: L. Alf. 49; Th. i. 58, 25: L. Eth. i. pref.; Th. i. 280, 4. Ðā fēng Æðelbald tō rīce on Mercium (Myrcum, MS. E.), Chr. 716; Erl. 44, 14. In Mercum preóst, 731; Erl. 47, 10. On Myrcean, L. C. S. 14; Th. i. 384, 1. On West-Sexan and on Myrcan and on Eást-Englan, 72; Th. i. 414, 14: Swt. A. S. Rdr. 100, 146. Hine on Mierce (Myrce, MS. E.) lǽddon, Chr. 796; Erl. 58, 12. Hē fōr ofer Mierce on Norþ-Walas, 853; Erl. 68, 10. Innan Mierce (Myrce, MS. E.) tō Snotengahām, 868; Erl. 72, 21. Of Wesseaxum on Merce, 853; Erl. 68, 22. v. Norþ-, Sūþ-Mirce; *and* mearc.

mirce; *adj.* I. *dark, murky*:—Ða mircan gesceaft (*Hell*), Exon. 116 a; Th. 446, 23; Dōm. 26. Gang ofer myrcan mōr *her course o'er the dark moor*, Beo. Th. 2814; B. 1405. II. in a metaphorical sense (of sin, crime, etc.) *dark, black, evil*:—Mircne mægencræft mānwomma gehwone *dark power, each sinful stain*, Exon. 26 b; Th. 78, 26; Cri. 1280. Þeáh ðū drype þolige, myrce mānslaga, Andr. Kmbl. 2437; An. 1220. Leahtras mirce māndǽde *crimes, black deeds of wickedness*, Exon. 62 b; Th. 229, 18; Ph. 457. Mircast mānweorca *blackest of crimes*, 73 a; Th. 272, 26; Jul. 505. [*Havel.* mirke: *Chauc. Piers P.* merke: *Prompt. Parv.* myrke *obscurus, tenebrosus*: *O. Sax.* mirki: *Icel.* myrkr: *Dan. Swed.* mörk.] v. mirc-apuldor, æl-myrca, Gūþ-myrce.

mirce, es; *n. Darkness*:—Se ðe hié of ðam mirce (*the fiery furnace*) generede, Cd. 196; Th. 244, 15; Dan. 448. Myrce (*or adv.?*) gescȳrded *shrouded with darkness*, Andr. Kmbl. 2628; An. 1315. [*Piers P.* men þat in *merke* sitten: *Scot.* mirk: *Icel.* myrkr; *n. darkness*; mjörkvi *darkness, thick fog*: *Dan.* mörke.]

mircels, es; *m.*: e; *f.* I. *a sign, mark, token*:—Ðū āsettest ðīnes wuldres myrecels on worlde, sete nū ðīn wuldres tācn in helle, Blickl. Homl. 87, 16. II. *a mark to aim at*:—Hē miste mercelses, and his mǽg ofscēt, Beo. Th. 4869; B. 2439. Hī setton hine tō myrcelse, and heora flān him on āfæstnodon, Homl. Skt. 5, 426. III. *a signet, seal*:—Gehealdenre mercelse *salvo signaculo*, Hpt. Gl. 501, 27. Insegle, mercelse *signaculo*, 504, 37. IV. *an ensign, a trophy*:—Ðā hēt se hǽðena cyning his heáfod of āsleán and his swīðran earme, and settan hī tō myrcelse, Swt. A. S. Rdr. 99, 135. Ðā ðū gehēte ðæt ðec hālig gǽst wið earfeþum eáðe gescilde for ðam myrcelse ðe (ðec?) monnes hond from ðīnre onsȳne āhwyrfde *when thou didst promise, that the Holy Spirit would easily shield you from troubles, on account of the ensign* (*the cross?*) *that would turn man's hand from thy face*, Exon. 39 a; Th. 129, 30; Gū. 429. V. *a marked spot*:—Hē hēt ða gebrōðru ādelfan ǽnne pytt, ðǽr ðǽr hē ǽr gemearcode ... Ða gebrōðru ðā eodon tō ðam mercelse, Homl. Th. ii. 162, 1–6.

Mircisc; *adj. Mercian*:—Be Merciscan āðe, L. O. 13; Th. i. 182, 18.

mire *a mare.* v. mere.

mirgan; *p.* de *To be merry, to rejoice, be glad*:—Fægniaþ and myrgaþ Gode mid wynsumre stemne *jubilate Deo in voce exultationis*, Ps. Th. 46, 1.

mirgen *that which causes delight, poetry* (?):—Him wæs lust micel ðæt hē ðiossum leódum leóþ spellode, monnum myrgen *great his* (*Alfred*) *delight was lays to relate, matter of mirth for men*, Bt. Met. Fox introd. 9; Met. Einl. 5. Cf. mirigness.

mirhþ. v. mirigþ.

mirige; *adj. Pleasant, delightful, sweet*:—Myrige leóþ *dulce carmen*, Hymn. Surt. 55, 17. Ðeós woruld deáh ðe heó myrige hwīltīdum geþuht sȳ *this world, though it seem at times pleasant*, Homl. Th. i. 154, 17. Ðeós woruld is hwīltīdum myrige on tō wunigenne, 182, 24. Gærs myrige on tō sittenne, 182, 15. Wǽre hit ðonne murge mid monnum, Bt. Met. Fox 11, 203; Met. 11, 102. Eall se eard wæs mirige (*or adv.?*) mid wætere gemenged, Gen. 13, 10. Dōmes dæg, ðæt is se myriga dæg, Wulfst. 244, 15. Hwæt ða woruldlustas myreges (myrges, MS. Cott.) brengaþ *quid habeat jucunditatis*, Bt. 31, 1; Fox 112, 4. Ne geleofaþ man nāht miriges ða hwīle ðe mon deáþ ondrǽt *one gets no pleasure from life, while one fears death*, Prov. Kmbl. 16. Mid merigum lofsange *dulci ymno*, Hymn. Surt. 141, 38. Him ða twigu þincaþ swā merge *the boughs seem so pleasant to them*, Bt. Met. Fox 13, 89; Met. 13, 45. Ða mergen *amoena*, Hpt. Gl. 409, 36. [*Laym. A. R.* murie: *Gen. and Ex.* mirie: *Prompt. Parv.* myry yn chere *letus, jocundus*; myry, mery weder *malacia*: *Chauc. Piers P.* murie, merie.] v. next word.

mirige; *adv. Pleasantly, sweetly, gladly*:—His mōdor gehȳrde hū myrge hē sang mid ðām munecum and hyre wæs myrge on hyre mōde *his mother heard how sweetly he sang with the monks, and she was glad at heart*, Wulfst. 152, 11–13.

mirig-ness, e; *f. Pleasantness, sweetness* (of sound), *music*:—Myrgnis *musica*, Wrt. Voc. ii. 114, 45. v. mirgen, mirige.

mirigþ, mirgþ, mirhþ, myrþ, e; *f. Pleasure, joy, delight, sweetness* (of sound):—Dæg byþ myrgþ eádgum and earmum *day is a delight to rich and to poor*, Runic pm. Kmbl. 344, 12; Rūn. 24. Wā him ðære mirigþe būte hē ðæs yfeles ǽr geswīce *alas for his delight, unless first he leave evil*, Hy. 2, 6; Hy. Grn. ii. 281, 6. Hē ādrǽfed wæs of neorxena wanges myrþe (*paradisum voluptatis*), Gen. 3, 24. For ðære mirhte (mergþe, MS. Cott.) ðæs sōnes, Bt. 35, 6; Fox 168, 11. On heofonan rīces mirhþe, Ælfc. T. Grn. 1, 11. Myrhþe, Homl. Th. i. 58, 4. Ða heorde tō heofonlīcre myrhþe (myrþe, MS. B.) lǽdan, L. C. S. 85; Th. i. 424, 11. Man byþ on myrgþe (*joyous*), Runic pm. Kmbl. 343, 11; Rūn. 20. Ðū ðǽr nāne myrhþe on næfdest ðā ðā ðū hié hæfdest *thou hadst no pleasure in them, when thou hadst them*; nec habuisse te in ea pulcrum aliquid, Bt. 7, 1; Fox 16, 17. Ðīn rīce ðǽr wē gemētaþ ealle mirhþe, Hy. 7, 31; Hy. Grn. ii. 287, 31. Ðǽr (*heaven*) syndan mihta, mǽrþa and myrhþa, Wulfst. 5, 5: 167, 9: 28, 7. Adam wearþ of myclum myrhþum bescofen tō hefigum geswincum, 104, 1. v. myrige, un-mirigþ.

mirra, merra, an; *m. One who leads astray, a deceiver*:—Merra *seductor*, Mt. Kmbl. Lind. 27, 63.

mirran, mierran, merran; *p.* de. I. *to be a stumbling-block to, to hinder, obstruct*:—Ðe ðone ungesceádwīsan mirþ (*scandali occasionem praebere*), Past. 59, 6; Swt. 453, 4. Sió ofersmeáung mirþ (*is a hindrance to*) ða unwīsan, 15, 5; Swt. 97, 17. Ðæt eów læst þinga mierþ *sine impedimento*, 51, 7; Swt. 401, 17. Ðæs andwearda wela āmerþ and lǽt (MS. Cott. myrþ and let) ða men ðe beóþ ātihte tō ðām sōþum gesǽlþum, Bt. 32, 1; Fox 114, 3. Merþ, tit. 32; Fox xvi, 12. Seó ungesceádwīsnes heora eágena hī myrþ (āmerraþ, Cott. MS.), 32, 2; Fox 116, 26. Gyf hī ðē myrraþ and lettaþ, Shrn. 185, 5. Hwī mirraþ git ðis folc fram heora weorcum *quare sollicitatis populum ab operibus suis?* Ex. 5, 4. God nolde ðæt hié ðone Cristendōm mierde leng *God would not that they should longer obstruct Christianity*, Ors. 6, 7; Swt. 262, 21. Gif hwā Godes lage wyrde oððe folclage myrre, L. I. P. 2; Th. ii. 306, 12. II. *to waste, squander*:—Ðȳ læs mon unnytlīce mierre ðæt ðæt hē hæbbe *ne, quae possident, inutiliter spargant*, Past. 44, 4; Swt. 325, 3. Ne myr ðū eal ðæt ðū hæbbe, ðȳ læs ðe geþearfe tō ōðres mannes ǽhtum, Prov. Kmbl. 73. Gif ðū ðīn āgen myrre, ne wīt ðū hit nā Gode, 51. Se hordere nā mynstres ǽhta ne ȳte, ne nā myrre, R. Ben. 55, 4. III. *intrans. To err*:—Gié merras ł geduellas *erratis*, Mt. Kmbl. Lind. 22, 29. [*Goth.* marzjan σκανδαλίζειν: *O. Sax.* merrian (*trans.* and *intrans.*): *O. Frs.* meria: *O. H. Ger.* marrian *impedire, scandalizare.*] v. ā-, ge-myrran.

mirrelse, an; *f. A hindrance, stumbling-block*:—Gif sōþfæstra þurh myrrelsan mōd ne ōðcyrreþ *if the mind of the righteous, through rock of offence, turn not aside*, Exon. 70 b; Th. 262, 25; Jul. 338.

mirring, e; *f.* I. *hindering, leading astray*:—Merrunga *seductiones*, Mk. Skt. p. 5, 8. Cf. mirra. [*O. Frs.* meringa *hindrance*: *O. H. Ger.* marunga *impedimentum.*] II. *waste, squandering* (v. mirran, II):—Oððe se gielpna for his gōda mierringe (mirringe, Cott. MSS.) gielpe and wēne ðæt hē sīe kystig and mildheort *aut cum effuse quid perditur, largum se glorietur*, Past. 20, 2; Swt. 149, 20. Ða uncystgan cysta lǽre hē, swā hē ða cystgan on merringe ne gebringe *sic tenacibus infundatur tribuendi largitas, ut prodigis effusionis frena minime laxentur*, 60; Swt. 453, 27. v. mann-mirring.

mirt, myrt *a mart, market*:—Cēping *mercatum*: scipmanne myrt þe (Wrt. se) cēping *teloneum*, Wrt. Voc. i. 37, 9–10.

mis-, miss-, mist-, misse- a prefix denoting *defect, imperfection*, *Goth.* missa- (*for* miþto- *a participial form connected with root meaning* to lose): *O. Sax. O. L. Ger. O. Frs.* mis-: *Icel. Da. Swed.* mis-: *O. H. Ger.* missa-, missi-: *M. H. Ger.* misse-: *Ger.* mis-, miss-.

mis-begān *to cultivate badly, waste, disfigure*:—Misbegāas onsióne hiora *exterminant facies suas* (cf. unrōtlīce dōþ *exterminant*, Wrt. Voc. ii. 30, 64), Mt. Kmbl. Lind. 6, 16.

mis-beódan; *p.* -beád, *pl.* -budon; *pp.* -boden *To do wrong to, to offend, abuse, ill-use*:—Hē misbeád his munecan on fela þingan *he ill-used his monks in many things*, Chr. 1083; Erl. 217, 3. Ðē læs ǽnig man ōðrum misbeóde *lest any do wrong to other*, L. I. P. 7; Th. ii. 312, 22: Chart. Th. 320, 13: 416, 13. Ne misbeóde ǽnig ōðrum, forðam eal ðæt ǽnig man ōðrum on unriht tō hearme gedēþ, eal hit sceal eft mænigfealdlīce derian him sylfum, Wulfst. 112, 7–11. Misbeódan, 157, 20. Gif him ǽnig man heálīce misboden hæbbe (cf. Who hath yow misboden, or offended, Chauc. Kn. T. 51), L. Edg. C. 5; Th. ii. 244, 18. [*Piers P.* mysbede nouȝte þi bondemen: *Icel.* mis-bjóða *to ill-use, offend.*]

mis-boren; *pp.* I. *mis-born, mis-shapen at birth, abortive*:—Gif cild misboren sȳ, Herb. 115, 3; Lchdm. i. 228, 10. (Cf. H. M. 33, 34: ȝif hit (the child) is mis-born, as hit ilome limpeð.) II. *degenerate*:—Misboren *degener*, Germ. 393, 130. v. mis-byrd, -byrdo.

mis-bregdan *to remove, draw aside* (?):—Misbroden [ic eom?] *disto* i. *differo*, Wrt. Voc. ii. 141, 50. [Cf. *Icel.* mis-brigði *deviation.*]

mis-byrd, e; *f. A mis-birth, abortion*:—Misbyrd *abortus*, Wrt. Voc. ii. 4, 13: 98, 17: Ep. Gl. 2 f, 4. [*Da.* mis-byrd *miscarriage, abortion.*]

mis-byrdo; *f. indecl. Imperfect nature* or *quality*:—Be wambe missenlīcre gecyndo oððe ðære misbyrdo, L. M. 2, 27; Lchdm. ii. 220, 14. Sió wamb sió ðe biþ cealdre gecyndo oððe misbyrdo, 222, 3. [Cf. *Da.* mis-byrd *mean birth.*]

mis-bysnian; *p.* ode *To set a bad example*:—Gif ða lāreówas wel tǽcaþ and wel bysniaþ ðonne beóþ hī gehealdene; gif hī mistǽcaþ, oððe misbysniaþ, hī forþǽraþ hī sylfe, Homl. Th. ii. 50, 3–5.

miscan, miscean *to injure, afflict*:—Hwī lǽtst ðū mē gān unrōtne ðonne mē mysceaþ mīne fȳnd *quare tristatus incedo, dum affligit me inimicus?* Ps. Th. 44, 11. [Cf. *Icel.* miski *a misdeed, offence.*]

mis-cealfian; *p.* ode *To cast a calf*:—Miscalfaþ *abortabit*, Wrt. Voc. ii. 62, 1.

miscian; *p.* ode *To mix, to mix in due proportion*:—Hē of ðæm heán hrōfe hit eall gesihþ and ðonan miscaþ and metgaþ ǽlcum be his gewyrhtum *qui, cum ex alta providentiae specula respicit, quid unicuique conveniat, agnoscit, et, quod convenire novit, accommodat*, Bt. 39, 9; Fox 226, 22. Gehwæðeres sceal mon nyttian and miscian ðæt ðone līchoman hǽle *each method* (*treatment by hot or by cold remedies*) *shall be used and applied in due proportion, that the body may be cured*, L. M. 1, 1; Lchdm. ii. 22, 7. [*O. H. Ger.* misken *mis ere*: *M. H. Ger. Ger.* mischen.]

mis-cirran *to pervert*:—Oft ic miscyrre cūðe sprǽce, Bt. Met. Fox 2, 15; Met. 2, 8. v. mis-fōn.

mis-crocettan *to make a horrible noise*:—Hī (*evil spirits*) miscrocetton on hāsrūnigendum stefnum, Guthl. 5; Gdwin. 36, 1. v. cræcetung.

mis-cweðan. I. *to speak amiss* or *incorrectly*:—Miscweden word *barbarismus*, Wrt. Voc. ii. 12, 46: Ælfc. Gr. 50, 21; Som. 51, 49. *Solocismus*, ðæt is miscweden word on endebyrdnysse ðære rǽdinge of ðam rihtan cræfte, 50, 22; Som. 51, 49. II. *to curse*; maledicere:—Se ðe miscweðes feder ł moeder *qui maledixerit patri aut matri*, Mk. Skt. Rush. 7, 10. Miscuēdon him *maledixerunt ei*, Jn. Skt. Lind. 9, 28. [Cf. *Goth.* missa-kwiss *dissension*: *Icel.* mis-kviðr *a slip in pleading.*]

mis-dǽd, e; *f. A mis-deed, evil action, transgression, offence, injury*:—Mīne misdǽda bióþ simle beforan mē *delictum meum coram me est semper*, Past. 53, 2; Swt. 413, 18. God him geunne ðæt his gōde dǽda swȳðran wearþan ðonne misdǽda, Chr. 959; Erl. 121, 6. Gif hund mon tōslīte æt forman misdǽde geselle vi scill . . . Gif æt ðissa misdǽda hwelcere se hund losige . . . Gif se hund mā misdǽda gewyrce, L. Alf. pol. 23; Th. i. 78, 3–6. Menn scamaþ for gōddǽdan swȳðor ðonne for misdǽdan, Wulfst. 164, 16. Forsyngod þurh mænigfealde synna and þurh fela misdǽda, 163, 20: L. Eth. vi. 52; Th. i. 328, 15: L. Alf. pol. 14; Th. i. 70, 16. Gif hwā lengctenbryce gewyrce . . . þurh ǽnige heálīce misdǽda, L. C. S. 48; Th. i. 404, 1. [*Goth.* missa-dēds: *O. L. Ger.* mis-dāt *delictum*: *O. Frs.* mis-dēd: *Da.* mis-daad: *O. H. Ger.* missa-, mis-tāt *offensio, delictum, culpa, injuria*: *Ger.* misse-that.]

mis-dōn *to act wrongly, offend, transgress*:—Gif hit geweorðeþ ðæt man unwilles ǽnig þing misdēþ, nā biþ ðæt nā gelīc ðam ðe sylfwilles misdēþ, and eác se ðe nȳdwyrhta biþ ðæs ðe hē misdēþ, L. Eth. vi. 52; Th. i. 328, 21: L. Edg. C. 4; Th. ii. 262, 6. Se ðe misdōeþ *qui male agit*, Jn. Skt. Lind. 3, 20. Se ðe misdyde, hē hit gebēte, L. I. P. 19; Th. ii. 328, 15. Tō fela is ðæra ðe misdydan, Wulfst. 270, 30. [Durste nān man misdōn wið ōðer on his tīme, Chr. 1135; Erl. 261, 7.] [*O. Frs.* mis-dūa: *O. H. Ger.* missa-, mis-tuon *delinquere, offendere, culpare.*]

mis-efesian *to cut the hair improperly* (of the tonsure):—Wē lǽraþ, ðæt ǽnig gehādod man his sceare ne helige, ne hine misefesian ne lǽte, L. Edg. C. 47; Th. ii. 254, 13.

mis-endebyrdan *to arrange improperly, put in wrong order*:—Gif preóst misendebirde ciriclīce geárþēnunga, L. N. P. L. 38; Th. ii. 296, 7.

misen-līc. v. missen-līc.

mis-fadian *to misconduct, order wrongly*:—Gif hē his līf misfadige *if he do not order his life aright*, L. Eth. ix. 29; Th. i. 346, 20. Gif preóst ordāl misfadige, L. N. P. L. 39; Th. ii. 296, 9.

mis-fadung, e; *f. Misconduct, irregularity*:—For oft hit getīmaþ ðæt sacu and ungeþwǽrnessa on mynstre āspringaþ þurh ðæs profostes misfadunge, R. Ben. 124, 5. Þurh ðis beóþ āwecte saca and tala, ungeþwǽrnessa and misfadunga, 124, 18. Misfadunga *exordinationes*, Wrt. Voc. ii. 145, 78.

mis-faran. I. *to go astray, to err, transgress*:—Oft for ðæs lāreówes unwīsdōm misfaraþ ða hiéremenn *per pastorum ignorantiam hi, qui sequuntur, offendant*, Past. 1, 4; Swt. 29, 4. Ðæt men for nytennysse misfaran ne sceolon, Homl. Th. ii. 314, 5. [Cf. If Joseph sag hise breðere misfaren His fader he it gan unhillen and baren, *Gen. and Ex.* 1911.] II. *to fare badly, have ill success*:—Sume secgaþ ðæt hī (*certain animals*) þurh bletsunge misfaraþ, and þurh wyrigunge, geþeóþ, Homl. Th. i. 100, 31. Þurh deófol fela þinga misfōr *by the devil's agency many things have gone on badly*, Wulfst. 104, 22. Se ðe Gode nele hȳran, witod hē sceal misfaran, 178, 21. [*O. Frs.* mis-fara *to act falsely*: *Icel.* mis-fara *to go astray, to transgress*; mis-farask einum *to go badly with one*: *Da.* mis-fare *to miscarry*: *O. H. Ger.* missa-faran *to transgress.*] v. mis-fēran.

mis-fēdan *to feed improperly*:—Misfēdeþ *glosses* de-pascet *in* Ps. Spl. T. 48, 14.

mis-fēran *to go astray, transgress*:—Hē (*Saul*) ðæt folc bewerode wið ða hǽðena leóda, ðeáh hē misfērde on manegum ōðrum þingum, Ælfc. T. Grn. 7, 4. [*Laym.* mis-ferde; *p. wandered: Havel.* mis-ferde; *p. acted ill.*] v. mis-faran.

mis-fôn *to fail to take, to mistake:*—Ic hwīlum gecoplīce funde ac ic nū gerādra worda misfō *once I readily invented, but now I fail to get appropriate words,* Bt. 2; Fox 4, 9. Be ðǽm ðe on cyricean misfōu. Gif hwylc brōðor wǽgþ and misfēhþ (*makes a mistake*) on boduncge sealma, R. Ben. 71, 4–5. Wīn gedēþ, ðæt furþon witan oft misfōþ and fram rihtum geleáfan būgan, 65, 5. Ðȳ læs ǽnig ðære tale brūce ðæt hē ðȳ dæge misfēnge (*mistook the day*), Lchdm. iii. 442, 3. [Mine songe þah he beó god me hine mai misfonge (*mis-apply, take wrongly*), O. and N. 1374: cf. *Icel.* mis-fangi *a taking one thing for another.*]

mis-gedwild, es; *n. Error:*—Ðæt wē sōðfæstra, þurh misgedwield, mōd oncyrren, Exon. 70 b; Th. 262, 1; Jul. 326.

mis-gehygd, es; *n. Evil mind* or *thought,* Andr. Kmbl. 1543; An. 773. [Cf. *Icel.* mis-huga *to think evil.*]

mis-gelimp, es; *n. Mishap, misadventure:*—Hē sende misgelimpu on manna bearn, Wulfst. 211, 30.

mis-gemynd, e; *f. Evil memory* or *memorial:*—Ȳweþ him earmra manna misgemynda *shews him the evil memories of wretched men,* Salm. Kmbl. 987; Sal. 495.

mis-gewider, es; *n. Bad weather:*—Hwanan sió ādl cume be misgewiderum, L. M. 2, 36; Lchdm. ii. 244, 11. v. mis-wider.

mis-gîman *to fail to take care, to neglect:*—Gif preóst sceare misgȳme beardes oððe feaxes, L. N. P. L. 34; Th. ii. 294, 27.

mis-grêtan *to affront, insult:*—Se gylda ðe ōðerne misgrēt . . . gebēte hē ðæt wið ðone man ðe hē mysgrētte, Chart. Th. 606, 22–27. Gif hwilc gegilda ōðerne misgrēte, 612, 18. Cf. mis-beódan.

mis-hæbbende *being ill:*—Alle mishæbbende *omnes male habentes,* Mt. Kmbl. Lind. 8, 16. Cf. yfel-hæbbende.

mis-healdsumness, e; *f. Want of observance, negligence:*—Be muneces mishealdsumnysse *de monachi inobservantia,* L. Ecg. P. iii. tit. 11; Th. ii. 196, 3.

mis-hîran *to pay no attention to a person speaking, to disobey:*—Se ðe eów gehȳrþ, hē gehȳrþ mē, and se ðe eów mishȳrþ, hē mishȳrþ mē, R. Ben. 19, 23. Mid ðām murcnerum ðe Gode mishȳrdon, 21, 5. Mancynn Gode mishȳrde, Wulfst. 104, 23. Mishȳrdan, 13, 13. Ūre bisceopas ðe wē nǽfre mishȳran ne scylon on nān ðara þinga ðe hī ūs tǽcaþ, L. Edg. S. 1; Th. i. 272, 19.

mis-hirness, e; *f. Disobedience, act of disobedience:*—Forlǽt mē hȳ on wīta lǽdan, and ða mishērnessa gewrecan, ðe hȳ wið ðē forworhtan, Wulfst. 256, 4.

mis-hwirfed; *pp. Perverted:*—Swā hit is mishweorfed *sic rerum versa conditio est,* Bt. 14, 2; Fox 44, 18. Mishwyrfedre *praepostero,* Hpt. Gl. 496, 41: 518, 19. v. next word.

mis-hworfen; *pp. Perverted, inverted:*—Tō mishworfenum *depravandam,* Wrt. Voc. ii. 26, 73: 85, 61. Mishworvenre tīde *tempore praepostero,* Hpt. Gl. 496, 42. [Cf. *O. H. Ger.* missa-huarpida *eversio;* missa-huarpari *eversor,* Grff. iv. 1236, 1237.]

mis-lǽdan *to mislead, lead astray:*—Gif hē lāre ne can, ne hē leornian nele, ac mislǽt his hȳrmen and hine silfne forþ mid, L. Ælfc. P. 46; Th. ii. 384, 22.

mis-lǽran *to teach wrongly, to persuade a person to do what is wrong:*—Ðā ongunnon heora māgas behreówsian ðæt hī ǽfre ða martyras mislǽran woldon, Homl. Skt. 5, 119. [Luþer men ðat hine mislerede, Laym. 4311.]

mis-lâr, e; *f. Bad teaching* or *doctrine,* Scint. 21: 78.

mis-libban *to lead a bad life:*—Biþ mannum sceamu ðæt hī mislybban sceolon, and ða nȳtenu healdaþ heora gesetnysse, Homl. Th. ii. 324, 18.

mis-, mist-, misse-lîc; *adj.* I. *wanting in likeness* or *unity, unlike, diverse, various:*—Sorh manig and mislīc, Frag. Kmbl. 2; Leás. 2. Hū ne sǽdon wē ðæt ðis andwearde līf nǽre nō ðæt hēhste gōd, forðam hit wǽre mistlīc (MS. Cott. mislīc), Bt. 34, 9; Fox 146, 17. Mistlīc *promiscuum, mixtum,* Hpt. Gl. 497, 5. Mistlīc bleó *discolor,* Wrt. Voc. i. 46, 35. Mistlīces bleós *discolor,* 77, 5. Gescȳ mistlīces cynnes *calceamenta diversi generis,* Coll. Monast. Th. 27, 31. Se hrōf wæs on mislīcre heánesse *the roof was of varying height,* Blickl. Homl. 207, 21. Se ðe micel inerfe and mislīc āgan wile, Bt. 14, 2; Fox 44, 10. Synna beóþ mislīce, Blickl. Homl. 43, 17. Mistlīce wōge wegas *divortia, diverticula,* Wrt. Voc. i. 37, 44. Mistlīcra (*variarum*) cræfta biggenceras, Coll. Monast. Th. 30, 1. Misselīcum sweccum *variis odoribus,* Kent. Gl. 1016. Mistlīcum *diversis,* Hpt. Gl. 522, 73. Ðæt geár wæs hefigtȳme on manegum þingum and mislīcum . . . þurh mistlīce coða, Chr. 1041; Erl. 169, 5–9. Mistlīce *varios, multimodos,* Hpt. Gl. 524, 33. II. *diverging from the usual course* (?), *erratic* (v. mis-līce, II):—Mistlīcum *errabundis, vagabundis,* Hpt. Gl. 493, 20. [*Goth.* missa-leiks *various: O. Sax.* mis-līc: *O. H. Ger.* missa-, mis-līh *varius, diversus, dispar, multiplex, multifarius.*]

mis-, mist-lîce; *adv.* I. *diversely, variously, in different ways:*—Godwine his geféran mislīce ofslōh *Godwine killed his companions in different ways,* Chr. 1036; Erl. 164, 33; Älf. Tod. 2: Exon. 107 b; Th. 411, 13; Rä. 29, 12. Hī his mistlīce (Cott. MS. mislīce) willnigen, Bt. 36, 3; Fox 176, 26. II. *in an irregular manner* (v. mis-līc, II):—Eádwine eorl and Morkere eorl hlupon ūt and mislīce fērdon (*went wandering about*) on wuda and on feldon ōþ ðæt Eádwine wearþ ofslægen fram his āgenum mannum, Chr. 1072; Erl. 210, 26. [Cf. Laym. 6270: fulle seouen ȝere heo misliche foren (*wandered about*).]

mis-lîcian *to displease:*—Gif heó mislīcaþ (*displicuerit*) ðam hlāforde, Ex. 21, 8. Se ðe him sylfum mislīcaþ tō ðī ðæt hē Gode gelīcige, Homl. Th. i. 512, 35. Ðonne eów mislīciaþ ða mettrumnessa ðe gē on ōðrum monnum geseóþ, Past. 21, 4; Swt. 159, 13. Hē him sylfum mislīcade, Bd. 5, 13; S. 632, 10. Ðeós ūre mynegung wile mislīcian eów wel manegum, L. Ælfc. P. 2; Th. ii. 364, 14. [*Icel.* mis-līka: *O. H. Ger.* misse-līchēn *displicere.*]

mis-, mist-lîcness, e; *f. Diversity, variety:*—Be swefena mistlīcnysse *de somniorum diversitate,* Lchdm. iii. 198, 4. Mislīcnysse *varietate,* Ps. Spl. 44, 11. Mistlīcnesse *varietates, diversitates,* Hpt. Gl. 431, 75. Ðās ylcan mislīcnyssa ðæra foresǽdra tīda, Homl. Th. ii. 76, 12.

mis-limp, es; *n. A mishap:*—Mislimp *excessus,* Wrt. Voc. ii. 145, 67. Mislimp tearte *casus asperos,* Hymn. Surt. 16, 5.

mis-limpan *to turn out unfortunately:*—Æfter ðæm ðe him swā oftrǽdlīce mislamp hié angunnan hit wītan heora lātteówum *iterum infelicius victi sunt; propter quod ducem suum exsulare jusserunt,* Ors. 4, 4; Swt. 164, 24. Nis nān wundor ðeáh ūs mislimpe *it is no wonder, though we have ill success,* Wulfst. 163, 16. Gif hit geweorðe ðæt folce mislimpe þurh here oððon hunger, L. I. P. 18; Th. ii. 324, 28. [*O. E. Homl.* him mai sone mislimpe.]

mis-micel; *adj. Wanting in greatness* or *quantity* (?), *few:*—On feorhgebeorh hæfde eallum eorþcynne ēce lāfe frumcneów gehwæs fæder and mōder tuddorteóndra geteled rīme mismicelra (misselīcra *or* missenlīcra ?) ðonne men cunnon *to preserve the life of all that lives on earth Noah had an everlasting remnant* (*one from which an endless line of descendants would come*), *an original pair, father and mother, of every one of the offspring-producers, few in number,* (*fewer indeed*) *than men know,* (or ? *of many kinds when reckoned up, more so than men know*), Cd. 161; Th. 201, 16; Exod. 373.

mis-rǽcan *to reach* or *touch wrongly,* metaph. *to apply abusive language to a person:*—Ðæt man biddendne þearfan misrǽce *to abuse a needy person who begs* (*is one of the lighter offences*), Homl. Th. ii. 590, 25. v. ge-rǽcan (*the last example there given*).

mis-rǽd, es; *m.* I. *evil advice* or *direction, mis-guidance:*—Hī beóþ geyrmede þurh unwīsne cyning on manegum ungelimpum for his misrǽde *they* (*a people*) *are made miserable through an unwise king, by many mischances, on account of his misguidance,* Homl. Th. ii. 320, 3. II. *evil conduct:*—God hī (*the Israelites*) betǽhte ðam hǽðenan folce feówertig geára for heora misrǽde, Jud. 13, 1. [Cf. *Icel.* mis-ræði *an ill-advised deed.*]

mis-rǽdan *to counsel amiss, give bad advice:*—Gif geférrǽden ðæne rǽd on gemǽnum geþeahte misrēdaþ (-rǽdaþ) and feáwa witena ðæs gefēres ða þearfe wīslīcor tōcnāwaþ stande ðara rǽd ðe mid Godes ege and wīsdōme ða þearfe geceósaþ *if the society in a general council act ill-advisedly* (*in the choice of an abbot*), *and a few wise men of the society with greater wisdom recognize what is necessary, let their counsel prevail, who with the fear and wisdom of God choose what is necessary,* R. Ben. 117, 19. [Cf. *Laym.* 'we adredeð ðat heo him mis-ræden.' Þa answerede þe abbed: 'Næi ac heo him radeþ god,' 13130: *Ayenb.* me him gyleþ and misret, 184, 31: *Icel.* mis-rāðit *ill-advised.*]

missan; *p.* miste. I. *to miss, fail to hit* (with gen. of object):—Hē miste mercelses, Beo. Th. 4869; B. 2439. II. *to escape the notice of a person* (with dat.): Beó se canon him ætforan eágum, beseó tō gif hē wille, ðȳ læs ðe him misse (*lest any part be omitted by him*), L. Edg. C. 32; Th. ii. 250, 25. [*Laym.* missen *to notice the absence of a person: Gen. and Ex.* missen *to lose, fail: Prompt. Parv.* missyn *careo: O. Frs.* missa *to be without: Icel.* missa *to fail to hit, to lack, to omit, to lose: O. H. Ger.* missan *carere.* The verb governs the gen. in the cognate dialects.]

mis-screnc e; *adj. Shrivelled up, distorted:*—Hī (*demons*) hæfdon wōge sceancan and misscrence tān, Guthl. 5; Gdwin. 36, 1. Cf. ge-screngce.

mis-scrȳdan *to clothe improperly:*—Bindaþ ðone misscrȳddan (*the man who had not on the wedding garment*), Homl. Th. i. 530, 13.

missen-, misen-, missend-lîc; *adj. Dissimilar, different, diverse, various, divers:*—Hwītes hiowes and eác missenlīces *candido versicolore,* Nar. 16, 1. Draca missenlīces hiwes, 43, 13. For missenlīce heora feaxes hiwe ōðer wæs cweden se bleaca Heáwold ōðer se hwīta (*pro diversa capillorum specie*), Bd. 5, 10; S. 624, 16. Misenlīco wilddeór him cōmon tō, Shrn. 88, 16. Wið misenlīce (misendlīce, MS. B.) leahtras, Herb. tit. 165, 3; Lchdm. i. 62, 8. Missendlīce cynno *diversitatem gentium,* Rtl. 32, 1. Hē gedǽleþ missenlīce (*or adv.?*) leoþocræftas londbūendum, Exon. 78 b; Th. 295, 4; Crā. 28. Hē ūs syleþ missenlīcu mōd, 89 a; Th. 334, 8; Gn. Ex. 13. Ealle yfelhæbbende missenlīcum ādlum (*variis languoribus*), Mt. Kmbl. 4, 24. Mid eallum missenlīcum āfēddum blōstmum *with all the various flowers that are brought forth,* Blickl. Homl. 7, 31. For missenlīcum intingan *diversis ex causis,* Bd.

4, 1; S. 564, 17. Mid missendlícum blóstmum *variis floribus*, 1, 7; S. 478, 22. v. mis-líc.

missen-líce; *adv. Variously, diversely, differently*:—Ðeáh hé hié mannum missenlíce dǽle, Blickl. Homl. 39, 18: Exon. 88 a; Th. 331, 6; Vy. 64: 79 b; Th. 299, 18; Crä. 104.

missenlíc-ness, e; *f. Variety, diversity*:—Ðanon him wæs eágena missenlícnes geseald *thence was given him variety of eyes*, Salm. Kmbl. 180, 14. Ðeós wyrt is gecweden *iris illyrica* of ðære missenlícnysse (*variegated character*) hyre blóstmena, for ðý ðe is geþuht ðæt heó ðone heofonlícan bogan mid hyre bleó geefenlǽce, Herb. 158, 1; Lchdm. i. 284, 14. Missenlícnesse *varietatibus*, Ps. Spl. T. 44, 16.

missere, missare, es; *n. A period of half a year* [cf. *Icel.* ár heitir tvau misseri, *but the word also means* a year: *as in the following examples the Icelandic word* (*also written* missari) *occurs generally in the plural*. v. Grmm. D. M. 716]:—Swá ic Hring-Dena hund missera (*fifty years*) weóld, Beo. Th. 3543; B. 1769: 3001; B. 1498. Fela missera *many a year*, 309; B. 153: 5234; B. 2620: Cd. 145; Th. 180, 23; Exod. 49. Hé forþ gewát misserum fród (*well stricken in years*), 83; Th. 104, 30; Gen. 1743. Missarum fród, 107; Th. 141, 16; Gen. 2345.

mis-spówan *to succeed badly*:—Hé sǽde ðæt hit ðæm cyninge læsse edwit wǽre, gif ðæm folce búton him misspeówe *if it went ill with the people when he was not with them*, Ors. 2, 5; Swt. 82, 34.

mis-sprecan *to murmur*:—Misspreca *murmurari*; missprécon *murmurabant*, Jn. Skt. Lind. 6, 43, 41.

mist, es; *m. Mist, dimness*:—Mist *vel* genip *nebula*, Wrt. Voc. i. 52, 61. Dymnys oððe myst *caligo*, Ælfc. Gr. 9, 3; Som. 8, 58. Ðá slóh ðǽr micel mist *facta est caligo tenebrosa*, Gen. 15, 17. Ǽr se þicca mist þinra weorðe, Bt. Met. Fox 5, 11; Met. 5, 6. Woruld miste oferteáh *covered the world with mist*, Exon. 51 b; Th. 178, 35; Gú. 1254. Tódríf ðone mist ðe nú hangaþ beforan úres módes eágum, Bt. 33, 4; Fox 132, 32. Ðone sweartan mist, módes þióstro, Bt. Met. Fox 23, 9; Met. 23, 5. Ða mistas ðe ðæt mód gedréfaþ, Bt. 5, 3; Fox 14, 17. On ðás sweartan mistas (*hell*), Cd. 21; Th. 25, 9; Gen. 391. *Dimness* (*of sight*):—Lǽcedómas wið eágna miste, L. M. 1, 2; Lchdm. ii. 26, 6. Of wlǽtan cymþ eágna mist, Lchdm. ii. 28, 1. Ðeós eáhsealf mæg wið ǽlces cynnes broc on eágon . . . wið mist, Lchdm. iii. 292, 2. [Cf. *Icel.* mistr *mist*.] v. eáh-, gedwol-, wæl-mist; mistian, mistrian.

mis-tǽcan *to teach wrongly*:—Gif ða láreówas wel tǽcaþ, ðonne beóþ hí gehealdene; gif hí mistǽcaþ, hí forpǽraþ hí sylfe, Homl. Th. ii. 50, 4. [*Gen. and Ex.* mis-tagte *mis-directed*.]

mistel, es; *m* (?). I. *basil*:—Mistel *ocimum*, Wrt. Voc. i. 68, 37: ii. 65, 51. Genim ðás wyrte ðe man *ocimum*, and óðrum naman mistel nemneþ, Herb. 119, 1; Lchdm. i. 232, 11. Heó hafaþ leáf neáh swylce mistel, 137, 1; Lchdm. i. 254, 12. v. eorþ-mistel. II. *mistletoe*:—Mistil *viscus*, Ep. Gl. 28 d, 21. Mistel, Wrt. Voc. ii. 123, 59. v. ác-mistel. [*Da.* mistel: *O. H. Ger.* mistil; *m. viscus*.] v. next two words.

mistel-lám, es; *n. Bird-lime made from the berries of the mistletoe*:—Mistellám *viscus*, Wrt. Voc. i. 289, 65.

mistel-tán, es; *m. Mistletoe*:—Mistiltán *viscarago*, Wrt. Voc. i. 31, 66. [*Icel.* mistil-teinn: *Da.* mistel-ten.] v. tán *a twig*.

mist-glóm *darkness caused by mist*:—Helle séceþ grundleásne wylm under mistglóme *seeks hell, bottomless burning, amid the misty gloom*, Exon. 97 a; Th. 363, 1; Wal. 47.

mist-helm, es; *m. A veil or covering of mist*:—Oft ic misthelme forbrægd eágna leóman *oft have I drawn a misty veil before the light of their eyes*, Exon. 72 b; Th. 270, 25; Jul. 470.

mis-þeón; *p.* -þáh *To succeed badly, to fail to improve, to degenerate*:—Ic misþeó *degenero*, Wrt. Voc. i. 39, 29. Misþihþ *degenerat*, ii. 138, 36. Misthágch *degeneraverat*, 106, 30. Misþáh, 25, 36: Exon. 95 a; Th. 354, 39; Reim. 58. [*O. H. Ger.* missi-díhan *deprimi*.] v. geþeón.

mist-hliþ, es; *n. A mist-covered hill-side*:—Ðá com of móre under misthleoþum Grendel gongan *then came from the moor, under the misty slopes, Grendel walking*, Beo. Th. 1425; B. 710. Ðis leóhte beorht (*the sun*) cymeþ morgna gehwam ofer misthleoþu wadan ofer wǽgas, Exon. 93 a; Th. 350, 8; Sch. 60.

mistian; *p.* ode *To grow dim*:—Mé mistiaþ míne eágan *caligo*, Ælfc. Gr. 36; Som. 38, 48. v. mistrian.

mis-tídan; *p.* de (*used impersonally*) *To turn out badly*:—Gif æt láde mistíde *if the attempt at exculpation prove a failure*, L. C. S. 57; Th. i. 406, 27. [Cf. *O. and N.* þu miht wene þat þe mistide, 1501.] Cf. mis-tímian.

mistig; *adj. Misty, covered with mist*:—Ofer mór mistig *super montem caliginosum*, Rtl. 18, 38. Hé heóld mistige móras, Beo. Th. 326; B. 162.

mis-tímian; *p.* ode *To happen amiss, to do amiss* (with dat. of person):—Gif ðú hwene gesihst geþeón on góde blissa on his dǽdum and gif him hwæt mistímaþ besárga his unrótnysse *if you see any one flourish in goodness, rejoice at his deeds, and if any mischance befall him* (or *if he do anything amiss?*) *sorrow for his disquietude*, Basil admn. 5; Norm. 44, 30. [Gyf ǽnie prusten mistímide on áþaran mynstre ne fóre hé náwider ac gesóhte hé his nágabúras and him þingadan *if there were misconduct on the part of any priest in either monastery, he would go no whither, but would seek his neighbours, and they would mediate for him*, Chart. Th. 324, 8. *A. R.* þe ueorðe is Gledschipe of his vuel, lauhwen oðer gabben, gif him misbiueolle (mistimes, MS. T.; mistimeð, MS. C.), 200, 21.]

mist-líc. v. mis-líc.

mistran; *p.* ede *To grow dim*:—His eágan ne mistredon *non caligavit oculus ejus*, Deut. 34, 7. v. mistian.

mis-tríwan *to mistrust, be diffident*:—Wé mistríwaþ *difidimus*, Rtl. 39, 32. [Cf. *Icel.* mis-trúa *to mistrust*: *O. H. Ger.* missa-trúén *diffidere*: *Ger.* miss-trauen.]

mis-tucian *to maltreat*:—Ðe abbot wolde hí (*the monks*) mistukian, and sende æfter lǽwede mannum, and hí cómon intó capitulan fullgewépnede, Chr. 1083; Erl. 217, 9.

mis-tyhtan *to incite* or *persuade to what is wrong, dissuade*:—Hig ðæt folc mistihton *murmurare fecerant multitudinem*, Num. 14, 36. Hé cwæþ tó ðám mágum ðe ða martyras mistihton (*urged them to renounce Christianity*), Homl. Skt. 5, 69. v. next word.

mistyhtend-líc; *adj. Dissuasive*:—Sume (*adverbs*) synd *deortativa*, ðæt synd forbeódendlíce oððe mistihtendlíce, Ælfc. Gr. 38; Som. 40, 8.

mis-weaxan *to grow in an improper way*:—Ðæt hí symle ða misweaxendan bógas of ásceádian, Homl. Th. ii. 74, 12.

mis-wendan; *p.* de. I. *trans. To pervert, apply to a wrong use, abuse*:—Ðá miswendon sume ða englas heora ágenne cyre, and hý sylfe tó deóflum geworhton *then some of the angels made an ill-use of the choice that was theirs, and made themselves devils*, Homl. Th. i. 112, 7. Hé begann tó þreágenne ða gebróðru ðe miswende wǽron *he began to rebuke the two brothers who were perverted*, 66, 34. Mid þweorum ðú bist miswend *cum perverso perverteris*, Ps. Lamb. 17, 27. II. *intrans. To turn in a wrong direction, be perverted*:—Gif seó gewylnung miswent, ðonne ácenþ he[ó] gýfernesse and forlygr and gítsunge, Homl. Skt. 1, 102. [*Ayenb.* hwanne he miswent and went to þe worse half al þet he yherþ, 62, 15: *O.H.Ger.* missa-wenten *evertere*; missa-wentit *transversus, obliquus*.]

mis-weorc, es; *n. An evil deed*:—Miswerc *mala opera*, Jn. Skt. Rush. 3, 19. [*Icel.* mis-verk.]

mis-weorþan *to turn out badly* (for a person, dat.):—Gif ða penegas teóþ swíðor ðonne ðæt gold ðonne miswyrþ ðam men hraðe *if the pennies weigh more than the gold, then will it soon prove a bad thing for the man*, Wulfst. 240, 4.

mis-weorðian, -wurðian *to dishonour, treat disrespectfully*:—Gif preóst circan miswurðige, ðe eal his wurðscipe of sceal árísan, gebéte ðæt, L. N. P. L. 25; Th. ii. 294, 10.

mis-wider, es; *n. Bad weather, storm*:—Gif hwæt fǽrlíces on þeóde becymþ, beón hit hereréǽsas, beón hit miswyderu oððon unwæstmas, Wulfst. 271, 2. v. mis-gewider.

mis-wissian *to mis-direct*:—Gif mæssepreóst folc miswissige æt freólse and æt fæstene, gylde xxx scill. mid Englum, L. E. G. 3; Th. i. 168, 8.

mis-wrítan *to write incorrectly, make a mistake in writing*:—*Barbarismus*, ðæt is ánes wordes gewæmmednyss, gif hit biþ miswriten, Ælfc. Gr. 50, 21; Som. 51, 48. On manegum wísum miswritene, 50, 23; Som. 51, 54.

míte, an; *f. A small insect, a mite*:—Míte *tamus*, Wrt. Voc. i. 24, 16. [*Chauc.* These wormes, ne these mothes, ne these mites Upon my paraille fret hem never a del: *O. Du.* mijte *acarus*: *O. H. Ger.* míza *culex*.]

mið. v. mid.

míðan; *p.* máð, *pl.* miðon; *pp.* miðen. I. *to conceal, dissemble* (a) *with gen.*:—Ðú mé tǽldesð forðon ic mín máð and wolde fleón ða byrðenne ðære hirdelecan giémenne *pastoralis curae me pondera fugere delitescendo voluisse reprehendis*, Past. proem.; Swt. 23, 11. Mé nǽfre næs ealles swá ic wolde ðeáh ic his miðe *it was never with me just as I would, though I dissembled the fact*, Bt. 26, 1; Fox 90, 28. (b) *with acc.*:—Ic on móde máð, monna gehwylcne, þeódnes þrymcyme, Exon. 51 a; Th. 177, 18; Gú. 1229. Hé ða wyrd ne máð, fǽges (*Guthlac*) forðsíð, 52 b; Th. 182, 33; Gú. 1319. Ðá hié ús gesáwon hié selfe sóna in heora húsum deágollíce hié miðan *visis nobis continuo inter tectorum suorum culmina delituerunt*, Nar. 10, 18. Ne sceal ic míne onsýn for eówere mengu míðan, Exon. 43 a; Th. 144, 18; Gú. 680. Ic míðan sceal monna gehwylcum síðfæt mínne, 127 b; Th. 491, 12; Rä. 80, 13. Ic monnan funde heardsǽligne mód míðendne *I found a man of hard fortunes, his thoughts concealing*, 115 a; Th. 442, 29; Kl. 20. (c) *case undetermined*:—Míðiþ *dissimulat*, Wrt. Voc. ii. 106, 42. Míðeþ, 25, 51. Fela gé fore monnum míðaþ, ðæs ðe gé in móde gehycgaþ, Exon. 39 a; Th. 130, 10; Gú. 436. Cyriacus hygerúne ne mâđ tô Gode cleopode *Cyriacus concealed not the secret of his mind, but cried to God*, Elen. Kmbl. 2196; El. 1099. Hwîlum biþ gôd tô mîđanne his hiéremonna scylda *aliquando subjectorum vitia prudenter dissimulanda sunt*, Past. 21, 1; Swt. 151, 8. Miđene *concealed*, Bd. 4, 27; S. 604, 24. II. *intrans. To be concealed, lie hid*:—Đonne biþ sôna sweotol æteówod on him đæt ǽr deágol mâđ *then at once will be made manifest in him what before lay hid*, L. M. 2, 66; Lchdm. ii. 298, 8. Monig þing ge egeslîce ge willsumlîce đe ôđre men miđon *multa, quae alios laterent, vel horrenda, vel desideranda*, Bd. 5, 12; S. 627, 30. Mîđende *dilitiscendo*, Wrt. Voc. ii. 140, 39. III. *to avoid, refrain from, forbear* (*with inst.* (?) *dat.* (?) or *intrans.*):—Ic þurh mûþ sprece . . . hleođre ne mîđe *I speak with my mouth . . . refrain not from sound*, Exon. 103 a; Th. 390, 20; Rä. 9, 4. Wulf on walde wǽlrûne ne mâđ, Elen. Kmbl. 56; El. 28. Ne mîđ đû for menigo *forbear not on account of the multitude*, Andr. Kmbl. 2419; An. 1211. Ne mæg ic đý mîđan, Exon. 125 a; Th. 481, 1; Rä. 64, 10. [*Havel.* his sorwe he couþe ful wel miþe (*conceal*), 948: *Gen. and Ex.* đog ðis folc miðe (*forbore*) a stund, 3807: *O. Sax.* mîđan (*with gen. acc.* and *intrans.*) *to avoid, forbear*: *O. H. Ger.* mîdan *vitare, cavere, latere, latitare, occultare, erubescere*: *Ger.* meiden: *O. Frs.* for-mîtha.] v. be-mîđan.

mitinc. v. mitting.

mitta, an; *m. A measure, both dry and liquid, as for corn, meal, ale, honey*; according to one passage it seems equal to two 'ambers':—Under mittan *sub modio*, Wrt. Voc. ii. 85, 9: Hpt. Gl. 505, 4. Under mitte (mytte, Rush), Mt. Kmbl. Lind. 5, 15. Mitta, Mk. Skt. 4, 21: mitto, Lk. Skt. Lind. 11, 33. Selle mon xxx ombra gôdes Welesces aloþ, đet limpaþ tô xv mittan, and mittan fulne huniges, ođđe twegen wînes, Chart. Th. 460, 22–28. Mittan *bata*, Wrt. Voc. ii. 11, 52: *chori*, 15, 82. His bigleofa wæs ǽlce dæg þrittig mittan clǽnes melowes and sixtig mittan ôđres melowes '*Solomon's provision for one day was thirty measures of fine flour, and threescore measures of meal*' (1 Kings 4, 22), Homl. Th. ii. 576, 31–32. Hund mittena *centum choros*, Lk. Skt. 16, 7. Wîf gehýdeþ in meolo mitto þrió *mulier abscondit in farinae sata tria*, Lind. 13, 21. [Cf. *Goth.* mitaþs, mitaþjô *a measure*: *O. H. Ger.* mezzo: *Ger.* metze.] v. an- (on-), cyric-, hand-mitta.

mittan; *p.* te *To meet with, find*:—Ne meahton ceastre weg cûđne mittan *viam civitatis non invenerunt*, Ps. Th. 106, 3. v. ge-mittan.

mitting, e; *f. A meeting*:—Đonne habbaþ wê gecweden đæt ûre mytting sîe þrîwa on xii mônþum *we have agreed that our meeting be thrice a year*, Chart. Th. 613, 25. Se mæssepreóst â singe twâ mæssan æt ǽlcere mittinge, 614, 5. v. gâr-, ge-, word-mitting.

mix. v. meox.

mixen, [n]e; *f. A mixen, dung-heap*; also *dung*:—On đære nyđemestan flêringe (*of the ark*) wæs heora gangpyt and heora myxen, Boutr. Scrd. 21, 7. Meoxine *sterculii*, Germ. 397, 449. Job sæt on his mixene, Homl. Th. ii. 452, 28. Nis hyt nyt ne on eorþan ne on myxene (mixen, Lind.: mixenne, Rush.) *neque in terram neque in sterculinium utile est*, Lk. Skt. 14, 35. Đeós wyrt biþ cenned on ealdum myxenum (myxennum, MS. H.), Herb. 14, 1; Lchdm. i. 106, 12. Meoxena *sterquilinia*, Hpt. Gl. 504, 2. Ic sendo micxseno (mixenne, Rush.), *mittam stercora*, Lk. Skt. Lind. 13, 8.

mixen-plante, an; *f. The mixen-plant*; '*solanum nigrum*, which is morella minor, and is often found on mixens. Otherwise *night-shade*,' Lchdm. iii. 338, col. 2:—Of đære wyrte đe man hâteþ myxenplante, L. M. 1, 58; Lchdm. ii. 128, 23.

môd, es; *n.* I. *the inner man, the spiritual as opposed to the bodily part of man*, e. g. đa ryhtæþelo biþ on đam môde, næs on đam flǽsce, Bt. 30, 2; Fox 110, 19. Đone blindan đe on lîchoman wæs gehǽled ge eác on môde, Blickl. Homl. 21, 10. Like the English *spirit, soul* it can be used to denote a person, e. g. đæt æđele môd (*St. Andrew*), Andr. Kmbl. 2486; An. 1244: (*St. Juliana*), Exon. 68 b; Th. 255, 4; Jul. 209. Đæt milde môd (*St. Guthlac*), 43 b; Th. 146, 17; Gû. 711; and throughout Alfred's translation *ðæt môd* represents Boethius, e. g. đâ đæt môd đillîc sâr cweþende wæs se wîsdôm him blîþum eágum on lôcude and hê for đæs môdes geómerunge næs nâuht gedrêfed *haec ubi continuato dolore delatravi, illa vultu placido, nihilque meis questibus mota*, Bt. 5, 1; Fox 8, 23–26. (a) with more especial reference to intellectual or mental qualities, *mind*:—Gesceád *ratio*, môd *mens*, Ælfc. Gr. 5; Som. 4, 48. Môd *vel* geþanc *animus*, Wrt. Voc. i. 42, 33. Seó sâwul is *animus*, đæt is môd, đonne heó wât; heó is *mens*, đæt is môd, đonne heó understent, Homl. Skt. 1, 184: Blickl. Homl. 229, 14, 18. Nû ic wât tela and ic onfêng gewit mînes môdes, Bd. 3, 11; S. 536, 34. Hit is ǽlces môdes wîse đæt sôna swâ hit forlǽt sôþcwidas swâ folgaþ hit leásspellunga *eam mentium constat esse naturam, ut quoties abjecerint veras, falsis opinionibus induantur*, Bt. 5, 3; Fox 14, 15. Hê ongeat đæs môdes ingeþancas, 7, 1; Fox 16, 5. Hâles môdes *sane mentis*, Mk. Skt. 5, 15. Hê đâ cwices môdes (*animi vivacis*) geornlîce leornade, Bd. 5, 19; S. 637, 37. Môdes snyttru, Exon. 17 b; Th. 41, 28; Cri. 662: 78 b; Th. 295, 14; Crä. 33: Cd. 52; Th. 66, 16; Gen. 1085. Heó cwæþ on hyre môde *dicebat intra se*, Mt. Kmbl. 9, 21. Nis mê on geþance *vel* on môde *non mihi est cordi*, Wrt. Voc. i. 54, 47. Ic hæfde mê êce geár ealle on môde *annos aeternos in mente habui*, Ps. Th. 76, 5. Gleáw on môde, Cd. 107; Th. 143, 2; Gen. 2373: 213; Th. 266, 14; Sat. 22. Môde gegrîpan *to comprehend*, Exon. 92 b; Th. 348, 10; Sch. 26. Môd *mentes*, Wülck. 253, 30. (b) with reference to the passions, emotions, etc., *soul, heart, spirit, mind, disposition, mood*:—God biþ đonne þearlwîsra đonne ǽfre ǽnig môd gewurde *God shall then be more severe than ever any soul might be*, Blickl. Homl. 95, 31. Đâ weóp hê sylf, and his môd wæs onstyred, 225, 22: Cd. 35; Th. 47, 10; Gen. 758. Him wæs murnende môd *sad hearts had they*, Beo. Th. 99; B. 50. Hî lǽrdon đæt hî him wǽpno worhton and môdes strengþo nâman *they* (*the Romans*) *urged them* (*the Britons*) *to make themselves weapons and to take courage*, Bd. 1, 12; S. 481, 5. In môdes heánnesse *in extasi*, Wrt. Voc. ii. 47, 20. On gnornunga môdes *in merore animi*, Kent. Gl. 517. Môdes heánes *loftiness of soul*, Blickl. Homl. 119, 20; 31, 34. Đæt is đînes môdes willa *the desire of thy heart*, 225, 19. Đa đe betran môdes wǽron *those who were better disposed*, 215, 11. His þegnas wǽron flǽsclices môdes (*carnally minded*), 17, 5: Ors. 4, 13; Swt. 212, 25: 5, 3; Swt. 222, 2: Ps. Th. 118, 60: 144, 5. Lufa đînne drihten mid ealre đînre heortan and mid eallum môde (*ex tota anima tua*), Deut. 6, 5: 13, 3. Forseó đisse worulde wlenco gif đû wille beón welig on đînum môde; forđam đa đe đâs welan gîtsiaþ, hî bîþ wædlan on hyra môde, Prov. Kmbl. 50. Hê wæs â on âenum môde and heofonlîce blisse mon mihte â on his môde ongytan *he was always the same, and heavenly joy might ever be seen in him*, Blickl. Homl. 223, 34. Đâ wǽron hié swîđe erre on heora môde *then were they very angry in their hearts*, 149, 28: Cd. 3; Th. 4, 33; Gen. 63: 16; Th. 20, 2; Gen. 302. God onsende on đara brôđra môd đæt hî woldan his bân geniman *God put it into the hearts* (in animo) *of the brethren to take his* (*Cuthbert's*) *bones*, Bd. 4, 30; S. 608, 28. Bêgan wê ûre môd from đære lufan đisse worulde, Blickl. Homl. 57, 22. Is mê nû swîđe earfeþe hiera môd tô âhwettane, nû hit nâwþer nyle beón, ne scearp ne heard, Ors. 4, 13; Swt. 212, 30. Hî hine on yrre môd gebrohtan *in ira concitaverunt eum*, Ps. Th. 77, 40: Cd. 3; Th. 4, 28; Gen. 60: 21; Th. 26, 7; Gen. 403. Hý se sylfa cyning lýsde þurh milde môd, Exon. 25 b; Th. 74, 23; Cri. 1211. Đa tydran môd, 43 b; Th. 147, 19; Gû. 729. Drihtnes weg gegearwian tô heora môdum, Blickl. Homl. 81, 8. Hê ûs syleþ missenlîcu môd (*different dispositions*), Exon. 89 a; Th. 334, 8; Gn. Ex. 13. Môde, *inst. with much the same force as the Romance suffix* -mente, -ment:—Unforhte môde *fearlessly*, Blickl. Homl. 67, 1. Untweógende môde *undoubtingly*, 171, 13. Erre môde, 189, 25. Sorgiende môde, Bd. 1, 15; S. 484, 8. Mid freó môde, 2, 5; S. 507, 32. II. a special quality of the soul, (a) in a good sense, *Courage, high spirit*:—Æfter đam đe his môd wæs mid đam bismre âhwæt hê fôr eft on Perse and hî geflýmde *after his courage had been sharpened by this disgrace, he again marched against the Persians, and put them to flight*, Ors. 6, 30; Bos. 126, 17. Heorte sceal đê cênre môd sceal đê mâre đê ûre mægen lytlaþ *heart shall the braver be, courage the higher, as our force dwindles*, Byrht. Th. 140, 64; By. 313. Đâ ongunnon hî môd niman *then they began to take courage*, Bd. 1, 16; S. 484, 15. Hê hæfde môd micel, Beo. Th. 2338; B. 1167. Woldon ellenrôfes môd gemiltan, Andr. Kmbl. 2785; An. 1395. (b) in a bad sense, *Pride, arrogance*:—Đæs engles môd, Cd. 1; Th. 3, 2; Gen. 29. Hyre môd âstâh *her* (*Hagar's*) *pride mounted up*, 101; Th. 134, 35; Gen. 2235: 205; Th. 253, 18; Dan. 597: Exon. 42 a; Th. 141, 27; Gû. 633. Cf. Hê wæs on swâ micle ofermêtto âstigen *efferatus superbia*, Ors. 6, 9; Swt. 264, 8. Næs mê for môde *it was not from pride in me*, 28 b; Th. 87, 22; Cri. 1429. Him se mǽra môd getwǽfde, bælc forbîgde, Cd. 4; Th. 4, 14; Gen. 53. Þurh đîn (*Lucifer's*) micle môd, 35; Th. 46, 2; Gen. 738. III. applied to inanimate things, *Greatness, magnificence, pride*:—Heriaþ hine æfter môde his mægenþrymmes *laudate eum secundum multitudinem magnitudinis ejus*, Ps. Th. 150, 2. Mycel môd and strang đînes mægenþrymmes *magnificentiam majestatis tuae*, 144, 5. Ne mihton forhabban werestreámes môd *they could not restrain the pride of the flood* (*of the Egyptians drowned in the Red Sea*), Cd. 167: Th. 208, 24; Exod. 448. [*Goth.* môds *anger*: *Icel.* móðr *wrath, grief*: *O. Sax. O. Frs.* môd *mind, heart, courage*: *O. H. Ger.* muot *mens, animus, anima, cor*: *Ger.* muth.] v. ofer-môd.

-môd *in composition of adjectives*. v. âcol-, an-, ân-, ǽttren-, ǽwisc-, blîđe-, deór-, dreórig-, eád-, eáđ-, forht-, freórig-, gâl-, gealg-, geómor-, gewealden-, glæd-, gleáw-, gûþ-, heáh-, heán-, heard-, hreóh-, hreówig-, hwæt-, irre-, lâđwende-, leóht-, meagol-, meaht-, micel-, ofer-, or-, reomig-, reónig-, rêđe-, rêđig-, rûm-, sârig-, sceóh-, stîđ-, styrn-, swîđ-, þancol-, þearl-, til-, torht-, torn-, wêrig-, wrâđ-môd.

môd-blind; *adj. Having the mind's eye darkened, undiscerning*:—Leóde ne cûđan, môdblinde men, Meotud oncnâwan, Exon. 25 a; Th. 73, 11; Cri. 1188: Andr. Kmbl. 1627; An. 815: Elen. Kmbl. 611; El. 306. [Cf. *O. H. Ger.* muot-plinti *coecitas animi*.]

môd-blissiende *rejoicing at heart*:—Môdblissiendra *laetantium*, Ps. Th. 67, 17.

mód-bysgung, e; *f. Anxiety of mind*:—Ðam ðe his synna sáre geþenceþ módbysgunge micle dreógeþ *to him who his sins with sorrow remembers, much anxiety suffers of mind*, Exon. 117 a; Th. 450, 7; Dóm. 84.

mód-cearig; *adj. Anxious at heart*, Exon. 76 b; Th. 286, 18; Wand. 2. [*O. Sax.* mód-karag.]

mód-cearu, e; *f. Sorrow of heart, grief*:—Ðæt gelumpe módcearu mǽgum, Exon. 35 a; Th. 114, 1; Gú. 166. Ic ǽfre ne mæg ðære módceare mínre gerestan, 115 b; Th. 443, 34; Kl. 40. Dreógeþ mín wine micle módceare, Th. 444, 22; Kl. 51. Hygesorge wæg, micle módceare, 47 b; Th. 162, 29; Gú. 983: 52 a; Th. 182, 26; Gú. 1316: Beo. Th. 3560; B. 1778: 3989; B. 1992. Higum unróte módceare mǽndon mondryhtnes cwealm *troubled in mind they mourned with sorrow of soul their lord's decease*, 6289; B. 3149. [*Laym.* heo þolede modkare, 3115: *O. Sax.* mód-kara.]

mód-cræft, es; *m. Mental power* or *skill*:—Ða ðe snyttro mid eów and módcræft habben, Elen. Kmbl. 815; El. 408. Módcræfte séc þurh sefan snyttro ðæt ðú wite, Exon. 14 a; Th. 28, 4; Cri. 441.

mód-cræftig; *adj. Possessing mental power, intelligent, skilled*:—Módcræftig smiþ, Exon. 79 a; Th. 297, 2; Crä. 62.

mód-cwánig; *adj. Sad at heart*:—Mengo módcwánige, Elen. Kmbl. 754; El. 377. v. cwánian.

móddor, móddrige. v. módor, módrige.

mód-earfoþ, es; *n. Travail of soul, distress of mind*:—Ic wonn (MS. þonc) módearfoþa má, Exon. 119 a; Th. 457, 19; Hy. 4, 86.

móde-líc, -wǽg, móder. v. módig-líc, -wǽg, módor.

mód-full; *adj. Proud, arrogant*:—Cild ácenned [biþ] weallende módful *a child born* (*on the eleventh day of the moon*) *will be turbulent and arrogant*, Lchdm. iii. 188, 26. [Oswi hæfde emes sunen þe weoren swiðe þrute gumen, and ma of his cunne þe weoren modfulle, Laym. 31464.]

mód-gehygd, es; *n. Thought*:—Ic tó ðé mid módgehygde clypade *I cried to thee in thought*, Ps. Th. 87, 13. Hine fyrwyt bræc módgehygdum *his thoughts were distracted by curiosity*, Beo. Th. 471; B. 233.

mód-gemynd, es; *n.*: e; *f. Mind, thought, intelligence*:—Ðá wæs módgemynd miclum geblissod hyge onhyrded *then was his mind much rejoiced, his heart confirmed*, Elen. Kmbl. 1676; El. 840. Ða ðe leornungcræft þurh módgemynd hæfdon *those who had knowledge through intelligence*, 761; El. 381: Andr. Kmbl. 1375; An. 688: Exon. 96 b; Th. 360, 9; Wal. 3.

mód-geómor; *adj. Sad at heart, of mournful mind*:—Ðæt eorlwerod módgiómor sǽt, Beo. Th. 5779; B. 2894. Þeód wæs módgeómre, Andr. Kmbl. 2227; An. 1115: 3412; An. 1710.

mód-geþanc, es; *m. n. Mind, thoughts, thought*:—Hé mid his eágum up tó heofenum lócade ðyder his módgeþanc á geseted wæs *with his eyes he looked up to heaven, whither his thoughts were ever directed*, Blickl. Homl. 227, 17: Exon. 50 a; Th. 173, 33; Gú. 1170. Módgeþonc, Bt. Met. Fox 31, 37; Met. 31, 19. Nǽron gé swá eácne ofer ealle men módgeþances *ye were not so gifted above all men with understanding*, Cd. 179; Th. 224, 16; Dan. 137. Mǽtra on módgeþanc *more humble in mind*, 207; Th. 256, 3; Dan. 635. Nú gé fyrhþsefan and módgeþanc mínne cunnon, Elen. Kmbl. 1067; El. 535. Nú wé sceolan herigean metodes módgeþanc (-gidanc) *nunc laudare debemus creatoris consilium*, Bd. 4, 24; S. 597, 20. Monnes módgeþonc, Beo. Th. 3462; B. 1729: Bt. Met. Fox 5, 45; Met. 5, 23. Ne þearf hé gefeón módgeþance *he need not rejoice in his heart*, Cd. 75; Th. 92, 5; Gen. 1524. On hige sínum, módgeþance, 107; Th. 141, 3; Gen. 2339. Ðá þeahtode þeóden úre módgeþonce, 5; Th. 6, 23; Gen. 93. Swá monig beóþ men ofer eorþan swá beóþ módgeþancas *quot homines, tot sententiae*, Exon. 91 b; Th. 344, 4; Gn. Ex. 168: 91 a; Th. 341, 11; Gn. Ex. 124.

mód-geþoht, es; *m. Mind, thought*:—Mihtigne on his módgeþohte *mighty of mind*, Cd. 14; Th. 17, 1; Gen. 253. [*O. Sax.* módgiþaht.]

mód-geþyldig; *adj. Patient of soul*, Andr. Kmbl. 1962; An. 983.

mód-gewinna, an; *m. A foe of the mind, care, anxiety*:—Lǽt ðé áslúpan sorge of breóstum, módgewinnan, Cd. 134; Th. 169, 9; Gen. 2797.

mód-glæd; *adj. Of gladsome mind*, Exon. 49 b; Th. 171, 23; Gú. 1131.

mód-gleáw; *adj. Wise of mind*, Salm. Kmbl. 361; Sal. 180.

mód-hete, es; *m. Hate*:—Ic hine wergþo on míne sette, and módhete, Cd. 83; Th. 105, 21; Gen. 1756.

mód-hord, es; *n. m. The mind*:—Módhord onleác weoruda dryhten and ðus wordum cwæþ, Andr. Kmbl. 344; An. 172.

mód-hwæt; *adj. Strong of soul, courageous, brave*:—Mægeþ módhwatu *a maiden strong of soul*, Exon. 122 b; Th. 470, 14; Hy. 11, 16. Nymðe hié módhwate Moyses hýrde *unless they with courage good obeyed Moses*, Cd. 148; Th. 185, 17; Exod. 124. Ða módhwatan *the courageous ones*, 191; Th. 238, 20; Dan. 357.

módig; *adj.* I. *of high* or *noble spirit, high-spirited, noble-minded*:—Ðis is se écea God módig and mægenróf *this is the eternal God, noble and mighty*, Cd. 156; Th. 195, 11; Exod. 275: Exon. 18 b; Th. 46, 32; Cri. 746: Rood Kmbl. 81; Kr. 41. Ðæt wæs módig cyn *that was a high-spirited race*, Cd. 173; Th. 216, 16; Dan. 7. Se fugel engla eard gesóhte, módig, meahtum strang, Exon. 17 a; Th. 40, 31; Cri. 647. Is se wyrhta módig meahtum spédig *of noble mind is the maker, abundant in might*, 56 a; Th. 198, 14; Ph. 10: 42 b; Th. 143, 26; Gú. 667. Ðæt is módig wuht *it* (*the bull*) *is a high-spirited creature*, Runic pm. Kmbl. 339, 12; Rún. 2: Elen. Kmbl. 2524; El. 1263. Hlóh ðá módi man (*Byrhtnoth*), Byrht. Th. 136, 6; By. 147. Se módiga (*Holofernes*), Judth. 10; Thw. 22, 7; Jud. 52. Se módega mǽg Higeláces (*Beowulf*), Beo. Th. 1630; B. 813. Se módga (*the Phenix*), Exon. 59 b; Th. 216, 3; Ph. 262. Geáta leód trúwode módgan (*Beowulf's*) mægnes, Metodes hylde, Beo. Th. 1344; B. 670. Unc módige ymb mearce sittaþ, þeóda þrymfæste, Cd. 91; Th. 114, 20; Gen. 1907. Módge maguþegnas, Exon. 77 a; Th. 290, 8; Wand. 62. II. *bold, brave, courageous* (physically or morally):—Wæs from se ðe lǽdde, módig magorǽswa, Cd. 145; Th. 181, 2; Exod. 55. Gǽþ se ðe mót tó medo módig *he that may shall go bold to the mead*, Beo. Th. 1212; B. 604: Andr. Kmbl. 481; An. 241. Ðæt wæs módig secg *a brave man was he*, Beo. Th. 3629; B. 1812: 3021; B. 1508. Næs ǽnig ðæs módig mon ofer eorþan . . . ðæt mec ðus bealdlíce bendum bilegde, Exon. 73 a; Th. 273, 8; Jul. 513. Sió hand gebarn módiges mannes, Beo. Th. 5329; B. 2698. Beówulfes síþ, módges merefaran, 1008; B. 502. Hægsteald módige, wígend unforhte, Cd. 160; Th. 198, 24; Exod. 327. III. *proud, arrogant*:—Módig *superbus* . . . eádmód *humilis*, Wrt. Voc. i. 76, 25, 27. Ne beó nǽnig man hér on worldríce tó módig, Blickl. Homl. 109, 27. Módig and medugál '*flown with insolence and wine*,' Judth. 10; Thw. 21, 19; Jud. 26. Mǽre and módig (*Nebuchadnezzar*), Cd. 177; Th. 222, 15; Dan. 105. Æfter ðæra módigra gásta hryre, Homl. Th. ii. 82, 11. Hé tóstæncte ða módigan *dispersit superbos*, Cant. Mar. 51. IV. *hearty, earnest, impetuous*; in a bad sense, *bold, headstrong, stubborn, wilful*:—Bidde ic monna gehwone . . . ðæt hé mec neódful . . . gemyne módig *I pray every man that diligently and heartily he bear me in mind*, Exon. 76 a; Th. 285, 28; Jul. 721. Merestreám módig *the impetuous flood* (v. mód, III; *and* módigian), Cd. 166; Th. 207, 17; Exod. 468. Módig *contumax*, Ælfc. Gr. 9, 60; Som. 13, 42. Gif ǽnig man hæbbe módigne sunu and rancne *si genuerit homo filium contumacem et protervum*, Deut. 21, 18. On óðre wísan sint tó manianne ða módgan (*protervi*), on óðre ða unmódgan (*pusillanimes*), Past. 32, 1; Swt. 209, 4. [*Goth.* módags *angry*: *Icel.* móðugr: *O. Sax.* módag: *M. H. Ger.* muotec: *Ger.* muthig.] v. fela-, ofer-, til-, un-módig.

módigian, módigan; *p.* ode. I. *to be* or *become proud, to glory, exult*:—Se unwæra oft módegaþ on gódum weorcum *the heedless is often proud of good works*, Homl. Th. ii. 222, 4. Se ríca módegode on his welum *the rich man gloried in his wealth*, i. 328, 19. Se deófol ðe módegode *the devil who grew proud*, 138, 11. Swá módgade wuldres cempa *thus exulted the soldier of glory* (*Guthlac*), Exon. 37 a; Th. 121, 25; Gú. 294. Bebeódaþ ðám rícum ðæt hí ne módigan on heora ungewissum welan, Homl. Th. i. 256, 25. Ðá begann hé (*Lucifer*) tó módigenne for ðære fægernesse ðe hé hæfde, 10, 22. Wá lá wá ðæt ǽnig man sceolde módigan swá, hine sylf upp áhebban, and ofer ealle men tellan, Chr. 1086; Erl. 222, 36. II. *to take offence through pride*:—Sum æþelboren cild heóld leóht ætforan his mýsan, and ongann módigian ðæt hit on swá wáclícum þingum him wícnian sceolde. Se hálga undergeat his módignysse, Homl. Th. ii. 170, 25. III. *to bear one's self proudly, impetuously*:—Flota módgade (*moved proudly*), Cd. 160; Th. 198, 32; Exod. 331. Ðǽr ǽr wegas lágon mere módgode (v. módig, IV) *where before ran the roads, now raged the sea*, 166; Th. 206, 27; Exod. 458. v. ofer-módigian.

módig-líc; *adj.* I. of persons, *Noble-mind, high-souled, courageous, brave*:—Eálá mín drihten! ðæt ðú eart ælmihtig, micel, módilíc, Bt. Met. Fox 20, 3; Met. 20, 2. Módiglíce menn síðfrome *brave men, bold in travel*, Andr. Kmbl. 491; An. 246. Ne seah ic elþeódige men módiglícran *no braver men from foreign lands have I seen*, Beo. Th. 680; B. 337. II. of things (v. mód, III), *Superb, magnificent*:—Nǽnig man nafaþ tó ðon módelíco gestreón hér on worlde, Blickl. Homl. 111, 24: 113, 6.

módiglíce; *adv. Boldly, bravely*:—Modelíce manega sprǽcon ðe eft æt þearfe (MS. þære) þolian noldon *many used brave words, who would fail at need*, Byrht. Th. 137, 42; By. 200. [ȝho mihhte modiȝlike onnȝæn Anndswerenn þuss, Orm. 2035.]

módig-ness, e; *f.* I. in a bad sense, *Pride*:—Módignys *superbia*, Wrt. Voc. i. 76, 26. Se eahteoða heáfodleahter is módignyss (þe ehtuðe sunne is ihatan *superbia*, þet is on englisc modinesse, O. E. Homl. i. 103, 33), Homl. Th. ii. 218, 22. Flǽsces tóbryte módignesse *carnis terat superbiam*, Hymn. Surt. 9, 22. Ða heofenlícan myrhþe ðe ða englas þurh módignysse forluron, Homl. Th. i. 360, 28. II. in a good sense, *Highmindedness, magnanimity, greatness of mind which does not resent injury*:—Eahta sweras syndon ðe rihtlícne cynedóm up wegaþ:

sôþfæstnys, môdignes (*patientia*), L. I. P. 3; Th. ii. 306, 28. [Þatt wǽre modiȝnesse ᴊ idell ȝellp, Orm. 12040: stiȝþ on heh þurh modinesse, O. and N. 1405.]

môdig-wǽg, es; *m. An impetuous wave:*—Môdewǽga mǽst (*the water that overwhelmed the Egyptians*), Cd. 167; Th. 209, 14; Exod. 499. v. môdig, IV.

môd-leás; *adj. Spiritless, dull;* excors, Kent. Gl. 400.

môd-leást, e; *f. Want of courage, pusillanimity:*—Ðá wearþ se wælhreówa wódlíce geancsumod, ðæt his mágas ne mihton his môdleáste ácuman, ac hêton ácwellan ðæt mǽden, Homl. Skt. 9, 125. [Þe sixte unþeau is þet þe ðe to lauerd bið iset þet he for modleste ne mei his monnan don stere, O. E. Homl. i. 111, 24.]

môd-leóf; *adj. Dear to the heart, beloved:*—Fæder lǽrde môdleófne mágan, Exon. 80 a; Th. 301, 32: Fä. 28.

môd-lufu, an; *f. Heart's love, affection,* Beo. Th. 3650; B. 1823: Exon. 26 a; Th. 77, 25; Cri. 1262: 71 a; Th. 264, 26; Jul. 370: 76 a; Th. 284, 18; Jul. 699: 123 a; Th. 473, 3; Bo. 9. [*O. H. Ger.* mót-luba *affectu.*]

môdor; *gen.* môdor, mêder; *dat.* mêder; *f. A mother* (of human beings or of animals):—Heó is ealra libbendra môdor, Gen. 3, 20. Hêr is ðín môdor, Mk. Skt. 3, 32. Ánes cildes môdor *mater;* manigra cilda môdur *materfamilias,* Wrt. Voc. ii. 59, 20, 21. Fæder and môdor, Exon. 103 a; Th. 391, 8; Rä. 10, 2. Môdur, Gen. 37. 10: Ps. Th. 108, 14. Ðæt is môddor monigra cynna, Exon. 112 a; Th. 428, 16; Rä. 41, 2: 128 a; Th. 492, 13; Rä. 81, 15. Þridde môder *proavia:* feówerþe môder *abavia:* fífte môder *tritavia,* Wrt. Voc. i. 51, 56, 58, 60. Wynburge þridde môdor, Chart. Th. 650, 23. Of his môdor (môderes, Lind.: moeder, Rush.) innoþe, Lk. Skt. 1, 15. Of môdur hrife, Ps. Th. 70, 5. From bearme môddor, Exon. 112 b; Th. 430, 27; Rä. 44, 15. Þurh geleáfan ðæs fæder and ðære mêder, Homl. Th. ii. 52, 2: 50, 35: 116, 13: i. 66, 21. Hê mín ne rǽcþ ne ðære mêder, Homl. Skt. 4, 313. Þurh þingunge his ðære eádigan mêder, Bd. 5, 19; S. 640, 42. Segþ his fæder and mêder, Mk. Skt. 7, 11: Ps. 130, 4: Wulfst. 119, 3: Cd. 50; Th. 64, 10; Gen. 1048: Exon. 8 b; Th. 3, 15; Cri. 36. Riht is ðæt ðæt bearn mêdder folgige, L. H. E. 6; Th. i. 30, 4: 99 a; Th. 370, 7; Seel. Ex. 53. Nim ðæt cild and his môdor, Mt. Kmbl. 2, 13. Gif mon cú oððe stôdmyran forstele, and folan oððe cealf of ádrífe forgelde . . . and ða môder be hiora weorðe, L. Alf. pol. 16; Th. i. 72, 1. Ealle fæderas and môddru, Homl. Th. ii. 34, 32: 124, 17. Heáp môddra *caterva matrum,* Hymn. Surt. 52, 5. Ðê læs hê ofsleá ðás môdra, Gen. 32, 11. [*The Gothic uses* aiþei, *the other dialects use a form corresponding to the English. O. Sax.* môdar: *O. Frs.* môder: *Icel.* móðir: *O. H. Ger.* muotar: *Lat.* mater: *Grk.* μήτηρ.] v. beó-, eald-, fôstor-, steóp-môdor.

môdor-cynd, e; *f. The nature derived from the mother:*—Hê wæs sôþ man þurh his mêdrengecynd (môdercynde, MS. H.), Wulfst. 17, 7.

môdor-leás; *adj. Motherless:*—Fylstan fæderleásum and môderleásum cildum, Wulfst. 228, 22.

môdor-líc; *adj. Maternal:*—Môderlíc *maternus,* Ælfc. Gr. 5; Som. 4, 57. Môderlícere stæððinysse *materna gravitate,* Hpt. Gl. 469, 37.

môdor-slaga, an; *m. A matricide;* matricida, Wrt. Voc. i. 85, 46.

môdren, môddren; *adj. Maternal:*—Môddrenum flǽsce ic brúce *materna carne vescor,* Ap. Th. 4, 12. v. mêdren.

môdrige, môderge, môddrige, an; *f.* I. *an aunt:*—Mín môdrige *matertera mea,* Wrt. Voc. i. 52, 25: 51, 53: Bd. 3, 8; S. 532, 21. Môdriæ, Kent. Gl. 1190. Bisceop næbbe on his húse nǽnne wífman búton hit sý his môdor . . . oððe môdrige, L. Ælfc. C. 5; Th. ii. 344, 14. Môddrie, Homl. Th. ii. 94, 32. Môdrigan sunu *fratrueles,* Wrt. Voc. ii. 39, 53: 55, 31. Môdrian sunu *consobrinus,* Ors. 3, 9; Swt. 130, 21: Ælfc. T. Grn. 16, 9. Môdergan sunu, Shrn. 93, 3. Môddrian sunu, Homl. Th. i. 58, 5: Wrt. Voc. i. 52, 2, 27, 28. II. *a cousin:*—Môderge *consobrinus,* Wrt. Voc. ii. 105, 31. Mínre môdrigan môder *matertera mea materna,* 55, 33. Tô ðǽre hire (*the Virgin Mary*) môddrian ðære hálgan Elizabethe, Blickl. Homl. 165, 28. [His moddrie sune, Laym. 30644.]

môd-sefa, an; *m.* [*a poetical word with much the same meaning as* môd, e. g. Swá bióþ ánra gehwæs monna môdsefan áwegede of hiora stede, Bt. Met. Fox 7, 47; Met. 7, 24 = swá ðæt mennisce môd biþ áweged of his stede, Bt. 12; Fox 36, 17: *and* Gif heora môdsefa meahte weorþan staþolfæst gereaht, 11, 195; Met. 11, 98 = gif heora môd wǽre gestaþelod, Bt. 21; Fox 74, 40.] *The inner man, mind, spirit, soul, heart:*—Ðæt ðín môdsefa mára wurde and ðín líchoma leóhtra micle *that thy mind would be mightier and far fairer thy body,* Cd. 25; Th. 32, 10; Gen. 501. Ðá wæs môdsefa miclum geblissod *greatly then was his heart gladdened,* Andr. Kmbl. 1783; An. 894: Elen. Kmbl. 1748; El. 876. Wæs môdsefa áfýsed on forþwege *my soul longed to be gone,* Rood Kmbl. 246; Kr. 124. Mê ðín môdsefa lícaþ *you please me,* Beo. Th. 3711; B. 1853. Ne gemealt him se môdsefa *his heart did not fail,* 5249; B. 2628. Helle gemundon in môdsefan *hell had they in mind,* 362; B. 182. Ic ne mêtte on môdsefan máran snyttro, Andr. Kmbl. 1107; An. 554. Ne sceal se Dryhtnes þeów in his môdsefan (*in his heart*) máre gelufian eorþan ǽhtwelan, Exon. 38 a; Th. 125, 22; Gû. 358: 66 b; Th. 247, 1; Jul. 72. Man cweþeþ on his môdsefan *dicet homo,* Ps. Th. 57, 10. On môdseofan, 115, 2. Môdsefan ásecgan *to open one's heart to another,* Exon. 76 b; Th. 287, 6; Wand. 10. Hê his môdsefan fæste trymede *he his soul surely stablished,* 46 b; Th. 159, 26; Gû. 933: Andr. Kmbl. 2420; An. 1211. Syððan hê môdsefan mínne cúðe *after he knew my heart,* Beo. Th. 4028; B. 2012: Exon. 54 a; Th. 188, 24; Az. 50. Beóþ môdsefan dálum gedǽled, sindon dryhtguman ungelíce, 83 b; Th. 314, 29; Môd. 21. [*O. Sax.* môdsebo: *Icel.* móð-sefi.]

môd-seóc; *adj. Sick at heart, with mind diseased, distressed:*—Unrôtne, môdseócne, Exon. 51 a; Th. 177, 30: Gû. 1235. [*O. H. Ger.* muot-siuh: cf. *Icel.* hug-sjukr *distressed.*]

môd-seócness, e; *f. Disease of the stomach:*—Môdseócnes *vel* [môd-] unmiht *morbus cordis* (*cardiacus*), Wrt. Voc. ii. 128, 66.

môd-snotor, -snottor; *adj. Prudent of mind, wise, sagacious:*—Fród fæder freóbearn lǽrde, môdsnottor, Exon. 80 a; Th. 300, 6; Fä. 2. In mæðle môdsnottera, 79 a; Th. 295, 31; Crä. 41: 100 a; Th. 374, 19; Seel. Ex. 128. Môdsnotra, Soul Kmbl. 249; Seel. Verc. 128.

môd-sorh; *gen.* -sorge; *f. Care or sorrow of mind, sorrow of soul:*—Eác is hearm Gode, môdsorg gemacod, Cd. 35; Th. 47, 3; Gen. 755. Hê môdsorge wæg hefige æt heortan *sorrow of soul bore he heavy at heart,* Exon. 48 a; Th. 165, 6; Gû. 1024: Elen. Kmbl. 122; El. 61. [Mid muchele modsorȝe (sorewe, 2nd MS.), Laym. 8692.]

môd-staþol, es; *m. The foundation on which the mind rests:*—Steðefæst môdstaþol biþ witena gehwilcum weorþlícre micle ðonne hê his wísan fágige tô swíðe *a firm foundation for the mind is much more honourable for every man of counsel, than an excessive variation of manners,* L. I. P. 10; Th. ii. 318, 38.

môd-staþolfæstness, -staþolness, e; *f. Stability of mind:*—Ongeán môdstaþolnysse (-staþolfæstnesse, MS. C.) and môdes strencþe se mánfulla deófol sendeþ wácmodnysse and lyðerne earhscype, Wulfst. 53, 10.

môd-swíð; *adj. Strong of mind or soul:*—Wec ðú in mê môdswíðne geþanc *crea in me spiritum rectum,* Ps. C. 50, 89; Ps. Grn. ii. 278, 89.

môd-þracu; *gen.* -þræce; *f. Impetuosity of mind, impetuous or daring courage:*—Ic ðæm gôdan (*Beowulf*) sceal for his môdþræce mádmas beódan, Beo. Th. 775; B. 385. [*O. Sax.* môd-thraka *conflict of mind, grief:*—Sind that môdthraka manno gehwilikumu, that hê farlâtan skal liobana herron, Hel. 4775.]

môd-þreá; *gen.* -þreán; *m. f. Pain or torment of mind:*—Egsa micel môdþrea *terror, great torment of mind,* Exon. 102 a; Th. 385, 25; Rä. 4, 50.

môd-þryðu (o); *indecl. f. Violence of mind:*—Môdþryðo wæg folces cwên *a violent heart bore the queen of the people,* Beo. Th. 3867; B. 1931.

môd-þwǽre; *adj. Gentle, meek, mild:*—Hê gerehþ môdþwǽre on dôme *diriget mansuetos in judicio,* Ps. Lamb. 24, 9.

môd-þwǽrness, e; *f. Gentleness, meekness, patience:*—Môdþwǽrnes (*patientia vel* geþyld, MS. E.), Wulfst. 69, 1.

môd-unmeaht, -miht. v. môd-seócness.

môd-welig; *adj. Rich in spiritual or mental gifts:*—Gregorius, Rômwara betest, monna môdwelegost, Past. Swt. 9, 12.

môd-wên, e; *f. Hope entertained by the mind:*—Forþ áscúfan ðæt mínes freán môdwên (ᚹ, MS.) freoþaþ middelnihtum *to push on what my lord's hopes favour at midnight* (*to carry out the plans which are thought on at night, and in which he hopes to succeed?*), Exon. 129 b; Th. 498, 3; Rä. 87, 7.

môd-wlanc; *adj. Proud, haughty, of high courage:*—Nis ðæs môdwlonc mon ofer eorþan ðæt hê á his sǽfôre sorge næbbe *no man upon earth is of courage so high, as on his sea-journey ne'er to feel fear,* Exon. 82 a; Th. 308, 13; Seef. 39. Môdwlonc meówle *haughty maiden,* 107 a; Th. 407, 18; Rä. 26, 7.

mohþe. v. moððe.

molcen, es; *n. Curdled milk:*—Molcen *lac coagolatum,* Wrt. Voc. i. 290, 29: ii. 52, 7. Swá þicce swá molcen, L. M. 3, 39; Lchdm. ii. 332, 18. Nim súr molcen, 1, 39; Lchdm. ii. 98, 25.

mold-ærn, es; *n. An earth-house, a grave:*—Þeáh mín líc scyle on moldærne molsnad weorþan, Exon. 64 a; Th. 235, 28; Ph. 564: Rood Kmbl. 130; Kr. 65: Andr. Kmbl. 1604; An. 803.

molda or molde, an; *m. or f. The top of the head:*—Ðæt galdor man sceal singan ǽrest on ðæt wynstre eáre ðænne on ðæt swíðre eáre ðænne ufan ðæs mannes moldan *the charm must first be sung into the left ear, then into the right ear, then on the top of the man's head,* Lchdm. iii. 42, 9. [Cf. Trev. v. 369, 7: Þe Longobardes used to schere of þe heere of hir heed from þe *molde* to þe nolle (from the toppe un to the hynder parte, MS. Harl.) *comam capitis a cervice usque ad occipitium tondebant.* Halliwell gives *mold* the suture of the skull.]

molde, an; *f.* I. *mould, dust, sand, earth:*—Molde *sabulum,* Wrt. Voc. i. 37, 24: *sablo,* ii. 119, 39: 89, 36. Of ðære moldan (*pulvere*) ðæs flôres monige untrume men gehǽlede wǽron. Ond heó bæd ðæt hyre man sumne dǽl ðære hálwendan moldan (*pulveris*) sealde, Bd. 3, 11; S. 536, 5-8: 3, 10; S. 534, 23, 29. Ða ðe for hund wintrum mid eorþan moldan (*pulvere terrae*) bewrogene wǽron, L. Ecg. P. iv. 66; Th. ii. 226, 23. Ðonne hit (*cadaver*) biþ on ða byrgenne set, ðonne wyrpeþ man moldan ofer hit, L. Ecg. C. 36; Th. ii. 162, 3. His þegnas mid moldan hit (*a cross*) gefæstnedon *adgesto a militibus pulvere, terrae figeretur*, Bd. 3, 2; S. 524, 19. Be moldan ða ðe on ðære stówe genumene wǽron, 3, 9; S. 533, 27. II. *ground, earth, land*:—Molde *vel* land *humus, rus, arvum*, Wrt. Voc. i. 41, 61: *humus*, 70, 12: Ælfc. Gr. 8; Som. 7, 53. Of ðære moldan tyrf *from the grass of the ground*, Exon. 56 b; Th. 202, 8; Ph. 66. God forþ áteáh of ðære moldan (*de humo*) ǽlces cynnes treów, Gen. 2, 9. Þeóda wealdend árás of moldan (*rose from the grave*), Hy. 10, 34; Hy. Grn. ii. 293, 34: Exon. 120 a; Th. 460, 24; Hö. 22. Ðonne of ðisse moldan men onwecniaþ, deáde of duste árísaþ, Cd. 227; Th. 302, 22; Sat. 604. Ða moldan ðe meolce and hunige flēwþ *humum lacte et melle fluentem*, Num. 14, 8. Mearh moldan træd *the steed trod the ground*, Elen. Kmbl. 109; El. 55. III. *earth* (the dwelling place of men):—Ne mihte ða on moldan man gerîman *no man on earth might number them*, Ps. Th. 104, 30: 127, 5: Cd. 202; Th. 251, 21; Dan. 567: Exon. 99 a; Th. 371, 13; Seel. 75. Of moldan on ða mǽran gesceaft *from earth to heaven*, Bt. Met. Fox 20, 561; Met. 20, 281. Men ofer moldan *men upon earth*, Rood Kmbl. 23; Kr. 12: Hy. 3, 12; Hy. Grn. ii. 281, 12: Exon. 50 b; Th. 176, 2; Gū. 1203. Meotud ða moldan gesette, 56 a; Th. 198, 15; Ph. 10. [*Goth.* mulda *dust*: *Icel.* mold *mould, earth*: *O. H. Ger.* molta *pulvis, humus, solum, terra.*] v. græs-molde.

mold-corn, es; *n.* '*The granular tuber of saxifraga granulata, and the plant itself*,' Cockayne:—Moldcorn *vulnetrum*, Wrt. Voc. i. 69, 8: Lchdm. iii. 18, 8.

mold-græf, es; *n. A grave*:—Wæs lǽded líc tō moldgræfe, Exon. 75 b; Th. 284, 1; Jul. 690. Ǽnra gehwylc from moldgrafum sēceþ Meotudes dōm, 63 b; Th. 233, 13; Ph. 524.

mold-hrērende *moving upon earth*:—Nis ðæt monnes gemet moldhrērendra *it is not within the compass of man, of those who move upon earth*, Exon. 92 b; Th. 348, 13; Sch. 27.

mold-hȳpe, an; *f. A heap of earth* or *dust*:—Ðonne biþ hit swylce hē sȳ mid sumere moldhȳpan ofhroren *it is as though he be overwhelmed by a heap of dust*, Homl. Th. i. 492, 33.

mold-stōw, e; *f. A place on the earth, a site*, or *a place in the earth, a grave*:—Moldstōwe, stōwlîcere moldan *situ* i. *sepulcro*, Germ. 391, 195.

mold-weg, es; *m. A way upon earth, earth*:—Gif wē on moldwege fundne weorþen *if we are found on earth*, Exon. 70 b; Th. 262, 18; Jul. 334: 48 a; Th. 164, 15; Gū. 1012: Elen. Kmbl. 931; El. 467.

mold-wyrm, es; *m. An earth-worm, a worm in the grave*:—Ðec (*the body*) sculon moldwyrmas monige ceówan, Exon. 99 a; Th. 371, 7; Seel. 72. [*O. H. Ger.* molt-wurm *stellio.*]

molegn, es; *n.* (?) *A thick substance made of curds*:—Molegn *calmum* (occurs under the heading *de mensa*), Wrt. Voc. i. 290, 34: ii. 17, 20: *galmum*, 40, 63: Ep. Gl. 10 f, 15: *galmilla*, 10 f, 32. Molegen *galmilla*, Wrt. Voc. ii. 40, 64. Moling *galmum*, Wülck. 24, 4.

molegn-stycce, es; *n. A portion of* molegn (?):—Molegnstycce *galmulum*, Wrt. Voc. ii. 109, 54.

molsnian; *p.* ode *To moulder, become corrupt, decay*:—Sōna hē molsnaþ and wyrþ tō ðære ilcan eorþan ðe hē ǽr of gesceapen wæs *soon it* (*the body*) *suffers corruption, and turns to the same earth from which before it was made*, Blickl. Homl. 21, 28. Ðonne hit (hūsl) molsnaþ tō þicgenne *cum prae mucore percipi non potest*, L. Ecg. P. iv. 48; Th. ii. 218, 8. Ðeáh mīn līc scyle on moldærne molsnad weorþan, Exon. 64 a; Th. 235, 29; Ph. 564. v. ā-, for-, ge-molsnian.

momna, Wrt. Voc. ii. 120, 82. v. mamor.

mon. v. man.

mōn *in the phrase* full mōn *plenilunium*:—Fullum mōne *plenilunio*, Wrt. Voc. ii. 67, 42. [Cf. *O. H. Ger.* -māni *in* niu-māni *neomenia*; uol-māni *plenilunium*; unter-māni *interlunium*, Grff. 2, 795.]

mōna, an; *m.*: *but also* mōne, an; *f.* I. *the moon*:—Se mōna and ealle steorran underfōþ leóht of ðære miclan sunnan, Lchdm. iii. 236, 19. Se mōna wæs æt fruman on ǽfen gesceapen, 264, 26. Sunna and mōne (*but* næs se mōna ðāgyt uppe, 29, 22), Nar. 28, 20: Bt. Met. Fox 29, 73; Met. 29, 37. Ðæs sunnan āsprungnis oððe ðære mōnan, Nar. 28, 10. Ðæs mōnan trendel *the moon's disc*, Lchdm. ii. 242, 4. II. *moon* as in new, full *moon*, the reference being to the stage reached in a lunar month:—Nīwe mōna *neomenia*, Wrt. Voc. i. 16, 51. Se nīwa mōna, Lchdm. iii. 264, 26. Mōna se forma, se ōðer, se þridda, etc., pp. 184–196. [Ful]les mōnan *plene lunae*, Kent. Gl. 210. Nǽfre būton on nīwum mōnan, Lchdm. iii. 242, 23. On ānre nihte ealdne mōnan . . . on tweigra nihta mōnan, etc., 154, 15–28, 156, 1–16. Hē gesette ðone mōnan fulne, 238, 27. Ðæt geár hæfþ twelf nīwe mōnan, 248, 25–26. [*Goth.* mēna; *m.*: *Icel.* māni; *m.*: *O. Sax.* māno; *m.*: *O. Frs.* mōna; *m.*: *Du.* maan; *f.*: *O. H. Ger.* māno; *m.*: *M. H. Ger.* māne; *m. also f.*; mānt, mānde: *Ger.* mond; *m.*]

Mōnan-ǽfen, es; *m. Monday-eve, the evening of Sunday*:—Gif esne ofer dryhtnes hǽse þeówweorc wyrce an Sunnanǽfen efter hire setlgange ōþ Mōnanǽfenes setlgang, L. Wih. 9; Th. i. 38, 19. v. Mōnan-niht.

Mōnan-dæg, es; *m. Monday*:—Ūtgangendum ðam mōnþe ðe we Aprelis hātaþ, se nȳhsta Mōnandæg & ingangendum ðam mōnþe ðe we Agustus hātaþ se ǽresta Mōnandæg . . . se ǽresta Monandæg æfter ūtgange ðæs mōnþes Decembris *the last Monday in April . . . the first Monday in August . . . the first Monday after the end of December*, Lchdm. iii. 76, 14–18. On Mōnandæg, Rubc. Jn. Skt. 2, 12: 7, 32. [*O. Frs.* mōna-, mōnan-dei: *O. H. Ger.* māno-tag: *Ger.* mon-tag: *Icel.* māna-dagr: *Dan.* man-dag.] v. Mōn-dæg.

Mōnan-niht, e; *f. Monday eve, the evening of Sunday*:—Hē ūs ðonne myngaþ ðæs Sunnandæges weorces and ðæs Sæternesdæges ofer nōn and ðære Mōnannihte, Wulfst. 210, 10. v. Mōnan-ǽfen.

mōnaþ, mōnþ, es; *pl.* mōnaþ, mōnþas; *m. A month, lunar* or *calendar*:—Ǽlce mōnþe seó sunne yrnþ under ān ðæra tācna . . . Ǽlc ðæra twelf tācna hylt his mōnaþ, and ðonne seó sunne hī hæfþ ealle underurnen, ðonne byþ ān geár āgān. On ðam geáre synd getealde twelf mōnþas . . . Ðæs mōnan mōnaþ is ðonne hē gecyrþ nīwe fram ðære sunnan ōð ðæt hē eft cume hyre forne āgeán, eald and āteorod, and eft þurh hī beó ontend. On ðam mōnþe synd geteald nigon and twentig daga and twelf tīda, ðis is se mōnelīca mōnaþ . . . Se mōnelica mōnaþ hæfþ ǽfre on ānum mōnþe xxx nihta, and on ōðrum nigon and xx. On swā hwilcum sunlīcum mōnþe swā se mōna geendaþ, se byþ his mōnaþ. Ic cweðe nū gewislīcor; gyf se ealda mōna geendaþ twām dagum binnan Hlȳdan mōnþe, ðonne byþ hē geteald tō ðam mōnþe, Lchdm. iii. 244–250. Ðā ān mōnuþ āgan wæs, Gen. 29, 14. Fullne mōnoþ, Num. 11, 20. Se teóþa mōnþ, October, Menol. Fox 360; Men. 181. On ðone seofenteóþan dæg ðæs mōnþes, Gen. 7, 11: Lev. 23, 5. Healfum mōnþe se mōna biþ weaxende, healfum hē biþ wanigende, Homl. Th. i. 154, 27. Ðȳ syxtan mōnþe ðæs ðe Sanctus Johannes on his mōdor bōsm onfangen wæs, Blickl. Homl. 165, 24. Æfter nigan mōnþa fæce, 9, 29. Feola mōnþa, Bd. 5, 19; S. 638, 19. On XII mōnþum, Chart. Th. 433, 10. Fīf, syx mōnþas, Lk. Skt. 1, 24: 4, 25. Feówer, eahta, seofon, nigon, twelf, feówertȳne mōnaþ, Ors. 6, 28; Swt. 278, 8: 6, 31; Swt. 286, 2: Blickl. Homl. 193, 13: 89, 19: 39, 15: Homl. Th. ii. 490, 25. The names of the months are as follows: Se æftera Geóla *January*, Sol-mōnaþ *February*, Hrēd- *or* Hlȳd-mōnaþ *March*, Eáster-mōnaþ *April*, Þrīmilci *May*, se ǽrra Līða *or* Sear-mōnaþ *June*, se æftera Līða *or* Mǽd-mōnaþ *July*, Weód-mōnaþ *August*, Hālig- *or* Hærfest-mōnaþ *September*, Winterfylliþ *October*, Blōt-mōnaþ *November*, se ǽrra Geóla *December*. See the several words for references, and Grmm. Gesch. D. S. c. VI for the month-names in Anglo-Saxon and related dialects. [*Goth.* mēnoþs: *Icel.* mānuðr: *Dan.* maaned: *Swed.* monad: *O. L. Ger.* mānuth: *O. Frs.* mōnath: *O. H. Ger.* mānod: *Ger.* monat.]

mōnaþ-ādl, e; *f. A disease that occurs at intervals of a month*:—Ða ðe ðonne on gewunon mōnaþādle numene beóþ . . . Ðæt wīf mid ðȳ heó ðone gewunan þrowaþ mōnaþādle *cum in suetis menstruis detinentur . . . Mulier dum consuetudinem menstruam patitur*, Bd. i. 27; S. 493, 40–43.

mōnaþādlig; *adj. Suffering from* mōnaþādl:—Gif hwylc man gangeþ tō mōnaþādligum wīfe *si quis vir ad menstruatam mulierem accedat*, Bd. 1, 27; S. 493, 42.

mōnaþ-blōd, es; *n. Menstruum*:—Mōnaþblōd *menstrum*, Wrt. Voc. ii. 59, 22: *menstrua*, i. 46, 13. [Cf. *O. H. Ger.* mānod-blōti *menstruus.*]

mōnaþ-bōt, e; *f. Penance extending over a month*:—Sumon geárbōte, sumon mā geára . . .; sumon mōnþbōte, sumon mā mōnþa; sumon wucubōte, sumon mā wucena, L. Pen. 3; Th. ii. 278, 12.

mōnaþ-fyllen, e; *f. The time of full moon*:—Mōnaþfylene *plenilunio*, Hpt. Gl. 525, 63.

mōnaþ-gecynd, e; *f. Menstruum*:—Gīf wīfe tō swīðe of flōwe sió mōnaþgecynd, L. M. 3, 38; Lchdm. ii. 330, 26, 13.

mōnaþ-līc; *adj.* I. *monthly*:—Ða mōnaþlecan *menstrua*, Wrt. Voc. ii. 57, 34. II. *lunar*:—Mōnoþlīces clywnes *lunaris luminis*, Hpt. Gl. 418, 15. [*O. L. Ger.* mōnoþ-līc: *O. H. Ger.* mānod-līh *menstruus.*] v. symbel-mōnaþlīc.

mōnaþ-seóc; *adj.* I. *lunatic, epileptic*:—Mōnaþseóc *lunaticus*, Wrt. Voc. i. 45, 65. *Comitiales* i. *garritores* ylfie *vel* mōnaþseóce, ii. 132, 26 (v. ilfig). Mōnaþseóce *lunaticos*, Mt. Kmbl. 4, 24: Herb. 10, 2; Lchdm. i. 100, 18. II. *suffering from* mōnaþādl:—Bearneácnigende wīf and mōnaþseóc, Homl. Th. ii. 94, 4. [*O. H. Ger.* mānodsiuh *lunaticus*: *and* cf. mānod-suhtig *menstruata.*] v. mōn-seóc.

mōnaþseóc-ness, e; *f. Lunacy*:—Wið mōnoþseócnysse, gyf man ðās wyrte ðam mōnoþseócan ligcgendon ofer ālegþ, sōna hē hyne sylfne hālne up āhefþ, Herb. 66, 2; Lchdm. i. 170, 4.

mond = (?) mōd, Exon. 40 b; Th. 134, 26; Gū. 514.

Mōn-dæg, es; *m. Monday*:—Ǣlce Mōndæge, L. R. S. 3; Th. i. 432, 21. v. Mōnan-dæg.

mōne-, **mōn-líc**; *adj. Lunar*:—Ðis is se mōnelīca [mōnlīca, MS. P.] mōnaþ, Lchdm. iii. 248, 20: 250, 1. Seó sunne biþ hwīltīdum þurh ðæs mōnelīcan trendles underscyte āþȳstrod, Homl. Th. i. 608, 32.

Mon-íg, e; *f. The Isle of Man* or *Anglesey*; Mona:—Ðā gehergodon hī Monīge [Mænīge] *then they harried the Isle of Man*, Chr. 1000 (ed. Thorpe). Monīge Brytta eáland Angelcynnes rīce hē underþeódde *Mevanias insulas imperio subjugavit Anglorum*, Bd. 2, 9; S. 510, 16. [*Icel.* Mön; gen. Manar *Isle of Man.*]

mōn-seóc; *adj. Lunatic, epileptic*:—Mōnsēk (fylleseóc, W. Sax.) hē is *lunaticus est*, Mt. Kmbl. Rush. 15. Mōnsēkæ *lunaticos*, 4, 24. v. mōnaþ-seóc.

mōr, es; *m.* I. *a moor, waste and damp land*:—Moor *uligo*, Wrt. Voc. i. 37, 23. Mōres græs *the grass of the field* (*which Nebuchadnezzar was to eat*), Cd. 203; Th. 252, 8; Dan. 575. On ðone hreódihtan mōr; of ðon mōre, Cod. Dip. Kmbl. iii. 121, 21: Beo. Th. 1424; B. 710. Ofer myrcan mōr, 2814; B. 1405. Ys on Breotoneland sum fenn unmǣtre mycelnysse . . . Ðǣr synd unmǣte mōras, Guthl. 3; Gdwin. 20, 1–4. Fennas and mōras *paludes*, Bt. 18, 1; Fox 62, 14. Sumra wyrta eard biþ on dūnum sumra on merscum sumra on mōrum *aliae herbae montibus oriuntur, alias ferunt paludes*, 34, 10; Fox 148, 24. Ofer burna and ofer mōras *super rivos et paludes*, Ex. 8, 5. Mistige mōras, Beo. Th. 326; B. 162: 207; B. 103. II. *high waste ground, a mountain*:—Licgaþ wilde mōras wið eástan . . . on ðǣm mōrum eardiaþ Finnas . . . Ðǣr hit (*Norway*) smalost wǣre, hit mihte beón þreora mīla brād tō ðæm mōre; and se mōr syððan, on sumum stōwum, swā brād swā man mæg on twām wucum oferfēran . . . Ðonne is tōemnes ðæm lande sūðeweardum, on ōðre healfe ðæs mōres, Sweóland (*Ohthere's description of Norway*), Ors. 1, 1; Swt. 18, 27–34, 19, 1–2. Ne munt ne mōr, Salm. Kmbl. 845; Sal. 422: 681; Sal. 340. In mōr hēh *in montem excelsum*, Mt. Kmbl. Lind. 4, 8: 5, 1. Swā unefne is eorþe þicce, syndon ðās mōras myclum āsprotene, Ps. Th. 140, 9. Ungefēredra mōra *inaccessorum montium*, Bd. 4, 26; S. 602, 20. In heágum mōrum and in hrēðum *in arduis asperisque montibus*, 4, 27; S. 604, 27: 3, 23; S. 554, 20. Of ðissum wēstum wīdum mōrum *a desertis montibus*, Ps. Th. 74, 6. Waldend scōp wudige mōras, Exon. 54 b; Th. 193, 12; Az. 120. [*O. H. Ger. M. H. Ger.* muor; *n. a marsh, bog.*]

mōraþ, mōrod, es; *n. A drink formed by boiling down and sweetening wine* (*with mulberries*), *a decoction of wine and herbs*:—Mōraþ *carenum* (cf. *carenum* æþele alu, ii. 23, 1), Wrt. Voc. i. 27, 64. Ne ete fersce gōs . . . ne fersc swīn ne nāht ðæs ðe of mōrode cume. Gif hē hwilc ðissa ete sīe ðæt sealt *do not let him eat fresh goose or fresh pork or aught of that which comes out of a decoction of wine and herbs* (*has been cooked with wine and herbs?*). *If he eat any of these, let it be salted*, Lchdm. ii. 88, 9. Āwylle on ealdum mōrode, 88, 14: 122, 16. Nim eald mōrod, iii. 14, 8. [*M. H. Ger.* mōraz *mulberry wine.* v. Du Cange, moratum.]

mōr-beám, es; *m. A mulberry tree* or *blackberry bush*:—Mōrbeám *morus* vel *rubus*, Wrt. Voc. i. 32, 60: *murus*, 80, 26. Mārbeámas *moros*, Ps. Surt. 77, 47. [Cf. Wick. mōr-tree.]

mōr-denu, e; *f. A swampy* or *fenny valley*:—Of ðam stocce inn on mōrdene; of mōrdene inn on ðere saltstrēt, Cod. Dip. Kmbl. iii. 384, 30. Cf. mōr-fæsten.

more, moru, an; *f.* (*also* mora *in cpds.* q. v.) *An* (*edible*) *root, a carrot, parsnip*:—Bētan more *a root of beet*, Lchdm. iii. 6, 19. Wylisc moru *carrot* . . . Englisc moru *parsnip*, L. M. 3, 8; Lchdm. ii. 312, 16, 21. Eolonan moran dust, doccan moran dust, 1, 54; Lchdm. ii. 126, 6. Mintan broþ oððe moran (*carrot*), 1, 18; Lchdm. ii. 62, 6: 2, 28; Lchdm. ii. 224, 25. Nim celeþonian moran and glædenan moran and hocces moran, 3, 41; Lchdm. ii. 334, 27. Ete wælwyrte moran, Lchdm. i. 354, 13. Nim Englisce moran, L. M. 1, 2; Lchdm. ii. 38, 15. Moran *pastinace*, Wrt. Voc. i. 69, 13. Genim ðæs scearpan þistles moran, L. M. 3, 12; Lchdm. ii. 314, 11. [*O.H.Ger.* moraha, morach *pastinaca, cariota*: *Ger.* möhre.] v. feld-, weal-, weald-more; ǣg-moran.

mōr-fæsten, es; *n. A place secure from attack from the swampy character of the country*:—Hē (*Alfred*) lytle werede uniéþelīce æfter wudum fōr, and on mōrfæstenum, Chr. 878; Erl. 78, 34.

morgen, es; *m.* I. *morning, morn*:—Ðā hyt morgen wæs *mane facto*, Mt. Kmbl. 27, 1: Blickl. Homl. 235, 18. Syððan morgen com, Beo. Th. 2159; B. 1077: Cd. 160; Th. 199, 29: Exod. 346. On morgene *mane*, Ps. Th. 91, 2. On morgenne *in matutino*, 100, 8. Æt ðære þriddan tīde on morgenne, Blickl. Homl. 201, 35: 203, 2. On morgne *at morn*, Exon. 50 b; Th. 175, 10; Gū. 1192: Th. 176, 29; Gū. 1217. On marne *mane*, Ps. Surt. 5, 4, 5: 54, 18: Bd. 2, 6; S. 508, 23. Bringþ morgen tō mannum Decembris, Menol. Fox 435; Men. 219. On morgen *mane*, Gen. 28, 18: Blickl. Homl. 69, 28: 231, 36. Swīðe ǣr on morgen, Ps. Th. 18, 5. Morgena gehwilce *every morning*, Cd. 40; Th. 52, 23; Gen. 848: Ps. Th. 58, 16. Morgna gehwam, Exon. 93 a; Th. 350, 7; Sch. 60. Morna, Beo. Th. 4892; B. 2450. Drince þrȳ morgenas *let him drink three mornings*, Lchdm. i. 88, 13. Nigon morgenas, ii. 118, 5. viiii morgnas . . . viii morgnas, 294, 1. Morghenas, iii. 6, 17. II. *the morning of the next day, morrow*:—Gā and cum tō morgenne *go, and come to-morrow*, Past. Swt. 325, 1. On morgne *on the morrow*, Beo. Th. 4961; B. 2484. On morne, Bd. 2, 6; S. 508, 7. Tō morgen *cras*, Ex. 8, 23: Mt. Kmbl. 6, 30: Kent. Gl. 54: Cd. 111; Th. 147, 12; Gen. 2438. Tō morhgen (morgen, MS. A.), Lk. Skt. 13, 32, 33. [*Gen. and Ex.* morgen, morwen: *A. R.* morwen: *Ayenb.* morȝen: *Chauc. Piers P.* morwe: *Laym.* morȝen, marȝen, morwe: *Goth.* maurgins: *Icel.* morginn: *O. Sax. O. L. Ger. O. H. Ger.* morgan: *O. Frs.* morn: *Dan. Du. Ger.* morgen: *Swed.* morgon.] v. ǣr-morgen, ǣrne, *and* mergen.

morgen-ceald; *adj. Chilled with the cold of early morning*:—Sceal gār wesan monig morgenceald, Beo. Th. 6036; B. 3022.

morgen-colla, an; *m. Dread* (?) or *rage* (?), *furious attack* (?) *which comes in the morning*:—Him fǣrspel bodedon, morgencollan, atolne ecgplegan, Judth. 12; Thw. 25, 6; Jud. 245. v. collen-ferhþ.

morgen-dæg, es; *m.* I. *morning, day-light*:—Ðā hit wæs tōforan dæges ðā cwōman fugelas . . . hī eft gewiton. Ðā hit on morgendæg wæs ðā . . ., Nar. 16, 24. II. *the morrow*:—Be ðan morgendæge þencean, Blickl. Homl. 213, 22. v. mergen-dæg.

morgen-drenc, es; *m. A drink* or *potion to be taken in the morning*:—Hē gesette gōdne morgendrænc wið eallum untrumnessum, Lchdm. iii. 70, 17. [Cf. *Icel.* morgin-drykkja.]

morgen-gifu, e; *f. The gift made by the husband to the wife on the morning after the consummation of the marriage*:—Morgengifu *dos*, Wrt. Voc. i. 20, 53. Hit (*five hides of land*) wæs hire morgengifu ðā heó ǣrest tō Aðulfe com, Chart. Th. 170, 24. Gif heó (*a widow*) binnan geáres fæce wer geceóse, ðonne þolige heó ðære morgengyfe, L. C. S. 74; Th. i. 416, 8 (cf. 522, 3: 576, 2). Ic cȳðe hwæt ic mīnum wīfe tō morgengife sealde, ðæt is Beadewan and Burgestede and Strātford and ða þreó hȳda æt Heánhealan, Chart. Th. 596, 31. Hig ðone cincg bǣdon ðæt heó mōste gesyllan hire morgengife intō Cristes cyrcean, 540, 18. Gif hió bearn ne gebyreþ fæderingmāgas āgan morgengyfe, L. Ethb. 81; Th. i. 24, 2. [*Gen. and Ex.* morgen-giwe: *A. R.* marhen-, marech-, morh-giue: *Laym.* mor-, mær-ȝeue *douaire*: *Prompt. Parv.* mor-yve *dos*: *Icel.* morgun-gjöf: *Dan.* morgen-gave: *O.H.Ger.* morgangeba: *Ger.* morgen-gabe.] v. Grmm. R. A. 441.

morgen-lang; *adj. Having a long morning*:—Eorlwerod morgenlongne dæg mōdgiómor sæt *sad at heart sat the warriors through a day whose evening seemed as if would never come*, Beo. Th. 5780; B. 2894.

morgen-leóht, es; *n. The morning light, morning*, Beo. Th. 1213; B. 604: 1839; B. 917. [*Laym.* morȝen-, more-liht: *O.H.Ger.* morganlioht *mane.*]

morgen-líc; *adj.* I. *morning*:—Morgenlīc *matutinus*, Wrt. Voc. ii. 116, 67. From gehæld morgenlīcum *a custodia matutina*, Rtl. 181, 1. Tō morgenlīcum tīdum *ad matutinas horas*, 36, 35. Ic beó ðȳs morgenlīcan dæge (*on the morning of this day*: St. Mary's death seems to have taken place on the day when she says this) gongende of līchoman, Blickl. Homl. 143, 2: 139, 18. II. *of to-morrow*:—Se morgenlīca dæg *crastinus dies*, Mt. Kmbl. 6, 34. [*Icel.* morgun-ligr *matutinus*: *O. H. Ger.* morgan-līh *matutinus.*] v. mergen-, myrgenlīc.

morgen-mete, es; *m. A morning meal, breakfast*:—On xii mōnþum ðū scealt sillan ðīnum þeówan men vii hund hlāfa and xx hlāfa, būton morgenmetum and nōnmetum, Salm. Kmbl. p. 129, 19. [ȝief he frend were me sceolde ȝief him his *morȝemete* (cf. 231, 19 where it is called *forme mete*) þat he þe bet mihte abide þane more mete, O. E. Homl. i. 237, 33.]

morgen-regn, es; *m. Rain that falls in the morning*:—Ðū þurh lyft lǣtest, leódum tō freme, mildne morgenrēn, Exon. 54 a; Th. 191, 2; Az. 82.

morgen-seóc; *adj. Sick in the morning*:—Him biþ ā sefa geómor, mōd morgenseóc, Exon. 119 a; Th. 458, 4; Hy. 4, 95.

morgen-spell, es; *n. A story* or *narrative told in the morning*:—Ðā wæs wīde lǣded mǣre morgenspel . . . ðæt Cristes rōd funden wǣre, Elen. Kmbl. 1936; El. 970.

morgen-sprǽc, e; *f. The periodical assembly of a guild held in the morning*, or *on the morrow after the guild-feast*:—Se gegilda ðe ne gesēce his morgenspǣce gilde his syster huniges *the member of a guild, who does not attend the assembly of the guild, shall pay a sester of honey*, Chart. Th. 613, 7. [Cf. And if any broþer be somound to any *morwespeche* . . . and wil nouht come, he scal paye a pound of wax, English Guilds (E. E. T. S.), p. 54. See also the Glossary for other references to the word, and Introduction, pp. xxxii–xxxiii, for remarks upon it. In the Promptorium morow-, morwe-, mor-speche = *crastinum colloquium*; cf. English Guilds, p. 30, where a meeting is held 'on morwe aftyr þe gylde day.']

morgen-steorra, an; *m. The morning star*:—Ðone beorhtan steorran ðe wē hātaþ morgensteorra *Lucifer*, Bt. 4; Fox 8, 3: 39, 13; Fox 234, 3: Bt. Met. Fox 4, 26; Met. 4, 13. [*Prompt. Parv.* morow-, morwyn-sterre *Lucifer*: cf. *Icel.* morgun-stjarna: *Ger.* morgen-stern.] v. ǽfen-steorra.

morgen-swég, es; *m. A sound made in the morning*:—Ðá wæs on úhtan Grendles gúþcræft gumum undyrne. Ðá wæs æfter wiste wóp up áhafen, micel morgenswég, Beo. Th. 258; B. 129.

morgen-tíd, e; *f. Morning-tide, morning*:—In morgentíd *in matutinis*, Ps. Surt. 100, 8. On morgentíd, Beo. Th. 973; B. 484: 1041; B. 518: Chr. 937; Erl. 112, 14. On ða morgentíd, Judth. 12; Thw. 25, 1; Jud. 236. Útgong margentíde *exitus matutini*, Ps. Surt. 64, 9. Tó margentíde *ad matutinum*, 29, 6. In margentíd *in matutino*, 72, 14. [*Gen. and Ex.* morgen-tid: *O.Sax.* morgan-tíd: *Icel.* morgun-tíðir *matins*.] v. mergen-tíd.

morgen-torht; *adj. Bright with the brightness of morning* (applied to the sun), Andr. Kmbl. 482; An. 241.

morgen-wacian; *p.* ode *To get up early in the morning*:—Morgenwacode *manicabat* (v. Lk. 21, 38), Wrt. Voc. ii. 73, 72: 56, 58.

mór-hǽþ, e; *f. A mountain-heath*:—Swá líg freteþ mórhǽþ *velut flamma incendat montes*, Ps. Th. 82, 10.

mór-heald (?):—Wǽron land heora lyfthelme beþeaht mearchofu mórheald, Cd. 145: Th. 181, 14; Exod. 61. *Grein takes the word to be an adjective = placed on a mountain slope*, cf. heald; *adj. But the word might be a noun*, cf. *O.H.Ger.* halda; *f. clivus*: *Icel.* hallr; *m. a slope*, '*their march-dwellings were the mountain-slope.*' *Or perhaps* heald, ge-heald *in the sense of* keeping *might be compared, as also* hald *fermum*, Wrt. Voc. ii. 147, 71, so mór-heald = *mountain-hold* or *fastness. Yet again*, heald *may be* [*a northern form* (?) *of*] *the verb* = heóld, '*the mountain guarded their march-dwellings.*' *Bouterwek and Thorpe read thus.*

mór-hop, es; *n. A pool in a marsh*:—Hé byreþ blódig wæl . . . mearcaþ mórhopu *he* (*Grendel*) *will bear the bloody corse . . . will mark the marshy pools* (*with the blood*), Beo. Th. 904; B. 450. Cf. fen-hop.

mórig; *adj. Marshy, fenny*:—On mórium lande *in locis palustribus*, Gen. 41, 2. v. mór-mǽd.

mór-land, es; *n. Moor-land, wild hilly country*:—Se ðe on wéstenne, méðe and meteleás, mórland trydeþ, Elen. Kmbl. 1221; El. 612. Hé wunede on ðám mórlandum (*in montanis*), Bd. 4, 27; S. 604, 33. Se ǽresta láreów on ðám mórlandum ða ðe syndon tó norþdǽle Pehta ríces *primus doctor transmontanis Pictis ad aquilonem*, 5, 9; B. 622, 40. Ofer alle mórlonda *super omnia montana*, Lk. Skt. Lind. Rush. i. 65.

mór-mǽd, e; *f. A marshy meadow*:—Tó mórmǽde norþhyrnan, Cod. Dip. Kmbl. iii. 449, 19. v. mórig.

morne, mórod. v. morgen, móraþ.

mór-pytt, es; *m. A marshy pool*:—On mórpyt, Cod. Dip. Kmbl. iii. 381, 9.

mór-sceaþa, an; *m. A bandit, a robber who takes refuge in the moors* (v. mór):—Ðone mórsceaþo (*Barabbas*), Mk. Skt. Lind. Rush. 15, 15, 11. Wæs Barabbas mórsceaþe (sceaþa, Rush.) *erat Barabbas latro*, Jn. Skt. Lind. 18, 40. Swá tó mórsceaþe (scaþe, Rush.) gié cwómun (*ad latronem*), Mt. Kmbl. Lind. 26, 55. Tuoge mórsceaþo *duo latrones*, Mk. Skt. Lind. 15, 27: Lk. Skt. Lind. 23, 33.

mór-seáþ, es; *m. A boggy, marshy pit*, Cod. Dip. Kmbl. iii. 378, 13.

mór-secg, es; *m. n. Sedge*:—Bedde hys bed myd mórsecge, Lchdm. iii. 140, 25.

mór-stapa, an; *m. A moor-stepper, traverser of the moors*:—Mǽre mórstapa (*the bull*), Runic pm. Kmbl. 339, 11; Rún. 2.

mortere, es; *m. A mortar*:—Mortere *mortariola*, Wrt. Voc. ii. 58, 28. Se ealra mǽsta mortere *girba*, 42, 22: i. 20, 25. Gepuna eall tósomne on ánum mortere, Lchdm. i. 216, 13: 142, 18.

morþ, es; *n. m.* I. *death, destruction, perdition*:—Hit wæs hæleþa forlor menniscra morþ ðæt hié tó mete dǽdon ofet unfǽle *it was men's ruin, our race's destruction, that for their food they took that evil fruit*, Cd. 33; Th. 45, 5; Gen. 722. Mid morþes cwealme *with death's pang*, 35; Th. 47, 9; Gen. 758. Ðæt micle morþ (*death which followed the eating of the forbidden fruit*), 30; Th. 40, 16; Gen. 640. Nys ús ná tó secgenne ðone sceamlícan morþ ðe ðǽr gedón wæs (*the mortality, attended with so many horrible circumstances, that happened at the siege of Jerusalem*), Ælfc. T. Grn. 21, 15. II. *that which causes death*:—Ðú (*the evil soul*) wǽre ðǽr (*in this world*) morþ and myrþra, ac ðú ne miht hér (*in the next world*) swá beón, Wulfst. 241, 9. Ic bidde ðæt man ðæs morþes (*deadly sin, marriage by men in orders*) heononforþ geswíce, L. I. P. 23; Th. ii. 334, 23. Hé (*the devil*) hogode on ðæt micle morþ (*the eating of the forbidden fruit*) men forweorþan, forlǽran and forlǽdan, Cd. 32; Th. 43, 15; Gen. 691. Man téh ðæt morþ (*apparently an image of the intended victim whose destruction was being attempted through witchcraft by a widow and her son*, v. III *and* morþ-dǽd) forþ of hire inclifan. Ðá nam man ðæt wíf and ádrencte hí æt Lundenebricge, Chart. Th. 230, 17. III. *murder*; (a) as a technical term, *slaying with an attempt at concealment of the deed*. Cf. the distinction in Icelandic law between *morþ* murder and *víg* manslaughter, 'þat er morþ ef maðr leynir eða hylr hræ ok gengr eigi í gegn,' but if declaration (*lýsing*) were made it was *víg*. v. Cl. & Vig. Dict. and Grmm. R. A. 625. Schmid. A. S. Gesetz. p. 633, suggests that *morþ* has particular reference to death caused by witchcraft or by poison, and refers to the connection in which the compounds *morþ-dǽd-*, *weorc*, *-wyrhta* occur: see the passages given under those words. See also the last passage under II:—Gif open morþ weorþe ðæt man sý ámyrdred ágife man mágum ðone banan and gif hit tihtle sý and æt láde mistíde déme se bisceop *if there be a death and it afterwards appear that the man was murdered, the* (*supposed*) *murderer being discovered, let the latter be given up to the kinsmen* (*of the slain man*), *and if the accusation be brought, and the attempt of the accused to clear himself fail, let the bishop pass sentence*, L. C. S. 57; Th. i. 406, 25. Ǽbere morþ æfter woruldlage is bótleás *slaying, which is proved to be murder, according to the secular law, cannot be compounded for*, 65; Th. i. 410, 5. (b) as a general term, *murder, homicide*:—Hí swylc geblót and swylc morþ dónde wǽron (*of Busiris sacrificing strangers to the gods*, Ors. 1, 8; Swt. 40, 26. Ðæs ðe hé blódgyte, wælfyll weres wǽpnum gespédeþ, morþ mid mundum, Cd. 75; Th. 92, 13; Gen. 1528. [*Laym.* morþ *destruction*: *O. Sax.* morð: *O. Frs.* morth: *Icel.* morð: *O. H. Ger.* mord: *Lat.* mort-.] v. morþor.

morþ-bealu, wes; *n. Deadly harm, murder*, Beo. Th. 272; B. 136. v. morþor-bealu.

morþ-crundel. v. crundel.

morþ-dǽd, e; *f. A deed which causes destruction*, (a) *of the body*:—Be ðǽm wiccecræftum and be liblácum and be morþdǽdum, gif man ðǽr ácweald wǽre (v. *last passage under* morþ, II, *and* morþ-weorc), L. Ath. i. 6; Th. i. 202, 11. (b) *of the soul, deadly sin, evil deed*:—Hé gewenede swá hine sylfne tó heora synlícum þeáwum and tó márum morþdǽdum mid ðam mánfullum flocce . . . Swá férde se cniht on his fraceþum dǽdum and on morþdǽdum micclum gestrangod on orwénnysse his ágenre hǽle, Ælfc. T. Grn. 17, 18–24. Wearþ ðes þeódscype swýðe forsyngod . . . þurh morþdǽda and þurh mándǽda, Wulfst. 163, 21. [Þonne scalt þu (*the body*), erming, up arisen imete þine morþdeden, Fragm. Phlps. 7, 37.]

morþor, es; *n. m.* I. *murder*:—Manige men wénaþ ðæt morþor sý seó mǽste synne; ac ús is tó witenne ðæt þreora cynna syndon morþras. Ðæt is ðonne ðæt ǽreste, ðæt man tó óðrum lǽþþe hæbbe, and hine hatige . . . Ða æfstigan men, ðéh hí sýn ðæs morþres scyldige, hí hit him tó nánre synne ne gelýfaþ, Blickl. Homl. 63, 34–65, 11. Ðara banena byre morþres gylpeþ, Beo. Th. 4116; B. 2055. Ðeáh hié (*cannibals*) morþres feala gefremed habben, Andr. Kmbl. 1950; An. 977. Morþres on luste, 2282; An. 1142. Draca morþre swealt *the dragon perished by the sword*, Beo. Th. 1789; B. 892. Ic on morþor ofslóh minra sumne hyldemága, Cd. 52; Th. 66, 32; Gen. 1093. Morþor sceal mon under eorþan befeolan, ðe hit forhelan þenceþ, Exon. 90 b; Th. 340, 23; Gn. Ex. 115. Morþer *homicidium* . . . fore morþre *propter homicidium*, Lk. Skt. Rush. 23, 19, 25. Ne ðú morþur ne fremme *non homicidium facies*, Mt. Kmbl. Rush. 19, 18: Lind. 27, 16. Morþur *homicidia*, 15, 19. II. *mortal sin, great wickedness*:—Wælhreówes árleásta fela, mán and morþor, misdǽda worn (cf. hwilc mán and hwilce ǽrleásnesse Neron weorhte, Fox 58, 2), Bt. Met. Fox 9, 13; Met. 9, 7. Morþres brytta (*Holofernes*), Judth. 10; Thw. 22, 33; Jud. 90: (*the devil*), Andr. Kmbl. 2342; An. 1142. Ðæt wé ðæs morþres meldan ne weorþen, hwǽr ðæt hálige treó beheled wurde, Elen. Kmbl. 855; El. 428: 1248; El. 626. Ðære synwræce sceoldon, morþres ongyldan, Exon. 45 a; Th. 153, 30; Gú. 833. Hú lange mánwyrhtan morþre gylpaþ *usque quo peccatores gloriabuntur*, Ps. Th. 93, 3. Seó sáwl sceal mid deóflum drohtnoþ habban in morþre and on máne, Wulfst. 187, 18. Morþor (*adultery*), Exon. 10 b; Th. 12, 29; Cri. 193. Ic andette mínes módes morþor, L. de Cf. 8; Th. ii. 262, 31: Salm. Kmbl. 82; Sal. 41. III. *torment, deadly injury, great misery*:—Swá hwæt swá wit morþres þoliaþ, hit is Adame forgolden, Cd. 35; Th. 47, 4; Gen. 755. Se hié of ðam morþre álýsde (*from the fiery furnace*), 196; Th. 244, 23; Dan. 452. God wearp hine on ðæt morþer innan (*into hell*), 18; Th. 22, 18; Gen. 342. Heó his mǽgwinum morþor fremedon (*greatly afflicted*), 149; Th. 187, 5; Exod. 146. Sceolde his wíte habban, ealra morþra mǽst, 16; Th. 19, 26; Gen. 297. Ðe ús monna mǽst morþra gefremede, sárra sorga, Judth. 11; Thw. 24, 10; Jud. 181. [*Goth.* maurþr φόνος.] v. morþ.

morþor-bealu, wes; *n. Deadly hurt, murder*:—Geseón morþorbealo mága, Beo. Th. 2162; B. 1079: 5477; B. 2742. v. morþ-bealu.

morþor-bedd, es; *n. The bed of death, the bed where a murdered man lies*:—Wæs ðam yldestan mǽges dǽdum morþorbed stréd (*of a man shot by his brother*), Beo. Th. 4864; B. 2436.

morþor-cofa, an; *m. A prison*, Andr. Kmbl. 2008; An. 1006.

morþor-cræft, es; *m. Deadly* or *murderous art* or *power*:—Ðǽr sylfǽtan (*the cannibal Mermedonians*) éðel healdaþ morþorcræftum, Andr. Kmbl. 353; An. 177.

morþor-cwealm, es; *m. Murder, slaughter*, Exon. 91 b; Th. 343, 4; Gn. Ex. 152.

morþor-hete, es; *m. Murderous, deadly hate*, Beo. Th. 2214; B. 1105.

morþor-hof, es; *n. A place of torment* or *extreme misery* (*hell*), Elen. Kmbl. 2603; El. 1303.

morþor-hûs, es; *n. A house of torment* (*hell*), Exon. 31 b; Th. 99, 15; Cri. 1625.

morþor-leán, es; *n. Recompense of sin* or *a terrible recompense*:—Ðǽr (*in hell*) sceolan þeófas and þeódsceaþan, leáse and forlegene, lîfes ne wênan, and mânsworan morþorleán seón, Exon. 31 b; Th. 98, 24; Cri. 1612.

morþor-scyldig; *adj. Guilty of murder* or *of grievous sin*, Andr. Kmbl. 3197; An. 1601.

morþor-slaga, an; *m. A murderer, homicide*:—Morþorslago *homicidas*, Mt. Kmbl. Lind. 22, 7. v. morþ-slaga.

morþor-slagu (?), e; *f. Murder, homicide*:—Morþurslaga *homicidium*, Mt. Kmbl. p. 14, 13. Morþorslago (morþurslagu, Rush.) *homicidia*, Mk. Skt. Lind. 7, 21.

morþor-slege, es; *m. Murder, homicide*:—Swâ hwylc swâ morþorslege þafaþ *quicunque ad homicidium consenserit*, L. Ecg. C. 22; Th. ii. 148, 14.

morþor-sliht, es; *m. Slaughter, the slain*:—Hwæt wæs on manrîme morþorslehtes, deádra gefeallen, Elen. Kmbl. 1297; El. 650. v. morþsliht.

morþor-wyrhta, an; *m. A worker of iniquity* or *of murder*:—Hêr syndan mânsworan and morþorwyrhtan, Wulfst. 165, 30. v. morþwyrhta.

morþ-slaga, an; *m. A murderer, an assassin*:—Sý ǽlc morþslaga âwirged *maledictus, qui clam percusserit proximum suum*, Deut. 27, 24. Oferfyll biþ mǽgbana and morþslaga, Wulfst. 242, 6. [*O. E. Homl.* morð-slaȝa: *pl.*] v. morþor-slaga.

morþ-sliht, es; *m. Murder, assassination*:—Be morþslihtum, L. Æðelst. iv. 6; Th. i. 224, 11, 12. v. morþor-sliht.

morþ-weorc, es; *n. An act which causes death* (*by witchcraft* or *poison*):—Hǽðenscipe biþ ðæt man . . . wiccecræft lufige oððe morþweorc gefremme (*causes death by witchcraft or poison*, v. morþ, III), L. C. S. 5; Th. i. 378, 21. Deóflîce dǽda on morþweorcum and on manslihtan, L. Eth. v. 25; Th. i. 310, 15: vi. 28; Th. i. 322, 16. [*O. Sax.* morð-werk.] Cf. morþ-dǽd *and next word.*

morþ-wyrhta, an; *m. One who causes death* (*by witchcraft* or *poison*):—Wiccan oððe wigleras, mânsworan oððe morþwyrhtan, L. E. G. 11; Th. i. 172, 20 (see note): L. Eth. vi. 7, 36; Th. i. 316, 21, 324, 11: L. C. S. 4; Th. i. 378, 7: Wulfst. 266, 25. v. morþ, III.

moru. v. more.

môr-wyrt, e; *f. Moor-wort*:—Wyrc hié (*a salve*) of ðære smalan môrwyrte (*drosera rotundifolia*, Cockayne), Lchdm. ii. 128, 8.

mos, es; *n. A moss, a marshy place*:—In ðæt micle mos; of ðæm mose, Cod. Dip. Kmbl. iii. 121, 19. Cf. Tô mossetena gemǽre, and swâ big mossetena gemǽre . . . Ðis syndon ðæs landes gemǽre æt mosleáge, Cod. Dip. B. ii. 56, 22, 28. [*N. of England and Scott.* moss (*as in* moss-trooper): *O. H. Ger.* mos *palus*: cf. *Icel.* mosi *a moss*: *Dan.* mose *a bog, moor.*]

môs, es; *n. Food, nourishment*:—Gê oftugon hrægles nacedum, môses meteleásum, Exon. 30 a; Th. 92, 11; Cri. 1507. Tô môse ł ǽte *ad edulium*, Hpt. Gl. 494, 66. Ðû his heáfod sealdest tô môse (*in escam*), Ps. Th. 73, 14. Tô môse *manducare*, 77, 25: Andr. Kmbl. 53; An. 27: 271; An. 136: Salm. Kmbl. 576; Sal. 287. Môse fêdan, Exon. 36 b; Th. 118, 26; Gû. 245. Wista ł môsa *epularum*, Hpt. Gl. 481, 15. [*O. L. Ger.* muos, môs *esca, cibus*: *O. H. Ger.* muos, môs *cibus, esca, edulium, coena, alimonia*: *Ger.* mus: cf. ge-müse.]

mot, es; *n. A mote, an atom*:—Mot *attomos*, Wrt. Voc. i. 284, 37: ii. 8, 10. Mote *atomo*, 9, 62. Tô hwî gesihst ðû ðæt mot (*festucam*) on ðînes brôðor êgan, Mt. Kmbl. 7, 3, 5. Ðû gesâwe gehwǽðe mot on ðînes brôðor eáge, R. Ben. 12, 3. Ðæt lytle mot . . . ðone mot, Lk. Skt. Lind. 6, 41, 42.

môt *a meeting, court.* v. folc-, ge-môt, *and compounds in which* môt *forms the first part.*

môt, e; *f.* (?) *Toll, tax*:—Môt ðæs cyninge[s] *nomisma census*, Mt. Kmbl. Lind. 22, 19. [*Goth.* môta *toll, custom*: cf. *Icel.* mûta *a fee*: *O. H. Ger.* mûta *toll*: *Ger.* mauth.]

mótan = (?) mêtan:—Gif man óðerne sace tihte and hê ðane mannan môte (*meet with*; Price translates *cite*, see his note) an medle oððe an þinge, L. H. E. 8; Th. i. 30, 11.

[**môtan**;] ic, hê môt, ðû môst; wê môton; *p.* môste (*from* môt-te). I. *to be allowed, may, mote*, (a) *with an infinitive*:—Môt ic drincan *licet mihi bibere*, ic môste *mihi licuit*, gif wê môstan *si nobis liceret*, beón âlýfed *licere*, Ælfc. Gr. 33; Som. 37, 15. Wê môton *nobis licet*, ðû môstest *tibi licuit*, 44; Som. 46, 29. Ðû môst heonon hûðe lǽdan, Cd. 98; Th. 129, 25; Gen. 2148: Beo. Th. 3347; B. 1671. Monna gehwylc geceósan môt swâ helle hiénþu swâ heofones mǽrþu, Exon. 16 b; Th. 37, 9; Cri. 590. Gif hê ûs geunnan wile ðæt wê hine grêtan môton, Beo. Th. 700; B. 347. Ne mâgon hié and ne môton (*are not able and are not permitted*) ðînne lîchoman deáþe gedǽlan, Andr. Kmbl. 2431; An. 1217. Ðæt hié on ðæt fǽgon, ðæt ic swâ lytle hwîle lifgean môste, Nar. 32, 21. Ðæt ðû wilwega wealdan môstest, Ps. Th. 90, 11. Môstes, Exon. 28 a; Th. 85, 10; Cri. 1389. Hê him âlýfde ðæt hî ærnan môstan, Bd. 5, 6; S. 618, 42. Ðæt ic gâst mînne âgifan môte, Andr. Kmbl. 2832; An. 1418. Ðæt ðû môte frætwa dǽlan, Cd. 136; Th. 171, 15; Gen. 2828. Ðæt hê ða yldu môte wendan tô lîfe, Exon. 58 b; Th. 210, 24; Ph. 190. Ðǽr wê môtun sêcan, 65 b; Th. 242, 8; Ph. 670. Môtan, 11 b; Th. 16, 1; Cri. 246. Môten, 13 a; Th. 23, 30; Cri. 376. (b) *with ellipsis of infinitive*, (1) *to be supplied from preceding clause*:—Ða ic for God wille gemundbyrdan gif ic môt, Cd. 114; Th. 149, 12; Gen. 2473. Blǽd biþ ǽghwæm ðæm ðe Hǽlende hêran þenceþ, and wel is þam ðe ðæt môt, 221; Th. 287, 11; Sat. 365. Uton fleón ða hwîle ðe wê môton, Homl. Th. ii. 124, 20. Nû cweþaþ oft preóstas ðæt Petrus hæfde wîf: fulsôþ hý secgaþ, forðam ðe hê swâ môste ðâ, L. Ælfc. C. 6; Th. ii. 344, 23. (2) *to be inferred otherwise*:—Ic him yfle ne môt *I may not be harmful to him*, Exon. 127 b; Th. 491, 5; Rä. 80, 9. Ðû of nêde môst (*mayst go*), Andr. Kmbl. 230; An. 115. Nǽfre hió tô helle môt, Exon. 110 a; Th. 421, 19; Rä. 40, 20. Hê begeat leáfe ðæt hê of ðam lande môste, Homl. Skt. 3, 328. Ðæt Metellus tô Rôme môste, Ors. 5, 9; Swt. 232, 25. Ðæt hê môste mid ðæm sunu wið Somnitum, 3, 10; Swt. 140, 17. II. *to be obliged, must*:—Man môt on eornost môtian wið his drihten, Ælfc. T. Grn. 15, 3. Londrîhtes môt monna ǽghwylc îdel hweorfan, Beo. Th. 5765; B. 2886. Ðæt hit sceaðen mǽl scýran môste, 3883; B. 1939. [This verb is one of the small class of verbs called preterite-present. The infin. does not occur in any of the dialects, but in the forms which are found the conjugation is the same as that of the A. S. verb. *Goth.* ga-môt; *p.* -môsta: *O. Sax.* môt; *p.* môsta: *O. Frs.* môt; *p.* môste: *O. H. Ger.* muoz, môz; *p.* muosi, muoste.]

môt-ærn, -ern, es; *n. A court-house*:—Môtern *praetorium*, Jn. Skt. Lind. 18, 28. v. gemôt-ærn.

môt-bell, e; *f. A bell rung to call an assembly together*:—Debent statim pulsatis campanis, quod Anglice vocant *mótbel*, convocare omnes et universos, quod Anglice dicunt *folcmóte*, L. Edw. Conf. Schmid, p. 509, § 4.

môtere, es; *m. One who addresses a meeting*:—Môtere *vel* maþelere *concionator*, i. *locutor*, Wrt. Voc. ii. 135, 31. On môtera ford; of môtera forde andlang môtera lace, Cod. Dip. Kmbl. iii. 313, 24. [*Prompt. Parv.* motare *or* pletare *disceptor*, p. 345, *and see note.*] v. môtian, II, III.

môt-gerêfa, an; *m. The* gerêfa *who presides at a court* or môt:—Swâ ðæt nân scýrgerêfe oððe môtgerêfe ðâr habban ǽne sôcne oððe gemôt bûton ðæs abbudes âgen hǽse (*nullus vicecomes vel praepositus*), Cod. Dip. Kmbl. iv. 200, 9. v. Kemble's Saxons in England, ii. 181, 155, note 2.

moððe, an; *f. A moth*:—Moððe *tinea*, Wrt. Voc. i. 24, 15: 78, 70. Ðǽr moððe (mohða, Lind. Rush.: mouȝþe, mouȝte, Wick.) hit fornimþ *ubi tinea demolitur*, Mt. Kmbl. 6, 19, 20: Lk. Skt. 12, 33. Moððe word fræt, Exon. 112 b; Th. 432, 4; Rä. 48, 1. Ðǽr moððan hit âwêstaþ, Wulfst. 286, 32. [*H. M.* mohðe: *Prompt. Parv.* mouȝte: *Chauc.* mouhtes; *pl.*: *Icel.* motti: *Ger.* motte.]

môt-hûs, es; *n. A house where a court* or *assembly is held*:—Dômhûs *vel* môthûs *epicausterium*, Wrt. Voc. i. 57, 52. Môthûses *prod[r]omi*, Hpt. Gl. 476, 61.

môtian; *p.* ode. I. *to address one's self, speak* (*to a person*), *converse* (v. môtung):—Man môt on eornost môtian wið his Drihten se ðe wyle ðæt wê sprecon mid weorcum wið hine *the Lord, who will have us speak to him by our deeds, must be addressed in all seriousness*, Ælfc. T. Grn. 15, 3. Ne hiwa ðû swilce ðû mid bilewitnysse mǽge ðê gân orsorh tô mǽdena hûsum and wið hî môtian ðæt ðîn môd ne beô ýfele besmiten þurh ða ýdelan spellunga *do not pretend, as if in innocency you can go secure to maidens' houses and converse with them, and your heart not be defiled through the idle conversations*, Basil admn. 7; Norm. 48, 11. Gif se munuc wyle gân tô wîfmanna hûsum and wið hý môtian, and gif ðǽm mǽdenum lîkiaþ hyra luftýman sprǽce, 48, 15. [Cf. Stille beo þu, ne schaltu motin wið me na mare, Marh. 17, 26.] II. *to address an assembly* (cf. môtere):—Herôdes hæfde gemôt . . . Mid ðam ðe hê swîðost môtode, on his dômsetle sittende (cf. Acts 12, 21: *Herod sat upon his throne, and made an oration*), Homl. Th. ii. 382, 30. III. *to discuss, dispute, moot a question* (cf. *a moot* point):—Ðû scealt gelýfan on ðone lifigendan God, and nâ ofer ðîne mǽðe môtian be him, Hexam. 3; Norm. 6, 17. [Cf. ge-môtod, *and Prompt. Parv.* mootyn *discepto, placito*; môtynge *disceptacio.*]

môt-lǽðu *in* Chart. Th. 433, 22. *The word occurs in a list of services due from the tenant of certain land, and seems to mean 'courts, assemblies'*:—Þreó môtlǽðu ungeboden on xii mônþum *the tenant must attend three courts a year without summons. In the same charter, in similar lists, occur two phrases which seem identical in meaning with that just given*, Þrîwa sêcan gemôt on xii mônþum, 433, 9, *and* iii gemôt on geáre, 433, 32. The charter is later than 1066, perhaps the *Icel.* leið *an assembly*, may be compared. Cf. also kynnis-leið *a visit to relations.*

môt-stôw, e; *f. A place of assembly, forum*:—Môtstôw on burge *forus* (*forum?*) *vel prorostra*, Wrt. Voc. i. 36, 43: 47, 22. v. gemôt-stôw.

mōtung, e; *f. Conversation, discourse:*—Of mōtunge *colloquio, sermocinatione*, Hpt. Gl. 511, 26. v. mōtian, I.

mōt-weorþ; *adj. Entitled to attend a* mōt:—Ealle ða men ða beón mōtwurðe, Cod. Dip. Kmbl. iv. 208, 32.

mucg-, mug-wyrt, e; *f.* A plant name *mug-wort*, (Scott.) *muggart, muggon*, also called *mother-wort*. In the Herbarium, Lchdm. i, three kinds of *mug-wort* are mentioned:—Mugcwyrt. Ðeós wyrt ðe man *artemisiam* and ōðrum naman mucgwyrt nemneþ (*Artemisia vulgaris*), 102, 1-3. *Herba artemisia tragonthes* ðæt is mugcwyrt (*Artemisia dracunculus tarragon*), 102, 18. Mucgwyrt. Ðeós wyrt þridde ðe wē *artemisiam leptefilos*, and ōðrum naman mucgwyrt nemdon (*Artemisia Pontica*), 104, 15-18. Mugwort was supposed to prevent weariness on a journey, v. Lchdm. i. 102, 3-7: ii. 154, 8-12. Mugwyrt *artemisia* vel *matrum herba*, Wrt. Voc. i. 36, 51: 66, 61. Mucgwyrt, ii. 8, 36. Mugwyrt *gagantes* (see above, Lchdm. i. 102, 18), i. 68, 78. Mucgwyrt, ii. 42, 40. See Lchdm. iii. 339 for other references, and Grmm. D. M. 1152.

mucxle, mūdrica. v. muscle, mȳdrece.

mūga, mūha, mūwa, an; *m. A mow* (as in barley-*mow*), *a heap* (of hay, corn):—Mūha *aceruus*, Wülck. 3, 10. Mūwan *acervum*, Wrt. Voc. ii. 6, 10. Mūwan, hreácas *acervos*, 9, 55. Gif fȳr bærne mūgan oððe standende æceras *si ignis comprehenderit acervos frugum sive stantes segetes in agris*, Ex. 22, 6. [Cf. Wrt. Voc. i. 154, 23 a mowe (reke, MS. Camb.) *une moye:* Sparewen grupen in þen *muȝen*, Laym. 29280: *Icel.* mūgi *a swathe.*]

mūl, es; *m. A mule:*—Mūl *mulus*, Wrt. Voc. i. 23, 25: 78, 10: 287, 49: ii. 56, 40. Ne beó gē nā swylce hors and mūlas, Ps. Th. 31, 10. [*From Lat.* mulus. *Icel.* mūll: *O. H. Ger.* mūl: *Ger.* maul (-thier, -esel).]

mūl-hirde, es; *m. A mule-keeper:*—Mūlhyrde *mulio*, Ælfc. Gr. 9, 3; Som. 8, 37.

munan (a pret. pres. verb); ic, hē man, ðū manst, wē munon; *p.* munde. I. *to remember, be mindful of, to be careful of:*—Til mon tiles and tomes meares *a good man thinks of, is careful of, a good and quiet horse*, Exon. 91 a; Th. 342, 12; Gn. Ex. 142. [Cf. *Icel.* muna *to remember with feelings of gratitude, hate*, etc.] II. *to consider, think:*—Fēdan hig swā swā hig sylfe wyrþe munon *let their meal be such as they consider suitable*, L. Ath. v. 8; Th. i. 236, 7. Ðæt hine God ðæs cynedōmes weorþne munde, Ps. C. 50, 150; Ps. Grn. ii. 280, 150. [*Goth.* ga-munan; *prs.* -man, *pl.* -munum; *p.* -munda *to remember: O. Sax.* far-munan; *prs.* -man, *pl.* -munun; *p.* -munsta *to despise: Icel.* muna; *prs.* man, *pl.* munum; *p.* mundi *to remember.*] v. ā-, ge-, of-, on-munan.

mund, e; *f.* I. *a hand:*—Hē cwehte mægenwudu mundum, Beo. Th. 477; B. 236: 6037; B. 3022. Merestrǣta mundum brugdon (*swam*), 1033; B. 514. Mundum brugdon scealcas of sceáðum scīrmǣled swyrd, Judth. 11; Thw. 24, 38; Jud. 229. Gif monna hwelc mundum sīnum aldre beneóteþ, Cd. 50; Th. 63, 31; Gen. 1040. Ic gefēng mid mundum mægenbyrðenne, Beo. Th. 6173; B. 3091. II. *a hand* (as a measure):—Stǣnen bedd þrȳm mundum hiérra ðonne ðæs hūses flōr, Shrn. 69, 4. III. (a) *protection* (cf. *to be in a person's hands, and* v. hand):—Wē woldon gesettan ðās bōc mannum tō getrymminge and tō munde ūs sylfum *we wished to compose this book to encourage other men, and to secure ourselves*, Homl. Skt. pref. 71. Gē orsorge wuniaþ on lande under mȳnre munde, Wulfst. 132, 16. Ða hǣðenan mid lācum heora leásra goda munde and gescyldnysse bǣdon, Homl. Th. i. 504, 19. Munde *patrocinium*, Hpt. Gl. 425, 19. Gif hȳ him syððan ne dōþ mete ne munde *if afterwards they do not feed or shelter him*, L. Edm. S. 1; Th. i. 248, 7. Gif mete and munde ðam ðe ðæs beþurfe, L. Pen. 15; Th. ii. 282, 25: Hy. 7, 48; Hy. Grn. ii. 288, 48. Hwī wēnst ðū ðæt hȳ habban nānege munde heora freónda on ðisse weorulde *why do you think that they* (*the good who are dead*) *afford no protection to their friends in this world*, Shrn. 202, 25. (b) in a technical sense, *Guardianship:*—Ðā betǣhte Ecgferþ land and bōc on cynges gewitnesse Dūnstāne arcebisceope tō mundgenne his lāfe and his bearna. Ðā hē geendod wæs ðā rād se bisceop tō ðam cynge myngude ðære munde and his gewitnesse *then Ecgferth delivered land and charter, with the witness of the king, to archbishop Dunstan, that he might act as guardian in respect to them, on behalf of his widow and children. When he died, the bishop rode to the king, and reminded him of the guardianship and his witness*, Chart. Th. 208, 10-18. (c) in a personal sense, *A protector, guardian* (cf. mund-bora, mundbyrdness, II):—Ðæt hē beó ðǣrtō geheald and mund under mē, Chart. Th. 391, 17. Ic wile ðæt Ælfhelm sȳ hire mund and ðæs landes, 545, 23. Ic wille ðæt Ælfrīc and Ælfhelm bēn mund and freónd intō ðære stōwe, 547, 37. Ic eom ðæs mynstres mund and upheald, Cod. Dip. Kmbl. iv. 232, 7. [Bē Alfrīc and Tofi and Ðrunni ðese quides mundes, Chart. Th. 567, 1.] IV. as a technical term in the laws, (a) *protection, guardianship* extended by the king to the subject, *the king's peace*, by the head of a family to its members:—Gif man his mæn freóls gefe freólsgefa āge munde ðare hīna *if a man give his slave freedom, let him who gives the freedom be the guardian of the freedman's family*, L. Wih. 8; Th. i. 38, 16. Ðonne ðæt gedōn sȳ ðonne rǣre man cyninges munde ðæt is ðæt hȳ ealle gemǣnum handum of ǣgðere mǣgþe on ānum wǣpne ðam sēmende syllan ðæt cyninges mund stande *when that is done, then let the king's peace be declared, that is, that they all of either kindred, with their hands in common upon one weapon, engage to the mediator that the king's peace shall not be broken*, L. E. G. 12; Th. i. 174, 20-22: L. Edm. S. 7; Th. i. 250, 19. Be munde. Hwīlum wǣron heáfodstedas and heálīce hādas micelre mǣþe and munde wyrþe and griðian mihton ða ðe ðæs beþorf[ton] (*they were entitled to afford protection, and might give 'grið' to those that needed it*), L. Eth. vii. 3; Th. i. 330, 7: Wulfst. 157, 19. Se ærcebiscop spæc tō mē ymbe Xp̄es circean freóls, ðæt heó hæfþ nū læsse munde ðonne hió hwīlan ǣr hæfde, Chart. Th. 308, 20. [Ich wille ðat hié habben alsuā hiere rigte ðane tūn mid alsuā muchele munde alsuā on mēseluen stant, Cod. Dip. Kmbl. iv. 204, 7.] (b) *the fine paid for violation of* mund, cf. mund-bryce, mund-byrd:—Mund ðare betstan widuwan eorlcundre, L. scillinga gebēte, L. Ethb. 75; Th. i. 20, 10. Gif man widuwan unāgne genimeþ, ii gelde seó mund sȳ, 76; Th. i. 20, 14. Heáfodmynstres griðbryce bēte man be cyninges munde, ðæt is mid .v. pundum (*let the fine be as in the case of breach of the king's* mund, cf. gif hwā cynges mundbrice gewyrce, gebēte ðæt mid .v. pundum, L. Eth. vii. 11; Th. i. 330, 29), L. Eth. ix. 5; Th. i. 342, 1: L. C. E. 3; Th. i. 360, 19. Gif hwā folces fyrdscip āwyrde, gebēte ðæt georne, and cyninge ða munde, L. Eth. vi. 34; Th. i. 324, 6. [*O. Sax.* mund *hand: Icel.* mund; *f. hand* (mostly poetry); also *hand* (a measure): *O. Frs.* mund *guardianship*; also *a guardian: O. H. Ger.* munt *palmus, cubitus; protectio; protector*, Grff. ii. 815: 813. v. Grmm. R. A. 447.] v. fēðe-mund. The word also is found in proper names, e. g. Eád-mund.

mund (?):—Hū ic fǣmnanhād mund inne geheóld and eác mōdor gewearþ Meotodes suna, Exon. 9 a; Th. 6, 32: Cri. 93.

mund-beorh, -beorges; *m. A sheltering hill:*—Hī (*Jerusalem*) synd mundbeorgas micle ymbūtan, Ps. Th. 124, 2.

mund-bora, an; *m.* I. *one who can give protection* (mund), *a protector, patron, guardian, advocate:*—Forspeca *vel* mundbora *advocatus, patronus* vel *interpellator*, Wrt. Voc. i. 57, 42. Mundbora *patronus*, ii. 67, 24: *subfragator*, 121, 55; Ep. Gl. 24 b, 31: *advocatus*, Hpt. Gl. 466, 73. (a) applied to the Deity:—Se ðe (*Christ*) is ūre mundbora, Homl. Th. i. 350, 25: Exon. 120 b; Th. 463, 24; Hö. 75: 68 a; Th. 251, 36; Jul. 156. Drihten ðīn mundbora *Dominus protectio tua*, Ps. Th. 120, 5. Ūres mundboran (*Christ*) lāre folgian, Blickl. Homl. 169, 17: (*God*), Exon. 40 b; Th. 134, 25; Gū. 514: 8 a; Th. 2, 33; Cri. 28. (b) to angels or saints:—Tō ðæm heáhengle Michaele, swā tō ðæm getreówestan mundboran, Blickl. Homl. 201, 27. Hē (*Dives*) ðone wolde habban him tō mundboran, ðam ðe hē nolde ǣr his cruman syllan, Homl. Th. i. 330, 27. (c) to earthly kings:—Wes ðū (*Hrothgar*) mundbora mīnum magoþegnum, Beo. Th. 2964; B. 1480. Eádmund cyning, māga mundbora, Chr. 942; Edm. 2. Eádgār, West-Seaxena wine, Myrcene mundbora, 975; Erl. 125, 17. Eást-Engla cyning and seó þeód gesōhte Ecgbryht him tō mundboran, 823; Erl. 62, 25: 921; Erl. 108, 14. Sceal him (*an ecclesiastic or a foreigner who was wronged*) cyng beón oððon eorl and bisceop for mǣg and for mundboran, L. E. G. 12; Th. i. 174, 8: L. Eth. ix. 33: Th. i. 348, 6: L. C. S. 40; Th. i. 400, 6. II. *a guardian* (of things):—Ðara māðma mundbora wæs, Beo. Th. 5552; B. 2779. [*O. Sax.* mund-boro: *O. L. Ger.* mundboro *municeps: O. H. Ger.* munt-poro *patronus, protector.*]

mund-bryce, es; *m.* I. *a breach of* mund (v. mund, IV):—Wē cwǣdon be mundbrice, se ðe hit dō, ðæt hē þolige ealles ðæs ðe hē āge, L. Edm. S. 6; Th. i. 250, 9. Gif hwā cynges mundbrice gewyrce, gebēte ðæt mid v. pundum, L. Eth. vii. 11; Th. i. 330, 29. On Centlande æt ðam mundbryce (*for the offence*), v. pund ðam cingce, and þreó ðam arcebiscope, L. C. E. 3; Th. i. 360, 20. II. *the fine paid for the offence to the authority whose* mund *was violated:*—Ðis syndon ða gerihta ðe se cyning āh ofer ealle men on Wessexan, ðæt is, mundbryce . . . , L. C. S. 12; Th. i. 382, 13. Gif hwā folces fyrdscip āmyrre ðæt hit ǣnote weorþe forgilde hit fullīce and cyninge ðone mundbrice (*pay the fine to the king for the offence*), L. Eth. vi. 34; Th. i. 324, 7. Bēte cynincge be fullan mundbryce, 42; Th. i. 400, 24: L. C. E. 2; Th. i. 360, 5. On Cantwara lage cyning and arcebiscop āgan gelīcne and efendȳrne mundbryce, L. Eth. vii. 6; Th. i. 330, 18. Myndbræcas and ǣlces wȳtes, Chart. Th. 333, 33.

mund-byrd, e; *f.* (v. mund, mund-bora). I. *protection, patronage, aid:*—Mundbyrd *suffragium*, Ep. Gl. 24 b, 32: *patrocinium*, Wrt. Voc. i. 288, 59: ii. 66, 53: 116, 3: Hpt. Gl. 497, 59. Hē þancaþ Gode his mundbyrde, ðonne hē hine of hwylcum earfoþum ālysed hæfþ, Ps. Th. 17, arg. Se ðe him ēcean Godes tō mundbyrde miht gestreóneþ *qui sperat in Domino*, 83, 13: Cd. 83; Th. 105, 14; Gen. 1753. Mundbyrde and fultome *presidio*, Wrt. Voc. ii. 67, 41. Under mundbyr[d]e *sub pretextu*, 79, 84: 84, 15. Ic mundbyrd on ðē hæfde *tu es meus protector*, Ps. Th. 70, 5. Heó funde mundbyrd æt ðam mǣran þeódne, Judth. 9; Thw. 21, 2; Jud. 3: Andr. Kmbl. 1447; An. 724: Exon.

35 a; Th. 113, 11; Gū. 113. Gif ðū ðē tō swā mildum (*heathen gods*) mundbyrd sēcest, 68 a; Th. 252, 29; Jul. 170. Ða mundbyrde (*patrocinium*) ðæs fērendan fæder tō Drihtne, Bd. 5, 22; S. 644, 41. Geornlīce mundbyrde gelȳfaþ tō ðære stōwe (*a church*), Blickl. Homl. 207, 3. Ðæt folc beág tō Eádwearde cyninge and sōhton his friþ and his mundbyrde, Chr. 921; Erl. 108, 2. Ūs gehǣl mid mundbyrdum *nos salva patrociniis*, Hymn. Surt. 111, 44. II. *the fine paid for a violation of* mund (v. mund, IV a, b; mund-bryce, II):—Cyninges mundbyrd .L. scillinga, L. Ethb. 8; Th. i. 6, 1: 15; Th. i. 6, 12. Ciricean mundbyrd .L. scill. swā cinges, L. Wih. 2; Th. i. 36, 17. Scyldig (*liable to pay*) cyninges mundbyrde, L. Alf. pol. 5 Th. i. 64, 11. Forgylde ðem mæn his mundbyrd (*the fine for violating the man's* mund *by fighting in his house*), L. H. E. 14; Th. i. 32, 15: L. Ath. iv. 4; Th. i. 224, 1. [*O. Sax. O. L. Ger.* mund-burd: *O. H. Ger.* mundi-burd.]

mundbyrdan. v. ge-mundbyrdan.

mundbyrdness, e; *f.* I. *protection*:—Ic fare swā hwyder swā ðū mē tō mundbyrdnysse gerecst *I will go whithersoever thou dost direct for my protection*, Glostr. Frag. 106, 24. II. in a personal sense (v. mund, III b), *A protector, patron, advocate*:—Ic ðē mē tō mundbyrdnysse geceóse wið ðīn āgen bearn *I choose thee for my advocate with thy own child*, 106, 19. Swā swā ic ǣr cwæþ ðīnre ðære līcwurþan mundbyrdnysse, 108, 16. III. *a protection of rights granted by charter*:—Ic wille ðæt ðeós mundbyrdnesse beó strang *volo ut haec confirmatio vim obtineat*, Cod. Dip. Kmbl. iv. 202, 20: 205, 7. Icc nelle ðat any man ðās mundbyrdnesse tōbreke, 213, 19.

mund-cræft, es; *m. Power of hand* or *power to protect*:—Cunne ic his mihta, his mægen, and his mihta, and his mundcræftas, Lchdm. i. 384, 13.

mund-gripe, es; *m. Hand-gripe, grasp*:—Ðæt hē þrittiges manna mægencræft on his mundgripe hæbbe, Beo. Th. 766; B. 380. Strenge getrūwode, mundgripe mægenes, 3072; B. 1534. Æfter mundgripe, 3880; B. 1938. Ðæt hē ne mētte middangeardes on elran men mundgripe māran, 1510; B. 753.

mund-heáls, -hāls, e; *f.* (?) *Safety which comes from the protection* (mund) *afforded by another* (?):—Ðā se ælmihtiga ācenned wearþ siððan hē Marian mundheáls geceás *when Christ was born, after he had chosen a safe retreat in Mary's protecting womb*, Exon. 14 a; Th. 28, 14; Cri. 446.

mundian; *p.* ode. I. *to protect, shelter, guard*:—Se ðe ðē mundaþ swā swā fæder, Homl. Th. i. 274, 6: Exon. 36 a; Th. 117, 28; Gū. 231. Baldwine geaf Ælfgife wununge on Bricge and hē hī mundode and heóld ða hwīle ðe heó ðǣr wæs, Chr. 1037; Erl. 167, 4. Cristenum cyninge gebyreþ ðæt hē Godes āre mundie, Wulfst. 266, 17. II. in a technical sense, *To act as guardian*. v. mund, III b. [*O. Sax.* mundōn: *O. H. Ger.* muntōn *defendere*.] v. ā-, ge-mundian.

mundiend, es; *m. A protector, guardian*:—Ic hine bidde ðæt hē mīn fulla freónd and mundiend beó on mīnum dege, Chart. Th. 525, 8.

mund-leów, (-leáw?), -laú, -leú, e; *f. A basin for washing the hands*:—Mundlaú *vescada* (among things belonging to the table), Wrt. Voc. i. 290, 68. Mundleú, ii. 123, 22: *conca* (cf. *Ital.* conca *a laver*: *Span.* cuenca *a wooden bowl*), 105, 7. Mundleów *conca, coclea*, 136, 15. [*Icel.* mund-laug *a basin for washing the hands, especially before and after a meal*.]

mund-rōf; *adj. Ready* or *active with the hands*:—Þegn mægenstrong and mundrōf, Exon. 129 a; Th. 495, 5; Rā. 84, 3.

munec, munecian, munecenu. v. munuc, munucian, mynecenu.

munt, es; *m.* [*from Lat.* mons] *A mount, hill, mountain*:—Munt *mons*, Wrt. Voc. i. 54, 4. Wæs se munt Garganus bifigende, Homl. Th. i. 504, 28. Tō Oliuetes muntes nyðerstige, Lk. Skt. 19, 37. Ofer ðæs muntes cnæpp, 4, 29: Ex. 19, 20. Ne mæg hūs on munte lange gelǣstan, Bt. Met. Fox 7, 36; Met. 7, 18. Munte *promontorio*, Hpt. Gl. 420, 6. Munt *Scyllam*, 529, 20. Ābūtan ðone munt, Ex. 19, 12. Ðæra munta cnollas, Gen. 8, 5. Tō ðām muntum, 14, 10. On heán muntum heortas wuniaþ, Ps. Th. 103, 17. On heálīcum muntum, Homl. Th. ii. 160, 29. Ðā ðā hē com tō muntum, ðā gemētten hine sceaþan, 502, 24. Tō Alpes ðǣm muntum, Ors. 4, 8; Swt. 186, 16. Ofer ða muntas ðe Caucaseas wē hātaþ, Bt. 18, 2; Fox 64, 10: Gen. 8, 4. v. fore-munt.

munt-ælfen, e; *f. A mountain-nymph*:—Muntælfen *oreades*, Wrt. Voc. i. 60, 14.

munt-geóf, -iōf, -giōp, es; *m. The Alps*:—Muntiōfes clifu *Alpes*, Wrt. Voc. ii. 9, 41. From muntgiōp ōð ðone mǣran wearoþ (cf. betwux ðām muntum and Sicilia, Bt. 1; Fox 2, 4), Bt. Met. Fox 1, 27; Met. 1, 14. Ðā wæs ofer muntgiōp monig ātyhted, 1, 15; Met. 1, 8. Hē com tō Alpis ðǣm muntum . . . and ðone weg geworhte ofer munt Iōf, Ors. 4, 8; Swt. 186, 18. Muntgeófa *Alpium*, Wrt. Voc. ii. 2, 27.

munt-land, es; *n. A hilly country*:—Fērde on muntland *abiit in montana*, Lk. Skt. 1, 39.

munuc, munec, es; *m.* [*Lat.* monachus] *A monk*:—Munuc *monachus*, Wrt. Voc. i. 42, 19. Ic Ælfrīc munuc and mæssepreóst, Homl. Th. i. 2, 12: Bd. 5, 12; S. 630, 41. Be ðām ðe munecum heora feoh būtan leáfe befæstaþ. Gif mon ōðres monnes munuce feoh ōðfæste, būtan ðæs munuces hlāfordes lēfnesse, L. Alf. pol. 20; Th. i. 74, 13–16. Swā swā dafnaþ munuce, Coll. Monast. Th. 35, 5. Ic eom geanwyrde monuc *professus sum monachum*, 18, 28. Godes þeówas, biscopas, abbudas, munecas, preóstas, L. Eth. v. 4; Th. i. 304, 26. Wē willaþ ðæt munecas regollīcor libban ðonne hī nū ǣr ðisan on gewunan hæfdon, ix. 31; Th. i. 346, 27. Muneca gehwylc ðe ūte sȳ of mynstre and regoles ne gȳme . . . gebūge georne intō mynstre, v. 5; Th. i. 306, 1. Be munuca cynne. Feówer synt muneca cyn, R. Ben. 9, 2–3. Syx synt muneca cynerena, 134, 3. Hē beád, ðæt nān his bearna ðæt menster leng mid preóstan gesette, ac ðæt hit ēfre mid munecan stōde, Chart. Th. 227, 17. Hē sende Godes þeów Agustinum and ōðre monige munecas, Bd. 1, 23; S. 485, 27. [*Icel.* mūnkr: *O. H. Ger.* munich.] v. mynster-munuc.

munuc-cild, es; *n. A boy that is being brought up to be a monk*:—Sum munuccild drohtnode on his mynstre, and hæfde micele lufe tō his fæder and tō his mēder. Swīðor for ðære sibbe ðonne for Godes dǣle wearþ ðā oflangod, and arn of mynstre tō his māgum, Homl. Th. ii. 174, 33. Ān munuccild wunode on Mauricius mynstre . . . hæfde ðæt munuccild swīðe mǣrlīce stemne, Wulfst. 152, 7–11: 22.

munuc-gegerela, an; *m. A monastic dress*:—Gegyrede hine mid his munucgegyrelan, Bd. 1, 7; S. 477, 10.

munuc-hād, es; *m. Monk-hood, the monastic state* (of women as well as of men):—Munuchād and abbudhād syndon on ōðre wīsan (*different from the seven orders previously mentioned*), L. Ælfc. C. 18; Th. ii. 348, 31. Ǣgðer ge preósthādes ge munuchādes menn *both the secular and regular clergy*, Homl. Th. ii. 126, 16. Wæs sum mæssepreóst munuchādes *quidam monachus*, Bd. 5, 12; S. 630, 41, MS. B. Hē weoruldhad forlǣte and munuchāde (*habitum monachicum*) onfēnge, 4, 24; S. 598, 2. Of munuchāde on bisceophāde gecorene *de monachorum collegio in episcopatus gradum adsciti*, 4, 12; S. 581, 21: Blickl. Homl. 219, 32. Seó ǣrest wīfa is sǣd in Norþanhymbra mǣgþe ðæt heó munuchāde and hāligrifte onfēnge *quae prima feminarum fertur in provincia Nordanhymbrorum propositum vestemque sanctimonialis habitus suscepisse*, Bd. 4, 23; S. 593, 23.

munuc-heáp, es; *m. A band of monks, the monks of a monastery*:—Ān abbod . . . mid eallum his munucheápe, Anglia viii. 325, 43.

munucian; *p.* ode *To make a person a monk*:—Hē hine mōt munecian *se monachum potest facere*, L. Ecg. C. 27; Th. ii. 152, 13.

munuc-līc; *adj. Monastic*:—On munuclīcre drohtnunge *in monachica conversatione*, Swt. A. S. Rdr. 96, 46: Bd. 4, 11; S. 579, 2: 4, 27; S. 603, 24. Hē wolde ārǣran on his biscoprīce munuclīcne regol, Homl. Skt. 6, 59. Healdan his munuclīce scrūdware, L. Eth. v. 6; Th. i. 306, 9. Hē heóld his munelīce ingehȳd swā ðeáh betwux mannum *he preserved the habit of mind which he had when a monk though mixing with men*, Homl. Th. ii. 506, 13. On munuclīcum hādum *in monachico habitu*, Bd. 5, 19; S. 636, 21.

munuc-līce; *adv. Monastically, after the manner of a monk*:—Hē munuclīce leofode betwux ðām lǣwedan folce, Swt. A. S. Rdr. 97, 67.

munuc-līf, es; *n.* I. *the monastic life*:—Monige of Breotone for intingan munuclīfes (*monachicae conversationis gratia*) gewunedon sēcan Francna mynstro, Bd. 3, 8; S. 531, 17. Hē in heardnesse munuclīfes lifde *in monachica districtione vitam duxit*, 4, 26; S. 602, 40. Man on munuclīfe gelǣred *viro monachica vita instituto*, 3, 21; S. 551, 40: (*of a woman*), 4, 23; S. 593, 1. Hē munuclīfe swīðor lifde ðonne lǣwedes mannes, Blickl. Homl. 213, 10. Hē ārǣrde mynster and munuclīf *he established a monastery and monastic discipline*, Homl. Skt. 6, 146. Munuclīf lǣdan, dōn *monachicam vitam ducere, agere*, Bd. 3, 27; S. 558, 7: (*of a woman*), 4, 23; S. 593, 19. Hē sundorlīf and munuclīf wæs foreberende *vitam privatam et monachicam praeferens*, 4, 11; S. 579, 8. II. *the place in which the monastic life is lived, a monastery*:—Hē ārǣrde him munuclīf . . . Ðæt mynster hē gelōgode mid wellybbendum mannum, ðæt wǣron hundeahtatig muneca, Homl. Th. ii. 506, 14. Hē ārǣrde six munuclīf on Sicilia lande, and ðæt seofoþe binnan Rōmāna burh getimbrode, on ðam hē sylf regollīce under abbodes hǣsum drohtnode, 118, 27: Ors. 6, 34; Swt. 290, 4. Munuclīfa *coenobiorum, monasteriorum*, Hpt. Gl. 412, 22. Aþelwold biscop æft ða lāre (*Latin*) on munuclīfum ārǣrde, Ælfc. Gr. pref.; Som. 1, 42. [Cf. *Icel.* mūnk-līfi *a monastery*.]

munuc-regol, es; *m.* I. *the rule of a monastic order*:—Basilius āwrāt munucregol, Homl. Skt. 3, 145. II. *the monastic order which observes a certain rule*:—Ic geann intō ǣlcum munucregole .i. pund, Chart. Th. 544, 12.

munuc-stōw, e; *f. A place for monks*; locus monachorum, Bd. 3, 24; S. 556, 42.

munuc-wīse, an; *f. The manner of monks*:—On munucwīsan gescrȳd, Homl. Skt. 6, 247.

mūr, es; *m. A wall*:—Burstan mūras and stānas, Exon. 24 b; Th. 70, 23; Cri. 1143. [*O. Sax. O. L. Ger.* mūra; *f.*: *O. Frs.* mūre; *f.*: *O. H. Ger.* mūra, murī; *f.*: *M. H. Ger.* mūre, mūr; *f.*: *Ger.* mauer; *f.*: *Icel.* mūrr; *m.* all from Latin *murus*.]

murcen (?); *adj. Sad, complaining*:—Ða ðe murcne ǣr hungur heardne geþoledan, Ps. Th. 145, 6. [v. murcian, murcnian, *and* cf. *for* *similar relation* murnan *and* un-murne, Ps. Th. 75, 4; *also* weoren Bruttes bliðe an mode þæ ær weoren *murne*, Laym. 16159.]

murcian; *p.* ode *To grieve, complain, repine*:—Hwī murcnast (MS. Bod. murcas) ðū wið mīn *quid tu reum me quotidianis agis querelis?* Bt. 7, 3; Fox 20, 3. Murcaþ forðȳ ðæt hē Gode nolde þeówian *gemunt homines quod Deo servire noluerunt*, Past. 36, 3; Swt. 250, 16. Ðæt hī him ondrǣden and murkien for hira unfullfremednesse *ut imperfectionis suae taedio tabescant*, 65, 6; Swt. 467, 13. Sōna swā ic ðē on ðisse unrōtnesse geseah ðus murciende (Cott. MS. murcniende) *cum te moestum lacrymantemque vidissem*, Bt. 5, 1; Fox 8, 27. v. murcung, murcnian.

murcnere, es; *m. One who murmurs*:—On ēcum wīte mid ðām murcnerum, R. Ben. 21, 5.

murcnian; *p.* ode *To murmur, complain, repine, grieve*:—Hwæt murcnast ðū æfter ðæm ðe ðū forlure oððe tō hwon fagnast ðū ðæs ðe ðū ǣr hæfdest *quid est, quod vel amissis doleas, vel laeteris retentis?* Bt. 14, 2; Fox 42, 31: 7, 3; Fox 20, 3 (v. murcian). Hī murcniaþ ł geómriaþ *murmurabunt*, Ps. Spl. 58, 17. Gē murcnodon *murmurastis*, Deut. 1, 27. Ne murcniaþ, Jn. Skt. 6, 43. Ðā ongunnon hig murcnian ongēn ðone hīrēdes ealdor, Mt. Kmbl. 20, 11. Ðonne onginþ hē tō murcnienne, and þincþ him tō lang hwænne hē beó genumen of ðyses līfes earfoþnyssum, Homl. Th. i. 140, 19. Ða Pharisēi gehȳrdon ða menigeo ðus murcnigende be him, Jn. Skt. 7, 32: Bt. 5, 1; Fox 8, 27 (v. murcian). v. be-murcnian.

murcnung, e; *f. Complaint, murmuring*:—Ðā gehȳrde Drihten folces murcnunge (*murmurationes*), Ex. 16, 11. Ic syngede þurh tale and þurh murcnunge (*per detractionem et per murmurationem*), Confess. Pecc. Wōplīcum murcnungum *flebilibus questibus*, Hpt. Gl. 518, 26. Hiófum, murcnungum *questibus*, 472, 64.

murcung, e; *f. Complaint, grief, murmuring*:—Hwæt is eówer murcung (*murmur*) wið unc? Past. 28, 6; Swt. 201, 5. Mid suā micelre murcunga his āgen mōd gedrēfþ *tanto mentem moerore conturbat*, 33, 7; Swt. 227, 19. Ðæt hié weorþen on murcunga and on ungeþylde *ad impatientiae murmurationem proruunt*, 45, 3; Swt. 341, 3. Hȳ ðē willaþ on murcunga gebringan ðonne hié ðē fram hweorfaþ *fortuna cum discesserit allatura moerorem*, Bt. 7, 2; Fox 18, 19 note.

murge. v. mirige.

murnan; *p.* de. I. *intrans. To mourn, be sad, be anxious*:—Gif ðū ðonne heora þegen beón wilt and ðē heora þeáwas līciaþ tō hwon myrnst ðū swā swīðe *si probas, utere moribus, ne queraris*, Bt. 7, 2; Fox 18, 7. Sēlre biþ ǣghwæm ðæt hē his freónd wrece, ðonne hē fela murne, Beo. Th. 2775; B. 1385. Ðæt mīn murnende mōd, Bt. 3, 1; Fox 4, 18: Beo. Th. 99; B. 50: Andr. Kmbl. 3332; An. 1669: Exon. 101 a; Th. 380, 28; Rä. 1, 15. Geómor sefa, hyge murnende, 15 a; Th. 31, 24; Cri. 500. Cwom seó murnende Maria, 119 b; Th. 459, 33; Hö. 9: 121 a; Th. 464, 22; Hö. 91. Bonan gnornedon, mǣndon murnende, 38 b; Th. 128, 8; Gū. 401. Murnan on mōde *to be sad at heart*, Cd. 35; Th. 45, 31; Gen. 735: Judth. 11; Thw. 23, 33; Jud. 154. Hī murnaþ on mōde, Cd. 169; Th. 212, 6; Exod. 535. Ne beó ðū on sefan tō forht, ne on mōde ne murn *be not fearful of mind, nor anxious of heart*, Andr. Kmbl. 197; An. 99. II. *with prepositions* for, æfter:—Ne mæg nā for feore murnan se ðe wrecan þenceþ freán *not for life must he care that his lord will avenge*, Byrht. Th. 139, 25; By. 259. Ne murn ðū for ðī mēce ðe wearþ māðma cyst, Wald. 1, 44; Vald. 1, 24. Hyge wæs oncyrred ðæt hié ne murndon æfter mandreáme *the mind was o'erthrown, so that after the glad life of men they longed not*, Andr. Kmbl. 73; An. 37. III. *trans.* (a) *To mourn, lament*:—Sum sceal murnan meotudgesceaft mōde gebysgad *the Maker's decree shall one mourn, troubled in mind*, Exon. 87 b; Th. 328, 19; Vy. 20: Salm. Kmbl. 971; Sal. 485. (b) *to care about, regard*:—Se ðe hiora welt ne murnþ nāuþer ne friénd ne fiénd ðē mā ðe wēdende hund *he that rules them regards neither friend nor foe any more than he would a mad dog* (cf. se hlāford ne scrīfþ freónde ne feónde, Met. 25, 15), Bt. 37, 1; Fox 186, 7. [*A.R.* murnen; *p.* murnede: *Laym.* murnede; *p.*: *Piers P.* mornede; *p.*: *Goth.* maurnan μεριμνᾶν: *O.Sax.* mornōn: *Icel.* morna: *O.H.Ger.* mornēn *moereo*; *part.* mornēnti *moestus*.] v. be-murnan, meornan.

murnung, e; *f. Grief, anxiety*, Bt. 7, 2; Fox 18, 19. v. murcung (last passage).

murra, myrra, an; *m. Cicely*:—Murra hātte wyrt, Lchdm. ii. 18, 3. Nim murran ða wyrt, iii. 8, 1. Myrran, 14, 20.

murre *myrrh*. v. myrre.

mūs, e; *f.* I. *a mouse*:—Muus *mus*, Wrt. Voc. ii. 114, 41. Mūs *sorex*, i. 23, 31: *mus* vel *sorex*, 78, 23. Ðeós mūs *hic mus*, Ælfc. Gr. 9, 33; Som. 12, 20. Gif gē gesāwen hwelce mūs ðæt wǣre hlāford ofer ōðre mȳs, Bt. 16, 2; Fox 52, 2. Mȳs *sorices*, Wrt. Voc. ii. 87, 73. [Ðæt gewrit beó geworpen mūsen tō gnagene, Chart. Th. 318, 28.] II. *a muscle*:—Mūs ðæs earmes *torus* vel *musculus* vel *lacertus*, Wrt. Voc. i. 43, 48. [*Icel.* mūs, *pl.* mȳss *a mouse*; also *a muscle*: *O. H. Ger.* mūs *mouse*; *muscle*: *Ger.* maus *mouse*; *muscle*: *Gk.* μῦς *mouse*; *muscle*.] v. hreáðe-, hrēre-, scirfe-, sise-mūs; mūse-pise.

muscelle, muscle, muxle, musle, an; *f.* [from Latin] *A muscle* or *mussel, a shell-fish*:—Muscle *muscula*, Wrt. Voc. ii. 57, 76. Muxle, i. 77, 71: *geniscula*, 281, 62. Mucxle, 65, 68: ii. 41, 19. Musclan scil *conca*, 15, 35. Of muscellan *de conca*, 26, 39: 75, 71: 89, 35. Musclan, Hpt. Gl. 417, 9. Hēr beóþ oft numene missenlīcra cynna muscule (muslena, note), Bd. 1, 1; S. 473, 17. Muslan *musculos*, Coll. Monast. Th. 24, 11. [*O.H. Ger.* muscula; *f.*]

musc-fleotan. v. must-fleóge.

mūse-pise, an; *f. Mouse-pea, a vetch*:—Mūsepise *vicia*, Wrt. Voc. i. 38, 55.

mūs-fealle, an; *f. A mouse-trap*:—Muusfalle *muscipula*, Wrt. Voc. ii. 114, 34. Mūsfealle *pelx*, 71, 28. [*Prompt. Parv.* mows-falle: *O. H. Ger.* mūs-falla; *f. muscipula*: *Ger.* mäuse-falle.]

mūs-fealu; *adj. Mouse-coloured*:—Mūsfealu, bleóreád *myrteus*, Wrt. Voc. ii. 58, 8. [*Ger.* mäuse-fahl.]

mūs-hafoc, es; *n. A mouse-hawk*:—Mūshafoc *siricarius*, Wrt. Voc. i. 62, 17: *suricarius*, 280, 21. Mūshabuc *soricarius*, ii. 120, 81.

must, es; *m.* (?) *Must, new wine*:—Must *mustum* (cf. nīwe wīn *mustum*, 27, 47), Wrt. Voc. i. 82, 36. Must mid hunig gemenged *inomellum*, 27, 45. Heortan manna must and wīndrinc myclum blissaþ *vinum laetificet cor hominis*, Ps. Th. 103, 14. Ne miht ðū wīn wringan on midne winter, deáh ðē wel lyste wearmes mustes, Bt. 5, 2; Fox 10, 32. Ðās men sindon mid muste fordrencte ('*these men are full of new wine*,' Acts 2, 13), Homl. Th. i. 314, 21. [*O. H. Ger.* most; *m.*: *Ger.* most; *m.* From Latin.]

must-fleóge, an; *f. A small fly found in wine*; bibio, parva musca quae in vino nascitur:—Mustfleógan (muscfleotan, Wrt.) *bibiones*, *mustiones*, Wrt. Voc. i. 23, 74. Cf. bibulus musti bibiones (Anglice *myntys*) arcet amurca, 176, 24.

mūþ, es; *m.* I. of persons, (a) *The mouth*:—Mūþ *os*, Wrt. Voc. i. 64, 52. Mūþes hrōf *palatum*, 64, 58. Gān[i]gende mūþe *hiulco rostro*, ii. 79, 34. Hē for ðȳ sāre ne mihte his hand tō mūþe gedōn *could not put his hand to his mouth*, Bd. 3, 2; S. 525, 4. Eall ðæt on ðone mūþ gǣþ, gǣþ on ða wambe, Mt. Kmbl. 15, 17. Mūþum *buccis*, Wrt. Voc. ii. 12, 16. (b) *the mouth* as an instrument of speech:—Be ǣlcon worde ðe of Godes mūþe gǣþ, Mt. Kmbl. 4, 4. Hē æt his sylfes mūþe gehȳrde, Bd. 3, 27; S. 558, 40. Mūþas ealle ða unriht sprecaþ *os loquentium iniqua*, Ps. Th. 62, 9. (c) *the face*:—Ic sprece tō him mūþe tō mūþe, Num. 12, 8. II. of things, *A mouth, opening, orifice*:—Ǣlces kynnes mūþ *orificium*, Wrt. Voc. i. 19, 57: Exon. 108 b; Th. 415, 10; Rä. 33, 9. Duru sceal on healle, rūm recedes mūþ, Menol. Fox 533; Gn. C. 37. Gif mon biþ on hrif wund . . . gif hē þurhwund biþ, æt gehweðerum mūþe twentig scill., L. Alf. pol. 61; Th. i. 96. 12. Beleác heofonrīces weard merehūses mūþ (*the door of the ark*), Cd. 69; Th. 82, 18; Gen. 1364. [*Goth.* munþs: *Icel.* munnr, mūðr: *O. Sax.* mūð: *O. Frs.* muth, mund: *O. H. Ger.* mund.]

mūþa, an; *m.* I. *the mouth of a river*:—Ðǣr ligeþ se mūþa ūt on ðone gārsecg ðære ié ðe mon hāteþ Gandis (*ostia fluminis Gangis*) . . . Be sūþan ðæm mūþan is se port Caligardamana . . . be norþan ðæm Gandes mūþan is se port Samera. Be norþan ðæm porte is se mūþa ðære ié . . . Ottorogorre, Ors. 1, 1; Swt. 10, 6-13. On Limene mūþan . . . Se mūþa is on eástweardre Cent . . . On ða eá hī tugon up hiora scipu ōþ ðone weald, iiii mīla fram ðæm mūþan ūtanweardum, Chr. 893; Erl. 88, 25-32. Ǣlc ceápscip friþ hæbbe ðe binnan mūþan cumau, L. Eth. ii. 2; Th. i. 284, 20: ii. 3; Th. i. 286, 6. Ofer Humbre mūþan, Chr. 867; Erl. 72, 7. On sūþhealfe Sæfern mūþan . . . ōþ Afene mūþan, 918; Erl. 104, 4-5: Bd. 5, 24; S. 647, 20. Ofer ðone mūþan *trans fretum*, Mt. Kmbl. 8, 18, 28. On hwelcum wæterum and on ǣghwelcra eá mūþum hī sculun sēcan fiscas, Bt. 32, 3; Fox 118, 19. II. *an opening, door*:—Recedes mūþan, Beo. Th. 1452; B. 724. [*Icel.* munni *mouth* (of a cave, etc.).] v. ge-mȳþe.

mūþ-ādl, e; *f. A mouth-disease*:—Mūþādl on gōman *mentedra* vel *oscedo*, Wrt. Voc. i. 43, 64: ii. 58, 7. v. mūþ-coþu.

mūþ-bana, an; *m. One who destroys with the mouth*:—Him Grendel wearþ tō mūþbonan, leófes mannes līc eall forswealg, Beo. Th. 4165; B. 2079.

mūþ-bersting, e; *f. A breaking out about the mouth*:—Mūþberstingc (*in a list of diseases*) *frenus* (cf. *frenusculi*, ulcera circa rictum oris, similia his quae fiunt jumentis asperitate frenorum, Isid. 4, orig. 8), Wrt. Voc. i. 20, 14. Mūþbersting, ii. 39, 17. Mūþberstung, 150, 56.

mūþ-coþu, e; *f. A mouth-disease*; oscedo (=oris ulcus), Wrt. Voc. i. 20, 13: ii. 64, 2.

mūþ-freó; *adj. At liberty to speak*:—Hwī ne synt wē mūþfreó? hū ne mōton wē sprecan ðæt wē willaþ, Ps. Th. 11, 4.

mūþ-hǣl, es; *n. Salutary words pronounced by the mouth*:—Mōdiges (*Moses*) mūþhǣl (cf. ēce rǣdas Moyses sægde, Th. 210, 15-17), Cd. 170; Th. 213, 14; Exod. 552.

mūþ-hrōf, es; *m. The roof of the mouth, palate*:—Mūþhrōfe *palato*, Hpt. 414, 22.

mūþ-leás, *adj. Without a mouth*:—Ic sceolde mūþleás sprecan, Exon. 123 a; Th. 472, 1; Rä. 61, 9.

mūtian. v. bi-mūtian.

mūtung, e; *f. A loan* (?):—Mūtung *vel* wrixlung *mutuum*, Wrt. Voc.

ii. 58, 60. Cf. lǽn *commodum*; wrixlung *mutuum*, i. 21, 1-3: *and* tō borge *mutuum*, Kent. Gl. 817.

mūwa, muxle. v. múga, muscelle.

mycel. v. micel.

mycg, mygg, es; *m.*: mycge (?), an; *f.* *A midge*:—Mygg *culix*, Wrt. Voc. ii. 105, 60: *sciniphes*, 120, 9. Mycg *culix*, 15, 55. Mygc, i. 281, 36. Micge (micgc?) *culex*, 24, 17. Mycgæs *cynomya*, Ps. Spl. T. 104, 29. Wiđ gnættas and micgeas, Lchdm. i. 54, 14. Heó gnættas and micgeas (micgas, MS. B.) ācwelleþ, 266, 2. [*O. L. Ger.* muggia; *f. culex*: *O. H. Ger.* mucca, mugga; *f. culex, conopis, scinifes*: *Ger.* mücke: *Icel.* mý; *n.*: *Dan.* myg: *Swed.* mygg.]

mycgern *fat about the kidneys*:—Micgern *exugium*, Wrt. Voc. i. 46, 10: *exugia*, ii. 30, 13. Micgerne *exugia* i. *minctura*, 146, 31. Rysele, mycgern *axungia*; micgern *arvina*, i. *adeps* ł *pinguedo*, Hpt. Gl. 471, 4-7. [*Leo suggests borrowing from Welsh* mychiryn *lard*.]

mycg-nett, es; *n.* *A mosquito-net*:—Fleóhnet *vel* micgnet *conopeum*, Wrt. Voc. i. 57, 24.

mydd, es; *n.* *A bushel;* modius:—Hannibal sende tō Cartaina þrió mydd gyldenra hringa his sige tō tācne *Annibal in testimonium victoriae suae tres modios annulorum aureorum Carthaginem misit*, Ors. 4, 9; Swt. 190, 12. [*O. L. Ger.* muddi: *O. H. Ger.* mutti *modius*.]

mȳdrece, an; *f.* *A chest*:—Mȳderce (mēderce, MS. J.) ođđe cyst *loculus*, Ælfc. Gl. Zup. 313, 15. Đǽs synt twā micle mȳdercan, and ān hræglcysđ, and ān lytulu towmȳderce, and eác twā ealde mȳdercan, Chart. Th. 538, 19-22. Heó becwiþ him twā mȳdrecan, and đǽr aninnan ān bedreáf, eal đæt tō ānum bedde gebyreþ, 536, 24: 537, 26. vi. mīdreca, 430, 2. Mūdrica *loculos*, Jn. Skt. Lind. 12, 6.

mȳgþ. v. mǽgþ.

myl *dust*:—Đæt đære ylcan stōwe myl wiđ fȳre wæs freomigende *ut pulvis loci illius contra ignem voluerit*, Bd. 3, 10, tit.; S. 534, 16. [*Prompt. Parv.* mul *pulvis*, p. 348, and note. Cf. *Icel.* mylja *to crush*.]

myldan, myldende. v. be-myldan, miltan I (a).

mylen, es; *m.* *A mill*:—Myln *molendenum*, Wrt. Voc. i. 83, 7. Mylen *mula*, ii. 58, 16: R. Ben. 127, 6. Se mylenham and se myln đǽrtō, Cod. Dip. Kmbl. iii. 189, 10. Of Eádweardes mylne, 438, 26: 439, 2. Ne mylnum nis ālȳfed tō eornenne (*on Sunday*), Wulfst. 227, 11. [Myln *molendinum*, Wrt. Voc. i. 235, 60: *A. R.* mulne: *Wick.* milne: *Icel.* mylna: *O. H. Ger.* mulīn; *f.*: *Du.* molen.]

mylen-brōc, es; *m.* *A mill-brook*:—On mylenbrōc; đonne andlang streámes, Cod. Dip. Kmbl. v. 198, 30.

mylen-ham[m], es; *m.* *An enclosure in which a mill stands*:—Hit (*the boundary*) cymþ nyđer tō đam mylenhammæ and se mylenham and se myln đǽrtō, Cod. Dip. Kmbl. iii. 189, 10.

mylen-hweogul, es; *n.* *A mill-wheel*:—Seó heofon ǽfre tyrnþ onbūtan ūs swiftre đonne ǽnig mylenhweól (-hweowul, MS. P.), Lchdm. iii. 232, 19.

mylen-pūl, -pōl, es; *m.* *A mill-pool*:—On mylepūl; of mylenpūlle in Afene streám, Cod. Dip. Kmbl. iii. 401, 8. In đone mylenpōl; of đam pōle tō đære portstrǽte, Cod. Dip. B. i. 418, 1.

mylen-scearp; *adj.* *Ground sharp*:—Heówan mēcum mylenscearpum, Chr. 937; Erl. 112, 24; Æđelst. 24. v. next word.

mylen-stān, es; *m.* *A stone for grinding*:—Feól ođđe mylenstān *lima*, Wrt. Voc. ii. 49, 75: i. 287, 2.

mylen-steall, es; *m.* *A mill*:—Tō myllnstealle, Cod. Dip. Kmbl. iii. 4, 14. Mylenstall, 169, 9. v. next word.

mylen-stede, es; *m.* *A mill-stead, mill*:—Đysne mylenstede đe đǽrtō gebyreþ æt Leóferes hagan, Cod. Dip. Kmbl. vi. 243, 10.

mylen-stīg, e; *f.* *A path to a mill*:—Æfter đam grēnan wege in tō đære mylnstīge; of đære mylenstīge, Cod. Dip. Kmbl. iii. 389, 9.

mylen-troh, -trog, es; *n.* *A mill-trough, the channel in which water comes to a mill-wheel*:—Mylentroh *canalis*, Wrt. Voc. ii. 128, 16.

mylen-waru, e; *f.* *A mill-dam* (? cf. *Icel.* vörr; *f.* *a fenced-in landing place*):—Andlang streámes on đa mylenware; of đare mylenware tō đare swēte apuldre, Cod. Dip. Kmbl. iii. 454, 7. Cf. mylen-wer.

mylen-weard, es; *m.* *A miller*:—Mylenwyrd *molendinarius* vel *molinarius*, Wrt. Voc. i. 34, 35. Myleweard *molendarus*, ii. 58, 17.

mylen-wer, es; *m.* *A mill-weir, mill-dam*:—Andlang streámes đæt it cymþ tō đam mylewere, Cod. Dip. Kmbl. iv. 92, 30.

mylma, an; *m.* *A retreat* (?); recessus, Germ. 398, 150.

myltan, mylte, myltestre. v. miltan, milte, miltestre.

-mynd. v. freónd-, ge-, weorþ-mynd.

myndgian; *p.* ode. I. *to bear in mind, recollect*:—Gē sweltaþ deáþe nymþe ic dōm wite sōđan swefnes đæs mīn sefa myndgaþ *ye shall die unless I know the import of the true dream, of which my mind is still conscious*, Cd. 179; Th. 224, 31; Dan. 144. Wē đæs hereweorces myndgiaþ (*recollect*), and đa wiggþræce on gewritu setton, Elen. Kmbl. 1311; El. 657. II. *to bring to the mind of another, recall, remind*:—Manaþ swā and myndgaþ mǽla gehwylce sārum wordum, Beo. Th. 4120; B. 2057. Ic wolde đē nū myngian (Cott. MS. myndgian) đære manigfealdan lāre đe đū mē ǽr gehēte, Bt. 40, 5; Fox 240, 11. v. gemyndigian, mynegian *and next two words*.

myndgiend, es; *m.* *One who reminds*:—Gyf Frysna hwylc đæs morþorhetes myndgiend wǽre, Beo. Th. 2215; B. 1105.

myndgung, e; *f.* *A reminding one of anything, admonition*:—Sió myndgung đara hāligra gewrita *divinae admonitiones verba*, Past. 22, 1; Swt. 169, 8.

myndig; *adj.* *Mindful*:—Myndig wæs Petrus wordes đætte cweden wæs him, Mk. Skt. Rush. 14, 72. v. ge-myndig.

mynd-leás; *adj.* *Senseless, foolish*:—Se wīsdōm hine sylfne ætbret fram myndleásum geþohtum, Homl. Th. ii. 326, 4. v. gemyndleás.

myne, es; *m.* I. *the mind*:—Mōd mægnade, mine fægnade, Exon. 94 b; Th. 353, 56; Reim. 33. II. *mind* (as in to have a *mind* for anything), *purpose, desire*:—Læssan hwīle đonne his myne sōhte *for a less time than he would have desired*, Beo. Th. 5138; B. 2572. Wæs him ūt myne fleón fealone streám *they had a mind to escape, to flee the yellow stream*, Andr. Kmbl. 3073; An. 1539. Gē holdlīce hyge staþeladon mid mōdes myne (*with full purpose of heart*), Exon. 27 b; Th. 83, 20; Cri. 1359. Hē lārum wile, þurh mōdes myne, mīnum hȳran, 71 a; Th. 265, 10; Jul. 379: 74 a; Th. 282, 2; Jul. 657. Nō hē đone gifstōl grētan mōste for Metode ne his myne wisse *he might not approach the throne because of the Lord, and knew not his purpose*, Beo. Th. 341; B. 169. III. *love*:—Hwǽr ic feor ođđe neáh findan meahte đone đe in meoduhealle mine wisse (*would feel love, would love*), ođđe mec frēfran wolde, Exon. 76 b; Th. 288, 7; Wand. 27. [Do þu þis mid gode mune (*intent*), þenne eart þu godes sune, O. E. Homl. i. 57, 53. *Goth.* muns *purpose, device, readiness*: *Icel.* munr *the mind; mind, longing; love*.] v. wīf-myne.

myne. v. mene, mine.

mynecenu, e; *f.* *The feminine form corresponding to masc.* munuc:—Mynecenu *monacha* vel *monialis*, Wrt. Voc. i. 42, 20: Homl. Th. ii. 26, 28. Munuc and mynecenu đe Gode sylfum beóþ gehālgode, and hyra gehāt Gode gehāten habbaþ, L. Ecg. P. iii. 11; Th. ii. 198, 32. Seó mynecynu *monacha*, iv. 9; Th. ii. 206, 16: Homl. Th. ii. 184, 1. Bysn be sumere mynecyne, 546, 26. Gif hwā mynecene, đe Godes brȳd biþ gehāten, him tō wīfe nimþ, beó heó āmānsumad, L. Ecg. P. ii. 19; Th. ii. 188, 21. Godes þeówas, munecas and mynecena, preóstas and nunnan, L. Eth. v. 4; Th. i. 304, 26. Munecas and mynecena, canonicas and nunnan, vi. 2; Th. i. 314, 17: L. C. E. 6; Th. i. 364, 7. Be mynecenan. Riht is đæt mynecena mynsterlīce macian, efne swā wē cwǽdon ǽror be munecan (v. *next paragraph where* preóstas and nunnan *are taken together*), L. I. P. 15; Th. ii. 322, 31-33. Eugenia hæfde āsteald mynecena mynster, Homl. Skt. 2, 311. Munecena mynstru, R. Ben. 136, 4. Đa forlǽtenan mynstru mid munecum gesettan and eác mid mynecenum, Chart. Th. 240, 17. Basilisca wearþ mōdor ofer manega mynecena, Homl. Skt. 4, 85. Mynecæna, Lchdm. iii. 440, 15. [Ealra đare landa đe intō đæ mynechina līfe æt Wiltūne forgifene synt, Cod. Dip. Kmbl. iii. 117, 25. *Laym.* munechene: *Piers P.* monchen: *Trev.* minchin.]

mynegian, myngian; *p.* ode (*with acc. of person and gen. of thing, or with a clause*). I. *to bring to one's own mind, recall*:—Dauid myngode đæra gyfa đe God his fædrum and his foregengum sealde, Ps. Th. 43, arg. II. *to bring to another's mind*, (a) *to remind*:—Drihten ūs đonne myngaþ đæs Sunnandæges weorces *the Lord will remind us then of the work done on Sunday*, Wulfst. 210, 9. Mec đæra nægla fyrwet myngaþ, Elen. Kmbl. 2156; El. 1079. Ic đē ǽr mynegode (Cott. MS. myndgode) đære ilcan sprǽce, Bt. 35, 3; Fox 160, 7. Hū ne mynegodest (Cott. MS. myndgodest) đū mē đære ilcan sprǽce, 35, 2; Fox 156, 14. Ic wolde đē myngian (Gott. MS. myndgian) đære manigfealdan lāre đe đū mē ǽr gehēte, 40, 5; Fox 240, 11. Wē willaþ eów myngian, đæt hit ne gange eów of gemynde, Homl. Th. i. 220, 3. (b) *to bring a duty to the mind, to admonish, exhort*:—Eów ic mynegie *vos moneo*, Ælfc, Gr. 15; Som. 18, 3. Mīne wylna ic mynegige *meas ancillas moneo*, 19, 6. Ic myngige and manige manna gehwylcne, Blickl. Homl. 109, 11. Ic myngie and lǽre, 107, 10. Manaþ ūs and myngaþ seó ār and seó eádignes, 197, 3. Mynegaþ, 161, 3. Menegaþ *instigat*, Hpt. Gl. 526, 63. Eádweard cyning myngode his wytan đæt hȳ smeádon hū heora friþ betere beón mæhte, L. Ed. 4; Th. i. 160, 23. Minga hine *hunc exhortare*, Deut. 1, 38. Ælc biscop đone cyning myngige (MS. B. myndgige) đæt ealle Godes cyrcan sȳn wel behworfene, L. Edm. E; Th. i. 246, 11. Ǽnne hyndenman, đe đa .x. mynige tō ūre ealre gemǽne þearfe, L. Æđelst. v. 3; Th. i. 232, 2. Wē willaþ myngian freónda gehwilcne, đæt gehwā hine sylfne beþence, L. Eth. vi. 42; Th. i. 326, 6. (c) *to remind of a debt, to ask for payment.* v. manian:—Myngaþ *exigit*, Wrt. Voc. ii. 144, 81. Sǽde on heortan hys ne myngeþ (*requiret*), Ps. Spl. T. 9, 15. Gif hē gelōmlīce þurh his bydelas his gafoles myngaþ *if he by his messengers often asks for his tribute*, L. Edg. S; Th. i. 270, 20. Heáhberht oft đæs myngode, ođđe đæs landes bæd, Chart. Th. 167, 6. Se đe nimþ đa þing đe đīne synt ne mynega đū hyra (*ne repetas*), Lk. Skt. 6, 30. III. *to have in the mind, to purpose, intend, determine*:—Menegiaþ, hogiaþ *conati sumus, decrevimus*, Hpt. Gl. 527, 66. [*A. R.* munegen: *Marh.* munegin:

Laym. munegie: *Piers P.* munge, menewe: *O. H. Ger.* bi-munigôn.] v. ge-mynegian.

mynegung, e; *f.* I. *admonition, exhortation* (v. mynegian, II b):—Mynegung *monitus*, Ælfc. Gr. 11; Som. 15, 16. Mynigung, 43; Som. 44, 53. Mynegunge *monitionem*, 15; Som. 18, 4. Þurh Albinus myngunge (*hortatu*), Bed. pref.; S. 472, 8. 'Ne ondrǽde gē eów' hē cwæþ . . . þurh ðās minegunge . . ., L. Ælfc. P. 13; Th. ii. 364, 26. Þurh ðæs apostoles mungunge (myngunge, MSS. O. F.; minegunge, MS. T.), R. Ben. 53, 1. Heó wolde þurh his mynegungum hire mōd getrymman, Homl. Th. ii. 146, 10. Æfter mynegungum Æðeluuoldes ðe mē oft manode, Chart. Th. 240, 30. Menegungum *hortamentis*, Hpt. Gl. 485, 52. II. *a demand for payment of what is due, a claim* (v. mynegian, II c):—Þurh ða gedurstegnysse ðe folces men wiðhæfton ðære gelōmlīcan mynegunge (myngunge, MS. F.) . . . ðe ūre lāreówas dydon ymbe ðæt neádgafol ūres Drihtnes, L. Edg. S; Th. i. 270, 25. Ne forlǽte hē ða mynegunge *let him not relinquish the claim*, L. Æðelst. v. 7; Th. i. 234, 26.

mynele, an; *f. Desire, longing*:—Ðæt hē tō his earde ǽnige nyste mōdes mynlan *so that he* (*Ulysses*) *felt no heart's desire for his native land*, Bt. Met. Fox 21, 133; Met. 26, 67. v. myne.

myne-līc; *adj. Pleasant, desirable*:—Oft hē geþah mynelīcne māþþum, Exon. 84 b; Th. 318, 25; Vīd. 4. [*O. Sax.* muni-līh: *Icel.* mun-ligr *pleasant*.] v. myne.

mynet, es; *n.* I. *a coin*:—Mynet *nummisma*, Wrt. Voc. i. 73, 48. Mynit *nomisma*, ii. 114, 75. Mynete *nummismate*, 61, 14: 96, 80. Genim pipores swilce ān mynet gewege, diles sǽdes swilce iiii mynet gewegen, Lchdm. ii. 192, 14. Ætgȳwaþ mē ðæs gafoles mynyt, Mt. Kmbl. 22, 19. Ðæt hī sceoldon ðæt gyldene mynet (*aureum illud numisma*) mid him geniman, Bd. 3, 8; S. 532, 1. Hē hēt ðæm cwelre syllan .xxv. gyldenra myneta, Shrn. 129, 12. II. *coinage, money*:—Ðæt ān mynet sȳ ofer eall ðæs cynges onweald, L. Ath. i. 14; Th. i. 206, 18: L. Edg. i. 8; Th. i. 268, 27. Ān mynet gange ofer ealle ðās þeóde būtan ǽlcon false, L. Eth. vi. 32; Th. i. 322, 28: L. C. S. 8; Th. i. 380, 15: Wulfst. 272, 2. [*O. L. Ger.* munita; *f. nomisma, moneta*: *O. H. Ger.* muniza, munizza; *f.*: *Ger.* münze. *From Latin* moneta.]

mynet-cȳpa, an; *m. A money-dealer*:—Se ðe him sylfum teolaþ on Godes gelaþunge, and ne caraþ ymbe Cristes teolunge, se biþ mynetcȳpa getalod, Homl. Th. i. 412, 16.

mynetere, es; *m.* I. *a moneyer, a money-changer, money-dealer*:—Mynetere *nummularius*, Wrt. Voc. i. 47, 15: *trapezita*, 57, 33: *trapezeta* vel *nummularius*, 73, 47. Miyniteri *numularius, nummorum praerogator*, ii. 115, 2. Mynetere *trapezita*, Ælfc. Gr. 7; Som. 6, 43. Mynetera *nummulariorum*, Wrt. Voc. ii. 60, 51. Munetera, 73, 8, 41. Ða setl ðara mynetera *the seats of the money-changers*, Blickl. Homl. 71, 19. Hyt gebyrede ðæt ðū befæstest mīn feoh mynyterum, Mt. Kmbl. 25, 27: Homl. Th. ii. 554, 8. Hē gemētte sittende myneteras, Jn. 2, 14. II. *a minter, one who coins*:—Mynetere *monetarius*, Wrt. Voc. i. 57, 33. Be myneterum . . . Nān man ne mynetege būtan on porte. And gif se mynetere fūl wurþe, sleá man of ða hand ðe hē ðæt fūl mid worhte, and sette upp on ða mynetsmiððan . . . On Cantwara byrig .vii. myneteras, L. Ath. i. 14; Th. i. 206, 17–26. Ǽlc mynetere ðe man tīhþ ðæt fals feoh slōge . . . gif hē fūl beó, sleá hine man, L. Eth. iii. 8; Th. i. 296, 12–15. Ða myneteras ðe inne wuda wyrcaþ oððe elles hwǽr; ðæt ða bión heora feores scyldige, iii. 16; Th. i. 298, 13. Godes feoh biþ befæst myneterum tō sleánne, Homl. Th. ii. 554, 14. Ic habbe geunnen Baldewyne abbode ōnne meonetere wiðinne Sæint Eádmundes byrg, Cod. Dip. Kmbl. iv. 223, 6. [*O. Sax.* muniteri *a money-changer*: *Icel.* myntari *a minter*: *O. H. Ger.* munizari, munizzari *numularius, monetarius, trapezita*: *Ger.* münzer.]

mynetian; *p.* ode *To mint, coin*:—Nān man ne mynetege būtan on porte, L. Ath. i. 14; Th. i. 206, 19. [*O. Sax.* gi-munitōd: *O. H. Ger.* munizōn *cudere*.]

mynet-smiððe, an; *f. A mint, place for coining.* v. mynetere, II.

myngian. v. mynegian.

mynian; *p.* ede (cf. myne, II) *To have as the object of desire* or *purpose, to intend, direct one's course to an object*:—Ðǽr mīn hyht myneþ tō gesēcenne *my heart's desire is to visit there*, Exon. 48 b; Th. 167, 17; Gū. 1601: Andr. Kmbl. 583; An. 294. Ic lǽre ǽlcne ðara ðe maga sī and manigne wǽn hæbbe ðæt hē menige tō ðam ilcan wuda *I advise every one that is able and has many a waggon, to direct his steps to that same wood*, Shrn. 163, 13.

mynster, es; *n.* I. *a monastery, a place where a body of monks* or *of nuns resided*:—Gif hit beón mæg, swā sceal mynster beón gestaþelod, ðæt ealle neádbehēfe þing ðǽr binnan wunian, ðæt is wæterscype, mylen, wyrtūn and gehwylce misenlīce cræftas ðe synd gōde tō begānne, R. Ben. 127, 4–7. Wæs se ǽrest abbod ðæs ylcan mynstres Petrus hāten, Bd. 1, 33; S. 499, 5: 2, 2; S. 502, 40. Mynstres aldor, L. Wih. 17; Th. i. 40, 13. Gif hwā gefeohte on cyninges hūse sīe hē scyldig ealles his ierfes . . . Gif hwā on mynstre gefeohte, hundtwelftig scill. gebēte, L. In. 6; Th. i. 106, 4. Gif hwā gefeohteþ on mynstre būtan circean gebēte . . . be mynstres mǽðe, L. Eth. vii. 10; Th. i. 330, 26. Muneca gehwylc ðe ūte sȳ of mynstre . . . gebūge georne intō mynstre, v. 5; Th. i. 306, 1–3. Gif hwā nunnan of mynstre ūt ālǽde, L. Alf. pol. 8; Th. i. 66, 15. Wæs heó . . . on ðam mynstre ðe on Franclande wæs getimbrad fram ðære abbadissan ðe Fara hātte . . . forðon on ða tīd ne wǽron monige mynstra getimbrade on Angelþeóde; forðon monige of Breotone gewunedon sēcan Francna mynstro, Bd. 3, 8; S. 531, 12–17. Mid ðȳ ðe wǽn ðā com, ðe ða bān on lǽded wæron, in ðæt foresprecene mynster, ðā ne woldan ða hīwan ðe on ðam mynstre wǽron him lustlīce onfōn, 3, 11; S. 535, 17. Se munuc ðe mynster næbbe, L. Eth. v. 6; Th. i. 306, 6. On mynstrum fæste gewunian and regollīce libban (*said of abbots*), ix. 32; Th. i. 348, 1. In mynsterum, Exon. 38 b; Th. 127, 16; Gū. 387. Coloman twā mynstro geworhte, Bd. 4, 4; S. 570, 30. Twā æðele mynstere, 4, 6; S. 574, 12. Mynstru, R. Ben. 139, 4. II. *a church, minster* (v. mynster-clǽnsung):—Ne sīn ealle circan nā gelīcre mǽðe worldlīce wyrðe . . . Heáfodmynstres griþbryce . . . bēte man be cyninges munde . . . and medemran mynstres mid hundtwelftigan scill., L. Eth. ix. 5; Th. i. 342, 1: L. C. E. 3; Th. i. 360, 21. Man āgife ǽlce teóþunge tō ðam ealdan mynstre (*ad matrem ecclesiam*) ðe seó hȳrnes tō hȳrþ, L. Edg. i. 1; Th. i. 262, 7. Ðæs mynstres mæssepreóst, i. 3; Th. i. 262, 25. (See also sections 2 and 5.) Ōswold fullworhte on Eferwīc ðæt ǽnlīce mynster ðe his mǽg Eádwine ǽr begunnen hæfde, Swt. A. S. Rdr. 98, 90. [*Laym.* munster *a monastery*: *Orm.* i þeȝȝre minnstre (*the temple*, cf. i þe kirrke, 1099), 1017: *O. H. Ger.* munustiri *monasterium*. From the Latin.] v. heáfod-, nunn-mynster.

mynster-clǽnsung, e; *f. Purification of a minster* (*within whose walls a man has been slain*):—Ðonne bēte man ðæt ciricgriþ intō ðære circan . . . and ða mynsterclǽnsunge begite (cf. gif ǽnig man Godes ciricgriþ swā ābrece ðæt hē binnon ciricwāgum manslaga weorþe, ll. 6–8), L. Eth. ix. 3; Th. i. 340, 18: L. C. E. 2; Th. i. 360, 6.

mynster-gang, es; *m. Going into a monastery, entering on a monastic life*:—Heó ðonne mōt gif heó wile ðæt forlǽtan and hyre mynstergang geceósan *tunc, si velit, licebit ei id derelinquere, et vitam monasticam sibi eligere*, L. Ecg. C. 20; Th. ii. 146, 23.

mynster-hām, es; *m. A monastic house, monastery*:—Gif hwā ðara mynsterhāma hwelcne, for hwelcre scylde gesēce, ðe cyninges feorm tō belimpe, oððe ōðerne freóne hiérēd, L. Alf. pol. 2; Th. i. 60, 23. Ðone oferēcan mon gedǽle gind mynsterhāmas tō Godes ciricum in Sūðregum and in Cent, Chart. Th. 482, 18.

mynster-hata, an; *m. A hater* or *enemy of monasteries*:—Hēr syndan sacerdbanan and mynsterhatan, Wulfst. 165, 28.

mynster-līc; *adj. Monastic*:—Man ārǽrde cyrcan on his rīce geond eall and mynsterlīce gesetnyssa (*monastic institutions*), Swt. A. S. Rdr. 97, 71. [*O. H. Ger.* munistri-līh *monasterialis*.]

mynster-līce; *adv. Monastically, in a manner suitable to a monastery*:—Riht is ðæt mynecena mynsterlīce macian (*act in accordance with monastic rules*), L. I. P. 15; Th. i. 322, 32. Hē æþele mynster getimbrede. Ðā hē ðā ðæt hæfde mynsterlīce ge þeáwlīce gesett, Bd. 3, 19; S. 549, 37.

mynster-līf; es; *n.* I. *monastic life*:—Gif hlāford nylle hire mynsterlīfes geunnan, oððа hiá siolf nylle, Chart. Th. 471, 2. Hē mynsterlīf ðam weoruldlīfe forbær *monasticam saeculari vitam praetulit*, Bd. 5, 19; S. 637, 7. Hē him sendan sceolde sume eáwfæste munecas ðe him mynsterlīf āstealdon, Homl. Skt. 6, 57. II. *a place in which the monastic life is lived*:—Mynsterlīf *coenobium* (cf. *hec cenobium* an abbay, i. 230, 8), Wrt. Voc. ii. 19, 47: 93, 32: *gurgustia*, 93, 33. Ic wille ðæt ðǽr ǽfre beó mynstrelīf and samnung (*a monastery and brotherhood*), Chart. Th. 391, 29. Cf. munuc-līf.

mynster-mann, es; *m. A man who lives in a monastery, a monk*:—Gif hit mynsterman sig *si monasticus sit*, L. Ecg. C. 40; Th. ii. 166, 10. Ðās bōc be ðæra hālgena līfe ðe mynstermenn mid heora þēnungum wurðiaþ, Homl. Skt. pref. 44: Swt. Rdr. 100, 148. Ðæt forme muneca cyn is mynstermanna, ðe gemǽnan līfe drohtniaþ on mynstre, R. Ben. 134, 5: 9, 3. Mynstermannum gedafenaþ ðæt hī on stilnysse heora līf ādreógan, Homl. Th. ii. 342, 29: Ælfc. Gr. pref.; Som. 1, 38.

mynster-munuc, es; *m. A monk who lives in a monastery*:—Ne þearf ǽnig mynstermunuc mid rihte fǽhþbōte biddan, L. Eth. ix. 25; Th. i. 346, 1. Ða mynstermunecas urnon tō, Homl. Th. ii. 176, 23. Benedictus mid his mynstermunecum, 178, 33: i. 532, 33.

mynster-prafost, es; *m. The provost of a monastery*:—Ælfnōd mynsterprauost, Chart. Th. 434, 4.

mynster-preóst, es; *m. A priest who conducts service in a minster*:—Wē lǽraþ ðæt mæssepreósta oððe mynsterpreósta ǽnig ne cume binnan circan dyre, ne binnan weohstealle būtan his oferslipe, L. Edg. C. 46; Th. ii. 254, 8.

mynster-scīr, e; *f. The management of a monastery*:—Hē gewāt tō his mynsterscīre *ad monasterii sui curam secessit*, Bd. 5, 19; S. 639, 13.

mynster-stōw, e; *f. A place where there is a minster, a town*:—Hē ferde geond ealle ge þurh mynsterstōwe ge þurh folcstōwe *per cuncta et urbana et rustica loca*, Bd. 3, 5; S. 526, 27.

mynster-þeáw, es; *m. A monastic custom*:—Cyriclīce þeáwas oððe mynsterþeáwas *ritus ecclesiastici sive monasteriales*, Bd. 5, 19; S. 637, 24.

mynster-þegnung, e; *f. Service done in a monastery*:—Ðeós foresceáwung sȳ gehealden . . . on eallum mynstres þēnungum (mynsterþēnungum, Wells Frag.), R. Ben. 85, 17.

mynster-wīse, an; *f. A custom or manner followed in a monastery*:—Se abbod ongeat sume ða mynsterwīsan tō gerihtanne *the abbot managed to correct some of the abuses practised in the monastery*, Glostr. Frag. 110, 27.

myntan; *p.* te. I. *to mean, intend, purpose, determine*, (a) *with infin.*:—Se ðe Gode mynteþ bringan beorhtne wlite, Exon. 23 b; Th. 65, 22; Cri. 1058. Mynte ic hié hāton yflian *I had a mind to order them to be punished*, Nar. 25, 27. Heó hī mynte for hȳ tō abbudissan gesettan *abbatissam eam pro se facere disposuerat*, Bd. 5, 3; 616, 19. Hē mynte hine sleán, Blickl. Homl. 223, 7, 9, 11, 16. Hē mynte mid his discipulum tō his mynstre fēran, 225, 11: Beo. Th. 1428; B. 712. Ðā mynton wē ūs gerestan, Nar. 14, 25: Bt. Met. Fox 26, 143; Met. 26, 72. (b) *with infin. to be supplied*:—Gif ðū seó riht cyning swā ðū ǣr myntest, Cd. 228; Th. 308, 8; Sat. 688. Mynte se mǣra hwǣr hē meahte ðanon fleón *the mighty one designed* (*to get*) *where he could flee thence*, Beo. Th. 1528; B. 762. [Cf. *Prompt. Parv.* myntyn or amyn towarde *attempto*.] (c) *with a clause introduced by* ðæt:—Gerēfa mīn mynteþ ðæt mē æfter sīe eaforan sīne yrfeweardas *my steward means his children to be heirs after me*, 100; Th. 131, 27; Gen. 2182. Hē mynte ðæt hē gedǣlde līf wið līce, Beo. Th. 1466; B. 731. (d) *with a case*:—Wit sculon sēcan ðæt ðæt wit ǣr mynton *sed quae proposuimus intueamur*, Bt. 35, 3; Fox 158, 11. Hī him sylfum rīce mynton, Wulfst. 145, 26. II. *to think, suppose*:—Mynton ealle, ðæt se brego and seó mægþ wǣron ætsomne, Judth. 12; Thw. 25, 10; Jud. 253. v. ge-myntan.

mynung (?) *admonition*:—Ūre hālige fæderes mid gelōmrǣdre menunge ūs gemenegiþ, Chart. Th. 316, 27. v. mynegung, manung.

Myrce, myrce, myrcels, myre, myrhþ, myrgan, myrige. v. Mirce, mirce, mircels, mere, mirigþ, mirgan, mirige.

myrgen-līc; *adj. Morning*:—Ðȳs myrgenlīcan dæge heó biþ gongende of līchoman *she will depart before evening*, Blickl. Homl. 141, 33. v. morgen-līc.

myrran, myrrelse, myrring. v. mirran, mirrelse, mirring.

myrre, myrra, an; *f. Myrrh*:—Hī him lāc brohton; ðæt wæs gold and rēcels and myrre, Mt. Kmbl. 2, 11. Seó myrre getācnode ðæt hē wæs deádlīc, Homl. Th. i. 116, 10. Myrra dēþ ðæt ðæt deáde flǣsc ne rotaþ, 118, 11. Murre *myrra*, Ps. Spl. 44, 10. Wīn gemenged mid myrran *myrratum vinum*, Wrt. Voc. i. 27, 59. Uton him bringan myrran, Homl. Th. i. 116, 25: 118, 17. [*O. Sax. O. H. Ger.* myrra.]

myrt. v. mirt.

myrten, es; *n. Flesh of animals that have died a natural death*:—Ne ǣnig man myrtenes ǣfre ne ābīte, Wulfst. 71, 1. Gif hē myrten ete *si morticinam ederit*, L. Ecg. C. 15; Th. ii. 142, 26. v. next word.

myrten; *adj. That has died by disease*:—Gif swȳn etaþ myrten flǣsc *si porci carnem morticinam ederint*, L. Ecg. C. 40; Th. ii. 164, 18. Grēcas myrten flǣsc nǣnigum men ne lȳfaþ ac ða hȳda ðæra myrtenra neáta hȳ heom dōþ tō scōn *Graeci carnem morticinam nulli permittunt, de pellibus tamen morticinorum animalium calceamenta sibi faciunt*, Th. ii. 166, 29-31.

myrþ. v. mirigþ.

myrþra, an; *m. A murderer, homicide*:—Se man biþ myrþra (*homicida*), se ðe his brōþor hataþ, L. Ecg. C. 24; Th. ii. 150, 10. Gif hwylc man for his mǣges wræce man ofsleá, dō (*do penance*) hē swā myrþra .vii. geár oððe .x., L. Ecg. P. iv. 68, 18; Th. ii. 230, 19, 21: Bd. 2, 9; S. 511, 37. Ðū (*the soul*) wǣre ðǣr (*in the world*) morþ and myrþra, Wulfst. 241, 9. Ðonne biþ hē ealra ðara manna deáþes sceldig and myrþra beforan ðæs ēcan Dēman heáhsetle, Blickl. Homl. 53, 7. Myrþran and mānswaran, 61, 13. Mīne myrþran and mānsceaþan (*the devils*), Exon. 42 a; Th. 141, 4; Gū. 622. Myrþra *homicidas*, Mt. Kmbl. Rush. 22, 7. [*Goth.* maurþrja: *O. H. Ger.* murdreo *latro*.] v. bearn-, mǣg-, self-myrþra.

myrþrian *to murder*. [*Goth.* maurþrjan: *O. H. Ger.* murdrian *jugulare*.] v. for-, of-myrþrian.

myrþrung, e; *f. Murder, homicide*:—Myrþrunge *parricidium*, Wrt. Voc. ii. 67, 30.

myrwa. v. mearu.

mysci; *pl. Flies*:—Sōna cwōman mysci manige *venit cynomyia*, Ps. Th. 104, 27. [From *Lat.* musca.]

mȳse *a table*. v. mēse.

mȳðe (?); *pl. The mouth of a stream*:—Andlang brōces on ða mȳðy; of ðes gemȳðon on Ceahhanmere, Cod. Dip. Kmbl. iii. 48, 25. v. gemȳðe.

mȳðe (?), an; *f. The mouth of a stream*:—Ǣrest fram mȳðan in cyrstilmǣl āc . . . eft in ða mȳðan, Cod. Dip. Kmbl. iii. 379, 20-380, 7. v. mūða.

myxen. v. mixen.

N.

N, like *m* (q. v.), in Anglo-Saxon generally corresponds to *n* in Gothic and in other cognate dialects, e. g. *net, hand, ān*; Goth. *nati, handus, ains*; O. H. Ger. *nezzi, hant, ein*; O. Sax. *net, hand, ēn*; but, like *m*, it falls away before *ð* and *s*, and the vowel which preceded the *n* is lengthened, e. g. *cūð, tōð, ōðer, mūð, hūsel, est*; Goth. *kunþs, tunþus, anþar, munþs, hunsl, ansts*; O. H. Ger. *chund, zand, andar, mund, anst*; O. Sax. *kūð, tand, ōðar, mūð, anst*. If, however, *n* and *s* come together by the loss of an intervening vowel the *n* remains, e. g. *winstre*; O. H. Ger. O. Sax. *winistar*. The character which appears in the Runic poem is ᚾ, and the verse, in which the name (cf. Icel. *nauð*) is given, is the following:—

Nȳd byþ nearu on breóste	oft tō helpe
niða bearnum,	and tō hǣle gehwæðre
weorðeþ heó ðeáh	gif hī his hlystaþ ǣror.

Runic pm. Kmbl. 341, 8-13.

nā, nō; *adv. No, not*; non. I. *qualifying a verb expressed or implied*, (a) *without any other negative particle*:—Nā cunne *nesciat*, Wülck. Gl. 257, 28. Fela gōdra hāma ðe wē genemnan nā cunnan, Chr. 1001; Erl. 136, 29. Fremde nā heom God setton on gesyhþe, Ps. Th. 53, 3. Nā ðū andwlitan ðīnne āwend fram mē, 101, 2. Swā sceal man dōn, ðonne hē gegān þenceþ longsumne lof, nā ymb his līf cearaþ, Beo. Th. 3077; B. 1536. Ealle hī scīnaþ, nā hwæðre ðeáh ealle efenbeorhte, Bt. Met. Fox 20, 460; Met. 20, 230. Gewīte ðes calic fram mē, ðeáhhwæðere nā swā swā ic wylle, Mt. Kmbl. 26, 39. Ða habbaþ twegen casus and nā mā on gewunan, Ælfc. Gr. 14; Som. 17, 3. Ðæt is se ēþel ðe nō geendad weorþeþ, Exon. Th. 100, 12; Cri. 1640. Ic gelȳfe nō ðæt him eorþwelan ēce stondeþ, 309, 33; Seef. 66. Nō ðæt ðīn aldor wolde Godes goldfatu in gylp beran, ne ðȳ hraðor hrēmde . . . ac ðæt oftor gecwæþ . . . ðæt hē wǣre āna Drihten, Cd. Th. 263, 34; Dan. 754. Nō seoððan ðæt hī mōsten in ðone ēcan andwlītan, 288, 8; Sat. 377: 304, 23; Sat. 634. (b) *with other negatives*:—Hyt nā ne feóll *non cecidit*, Mt. Kmbl. 7, 25. Ne eom ic nā Crist, Jn. Skt. 1, 20. Rāde ðe mon nā ne rīmde, Chr. 871; Erl. 76, 12. Næs ðæt nā ðæt hē nyste, Blickl. Homl. 19, 33. Ne hē hine nā ne onstyreþ, 21, 27. Ðæt ðās lāreówas ne sceolan Godes dōmas nāwðer ne nā wanian, ne ne ēcan, 81, 4. Ne wandige nā se mæssepreóst nō for rīces mannes ege, 43, 9. Nǣron gē nō mīn gemunende, ne gē nō geþohton, Past. 21; Swt. 151, 21. Swā nān ōðer nā dēþ, Menol. Fox 392; Men. 197. Nabbaþ ðās naman nā ōðre gebīgednysse, Ælfc. Gr. 11; Som. 15, 24. Nis nā mā casa on gewunan . . . nis nā mā mislīcra casa, 14; Som. 17, 4-7. Ne behōfaþ nāðor ðyssera pronomina nā mā stemna būton twegra, 15; Som. 17, 38. Ne synd nā mā namanspeligende būtan ðās fīftēne, Som. 17, 46: Blickl. Homl. 35, 24. Nō mā, Exon. Th. 441, 25; Kl. 4. Telle ic ða weorþmynd ðæm wyrhtan, næs nā ðē, Bt. 14, 1; Fox 42, 19. Næs nā for ðam ðe ðæs landes swā fela wǣre, ac for ðam ðe se Wendelsǣ hit hæfþ swā tōdǣled, Ors. 1, 1; Swt. 24, 25. Lufian wē hine . . . næs nō on gesundum þingum ānum, ac eác swylce on wiðerweardum þingum, Blickl. Homl. 13, 7. II. *qualifying* (a) *an adjective*:—Mid langum scipum nā manegum, Chr. Erl. 3, 7. Ðȳ ilcan sumera forwearþ nō læs (= *not a smaller number*) ðonne xx scipa, 897; Erl. 96, 14. Wīse sweltende samod nā wīs *sapientes morientes, simul insipiens*, Ps. Spl. 48, 9. (b) *an adverb or adverbial phrase*:—Nis nō ðæt ān . . . ac eác *not only . . . but also*, Blickl. Homl. 85, 15. Næs hit nā ðæt ān ðæt ðū on ungemetlīcum ungesǣlþum wǣre, ac eác ðæt ðū fulneáh mid ealle forwurde, Bt. 5, 3; Fox 14, 6. Ðe nā ðæt ān mē, ac eác swylce mīne gefēran, mæg besencan, Coll. Monast. Th. 24, 31: L. Ecg. P. iii. 1; Th. ii. 196, 13. Nā ðā git *non dum*, Wrt. Voc. ii. 59, 55. Nā swā *numquam ita*, Wülck. Gl. 248, 9. Nā lancge *non diu*, Coll. Monast. Th. 28, 31. Nā elles *haud secus*, Ælfc. Gr. 38; Som. 42, 3. Ðū hit nā hū elles begitan ne miht, Bt. 32; Fox 114, 8. Ne mæg hē nō ðē raþor, Bt. tit. 32; Fox xvi, 15. Næs him nō ðȳ læs underþeóded eall ðes middangeard, 16, 4; Fox 58, 10. Ðā nā ðē læs beseah Lothes wīf underbæc, Scrd. 22, 42. Nō ðȳ fægra wæs, Cd. Th. 203, 6; Exod. 399. Nō ðȳ sēl dyde, 246, 35; Dan. 489. Ne sȳ nā tō ðæs hwōn (*on no account*) geendod nāðer ne dægrēdsang ne ǣfensang būtan ðam drihtlīcan gebede, R. Ben. 38, 14: 87, 1, 10: 95, 7. Nā tō hwōn (nā tō ðæs hwōn, MS. T.), 111, 10. v. lytes-nā.

nabban (= ne habban, *the verb is conjugated throughout*) *not to have, to be without*:—Næbbe ic synne gefremed, Cd. Th. 160, 15; Gen. 2650. Næbbe ic welan, Andr. Kmbl. 601; An. 301. Nafast hlāfes wiste, 621; An. 311. Ðū næfst nān þing, Jn. Skt. 4, 11. Næft ðū, Bt. Met. Fox 20, 71; Met. 20, 36. Hē nǣnige mehte nafaþ, Blickl. Homl. 31, 33. Hē wilnaþ . . . ðæs ðe hē næft, Bt. 11, 1; Fox 34, 2. Næfþ, Ps. Th. 71, 12. Wē nabbaþ, Mk. Skt. 9, 13. Earmra manna gehelpan ðe sylfe nabbaþ and ðæra myhta nabbaþ ðæt hié wyrcen māgon, L. E. I. 3, Th. ii. 404, 22. Hī heora nabbaþ mā ðonne hī heora habban, Bt. 26, 1;

Fox 90, 19. Đonne đū hæfdest đæt đū noldest odđe næfdest đæt đū woldest, Fox 90, 31. Næfde heó nôht on hire, Blickl. Homl. 147, 15. Næfde gē, Jn. Skt. 9, 41. Nafa đū fremde godas, Deut. 5, 7. Đonne gē faran næbbe gē mid eów hlāf, Blickl. Homl. 233, 17. Gif hē wīf næbbe, Ex. 21, 4. Ne mæg đæt nā beón đæt đa bearn langunga nabban, Blickl. Homl. 131, 26. Næbben, Beo. Th. 3705; B. 1850. Hēt mē fremdne god hergan, odđe hī nabban, Exon. Th. 247, 12; Jul. 77. Sint hī đē pliólīcran hæfd đonne næfd, Bt. 14, 1; Fox 42, note 10. [*O. Frs.* combines the negative with the verb in the same way.] v. ge-næfd.

nabo-gâr, nabula. v. nafo-gâr, nafola.

naca, an; *m. A boat, bark, ship, vessel:*—Ne hié scip fereþ, naca, Exon. Th. 439, 17; Rä. 59, 5. Sǣgeáp naca, Beo. Th. 3797; B. 1896. Heáhstefn naca, Andr. Kmbl. 532; An. 266. Of nacan stefne, 582; An. 291: Exon. Th. 306, 14; Seef. 7. On bearm nacan, Beo. Th. 433; B. 214. Nēđan on nacan tealtum, Runic pm. 343, 22; Rūn. 21. Flotan nīwtyrwydne, nacan, Beo. Th. 596; B. 295: Exon. Th. 474, 31; Bo. 39. [*O. Sax.* nako: *O. H. Ger.* nacho: *Icel.* nökkvi.] v. hring-, sǣ-, ȳđ-naca.

nacian; *p.* ode *To strip* (*the clothes off a person*):—Đā hē đæt nolde hē wæs nacod and on carcern onsænded *when he would not do that* (*deny Christ*), *he was stripped and sent to prison*, Shrn. 51, 12. [The shenship of his flesh he shal *nakyn*, Wick. Lev. xx, 19; he *nakide* (later version, *made nakid*) the hous of the pore man, Job xx, 19: O nice men, whi *nake* ye youre bakkes, Chauc. Boeth. l. 4288: *Prompt. Parv.* nakyn *nudo, denudo*, v. p. 351, note 1. The verb *to nake* occurs as late as Tourneur who has '*nake* your swords;' v. Skeat Dict. s. v. naked.] v. be-nacian, nacod.

nacod, næcad; *adj.* I. *naked, bare;* nudus:—Nacod *exertum*, Wrt. Voc. ii. 144, 70. Næcad *exerta*, 107, 78. (a) of persons, *without clothing:*—Nacod and ceald *nuda*, 61, 65. Nacod plegere *gymnosophista*, i. 17, 10. Ic eom nacod (*nudus*), Gen. 3, 10, 11. Đā sæt đǣr sum þearfa nacod, bæd him hrægles, Blickl. Homl. 213, 33: Cd. Th. 255, 32; Dan. 633. Ic wæs nacud and gē mē scrȳddon, Mt. Kmbl. 25, 36: Cd. Th. 207, 29; Exod. 474. Gif đū earm gewurđe, geþenc đū đæt đīn mōder đē nacodne gebær, Prov. Kmbl. 15. Nacode wē wǣron ācennede, and nacode wē gewītaþ, Homl. Th. i. 64, 28. Gē gēfon hrægl nacedum, Exon. Th. 83, 13; Cri. 1355. Nacode scrȳdan, Blickl. Homl. 213, 18. Se feónd swā micle iédlīcor đæt mōd gewundaþ swā hē hit ongiet nacodre đære byrnan wærscipes, Past. 56; Swt. 431, 10. (b) of an animal, *unsaddled, bare-backed:*—Hē nolde on nacedum assan rīdan, Homl. Th. i. 210, 27. (c) of a sword, *naked, unsheathed:*—Him ne hangaþ nacod sweord ofer đam heáfde, Bt. 29, 1; Fox 102, 27: Beo. Th. 1082; B. 539. II. *bare* in a metaph. sense, (a) of persons, *destitute, stripped of property:*—Se nacoda wegfērend *vacuus viator*, Bt. 14, 3; Fox 46, 29. Đū (*Adam*) scealt on wræc hweorfan, nacod niédwædla, neorxna wanges dugeþum bedǣled, Cd. Th. 57, 16; Gen. 929. Đū (*Laban*) mē (*Jacob*) woldest forlǣtan nacodne, Gen. 31, 42. (b) of words, *not accompanied by deeds:*—God nele đæt đū hine lufie mid nacodum wordum ac mid rihtwīsum dǣdum, Basil admn. 4; Norm. 40, 18. [*Goth.* nakwaþs: *Icel.* nökviðr: *O. Frs.* nakad: *O. H. Ger.* nachot, nahhut: *Ger.* nackt.] v. eall-, lim-nacod; nacian.

nacodian. v. ge-nacodian. [*O. H. Ger.* gi-, ant-nachatōn.]

nǣcan *to kill:*—Ic nǣce (other MSS. knǣce, nǣte) odđe ic ācwelle *neco*, Ælfc. Gr. 24; Som. 25, 56. [Cf. *O. H. Ger.* neihan *immolare*, Grff. 2, 1015.]

næced, e; *f. Nakedness:*—Gif hwylc man stele mete odđe clāđas and hine hungor odđe næced đǣrtō drife (*fames vel nuditas eum coegerit*), L. Ecg. P. iv. 25; Th. ii. 212, 4. Drihten āsent hungor on eów and þurst and næcede, Deut. 28, 48. [*Goth.* nakwadei: *Icel.* nekt *nakedness.*]

næcedness, e; *f. Nakedness:*—Swā đæt hig ne gesāwon heora fæder næcednesse, Gen. 9, 23. Đē ne sceamaþ đīnre næcednysse, Homl. Th. i. 432, 5.

næct, nædder-, næddre, nǣdel. v. niht, næder-, nædre, nǣdl.

næder-bīta, an; *m. An ichneumon:*—Næderbīta *hinc neomon* (=*ichneumon*), Wrt. Voc. ii. 43, 49. Nædderbīta *cicidemon*, 131, 40.

næder-winde, an; *f.* The name of a plant, *adder-wort:*—Næddrewinde *viperina*, Wrt. Voc. i. 63, 26. v. next word.

næder-, nædre-wyrt, e; *f. Adder-wort;* polygonum bistorta:—Nædderwyrt *uiperina*, Wülck. Gl. 300, 23. Nædrewyrt. Đeós wyrt đe man *uiperinam* and ōđrum naman nædderwyrt nemneþ, Lchdm. i. 96, 11. Nædderwyrt. Đeós wyrt đe man *basilisca* and ōđrum naman nædder- (næddre-, MS. O) wyrt nemneþ, 242, 7: iii. 8, 24. Genim næderwyrte, ii. 110, 25. [v. E. D. S. Pub. Plant Names, *adderwort*, and Lchdm. ii. Glossary.]

nǣdl, e; *f. A needle:*—Nǣdl *acus*, Wrt. Voc. i. 85, 4: Ælfc. Gr. 11; Som. 15, 18. Hwanon seámere nǣdl *unde sartori acus*, Coll. Monast. Th. 30, 33. Þurh nǣdle (nēdle, Rush.) eáge *per foramen acus*, Mt. Kmbl. 19, 24: Lk. Skt. 18, 25. Þurh nǣdle þyrel, Mk. Skt. 10, 25: Wrt. Voc. ii. 73, 1. Nǣdle sceorpran, Soul Kmbl. 230; Seel. 116. Mid nēdle *acu*, Wrt. Voc. ii. 117, 37. Mid naeđlae, Ep. Gl. 19 f, 30. [*Goth.* nēþla: *O. Sax.* nādla: *O. Frs.* nēdle: *O. H. Ger.* nādala: *Icel.* nál.] v. feax-, hǣr-nǣdl.

nædre, næddre, an; *f. Any kind of serpent, adder, viper:*—Nædre *gipsa*, Wrt. Voc. ii. 41, 55: *natrix*, 97, 36: 60, 77. Snaca odđe nædre *coluber*, 16, 75. Gerumpenu, gehyrnedu nædre *coluber cerastis*, 15, 68: 16, 2. Mē nædre beswāc, Cd. Th. 55, 20; Gen. 897. Næddre *vipera* vel *serpens* vel *anguis*, Wrt. Voc. i. 78, 55. Fleónde næddre, 24, 1. Đære nædran *basilisci*, ii. 12, 2: 86, 58. Efter gelīcnisse nedran (*serpentes*), Ps. Surt. 57, 5: Cd. Th. 271, 8; Sat. 102. Đære scortan næddran *spalangii*, Hpt. Gl. 450, 25. Nedran *colubri*, Kent. Gl. 1095. God cwæþ tō đære næddran (*ad serpentem*), Gen. 3, 14. Nædran *celidrum*, Wrt. Voc. ii. 21, 21. Nædran *hilidros*, i. *celidros*, 43, 38. Swā swā Moyses āhōf đa næddran . . . Đā sende God fȳrene næddran . . . God bebeád Moyse đæt hē geworhte āne ǣrene næddran, and sette up tō tācne, and đæt hē manode đæt folc đæt swā hwā swā fram đām næddrum ābiten wǣre, besāwe up tō đære ǣrenan næddran, Homl. Th. ii. 238, 4–19. Nædran *serpentes*, Ps. Th. 139, 3. Gif mon hine (gagates) on fȳr dēþ, đonne fleóþ đǣr neddran onweg, Bd. 1, 1; S. 473, 25. Nædrena *draconum*, Wrt. Voc. ii. 27, 71. Næddrena āttor *venenum aspidum*, Deut. 32, 33. Lā næddrena (ætterna, Lind.; nedrana, Rush.) cyn *progenies viperarum*, Mt. Kmbl. 3, 7: 12, 34. Hig wurpon ealle hira gyrda nyđer and hī wurdon tō næddrum (*versae sunt in dracones*), Ex. 7, 12. [*Goth.* nadrs: *Icel.* naðr (*in poetry*); *m.*; naðra; *f.*: *O. Sax.* nadra: *O. H. Ger.* natra, natara; *f.*: *Ger.* natter.] v. hilde-, mere-, wæternædre.

næfde = ne hæfde. v. nabban.

næfig; *adj. Not having means, poor:*—Þarfa ɫ næfga (næfge, Lind.) *mendicus*, Jn. Skt. Rush. 9, 8. Næfigum (næfigum, Lind.) *egenis*, 13, 29. Næfigum, Lind. 12. 5.

nǣfre (=ne ǣfre); *adv. Never.* I. alone:—Nǣfre ætȳwde swylc, Mt. Kmbl. 9, 33. Nǣfre ic māran geseah eorl ofer eorþan, Beo. Th. 500; B. 247. Nǣfre gē mid blōde beódgereordu eówre þicgeaþ, Cd. Th. 91, 26; Gen. 1518. Eádig biþ se đe in his ēþle geþīhþ; earm se him his frȳnd geswīcaþ; nēfre (?) sceal se him his nest āspringeþ (*never shall he thrive whose provision fails him* (?). Grein takes *nefre*=infirmus), Exon. Th. 335, 23; Gn. Ex. 38. II. with another negative:—Ne hit nǣfre ne gewurđe *nec unquam fiat*, Ælfc. Gr. 38; Som. 40, 14. Đæt hī nǣfre ne gedōþ, Bt. 14, 2; Fox 44, 15. Nǣfre siđan Rōmāne ne rīcsodon on Bretone, Chr. 409; Erl. 10, 7. Hié nǣfre his banan folgian noldon, 755; Erl. 50, 20. Nān man ne dorste sleán ōđerne man, næfde hē nǣfre swā mycel gedōn wid đone ōđerne, 1086; Erl. 222, 6.

nǣgan, nēgan; *p.* de *To address, accost, speak to:*—Nigeþan sīþe nǣgde se gomola, sǣgde eaforan worn, Exon. Th. 304, 5; Fä. 65. *But generally the verb is accompanied by* wordum:—Đū mē wordum nǣgest, fūsne frignest, 175, 26; Gū. 1200. Hine weroda God wordum nǣgde, Cd. Th. 179, 4; Exod. 23. Hē đone wīsan wordum nǣgde (hnǣgde, MS.) freán Ingwina, Beo. Th. 2641; B. 1318. Ongan đā wīf weras wordum nēgan, Elen. Kmbl. 574; El. 287: 1115; El. 559. v. ge-nǣgan.

nægel, nægl, es; *m.* I. *the nail of a finger* or *toe:*—Nægel *unguis;* næglas *ungues*, Wrt. Voc. i. 43, 60. Fingras *digiti* . . . nægel *ungula*, 65, 4. Nægl, 283, 25. Nægl *unguana*, ii. 124, 10. Gif nægl of honda weorđe *if a nail come off a hand*, Lchdm. iii. 58, 7: ii. 80, 20. Gif þuman nægl of weorđeþ, .iii. scill. gebēte . . . Æt đām neglum gehwylcum scilling *if a thumb-nail come off* (*from a blow*) *the* bōt *shall be* iii *shillings . . . For each finger-nail a shilling* (cf. L. Alf. pol. 56–60; Th. i. 94, 96 *where the* bōt *for the thumb-nail is* 5 *shillings, for the nail of the fore-finger and for that of the ring-finger* 4 *shillings each, for that of the middle finger* 2 *shillings, and for that of the little finger one shilling*), L. Ethb. 54, 55; Th. i. 16, 9–14. Wid scurfedum nægle; nim gecyrnadne sticcan, sete on đone nægl, Lchdm. ii. 150, 4: i. 370, 9: iii. 114, 21. Deóplīc dǣdbōt biþ . . ., đæt īren ne cume on hǣre ne on nægle, L. Edg. C. 10; Th. ii. 280, 21. God of đam lāme flǣsc worhte and blōd, bān and fell, fex and næglas, Homl. Th. i. 236, 16. II. *a nail, peg:*—Nægl *clavus*, Wrt. Voc. ii. 22, 10. Nægl *paxillum, palum*, 116, 27. Nægles *epigri* vel *clavi*, i. 39, 63. Nægle *cuspide*, ii. 21, 24. Đǣr hȳdde wǣron næglas (*the nails by which Christ was fastened to the cross*) on eorþan, Elen. Kmbl. 2216; El. 1109: 2227; El. 1115: 2344; El. 1173. Ne gelȳfe ic būton ic geseó đæra nægela (*clavorum*) fæstnunge on his handa, and ic dō mīnne finger on đære nægela stede, Jn. Skt. 20, 25. Đæt fȳr eode andlang đara nægla đe seó studu mid gefæstnad wæs tō đam wāge, Bd. 3, 17; S. 544, 31, col. 1. Mid næglum þurhdrīfan đa hwītan honda, Exon. Th. 68, 27; Cri. 1110: Rood Kmbl. 91; Kr. 46. Hié nāmon treówu, and slōgon on ōđerne ende monige scearpe īsene næglas, Ors. 4, 1; Swt. 158, 5. Heó lǣdde tō hire suna đa īsenan næglas đe wǣron ādrifene þurh Cristes folman, Homl. Th. ii. 306, 15. Nægelas geseón anxsumnysse getācnaþ, Lchdm. iii. 212, 24. III. *an instrument for striking the strings of a harp*, v. hearpenægel, Exon. Th. 332, 12; Vy. 84. [*O. Sax.* nagal (*in both senses*): *O. Frs.* neil (*in both senses*): *O. H. Ger.* nagal *unguis, clavus. paxillus*: *Icel.* nagl *unguis;* nagli *clavus*: cf. *Goth.* ga-nagljan.] v. hearpe-, scōh-, steór-nægel.

nægel-seax, es; *n. A knife for cutting the nails*:—Næglsex *novaculum*, Wrt. Voc. i. 35, 22: *novacula*, 86, 22. [*Laym.* nail-sax (-sex).]

nǽgen=ne mǽgen:—Gedó ðæt hý nægen dón ðæt yfel ðæt hý þencaþ *make them unable to do the evil that they devise*; decidant a cogitationibus suis, Ps. Th. 5, 11.

nægled-bord. v. næglian.

nægled-cnearr, es; *m. A vessel the planks of whose sides are nailed together*:—Gewitan him ðá Norþmen nægledcnearrum, Chr. 937; Erl. 115, 2; Æðelst. 53.

næglian; *p.* ode, ede *To nail, fasten with nails*:— Hí dulfon ꝉ nægledun handa míne and fét míne *foderunt manus meas, et pedes meas*, Ps. Lamb. 21, 17. Siæ nægled on róde *crucifigatur*, Mt. Kmbl. Rush. 27, 23. Ne hié scip fereþ naca nægled bord (*or* nægled-bord; adj.?) *nor does ship carry her, vessel, nailed plank* (or *with nail-fastened sides*), Exon. Th. 439, 17; Rä. 59, 5. Siððan nægled bord, fær séleste, flód up áhóf, Cd. Th. 85, 22. Hwonne hié of nearwe ofer nægled bord stæppan mósten *when from durance over the vessel's* (*the ark*) *nail-fastened side they might step*, 86, 20; Gen. 1433. Hió [næ]gled sinc hæleþum sealde (*bracelets fastened with rivets* or *studs*), Beo. Th. 4051; B. 2023. Næglede (ætlede, Th.) beágas, Exon. Th. 474, 22; Bo. 34. Nægledne, 400, 7; Rä. 20, 5. [*Goth.* ga-nagljan: *Icel.* negla: *O. Sax.* neglian; negilid sper, neglit skip: *O. H. Ger.* nagalian.] v. ge-nægled.

Nægling *the name of Beowulf's sword*:—Nægling forbærst, sweord Beówulfes, Beo. Th. 5354; B. 2680.

nǽh, næht, nǽht, nǽm, nǽman, nǽmne. v. neáh, niht, náht, níd-nǽm, be-, míd-nǽman, nemne.

nǽming, e; *f. Acceptance, agreement, bargain*:—Ceáp *distractio*; sala *venditio*; nǽmingce *contractio* vel *contractus*, Wrt. Voc. i. 55, 54-56.

nǽnig (=ne ǽnig). I. used as an adjective, *not any, none, no*, (a) without another negative:—Nǽnig óðer hý ǽfre má eft onlúceþ, Exon. Th. 20, 27; Cri. 324. Ðeáh ðe nǽnegu néðþearf wǽre, Met. 20, 25. Ðǽr nǽngu biþ niht on sumera, 16, 13. Naenge earbeðe *nullo negotio*, Wrt. Voc. ii. 115, 5. Nǽnigne ic sélran hýrde hordmádmum, Beo. Th. 2398; B. 1197. Hafaþ tóþ nǽnigne, Exon. Th. 439, 24; Rä. 59, 8: Cd. Th. 272, 20; Sat. 122. Him ðæs nǽnige bót dydon, Blickl. Homl. 201, 23. (b) with other negatives:—Nǽnig mon ne sceal lufian ne ne géman his gesibbes, 23, 16. Ðæt wíte ðe nǽfre nǽnig ende ne becymeþ, 51, 31. Ne hé nǽnigne man unrihtlíce fordémde, ne hine nǽnig man yrne ne funde, 223, 32. Ðǽr him nǽnig wæter wihte ne sceþede, Beo. Th. 3032; B. 1514. Óðer nǽnig sélra nǽre, 1723; B. 859. Nis nǽnigu gecynd, Salm. Kmbl. 839; Sal. 419. Ne sý eów nǽnigu cearo, Blickl. Homl. 145, 8. Ne hié nǽnigo firen ne gewundode, 161, 33. Næs nǽnig ylding, 87, 17. Nis nǽnig máre mægen, 31, 30. Eów nǽnig wuht ne deraþ, And. 14, 8. God ðonne ne gýmeþ nǽnges mannes hreówe, Blickl. Homl. 95, 29. Nǽnges þinges máre þearf nǽre, 175, 8. Hé nǽfre nǽnigum woruldrícum men onbúgan nolde, 223, 27. Warna ðé ðæt ðú hyt nǽnegum men ne secge, Mt. Kmbl. 8, 4. Ðæt hé nǽnigum óðrum men ne sǽde, Bd. 5, 9; S. 623, 3: Blickl. Homl. 221, 16. Hié eów tó nǽnigre áre ne belimpeþ, Blickl. Homl. 41, 23: 179, 15. Hí ne mihtan ðære heorde nǽnige góde beón, 45, 16. Hé nǽnige mehte wið ús nafaþ, 31, 33: 79, 7. Ne bideþ hé æt ús nǽnig óðor edleán, 103, 21. Ne ðǽr nǽnige þingunga ne beóþ, 95, 30: 157, 13: 185, 9. Hé nǽfre nǽnige godcunde englas næfde, 181, 28. II. as a substantive, *no one, not any one*, (a) without another negative:—Nǽnig bihelan mæg wom unbéted, Exon. Th. 80, 23; Cri. 1311: 294, 20; Crä. 18: Beo. Th. 3870; B. 1933. Nǽnig óðerne freóþ, Frag. Kmbl. 69; Leás. 36: Exon. Th. 491, 29; Rä. 81, 6. Nǽnegum þuhte dæg on þonce, Met. 12, 15. Se ðe nǽngum scód, Exon. Th. 90, 1; Cri. 1467. Nǽnige *neminem*, Hpt. Gl. 457, 57. Ðǽr hé nǽnige forlét bendum fæstne, Andr. Kmbl. 2074; An. 1039. (b) with other negatives:—Nis nǽnig swá snotor nymþe God seolfa, Cd. Th. 286, 8; Sat. 349. Ðone nǽnig heonon ne sceáwaþ, Blickl. Homl. 31, 9. Nǽnigne tweógean ne þearf, 83, 9. III. with partitive gen. (a) without another negative:—Nǽnig fira ðæs fród leofaþ, Exon. Th. 351, 6; Sch. 76. Nǽnig wera gewiste, 412, 13; Rä. 30, 13. Nǽnig manna is, Andr. Kmbl. 1088; An. 544: Salm. Kmbl. 120; Sal. 59. Him nǽnig wæs ǽlǽrendra óðer betera, Elen. Kmbl. 1008; El. 505. Nǽnig heora þohte, Beo. Th. 1385; B. 691. Nǽnegum áraþ leóde Deniga, 1201; B. 598. Ic nǽngum sceððe burgsittendra, Exon. Th. 407, 9; Rä. 26, 2. Mid ðý se cyning nǽnige þinga (*nulla tenus*) his bénum geþafian wolde, Bd. 3, 24; S. 556, 11. (b) with other negatives:—Ne ðǽr nǽnig wihte wénan þorfte, Beo. Th. 316; B. 157: 490; B. 242. Nǽnig gumena ongitan ne mihte, Andr. Kmbl. 1971; An. 988; Salm. Kmbl. 867; Sal. 433. Nǽniges Godes háligra gebyrd, ne his heáhfædera ... ciricean ne mǽrsiaþ nemþe ..., Blickl. Homl. 161, 9. Nis ðæt mín miht ne nǽniges úres (=úre nǽniges), 151, 29. Be ðare nǽnigum gecweden beón ne mihte, 161, 22. Ne eart ðú ðon leófre nǽngum lifgendra, Exon. Th. 370, 5; Seel. Ex. 54. Ðeós dǽd nǽnige þinga forholen ne wurþe, Lchdm. iii. 60, 24: Met. 10, 16: 19, 37. Ne sculon mæssepreóstas náteshwón nǽnig þinga bútan óðrum mannum mæssan syngan, L. E. I. 7; Th. ii. 406, 21.

nǽnig-wiht; *adv. Nothing, not, not at all*:—Andreas nǽnigwuht ðú gefirnodest *Andrew, thou hast nothing sinned*, And. 10, 20. v. nán-wiht.

nǽniht. v. nán-wiht.

nǽp, es; *m. Turnip, rape*:—Nǽp *napus, rapa*, Wrt. Voc. i. 31, 44, 51: *napis*, 68, 18: 286, 26: ii. 114, 56. Wilde nǽp *nap silvatica*, i. 31, 27: *diptamnus* vel *bibulcos*, 32, 5. Nim Ænglisce nǽp, Lchdm. iii. 12, 14. Nim smælne nǽp, 40, 5. Healde hine wið nǽpas, and wið ða þing ðe windigne ǽþm on men wyrcen, ii. 214, 3. [Nepe *bacar*, Wrt. Voc. i. 191, 39: nepe *coloquintida, cucurbita*, Prompt. Parv. 353. See also E. D. S. Plant Names, *nape, nep*: *Icel.* næpa; *f. a turnip*.]

nǽp-sǽd, es; *n. Seed of turnip* or *of rape*:—Genim senepes sǽdes dǽl and nǽpsǽdes, Lchdm. ii. 24, 15. Nim senepsǽd and nǽpsǽd, iii. 88, 15.

næpte, nǽre, nǽron. v. nepte, næs.

næs=ne wæs *was not*:—Wǽre ðú tódæg on huntnoþe? Ic næs, Coll. Monast. Th. 22, 1: 34, 9. Ðú nǽre mildsiend ofer heora cild, Blickl. Homl. 249, 6. Man næs, ðe ða eorþan worhte, Gen. 2, 5. Nǽron ðá welige hámas, ne diórwyrþra hrægla hí ne girndan, forðam hí ðá git nǽran, Bt. 15; Fox 48, 4-6. Ða cyningas Rómeburg begeáton ðǽr Mutius nǽre (*if it had not been for Mucius*), Ors. 2, 3; Swt. 68, 20. Gif hé nǽre yfeldǽde, ne sealde wé hine ðé, Jn. Skt. 18, 30. Hié wýscaþ ðæt hié nǽfre nǽron ácennede Blickl. Homl. 93, 28. [*O. Frs.* nas=ne was; nére=ne wére.]

næs; *adv. Not*. I. alone:—Búton hit riht sprǽc sý and behéfe næs ídel *nisi recta locutio sit et utilis, non anilis*, Coll. Monast. Th. 18, 16. Ic wylle mildheortnesse næs onsægdnesse, Mt. Kmbl. 9, 13. Gif hit fæger is, ðæt is of heora ágnum gecynde, næs of ðínum; heora fæger hit is, næs ðín, Bt. 14, 2; Fox 42, 33. Heó wæs ful cweden, næs æmetugu, Blickl. Homl. 5, 5. Ic cýðe mid dǽdum, næs mid wordum ánum, 181, 25: Ps. Th. 48, 12. Næs hié ðære fylle gefeán hæfdon, Beo. Th. 1128; B. 562: 6140; B. 3074. II. with another negative:—Ábréd of ða fiðeru, næs ne cerfe, Lev. 1, 17. Ic ondrǽde ðæt hé wirige mé, and næs ná bletsige, Gen. 27, 12. Ðonne telle ic ða weorþmynd ðæm wyrhtan, næs ná ðé, Bt. 14, 1; Fox 42, 19. Gif ðú gesáwe þeóf, ðú urne mid him, næs ná ongeán hine, Ps. Th. 49, 19. Gesceapene tó ðon écan lífe, næs ná tó ðon écan deáþe, Blickl. Homl. 61, 8. Næs ná mid golde, ac mid gódum dǽdum, 95, 19. Lufian wé hine næs nó on gesundum þingum ánum, ac eác swylce on wiðerweardum þingum, 13, 7. [*O. Frs.* nas.]

næsc *fawn-skin*:—Fel *pellis*, hýd *cutis* vel *corium*; næsc *nebris*, Wrt. Voc. i. 86, 37-39. Gefóh fox, ásleah of cucum ðone tuxl, lǽt hleápan áweg, bind on næsce, hafa ðé on, Lchdm. ii. 104, 13: 140, 10. Dó on næsc, 36, 8. Naescum *tractibus* (cf. tracta; *pl. in mulomedicina emplastrum ex variis medicamentis compositum, et in tela linea distentum*, Forcellini.), Wrt. Voc. ii. 122, 77.

næse. v. nese.

næs-gristle *the gristle* or *cartilage of the nose*: — Naesgristlae *cartilago*, Ep. Gl. 7 b, 5. Naesgristle, Wrt. Voc. ii. 102, 45. Næsgristle, 13, 10. [Þe laðe helle wurmes þe freoteð ham ut te ehnen ant te nease gristles, O. E. Homl. i. 251, 16.] v. nos-gristle.

næss, ness, es; *m.* I. *a ness, land running out into water, headland, promontory*. [The word *ness* found in English local names is mostly of Scandinavian origin, *Icel.* nes; but, in a charter of 778, Cod. Dip. Kmbl. iii. 382, 28, Tucingnæs occurs, and in another of 801 is the passage, 'adjecto uno piscatorio on Taemise fluuio ubi dicitur Fiscnaes,' i. 216, 25. Other instances in the charters are, Herces næs, iii. 437, 1: on scearpan næsse, 438, 22. Earna næs *Eagles-ness*, Beo. Th. 6055; B. 3031, Hrones næs *Whales-ness*, 5603; B. 2805, are examples of the word in foreign local names]:—Æt brimes næsse *at the sea-headland*, Andr. Kmbl. 3417; An. 1712. Beorh wæterýðum neáh, be næsse, Beo. Th. 4478; B. 2243. Gesæt on næsse cyning, 4825; B. 2417. Wearþ on næs (*of a lake*) togen wundorlíc wǽgbora, 2883; B. 1439: 3205; B. 1600. Se ðe næs (*by the sea*) geràd, 5789; B. 2898. Windige næssas *wind-swept headlands*, 2721; B. 1358. Neowle næssas *headlands that plunge into the water*, 2826; B. 1411. Hié Geáta clifu ongitan meahton, cúþe næssas, 3828; B. 1912. II. in connection with *under, niðer*, and often in pl. *ground* (as in under-*ground*):—Ongan ðá eorþan delfan, ðæt hé on twentigum fótmǽlum feor funde behelede under neólum niðer næsse gehýdde in þeóstorcofan (*he found the cross hidden twenty feet underground*), Elen. Kmbl. 1661; El. 832. Gǽst ellor hwearf under neowelne næs (*underground*, i. e. *to hell*), Judth. Thw. 239; Jud. 113. Sunne gewát tó sete glídan under niflań næs (*sink beneath the horizon*), Andr. Kmbl. 2611; An. 1307. Fyrgenstreám under næssa genipu niðer gewíteþ (*the stream disappears in a dark chasm*), flód under foldan, Beo. Th. 2724; B. 1360. Hí (*the fallen angels*) gedúfan sceolun niðær undær nessas (*to hell*) in ðone neowlan grund, Cd. Th. 266, 32; Sat. 31: 270, 15; Sat. 91. Ingong in ðæt atule hús (*hell*) niðer under næssas, neóle grundas, Exon. Th. 136, 2; Gú. 535. v. sǽ-næss *and next word*.

næsse, an; *f. A headland, promontory, cape*:—Óþ ða norþmestan næssan on eorþan *to the most northerly cape on earth*, Met. 9, 43. Næssun (-an?) *litora*, Germ. 400, 488. v. næss.

næss-hliþ, es; *n. The slope of a headland* :—Gesāwon on næshleoþum nicras licgean, Beo. Th. 2858; B. 1427.

nǽstan. v. ge-nǽstan.

næster *cancale* (=? καυκαλίς *wild carrot*), Wrt. Voc. ii. 129, 74.

næs-þyrel, -þyrl, es; *n. A nostril*:—Næsþyrel *pennula*, Wrt. Voc. i. 282, 66: *nares*, ii. 62, 5. Dō on ðæt næsþyrl, Lchdm. i. 352, 4. On næsþyrl bestungen, 348, 4. His (*the dead man*) næsþyrlo beóþ belocene, Blickl. Homl. 59, 14. Wið næsþyrla (næsþurla, 14, 11) sāre, Lchdm. i. 114, 19. Blōdryne of næsþyrlon, 282, 12. Mid hundes lūsum, ða flugon intō heora mūðe and heora næsþyrlum, Homl. Th. ii. 192, 22. Hit gǽþ þurh eówre næsþyrlu *exeat per nares vestras*, Num. 11, 20: Ps. Spl. 113, 14. Dō on ða næsþyrlu, Lchdm. i. 72, 21. [*Wick.*: *Prompt. Parv.* nese-þirl.] v. nos-þyrel.

nǽtan; *p.* te *To trample upon, crush, subdue*:—Oft ic cwice bærne nǽte mid nīþe *oft the living I burn, painfully oppress them*, Exon. Th. 389, 7; Rä. 7, 4. Hē sceal weorðan his līfe tō nytte mid ðȳ ðæt hē nǽte his unþeáwas *mores pravorum premere, vitae prodesse*, Past. 46, 5; Swt. 353, 10. Nǽtendne *proterentem*, Wrt. Voc. ii. 118, 3: Ep. Gl. 18 b, 27. v. ge-nǽtan *and next word*.

nǽting, e; *f. Blaming, upbraiding*:—Ac hū wēne wē hū micel scyld ðæt sīe ðæt monn āþreóte ðære nǽtinge yfelra monna and nime sume sibbe wið ða wierrestan *pensandum ergo est, quando ab increpatione quiescitur, quanta culpa cum pessimis pax tenetur*, Past. 46, 6; Swt. 353, 11. [Cf. *Goth.* naiteins *blasphemy*.]

nafa *a nave*. v. nafu: nafa = ne hafa. v. nabban.

nafela, an; *m. The navel*:—Nabula *umbilicus*, Wülck. Gl. 54, 13. Navela, Wrt. Voc. i. 44, 50. Ðīnum nafelan, Kent. Gl. 32. Hē (*Minutius*) hiene (*the elephant*) on ðone nafelan ofstang, Ors. 4, 1; Swt. 156, 11. [*O. Frs.* navla: *Icel.* nafli: *O. H. Ger.* nabalo.]

nafel-sceaft, e; *f. The navel*:—Ðisne lǽcedōm man sceal dō ðan manne se his nafulsceaft in tȳhþ, Lchdm. iii. 124, 22.

nafeþa, an; *m. A nave*:—Naveþa *modiolus*, Wrt. Voc. i. 16, 22.

nafu, e; *f.*: nafa (?), an; *m. A nave*:—Nafu *modialis*, Wrt. Voc. i. 284, 55. Sió nafa (nafu, Cott.) nēhst ðære eaxe, Bt. 39, 7; Fox 220, 29. Sió nafu, Fox 222, 1. Se nafa, 222, 12. Fæst on ðære nafe, 222, 3, 8, 9, 11, 12. [*Icel.* nöf: *O. H. Ger.* naba *modiolus*.]

nafu-gār, es; *m. An auger*:—Nabogaar *terebellus*, Wrt. Voc. ii. 122, 21. Nabogār *rotrum*, 119, 31. Nafogār *foratorium*, 149, 74: *foratorium* vel *terebellum*, 38, 50. Navegār *terebrum*, i. 16, 12: 84, 63. [Wymble, nauger *terere*, 170, 17: *O. H. Ger.* naba-gēr *terebellus, terebellum, terebrum*: *Icel.* nafarr: *Du.* ave-gaar.]

-nāg. v. ge-nāg.

nāgan = ne āgan. I. *not to have*, (a) with acc.:—Nāh se sacerd nāne þearfe (*sacerdoti non opus est*), ðæt hē forwyrne ðam men rihtre andetnysse, L. Ecg. P. i. 2; Th. ii. 172, 11. Gif hē nāh his selfes geweald, Met. 16, 21. Helle hlinduru nāgon hwyrft, Exon. Th. 364, 29; Wal. 78. Ðeáh ðū hī nǽfre nāhtest, Bt. 14, 2; Fox 44, 1. Hē nāhte his līchoman geweald, Blickl. Homl. 223, 11. Nāhton hié nāðer ne mete ne freónd, Ors. 2, 8; Swt. 92, 34. Sī on cynges dōme hwæðer hē līf āge ðe nāge, L. Eth. vii. 9; Th. i. 330, 25. (b) with gen.:—Nāgan wē ðæs heolstres, ðæt wē ūs gehȳdan māgon, Cd. Th. 271, 5; Sat. 101. II. *not to be allowed, ought not*:—Nāh nāðer tō farenne ne Wylisc man on Ænglisc land, ne Ænglisc man on Wylisc, L. O. P. 6; Th. i. 354, 23. Nāge hē hié ūt on elþeódig folc tō bebycgganne *it shall not be allowable for him to sell her abroad into a foreign people*, L. Alf. 12; Th. i. 46, 13. On ða gerād ðæt hine nāge nān man of tō āceápienne, Chart. Th. 151, 13. Ðæt hit nāge nān man fram ðære stōwe tō dǽlanne, 157, 6.

náht. v. nā-wiht.

nā-hwǽr, -hwār, -wēr; *adv.* I. *no-where, in no place*:—Nāhwǽr *nusquam*, Ælfc. Gr. 38; Som. 41, 55. Ðū ne ætstande nāhwār on ðisum earde *nec stes in omni circa regione*, Gen. 19, 17. Hē sōhte his wǽpnu, ac hē ne geseah hī nāhwǽr, Homl. Skt. 3, 257: Blickl. Homl. 59, 20: 181, 23. Ðeáh hē hire nāwēr ne geneálǽce on ǽlcere stōwe hē is hire emneneáh *though the sky nowhere approach the earth, it is everywhere equally near to it*, Bt. 33, 4; Fox 130, 22. II. *in no case, never*:—Ðās *prepositiones* ne beóþ nāhwār āna, ac beóþ ǽfre tō sumum ōðrum worde gefēgede, Ælfc. Gr. 47; Som. 48, 50. Ne heard sweopu hūse ðīnum nāhwǽr sceþþan [māgon], Ps. Th. 90, 10. Ðū mē nāhwār forlēte *thou didst never forsake me*, Homl. Th. i. 74, 32. III. *in no respect, not at all*:—Eall moncynn and ealle nētenu ne notigaþ nāwēr neáh feórþan dǽles ðisse eorþan *men and animals do not use anywhere near a fourth part of this earth*, Bt. 18, 1; Fox 62, 8: 18, 2; Fox 64, 6. Nese lā nese ne nāwēr neáh, Shrn. 196, 28. Ne trūige ūs swā wel, ne nāwēr neáh swā ðām, 197, 13. [Cf. *Icel.* hvergi nær.]

nā-hwǽrn (?), -wērn; *adv. No-where*:—Nāwern *non usquam*, Wrt. Voc. ii. 61, 9: 95, 8. Cf. ǽgwērn, Ors. Swt. 154, 22.

nā-hwæðer, nāwðer, nāðer, nōðer; *pron. Neither*:—Nāðor *neuter, neutra, neutrum*; nāðres *neutri*; nāðrum *neutro*, Ælfc. Gr. 18; Som. 21, 49. Getācnigende oððe sum þyngc tō dōne, oððe sum þingc tō þrowigenne, oððe nāðor, 19; Som. 22, 23, 25. Nāuðær næ sīe tō ðon gedurstig ne cyning næ bisceop ne nānes hādes man *nullus rex aut episcopus, vel aliquis alius potens, sit tam audax*, Cod. Dip. Kmbl. v. 218, 26. Ne fornime nōder ōðer ofer will *let neither of you deprive the other against his or her will*, Past. 51; Swt. 399, 34. Hī gecȳðaþ ðonne hié endiaþ ðæt hié nāwðer ne bióþ, 16, 3; Fox 56, 27. Ða þing ða ðe nāuðer ne sint, ne getrēwe tō habbenne ne eác ēðe tō forlǽtanne, 7, 2; Fox 18, 15. Dydon swā hwæðer swā hȳ dydon ne dohte him nāwðer *whichever of the two they did, neither did them any good*, Bt. 29, 2; Fox 106, 2: Exon. Th. 12, 22; Cri. 189. His rihtwīsnys nolde hī neádian tō nāðrum Homl. Th. i. 112, 3. Godes gelaþung nis būton nāðrum ðæra (*the strong and the weak*), ii. 390, 29. Swā mīn sāwl bād ðæt ðū swylce heó for nāhwæðer nōwiht hǽle *sicut expectavit anima mea, pro nihilo salvos facies eos*, Ps. Th. 55, 6. Ðæt se yfela mǽge dōn yfel ðeáh hē gōd ne mǽge, and se deáda ne mǽge nāuðer dōn, Bt. 36, 7; Fox 182, 25. Hié nāðer (nāwðer, Cott. MS.) ne māgon, ne ðīn helpan ne heora selfra, 14, 1; Fox 42, 9. Hié nāðer næfdon siððan, ne heora namon ne heora anweald, Ors. 3, 1; Swt. 98, 7. Se ðe nāðor nele, ne leornian ne tǽcan, Ælfc. Gr. pref.; Som. 1, 34. v. next word.

nā-hwæðer, nāwðer, nāðor; *conj. Neither*:—Ðā ðā wē hit nōhwæðer ne selfe ne lufodon ne eác ōðrum monnum ne lēfdon *when we neither loved it ourselves nor allowed it to other men*, Past. Swt. 5, 6. Wē nōhwæðēr ne hit witan nyllaþ ne hit bētan nyllaþ, ne furðum ne rēcaþ hwæðer wē hit ongieten, 28; Swt. 195, 5. Nāwðer ne ða wōhhǽmendan, ne ða ðe diófulgieldum þiówiaþ, ne ða unfæsðrādan, ne ða þiófas, ne ða giétseras, ne ða reáferas Godes rīce ne gesittaþ, 51; Swt. 401, 26. Nǽron nāwðer ne on Fresisc gescæpene, ne on Denisc, Chr. 897; Erl. 95, 15: Blickl. Homl. 45, 14. Lāreówas ne sceolan Godes dōmas nāwðer ne nā wanian, ne ne ēcan, 81, 4. Hié nāwðer ne him sylfum helpan ne mihton, ne nānum ðara ðe tō him āre wilnodan, 223, 2: Bt. 29, 2; Fox 106, 5. Ðā nolde hē āsendan nāðor ne engel, ne heáhengel, ne wītegan, ne apostolas, Homl. Th. ii. 6, 15. v. preceding word.

nā-hwanon; *adv. From nowhere*:—Sió his gesǽlþ him nāhwonan ūtane ne com, ac wæs simle on him selfum, Bt. 34, 7; Fox 144, 20.

nā-hwider; *adv. No-whither, to no place*:—Hȳ nāhwider faraþ būtan ðæs abbodes rǽde, R. Ben. 137, 10.

nalas (-læs, -les), nalles. v. nealles.

nām, e; *f. Seizure of property belonging to one which is in the hands of another*:—Be naame. Ne nime nān man nāne nāme, ne innan scīre ne ūt of scīre, ǽr man hæbbe þrīwa on hundrede his rihtes gebeden; (*but on the failure of legal means*) nime ðonne leáfe ðæt hē mōte hentan æfter his āgenan, L. C. S. 19; Th. i. 386, 9–17. Cf. Nullus *namium* capiat... accipiat licenciam *namium* capiendi, L. W. I. 45; Th. i. 485, 13–17: L. H. I. 29, 2; Th. i. 533, 7. Nulli sine judicio vel licencia *namiare* liceat alium in suo vel alterius, 51, 3; Th. i. 550, 5. [Cf. *Icel.* land-nām in Norse law *an unlawful holding of another man's land*, and hence a *fine* for trespassing on another man's land; in Icel. *the taking possession of land as a settler*: nes-nām *in phrase* nema nesnām *to land on a ness and seize cattle*: nām *a seizing by the mind, learning*: *O. H. Ger.* nāma; nōt-nāma *rapina*.]

nama, an; *m.* I. *a name*:—Sumum men, ðam is Æþelm nama, Cod. Dip. Kmbl. ii. 383, 24. Wæs ðæm hæftmēce Hrunting nama, Beo. Th. 2919; B. 1457. Ðære (eá) is Geon noma, Cd. Th. 15, 9; Gen. 230. *Ego hoc feci*, ic dyde ðis, ðon stent se ic on ðīnes naman stede, Ælfc. Gr. 5; Som. 3, 33. Naman *titulo*, Hpt. Gl. 509, 4: *vocabulo*, 517, 61. Hē nemþ his āgene sceáp be naman *propias oves vocat nominatim*, Jn. Skt. 10, 3. Be naman cīgean, Ps. Th. 146, 4. Ðone ilcan wē hātaþ ōðre naman ǽfensteorra, Bt. 4; Fox 8, 3: 33, 4; Fox 128, 27. Ðū nemdest eall mid āne noman, Met. 20, 56. Him se pāpa Petrus tō noman scōp, Bd. 5, 7; S. 620, 43. God him sette naman Adam, Homl. Th. i. 12, 31. Hī him naman gesceópon, 92, 27. Hit ofetes noman āgan sceolde, Cd. Th. 44, 34; Gen. 719. II. *a noun*:—*Nomen* is nama, mid ðam wē nemnaþ ealle þing... *Pronomen* is ðæs naman speliend... *Amans* lufigend cymþ of ðam worde *amo*, ic lufige; ðon nymþ hē of ðam naman him ealle ða six casus, Ælfc. Gr. 5; Som. 3, 26–46. Sume synd āgene naman, swā swā is Eádgār, Dūnstān. Sume gemǽnelīce, kyningc, biscop, Som. 4, 10–11. [*Goth.* namō: *Icel.* nafn: *O. Sax.* namo: *O. Frs.* noma: *O. H. Ger.* namo.] v. freó-, heáh-nama.

nam-bōc; *f. A book in which names are written, a register*:—Nombēc *albo*, Wrt. Voc. ii. 3, 1.

nam-bred, es; *n. A tablet on which names are written, a register*:—Nombred *albo*, Wrt. Voc. ii. 81, 35.

nam-cūþ; *adj. Having the name well-known, celebrated, famous, of note, of renown*:—Nabochodonossor se namcūþa cining, Ælfc. T. Grn. 8, 15. Ǽlcre namcūþre wyrte dǽl *a bit of every well-known plant*, Lchdm. i. 398, 9. Twegen sacerdas ðe ǽr on līfe wǽron swīðe namcūþe, Homl. Th. ii. 342, 3. Heáhfæderas namcūþe weras (*the twelve patriarchs*), Ælfc. T. Grn. 5, 2: R. Ben. 33, 20. On ðām gemōtan ðeáh rǽdlīce wurðan on namcūðan stōwan *in those assemblies, though advisedly they were made in places of note*, L. Eth. ix. 37; Th. i. 348, 18. Se rīca biþ namcūðre on his leóde ðonne se þearfa *the name of the rich man is better known in his country than that of the poor man*, Homl. Th. i. 330, 5. [Sodome and Gomorre, and alle þe nomecuðe buruhwes (*famous cities*) A. R. 334, 25. Cf. *Icel* nafn-kunnigr *famous*.]

namcūþlīce; *adv. By name:* — Ūre mǣþ nis ðæt wē ealle Godes gecorenan eów namcūðlīce gereccan *it is not within our power to recount to you by name all God's elect*, Homl. Th. ii. 72, 2. Hē gehwilce eardas namcūðlīce on gemynde hæfde, i. 558, 25. [Þurh him and ðurh ealle his freónd namcūðlīce, Chr. 1127; Erl. 256, 12.]

namian; *p.* ode. I. *to name, mention the name of, mention:*— Git ðū namast Crist *dost thou still name the name of Christ?* Homl. Skt. 8, 165. Ða twā tabelan getācnodon ða twā bebodu ðe ic nū namode, Homl. Th. ii. 204, 21. On ðære ylcan byrig ðe wē ǣr namodon, 296, 32. Namedon, Ælfc. Gr. 8; Som. 7, 7. Ðæt ðū nānne brȳdguman nǣfre mē ne namige *that you never mention the name of any bridegroom to me*, Homl. Skt. 9, 37. Ðeáh ðe wē ðās sinderlīce namian *though we mention the names of these in particular*, Homl. Th. ii. 432, 23. II. *to name, appoint by name to a particular duty, nominate:*—Gif hē ne mehte, ðonne namede him man six men, L. Ed. 1; Th. i. 158, 21. Beforan his witum ðe se cyng silf namode, L. Æðelst. v. 10; Th. i. 240, 6. III. *to name, give a name to:*— Hwī namode Crist Abel rihtwīsne? Boutr. Scrd. 18, 6. [*O. Frs.* nomia: *O. H. Ger.* namōn.] v. ge-namian.

nam-mǣlum; *adv. Name by name:*—Nammǣlum *nominatim, per singula nomina*, Hpt. Gl. 427, 28.

namnian; *p.* ode *To name, call by name:* — Se namnode ðone Hǣlend be his naman, Ælfc. T. Grn. 10, 16. [*O. Frs.* namna, nanna.] v. nemnan.

nām-rǣden[n], e; *f. Learning, erudition:*—Nāmrǣdenne *litterature*, Wrt. Voc. ii. 50, 19. [Cf. *Icel.* nām *learning, study.*]

nān [=ne ān]; *pron.* I. as adjective, *not one, none, no*, (a) without other negatives:—Nān mǣrra man wurde ācenned, Menol. Fox 319; Men. 161. Hit is nānum men getiohhod ac is eallum monnum *it is not intended for one man, but for all men*, Bt. 37, 2; Fox 188, 15. (b) with other negatives:—Ne nān heora ān nis nā læsse ðonne eall seó þrynnys *and no one of them is less than all the Trinity*, Homl. Th. i. 284, 1. Nān heort ne onscunode nǣnne león, ne nān hara nǣnne hund, ne nān neát nyste nǣnne andan ne nǣnne ege tō ōðrum, 35, 6; Fox 168, 9-11. Nān swylc ne cwom . . . brȳd, Exon. Th. 18, 28; Cri. 290. Swā nān ōðer nā dēþ mōnaþ, Menol. Fox 392; Men. 197. Nān þing ðæs folces belyfen næs *there was nothing left of the people*, St. And. 34, 13. Næs ðæt nān þing wundor ðæt . . . *it was no wonder that*, Deut. i. 37. Ða cild ðe niton nānes þinges nān gesceád ne gōdes ne yfeles, 1, 39. Seó leáse wyrd ne mæg ðam men dōn nǣnne dem, forðam heó nis nānes lofes wyrðe, Bt. 20; Fox 70, 22-24. Ne cyning næ bisceop ne nānes hādes man *nullus rex aut episcopus, vel aliquis alius potens*, Cod. Dip. Kmbl. v. 218, 28. Hié nǣfre tō nānum men ne becumaþ, Bt. 11, 1; Fox 30, 27. Hē on nāne wīsan ne mæg forbūgan *he can in no wise avoid*, 16, 2; Fox 54, 5. Ðā ne mihton hig him nān word andswarian ne nān ne dorste hyne nān þing māre āxigean, Mt. Kmbl. 22, 46. Ne sǣdon hyt mē nāne swā sōðfeste men, Shrn. 204, 22. II. as predicate:— Forhwī ðē hātan dysige men wuldor nū ðū nāne eart (nān neart, MS. Cott.) *why do foolish men call thee glory, when thou art none*, Bt. 30, 1; Fox 108, 3. III. as substantive, (a) absolutely, *none, no man, nothing:*—Nān mihtigra ðē nis, ne nān ðīn gelīca, 33, 4; Fox 128, 11. Nān in nearowe nēþan mōste, Exon. Th. 436, 12; Rä. 54, 13. Ðam wæs nān tō gedāle, Cd. Th. 84, 20; Gen. 1400. Hē nolde nǣnne forlǣtan ðe him fylgian wolde, Hy. Grn. 10. 38. Deáþ nāne forlēt, Met. 10, 66. (b) with partitive genitive:— Næs ǣnig engel geworden, ne ðæs miclan mægen-þrymmes nān, Exon. Th. 22, 17; Cri. 352. Him ne mæg ealdfeónda nān ātre sceþþan, 229, 2; Ph. 449. Gūþbilla nān, Beo. Th. 1610; B. 803: 1980; B. 988. Næs heora neáta nān geyfelad *jumenta eorum non sunt minorata*, Ps. Th. 106, 37. Ne þearf hæleþa nān wēnan, Met. 7, 6. Hwæt wille gē cueðan hwæs oððe hwæs gē sīen? gē habbaþ gecȳðed ðæt gē ūres nānes (=ūre nānes) ne siendon *quid vos hujus vel illius dicitis, qui nullius vos esse monstratis?* Past. 32, 1; Swt. 211, 14. Nānne ne sparedon ðæs herefolces, Judth. 11; Thw. 24, 40; Jud. 233. Nāne þinga beór ne drince *on no account let him drink beer*, Lchdm. ii. 88, 10. [*Icel.* neinn: cf. *O. Sax.* nēn: *O. H. Ger.* nein (*particle of negation*).] v. nǣnig.

nān-wiht, nān-uht. I. as subst. *nothing:*—Nānwiht *nihil*, Wrt. Voc. i. 47, 32. Heó hire self gecȳþ ðæt heó nānwuht ne biþ *she herself shews that she is nothing*, Bt. 20; Fox 70, 24. Ðū wēndest ðæt ðē nānwuht unrihtlīces on becuman ne mihte, 7, 3; Fox 22, 15: 16, 3; Fox 56, 31: 38, 2; Fox 198, 6. Ðæt gecynd nyle nǣfre nānwuht wiðerweardes lǣtan gemengan, 16, 3; Fox 54, 36. Hió nānwuht elles ne lufaþ būtan ðē, 10; Fox 28, 24. Hē nānwuht ealles (*nothing at all*) næbbe ymbe tō sorgienne, 11, 1; Fox 32, 12. Hié hiora nānwuht ongiotan ne meahton, Past. Swt. 5, 12. Ðone ðe ðū nānwiht yfles on nystest, Blickl. Homl. 85, 36. Nānuht berendes, ne wīf ne niéten, ne mehton nānuht libbendes geberan, Ors. 4, 1; Swt. 158, 18. Nānuht āgiefan nolde ðæs ðe hié bēna wǣron, 3, 11; Swt. 146, 35. Gē nānuht nabbaþ fæstes ne stronges, 2, 4; Swt. 74, 28. *The Northern gospels have* nǣniht (*from* nǣnig?):—Nǣniht unmæht biþ *nihil impossibile erit*, Mt. Kmbl. Lind. 17, 20. Tō nōwihte ł nǣnihte *ad nihilum*, 5, 13. Bibeód him ðæt nǣniht (ne ǣniht, Lind.) hiǣ gilǣdde on woeg *praecepit ne quid tollerent in via*, Mk. Skt. Rush. 6, 8. Nǣneht ł ne ōht (nǣniht ł nōht, Rush.) *nullam*, Lk. Skt. Lind. 23, 22. II. as an adverb, *nothing, not at all, no whit:*—Hē his godcundnesse nānwiht ne gewanode *he no whit diminished his divinity*, Blickl. Homl. 91, 9. Ne gefyrenodest ðū nānwuht *thou hast done no sin*, 235, 34. v. nā-wiht.

nāpan. v. ge-nāpan *and* nīpan.

nard, es; *m. Spikenard;* nardus:—Sealfbox deórwyrþes nardes *alabastrum ungenti nardi spicati praetiosi*, Mk. Skt. 14, 3. Nardys, Lchdm. i. 184, 19. Ete nardes eár, 354. 12. Ele ðe sȳ of nardo, 246, 20. Nardes stenc, Exon. Th. 423, 28; Rä. 41, 29. [*Goth.* nardus: *O. H. Ger.* narda. *From Latin.*]

naru. v. ealdor-, feorh-, līf-naru.

nāst. v. nytan.

nasu; *f. The nose:*—Nasu *naris;* eall seó nasu *columpna;* forewerd nasu *pirula*, Wrt. Voc. i. 282, 63-65. Gif nasu þyrel weorþ, L. Ethb. 45; Th. i. 14, 10: 48; Th. i. 14, 13. Gif man ōðerne mid fyste in naso slæhþ, 57; Th. i. 16, 17. [*Icel.* nös: *O. H. Ger.* nasa.] v. nosu.

nāt. v. nytan.

nātes-hwōn; *adv. Not at all, by no means:*—*Haud, adverbium*, ðæt is on Englisc nātes-hwōn, Ælfc. Gr. 50, 16; Som. 51, 25. Nāteshwōn *haud, minime, nullatenus*, 38; Som. 40, 13-15: *nequaquam*, Som. 41, 55: *nequaquam, nullo modo*, Hpt. Gl. 433, 60: *haud*, 466, 70: *minime*, 470, 24. Ne eart ðū nāteshwōn wacost burga *thou art by no means least of towns*, Homl. Th. i. 78, 14. Ne mæg ic nāteshwōn būton mynstre nihtes wunian, ii. 182, 33: 80, 16. Sume teolunga sind ðe man earfoþlīce mæg oððe nāteshwōn (*hardly or not at all*) būton synnum begān, 288, 22: Homl. Skt. 7, 104. Hē ne āwyrpþ nāteshwōn his wǣpna him fram, ǣr ðam ðe ðæt gewinn wurðe geendod, Basil admn. 2; Norm. 36, 9. Ne sculon mæssepreóstas nāteshwōn būtan ōðrum mannum mæssan syngan, L. E. I. 7; Th. ii. 406, 21. v. nā-wiht.

nāðor. v. nā-hwæðer.

nāt-hwǣr; *adv. In some place unknown*, Exon. Th. 480, 8; Rä. 63, 8: 407, 14; Rä. 26, 5.

nāt-hwæt; *pron. indef. Something unknown:*—Rūwes nāthwæt *something rough, but what I know not*, Exon. Th. 479, 17; Rä. 62, 9: 436, 23; Rä. 55, 5: 499, 25; Rä. 88, 21.

nāt-hwilc; *pron. indef. Some one, I know not who:*—Hæleþa nāthwylc *some man, I know not who*, Elen. Kmbl. 146; El. 73. Hē, gumena nāthwylc, Beo. Th. 4459; B. 2233. Ðara banena byre nāthwylces *the child of one of those murderers, but I know not of which*, 4113; B. 2053: 4451; B. 2224. Þurh nāthwylces . . ., Exon. Th. 12, 21; Cri. 189. Hē in nīþsele nāthwylcum wæs *in some unknown hall was he*, Beo. Th. 3031; B. 1513. (Cf. sceaða ic nāt hwylc, 554; B. 274.)

nāuht. v. nā-wiht.

nāwa [=ne āwa]; *adv. Never:*—Ðæt is swīðe strang ðam ðe ðæt nāwa ǣr þigde *it is very strong for him who never before tasted it*, Lchdm. ii. 252, 14. [Cf. *O. Sax. O. H. Ger.* nēo: *Goth.* ni aiw.] v. āwa.

nā-wērn. v. nā-hwǣrn.

nā-wiht, nō-wiht, nā-uht, nāwht, nāht, nōht. I. as subst. *with gen.* es; *n.* (a) *nothing, naught, a thing of no value, an evil thing:*—Is tō cȳðanne hwelc nāwuht (nāuht, Cott. MSS.) ðes woruldgielp is *intimandum est, quam sit nulla temporalis gloria*, Past. 41, 1; Swt. 299, 6. Nāwuhtes cearu ofer ða ryhtwīsnesse *care for nothing besides righteousness*, Swt. 302, 9. Ðū hī miht tō nāwihte (*ad nihilum*) forniman, Ps. Th. 72, 16, 17: 107, 12. Spoede mīne swē swē nōwiht beforan ðē biþ *substantia mea tanquam nihil ante te est*, Ps. Surt. 38, 6. Tō nōwihte, 14, 4: 80, 15. Fore nōwihte *pro nihilo*, 55, 8. Hē nōwiht ne fremede *nec ipse aliquid profecisset*, Bd. 5, 9 tit.; S. 622, 6. Hē nōwiht elles ne dyde, 2, 14; S. 518, 8. Yfel is nāuht. Ðǣr yfel āuht wǣre, ðonne mihte hit God wyrcan. For ðȳ hit is nāuht, Bt. 35, 5; Fox 164, 10-11. Heore þincþ eall nāuht (nōht, Cott. MS.) ðæt heó hæfþ, 10; Fox 28, 28. Hū ne is se anweald ðǣr nāuht? 16, 2; Fox 54, 7. Hū ne wāst ðū ðæt hit nis nāuht gecynde ne nāuht gewunelīc ðæt ǣnig wiðerweard þing bión gemenged wið ōðrum wiðerweardum *do you not know that it is not a natural or usual thing, for contraries to be mingled with other contraries*, 16, 3; Fox 54, 11. Ne eart ðū nō eallunga tō nāuhte gedōn *thou art not altogether brought to naught*, 10; Fox 30, 4. Weorðan tō nāuhte *to come to naught*, Met. 11, 87. For nāuht tō habbene *to be considered worthless*, Bt. 30, 1; Fox 108, 17. Mon ongiet mid hwelcum stæpum ðæt nāwht (nāuht, Cott. MSS.) wæs þurhtogen *quibus vestigiis nequitia sit perpetrata*, Past. 35, 3; Swt. 241, 18. Nāht *nichil*, Wrt. Voc. i. 83, 68: *nihili*, 47, 33; *nihil*, Ælfc. Gr. 9, 8; Som. 9, 13. Nāht mē wana biþ *nihil mihi deerit*, Ps. Spl. 22, 1. Nis ðæs mannes fæsten nāht, ðe hine sylfne on forhæfednysse dagum fordrencþ, Homl. Th. ii. 608, 23. Heora dȳre gold ne biþ nāhte wurð wið ða foresǣdan mādmas *their precious gold will be worth nothing in comparison with the aforesaid treasures*, Glostr. Frg. 2, 29. Tō nāhte *ad nihilum*, Ps. Spl. 14, 5: Ps. Th. 59, 11. Ne ðæt tō nāhte nyt ne biþ *it is to no purpose*, Blickl. Homl. 57, 5. Hig tellaþ mīn wedd for nāht *irritum facient pactum meum*, Deut. 31, 20. For nāhtum *pro nihilo*, Ps. Lamb. 80, 15. Ungeleáfsumum nōht biþ clǣne *infidelibus* *nihil est mundum*, Bd. 1, 27; S. 494, 40. Mon nôhtes wyrþe his sâule ne dêþ ne his goldes ne his seolfres *a man does not make his soul worthy of anything, of his gold or of his silver*, Blickl. Homl. 195, 5. Næfdon heó nôht on hire, bûton ðæt ân ðæt heó hæfde mennisce onlîcnesse, 147, 15. Ne forstent hit him nôht, ne him nôhte ðon mâ ne beóþ forlǽtna his âgna synna, Past. 21; Swt. 163, 19. ¶ genitive used as predicate:—Ða sǽlþa ðe hê ǽr wênde ðæt gesǽlþa beón sceoldan, nâuhtas nǽran (*were worthless*), Bt. 10. tit.; Fox xii. 6. Eówer godas ne synd nâhtes, Homl. Skt. 7, 205. (b) with a genitive:—Eallinga nâwiht mægenes hæfeþ seó ǽfæstnys *nihil omnino virtutis habet religio illa*, Bd. 2, 13; S. 516, 3. Ic ðæs nôwiht wât, Exon. Th. 393, 5; Rä, 12, 5. Ealles nâuht *nothing at all*, Bt. 36, 6; Fox 182, 8. Nâuht elles *nothing else*, 3, 2; Fox 6, 11. Hê ne mæg ûtane nâuht âgnes habban, 27, 2; Fox 98, 8. Ðes nâht yfeles ne dyde *hic nihil mali gessit*, Lk. Skt. 23, 41. Nâht elles bûton *nothing but*, Blickl. Homl. 215, 3. Nôht elles ne wunaþ, bûton ðæt ân, 101, 4. Gif wê yfles nôht gedôn habbaþ, Exon. Th. 262, 8; Jul. 329. II. as an adverb, *not*:—Hit gelamp neâht micelre tîde æfter his slæge (*non multo exacto tempore*), Bd. 3, 9; S. 533, 30. Nâht feor eást, 2, 13; S. 517, 15: Blickl. Homl. 43, 26. Mannum ðe nâht swîðe God ne lufiaþ, 53, 18: Wrt. Voc. ii. 55, 27. Ic wât ðæt ðû nâht (âuht, Cott. MSS.) ne forslâwodest, Bt. 10; Fox 28, 15. Heó nôht lata ne wæs, Blickl. Homl. 163, 8. Ne þurfan gê nôht besorgian hwæt gê sprecan, 171, 18. Ne wæs hê nôht feor on oferhygd âhafen, 215, 32. Nôht longe ofer ðis, Exon. Th. 172, 15; Gû. 1144. Æfter nôht langre tîde, Bd. 5, 11; S. 626, 10. Ic nôht ðon ǽr ðære ærninge blon, 5, 6; S. 619, 15. [*O. Frs.* nâ-wet: *O. Sax. O. H. Ger.* neô-wiht.] v. nâtes-hwôn *and following words.*

nâwiht-, nâht-fremmend, es; *m. One who does evil*:—Genere mê fram nîðe nâht-fremmendra *eripe me de operantibus iniquitatem*, Ps. Th. 58, 2.

nâwiht-, nâwht-, nâuht-gîtsung, e; *f. Wicked avarice*:—Ðonne hié wilniaþ þurh ða nâwhtgîtsunga (nâuhtgîdsunga, Cott. MSS.) ðæt hié hira woruldspêda îcean *dum per avaritiae nequitiam multiplicari appetunt*, Past. 44, 10; Swt. 333, 5.

nâwiht-, nâht-lîc; *adj. Good for nothing, worthless, naughty*:—Seó hæfde nigon dohtra, nâhtlîce and fracode, Homl. Skt. 8, 11. Manna rǽdas syndon nâhtlîce ongeán Godes geþeaht *men's plans are of no avail against God's counsel*, Chr. 979; Erl. 129, 27. Ða hê geceás ðe dyselîce and nahtlîce geþuhte synt *he chose those that seemed foolish and of no account*, R. Ben. 138, 30. v. next word.

nâwiht-, nôht-lîce; *adv. Worthlessly, evilly*:—Ðætte nôhtlîce ðû dôe *ut nequiter facias*, Ps. Surt. 36, 8, 9.

nâwiht-, nâht-ness, e; *f. Worthlessness, cowardice*:—Heom seggan Brytwalana nâhtnesse (MS. E. nâhtscipe. Cf. secgan Brytta yrgþo (*segnitia*), Bd. 1, 15; S. 483, 15), Chr. 449; Erl. 12, 6.

nâwiht-, nâuht-wela, an; *m. False wealth, wealth that is not really wealth*:—Gê wênaþ ðæt eówre nâuhtwelan (nôht-, Cott. MS.) sîen eówra gesǽlþa, Bt. 14, 2; Fox 44, 37.

nâwðer. v. nâ-hwæðer.

Nazarenisc, Nazaresc; *adj. Of Nazareth*:—Se Nazareniscea (Nazaresca, Lind.) Hǽlend, Mk. Skt. 10, 47: 14, 67. Ðone Nazareniscean (Natzarenisca, Lind.) Hǽlend, Jn. Skt. 18, 5.

ne. I. *adv.* (a) *Not*; non, ne:—Ic ne dyde *non feci*, Ælfc. Gr. 38; Som. 40, 13. Nis hit swâ hit nys *non, non*, 40, 23. Warna ðæt ðû ðæt ne dô *cave ne hoc facias*, 40, 9. Hwî forbeád God eów, ðæt gê ne ǽton of ǽlcum treówe? Gen. 3, 1. Hî nyllaþ geswîcan ðæt hî ôðre men ne reáfigen, Past. 45, tit; Swt. 335, 4. Ne gǽst ðû ðanone *non exies inde*, Lk. Skt. 12, 59. Ne sleh ðu. Ne synga ðû. Ne stel ðû, Ex. 20, 13–15. (b) *no, nay*:—Ne secge ic eów *I tell you, Nay*, Lk. Skt. 12, 51: 13, 5. Ne secge ic nâ, 13, 3. II. *conj. Nor, neither*; ne, neque, nec:—Ne tunge ne handa oððe eágan syngion *ne lingua nec manus oculive peccent*, Ælfc. Gr. 44; Som. 45, 47. Ne ic ne herige ne ic ne tǽle *nec laudo, nec vitupero*, 45, 49. Ne ic ne dyde ne ic ne dô *neque feci, neque faciam*, 38; Som. 40, 9. Ne fare gê ne ne fyliaþ, Lk. Skt. 17, 23. Ne hig ne cweðaþ *neque dicent*, 17, 21. Ne him eác nǽfre genôg ne þincþ ǽr hê hæbbe eall ðæt hine lyst, Bt. 33, 2; Fox 124, 6. Suelcum ingeþonce gerîst ðæt hê for lîcuman tiedernesse ne for woroldbismere ânum wið ða scîre ne winne, ne hê ne sîe giétsiende ôðerra monna ǽhta, Past. 10; Swt. 61, 9–11. Ða ðe nôhwæðer ne ôðerra monna ne wilniaþ, ne hiora âgen nyllaþ sellan, Past. 45, tit.; Swt. 335, 1. *The word often occurs with other negatives.* v. nâ, nâ-wiht, nâ-hwæðer; *it also coalesces with many words beginning with a vowel, with* w *or with* h. v. nabban, nâgan, næs, neom, nic, nyllan, nytan; nân, nâ-, nât-, nǽfre, nǽnig. [*Goth.* ni: *O. Sax.* ne, ni: *O. Frs.* ne: *O. H. Ger.* ni.]

nê-, neá-, neád. v. neó-, neáh-, nîd.

neádian; *p.* ode (v. nîd, VI) *To force, compel, constrain*:—Neádaþ forlǽtan *cogit intermittere*, Hymn. Surt. 56, 13: 84, 17. Ûtlagan ûs wêpan neádiaþ *exules nos flere cogunt*, 56, 3. Se ðe ôðerne neádaþ ofer his mihte tô drincenne, Ælfc. T. Grn. 21, 31. God hine ne neádode on nâðre healfe, ac lêt hine habban his âgene cyre, Hexam. 15; Norm. 22, 30. Ne neádige hine man tô fæstene *ne cogatur ad jejunium*, L. Ecg. P. iv. 25; Th. ii. 212, 5: L. Ælfc. C. 29; Th. ii. 352, 29. Neádede *cogeret*, Hpt. Gl. 519, 19. Neádiendum *cogente*, 503, 39. His deópe rihtwîsnys nolde hî neádian tô nâðrum, Homl. Th. i. 112, 3. v. ge-, of-neádian, nîdan.

neádian, neódian; *p.* ode (v. nîd, IV) *To be necessary*:—On cealdum eardum neódaþ (is neód, W. F.), ðæt ðæs reáfes mâre sŷ, on hleówfæstum læs. Ðæs abbodes forsceáwung sceal beón be ðysum, hû ðæs neódige, R. Ben. 89, 6, 8.

neádigness, e; *f. Obligation*:—Neádinysse ł neóde *debitum*, Hpt. Gl. 456, 14.

neádlunga; *adv. Forcibly, against one's will*:—Manega gewilniaþ ôðres mannes wôlîce and hî beóþ benǽmede neádlunga hyra âgenes *many covet another man's goods, and they shall be forcibly deprived of their own*, Basil admn. 9; Norm. 52, 20. v. nîdlinga *and next two words.*

neádung, e; *f. Force* or *violence used against any one, compulsion, necessity*:—Ðeós neádung *haec vis*, Ælfc. Gl. 9, 29; Som. 11, 62. Of ðisum leahtre (gîtsung) beóþ âcennede reáflâc, stala, unmǽþlic neádung, Homl. Th. ii. 220, 12. Hê nolde geniman ûs neádunge of deófles anwealde, i. 26, 30. Hine betellan swilce hê neádunge gefremode ðæt fâcn *to excuse himself, as if he committed that crime of necessity*, H. R. 105, 26. Neádunge *vim*, Hpt. Gl. 435, 70. [*Icel.* nauðung *compulsion.*] v. next word.

neádunga(-inga); *adv. Forcibly, not willingly, under compulsion, of necessity*:—Hê nolde niman mancyn neádunga of ðam deófle bûton hê hit forwyrhte *he would not have taken mankind by force from the devil, unless he had forfeited it*, Homl. Th. i. 216, 5. Ðone cniht ðe hê neádinga genam (*rapuisset*), Ors. 1, 8; Swt. 42, 10. Hî hine neádunga mid him lǽddon *invitum duxerunt*, Bd. 3, 18; S. 546, 22. Gif lǽweda man neádinga (*invite*) man ofsleá, L. Ecg. P. ii. 1; Th. ii. 182, 16. Neádunga, L. M. I. P. 6; Th. ii. 266, 27. Gif hê (*man*) wǽre neádunga (*without power of choice, necessarily*) Gode underþeód, ðonne næfde hê nân wuldor for gôdum weorcum, Boutr. Scrd. 17, 26. Sió leáse gesǽlþ tîhþ on lâst neádinga (*inevitably*) ða ðe hiere tô geþeódaþ from ðǽm sôðum gesǽlþum; seó wiðerweardnes full oft ealle ða ðe hiere underþeódde bióþ, neádinga getîhþ tô ðâm sôðum gesǽlþum, swâ swâ mid angle fisc gefangen biþ, Bt. 20; Fox 72, 7–11. v. nîdinga *and preceding word.*

neáh; *adj.* I. *nigh, near*:—On ðam neáhgum mynstre [neáhnunnan-mynstre] *de vicino virginum monasterio*, Bd. 4, 1; S. 564, 4 note. Neágum *proximis* (cf. *O. L. Ger.* nâan *proximum*), Germ. 399, 409. Seó ûs neárre Ægyptus, Ors. 1, 1; Swt. 14, 3. Seó ûs neárre Ispania, Swt. 22, 31: 24, 9. Sîe se lâreów eallum monnum se niéhsta and eallum monnum emþrowiende on hira gesuincum *sit rector singulis compassione proximus*, Past. 16; Swt. 97, 22. Seó mǽgþ is seó nŷhste on sûþhalfe Humbre streámes *provincia (Lindissi) quae est prima ad meridianam Humbrae fluminis ripam*, Bd. 2, 16; S. 519, 19. Nîhsta *proxima*, Ps. Spl. 21, 10. Sió nêste hond *the nearest relative*, Chart. Th. 481, 21. Gif hwylc man wîfige on his nêhstan mâgan (*proximam cognatam*), L. Ecg. P. ii. 18; Th. ii. 188, 16. Hiera niéhstan friénd, Past. 49; Swt. 377, 1. Heora nŷhstan mâgas, L. Eth. ii. 6; Th. i. 286, 32. II. in cpve. *later, latter*; superl. *last, latest*. v. ende-nêhst:—Se æftera ł nǽrra *novissimus*, Mt. Kmbl. Rush. 21, 31. His ða nêrran tîde wǽron wyrsan ðâm ǽrran *habuit posteriora pejora prioribus*, Bd. 2, 15; S. 518, 31. Cedd and Adda and Bete and Dema, se nŷhsta wæs Scyttysces cynnes, 3, 21; S. 551, 15. Ðis is Byrhtrîces nîhsta cwide (*last will*), Chart. Th. 500, 24. Ôðer is se ǽresta apostol, ôðer se nêhsta, Blickl. Homl. 171, 9. On ðæm nêhstan dæge *on the last day*, 21, 35. On ða nêhstan tîd ðisse worlde, on dômes dæge, 123, 32. Ôþ ða nŷhstan orþuncge *until his latest breath*, L. Ælfc. E.; Th. ii. 392, 9. From Ninuse hiora ǽrestan cyninge ôþ Sardanapolim heora nîhstan, Ors. 6, 1; Swt. 252, 8. Be ðâm neáhstan twâm is æfter tô cweþanne *de ultimis infra dicendum est*, Bd. 4, 23; S. 594, 12. Monige beóþan ða ǽrestu nǽhstu and ða nǽhstu ǽrestu, Mt. Kmbl. Rush. 19, 30. From ðǽm nǽhstum ôþ ðe ǽrestum, 20, 8. Æt neáhstan *postremo*, Bd. 2, 6; S. 508, 19. Æt nêhstan (Rush. nîhsto) *novissime*, Mt. Kmbl. 25, 11: Blickl. Homl. 85, 1. Æt nêxtan, Homl. Th. i. 66, 23. Æt niéhstan, Cd. Th. 84, 19; Gen. 1400. Æt nîhstan, Ors. 4, 9; Swt. 192, 35. Æt nŷhstan, Bd. 2, 12; S. 513, 4. Æt nŷxtan, Chr. 994; Erl. 133, 20: 1010; Erl. 144, 9. v. nîhsta *and next word.*

neáh, nêh *nigh, near.* I. *as adv.* (1) of place:—Ealle hire mâgas ða ðe ðǽr neáh wǽron, Blickl. Homl. 139, 16. Ic wât heáhburh hêr âne neáh, Cd. Th. 152, 9; Gen. 2517. Feor oððe neáh, 63, 8; Gen. 1029. Ge neáh ge feor, Bd. 4, 4; S. 571, 7. Ge nêh ge feor, Andr. Kmbl. 1083; An. 542. Gâ hider neár *accede huc*, Gen. 27, 21. Mid ðŷ ic ðâ wolde neár geseón *quos cum adire vellemus vicinius*, Nar. 22, 11. Swa fyr swâ nŷr, L. I. P. 21; Th. ii. 332, 16. Ðǽr ðǽr hê niéhst rŷmet hæfde, Chr. 894; Erl. 90, 9. (2) of time:—Ðisses middangeardes ende (*or dat.?*) swîðe neáh is, Blickl. Homl. 107, 23. Eall ðâs getimbro neáh is ðæt hî eall fŷr fornimeþ and on axsan gehwyrfeþ *cuncta haec aedificia, in proximo est ut ignis absumens in cinerem convertat*, Bd. 4, 25; S. 600, 33. Nemnan ðæt ûs neáh (*lately*) geweard gecŷþed, Exon. Th. 107, 26; Gû. 64. Ðâ ic hine nêhst geseáh *when I last saw him*, Cd.

Th. 34, 12; Gen. 536. Đonan hȳ God nȳhst eágum sēgun, Exon. Th. 34. 1; Cri. 535. (3) of degree, *near, nearly, about*:—Heó hafaþ leáf neáh swylce mistel, Lchdm. i. 254, 12. Đa Finnas and đa Beormas sprǽcon neáh ān geþeóde, Ors. 1, 1; Swt. 17, 34. Hié æt nīhstan hæfdon ealra đara anwald đe ǽr nēh heora hæfdon *in the end they had dominion over all those who before nearly had dominion over them*, 4, 9; Swt. 192, 35. Swā neáh wæs þūsend āurnen *so nearly had a thousand years passed* (*all but twenty-seven*), Chr. 973; Erl. 124, 23. Swīđe neáh đū ongeáte đæt riht, Bt. 34, 12; Fox 154, 10. Nihtscūwan neáh ne mihton (*could not nearly*) heolstor āhȳdan, Col. Th. 184, 29; Exod. 114. Hī ne notigaþ nāwēr neáh feórþan dǽles đisse eorþan *they do not use anywhere near a fourth part of the earth*, 18, 1; Fox 62, 9. Đæt gē dōn ne māgon, ne furþum nāwēr neáh, 18, 2; Fox 64, 6: Shrn. 196, 28: 197, 13. Ne mæg hió đeáh gescīnan āhwǽrgen neáh ealla gesceafta *the sun cannot reach with its rays anywhere near all creatures*, Met. 30, 10. Ús is þearf đæt wē geþencen hwæt Dauid cwæþ and eác đon dōn swā wē nȳhst mǽgan *we must consider what David said, and besides that act as nearly as we can accordingly*, L. E. I. 30; Th. ii. 426, 38. II. *as prep. with dat.* (1) of place:—Neáh helle *secus infernum*, Ps. Spl. 140, 9. Neáh [Lind. Rush. nēh] đam tūne *juxta praedium*, Jn. Skt. 4, 5. Seó flōweþ neáh đære ceastre wealle, Bd. 1, 7; S. 478, 5. Him wæs engel neáh, Exon. Th. 112, 14; Gū. 143. Đæt nān ne sǽte hiere x mīlum neáh *that no one should settle within ten miles of it* (*Carthage*), Ors. 4, 13; Swt. 210, 22. Tō đæm tūne nēh Oliuetes dūne, Blickl. Homl. 69, 33. Gang mē neár hider *come hither nearer to me*, 179, 30. Seó Ægyptus đe ūs neár is, Ors. 1, 1; Swt. 12, 16. Swā hē biþ đære sunnan neár swā biþ hire fyrr *whether it* (*the moon*) *is nearer to the sun or farther from it*, Shrn. 64, 32. Swā neár ende đyssere woruld swā māre ehtnys đæs deófles *the nearer to the end of the world, the greater the devil's persecution*, Homl. Th. ii. 370, 15. Ne biþ hió merestreáme đē neár đe on midne dæg, Met. 28, 37. Đā se swēg mē nȳr wæs, Bd. 5, 12; S. 628, 31. Swā swā sió nafu fērþ nēhst (Cott. MS. neáhst) đære eaxe, Bt. 39, 7; Fox 222, 1. Sceall beón se læsta dǽl nȳhst đæm tūne, Ors. 1, 1; Swt. 20, 33. (2) of time:—Ne đīnre forþfōre swā neáh is *neque mori adhuc habes*, Bd. 4, 24; S. 598, 37, 32: 3, 8; S. 531, 36. Đære tȳde is neáh, đæt Godes cyrce hafaþ sybbe on eorþan, Shrn. 154, 33. Biþ nēh đæm seofoþan dæge, Blickl. Homl. 95, 11. Hié wēndon đæt hit neár worulde endunge wǽre đonne hit wǽre, Past. 32; Swt. 213, 6. (3) of manner:—Ic dō neáh đam đe đū cwǽde *juxta verbum tuum faciam*, Ex. 8, 10. Neáh (*juxta*) eallon đām þingum, đe Drihten bebeád, Num. 1, 54: 8, 20. Neáh andefene *prope modum*, Wrt. Voc. ii. 66, 73. Āgnung biþ nēr đam đe hæfþ đonne đam đe æfter sprecþ *possession is nine points of the law*, L. Eth. ii. 9; Th. i. 290, 20. Ús sylfe gerihtlǽcan swā neáh swā wē nȳhst māgon đam rihte *to direct ourselves as much according to right as we possibly can*, Chart. Th. 615, 24. [*Goth.* nēhw; *adv.*; *cpve.* nēhwis: *Icel.* nā- (*in cpds.*); nær; *adv.* (*pos. and cpve.*): *O. Sax.* nāh; *adv. prep. with dat.*; *cpve.* nāhor: *O. Frs.* nī, nei; *adv.*: *O. H. Ger.* nāh; *adv. prep. with dat.*; nāh; *adj. contiguus, vicinus.*] v. efen- (emn-), un-neáh, *the preceding word, the cpds. with* neáh-, *and* neáwung.

-neah. v. be-, ge-neah.

neáh-būend, es; *m.* *A near-dweller, a neighbour*:—Ic eom neáhbūendum nyt, Exon. Th. 407, 8; Rä. 26, 2.

neáh-būr. v. neáh-gebūr.

neáh-dūn, e; *f.* *A neighbouring hill*:—Of đǽm neáhdūnum and scrafum *ex vicinis montium speluncis*, Nar. 14, 6.

neáh-eá; *f.* *A neighbouring river*:—Hié of đǽm neáhēum and merum đa hronfiscas up tugon and đa ǽton, Nar. 22, 9.

neáh-eáland, es; *n.* *A neighbouring island*:—On đysum neáheálande đæt is nemned Ulcani, Shrn. 86, 1.

neáh-freónd, es; *m.* *A near friend* or *relation*:—Đǽr wæs mycel menigo manna gegaderod his māga and eác ōđra his nēhfreónda, Guthl. 12; Gdwin. 56, 22. [*Icel.* nā-frændi *a near kinsman.*]

neáh-, nēh-gebūr, nēhche-, nēhhe-, nēche-, nēhe-būr, es; *m.* *A neighbour*:—Nēhgebūr *adfinis*, Wrt. Voc. ii. 9, 68: *convical*, 135, 56. Mīne frȳnd and mīne māgas and mīne neáhgebūras *amici mei, et proximi mei*, Ps. Th. 37, 11. His neáhgebūras (nēhebūras, Lind.: nēhgibūras, Rush.) *vicini*, Jn. Skt. 9, 8. Hyre nēhchebūras (nēhhebūras, MS. A.: nēhebūras, Lind.: nēhgibūras, Rush.), Lk. Skt. 1, 58, 65. Nēhhebūras, 14, 12: 15, 6. Neapolite đa heora nēhgebūras, Blickl. Homl. 201, 19. Nēchebūrena gefeoht *intestinum bellum*, Wrt. Voc. i. 35, 16. V. men his neáhgebūra (nēhbūra), L. Ath. i. 9; Th. i. 204, 11. On his nēhebūra gewitnesse, v. 8, 7; Th. i. 238, 3. Se đe æfter ǽnegum ceápe rīde, cȳþe his neáhgebūrum ymbe hwæt hē rīde, L. Edg. S. 7; Th. i. 274, 20: Ps. Th. 30, 13. Ne lađa đū đīne welegan neáhgebūras, Past. 44; Swt. 323, 21. [Cf. *Icel.* nā-būi *a neighbour.*] v. next two words.

neáh-gebȳrild, es; *m.* *A neighbour*:—Nēhebȳrildas *vicinas*, Lk. Skt. Lind. 15, 9. v. next word.

neáh-gebȳren, e; *f.* *A neighbour*:—Heó clypaþ hyre frȳnd and nēhhebȳryna (-byrna, MS. A.) *convocans amicas et vicinas*, Lk. Skt. 15, 9. v. neáh-gebūr.

neáh-gehūsa, an; *m.* *A neighbour*:—Nēhgehūsum mīnum *vicinis meis*, Ps. Surt. 30, 12: 78, 4, 12: 79, 7.

neahhige; *adv.* *Abundantly, frequently*, Ps. Th. 138, 9. v. ge-neahhie.

neáh-, neá-lǽcan; *p.* -lǽhte, -lǽcte *To draw nigh, approach*:—Đis fȳr mē swīđe neálǽceþ *ignis mihi adpropinquat*, Bd. 3, 19; S. 548, 24: Exon. Th. 164, 4; Gū. 1006. Deáþ neálǽcte, 170, 16; Gū. 1112. Hē neálǽhte *accessit*, Gen. 27, 27. On đære tīde đe neálǽhte niđđa bearnum, Cd. Th. 77, 32; Gen. 1284: Judth. Thw. 21, 25; Jud. 34. Hī neáhlǽhton tō đære ceastre *adpropinquantes civitati*, Bd. 1, 25; S. 487, 21. Hī đam mynstre neálǽctan, 4, 25; S. 600, 28. Tō him neálǽcan, 4, 3; S. 567, 43. v. ge-, tō-neáhlǽcan.

neáh-, neá-lǽcung, e; *f.* *A drawing nigh, approach*:—Đā đā hē gefrēdde his deáþes neálǽcunge *when he was sensible of the approach of his death*, Homl. Th. i. 88, 8. Hȳ sylfe fram manna gesyhþe āscyriende đara manna neálǽcynge nā underfōþ *cutting themselves off from the sight of men they do not admit the approach of men*, R. Ben. 135, 1. v. ge-neálǽcing.

neáh-līc; *adj.* *Near*:—Unrōtnysse neáhlīce *tribulatio proxima*, Ps. Lamb. 21, 12. [*Icel.* nā-ligr *near, close at hand.*] v. next word.

neáh-, neá-līce; *adv.* *Nearly, about*:—Hié neálīce swā fela (*tot pene*) þearfena ofsleáþ swā hié īđelīce mid hiera ælmessan gehelpan meahton, Past. 45, 1; Swt. 335, 15. Hȳ blōwaþ đonne neálīce (*just about when*) ōđre wyrta scrincaþ, Lchdm. i. 204, 13. [*Icel.* nā-liga *nearly, almost*: *O. H. Ger.* nāh-līcho *ferme.*] v. ge-nēhlīce.

neáh-, neá-, nēh-mǽg, es; *m.* *A near kinsman*:—His gebrōđru and his neámāgas *fratres ejus omnisque cognatio illa*, Ex. 1, 6. Neáhmāga *adfinium*, Wrt. Voc. ii. 3, 8. His nēhmāga sum and his worldfreónda, Blickl. Homl. 113, 9. Se man leóf his nēhmāgum and his worldfreóndum, 111, 27. Wīfe and cildan and nēhmāgon (MS. B. neáhmāgum), L. C. S. 71; Th. i. 414, 1. [*Icel.* nā-māgr *a near kinsman by marriage.*]

neáh-mǽgþ, e; *f.* *A neighbouring province* (v. mǽgþ, **IV.** c):—On đa neáhmǽgþe *in proximam provinciam*, Bd. 4, 16; S. 584, 23. Đæra neáhmǽgþa *finitimarum provinciarum*, 3, 24; S. 557, 15.

neáh-, nēh-mann, es; *m.* *A neighbour*:—Him se gesīþ eác fultumade and ealle đa neáhmenn *juvante etiam comite ac vicinis omnibus*, Bd. 4, 4; S. 571, 14. Đa nēhmen *vicini*, 1, 33; S. 499, 10. Ūrum neáhmannum *vicinis nostris*, Ps. Th. 79, 6: Shrn. 73, 35.

neáh-munt, es; *m.* *A neighbouring mountain*:—Of đæm neáhmunte (*ex vicino monte*) wealleþ wæter, Nar. 31, 7.

neáhness, e; *f.* *Nearness, neighbourhood*:—Hwylc tōweard yfel đū đē on neáhnysse forhtast *quae ventura tibi in proximo mala formidas*, Bd. 2, 12; S. 514, 1. On nēhnesse his cytan *in vicinia cellae illius*, 5, 12; S. 630, 42.

neáh-nunnan-mynster. v. neáh, **I.**

-neáhsen. v. ge-neáhsen.

neáh-sibb, e; *f.* *Relationship*:—Nēhsibbe *propinquitatis*, Wrt. Voc. ii. 66, 36.

neáh-sibb; *adj.* *Related*:—Wē lǽraþ đæt ǽnig cristen man ǽfre ne gewīfie on his mǽges lāfe đe swā neáhsib (neáh sib, Th.) wǽre, L. C. E. 7; Th. i. 364, 24. Nān man ne wīfige on neáhsibban (neáh sibban, Th.) nēr (m', Th.) đonne wiđūtan đam .iiii. cneówe *let no one take a wife among his relations nearer of kin than beyond the fourth degree*, L. N. P. L. 61; Th. ii. 300, 14.

neáhsta *a neighbour.* v. nīhsta.

neáh-stōw, e; *f.* **I.** *a neighbouring place*:—Ealle đa neáhstōwa đǽr ymbūtan, Bt. 15; Fox 48, 22. **II.** *neighbourhood*:—On đære circean ođđe on hire neáhstōwe, Shrn. 81, 24.

neaht. v. niht.

neáh-þeód, e; *f.* *A neighbouring people*:—Europe ne Asia ne ealle đa neáhþeóda, Ors. 1, 10; Swt. 46, 28. Ægđer ge hié self wēndon ge ealle đa neáhþeóda đæt hié ofer hié ealle mehte anwald habban, 3, 1; Swt. 96, 6.

neáh-tīd, e; *f.* *A time close at hand*:—Đæt heó tō đon đider com đæt heó hire sǽde đa neáhtīde hire geleórnesse *quod ipsa ei tempus suae transmigrationis in proximum nunciare venisset*, Bd. 4, 9; S. 577, 33.

neáh-tūn, es; *m.* *A neighbouring town*:—Sum eald man wæs in đam nēhtūne đǽr ic wæs đæs nama wæs Malchus *there was an old man in the town near where I was, whose name was Malchus*, Shrn. 36, 6.

neáh-wæter, es; *n.* *A piece of water that is near*:—Wē gewīcodon be đǽm neáhwætrum, Nar. 22, 24.

neáh-west, -wist, e; *f.*: es; *m.* **I.** *nearness, neighbourhood*:—Hē ne dorste his neáwiste geneálǽcan *he dare not come into his neighbourhood*, Homl. Th. i. 88, 21. Ungewuniendlīc for đære sunnan neáweste *uninhabitable on account of the nearness of the sun*, Lchdm. iii. 260, 21. On đære neáwiste næs nān wæterscipe, Jud. 15, 18. In đara neáwiste *in quorum vicinia*, Bd. 5, 14; S. 634, 28. Hig on neáwiste (*in vicino*) eardodon, Jos. 9, 16: Elen. Kmbl. 133; El. 67. Wæs đǽr on neáweste (*in proximo*) hūs, Bd. 4, 24; S. 598, 27: Blickl. Homl. 197, 20: Chr. 924; Erl. 110, 13. Đā wīcode se cyng on neáweste đære byrig, 896; Erl. 94, 5. Swā feala earmra manna swā on đæs rīcan neáweste sweltaþ, Blickl. Homl. 53, 5. Ða ðe on hire neáwiste lifgeaþ, 43, 2. Ne [mãgon] hũse ðínum on neáweste nãhwǽr sceþþan *flagella non appropiabunt tabernaculo tuo*, Ps. Th. 90, 10. Ealle ða wǽpnedmen ðe him on neáweste wǽron, Ors. 1, 10; Swt. 46, 2. Ealle ða rícu ðe him under beóþ oððe on neáweste, Bt. 16, 1; Fox 50, 3. Tõ ðæs ríces neáwiste belimpeþ seó stõw *ad cujus vicina pertinet locus ille*, Bd. 5, 12; S. 630, 22. II. *the being with another, presence, society, fellowship:*—Hwæt is betere ðonne ðæs cyninges folgaþ and his neáwest (cf. ðæs cyninges geférrǽden, l. 2) *what is better than to serve and be with the king?* Bt. 29, 1; Fox 102, 7. Hwelc is ǽngum men mãre daru ðonne hē hæbbe on his geférrǽdenne and on his nēweste feónd on freóndes anlícnesse, 29, 2; Fox 106, 14. Þincþ his neáwist (*the presence of the dead body*) láþlíco and unfæger, Blickl. Homl. 111, 30. Ne cume hē nã on ðæs cyninges neáwiste (ansýne, MS. H.), L. Edm. E. 3; Th. i. 246, 3. Se sacerd dēmde ðæt hē sceolde beón ãscyred fram manna neáwiste *the priest judged that he (the leper) should be separated from the society of men*, Homl. Th. i. 124, 25. Hē fērde tõ folces neáwiste and bodade, 352, 11. From alre nēweste geleáfulra sýn heó ãsceádene, Chart. Th. 29, 19. Mid ðý ic wæs him on neáwiste, hē ðus wæs sprecende, Bd. 3, 13; S. 538, 23. Forlǽt mec englas geniman on ðínne neáwest (*into thy presence*), Exon. Th. 455, 13; Hy. 4, 49. Ic forboden ǽlcon bisceope and mæssepreóste ðæt hig nãnes wífmannes neáweste mid him næbbon (*ne mulieris alicujus societatem secum habeant*), L. Ecg. P. ii. 6; Th. ii. 198, 8. Wē lǽraþ ðæt ǽnig preóst ne lufige wífmanna neáwiste, L. Edg. c. 60; Th. ii. 256, 21. Hí wífes neáwiste forlēton, L. Ælfc. C. 1; Th. ii. 342, 14: Homl. Skt. 10, 204. Libia and Agrippina wurdon swã gelýfede ðæt hí forbugon heora wera neáwiste, Homl. Th. i. 374, 33. Ne can ðara idesa õwðer þurh gebedscipe beorna neáwist, Cd. Th. 148, 36; Gen. 2467. [*Laym.* ne-, neo-weste (-uste): *Icel.* nã-vist *presence*: *O. H. Ger.* nãh-wist *praesentia*.]

nealles, nalles, nallæs, nallas, nales, nalæs, nalas; *adv. Not, not at all:*—(a) in the second clause of a sentence. Ðonne telle ic ða weorþmynd ðæm wyrhtan, nealles ðē *I ascribe the honour to the maker, not to thee*, Bt. 14, 1; Fox 42, 19 note. Swã sceal mǽg dõn, nealles inwitnet õðrum bregdan, Beo. Th. 4340; B. 2167: 4365; B. 2179. Hē spræc þurh feóndscipe, nalles hē hié freme lǽrde, Cd. Th. 38, 22; Gen. 610: 14, 2; Gen. 212. Hēt hine ðære sweartan helle grundes gýman, nalles wið God winnan, 22, 26; Gen. 346. Nallæs, Soul Kmbl. 206; Seel. Verc. 104. Hwæðere him on ferhþe greów breósthord blõdreów, nallas beágas geaf, Beo. Th. 3443; B. 1719: 3503; B. 1749. Ic feówer men geseó tõ sõðe, nales mē selfa [sefa?] leógeþ, Cd. Th. 242, 9; Dan. 416. Ðǽr heó brynewelme bídan sceolden, nales swegles leóht habban, 266, 27; Sat. 28. Waraþ hine wræclãst, nales wunden gold; ferþloca freórig, nalæs foldan blǽd, Exon. Th. 288, 16–19. Ðis ic cweþe æfter forgifenysse nalæs æfter bebode *hoc autem dico secundum indulgentiam, non secundum imperium*, Bd. 1, 27; S. 495, 45. Hí ãwendan ãweg, nalæs wel dydan, Ps. Th. 77, 57: Andr. Kmbl. 92; An. 46. Ðũ eart geong, nalas wintrum frõd, 1012; An. 506: Beo. Th. 2991; B. 1493: Blickl. Homl. 207, 17. (b) in the first clause:—Nealles him handgesteallan ymbe gestõdon, ac hý on holt bugon, Beo. Th. 5185; B. 2596: 4296; B. 2145: 4446; B. 2222. Nealles ... hwæðre, 5738; B. 2873. Heó nalles on goldes wlite ne scíneþ, ac on sundorweorþunge heó gewuldrad stondeþ, Blickl. Homl. 197, 8: Cd. Th. 173, 19; Gen. 2863: 249, 14; Dan. 530. Nales, Exon. Th. 60, 1; Cri. 963: 111, 3; Gũ. 121. Nalæs ... ðãgyt, Beo. Th. 85; B. 43. Nalas ... ah, Blickl. Homl. 121, 11: Andr. Kmbl. 3180; An. 1593. Nales ðæt ãn ðæt ... ac eác swelce *not only ... but also*, Ors. 1, 2; Swt. 30, 27: 1, 7; Swt. 40, 4. Nalæs ðæt ãn ðæt ... ac swylce eác, Bd. 3, 13; S. 538, 4: 1, 14; S. 482, 24: 4, 29; S. 608, 17. Nalæs ðæt ãn ... ac eác, 2, 12; S. 514, 8. Ēcan gesǽlþa sõhtan nallas þurh ðæt ãn ðæt hí wilnodon ðæs líchomlícan deáþes, ac eác manegra sãrlícra wíta hié gewilnodon, Bt. 11, 2; Fox 36, 3. (c) with an adjective or adverb:—Nealles swǽslíce, Beo. Th. 6169; B. 3089. Nalles hõlinga, 2156; B. 1076. Nalles hneáwlíce, Cd. Th. 108, 20; Gen. 1809. Nales feám síðum, Elen. Kmbl. 1633; El. 818. Nales hõlunge, Cd. Th. 61, 14; Gen. 997. Nales swã wíde, Wrt. Voc. ii. 60, 55. Nales [nalles, 60, 69] ungerãde *non dissona*, 86, 12. Monge, nales feá, Exon. Th. 72, 11; Cri. 1171. Nalæs æfter myclum fæce *non multo post*, Bd. 1, 14; S. 482, 33. Nalæs æfter mycelre tíde, 4, 23; S. 593, 24. Oft, nalæs seldan, Ps. Th. 74, 4.

neán; *adv.* I. *from near:*—Neán and feorran *from near and far*, Cd. Th. 14, 28; Gen. 225. Feorran oððe neán, 64, 8; Gen. 1047. Somnaþ sũþan and norþan, eástan and westan, faraþ feorran and neán, Exon. Th. 220, 26; Ph. 326: Beo. Th. 1683; B. 839. Ic eów wísige ðæt gē genõge neón sceáwiaþ beágas *I will guide you so that from near ye may gaze on rings in abundance*, Beo. Th. 6200; B. 3104. II. *near, close at hand:*—Gif ðũ Grendles dearst neán bídan *if thou durst here await Grendel*, 1061; B. 528. Wæs ðæs wyrmes wíg wíde gesýne, neán and feorran, 4624; B 2317. Hí ðære eaxe ũtan ymbhwerfaþ, ðone norþende neán ymbcerraþ (cf. hí sint swã neáh ðam norþende ðære eaxe, Fox 214, 20), Met. 28, 14. III. *nearly, about:*—Neán twelfwintre *fere annorum duodecim*, Lk. Skt. 8, 42. Ðã wæs geworden æfter ðam wordum neán (MS. A. neáh) eahta dagas, 9, 28. Ðã wæs neán seó syxte tíd *erat autem fere hora sexta*, 23, 44. Wē ðæs hereweorces neán myndgiaþ *we bear that warlike deed in mind nearly as it happened, have an accurate remembrance of it*, Elen. Kmbl. 1311; El. 657. v. for-neán.

neap *a cup*, Lchdm. i. 374, 23. v. hnæpf.

Neapolite; *pl. The Neapolitans*, Blickl. Homl. 201, 19.

neár; neara, nearo. v. neáh; nearu.

nearu; *adj.* I. *narrow, strait, confined, not spacious:*—Neara scræf *gurgustulum*, Wrt. Voc. i. 58, 29. Neare pyt *puteus angustus*, Kent. Gl. 901. Gangaþ inn þurh ðæt nearwe (MS. B. nearuwe: Lind. nearuo: Rush. naarwe) geat ... Eálã hũ neara (MS. A. nearu: Lind. naruu: Rush. naru) is ðæt geat *intrate per angustam portam ... Quam angusta porta*, Mt. Kmbl. 7, 13–14: Lk. Skt. 13, 24. Se sǽ ðe ǽgðer is ge nearo ge hreóh, Ors. 1, 1; Swt. 28, 12. Alexander him ðæt ondrēd for ðære nearwan stõwe ðæt hē ðã on wæs *timens angustias quibus inerat locorum*, 3, 9; Swt. 124, 25. In ãn nearo fæsten ungeféredra mõra *in angustias inaccessorum montium*, Bd. 4, 26; S. 602, 20. Nearo wíc *mansionem angustam*, 4, 28; S. 605, 23. Tõbrǽdan ofer ða nearwan eorþan (cf. ofer ðãs nearowan eorþan sceátas, Met. 10, 16), Bt. 19; Fox 68, 25. Binnon nearwum gemǽrum *intra fines angustiores*, Bd. 4, 26; S. 603, 9. Nearewum *artis*, Wrt. Voc. ii. 5, 67. Mid ða nearwan *arta*, 5, 57. Ofereode stíge nearwe, enge ãnpaðas, Beo. Th. 2823; B. 1409. II. *narrow, limited, poor, restricted:*—Hũ ne ongite gē hũ neara (Cott. MS. nearo) se eówer hlísa beón wile, Bt. 18, 2; Fox 64, 14. Swíðe nearewe (Cott. MS. nearwa) sent and swíðe heánlíce ða menniscan gesǽlþa, 11, 1; Fox 30, 25. Hēt hié from hweorfan neorxna wange on nearore líf, Cd. Th. 58, 11; Gen. 944. III. *strait, oppressive, causing anxiety* (of that which restricts free action of body or mind):—Nýd byþ nearu on breóste niða bearnum *need straitens the breast of man*, Runic pm. Kmbl. 341, 8; Rũn. 10. Nearo nihtwaco *the anxious night watch*, Exon. Th. 306, 13. In hæft under nearone clom (*under confining fetter*), Exon. Th. 138, 2; Gũ. 570. Ðone nearwan níþ onfõn, Cd. Th. 43, 27; Gen. 697: 304, 22; Sat. 634. Of ðǽm nearwum bendum, Homl. Skt. 3, 197: Exon. Th. 435, 6; Rä. 53, 3. Under nearwum clommum, 134, 22; Gũ. 511. Hié wilnodan ðæt hē hié of ðǽm nearwan þeóstrum ãlēsde, Blickl. Homl. 103, 13. IV. *oppressed, not having free action:*—Wið nearwre sworetunge *for difficult breathing*, Lchdm. i. 340, 11. Hym beóþ on hyra brõsten nearuwe (*people with asthma*), iii. 116, 23. V. *strict, severe:*—Ðæt hié ne þyrfen bión gesewene æt ðæm nearwan dõme *ut a districta judice videri non debeant*, Past. 53, 2; Swt. 413, 16. [*O. Sax.* naru.]

nearu, we; nearu (o); *indecl. f.* I. *confinement, durance, prison:*—Hwonne hié of nearwe stæppan mõsten, of enge ũt ǽhta lǽdan (*when they might come out of the ark*), Cd. Th. 86; Gen. 1433. Hió bebeád ðæt hine man of nearwe and of nýdcleofan, fram ðam engan hofe forlēte, Elen. Kmbl. 1418; El. 711. Næglas of nearwe scínende *the nails shining from the hole where they had been hidden*, 2227; El. 1115. Neb wæs mín on nearwe *my face was in confinement*, Exon. Th. 392, 1; Rä. 11, 1. Siððan mē nioþan upweardne on nearo fēgde *afterwards fixed me upside down in durance*, 479, 12; Rä. 62, 6: 480, 8; Rä. 63, 8. II. *a strait, difficulty:*—On nearwe *in a strait*, Elen. Kmbl. 2203; El. 1103. Nearwe genýddon on norþwegas wiston him be sũþan Sigelwara land *the difficulties of the situation forced them to the north for they knew that to the south of them lay the land of the Ethiopians*, Cd. Th. 181, 29; Exon. 68. Nearu, nearo þrowian *to be in straits*, Andr. Kmbl. 828; An. 414: Beo. Th. 5182; B. 2594. Hē ǽr fela nearo nēþende níða gedígde *from many straits and strifes had he come safely*, 4689; B. 2350. Hine of nearwum ũt forlēt, Vald. 2, 8. In nearowe nēþan *to venture into difficulties*, Exon. Th. 436, 12; Rä. 54, 13.

nearu-bregd, es; *n. A wile or trick that brings others into straits* (v. *preceding word and* nearu, III):—Nēþde ic nearobregdum, ðǽr ic Neron biswãc, ðæt hē ãcwellan hēt Cristes þegnas, Exon. Th. 260, 24; Jul. 302.

nearu-cræft, es; *m. An art that confines or imprisons* (?):—Beorh wunode on wonge nearocræftum fæst ðǽr on innan bær eorl gestreóna ... feá worda cwæþ: Hold ðũ nũ hrũse eorla ǽhte *the mound stood on the plain firm in its prisoning powers (able to keep in durance the treasure entrusted to it); therein bore the earl treasures ... few words he spake: Hold thou now, earth, the possessions of earls*, Beo. Th. 4475–4488; B. 2241–2248. v. nearu; *f.* I.

nearu-fáh; *adj. Disastrously hostile, bearing enmity the result of which is to reduce others to straits:*—Wæs ðæs wyrmes wíg wíde gesýne, nearofãges níð, hũ se gũþsceaþa Geáta leóde hatode and hýnde, Beo. Th. 4623; B. 2317.

nearu-grãp, e; *f. A close grasp:*—Ãn wiht is ... hreóh and rēþe hafaþ ryne strongne ... and be grunde faraþ ... neól is nearogrãp, Exon. Th. 491, 28; Rä. 81, 6. v. grãp.

nearu-líc; *adj. Oppressive, distressing, grievous:*—Feala mē se Hǽlend hearma gefremede, níða nearolícra, Elen. Kmbl. 1822; El. 913. v. next word.

nearulíce; *adv.* I. *narrowly, within narrow limits, briefly:*—

Nearolîce *strictim*, Ælfc. Gr. 38; Som. 41, 60. Ys seó foresǽde bôc (*Genesis*) on manegum stôwum swîđe nærolîce gesett (*is a mere narrative of events*), and đeáh swîđe deóplîce on đam gâstlîcum andgite, Ælfc. Gen. Thor. 4, 3. II. *oppressively, grievously*:—Đa đe nearwlîcast cûđan swician *those who knew how to cheat in most oppressive manner*, L. I. P. 12; Th. ii. 320, 24. III. *narrowly, exactly, strictly*:—Manegu dîglu þing sindon nearolîce (*subtiliter*) tô smeáganne *many secret things are to be narrowly examined*, Past. 21, 3; Swt. 153, 13. Swâ swŷđe nearwelîce hê hit lêtt ût âspyrian (*of the enquiry which was made when Doomsday Book was compiled*), Chr. 1085; Erl. 218, 34. [He nule nout so neruhliche demen ase ȝe siggeð, A. R. 334, 14.]

nearuness, e; *f.* I. *a strait*:—Mid longre nearonesse be eástan Constantinopolim ligeþ *juxta Constantinopolim longae mittuntur angustiae*, Ors. 1, 1; Swt. 8, 21. II. *oppression, distress* (of body):—Nearones breósta *oppression of the chest*, Lchdm. ii. 204, 27. Đæt (*asthma*) ys nearunyss . . . and breóst byþ inne mid micle nearnysse, iii. 116, 23–26. III. *distress* (of mind), *anxiety, tribulation, trouble, grief*:—Hêr is seó lǽnlîce winsumnes ac đǽr is seó syngale nearones *in this world is the transient delight, in the next is the perpetual distress*, L. E. I. introd.; Th. ii. 394, 8. Hû ne witon wê đæt nân nearewnes ne nân unrôtnes nis nân gesǽlþ *nam non esse anxiam, tristemque beatitudinem quid attinet dicere?* Bt. 24, 4; Fox 86, 20. Hê on swâ micelre nearanesse becom *he fell into so great trouble* (*was imprisoned*), 1; Fox 2, 27. Swâ hwâ swâ đa flǽsclîcan unþeáwas forlǽtan wile hê sceal geþolian micele nearanesse *corporis voluptatum appetentia plena est anxietatis*, 31, 1; Fox 110, 26. Seó hreówsung ne beoþ nâ bûtan sorge and bûton nearonesse, Fox 110, 29. On swâ micelre môdes unrêto and nearonisse *anxietate*, Nar. 30, 24. Nearonessa *angustia*, Ps. Th. 118, 143. On mînum earfoþum and nearonessum *in tribulatione*, 4, 1. Of nearonessum heora *de necessitatibus eorum*, Ps. Lamb. 106, 6. Nearonessum môdes *mentis angoribus*, Bd. 2, 12; S. 513, 33 note.

nearu-nîd, -nêd, e; *f. Sore need, grievous trouble*:—Đa menigo đe đê mid wuniaþ on nearonêdum [*or* (?) on nearo nêdum *in confinement by force*], Andr. Kmbl. 203; An. 102. From naronêđe *de angusta* (as if *angustia?*), Lk. Skt. p. 8, 6.

nearu-searu, we; *f. A wile that causes restraint* or *confinement* (?):—Hŷdde wǽron þurh nearusearwe næglas on eorþan (*of the nails in the cross that had been buried*), Elen. Kembl. 2215; El. 1109.

nearu-sorh, -sorg, e; *f. Oppressive care, grievous trouble*:—Nearusorge dreáh, Elen. Kmbl. 2520; El. 1261.

nearu-þanc, es; *m. Illiberal thought, wickedness*:—Feóndlîcra nearaþanca *spiritalium nequitiarum*, Hpt. Gl. 426, 61. Syle heom æfter nearuþancum (nearoþancnysse, Ps. Lamb. 27, 4), widmêtednyssa heora *da illis secundum nequitiam adinventionum ipsorum*, Ps. Spl. 27, 5.

nearu-þancness. v. preceding word.

nearu-þearf, e; *f. Pressing need*:—Ic on ŷđum slôg niceras nihtes, nearoþearfe dreáh, Beo. Th. 849; B. 422: Exon. Th. 5, 14; Cri. 69.

nearu-wrenc, es; *m. A trick* or *wile that causes anxiety* or *trouble*, Exon. Th. 316, 5; Môd. 44.

nearwe; *adv.* I. *straitly, strictly, closely*:—Nearwe gebunden *straitly bound*, Exon. Th. 463, 2; Hö. 64. Hyne sâr hafaþ nearwe befongen, Beo. Th. 1957; B. 976: Elen. Kembl. 2550; El. 1276: Met. 21, 5. II. *narrowly, strictly, exactly* (of enquiry):—Þeódcwên ongan georne sêcan nearwe, tô hwan hió đa næglas gedôn meahte, Elen. Kmbl. 2313; El. 1158: 2476; El. 1240. III. *oppressively, forcibly*:—Đonne hine æt niéhstan nearwe stilleþ G, Salm. Kmbl. 268; Sal. 133. Nearwe gebêged, Cd. Th. 292, 26; Sat. 446. IV. *anxiously, in a manner causing trouble*:—Hyge gnornende nihtes nearwe *the mind mourning in anguish at night*, Exon. Th. 174, 25; Gû. 1183. Ferþ gebysgad, nearwe genǽged, 162, 35; Gû. 986. Đâ heó nearwe beswâc yldran ûsse *when the serpent deceived our first parents to their hurt*, 226, 30; Ph. 413: Frag. Kmbl. 51; Leás. 27.

nearwe-lîce. v. nearu-lîce.

nearwian; *p.* ode. I. *to make narrow, straiten, compress*:—Se đe mec nearwaþ, Exon. Th. 407, 25; Rä. 26, 10. II. *to become narrow, contracted*:—Sefa nearwode (*of Noah when drunk*), Cd. Th. 94, 32; Gen. 1570. Sinc searwade, sib nearwade, Exon. Th. 353, 63; Reim. 37. v. ge-nearwian, nirwan.

neát, es; *n. A neat, an ox* or *a cow, cattle, beast, animal*:—Gif neát mon gewundige, weorpe đæt neát tô honda ođđe foreþingie, L. Alf. pol. 24; Th. i. 78, 9. Nân neát nyste nǽnne andan tô ôđrum, Bt. 35, 6; Fox 168, 10. Ne ligeþ hê eallinga on đære eorþan suâ đa creópendan wuhta, ac biþ hwæthwugu upâhæfen suâ đæt neát from eorþan, Past. 21, 3; Swt. 157, 1. Fugel ođđe fisc on sǽ ođđe eorþan neát, feldgongende feoh bûtan snyttro, Exon. Th. 371, 23; Seel. 80. Foldan neát, Salm. Kmbl. 436; Sal. 218. Ic eom anlîc ânum neáte *ut jumentum factus sum*, Ps. Th. 72, 18. Sealde heora neát (*jumenta*) hæglum, 77, 48. Deór and neát *bestiae et universa pecora*, 148, 10. Đa dumban neát, Andr. Kmbl. 134; An. 67. Tô neáta scypene *ad stabula jumentorum*, Bd. 4, 24; S. 597, 9. Nǽnig mann scypene his neátum ne timbreþ, 1, 1; S. 474, 32. Đâm monnum đe beóþ neátum gelîce, Bt. 14, 1; Fox 42, 3 note: 41, 5; Fox 254, 5. [*O. Frs.* nât: *Icel.* naut *cattle, oxen*: *O. H. Ger.* nôz *jumentum*.] v. sleg-neát.

Neátan-leáh (?) *Netley*, Chr. 508; Erl. 14, 18.

neáten, neá-west. v. nîten, neáh-west.

neáwung, e; *f. Nearness, coming near*:—In neáwung sîe sumer *in proximo sit aestas*, Mk. Skt. Lind. 13, 28.

nebb, es; *n.* I. *a neb* (dialect.), *nib, a beak, a beak-shaped thing*:—Neb *rostrum*, Wrt. Voc. ii. 119, 25. Đæt nebb (*of the Phœnix*) lîxeþ swâ glæs ođđe gim, Exon. Th. 218, 24; Ph. 299. Neb (*of a ship*), 392, 1; Rä. 11, 1. Neb (*of a plough*), 403, 1; Rä. 22, 1. Nebb (*of a rake*), 416, 23; Rä. 35, 3. Neb (*of a musical instrument*), 413, 16; Rä. 32, 6. Ic (*a key*) bregde nebbe, 498, 6; Rä. 87, 8. Ic (*a helm*) hæbbe heard nebb, 489, 29; Rä. 79, 1. II. *a nose, the gristle of the nose*:—Neb *internasum* (cf. nose gristle *internasus*, 43, 20), Wrt. Voc. i. 64, 50. Gif mon ôđrum đæt neb (nebb, MSS. B. H.: næb, MS. G.) of âsleá, gebête him mid. lx. scill., L. Alf. pol. 48; Th. i. 94, 8. III. *the face, countenance*:—Neb *facies*, Wrt. Voc. i. 42, 51: *vultus*, Hpt. Gl. 475, 6. Hys nebb (*facies*) wæs mid swâtlîne gebunden, Jn. Skt. 11, 44. Neb, Met. 31, 23. Be blǽdrum đe on mannes nebbe sittaþ . . . smyre đæt neb mid, Lchdm. i. 86, 5–8. Mid đam wlitegostan nebbe, Homl. Th. i. 430, 14. Đonne wê wendaþ ûre neb tô eástdǽle, 262, 10: ii. 102, 16. Heó helode hire nebb (*vultum*), Gen. 38, 15: Ex. 3, 6. Spǽte đæt wîf on his nebb (*faciem*), Deut. 25, 9: Num. 12, 14. Đâ forceáw hê his âgene tungan and wearp hine on đæt neb foran (*in os tyranni abjecit*), Bt. 16, 2; Bt. 52, 25. Hŷ habbaþ twâ neb on ânum heáfde *duas in uno habentes capite facies*, Nar. 35, 24. [*Icel.* nef (*gen. pl.* nefja) *the nose*; *the beak of a bird*.]

nebbian; *p.* ode *To turn the face towards anyone* (?), *to retort upon anyone* (?):—Se rîca besihþ on his pællenum gyrlum, and cwyþ: 'Nis se loddere mid his tættecon mîn gelica.' Ac se apostol Paulus hine nebbaþ mid đisum wordum (*retorts upon him, meets him, with these words*): 'Ne brohte wê nân þing tô đisum middangearde, ne wê nân þing heonon mid ûs lǽdan ne mâgon, Homl. Th. i. 256, 7–12.

neb-corn, es; *n. A pimple on the face*:—Gif nebcorn on wîfmannes nebbe weaxan . . . hit âfeormaþ of ealle đa nebcorn, Lchdm. i. 118, 22–25.

neb-gebræc, es; *n. A defluxion from the head, mucus of the nose*:—Nebgebræc *coriza* (=κορυζα), Wrt. Voc. i. 19, 28: ii. 135, 77.

Nebrond, es; *m. Nimrod*:—Freónd Nebrondes, Salm. Kmbl. 426; Sal. 213. v. Nefrod.

nebwlât-ful; *adj. Bold, impudent, shameless*:—Nebwlâtful, scamleás *frontosa*, Hpt. Gl. 506, 78. v. *next word and* wlâtian.

neb-wlátung, e; *f. Boldness, impudence*; frontositas, Lye (from a vocabulary in the Cotton library). v. preceding word.

neb-wlatung, e; *f. Dejection*; vultus demissio, Lye.

neb-wlitu, e; *f. The form of the face, the face, countenance*:—Heora nebwlitu sceán swâ swâ sunne, Homl. Th. ii. 426, 10. Ic ne mæg on his nebwlite beseón, Homl. Skt. 7, 104. Hî gesâwon his nebwlite swylce sumes engles ansŷne, Homl. Th. i. 46, 5. Sege ûs his nebwlite *describe his face to us*, 456, 15. Ne behealde gê heora nebwlite, ii. 404, 28.

nêchebúr, necte-gale, nêd-. v. neáh-gebûr, nihte-gale, nîd-.

nediende (?) *abominandum, execrandum*, Hpt. Gl. 515, 40.

nefa, an; *m.* I. *a nephew*; nepos:—Brôđer sune *vel* suster sune đæt is nefa, Wrt. Voc. i. 51, 71. Neva *nepos*, 72, 35. Hlôþhere Ægelbrhytes nefa (cf. hê him onsende Leutherium his nefan (*nepotem*), Bd. 3, 7; S. 530, 29), Chr. 670; Erl. 34, 29: 789; Erl. 57, 34: Ælfc. Gr. 9, 31; Som. 11, 69. Eám and nefa, Exon. Th. 431, 35; Rä. 47, 6. Heó wæs Êdwines nefan (*nepotis*) dohtor, Bd. 4. 23; S. 593, 2. Hê swylces hwæt secgan wolde eám his nefan, Beo. Th. 1766; B. 881. II. *a grandson*:—Nefena bearnum *pronepotibus, filiis nepotum*, Hpt. Gl. 426, 50. Ealdra nefena *pronepotum*, 445, 56. III. *a step-son*:—Nefa *prifignus*, Wülck. Gl. 41, 28. [*Icel.* nefi *a cognate kinsman, a nephew*: *O. Frs.* neva: *O. H. Ger.* nefo *nepos, sobrinus*: *Ger.* neffe.] v. for-, ge-nefa.

nefene, an; *f. A niece* or *grand-daughter*:—Brôđer dochter *vel* suster dohter, nefene *neptis*, Wrt. Voc. i. 51, 72. Nefenu[m] *nepotibus* (*neptibus?*), Hpt. Gl. 485, 42.

nefne, nemne. I. *conj.* connecting clauses, *Unless, except*:—Hê hyra mâ âcwellan wolde, nefne him witig God forstôde, Beo. Th. 2116; B. 1056: 6101; B. 3054: Exon. Th. 340, 5; Gn. Ex. 106: 345, 11; Gn. Ex. 186. Hî sǽdon, nemne (*nisi*) hî him mâran andlyfne sealdon, đæt hî woldan him sylfe niman, Bd. 1, 15; S. 483, 37. Hê læg swâ swâ deád mon nemne đynre êđunge ânre ætŷwde đæt hê lîfes wǽre *quasi mortuus jacebat, halitu tantum pertenui quia viveret demonstrans*, 5, 19; S. 640, 24. Nymne, 1, 27; S. 493, 38. Nô hê fôddor þigeþ, nemne meledeáwes dǽl gebyrge, Exon. Th. 215, 29; Ph. 260: 124, 12; Gû. 338: 249, 10; Jul. 109: Beo. Th. 3108; B. 1552: 5302; B. 2654. Næfne, 506; B. 250. On weres wæstmum, næfne (*except that*) hê wæs mâra đon ǽnig man ôđer, 2710; B. 1353. Hwæt hæfde seó godcunde þurh đa menniscan nemne bûton đæt heó mihte beón âcenned, Blickl. Homl. 19, 22. II. connecting words in the same case (contracted clauses, the verb of the second clause being the same as that in the first, and not expressed :—Ne gehȳrde nǣnig man on his mūþe ōht elles nefne Cristes lof and nytte sprǣce, 223, 36: Exon. Th. 308, 28; Seef. 46. Nǣneg dorste nefne sinfreá, Beo. Th. 3873; B. 1934. Ic lyt hafo heáfodmāga nefne đec, 4309; B. 2151. Đǣt unc ne gedǣlde nemne deáþ āna ōwiht elles, Exon. Th. 442, 34; Kl. 23: Andr. Kmbl. 1327; An. 664. III. *prep. Except* :—Nemne feáum ānum, Beo. Th. 2167; B. 1081.

nefre. v. nǣfre.

Nefrod, es; *m. Nimrod* :—Nefrod se gigant; se Nefrod wæs Chuses sunu, Bt. 35, 4; Fox 162, 17. v. Nebroud.

nefte. v. nepte.

nē-fugol, nēgan, nēh, nēhsta, neht, nele, nellan. v. neó-fugol, nǣgan, neáh, nīhsta, neht, nyllan.

nemnan, nemnian; *p.* nemde. I. *to name, give a name to a person* or *thing* :—Đū cennest sunu đone đū nemnest Hǣlend, Blickl. Homl. 7, 19. Đū nemdest mid āne noman ealle tōgædere woruld, Met. 20, 55. Đa hē nemde (*nominavit*) apostolas; Simonem đæne hē nemde (*cognominavit*) Petrus, Lk. Skt. 6, 13–14. Hē đone yldestan Noæ nemde, Cd. Th. 75, 4; Gen. 1235. Hig nemdon (*vocant*) hyne hys fæder naman Zachariam, Lk. Skt. 1, 59. Đysne dæg hié nemdon siges dæg, Blickl. Homl. 67, 13. II. *to use such and such a name* or *title in speaking of a person* or *thing* :—Đone wē wifel wordum nemnaþ *which we call beetle, when we speak of it*, Exon. Th. 426, 14; Rä. 41, 73. Hine tō sylfcwale secgas nemnaþ *men speak of him as a suicide*, 330, 25; Vy. 56. Eác hī ōđre worde beornas Bađan nemnaþ *men also use the name Bath in speaking of it*, Chr. 973; Erl. 124, 13: 975; Erl. 124, 32. David sylf nemde hine drihten *ipse David dicit eum dominum*, Mk. Skt. 12, 37. Heó sylf hié þeówen nemde, Blickl. Homl. 13, 13. Drihten đa cynelīcan burh forhogodlīce naman nemde *the Lord used a contemptuous name* (wīc) *in speaking of the royal city*, 77, 23, 26. Đis andwerde līf hē nemde for weg *this present life he spoke of as a way*, L. E. I. 35; Th. ii. 432, 23. Đone hwītan hlāf (*the eucharistic bread*) đone đū sealdest Saban ūssum fæder nemdon heó hine swā (*sic eum appellare consuerant*), Bd. 2, 5; S. 507, 15. Ne gyrne gē đæt eów man Lāreówas nemne *nolite vocari Rabbi*, Mt. Kmbl. 23, 8: Ps. Th. 82, 4. Đēh đe gewrito oft nemnen eal đa lond Mēđia, Ors. 1, 1; Swt. 10, 24. Đeáh mon anweald and genyht tō twǣm þingum nemne đeáh hit is ān *though power and abundance be spoken of as two things, yet are they one*, Bt. 33, 1; Fox 120, 21. Hī gewunedon hī mōder cȳgean and nemnian (tō hātenne and tō nemnenne, MS. B.) *quam matrem vocare consueverant*, Bd. 4, 23; S. 594, 39. Đæs fæder wæs Wōden nemned, 1, 15; S. 483, 30: Blickl. Homl. 81, 1. On đǣm bōcum đe nemned is *Actus Apostolorum*, 133, 11: 137, 31. Đæt wæs swīđe heálīc nama đæt Sanctus Johannes engel wæs nemned, 167, 32. Đam is tō naman nemned Drihten *Dominus nomen est ei*, Ps. Th. 67, 4. III. *to call upon the name of, address by name, to invoke* :—Ne nemn đū Drihtnes naman on ȳdel ne byþ unscyldig se đe his noman on ȳdel nemþ *non assumes nomen Domini Dei tui in vanum! nec enim habebit insontem Dominus eum, qui assumpserit nomen Domini frustra*, Ex. 20, 7. Ic naman đīnne nemde, Dryhten, Ps. Th. 118, 55. Hē nemde mē mīnne noman *vocavit me nomine meo*, Bd. 5, 6; S. 619, 37. Hine se ǣr be naman nemde, Elen. Kmbl. 155; El. 78. Se nemde God niþþa bearna ǣrest ealra, Cd. Th. 69, 13; Gen. 1135. God nemdon and hine bǣdon, 48, 22; Gen. 779. Ongan swegles weard be naman nemnan, Judth. Thw. 22, 27; Jud. 81. IV. *to mention by name, to mention, relate* :—For mīne brōđru ic bidde, and mīne đa neáhstan nemne swylce, Ps. Th. 121, 8. Đǣm unþeáwum đe ic ǣr nemde, Met. 25, 62. Ealle đa ōđru gōd đe wē ǣr nemdon, Bt. 24, 3; Fox 84, 24: Cd. Th. 288, 20; Sat. 383. Sege hwæt ic þence, nemn gif đū hit gereccean mǣge, Blickl. Homl. 181, 14. Māgun wē nemnan *we can tell*, Exon. Th. 107, 25; Gū. 64. Đeáh đe ic hȳ nīhst nemnan sceolde *though I should mention their names last*, 326, 10; Vīd. 126. *Pronomen* spelaþ đone naman đæt đū ne þurfe tuwa hine nemnan *the pronoun represents the noun so that you need not mention it* (*the noun*) *twice*, Ælfc. Gr. 5; Som. 3, 30. Swā on đære ilcan lāre nemned (*mentioned*) is, Blickl. Homl. 133, 34. V. *to name, nominate* :—Gif landāgende man ætsace, đonne nemne man him his gelīcan ealswā micel Wente swā cyninges þegne, L. N. P. L. 52; Th. ii. 298, 10. [*Goth.* namnjan: *O. Sax. O. H. Ger.* nemnian: *Icel.* nefna.] v. ge-nemnan, namnian, namian.

nemne. v. nefne.

nemnigend-līc; *adj. Nominative* :—*Nominativus* is nemnigendlīc, mid đam casu wē nemnaþ ealle þing, Ælfc. Gr. 7; Som. 6, 17.

nemþe. v. nimþe.

Nen *the river Nen in Northamptonshire* :—Đæt water, đæt man cleopeþ Nen, Chr. 963; Erl. 122, 17.

neó *a corpse.* v. dryht-nē, neó-bedd, -fugol, -sīđ. [*Goth.* naus: *Icel.* nār.]

neó-bedd, es; *n. A bed for a corpse* :—Ic in mīnum neste neóbed ceóse '*I shall die in my nest*' (A. V.), Exon. Th. 235, 7; Ph. 553. God wearp hine niđer on đæt neóbedd (*that couch of corpses, Hell*; cf. Milton '*that fiery couch*'; *and Icel.* nā-strōnd *the place where the dead came, who had not fallen in battle*), Cd. Th. 22, 19; Gen. 343.

neód, nēd, niéd, nȳd, e; *f. Desire, eagerness, diligence, earnest endeavour* :—Wæs him neód micel đæt hié tōbrugdon fira flǣschoman him to fōdderþege *great was their desire to rend the bodies of men for their repast*, Andr. Kmbl. 316; An. 158. Biþ him neód micel đæt hē đa yldu mōte wendan tō līfe feorg geong onfōn *it is most eager to turn old age to life, to receive youth*, Exon. Th. 210, 22; Ph. 189: 228, 3; Ph. 432. (Cf. *O. Sax.* was im niud mikil that sie selbon Krist gisehan mōstin *they desired eagerly to see Christ.*) Ūs is eallum neód đæt wē đīn mēdrencynn mōtan cunnan *we all desire to know thy descent on the mother's side*, 15, 33; Cri. 245. Wundorlīc is geworden đīn wīsdōm ne mæg ic him on neóde ā neáh cuman (*I cannot with all my endeavours come near it*), Ps. Th. 138, 4. Noe tealde đæt hē on neód hine gif hē land ne funde sēcan wolde *Noah reckoned that if the raven did not find land it would eagerly seek him*, Cd. Th. 87, 4; Gen. 1443. Hié God herigaþ, and him be namon gehwam on neód (*earnestly*) sprecaþ, 242, 25; Dan. 424. Ic đīnne naman on neód secge *confitebor nomini tuo*, Ps. Th. 137, 2. Sōđfæste đīnne naman willaþ þuruh neód herigean *justi confitebuntur nomini tuo*, 139, 13. Se đe naman đīnne þurh neód forhtaþ *he that is earnest in reverencing thy name*, 60, 4. ¶ *The instrumental with adverbial force occurs very frequently in the Psalms.* Neóde, nēde, niéde, nȳde *earnestly, diligently, eagerly* :—Weoroda mǣst fore Waldende gǣþ neóde and nȳde (*the good will go eagerly, the wicked only on compulsion*), Exon. Th. 66, 15; Cri. 1072. Oft hē hǣþengield gesōhte neóde geneahhe (*very diligently*), 244, 7; Jul. 24: Ps. Th. 82, 12, 13. His naman neóde heriaþ, 67, 4. His naman neóde lufiaþ, 68, 37. Hī hyrdnesse neóde begangaþ *they diligently keep watch*, 89, 5: 112, 2: 121, 6. Nēde, 105, 36: 118, 55. Nȳde, 118, 132: 114, 4. Niéde, Ps. Ben. 43, 27. Þurh đīnra neóda (niéda, MS. Verc.), lust *by the pleasure of thy passions*, Exon. Th. 369, 29; Seel. Ex. 48. Hē ūs on hæft nimeþ ofer ūsse neóde lust (*contrary to our desires*), 16, 30; Cri. 261. Wē đǣrinne andlangne dæg nióde nāmon *in the hall the live long day we took our pleasure*, Beo. Th. 4238; B. 2116. [*O. Sax.* niud: *O. Frs.* niod: *O. H. Ger.* niot; *m. desiderium, cupido.*] v. next word.

neód (= neád) *necessity. The distinction in form between the word = Goth.* nauþs, *and the preceding word seems not to have been observed in A. S. MSS. See the passages under* nīd.

neód-fracu, e; *f. Desire, appetite, the object of desire* or *of appetite* :—Wuhta gehwilc hnipaþ of dūne, wilnaþ tō eorþan, sume nēdþearfe, sume neódfræce (cf. ealle beóþ of dūne healde wiđ đære eorþan and đider wilniaþ ođđe đæs đe hī lyst ođđe đæs đe hī beþurfon, Bt. 41, 6; Fox 254, 28), Met. 31, 15.

neód-freónd. v. nīd-fréond.

neód-ful; *adj. Earnest, zealous* :—Bidde ic monna gehwone đe đis gied wræce, đæt hē mec neódful gemyne, Exon. Th. 285, 26; Jul. 720.

neódian *to be necessary.* v. neádian.

neód-lađu; *f. Earnest, hospitable invitation* :—Hē frægn gif him wǣre æfter neódlađu niht getǣse *Beowulf asked if to Hrothgar the night had been pleasant after the hospitality of the preceding evening* (?) (cf. him wæs ful boren and freóndlađu wordum bewægned, 2389; B. 1192), Beo. Th. 2644; B. 1320.

neód-līce; *adv. Diligently, sedulously, zealously, eagerly, earnestly* :—Smire đa sīdan mid đȳ neódlīce *smear the sides with it diligently*, Lchdm. ii. 262, 11. Đā éfste se abbud wiđ đæs muneces, and neódlīce (*eagerly, anxiously*) cwæþ: 'Hwǣr is se đe đū feredest?' Homl. Th. i. 336, 22: ii. 26, 5. Lustlīce gehyrdon đa đe him gelǣrde wǣron and eác swylce neódlīce mid dǣdum lǣston đa đe hī ongitan mihton *libenter ea quae dicerentur, audirent; libentius ea quae intelligere poterant, operando sequerentur*, Bd. 4, 27; S. 604, 18. Gōd is đæt man neódlīce Drihtnes naman āsinge, Ps. Th. 91, 1: 128, 6: 133, 3: 148, 12. Neódlīce on naman đīnum ealle eorþbūend egsan habbaþ *greatly do all dwellers on earth stand in awe of thy name*, 101, 13. Mē neódlīce tō forsceape scȳhte, Cd. Th. 53, 21; Gen. 897. Nǣnig đīnra þegna neódlucor ne gelustfullīcor hine sylfne underþeódde tō ūra goda bigange đonne ic *nullus tuorum studiosius quam ego culturae deorum nostrorum se subdidit*, Bd. 2, 13; S. 516, 5. Nȳdlīcor *libentius*, 4, 13; S. 583, 4. [*O. Sax.* niud-līko.]

neód-lof, es; *n. Diligent praise* :—Herian naman Drihtnes mid neódlofe (cf. hebbaþ neódlīce eówre handa on hālig lof, 133, 3), Ps. Th. 148, 12.

neód-spearuwa, an; *m. An active, restless sparrow* (cf. (?) sparuwe is a cheaterinde brid; cheatereð euer ant chirmeð, A. R. 152), Ps. Th. 123, 6.

neód-weorþung, e; *f. Great honouring* :—For naman đīnes neódweorþunge *propter nomen tuum*, Ps. Th. 142, 11.

neó-, nē-fugol, es; *m. A bird that feeds on carrion, a vulture* or *crow* :—Nēfuglas sittaþ þeódherga wæl þicce gefylled *carrion-birds sit gorged with the slain*, Cd. Th. 130, 12; Gen. 2158.

neól. v. neowol.

neom, neam, nam = ne eom *am not*, nis = ne is *is not* :—Đæs gescȳ neom (nam, Lind.: næm, Rush.) ic wyrđe tō berenne, Mt. Kmbl. 3, 11. Neam ic *non sum*, Ps. Surt. 118, 30. Sī eówer sprǣc: Hyt ys, hyt ys:

nyt nys, hyt nys, Mt. Kmbl. 5, 37. Nis âlýfed *it is not allowed*, Homl. Th. i. 94, 29.

neómian (?) *to produce harmonious sounds*:—Nægl (*plectrum*) neómigende (MS. neome cende), Exon. Th. 332, 12; Vy. 84. [Grein compares the word with *O. H. Ger.* niumôn *jubilare, psallere*; there is also the noun niumo *modulatio, sonus, canticum*.]

neón. v. neán.

neorxna wang, es; *m. Paradise*:—*Paradisum* ðæt wē hâtaþ on Englisc neorxna wang, Hexam. 16; Norm. 14, 5: Cd. Th. 13, 26; Gen. 208: Blickl. 17, 15: Homl. Th. i. 12, 32. Gif hē beget and yt rinde sió ðe cymþ of neorxna wonge, ne dereþ hīm nān âtter. Đonne cwæþ se ðe ðās bōc wrāt hió wǣre torbegete, Lchdm. ii. 114, 4. Neorxena wang, Gen. 2, 9: 3, 8. Neorxnewong, Hpt. Gl. 447, 2. Nearxnewang, Hy. Surt. 64, 25. Nerxnewang, 47, 12. Nercsna ([n]erexna, Rush.) wong, Lk. Skt. Lind. 23, 43. Neirxna wong, Mt. Kmbl. p. 8, 5: Rtl. 124, 7. Nerxna wong, 124, 3.

neósan; *p.* de (?) *with gen. acc. or clause*. I. *to search out, find out by enquiry*:—Wolde ic ânes tō ðē cræftes neósan ðæt ðū mē getǣhte hū ðū sǣhengeste sund wīsige *one art would I find out by enquiry of thee; that thou wouldest teach me how for the sea-horse thou guidest its swimming*, Andr. Kmbl. 968; An. 484. Hý neósan cwōman, hwæðere him ðæs wonges wyn sweðrade, Exon. Th. 123, 12; Gū. 321. II. *to seek, visit* (a) a place:—Gewât his beddes neósan *Holofernes sought his couch*, Judth. Thw. 22, 15; Jud. 63: Beo. Th. 3587; B. 1791. Setles neósan, 3576; B. 1786. Ceóles neósan, 3617; B. 1806: Andr. Kmbl. 620; An. 310. Êðles neósan, 1660; An. 832: 2050; An. 1027. Burga neósan, Elen. Kmbl. 304; El. 152. Wīca neósan, Beo. Th. 251; B. 125: Exon. Th. 184, 5; Gū. 1339. Þȳstra, wīta neósan *to seek hell*, 275, 23; Jul. 554: 280, 18; Jul. 631. Hâmes niósan, Beo. Th. 4722; B. 2366: 4765; B. 2381. Êce staðulas neósan, Cd. Th. 207, 30; Exod. 474. (b) a person:—Ûser neósan, Beo. Th. 4155; B. 2074. Com ðā hǣðenra hlōþ hâliges neósan, Andr. Kmbl. 2778; An. 1391: Exon. Th. 170, 30; Gū. 1119. Ic his neósan wille, 145, 8; Gū. 691. Word âres oft neósendes (ðîn), 175, 6; Gū. 1190. III. *to seek with hostile intent* (cf. sēcan):—Wyrm yrre cwom fiónda niósan, lāðra manna, Beo. Th. 5336; B. 2671. [*Goth.* bi-niuhsjan *to spy out*: *Icel.* nȳsa *to pry, enquire*: *O. Sax.* niusian: *O. H. Ger.* niusian *niti, conari*.] v. next word.

neósian; *p.* ode *with gen. acc.* or *clause*. I. *to search out, find out by enquiry* or *inspection, to inspect*:—Wolde neósian Nergend, hwæt his bearn dyde, Cd. Th. 53, 2; Gen. 855. Gewât neósian heán hūses hū hit Hring-Dene gebūn hæfdon *he came and inspected the lofty house, how the Hring-Danes had ordered it*, Beo. Th. 230; B. 115. II. *to seek, visit* (a) a place:—Wæs his gewuna ðæt Norþanhymbra mǣgþe sōhte and neósode *solebat Nordanhymbrorum provincian revisere*, Bd. 3, 23; S. 554, 7. Gewiton him wīgend wīca neósian, Frysland geseón, Beo. Th. 2255; B. 1125. (b) a person:—Mannes sunu ðe ðū neósast (*visitas*), Ps. Th. 8, 5. Neósode hē mīn eft *me revisens*, Bd. 5, 6; S. 619, 43. Se hine ǣghwylce daga neósade, Exon. Th. 162, 11; Gū. 974. Hwīlum mennisce âras neósedon (hine *or* his), 157, 16; Gū. 892. Ic wæs on ðæm carcerne and gē mīn neósodon, L. E. I. 32; Th. ii. 428, 29. Se leófa cuma se ðe gewunade ūre brōðer neósian (*visitare*), Bd. 4, 3; S. 568, 17. Đone ðe hī untrumne neósian cōman, 4, 11; S. 579, 40: R. Ben. 17, 2. Đonne Drihten ūre hwylces neósian wille, Blickl. Homl. 125, 13. III. *to seek with hostile intent* (cf. sēcan), *to visit with calamity, disease*, etc.:—Leomu hefegedon, hē gecneów ðæt hine ælmihtig ufan neósade (cf. the phrase *the visitation of God*), Exon. Th. 159, 24; Gū. 931. Đǣr Ongenþeów Eofores niósade (MS. niosað), Beo. Th. 4966; B. 2486. [*O Sax.* niusôn.] v. ge-neósian *and preceding word*.

neó-sīþ, es; *m. Death*:—Se sceal æfter neósīþum wunian wītum fæst Exon. Th. 316, 27; Mōd 55.

neósung, e; *f. A visiting, visitation*:—Synna forgyfenys, hūselgang and Godes neósung sind eallum gemǣne, Homl. Th. i. 64, 32. Johannes wearþ on ðysum dæge tō heofenan rīces myrhþe þurh Godes neósunge genumen, 58, 4. Mid ðȳ ðā æfter langre tīde com tō him for neósunge intingan (*gratia visitationis*), Bd. 4, 3; S. 569, 41. Būton niósunga *absque visitatione*, Kent. Gl. 710. v. ge-neósung.

neótan, niótan; *p.* neát, *pl.* nuton *To enjoy, have the benefit of, make use of*, (a) with gen.:—Brūc ðisses beáges and ðisses hrægles neót,' Beo. Th. 2439; B. 1217. Nióta þ inc ðæs ōðres ealles *all other take for your use*, Cd. Th. 15, 18; Gen. 235. Līfes, feores neótan *to live*. Hwylc is manna ðæt feores neóte *quis est homo, qui vivet*, Ps. Th. 88, 41: Exon. Th. 328, 14; Vy. 17. Niótan, Cd. Th. 31, 17; Gen. 486: 26, 4; Gen. 401. Mīnes ēðelrīces eádig neótan, Exon. Th. 89, 25; Cri. 1462: 223, 18; Ph. 361: 356, 14; Pa. 11. Geofona neótan, 225, 5; Ph. 384: 152, 6; Gū. 804. Willum neótan blǣdes and blissa, 184, 21; Gū. 1347: 82, 26; Cri. 1344. Đæt hē ðǣr brūcan mōt wonges mid willum, and welan neótan līfes and lissa, 208, 2; Ph. 149. Sēcan swegles dreámas and (ðara dreáma) willum neótan, Andr. Kmbl. 1620; An. 811. Wǣpna neótan *to make good use of his weapons*, Byrht. Th. 140, 55; By. 308. (b) with acc.:—Ic ðē on ða fægran foldan gesette tō neótenne neorxna wonges beorhtne blǣdwelan, Exon. Th. 85, 14; Cri. 1391. [*Goth.* niutan: *O. Sax.* niotan: *O. Frs.* niata: *Icel.* njóta: *O. H. Ger.* niuzan (*with gen. and acc.*) *uti, frui*.] v. be-, (bi-)neótan.

neóten. v. nīten.

neoþan; *adv. Down, beneath, from beneath*:—Nyþan (niþan, neoþan) *dedeorsum*, Ælfc. Gr. 38; Zup. 238, 10. On heofenum and on eorþan neoþan *in coelo sursum et in terra deorsum*, Jos. 2, 11. Ealle stōwa hē neoþan underwreþeþ, Blickl. Homl. 23, 20. Đæt wæter wæs sweart under ðæm clife neoþan, 211, 2: Cd. Th. 20, 18; Gen. 311. Wrætlīc is seó womb neoþan, Exon Th. 219, 14; Ph. 307: 392, 2; Rä. 11, 1: 407, 14; Rä. 26, 5: 414, 14; Rä. 32, 20. Đū mē of neowelnesse neoþan âlȳsdest, Ps. Th. 70, 19: 103, 7: Elen. Kmbl. 2228; El. 1115. Neoþan, Exon. Th. 479, 11; Rä. 62, 6. v. be-, wið-neoþan, *and next word*.

neoðane; *adv. Beneath, below*:—Hēr is fȳr micel ufan and neoþone, Cd. Th. 24, 8; Gen. 375. Ufane and neoþane, Met. 20, 141. [*O. Sax.* niðana: *O. H. Ger.* nidana *subtus, subtu*.]

neoþan-weard; *adj. Low in position*:—Nioþanweard hype *ilia*, Wrt. Voc. ii. 110, 54.

neoþemest. v. *next word and* neoþor.

neoþera, niþera; *adj.* (*without a positive form*) *Lower*:—Neoþera welor *albrum* (= *labrum*), Wrt. Voc. ii. 7, 79: i. 282, 71. Niþera lippe *labrum*, 43, 25. Đū genēredest mīne sâule of ðære neoþeran helle, Blickl. Homl. 89, 28. Neoþran, Ps. Spl. 85, 12. On seáðe ðam neoþeran *in lacu inferiori*, 87, 6. Cyng âh ðone uferan and bisceop ðone nyþeran, L. E. G. 4; Th. i. 168, 16. On nyþerum eorþan *in inferioribus terrae*, Ps. Spl. 138, 14. On ða neoþran eorþan, 62, 9. On ðās niþeran dǣlas ðisse ceastre, Blickl. Homl. 239, 6. Yfemest is eallra gesceafta fȳr ofer eorþan, folde neoþemest, Met. 20, 85. On ðære nyþemystan (*lowest*) bytminge, Homl. Th. i. 536, 10. Đa niþemestan ic gebrenge æt ðām hēhstan, and ða hēhstan æt ðām niþemestan, Bt. 7, 3; Fox 20, 35. Gē underþiódaþ eówre hēhstan medemnesse under ða eallra nyþemestan gesceafta, 14, 2; Fox 44, 34. On ða neoþemestan helle wītu, Blickl. Homl. 185, 6.

neoþe-, nioþo-, niþe-weard; *adj. Low, situated beneath, bottom of* (the noun with which the adjective agrees):—Niþeweard fōt *planta*; hōh niþeweard *calx*, Wrt. Voc. i. 283, 73, 75. Is se hals grēne nioþoweard and ufeweard, Exon. Th. 218, 23; Ph. 299. On nyþewerdum ðam munte *ad radices montis*, Ex. 19, 17. Hē (*Noah's ark*) wæs on nyþeweardan wīd, and on ufeweardan nearo, Homl. Th. i. 536, 9. Wyrc hié of nioþoweardre netlan, Lchdm. ii. 128, 6. Wyl neoþewearde netelan, 312, 5. Lege on ðone pyt neoþeweardne *lay it at the bottom of the pit*, i. 398, 22. Neoþouard *crepidinem*, Wrt. Voc. ii. 98, 5. Tōsliten of ufewerdum ōþ neoþewerd (nioðuord, Lind.: nioþawordum, Rush.), Mk. Skt. 15, 38. Nyþeweard (nioþaweard, Lind.: neoþewearde, Rush.), Mt. Kmbl. 27, 51. Of neoþeweardum *imis*, Wrt. Voc. ii. 43, 57. Fram his hnolle ufewerdan ōþ his ilas neoþewerde *from the crown of his head to the soles of his feet*, Homl. Th. ii. 452, 27.

neoþor, nioþor, niþor; *adv.* (*without a positive form*) *Lower, in an inferior position*:—Niþor *inferius*, nyþemyst *infime*, Ælfc. Gr. 38; Som. 42, 14. Se ðe wæs neoþor on endebyrdnysse wearþ fyrmest on þrowunge *he* (*Stephen*) *that was lower in order, was first in suffering*, Homl. Th. i. 50, 4. Đā heó ðā hié in ðæm gefeohte neoþor gesēgon *qui dum se inferiores in bello conspicerent*, Bd. 3, 18; S. 546, 16. Đē læs ðe ðæt mōd sȳ neoþer ðonne se līchoma, Homl. Skt. 1, 58. Nioþoror, Bt. 41, 6; Fox 254, 31. Sió eorþe is nioþor ðonne ǣnig ōðru gesceaft, Bt. 33, 4; Fox 130, 20. Nioþor hwēne, Beo. Th. 5392; B. 2699. Đæt mōd glīt nioþor and nioþor (niþor and niþor, Hatt. MS.) stæpmǣlum, Past. 38, 7; Swt. 278, 2. Hine nyþor âsette Metod *the Lord humbled him* (*Nebuchadnezzar*), Cd. Th. 247, 7; Dan. 493.

neówan, neówe, neowel, neówian, neówinga, neówness. v. nīwan, nīwe, neowol, nīwian, nīwinga, nīwness.

neowol, nifol, nihol, nihold, neól, niwol; *adj.* I. *prone, prostrate*:—Nihol *pronus*, Ep. Gl. 20 b, 2. Nihold, Wrt. Voc. ii. 118, 20. Hwī līst ðū neowel on eorþan *cur jaces pronus in terra?* Jos. 7, 10. Hē feóll niwel on ða eorþan, Gen. 33, 3. Niwol, Bt. 1; Fox 4, 3. Neowol, Met. 1, 80. Đǣrrihte fērde eall seó heord myclum onrǣse niwel on sǣ *ecce impetu abiit totus grex per praeceps in mare*, Mt. Kmbl. 8, 32. Neól ic fēre, Exon. Th. 403, 2; Rä. 22, 1. Hīt swā niowul (*prostrate*) up ârǣrde, Bt. 3, 1; Fox 4, 26. Neowle nihtscūwan *the shades of night that had settled down upon earth*, Cd. Th. 184, 28; Exod. 114. Đa neowelan *cernua*, Wrt. Voc. ii. 18, 14: 78, 59. Neóle *cernuas*, 83, 3. Nióle, 18, 42. Nifle nædran cynn *serpentes*, Ps. Th. 148, 10. II. *deep down, low, profound* (v. neowolness):—Niól *infima*, 110, 73. Under neólum niþer næsse *deep underground*, Elen. Kmbl. 1660; El. 832. In ðam neólan scræfe *in that deepest den* (*hell*), Exon. Th. 283, 23; Jul. 684. In ðissum neowlan genipe (*hell*), Cd. Th. 271, 7; Sat. 102. In ðone neowlan grund *to that profound abyss*, 267, 1; Sat. 31: 270, 16; Sat. 91. In ðis neowle genip, 275, 31; Sat. 180: 292, 25; Sat. 446. Drihten for ðē of ðæm heán heofone on ðās neowlan gesceaft niðer âstāh *for thee the Lord descended from the high heaven to this lower world*, L. E. I. prm.; Th. ii. 396, 2. Gē beóþ forǣltene on ðone neowlan helle seáð *ye shall be dismissed to the bottomless* *pit*, 396, 18. Gǽst ellor hwearf under neowelne næs, Judth. Thw. 23, 9; Jud. 113. Sunne gewât tô sete glîdan under niflan næs, Andr. Kmbl. 2611; An. 1307. Nyþer gefeallaþ under neowulne grund *descendunt usque ad abyssos*, Ps. Th. 106, 25. Neowle næssas *low-lying headlands*, Beo. Th. 2826; B. 1411; Niþer under næssas, neóle grundas (*hell*), Exon. Th. 136, 3; Gû. 535.

neowol-líc; *adj. Profound*:—Hê siccetunga teáh of niwellîcum breóste *he heaved sighs from the depths of his breast*, Homl. Skt. 7, 66.

neowolness, e; *f. A deep place, an abyss*:—Neowelnys *abyssus*, Ps. Spl. 35, 6. Seó neólnes cliopaþ tô ðære neólnesse *abyssus abyssum invocat*, Ps. Th. 41, 8. Ealle wyllspringas ðære micelan niwelnesse, Gen. 7, 11: 1, 2. Of neowelnesse *de abyssis terrae*, Ps. Th. 70, 19. In neólnesse, in sûsla grund, Elen. Kmbl. 1882; El. 943 Ealle neowelnessa *omnes abyssi*, Ps. Th. 148, 7. Neowelnyssa, Cant. Moys. 5. Neólnessa, Blickl. Homl. 93, 12. On þa neowolnesse ðæs seáþes *in profunda*, Bd. 5, 12; S. 628, 21. Neólnisse *abyssos*, Ps. Surt. 32, 7, Nywolnessa, Ps. Th. 103, 7.

nêp; *adj. Lacking, scanty* (?):—Mægen wæs on cwealme fæste gefeterod forþganges nêp *the force of the Egyptians was fast fettered in death, they could make no advance* (*when they were overwhelmed in the Red Sea*), Cd. Th. 207, 20; Exod. 469. v. next word.

nêp-flôd, es; *m. A neap-tide, a very low tide*:—Nêpflôd *vel* ebba *ledona*, Wrt. Voc. i. 57, 11: *ledo*, 63, 74: ii. 98, 22. On ǽlcum ânum geáre weaxeþ ðæt flôd ðæs sǽs feówer and twentigum sîða, and swâ oft wanaþ; fylleþflôd biþ nêmned on lǽden *malina*, and se nêpflôd *ledo*, Shrn. 63, 31. [Cf. Eng. Gilds (E. E. T. S.), p. 425, 30, where '*neep* sesons' are mentioned, the times of neap-tides.]

nepte, nefte, an; *f. Nep* or *nip* (v. E. D. S. Plant-Names), *cat's mint*:—Nepte *nepita*, Wrt. Voc. ii. 62, 40. Næpte, i. 30, 21. Nepte. Ðâs wyrte man *nepitamon*, and ôðrum naman nepte nemneþ, and eác Grêcas hŷ *mente orinon* hâtaþ, Lchdm. i. 208, 7-9. Nefte, ii. 122, 13: 316, 5: 318, 12. Neptan sǽd, iii. 72, 11. Wyl neftan, ii. 62, 25: 76, 19: 142, 3: 266, 11. [*Prompt. Parv.* nepte *nepta*.]

ner, es; *n. A refuge*:—Geworden is [Dryhten] ner oððe rôtnes ðam þearfan *factus est Dominus refugium pauperi*, Ps. Lamb. 9, 10. v. ge-ner.

nergend, nerigend, neriend, es; *m. A saviour, preserver*:—Ðec, mihtig God, nergend, Cd. Th. 239, 24; Dan. 375. Crist nergend, Hy. Grn. ii. 291, 39. Dryhten God, nerigend fira, Andr. Kmbl. 2573; An. 1288. Neregend, 581; An. 291. Se Godes cwide is folces nerigend (MS. B. neriend), Salm. Kmbl. 162; Sal. 80. Nergendes hǽs *God's command*, Cd. Th. 173, 19; Gen. 2863. Nergende leóf, 77, 35; Gen. 1285. Ealra fǽmnena cwên cende ðone sôþan Scyppend and ealles folces Fêrfrend, and ealles middangeardes Hǽlend, and ealra gâsta Nergend, and ealrasâula Helpend, Blickl. Homl. 105, 18. [*O. Sax.* neriand (*Christ*).]

nerian; *p.* ede *To save*:—Wyrd oft nereþ unfǽgne eorl *if a man's death be not doomed, oft destiny saves him*, Beo. Th. 1149; B. 572. Of neádum heora hê nerode (*eripuit*) hig, Ps. Spl. 106, 6. Hié hâlig God nerede, Cd. Th. 84, 13; Gen. 1397: 90, 6; Gen. 1491. Hî freá nerede fram hellcwale, Exon. Th. 73, 14; Cri. 1189. Ðîn ealdor nere, Cd. Th. 151, 2; Gen. 2502. Ðæt ðû nerige (*eruas*) mê, Ps. Spl. 39, 18. Se ðe wyle oððe sceall nerian *eruiturus*, Ælfc. Gr. 41; Som. 44, 26. Hyne God wolde nergan wið nîþum, Exon. Th. 135, 16; Gû. 525. Gewiton feorh heora fleáme nergan, Cd. Th. 120, 126; Gen. 2000. Nergean, 151, 16; Gen. 2509. Tô nergenne, 234, 1; Dan. 285. Tô nerganne, Exon. Th. 185, 11; Az. 6. Neriende Crist (cf. *O. Sax.* neriendi Krist), Hy. Grn. ii. 286, 4, 28. Nerigende, Cd. Th. 238, 15; Dan. 355. Nergende Crist, 300, 25; Sat. 570. [*Goth.* nasjan: *O. Sax.* nerian: *O. Frs.* nera: *O. H. Ger.* nerian *alere, pascere, sustentare, salvare*: *Ger.* nähren: cf. *Icel.* næra *to nourish*.] v. ge-nerian.

nering, e; *f. Protection, defence*:—Nerin[ge] *presidio, protectionis*, Hpt. Gl. 527, 68.

Neron, es; *m. Nero*:—Neron cwæþ, Blickl. Homl. 175, 33. Nerones wîf Libia, 173, 13. Tô Nerone, 173, 10.

nerwet. v. nirwett.

nesan; *p.* næs; *pl.* nǽson; *pp.* nesen *To be saved from, to escape from*:—Ðam ðe mid sceolon mereflôd nesan *those who are to be saved with you from the flood* (*the living creatures in the ark with Noah*), Cd. Th. 81, 7; Gen. 1341. v. ge-nesan.

nese (=ne sî); *adv. No* (*the opposite of* gese):—Wylt ðû ðis? Nese *vis hoc? Non*, Ælfc. Gr. 38; Som. 40, 13. Wylt ðû wê gadriaþ hig? Ðâ cwæþ hê, Nese (*non*), Mt. Kmbl. 13, 29. Syllaþ ûs of eówrum ele ... Ðâ andswarudun ða gleáwan, Nese, 25, 9. Ðâ cwæþ hê: Nese (Lind. næsæ) fæder Abraham, Lk. Skt. 16, 30. Sume cwǽdon, he is gôd; ôðre cwǽdon, nese (Lind. næse), ac hê beswîcþ ðis folc, Jn. Skt. 7, 12. Næsi, Jn. Skt. Lind. 21, 5. Hwæðer ðû swelces âuht geworhtes habbe. Nese, nese, Bt. 14, 1; Fox 40, 26, 33.

-nes[s], -nes[s], -nys[s], a frequently occurring suffix of feminine abstract nouns, cf. *Goth.* -assus, e. g. ufar-assus: *O. H. Ger.* -nessî; *f.* nessi; *n.*; -nissa, -nissi; *f.* -nissi; *n.* v. Grimm. Gram. ii. 321 sqq.

ness. v. næss.

nest, es; *n. A nest*; also *the young birds in the nest*; nidus:—Nest *nidus*, Wrt. Voc. i. 77, 39: Ælfc. Gr. 8; Som. 7. 30. Ic in mînum neste neóbed ceóse, '*I shall die in my nest*,' Exon. Th. 235, 6; Ph. 553: 212, 25; Ph. 215. Nest timbran, gearwian, getimbran, wyrcan *to build a nest*, 210, 20, 21; Ph. 189: 228, 2; Ph. 432: 229, 6; Ph. 229. Ðîne bearn gegaderian swâ se fugel dêþ his nest (*nidum*) under his fiðerum, Lk. Skt. 13, 34. Heofones fuglas habbaþ nestþ (MS. A. nest: Lind. nesto) *volucres coeli habent nidos*, 9, 58. Nest (Lind. nestas ł nesto), Mt. Kmbl. 8, 20: Homl. Th. i. 160, 34. [*O. H. Ger.* nest *nidus*.] v. nistian, nestlian.

nest, es; *n.* I. *provisions, victuals*:—Se him his nest âspringeþ *he whose provisions fail him*, Exon. Th. 335, 23; Gn. Ex. 38. Sum sceal on feorwegas gongan, and his nest beran, 329, 3; Vy. 28. On ðæm fætelse ðe hyre foregenga hyra begea nest þyder lǽdde, Judth. Thw. 23, 19; Jud. 128. II. *provisions served out at fixed times, rations*:—Nest *epimenia* (ἐπιμήνια, cf. fôstraþas *epimoenia*, 32, 41. *Epimenia* expensae vel exennia vel tributa quae dantur per singulos menses, Ducange), Wrt. Voc. ii. 107, 32. Ða cempan cwǽdon: Hwæt dô wê? Ðâ sǽde hê him: Beóþ êðhylde on eówrum andlyfenum (Lind. Rush. nestum=*stipendiis*), Lk. Skt. 3, 14. [*Icel.* nest; *n. provisions*: *O. H. Ger.* wega-, fart-nest *viaticum*.] v. weg-nest, nest-pohha.

nêst, nêsta. v. neáh, nîhsta.

nestan; *p.* te *To spin*:—Ne wynnes and ne nestas *non laborant neque nent*, Mt. Kmbl. Lind. 6, 28. Nestaþ, Lk. Skt. Lind. Rush. 12, 27. [Cf. *Icel.* nist *a pin*; nista *to pin*: *O. H. Ger.* nestilo, nestila *vitta, funiculus, redimiculum, vitta, fibula, ansa*: *Ger.* nestel.]

nestlian; *p.* ede *To make a nest*:—Ðâr spearwan nestliaþ *illic passeres nidificabunt*, Ps. Lamb. 103, 16. [Þar nestleþ (1st MS. næstieþ) hearnes, Laym. 21753. Nestlyñ *nidifico*; nestlyd *nidificatus*; nestelynge *nidificatio*, Prompt. Parv. 354.] v. nistian, nistlan.

nest-pohha, an; *m. A bag for food, wallet*:—Nestpoha *pera*, Mt. Kmbl. Lind. 10, 10. [Cf. *Icel.* nest-baggi *a wallet*.]

neta, an; *m. A caul*:—Inilve *intestinum*; midhryþre *onentem*; neta *disceptum*; blind þearm *cecum*, Wrt. Voc. i. 284, 2-5. v. nette.

netele, netle, netel, an; *f. A nettle*:—Netele *urtica*, Wrt. Voc. i. 289, 43: ii. 65, 49. Netle, i. 31, 60: 68, 25. Netel (netele, netle) *urtica*; blind netel (netele, netle) *archangelica*, 79, 30, 31. Netle, blinde netle, Lchdm. ii. 66, 4. Netele. Genim ðysse wyrte seáw ðe man *urticam*, and ôðrum naman netele nemneþ, i. 310, 14-16. Seó reáde netele *lamium purpureum*, iii. 52, 11: ii. 58, 10: 92, 10. Netelan sǽd, i. 228, 24: ii. 94, 12. Of nioþoweardre netlan, 128, 7. Nim netelan, 152, 10: 312, 5. Ða greátan netlan (*urtica dioica*), 86, 12. Smale netelan (*urtica urens*), 68, 4. Netlan *verticeta*, Wrt. Voc. ii. 124, 20. [*O. H. Ger.* nezila] v. worþig-netele.

nêten, neteness. v. nîten, nytenness.

nêðan; *p.* de *To have courage to do, to dare to do, to venture*:—Nêþeþ hwîlum meówle ðæt heó on mec grîpeþ *the maiden has at times the courage to lay hold on me*, Exon. Th. 407, 15; Rä. 26, 5. Nêðde ðǽr ic Neron beswâc *I dared to go where I deceived Nero*, 260, 24; Jul. 302. Hê in ðæt bûrgeteld nêðde *he ventured into the pavilion*, Judth. Thw. 25, 25; Jud. 277. Git on deóp wæter aldrum nêðdon *ye ventured into deep water at the risk of your lives*, Beo. Th. 1024; B. 510: 1080; B. 538. Ic nêðan gefrægn hæleþ tô hilde *I have heard that warriors dared to do battle*, Cd. Th. 124, 9; Gen. 2060. Nêðan on nacan tealtum *to venture upon the unsteady vessel*, Runic pm. Kmbl. 343, 21; Rûn. 21. In nearowe nêðan, Exon. Th. 436, 13; Rä. 54, 13. [*Goth.* ana-nanþjan *to be bold*: *Icel.* nenna *to strive, have a mind to*: *O. H. Ger.* nendjan *insurgere*; gi-nendjan *audere*.] v. ge-nêðan.

nêðing, e; *f. Daring, audacity*:—Ðæt hê þurh nêðinge wunne, Exon. Th. 109, 33; Gû. 99. Ða swâ swîðe hiene ondrêdan ðe on westeweardum ðisses middangeardes wǽron ðæt hié on swâ micle nêðinge ... hiene æfter friþe sôhton on eástweardum ðeosan middangearde *those who were in the west of this earth feared him* (*Alexander*) *so much, that they had the courage to visit him in search of peace in the east of this earth*, Ors. 3, 9; Swt. 136, 24. [*Icel.* nenning *activity, energy*: cf. *O. H. Ger.* nendigî *audacia*.]

net-gearn, es; *n. Net-yarn, string for making nets*:—Ân cliwen gôdes nettgernes, Cod. Dip. Kmbl. iii. 451, 7.

net-râp, es; *m. A toil*:—Netrâpas *plagas*, Wrt. Voc. i. 48, 26: 57, 21.

nett, es; *n.* I. *a net* (for fowling, fishing, or hunting):—Net *rete*, Wrt. Voc. i. 285, 16. Nyt, 73, 41. Ned *cassis*, ii. 14, 3. Hyra net wæs tôbrocen, Lk. Skt. 5, 6. Ûres fisceres nett *nostri piscatoris rete*, Ælfc. Gr. 15; Som. 19, 57. Feallaþ on nette his *cadent in retiaculo ejus*, Ps. Spl. 140, 11. Ic mîn nett ût lǽte *laxabo rete*, Lk. Skt. 5, 5: Mt. Kmbl. 4, 18. Lǽtaþ ðæt nett on ða swîðran healfe, Jn. Skt. 21, 6. Ic brêde nett *plecto*, Ælfc. Gr. 28; Som. 32, 8. Ôþ ðæt ðe hig (wildeór) cuman tô ðâm nettan ... Ne canst ðû huntian bûton mid nettum? Coll. Monast. Th. 21, 15-21: 22, 11. On feala wîsan ic beswîce fugelas, hwîlon mid nettum, 25, 11. Hî forlêton hyra nett (netta, Lind.) *relictis retibus*, Mt. Kmbl. 4, 22: Homl. Th. i. 578, 21. II. *a mosquito-net*:—Nette, fleógryfte *conopio*, Wrt. Voc. ii. 19, 18. III. *net-*

work, web:—Swâ tedre swâ swâ gangewifran nett, Ps. Th. 38, 12. Ðonne hió (*the spider*) geornast biþ ðæt heó âfǽre fleógan on nette, 89, 10. Folc gescylde hâlgan nette (*with a net-work of clouds*), Cd. Th. 182, 11; Exod. 74. [*Goth.* nati: *O. Sax.* netti, (fisk-)net: *O. Frs.* nette: *Icel.* net; *gen. pl.* netja: *O. H. Ger.* nezzi *rete.*] v. ǽl-, boge-, breóst-, deór-, dræg-, feng-, fisc-, fleóh-, here-, hring-, inwit-, mycg-, searo-, wæl-nett, *and next word.*

nette, an; *f. The net-like caul:*—Nette (*under the heading* de membris hominum) *disceptum* i. *reticulum* (cf. hoc reticulum, pinguedo circa jecur, 704, 7), Wülck. Gl. 293, 6. Nettae *oligia*, 35, 34. Nytte *obligia*, Wrt. Voc. i. 45, 18. Nette, ii. 63, 39: *disceptum*, 26, 19. [*Icel.* netja *the caul:* cf. *O. H. Ger.* nezzi *adeps intestini; pl. intestina.*] v. neta.

neurisn, e; *f. A kind of paralysis:*—Wiđ paralisin and wiđ neurisne, Lchdm. i. 12, 21: 130, 11.

newe-, niwe-, nu-seóđa, an; *m. The pit of the belly:*—Be ðam nafolan and bæcþearme and neweseóđan, Lchdm. ii. 232, 1. Niweseóđan, 164, 8. Sió biþ on ða swîđran sîdan âþened óþ ðone neweseóđan, 198, 1: 242, 19: 258, 6. Nuseóđan, 160, 12. Cf. (?) seód.

nê-west, nêxt, nêxta. v. neáh-west, neáh, nîhsta.

nî-. v. nîw-.

nic=ne ic *not I:*—Wilt ðû fôn sumne hwæl? Nic *vis capere aliquem cetum? Nolo*, Coll. Monast. Th. 24, 17. Eart ðû wîtega? Hê cwæþ nic, Jn. Skt. 1, 21. Eart ðû of ðysses leorningcnihtum? Ðâ cwæþ hê: Nicc, ne eom ic, 18, 17.

nî-cend, -cumen. v. nîw-cenned, -cumen.

nicor, es; *m.* I. *a hippopotamus:*—Him wǽron ða breóst gelîce niecres breóstum *hypopotami pectore*, Nar. 20, 29. Nicoras *hypopotami*, 11, 11. II. *a water-monster:*—Sanctus Paulus wæs geseónde on norþanweardne ðisne middangeard, ðǽr ealle wætero niþer gewîtaþ, and hê ðǽr geseah ofer ðæm wætere sumne hârne stân . . . and under ðæm stâne wæs niccra eardung and wearga. And hê geseah . . . manige swearte sâula . . . and ða fŷnd on nicra onlîcnesse heora grîpende wǽron . . . gewitan ða sâula niþer and him onfêngon ða nicras, Blickl. Homl. 209, 29–211, 5. On nicera mere, Beo. Th. 1695; B. 845. Ic on ŷđum slôg niceras nihtes, 848; B. 422: 1154; B. 575. Nicras, 2859; B. 1427. [*Icel.* nykr *a sea-goblin; a hippopotamus: O. H. Ger.* nichus *a crocodile.* v. Grmm. D. M. 135, 146.]

nicor-hûs, es; *n. The abode of a 'nicor,'* Beo. Th. 2827; B. 1411.

nîd, neád, nêd, neód, niéd, nŷd, es; *n.:* e; *f.* I. *necessity, inevitableness:*—Neód (nêd, Lind. Rush.) ys ðæt swycdômas cumon *necesse est ut veniant scandala*, Mt. Kmbl. 18, 7: Homl. Th. i. 514, 33. Gif ðæt nŷd âbǽdeþ *cum ipsa necessitas compellit*, Bd. 1, 27; S. 497, 1. Nenne hwylc nŷd mâre âbǽdde, 3, 5; S. 526, 28. Swâ hyne nŷd fordrâf, Judth. Thw. 25, 25; Jud. 277. Nŷd biþ wyrda heardost, Salm. Kmbl. 622; Sal. 310. Eádfriþ for neóde (neáde, MS. T.: nŷde, MS. B.) tô Pendan gebeáh *Eadfrid necessitate cogente ad Pendam transfugit*, Bd. 2, 20; S. 521, 15: Chr. 1016; Erl. 154, 11. Mid nŷde gebǽded *necessitate cogente*, Bd. 3, 24; S. 556, 7. Nŷde genŷdde *forced by necessity*, Beo. Th. 2014; B. 1005. II. *necessity, need, urgent requirement:*—Ne nêd is ðê ðætte hwelc ðec gifregne *non opus est tibi ut quis te interroget*, Jn. Skt. Rush. 16, 30. Mê is neód *necesse habeo*, ic habbe neóde *necesse habeo*, Ælfc. Gr. 38; Som. 41, 38. Nis Gode nân neód ûre ǽhta, Homl. Th. i. 140, 24. Nis Gode nân neód ðæt wê gôd wyrcan, ne hê nân þing ne hǽt for his âgenre neóde, Homl. Skt. 11, 299. Seó þearlwîsnes ðæs heardan lîfes him ǽrest of nŷde becom for bôte his synna ac forþgangendre tîde ðæt hê ðæt nŷd on gewunon gecyrde . . . *ex necessitate obvenerat, sed . . . necessitatem in consuetudinem verterat*, Bd. 4, 25; S. 599, 32. Nabbaþ hî neóde tô farenne, Mt. Kmbl. 14, 16: Lk. Skt. 14, 18. III. *a necessary business, duty:*—Neád *debita*, Wrt. ii. 139, 68. Ús is neód (*it is our bounden duty*) ðæt wê ða hâlgan eástertîde be ðam sôđan regole healdon, Lchdm. iii. 256, 17. Ús is twŷfeald neód on bôclîcum gewritum. Ânfeald neód ûs is, ðæt wê ða bôclîcan lâre mid carfullum môde smeágan; ôđer ðæt wê hî tô weorcum âwendan, Homl. Th. ii. 284, 23. Hê fêrde embe sumere neóde *he was going about some necessary business*, 508, 15. Nolde Maurus of ðam mynstre faran for nânre neóde, bûtan hê nŷde sceolde, Homl. Skt. 6, 290. Eádsige hine wel lǽrde and tô his âgenre neóde and ealles folces manude (*exhorted him with regard to his duty as king*), Chr. 1043; Erl. 168, 5. Hê wolde gân embe his neóde forþ, Homl. Th. i. 290, 18. Gafele ł nêdde (neáde?) *debito, necessitate*, Hpt. Gl. 440, 29. Neóde *debitum*, 456, 14. On ðam tôweardan lîfe ne beóþ ðâs neóda (*the duties of feeding the hungry, etc.*), ne ðâs þênunga Homl. Th. ii. 442, 18. Neódum *causis*, Hpt. Gl. 412, 57. IV. *need, what one wants:*—Ðæt man underfô mâre ðonne his lîchaman neód sŷ, Homl. Th. ii. 590, 21. Mid ðŷ hî ðâ ðæt scyp gehlæsted hæfdon mid ðâm þingum ðe swâ mycles sîþfætes nŷd âbǽdde *cum navi imposuissent quae tanti itineris necessitas poscebat*, Bd. 5, 9; S. 623, 18. Ne lufode hê woruldlîce ǽhta for his neóde âna (*to supply his own needs only*), ac tô dǽlenne eallum wædliendum, Homl. Th. ii. 340, 21. Gylde se tûnscipe tô ðǽre muneca neóde (*ad usus*), Chart. Th. 307, 26. Tô ðæs minstres neóde, 362, 7. Ðû hogast embe ðîne neóde, Homl. Th. i. 488, 24. Ðâm mannum ðe heora neóde habbaþ *who have what they want*, ii. 106, 18. Hê sylþ him his neóde *he gives him what he wants*, Lk. Skt. 11, 8. God dæghwamlîce ûs dêþ ûre neóde *God daily supplies our needs*, Basil Admn. 4; Norm. 40, 29: Homl. Th. i. 516, 9. Ealle ûre neóda ǽgđer ge gâstlîce ge lîchamlîce, 272, 16. V. *necessity, need, difficulty, hardship, distress:*—Lust hæfþ wîte and neád wuldorbeáh gegearwaþ *pleasure hath punishment and hardship is a preparation for a crown*, R. Ben. 26, 9. Ðâ cwǽdon hié ðæt him leófre wǽre ðæt hié an swelcan niéde deáþ fornôme ðonne hié mid swelcan niéde friþ begeáte *tutius rati sese armatos mori quam miseros vivere*, Ors. 4, 6; Swt. 174, 25–27. Sume men ða wǽtan for ðæm nŷde þigdon *suam urinam vexatos ultimis necessitatibus haurientes*, Nar. 9, 22. Moises sǽde Drihtne ðæs folces neóde, Ex. 15, 25. Of neádum mînum genera mê *de necessitatibus meis erue me*, Ps. Spl. 24, 18: 106, 6. Nêdum, 30, 9. Niédum, Andr. Kmbl. 2754; An. 1379. VI. *force, compulsion:*—Rîccra manna need *vis potestatis*, Wrt. Voc. i. 21, 28. Ne eom ic nânre neáde gecnêwe, Chart. Th. 296, 1. Him beóþ ealle mid nêde (*by force*) on genumene, Blickl. Homl. 49, 26. Mid nǽnigum nêde gebǽded, 83, 32. Ða kyningas ðe ic mid nêde tô hŷrsumnesse gedyde, Nar. 32, 19. Mâ hreósende for ealddôme ðonne of ǽniges cyninges niéde, Ors. 2, 4; Swt. 76, 3. Heofena rîce þolaþ neád (*vim*), Mt. Kmbl. 11, 12. Nêd, Ps. Surt. 37, 13. Nŷd, Ps. Spl. 37, 12. VII. *the name of the rune*, ᚾ, N; hence the symbol is sometimes put instead of writing the word, Runic pm. Kmbl. 341, 8; Rûn. 10: Exon. Th. 429, 22; Rä. 43, 8: 50, 14; Cri. 800: 284, 28; Jul. 704: Elen. Kmbl. 2519; El. 1261. [*Goth.* nauþs: *Icel.* nauð, neyð: *O. Sax.* nôd: *O. Frs.* nêd: *O. H. Ger.* nôt *vis, violentia, exactio, necessitas, tribulatio, angor.*] v. hæft-, nearo-, ôht-, þeów-, þreá-nîd; nêde, nêdes, *and* neód.

nîdan; *p.* de *To force, compel, urge:*—Ic nŷde *cogo*, Ælfc. Gr. 28; Som. 32, 14. Hê ûs ne nêt (Cott. MS. nêd) tô ðam ðæt wê nêde scylen gôd dôn, Bt. 41, 4; Fox 252, 3. Hê nŷt (*compellet*) eów ðæt gê faron ût, Ex. 11, 1. Hié hié selfe nîdaþ (Cott. MSS. niédaþ) tô healdonne swîgean, Past. 38, 1; Swt. 271, 16. Se pâpa nêdde Adrianus ðæt hê biscophâde onfênge, Bd. 4, 1; S. 564, 6. Gif gê gesâwen hwelce mûs ðæt wǽre hlâford ofer ôđre mŷs and nîdde (Cott. MS. nêdde) hié æfter gafole (*exacted tribute from them*), Bt. 16, 2; Fox 52, 3. Hê nŷdde his leorningcnihtas on scyp stîgan, Mk. Skt. 6, 45. Ne nŷdde hê nâ ðæt folc tô his cwale *he did not force the people to kill him*, Homl. Th. i. 216, 1. Ðâ nŷdde hê ðone unclǽnan gâst ût, Lk. Skt. 9, 42. Hê hié nŷdde in fæđm fŷres, Cd. Th. 230, 14; Dan. 233. Ða Egiptiscan nŷddon (*urgebant*) ðæt folc ût of hira lande, Ex. 12, 33. Ðâ nŷddon hine his yldran tô ðæm ðæt hê sceolde woroldlîcum wǽpnum onfôn, Blickl. Homl. 213, 1. Ðone hig nŷddon ðæt hê bǽre hys rôde, Mt. Kmbl. 27, 32. Nŷd *compelle*, Lk. Skt. 14, 23: Homl. Th. ii. 376, 14. Ne niéde (MS. H. nŷde) ðû hine *you shall not press him* (*the debtor*), L. Alf. 35; Th. i. 52, 22. Hwæđer seó godcunde foretiohhung ođđe sió wyrd ûs nêde tô ðam ðe hî willen, Bt. 40, 7; Fox 242, 15. Nêdendum dôme *urgente decreto*, Hpt. Gl. 488, 68. Ic eom nŷded, Bd. 3, 13; S. 538, 26. [*Goth.* nauþjan: *Icel.* neyđa: *O. Sax.* nôdian: *O. Frs.* nêda: *O. H. Ger.* nôtian.] v. ge-nŷdan, neádian.

nîd-bâd, e; *f. An exaction, a due, toll:*—Ic Æđelbald Myrcna cincg wæs beden from bisceope Milrêde ðæt ic him âlêfde alle nêdbâde tuegra sceopa, Chart. Th. 28, 25: 29, 8. Hê nymeþ nŷdbâde *he* (*Grendel*) *takes toll*, Beo. Th. 1200; B. 598. v. bâdian, bǽdan, nîd *debitum*, nîdgafol, *and next word.*

nîd-bâdere, es; *m. One who exacts toll:*—Ic him âlŷfde alle nêdbâde tuegra sceopa, ða ðe ðǽr âbǽdde beóþ from ðǽm nêdbâderum in Lundentûnes hŷđe, ond nǽfre ic ne mîne lâstweardas ne ða nêdbâderas geþrîstlǽcen ðæt heó hit onwenden, Chart. Th. 29, 7–14. v. preceding word.

nîd-bebod, es; *n. An urgent command, mandate:*—Healdeþ nŷdbibod hâlgan Dryhtnes, Exon. Th. 350, 32; Sch. 72.

nîd-behêfe; *adj. Necessary, needful:*—Neádbehêfe *necessarium*, Hpt. Gl. 524, 65. Ân þing is niédbehêfe, Lk. Skt. 10, 42. Is ðeáh niédbehêfe ungelǽredum woroldmonnum, Lchdm. iii. 440, 32. Se man wæs ðam dêman þearle nŷdbehêfe, Homl. Skt. 4, 144. On eallum ðissum þingum is geþyld nŷdbehêfe, Homl. Th. i. 470, 31. Seó hand getâcnaþ ûrne nŷdbehêfan freónd, ðe ûs ûre neóde dêþ, 516, 8. Synd gesealde from ðam abbode ealle neádbehêfe þing, R. Ben. 92, 2: 127, 5. In Godes lofe and in nŷdbehêfum weorcum wê sceolon gewunigan, L. E. I. 42; Th. ii. 438, 31. Wê habbaþ ða nŷdbehêfestan ânunga âwritene, Boutr. Scrd. 23, 12. v. nîd-behôf *and next word.*

nîd-behêfe (?) *necessity:*—Ðâ hnêdbihoefe (Lind. nêd) hæfde *quando necessitatem habuit*, Mk. Skt. Rush. 2, 25.

nîd-behôf; *adj. Necessary, needful:*—Ân þing is nŷdbehôf, Homl. Th. ii. 440, 9. v. nîd-behêfe.

nîd-behôflîc; *adj. Necessary:*—Hê sǽde ðæt him wǽre his lîf nŷdbehôflîc *quia multum necessaria sibi esset vita ipsius*, Bd. 5, 5; S. 618, 3.

nîd-beþearf; *adj. Necessary:*—Sumæ bêc ða ðe niédbeþearfosta (nîdbeþyrfesta, Cott. MSS.) sîen, Past. præf.; Swt. 7, 7.

nîd-boda, an; *m. One who announces violence or distress* (v. nîd, V,

VI):—Sincalda sǽ, nýdboda (*the Red Sea which overwhelmed the Egyptians*), Cd. Th. 207, 29; Exod. 474.

níd-brýce, es; *m. Necessary use, requirement, need*:—Ðá wolde se hálga sum hús timbrian tó his nédbrícum, Homl. Th. ii. 144, 31.

níd-bysig; *adj. Troubled by distresses*:—Ðǽr (*in hell*) ðú (*the devil*) nýdbysig fore oferhygdum eard gesóhtes, Exon. Th. 267, 31; Jul. 423.

níd-bysigu, -bysgu; *f. Distress, trouble*:—Nýdbysgum neáh, Exon. Th. 354, 11; Reim. 44.

níd-clamm, -clomm, es; *m. Necessity, need, distress*:—Of neádclammum heora hé álǽdde *de necessitatibus eorum eduxit*, Ps. Lamb. 106, 28.

níd-cleofa, -clafa (?), an; *m. A prison*:—Ðæt hine man of nearwe and of nýdcleofan fram ðam engan hofe up forléte, Elen. Kmbl. 1419; El. 711. In nédcleofan nearwe geheaðrod, 2249; El. 1276. Ðá wæs carcernes duru behliden . . . symle heó wuldorcyning herede in ðam nýdclafan, Exon. Th. 256, 31; Jul. 240. v. next word.

níd-cofa, an; *m. A prison*:—Se hálga wæs lǽded in ðæt dimme ræced, sceal ðonne in neádcofan nihtlange fyrst wunian, Andr. Kmbl. 2619; An. 1311.

níd-costing, e; *f. A distressing trial, affliction*:—Nearwum genǽged nýdcostingum, Exon. Th. 171, 14; Gú. 1126.

níd-dǽda, an; *m. One who does something under compulsion*:—Gif hé æfter sunnan upgonge ðis dēþ (*kills the housebreaker*), hé biþ mansleges scyldig, and hé ðonne self swelte, búton hé niéddǽda (nýd-, MS. H.) wǽre (*unless he were forced to do it in self-defence*), L. Alf. 25; Th. i. 50, 21. Cf. Se ðe hine nédes ofslóge oððe unwillum oððe ungewealdes, 13; Th. i. 46, 22. v. níd-wyrhta.

níde, neáde, neóde, níde, niéde, nýde; *adv.* (*a case of* níd, q. v.). I. *of necessity, as a natural, inevitable consequence, from force of circumstances*:—Gif gé neáde swá dón sceolon (*si sic necesse est*), dóþ swá gé wyllon, Gen. 43, 11. Wegférende móton for neóde mete neáde ferian and for unfriþe man mót freólsǽfenan nýde fulfaran betweonan Eferwíc, and six míla gemete *travellers may, when compelled by circumstances, carry food to supply their needs; and on account of war, a man may, on the eve of a festival, when compelled by circumstances, travel between York and a distance of six miles*, L. N. P. L. 56; Th. ii. 298, 25–27. Forðamðe wé witon ðæt án wealdend is eallra þinga wé sceolon beón néde geþafan (*we must inevitably assent to the conclusion*) ðæt hé síe se héhsta hróf eallra góda, Bt. 34, 12; Fox 154, 7. Ðes middangeard néde (*as the result of natural, inevitable laws*) on ðás eldo endian sceal, Blickl. Homl. 117, 35. Wæs his fæder cininges þegna aldorman. Ðá sceolde Sanctus Martinus néde (*as an inevitable result*) beón on his geógoþháde on ðære gefērǽdenne cininges þegna, 211, 22. Niéde sceal bión gebrocen ðæt mód ðara hiéremonna, gif se láreów ágiémleásaþ ðæt hé hiera útan ne helpe, Past. 18; Swt. 137, 13: Ors. 5, 2; Swt. 218, 20. Ðǽr ðǽr ðú neóde irsian scyle, gemetiga ðæt ðeáh, Prov. Kmbl. 24. Hit is on worulde swá leng swá wyrse, and swá hit sceal nýde ǽr Antecristes tócyme yfelian swíðe, Wulfst. 156, 4: 157, 8. II. *of necessity, because a law, natural, moral or human, is to be satisfied*:—Ðis sceal se mæssepreóst néde bebeódan *the priest is bound by his duty to proclaim this*, Blickl. Homl. 49, 6. Ðone andleofan ðe hé néde big lifgean sceolde (*the provision that nature required*), 213, 20. Ðás béc sceal mæssepreóst néde habban (*these books are indispensable*), and hé ne mæg bútan beón, L. Ælfc. C. 21; Th. ii. 350, 15. Niéde hé sceolde him forgyfan ánne (*custom required it*), Lk. 23, 17. III. *from force, under compulsion, without free-will*:—Nán nyle onginnan ðæt ðæt hé nele, búton hé néde scyle (*unless he is forced*), Bt. 36, 3; Fox 176, 9: 41, 4; Fox 252, 3. Sceal néde riht wyrcean se ðe ǽr nolde, L. O. D. 3; Th. i. 354, 9. Néde oððe lustum héran, Met. 9, 44. Niéde sceoldon gombon gieldan, Cd. Th. 119, 10; Gen. 1977. v. next word.

nídes; *adv. Of necessity, not willingly*:—Se ðe hine nédes (nýdes, MS. G.) ofslóge, L. Alf. 13; Th. i. 46, 22. v. níd-dǽda *and preceding word*.

níd-, nýd-fara, an; *m. One who journeys under compulsion, who is forced to march*, Cd. Th. 191, 1; Exod. 208. v. *next word and* níd-genga, -dǽda.

níd-faru, e; *f. A journey one is forced to take, death*:—Fore there neidfaerae naenig uuirthit thoncsnotturra than him tharf síe, Archaeologia, vol. xxviii. p. 357. v. níd-gedál.

níd-freónd, es; *m. One closely connected by relationship* or *friendship*:—Hé wæs pápan ǽhte bifealden Enagrius his neódfreóndes, Shrn. 36, 4. [*O. H. Ger.* nōt-friunt; *pl. necessarii.*] v. níd-gestealla, -mǽg.

níd-gafol, es; *n. A tax that must be paid, tribute*:—Nédgaefel ðæm cásere *tributum Caesari*, Mt. Kmbl. p. 18, 2. Ymbe ðæt neádgafol úres Drihtnes, ðæt sýn úre teóþunga and cyricsceattas, L. Edg. S.; Th. i. 270, 26, 13. v. níd-gild.

níd-gedál, es; *n. An inevitable parting, the parting of body and soul*:—Nis nú swíðe feor ðam ýtemestan endedógor nýdgedáles, Exon. Th. 172, 9; Gú. 1141. Se Dryhtnes dóm wísade tó ðam nýhstan nýdgedále, 129, 5; Gú. 416. Þurh nýdgedál, 158, 9; Gú. 906.

níd-genga, an; *m. One who is forced to go* or *one who goes in misery*:—Nacod nídgenga (*Nebuchadnezzar*), Cd. Th. 255, 32; Dan. 633. v. níd-fara.

níd-gestealla, an; *m. One who is closely bound to another by the ties of comradeship*:—Hié á wǽron æt níða gehwam nýdgesteallan, Beo. Th. 1769; B. 882. v. níd-freónd.

níd-geweald, es; *n. Power that is forcibly exercised* or *that causes distress, tyranny*:—Of deófles nýdgewealde genered, Exon. Th. 89, 2; Cri. 1451.

níd-gewuna, an; *m. A necessary, suitable custom* (v. néd, IV):—Neádgewuna *debitus usus*, i. *congruus*, Wrt. Voc. ii. 139, 72.

níd-gild, es; *n. Enforced payment, tribute, exaction*:—Scandlíce nýdgild ús sind gemǽne, Wulfst. 162, 11. [*Icel.* nauð-gjald.] v. níd-gafol.

níd-gilda, an; *m. One who is forced to pay*:—Neádgilda *debitor* i. *obnoxius, reus*, Wrt. Voc. ii. 139, 74.

níd-gripe (?) *a violent grasp*:—Hyne (*Grendel*) sár hafaþ in nídgripe (MS. mid gripe; Th. níþgripe) nearwe befongen, Beo. Th. 1956; B. 976.

níd-hád, es; *m. Force, compulsion*:—Neádháde *vim*, Wrt. Voc. ii. 72, 54.

níd-, néd-, niéd-, nýd-hǽmed, es; *n. Rape*, L. Alf. pol. 25, 26; Th. i. 78, 11–18.

níd-hǽmestre, an; *f. A woman who has been violated, a mistress*:—Nédhǽmestran *amatricis*, Hpt. Gl. 509, 70.

níd-hǽs, e; *f. A command which is attended by compulsion*:—Man for cyning gebidde and hine búton neádhǽse heora willum weorðigen *let people pray for the king, and honour him without injunction, of their own accord*, L. Wih. 1; Th. i. 36, 16.

níd-help; *m. f. Help in need, needful help*:—On wísum scrifte biþ swíðe forþ gelang forsyngodes mannes nýdhelp, L. Pen. 1; Th. ii. 278, 3.

níd-hírness, e; *f. Enforced obedience, servitude*:—In nédhérnesse ic bégo *in servitutem redigo*, Rtl. 6, 9.

níding. v. neádung *and next word*.

nídinga (-unga); *adv. By force, against a person's will*:—Nédunga *violenti*, Mt. Kmbl. Lind. 11, 12. Ðý læs nédunga genom Crist menn *ne raperet Christus homines*, Rtl. 197, 35. Woldon hine dón niédenga (nídenga, Cott. MSS.) tó cyninge, Past. 3, 1; Swt. 33, 14. Ðá tugon heó hine nýdinga of ðam mynstre *illum invitum monasterio duxerunt*, Bd. 3, 18; S. 546, 22. Gif hwá mǽden nýdinga nimþ *si quis puellam invitam ceperit*, L. Ecg. P. ii. 130; Th. ii. 186, 20. v. neádunga, nídlinga.

-nídla, -nýdlíc. v. þreá-nídla, -nídlíc.

nýd-líce. v. neód-líce.

nídling, es; *m.* I. *one who serves of necessity, a slave, bondman*:—Gif ðú fioh tó borge selle ðínum geféran ðe mid ðé eardian wille, ne niéde ðú hine swá niédling (MS. H. nýdling), L. Alf. 35; Th. i. 52, 22. Hié on cnihtháde wǽron óðerra manna niédlingas *in youth they had been the bondmen of others*, Ors. 2, 2; Swt. 66, 17. Se æðeling bebeád ðæt hié ða consulas and witan him beforan drifen swá swá niédlingas, ðæt heora bismer ðý máre wǽre, 3, 8; Swt. 122, 7. Hý ealle tó nýdlingum him gedydon, 1, 5; Swt. 34, 34. Wæterberere oððe nédlungum *lixarum*, Wrt. Voc. ii. 52, 73. II. *one who has to serve on board ship, a sailor*:—Nédling *nauta*; nédlingas *nauticos*, 60, 30, 29. Ðá ongunnon ða nýdlingas and ða scypmen ða ancras on ðone sǽ sendan woldon ðæt scyp mid gefæstnian *tentabant navitae anchoris in mare missis navem retinere*, Bd. 3, 15; S. 541, 40.

nídlinga; *adv. By force, against a person's will*:—Gif hwá mǽden nýdlinga nimþ *si quis puellam invitam ceperit*, L. Ecg. P. ii. 13; Th. ii. 186, 20 note. v. neádlunga.

níd-mǽg, es; *m. A near kinsman, a cousin*:—Iohannes úres Drihtenes nýdmǽg, L. Ælfc. P. 9; Th. ii. 366, 37. v. níd-máge, -freónd, -sibb; *and* cf. *Icel.* nauð-maðr *a near kinsman*.

níd-mægen, es; *n. Force, violence*:—Nédmægn *vim*, Rtl. 117, 25.

níd-máge, an; *f. A near kinswoman, a cousin*:—Ǽfre ne geweorðe ðæt cristen man gewífige on ðæs wífes nýdmágan ðe hé ǽr hæfde, L. Eth. vi. 12; Th. i. 318, 16. Nédmágan, L. C. E. 7; Th. i. 364, 24. v. níd-mǽg.

níd-micel; *adj. Very important, urgent*:—Nédmycel (medmycel, MS. B.) ǽrende wé ðider habbaþ, and ús is þearf ðæt wé hit gefyllon, St. Andr. 6, 20.

níd-nǽm, e; *f. A taking by force, rapine*:—Nǽnigum biscope álýfed sí ówiht of heora ǽhtum þurh nýdnǽme him on geniman (*violenter abstrahere*), Bd. 4, 5; S. 572, 36. Gif hwá binnan ðám gemǽrum úres ríces reáflác and niédnǽme dó, L. In. 10; Th. i. 108, 9. [Cf. *O. H. Ger.* nōt-numft *violentia, rapina*.] v. next word.

níd-nǽman; p. de *To take by force, to force a woman, to ravish*:—Gif hwá nunnan gewemme oððe wydewan nýdnǽme, L. Eth. vi. 39; Th. i. 324, 25: L. C. S. 53; Th. i. 406, 2, 3. v. níd-niman.

nídness, e; *f. Necessity*:—Ðeáhhwæðere mid nýdnysse hire man mót lýfan ðæt heó mid ðam sig *tametsi si necesse est, licet viro ejus ei permittere secum esse*, L. Ecg. C. 33; Th. ii. 158, 10.

níd-nima, an; *m. One who takes by force*:—Nēdniomu *violenti*, Mt. Kmbl. Rush. 11, 12. Nēdnioma (-niomo, Lind.) *raptores*, Lk. Skt. Rush. 18, 11. [Cf. *O. H. Ger.* nōt-nemo *rapidus*; nōt-numeo *raptor*.]

níd-niman; *pp.* -numen *To take by force, ravish*:—Ðeáh heó nȳdnumen (neád-, MS. B.) weorðe, þolige ðæra ǽhta, būton heó fram ðam ceorle wille eft hām ongeán and nǽfre eft his ne weorðe, L. C. S. 74; Th. i. 416, 13. v. nīd-nimung, -nǽman.

níd-nimu (?), e; *f. A taking by force, rapine*:—Fulle sint nēdnima (-nimende, Rush.) *pleni sunt rapina*, Mt. Kmbl. 23. 25. Full is mið nēdnime, Lk. Skt. Rush. 11, 39. Nēdnioma *rapinam*, Rtl. 21, 18. v. nīd-nǽm.

níd-nimung, e; *f. A taking by force, rapine*:—Wīfa nȳdnimung *stuprum, raptum*, Wrt. Voc. i. 21, 32. Full is mið nēdniminc*g* *plenum est rapina*, Lk. Skt. Lind. 11, 39.

níd-riht, es; *n.* (v. nīd, III). I. *a duty that must be performed, service, office*; officium, debitum:—Nēdreht *debitum*, Rtl. 89, 26. Godcund þeówdōm is gesett on cyriclīcum þēnungum æfter canoneclīcan gewunan tō niédrihte eallum gehādedum mannum. On ǽlcne tīman man sceal God herian . . . Ac ðeáhhwæðere sindon gesette tīman synderlīce tō ðam ānum, ðæt gif hwā for bisgan oftor ne mæge, ðæt hē hūru ðæt niédriht dæghwamlīce gefylle, Btwk. 194, 3–8. II. *a due, what must be paid*:—Eallum ǽhtemannum gebyreþ midwintres feorm and Eástorfeorm . . . tōeácan heora nȳdrihte, L. R. S. 9; Th. i. 438, 2. v. next word.

níd-scyld, e; *f. Bounden duty*:—Sōna swā hē tō ðære āre cymþ, swā þyncþ him ðæt se hié him niédscylde sceolde se se hié him sealde *as soon as he comes to the honour, it seems to him that he who gave it him was bound to grant it as a matter of right*; repente perveniens jure sibi hoc debitum, ad quod pervenerit, putat, Past. 9; Swt. 57, 6. v. preceding word.

níd-sibb, e; *f. Relationship*:—Neádsibba *necessitudinum*, Wrt. Voc. ii. 61, 15. v. nīd-mǽg.

níd-syn[n] (?), e; *f. A sin of violence*:—Hū ic becwom in ðis neowle genip nīdsynnum (MS. mid synnum: Grein, nīþsynnum) fāh, Cd. Th. 275, 32; Sat. 180.

níd-syndrig; *adj. Quite apart* (?):—Hī sylfe ða munecas nǽdsyndrige (*monachos*) *seipsos*, Cod. Dip. B. i. 154, 12.

níd-þearf, e; *f.* I. *necessity, inevitableness*:—Sum hit sceal geweorþan unāwendendlīce, ðæt biþ ðætte ūre nȳdþearf (nēd-, Cott. MS.) biþ, and his willa biþ. Ac hit is sum swā gerād ðæt his nis nān neódþearf (nēd-, Cott. MS.), and ðeáh ne deraþ nō ðeáh hit geweorþe, Bt. 41, 3; Fox 250, 1–4. II. *necessity, constraint*:—Ðē nān neódþearf ne lǽrde tō wyrcanne ðæt ðæt ðū worhtest, ac mid ðīnum āgenum willan ðū ealle þing geworhtest, 33, 4; Fox 128, 11. III. *need (for something)*:—Nis him nānes þinges nēdþearf, 42; Fox 258, 8. Him biþ nīdþearf (niéd-, Cott. MSS.) ðæt hē fleó, Past. 21; Swt. 167, 16. Is suīðe micel niédþearf ðæt . . . , Swt. 159, 2. Ðē heora nān nȳdþerf nis eft on mē tō nimene *bonorum meorum non eges*, Ps. Th. 15, 1. Nēdþearf, Met. 20, 20. Mycel is nȳdþearf manna gehwylcum ðæt . . . , Wulfst. 157, 10. Hē wæs fram him eallum ārǽfned fore nȳdþearfe his ūtran weorca (*ob necessitatem operum ipsius exteriorum*), Bd. 5, 14; S. 634, 13. Him nānes ne biþ wana, ne hē nānes neódþearfe næfþ, Bt. 24, 1; Fox 80, 22. Wē habbaþ nēdþearfe ðæt wē ongyton, Blickl. Homl. 23, 1: 81, 36. IV. *a necessary thing, what a person needs*:—Wuhta gehwylc wilnaþ tō eorþan, sume nēdþearfe (cf. ealle ðider (*earthwards*) willniaþ . . . ðæs ðe hī beþurfon, Bt. 41, 6; Fox 254, 29) sume neódfræce, Met. 31, 15. Hē wirþ swā earm ðæt hē næfþ furþum ða neódþearfe āne (*fit ut necessariis egeat*), ðæt is wist and wǽda; wilnaþ ðonne ðære neádþearfe, næs ðæs anwealdes, Bt. 33, 2; Fox 124, 15–18. Seó gītsung ne cann gemet, ne nǽfre ne biþ gehealden on ðære nīdþearfe, ac wilnaþ simle māran ðonne hē þurfe, 26, 2; Fox 94, 6. Se cyning his lāreówum sealde heora nȳdþearfe on missenlīcum ǽhtum (*necessarias in diversis speciebus possessiones*), Bd. 1, 26; S. 488, 20. V. *need, distress, trouble*:—Hwī noldest ðū cuman tō ūs tō ðære tīde ðe ūs nȳdþearf wæs *quid recessisti longe in tribulatione?* Ps. Th. 9, 20. Ðæt gē mē ne forseón on ðisse mycclan nēdþearfe tīde, Blickl. Homl. 151, 23. Gedō ðæt ðū mē gefriðie æt mīnre nȳdþearfe *de necessitatibus meis eripe me*, Ps. Th. 24, 15. Fylston eów æt nȳdþearfe *in necessitate vos protegant*, Deut. 32, 38. Seldon būtan māran nȳdþearfe (*praeter arctiorem necessitatem*) mā ðonne ǽne sīþe on dæge ðæt heó wolde mete þicgan, Bd. 4, 19; S. 588, 11. VI. *a necessary business*:—Ðā cwǽdon hī ðæt hī wǽron on heora nȳdþearfum swȳðe geswencte, Guthl. 14; Gdwin. 64. 3. [*O. H. Ger.* nōt-duruft *necessitas, necessarium*: *Ger.* noth-durft.] v. nīd *and next word.*

níd-þearf; *adj. Necessary, needful*:—Ys cræft mīn behēfe þearle eów and neódþearf *est ars mea utilis valde vobis et necessaria*, Coll. Monast. Th. 27, 27: 29, 17. Is eallum mannum nēdþearf and nytlīc ðæt hié heora fulwihthādas wel gehealdan, Blickl. Homl. 109, 25. Behōflīc ł nēdþarf *necessarius*, Mk. Skt. Lind. Rush. 11, 3. Ān is nēdþarf ł behōflīc *unum est necessarium*, Lk. Skt. Lind. Rush. 10, 42. Nēdþærfo tīdo ymbhuoerfnise undercymende *necessaria temporum vicissitudine succedente*, Rtl. 37, 35. Habban gōde geferan and þearle neódþearfe (*necessarios*), Coll. Monast. Th. 29, 31. v. *preceding word and* nīdþearfness.

nídþearf-líc; *adj. Necessary, needful, useful*:—Neádþearflīc *operae pretium*, Hpt. Gl. 433, 25: 506, 29: *operae pretium, necessarium, utile, justum*, 499, 78: *debitum, necessarium*, 424, 51. Is swȳðe nȳdþearflīc (*necessaria*) gesceád, Bd. 1, 27; S. 496, 35. Gif ic sīe ðīnum folce nēdþearflīc tō hæbbene, Blickl. Homl. 225, 26. Būtan tō his neódþearflīcre þēnunge *nisi ad usum necessarium*, Bd. 2, 16; S. 520, 8. Be monigum sōcnum ða ðe him nȳdþearflīce (*necessariae*) gesewen wǽron, 1, 27; S. 488, 33. Ða þing ðe heora andlyfene nēdþearflīco gesawen wǽron, 1, 26; S. 487, 35. Nȳdþearflīcu, 5, 9; S. 622, 26: 4, 3; S. 567, 31. Be ðām nȳdþearflīcan þingum, intingum, Bd. 1, 27; S. 488, 24: 2, 4; S. 505, 30. Neádþearflīcum gestreónum *debito emolumento*, Hpt. Gl. 432, 69. Ða nēdþearflīcan hūs, Bd. 4, 28; S. 605, 25.

nídþearflíce; *adv. Necessarily*:—Nēdþearflīce (nīd-, nȳd-, neád-) *necessario*, Ælfc. Gr. 38; Som. 41, 37.

nídþearfness, e; *f.* I. *necessity, compulsion*:—Mid rihtre nȳdþearfnysse gebǽded *justa necessitate compulsus*, Bd. 2, 2; S. 502, 27. II. *necessity, need (for something)*:—Mycel nȳdþearfnys is ðæt ðæt gesceád . . . *necessaria est magna discretio*, 1, 27; S. 497, 17. III. *need, trouble, distress*:—Wæs biddende ðætte hē on swā mycelre neódþearfnysse his bigengum gehulpe *deprecatus est ut in tanta rerum necessitate suis cultoribus succurreret*, 3, 2; S. 524, 15: Cant. M. ad fil. 38. Of nēdþearfnessum *de necessitatibus*, Ps. Surt. 30, 8: 24, 17. On neádþearfnessum *in opportunitatibus*, Ps. Lamb. second 9, 1. Nȳdþearfnyssum, Ps. Spl. C. 106, 6. Ymb heora nēdþearfnesse *in necessitatibus suis*, Bd. 4, 23; S. 594, 1.

níd-þeów, es; *m. A slave, thrall*:—Wē ðē, Hǽlend, biddaþ, ðæt ðū gehȳre hæfta stefne ðīnra niédþiówa, Exon. Th. 22, 33; Cri. 361. Ne derige se hlāford his mannum, ne forðan his nȳdþeówan, L. I. P. 7; Th. ii. 314, 3. v. next word.

níd-þeówetling, es; *m. One who is forced into slavery (for an unsatisfied claim)*:—Hēr kȳð on ðissere bēc ðæt Ælfrīc wolde þeówian Putraele him tō nȳdþeówetlinge (*the enslavement was abandoned at the intercession of Bora, Ælfric's brother, on payment to Ælfric of eight oxen; Bora received sixty pence for his mediation*), Chart. Th. 628, 11–26.

níd-þeówian; *p.* ode *To reduce to servitude, to compel service from*:—Gif man cirican nȳdþeówige (cf. ǽnig man heonan forþ cirican ne þeówige, L. Eth. v. 10; Th. i. 306, 27: vi. 15; Th. i. 318, 26), L. N. P. L. 21; Th. ii. 294, 1.

níd-þing, es; *n. A necessary thing*:—Ealra neádþinga hē (*the monk*) sceal hihtan and wilnigan fram his mynstres fæder (*the abbot*), R. Ben. 57, 3.

níd-wædla, an; *m. A needy person*:—Ðū scealt on wræc hweorfan nacod niédwædla, neorxna wanges dugeþum bedǽled, Cd. Th. 57, 16; Gen. 929.

níd-wís; *adj. Necessary, due*:—Lof neádwīs *laus debita*, Hy. Surt. 49. 29. Neádþearflīc ł neádwīs *debitum, necessarium*, Hpt. Gl. 424, 52. Swā swā se līchama biþ ontend þurh unālȳfede lustas, swā eác byrnþ seó sāwul þurh neádwīs wīte, Homl. Th. ii. 338, 19. Neádwīsum ł neádþearflīcum gestreónum *debito emolumento*, Hpt. Gl. 432, 68. Þances hit āgylde neadwīse *grates rependat debitas*, Hy. Surt. 27, 21. Lofu neádwīse *laudes debitas*, 86, 33. v. nīd, III.

nídwíslíce; *adv. Of necessity*:—Hē sylf wæs ðære hālgan ǽ underþeód, ðæt hē ða ālȳsde ðe neádwīslīce ðære ǽ underþeódde wǽron, Homl. Th. i. 94, 16.

nídwísness, e; *f. Necessity*:—Neádwīsnysse *debitum*, Hpt. Gl. 462, 69.

níd-wraca, an; *m. One who is forced to be an avenger, who avenges an affront*:—Gif ǽnig gilda hwilcne man ofstleá, and hē neádwraca sī, and his bismer bēte, fylste ǽlc gegylda, Chart. Th. 611, 29. v. nīd-dǽda, -fara.

níd-wracu, e; *f. Violence, misery caused by violence*:—Wæs ðæt gewin lāð and longsum, ðe on ða leóde becom, nȳdwracu nīþgrim, nihtbealwa mǽst, Beo. Th. 388; B. 193. Hyne God wolde nergan wið nīþum, and hyra nȳdwræce deópe dēman, Exon. Th. 135, 17; Gū. 525.

níd-wyrhta, an; *m. One who acts from necessity, an involuntary agent*:—Se ðe nȳdwyrhta biþ ðæs ðe hē misdēþ, se biþ ðȳ beteran dōmes symle wyrðe, ðe hē nȳdwyrhta wæs ðæs ðe hē worhte, L. Eth. vi. 52; Th. i. 328, 23–25. On mænigre dǽde ðonne man biþ nȳdwyrhta, ðonne biþ se gebeorges ðē bet wyrðe ðe hē for neóde dyde ðæt ðæt hē dyde, L. C. S. 69; Th. i. 412, 12–14. v. nīd-dǽda.

niéd, niéten. v. nīd, nīten.

nifol. v. neowol.

nift, e; *f. A niece, grand-daughter*, or *a step-daughter*:—Nift *privigna, filia sororis*, Ep. Gl. 18 b, 6. Nift *privigna*, Wrt. Voc. ii. 117, 80. Seó wæs nift ðæs hīna ealdres (*neptem patris familias*), Bd. 3, 9; S. 534, 5. Ic an mīne lāuedy half marc goldes an mīne nifte ānn ōre wichte goldes, Chart. Th. 556, 27. [*Prompt. Parv.* nypte, nifte *neptis*;

nypt, broderys douter *lectis:* Rebecca was ford nefte (*great niece*) of Abraham, Gen. a. Ex. 1386: *O. Frs.* nift *niece: Icel.* nipt *a female relative, sister, daughter, niece: O. H. Ger.* nift *neptis, privigna.*] Cf. nefa.

nîg-. v. nîw-.

nîgan (?):—Đonne ic bûgendre stefne styrme, stille on wîcum siteþ nîgende (*one who listens* [?]), Exon. Th. 390, 27; Rä. 9, 8.

nigon *nine.* I. *as subst.*:—Hwǽr synt đa nigone (nygene, MS. A: nigona, Lind.: nióne, Rush.), Lk. Skt. 17, 17. Đâ hêt se cyng faran mid nigonum đara nîwena scipa, Chr. 897; Erl. 95, 20. II. *as adj.*:—Harold wes gewend mid nigon scipon, 1052; Erl. 183, 18. Nigon nihtum ǽr middum sumere, 898; Erl. 96, 19. Ic ofslôh niceras nigene, Beo. Th. 1154; B. 575. [*Goth. O. H. Ger.* niun: *O. Sax. O. Frs.* nigun: *Icel.* níu.]

nigon-feald; *adj. Nine-fold*:—Nigonfeald *novenarius,* Ælfc. Gr. 49; Som. 50, 17.

nigonteóþa *nineteenth*:—Se niganteóþa getælcircul *circulus decennovenalis,* Wrt. Voc. ii. 131, 33. Nigonteóþe healf geár, Chr. Erl. 4, 7: 855; Erl. 68, 33. Đý nigonteóþan geáre mînes lîfes, Bd. 5, 24; S. 647, 28.

nigontig *ninety*:—Ofer nigon and nigontigum rihtwîsra, Lk. Skt. 15, 7. v. hund-nigontig.

nigontîne *nineteen*:—Embe nigontýne niht, Menol. Fox 141; Men. 71.

nigontîn-lîc; *adj. Containing the number nineteen*:—Đa nigontýnlîcan hringas rihtra Eástrana *circuli Paschas decennovenales,* Bd. 5, 21; S. 643, 26.

nigon-wintre; *adj. Nine years old*:—Đâ hê nigonwintre cniht wæs *cum esset novem annos natus,* Ors. 4, 8; Swt. 186, 10.

nigoþa *ninth*:—Embe đa nigoþan tîde, Mt. Kmbl. 20, 5. Fram đære sixtan tîde ôþ đa nigoþan tîde. Ymbe đa nigoþan tîd clypode se Hǽlend, 27, 45, 46. Đý nigeþan dæge, Bd. 5, 23; S. 645, 9. Nigend half *eight and a half,* Cod. Dip. Kmbl. iv. 194, 11. Nigende, vi. 203, 15. Nióþa, Mt. Kmbl. p. 3, 16: 11, 8.

nihol, nihold. v. neowol.

nîhsta, an; *m. A neighbour; proximus*:—Se đe his neáhstan yfeles nân þing ne dyde, and se đe hosp on his neáhstan ne sette, R. Ben. 3, 20–22. Ne girn đû đînes neáhstan wîfes (*uxorem proximi tui*), Deut. 5, 21. Gif đû wed nime æt đînum nǽhstan, Ex. 22, 26. Gif hwâ ofslihþ his nêhstan, 21, 14. Lufa đînne nêhstan (Lind. nêsta), Mt. Kmbl. 19, 19. Hwylc is mîn nêhsta (neestæ, Lind.)? Lk. Skt. 10, 29. Lufa đînne nêxtan (nêste, Lind: nêxstan, Rush.), Mt. Kmbl. 5, 43. Hwâ is ûre nêxta? Homl. Th. ii. 318, 1. Hwelc đara niéhstena (nîhstena, Cott. MSS.) đæs ofslægenan, Past. 21; Swt. 167, 3. Tô nýhstan his, Ps. Spl. 11, 2: Ps. Th. 11, 2. v. neáh.

nihstig, nistig, nestig; *adj. Fasting*:—Gedrinc his on niht nistig, Lchdm. i. 74, 1, 6: 76, 7, 13. Nyhstig, iii. 48, 2. Nibstig, 48, 15: 50, 21: i. 82, 14: 84, 16. v. niht-nihstig.

nihstnig *fasting* (?):—Eft hý (*monks*) gaderiaþ hý on nixtnig, đæt hý raca gehýren æt heora fæder . . . Hý siđđan heora lîchoman gereordaþ, R. Ben. 138, 2–8.

niht, næht, næct, neaht, neht, nyht, e; *f.: but also with gen.* es. I. *night* (as opposed to day):—Niht is gesett mannum tô reste on đysum middanearde . . . Ûre eorþlîce niht (nyht, MS. M.) cymþ þurh đære eorþan sceade . . . Seó niht hæfþ seofan dǽlas fram đære sunnan settlunge ôþ hire upgang. Ân đæra dǽla is *crepusculum,* ôđer is *vesperum,* þridde is *conticinium,* feórþa is *intempestum,* đæt is midniht, fîfta is *gallicinium,* syxta is *matutinum vel aurora,* seofoþa is *diluculum,* Lchdm. iii. 240, 10–244, 5. Hê hine micelre tîde đære deáhlan neahte swong, Bd. 2, 6; S. 508, 13. Scînaþ þurh đa scîran neaht, Met. 20, 229. Niht (næht, Lind. Rush.) cymþ đonne nân man wyrcan ne mæg, Jn. Skt. 9, 4: 13, 30. Fira bearnum neálǽhte niht seó þýstre, Judth. Thw. 21, 25; Jud. 34. Hê com tô him ânes nihtes, Shrn. 16, 27. Næs nǽnig man đe ǽfre nihtes tîdum dorste on đære ciricean cuman, Blickl. Homl. 207, 34. Wacana næhtes *vigilia noctis,* Lk. Skt. Lind. Rush. 2, 8: Mt. Kmbl. Lind. Rush. 14, 25. Swâ swâ se beorhta dæg tôdrǽfþ đa dimlîcan þeóstru đære sweartan nihte, Homl. Th. i. 604, 2. On dæge and nâ on nihte, 36, 28. Hê fealh đære ilcan niht of đǽm bendum, Ors. 5, 11; Swt. 236, 12: Bd. 1, 33; S. 499, 9: Blickl. Homl. 215, 15. Tô niht *hac nocte,* Num. 22, 19. On næht *nocte,* Ps. Surt. 16, 3. On niht ǽr hê ræste, Blickl. Homl. 47, 18. Feówurtig daga and feówurtig nihta (Lind. næhta), Mt. Kmbl. 4, 2. Þreó niht and dagas, Cd. Th. 20, 12; Gen. 307. Dagum and nihtum, Met. 20, 213. II. *night, darkness* (as opposed to light):—Seó swearte niht đære êcan geniþerunge, Homl. Th. i. 530, 23. Dryhten đe ûs of duste geworhte, nergend of nihtes sunde, Salm. Kmbl. 675; Sal. 337. III. *night* (as in se'n-*night,* fort-*night;* cf. Tacitus' Germania, c. xi: 'Instead of reckoning by days as we do, they reckon by nights.'):—Be ânre nihtes (MS. B. nihte) þiéfþe, L. In. 73; Th. i. 148, 11. Hê fôr ymb âne niht tô Îgleá, and đæs ymb âne tô Êþandûne . . . and đǽr sæt xiiii niht . . . and hê was xii niht mid đam cyninge, Chr. 878; Erl. 80, 12–24. Embe seofon niht, Blickl. Homl. 45, 31. Emb tên niht, 117, 16. On twâm nihtum biþ mannes sunu geseald on synfulra hand, 73, 1. For tên nihtum *ten days ago,* 131, 10. Mid đon dæge wæs gefylled se dæg đe is nemned Pentecosten ymb fiftig nihta æfter đære gecýþdan ǽriste, 133, 14. [*Goth.* nahts: *O. Sax.* naht: *O. Frs.* nacht: *Icel.* nâtt, nôtt: *O. H. Ger.* naht.] v. Eáster-, efen- (emn-, em-), Frige-, mæsse-, mid-, middel-, mônan-, sæter-, sin-, sunnan-, þunres-, Tîwes-, Wôdnes-niht; nihtes.

niht-bealu, wes; *n. Bale* or *hurt that comes at night,* Beo. 389; B. 193.

niht-buttorfleóge, an; *f. An insect that flies at night; blatta,* Wrt. Voc. i. 23, 65.

niht-eáge, -êge; *adj. Able to see at night*:—Nihteáge *nyctalmus,* Wrt. Voc. ii. 62, 23. Nihtêge *nictalmus,* i. 20, 8.

niht-eald; *adj. A day old*:—Gif hit biþ nihteald þiéfþ *if it is a theft a day old,* i. e. *if a day passes between the commission of the crime and the capture of the thief,* L. In. 73; Th. i. 148, 10.

niht-egesa, an; *m. Terror by night*:—Ne đû đê nihtegsan ondrǽdest *non timebis a timore nocturno,* Ps. Th. 90, 5. [Cf. *O. H. Ger.* naht-forhta *timor nocturnus.*]

nihte-gala, an; *m. A nightingale*:—Nihtegala *luscinia,* Wrt. Voc. i. 62, 25. v. next word.

nihte-gale, an; *f. A bird whose note* (v. galan) *is heard at night.* I. *the night-raven*:—Naechthraebn, *ali dicunt* nectigalae *noctua,* Ep. Gl. 16 b, 15; *but more generally* II. *the nightingale*:—Naectegale *luscinia,* Wrt. Voc. ii. 113, 30: *roscinia,* 119, 23. Nectægälae *roscinia,* Ep. Gl. 22 b, 27. Nictigalae *achalantis,* 1 f, 6. Nehtegale *achalantis* vel *luscinia* vel *roscinia,* Wrt. Voc. ii. 99, 3. Nihtegale, 4, 24: *luscinia,* 51, 27: *philomela,* i. 63, 23. Nightegale *lucinia* vel *philomela,* 29, 12. [*O. L. Ger.* nahti-gala *luscinia, acredula: O. H. Ger.* nahti-gala *luscinia, filomela;* also *corax, nocticorax, noctua.*]

nihte-lîc. v. niht-lîc.

nihterne, neahterne; *adj. Nocturnal*:—Þurh nihterne besmitenesse *per nocturnam pollutionem,* Confess. Peccat. v. next word.

nihterne, neahterne, nihternum; *adv. For a night*:—Đæs gâst wæs neahterne of lîchoman âlǽded *his* (*Fursey*) *spirit was for a night taken from his body,* Shrn. 51, 30. Lǽt standan neahterne, Lchdm. ii. 24, 21: 32, 25. Lǽt licgean neahterne, 66, 12. Bind on đa eágan nihterne, 34, 23. Lǽt beón nihterne, 74, 14: 270, 8. Lǽt standan nyhternum, iii. 16, 17. v. *preceding and following words, and* dægþerne.

nihternness, e; *f. Night-time*:—Đonne gescylt đê God wiđ unswefnum đe nihternnessum on menn becumaþ *then will God protect thee against evil dreams that come to men at nights,* Lchdm. iii. 288, 22. v. preceding word.

nihtes (*gen.* of niht, q. v.); *adv. At night, night*:—Ne mæg ic bûton mynstre nihtes wunian *I cannot stop out of the monastery at night,* Homl. Th. ii. 182, 34. Đâ gestôd hê æt ânum êhþyrle ôþ forþ nihtes (*far on into the night*), 184, 27. Hys leorningcnihtas cômon nihtes (*nocte*), Mt. Kmbl. 28, 13. Đæra eágan scînaþ nihtes, Nar. 34, 14. Se biþ dæges hât and nihtes ceald, 36, 27. Dæges and nihtes *die et nocte,* Ps. Th. 1, 2: Mk. Skt. 4, 27: Blickl. Homl. 47, 11: 127, 30: 137, 22. Deges and naehtes, Ps. Surt. 31, 4. [*O. Sax.* nahtes: *O. Frs.* nachtes: *O. H. Ger.* nahtes: *Ger.* nachts.]

niht-feormung, e; *f. Entertainment for the night*:—Hê (*Lot*) đâm rincum (*the angels*) beád nihtfeormunge, Cd. Th. 147, 2; Gen. 2433.

niht-genga, an; *m. A creature that goes at night, a goblin, evil spirit*:—Wiđ feóndes costunga and nihtgengan and maran, Lchdm. ii. 306, 12. Wyrc sealf wiđ nihtgengan, 342, 1. Wiđ ælfcynne and nihtgengan and đâm mannum đe deófol mid hǽmþ, 344, 7. Gif men hwylc yfel costung weorþe ođđe ælf ođđe nihtgengan, 344, 16. Hió (*betony*) hyne scyldeþ wiđ unhýrum nihtgengum and wiđ egeslîcum gesihþum and swefnum, i. 70, 5.

niht-genge, an; *f. A night-goer, an animal that prowls at night, a hyena*:—Naectgenge *hyna,* Wrt. Voc. ii. 110, 41. Nihtgenge *hyna,* 43, 6.

niht-gerîm, es; *n. Reckoning by days* (v. niht, III), *number of days*:—Æfter seofontýnum nihtgerîmes *after seventeen days,* Menol. Fox 52; Men. 26: 110; Men. 55: Andr. Kmbl. 229; An. 115: 315; An. 158. Ealra hæfde v. and syxtig đâ hê forþ gewât and nigon hund eác nihtgerîmes *in all the number of his days when he died was nine hundred and sixty-five years,* Cd. Th. 72, 28; Gen. 1193. [Cf. dôgorgerîm, *and Icel.* nâttar-tal: *Chauc.* nighter-tale.]

niht-gild, es; *n. A service, sacrifice celebrated at night*:—Nihtgild *nyctilia,* Wrt. Voc. ii. 61, 18. Blôstmfreólsas and nihtgilda *floralia nictelia* (cf. blôstmgeld *floralia,* Wrt. Voc. ii. 37, 52), Hpt. Gl. 515, 18.

niht-glôm, es; *m.* (?) *The darkness of night*:—Wæs đam bâncofan æfter nihtglôme (*when the shades of night prevailed*) neáh geþrungen, Exon. Th. 158, 27; Gû. 916. v. ǽfen-glôma.

niht-helm, es; *m. The covering of night, night's curtain*:—Nihthelm geswearc deorc ofer dryhtgumum *night's curtain dark was drawn over men,* Beo. Th. 3583; B. 1789.

niht-hræfn, es; *m. The night-raven, night-jar, night-owl*:—Naechthraebn *noctua, nocticorax*, Ep. Gl. 16 b, 15, 18. Naehthraefn *noctua*, Wrt. Voc. ii. 114, 76. Nihthræfn *nycticorax*, i. 63, 12. Niht-hrefn, 281, 42. Nihthremn, ii. 60, 36. Nihtremn, i. 29, 35. Niht-hrefne (nihtrefen, Ps. Spl.; næhthrefn, Ps. Surt.; nihthræm, Ps. Lamb.) gelīc, Ps. Th. 101, 5. [*Icel.* nātt-hrafn: *O. H. Ger.* naht-hraban *nocticorax, noctua, bubo*.]

niht-hrōc, es; *m. The night-rook, raven*:—Nihtrōc *nycticorax*, Ps. Lamb. 101, 7.

niht-lang; *adj. Night-long, a night in length*:—Nafa đū nānes þearfan wedd mid đē nihtlangne fyrst *si pauper est proximus tuus, non pernoctabit apud te pignus*, Deut. 24, 12: Cd. Th. 191, 2; Exod. 208: Andr. Kmbl. 1668; An. 836: 2620; An. 1311: Elen. Kmbl. 134; El. 67. Nihtlongne fyrst, Beo. Th. 1060; B. 528. [*Icel.* nātt-langt *for a night*.] v. next word.

niht-langes; *adv. For the night*:—Ic bidde eów đæt gē gecirron tō mīnum hūse and đǣr wunion nihtlanges, Gen. 19, 2. [Ne moste niht-longes istonden, Laym. 15564.] v. preceding word.

niht-līc; *adj. Nightly, of the night, nocturnal*:—Fram ege niht-līcum *a timore nocturno*, Ps. Spl. 90, 5. For nihtlecum ege, Past. 56; Swt. 433, 11. Hī swuncon on nihtlīcum rēwette, Homl. Th. ii. 384, 24. Đa steorran sint mannum tō nihtlīcere līhtinge gesceapene, i. 110, 15. On nihtlīcre tīde *at night*, Lchdm. iii. 234, 21: 270, 26. On nihtlīcre gesyhþe *in a vision of the night*, Bd. 5, 10; S. 625, 12. Hine drehton nihtlīce gedwimor, Homl. Th. i. 86, 18. Đæs synfullan līf is wiđmeten nihtlīcum þeóstrum, ii. 200, 33. Nihtlīcum tīdum *in the night seasons*, Bd. 3, 11; S. 536, 11. Þerh næhtlīco mysto *per nocturnas caligines*, Rtl. 171, 39. [*Icel.* nātt-ligr: *O. H. Ger.* naht-līh *nocturnus*.]

niht-nihstig, -nestig; *adj. Fasting for a night*:—Sele nihtnestig drincan, Lchdm. ii. 64, 18. Gedrinc ǣlce dæge neahtnestig, 30, 26. Drince iii morgenas neahtnestig, 296, 12. Mid his selfes nihtnestiges migoþan, 42, 1. Sele nihtnestigum drincan, 64, 9, 19: 186, 5. Syle on morgenne đam seócum men neahtnestigum, 286, 11.

niht-rest, e; *f. The couch on which one rests at night*:—Abram sīne nihtreste ofgeaf, Cd. Th. 173, 18; Gen. 2863.

niht-rīm, es; *n. A number of days*:—Nihtrīm scridon, Exon. Th. 167, 35; Gū. 1070.

niht-sang, es; *m.* I. *the service at the seventh of the canonical hours, compline*:—Nū gebyraþ mæssepreóstum đæt hī đa seofon tīdsangas gesyngon . . . nihtsang seofoþan, L. Ælfc. C. 19; Th. ii. 350, 3-7: R. Ben. 40, 7. Hwænne wylle gē singan nihtsangc (*completorium*), Coll. Monast. Th. 34, 3. II. *a copy of the service*:—Sind .ii. fulle sangbēc and .i. nihtsang . . . Hē ne funde nā mā būton āne capitulare and .i. forealdodne nihtsang . . ., Chart. Th. 430, 8, 28. [*Icel.* nātt-söngr.]

niht-scada (-sceadu?) *night-shade* (plant name):—Nihtscada *strumus* vel *uva lupina*, Wrt. Voc. i. 31, 18.

niht-scūa, -scūwa, an; *m. The darkness, shades of night*:—Đonne nīpeþ nihtscūa, Exon. Th. 292, 24; Wand. 104: 307, 29; Seef. 31. Æfter nihtscūan, 162, 5; Gū. 971. Under nihtscūwan, Cd. Th. 124, 10; Gen. 2060. Neowle nihtscūwan, 184, 28; Exod. 114.

niht-slǣp, es; *m. Sleep during the night*:—Đæt ilce geþanc đe heom amang đam nihtslǣpe wæs on heora heortan, eall đā hī āwac. Odon hī đæt sylfe geþohton, Homl. Skt. 23, 442.

niht-wacu (o); *f. A night-watch*:—Mec oft bigeat nearo nihtwaco æt nacan stefnan, Exon. Th. 306, 13; Seef. 7. v. next word.

niht-wæcce, an; *f. A night-watch, vigil*:—Nihtwæccan *vigiliae*, Wrt. Voc. i. 18, 22. Hyrdas wǣron waciende and nihtwæccan (-wæcan, MS. C.) healdende *pastores erant vigilantes et custodientes vigilias noctis*, Lk. Skt. 2, 8. [*Icel.* nātt-vaka: *O. H. Ger.* naht-wacha *vigilia*.]

niht-waru, e; *f. Night-wear*:—Genōh byþ đam munuce đæt hē hæbbe twā cūlan and twegen syricas for đære nihtware and for đæs reáfes þweále, R. Ben. 90, 4.

niht-weard, es; *m. A guard who keeps watch at night*:—Heofon-candel (*the fiery pillar*) barn, nīwe nihtweard, Cd. Th. 185, 1; Exod. 116.

niht-weorc, es; *n. A work done at night*:—Nihtweorce (*the defeat of Grendel*) gefeh, Beo. Th. 1659; B. 827.

nillan. v. nyllan.

nima. v. nīd-nima.

niman; *p.* nam, *pl.* nāmon; *pp.* numen (*kept in the slang word* nim = *steal*. Cf. Shakspere's Corporal Nym). I. *to take, receive, get*; sumere, accipere:—Nimþ *sumpserint*, Kent. Gl. 1056. Hwār nime wē (hwonon ūs tō niomane, Rush.) swā fela hlāf? Mt. Kmbl. 15, 33. Cristes onsægdnesse đe wē æt đæm weofode nimaþ, Blickl. Homl. 77, 5. Đæt (*food*) hē ǣr tō blisse nam, 57, 7. Đā nam Petrus and đa ōđre apostolas hié (*Mary*), and hié āsetton ofer hire bǣre, 149, 5. Hié nāman blōwende palmtwigu and bǣron him tōgeánes, 69, 30. Nim and telle Israhēla folc, Num. 1, 2. Nim ǣnne ođđe twegen tō đē *adhibe tecum unum vel duos*, Mt. Kmbl. 18, 16. Nim đē đis ofæt on hand, Cd. Th. 33, 11; Gen. 518. Đæt đū nǣfre ne nyme wīf mīnum suna of đisum mennisce, Gen. 24, 3. Nān man ne sceal sceattas niman for Godes cyrcan, Homl. Th. ii. 592, 21. Hē lǣrde tō healdenne reogollīces līfes þeódscipe swā swīđe swā đa nīwan Cristenan hit niman (*capere*) mihton, Bd. 3, 22; S. 553, 11. Hēht his sweord niman, Beo. Th. 3621; B. 1808. II. *to take, keep, hold*; tenere:—Nimþ mē seó swȳđre đīn *tenebit me dextera tua*, Ps. Spl. 138, 9. Đū nǣme (*tenuisti*) hand đa swȳđran, 72, 23. Hē đæt wolcn him beforan nam *he had the cloud before him*, Blickl. Homl. 121, 14. Hī oferhygd nam (*tenuit*), Ps. Th. 72, 5. Hī hī be handum nōman *junctis manibus*, Bd. 4, 13; S. 582, 31. III. *to take, catch*:—Hēr beóþ oft numene missenlīcra cynna weolcscylle, 1, 1; S. 473, 17. IV. *to contain*:—Nō swā đæt heó (*the coffin*) đone līchoman neoman mihte, 4, 11; S. 580, 7. V. *to take* (*with one*), *carry, bring*:—Đā nam hē fīf stānas on his herdebelig, Blickl. Homl. 31, 17. Nāmon wē hlāfas mid ūs, Mt. Kmbl. 16, 7. VI. *to take* (*to one*), *give*:—Hāt đē niman Pilatus ǣrendgewrit, Blickl. Homl. 177, 2. VII. *to take forcibly, seize, take away, carry off*; tollere, capessere, auferre, rapere:—Ic nyme *tollo*, Ælfc. Gr. 28; Som. 32, 53. Đam đe đīn reáf nymþ *qui auferet tibi vestimentum*, Lk. Skt. 6, 29. Se đe hine deáþ nimeþ, Beo. Th. 887; B. 441. Gūþ nimeþ freán eówerne, 5066; B. 2536. Þeófas đe on mannum heora ǣhta on wōh nimaþ, Blickl. Homl. 61, 22. Manige men đa moldan neomaþ on đǣm lǣstum, 127, 11. Nimaþ *capessunt*, Wrt. Voc. ii. 23, 33. Nam *capessit*, 20, 8. Hē nam *tulit*, Kent. Gl. 209. Nam mid handa rinc on ræste, Beo. Th. 1496; B. 746. Đæt hē mōste niman đæs Hǣlendes līchaman . . . Đā com hē and nam đæs Hǣlendes līchaman *ut tolleret corpus Jesu . . . venit ergo et tulit corpus Jesu*, Jn. Skt. 19, 38. Đæt flōd com and nam (*tulit*) hig ealle, Mt. Kmbl. 24, 39. Nimaþ đæt pund fram him *auferte ab illo mnam*, Lk. Skt. 19, 24. Nis nānum men ālȳfed đæt hē nime on his þeówe ǣnig feoh *nemini licet servo suo pecuniam aliquam auferre*, L. Ecg. P. addit. 35 note; Th. ii. 238, 11. Gif mec hild nime, Beo. Th. 909; B. 452. Mē sceal wǣpen niman, Byrht. Th. 139, 11; By. 252. Ne biþ ālȳfed æt đam þeówan his feoh tō nimanne *non licet pecuniam suam servo auferre*, L. Ecg. P. addit. 35; Th. ii. 238, 6. VIII. in phrases in a metaphorical sense:—Andan niman *to take umbrage, offence*. Đā nam đæt folc micelne andan ongeán his lāre, Homl. Th. i. 26, 21. Tō đon ealdfeóndas ondan nōman, Exon. Th. 115, 14; Gū. 189. Bysne niman be, æt *to take example by, from*. Nime heó bysne be đisre wudewan, Homl. Th. i. 148, 5. Hī nāmon đa bysne đæs fæstenys æt đam Niniveiscan folce, 244, 23. Casum niman *to take a case* (of the government of verbs), Ælfc. Gr. 41; Som. 43, 57. Eard niman *to take up one's abode*. Đǣr ic eard nime *hic habitabo*, Ps. Th. 131, 15. Heofones cyning sylf cymeþ, nimeþ eard in đē, Exon. Th. 5, 1; Cri. 63. Freónd-rǣdene niman *amicitias jungere*, Ex. 34, 12. Friþ niman wiđ *to make peace with*, Chr. 867; Erl. 72, 17: 868; Erl. 72, 29 (often in the Chronicle). Geleáfan niman *to believe*, Cd. Th. 41, 2; Gen. 650. Geþeódrǣdene niman wiđ *to associate with*. Gif hwylc brōđor gedyrst-lǣcþ đæt hē on ǣnige wīsan geþeódrǣdene nime wiđ đone āmānsumedan, R. Ben. 50, 11. Graman niman *to take offence, feel angry*. Đā nam hē micelne graman and andan tō đām mannum, Homl. Th. i. 16, 30. Lāre niman *to accept teaching*. Hȳ leng mid him lāre ne nāmon, Salm. Kmbl. 926; Sal. 462. Lufe niman tō *to take an affection for*. Māran lufe nimþ-se heretoga tō đam cempan, đe æfter fleáme his wiđerwinnan þegenlīce oferwinþ, Homl. Th. i. 342, 2. Mōd niman *to take courage*, Bd. 1, 16; S. 484, 15. On niman *to take effect on*, Lchdm. ii. 84, 6: 234, 5: 282, 22. On gemynd niman *to bear in remembrance*, Elen. Kmbl. 2464; El. 1233. On hæft niman *to take captive*, Exon. Th. 16, 29; Cri. 260. Sibbe niman wiđ *to make terms with*. Ne nim đū nāne sibbe wiđ đæs landes menn *ne ineas pactum cum hominibus illarum regionum*, Ex. 34, 15. Sige niman *to gain the victory*, Chr. 871; Erl. 74, 8 (and often). Tō gemæccan niman *to take to wife*, Cd. Th. 76, 17; Gen. 1258. Tō suna niman *to adopt as a son*, Ors. 1, 12; Swt. 52, 16. Wæpna niman *to take up arms*, 1, 10; Swt. 44, 32. Ware niman *to take care*. Hē ne nom nāne ware hūlīce hié wǣron, 5, 4; Swt. 224, 21. Weg niman *to take, go one's way*, Cd. Th. 80, 16; Gen. 1329. Wīcstōwa niman *to pitch a camp*, Ors. 4, 10; Swt. 200, 8. [*Goth.* niman: *O. Sax.* niman: *O. Frs.* nima, nema: *Icel.* nema: *O. H. Ger.* neman *tollere, carpere, vellere, rapere, capere*.] v. ā-, æt-, be- (bi-), dǣl-, for-, ge-, of-, ofer-, under-niman.

nimþe, nemþe, nymþe; *conj. Unless, except*:—Nimþe *nisi*, Wülck. Gl. 249, 9. Nimþe wēn wǣre *ni forsan*, Wrt. Voc. ii. 61, 4: 93, 3. I. connecting clauses:—Ne hine mon on ōđre wīsan his bēne tȳþigean wolde, nemþe hē Cristes geleáfan onfēnge, Bd. 3, 21; S. 550, 43. Ne sceal nǣfre his torn tō rycene beorn ācȳđan, nemþe hē ǣr đa bōte cunne, Exon. Th. 293, 9; Wand. 113. Nymþe mē Drihten gefultumede, wēnincga mīn sāwl sōhte helle, Ps. Th. 93, 16: Beo. Th. 3321; B. 1657. II. connecting words in the same case (contracted clauses, the verb of the second clause being the same as that in the first, and not expressed):—Nǣnig ōđerne freóþ in fyrhþe, nimþe feára hwylc (freóþ), Fragm. Kmbl. 71; Leas. 37. Næs monna gemet, ne mægen engla đæt eów mihte helpan, nimþe Hǣlend God, Cd. Th. 295, 27; Sat. 403. Nǣniges Godes hāliga gebyrd ciricean ne mǣrsiaþ, nemþe Cristes sylfes and đyses Johannes, Blickl. Homl. 161, 11. Ne wē ūs nāht elles ne wēnden nemþe deáþes sylfes, Bd. 5, 1; S. 613, 26. Unc gemǣne ne sceal elles āwiht nymþe lufu langsumu, Cd. Th. 114, 17; Gen. 1905: 252, 8; Dan. 575. Nis đē wiđerbreca man on moldan, nymþe Metod āna, 251, 22; Dan. 567. Hwā is đæt đē cunne, nymþe ēce God, 266, 7; Sat. 18. Nis nǣnig swā snotor, nymþe God seolfa, 286, 11; Sat. 350. Ic nǣngum sceþþe nymþe bonan ānum, Exon. Th. 407, 11; Rä. 26, 3. Nabbaþ wē tō hyhte nymþe cyle and fȳr, Cd. Th. 285, 10; Sat. 335. Eaforan syndon deáde nymþe feá āne, 128, 30; Gen. 2134. Cf. nefne.

nimung, e; *f. A taking, plucking:*—Niming hēra *vulsio spicarum*, Lk. Skt. p. 5, 3. v. nīd-nimung.

nió-bedd, nióđ, niól, niowol, niótan, nioþan, -nip. v. neó-bedd, neód, nīd, neowol, neótan, neoþan, ge-nip.

nip (?):—Nipum *rudente*, Germ. 399, 451.

nīpan; *p.* nāp, *pl.* nipon; *pp.* nipen *To grow dark:*—Đonne won cymeþ, nīpeþ nihtscūa, Exon. Th. 292, 24; Wand. 104. Nāp nihtscūa, 307, 29; Seef. 31. Nīpende niht, Beo. Th. 1098; B. 547: 1302; B. 649. v. ge-nīpan, ge-nip.

nirwan, nirwian; *p.* de, ode *To constrain, repress, blame, threaten:*—Moyses onfēng scīnendum wulderhelme forđon hē symle đa nyrugde đe God oferhogodan *Moses received a shining crown, because he ever repressed those that despised God*, Blickl. Homl. 49, 12. Hī fȳrene tangan him on handa hæfdon and mē nyrwdon and mē tōbeótodan đæt hī mē mid đām gegrīpon woldon *forcipibus igneis quos tenebant in manibus, minitabantur me comprehendere*, Bd. 5, 12; S. 628, 43. Ne ne on đīnum yrre ne nyrwa đū mē *neque in ira tua corripias me*, Ps. Spl. 37, 1. v. ge-nyrwian, nearwian.

nirwett, es; *m.* I. *narrowness:*—Ic hit gefēran ne mehte for đara wega nerwette (*propter angustas semitas*), Nar. 25, 5. II. *a narrow place, pass:*—Se engel eode intō ānum nyrwette *angelus ad locum angustum transiens*, Num. 22, 26. III. *oppression of the chest, difficulty of breathing:*—Hit fremaþ myclum gedruncen wiđ nyrwyt, Lchdm. i. 140, 1: 144, 17. v. nearuness *and next word.*

nirwþ, e; *f. Confinement, a prison:*—Nirwþa *ergastula*, Wrt. Voc. ii. 33, 24.

nis. v. neom.

nistan, nistian *to build a nest:*—Đǣr sperwan nistiaþ *illic passeres nidificabunt*, Ps. Spl. 103, 18. Nistaþ (MS. nistađađ), Ps. Surt. 103, 17. [*O. H. Ger.* nistian, nistōn *nidificare.*] v. nistlan.

nistig. v. nihstig.

nistlan *to make a nest:*—On đam spearwan nystlaþ, Ps. Th. 103, 16. Nistlaþ, 83, 3. v. nestlian, nistan.

nitan, nitenness. v. nytan, nytenness.

nīten, niéten, neáten, nȳten, es; *n. An animal, beast, cattle:*—Ǣlc cuce þing *vel* nȳten *animal:* ǣlces kynnes nȳten *pecus, jumentum*, Wrt. Voc. i. 22, 37, 38: 78, 49. Rēđe nȳten *feralis bestia*, ii. 147, 54. Đis nȳten *haec pecus*, Ælfc. Gr. 9, 32; Som. 12, 10. Đis nȳten *istud animal;* đyses nȳtenes *istius animalis;* đās nīhtenu *ista animalia*, 15; Som. 18, 34–36. Swā nȳten geworden eom *ut jumentum factus sum*, Ps. Spl. 72, 22. Sum nȳten is đe wē nemnaþ broc, Lchdm. i. 326, 11. Nēten, Met. 20, 191. Niéten, Salm. Kmbl. 44; Sal. 22. Hē hine on his nȳten (nētne, Lind.) sette, Lk. Skt. 10, 34. Nȳtenu and deór fixas and fugelas God gesceóp on flǣsce būtan sāwle. Đa nȳtenu hē lēt gān ālotene, and hē forgeaf đām nȳtenum gærs, Homl. Th. i. 276, 3–6. Men and nȳtenu sweltaþ *homines et jumenta morientur*, Ex. 9, 19. Swā stunte nȳtenu *sicut bruta animalia*, Coll. Monast. Th. 32, 19. Đa ungesceádwīsan neótena, Bt. 14, 2; Fox 44, 21. Nētenu, 34, 11; Fox 152, 6. Đām monnum đe beóþ neátenum gelīce, 14, 1; Fox 42, 3. Lǣde seó eorþe forþ cuce nītenu, Gen. 1, 24. v. neát.

nīten-līc; *adj. Animal, after the manner of a brute:*—Gē nētelīcan (nētenlīcan, Cott. MS.) men *O! terrena animalia*, Bt. 16, 2; Fox 50, 35.

niþ[þ] *a man.* v. niþþas.

niþ, es; *n. A place low down, an abyss:*—Lǣdaþ in đæt sceađena scræf, scūfaþ tō grunde in đæt nearwe niþ, Cd. Th. 304, 22; Sat. 634. v. nīþ-sele, -wundor.

nīþ, es; *m.* I. *envy, hatred, enmity, rancor, spite, ill-will, jealousy:*—Đis synt đa īdelnyssa đisse worlde . . . nīþ and æfēsta and hātheortnys *hae sunt vanitates hujus mundi . . . odium et invidiae et furor*, L. Ecg. P. i. 8; Th. ii. 174, 32. Ne mehte se nīþ betux him twǣm gelicgean *the enmity between the two could not die out*, Ors. 3, 11; Swt. 152, 14. Gif him þince đæt hē næddran geseó đæt biþ yfeles wīfes nīþ *if he fancies he sees a snake, that means a bad woman's spite*, Lchdm. iii. 174, 17. Blātende nīþ *livid envy*, Cd. Th. 60, 14; Gen. 981: Andr. Kmbl. 1536; An. 769. Nīþ wiđ God *enmity with God*, Exon. Th. 302, 23; Fä. 40. Āhrede mē hefiges nīþes feónda mīnra *eripe me de inimicis meis*, Ps. Th. 58, 1. Genere mē fram nīþe nāhtfremmendra, 58, 2. Paulus ehte cristenra manna, nā mid nīþe (*rancorously*), swā swā đa Iudēiscan dydon, ac hē wæs bewerigend đære ealdan ǣ, Homl. Th. i. 388, 31. Hió mid wīflīce nīþe wæs feohtende on đæt underiende folc *she* (*Semiramis*) *with a woman's rancor was carrying on war against that harmless people*, Ors. 1, 2; Swt. 30, 19. Đæt gē eówer mōd gemetgien on đæm nīþe *ut in increpationis zelo se spiritus temperet*, Past. 21, 4; Swt. 159, 15. Đǣr is friþ būtan æfēstum, sib būtan nīþe, Exon. Th. 101, 18; Cri. 1660. Hē slōh hildebille đæt hit on heafolan stōd nīþe genȳded *he smote with his battle-blade, that, forced on by hate, it stuck in the* (*dragon's*) *head*, Beo. Th. 5353; B. 2680. Đa hwīle đe hē nȳþ odđe andan hæbbe on his heortan wiđ his đone nēhstan *quamdiu invidiam vel malitiam in corde suo cum proximo suo habet*, L. Ecg. P. ii. 27; Th. ii. 192, 27. Siđđan genam Saul micelne nīþ tō Davide, Homl. Th. ii. 64, 16. Hannibal gecȳþde đone nīþ and đone hete (*odium*) đe hē beforan his fæder swōr, Ors. 4, 8; Swt. 186, 9. Hē him forgeaf đone nīþ đe hē tō him wiste *he* (*Augustus*) *forgave them* (*the Germans who had slain Varus*) *the ill-will he felt towards them*, 5, 15; Swt. 250, 15. Hē ne rōhte heora eallra nīþ, Chr. 1086; Erl. 222, 32. Ic hine on sette mōdhete, longsumne nīþ, Cd. Th. 105, 22; Gen. 1757: 47, 30; Gen. 768. Nīþa gebǣded *forced by feelings of hatred*, Exon. Th. 254, 27; Jul. 203: 270, 9; Jul. 462. II. *action which arises from hatred, strife, war, hostility:*—Hē cwæþ nīþes ofþyrsted đæt hē on norþdǣle heáhsetl heofena rīces āgan wolde *all too eager for strife he said that in the north of heaven a throne he would own*, Cd. Th. 3, 7; Gen. 32: 120, 15; Gen. 1995. Gūþbill nacod æt nīþe *the blade bared in battle*, Beo. Th. 5163; B. 2585. Nīþe rōf *bold in battle*, Judth. Thw. 22, 7; Jud. 53. Nīþ āhebban wiđ *to strive against*, Elen. Kmbl. 1672; El. 838. Nīþa ofercumen, fǣge and geflȳmed, Beo. Th. 1694; B. 845. Æt nīþa gehwam nȳdgesteallan, 1768; B. 882. Nīþa cræftig, 3929; B. 1962: 4346; B. 2170. Hē nīþa gedīgde, hildehlemma, 4690; B. 2350: 4785; B. 2397. III. *the effect of hatred, persecution, trouble, vexation, annoyance, affliction, tribulation, grief:*—Đā wæs wyrmes wīg wīde gesȳne nearofāges nīþ (*the disastrous effects of the dragon's malice*), 4623; B. 2317: Cd. Th. 83, 22; Gen. 1383. Oft đǣr brōga cwom ealdfeónda nīþ *oft came terror there, trouble from the hate of ancient foes*, Exon. Th. 110, 24; Gū. 112: 125, 29; Gū. 361: 345, 25, 30; Gn. Ex. 195, 197: 346, 4; Gn. Ex. 200. Him leófre wǣre đæt hié an swelcan niéde (MS. C. nēđe) deáþ fornōme đonne hié mid swelcan niéde friþ begeáte *cum intolerabiles conditiones pacis audissent, tutius rati sese armatos mori quam miseros vivere*, Ors. 4, 6; Swt. 174, 26. Hæfde hē sele Hrōđgāres genered wiđ nīþe, Beo. Th. 1658; B. 827: Andr. Kmbl. 2073; An. 1039. Hié habban sceoldon hellgeþwin, đone nearwan nīþ, Cd. Th. 43, 27; Gen. 697: 48, 13; Gen. 775. Ic wræc Wedera nīþ, Beo. Th. 850; B. 423. Scyld đū đē nū đū đysne nīþ genesan mōte, Lchdm. iii. 52, 17. Đæt đū mē generige nīþa gehwylces *eripe me*, Ps. Th. 118, 170: Exon. 230, 8; Ph. 469. Fela mē se Hǣlend hearma gefremede, nīþa nearolīcra, Elen. Kmbl. 1822; El. 913. Nīþa georn, bealwes beald, Blickl. Homl. 109, 28. Hǣle wiđ deófla nīþum, 171, 30. Hē mec wile wiđ đām nīþum genergan, Exon. Th. 116, 24; Gū. 212: 140, 34; Gū. 620. Ofer đa nīþas đe wē nū dreógaþ, 105, 8; Gū. 20. Ic mē forhtige fyrenfulra fǣcne nīþas *conturbatus sum a tribulatione peccatoris*, Ps. Th. 54, 2. Helle heáfas, hearde nīþas, Cd. Th. 3, 20; Gen. 38. IV. *evil, wickedness, malice:*—Nīþ synfulra *nequitia peccatorum*, Ps. Surt. 7, 10. On đara ācorenra monna heortan sceal đære nædran lytignes and hire nīþ đære culfran biliwitnesse gescirpan *in electorum cordibus debet simplicitatem columbae astutia serpentis acuere*, Past. 35, 1; Swt. 237, 22. Mid đȳ nīþe yfles ingeþonces *malitiae peste*, 33, 5; Swt. 220, 19. Nīþe *nequitiae*, Ps. Spl. 54, 17. Þurh næddran nīþ *through the serpent's malice*, Cd. Th. 290, 8; Sat. 412: Exon. Th. 226, 29; Ph. 413. Nīþa geblonden (*Holofernes*), Judth. Thw. 21, 25; Jud. 34. Nīþa efter nīþum teolunge heara *secundum nequitias studiorum ipsorum*, Ps. Surt. 27, 4. Æfter nīþas, Ps. Spl. C. 27, 5. [*A. R. Orm. Laym.* niþ: *Gen. and Ex.* niđ and strif: *Goth.* neiþ *φθόνος*: *O. Sax.* nīđ: *O. Frs.* nīth: *Icel.* nīđ *a libel, lampoon:* *O. H. Ger.* nīd *invidia, rancor, discidium, invidentia, iniquitas.*] v. bealu-, fǣr-, gār-, helle-, here-, hete-, inwit-, orleg-, searo-, sin-, spere-, wæl-nīþ.

nīþ; *adj.* (?) *Vexatious, rancorous:*—Æfǣstum onǣled, nīþum nearowrencum (*or* nīþum *from preceding word?*), Exon. Th. 316, 5; Mōd. 44. [Cf. he fell off heffne dun Inntill niþ hellepine, Orm. 13677.]

nīþ-cwalu, e; *f. Grievous destruction:*—Hē hȳ generede from nīþcwale, and eác forgeaf ēce dreámas, Exon. Th. 77, 18; Cri. 1258.

nīþ-cwealm, es; *m. Violent death, destruction:*—Heora neát niþcwealm forswealh *jumenta eorum in morte conclusit*, Ps. Th. 77, 50.

nīþ-draca, an; *m. A hostile, malicious dragon*, Beo. Th. 4538; B. 2273.

niþemest. v. neoþera.

niþer; *adv. Down, beneath, below:*—Niþer *deorsum*, Ælfc. Gr. 38; Som. 40, 6. Đē wearþ helle seáþ niþer gedolfen *beneath was the pit of hell dug for thee*, Exon. Th. 267, 30; Jul. 423. Đā hē nyþer ābeáh *cum se inclinasset*, Jn. Skt. 20, 5. Ic nyþer ālǣte *submitto*, Ælfc. Gr. 28; Som. 31, 41. Hē nyþer ālēde *deposuit*, Lk. Skt. 23, 53. Nyþer āsceótan *to cast down*, Homl. Th. i. 170, 23. Hē niþer āsette đa mihtigan *deposuit potentes*, Cant. Mar. 52. Đonne heó nyđer byþ āstigen, Anglia viii. 319, 19. Đæt hī hine nyþer bescufon *ut praecipitarint eum*, Lk. Skt. 4, 29. Se đe nyþer com of heofonum *qui descendit de caelo*, Jn. Skt. 3, 13. Đū niþer færst (*descendes*) ōþ helle, Mt. Kmbl. 11, 23. Niþer feallaþ *procident*, Ps. Lamb. 71, 9: 94, 6. Niþer fylþ *decidat*, 89,

6. Gā nyþer *descende*, Mt. Kmbl. 27, 40. Hē nyþer ne eode, Ex. 32, 1. Gang niþer, Deut. 9, 12. Niþer gewītan *descendere*, Bd. 5, 12; S. 628, 21. Hwearf him eft niþer (*to hell*) boda bitresta, Cd. Th. 47, 18; Gen. 762. Niþer stīgan *descendere*, Ps. Lamb. 27, 1: Lchdm. iii. 210, 17. Hē sceal mā þencan up đonne nyþer *he must direct his thought upwards rather than downwards*, Bt. 41, 6; Fox 254, 31. [*Laym.* niđer: *O. E. Homl. Marh.* neoþer: *Gen. and Ex.* neđer: *O. Sax.* niđar: *O. Frs.* nither: *Icel.* niđr: *O. H. Ger.* nidar *deorsum*: *Gen.* nieder.] v. niþere.

niþera. v. neoþera.

niþer-bogen *down-bent*:—Tō đære niþerbogenan āc, Cod. Dip. Kmbl. iv. 72, 1. [Cf. *Icel.* niđr-bjúgr.]

niþer-dǣl, es; *m. A lower part*:—On niþerdǣlum eorþan *in inferioribus terrae*, Ps. Th. 138, 13.

niþere, niþre; *adv. Down, beneath, below*:—Læg mīn flǣschoma in foldan bigrafen, niþre gehȳded in byrgenne, đæt đū meahte beorhte uppe on roderum wesan, Exon. Th. 89, 34; Cri. 1467. Uppe ge niþre, 360, 3; Pa. 74. [*O. H. Ger.* nidare, nidere: *Icel.* niđri.]

niþer-gang, es; *m. Descent*:—Mid hyra upgange ođđe nyþergange, Lchdm. iii. 246, 8. [*Icel.* niđr-gangr, -ganga.]

niþer-heald; *adj. Bent downwards*:—Nis đæt gedafenlīc, đæt se mōdsefa monna ǣniges niþerheald wese, and đæt neb upweard, Met. 31, 23. [Cf. Hie mugen lihtliche cumen mid þare niđerhelde (*the downward slope*), O. E. Homl. ii. 230, 347: *O. H. Ger.* nidar-haldig *reclinus*.]

niþerian, niþrian; *p.* ode. I. *to bring low, humiliate*:—Se đe hine nyþeraþ *qui se humiliat*, Lk. 14, 11. Hī nyþerodon *humiliaverunt*, Ps. Spl. 93, 5. II. *to accuse, condemn*:—Ne ǣnig mon đec niþraþ (*condemnavit*), Jn. Skt. Rush. 8, 10. Hī niþeriaþ *condemnabunt*, Ps. Spl. 93, 21. Niþrigaþ *condemnabunt*, Mt. Kmbl. Rush. 12, 41. Đæt hiǣ niþradun (*accusarent*) hine, Mk. Skt. Rush. 3, 2. Niþrad *damnatus*, Mt. Kmbl. Rush. 27, 3. Wæs neþored *damnatur*, Hpt. 495, 2. [*Orm.* niþþrenn: *Laym.* neoþered: *Icel.* niđra *to put down, lower*: *O. H. Ger.* niderren *humiliare, accusare, condemnare*.] v. ge-niþerian.

niþerigend-līc; *adj. Deserving condemnation*:—Þurh gōdne willan herigendlīc ođđe of yflum willan nyþergendlīc, Boutr. Scrd. 20, 1.

niþer-līc; *adj.* I. *low* (of position):—Ān þeósterful dene swīđe niþerlīc, Homl. Th. ii. 338, 5. Heortan niþerlīcan *cordis ima*, Ps. Surt. ii. p. 202, 5. On nyþerlīcum eorþan *in inferioribus terrae*, Ps. Lamb. 62, 10. Tō nyþerlīcum *ad inferos*, Cant. An. 6. Hē his eágan bīgde on đās nyþerlīcan þing *oculos in inferiora deflectens*, Bd. 3, 19; S. 548, 8. II. *low, humble, inferior*:—In đisse nyþerlīcan worulde *in this lower world*, Shrn. 123, 10. Đa nyþerlīcan *humilia*, Blickl. Gl. Gē sēcaþ đære heán gecynde gesǣlþa tō đām niþerlīcum and tō đām hreósendlīcum þingum, Bt. 14, 2; Fox 44, 30: Homl. Th. ii. 522, 30.

niþerness, e; *f. Lowness, a low position, the bottom*:—Đā geseah hē swā þȳstre denę under him in nyþernesse gesette *vidit quasi vallem tenebrosam subtus se in imo positam*, Bd. 3, 19; S. 548, 9.

niþer-scyfe, es; *m. A pushing down, falling down, hasty downward movement*:—Niþerscyfe *per praeceps*, Hpt. Gl. 468, 74. v. scyfe.

niþer-sige, es; *m. A going down, setting*:—Sunne oncneów niþersige (*occasum*) hire, Ps. Lamb. 103, 19: 113, 3. Ofer niþersi[g]e *super occasum*, 67, 5.

niþer-stige, es; *m. A descent*:—Se upstige and se niþerstige *the ascent and descent* (*of the angels seen by Jacob in his dream*), R. Ben. 23, 7. Tō Olivetes muntes nyþerstige *ad descensum montis Oliveti*, Lk. Skt. 19, 37. [Cf. *Icel.* niđr-stiga *a descent*: *O. H. Ger.* nidar-stiga.]

niþerung, e; *f.* I. *a bringing low, humiliation, overthrow*:—Ic salde..iów mæhte hēnnisse ł niþrunge ofer nedre *dedi vobis potestatem calcandi supra serpentes*, Lk. Skt. Rush. 10, 19. Ǣttrige niþerunge *venenata detrimenta*, Hpt. Gl. 450, 39. II. *damnation, condemnation*:—Niþrung *damnatio*, Lk. Skt. Lind. 23, 40: 24, 20. Hē hī fram yrmþum ēcre niþerunge generede, Bd. 4, 13; S. 582, 26: 5, 13; S. 633, 14. In niþrunge *in condemnatione*, Rtl. 24, 19. For đæs dæges nyþerunge *ad damnationem diei*, L. Ecg. P. add. 22; Th. ii. 236, 4: Bd. 5, 14; S. 635, 2. [*O. H. Ger.* nidarunga *damnatio*: cf. *Icel.* niđran *degradation*.]

niþer-weard; *adj. Downward, turned downwards*:—Neb is mīn niþerweard, Exon. Th. 403, 1; Rä. 22, 1: 416, 24; Rä. 35, 3. Niþerwearþ, 413, 15; Rä. 32, 6.

niþer-weardes, -weard; *adv. Downwards, in a downward direction*:—Niþerweardes *per praeceps*, Mt. Kmbl. Rush. 8, 32. Nyþerwerd *deorsum versum*, Ælfc. Gr. 38; Som. 41, 63. Niþerwurd *in praeceps, deorsum*, Hpt. Gl. 499, 66.

niþe-weard. v. neoþe-weard.

nīþ-full; *adj. Envious, malicious*:—Ǣfre biþ se nīþfulla (*envious*) man on gedrēfednysse, forđan đe se anda his mōd ǣlcere gāstlīcere blisse benǣmþ, Homl. Th. i. 606, 2. Se nīþfulla wer ... se gesibsuma wer *the malicious man ... the man that loves peace*, Basil admn. 6; Norm. 46, 20, 22, 30. Feóndes nīþfulles fācne *hostis invidi dolum*, Hymn. Surt. 3, 21. Đeós costung is of đam nīþfullan deófle, Boutr. Scrd. 23, 10. Nīþfullum *rancida, amara*, Hpt. Gl. 475, 73. Đā geseah se hālga wer đæs ārleásan preóstes nīþfullan ehtnysse, Homl. Th. ii. 162, 34. Nīþfulra *lividorum*, Hpt. Gl. 519, 69.

nīþful-līce; *adv. Maliciously, enviously*:—Gē đone rihtwīsan Crist nīþfullīce ācwealdon, Homl. Th. i. 46, 25.

nīþ-gæst, es; *m. A malicious, malignant guest*:—Hē đone nīþgæst (*the dragon*) slōh, Beo. Th. 5391; B. 2699. Under nīþgysta (*the devils who persecuted Guthlac*) nearwum clommum, Exon. Th. 134, 21; Gū. 511.

nīþ-geteón, es; *n. Injurious malice*:—Sigor āhwearf of norþmanna nīþgeteóne (*when Abraham defeated those who carried away Lot*), Cd. Th. 124, 26; Gen. 2068.

nīþ-geweorc, es; *n. Malicious, evil work*:—Đeáh hē (*Grendel*) rōf sīe nīþgeweorca, Beo. Th. 1370; B. 683.

nīþ-grim[m]; *adj. Savage, cruel*:—Nȳdwracu nīþgrim, nihtbealwa mǣst, Beo. Th. 388; B. 193. Mē beþeahton þeóstru nīþgrim, Ps. Th. 54, 5. Cf. hete-grim.

nīþ-gripe (?), es; *m. A hostile grasp*:—Hyne (*Grendel*) sār hafaþ in nīþgripe (MS. mid gripe, nīdgripe [?]) nearwe befongen, Beo. Th. 1956; B. 976.

nīþ-heard; *adj. Bold in battle, audacious*:—Nīþheard cyning (*Constantine*), Elen. Kmbl. 389; El. 195: (*Beowulf*), Beo. Th. 4826; B. 2417. Đā wearþ sum tō đæs ārod đara beadorinca, đæt hē in đæt būrgeteld nīþheard nēđde, Judth. Thw. 25, 25; Jud. 277. [Cf. *O. H. Ger.* Nīdhart (*proper name*).]

nīþ-hete, es; *m.* I. *rancorous hate, enmity*:—Āwehte đone wælnīþ Nabochodonossor þurh nīþhete, Cd. Th. 219, 2; Dan. 48. II. *affliction, grievous trouble*:—Đe hié generede wiđ đam nīþhete (*the fiery furnace*), 233, 22; Dan. 279. III. *malice, wickedness*:—Ǣfter nīþhete wiđmētednyssa heora *secundum nequitiam adinventionum ipsorum*, Ps. Spl. T. 27, 5. Cf. hete-nīþ.

nīþ-hete, es; *m. A malignant foe*:—Lēton đone hālgan bīdan burhwealle nēh, his nīþhetum, nihtlangne fyrst, Andr. Kmbl. 1667; An. 836. Cf. scyld-hete.

nīþ-hycgende *having hatred* or *malice in the heart*:—Slōgon eornoste Assiria oretmæcgas nīþhycgende nānne ne sparedon *with hate in their hearts Assyria's warriors they* (*the Hebrews*) *hewed, not one did they spare*, Judth. Thw. 24, 40; Jud. 233. Him (*Christ*) mid næglum þurhdrifan nīþhycgende đa hwītan honda, Exon. Th. 68, 28; Cri. 1110.

nīþ-hygdig; *adj. Having the mind disposed to strife, bold*:—Hyrsta swylce on horde ǣr nīþhȳdige men genumen hæfdon, Beo. Th. 6311; B. 3166. [*O. Sax.* nīđ-hugdig *maliciously disposed* (*applied to Herod and to the devil*).] Cf. nīþ-heard.

nīþing, es; *m. A villain, one who commits a vile action*:—Walreáf is nīþinges dǣde, L. Ath. iv. 7; Th. i. 228, 3. Se cing and eall here cwǣdon Swegen for nīþing (*Swegen had treacherously put Beorn to death*), Chr. 1049; Erl. 174, 31. [*Icel.* nīđingr *a villain*. v. Cl. & Vig. Dict.] v. un-nīþing.

nīþ-līce; *adv. Cowardly, meanly*:—Earhlīce ł nīþlīce *muliebriter*, Hpt. Gl. 424, 1.

nīþ-loca, an; *m. A place where one is shut up in misery*:—Under nīþloc[an] gebunden, under bealuclommum, Exon. Th. 463, 3; Hö. 64.

niþor. v. neoþor.

nīþ-plega, an; *m. Battle*, Andr. Kmbl. 827; An. 414.

niþre. v. niþere.

nīþ-sceađa, an; *m. A malignant foe*, Exon. Th. 397, 23; Rä. 16, 24.

nīþ-sele, es; *m. A hall where one is exposed to the hatred of a foe*:—[*Grein reads* niþ-sele *a hall low down, beneath the water*.] Hē [in] nīþsele nāthwylcum wæs, đǣr him nǣnig wæter wihte ne sceþede, Beo. Th. 3030; B. 1513.

nīþ-syn. v. nīd-syn.

niþþas, niþas; *pl. m.* (a poetical word used only in the plural) *Men*:—Niþþas findaþ gold, gumþeóda bearn, Cd. Th. 14, 27; Gen. 225. Niþþa bearna ǣrest ealra, 69, 14; Gen. 1135: 77, 33; Gen. 1284: Beo. Th. 2015; B. 1005: Exon. Th. 167, 34; Gū. 1070. Niþþa nergend, 140, 18; Gū. 612. Niþþa gehwylcum, 360, 15; Wal. 6. Geneósian niþa bearna ealra þeóda *ad visitandas omnes gentes*, Ps. Th. 58, 5: 65, 3: 71, 17. Niþa nāthwilc, Beo. Th. 4436; B. 2215. Niþa gehwam unāsecgendlīc, Elen. Kmbl. 928; El. 465. Hē from sceolde niþþum hweorfan *he must die*, Cd. Th. 74, 16; Gen. 1223: 75, 5; Gen. 1235. Hē is niþum swǣs, is đīn milde mōd ofer manna bearn, Ps. Th. 99, 4. Neáh is Drihten niþum eallum đe hine mid sōþe hige sēceaþ *prope est Dominus omnibus invocantibus eum in veritate*, 144, 19. Đū eart mihtum swīđ niþas tō nergenne, Cd. Th. 234, 1; Dan. 285. [*Goth.* nithjis *a kinsman*: *Icel.* niđr; *pl.* niđjar *a son, kinsman*.]

nīþ-weorc, es; *n. Battle, conflict*:—Nīþweorca heard *brave in battle*, Chr. 973; Erl. 124, 26.

nīþ-wracu; *gen.* -wræce; *f. Severe punishment*:—Đa fǣmnan hēt þurh nīþwræce nacode þennan, and mid sweopum swingan, Exon. Th. 253, 28; Jul. 187. Cwom Nabochodonossor of nīþwracum (*his exile among the beasts of the field*), Cd. Th. 257, 28; Dan. 664.

nīþ-wundor, es; *n. A wonder that bodes evil, a portent*:—Đǣr mæg nihta gehwæm nīþwundor (niþ-, Grein) seón, fȳr on flōde, Beo. Th. 2735; B. 1365.

níwan, neówan, neón; *adv. Recently, lately, newly*:—Níwan, neówan, *nuper*, Ælfc. Gr. 38; Som. 39, 58. Secgeaþ hí ðæt sume dæge ðider níwan (*nuper*) cóme cýpemen, Bd. 2, 1; S. 501, 4. Ða þing ðe ús níwan bodade syndon *ea quae nunc nobis nova praedicantur*, 2, 13; S. 516, 11. Ðonne man níwan wíf nymþ *cum acceperit homo nuper uxorem*, Deut. 24, 5. Ðone consul ðe hié ðá níwan geset hæfdon, Ors. 2, 6; Swt. 86, 32. Gif hwelc man biþ wíteþeów níwan geþeówad, L. In. 48; Th. i. 132, 7. Ic eom se ðe nú níwan com. Swilce hē swā cwǣde: Ic wæs geswutelod nū níwan, Glostr. Fragm. 10, 2-4. For ðære swīðlīcan ehtnysse ðe ðā níwan āsprang æfter Carines slege *on account of the fierce persecution that just then had sprung up after the murder of Carinus*, Homl. Skt. 5, 326. Gif hwā níwan tō mynstres drohtnunge gecyrran wyle *if a man's wish to turn to a monastic life is but newly formed*, R. Ben. 96, 3. Gelamp nýwan *it happened lately*, Nicod. Thw. 8, 27: 19, 37. Seó nūgyt neówan is becumen and gelǣded tō Godes geleáfan *quae* (*ecclesia Anglorum*) *nuper adhuc ad fidem adducta est*, Bd. 1, 27; S. 489, 12. Hē eów neón gesceód *lately he harmed you*, Andr. Kmbl. 2354; An. 1178. [Cf. *O. H. Ger.* níwanes *nuper.*] v. níwane.

níwan-ācenned *new-born*:—Ðā wæs broht tō fulwihte níwanācenned cild, Shrn. 130, 7. Cf. níw-cenned.

níwan-cumen *recently come* (*to a particular belief*), *a neophyte*:—Níwancumen *neofitus*, Wrt. Voc. ii. 59, 68. Cf. níw-cumen.

níwane; *adv. Lately, recently*:—Wēnaþ ðæt ðæt ne sīe eald gesceaft, ac síe geworden níwane, Bt. 39, 3; Fox 216, 4. v. níwan.

níw-bacen; *adj. New-baked*:—Wē mid ūs nāmon nīgbacene hlāfas *panes calidos sumpsimus*, Jos. 9, 12.

níw-cealct, -cilct *newly white-washed*:—On ānum nīcealtan (nīwcilctan, MS. C.) hūse *in cubiculo nuper calce illito*, Ors. 6, 32; Swt. 286, 30.

níw-cenned, -cend *new-born*:—Mid hyre nīcendum cilde *cum recens nato parvulo*, Bd. 2, 16; S. 520, 1.

níw-cumen *newly come* (*to a particular belief*), *a neophyte*:—Nīcumen *neophytus*, Hpt. Gl. 480, 12. Se sylfa nīgcumena (nīcumena, nīgcumene) brōðor, R. Ben. 101, 15. Be nīgcumenra (nīcumenra, Wells, Frag.) gebrōðra andfenge, 97, 2. Tǣce him mon siððan tō nīgcumenra manna hūse, 97, 11. v. níwan-cumen.

níwe, neówe; *adj.* I. *new, not yet used*:—Ne āsend nān scyp of níwum reáfe on eald reáf; elles ðæt níwe slít, and se níwa scyp ne hylp ðam ealdan, Lk. Skt. 5, 36. Smyre mid níre (MS. B. ānre) feþere, Lchdm. i. 234, 13. Hē lēde hyne on hys níwan byrgene, Mt. Kmbl. 27, 60. Gē ðǣr gemētaþ níwe byrgenne, Blickl. Homl. 147, 30. II. *new, recent, not of long standing, not long made*:—Nān man ne sent níwe wīn on ealde bytta; elles ðæt níwe wīn brycþ ða bytta . . . Ac níwe wīn is tō sendenne on níwe bytta . . . And ne drincþ nān man eald wīn and wylle sōna ðæt níwe, Lk. Skt. 5, 37-39. Ðā hē (*the Roman name*) com ǣrest tō Parþum, and wæs ðǣr swīðe níwe, Bt. 18, 2; Fox 64, 13. Níwe mōna *neomenia*, Wrt. Voc. i. 16, 51. Se níwa *neophytus*, ii. 60, 64. Seó (*the English Church*) nūgyt is níwe on geleáfan, Bd. 489, 41. Ðý læs se steall swā níwre cyricean tealtrian ongunne, 2, 4; S. 505, 11. Ðis gelimpþ seldon, and nǣfre būton on níwum mōnan, Lchdm. iii. 242, 23. Nō on níwan wylme, ac on lancsumere mynsteres drohtnunge, R. Ben. 9, 6. Hē ðone winter mid ðý níwan folce (*the newly converted Frisians*) wunode, Bd. 5, 19; S. 639, 26. Níwan stefne *anew*, Cd. Th. 94, 1; Gen. 1555: Andr. Kmbl. 245; An. 123. Nióẃan, Beo. Th. 3582; B. 1789. On swā nióẃan gefeán, Andr. Kmbl. 3336; An. 1672. Ðā sceáwode Scyppend ūre his weorca wlite, níwra gesceafta, Cd. Th. 13, 25; Gen. 208: 55, 4; Gen. 889. On ðisum níwum dagum *in these modern times*, Homl. Th. i. 608, 23: Homl. Skt. 13, 177. Brembel ðe síen begen endas on eorþan; genim ðone neówran wyrttruman, Lchdm. ii. 292, 1. III. *new* (*to anything*), *inexperienced*:—Swā swīðe swā ða níwan Cristenan hit niman mihte *in quantum rudes capere poterant*, Bd. 3, 22; S. 553, 10. Ðǣm níwum *neotericis*, Wrt. Voc. ii. 60, 58. Ðæt is ðæt mon ða earce bere on ðǣm saglum ðætte ða gōdan lāreówas ða hālgan gesomnunge lǣrende ða níwan (niéwan, Cott. MSS.) and ða ungeleáffullan mōd mid hira lāre gelǣde tō ryhtum geleáfan *vectibus arcam portare est bonis doctoribus sanctam ecclesiam ad rudes infidelium mentes praedicando deducere*, Past. 22, 2; Swt. 171, 13. Níwa lāre *rudimenta*, Rtl. 80, 3. IV. *new, novel, different from what has gone before*:—Ārās níwe cing ðe nyste hwæt Iosep wæs, Ex. 1, 8. Hasterbal se níwa cyning *Asdrubal novus imperator*, Ors. 4, 6; Swt. 176, 33. Hwæt is ðeós níwe lār, Mk. Skt. 1, 27. Níwe circhālgung (v. cyric-hālgung) *encenia*, Wrt. Voc. i. 16, 52. Calic níwre ǣ (*novi testamenti*), Mt. Kmbl. 26, 28. Nemde níwan stefne; nama wæs gecyrred, Elen. Kmbl. 2119; El. 1061. Him ne wæs nǣnig earfoþe ðæt līchomlīce gedāl on ðære neówan wyrde (*in their new condition*), Blickl. Homl. 135, 31. Ic eów sylle níwe bebod, Jn. Skt. 13, 34. Singaþ Drihtne neówne sang, Ps. Th. 149, 1: Ps. Surt. 32, 3. Hí hæfdon neówne gefeán gemēted, Elen. Kmbl. 1737; El. 870. Fægere word ðis synd . . . ac forðon hí níwe syndon and uncūþe, Bd. 1, 25; S. 487, 9. Lyt swīgode níwra spella, se ðe næs gerād, Beo. Th. 5788; B. 2898. Hí sprecaþ níwum tungum, Mk. Skt. 16, 17. Gelǣrdan biscepas swelce níwe rǣdas swelce hié fol oft ǣr ealde gedydan, Ors. 4, 7; Swt. 184, 2. Singaþ sangas neówe, Ps. Th. 95, 1. [*Goth.* niujis: *O. Sax.* níwi: *O. Frs.* níe: *O. H. Ger.* niuwi, níwi *novus, recens, rudis, modernus.*] v. ed-níwe.

níwe, níge; *adv. Newly, recently*:—Wē níwe syndon tō ðissum geleáfan gedōn *we are newly turned to this faith*, Blickl. Homl. 247, 34. Syððan heó níge cealfod hæfþ *after it* (*a cow*) *has recently calved*, L. R. S. 13; Th. i. 438, 19. Sceal mon lācnian swilce ādle mid cū meolcum oððe gāte swā níge molcene drince (*or let him drink goat's milk as newly milked as possible*), Lchdm. ii. 218, 22: 222, 13. v. níwan.

niwel. v. neowol.

níw-fara, an; *m. A new-comer, a stranger*:—Ic eom nífara hider on eorþan beforan ðē and ælþeódig *incola ego sum apud te in terra, et peregrinus*, Ps. Th. 38, 15.

níw-gecirred *newly converted*:—Nīgecerred *neophytus, novellus*, Hpt. 488, 4.

níw-gehālgod *newly consecrated*:—Hieu se nīgehālgode (nīghālgoda) cynincg, Homl. Skt. 18, 326.

níw-gehwirfed *newly converted*:—Ðæt hē ða nīgehwyrfedan (nīghwurfedan, MS. C.; nīghwerfdan, MS. V.) mid fulluhte āþwōge, Homl. Skt. 5, 126.

níw-hwirfed *newly converted*:—Nīhwurfed ł nīlǣred *neophytus*, Hpt. Gl. 480, 13. v. preceding word.

níw-hworfen *newly converted*:—Betwux ðam nīghworfenum folce (*the recently converted people of Kent*), Homl. Th. ii. 130, 27.

níwian; *p.* ode *To renew, renovate, restore*:—Nū mē Sethes bearn torn níwiaþ, Cd. Th. 76, 16; Gen. 1258. Hē níwade Cnutes lage (v. Freeman's Old English History, p. 241), Chr. 1064; Erl. 196, 2. Ne wrec ðū ða ǣrran yflu, būton hí mon eft níwige, Prov. Kmbl. 35. Swā ðæt ðū ǣghwylce dæg ðone drenc níwie (níwige, MS. B.), Lchdm. i. 192, 15. Burh rǣran, and sele settan, salo níwian, Cd. Th. 113, 3; Gen. 1881. Sār níwigan, Elen. Kmbl. 1878; El. 941. Eft níwige *emendare*, Mt. Kmbl. p. 2, 12. Wǣren ǣrendracen gesend tō Ængla lande tō níwianne ðone geleáfan, Chr. 785; Erl. 57, 17. Eorþan neówiende anseón *terrae novas faciem*, Hymn. Surt. 97, 34. [*Chauc.* newe: *Goth.* ana-niujan: *O. Sax.* níwian: *O. H. Ger.* niuwōn, níwōn *novare.*] v. ed-, ge-níwian.

ni-wiht *nothing*:—Tō niwihte *ad nihilum*, Ps. Surt. 59, 14. v. nā-wiht.

níwinga, níw-lǣred. v. níwunga, níw-hwyrfed.

níw-líc; *adj. New, fresh*:—Bearn ðīne swā swā nýwlīcra elebergena *filii tui sicut nouellae oliuarum*, Ps. Lamb. 127, 3.

níwlíce; *adv. Newly, recently*:—Níwan *nuper*, níwlīcor *nuperius*, níwlīcost *nuperime*, Ælfc. Gr. 38; Som. 42, 11. Hēr cumaþ tō eów níwlīce twegen men, Homl. Th. ii. 494, 7. Hí hæfdon níwlīce gesett *they had recently decreed*, Ors. 4, 10; Swt. 202, 26. Hió ðā wæs níwlīce cristen, 6, 4; Swt. 260, 12.

níwness, e; *f. Newness, novelty*:—Ne sceal him mon ānne mete gebeódan, ac missenlīce, ðæt seó nióẃnes ðara metta mǣge him gōde beón, Lchdm. ii. 240, 15. Ðæs mōnan níwnys, Anglia viii. 310, 38. Ðā wæs se dēma mid ða neównysse (*novitate*) swā monigra heofonlīcra wundra swýðe gedrēfed, Bd. 1, 7; S. 478, 44. Míne níwnysse *juventutem meam*, Ps. Lamb. 42, 4.

niwol. v. neowol.

níw-tirwed *new-tarred*:—Flotan níwtyrwdne, Beo. Th. 595; B. 295.

níwung, e; *f. A beginning, rudiment*:—Níwunge *rudimenta*, Hpt. Gl. 428, 18. v. níwe, III.

níwunga; *adv. Anew*:—Níwunga (nióẃunga, Rush.) *denuo*, Mk. Skt. Lind. 14, 40. Niúnge (nióẃunga, Rush.), Jn. Skt. 3, 3. Neówinga, Andr. Kmbl. 2787; An. 1396. v. ed-níwinga.

níwerne; *adj. Young, tender*:—Sum wíf mid hire nýwerenan (MS. Bodl. niwernan, *glossed by* tenero) cilde, Homl. Th. i. 566, 5.

nixtnig. v. nihstnig.

nō, nōh, nōht, nolde, nom-, noma. v. nā, ge-nōh, nā-wiht, nyllan, nam-, nama.

nōn, es; *n.* I. *the ninth hour*; hora nona:—Prím *prima*; undern *tertia*; middæg *sexta*; nōn *nona*; ǣfen *vesperum*, Wrt. Voc. i. 53, 10-15: R. Ben. 40, 13. Ða nigoþan tīde ðe wē nōn hātaþ, Homl. Th. ii. 256, 35. Ðā com nōn dæges, Beo. Th. 3204; B. 1600. Hí him tō gewunon nāman ðæt hí fæston tō nōnes (*ad horam nonam*), Bd. 3, 5; S. 527, 9. Tō hwīl nōnes *ad horam nonam*, Mt. Kmbl. Lind. 27, 45, 46. On tīde nōnes, Mk. Skt. Rush. 15, 33, 34. Tō underne and tō nōne . . . and tō middæge, Lchdm. iii. 218-222, often. Fram middæge ōþ nōn, H. R. 107, 9. Sele drincan on undern, on middæg, on nōn, Lchdm. ii. 140, 2. II. *the service held at the ninth hour, nones*:—Wē sungon nōn *cantavimus nonam*, Coll. Monast. Th. 33, 35. [*O. Sax.* nōn, nuon: *Icel.* nōn; *n. nones, about three o'clock.*] v. ofer-nōn.

non, es; *m. The title given to the older by the younger monks*:—Ða yldran hyra gingran brōðor nemnen, and ða gingran hyra yldran nonnos (nonas, Wells, Frag.) nemnen, R. Ben. 115, 19. v. nunne.

nōn-gereord, es; *n. A repast after the service of nones*:—Siððan hý đone forman cnyl tō nōne gehȳren, gangen hȳ ealle from hyra weorce and dōn hȳ gearuwe, đæt hȳ māgon tō cirican gān, đonne mon eft cnylle. Đonne eft æfter heora nōngereorde rǽdan hȳ eft heora bēc, R. Ben. 74, 8.

nōn-mete, es; *m. An afternoon meal*:—Nōnmete *merenda*, Wrt. Voc. i. 38, 14: *annona*, 291, 2: ii. 8, 67. On xii mōnþum đū scealt sillan đīnum þeówan men vii hund hlāfa and xx hlāfa, būton morgenmetum and nōnmetum, Salm. Kmbl. p. 192, 19. [*Prompt. Parv.* nunmete *merenda*, p. 360. v. note there.]

nōn-sang, es; *m. The service held at the ninth hour, nones*:—Đa seofon tīdsangas . . . nōnsang, L. Ælfc. C. 19; Th. ii. 350, 7. *De officio nonae horae* (nōnsang), Btwk. 216, 31: R. Ben. 39, 19: 40, 7. Nōnsang wē singaþ *nonam psallimus*, Hymn. Surt. 60, 35.

nōn-tīd, e; *f. The ninth hour*:—On undern, on midne dæg, on nōntīde, Homl. Th. ii. 74, 9.

nōn-tīma, an; *m. The ninth hour*:—On nōntīman wē sculon God herian, forđam on đone tīman Crist gebæd for đām đe him deredon, and siđđan his gāst āsende, Btwk. 216, 31.

Normandīg, e; *f. Normandy*:—Willelm cyng fōr ofer sǽ tō Normandīg, and Eádgār cild com of Scotland tō Normandīge, Chr. 1074; Erl. 212, 3–4.

Nor-men. v. Norþ-mann.

Norren, Noren; *adj. Norse, Norwegian*:—Se Norrena cyng, Chr. 1066; Erl. 201, 12. Ōlaf đæs Norna cynges sunu, 201, 34. [*Icel.* Norrœnn, Norœnn.]

[norþ]; *adj. In a northerly position*:—Đæt folc đe tō đære norþerran byrig hiérde, Chr. 922; Erl. 108, 19. Hēt Eádweard cyning ātymbran đa norþran burg, 913; Erl. 100, 34. On đǽm dagum wæs đæt norþmeste [rīce] micliende, Ors. 6, 1; Swt. 252, 12. Sciþþie đa norþmestan 1, 7; Swt. 40, 6. Ōþ đa norþmestan næssan on eorþan, Met. 9, 43. [*Icel.* nyrđri, norđari; nyrđstr, norđastr.] *See the compounds of which* norþ *forms the first part.*

norþ; *adv. In a northerly direction* or *position*:—Đæt is norþ ehta hund mīla lang, Bd. 1, 1; S. 473, 11. Hié Baldred norþ ofer Temese ādrifon, Chr. 823; Erl. 62, 20. Hié fōron norþ ymbūtan, 894; Erl. 91, 6. Symle swā norþor swā smælre *ever the further north, the narrower*, Ors. 1, 1; Swt. 18, 29. Hē ealra Norþmonna norþmest būde, 17, 2. [*O. Sax.* nord: *O. Frs.* north: *Icel.* norđarr; *cpve.*; norđast; *super.*]

norþan; *adv. From the north*:—Se wind se đe ǽr sūþan bleów, hine norþan āwearp, Bd. 2, 7; S. 509, 28. Gif hēr wind cymþ westan ođđe eástan, sūþan ođđe norþan, Cd. Th. 50, 11; Gen. 807. See following words.

norþan-eástan; *adv. From the north-east*:—Đonne se stearca wind cymþ norþan-eástan, Bt. 9; Fox 26, 19.

norþan-eástan *in* be norþan-eástan *to the north-east*, Ors. 1, 1; Swt. 24, 10: 16, 18.

norþan-eástan-wind *a north-east wind*; eurus, euroauster, circius, Wrt. Voc. 1, 36, 13, 17. [Cf. *O. H. Ger.* nordōstir-wint *aquilo*.]

Norþan-hymbre; *pl. The Northumbrians, Northumbria, the people* or *province north of the Humber*:—Hēr Ida fēng tō rīce, đonon Norþanhymbra cynecyn onwōc, Chr. 547; Erl. 16, 7. Đǽr wæs ungemetlīc wæl geslægen Norþanhymbra, 867; Erl. 72, 15. Norþanhymbra mǽgþ đe Ceólwulf ofer is, Bd. 5, 24; S. 646, 28. Hēr fōr se here of Eást-Englum on Norþanhymbre, Chr. 867; Erl. 73, 7. v. Norþ-hymbre.

norþan-weard; *adj. Northward*:—Sanctus Paulus wæs geseónde on norþanweardne đisne middangeard, Blickl. Homl. 209, 30. Đa Pyhtas gefērdon đis land norþanweard *the Picts occupied the north of this land*, Chr. Erl. 3, 13.

norþan-westan; *adv. From the north-west*; a circio, Hpt. Gl. 512, 11: Wrt. Voc. ii. 3, 44: 98, 40.

norþan-westan *in* be norþan-westan *to the north-west*, Ors. 1, 1; Swt. 16, 5.

norþan-westan-wind *a wind from the north-west*; corus, aquilo *vel* boreas, Wrt. Voc. i. 36, 16, 18. [Cf. *O. H. Ger.* nortwesterwint *circius*.]

norþan-wind *a wind from the north*:—Norþanwind *septentrio*, Wrt. Voc. i. 36, 11. Đæs norþanwindes ȳst, Bt. 9; Fox 26, 20. Stearc stormas and norþanwindas, 23; Fox 78, 27. v. norþ-wind.

norþ-dǽl, es; *m.* I. *a northern part*:—Middaneardes norþdǽl *Europa*, Hpt. Gl. 512, 20. Sió hǽte hæfþ genumen đæs sūþdǽles māre đonne se cyle đæs norþdǽles hæbbe, Ors. 1, 1; Swt. 24, 29. Nū hæbbe wē āwriten đære Asian sūþdǽl; nū wille wē fōn tō hire norþdǽle, Swt. 14, 6. Sittan on đam norþdǽle heofenan rīces, Homl. Th. i. 10, 25: Cd. Th. 3, 8; Gen. 32. Norþdǽl *aquilonem*, Ps. Th. 89, 11. Hē wæs mid firde farende on Sciþþie on đa norþdǽlas, Ors. 1, 10; Swt. 44, 7. Peohtas ongunnon eardigan đa norþdǽlas đysses eálondes, Bd. 1, 1; S. 474, 18. II. *the north*:—Breoton is geseted betwyh norþdǽle and westdǽle *Britannia inter septentrionem et occidentem locata est*, S. 473, 9. Đonne āstīgeþ blōdig wolcen from norþdǽle, Blickl. Homl. 91, 32.

Norþ-Dene; *pl. The North-Danes*, Beo. Th. 1571; B. 783: Ors. 1, 1; Swt. 16, 25, 27.

norþ-duru *a door on the north side of a building*:—Beforan đære norþdura, Blickl. Homl. 203, 34. [*Icel.* norđr-dyrr; *n. pl.*]

norþ-eást; *adv. North-east.* v. following words.

norþeást-ende *the north-east end*:—Ōþ đone norþeástende đisses middangeardes, Ors. 1, 1; Swt. 14, 14.

norþeást-lang; *adj. Long in a north-easterly direction*:—Brittania is norþeástlang *Britannia per longum in boream extenditur*, Ors. 1, 1; Swt. 24, 12.

norþ-ende *the north end* or *part*:—Đȳ þriddan dæge seó eorþe on đæm norþende and on đam eástende sprecaþ him betweónum, Blickl. Homl. 93, 11. Đone norþende đære eaxe (*the north-pole*), Met. 28, 14.

Norþ-Engle; *pl. The inhabitants of the north of England*:—On Norþ-Engla lage stent . . . be Norþ-Engla lage, L. Eth. vii. 13; Th. i. 332, 7–10.

norþerne; *adj.* I. *northern*:—Norþerne ȳst, Met. 6, 14. Norþerne wind *africum*, Ps. Lamb. 77, 26. Of Japhet com đæt norþerne mennisc be đære norþsǽ . . . Europa on norþdǽle [is gedǽled] Japhetes ofspringe, Ælfc. T. Grn. 4, 37. Hine gelǽhton sume đæs norþernan folces *some of the Northumbrians seized him* (*after a battle between Northumbrians and Mercians*), Homl. Th. ii. 356, 29. Đa norþerne men *the men from the north of England*, Chr. 1064; Erl. 196, 2. II. applied to the Scandinavians:—Guma norþerna (guman norþerne, other MSS.), 937; Erl. 112, 18. Godrum se norþerna cyning, 890; Erl. 86, 27.

norþe-weard; *adj. Northward, north*:—Norþeweard, đǽr hit smalost wǽre, hit mihte beón þreora mīla brād tō đæm mōre *the northern part of Norway, where it was narrowest, might be three miles broad to the mountains*, Ors. 1, 1; Swt. 18, 31. Đonne is tōemnes đæm lande sūþeweardum Sweóland, ōþ đæt land norþeweard; and tōemnes đæm lande norþeweardum Cwēna land *alongside the south of the country* (*Norway*), *up to its northern part, lies Sweden; and alongside its northern part the country of the Fins*, Swt. 19, 1–3. Đæt Babylonicum wæs đæt forme, and on eásteweardum; đæt æfterre wæs đæt Crēcisce, and on norþeweardum, 2, 1; Swt. 60, 3. Æt Baddanbyrg westeweardre and norþeweardre . . . of foxhylle norþeweardre, Cod. Dip. Kmbl. ii. 249, 26, 34. From easteweardan đisses middangeardes ōþ westeweardne, and fram sūþeweardum ōþ norþeweardne, Bt. 18, 1; Fox 62, 2. v. norþ-weard.

norþ-folc, es; *n. The northern division of a people*; (a) *the people of the north of England*:—Humbre tōsceádeþ sūþfolc Angelþeóde and norþfolc, Bd. 1, 25; S. 486, 18. (b) *the people of Norfolk, Norfolk*:—Hē wæs geboren on Norþfolce. Đā geaf se cyng his sunu đone eorldōm on Norþfolc and Sūþfolc, Chr. 1075; Erl. 213, 4–5: 1085; Erl. 218, 21.

norþ-gemǽre *a boundary to the north*:—Đara landa norþgemǽro sindon æt đǽm beorgum Caucasus, Ors. 1, 1; Swt. 10, 26, 33.

Norþ-Gyrwas; *pl. The northern division of the Gyrwas*:—Norþ-Gyrwa syxhund hȳda, Cod. Dip. B. i. 414, 19.

Norþhāmtūn *Northampton*:—Ne innan Lægreceastre scīre, ne innan Norþhāmtūne, Chr. 1087; Erl. 224, 36.

norþ-healf, e; *f. The north-side, the north*:—Æt đæs weofudes sīdan đe ys on norþhealfe *ad latus altaris, quod respicit ad aquilonem*, Lev. 1, 11: Blickl. Homl. 209, 1: Ps. 47, 2: Ors. 1, 1; Swt. 12, 13: Swt. 22, 13. [*Icel.* norđr-hālfa *northern region*: *O. H. Ger.* nord-halba *the north side*.]

norþ-here, es; *m. An army belonging to the north*:—Heó (*the English force*) gehergade swīđe micel on đæm norþhere, ǽgđer ge on mannum ge on gehwelces cynnes yrfe, and manega men ofslōgon đara Deniscena, Chr. 910; Erl. 100, 13.

Norþ-hymbre; *pl. The Northumbrians, Northumbria, the people* or *province north of the Humber*:—Norþhymera cyning, Homl. Th. ii. 356, 23. Norþhymbra cining, Chr. 761; Erl. 53, 15. Hēr bræc se here on Norþhymbrum đone friþ, 911; Erl. 100, 16. Hēr fōr se here on Norþhymbre, 867; Erl. 72, 7: 873; Erl. 76, 18. v. Norþan-hymbre.

Norþ-hymbre; *adj. Northumbrian*:—Đa Norþhymbran leóde, Swt. A. S. Rdr. 95, 9.

Norþ-hymbrisc; *adj. Northumbrian*:—Tō Norþhymbriscum gereorde, Swt. A. S. Rdr. 97, 58.

norþ-land *a northern land*:—Hē fōr on Sciđđie đa norþland, Ors. 1, 2; Swt. 30, 3.

norþ-lane *a north lane*:—Ōþ norþlanan tō strǽte, Cod. Dip. Kmbl. i. 1, 15.

norþ-leóde; *pl. The north-folk of England, Angles*:—Norþleóda cynges gild (đæs cyninges wergyld mid Engla cynne), L. Wg. 1; Th. i. 186, 2.

norþ-līc; *adj. Northern*:—Đære norþlīcan *boreali*, Wrt. Voc. ii. 12, 46.

Norþ-mann, es; *m. A man belonging to a northern country.* I. *a Norseman, Norwegian* or *Dane*:—Ealle đa đe on Norþhymbrum būgeaþ, ǽgþer ge Englisce ge Denisce ge Norþmen, Chr. 924; Erl. 110, 17. Gewitan him đā Norþmen nægledcnearrum, 937; Erl. 115, 2. Đa Cwēnas hergiaþ hwīlum on đa Norþmen (*Norwegians*) ofer đone mōr, hwīlum da Norþmen on hý, Ors. 1, 1; Swt. 19, 3–5: 16, 36. Ða Normen âhton sige, Chr. 1066; Erl. 199, 40: 200, 26. Hé sǽde ðæt Norþmanna land (*Norway*) wǽre swýðe lang and swýðe smæl, Swt. 18, 24. Hé (*Ohthere from Halgoland*) ealra Norþmonna norþmest búde, 17, 2. On his dagum cómon ǽrest iii scipu Norþmanna . . . Ðæt wǽron ða érestan scipu Deniscra manna ðe Angelcynnes land gesóhton, Chr. 787; Erl. 57, 21–25. Ðǽr geflémed wearþ Norþmanna bregu, 937; Erl. 112, 33. Wǽran ǽr under Norþmannum, 942; Erl. 116, 15. *The word occurs as a proper name*:—Norþman Leófwines sunu, 1017; Erl. 161, 6. II. referring to other countries:—Norþmen (*those who attacked Sodom*), Cd. Th. 120, 16; Gen. 1995. Norþmonna, 124, 25; Gen. 2068. Norþmonnum, 119, 9; Gen. 1977. [*Icel.* norð-maðr *a Norwegian*: *O. H. Ger.* nord-man.]

norþmest. v. norþ; *adj. adv.*

Norþ-Mirce; *pl. The North-Mercians*:—Wið Norþ-Myrcum, Bd. 3, 24; S. 557, 37.

norþ-portic *a north-porch*:—On ðære cyricean norþportice *in porticu aquilonali*, Bd. 2, 3; S. 557, 37.

Norþriga, an; *m. A Norwegian*:—Cnut cyningc ealles Engla landes cyningc, and Dena cyningc, and Norþrigena cyningc, L. C. E. pref.; Th. i. 358, 4.

norþ-rihte; *adv. Due north*:—Ðá fór hé norþryhte be ðæm lande *he sailed due north along the coast*, Ors. 1, 1; Swt. 17, 9, 12.

norþ-rodor *the north part of the sky*, Exon. Th. 178, 33; Gú. 1253.

norþ-sǽ *a northern sea*:—Norþsǽ *mare arctoum*, Wrt. Voc. i. 41, 66. Of Japhet com ðæt norþerne mennisc be ðære norþsǽ, Ælfc. T. Grn. 4, 38. Án geweorc on Defnascíre be ðære norþsǽ, Chr, 894; Erl. 91, 8. [*Icel.* norðr-sjór.]

norþ-sceáta *a northern promontory*, Ors. 1, 1; Swt. 28, 3.

Norþ-Scottas *the Northern Scots*, Bd. 3, 3; S. 526, 12.

norþ-þeód *a northern people*:—Hergung ðara norþþeóda (*the peoples who harried Britain after the Romans went*), Bd. 1, 14; S. 482, 38.

Norþ-Walas, -wealas; *pl. The Welsh, Wales*:—Ða cyningas on Norþ-Wealum, Howel and Cledanc, Chr. 922; Erl. 108, 27. Se here . . . hergodon ǽgðer ge on Cornwealum and on Norþ-Wealum, 997; Erl. 134, 9. Ælfgár eorl gesóhte Griffines geheald on Norþ-Wealan, 1055; Erl. 190, 3. Ecgbryht lǽdde fierd on Norþ-Walas, 828; Erl. 64, 12: 853; Erl. 68, 10. Hí hergodon on Norþ-Wealas, 918; Erl. 102, 25.

Norþ-Wealh-cynn, es; *n. The Welsh*, Chr. 922; Erl. 108, 28. Sum dǽl ðæs Norþ-Wealcynnes, 894; Erl. 92, 21.

norþ-weard; *adj. North*:—Hé búde on ðæm lande norþweardum, Ors. 1, 1; Swt. 17, 3. v. norþe-weard.

norþ-weard; *adv. Northward*:—Hé éfste norþweard, Chr. 1016; Erl. 154, 28.

norþweardes; *adv. Northwards*:—Hié ða herehýþ woldon ferian norþweardes ofer Temese, Chr. 894; Erl. 90, 23.

norþ-weg *a way going to the north*:—Nearwe genýddon on norþwegas wiston him be súþan Sigelwara land, Cd. Th. 181, 29; Exod. 68. [*Icel.* norðr-vegar; *pl.*]

norþ-west; *adv. North-west*:—Se þridda [gâra líþ] norþwest, Ors. 1, 1; Swt. 24, 5.

norþwest-ende *the north-west end*:—Thyle is on ðam norþwestende ðisses middaneardes, Bt. 29, 3; Fox 106, 24: Ors. 5, 3; Swt. 220, 23.

norþwest-gemǽre *a north-west boundary*:—Ðære Affrica norþwestgemǽre is æt ðæm ilcan Wendelsǽ, Ors. 1, 1; Swt. 8, 31.

Norþ-wíc *Norwich*:—Hér com Swegen tó Norþwíc . . . Ðá gerǽdde Ulfkytel wið ða witan on Eást-Englum, Chr. 1004; Erl. 139, 17. Ðá geaf se cyng his sunu ðone eorldóm on Norþfolc and Súþfolc; ðá lǽdde hé ðæt wíf tó Norþwíc, 1075; Erl. 213, 6.

norþ-wind *a north wind*:—Twegen norþwindas *circius et boreus*, Wrt. Voc. ii. 21, 55. [*O. H. Ger.* nord-wind *aquilo, boreas.*] v. norþan-wind.

Norweg, es; *m.* [*The plural seems the more usual form.*] *Norway*:—Sume férdon tó Norwæge, Chr. 1070; Erl. 209, 30. Hér fór Cnut cyng tó Norwegum (Norwegon, Erl. 162, 37), 1028; Erl. 163, 13. Hér com Óláf cyng eft intó Norwegum, 1030; Erl. 163, 16. Harold cyng of Norwegon, 1066; Erl. 199, 37. Com Harold of Norwegan, Erl. 200, 12. Harold cyng on Norwegan, 200, 18, 27, 34, 40. [*Icel.* Noregr, *occasionally* Norvegr (vegr = *way*).]

nose. v. nosu.

nos-, nosu-gristle *the gristle* or *cartilage of the nose*:—Nosgrisele *internasus*, Wrt. Voc. ii. 48, 31. Nosugrisle *cartilago*, i. 64, 49. v. *under* nosu.

nosle. v. nostle.

nos-þyrel, -þyrl, -terl, es; *n. A nostril*:—Dó on ðæt næsþyrl (nos-, MS. B.), Lchdm. i. 352, 4. Nosþyrla *nares*, Wrt. Voc. i. 43, 19. Úteweard nosterle *pinnulae*, 43, 22. Nosterla hǽr *vibrissae*, 21, 52. Se brǽþ on heora nosþyrlum, Homl. ii. 98, 9. Dó on ða næsþyrlu (nos-, MS. B.), Lchdm. i. 72, 21. [*Chauc.* nose-thirl, -þril: *Wick.* nose-, nese-þirl, -þril: *Prompt. Parv.* nese-thyrlys, *naris*: *O. Frs.* nosterle.] v. næs-þyrel.

nostle, nosle, an; *f. A fillet, band*:—Nostle *fascia*, Wrt. Voc. i. 26, 8: *ansa*, ii. 6, 34. Nosle *vel* sárcláþ *fasciola*, i. 40, 62. Nostlena *vittarum*, ii. 87, 65. Mid nostlum (noslum, Hatt. MS.) gebunden, Past. 13, 2; Swt. 86, 10.

nosu, neosu; *gen.* a *and* e; *also* an; *f.* I. *the nose*:—Nosu *nasus*, Wrt. Voc. ii. 62, 4: i. 43, 17: 64, 48: *naris*, ii. 60, 37: *nasus* vel *naris*, i. 70, 29. Eal ufweard nosu *columna*; foreweard nosu *pirula*, 43, 18, 21. Eal nosu *columna*, ii. 16, 49. Nose grystle *internasus* vel *interfinium*, i. 43, 20. *Odoratus* stænc on ðæra nosa, Homl. Skt. 1, 198. Wið ðæt hwam on nosa (nosan, MS. B.) wexe, Lchdm. i. 116, 11. Se ðe hæfþ miccle nosu *nasatus*, Ælfc. Gr. 43; Som. 45, 10: Past. 11, 1; Swt. 65, 3–4. Hé hæfþ medemlíce nosu, Homl. i. 456, 18: 568, 33. Hé hæfde midmycle nosu þynne, Bd. 2, 16; S. 519, 34. Wið blódryne of nosum, Lchdm. i. 72, 17: 352, 3. Gif hwylcum weargbrǽde weaxe on ðám nosum, 86, 1. Wé gestincaþ mid úrum nosum, Past. 56; Swt. 433, 20: Bd. 5, 12; S. 628, 42. Ða telgran habbaþ ǽgðer ge eágon ge nosa (nosan, MS. B.), Lchdm. i. 318, 11. Nose hí habbaþ *nares habent*, Ps. Th. 134, 17: 113, 14. II. *a ness, a piece of land projecting into water*:—Of hliþes nosan, Beo. Th. 3789; B. 1892. Æt brimes nosan, 5599; B. 2803. Cf. næss, næssa. [*Laym.* neose, nose: *O. E. Homl.* nease: *A. R.* neose: *Havel.* nese: *Prompt. Parv.* nese, nose: *Chauc.* nose: *O. Frs.* nose: *Icel.* nös: *O. H. Ger.* nasa.] v. nasu.

not, es; *m. A mark, sign*:—Mé þingþ wynsumlíc ðæt ic ðæra preósta notas ðám bócerum gekýðe ðé læs ðe hig witan ðæt ða rímcræftige weras sýn bútan cræftigum getácnungum, Anglia viii. 333, 17–19. v. wæl-not.

-note. v. ǽ-note.

notere, es; *m. One who makes notes*:—Notera ł wrítera *notariorum*, Hpt. Gl. 473, 12. v. not-writere.

nóþ, e; *f.* I. *temerity, presumption, boldness, daring*:—Ðú sylfa meaht gecnáwan ðæt ic ðisse nóþe wæs nýde gebǽded ðæt ic ðé sóhte *thyself may'st know, that I was by need compelled to the presumption of visiting thee*, Exon. Th. 263, 1; Jul. 343. II. *an adventurous band* (?):—Semninga on sealtne wǽg mid ða nóþe (*the sailors who have landed on the whale thinking it an island*) niþer gewíteþ gársecges gæst (*the whale*), 361, 31; Wal. 28. [*O. H. Ger.* nand *temeritas, praesumtio.*] v. néþan.

nóþ *occurs often as a component of proper names.* v. Txts. 642.

nóðer. v. ná-hwæðer.

notian; *p.* ode. I. *to make use of, employ, enjoy*; (a) *with gen.*:—Gif ðú his wel notast hwæt biþ wæstmbǽrre *if you make good use of it* (*dung*), *what is more productive?* Homl. Th. ii. 408, 34. Ða ðe ðisses middangeardes notigaþ swelce hí his nó ne notigen *qui utuntur hoc mundo, tanquam non utantur*, Past. 50, 2; Swt. 389, 1–2. Eall moncyn and ealle nétenu ne notigaþ náwér neáh feórþan dǽles ðisse eorþan, Bt. 18, 1; Fox 62, 8. Ðæt hý (*garments*) synd gemǽte ðám ðe hyra notiaþ, R. Ben. 89, 19. Nota ðæs wísdómes ðe ðú habbæ, Shrn. 189, 18. Gif hé þurh ða gebedu gehǽled ne biþ, notige ðonne se abbod cyrfes, R. Ben. 52, 19. Notian ðara (*the garments*), ðe for hwylcere neóde on ýtinge faraþ, 91, 12. Betǽce ðǽm ðe heora (*tools*) notian sceolan, 56, 6. Ic wille mid ðære geferǽdene libban and ðære áre mid him notian (*enjoy with them the property given to them*), Cod. Dip. Kmbl. iii. 344, 26. (b) *with dat.*:—Hwilc eówer ne notaþ cræfte mínon *quis vestrum non utitur arte mea?* Coll. Monast. Th. 31, 9. Hý scylun lǽca þeáwe notian, R. Ben. 51, 2. (c) *with acc.*:—Gold and seolfor sind góde, gif ðú hí wel notast: gif ðú sylf yfel bist, ne miht ðú hí wel notian, Homl. Th. ii. 410, 8–9. (d) case undetermined:—Man ða reáf nime, ðe hé ǽr notode, R. Ben. 101, 24. Nota ðenna neód sig *use the medicine when need be*, Lchdm. i. 378, 18. II. *to discharge an office*:—Búton hé forworhte, ðæt hé ðære hádnote notian ne móste, L. R. 7; Th. i. 192, 16. [*A. R.* notien: *O. and N.* ich notie: *Orm.* þu notesst: *Ayenb.* noteþ: *Icel.* nota *to make use of.*] v. be-, ge-notian; nyttian.

notu, e; *f.* I. *use, profit, advantage*:—Nittung *vel* notu *usus*, Wrt. Voc. i. 21, 39. Hæbbe se abbod á mid him gewrit ealra ðæra ǽhta; ðonne seó notu (*the use of tools, etc.*) on gebróðra gewrixle biþ, sý ðæt gewis á mid ðam abbode, ðæt hé wite, hwæt betǽht sý and hwæt underfangen, R. Ben. 56, 8. Hí tó ðínre note gelǽnde wǽron, Bt. 14, 2; Fox. 44, 2. Ðæt se man tó note (*to profit*) wyrcean wille, Btwk. 222, 8. Hit læg wéste and gé his náne note ne hæfdon *it lay waste and you got no good from it*, Ors. 1, 10; Swt. 48, 25. Gif Drihten tó lytele note and nytwyrðnesse on his heorde angyt, R. Ben. 11, 2. [Se ðe ðaren bróðren note gewanie, God gewani his dages hér on werlde, Cod. Dip. Kmbl. iv. 215, 21.] II. *an office, employment*:—Ne nán gehádod man ne sceal him tó geteón ðæt hé Crist spelige ofer his hálgan híréd, búton him seó notu fram Godes láreówum betǽht sý, Homl. Th. ii. 592, 30. Hé geset ðé tó ðære ylcan note (*to the office of butler*), Gen. 40, 13. Ða hwíle ðe hié tó nánre óðerre note ne mǽgen *while they are fit for no other employment*, Past. pref.; Swt. 7, 12. Ne rǽden gebróðru, ne ne singen be nánre endebyrdnesse, ac ða sýn gecorene tó ðære note, ðe hit dón cunnon, R. Ben. 63, 6: 49, 18. Cristes gespelia hé is and his note and spelinge on mynstre healt, 10, 12. Ealne dæg hí fleardiaþ and nǽnige note dreógaþ *they trifle all day, and exercise no useful employ-*

ment, L. I. P. 14; Th. ii. 322, 25. On eallum betǣhtum notum, R. Ben. 29, 5. III. *the discharge of an office, conduct of business*:—Gif hit beón mæg swylc notu þurh decanonas on mynstre sȳ gefadod . . . ðæt nā nān ǣnlīpig ne mōdige ðonne mynstres notu manegum biþ betǣht *if possible, let such a conducting of its business by deans be arranged in the monastery, that no single person grow proud, when the conduct of business is committed to many*, 125, 8–11. [*O. E. Homl.* note *profit, use*: *O. and N.* note *office*: *Chauc.* note *business*: *Prompt. Parv.* note *opus, occupacio*: *O. Frs.* note *usus*: cf. *Icel.* not; *pl. use, utility.*] v. nytt.

not-wrītere, es; *m. One who writes notes*:—Notwrītera *notariorum*, Wrt. Voc. ii. 59, 66. v. notere.

nō-wiht. v. nā-wiht.

nū. I. *adv. Now, at this time*:—Nū *nunc* vel *modo*, Wrt. Voc. i. 76, 70. Ǣr oððe nū *dudum*, ii. 27, 56. Nū *nunc*, Ælfc. Gr. 38; Som. 39, 59. Ic hæbbe sumne cnapan, ðe nū (*modo*) hās ys for hreáme, Coll. Monast. Th. 19, 29. Hū him ðā speów mid wīsdōme . . . and hū man ūtanbordes wīsdōm and lāre hieder on lond sōhte, and hū wē hié nū sceoldon ūte begietan gif wē hié habban sceoldon, Past. Pref.; Swt. 3, 8–13. Understandaþ, ðæt deófol ðās þeóde nū fela geára dwelode, Wulfst. 156, 8. Babylonia, seó ðe mǣst wæs and ǣrest ealra burga, seó is nū læst and wēstast, Ors. 2, 4; Swt. 74, 23. Nǣron nāðer gōde ne ðā, ne nū, 2, 5; Swt. 86, 12. Wā eów ðe nū hlihaþ, forðon gē eft wēpaþ, Blickl. Homl. 25, 23. Ðū meaht geseón nū gēn (*still*) swātge wunde, Exon. Th. 89, 17; Cri. 1458: Beo. Th. 5711; B. 2859. Micel is nū gēna lād ofer lagustreám, Andr. Kmbl. 844; An. 422: 950; An. 475. Nū gyt (*adhuc*) lytel fæc and nā biþ synfull, Ps. Spl. 36, 10. Nū giet, Ors. 2, 4; Swt. 76, 1. Ne þearft ðū ðē ondrǣdan feorhcwealm nū giet (*as yet*), Cd. Th. 63, 26; Gen. 1038. Ic wāt manig nū gyt micel mǣre spell, Andr. Kmbl. 1628; An. 815. Ðās tācno ðe ic nū hwīle big sægde *the signs that I have just now spoken of*, Blickl. Homl. 109, 6. Hē nū hwonne (*quandoque*) biþ on wuldre ārīsende, Bd. 2, 1; S. 500, 16. Swā swā wē nū rihte (*straightway, directly*) secgaþ, Ælfc. Gr. 15; Som. 17, 53. *Futurum tempus* is tōwerd tīd, *stabo* ic stande nū rihte, 20; Som. 23, 9. *Modo* nū ðā oððe hwīltīdum, 38; Som. 41, 37. Nū ðā *nunc*, Ps. Spl. 11, 5. Ðǣr sitt nū ðā mid his hālgum, Homl. Th. i. 182, 30: Beo. Th. 857; B. 426: Cd. Th. 51, 24; Gen. 831. II. *conj. Now, since, when*:—Nū ðonne nū ǣlc gesceaft onscunaþ ðæt ðæt hire wiðerweard biþ *since, then, every creature shuns that which is contrary to it*, Bt. 16, 3; Fox 56, 4: Ors. 2, 4; Swt. 74, 26. Ðeáh hī nū eall hiora līf āwriten hæfdon . . . hū ne forealldodon ða gewritu ðeáh *now though they had written all their life, yet would not the writings wax old?* Bt. 18, 3; Fox 64, 36. Forhwī ðē hātan dysige men wuldor, nū ðū nāne eart, 30, 1; Fox 108, 2. Ond nū (*since*) ðeós hālige tīd englum tō blisse wearþ, ðonne . . ., Blickl. Homl. 123, 1. Wē māgon geþencean, nū (*since*) ða sint Godes bearn genemned ðe sibbe wyrcaþ, Past. 47; Swt. 359, 12. Hū mæg hē hira bión orsorg, nū (*when*) se hierde cwæþ, 54; Swt. 427, 5. Nū . . . nū (*in principal and dependent clauses*):—Wē wyllaþ nū eów gereccan ōðres mannes gesihþe nū se apostol Paulus his gesihþe mannum āmeldian ne mōste, Homl. Th. ii. 332, 26: Cd. Th. 26, 8–9; Gen. 403–404: Beo. Th. 857–865; B. 426–430. Ðonne is nū tō geþencenne on ðās hālgan tīd, nū wē ūrne līchoman clǣnsiaþ, Blickl. Homl. 39, 1. Nū ic sceal geendian earmlīcum deáþe, nū wolde ic gebētan, Swt. A. S. Rdr. 101, 205. Nū ðonne nū ða līchomlīcan lǣcas ðus scyldige gerehte sint, nū is tō ongietanne . . ., Past. 49; Swt. 377, 21. III. *interj.*:—Nū is seóc se ðe ðū lufast *ecce quem amas infirmatur*, Jn. Skt. 11, 3. Sume syndon *ortativa* . . . *heia* nū lā, *age* nū lā; ðis is eác menigfealdlīce, *agite* nū gē lā, Ælfc. Gr. 38; Som. 40, 27–28. Nū lā *age jam*, Wülck. Gl. 252, 43. [*Goth. Icel. O. Sax. O. Frs. O. H. Ger.* nu, nū.]

-nugan. v. be-, ge-nugan.

-numa. v. irfe-numa.

Numantie, Numentie, Numentīne, Numentīnas; *pl. The Numantians*:—Se consul fōr on Numentīne, Ispania folc, Ors. 5, 2; Swt. 218, 29. Numentie āhnescaden, 5, 3; Swt. 222, 15. On Numantie, 220, 22. Numantia duguþ, 222, 8. Numentia fæsten, 5, 2; Swt. 218, 32. On Numantium, 5, 3; Swt. 220, 19. On Numentīnas, Ispania þeóde, 5, 2; Swt. 218, 13.

Numentisc; *adj. Of Numantia*:—Se wæs Numentisc, Ors. 5, 3; Swt. 222, 14.

nume-stān, es; *m. A pebble*:—Cealc, numestān *calculus*, Wrt. Voc. ii. 13, 6.

Numeðe; *pl. The Numidians*:—Numeðe, Ors. 4, 10; Swt. 200, 9. Numeðia cyning *Numidarum rex*, 5, 7; Swt. 228, 6.

numol; *adj. Able to take* or *contain much*:—Numol *capax*, Ælfc. Gr. 9, 60; Som. 13, 41. Numul, gripul *capax, qui multum capit*, Wrt. Voc. ii. 128, 29. v. scearp-, teart-numol.

nūna; *adv. Now*:—Nūna *nunc*, Wülck. Gl. 254, 24. [*Icel.* nūna.]

nunne, an; *f. A nun, a vestal*:—Ārwurðe wudewe *vel* nunne *nonna*, Wrt. Voc. i. 42, 30. Nunna, 72, 3. Nunne *sanctimonialis*, 284, 68. Wæs on ðam sylfan mynstre sum hālig nunne *erat in ipso monasterio quaedam sanctimonialis femina*, Bd, 4, 23; S. 595, 36. Caperronis wæs hātenu heora goda nunne (*virgo vestalis*), Ors. 4, 4; Swt. 162, 31. Se ðe mid nunnan hǣme, gehālgodre legerstōwe ne sȳ hē wyrðe, L. Edm. E. 3; Th. i. 246, 6. Ǣfre ne geweorðe, ðæt cristen man gewīfige on gehālgodre ǣnigre nunnan, L. Eth. vi. 12; Th. 318, 17. Gif hwā wið nunnan forlicge, sī ǣgðer his weres scildig, ge hē ge heó, L. N. P. L. 63; Th. ii. 300, 20. Be nunnan hǣmede. Gif hwā nunnan of mynstre ūt ālǣde būtan kyninges lēfnesse geselle hundtwelftig scill. . . . Gif heó leng libbe ðonne se ðe hié ūt ālǣdde, nāge hió his ierfes ōwiht. Gif hió bearn gestriéne, næbbe ðæt ðæs ierfes, L. Alf. pol. 8; Th. i. 66, 14–20. Be nunnena onfenge. Gif hwā nunnan mid hǣmedþinge, oððe on hire hrægl, oððe on hire breóst būtan hire leáfe gefō sȳ hit twȳbēte, 18; Th. i. 72, 7–10. Nunnan regollīce libban *let nuns live according to their rule*, L. Eth. v. 4; Th. i. 304, 27. Sum fǣmne of ðæra nunnena rīme *quaedam de numero virginum*, Bd. 5, 3; S. 616, 3. Nunnena pōl, Cod. Dip. Kmbl. iii. 313, 26. [*Icel.* nunna: *O. H. Ger.* nunna, *from Lat.* nonna.]

nunn-hīred, es; *m. A nunnery*:—Ðe ǣr ðes nunhīredes wes, Chart. Th. 232, 6.

nunn-, nunnan-mynster, es; *n. A nunnery*:—Ðæt nunmynster (*monasterium virginum*) ðæt mon nemneþ Coludesburhg, Bd. 4, 25; S. 599, 19: 5, 3; S. 615, 41. In tō nunnanmynstre, Chart. Th. 231, 35. [Cf. *Icel.* nunnu-klaustr *a nunnery.*] v. neáh-nunnan-mynster.

nunn-scrūd, es; *n. The habit of a nun*:—Finde Æþelflæd ān hyre nunscrūde, lōce hwæt hió betsð mǣge, Chart. Th. 538, 12.

nȳd, nȳhst. v. nīd, nīhst.

nyhtness, e; *f. Abundance*:—Of nyhtnisse *ex abundantia*, Mt. Kmbl. Rush. 12, 34. v. ge-nyhtsum.

nyllan = ne willan:—Nylle ic ūt wītan, Met. 24, 52. Ic nelle *nolo*, ðū nelt *non vis*, hē nele *non vult*, wē nellaþ *nolumus* . . . nelle ðu *noli*, nelle gē *nolite*, . . . nellan *nolle*, Ælfc. Gr. 32; Som. 36, 16–19. Ðū nelt, Exon. Th. 250, 12; Jul. 126. Nyle hē, Ps. Th. 74, 8. Nān eówer nele *nemo vestrum vult*, Coll. Monast. Th. 28, 1. Nellaþ *nolunt*, 29, 3. Nyllaþ, Past. 5; Swt. 45, 18. Nolde, Jn. Skt. 7, 1. Nalde, Ps. Surt. 35, 4. Noldon, Mt. Kmbl. 22, 3. Gif ðæt wīf nele *si noluerit mulier*, Gen. 24, 5. Sam wē willan, sam wē nyllan, Bt. 35, 12; Fox 154, 7. Nyllan gē *nolite*, Ps. Th. 61, 11. Nellaþ, 61, 10. Būtan nellendes andsware, R. Ben. 20, 19.

nymne, nymþe, nȳr, nyrwan, nyrwian, nyrwet, nyt. v. nefne, nimþe, neáh (*adv.*), nirwan, nirwet, nett, nytt.

nytan = ne witan:—Ic nāt *nescio*, Jn. Skt. 9, 25. Nāt ic hwilc wundorlīc þing, Shrn. 36, 18. Gif ðū nāst *if you do not know*, Ælfc. Gr. 50, 17; Som. 51, 34. Gyt nyton hwæt gyt biddaþ, Mk. Skt. 10, 38. Wē witon ðæt God spæc wið Moyses; nyte wē hwanon ðes is, Jn. Skt. 9, 29. Wē nyton (nutu wē, Lind.: niton wē, Rush.), Mt. Kmbl. 21, 27. Gē neton, Exon. Th. 282, 9; Jul. 660. Ic wiste ðæt ðū ūt āfaren wǣre, ac ic nyste hū feor, Bt. 5, 1; Fox 8, 33. Ðæt ðæt ic ǣr sǣde ðæt ic nyste (Cott. MS. nesse) . . . Ðū sǣdest ðæt ðū nystest (Cott. MS. nesse), 34, 12; Fox 154, 12–13. Ðū nysstest (Cott. MS. nesse) . . . ic nyste (Cott. MS. nysse), 35, 2; Fox 156, 33–34. Ðū nestest, 5, 3; Fox 12, 34. Hē nyste, Past. 15; Swt. 91, 13. Hī nysðon (nyston, MS. A.), Mt. Kmbl. 24, 39. Wē neston, Blickl. Homl. 17, 12. Wēnst ðū ðæt ic nyte, Bt. 5, 3; Fox 12, 17. Ðæt hē nān ryht andwyrde nyte, 35, 1; Fox 156, 8. Nyte ðīn wynstre hwæt dō ðīn swȳðre, Mt. Kmbl. 6, 3. Nytende, Lchdm. i. 164, 5. Him nytendum, 228, 1. Nytendum weardmannum *clam custodibus*, Ælfc. Gr. 47; Som. 47, 58. v. nāt-.

nyten; *adj. Ignorant*:—Ðæt ðās nytenan menn ðīne mihta oncnāwon, Homl. Th. i. 62, 14. v. nytenness.

nȳten. v. nīten.

nytenness, e; *f.* I. *ignorance*:—Hwæt getācnaþ seó midniht būtan seó deópe nytennys, Homl. Th. ii. 568, 5. Ðæt men for nytennysse misfaran ne sceolon, 314. 5. Ðū cniht ne cūðest manna Hǣlend . . . Nū ic for ðīnre nytennysse geornlīce bæd, i. 66, 30. Se ðe tōdrǣfde ealle nytennysse ðære ealdan nihte, 36, 29. Crist mæg ðīne nytennysse (MSS. C. V. nyte-) onlīhtan, Homl. Skt. 5, 200. Gif folces man syngaþ þurh nytenysse *per ignorantiam*, Lev. 4, 27. Ðæt hyra nān þurh nytennesse hine belādian ne mǣge, R. Ben. 127, 10. II. *laziness, desert, disgrace, ignominy*:—Netenes ðam se ðe forlēt *ignominia ei qui deserit*, Kent. Gl. 454. On his netenesse *in ignominia sua*, 615. For mōdes mīnes nytenysse *propter mentis meae ignaviam*, Coll. Monast. Th. 25, 7.

nyt-līc; *adj. Useful, profitable, beneficial*:—Ǣghwæðer (*the male and female pennyroyal*) ys nytlīc (MS. H. netlīc) . . . and hī on him habbaþ wundorlīce mihte, Lchdm. i. 204, 11. Mōna se feórþæ wercū onginnan nytlīc ys *the fourth day of the moon is advantageous for beginning works*, iii. 184, 28. Mǣden (*a girl born on the eighth day of the moon*) is nytlīce, 188, 6. Is eallum mannum nytlīc, ðæt hié heora fulwihthādas wel gehealdan, Blickl. Homl. 109, 26. Ic ne gȳmde ðara nytlīcra geþeahta mīnra freónda *utilia consilia spreveram amicorum*, Nar. 6, 26. Monig nytlīco þing *multa utilia*, Bd. 5, 20; S. 642, 19. [*O. H. Ger.* nuz-līh *utilis.*] v. un-nytlīc.

nytlīcness, e; *f. Usefulness, utility, useful property*:—Ic bidde ðē *vica pervica* manegum nytlícnyssum tō hæbenne *te precor vica pervica multis utilitatibus habenda*, Lchdm. i. 314, 8.

nytness, e; *f. Use, utility, advantage, profit*:—Hwylc nytnys on blóde mínum *quae utilitas in sanguine meo*, Ps. Spl. 29, 11. Náwiht nytnesse (*nihil utilitatis*) hafeþ seó ǽfæstnys ðe wē óþ ðis hæfdon, Bd. 2, 13; S. 516, 3. Mid micelre nytnysse (*magna utilitate*) ǽghwæðeres folces, 3, 24; S. 557, 13: 5, 10; S. 623, 38. Tō líchoman nyttnesse *for the advantage of the body*, Blickl. Homl. 57, 8. Mid allum ðǽm nytnessum ge on fixnoþum ge on mēdwum ðe ðǽrtō belympaþ, Cod. Dip. Kmbl. v. 186, 5, 9.

nyt[t], e; *f.* I. *use, advantage, profit*:—Nyt *commodum*, Wrt. Voc. ii. 24, 63. Hundteóntig hí him sylfum tō nytte dydon *centum in suos usus habebant*, Bd. 4, 13; S. 583, 3: Ors. 2, 4; Swt. 72, 6. Niþum tō nytte, Exon. Th. 409, 10; Rä. 27, 27. Nebb biþ hyre æt nytte *it has a face for use*, 416, 23; Rä. 35, 3. Tō nyttum *ad pensas*, Wrt. ii. 4, 40: *ad expensas*, 7, 30: *ad penses*, 99, 23. II. *office, duty*:—Ðegn nytte beheóld, se ðe on handa bær hroden ealowǽge, Beo. Th. 993; B. 494: 6228; B. 3118. [Bruttes neoren noht to nuttes, Laym. 13428: *Icel.* nyt; *gen.* nytjar; *f. use, enjoyment*: *O. H. Ger.* nuzzi.] v. cyric-, sund-, sundor-nytt.

nyt[t]; *adj. Useful, profitable, advantageous, beneficial*:—Hē moneg-um nyt wæs *multis utilis fuit*, Bd. 3, 23; S, 555, 33. Ic nát, hū nyt ic ða hwíle beó, ðe ic ðás word sprece, būtan ðæt ic mín geswinc ámirre, Ors. 4, 13; Swt. 212, 25. Wē næfdon ða gesēlþa, ðæt seó scipfyrd nytt wǽre ðisum earde, Chr. 1009; Erl. 141, 26. Tō náhte nyt, Blickl. Homl. 57, 5. Hū nyt biþ ðæm men, ðéh hē geornlíce gehýre ða word ðæs hálgan godspelles, gif hē ða nel on his heortan habban, 55, 6: Bt. 38, 5; Fox 206, 10 note. Nyttre fōre, Exon. Th. 393, 4; Rä. 12, 5. Ðæt hí hæfdon nyt ǽrend and nytne intingan sumne (*aliquid legationis et causae utilis*), Bd. 5, 10; S. 624, 21. Ðysne nyttan cræft ðéh hē árlíc nǽre *hanc utilem magis quam nobilem victoriam*, Ors. 2, 8; Swt. 92, 2. Ne gehýrde nǽnig man on his mūþe óht elles nefne nytte sprǽce, Blickl. Homl. 225, 1. Hē ðone gōdan cræft dō nytne ōðrum mannum, Ælfc. Gr. pref.; Som. 1, 29. Ðæt land hyre nytt gedōe, Chart. Th. 470, 8: 472, 10. Nǽron Metode wíd lond ne wegas nytte, Cd. Th. 10, 13; Gen. 156: Beo. Th. 1592; B. 794. Nis nǽnig mǽre mægen, ðisse menniscan tydernesse nyttre, Blickl. Homl. 31, 30. Hē cwæþ, ðæt nyttre wǽre ðæt hié man gesealde, 75, 22. Wē māgon beón nyttran æt him, Past. 32; Swt. 211, 21. Rǽd biþ nyttost, Exon. Th. 341, 1; Gn. Ex. 119. [Is þe man nut þe sæhtnesse wurcheþ, Laym. 9470: *Goth.* [un-]nutis: *Icel.* nytr: *O. H. Ger.* nuzzi *utilis*.] v. un-nytt.

nytte. v. nette.

nyttian; *p.* ode; *with gen. To make use of, enjoy*:—Ic nyttige *fungor, utor, perago*, Wrt. Voc. ii. 152, 22. Wuda and wætres nyttaþ, Exon. Th. 340, 12; Gn. Ex. 110. Sume ðæs seáwes ánlípiges nyttiaþ *some make of the juice only*, Lchdm. ii. 30, 16. Nyttade Noe sídan ríces, Cd. Th. 96, 21; Gen. 1598. Ðises ðū nytta ge on ǽfenne ge on underne, Lchdm. ii. 184, 25: 28, 16: 32, 25. Nyttigen baþes, 240, 24. Gehwæðeres (*both methods of cure*) sceal mon nyttian, 22, 7. [*A. R. O. E. Homl. Marh.* nutten: *Orm. Havel.* nitten: *O. H. Ger.* nuzzan.]

nyttol; *adj. Useful, advantageous, beneficial*:—Ðæt ilce (*the same treatment*) biþ nyttol wið hundes slite, Lchdm. ii. 86, 2.

nyttung, e; *f. Profit, advantage*:—Nittung *usus*, Wrt. Voc. i. 21, 39.

nyt-weorð, -wirðe; *adj. Useful, advantageous, profitable*:—Eálā ðū mín wyln beó nytwyrðe *O mea ancilla, esto utilis*, Ælfc. Gr. 15; Zup. 101, 4. Hū se lāreów sceal beón nytwierðe (MS. Hatt. -wyrðe) on his wordum *ut sit rector utilis in verbo*, Past. 15; Swt. 88, 3. Ðā stōd ðǽr sum nytwyrðe hūs, Blickl. Homl. 221, 7. Se biþ on eallum þingum nytwurðe, Lchdm. iii. 158, 6. Nytwyrðe, 188, 14. Se nytwyrða brōðor, R. Ben. 24, 18. Fleóþ ðonne ða nytwierðan (nyttwyrðan, Hatt. MS.) hiérsumnesse ðære lāre, and nyllaþ ðæs þencean hū hié mǽgen nytwierðuste (nyttweorðuste, Hatt. MS.) bión hiera níhstum, Past. 5, 3; Swt. 44, 17–19. Ic gehýrde fela nytwurðe (-wyrðe, -werðe, -wyrða) þing (*multa utilia*), Ælfc. Gr. 15; Zup. 95, 18. Seó wiðer-wearde wyrd byþ ǽlcum men nytwyrðre ðonne seó orsorge *plus hominibus reor adversam, quam prosperam prodesse fortunam*, Bt. 20; Fox 70, 29. Ða scipu nǽron on Fresisc gescæpene, būte swā him selfum þūhte ðæt hié nytwyrðoste beón meahten, Chr. 897; Erl. 95, 16.

nytweorð (-wirð) -líc; *adj. Useful*:—Nytwurðlíc (-wyrð-, -weorð-) *utilis*, Ælfc. Gr. 9, 28; Zup. 55, 5. Tō ðæs munstres nitwurðlícre þearfe *for the useful requirements of the monastery*, Chart. Th. 369, 28.

nytweorð (-wirð) -líce; *adv. Usefully*:—Nytwurðlíce (-wyrð-, -wirð-) *utiliter*, Ælfc. Gr. 38; Zup. 238, 15. Ða ðonne sint tō manianne ðe nytwyrðlíce (nyttweorðlíce, Hatt. MS.) lǽran meahton (*qui praedicare utiliter possent*), Past. 49, 1; Swt. 374, 21. Nytwierðlecust (nyttwyrð-lícost, Hatt. MS.), 15; Swt. 91, 22.

nytweorþ (-wirð) -ness, e; *f. Usefulness, utility*:—Nytweorðnes *commoditas* i. *utilitas*, Wrt. Voc. ii. 132, 5. Hwæt wyrcst ðū ūs nytwyrð-nesse *quid operaris tu nobis utilitatis*, Coll. Monast. Th. 27, 25.

nywol, nýxt. v. neowol, neáh.

O

Ō *ever*. v. á.

ōb. v. ō-web.

ob, ober, obet. v. of, ofer, ofet.

oc, ōcusta. v. ac, ōhsta.

oden, e; *f. A threshing-floor*:—Frymþa odene ðínre *primitias areae tuae*, Scint. 29. Beóþ sume on būre, sume on healle, sume on ódene, sume on carcerne, and lybbaþ ðeáh ealle be ānes hlāfordes āre, Shrn. 187, 23. On odene cylne macian, Som.

of; *prep. with dat.*, or *adv. Of, from, out of, off.* I. with the idea of motion, (*a*) as the opposite of *in, into*:—Se wyll āstāh upp of ðære eorþan *fons ascendebat e terra*, Ælfc. Gr. 47; Som. 47, 61. Hē āstāh of ðam wætere *ascendit de aqua*, Mt. Kmbl. 3, 16. 'Drihten āsette on sunnan his hūs, and of ðæm ūt eode swā swā brýdguma of his brýdbūre.' Ðæt wæs ðonne ðæt se wuldorcyning on middangeard cwom forþ of ðæm innoþe ðære ā clǽnan fǽmnan, Blickl. Homl. 9, 30–33. Faran of stōwe tō ōðerre, 19, 23: Gen. 12, 4. (*β*) as the opposite of *on*:—Moises eode nyðer of ðam munte tō ðam folce, Ex. 19, 14. Crist of heofona heáness-um on ðínne innoþ āstígeþ, Blickl. Homl. 5, 13. II. with the idea of direction from, but at the same time continuous connection with an object from which an act or thing proceeds:—Drihten lōcaþ of heofenum *Dominus de caelo prospexit*, Ps. Th. 13, 3. Of wealle geseah weard Scyldinga, Beo. Th. 463; B. 229. Of ðam leóma stōd *from it stretched a ray*, 5532; B. 2769. Ic geseah Drihten of ansíne tō ansíne, Gen. 32, 30. On ðæm dæge plegedon hié of horsum, Ors. 3, 7; Swt. 118, 29: 3, 9; Swt. 132, 19. III. with the idea of origin or source:—Ða nítenu of eallum cinne and of eallum fugelcynne, Gen. 7, 8. Ðā feóllon ða ciningas ofslagene of Sodoman and Gomorran *rex Sodomorum et Gomorrhae ceciderunt ibi*, 14, 10. Sum wer of Sceotta þeóde, Bd. 4, 25; S. 599, 27. Ða ōðre seofan syndon *derivativa*, ðæt is ðæt hí cumaþ of ðām ōðrum, Ælfc. Gr. 15; Som. 17, 44. Of Geáta fruman syndon Cantware ... Of Seaxum cōman Eást-Seaxan and Sūþ-Seaxan and West-Seaxan, Bd. 1, 15; S. 483, 21–24. Ða men of Lundenbyrig, Chr. 896; Erl. 94, 17. Ðās woruldgesǽlþa of heora āgnum gecynde and heora āgnes gewealdes nāuht gōde ne sient, Bt. 16, 3; Fox 54, 17. Wæs sió bysen of him (*the example that had its origin with them*) ofer ealle world, Ors. 1, 5; Swt. 34, 31. Hié woldon of ǽlcerre byrig him self anwald habban (*imperare singulae cupiunt*) ... Ðā bǽdan hié Philippus ǽrest of ānre byrig, ðonne of ōðerre, ðæt hē him on fultume wǽre, 3, 7; Swt. 112, 19–23. Mē of brýde bearn ne wōcon, Cd. Th. 131, 30; Gen. 2184: Exon. Th. 433, 26; Rä. 51, 2. Him stent ege of ðē *timebunt te*, Deut. 28, 10. Wendan on Englisc, hwílum word be worde, hwílum andgit of andgite, Past. Swt. 7, 20. Hwæðer ǽnig man wǽre ðe ǽnige mǽrþa of ðam Hǽlende hæfde, St. And. 36, 31. Sōðfæstnesse, ða ðe ic gehýrde of Gode, Jn. Skt. 8, 40. IV. denoting the agent from whom an action proceeds, *by*:—Æþelstān wæs gecoren tō cynge of Myrcum, Chr. 924; Erl. 111, 34. Hēr wearþ Eádward cing gecoren tō hlāfuorde of Scotta cinge and of Scotton and of eallum Norðhumbrum, Erl. 111, 11. Hē wæs of cilda mūþe gecnāwen and weorþad, Blickl. Homl. 71, 33. V. denoting the instrument:—Weorþian wē ða clāþas his hādes, of ðǽm wæs ūre gecynd geedneówod, 11, 9. Hē of .v. hlāfon and of twām fixum fíf þūsend manna gefylde, St. And. 28, 32. VI. denoting material or substance:—Reáf of olfenda hǽrum, Mt. Kmbl. 3, 4. Gyld of golde *an idol of gold*, Cd. Th. 226, 22; Dan. 175. Adam ðe wæs of eorþan ge-worht, 23, 26; Gen. 365. Hæfdon of ðæm hreóde on scipwísan geworht *factis ex harundine naviculis*, Nar. 11, 18. Offrunga of nýtenum, Lev. 1, 2. Ne biþ on hlāfe ānum mannes líf, ac of eallum ðæm worde ðe gǽþ of Godes mūþe, Blickl. Homl. 27, 9. VII. denoting removal, separation, or privation:—Of slǽpe āwreht, Homl. Th. i. 60, 19. Ðæt ðū of deáþe āríse, 66, 30. Ālýs ūs of yfele, Mt. Kmbl. 6, 13. Beó of ðysum hāl, Mk. Skt. 5, 34. Hē gehǽlde manega of ādlum ge of wítum and of yfelum gāstum, Lk. Skt. 7, 21. Sundor of ðæm weorode *apart from the multitude*, Blickl. Homl. 15, 7. Āsceofene of géfeán neorxna wanges, 17, 15. Wæs ādǽled wæter of wætrum, Cd. Th. 10, 5; Gen. 152. Dyde him of healse hring gyldenne, Beo. Th. 5610; B. 2809. Ðone cynelícan naman of Rōme byrig ādydon, Bt. 16, 1; Fox 50, 9. Ne þincþ mē nāuht ōðres of (*nothing different from*) ðínum spellum, 36, 4; Fox 178, 24. Fixas cwelaþ gyf hí of wætere beóþ, Lchdm. iii. 272, 25. VIII. *as regards, about*:—Fela spella him sǽdon ða Beormas ǽgðer ge of hiera āgnum lande ge of ðǽm landum ðe ymb hié ūtan wǽron, Ors. 1, 1; Swt. 17, 31. IX. partitive:—Ic nyme of ðínum gāste, Num. 11, 17. Heó genam of ðæs treówes wæstme, Gen. 3, 6: Lk. Skt. 20, 10. Syllaþ ūs of eówrum ele, Mt. Kmbl. 25, 8. Ic ne drince of ðysum eorþlícan wíne, 26, 29. Se Peohta þeóde of myclum dǽle (*in great part*) geeode, Bd. 2, 5; S. 506, 20. Swā ān of ðyson, Mt. Kmbl. 6, 29. Ān eá of ðām hātte Fison, Gen. 2, 11. Ðū ne gesihst ǽnigne of Godes ðām hālgum, St. And. 16, 8: Exon. Th. 154, 5; Gū. 838. X. marking time:—Of ðam dæge; Jn. Skt. 11, 53. Of sunnan upgange,

Swt. A. S. Rdr. 98, 96. Of ðyssan forþ áwa tó worulde, Ps. Th. 112, 2. Of cildháde, Elen. Kmbl. 1826; El. 915. **XI.** adverbially (a) denoting separation, removal, privation:—Ic ðé ðíne téþ of ábeáte *I knock out your teeth for you*, Lchdm. i. 326, 15. Búton hé him wille fǽhþe of áceápian *unless he will buy off the feud from himself*, L. In. 74; Th. i. 150, 2. Petrus ácearf him of ðæt swýðre eáre, Jn. Skt. 18, 10. Ðonne án tweó of ádón biþ, Bt. 39, 4; Fox 216, 19. Gif man cealf of ádríſe, L. Alf. pol. 16; Th. i. 72, 1. Hé áslóh of ánys ðæra sacerda ealdres þeówan eáre, Mt. Kmbl. 26, 51. Átió of ða þornas, Bt. 23; Fox 78, 22. Gif ðara lima hwilc of biþ, 37, 3; Fox 190, 27. Ceorf of ðæt lim, Homl. Th. i. 516, 4. Ealles ðæs ðe ðenne on biþ, bútan ðæt man scel for hyre sáulle of dón, Chart. Th. 534, 7. Ða reáf ðe hé him of dyde, R. Ben. 103, 1. Seó eádmódnys heáwþ of ðære módinysse heáfod *humilitas amputat caput superbiae*, Gl. Prud. 36 b. Him mon slóg ða handa of, ðá ðæt heáfod, Ors. 4, 5; Swt. 168, 5. Wring of ða wyrta, Lchdm, iii. 58, 30. (b) denoting motion:—Man sceolde mid sáre on ðás world cuman, and mid sáre of gewítan, Blickl. Homl. 5, 29. Ðonne hwá on ða leásunga beféhþ, ðonne ne mæg hé of, Past. 35; Swt. 239, 17. (c) denoting direction:—Stód se leóma him of swylce fýren þecelle, Bd. 5, 23; S. 645, 29. (d) denoting origin or source:—Ðære þeóde ðe hé of com, 5, 19; S. 639, 37. On ðære béc ðe wé ðás of álesan, 4, 10; S. 578, 15. Hé ǽnne calic sealde his gingrum of tó súpenne, Homl. Th. ii. 244, 13. [*Goth. Icel. O. Sax.* af: *O. Frs.* of: *O. H. Ger.* ab.]

of- *as a prefix modifies the words to which it is attached in many ways. Amongst these may be noticed* (1) its intensive force *in such words as* of-georn, of-langod, of-lysted, of-calen, of-hyngrod, of-þyrsted. (2) its unfavourable force *in* of-lícian, of-unnan, of-þyncan. (3) the idea of attainment *which it gives to* (a) *verbs of motion as* of-faran, of-féran, of-irnan, of-rídan: (b) *verbs of inquiring, calling, etc., as* of-áxian, of-clypian, of-spyrian. (4) the force of (a) killing *which it gives to verbs of striking, throwing, falling, etc., as* of-feallan, of-hnítan, of-hreósan, of-sceótan, of-stician, of-stingan: (b) injury *which it gives to verbs denoting rest as* of-licgan, of-sittan, *or those denoting action as* of-settan, of-tredan.

ofæt. v. ofet.

of-áxian, -ácsian; *p.* ode *To find out by asking, to learn*:—Ðá hé ofáxode (*didicisset*) hwæt his suna him dydon, Gen. 9, 24: Chart. Th. 340, 27. Hé his bróðor slege ofáxode, Homl. Th. ii. 358, 5. Hé ofáxode æt ðám láreówum, ðæt Cristes þeówdóm ne sceal b-ón geneádod, 130, 14. Hé ofácsode (*suspicabatur*) ðæt hé hæfde ǽrendo, Bd. 4, 1; S. 564, 48 note. Hit wearþ gecweden, ðæt man ofáxode on eallum his ríce, gif ǽnig mǽden mihte beón áfunden swá wlitiges hiwes, Anglia ix. 29, 71. Ic ðé bidde ðæt ðú ofáxie ða næglas, H. R. 15, 23. Ðá sænde hé his móder tó Hierusalem, tó ðam ðæt hió ðǽr ofáxian scolde ða hálgan róde, 7, 4. Cf. of-spyrian.

of-beátan; *p.* -beót; *pp.* -beáten *To kill by beating, to beat to death, to beat to pieces*:—Wé hit uneáþe mid ísernum hamerum ofbeóton *quam ferreis vix comminuimus malleis*, Nar. 21, 6. Claudium mid saglum ofbeótan *they beat Claudius to death with clubs*, Ors. 2, 6; Swt. 88, 26. Ðæt hí ofbeátun *ut trucident*, Ps. Lamb. 36, 15. Hét se cásere ðone cempan mid saglum ofbeátan, Homl. Skt. i. 5, 455. Mid billum ofbeátan, Met. 9, 30. Sume wǽron mid wǽpnum ofslagene óðre mid swipum ofbeátene *some were slain with weapons, others scourged to death*, Homl. Th. i. 542, 27.

of-blindian *to make blind*:—Ofblindade égo hiora *excaecavit oculos eorum*, Jn. Skt. Lind. Rush. 12, 40.

of-brǽdels. v. ofer-brǽdels.

of-brytsig (?); *adj. Very broken*:—Ofbyrtstigum (? ofbrytsigum) *praeruptis, fractis*, Hpt. Gl. 454, 44.

of-calen *very cold*:—Petrus stód ofcalen on ðam cauertúne, Homl. Th. ii. 248, 27. v. calan.

of-clipian; *p.* ode *To obtain by calling*:—Ðá wolde se hálga habban gewitan ðære wunderlícan gesihþe and ofclypode his diácon him hrædlíce tó (*the deacon was called and came*), Homl. Th. ii. 184, 33. Heó mid hreáme hyre hræddinge ofclypode *she had obtained help by her cries*, Homl. Skt. i. 2, 219.

of-cumende *derivative*:—Eahta synd frumcennede, and seofan ofcumende, Ælfc. Gr. 15; Som. 17, 34.

of-cyrf, es; *m.* I. *a cutting off, amputation*:—Hwæt getácnaþ ðæs fylmenes ofcyrf, Homl. Th. i. 94, 32. II. *that which is cut off*:—Hé tócearf his basing on emtwá, and sealde óðerne dǽl ðam earman wædlan, and mid ðam ofcyrfe hine eft bewǽfde (*wrapped himself in the remaining portion of the cloak*), Homl. Th. ii. 500, 27. Heó (*the cross*) is wíde tódǽled mid gelómlícum ofcyrfum (*by the bits often cut off it*), H. R. 105, 14.

of-dæl; *adj. Tending downwards, inclined to anything inferior*:—Hit biþ ámerred mid ðám lǽnum gódum forðam hit biþ ofdælre ðǽrtó *it is led astray by the transitory goods, because it is more inclined to them*; ad falsa devius error abducit, Bt. 24, 2; Fox 82, 2. v. next word.

of-dæle, an (?); *n. A downward slope, descent, incline*:—Hié nyllaþ gepyndan hiera mód swelce mon deópne pól gewerige ac hé lǽt his mód tóflówan on ðæt ofdæle (ofdele, Hatt. MS.) giémeliéste and ungesceádwísnesse *they will not dam up their minds, as one banks up a deep pool, but he lets his mind flow away to the downward slope of carelessness and folly*; quia (anima) se ad superiora stringendo non dirigit, neglectam se inferius per desideria expandit, Past. 39, 1; Swt. 282, 15. Hí síen on ðæt ofdæle ásigen tó yfele and ðider healde, Bt. 24, 4; Fox 84, 28. Sió sunne scýft on ofdæle *the sun descends*, Met. 13, 58. [Cf. *Goth.* at ibdaljin this fairgunjis *ad descensum montis*, Lk. 19, 37: *O. Sax.* te dale: *O. H. Ger.* ze tale *downwards*.] v. preceding word.

of-drǽd[d] *terrified, afraid*:—Ic férde ofdrǽd *timens abii*, Mt. Kmbl. 25, 25. Befrán se sceaþa hwæt hé manna wǽre, oððe wǽre ofdrǽd, Homl. Th. ii. 502, 28. Hé ofdrǽdd wæs for his morþdǽdum, Ælfc. T. Grn. 18, 38. Hié beóþ mid ðæm ymbeþonce ofdrǽdde, Past. 35, 2; Swt. 238, 7: Homl. Skt. i. 23, 300. [*Laym. A. R.* (swiþe, sore) of-dred: *Orm.* off-dredd: *O. and N.* of-drad.]

of-dúne; *adv. Down*:—Ofdúne stígan, gestígan *to descend*, Mt. Kmbl. Lind. 3, 16: 11, 23: Rtl. 28, 9. Hé gefeóll ofdúne on ða flór, Bt. 1; Fox 4, 3. Nis hire ǽþre tó feallanne ofdúne ðonne up, 33, 4; Fox 130, 38. Ðeáh ðú teó hwelcne bóh ofdúne tó ðære eorþan, 25; Fox 88, 22. Hié léton hiera hrægl ofdúne tó fótum, Ors. 3, 5; Swt. 106, 19. 'Wendaþ mín heáfod ofdúne, forðon ðe mín Drihten of heofenum ádúne tó eorþan ástág.' Ðá fæstnedan hié ða fét up and ðæt heáfod ofdúne, Blickl. Homl. 191, 2-9.

of-earmian; *p.* ode *To have pity* or *compassion*:—Rihtwísa ofearmaþ *justus miseretur*, Ps. Spl. 36, 22. Ofearmian *misereri*, 76, 9.

of-earmung, e; *f. Pity, compassion*:—On ofearmunga *in miseratione*, Blickl. Gl.

ofen, ofn, es; *m. An oven, a furnace*:—Ofen *fornax* vel *clibanus*, Wrt. Voc. i. 83, 14. Ofn, 34, 40. Se ofn (*caminus*) ðære singalan costnunge, Bd. 4, 9; S. 576, 29. Ða fúlnessa ðæs þýstran ofnes (*fornacis*), 5, 12; S. 629, 21: Cd. Th. 245, 13; Dan. 462. Axan of ðam ofene (*camino*), Ex. 9, 8. Ðás þrí cnihtas hét se cyning áwurpan intó byrnendum ofne (*the fiery furnace*), Ælfc. T. Grn. 8, 26. Geond ðone ofen, Cd. Th. 238, 13; Dan. 354. On fýres ofen (ofn, Lind.) *in caminum ignis*, Mt. Kmbl. 13, 42. Gif hwylc wíf seteþ hire bearn on ofen (*in fornacem*), L. Ecg. C. 33; Th. ii. 156, 35. On ofon (*clibanum*) gisended, Lk. Skt. Rush. 12, 28. Hí gáþ on ðíne ofnas (*furnos*), Ex. 8, 3. Ðæt man ða ofnas ontende, Homl. Skt. i. 5, 294. [*Goth.* auhns: *Icel.* ofn *and* ogn: *Dan.* ovn: *Swed.* ugn: *O. Frs.* oven: *O. H. Ger.* ovan.] v. hláf-ofen (-ofn).

ofen-bacen; *adj. Baked in an oven*:—Ofenbacen hláf *formentum*, Wrt. Voc. ii. 38, 60: *fermentum*, i. 27, 24: *clibanius panis*, 41, 21. Genim ðone cruman of ofenbacenum hláfe, Lchdm. i. 132, 19. Bring clǽne ofenbacene hláfas *sacrificium coctum in clibano, panes*, Lev. 2, 4.

ofen-raca, an; *m. An oven-rake, an instrument for clearing out an oven* or *furnace*:—Ofenraca *rotabulum*, Wrt. Voc. i. 16, 34: 27, 10.

of-eode. v. of-gán.

ofer, ofor; *prep. adv.* I. *with dat.* generally with the idea of rest; (1) *above, over*:—Wæs hálig leóht ofer wéstenne, Cd. Th. 8, 16; Gen. 125. Beheóld ofer leódwerum byrnende beám, 184, 20; Exod. 110. Mæst hlifade ofer Hróþgáres hordgestreónum, Beo. Th. 3802; B. 1899. Wígláf siteþ ofer Biówulfe, 5806; B. 2907. (2) denoting contact with anything, *upon, on*:—Hé gesette ofer stáne fét míne, Ps. Lamb. 39, 3. Hwonne hié ofer streámstaðe stæppan mósten (*might set foot on shore*), Cd. Th. 86, 21; Gen. 1434. Wind ofer ýðum *the wind on the waves*, Beo. Th. 3819; B. 1907. Ánra gehwylc hæfde sweord ofer his hype, Blickl. Homl. 11, 18. Sittende ofor eoselan folan, 71, 5. Úre Dryhten sæt ofer winda fiðerum, Salm. Kmbl. p. 198, 16. (3) denoting extension over, *throughout, in, on*:—Hé wolde ǽgðær ge ofer heofenum ge ofer eorþan ús his miltse gecýðon, Blickl. Homl. 39, 22: Gen. 4, 11. (4) denoting a higher degree, *beyond, more than*:—Ofer snáwe scínende, Ps. C. 50, 75; Ps. Grn. ii. 278, 75. (5) denoting the cause of an emotion, *over* (as in to rejoice *over*, etc.):—Byþ on heofone blis be ánum synfullum ðe dǽdbóte déþ, má ðonne ofer nigon and nigontigum rihtwísra, Lk. 15, 7. Ic blissige ofer ðínre sprǽce, Ps. Th. 118, 162. (6) denoting the object over which power is exercised:—Ðæt mód ðe ofer ðæm flǽsce sitt and his wealdan sceolde *mens carni praesidens*, Past. 36, 7; Swt. 257, 3. Ofer deóflum wealdeþ, Cd. Th. 263, 20; Dan. 765. (7) with the idea of movement, where the accusative might be expected:—Hleó wand ofer wolcnum, Cd. Th. 182, 23; Exod. 80. Up gewát líg ofer leófum, 231, 18; Dan. 249. Ofer ðære Reádan Sǽ eode Israela folc, Salm. Kmbl. p. 198, 20. (8) marking time, *after, beyond*:—Ðá undergeat heó ðæt se bróðer ne móste his lífes brúcan ofer ðam ánum geáre, Homl. Th. ii. 146, 17. Se dæg biþ ofer eástrum, H. R. 99, 15. II. *with acc.* generally with the idea of movement. (1) denoting motion in a definite direction across, to the other side of an object:—Ofer sǽ *citra pontum*, Wrt. Voc. ii. 18, 68. Ofer landgemǽru *extra terminum* . . . ofer ðone ford *trans vadum*, ofer sǽ *trans mare*, Ælfc. Gr. 47; Som. 47, 29, 38. Ðá cómon hí ofer ðære sǽs múþan, Mk. Skt. 5, 1. Hié ofer sǽ gewiton, Chr. 885; Erl. 82, 25. Hié eodon ofer land *they went across the country*, 896; Erl. 94, 14: Andr.

Kmbl. 2460; An. 1231. Ofer eástreámas ís brycgade *the ice threw a bridge across the rivers*, 2523; An. 1263. Hí wurpon heora waru ofor bord *they cast their wares overboard*, Homl. Th. i. 246, 2, 9. Ofer clif *per praeceps* (v. Mt. 8, 32, where the swine go over the cliff's edge), Wrt. Voc. ii. 72, 35. Ic út gange ofer mínre burge weall *transgrediar murum*, Ps. Th. 17, 28: Cd. Th. 90, 12; Gen. 1494. Ic cume ofer langne weg, 35, 13; Gen. 554. Se eádega bewlát ofer exle, 177, 7; Gen. 2926. (2) denoting motion which is diffused over a surface:—Streám út âweóll, fleów ofer foldan, Andr. Kmbl. 3046; An. 1526. Wíde ofer woruld ealle geseón, Cd. Th. 36, 2; Gen. 565: 42, 17; Gen. 675. Hé ofer ealle þeóde eágum wlíteþ, Ps. Th. 65, 6. Âlǽd upp ða froxas ofer eall Egipta land, Ex. 8, 5. Wǽron gewurden þýstru ofer ealle eorþan, Mt. 27, 45: Blickl. Homl. 93, 18. Bufan ðæm máran wealle ofer ealne ðone ymbgong hé is mid stǽnenum wíghúsum beworht, Ors. 2, 4; Swt. 74, 20. Mann ús ofer eall (cf. *Ger.* überall) sóhte, Homl. Skt. i. 23, 450. Ða weorcstánas lágon ofer eall *lay scattered in all directions*, 23, 490. (3) denoting extension through a space, *throughout, among*:—Se wæs mǽrost ofer werþeóde, Beo. Th. 1802; B. 899. Heó wæs seó eádgeste ofer eall wífa cynn *she was most blessed among all the race of women*, Blickl. Homl. 13, 15. Se sceal beón gehered ofor ealle þeóda, 71, 16. Hét hé beódan ofer ealle ða fird ðæt hié fóron ealle út ætsomne, Chr. 905; Erl. 98, 22. Wilnung leáses gilpes ofer eall folc, Bt. 18, 1; Fox 60, 24. (4) denoting motion from below, *over, above*:—Hefe upp ðíne hand ofer eall ðæt flód, and ofer burna and ofer móras, Ex. 8, 5. Mín unriht mé hlýpþ ofer heáfod, Ps. Th. 37, 4. Hié him âsetton segen gyldenne ofer heáfod, Beo. Th. 95; B. 48. Man slóh án geteld ofer ða hálgan bán, Swt. A. S. Rdr. 100, 150. Iudas up âhóf ðara róda twá ofer ðæt fǽge hús, Elen. Kmbl. 1759; El. 881. Se ðe âstáh ofer heofenas *qui ascendit super caelos*, ofer heálíce dúne âstíh ðú *super montem excelsum ascende tu*, Ælfc. Gr. 47; Som. 48, 23. (5) denoting motion from above, *upon, on*:—Se hys hús ofer stán getimbrode, Mt. Kmbl. 7, 24. Hé hine âsette ofer ðæs temples scylf, Blickl. Homl. 27, 11. Feallaþ ofor ús, 93, 33: Elen. Kmbl. 2267; El. 1135. (6) denoting the object upon which an action or feeling takes effect:—Andreas sette his hand ofer ðara wera eágan ... And eft hé sette his hand ofer hiora heortan, St. And. 12, 34–35. Sleáþ synnigne ofer seolfes múþ (*smite him over the mouth*), Andr. Kmbl. 2602; An. 1302. Sý hys blód ofer ús and ofer úre bearn *his blood be upon us, and upon our children*, Mt. Kmbl. 27, 25. Mín hand byþ ofer ðíne æceras and ofslihþ ðíne hors mid hefegum cwealme, Ex. 9, 3. Ða tácna ðe hé worhte ofer ða untruman men *the miracles he wrought upon the sick*, Homl. Th. i. 182, 1. Eftwyrd cymþ ofer middangeard, Cd. Th. 212, 17; Exod. 540. Se tán gehwearf ofer (*the lot fell upon*) ǽnne ealdgesíþa, Andr. Kmbl. 2209; An. 1106. Gé onfóþ ðæm mægene Hálges Gástes, se cymeþ ofor eów, Blickl. Homl. 119, 12. Ðín mildheortnes is mycel ofor mé, 89, 27. (7) denoting the object over which power is exercised:—His mægen wealdeþ ofer eall manna cyn, Ps. Th. 65, 6. Forðam ðe ðú wǽre getrýwe ofer lytle þing, ic gesette ðé ofer mycle, Mt. Kmbl. 25, 21. Ðú byst andweald hæbbende ofer týn ceastra ... Beó ðú ofer fíf ceastra, Lk. Skt. 19, 17–19. Se hæfde mægen ofer ealle gesceafta, Blickl. Homl. 9, 15. Ríce ofer heofenstólas, Cd. Th. 1, 15; Gen. 8. Cræft móda gehwylces ofer líchoman, Met. 26, 106. Deáþ rícsade ofer foldbúend, Exon. Th. 154, 17; Gú. 843. (8) denoting degree (*a*) *above, more than*; supra, super:—Ioseph wæs gleáwra ofer hí ealle, Ors. 1, 5; Swt. 34, 1. Hé lufode Iosep ofer his suna *he loved Joseph more than all his children*, Gen. 37, 3: 44, 20. Ne lufige ic nánwiht ðisses andweardan lýfes ofer ðæt (éce líf), ne furðum ðam gelíce, Shrn. 177, 14. Ða stówe ofer ealle óðre ic geceás, Blickl. Homl. 201, 7. Nys se leorningcniht ofer his láreów, ne þeów ofer hys hláford, Mt. Kmbl. 10, 24: Exon. Th. 105, 35; Gú. 33. Hit is áwriten, ðæt seó góde antswaru sý ouer ða sélestan selene, R. Ben. 55, 8. Ðæs biscepes weorc sceolon bión ofer óðra monna weorc *debet actionem populi actio transcendere praesulis*, Past. 12; Swt. 75, 3. Is án steorra ofer óðre beorht, Met. 29, 19. Moises wæs se bilewitusta mann ofer ealle men, Num. 12, 3. Fram twentig wintrum and ofer ðæt *a vigesimo anno et supra*, 1, 3. (*β*) *beyond, besides*; ultra:—Ofer ðæt (*ultro*) gé ne lǽtaþ hine ǽnig þing dón, Mk. Skt. 7, 12. Ne ofer ðæt (*ultra*) sweltan ne mágon, Lk. Skt. 20, 36. Ne lǽteþ hé ús nó costian ofer gemet, Blickl. Homl. 13, 9. Ðú sprycst ofer mǽþe úre *ultra etatem nostram*, Coll. Monast. Th. 32, 11. Ðæt héhste gód [is] ðætte man ne þurfe nánes óðres gódes ne eác ne récce ofer ðæt siððan hé ðæt hæbbe *id est bonum, quo quis adepto, nihil ulterius desiderare queat*, Bt. 24, 1; Fox 80, 13. Siððan ðú hí gecnáwan miht ðonne wát ic ðæt ðú ne wilnast nánes óðres þinges ofer ða (*you will desire nothing further*), 23; Fox 80, 3. Hié lícettaþ ðæt him ne síe náwuhtes cearu ofer ða ryhtwísnesse, Past. 41; Swt. 302, 10. Se ðe godgeldum onsæcge ofer (*besides*) God ánne, L. Alf. 32; Th. i. 52, 12. (9) denoting the passing over moral bounds, *in violation of, in opposition to, contrary to, against*:—Ofer Godes ǽ hé déþ *extra legem Domini facit*, Ælfc. Gr. 47; Som. 47, 29. Se wæs ofslagen ofer áþas and treówa *contra fidem jusjurandi peremptus est*, Bd. 2, 20; S. 521, 17: Chr. 894; Erl. 90, 5. Ætsǽton ða Centiscan beæftan ofer his bebod, 905; Erl. 98, 24: Blickl. Homl. 91, 16: Exon. Th. 244, 5; Jul. 23. Wite hé ðæt hé hit dé ófer Godes ést, and ofer ealra his háligra, and eác ofer monna godcundra háda and woruldcundra, Chart. Th. 131, 36: Exon. Th. 226, 10; Ph. 403: Cd. Th. 76, 2; Gen. 1251. Hié ǽr ofer hiera willan him tó gecierdon, Ors. 2, 5; Swt. 82, 10. Gecuron Brettanie Maximianus him tó cásere ofer his willan, 6, 35; Swt. 292, 15. (10) with words implying rest:—Standende ofer hig, Lk. Skt. 4, 39. Ne biþ forlǽten stán ofer stán, Blickl. Homl. 79, 1. Hé fyrgenbeámas ofer hárne stán hleonian funde, Beo. Th. 2834; B. 1415. Æþelingas ofer heánne hróf hand sceáwedon, 1970; B. 983. (11) denoting the subject of discourse (cf. to talk *over*):—Hé ofer benne spræc, wunde wælbleáte, 5442; B. 2724. Ofer Ysmahel ic gehírde ðé, Gen. 17, 20. (12) denoting the cause of an emotion (cf. I. 5):—Heó hæfþ genóh on ðís andweardan lífe, ac heó hit hæfþ eall forsewen ofer ðé ánne (*simply on your account* [?]), Bt. 10; Fox 28, 26. (13) *without*:—Gif hé gesécean dear wíg ofer wǽpen, Beo. Th. 1374; B. 685. (14) with words expressing time, (*a*) *after*:—Ofer middæg *post meridiem*, Gen. 3, 8. Ofor undern, Blickl. Homl. 93, 15. Ofer ealle tíd tó sáwenne *ultra omne tempus serendi*, Bd. 4, 28; S. 605, 39, 8. Ofer hyre deg ... ofer mínnæ dæg (cf. æfter hæora dæge, 12), Chart. Th. 520, 7–34. Ne onbirigdon ðæs bigleofan ofer ðæt (*ultra*), Jos. 5, 12. Hé ne oncnáweþ ofer ðæt stówe *non cognoscet amplius locum*, Ps. Lamb. 102, 16. Hé ofer ðæt (*ultra*) deófulgyldum ne þeówde, Bd. 2, 9; S. 512, 7: Ors. 5, 7; Swt. 230, 7: R. Ben. 53, 16. Longe ofer ðis, Exon. Th. 172, 15; Gú. 1144. Ofer ða niht, Beo. Th. 1476; B. 736. (*β*) expressing duration, *through, during*:—Ofer ealle ða niht ðe wé férdon *during the whole night that we marched*, Nar. 12, 2. Hé hié slóg ofer ealne ðone dæg, Ors. 4, 10; Swt. 200, 21. Ða steorran ðe ofer ealne winter scínaþ ... Ofer ealne sumor hí gáþ on nihtlícre tíde under ðissere eorþan, Lchdm. iii. 270, 24–26. Hí wunodon mid ðæm biscope ofer geár, and siðan gewendon tó Antiochia, Homl. Skt. i. 3, 81. Ða sylfan sealmas sýn dæghwamlíce geedlǽhte ofer ealle wucan, R. Ben. 43, 1. III. adverbially, or not followed by a case:—Ðæt ðú ne mihtst nǽnne weg findan ofer, Bt. 34, 4; Fox 138, 28. Hé eode tó ðære burge wealle, and fleáh út ofer, Ors. 5, 12; Swt. 244, 3. Ðonne cépþ hé hwǽr se weall unhéhst sý, and ðǽr ofer scýt (oferscýt?) *he observes where the wall is lowest, and over there he rushes*, Homl. Th. i. 484, 11. Án fiscere uneáþe hiene ǽnne ofer brohte, 2, 5; Swt. 84, 10. Mid Angelþeóde ðe hé ofer cyning wæs, Bd. 3, 6; S. 528, 3. Sió giémen ðære cirícean síe ðæm beboden ðe hié wel ofer mǽge, Past. 5; Swt. 45, 1. Wese ús beorhtnes ofer Drihtnes úres, Ps. Th. 89, 19. Se cwellere him ofer stód *illi instante carnifice*, Bd. 4, 16; S. 584, 36: Homl. Th. ii. 494, 27. Eall ðæt ofer biþ tó láfe is tó syllanne, swá swá Crist lǽrde: '*Quod superest date eleemosynam*:' ðæt ofer sí and tó láfe sellaþ ælmessan, Bd. 1, 27; S. 489, 26–30. Wé nú gehýrdon ðis hálige godspel beforan ús rǽdan, and ðéh wé hit sceolan eft ofer cweþan (*we must say it over again*), ðæt wé ðé geornor witon ðæt hit ús tó bysene belimpeþ éces lífes, Blickl. Homl. 15, 31. Ealle ðe ðǽr ofer beóþ getealde wintra, ða beóþ gewinn and sár, 89, 11. Hú þicke se hefon wǽre oððe hwæt ðǽr ofer wǽre, Bt. 35, 4; Fox 162, 23. Ofer ufa *desuper*, Mt. Kmbl. Rush. 21, 7. Ofer uppan *up above*, Met. 24, 27. [*Goth.* ufar: *O. Sax.* obar: *O. Frs.* over: *Icel.* ofr-; *and* cf. yfir: *O. H. Ger.* ubar.]

ófer, ófor, es; *m.* I. *an edge, border, margin*:—Óbr *margo*, Wrt. Voc. ii. 113, 45. Ófor, 55, 6. Ófer, Ælfc. Gr. 6; Som. 5, 51. On ðære lifre ófrum, Lchdm. ii. 204, 24. Smire ða ófras (*the borders of a cancer*) ðǽr hit reádige, 108, 20. II. *the land bordering on water, a river-bank, sea-shore, over* in local names, e. g. Over in Cambridgeshire, Wendover:—Strand *litus*, brerd *vel* ófer *crepido*, Wrt. Voc. i. 54, 24–25. On ðone ófer; ondlong ófres ðæt on Stánford, Cod. Dip. Kmbl. iii. 378, 20. Ondlong strǽte, ðæt on reádan ófer, iii. 52, 17. On ðære eá ófre, Nar. 10, 14: Byrht. Th. 132, 39; By. 28. On ófre ðæs forespreecenan streámes, Bd. 2, 3; S. 504, 18. Of sǽs ófre, 4, 13; S. 582, 32. On ðam sealtum ófre, Homl. Th. ii. 146, 6. On (meres) ófre, Beo. Th. 2746; B. 1371. Ófras heá, streámas stronge, Exon. Th. 404, 14; Rä. 23, 7. On wǽtum stówum and on ófrum, Lchdm. i. 222, 19: Hpt. Gl. 516, 70. Óbras, ófras *oras*, sǽ *marmora*, Wrt. Voc. ii. 91, 72: 64, 42. [*Laym. Havel.* over: *M. H. Ger.* uover: *Ger.* ufer: *O. Du.* oever.] v. eá-ófer.

ofer-ǽt, es; *m.* I. *over-eating, gluttony, excess in eating*:—Oferǽt *ingluvies*, Ælfc. Gr. 12; Som. 15, 54. Se oferǽt wierþ gehwierfed tó fierenluste *edacitas usque ad luxuriam pertrahit*, Past. 43, 2; Swt. 309, 14. Behealdaþ eów ðæt gé ne gehefegien eówer heortan mid oferǽte (*in crapula*), 18, 2; Swt. 129, 19. Ða téþ ðe nú on oferǽte blissiaþ, Homl. Th. i. 530, 32. Hine wið oferǽt beorge, L. E. I. 24; Th. ii. 422, 3. Þurh oferǽt *per commessationem*, Confess. Peccat. II. *rioting, feasting, an entertainment where excessive eating takes place*:—Ða hús ða ðe on tó gebiddenne geworhte wǽron ða syndon nú on hús gehwyrfed oferǽta (*commessationum*), Bd. 4, 25; S. 601, 13. Oferétum *comessationibus*, Kent. Gl. 888. [Cf. ofer-etes = *comessationes* (in Rom. 13, 13), Rel. Ant. i. 131, 32: *O. L. Ger.* ovar-ât: *O. H. Ger.* ubar-âzi, -âzzi; *f. crapula, commessatio.*]

ofer-ǽte; *adj. Given to excess in eating, gluttonous*:—Ne sceal mon beón druncengeorn, ne oferǽte, R. Ben. 17, 15.

ofer-bæc *the upper part of the back.* v. next word.

oferbæc-getéung, e; *f. Contraction of the muscles at the back of the neck, tetanus* (cf. Lchdm. iii. 110, 16 sqq.:—Ðisne lǽcecræft man sceal dón mannum ðe hyra swyran mid ðám sinum fortogen beóþ, ðæt hē hys nǽn geweald nāh, ðæt Grēcas hātaþ *tetanicus*):—Oferbæcgetēung *titanus*, Wrt. Voc. i. 19, 22.

ofer-bebeódan *to command, rule*:—Ic wealdige *vel* oferbebeóde *imperito*, Wrt. Voc. i. 54, 52.

ofer-becuman *to supervene*:—For ðī ðe oferbecymþ gedēfnes *quoniam supervenit mansuetudo*, Ps. Lamb. 89, 10.

ofer-bīdan *to outlast, outlive, survive*:—Gif hwylces weres forme wīf biþ deád, ðæt hē be leáfe ōðer wīf niman mōte; and gif hē ða oferbȳt (*si supersit ei*) wunige hē ā syððan wīfleás, L. Ecg. P. ii. 20; Th. ii. 190, 3. Yldo oferbīdeþ stānas, Salm. Kmbl. 599; Sal. 299. Ðā oferbād (*survived*) Ælfēh his brōðor, Chart. Th. 272, 12. Gif ic hire ouerbīde . . . gif heó mē ouerbīde, 583, 5–10. Hē ða bysgu oferbiden hæfde, Exon. Th. 135, 3; Gū. 518.

ofer-biterness, e; *f. Excessive bitterness; amaritudo*, Ps. Spl. 13, 6.

ofer-blice (?), an; *f. A superficies, surface*:—Oferbliocan *superficiem*, Txts. 181, 44.

ofer-blīðe; *adj. Over-cheerful*:—Ðǽm oferblīðum (*laetis*) is tō cȳðanne ða unrōtnessa ðe ðǽræfter cumaþ, and ðām unblīðum sint tō cȳðanne ða gefeán ðe him gehātene sindon, Past. 27; Swt. 187, 15: 189, 4: 61; Swt. 455, 22.

ofer-bord. v. ofer, II. 1.

ofer-brǽdan. I. *to overspread, overshadow, act as a covering over*:—Ðæt land biþ eal unnyt swā se fiicbeám hit oferbrǽt, Past. 45; Swt. 337, 13–15. Oferbrǽdeþ, Met. 7, 13. Heofonlīc leóht com ofer hī ealle and hī swā swā mycel scȳte hī ealle oferbrǽdde, Bd. 4, 7; S. 575, 7. Wolcen oferbrǽdde hiǽ *nubis obumbrans eos*, Mk. Skt. Rush. 9, 7: Lk. Skt. Rush. 9, 34. Sticmǽlum mid wuda oferwexen, sticmǽlum mid grēnum felda oferbrǽded, Homl. Th. i. 508, 24. Mid ðȳ feó oferbrǽded and beþeaht, Blickl. Homl. 199, 3. Bewrigen and oferbrǽded mid baswe godwebbe, 207, 16. Apollonius mid rōsan rude wæs eal oferbrǽded, Ap. Th. 22, 4. II. *to overspread, put a covering over*:—God oferbrǽdde byrnendne heofon nette, Cd. Th. 182, 9; Exod. 73. [*Laym.* mid palle overbræd.]

ofer-brǽdels, es; *m. A covering, veil, garment*:—Cyrtel *vel* oferbrǽdels *palla*, Wrt. Voc. i. 16, 56. Oferbrēdels *operimentum*, Kent. Gl. 853. Swā swā oferbrǽdels (*opertorium*) ðū āwenst hyg, Ps. Lamb. 102, 27. On oferbrǽdelse (*velamento*) fyðera ðīnra, Ps. Spl. 62, 8. Hē þencþ on ðam oferbrǽdelse (*surface*) his mōdes ðæt hē sciele monig gōd weorc wyrcan, and hē þencþ mid innewearde mōde ðæt hē gierneþ for gilpe . . . on hiera mōdes rinde . . . ac on ðam piðan . . . , Past. 9, 1; Swt. 55, 18–23. Oferbrǽdels *superhumeralis*, 14, 3; Swt. 83, 21. Hī āhōfen ðone oferbrǽdels (*the veil*) of ðære byrgene, Homl. Skt. i. 8, 227. vii. of[er]brǽdelsas, Chart. Th. 429, 26. [*Icel.* yfir-breizl *a coverlet.*]

ofer-brǽw, -brāw, es; *m. An eye-brow*:—Hæfþ mǽden tācn on oferbrāwe, Lchdm. iii. 188, 5. [*O. H. Ger.* uber-brāwa *supercilium.*] v. ofer-brū.

ofer-brecan *to infringe, violate* (*an agreement*):—Hē oferbræc heora gecwedrǽdenne, Ors. 3, 6; Swt. 108, 8: 5, 12; Swt. 242, 8.

ofer-bregdan, -brēdan. I. *v. trans. To overspread, cover, draw a covering over*:—Se ða burh oferbrægd blācan līge, Andr. Kmbl. 3080; An. 1543. Niht oferbrǽd beorgas steápe, 2613; An. 1308. II. *intrans. To break out over a surface*:—Scamoniam geceós ðus brec on tū dō hwōn on ðine tungan gif hió hwīte oferbregdeþ swā meluc ðonne hió biþ gōd *choose scammony thus; break it in two, put a bit on your tongue, if it breaks out all over white as milk, it is good*, Lchdm. ii. 272, 18.

ofer-brū; *gen.* -brūwe; *f. An eye-brow*:—Mǽden (hæfþ) tācn on oferbrūwe swīðran, Lchdm. iii. 186, 25: 192, 28. Oferbrūa *supercilia*, Wrt. Voc. i. 42, 69. Oferbrūwa *supercilium*, 64, 33: 70, 40: 282, 47. Betwux oferbrūan and brǽwum *intercilium*, 43, 4. Oferbrūum *supercili*[*i*]*s*, Txts. 172, 33. v. ofer-brǽw.

ofer-brycgian *to overbridge, make a bridge over*:—Ðā hēt Maxentius oferbrycgian ða eá mid scipum, Homl. Th. ii. 304, 22.

ofer-būgan (?) *to avoid, shun*:—Hié sindon suā micle wærlīcor tō oferbūganne [ferbūgonne, Cott. MSS.] suā mon ongiet ðæt hié on māran ungewitte beóþ *tanto caute declinandi sunt, quanto insane rapiuntur*, Past. 40, 5; Swt. 295, 21. [*Ofer* is probably a mistake for *fer.* v. note on this passage, and *for-būgan.*]

ofer-cæfed *covered with ornamental work*:—Ofercæfedu *innexa*, Germ. 394, 353. Cf. be-cæfed *falerata*, Wrt. Voc. ii. 34, 67; cæfing *discriminale* (ornamentum capitis mulieris, Wülck. Gl. 656, 13), 141, 1: *and see* ymb-cæfed.

ofer-ceald; *adj. Excessively cold*, Runic pm. Kmbl. 341, 14; Rūn. 11. [Cf. *Icel.* ofr-kuldi *excessive cold.*]

ofer-cīdan *to censure, reprove*:—Ða ðe wyrceaþ Sunnandæge æt ðam forman cyrre Grēcas hȳ ofercīdaþ (*arguunt*), L. Ecg. C. 35; Th. ii. 160, 31. Ðū ofercīddest *increpasti*, Ps. Spl. T. 118, 21.

ofer-cirr, es; *m. A passing over*:—Ofercerr *transmigratio*, Mt. Kmbl. Lind. 1, 11.

ofer-climban, -climman *to ascend, climb upon*:—Alexander ðone weall oferclom *cum murum escendisset*, Ors. 3, 9; Swt. 134, 13.

ofer-cræft, es; *m. Craft, fraud*:—Gif hwā mid his ofercræfte (*per fraudem*) wīf nȳdinga nimþ, L. Ecg. P. ii. 13; Th. ii. 186, 20.

ofer-cuman. I. *to overcome, vanquish, subdue*:—Ofercymeþ hē ælle his feónd, Lchdm. iii. 170, 19. Ofercymþ *deicit, confudit*, Wrt. Voc. ii. 133, 68. Ofercom *obpressit*, 65, 35. Æþelfriþ Scotta þeóde mid gefeohte ofercom (*praelio conterens*), Bd. 1, 34; S. 499, 17: Cd. Th. 178, 33; Exod. 21. Hē ðone feónd ofercwom, Beo. Th. 2551; B. 1273. Hié feónd heora þurh ānes cræft ofercōmon, 1403; B. 699. Ðæm wergan gāste wiðstondan and ofercuman, Blickl. Homl. 135, 11: 119, 21. Beswicen and ofercumen, 179, 5. Ðonne hié hwelc folc mid gefeohte ofercumen hæfdon, Ors. 2, 4; Swt. 70, 23. Nīða ofercumen, Beo. Th. 1694; B. 845. Ofercumen *obpressus*, Wrt. Voc. ii. 65, 34. Ofercymen wæs *obstipuit*, 63, 9. Ðū mē hæfst ofercumenne mid ðīnre gesceádwīsnesse, Bt. 22, 1; Fox 76, 12. Hē ongitt hine selfne ofercumenne (-cymenne, Hatt. MS.), Past. 34, 1; Swt. 228, 20. Ðās men geseóþ ðæt hié synt ofercumene, Blickl. Homl. 189, 5. Ofercymene *consternati*, Wrt. Voc. ii. 91, 10. Ofercumenum leahtrum *devictis vitiis*, Prud. 28 a. II. *to come upon, reach, obtain*:—Ofercuom *obtinuit*, Wrt. Voc. ii. 115, 29. Ofercom, 63, 26. Nānne ne sparedon cwicera manna ðe hié ofercuman mihton (*spared none that they could come up with*), Judth. Thw. 24, 41; Jud. 235. His gefēran ðȳ ofercumendan wōle (*pestilentia superveniente*) fordilgode wǽron, Bd. 4, 1; S. 563, 26.

ofer-cyme, es; *m. A coming upon, arrival*:—Ǽr ðon ðe hē mid ofercyme semninga deáþes ealle tīd hreówe forlure *priusquam subito mortis superventu tempus omne poenitendi perderet*, Bd. 5, 13; S. 632, 12.

ofer-cȳðan *to bring stronger testimony than another*:—Wē cwǽdon be mannum . . . gif āþ burste oððe ofercȳðed wǽre (*if the oath were not supported by a sufficient number of compurgators, or were disproved by testimony more strongly supported by oath.* Cf. mid āþe cȳðan, gecȳðan), ðæt hȳ siððan āþwyrðe nǽron, L. Ed. 3; Th. i. 160, 20.

ofer-dōn *to overdo, do to excess*:—Ðonne sceal his steór beón mid lufe gemetegod, nā mid wælhreáwnysse oferdōn, Homl. Th. ii. 532, 13. Ealle oferdōne þing dæriaþ *omnia nimia nocent*, Homl. Skt. i. 1, 163.

ofer-drenc, es; *m. Excessive drinking, drunkenness*:—Ða heáfodleahtras sind . . . singal oferdrenc . . . , Homl. Th. ii. 592, 6. Ðū woldest mē laðian, ðā ðā ic wæs mid ðē, ðæt ic swīðor drunce swilce for blisse ofer mīne gewunan . . . Ūre Hǽlend on his hālgan godspelle forbeád ðone oferdrenc eallum gelȳfendum mannum . . . and ða hālgan lāreówas æfter ðam Hǽlende ālēdon ðone unþeáw . . . for ðan ðe se oferdrenc fordēþ ðæs mannes sāwle and his gesundfulnysse, Ælfc. T. Grn. 21, 29–37. v. ofer-drync.

ofer-drencan *to overdrench, give a person too much to drink, to inebriate, intoxicate*:—Se ðe þurh fācn ōðerne oferdrencþ (*inebriaverit*), fæste .xl. daga, L. Ecg. P. iv. 37; Th. ii. 214, 20: Past. 36; Swt. 261, 14. Ðū oferdrenctest hig *inebriasti eam*, Ps. Spl. 64, 9. Hié hié selfe mid ealoþ oferdrencton, Ors. 5, 3; Swt. 222, 6. Se ðe ne wirnþ ðæs wīnes his lāre ða mōd mid tō oferdrencanne . . . hē biþ oferdrenced mid ðæm drence mislīcra giefa, Past. 49; Swt. 381, 5–6: Bt. 24, 4; Fox 84, 33. Hȳ beóþ oferdrencte (*inebriabuntur*) on ðære genihte ðīnes hūses, Ps. Th. 35, 8: Judth. Thw. 21, 22; Jud. 31. [*O. H. Ger.* ubar-trenkjan *inebriare.*]

ofer-drettan (?) *to take with violence*:—Wē oferdryttan *praeoccupemus*, Ps. Spl. 94, 2. v. ge-drettan, -dreccan.

ofer-drīfan. I. *to cover by drifting*:—Ðeáh hit wind oððe sǽs flōd mid sonde oferdrīfen *though the wind or sea cover it by driving the sand over it*, Ors. 1, 7; Swt. 40, 1. II. *to overcome, refute, repel, defeat*:—Ðū ðe þióstro giduoles oferdrīfest (*depellis*), Rtl. 38, 17. Se Hǽlend ne geswutulode nā him his mihte ac oferdrāf hine geþyldelīce mid hālgum gewritum *the Saviour did not display his power to him* (*the devil*) *but overcame him patiently by the holy scriptures*, Homl. Th. i. 176, 11. Marcellus folgode ðam sceandlīcan drȳ ōððæt Petrus ðone ārleásan oferdrāf, Homl. Skt. i. 10, 197. Onsage oferdrīfan *to refute an accusation*, 2, 206. Wē syndon fram ðē oferswȳðde, ac wē ācsiaþ: Hwæt eart ðū swā wunderlīc on ānes mannes hiwe ūs tō oferdrȳfenne, Nicod. Thw. 16, 20. Gif hig sacan stande ðæt hig .viii. secgaþ and ða ðe ðǽr oferdrifene beóþ gilde heora ǽlc .vi. healfmarc *if they* (*the twelve*) *disagree, that which eight of them say shall stand: and those that in such case are out-voted shall each pay six half-marks*, L. Eth. iii. 13; Th. i. 298, 4.

ofer-drinc. v. ofer-drync.

ofer-drincan *to overdrink* (*one's self*):—Ne oferdrincaþ gē eów wīnes, L. E. I. 40; Th. ii. 438, 19. Gif hwylc bisceop hine oferdrince (*se inebriet*), L. Ecg. P. iv. 33; Th. ii. 214, 12. Beón oferdruncen *inebriari*, Lk. 12, 45. Ðæt mōd, ða hwīle ðe hit biþ oferdruncen ðæs ierres, Past. 40; Swt. 295, 3. Swā hwā swā ōðerne drencþ, hē wirþ self oferdruncen, 49; Swt. 381, 4. Swā swā mihti oferdruncon (*crapulatus*) fram wīne, Ps. Spl. 77, 71. Swā swā oferdruncen man wāt ðæt hē sceolde tō his hūse, and ne mæg ðeáh ðider āredian, Bt. 24, 4; Fox 84, 30. [*O. H. Ger.* ubar-trinkan.]

ofer-druncen, es; *n. Drunkenness, inebriety*:—Ne gerīseþ ǣnig unnytt mid bisceopum, ne doll ne dysig, ne tō oferdruncen, L. I. P. 9; Th. ii. 314, 31. Ðæt preóstas beorgan wið oferdruncen, and hit beleán ōðrum mannum, L. Edg. C. 57; Th. ii. 256, 13. Gif preóst lufige oferdruncen, L. N. P. L. 41; Th. ii. 296, 11. [*O. H. Ger.* ubar-trunkani *ebrietas, crapula.*]

ofer-druncenness, e; *f. Drunkenness, intoxication, rioting*:—Oferdruncennys *ebrietas*, L. Ecg. P. iv. 64; Th. ii. 224, 30. Gif munuc for oferdruncennysse (*ex ebrietate*) spīwe, iv. 34–36; Th. ii. 214, 14–19. Ne gewunigen gē tō oferdruncennisse (*non in ebrietatibus*), Past. 43, 9; Swt. 317, 18. Ða ofordruncennessa ðe hē lufode, Blickl. Homl. 195, 15.

ofer-drync, es; *m.* I. *excessive drinking, drunkenness*:—Behealdaþ eów ðæt gē ne gehefgien eówre heortan mid oferdrynce (*ebrietate*), Past. 18, 2; Swt. 129, 19. Hī fērdon tō sumre wydewan hām and ðǣr wǣron ondrencte mid oferdrynce, Guthl. 14; Gdwin. 62, 20. II. *an entertainment where excessive drinking takes place* (cf. ge-drinc):—Hē begǣþ unǣtas and oferdrincas *comessationibus vacat atque conviviis*, Deut. 21, 20. [*O. H. Ger.* ubar-trunk *ebrietas*: cf. *O. L. Ger.* obardrank.]

ofer-dyre *a lintel*; superliminare, Wrt. Voc. i. 290, 17. [*O. H. Ger.* ubar-turi *superliminare.*] Cf. ofer-gedyre.

ofere; *adv. From above*; desuper, Ps. Spl. 77, 27.

ofer-eáca, an; *m.* I. *an over-plus, a surplus, what remains over when a part has been taken*:—Ðone mǣstan dǣl ðæs folces hī ofslōgon, and ðone ofereácan āweg gelǣddon, Homl. Th. ii. 66, 4. Ða seofon mynstru hē gegōdode, ðone ofereácan his ǣhta hē āspende on Godes þearfum, 1118, 31. Oferēcan, Chart. Th. 482, 17. Ofæreácan, 554, 32. Wē niman eall ðæt hē āge, and niman ǣrest ðæt ceápgyld of ðam yrfe, and dǣle man syððan ðone ofereácan on .ii., L. Ath. v. 1, 1; Th. i. 228, 16: v. 6, 1; Th. i. 232, 28: v. 6, 3; Th. i. 234, 6. Ðæs geáres ofereácan fæste hē *reliquum anni jejunet*, L. Ecg. P. ii. 29; Th. ii. 194, 13. II. *an addition, augmentation*:—Oferēce *augmentum*, Rtl. 85, 33.

ofer-eald; *adj. Exceedingly old*:—Ðeáh hit gecyndelīc sȳ on menniscum gewunan, ðæt man mildheortnesse cȳðe ðām oferealdum and ðām cildgeongum, R. Ben. 61, 12.

ofer-ealdormann, es; *m. A chief officer*:—Hē wæs hyre þēna hire hūses and hire gefērscipes oferealdormann *erat primus ministrorum et princeps domus ejus*, Bd. 4, 3; S. 567, 22.

ofer-eode. v. ofer-gān.

ofer-etol, -ettol; *adj. Given to excess in eating, gluttonous*:—Ofereotol *edax* vel *glutto*, Wrt. Voc. i. 86, 49. Se mynstres hordere sī . . . wīs, sȳfre and nā oferettol (-etol, MS. T.), R. Ben. 54, 8. Ðes oferetola man *hic comedo*, Ælfc. Gr. 36; Som. 38, 47. Gehiéren ða oferetolan ða word ðe Krist cuæþ: Behealdaþ eów ðæt eówre heortan ne sīn gehefegode mid oferǣte, Past. 43, 9; Swt. 317, 8, 16.

ofer-etolness, e; *f. Excess in eating, gluttony*:—Ne gewunigen gē tō oferetolnisse *non in comessationibus*, Past. 43, 9; Swt. 317, 18.

ofer-fær *a passing over*; transmigratio, Mt. Kmbl. p. 12, 13: Lind. 1, 17.

ofer-færeld, es; *m. n. A going across, passage, transit*:—Galilea is gecweden oferfæreld, Homl. Th. i. 224, 10. Pasca getācnaþ oferfæreld, Anglia viii. 322, 2. Crist gewāt þurh oferfæreld of deáþe tō līfe, 330, 9. Heore is ðæt scip and se ouerfæreld ðare hæuene *eorum* (the monks of Christchurch) *est navicula et transfretatio portus*, Chart. Th. 317, 38. Æfter oferfærelde sǣ reádre *post transitum maris rubri*, Hymn. Surt. 82, 7.

ofer-fæðman; *p.* de *To cover in an embrace, to overspread, to envelope*:—Swilce hē oferfæðmed ealne middangeard *as if it* (*the tree of Nebuchadnezzar's vision*) *would cover with embracing boughs all the world*, Cd. Th. 247, 24; Dan. 502. Þȳstre oferfæðmed *enveloped in darkness*, Exon. Th. 470, 12; Hy. 11, 14.

ofer-fǣtt; *adj. Too fat, obese*:—Oferfǣt *obesus*, Wrt. Voc. i. 51, 10.

ofer-faran. I. *intrans. To pass, go off*:—Ælþeódiglīce ic oferfare *peregre transeo*, Ælfc. Gr. 38; Som. 41, 28. Oferfare on munt swā swā spearwa *transmigra in montem sicut passer*, Ps. Spl. 10. 1. II. *trans.* (*a*) *to pass, cross* (*a river, boundary*, etc.):—Ic Iordane eft ongeán oferfare mid twām floccon, Gen. 32, 10. Gyf ðū Iordanem oferfærst, Glostr. Frag. 108, 19. Moyses oferfōr ða Reádan Sǣ, Wulfst. 210, 12. Oferfōren *egrederentur*, Hpt. Gl. 464, 64. Ðā gebeótode ān his þegna ðæt hē mid sunde ða eá oferfaran wolde, Ors. 2, 4; Swt. 72, 29: Bd. 1, 7; S. 478, 9. Ne ða ebban foldes mearce oferfaran mōton, Met. 11, 70. (β) *to pass through, traverse*:—Hī forþ oferfōran folcmǣro land, Cd. Th. 108, 4; Gen. 1801. Siððan ðū ðone up āhafast forþ oferfarenne, Met. 24, 26. (γ) *to pass through* (*a danger*):—Ða hyssas fǣrgryre fȳres oferfaren hæfdon, Cd. Th. 245, 15; Dan. 463. (δ) *to pass through, penetrate*:—Oferfarende *penetrans*, Hpt. Gl. 493, 30. (ε) *to come upon, come across, meet with*:—Se here . . . slōgon and bærndon swā hwæt swā hī oferfōron *the Danes slew and burnt whatever they came across*, Chr. 1016; Erl. 157, 2.

ofer-feallan *to fall upon, to attack*:—Hié oferfeóllan ða ðe ða yrmþo genǣson, Blickl. Homl. 203, 19. [*Ger.* über-fallen.]

ofer-feng, es; *m. A clasp, buckle, latchet of a shoe*:—Oferfeng *fibula*, Wrt. Voc. i. 40, 53. Oferfengc, 74, 60: *ligulam, fibulam*, Hpt. Gl. 523, 2. v. ofer-fōn.

ofer-feohtan *to conquer, vanquish*:—Oferfehtaþ *debellant*, Ps. Surt. 55, 4. Hī feónd oferfeohtaþ, Exon. Th. 150, 7; Gū. 775. Oft hī ofyrfuhtun (*expugnaverunt*) mē, Ps. Spl. C. 128, 2. Hæfde Drihten feónd oferfohten, Cd. Th. 289, 29; Sat. 405. Sió burg biþ micle ðē iéðre tō oferfeohtanne ðe hió self fieht wið hié selfe *tanto ille sine labore superat, quanto et ipsa, quae vincitur, contra semetipsam pugnat*, Past. 38, 6; Swt. 277, 25. [*O. H. Ger.* ubar-fehtan *expugnare, devincere.*]

ofer-fēran. I. *to pass over* or *through, to cross, traverse*:—Ic oferfērde (*transivi*) Iordane, Gen. 32, 10. Seó sǣ ðe se Hǣlend oferfērde, Homl. Th. i. 182, 25. Oberfoerde *emenso*, Wrt. Voc. ii. 107, 22. Oferfērde, 29, 33. Mid ðȳ wit oferfērdon (*transissemus*) ðās wununesse ðara eádigra gāsta, Bd. 5, 12; S. 629, 31. Ðet hī ne oferfērdan *ne transirent*, Kent. Gl. 275. Se mōr swā brād swā man mæg on twām wucum oferfēran, Ors. 1, 1; Swt. 18, 34. II. *to come upon* or *across, meet with*:—Se here fērde intō Myrcean and fordydon eall ðæt hē oferfērde, Chr. 1016; Erl. 157, 12. v. ofer-faran.

ofer-fēre. v. un-oferfēre *and next word.*

ofer-fērness, e; *f. Possibility of being crossed*:—On twām stōwum is oferfērnes *duobus tantum in locis est transmeabilis*, Bd. 1, 25; S. 486, 21.

ofer-firr, e; *f. Too great distance*:—Hit is feáwum mannum cūð for ðære oferfyrre *insula Thule, quae per infinitum a ceteris separata, vix paucis nota habetur*, Ors. 1, 1; Swt. 24, 21.

ofer-flēdan *to overflood, overflow, inundate, cover with water*:—Seó eá Nilus oferflētt (-flēd, MS. M.: -flēt, MSS. P. L.) eall ðæt Egiptisce land, and stent oferflēde hwīlon mōnaþ hwīlon leng *the river Nile floods all the land of Egypt, and continues in a state of overflow sometimes a month, sometimes longer*, Lchdm. iii. 252, 23. [*Ger.* über-fluthen.]

ofer-flēde; *adj. Overflowing its banks.* v. preceding word. [Cf. *O. H. Ger.* ubar-fluatida *superfluitas*: *Ger.* über-fluth *overflowing* (*of a river*).]

ofer-fleón *to fly over*:—Ic oferfleó *supervolo*, Ælfc. Gr. 47; Som. 48, 46. [*In* Beo. Th. 5043; B. 2525 *it might be better to take* ofer *separate from* fleón:—Nelle ic beorges weard ofer fleón fōtes trem *I mean not to flee the dragon* [*by retiring*] *over even part of a foot's space.*]

ofer-flītan *to overcome in a contest, to confute*:—Hē ðē æt sunde oferflāt, hæfde māre mægen, Beo. Th. 1039; B. 517. Ymb done tīman wæs gegaderad iii. hund biscepa and eahtatiéne hiene tō oferflītanne (*to confute Arius*), Ors. 6, 30; Swt. 284, 1.

ofer-flōwan. I. *to overflow, cover with water*:—Seó eá ðæt land middeweard oferfleów mid fōtes þicce flōde, Ors. 1, 3; Swt. 32, 6. II. *to overflow, pass beyond bounds*:—Gōd gemet, geheápod and oferflōwende hig syllaþ on eówerne bearm, Lk. Skt. 6, 38.

ofer-flōwend; *adj. Superfluous*:—Īdel and oferflōwend byþ eal ðæt tōforan ðysum is, R. Ben. 91, 4.

ofer-flōwendlīce; *adv. Superfluously*:—Oferflōwenlīce *superflue*, Hpt. Gl. 527, 57.

ofer-flōwend-, flōwed-, flōwen-ness, e; *f. Superfluity, exuberance*:—Oferflōwenes *superfluitas*, Wrt. Voc. i. 17, 9. Oferflōwendnys *affluentia*, 41, 10. Eall hit byþ oferflōwendnyss and īdel tōforan ðisum, R. Ben. 90, 5. Mid heora ouerflōwednesse ne gedrīfen ða gebrōðru, 60, 17: 108, 5. Gif hit gelimpþ for oferflōwennysse metes (*ex superfluitate cibi*), L. Ecg. P. iii. 14; Th. ii. 200, 30. Hē ne dranc mid oferflōwendnysse, Homl. Th. i. 168, 12: ii. 218, 30. Wē nellaþ habban ūs tō līfes bricum, ac tō oferflōwednyssum, 540, 11.

ofer-flōwness, e; *f. Superfluity, overflowing*:—Oferflōwnes *superfluitas*, Wrt. Voc. ii. 149, 69. Oferflōuwnys (*superfluitas*) ðæs gecyndes, Bd. 1, 27; S. 494, 1. Of oferflōwnysse, S. 496, 37. His līchoma mid oferflōwnessum gefrætwod wæs, Blickl. Homl. 195, 12.

ofer-fōn *to seize*:—Oferfēng *obuncabat*, Wrt. Voc. ii. 62, 69. Þeódrīc ðone þegn oferfēng, hēht healdan ðone hererinc, Met. 1, 69. Ðā genāman him ǣfest tō ða ealdormen ðara sacerda, and hine sylfne oferfēngon, Blickl. Homl. 177, 21. Hē hiene oferfōn hēt, and āhōn, Ors. 4, 4; Swt. 164, 32. Oferfangen *comprehensus*, Wrt. Voc. ii. 133, 8. [*O. H. Ger.* ubar-fāhan *rapere.*] v. ofer-feng.

ofer-froren *frozen over*:—Ðā wæs Donua seó eá swīðe oferfroren, Ors. 4, 11; Swt. 208, 1: 1, 1; Swt. 21, 17.

ofer-full; *adj. Over-full*:—Oferfull *crapulatus*, Ps. Lamb. 77, 65. [*Goth.* ufar-fulls: *O. H. Ger.* ubar-foll *crapulatus.*]

ofer-fylgan, -fylgean; *p.* de *To pursue, persecute, attack*:—Gif ðæm mōde mon tō ungemetlīce mid ðære þreápunga oferfylgþ *si mentem immoderata increpatio affligit*, Past. 21, 7; Swt. 167, 15. Ðonne ða iersigendan menn ōðrum monnum oferfylgeaþ tō ðon suīðe ðæt hit mon forberan ne mæg *cum ita iracundi alios impetunt, ut declinari non possint*, Past. 40, 5; Swt. 295, 10. Assael hine unwærlīce mid anwealde þreátode and him oferfylgde *hunc* (*Abner*) *cum Asael vi incautae praecipitationis impeteret*, Swt. 295, 14.

ofer-fyll, e; -fyllu (o); *indecl. f. Overfulness, repletion, surfeit, excess in eating* or *in drinking*:—Gȳfernys vel oferfil *gastrimargia*, Wrt. Voc.

i. 27, 21. Oferfyl *aplestia*, ii. 10, 12. Ǽlc oferfyl fēt unhǽlo, Prov. Kmbl. 61. Nǽfre oferfyl ne filige, forđī nis cristenum monnum nān þing swā wiđerweardlīc swā swā oferfyl, R. Ben. 63, 19-21. Seó oferfyll simle fēt unþeáwas, Bt. 31, 1; Fox 110, 27: Blickl. Homl. 37, 14. Wiđ manegum ādlum đa đe cumaþ of oferfyllo, Lchdm. ii. 178, 10: 244, 4. Hit gelimpeþ of oferfylle... for oferfyllo (*ex crapula*), Bd. 1, 27; S. 496, 36-42. On oferfylle (oferfyllo, Lind. Rush.) *in crapula*, Lk. Skt. 21, 34: Blickl. Homl. 159, 18. Đū scealt druncen fleón, and đa oferfylle ealle forlǽtan, Dōm. L. 32, 75. Nīwes wīnes oferfelle *musti crapulam*, Hymn. Surt. 97, 18. Þurh oferfylla and mænigfealde synna heora eard hȳ forworhton, Wulfst. 166, 29. [*Goth.* ufar-fullei: *O. H. Ger.* ubarfullī *crapula*.]

ofer-fyllan *to fill to overflowing*, (of eating) *to feed to excess*:—Oferfylled *crapulatus*, Wrt. Voc. ii. 136, 56. Hȳ beóþ oferfyllede ōþ spīweþan, R. Ben. 136, 25. [*Goth.* ufar-fulljan.]

ofer-gǽgan *to transgress*:—Hwī ofergǽge gē Godes word *cur transgredimini verbum Domini?* Num. 14, 41. v. for-gǽgan *and next word.*

ofer-gǽgedness, e; *f. Transgression*:—Wē sceolon mid geswince ūs metes tilian for Adames ofergǽgednysse, Homl. Th. ii. 462, 12: 486, 26: Boutr. Scrd. 18, 13. v. for-gǽgedness *and preceding word.*

ofer-gān; *p.* -eode; *pp.* -gān. I. *to overspread*:—Seó lyft ofergǽþ ealne middaneard, Lchdm. iii. 272, 17. II. *to overrun* (*a country, as a victorious army does*), *to conquer*:—Se here fōr tō Sandwīc, and swā đanon tō Gipeswīc, and đæt eall ofereode, Chr. 993; Erl. 132, 4. Wǽndon đæt hē sceolde đet land ofergān, 1070; Erl. 207, 24. Hī hæfdon đā ofergān .i. Eást-Engle, and .ii. Eást-Sexe..., 1011; Erl. 144, 33. III. *to pass a point* or *limit*:—Ic ofergaa wall *transgrediar murum*, Ps. Surt. 17, 30. Hē ofergǽþ đone sūđran sunnstede, Lchdm. iii. 252, 14. Gemǽre đū settest đæt nā hī ofergāþ (*transgredientur*), Ps. Spl. 103, 10. Ofereode *excederit*, Wrt. Voc. ii. 30, 41. III a. *to pass a moral limit, to transgress*:—Forhwon leorneras đīne ofergǽþ gesetnisse đara ældra, Mt. Kmbl. Rush. 15, 2. IV. *to pass across, traverse, cross*:—Hē ofereode steáp stānhliþo, Beo. Th. 2820; B. 1408. Hī đa Reádan Sǽ ofereodon, Homl. Th. ii. 200, 27: Beo. Th. 5911; B. 2959. V. *to pass, pass off* or *away, be over, come to an end*:—Hū hrædlīce se eorþlīca hlīsa ofergǽþ, Past. 59, 1; Swt. 447, 30. Đæt ilce yfel ofereode būtan geblōte *pestilentia sine ullis sacrificiorum satisfactionibus sedata est*, Ors. 5, 2; Swt. 218, 3. Đa geswinc đe ofergān sculon *quod transeundo laboratur*, Past. 52, 5; Swt. 407, 31. V a. *impers. with gen. To be over* (*with anything*):—Đæs ofereode đisses swā mæg *it is all over with that, so may it be with this, that trouble is over, so may this be*, Exon. Th. pp. 377-379; Deór. 7, etc. VI. *to come upon, attack* (of disease, sleep, etc.):—Wæterseócnyss hine ofereode, Homl. Th. i. 86, 9. Hine slǽp ofereode, Andr. Kmbl. 1640; An. 821. v. ofer-gangan.

ofer-gangan. I. *to cross* (*a boundary*):—Ic ofergange (*transgrediar*) weall, Ps. Spl. 17, 31. Heora ǽnig ōđres ne dorste mearc ofergangan, Met. 20, 71. II. *to conquer*:—Gē feónda gehwone ofergangaþ, Cd. Th. 213, 33; Exod. 561 [cf. Orm. 10228: To werenn hemm wiþþ wiþerrþeod þatt wollde hemm oferrganngenn]. III. *to pass, pass off, be over*:—Hié gebidon đæt se ege ofergongen wæs, Ors. 4, 2; Swt. 160, 31. IV. *to come upon* (of sleep):—Mec slǽp ofergongeþ, Exon. Th. 422, 23; Rä. 41, 10. [*Goth.* ufar-gaggan.] v. ofer-gān.

ofer-gapian *to neglect, disregard*:—Ne hē þurh đone trūwan his sacerdhādes ofergapige (ofergumige, other MS.) his gehȳrsumnysse *let not the priest through trust in his priesthood be careless of his obedience*, R. Ben. 112, 2. [Cf. *O. H. Ger.* geffida *consideratio*.]

ofer-geáre; *adj. Old, superannuated*:—Gif wyrm ete đa tēþ genim ofergeáre holenrinde, Lchdm. ii. 50, 14. [Cf. *Ger.* über-jährig *superannuated*.] Cf. þrī-geáre.

ofer-geatu, e; *f. Oblivion*:—Đa his cwide weoldan on ofergeate hæbben (*would have it buried in oblivion*, cf. *O. H. Ger.* habe in āgezze *obliviscere*, Grff. iv. 279), Ps. Th. 128, 6. Cf. be-geatu.

ofer-gedrync, es; *n. Excessive drinking* or *feasting*:—Hié hæfdon wiste and plegan and oforgedrync, Blickl. Homl. 99, 21. v. ofer-drync.

ofer-gedyre, es; *n. A lintel*:—Smīton on ǽgđer gedyre and on đa ofergedyru *ponent super utrumque postem et in superliminaribus domorum*, Ex. 12, 7. v. ofer-dyre.

ofer-gemet, es; *n. Excess*:—Suā oft suā wē ūre hand dōþ tō ūrum mūþe for giéfernesse ofergemet (*per immoderatum usum*), Past. 43, 5; Swt. 313, 14. [Cf. *O. H. Ger.* ubar-gamez; *adj. supervacuus*.]

ofer-genga, an; *m. One who goes over* or *beyond*:—Gif hē biþ on .xi. nihta ealdne mōnan se biþ landes ofergenga *if he is born on the eleventh of the month, he will be a traveller about the land*, Lchdm. iii. 158, 1: 160, 30.

ofer-geong, es; *m. A going across*; transmigratio, Mt. Kmbl. p. 12, 13. Cf. forþ-geong.

ofer-geótan *to cover by pouring, to suffuse*:—Đara deófla þeóstro hē oforgeát mid his đæm scīnendan leóhte *he overcame the darkness of the devils by pouring upon it his shining light*, Blickl. Homl. 85, 8. Dreórige hleór sealtum dropum ofergeótaþ *suffuse the mournful face with tears*, Dōm. L. 4, 36. Đæt scyp wearþ ofergoten (*operiretur*) mid ȳđum, Mt. Kmbl. 8, 24. Mid swāte ofergoten, Glostr. Frag. 104, 17. Mid wōpe ofergoten, Ælfc. T. Grn. 18, 2.

ofer-geotol, -geotolian. v. ofer-gitol, -gitolian.

ofer-gesett *placed above* (*others*):—On ōđre wīsan sint tō manianne đa underþióddan on ōđre đa ofergesettan *aliter admonendi sunt subditi, atque aliter praelati*, Past. 28, 1; Swt. 189, 15, 23.

ofer-getimbran *to raise a building*:—On đæm stāne hī ciricean ofergetimbredon *they raised a church on that rock*, Blickl. Homl. 205, 5.

ofer-geweorc, es; *n.* I. *a superstructure*:—Đæs heáhaltares ofergeweorc *cibborium*, Wrt. Voc. ii. 23, 15. II. *a tomb, mausoleum*:—Mētton ofergeweorke *depicto mausoleo*, Coll. Monast. Th. 32, 35. Gē sind gelīce gemēttum ofergeweorcum, Homl. Th. ii. 404, 17. v. ofer-weorc.

ofer-gewrit, es; *n. A superscription, an inscription*:—Hwæs anlīcnys, ys đis and ofergewrit (*suprascribtio*), Mt. Kmbl. 22, 20: Homl. Skt. i. 23, 475. Ofergewritum *epigrammatibus*, Wrt. Voc. ii. 33, 23.

ofer-gīfre; *adj. Over-greedy, gluttonous*; gulae deditus, Past. 23; Swt. 177, 4: 43; Swt. 308, 16.

ofer-gīman *to neglect, disregard*:—Gif hwā đis ofergȳme, R. Ben. 129, 9. Gif hē āđor dyde, ođđe ofergīmde, ođđe forgeat, 71, 15. Đæs git ofergȳmdon Hǽlendes word, Cd. Th. 295, 14; Sat. 486. Cf. ofergumian.

ofer-gīmness, e; *f. Watching over, observation*:—Miđ ofergēmnise *cum observatione*, Lk. Skt. Lind. 17, 20.

ofer-gitan *to forget, neglect*:—Ealle þeóda đa đe ofergitaþ (*obliviscuntur*) God, Ps. Spl. 9, 18. Ic ofergeat (*oblitus sum*) etan, 101, 5. Sum wȳf ofergeat hyre cyld slǽpende, Shrn. 150, 30. Hī ofergēton (-geáton, MS. A.) (*obliti sunt*) đæt hī hlāfas ne nāmon, Mk. Skt. 8, 14. Hié ofergeáton Godes dōmas, Cd. Th. 155, 32; Gen. 2581. Spec... đæt hié ofergieton (sȳn ofergytende, MS. B.) đisse sǽwe ege, St. And. 8, 15. Ne ofergit đū þearfan, Ps. Spl. 9 second, 14. Ofergyt, 73, 24. Oferget, Ps. Surt. 73, 23. Nylle đū ofergiten *noli oblivisci*, Ps. Spl. 102, 2. Ofergeotan, Nar. 45, 7. Wǽre đū ofergeotende mīnre bysne, Bd. 2, 6; S. 508, 17. Ān nis of đām ofergyten, Lk. Skt. 12, 6.

ofer-gitness, e; *f. Forgetfulness, oblivion*:—On đam lande đe ofergytnes on eardige (this seems to correspond to *in terra oblivionis*, v. 12), Ps. Th. 87, 11. On ofergetnisse *in oblivione*, Lk. Skt. Rush. 12, 6.

ofer-gitol, -geotol; *adj. Forgetful, oblivious*:—Ne eom ic ofergitol (-gittul, Ps. Th.) *non sum oblitus*, Ps. Spl. 118, 61: 9, 19: 9 second, 13. Ofergittol, Ps. Th. 118, 41. Worda đīnra ofergittul, 118, 15. Ofergyttol, 118, 43. Ne sȳ ofergyttol ac gemyndig, R. Ben. 24, 1. Nā ofergeotol đara gebeda his þearfena, Ps. Th. 9, 12. Ofergeottul, 102, 2. Ofergeatul *obliviosus*, Rtl. 29, 7. Ofergeotele wē ne sind *obliti non sumus*, Ps. Surt. 43, 18. Ofergeotulæ (-geotole, Ps. Th.), 43, 21. Ofergeotole, Mt. Kmbl. Lind. 16, 5.

ofer-gitolian; *p.* ode *To forget, be forgetful of*:—Nō ofergeoteliu word đīn *non obliviscar sermones tuos*, Ps. Surt. 118, 16. Ofergeotulas đū *oblivisceris*, 12, 1. Ofergeoteliaþ *obliviscimini*, 49, 22. Alle þeóde đa đe ofergeoteliaþ Dryhten, 9, 18. Ne ofergeotela đū, 9, 33. Ofergeotelien *obliviscantur*, 58, 12.

ofer-gitolness, e; *f. Forgetfulness, oblivion*:—Ofergitolnys (-geotulnis, Ps. Surt.) *oblivio*, Ps. Spl. C. T. 9, 19. Wiđ đa ādle đe man litargum hāteþ, đæt ys on ūre geþeóde ofergytulnys (-gittolnes, MS. H.), Lchdm. i. 200, 8. In eorþan ofergytolnysse *in terra oblivionis*, Ps. Spl 87, 13. Đa unþeáwas oft ābisegien đæt mōd mid ofergiotulnesse, Bt. 35, 1; Fox 154, 32. Ic eom myd earmlīcre ofergiotolnesse ofseten, Shrn. 198, 21. On ofergeotolnisse, Blickl. Homl. 103, 16. Ofergeottolnisse *oblivionem*, Rtl. 61, 14. Ofergiottulnisso *ignorantias*, 167, 31.

ofer-glenged; *part. Over-ornamented, too much adorned*:—Ne mōt nān preóst beón on his girlum tō ranc, ne mid golde oferglængced, L. Ælfc. P. 49; Th. ii. 386, 10.

ofer-grǽdig; *adj. Over-greedy, too covetous*:—Menn beóþ ofergrǽdige woruldgestreóna, Wulfst. 81, 13.

ofer-gumian; *p.* ode *To neglect, be careless about*:—Ne hē ofergumige đa hȳrsumnesse đæs hālgan regoles, R. Ben. 113, 2. [Cf. *Icel.* guma at einu *to take heed to a thing*: *O. Sax.* far-gumōn *to neglect*.] v. ofer-gīman.

ofer-gyldan *to cover* or *ornament with gold*:—Ic ofergylde *auro*, Ælfc. Gr. 36; Som. 38, 39. Ealle đa græftas gē ofergyldaþ mid cræfte, Homl. Skt. i. 8, 61. On ofergildum hrægle *in vestitu deaurato*, Ps. Lamb. 44, 10: Homl. Th. ii. 586, 16. ii. sylure candelsticcan and ii. ouergylde, Cod. Dip. Kmbl. vi. 101, 26. Đa ofergyldan saglas sceolden stician on đǽm gyldnum hringum, Past. 22; Swt. 171, 22.

ofer-gylden; *adj. Gilded, covered with gold*:—Gif hē begytaþ đæt hē hæbbe byrne and helm and ofergyldene (cf. golde fæted, ll. 8-9) sweord, L. Wg. 10; Th. i. 188, 21.

ofer-gyrd *overgirt*:—Ofergyrdum *recincta*, Germ. 394, 236.

ofer-habban (?) *to command, govern*:—Hȳ mōstan đām læppan friþ gebicgean đe hȳ under cyngces hand oferhæfdon [geweald ofer hæfdon (?)], L. Eth. ii. 1; Th. i. 284, 14.

ofer-hacele, an; *f. A cope, hood;* cappa, L. Ecg. C. 10, note; Th. ii. 140, 22. [Cf. *Icel.* yfir-hökull *a surplice.*]

ofer-heáfod; *adv. Generally, in every case:*—Ǽlc man oferheáfod sceolde cennan his gebyrde and his āre on ðære byrig ðe hē tō gehȳrde, Homl. Th. i. 30, 4. [*Ger.* über-haupt.]

ofer-heáh; *adj. Excessively high:*—Æsc byþ oferheáh, Runic pm. Kmbl. 344, 23; Rūn. 26.

ofer-healdan *to hold over, delay to do, neglect:*—Gif se gereáfa ðis ofer-heald, gebēte .xxx. scill., L. Ath. i. prm.; Th. i. 198, 11. Cf. ofer-hebban.

ofer-healfheáfod *the upper half of the head:*—Forheáfod *anciput,* æfte-weard heáfod *occiput,* oferhealfheáfod *sinciput,* Wrt. Voc. i. 42, 42–44.

ofer-hebban *to pass by, neglect, omit:*—Gif hit (*the holding a gemōt*) hwā oferhebbe (-habbe, MS. B.) bēte swā wē ǽr cwǽdon, L. Ed. 11; Th. i. 164, 23. Gif hē āht ðæs oferhæbbe ðe on ūrum gewritum stent, L. Ath. v. 8, 5; Th. i. 236, 33. Ic wāt ðæt ic his sceal fela ofer-hebban *ego cogor fateri me praeterire plurima,* Ors. 1, 8; Swt. 42, 1. Hit þencþ fela gōdra weorca tō wyrcanne, gif hē worldāre hæbbe, and wile hit oferhebban, siððan hē hié hæfþ, Past. 9; Swt. 55, 16. [For ever hem (*the poor*) thou overhaf, Mapes 341, 1: *O. H. Ger.* ubar-hevan *praeterire, transire.*] Cf. ofer-healdan.

ofer-helian *to cover over, conceal:*—Neahte þeóstru ðū oferhelast (*detegis*), Hymn. Surt. 12, 12. Oferhelaþ *contegit,* 23, 11. Se ceác oferhelede ða oxan, Past. 16, 5; Swt. 105, 4. Gif hwā pytt ādelfe and hine ne oferhelie (*operuerit*), Ex. 21, 33. Tō oferhelianne, Glostr. Frag. 102, 2. Beón oferheled *obtegi,* Germ. 389, 22. Nis nān þing oferheled (*opertum*) ðe ne beó unheled, Lk. Skt. 12, 2.

ofer-helmian *to overshadow:*—Wudu wæter oferhelmaþ, Beo. Th. 2733; B. 1364.

ofer-heortness, e; *f. Excessive feeling:*—Mid oferheortnesse hē him wæs wānigende ǽgðer ge his āgene heardsǽlþa ge ealles ðæs folces *with bursting heart he was bewailing both his own and the people's hard fortune,* Ors. 4, 5; Swt. 166, 20.

ofer-hergian *to ravage:*—Ceólwulf oferhergeade (-ode, MS. E.) Cant-ware, Chr. 796; Erl. 58, 10: 865; Erl. 70, 34. Eádweard oferhergade eall hira land, 905; Erl. 98, 20: 933; Erl. 110, 28. Hǽþne men ofer-hergeadon (-odon, MS. E.) Sceápīge, 832; Erl. 64, 18. Ða Gotan eów hwōn oferhergedon, Ors. 1, 10; Swt. 48, 20. Heora land tō bismere oferhergodan, Blickl. Homl. 201, 23.

ofer-hīdig, -higd, -hige. v. ofer-hygdig, -hygd, -hyge.

ofer-higian *to overreach* (?):—Sinc eáþe mæg gold on grunde gum-cynnes gehwone oferhigian hȳde se ðe wylle *easily may treasure, gold in the ground, overreach every man* (i. e. *make the effort at concealment vain*), *hide it who will,* Beo. Th. 5525; B. 2766.

ofer-hīran. I. *not to listen to, to disregard, disobey:*—Ðē ealle gesceafta heórsumiaþ . . . būtan men ānum, se ðē oferheórþ, Bt. 4; Fox 8, 10. Swā weorþlīce sige hæfde swā hē ǽr unweorþlīce ðara goda biscepum oferhīrde (*he disregarded the prohibition of the augurs*), Ors. 3, 10; Swt. 140, 4. Hié þurh his lāre oferhiérdon ðǽm godum, 4, 12; Swt. 210, 2. II. *to overhear, hear:*—Swā ic mid mīnum eárum oferhȳrde, L. O. 8; Th. i. 180, 29: L. C. S. 23; Th. i. 388, 24. Se oþeling (*Phalaris*) ǽgðer hæfde, ge his plegan ge his gewill, ðonne hē ðara manna (*those shut up in the brazen bull*) tintrego oferhiérde, Ors. 1, 12; Swt. 54, 28. Gē sylfe swutele gesāwon, and eác oferhȳrdan ða bletsunge, Wulfst. 176, 4.

ofer-hīre; *adj. Disobedient, regardless:*—Gif preóst on his scriftscīre ǽnigne man wite Gode oferhȳre, oððe on heáfodleahtrum yfele befeal-lene, L. Edg. C. 6; Th. ii. 244, 22.

ofer-hīrness, e; *f. Disobedience, disregard, neglect, contempt:*—Ungelimp mid oferhȳrnysse Godes beboda geearnod, L. Edg. S. 1; Th. i. 270, 12. But it occurs chiefly as a legal term *the disregard of an authoritative enactment* or *the fine for such disregard,* amounting to 120 shillings. Some of the offences to which it applies may be seen from the following passages:—Gif hwā būtan porte ceápige, ðonne sȳ hē cyninges oferhȳrnesse scyldig, L. Ed. 1; Th. i. 158, 14. Ðæt se wǽre, ðe rihtes wyrnde, scyldig æt þriddan cyrre cyninges oferhȳrnesse ðæt is .cxx. scill., 2; Th. i. 160, 16. Ne underfō nān man ōðres mannes man būtan ðæs leáfe ðe hē ǽr fyligde. Gif hit hwā dō, bēte mīne oferhȳrnesse, 10; Th. i. 164, 18. Gif hwā gemōt forsitte þrīwa, gilde ðæs cynges ofer-hȳrnesse . . . Gif hē nylle ða oferhȳrnesse syllan, ðonne rīdan ða yldestan men . . . Gif hwā nylle rīdan mid his geféran, gilde cynges oferhȳr-nesse, L. Ath. i. 20; Th. i. 208, 26–210, 1. Gif hwā hreám gehȳre and hine forsitte, gylde ðæs cynges oferhȳrnysse, L. C. S. 29; Th. i. 392, 18. Ne quis pecuniam puram et recte appendentem sonet, mone-tetur in quocunque portu monetetur, in regno meo, super overhyrnessam meam, L. Eth. iv. 6; Th. i. 302, 15. Gē (gerēfan) hīraþ, cwæþ se cyngc, hwæt gē gelǽstan sculan be (*on pain of incurring*) mīnre ofer-hȳrnysse, L. Ath. i. prm.; Th. i. 196, 15. See Schmid. A. S. Gesetz. s. v. [Cf. *Goth.* ufar-hauseins *disregard, disobedience.*]

ofer-hlæstan *to overload:*—Mid ðære herehȳþe Rōmāne oferhlæstan heora scipa, Ors. 4, 6; Swt. 176, 18, 27. Hié (*the ships*) mon ne mehte mid monnum oferhlæstan, 5, 13; Swt. 246, 11.

ofer-hleápan *to overleap, pass by jumping:*—Ic oferhleápe *transitio,* Wrt. Voc. i. 60, 40. *Saltus lunae,* ðæt is, ðæs mōnan hlȳp, for ðan ðe hē oferhlȳpþ ǽnne dæg, Lchdm. iii. 264, 24. Ðæt hors slōg on ðam wege oferhleóp, Bd. 5, 6; S. 619, 17. All eorþlīc þing wæs oferhleápende (*transiliens*), 2, 7; S. 509, 14. v. next word.

ofer-hleápend, es; *m. One who overleaps;* transilitor, Wrt. Voc. i. 60, 41.

ofer-hleóðor; *adj. Not hearing, inattentive to sound:*—Se ðe ǽrest eáran worhte hū se oferhleóður ǽfre wurde *qui plantavit aurem, non audiet?* Ps. Th. 93, 9.

ofer-hleóðrian. I. *to outsound, exceed in sound:*—Ðeáh ānra gehwylc hæbbe gyldene bȳman, and ealra bȳmena gehwylc hæbbe .xii. hleóðor, and hleóðra gehwylc sȳ heofone heárre and helle deópre, ðonne ðæs hālgan cantices se gyldena organ hē hȳ ealle oferhleóðraþ, and ealle ða ōðre hē ādȳfeþ, Salm. Kmbl. p. 152, 12. II. *to exceed* (?):—Ne frign ðū unc nōhtes mā for ðon wit habbaþ oferhleóðred [-leóred (?)] ðæt gemǽre uncres leóhtes *cave ne nos ulterius sciscitaris jam excede ter-minos luci nostri,* Nar. 32, 7.

ofer-hlifian. I. *to tower above, rise high above:*—Sōna swā seó sunne sealte streámas heá oferhlifaþ, Exon. Th. 206, 3; Ph. 121. II. *to exceed, surpass, excel:*—Ofer[h]lyfaþ *praecellat, supereemineat,* Hpt. Gl. 413, 48. Hē ōðre oferhlifaþ *ceteris praeeminet,* Past. 17, 3; Swt. 111, 1. Iohannes ealle heáhfæderas and Godes wītgan oferhlifaþ, Shrn. 95, 10. III. *to tower over in a threatening manner:*—Oferhlifode ege heora ofer hig *incubuit timor eorum super eos,* Ps. Spl. M. 104, 36. Ofer[h]lifiende *minaci,* Wrt. Voc. ii. 85, 47.

ofer-hlifung, e; *f. Eminence, sublimity, excellence:*—Oferhlifung *eminentia, sublimitas, celsitudo,* Wrt. Voc. ii. 143, 37. Oferhlifinge *excel-lentiae,* Germ. 393, 52.

ofer-hlūd; *adj. Over-loud, noisy, clamorous:*—Oferhlūd *clamosa,* Wrt. Voc. ii. 131, 61. v. next word.

ofer-hlȳde; *adj. Over-loud, noisy:*—Hē ne sȳ oferhlȳde on stefne, R. Ben. 30, 14. v. preceding word.

ofer-hlȳp, es; *m. A leap across* or *over, a bound:*—Ðes *saltus,* ðæt is ðes mōnan oferhlȳp, Anglia viii. 308, 24. For ðæs mōnan oferhlȳpe *id est, propter saltum,* 316, 43. [Cf. *Icel.* yfir-hlaup.]

ofer-hlȳttrian *to clarify, strain:*—Ic oferhlȳttrige *eliquo,* Ælfc. Gr. 37; Som. 39, 42.

ofer-hoga, an; *m. One who despises, a contemptuous, proud person:*—Se biþ Godes oferhoga ðe Godes bodan oferhogiaþ, L. I. P. 5; Th. ii. 308, 31. Hēr sȳn on earde oferhogan godcundra rihtlaga, Wulfst. 164, 12. Oferhogan *superbi,* Ps. Surt. 118, 122: 139, 6. Oferhogum *super-bis,* 122, 4. Oferhogan *superbos,* ii. p. 200, 16.

ofer-hogian *to despise, contemn, scorn, disdain:*—Moyses symle ða nyrugde ðe God oferhogodan. Se ðe Godes bebod oferhogaþ, hē biþ on hǽðenra onlīcnesse, Blickl. Homl. 49, 12–13. Sum fearhrȳðer ðæs ōðres ceápes geférscipe oferhogode, 199, 4. Hē ǽlce unsīuernysse oferhogode Chr. 1067; Erl. 204, 36. Ðā oferhogode hē ðæt hē āðer dyde, Ors. 6, 34; Swt. 290, 21: Beo. Th. 4679; B. 2345. Hié ealle worlde weán oforhogodan, Blickl. Homl. 119, 16, 20. Oferhoga hī, and ādrīf hī fram ðē, Bt. 7, 2; Fox 18, 8. Warniaþ ðæt gē ne oferhogian ǽnne of ðysum lytlingum, Mt. Kmbl. 18, 10. Ða gȳmeleásan and ða oferhogiendan hē sceal mid wordum þreágan, R. Ben. 13. 15. v. *preceding and next words and* ofer-hycgan.

ofer-hogiend, es; *m. A despiser, contemner:*—Gyf hwylc brōðor ongyten biþ his yldrena geboda oferhogiend, R. Ben. 48, 6.

ofer-holt *a forest of spears which rise over the heads of those who bear them* (?):—Hié gesāwon fyrd Faraonis forþ ongangan oferholt wegan eóred līxan *they* (*the Israelites*) *saw Pharaoh's host advance, saw a forest of spears move* (or *saw them bearing a forest of spears*), *saw the band glit-ter,* Cd. Th. 187, 27; Exod. 157.

ofer-hragan *to come in storms* (?):—Wǽtum hē oferhrægeþ, gebryceþ burga geatu *it* (*snow*) *comes in damp storms on cities' gates, and breaks them,* Salm. Kmbl. 612; Sal. 305. [Cf. *Icel.* hragla *to sleet;* hregg *a storm.*]

ofer-hrēfan *to roof over, cover with a roof, cover:*—Ðē oferhrēf ufan mid hwītle *cover yourself over from above with a cloak,* Lchdm. ii. 76, 22. Porticas ealle swīðe fægere oferhrȳfde, Blickl. Homl. 125, 25.

ofer-hrēran *to overthrow:*—Oferhrȳred *dirute,* Wrt. Voc. ii. 26, 13. Oferhrērede *obrutos,* 62, 71.

ofer-hrops *voracity:*—Ic brūce ðisum mettum mid sȳfernysse swā swā dafnaþ munuce næs mid oferhropse *vescor his cibis cum sobrietate, sicut decet monacho, non cum voracitate,* Coll. Monast. Th. 35, 5.

ofer-hrȳfan, -hrȳred. v. ofer-hrēfan, -hrēran.

ofer-hycgan *to despise, contemn, disdain, scorn:*—Gif hē ðis (*lying at the feet of his superior*) oferhigþ and hit dōn nelle, R. Ben. 131, 7. Ðonne se mon oferhygþ (Hatt. MS. oferhȳþ) ðæt hē bió gelīc ōðrum monnum *dum homo hominibus esse similis dedignatur,* Past. 17, 4; Swt. 112, 3. Wē hine mid swā micle māran unryhte oferhycgeaþ swā hē læs forhogaþ ðæt hē ūs ðonne giet tō him spane, siððan wē hiene oferhycggeaþ *tanto graviori improbitate contemnitur, quanto contemtus adhuc vocare non dedignatur,* 52, 4; Swt. 407, 17–19. Ðeáh hī hine oferhogden, ne forhogde hē hī nō, Swt. 405, 31. Ða lytegan sint tō manianne ðæt hī oferhycggen (-hycgen, Cott. MSS.) ðæt hié wieton, 30, 1; Swt. 203, 7. Oferhige hī and ādrīf hī fram ðē, Bt. 7, 2; Fox 18, 8 note. Utan oferhycgan helm ðone miclan, Cd. Th. 280, 7; Sat. 252: 283, 15; Sat. 305. [*O. H. Ger.* ubar-hugjan *contemnere, aspernere*: cf. *Goth.* ufar-hugjan *to be puffed up.*] v. ofer-hogian.

ofer-hȳd, -hȳdig. v. ofer-hygd, -hygdig.

ofer-hygd, -hȳd, e; *f.*: es; *n.*: -hygdu, -hȳdu (o); *indecl. f.* [the plural is used with singular meaning, cf. ofer-mēde, -mēttu]. I. in a bad sense, *pride, arrogance*:—Hæfde hig ofyrhigd (-hȳd, MS. T.) *tenuit eos superbia*, Ps. Spl. 72, 6. Oferhigd *supercilio*, Wrt. Voc. ii. 76, 20. Oferhygd, Cd. Th. 21, 22; Gen. 328. Wlenco, oferhȳd, 258, 21; Dan. 679. Ðæs oferhȳdes ord, 272, 3; Sat. 114. Se is kyning ofer eall ða bearn oferhygde (-hȳde, Cott. MSS.) *ipse est rex super universos filios superbiae*, Past. 17, 4; Swt. 111, 22. In oferhygde *in superbia*, Ps. Surt. 16, 10: 58, 13. Hū mycel yfel ðē gelamp for ðīnre gītsunga and oforhȳdo and for ðīnum īdlan gilpe, Blickl. Homl. 31, 14. Hī druncennesse and oferhȳdo wǣron heora swiran underþeóddende *ebrietati, animositati, sua colla subdentes*, Bd. 1, 14; S. 482, 26. Sum on oferhygdo þrinteþ, Exon. Th. 314, 33; Mōd. 23. Nō wē oferhygdu (*or pl.?*) ānes monnes māran fundon, 118, 15; Gū. 240. Ðæt heofenlīce rīce ðæt ða ǣrestan men forworhtan þurh heora gīfernesse and oferhygde, 25, 1. Se dōeþ oferhygde *qui facit superbiam*, Ps. Surt. 100, 7. Ða dōeþ oferhygd, 30, 24. Ðās þing wē sculon forgān oferhȳd gȳtsunge ... *ab his debemus nos abstinere, a superbia, et avaritia* ..., L. Ecg. P. iv. 64; Th. ii. 224, 28. Næfde hē on him nāðer ne yrre ne oferhȳd, Bd. 3, 17; S. 545, 8. Him oninnan oferhygda dǣl weaxeþ, Beo. Th. 3485; B. 1740. Oferhȳda, 3525; B. 1760. Ða setl ðe deófol for his oforhygdum of āworpen wæs, Blickl. Homl. 121, 35. For oferhygdum, 156, 13: Cd. Th. 268, 4; Sat. 50: 269, 6; Sat. 69. Ne gedafenaþ ðē ðæt ðū andsware mid oferhygdum sēce, Andr. Kmbl. 638; An. 319. Hwæt is wuldor ðīn ðe ðū oferhygdum upp ārǣrdest, 2637; An. 1320. Þurh oferhygda, Exon. Th. 316, 23; Mōd. 53. Hē oferhȳda āgan wolde *he would give way to pride*, Cd. Th. 287, 20; Sat. 370. II. in a good sense, *honourable pride* (?), *high spirit*:—Gif ðū gesāwe sumne swīðe wīsne man ðe hæfde swīðe gōda oferhȳda and wǣre ðeáh swīðe earm hwæðer ðū woldest cweþan ðæt hē wǣre unwyrþe anwealdes and weorþscipes *si quem sapientia praeditum videres, num posses eum vel reverentia, vel ea, qua praeditus est, sapientia, non dignum putare?* Bt. 27, 2; Fox 96, 24. [*O. H. Ger.* ubar-huht, -hucti *superbia.*]

ofer-hygd; *adj. Proud*:—Oferhygdum ēgan *superbo oculo*, Ps. Surt. 100, 5. Oferhygde (sic MS.) *superbi*, Ps. Th. 139, 5. Ða oferhygdan *superbi*, Ps. Surt. 118, 78: 118, 21. Āgyld edleán oferhygdum *redde retributionem superbis*, Ps. Spl. C. 93, 2. Tōstrægd oferhygd *dispersit superbos*, Lk. Skt. Rush. 1, 51.

ofer-hygdig, -hȳdig, es; *n. Pride*:—Ðonne hī oferhȳdig up āhōfan and him wōhgodu worhtan and grōfun *in sculptilibus suis emulati sunt eum*, Ps. Th. 77, 58.

ofer-hygdig, -hȳdig; *adj. Proud, arrogant, haughty*:—Hē eode tō reordum mid tōcumendum mannum. Ðā tǣlde hine ān oferhȳdig bisceop for ðon, Shrn. 129, 28. Ðone oferhygdgan *superbum*, Ps. Surt. 88, 11. Ðā wǣron hī æfter æþelborennysse oferhȳdige, Homl. Th. ii. 174, 8. Ða oferhȳdegan, Ps. Th. 118, 78. Ēgan oferhygdigra *oculos superborum*, Ps. Surt. 17, 28: 118, 69. Ofyrhȳdigra, Ps. Spl. 118, 69. Ðū eallum oferhȳdigum eáþmōdnesse forgifest, Blickl. Homl. 141, 12. Oferhȳdegum eágum *superbo oculo*, Ps. Th. 100, 5. Fyll ða oferhȳdigan, 73, 22. Ða oferhygdego *superbos*, Lk. Skt. Lind. 1, 51. [*O. H. Ger.* ubar-huctig *superbus.*]

ofer-hygdigian *to be proud*:—Ðonne oferhygdgaþ se ārleása *dum superbit impius*, Ps. Surt. 9, 23.

ofer-hyge (?), es; *m. Pride, arrogance*:—Ðū mē oferhige (*or* ofer hige? mē ofer corresponding to *super me* in the Latin) on ealle gelǣddest *omnes elationes tuas super me induxisti*, Ps. Th. 87, 7.

ofer-hylmend, es; *m. One who conceals, who does not act openly*:—Ic oferhylmend ealle getealde ða on eorþan yfele wǣron *praevaricantes reputavi omnes peccatores terrae*, Ps. Th. 118, 119. [Cf. *Icel.* hylma yfir *to hide, conceal* (as a law phrase); yfir-hylma *to hide, cloak*; yfir-hylming *a hiding, cloaking.*]

ofer-hȳran, -hȳre, -hȳrness. v. ofer-hīran, -hīre, -hīrness.

ofer-hyrned; *adj. Having horns above*:—Ūr bȳþ oferhyrned, Runic pm. Kmbl. 339, 8; Rūn. 2.

oferian; *p.* ode *To exalt*:—Geoferode *sublimati, exaltati*, Hpt. Gl. 428, 47.

ofer-ild, e; *f. Very great age*:—Him se deáþ geneálǣcþ for ðære oferylde, Wulfst. 147, 27.

ofering, e; *f. Superfluity*:—Gif ðū ofer gemet itst oððe drincst oððe clāþa ðē mā on hæfst ðonne ðū þurfe seó ofering ðē wurþ tō sāre *cujus satietatem si superfluis urgere velis, quod infuderes fiet noxium*, Bt. 14, 1; Fox 42, 16. Hē wilnigen mid oferinge hiora gītsunga gefyllan *qui abundantiam suam ambitus superfluitate metiantur*, 14, 2; Fox 44, 14.

ofer-irnan. I. *to pass by running, cross*:—Ða hwīle ðe se mōna ðære sceade ord oferyrnþ *while the moon is crossing the point of the shadow*, Lchdm. iii. 240, 26. II. *to run over, go over a subject*:—Nū wille wē eft oferyrnan ða ylcan godspellīcan endebyrdnysse, Homl. Th. i. 104, 7. Wē wyllaþ scortlīce oferyrnan ða dīgelystan word, 202, 29. III. *to come upon with violence, overwhelm, to come upon with surprise*:—Seó sǣ oferarn Pharao and ealle his cræftu, ii. 194, 27. Mē slǣp oferarn *cum mihi somnus obrepsisset*, Bd. 5, 9; S. 622, 33.

ofer-lād, e; *f. A carrying across, translation*:—Oferlād *translationem*, Rtl. 62, 19. v. lād, III.

ofer-lǣdan *to oppress*:—Ðā wæs se munt mid mycelum brōgan eall oferlǣded; and unhiérlīc storm of ðæm munte āstāg, Blickl. Homl. 203, 7. [Shal neither kynge ne knyȝte, constable ne meire ouerlede þe comune, Piers. P. 3, 314: *Prompt. Parv.* ovyrledyn̄ *opprimo*; ovyrledare *oppressor*; ovyrledynge *oppressio.*]

ofer-læg, es; *n. A cloak*:—Oberlagu *amfibula* (amfibulum *birrum villosum*, Isidore), Txts. 111, 1.

ofer-leóf; *adj. Exceedingly dear*:—Ēðel byþ oferleóf ǣghwylcum men, Runic pm. Kmbl. 344, 3; Rūn. 23.

ofer-leóran. I. *to pass, pass away, pass by*:—Hē oferlióræs (-lióraþ, Rush.) from deáþe in līfe *transiet a morte in vitam*, Jn. Skt. Lind. 5, 24. Oferleóraþ *transeant*, p. 4, 10. Oferhlióras *transibunt*, Mk. Skt. Lind. 13, 31. Ðætte oferleórade (*transiret*) ðió tīd, 14, 35. Tīd ðætte hē oferliórde of ðissum middengeorde, Jn. Skt. Rush. 13, 1. Oferleórdun *transierunt*, Ps. Surt. 118, 136. Oferleór *transfer*, Lk. Skt. Lind. 22, 42. Oferlióra *transire*, Mt. Kmbl. Lind. 26, 42. II. *to pass moral bounds, deviate from right, transgress*:—Hæftas heársume ðæs hālgan word lyt oferleórdun, Exon. Th. 145, 21; Gū. 698. Oferliórende *praevaricantes*, Ps. Surt. 118, 119. Ofyrleórynde, -liórende, Ps. Spl. C. T. 118, 119. v. next word.

ofer-leórness, e; *f. Deviation from right, transgression*:—Dōnde oferleórnisse *facientes praevaricationes*, Ps. Surt. 100, 3.

ofer-libban *to outlive, survive*:—Wes ðet lond becueden his brōðar, gif hē Cyneþrȳðe oferlifde, Chart. Th. 465, 19. Lāf oððe oferlibbende *superstes*, Gr. 9, 26; Som. 11, 7. [*O. H. Ger.* ubar-lebēn.]

oferlīce; *adj. Excessively*:—Hī mid heora synnum swā oferlīce swȳðe God gegræmedon, ðæt hē lēt Engla here heora eard gewinnan, Wulfst. 166, 18: 83, 14. [Cf. *Icel.* ofr-ligr *excessive.*]

ofer-līhtan *to outshine*:—Seó sunne oferlīht ealle ōðre steorran and geþióstraþ mid hire leóhte, Bt. 9, tit.; Fox xii. 2.

ofer-līðan *to cross* (*water*), *sail across*:—Āstīgende on scipe oferlāð (*transfretavit*) ðone sǣe, Mt. Kmbl. Rush. 9, 1: Shrn. 88, 28: Cd. Th. 200, 26; Exod. 362. Oferlīðan *transire, transfretare*, Hpt. Gl. 492, 50. [*Goth.* ufar-leiþan.]

ofer-lufu, e, an; *f. Excessive love*:—Seó oferlufu eorþan gestreóna, Wulfst. 149, 4: 263, 24.

ofer-mæcga, an; *m. A man superior to others, an illustrious person*:—Ofermæcga spræc dȳre Dryhtnes þegn (*the angel sent to save Guthlac*), Exon. Th. 143, 21; Gu. 664. [Cf. *Icel.* ofr-menni *a mighty champion.*]

ofer-mægen, es; *n. Superior* or *overwhelming force*:—Wið ofermægenes egsan, Cd. Th. 127, 27; Gen. 2117. Hē hæfde wīgena tō lyt wið ofermægene, Elen. Kmbl. 128; El. 64. Hyne Hetware hilde gehnǣgdon mid ofermægene, Beo. Th. 5827; B. 2917. Forst and snāw mid ofermægene eorþan þeccaþ, Exon. Th. 215, 6; Ph. 249. Him on swaðe fylgeþ A ofermægene, Salm. Kmbl. 187; Sal. 93. [Cf. *O. H. Ger.* ubar-meginōn *praevalere*: *Ger.* über-macht: *Icel.* ofr-efli *overwhelming force.*]

ofer-mǣned (?) *made too common* (?), *trite*:—Ofermēned *contrita*, Wrt. Voc. ii. 19, 43: 92, 37.

ofer-mæstan *to over-fatten*:—Swā ðæt ūre līchama ne wurþe ofermæst tō īdelum lustum, Bd. Whelc. 228, 25.

ofer-mǣte; *adj. Beyond measure, excessive, immoderate, immense*:—Ofermǣte *insolens*, Hpt. Gl. 526, 10. Moyses behelede ða ofermǣtan bierhto his ondwlitan, Past. 63; Swt. 459, 19. God hyra ofermǣtan ofermētto genyðerode, Ors. 1, 7; Swt. 38, 27. Hē hēt ða ofermǣtan brycge mid stāne ofer gewyrcan, 2, 5; Swt. 84, 3. Æt ðām ofermǣtum wæterum *de multitudine aquarum*, Ps. Th. 17, 17. Ȳða ofermǣta, Exon. Th. 53, 23; Cri. 855. [Cf. *Icel.* ofr-māta *excessively*: *Ger.* über-mässig.]

ofermǣt-lic; *adj. Immense*:—Ðonne swā ofermǣtlīcu rīcu onstyrede wǣron *ubi tot et talia regna mutata sunt*, Ors. 1, 12; Swt. 52, 10.

ofer-mǣtu (o); *indecl. f. Excess, presumption*:—Ādrīf fram mē dysig and ofermǣto and sile mē wīsdōm, Shrn. 169, 16.

ofer-māðum, es; *m. A very valuable treasure, a treasure of surpassing worth*, Beo. Th. 5979; B. 2993.

ofer-mēde, es; *n.*: -mēdu; *f.* [the plural form is used with singular meaning, cf. ofer-hygd, -mēttu] *Pride*:—His ofermēdu is fruma ūres forlores, Past. 41; Swt. 301, 8. Ofermēdes *elationis*, Hpt. Gl. 433, 31. His engyl ongan ofermēde micel āhebban, Cd. Th. 19, 19; Gen. 293. Ðæt hié ne āstigan on ofermēdu, Blickl. Homl. 185, 14. Se ðe on ofermēdum leofaþ, Exon. Th. 317, 33; Mōd. 75. [*O. H. Ger.* ubar-muoti *superbia, elatio, animositas.*] v. ofer-mōd, -mēttu.

ofer-mēde; *adj. Proud, arrogant, presumptuous*:—Cyning gefeaht wið ðone ofermēdan (-mōdigan, MS. E.) aldorman, Chr. 750; Erl. 48, 10. [*O. H. Ger.* ubar-muoti *superbus.*]

ofer-mēdla, an; *m.Pride:*—Eahta syndan heáfodlīce synna... eahtoþa is ofermēdla, L. E. I. 31; Th. ii. 428, 8. Sōna swā ic mīnes ofermēdlan geswīce, 36; Th. ii. 436, 1. Gif hē on ofermēdlan and on ōðrum unþeáwum his līf lyfaþ, 32; Th. ii. 428, 33: Cd. Th. 257, 14; Dan. 657.

ofer-mēdu. v. ofer-mēde.

ofer-mete, es; *m. Food in excess, a feast where food is in excess:*—Se ofermete ne befæst ūs nǣfre Gode *esca nos non commendat Deo*, Past. 43, 9; Swt. 316, 19. Ofermettas *commessationes*, Bd. 4, 25; S. 601, 13 note.

ofer-mēttu (o); *indecl. in sing.; but declined in pl., where it is used with singular meaning*, cf. ofer-hygd, -mēde: *perhaps all the instances which follow may belong to the plural, since eáþmētto takes a verb in the plural; f. Pride, arrogance, haughtiness:*—Hine his hyge gespeón and his ofermētto ealra swīðost, Cd. Th. 22, 35; Gen. 351. Þurh heora miclan mōd, and þurh ofermētto, 22, 7; Gen. 337: 21, 30; Gen. 332. Hē biþ on ofermēttu (-mētto, Cott. MSS.) āwended... hē āstāg on ofermētto *in elationem permutatur... intumuit*, Past. 3, 2; Swt. 35, 13–16. On ofermētto *in superbiam*, 19, 3; Swt. 147, 3: Bt. 6; Fox 14, 34. God hyra ofermǣtan ofermētto genyðerode, Ors. 1, 7; Swt. 38, 28. God ða mǣstan ofermētto gewræc on ðam folce, 6, 2; Swt. 256, 5. Ðe ofermētto dōþ *qui faciunt superbiam*, Ps. Th. 30, 27. Ofermētto *fastu*, Wrt. Voc. ii. 33, 62. Ðis synt ða īdelnyssa ðisse worulde: ǣrest is ofermētta (*arrogantia*), L. Ecg. P. i. 8; Th. ii. 174, 32. Ne gerīsaþ heom prīta, ne micele ofermētta, L. I. P. 10; Th. ii. 318, 32. Heora eáþmētto ne mihton nāuht forstandan, ne hūru heora ofermētta, Bt. 29, 2; Fox 106, 1. Ðonne weaxaþ ða ofermētta (cf. ðonan mǣst cymeþ yfla ofermēta, Met. 25, 44), 37, 1; Fox 186, 19. Mid his āgnum wordum ðone swiran gebiége his āgenra ofermētta *suo judicio superbiae cervicem calcat*, Past. 26, 3; Swt. 185, 15. On heora ofermēttum *in superbia*, Ps. Th. 30, 20. On ofermēttum āþunden, Past. proem.; Swt. 25, 6. Biscopum gebiraþ ealdlīce wīsan būton ofermēttum, L. I. P. 10; Th. ii. 318, 31. Lēt befeallan on ðæt ēce fȳr ðe him gegearcod wæs for heora ofermēttum, Homl. Th. i. 12, 4: Met. 5, 32: Bt. 16, 1; Fox 50, 9–11. Mid ofermētum *superbia*, Past. 42, 2; Swt. 307, 7. Ne mæg hē wið ofermētta, Bt. 12; Fox 36, 10. Mūþ heora spræc ofermētta (*superbiam*), Ps. Lamb. 16, 10: Met. 7, 8.

ofer-micel; *adj. Over-much, excessive:*—On ðære tīde wæs sió ofermycelo hǣlo on ealre worulde, Ors. 1, 7; Swt. 40, 3. Būtan hȳ ouermicel geswinc habben, R. Ben. 65, 17. [*Prompt. Parv.* ovir-mikel *nimius*: *Icel.* ofr-mikill.]

ofer-micelness, e; *f. Over-greatness, excess:*—Nāht framaþ eallum dæge lang ādreógan fæsten gif æfter ðam metta oferfylle oððe ofermicelnysse (*nimietate*) sāwl byþ ofersȳmed, Scint. 13.

ofer-mōd, es; *n.* I. *pride, arrogance, over-confidence:*—Feala worda gespæc se engel ofermōdes, Cd. Th. 18, 12; Gen. 272. Ðā se eorl ongan for his ofermōde ālȳfan landes tō fela lāðere þeóde, Byrht. Th. 134, 25; By. 89. [Gif hwa nulle for his ouermoð, oðer for his prude... his scrift ihalden, O. E. Homl. i. 9, 30.] II. *a high style* (?):—Ofermōd *coturnus*, Wrt. Voc. i. 19, 5. [*O. H. Ger.* ubar-muot *superbia*: *Ger.* über-muth.] v. ofer-mēde, -mētto.

ofer-mōd; *adj. Proud, arrogant, presumptuous:*—Ne sceal mon beón ofermōd, R. Ben. 17, 15. Cild ācenned ofermōd him sylfum gelīcigende *a child born on the thirteenth day of the moon will be arrogant, pleasing himself*, Lchdm. iii. 190, 14. Se ofermōda cyning (*Lucifer*), Cd. Th. 22, 9; Gen. 338. On Torcwines dagum ðæs ofermōdan cyninges *in the days of Tarquinius Superbus*, Bt. 16, 1; Fox 50, 8. Ðū ne scealt nǣfre gelīce dēman ðam eádmōdan and ðam ofermōdan, L. de Cf. 3; Th. ii. 260, 25. Hig wǣron ōfermōde ongēn hig *superbe egerint contra illos*, Ex. 18, 11. Ða ðe wǣron ofermōde on heora heortan, Blickl. Homl. 159, 10. On ōðre wīsan ða ofermōdan on ōðre ða wācmōdan *aliter protervi, aliter pusillanimes*, Past. 23; Swt. 175, 18: 32; Swt. 209, 1. Ða eágan ðara ofermōdena (*superborum*) ðū geeáðmētst, Ps. Th. 17, 26. Spell be ðām ofermōdum cyningum, Bt. 37, 1; Fox 186, 1. Ofermōdum *superbis*, Ps. Spl. 93, 2. Se Scyppend oft ða ofermōdan geeádmētte, Homl. Th. ii. 432, 20. [*O. Sax.* oðar-mōd.] v. ofer-mēde.

ofer-mōdig; *adj. Proud, arrogant, saucy, wanton:*—Mǣden biþ ofermōdig *a girl* (*born on the thirteenth day of the moon*) *will be saucy*, Lchdm. iii. 190, 16. Ofermōdige *superbi*, Ps. Th. 118, 51. Ofermōdigra *superborum*, Ps. Spl. 118, 69. Ofermōdigum *superbis*, 122, 5. Ða ofermōdegan *superbos*, Bd. 3, 17; S. 545, 12. Tarcuinius ðe hira eallra wæs ofermōdgast *Tarquinius Superbus*, Ors. 2, 2; Swt. 66, 28. [*O. Sax.* oðar-mōdig: *O. H. Ger.* ubar-muotig *contumax*: *Ger.* über-müthig.]

ofer-mōdigian, -mōdgian, -mōdigan *to be proud* or *haughty, to be puffed up with pride:*—Ðonne se unrihtwīsa ofermōdegaþ (-mōdgaþ, Ps. Spl.) *dum superbit impius*, Ps. Th. 9, 21. Hwī ofermōdige gē ofer ōðre men for eówrum gebyrdum, Bt. 30, 2; Fox 110, 15: 42; Fox 258, 15. Hī ofermōdigaþ for ðæm welan, 39, 11; Fox 230, 23. Ne ofermōdgiaþ (*superbiunt*) ða scīrmenn nā for ðȳ, Past. 17, 2; Swt. 109, 17. Hié wið Gode ofermōdgiaþ *contra Deum superbiunt*, 29; Swt. 201, 16. Ðē læs ðe hira fȳnd ofermōdegodun *ne forte superbirent hostes eorum*, Deut. 32, 27. Hwȳ gē ofer ōðre men ofermōdigen, Met. 17, 16. [Cf. *O. H. Ger.* ubar-muotōn *superbire*.]

ofer-mōdigness, e; *f. Pride, arrogance:*—Ofermōdignis *superbia*, Ps. Spl. 72, 6: 30, 22: 16, 11: 100, 8. Seó eáðmōdnes of ācearf heáfod ðære ofermōdignesse *humilitas amputat caput superbiae*, Gl. Prud. 36 a; 37 a: 38 a. Ofermōdinysse *arrogantiae, inflationis*, Hpt. Gl. 523, 52. Ofermōdignysse *insolentiam*, 526, 8. Ofermōdignessa *superbia*, Mk. Skt. 7, 22.

ofer-mōdigung, -mōdgung, e; *f. The being proud, pride:*—Hit is ungecyndlīcu ofermōdgung *contra naturam superbire est*, Past. 17, 2; Swt. 109, 11.

ofermōd-līc; *adj. Proud, arrogant, presumptuous:*—Mid ofermōdlīcum gilpe, Bt. 18, 4; Fox 66, 31. Hē sceal ða ofermōdlīcan word mid eáðmōdlīcum wordum gemetgian *ut verba praemissae superbiae verbis subjectae humilitatis impugnet*, Past. 54, 5; Swt. 423, 36. [*O. H. Ger.* ubarmuot-līh *sublimis*.]

ofermōdlīce; *adv. Proudly, arrogantly, insolently:*—Hī sprecaþ swīðe ofermōdlīce *os eorum locutum est superbiam*, Ps. Th. 16, 9. Hit ofermōdlīce fērde, Blickl. Homl. 199, 17: 201, 24. [*O. H. Ger.* ubarmuotlīho *superbe, proterve, elate, hyperbolice*.]

ofer-mōdness, e; *f. Pride:*—Ofermōdnys *superbia*, Ps. Spl. 73, 24, 4. Ofermōdnes eáðmōdnes *superbia... humilitas*, Gl. Prud. 31 a: 29 a: 30 a: 32 a: 33 a. Bebeorh ðē wið ofermōdnysse *cave te a superbia*, L. Ecg. C. proem.; Th. ii. 132, 10.

ofer-nīd, -neód, e; *f. Extreme need:*—Gif hit oferneód beó *si valde necesse sit*, L. Ecg. P. iii. 14; Th. ii. 200, 33.

ofer-niman. I. *to take by violence, to violate:*—Be ðam men ðe wīf oððe mǣden ofernimþ mid unrihtum þingum *de homine qui mulierem vel puellam per fraudem constuprat*, L. Ecg. P. ii. 13 tit.; Th. ii. 180, 22. [*The section to which the title refers is as follows:*—Gif hwā mid his ofercræfte wīf oððe mǣden nȳdinga nimþ tō unrihthǣmede, Th. ii. 186, 20.] Gif ǣnig man ofernyme unbeweddod mǣden *si invenerit vir puellam virginem, et apprehendens concuberit cum illa*, Deut. 22, 28. Hē eode in tō mē ðæt hē mē ofernāme *ingressus est ad me, ut coiret mecum*, Gen. 39, 14. II. *to take away, carry off:*—Sōna wæs ðæt ǣtter ofernumen *vidimus rasuram totam vim veneni absumisse*, Bd. 1, 1; S. 474, 39. [*O. H. Ger.* ubar-neman *to take away*.]

ofer-nōn *the latter part of the day, afternoon:*—Middæg *sexta*: nōn *nona*: ofernōn oððe geloten dæg *suprema*: ǣfen *vesperum*, Wrt. Voc. i. 53, 12–15.

ofer-rǣdan. I. *to read over* or *through:*—Ic oferrǣde *perlego*, Ælfc. Gr. 28, 6; Som. 32, 15. Oferrǣdan *perlegere*, Hpt. Gl. 439, 4: Homl. Th. i. 166, 7. Ðā heó ða gewrita oferrǣd hæfde, Ap. Th. 20, 20: 21, 12. II. *to consider:*—Oferrǣdan ł hycgean *coniici*, Hpt. Gl. 439, 4.

ofer-ranc; *adj. Over-luxuriant, extravagant, sumptuous:*—God lǣteþ reáfian eówere dohtra heora gyrla and tō oferrancra heáfodgewǣda, Wulfst. 46, 1.

ofer-reccan *to convince, confute, convict:*—Gif hine mon oferricte ðæt hē ne mōste londes wyrþe beón *if it should be proved against him that he was disqualified for holding land*, Chart. Th. 141, 11. Forðon hē ðus cwæþ ðæt hē ða lotwrencas oferwunne and oferreahte *quatenus et illos victrix ratio frangeret*, Past. 30; Swt. 205, 17. Ðū hæfst mē swīðe rihte oferreahte (-rehtne, MS. Bod.) *thou hast completely convinced me*, Bt. 34, 3; Fox 138, 11. Ðonne is betere ðæt hié mid ryhtre race weorðen oferreahte and mid ðære race gebundene and ofersuīðde *prodest, ut in suis allegationibus victi jaceant*, Past. 30; Swt. 205, 3. Ðȳ læs ðonne hié oferhyggaþ ðæt hié sīen oferreahte ūtane mid ōðerra manna ryhtum lārum hié ðonne sīen innan gehæfte mid ofermētum *ne dum rectis aliorum suasionibus foris superari despiciunt, intus a superbia captivi teneantur*, 42, 2; Swt. 307, 6. Cf. ofer-stǣlan.

ofer-renc[u], e; *f. Over-luxuriance, extravagance:*—Manege ðe mid oferrence glengdan hȳ sylfe, Wulfst. 46, 2.

ofer-rīcsian *to dominate, rule over:*—Hē him geþafode ðæt hit mid anwalde him mōste oferrīcsian, Past. 17, 8; Swt. 119, 19.

ofer-rīdan *to cross on horseback:*—Sealde hē ðæt betste hors Aidane, ðæt hē on ðam mihte fordas oferrīdan, Bd. 3, 14; S. 540, 18.

ofer-rōwan *to cross by rowing:*—Ðā hēt hē his leorningcnihtas faran tō scipe, and oferrōwan ðone brym, Homl. Th. ii. 384, 19.

ofersǣ-līc; *adj. Transmarine:*—On ðām ofersǣlīcum dǣlum *in transmarinis partibus*, Bd. 3, 28; S. 560, 13. Cf. ofersǣwisc.

ofer-sǣlig; *adj. Exceedingly fortunate, more than happy:*—Se biþ gesǣlig and ofersǣlig ðe swylce cwyldas mæg forbūgon, Dōm. L. 16, 246.

ofer-sǣlþ, e; *f. Pleasure* or *happiness that exceeds due bounds:*—Gif ðū wilnast ðæt ðū wel mǣge ðæt sōðe leóht sweotole oncnāwan ðū forlǣtan scealt īdle ofersǣlþa unnytne gefeán (cf. gif ðū wilnige ðæt sōðe leóht oncnāwan āfyr fram ðē ða yfelan sǣlþa and ða unnettan, Bt. 6; Fox 14, 32) *tu si vis cernere verum, gaudia pelle*, Met. 5, 27.

ofersǣwisc; *adj. From beyond the sea, transmarine:*—Ofersǣwisc rind *bark from beyond the sea* (*cinnamon*), Lchdm. ii. 52, 3. Landferþ se ofersǣwisca hit gesette on Lēden, Glostr. Frag. 10, 21. Hē (*Benedict of Wearmouth*) ða cirícean gefretwade mid godcunde wīsdōme and mid woroldlīcum frætwum ofersǣwiscum, Shrn. 50, 32.

ofer-sāwan *to oversow:*—Ðā com his feónda sum and oferseów (*superseminavit*) hit mid coccele, Mt. Kmbl. 13, 25. [*O. H. Ger.* ubar-sāan.]

ofer-sceadwian *to cover with a shadow, overshadow*:—Ic ofersceadewige *obumbro*, Wrt. Voc. i. 54, 59. Ðæs Heáhstan miht ðē ofersceadaþ, Lk. Skt. 1, 35. Genip ofersceadude hig, 9, 34. Seó lyft hī ofersceadewude, Mk. Skt. 9, 7. Ðū oferscadudest (-sceaduwedest, Ps. Lamb.) *obumbrasti*, Ps. Spl. 139, 8. Ofersceadwa *obumbra*, Ps. Surt. 139, 8. [*Goth.* ufar-skadwjan.]

ofer-sceatt, es; *m. Money in excess (of a loan), interest*:—Ic onfēnge ðæt ðe mīn is mid ofersceatta (*cum usura*), Mt. Kmbl. Rush. 25, 27.

ofer-sceáwian *to overlook, superintend*:—Preóstum gedafenaþ, ðæt hī heora biscope beón eádmōdlīce underþeódde, and hē hī ofersceáwige, and heora wīsan begīme, swā swā his nama swēgeþ: his nama is gecweden *episcopus*, and ofersceáwigend on Englisc, ðæt hē ofersceáwige symle his underþeóddan, L. Ælfc. P. 37; Th. ii. 378, 25-30. [*Episcopus* . . . is on Englisc scawere, for he is iset to þon þet he scal ouerscawian mid his ȝeme þa lewedan, O. E. Homl. i. 117, 7.]

ofer-sceáwigend *a superintendent*; episcopus. v. preceding word.

ofer-sceótan. v. ofer, III.

ofer-scīnan *to cover with light, illumine*:—Næs nā ðæt ān ðæt ðæt leóht ða dūne āne oferscīneþ, ac eác swylce ða burh, Blickl. Homl. 129, 2. Beorht wolcn hig oferscean *nubes lucida obumbravit eos*, Mt. Kmbl. 17, 5. Ðonne his (*the moon's*) leóma ealne middaneard oferscīne, Anglia viii. 323, 7.

ofer-scūwan, -scūan *to overshadow*:—Wolken oferscūade (-scȳade, Lind.) hiæ, Mt. Kmbl. Rush. 17, 5. [*Icel.* yfir-skyggja.]

ofer-seám, es; *m. A bag*:—Oferseámas *sacculos*, Lk. Skt. Lind. 12, 33.

ofer-sēcan *to make too great demands upon, put to too severe a trial, press too hard*:—Wæs sió hond tō strong seó (MS. se) ðe mēca gehwane swenge ofersōhte *the hand was too strong, which with its stroke put every blade to too severe a trial*, i. e. Beowulf struck so hard that any sword would be broken, Beo. Th. 3655; B. 2686. [*O. H. Ger.* ubar-suochian, Grff. vi. 84.]

ofer-segl, es; *m. A top-sail*:—Oversegl *artemon*, Wrt. Voc. ii. 100, 76.

ofer-seglian *to cross by sailing*:—Ðā āstāh hē on scyp and oferseglode (*transfretavit*), Mt. Kmbl. 9, 1.

ofer-sendan *to transmit*:—Ic ofersende *transmitto*, Ælfc. Gr. 28, 4; Som. 31, 40.

ofer-seócness, e; *f. Extreme sickness*:—Unfæstende man hūsles ne ābirige, būton hit for oferseócnesse sī, L. Edg. C. 36; Th. ii. 252, 2: 30; Th. ii. 250, 20.

ofer-seolfrian *to cover with silver*:—Hié eall heora wǣpn ofersylefredan *deargentatis armis*, Ors. 3, 10; Swt. 138, 31. Eall heora wǣpn wǣron ofersylefreda, 3, 11; Swt. 146, 23. Ofersylfrede (-seolfrade, Ps. Lamb.) *deargentatae*, Ps. Spl. 67, 14.

ofer-seón. I. *to observe, survey, see*:—Ðū ðe ealle gesceafta ofersihst *thou that dost survey all creatures*, Bt. 4; Fox 8, 20. Æfter ðære wīsan ðe ic hit oferseah *quemadmodum inspexi*, Nar. 2, 9. Swā ic mid mīnum ēgum oferseah, and mīnum eárum oferhȳrde, L. O. 8; Th. i. 180, 29: L. C. S. 23; Th. i. 388, 24. Ðū ealle mīne fȳnd eágum ofersāwe *super inimicos meos respexit oculus tuus*, Ps. Th. 53, 7. Ðæt hié heora sylfra eágon oforsēgon and heora eáron gehȳrdon *what they had seen with their own eyes and heard with their ears*, Blickl. Homl. 121, 1. Oft wē ofersēgon þeóda þeáwas, Exon. Th. 118, 9; Gū. 237. Selfe ofersāwon ðā ic cwom, Beo. Th. 842; B. 419. Ofersewen *respectus*, Ps. Spl. 72, 4. [*O. H. Ger.* ubar-sehan *respicere, superspicere.*] II. *to overlook, neglect, despise*:—Ða ðe tō ðam þriste sȳn, ðæt hig God oferseóþ and swā mæniges hāliges mannes dōm, Wulfst. 270, 23.

ofer-sīman *to overload, oppress*:—Gif metta oferfylle sāwl byþ ofersȳmed *si ciborum satietate anima obruatur*, Scint. 13. Warniaþ ðæt eówere heortan ne sȳn ofersȳmede mid oferfylle, R. Ben. 64, 1: 138, 11. Ðæt ða unstrangan ofersȳmede heora þeówdōm ne forfleón, 121, 23. [Þe burden ðe hē haddeus mide ouersemd, O. E. Homl. ii. 65, 4.]

ofer-sittan. I. *to sit upon, occupy, take possession of*:—Ofersēton *obsederunt*, Ps. Surt. 21, 13. Ofersētun sāwle mīne *occupaverunt animam meam*, 58, 4. Ðone mǣstan dǣl his hæfþ sǣ oferseten *the greatest part of it the sea has occupied*, Bt. 18, 1; Fox 62, 11. [We maȝen ouersitten þis lond, Laym. 8035.] II. *to desist from, abstain from*:—Ic ofersitte *supersideo*, Ælfc. Gr. 47; Som. 48, 45. Ic gylp ofersitte *I abstain from boasting*, Beo. Th. 5050; B. 2528. Wit sculon secge ofersittan *we shall abstain from the sword, not make use of swords*, 1372; B. 684. [Cf. *Prompt. Parv.* ovyrsyttynge of dede or time *omissio.*]

ofer-slǣp, es; *m. Excessive sleep*:—Wið overslǣpe, Lchdm. i. 342, 14.

ofer-sleán *to reduce, subdue*:—Ðæt ða munecas furþor restan ðonne healfe niht ðæt seó dæges þigen tōfered sȳ on ðære nihtlīcam reste and seó hǣte ðære þigene oferslegen *that the monks may rest more than half the night, so that the food of the day may be distributed through the body in the nightly rest and the heat of the food subdued*, R. Ben. 32, 15.

ofer-slege, es; *n. A lintel*:—Oferslege oððe þrexwold *limen*, Ælfc. Gr. 9, 12; Som. 9, 28. Ofershæge, Wrt. Voc. i. 85, 65. Sprengaþ on ðæt oferslege (*superliminare*) . . . ðonne hē gesihþ ðæt blōd on ðam oferslege, Ex. 12, 22-23. On hyra gedyrum and oferslegum, Homl. Th. i. 310, 29: ii. 40, 12: 264, 1: 266, 8. [*Prompt. Parv.* ovyrslay of a dore *superliminare.*] v. ofer-dyre, -gedyre.

ofer-slop, es; *n. An over-garment, surplice*:—Oferslop hwīt habban, blisse getācnaþ. Oferslop bleófāh habban ǣrende fūllīc getācnaþ, Lchdm. iii. 200, 5-7. On oferslopum *in stolis*, Lk. Skt. Lind. 20, 46. [His (the canon's) oversloppe nis nat worth a myte, Chauc. Group G. 633: *Icel.* yfir-sloppr.] v. next word.

ofer-slype, es; *m. An over-garment, surplice*:—Ðæt mæssepreósta ǣnig ne cume binnan circan dyre būton his oferslipe (-slope), L. Edg. C. 46; Th. ii. 254, 10. Hē is ymbscrȳd mid hwītum oferslype *he is clad in a white upper garment*, Homl. Th. i. 456, 19.

ofer-smeáung, e; *f. Excessive consideration of a subject*:—Sió ofersmeáung mirþ ða unwīsan, Past. 15, 6; Swt. 97, 17.

ofer-sprǣc, e; *f. Excessive speaking, loquacity*:—Ne biþ nǣfre sió ofersprǣc būtan synne *in multiloquio non deerit peccatum*, Past. 38, 8; Swt. 279, 23. Āīdlode on ofersprǣce *multiloquio vacantes*, 38, 1; Swt. 271, 10. On īdle ofersprǣce *supervacuis verbis*, 38, 6; Swt. 277, 11. Ðonne mon mid ungedafenlīcre and unwærlīcre ofersprǣce ða heortan gedweleþ ðara ðe ðǣrtō hlystaþ and eác se lāriów biþ gescinded mid ðære ofersprǣce *cum apud corda audientium loquacitatis incauta importunitate laevigatur, et auctorem suum haec eadem loquacitas inquinat*, 15, 5; Swt. 95, 19-21. Gelimpeþ ðæt his word beóþ gehwyrfedo tō unnyttre ofersprǣce *contingit, ut magistri lingua usque ad excessus verba pertrahatur*, 21, 7; Swt. 165, 18. [*O. H. Ger.* ubar-sprāhhi.]

ofer-sprǣce; *adj.* I. *speaking too much, talkative, loquacious*:—Se ðe ofersprǣce biþ *multiloquio subditus*, Past. 15, 6; Swt. 97, 6. Se ofersprǣcea wer *vir linguosus*, 38, 8; Swt. 279, 21. Ne beó ðū tō ofersprēce ac hlyst ǣlces monnes worda swīðe georne '*give every man thy ear, but few thy voice*,' Prov. Kmbl. 58. Salamon cwæþ, ðæt sēlre wǣre tō wunigenne mid león and dracan ðonne mid yfelan wīfe and ofersprǣcum, Homl. Th. i. 486, 33. Ða . . . ofersprǣcean *multiloquio vacantes*, Past. 38, 6; Swt. 277, 3: 38, 1; Swt. 271, 14. [Cf. *O. H. Ger.* ubarsprācha zungun *linguam magniloquum.*] II. *saying more than is just* or *true* (v. ofer-sprecan):—Ða fācnes fullan weoloras and ða ofersprǣcan *labia dolosa*, Ps. Th. 11, 3. Ða ofersprēcan ðe mē yfel cweðaþ *qui maligne loquuntur adversum me*, 34, 24.

ofer-sprǣdan *to overspread, cover*:—Beón ðǣr (*in the house for strangers*) symble bedd genihtsumlīce ofersprǣdde, R. Ben. 84, 23.

ofer-sprecan. I. *to say too much, use too many words*:—Ne flȳt ðū wið ānwilne man ne wið ofersprecenne *don't dispute with an obstinate man, or with one using too many words*, Prov. Kmbl. 5. II. *to say too much, more than is just*:—Ofersprecendes *obloquentis*, Ps. Lamb. 43, 17. [*O. H. Ger.* ubar-sprehhan *blasphemare.*]

ofer-sprecol; *adj.* I. *given to talk too much, talkative, loquacious*:—Se ðe ofersprecol biþ *multiloquio serviens*, Past. 38, 8; Swt. 279, 20. Se ofersprecola wer *vir linguosus*, R. Ben. 30, 5. II. *given to extravagant, inconsiderate speech*:—Ofersprecelum *procacibus, imprudentibus*, Hpt. Gl. 452, 14: 507, 24.

ofer-sprecolness, e; *f. Talkativeness, loquacity*; superfluitas locutionis, Past. 43, 1; Swt. 308, 16.

ofer-stǣlan *to confute, convince, convict*:—Ic oferstǣle *confuto*, Wrt. Voc. i. 34, 15. Oberstaelid *confutat*, ii. 105, 32. Oferstǣleþ, 15, 31. Ic eom geþafa ðæt ic eom swīðe rihte oferstēled, and ic beó ealne weig micle gefegenra ðonne ðū mē myd þillīcum ofærstǣlest, ðonne ic ǣfre wēræ ðonne ic ōðerne man oferstǣlde *I allow that I am very properly confuted, and I am always much more pleased when you confute me with such arguments, than I ever should be when I confuted another man*, Shrn. 197, 32-35. Ne beó ðū tō ānwille; forðam ðe is gerisenlīcre ðæt ðū sī mid rihte oferstēled, ðonne ðū oferstēle ōðerne man mid wōge, Prov. Kmbl. 8. Ðæt hī ðæs deófles leásunge mid Godes sōðfæstnysse oferstǣlan, Homl. Th. ii. 100, 9. Oberstaelende *convincens*, Wrt. Voc. ii. 104, 37. Oferstǣlende, 14, 60: *confutans*, 23, 45: Hpt. Gl. 436, 37. Oberstaeled *convicta*, Wrt. Voc. ii. 104, 45. Ðonne hē oferstǣled biþ *when he is convinced*, Past. 6; Swt. 46, 16. Hē biþ ðonne oferstǣled ðæt hē Godes feónd is *he will then be convicted of being God's foe*, Homl. Th. i. 612, 24. Gif hwā mǣne āþ on hāligdōme swerige, and hē oferstǣled weorðe *if a man commit perjury on a relic, and he be convicted*, L. C. S. 36; Th. i. 398, 5: 37; Th. i. 398, 12. Oferstǣlede *confutati, superati, convicti, redarguti*, Hpt. Gl. 475, 19.

ofer-steall, es; *m. Opposition*:—Gif ic ðīsum dracan tō forswelgenne geseald eom hwī sceal ic elcunge þrowian for eówerum ofersteallе (*the opposition which was offered by the prayers said at the speaker's bedside*), Homl. Th. i. 534, 20. Cf. wiðer-steall.

ofer-stealla, an; *m. A survivor*:—Heó wȳscte ðæt heó nānne æfter hyre ne forlēte, ðē læs gif hyra hwylc wǣre hyre ofersteallа, ðæt se ne myhte on heofenum beón hyre efngemæcca, Shrn. 151, 13.

ofer-stellan *to cross*:—Hit sum slōg oferhleóp and oferstælde (*transiliret*), Bd. 5, 6; S. 619, 17.

ofer-steppan *to over-step, to cross, exceed*:—Ic ofersteppe weall *transgrediar murum*, Ps. Lamb. 17, 30. Ðū oferstōpe *tu supergressa es*, Kent. Gl. 1151. Ne oferstepe ðū ealde gemēro *ne transgrediaris terminos antiquos*, 854. Seó sǣ ne mōt ðone þeorscwold oferstæppan (-steppan, Met. 11, 69) ðære eorþan, Bt. 21; Fox 74, 26. [*O. H. Ger.* ubar-stephen *transgredi, excedere.*]

ofer-stīgan. I. *to mount, scale, surmount, rise above*:—Ic heofonas oferstīge, Exon. Th. 482, 24; Rä. 67, 6. Sume ða ȳða hē becerþ mid ðȳ scipe sume hit oferstīgþ *some of the waves the steersman avoids with the ship, some it surmounts*, Past. 56, 3; Swt. 433, 3. Heó ða þȳstre ðysses andweardan middangeardes oferstāh *praesentis mundi tenebras transiens*, Bd. 3, 8; S. 532, 3. Hē on ānre diégelre stōwe ðone munt oferstāg, Ors. 4, 6; Swt. 172, 21. Breóst oferstāg brim weallende eorlum ōþ exle *the boiling sea rose above the breast up to men's shoulders*, Andr. Kmbl. 3146; An. 1576. Eles gecynd is ðæt hē wile oferstīgan ǣlcne wǣtan, Homl. Th. ii. 564, 12. II. *to transcend, surpass, excel, overcome, exceed*:—Ic oferstīge *excelleo*, Ælfc. Gr. 26; Som. 28, 45. Ðū ealle ðīne yldran on rīce feor oferstīgest (*transcendas*), Bd. 2, 12; S. 514, 9. Hē ealra ōðerra heáhfædera mægen oferstīgeþ, Blickl. Homl. 167, 23. Yldo oferbīdeþ stānas, heó oferstīgeþ stȳle, Salm. Kmbl. 600; Sal. 299. Oferstīhþ *excedit*, i. *superat*, Wrt. Voc. ii. 145, 71. Ðæs gebodes micelnes his mihta oferstīhþ, R. Ben. 128, 14. Hē ongeat ðæt hē oferstāg hine selfne *semetipsum noverat transcendere*, Past. 16, 2; Swt. 101, 13. Oforstāg, Blickl. Homl. 163, 28. Oferstāh, Homl. Th. i. 70, 11. Hī swīðra oferstāg weard *a stronger guard overcame them*, Exon. Th. 116, 3; Gū. 201. Oferstīge *excedat*, Wrt. Voc. ii. 145, 72. Ǣr ðan ðe ðæs dæges lenge oferstīge ða niht, Lchdm. iii. 256, 13. Oferstigan *percellerent, supereminerent*, Hpt. Gl. 489, 27. Ða yldo mid þeáwum oferstīgende *aetatem moribus transiens*, Bd. 5, 19; S. 637, 4. Ða oferstīgendan lufe *the surpassing love*, Homl. Th. ii. 408, 22. [*Goth.* ufar-steigan: *O. H. Ger.* ubar-stīgan *transcendere, transire, exsuperare*: *Icel.* yfir-stiginn *overcome.*]

ofer-stige, es; *m. Astonishment, extasy*:—Hē cwæþ tō him sylfum: 'Nū ic wæs of ðam rihtan wege mīnes ingeþances, ac betere hit biþ ðæt ic eft fare ūt of ðysum porte, ðȳ læs ðe ic tō swīðe dwelige . . . gewislīce ic hēr ongyten hæbbe ðæt mē hæfþ gelǣht fæste mīnes mōdes oferstige, ðæt ic nāt nā forgeare hū ic hit ðus macige,' Homl. Skt. i. 23, 551–556. v. ofer-stigenness.

oferstīgend-līc; *adj. Superlative*:—Sume synd *superlativa*, ðæt is oferstīgendlīce, Ælfc. Gr. 5; Som. 4, 63.

ofer-stigenness, e; *f. A passing over*:—Geleórednysse ɫ oferstigenysse *extaseos, transgressionis*, Hpt. Gl. 413, 9. v. ofer-stige.

ofer-swimman *to cross by swimming*:—Oferswam ða sioleþa bigong sunu Ecgþeówes, Beo. Th. 4723; B. 2367. [*O. H. Ger.* ubar-swimman *tranare.*]

ofer-swīðan; *p.* -swīðde, *but also* -swāð *To prove stronger than* or *superior to another, to overcome, overpower, conquer, surpass*:—Obersuīðo *vinco*, Wrt. Voc. ii. 123, 69. Ic oferswīðe *vinco*, Ælfc. Gr. 28; Som. 32, 17. Ic nardes stenc oferswīðe mid mīnre swētnesse, Exon. Th. 423, 29; Rä. 41, 29. Ðū ðe ūre wiðerwinnan oferswīðst, Homl. Skt. i. 11, 233. Ðū oferswīðest deáþ, Blickl. Homl. 141, 13. Hē on his mægenes weorþunga oferswīð ealra ōðerra Godes martira wuldor, 167, 25. Gyf strengra hine oferswȳð (-swīð, MSS. B. C.) *si fortior vicerit eum*, Lk. Skt. MS. A. 11, 22. Oferswȳðeþ, Beo. Th. 564; B. 279. Ðū oferswīðdest ðone deófol, Homl. Skt. i. 3, 436: Blickl. Homl. 157, 4. Hē ðone ealdan gedwolan oforswīðde, 7, 13. Gaius Julius se cāsere Brettas oferswīðde, Chr. Erl. 4, 24: Ors. 1, 2; Swt. 30, 22. Hē þurh Godes mihte ðone cwelmbǣran drenc oferswīðde, Homl. Th. i. 72, 12. Heó þurh martyrdōm ðisne middaneard oferswāð, Homl. Skt. i. 2, 4. Hē ðone feónd oferswāð, Shrn. 13, 30. Ða ðe mid sygefæstum deáþe middangeard oferswīðdon, Homl. Th. i. 84, 31. Oferswīð ðās cristenan þurh tearte wīta, Homl. Skt. i. 11, 137. Ðonne hē ðone āwyrgdan gāst oferswīðe, Blickl. Homl. 31, 31. Deófol oferswīðan, 29, 1: Elen. Kmbl. 2354; El. 1178. Mid swinglan oferswīðan, Bd. 1, 7; S. 478, 1: 1, 25; S. 487, 1. Mid gedwylde lāre oferswīðan, Homl. Th. i. 44, 26. Ðæt geþyld oferswīðende *patientia victrix*, Prud. 25 a. Hī habbaþ deófol oferswīðed, Blickl. Homl. 35, 4. Oferswīðod, Homl. Skt. i. 1, 8: 4, 57. Is betre ðæt hié weorðen gebundene and oferswīðde, Past. 30; Swt. 204, 4; Blickl. Homl. 145, 13. Wit sȳn oferswīðede, 181, 30. Oferswīðdum leahtrum *devictis vitiis*, Prud. 28 b. v. un-oferswīðende.

ofer-swīðe; *adv. Over-much, too much*:—Sȳ hē snotor and nā oferswīðe ne þreáge, R. Ben. 121, 3. Ða heáfodmen lufedon swīðe and oferswīðe gītsunge on golde and on seolfre, Chr. 1086; Erl. 220, 5. [Ouermuchel and ouerswuðe ivonded, A. R. 178, 9.]

ofer-swīðestre, an; *f. A conqueror*; victrix, Wrt. Voc. ii. 141, 68.

ofer-swīðness, e; *f. Oppression, distress*:—Oferswīðnisse *pressura*, Lk. Skt. Rush. 21, 25: Jn. Skt. Rush. 16, 33.

ofer-swīðrian *to prevail, conquer*:—Ic oforswīðrode ongēn hine *praevalui adversum eum*, Ps. Lamb. 12, 5. Wē oferswīðredon (-swīðdon MS. F.) on ðysum eallum þurh ðone ðe ūs lufode '*in all these things we are more than conquerors through him that loved us*' (Rom. 8, 37), R. Ben. 27, 12.

ofer-swīðung, e; *f. Oppression, distress*; pressura, Jn. Skt. Lind. 16, 21, 33: p. 7, 17.

ofer-swōgan *to cover thickly*:—Mid þȳstro genipum ðæs muntes cnoll eall oferswōgen wæs, Blickl. Homl. 203, 9. v. ā-swōgan, ge-swōgen.

ofer-tæl, es; *n. An odd number*:—Ðæra pipercorna sȳ ofertæl, ðæt ys ðȳ forman dæge ān and þrittig, and ðȳ ōðrum dæge seofontȳne, and ðȳ þriddan dæge þreótȳne, Lchdm. i. 288, 8.

ofer-teldan *to cover with an awning*:—Segle ofertolden, Cd. Th. 182, 26; Exod. 81. [Al þe cure ouertild, Jul. 9, 8.]

ofer-teón. I. *to draw one thing over another, to cover by drawing one thing over another*:—Ðonne ic oferteó heofenan mid wolcnum *cum obduxero nubibus coelum*, Gen. 9, 14: Homl. Th. i. 22, 11. Woruld miste oferteáh, þȳstrum biþeahte, Exon. Th. 178, 35; Gū. 1254. Hē nǣfre eft nolde ealne middaneard mid nānum flōde oferteón, Scrd. 21, 21. Ðonne se fulla mōna wyrð ofertogen mid þȳstrum, Bt. 39, 3; Fox 214, 29: Met. 9, 16. II. *to bring to an end, finish*:—Ofertogen *finitum*, Wrt. Voc. ii. 134, 4.

ofer-þearf, e; *f. Extreme need*:—Gif ðæs oferþearf sīe ǣr mete, ðæt hē spīwan mǣge, Lchdm. ii. 226, 9: Wulfst. 134, 21. Āgan ða yldran ðæs oferþearfe, ðæt hī heora gingran Gode gestrȳnan, 38, 23. For oferþearfe ilda cynnes, Elen. Kmbl. 1039; El. 521. Ða unþeáwas habbaþ oferþearfe hreówsunga, Bt. 31, 1; Fox 110, 27.

ofer-þearfa, an; *m. One in extreme need*:—Is seó bōt gelong æt ðē ānum oferþearfum *on thee alone depends the remedy for those in dire need*, Exon. Th. 10, 17; Cri. 153.

ofer-þeccan *to cover*:—Blōdig wolcen oforþecþ ealne ðysne heofon, Blickl. Homl. 91, 33: 93, 2. Eall eorþe biþ mid þeóstrum oforþeaht, 93, 6. Mid forste oferþeaht *covered with ice*, Homl. Skt. i. 11, 143. Þicce vel oferþeaht *condensa*, i. *spissa, secreta*, Wrt. Voc. ii. 135, 65. Hē onwreáh ða eorþan ðe ǣr wæs oferþeaht mid feóndum *revelabit condensa*, Ps. 28, 7. Mid þeóstrum oferþeht, Homl. Th. ii. 350, 17. Scip mid ȳðum oferþeht, 378, 15: Hexam. 6; Norm. 10, 18: Exon. Th. 353, 10; Reim. 10. [*Ger.* über-decken.]

ofer-þeón; *p.* -þāh, -þeáh; *pl.* -þugon, -þungon; *pp.* -þogen, -þungen *To thrive beyond others, to excel, surpass*:—Ic oferþeó *excello*, Ælfc. Gr. 37; Som. 39, 28. Oft on lǣwedum hāde mid gōdum weorcum man oferþīhþ ðone munuchād, Past. 52, 10; Swt. 411, 36. Oferþȳhþ, R. Ben. 12, 16. Hē oferþeáh biscopes, Shrn. 17, 11. Būtan hwylc ōðerne mid geearnunge oferþeó, R. Ben. 12, 21. Bonan mǣndon ðæt hȳ monnes bearn oferþunge, Exon. Th. 128, 10; Gū. 402. Oferþuge *praestaret, superaret, superexcelleret*, Hpt. Gl. 480, 1. Oferþeón *praestare, antecellere*, 417, 62: *melior esse*, 418, 67. Ic hæbbe ðē oferþogen, Homl. Th. i. 448, 34: Homl. Skt. i. 3, 209. Seó hæfþ ealle ōðru wīf oferþungen mid clǣnnesse, Bt. 10; Fox 28, 21: 33, 4; Fox 132, 7: Met. 20, 194: Past. 32, 2; Swt. 213, 11. Hē wēnþ ðæt hē hæbbe hié oferþungne on his lifes geearnunge *transcendisse se vitae meritis credit*, 17, 3; Swt. 111, 15. [*Goth.* ufar-þeihan.]

ofer-þrymm, es; *m. Exceeding power*:—Ǣr ðon se wlonca dæg bodige þurh bȳman brynehātne lēg egsan oferþrym *ere that august day* (*doom's day*) *announce by the trumpet fire burning-hot, over-powering terror*, Exon. Th. 448, 10; Dōm. 52.

ofer-þungen. v. ofer-þeón.

ofer-togenness, e; *f. The condition of being covered*:—Wið eágena ofertogennysse *ad albuginem oculorum*, Lchdm. i. 176, 16. v. ofer-teón.

ofer-trahtnian *to comment upon, expound*:—Langsum hit biþ ðæt wē ealne ðisne lofsang ofertrahtnian, Homl. Th. i. 202, 28.

ofer-tredan *to trample upon, tread under foot*:—Se geleáfa ofertret ðæt deófolgyld *fides conculcat idolatriam*, Prud. 9 a. Seó gȳtsung manega ofertret *avaritia multos sternit*, 58 a. Seó rūmgyfolnes ða gȳtsunge mid cneówum and mid fōtum ofertræd *largitas avaritiam genibus et calcibus perfodit*, 68 a. [Þe Laferrd oferrcomm ⁊ oferrtradd te deofell, Orm. 12493.]

ofer-trūwa, an; *m. Over-confidence*:—For ðam ofertrūwan on ðam friþe *from over-confidence in the truce*, L. Ath. v. 8, 7; Th. i. 238, 5.

ofer-trūwod *possessed by over-confidence, over-confident*:—Ðæm lāreówe is swīðe smeálīce tō underseceanne be ðǣm weorcum ðara ofertrūwudena *subtiliter ab arguente discutienda sunt opera protervorum*, Past. 32, 1; Swt. 208, 13.

ofer-wacian *to keep watch over, act as a guard*:—Julianus wȳcode wið ða eá Eufraten, and him oferwacedon syfanfealde weardes, Homl. Skt. i. 3, 271.

ofer-wadan *to cross by wading*:—Ðā gebeótode Cirus ðæt hē his þegn on hire swā gewrecan wolde ðæt hié mehte wīfmon be hiere cneówe oferwadan *rex iratus ulcisci in amnem statuit, contestans eum feminis vix genua tingentibus permeabilem relinquendum*, Ors. 2, 4; Swt. 72, 33. [*O. H. Ger.* ubar-watan *pertransire.*]

ofer-wealdend, es; *m. One who rules over others, ruler, governor*:—Ealles oferwealdend, Elen. Kmbl. 2469; El. 1236.

ofer-weaxan *to cover by growing, over-grow*:—Hǣlend wæs sprecende tō Abrahame and wæs cweðende ðæt his sǣd oferweóxe ealle ðās woruld, Blickl. Homl. 159, 26. Mid wuda oferwexen, 207, 27: Homl. Th. i. 508, 23.

ofer-weder, es; *n. Storm, tempest*:—Heora scipu sume þurh oferweder wurdon tōbrocene, Chr. 794; Erl. 59, 22.

ofer-wenian *to become insolent*:—Oberwenide *insolesceret*, Wrt. Voc. ii. 111, 34. Oberwaenidae, Ep. Gl. 12 d, 20.

ofer-weorc, es; *n. A superstructure, a tomb*:—Oferwurces *sarcophagi, tumba*, Hpt. Gl. 488, 51. [Oferr þatt arrke wuss An oferwerrc wel timmbredd (*the mercy-seat*), Orm. 1035.] v. ofer-geweorc.

ofer-weorpan. I. *to overthrow, throw down*:—Nim eorþan, oferweorp mid đînre swîđran handa under đînum swîđran fêt, Lchdm. i. 384, 19. Gif hê hié oferweorpe, mid x scill. gebête, L. Alf. pol. 11; Th. i. 68, 15. Đý gewunelîcan þeáwe horsa æfter wêrinysse hit (*the horse*) ongan walwian and on gehwedære sîdan hit oferweorpan *consueto equorum more, quasi post lassitudinem in diversum latus vicissim sere volvere coepit*, Bd. 3, 9; S. 533, 40. Mid đý storme onwend and oferworpen *tempestate convulsa*, Past. 26; Swt. 181, 11. II. *to throw* (*water*, etc.) *upon, to sprinkle*:—Oferwurpe đû mid đý wætere ealle burgwaran, Exon. Th. 467, 3; Hö. 133. Se đe mid wætere oferwearp wuldres cynebearn, Menol. Fox 315; Men. 159. III. *intrans. To fall down*:—Oferwearp đâ wêrigmôd, wîgena strengest, đæt hê on fylle wearđ, Beo. Th. 3090; B. 1543. [Uorte holden þet schip, þet uđen ne stormes hit ne ouerworpen, A. R. 142, 11. He oferrwarp þeȝȝre bordess, Orm. 15567 note.]

ofer-wîgan *to overcome in fight, conquer*:—Yldo oferwîgeþ wulf, heó oferbîdeþ stânas, Salm. Kmbl. 598; Sal. 299.

ofer-willan. I. *to boil so that a liquid is reduced in quantity*:—Oferwylle ôþ đone þriddan dǽle, Lchdm. ii. 216, 3, 4: 228, 18: 238, 10. II. *to overboil, boil too much*:—Nim đæt wæter đe pyosan wǽran on gesodene oferwilleda, 286, 29.

ofer-winnan *to overcome, conquer, vanquish, subdue*:—Se đe his môd gewylt is betera đonne se đe burh oferwinþ, Homl. Th. ii. 544, 10. Oferwinnaþ *debellant*, Blickl. Gl. Gif ûre fýnd ûs oferwinnaþ *expugnatis nobis*, Ex. 1, 10. Hê Soroastrem oferwann and ofslôh *Zoroastrem pugna oppressum interfecit*, Ors. 1, 2; Swt. 30, 11. Oferwan, 1, 6; Swt. 36, 17. Iudith seó wuduwe đe oferwann Holofernem, Ælfc. T. Grn. 11, 15, 44. Hî oferwunnon mê *expugnaverunt me*, Ps. Spl. 128, 1. Oferwin onwinnende *expugna inpugnantes*, Blickl. Gl. Hê đus cwæđ đæt hê đa lotwrenceas oferwunne, Past. 30, 2; Swt. 205, 17. Gif đû wille ǽnige buruh oferwinnan (*expugnare*), Deut. 20, 10: Jos. 10, 4. Đæt hî mihton heora fýnd oferwinnan, Bd. 1, 12; S. 480, 28. Seó ylce þeód wæs oferwunnen fram Eald-Seaxum, 5, 11; S. 626, 10, On đǽm xxv. wintrum đe hê winnende wæs hê nâ oferwunnen ne wearđ, Ors. 3, 7; Swt. 114, 6. Se mon hafaþ weán oferwunnen, Exon. Th. 475, 5; Bo. 43. Synd đa fýnd oferwunnene, Gen. 14, 20. Oferwunnenum feóndum *devictis hostibus*, Prud. 4 a. [*O. H. Ger.* ubar-winnan *expugnare, superare, devincere*: *Icel.* yfir-vinna.]

ofer-wintran *to winter, pass the winter*:—Nân eówer nele oferwintran (*hiemare*) bûton mînum (*the shoemaker*) cræfte, Coll. Monast. Th. 28, 1. [*Ger.* über-wintern.]

ofer-wist, e; *f. Excess in eating*:—Sint tô manianne đa ofergîfran đeáh hié ne mǽgen đone unþeáw forlǽtan đære gîfernesse and đære oferwiste đæt hê hûru hine selfne ne þurhstinge mid đý sweorde unryhthǽmedes, ac ongiete hû micel ofersprǽc cymeþ of đære oferwiste *admonendi sunt gulae dediti, ne in eo, quod escarum delectationi incubant, luxuriae se mucrone transfigant, et quanta sibi per esum loquacitas insidietur, aspiciant*, Past. 43, 5; Swt. 313, 6–10. Hî lufiaþ oferwiste and îdele bliese, L. I. P. 14; Th. ii. 322, 24.

ofer-wistlîc glosses *supersubstantialis*, Mt. Kmbl. Lind. 6, 11.

ofer-wlenced *possessed of superabundant means, very opulent*:—Hié andwyrdon đæt hit gemâlîc wǽre đæt swâ oferwlenced cyning sceolde winnan on swâ earm folc swâ hié wǽron *responderunt, stolide opulentissimum regem adversus inopes sumsisse bellum*, Ors. 1, 10; Swt. 44, 12.

ofer-wlencu (o); *f. Ostentation, superabundant means*:—Đa đe hyra lîfes þurh lust brûcan îdelum ǽhtum and oferwlencum, gierelum gielplîcum, Exon. Th. 127, 21; Gû. 389. v. preceding word.

ofer-wrecan *to overwhelm*:—Oberurecan *obruere*, Wülck. Gl. 35, 14.

ofer-wreón; *p.* -wráh, -wreáh, *pl.* -wrigon, -wrugon; *pp.* -wrigen, -wrogen *To cover, cover over, veil, hide, conceal, overspread*:—Ic oferwreó *nubo*, Ælfc. Gr. 28; Som. 31, 19: *cooperio*, 30; Som. 34, 43. Đû đe oferwrîhst mid wæterum đa uferan hire *qui tegis aquis superiora ejus*, Ps. Lamb. 103, 3. Geswinc welera heora oferwrîhþ (-wrîđ, Ps. Surt.: -wrýhþ, Ps. Spl.) hî *labor labiorum ipsorum operiet eos*, 139, 10. Oferwrîhþ (-wrîđ, Ps. Surt.: -wrýcþ, Ps. Spl.) *operit*, 146, 8. Oferwrîhþ *operit*, Kent. Gl. 323. Seó sôđe lufu Godes and manna oferwrýhþ đa mengo synna *charity covereth a multitude of sins*, L. E. I. 36; Th. ii. 434, 39, 37. Mycel mægen đone heofon oforþecþ and oforwrýhþ, Blickl. Homl. 93, 3. God ǽlce stôwe gefylþ and ufan oforwrýhþ, 19, 27. Seó sunne scînþ geond ealle eorþan gelîce, and ealre eorþan brâdnysse endemes oferwrýhþ, Lchdm. iii. 236, 13. Unrehtwîsnesse mîne ic ne oferwrâh (-wreáh, Ps. Spl. C. T.), Ps. Surt. 31, 5. Đû oferwrige *operuisti*, 84, 3. Oferwrâh (-wreáh, Ps. Spl.) *operuit*, 43, 17: 68, 8. Seó sǽ ealle his cræftu and riddan mid ýđan oferwreáh, Homl. Th. ii. 194, 28. Þicce genip oferwrêh đone munt, Ex. 19, 16. Oferwreogan (*contexerunt*) mê þýstru, Ps. Lamb. 54, 6. Ne ne beóþ gecyrred oferwreón (tô oferwreónne, Ps. Lamb.: oferwreán, Ps. Surt.) eorþan *neque convertentur operire terram*, Ps. Spl. 103, 10. Sume âgunnon oferwreón (*velare*) his ansýne, Mk. Skt. 14, 65. Nacode wê sceolan oferwreón, L. E. I. 32; Th. ii. 428, 25. Næs Salomon oferwrigen (*coopertus*) swâ swâ ân of đyson, Mt. Kmbl. 6, 29. Đæt dysig đæt hit ǽr mid oferwrigen wæs, Bt. 39, 3; Fox 216, 6. Sýn oferwrigene *operiantur*, Ps. Lamb. 70, 13. Synna beóþ oferwrigenne for dǽdbôte, L. E. I. 36; Th. ii. 434, 22. Đǽr stôd ân æmtig cýf oferwrogen, Homl. Th. ii. 178, 34. Se đe wæs hwîlon gescrîd mid golde, hê læg đâ oferwrogen mid moldan, Chr. 1086; Erl. 221, 3. Hwîtum gegyrlan oferwrohne (-wrogenne, MS. A.), Mk. Skt. 16, 5. Mid hwam beó wê oferwrogene? Mt. Kmbl. 6, 31. Oferwrogne *contecta*, Hpt. Gl. 417, 48.

ofer-wrîgels, es; *n. A covering*:—Ofyrwrîgyls *opertorium*, Ps. Spl. C. 101, 28. Oferwrîgelsum *operculis*, Wrt. Voc. ii. 62, 55.

ofer-writ *a writing upon a subject, a letter*:—In oferwurit his *in epistola sua*, Mt. Kmbl. p. 8, 20.

ofer-wundenness, e; *f. Experiment, proof*:—Oferwundennyssum *experimentis*, Hpt. Gl. 419, 38.

ofer-wyrcan *to cover by working, to work a covering over something, to overlay*:—Hê hit him eft hâm bebeád on ânum brede âwriten and siđđan hit âwriten wæs hê hit oferworhte mid weaxe *qui omnia civibus suis per tabellas scriptas, et post cera superlitas, enunciabat*, Ors. 4, 5; Swt. 168, 14. Nǽfre nǽnig man đa lǽstas sylfe ufan oferwyrcean ne mihte, ne mid golde, ne mid seolfre, Blickl. Homl. 125, 35. Hûs (*the temple*) oferworht mid golde and mid hwîtan seolfre, Ælfc. T. Grn. 7, 35: Blickl. Homl. 125, 25. Hê wæs bebyrged and oferworht syđđan (*a tomb was erected*), Homl. Skt. i. 21, 19.

ofer-ýđ, e; *f. An excessive wave, wave of a tempestuous sea*:—Nâ selleþ on êcnysse oferýđe rihtwîse *non dabit in aeternum fluctuationem justo*, Ps. Spl. 54, 25.

ofesc, e; *f. A border* (?):—Đis syndon đæs landes gemǽru ... Ǽrest of Seferne be hîgna gemǽre ... and swâ be đære alra ofesce (*along the border of elders?*) on đa neówan dîc, Cod. Dip. Kmbl. iii. 393, 11. v. owisc.

ôfest. v. ôfost.

ofet, es; *n. Fruit, pulse*:—Obet *fraga*, Wrt. Voc. ii. 109, 20. Ofet *fraga* (cf. streówberge *fraga*, 59), 36, 9: 150, 28. Ofet, wæstm *fruges, frumenta*, 151, 31. Ofet *legumen*, i. 38, 54. Đis ofet *the fruit of the tree of knowledge*, Cd. Th. 46, 12; Gen. 655. Ofæt, 33, 11; Gen. 518. Ofett, Exon. Th. 202, 29; Ph. 77. Ofetes wôs *ydromellum*, Wrt. Voc. i. 27, 43. Hit ofetes noman âgan sceolde, Cd. Th. 44, 34; Gen. 719. Ofætes, 30, 4; Gen. 461. Bergena ođđe ofeta *bacciniorum*, Wrt. Voc. ii. 87, 29. Ofætum ł wurtum *leguminibus*, Hpt. Gl. 444, 71: *holusculis, leguminibus*, 494, 47. [*Ayenb.* Þet ovet of þine wombe: *O. H. Ger.* obaz, obez *pomum, grosa*: *Ger.* obst.]

of-faran *to come up with those who are pursued, to overtake, to get near enough to attack, to reach and attack*:—Đâ Philippus wæs cirrende đâ offôr hiene ôđere Sciđđie Triballe wǽron hâtene *revertenti Philippo Triballi bello obviunt*, Ors. 3, 7; Swt. 118, 1. Đâ cômon Tarentîne tô heora âgnum scipum, and đâ ôđre hindan offôran, and hié ealle him tô gewildum gedydan bûton v *Tarentini Romanam classem praetereuntem hostiliter invaserunt, quinque tantum navibus per fugam elapsis*, 4, 1; Swt. 154, 6. Đâ offôron hié đone here hindan æt Buttingtûne and hine đǽr besǽton *they pursued and came up with the Danes at Buttington, and there besieged them*, Chr. 894; Erl. 92, 22. Hié offôron đone here hindan, đâ hê hâmweard wæs, and him đâ wiđ gefuhton, 911; Erl. 100, 26. Đâ ne mehte seó fird hié nâ hindan offaran, ǽr hié wǽron inne on đan geweorce, 894; Erl. 93, 7. Se cyng ofslôh heora swâ feala swâ hê offaran mihte, 1016; Erl. 157, 8. Ic tô fare *adeo*, ic eom offaren *adeor*, Ælfc. Gr. 37; Som. 39, 1. v. of-fêran, -fylgan, -irnan, -rîdan.

of-feallan *to fall upon, kill by falling, destroy*:—Hit hreás underbæc and forneán offeóll đa đe hit ǽr forcurfan *the tree fell backwards, and by its fall very nearly killed those who before were cutting it down*, Homl. Th. ii. 510, 2. Sigferþ cyning hine offeóll and his lîc ligþ æt Wimburnan *King Sigferth laid violent hands on himself, and his body lies buried at Wimborne*, Chr. 962; Erl. 120, 4. Hê geslôg xxv dracena and hine đâ [of] deáþ offeóll *he slew 25 dragons and then death fell upon him*, Salm. Kmbl. 430; Sal. 216. Seó môdinys wyle offeallan đa eádmôdnysse *superbia inruere vult super humilitatem*, Prud. 32 b. Ǽfter his fielle wearþ đara câsera mǽgþ offeallen *caesarum familia consumta est*, Ors. 6, 6; Swt. 262, 6. v. of-fillan.

of-fellan. v. of-fillan.

of-fêran *to overtake* (*an enemy*):—Pharao tengde æfter mid eallum his here and offêrde hî æt đære Reádan Sǽ *Pharaoh pressed after with all his host, and overtook the Israelites at the Red Sea*, Homl. Th. ii. 194, 16: Chr. 948; Erl. 118, 19. Se cyng fêrde him (*the Danes*) æt hindan, and offêrde hî innan Eást-Seaxan, and đǽr tôgædere heardlîce fêngon, 1016; Erl. 158, 1. v. of-faran.

of-ferian *to bear off*:—Hê fræt fîftýne men, and ôđer swylc ût offerede lâđlîcu lâc, Beo. Th. 3171; B. 1583.

of-fillan *to kill by felling, to kill by causing to fall, to destroy*:—Gif mon ôđerne æt gemǽnum weorce offelle (-fealle, MSS. B. H.), L. Alf. pol. 13; Th. i. 70, 9. Hî woldon heó sylfe offyllan ođđe âdrencan *ruina perituri aut fluctibus absorbendi*, Bd. 4, 13; S. 582, 33. Đâ hêt se dêma đæt wîf weorpan on seáþ and đǽr mid stânum offellan, Shrn. 89, 29. Cf. of-feallan.

offrian; *p.* ode, ede *To offer, bring a sacrifice* or *gift in honour of another*:—Ic offrige onsægednyssa *immolavi hostiam*, Ps. Spl. 26, 10.

Onsegdnisse ic offriu ðē *holocausta offeram tibi*, Ps. Surt. 65, 15. Ðū offrast ān celf, Ex. 29, 10, 18, 20. Offrede *litarat, sacrificabat*, Hpt. Gl. 415, 13. Hió offrede hiore ansegednesse *immolavit victimas suas*, Kent. Gl. 285. Hē offrude lāc Gode his fæder *mactatis victimis Deo patris sui*, Gen. 46, 1. Offrode, Homl. Th. ii. 456, 34. [Hē offrede hit (*the body of St. Florentine*) Crist and sc̄e Peter, Chr. 1013; Erl. 149, 21.] Hī offrodon (*immolaverunt*) twelf cealfas, Ex. 24, 5. Mesiane noldon ðæt Læcedemonia mægdenmenn mid heora ofreden, Ors. 1, 14; Swt. 56, 16. Ðē ofreden (*offerent*) cyningas gefe, Ps. Surt. 67, 30. Lǣtaþ ūs faran and offrian (*sacrificemus*) ūrum Gode, Ex. 5, 17. Tō offrienne *litaturus*, Hpt. Gl. 522, 25. [*O. Frs.* offria: *O. L. Ger.* offrōn: *Icel.* offra: *O. H. Ger.* opfarōn: *from Lat.* offerre.] v. ge-offrian.

offrung, ofrung, e; *f.* I. *the offering of a sacrifice* or *gift*:—Hit wæs gewunelīc on ealdum dagum, ðæt man Gode ðyllīce lāc offrode on cucan orfe; ac seó offrung is nū unālȳfedlīc, Homl. Th. ii. 456, 35. II. *an offering, sacrifice*:—Ic āxige hwǣr seó offrung (*victima*) sig . . . God foresceáwaþ ða offrunge, Gen. 22, 7–8. Hwæðer is māre, ðe offrung (ofrung, MS. A.), ðe ðæt weofud ðe gehālgaþ ða offrunge (ofrunge, MS. A.)? Mt. Kmbl. 23, 19. Melu oððe offrung *ador*, Ælfc. Gr. 9, 21; Som. 10, 32. Offrung *sacrificium*, Wrt. Voc. i. 28, 49. Ofrung *oblatio*, 28, 43. Wylt ðū ūs syllan offrunge *hostias quoque et holocausta da nobis*, Ex. 10, 25. Ofrunga *libamina, sacrificia*, Hpt. Gl. 487, 72. Offrunga *holocausta*, 509, 61: *holocaustomata*, 521, 71. [*O. L. Ger.* offrenga: *O. H. Ger.* opfarunga.]

offrung-disc, es; *m. A paten* [? v. hūsel-disc]:—Ānnæ offringdisc intō Nunnamynstær (*she gives*) *one paten to the Nuns' monastery*, Chart. Th. 553, 17.

offrung-hlāf, es; *m. Sacrificial bread, the shew-bread*:—Hē æt ða offringhlāfas *panes propositionis comedit*, Mt. Kmbl. 12, 4.

offrung-sang, es; *m. A hymn sung when an offering is made*:—Nū sceole wē healdan ūrne palm, ōþ ðæt se sangere onginne ðone offringsang, and geoffrian ðonne Gode ðone palm, Homl. Th. i. 218, 9.

of-fylgan, -fyligan *to come up with, overtake by pursuit*; assequi, Lk. Skt. Lind. Rush. 1, 3.

of-fyllan. v. of-fillan.

of-gān. I. *to demand what is due, seek satisfaction for, require, exact*:—Ic ofgā his blōdes gyte æt ðīnum handum *I will require the shedding of his blood at thy hands*, Homl. Th. ii. 340, 24. God ofgǣþ his feoh æt eów, 554, 19. Ic wille ofgān æt ðē his blōd, i. 6, 27. Ic wille ofgān ða scēþ æt eówrum handum, 242, 11. Ic wolde mīn āgen ofgān mid ðam gafole, ii. 554, 9. Ofgān *exigere*, Wülck. Gl. 257, 29. II. *to require what is not due, to exact with violence, extort*:—Ic wille mid tintregum æt ðē ofgān ðises þinges insiht *I will extort from thee with torments an account of this thing*, Homl. Th. i. 590, 22. Mid ðām tintregum hē wolde his ǣhta æt him ofgān, ii. 180, 18. III. *to require what is not one's due but is granted as a favour or for a fair equivalent, to obtain, hold by allowance of another*:—His brōðer wearþ his yrfenuma swā swā hē hit æt ðam cynge ofeode *his brother was his heir, according to the concession he had obtained of the king*, Chr. 1098; Erl. 235, 8. Gif ōðres mynstres ār on ōðres mynstres rȳmette lēge ðæt ðes mynstres ealdor ðe tō ðam rȳmette fēnge ofeode ðǣs ōðres mynstres āre mid swilcum þingum swylce ðam hīrēde ðæ ða āre āhte gecwēme wǣre *if one monastery's property lay in the space allotted to another, that the chief of the monastery that accepted the space should hold the other monastery's property on such conditions as should be agreeable to the society that owned that property*, Chart. Th. 231, 10–18. Hē beád ǣlcon his þegna ðe ēnig land on ðan lande hafde ðæt hī hit ofeodon be ðes biscopes gemēdon oððe hit āgēfon *that they should hold it in accordance with the bishop's pleasure, or give it up*, 295, 11. [Ich wille ðæt hit cume in ongeǽn, ōðer ðæt man hit ofgō on hise gemōð, 387, 22.] Eádmund æþeling bæd ðone hīrēd ðæt hē mōste ofgān (*have, hold*) ðæt land . . . Ðā cwæþ se cing ðæt hē nolde ðæt ðæt land mid ealle ūt āseald wǣre, ac ðæt ðæt land eft intō ðære hālgan stōwe āgifen wǣre, 300, 13–33. Ofgān tō rihtan gafole *to hold at a fair rent*, 355, 23: 478, 21. Ofgān land wið gersumen, 587, 7. God wile ðæt wē mid gemāglīcum bēnum his mildheortnesse ofgān *God wishes us to seek for his mercy by importunate prayers*, Homl. Th. ii. 126, 5. Wē sceolon mid hālgum mægnum ðone eard ofgān ðe wē þurh leahtras forluron *with holy virtues must we obtain the country, that we lost through vices*, i. 118, 33. [Ich hit wulle uorto ofgon (*gain*) þine heorte, A. R. 390, 13. To ofgon her lyflode, Piers P. 9, 106.] IV. *to start off, make a beginning of anything*:—Se ðe hine belecge ofgā his sprǣce mid forāðe *let him start his suit with a preliminary oath*, L. O. D. 6; Th. i. 354, 30: L. Ath. i. 23; Th i. 212, 4: L. C. S. 22; Th. i. 388, 14, 17: 30; Th. i. 394, 4. v. next word.

of-gangan. I. *to require*:—Ic ofgange *exigo*, Ælfc. Gr. 28, 6; Som. 32, 13. Eówer blōd ic ofgange (*requiram*) æt eallum wilddeórum and eác æt ðam men; of ðæs weres handa ic ofgange ðæs mannes līf, Gen. 9, 5. II. *to extort, exact what is not due*:—Ofgang ða mādmas *extort* (from St. Lawrence) *the treasures* (of the church, about which he would say nothing), Homl. i. 420, 26. III. *to acquire, obtain*:—Syle mē ðinne wīneard . . . ic ðē (*Naboth*) ōðerne finde oððe mid feó ofgange *give me thy vineyard . . . I will find thee another or will acquire it by purchase*, Homl. Skt. i. 18, 175. Ne sȳ nān man ðe ðyses landes ǣniges dǣles brūke, būtan hē hit ofgange æt ðām hīwum mid rihtum landrihte, Cod. Dip. Kmbl. iii. 435, 34. v. preceding word.

of-gangende *derivative*:—*Dirivativum*, ðæt is ofgangende, Ælfc. Gr. 18; Som. 20, 58. Sume (*pronouns*) synd *derivativa*, ðæt synd ofgangende, 15; Som. 17, 33. Hwæt sī betwux ðām genitvum ðæra frumcennedra pronomina and ðæra ofgangendra, Som. 19, 41.

ofgangend-līc *derivative*:—*Dirivativa*, ðæt is ofgangendlīc, Ælfc. Gr. 14; Som. 17, 4: 17; Som. 20, 35.

of-georn; *adj. Too eager, elated*:—Ofgeorn[um] *subnixis*, Hpt. Gl. 485, 45.

of-geótan. I. *to moisten by pouring, souse, soak*:—Ofgeót mid ealaþ *moisten the plants by pouring ale on them*, Lchdm. ii. 140, 15: iii. 28, 16. Ofgeót mid wætere, 48, 5. Ofgeót hȳ āne niht mid wȳne ðanne on morgen nim ða leáf cnuca hȳ . . . and ofgeót hȳ mid ðan ylcan wīne ðe hȳ ǣr ofgotene wǣron *soak them a night with wine, then in the morning take the leaves, pound them . . . and soak them with the same wine that they were soaked with before*, 130, 30–132, 2. Sele wermōd on wearmum wætere ofgotenne, ii. 182, 6. II. *to put out a fire by pouring water on it*:—Hit biþ gelīc, ðæt man mid wætere ðone weallendan welm (līg, MS. D.) ofgeóte, ðæt hē leng ne mōt rīxian, swā man mid ælmessan synna ealle ālȳseþ, Wulfst. 257, 21. Hī woldon ðæt fȳr mid wætere ofgeótan, Homl. Th. ii. 166, 7.

of-gerād; *adj. Appropriate*:—Ðeáh ic hwīlum gecoplīce funde, ic nū wēpende ofgerādra worda misfō, Bt. 2; Fox 2, 9.

of-gesleán *to slay*:—Hī ðǣr ofgeslōgan (ofslōgon, MS. E.) micel wæl, Chr. 992; Erl. 130, 35. v. of-sleán.

of-gestīgness, e; *f. Descent*:—Ofgestīgnisse *descensionis*, Mt. Kmbl. p. 8, 4.

of-gifan *to give up, leave, abandon*:—Obgibeht (=ofgifeþ) *destituit*, Wrt. Voc. ii. 105, 77. Hē Dena land ofgeaf *he left the Danes' land*, Beo. Th. 3813; B. 1904. Hē ðās woruld ofgeaf *he died*, Cd. Th. 72, 30; Gen. 1194. Hē ðone beám ofgeaf *he* (*Christ*) *left the cross* (*when he was taken to be buried*), Exon. Th. 45, 35; Cri. 729. Hī flet ofgeáfon *they gave up their halls* (*when they died*), 290, 7; Wand. 61. Mec deádne ofgeáfun fæder and mōder, ne wæs mē feorh ðāgēn in innan, 391, 7; Rä. 10, 1. Hī heora land ofgeáfan *patria profugi*, Ors. 1, 4; Swt. 32, 20. Ofgǣfon, Cd. Th. 6, 8; Gen. 85. Ne ofgif ðū mē *ne elonges a me*, Ps. Th. 70, 11. Hē ða goldburg ofgifan (*leave*) wolde, Andr. Kmbl. 3309; An. 1657. Ofgefen *distitutum*, Wrt. Voc. ii. 106, 58. Ofgifene, 25, 59: Bd. 4, 9; S. 577, 3. [*O. H. Ger.* aba-geban *destituere*: *O. Sax.* af-geƀan.]

of-habban *to keep from, hold back, restrain*:—Gif ðū ðæt (*letting the people go*) git dōn nelt and ðæt folc ofhæfst (*retines*), Ex. 9, 2. [*Goth.* af-haban.] Cf. of-healdan.

of-hagian *to be inconvenient*:—Gif his scrifte ofhagie, sēce man tō ðam leódbiscope, Wulfst. 275, 5. Cf. on-hagian.

of-healdan *to withhold, keep back, retain*:—Hē lēt niman of hyre ealle ða betstan gærsuma ðe heó ofhealdan ne mihte *he had all the best valuables, that she could not keep back, taken from her*, Chr. 1035; Erl. 164, 23. Mī gauil hē hauiþ ofhealden *my rent he has withheld*, Chart. Th. 427, 30. [*Ayenb.* to ofhealde *to retain*.] v. of-habban.

of-hearmian; v. *impers. To cause grief*:—Ðā ofhearmode (ofearmode? v. of-earmian) Gode heora yrmða *God was grieved at their miseries*, Jud. 11, 1. [Cf. *Icel.* harmr *grief, sorrow*; harmar einum *it vexes one.*]

of-hende; *adj. Out of one's hand, taken away, lost to one*:—Gif him ǣnig ðara ofhende wyrþ *if any one of them is lost to him*, Met. 25, 34. [*Icel.* af-hendr.] v. on-hende.

of-hnītan *to kill by butting, to gore to death*:—Gif se oxa wer oððe wīf ofhnīt *if an ox gore a man or woman, that they die*, Ex. 21, 29: L. Alf. 21; Th. i. 48, 27.

of-hreósan. I. *to overwhelm, cover, bury*; obruere:—Oft eorþstyrung fela burhga ofhreás, Homl. Th. i. 608, 26. Ðæt ne ða sleacgiendan hē (*sompnolentia*) ofhreóse (*obruat*), Hymn. Surt. 18, 15. Swylce hē sȳ mid moldhȳpan ofhroren, Homl. Th. i. 492, 33. Sume (*martyrs*) mid stānum ofhrorene, 542, 30. Mid sande ofhrorene *operti humo* Num. 16, 33. Ofhrorenne *obrutum*, Hpt. Gl. 487, 25. Ofrorene *obruti*, 506, 7: *obrutos*, 478, 77. II. *to fall down*:—Heofonas berstaþ, tungol ofhreósaþ, Exon. Th. 58, 12; Cri. 934.

of-hreówan. I. *to cause grief* or *pity* (a) *impers. with dat. of pers. and gen. of the cause*:—Mē ofhrīwþ *me miseret*, Ælfc. Gr. 33; Som. 37, 24. Ðæs sceápes untrumnesse him ofhreáw (-hreów, MS. F.), R. Ben. 51, 20. Him ofhreów ðæs mannes *he was sorry for man*, Homl. Th. i. 192, 16. (b) *with dat. of pers. and nom. of cause, or a clause introduced by* ðæt:—Ðā ofhreów ðam munece ðæs hreófian mægenleást *the powerlessness of the leper excited the pity of the monk*, 336, 11. Mē ofhreów ðæt hī nē cūðon ða godspellīcan lāre, 2, 22. II. *to feel pity*:—Se mæssepreóst ðæs mannes ofhreów, Swt. A. S. Rdr. 102, 216. Iohannes ofhreów ðære mēder dreórignysse, Homl. Th. i. 66, 21.

of-hyngrod *very hungry*:—Eádige beóþ ða ðe sind ofhingrode rihtwīsnysse, Homl. Th. i. 204. Ofhingrod æfter rihtwīsnysse, 550, 34–

35. [Gif þu ert ofhungred efter þe swete, A. R. 376, 18: *Laym.* offingred: *Piers P.* afingred.]

of-irnan. I. *to overtake (by running)*:—Færþ hē (*the evening star*) æfter ðære sunnan, óþ hē ofirnþ ða sunnan hindan, Bt. 39, 13; Fox 234, 2. Ðæs wītegan cnapa, Gyezi, ofarn Naaman, Homl. Th. i. 400, 17. [Þe abbed æfter Uortiger rad & sone gon ofærne Uortigerne, Laym. 13149.] II. *to tire with running*:—Hē wæs swīðe ofurnen *he was very tired with running*, Jud. 4. 19.

of-lǽtan. I. *to give up, relinquish*:—Gif ðū ǽr ðonne hē worold oflǽtest *if you die before him*, Beo. Th. 2371; B. 1183. Ðā se ellorgāst oflēt līfdagas and ðās lǽnan gesceaft, 3248; B. 1622. Līf oflǽtan, Cd. Th. 65, 28; Gen. 1073. [*Goth.* af-lētan ahman *to give up the ghost.*] II. *to let off, cause (blood) to flow*:—Ðæt him (hine, Cott. MS.) mon ofiēte blōdes on ðam earme, Bt. 29, 2; Fox 104, 23. [*Goth.* af-lētan *to let off, forgive, dismiss*: *Ger.* ab-lassen.]

oflǽte, -lāte, -lēte, an; *f.* I. *an oblation, offering*:—Oflǽtan *oblationem*, Ps. Spl. C. 39, 9. Oflātan *oblationes*, Ps. Surt. 50, 21. II. *a sacramental wafer*:—Eal ðæt tō hūsle gebirige, ðæt is, clǽne oflēte, clǽne wīn, and clǽne wæter, L. Edg. C. 39; Th. ii. 252, 13. Behealde hē ðæt his oflētan ne beón ealdbacene, L. Ælfc. C. 36; Th. ii. 360, 26. Benedictus āsende āne ofelētan, and hēt mid ðære mæssian, Homl. Th. ii. 174, 26. III. *a wafer like the sacramental wafer*:—Man sceal niman .vii. lytle oflǽtan swylce man mid ofraþ, Lchdm. iii. 42, 3. [Erest þat husel beð ouelete and win, O. E. Homl. ii. 97, 33. *Icel.* oblāta, oblāt *a sacramental wafer*: *O. H. Ger.* oblāta *oblatio*: *Ger.* oblate *wafer*. *From Mid. Lat.* oblāta.]

of-langod; *part. Seized with an excessive longing* or *desire*:—For ðære sibbe hē wearþ oflangod ungemetlīce *he was seized with an immense longing on account of the love he bore his father and mother*, Homl. Th. ii. 176, 1. Oflongad, Exon. Th. 443, 13; Kl. 29. [*Laym.*: *O. and N.* of-longed.]

oflāte. v. oflǽte.

of-lecgan *to lay down*:—Eom ic on lāme oflegd *infixus sum in limo*, Ps. Th. 68, 1. [*Goth.* af-lagjan *to lay down, put away.*]

of-leógan *to lie, be false*:—Ða ælþeódgan bearn mē oflugon *filii alieni mentiti sunt mihi*, Ps. Th. 17, 43.

of-licgan *to oppress, to hurt by lying upon*:—Gif hwā on slǽpe his bearn oflicge ðæt hit deád wurðe *si quis in somno infantem suum oppresserit, et mortuus sit*, L. M. I. P. 41; Th. ii. 276, 10.

of-līcian *to displease, be displeasing*:—Gode swȳðe oflīcaþ heora ceorung, Homl. Skt. i. 21, 240. Swā hwæt swā him oflīcaþ ðeáh hit hālig sȳ hié hit lǽtaþ unālȳfed *whatever they do not like, though it be holy, they profess that it is not permitted*, R. Ben. 9, 19. Ðā oflīcode mē þearle ðæt ic eft tō ðam līchaman sceolde, Homl. Th. ii. 354, 10. Gif hwam seó lār oflīcige, 216, 23.

of-linnan *to cease, leave off*:—Ðæt wæter oflan and mā of heora mūþe hit ne eode *the water stopped, and it no longer came out of the mouth of the image*, Blickl. Homl. 247, 8. [*Goth.* af-linnan *discedere.*]

of-lysted, -lyst; *part. Possessed with a very strong desire, very desirous for* (with gen. of object):—Eubolus wearð swā mycclum oflyst Basilies lāre, ðæt him ne lyste nānes metes, Homl. Skt. i. 3, 42: Bt. 35, 6; Fox 168, 23. Ðā wæs ðes man swīðe oflyst ðæs Hǽlendes tōcymes, Homl. Th. i. 136, 6. Þeód wæs oflysted metes, Andr. Kmbl. 2226; An. 1114: 2454; An. 1228. Ðā wæs hē swȳðe oflysted ðæt hē ðæs eádigan weres blōd āgute *he was possessed with a very strong desire to shed the holy man's blood*, Guthl. 7; Gdwin. 44, 22. Ða ðe sind oflyste rihtwīsnysse, Homl. Th. i. 204, 1: Exon. Th. 464, 3; Hö. 81. [Oflust æfter deores flæsce, Laym. 30554.]

of-manian *to exact a fine* or *due*:—Ofmanige se bisceop ða bōte tō ðæs cynges handa, L. Edg. ii. 3; Th. i. 266, 19, note.

of-munan *to recall to mind, recollect*:—Ðonne hē hit eft ofman æfter lytlum fæce *cum post paululum haec ipsa ad memoriam revocant*, Past. 33, 7; Swt. 225, 19. Ne ofman hē nǽfre nānwuht forðæm nǽfre nāuht hē ne forgeat *he never recalls anything, for he never forgot anything*, Bt. 42; Fox 356, 30. Ic wāt æác ðæt ic hyt hæfde swā clēne forgeten ðæt ic hyt nǽfre eft ne ofmunde *I know too that I should have so clean forgotten it, that I should have never again recalled it*, Shrn. 198, 4.

of-myrðrian *to murder*:—Men hine ofmyrðrodon, Chr. 979; Erl. 129, 7.

ofn. v. ofen.

of-neádian *to obtain by force, extort*:—Nū cȳdde man mē ðet Æþelwold and ic sceoldon ofneádian ða bōc æt Leófrīce *I have been informed that Athelwold and I must have obtained the charter from Leofric by force*, Chart. Th. 295, 32. [*O. Frs.* of-nēda: cf. *Ger.* ab-nöthigen.]

ofnet *a closed vessel*:—Geseóþ ofnete *seethe in a closed vessel* (*vasculo clauso vel operto*), Lchdm. ii. 30, 24.

of-niman *to fail*:—Be ðam ðe him his sprǽc ofnimþ *de eo cui sermo deficit*, L. Ecg. P. i. tit. 3; Th. ii. 170, 6. [*Ger.* ab-nehmen *to decrease, wane.*]

ōfost, ōfest, ōfst, e; *f. Haste, speed*:—Ōfost is sēlost tō gecȳðanne hwanon eówer cyme sȳ *the quicker you make known where you come from the better*, Beo. Th. 518; B. 256: 6007; B. 3007. Ōfest, Cd. Th. 196, 18; Exod. 293. Ōfst and hradung, R. Ben. 3, 11. Swā hwylc preóst swā wyrne (*refuses to baptize a man*) for ōfste his fōre *quicunque presbyter festinandi itineris sui causa deneget*, L. Ecg. C. 6; Th. ii. 138, 21. Se cnapa hit mid ōfste gegearcode *puer festinavit et coxit illum*, Gen. 18, 7. Mid ōfste (oefeste, Lind.) *cum festinatione*, Mk. Skt. 6, 15: Lk. Skt. 1, 39: Jn. Skt. 11, 31. Wē secgaþ nū mid ōfste ðās endebirdnisse, for ðan ðe wē oft habbaþ ymbe ðis āwriten, Ælfc. T. Grn. 3, 30. Ðeós worald is on ōfste *this world is hurrying on* (*to its end*), Wulfst. 156, 5: Cd. Th. 191, 32; Exod. 223. Beó ðū on ōfeste *hasten*, Beo. Th. 777; B. 386. On ōfoste, 5487; B. 2747. Þorh ōfst *per anticipationem*, Wrt. Voc. ii. 116, 77. Ōfestum *hastily*, Cd. Th. 140, 32; Gen. 2336. Ōfestum miclum, 177, 15; Gen. 2930. Ōfstum, 153, 8; Gen. 2535: 161, 29; Gen. 2672. [*Laym.* ovest.]

ōfostlīce; *adv. Hastily, speedily, in haste*:—Hē stōp ōfostlīce tōforan ðam biscope and feól tō his fōtum *festinus accedens ante pedes episcopi conruit*, Bd. 3, 14; S. 540, 36. Ongan ōfostlīce ðæt hof wyrcan, Cd. Th. 79, 24; Gen. 1316. Gewīt ðū ōfestlīce fēran, 172, 24; Gen. 2849. Mē ōfestlīce gehȳr *velociter exaudi me*, Ps. Th. 101, 2. Ōfstlīce *cursim, velociter*, Hpt. Gl. 446, 48. Ēfstende wē sceolon etan ūre eásterlīcan blisse, and ōfstlīce wē sceolon Godes bebodu healdan, Anglia viii. 323, 36: Cd. Th. 150, 6; Gen. 2487. Ōfostlīcor, Exon. Th. 17, 18; Cri. 272. [*O. Sax.* ōbast-, ōfst-līko.]

of-rīdan *to overtake by riding, overtake*:—Ēfstaþ ardlīce and gē hig ofrīdaþ *persequimini cito, et comprehenditis eos*, Jos. 2, 5. Abram ēfste wið ðæs heres óþ ðæt hē hig ofrād, Gen. 14, 14. Se cyng hēt rīdan æfter, and ne mehte hine mon ofrīdan, Chr. 901; Erl. 98, 1: 877; Erl. 78, 21. v. of-faran.

of-sacan *to deny a charge*:—Gif hwā ofsacan wille, dō ðæt mid eahta and feówertig fulborenra þegena, L. Ath. iv. 7; Th. i. 228, 3. [I ne mai hit noȝt ofsake, P. L. S. 15, 60. Cf. *Icel.* af-saka *to exculpate.*]

of-sceacan *to shudder, shake with fear*:—Ofscōc *exhorruit*, Hpt. Gl. 504, 10.

of-sceamian *to put to shame*:—Gif ðū ðē ofsceamian (onsceamian, MS. Cott.) wilt ðīnes gedwolan, Bt. 3, 4; Fox 6, 16. Hē wearþ ofsceamod, Homl. Skt. i. 12, 214. Se drȳ stōd eádmōd and ofsceamod *the sorcerer stood humble and ashamed*, Homl. ii. 416, 30. Hī gecyrdon him hām hearde ofsceamode, 518, 31. [*O. and N.* of-schomed: *R. Glouc.* of-ssamed.]

of-sceótan. I. *to wound* or *kill by shooting an arrow* or *by hurling a weapon*:—Wulfstān ðone forman man mid his francan ofsceát, Byrht. Th. 134, 1; By. 77. Hǽþcyn his mǽg ofscēt blōdigan gāre, Beo. Th. 4870; B. 2439. Hē hiene ne meahte ofsceótan mid ðæm bismere *quem commovere in ipsa contumeliarum jaculatione non potuit*, Past. 33, 7; Swt. 227, 9. Hē mid geǽttrode flāne hine ofsceótan wolde, Homl. Th. i. 502, 18. Hē wearð ofscoten mid ānre flāne *sagitta ictus interiit*, Ors. 1, 2; Swt. 30, 13. Ðǽr wearð Leostenas mid ānre flān ofscoten *ibi Leosthenes telo e muris jacto perfossus occiditur*, 3, 11; Swt. 144, 27. Mid fȳrenum flānum ofscotene (ofsceotene, 7), Homl. Th. i. 506, 1. II. Ofscoten *elf-shot, diseased from an elf's shot*, Lchdm. ii. 156, 25: 290, 21. The disease consists in an over-distension of an animal's stomach from the swelling up of clover and grass, when eaten with the morning dew on it. See the Glossary and Jamieson's Scottish Dictionary *elf-shot*. v. next word.

of-scotian *to shoot, wound* or *kill with an arrow, spear,* etc.:—Hē hēt hine mid strǽlum ofscotian, ðæt hē wæs ðara swā full swā igl biþ byrsta, Shrn. 55, 8. Ne ofsleá hine nān man mid his handa ac sī hē mid stānum oftirfod oððe mid flānum ofscotod *manus non tanget eum, sed lapidibus opprimetur aut confodietur jaculis*, Ex. 19, 13. Mid flānum ofscotod and mid stānum oftorfod *sagittis, saxis contriti*, Ors. 4, 11; Swt. 206, 14. v. preceding word.

of-sendan *to reach by sending, send for, summon*:—Ofsænd se cyng Godwine eorl *the king sent for earl Godwin*, Chr. 1048; Erl. 178, 7. Ðā sende se cyng æfter ðām scypon ðe hē ofsendan mihte *the king sent after the ships that his summons could reach*, 1049; Erl. 172, 39. [Heo him radden ðat he ofsende magan, Laym. 15748. Þis kyng ys knyȝtes let ofsende, R. Glouc. 122, 21.] v. of-faran.

of-seón *to see, observe*:—Ðā ofseah hig Godes engel *cum invenisset eam angelus Domini*, Gen. 16, 7. Ðā ofseah hē ǽnne geongne man, Homl. Skt. i. 23, 545. Se hālga wer oferseah ealne middaneard, and ofseah lǽdan ānes biscopes sāwle tō heofenum, Homl. Th. ii. 184, 30. Se apostol ofseah hwǽr sum ūþwita lǽdde twegen gebrōðru, i. 60, 22. Ofsión, Met. 21, 38.

of-setenness, e; *f. Siege*:—Ofsetenesse *obsidione*, Wrt.Voc. ii. 63, 13. v. of-sittan.

of-settan *to beset, press hard, oppress*:—Hē hig ofsette and geswenct *he oppressed and afflicted them*; servierunt ei, Jud. 3, 8. Fearras fǽtt ofsetton ł ymbsǽton (*obsederunt*) mē, Ps. Lamb. 21, 13. Feónd ūrne ofsete (*comprime*), Hymn. Surt. 11, 33. Mid untrumnesse oððe bysegum ofset, R. Ben. 58, 15: 59, 3. Mid weorces geswince ofsette, 63, 17: Homl. Th. ii. 120, 8. Se ðe on wræcsīt gesihþ mid micelum gyltum heom ofsett getâcnaþ *if a man dreams of being in exile, it betokens that he will be weighed down with great crimes*, Lchdm. iii. 212, 23. Swête etan on manegum leahtrum biþ ofsett hit getâcnaþ *to dream of eating sweets betokens a man will be sunk in many faults*, 202, 25. Ofsettum *obsessis*, Wülck. Gl. 251, 5. v. next word.

of-sittan. I. *to sit upon, press down by sitting* :—Heó ofsæt ðone selegyst *she* (*Grendel's mother*) *pressed down the hall-guest* (*Beowulf, who had fallen*), Beo. Th. 3094; B. 1545. Nû sceal se ðe wile sittan æt Godes gereorde ðæt gærs ofsittan, ðæt is, ðæt hê sceal ða flǽsclîcan lustas gewyldan, Homl. Th. i. 188, 26. II. *to sit upon, oppress* :—Gif hê (*a king*) his folc ofsit, ðon biþ hê *tyrannus*, Ælfc. Gr. 50, 20; Som. 51, 47: Homl. Th. i. 242, 4. Swongornes hî ofsit, and hî mid slǽwþe ofercymþ, Bt. 36, 6; Fox 180, 33. Godes fýnd ðe ða earman ofsittaþ, Jud. Thw. 156, 5. Ðû wilt cweþan ðæt ungemetfæstnes hî ofsitte, Bt. 36, 6; Fox 182, 2. Ete ælþeódig folc ðîne tilinga and ðê mid bismore ofsittan *sis calumnian sustinens*, Deut. 28, 33. Ofseten mid ðǽm ðîstrum ðisses andweardan lîfes *praesentis vitae tenebris pressus*, Past. 11, 1; 65, 7. Ic eom mid earmlîcre ofergiotolnesse ofseten, Shrn. 198, 21. Ðæt môd sǽde ðæt hit wǽre ofseten (cf. ofþrycced, Fox 24, 14) mid ðæs lâðes sâre, Bt. 8, tit.; Fox x. 19. III. *to sit upon, occupy, take possession of* (with idea of force or wrong) :—Ðæt sió oferflôwnes ðæra geþohta ne meahte ofsittan ðæs sacerdes heortan *quatenus sacerdotale cor nequaquam cogitationes fluxae possideant*, Past. 13, 1; Swt. 77, 11. Eall ðæt seó sǽ his ofseten hæfþ *quantum maria premunt*, Bt. 18, 1; Fox 62, 12. IV. *to sit about, besiege* :—Fearas mê ofsǽton (*obsederunt*), Ps. Th. 21, 10, 14. V. *to repress, check, prevent motion*; cf. of-standan :—Ðus ðû scealt ða yfelan ofsetenan wǽtan ût âdôn *thus shalt thou remove the evil, repressed humours*, Lchdm. ii. 24, 7. v. preceding word.

of-sleán *to kill or wound by a blow, to kill, slay* :—Ic ofsleah wildeór *ego jugulo feras*, Coll. Monast. Th. 21, 19. Ic on morgenne ofsleá mânes wyrhtan *in matutino interficiebam omnes peccatores*, Ps. Th. 100, 8. Gif man mannan ofslæhþ, L. Eth. 21; Th. i. 8, 3. Ofsleahþ, 6; Th. i. 4, 6. Ofslehþ, 7; Th. i. 4, 9. Gif hwâ his cild ofslihþ tô deáþe, L. M. I. P. 8; Th. ii. 268, 1. Se gerêfa nyste hwæt hié wǽron, and hiene mon ofslôg, Chr. 787; Erl. 56, 15. Hê (*the elephant*) ofslôg micel ðæs folces, Ors. 4, 1; Swt. 156, 12. Ofslôh, Cd. Th. 60, 18; Gen. 983. Ðû ofslôge (*percussisti*) ealle ða ðe mê wiðerwearde wǽron, Ps. Th. 3, 6. Hî willaþ mê ofsleán *interficient me*, Gen. 20, 11. Eall his weorod ofslegen wæs, Bd. 1, 34; S. 499, 33. Wurdon begen ofslægene ða aldormen, Chr. 800; Erl. 60, 8. Fela þûsenda ofslægenra, 871; Erl. 74, 24. [*Goth.* af-slahan *to slay*.]

of-slegenness, e; *f. Killing, destruction* :—Sceáp ofslegennysse *oves occisionis*, Ps. Spl. 43, 25.

of-slîtan *to wound by the bite* (of a snake, dog, etc.) :—Ða ðe ofslitene wǽron (*the Israelites who were bitten by the serpents*), Num. 21, 9.

of-smorian *to choke, strangle, suffocate* :—Hiene ofsmorode his ealdormon *dolo comitis sui strangulatus*, Ors. 6, 36; Swt. 294, 9. Mid ðæm brǽþe ofsmorod (*suffocatus*), 6, 32; Swt. 288, 2.

of-sniðan *to kill by cutting, to slaughter* (an animal) :—Ðæt lamb ðe se ealda Israhel ofsnâð, Homl. Th. ii. 264, 28: Gen. 22, 13. Ðâ nâmon hig ân biccen and ofsnidon hit, 37, 31. Swilce se sunu wǽre geoffrod and se ramm ofsniden, Homl. Th. ii. 62, 27.

of-sprǽc, e; *f. An outspeaking, utterance* :—Gydde ł ofsprǽce *elogio, textu, locutione*, Hpt. Gl. 460, 65.

of-spring, es; *m. Offspring, progeny, posterity, descendants* :—Ofspring *styrps*, Ælfc. Gr. 9, 58; Som. 13, 36. Ofsprincg *progenies*, 12; Som. 15, 53. Eall heora ofspring ðe him of com, Ælfc. T. Grn. 3, 11. Eall heora ofsprinc boren and unboren, Cod. Dip. Kmbl. iv. 263, 29. Gif his sunu and sunu-sunu swâ micel landes habban, siððan biþ se ofsprinc (cf. hiora æftergengas, 24) gesîðcundes cynnes, L. Wg. 11; Th. i. 188, 11. Ic sette feóndrǽdene betweox ðînum ofspringe and hire ofspringe, Gen. 3, 15. Ðînum ofspringe (*semini tuo*) ic forgife ðis land, 12, 7: 13, 15. Ic dô ðînne ofspring swâ menigfealdne swâ ðære eorþan dust, 13, 16. Hî gesworen habbaþ ge for hý sylfe ge for heora ofspryng (gingran, MS. B.), L. A. G. tit.; Th. i. 152, 17. Ðis sý gedôn for Sîferþ and for his ofsprincg tô hyra sâwle þearfe, Cod. Dip. Kmbl. ii. 300, 15. [*Icel.* af-springr.]

of-spyrian *to find out by inquiry or search* :—Se ðe hit ofspyraþ, hê âh ðæt meldfeoh, L. In. 17; Th. i. 114, 4. Cf. of-âxian.

ôfst. v. ôfost.

of-standan *to remain standing, keep* (*trans.* or *intrans.*) *in the same place* or *condition, stop in a place* :—Swâ raðe swâ ðæt scrîn in biþ geboren, swâ ofstint (oft stint, Thw.) se streám *aquae in una mole consistent*, Jos. 3, 13. Gif him ofstondeþ on innan ǽnigu ceald wǽte *if any cold humour stops in them*, Lchdm. ii. 194, 15. Sele him on hâtum wætre gewlecedum ða wyrta drincan ðý læs ðæt pic ofstande mid ðý ôðre duste *give him the herbs to drink in hot water made lukewarm, lest the pitch be left sticking with the other dust*, 252, 4. Ðæt ofstandene þicce horh *the thick foulness that has refused to move*, 194, 21. Wâg ofstonden unde stormum *a wall unmoved amid storms*, Exon. Th. 476, 21; Ruin. 11. Ofstondene beóþ *sive* ofstonden feoh *integri restitutione*, Wrt. Voc. ii. 49, 34–35. [Cf. *O. Sax.* is (*of the temple*) afstandan ni skal stên obar ôðrumu.]

of-steppan *to trample upon* :—Ofstæppaþ heora swuran swîðe mid fôtum. Ðâ dydon ða ealdormen swâ, swâ him dihte Josue, and ðæra cynega swuran forcûðlîce trǽdon, Jos. 10, 24. v. of-tredan.

of-stician *to wound* or *kill by a thrust, to stab, pierce, transfix* :—Ofsticoþ *configet*, Kent. Gl. 844. Ic ofstikode hyne *jugulavi aprum*, Coll. Monast. Th. 22, 17. Antonius hiene selfne ofsticade *Antonius sese ferro transverberavit*, Ors. 5, 13; Swt. 246, 30. Se kâsere âlýfde ðâm cnihtum ðæt hî hyne (*St. Casianus*) ofslôgen mid heora writbredum, and hine ofsticodon mid hira writýrenum, Shrn. 117, 29. Ðâ hêt hê ðone pâpan (*Alexander*) ofstician, 79, 8. Ofstikian bâr *jugulare aprum*, Coll. Monast. Th. 22, 13. Hê swealt ofsticod fram him sylfum, Chr. 2; Erl. 5, 19. [*Ger.* ab-stechen.] v. of-stingan.

ôfstig; *adj. Hasty, swift* :—Ôfstige *percita, velocissima*, Germ. 392, 73.

of-stingan *to wound* or *kill by a thrust, to stab, pierce* :—His ealdgefâna sum hiene ofstang *a Pausania occisus est*, Ors. 3, 7; Swt. 118, 34. Hê hiene (*the elephant*) on ðone nafelan ofstang, 4, 1; Swt. 156, 11. Hê (*Pilate*) hiene selfne ofstong *sua se transverberans manu*, 6, 3; Swt. 258, 10: Shrn. 33, 5. Hê wolde ofstingan Eádwine, ac hê ofstang Lillan his þegn, Chr. 626; Erl. 23, 29: 755; Erl. 48, 23. Ne ofstong Æfner hiene nô mid ðý speres orde ac mid hindewerdum ðam sceafte *Abner non eum recta, sed aversa hasta transforavit*, Past. 40, 6; Swt. 297, 10. Sunu gif hê (*an ox*) ofstinge (*gore*), L. Alf. 21; Th. i. 50, 2. Hêt Fabianus ðæt hî man begen ofstunge, Homl. Skt. i. 5, 405. Ðæt ic ðê ne dyrre ofstingan *ne compellar confodere te in terram*, Past. 40, 5; Swt. 295, 16. Hêr Ædmund cyning wearð ofstungen, Chr. 948; Erl. 117, 8. v. of-stician.

ôfstlîce. v. ôfostlîce.

of-swelgan *to swallow up, devour* :—Deáþ forsiehþ ða æþelo, and ðone rîcan gelîce and ðone heánan ofswelgþ, Bt. 19; Fox 68, 33. Cf. forswelgan.

of-swingan *to scourge to death* :—Sume hié ofslôgon sume ofswungon sume wið feó gesealdon *omnes bello utiles caesi, reliqui pretio venditi sunt*, Ors. 4, 1; Swt. 154, 8.

oft; *adv. Oft, often* :—Oft (*saepe*) hê fylþ on fýr, and gelômlîce (*crebro*) on wæter, Mt. Kmbl. 17, 15. Oft (oftust, Lind. Rush.) *sepe*, Mk. Skt. 5, 4: *interdum*, Wrt. Voc. ii. 48, 38. Hû oft *quotiens*, Lk. Skt. 13, 34. Swâ oft swâ ða ôðre hergas ût fôron, ðonne fôron hié, Chr. 894; Erl. 90, 5. Hî beóþ ðæs ðe lator ðe hî oftor ymbþeahtiaþ, Past. 56; Swt. 435, 2. Hwîlum hê wæs on horse sittende, ac oftor on his fôtum gongende, Bd. 4, 27; S. 604, 12. Hê oftust on gebedum âwunode, 3, 12; S. 537, 22. Oftost, Met. 4, 28. [*Goth.* ufta: *O. Sax.* oft, ofto: *O. Frs.* ofta: *Icel.* oft, opt: *O. H. Ger.* oft, ofto.] v. for-oft.

of-talu, e; *f. The successful defence made against a claim* :—Seó sprǽc wearð ðam cynge cûð. Ðâ ðâ him seó talu cûð wæs, ðâ sende hê gewrit tô ðam arcebisceope, and beád him ðæt hê and hys þegenas hý on riht gesêmdon be ontale and be oftale *the suit became known to the king. When the claim was known to him, he sent a writ to the archbishop, and commanded him that he and his thanes should settle it rightfully according as the claim was to be allowed or rejected, according as the verdict was for or against the claim* (cf. *Icel.* bera kvið â einn, af einum *to give a verdict for, against a person*), Chart. Th. 302, 14–22.

of-teón; *pp.* -togen *and* -tigen. I. *to withdraw* :—Hê hine ofteáh ðære fôre *subtraxit se illi profectioni*, Bd. 5, 9; S. 623, 23. II. *to take away what a person has, deprive a person of anything* (with dat. or acc. of person, gen. of thing, or dat. of person and acc. of thing) :—Ic ofteó *derogo*, Wrt. Voc. i. 39, 27. Gif mon him oftîhþ ðara þênunga and ðæs anwealdes *detrahat si quis superbis vani tegmina cultus*, Bt. 37, 1; Fox 186, 10. Oft ic sýne ofteáh, âblende beorna unrîm, Exon. Th. 270, 21; Jul. 468. Wê oftugon ðê londes wynna, 130, 15; Gû. 438. Bûton seó *syncopa* ðone *i* (*of the gen. pl.*) ofteó, Ælfc. Gr. 10; Som. 14, 55. Nô Ælmihtig ealra wolde Adam and Eve ârna ofteón, Cd. Th. 58, 29; Gen. 953. Gif him gebyreþ ðæt him wyrþ ðara þênunga oftohen (oftogen, Met. 25, 31), Bt. 37, 1; Fox 186, 14. Ðê biþ seó bodung oftogen, Homl. Th. ii. 530, 30. Oftigen biþ him torhtre gesihþe *he shall be deprived of clear sight*, Exon. Th. 335, 29; Gn. Ex. 41. III. *to withhold, keep back, deny a person anything* :—Ic ðê ofteó mînne fultum ... Ic ofteó mîne rênscûras *I will withhold from thee my help ... I will withhold my rain-showers*, Homl. Th. ii. 102, 32–33. Gehelp ðû earmra manna mid ðam dǽle ðe ðû ðê sylfum oftîhst, i. 180, 12. For synnum oftîhþ se Ælmihtiga Wealdend hwîlon mannum bigleofan, ii. 462, 21. Gif wê Godes lâre eów ofteóþ, 554, 18. Hond feorhsweng ne ofteáh *the hand refused not to strike a fatal stroke*, Beo. Th. 4972; B. 2489: 3045; B. 1520. Gê him ǽghwæs oftugon hrægles nacedum môses meteleásum *ye withheld from them everything, raiment from the naked, food from the hungry*, Exon. Th. 92, 8; Cri. 1505. [And wô sô mîne cwyde oftê God him oftê heuenrîches *and whoso refuses to carry out my testament, may God refuse him the kingdom of heaven*, Chart. Th. 515, 30.]

Hē hēt hire ofteón ǽtes and wǽtes, Homl. Skt. i. 8, 129: Blickl. Homl. 37, 28. Ðæt ðām gōdum, ðe hit (*doctrine*) gehealdan willaþ, ne sȳ oftogen seó gāstlīce deópnyss, Homl. Th. ii. 96, 4: i. 370, 8. Swelce snytro swylce ōðrum ieldran gewittum oftogen is *negatas senibus dignitates*, Bt. 8; Fox 24, 29. [*Goth.* af-tiuhan: *O. H. Ger.* aba-ziohan *abstrahere.*]

of-þænnan *to moisten*:—Gegnīd on wīn, ofþæne wel, Lchdm. ii. 90, 7. Ofþæne mid ecede, 184, 15. Obðaenit *madidum*, Wrt. Voc. ii. 113, 72. Ofðæned *madefactus*, 80, 48. Ofþænda and gesodena on ecede, Lchdm. ii. 180, 15. Mid hlāfes cruman ofþendum mid cealdwætre, 82, 7.

of-þecgan *to consume, destroy*:—Æþelinga bearn ecgum ofþegde *consumed by the sword*, Cd. Th. 120, 30; Gen. 2002.

of-þencan *to remember*:—Gif ðū ofþence hwæthwugu ðæs ðe ðīn niéhsta ðē wiðerweardes gedōn hæbbe *si recordatus fueris, quia frater tuus habet aliquid adversum te*, Past. 46, 4; Swt. 349, 10.

of-þinen *too moist* (?):—Hig wǽron gemyndige ðæs tōweardan hungres ðȳ læs ða ofþinenan corn in brord gehwyrfden and hig forcurfon ða sǽd *they* (*the ants*) *were mindful of future hunger, and lest the grains that were too moist should sprout, they bit them*, Shrn. 41, 5. Cf. ofþænnan.

of-þistrian *to darken, obscure*:—Ða ðe ofþȳstrode synd *qui obscurati sunt*, Ps. Spl. 73, 21.

of-þringan *to throng, crowd, press upon*:—Ðeós menigu ðe ofþrincþ '*the multitude throng thee and press thee*' (A. V.), Homl. Th. ii. 394, 15. Ðæt hī hine ne ofþrungon '*lest they should throng him*' (A. V.), Mk. Skt. 3, 9.

of-þriton, Jud. 4, 24. v. next word.

of-þryccan *to press, oppress, repress, cumber, occupy forcibly*:—Ic ofþricce *premo*, Ælfc. Gr. 28, 4; Som. 31, 14. Hwī ofþricþ hē ðæt land *quid terram occupat ficulnea*, Lk. Skt. 13, 7. Ofþrect *comprimit*, Kent. Gl. 654. Ofþrecþ *exprемit*, 1120. Se draca mē þearle ofþryhþ, Homl. Th. i. 534, 25. Ymbhīdignyssa ofþriccaþ ðæt mōd, ii. 92, 15. Ofþrihte *compressit*, Hpt. Gl. 465, 21. Mīne sāwle feóndas mīne ofþryhtum (*occupaverunt*), Ps. Th. 58, 3. Ofþrihton, Blickl. Gl. Hig hine ofþriton (-þrihton?) *opprimebant eum*, Jud. 4, 24. Ofþriccetan mē grynu deáþes *praeoccupaverunt me laquei mortis*, Ps. Lamb. 17, 6. Feónd ūrne ofþrece (*comprime*), Hymn. Surt. 11, 33. Ofþrice *reprime*, 13, 7. Ofþreccan *comprimant*, 17, 32. Wē ofþriccan *praeoccupemus*, Ps. Spl. M. 94, 4. Ofþriccende *deprimentes*, 88, 41. Mid unrōtnessum ofþrycced, Ps. Th. 38, arg.: Bt. 8; Fox 24, 14. Biþ ofþreced *opprimitur*, Kent. Gl. 974. Beón ofþryht *deprimi*, Rtl. 66, 25. Ofþrihte *compressa*, Hpt. Gl. 490, 13.

of-þryccedness, e; *f. Distress, trouble*:—Biþ mycel ofþriccednys (*pressura*) ofer eorþan, Lk. Skt. 21, 23: Homl. Th. i. 608, 24. Fram ofþriccednysse (*a refuge*) *from trouble*, Blickl. Gl.

of-þryccness, e; *f. Oppression, repression*:—Swā þrycce se magister ða belde on ðæm oferblīðum ðæt ðǽr ne weaxe on him sió ofþrycnes ðæs eges ðe cymþ of ðæs yflan blōdes flōwnesse *sic in illo reprimatur repente oborta praecipitatio, ut non convalescat impressa ex conspersione formido*, Past. 61, 1; Swt. 455, 22. Seó Sūþ-Seaxna mǽgþ for ðære grimman feónda ofþrycnesse āgenne biscop habban ne mihte *the people of Sussex on account of the cruel oppression of their foes could not have a bishop of their own*, Bd. 4, 13 tit.; S. 581, 38.

of-þryscan *to beat down, repress, suppress*:—*Concutit* i. *turbat, terreat* tōscæcþ, ofþrysceþ *percutit*, Wrt. Voc. ii. 136, 48. Ða ðe ofþryscaþ ða styringe ðæs flǽsclīcan lustes *qui compressis motibus carnis*, Past. 52, 6; Swt. 409, 1. Ða hié suīðe stīðlīce ārāsigeaþ and mid ealle ofþrysceaþ *hos asperitate rigidos semper invectionis premunt*, Past. 19, 2; Swt. 145, 1. Ðæt hē on him selfum ofþrysce ða lustas his unþeáwa *in semetipso suggestiones vitiorum reprimat*, 14, 5; Swt. 85, 12. [Cf. *O. H. Ger.* druski *excute*, Grff. 5, 265.] v. ge-þryscan.

of-þrysman, -þrysmian *to destroy by choking*:—Gewilnunga ðæt word ofþrysmaþ (-þrysmiaþ, MS. A.) *concupiscentiae verbum suffocant*, Mk. Skt. 4, 19.

of-þyncan *with dat. of pers. and* (a) *gen. of cause*, (b) *nom. of cause*, (c) *cause given by a clause*. I. *to cause regret* or *sorrow*:—Mē ofþincþ *penetet*, Ælfc. Gr. 33; Som. 37, 21. Mē ofþincþ ðæt ic hig worhte *poenitet me fecisse eos*, Gen. 6, 7. Hit mē ofþincþ, Lk. Skt. 17, 4. Ofþinceþ ðē ealles ðe ðū tō yfele hæfst geworht? L. Ecg. C. proem.; Th. ii. 130, 43. Ðā ofþūhte Pharao ðæt hē ðæt folc swā freólīce forlēt, Homl. Th. ii. 194, 15. II. *to cause displeasure* or *offence*:—Ðonne him hira scylda nā ne ofþyncþ *si minus contra culpas accenditur*, Past. 21, 5; Swt. 161, 2. Hine drehton nihtlīce gedwimer swā ðæt him ðæs slǽpes ofþūhte *so that sleep was displeasing to him*, Homl. Th. i. 86, 19. Ðā ofþūhte heora ceorlum ðæt mon ða þeówas freóde, Ors. 4, 3; Swt. 162, 15. Ðā ofþūhte ðæt ānum ðæs cyninges geféran, Lchdm. iii. 424, 16. Ðā ðæs ofþūhte, ðæt se þeóden wæs strang, Cd. Th. 279, 32; Swt. 247. Ðā sceolde ðām gigantum ofþincan þæt hē hæfde hiera rīce *it is said that the giants were displeased at his having their kingdom*, Bt. 35, 4; Fox 162, 11. Mæg ðæs ofþyncan þegna gehwam, Beo. Th. 4070; B. 2032. Hit wæs swīðe ofþyncende ðām ōðrum consulum *it gave great offence to the other consuls*, Ors. 5, 9; Swt. 232, 21. Mid ðon ðe hē geweóx, him ðā ofþyncendum and ðǽm Perseum ðæt hié on his eámes anwalde wǽron, Ors. 1, 12; Swt. 52, 18. Him ða ofþyncendum ðæt his folc swā forslagen wæs, 2, 5; Swt. 80, 23.

of-þyrsted, -þyrst; *part. Possessed with exceeding thirst, very thirsty, athirst*:—Hē wearþ swīðe ofþyrst *sitiens valde*, Jud. 15, 18. Eádige beóþ ða ðe sind ofhingrode and ofþyrste æfter rihtwīsnysse, Homl. Th. i. 550, 34. Nīþes ofþyrsted *thirsting for strife*, Cd. Th. 3, 7; Gen. 32. Ofþyrsted gāstes dryncеs, Soul Kmbl. 80; Seel. 40. [Cf. *Goth.* afþaursiþs *thirsty*.]

of-tige. v. of-tyge.

of-torfian *to stone, to kill by casting stones* or *similar missiles*:—Hī ūs oftorfiaþ mid stānum *lapidibus nos obruent*, Ex. 8, 26. Hī hine oftorfodon mid bānum and mid hrȳðera heáfdum, Chr. 1012; Erl. 146, 18. Hig wyllaþ mē oftorfian *populus lapidabit me*, Ex. 17, 4. Mid stānum oftorfian *lapidibus opprimere*, Num. 14, 10: *lapidare*, Jn. Skt. 8, 5: Homl. Th. i. 48, 2: 196, 12. Fela mid stānum oftorfod *saxis contriti*, Ors. 4, 11; Swt. 206, 15. Hēr wæs sċs Stephanus oftorfod, Chr. 34; Erl. 6, 15: Ælfc. T. Grn. 9, 31. v. of-tyrfan.

oft-rǽde; *adj.* I. *frequent*:—Hæglas and snāwas and se oftrǽda rēn leccaþ ða eorþan on wintra, Bt. 39, 13; Fox 234, 16. II. *ready at many times*:—Gafolswān sceal beón swā ic ǽr be beócere cwæþ (cf. l. 3, beóceorl sceal *hwīltīdum geara* beón on manegum weorcum tō hlāfordes willan) oftrǽde tō gehwilcon weorce *the swain must be, as I said before of the beekeeper, generally ready for any work*, L. R. S. 6; Th. i. 436, 18. Bydele gebyraþ ðæt hē sȳ weorces frigra ðonne ōðer man forðan hē sceal beón oftrǽde *he must be always ready*, 18; Th. i. 440, 7.

oftrǽd-līc; *adj. Frequent*:—Ðis syndon ða wǽpena ðe deófol mid oferswīðed biþ, ofthrǽdlīce rǽdinga hāligra bōca and gelōmlīce gebedu, L. E. I. 2; Th. ii. 404, 2. Hié Alexander uneáðe oferwonn ǽgðer ge for ðære sumorhǽte ge eac for ðǽm oftrǽdlīcan gefeohtum, Ors. 3, 9; Swt. 132, 32. Oftrǽdlīca gefeoht *crebra bella*, 6, 30; Swt. 282, 31.

oftrǽdlīce; *adv. Frequently, often, habitually*:—Oftrǽdlīce *crebro, frequenter*, Wrt. Voc. ii. 136, 81. Se Hǽlend oftrǽdlīce (*frequenter*) com ðyder, Jn. Skt. 18, 2. Gif man hine oftrǽdlīce (*ex consuetudine*) ofer drince, L. Ecg. P. iv. 33; Th. ii. 214, 12. Ǽghwæðer ōðerne oftrǽdlīce ūt drǽfde, Chr. 887; Erl. 86, 12. Hē oftrǽdlīce fōr mid miclum gefeohtum on Sciððie, Ors. 1, 2; Swt. 30, 2: 4, 12; Swt. 208, 33.

of-tredan *to tread down, trample upon, injure* or *destroy by treading*:—Ða ȳða ārison ac Drihten hī oftræd . . . Ðeáh ðe ārleáse woruldmenn ārīson ongeán ūs swā ðeáh Crist oftret heora heáfod, Homl. Th. ii. 388, 18–22. Iii hit oftræd and hié tō loman gerēnode *duos et .l. calcatos inutiles fecit*, Nar. 15, 25. Ða hors hī (*Jezabel*) oftrǽdan huxlīce under fōtum, Homl. Skt. i. 18, 347. Oftredan ðæt gærs and ofsittan, Homl. Th. i. 188, 25. Swā hwæt swā ðæs gōdan sǽdes on swylcum wege befylþ, biþ mid yfelum geþohtum oftreden, ii. 90, 19. Ðǽr wǽron xxx M ofslagen and æt ðæm geate oftreden *triginta millia caede prostrata et compressione suffocata*, Ors. 6, 4; Swt. 260, 18. [*Orm.* off-tredenn (gluterrnesse).]

oft-sīþ, es; *m. A time that often occurs*:—Hwæt hē hæfde Godes þeówum on oftsīþas tō lāðe gedōn *what he had ofttimes done to hurt God's servants*, Ors. 6, 34; Swt. 290, 29. [*A. R.* ofte-siðen: *Chauc.* ofte-siþes: *Ayenb.* ofte-ziþes: *Icel.* opt-sinnis, -sinnum *ofttimes.*]

of-tyge, es; *m. A holding back, withholding* (v. of-teón, III):—Ungelimp mid synnum geearnod, swīðost mid ðam oftige ðæs neádgafoles ðe Cristene men Gode gelǽstan sceoldon on heora teóþingsceattum *misfortune merited through sins, especially through the keeping back of the tax that Christian men ought to pay to God in their tithes*, L. Edg. S. 1; Th. i. 270, 13. Mid ǽnigum oftige Godes gerihta, 270, 30.

of-tyrfan *to stone*:—Hiene oftyrfdon his āgene geféran *ab exercitu suo lapidibus coopertus interiit*, Ors. 4, 6; Swt. 172, 28. v. of-torfian.

of-unnan. I. in a bad sense, *to begrudge a person* (dat.) *anything* (gen.), *wish to deprive a person of anything*:—Se biþ ðæm īsene gelīc se ðe ofan his nīhstan his līfes *ferro utitur, qui vitae proximi insidiatur*, Past. 37, 3; Swt. 269, 7. Se ðe (*the devil*) him (*hermits*) līfes ofonn, Exon. Th. 107, 10; Gū. 56: 265, 7; Jul. 377. II. *to refuse to grant*:—Ðām ðe gē forgifenysse ofunnon him biþ oftogen seó forgyfenys *to whom ye refuse forgiveness, from them shall forgiveness be withheld*, Homl. Th. i. 370, 8. [*O. Sax.* af-unnan: cf. *O. H. Ger.* ab-unst *invidia, livor*: *Ger.* ab-gunst: *Icel.* af-und (ōfund).]

of-weorpan *to kill by casting* (*a stone*, etc.), *to knock down and kill by a missile*:—David nam fīf stānas and ðeáhhweðere mid ānum hē ðone gigant ofwearp, Blickl. Homl. 31, 18. David mid his liðeran ofwearp ðone geleáfleásan ent, Ælfc. T. Grn. 7, 18: Homl. Skt. i. 18, 18, 23. Hē wearð mid āne stāne ofworpen *saxo ictus occubuit*, Ors. 4, 1; Swt. 158, 32. Gif oxa wer ofslōge, sīe hē mid stānum ofworpen, L. Alf. 21; Th. i. 48, 32 note: 50, 5 note. [*Goth.* af-wairpan stainam *lapidare*: *Ger.* abwerfen.]

of-worpian *to kill by casting* (*stones*, etc.):—Mid stānum ofworpod, L. Alf. 21; Th. i. 48, 28, 32: 50, 5. v. preceding word.

of-wundrian *to be astonished*:—Ðætte ofwundradun alle *ut ammirarentur omnes*, Mt. Skt. Rush. 2, 12. v. next word.

of-wundrod *astonished*:—Sarra cwæþ ðā ofwundrod, Gen. 21, 6. Ic eom swīðe ungemetlīce ofwundrod hwī eów þince ... *vehementer admiror*, Bt. 13; Fox 40, 5. Seó cwēn wæs tō ðan swīðe ofwundrod, ðæt heó næfde furþor nǣnne gāst, Homl. Th. ii. 584, 18. Maria and Ioseph wǣron ofwundrode ðæra worda, i. 144, 15. [Wurþen men swīðe ofwundred and ofdrēd, Chr. 1135; Erl. 261, 1.]

ōga, an; *m.* I. the feeling which is excited in a person, *terror, dread, horror, great fear*:—Ōga *horror*, Ælfc. Gr. 9, 21; Som. 10, 26: *metus*, 11; Som. 15, 12: *pavor*, Hymn. Surt. 3, 23. Micel ōga (*horror*) him becom, Gen. 15, 12. Būtan ōgan (*absque terrore*) hē hine gerest, Ælfc. Gr. 47; Som. 48, 4. Ðā clypode hē mid micclum ōgan, Homl. Th. ii. 98, 3. II. the exciting cause of such a feeling:—Beó eówer ege and ōga ofer ealle nītenu *terror vester ac tremor sit super cuncta animalia*, Gen. 9, 2. On līgette is ōga, Homl. Th. i. 222, 32. For hellewītes ōgan (*on account of the terror which hell-torment causes*), oððe for ðæs ēcan līfes wuldre, R. Ben. 19, 17. III. *an object which excites fear, a terrible, horrible thing*:—Hē hēt Ðeódolum standan æt ðam mūþe (*of the fiery furnace*) ðæt hē for ðam ōgan (*on account of the terrible spectacle*) him ābūgan sceolde, Homl. Th. ii. 310, 33. Ōgan (egsan, Lk. Skt. 21, 11) of heofenum and micele tācna *terrores de caelo et signa magna*, 538, 32. Ōgana *terribilium*, Blickl. Gl. God him sende swīðlīce ōgan (*the ten plagues*), Ælfc. T. Grn. 5, 18. [Cf. *Goth.* ōgan *to fear*; ōgian *to terrify*: *Icel.* ōgn *dread, terror*; œgja *to frighten*; œgi-ligr *terrible*.] Cf. ege.

ō-gengel *a bar, bolt*; obex, Wrt. Voc. ii. 63, 28: 115, 32. [Ō = on? v. next word.]

ō-heald, -hilde; *adj. Sloping, inclined*:—Ōhældi (ōhaeldi, Ep. Gl. 21 d, 16) *pendulus*, Wrt. Voc. ii. 117, 19. Ōhylde, 68, 10. Clifig ł ōhyld (*not* tōhyld) *clivosus*, i. 19, 4. Ōheal[d?] *clivosa, tortuosa*, Germ. 392, 53. Hōhyldo *prona*, 400, 118. [*O. H. Ger.* uo-hald, -haldi *proclivus*. *For the prefix* ō-, cf. on-, ā-hildan.]

ōhsta, an; *m. The arm-pit, oxter* (in northern dialects, e. g. Yorkshire, Cumberland, Scotland):—Ōhsta *ascella*, Wrt. Voc. ii. 10, 5. Ōcusta, Ep. Gl. 2 b, 19. Ōxtan *ascilla*, Wrt. Voc. i. 283, 9. Cf. ōxn.

ōht. v. āht.

ōht, e; *f. Fear, terror* (? cf. ōga and *Icel.* ōtti *fear*), or *hostile pursuit, persecution, active enmity* (? cf. ēhtan and *O. H. Ger.* āhta *persecutio*, āhtunga *persecutio*):—Wǣron ðā gesōme ða ðe swegl būan wrōht wæs āsprungen ōht mid englum and orlegnīð *then were at peace the dwellers in heaven, discord was at an end among angels, and enmity* (or *fear?*) *and war*, Cd. Th. 6, 5; Gen. 84. Ðǣr on fyrd hyra fǣrspell becwom, ōht inlende (*the pursuit by the Egyptians*, or *the terror which their coming caused*); egsan stōdan wælgryre weroda, 186, 9; Exod. 136.

oht-rīp (?) *harvest*; messis, Mt. Kmbl. Lind, 9, 38: Lk. Skt. Lind. 10, 2.

ō-hwǣr, -hwanon, -hylde. v. ā-hwǣr, -hwanon, ō-heald.

ō-leccan, -liccan, -læcan; *p.* -lecte, -lehte, -læhte. I. *to treat gently, to soothe, caress*:—Ic ōlæce *blandior*, Ælfc. Gr. 31; Som. 35, 51. Ōlecceþ *favet*, Wrt. Voc. ii. 147, 19. Ōlehte *delinuit*, 138, 50. Hē him ōlecte ðā hē cuæþ *cui blandiens dicit*, Past. 26, 1; Swt. 181, 10. God hwīlon geōlæhþ, and hwīlon beswingþ. Nǣre nān tihting, gif hē ūs ne ōlæhte, Homl. Th. ii. 330, 3. Ōlecce *demulceat, blanditur*, Wrt. Voc. ii. 138, 68. Ōleccende *blandiens*, 127, 8. Ōleccendra *palpantum*, 116, 51. II. *to be obsequious, pay court to, fawn upon, flatter, to try to gain a person's good will by unworthy means*:—Ōleccaþ *adolatur*, Wrt. Voc. ii. 127, 7. Þeófum ðū ne ōlæce, ne yfeldǣdum ne geþwǣrlǣce, Homl. Skt. i. 21, 361. Hē nolde ōlæcan ǣnigum rīcan mid geswǣsum wordum, Homl. Th. ii. 514, 13. Gif ðū wille ðæt ðē monige ōlæcan ðonne ōlæce ðū ānum swīðe georne *if you wish many to pay court to you, do you sedulously pay court to one*, Prov. Kmbl. 79: 80. Mē riht ne þinceþ ðæt ic ōleccan þurfe Gode æfter gōde ǣnegum, Cd. Th. 19, 12; Gen. 290. III. *to gain good will by worthy means, to propitiate, be submissive*:—Ðæm (*God*) ōleccaþ ealle gesceafte ðe ðæs ambehtes āwuht cunnon (cf. ðam þeówiaþ ealle ... ða ðe cunnon, Bt. 21; Fox 72, 30), Met. 11, 8. Ōlæce Gode ānum *try to please God only*, Prov. Kmbl. 80. Hē wolde onginnan him ōleccan mid his hearepan *he* (*Orpheus*) *would attempt to propitiate them* (*the gods of Hell*) *with his harp*, Bt. 35, 6; Fox 168, 14: Cd. Th. 118, 3; Gen. 1959. Uton wē Gode ōliccan, Exon. Th. 366, 15; Reb. 12. IV. of things *to gratify, charm, give pleasure*:—Ealle ða ōðru gōd ōleccaþ ðam mōde and hit rēt se lust āna ōlecþ ðam līchoman ānum swīðost *cetera omnia jucunditatem animo videantur afferre*, Bt. 24, 3; Fox 84, 23–25. Swilce hȳ wǣron rihte ðā hī ðē mǣst geōleccan swilce hī nū sindon ðeáh ðe hȳ ðē ōleccan on ða leásan sǣlþa *talis erat, cum blandiebatur, cum tibi falsae illecebris felicitatis alluderet*, 7, 2; Fox 18, 2.

ōleccere, es; *m. A flatterer*:—Leás ōlecere *parasitus*, Wrt. Voc. i. 74, 36. Hē geliéfþ ðæt hē suelc sīe suelce hē gehiérþ ðæt his ōlicceras secgaþ ðæt hē sīe, Past. 17, 3; Swt. 111, 11.

ōleccung, e; *f.* I. *soothing, caressing, gentleness of treatment*:—Ōlæcung *delinimentum*, Wrt. Voc. i. 54, 69. Ōlæcunge *blandimentorum*, Hpt. Gl. 485, 48. Hū gesceádwīs se reccere sceal biōn on his þreáunga and on his ōleccunga *quae esse debet rectoris discretio correptionis et dissimulationis*, Past. 21, tit.; Swt. 151, 6. Ðā āhsode heó hine georne mid hire ōlæcunge, on hwam his miht wǣre, Jud. 16, 6. Ōlæcunga *blanditiae*, Ælfc. Gr. 13; Som. 16, 17. II. *flattery, fawning, adulation*:—Ōlæcung *adulatio*, Hpt. Gl. 527, 40. Wyrð ðæt mōd besuicen mid ðæra ōlicunga (ōliccunga, Cott. MSS.) ðe him underþiédde beóþ, Past. 17, 3; Swt. 111, 7. Ne wilna nānes monnes ōlæcunga, Prov. Kmbl. 80. Hē nǣfre nǣnigum woruldrīcum men þurh leáse ōlecunga onbūgan nolde, Blickl. Homl. 223, 28. Ðonne hit hæfþ gewunnen ðæs folces ōlecunga (*favor popularis*), Bt. 24, 3; Fox 82, 23. III. of things, *charm, allurement*:—Ōliccung *jocunda*, Wrt. Voc. ii. 127, 2. Ne hine ne geloccige nān ōliccung (ōlicung, Cott. MSS.) tō hiere willan *non blanda usque ad voluptatem demulceant*, Past. 14, 3; Swt. 83, 18. Forsió hē ǣlce ōlicunge (ōliccunge, Cott. MSS.) ðisses middangeardes *blandimenta mundi despiciat*, 14, 2; Swt. 83, 6. Hit gewarenaþ ǣgðer ge wið heora þreáunga ge wið ōlecunga *nec formidandas fortunae minas, nec exoptandas facit esse blanditias*, Bt. 7, 2; Fox 18, 24. v. leás-ōlecung.

ōleht-word, es; *n. A flattering speech*:—Hwǣr syndon ða ðe hié heredan, and him ōlyhtword sprēcan?, Blickl. Homl. 99, 26.

ōl-fæt (= āl-fæt. v. Wrt. Voc. ii. 135, 39), es; *n. A cooking vessel; coculum*, Wrt. Voc. i. 24, 41.

olfend, es: olfenda, an; *m. A camel*:—Olfend *camelus* vel *dromeda*, Wrt. Voc. i. 22, 58: *camelus*, 78, 8. Āfȳred olbenda *dromidus*, ii. 106, 66. Ōfȳrit olfenda, 25, 68. Under ānes olfendes (*cameli*) seáme, Gen. 31, 34. Gescrȳd mid oluendes hǣrum, Mk. Skt. 1, 6. Gē drincaþ ðone olfend (olbendu, Rush.), Mt. Kmbl. 23, 24. Of olfenda hǣrum āwunden, Blickl. Homl. 169, 2. Hē nam tȳn olfendas (*camelos*), Gen. 24, 10. [*Orm.* olfent *a camel*: *Goth.* ulbandus; *m.*: *O. Sax.* olbundeo; *m.*: *O. H. Ger.* olpenta; *f.*: *Icel.* ūlfaldi; *m.*]

olfend-mere, an; *f. A she-camel*:—Þrītig gefolra olfendmyrena mid heora coltum *camelos foetas cum pullis suis triginta*, Gen. 32, 15.

ōliccan. v. ōleccan.

oll *contempt, insult, contumely* (in the phrase mid olle):—Se deófol cwæþ mid olle ðæt hē wolde æt ðam weorce gecuman, Homl. Th. i. 166, 15. Hē āxode ðā mid olle (*contemptuously*): Eart ðū lā God? Homl. Skt. i. 9, 72. Man tǣleþ and mid olle gegrēteþ (*insults*) ealles tō gelōme ða ðe riht lufiaþ, Wulfst. 164, 19.

ōl-þwang (*better?* āl-, cf. ōl-fæt), es; *m. A strap*:—Ōlþwongas *corrigie*, Wrt. Voc. ii. 22, 47. [*Icel.* āl (mod. ōl) *a strap*.]

ōm *rust*:—Oom *rubigo*, Wrt. Voc. ii. 119, 34. Ōm *erugo, vitium ferri*, 144, 3: Ælfc. Gr. 9, 3; Som. 8, 58. Ðǣr ōm (*aerugo*) hit fornimþ, Mt. Kmbl. 6, 19, 20. Ōmm, Homl. Th. ii. 104, 29. Yldo ābīteþ īren mid ōme, Salm. Kmbl. 601; Sal. 300. v. brand-(brond-)ōm.

om-. v. am-.

ōman; *pl. f. Erysipelas, erysipelatous inflammations*:—Ōman *ignisacrum*, Wrt. Voc. ii. 45, 34: 110, 52. Lǣcedōmas wið ǣlces cynnes ōmum, Lchdm. ii. 98, 21. *In the section of which this is the heading the word frequently occurs.* Of hōmena stiéme cymþ eágna mist, 26, 26. Wið hōmum, nim gāte horn ... dō on ða hōman, i. 350, 17–20. Wið hōmum (ōman, MS. O.), bāres scearn ... ða hōman hyt bēteþ, 360, 10–11. [*Icel.* āma; *f.* and āmu-sōtt *erysipelas*.] v. next word.

ōm-cynn, es; *n. Corrupt humour*:—Ðū meaht clǣnsian ðæt ōmcyn, Lchdm. ii. 82, 18. v. ōmig.

omer *a bird's name, hammer* (in yellow-*hammer*):—Omer (emer, Ep. Gl. 23 e, 31) *scorelus*, Wrt. Voc. ii. 120, 6. Amore *scorellus*, i. 281, 18. In Cd. Dip. Kmbl. iii. 118 *omer*lond occurs. [*O. H. Ger.* amero: *Ger.* ammer.] v. clod-hamer.

ō-middan. v. on-middan.

ōmig; *adj.* I. *rusty* (v. ōm), *rust-coloured*:—Ðǣr wæs helm monig eald and ōmig, Beo. Th. 5519; B. 2763. Dȳre swyrd ōmige þurhetene, 6090; B. 3049. Ðȳ læs ðæt ōmige fæt mid ealle tōberste, gif hē mid ungemete scæfþ, R. Ben. 121, 3. Anfiltes hōmiges *incudis*, Hpt. Gl. 417, 64. Ōmigum *vel* īsengrǣgum *ferrugineo*, Wrt. Voc. ii. 147, 66. II. *inflammatory* (v. ōman):—Wyrð gegaderodu ōmig wǣte on ðære wambe, Lchdm. ii. 218, 16. On ðam magan ōmigre wǣtan gefylled, 178, 9. v. next word.

ōmiht; *adj. Full of inflammation*:—Þis sint tācn ðæs hātan magan ōmihtan ... Ðæs hātan magan tācn sindon ðonne hē biþ mid ōmum geswenced, Lchdm. ii. 192, 24. Ða ōmihtan þing *the inflammatory symptoms*, 82, 21.

on, an; *prep. adv.* A. *with dat. or inst.* I. expressing local relations, (1) rest upon and contact with an object, *on*:—Hig stōdon on nyðewerdum ðam munte, Ex. 19, 17. Hē on dōmsetle sittende wæs, Bd. 5, 19; S. 639, 43. Him on bearme læg mādma mænigo, Beo. Th. 80; B. 40. On him byrne scān, 815; B. 405. Se on foldan læg, Byrht. Th. 138, 29; By. 227. Hē on meare rād, 138, 53; By. 239. *And metaphorically*:—On eów scyld siteþ, Exon. Th. 131, 2; Gū. 449. (2) dependence upon an object:—Hié hine on rōde āhēngon, Blickl. Homl. 7, 11. Ðæs on ðam beáme geweóx, Cd. Th. 31, 11; Gen. 483: Exon. Th. 202, 27; Ph. 76. (3) extension over a surface:—Deófles rīce on ðyssum middangearde, Blickl. Homl. 7, 13. Ðæt mycel hǣto wǣre Cristes geleáfan on Norþanhymbra þeóde, Bd. 2, 14; S. 518, 5: Exon. Th. 201, 2; Ph. 50. (4) nearness:—Hī nāmon him wintersetl on Temesan, Chr. 1009; Erl. 143, 4. (5) *in* or *at* a place, or *with* a person, cf. æt:—Ða đe wǣron on đam mynstre Æbbercurnig, đæt is geseted on Engla-lande, Bd. 4, 26; S. 602, 35. Hē on sinoþe sittende wæs, 5, 19; Bd. 639, 43. Gewundad on gefeohte, 4, 26; S. 603, 14. Hī đone līchoman on cneówum bēgde, 4, 11; S. 580, 10. On đam dōme standeþ, Exon. Th. 95, 22; Cri. 1561. On beóre *at a feast*, 330, 14; Vy. 51. Hē ānne cnapan gesette on hyra middele, Mk. Skt. 9, 36: Lk. Skt. 21, 21. Ða clǣnan heortan God geseóþ. On đære gesihþe wesaþ ealle geleáffulle, Blickl. Homl. 13, 27. Ða sǣton on portum *qui sedebant in porta*, Ps. Th. 68, 12. Ic mundbyrd on đē hæfde, 70, 5. Is mildheortnisse miht on (*apud*) Drihtne, 129, 7. ¶ *Like Icelandic* á *it occurs in names of places*:—On his mynstre đe is cweden on Hripum, Bd. 5, 18; S. 636, 45. (6) with verbs of motion:—Se đe on heofenum cuman ne mōt, Homl. Th. ii. 452, 4. (7) rest where one object is contained in another, or is surrounded by others, *within, among*; and metaphorically *in* (the power of, etc.):—Drihten wæs uppan him on fȳre, Ex. 19, 18. Drihten is on đīnre heortan, and on đīnum innoþe, Blickl. Homl. 5, 11. Sum mon scīnende on hwītum gegyrelan, Bd. 5, 19; S. 640, 39. Twegen weras on hwītum reáfe, Lk. Skt. 24, 4. Ic wāt đæt ic (đæt Mōd) on libbendum men eom, and đeáh on deádlīcum, Bt. 5, 3; Fox 12, 27. Gif hit on heora anwealde wǣre, 11, 1; Fox 32, 2. Ic hī on lufan mīnre hæfde *quae dilexi*, Ps. Th. 118, 47. On þeóstre, Exon. 94, 27; Cri. 1546. On Juda ealdrum *among the princes of Judah*, Mt. Kmbl. 2, 6. Đū eart gebletsud on wīfum, Lk. Skt. 1, 28. (8) marking the seat of feeling, thought, etc., *in, within, at*:—Đā ongan hē smeágan on him selfum, Bt. 1, 1; Fox 2, 18. Ða fōre đe hē on his mōde gelufad hæfde, Bd. 5, 19; S. 637, 27. Yr on mōde, Cd. Th. 4, 33; Gen. 63. Murnan on mōde, 45, 31; Gen. 735. Se unrihtwīsa cwyþ on his mōde, Ps. Th. 13, 1: 54, 6. II. expressing temporal relations, (1) marking a point of time, *on, at, in*:—On đære tīde Drihten cwæþ tō mē, Deut. 10, 1. Đonne cymþ đæs weles hlāford on đam dæge đe hē nā ne wēnþ, and on đære tīde đe hē nāt, Mt. Kmbl. 24, 50. Swā byþ on worulde endunge, 13, 40. On anginne *in principio*, Gen. 1, 1. On mergen, St. And. 18, 28. On ǣfenne, 20, 14. (2) marking a period, past or future, *within, in the course of, in, during*:—Đes tōwyrpþ Godes templ, and on þrīm dagum (*in triduo*) hyt eft getimbraþ, Mt. Kmbl. 27, 40: Cd. Th. 266, 1; Sat. 15: Lchdm. iii. 262, 23. Gē sweltaþ on litelre hwīle, Deut. 30, 18. Hē nōwiht elles dyde on eallum đām dagum, Bd. 2, 14; S. 518, 8. On đæs biscopes tīde, 4, 12; S. 580, 34. On đissum geáre, Chr. 889; Erl. 86, 22. On đȳ ylcan gēre, 896; Erl. 93, 34. On geóguþe, Exon. Th. 288, 22; Wand. 35. On đissum līfe, 448, 12; Dōm. 53. On đīs andweardan līfe, Bt. 10; Fox 28, 25: 11; Fox 30, 23. On sumera sunne scīneþ, Cd. Th. 233, 15; Dan. 276. On geárdagum, 287, 16; Sat. 368. On fyrndagum, Exon. Th. 313, 17; Mōd. 1. Đæt feoh đe mon đām ferdmonnum on geáre sellan sceolde, Bt. 27, 4; Fox 100, 14. Þriwa on gēre *tribus vicibus per singulos annos*, Ex. 23, 14. Ic fæste tuwa on wucan, Lk. Skt. 18, 12. Đæt hridder tōbærst on đære lǣne *the sieve broke during the loan*, Homl. Th. ii. 154, 16. Heó cwæþ đæt heó wǣre wydewe on đam geáre *she said that she had been a widow during the last year*, Homl. Skt. i. 2, 154. On đam đe Godwine eorl and Beorn eorl lāgon on Pevenseá, Chr. 1050; Erl. 175, 14. III. expressing other relations, (1) *on, a-* (as in *a*-foot):—Heó on hire fōtum gesund hām hwearf, Bd. 3, 9; S. 534, 14. Sceal on ānum fēt fēran, Exon. Th. 415, 5; Rä. 33, 6. Đū gǣst on đīnum breóste, Gen. 3, 14. (2) with verbs of taking, depriving, etc., *from* (cf. æt):—Đone mǣstan dǣl đæra ǣhta đa đe on đē genumene wǣron, Bd. 5, 19; S. 640, 46 note: Bt. 7, 3; Fox 20, 29. Se đe gold on ōđrum reáfaþ, 13; Fox 38, 13. Đæt (*what*) hē on him gereáfade (bereáfode, MS. C.), Ors. 3, 11; Swt. 146, 30. Ða ǣrestan cyningas đe West-Seaxna lond on Wealum geeodon, Chr. Erl. 2, 10: Exon. Th. 118, 20; Gū. 242. Nāđer ne mehte on ōđrum sige gerǣcan, Ors. 3, 1; Swt. 96, 33. Hwæđer heora sceolde on ōđrum sige habban, 4, 1; Swt. 156, 1. (3) marking the object of thought, feeling, etc., *on, in, at*:—Manege wundrodon on his lāre (*or acc.?*), Mk. Skt. 6, 2. Ic on đīnum bebodum mōte gemetegian, Ps. Th. 118, 47. (4) marking the means or instrument, *by, with*:—Ic hæfde gemynt đē tō ārwurđienne on ǣhtum and on feó, Num. 24, 11. On tympanis, Ps. Th. 67, 24. Ic on mīnum mūþe mihta Drihtnes andette, 108, 29. Hē nōwiht fremian mihte on his lāre đære þeóde, Bd. 3, 5; S. 527, 24. Heó geleornod hæfde on onwrihgennysse, 3, 8; S. 531, 35. On đæs engles wordum wæs gehȳred đæt þurh hire beorþor sceolde beón gehǣled eall wīfa cynn, Blickl. Homl. 5, 22. On đæm upstige đære rōde eall ūre līf Drihten getremede, 9, 35. Hī wurdon on fleáme generede, Chr. 894; Erl. 92, 33. Se deófol wæs oferswīđde on đām ylcum gemetum đe hē ǣr Adam oferswīđde, Homl. Th. i. 178, 1. (5) marking the material or components of which a thing is made, *of, consisting of* or *in*:—Mycelne aad on beámum and on ræftrum and on wāgum and on watelum and on þacum, Bd. 3, 16; S. 542, 22. Lāc on mæssereáfum and on bōcum, Homl. Th. ii. 132, 7: Gen. 21, 27. Đæt gafol biþ on deóra fellum, and on fugela feđerum, Ors. 1, 1; Swt. 18, 17. Unrīm getæl on horsum and on mūlum and on olfendum and on elpendum.

Nar. 9, 14. Swā micel ungewiss, ǣgđer ge on sǣs fyrhto, ge on wēstennum wildeóra, ge on þeóda gereordum, Ors. 3, 9; Swt. 136, 24. (6) marking that *in* which a quality or property resides, *in respect to, in the matter of, in*:—Se wæs in bōccræftum and on woruldþeáwum se rihtwīsesta, Bt. 1, 1; Fox 2, 13. Hē āxode gif hē cūđe āht on lǣcecræfte. Apollinaris him cwæþ tō: 'Ne cann ic nāht on lācnunge,' Homl. Skt. i. 22, 40–41. Æþele on geƀyrdum, 11, 1; Fox 30, 31. On dǣde unæþele, Bd. 2, 15; S. 518, 37. On rīce gestrangod, 4, 26; S. 603, 19. On wīsdōme þeónde, Homl. Th. ii. 154, 11. Foremihtig on fēþe, Beo. Th. 1944; B. 970. Spēdig on đām ǣhtum đe heora spēda on beóþ, Ors. 1, 1; Swt. 18, 8. Wæstmberende on ǣlces cynnes blǣdum, 1, 3; Swt. 32, 13. Beorht on blǣdum, Cd. Th. 247, 20; Dan. 500. (7) marking state, condition, occupation, *in, of*:—Heora līc biþ on marmorstānes hwītnysse, Nar. 38, 9. Đū forþfærst on sybbe, đonne se tīma cymþ, on gōdre ylde, Gen. 15, 15: Bd. 2, 15; S. 519, 14: 5, 19; S. 641, 14. Ða welegan hē forlǣteþ on īdelnesse . . . Drihten is on đīnum fultume, Blickl. Homl. 5, 9–12. Þurhwunian on rihtum geleáfan and on fulfremedlīcum weorcum, 77, 19. On sorhgum beón, 5, 29. On stilnesse, Bt. 7, 2; Fox 18, 11. Gif hē wyrþ on ungeþylde, 11, 1; Fox 32, 33. Đā wæs cyning on hreón mōde, Beo. Th. 2619; B. 1307. On ungearwe *at unawares*, Ors. 1, 10; Swt. 46, 34. Eal đæt folc wæs on blǣdran, 1, 7; Swt. 38, 6. Job sæt on ānre wunde, Homl. Th. ii. 452, 27. Đā wearþ hē on slǣpe, Glostr. Frag. 6, 26. Hī wǣron on đan mǣstan hungre, Ors. 1, 5; Swt. 32, 26. Hē wēnde đæt hié wolden Hannibale on fultume beón, 4, 10; Swt. 196, 7. On feáwum stōwum wīciaþ Finnas, on huntoþe on wintra, and on sumera on fiscaþe, 1, 1; Swt. 17, 5. Sum man wæs betogen đæt hē wǣre on stale, Homl. Skt. i. 21, 265. (8) marking measure, *at* (*a distance*), *of* (*the weight of*), etc.:—Weđeras on oxna micelnesse, Nar. 33, 16: Lchdm. i. 314, 21. Six wæterfatu . . . ǣlc wæs on twegra sestra gemete (*capientes singuli metretas binas*), Jn. Skt. 2, 6. Ic geseah sumne gildenne dalc on fīftigum entsum, Jos. 7, 21. Ān æstel on fīftegum mancessa, Past. pref.; Swt. 9, 1. Hī đæt feoh gesetton on þrittig scillingum *they fixed the money at thirty shillings*, Homl. Th. ii. 242, 18. Se gewāt on wēsten đā hē wæs on twentigum geára, and on đæm hē wunode ōþ đæt hē wæs on fīf and hundteóntig geára, Shrn. 52, 16–18. Hig flugon on twegra elna heáhnisse bufan eorþan, Num. 11, 31. Wæs seó stōw hwæthwugu on healfre mīle fram đære ceastre wealle, Bd. 1, 7; S. 478, 31. Is đæt eálond fram đære ylcan cyricean feor ūt on gārsecge seted hūhugu on nygan mīlum, 4, 27; S. 603, 30: 2, 3; S. 504, 26: Shrn. 29, 31. Ālecgaþ hit on ānre mīle đone mǣstan dǣl fram đæm tūne, đonne ōđerne, đonne đæne þriddan, ōþ đe hyt eall ālēd biþ on đære ānre mīle (*within the one mile*); and sceall beón se lǣsta dǣl nȳhst đæm tūne, Ors. 1, 1; Swt. 20, 30–33. Hī hine bebyrgdon on đære æfteran mīle fram đære ceastre, Shrn. 115, 16: Blickl. Homl. 193, 19. (9) marking degree:—On swīđe lytlon hiera hæfþ seó gecynd genōg, on swā myclum heó hæfþ genōg swā wē ǣr sprǣcon, Bt. 14, 1; Fox 42, 10–11. (10) marking manner, *with, in*:—Hlāfas on lilian beorhtnysse scīnende, and on hrōsan brǣđe stȳmende, Homl. Th. ii. 136, 28. His gewǣda scinon on snāwes hwītnysse, 242, 7. Hī cōmon on þrīm floccum, Homl. Th. ii. 450, 13. Se on hrædnesse mycele menigo fornom, Bd. 1, 14; S. 482, 30. (11) denoting end, purpose:—Āsceacaþ đæt dust of eówrum fōtum him on gewitnysse, Mk. Skt. 6, 11. 'Mīn blōd, đæt đe biþ āgoten on synna forgifennysse' . . . Hī hālgodon hlāf and wīn on his gemynde, Homl. Th. ii. 268, 1–3. (12) *in accordance with*:—Đæt hē irne on his willan, Bt. 11, 1; Fox 32, 21. (13) *of* (*such and such a name*):—Wæs sum man on naman Zacheus, Lk. Skt. 19, 2: 23, 50. Castel on naman Emaus, 24, 13. (14) *in* (*the name of*):—Hē him geswōr on his goda noman, Ors. 4, 6; Swt. 178, 11. (15) without a case following:—Deófol đē sticaþ on, Jn. Skt. 7, 20. Seó wyrd (hit) đē on genimian ne mihte, Bt. 11, 2; Fox 34, 14. Swelce him nǣfre gelīc yfel an ne become, Ors. 3, 10; Swt. 140, 10. For đæm ungemetlīcan feóndscipe đe ūre ēhtende on sindon, 2, 5; Swt. 80, 36. Đæt him mon sceolde an mā healfa on feohtan đonne on āne, Swt. 80, 27. Him man on līhþ, Bt. 30, 1; Fox 108, 8: Prov. 70. On secgan *to bring a charge against*, Deut. 19, 16: Mt. 26, 62. B. with acc. I. expressing local relations. (1) motion, actual or figurative, which is external to the object expressed by the word which *on* governs, *upon, on, on to, to*:—Hē āstāh on đone munt, Mt. Kmbl. 5, 1. Se deófol lǣdde hine on swīđe heáhne munt, 4, 8: Cd. Th. 220, 11; Dan. 69. Speón hine on đa dimman dǣd, 43, 3; Gen. 685. Gewāt Abraham on đa wīgrōde, 125, 24; Gen. 2084. Se wuldorcyning on middangeard cwom, Blickl. Homl. 9, 32. Āhōn on heánne beám, Exon. Th. 261, 3; Jul. 309. Com hungur on Bryttas, Bd. 1, 14; S. 482, 15. Hē wæs ādrifen đæt hē com up on Frysena land *pulsus est Fresiam*, 5, 19; S. 639, 20. Hē his āgene tungan wearp hine on đæt neb foran *linguam in os tyranni abjecit*, Bt. 16, 2; Fox 52, 25. Hī spǣtton on hyne, Mt. Kmbl. 27, 30. On đone andwlitan men slōgun, Exon. Th. 69, 19; Cri. 1123. Wē wyllaþ fōn on đone traht đissere rǣdinge, Homl. Th. i. 206, 21. (2) marking motion from without to the inside, *into, among*:—Sume feóllon on þornas, Mt. Kmbl. 13, 7. Sume feóllon on gōde eorþan, 13, 8. Đā cōmon hig on đa stōwe đe ys genemned Golgotha, 27, 33. Crist of heofona heánessum on ðínne innoþ ástígeþ, Blickl. Homl. 5, 14. On ðás world cuman, 5, 28. Gelǽded on his ðæt ǽrre mynster, Bd. 5, 19; S. 641, 17. Hē on scip eode, S. 639, 19. Gōd geár com on Breotone land, 1, 14; S. 482, 21. Gǽstas hweorfaþ on ēcne eard, Exon. Th. 64, 31; Cri. 1046. On ðæt micle morþ men forweorpan, Cd. Th. 43, 15; Gen. 691. Sum man becom on ða sceaþan, Lk. Skt. 10, 30, 36. On ealle þeóda *among all nations*, 24, 47. Hē on ða duru eode, Chr. 755; Erl. 48, 32. (3) marking position or direction:—Ic stande on ðás healfe *ego in hac parte sto*, Ælfc. Gr. 47; Som. 47, 50. On ða swýðran healfe, Mt. Kmbl. 26, 64. Ān on ða swýðran healfe, and óðer on ða wynstran, 27, 38. On healfa gehwone, Beo. Th. 1604; B. 800. On ðæt steórbord ... on ðæt bæcbord *on the starboard ... on the larboard*, Ors. 1, 1; Swt. 17, 10–11. (4) denoting conjunction (*in the phrase* on ān), *continuously, together, anon, at once*:—Feówertig daga and feówertig nihta on ān, Gen. 7, 12: Homl. Th. i. 178, 5. On ān gesworene *conjurati*, Wrt. Voc. ii. 20, 22. Ealle deáde men sculon ðone mýclan dōme gesēcan, and ða synfullan sculon ðanon on ān tō helle faran, Wulfst. 126, 20. In ðone ealdan secgmōr; of ðam on ān betwēnan ācwudu and wulleleáh; and swā ǽfre betwyx ðām twām wudan, Cod. Dip. Kmbl. vi. 218, 23. (5) with verbs denoting division or separation:—Ūre ieldran ealne ðisne ymbhwyrft ðises middangeardes on þreó tōdǽldon; and hié ða þrié dǽlas on þreó tōnemdon, Ors. 1, 1; Swt. 8, 1–4. Tōsliten on twegen dǽlas, Mt. Kmbl. 27, 51: Chr. 894; Erl. 90, 16. Hit tōbærst on emtwā, Homl. Th. ii. 154, 16. II. expressing temporal relations. (1) marking a point of time, *on, in, at*:—On ðone dæg (*in die*) ðe God gesceóp man, Gen. 5, 1. On midne dæg *in meridie*, Deut. 28, 29. On ǽlcne tīman *omni tempore*, 11, 1: 14, 23. On ealle tīd, Ex. 18, 22, 26. On dægrēd *diluculo*, 8, 20. On ða tīd *tunc*, Bd. 4, 26; S. 603, 3: *eo tempore*, 2, 16; S. 519, 38. On ðone forman Eásterdæg, 5, 23, tit.; S. 645, 3. Ðā hit ðā on morgendæg wæs, Nar. 16, 21: 22, 1. Heora wīse on nǽnne sǽl (*on no occasion*) wel ne gefōr, Ors. 4, 4; Swt. 164, 13. Eten ða gebrōðru on twā mǽl, R. Ben. 65, 14. (2) marking a period of time:—On ēcnesse *for ever*, Blickl. Homl. 13, 30. On ðās lǽnan tīd *in this life*, Exon. Th. 364, 1; Wal. 64. On sumeres tīd, 212, 12; Ph. 209. On nānes cynges dæg, Chr. 1009; Erl. 141, 22. III. in metaphorical expressions. (1) *into* (one's power, etc.):—Gif hig on hand gāþ *if they submit*, Deut. 20, 11: Bd. 1, 14; S. 482, 16. Hine sylfne on þeówdōm gesealde ðara muneca, 5, 19; S. 637, 12. Hē ealle Assirie on Persa anwald gedyde, Ors. 2, 1; Swt. 62, 3. (2) expressing hostile action, *against*:—Hē wonn on Sciððie, 2, 5; Swt. 78, 3. Ðā gelǽdde hē here on Peohtas, Bd. 4, 26; S. 602, 19. Ne dō ūs swā swā wē dydon on ðisne ælþeódigan, St. And. 22, 21. Óðer biþ tō ungemetlīce ātyht on ðæt ðe hió mid ryhte irsian sceal, óðer on ðæt ðe hió ne sceal biþ tō swīðe onbærned, Past. 40, 4; Swt. 293, 12–14. Hié ealle on ðone cyning wǽrun feohtende, Chr. 755; Erl. 48, 35. (3) expressing agreement, *in accordance with*:—Hē hēt sumne biscep secgan on his gewill hwā his fæder wǽre, Ors. 3, 9, tit.; Swt. 3, 13. Heó on his willan spræc, Cd. Th. 44, 1; Gen. 701. On riht *a-right*:—Ðæt hié healdan Godes ǽwe on riht, Blickl. Homl. 45, 9: 47, 35. (4) denoting change from one state to another:—Ðā wendon hié hié on hiora āgen geþióde, Past. pref.; Swt. 7, 2. Wendan on Englisc, Swt. 7, 18. Wēsten hē geworhte on wīdne mere, Ps. Th. 106, 34. Hē wendeþ stān on wīdne mere, 113, 8. Hī on heora āgen dust hweorfaþ, 103, 27. (5) marking the object of thought, emotion, speech, trust, sight:—Ne gladige on ðæt nōðer ne cyning ne woruldrīca, Lchdm. iii. 442, 35. Hē getrūwode on īdel gylp, 51, 6. Ða ðe on Drihten getreówaþ, 124, 1: 70, 13. On hine gelýfende, Homl. Th. ii. 130, 18. Gōd ys on Drihten tō þenceanne, Ps. Th. 117, 8. Sete on Drihten ðīn gehygd, 54, 22. Hycgan on ellen, Cd. Th. 191, 22; Exod. 218. On ðæt wundor seón, 261, 25; Dan. 731. On ðæt bearn starian, Exon. Th. 21, 27; Cri. 341. Hē on ðone æþeling lōcude, Chr. 755; Erl. 48, 33. Se deófol ðe andode on ðæs munuces sōðan lufe, Homl. Th. ii. 156, 8. Hwæt gōdes māgan wē secgan on ða flǽsclīcan unþeáwas, Bt. 31, 1; Fox 110, 24. Higeteónan spræc on fǽmnan, Cd. Th. 136, 22; Gen. 2262. Ne sceal nān mann secgan on hine sylfne ðæs ðe hē wyrcende næs, Homl. Skt. i. 12, 177, 195. (6) marking the object in relation to which an action takes place:—Ðæt ða woruldsǽlþa on ðē (*erga te*) onwenda sint, Bt. 7, 2; Fox 16, 29. (7) marking end or purpose:—Ic wylle gān on fiscaþ, Jn. Skt. 21, 3. Hī him on fultum cýgdon ða godcundan ārfæstnesse, Bd. 4, 26; S. 602, 9. (8) marking price:—On gold bebycgean, 2, 12; Bd. 514, 39. Hē bebohte bearn Wealdendes on seolfres sinc, Cd. Th. 301, 7; Sat. 578. (9) marking manner:—Nemned on Lǽden *Pastoralis*, and on Englisc Hierdebōc, Past. pref.; Swt. 7, 19. Hēr sýn on earde on mistlīce wīsan hlāfordswican manege, Wulfst. 160, 7. On ýdel *necquicquam*, Wülck. Gl. 256, 14. (10) *in* (*the name of*), *by* (in adjuration):—Ic eów hālsige on ðone Drihten, ðe gescōp heofenas and eorþan, and on ða Hālgan Þrynnesse and on ða twelf apostolas and on ealle Godes hālgan and on ða cyrcan, ðe gē tō gelýfaþ, and on ðæt hālige fulluht, Wulfst. 232, 12–16. (11) not followed by a case, or as adverb:—Hī gegearwodon wægen and on āsetton ða fǽmnan, Bd. 3, 9; S. 534, 9. Fæht hine on Penda, 3, 14; S. 539, 18. On ðæm dǽle ðe Decius on ofslagen wæs, Ors. 3, 10; Swt. 138, 15. Hē on ða sunnan mæg on lōcian, Met. 22, 20. Ðā fērde hē tō heofonum, him on lōcigendum *while they looked on*, Homl. Th. i. 294, 1. Dēþ hē wyrplas on, Exon. Th. 332, 19; Vy. 87. Hine on cymeþ wracu, Cd. Th. 63, 33; Gen. 1041. Hine Abraham on his āgene hand sette, 167, 17; Gen. 2767. Rǽsdon on sōna, Andr. Kmbl. 2670; An. 1336. *The word is often used in translating Latin words with the prefix* in-, thus on belǽdan *inferre*, on gebringan, on heápian *ingerere*, on gehreósan *ingruere*. (12) with other adverbs:—Ðǽr stōd disc on, Bd. 3, 6; S. 528, 14. Ne ic ðǽr nān þing on ne cann, St. And. 28, 24: 40, 3. Ðǽr wæs on Leo (*at the synod*), Chr. 1046; Erl. 171, 12. Ealles ðæs ðe ðǽr ðenne on biþ, Chart. Th. 534, 5. Swā swā Drihten cwæþ on ǽr, Jos. 11, 23: Gen. 6, 6. Hē cýðde his forþsīþ on ǽr *he foretold his death*, Homl. Th. ii. 186, 23. Hió þyrstende wæs on symbel (*for ever*) mannes blōdes, Ors. 1, 2; Swt. 30, 27. Hē nyste būtan hī sungon ðone lofsang forþ on, Homl. Skt. i. 21, 236. [*Goth.* ana: *O. Sax. O. Frs. O. H. Ger.* an: *Icel.* ā.]

on-. The prefix, when used with verbs, for the most part corresponds with the *O. H. Ger.* int-, *Ger.* ent-, e. g. on-līsan, -lūcan, -týnan, -wreón.

on-ǽht, e; *f. Possession*:—Ic sellu ðē þeóde erfeweardnisse ðīne and onǽhte ðīne gemǽru eorþan *dabo tibi gentes hereditatem tuam et possessionem tuam terminos terrae*, Ps. Surt. 2, 8.

on-ǽlan; p. de. I. *to set fire to, to ignite, kindle* (lit. and figurative):—Hū ne onǽlþ (*accendit*) heó hyre leóhtfæt? Lk. Skt. 15, 8. Hē hiene onǽlþ mid ðam tapure ðæs godcundan liéges, Past. 36; Swt. 259, 12. Ne byrnþ on ðē ðæt ðæt ðū on līfe ne onǽldest þurh leahtras, Homl. Th. ii. 338, 16: 344, 26. Ne onǽl ðū ðē sylfum ðæt ēce fýr, i. 594, 27. Ne onǽle gē nān fýr on ðam dæge *non succendetis ignem per diem sabbati*, Ex. 35, 3. Ðā hēt se ealdorman onǽlan ormǽte ād, Homl. Th. ii. 484, 7: Exon. Th. 277, 13; Jul. 580. Drihtenes fýr wearþ onǽled (*accensus*), Num. 11, 1, 3. Cola onǽlde synd *carbones succensi sunt*, Ps. Spl. 17, 10. II. *to burn* (cf. *anneal*), *consume by burning*:—Ðās fýr onǽlaþ manna sāwla ... Ðis fýr onǽlþ ǽlcne be his gewyrhtum, Homl. Th. ii. 338, 6–17. Ðā nāmon Nadab and Abiud hīra stōrcillan and onǽldon ðǽron ungehālgod fýr, Lev. 10, 1. Nim fela tunnan and dō hī ðǽr on innan, onǽl hī siððan ealle, Homl. Skt. i. 4, 260. III. *to make hot with fire*:—Hē hēt onǽlan ðone ofen swīðe þearle, Homl. Th. ii. 20, 1. IV. *to make hot* (in a metaphorical sense), *to inflame, to excite intense feeling, to kindle passions*:—Ic (*the devil*) hine ðæs swīðe synnum onǽle, ðæt hē byrnende from gebede swīceþ, Exon. Th. 264, 31; Jul. 372. Onǽled *incensum*, Wrt. Voc. ii. 133, 18. Mid ðære lufe onǽled ðara worda, Ap. Th. 18, 27. Onǽled mid ðæm andan his hiéremonna unþeáwa, Past. 21; Swt. 159, 8. v. in-ǽlan.

on-ǽlet, es; *n. Lightning*:—Onǽletu ł līgetu *fulgura*, Ps. Lamb. 143, 6.

on-æðele; *adj. Natural, in accordance with the nature of a thing*:—Eallum treówum, ðe him onæðele biþ, ðæt hit on holte hýhst geweaxe (cf. ðām treówum ðe him gecynde biþ up heáh tō standanne, Bt. 25; Fox 88, 21), Met. 13, 51.

on-āl, es; *n. A burning, kindling*; also *what is burnt*:—Hē nemde ðære stōwe naman 'onāl' (*incensio*), for ðam ðe Drihtenes fýr wæs ðǽr onǽled, Num. 11, 3. Mid onāle ramma *cum incenso arietum*, Ps. Lamb. 65, 15. Onāl *incensum*, 140, 2. Onāl *incensa*, 79, 17: *incendia*, Hpt. Gl. 510, 18. Cf. āl- (aal-) geweorc *ignarium*, *and see* on-ǽlan.

on-āscunung, e; *f. Abomination, detestation*:—Fram onāscununga *abominationem*, Ps. Spl. 87, 8.

on-āsendedness *glosses* immisio, Ps. Lamb. 77, 49.

on-bæc; *adv. A-back, backward, behind*:—Gang ðū sceocca onbæc, Mt. Kmbl. 4, 10. Nā gewāt onbæc heorte ūre *non recessit retro cor nostrum*, Ps. Spl. 43, 21. v. next word.

on-bæcling; *adv. Back, backward, behind*; retrorsum:—Gān onbæcling *to go back, retire*, Blickl. Homl. 27, 20: 31, 12: Ps. Th. 43, 19. Cer ðē onbæcling *get thee behind*, Cd. Th. 308, 26; Sat. 698. Forhwī gengdest ðū onbæcling *quare conversus es retrorsum*? Ps. Th. 113, 5. Ðū hæfst ūs gehwyrfde onbæclincg *avertisti nos retrorsum*, 43, 12. Ðā feól hē fǽringa onbæcling, Blickl. Homl. 223, 11.

on-bærnan; p. de. I. *to set fire to, to light* (a fire), *to kindle* (a) literal:—Hió hié mid flexe bewundon and onbærndon hit *they wrapped them round with flax, and set fire to it*, Ors. 4, 1; Swt. 158, 6. Ðā hēton ða dēman micel fýr onbærnan, Shrn. 53, 15: Exon. Th. 277, 11; Jul. 579. Lyft biþ onbærned, 64, 26; Cri. 1043. (b) figurative:—Hē on monigra geleáfsumra heortan ðæs gāstlīcan leóhtes gyfe onbærnde, Bd. 2, 2; S. 502, 30. Ðæt fýr ðæt ðū sylfa on ðē onbærndest, Guthl. 5; Gdwin. 38, 18. Is onbærned ðīn yrre, Ps. Th. 78, 5. II. *to burn, consume by burning*:—Fýr onbærneþ, 79, 15. III. *to heat, inflame*:—Mid ðisse pannan hierstinge wæs Paulus onbærned *Paulus hujus sartaginis urebatur frixura*, Past. 21, 6; Swt. 165, 3. Óðer on ðæt ðe hió ne sceal irsian biþ tō swīðe onbærned (*inflammatur*), 40, 4; Swt. 293, 14. Mid hātheortnesse onbærnedne, 40, 6; Swt. 295, 25. Hié beóþ onbærnde mid ǽfēste, Blickl. Homl. 25, 7. IV. *to kindle desire for anything, to incite*:—Monigra monna mōd tō worulde forhogenesse onbærnde (*accensi*) wǽron, Bd. 4, 24; S. 596, 37.

on-bærnness, e; *f. Incense*:—Mid onbærnysse ramma *cum incenso arietum*, Ps. Spl. 65, 14. v. an-, in-bærness.

on-béru; *f.* [on = un?] *Wrong behaviour, vexation, anger*:—Hē ðæs onbǽru habban ne meahte ac hē hāte lēt teáras geótan *he could not be vexed at it* (*Guthlac's death*), *but he shed hot tears*, Exon. Th. 165, 12; Gū. 1827. [Cf. (?) *O. H. Ger.* un-gipārida *fastidium, ira, rabies.*]

on-bāsnung, e; *f. Awaiting, expectation*; expectatio, Rtl. 4, 34.

on-bēgness. v. on-bīgness.

on-bēn, e; *f. A prayer asking for something* (*evil*) *to come upon a person, an imprecation*:—Hī ūs mid heora wiðerwordum onbēnum and wyrinessum ēhtaþ *qui adversis nos imprecationibus persequuntur*, Bd. 2, 2; S. 504, 4.

on-beódan; *p.* -beád; *pl.* -budon; *pp.* -boden. I. *to bid, order*:—Ðū onbude hǽlu *qui mandas salutem*, Ps. Surt. 43, 5: 118, 138. Hē onbeád *ipse mandavit*, 148, 5. Ðā onbeád Basilla and cwæþ, Shrn. 86, 17. Ðā onbeád heó him ðæt hē hire tō onsænde all ða gesīðwīf, 87, 20. Hē onbeád ðæt hē of Rōme cōme, Bd. 1, 25; S. 486, 25. II. *to announce, tell, proclaim, send word*:—Hē hit him hām bebeád (onbeád, MS. C.) *he sent them home word of it*, Ors. 4, 5; Swt. 168, 13. Him Pilatus onbeád ymbe Cristes tācnunga *Pilatus ad Tiberium repulit de Christi virtutibus*, 6, 2; Swt. 254, 23. Word unreht onbudun (*mandaverunt*) wið mē, Ps. Surt. 40, 9. Eác beámas onbudon, hwā hȳ sceóp, Exon. Th. 72, 9. Agustinus hēt him onbeódan ðæt hēr wǽre mycel riip, Bd. 1, 29; S. 498, 4. [*Goth.* ana-biudan: *O. Sax.* an-beodan: cf. *O. H. Ger.* in-piotan.]

on-beornan, -brinnan; *pp.* -burnen. I. *to set fire to, to kindle*:—Abraham ādfȳr onbran, Cd. Th. 203, 4; Exod. 398. II. *to inflame*:—Se innoþ wyrþ onburnen, Lchdm. ii. 278, 9. Wǽte onburnenu, 218, 14.

on-beran; *pp.* -boren *To diminish, enfeeble, impair, destroy*:—Onboren *inminutus*, Wrt. Voc. ii. 49, 60. Wæs ðam bāncofan neáh geþrungen breósthord onboren wæs se blīða gǽst fūs on forþweg *disease pressed the body hard, the mind was enfeebled, the glad spirit was eager for departure*, Exon. Th. 158, 29; Gū. 917. Ðā wæs hord rāsod onboren beága hord *the hoard was explored, the treasure of rings rifled*, Beo. Th. 4557; B. 2284. Ǽghwylc gecwæþ ðæt him heardra nān hrīnan wolde īren ǽrgōd ðæt ðæs aglǽcan blōdge beadufolme onberan wolde *everyone agreed that no weapon would wound Grendel's claws, no sword would destroy* (or *harm*) *the monster's hand*, Beo. Th. 1985; B. 990.

on-bīd (-bid?), es; *n. Awaiting, expectation*:—Næs ðæt onbīd long ðæt ... *it was not long to wait, before* ..., Exon. Th. 156, 18; Gū. 876. Long is ðis onbīd worulde līfes *long in this life is this waiting for the next*, 164, 30; Gū. 1019. Hē on tweógendlīcan onbīde wæs hwæðer hē wið Rōmānum winnan dorste *he was waiting in doubt* (cunctans) *whether he durst fight with the Romans*, Ors. 4, 11; Swt. 204, 29. v. an-bīd, onbīd-stōw.

on-bīdan; *p.* -bād; *pl.* -bidon; *pp.* -biden. I. *to abide, wait, remain*:—Onbād ōþ ðæt ǽfen cwom, Beo. Th. 4594; B. 2302. Hē onbād ðæt feówertig wintra hweðer hié gecyrran woldan *he waited the forty years to see whether they would change*, Blickl. Homl. 79, 4. Onbīd hēr seofon and twentig nihta, 231, 5: 237, 33. Hēr sceolon hī onbīdan, Soul Kmbl. 121; Seel. 61. II. *to wait for, expect*, with gen.:—Ic uncres gedāles onbād, 75; Seel. 37. Ic ðīn onbād, Ps. Th. 118, 116. Gif wīfes wer sig on hæftnȳde gelǽded, onbȳde (*expectet*) heo his .vi. winter, L. Ecg. C. 26; Th. ii. 152, 4. Wē sculon ōðres onbīdan, Lk. Skt. 7, 20. Willaþ gē mīn onbīdan? Blickl. Homl. 233, 30, 27. III. *to wait on, attend upon*:—Onbīdendum *prestulanti*, Wrt. Voc. ii. 65, 58.

on-bidian *to wait*:—Onbidedon, Chr. 1006; Erl. 140 note 8. v. an-bidian.

onbīd-stōw, e; *f. A place in which to wait*:—On hwylcere anbīdstōwe ðīn sāwl bīdan mōte dōmes dæges *in quo commorationis loco animae tuae expectare liceat diem judicii*, L. Ecg. P. iv. 65; Th. ii. 226, 8.

on-bīdung. v. an-bīdung.

on-bīgan; *p.* de *To cause to bend, to subdue*:—Heó mīne sāwle onbīgdon *incurvaverunt animam meam*, Ps. Th. 56, 7. Heora mōdes heánesse ealle eorþcyningas onbēgan mihton *their loftiness of soul could make all the kings of the earth to bend*, Blickl. Homl. 119, 21. v. onbūgan.

on-bīgness, e; *f. Bending, curvature*:—Onbēgnes *curvatura*, Wrt. Voc. ii. 64, 25: 79, 2.

on-bindan; *p.* -band; *pp.* -bunden *To unbind, set free, disclose*:—Seó wiðerwearde wyrd onbint and gefreóþ ... mid ðam hió geopenaþ hū tiedre ðās andweardan gesǽlþa sint, Bt. 20; Fox 72, 2. Hē onband beadurūne, Beo. Th. 1006; B. 501. Ǽfter ðon onbind, Lchdm. ii. 250, 20. Wæs onbunden *enodaretur*, Hpt. Gl. 490, 73. Onbund[en?]um *exertis*, Wrt. Voc. ii. 31, 50. v. un-bindan.

on-birgan; *p.* de (*with gen. and acc.*) *To taste of, taste, take* (*food*):—Gif hē bitres onbyrgeþ, Met. 12, 11: 13, 23. Onbirigþ, Bt. 23; Fox 78, 26: 25; Fox 88, 11. Sume ðe deáþ ne onbyrigeaþ (-byrgeaþ, MS. A.: -byrigaþ, MS. B.), Mt. Kmbl. 16, 28. Onbyrigeaþ (-byrgaþ MS. A.), Mk. Skt. 9, 1. Nān ðara manna ne onbyrigeaþ (-byriaþ, MS. A.) mīnre feorme, Lk. Skt. 14, 24. Hē his (*the water*) onbergde, Shrn. 64, 9. Onbyrigde (-byrgde, MS. A.), Mt. Kmbl. 27, 34: Jn. Skt. 2, 9: Homl. Th. i. 136, 8. Onberede, Bt. 23, tit.; Fox xiv, 9. Ne hī siððan ne onbirigdon ðæs bigleofan, Jos. 5, 12: Homl. Th. ii. 168, 2-3. Onbyrigdon, i. 18, 1: Blickl. Homl. 209, 8. Onbyrgaþ *gustate*, Ps. Spl. 33, 8. Ic hæbbe bōca onbyrged, Salm. Kmbl. 3; Sal. 2.

on-birging, e; *f. Tasting, taking* (*food*):—Wið āttres onbyrgingce, Lchdm. i. 136, 12.

on-birgness, e; *f. Taste, tasting*:—Seó wæs wynsumu on ðære onbyrignesse ... Manige men þurh ðyses wǽtan onbyrignesse wurdan gehǽlde, Blickl. Homl. 209, 9-12.

on-birhtan *to illumine*:—God hié onbyrhte mid andgite, Blickl. Homl. 105, 31.

on-bītan; *p.* -bāt; *pp.* -biten (*with gen.*) *To taste of, partake of*:—Se ðæs wæstmes onbāt, Cd. Th. 30, 21; Gen. 470: 42, 22; Gen. 677. Gif wulf ǽniges cynnes orf tōslīte, and hit forðon deád beó, ne onbīte (*gustet*) his nān Cristen man, L. Ecg. P. iv. 29; Th. ii. 212, 26. Anbīte, iv. 28; Th. ii. 212, 23. Gecȳðan ðæt heó ðæs forstolenan ne onbite, L. In. 57; Th. i. 138, 10. Ne sceal hē huniges onbītan, Lchdm. ii. 222, 20. Ne hit se mon drincan meahte, ne his ǽnig neát onbītan ne meahte, Nar. 8, 32. Nǽnigre wǽtan onbītan, Guthl. 2; Gdwin. 16, 24. [*O. Sax.* an-bītan: *O. H. Ger.* en-bīzan.]

on-blǽstan *glosses* inrumpere, Wrt. Voc. ii. 48, 49.

on-blandan *to intermingle, to infect* (*with moral evil*):—Hē lungre āhōf wōðe wiðerhȳd g weán onblonden *he raised at once his voice, hostile and harmful* (cf. *the use of* geblanden *in similar phrases*), Andr. Kmbl. 1350; An. 675.

on-blāwan *to breathe into, inspire, inflate*:—Onblǽwþ *litrat* (?), Wrt. Voc. ii. 53, 60. Onblā[wende] *inspirans, inflans*, Hpt. Gl. 442, 29. Mid elreordre dysignesse onblāwne *barbara inflati stultitia*, Bd. 2, 5; S. 507, 13.

on-blāwness, e; *f. Inspiration*:—Seó onblāwnes ðære heofonlīcan onfæþmnesse, Blickl. Homl. 7, 26.

on-blōtan *to offer, sacrifice*:—Abraham onbleót ðæt lāc Gode, Cd. Th. 177, 21; Gen. 2933.

on-bregdan, -brēdan; *p.* brægd, -brǽd, *pl.* brugdon, -brudon. I. *with dat. acc.* (?), *To move quickly*:—Heáfde onbrygdeþ þriwa āscæceþ *the Phenix thrice moves its head* (*bowing to the sun*; igniferum caput ter venerata), Exon. Th. 207, 18; Ph. 143. Onbrǽd recedes mūþan raþe æfter ðon on flōr treddode *Grendel opened the door violently and stepped on to the floor of the hall*, Beo. Th. 1450; B. 723. II. *intrans. To move* (*oneself*) *quickly, to start* (*from sleep*):—Ðā on morgne mid ðȳ hit dagode ðā onbrǽd ic *postero die matutino expergefactus diluculo*, Nar. 30, 30: Bd. 3, 27; S. 559, 16. Ðā onbrǽd Gūþlāc of ðam slǽpe, Guthl. 6; Gdwin. 42, 13. Hē of slǽpe onbrægd, Elen. Kmbl. 150; El. 75. Swā hē of hefigum slǽpe onbrude, Bd. 5, 19; S. 640, 27.

on-bring, es; *m. Instigation*:—Se man ðe hine sylfne ofslihþ mid wǽpne oððe mid (for, MS. X.) hwylcum mislīcum deófles onbringe (*instigatione*), L. Ecg. P. ii. 5; Th. ii. 184, 5.

on-brinnan. v. on-beornan.

on-brucol; *adj. Rugged*:—Anbrucolne *preruptam*, Germ. 402, 85.

on-bryce, es; *m. An irruption, attack*:—Onrǽs, onbryce *irruptionem, ingressionem*, Hpt. Gl. 464, 66.

on-bryrdan; *p.* de. I. *to instigate, stimulate, incite, inspire, animate*:—Onbryrde *instigavit*, Wrt. Voc. ii. 44, 82. Hē hī tō geleáfan onbryrde, Blickl. Homl. 107, 2. Hī se hēhsta Dēma mid elne onbryrde *inspired her with courage*, Judth. Thw. 22, 37; Jud. 95. Git mid fullwihte onbryrdon ealne ðisne middangeard, Exon. Th. 467, 10; Hö. 136. Onbryrdan beorman mīne *to leaven with my leaven*, 266, 10; Jul. 396. Hit nis git se tīma ðæt ic þē heálīcor mǽge onbryrdan *firmioribus remediis nondum tempus est*, Bt. 5, 3; Fox 14, 14. Onbryrdendum (*instigante*) feónde ealra gōda, Bd. 3, 22; S. 553, 14. Onbryrd (*compunctus*) mid lufan ðæs upplīcan rīces, 4, 12; S. 580, 36. Wearþ Johannes swā onbryrd þurh ðæt tācen, ðæt hē his brȳde on mægþhāde forlēt, Homl. Th. i. 58, 16. Him wearþ onbryrded breóstsefa, Exon. Th. 122, 15; Gū. 306. Ǽfter heora lāre ða ðe wǽron godcundlīce onbryrde *juxta divinitus inspiratam doctrinam*, Bd. 4, 17; S. 585, 34. Sceolan wē beón āwehte and onbryrde tō godcundre lāre, Blickl. Homl. 33, 23. II. *to excite to a feeling of compunction*:—Hē wæs onbryrded (*compunctus*) mid gemynde his synna and weóp, Bd. 3, 27; S. 559, 2. Ðǽr mon ðæt godspel sægþ maniges mannes heorte biþ onbryrded, Blickl. Homl. 47, 32. v. in-bryrdan.

on-bryrding, e; *f. An exciting, a stimulus*:—Onbryrdinge *instinctu*, Wrt. Voc. ii. 44, 34.

on-bryrdness, e; *f. Instigation, stimulus, inspiration, compunction*:—Mid wīne onbryrdnysse *vino compunctionis*, Ps. Spl. 59, 3. Mid onbryrdnysse ðæs upplīcan ēðles *with the stimulus that is given by the land on high*, Homl. Th. ii. 550, 19. Mid godcundre onbryrdnysse monad *divino admonitus instinctu*, Bd. 1, 23; S. 485, 24: 4, 32; S. 611, 39. Mid ða godcundan onbryrdnesse monad, 5, 6; S. 620, 1. Þurh ðæs sóþan Godes onbryrdnysse *inspirante Deo vero*, 2, 13; S. 517, 17: Blickl. Homl. 119, 18. v. in-bryrdness.

on-búgan; *p.* -beáh. I. *to bend*:—Ðonne ic onbúge *when I (a bow) bend*, Exon. Th. 405, 16; Rä. 24, 3. II. *to bend in reverence* or *submission, to bow*:—Heó tó hyre módor cneówum onbeáh, Lchdm. iii. 428, 13. Hís gebróðru onbugon tó him (*proni adorantes*), Gen. 50, 18. Ða ðe nolden tó his libbendum líchaman onbúgan, ða nú eádmódlíce on cneówum ábúgaþ tó his deádum bánum, Chr. 979; Erl. 129, 20: Ors. 6, 9; Swt. 264, 9. III. *to submit, yield*:—Ðú eart rihtwís and nánum ne onbíhst, Homl. Th. ii. 298, 33. Hé nǽnigum woruldrícum men þurh leáse ólecunga swíðor onbúgan nolde, ðonne hit riht wǽre, Blickl. Homl. 223, 28. Beó ðú onbúgende ðínum wiðerwinnan, Mt. Kmbl. 5, 25. IV. *to bend aside, deviate*:—Ic onbúgan ne mót of ðæs gewealde ðe mé wegas tǽcneþ, Exon. Th. 383, 24; Rä. 4, 15. v. an-búgan, on-bígan.

on-bútan; *prep.* (*adv.*) *with dat. acc. About.* I. of place:—Gewríðe onbútan (MS. H. ábútan) ðæs mannes swyran, Lchdm. i. 160, 23. Feówer circulas onbútan ðære sunnan, Chr. 1104; Erl. 239, 18. Se here sceolde bión getrymed onbútan Hierusalem, Past. 21; Swt. 161, 25. Seó eá gǽþ onbútan ðæt land, Gen. 2, 11. Ðæt folc him sáh eall onbútan, Homl. Skt. i. 23, 651. II. of time:—Onbútan Martines mæssan and gyt lator, Chr. 1089; Erl. 226, 19. III. *with* ðǽr:—Æt Hocneratúne and ðǽr onbútan, 917; Erl. 102, 14. Ofer eall ðǽr onbútan, Homl. Skt. i. 23, 490, 660.

on-býgan, -byrgan. v. on-bígan, -birgan.

on-cennan; *p.* de *To bear* (*a child*), *bring forth*:—Mǽden sceal oncennan sunu, Ælfc. T. Grn. 9, 11. Sí oncenned *nascatur*, Kent. Gl. 984. v. á-cennan.

on-cígung, e; *f. Invocation, invoking*:—Ðerh onceigunge *per invocationem*, Rtl. 114, 3: 122, 3. Onceigince, 147, 27.

on-cirran, -cerran, -cyrran; *p.* de. A. in a physical sense. I. (a) *to turn* (*trans.*) *make a change in position* or *direction*:—Hé oncyrde hine tó Paule *he turned to Paul*, Blickl. Homl. 183, 30: 185, 36. Ðæt hié hine móston on óðre sídan oncyrran, 227, 19. Andwlitan út oncyrran *faciem avertere*, Ps. Th. 131, 10. Wénst ðú ðæt ðú ðæt hwerfende hweól ðonne hit on ryne wyrþ mǽge oncyrran *tu vero volventis rotae impetum retinere conaris?* Bt. 7, 2; Fox 18, 36. Oncerran, Met. 10, 39. Oncirredre *prepostero*, Wrt. Voc. ii. 67, 23. (b) *to turn* (*into another form*):—Ða lástas on óðerne mǽgwlite oncyrran, Blickl. Homl. 127, 19. II. *to turn* (*intrans.*) *to go*:—Ðá oncerde se wind from ðære byrig, Bd. 3, 16; S. 543, 7. Hé þyder oncirde, Beo. Th. 5933; B. 2970: 5895; B. 2951. Ýða ongin eft oncyrde, Andr. Kmbl. 932; An. 466. B. in a metaphorical sense. I. (a) *to turn, make a person adopt a line of conduct*, etc.:—Se nýdde Clementem ðæt hé Cryste wiðsóce, ðá ne mihte hé hyne oncyrran *he could not turn him*, Shrn. 150, 18. Angan þencean hú hé þider meahte Crécas oncerran, Met. 1, 61. (b) *to turn, change*:—Ðú ða wyrde oncyrrest *fata mutabis*, Nar. 31, 24. Hí mé ðæt on edwít eft oncyrdan *factum est mihi in opprobrium*, Ps. Th. 68, 10. Nergend him naman oncyrde, Elen. Kmbl. 1004; El. 503. Ne meahte hé ðæs wealdendes willan oncirran, Beo. Th. 5707; B. 2857. Hí woldon his mód oncyrran, Andr. Kmbl. 2921; An. 1463. Hé ne meahte hire mód oncyrran *he could not make her change her mind*, Exon. Th. 256, 4; Jul. 226. (c) *to turn from good to bad, to pervert*:—Ðus ic sóðfæstum mód oncyrre, 264, 13; Jul. 363. Ðæt wé þurh misgedwield mód oncyrren, 262, 2; Jul. 268. Hyge wæs oncyrred (*by a magical drink*), Andr. Kmbl. 72; An. 36. Ðú miht ongiton hú se mín weorþscipe for worulde is oncerred *quantum decus ornamentis nostris decesserit, vides*, Bt. 10; Fox 30, 15. (d) *to turn aside, avert*:—Ðín yrre fram ús oncyrre, Ps. Th. 84, 4. Oncyrran, 78, 5. Oncyrran mód from his Meotude, Exon. Th. 124, 8; Gú. 336. (e) *to turn back, reverse* (*a sentence*), *revoke*:—Ðú yrre ðín eft oncyrdest, Ps. Th. 70, 19. Hé ða yrmðu eft oncyrde æt his upstige, Exon. Th. 38, 30; Cri. 614. Ða word oncyr *retract the words*, 251, 13; Jul. 144. Wæs se dóm oncyrred Euan ungesǽlignesse, Blickl. Homl. 3, 8. Wearþ se sárlíca cwide eft oncerred, 123, 7. II. *to turn* (*intrans.*):—Hié fram heora unrihtum oncyrron, Blickl. Homl. 109, 20.

on-clifiende; *adj. Sticking to, persistent*:—On forhæfednysse and on clǽnnysse fæsthafule and onclyfiende *in abstinence and purity constant and persistent*, Cod. Dip. B. i. 154, 37. v. clifian.

on-clipian *to invoke*:—Enos ongan ǽrest onclypian (*invocare*) Drihtnes naman, Gen. 4, 26.

on-cnǽwe; *adj. Known, recognised*:—Oncnǽwe *cognitum*, Ps. Spl. T. 33, 5. Cf. ge-cnǽwe.

on-cnáwan; *p.* -cneów; *pp.* -cnáwen *To know;* noscere, cognoscere, agnoscere:—Ic oncnáwe *nosco, cognosco*, ic ancnáwe *agnosco*, Ælfc. Gr. 28, 1; Som. 30, 31–32. Tó angitanne and tó oncnáwenne *animadverti*, Wrt. Voc. ii. 2, 44. Beón oncnáwen *conici* (cf. 23, 50), 23, 78. I. *to know, recognise*, (1) *to identify an object through being acquainted with its characteristics, to distinguish*, (a) of persons:—Se oxa oncneów his hláford, Homl. Th. i. 42, 25. Hí hine (*Jesus*) on ðam gereorde oncneówon, ðone ðe hí ne mihton on onwrigennysse háliges gewrites oncnáwan, 284, 33–34. Ðæt is éce líf, ðæt hí ðé oncnáwon sóðne God, and ðone ðe ðú ásendest, 42, 14: ii. 362, 22. Frán hwæðer hit oncneówe his fóstermódor, Bt. 3, 1; Fox 4, 28. Ðeáh ðe hé wundra fela gecýðde, synnige ne mihton oncnáwan ðæt cynebearn, Andr. Kmbl. 1131; An. 566. Hé is ancnáwen *dinoscitur, agnoscitur*, Hpt. Gl. 440, 32. Ðú wǽre ǽfre fǽmne oncnáwen, Glostr. Frag. 106, 8. Biþ oncnáwen Drihten dómas wyrcende *cognoscetur Dominus judicia faciens*, Ps. Spl. 9, 17. (b) of things:—Heáh feorran hé oncnáwaþ *alta a longe cognoscit*, 137, 7. Ná ic hit swá oncneów swá hit ðín ǽ hafaþ *I did not recognise it* (*what was said*) *as what is in thy law*, Ps. Th. 118, 85. Ic his word oncneów, ðéh hé his mǽgwlite bemiðen hæfde, Andr. Kmbl. 1710; An. 857: Beo. Th. 5102; B. 2554. Se assa oncneów his hláfordes binne, Homl. Th. i. 42, 25. Ðæt ðú oncnáwe (*cognoscas*) ðara worda sóðfæstnesse, Lk. Skt. 1, 4. Ðæt ðás nytenan menn ðíne mihta oncnáwon, Homl. Th. i. 62, 14. Hié ðæt ongeotan ne cúðan, ðæt hié gehýrdon, ne ðæt oncnáwan ne mihton ðæt hié gesáwon, Blickl. Homl. 105, 29: 95, 10. Ðú meaht sóða gesǽlþa sóna oncnáwan, Met. 12, 30: Elen. Kmbl. 790; El. 395. Oncnáwan hwǽr wé sǽlan sceolon sundhengestas, Exon. Th. 54, 1; Cri. 862. Ðíne fótswaða nǽron oncnáwene, Ps. Lamb. 76, 20. (2) *to recognise a fact* (which is generally stated in a clause beginning with *ðæt*:—Wundra weorc ðíne and sáwle mín oncnáweþ (*knows that thy works are wonderful*), Ps. Spl. 138, 13. Be ðam oncnáwaþ ealle men, ðæt gé synt míne leorningcnihtas, Jn. Skt. 13, 35. Ic oncneów (*cognovi*) ðæt ðú ondrǽtst swýðe God, Gen. 22, 12. Ðá se déma ðæt oncneów and ongæt (*persensit*), ðæt hé hine oferswíðan ne mihte, Bd. 1, 7; S. 478, 1: 5, 9; S. 623, 21. Ðá cwæþ eal folc ðæt hé Godes sunu wǽre, and ðæt fulfremedlíce oncneówan, Blickl. Homl. 177, 20. Hig oncneówon, ðæt hig nacode wǽron, Gen. 3, 7: Mk. Skt. 12, 12. Oncnáw ðæt míne welan syndon gewitene, Blickl. Homl. 113, 24. Tó ðam earde ðe fléwþ meolce and hunige, swá swá gé of ðissum wæstmum oncnáwan mágon, Num. 13, 28. Geseón and oncnáwan and swíðe gearelíce ongeotan ðæt ðisses middangeardes ende neáh is, Blickl. Homl. 107, 22: 115, 5. Be ðam man mihte oncnáwan ðæt se cniht nolde wácian æt ðam wíge, Byrht. Th. 131, 16; By. 9. II. *to know, understand, attain to a knowledge of*:—Gyt gé ne oncnáwaþ ne ne ongitaþ, Mk. Skt. 8, 17. Ðú míne geþohtas oncneówe *intellexisti cogitationes meas*, Ps. Th. 138, 2, 3. Ðá oncneówon hig be ðam worde *cognoverunt de verbo*, Lk. Skt. 2, 17: Homl. Th. i. 30, 32. Hé ða yldestan lǽrde, ðæt heó wísdómes word oncneówan, Ps. Th. 104, 18. Ða mægnu tweónedon be ðære gýtsunge, ðæt hió fullíce hió ne oncnéwon, Gl. Prud. 64 a. Oncnáwaþ ða ðing ðe eówre bearn nyton, Deut. 11, 2. Dysige ðæt oncnáwan *stulti sapite*, Ps. Th. 93, 8. Ic ðínra worda ne mæg wuht oncnáwan, Cd. Th. 34, 8; Gen. 534. Oncnáwan, hú hine lýgnedon leáse, Exon. Th. 69, 12; Cri. 1119. III. *to know, learn by observation, observe, perceive*:—Gif ic mé unrihtes oncneów áwiht on heortan *iniquitatem si conspexi in corde meo*, Ps. Th. 65, 16. Oncnáw onsýne Cristes ðínes *respice in faciem christi tui*, 83, 9. Oncnáw paþas míne *cognoscite semitas meas*, Ps. Spl. 138, 22. Ða deóflu æteówiaþ ðære synfullan sáwle hyre mánfullan dǽda, ðæt heó oncnáwe mid hwilcum feóndum heó ymbset biþ, Homl. Th. i. 410, 9. IV. *to acknowledge*, (1) *make acknowledgment of a fault*:—Wé oncnáwaþ eal ðæt wé geworhton on worldríce, ne mágon we hit dyrnan, Hy. Grn. 7, 90. Ðæt hé mihte oncnáwan his mánfullan dǽda on ðam hæftnéde, Ælfc. T. Grn. 8, 21. (2) *to acknowledge a greeting*:—Iosep hig oncneów árfullíce *clementer resalutatis eis*, Gen. 43, 27. (3) *to acknowledge the power of another* (?):—Elias eorl ðe ða Mannie of ðam cynge geheóld and oncneów (-cweow, MS.), Chr. 1110; Erl. 243, 11.

on-cnáwenness, e; *f.* I. *recognition, knowledge* (*that an object is what it really is*):—Wé habbaþ ðæt éce líf þurh geleáfan, and oncnáwennysse ðære Hálgan Þrynnesse, gif wé ða oncnáwennysse mid árwurþnysse healdaþ. Witodlíce gif Godes oncnáwennys ús gearcaþ ðæt éce líf, swá miccle swíðor wé éfstaþ tó lybbenne swá micclum swá wé swíðor on ðissere oncnáwennysse þeónde beóþ. Sóðlíce ne swelte wé on ðam écan lífe; ðonne biþ ús Godes oncnáwennys fulfremed. . . . Ac wé sceolon on andwerdum lífe leornian Godes oncnáwennysse . . . ðæt wé móton becuman tó his fulfremedan oncnáwennysse, Homl. Th. ii. 362, 32–364, 9. Hé nolde him æteówian his oncnáwennysse *he would not let them recognise him* (cf. l. 16, hé him ne geswutelode hwæt hé wæs), 284, 12. Ða deóflu æteówiaþ ðære synfullan sáwle hyre mánfullan dǽda . . . Tó eorþan heó biþ ástreht þurh hire scylda oncnáwennysse (*on recognising her guilt*), i. 410, 12. II. *acknowledgment, recognition of a claim*:—Ðonne ys ðis seó oncnáwennis ðe hé hæfþ God mid gecnáwen . . . on circlícum mádmum, Chart. Th. 429, 7.

on-cnáwness, e; *f. Knowledge, conception*:—Hé hiene bedǽlþ ðære oncnáwnesse ðæs uplecan leóhtes *a luce se supernae cognitionis excludit*, Past. 11, 4; Swt. 69, 24.

on-cnyssan *to cast down*:—Ðú mé yfela feala oft oncnyssedest *thou didst strike me down with many evils*, Ps. Th. 70, 19. Oncnyssyde *depulsae*, Ps. Spl. C. 61, 3.

on-cunnan; *p.* -cúðe; *pp.* -cunnen *To accuse a person* (acc.) *of something* (gen., clause beginning with *ðæt*, or with prep. *be, for*), *to blame, charge, lay to a person's charge*:—Ðonne oncann hé hiene selfne for ðære hrædhýdignesse ðe hé ǽr tó fela sealde *occasionem contra se im-*

patientiae enquirit, Past. 44, 4; Swt. 325, 16. Ic him mīn wedd beád, ðæt ic hyra nǣfre nǣnne ne oncūðe, for ðon ðe hȳ on riht sprǣcon, Chart. Th. 486, 21. Mē mīne āgen word sōcon swȳðe oncūðan *verba mea execrabantur*, Ps. Th. 55, 5. Ðonne oncūðon (*impugnabant*) hié mē būtan scylde, Past. 46, 7; Swt. 355, 15. Hié sylfe be ðon oncūðon, ðæt hié swā ne dydon, Blickl. Homl. 215, 12. Gif hwā ōðerne godborges oncunne, L. Alf. pol. 33; Th. i. 82, 5. Ðȳ læs ðec Meotud oncunne, ðæt ðū sȳ wommes gewita, Exon. Th. 301, 13; Fä. 18. Ðæt ūs God ne þurfa oncunnan for ðæræ waniungæ *nec nobis Deus debeat imputare hanc imminutionem*, Chart. Th. 163, 25. Oncunnen *notatus*, Wrt. Voc. ii. 114, 81. Hē wæs oncunnen (*accusatus*) fram ðam ylcan cyninge, Bd. 5, 19; S. 640, 9. Tō oncunnyne oncunnysse *ad excusandas excusationes*, Ps. Spl. M. C. 140, 4. v. next word.

on-cunness, e; *f. An accusation* (?), *excuse* (?):—Tō ācunnenne oncunnisse *ad excusandas excusationes*, Ps. Surt. 140, 4. v. on-cunnan.

on-cunning, e; *f. An accusation*:—Mid gelōmlīcum oncunningum *crebris accusationibus*, Bd. 3, 19; S. 548, 3.

on-cweðan. I. of animate beings, *to reply, respond*:—Oft mec slǣpwērigne secg grētan eode, ic him oncweðe, Exon. Th. 387, 18. Him Andreas oncwæð, Andr. Kmbl. 540; An. 470: 1109; An. 555. Him Babilone weard andswarode and oncwæð, Cd. Th. 229, 3; Dan. 211: 53, 23; Gen. 865. Judas cwæð . . . him oncwæð cāseres mǣg, Elen. Kmbl. 1334; El. 669. Stormas stānclifu beótan, him stearn oncwæð, Exon. Th. 307, 14; Seef. 23. Swilce ealle ða anlícnyssa ðe on ðære byrig tō godon gesette wǣron, ðæt hī ealle ætgædere oncwǣdon and ānre stemne clypedon, ðæt hī āweg ðanon woldon . . . and swilce ða strǣta ealle eác oncwǣdon, Homl. Skt. i. 23, 93–98. Ne sculon mæssepreóstas būtan ōðrum mannum mæssan syngan, ðæt hē wite hwone hē grēte, and hwā him oncwæðe, L. E. I. 7; Th. ii. 406, 23. Ðæt hió ðære cwēne oncweðan meahton . . . swā hió him tō sōhte, Elen. Kmbl. 648; El. 324. II. of inanimate things, *to echo back, give back a sound, reply*:—Oncwyð *remugiet*, Hpt. Gl. 513, 12. Scyld scefte oncwyð, Fins. Th. 12; Fin. 7. Ðæt him se weald oncwyð . . . wudu eallum oncwyð, Met. 13, 46–50: Bt. 25; Fox 88, 20. Oft oncwæð ȳð ōðerre, Andr. Kmbl. 884; An. 442.

on-cȳð[ð], e; *f. Grief, distress*:—Denum eallum wæs weorce on mōde, oncȳð eorla gehwæm, syððan Æscheres hafelan mētton, Beo. Th. 2844; B. 1420. Hæfde Eást-Denum gilp gelǣsted, swylce oncȳððe ealle gebētte, 1664; B. 830.

on-cȳðan *to make known, announce*:—Ðā ðā ic on eard com ic oncȳðde ealle folce hwæt ic on Rōme gedōn hæfde, Chart. Th. 117, 1.

oncȳð-dǣd, e; *f. A deed causing distress, an injury*:—Oncȳðdǣda wrecan, Andr. Kmbl. 2360; An. 1181.

on-cȳðig; *adj. Suffering from the want of something* (?), *not acquainted with, a stranger to anything* (?); cf. un-cȳðig:—Elnes oncȳðig *suffering from weakness* (?) or *a stranger to strength* (?), Elen. Kmbl. 1446; El. 725. *The term is used of Judas, to whom the previous lines* 1392–3 *refer*:—Mēðe and meteleás, mægen wæs geswiðrod.

ond, ond-. v. and, and-.

on-dǣlan *to impart, infuse*; infundere, Rtl. 17, 11: 85, 39: Lk. Skt. Lind. 10, 34.

on-dǣlend, es; *m. One who imparts*:—Mægna sellend and bloedsunga ondǣlend *virtutum dator et benedictionum infusor*, Rtl. 103, 38.

ond-efen, on-derslīc, -deslīc, -desn. v. and-efn, on-dryslīc, -drysnu.

on-dōn *to undo, open*:—Ondēst *solvat*, Wrt. Voc. ii. 120, 79. Ðonne andydan hié ða duru, Ors. 3, 5; Swt. 106, 14. Siont ondōne *aperientur*, Kent. Gl. 232.

on-dōung, e; *f. A putting in, injection*:—Mid ondōunge wyrtdrences þurh horn sió wamb biþ tō clǣnsianne, Lchdm. ii. 260, 11.

on-drǣdan; *p.* -drēd, -drǣd, -dreard, -dreord; *pp.* -drǣd *to dread, fear*; timeo. I. with construction undetermined:—Ondrēt *obstupuit*, Hpt. Gl. 510, 23. Ondreard *timuit*, Mt. Kmbl. Lind. 2, 22. Ic ondreord *timui*, Ps. Surt. 118, 120. Ondreord *timuit*, 63, 10. Ondreordun, 63, 6. Ondreardon *timuerunt*, Mt. Kmbl. Lind. 9, 8. Ondreardon (-dreordun, Rush.), Mk. Skt. 10, 32: 11, 18. II. with acc. or gen. of object, and (a) with a reflexive dative:—Ic ondrǣde mē God *Deum timeo*, Gen. 42, 18. Ic mē ondrǣde *timeo, metuo*. Se ðe him ondrǣt, sumes þinges hē him ondrǣt, *timeo Deum* ic mē ondrǣde God; *timeor* ic eom ondrǣd, ðæt is, ðæt sumum menn stent ege fram mē, Ælfc. Gr. 19; Som. 22, 62–64. Ne ðū ðē nihtegsan ondrǣdest, Ps. Th. 90, 5. Se ðe him ǣlc wolcn ondrǣdt, ne rīpþ se nǣfre, Past. 39; Swt. 285, 18. Hē him ondrǣt his deáþes, Homl. Skt. i. 12, 87. Hwā him ne ondrēde ðæs cyninges irre? Ap. Th. 2, 18. (b) without the reflexive dative:—Ic hine swīðe ondrǣde, Gen. 32, 11. Ðū ondrǣtst swȳðe God, 22, 12. Se ðe ǣgðer ondrǣt, ge ðone ðe hine ondrǣt, ge ðone ðe hine nā ne ondrǣt, Bt. 29, 1; Fox 104, 5–6. Herodes ondrēd (-dreard, Lind.: -dreord, Rush.) Johannem, Mk. Skt. 6, 20. Ðæt hig hine ondrēdon, swā swā hig ondrēdon Moysen, Jos. 4, 14. III. with the prep. *from*:—Swā egefull wæs Alexander ðā ðā hē wæs on eásteweardum ðissum middangearde, ðætte ða from him ondrēdan ðe wǣron on westeweardum, Ors. 3, 9; Swt. 136, 7. Hié alle from him ondrēdon, ðæt hī hié mid gefeohten, 1, 10; Swt. 48, 16. IV. without an object, and with reflexive dative, *to be afraid*:—Hié word Drihtnes gehȳrdon and ondrēdon him, Cd. Th. 53, 15; Gen. 861. Ða weras ðā ðæt gesāwon hié him swīðe ondrǣdon, and cwǣdon, Blickl. Homl. 247, 16. Ne ondrǣd ðū ðē, Elen. Kmbl. 162; El. 81. Ne wilt ðū ðē ondrǣdan Zacharias, Blickl. Homl. 165, 7. Him ðā ondrǣdendum ðǣm gebrōðrum, Ors. 1, 5; Swt. 34, 1.

on-drǣdendlīc; *adj. To be feared, terrible*:—Hē wǣs swīðe strang and swīðe ondrǣdendlīc *he (William Rufus) was very severe, and very terrible*, Chr. 1100; Erl. 235, 39. Gif ðes bealdwyrda biscop ācweald ne biþ, siððan ne biþ ūre ege ondrǣdendlīc, Homl. Th. i. 420, 3. Ðises godspelles geendung is swīðe ondrǣdendlīc: 'Fela sind geladode, and feáwa gecorene,' ii. 82, 3.

on-drǣding, e; *f. Dread, terror*:—Hié selfe wǣron on ðære ondrǣdinge hwonne hié on ða eorþan besuncene wurden, Ors. 2, 6; Swt. 88, 14. Hē sume hwīle wēnde ðæt hine mon gefōn sceolde, and hē for ðære ondrǣdinge ðæs ðe swīðor on ðæt weorod þrong, 5, 12; Swt. 244, 12.

on-drencan *to inebriate*:—Hī wǣron ondrencte mid oferdrynce, Guthl. 14; Gdwin. 62, 20. v. in-drencan.

on-drincan *to drink of* (with gen.):—Ða ðe on wege weorðaþ wætres æt hlimman deópes ondrincaþ *de torrente in via bebet*, Ps. Th. 109, 8. Ðā ondranc se ðæs wætres, and sealde hit ðǣm brēðer . . . and se ondranc eác ðæs wætres, Shrn. 64, 11–12. Bæd ðæt hē him onsende wīnes ondrincan, Bd. 5, 5; S. 618, 11. Sioððan hié hæfdon ondruncen ðæs wætres *potata aqua*, Nar. 13, 28.

on-drislīc. v. on-dryslīc.

on-druncnian *to get drunk*:—Beóþ ondruncniende *inebriabuntur*, Ps. Spl. T. 35, 9.

on-dryslīc, -drystlīc, -dyrstlīc, -deslīc; *adj. Terrible, dreadful*:—Ūs is tō geþencanne hū onþrislīc (-dryslīc: egeslīc, other MS.) hit on bōcum gecweden is, L. Ath. i. prm.; Th. i. 196, 4. Cwæð ðæt se mon wǣre ondrysenlīc (onderslīc, MS. T.: ondrislīc, MS. B.) on tō seónne (*terribilis aspectu*), Bd. 2, 16; S. 519, 35. Ondeslīc *terribilis*, Rtl. 69, 4: *orror* (?), 162, 28. Ācwellan ondryslīcum wītum, Shrn. 111, 10. Þreágan mid ondrystlīcum wītum, 104, 16. Gif hwilc mon sīe on ondyrstlecum wīsum (*in dreadful straits*), and hē sȳ mīnes naman gemyndig, Drihten, gefriða ðū hine from ðǣm brōgan, 101, 30. Sum sume swīðe ondryslīcu (*tremenda*) secgende wæs, Bd. 5, 12 tit.; S. 627, 3. v. following words.

on-drysne; *adj.* I. applied to that which is evil, *terrible, dreadful, awful*:—Firen ondrysne *terrible crime*, Beo. Th. 3869; B. 1932. II. applied to that which is good, *awful, exciting awe* or *reverence, venerable*:—Him wæs freán engla word ondrysne, Cd. Th. 173, 14; Gen. 2861. Wæs hē for his ārfæstum dǣdum eallum his geferum leóf and weorð and ondrysne *he was beloved, honoured and reverenced by all his companions for his pious deeds*, Blickl. Homl. 213, 12. Ðæt hȳ messan singan and ða andrysnan þēnunge mid ārwyrþnesse gefyllen, R. Ben. 140, 5. *See other examples under* an-drysne.

on-drysness, -desness, e; *f. Fear*:—Ondesnisse *timoris*, Rtl. 3, 24.

on-drysnlīc, -drysenlīc; *adj. Terrible*:—Mē ætȳwde ondrysnlīco gesihþ *visio mihi tremenda apparuit*, Bd. 5, 19; S. 640, 36. Ondrysenlīc *terribilis*, 2, 16; S. 519, 35. Ðā ætȳwde hire micel mon and ondrysnlīc, Shrn. 106, 9. Hē wæs of līchoman ālǣded, and hē geseah mā ondrysnlīces and eác wundorlīces ðonne hē mihte āsecgan, 51, 31. v. on-dryslīc, *and see other examples under* an-drysenlīc.

on-drysnu, -desnu; *f.* I. *fear*:—Fore ondesne (ondesnum, Rush.) *propter metum*, Jn. Skt. Lind. 19, 38: 20, 19. Ðætte sió forsewennes him ege and ondrysnu on gebringe *ut ostensa desperatio formidinem incutiat*, Past. 37, 2; Swt. 265, 19. Hē wolde ðǣm fortrūwodum monnum andrysno hālwendes eges on gebrengean *ut praecipitatis vim saluberrimi timoris infunderet*, 49, 5; Swt. 385, 16. Ðonne esne ondrysnum his hlāforde cwemeþ, Ps. Th. 122, 2. II. *reverence*:—Hié hæfdan miccle lufan and geleáfan tō ðære ciricean, ond eác heálīco ondrysnu (*profound reverence for the church*), Blickl. Homl. 205, 9. v. an-drysno.

on-drystlīc, -dyrstlīc. v. on-dryslīc.

on-dwæscan *to extinguish*:—Se mōna ðe byþ andwæsced oððe āteorod, Anglia viii. 316, 38. v. ā-dwæscan.

on-ealdian *to grow old*:—Onealdodon bān mīne *inveteraverunt ossa mea*, Ps. Spl. 31, 6.

on-eardian *to inhabit*:—Oneardiaþ on ðam *inhabitabunt in ea*, Blickl. Gl. Rihtwīse oneardiaþ (*inhabitabunt*), Ps. Spl. 36, 31. Onearda *inhabita*, 36, 28. Ealle oneardigende ymbhwyrft *omnes inhabitantes orbem*, 32, 8.

on-eardiend, es; *m. An inhabitant*:—Ne on heora ēðele ne sy þinc oneardiendes *et in tabernaculis eorum non sit qui inhabitet*, Ps. Th. 68, 26.

on-efn, -emn, -em *by, near*:—Hī gemētton fȳr, and hlāf onem *they found a fire, and bread close by*, Homl. Th. ii. 262, 5. Onefen ðone hagan . . . norþ onefen ðæt gelād, Cod. Dip. Kmbl. ii. 150, 10–13.

Onemn ðæm *at the same time*, Ors. 3, 9; Swt. 128, 33. *See* efn, emn *for other examples.*

on-égan; *p.* de *To fear*:—Sǽton him at wíne, wealle belocene, ne onégdon ná orlegra níð, Cd. Th. 259, 25; Dan. 697. Ic mé onégan (onagen, MS.) mæg, ðæt mé wráðra sum wǽpnes ecge feore beneóte, 109, 28; Gen. 1829. Ni anoegun (anoegu ná?) ic mé aerigfaerae egsan brógum, Txts. 151, 13. Cf. óga.

on-erian *to plough up*:—Wé má lufiaþ ðone æcer ðe ǽr wæs mid þornum áswógen and æfter ðæm ðe ða þornas beóþ áheáwene and se æker biþ onered bringþ gódne wæsðm *plus terram diligimus, quae post spinas exarata fructus uberes producit*, Past. 52, 9; Swt. 411, 18.

on-éðung, e; *f. In-breathing, inspiration*:—From onoeðunge gástes, Ps. Surt, 17, 16.

onettan; *p.* te. I. *to hasten, move rapidly*:—Ǽlc wlite tó ende éfsteþ and onetteþ, Blickl. Homl. 57, 28. Tó ðam onet Egeas unforwandodlíce, Homl. Th. i. 592, 17. Deáþ eów ǽlce dæg tóweardes onet, Bt. 39, 1; Fox 210, 28. Eall moncynn irnaþ and onettaþ, 37, 2; Fox 188, 14. Hé onette on ðære byrig him tó fultume, Jos. 10, 33. Hé wið mín onette, Homl. Th. ii. 352, 4. Wið ðæs fæstengeates folc onette, Judth. Thw. 23, 39; Jud. 162. Ðá onette Abrahames mǽg tó ðam fæstenne, Cd. Th. 153, 3; Gen. 2533. Éfste ðá swíðe and onette forþ foldwege, 174, 3; Gen. 2872. Hié swíðe on ða úre wíc onetton and in ða feóllon *ad castra confluxere*, Nar. 13, 14. Onettad *agitate*, Wrt. Voc. ii. 99, 56. Onettendum (*festinantibus*) cretum, 147, 80. II. *to make a quick movement, to anticipate*:—Onette *occupavit*, 63, 30. Hé gebrægd his swurd and wolde mé ofsleán ðǽr ic him ne onette and ic ðæt wíf gegripe be hire earme and mé tóforan ábrǽd and ðǽr ðis nǽre ðonne wǽre mín blód instæpe ágoten *he drew his sword and would have slain me, if I had not anticipated him, and had seized the woman by her arm, and drew her before me; and if it had not been for this, my blood would have been straightway shed*, Shrn. 39, 16. III. *to be quick in one's movements* or *actions, be active, quick* or *busy*:—Byrig fægriaþ wongas wlitigaþ woruld onetteþ *fair grow the towns, beauteous the plains, the world is quickened* (*in the spring*), Exon. Th. 308, 34; Seef. 49. Lég onetteþ *busy shall the flame be* (*at the day of judgment*), 448, 17; Dóm. 55: 212, 29; Ph. 217. Sceal onettan se ðe ágan wile líf æt Meotude ðenden him leóht and gǽst somod fæst seón *diligent must he be, while light and spirit hold fast together, who life will receive at the hands of the Lord*, 96, 24; Cri. 1529. Rǽd sceal mon secgan, dæges onettan (cf. *the night cometh, when no man can work*), 342, 11; Gn. Ex. 141. [Cf. *O. H. Ger.* anazzan *sollicitare, excitare, inflammare, hortari, instigare.*]

onettung, e; *f. Hastening, haste, precipitation*:—Oft ða oferblíðan weorðaþ gedréfde for ungemetlícre onettunga *gravatur usu immoderatae praecipitationis*, Past. 61, 1; Swt. 455, 15.

on-fægnian *to shew gladness*:—Ðære helle hund ongan onfægnian mid his steorte *Cerberus shewed his gladness by wagging his tail*, Bt. 35, 6; Fox 168, 17 note.

on-færeld, es; *n. An in-going, entrance*:—Gesáwon onfæreldu *viderunt ingressus*, Ps. Spl. 67, 26. v. an-, in-færeld.

on-fæstnian *to transfix, pierce*:—Hig geseóþ on hwæne hig onfæstnodon *videbunt in quem transfixerunt*, Jn. Skt. 19, 37. Onfæstna (*confige*) ege ðínum flǽsc míne, Ps. Spl. 118, 120.

on-fæðmness, e; *f. Embrace*:—Seó onbláwnes ðære heofonlícan onfæðmnesse sý gewindwod on ðé (*the Virgin Mary*), Blickl. Homl. 7, 26.

on-fangenness, e; *f. Receiving, reception, acceptance*:—Mid Gode nis anfangenness (onfangenes, MS. T.) nánra háda bútan geearnunge ánre (cf. *God is no respecter of persons, but he that worketh righteousness is accepted with him*, Acts 10, 34–35), R. Ben. 13, 4. Seó onfangenes ðæs ríces is of Godes gódnysse, Homl. Th. ii. 80, 23. Nán ásolcen man nis orsorh be onfangennysse Godes feós, 556, 24, 33. Mid onfangennesse (*perceptione*) ðæs Drihtenlícan líchoman, Bd. 4, 3; S. 568, 39. For onfangenysse (*susceptionem*) gesta, 1, 27; S. 489, 8. v. on-fengness.

on-fealdan; *p.* -feóld *To unfold, unwrap*:—Hé onfeóld hys hrægl æt hys sceoldrum, Shrn. 98, 17. v. un-fealdan.

on-feall *a swelling, fellon*:—Wið onfealle, gefóh fox, ásleah of cucum ðone tuxl, lǽt hleápan áweg, bind on næsce, hafa ðé on, Lchdm. ii. 104, 12. Drenc wið onfealle, 102, 27: 104, 1, 3, 4, 6. Lǽcedomas wið ǽlces cynnes ómum ond onfeallum and báncoþum, 98, 21: 102, 20. Wið innanonfealle, 106, 9. Onfelle, 106, 10.

on-feallende; *part. On-rushing*:—From ðære onfeallendan *ab ingruenti*, Wrt. Voc. ii. 3, 34. Ða unstillnesse ðara onfeallendra menigeo *tumultus irruentium turbarum*, Bd. 3, 19; S. 549, 32.

on-feng, es; *m.* [v. fón (on)]. I. *laying hold of, seizing*:—Be cirliscre fǽmnan onfenge. Gif mon on cirliscre fǽmnan breóst gefó, L. Alf. pol. 11; Th. i. 68, 13. Be nunnena onfenge (andfengum, MS. B.: anfenge, MS. H.), 18; Th. i. 72, 7. Be þeófes onfenge æt þiéfþe, L. In. 28; Th. i. 120, 4. Secg wundaþ beorna gehwylcne ðe him ǽnigne onfeng gedéþ *sedge cuts every one that lays hold of it*, Runic pm. 15; Kmbl. 342, 14. II. *taking*, with the idea of wrongful taking:—Be wuda onfenge (andfenge, MS. H.: anfenge, MS. B.) bútan leáfe, L. In. 44; Th. i. 130, 1. Be unáliéfedes mæstennes onfenge, 49; Th. i. 132, 11. III. *defence, protection* (cf. and-fenga):—Wǽron ða hálgan on onfenge manna sáulum, Blickl. Homl. 209, 29. IV. *attack, onset, assault*:—Wurdon hié on ðam onfenge forhte, and on fleám numen, Andr. Kmbl. 2679; An. 1341. Hé hine scilde wið onfengom earmra gǽsta, Exon. Th. 126, 24; Gú. 376; 133, 15; Gú. 490. v. an-feng.

on-fenge, es; *m. A receptacle*:—Anfengce *receptaculum*, Hpt. Gl. 498, 32. Anfencgas *receptacula*, 408, 51.

on-fenge; *adj. Taken, accepted*:—Onfenge *adsumtus*, Mk. Skt. Lind. 16, 19. Mið ðý onfenge woeron *assumtis*, Lk. Skt. Lind. 9, 10: *acceptis*, 9, 16. Án geonfenge (onfenge, Rush.) biþ *una assumetur*, 17, 35. Onfengo *suscepta*, Rtl. 9, 7. v. and-fenge.

on-fengness, e; *f. Reception, acceptance*:—Seó onfengnes Cristes geleáfan, Bd. 2, 9; S. 510, 12. Be ðære onfengnysse Cristes geleáfan *de percipienda fide Cristi*, 2, 13 tit; S. 515, 33. Ymb xl nihta ðæs sǽdes onfengnesse *xl dies post semen receptum*, L. Ecg. C. 30, note; Th. ii. 154, 36. Þurh ða onfengnesse ðæs Hálgan Gástes, Blickl. Homl. 135, 35. v. and-fengness.

on-findan; *p.* -fand, -funde. I. *to find out, discover, detect*:—Ic anfinde *deprehendo*, Wrt. Voc. ii. 25, 32. Gif mec onfindeþ wíga, ðǽr ic búge, Exon. Th. 396, 20; Rä. 16, 7. Ic mé sylf onfand ðæt . . . *I discovered that* . . . , Blickl. Homl. 177, 6. Ic hine onfand, and hine onbændan hét, Salm. Kmbl. 550; Sal. 274. Ne ic culpan in ðé ǽfre onfunde, Exon. Th. 11, 30; Cri. 178. Hú Boetius hí wolde berǽdan, and Þeódríc ðæt anfunde, Bt. 1, tit.; Fox x. 2. Onfundan *deprenderint*, Wrt. Voc. ii. 25, 33. Gif hé wæccende weard onfunde búan on beorge, Beo. Th. 5675; B. 2841. Gif hwylc bróðor on lytlum gyltum byþ onfunden, R. Ben. 49, 2. II. *to find out from experience, become aware of, perceive, be sensible of*:—Ic onfinde *experiar*, Wrt. Voc. ii. 32, 7. Hé ðæt ðonne onfindeþ, ðonne se fǽr cymeþ *he will find it out, when the peril comes*, Exon. Th. 449, 18; Dóm. 73. Ðá se gist onfand ðæt se beadoleóma bítan nolde, Beo. Th. 3049; B. 1522. Landweard onfand (*became aware of*) eftsíð eorla, 3785; B. 1890. Onfunde, 1504; B. 750: 1622; B. 809. Ðá hé ðá onfunde, ðæt hé deád beón sceolde, Bt. 29, 2: Fox 104, 20. Onfunde *comperit*, i. *intellexit, cognovit, invenit*, Wrt. Voc. ii. 132, 63. Ǽr hine ða men onfunden ðe mid ðam cyninge wǽrun, Chr. 755; Erl. 48, 31. On ðæs wífes gebǽrum onfundon ðæs cyninges þegnas ða unstilnesse, Erl. 50, 2. Hú fela onfundun (*were sensible of*), ða gefélan ne mágun, Dryhtnes þrowinga, Exon. Th. 72, 27; Cri. 1179. Onfindaþ ðæt and ongeotaþ *intelligite*, Ps. Th. 93, 8. Onfinden *sapiant*, Germ. 389, 16. Onfinden *experiamur*, Wrt. Voc. ii. 31, 42. Onfindende *expertur*, 31, 62. Onfunden, ongeten *expertus, cognitus*, i. *probatus, inventus*, 145, 47. Heó onfunden wæs *men were aware of her presence*, Beo. Th. 2591; B. 1293. III. *to meet with, experience, suffer*:—Hé weán oft onfond, Exon. Th. 377, 16; Deor. 4.

on-findend, es; *m. One who finds out; inventor*, Germ. 391, 1.

on-flǽscness, e; *f. Incarnation*:—On ðære sóþan onflǽscnesse, Blickl. Homl. 81, 29.

on-flígen, es; *n. Infectious disease*:—Nú mágon ðás .viiii. wyrta wið .viiii. áttrum and wið nygon onflýgnum, Lchdm. iii. 36, 16. v. next word.

on-flyge, es; *m. Infectious disease, disease which, as it were, flies at people*:—Ðú miht wið áttre and wið onflyge, Lchdm. iii. 32, 2, 16, 30. v. *preceding word and* ongeflogen; *and* cf. *Icel.* á-flog, *flying at a person, fighting.*

on-fón; *p.* -féng; *pp.* -fangen (*with gen. dat. acc.*). I. *to take*:—Calic hǽlu ic onfóu, Ps. Surt. 115, 13. Hé mycelne dǽl ðæs landes on anweald onféng, Bd. 1, 3; S. 475, 12. Mód Bryttas onféngon *they took courage*, 1, 16; S. 484, 19. Se Ǽlmihtiga onféng ðæt hiw úre tyddran gecynde. Geþencean wé, gif óðer nýten wǽre tó háligienne, ðonne onfénge hé heora hiwe, ac hé wolde úrum hiwe onfón, Blickl. Homl. 29, 2–6. Ðá nýddon hine hys yldran tó ðæm ðæt hé sceolde woroldlícum wǽpnum onfón, 213, 2. Se hálga héht his heorþwerod wǽpna onfón, Cd. Th. 123, 5; Gen. 2040. Wífe onfón *uxorem ducere*, L. Ecg. C. 26; Th. ii. 152, 3. II. *to take what another appoints* or *grants, to receive, have given* (a) of material things:—Seó sául onféhþ hire líchoman, Blickl. Homl. 57, 16. Adames cynn onféhþ flǽsce, Exon. Th. 63, 33; Cri. 1029. Ðá onféngon hig syndrige penegas, Mt. Kmbl. 20, 10. (b) of non-material things:—Ic ne onfó gewitnesse fram menn, Jn. Skt. 5, 34. Se ðe Godes word mid blisse onféhþ, Mt. Kmbl. 13, 20. Gé onfóþ ðæm mægene Hálges Gástes, Blickl. Homl. 119, 11. Hé onféng for worlde mycelne noman, 43, 34. Hí léfnysse onféngon, Bd. 1, 26; S. 488, 5. Hé ðonne mid lǽwedum mannum onfó ðæs heardestan þeówdómes *let the hardest service be assigned to him among laymen*, Blickl. Homl. 49, 5. Onfón synna forgifnesse, 45, 7. Méde onfóu 83, 15. Freódóm onfón, Ap. Th. 5, 19. Hé ðam upplícan ríce gehyhte tó anfónne, Bd. 3, 6; S. 528, 5. III. *to take what another offers, receive favourably, accept*:—Gif ðú on God gelýfan wilt, ic ðæs drences onfó, Homl.

Th. i. 72, 17. Se yfela dēma onfēhþ feó, Blickl. Homl. 61, 30. Dryhten onfēhþ eallum đǽm gōdum đe ǽnig man gedēþ his đæm nēhstan of ārfæstre heortan, 37, 25. Onfōh đissum fulle, Beo. Th. 2342; B. 1169. Ic bidde đē đæt đū onfō đissa lāca, Gen. 33, 10. Gif hī sibbe mid Godes mannum onfōn ne woldan, đæt hī wǽron unsibbe fram heora feóndum onfōnde, Bd. 2, 2; S. 503, 30. IV. *to receive a person* (a) *for entertainment, assistance* or *protection;* v. on-fōnd:—Swā hwylc swā ānne lytling onfēhþ, se onfēhþ mē, Mt. Kmbl. 18, 5. Israhel onfēhþ eallum his cnihtum *suscepit Israhel*, Blickl. Homl. 159, 20. Martha onfēng Crist on hire hūs, 73, 9. Onfōh ūs on đæt scip, 233, 7. Onfōþ mīnre mēder on neorxna wonge, 157, 32. Onfōh đū đīnum esne, Ps. Th. 118, 122. Đæt hē onfēnge đære eádigan Marian sāwle, Blickl. Homl. 155, 12. His đā đa onfōn noldon, đe hiene mon tō brohte, Ors. 5, 2; Swt. 218, 34. Conon mid micle gefeán onfangen wæs, 3, 1; Swt. 98, 25. (b) in a special sense of receiving at the baptismal font, or at confirmation, *to stand sponsor to a person:*—His (*Godrum*) se cyning onfēng æt fulwihte, Chr. 878; Erl. 80, 22. Æt đam fulwihte hyre onfēng sum Godes þeów, Shrn. 140, 22. Hine onfēng æt fulluhtbæþe him tō godsuna Æþelwald, Bd. 3, 22; S. 553, 44. Ne hē nāh mid rihte ōđres mannes tō onfōnne æt fulluhte ne æt bisceopes handa, L. C. E. 22; Th. i. 374, 2. Ic his hæfde ǽr onfongen æt biscopes handa, Ch. Th. 169, 27. V. *to undergo a rite, undertake a duty:*—Hié fulwihte onfēngon, Blickl. Homl. 203, 24. Đonne wile hē onfōn rihtre ondetnesse, 155, 1. VI. *to conceive:*—Gif heó bearn onfēhþ *si infantem conceperit*, L. Ecg. 6, 19; Th. ii. 146, 29. Seó unwæstmfæstnes fram him fleáh, and seó clǽnnes onfēng, Blickl. Homl. 163, 19. Ic wæs mid unrihtwīsnesse onfangen *in iniquitatibus conceptus sum*, Ps. Th. 50, 6. VII. *to take to, to begin;* incipere [cf. *O. H. Ger.* ana-fāhan: *Ger.* an-fangen]:—Đonne đæt vers geendaþ on đam naman đe hit eft onfēhþ, Anglia viii. 331, 24. Ǽrest on cattes stān . . . eft on cates stān đǽr hit (*the boundary*) ǽr onfēng, Cod. Dip. Kmbl. iii. 313, 33. v. ā-fōn.

on-fōnd, es; *m. One who undertakes* or *supports:*—Onfōnd mīnre hǽle *susceptor salutis meae*, Ps. Lamb. 88, 27. v. on-fōn, IV.

on-foran. I. *prep. Before, afore:*—Onforan winter, Chr. 895; Erl. 93, 30. II. *adv. Before, in front:*—Beóþ onforan eágan, Ps. Th. 113, 13.

on-fordōn; *part. Destroyed:*—Bearn onfordōnra *filios interemptorum*, Ps. Lamb. 101, 21. Cf. on-forwyrd.

on-foreweardan; *prep. adv. In front, in the front of, in the earlier part of:*—Onforeweardan đysre race *in the earlier part of this narrative*, Homl. Skt. i. 23, 790. Malchus eode onforeweardan (*led the way*) in tō his đām hālgan gefēran, 23, 752.

on-forht. v. an-forht.

on-forhtian *to fear, be afraid:*—Ne ondrǽdaþ gē eów ne gē ne onforhtion *nolite timere ne paveatis*, Deut. 31, 6. Onforgtigan *timere*, Germ. 388, 40. v. ā-forhtian.

on-forwyrd, es; *n. Destruction:*—Fornam hine eofor (onforwyrd, MS. T.) of wuda *exterminavit eam aper de sylva*, Ps. Spl. 79, 14. God gelǽdeþ hī on pitt onforwyrdes *in puteum interitus*, 54, 26.

on-fundelness, e; *f. Experience, proof:*—Đysse wyrte onfundelnysse manega ealdras gesēđaþ *many authorities testify to the efficacy of this plant from experience*, Lchdm. i. 140, 9. Hyt dēþ onfundelnysse đæs sylfan þinges *it will give proof of the same thing, the second method will prove as efficacious as the first*, 162, 1.

on-fundenness, e; *f.* I. *experience, experiment:*—Onfundenness *experimentum*, i. *testamentum*, Wrt. Voc. ii. 145, 49: *experientia*, 145, 52. II. *finding out, discovery:*—Đū āsettest rǽdels gehȳr đū đa onfundennesse ymbe đæt đū cwǽde *you have set a riddle, hear the meaning discovered of what you have said*, Ap. Th. 4, 22.

onga [*should have been given under* anga], an; *m. A sting:*—Onga *aquilium*, Wrt. Voc. ii. 100, 59: 7, 12. Mē of bōsme fareþ ǽttren onga (*an arrow*), Exon. Th. 405, 18; Rä. 24, 4. [*O. H. Ger.* ango *aculeus: Icel.* angi *a spine, prickle.*]

on-gægum (?) *towards:*—Ongægum west *towards the west*, Ch. Th. 70, 18.

on-galan *to charm:*—Stefne ongalendra *vocem incantantium*, Ps. Spl. 57, 5: Blickl. Gl.

on-gang, es; *m.* I. *an entrance:*—Ongongas *ingressus*, Ps. Spl. C. 67, 26. II. *an irruption, attack, a going with violence:*—Ongong *incursus*, Wrt. Voc. ii. 111, 44: *irruptio*, 111, 47. Ongeong (-gong, Rush.), *impetus*, Mk. Skt. Lind, 5, 13.

on-geador; *adv. Together:*—Ongeador sprǽcon, Beo. Th. 3195; B. 1595.

on-geagn, -gegen, -gægn, -gegn, -geán, -gān, -geǽn, -gēn. A. *prep. often following a case.* I. *with dat.* (1) marking position, *opposite, over against, against:*—Breoton . . . đām mǽstum dǽlum Eurōpe myccle fæce ongegen (-gēn, MS. C.: -geán, MS. B.) *Britannia . . . maximis Europae partibus multo intervallo adversa*, Bd. 1, 1; S. 473, 10. Nebo on đam lande Moab ongeán (*over against*) Iericho, Deut. 32, 49. Gangaþ on đās ceasterwīc đe inc ongeán standeþ, Blickl. Homl. 69, 35. Đā arn hē and gestōd ongeán (*opposite*) đam lēge, 221, 11. Wæs ongeán đyssum wæterscipe glæsen fæt *a glass vessel was placed so that the water ran into it*, 209, 4. Mīn syn biþ symble ongeán mē *my sin is ever before me*, L. E. I. 30; Th. ii. 426, 40. (2) marking motion, *towards, in the direction of, to meet, in the way of:*—Hēht his þegnas hine beran ongeán đæm fȳre *jussit se obviam ignium globis efferi*, Bd. 2, 7; S. 509, 24. Bæd đæt him mon brohte đone triumphan ongeán, Ors. 5, 12; Swt. 240, 2: Shrn. 129, 21. Him com seó menio ongeán (-gægn, Lind. Rush.), Jn. Skt. 12, 18. Fērdon ongeán đǽm hǽđnum *they marched against the heathens*, Blickl. Homl. 203, 2. (3) marking opposition, hostility in action or feeling, *against:*—Swā se wind swīđor slōg on đone lēg, swā bræc hē swīđor ongeán đæm winde, 221, 13. Hē hié lǽrde, đæt hié hié forþ trymedan ongeán heora feóndum, 201, 36. Ic niste đæt đū stōde ongeán mē *I knew not that you opposed me*, Num. 22, 34. Ne hit for đæm bryne wandode đæs hātan lēges đe him wæs ongeán, Nar. 15, 21. Đonne storm cyme mīnum gǽste ongegn, Exon. Th. 455, 33; Hy. 4, 59. (4) denoting waiting for what is coming, *against, for the reception of, to receive:*—Ongeán gramum gearowe stōdon *stood ready for the attack of the foes*, Byrht. Th. 134, 46; By. 100. Biþ sūsla hūs open ongeán āđlogum *open against the coming of the perjurers*, Exon. Th. 98, 10; Cri. 1605. Him biþ fȳr ongeán *fire awaits them*, 446, 7; Dōm. 18. (5) marking direction where no actual motion takes place:—Seó eádge biseah ongeán gramum, 280, 12; Jul. 628. (6) *in reply to:*—Hīg cwǽdon mē ongeán, St. And. 40, 14. (7) denoting contrast:—Ongeán đam *e contra* . . . Ongeán đyssum spelle, Bd. 5, 13; S. 632, 2–4. Swā wē oftor hig (*our sins*) gemunaþ, swā forgyt God hyra hrađor . . . Đonne ongeán đon (*on the contrary*) swā wē oftor misdǽda forgytaþ, swā gemon hig God geornor, L. E. I. 30; Th. ii. 426, 36. (8) *in return for, as an equivalent for:*—Hē hine on eorþan streccan ongan, ongeán đam heó eác hī āstrehte, Glostr. Frag. 102, 6. Ongeán đam andgyte se deófol forgifþ stuntnysse, Wulfst. 59, 6–19. Cf. II. 7. II. *with the acc.* (1) marking position, *opposite, over against* (v. foran):—Ān đæra gārena līþ ongeán đæt īgland đe Gades hātte, ōđer ongeán đæt land Narbonense, se þridda . . . ongeán đæne mūđan, Ors. 1, 1; Swt. 24, 3–6. Hē sæt đǽr ihm getǽht wæs ongeán đone cyngc, Ap. Th. 14, 13. Đā sæt se Hǽlend ongēn (-geán, MS. A.: -gægn, Lind.: -gegn (*with dat.*), Rush.) đone tollsceamol, Mk. Skt. 12, 41. (1a) *to meet* that which is moving:—Gif đū đīnes scipes segl ongeán đone wind tōbrǽdst, Bt. 7, 2; Fox 18, 32. (2) marking motion, *towards, in the direction of, to meet:*—Se man đe ongeán ūs (*dat.?*) gǽþ, Gen. 24, 65. Seó eá gǽþ ongeán đa Assiriscan, 2, 14. Moises hig ūt ālǽdde ongēn Drihten, Ex. 19, 17. Đā gegaderode đæt folc tōgædere ongēn Moises, 16, 2. Hī fērdon ongēn (-geaen, Lind.: -gægn, Rush.) đone brȳdguman, Mt. Kmbl. 25, 1, 6. Woldon ferian đa herehȳđ ongeán đa scipu, Chr. 894; Erl. 90, 24. Đā flugon đa lēgetu ongeán đa hǽđnan leóde, Blickl. Homl. 203, 10. (2a) *against, in a direction opposite to:*—Ongeán streám *in a direction opposite to that in which the stream flows*, Cod. Dip. B. i. 502, 3: ii. 374, 10. (3) denoting hostility, resistance, or opposition in action or feeling, *against, with, contrary to, in opposition to:*—Se lēg ongan sleán and brecan ongeán đone wind, Blickl. Homl. 221, 12. Æfter hǽđenum gewunan, ongeán heora cristendōm, Homl. Th. i. 100, 20. Ongǽn þūsendfealde deriende cræftas *contra mille nocendi artes*, Wrt. Voc. ii. 135, 29. Ongién allo ūs wiđerwordnisse swīđre girǽc *contra cuncta nobis adversaria dexteram extende*, Rtl. 14, 38. Him lāđ wǽre đæt hī ongeán heora cynehlāford standan sceoldan, Chr. 1048; Erl. 178, 31. Wearþ swīđe gestired se here ongeán đone biscop, 1012; Erl. 146, 13. Đæt heó yrsige ongeán leahtras (-es, MS.), Homl. Skt. i. 1, 104. Hē gewāt yrre ongēn hig, Num. 12, 9. Đæt folc . . . ceorodon ongeán God . . . Wē sprǽcon ongeán God, 21, 5–7. Hwylce wrōhte bringe gē ongeán đysne man, Jn. Skt. 18, 29. Næfst đū nāne mihte ongeán (*adversum*) mē, 19, 11. Ic ne mǽg nō wiđcweþan ne furþum ongeán đæt geþencan *I cannot contradict, I cannot even have a conception contrary to it*, Bt. 34, 1; Fox 134, 29. (4) marking direction where no actual motion takes place:—Hī elciaþ ongeán đone deáþ, and mid ealle ne forfleóþ . . . Ūre Ālȳsend ne elcode nā ongeán đone deáþ ac hē hine oferswīđde *Enoch and Elias delay to meet death, and do not at all avoid it . . . Our Redeemer did not delay to meet death, but he overcame it*, Homl. Th. i. 308, 2–8. Hē ne dorste beseón ongēn God, Ex. 3, 6. Hē fægnaþ ongeagn (-geán, Cott. MSS.) đara ōđerra word *he rejoices at the words of the others*, Past. 17, 3; Swt. 111, 10. Đæt cild ongeán his Hlāford hyhte and hine hǽlette *the hope of the child went out to meet his Lord, and he hailed him*, Blickl. Homl. 165, 29. (5) *in reply to:*—Ne andwyrtst đū nān þing ongēn đa đe điss đē onsecgeaþ, Mt. Kmbl. 26, 62. (6) denoting contrast or comparison:—Seó næddre is geset on đam godspelle ongeán đone fisc *in the gospel the serpent is put in contrast to the fish*, Homl. Th. i. 252, 1. Feáwa ongeán getel đæra wiđercorena *few in comparison with the number of the reprobate*, 536, 32. (7) *against* as in to set one thing *against* another, *as an equivalent for, in return for, in exchange for:*—Þolige cyle ongeán (*in atonement for*) đa hlīwþe, L. Pen. 16; Th. ii. 284, 5. Hē gesealde twā gegrynd ongēn đes mynstres mylne, Ch. Th. 231, 24: 232, 3. Ælfrīc sealde đæt land æt Hacceburnan ongeán đæt land æt Deccet, 288, 12. Hig of đām Iūdeum for ãnum penige xxx gesealdon, ongeán ðæt ðæt ða Iūdeas ūrne Hǣlend mid xxx penegum gebohton, St. And. 36, 26. (8) marking readiness for a coming event, *against, ready for*:—Hīg lēdon forþ hira lāc ongeán ðætte Iosep in eode *they made ready their presents against Joseph came*, Gen. 43, 25. Ðonne sceolde fyrd ūt ongeán ðæt hī up woldon, Chr. 1010; Erl. 144, 4. (9) marking time, *towards*:—Fela ongeán winter hām tugon, Chr. 1096; Erl. 233, 22. **B.** *as an adverb.* (1) marking position, *opposite*:—Ic stande on ðās healfe and ðū ongeán *ego in hac parte sto, tu contra*, hēr is se *contra* adverbium, Ælfc. Gr. 47; Som. 47, 50. Is Gotland on ōðre healfe ongeán, Ors. 1, 1; Swt. 19, 20. Se hundredman ðe ðār stōd āgēn (ongeán, MS. A.: ongægn, Lind. Rush.) *ex adverso stabat*, Mk. Skt. 15, 39. (2) marking motion:—Ðā com mycel windes blǣd foran ongeán (*in the opposite direction*), Blickl. Homl. 199, 21. Ætstōd se streám and ongan tō þindenne ongeán (*in the direction opposite to that in which had come*), Jos. 3, 16. (3) denoting return, reversal of a previous action, *again, back; Lat.* re-:—Ða bodan ongeán cōmon tō Jacobe, Gen. 32, 6. Ic fare eft ongeán, Num. 22, 34. Hē gewende ongeán tō ðam cynge, Chr. 1048; Erl. 178, 5. Ongeán cirran *reverti*, Gen. 8, 7. Ongeán fleón *refugere*, Ælfc. Gr. 28, 6; Som. 32, 47. Ongēn sceát, ongeán hwyrfde *retrorsit*, Hpt. Gl. 505, 59. (4) with verbs of speaking, *in reply*:—Sōhte gylpword ongeán, Cd. Th. 17, 23; Gen. 264. Ða wergendan ne sceal mon nā ongeán werian, R. Ben. 17, 13. Brimmanna boda, ābeód ongeán, Byrht. Th. 133, 13; By. 49. (5) marking direction without actual motion, *towards*:—Ðonne hē sīþ ongān *cum viderit*, Ps. Th. 57, 9. Hié ongeán lōcian ne mihton, Blickl. Homl. 203, 11. (6) denoting opposition or resistance:—Ðā stōd Grantabrycgscīr fæstlīce ongeán, Chr. 1010; Erl. 143, 20. Nolde seó burhwaru ābūgan, ac heóldan mid fullan wīge ongeán, 1013; Erl. 148, 12. Ealle ða yldestan menn on West-Seaxon lāgon ongeán swā hī lengost mihton ac hī ne mihton nān þing ongeán wealcan *all the chief men of Wessex resisted as long as ever they could, but they could not offer any effectual opposition*, 1036; Erl. 165, 1-3. Ongēn sette *objecte*, Wrt. Voc. ii. 115, 25. (7) marking contrast, *on the other hand*:—God sette beforan eów līf and gōd, and ðǣr ongēn deáþ and yfel, Deut. 30, 15. (8) marking repetition, *again*:—Drihten cwæþ: Dō ðīne hand on ðīnne bōsum . . . Ðā cwæþ hē: Teóh eft ðīne hand on ðīnne bōsum. Ðā teáh hē hig ongeán, Ex. 4, 6-7. [*O. Sax.* an-gegin: *O. H. Ger.* in-gagan *and* in-gegin, -gegini: *Ger.* ent-gegen: *Icel.* ī-gegn *and* cf. gagn-.]

ongeán-cirrendlīc; *adj. Relative*:—*Relativum* ðæt is ongeáncyrrendlīc, Ælfc. Gr. 38; Som. 40, 62.

ongeán-cyme, es; *m. A return*:—Ūtfæreld his fram fæder, ongeáncyme (*regressus*) his tō fæder, and utrene tō helle, ongeáncyme (*recursus*) tō setle Godes, Hymn. Surt. 44, 17, 23.

ongeán-flōwende *refluent*:—Ongēntflōwende ȳða *reciproca*, Hpt. Gl. 418, 41. Ongēndflōwendum wæterum *reciprocis fluentis*, 462, 1.

ongeán-weard; *adj. Going against* or *towards*:—Hē him ongeánweard wæs *he was on his way to meet him*, Ors. 6, 31; Swt. 284, 32. Ongeánwurde *obvia*, Hpt. Gl. 499, 65.

ongeánweard-līc; *adj. Adversative*:—*At* (*the conjunction*) is ongeánweardlīc, Ælfc. Gr. 44; Som. 45, 40.

ongeánweardlīce; *adv. Adversatively*, Ælfc. Gr. 44; Som. 45, 50.

on-geboren; *adj. In-born*:—Ongeborene *ingenitam*, Hpt. Gl. 514, 2.

on-gebroht; *adj. Imposed*:—Be ongeb[r]ohtum *de inrogata*, Hpt. Gl. 514, 62.

on-gecīgung, e; *f. Invocation*:—Þerh ongiceiging *per invocationem*, Rtl. 99, 28.

on-gefeoht, es; *n. Attack, assault*:—From ǣlcum ongifeht *ab omni impugnatione*, Rtl. 98, 26: 122, 5.

on-geflogen; *part. Attacked with disease*:—Gif men his leoþu acen oððe [hē] ongeflogen sȳ, Lchdm. i. 86, 21. Cf. on-flyge.

on-gefremming, e; *f. Imperfection*:—Ongefremminge mīne (*imperfectum meum*) gesāwon eágan ðīne, Ps. Spl. 138, 15.

on-gegen, -gegn. v. on-geagn.

Ongel. v. Angel.

on-gemang. I. *prep. with dat. Among*:—Ongemong ōðrum mannum, Bt. 35, 6; Fox 168, 6. Ðā ongan ic ongemang ōðrum mislīcum and manigfealdum bisgum ða bōc wendan on Englisc, Past. pref.; Swt. 7, 17. Eác ðæm golde and ðæm līne wæs ongemang *purpura*, 14; Swt. 85, 9. Ongemang ðæm ðe *whilst*, 45; Swt. 339, 24. Ongemang ðam *meanwhile*, Jn. Skt. 4, 31. II. *adv.*:—Gif wē Sanctus Paulus lāre sume ongemong secgaþ *if we introduce some of St. Paul's teaching*, 40; Swt. 291, 13. Gif wē Æfneres dǣda sume hēr ongemong secgaþ, Swt. 295, 13. [*O. Sax.* an-gemong (*as adv.*).] v. gemang.

on-gemet; *adj. Immense*:—Ongemetum *immensis*, Wülck. Gl. 250, 23. v. un-gemet.

ongemet-hāt; *adj. Exceedingly hot*:—Wyl on wætere, beþe hine mid ongemethātum *boil in water, foment him with it exceedingly hot*, Lchdm. ii. 338, 22.

ongend = (?) ongēn (cf. *the form of the word under* ongeán-flōwende), Exon. Th. 323, 28; Vīd. 85.

on-geótung, e; *f. Pouring in*:—Clǣnsa ǣrest ða wambe mid drences ānfealddre ongeótunge, Lchdm. ii. 234, 26.

on-geþwǣre. v. un-geþwǣre.

on-gewiss; *adj. Uncertain*:—Ongewissu *incerta*, Ps. Spl. 50, 7. v. un-gewiss.

on-gifan. I. *to give back*:—Nime man ðīnne assan and hine nā ne ongife *asinus tuus rapiatur, et non reddatur tibi*, Deut. 28, 31. II. *to forgive, pardon*:—Ðū ðe ongæfest *qui ignoscis*, Rtl. 40, 33. v. ā-gifan.

on-gildan. I. *to pay* (*a penalty for*), *to be punished for* (with gen. acc. of crime *or* clause):—Banan heardlīce grimme ongildaþ, ðæs hié oft gilp brecaþ, Salm. Kmbl. 265; Sal. 132. Hē ðæs wraðe ongeald, Cd. Th. 111, 26; Gen. 1861: 253, 20; Dan. 598. Hū eall moncyn angeald ðæs ǣrestan monnes synna mid miclum teónum and wītum *ab initio et peccare homines et puniri propter peccata*, Ors. 5, 15; Swt. 250, 27. Hū swīðe hī his anguldon from heora āgnum cāsere *ut Caesare punirentur*, 6, 2; Swt. 256, 6. Weorces onguldon deópra firena þurh deáþes cwealm, Exon. Th. 153, 22; Gū. 829: 226, 23; Ph. 410. Ðæs ða byre siððan grimme onguldon gafulrǣdenne, 161, 15; Gū. 959. Sceal wearh ongildan, ðæt hē ǣr fācen dyde *he shall pay the penalty for previous wrong-doing*, Menol. Fox 573; Gn. C. 56. Sceolde hē ða dǣd ongyldan, Cd. Th. 19, 23; Gen. 295. Monig sceal ongieldan sāwel sūsles *shall be tormented*, Exon. Th. 304, 17; Fä. 71. II. *to pay*:—Hwylc hira ōðrum sceolde tō fōddurþege feores ongildan *which should pay for the others' food with his life*, Andr. Kmbl. 2204; An. 1103. III. *to give an offering, to offer*:—Ðǣr hǣðene men deóflum onguldon, Blickl. Homl. 221, 3. [Cf. *O. Sax.* a-, ant-(an-) geldan: *O. H. Ger.* ant-(en-, in-)geltan: *Ger.* ent-gelten.] v. ā-, an-gildan.

on-gin[n], es; *n.* I. *a beginning*:—Ðæs weges ongin, ðe tō Criste lǣt, ne meg beón begunnen on fruman būtan sumre ancsumnysse, R. Ben. 5, 16. Næs his frymþ ǣfre, eádes ongyn, Exon. Th. 240, 13; Ph. 638. His rīces ongin (*original condition*) nǣfre gewonaþ, Blickl. Homl. 9, 16. II. *an attempt, undertaking, enterprise*:—Micel is ðæt ongin ðīnre gelīcan ðæt ðū forhycge hlāford ūrne *it is a great undertaking for the like of thee to despise our lord*, Exon. Th. 250, 15; Jul. 127. Gif ðū gewītest āna from ēþele, nis ðæt ongin wiht, 119, 2; Gū. 248. Ongin, 123, 22; Gū. 326. Be ðam onginne ðe hē ongan, ðæt wēsten swā āna eardigan, Guthl. 4; Gdwin. 28, 7. Ðū miht æt Gode ābiddan ðæt ðū wilt wið ðæs drȳg onginne, Blickl. Homl. 187, 19. Onginnum *incoeptis*, Hpt. Gl. 515, 15. III. *action, proceeding*:—*Gesticulatio* angin *jocus* ł *actus*, 473, 61. Wrætlīc þūhte stānes ongin (*the stone spoke*), Andr. Kmbl. 1482; An. 742. Ȳða ongin *the violent action of the waves*, 931; An. 466. IV. *action, activity, active life, actions, endeavours*:—Ðǣr wæs wuldres wynn, wīgendra þrym, æðelīc onginn, næs ðǣr ǣnigum gewinn, 1775; An. 890. Ðæt se ǣresta dǣl his onginnes and līfes wǣre tō geleáfan gecyrred, Blickl. Homl. 211, 30. Drihtne ūres anginnes nān þing dīgle ne biþ . . . 'Beforan ðē is eall mīn gewilnung,' R. Ben. 25, 9. [*O. Sax.* ana-, an-gin: *O. H. Ger.* ana-gin, -ginni.] v. an-gin.

on-ginnan; *p.* -gan[n]; *pl.* -gunnon; *pp.* -gunnen. I. *to begin, set about, set to work*:—Ic onginne *inchoo*, Ælfc. Gr. 24; Som. 25, 39: *incipio*, 28, 6; Som. 32, 42: *ineo*, 37; Som. 39, 1. Wæs ongunnen *ordiretur*, Hpt. Gl. 494, 11. (a) where the action begun is given by the verb in the infin. or in the gerund.:—Ic onginne tō wearmigenne *calesco*, 35; Som. 38, 4. Hē onginþ (*incipiet*) tō ālȳsenne his folc of þeówte, Jud. 13, 5. Ðā ongan ic ða bōc wendan on Englisc, Past. pref.; Swt. 7, 17. Ðū ðe ongunne (*coepisti*) ætȳwan ðīne mǣrþe, Deut. 3, 24. Se ongan ǣrest onclypian Drihtnes naman, Gen. 4, 26. Ongan se Hǣlend bodian, Mt. Kmbl. 4, 17. Ðā ongan hine langian on his cȳþþe, Blickl. Homl. 113, 14. Ongan se Hǣlend him andswarigende tō cweþan, Mk. Skt. 13, 5. Hī ongunnon ða eár pluccigean, 2, 23. (b) where a case follows:—Se mon ðe gōd onginneþ and ðonne āblinneþ . . . Se ðe gōd onginneþ and on ðon þurhwunaþ, Blickl. Homl. 21, 34-36. Freme ðæt ðū ongunne, 189, 3. Raðe ðæs hié ōðer ongunnon wið Macedonie *cui Macedonicum bellum continuo successit*, Ors. 4, 11; Swt. 202, 32. Ongin ðæt ðū onginnest, Blickl. Homl. 187, 22. Ðæt fæsten ongunnen wæs instepes ðæs ðe hē of ðæm fulwihte āstāg, 35, 5. (c) where the verb is used intransitively:—Ða six onginnaþ of ðam stæfe e, and geendiaþ on him sylfum; x āna onginþ on ðam stæfe i, Ælfc. Gr. 2; Som. 2, 57-58. II. *to attempt, endeavour* (with infin.):—Ic onginne *conabor*, Wrt. Voc. ii. 24, 77: *nitar*, 60, 3. Ðæt ic geseó ða mē onginnaþ dōn ða werrestan tintrega *that I may see those who are trying to inflict on me the worst tortures*, Blickl. Homl. 229, 24. Hiene Hannibal āspōn ðæt hē ðæt gewin leng[ne] ongan *Hannibal induced him to carry on the struggle longer*, Ors. 4, 11; Swt. 204, 31. Se nāht freomlīces ongan on ðære cynewīsan *nihil omnino in re militari ausus est*, Bd. 1, 3; S. 475, 20. Ðā ongunnon (*tentabant*) ða scypmenn ða ancras upp teón, 3, 15; S. 541, 40. Ōþ hē ongite ðæt hē mǣge ābiddan æt Gode ðæt hē ongiene (-ginne, MSS. Cot.) *until he finds that he can obtain by prayer from God what he endeavours to get*, Past. 10; Swt. 61, 22. Ðæt ic dorste ðis weorc ongynnan *ut hoc opus adgredi auderem*, Bd. pref.; S. 472, 12. Hē wolde onginnan him ōleccan, Bt. 35, 6; Fox 168, 13. **III.** *to act strenuously*:—Hí on ðam gewinne werlīce ongunnon, Homl. Th. ii. 502, 5. Onginnaþ werlīce, i. 188, 31. Onginnaþ esnlīce *viriliter agite*, Deut. 31, 6. **IV.** *to make an attempt upon, to attack*:—Gramhȳdige mē mid unrihte oft onginnaþ *injusti insurrexerunt in me*, Ps. Th. 85, 13. Ðonne ūs mānfulle menn onginnaþ (*insurgerent*), 123, 2. Ðonne yfle unmǣgas onginnaþ, mēcum gemētaþ, swā gē mē dydon, Vald. 2, 23. Mē strange ongunnon *irruerunt in me fortes*, Ps. Th. 58, 3: 61, 3. Gif hī sceoldon eofor onginnan, Exon. Th. 344, 20; Gn. Ex. 176. [*O. H. Ger.* in-ginnan *inchoare, incipere, conari, moliri, niti.*]

on-ginnendlīc; *adj. Inchoative*:—Ōðer hiw is gehāten *inchoativa*, ðæt is onginnendlīc, forðan ðe hit getācnaþ weorces anginn, Ælfc. Gr. 35; Som. 38, 2.

on-ginness, e; *f. A beginning, undertaking*:—Onginnissum *inceptis*, Wrt. Voc. ii. 86, 26. Hine hēt ðæt hē ðām hālwendan ongynnessum georne befulge *eum coeptis insistere salutaribus jussit*, Bd. 5, 19; S. 637, 11.

on-girwan; *p.* -girede *To divest, strip*:—Hē hine middangeardes þingum ongyrede and genacodade *se mundi rebus exuit*, Bd. 4, 3; S. 567, 24. Ongyrede hine ða geong hæleþ . . . gestāh hē on gealgan heánne, Rood Kmbl. 77; Kr. 39. Hē wæs līchoman ongyrwed *corpore exutus*, Bd. 3, 19; S. 547, 34: 5, 12; S. 631, 5. Ongered *exuta*, Ps. Surt. ii. p. 202, 17. Ongirede *exutas*, Wrt. Voc. ii. 33, 18.

on-git, es; *n. Understanding*:—Ongit (ondgit, Cott. MSS.) wīsdōmes, Past. 14; Swt. 85, 3. Ongyt *intellectum*, Ps. Spl. 31, 10. v. and-git.

on-gitan, -gietan, -giotan, -geotan; *p.* -geat, -get; *pl.* -geáton, -gēton; *pp.* -giten, -gieten *To perceive*:—Ic ongite *comperio*, Ælfc. Gr. 30; Som. 34, 46. Ongiotaþ *animadvertite*, Kent. Gl. 230. Ðā hē ongitende wæs *animadverterit*, Wrt. Voc. ii. 3, 9. Ongeten, onfunden *expertus, cognitus*, i. *probatus, inventus*, 145, 47. **I.** *to perceive, see*:—Gif ðū gesihst hwylcne ungesǣligne mon and ongitst hwæthwegu gōdes on him, Bt. 38, 3; Fox 200, 15. Hī ðǣr hwīlum synne ongytaþ ðǣr ðe syn ne biþ, Bd. 1, 27; S. 494, 26. Gif hī hwilcne mon on ðām landum ongytaþ oððe geseóþ ðonne feorriaþ hī and fleóþ *sed hominem cum viderint longe fugiunt*, Nar. 36, 21. Ðīn wuldor ongitaþ woruldcyningas, Ps. Th. 101, 13. Siððan hē beácen (*the miracle of the fiery furnace*) onget, Cd. Th. 246, 33; Dan. 488. Ðæt ic ǣrwelan ongite, gearo sceáwige, Beo. Th. 5489; B. 2748. Ðæt hié Geáta clifu ongitan meahton, 3827; B. 1911. Gefeán mon mihte on his andwleotan ongytan, Blickl. Homl. 223, 35. **II.** *to perceive by hearing*:—Ic ðæs þeódnes word ongeat, Exon. Th. 175, 11; Gū. 1193. Gif ðū sanges stæfne gehȳrdest and ðū heofonlīc weorud ongeáte ofer ūs cuman, Bd. 4, 3; S. 568, 31. Hié horn galan ongeáton, Beo. Th. 5880; B. 2944. **III.** *to perceive, feel* (*pain*, etc.):—Ðonne ne ongitest ðū ǣnig sār, Lchdm. i. 368, 26. Ðonne ne ongyt hē nā mycel tō geswynce ðæs sīdes, 102, 6. Ongæt gumena aldor hwæt him Waldend wræc wīteswingum, Cd. Th. 111, 29; Gen. 1863. Swā ðæt se seóca ðone stenc ne ongite, Lchdm. i. 304, 23. **IV.** *to feel, be of opinion, judge*:—Ðeáh ðe be ðyssum willan misenlīce cynn monna missenlīce ongite *quamvis de hac re diversae hominum nationes diversa sentiant*, Bd. 1, 27; S. 495, 14. **V.** *to know, hear of, find out*:—Wē witon manige foremǣre weras forþgewitene ðe swīðe feáwa manna ā ongit *that very few men ever hear of*, Bt. 19; Fox 70, 13. Wē oft ongytaþ ðæt ārīseþ þeód wið þeóde *we often hear of nation rising against nation*, Blickl. Homl. 107, 27. Eall ðæt hē oððe on gewritum oððe on ealdra manna sægenum ongeat (*cognoverat*), Bd. prep.; S. 471, 27. Sumu ða ðe ic sylf ongitan (*cognoscere*) mihte þurh gesægene, S. 472, 30. Ne mæg ic nāne cwica wuht ongitan . . . ðe ungenēd lyste forweorþan *si animalia considerem . . . nihil invenio, quod, nullis extra cogentibus, ad interitum sponte festinet*, Bt. 34, 10; Fox 148, 13. Miht ðū ongitan hwæðer ðū āuht ðē deórwyrþre habbe ðonne ðē sylfne *do you know whether you have anything more precious to you than yourself?* 11, 2; Fox 34, 9. **VI.** *to perceive, understand*:—Ǣlc ðæra ðe Godes word gehȳrþ and ne ongitt (*intelligit*), Mt. Kmbl. (MS. A.) 13, 19. Ongyte (ongete, Lind.) gē ealle ðās þing? Ðā cwǣdon hig: Wē hit ongytaþ, 13, 51. Ne ongyte gē gyt *nondum intellegitis?* Mk. Skt. 8, 21. Onfindaþ ðæt and ongeotaþ *intelligite*, Ps. Th. 93, 8. Ðȳ læs hig mid heortan ongyton (ongeton, Rush.) *ne corde intelligant*, Mt. Kmbl. 13, 15. Hié hiora (*books*) nānwuht ongiotan (ongietan, Cott. MSS.) ne meahton, Past. pref.; Swt. 5, 12. Ðæt wē ðȳ geornor ongietan meahton tācen, ðæt se fugel þurh bryne beácnaþ, Exon. Th. 236, 13; Ph. 573. Ongeotan, Blickl. Homl. 15, 13: 131, 23: 105, 28. **VII.** *to recognise, know*, (a) *to take a person* or *thing to be what it really is*:—Gif ðū sōðne God lufast and ongietest gǣsta hleó, 245, 23; Jul. 49. Wið ðæs ðū wilt higian ðon ǣr ðe ðū hine ongitest *towards that thou wilt strive as soon as thou dost recognise it*, Bt. 11, 2; Fox 34, 8. Se man ðe swereþ mān and eft his gilt onget, Lev. 5, 4: Met. 22, 16. Ða neát ongitaþ hira gōddēnd *the brutes know their benefactors*, Elen. Kmbl. 717; El. 359. Hē Godes good on ðære his dǣde ongeat *he recognised the goodness of God in that deed of his*, Blickl. Homl. 215, 33. Witon wē ðæt ūre Drihten mid ūs wæs on ðæm scipe, and wē hine ne ongeáton, 235, 22. Ongytaþ Godes mildheortnesse seó is nū mid ūs geworden *recognise in this the mercy of God that has been now shewn to us*, 235, 20. Ne mē ǣnig ongitan wolde *non erat qui agnosceret me*, Ps. Th. 141, 4. Ðēh ic engla þeóden ongitan ne cūðe, Andr. Kmbl. 1802; An. 903. Nū wē māgon ongytan hwæt ðæt gerȳne getācnaþ *now we know what the mystery means*, Blickl. Homl. 17, 13. Wē māgon ongytan on ðæm ūre tydran gecynd *we may see in that* (the temptation of Christ by the devil) *our weak nature*, 33, 35: 95, 11. Ne mæg ic fullīce ongitan æfter hwæm ðū spyrast *I don't quite know what you are asking for*, Bt. 34, 9; Fox 148, 1. Nū ðū hæfst ongyten ða wanclan treówa ðæs blindan lustes, 7, 2; Fox 18, 2. Heó (*a woman dressed in man's clothes*) wæs fram hire fæder ongitenu *she was recognised by her father*, Shrn. 31, 15. (b) *to recognise a fact* or *circumstance*, (1) the fact stated in a clause:—Ðū ongitst ðætte ðū git hæfst ðone mǣstan dǣl ðīnra gesǣlþa, Bt. 10; Fox 28, 6. Ðonne ongit hē, hū lytel hē biþ, 12, 1; Fox 60, 28. Ðā se dēma oncneów and ongæt, ðæt hē hine mid swinglan oferswīðan ne mihte, Bd. 1, 7; S. 478, 1. Oferswīðan ða men ðe hié ongeáton ðæt wiðer-wearde wǣron, Blickl. Homl. 135, 12. Leóde ongēton, ðæt ðǣr Drihten cwom, Cd. Th. 183, 12; Exod. 90. Hē wolde ðæt hē on ðon ongeáte, ðæt ðæt mon ne wæs, se ðe him ætȳwde, Bd. 2, 12; S. 514, 25. Ic wundrige hwī ðū ne mǣge ongitan, ðæt ðū eart nū git swīðe gesēlig, Bt. 10; Fox 28, 34. Ðæt is tō ongytanne ðæt ācennede wǣron wæstmas gōdra dǣda, Bd. 3, 23; S. 554, 23. Ðū hæfdest ongiten, ðæt mē selfum þūhte, ðæt ic hæfde forloren ðæt gecyndelīce gōd, Bt. 35, 2; Fox 156, 17. Heó ongieten hæfde, ðæt heó eácen wæs, Exon. Th. 378, 3; Deór. 10. (2) the fact referred to by the pronoun *ðæt*:—Fȳren wolc[en] āstāh of heofonum, and hit ymbsealde ealle ða ceastre. Mid ðȳ ðæt (*the circumstance just related*) ongeat Andreas, Blickl. Homl. 245, 32. Hié ðæt ongeáton, ðæt hē leng mid him wunian nolde, 135, 22. (3) the fact given by accus., (a) with infin.:—Ðæt hié ongieton mīn mægen on ðē wesan, 241, 14. (b) without infin.:—Hē ongeat Titum hwēne mon-þwǣrran ðonne hē sceolde, and Timotheus hē ongeat hātheortran ðonne hē sceolde, Past. 40; Swt. 291, 21-23: Blickl. Homl. 219, 5. Hit ongeat his lāre swīðe tōtorenne, Bt. 3, 1; Fox 4, 31. Ðæt Mōd sǣde ðæt hit hit ǣghwonan ongeáte scyldig (cf. Ic mē ongite ǣghwonan scyldigne, 8; Fox 24, 13), tit.; Fox 10, 19. (4) with the passive:—Hē wæs tō cinge ongyten *he was recognised as king*, Blickl. Homl. 71, 32. Ðonne hē biþ ongieten æfstig, Past. 13; Swt. 79, 12. **VIII.** *to know* (of sexual intercourse):—Ic nǣnigne wer ne ongeat, Blickl. Homl. 7, 22. v. an-gitan.

on-gitenness, e; *f.* **I.** *understanding, knowledge*:—Hē wæs gefeónde ðære ongytenesse (*agnitione*) ðæs sōðan Godes biganges, Bd. 2, 13; S. 517, 13. Tō ongytenysse (*ad agnitionem*) ðæs sōðan Godes, 2, 9; S. 511, 3. **II.** *meaning, purport* (cf. and-git, III):—Ðeós ongitenys (þes ongitenysse, MS.) mīnre untrumnysse ys ðæt of ðisum līchaman sceal beón se gāst ālǣded *the meaning of my illness is, that the spirit shall be taken away from the body*, Guthl. 20; Gdwin. 80, 22.

on-gitness, e; *f. The understanding, intellect*:—Of alre ongetnisse *ex toto intellectu*, Mk. Skt. Rush. 12, 33.

ongnere, es; ongnora (?), an; *m. The corner of the eye* (?):—Eághyll from ðam ongnoran *glebenus*, Wrt. Voc. ii. 42, 7. Ongneras *irqui*, 46, 30.

on-gripe, es; *m. Attack, assault*:—Ðæra wyrma ongrype and ðæra sorhwīta mǣst, Wulfst. 187, 2. [*O. H. Ger.* ana-griffe (*dat.*) *tactu*, Grff. iv. 318: *and cf. Icel.* ā-grip *in the phrase* lītill āgripum].

on-grisla, an; *m. Dread, horror*:—Wæs se munt mid mycelum brōgan and mid ongryslan eall oferlǣded, Blickl. Homl. 203, 7.

on-grislīc; *adj. Horrible, dreadful*:—Ðā becwom sum ongrislīc wīse (*horrenda res*) on hié, Nar. 10, 32. Ðæt ongrislīce gemōt *the last day*, Wulfst. 186, 15. Angryslīc, Dōm. L. 14, 225. Ongrislīces andwlitan *horrido vultu* . . . ongrislīcre ansīne *horrendae visionis*, Bd. 5, 13; S. 633, 1-5. On ðære angrislīcan gesihþe *horridae visionis*, 5, 12; S. 628, 19. Ongrislīco hǣr *horridi crines*, 5, 2; S. 615, 1. Ongristlīce on stefne, Guthl. 5; Gdwin. 34, 26.

on-gryrelīc; *adj. Horrible*:—Hī hine lǣddon on ðām ongryrlīcan (-gryslīcan?) fiðerum, Guthl. 5; Gdwin. 36, 24.

on-gunnenness, e; *f. An undertaking*:—Hē bæd ðæt hē ða ārfæstan ongunnennysse gefylde *petiit eum pia coepta complere*, Bd. 3, 23; S. 554, 40.

on-gyldan, -gynness, -gyrede, -gytan. v. on-gildan, -ginness, -girwan, -gitan.

on-hādian *to degrade from holy orders*:—Gif preóst ōðerne man ofsleá . . . hine biscep onhādige, L. Alf. pol. 21; Th. i. 76, 1.

on-hǣle; *adj. Whole, entire*:—Gemengde beóþ onhǣlo gelāc engla and deófla *the entire hosts of angels and devils shall be joined together*, Exon. Th. 56, 5; Cri. 896.

on-hǣle; *adj. Secret, hidden*:—Ne lǣt ðū ðīnne ferþ onhǣlne, dēgol ðæt ðū deópost cunne, nelle ic ðē mīn dyrne gesecgan, gif ðū mē ðīnne hygecræft hylest, Exon. Th. 333, 9; Gn. Ex. 1. Gif mec onhǣle ān onfindeþ, ðǣr ic wīc būge (cf. gif ic mǣgburge mōt mīne gelǣdan on dēgolne weg, 397, 15-17), 396, 19; Rä. 16, 7. Wīd is ðes wēsten, wræcsetla fela, eardas onhǣle earmra gǣsta, 121, 7; Gū. 268: 123, 13;

Gū. 322. Wiđ onhǣlum ealdorgewinnum *against secret and deadly foes*, 134, 9; Gū. 505.

on-hǣled *infirm, ill*:—Ða đe on unhǣle (onhǣlede, MS. C.) wǣron, Ors. 4, 4; Bos. 80, 40.

on-hǣtan. I. *to heat*:—Hēt hē đone stān onhǣtan, Ors. 4, 8; Swt. 186, 19. Blōd onhǣtan, Salm. Kmbl. 88; Sal. 43. Ofn onhǣtan, Cd. Th. 229, 31; Dan. 225. Onhǣted, 231, 7; Dan. 243. Ðā đæt (*the brazen bull*) onhǣt wæs, Ors. 1, 12; Swt. 54, 28. II. of violent emotion, *to inflame*:—Hira mōd ne beóþ onhǣt mid nānre manunge, Past. 52; Swt. 411, 7. Heorte is onhǣted, Judth. Thw. 22, 30; Jud. 87.

on-hagian; *p.* ode; *v. impers. with dat. or acc. of pers. To be within a person's power* or *means, to be in accordance with a person's will* or *convenience*:—Eádig byþ se đe đam þearfan gefultumaþ, gif hine tō onhagaþ (*if it be in his power*); gif hine ne onhagaþ, đonne ne līcaþ him his earfoþu, Ps. Th. 40, 1. Mē ne onhagaþ nū đa bōc ealle tō asmæáganne, Shrn. 200, 22. Ðonne hit (*the mind*) onhagaþ tō đǣm ūteran *si facultas exterior suppetat*, Past. 53, 6; Swt. 17, 13. Ne anhagode heora cyninge đæt hē wiđ hié mehte būton fæstenne gefeohtan, Ors. 4, 5; Swt. 168, 21. Hié hergodon ǣghwǣr be đam sǣ đǣr hié onhagode (*wherever it suited them*), Chr. 918; Erl. 102, 25. Ðā seó fyrd gesomnod wæs đā ne onhagode heom đārtō būton đæt wǣre đæt se cyng đǣr mid wǣre *they would not be satisfied unless the king were there too*, 1016; Erl. 153, 27. Ðæra hālgena þrowunga đe mē tō onhagode on Englisc tō āwendene *that I have had the opportunity of translating into English*, Homl. Skt. i. pref. 37. Gelǣste binnan twelf mōnþum būton hire ǣr tō onhagige *unless it be convenient to pay earlier*, L. C. S. 74; Th. i. 416, 17. Gif hine tō swā mycelum ne onhagige *si tantum facultatis ei non suppetat*, L. Ecg. P. iv. 60; Th. ii. 222, 3. Gif hine onhagige (*si facultatem habeat*), gefreóge ǣnne man, ii. 24; Th. ii. 192, 12: L. Pen. 14; Th. ii. 282, 9–12: Homl. Th. i. 180, 12. Ðone dǣl đe him tō onhagige, 398, 17. Gif đē onhagige, đæt đū hit (*the law*) healdan mǣge, far đū in; gif đē ne onhagige, far đē freoh đider đū wille, R. Ben. 97, 23. Ða hȳrsumnesse beginne đeáh hine hwōn onhagige *though he have little power* (or *inclination*), 128, 19. Gif mon tō gōdum weorcum ne onhagie habban gōdne willan *if people have not the means for good works, let them have good will*, Bt. 41, 2; Fox 246, 10.

on-hātan *to promise*:—Hyre nales frætwe onhēht, Exon. Th. 249, 28; Jul. 118. Ðæt ic deófolgieldum gaful onhāte, 251, 27; Jul. 151. [Cf. *O. H. Ger.* ant-heizan *vovere, spondere, polliceri*: *O. Sax.* ant-hētan.]

on-hātian *to grow hot*:—Onhātode *incanduisset*, Wrt. Voc. ii. 47, 4.

on-heáw, es; *m. A block to hew on*:—Onheáwas *codices*, Wrt. Voc. ii. 104, 38: 135, 60: 14, 62. [*M. H. Ger.* ane-hou *incus*.]

on-hebban; *p.* -hōf (*the weak form* -hefde *also occurs*); *pp.* -hafen. I. *to lift up, raise* (the eyes, voice):—Ðonne ic mec onhæbbe, and hī onhnīgaþ tō mē, Exon. Th. 412, 28; Rä. 31. 7. Ðā onhōf Laurentius his ēgan up, Shrn. 116, 4. Petrus onhōf his stefne, Blickl. Homl. 149, 21. II. *to raise* (as barm does), *to leaven*:—Ne ete gē nān þing onhafenes, Ex. 12, 19. III. *to take up, begin* (cf. *Icel.* hefja *to begin*):—Ic đās unhȳrlīcan fers onhefde mid sange, Dōm. L. 2, 11. IV. *to take away*:—Ōþ đæt onhafen biþ (*auferatur*) se mōna, Ps. Spl. 71, 7. V. metaph. *to lift up, exalt* (generally in a bad sense):—Ǣlc đæra đe hine onhefþ, hē sceal beón geeádmēt, Homl. Th. i. 202, 33. Ǣlc đe hine anhefþ, hē biþ geneoþerad, and ǣlc đe hine geneoþeraþ, hē biþ mid weorþmynte onhafen. . . . Ac hwæt gif ic mīn mōd on mōdignesse anhōfe? R. Ben. 22, 11–19. Ða de God ondrǣdaþ, and hȳ þurh heora gōdan dǣda ne anhebbaþ, 4, 2. Hē ēđelþrym onhōf, rȳmde and rǣrde, Cd. Th. 98, 23; Gen. 1634. Ic tǣhte đām rīcan, đæt hī ne onhōfon hī, Homl. Th. i. 378, 18. Ne onhebbe hine nān man on his weorcum, ii. 80, 29. v. an-, ā-hebban, -hefan, *and next word.*

on-hefedness, e; *f. Exaltation*:—Gif wē đone hrōf đære heálīcan eáđmōdnesse getellan willaþ and tō đære heofonlīcan anhefednesse cuman þencaþ, R. Ben. 23, 2.

on-heldan, -heldedness. v. on-hildan, -hildedness.

on-hende; *adj. On hand, demanding attention*:—Hié forgeátan đara ūtera gefeohta đe him anhende wǣron, Ors. 2, 6; Swt. 88, 24. [Cf. *Icel.* ā-hendr *within reach*.] v. of-hende.

on-herian, -hering. v. on-hyrian, -hyring.

on-hetting, e; *f. Persecution*:—Onhettincga *persecutiones*, Hpt. Gl. 476, 17. v. hettend.

on-hildan, -hieldan, -heldan, -hyldan. I. *trans.* (1) of actual motion, *to lean, incline, recline, bend down*:—Onheldeþ hine and falleþ *inclinabit se et cadet*, Ps. Surt. 9, 31. Se biscop hine onhylde tō ānre đære studa, Bd. 3, 17; S. 543, 37: 4, 9; S. 577, 7. Hē his heáfod onhylde swā swā hē slāpan wolde, 3, 11; S. 536, 30: 4, 24; S. 599, 6: Exon. Th. 178, 14; Gū. 1244. Walle onhældum *parieti inclinato*, Ps. Surt. 61, 4. Onhylded *reclinem*, Wrt. Voc. ii. 78, 80. (2) metaphorically (a) with the idea of favourable disposition towards a person or thing, *to incline*:—Tō mē đīn eáre onhyld, Ps. Th. 101, 2. His breósđ sīen onhielde tō forgiefnesse, Past. 10, 1; Swt. 61, 12. Onhelded wiđ đæs gecyndes, Met. 13, 11. (b) with the idea of subjection, *to bow, bend*:—Mid hwelcum monnum māgon gē onheldon eówra feónda swyrbān, Shrn. 86, 22. (c) *to turn from the right course*:—Hié onhældon in đē yfel *declinaverunt in te mala*, Ps. Surt. 20, 12. (d) *to cause to sink*:—Onhælde sind rīce *inclinata sunt regna*, 45, 7. II. *intrans. To decline, deviate, incline, sink*:—Heofones gym west onhylde, Exon. Th. 174, 32; Gū. 1186. Onhylde (onhældeþ, Ps. Surt.) of đysum on đys (*inclinavit*), Ps. Spl. 74, 8. Alle onhældon *omnes declinaverunt*, Ps. Surt. 13, 3. Onheldan *declinare*, 16, 11. Onhældende *declinantes*, 100, 4.

on-hildedness, e; *f. Declining*:—Onheldednis *declinatio*, Ps. Surt. 72, 4.

on-hindan; *adv. Behind*:—Womb wæs onhindan āþrunten, Exon. Th. 419, 6; Rä. 38, 1. Ǣtterne tægel hafaþ onhindan, Fragm. Kmbl. 38; Leas. 21.

on-hinder. v. hinder.

on-hinderling; *adv. Back*:—Onhinderling hweorfaþ mīne feóndas *convertentur inimici mei retrorsum*, Ps. Th. 55, 8: 69, 3. v. on-bæcling.

on-hirdan *to comfort, strengthen, encourage*:—Manegum wearþ hige onhyrded þurh his hālig word, Apstls. Kmbl. 105; Ap. 53: Elen. Kmbl. 1678; El. 841.

on-hiscan. v. on-hyscan.

on-hlīdan; *p.* -hlād. I. *trans. To open, unclose*:—Onhlīdest (*aperis*) đū đīne handa, Ps. Th. 144, 17. Undōþ eówre geatu, and onhlīdaþ đa ēcan geata, 23, 7, 9. Deáþræced heolstorcofan onhliden weorþaþ, Exon. Th. 201, 1; Ph. 49. Ðǣr biþ open eádgum tōgeánes, onhliden hleóđra wyn, heofonrīces dura, 198, 18; Ph. 12. Carcernes duru opene fundon, onhliden hamera geweorc, Andr. Kmbl. 2155; An. 1079. II. *intrans. To be disclosed, to appear*:—Ōþ đæt wuldres gim onhlād *until the sun shewed itself*, 2539; An. 1271.

on-hnīgan. I. *trans. To bend down, bow, press down*:—Onhnīgaþ *incumbunt*, Wülck. Gl. 255, 11. Onhnīgendre *grassante*, Hpt. Gl. 421, 19. Biþ wuhta gehwilc onhnigen tō hrūsan, Met. 31, 13. Onhnigenum heáfde simle his gesyhþa ādūna on eorþan besette, R. Ben. 31, 8. II. *intrans. To bend down, bow*:—Hī onhnīgaþ tō mē, Exon. Th. 412, 29; Rä. 31, 7. Ealle eáđmōdlīce tō Criste sylfum onhnigan, Blickl. Homl. 203, 23: Cd. Th. 227, 3; Dan. 181. Man mæg tō đǣm lāstum onhnīgan, and đa cyssan, Blickl. Homl. 127, 10.

on-hnyscan. v. on-hyscan.

on-hohsnian (?) *to abominate, detest*:—Ðæt onhohsnode (MS. onhohsnod, *the* s *has been afterwards inserted between the* h *and* n) Hemninges mǣg, Beo. Th. 3892; B. 1944. Cf. on-hyscan.

on-hrægel, es; *n. A covering, sheet*:—Wæfelsum, onhræglum *sabanis*, Hpt. Gl. 490, 43.

on-hrǣs. v. on-rǣs.

on-hreódan *to adorn* (?). v. on-reódan.

on-hrēran. I. of actual movement, *to stir, agitate, move violently*:—Ðonne hī (*the waves*) wind onhrēreþ, Ps. Th. 88, 3: Met. 7, 27. Ðonne micla ȳsta onhrēraþ hronmere, 5, 10. Fiscas đe onhrēraþ hreó wǣgas, Exon. Th. 194, 19; Az. 141. Eorþan đū onhrērdest *commovisti terram*, Ps. Th. 59, 2. Onhrērdan, 76, 15. Ðonne hine mon drincan welle, onhrēre eft, Lchdm. ii. 270, 13. Ne mæg him se flǣschoma hond onhrēran, Exon. Th. 311, 22; Seef. 96. Eorþe biþ onhrēred of hire stōwe, Blickl. Homl. 91, 36. Lyft wæs onhrēred, Cd. Th. 208, 13; Exod. 482. Grund is onhrēred, deópe gedrēfed, Andr. Kmbl. 786; An. 393. II. metaph. *to move, disturb, agitate*:—Ðone ungeþyldegan swīđe lytel scūr đære costunga mæg onhrēran (-hrēran, Hatt. MS.), Past. 33; Swt. 224, 5. Ne mǣg hine ǣnig onhrēran (*non commovebitur*), đe eardfæst byþ on Hierusalem, Ps. Th. 124, 1. Eall heofena mægen biþ onwended and onhrēred, Blickl. Homl. 91, 28. III. of emotions, *to stir up, arouse, excite*:—Mægen wæs onhrēred, Cd. Th. 192, 4; Exod. 226. Wæs merefixa mōd onhrēred, Beo. Th. 1103; B. 549. Hete wæs onhrēred, 5101; B. 2554: Andr. Kmbl. 2606; An. 1304: 2788; An. 1396.

on-hrīnan; *with gen. dat. To touch*:—Sió sunne ne onhrīnþ nō đæs dǣles đæs heofenes đe se mōna on irnþ, ne se mōna nō ne onhrīnþ đæs dǣles đe sió sunne on irnþ, Bt. 39, 13; Fox 232, 27–29. Ða hundas . . . his nāne onhrinon, Shrn. 145, 5. Ðā ne onhrān đæt fȳr him, 53, 24. Onhrīn đissum muntum *tange montes*, Ps. Th. 143, 6.

on-hrine (?), es; *m. Touch*:—Ne đe ǣniges yfeles onhrine (onryne, MS. B.) dereþ, Lchdm. i. 328, 1. Cf. æt-hrine.

on-hrōp, es; *m.* I. *importunate clamour, importunity*:—For his onhrōpe hē ārīst and sylþ him his neóde *propter inprobitatem surget, et dabit illi quod habet necessarios*, Lk. Skt. 11, 8: Homl. Th. i. 248, 32. Se brōđor đe hine synderlīce gebiddan wile, ne sȳ gelet mid (þurh, W.F.) ǣniges ōđres onhrōpe, R. Ben. 81, 9. II. *abusive language, reproach*:—Hosp ł onhrōp *improperium*, Ps. Lamb. 68, 20. [Cf. *O. H. Ger.* ana-ruof *appetitio*.] v. hrōp.

on-hupian *to draw back, recoil*:—Ðonne đæt mōd ongit hine selfne on swelcne spild forlǣd đonne wiđtremþ hē and onhupaþ and ondrǣt him ðæt ðæt hē ǣr lufode *dum mens sese in praecipitium pervenisse deprehendit, gressum post terga revocet, pertimescens quae amaverat*, Past. 58, 2; Swt. 441, 28. [Cf. *Icel.* hopa aptr, ā hæl, undan *to draw back.*]

on-hwelan *to resound*:—Onhwileþ *reboat*, Wrt. Voc. ii. 94, 74. v. hwelan.

on-hweorfan; *p.* -hwearf. I. *trans. To change, reverse*:—Metod onhweorfeþ heortan ðīne (*of Nebuchadnezzar's transformation*), Cd. Th. 251, 27; Dan. 570. Hē cwide (*the curse pronounced against Adam*) eft onhwearf, Exon. Th. 39, 7; Cri. 618. Eft is ðæt onhworfen, is nū swā hit nō wǣre freóndscipe uncer, 443, 2; Kl. 23. Hwȳ is ðis gold ādeorcad and ðæt æðeleste hiew hwȳ wearþ hit onhworfen *quomodo obscuratum est aurum, mutatus est color optimus*, Past. 18, 3; Swt. 133, 11. II. *intrans. To change, turn, revert*:—Manegum cyninge onhwearf se anweald and se wela ōþ ðæt hē eft wearþ wædla *qui reges felicitatem calamitate mutaverint*, Bt. 29, 1; Fox 102, 13. Hē (*Nebuchadnezzar*) eft onhwearf wōdan gewittes, Cd. Th. 255, 21; Dan. 627. v. next word.

on-hwirfan; *p.* de. I. *to turn* (of actual motion), (a) *trans.*:—Ic mē wille nū onhwyrfan tō ðisse bǣre, Blickl. Homl. 151, 14. (b) *intrans.*:—Swā swā hweól onhwerfþ, Bt. 33, 4; Fox 132, 13. II. *to invert, transpose*:—Agof (boga) is mīn noma eft onhwyrfed, Exon. Th. 405, 13; Rä. 24, 1. III. *to change, turn*:—Mē onhwyrfdon ða mē grome wurdon of ðære gecynde ðe ic ǣr cwic beheóld, 485, 24; Rä. 72, 2. Ðū geómrast forðam ðe seó woruldsǣlþ onhwyrfed is, Bt. 7, 1: Fox 16, 9. v. preceding word.

on-hwirfedness, e; *f. Change, mutation*:—Sōð God būton ǣlcere onhwerfednesse, Shrn. 167, 34.

on-hyldan. v. on-hildan.

on-hyreness, e; *f. Imitation*:—Ðone weg ðære onhyrenesse *viam imitationis*, Past. 16, 4; Swt. 103, 14. Tō onhyrenesse (*ad imitationem*) ðæra eádigra apostola, Bd. 4, 28; S. 606, 26: 1, 27; S. 492, 23.

on-hyrian; *p.* ede *To imitate, emulate* (with dat. acc.):—Hwīlum ic onhyrge gūþfugles hleóþor, Exon. Th. 406, 20; Rä. 25, 4: 391, 2; Rä. 9, 10. Mon onhyreþ dysegum neátum *homo comparatus est jumentis insipientibus*, Ps. Th. 48, 11. Se ðe hit gehȳreþ hē onhyreþ ðam *ad imitandum bonum auditor sollicitus instigatur*, Bd. pref.; S. 471, 15: Bt. 41, 5; Fox 254, 5. Ða cild onhyriaþ ealdum monnum, 36, 5; Fox 180, 10. Ðonne wē onhyrigaþ Criste, Past. 51; Swt. 397, 1. Ðæt hȳ ne onhyredon ðǣm yfelwillendum, Ps. Th. 36, arg. Ne onhyre (*emulatus fueris*) ðam ðe byþ orsorh, 36, 7. Onhyriaþ, 36, 1. Ne ðū ne onhere *ne emuleris*, Kent. Gl. 58. Ne onherie *ne emuletur*, 885. Ðæt wē onhyrigen ðǣm þeáwum, Past. 34; Swt. 231, 3: Swt. 229, 15. Onhyrgean wē ðone blindan, Blickl. Homl. 21, 9. Wē sceolan onherian Marian ðære ðe smerede Hǣlendes fēt, 75, 11. Onhyrian (-hirian, Cott. MS.), Bt. 40, 4; Fox 240, 4: Bd. 1, 7; S. 477, 2. Ðæt onhyrian woldan, 4, 3; S. 569, 43. Heora līf onhyrian wolde, 4, 13; S. 582, 24: 5, 9; S. 622, 12. Onhyrigean, 1, 26; S. 487, 32. Onhyrgan, 3, 18; S. 545, 43. Hē ðære frymþelīcan cyrican līf wæs onhyrigende, 1, 26; S. 487, 28: 4, 23; S. 593, 15. Onhyrgende, L. Ecg. P. iv. 68, 8; Th. ii. 228, 29.

on-hyriend, es; *m. One who imitates* or *emulates*:—Onhyrgend *emulatores*, Wrt. Voc. ii. 31, 28. Onhyrgend[r]as, 85, 25.

on-hyring, e; *f. Imitation, emulation*:—Anhering *emulatio*, Wrt. Voc. ii. 143, 48. Gōd anda and anhering āscyreþ fram synna leahtrum, and lǣt tō Gode, R. Ben. 131, 13. Ðonne wē onhyrigaþ Criste and eác ða onhyringe gefyllaþ *tunc legem Christi imitando complemus*, Past. 51, 3; Swt. 397, 2.

on-hyscan; *p.* te. I. *to mock, make a jest of*:—Drihten onhnyscþ (? -hyscþ, MS. T.) hine *Dominus irridebit eum*, Ps. Spl. 36, 13. Ic wēnde ðæt hī mec onhyscte *illudi me a senibus existimavi*, Nar. 25, 22. II. *to reproach, abuse, speak ill of*:—Ðonne men eów onhiscaþ (*exprobaverint*), Lk. Skt. 6, 22. Gebiddaþ for ða ðe eów onhyscaþ (-hisceaþ) *pro calumniantibus vos*, 6, 28. Ðæt man ða onhisce swȳðe for worulde and hȳ unweorðige, Wulfst. 168, 6: 70, 12. III. *to detest*:—Ic unrihta gehwylc onhyscte *iniquitatem abominatus sum*, Ps. Th. 118, 163. Hī onhysctan ǣghwylcne mete *omnem escam abominata est anima eorum*, 106, 17.

on-in *within*:—Onin mē *intra me*, Ps. Spl. 38, 4.

on-innan. v. innan, V.

on-irnan *to yield, give way*:—Duru sōna onarn fȳrbendum fæst, syððan hē hire folmum [hrān], Beo. Th. 1447; B. 721. Duru sōna onarn þurh handhrine hāliges gāstes, Andr. Kmbl. 1998; An. 1000. [*O. H. Ger.* int-rinnan *evadere, abire, profugere.*]

on-irning, e; *f. Attack, assault*:—Diówlīca onerninge tōsliteno beón *diabolica incursione lacerari*, Rtl. 36, 1.

on-īwan *to shew*:—Drihten ūs līfes wegas anȳweþ, R. Ben. 3, 5. Ic ðē bidde ðæt ðū mē ðē onȳwe, St. And. 10, 14. Seó hlǣdder ðe Jacobe on swefne wearþ anȳwed, R. Ben. 23, 5.

on-lǣnan; *p.* de; *with gen.* or *acc. of the loan.* I. *to lend, grant*:—Ic eów onlǣne ðās gewītendan, and ic eów geselle ða þurhwuniendan, Past. 46, 5; Swt. 351, 13. Se cræft ðe him Crist onlǣnþ, Met. 10, 37. Hē ūre ðē onlǣnde æfter his bebodum tō brūcanne, Bt. 7, 5; Fox 24, 9. Gif hwā his wǣpnes ōðrum onlǣne, L. Alf. pol. 19; Th. i. 74, 3: L. In. 29; Th. i. 120, 10, 12, 14. Hī ðē onlǣnde wǣron, Bt. 7, 3; Fox 20, 6. II. *to lease, let*:—Denewulf and ða hȳwan on Wintanceastre ænlǣnaþ Ælfrēde his deg XL. hīda landes, Chart. Th. 147, 27. Cf. on-león.

on-lǣtan. I. *to release, relax*:—Ðonne forstes bend Fæder onlǣteþ, Beo. Th. 3223; B. 1609. Ðonne him sigera weard his gewealdleðer wille onlǣtan, Met. 11, 28, 75. II. *to let a thing go on, to continue*:—Tō anlǣtenne *continuanda*, Wrt. Voc. ii. 135, 19. Fæstan twegen dagas on ðære wucan, būtan hȳ ouermicel geswinc habben. Gif hȳ ūt an æcere wurc habben, ðæs middæges gereord is singallīce tō anlǣtenne (on-, MS. T.), R. Ben. 66, 1.

on-lang; *prep. Along*:—Onlong Mǣse, Chr. 882; Erl. 82, 7. v. and-lang.

on-lēc, es; *m. On-look, regard*:—Onlēce *respectu, intuitu*, Hpt. Gl. 487, 50. v. lēc.

on-leccan (?) *to reproach, blame*:—Onlehton (bysmrydon, MS. C.) *irritaverunt*, Ps. Spl. T. 105, 8. Cf. hosp (on leccungæ, MS. T.: tō bysmre, MS. C.) *irrita*, 88, 34, *and see* læcing.

on-lecgende *on-lying*:—Wyrc him onlecgende sealfe, Lchdm. ii. 200, 8.

on-legen, e; *f. An on-laying*, (*medicinal*) *application*:—Onlegen (ἐπίθεμα) tō trymmanne ðone magan, Lchdm. ii. 180, 24. Mid onlegene swā swā mon of swelcum þingum wyrcþ... Lācna mid onlegena beres, 82, 14–24. Gesodene wuduæpla and hlafes cruman and swilce onlegena, 190, 15.

on-leóhtan. v. on-līhtan.

on-leóhtness, e; *f. Illumination*; illuminatio, Ps. Lamb. 138, 11. v. on-līhtness.

on-león; *p.* -lāh, -leáh; *pl.* -ligon; *pp.* -ligen. I. *to grant the loan of something* (gen. of loan):—Gielde se ðæs wǣpnes onlāh, L. Alf. pol. 19; Th. i. 74, 6: Beo. Th. 2939; B. 1467. Onligenre *inpactae*, Wrt. Voc. ii. 111, 31. II. *to grant, bestow*:—Sum ǣhta onlīhþ, sum biþ wonspēdig, Exon. Th. 295, 9; Crä. 30. Metod onlāh Mēdum aldordōmes, Cd. Th. 258, 25; Dan. 681. Ungelīc ðam ōðrum stede ðe mē mīn hearra onlāg, 23, 12; Gen. 358. Hē mē lāre onlāg, Elen. Kmbl. 2489; El. 1246. God hyre sigores onleáh, Judth. Thw. 23, 16; Jud. 124.

on-lēsan, -lēsness. v. on-līsan, -līsness.

on-līc; *adj. Like, similar*:—Heáp synnigra hīge onlīc, Ps. Th. 91, 6. Gelamp ōðer wundor ðissum onlīc, Blickl. Homl. 219, 7: 223, 14. Eal hē ǣr on onlīc weorc āteáh, 215, 5. Manigfeald onlīc wundor ðysum ðǣr wǣrom æteówed, 209, 14. Monige sindon mē suīðe onlīce on ungelǣrednesse, Past. proem.; Swt. 25, 7. Se is lyfte onlīcusð on hiwe, 14; Swt. 85, 5. Se fugel is onlīcost peán, Exon. Th. 219, 25; Ph. 312. Onlīcust, 189, 20; Az. 62. v. an-līc.

on-līce; *adv. Like, in like manner*:—Ealle ða rīca forheregian... swīðe onlīce ðam micclan flōde, Bt. 16, 1; Fox 50, 6: Met. 8, 47: Elen. Kmbl. 197; El. 99. Onlīcost dydon swelce him nǣfre ǣr ðǣm gelīc yfel an ne becōme, Ors. 3, 10; Swt. 140, 10: Past. 17; Swt. 123, 7. v. an-līce.

on-līcness, e; *f. Likeness, image*:—Idese onlīcnes *the form of a woman*, Beo. Th. 2706; B. 1351: Andr. Kmbl. 1461; An. 731. Hē hæfþ mon geworhtne æfter his onlīcnesse, Cd. Th. 25, 19; Gen. 396: Exon. Th. 424, 10; Rä. 41, 37. v. an-līcness.

on-liésan. v. on-līsan.

on-līhtan, -leóhtan. I. of places or things, *to illumine, make bright, cause to shine*, (a) literally:—Mycel leóht onleóhte ðæt carcern, St. And. 4, 4. Ōþ ðæt ðære sunnan leóman hine (*the moon*) eft onlīhton, Lchdm. iii. 240, 27. Onleóhtende *inluminans*, Hymn. Surt. 15, 22. Ealle steorran weorþaþ onlīhte and gebirhte of ðære sunnan, Bt. 34, 5; Fox 140, 5. (b) metaph.:—God onlȳhteþ (*illuminet*) andwlitan his ofer ūs, Ps. Spl. 66, 1. Onlȳht (*inlustra*) ansīne ðīn ofer þeów ðīnne, 30, 20. Tō hwon yldestū middangeard tō onlȳhtenne, Blickl. Homl. 7, 33. II. of persons, (a) *to give sight to, make the sight clear*:—Drihten blinde on heora eágum onleóhteþ *Dominus illuminat caecos*. Ps. Th. 145, 7. Heó gegōdaþ and onlīht ðæra eágena scearpnysse, Lchdm. i. 72, 15. Ðæt se ylca ða dohter ðæs ealdormannes blinde onlīhte, Bd. 1, 18; S. 484, 30. Ðæt wundor worhte, ðæt hē ðone blindan onlȳhte, Blickl. Homl. 19, 19. Mon geseah hine blinde onlȳhtende, 177, 15. Ðā geseah hē sōna gesundfullum eágum, þurh ðone ylcan onlīht ðe hine ǣr āblende, H. R. 107, 28: Homl. Skt. i. 21, 275. (b) *to clear the mental vision, to enlighten*:—Sōð leóht ðæt onlȳht ǣlcne man, Jn. Skt. 1, 9. Se hālga Gāst ealle ða englas onlīht, Ælfc. T. Grn. 2, 14. Worda mē ðīnra wīse onleóhteþ, Ps. Th. 118, 130. Ne onlīhtaþ hī nāuht ðæs mōdes eágan, Bt. 34, 8; Fox 144, 32. Ðū simle mīne sāwle onlīhtest, Homl. Th. i. 74, 31. Hē hió onlȳhte mid ðæs Hālgan Gāstes gife, Blickl. Homl. 145, 6. Onliht ða eágan ūres mōdes mid ðīnum leóhte, Bt. 33, 4; Fox 132, 33: Ps. Th. 12, 4. Onleóht heorte manna, Hymn. Surt. 23, 1. Crist mæg ðīne nytennysse onlīhtan, Homl. Skt. i. 5, 200. Manegum wearþ mōd onlīhted, Apstls. Kmbl. 104; Ap. 52. Wē wurdon onlīhte þurh geleáfan, Homl. Th. i. 154, 21. Onlȳhte, Blickl.

Homl. 161, 14. **III.** *to give light* (with dat.):—Ðæt hit onlīhte eallum ðe on ðam hūse synt, Mt. Kmbl. 5, 15. Onlīhtan ðām ðe on þȳstrum sittaþ, Lk. Skt. 1, 79. **IV.** *intrans. To shine*:—Ic onlīhte oðđe scȳne *luceo*, Ælfc. Gr. 35; Som. 38, 8. Sæterdæg onlȳhte (*inlucescebat*), Lk. Skt. 23, 54. Onlīhton (*illuxerunt*) līgrascas ðīne, Ps. Spl. 76, 18: 96, 4. Heora wegas onlīhton, Blickl. Homl. 137, 2. Swā onlīhte (*luceat*) eówer leóht, Mt. Kmbl. 5, 16. Onlióhte *inlucescat*, Kent. Gl. 206.

on-līhting, e; *f. Illumination, enlightening*:—Onlȳhtinga *illuminatio*, Ps. Spl. 43, 5. Onlīhtinge, Ps. Lamb. 26, 1. Onlīhting, 138, 11. On onlīhtinge fȳres, 77, 14.

on-līhtness, e; *f. Illumination*:—Onlȳhtnes (-līhtnes, Ps. Lamb.) *illuminatio*, Ps. Spl. 26, 1: 43, 5. Seó onlȳhtnes Cristes godspelles, Bd. 2, 9; S. 511, 10: 2, 2; S. 502, 29. v. on-leóhtness.

on-līsan. **I.** *to unloose* (real or metaphorical bonds):—Ðæt bearn benda onlȳseþ, Exon. Th. 5, 12; Cri. 68. Hē ða tungan onlȳsde, Blickl. Homl. 167, 10. Hire bendas wǣron onlȳsede, 89, 25. Onlȳsde, 87, 36. **II.** *to release, deliver, liberate*:—Mīn līf of ðære ēcean forwyrde ðū onlȳsdest, 89, 4. Cyning onlēsde (*solvit*) hine, Ps. Surt. 104, 20. Tō onliésanne ða gehæftan on helle, Past. 58; Swt. 443, 10. Siððan seó sāwl of ðam carcerne ðæs līchoman onliésed biþ, Bt. 18, 4; Fox 68, 15. Onlēsed, unsǣled *desolutus*, i. *liberatus*, Wrt. Voc. ii. 139, 29: 138, 50. Swā hwylce swā hē on eorþan ālȳsde, ðæt se wǣre on heofonum onlȳsed, Blickl. Homl. 49, 18. Fram swā myclum cwylmnessum onlȳsed beón, Bd. 4, 9; S. 577, 10: 5, 19; S. 639, 42. Onlȳsed ðȳ līchaman *solutus corpore*, 3, 19; S. 548, 29.

on-līsness, e; *f. Deliverance, redemption*:—Ða ðe on helle synt biddaþ ðīnre onlēsnesse *ask for deliverance by thee*, Blickl. Homl. 81, 23: 67, 3. Onlēsnisse *redemtio*, Lk. Skt. Lind. Rush. 21, 28.

on-līðian *to become pliant, to yield*:—Sceal hira ānra gehwylc onlūtan and onlīðigan ðe hafaþ læsse mægen, Salm. Kmbl. 713; Sal. 356.

on-lōciend, es; *m. An on-looker, spectator*:—Heó wæs swīðe lufigendlīc eallum onlōciendum, Anglia ix. 30, 97.

on-lūcan. **I.** literally, *to unlock, open*:—Ðæs ceasterhlides onlūcan . . . ða fæstan locu nǣnig ōðer eft onlūceþ, Exon. Th. 20, 7–20. Onlaec *reserat*, Wrt. Voc. ii. 119, 2. Suelce ic gesāwe sume duru onlocene, Past. 21, 3; wt. 155, 6. **II.** metaph. *to open, disclose, reveal*:—Ðæt word ðære þreáunge is cǣg forðam hit oft onlȳcþ (anlȳcþ, Hatt. MS.) and geopenaþ ða scylde *clavis est sermo correptionis; quia culpam detegit*, Past. 15, 2; Swt. 90, 11. Hié ne ongietaþ nā hū suīðe hié onlūcaþ hiera mōd mid ðæm unþeáwe ofermētta *quantum se vitiis superbiendo aperiat, non agnoscit*, 38, 1; Swt. 271, 22. Mōdhord onleác and ðus wordum cwæþ, Andr. Kmbl. 344; An. 172. Leóþucræft onleác, Elen. Kmbl. 2499; El. 1251. Wordhord onleác, Beo. Th. 524; B. 259. Engla helm tuddorspēd onleác (*revoked the sentence of barrenness*), Cd. Th. 166, 24; Gen. 2752. Hwylc ðæs hordgates, cǣgan cræfte, ða clamme onleác, Exon. Th. 429, 30; Rā. 43, 12. Wærc in gewōd līchord onleác *pain hath invaded me, hath opened to itself a way within my body*, 163, 31; Gū. 1002: 170, 26; Gū. 1117. Ðæt mon onlūce ða heardan heortan *duritiam cordis aperire*, Past. 21, 3; Swt. 155, 2. Onlūcan gāstes cǣgon, Cd. Th. 211, 6; Exod. 522. Ic hæbbe lārcræftas onlocen, Salm. Kmbl. 5; Sal. 3.

on-lūtan *to lout, bend down, bow*:—Hē onlȳtt tō ðissum eorþlīcum, suā ðæt neát for gīfernesse onlȳt tō ðære eorþan, Past. 21, 3; Swt. 157, 2–4. Ælc gesceaft ealle mægene symle onlȳt wið his gecyndes, Met. 13, 66. Hié him tō onluton and hine weorþodan swā cinige gerīseþ, Blickl. Homl. 69, 31: 87, 7. Anlūte him eáðmōdlīce tō mid ðam heáfde, R. Ben. 83, 11. Hira sceal ānra gehwylc onlūtan, ðe hafaþ læsse mægen, Salm. Kmbl. 713; Sal. 356. Ælc gesceaft biþ heald onloten (-locen, Fox) wið hire gecynde, Bt. 25; Fox 88, 7.

on-lȳhtan, -lȳhting, -lȳhtness, -lȳsan. v. on-līhtan, -līhting, -līhtness, -līsan.

on-mǣdla. v. on-mēdla.

on-mǣlan *to address*:—Him Babilone weard yrre andswarode, eorlum onmǣlde, grimme ðām gingum oncwæþ, Cd. Th. 229, 1; Dan. 210.

on-mang; *prep. with dat. Among*:—Onmang folce, Lev. 24, 10: Homl. Skt. i. 23, 92. Onmang ōðrum mannum, 23, 478. Onmang ðam ðe hī on wōpe wǣron *whilst they were weeping*, 23, 246.

on-mearc. v. mearc.

on-mearcung, e; *f. An inscription*:—Onmercunge *inscribtionem*, Lk. Skt. Rush. 12, 24.

on-mēdan (?) *to take upon one's self, to presume* (*the following passage should be given under* mēdan):—Ondsware ȳwe se hine on mēde wordum secgan hū se wudu hātte *let him give answer, who will take upon himself to say in words, what the name of that wood is*, Exon. Th. 437, 30; Rā. 56, 15. v. next word.

on-mēdla (-medla, Grimm, Grein), an; *m.* **I.** *pride, glory, magnificence*:—Ald onmēdla is gecyrred *the glory of earlier times is changed*, Elen. Kmbl. 2529; El. 1266. Ðæt geó guman heóldan, ðenden him on eorþan onmēdla wæs, Exon. Th. 51, 13; Cri. 815. Dagas sind gewitene, ealle onmēdlan eorþan rīces, 310, 27; Seef. 81. **II.** *pride, arrogance, presumption*:—For onmēdlan, Beo. Th. 5844; B. 2926. Him for onmǣdlan eorre geworden, Cd. Th. 291, 11; Sat. 429. **III.** *courage, boldness*:—For hwam ne mōton wē ealle mid onmēdlan (*boldly*) gangan in Godes rīce, Salm. Kmbl. 704; Sal. 351. v. an-medla.

on-mētan *to paint, cover as with colour*:—Ðū mid sārlīcre sceame onmēttest (-meltest, Th.) *perfudisti eum confusione*, Ps. Th. 88, 38. v. ā-mētan.

on-middan; *prep. Amid, in the middle of*:—Onmiddan ðæm hwǣte *in medio tritici*, Mt. Kmbl. 13, 25. Onmiddan ðām þȳstrum, Bd. 5, 12; S. 628, 19. Onmiddan ðære byrig, Homl. Skt. i. 23, 609. Ōmiddan eówrum sceáfum, Gen. 37, 7. v. ā-middan, midde.

on-mirran *to hinder, obstruct, disturb*:—Ic bebeóde ðæt ðisne freóðōm nǣnig mīnra æfterfylgendra eft ne onwende, ne on nǣnigum dǣlum hyne ne onmyrdon, Chart. Th. 390, 31. v. ā-myrran.

on-mitta, an; *m. A measure*; exagium, Wrt. Voc. ii. 30, 49: 144, 45. v. an-mitta.

on-mōd; *adj. Bold, courageous*, Exon. Th. 146, 29; Gū. 717. v. an-mōd.

on-munan *to esteem, consider* (*worthy*), *think* (*highly of*). (a) with acc. of person and adj. denoting worth:—Būton ic openlīce gecȳþe ðæt ic God sylfa sȳ, ne onmun ðū mē nānre āre wyrþne, Blickl. Homl. 181, 36. Ælc ðara ðe sīe under ðæm gioke hlāfordscipes hē sceal his hlāford ǣghwelcre āre wierþne onmunan *quicumque sunt sub jugo servi, dominos suos omni honore dignos arbitrentur*, Past. 29; Swt. 201, 23. (b) with acc. of person alone:—Hē ūsic on herge geceás tō ðyssum sīðfæte, onmunde ūsic mǣrþa *he thought us fit for great deeds*, Beo. Th. 5273. Ðā cuǣdon hié ðæt hié hié ðæs ne onmunden ðon mā ðe eówre gefēran *then they said, that they did not consider themselves entitled to accept the offer, 'any more than your comrades did,'* Chr. 755; Erl. 50, 24. Miclum geblissod ðæt hié God wolde onmunan swā micles ofer menn ealle *Andrew was greatly rejoiced that God deemed his disciples worthy of such high regard beyond all men* (*in granting them the vision they had seen*), Andr. Kmbl. 1789; An. 897.

on-nytt *useless*:—Onnitte *inutiles*, Ps. Spl. 13, 4. v. un-nytt.

ono *if*:—Ono nū ðæt wīf wel gedyrstgade *si igitur bene praesumsit*, Bd. 1, 27; S. 494, 19. Ono hē wiste hine on wōnyssum geeácnodne, hē ðā geómrade hine fram scylde ācennedne *qui enim in iniquitatibus conceptum se noverat, a delicto se natum gemebat*, S. 495, 24. Ono (ond ?) gif (*si autem*) hē gehæfted wæs, hwæt hē ðonne ne feaht, S. 497, 37: 3, 24; S. 557, 29. [Cf. (?) *Goth.* an: *O. H. Ger.* inu, enu.]

on-orettan *to perform with effort, to accomplish* (*a difficult undertaking*):—Nō hē ofer Offan eorlscype fremede (*he did not excel Offa*), ac Offa geslōg cynerīca mǣst; nǣnig efeneald him eorlscipe māran onorette āne sweorde *no one of equal age had done such heroic deeds*, Exon. Th. 321, 4; Vīd. 41. Iudiscfēða ān onorette uncūð gelād *the tribe of Judah by itself performed the difficult and unknown course* (*the passage of the Red Sea*), Cd. Th. 197, 25; Exod. 313.

on-orþung, e; *f. A breathing in* or *on*:—Fram onorþunge (*inspiratione*) gāstes yrres ðīnes, Ps. Lamb. 17, 16.

onoþa, an; *f. Fear*:—Onoþa *formido*, Wrt. Voc. ii. 35, 75. Anoþa, 109, 3. [Cf. anathe *sollicitudine*, *cura* in Papias, quoted by Graff. i. 267.]

on-pennian *to unpen, open*:—Ðæt wæter, ðonne hit biþ gepynd, hit miclaþ . . . Ac gif sió pynding wierþ onpennad, ðonne tōflēwþ hit eall, Past. 38, 6; Swt. 277, 8.

on-rād, e; *f. Riding on horseback*:—Sēcen hié him broc on onrāde and on wǣne *let them seek for themselves fatigue in riding on horseback and in a carriage*, Lchdm. ii. 184, 13.

on-ræfniendlīc; *adj. Intolerable*; intolerabilis, Ps. Spl. 123, 4.

on-rǣs, es; *m. On-rush, attack, assault, violent motion*:—Onrǣs *impetus*, Ælfc. Gr. 11; Som. 15, 12. Flōdes onrǣs *fluminis impetus*, Ps. Spl. 45, 4: Ps. Surt. ii. 189, 40. Hyne þurhþȳdde mid egeslīcum onhrǣse, Homl. Skt. i. 3, 274. Onrǣs *irruptionem*, Hpt. Gl. 464, 66. Ðone onrǣs his hātheortnesse *fervoris sui impetu*, Past. 40, 5; Swt. 297, 20.

on-rǣsa (?), an; *m. Attack, irruption*:—Onrǣsan *inruptiones*, Wrt. Voc. ii. 45, 1.

on-rǣsan. v. rǣsan.

on-reádan; *p.* -reód *To redden, stain*:—Onreód *inbuit*, Wrt. Voc. ii. 111, 65. v. on-reódan.

onred, es; *m.* (?) *The name of some plant*:—Onred, hāmwyrt . . . onredes emfela, Lchdm. ii. 104, 14–15. Genim onred, 270, 26.

on-reódan; *p.* -reád *To redden*:—Brynegield onreád (-hread, MS.) rommes blōde, Cd. Th. 177, 18; Gen. 2931. v. reódan.

onrettan. v. orrettan.

on-riht; *adj. Right, proper*:—Se wuldorcyning gesette ȳðum heora onrihtne ryne, Cd. Th. 10, 35; Gen. 167. v. on-rihtlīce *and next word*.

on-riht, es; *n. A right* (?):—Hālige þeóde, Israēla cyn, onriht Godes *God's peculiar people*, Cd. Th. 200, 18; Exod. 358. [Cf. *Icel.* eiga rētt ā einum *to have rights over a person*.]

on-rihtlīce; *adv. Rightly, duly*:—Ða lāreówas sceolan synfullum mannum tǣcan, ðæt hió heora synna cunnon onrihtlīce geandettan, Blickl. Homl. 43, 16.

on-rihtwísness, e; *f. Unrighteousness, iniquity:*—Onrihtwísnyssum *iniquitatibus*, Ps. Spl. 52, 2.

on-rísan *to arise:*—Mín yrre onríst ongēn hig *irascetur furor meus contra eum*, Deut. 31, 17.

on-ryne, es; *m.* I. *a running on, course:*—Onryne tíde *cursu temporis*, Hymn. Surt. 36, 8. II. *a running on* or *against, an attack:*—Ne đē ǽniges yfeles onryne (anryne, MS. H.) dereþ, Lchdm. i. 328, 1, MS. B.

on-sacan. I. *to attack, strive against:*—Ne biþ cwēnlíc þeáw đætte freoþuwebbe feores onsæce leófne mannan (*to strive with a man for his life*), Beo. Th. 3889; B. 1942. II. *to resist, refuse to comply with a demand:*—Đeáh đū onsōce đæt đū sōþ godu lufian wolde *though you have refused to love the true gods*, Exon. Th. 254, 8; Jul. 194. Hē ne trūwode đæt hē sǽmannum onsacan mihte, hord forstandan bearn and brȳde, Beo. Th. 5901; B. 2954. III. *to deny*, (a) of persons, *to declare that one has no knowledge of a person:*—Ne đē onsæco (-sæcco, Lind.) ic *non te negabo*, Mk. Skt. Rush. 14, 31. Đū mē onsæces *me negabis*, 14, 72. Se đe mē onsaekeþ (-sæccas, Lind.) beforan monnum, onsaece ic đone beforan fæder mínum, Mt. Kmbl. 10, 33. (b) *to refuse a person what he wants:*—Gif huā wil æfter meh gecyme onsæcæ (andsæce, Rush.) hine seolfne *abneget semetipsum*, 16, 24. (c) *to refuse to acknowledge a claim, not to allow the truth of a statement*, in a legal sense *to deny a charge:*—Ne onsace ic nāuht, đæt seó eádignes síe đæt hēhste gōd đises andweardan lífes, Bt. 24, 3; Fox 84, 14. Đā onsōc se ōđer, and cwæþ hē him nān feoh ne sealde, Shrn. 127, 26. Hē onsōc (andsōc, Rush.) mid aađ, đæt ic ne conn đone monno, Mt. Kmbl. Lind. 26, 72, 70. Forđam hié his cræftas onsōcon (*they would not acknowledge his powers, would not bow down to the golden image*), Cd. Th. 230, 1; Dan. 226. Se đæs onsōce, đætte sōþ wǽre Waldend, se hié ālȳsde, 244, 20; Dan. 451. Đonne sceal hē be .LX. hȳda onsacan đære þiéfþe gif hē āđwyrđe biþ. Gif Englisc onstal gā forþ, onsace be twȳfealdum, L. In. 46; Th. i. 130, 13–15: Th. i. 132, 1: 28; Th. i. 120, 8. IV. *to make excuse:*—Ongunnun alle onsaca (-sacca, Lind.) *coeperunt omnes excusare*, Lk. Skt. Rush. 14, 18. Cf. of-sacan. V. *to sacrifice* (v. on-secgan):—Onsacende *litaturus*, Wrt. Voc. ii. 53, 57.

on-sæc; *adj.* I. *freed from a charge, excused* (cf. *Icel.* sekr):—Hæfe mec onsæcne *habe me excusatum*, Lk. Skt. Lind. Rush. 14, 18. II. *denying:*—Mec đū bist onsæcc (-sæcen, Rush.) *me es negaturus*, Mk. Skt. Lind. 14, 30. Mec đū bist onsæc *me negabis*, 14, 72.

on-sǽgan *to cause to sink down, to prostrate:*—Ǽrđon hine deáþ onsǽgde, Exon. Th. 171, 32; Gū. 1135. Hū hí (*hell*) būtan ende ēce stondeþ, đæm đe đǽr for his synnum onsǽgd weorþeþ, 446, 27; Dōm. 28. Selegesceotu synd onsǽgd (?), Ps. Th. 82, 6.

on-sǽge; *adj. Falling upon, assailing, attacking:*—Wē ǽr đysan oftor brǽcan, đonne wē bēttan, and đȳ is đisse þeóde fela onsǽge. Ne dohte hit nū lange inne ne ūte, ac wæs here and hunger, bryne and blōdgyte on gewelhwylcon ende, Wulfst. 159, 7: 128, 14: 243, 2. Hǽđcynne wearþ gūþ onsǽge *war had come upon Hæthcyn*, Beo. Th. 4960; B. 2483: 4159; B. 2076. [*O. H. Ger.* ana-seigi *infestus*.]

on-sægedness, e; *f.* I. *the rite, act of sacrifice* or *offering:*—Onsægednys lofes ārwurþaþ mē *sacrificium laudis honorificabit me*, Ps. Spl. 49, 24. Đonne sceal hē hine āhabban fram onsægdnysse (*immolatione*) đæs hālgan gerȳnes, Bd. 1, 27; S. 497, 4. Hē ricels bærnde in Godes ansægdnesse, Shrn. 133, 29. Ic wille mildheortnesse næs onsægdnesse (-sægednesse, MS. A.), Mt. Kmbl. 9, 13. Aarone tō fylste tō đām ǽlícum onsægednyssum, Num. 18, 2. Onsægdnyssum and offrungum, Mk. Skt. 12, 33. Onsægdnessa *cerimonias*, Wrt. Voc. ii. 15, 81. II. *what is offered at the rite, a sacrifice, oblation:*—Nis nā tō onfōnne seó hālige onsægdnes (*eucharistiam accipere*), L. Ecg. C. 35; Th. ii. 160, 37. Gif seó onsægednys on eorþan fealle, L. Ecg. P. iv. 15; Th. ii. 216, 15. Ne offra đū đínre onsægdnysse (*victimae*) blōd uppan beorman, Ex. 23, 18. Þurh lāc đære hālwendan onsægdnesse (*hostiae*), Bd. 4, 22; S. 592, 22. Gode onsægdnesse beran, S. 592, 25: 5, 10; S. 624, 32. Đa onsægdnysse đa đe fram eów deóflum wǽron āgoldene, 1, 7; S. 477, 36. Onsægdnisse onsæcgan *victimis placare*, Nar. 20, 5. Ic đē onsegednesse brohte, Ps. Grn. ii. 279, 120. Onsegednesse *victimas*, Wülck. Gl. 61, 8: 71, 40.

on-sægness, e; *f. A sacrifice:*—Onsægnessa *holocausta*, Blickl. Gl.

on-sægung, e; *f. An offering in sacrifice; immolatio:*—Onsægung, Wrt. Voc. i. 28, 48. Onsægcgiung, ii. 49, 45.

on-sǽlan *to untie, unfasten:*—Onsǽl meoto sigehrēđ secgum, Beo. Th. 983; B. 489. Đonne gemēte gyt eoselan gesǽlede and hire folan; onsǽlaþ hié, Blickl. Homl. 69, 36. Onsaelid *desolutus*, Wrt. Voc. ii. 105, 80. Hæft wæs onsǽled, Cd. Th. 215, 15; Exod. 583.

on-sagu, e; *f. A charge brought against a person, accusation:*—Ā biþ andsæc swíđere đonne onsagu, i. e. *in a case where a charge is brought against a person, and it is met with a denial attested by the proper legal formalities, the case against him fails*, L. Eth. ii. 9; Th. i. 290, 17. [Cf. the somewhat similar principle which follows:—Āgnung biþ nēr đam đe hæfþ đonne đam đe æfter sprecþ. See also Grmm. R. A. 856.] Đā cwæþ Eugenia đæt heó eáþe mihte Melantian onsage oferdrífan (*refute the charge*), Homl. Skt. i. 2, 206. Manega mid leásum onsagum geneálǽhton *multi falsi testes accessissent*, Mt. Kmbl. 26, 60. v. onsecgan.

on-sand, e; *f. A sending to another:*—Onsande *immissiones*, Ps. Spl. 77, 54. Onsanda, Blickl. Gl.

on-sāwen *sown:*—Sǽd onsāwen, Exon. Th. 215, 14; Ph. 253.

on-scǽgan (?) *to mock, deride, reproach:*—Hí tǽldon ł onscǽgdon (onsægdon?) ł hig hyspton mē *subsannaverunt me*, Ps. Lamb. 34, 16.

on-sceacan. I. *to shake:*—Heó fеđera onsceóc, Cd. Th. 88, 26; Gen. 1471. Onscacene *concusa*, Wrt. Voc. ii. 15, 80. II. *to shake off, remove:*—Onscacan (-seacan, Wrt.) *detestare*, Wrt. Voc. ii. 106, 28. Onsceæcannæ onsceacnessum (ob-, MS.) *excusandas excusationes*, Ps. Spl. T. 140, 4. Cf. ā-sceacan.

on-sceacness. v. preceding word.

on-sceamian, -sceoniendlíc, -sceonung. v. of-sceamian, on-scuniendlíc, -scunung.

on-sceortian *to grow short:*—Swā đa dagas forþ onsceortiaþ *as the days go on shortening*, Shrn. 96, 3. Cf. ā-sceortian.

on-scunian, -scynian, -sceonian. I. *to regard with loathing, to abhor, detest, execrate:*—Ic onscunige (-sceonige) *abhominor, detestor*, Ælfc. Gr. 25; Som. 26, 63. Drihten onscunaþ (*abominatur*) ealle đās þing, Deut. 18, 12. Ealle Egiptisce onscuniaþ (*detestantur*) scēphyrdas, Gen. 46, 34. Onscuniaþ *abhominentur*, Wrt. Voc. ii. 3, 59. Ic hit swíđe onscunode *multum detestans*, Bd. 3, 17; S. 545, 3. Word mín onscunedon (*execrabantur*) wiđ mē, Ps. Surt. 55, 6. Đā anscunedon hiene his āgene leóde, and monige from him cirdon, Ors. 3, 11; Swt. 152, 12. Đonne hē biþ æfstig wiđ ōđra manna yfelu anscunige eác his āgenu *cum contra aliena vitia aemulatur ostenditur, quae sua sunt, exequatur*, Past. 13, 2; Swt. 79, 12. Đā wæs ic đæt swíđe onscuniende, and mē lāþ wæs, Bd. 5, 12; S. 630, 32. Onscunigende gefeoht *exosus bella*, Ælfc. Gr. 41; Som. 44, 12. Onscunede *exosam*, Wülck. Gl. 55, 18. II. *to regard with disfavour, to refuse, reject, shun:*—Ǽlc gesceaft onscunaþ đæt đæt hire wiđerweard biþ *quae sunt adversa, depellit*, Bt. 16, 3; Fox 56, 4. Se đe đis gewrit gehȳreþ hē flȳhþ đæt yfel and onscunaþ *devitando quod noxium est*, Bd. pref.; S. 471, 16. Đā onscunode hē đæt and cwæþ *qui renuens ait*, Gen. 48, 19. Hē onscunede unrihthǽmed *ille recusabat stuprum*, 39, 10. Gē onscunedon (*rejected*) đone Scippend, and gedwolan fylgdon, Elen. Kmbl. 739; El. 370. Onscuna đū leásunga (cf. fleóh leasunga, Ex. 23, 7), L. Alf. 44; Th. i. 54, 14. Godes willan onscunian *Dei voluntate resistere*, Gen. 50, 19. Heora ealde þeáwas onscunian and forlǽtan *priscis abdicare moribus*, Bd. 2, 2; S. 502, 35. Nis nā tō onsceonienne seó sōđe gecyrrednys *non est rejicienda vera conversio*, L. Ecg. P. i. 2; Th. ii. 172, 10. III. *to regard with fear:*—Ondrēdeþ ł onscynaþ *formidet*, Jn. Skt. Lind. 14, 27: *metuit*, Rtl. 125, 25. Onscyniaþ *opriant* (= *aporiant*), Wrt. Voc. ii. 65, 16. Onscunode *exorruit*, 33, 14. Đeáh hí men ođđe hundas wiđ eodan, hí hí nā ne onscunedon . . . and nān heort ne onscunode nǽnne león *though men or dogs went against them* (*wild beasts*), *they were not afraid of them . . . and the hart was not afraid of the lion*, Bt. 35, 6; Fox 168, 2–9. Gif đū heora untreówa onscunige *si perfidam perhorrescis*, 7, 2; Fox 18, 8. Onscunien (*revereantur*) feónd míne, Ps. Surt. 34, 4, 26. Se onscunienda þystel *carduus orrens*, Wrt. Voc. ii. 22, 43. Onscuniende *aporians*, 2, 23: 4, 74. Onscunigende, 78, 30. Anscungendi *aporiens*, 100, 41. IV. *to irritate:*—Ābealg *vel* onscunede *exacerbavit*, i. *provocavit, adflixit*, 144, 56. Onscynedun *exacervaverunt*, Ps. Surt. 106, 11.

on-scuniend, -scunigend (?), es; *m. One who detests* or *shuns:*—Nān (*no friend of the dead man*) hine tō đæs swíđe ne lufaþ, đæt hē sōna syđđan ne sȳ onscungend, seođđan se líchoma and se gāst gedǽlde beóþ, Blickl. Homl. 111, 29.

on-scuniendlíc, -scunigendlíc, -sceoniendlíc; *adj. Abominable, detestable, execrable:*—Onscunigendlíc *perosus*, Ælfc. Gr. 33; Som. 36, 62: *detestabilis*, Bd. 3, 9; S. 533, 9. Cristendōm wæs đǽr onscunigendlíc, Homl. Skt. i. 2, 330. Onscuniendlíc *execrandum*, Wrt. Voc. ii. 33, 20. Đa onscuniendlecan *execranda*, 33, 5. Onscuniendlícan *probrosas*, 66, 31. Onscuniendlíce (*abominabiles*) gewordene synd, Ps. Spl. 13, 2: Ps. Surt. 52, 2. Onsceoniendlíce, Ps. Th. 52, 1. Đa anlícnessa ealra onscuniendlícra nīetena *omnis animalium abominatio*, Past. 21, 3; Swt. 155, 14. Anscunigendlícra (anscunigendra, Cott. MSS.), Swt. 153, 22.

on-scunung, -sceonung, e; *f.* I. *abomination, execration:*—Of onscununge *execratione*, Ps. Spl. C. 58, 14. Hí setton mē on onscununge (*abominationem*) him, 87, 8. Đonne gē geseóþ đa onsceonunge (*abominationem*) đære tōworpennysse, Mt. Kmbl. 24, 15. II. *irritation, exasperation:*—In onscununge *in exacervatione*, Ps. Surt. 94, 9.

on-scynian. v. on-scunian.

on-scyte, es; *m.* I. *an attack, assault:*—Salomon đæt mǽre hūs Gode betǽhte, him and his folce tō gescȳldnysse wiđ ǽlces yfeles onscyte *as a protection against the assault of every evil*, Homl. Th. ii. 578, 23. II. *an attack in words, a calumny, backbiting:*—Mǽst ǽlc ōđrum derede wordes and dǽde; and hūru unrihtlíce mǽst ǽlc ōđerne æftan heáweþ mid scandlícan onscytan [and mid wrōhtlācan, MS. E.], Wulfst. 160, 5. For ídelan onscytan hȳ scamaþ, đæt hȳ bētan heora misdǽda, 165, 7.

on-sēcan *to require something* (gen.) *of a person* (acc.):—Ne onsēcþ *non quaeret*, Ps. Spl. T. 9 second, 4. Ðǣr .xxx. wæs and feówere eác feores onsōhte þurh wǣges wylm *then was life required of thirty-four by the rage of the wave* (cf. *under* ā-sēcan, Ps. 118, 95), Exon. Th. 283, 13; Jul. 679.

on-secgan. I. *to sacrifice, offer*:—Ic onsecge *sacrificabo*, Ps. Surt. 53, 8. Ic ðē tifer onsecge, Ps. Th. 65, 12. Gif man medmycles hwæthwega deóflum onsægþ (*immolaverit*), L. Ecg. C. 32; Th. ii. 156, 15. Hē lāc onsægde, Cd. Th. 107, 21; Gen. 1792. Hē gild onsægde, 172, 11; Gen. 2842. Hē lāc onsægde (*of Christian service*), Exon. Th. 168, 28; Gū. 1084. Mesiane noldon ðæt Læcedemonia mægdenmenn mid heora ofreden and heora godum onsægden, Ors. 1, 14; Swt. 56, 16. Hié Gode eáðmōdlīce lāc onsægdon, Blickl. Homl. 201, 14. Onsecggaþ gē him mid sōðfæstnesse wæstmum, 41, 10. Ne yld ðū ðæt ðū ðām myclan godum mid ūs onsecge *diis magnis sacrificare ne differas*, Bd. 1, 7; S. 477, 36. Se ðe godgeldum onsæcge ofer God āne, L. Alf. 32; Th. i. 52, 12. Gif ðū onsecgan nelt sōðum godum, Exon. Th. 253, 3; Jul. 174. Ðu scealt Isaac mē onsecgan, Cd. Th. 172, 30; Gen. 2852. Ðǣm godum onsægdnisse onsæcgan *victimis placare*, Nar. 20, 5. Ongunnan heora bearn blōtan feóndum, sceuccum onsæcgean *immolaverunt filios suos, et filias suas daemoniis*, Ps. Th. 105, 27. Onsægd sīe *turificatur*, Wrt. Voc. ii. 88, 51. [Cf. *O. H. Ger.* insaket *litat*; insaket *delibatus*; insaget pim *delibor, sacrificio*.] II. *to deny, renounce, abjure* (*O. H. Ger.* antsagēn *renunciare, abjurare, excusare*: *Ger.* ent-sagen):—Gif mon sīe dumb oððe deáf geboren ðæt hē ne mǣge his synna onsecggan (-sæcgan, MS. H.; ætsacan, MS. B.) ne andettan, bēte se fæder his misdǣda, L. Alf. pol. 14; Th. i. 70, 15.

on-segedness. v. on-sægedness.

on-sendan. I. *to send off, despatch* (*an emissary*):—Onsende *direxit*, Wrt. Voc. ii. 27, 19. Him his sunu hām onsende *filium remisit*, Ors. 4, 11; Swt. 206, 2. Hine God ūs onsende, Beo. Th. 770; B. 382. Se ðisne ār hider onsende, Andr. Kmbl. 3207; An. 1606. Ðā onbeád heó him ðæt hē hire tō onsænde all ða gesīðwīf, Shrn. 87, 21. Ðæt hē Angelþeóde onsende lāreówas, Bd. 2, 1; S. 501, 29. Hwylcne Arcebiscop hē onsendan mihte on Angolþeódes cyricum, 4, 1; S. 563, 29. Tō ǣlcum biscepstōle on mīnum rīce ic wille āne (*a copy of the translation*) onsendan, Past. pref.; Swt. 9, 1. Onsended *distinatus*, Wrt. Voc. ii. 26, 64: 28, 15. Ic wæs hider onsended, Blickl. Homl. 9, 20. Hē wæs of heofenum onsended, 131, 13: Chr. 430; Erl. 10, 18. Onsendum gewritum *missis literis*, Bd. 2, 10; S. 512, 17. II. *to send forth* or *out*, (a) literal:—Ðǣr wǣron on carcerne ccxlviii wera and xlix wīfa, ða Andreas ðanon onsende, Blickl. Homl. 239, 15. (b) metaph. *to emit* (*an odour*, etc.):—Of ðære stōwe mycel swētnes onsended wæs, Bd. 5, 12; S. 629, 35. Seó beorhtnes ðæs onsendan leóhtes, 4, 7; S. 575, 9. (c) *to send forth* (*the spirit*), *to give up* (*the ghost*):—Sōna swā hē ðās word gecwæþ, hē his gāst onsende, Blickl. Homl. 191, 29. Heó hire gāst onsænde, and hire līchoma resteþ on Ðæssalonica ðære ceastre, Shrn. 70, 28. Heó onsænde hire gāst tō Gode, 107, 31. Hē sceal þurh gāres gripe gāst onsendan, Andr. Kmbl. 374; An. 187.

on-seón. v. an-sȳn.

on-seón *to regard, look on*:—Wliteseón wrætlīc weras onsāwon, Beo. Th. 3305; B. 1650. Freónd onsigon (feónd onsēgon?) lāðum eágan landmanna cyme, Cd. Th. 189, 2; Exod. 178. [*O. H. Ger.* ana-sehan *intueri*: *Ger.* ansehen.]

on-setenness, e; *f. Laying on, imposition*:—Ðæm gāste ǣghwelc gefullwad man onfēhþ þurh biscopa handa onsetenesse, Shrn. 85, 19.

on-setness, e; *f.* I. (cf. settan) *constitution, appointment*:—From onsetnisse middangeardes *a constitutione mundi*, Lk. Skt. Lind. Rush. 11, 50. II. (cf. sittan) *ambush, artifice, plot*:—Allo onsetnisse fióndes *omnes insidias inimici*, Rtl. 121, 40. v. next word.

on-setnung, e; *f. Plot, wile*:—Onsettnungo diúbles *insidias diaboli*, Rtl. 147, 13.

on-settan *to oppress, bear down*:—Hē hig yfele onsette *vehementer oppresserat eos*, Jud. 4, 3. Ða Cristenan him mid heora wǣpnum hȳndon and onsetton, Blickl. Homl. 203, 17. v. settan, on-sittan.

on-sīcan; *p.* -sāc *To sigh, groan*:—Ðā onsāc se wīsdōm and cwæð; Eálā, Bt. 26, 2; Fox 92, 24: 40, 3; Fox 238, 7.

on-sién. v. an-sȳn.

on-sīgan. I. of gentle, gradual movement, *to sink, decline, descend*:—Ðonne se dæg gewīt, and seó niht onsīhþ tō wērium mankynne, Anglia viii, 320, 2. Simbel onsāh dæg *sollempnis urgebat* (*vergebat?*) *dies*, Hymn. Surt. 96, 1. Ðeáh seó sunne ofer midne dæg onsīge and lūte tō ðære eorþan, Bt. 25; Fox 88, 25. Wǣre onsigen *vergeretur*, Wrt. Voc. ii. 81, 27. Onsīgendum (*vergente*) ǣfene, Hymn. Surt. 34, 28. Fornumen mid onsīgendre ylde *with declining years*, Basil admn. 8; Norm. 50, 20. II. of violent movement:—Gif hī oncneówon ða geniðerunge ðe him onsīhþ, Homl. Th. i. 408, 8. Swearte gāstas mid micclum þreáte him onsigon, ðæt hī his sāwle gegripon, 414, 10. Hē bodode ðæt him wæs Godes grama onsīgende, 246, 17. Mē wæs onsīgende se stranga wynd, St. And. 28, 13. Onsīgendum *ingruenti*, Hpt. Gl. 503, 32.

on-sīn, -sién, -sȳn, e; *f. Lack, want*:—Ðæt eów nǣfre ne biþ þurh gife mīne gōdes onsién, Exon. Th. 30, 16; Cri. 480. Him nǣnges wæs willan onsȳn, ne welan brosnung, 151, 24; Gū. 800. Nis on ðæm londe ne sār wracu ne wædle gewin ne welan onsȳn *luctus acerbus abest, et egestas obsita pannis*, 201, 13; Ph. 55. Ðǣr him nǣnges wæs eádes onsȳn, 225, 32; Ph. 398.

on-sīne, -sȳne; *adj. Visible*:—Hē mē fore eágum onsȳne wearþ, Exon. Th. 177, 17; Gū. 1228: Andr. Kmbl. 1820; An. 912. Cf. gesȳne.

on-sinscipe (?), es; *m. Wedlock*:—Ðyssum mānfullum onsinscype (gesinscipum, MS. T.) wǣron sǣde gemengde *huic nefando conjugio dicuntur admixti*, Bd. 1, 27; S. 491, 22. [*Perhaps* on *should be written before* ðyssum *instead of being a prefix*. v. sinscipe.]

on-sittan. I. *to occupy*:—Ic onsitte *insideo*, Ælfc. Gr. 26; Som. 29, 6. Ðō þrē acres ðe hē onsit, Cod. Dip. Kmbl. iv. 259, 20. Ðone hagan ðe hē sylf onsæt, 39, 13. Hit wæs his lǣn ðæt hē onsǣte, Chart. Th. 173, 5. Onsite sǣnacan, Exon. Th. 474, 7; Bo. 26. II. *to oppress* (cf. colloquial *to sit on a person*):—For ðām heardum weorcum ðe him onsæt, Ex. 6, 9. Gehreás ł onsæt egsa heora ofer hig *incubuit timor eorum super eos*, Ps. Lamb. 104, 38. Hē ālȳseþ þearfan ðæt him se welega ne mæg wiht onsittan *liberavit pauperem a potente*, Ps. Th. 71, 12. III. (with a different prefix, cf. *O. H. Ger.* int-sizzen *metuere*: *Goth.* and-sitan *to regard*) *to fear* (*taking like* ondrǣdan *a reflexive dative*):—Nō ic mē onsitte *non vereor*, Wrt. Voc. ii. 61, 46. Ne ic mē herehlōþe helle þegna swīðe onsitte, Exon. Th. 166, 15; Gū. 1043. Ðæt is ðæt ān ðæs ic eallan dæg mē onsitte, Homl. Skt. i. 23, 730. Hī onsǣton and ondrēdon ðæt wē heom grame beón woldon, 23, 273. Godes him ondrēdon hete, heofoncyninges nīþ swīðe onsǣton, Cd. Th. 48, 1; Gen. 769. Ðonne ðū ðē selfum swīðost onsitte, Met. 5, 38. Ðū ðē lāðra ne þearft hæleþa hildþræce onsittan, Cd. Th. 130, 10; Gen. 2157: Beo. Th. 1198; B. 597: Exon. Th. 397, 22; Rä. 16, 23. Hē wæs him onsittende ðæt hine sum man gecneówe, Homl. Skt. i. 23, 494.

on-slæge. v. on-slege.

on-slǣpan, -slēpan; *p.* te *To sleep, fall asleep*; obdormire:—Wērig gesette his leomu tō restenne and hwæthwugo onslēpte (slēp, MS. B.), Bd. 2, 6; S. 508, 11. Onslǣpte (slēp, MS. B.), 4, 11; S. 579, 33: S. 580, 2: 4, 24; S. 597, 11: S. 599, 7: 4, 31; S. 610, 31. v. next word.

on-slāpan; *p.* -slēp *To sleep, fall asleep*:—Heó hwōn onslēp, forðon ðe heó wæs on ðære sǣ swīðe geswenced, Shrn. 60, 17. Andreas āsette his heáfod ofer ǣnne his discipula and hē onslēp, Blickl. Homl. 235, 13. [*Goth.* ana-slēpan: *O. H. Ger.* int-slāfan: *Ger.* ent-schlafen.] v. ā-slāpan *and preceding word*.

on-slege, es; *m. A blow struck on something*:—Onslægiun *inflictis*, Wrt. Voc. ii. 92, 53. Onslægum, 47, 27.

on-spannan. I. literally, *to unfasten, unclasp*:—Þegn winedryhten his wætere gelafede, and his helm onspeón, Beo. Th. 5440; B. 2723. II. metaph. *to open the mind, to speak, disclose the thoughts*:—Ongan reordigan, wordlocan onspeónn, Andr. Kmbl. 940; An. 471. Onspeón, 1342; An. 671: Elen. 172; El. 86: Exon. Th. 247, 16; Jul. 79.

on-sprǣc, e; *f. A suit involving a claim* or *accusation, claim, charge*:—Se mōste his hlāford āspelian, and his onspǣce gerǣcan, L. R. 3; Th. i. 192, 3. Bǣdon ðæt heó mōsten gesyllan hire morgengyfe wið ðan ðe se cing ða egeslīcan onspǣce ālēte (*the charge is previously stated*: ðæt hē wǣre on ðam unrǣde, ðæt man sceolde on Eást-Sexon Swegen underfōn), Chart. Th. 540, 21.

on-spreca, an; *m. One who brings a claim* or *charge*:—Ðone āþ funde ðe se onspeca (*claimant*) on gehealden wǣre, L. Ed. 1; Th. i. 158, 20. v. sprecan.

on-spreccan *to enliven, to make sprack* (?) [Sprack *lively, active*, Halliw. Dict.: *Icel.* sprækr *active*.]:—Ðā wæs wæstnum āweaht world onspreaht (-spreht, MS.), Exon. Th. 353, 8; Reim. 9. [Cf. (?) ich sprechi in ham sprekes of lustes swa luðere ðæt ha forberneþ, Marh. 15, 21.]

on-sprecend, es; *m. An accuser, plaintiff*:—Ðā ongon Higa him specan on mid ōðran onspecendan, Chart. Th. 169, 22.

on-springan. I. *to burst asunder*:—Seonowe onsprungon, burston bānlocan, Beo. Th. 1639; B. 817. II. *to spring* or *burst forth*, (of streams), *to rise*:—Ðǣr lagustreámas, wyllan onspringaþ, Exon. Th. 202, 2; Ph. 63. Ðǣr se flōd onsprang, Andr. Kmbl. 3269; An. 1637. Ealle eorþan ǣddre onsprungon ongeán ðam heofonlīcan flōde, Wulfst. 206, 18. [*Ger.* ent-springen.]

on-sprungenness, e; *f. Defect, want*:—Onsprungennes *eclipsis*, i. *solis vel lunae defectio*, Wrt. Voc. ii. 142, 22. v. ā-sprungenness.

on-stæl, es; *m. Arrangement, disposition*:—Ðā (*at the creation of man*) wæs fruma nīwe ælda tudres, onstæl wynlīc, fæger and gefeálīc fæder wæs ācenned Adam ǣrest, Exon. Th. 151, 17; Gū. 796. v. on-steall.

on-stæpe, es; *m. Entrance, ingress*:—Onstæpas *ingressus*, Ps. Spl. 67, 26.

on-stâl, es; *m.* (?) *A charge, accusation*:—Gif Englisc onstâl gâ forþ . . . Gif hit biþ Wilisc onstâl, L. In. 46; Th. i. 130, 15-16. Onstâles *invectionis, illationis*, Hpt. Gl. 448, 53. v. stǽlan.

on-steall, es; *m. Institution, provision*:—Gode ælmiehtigum sî þonc ðætte wê nû ǽnigne onstal habbaþ lâreówa, Past. pref.; Swt. 4, 1. v. on-stæl *and* on-stellan.

on-stedfullness, e; *f. Instability*:—Onstydfullnisse *instabilitas*, Rtl. 192, 19.

on-stellan *to institute, give rise to, set on foot, bring in, be the author of, set* (*an example*):—Ðû scealt greót etan swâ ðû wrôhte onstealdest *thou* (*the serpent*) *hast brought sin into the world*, Cd. Th. 56, 12; Gen. 911: 57, 22; Gen. 932. Hê in wuldre wrôhte onstalde, 287, 19; Sat. 369. Ðâ onstealdon ða heretogan ǽrest ðone fleám *the leaders were the first to fly*, Chr. 993; Erl. 132, 15. Swâ hit (*persecution*) Nero onstealde, Ors. 6, 6; Swt. 262, 12. Crêca gewinn ðe of Læcedemonia ǽrest onsteled (stæled, MS. C.) wæs *dominandi Lacedaemoniorum cupiditas, quantas causas certaminum suscitavit*, 3, 1; Swt. 100, 11. Hê wuldres gehwæs ord onstealde *omnium miraculorum auctor exstitit*, Bd. 4, 24; S. 597, 21. Se ðæs orleges or onstealde, Beo. Th. 4806; B. 2407. Ðe ðæs oferhŷdes ord onstaldon, Cd. Th. 272, 4; Sat. 114. Abraham bysene onstealde geleáffullum *Abram exemplum credentium fuit*, Gl. Prud. 1: Blickl. Homl. 7, 9: 23, 16. Ða lâreówas sceolan gôdes lîfes bysene onstellan ðǽm ðe him æfter fylgeon, 81, 6. Wolde ic eów on ðon bysne onstellan, Andr. Kmbl. 1942; An. 973. Ða godcundan leán mînre sâule mid gerêce, swǽ hit mîne ærfenuman onstellen (*appoint*), Chart. Th. 477, 12. Onstaelde (ox-, Wrt.) *idoneus*, Wrt. Voc. ii. 110, 51.

on-stêpan *to raise*:—Onstêp mînne hige in gearone rǽd, Exon. Th. 454, 25; Hy. 4, 38.

on-steppan *to walk, go*:—Ðû onstæpst *gradieris*, Ps. Spl. 31, 10. Lege on lange hwîle ôþ ðæt hê onstæppe, Lchdm. ii. 126, 17. v. steppan.

on-stîgend, es; *m. One who ascends* or *mounts*:—Hors and onstîgend âwearp in sǽ *equum et ascensorem projecit in mare*, Ps. Surt. ii. 187, 4.

on-sting, es; *m. Authority*:—Icc nelle geþafian ðæt ǽnig mann ǽnigne onstingc habbe on ǽnigum þingum oððe on ǽnigum tîman bûtan se abbod, Chart. Th. 362, 3. Ǽnige onsting, 369, 24. Ic nelle geþafian ðæt ǽni man ǽnine onstyngc hæbbe *nolo permittere ut quis jus habeat*, Cod. Dip. Kmbl. iv. 202, 17. Ðæt gê nân onsting ne hauuen of ðat mynstre bûton swâ micel swâ ðone abbot wille *ut nec tu nec quisquam successorum episcoporum quicquam hujus aecclesiae usurpet praeter abbatis uoluntatem*, v. 29, 20.

on-stiran *to govern*:—Rîcsiendum on êcnysse and onstŷrendum his cyricean ðam ilcan Drihtne *regnante in perpetuum et gubernante suam ecclesiam eodem Domino*, Bd. 4, 5; S. 572, 4.

on-stîðian *to make hard*:—Onstîðade (*induravit*) hiora hearta, Jn. Skt. Lind. Rush. 12, 40.

on-stregdan *to sprinkle*:—Ðû onstrigdes (*asparges*) mec mid ysopan, Ps. Surt. 50, 9.

on-styreness, e; *f. Movement*:—Nalæs ðæt ân ôðra lima ac swylce eác ðære tungan onstyrenesse *non solum caeterorum membrorum, sed et linguae motu*, Bd. 4, 9; S. 577, 17.

on-styrian. I. *to move, stir* (of physical motion):—Se lîchoma nâ ne onstyreþ siððan seó sâwl him of biþ, Blickl. Homl. 21, 27. Onstyredan, drifan *agitabant*, Wrt. Voc. ii. 3, 39. Heó nǽnig lim onstyrian mihte, Bd. 4, 9; S. 577, 4: Onstyrgan (*commoveri*) foet mîne, Ps. Surt. 65, 9. II. *to move, stir up, excite*:—Hî mycle fyrhto onstyredon ðâm monnum ðe hî sceáwodon, Bd. 5, 23; S. 645, 23. Unsibbe onstyrian, Cd. Th. 281, 14; Sat. 271. III. *to move, disturb, agitate* (a person):—Seó gedrêfednes mæg ðæt môd onstyrian, Bt. 5, 3; Fox 12, 24. Se ðe mæg eorþware onstyrian, Ps. Th. 98, 1. Hŷ fægniaþ gif ic onstyred beó *exultabunt si motus fuero*, 12, 5: 32, 7. Hwæt arun gê onstyred *quid turbamini*, Mk. Skt. Rush. 5, 39. Onstyred and onǽled mid andan, Past. 21; Swt. 159, 7: Blickl. Homl. 199, 16. Onstyred mid heora wordum, 225, 23. Eal seó burh wæs onstyred, 71, 13. Hié beóþ on heora môde mid mislîcum geþohtum onstyrede, 19, 9.

on-sund; *adj.* I. of persons, *sound, whole, uninjured*:—Sum cild wearþ tô deáþe tôcwŷsed. Seó môder bær ðæs cildes lîc tô ðam gemynde ðæs hâlgan Stephanes, and hit sôna geedcucode and ansund æteówode, Homl. Th. ii. 26, 28. Onsund, Exon. Th. 278, 5; Jul. 593. Heó ârâs andsund of ðam bedde, Homl. Skt. i. 22, 52. Âbeád ðæt hié hine ealles onsundne eft gebrohten of ðære folcsceare *the king ordered that Abraham should be brought again out of Egypt safe and sound*, Cd. Th. 112, 15; Gen. 1871. Hê âlêde his tunecan uppon ðâm deádum, and hî ansunde ârison, Homl. Th. i. 74, 3: Andr. Kmbl. 2023; An. 1014: 3244; An. 1625. II. of things, *sound, entire, perfect, without flaw* or *injury*:—Ne wearm weder ne winterscûr wihte gewyrdan, ac se wong seómaþ onsund, Exon. Th. 199, 3; Ph. 20: 200, 21; Ph. 44. Nân cynerîce ne stent nâne. hwîle ansund, gif hî gesôme ne beóþ, Homl. Skt. i. 13, 238. For ðære clǽnnysse his ansundan mægþhâdes. Hê on êcnysse on ungewemmedum mægþhâde þurhwunode, Homl. Th. i. 58, 7. Hine getâcnode God tô ansundre hǽle, ii. 512, 13. Ansundre *integro*, Hpt. Gl. 525, 61. God hine (*Enoch*) genam mid ansundum lîchaman of ðissum lîfe, Ælfc. T. Grn. 3, 42. Ðenden gǽst and lîc geador sîþedan onsund on earde, Exon. Th. 285, 16; Jul. 715. Ðâ wurdon ða gymstânas swâ ansunde, ðæt nân tâcen ðære ǽrran tôcwŷsednesse næs gesewen, Homl. Th. i. 62, 16. v. an-sund.

on-sundness, e; *f. Soundness, freedom from physical* or *moral flaw*:—Andsumnysse (ansundnysse?) *integritatis, virginitatis*, Hpt. Gl. 444, 53. Gefêg ðâs bricas tô ansundnysse *join these broken gems together so that they may again be whole*, Homl. Th. i. 62, 8. v. ansundness.

on-sundrian *to separate, take apart*:—Nǽnig heora, of ðâm ðe hî âhton, ôwiht his beón onsundrad cwæþ *none of them said that anything they owned was his separate property*, Bd. 1, 27; S. 489, 15 note. v. â-sundrian.

on-sundrum, -sundran, -sundron; *adv.* I. *separately, severally, separated one from the other, apart*:—Onsundron *separatim*, onsundron hê sit *singillatim sedet*, Ælfc. Gr. 38; Som. 40, 39. Onsundran *altrinsecus, hinc et inde*, Hpt. Gl. 410, 2. Uton biddan onsundron æt Gode, ic æt mînum Gode . . . and gê eác swâ dôn *let each pray severally to his own God*, Homl. Skt. i. 18, 107. Ðâ nâ gestôd hê nâ ǽlcne onsundran (*each separately*), 23, 177. Hié sǽton onsundran *they* (*Adam and Eve*) *did not sit together*, Cd. Th. 52, 11; Gen. 842. Stande hê ealra ŷtemest, oððe on ðam stede, ðe se abbod swâ gêmeleásum monnum tô stealle onsundrum betǽht hæfþ . . . Wê forðî tǽhton ðæt hŷ on ûteweardan oððe onsundrum standen, ðæt . . ., R. Ben. 68, 10-17. Nǽnig heora, of ðâm ðe hî âhton, ôwiht his beón onsundran cwæþ, Bd. 1, 27; S. 489, 15. Ðeáh bûtû on ânum men sîen, ðeáh biþ ǽgðer him onsundron, Bt. 16, 3; Fox 54, 35. Ǽlc ðæra gesceafta hæfþ his âgenne eard onsundron, 33, 4; Fox 130, 24. For ǽghwylc onsundran riht âgieldan, Exon. Th. 372, 24; Seel. 97. II. *in retirement from others, apart*:—Ðâ fêrde hê onsundron *secessit*, Mt. Kmbl. 14, 13. Hê lǽdde hig onsundron (*seorsum*), 17, 1. Hê nam his leorningcnihtas onsundron *assumsit discipulos secreto*, 20, 17. Uton gân onsundron (*seorsum*) . . . Hî fôron onsundran, Mk. Skt. 6, 31-32. III. making distinction from others, *especially*:—Ic onsundrum ða stôwe lufige, and ofer ealle ôðre ic hié geceás, Blickl. Homl. 201, 6.

on-swætende, Wrt. Voc. ii. 47, 31. v. sprecan.

on-swâpan. v. swâpan.

on-swebban *to put to sleep* (but generally of the sleep of death), *lay to rest* (*in the grave*):—Onsuebbaþ *sepeliant*, Wrt. Voc. ii. 120, 44. Onsuebdum *sopitis*, 120, 73. [*O. Sax.* an-swebian: *O. H. Ger.* in-, intsueppen *sopire*.] v. â-swebban.

on-swêgan. v. swêgan.

on-swîfan. I. *to swing, turn*:—Bordrand onswâf wið ðam gryregieste Geáta dryhten *Beowulf turned his shield against the approaching fire-drake*, Beo. Th. 5112; B. 2559. II. *to turn aside, divert*:—Ne mæg mon ǽfre ðŷ êð ǽnne his cræftes beniman, ðe mon oncerran mæg sunnan onswîfan and ðisne swiftne rodor of his rihtryne, Met. 10, 40.

on-swôgan. v. swôgan.

on-symbelness, e; *f. A solemn festival*:—Mid ðŷ heó gesêgon ðone biscop mæssan (mæssena, MS. B.) onsymbelnesse mǽrsian (*celebratis missarum sollemniis*), Bd. 2, 5; S. 507, 12.

on-sŷn. v. on-sîn.

on-talu, e; *f. A successful claim, a charge that is established.* v. of-talu.

on-tênan. v. on-tŷnan.

on-tendan; *p.* -tende; *pp.* -tended, -tend. I. *to kindle, set fire to, to fire*:—Gif fŷr sîe ontended . . . gebête ðone æfwerdelsan se ðæt fŷr ontent, L. Alf. pol. 27; Th. i. 50, 27-28. Ontend þreó candela, Lchdm. iii. 286, 6. Ðe ðæt fŷr ontende *qui ignem succenderit*, Ex. 22, 6. Ða hâlgan tihton ðæt man ða ofnas ontende (-tænde, MSS. C. V.), Homl. Skt. i. 5, 294. Hî on ða burh feohtende wǽron, and eác hî mid fŷre ontendan woldon, Chr. 994; Erl. 133, 12. Ðonne hê (*the moon*) of hyre (*the sun*) ontend byþ, Lchdm. iii. 242, 12. Ontend *succensus*, Hpt. Gl. 507, 17. Antend, 471, 22. Antendne *succensam, ardentem*, 464, 36. II. *to kindle emotion* or *passion, to excite, inflame*:—Sume se deófol ontent tô gŷtsunge, Homl. Th. i. 240, 25. Ðîne gebedu geancsumiaþ mê and ontendaþ, 458, 4. [*O. E. Homl. A. R. Jul. Marh.* ontenden: *Goth.* tandjan *to kindle, light*; in-tandjan *to consume with fire*.]

on-tendness, e; *f.* I. *a burning, fire*:—Hê hêt gearcian ða tunnan tô heora bærnette . . . Hî wurdon gebrohte tô ðâm tunnum and tô ðære ontendnysse, Homl. Skt. i. 4, 307. Ontendnyssa *incendia*, Hpt. Gl. 499, 42. Antendnyssum *globis*, 489, 68. Ontyndnissum *incendiis*, 440, 4. II. metaph. *fire, that which kindles passion*:—Eugenia cwæþ ðæt heó wǽre gâlnysse ontendnyss, Homl. Skt. 2, 173. III. *passion, vehement desire*:—Ðære forligerlîcere ontendnysse *adulterinae titillationis*, Hpt. Gl. 505, 68. [illegible]yndnysse, 520, 33. Hê uneáðe ðære lîchamlîcan ontendnysse wiðstandan mihte, Homl. Th. ii. 156, 26.

Geangsumod mid ðæra ormǽtan ontendnysse and hrȳmende . . . 'Forgif mē ðam men ðe mīn mōd mē tō spenþ, Homl. Skt. i. 3, 387: 3, 397. Ic on ðē ādwesce ealle ontendnysse, 4, 171. IV. *burning sensation, inflammation*:—Hē unscrȳdde hine ealne, and wylode hine sylfne on ðām þiccum bremlum and þornum and netelum . . . and swā þurh ðære hȳde wunda ādwæscte his mōdes wunda; for ðan ðe hē āwende ðone unlust tō sārnysse, and þurh ða ȳttran ontendnysse ācwencte ða inran, Homl. Th. ii. 156, 27–33.

on-þanc, Wrt. Voc. ii. 132, 40. v. or-þanc.

on-þenian *to extend, stretch, bend (a bow)*:—Hī onþeneden (*intenderunt*) boga, Ps. Spl. T. 63, 3. v. ā-þenian.

on-þeón. I. *to prosper*:—Se wæs wreccena wīde mǽrost ofer werþeóde wīgendra hleó ellendǽdum; hē ðæs ǽr onþāh (*so at first he prospered*), Beo. Th. 1805; B. 900. II. *to be successful in one's efforts, to prove serviceable*:—Gamele ne mōston hilde onþeón *the aged might not be of service in battle* (in the preceding lines it is mentioned that the very young were excluded from the army), Cd. Th. 193, 5; Exod. 241. Oft ic secga seledreáme sceal fægre onþeón ðǽr guman drincaþ *oft must I prove of excellent service to festivity in hall, where men drink*, Exon. Th. 480, 14; Rä. 64, 2.

on-þracian (-þrācian ?); *p.* ode *To fear, dread*:—Ic anþracige (and-, MS. F.: ā-, MS. O.) *vereor*, Ælfc. Gr. 27; Zup. 162, 1. Ic andþracige (onþracie, MS. T.) *horreo*, ic onginne tō onþracigenne (and-) *horresco*, 35; Zup. 212, 3–4. Sum dēma wæs se God ne ondrēd ne nānne man ne onþracude (*reverebatur*) . . . Ðā cwæþ hē: Ðeáh ic God ne ondrǽde ne ic man ne onþracige (*revereor*), Lk. Skt. 18, 2–4. Ðū ne onþracedest (*horruisti*) mǽdenes innoþ, Hymn. L. 16. Ða ðe middaneard anþracode (*inhorruit*) Hymn. Surt. 132, 10. Ðā wearþ hē myccluм āfyrht and anþracode ðæt his rīce feallan sceolde, Homl. Th. i. 82, 5. Anþracian *revereantur*, Ps. Spl. 69, 2.

on-þræc (-þrǽce ?); *adj. Horrible, dreadful*:—Iulianus mid anþræcum hreáme forswealt, Homl. Th. i. 452, 16. Mid unāsecgendlīcum wītum āfyllede and mid anþræcum stencum, 68, 6. Ðā cwæþ ðæt wīf betwux ðām anþræcum wītum, Homl. Skt. i. 12, 191.

on-þringan (?):—Beofode ðæt eálond foldwong onþrong [onsprong *the earth cracked with the shaking* (?)], Exon. Th. 181, 28; Gū. 1300.

on-þunian (?) *to swell out, exceed due bounds*:—Ic eom ufor ealra gesceafta ðara ðe worhte Waldend ūser; se mec āna mæg geþeón þrymme, ðæt ic onrinnan (onþunian *is suggested by Grein*) ne sceal, Exon. Th. 427, 15; Rä. 41, 91.

on-þweán *to wash, cleanse by washing*:—Wē nǽron mid fulwihte hēr on eorþan onþwægen, Shrn. 53, 21. Gif gē willaþ onþwegene beón *si vultis ablui*, Bd. 2, 5; S. 507, 16.

on-þyncan *to seem, appear*:—Ðȳ læs ðæt eów seó sægen monigfealdlīcor biþ onþūhte tō wrītanne *ne sim scribendi multiplex*, Nar. 3, 29.

on-tīgan *to untie, set free*:—Seó sāwl færþ swīðe freólīce tō heofonum siððan heó ontīged biþ and of ðam carcerne ðæs līchoman onliésed biþ, Bt. 18, 4; Fox 68, 14.

on-tige. v. on-tyge.

on-timber, es; *n.* I. *material*:—Ðæt ōðer antimber *materia*, Wrt. Voc. ii. 57, 42. Ðæt antimber ðe hē of gesceóp gesceafta, Hexam. 4; Norm. 6, 22. Nis hit nān wundor ðeáh mon swilc ontimber gewirce, Shrn. 164, 1. II. metaph. *reason, occasion*; materia:—Swilce him gerȳmed sȳ and antimber geseald, ðæt hē God bereáfige, Lchdm. iii. 444, 1. For ðisum antimbre ic gedyrstlǽhte ðæt ic ðās gesetnysse undergann, Homl. Th. i. 2, 26. v. and-timber.

on-timberness, e; *f. Instruction*:—Tō ontimbernesse ðæra æfterfyligendra *ad instructionem sequentium*, Bd. 4, 17; S. 585, 16. v. next word.

on-timbran *to instruct, edify*:—Hē monig þūsendo heora mid sōðfæstnesse worde wæs ontimbrende (*instituens*), Bd. 5, 19; S. 639, 23. Æþellīce ontimbred and gelǽred *nobiliter instructus*, 5, 23; S. 646, 19: 5, 19; S. 637, 36: 5, 22; S. 644, 18. Hē wolde mid his lāre and mid his līfes bysene beón ontimbred, Blickl. Homl. 217, 14.

on-tīned (-tīmed ?) *well-supplied*:—Gif .vii. dæge sunne scīneþ, mycele wæstmas on treówum beóþ . . . Gif ðī .x. dæge sunne scȳneþ, ðonne byþ sē and ealle sǽ mid fixum ontīned, Lchdm. iii. 166, 13.

ontre, an; *f. Radish*, Lchdm. ii. 78, 26: 76, 5. v. antre.

on-tydran *to nourish, support*:—Hū þyncþ eów hū seó sibb gefæstnad wǽre, hwæðer hió sīe ðæm gelīcost ðe mon nime ǽnne eles dropan, and drȳpe on ān micel fȳr, and þence hit mid ðæm ādwæscan? ðonne is wēn, swā micle swīðor swā hē þencþ ðæt hē hit ādwæsce, ðæt hē hit swā micle swīðor ontydre *pax ista an incentivum malorum fuit? stillicidium illud olei, in medium magnae flammae cadens exstinxit fomitem tanti ignis, an aluit?* Ors. 4, 7; Swt. 182, 22–26.

on-tydre; *adj. Weakened, debilitated, effete*:—Ontudri *effetum*, Wrt. Voc. ii. 106, 82. Ontydre *effeto*, i. *sine foetu, ebetato, debilitato, evacuato, exinanito*, 142, 46.

on-tyge, es; *m. What one takes upon one's self, an undertaking*:—Gif hwylc abbod geþafaþ ðæt mæssepreóst oððe diácon in tō mynstre gange tō ðȳ ðæt hȳ messan singan . . . hȳ nān þing gedyrstlǽcen ne nǽnne ontige on ðam mynstre būtan ðære mæssan ānre *if any abbot permit a mass-priest or deacon to enter a monastery for the purpose of celebrating mass . . . they shall not presume to do anything or take anything upon themselves except only the mass*, R. Ben. 140, 3–10. v. teón (on), tyge.

on-tyhtan *to incite, instigate, impel*:—Wæs ðæt gifeðe tō swīð ðe ðone ðyder ontyhte, Beo. Th. 6164; B. 3086.

on-tȳnan *to open.* I. of places or things, (a) *to make an opening in*:—Seó eorþe hié ontȳnde and hió forswealh ðæt wæter, Blickl. Homl. 247, 15. (b) *to open, allow to burst forth*:—Hē ūs ontȳneþ heofenes þeótan, 39, 31. (c) *to open* so as to admit of ingress or egress:—Him se āwyrgda ongeán helle ontȳneþ, Exon. Th. 364, 10; Wal. 68. Ðæt hī Godes cyricean ontȳndon (*aperirent*), Bd. 3, 30; S. 562, 16. Ðē is neorxna wang ontȳned, Andr. Kmbl. 209; An. 105. (d) *to open (a door)*:—Geatu ontȳnaþ, Exon. Th. 36, 15; Cri. 576. Gif sió duru ontȳned biþ . . . būton ðū ða duru ontȳne, Past. 21; Swt. 157, 15–19. Sīe manna gehwam behliden helle duru, heofones ontȳned, ēce geopenad engla rīce, Elen. Kmbl. 2458; El. 1230. Heofonrīces duru sceal þurh ðē ontēned beón, Blickl. Homl. 9, 3. (e) *to open* the mouth, lips, *to speak*:—Ic antȳne (ontȳne, MS. C. T.) on bigspellum mūþ mīnne, Ps. Spl. 77, 2. Ðā ontȳnde Hǽlend his mūþ, and wæs sprecende, Blickl. Homl. 159, 25. Ontȳn weoloras mīne, Ps. Grn. ii. 279, 116. (f) *to open* the eyes (one's own), *to look*, (another's), *to give sight to*:—Ðā ontȳnde ic mīne eágan, lōcade on hine, Bd. 5, 6; S. 619, 39. Hē his eágan ontȳnde, biseah tō heofones rīce, Exon. Th. 180, 6; Gū. 1275. Þweah ða eágan and ontȳne, Lchdm. ii. 26, 25. Blindra manna eágan ontȳnan, Jn. Skt. 10, 21. Hyra eágan wǽrun ontȳnede, Mt. Kmbl. 9, 30. (g) *to open* the ears, *to listen to a person*:—Hē him mildheortnesse eáron ontȳnde, Blickl. Homl. 107, 1. Ontȳn eárna hleóþor, Ps. Grn. ii. 278, 77. II. *to disclose, reveal, display*:—Se ðe līf ontȳneþ, Exon. Th. 2, 15; Cri. 19. Forðæm wæs gecweden tō ðæm lytegan feónde ðe ðæs ǽrestan monnes mōd ontȳnde on ðæs æples gewilnunge *unde hosti callido, qui primi hominis sensum in concupiscentia pomi aperuit*, Past. 43, 2; Swt. 309, 17. Þīn tunge ontȳnde fācn, Ps. Th. 49, 20. Ðū mē ðīnre snetera hord selfa ontēndes, Ps. Grn. ii. 278, 71. David his synna hord selfa ontēnde, 277, 28. Hwonne ūs līffreá leóht ontȳne, Exon. Th. 2, 31; Cri. 27. Ðæt ic mōte ðis gealdor tōþum ontȳnan *that I may utter this incantation*, Lchdm. i. 400, 5. Ūs is wuldres leóht ontȳned, Cd. Th. 299, 28; Sat. 557: Exon. Th. 102, 17; Cri. 1674: Andr. Kmbl. 3222; An. 1614. Ðǽr is wuldres blēd ontȳned, Cd. Th. 302, 5; Sat. 594.

on-tȳnan (?) *to cover*:—Ða stōwe wæs ontȳnende *ea loca operiens* (did the translator read *aperiens?*), Bd. 4, 7; S. 575, 12.

on-tyndness. v. ontendness.

on-tȳnness, e; *f.* I. *an opening, aperture*:—Se heofon tōbyrst and eall engla cynn lōciaþ þurh þa ontȳnnesse on manna cynn, Blickl. Homl. 93, 24. II. *discovery*:—Be cierlisces monnes ontȳnesse (betogenesse, MSS. B. H. Schmid takes *ontȳnesse = ontigenesse*, and Thorpe translates 'of accusing a "ceorlish" man;' but the section deals with the discovery of the theft. Cf. too, L. In. 18; Th. i. 114, 5, which is a section to the same effect as the present one: Be cirliscum þeófe gefongenum) æt þiéfþe. Se cierlisca mon se ðe oft betygen wǽre þiéfþe, and ðonne æt sīðestan synnigne man gefō, L. In. 37; Th. i. 124, 20.

on-ufan; *prep. with dat. adv.* I. of place, *upon, on*:—Ðæt preóst ne mæssige būton onufan gehālgodon weofode, L. Edg. C. 31; Th. ii. 250, 22. Ða forwurdon ðe him (*the elephant*) onufan wǽron, Ors. 4, 1; Swt. 156, 13. Ða men ðe him onufan gāþ, Lk. Skt. 11, 44. Hī ðone Hǽlend onufan setton, 19, 35. II. of time, *beyond, after*:—Fēr Eádweard cyning onufan hærfest, Chr. 923; Erl. 110, 1. v. ufan.

on-unspēd (?), e; *f. Indigence, poverty*:—For hwȳ ofergytest onunspēde (*inopiae*) ūre, Ps. Spl. 43, 27.

on-unwīs (?); *adj. Foolish, ignorant*:—Wiðmeten is nītenu[m] onunwīsum (*insipientibus*), Ps. Spl. 48, 12. v. next word.

on-unwīsdōm, es; *m. Folly, ignorance*:—Ic wæs unwīsum nētenum gelīc geworden. Ac ðū Drihten onunwīsdōmes ne wes ðū gemyndig, Blickl. Homl. 89, 10. v. preceding word.

on-uppan; *prep. with dat. adv.* I. *upon, on*:—Se Hǽlend rād onuppan ðam assan, Jn. Skt. 12, 14. Stōd ǽren ceác onuppan twelf ǽrenum oxum, Past. 16; Swt. 105, 2. Hē wearþ bebyrged, and him læg onuppan fela byrðena eorþan, Homl. Skt. i. 12, 56: 14, 114. Hē sæt ðǽr onuppan, 13, 25. Ðonne man bringe offrunge nime smedeman and geóte ele onuppan, Lev. 2, 1. Hī lēdon hyra reáf uppan hig, and setton hyne onuppan, Mt. Kmbl. 21, 7. Hī gemētton fȳr and fisc onuppon, Homl. Th. ii. 292, 4. II. *besides, over and above*:—Hē hēt ācwellan ða rīcostan witan, and onuppan āgenne brōðor and his mōdor ofbeátan, Met. 9, 28. v. uppan.

on-wacan. I. *to awake, cease to sleep*:—Sōna ðæs ðe heó onwōc *ubi vigilavit*, Bd. 3, 9; S. 534, 11: 4, 31; S. 610, 37. Ðā of slǽpe onwōc, swefn wæs æt ende, eorþlīc æðeling, Cd. Th. 249, 2; Dan.

534. Se wyrm onwôc, Beo. Th. 4563; B. 2287. Ða men onwôcan, and ût urnon, Ors. 4, 2; Swt. 160, 22. II. *to arise, spring, be derived, be born*:—Ðû wâst ðæt ðû of mînre (*the speaker is Eve*) dehter, Drihten, onwôce, Blickl. Homl. 89, 20: Cd. Th. 292, 12; Sat. 439. Hēr Ida fēng tō rîce, ðonon Norþanhymbra cynecyn onwôc, Chr. 547; Erl. 16, 8. Him onwôc heáh Healfdene, Beo. Th. 112; B. 56. Beornas onwôcan, cynn æfter cynne cende wǽron, Ps. Th. 104, 11. Hwǽr ûs hearmstafas onwôcan, Cd. Th. 58, 2; Gen. 940. Hié begeton feówertig bearna ðæt ðonon menio onweócon, 294, 25; Sat. 476.

on-wacan, -waccan, e; *f. An awakening, arousing, incentive*:—Onwaccano mægna *incitamenta virtutum*, Rtl. 74, 24. v. wacan.

on-wacnian; *p.* ode *To wake up, rouse one's self*:—Onwacnigeaþ nû, wîgend mîne, Fins. Th. 28; Fin. 10. v. on-wæcnan.

on-wadan. I. *to make one's way into, to penetrate*:—Oft hira môd onwôd under dimscûan deófles lârum, Andr. Kmbl. 280; An. 140. II. *to enter with irresistible force, to make one's self master of, take possession of*:—Wîfa wlite onwôd folcdriht wera *the beauty of the women made its way to the hearts of the men*, Cd. Th. 76, 20; Gen. 1260. Hié wlenco onwôd, 155, 27; Gen. 2579. v. an-wadan.

on-wǽcan *to soften, mollify, cause relaxation of severity*:—Ðæt wē mihtiges Godes môd onwǽcen, Cd. Th. 26, 7; Gen. 403.

on-wæcnan; *p.* ede. I. *to awake*:—Hit ne onwæcneþ tō ðon ðæt hit eft on ierne mid hreówsunga. Ac hit wilnaþ ðæt hit tō ðon onwæcne, ðæt hit mǽge eft weorþan oferdruncen, Past. 56; Swt. 431, 22–25. Ðonne onwæcneþ eft winleás guma, Exon. Th. 289, 8; Wand. 45. Ðā hî onwæcnedun *vigilantes*, Lk. Skt. 9, 32. 'Nû us is tîma ðæt wē onwæcnen of slǽpe.' Ond eft hē cwiþ: 'Onwæcnaþ, gē ryhtwîsan,' Past. 63; Swt. 459, 33–461, 1. Fordytte ðæt eáre mid ðære wulle ðonne ðû slāpan wille, and dō eft of ðonne ðû onwæcne, Lchdm. ii. 42, 26. II. *to rise, spring, be derived*:—Ðonne hē (*the Phenix*) of ascan onwæcneþ, Exon. Th. 240, 34; Ph. 648. Monig sceal siððan wyrt onwæcnan, 191, 4; Az. 83. Ðanon ǽtorcyn ǽrest gewurdon onwæcned, Salm. Kmbl. 439; Sal. 220. v. next word.

on-wæcnian, -wecnian; *p.* ode *To awake, arise, be roused, be raised*:—Of mistlîcum dryncum onwæcnaþ sió wôde þrāg ðære wrǽnnysse, Bt. 37, 1; Fox 186, 17. Ðonne (*at the sound of the archangel's trumpet*) of ðisse moldan men onwecniaþ, deáde of duste ârîsaþ, Cd. Th. 302, 23; Sat. 604. v. on-wacnian, -wæcnan.

on-wæmme. v. un-wemme.

on-wǽre (?) *unripe*:—Genim onwǽre slāh ðæt seáw, and wring þurh clāþ on ðæt eáge, sôna gǽþ of (*the white spot will go off*) gif sió slāh biþ grēne, Lchdm. ii. 32, 18.

on-wæstm *increase, increment*:—Onwæstem *incrementum*, Rtl. 69, 19.

on-wæterig. v. un-wæterig.

on-wald, -walh. v. on-weald, -wealh.

on-wealcan; *v. trans. To roll*:—Dryhtnes bibod geofonflôda gehwylc georne behealdeþ ðonne merestreámas wæter onwealcaþ *each ocean flood carefully observes the Lord's command, when the sea-streams make the water roll*, Exon. Th. 193, 25; Az. 127. Cf. Sôna swā ðû geseó ðæt ðû hyre (*the mandrake*) geweald hæbbe, genim hȳ sôna on hand, swā andwealc hî, and gewring ðæt wôs of hyre leáfon, Th. An. 116, 22.

on-weald, es; *m. Power*:—Sȳ him âr and onwald *to him be honour and power*, Exon. Th. 241, 28; Ph. 663. Hié hiere onwaldes hié (*Rome*) beniman woldon; and heó hwæðere onwealg on hiere onwalde æfter þurhwunade, Ors. 2, 1; Swt. 62, 22–24. Se geeode ðæt eálond and Rômâna onwealde underþeódde, Bd. 1, 3; S. 475, 18. Ne lǽt âwyrgde ofer ûs onwald âgan, Exon. Th. 10, 28; Cri. 159. Ða kyningas ðe ðone onwald hæfdon ðæs folces . . . hié heora onweald gehióldon, Past. pref.; Swt. 3, 5–7. Ðû âhtest alra onwald (*power over all*), Cd. Th. 268, 24; Sat. 60. Ðæt gē mîn onweald âgan môsten, Exon. Th. 131, 9; Gû. 453. Ûs âlēfan ēcne onwald, Cd. Th. 272, 11; Sat. 118. Wē hine oferswȳððon and ûs in onweald geslôgon eal his londrîce *regi superato acceptaque in conditiones omni ejus regione*, Nar. 3, 22. Wē ealle his þeóde on onwald onfēngon, 4, 6. v. an-, and-weald, on-wealda.

on-weald (?); *adj. Powerful*:—Ðā Dryhten of deáþe ârās onweald (-wealh?) of eorþan, Exon. Th. 168, 9; Gû. 1075.

on-wealda, an; *m. One who has power, a ruler*:—Ic gelȳfe in ēcne onwealdan ealra gesceafta, Exon. Th. 140, 14; Gû. 610. [*O. H. Ger.* ana-walto: *Ger.* an-walt. In *O. H. Ger.* ana-walton (*gen. dat. pl.*) also translates *potestatum, potestatibus*, v. Grff. i. 813. Cf. on-weald.] v. an-wealda.

on-wealg. v. next word.

on-wealh, -walh; *adj. Whole, entire*:—Onwalh *integer*, Wrt. Voc. ii. 44, 25. Of anwealhre *integro*, Hpt. Gl. 525, 61. I. literal, *sound, uninjured, uncorrupted*:—Ealne his lîchoman gemētton onwealhne and gesundne (*integrum*), Bd. 4, 30; S. 608, 37. Ealle ða scȳtan ðe se lîchoma mid bewunden wæs onwealge ætȳwdon *linteamina omnia quibus involutum erat corpus integra apparuerunt*, 4, 19; S. 589, 21. Ða lāstas â onwalge beóþ and on ðære ilcan onsȳne ðe hié on forman on ða eorþan bestapene wǽron, Blickl. Homl. 127, 20. II. metaph.:—Heó onwealg on hiere onwalde æfter þurhwunade *regnat incolumis*, Ors. 2, 1; Swt. 62, 23. Wæs hyre mægdenhād onwalg, Exon. Th. 87, 6; Cri. 1421. Ðæt gecyndelîce gewitt biþ anwalg untôsliten, Past. 52, 2; Swt. 405, 5. Ða ôðre stondaþ on anwalgre hǽlo, Swt. 403, 23. Andswarede ðæt hē on ðyssum hæfde fæstne geleáfan and onwalhne *integram se in hoc habere fidem respondebat*, Bd. 3, 13; S. 539, 4. Geleáfan onwealhne and unwemmedne heóldan, 1, 4; S. 475, 33: 4, 10; S. 578, 27. III. of time, *whole, entire*:—Onwalhge wican *ebdomade integra*, 4, 27; S. 604, 31. Geár onwealh *anno integro*, 3, 1; S. 523, 28. Onwalhge niht *noctes integras*, 4, 25; S. 599, 30. [*O. H. Ger.* ana-walg *absolutus*.]

on-wealhlîce; *adv. Entirely*:—Ða mægenu ðæs gôdes weorces ðe hē Gode ûtan anwealglîce forgeaf *tantae virtutis sacrificium, quod integrum foras immolant*, Past. 33, 5; Swt. 220, 22.

on-wealhness, e; *f. Wholeness, soundness, integrity.* I. literal:—Þurh ða heora onwalhnesse gecȳðed is *it is made evident by the unchanged condition of the footsteps*, Blickl. Homl. 127, 27. II. metaph. *purity, chastity, integrity*:—Andwealhnys *integritas, religio sanctitas*, Hpt. Gl. 433, 50. Andhwælhnysse *integritatis*, 414, 74. Andwealcnysse, 432, 47. Andwealhnysse, 452, 32. Anhwealhnysse, 461, 46. Andwealhnysse *integritatis, castitatis*, 465, 71. Onwealhnesse *integritatis*, Wrt. Voc. ii. 44, 24. Mid ēcre onwalhnesse (*integritate*) mægþhādes, Bd. 4, 19; S. 587, 25. Anwalhnysse, Homl. Th. ii. 564, 6. Andwælhnysse *integritatem, pudicitiam*, Hpt. Gl. 463, 57.

on-weard; *adj. Proceeding against, taking action against*:—Warnige se abbod ðæt hē þurh andan ne sȳ onweard ðam profaste *let the abbot take heed that he be not acting against the provost from hatred*, R. Ben. 126, 11.

on-wecnian. v. on-wæcnian.

on-weg; *adv. Away, off.* I. with verbs of motion:—Ôðer þing wiston ða wîfmenn ðā hȳ onweg cyrdon *when they went away* (*from the sepulchre*), Exon. Th. 460, 13; Hö. 16. Gif ðû onweg cymest *if you come away* (*alive from the fight*), Beo. Th. 2769; B. 1382. Fēran onweg, Exon. Th. 373, 4; Seel. 103. Onweg (âweg) fleón, Ors. 4, 2; Bos. 79, 15: Bd. 4, 22; S. 591, 11. Onweg gewîtan, Blickl. Homl. 117, 1. Onweg hweorfan, Beo. Th. 534; B. 264. Hē onweg ðanon feorhlāstas bær, 1693; B. 844. II. with verbs of taking, removing, separating, etc.:—Onweg âceorfan *amputare*, Ps. Spl. T. 118, 39. Onweg âdôn *to put away*, Bd. 3, 1; S. 524, 3. Onweg âdrîfan *to drive away, expel*, 2, 5; S. 507, 28. Onweg âhebban *to remove*, 1, 27; S. 493, 7. Onweg âlǽdan, 5, 3; S. 616, 36. Onweg âniman, Blickl. Homl. 55, 9. Onweg âteón *to withdraw, subtract*, Bd. 4, 17; S. 586, 9. v. â-weg.

onweg-âcirredness, e; *f. A turning away* (*from right belief*), *apostasy*:—Seó onwegâcerrednes fram Cristes geleáfan Angelcyninga *apostasia regum Anglorum*, Bd. 3, 9; S. 533, 8.

onweg-âlǽdness, e; *f. A taking away, removal*:—Ond for ðære gelômlîcum onwegâlǽdnesse (*frequenti ablatione*) ðære hâlgan moldan wæs mycel seáþ geworden, Bd. 5, 18; S. 635, 31.

onweg-gewite, es; *m. A going forth*:—In onweggewite *in excessu*, Ps. Surt. 115, 11.

onweg-gewitenness, e; *f. Going forth, departure*:—Æfter his onweggewitenesse (*abscessum*) of Breotene, Bd. 3, 7; S. 530, 12. v. âweg-gewitenness.

on-wendan. I. *to turn, change*:—Ðû hî onwendest *mutabis ea*, Ps. Th. 101, 23. Hē onwendeþ his hiw, Lchdm. ii. 204, 9. Werþióde his (*the morning-star*) noman onwendaþ, hâtaþ hine ǽfenstiorra, Met. 29, 29. Mē onhwyrfdon of ðære gecynde ðe ic ǽr beheóld, onwendan mîne wîsan, Exon. Th. 485, 29; Rä. 72, 5. Onwend ðec in gewitte *think differently*, 251, 12; Jul. 144. On ðæs bisceopes anwealde ðæt biþ hwæðer hē hit onwende ðe nā *utrum mutet an non*, L. Ecg. C. 33; Th. ii. 158, 13. Ða menn ðeáh wisston ðæt hió mid ðam drȳcræfte ne mihte ðara manna môd onwendan ðeáh hió ða lîchoman onwende *nec potentia gramina, membra quae valeant licet, corda vertere non valent*, Bt. 38, 1; Fox 196, 8–10: Met. 26, 101–104. Ðû ne meaht hiora sidu and heora gecynd onwendan, 7, 2; Fox 18, 31. Nis mē tîd mîn lîf tō onwendenne *non est mihi tempus vitam mutandi*, Bd. 5, 14; S. 634, 32. Onwended ne biþ ǽfre tō ealdre, Exon. Th. 203, 11; Ph. 82. Nân gewuna ne mæg nânum men beón onwended, Bt. 7, 1; Fox 16, 23. Gif ðû wēnst ðæt hit on ðē gelong sē ðæt ða woruldsǽlþa on ðē swā onwenda sint ðonne eart ðû on gedwolan *tu, fortunam putas erga te esse mutatam? erras*, 7, 2; Fox 16, 30. II. *to change one thing for another, to exchange*:—Heó wæs genumen of middanearde and eall ðæt sâr and ðone deáþ mid ēcre hǽlo and lîfe onwende, Bd. 4, 19; S. 589, 7. III. *to turn, change a direction, to avert, divert, turn aside*:—Nǽfre gē mec of ðissum wordum onwendaþ ðendan mec mîn gewit gelǽsteþ, Exon. Th. 124, 33; Gû. 347. 'Onwend ðē tō ðē sylfum' . . . Hē hine ðā onwende from ðisse worlde begangum, Blickl. Homl. 113, 26–30. Onwende hē his neb âweg, Lchdm. ii. 284, 15. Nǽfre ðû ðæs swîðlîc sâr gegearwast ðæt ðû mec onwende ðissa worda, Exon. Th. 246, 5; Jul. 57. Wēnst ðû ðæt ðû ðæt hwerfende hweól, ðonne hit on ryne wyrþ, mǽge oncyrran? Ne miht ðû ðon mā ðara woruldsǽlþa hwearfunga onwendan, Bt. 7, 2; Fox 18, 37. Ne mihte hæleþ weán onwendan, Beo. Th. 384; B. 191: Exon. Th. 130, 19; Gû. 440. Ðara unstillena gesceafta styring ne mæg nô weorþan onwend of ðam ryne ðe him geset is, Bt. 21; Fox 74, 4. Brôc biþ onwended of his rihtryne, Met. 5, 19. Biþ him se wela onwended, and wyrþ him wîte gegearwod, Cd. Th. 28, 5; Gen. 431: Blickl. Homl. 195, 28. Sýn hié from heora wônessum onwende, 109, 20. IV. *to change the position of a thing, to invert, turn upside down*, (a) literal:—Sceal mîn rôd onwended beón; mîn heáfod sceal beón on eorþan gecyrred, and mîne fêt tô heofenum gereahte, Blickl. Homl. 191, 5. Onwendedre endebyrdnysse *ordine prepostero*, Wrt. Voc. ii. 64, 33. (b) figurative, *to subvert, disturb, upset*:—Hond synfulra ne onwendeþ (*moveat*) mec, Ps. Surt. 35, 12. Ðis is ðæt mennisc ðe ealle mîne dǽda mid heora wordum (*destroyed by their words the effect that my actions should produce*), ðæt hié mê ne gelýfdon, Blickl. Homl. 175, 25. Næ sîe tô ðon gedurstig, ne cyning, næ bisceop, ðæt ðǽs mînæ gife onwændæ (*commoveat*), Cod. Dip. Kmbl. v. 218, 28. Nǽfre ic ne mîne lâstweardas geþrîstlǽcen ðæt heó hit (*the grant of certain dues*) onwenden, Ch. Th. 29, 14: Cd. Th. 26, 11; Gen. 405. Hwæt miht ðû his onwendan? Nû hê hafaþ ealle ðîne þeóstro geflêmed, Blickl. Homl. 85, 21. Sibb ǽfre ne mæg wiht onwendan ðam ðe wel þenceþ *nothing can destroy the ties of kindred in the case of a right-minded man*, Beo. Th. 5195; B. 2601. Hê (*Julian*) wolde ðone Cristendôm onwendan, Ors. 6, 31; Swt. 286, 3. Hié ealle ða worold on hiora âgen gewill onwendende (*evertendo*) wǽron, 1, 10; Swt. 48, 10. Eall heofona mægen biþ onwended and onhrêred, Blickl. Homl. 91, 27: 93, 13. Biþ se maga onwent and tôbrocen, Lchdm. ii. 218, 18. V. *to cause to change for the worse, to give a wrong direction, pervert*:—Se yfela dêma onwendeþ ðone rihtan dôm for ðæs feós lufon, Blickl. Homl. 61, 31. Hié (*bribes*) wîsra monna word onwendaþ, L. Alf. 46; Th. i. 54, 18. Beorht wǽron burgræced . . . meodoheall monig mandreáma full ôþ ðæt ðæt onwende wyrd seó swîðe *until fate wrought disastrous change*, Exon. Th. 477, 15; Ruin. 25. Drync unheórne, se onwende gewit wera, Andr. Kmbl. 69; An. 35. Mid ðý ðe hié ðone drenc druncon, hraþe heora môd wæs onwended, Blickl. Homl. 229, 14. Is mîn flǽsc frêcne onwended *caro mea immutata est*, Ps. Th. 108, 24. VI. *intrans. To return*:—Heora gâst gangeþ onwendeþ on ða eorþan ðe hî of cômon *exiet spiritus ejus, et revertetur in terram suam*, 145, 3. v. â-wendan.

on-wendedlîc; *adj. Changeable*:—Gyf se midwinter byþ on Frigendæge, ðonne byþ onwendedlîc winter, Lchdm. iii. 164, 8. v. â-wendedlîc.

on-wendedness, e; *f. Change, alteration*:—Nis him onwendednes *non est illis commutatio*, Ps. Th. 54, 20. Onwendednis *inmutatio*, Ps. Surt. 76, 11. In onwendednissum *in commutationibus*, 43, 13. v. next word.

on-wendness, e; *f.* I. *change*:—Ðære godcundnesse nǽnig onwendnesse on carcerne wæs of ðære menniscan gecynde, Blickl. Homl. 19, 24. II. *turning, movement* (v. onwendan, IV):—Onwendnisse heáfdes *commotionem capitis*, Ps. Surt. 43, 15. v. preceding word.

on-weorpan *to throw aside, turn aside*:—Hine se wind onwearp fram ðære byrig *mutati ab urbe venti*, Bd. 3, 16; S. 543, 8. [Cf. *O. H. Ger.* int-werfan *dissociare.*]

on-weorpness, e; *f. A throwing on*:—Ðæt lêg swîðe weóx and him nǽnig mon mid wætra onweorpnesse (*injectu*) wiðstondan meahte, Bd. 2, 7; S. 509, 20.

on-wêstan *to lay waste, desolate*:—Sý wunung heora onwêst (*deserta*), Ps. Spl. 68, 30. v. â-westan.

on-wîcan *to yield, retreat*:—Onwican *cessere*, Wrt. Voc. ii. 14, 23. [Cf. *O. H. Ger.* int-wîchan *cedere, recedere*: *Ger.* ent-weichen.]

on-willan *to cause to boil*; fig. *to cause passion* or *emotion to be violent*:—Ðâ wæs eft swâ ǽr ealdfeónda nîþ onwylled *then again as before hot waxed the hate of former foes*, Exon. Th. 125, 30; Gû. 362. v. â-wellan, -wyllan.

on-wille; *adj. Desired*:—'Ac gê hine gesundne âsettaþ ðǽr gê hine sylfne genôman' . . . Ongon ðâ leófne sîð dragan Dryhtnes cempa tô ðam onwillan eorþan dǽle *to the hermitage to which he* (*Guthlac*) *desired to go, and from which the fiends had removed him*, Exon. Th. 145, 25; Gû. 700.

on-windan. I. *to unwind, unfasten, loosen*:—Ðonne forstes bend Fæder onlǽteþ, onwindeþ wælrâpas, Beo. Th. 3224; B. 1610. Bâncofan onband, breóstlocan onwand, Elen. Kmbl. 2498; El. 1250. II. *to retire, retreat*:—Hærn eft onwand . . . wædu swæðorodon, Andr. Kmbl. 1062; An. 531.

on-winnende *assailing, attacking*:—Se onwinnenda here *the attacking army*, Homl. Th. ii. 432, 4. Mîne geféran mê betǽhton ðâm onwinnendum feóndum, Homl. Skt. i. 7, 351. v. winnan.

on-wist, e; *f. The being in a place, dwelling, habitation*:—Gesealde sigora waldend onwist êðles Abrahames sunum *God granted to Abraham's descendants to live in a country*, Cd. Th. 178, 27; Exod. 18. Cf. onwunung.

on-wlât (?) *form, appearance*:—Anwlâten (-es?) *formae*, Hpt. Gl. 523, 61.

on-wlite, es; *m. Face*:—Onwlite *patham*, Txts. 172, 17. v. and-wlite.

on-wôh. v. wôh.

on-worpenness, e; *f. An injection*; fig. of a feeling which has been inspired:—Ðâ ic getihtode bi ðære gîtsunge onworpennesse and ðâ wæs ic gesprecende ðone man and sêcende wæs ðæs þinges cûðnesse æt him, Shrn. 36, 19.

on-wrecan *to avenge*:—Ðý læs on him gesewen sî ðâs þing onwrecen beón *ne in eis illa ulcisci videantur*, Bd. 1, 27; S. 491, 28. v. â-wrecan.

on-wreón *to uncover, disclose*:—Ne onwrîh ðû *ne reveles*, Kent. Gl. 960. Onwreónde *discooperiens*, Wrt. Voc. ii. 25, 73. I. literal, *to uncover, open, remove a covering*:—Hê his hrægl onwrâg *retecto vestimento*, Bd. 2, 6; S. 508, 23. Ðâ onwrigon hî hire ondwliton *discooperto vultus indumento*, 4, 19; S. 589, 16. Onwreóh (-wrîh, Ps. Surt.) eágan mîne, Ps. Spl. T. 118, 18. Onwreón ða duru ðæs geteldes, Bd. 4, 19; S. 589, 14. II. figurative, *to make known, shew forth, reveal, discover*:—Heó onwrîhþ hire ǽwelm, donne heó geopenaþ hiore þeáwas, Bt. 20; Fox 70, 25. Hê his miltse onwreáh, Blickl. Homl. 107, 20. Ðâ com yrnan sum olbenda, and se cwæþ . . . 'Ne tôdǽlaþ gê ðara hâligra lîchoman' . . . ðâ dydon hý swâ him ðæt dumbe neát onwreáh, Shrn. 136, 2. Ic ðê hâte ðæt ðû ðâs gesyhþe secge mannum, onwreóh wordum ðæt hit is wuldres beám, Rood Kmbl. 191; Kr. 97. Bæd ðæt hê him on spellum gecýðde, onwrige worda gongum, hû . . ., Exon. Th. 171, 29; Gû. 1134. Iudas ðê mæg sôð gecýðan, onwreón wyrda gerýno, Elen. Kmbl. 1174; El. 589. Ðû scealt biddan ðæt môte beón open and onwrigen hwæt hê sý, Blickl. Homl. 185, 4: Bd. 2, 12; S. 512, 32. Is onwrigen wyrda bigang, Elen. Kmbl. 2245; El. 1124. III. *to shew the* (*hidden*) *meaning of anything, to explain*:—Ic wêne ðæt ðâs word ne sind eów fullcûðe, gif wê hî openlîcor eów ne onwreóþ, Homl. Th. i. 580, 27. Augustinus ûs onwreáh ðissere rǽdinge andgit, ii. 384, 21. Ðâs word sind sceortlîce gesǽde, and eów is neód ðæt wê hî swutelîcor eów onwreón, i. 278, 14. Onwrión *explicare*, Kent. Gl. 1152. IV. *to shew, display* so as to avoid concealment:—Ðâ seó fǽmne onwrâh ryhtgerýno, Exon. Th. 12, 34; Cri. 195. Onwreóh (-wrîh, Ps. Surt.) Gode ðîne wegas, Ps. Th. 36, 5. Gif his sâule gyltas ôðerum monnum dîgle beóþ and him sylfum cûðe, mid his andetnesse onwreó ða his abbode, R. Ben. 72, 5. V. *to display what is bad, to expose*:—God hine (*the sorcerer*) onwrýhþ gyt, ðeáh ðe wit hine ne geopenian, Blickl. Homl. 187, 17. Seó hâlige ǽ forbeódeþ ða sceondlîcnysse onwreón mǽgsibba . . . Ne onwreóh ðû sceondlîcnysse ðînes fæder . . . se ðe gedyrstigaþ onwreón ða sceondlîcnysse his steópmêder . . . se onwrîhþ his fæder sceondlîcnysse, Bd. 1, 27; S. 491, 6-16. Womdǽda onwreón, Exon. Th. 270, 18; Jul. 467. VI. of the operations of the Deity, *to reveal*:—Dryhten ðû ðe ðâs þing onwrige lytlingum, Mt. Kmbl. 11, 25. Hit ðê ne onwreáh flǽsc ne blôd, ac mîn Fæder, 16, 17: Bd. 2, 12; S. 512, 24. Âne bôc on his wîtegunge, ðe him God sylf onwreáh, Ælfc. T. Grn. 9, 44. Ðeáh ðe him God onwrîge wîsdômes gǽst, Exon. Th. 273, 14; Jul. 516. Ðam ðe se sunu wyle ðone Fæder onwreón, Mt. Kmbl. 11, 27. Drihten hire forþfôre wæs geeáþmôdad tô onwreónne, Bd. 4, 23; S. 595, 36. Sum gesihþ ðe God ðysan menn onwreogan hæfþ, Homl. Skt. i. 23, 747. [*O. H. Ger.* int-rîhan *revelare.*]

on-wrigenness, e; *f. An uncovering, discovery*:—Onwrigenys *apocalypsis*, Hpt. Gl. 435, 43. I. *a removal of that which obscures* or *conceals*:—Leóht tô onwrigennysse þeóda *lumen ad revelationem gentium*; a light to lighten the Gentiles, Homl. Th. i. 136, 22. II. *an explanation, exposition* (v. on-wreón, III):—Circlîcere anwrigenisse *ecclesiasticae traditionis, expositionis*, Hpt. Gl. 410, 36. Hæbben ða ungelǽredan inlendisce ðæs hâlgan regules cýððe þurh âgenes gereordes anwrigennesse *by means of an explanation* (*translation*) *in their own tongue*, Lchdm. iii. 442, 9. III. *an exposure* of a person's real character (v. on-wreón, V):—Nû neálǽceþ ǽgðer ge ðîn onwrigennes ge uncer gecýðnes *the vanity of your pretensions will be exposed, and the reality of our claims will be made manifest*, Blickl. Homl. 187, 23. IV. *a revelation, manifestation made to the eye* or *to the ear by divine power* (v. on-wreón, VI):—Heó sægde ðæt heó geleornod hæfde on onwrihgennysse (MS. T. onwrignesse) ðæt hire forþfôre wǽre swîðe neáh. Sǽde heó him ðæt seó onwrihgnes ðyslîc wǽre. Cwæþ ðæt heó gesâwe micelne þreát, Bd. 3, 8; S. 531, 35-38. Se Hǽlend geswutelode him ða tôweardan onwrigenysse (*a revelation of the future*), be ðære hê âwrât ða bôc ðe is gehâten Apocalipsis, Homl. Th. i. 60, 1. Helena hî (*the cross*) âfunde þurh Cristes onwrigennesse *through a revelation made by Christ*, H. R. 99, 8. Him ða upplîcan onwrigenesse wiðstôdon *superna illi oracula restiterunt*, Bd. 5, 9; S. 622, 21.

on-wrigness, -wrihness, e; *f. Revelation*:—Of onwrihnesse geendad *revelatione saturatus*, Mt. Kmbl. p. 9, 6. v. on-wrigenness, IV.

on-wrîðan *to unwrap, to release from a covering*:—Seó hêt heáfod onwrîðan *she bade take the head* (*of Holofernes*) *from the bag in which it had been put*, Judth. Thw. 24, 5; Jud. 173.

on-wrîðung, e; *f. A band*:—Onwrîðung (-wrîtung, Wrt.) *ligamentum*, Wrt. Voc. ii. 53, 76.

on-wrîting, e; *f. An inscription*; inscriptio Lk. Skt. Rush. 20, 24.

on-wunian *to dwell, inhabit*:—Ic onwunige (*inhabitabo*) on ðînum getelde, Ps. Lamb. 60, 5. Ðæt ic onwunige (*inhabitem*) on hûse Drihtnes

Ps. Spl. 26, 7. Ðú onwunast (*habitabis*) on heom, 5, 13. Hí onwuniaþ *inhabitabunt*, 55, 6. Hig onwuniaþ on worlde *inhabitabunt in saeculum*, Ps. Lamb. 36, 29. Onwuna on geladunge *inhabita terram*, 36, 3.

on-wunung, e; *f.* I. *a habitation, dwelling*:—Gewurde him wēste eall his onwunung *fiat habitatio ejus deserta*, Ps. Th. 108, 7. Gewȳt fram mē, and far ūt of mȳnre onwununge, Nicod. 27; Thw. 15, 11. Ðonne forlǣt se hālga gāst ða onwununge, and dǣr sōna wyrþ deófol inne, Wulfst. 280, 9. II. *persistence, perseverance*:—Mid singalre ānrǣdnesse ł onwununge *assidua* (*perpetua*) *instantia*, Hpt. Gl. 407, 66.

on-wyllan, -ȳwan. v. on-willan, -īwan.

on-ȳdan *to pour in*:—Tunge witan swylce lagoflōd onȳdaþ *lingua sapientis quasi diluvium inabundabit*, Scint. 65.

oo-. v. ō-.

open; *adj. Open.* I. *not shut*, (a) *allowing ingress* or *egress*:—Heofen biþ open on sumum ende . . . and mycel mægen forþ cymeþ þurh đone openan dǣl, Blickl. Homl. 93, 1. Open scræf, Cd. Th. 212, 10; Exod. 537. Open wæs đæt eorþærn (*the sepulchre*), Exon. Th. 460, 18; Hö. 19. Ðín carcern open wē gemētton, Blickl. Homl. 239, 27. Gē geseóþ opene heofenas (*caelum apertum*), Jn. Skt. 1, 51. (b) of a door:—Ðonne andydan hié đa duru đe on đa healfe open wæs (*the door that opened on that side*) . . . and mid đæm đe hié đara dura hwelce opene gesāwon, Ors. 3, 5; Swt. 106, 14–16. Biþ oft open eádgum tōgeánes onhliden heofonrīces duru, Exon. Th. 198, 16; Ph. 11. Hié gemētton đæs carcernes duru opene, Blickl. Homl. 239, 24. (c) of the eyes:—Mid openum eágum gesión, Met. 20, 257. (d) of wounds, *not closed up*:—Ða openan dolg, Exon. Th. 68, 24; Cri. 1108; Rood Kmbl. 93; Kr. 47. II. *not covered, not protected*:—Seó cirice is ufan open and unoferhrēfed, Blickl. Homl. 125, 26, 30. Open burh *urbs patens*, Kent. Gl. 975. III. *declared, public*:—Ða bēc (*of the Old Testament*) synd gehātene seó ealde gecȳdnyss and seó ealde ǣ, đæt is, open lagu đe God gesette Israhēla folce, Hexam. 1; Norm. 2, 19. IV. *not secret, not concealed, discovered, brought to light* (in reference to things where concealment is desired):—Hwanon ys đis word open geworden (*palam factum*), Ex. 2, 14. Ne dēþ nān man nān þing on dīglum ac sēcþ đæt hit open sȳ (*in palam esse*), Jn. Skt. 7, 4. Ðæt mōte beón open and onwrigen hwæt hē sȳ, Blickl. Homl. 185, 4. Se đe mānāþ swerige and hit him on open wurđe *he that commits perjury, and the crime is clearly proved against him*, L. Ath. i. 25; Th. i. 212, 18. Gif open morþ weorđe āgife man māgum đone banan *if in a case of murder the murderer be discovered, let him be given up to the kinsmen of the murdered man*, L. C. S. 57; Th. i. 406, 25. Æt openre þȳfþe *in case of discovered theft*, 26; Th. i. 392, 3. Opene weorđaþ monna dǣde *the deeds of men shall be brought to light* (*at the last day*), Exon. Th. 64, 32; Cri. 1046. V. *without attempt at concealment*:—Antonius him (*Octavianus*) onbeád gewin and openne feóndscipe, Ors. 5, 13; Swt. 246, 1. Blisse on openum, Lchdm. iii. 200, 8. On đa openan tīd *the last day when nothing is concealed*, Exon. Th. 96, 9; Cri. 1571. VI. *manifest, clear, plain, evident*:—Đā cwæþ hē: 'Genōg sweotol đæt is đætte for đȳ sint gōde men gōde đe hí gōd gemētaþ.' Đā cwæþ ic: 'Genōg open hit is' *certum est, adeptione boni, bonos fieri. Certum*, Bt. 36, 3; Fox 176, 29. Se đe unwīslīce leofaþ biþ open sott, đeáh him swā ne þince, Homl. Skt. i. 13, 132. Is seó wyrd mid eów open orgete, Andr. Kmbl. 1517; An. 760. Đā āgann Landfranc atȳwian mid openum gesceáde (*with manifest reason*), đæt hē mid rihte crafede đās đa hē crafede, Chr. 1070; Erl. 208, 17. [*O. Sax.* opan: *O. Frs.* epen: *Icel.* opinn: *O. H. Ger.* offan.]

open-ears, -ærs, es; *m. A medlar*; mespila, Wrt. Voc. i. 32, 50. (v. *Halliw. Dict.* openers.)

openere, es; *m. One who opens*:—Aprilis quasi aperilis . . . swylce hē sȳ openere. On his tīman beóþ geopenade trȳw tō blōwanne, Anglia viii. 326, 5.

openian; *p.* ode. I. *intrans.* (a) *to open, to become open*:—Openaþ *patebit*, Kent. Gl. 401. Byrgenu openodon, Homl. Th. ii. 258, 5. Openige nū đīn fæđm, Blickl. Homl. 7, 24. Byrgen opnigende (*patens*) is race heora, Ps. Spl. 5, 10. Openiendum heofonum *caelis patentibus*, Bd. 4, 9; S. 576, 37. Opniendum, Hpt. Gl. 514, 55. (b) *to become manifest*:—Ðæs līf mid heálīcum tācnum heofonlīcra wundra openode *cujus vita sublimis crebris miraculorum patebat indiciis*, 4, 30; S. 608, 26. II. *trans.* (a) *to open, unclose*:—Openast (*aperis*) đū hand đīne, Ps. Spl. 144, 17. Seáþ hē openode *lacum aperuit*, 7, 16. Opnyaþ mē gatu rihtwīsnysse, 117, 19. (b) *to disclose, manifest*:—Gefeohtu gesihþ blisse hit openaþ *if he sees fights, it is a sure sign of joy*, Lchdm. iii. 200, 8. Hē cȳđde and openade đæt hē Cristen wǣre *se Christianum esse prodiderat*, Bd. 1, 7; S. 477, 22. Ðæt hē nǣnigum mā openade ne cȳđde (*patefaceret*), 5, 9; S. 623, 15. Hord openian *to discover the treasure*, Beo. Th. 6105; B. 3056. Openiende *propalat*, Wrt. Voc. ii. 66, 17. [*O. Sax.* oponōn: *O. H. Ger.* offanōn: *O. Frs.* epenia: *Icel.* opna.] v. ge-openian.

open-līc; *adj. Open, public*:—Openlīc *publicum*, Germ. 398, 45. Openlecre *puplica*, Wrt. Voc. ii. 66, 55. Openlecum (opanletet, Wrt. ii. 3, 61) *a puplicis*, Wülck. Gl. 343, 28. [*O. H. Ger.* offan-līh *publicus*.]

open-līce; *adv. Openly.* I. *publicly, in a way by which not a few only are affected*:—Eft cymþ God swīđe openlīce (*in a way to be seen by all*), Ps. Th. 49, 3. Hié openlīce đæt gesetton (*they publicly decreed*) đæt hē swungen wǣre ōþ đæt hē swylte, Blickl. Homl. 193, 3. Wæs đis đara wundra ǣrest đe đes eádiga wer openlīce beforan ōđrum mannum geworhte, 219, 3: Homl. Th. i. 58, 15. Hē funde āne tabulan eall āwritene and hī openlīce rǣdde (*read it out to the by-standers*), Homl. Skt. i. 23, 767. II. *without concealment, without reserve, freely*:—Hē spræc openlīce (*palam*), Mk. Skt. 8, 32. Nān man spæc openlīce be him for đæra Iudēa ege, Jn. Skt. 7, 13. Đā fōr hē næs nā openlīce ac dȳgollīce, 7, 10. Monige scylda openlīce wietena (*aperte cognita*), Past. 21, 2; Swt. 152, 1. Ða dīglan gyltas man sceal dīgelīce bētan, and đa openan openlīce, Homl. Th. i. 498, 10. III. *plainly, evidently, clearly, manifestly*:—Swelce hē open, līce cuǣde *si aperte dicat*, Past. 21, 2; Swt. 153, 11: Blickl. Homl. 81; 19. Būton ic openlīce gecȳþe đæt ic God sylfa sȳ *unless I make it evidently appear that I am God himself*, 181, 36. Se wæs openlīce ūþwita, Bt. 19: Fox 70, 8: Met. 13, 72. Hū ne is đē genōg openlīce geeówad, Bt. 24, 3; Fox 84, 19: 32, 2; Fox 116, 33. Ic ongite openlīce . . . Ic wolde đeáh hit fullīcor and openlīcor of đē ongitan *video . . . sed ex te cognoscere malim apertius*, 33, 1; Fox 120, 2–9: 39, 2- Fox 212, 11. Openlīce *manifeste*, Hpt. Gl. 460, 59. Sume sindon openlīce forgitene *some plainly are forgotten*, Met. 10, 60. IV. *without obstruction, at large*:—Wolde openlīcor (*latius*) ætȳwan seó godcunde ārfæstnyss on hū myclum wuldre Cūþbyrht æfter his deáþe lifede, Bd. 4, 30; S. 608, 24. Ic wēne đæt đū nyte hwæt đis gemǣne, būton wē of ōđrum bōcum đis openlīcor secgan (*give a fuller account*), Boutr. Scrd. 18, 27. Ðās þing wē willaþ openlīcor gecȳđan đonne đæt lȳden dō, Anglia viii. 298, 25: Chr. 1106; Erl. 240, 35. [*O. Sax.* opanlīko: *O. H. Ger.* offanlīhho *palam, publice, evidenter*.]

openness, e; *f. Openness, publicity*:—Gend openysse *per publicum*, Hpt. Gl. 524, 5. [*O. H. Ger.* offannussi *apocalypsis*.]

openung, e; *f. Manifestation, revelation*:—Seó openung đæs dæges (*the day of judgment*) is swīđe egesfull eallum gesceaftum, Blickl. Homl. 91, 19. [*O. H. Ger.* offenunga *manifestatio, declaratio*.]

ōr. I. *beginning, origin*:—Ōr ł fruma *initium*, Mk. Skt. Lind. 13, 8. Dæges ōr onwōc geleáfan *the day-spring of belief awoke*, Apstls. Kmbl. 130; Ap. 65. Næs him fruma ǣfre ōr geworden, Cd. Th. 1, 11; Gen. 6. Đǣr wæs yfles ōr, Andr. Kmbl. 2763; An. 1384. On đæm wæs ōr writen fyrngewinnes, Beo. Th. 3381; B. 1688. Ōr and ende, Exon. Th. 492, 6; Rä. 81, 10. Cwealmes on ōre *at the beginning of the destruction*, Cd. Th. 153, 32; Gen. 2547. Gif đū his ne meaht ōr āreccan *if you cannot tell even the beginning of your dream*, 224, 9; Dan. 133. Secgan ōr and ende *to tell from first to last*, Andr. Kmbl. 1297; An. 649. Ic đē yfla gehwylces ōr gecȳđe ōþ ende forþ, Exon. Th. 263, 21; Jul. 353. Suē hē wundra gihuaes ōr āstelidæ (cf. ord onstealde, Bd. 4, 24; S. 597, 21) *quomodo ille omnium miraculorum auctor exstitit*, Txts. 149, 4. Orleges ōr onstellan, Beo. Th. 4806; B. 2407: Exon. Th. 386, 10; Rä. 4, 59. Ne can ic Abeles ōr ne fōre hleómǣges sīđ *I know not Abel's life from its beginning or its later course*, Cd. Th. 61, 33; Gen. 1006. II. *front, van*:—Wæs on ōre heard handplega, 198, 22; Exod. 326: Beo. Th. 2087; B. 1041. Heriges on ōre, Andr. Kmbl. 2213; An. 1108. Cf. ord.

or. This form occurs in A. Sax. only as a prefix, but in Goth. *us*, in Icel. *or, ur*, in O. H. Ger. *ur* it is found also as a preposition. It has the meaning *without*, e. g. or-mōd; also that of *original, early*, e. g. or-eald.

ōra, an; *m. A border, edge, margin, bank* (mostly in place names, -*or* in Windsor, Bognor. v. Cod. Dip. Kmbl. iii. xxxv: Leo, A. S. Names, p. 92):—In đone stede đe is gecueden Cerdices ōra, Chr. 495; Erl. 14, 10: 514; Erl. 14, 21. Æt Cerdices ōran, Erl. 2, 3. Ðonan on đone ōran foran wiđ-eástan Ecgulfes setl west be đam ōran eft tōweard setle, Cod. Dip. Kmbl. ii. 216, 2–3. Siđđan đū gehȳrde on hliþes ōran galan geác on bearwe, Exon. Th. 473, 28; Bo. 21. On ōra[n] his hrægles *in oram vestimenti ejus*, Ps. Spl. 132, 3.

ōra, an; *m. Ore, metal in an unreduced state*:—Ǣlces kynnes wecg vel ōra *metallum*, Wrt. Voc. i. 34, 67. Seolfor đe byþ seofon sīđon āmered syđđan se ōra ādolfen byþ, Ps. Th. 11, 7. Gedolfene ōran *effossa rudera*, Germ. 396, 190. Hit is eác berende on wecga ōrum āres and īsernes leádes and seolfres *quae etiam venis metallorum, aeris, ferri, et plumbi et argenti faecunda*, Bd. 1, 1; S. 473, 23. Seó eorþe is cennende wecga ōran *terra parens metallorum*, Nar. 2, 15. Goldōrum ł-wecgum *auri metallum*, Hpt. Gl. 449, 14. [Cf. golt, seluer, stel, irn, copper, mestling breas: al is icleopet or, A. R. 284, note b.] v. ōre.

ōra, an; *m. A species of money introduced by the Danes* (cf. Icel. *eyrir*, the eighth part of a mark):—Þolie twelf ōrena mid Denum and .xxx. scill. mid Englum, L. E. G. 7; Th. i. 170, 16. Bēte man đæt æt deádum menn mid .vi. healfmarce, and æt cwicon mid .xii. ōran, L. Eth. iii. 1; Th. i. 292, 11. Ita quod xv. (xvi?) ore libram faciant, iv. 9; Th. i. 303, 9. In the Law of the Northumbrian Priests, Th. ii. 290 sqq., this money is often mentioned. Ōro *mnas*, Lk. Skt. Lind. Rush. 19, 13: Rush. 19, 16.

oraþ. v. oroþ.

or-blēde; *adj. Bloodless*:—Orblēde *exsangues*, Wrt. Voc. ii. 32, 39.

orc, es; *m. A cup, can, tankard, flagon*:—Orc *orca* (cf. orca *a tankard*, Wülck. Gl. 599, 16: *a cane*, 771, 29), Wrt. Voc. i. 25, 4. Blōt-(blōd-)orc *uas in quo sacrificabant res impias*, Germ. 307, 514. Orce *calice*, Hpt. Gl. 435, 39. Bollan steápe, swylce eác orcas, Judth. Thw. 21, 15; Jud. 18: Beo. Th. 6087; B. 3047. Hē geseah orcas standan, fyrnmanna fatu, 5514; B. 2760. Orcas *crateras*, Ex. 24, 6. [*Goth.* aurkeis *a cup*: *O. Sax.* ork.]

orc, es; *m. The infernal regions* (orcus):—Orc *orcus*, Ep. Gl. 16 f, 36: Wrt. Voc. ii. 115, 61. Orcþyrs oððe heldeófol *Orcus* (*the god of the infernal regions*), 63, 49.

or-ceápe, -ceápes, -ceápunga, -ceápungum; *adv. Without payment, without cause, for nothing, gratis, gratuitously*:—Ne þurfon gē wēnan ðæt gē ðæt orceápe sellon, ðæt gē under Drihtnes borh syllaþ, þēh gē sōna ðære mēde ne ne onfōn, Blickl. Homl. 41, 12. Orceápes *gratis*, Hpt. Gl. 478, 42. Beó hē frióh orceápunga, L. Alf. 11; Th. i. 46, 3. Hí onwunnon mē orceápunga (*gratis*), Ps. Spl. M. 119, 6. Orceápungum, Ps. Lamb. 108, 3.

orc-eard, -geard. v. ort-geard.

or-ceás; *adj. Free from complaint, not chargeable* (*with a fault*):—Orceás *inmunis*, Wrt. Voc. ii. 91, 50; *inmunes*, 111, 14. Orcǽsne *immunem, immaculatum, castum*, Hpt. Gl. 474, 72. Orceáse ł unwemme *immunes, incontaminati, inviolatas*, 447, 43. v. ceás, ceást, *and next word*.

or-ceásness, e; *f. Immunity, freedom from fault*:—Orceásnes *inmunitas*, Wrt. Voc. ii. 46, 59: 77, 34. Seó orceásnys, Hpt. Gl. 433, 57. Orceásnysse ł uniwemnysse *immunitatis*, 434, 27. Orceásnysse *immunitatem, castitatem*, 461, 41.

orcen (?) *a sea-monster*:—Ðanon untydras ealle onwōcon, eotenas and ylfe and orcneas [orcenas (?). *Grein reads* orc-nēas, *with which compare* orc-þyrs *under* orc] swylce gigantas, Beo. Th. 225; B. 112. [Cf. (?) *Icel.* orkn (örkn) *a kind of seal.*]

or-cnāwe, -cnǽwe; *adj. Recognisable, evident*:—Ðǽr orcnāwe (wearþ) þurh teóncwide tweógende mōd, Andr. Kmbl. 1540; An. 771. Ðā wæs orcnǽwe (on-, Kmbl.) idese sīðfæt, Elen. Kmbl. 457; El. 229. v. ge-, on-cnǽwe.

orc-þyrs. v. orc.

ord, es; *m.* I. *a point*, (a) of a weapon:—Ǽlces wǽpnes ord *mucro*, Wrt. Voc. i. 35, 35. Se ord (ðæs speres), L. Alf. pol. 36; Th. i. 84, 17. Seaxes ord, Exon. Th. 472, 6; Rä. 61, 12. Wordes ord breósthord þurhbræc, Beo. Th. 5576; B. 2791. Ne ofstong hē hiene mid ðȳ speres orde. Ðæt is ðonne swelc mon mid forewearde orde stinge ... suā suā Assael wæs deád būtan orde *non cum recta, sed aversa hasta transforavit ... quasi sine ferro moriuntur*, Past. 40, 5; Swt. 297, 10–23. Mid gāres orde, Cd. Th. 92, 2; Gen. 1522. Hē sette his swurdes ord tōgeánes his innoþe, Homl. Th. ii. 480, 14. Ðæt gebearh feore wið ord and wið ecge (cf. *Icel.* með oddi ok eggju) *it protected life from thrust and cut*, Beo. Th. 3102; B. 1549. (b) putting a part for the whole, *a spear, pointed weapon*:—Mē sceal wǽpen niman, ord and īren (*spear and sword*), Byrht. Th. 139, 12; By. 253. Hwā ðǽr mid orde mihte on fǽgean men feorh gewinnan, wīgan mid wǽpnum, 135, 31; By. 124. Hit is mycel nēdþearf ðæt hié man forspille, and mid īrenum þislum and ordum hié man sleá, Blickl. Homl. 189, 30. Hildesercum, bordum and ordum, Elen. Kmbl. 469; El. 235. (c) of other point-shaped, conical things:—Ord *apicem*, Wrt. Voc. ii. 73, 64. Ða hwīle ðe se mōna ðære sceade ord (*the shadow of the earth*) ofer yrnþ, Lchdm. iii. 240, 26. Hafaþ tungena gehwylc xx orda, hafaþ orda gehwylc engles snytro, Salm. Kmbl. 461–464; Sal. 231–232. (d) of persons, (1) *one who is at the topmost point, a head, chief, prince*:—Ǽþelinga ord *Christ*, Exon. Th. 32, 19; Cri. 515: 46, 22; Cri. 741: 53, 5; Cri. 846: Elen. Kmbl. 785; El. 393. Burgwarena ord, 462, 22; Hö. 56. (2) of position, *head, front*:—Se ðe on orde geóng *he who went at the head of the band*, Beo. Th. 6242; B. 3125. II. *line of battle, forefront*:—Se ord on here *acies*, Ælfc. Gr. 5; Som. 4, 14. Hī Pantan streám bestōdon, Eást-Seaxena ord and se æschere, Byrht. Th. 133, 52; By. 69. Elamitarna ordes wīsa, Cd. Th. 121, 3; Gen. 2004. On orde stōd Eádweard *Edward stood in the forefront of the battle*, Byrht. Th. 139, 52; By. 273. III. *the beginning, origin, source* (applied to persons and things):—Se ðe (*the devil*) is ord ǽlcere leásunge and yfelnysse, Homl. Th. i. 4, 29. Se leahter (*pride*) is ord and ende ǽlces yfeles, ii. 220, 34. Ord moncynnes (*Adam*), Cd. Th. 68, 2; Gen. 1111. Dæges ord *day-break*, 174, 10; Gen. 2876. Sume ūre þeningbec onginnaþ on Aduentum Domini; nis ðeáh ðǽr forðȳ ðæs geáres ord, Homl. Th. i. 98, 27. From orde ōþ ende forþ, Elen. Kmbl. 1176; El. 590. Hē folcmǽgþa fruman āweahte, æþelinga ord, ðā hē Adam sceóp, 77, 20; Gen. 1278. Sōna ongeat cyning ord and ende ðæs ðe him ȳwed wæs, 225, 30; Dan. 162. Ord onstellan *to make a beginning, be the source of*, 272, 4; Sat. 114: Bd. 4, 24; S. 597, 21. Ðæt ðīn sprǽc hæbbe ǽgðer ge ord ge ende, Past. 49; Swt. 385, 13. [*Laym., A. R., O. and N.* ord: *Orm.* ord and ende: *O. Sax. O. L. Ger. O. Frs.* ord: *O. H. Ger.* ort *angulus, aculeus, acies, initium*: *Icel.* oddr *the point of a weapon, head of a troop, leader.*]

or-dǽle; *adj. Not having* or *taking part* in a thing, *not participating*:—Ordǽle *expers*, Wrt. Voc. ii. 31, 48: 90, 67. Ordǽla *expers*, i. *ignarus, alienus, sine parte, imperitus, inscius, privatus*, Wülck. Gl. 232, 23.

or-dāl, -dēl; *generally neuter, but an apparently fem. acc. pl.* ordēla *occurs*, L. Edg. C. 24; Th. ii. 248, 28. (Cf. *O. H. Ger.* which has fem. and neut. forms.) In the sense of *judicial decision, judgment* the word is used by *O. Frs. O. Sax. O. H. Ger.* (v. Richthofen, the Heliand and Graff), but in *A. Sax.* it is found only in the special sense, which belongs also to the *O. Frs.*, of a decision which follows an appeal to the Deity. The ordeal was thus connected with religion, and attended by religious ceremonies. In L. Ath. i. 23; Th. i. 210, 26, it is said with respect to the person who is to undergo the ordeal 'fēde hine sylfne mid hlāfe and mid wætere and sealte and wyrtum ǽr hē tō gān scyle, and gestande him mæssan ðæra þreora daga (*the three days preceding the ordeal*) ǽlcne, and geoffrige tō, and gā tō hūsle ðȳ dæge ðe hē tō ðam ordāle gān scyle, and swerige ðonne ðane āþ, ðæt hē sȳ unscyldig ðære tihtlan ǽr hē tō ðam ordāle gā.' Before taking the Eucharist and going to the ordeal a solemn form of adjuration was addressed to the person concerned, that unless he was conscious of innocence he should desist. v. Rtl. 114, 13–23. The further proceedings in connection with the ordeal by hot water or by hot iron are detailed in L. Ath. iv. 7; Th. i. 226, 8. After the fire to be used in heating was carried into the church, none were to enter but the priest and the accused. When the iron was hot or the water boiled, two men for the accused, two for the accuser, were admitted, to see that the proceedings were fairly conducted. When hot water was employed, if it were a case of *ānfeald tihtle*, the hand was plunged in up to the wrist, if of threefold, up to the elbow. When the hot iron was used, a weight of one pound or of three pounds, according to the case, had to be carried nine feet. The hand was then sealed up, and its condition, when unwrapped at the end of three days, determined the guilt or innocence of the accused. See also L. Ath. i. 23; Th. i. 212, 2–10. Further reference to the difference in degree is made in Ath. iv. 6; Th. i. 224, 13: L. Edg. H. 9; Th. i. 260, 18. Among those who were to be subjected to this form of trial are mentioned convicted perjurors, who after conviction are not 'āþwyrðe ac ordāles wyrðe,' L. Ed. 3; Th. i. 160, 18–21: the man who was charged with plotting against his lord, or with being guilty of 'cyricbryce,' or with practising witchcraft and similar illicit arts underwent the threefold ordeal, L. Ath. i. 4–6; Th. i. 202, 1–17; and the same trial was appointed in the case of incendiaries, L. Ath. iv. 6; Th. i. 224, 11–19, and of coiners, L. Ath. i. 14; Th. i. 206, 17–25: L. Eth. iii. 8; Th. i. 296, 12–16. The ordeal is also mentioned as being the only method of meeting an accusation in a case between English and Welsh, 'ne stent nān ōðer lād æt tihtlan būte ordāl betweox Wealan and Englan,' L. O. D. 2; Th. i. 354, 1–2. The ordeal must take place in a king's burgh, 'Ǽlc ordāl beó on ðæs kyninges byrig, L. Eth. iii. 6; Th. i. 296, 4, and upon fastdays and festivals could not be used, 'ordēl and āþas syndan tōcwedene freólsdagum and rihtfæstendagum,' L. E. G. 9; Th. i. 172, 10: L. Eth. v. 18; Th. i. 308, 24–27: vi. 25; Th. i. 320, 24–27: L. Edg. C. 24; Th. ii. 248, 27. Wē forbeódaþ ordāl and āþas freólsdagum and ymbrendagum and lenctendagum and rihtfæstendagum and fram *aduentum domini* ōþ *octabas epiphanie* and fram *septuagesima* ōþ fīftēne niht ofer eástran, Wulfst. 117, 14. See Schmid. A. S. Gesetz., Grmm. R. A. pp. 863 sqq., 908 sqq., and cf. cor-snǽd. As an instance of the occurrence of the word elsewhere than in the Laws, see Chart. Th. 432, where the phrase *āþ and ordēl* occurs several times. [*O. Frs.* or-, ur-dēl: *O. Sax.* ur-deili: *O. H. Ger.* ur-teil, -teila, -teili *judicium, sententia.*] v. īsen-, wæter-ordāl.

ordāl-īsen, es; *n. The iron used in the ordeal*, L. Ath. iv. 6; Th. i. 224, 14.

ord-bana, an; *m. One who slays with* (*the point of*) *a weapon* (ord, cf. ecg-bana), *a murderer*:—Ic fylde mid folmum ordbanan Abeles (*Cain*), Cd. Th. 67, 7; Gen. 1097.

ord-ceard. v. ort-geard.

ord-fruma, an; *m.* I. of things, *source, origin*:—Ordfruma *origo*, Ælfc. Gr. 9, 3; Som. 8, 58. Ōs byþ ordfruma ǽlcere sprǽce, Runic pm. Kmbl. 340, 5; Rūn. 4. II. of persons, (1) *author, source*, (a) applied to the Deity:—Crist, ordfruma ǽlcere gife, Homl. Th. ii. 526, 7. Ordfruma ealre clǽnnesse, Blickl. Homl. 13, 21. Drihten is ordfruma (*auctor*) ealra eádignesse, Bd. 4, 30; S. 609, 16. God, līfes ordfruma, Exon. Th. 14, 30; Cri. 227. Ordfruma ealra gescafta, Cd. Th. 292, 17; Sat. 442. (b) applied to others:—Se wæs ordfruma (*auctor*) ðæs gefeohtes, Bd. 3, 24; S. 556, 32. Danaus ðæs yfeles ordfruma *scelerum fabricator Danaus*, Ors. 1, 8; Swt. 40, 16: Nicod. 6; Thw. 3, 14: 29; Thw. 17, 4. (2) *chief, head, prince*:—Wæs mīn fæder æþele ordfruma, Beo. Th. 531; B. 263. Daniel wæs ordfruma earmre lāfe, Cd. Th. 225, 10; Dan. 152. Ðonne beóþ ða synfullan genyðerade mid heora ordfruman, swā hē genyðerad wearþ, Blickl. Homl. 33, 1. [*O. Sax.* ord-frumo: *O. H. Ger.* ort-frumo *auctor.*]

ord-stapu; *gen.* -stæpe; *f. A step of a pointed instrument, the prick* or *wound made by a sharp point*:—Oft mec īsern scōd sāre on sīdan; ic nǽfre meldade monna ǽngum, gif mē ordstæpe egle wǽron, Exon. Th. 485, 19; Rä. 71, 16.

ord-wíga, an; *m. A warrior who fights with a pointed weapon* (? cf. gár-wíga), or *one who fights in the van* (? v. ord, II):—Ordwýga! ne lǽt ðín ellen gedreósan tó dæge, Wald. 9; Vald. 1, 6.

óre, an; *f. A mine, place in which ore is dug*:—Ísern óre *ferri fodina, in quo loco ferrum foditur*, Wrt. Voc. ii. 148, 11. v. óra *ore*.

or-eald; *adj. Of great age*:—Caron wæs swíðe oreald, Bt. 35, 6; Fox 168, 20. [*O. H. Ger.* ur-alt *valde senex, grandaevus, veteranus, decrepitus.*]

or-eldo. v. or-ildu.

orel, es; *n.*: orl, es; *m. A garment, veil, mantle*:—Orel, ryft *cycla[s]*, Wrt. Voc. ii. 131, 38. Orelu *oraria*, 65, 5. Winpel *vel* orl *ricinum*; orl *orarium* vel *ciclas*, i. 17, 1-3: *stola* vel *ricinum*, 40, 34. Orlas *ciclas* vel *oraria*, 59, 40. Hé geglængde mé mid orle (*the monastic veil?*), Homl. Skt. i. 7, 36. Wimplum ł orlum *cycladibus*, Hpt. Gl. 486, 47: *velaminibus*, 526, 54. [*Goth.* aurali *a napkin*: *O. H. Ger.* oral *strophium, peplum, flammeolum.* From *Lat. orale.*]

orenum, Nar. 24, 2. v. or-wéne.

oreþ, oreþian. v. oroþ, orþian.

oret, es; *n.* (?) *Struggle, labour*:—Ðonne ðú ðínes gewinnes wæstme byrgest etest oretes *labores fructuum tuorum manducabis*, Ps. Th. 127, 2. v. following words.

oreta. v. oretta.

oret-mæcg, es; *m. A combatant, warrior, champion*:—Hí (*the Jews*) slógon eornoste Assiria oretmæcgas (*the army of Holofernes*), Judth. Thw. 24, 39; Jud. 232. Oretmecgas (*Beowulf and his band*), Beo. Th. 669; B. 332: 732; B. 363: (*Hrothgar's men*), 967; B. 481. Orettmæcgas (*the disciples*), Andr. Kmbl. 1328; An. 664. Weóld Walum and Scottum and Bryttum eác byre Æðelrédes, Englum and Sexum, oretmæcgum, Chr. 1065; Erl. 196, 30. v. next word.

oret-mæcga, an; *m. A combatant, athlete*:—Oretmæcga *agonista*, Wrt. Voc. ii. 1, 2. Oretmæcgan *anthletae*, 3, 3.

oret-stów, e; *f. A place where a struggle is carried on, a place for wrestling*:—Oretstówe ł winstówe ł plegstówe *scammatis*, Hpt. Gl. 405, 39. Oredstówe *in scammate*, 478, 48.

oretta, an; *m. One who strives, a combatant, warrior, champion*:—Wearp ðá wunden mǽl yrre oretta (*Beowulf*), Beo. Th. 3068; B. 1532: 5070; B. 2538. David, eádig oretta, Andr. Kmbl. 1757; An. 881. Beorn beaduwe heard . . . ánrǽd oretta . . . Cristes cempa (*St. Andrew*), 1965; An. 985. Þegnas lǽrde eádig oreta (*St. Andrew*), eorlas trymede, 925; An. 463. Eádig oretta andwíges heard (*Guthlac*), Exon. Th. 112, 21; Gú. 147. Swá sceal oretta compian, 122, 33; Gú. 315. Godes orettan swencan, 136, 15; Gú. 541.

orettan. v. on-orettan.

orf, es; *n. Cattle, live stock*:—Ǽlce geáre byþ orf ácenned, and mennisce menn tó mannum ácennede, ða ðe God gewyrcþ swá swá he geworhte ða ǽrran, Hexam. 12; Norm. 20, 20. Cuce orf, L. Edg. S. 8; Th. i. 274. 25. Swá mycel orfes wæs ðæs geáres forfaren, swá nán man ǽr ne gemunde, Chr. 1041; Erl. 169, 7. Hé nam him on orfe and on mannum and on ǽhtum swá him gewearþ, 1052; Erl. 183, 22. Hé hæfde on orfe micele ǽhte *fuerunt ei oves et boves*, Gen. 12, 16. Ǽlces cynnes orf *animantia diversi generis*, Ex. 12, 38. Habbaþ ðæt orf eów gemǽne *omnia animantia diripiens vobis*, Jos. 8, 2. Hí námon eall ðet orf ðe hí mihton tó cuman, ðæt wæs fela þúsend, Chr. 1064; Erl. 196, 5. Drífaþ hider eówre orf *adducite pecora vestra*, Gen. 47, 16.

orf-cynn, es; *n. Cattle*:—Næs orfcynnes nán máre búton vii. hrúðeru, Chart. Th. 429, 5. Of eallum orfcinne *de jumentis in genere suo*, Gen. 6, 20.

orf-cwealm, es; *m. Pestilence among cattle, murrain*:—On ðisum geáre wæs swá mycel orfcwealm swá man ne gemunde fela wintrum ǽr, Chr. 1054; Erl. 188, 5. Ús stalu and cwalu, stric and steorfa, orfcwealm and uncoþu . . . derede swýðe þearle, Wulfst. 159, 10.

or-feorm; *adj. Unprovided, destitute, worthless*:—Ðæt biþ feóndes bearn, hafaþ grundfúsne gǽst Gode orfeormne (of feormne, MS.) wuldorcyninge (*a godless spirit*), Exon. Th. 316, 16; Mód. 49. Ða (*the heathen gods*) sind geásne góda gehwylces, idle, orfeorme, unbiþyrfe, 255, 20; Jul. 217. Hwider hweorfaþ wé hláfordleáse, góde orfeorme, synnum wunde (cf. gif wé gewítaþ fram ðé, ðonne beó wé fremde from eallum ðǽm gódum ðe ðú ús gegearwodest, Blickl. Homl. 233, 31-33), Andr. Kmbl. 812; An. 406. Gástæs góde orfeorme, wuldre bescyrede, 3233; An. 1619: Judth. Thw. 25, 21; Jud. 271.

or-feormness, e; *f. Want of cleanliness* (v. feormian *to cleanse*), *squalor*:—Orfeormnisse *squalores*, Wrt. Voc. ii. 121, 8. v. or-firme.

orf-gebitt, es; *n. Grazing*; herbitum, Wrt. Voc. i. 39, 24.

or-firme; *adj. Uncleanly, squalid*:—Hí wǽron fúlíce and orfyrme on heora beardum, Guthl. 5; Gdwin. 34, 22. v. or-feormness *and next word.*

or-firm[u]; *f. Squalor*:—Orfiermae, orfermae *squalores*, Txts. 96, 933. v. preceding word.

or-gálscipe (?), es; *m. Wantonness*:—Orgálscype (on gálscype (?), orgelscipe (?)), wrénscipe *petulantia*, Hpt. Gl. 525, 74.

organ, es; *m. A song*:—Se organ *the Pater Noster* (cf. v. 47, where it is called *cantic*), Salm. Kmbl. 107; Sal. 53. Gif hé ðæs organes ówiht cúðe, 65; Sal. 33. Organa swég ðe from englum biþ sungen, L. E. I. pref.; Th. ii. 400, 11. v. organian.

organe (organa (?); cf. *O. H. Ger.* organa; *f.*), an; *f.*: organon; *pl.* organa; *n. A musical instrument*:—Organon, Exon. Th. 207, 4; Ph. 136. Ða organa wǽron getogene, and ða bíman gebláwene, Th. Ap. 25, 15. Organan *organo*, Ps. Surt. 150, 4. On salig wé úre organan up áhengan *in salicibus suspendimus organa nostra*, Ps. Th. (Spl. T., Surt.), 136, 2. Iubal wæs fæder herpera and ðæra ðe organan macodun *Iuba, fuit pater canentium cithara et organo*, Gen. 4, 21. [*Icel.* organ; *n.*]

organe, an; *f. Marjoram*; origanum vulgare:—Organe. Ðeós wyrt ðe man *origanum* and óðrum naman ðam gelíce organan nemneþ, Lchdm. i. 236, 9-11: 282, 23.

organian, orgnian *to sing to the accompaniment of a musical instrument*:—Ic orgnige (organige, MS. H.), Ælfc. Gr. 28, 7; Som. 32, 62.

orgel *pride*:—Hwǽr is heora prass and orgol búton on moldan beþeaht and on wítum gecyrred? Wulfst. 148, 32. [Woreldes richeise wecheð orgel on mannes heorte, O. E. Homl. ii. 43, 17. *The form* orguil *occurs*, p. 63. Heó leapeð into horel (orhel, MS. T.: orȝel, MS. C.), A. R. 224, 2. Cf. *French* orgeuil (*to which Brachet assigns a German origin*): *Ital.* orgoglio.] v. orgel-líc.

orgel-dreám, es; *m. The sound of a musical instrument*:—Orgeldreáme *organo*, Blickl. Gl.

orgele (? cf. *O. H. Ger.* orgela: *Ger.* orgel; *f.*: orgles, Alis. 191) *an organ, a musical instrument.* v. preceding word.

orgel-líc; *adj.* I. *proud, arrogant, disdainful* (v. next word). II. *deserving scorn* or *disdain*:—Hwý sceal ǽnigum menn þyncean tó orgellíc ðæt hé onbúge tó óðres monnes willan *qua conscientia dedignatur homo alienae voluntati acquiescere?* Past. 42, 2; Swt. 307, 15.

orgel-líce; *adv. Proudly, arrogantly, haughtily, insolently*:—Hé hine swá orgellíce up áhóf and bodode ðæs ðæt hé úþwita wǽre ne cýðde hé hit mid nánum cræftum ac mid leásum and ofermódlícum gilpe *hominem, qui non ad verae virtutis usum, sed ad superbam gloriam falsum sibi philosophi nomen induerat*, Bt. 18, 4; Fox 66, 29. Ðá áxode Pilatus hine orgollíce, Homl. Th. ii. 250, 29. Orgellíce, Homl. Skt. i. 9, 76. Hé cwæþ orgællíce, 5, 449. Hé forþ stæpþ wel orglíce swylce hwylc cyng of his giftbúre stæppe geglenged, Anglia viii. 298, 34.

orgelness, e; *f. Pride, elation*:—Orgelnysse *elationis*, Hpt. Gl. 432, 54.

orgel-word, es; *n. An arrogant, insolent speech*:—Ðá cwæþ se ealdorbiscop mid orgelworde, Homl. Th. ii. 248, 21.

or-gete, -gyte, -geate; *adj. To be perceived, manifest*:—Ðæt tácn núgyt is orgyte (*pervidetur*), Ors. 1, 7; Swt. 38, 34. Orgeate, Exon. Th. 76, 12; Cri. 1238: 347, 6; Sch. 8. Tácen orgeatu, 75, 3; Cri. 1216. Is gesýne sóþ orgete cúð oncnáwen, ðæt ðú cyninges eart þegen geþungen, Andr. Kmbl. 1052; An. 526. Is seó wyrd mid eów open orgete, 1517; An. 760. Andrea orgete wearþ folces gebǽro, 3137; An. 1571. Ic eów secgan mæg sóþ orgete, 1702; An. 853. Ðú meaht geseón orgete on mínre sídan swátge wunde, Exon. Th. 89, 17; Cri. 1458.

or-gilde; *adj. Unpaid for*, applied to one for whom the wergild is not paid:—Gif hine (*the man who has broken his pledge, and will not submit to the penalty*) mon ofsleá, licgge hé orgilde, L. Alf. pol. 1; Th. i. 60, 15. v. ǽ-gilde.

orglíce, or-gyte. v. orgellíce, or-gete.

orgol. v. orgel.

or-hlyte; *adj. Having no share of, not participating in, free from, without*:—Orhlyte oððe bedǽled *expers*, Ælfc. Gr. 9, 43; Som. 13, 1: 47; Som. 48, 44. Orhlita *exsors*, Wrt. Voc. i. 51, 48. Wá ðære sáwle ðe orhlyte hyre líf ádríhþ ðæra háligra mihta, Homl. Th. i. 346, 25. Orhlyte ýðeles gylpes, ii. 286, 28. Ne bist ðú orhlyte eallunge ðæra wítena *you shall not altogether escape those torments*, 310, 27. Ðæt gé eallunge ðæs andgites orhlyte ne sýn, 188, 28. Eádiges orhlyte, Andr. Kmbl. 1359; An. 680. [*O. H. Ger.* ur-hlozi, -hlozzo *exsors.*] Cf. wan-hlyte.

orige (?) *in the following passage*:—Se ðe þeóf geféhþ hé áh .x. scill. . . . Gif hé ðonne óþierne and orige (orrige, MS. H.) weorðe ðonne biþ hé wítes scyldig *he who catches a thief shall have ten shillings . . . If he (the thief) run away, and gets clear off* (?), *then shall he (the captor.* For the responsibility of one who lets a thief escape, see L. In. §§ 36, 72) *be liable to fine*, L. In. 28; Th. i. 120, 7.

or-ildu (o); *f. Extreme old age*:—Hine (*death*) gelettan ðæt hé ðý lator cymþ, ge furþum óþ oreldo hí hine hwílum lettaþ (*put off death until extreme old age*), Bt. 41, 2; Fox 246, 9. Á ic wundor ðín weorðlíc sægde and ic ðæt wið oryldu áwa fremme *usque nunc pronuntiabo mirabilia tua, et usque in senectam et senium*, Ps. Th. 70, 16. v. or-eald.

orl. v. orel.

or-læg, -leg, es; *n.* (?) *Fate*:—Nó ic (*Daniel*) wið feohsceattum ofer folc bere Drihtnes dómas, ac ðé (*Belshazzar*) unceápunga orlæg secge, worda gerýnu *I will tell thee thy fate (by explaining the writing on the wall)*, Cd. Th. 262, 19; Dan. 746. Hé ðonne á tó ealdre orleg dreógeþ *he then for ever and ever undergoes his fate in hell* (cf. *Icel.* drýgja örlög, to 'dree' one's 'weird'), Exon. Th. 446, 29; Dóm. 29. [*O. H. Ger.* ur-lag; *m. fatum*: *Icel.* ör-lög; *n. pl. fate*; also *war.*] v. or-lege.

orlæg-gífre; *adj. Eager to cause death* (?):—Ismahel biþ unhýre orlæggífre wiðerbreca wera cneórissum, Cd. Th. 138, 6; Gen. 2287.

or-leahter = *dis-crimen* :—Orleahter *discrimen*, i. *periculum*, *damnum*, Wrt. Voc. ii. 140, 82. Orhlættras *discrimina*, Hpt. Gl. 450, 43.

or-leahtre; *adj. Blameless, faultless* :—Ðæt wæs ân cyning ǽghwæs orleahtre, Beo. Th. 3776; B. 1886. Ǽghwylc mennisc leahter on ðǽm eádigan Sancte Iohanne cennendum gestilled wæs, and hié on eallum heora lîfe orleahtre gestôdan, Blickl. Homl. 163, 17.

orleg-ceáp, es; *m. Battle-bargain, fighting* (?) :—Ðǽr wæs eáðfynde eorle orlegceáp se ðe ǽr ne wæs nîðes genihtsum *there might fighting be easily found for the man that before had not had enough of war*, Cd. Th. 120, 13; Gen. 1994.

or-lege, es; *n.* I. *war, strife, hostility* :—Ðâ wæs orlege eft onhrêred, nîð upp ârâs, Andr. Kmbl. 2605; An. 1304. Ic ðæs orleges or anstelle (*speaking of the strife of the elements*), Exon. Th. 386, 9; Rä. 4, 59. Se ðæs orleges or onstealde, Beo. Th. 4805; B. 2407. Ðonne wê on orlege hafelan weredon, ðonne hniton fêþan, 2657; B. 1326. Nalæs late wǽron eorre æscberend tô ðam orlege, Andr. Kmbl. 94; An. 47: 2411; An. 1207. Hêt wǽpen on ðam orlege formeltan, 2293; An. 1148. Hý hine brêgdon, budon orlege, egsan and ondan, Exon. Th. 136, 5; Gû. 536. Ðû hafast þurh ðîn orlegu ofer witena dôm wîsan gefongen, wiðsæcest tô swîðe ðînum brýdguman *thou hast by thy hostile proceedings acted contrary to the judgement of wise men, dost reject too violently thy suitor*, 248, 17; Jul. 97. II. *a place where hostility is shewn* :—Cwǽdon ðæt hê on ðam beorge byrnan sceolde ... gif hê monna dreám of ðam orlege eft ne wolde sylfa gesêcan, 114, 3; Gû. 167. Ðâ ðû heán and earm on ðis orlege ǽrest cwôme, 129, 24; Gû. 426. (In both passages the word seems to mean the place which Guthlac had selected for his dwelling, and from which the evil spirits, that before occupied it, wished to drive him.) Hafaþ nû se hâlga helle bireáfod ealles ðæs gafoles ðe hî geárdagum in ðæt orlege swealg, 35, 18; Cri. 560. [Cf. *O. Sax.* orlegas (-lages, -lagies) word *battle-cry* : *O. Frs.* or-loch *war* : *O. H. Ger.* or-loge, -liugi *bellum*, Grff. ii. 137: *Icel.* or-lygi *fate, battle* : *Dan.* or-log *warfare at sea* : *Du.* or-log *war*. v. Grmm. D. M. 381, 817.] v. or-læg *and next word*.

or-lege; *adj. Hostile* :—Wêpaþ and heówaþ eall orlegu folc, for ðam ûre God eów hæfþ ofercumen ... orlega þeóda hê âlêde under ûre fêt, Ps. Th. 46, 1–3. Ne onêgdon nâ orlegra nîð, ðeáh ðe feónda folc fêran cwôme, Cd. Th. 259, 26; Dan. 697.

orleg-from; *adj. Stout in battle* :—Oft ic gǽstberend cwelle compwǽpnum; cyning mec ... hwîlum lǽteþ sceacan orlegfromne, Exon. Th. 401, 21; Rä. 21, 15.

orleg-hwîl, e; *f. Battle-time, time of war* :—Nû is leódum wên orleghwîle, Beo. Th. 5814; B. 2911. Fela ic gûþrǽsa genæs, orleghwîla, 4845; B. 2427. [Cf. *O. Sax.* orlag-hwîla *the hour of death*.]

orleg-nîð, es; *m. Hostility, strife*, Cd. Th. 6, 6; Gen. 84: 56, 20; Gen. 915.

orleg-stund, e; *f. A time of trouble, time when the unfavourable decree of fate is carried out* :—Dreógeþ earfoþu orlegstunde, Salm. Kmbl. 750; Sal. 374.

orleg-weorc, es; *n. War-work, action* :—Se ðæt orlegweorc (*the defeat of the people of Sodom*) gecýðde, Cd. Th. 122, 2; Gen. 2020.

or-mǽte; *adj. Immense, excessive* :—Ormǽte *gigas*, Hymn. Surt. 44, 13. Ormǽde, 112, 23. Ðǽr læg sum ormǽta stân, Homl. Th. ii. 164, 29. Duru ormǽte, Exon. Th. 19, 32; Cri. 309. Þreát ormǽte, 270, 14; Jul. 465. Þreá ormǽte, Andr. Kmbl. 2333; An. 1168. Hê mid ormǽtre angsumnysse wæs gecwylmed, Homl. Th. i. 88, 5. Bifigende mid ormǽtre cwacunge, 504, 28. For ðære ormǽtan êhtnysse, ii. 542, 20. Hié woldon ormǽte feoh gegaderian, Bt. 24, 2; Fox 82, 17. Ðâ gesomnode man ormǽte fyrde, Chr. 1001; Erl. 137, 10. Ða ormǽtan *minacem*, Wrt. Voc. ii. 55, 1. Ormǽte buccan *magnicaper*, i. 23, 58. Legcan him onuppan ormǽte (*ingentia*) weorcstânas, Jos. 10, 27. Ic dreág yfel ormǽtu, Exon. Th. 280, 10; Jul. 627. Þurh ða ormǽtan êhtnyssa, Homl. Th. i. 6, 2. [*Orm.* orr-mete.]

or-mǽte; *adv. Excessively, exceedingly, without measure* :—Mê ðînes hûses heard ellenwôd æt ormǽte (*or adj.*?), Ps. 68, 9.

[**ormǽt-lîc**; *adj. Excessive* :—Ðises geáres wurdon ormǽtlîca wædera, Chr. 1117; Erl. 246, 14.]

ormǽtness, e; *f. Excess, immensity* :—Hâtheorte lâreówas þurh wôdnysse hâtheortnysse lâre gemet tô ormǽtnysse wælhreównysse gecyrraþ *iracundi doctores per rabiam furoris disciplinae modum ad inmanitatem crudelitatis convertunt*, Scint. 32. Þurh ormǽtnysse ðæs godcundlîcan leóhtes, Homl. Th. ii. 186, 15. Micelre ormǽt[nysse] *mirae magnitudinis*, Hpt. Gl. 454, 77. Nâht elles gestincan bûton unstenca ormǽtnessa, Wulfst. 139, 8.

or-met (?) *a very great mass, something immense* :—Ormetum *molibus*, Wrt. Voc. ii. 55, 75: 114, 20. Cf. ge-met.

or-met[t], -mete; *adj. Excessive, without measure* :—Ymbhogena ormete rên (cf. se rên ungemetlîces ymbhogan, Bt. 12; Fox 36, 19), Met. 7, 36. Hê mid ormettum mynum mê gefretewode *he decked me with priceless jewels*, Homl. Skt. i. 7, 37.

or-môd; *adj. Without courage, hopeless, despairing* :—Ðis folc is geirged and ormôd ongên eów *elanguerunt omnes habitatores terrae*, Jos. 2, 9. Se ðe hine forþencþ, se biþ ormôd, Bt. 8; Fox 24, 18. Wæs ðâ ormôd eorl, âre ne wênde, ne on ðam fæstene frôfre gemunde, Met. 1, 78: 5, 30. Mîn sylfes gâst wæs ormôd worden *defecit spiritus meus*, Ps. Th. 76, 4. Ðý læs hê ormôd sý ealra þinga, Exon. Th. 294, 12; Crä. 14. Ne beó ðû tô ormôd ðeáh ðe sî on unriht gedêmed *be not too much discouraged, though judgement be given wrongfully against thee*, Prov. Kmbl. 34. Ða lytelmôdan ðonne hié ongietaþ hiera unbældo, hié weorðaþ oft ormôde (*in desperationem cadunt*), Past. 32, 1; Swt. 209, 8: Homl. Th. i. 536, 6: Nar. 32, 23. Hig ormôde (orwêne, MS. D.) ne gedô, L. de Cf. 1; Th. ii. 260, 14. [*O. H. Ger.* ur-môt *disperatus*.]

or-môdness, e; *f. Desperation, despair* :—Ormôdnes *disperatio*, Wrt. Voc. ii. 140, 72. Mid ðý hê ûs geseah on ormôdnesse (*in desperatione*) gesette, Bd. 5, 1; S. 614, 5. Ðâ se earma man ðus mid ormôdnesse sprecende wæs *sic loquebatur miser desperans*, 5, 13; S. 633, 21. Tô ormôdnesse *ad desperationem*, Past. 14, 3; Swt. 83, 19: 21, 7; Swt. 165, 19. Hæfde hine seó deófollîce strǽl mid ormôdnysse gewundodne: wæs se eádiga wer Gûðlâc mid ðære ormôdnysse þrî dagas gewundod, ðæt hê sylfa nyste hwider hê wolde mid his môde gecyrran, Guthl. 4; Gdwin. 28, 13–17. Ic habbe ongiten ðîne ormôdnesse ... ðû sǽdest ðæt ðû wǽre bereáfod ǽlces gôdes, Bt. 5, 3; Fox 12, 31. Ic eom geunrôtsod fulneáh ôþ ormôdnesse, 41, 2; Fox 246, 14.

orne; *adj. Unhealthy, harmful* :—Mid Godes fultume ne wyrð him nân orne *with God's help no harm will be done him*, Lchdm. iii. 16, 5. Wið ornum ûtgange, 70, 25. v. un-orne.

ornest, es; *n. Trial by battle* :—Gif Englisc man beclypaþ ǽnigne Frænciscne mann tô orneste for þeófte ... oððe for ǽnigan þingan ðe gebyrige ornest for tô beónne ... hæbbe hê fulle leáfe swâ tô dônne. And gif se Englisca forsæcþ ðæt ornest, W. ii. 1; Th. i. 489, 5–9: ii. 2–3; Th. i. 489, 11–25. v. eornost, orrest.

oroþ, orþ, es; *n. Breath, breathing* :—Oroþ oððe gâst *flamen*, Wrt. Voc. ii. 37, 11: *flatus*, *spiritus*, 149, 32: *anhela*, Rtl. 192, 21. Hê oroþ stundum teáh ... swâ wæs ôþ ǽfen oroþ up hlæden, Exon. Th. 178, 17–30; Gû. 1245–1252. Heora oruþ biþ swylce lîg *ignem et flammam flantes*, Nar. 34, 32: Beo. Th. 5107; B. 2557. Orþ *spiraculum* (cf. lîfes orþung *spiraculum vitae*, Gen. 2, 7), Kent. Gl. 757. Orþas ł hfæstes (= orþes ł fnæstes) *spiritus*, Hpt. Gl. 464, 24: 454, 66. Oreþe *aura*, Wrt. Voc. ii. 6, 56: *flatu*, 38, 9. Wið âttorsceaþan (*dragon*) oreþe, Beo. Th. 5671; B. 2839. Eallinga gewǽced and ðam orþe belocen, Glostr. Frag. 102, 13. Hê mid langre swôretunge ðæt orþ of ðam breóstum teáh, Guthl. 20; Gdwin. 84, 20. Þurh âttres oraþ, Salm. Kmbl. 441; Sal. 221. Ðû him on âðdest oruþ and sâwul, Hy. Grn. 9, 55. Oroþo *anhelae*, Rtl. 192, 25.

orped; *adj. Grown up, of full strength, stout, active, bold* :—Lâ orpeda cleric, gif ðû wylle witan ða terminos ðe wê ymbe sprǽcon, wite hwylc gêr hyt sý ðæs mônan ðæt man hǽt *lunaris*, Anglia viii. 325, 5. Swâ gedafenaþ esnum ðam orpedan, ðonne hê gôd weorc ongynþ, ðæt hê ðæt geornlîce beswynce, 324, 17. Orped[n]e, snellne *adultum*, Hpt. Gl. 485, 25. [Orpud *audax*, *bellipotens*, Promp. Parv. 371, v. *note for other examples of the word*. Þe guode kniȝt and orped, þet heþ guod herte and hardi, Ayenb. 183, 6. *Jamieson gives* orpit *proud*.] v. next word.

orpedlîce; *adv. Boldly, in full force* :—Wê willaþ âmearkian ðâs epactas and eác ða regulares lunares, ðæt hig openlîc[r]e and orpedlîce standun beforan ðæs preóstes gesyhþe *that they may stand out clearly and boldly in sight of the priest*, Anglia viii. 301, 31. [Cf. But for þe emperour hadde out of his companye þe orped man (*virum strenuum*) Bonefacius, þe emperour dede noþing orpedliche (*nihil strenue egit*), Trev. v. 231, 13–15. He orpedly strydeȝ, Bremly broþe, Gaw. 2232. Þenne orppedly in to his hous he hyȝed to Sare, Allit. Pms. 56, 623.]

orrest *battle* :—Hê hine on orreste ofercom, Chr. 1096; Erl. 233, 4. [A Danish form, *Icel.* orrosta *battle*. *Orm.* he wass Inn orresst ȝæn þe deofell.]

orretscipe, es; *m. Infamy, disgrace* :—Ðæs unhlîseádgan orretscipe *infamis*, Wrt. Voc. ii. 44, 49. Orretscipe *infamis*, 85, 11.

orrettan *to disgrace, put to shame, cover with confusion* :—Orretteþ *turpabat*, Wrt. Voc. ii. 91, 18: *subfundit*, 78, 19. Onretteþ (or-?) *deturpans*, 26, 56: 82, 56. Cf. georrettan *infamare*, 47, 26: 92, 33. v. ge-orettan.

or-sâwle; *adj. Without soul, lifeless* :—Orsâule *exsangue*, Wrt. Voc. ii. 33, 28. Næs ðâ deád ðâ gyt, ealles orsâwle, Judth. Thw. 23, 6; Jud. 108. Saga ðæt heó lâme bilûce lîc orsâwle in þeóstorcofan, Exon. Th. 173, 28; Gû. 1167.

or-sceattinga; *adv. Gratuitously, free of charge* :—Hî lâreówas orsceattinga sealdon *magisterium gratuitum praebere curabant*, Bd. 3, 27; S. 558, 27. Cf. or-ceápe, -ceápunga.

or-sorg, -sorh; *adj. with gen.* I. *free from care, without anxiety, secure, prosperous* :—Orsorh *securus*, Kent. Gl. 365: Wrt. Voc. i. 83, 59. Orsorg *lentus*, ii. 96, 62: *consors*, 15, 23: 105, 18. Orsorh wǽpna *securus armorum*, Ælfc. Gr. 41; Som. 44, 9. Se tô ânra ðara burga (*the cities of refuge*) gefliéhþ ðonne mæg hê beón orsorg ðæs monnsliehtes *he may be without anxiety as to the manslaughter he has committed*; reus perpetrati homicidii non tenetur, Past. 21, 7; Swt. 167, 20. Ne þorftest ðû ðê nânwuht ondrǽdan ... Ðonne ðû ðonne orsorg wǽre, Bt. 14, 3;

Fox 46, 30. Næs ic nǽfre swâ emnes mōdes ðæt ic eallunga wǽre orsorg, ðæt ic swâ orsorg wǽre ðæt ic nâne gedrēfednesse næfde, 26, 1; Fox 90, 26. Seó wiðerwearde wyrd byþ ǽlcum men nytwyrðre ðonne seó orsorge (*prospera*), 20; Fox 70, 30. Orsorg lîf lǽdaþ woruldmen wîse, ðonne hē forsihþ eorþlîcu gōd and ðara yfela orsorh wunaþ, Met. 7, 43. Hē furþon orsorh ne brîcþ his genihtsumnysse *he does not enjoy even his abundance without anxiety*, Homl. Th. i. 64, 34. Uton lǽtan bión ðâs sprǽce and bión unc ðæs orsorge *secure concludere licet*, Bt. 34, 7; Fox 144, 18. Tō upâhafen for orsorgum woruldgesǽlþum (cf. on ðînre orsorgnesse, Fox 14, 35) *too much uplifted on account of untroubled earthly felicity*, Met. 5, 33. II. *secure from danger, safe*:—Orsorg *tuta*, Wrt. Voc. ii. 123, 2. Samson eode him swâ orsorh of heora gesihþum, Jud. 16, 3. Hē ūs sealde orsorh wuldor (*glory secure from the assaults of men*), Blickl. Homl. 151, 12. Ða hâlgan martyras orsorge becōmon tō wulderbeáge ðæs ēcan lîfes, Homl. Th. i. 416, 9. Wit begra ǽr wǽron orsorge *we before were safe from both* (*hunger and thirst*), Cd. Th. 50, 5; Gen. 804. Wē beóþ for eów and eów orsorge gedōþ (cf. wē gedōþ eów sorhleáse *securos vos faciemus*; we will secure you, Mt. Kmbl. 28, 14), Nicod. 17; Thw. 8, 23. [*O. H. Ger.* ur-sorg *securus*.]

orsorg-lîc; *adj. with gen. Secure*:—Ðæt lîf ðara gesinhîwena mæg bión orsorglîc ǽlcra wîta *conjugalis vita a suppliciis secura est*, Past. 51, 6; Swt. 399, 22.

orsorglîce; *adv.* I. *without anxiety*:—Geoffra Gode ðone ðe ðū getuge, ðæt ðū ðȳ orsorglîcor becume tō ðam æðelan wulderbeáge *offer to God him whom thou hast brought up, that with the less anxiety thou mayest come to the noble crown of glory*, Homl. Th. i. 418, 5. II. *carelessly, rashly*:—Ðæt hiera nân ne durre grîpan suâ orsorglîce on ðæt rîce, Past. 4, 2; Swt. 41, 5. III. *securely, safely*:—Forðam ðe hit swâ earfoðe is ǽnegum menn tō witanne hwonne hē geclǽnsod sîe, hē mæg ðȳ orsorglîcor (*tutius*) forbūgan ða þegnunga, 7, 2; Swt. 51, 6. Hî woldon ðȳ mâran anweald habban, ðæt hȳ mihton ðȳ orsorglîcor ðissa woruldlusta brūcan, Bt. 24, 2; Fox 82, 15. Sió nafu færþ micle fæstlîcor and orsorglîcor ðonne ða felgan, 39, 7; Fox 220, 30.

orsorgness, e; *f.* I. *freedom from care* or *anxiety, tranquillity*:—Caru *cura*, orsorhnys *securitas*, Wrt. Voc. i. 83, 60–61. Sibb and orsorhnes *pax et securitas*, Bd. 4, 25; S. 601, 29. II. *prosperity*:—Dysigra monna orsorgness (*prosperitas*) hî fordēþ, Past. 50, 2; Swt. 387, 34. Ða mîne sǽlþa and seó orsorgnes *prosperitas mea*, Bt. 10; Fox 26, 26. Seó orsorhnes... seó wiðerweardnes *prospera fortuna... adversa* 20; Fox 72, 4. Ðæt ðū ðē ne anhebbe on ðînre gesundfulnesse and on ðînre orsorgnesse, 6; Fox 14, 35. Cuman tō ræste and tō orsorgnesse, 25; Fox 88, 31. Hū forht hē sceal beón for ǽlcre orsorgnesse *prospera formidanda*, Past. 3; Swt. 33, 5: Swt. 35, 1, 2, 8. Ðe ðisses middangeardes orsorgnesse ne gîmþ, ne him nâne wiðerweardnesse ne andrǽt *qui prospera mundi postposuit, qui nulla adversa pertimescit*, 10, 1; Swt. 61, 8. Orsorgnesse *prosperitatem*, 50, 1; Swt. 387, 22.

ort-geard, es; *m. An orchard, garden*:—Orcyrd *hortus*, Wrt. Voc. i. 84, 51. Orceard, orcird, orcyrd, orcgyrd, ordceard, Ælfc. Gr. 8; Zup. 28, 11. Se ordceard, Cod. Dip. Kmbl. iv. 72, 5. Of ǽlcum treówe ðises orcerdes, Gen. 2, 16. Ðū ðe eardast on frióndes ortgearde (orcgearde, MS. Hat.), Past. 49, 2; Swt. 380, 14. Suâ se ceorl dēþ his ortgeard, 40, 3; Swt. 293, 4. God âplantode wynsumnisse orcerd (*the garden of Eden*), Gen. 2, 8. Beóþ hyra orcerdas mid æpplum âfyllede, Lchdm. iii. 252, 22. Seó eorþe stōd mid holtum âgrōwen... mid æppelbǽrum treówum and mid orcgeardum, Hexam. 6; Norm. 12, 6. [*Goth.* aurti-gards.]

ortgeard-weard, es; *m. A gardener*:—Orcerdweard *ortulanus*, Wrt. Voc. i. 84, 52.

orþ. v. oroþ.

or-þanc, es; *m. n. Original, inborn thought.* I. *mind, genius, wit, understanding*; ingenium:—Orþanc *ingenium*, cræftica *artifex*, Wrt. Voc. i. 47, 8–9. Lîflîces orþa[nces] *vivacis ingenii*, Hpt. Gl. 407, 40–43. Hē genam þurh heora lâre on his orþance ða egeslîcan dǽda, Ælfc. T. Grn. 17, 21. Nū wolde ic ðæt ða æðela[n] clericas âsceócon fram heora andgites orþance ǽlce sleacnysse, Anglia viii. 301, 4. Gif ðonne [man] mid orþonce (*skilfully*) ðisses þinges fundian wille, Lchdm. i. 100, 6. Yfele orþance *malo ingenio*, Wrt. Voc. ii. 56, 8. Orþancas *ingenia*, Germ. 397, 423. Orþancum *ingeniis*, Wülck. Gl. 250, 5. II. *a skilful contrivance* or *work, artifice, device, design*:—Orþanc *molimen* (cf. searo *molimen*, Wrt. Voc. ii. 54, 29), Ælfc. Gr. 9, 12; Som. 9, 32. His ofermēdu is fruma ūres forlores and se orþonc (*argumentum*, cf. searwe *argumenta*, Wrt. Voc. ii. 84, 69) ðe wē mid âliésde siendon is Godes eáðmōdnes, Past. 41, 1; Swt. 301, 9. Mid orþance *argumento*, Hpt. Gl. 439, 3: Wrt. Voc. ii. 9, 12. Orþonce, gleáwnysse *argumento*, 2, 11. Hwâ is ðæt ðe cunne orþonc clǽne (*the creation*) nymðe ēce God? Cd. Th. 266, 6; Sat. 18. Orþancas *argumenta, commenta*, Hpt. Gl. 479, 68. Orþanc *commenta*, i. *machinamenta, excogitata, astutia, argumenta, machinationes, ficta, fraudes*, sarwa *dicta, mendacia*, Wülck. Gl. 206, 42–46. Orþonc *machinamenta*, Wrt. Voc. ii. 113, 74. Orþoncum, searwum *commentis*, 14, 82. Orþancum *machinamentis*, Hpt. Gl. 477, 9: *argumentis*, 486, 19. Stān in goldfate smiþa orþoncum biseted, Exon. Th. 219, 8; Ph. 304: Beo. Th. 817; B. 406. Ealle ða orþancas tōslîteþ, Salm. Kmbl. 145; Sal. 72. ¶ Orþoncum *skilfully, cunningly, ingeniously, with art*:—Orþanc[um?] *subtiliter, sagaciter*, Hpt. Gl. 407, 21. Is se sweora orþancum geworht (*cunningly wrought*), Exon. Th. 483, 15; Rä. 69, 3: Beo. Th. 4180; B. 2087. Ðæt orþancum ealde reccaþ, Cd. Th. 200, 19; Exod. 359. [*O. H. Ger.* ur-dank *argumentum, commentum.*]

or-þanc, es; *m.* [or *without*] *Thoughtlessness, want of thought*:—Nǽnig man scile oft orþances (*heedlessly*) ūt âbrēdan wǽpnes ecgge, Salm. Kmbl. 329; Sal. 164.

or-þanc; *adj. Cunning, skilful*:—Ceastra beóþ feorran gesȳne, orþanc enta geweorc, wrǽtlîc weallstâna geweorc, Menol. Fox 463; Gn. C. 2. Orþonc ǽrsceaft, Exon. Th. 477, 1; Ruin. 16. Mē þurh hrycg wrecen hongaþ under ân orþonc pîl, ōðer on heáfde, Exon. Th. 403, 23; Rä. 22, 12. Hwǽr com heora snyttro and seó orþonce glâunes, and se ðe gebregdnan dōmas dēmde? Blickl. Homl. 99, 31.

orþanc-bend; *m. f. A skilfully contrived band*:—Bewrigene orþoncbendum, Exon. Th. 429, 35; Rä. 43, 15.

orþancscipe, es; *m. Art, mechanical art, mechanics*:—Orþancscipe *mechanica* (*the word occurs at the end of a list of the arts.* Cf. *in a similar list* searocræft *mechanica*, Wrt. Voc. ii. 81, 61), Hpt. Gl. 479, 61. Orþancscipe *mechanicam*, i. *peritiam* ł *fabricam rerum*, 528, 65. Searwa, orþanscipes (-as?) *molimina, ingenia*, 502, 54.

orþian; *p.* ode *To breathe, pant*:—Ic orþige *spiro*, Ælfc. Gr. 19; Som. 22, 42. Ic on orþige *inspiro*, 47; Som. 48, 44. *Animal* is ǽlc þing ðæt orþaþ, 5; Som. 4, 41. Ðonne se sacerd cristnaþ, ðonne orþaþ hē on ðone man, Wulfst. 33, 18. Gâst oreþaþ *spiritus spirat*, Jn. Skt. 3, 8. Þurh ðæt lyft wē orþiaþ and eác ða nȳtenu, Hexam. 4; Norm. 8, 18. Ǽlc þing ðe orþode *omne quod spirare poterat*, Jos. 10, 40. Orþode *palpitavit* (*palpavit*, MS.), Germ. 402, 73. Orþige *palpitet*, 398, 116. Hē ne gedyrstlǽceþ ðæt hē furþon orþige *he dare not even breathe*, Homl. Th. i. 456, 10. Hē earfoþlîce orþian mihte, 86, 8. Ðâ ongann hē tō ēðele ðæs upplîcan lîfes mid eallum gewilnungum orþian *then began he to pant for the country of the life above with all his desires*, ii. 118, 26. Orþiende swētnyssa *spirans balsama*, Hymn. Surt. 98, 19.

orþung, e; *f.* I. *breathing, breath*:—Ðæra dracena orþung âcwealde ðæt earme mennisc, Homl. Th. ii. 474, 6. *Syllaba* is stæfgefēg on ânre orþunge geendod, Ælfc. Gr. 3; Som. 3, 13. Of orþunga gâstes graman ðînes *ab inspiratione spiritus irae tuae*, Ps. Spl. 17, 18. Nân mann ne nȳten næfþ nâne orþunge būton þurh ða lyfte, Lchdm. iii. 272, 22. Ōþ ða nȳhstan orþuncge *until his latest breath*, L. Ælf. E. 4; Th. ii. 392, 10. God on âbleów on hys ansîne lîfes orþunge (*spiraculum vitae*), Gen. 2, 7. II. *a breathing-hole* (? cf. preceding passage), *a pore*:—Orþung *spiramentum* vel *porus*, Wrt. Voc. i. 54, 67. v. on-orþung.

or-treówe, -triéwe, -trȳwe; *adj.* I. *despairing, hopeless*:—Ðâ him eorla mōd ortrȳwe wearþ, Cd. Th. 187, 21; Exod. 154. Wē tō wâce hȳraþ ūrum Drihtne, and wē tō ortreówe (-trȳwe, MS. A.: -trūwe, MS. C.) syndan Godes mihta and his mildheortnesse, Wulfst. 91, 14. Hié æt nîhstan wǽron ortriéwe (-treówe, MS. C.) hwæðer him ǽnig moneáca cuman sceolde, Ors. 4, 1; Swt. 158, 19. II. *faithless, perfidious*:—Ortrūes cyuesdōmes *perfidi pellicatus*, Hpt. Gl. 521, 33. Ortreówra cempena *perfidorum militum*, 415, 48.

or-treówness, e; *f. Want of faith* or *confidence, mistrust*:—Ortreównes *diffidentia, desperantia*, Wrt. Voc. ii. 140, 18. Hē æteówde ða wunda ðǽm ungeleáffullum mannum, forðon ðe hē nolde ðæt ǽnig ortrȳwnes wǽre embe his ǽriste, Blickl. Homl. 91, 3.

or-trūwian; *p.* ode *To be without hope of, to despair of*:—Hē ortrūwode his Drihtnys mildheortnysse *he despaired of his Lord's mercy*, Ælfc. T. Grn. 17, 25. Tō ortrūwienne *desperandum*, Wülck. Gl. 250, 36. v. *next two words and* ge-ortrūwian.

or-trūwung, e; *f. Despair*:—Se ðe forgyfenysse be synne ortrūwaþ swȳðor be ortrūwunge ðænne be synne âfealþ. Ortrūwung geȳcþ synne *qui veniam de peccato desperat plus de desperatione quam de peccato cadit. Desperatio auget peccatum*, Scint. 34.

or-trȳwan *to despair of*:—Ne ortrȳwan hig Godes mildheortnysse *ne desperent illi de misericordia Dei*, L. Ecg. P. ii. 20; Th. ii. 190, 7.

or-trȳwe. v. or-treówe.

or-tydre; *adj. Without offspring, barren*:—Ontydre (*Wülcker reads* ortydre) *effeto, sine foetu*, Wrt. Voc. ii. 142, 46. v. on-tydre.

oruþ. v. oroþ.

or-wearde; *adv. Without guard, in an unprotected condition*:—Syððan orwearde ǽnigne dǽl secgas gesēgon on sele wunian, lǽne licgan *after men saw any part* (*of the dragon's hoard*) *lying there without its warder*, Beo. Th. 6245; B. 3127.

or-wegness, e; *f. Inaccessibility, remoteness*:—Orwegnes *devia*, s. *loca secreta et abdita, quasi extra via, vel invia, sine via*, Wrt. Voc. ii. 139, 55.

orweg-stîg, e; *f. A path difficult of access*:—Orwegstîg *devia callis* (-*us*, MS.), Wrt. Voc. ii. 139, 57. Horwegstîg (*but* cf. horu-weg), 25, 25.

or-wēna; *adj. with gen. Hopeless, despairing*:—Ðâ wearþ his âgen sunu yfele geuntrumed, and orwēna lîfes læg æt forþsîðe, Homl. Skt. i. 3, 301: Beo. Th. 2008; B. 1002: 3134; B. 1565: Exon. Th. 329, 27; Vy. 40. Friþes orwēna, 261, 25; Jul. 320. Ic eom orwēna, ðæt...,

Cd. Th. 134, 10; Gen. 2222. Wǽron orwênan êdelrihtes, 191, 7; Exod. 211. Sindon gê firenum bifongne, feores orwênan, Exon. Th. 139, 27; Gû. 599. v. next word.

or-wêne; *adj. with gen.* I. *not having ground for hope, without hope, despairing*:—Biþ orwêne ðæt hê ne mǽge ða bôte âberan *desperet posse se emendationem perferre*, L. Ecg. P. i. 4; Th. ii. 172, 23. Hê wearþ his lîfes orwêne, Homl. Th. i. 86, 28. Hê læg his lîfes orwêne, Homl. Skt. i. 21, 301: Glostr. Frag. 6, 18: Chart. Th. 339, 22. Hié ðæs êcan lîfes orwêne wǽron, Blickl. Homl. 85, 27. Hié wǽron orwêne hwæðer . . ., Ors. 4, 9; Swt. 192, 4. II. *not giving ground for hope, desperate, despaired of*:—Wênstû ðæt ic sceole sprecan tô ðissum treówleásan men and tô ðissum orwênan drý (*this desperate sorcerer*), Blickl. Homl. 183, 32. Æt orwênum lîfe *when life is despaired of*; in extremitate vitae, L. Ecg. P. i. tit. x; Th. ii. 170, 18. Wê ðâ bûtan orenum (orwênum ?) þingum mete þigdon *ab securis nobis epule capiuntur*, Nar. 24, 2. See preceding word.

or-wênness, e; *f. Despair, hopelessness*:—Ðonne biþ him seó orwênnys (*desperatio illa*) tô mâran synne geteald, L. Ecg. P. i. 4; Th. ii. 172, 24. Hwî sprecst ðû mid swâ micelre orwênnysse? Homl. Th. i. 534, 22. On orwênnysse his âgenre hǽle *in despair of his own salvation*, Ælfc. T. Grn. 17, 24. Woldon hý geteón in orwênnysse Meotudes cempan, Exon. Th. 136, 27; Gû. 547.

or-weorð, -wurð, es; *n. Ignominy, shame*:—Gefyl ansýne heora of orwurðe (*ignominia*), Ps. Spl. C. 82, 15. v. or-wirðu.

or-wîge; *adj.* I. *defenceless, without power of fighting*:—Orwîge *inbellem*, Wrt. Voc. ii. 45, 69: 111, 81. Ofsleán mê mîne fýnd orwîgne *decidam merito ab inimicis meis inanis*, Ps. Th. 7, 4. Saga hû ðû wurde ðus wîgþrîst ðæt ðû mec ðus fæste gebunde ǽghwæs orwîgne (*without any power of resisting*), Exon. Th. 268, 18; Jul. 434. II. *not liable to a charge of homicide*, said of one who, under the circumstances mentioned in the following passages, caused a person's death, but was not exposed on that account to the consequences which usually followed homicide (cf. *Icel.* víg *homicide*):—Wê cweþaþ ðæt mon môte mid his hlâforde feohtan orwîge (onwîge, MS. H.), gif mon on ðone hlâford fiohte; swâ môt se hlâford mid ðý men feohtan (cf. Unicuique licet domino suo sine wita subvenire, L. H. I. 82, 3; Th. i. 590, 2). Æfter ðære ilcan wîsan mon môt feohtan mid his geborene mǽge, gif him mon on wôh on feohteþ. And mon môt feohtan orwîge, gif hê gemêteþ ôðerne æt his ǽwum wîfe, betýnedum durum oððe under ânre reón, oððe æt his dehter ǽwum-borenre, oððe æt his swister, oððe æt his mêdder ðe wǽre tô ǽwum wîfe forgifen his fæder, L. Alf. pol. 42; Th. i. 90, 20–30. (Cf. L. H. I. 82, 4–8; Th. i. 590, 5–22.)

or-wirðed *disgraced*, cf. ge-oruuierdid *traductus*, Txts. 100, 990. Georuuyrde, 103, 2042. Georwyrðed *traducta*, Wrt. Voc. ii. 85, 14.

or-wirðlîc; *adj. Ignominious, shameful*:—God hine forlêt in ðisse nyþerlîcan worulde swâ orwyrþlîcne dêþ þrowian, ðæt hê hine wolde in ðære heán worulde gelǽdan, Shrn. 123, 10.

or-wirðu, *indecl.*; -wirð, e; *f. Ignominy, shame, dishonour*:—Gefyl onsiéne heara mid orwyrðe *imple facies eorum ignominia*, Ps. Surt. 82, 17. Mê ðîn dohtor hafaþ geýwed orwyrðu *thy daughter hath shewn me dishonour*, Exon. Th. 246, 29; Jul. 69.

or-yldu. v. or-ildu.

ôs *a divinity, god*, the Anglo-Saxon form of a word whose existence in Gothic is inferred from a passage in Jornandes, 'Gothi proceres suos quasi qui fortuna vincebant non pares homines sed semideos, id est, *Anses* vocavere.' The Icelandic, which throws out *n* before *s*, as the Anglo-Saxon does (cf. *Icel.* gâs: *A.S.* gôs), has *áss*; *pl. æsir*, a term which has an application in the opening chapters of the Yngling Saga very similar to that attributed to *anses* among the Goths: Odin, Thor, and other personages of the Scandinavian mythology are the Æsir. Particularly apparently did the term refer to Thor, so that the proper name Âs-björn is used as the equivalent of Þor-björn. As the first part of Scandinavian proper names it occurs frequently, and it is in the same dependent character that it mostly, if not exclusively, is found in Anglo-Saxon and O. H. German. Thus Ôs-beorn, Ôs-lâc, Ôs-wine, Ôs-weald preserve the word which is found in Âs-björn, Âs-lâkr, Âs-mundr, and this is certainly the independent *áss*. The *O. H. Ger.* Ans-gâr shews the same word. Whether *ôs* in the sense of *god* occurs as an independent word is doubtful. It is the name of the Rune ᚩ, which in the Runic poem is accompanied by the following verse:—

> 'Ôs byþ ordfruma ǽlcre sprǽce
> Wîsdômes wraðu and witena frôfur
> And eorla gehwam eádnis and tôhyht.'
> Runic pm. Kmbl. 340, 5–10; Rûn. 4.

Kemble translates ôs by mouth (as if the Latin word had been taken ?), but if the verse is old, the reference might be to Woden. Cf. the account of Óðinn in the Ynglinga Saga: þar þóttust Óðins menn eiga alt traust, er hann var, c. 2. Óðinn var göfgastr af öllum, ok af honum námu þeir allir íþróttirnar: því at hann kunni fyrst allar ok þó flestar. . . . Hann ok hofgoðar hans heita ljóðasmiðir, því at sú íþrótt hófst af þeim í norðrlöndum, c. 6. See also c. 7, and Salm. Kmbl. p. 192: Saga mê hwâ ǽrost bôcstafas sette? Ic ðê secge Mercurius (= *Woden*) se gygand. Further in Lchdm. iii. 54, in a charm, occurs a genitive pl. *êsa*:—Gif hit wǽre êsa gescot, oððe hit wǽre ylfa gescot, oððe hit wǽre hægtessan gescot, nû ic wille ðîn helpan. Ðis ðê tô bôte êsa gescotes, &c. . . . But though on the comparison of other forms, a nom. pl. ês might be inferred for *ôs*, the change of vowel would not occur in the genitive, which should be *ôsa*. *Ésa* would point to a singular ês (cf. êst; *Goth.* ansts). The meaning however of the word is that given to *ôs*. See Grmm. D. M. p. 22.

ôsle, an; *f. An ousel, blackbird*:—Ôslae *merula*, Txts. 78, 665: Wrt. Voc. ii. 114, 1. Ôsle, i. 281, 17. [*O. H. Ger.* amsala, amisala: *Ger.* amsel.]

osogen = â-sogen (?):—Osogen wǽre *sugillaretur* [cf. wǽre forsocen (*in margin* forgnegen), *sugillaretur*, Hpt. Gl. 484, 68], Wrt. Voc. ii. 82, 23.

ôst, es; *m.* (?) *A knot, knob*:—Ôst *nodus*, Txts. 80, 688: Wrt. Voc. ii. 60, 66. Copses, ôstes *cippi*, Hpt. Gl. 482, 61. Yfele treówes on ôste yfel nægel oððe wecg on tô fæstnigenne ys *male arboris nodo malus clavus aut cuneus infingendus est*, Scint. 27. Of ðǽm ôstum ðæs treówes flôweþ ût swêtes stences wǽte, Shrn. 67, 29.

oster-hlâf, es; *m. An oyster-patty*:—Osterhlâfas sint tô forbeódanne, Lchdm. ii. 210, 28. See Lchdm. iii. Glossary.

oster-scill, e; *f. An oyster-shell*:—Mid ostorscyllum gecnucud and gemenged, Lchdm. i. 338, 16.

Ôst-Gotan; *pl. The Ostrogoths*:—Þeódorîc Ôstgotona cyning, Shrn. 85, 26.

ôstig; *adj. Knotty, rough, scaly*:—Ôstig gyrd *scorpio*, Wrt. Voc. i. 21, 17. Ôstig *nodosus*, ôstigre *nodosa*, ôstigum *nodosis*, Hpt. Gl. 483, 66, 65, 57. Ôsties, rûches *nodosi*, 482, 60. Ôstie *squamigeros*, *scabrosos*, 464, 45. Þý ôstihan *nodosa*, Wrt. Voc. ii. 93, 37.

ôstiht; *adj. Knotty, rough*:—Ôstihtum *nodosi*, Wrt. Voc. ii. 82, 2: 60, 65.

ostre, an; *f. An oyster*:—Ostre *ostrea*, Wrt. Voc. ii. 63, 71: i. 65, 67: *ostrea* vel *ostreum*, 77, 70. Ðonne cumaþ ða oftost of mettum and of cealdum drincan swâ swâ sindon cealde ostran and æpla, Lchdm. ii. 244, 2: Coll. Monast. Th. 24, 9. [From Latin.]

Ôst-sǽ *the Baltic with the Cattegat*, the water east of Denmark and of the Scandinavian peninsula as that on the western coast is called Westsǽ, Ors. 1, 1; Swt. 17, 3:—Be norþan Sûþdenum is ðæs gârsecges earm ðe mon hǽt Ôstsǽ . . . Norþdene habbaþ be norþan him ðone ilcan sǽs earm ðe mon hǽt Ôstsǽ, Ors. 1, 1; Swt. 16, 23–28. [*Ger.* Ost-see *the Baltic*: cf. *Icel.* fara â Austrveg, a phrase used of trading or piratical expeditions in the Baltic.]

ôt-. v. ôþ.

oter, otr, es; *m. An otter*:—Otr *lutrus*, Txts. 74, 585. Otor, Wrt. Voc. ii. 51, 18: *lutria*, i. 22, 49. Ottor *sullus*. 121, 51. Oter *lutrius*, i. 78, 15. Of oteres hole, Cod. Dip. Kmbl. iii. 418, 17. [*Icel.* otr: *O. H. Ger.* ottar, oter.]

oter-hola, an; *m. An otter's hole*:—Of ðam oterholan, Cod. Dipl. Kmbl. iii. 23, 30.

ôþ; *prep.* I. *with dat.* (1) local, marking a point reached, *to, unto, as far as*:—Fram eástdǽle ôþ westdǽle, and fram sûþdǽle ôþ norþdǽle, Gen. 28, 14. (2) referring to time, *until*:—Fram Davide ôþ Daniele ðam wîtegan, Ælfc. T. Grn. 7, 13. (3) marking extent, degree, so *much as*:—Nis se ðe dô gôd, nis ôþ ânum (*usque ad unum*), Ps. Spl. 13, 2: 52, 4. II. *with acc.* (1) local, marking a point reached, *to, up to, as far as*:—Ôþ eorþan endas, Deut. 28, 64: Ps. Th. 71, 8. Ðû nyðer færst ôþ helle, Mt. 11, 23. Hê him æfter râd ôþ ðæt geweorc, Chr. 878; Erl. 80, 15. Hê him æfterfylgende wæs ôþ v mîla tô ðære byrig Cartanense *ad quintum lapidem a Carthagine statuit*, Ors. 4, 5; Swt. 168, 32: 3, 4; Swt. 104, 2: 4, 10; Swt. 194, 7. Ôþ Eufraten, Cd. Th. 133, 6; Gen. 2206. (1 a) in phrases marking extent, degree or measure:—Ôþ ðæt *eatenus* vel *eotenus*, Wrt. Voc. i. 61, 30. Ôþ hielt *capulo tenus*, Wrt. Voc. ii. 19, 7. Ôþ ða hylta, Ælfc. Gr. 47; Som. 48, 7. Hî druncan ôþ ða drosna *usque ad feces biberunt*, Som. 47, 45. Ôþ mannes breóst heáh *as high as a man's breast*, Blickl. Homl. 127, 6: 245, 33. Hié ðæt gild gefyldan eal ôþ grund, 221, 33. Ðæt hî ôþ forwyrd fordiligade ne wǽron, Bd. 1, 16; S. 484, 17. Se Ægipta slôh frumbearn ǽghwylc ealra ôþ ða nýtenu (*down to the very beasts*), Ps. Th. 134, 8. Seóð ðonne ôþ huniges þicnesse, Lchdm. ii. 30, 7. (2) temporal, *until, to, unto*:—Ôþ ðisne dæg *usque in praesentem diem*, Gen. 32, 4. Ôþ ðâs dagas, Ex. 9, 18. Nû ôþ ðis *hactenus*, Bd. 4, 22; S. 591, 15: Blickl. Homl. 175, 12. On ðære hwîle ôþ ðæt *up to the present time*, Homl. Skt. i. 4, 265. Ôþ ǽfen *usque ad vesperum*, Ælfc. Gr. 47; Som. 47, 46. Ôþ ende his lîfes, Blickl. Homl. 21, 36. Ôþ ðone deáþ, 59, 30. Ôþ ðæt *until*:—Ôþ ðæt (*donec*) hê forgite ða þing ðe ðû him dydest, Gen. 27, 45: Beo. Th. 4084; B. 2039: Andr. Kmbl. 535; An. 268. Ôþ ðæt hiene ân swân ofstang, Chr. 755; Erl. 48, 22. Ôt ðet *donec*, Ps. Surt. 70, 18. Ôþ ðe *until*:—Fôron forþ ôþ ðe hié cômon tô Lundenbyrig, Chr. 894; Erl. 91, 13. Ôþ ðe hê eall forweorðeþ, Ps. Th. 139, 11: Beo. Th. 1302; B. 649. (2 a) with other prepositions:—Ôþ in ældu *usque in senecta*, Ps. Surt. 70, 18. Ðâ gestôd hê æt ânum êhþyrle ôþ forþ nihtes, Homl. Th. ii. 184, 27. Ôþ tô dæge *usque hodie*, Bd. 1, 15; S. 483, 27. Ôþ gyt tô dæge, 4, 4; S. 571, 16. [Cf. *Goth.* und; *prep.;* unte *conj.: O. Sax.* unt; *prep.;* und; *conj.: Icel.* unz *conj.: O. H. Ger.* unz, v. Grff. i. 363-366.] v. next word.

ōþ; *conj. Until:*—Wuna mid him, ōþ đīnes brōđur yrre geswīce, Gen. 27, 44: Mt. Kmbl. 10, 11. Hē hæfde đa, ōþ hē ofslōg đone aldorman, Chr. 755; Erl. 48, 20. Đæt mōd glīt niđor and niđor, ōþ hit mid ealle āfielþ, Past. 38; Swt. 279, 3: Cd. Th. 22, 14; Gen. 340. v. preceding word.

ōþ- as a prefix of verbs, *from, away.* Cf. *æt* for similar meaning. [Cf. *Goth. untha*-thliuhan to *escape.*]

ōþ-beran *to bear forth, bear away* (cf. æt-beran):—Nō ic eów sweord ongeán ōþberan þence, Exon. Th. 120, 20; Gū. 274. Mec sǣ ōþbær on Finna land *the sea bore me forth to the land of the Fins,* Beo. Th. 1163; B. 579: Exon. Th. 404, 20; Rā. 23, 10. Sumne fugel ōþbær (*bore off*) ofer heánne holm, 291, 13; Wand. 81.

ōþ-berstan *to break away, escape:*—Hē ōþbærst tō wuda, Cod. Dip. Kmbl. iii. 291, 17. [Rannulf ūt of đam tūre on Lunden nihtes ōþbærst, đǣr hē on hæftneþe wæs, Chr. 1101; Erl. 237, 40.] Gif se bana ōþbyrste, L. H. E. 2; Th. i. 28, 1. Cf. æt-berstan.

ōþ-bregdan, -brēdan *to take away, carry off:*—Đa burgleóde ōþbrūdon đa snore mid hiere suna, and hī sendon on ōđer fæstre fæsten, Ors. 3, 11; Swt. 148, 21. Hæbbe hē Godes unmiltse, se đe đis āwende and đere stōwe ōþbrēde, Cod. Dip. Kmbl. ii. 4, 3. Hē (*Nero when Rome was burning*) bebeád his āgnum monnum đæt hié gegripen đæs licgendan feós swā hié mǣst mehten, and tō him brohten, đonne hit mon ūt ōþbrūde, Ors. 6, 5; Swt. 260, 32. Siđđan wearþ Adame eardrīca cyst ōþbrōden, Exon. Th. 153, 15; Gū. 826. Ōþbrog[d]en *ademptam,* Wrt. Voc. ii. 9, 18. Ōþbrōdenum hwelpum *raptis fetibus,* Kent. Gl. 607. v. æt-brēdan.

ōþ-cirran *to turn away, be perverted:*—Gif sōđfæstra þurh myrrelsan mōd ne ōþcyrreþ (neod cyrreþ, MS.) *if by seduction the mind of the righteous is not perverted,* Exon. Th. 262, 26; Jul. 338. Cf. on-cirran; *intrans.*

ōþ-clīfan *to cleave to, adhere:*—Him sār ōþclīfeþ, Exon. Th. 78, 1; Cri. 1267.

ōþ-cwelan *to die:*—Gif sió hond sié ōþcwolen *if the person be dead,* L. In. 53; Th. i. 134, 17.

ōþ-dōn *to put out:*—Gif hwā ōđrum his eáge ōþdō (of dō, MS. H.), L. Alf. 19; Th. i. 48, 20. Cf. æt-dōn.

ōþ-eáwan. v. ōþ-īwan.

ōþ-ēhtian *to drive away:*—Se đe đis feoh ōþfergean þence, odđe đis orf ōþēhtian þence *he that thinks of carrying off this cattle, or of driving it away,* Lchdm. i. 384, 15.

ōđel, es; *m. Home, native country:*—Abraham ferede æđelinga bearn ōđle niór, mægeþ heora māgum, Cd. Th. 126, 7; Gen. 2091. v. ēđel.

Ōđen, es; *m. Odin* (the Scandinavian form of the word which appears in Anglo-Saxon as *Wōden*):—Đes gedwolgod (*Mercurius*) wæs ārwurđe betwux eallum hǣđenum on đām dagum, and hē is Ōđon gehāten ōđrum naman on Denisce wīsan. Nū secgaþ sume đa Denisce men on heora gedwylde, đæt se Iouis wǣre, đe hȳ Þōr hātaþ, Mercuries sunu, đe hī Ōđon namiaþ, Wulfst. 107, 6-11. Þōr and Ōwđen (Oþen, MS. F.), 197, 19.

ōþ-eode, -eówan. v. ōþ-gān, -īwan.

ōđer; *indef. prn. and ordinal, used as adj. and as subst., always of strong declension.* I. when two definite objects are referred to, (1) *one of two:*—Him wearþ ōđer eáge mid ānre flān ūt āscoten *ictu sagittae oculum perdidit,* Ors. 3, 7; Swt. 112, 15. Hē hyne onsende myd twām mæssepreóstum . . . đā forþfērde đæra mæssepreósta ōđer, Shrn. 98, 28. Him bærst micel wund on ōđrum þeó *in one of his thighs,* 109, 14. Đā gewearþ him đæt hī twegen tō ānwīge eodon . . . ealle gecwǣdon, đæt gif ǣnig man wolde heora ōđrum (*either of them*) fylstan, đæt man hine sōna gefēnge, H. R. 101, 21. Đǣr wearþ Pirrus wund on ōđran earme (*transfixo brachio*) . . . Hī nāmon treówu, and slōgon on ōđerne ende īsene næglas, Ors. 4, 1; Swt. 158, 2-5. Þurhscoten underneođan ōđer breóst, 3, 9; Swt. 134, 23. Wund þurh đæt ōđer cneów, 4, 6; Swt. 180, 6. Ān strǣl hyne gewundode on hys ōđer gewenge, Shrn. 97, 14. Se đe hæbbe twā tunecan, selle ōđre đam đe nāne næbbe, Blickl. Homl. 169, 13. Ōđer twega, đara, *or without these forms, one of two alternatives:*—For đam ōđer twega, odđe hié nǣfre tō nānum men ne becumaþ, odđe hié nǣfre fæstlīce ne þurhwuniaþ, Bt. 11, 1; Fox 30, 26. Đa wilniaþ ōđer twega, odđe . . . , odđe, 24, 2; Fox 82, 8. Wite hē đæt ōđer đara, odđe hē sceal đæs hādes þolian, odđe hit gebētan, L. E. I. 14; Th. ii. 412, 1: 9; Th. ii. 408, 11. Đæt hió ōđer đara dydon, odđe . . . odđe . . . , Chart. Th. 167, 22: Ors. 3, 7; Swt. 114, 23. Him sǣdon đæt hié ōđer dyden, odđe hām cōmen odđe hié him woldon ōđerra wera ceósan, 1, 10; Swt. 44, 21. (2) *the second of two, other:*—Se ōđer consul Duilius *Duilius, alter consul,* 4, 6; Swt. 172, 8. Hē for đære geómrunga đæs ōđres deáþes leng on đam lande gewunian ne mihte, Blickl. Homl. 113, 11. Ān mann hæfde twegen suna. Đā cwæþ hē tō đam yldran . . . Đā cwæþ hē ealswā to đam ōđrum, Mt. 21, 30. Đæt mon ierne from geate tō ōđrum, Past. 49; Swt. 383, 8. Fram ende ōþ ōđerne *from one end of the church to the other,* Glostr. Frag. 12, 17. Hafa đās (*Leah*) tō gemæccan, and ic gife đē đa ōđre (*Rachel*), Gen. 29, 27. Hē sette his ǣnne sunu tō ealdormen, and ōđerne tō cyninge, Homl. Th. ii. 480, 21. (3) when *ōđer* is applied to each of two:—Đara ōđer bewiste his byrlas, ōđer his bæcestran, Gen. 40, 2. Ōđer is se ǣresta apostol, ōđer se nēhsta, Blickl. Homl. 171, 8. Đæt se ōđer beó ārǣred from đæm ōđrum *ut alter regatur ab altero,* Past. 17, 1; Swt. 107, 23. On twǣm gefylcum, on ōđrum wǣron đa hǣđnan cyningas, on ōđrum đa eorlas, Chr. 871; Erl. 74, 16-18. Ǣgđer ōđerne ofslōg, Ors. 2, 3; Swt. 68, 18. Uncer lāþette ǣgđer ōđer đeáh đe hē hit ōđrum ne sǣde, Shrn. 39, 22. II. when the reference is not limited to two objects. (1) marking a sequence, *other, second in a series, next, following* an object already mentioned:—Se forma . . . se ōđer, and se þrydda ōþ đone seofoþan, Mt. 22, 25, 26: Ælfc. Gr. 49; Som. 49, 55. Wæs đis đara wundra ǣrest . . . Eft gelamp ōđer wundor, Blickl. Homl. 219, 6: 221, 18: 223, 13. Đære ōđre eá naman *nomen fluvii secundi,* Gen. 2, 13. Fram dæge tō ōđrum *from day to day,* Blickl. Homl. 107, 25. Faran of stōwe tō ōđerre, 19, 23. Ān æfter ōđrum, Cd. Th. 266, 22; Sat. 26. Hē sette hine on his ōđer cræt (*currum suum secundum*), Gen. 41, 43. Ǣrest . . . ōđre sīþe . . . þriddan sīþe, Blickl. Homl. 47, 16. Ōþre dæge *next day,* 175, 18. Đā fōr hē swā feor swā hē meahte on đǣm ōđrum þrīm dagum (*in the next three days*) gesiglan, Ors. 1, 1; Swt. 17, 13. Wearþ syfan geár se ungemetlīca eorþwela, and hī æfter đǣm wǣron on đan mǣstan hungre ōđre syfan geár, 1, 5; Swt. 32, 26: Gen. 29, 27. (1 a) *with* swilc, *another such,* a repetition of what has preceded:—Đā com ungemetlīc rēn . . . eft wearþ ōđer swelc rēn, Ors. 4, 10; Swt. 194, 20. Medmicel pipores, ōđer swilc cymenes, Lchdm. ii. 256, 5. His māgas hine wiđ ōđær swilc (*contra simile quid*) gescyldan, L. Ecg. P. addit. 29; Th. ii. 236, 31. (2) marking difference from the subject, or from something already referred to, *other, different, somebody else, something else:*—Đū nimst wīf and ōđer man līþ mid hire, Deut. 28, 30. Ne þearf nān mon wēnan đæt hine ōđer mon mǣge ālēsan, Blickl. Homl. 101, 13. Gif ūtancymene oxa ōđres oxan gewundaþ, Ex. 21, 35. Eart đū đe tō cumenne eart, odđe wē ōđres sceolon ābīdan, Mt. Kmbl. 11, 3. Gif wē willaþ on ōđres gōde beón gefeónde, Blickl. Homl. 75, 20. Leófre mē ys, đæt ic hig sylle đē đonne ōđrum men, Gen. 29, 19. Đæt man tō ōđrum lǣđđe hæbbe, Blickl. Homl. 63, 36. Đæt ǣlc stān ne sȳ fram ōđrum ādōn, 79, 1. Heora ongon ǣlc cweđan tō ōđrum, 149, 29. Đa lǣstas on ōđerne mǣgwlite oncyrran, 127, 19. On ōđre wisan, 205, 21. Nū hæbbe wē broht ōđer sylfor (*aliud argentum*), Gen. 43, 22. Seó wyrd oft oncyrreþ and on ōđer hworfeþ, Nar. 7, 28. Mid hire syndan Godes apostolas and ōđre, Blickl. Homl. 143, 10. Petrus and ōđre Cristes þegnas, 145, 27. Đa đe wōhhǣmed begangaþ mid ōđerra ceorla wīfum, 61, 14. Sceattas ge on lande, ge on ōđrum þingum, 51, 7. Hē gesett hys wīngerd myd ōđrum tilion, Mt. Kmbl. 21, 41. Hē him tō genymþ seofun ōđre gāstas, 12, 45. (2 a) ōđer . . . ōđer *other . . . than, different from:*—Nū is *participium* of worde and of worde cymþ, biþ swā đeáh ōđer dǣl and ōđer þing ōđer his ealdor biþ, Ælfc. Gr. 41; Som. 43, 14. Đonne gā heó in ōđer hūs ōđer heo ūt ofeode, Lchdm. iii. 68, 21. Gif đū wilnast đæt heó ōđre þeáwas nimen ōđre (ōđer, Cott. MSS.) heora willa and heora gewuna is, Bt. 7, 2; Fox 18, 28. (2 b) with the indefinites *sum, ǣnig,* etc.:—Helias odđe sum ōđer wītega, Homl. Th. i. 364, 18. Wæs his nēhmāga sum đæt hine swȳđor lufode đonne ǣnig ōđor man, Blickl. Homl. 113, 10. Māran wræce đonne ǣfre ǣr ǣnigu ōđru gelumpe, 79, 10. Wæs đæt wæter biterre đonne ic ǣfre ǣnig ōđer bergde, Nar. 8, 30. Hē nǣnigum ōđrum ærne sceþþan ne mihte, Blickl. Homl. 221, 16. Ne bideþ hē æt ūs nǣnig ōđor edleán būton . . . , 103, 21. Nǣnige ōđre būton đa ǣne, 185, 9. Đara ōđerra manna nān ārian wolde, 215, 1. Mid manegum ōđrum gāstlīcum mægenum, 73, 28. Đæt geleáfulle folc Iudēa, and eác ōđor manig đa đe beóþ Gode underþeódde, 79, 31. Đās wundor and manig ōđer, 219, 22. Ōđre wundro manega, 177, 18. Augustinum and ōđre monige munecas, Bd. 1, 23; S. 485, 27. Lufian wē ūrne Drihten ofer ealle ōđru þing, Blickl. Homl. 11, 33. Sanctus Iohannes gǣþ beforan eallum ōđrum wītgan and ealra ōđerra heáhfædera mægen hē oferstīgeþ, 167, 22. (3) denoting that part of a whole which is not yet mentioned, *other, the rest, remaining:*—Micel đæs folces hié ofer sǣ ādrǣfdon, and đæs ōđres đone mǣstan dǣl hié geridon, Chr. 878; Erl. 78, 31. Sum fearhrȳđer đæs ōđræs ceápes geférscipe oferhogode, Blickl. Homl. 199, 4. Seó hand wæs gelīc đam ōđrum flǣsce *erat similis carni reliquae,* Ex. 4, 7. Đa ōđre nigon *consonantes* synd gecwedene *mutae,* Ælfc. Gr. 2; Som. 3, 1. Đa ōđre (*ceteri*) cwǣdon, Mt. 27, 49. Petrus and đa ōđre apostolas, Blickl. Homl. 149, 5. Wæs heora sum rēđra đonne đa ōđre, 223, 7. Wyrtruma ealra ōđerra synna, 65, 3. Đæt deófol cwæþ tō đām ōđrum deóflum, 243, 10. Hig cȳđdon eall đis đām endlufenum and eallum ōđrum (*ceteris omnibus*), Lk. Skt. 24, 9. [*Goth.* anþar: *O. Sax.* ōđar: *O. Frs.* ōther: *O. H. Ger.* andar: *Icel.* annarr.]

ōđerlīce; *adv. Otherwise, differently:*—Se đe ōđerlīcor gedyrstlǣce underhnīge đære regullīcan þreále *que autem aliter presumpserit, discipline regulari subjaceat,* R. Ben. 87, 19. [*Goth.* anþarleiko *otherwise:* cf. *O. Sax.* ōđar-līk: *O. H. Ger.* andar-līh: *Icel.* annar-ligr.]

ōþ-ēwan. v. ōþ-īwan.

ōþ-fæstan. I. *to entrust, commit to the charge of another:*—Ōþ đæt ic mē gebidde tō him and mīn gāst ōþfæste *I commit my spirit* *into his hands*, Nar. 46, 34. Heó hyre mægþhād Gode ōþfæste, 40, 16. Gif hwā ōþfæste his friénd feoh, L. Alf. 28; Th. i. 50, 29: L. Alf. pol. 20; Th. i. 74, 15. Gif hwā ōðrum his unmagan ōþfæste, and hē hine on ðære fæstinge forferie, 17; Th. i. 72, 4. Se ðe wile hwilc sǣd ōþfæstan ðām drīum furum, Bt. 5, 2; Fox 10, 30. Þæt hié sīen tō liornunga ōþfæste, Past. pref.; Swt. 7, 12. **II.** *to inflict, impose* (pain, punishment. Cf. æt-fæstan):—Ne meahton hié deáþ (*Kemble has* deáþe, *in which case the verb belongs to* I) ōþfæstan *they could not inflict death* (*on Christ*), Elen. Kmbl. 952; El. 477. Drihten hæfde wītes clomma[s] feóndum ōþfæsted *the Lord had imposed penal chains on the fiends*, Cd. Th. 292, 23; Sat. 445.

ōþ-faran *to escape*:—Siððan hié feóndum ōþfaren hæfdon, Cd. Th. 181, 21; Exod. 64.

ōþ-feallan. **I.** *to fall away, cease to have connection with*:—Ōþfealle se wer (*in the case of a man who, upon a charge of theft, being forsaken by his kinsmen, forfeits his freedom*) ðām māgum *the kinsmen shall have no further concern in the 'wer*,' L. Ed. 9; Th. i. 164, 13. Cf. æt-feallan. **II.** *to fall away, fail, decay*:—Gif hwam seó sprǣc ōþfylþ *if speech fail a man*, Lchdm. ii. 288, 18. Æfter his fielle wearþ ðara cāsera mǣgþ offeallen (ōþ-, MS. C.) *Caesarum familia consumta est*, Ors. 6, 5; Swt. 262, 6. Swā clǣne hió (*learning*) wæs ōþfeallenu on Angelcyn *so utterly was learning decayed in England*, Past. pref.; Swt. 3, 13.

ōþ-feolan *to cleave, stick*:—Ōþfealh *heresceret*, Wrt. Voc. ii. 42, 46. Cf. æt-feolan, -felgan.

ōþ-ferian *to bear off*:—Ic unsōfte ðonan feorh ōþferede næs ic fǣge ðāgyt *not easily thence* (*the conflict with Grendel's mother*) *did I bring away life, but not then had my hour come* (cf. *last passage under* ōþ-lǣdan), Beo. Th. 4288; B. 2141. Ðæt hē nǣfre nabbe foldan ðæt hit ōþferie . . . Se ðe ðis feoh ōþfergean (*carry off, steal*) þence, Lchdm. i. 384, 9–15. Hī willaþ ōþfergan, ðæt ic friþian sceal; ic him ðæt forstonde, Exon. Th. 398, 13; Rä. 17, 7. Cf. æt-ferian.

ōþ-fleógan *to fly away*:—Se ānhoga ōþfleógeþ feðerum snel, Exon. 222, 11; Ph. 347.

ōþ-fleón *to flee away, escape*:—Favius heánlīce hāmweard ōþfleáh, Ors. 3, 10; Swt. 140, 14. Ða ðe tō him mid scypum ōþflugon tō ðǣm beorgum *ad se ratibus confugientes*, 1, 6; Swt. 36, 11: 2, 8; Swt. 94, 8. Sume binnan ðæt fæsten ōþflugon, Swt. 92, 23. Ða ðe him (*Joshua*) ōþflugon, ðām feóllon stānas on uppan, and hī fordydon, Homl. Th. ii. 214, 2. Ðām monnum ðe ōþflugon ofer ðone weall, Chr. 921; Erl. 107, 12. Uneáðe mehte ǣnig ðǣm Gallium ōþfleón, Ors. 2, 8; Swt. 94, 11. Wilniende ðæt hī ǣlcum gewinne ōþflogen hæfdon, 1, 4; Swt. 32, 21.

ōþ-flītan *to get from another by litigation*:—Ðā ongon Higa him specan sōna on, and wolde him ōþflītan ðæt lond *then Higa at once began the case against him, and wanted to get the land from him by the litigation*, Chart. Th. 169, 23.

ōþ-gān *to go away, escape*:—Ōþeodon, Beo. Th. 5860; B. 2934.

ōþ-glīdan *to glide away*, Salm. Kmbl. 804; Sal. 401.

ōþ-grīpan *to snatch away*:—Gif wēn wǣre ðæt hē ðǣr hwylce mihte deófle ōþgrīpan and tō Criste gecyrran *si quos forte ex illis ereptos Satanae ad Christum transferre valeret*, Bd. 5, 9; S. 622, 19.

ōþ-healdan *to withhold, keep back*:—Gif hwelc folc biþ mid hungre geswenced, and hwā his hwǣte gehȳt and ōþhielt hū ne wilt hē ðonne hiera deáþes *si populos fames attereret, et occulta frumenta ipsi servarent, auctores proculdubio mortis existerent*, Past. 49, 1; Swt. 377, 9. Ðæt hē nǣfre nabbe hūsa ðæt hē hit (*stolen property*) ōþhealde, Lch. i. 384, 10.

ōþ-hebban *to elevate, exalt, lift up*:—Ða welan ðe ǣlcne ofermōdne ōþhebbaþ *abundantia, quae sublevat*, Past. 26, 2; Swt. 183, 18. Hē hine ōþhōf (ot-, Cott. MSS.) innan his geþohte eallum ōðrum monnum *cunctis in cogitatione se praetulit*, 4, 2; Swt. 39, 15. Ða ofersettan mon sceal swā manian ðæt se hiera folgoþ hī ne ōþhebbe *admonendi sunt praelati, ne eos locus superior extollat*, 28, 1; Swt. 189, 17.

ōþ-hilde; *adj. Content*:—Ānum were ōþhylde heó ne biþ *she will not be content with one man*, Lchdm. iii. 188, 6. Ōþhelde (cf. ēþhylde, l. 1), 194, 14. v. eáþ-, ēþ-hylde.

ōþ-hleápan *to run away, escape*:—Gif hē ūt ōþhleápe, L. Eth. i. 1; Th. i. 282, 11. Cf. æt-hleápan.

ōþ-hȳdan *to hide away*:—Uneáðe mehte ǣnig ðām Gallium ōþfleón oððe ōþhȳdan *hardly could any one escape or hide from the Gauls*, Ors. 2, 8; Swt. 94, 11.

ōþ-īcan *to add to*:—Ōtēctun *addiderunt*, Ps. Surt. 68, 27. Cf. æt-ȳcan.

ōþ-irnan *to run away, escape*:—Hē ðære eorþan ǣfre ne ōþrineþ, Met. 20, 138. Gif hē ōþierne, L. In. 28; Th. i. 120, 7. v. æt-irnan.

ōþ-īwan, -ēwan, -eáwan, -eówan, -iéwan, -ȳwan. **I.** *to shew*:—Ic ōþeówe *ostendam*, Ps. Spl. 49, 24. Ne ðū mē ōþiéwest ǣnig tācen, Cd. Th. 34, 19; Gen. 540. Ōteáweþ *ostendit*, Ps. Surt. 4, 6. Hē ōþēwde openlīce ðæt hē ǣr gehȳd hæfde, Ors. 6, 34; Swt. 288, 32. Ōþīwde, Ps. Spl. 77, 14. Ōþiéwde, Cd. Th. 44, 24; Gen. 714. Hēr cometa hiene ōþiéwde, Chr. 729; Erl. 46, 5. Ðæt ðū mē ōþēwe, Bt. 22, 2; Fox 78, 11. Wearþ ōþiéwed ān īgland, Ors. 6, 4; Swt. 260, 14. Ōþēwed, Met. 29, 34. Open and ōþeáwed, Exon. Th. 98, 9; Cri. 1605. Ōþȳwed, 52, 25; Cri. 839. **II.** *to shew one's self, to appear*:—Ic ōteáwu *apparebo*, Ps. Surt. 16, 15. Sió sunne eldum ōþēweþ, Met. 13, 60. Ōþȳweþ, Exon. Th. 56, 24; Cri. 905. Ic ōþeówde *apparui*, Ps. Spl. 62, 3 Met. 28, 74. Hēr ōþiéwde cometa se steorra, Chr. 678; Erl. 40, 5: 773; Erl. 52, 23. Ōþȳwde, Elen. Kmbl. 325; El. 163. Ōteáwdon *apparuerunt*, Ps. Surt. 17, 16. Ōþeówdun, Exon. Th. 28, 17; Cri. 448. In bōcum ne cwiþ ðæt hȳ in hwītum hræglum ōþȳwden, 28, 30; Cri. 454. Cf. æt-ȳwan.

ōþ-lǣdan *to lead away, carry off*:—Hē Israhēlas ealle ōþlǣdde *eduxit Israel*, Ps. Th. 135, 11. Ālȳs mē and ōþlǣd lāðum wætrum *eripe me et libera me de aquis*, 143, 12. Ic þence ðis feóh tō lufianne, næs tō ōþlǣdanne . . . hē nǣfre nabbe landes ðæt hē hit ōþlǣde, Lchdm. i. 384, 4–9. Ic eom ōþlǣded gōdum *excussus sum*, Ps. Th. 108, 23. Hié ōþlǣded hæfdon feorh of feónda dōme *life had they withdrawn from the foes' power* (cf. Beo. Th. 4288 *under* ōþ-ferian), Cd. Th. 214, 15; Exod. 569. Cf. æt-lǣdan.

Ōðon. v. Ōðen.

ōþ-rīdan *to ride away*:—Cyning in ōþrād forþ onette *the king* (*Christ after the doors of Hell had opened*) *rode away into Hell, hastened on*, Exon. Th. 461, 24; Hö. 40.

ōþ-rōwan *to row off*:—Hió ūt ōþreówon *they rowed out and away*, Chr. 897; Erl. 96, 7.

ōþ-sacan (*with gen.*). **I.** *to deny* (a statement):—Hwā ōþsæcþ ðæs? Bt. 26, 2; Fox 92, 21. Ne mæg ic ðæs ōþsacan, forðam ðe ic his wæs ǣr geþafa, 34, 3; Fox 138, 15: 33, 1; Fox 122, 2: 34, 9; Fox 146, 34. Nān mon ne mæg ōþsacan ðæt sum gōd ne sīe ðæt hēhste, 34, 1; Fox 134, 9. **II.** *to deny* (an obligation, a charge, etc.):—Gange feówra sum tō and ōþsace (*deny a charge of robbing*), L. Eth. ii. 4; Th. i. 286, 18. Borges mon mōt ōþsacan gif hē wāt ðæt hē ryht dēþ, L. In. 41; Th. i. 128, 2. Cf. æt-sacan.

ōþ-sceacan *to run away, escape*:—Gif hē ōþsceóce (-seoce, MS.), L. Ath. v. 6; Th. i. 234, 11.

ōþ-sceótan *to shoot away, escape, turn aside, hurry off*:—Swā hwā swā ōþscȳt fram ānnysse ðæs geleáfan *whoever turns aside from the unity of the faith*, Homl. Th. i. 370, 17. Man gehylt ðæt hē hæfþ gif hē him ondrǣt ðæt hit him ōþsceóte *a man guards what he has, if he is afraid that it will escape from him*, Prov. Kmbl. 18.

ōþ-scūfan *to push* (intrans.) *away, move away*:—Hē geseceþ (-aþ, MS.) Syrwara lond corðra mǣste. Him se clǣna ðǣr ōþscūfeþ scearplīce (*the Phenix moves off quickly from the attendant birds*) ðæt hē in scade weardaþ on wudubearwe wēste stōwe biholene and bihȳdde hæleþa monegum *dirigit in Syriam celeres longaeva volatus, secretosque petit deserta per avia lucos, hic ubi per saltus silva remota latet*, Exon. Th. 209, 9; Ph. 168.

ōþ-seóce. v. ōþ-sceacan.

ōþ-spurnan, -spornan *to strike against, stumble*:—Hió ōþsper[n]þ *impingetur*, Kent. Gl. 769. Ðē læs ðīn fōt ōþsporne, Blickl. Homl. 27, 14. Næs gecweden ðæt his fōt æt stāne ōþspurne, 29, 31. Cf. æt-spurnan.

ōþ-spyrning, e; *f. An offence, a stumbling-block*:—Būto ōtspernince *absque offendiculo*, Kent. Gl. 528. Cf. æt-spyrning.

ōþ-standan. **I.** *to stop in one's course, to come to a standstill*:—Ðonne ōþstandeþ se blōdgyte sōna, Lchdm. i. 88, 10. Sōna ðæt blōd ōþstænt, 180, 3. Ðæt unstille hweól ōþstōd, Bt. 35, 6; Fox 168, 32. **I a.** metaphorically, *to cease to act*:—Gif se hlyst ōþstande, ðæt hē ne mǣge gehiéran, L. Alf. pol. 46; Th. i. 92, 23. **II.** *to remain standing, remain*:—Uneáþe ǣnig grot staþoles ōþstōd, Ors. 6, 1; Swt. 252, 23. Ðæt is lang tō sæcganne, hū ða wurdon generede in ðære Noes earce, ða ðe ðǣr tō lāfe ōþstōdon, Wulfst. 206, 30. **III.** *to remain standing and so prove an obstacle*:—Ðæt swefn swīðe ōþstōd manegum mīnra leóda (*the dream interpreted by Daniel*), Cd. Th. 246, 23; Dan. 483. Cf. æt-standan.

ōþ-stillan *to put a stop to, to stop*:—Ðonne biþ hit (*hæmorrhage*) sōna ōþstilled, Lchdm. i. 82, 5. Cf. æt-stillan.

ōþ-swerian *to abjure, deny on oath*:—Ðā ōþswōran hié mid ðam bismerlīcestan āðe ðæt hié him nǣfre on fultume nǣre ðēh ðe ða āðas wǣren neár māne ðonne sōðe *turpissimam rupti foederis labem adcumulavere perjurio*, Ors. 4, 3; Swt. 162, 10. Gif hlōþ ðis gedō and eft ōþswerian (æt-, MS. B.) wille, L. Alf. pol. 31; Th. i. 80, 16. Gif mon tō ðam men feoh getēme ðe his ǣr ōþswaren (ætsworen, MS. B.) hæfde, and æft ōþswerian wille, ōþswerige (æt-, MS. B.) be ðam wīte . . . Gif hē ōþswerian nylle . . ., L. In. 35; Th. i. 124, 10–12.

ōþ-swīgan *to stop speaking, become silent*:—Hē spræc tō his liornæra sumum, and ðā fǣringa ōþswīgde hē suā hē hwæshwegu hercnade, Shrn. 72, 24.

ōþ-swimman *to swim off*:—Ða āne ðe ūt ōþswymman mihton (æt-swummon, MS. A.) tō ðām scipum, Chr. 915; Erl. 105, 11.

ōþ-teón *to take away*:—Him biþ slǣp ōþtogen *sleep deserts them*, Lchdm. ii. 232, 14.

oððe; *conj.* **I.** *or*:—Gif seó offrung beó of sceápon oððe of gātum, Lev. 1, 10. Geeácnode ic hig ealle oððe ācende ic hig, Num. 11, 12. Hwā geworhte mannes mūþ oððe hwā geworhte dumne oððe deáfne and blindne oððe geseóndne? Ex. 4, 11. **I a.** *in conjunction with* ōđer :—Hí woldon ōđer twega, lîf forlǣtan ođđe leófne gewrecan, Byrht. Th. 137, 59; By. 207: Wald. 1, 16. II. ođđe . . . ođđe . . . *either . . . or* (a) :—Ođđa (ođđe, MS. B.) mid freóndscipe ođđa mid gefeohte *vel amicitia vel ferro*, Bd. 1, 1; S. 474, 26. Đonne fōron hié ođđe mid ođđe on heora healfe, Chr. 894; Erl. 90, 6. Đa scipu eall ođđe tōbrǣcon ođđe forbærndon ođđe tō Lundenbyrig brohton ođđe to Hrōfesceastre, Erl. 91, 25. (b) *with* ōđer, āđer :—Hē sǣde đæt hē wolde ōđer, ođđe đǣr libban ođđe đǣr licgan, 901; Erl. 96, 32. Hēt đæt hié ōđer sceolden, ođđe đæt lond æt him ālēsan, ođđe hē hié wolde fordōn, Ors. 1, 10; Swt. 44, 9: 44, 21. Hié ōđer forleósan woldon, ođđe hira āgen lîf ođđe Porsennes, 2, 3; Swt. 68, 28. Nū đonne ōđer twega, ođđe đara nān nis, ođđe hî nānne weorþscipe nabbaþ, Bt. 27, 4; Fox 100, 16. Gif onfunden biþ đæt hē āđer ođđe . . . ođđe . . ., L. E. I. 16; Th. ii. 412, 11.

ōþ-þeódan *to disjoin, dismember* :—Đū đæt gehēte đæt ūs heterōfra hild ne gesceóde, ne lîces dǣl ōþþeóded, ne sinu ne bān on swađe lāgon, ne loc of heáfde tō forlore wurde, Andr. Kmbl. 2842; An. 1423.

ōþ-þicgan *to take from* :—Him frumbearnes riht freóbrōđor ōþþah, Cd. Th. 199, 14; Exod. 338.

ōþ-þingian *to get from another on unfair conditions* :—Gif hwylc mæssepreóst onfunden biþ đæt hē . . . ǣnige mēdsceat selþ ođđe sealde, for đî đe hē wilnige ōđres preóstes cyrcean ōþþingian, L. E. I. 16; Th. ii. 412, 13.

ođđon; *conj. Or* :—On cyriclîcum þingum ođđon on earmra manna hyđđum ođđon on hernumena bygenum ođđon on sumum þingum, L. I. P. 19; Th. ii. 328, 10–12. Swā oft swā man fullaþ ođđon hūsel hālgaþ, 328, 21.

ōþ-þringan *to force away from one* (*oftenest in phrases* lîf, feorh, etc., ōþþringan *to take a person's life*) :—Đā geleornedon his byrelas hū hié him mehten đæt lîf ōþþringan, and him gesealdon ātor drincan, Ors. 3, 9; Swt. 136, 15. Se đe mid gāres orde ōđrum aldor ōþþringeþ, Cd. Th. 92, 3; Gen. 1523: Exon. Th. 330, 11; Vy. 49. Ecghete fǣgum feorh ōþþringeþ, 310, 8; Seef. 71. Đām ic ealdor ōþþrong, 272, 17; Jul. 500: Judth. Thw. 24, 12; Jud. 185. Hū hē Israēlum eáþost meahte guman ōþþringan *how he might most easily force away men from Israel* (*carry the Israelites captive*), Cd. Th. 219, 8; Dan. 51. Unc māgas uncre sculon eard ōþþringan *our kinsmen shall take our home from us*, Exon. Th. 496, 9; Rä. 85, 11. Cf. æt-þringan.

ōþ-wendan *to turn away, divert* :—Uton ōþwendan hit (*the kingdom of heaven*) monna bearnum, Cd. Th. 26, 8; Gen. 403.

ōþ-windan *to get away, escape* :—Ān scip ōþwand, Chr. 897; Erl. 95, 27. Cf. æt-windan.

ōþ-wîtan *to reproach with a fault, lay to a person's charge, to taunt* :—Ōþwîteþ *improperabit*, Ps. Spl. M. 73, 11. Hwȳ ōđwîte gē wyrde eówre, đæt hió geweald nafaþ? Met. 27, 4. Wē sindon cumen tō đǣm gōdan tîdun đe ūs Rōmāne ōþwîtaþ *we are come to the good times that the Romans taunt us with*, Ors. 4, 7; Swt. 182, 15. Ōþwāt *improperavit*, Ps. Spl. M. 73, 19. Ōþwiton *exprobaverunt*, 88, 11. Dryhten him swelc ōþwāt *the Lord charged them with such a fault*, Past. 1, 2; Swt. 27, 13: 15, 1; Swt. 89, 16. Đæt wē him sume opene scylde ōþwiéten, 32, 1; Swt. 209, 22. Đæt hē mē đæt ne ōtwîte *ut non hoc nobis imputet*, Bd. pref.; S. 472, 32. Uton gangan đæt wē bysmrigen bendum fæstne, ōþwîton him his wræcsîđ *let us go and insult the captive, taunt him with his misery*, Andr. Kmbl. 2715; An. 1360. Ne meaht đū đînre wyrde nāuht ōþwîtan ne đîn lîf nō getǣlan, Bt. 10; Fox 30, 3: Beo. Th. 5983; B. 2995. Cf. æt-wîtan.

ōþ-wyrcan *to do harm to* (?) :—Ic þence đis feoh tō witanne næs tō ōþwyrceanne *I intend to keep this cattle not to harm it* (?), Lchdm. i. 384, 5.

ōþ-yrnan, -ȳwan, otor. v. ōþ-irnan, -îwan, oter.

otor *for* ofer (?), Cd. Th. 220, 19; Dan. 73.

ō-wæstm, es; *m. A shoot, sprout, branch* :—Ōwestem *propago*, Ps. Surt. ii. p. 195, 13. Ōwæstm *surculus*, Wrt. Voc. ii. 121, 48. Ōwæstmas *antes*, 9, 21. Ōwæstmum *stirpidum*, 75, 70. Ōwæsmum *stirpis*, 89, 20. Đa ōwæstmas beóþ swā mycle, and swā fægere swā swā đæs deóres bearn đe unicornus hātte, Ps. Th. 28, 5. v. on-wæstm.

ō-web, -wef, es; *n. Woof* :—Ōweb *vel* āb (ōb, Wülck. Gl. 188, 12) *trama* vel *subtemen*, Wrt. Voc. i. 59, 50: *cladicla*, ii. 139, 59. Ōwef *cladica*, 104, 13: 14, 43. [Cf. trama . . . est filum inter stamen discurrens, *abbe*, Wülck. 617, 13.]

ō-wēr = ō-hwǣr.

ō-wērn; *adv. Anywhere*, Th. An. 101, 16. (*Smith's Bede*, 595, 3, *has* ōwhwǣr.)

ō-wiht. v. ā-wiht.

owisc, e; *f. A margin* (?) :—Đanon tō grāfes owisce, andlang owisce tō wege, Cod. Dip. Kmbl. iii. 388, 25.

Ōwđen. v. Ōđen.

oxa, an; *m. An ox* :—Oxa *bos* . . . oxa on đam forman teáme *unus*, on đam æfteran teáme *binus*, Wrt. Voc. i. 23, 39, 47–48: ii. 48, 36. Oxa *bova*, i. 287, 54. Wilde oxa *bubalus*, 22, 46. Oexen *boves*, Ps. Surt. 49, 10: ii. p. 191, 11. Ān getȳme oxena, Lk. Skt. 14, 19. Oxna hyrde *aubobulcus*, Wrt. Voc. i. 287, 63. iiii oxnum gers mid cyninges oxnum, Cod. Dip. Kmbl. ii. 64, 29. Đā genam Abimelech oxan and scēp, Gen. 20, 14. ¶ The value of an ox as given in the Laws was 30 pence :—Oxan mon sceal gyldan mid .xxx. p̄., L. O. D. 7; Th. i. 356, 4. Oxan tō mancuse, L. Ath. v. 6, 2; Th. i. 234, 1. .xxx. pæñ scyldig ođđe ānes oxan, v. 8, 5; Th. i. 236, 31. [*Goth.* auhsa: *Icel.* uxi: *O. H. Ger.* ohso.] v. feld-, steór-oxa. The word is found in many place-names; see e. g. Cod. Dip. Kmbl. vi. 320.

oxan-slyppe, an; *f. Oxlip*; primula veris elatior, Lchdm. ii. 32, 26: iii. 30, 8.

ōxn, e; *f. The arm-pit* :—Ōxn *ascella*, Wrt. Voc. i. 43, 65: 64, 70. Under his ōxne *sub ascella sua*, Kent. Gl. 992. Heó đone fūlan stenc đæra ōxna āfyrreþ, Lchdm. i. 284, 7. [*O. H. Ger.* uohsana *ascella.*] Cf. ōhsta.

Oxna-ford *Oxford* :—Tō Oxnaforda, Chr. 912; Erl. 100, 31. On Oxonaforda, 1015; Erl. 151, 17.

oxna-lyb *ox-heal*; helleborus foetidus and h. viridis, Lchdm. iii. Glossary.

ōxta. v. ōhsta.

P.

For the Runic ᚹ, see *peorđ*.

pād, e; *f. An outer garment, coat, cloak* :—Paad *pretersorium*, Wrt. Voc. ii. 118, 34, 15: 68, 40–41. [*Goth.* paida: *O. Sax.* pēda: *O. H. Ger.* pheit *camisa, indusium.*] v. here-pād, hōp-pāda; hasu-, salu-, salowig-pād, -pāda.

pǣca, an; *m. A deceiver* :—Se đe sægþ đæt hē lufie God, and his beboda ne healdeþ, hē biþ đonne him sylf leás, and biþ his āgen pǣca, Basil admn. 4; Norm. 40, 21.

pǣcan; *p.* pǣhte; *pp.* pǣht *To deceive* :—Swylce hié mid sceare and munuces hiwe God pǣcen (pǣcean, MS. T.) *as if deceiving God with the tonsure and the appearance of a monk*, R. Ben. 9, 15. Hȳ ōđer specaþ, ōđer hȳ þencaþ, and lǣtaþ đæt tō wærscype, đæt hȳ ōđre māgan swā swicollîce pǣcan, Wulfst. 55, 3. Pǣcht *decepta, seducta*, Hpt. Gl. 449, 42. v. ā-, be-pǣcan.

pægel *a wine-vessel, a pail* :—Pægel (Wright gives *wægel*, but see Anglia viii. 450) *gillo*, Wrt. Voc. i. 25, 26. [Cf. *Dan.* pægel *half a pint.*]

pæll, pell, es; *m.* I. *a pall, covering, cloak, costly robe* :—Pæl (pell) *pallium*, mid pælle (pelle) gescrȳd *palliatus*, Ælfc. Gl. Zup. 257, 3–4. Pæl *pallium*, Blickl. Gl. Weofod mid reádum pælle gescrȳd (*the altar was in the church dedicated to St. Michael.* v. next passage), Homl. Th. i. 508, 16. Mid hāligdōme of đæs Hǣlendes rōde and of Marian reáfe and of Michaheles pelle, Homl. Skt. i. 6, 73. Volosianus đone pæll āstrehte đe Dryhtnes andwlytan on wæs befealden, St. And. 46, 13. iiii. pellas, and iiii. cuppan, Chart. Th. 519, 23. Mycel đǣr wæs gegaderod on golde and on seolfre and on faton and on pællan, Chr. 1086; Erl. 223, 30. II. *purple, a purple garment* :—Of đam biþ geweorht se weolocreáda pæl *quibus tinctura coccinei coloris conficitur*, Bd. 1, 1; S. 473, 20 note. Pællas *purpuram*, Coll. Monast. Th. 27, 7. [*Icel.* pell *costly stuff. From Lat.* pallium.] v. next word.

pællen, pellen; *adj. Purple, rich* or *costly* (of garments) :—Hē hyne on pællenre scȳtan befeóld, St. And. 42, 13. V. pællene weofodsceátas, Chart. Th. 429, 25. Bicgaþ eów pællene cyrtlas, đæt gē tō lytelre hwîle scînon swā swā rōse, Homl. Th. i. 64, 13. Se cyning gesȳmde gold and seolfor and deórwurđe gymmas and pællene gyrlan uppon olfendas, 458, 24. Se rîca on his pællenum gyrlum cwyþ: 'Nis se loddere mid his tættecon mîn gelîca,' 256, 8. Se cāsere dyde of his purpuran and his pellenan gyrlan, H. R. 103, 18. [*Laym.* pallen (curtel).]

pælme, pǣran. v. palm, ā-, for-pǣran.

pærl (?) The word, which occurs in a list of terms connected with writing, is glossed by *enula*, which elsewhere glosses *horselene* :—Pærl *enula*, bōcfel *pergamentum*, Ælfc. Gr. Zup. 304, 7.

pæþ, paþ, es; *m.*: e; *f.* (?) *A path, track* :—Pæþ, paþ *semita*, Ælfc. Gr. 7; Zup. 25, 3. Manna paþ *semita*, deóra paþ *callis*, Wrt. Voc. i. 37, 41–42. Pæþ *semita*, 80, 37. Wegleás pæþ *invium*, 53, 61. Pæþ *callis, iter pecudum*, Wrt. Voc. ii. 127, 58. Paþ *callis*, 14, 10. Paat, 103, 48. Andlang oxna pæþes, Cod. Dip. Kmbl. v. 215, 10. Đone kyng gerihtan of đam dweliandan pæþe (*from the path of error*), Chr. 1067; Erl. 204, 30. Ne mihton forhabban helpendra paþ merestreámes mōd (*they could not stop the course of the rushing water*), Cd. Th. 208, 23; Exod. 487. Gerece mē on rihtne pæþ (*semitam*), Ps. Th. 26, 13. Lǣr mē đîne paþas (*semitas*), 24, 3: Ps. Spl. 8, 8: Homl. Th. i. 360, 32: 362, 16. Đeáh willniaþ ealle þurh mistlîce paþas cuman tō anum ende, Bt. 24, 1; Fox 80, 8. Ic ondrǣde đæt ic đē lǣde hidres đidres on đa paþas of đinum wege, 40, 5; Fox 240, 21. On paþum (*semita*) beboda đînra, Ps. Spl. 118, 35. *The word seems feminine in the following* :—Andlang paþæ . . . ǣc đæ standaþ in on đær paþæ, Cod. Dip. Kmbl. iii. 175, 36–176, 6. *In the Northern Gospels* pæþ *is an alternative gloss with* dene :—Pæþ ł dene *uallis*, Lk. Skt. Lind. Rush. 3, 5: *chaos*, 16, 26. [*O. Frs.* path, paed: *O. H. Ger.* pfad *callis, semita.*] v. ān-, flet-, gegn-, here-, mearc-, mîl-pæþ.

pæþþan; *p.* de *To tread* (*a path*), *to traverse*:—Tungol gársecges grundas pæþeþ *the sun* (*after it has set*) *treads ocean's depths as its path*, Exon. 350, 29; Sch. 71. Eorþgræf pæþeþ *it makes its way along a trench*, 439, 26; Rä. 59, 9. Sume fótum twám foldan peþþaþ, sume fiérféte, Met. 31, 10. Ic mearcpaþas træd, móras pæþde, Exon. 485, 8; Rä. 71, 10. [Cf. *O. H. Ger.* pfadón *to go along a path*, Grff. 3, 326.]

pætig. v. prættig.

pál, es; *m.* I. *a pale, pole, stake*:—Pál *palus*, Wrt. Voc. i. 84, 69. II. *a kind of hoe* or *spade*:—Delfísen *vel* spadu *vel* pál *fossorium*, 16, 14. [*Icel.* páll *a kind of hoe* or *spade*; *a pale*: *O. H. Ger.* pfál *palus*. From Latin.]

palent, es; *m.*: palente, palendse, an; *f. A palace*:—On ðam mǽran palente ðǽr ðǽr se cyning wæs oftost wunigende, Anglia ix. 28, 31. Ðæt seó cwén ne cume nǽfre heononforþ intó ðínum pallente, 29, 64. On stréte oððe on palentan, Lchdm. iii. 206, 6. Æt ðæs cáseres palendsan (palentsan, Bos.), Ors. 6, 21; Swt. 272, 23. Hé bræc ðæne palant (ða palentan, MS. D.), Chr. 1049; Erl. 172, 21. [*O. Frs.* palense: *O. Sax.* palencea: *O. H. Ger.* pfalanza, pfalinza *basilica, praetorium, aula, palatium*. From a Mid. Lat. form *palantium*. v. Kluge Dict. s. v. pfalz.]

palent-líc; *adj. Relating to a palace*:—Tó ðǽm palentlícum *ad palatinas*, Wrt. Voc. ii. 2, 67. [*O. H. Ger.* pfalenz-líh *palatinus*.]

palm, es; palma, an (?); *m.*: pælme, an; *f. A palm*:—Palm *palma*, Wrt. Voc. i. 32, 61. Se palm is sigebeácen, Homl. Th. ii. 402, 10: i. 218, 10. Swé swé palma *ut palma*, Ps. Surt. 91, 13. Swælce pælme *quasi palma*, Rtl. 65, 33. Pælmana *palmarum*, 95, 8. Palmana, Jn. Skt. Lind. Rush. 12, 13. [*O. Sax. O. H. Ger.* palma: *Icel.* pálmr *a palm-tree*.]

palm-æppel *the fruit of the palm, a date*:—Palmæppel *dactulus*, Wrt. Voc. ii. 26, 63: 89, 33. Palmæppla *nicolaos*, 83, 55. Palmǽpla, 60, 67.

palm-bearu *a palm-grove*:—Palmbearwes *palmeti*, Wrt. Voc. ii. 75, 77.

Palm-sunnandæg *Palm Sunday*:—Gyf se terminus becymþ on ðone Sunnandæg ðonne byþ se dæg Palmsunnandæg, Lchdm. iii. 244, 16. On Palmsunnandæg, Rub. Lk. Skt. 19, 29. [*Icel.* pálmsunnudagr.]

palm-treów *a palm-tree*:—Palmtreów *palma*, Ps. Lamb. 91, 13. Palmtreó *palmes*, Jn. Skt. Lind. Rush. 15, 4. Ðǽr wǽron hundseofontig palmtreówa (*palmae*), Ex. 15, 27. Palmtreówa (-trýwa) twigu *ramos palmarum*, Jn. Skt. 12, 13.

palm-twig *a palm-branch*:—Palmtwig *palma*, Wrt. Voc. i. 32, 61: Blickl. Gl. Onfóh ðissum palmtwige, Blickl. Homl. 137, 25. Heó álegde ðæt palmtwig ðe heó ǽr onféng, 139, 4. Se gewuna stent ðæt gehwǽr on Godes gelaþunge se sacerd bletsian sceole palmtwigu on ðisum dæge (*Palm Sunday*), Homl. Th. i. 218, 3.

palmung *glosses* palmes, Jn. Skt. Lind. Rush. 15, 2.

palm-wicu *the week which begins with Palm Sunday*:—On ðære palmwucan, Rub. Lk. Skt. 22, 1: Rub. Jn. Skt. 12, 1, 24.

palstr *a spike* or *something with a point*:—Palester, plaster, palstr *cospis*, Txts. 50, 225. Palstre *cuspite*, Wrt. Voc. ii. 21, 58.

pan-mete *cooked food*:—Ǽlces cynnes panmete *ferculum*, Wrt. Voc. ii. 38, 59. Ponmete *vivertitum*, i. 290, 42.

pang, Wrt. Voc. i. 289, 52, *an error for* þung (?).

panic, es; *n.* (?) *A sort of millet*; panicum:—Panecis fíf scillinga gewyht, Lchdm. iii. 124, 8. Nym panic, 118, 28. [*O. L. Ger.* penik: *M. H. Ger.* pfenich.]

panne, an; *f. A pan*:—Panne *patella*, Wrt. Voc. i. 24, 51. Mid ðisse pannan hierstinge wæs Paulus onbærned, Past. 21; Swt. 165, 3. Of brádre pannan *de sartagine*, Wrt. Voc. ii. 26, 11. Wyl on pannan, Lchdm. ii. 308, 28. Ðǽr wǽron inne geseted hweras and pannan, and hé clypte ða hweras and cyste ða pannan, ðæt hé wæs eall sweart, Shrn. 69, 27-29. [*O. H. Ger.* pfanna: *O. Frs.* panne: *Icel.* panna.] v. bräd-, brǽde-, brǽding-, bræg-, cócer-, fýr-, heáfod-, hearste-, holo-, hyrsting-, ísen-panne.

Pante, an; *f. The river Blackwater in Essex*:—Hí Pantan streám bestódon, Eástseaxena ord and se æschere, Byrht. Th. 133, 50; By. 68. Wódon wælwulfas ofer Pantan, 134, 41; By. 97. Seó ǽreste stów is on Pante staþe ðære eá *prior locus est in ripa Pentae amnis*, Bd. 3, 22; S. 553, 8.

pápa, an; *m. A pope*:—Ðá wæs on ða tíd Vitalianus pápa ðæs apostolican setles ealdorbiscop *sede apostolicae tempore illo Vitalianus praeerat*, Bd. 4, 1; S. 563, 23. Gregorius se hálga pápa, Homl. Th. ii. 116, 24. Æfter ðæs pápan geendunge, 122, 18. Tó pápan gecoren, 122, 31. Tó pápan gehálgod, 124, 1. [*Icel.* páfi. *From Latin* papa.]

pápan hád, es; *m. The papal dignity*:—Gregorius pápanhád onféng, Homl. Th. ii. 126, 24.

páp-dóm, es; *m. The papacy*:—Gregorius féng tó pápdóme, Chr. 592; Erl. 19, 33. [*Icel.* páfa-dómr.]

paper, es; *m.* (?) *Papyrus*:—Paper *papirus*, Wrt. Voc. ii. 92, 12.

papig. v. popig.

papol-stán, es; *m. A pebble-stone, pebble*:—Gǽþ tó ðære sǽstrande and feccaþ mé papolstánas, Homl. Th. i. 64, 3. Popelstánas *lapillulos*, Hpt. Gl. 449, 18. [*Wick.* pibbil-ston.]

páp-seld, es; *n. The papal see*:—Hé hié lǽrede ðæt hié raðost tó Róme sendon tó ðæm pápan, and ðone pápan and ðæt pápseld ðæt hié beáhsodan hwæt him ðæs tó rǽde þúhte, Blickl. Homl. 205, 20.

páp-setl, es; *n. The papal throne*:—Hé sæt on ðam pápsetle ændlefen geár, Shrn. 49, 17.

part, es; *m. A part*:—Ðes part oððe ðes dǽl, Ælfc. Gr. 41; Som. 43, 2. Ðisses partes, 16; Som. 20, 11. On ðisum parte, 17; Som. 20, 32.

Parthe; *pl. The Parthians*:—Parthe forhergodon Mesopotamian, Ors. 6, 24; Swt. 276, 6. Partha cyning, 5, 11; Swt. 236, 3. Partha gewin, Swt. 236, 26. Hié hæfdon gewin wið Parthe, 6, 13; Swt. 268, 6, 8. Hé com ǽrest tó Parþum, Bt. 18, 2; Fox 64, 12.

paþ. v. pæþ.

páwa, peá, an; *m.*: páwe, an; *f. Peacock, peahen*:—Páwa *pavo*, Ælfc. Gr. 9, 3; Som. 8, 34. Pauua, Txts. 90, 826. Pawa, Wrt. Voc. i. 77, 24. Páwe, *pavo, pavus*, 29, 4. Fuglas ða ðe heard flǽsc habbaþ, páwa, swan, æned, Lchdm. ii. 196, 19. On ðære ylcan stówe byþ óðer fugelcynn fenix hátte ða habbaþ cambas on heáfde swá páwan *in eo monte est avis fenix que habet cristas quasi orbes pavonis*, Nar. 39, 4. Se fugel (*the phenix*) is onlícost peán, Exon. Th. 219, 25; Ph. 312. [A pruest proud as a *po*, Pol. Songs, 159, 15: *Wick.* poos; *pl.*: *O. H. Ger.* pfáwo: *Icel.* pá or pái (*as a nickname*). From Latin.]

Peác-land *the Peak of Derbyshire*:—Eádweard cyning fór ðonan (*from Nottinghám*) on Peácland tó Badecan wiellon (*Bakewell*), Chr. 924; Erl. 110, 11. v. next word.

Peác-, Péc-sǽtan; *pl. The occupiers of the Peak*:—Pécsǽtna [land is] twelf hund hýda, Cod. Dip. B. i. 414, 17.

pearroc, es; *m. An enclosure*:—Pearroc, pearuc *clatrum*, Txts. 50, 224. Pearruc, Wrt. Voc. i. 34, 7. Pearruc *cauea*, Germ. 400, 62. On ðisum lytlum pearroce búgiaþ swíðe manega þeóda *hoc ipsum brevis habitaculi septum plures incolunt nationes*, Bt. 18, 2; Fox 62, 27. Ðis sindon ða landgemǽro. Ǽrest ... on Bogeles pearruc; of Boceles pearruce, Cod. Dip. Kmbl. v. 277, 11. Hié (*the English*) bedrifon hié (*the Danes*) on ánne pearruc, and besǽton hié ðǽr útan, Chr. 918; Erl. 102, 35. Pearruca *clatrorum*, Hpt. Gl. 489, 75. Pearroca, Wrt. Voc. ii. 18, 63. Of pearrocum *de clatris*, 26, 52: 18, 62. Of pearrucum, Hpt. Gl. 484, 44: 508, 29. Ðæs gemǽre is on eásthealfe spachrycg, on súðan plumwearding pearrocas, Cod. Dip. Kmbl. i. 258, 12. [*O. H. Ger.* pferrih, pfarrih. From Celtic: *Welsh* parwg.]

Pedrida, Pedreda (e ?) *the river Parret*:—Æt Pedridan (Pedredan, MS. E.) múþan, Chr. 845; Erl. 66, 23: 658; Erl. 34, 2.

pell, pellen. v. pæll, pællen.

pellican, es; *m. A pelican*:—Ic geworden eom pellicane gelíc se on wéstene wunaþ, Ps. Th. 101, 5.

pending. v. pening.

Péne; *pl. The Carthaginians*; Poeni:—Ðæt hié wið Péna folce mehte ... Ðá flugon Péne ... Hanna, Péna cyning, Ors. 4, 6; Swt. 170, 21-25.

pening, penning, pending, penig, pennig, es; *m. A penny* (1) referring to other than English coinage:—Ðes peningc (pening, penig) *hic as*, Ælfc. Gr. 9, 25; Zup. 50, 14. Fals pening *paracaraximus*, Wrt. Voc. i. 57, 34. Penninge *hymenis* (?), ii. 96, 71. Peninge, 43, 27. Bringaþ mé ðone pening (*denarium*), Mk. Skt. 12, 15. Ðá brohton hí him ǽnne peninc (penig, MS. A.: penning, Lind.), Mt. Kmbl. 22, 19. Hé sealde ǽlcon ǽnne penig (penning, Lind.) ... Ðá onféngon hig ǽlc his pening (suindrigo penningas, Lind.) ... syndrige penegas *singulos denarios*, 20, 2-10. Pening, Homl. Th. ii. 78, 27. Mé sind wana penegas *desunt mihi nummi*, Ælfc. Gr. 32; Som. 36, 37. Wé eác wiernaþ úrum cildum úrra peninga mid tó plegianne *pueris nummos subtrahimus*, Past. 50, 4; Swt. 391, 27. Hig sealdon hine wið þrítigum penegum, Gen. 37, 28. (2) of English coinage, a silver coin, the 240th part of a pound:—Fíf penegas gemaciaþ ǽnne scillingc, and xxx. penega ǽnne mancs, Ælfc. Gr. 50; Som. 52, 8. Gá seó wǽge wulle tó .cxx. p̄. (tó healfan punde, MS. G.), L. Edg. ii. 8; Th. i. 270, 3. Tén hund (pund ?) peñd ... Gedǽle hé ǽlcum Godes þiówe peñd ... þreóténe hund (pund ?) pending, Chart. Th. 471, 5-26. xiii. pund pendingæ, 474, 9. Mid .v. pundum mǽrra pæninga (*denarii meri*), L. Alf. pol. 3; Th. i. 62, 10. Gif mon men eáge of ásleá, geselle him mon .LX. scill. and .VI. scill. and .VI. pæningas and þriddan dǽl pæninges (peniges, MS. H.) tó bóte, 47; Th. i. 94, 3-5. Hire mægþhádes wurð, ðæt synd twelf scillingas be twelf penigon (cf. Se rihtscylling byþ á be .xii. penegum *legitimus solidus semper est .xii. denariorum*, L. Ecg. P. iv. 60; Th. ii. 222, 7), Ex. 21, 10. (3) as a weight, *pennyweight*:—Án *uncia* stent on feówer and twentig penegum. Twelf sídon twelf penegas beóþ on ánum punde, Anglia viii. 335, 17. Pund ealoþ gewihþ .vi. penegum máre ðonne pund wætres, and .i. pund wínes gewihþ .xv. penegum máre ðonne .i. pund wætres, etc., Lchdm. ii. 298, 16-26. Gegníd on mortere ðætte pening gewege, 18, 3: 134, 25. Swylce swá .iii. penegas gewegen, 52, 13: 110, 17. Wið lúsum; cwic seolfor, án pening seolfres, 124, 24. Drenc biþ on peninge *the dose will be a pennyweight*, 272, 24. Ceorf nygan penegas *cut up nine pennyweights*, iii. 8, 2. Man ðysses wyrttruman genime týn penega gewihte, i. 260, 17. Hý man wegeþ, swá man déþ gold wið penegas, and gif ða penegas teóþ swíðor ðonne ðæt gold, ðonne miswyrþ ðam men hraðe,

Wulfst. 240, 2-4. [*O. L. Ger.* penning: *O. Frs.* panning: *O. H. Ger.* pfenning, pfenting: *Icel.* penningr.] v. ælmes-, healf-, heorþ-, hundred-, Rōm-, seám-pening.

pening-hwirfere, es; *m. A money-changer:*— Pennighwyrfere *mensularius*, Wrt. Voc. i. 57, 31.

pening-mangere, es; *m. A money-dealer:*—Pennigmangere *collybista*, Wrt. Voc. i. 57, 32. Peningmongere, ii. 22, 36.

pening-sliht, es; *m. The striking of money:*—Gæfil ꞇ penningslæht *tributum vel censum*, Mt. Kmbl. Lind. 17, 25.

pening-wǣg, e; *f. A penny-weight:*—Wiđ lūsum; cwic seolfor and eald butere; ān pening seolfres, and tū peningwǣge buteran, Lchdm. ii. 124, 24.

pening-weorþ, -wurþ, es; *n. A penny-worth:*—Hafa ān penigweorþ swefles, Lchdm. iii. 38, 28. Æt ǣlcon gegyldan ǣnne peningc odđe ān peningcwurþ weaxes, Chart. Th. 605, 26. Twā hund peningweorþ hlāfes, Homl. Th. i. 182, 9.

penn, es; *m. A pen, fold:*—On penn; of đam penne, Cod. Dip. Kmbl. iii. 456, 3-4: 25, 21. On hacapenn foreweardne, 412, 13.

penn *a disease of the eye, pin, a kind of cataract:*—Đis is seó sēleste eáhsalf wiđ ēhwærce and wiđ miste and wiđ penne, Lchdm. i. 374, 2.

pennian. v. on-pennad. [Cf. Þe pit tineþ his muð ouer þe man þe liđ on fule synnen . . . gif ure ani is þus penned, O. E. Homl. ii. 43, 27.]

Pentecosten, es; *m.* (?) *Pentecost, the fiftieth day after the resurrection, Whitsuntide:*—On Pentecostenes dæg com se Hālga Gāst ofer đa apostolas, Btwk. 214, 29. On đære Pentecostenes wucan, Rubc. Lk. Skt. 5, 17: 8, 40. On ōđerne Pentecostenes mæssedæg, Rubc. Jn. Skt. 3, 16. On Pentecostenes mæsseǣfen, 14, 15.

Penwiht-steort, es; *m. The Land's End in Cornwall:*—Se here . . . wendon eft ābūtan Penwiht-steort (Penwiđ-, MS. C.: Penwæđ-, MS. D.) on đa sūþhealfe, and wendon in tō Tamermūþan, Chr. 997; Erl. 135, 10. [The Welsh form is *Pengwayd*, v. Earle's note.]

Peohtas; *pl. The Picts:*—Đā fērdon Peohtas in Breotone . . . Mid đȳ Peohtas wīf næfdon . . . đæt is mid Peohtum healden . . . Đridde cynn Breotone onfēng on Pehta dǣle, Bd. 1, 1; S. 474, 17-25. On Peohta gereorde, S. 474, 4. Pehta cynn, 5, 24; S. 646, 33. Hī sceoldon feohton wiđ Pyhtas (Pihtas, MS. A.). Heó đā fuhton wiđ Pyhtas, Chr. 449; Erl. 13, 6.

peonia, an; *m.* (?) *Peony:*—Peonia *peonia*, Wrt. Voc. i. 69, 22. Đeós wyrt đe man peonian nemneþ, Lchdm. i. 168, 14. [The Latin form of the accusative, *peoniam*, occurs, 170, 4.]

peorđ *the name of the Runic p.* Its meaning is doubtful. Grimm notices the name for *f* in the old Sclavonic alphabet, *fert*, and the Persian name for one of the figures on the chess-board, *ferz*. Kemble seems to take the latter, translating the word by *chess-man;* but it is doubtful whether the knowledge of chess was early enough among the Teutons to allow of this interpretation. v. Zacher Das Runenalphabet, pp. 7-9. The verse which accompanies the Rune in the Runic poem is the following:—Peorđ byþ symble plega and hlehter wlancum đǣr wīgan sittaþ on beórsele blīđe ætsomne, Runic pm. Kmbl. 341, 1-6; Rūn. 14.

pere(u), an; *f. A pear:*—Seó peru *hoc pirum*, Ælfc. Gr. 6; Som. 5, 59. Pere, Wrt. Voc. i. 285, 59. Healfreáde peran *crustumie* vel *volemis* vel *insana* vel *melimendrum*, 39, 25. (Cf. *hec volemus* a[e] permayn-tre, 191, col. 2: *hoc volemum* a[e] permayne, 192, col. 2.) Peran, Lchdm. ii. 176, 18. [*Icel.* pera: *O. H. Ger.* bira.]

pere-wōs, es; *n. Perry, a drink made from pears:*—Perewōs *sapa*, Wrt. Voc. i. 27, 50. (The word occurs in a list of drinks.)

persa. v. medema.

Persc-ware; *pl. The Persians:*—Of Perscwara mǣgþe, Shrn. 55, 32.

Perse, Persēas; *pl. The Persians:*—Đā wǣron đa Perse geegsade, Ors. 2, 5; Swt. 78, 13: 3, 1; Swt. 98, 30. Persa cyning, 2, 4; Swt. 74, 29. Persa rīce . . . Persēa rīce, 2, 5; Swt. 78, 2, 31. Wiđ Persum, Swt. 82, 23. On Persēum, 78, 30. Hié sendon on Perse, 3, 1; Swt. 98, 19.

Persida *Persia:*—Tō đam earde đe is gehāten Persida, Homl. Th. ii. 482, 2.

Persisc; *adj. Persian:*—Seó reáfung đæs Persiscan feós, Ors. 2, 5; Swt. 84, 21: Jud. Thw. 162, 23.

persoc, es; *m. A peach;* malum persicum:—Genim persoces leáf, Lchdm. iii. 58, 27. Æppla and peran and persucas, ii. 176, 18. [*M. H. Ger.* pfersich.]

persoc-treów, es; *n. A peach-tree:*—Persoctreów *persicarius*, Wrt. Voc. i. 32, 52.

peru. v. pere.

pervince, an; *f. Periwinkle* (plant):—Pervincæ *vinca*, Wrt. Voc. i. 31, 65. Pervince, 79, 34.

petersilige, an; *f. Parsley:*—Petersilie. Đās wyrte man *petroselinum* nemneþ, Lchdm. i. 240, 6. Petresilige, iii. 24, 9. Petorsilian sǣd, ii. 314, 29: 228, 26. Đa wyrt petersilian, 206, 27: 234, 8. [*O. H. Ger.* petarsile: *Ger.* petersilie.]

peþþan, petig. v. pæþþan, prættig.

Petrus; *gen.* Petres; *m. The apostle Peter:*—Đā genam Petrus hyne . . . Đā beseah hē hyne and cwæþ tō Petre, Mt. Kmbl. 16, 22-23. Se Hǣlend com on Petres hūse, 8, 14. Hē sceare (Petres mearce, MS. B.) onfēng, Bd. 3, 18; S. 546, 10. Be Peteres mæssan, Wulfst. 272, 9.

philosoph, es; *m. A philosopher:*—Paminunde đæm strongan cyninge and đæm gelǣredestan philosophe, Ors. 3, 7; Swt. 110, 22. Hié sealdon Demostanase đæm philosophe licgende feoh, 3, 9; Swt. 124, 1.

pic, es; *n. Pitch:*—Đis pic *haec pix*, Ælfc. Gr. 9, 63; Som. 13, 54: Wrt. Voc. ii. 117, 39. Hlūttor pic *resin*, Lchdm. ii. 44, 24: 72, 25. Genim pices lytel, 96, 12. Weallendes pices, 252, 1: Dōm. L. 14, 199. Heó smirode hine mid tyrwan and mid pice, Ex. 2, 3. Đā hēt se cāsere meltan on hwere leád and scipteoran and pic, Shrn. 91, 7: Lchdm. ii. 318, 4. [*O. L. Ger.* pik: *O. H. Ger.* peh: *Icel.* bik.]

pīc, es; *m. A point, pointed instrument, pike:*—Piic *acisculum*, Wrt. Voc. ii. 98, 39. Pīc, 4, 23: i. 17, 31. [Cf. his pic he nom on honden & helede hine under capen . . . þene pic he bilæfde, Laym. 30849. A Celtic word.] v. horn-pīc.

pīcan *to use a pīc, to remove by means of a pīc, to pick:*—Lēt him pȳcan ūt his eágan, and ceorfan of his handa, Chr. 796; Erl. 58, 33. [Pykyn *purgo*, Prompt. Parv. 397: to piken and to weden, Piers P. 16, 17.]

pic-bred (?) *glosses* glans, Wrt. Voc. i. 33, 58 (at the end of a list of names of trees).

picen; *adj. Pitchy, of pitch:*—Picen hell *piceus Tartarus*, Hymn. Surt. 142, 30. On đære picenan eá, Blickl. Homl. 43, 28.

pician; *p.* ode *To pitch, cover with pitch:*—Crocca gepicod ūtan, Lchdm. ii. 26, 23.

pīcung, e; *f. A pricking:*—Pīcung *stigmata*, Wrt. Voc. ii. 121, 39. v. pīc.

pīe; *f. An insect:*—Hundes pīe (pēo, Ps. Spl. C.) *cynomia*, Ps. Surt. 104, 31. Lūs *pedučla*, hnitu *ascarida*, pīe *ladasca*, Wrt. Voc. i. 287, 45-47. *Ladasca* pīae, *briensis* hondwyrm, Wrt. Voc. ii. 112, 48.

pihment *a pigment, drug:*—Of ōþþrum pyhmentum, Lchdm. iii. 136, 29. Cf. next word.

pihten *part of a loom:*—Pihten, Anglia ix. 263, 12. Pihtine *pectine*, Hpt. Gl. 494, 26.

pīl, es; *m. A stick with a point, something pointed:*—Dægmǣles pīl *gnomon*, Wrt. Voc. i. 86, 42. Đa Walas ādrifon sumre eá ford ealne mid scearpum pīlum (stængum, MS. D.) greátum innan đam wetere (cf. Cassobellannus ripam fluminis ac pene totum sub aqua vadum acutissimis sudibus praestruxerat, Bd. 1, 2), Chr. Erl. 5, 10. Heó (*sea-holly*) hafaþ stelan hwītne, on đæs heáhnysse ufeweardre beóþ ācennede scearpe and þyrnyhte pīlas (*sharp and thorny prickles*), Lchdm. i. 304, 1. Hē gehæfte hī on ānum micclum stocce, and mid īsenum pīlum heora īlas gefæstnode, Homl. Skt. i. 5, 388. [*O. H. Ger.* pfīl *pilum, arundo*. From Lat. *pilum*.] v. hilde-, orþanc-, searo-, wæl-pīl; and dægmǣls-pīlu.

pīle, an; *f. A stake.* v. temes-pīle.

pīle, an; *f. A mortar:*—Đeáh đū portige đone dysegan on pīlan swā mon corn dēþ mid piilstæfe ne meaht đū his dysig him from ādrīfan *si contuderis stultum in pila, quasi ptisanas feriente desuper pilo, non auferetur ab eo stultitia ejus*, Past. 37, 2; Swt. 267, 1. Swilce hit on pīlan gepīlod wǣre *quasi pilo tusum*, Ex. 16, 14. [From Latin *pila*.]

pile *a pillow.* v. pyle.

pilece, an; *f. A robe of skin, pelisse:*—Pylece *pellicie*, Wrt. Voc. i. 81, 68. Hwī worhte God pylcan Adame and Eve æfter đam gylte? Đæt hē geswutelode mid đām deádum fellum đæt hī wǣron đā deádlīce, Boutr. Scrd. 20, 28. [He to-rendeđ þe olde pilche of his deadliche uelle, A. R. 362, 29. Pylche *pellicium, pellicia*, Prompt. Parv. 397; see the note, where many instances of the word are given. *O. H. Ger.* pelliz: *Icel.* piliza, pilla *a fur coat.* From Latin.]

pīlere, es; *m. One who pounds in a mortar:*—Pīlere *pilurius*, Wrt. Voc. i. 34, 52. v. next word.

pīlian; *p.* ode *To pound in a mortar:*—Se đe pīlaþ *vel* tribulaþ *pilurus* vel *pistor*, Wrt. Voc. i. 20, 26. v. *preceding word and* pīle, pīl-stampe, -stoc.

pillan (?) *to peel* (of skin):—Đis lācecræft sceal tō đan handan đe đæt fell of pyleþ, Lchdm. iii. 114, 13.

pill-sāpe, an; *f. Silotrum* (?), Wrt. Voc. i. 27, 32.

pīl-stæf. v. pīle.

pīl-stampe, an; *f. A pestle;* pilum, Wrt. Voc. i. 34, 51.

pīl-stocc, es; *m. A pestle;* pila, Wrt. Voc. i. 86, 6.

pīlstre, an; *f. A pestle;* pila, Wrt. Voc. i. 34, 50.

pīn-beám, es; *m. A pine-tree:*—Se hālga wolde āheáwan ǣnne pīnbeam, Homl. Th. ii. 508, 24.

pinca. v. pynca.

pīnere, es; *m. One who torments:*—Hlāferd his gesalde hine đǣm pīnerum (*tortoribus*), Mt. Kmbl. Lind. 18, 34: Germ. 399, 265.

pinewincle. v. winewincle.

pīn-hnutu; *gen. dat.* -hnyte; *pl.* -hnyte; *f. A pine-nut, fir-cone:*—Seó eorþe stent on gelīcnesse ānre pīnnhnyte, Lchdm. iii. 258, 6. Genim of pīnhnyte .xx. geclǣnsodra cyrnela, ii. 180, 19. [*Prompt. Parv.* pynote *pinum*.]

pīnian; *p.* ode *To torment, torture:*—Đā pīneden hié hiene mid đæm đæt hié his hand forbærndon, ānne finger and ānne, Ors. 2, 3; Swt. 68, 22. Pīnedon *excruciabant*, 6, 11; Swt. 266, 15. Đæt hē his heortan and his mōd mid hreówsunga suīđe pīnige *ut per afflictionem poenitentiae cor prematur*, Past. 28, 6; Swt. 199, 25. Đā hēt hē hī pīnian (pīnigan, MS. C.), Homl. Skt. i. 5, 371. Đonne onginþ hē hȳ tō pīniaunne on mistlícre wísan, Wulfst. 195, 1. Gnættas ǽgðer ge ða men ge ða nýtenu píniende wǽron, Ors. 1, 7; Swt. 36, 31. Píniendum *cruciante*, Hpt. Gl. 503, 36. [*O. H. Ger.* pínôn: *Icel.* pína. From Latin.]

pinn. I. *a pin, peg*:—Ne sceolde hé nán þing forgýman ðe ǽfre tó note mehte; ne músfellan, ne ðæt git læsse is, tó hæpsan pinn, Anglia ix. 265, 10. [From Latin *pinna.*] II. *an instrument for writing, a pen*:—Mið pinn ł urittsæx *calami*, Mt. Kmbl. p. 2, 17. [From *penna*? or *pinna*?]

pinne (?), an; *f. A flask, bottle*:—Ic (*sutor*) wyrce of him (*cutes et pelles*) flaxan (pinnan) *facio ex iis flascones*, Coll. Monast. Th. 27, 35.

pínness, e; *f. Torment, pain*:—Tó ðare helware stíðe pínnesse, Chart. Th. 369, 34.

pinsian; *p.* ode *To weigh, judge, estimate, consider, examine*:—Geþænce ǽlc man hú swíðe man pinsaþ ða sáwle on dómes dæg, ðonne man sett ða synne and ða sáwle on ða wǽge and hý man wegaþ, swá man déþ gold wið penegas, Wulfst. 239, 26. Hé holrede ł pinsode *pensavit, cogitavit*, Hpt. Gl. 443, 76. Hé sceáwode hine selfne and pinsode *he observed and weighed himself*, Past. 7, 2; Swt. 51, 15. Pinsige ǽlc mon hiene selfne georne, 10, 2; Swt. 63, 18. Pinsiende *inquirendo, scrutando*, Hpt. Gl. 411, 26. [*Lat.* pensare.] v. á-pinsian.

pinsung. v. á-pinsung, Hpt. Gl. 447, 73.

pintel *virilitas, membrum virile*, Wrt. Voc. i. 65, 29. [Pyntyl *veratrum, tentigo, priapus*, 184, 11. Pyntylle *veretrum*, 186, col. 2. Pyntyle, 208, col. 1. Also see Cath. Angl. p. 281. s. v. *pyntelle*, and the note. Leo 200, 41 gives a Platt-deutsch *pint* with the same meaning.]

pín-treów, es; *n. A pine-tree*:—Píntreów *pinus*, Wrt. Voc. i. 32, 54: 79, 80: 285, 60. Þúfbǽres píntreówes *frondentis pini*, Hpt. Gl. 458, 68: Lchdm. ii. 216, 5. Ðæt man píntreów bærne tó glédum and ðonne ða gléda sette tóforan ðam seócum men, 284, 12.

pín-treówen, -tríwen; *adj. Belonging to a pine-tree*:—Cyrnlu of píntrýwenum (-treów-, MS. O.) hnutum, Lchdm. i. 250, 9.

pínung, e; *f. Torment, torture, pain*:—Ród[e] pínung *crucis tormentum*, Rtl. 24, 11. Tó pínunge *ad poenam*, 103, 17. For his gylta pínunga *in criminum suorum cruciatum*, L. Ecg. P. ii. 5; Th. ii. 184, 8. Pínunge, L. Edg. C. 13; Th. ii. 268, 19. Mid ungemetlícre pínunge hé (*Phalaris*) wæs ðæt folc cwielmende, Ors. 1, 12; Swt. 54, 18. Pínunge *tormento*, Hpt. Gl. 503, 20. Pínungum *cruciatibus*, 502, 70.

pínung-tól, es; *n. An instrument of torture*:—Decius hét gearcian eall ðæt pínungtól, Homl. Th. i. 428, 18. Mid eallum ðisum pínungtólum getintregod, 424, 22.

pipat (?) *glosses* accipiter, Wrt. Voc. ii. 10, 36.

píp-dreám, es; *m. The sound of the pipe*:—Pípdrám singan gehýreþ gehende blisse *to hear (in a dream) the sound of the pipe shews joy at hand*, Lchdm. iii. 208, 22.

pípe, an; *f. A pipe.* (1) as a musical instrument:—Pípe oððe hwistle *musa*, Wrt. Voc. i. 73, 60. Hearpe and pípe drémaþ eów on beorsele, Wulfst. 46, 16. i. silfren pípe, Chart. Th. 429, 20. (2) of other tubes:—In pípan; of pípan in wiði bróc, Cod. Dip. Kmbl. iii. 380, 2. Dó mid pípan on, Lchdm. ii. 126, 3. Mid ondóunge wyrtdrences þurh horn oððe pípan, 260, 11: 224, 28. [*O. L. Ger.* pípa: *Icel.* pípa: *O. H. Ger.* pfífa *fistula, calamus, camena.*] v. sang-pípe.

pípere, es; *m. A piper, player on the flute*:—Pípere *tibicen*, Wrt. Voc. i. 73, 59: 289, 55. Reódpípere *auledus*, 60, 46. Se Hǽlend geseah hwistleras (píperas, Rush.), Mt. Kmbl. 9, 23. [*Icel.* pípari: *O. H. Ger.* pfífari *tibicen.*]

pípfan; *p.* te *To breathe, blow*:—Pípfendes *spirantis, sufflantis*, Hpt. Gl. 450, 76. Út á-pýfhte (-pípfte?) *exhalavit, exspiravit*, 472, 42.

piplian *to grow pimply*:—Wið teter and pypylgende (pipligende, MS. B.) líc, Lchdm. i. 234, 10. Wið pypelgende (pipligende, MS. B.) líc ðæt Grécas erpinam (ἕρπης) nemnaþ, 266, 20. [*Lat.* papula a *pimple.*]

pipor, es; *m. Pepper*:—Piper (*other MSS.* pipor) *piper*, Ælfc. Gr. 9, 18; Zup. 44, 2. On ðám londum biþ pipores genihtsumnys . . . Ðone pipor mon swá nimeþ, Nar. 34, 21–23. Genim langes pipores .x. corn, Lchdm. ii. 186, 8. Of blacum pipore, 234, 2. Genim gebeátenne pipor, 186, 4. [*Icel.* pipar: *O. H. Ger.* pfeffar. From Latin.]

pipor-corn, es; *n. A pepper-corn*:—Genim .xvii. piporcorn, Lchdm. i. 74, 4. Ðæra pipercorna sý ofertæl, 288, 8.

pipor-horn, es; *m. A horn for holding pepper*:—Man sceal habban . . . sealtfæt . . . piperhorn, Anglia ix. 264, 19.

piporian; *p.* ode *To pepper*:—Pipra hit syððan swá swá man wille, Lchdm. iii. 76, 9. Cf. Gepipera mid .xx. corna, ii. 182, 21. Gepiporod wyrtdrenc, 182, 7. [*Icel.* pipra.]

pir-gráf, es; *m. An orchard of pear-trees*:—On pirgráf, Cod. Dip. Kmbl. v. 284, 23.

pirige, an; *f. A pear-tree*:—Ðeós pirige *haec pirus*, Ælfc. Gr. 6; Som. 5, 59: Wrt. Voc. i. 32, 51: 80, 9. Pirge, ii. 117, 35. On gerihte tó ðære pirigan, Chart. Th. 145, 28. Ðis sindon ða londgemǽra . . . ǽrest of Piriforda on ða díc; andlang díc on ða pyrigan; of ðære pyrigan . . ., Cod. Dip. Kmbl. iii. 76, 27–30. Æt ðære pirian, 52, 18. On ða pyrian, ii. 205, 15. *The word, as in* Piriford, *is found in local names*, e. g. Pirigfliát, Pyrihom, Pirigtún, vi. 322, col. 2. [*Chauc. Piers P.* pirie.]

pís; *adj. Heavy, weighty*:—Byrðenna hefiga ł písa *onera gravia*, Mt. Kmbl. Lind. 23, 4. [From Latin *pensus.*] v. pinsian, pís-líc, písian.

pise, an; *f. A pea*:—Pise *lenticula*, Wrt. Voc. ii. 50, 75. Piose, 112, 63. Pysan *lentis*, 51, 50. Pisan hosa *siliqua*, 120, 58: Lk. Skt. Lind. 15, 16. Heó hafaþ sǽd on ðære mycele ðe pysan, Lchdm. i. 316, 10. Beán, pisan *cicer*, Wrt. Voc. ii. 14, 37. Pisan gesodena on ecede, Lchdm. ii. 180, 15. Geseáwe pysan *juicy peas*, 254, 15. Nim ðæt wæter ðe pyosan wǽran on gesodene, 286, 29. Ðonne sceal man ða langnysse (*of the root*) tóceorfan on pysena gelícnysse, i. 260, 15. On pysena wóse, 260, 25. Pysena seáw, ii. 220, 10. Pysena broþ, 278, 18. Healde hí hine wið pisan and wið ða þing ðe windigne ǽþm on men wyrcen, 214, 2. v. múse-pise.

pise-cynn, es; *n. A kind of pea*:—Sum pysecynn hátte lenticulas, Lchdm. ii. 190, 16.

písian (?) *to weigh*:—Geþænce ǽlc man hú swíðe man pinsaþ (pysæþ, MS. H.) ða sáwle, Wulfst. 239, 26. v. pís.

pisle, an; *f.* (?) *A warm* (?) *chamber*:—*Scriptorium* pisle, fer-(fýr-?) hús (or? *pis(a)le* fýrhús), Wrt. Voc. i. 58, 58. [Cf. *O. Frs.* pisel *a chamber*: '*pisel, pesel* ist in Niedersachsen, Dietmarschen, Nordfriesland und Süddänemark, *phiesel* in Baiern für verschiedene arten von gemächern noch gangbar,' Richthofen. *O. H. Ger.* pfisel *pisalis, pisale, pirale*, Grff. 3, 352. '*Pisalis* videtur fuisse vestiarium seu vestiaria theca,' Du Cange.]

pís-líc; *adj. Heavy*:—Woeron égo hiora píslíco ł hefigo (*ingravati*), Mk. Skt. Lind. Rush. 14, 40. v. *next word and* pís.

píslíce; *adv. Heavily*:—Píslíce ł hefiglíce, *graviter*, Mt. Kmbl. Lind. 13, 15: Lk. Skt. Lind. Rush. 11, 53. v. preceding word.

pistol, es; *m. An epistle, letter*:—Be ðam spræc se pistol æt ðyssere mæssan, Homl. Th. ii. 330, 13. Ðone pistol ðe Hieronimus sette be forþsíðe Marian, 438, 3. Se apostol Iacob áwrít on his pistole, Boutr. Scrd. 22, 47. Iacob se rihtwísa áwrát ánne pistol, Ælfc. T. Grn. 14, 9, 13. Petrus áwrát twegen pistolas, 14, 7, 12, 16, 19. [*Icel.* pistil. From Latin.]

pistol-bóc; *f. A book containing the Epistles*:—Hé (*the priest*) sceal habban ða wǽpna tó ðam gástlícum weorce . . . ðæt synd ða hálgan béc, saltere and pistolbóc, godspellbóc and mæssebóc, L. Ælfc. C. 21; Th. ii. 350, 11–13. Hé (*bishop Leofric*) hæfþ ðiderynn (*St. Peter's minster at Exeter*) gedón . . . ii. pistelbéc . . . Hé ne funde on ðam mynstre ðá hé tó féng bóca ná má búton . . . .i. pistelbóc . . . , Chart. Th. 430, 8–29. [Cf. *Icel.* pistla-bók.]

pistol-rǽdere, es; *m. He who reads the epistle in church*, R. Conc. 5.

pistol-rǽding, e; *f. A lesson in the church-service*:—Lucas ús manode on ðisre pistol-rǽdinge, Homl. Th. i. 294, 13: ii. 380, 23. (Both passages refer to the Acts of the Apostles.)

pistol-rocc, es; *m. The vestment worn when reading the epistle*:—v. fulle mæssereáf, ii. dalmatica, iii. pistolroccas, Chart. Th. 429, 22.

piþa, an; *m. Pith, the soft inner part of the stem of a plant*:—Eall se dǽl se ðe ðæs treówes on twelf mónþum geweaxeþ, hé onginþ of ðám wyrtrumum, and swá upweardes gréwþ óþ ðone stemn, and siððan andlang ðæs piþan and andlang ðære rinde óþ ðone helm, Bt. 34, 10; Fox 150, 2. Þeahtigaþ on hiera módes rinde monig gód weorc tó wyrcanne, ac on ðam piþan biþ óðer gehýded, Past. 9; Swt. 55, 23. Nim ellenes piþan, Lchdm. iii. 90, 2.

plæce, plæse, an: plæts, e; *f. A place, an open space, a street*:—In huommum ðara plæcena *in angulis platearum*, Mt. Kmbl. Lind. 6, 5. On plæcum (on plætsa, Rush.) *in plateas*, Lk. Skt. Lind. 10, 10: 14, 21. In plaecum *in plateis*, 13, 26. In plæcum (plæsum, Rush.), Mk. Skt. Lind. 6, 56. In plægiword ł on plæcum *in plateis*, Rtl. 36, 7. In plæcum, 65, 37. [*Prompt. Parv.* plecke *or* plotte *porciuncula*. 'Pleck is given by Cole, Ray, and Grose as a North-country word, signifying a place;' note, p. 405. *Icel.* pláz; *n.*: *M. H. Ger.* platz, *m.*: (*both introductions of the end of thirteenth century*). From Latin.]

plægan, plægi-word (plæce-worþ), plæts. v. plegan, plæce.

plætt *a sounding blow, a smack*: in the compound *eár-plætt*:—Drihten ús sealde hǽlu þurh ðám eárplættum, Homl. Th. ii. 248, 25. [Plat *a blow with the fist*, Jamieson's Dict.] v. next word.

plættan; *p.* te *To give a sounding blow, to smack*:—Hí plætton hyne mid hyra handum *dabunt ei alapas*, Jn. Skt. 19, 3. [He come plattinde (*tramping, making a noise with the feet*), Havel. 2282. Plette; *pl. hurried*, 2613. His heued of he plette (*struck*), 2626. Plat, 2755. Platch *to make a heavy noise in walking, with quick short steps*, Jamieson's Dict. *O. Du.* platten, pletten: *M. H. Ger.* blatren, platren *to strike noisily*: *Ger.* platzen. Of onomatopoetic origin; cf. *smack.*] v. eár-plættan *and preceding word.*

plagian. v. plegan.

plante, an; *f. A plant, shoot*:—Swé swé niówe plant[e] *sicut novella*, Ps. Surt. 43, 12. Gesáwena plantan *plantaria*, Wrt. Voc. i. 39, 13. Ðæt is sió hálige gesomnung ðæt eardaþ in æppeltúnum ðonne hié wel begáþ hira plantan and hiera impan óþ hié fulweaxne beóþ *ecclesia quippe in hortis habitat, quae ad viridatem intimam exculta plantaria virtutum servat*, Past. 49, 2; Swt. 381, 17. [*Icel.* planta: *O. H. Ger.* pflanza. From Latin.] v. mixen-plante.

plantian; *p.* ode *To plant*:—Ðú plantast (*plantes*) wíneard and ne brícst his, Deut. 28, 30. Gé plantiaþ, 28, 39. Gé plantigeaþ, Lev. 19, 23. Hí heora heortan wyrtruman on ðisum andwerdum lífe plantiaþ,

Homl. Th. ii. 132, 7. Abraham plantode ǽnne holt, Gen. 21, 33: Mt. Kmbl. 15, 13. Hwæðer se anweald hæbbe ðone þeáw ðæt hē unþeáwas āwyrtwalige of rīcra manna mōde, and plantige ðǽr cræftas on? Bt. 27, 1; Fox 94, 24. Sanctus Paulus underfēng ða hālgan gesomnunga tō plantianne, suā se ceorl dēþ his ortgeard, Past. 40; Swt. 293, 3. [*Icel.* planta: *O. H. Ger.* pflanzōn.] v. ā-, ge-plantian.

plant-sticca, an; *m.* *A gardening-tool, a dibble* (?):—Plantsticca *pastinatum*, Wrt. Voc. i. 16, 13. [Cf. *Ital.* pastinare *to dig.*]

plantung, e; *f.* I. *planting*:—Wīntwiga plantung *propaginatio*, Wrt. Voc. i. 39, 5. II. *what is planted, a plant*:—Ǽlc plantung (*plantatio*) ðe mīn heofenlīca fæder ne plantode byþ āwurtwalod, Mt. Kmbl. 15, 13. Plontung rōsæs *plantatio rosae*, Rtl. 65, 35. Ðara bearn swā swā æðele plantunga, Ps. Spl. 143, 14: Blickl. Gl. Plantunga seten *plantaria*, Wrt. Voc. ii. 65, 76. [*O. H. Ger.* pflanzunga *propagatio, plantarium, plantatio.*]

plaster, es; *n.* (?) *A plaster*:—Tō plastre gewyrc, Lchdm. i. 272, 23: 304, 20. Hwī ne bidst ðū ðē beþunga and plaster līfes lǽcedōmes æt līfes freán *cur tibi non oras placidae fomenta medelae?* Dōm. L. 6, 80. [*O.H. Ger.* pflastar; *n. cataplasma, cementum.* From Latin [*em*]*plastrum.*]

platian; *p.* ode *To cover with plates*: in the compound ā-platian:—Āplatad *obryzum, nitidum*, Hpt. Gl. 417, 18. Āplatedum *obryzo*, 456, 47. v. next word.

platung, e; *f. A plate, thin piece of metal*:—Platung (? platum, Btwk.), smǽte gold *obrizum*, Hpt. Gl. 489, 34. Platungum *brateolis, laminis*, Wrt. Voc. ii. 127, 17. v. preceding word.

plega, an; *m.* I. *play, quick movement*:—Plega *gesticulatio*, Wrt. Voc. ii. 41, 36. Plegan *gestum*, Hpt. Gl. 474, 10. II. *play,* (*athletic*) *sport, game*; often in poetry applied to fighting, see the compounds:—Plega *ludus*, Ælfc. Gr. 8; Som. 7, 30. Ðes plega *hic jocus*, 13; Som. 16, 27: Wrt. Voc. i. 85, 30. Plaega *palestra*, ii. 116, 5. Mid ðām þiówum wæs on symbel mīn plega *hunc continuum ludum ludimus*, Bt. 7, 3; Fox 20, 34: Exon. Th. 46, 27; Cri. 743. Ealle ða hwīle ðe ðæt līc biþ inne, ðǽr sceal beón gedrync and plega, Ors. 1, 1; Swt. 20, 26. Ðǽr wæs heard plega wælgāra wrixl (*the battle between the four kings and the five*), Cd. Th. 120, 4; Gen. 1989. Plæges *saltationis*, Mk. Skt. p. 3, 11. Ic mē tō ðam plegan gemengde *ludentibus me miscui*, Bd. 5, 6; S. 619, 11. Bebudon Rōmāna godas ðæm senatum ðæt mon theatrum worhte him tō plegan, Ors. 4, 12; Swt. 208, 33. Ðā hió æt hiora theatrum wǽron mid heora plegan . . . heora plegan begān, 6, 2; Swt. 256, 10–14. Ða cild rīdaþ on heora stafum, and manigfealde plegan plegiaþ, Bt. 36, 5; Fox 180, 9. Wē forbeódaþ ǽgðer ge plegan, ge unnytta word, ge gehwylce unnyttnesse in ðām hālgan stōwum tō dōnne, L. E. I. 10; Th. ii. 408, 22. Hié wǽron welige . . . and heora plegan wǽron genihtsume . . . Hió hæfdon wiste and plegan and oforgedrync, Blickl. Homl. 99, 17–21. Plegan *allusiones*, Wrt. Voc. ii. 9, 44: *colludia*, 20, 71. Plegena *ludorum*, 50, 25. III. *clapping with the hands, applause* (v. plegan, IV):—Ðæm plegan *plausu*, Wrt. Voc. ii. 67, 26. v. æsc-, ecg-, gilp-, gūþ-, hand-, hearm-, hyht-, lind-, nīþ-, secg-, stæf-, sund-, sweord-, wīg-plega, *next word, and the compounds with* pleg-.

plegan, plægan, plegian, plagian, plægian; *p.* de, ede, ode *To play*; ludere:—Ic plege *ludo*, Ælfc. Gr. 28, 4; Som. 31, 23: Wrt. Voc. ii. 53, 29. Plegade *lusit*, 53, 28. Plegende *ludens*, Kent. Gl. 279: 995. I. *to play, move about sportively, frolic, dance*:—Hornfisc plegode, glād geond gārsecg, Andr. Kmbl. 740; An. 370. Hlōh ðā and plegode boda bitre gehugad, Cd. Th. 45, 10; Gen. 724. Plægede *saltasset*, Mk. Skt. Lind. Rush. 6, 22. Pleagade *saltavit*, Mt. Kmbl. Rush. 14, 6. Ne plægde gē, Lind., gē ne plagadun, Rush. *non saltastis*, 11, 17. Ðæt folc sæt and æt and dranc, and ārison and plegedon, Ex. 32, 6. Ðæt folc . . . eodon him plegean, Past. 43; Swt. 309, 14. Men willaþ binnan Godes hūse bysmorlīce plegian, L. Ælfc. C. 35; Th. ii. 357, 2 note. Gesión sǽmearh plegan, Elen. Kmbl. 490; El. 245. Ðæt wīf geseah Ismael plegan, Cd. Th. 168, 6; Gen. 2778. Ðā geseah hē plegan micel cnihta weorod be ðæs sǽs waroþe, Shrn. 78, 27. Ān plegende cild arn under wǽnes hweowol, 32, 11. Swā plegende lamp *quasi agnus lasciviens*, Kent. Gl. 214. Seofon nacode wīmmen urnon plegende on heora gesihþum, Homl. Th. ii. 162, 32. II. *to play, to divert or amuse one's self*:—Ða ðe dwollīce plegaþ æt deádra manna līce, and ǽlce fūlnysse ðǽr forþteóþ mid plegan, Homl. Skt. i. 21, 308. Tarentīne ðæt folc plegedon binnan heora byrg æt heora þeatra *the Tarentines were taking their amusement at the theatre*, Ors. 4, 1; Swt. 154, 2. Wē lǽraþ ðæt preóst ne beó hunta ne hafecere ne tæflere ac plege on his bōcum *we enjoin that a priest be neither a hunter nor a hawker nor a gamester, but let him find his amusement in his books*, L. Edg. C. 64; Th. ii. 258, 8. II a. *to play* (*a game*), *exercise one's self in any way for the sake of amusement*:—Ða cild rīdaþ on heora stafum, and manigfealdne plegan plegiaþ, Bt. 36, 5; Fox 180, 9. Samson plegode him ætforan *ludens Samson*, Jud. 16, 27. On ðæm dæge plegedon hió of horsum, Ors. 3, 7; Swt. 118, 29. II b. *to play* (*with anything*):—Hē mid bǽm handum upweard plegade *he waved both hands aloft*, Elen. Kmbl. 1609; El. 805. Ðā pleogede hē mid his wordum, Bd. 2, 1; S. 501, 25. Wē wiernaþ ūrum cildum ūrra peninga mid tō plegianne, Past. 50; S. 361, 27. II c. *to play with a person, toy*; in a bad sense, *to make sport of*:—Sarra beheóld, hū Agares sunu wið Isaac plegode, Gen. 21, 9. Ðære helle hund ongan fægenian mid his steorte and plegian wið hine (*Orpheus*), Bt. 35, 6; Fox 168, 17. Plegan, Exon. Th. 429, 10; Rä. 43, 2. II d. *to play* (*for something*), *strive after*:—Ðis is se ilca ðe ðū longe for his deáþe plegodest *this is the same for whose death thou hast long played*, Blickl. Homl. 85, 19. III. *to play on an instrument*:—Plægiendra (plegiyndra, Ps. Spl. C.) timpanan *tympanistriarum*, Ps. Surt. 67, 26. IV. *to clap the hands in applause* (v. plega, III):—Flōdas plægiaþ (plegiaþ, Ps. Spl. C.) *flumina plaudent*, Ps. Surt. 97, 8. Plagiaþ (plegaþ, Ps. Spl. C.) *plaudite*, 46, 2. v. plega.

plegere, es; *m. A player, athlete, wrestler*:—Nacod plegere *gimnosophista* (*the glosser seems to have misunderstood the word, which is rendered by* heáhlāreów, Wrt. Voc. ii. 40, 40, *and by* weoroldsnottor, 81, 52), Wrt. Voc. i. 17, 10. v. pleg-mann.

pleg-hūs, es; *n. A play-house, theatre*:—Ðæs heofenlīcan pleghūses *coelestis theatri*, Hpt. Gl. 447, 62.

plegian. v. plegan.

pleg-līc; *adj. Relating to play of any kind*:—Ðæs pleglīcan *olimpiaci*, Wrt. Voc. ii. 64, 20. Pleglīcum *scenico*, Hpt. Gl. 474, 6: *palaestrico*, 489, 60. Ðȳ pleglīcan plegan *scenica ludicra*, Wrt. Voc. ii. 90, 54. Ða pleglīcan *theatrales*, 75, 17. Pleglīcum *palaestricis, gymnicis*, Hpt. Gl. 405, 6, 9.

pleg-mann, es; *m. A player, athlete, wrestler*:—Plegmanna *gymnicorum*, Hpt. Gl. 407, 39. Þurh plegemen ł gligmen ł gleáwe *per gymnosophistas*, 406, 72. Swilce wittige ł gleáwe leorneras ł plegmen *velut sagaces gymnosophistas*, 404, 78. Plegmen *gimnosophistas*, ðǽm wærstlīcum *palestricis*, Wrt. Voc. ii. 74, 53–54. v. plegere.

plegol; *adj. Playful, sportive, jocose*:—Hwīlon wacodon menn ofer ān deád līc, and ðǽr wæs sum dysig mann plegol ungemetlīce, and tō ðām mannum cwæþ swylce for plegan, ðæt hē Swȳðun wǽre, Homl. Skt. i. 21, 292.

pleg-scild, es; *m. A small shield*:—Plegscylde *pelta*, Wrt. Voc. ii. 65, 69. [Cf. lytel scyld *pelta*, ða læssan scyldas *peltae*, i. 35, 28, 59.] Truman pleigscelde *tuta pelta*, Hpt. Gl. 424, 38.

pleg-scip, es; *n. A small ship, a yacht* (?); parunculus, Wrt. Voc. i. 56, 35. v. next word.

pleg-stōw, e; *f. A place for play, a gymnasium, wrestling-place, amphitheatre*:—Oretstōwe ł winstōwe ł plegstōwe *scammatis*, Hpt. Gl. 405, 41. Plegstōwe *amphitheatri*, Wrt. Voc. ii. 3, 13. On plegstōwe (bleg-, MS.) oððe on wafungstōwe andbidian hine gesihþ styrunge sume getācnaþ *if a man in a dream sees himself waiting in an amphitheatre or theatre it betokens some disturbance*, Lchdm. iii. 206, 15. Plegstōw[a] ł winstōwe *palaestrarum*, Hpt. Gl. 478, 50. Plegstōwa *palestrarum*, Wrt. Voc. ii. 66, 50. On plegestōwum *in gymnasio*, 40, 20.

pleoh; *gen.* pleós; *n. Danger, hurt, peril, risk*:—Nys ðæt nǽnig pleoh *nullum ei est periculum*, L. Ecg. C. 40; Th. ii. 166, 5. Swylce hit nān pleoh ne sȳ, ðæt se preóst libbe swā swā ceorl, L. Ælfc. C. 6; Th. ii. 344, 18: Wulfst. 269, 28. Læsse pleoh byþ ðam men, ðæt hē flǽsces brūce on Lenctenfæstene, ðonne hē wīfes brūce, 286, 3: Homl. Th. i. 178, 34. Ðæt wæs swīðe micel pleoh ðæt ðū swā wēnan sceoldest, Bt. 5, 3; Fox 14, 5. Hit biþ his pleoh nā mīn, Ælfc. Gr. pref.; Som. 2, 2. Wēnaþ sume menn ðæt nān pleoh ne sȳ on deórwurðum gyrlum, Homl. Th. i. 328, 25. Hē būton pleó tō his fixnoþe gecyrde, ii. 288, 26. Pleó *periculo*, Hpt. Gl. 457, 40. Gif hié sīen gelīc ord and hindeweard sceaft ðæt sīe būtan pleó (cf. si cuspis et acies lancee pari sustentacione respondeant, sine culpa sit, L. H. I. 88, 3; Th. i. 595, 12–14), L. Alf. pol. 36; Th. i. 84, 19. Philippus Mæcedonia rīce ealle hwīle on mician pleó and on miclan earfeþan hæfde, Ors. 3, 7; Swt. 110, 28. Gif ðū ofer gemet itst . . . seó ofering ðē wurþ oððe tō sāre . . . oððe tō plió *cujus satietatem si superfluis urgere velis, aut injucundum, quod infuderis, fiet, aut noxium*, Bt. 14, 1; Fox 42, 17. Hwā mæg ǽhta wilnian būtan plió nū se swelc plioh ðǽron gefōr se ðe his nō ne wilnode *quis opes quaerat innoxie, si et illi extiterunt noxia, qui haec habuit non quaesita*, Past. 50, 4; Swt. 393, 9. Hwelc māgon beón māran gehāt ðonne mon gehāte for his freónd ðæt hē underfoo his sāule on his pleoh *spondere pro amico est alienam animam in periculo suae conversationis accipere*, 28, 3; Swt. 193, 7. [*O. Frs.* plē, plī *danger.*] v. pliht.

pleó-līc; *adj. Dangerous, perilous, hurtful, hazardous*:—Hit swȳðe pleólīc is, ðæt man on ðām hālgum stōwum āðer oððe ðæt dō oððe ðæt sprece ðæt ðǽm stōwum ne gedafenaþ, L. E. I. 10; Th. ii. 408, 27. Mē þincþ ðæt ðæt weorc (*translating Genesis*) is swīðe pleólīc (*dangerous, because a foolish person might misapply what he read*), Ælfc. T. Grn. 22, 8. Ne becymst ðū nǽfre tō ðam pleólīcum leahtre, Homl. Th. ii. 208, 31. Gif hié (seó menigo ðīnra monna) yfele sint ðonne sint hié ðē pleólīcran and geswincfulran gehæfd ðonne genæfd *si vitiosi moribus sunt, perniciosa domus sarcina*, Bt. 14, 1; Fox 42, 22. Hiora ingewinn him wǽron forneáh ða mǽstan and ða pleólecestan, Ors. 2, 6; Swt. 88, 29. v. un-pleólīc.

pleón; *p.* pleah; *with gen. To risk, expose to danger*:—Se ilca David miclum his ágenes herges pleah (pleh, Cott. MSS.) *the same David exposed his host to great danger*, Past. 3, 2; Swt. 37, 7. Se đe on đæm gefeohte đisses andweardan lífes nile suincan ne his selfes plión, 34, 1; Swt. 229, 20. v. pleoh, pliht.

plett, e; *f.* (?) *A fold*:—Óđre scíp ic hafo đa đe ne sindun of đisse pletta (from đissum plette, Lind.) . . . biþ ân pletta (ân plette, Lind.), Jn. Skt. Rush. 10, 16. In scípa plett ł locc *in ouile ouium*, Lind. 10, 1. [From Latin *plecta* a hurdle. Cf. hyrdle ł bige *plecta*, Hpt. Gl. 497, 71.]

plicettan (?) *to expose to danger*:—Plicet *adludit* (*adlidit?*), Germ. 397, 20. Cf. pliht.

plicgan *to scrape, scratch*:—Plicged (plicgeđ?) *scalpit*, Germ. 396, 255. [Cf. (?) *Chauc. p.* plighte; *pp.* plight *plucked*.]

pliht, es; *m.*: e; *f. Danger, damage*:—Mid micclan plihte *cum magno periculo*, Coll. Monast. Th. 26, 37. Ne biþ ǽnig gewemmed líchama tó plihte (*dangerously, harmfully*), gif hit ne lícaþ đam móde, Homl. Skt. i. 9, 85. Gyf hit (*stolen property*) on hýdelse funden sý, đonne mæg đæt forfangfeoh leóhtre beón, forđam [hit] biþ on læsse plihte (*with less danger than when taken from the thief*) begytan, L. Ath. iv. 6; Th. i. 226, 6. Plihtas *pericula*, Ps. Surt. 114, 3. [*Laym.* pliht *harm, danger*; e. g. him muchel plihte ilomp (*he was murdered*), 4003: *O. Frs.* plicht *periculum*: *O. H. Ger.* pfligida *periculum*.] v. next word.

plihtan; *p.* te *To bring danger upon* an object (*dat.*), *to compromise* [*To plight* has later the meaning of to promise under peril of forfeiture, to make a solemn engagement for which one has to answer]:—Gif hwá bútan leáfe of fyrde gewende đe se cyng sylf on sý plihte him sylfum and ealre his áre *it shall be at the peril of life and property*, L. Eth. v. 28; Th. i. 310, 29: vi. 35; Th. i. 324, 10. Gif ǽnig ámánsumad man . . . on đæs cynges neáweste gewunige, ǽr đam đe hé hæbbe godcunde bóte georne gebogene, đonne plihte him sylfum and eallan his ǽhtan, v. 29; Th. i. 312, 3. Plihte hí heora áre and eallon heora ǽhton, vi. 36; Th. i. 324, 14. Gif hwá útlahne hæbbe and healde plihte him sylfum and ealre his áre, L. C. S. 67; Th. i. 410, 18. Plihte tó him sylfum and ealre his áre, L. Eth. ix. 42; Th. i. 350, 2.

plihtere (?) *one that watches in the prow of a ship*:—Pliclitere (plihtere?) ł ancremen *proreta*, Hpt. Gl. 406, 55. [Cf. *O. H. Ger.* pfliht *prora*, Grff. 3, 360.]

pliht-líc; *adj. Dangerous*:—Plyhtlíc þingc hit ys gefón hwæl *periculosa res est capere cetum*, Coll. Monast. Th. 24, 21. Đrý dagas syndon on geáre đe wé *egiptiaci* hátaþ, đæt is on úre geþeóde plihtlíce dagas; on đám ná tó đæs hwón for nánre neóde ne mannes ne neátes blód sý tó wanienne, Lchdm. iii. 76, 11–14.

plóg, es; *m. A plough*; with this meaning the word occurs in *Icel.* and *O. H. Ger.*, but in *A. S.* it seems to mean *land, a plough of land* (cf. Cath. Angl. p. 284:—a ploghe of land *carrucata*. In the *Tale of Gamelyn*, the knight, bequeathing his estate says:—

'Johan myn eldeste sone shall have *plowes* fyve,
And my myddeleste sone fyf *plowes of lond*.'

Plowlond *carrucata*, þat a plow may tylle on a day, Prompt. Parv. 405. In Ælfric's Colloquy the ploughman says: Ǽlce dæg ic sceal erian fulne æcer ođđe máre. *Pleuch* a quantity of land for caring for which one plough suffices, Jamieson's Dict.), the word *sulh* being used to denote the implement:—Ic hit (*property*) ágnian wille tó ágenre ǽhte, đæt đæt ic hæbbe, and nǽfre đé myntan ne plot ne plóh, ne turf ne toft, ne furh ne fótmǽl, L. O.; Th. i. 184, 6. [*Icel.* plógr; *m. a plough*; plógs-land *an acre*: *O. H. Ger.* pfluoc *aratrum*.]

plot *a plot of ground*. v. preceding word. [*Prompt. Parv.* plotte *porciuncula*.]

pluccian, ploccan; *p.* ode *To pluck, pull away, tear*:—Ic tótere ođđe pluccige ođđe tǽse *carpo*, ic of ápluccige *excerpo*, Ælfc. Gr. 28, 4; Som. 31, 21. Plucciaþ *carpunt, vellint*, Wrt. Voc. ii. 128, 77. Ploccaþ *disceptant, lacerant*, 140, 59. Pluc[ciaþ] *decerpint*, Hpt. Gl. 408, 37. Đa đe đæra treówa bógas heówon . . . sind đa láreówas on Godes cyrcan, đe plucciaþ đa cwydas đæra apostola, Homl. Th. i. 212, 35. His leorningcnihtas đa eár pluccedon (*uellebant*), Lk. Skt. 6, 1. Pluccian *plumemus* (cf. scecele sceccen wé *plectro plumemus*, Wrt. Voc. ii. 66, 79–80: 83, 77–78), Hpt. Gl. 497, 73. Pluccian (*later MS.* plockien) *vellere*, Mt. Kmbl. 12, 1. Pluccigean, Mk. Skt. 2, 23. Ic wolde gadrian (pluccian, MS. M.) sum gehwǽde andgyt of đære béc đe Beda se snotera láreów gesette, Lchdm. iii. 232, 2. [*Icel.* plokka, plukka: *M. H. Ger.* pflücken: *Du.* plukken.]

plúm-blǽd, e; *f. Fruit of the plum-tree*:—Plúmblǽda ete neahtnestig *let him eat plums after his night's fasting*, Lchdm. ii. 230, 13.

plúme, an; *f. A plum* (fruit or tree):—Seó plúme *hoc prunum*, Ælfc. Gr. 6; Som. 5, 60. Plumae *prunus*, Txts. 88, 822: *plumum*, 87, 1600. [*Prompt. Parv.* plowme *prunum*: *Icel.* plóma: *M. H. Ger.* pflûme. From Latin.] v. plýme, plúm-treów.

plúm-feđer, e; *f. Down*:—Plúmfeđera hnescnyss geonglíce lima ná gehlýwe *plumarum mollities iuuenilia membra non foveat*, Scint. 43.

plúm-seáw, es; *n. Plum-juice*:—Nim plúmsēwes ánes scyllinges gewyht, Lchdm. iii. 114, 21.

plúm-slá *a sloe, wild-plum*; pruniculus, Wrt. Voc. i. 33, 28.

plúm-treów, es; *n. A plum-tree*:—Đis plúmtreów *haec prunus*, Ælfc. Gr. 6; Som. 5, 60: Wrt. Voc. i. 32, 55: 33, 33: 80, 10: *plummus*, 285, 56. Plúmtreū *plunas*, ii. 117, 44. Nim plúmtreówes leáf, Lchdm. ii. 310, 19.

plýme, an; *f. A plum* (fruit or tree):—Plýme *prunum*, Wrt. Voc. i. 285, 57: *prunus*, ii. 68, 45. v. plúme.

poc-ádl. v. next word.

pocc, es; *m. A pock, pustule, ulcer*:—Poccas *ulcera*, Wrt. Voc. ii. 90, 73. Gif poc sý on eágan, Lchdm. iii. 4, 1: 14, 31. Wiđ ómena geberste . . . sleah feówer scearpan ymb đa poccas útan, and lǽt yrnan đa hwíle đe hé wille, 44, 1: ii. 100, 4. Wiđ pocádle . . . Mid hunige smire đǽr hit út sleá on đone poc . . . Sealf wiđ pocádl . . . Drenc wiđ poccum . . . Wiđ poccum swíđe sceal mon blód lǽtan . . . gif hié út sleán ǽlcne man sceall áweg ádelfan mid þorne, and đonne wín ođđe alordrenc drýpe on innan, đonne ne beóþ hý gesýne, 104, 14–106, 6. See the note on this section. [*Prompt. Parv.* pokke, sekenesse *porrigo, variolus*: *Piers P.* 20, 97: Kynde come after wiđ many kene sores, As pokkes and pestilence.]

pohha, poha, pohcha, pocca, an; *m. A poke, pouch, bag*; as a medical term *sinus*:—Pohha (poha, Lind.) *pera*, Mk. Skt. Rush. 6, 8. Pohha (pocca, Lind.), Lk. Skt. 9, 3. Đý læs đider in yfel pohha (*sinus*) gesíge, Lchdm. ii. 208, 18. Sift đonne, dó on pohhan (*bag*), lege under weofod, 138, 27. Dó on ǽnne pohchan, iii. 48, 5. 'Se đe médsceattas gaderaþ, hé legeþ hié on þyrelne pohchan (*sacculum*).' An þyrelne pohchan se legþ . . . , Past. 45, 4; Swt. 343, 20. [*Prompt. Parv.* pooke *sacculus*: *Chauc. Piers P.* poke: *Icel.* poki: *O. Du.* poke. *A Celtic word, Irish* poc, *Gaelic* poca *a bag*.] v. nest-pohha *and next word*.

pohhed; *adj. Baggy, loose*:—Hý gelyst ǽlces (ealces, MS.) ýdeles habbaþ síde earmellan and pohhede hosa stíþe reáf hý anscuniaþ *they take pleasure in every vanity, they have wide sleeves and loose hose, close-fitting garments they avoid*, R. Ben. 136, 23.

pól, es; *m. A pool*:—Salamon sǽde đætte swíđe deóp pól wǽre gewered on đæs wísan monnes mód *aqua profunda verba ex ore viri*, Past. 38, 7; Swt. 279, 15. Hié nellaþ gepyndan hiora mód, swelce mon deópne pool gewerige, 39, 1; Swt. 283, 14. Maurus þurh Godes mihte eode uppon yrnendum wætere, on ánum wídgyllan póle, Homl. Skt. i. 6, 12. Tó đæm póle *ad natatoriam*, Jn. Skt. 9, 11. In tó póle, Cod. Dip. Kmbl. iii. 424, 17. On pól; of póle út on Auene, 456, 1–2. In póll, 399, 14. Út on hreódpól, ii. 29, 10. [*O. H. Ger.* pfuol *palus*.] v. fisc-, hwirf-, mylen-pól, *and* pull.

polente (?), an; *f. Parched corn*:—Hig ǽton polentan (*polentam*), Jos. 5, 11.

pollegie, polleie, an; *f. Pennyroyal*; mentha pulegium:—Polleie, Lchdm. ii. 296, 23: 350, 26. Pollege, đæt on englis dwyrcge dwosle, i. 380, 10. Genim polleian, 118, 4: ii. 318, 7. Genim pollegian, 138, 26: iii. 4, 9: 16, 10. Pollegan, 28, 26: 48, 9. [*O. H. Ger.* polei, pulei: *Ger.* polei. From Latin.]

pollup, es; *m. A scourge* (?):—Mistlíce þreála gebyriaþ for synnum, bendas ođđe dyntas ođđe pollupas ođđe carcernþýstra, lobban ođđe bælcan, L. Pen. 3, note; Th. ii. 278, 26.

popig *poppy*:—Papig *papaver*, Ælfc. Gr. 9, 18; Som. 9, 62. Popig, Wrt. Voc. i. 31, 7: 68, 56. Popei, ii. 116, 48. Baso popig *astula regia*, i. 66, 65. Popaeg, Txts. 90, 824. Popeg *cucumis*, 52, 253. Popig, Wrt. Voc. ii. 15, 54. Popi *cucumus*, 17, 27. Wilde popig *saliunca*, i. 31, 8. Popig . . . đe Grécas *moecorias* and Rómáne *papauer album* nemnaþ and Engle hwít popig hátaþ, Lchdm. i. 156, 17–20. Him is tó sellanne lactucas and súþerne popig inneweard, ii. 212, 12.

popul *a poplar* (?; but cf. popylle *lolium*, Wrt. Voc. i. 234, 2), *in* popul-finig:—Of đam ellene tó populfinige; of populfinige tó Lambhyrste, Cod. Dip. Kmbl. iii. 219, 8. The second part of the compound occurs again v. 194, 2–3: 195, 10. [*Prompt. Parv.* popul-tre.]

por-leác, es; *n. A leek*:—Porleác *porrus*, Wrt. Voc. i. 31, 2. Wé hæfdon cucumeres and pepones and porleác *in mentem nobis veniunt cucumeres et pepones porrique*, Num. 11, 5. v. next word.

porr, es; *n.* (?) *A leek*:—Por *porrum*, Wrt. Voc. i. 286, 12. Nim merwes porres leáf, Lchdm. ii. 84, 31. Heáfdehtes porres, 230, 10. Dó sealt and merce tó, and porr, 284, 2. Por, 186, 19: 278, 19. [*O. H. Ger.* pforro: *Icel.* pors.]

port, es; *m. n.* I. *a port, haven*:—Wiđ đone gársecg is se port đe mon hǽt Caligardamana, and be súþaneástan đæm porte is đæt ígland Deprobane, and be norþan đæm Gandes múþan . . . is se port Samera. Be norþan đæm porte is se múþa đære ié Ottorogorre, Ors. 1, 1; Swt. 10, 8–13. Đonne is án port on súþeweardum đæm lande, đone man hǽt Sciringes heal . . . Of Sciringes heale hé seglode on fíf dagan tó đæm porte đe mon hǽt æt Hǽþum, Swt. 19, 10–23. Hé hine gelǽdde tó đam porte (*ad portum*) đe is nemned Cwentowíc, Bd. 4, 1; S. 564, 44. II. *a town*:—Port *castellum*, Wrt. Voc. i. 36, 28. Wíc ođđe lytel port *castellum*, 84, 42. Hwæt fremaþ đære burhware đeáh đe đæt port (*the town*) beó trumlíce on ǽlce healfe getimbrod, gif đǽr biþ án hwem open forlǽten, đæt se onwinnenda here þurh đam infær hæbbe? Homl. Th. ii. 432, 3. On ǽlche healfe đæs portes, Chart. Th. 226, 25. Hwá rít intó đam port *quis equitat in civitatem?* Ælfc. Gr. 5; Som. 3, 52. In burug ł in port *in civitate*, Mt. Kmbl. p. 15, 19. Gif đū hēr on porte (*Ephesus*) geboren wǽre, hwǽr synt đīne māgas đe đē āfēddon, Homl. Skt. i. 23, 679. Ic wille đæt nān man ne ceápige būtan porte, ac hæbbe đæs portgerēfan gewitnesse ođđe ōđera manna đe man gelȳfan mǽge. And gif hwā būtan porte ceápige, đonne sȳ hē cyninges oferhȳrnesse scyldig, L. Ed. 1; Th. i. 158, 10–14. Wē cwǽdon đæt man nǽnne ceáp ne ceápige būtan porte ofer .xx. penega, ac ceápige đǽr binnan on đæs portgerēfan gewitnesse, L. Ath. i. 12; Th. i. 206, 8–10. Ælc ceáping sȳ binnan porte, i. 13; Th. i. 206, 16. Nān man ne mynetege būtan on porte, i. 14; Th. i. 206, 19. Lecge ān .c. tō wedde, healf landrīcan and healf cinges gerēfan binnan port, L. Eth. iii. 7; Th. i. 296, 8. Đā com se here tō Hamtūne (*Northampton*) and đone port forbærndon, Chr. 1010; Erl. 144, 14. Burgas ł portas *civitates*, Mt. Kmbl. p. 16, 10. Portas *castella*, Mk. Skt. Lind. Rush. 6, 6. [Latin *portus*. '*Portus* est conclusus locus quo importantur merces et inde exportantur. Est et statio conclusa et munita,' Du Cange. Cf. Port- *in place-names*, e. g. Port-strǽt, Cod. Dip. Kmbl. vi. 323.]

port, es; *m. A gate, entrance:*—Port ł dure ł gæt *portam*, Mt. Kmbl. 7, 13. Eode đe Hǽlend in tempel in đone port (*in porticu*) Salamonnes, Jn. Skt. Rush. 10, 23. Fīf portas *quinque porticos*, Lind. Rush. 5, 2. Đa him sǽton sundor on portum *qui sedebant in porta*, Ps. Th. 68, 12. [*O. Frs.* porte: *O. Sax.* porta: *O. H. Ger.* pforta; *f.*: *Icel.* port; *n.* From Latin *porta*.]

Port, es; *m. The name attributed to one of the Saxon invaders of Britain, apparently an inference from a place-name:*—Hēr cuom Port on Bretene ... on đære stōwe đe is gecueden Portesmūþa, Chr. 501; Erl. 14, 12.

port-cwēn, e; *f. A harlot, woman of the town:*—Portcuoene ł synnful *peccatrix*, Lk. Skt. Lind. 7, 37, 39. Miđ portcuoenum *meretricibus*, 15, 30. Portcuoenes *meretricis*, Rtl. 106, 28. Portcuoene *meretrici*, 106, 30. Portcuoeno *meretrices*, Mt. Kmbl. Lind. 21, 31, 32. [Cf. *Icel.* port-kona *a harlot*; port-hūs *a brothel*; port-līfi *prostitution*.]

Portes-mūþa. v. Port.

port-geat, es; *n. The gate of a town:*—Portgeat *porta*, Wrt. Voc. i. 36, 37: 84, 38. Fare đæt wīf tō đam portgate *perget mulier ad portam civitatis*, Deut. 25, 7. Đā đā hē geneálǽhte đam portgeate (cf. đære ceastre gate, Lk. Skt. 7, 12), Homl. Th. i. 490, 30. Đæt portgeat getācnaþ sum līchamlīc andgit đe menn þurh syngiaþ, 492, 13. Hē đa portgeatu ealle beeode, Homl. Skt. i. 23, 507.

port-gerēfa, an; *m. A port-reeve* (v. port, II):—Portgerēfa ođđe burhwita *municeps*, Wrt. Voc. i. 18, 41. Đes portgerēfa *hic prefectus urbis*, Ælfc. Gr. 14; Som. 16, 56. Man cȳđde đam portgerēfan (*the case is one of buying in the market at Ephesus*), Homl. Skt. i. 23, 643. Port-reeves of London, Canterbury, Bodmin, and Bath are mentioned in the charters, and from the Laws (v. under *port*, II) it is seen that one of the duties of such officials was to witness all transactions by bargain and sale effected within the *port*. See Kemble's Saxons in England, ii. c. 5. [Robert of Gloucester mentions two portreeves of Oxford, 'William the Spicer and Geffray of Hencsei that tho were Portreven,' p. 540.] [*Icel.* port-greifi.]

port-geriht, es; *n. A town-due, due paid by a town:*—Đæs tūnes cȳping and seó innung đara portgerihta *uillae mercimonium censusque omnis civilis*, Cod. Dip. Kmbl. iii. 138, 10.

portian; *p.* ode *To pound, bray in a mortar:*—Đeáh đū portige đone dysegan on pīlan swā mon corn dēþ mid piilstæfe ne meaht đū his dysi him from ādrīfan *si contuderis stultum in pila, quasi ptisanas feriente desuper pilo, non auferetur ab eo stultitia ejus*, Past. 37, 2; Swt. 265, 25. v. pyrtan.

portic, es; *m.* I. *a porch, covered entrance, portico:*—Portic *porticus*, Ælfc. Gr. 11; Som. 15, 22: Wrt. Voc. i. 58, 2. Se mere hæfþ fīf porticas. On đām porticon læg mycel menigeo geādludra, Jn. Skt. 5, 2–3. II. *an enclosed place, a place roofed in:*—Sinewealt cleofa *vel* portic *absida*, lytle porticas *cancelli*, Wrt. Voc. i. 58, 34, 37. Ic Eádwine munek læi innan mīnre portice (*cell*) anbūtan nōntīde, Chart. Th. 321, 31. Portic *abscidam* (*absidam*), Wrt. Voc. ii. 9, 45. III. *part of a church, porch, vestibule*; also *an arched recess.* '*Porticus* aedis sacrae propylaeum in porticus formam exstructum, in quo consistebant Catechumeni et Poenitentes: improprie pro sanctuarium, seu orientalis ecclesiae pars in qua majus altare erigi solet,' Du Cange:—Hālig portic *sanctuarium*, Ps. Surt. 72, 17: 73, 7: 82, 13. Of đæs portices dura þærscwolde wæs gesȳne đæt đa swađo wǽron ǽrest ūtwearde ongunnen ... Đeós circe mid đȳs portice mihte hūhwego fīf hund manna befōn, Blickl. Homl. 207, 10–14. His līchaman Eorcenwald on portice (*in porticu*) his cyrcan sumre geheóld ... Đā dydon hī his līchaman up of đam portice and on cyrcan neáh weofode byrgan wolde, Bd. 3, 19; S. 550, 5–10. Wæs hē bebyriged on Sc̄e Paules portice (*porticu*), se is on Sc̄e Andreas cyricean, 5, 23; S. 645, 18. His līchoma on đære cyricean norþportice (*porticu aquilonali*) wæs bebyriged; in đam eác swylce ealra đæra æfterfylgendra ærcebiscopa līchoman syndon bebyrged būtan twegra; heora līchaman sindon on đære cyricean sylfre gesette, forđan đe on đone forecwedenan portic mā ne mihte, 2, 3; S. 504, 34–38. Đæt hē wībedas sette and porticas worhte and tōdǽlde binnan đære cyricean weallum *ut poneret altaria, distinctis porticibus intra muros ecclesiae*, 5, 20; S. 641, 42. Synd þrȳ porticas emb đa ciricean ūtan geworhte, and đa ealle fægere ufan oferworhte and oferhrȳfde, Blickl. Homl. 125, 23. [*O. H. Ger.* pforzih *porticus, vestibulum, peribolus, atrium*.] v. hūsel-, norþ-, sūþ-portic.

port-mann, es; *m. A towns-man, citizen:*—Portman *civis*, Wrt. Voc. i. 84, 39. Eádgār æþeling com mid eallum Norþhymbram tō Eoferwīc, and đa portmenn wiđ hine griđedon, Chr. 1068; Erl. 207, 2. Se portgerēfa and đa yldostan portmenn (*of Ephesus*), Homl. Skt. i. 23, 749.

port-strǽt, e; *f. A town-road, public way:*—In đære portstrǽt; and swā æfter đære strǽte, Cod. Dip. Kmbl. iii. 36, 22. Of đære portstrǽte, 52, 20. Portstreet occurs as a proper name, vi. 323, col. 2.

port-wara, an; *m. A citizen:*—Lulla gebohte đis lond miþ ealra đeassa portweorona gewitnesse, Cod. Dip. Kmbl. ii. 3, 11.

port-weall, es; *m. A town-wall:*—Man gengde ābūtan đone portweall, Homl. Skt. i. 23, 267. Đa heáfodleásan man hēngc on đa portweallas, and man sette heora heáfda būton đām portweallon on đām heáfodstoccum, and đǽr flugon hrōcas and hremmas intō đære byrig geond đa portweallas, and tōsliton đa hālgan Godes dyrlingas, 23, 73–80.

port-wer, es; *m. A citizen*; civis, Rtl. 187, 23.

posa. v. pusa.

posel *a small lump, a pill:*—Gǽten smeoro geþȳd tō poslum swelge *let him swallow goat's grease squeezed to pills*, Lchdm. i. 354, 9. v. next word.

posling, es; *m. A pill:*—Wyrc lytle poslingas feówer *make four little pills*, Lchdm. i. 76, 23. v. preceding word.

post, es; *m. A post, pedestal:*—Post *basis*, Wrt. Voc. i. 47, 20: *postis*, 86, 29: Ælfc. Gr. 9, 28; Som. 11, 45. Under đām sylfum postum *sub ipsos postes*, 47; Som. 48, 17. Hē āhēng đæt dust on ǽnne heáhne post ... Đæt hūs wearđ đā forburnen būton đam ānum poste, Swt. A. S. Rdr. 101, 186–191. [*O. H. Ger.* pfosto. From Latin.]

postol, es; *m. An apostle:*—Đara postolra *apostolorum*, Lk. Skt. p. 2, 2. Đa đe cwēdun đās tō đǽm postolum *quae dicebant apostolas haec*, Rush. 24, 10. [*Icel.* postuli: *O. H. Ger.* postul.] v. apostol.

potian *to push, thrust, strike, butt:*—Hwæt wǽron hī, būton fearra gelīcan, đā đā hī, mid leáfe đære ealdan ǽ, heora fȳnd mid horne līchamlīcere mihte potedon? Homl. Th. i. 522, 25. Đa deóflu hȳ potedon and þoddetton đa earman sāwle and hēton hȳ ūt faran rađe of đam līchaman swīđe heardlīce, Wulfst. 235, 15. [From Celtic, *Gael.* put *to push, thrust*: *Welsh* pwtio *to push, poke*.]

pott, es; *m. A pot:*—Dō on ǽnne neówna pott, Lchdm. i. 378, 21. [From Celtic, Welsh *pot*.]

prætt, es; *m. Craft, art, wile, trick:*—Præt, prætt *astu*, Ælfc. Gr. 43; Zup. 257, 8. Wō dōmas and prættas, Anglia viii. 336, 40: Wulfst. 245, 2. Prættum *artibus*, Hpt. Gl. 459, 23. Ongeán þūsendfealde derigende prattas *contra mille nocendi artes*, 424, 46. [Prat, pratt *a trick, wicked action*, Jamieson's Dict.: cf. *Laym.* mid pretwrenche, 81: mid prætwrenchen (2nd MS. felle wrenches), 5302: *Icel.* prettr *a trick*.] v. next word.

prættig, pætig; *adj. Wily, crafty, astute:*—Præt *astu*, pætig *astutus*, Ælfc. Gr. 43; Zup. 257, 8. Ic beó pætig *callidus fio*, 26, 2; Zup. 154, 11. Pætig *callida*, Germ. 389, 21: *astutus*, Wrt. Voc. i. 76, 14. Petig *sagax* vel *gnarus* vel *astutus* vel *callidus*, 47, 36. Næddre seó pætige *serpens ille callidus*, Hymn. Surt. 61, 32. Wille gē wesan prættige (*versipelles*), Coll. Monast. Th. 32, 27. Prættigustan deóre *callidissime bestiole*, Wrt. Voc. ii. 127, 50. [*Scot.* pratty *and* ill-pretty *tricky*: cf. *Orm.* nis he nohht hinnderrȝæp ne pratt. In *Prompt. Parv.* praty *elegans, formosus*. *Icel.* prettugr, prettōttr *deceitful, tricky*; pretta *to deceive*. Perhaps of Celtic origin. Cf. Cornish *prat* an act or deed, a cunning trick.] v. preceding word.

prāfost, prōfost, es; *m.* I. *an officer:*—Gerēfa ođđe prāfost *prepositus*, Wrt. Voc. i. 72, 67. Valerianus Decies prāfest đæs cāseres *Valerian, officer of the emperor Decius*, Shrn. 117, 12. Valerianus se prāuost, 117, 16. Pharaones þēnas swungon đa đe bewiston Israēla folces ... Đā cōmon Israēla folces prāfostas (*praepositi*) *the officers of the children of Israel* (A. V.), Ex. 5, 14–15. II. *an officer of a monastery*; praepositus: v. Smith's Dict. of Christian Antiquities, '*praepositus* the second in command under the abbot in a monastery, the *prior claustralis*;' also 'that member of a chapter who takes charge of the administration of the capitular estates:'—Be mynstres prāfaste. For oft hit getīmaþ, đæt swȳđe hefigtȳme ungeþwǽrnessa on mynstre āspringaþ þurh đæs geendebyrdan prōfostes misfadunge ... him þincþ, đæt hē sȳ ōđer abbod ... đis gelimpþ swīđust on đām stōwum, đǽr se prōfost on gȳmenne biþ geset fram đām ylcan biscopum ođđe abbodum, đe đone abbod ... on đam weorđmente settan ... Him þincþ, đæt hē đam abbode ne þyrfe hȳran ... Wē forđī foresceáwiaþ ... đæt eal mynstres fadung on đæs abbodes dōme and tǽcinge simle stande ... Gif ... hit đam abbode rǽd þince, swā hwilcne swā se abbod geceóse mid geþeahte đara brōđra đe God ondrǽdaþ, sette đæne him tō prāuoste. Se sylfa prāuost dō mid ārweorđnesse eal đæt him fram đam abbode getǽht biþ

. . . forđí swá miclan swá hé furđur on weorđmynte forlǽten biþ, swá miclan hé sceal geornlícor healdan regules beboda, R. Ben. pp. 124-125: 46, 21. Đá æteówde Benedictus on swefne hine sylfne đam munece đe hé tó ealdre geset hæfde ofer đam mynstre, and his prófoste samod, Homl. Th. ii. 172, 15. Đá hé đá monig geár biscophád þegnode and swylce eác đysses mynstres gémyne dyde, and đǽr práuast and ealdormen gesette *qui cum annis multis episcopatum administraret, et hujus quoque monasterii statutis propostis curam gereret*, Bd. 3, 23; S. 555, 7. [*Icel.* prófastr: *O. H. Ger.* próbist *praepositus, economus.* From Latin forms *praepostus, propostus.*] v. mynster-práfost.

práfost-folgoþ, es; *m. The office of provost:*—Gif se práfast þurh þreále nele gerihtan, hé sý áworpen of đam práfastfolgoþe (*de ordine prepositure*), R. Ben. 126, 5.

práfost-scír, e; *f. Provostship:*—Đa sylfan him (*the provost*) práfostscíre (prófost-, MSS. O. F.) betǽhtan, đe đæne abbod tó abbodháde gecuran, R. Ben. 124, 16.

pranga, Wrt. Voc. i. 56, 50, *read* wranga.

prass *pomp, array, parade:*—Hwǽr syndon démra dómstówa? hwǽr ys heora rícetere and heora prass and orgol, búton on moldan beþeaht and on wítum gecyrred? Wulfst. 148, 32. Se cásere fór intó Efese mid đrymme and mid prasse, Homl. Skt. i. 23, 26. Hí Pantan streám mid prasse bestódon, Eást-Seaxena ord and se æschere *they stood by Panta's stream in proud array, the East-Saxon line and the host of the ashen boats*, Byrht. Th. 133, 51; By. 68.

predicere, es; *m. One who announces, a preacher:*—Praedico ic bodige ođđe foresecge, *praedicator* prydecere (predicere, MSS. C. U.), Ælfc. Gr. 47; Zup. 276, 1. [*O. H. Ger.* predigari: *Icel.* prédikari.]

predician; *p.* ode *To preach:*—Hé férde Godes ríce prediciende (*euangelizans*), Lk. Skt. 8, 1. [*O. L. Ger.* predikón: *O. H. Ger.* predigón: *Icel.* prédika. From Latin *praedicare.*]

prénan. v. be-prénan.

preón, es; *m. A pin, brooch, fastening:*—Preón *vel* oferfeng *vel* dalc *fibula*, Wrt. Voc. i. 40, 53. Dolc ođđe preón *spinther*, 74, 59. Hió becwiþ hyre ealdan gewíredan preón is an .vi. mancussum, Chart. Th. 537, 35. Ic geann mínre yldran dehter . . . ánes bendes and twegea preóna[s] and ánes wífscrúdes ealles, 530, 21. Menum ɫ preónum *monilibus*, Hpt. Gl. 434, 71. Mynas, preánas *lunulas*, 458, 30. [Þe vikelare ablent þene mon and put him preon in eien, A. R. 84, 2. Gol prenes and ringes, Gen. and Ex. 1872. *Scot.* preyne, prene, prin *a pin made of wire*: *Icel.* prjónn (Vigfusson compares with Gael. prine) *a pin, knitting-pin*: *M. H. Ger.* pfrieme: *Ger.* pfriem: *Du.* priem. Cf. also *M. English* prene *to stick with a pin*: *Yorkshire Dialect* prin-cod *a pin-cushion*: *Scot.* prein *to pin*; prein-cod, -head *pin-cushion, -head*: *Icel.* prjóna *to knit.*] v. eár-, feax-, mentel-preón.

preóst, es; *m. A priest:*—Preóst *clericus*, Wrt. Voc. i. 42, 24: 71, 77. Hé wæs tó preóste besceoren fram him *attonsus est ab eo*, Bd. 5, 19; S. 638, 21. (v. be-sceran.) Riht is đæt preóstas regollíce libban, L. I. P. 16; Th. ii. 324, 2. Wé lǽraþ đæt preóstas geóguþe geornlíce lǽran, L. Edg. C. 51; Th. ii. 254, 25. Wé lǽraþ đæt preósta gehwilc, tóeácan láre, leornige handcræft georne, 11; Th. ii. 246, 16. [*O. L. Ger.* préstar: *O. Frs.* préstere: *O. H. Ger.* priestar, préstar: *Icel.* prestr. From Latin *presbyter.*] v. hand-, híréd-, mæsse-, mynster-preóst.

preóst-hád, es; *m. Priest-hood:*—Sumne Godes mann preósthádes *clericum quendam*, Bd. 1, 7; S. 476, 36. Gé sint ácoren kynn Gode and kynelíces preósthádes *vos autem genus electum regale sacerdotium*, Past. 14, 5; Swt. 85, 19. Iulianus nolde gehealdan his preósthád on riht, Homl. Skt. i. 3, 290.

preóst-heáp, es; *m. A band of priests, the clergy:*—On preóstheápe *in clero*, Wrt. Voc. ii. 45, 22.

preóst-lagu, e; *f. Law affecting priests:*—Norþhymbra preósta lagu . . . Ælc preóst finde him .xii. festermen đæt hé preóstlage wille healdan mid rihte, L. N. P. L. 2; Th. ii. 290, 1-16.

preóst-scír, e; *f. The district in which a priest exercises his duties, a parish:*—Ne spane nán mæssepreóst nánne mon of óđre cyrcean hýrnysse tó his cyrcan, ne of óđre preóstscýre lǽre, đæt mon hys cyrcan geséce, L. E. I. 14; Th. ii. 410, 31.

preówt-hwíl, e; *f. The time taken to close and open the eye, the twinkling of an eye:*—Preówthwíle, beorht (bearhtme?) *atomo* (ἐν ἀτόμῳ *in an instant. See also* Anglia viii. 318, 43:—564 *atomi* wyrcaþ án *momentum*, 4 *momenta* gefyllaþ *minutum*, 2½ *minuta*, gewyrcaþ ánne prican, 4 prica gewyrceaþ áne tíd), Hpt. Gl. 462, 9. On ánre preówthwíle on đære endenéxtan býman *in ictu oculi, in nouissima tuba*, Homl. Th. ii. 568, 23. Cf. be-príwan *to wink with the eye*, Wulfst. 148, 13.

press, e; *f. A press* (in a list of requisites for spinning), Anglia ix. 263, 12. Cf. *Pannicipium* a presse, Wülck. 600, 14: *vestiplicium*, 619, 10.

prica, an; *m.* pricu (e), an, e (?); *f.* I. *a point, spot, dot:*—Prica *punctus*, Ælfc. Gr. 28, 7; Som. 32, 57. Se forma prica on đam ferse is geháten *media distinctio*, đæt is, onmiddan tódál, 50; Som. 51, 15. Mǽltanges prica *centrum*, Wrt. Voc. i. 39, 62. Án i ođđe án prica ne gewít fram đære ǽ *iota unum aut unus apex non praeteribit a lege*, Mt. Kmbl. 5, 18. Đonne miht đú ongitan đæt eorþan ymbhwyrft is eall wiđ đone heofon tó mettanne swylce án lytel pricu (lytlu price, Cott. MS.) on brádan brede *omnem terrae ambitum ad coeli spatium puncti constat obtinere rationem*, Bt. 18, 1; Fox 62, 4. Swilce án prica (price, Cott. MS.), Fox 62, 20. Hé sǽde đæt eal đes middaneard nǽre đé máre dríges landes ofer đone mycelan gársecg, đonne man ǽnne prican ápricce on ánum brádum brede, Wulfst. 146, 21. Heó hæfþ on ǽghwylcum leáfe twá endebyrdnyssa fægerra pricena, and đa scínaþ swá gold, Lchdm. i. 188, 14. II. *a very small portion* (cf. *Fr.* ne point) (a) of space:—Ne gǽþ heora náđer ǽnne prican ofer đam đe him gesette is, Lchdm. iii. 252, 17. (b) of time, *the fourth or fifth part of an hour:*—Feówer *puncti*, đæt synt prican, wyrcaþ áne tíd on đære sunnan ryne, and forđan ys se prica gecweden forđan seó sunne ástíhþ pricmǽlum on đam dægmǽle . . . Syx and hundnigontig prican beóþ on đam dæge, and đa prican habbaþ *minuta* twá hund and feówertig, Anglia viii. 317, 16-24. Se án dæg hæfþ syx and hundnigontig prica (?) . . . feówer prica (?) gewyrceaþ áne tíd, 318, 10, 46: 320, 12 (cf. prican, l. 20). In Lchdm. iii. 222 the *prica* is a fifth of an hour:—On ánre nihta eald móna, and on .xxix. scínþ .iiii. pricena lengce. On twegra nihta eald móna, and on .xxviii. scínþ áne tíd and iii pricena, etc.: cf. with the calculations on this page the statement at 242, 7:—Dæghwamlíce đæs mónan leóht byþ weaxende ođđe waniende feówer prican. See also Homl. Th. i. 102, 30.

pricel, es; *n.* (?) *A prickle, sharp point:*—Seó rǽding pingþ đæne scoliere mid scearpum pricele, Anglia viii. 308, 1. Wiđ priclom *contra stimulos*, Lk. Skt. p. 3, 6. [*Prompt. Parv.* prykyl *stimulus, aculeus*: *Du.* prikkel.] v. pricels.

pricele (a ?), an; *f. m.* (?) *A point, very small thing:*—Foruord ɫ pricle *iota*, pricle ɫ stæfes heáfod *apex*, Mt. Kmbl. 5, 18. Đone hlætmesto pricclu (pricla, Rush.) *nouissimum minutum*, Lk. Skt. Lind. 12, 59.

pricels, es; *m.* (?) *A sharp point:*—Pricelsum *stimulis*, Hpt. Gl. 514, 13. v. pricel.

prician, priccan *to prick:*—Ic pricige *pungo*, Ælfc. Gr. 28, 5; Som. 31, 59: 28, 7; Som. 32, 57. *Punctus a pungendo dicitur*, forđan ys se prica gecweden, forđan hé pricaþ, Anglia viii. 317, 18. Đornas priciaþ, Homl. Th. ii. 88, 20. Hé hét đæs pápan lima gelóme prician, 312, 11. Đonne man ǽnne prican ápricce on ánum brádum brede, Wulfst. 146, 21.

pric-mǽlum; *adv. By points.* v. prica, II b.

pricung, e; *f. Pricking:*—Đornas priciaþ and đa welan gelustfulliaþ. Hí sind þornas đonne hí đa sáwla tóteraþ mid pricungum mislícra geþohta, Homl. Th. ii. 88, 22.

prím *prime, the first hour, six o'clock*; also *the service held at that hour*, v. prím-sang:—Prím *prima*, undern *tertia*, middæg *sexta*, Wrt. Voc. i. 53, 10-12. Onginnaþ heáfudcwido tó prím (*ad primam*), Rtl. 166, 17. Gibedd tó prím, 171, 27. On đysum tídum wé herien úrne scyppend . . . on dægréd, on prím, on undern, on middæg, on nón, on ǽfen, on nihtsange, R. Ben. 40, 13. Ic sang prím and seofon seolmas, Coll. Monast. Th. 33, 27. [*Icel.* prími; *m.*: príma; *f.*: prím; *n.*]

prím-sang, es; *m. Prime-song, the service at the first hour:*—Đa seofon tídsangas . . . prímsang . . . , L. Ælfc. C. 19; Th. ii. 350, 6: R. Ben. 40, 6. Ælce Sunnanniht bútan Lenctene . . . dægrédsang, prímsang . . . mid alleluian sýn gesungene, 39, 18.

princ (?) *a prick:*—On prince *in ictu, in puncto*, Hpt. Gl. 462, 8. [Jamieson gives prink *to prick.*]

prior, es; *m. A prior:*—Hine God geuferade đæt hé weard prior, Chart. Th. 445, 34.

prít. v. prýt.

príwan. v. be-príwan, preówt-hwíl.

prod-bor (?):—On prodbore *in foro*, Mt. Kmbl. Rush. 11, 16. On protbore, 20, 3. [Cf. (?) bor *and* prod a *pointed instrument*; to prod *to prick*, Jamieson, and common in many parts of England, as if *foro* were connected with *forare.*]

prófast. v. práfost.

prófian; *p.* ode *To esteem* or *regard as:*—Gif feorrancumen man búton wege gange, and hé đonne náwđer ne hrýme ne hé horn ne bláwe, for þeóf hé is tó prófianne *he is to be regarded as a thief*, L. Wih. 28; Th. i. 42, 25: L. In. 20; Th. i. 116, 2. [Cf. *Icel.* prófađr *convicted of*: nema þeir fengi af sér prófat *unless they can clear themselves of it.*]

prút; *adj. Proud, arrogant:*—Mægen prútes unnytt Gode *virtus superbi inutilis Deo*, Scint. 17. Sáwl prútes (*superbi*) byþ forlǽten fram Gode, 17. Wiđerwyrdnyss prúte (*sublimes*) geniþerude, 46. Đǽr mihton geseón Winceastre leódan rancne (prútne, MS. F., v. note, p. 336) here and unearhne, đæt hí be hyra gate tó sǽ eodon, Chr. 1006; Erl. 140, 26. [Þa iward þe king on mode prut, Laym. 8828. Prud (*the opposite of* edmod), A. R. 176, 17. *Icel.* prúđr *gallant, brave, magnificent.*] v. prút-líce, -scipe, prútung, prýt.

prutene, an; *f.* A plant-name, *artemisia abrotanon:*—Đone súþernan wermód, đæt is prutene, Lchdm. ii. 236, 20.

prútlíce; *adv. Proudly, in a stately manner, magnificently:*—Wel gelóme hig áspyriaþ đæs solecismus unþeáwas . . . and eác hig prútlíce gýmaþ đæs miotacismus gefleard, Anglia viii. 313, 25. Wé prútlíce (*in splendid fashion*) gecýđaþ uplendiscum preóstum đæt wé be đissum circul gerǽdd habbaþ, 325, 40. [*Icel.* prúðliga *stately, magnificently.* Cf. prúð-leikr *show, ornament.*]

prūt-scipe, es; *m. Pride, arrogance*:—Prūtscipes *arrogantiae, superbiae*, Hpt. Gl. 432, 50. Múþ heora spræc prūtscipe (*superbiam*), Ps. Lamb. 16, 10.

prūtung, e; *f. Pride, haughtiness*:—Prūtunge *fastu, elatione, superbio*, Hpt. Gl. 434, 13.

prȳd, prȳde, prydecere. v. prȳt, prȳte, predicere.

prȳt, e; *f. Pride, pomp*:—Mōd ofermōdignysse mid prȳte byþ gewemmed *animus superbiae tumore corrumpitur*, Scint. 13. Mid nānre prȳte ðū ofermōdiga *nulla elatione superbias*, 46. Ne gerīsaþ heom prīta ne īdele rænca ne micele ofermētta, L. I. P. 10, note; Th. ii. 318, 31. Riht is ðæt abbodas nǽfre ymbe woruldcara ne īdele prȳda ne carian tō swȳðe, 13; Th. ii. 320, 35. [We ne beoð iboren for to habbene nane prudu ne nane oðre rencas, O. E. Homl. i. 7, 27.] v. woruld-prȳt *and next word.*

prȳte, an; *f. Pride, haughtiness*;—Of ȳdelum gylpe biþ ācenned prȳte, Homl. Th. ii. 220, 32. Prȳte heáge ūt āwyr[p]þ *elatio excelsos deiecit*, Scint. 46. Gelīce ðām dwæsan ðe for heora prȳtan lēwe (sāre, MS. C.), (*on account of the infirmity of pride in them*) nellaþ beorgan, Wulfst. 165, 9. Se ðe for his prȳdan Gode nele hȳran . . . hē sceal misfaran, 178, 19. Sume men for heora prȳtan forhogiaþ ðæt hī hȳran godcundan ealdran, L. Eth. vii. 21; Th. i. 332, 33. [Þat ece fer þe ham ȝearcod was for hare prede, O. E. Homl. i. 221, 1. *Laym.* prude, prute: *R. Glouc.* prute: *Ayenb.* prede: *Icel.* prȳði; *f. an ornament;* also *pride, pomp, bravery.*] v. preceding word.

prȳtian *to be* or *make proud, shew pride*:—Prītigeaþ *pipant*, Wrt. Voc. ii. 88, 80. [Þe luttele mon . . . bute he mote himseluen *pruden*, he wole maken fule luden, Salm. Kmbl. p. 247, 25. Ofte onder þe uayre robes is þe zaule dyad be zenne, and mameliche ine þan þet ham *predeþ*. Yef þe pokoc him *prette* uor his uayre tayle, and þe coc uor his kombe hit ne is no wonder. . . . Ac man . . . ne ssel him naȝt *prede*, Ayenb. 258, 20–27. Prydyn or wax prowde *superbio*, Prompt. Parv. 413.]

psalm, psealm. v. sealm.

pūcel, es; *m. A goblin, demon*:—Wudewāsan *faunos*, pūcelas *priapos*, Germ. 394, 242. [Halliwell gives *puckle* a spirit or ghost. Cf. He wurþ bitauht þe *puke*, Misc. 76, 120. He shulde putten of so þe pouke (*the devil*), Piers P. 14, 190. *Icel.* pūki *a devil, imp*: *Dan.* pokker *devil, deuce*: *Welsh* pwca: *Irish* pūca *sprite, hobgoblin*, hence Puck in Shakspere.]

pucian *to poke* (?), *strike*:—Pucigende *repens*, Germ. 397, 493.

pudd, es; *m. A ditch, furrow*:—Puddas *sulcos*, Germ. 399, 338 [cf. puddle].

puduc, es; *m. A wen*:—Puducas *strumas*, Germ. 396, 258.

puerisc; *adj. Boyish*:—Ðȳ pueriscan *puerio*, Wrt. Voc. ii. 94, 48.

Pulgare; *pl. The Bulgarians*:—Hiliricos ðe wē Pulgare hātaþ, Ors. 3, 7; Swt. 110, 33.

pull, es; *m.*: e; *f. A pool, creek*:—Ondlong ðære strǽt tō māwpul; andlang pulles, Cod. Dip. Kmbl. iii. 79, 30–31. Of seges mere in ðæs pulles heáfod . . . of þornbrycge in ðone pull, and æfter ðam pulle in baka brycge . . . in dodhǽma pull, of ðam pulle in streám, 386, 12–19. Tō crampulle, 79, 12. Andlang Osrīces pulle, 18, 18: 19, 3. On æstege pul, 444, 7. [*Icel.* pollr. A Celtic word: *Welsh* pwll: *Irish* poll, pull.] v. pyll.

pullian; *p.* ode *To pull, pluck*:—Ða hreáþemȳs on ūre ondwlitan sper[n]don and ūs pulledon *vespertiliones in ora uultusque nostros ferebantur*, Nar. 15, 7. Gif him þince ðæt hē sceáp pullige, ne biþ ðæt gōd, Lchdm. iii. 176, 7. v. ā-pullian.

pull-spere, es; *n. A pool-spear, a reed* (*such as grows by pools*, cf. hreód-pōl *under* pōl):—Pulsper *harundinem*, Mt. Kmbl. Lind. 11, 7.

pumic, es; *m.* (?) *Pumice*:—Of felle āscafen mid pumice, Lchdm. ii. 100, 15. [*O. H. Ger.* pumiz *pumex.*] v. next word.

pumic-stān, es; *m. Pumice-stone*; pumex, Wrt. Voc. i. 38, 26.

pund, es; *n. A pound.* I. as a weight without reference to money:—Ān *uncia* stent on feówer and twentig penegum; twelf sīðon twelf penegas beóþ on ānum punde, Anglia viii. 335, 18. *Libra* is pund on Englisc, Ælfc. Gr. 50, 30; Som. 52, 8. Pund *praesorium* (*pressorium*), Wrt. Voc. ii. 118, 25. Maria nam ān pund (*libram*) deōrwyrðre sealfe, Jn. Skt. 12, 3. Ðæt īsen ðe biþ tō þrīmfealdum ordāle, ðæt wege .iii. pund, and tō ānfaldum ān pund, L. Edg. H. 9; Th. i. 260, 13. II. as a money-denomination, (a) of English money; *a pound, 240 pence*:—.xx. scillingas beóþ on ānum punde, and twelf sīðon twentig penega byþ ān pund, Anglia viii. 306, 35. Gā seó wǽge wulle tō .cxx. p̄. (tō healfan punde, MS. G.), L. Edg. ii. 8; Th. i. 270, 3. (b) of other money:—Ānum hē sealde fīf pund (*talenta*), Mt. Kmbl. 25, 15, 16, 20, 22. Hē sealde tȳn pund (*mnas*), Lk. 19, 13. Tȳn þūsend punda *decem millia talenta*, Mt. Kmbl. 18, 24. Pundes *libelli*, Wrt. Voc. ii. 52, 53: 91, 44. III. as a measure (cf. wæter-pund *norma*, Wrt. Voc. i. 39, 60) *a pint*, 'that is, a pound of water is a pint of water, and a pint of water is a pint for all liquids,' Lchdm. ii. 402:—Pund eles gewihþ .xii. penegum læsse ðonne pund wætres, and pund ealoþ gewihþ .vi. penegum māre ðonne pund wætres, etc., Lchdm. ii. 298, 16–26. [*O. L. Ger.* punt: *O. Frs.* pund: *O. H. Ger.* pfunt: *Goth. Icel.* pund. From Latin *pondo.*]

pund *a pound, an enclosure.* Cf. Si pundbreche, i. infractura parci, fiat, L. H. I. 40; Th. i. 540, 5. See also pyndan.

pundar, pundur *a plumb-line*:—Pundar *perpendiculum, modica petra de plumbo, quam ligant in filo quando aedificant parietes*, Txts. 112, 36. [Cf. punder *librilla*, 'librilla est baculus cum corrigia plumbata, ad librandum carnes,' Prompt. Parv. 416. Halliwell gives *punder*, to balance evenly, as an East-country word. *Icel.* pundari *a steel-yard.*]

pundere, es; *m. One who weighs*:—From boecerum ł punderum *a librariis*, Mt. Kmbl. p. 2, 2.

pundern. v. wǽg-pundern.

pundern-georn (?); *adj. Desirous of weighing* or *considering* (?):—Punderngeō *ponderator*, Kent. Gl. 545.

pund-mǽte; *adj. Weighing a pound*:—Gif hȳ on twā mǽl etaþ, sȳ gehealden ðæs pundmǽtan hlāfes se þridda dǽl tō ðam ǽfengifle, R. Ben. 63, 16.

pund-wǽg, e; *f. A pound-weight, a pound*:—Mon sceal simle tō beregafole āgifan æt ānum wyrhtan six pundwǽga, L. In. 59; Th. i. 140, 6. .xx. pundwǽga (-wēga, MS. B.) fōðres, 70; Th. i. 146, 19.

pung, es; *m. A small bag, purse*:—Pung *cassidele*, Txts. 54, 297: Wrt. Voc. i. 291, 19: ii. 13, 39. [*Goth.* puggs *a purse*: *Icel.* pungr: *O. H. Ger.* scaz-pfung *marsupium.*]

pungetung, e; *f. A pricking*:—Sió wamb gefēlþ sār ðonne se mon mete þigeþ and pungetunga and unlust metes, Lchdm. ii. 216, 21. v. pyngan.

punian; *p.* ode *To pound, beat, bray*:—Puna *pound* (*the roots*), Lchdm. iii. 292, 19. [Cf. Wicklif, Mt. 21, 44: it shal to gidre poune (*conteret*) hym. Halliwell gives *pun* as a West-country word, and quotes Florio: 'to stampe or punne in a morter.'] v. ge-punian.

Pūnice; *pl. The Carthaginians*:—Him cōmon ongeán Pūnice mid swā fela scipa *eo Carthaginienses cum pari classe venerunt*, Ors. 4, 6; Swt. 176, 11: 172, 25: 180, 5. Wæs geendad Pūnica ðæt æfterre gewinn *bellum Punicum secundum finitum est*, 4, 11; Swt. 202, 31. Ðiss gewearþ Pūnicum on ðæm teóþan geáre heora gewinnes, 4, 6; Swt. 176, 5. Claudius fōr eft an Pūnice, Swt. 178, 31.

punt *a punt, flat-bottomed boat*:—Punt *pontonium*, Wrt. Voc. i. 47, 63: *caudex*, 56, 26: *trabaria* vel *caudex*, 63, 36. [From Latin *ponto.*]

pur *a bittern* (?):—Hæferblǽte *vel* pur *bicoca*, Wrt. Voc. i. 21, 42. Rāradumbla, ðæt is pur *onocrotalus*, 62, 21. [*Purre* two sea-birds, the tern and the black-headed gull; pirre-, pyr-maw *a sea-bird*, E. D. S. Publ. Antrim and Down Glossary.]

pur-lamb, es; *n. A pur-lamb* (pur-lamb *a wether-lamb*, West of England, E. D. S. Publ. Old Farming Words, No. 6):—Ðæt lamb sceal beón ānwintre purlamb clǽne and unwemme *erit agnus absque macula, masculus, anniculus*, Ex. 12, 5.

purpure, an; *f. A purple garment*:—Constantinus hiene benǽmde ǽgðer ge ðæs onwaldes ge ðære purpuran ðe hē werede, Ors. 6, 31; Swt. 284, 23. Hī scrȳddon hine mid purpuran *induunt eum purpura*, Mk. Skt. 15, 17. Hē gemētte his āgenne sunu mid purpurum gegieredne (*purpuratus*) . . . hit næs þeáw ðæt ǽnig ōðer purpuran werede būton cyningum, Ors. 4, 4; Swt. 164, 30–35. Hiene hēt iernan on his āgenum purpurum, 6, 30; Swt. 280, 12. Hié woldon ða onwaldas forlǽtan, and ða purpuran ālecgan ða hié weredon *purpuram imperiumque deponerent*, Swt. 280, 21. [*Goth.* paurpaura: *Icel.* purpuri. From Latin.]

purpuren; *adj. Purple*:—Purpuren hrægl *clavus* vel *purpura*, Wrt. Voc. i. 40, 13.

pusa, posa, an; *m. A bag, scrip*:—'Nolite portare sacculum ne peram:' 'Ne bere gē mid eów pusan oððe codd' . . . Hwæt mǽnþ se pusa būton woruldlīce byrþene, Homl. Th. ii. 532, 19–24. Se rīca berþ māre ðonne hē behōfige tō his fōrmettum, se þearfa berþ æmtigne pusan, i. 254, 31. Āwurp stānas in tō ðām pusum, and besenc hȳ on sǽlīcum ȳþum, ii. 418, 6. Posa *peram*, Mk. Skt. Lind. 6, 8: Lk. Skt. Lind. 9, 3: 10, 4. [*O. H. Ger.* pfosa *marsupium, bursa*: *Icel.* posi *a bag*; cf. pūss.]

puslian *to pick out the best bits*:—Wyl on meolcum ōþ ðæt hié sȳn wel mearuwe, pusla snǽdmǽlum *pick them out by a bit at a time*, Lchdm. ii. 356, 13. 'Peuselen *summis digitis varia cibarria carpere*,' Kilian.

pȳcan, Pyhtas, pylece. v. pīcan, Peohtas, pilece.

pyle, es; *m.* (?) *A pillow*:—Pyle *cervical*, Ælfc. Gr. 9, 5; Som. 9, 2: *pulvillus*, Wrt. Voc. i. 284, 60: *pulvinar*, 81, 60. Lytel pile *pulvillus*, 25, 48. Wā ðǽm ðe willaþ under ǽlcne elnbogan leccgean pyle and bolster under ǽlcne hnecean. . . . Se legeþ pyle under ǽlces monnes elnbogan . . . *vae his qui consuunt pulvillos sub omni cubito manus, et faciunt cervicalia sub capite universae aetatis. . . . Pulvillos sub omni cubito manus ponere est* . . ., Past. 19, 1; Swt. 143, 13–15. Hit wæs þeáw mid him ðæt mon ymbe .xii. mōnaþ dyde ǽlces consules seti āne pyle hiérre ðonne hit ǽr wæs, Ors. 5, 11; Swt. 236, 7. [*Prompt. Parv.* pyliwe: *O. H. Ger.* pfuliwi; *n.* From Latin *pulvinus.*]

pyll, es; *m. A pool, pill* ('*Pill*, a small creek, *Hereford.* The channels through which the drainings of the marshes enter the river are termed *pills*,' Halliwell. *Pill*, a pool, a creek, E. D. S. Publ. Cornish Gloss. See also Seebohm's English Village Community, pp. 149–150):—

Andlang díce west on pull; of pylle on ford . . . eft on gerihte innan mycela pyll; of mycela pylle on smala pyll; andlang pylles . . . on ða díc innan holapyll; andlang holapylles, Cod. Dip. Kmbl. iii. 449, 11–22. v. pōl, pull.

pynca, an; *m. A point*:—On pincan *in puncto*, Hpt. Gl. 492, 77. Cf. pyngan.

pyndan *to shut up, dam.* [Moni punt hire word uorte leten mo ut, as me deþ water and ter mulne cluse, A. R. 72, 10. To pynde *includere*, Cath. Angl. 280.] v. for-, ge-pyndan; pynding.

pynding, e; *f. A dam*:—Ðæt wæter, ðonne hit biþ gepynd, hit miclaþ . . . ac gif sió pynding wierð onpennad, ðonne tōflēwþ hit eall, Past. 38, 6; Swt. 277, 8.

pyngan; *p.* de *To prick*:—*Punctus a pungendo dicitur*; forðan ys se prica gecweden, forðan hē pingþ oððe pricaþ, Anglia viii. 317, 18. Seó rǣding pingþ ðæne scoliere mid scearpum pricele, 308, 1. Hē wærlíce hine pynge mid sumum wordum *animum pungant*, Past. 40, 5; Swt. 297, 8. [Arthur up mid his spere . . . and pungde uppen Frolle þar he was on grunde, Laym. 23933. From Latin *pungere*.]

pyretre, an; *f. Bertram*; pyrethrum parthenium, Lchdm. iii. 12, 19.

pyrige. v. pirige.

pyrtan; *p.* te *To strike, beat*:—Wæs sceacen *vibratur*, pyrte *ferit*, Germ. 401, 47. v. portian.

pyse. v. pise.

pytt, es; *m.* I. *a pit, hole in the ground, a grave*:—Pyt *puteus*, Wrt. Voc. i. 84, 58. *Scrobs* ys pytt oððe díc, Ælfc. Gr. 9, 51; Zup. 66, 10. Heora mōd ys swā deóp swā grundleás pytt *sepulcrum patens est guttur eorum*, Ps. Th. 5, 10. Gif hwā pytt (*cisternam*) ādelfe and hine ne oferhelie and ðǣr fealle on oxa oððe assa, gilde ðæs pyttes hlāford ðæra nýtena wurð, Ex. 21, 33–34. Pytte *baratrum*, Wrt. Voc. ii. 11, 68. On fūlan pyt; of ðam pytte on dene, Cod. Dip. Kmbl. iii. 77, 20. On wulfputt; of ðam pytte on ða wōgan ǣc, 449, 31–32. Tō wulfpytte, Cod. Dip. B. i. 280, 20. Gelǣste man ā ðone sāwelsceat æt openum pytte (cf. æt openum græfe, L. Eth. v. 12; Th. i. 308, 5), Wulfst. 118, 7. Uton dōn hine on ðone ealdan pytt (*cisternam*), Gen. 37, 20. Ic wæs on pytt beworpen *in lacum missus sum*, 40, 15. Hē ādylfþ ðone pytt *lacum aperuit*, Ps. Th. 7, 15. Hwylces eówres assa befealþ on ānne pytt (*puteum*), Lk. Skt. 14, 5. Hē hēt ādelfan ǣnne gehwǣdne pytt, Homl. Th. ii. 162, 2. On hiere bryne gemulton ealle ða onlícnessa tōgædere and on pyttas besuncan, Ors. 5, 2; Swt. 216, 3. II. *a pit* (as in *pitted* with small-pox):—Pyt ful wyrmses *serpedo* (cf. *serpedo* a mesylle, 224, 9: a tetere, 267, 48), Wrt. Voc. i. 20, 4. [*O. H. Ger.* pfuzzi, pfuzza *puteus, cisterna*: *Ger.* pfütze: *Icel.* pyttr. From Latin *puteus*.] v. gang-, hor-, lām-, mōr-, rysc-, wæter-pytt, *and next word.*

pytted *pitted* (v. pytt, II), *marked with hollows*:—Ic gean mínon brēðer ðæs swurdes mid ðām pyttedan hiltan, Chart. Th. 559, 23.

Q

This letter occurs but seldom in Anglo-Saxon; in those native words where *qu* is now found, e. g. *quick, quoth, cw* or *cu* was written, *cwic, cuic, cwæþ, cuæþ*. In the glossary (belonging to the eighth century) given in Wrt. Voc. ii. 98 sqq. are six instances of words beginning with *qu*, and four others occur in the same volume; in the Blickling Gloss the form *quēmde* glosses *complacebam*, and the foreign word *reliquias* retained its original form.

R

rā, rāha; *gen.* rān; *m. A roebuck, a roe*:—Rāha *capria*, Wrt. Voc. ii. 103, 19. Raa *capriolus*, 129, 58: *capia* (=*caprea*), 128, 47. Rā *caprea*, 16, 79: i. 288, 15. Gyf man on huntuþe rān oððe rǣgean mid flāne gewǣceþ, Lchdm. i. 166, 24. Mǣre on huntunge heorta and rāna *cervorum caprearumque venatu insignis*, Bd. 1, 1; S. 474, 41. Ic gefeó heortas and rānn *capio cervos et damas*, Coll. Monast. Th. 21, 31. Rā ł gǣt *capras*, Rtl. 119, 16. *The word is found in names of localities*, e. g. On rāhweg: ðæt ondlong rāhweges on rāhdene, Cod. Dip. Kmbl. iii. 378, 22. Ðonan wið heortsolwe; ðonne wið rāhgelega, 391, 32. [*Prompt. Parv.* roo *capreus, capreolus*: *O. H. Ger.* rēho *capreolus*: *Icel.* rā *a roe*.] v. rāh-deór, rǣge.

rabbian; *p.* ode *To rage*:—God lǣt ðone deófol Antecrist rabbian and wēdan sume hwíle, Wulfst. 84, 11. [From Latin.]

raca, an; *m. A rake*:—Raca *rastrum* vel *rastellum*, Wrt. Voc. i. 15, 10. [*O. H. Ger.* rehho *rastellum*.] v. ofen-raca, racu, ræce.

-raca. v. ǣrend-raca.

racca, an; *m. A cord, which forms part of the rigging of a ship*; cf. *Icel.* rakki *the ring by which the sailyard moves round the mast*:—Racca *anguina* (cf. cops *anguina*, 56, 56: bogen streng *anguina*, 35, 26. The word occurs among a list of names for ropes under the heading *de nave et partibus ejus*), Wrt. Voc. i. 63, 63.

racente, an; *f. A chain, fetter*:—Licgaþ mē ymbe írenbendas, rídeþ acenntan sāl, Cd. Th. 24, 3; Gen. 372. Gebunden mid gyldenre racentan *vinctum compedibus aureis*, Ors. 3, 9; Swt. 128, 12. Gerǣped mid his racentan, Met. 13, 8: 25, 37: 26, 78. Racentan slítan, 13, 29. Sleán on ða raccentan and on copsas, Bt. 38, 1; Fox 194, 32. Geseah hē his sylfes ungesǣlige stōwe and carcern (racetan, MS. B.) *videt suum infelix carcerem*, Bd. 5, 14; S. 635, 3. Hié hine hæfdon geþreátodne mid fýrenum racentum, Blickl. Homl. 43, 31. Ðonne hié mon on racentum beforan hiera triumphan drifon *regibus catenatis ante currum actis*, Ors. 5, 1; Swt. 214, 16. Restan on racentum, Cd. Th. 28, 11; Gen. 434. [*O. H. Ger.* rahhinza *baga*: *Icel.* rekendr; *pl. f. a chain*.] v. next two words.

racent-teáge, an; *f. A chain*:—Se ðe tōbræc ða raceteágan ymbūtan eówrum swuran *qui confregi catenas cervicum vestrarum*, Lev. 26, 13. v. next word.

racent-teáh; *gen.* -teáge; *f. A chain, fetter*:—Racenteáh *catena*, Wrt. Voc. i. 86, 30. Glæsen fæt on seolfenre racenteáge āhangen, Blickl. Homl. 209, 5. Unforedlícre racentāgæ *inextricabili collario*, Hpt. Gl. 455, 10. Mid rūmre racenteáge, Salm. Kmbl. 587; Sal. 293. Fæste mid ísenum racenteágum gewriðen, Homl. Th. i. 456, 9. Hē wæs mid racenteágum (raccentēgum, Lind.) gebunden *vinciebatur catenis*, Lk. Skt. 8, 29. Hine nān man mid racenteágum (raceteágum, MS. A.: racantēgum, Rush.) ne mihte gebindan. For ðam hē oft mid racenteágum (racontēgum, Rush.) gebunden tōslāt ða raceteága (racontēge, Rush.), Mk. Skt. 5, 3–4. Gebundenne on heardum raceteágum *vinctum catenis*, Jud. 16, 21. [*Laym.* raketeȝe: *O. E. Homl.* raketehe.] v. sweor-racentteáh *and preceding words.*

racete, raceteáh. v. racente, racent-teáh.

racian; *p.* ode. I. *to direct, rule* (cf. reccan):—Ðæt is ðæt hēhste gōd ðæt eallum swā gereclíce racaþ and swā eáðelíce hit eall set *est summum bonum, quod regit cuncta fortiter, suaviterque disponit*, Bt. 35, 4; Fox 162, 1. Gif hí næfdon ǣnne God ðe him eallum stiórde and racode and rǣdde, 34, 12; Fox 154, 5. Hē sceal rǣdan and racian (reccean, MS. T.) ōðra manna sāulum, R. Ben. 14, 6. Hē þeódum sceal racian (rǣdan, Kmbl.) mid rihte, Andr. Kmbl. 1041; An. 521. II. *to take a course* or *direction, to run* (cf. racu *a 'rake'*):—Hē his tungan gehealde ðæt hió ne racige on unnytte sprǣca *ne lingua per verba inutiliter defluat*, Past. 38, 5; Swt. 275, 19. Ne biþ nā gebeorhlíc, ðam ðe wið God hæfþ forworht hine sylfne, ðæt hē tō hrædlíce intō Godes hūse æfter ðam racige, ac stande ðǣr ūte, Wulfst. 155, 21. [Cf. (?) *Scott.* raik *to move expeditiously*; rack *a swift pace*: *Chauc.* rakel *hasty*: *Icel.* rakr *straight*; rak-leið, -leiðis *straightway*: *Swedish* raka *to run hastily*.]

racsan, raxan *to stretch one's self after sleep*:—Swā hē of hefegum slǣpe raxende āwōce, Guthl. 12; Gdwin. 60, 6. [Cf. Après dormer il ço espreche *raskyt hym*, Wrt. Voc. i. 152, 25. He (*sloth*) his brest knocked and roxed (raxed, MS. W.: roskid, MS. B.) and rored, Piers P. 5, 398. *Scott.* rax *to stretch the limbs*.]

racsian (?):—Racsode *libet*, Wrt. Voc. ii. 53, 62.

racu, e; *f.* I. *an exposition, explanation, orderly account, narrative*:—Racu *historia*, Wrt. Voc. ii. 42, 56. Geþeahtung, gesceád *vel* racu *conlatio*, i. *conductio, comparatio, conciliatio*, i. *datio, contentio*, 134, 44. Gesytnys ł racu *textus*, Hpt. Gl. 505, 61. Ūs ne segþ nā seó racu (*the narrative*), tō hwam hē hine sette, Ælfc. T. Grn. 19, 3: Jud. Thw. 156, 10. Ðætte on Arones breóstum sceolde beón āwriten sió racu ðæs dōmes *ut in Aaron pectore rationale judicii imprimatur*, Past. 13, 1; Swt. 77, 9. Ðære býcnendlícan race *allegoricae expositionis*, Bd. 5, 24; S. 647, 42. Race *historiae*, Hpt. Gl. 459, 68: *prosae*, 528, 1. Of racu *relatione*, 480, 24. Ic eom geþafa ðæs ðe ðū segst forþam ðe ðū hit hæfst gesēþed mid gesceádwíslícre race *assentior, cuncta enim firmissimis nexa rationibus constant*, Bt. 34, 9; Fox 146, 8. Ðū spenst mē on ða mǣstan sprǣce and on ða earfoþestan tō gereccenne. Ða race (*the explanation*) sōhton ealle ūþwitan, 39, 4; Fox 216, 15. Ic wolde reccan sume race, 41, 4; Fox 252, 14. Race *narrationem*, Hpt. Gl. 522, 54: Lk. Skt. 1, 1. Raca *conlationes*, Wrt. Voc. ii. 134, 47. Racum *relatibus*, Hpt. Gl. 529, 39. Hit is gerǣd on gewyrdelícum racum *in historical narratives*, Homl. Th. i. 58, 10. Rǣde him mon ða raca oððe líf ðæra heáhfædera, R. Ben. 66, 17. II. *comedy*:—Racu, tūnlíc spǣc *comedia*, Wrt. Voc. i. 27, 13: 82, 63. III. *the art of exposition, rhetoric*:—Swā gedēþ se dreámcræft ðæt se mon biþ dreámere and seó racu dēþ ðæt hē biþ reccere *sic musica musicos, rhetorica rhetores facit*, Bt. 16, 3; Fox 54, 32. IV. *an account, reckoning*:—Ðǣr wæs uneten racu unc gemǣne; ic onfēng ðín sār ðæt ðū mōste gesǣlig mínes ēðelríces eádig neótan, Exon. Th. 89, 20; Cri. 1460. [*O. H. Ger.* rahha *res, causa, ratio, fabula, circumlocutio*.] v. martyr-, riht-, swefn-racu; reccan.

racu, e; *f. A rake*:—Hē sceal habban race (cf. man sceal habban ofnrace, 265, 2), Anglia ix. 263, 7. v. raca, ræce.

racu, e; *f. A 'rake'* (*rake* a mountain track across a steep, Cumberland Gloss. e. g. the Lord's rake on Sca-fell), *a hollow path, bed of a stream*:—Cf. Andlang brōces; ðanon . . . on ða ealdan éarace, Cod. Dip. Kmbl. v. 122, 15; *and see* streám-racu. [Ryde doun þis ilk *rake*, bi ȝon rokke syde, Gaw. 2144. Out of the *rake* of riȝtwisnes renne suld he nevire, Alex. 3384.]

racu, e; *f. Rack* (?), *cloud, storm*:—Ic wille ǽhta and ágend eall ácwellan ða beútan beóþ earce bordum ðonne sweart racu (*the black clouds that overspread the sky at the Deluge*) stígan onginneþ, Cd. Th. 81, 34; Gen. 1355. [Cf. (?) In rede rudede upon *rak* rises þe sunne, Gaw. 1695. A *rak* and a royde wynde rose in hor saile, A myst and a merkenes was meruell to se, Destr. Tr. 1984. *Or* cf. (?) *Icel.* raki *wet*, rakr; *adj. wet.*]

Raculf, Ræculf, Reaculf, Reculf, Raculf-ceaster *Reculver* in Kent; Regulbium:—In ðam mynstre ðe is Reaculf nemned, Bd. 5, 8; S. 621, 33. Abbot on Raculfe, Chr. 692; Erl. 43, 13. Reculf, 669; Erl. 34, 26. See Cod. Dip. Kmbl. vi. 324.

rád, e; *f.* I. *riding, going on horseback* or *in a carriage.* v. rǽd-wægen:—Þeáw wæs ðam ylcan biscope ðæt hé ðæt weorc ðæs godspelles má þurh his fóta gange fremede ðonne on his horsa ráde *moris erat eidem antistiti opus evangelii magis ambulando per loca quam equitando perficere*, Bd. 4, 3; S. 566, 32. Nán mon for ðý ne rít ðe hine rídan lyste, ac rít for ðý ðe hé mid ðære ráde earnaþ sume earnunga. Sume mid ðære ráde earniaþ ðæt hié síen ðý hálran, Bt. 34, 7; Fox 144, 5-8. Ðá wearð his hors gesíclod, and feóll wealwigende geond ða corþan . . . Hé begann ðá tó gereccenne hú him on ráde getímode, Swt. A. S. Rdr. 101, 178. Gif mon on mycelre ráde oððe on miclum gangum weorðe geteorad, Lchdm. i. 76, 4. Ðæt man funde ǽnne man tó ráde oððe tó gange, L. Ath. v. 4; Th. i. 232, 15. Rynestrong on ráde, Exon. Th. 400, 9; Rä. 20, 7. I a. *going in a ship*:—Sió cwén bebeád áras fýsan tó ráde, sceoldon Rómwarena ofer heánne holm hláford sécean, Elen. Kmbl. 1960; El. 982. II. *an expedition on horseback*; in a hostile sense *a raid*:—Ðonne rídan ða yldestan men tó . . . and nimon eall ðæt hé áge, and fó se cyning tó healfum, tó healfum ða men ðe on ðære ráde beón, L. Ath. i. 20; Th. i. 210, 7. Gif áðor oððe mǽg oððe fremde ða ráde forsace, L. C. S. 25; Th. i. 390, 24. Cyninges þegnas oft ráde onridon, Chr. 871; Erl. 76, 11. III. *a road*; *in the compounds* brim-, hran-, hweogol-, segl-, streám-, swan-, wíg-rád. IV. *the name of the Runic R.* v. Exon. Th. 440, 10; Rä. 59, 15. *See also next word.* [*Icel.* reið *riding*; *a raid.*] v. mid-, on-, setl-, swegl-, þunor-rád.

rád, e; *f. Furniture* (*of a house*), *harness* (*of a horse*):—Rád byþ on recyde rinca gehwylcum sēfte and swíðhwæt ðam ðe sitteþ onufan meare mægenheardum ofer mílpaþas *in the house is for each man furniture soft, and* (*the furniture for the horse, the harness*) *very strong for him that sits on the stout steed, traversing the roads*, Runic pm. Kmbl. 340, 11; Rún. 5. [Cf. *Icel.* reiða *implements, outfit*; reiði; *n. harness*; reiði; *m. tackle, harness.*] v. brand-rád, ge-rǽde, rǽde-sceamol.

rád, L. Wih. 10; Th. i. 38, 21. v. rǽd.

-rád. v. ge-, sam-rád.

rád-cniht, es; *m. A title equivalent to that of* sixhynde man:—Si autem talis occiditur qualem supra nominavimus rádcniht, et quidam Angli vocant sixhændeman, Text. Roff. p. 38. In domo hominis, quem Angli vocant rádcniht, alii vero sexhendeman, Schmid. A. S. Gesetz. 93, note 6.

rád-here, es. v. rǽde-here.

rád-hors, es; *n. A horse for riding, a saddle-horse*:—Man sceal lǽtan hine rídan on ðæs cyninges rádhorse, Anglia ix. 35, 235. [*Wick.* rood-hors *a horse for a chariot*: *O. H. Ger.* reit-hros *currilis equus.*]

-rádian, rador, v. ge-rádian, rodor.

radre *glosses* bovistra, Wrt. Voc. ii. 11, 26: 102, 10.

rád-stefn, e; *f. A term of service performed by a mounted person* (?):—Gif þegen geþeáh ðæt hé þénode cyning, and his rádstefne rád on his híréde, L. R. 3; Th. i. 190, 19. v. stefn.

rád-wægen. v. rǽd-wægen.

rád-wérig; *adj. Weary with riding* or *journeying*, Exon. Th. 401, 19; Rä. 21, 14.

rǽcan; *p.* rǽhte. I. *intrans. To reach, extend, stretch forth*:—Ic wíde rǽce ofer engla eard, Exon. Th. 482, 26; Rä. 67, 7. Yldo rǽceþ wíde, Salm. Kmbl. 588; Sal. 294. Heó rǽhte mid handum tó heofoncyninge, Cd. Th. 292, 7; Sat. 437: Beo. Th. 1499; B. 747. Rǽhton wíde geond werþeóda wróhtes telgan, Cd. Th. 61, 1; Gen. 990. Ne hé sóðfæste lǽteþ ðæt hí tó unrihte willen handum rǽcean *ut non extendant justi ad iniquitatem manus suas*, Ps. Th. 124, 4. II. *trans. To reach, hold forth, offer, present*:—Ic rǽce *porrigo* vel *porgo*, Ælfc. Gr. 28, 5; Som. 31, 46. Hé ys se ðe ic rǽce (*porrexero*) hláf, Jn. Skt. 13, 26. For hwon ne rǽcst (*porrigis*) ðú ús ðone hwítan hláf? Bd. 2, 5; S. 507, 14. Rǽcþ (*porrigit*) hé him scorpionem? Lk. Skt. 11, 12. Ðǽr (*in hell*) hý leomu rǽcaþ (*stretch forth*) tó bindenne, Exon. Th. 99, 8; Cri. 1621. Eall ða weoruldgód hé gefeónde þearfum rǽhte and sealde *cuncta pauperibus erogare gaudebat*, Bd. 3, 5; S. 526, 26. Hé hláf bræc and him rǽhte, Lk. Skt. 24, 30. Se óðer rǽhte forþ (*protulit*) his hand, Gen. 38, 28. Heó rǽhte hire handa him tó, Th. Ap. 27, 1: Past. 36, 1; Swt. 247, 21. Ðara ánra ðe for neóde him þénunge æt ðæs mynstres ingange rǽcan scylon, R. Ben. 139, 11. Se gebúr sceal erian healfne æcer and rǽcan (cf. on bærene gebringan, Chart. Th. 145, 1) ðæt sǽd on hláfordes berne, Cod. Dip. Kmbl. iii. 450, 35. [*O. Frs.* réka: *O. H. Ger.* reihhen.] v. á-, ge-, mis-rǽcan.

ræcc, es; *m. A dog that hunts by scent*:—Ræcc *bruccus*, Wrt. Voc. i. 288, 29. [*Rache* a dog that discovers and pursues his prey by the scent, Jamieson. Rihht alls an hunnte takeþþ der wiþþ hise ȝæpe racchess, Orm. 13505. See other passages in Halliwell's Dict. *Icel.* rakki *a dog.*]

ræce, an; *f. A rake*:—Raece *rastrum*, Wrt. Voc. ii. 98, 28. v. raca.

ræced, reced, es; *m. n. A house, hall, palace*:—Reced sélesta (*Hrothgar's hall*), Beo. Th. 828; B. 412: 1545; B. 770. Ræced, 3603; B. 1799. Wið ðæs recedes weal, 658; B. 326: 1452; B. 724. His (*Lot*) recedes hleów, Cd. Th. 147, 18; Gen. 1441. Se beorn (*Noah*) reste on recede, 95, 25; Gen. 1584. In ræcede, Exon. Th. 314, 21; Mód. 17: 413, 11; Rä. 32, 3. Recyde, Runic pm. Kmbl. 340, 11; Rún. 5. Ic seah rǽplingas in ræced fergan, Exon. Th. 435, 2; Rä. 53, 1. Con hé sídne ræced fæste gefégan, 296, 7; Crä. 47. In ðæt dimme ræced (*a prison*), Andr. Kmbl. 2618; An. 1310. Reced, Beo. Th. 2479; B. 1237. Hwearf geond ðæt síde reced, 3966; B. 1981. Ðæt (*Hrothgar's hall*) wæs foremǽrost receda, 625; B. 310. Receda wuldor, Salomones templ, Cd. Th. 219, 23; Dan. 59. Hió on Sodoman wlítan meahton, gesáwon ofer since salo hlifian, reced ofer reádum golde, 145, 11; Gen. 2404. Ræced, Exon. Th. 381, 4; Rä. 2, 6. [*O. Sax.* rakud *used of the Temple.*] v. burg-, deáþ-, eorþ-, gim-, heáh-, heal-, hlín-, horn-, sund-, wín-ræced, *and next word.*

ræced-líc; *adj. Pertaining to a palace, palatine*:—Ræcedlíce *palatina*, Wrt. Voc. ii. 116, 7.

rǽcing, e; *f. Reaching, holding out, offering, presenting, extending*:—Hláfes mið rǽcing *panis porrectione*, Jn. Skt. p. 7, 3. Mið rácing honda *extensione manuum*, 8, 11.

rǽd, es; *m.* I. *counsel, advice*:—Rǽd *consilium*, Wrt. Voc. i. 73, 23. Ðæt hit nǽfre næs náðer ne his gewile, ne his geweald, ne his rǽd, L. C. S. 76; Th. i. 418, 12. Is micel þearf ðisse þeóde helpes and rǽdes, Wulfst. 243, 5: Elen. Kmbl. 1103; El. 553. Sum woruldwita wæs swýðe wís on rǽde Acitofel geháten . . . Ðá wæs se Acitofel mid Absalone on rǽde and rǽdde him hú hé mihte beswícan his fæder, Homl. Skt. i. 19, 196-203. Ðíne heortan tó rǽde gecyr *turn thine heart to listen to good advice*, Blickl. Homl. 113, 27. On ðone Drihten næs ic æt rǽde ne æt dǽde, ðǽr man mid unrihte N. orf ætferede, L. O. 3; Th. i. 178, 17. Gyf mon ðone hláford teó ðæt hé (*the accused person*) be his rǽde út hleópe, L. Eth. i. 1; Th. i. 282, 5, 12. Gif þeów ete his sylfes rǽde *if a slave eat flesh during a fast of his own accord* (i. e. *when his master does not give the meat.* v. the paragraph which precedes), L. Wih. 15; Th. i. 40, 11. Ráde, 10; Th. i. 38, 21. Ic ðá féng on mínne ágenne réd, Chart. Th. 322, 10. Gehýr míne word and mínne rǽd, Ex. 18, 19. Ðæt hí ðæs cynges rǽd hæfdon and his fultum and ealra witena, Chr. 1048; Erl. 178, 22. Rǽd gelǽran *to give good advice* (cf. sellan hálwende geþeahte, Bd. 1, 1; S. 474, 14), pref.; Erl. 3, 10. Rǽd sóhtan *consulunt*, Wrt. Voc. ii. 21, 3. II. *counsel, prudence, intelligence*:—Nis nán wísdóm ne nán rǽd náht ongeán God, Homl. Th. i. 82, 14. Ongeán ðam wíslícan rǽde ðe of Godes ágenre gyfe cymþ, se wiðerrǽda deófol sǽwþ réceleásnesse, Wulfst. 53, 6. Se man ána hæfþ gesceád and rǽd and andgit, Homl. Skt. i. 1, 99. III. *counsel, course of action that results from deliberation, plan, a resolution taken after deliberation, ordinance, decree*:—Sý ðes rǽd gemǽne eallum leódscipe, L. Edg. S. 2; Th. i. 272, 33. Se rǽd wæs ǽfre on his rǽdfæstum geþance, ðæt hé wircan wolde ða wunderlícan gesceafta, Ælfc. T. Grn. 2, 4. Hé him tó rǽde genom ðæt . . . *cui rei consilium utile ratus est, ut* . . . Ors. 4, 5; Swt. 166, 27. Hé Rómánum tó rǽde gelǽrde, ðæt hié fóren on Hannibales land, 4, 10; Swt. 200, 1. On ðisum rǽde (*the conspiracy against William Rufus*) wæs Oda, Chr. 1087; Erl. 224, 5. Ðæne rǽd (*paying the Danes*) gerǽdde Síríc, 991; Erl. 131, 19. Rǽd geþencean, Cd. Th. 19, 4; Gen. 286: 35, 28; Gen. 561. Rǽd áhicgan, 122, 24; Gen. 2031: 131, 24; Gen. 2181. Rǽdas *consulta*, Wrt. Voc. ii. 19, 54: *consulta, consilia*, 133, 80: Hpt. Gl. 504, 75: *decreta, judicia, edicta*, 433, 19. Gelǽrdan biscepas swelce níwe rǽdas swelce hié fol oft ǽr ealde gedydan, Ors. 4, 7; Swt. 184, 2. Manna wísdóm and heore rǽdas syndon náhtlíce ongeán Godes geþeaht, Chr. 979; Erl. 129, 26. IV. *what is advisable, benefit, advantage*:—Rǽd *opere pretium*, Wrt. Voc. ii. 64, 31. Rǽd biþ gif hé nimþ mealwan *it will be worth his while to take mallow*, Lchdm. ii. 238, 13. Biþ nú micel rǽd, ðæt hé him gebycge ðæt éce líf, Homl. Skt. i. 12, 122. Ðonne biþ hire rǽd ðæt frýnd ða forword habban, L. Edm. B. 7; Th. i. 256, 2. Ðæt heó ús sý þingere ondweardes rǽdes and éces wuldres *that she be for us an advocate for present profit and eternal glory*, Blickl. Homl. 159, 34. Hí him tó rǽde and tó frófre fundon *aliquid commodi adlaturum putabant*, Bd. 1, 12; S. 481, 7: 2, 5; S. 507, 31. Ðis him tó rǽde gecuron *hoc esse tutius decernebant*, 1, 23; S. 485, 34. Tó rǽde Angelcynne *to the advantage of the English*, 2, 1; S. 501, 39: Blickl. Homl. 199, 30: 205, 12. Tó hǽle and tó rǽde, 227, 4. Ðam þeódscype tó langsuman rǽde *to the lasting benefit of the nation*, L. I. P. 4; Th. ii. 308, 6. Eów sylfum tó rǽde, Ælfc. T. Grn. 12, 2. Rǽd árediam *to determine what is advisable*, L. Eth. vi. 40; Th. i. 324, 28. Ða ðe heora sylfra rǽd forlǽtaþ *those who forsake their own advantage*, Blickl. Homl. 103, 16. Rǽda fyrmest ðæt manna gehwylc ofer ealle óðre þinc ǽnne God lufige, L. I. P. 24; Th. ii.

338, 1. V. *a council*:—Hē eode tō ðæra Judēiscra rǣde and befrān, hwæt hī him feós geūðon, Homl. Th. ii. 242, 16. Se cyng beád heom ðæt hī cōmon mid. xii. mannum intō ðæs cynges rǣde, Chr. 1048; Erl. 180, 11. VI. *as a part of proper names, generally under the form* rēd (red ?). For a list of such names v. Txts, 603 sqq., and for similar *O. H. Ger.* names v. Grff. ii. 463. [*O. Sax.* rād: *O. Frs.* rēd: *O. H. Ger.* rāt: *Icel.* rāð.] v. feorh-, folc-, mis-, un-rǣd.

rǣd[e] *in composition of adjectives*, v. ān-, fæst-, heard-, hwæt-, læt-, wiðer-rǣd[e].

rǣdan. *Two verbs originally distinct seem to coalesce under this form, the strong* rǣdan; *p.* reórd, rēd; *pp.* rǣden: *Goth.* ga-rēdan: *O. Sax.* rādan; *p.* rēd, ried: *O. Frs.* rēda; *p.* rēd: *O. H. Ger.* rātan; *p.* riet, riat: *Icel.* rāða; *p.* rēð, *and the weak* rǣdan; *p.* rǣdde: *Goth.* ga-raidjan: *O. H. Ger.* ant-reitjan *ordinare*: *Icel.* g-reiða. *The strong forms are rare.* I. *to counsel, give advice*:—Ic rǣde ðē *consulo tibi*, Wrt. Voc. i. 49, 37. Girwan Godes tempel, swā hire gāsta weard reórd, Elen. Kmbl. 2043; El. 1023. Hē rād and rǣdde, rincum tǣhte hū hī sceoldon standan, Byrht. Th. 132, 18; By. 18. Ðæt folc eall hrȳmde, swā swā Josue him rǣdde, Jos. 6, 5 (20, Grn.). Rǣdende *consulentes, consilium dantes*, Hpt. Gl. 491, 20. II. *to ask advice, consult a person*:—Ic frīne *vel* ic rǣde *consulo*, i. *inquiro* (cf. ic frīne ðē *consulo te*, i. 49, 38), Wrt. Voc. ii. 133, 79. II a. *to consult, deliberate, take counsel upon a matter* (acc.) *with* (wið) *a person*:—Justinus rǣdde wið ða cristenan, hwæne hī tō bisceope ceósan wolde, Homl. Th. i. 434, 28. Wið ðone rǣdde Chromatius, and be his rǣde underfēng ealle ða cristenan, Homl. Skt. i. 5, 323. Him þūhte and ðǣm ðe hē hit wið rǣdde, L. Ath. v. 12; Th. i. 240, 27. Hī gamenlīce rǣddon *callide cogitantes*, Jos. 9, 4. Ðā gesomnedon hī gemōt and þeahtedon and rǣddon hwæt him tō dōnne wǣre *initum est consilium quid agendum*, Bd. 1, 14; S. 482, 36. Ðā rēdon (rǣddan, MSS. C.) hī him betweónum *consultatione habita*, Ors. 1, 14; Swt. 56, 20. Ðā ongunnon ða Pharisēi rǣdan *consilium inierunt*, Mt. Kmbl. 22, 15. Bisceopum gebyreþ ðæt symle mid heom wunian wel geþungene witan, ðæt hī wið rǣdan māgan, L. I. P. 10; Th. ii. 316, 23. Man rǣdan sceolde hū man ðisne eard werian sceolde, Chr. 1010; Erl. 144, 7. II b. *to debate, speak in council* (or (?) *to read.* v. VI b):—Rādaþ (rǣdaþ) ł maðeliaþ *concionantur, sermocinantur, loquuntur*, Hpt. Gl. 461, 1. Rǣdende ł wordiende *concionandi, loquentes*, 461, 35. II c. *to deliberate for the good of any one, look to, provide for*:—Mīnre sāwle rǣd on ēcnysse *animae meae in aeternum consules*, L. Ecg. P. iv. 67; Th. ii. 228, 3. Rǣdende *consulens*, i. *consilium tenens, providens*, Wrt. Voc. ii. 133, 77. Rǣdende *consulentes, succurrentes*, Hpt. Gl. 491, 20. III. *to resolve after deliberation, to determine, decide*:—Ðæt folc rǣdde be him ðæt hī woldon hine āhebban tō cyninge ... Ðā ðā Crist ongeat ðæs folces willan, Homl. Th. i. 162, 3–6. Ac ðeáh man hwæt rǣdde, ðæt ne stōd furðon ǣnne mōnaþ, Chr. 1010; Erl. 144, 9. Hī rǣddon ðæt hī woldon ðone cyng gesettan ūt of Englalandes cynedōme, 1075; Erl. 213, 10. Hī ealle ānmōdlīce rǣddon ðæt ealle his gesetnyssa āȳdlode wǣron, Homl. Th. i. 60, 4. Rǣdan *decernere*, Wrt. Voc. ii. 27, 67. III a. rǣdan on (cf. *Icel.* rāða ā einn *to attack one*) *to proceed against, take action against a person*:—Wæs ðam eorle Godwine and his sunan gecȳdd, ðæt se cyng and ða menn ðe mid him wǣron woldon rǣdon on hī, Chr. 1048; Erl. 178, 30. IV. *to rule, govern, direct* (with dat. or inst.):—Ðū ðe Israēla ǣðelum cynne reccest and rǣdest *qui regis Israel*, Ps. Th. 79, 1. Hē rǣt ūs and recþ *ipse reget nos*, 47, 12. Drihten mē rǣt (*regit*), 22, 1. God ðe rǣt and gewissaþ eallum gesceaftum, Chart. Th. 239, 34. Hē reht and rǣt eallum gesceaftum, swā swā gōd steóra ānum scipe, Bt. 35, 3; Fox 158, 25. God ðe him stiórde and racode and rǣdde, 34, 12; Fox 154, 6. Ðætte God rǣdde and weólde ealles middaneardes, 35, 2; Fox 156, 31. Ðæt hē (*the abbot*) sceal rǣdan and racian ōðra manna sāulum, R. Ben. 14, 6. Hwā meahte iéð monnum rǣdan būtan scylde *quis principari hominibus tam sine culpa potuisset?* Past. 3, 1; Swt. 33, 16. Ðam ðe hié (*the Church*) wel ofer mǣge and hiere wel rǣdan cunne *ei qui hanc bene regere praevalet*, 5, 2; Swt. 45, 1. Ic mæg rǣdan on ðīs rīce, Cd. Th. 19, 10; Gen. 289. Ða ðe ðȳ rīce rǣdan sceoldon, 259, 4; Dan. 686. Wolde dōm Godes dǣdum rǣdan gumena gehwylcum *the decree of God would govern the deeds of every man*, Beo. Th. 5709; B. 2858. V. *to have the disposal of, have possession of*:—Ðone māððum ðe ðū mid rihte rǣdan sceoldest, 4119; B. 2056. Ðenden hié ðȳ rīce rǣdan mōston, Cd. Th. 216, 18; Dan. 8. Būtan hȳ ðȳ reáfe rǣdan mōtan, Exon. Th. 110, 6; Gū. 103. VI. *to read* (a) as in *to read* a riddle, *to explain*; conjicere:—Ic rǣde swefn *conicio*, Ælfc. Gr. 28, 6; Som. 32, 40. Mōdor ne rǣdoþ (-aþ, MS.) ðonne heó magan cenneþ, hū him weorðe geond woruld sceapen *a mother cannot read a boy's fate at his birth*, Salm. Kmbl. 741; Sal. 370. Rǣde se ðe wille hū wunda cwǣden, Exon. Th. 441, 11; Rä. 60, 16. Rǣd hwæt ic mǣne, 479, 18; Rä. 62, 9. Ðā ongan hē mid gleáwe mōde rǣdan *coepit sagaci animo conjicere*, Bd. 3, 10; S. 534, 21, MS. B. (b) *to read a book*; legere:—Ic rǣde *lego*, ðū rǣtst *legis*, Ælfc. Gr. 22; Som. 24, 1. Rǣtt *legit*, 44; Som. 45, 49. On hwylcum dæge man rǣt .ix. kl'. apr. swā fela beóþ *concurrentes* ... gif man rǣt ðæne daturum on Sunnandæg ðænne byþ ān, Anglia viii. 302, 19–20. Se ðe rǣt (rǣdæ, Rush.), Mt. Kmbl. 24, 15. Hē rǣdde his bōc ðam folce, Ex. 24, 7. Hē him gebæd and his bēc rǣdde, Bd. 4, 3; S. 567, 4. Ne rǣdde gē (gē hreórdeþ, Rush.) hwæt Dauid dyde, Mt. Kmbl. 12, 3. Ne rǣdde gē (gē ne reórdade, Rush.), 19, 4. Rǣddon (reórdadun, Rush.), 21, 16. Rǣdde (reórdun, Rush.), 21, 42. Mē lyst rǣdan *lecturio*, Ælfc. Gr. 34; Som. 37, 56. Rēða *to read*, Mt. Kmbl. p. l, 8. Hē ārās tō rēdanne, Lk. Skt. Rush. Lind. 4, 16: Rtl. 195, 16. Hē mē sealde bōc tō rǣdanne, Bd. 5, 13; S. 632, 37. Ðæt gewrit wæs rǣded beforan ðam cyninge, 5, 21; S. 643, 11. Ðā ðæt godspel rǣdd wæs, Blickl. Homl. 161, 9. Wē gehȳrdon ðā ðā Esaias se wītga rǣden wæs, 167, 28. VII. *to prepare* (?):—Hē sceal ǣlcre wucan erian .i. æcer and rǣdan sylf ðæt sǣd on hlafordes berne, L. R. S. 4; Th. i. 434, 15. (Cf. *last passage under* rǣcan.) v. ā-, be-, for-, ge-, mis-, ofer-rǣdan.

rǣd-bana, an; *m. One who contrives a person's death, but is not the actual perpetrator*:—Gif man secge ðæt hē wǣre dǣdbana oððe rǣdbana *if he be said to be the actual perpetrator of homicide, or the deviser of it*, L. Eth. ix. 23; Th. i. 344, 26. Cf. Qui ad occidendum aliquem innoxium redbana vel dedbana fuerit, L. H. I. 85, 3; Th. i. 592, 13. [*Icel.* rāð-bani: *see also* bana-rāð *the planning a person's death*; rāða einum bana *to plot a person's death*. v. Grmm. R. A. 626.]

rǣd-bora, an; *m. A counsellor*; also translates *consul*:—Rǣdbora *consiliarius*, Wrt. Voc. i. 73, 22. Hē (*the Messiah*) biþ gehāten wundorlīc, rǣdbora, strang God, Homl. Th. ii. 16, 7: Dōm. L. 42, 38. Aðelwold ðe is mīn rǣdbora *a secretis noster Athelwoldus*, Chart. Th. 241, 27: Beo. Th. 2655; B. 1325. God næfþ nǣnne rǣdboran, Ælfc. T. Grn. 24, 24. Hī hæfdon him Consulas ðæt wē cweðaþ Rǣdboran, Jud. Thw. p. 161, 22. Seó gerǣdnes ðe Angelcynnes witan and Wealhþeóde rǣdboran gesetton, L. O. D. tit.; Th. i. 352, 2. Rǣdboran *jurisperiti*, Wrt. Voc. ii. 46, 41. Rēdboran, 112, 13. Rǣdborena *juris peritorum*, Hpt. Gl. 524, 68. Cf. rǣd-gifa.

rǣde (?), an; *f. A reading, lesson*:—Ðiós rēdo *haec lectio*, Lk. Skt. p. 11, 16. Ðió rēdo *quae lectio*, 11, 5. Rēdes *lectionis*, Mt. Kmbl. p. 10, 16. Ðara rēda *lectionum*, 13, 13. Tō rēde *ad lectionem*, Rtl. 126, 1. Hālige rǣdan (rǣdincge, MS. T.) hē sceal lustlīce gehȳran, R. Ben. 18, 9.

-rǣde. v. ge-rǣde; *n.*

rǣde; *adj. Ready, prompt*:—On hwan mæg se iunga on gōdne weg riht[r]an ne (ðe ?) rǣdran rǣd gemittan ðonne hē ðīne wīsan word gehealde *in quo corrigit junior viam suam? in custodiendo sermones tuos*, Ps. Th. 118, 9. Rǣdan (?) biionges *exercitationis*, Wrt. Voc. ii. 29, 59. v. ge-rǣde, rǣde-gafol, rǣde-sceamol, rǣdness.

rǣde; *adj. Mounted*:—Rǣdum here *equitatu*, Hpt. Gl. 525, 25. v. rǣde-cempa, -here, -mann.

rǣde-cempa, an; *m. A mounted soldier*:—Rǣdewīga *vel* [rǣde]-cempa *equester, qui equitat*, Wrt. Voc. ii. 143, 66. v. rǣde-here.

rǣde-gafol, es; *n. Rent that can be paid all at once, as opposed to rent that is discharged by service rendered, and consequently takes time for its payment*:—Gif mon geþingaþ gyrde landes oððe māre tō rǣdegafole and geereþ gif se hlāford him wile ðæt land ārǣran tō weorce and tō gafole ne þearf hē him onfōn gif hē him nān botl ne selþ *if a man takes a yard of land or more at a fixed rent and ploughs it, if the lord wants to get service as well as rent, the tenant need not take the land, if the lord does not give him a dwelling*, L. In. 67; Th. i. 146, 3. [Cf. *Icel.* reiðu-penningar *ready money*.]

rǣde-here, es; *m. A mounted force, cavalry*:—Rǣdehere *cerethi*, Wrt. Voc. ii. 15, 76: *cerethei*, 130, 15. Of rādehere *equitatu*, Hpt. Gl. 525, 25. Alexandres næs nā mā geslægen ðonne hundtwelftig on ðæm rǣdehere *in exercitu Alexandri centum et viginti equites defuere*, Ors. 3, 9; Swt. 124, 21. Ǣgðer ge an gangehere ge on rǣdehere (rād-, MS. C.), 4, 1; Swt. 154, 24. Earnulf gefeaht wið ðæm rǣdehere (rāde-, MS. B.: rād-, MS. D.), Chr. 891; Erl. 88, 2.

rǣdelle. v. next word.

rǣdels, es; *m.*: e; *f.*: rǣdelse, rǣdelle (?), an; *f.* I. *counsel, consideration*:—Seó rēdelse and ðæt geþeaht ūrra feónda geteorode, Ps. Th. 9, 6. II. *debate, speech in council* (v. rǣdan, II b):—Rǣdelse *concionis, locutionis*, Hpt. Gl. 461, 4. III. *conjecture, imagination, interpretation* (v. rǣdan, VI a):—Rǣswung *vel* rǣdels *conjectura*, i. *opinatio, estimatio, interpretatio*, Wrt. Voc. ii. 133, 53. Ðeáh se leása wēna and sió rǣdelse ðara dysigena monna tiohhie ðæt se anweald sīe ðæt hēhste gōd (*hominum fallax opinio*), Bt. 27, 3; Fox 98, 32. Eall ðis ðū gerehtest tō sōðe swīðe gesceádwīslīce būton ǣlcre leásre rǣdelsan *haec nullis extrinsecus sumtis, sed altero ex altero fidem trahente, insitis domesticisque probationibus explicabas*, 35, 5; Fox 164, 31. Hrǣdelse *conjectura, argumentatione*, Hpt. Gl. 443, 19. Of rǣdelse *conjectura*, 460, 11. III a. *the imaginative faculty*:—Hē (*man*) hine ongit þurh his rǣdelsan (*imaginatio*) synderlīce, þurh his gesceádwīsnesse (*ratio*) synderlīce, Bt. 41, 5; Fox 252, 19. IV. *a dark saying, enigma, riddle*:—Rǣdels *aenigma*, Ælfc. Gr. 9, 1; Som. 8, 23. Hē āsette rǣdels ðus cweðende: Swā hwilc man swā mīnne rǣdels riht ārǣde onfō se mȳnre dohtor tō wīfe, and se ðe hine misrǣde, sȳ hē beheáfdod, Ap. Th. 3, 8–11. *The riddle is given on* p. 4. Ða clamme ðe ða rǣdellan (rǣdelsan?) wiđ rȳnemenn heóld, Exon. Th. 423, 31; Rä. 43, 13. Ic sprece tō him openlīce næs þurh rēdelsas (*per aenigmata; dark speeches*, A. V.), Num. 12, 8. [*Wick.* redels: *Piers P.* redel, ridel: *Prompt. Parv.* rydyl or probleme *enigma*: *M.H. Ger.* rātsal: *M.L. Ger.* rēdelse.] v. rǣsele.

rǣdelse. v. preceding word.

rǣde-mann, es; *m. A horseman*:—Nāwđer ne đam horse ne đæm rǣdemen ne wyrđ geborgen of his āgnum cræfte, Ps. Th. 32, 15. [*Icel.* reiđ-mađr.]

rǣden[n], e; *f.* I. *a condition, stipulation*:—Rǣden *conditio*, Hpt. Gl. 436, 1. Rēdin *condicio*, Wrt. Voc. i. 288, 44: ii. 17, 10. Ǣlc gebūr sylle .vi. hlāfas đam inswāne đonne hē his heorde tō mæstene drīfe, on đam sylfum lande đe đeós rǣden on stænt, L. R. S. 4; Th. i. 434, 22. Rǣdenne *condicione*, Wrt. Voc. ii. 104, 59. Đan (on đa?) rǣdenne *ea conditione*, Hpt. Gl. 492, 8. On đa rǣdenne đe hē him gā tō honda, L. In. 62; Th. i. 142, 3. Đū bist Godes bearn þurh đa rǣdenne đæt đū đīnne feónd lufige, Homl. Th. i. 56, 7. Raedinnae *condiciones*, Ep. Gl. 7 f, 13. II. *rule, direction* (v. rǣdan, IV):—Hæfdon sume mid āþum gefæstnod đæt hié on hire rǣdenne (rǣdinge, 193, col. 2) beón woldan *would be under her rule*, Chr. 918; Th. i. 192, 12. III. *a reckoning, estimating*:—Raedinne *taxatione*, Wrt. Voc. ii. 122, 1. The word occurs as the second part of many nouns, when its force is much the same as that of the suffixes *-ship, -hood, -red*, denoting *a state, condition*. v. bed-, brōđor-, burh-, camp-, feónd-, folc-, freónd-, gafol-, gebed-, gecwid-, gefēr-, heord-, hīw-, hūs-, land-, mǣg-, mann-, meodo-, nām-, teón-, þing-, treów-, un-, weorc-, wīg-, worold-rǣden[n].

rǣdend, es; *m. A ruler, one who possesses control over anything* (v. rǣdan, IV):—Rodera rǣdend *the Deity*, Chr. 975; Erl. 126, 17: Beo. Th. 3114; B. 1555: Andr. Kmbl. 1253; An. 627. Dreáma rǣdend, Exon. Th. 358, 34; Pa. 55. [*O. Sax.* rādand (*Christ*).] v. mago-, sele-rǣdend.

rǣdend-līc; *adj. Pertaining to a decree* or *statute* (v. rǣdan, III):—Đǣm rǣdendlīcum *decretalibus*, Wrt. Voc. ii. 26, 45.

rǣden-gewrit, es; *n. A writing containing a condition* or *stipulation, a written agreement, a note of hand*:—Ic him sealde ūre āgen rǣden-gewrit, đæt wǣre him tō đam gerāde đæt land tō lǣten, đe mon ǣlce gēre gesylle fīftēne scillingas clǣnes feós đam bisceope, Chart. Th. 168, 12. Rǣdinggewrit (rǣden-?) *cirographum*, Wrt. Voc. i. 20, 51.

rǣdere, es; *m.* I. *a reader, one who reads*:—Rǣdere *lector*, Wrt. Voc. i. 72, 6: Ælfc. Gr. 9, 21; Som. 10, 40. Be đære wucan rǣdere (rēdere, 7, 23). Gebrōđra gereorde ne sceal beón būtan hāligre rǣdinge. Ne nān ne gedyrstlǣce, đæt hē fǣrlīce bōc gelæcce and đǣr būtan foresceáwunge onginne tō rǣdenne, ac đære wucan rǣdere on đone Sunnandæg mid bletsunge hit beginne ... Nānes mannes stefn gehȳred ne sȳ būtan đæs rǣderes ānes, R. Ben. 62, 2-15. II. *a reader, scholar*:—Swā swā đa geleáfullan rǣderas hit gesetton, Lchdm. iii. 256, 21. III. *a reader, lector, the second of the seven orders*:—Seofon hādas syndon gesette on cyrcan ... ōđer is lector .... *Lector* is rǣdere, đe rǣd on Godes cyrcan, and biþ đǣrtō gehādod đæt hē bodige Godes word, L. Ælfc. C. 10-12; Th. ii. 346, 25-32. Rēdere rēderes forlonge foreboderes ł ceigeras fruma from wītgum đǣm is gecuoedin ceig *lector; lectores dudum praecones vel clamatores, initium a prophetis, quibus dicitur, Clama*, Rtl. 194, 1-4. IV. *a reader of riddles, a diviner* (v. rǣdan, VI a):—Wiccum, fram rǣderum *pythonibus*, Hpt. Gl. 504, 67. v. bōc-rǣdere.

rǣde-sceamol, es; *m. A reading-bench* (?); *a 'ready,' prepared bench, bench with furniture, a couch*, cf. *Icel.* reiđu-stōll, *and see* rād:—On rǣdescamole *in pulpito*, Wrt. Voc. ii. 45, 3. Rǣdescamelas *fulchra* (cf. *fulcra* eal bedreáf, Wrt. Voc. i. 59, 33: *fulcris, thoris, lectis*, Wülck. Gl. 245, 28), 36, 36.

rǣdes-mann, es; *m.* I. *a counsellor, adviser, councillor*:—Ealle đæs cynges rǣdesmen, Chart. Th. 330, 8: Chr, 1039; Erl. 167, 19. II. *a steward, manager*:—Æt Steorran đe đā wæs đæs kinges rǣdesman, Chart. Th. 339, 12. [*Icel.* rāđs-mađr *a manager, counsellor, steward.*]

rǣdesn (?), e; *f. A cluster of grapes*; bacido [cf. clyster *bacido, botrus*, Wrt. Voc. i. 33, 31]:—Rēdisn *vacedo* (in a list *de lignis*), Wrt. Voc. i. 285, 43. Rēdisnae *bacidones* (cf. raedinne *bacidones*, 43, 260: rǣdenne, Wrt. Voc. ii. 10, 59), Txts. 44, 1.

rǣdestre, an; *f. A female reader*:—Rēdestre, Ælfc. Gr. 9, 21; Som. 10, 40. Rǣdystre, 9, 64; Som. 13, 63. Rǣdistre, Wrt. Voc. i. 72, 7.

rǣde-wiga. v. rǣde-cempa.

rǣd-fæst; *adj. Wise, prudent*:—Se deófol gemacaþ đæt se man þurh leáse hiwunge dēþ swylce hē rǣdfæst sȳ đe rǣdes ne gȳmeþ *the devil causes the man by a false show to act as if he were wise, who cares not for wisdom*, Wulfst. 53, 9. Đæt ic on đīnum rihte rǣdfæst lifige, Ps. Th. 142, 11. Đīnes rīces rǣdfæst wulder *gloriam magnificentiae regni tui*, 144, 12. Him in gāst becwom rǣdfæst sefa, Cd. Th. 257, 3; Dan. 652: Exon. 468, 23; Hy. 5, 4. Se đe symle byþ rǣdfest, Wald. 108; Vald. 2, 26: Cd. Th. 90, 20; Gen. 1498. Ārīs and gereorda đē mid rǣdfæstum mōde, Homl. Skt. i. 18, 185. Se rǣd wæs ǣfre on his rǣd-fæstum geþance, Ælfc. T. Grn. 2, 5. Đæt hig māgon ārīsan, gif hig rǣdfæste beóþ, 19, 5. Rincas rǣdfæste, Exon. Th. 347, 15; Sch. 13. Cf. rǣd-leás.

rǣdfæstlīce. v. un-rǣdfæstlīce.

rǣdfæstness, e; *f. Readiness to follow good counsel, adherence to right courses*:—Eahta sweras syndon đe rihtlīcne cynedōm up wegaþ ... rǣdfæstnes (*persuabilitas*), L. I. P. 3; Th. ii. 306, 20.

rǣd-findende *furnishing counsel, advising*:—Rǣdfindende *consulentes*, Wrt. Voc. ii. 24, 29. Cf. rǣd-hycgende.

raedgasram *glosses* hyadas, Txts. 69, 1035.

rǣd-geþeaht, es; *n. Counsel*:—*Consilium*, đæt is rǣdgeþeht on Englisc, Wulfst. 51, 6. Elene hēht Eusebium on rǣdgeþeaht gefetian, Elen. Kmbl. 2101; El. 1052. Hēht gefetigean tō rūne đone đe rǣd-geþeaht þurh gleáwe miht georne cūđe, 2322; El. 1162.

rǣd-gifa, an; *m. One who gives counsel, a counsellor, councillor, adviser*; mostly of the king's advisers; it also translates *consul*:—Rǣdgifa *consiliator*, Wrt. Voc. i. 50, 1. Stīgand đe wæs đæs cinges rǣdgifa and his handprēst, Chr. 1051; Th. i. 317, col. 2. Rǣdgifan *consulem*, Germ. 397, 560. Đis sindon đa gerǣdnessa đe Engla rǣd-gifan gecuran and gecwǣdan, L. Eth. vi. 1; Th. i. 314, 3. Ealle đæs kyninges rǣdgyfan (*conciliarii*), Chart. Th. 326, 7. Đone rǣd đe ic mid mīnum rǣdgyfum gerǣdd hæbbe, 307, 10. Rǣdgifena *juris peritorum*, Hpt. Gl. 524, 69. [Cleope nu to ræde þine rædȝiuen gode, Laym. 11615. *O. Sax.* rād-gebo: *O. Frs.* rēd-jeva: *O. H. Ger.* rāt-gebo: *Icel.* rāđ-gjafi.] Cf. rǣd-bora *and next word.*

rǣd-gift *glosses* consulatus, senatus *in the following instances*:—Rǣd-giftes *consulatus*, Hpt. Gl. 412, 64. Rǣdgyft *senatu*, Hymn. Surt. 105, 34. Rǣdgifte *senatum*, Germ. 398, 108.

rǣd-hycgende; *part. Having wise counsel in the mind, prudent, sagacious*:—Đū đē ānne genim tō gesprecan symle rǣdhycgende, Exon. Th. 301, 28; Fä. 26.

rǣdic (rædic?), es; *m. A radish*:—Rǣdic *raphanum* vel *radix*, Wrt. Voc. i. 31, 37: *vermenaca*, 68, 65: *hierobotanim*, ii. 43, 52. Rēdic, Lchdm. ii. 276, 10. Syle đane rǣdic tō þicganne ... se rǣdic, 286, 10-14. Hrǣdic, iii. 20, 26. Genim hrǣdic nyđeweardne, 46, 1. [*O. H. Ger.* rātih, retih: *M. H. Ger.* retich: *Ger.* rettich. *From Lat.* radic-em.]

rǣding, e; *f.* I. *reading*:—Bisceopes dægweorc. Đæt biþ mid rihte his gebedu ǣrest, and đonne his bōcweorc, rǣding, L. I. P. 8; Th. ii. 314, 19. Æmtigaþ eów tō rǣdinge *vacate lectioni*, hē begǣþ his rǣdinge *vacuus est lectionibus*, Ælfc. Gr. 33; Som. 37, 14. Đæs đe ic on rǣdinge ne mihte fullīce āsmeágan, Wulfst. 65, 22. Beó đū ābisgad ymbe rǣdinge *attende lectioni*, Past. 22, 1; Swt. 169, 17. I a. *a reading, a single act of reading*:—Ofthrædlīce rǣdinga hāligra bōca, L. E. I. 2; Th. ii. 404, 2. Capitula rǣdinga, R. Ben. 43, 2. II. *what is read, reading, a passage in a book, a lesson*:—Đis Englisc ǣtȳwþ hwæt seó foresette rǣding (*passage*) mǣnþ, Anglia viii. 298, 9. Seó rǣding cwyþ đæt đǣr ys gyt on ǣlcum tācne healftīd, 298, 31: 300, 32: 309, 1. Sȳ ān rǣdincg gerǣd of đære ealdan cȳđnesse *let one lesson from the Old Testament be read*, R. Ben. 34, 12. Agustinus ūs onwreáh đissere rǣdinge (*the lesson for the day*) andgit, Homl. Th. ii. 384, 21. Swā swā gē gehȳrdon on đissere rǣdinge (*the homily which precedes*), Homl. Skt. i. 11, 284. Hē lufode hālige rǣdinge ... ealle his gefēran sceolde sealmas leornian ođđe sume rǣdinge, Swt. A. S. Rdr. 97, 62-65. Gē sculon singan sunnanūhtan ǣfre nigon ræpsas mid nigon rǣdingum, L. Ælfc. P. 44; Th. ii. 384, 5. Man þreó rǣdinga rǣde, R. Ben. 33, 14. Wē willaþ on đisre stōwe đa seofon rǣdinga (*passages*) āwrītan đe ymbe đa seofon geár synd gedihte ... Đās rǣdinga syndon wīde cūđe, Anglia viii. 314, 18-22. III. *rule, government* (v. rǣdan, IV):—Hæfdon sume mid āþum gefæstnod đæt hī on hire rǣdinge (rǣdenne, other MSS.) beón woldon, Chr. 918; Erl. 105, 30. v. bēc-, bōc-, pistol-rǣding.

rǣding-bōc; *f. A book containing the lessons, a lectionary*:—Se mæssepreóst sceal habban đa wǣpna tō đam gāstlīcum weorce ... đæt synd đa hālgan bēc ... rǣdingbōc, L. Ælfc. C. 21; Th. ii. 350, 14. ii. for-ealdode rǣdingbēc swīđe wāke (cf. ii. sumerrǣdingbēc and i. winter-rǣdingbōc, 16), Chart. Th. 430, 30. v. Maskell's Monumenta, vol. i. c. 3.

rǣding-gewrit, rǣdistre. v. rǣden-gewrit, rǣdestre.

rǣd-leás; *adj.* I. *without counsel, unwise, inconsiderate, rash, ill-advised*:—Rēdeleás *preceps*, Ælfc. Gr. 9, 55; Som. 13, 27. Gleáw ne wæs gumrīces weard, rēđe and rǣdleás, Cd. Th. 226, 26; Dan. 177. II. *without wise direction, in confusion*:—Đā đis (*the destruction of certain ships*) cūđ wæs tō đām ōđrum scipon ... wæs đā swilc hit eall rǣdleás wǣre *it was as if there were no counsel anywhere, as if everything was in confusion*, Chr. 1009; Erl. 142, 9. III. *lacking what is advantageous* or *beneficial, miserable, desolate* (v. rǣd, IV):—Gē Godes cræfta nān þing ne gȳmaþ, đȳ is folces forfaren māre đonne scolde ođđe þearf wǣre, and for đam hit wearđ swā rǣdleás đe hit Godes beboda forgȳmde *the people is become so miserable, because it neglected God's commandments*, Wulfst. 46, 20. Đæt rǣdleáse hof (*hell*), Cd. Th. 3, 32; Gen. 44. [Nabbich in me wisdom ... and am redleas ... Drihten ase þu ert redlease (*gen. pl.*) red, red me þet am redles

O. E. Homl. i. 211, 32-213, 1. Nis nevre mon redles Ar his heorte beo witles, O. and N. 691.] [*O. H. Ger.* râti-lô *sabsque consilio*: *Ger.* rat-los: *Icel.* rāð-lauss *shiftless, confused, foolish.*]

rǣd-līc; *adj. Advisable*:—Him ða rǣdlecre geþūhte ðæt hē wið ōðerne here friþ genāme ðæt hē ðone ōðerne ðē iéð ofercuman mehte *proviso ad tempus consilio, unum denuntiato bello adpetit, alterum pacta pace suspendit*, Ors. 3, 1; Swt. 96, 15: 4, 13; Swt. 212, 16. Tō smeágenne wið his witan hwet heom eallum rǣdlīcost þūhte, Chr. 1006; Erl. 141, 4. [*Icel.* rāð-ligr.]

rǣd-līce; *adv.* I. *wisely, skilfully, cleverly*:—Hē rǣdlīce slōh swā hē hine (*the ball*) nǣfre feallan ne lēt, Ap. Th. 13, 5. Ðæt hē meahte ðæt folc ðȳ wīslīcor and ðȳ rǣdlīcor lǣran, Past. 18, 2; Swt. 131, 18. II. *advisedly, deliberately, designedly, on purpose*:—Rǣdlīce *consulto*, Ælfc. Gr. 38; Som. 41, 35. On ðām gemōtan ðeáh rǣdlīce wurðan on namcūðan stōwan, L. Eth. ix. 37; Th. i. 348, 17. [*Icel.* rāðliga *cleverly.*] v. ān-, fæst-, un-rǣdlīce.

rǣd-mægen, es; *n. Beneficial force* (?), *force that is productive of good* or *abundant good* (?), cf. lof-mægen (v. rǣd, IV):—Ðā wæs wæstmum āweaht world onspreht . . . rǣdmægne oferþeaht *the world was aroused to fruitful life, and overspread by productive force*, Exon. Th. 353, 10; Reim. 10.

rǣdness, es; *f.* I. *readiness, promptness*:—Rǣdnis (hrædnis?) *pernicitas*, Txts. 182, 75. On rǣdnysse *in maturitate*, Blickl. Gl. Ðone þōþor mid swiftre rǣdnesse geslegene ongeán gesænde tō ðam plegendan cynge, Ap. Th. 13, 4. Rǣdnisse (hrædnisse?) *concursionibus*, Wrt. Voc. ii. 105, 24. Rǣdnessum, 15, 26. II. *an arrangement, agreement, condition*:—Ðæt ðeós gerǣdnis stondon mōte in ēcnesse, and ðis syndon ðara manna naman ðe æt ðære rēdnisse wǣron, Chart. Th. 168, 30. v. ge-rǣdness, rǣde.

rǣd-rīpe (hræd-?); *adj. Soon ripe, premature*:—Rǣdrīpe wæstm *praecoquus fructus*, Wrt. Voc. i. 39, 22. Rǣdrīpe wīnberige *praecoquae*, 38, 61.

rǣd-snotor; *adj. Wise in counsel, prudent, sagacious*:—Nǣfre ic sǣlidan sēlran mētte rǣdsnotteran, Andr. Kmbl. 946; An. 473. [*Icel.* rāð-snotr *sagacious.*]

rǣd-þeahtende; *part. Consulting, deliberating*:—Gesǣton sigerōfe rǣdþeahtende ymb ða rōda þreó, Elen. Kmbl. 1734; El. 869: 895; El. 449. Cf. rǣd-hycgende *and next word.*

rǣd-þeahtere, es; *m. A counsellor, adviser*:—Ða (*the senators*) wǣron simbel binnan Rōmebyrg wuniende, tō ðon ðæt hié heora rǣdþeahteras wǣron, Ors. 2, 4; Swt. 72, 3. Ðara twentigra monna ðe hē him tō fultume hæfde ācoren, ðæt his rǣdþeahteras wǣron *viginti viros sibi consilii causa legerat*, 6, 2; Swt. 256, 3.

rǣd-þeahtung, e; *f. Counsel*:—Hē wæs gemǣrsad ofer ealle ōðere cyningas ǣgðer ge mid his miclan fultume ge mid his rǣdþeahtunge ge mid his wīgcræfte *ob magnitudinem virium consiliorumque summam belli nomenque traduxit*, Ors. 4, 1; Swt. 154, 27.

rǣd-wægn, es; *m. A vehicle, chariot*:—Hē hiene hēt iernan beforan his rǣdwǣne *ante vehiculum ejus*, Ors. 6, 30; Swt. 280, 13. Cf. *Icel.* reið-skjótr, *but see also* hræd-wægn.

rǣd-wita, an; *m. A counsellor, one wise in counsel*:—Rīce rǣdwitan, Dom. L. 18, 298.

rǣfan (?); *p.* te *To involve, wrap*:—Hī weorþaþ gerǣfte (gerǣpte (?) cf. gereæped (-rǣped?) Met. 25, 48) mid ðære unrōtnesse, Bt. 37, 1; Fox 186, 21. [*Icel.* reifa *to swaddle.*] v. rāfian.

ræfnan; *p.* de. I. *to endure, suffer, undergo*:—Ræfnde *perpetitur*, Wrt. Voc. i. 66, 66. Ðeáh hē deáþes cwealm ræfnan sceolde, Exon. Th. 240, 24; Ph. 643. II. *to do, perform, accomplish, carry out*:—Ða ðe ræfnaþ hēr wordum and weorcum wuldorcyninges lāre, 149, 20; Gū. 764: 139, 17; Gū. 594. Neáh is Drihten eallum ðe his willan hēr wyrceaþ georne and his hyge swylce elne ræfnaþ, Ps. Th. 144, 19. Hié ðæt ōfstum miclum ræfndon, Judth. Thw. 21, 9; Jud. 11. Ræfn elne ðis, ðæt ðū nǣfre fǣcne weorð freónde ðīnum, Exon. Th. 302, 3; Fä. 30. v. ā-ræfnan *and* cf. dreógan *for the same two meanings.*

ræfnendlīc, ræfnian, ræfniendlīc, ræfsan. v. un-āræfnendlīc, ā-ræfnian, on-ræfniendlīc, ræpsan.

ræfter, es; *m. A rafter, beam*:—Ræfter *tignum*, Wrt. Voc. i. 26, 40: 82, 14: 290, 5. Reftras *amites*, Txts. 36, 11. Ræftras, Wrt. Voc. ii. 6, 58: *anses*, 10, 56. Reafteres *vel* !atta *asseres*, i. 58, 35. Mycelne aad on beámum and on ræftrum and on wāgum and on watelum and on þacum *congeriem trabium, tignorum, parietum, virgeorum & tecti fenei*, Bd. 3, 16; S. 542, 22. Ǣrest man āsmeáþ ðæs hūses stede, and eác man ðæt timber beheáwþ, and ða syllan man fægere gefēgþ, and ða beámas gelegþ, and ða ræftras tō ðære fyrste gefæstnaþ, Anglia viii. 324, 7-9.

rǣge, an; *f. A roe, a wild she-goat*:—Rǣge *caprea*, Wrt. Voc. i. 78, 31: *capriole*, ii. 129, 59. Hrǣge *damula* vel *caprea*, i. 22, 65. Rāge, ii. 16, 80. Mȳnster ðe is nemned æt Hrēge heáfde (*ad Caprae caput*), Bd. 3, 21; S. 551, 18. Ic gefeó rǣgan *capio capreas*, Coll. Monast. Th. 21, 31. Rǣgean (rǣgan, MS. B.), Lchdm. i. 166, 24. [*O. H. Ger.* reia *caprea.*] v. rā.

rægo-reósa, an; *m.*: -reóse (?); *f. A ridge of muscles at the side of the spine running up the back*:—Lǣcedōmas wið rægereósan sāre, Lchdm. ii. 14, 26. Wið rægereósan, rūdan swā grēne, seóþ on ele and on weaxe, smire mid ðone rægereósan. Eft nim gāte hǣr, smēc under ða brēc wið ðās rægereósan, 146, 1-3. Be ðam nafolan and ðam rægereósan and bæcþearme, 230, 26. Biþ ðæt sār fram ðam nafolan ōþ ðone milte and on ða winestran rægereósan, and gecymþ æt ðam bæcþearme, 232, 3-6. v. Lchdm. ii. Glossary.

rǣg-hār; *adj. Grey like the goat* (v. rǣge):—Oft ðæs wāg gebād rǣghār and reádfāh rīce æfter ōðrum *oft did its wall, grey and redstained, see change of rule*, Exon. Th. 476, 19; Ruin. 10.

rægiming (?):—*A clapping of the wings* (?):—*Pullorum* cocca, *plausu* blisse *laetitiae* fiðerslehte (*in margin*) rægiminge, Hpt. Gl. 518, 51-54.

rægu. v. ragu.

rǣman. v. ā-rǣman.

rǣming (?):—Heofenlīcre rǣminge *celibea Tempe*, Wrt. Voc. ii. 130, 54.

rænc. v. renc.

rǣpan; *p.* te *To bind* (*with a rope*), *make captive*:—Hī fērdon ǣghwiðer and ūre earme folc rǣpton (rȳpton, MS. C.) and slōgan (cf. rǣpling), Chr. 1011; Erl. 145, 6. Cyspan and mid racentan rǣpan, Met. 26, 78. [*Icel.* reipa *to fasten with a rope.*] v. ge-rǣpan.

rǣping. v. next two words.

rǣpling, rǣping, es; *m. One bound, a captive, prisoner, criminal*:—Wæs ðā rǣpling se ðe ǣr wæs Angelcynnes heáfod (*of archbishop Ælfheah taken captive by the Danes*), Chr. 1011; Erl. 145, 19. Hē (*St. Paul*) wæs ðyder (*to Rome*) rǣpling gelǣded, Blickl. Homl. 173, 7. Rǣplinga *damnatorum*, Wrt. Voc. ii. 26, 54. Se wæs gebunden mid ðām rǣplingum *qui cum seditiosis erat vinctus*, Mk. Skt. 15, 7. On cweartern ðǣr man ðæs cyninges rǣplingas heóld, Gen. 39, 20. Rǣplingas his *vinctos suos*, Ps. Spl. 68, 32. Rǣplingas unbindan, Dōm. L. 4, 48. Ic geseah rǣpingas in ræced fergan . . . ða wǣron genamne nearwum bendum, gefeterade fæste tōgædre (*two buckets of a draw-well*), Exon. Th. 435, 1; Rä. 53, 1.

rǣpling-weard, es; *m. A keeper of prisoners*:—Rēplingcweardes *collegiati*, Wrt. Voc. i. 18, 45. Rǣpingweardas *collegiati*, ii. 134, 52.

ræps, reps, es; *m. A response* (*in the service of the church*):—Ǣfengebed *vespertinum officium*, reps *responsorium*, rǣding *lectio*, Wrt. Voc. i. 28, 32. Sȳ ān rǣding gerǣd, and ān swȳðe scort ræps æfterfylige, R. Ben. 34, 13. Ān rǣding, æfter ðam reps (ræps, MSS. O. F.: ryps, MS. T.), ymen, fers and lofsang, 36, 21. Ǣfter ðæm glorian ðæs feórþan repses (ræpses, MS. O.), 35, 18. Man þreó rǣdinga rǣde and þrȳ ræpsas. Æt ðam þriddan repse singe se sangere 'Gloria Patri,' 33, 14-16: 35, 8-10. On ðisum dagum wē forlǣtaþ on ūrum repsum 'Gloria Patri,' Homl. Th. ii. 224, 26. Gē sculon singan sunnanūhtan ǣfre nigon ræpsas mid nigon rǣdingum, L. Ælfc. P. 44; Th. ii. 384, 5.

ræpsan; *p.* te *To seize* (?), *to reprove* (?):—Raebsid uuaes, repset uaes, ræpsit wæs *interceptum est* (cf. ā-raepsid, -repsit *interceptum*, 511), Txts, 68, 523. Raefsed, refset, raefsit *interpellari*, 70, 526. Refsede *intercepit*, 69, 1082. Cf. Fornoom *intercepit*, 71, 1083. Ārǣsed *interceptum*, 69, 1067. Ārǣsed wæs *interceptus est*, Wrt. Voc. ii. 46, 31. [*O. H. Ger.* refsan; *p.* rafsta *corripere, increpare, arguere, reprehendere.*]

ræpsung, e; *f.* I. *seizing* (?), *reproving* (?):—Raepsung *interceptio* (v. *preceding word, and* cf. *O. H. Ger.* rafsunga *correptio, invectio, increpatio*), Txts. 69, 1068. II. *an interval*:—Seó niht hæfþ seofan dǣlas . . . Ōðer is *uesperum*, ðæt is ǣfen, ðonne se ǣfensteorra betwux ðære repsunge æteówaþ, Lchdm. iii. 244, 1. *Vesperum* ðæt ys ǣfen oððe hrepsung, Anglia viii. 319, 28.

rǣran; *p.* de *To cause to rise, to rear, raise.* I. *to lift up, move from a lower to a higher position*:—Hē ūs tō roderum up hlǣdre rǣrde, Exon. Th. 437, 11; Rä. 56, 6. Hī tō heofenum up hlǣdræ rǣrdon, Cd. Th. 101, 1; Gen. 1675. Hié tō gūþe gārwudu rǣrdon, 198, 20; Exod. 325. Rǣre up ðīn heáfod and geseoh ðis ðæt Simon dēþ, Blickl. Homl. 187, 35. II. *to raise* (*a building*):—Ðū rǣrst hūs *domum aedifices*, Deut. 28, 30. Hī wībed setton neáh ðam ðe Abraham ǣror rǣrde, Cd. Th. 113, 7; Gen. 1883. Ðæt beácen (*the tower of Babel*) ðe rǣran ongunnon Adames eaforan, 101, 13; Gen. 1681. Ongunnon him bytlian and heora burh rǣran, 113, 1; Gen. 1880. III. *to set up, establish* (*a law, institution, etc.*):—God sibbe rǣreþ ēce tō ealdre engla and monna, Exon. Th. 43, 16; Cri. 689. Hē Cristes cyricean on his rīce geornlīce timbrede and rǣrde *ecclesiam Christi in regno suo multum diligenter aedificare ac dilatare curavit*, Bd. 3, 3; S. 525, 37. Man unriht rǣrde and unlaga manege, Wulfst. 156, 13. Ðonne rǣre man cyninges munde, ðæt is ðæt hȳ ealle ðam sēmende syllan ðæt cyninges mund stande, L. E. G. 13; Th. i. 174, 20. Se ðe unlage rǣre oððe undōm gedēme, L. C. S. 15; Th. i. 384, 9. Ys his handgeweorc ryhte dōmas ða hē rǣran wyle *opera manuum ejus judicium*, Ps. Th. 110, 5. IV. *to raise, offer* (*a prayer*):—Hyra þeódnes dōm ðæt hié to ðam beácne (*the golden image*) gebedu rǣrde, Cd. Th. 227, 24; Dan. 191. V. *to raise, begin, give rise to, excite* (*ill-feeling*):—Rǣrde *exagitabat*, Wrt. Voc. ii. 30, 22. Oft hī þræce rǣrdon . . . feóndscype rǣrdon *oft were their violence and enmity roused*, Exon. Th. 243, 18-22; Jul. 12-14. Hāteþ þræce rǣran . . . ðæt hī ūsic binden and in bælwylme swingen, 262, 16; Jul. 333. Fǽhþe rǽran, 113, 14; Gú. 157. Ne cúðon firena fremman . . . elles ne ongunnon rǽran on roderum nymþe riht and sóð, Cd. Th. 2, 18; Gen. 21. Geflitu rǽran, Elen. Kmbl. 884; El. 443. Sæce rǽran, 1879; El. 941. VI. *to rouse, excite*:—Saga hwā mec rǽre ðonne ic restan ne mōt, oððe hwā mec stæððe ðonne ic stille beom, Exon. Th. 387, 2; Rä. 4, 73. VII. *to raise, elevate, exalt, promote*:—Gif ðú sóðne God lufast and his lof rǽrest, 245, 22; Jul. 48: 103, 17; Cri. 1681: 111, 23; Gú. 131. Se ǽrest æðelinga éðelþrym rýmde and rǽrde, Cd. Th. 98, 24; Gen. 1635. Uton beón ā úrum hlāforde holde, and ǽfre ealllum mihtum his wurðscipe rǽran, L. C. E. 20; Th. i. 372, 9: Wulfst. 119, 14. Hū neáh ðære tíde wǽre ðætte ða bróðru árísan sceolden and Godes lof rǽran and heora úhtsang singan *quam prope esset hora qua fratres ad dicendas Domino laudes nocturnas excitari deberent*, Bd. 4, 24; S. 599, 4. [*Goth.* raisjan: *Icel.* reisa.] v. ā-rǽran.

rǽrend, rǽrness. v. ā-rǽrend, -rǽrness.

rǽs, es; *m.* I. *a race, swift* or *violent running, rush*:—Wæs se þridda hlýp, rodorcyninges rǽs ðā hē on róde āstāg, Exon. Th. 45, 30; Cri. 727. Micle rǽse (*magno impetu*) worn tódrifen wæs on sǽ, Mk. Skt. Rush. 5, 13. Mycelum rǽse, Lk. Skt. 8, 33. Ðæt hors sum slōg on ðam wege mid swíðran rǽse (*valentiore impetu*) oferhleóp, Bd. 5, 6; S. 619, 17. Ongeán ðam rǽse ðæs forþgotenan streámes *contra impetum fluvii decurrentis*, 5, 10; S. 625, 7. Hē hēt hwílon ða hundas ætstandan ðe urnon on ðam rǽse deórum getenge *he sometimes ordered the dogs to stop that were running at full speed close upon the game*, Homl. Th. ii. 514, 25. II. *an onset, attack*:—Beadumægnes rǽs, Cd. Th. 198, 28; Exod. 329. Hit ofslōh mínra þegna xxvi. āne rǽse (*in one onslaught*), Nar. 15, 25. Ðā wearð líg tólýsed, leád wíde sprong, hæleþ wurdon acle for ðý rǽse, Exon. Th. 277, 27; Jul. 587. Hē gúðe rǽs mid his freádryhtne fremman sceolde, Beo. Th. 5246; B. 2626. Gúðe rǽsum, 4702; B. 2356. [*Laym.* ræs, res, reas *an attack, onslaught*: *Allit. Pms.* to run in on a res *to rush in*: *Icel.* rās; *f. a race, running.*] v. beadu-, deáþ-, feónd-, gār-, gúþ-, hand-, heaðo-, hilde-, mǽg-, mægen-, on-, scyte-, sweord-, syn-, wæl-rǽs.

rǽs (?), -we; *f. Counsel, deliberation*:—Ðonne merestreámas meotudes rǽswum (*or from* rǽswa?) onwealcaþ, Exon. Th. 193, 24; Az. 126. *And see* rǽs-bora, rǽswian.

rǽsan; *p.* de *To rush, move violently* or *impetuously*; inruere:—Rǽsde *inruit*, Wrt. Voc. ii. 111, 56. I. of actual movement:—Seó hǽtu rǽsde on ða ðe ðæt fýr ǽlde, Bd. 3, 16; S. 543, 9. Hē, getogene ðý wǽpne, rǽsde on ðone cyning, 2, 9; S. 511, 21. Hē út rǽsde on ðone æþeling, Chr. 755; Erl. 48, 34. Se stranga wind ðǽr on rǽsde, Shrn. 81, 32. Hit on ús and on úre wícstówe rǽsde, Nar. 15, 20: Beo. Th. 5373; B. 2690. Hiá rǽsdon (*inruerent*) on hine, Mk. Skt. Lind. Rush. 3, 10. Hundas rǽsdon on ðone apostol, Blickl. Homl. 181, 21. Hié rǽsdon on gífrum grāpum, Andr. Kmbl. 2670; An. 1336. Wǽron hý reówe tō rǽsanne gífrum grāpum, Exon. Th. 126, 27; Gú. 377. Rǽsed eode *impetu abiit*, Mt. Kmbl. Rush. 8, 32. II. of violent action, *to proceed against with violence, to assault, attack*:—Se hlāford ne scrífþ freónde ne feónde, ac hē rēðigmōd rǽst on gehwilcne wēdehunde gelícost (cf. se ne murnþ nāuþer ne friénd ne fiénd ðe mā ðe wēdende hund, Bt. 37, 1; Fox 186, 7-8), Met. 25, 17. Hine (deáþ) rǽseþ on gífrum grāpum, Exon. Th. 161, 34; Gú. 968. Hū longe on rǽsaþ (*inruitis*) gē on men, Ps. Surt. 61, 4. On rǽsdun (*inruerunt*) in mē stronge, 58, 4. Ðæs burhgerēfan sunu wolde rǽsan on hí on ðæm scandhúse and hí bysmrian, Shrn. 56, 11. III. of precipitate action, *to rush* (*into anything*):—Oft mon biþ suíðe rempende, and rǽsð suíðe dollíce on ǽlc weorc and hrædlíce, Past. 20; Swt. 149, 12. Geþence se láriów ðæt hē unwærlíce forþ ne rǽse on ða sprǽce, 15; Swt. 95, 9. v. be-, ge-, in-, þurh-rǽsan; fǽr-rǽsende.

rǽs-bora, an; *m. A counsellor, one who takes thought for the public good, a leader, chief*:—Rǽsbora (*Abraham*), Cd. Th. 108, 24; Gen. 1811. Andreas þanc gesægde rícum rǽsboran (*the Deity who in disguise had guided Andrew's ship*), Andr. Kmbl. 769; An. 385. Rēðe rǽsboran (*the chiefs of the Mermedonians*), 277; An. 139. Rǽfborena [rǽs- (?), rǽd- (?)] *jurisperitorum*, Wrt. Voc. ii. 87, 38. v. rǽs, *and* cf. rǽd-bora.

ræsc. v. líg-ræsc.

ræscan; *p.* te *To move quickly* (cf. *rash*), *to quiver* (*of light*), *to glitter*:—Fēr ræscendum leóhte *ignis vibrante lumine*, Hymn. Surt. 94, 1. v. ræsc, ræscettan.

ræscettan; *p.* te *To crackle, make a crackling noise as fire does, to sparkle*:—Fýren líg braslaþ, ræsct and ēfesteþ, Dóm. L. 10, 152. Ðæt rēðe flód ræscet fýre, 12, 165. Ræsceteþ *crepitat*, Wrt. Voc. ii. 94, 66. Ræsceteþ, cyrmþ, scylþ *crepitat*, i. *resonat*, 136, 73. Ræscettan *crepitarent*, ræscettende *crepitantes*, 18, 9-10. Ræscetende *crepitantes*, 78, 10. [*O. H. Ger.* raskezzan *scintillare, singultare.*] v. preceding word.

ræscet[t]ung, e; *f. Sparkling, gleaming, coruscation*:—Hræscetunga *coruscationes*, Hpt. Gl. 509, 31. v. líg-ræscetung *and preceding word.*

rǽsele, an; *f. A conjecture, solution of a riddle*:—Gif ðú mǽge rēselan gesecgan, Saga hwæt hió hātte, Exon. Th. 421, 34; Rä. 40, 28. v. rǽswan, *and* cf. rǽdels, III.

ræsn, es; *n. A plank, a ceiling*:—Ræsn *asser*, Ælfc. Gr. 9, 18; Som. 9, 59. Ræfter *tignus*, beám *trabs*, wāh *paries*, ræsn *laquear*, Wrt. Voc. i. 290, 5-8: ii. 52, 4. [*Goth.* razn *a house*: *Icel.* rann.]

ræst, ræstan. v. rest, restan.

rǽswa, an; *m.* (a word used only in poetry). I. *a counsellor*:—Cwæð ðā se ðe wæs cyninges rǽswa (cf. 'the king spake unto his counsellors . . . They answered and said unto the king,' Dan. 3, 14), wís and wordgleáw, Cd. Th. 242, 11; Dan. 417. II. *one who takes thought* (*for the public good*), (a) *a prince, king*:—Se rǽswa (*Nebuchadnezzar*), 256, 14; Dan. 640. Werodes rǽswa, Babilone weard, 246, 31; Dan. 487. Folca rǽswa, Caldea cyning, 257, 34; Dan. 667. Ealwealdan Gode, þeóda rǽswan, Andr. Kmbl. 3243; An. 1624, Folccyningas, leóde rǽswan, Cd. Th. 125, 6; Gen. 2075. (b) *a leading man, chief person, leader*:—Ðā wearð forht manig folces rǽswa *many a chief man among the Mermedonians*, Andr. Kmbl. 2174; An. 1088. Gesetton Sennar leóda rǽswan leófum mannum heora, 99, 34; Gen. 1656: 100, 25; Gen. 1669. Folces rǽswan (*the chief men with Holofernes*), Judth. Thw. 21, 10; Jud. 12. Leóda rǽswan (*the chief men of Bethulia*), 24, 8; Jud. 178. Hæleþa rǽswan, dugoþ dōmgeorne (*the high priest and his fellows*), Andr. Kmbl. 1384; An. 692. Mōdgleáwe men, middangeardes rǽswan, Salm. Kmbl. 362; Sal. 180. Rǽswan herges, *the leaders of the host*, Cd. Th. 192, 20; Exod. 234. Hē beforan fremede folces rǽswum (*the chief men among the Jews*), Andr. Kmbl. 1238; An. 619. [*Icel.* ræsir *chief, captain, king.*] v. ge-, here-rǽswa, rǽs-bora, *and next word.*

rǽswan, rǽswian, rǽsian, rēsian; *p.* ede, ode *To think, suppose, suspect, consider, conjecture*:—Tō ðǽm sóðum gesǽlþum ðe ðín mōd oft ymbe rǽsweþ *ad veram felicitatem, quam tuus somniat animus*, Bt. 22, 2; Fox 78, 7. Rēsiaþ *comminiscimus*, Wrt. Voc. ii. 18, 7. Rēsiat, 77, 24. Hié eallneg rǽswaþ and ondrǽdaþ ðæt hí mon tǽlan wille *they are always suspecting and dreading that people want to blame them*, Past. 35, 2; Swt. 239, 6. Ðú rǽswedest (*existimasti*) swíðe unryhte ðæt ic wǽre ðín gelíca, Ps. Th. 49, 22. Hē rēsade (*suspicabatur*) ðæt hē hæfde ðæs Cāseres ǽrendo sum tō Breotone cyningum . . . Ðā hē ongeat ðæt hit swā ne wæs swā hē rēsade, Bd. 4, 1; S. 564, 48-565, 3. Rǽswodan, spǽcan, wǽron gemunende *comminiscuntur*, Wrt. Voc. ii. 24, 1. Ne réccaþ hwæt him mon ymbe rǽswe *mala de se opinari permittunt*, Past. 59, 1; Swt. 447, 28. Ðā ongan hē mid gleáwe mōde þencan and rǽsian (rēsian, MS. C.) *coepit sagaci animo conjicere*, Bd. 3, 10; S. 534, 21 note. Rēsigan *opinare*, Wrt. Voc. ii. 115, 55. Rǽswian *conici, conari*, 131, 79. Rēsenðe ic eom *suspicatus sum*, Ps. Surt. 118, 39. v. next word.

rǽswung, rēsung, e; *f. Supposition, conjecture*:—Rǽswung *vel* rǽdels *conjectura*, i. *opinatio, estimatio, interpretatio*, Wrt. Voc. ii. 133, 53. Rēsung *conjectura*, 104, 35. Rēsong, 77, 72. Rēsunge *ratiunculus*, 119, 14.

ræt *a rat*:—Ræt *raturus* (in a list of animals), Wrt. Voc. i. 22, 48. [*O. Du.* ratta: *O. H. Ger.* rato; *m.* ratta; *f.*: *Icel.* rotta; *f.*]

rǽw, rāw, e; *f. A row, line*:—Ðonon on ða rǽwe (*hedge-row*); of ðære reáwe on Temese, Cod. Dip. Kmbl. v. 275, 20. Sele ðonne drincan sume on (on sume, MS.) rāwe nigon dagon *nine days in succession*, Lchdm. ii. 238, 10. Cf. He sende hem so muche honger and luþer geres a-rewe, R. Glouc. 252, 2. Is seid of euerich on a-rewe, A. R. 90, 10. For þre niȝtes a-rowe he seiȝ þat same siȝt, Chron. Vilod. 68 (in Stratmann). *The word also occurs in* hæsel-, hege-, hlinc-, stān-, wiðig-rǽw, Cod. Dip. Kmbl. iii. xxxv. Cf. *also* gerǽwud fēða *acies*, Wrt. Voc. i. 18, 26. Standaþ on gerēwe, Cod. Dip. Kmbl. iii. 424, 8. Hí on gerǽwe sǽton, Homl. Skt. i. 23, 779.

rafan. v. be-rafan.

rāfian *to involve, wrap up* (?) cf. *Icel.* reifa *to swaddle*; or *to unloose, disclose*, cf. *Icel.* reifa *to rip up, disclose.* v. ā-rāfian, rǽfan.

rāge. v. rǽge.

raggig; *adj. Shaggy, bristly, ragged* as applied to the rough coat of a horse:—Raggie *setosa*, Hpt. Gl. 524, 16. [*Icel.* rögg *shagginess*; *a tuft* (cf. *rug-headed kernes* in Macbeth); raggaðr *tufted*: *Swed. Dan. dial.* ragg *rough hair*: *Swed. dial.* raggig *shaggy*: *Dan. dial.* raggad *shaggy.*]

ragu, e; *f. Lichen*:—Ragu *mosilicum*, Wrt. Voc. i. 67, 63: *mosiclum*, 287, 33: ii. 114, 18: *mossiclum*, 55, 74: *mosicum*, 114, 26. Rægu *sedulium*, 120, 46. Hæseles ragu *the lichen of hazel*, Lchdm. ii. 96, 2. Cristes-mǽl-ragu *lichen off a crucifix*, 346, 23. Ragu and meós (*rubigo*) fornymþ ealle eówre landes wæstmas, Deut. 28, 42. v. berc-, slāhþornragu.

ragu-finc, es; *m. The name of some bird*:—Ragofinc *scutatis, scutatus*, Wrt. Voc. i. 62, 44: 281, 15: *barrulus*, ii. 10, 79. Reagufinc *barilus*, 101, 62.

rāha. v. rā *and next word.*

rāh-deór, es; *n. A roe-buck*:—Rāhdeór *capreus*, Wrt. Voc. i. 22, 66: *capreolus*, 78, 30. Rāhdeóres mearh, Lchdm. iii. 2, 25.

ram. v. ramm.

ram-gealla, an; *m. Ram-gall* (a plant name); menyanthes trifoliata:—Ramgeallan ðone fāgan, Lchdm. ii. 124, 13. Hramgeallo, 140, 13.

ram-hund (?) :—De canibus quos ramhundt vocant, L. C. F. 32; Th. i. 430, 7.

ramm, es (*a wk. gen. pl. occurs*); *m.* I. *a ram*:—Ramm *aries*, Wrt. Voc. i. 23, 52. Ram, 78, 46. Rom *berbex*, ii. 12, 71: 126, 3. Rommes blōd, Cd. Th. 177, 20; Gen. 2932. Geoffra mē ǽnne þrīwintre ramm, Gen. 15, 9: 22, 13. Beorgas wǽron blīðe swā rammas, Ps. Th. 113, 6. Bringaþ him eówra ramma bearn, 28, 1: Ps. Spl. 65, 14. Twentig rammena *arietes viginti*, Gen. 32, 14. Rammum gelīce, Ps. Th. 113, 4. II. *an instrument for pounding* or *battering*:—*Aries* biþ ram betwux sceápum and ram tō wealgeweorce, Ælfc. Gr. 5; Som. 4, 15. Ram tō wurce *aries*, Wrt. Voc. i. 34, 57. Ram *aries*, andweorc tō wealle *cimentum*, wealwyrhta *cimentarius*, 85, 26–28. Þerscaþ ðone weall mid rammum, Past. 21; Swt. 161, 6. 'Gāþ tō mid rammum'... Hē bierþ rammas ymbūtan ðæt mōd his hiéremonna, ðonne hē him gecȳð mid hū scearplīcum costungum wē sint ǽghwonon ūtan behringde, and se weall ūres mægenes þurhþyrelað mid ðan scearpan ramman (ðǽm scearpan rammum, Cott. MSS.) ðara costunga, Swt. 163, 10–18. [*O. H. Ger.* ramm *aries, vervex.*]

rān, es; *n. Unlawful seizure of property, robbing*:—*Rān* quod dicunt apertam rapinam, L. W. iii. 12; Th. i. 493, 6. [*Icel.* rān.]

rān *rained.* v. rīnan.

ranc; *adj.* I. *proud, haughty, arrogant, insolent*: the word remains with a somewhat different meaning in *rank*, used of coarse but fertile growth:—Gif ǽnig man hæbbe mōdigne sunu and rancne (*protervum*) ðe nelle hīran his fæder and his mēder, Deut. 21, 18. Ne beón gē tō rance ne tō gylpgeorne, Wulfst. 40, 19: 81, 15. Sume munecas synd tō wlance and ealles tō rance, L. I. P. 14; Th. ii. 322, 12. Hī taliaþ ðē wyrsan for heánan gebyrdan ða ðe heora yldran on worolde ne wurdan welige ne wlance ne on lǽnan līffæce rance ne rīce *they account the worse for humble birth, those whose forefathers were not of great wealth or of high estate in the world, nor in this poor life-space proud or rich*, L. Eth. vii. 21; Th. i. 334, 4. [Forr þatt teȝȝ shollden Crist forseon þurrh þeȝȝre modignesse, þatt follc, þatt haffde beon til þa heh follc and rannc on eorþe, Orm. 9622. So were theih daungerouse for wlaunke; And siththen bicom ful reulich, that thanne weren so ranke, Pol. Songs 341, 390.] II. applied to dress, *showy* (cf. *brave* in Shakspere):—Witaþ ðæt ne mōt mid rihte nān preóst beón ne on his girlum tō ranc ne mid golde oferglæncged, L. Ælfc. P. 49; Th. i. 386, 10. Ne gē ne sceolon beón rance mid hringgum geglengede, L. Ælfc. C. 35; Th. ii. 358, 5. v. ofer-ranc. III. *bold, valiant* (*Icel.* rakkr *courageous, bold*):—Ðǽr mihton geseón Winceastre leódan rancne here and unearhne *a host bold and fearless*, Chr. 1006; Erl. 140, 26.

ranclīce; *adv.* I. *showily* (v. ranc, II):—Ne eówer reáf ne beó tō ranclīce gemacod, L. Ælfc. C. 35; Th. ii. 358, 6. II. *boldly* (v. ranc, III):—Ymbe ða feówer tīman wē wyllaþ cȳðan iungum preóstum mā þinga ðæt hig māgon ðē ranclīcor ðās þing heora clericum geswutelian, Anglia viii. 312, 18. [*Icel.* rakk-liga *boldly, valiantly.*]

ranc-strǽt, e; *f. A road in which bravery is displayed* (?):—God ðē wǽpnum lǽt rancstrǽte forþ rūme wyrcan *God let thee with weapons work an ample road where thy bravery was shewn* (*of Abraham's rescuing Lot*), Cd. Th. 127, 17; Gen. 2112. v. ranc.

rand, es; *m.* I. *a brink, edge, margin, shore*:—Ārās ðā bī ronde rōf oretta (cf. gesæt ðā on næsse nīðheard cyning, Beo. Th. 4825: hlǽw holmwylme neáh, 4814), Beo. Th. 5069; B. 2538. Of ðam fūlan brōce wið westan randes æsc *to the west of the ash tree on the bank* (?), Cod. Dip. B. ii. 259, 8. [Cf. *later English* rand *border, strip, slice*:—Raweȝ and randeȝ, Allit. Pms. 4, 105. Randes of bakun, Piers P. Crede 763. Rand *a narrow stripe*, Jameson. Rand *the edge of the upper leather, a seam of a shoe*, Bailey. *Icel.* rönd *a stripe*: *Ger.* rand *border, edge, margin.*] II. the word however is used generally of a shield, denoting the whole or part of it. (1) Denoting a part, *the boss of a round shield*, cf. rand-beáh *and O. H. Ger.* rant *umbo*. The word seems to have a different meaning in Icelandic: 'ā fornum skjöldum var tītt at skrifa rönd þā er baugr var kallaðr, ok er við þann baug skildir kenndir.' v. Cl. and Vig. s.v. baugr. Grein gives *margo clypei* as the meaning in the following passages, but *umbo* suits the sense: see too Worsaae's Primeval Antiquities of Denmark, pp. 31–2: 51–3, where instances of early shields are given:—Rand sceal on scylde fæst fingra gebeorh *a boss must be on a shield, a sure protection for fingers* (*which grasped the shield just behind the boss*), Menol. Fox 534; Gn. C. 37. Līgȳðum forborn bord wið rond *the buckler against the boss burned with the flames*, Beo. Th. 5339; B. 2673. (2) Denoting the whole, *a shield, buckler* [*Icel.* rönd *a shield*]:—Rand dynede, campwudu clynede, Elen. Kmbl. 100; El. 50. Ðonne rond and hand on herefelda helm ealgodon, Andr. Kmbl. 18; An. 9: 824; An. 412. Hē under rande gecranc *slain he sank under his shield*, Beo. Th. 2423; B. 1209. Ðæt hē mē ongeán sleá, rand geheáwe, 1368; B. 682. Siððan ic hond and rond hebban mihte *since I could bear arms*, 1316; B. 656. Hond rond gefēng geolwe linde, 5212; B. 2609. Scyldes rond fæste gefēgan wið flyge gāres *to join together firmly the shield's disk against the flight of javelin*, Exon. Th. 297, 11; Crā. 65. Beorhte randas, Beo. Th. 468; B. 231. Rondas regnhearde, 657; B. 326. Ðā hī on ðone Reádan Sǽ randas bǽron, Ps. Th. 105, 8; Cd. Th. 199, 2; Exod. 332. Rincas randas wǽgon, 123, 22; Gen. 2049. Bæd ðæt hyra randan (randas?) rihte heóldon, Byrht. Th. 132, 22; By. 20. v. bord-, calc-, gafol-, geolo-, hilde-, sīd-rand.

rand-beáh, -beág, es; *m. The boss of a shield* or *the shield itself*; buculus, bucula (cf. bucula *the boss of a shield*, Isidore), bucularis, umbo, testudo (cf. scyld *testudo, clipeus*, Wrt. Voc. i. 35, 57):—Randbeáh *umb*[*r*]*o*, Wrt. Voc. i. 84, 33: Ælfc. Gr. 9, 3; Som. 8, 34. Īsen randbeág *ferreus umbo*, ii. 147, 79. *Umbo* randbēh *vel bucula*, i. 35, 29. Randbeáh *buculus*, 288, 13. Rondbeág, ii. 11, 37. Rondbaeg, 102, 29. Randbeág *buculus* vel *bucularis*, 126, 65. Randbeáh *testudo*, Ælfc. Gr. 9, 3; Som. 8, 60. Swilce lytel pricu on brādan brede oððe rondbeáh on scilde, Bt. 18, 1; Fox 62, 5. Randbeáges *umbonis*, Wrt. Voc. ii. 86, 83: Hpt. Gl. 521, 8. Hrandbeága *testudine*, 495, 47. Under þiccum randbeáge *subter densa testudine*, Ælfc. Gr. 47; Som. 48, 29. Randbeág *testudinem*, Hpt. Gl. 423, 58. Randbeágum *umbonibus*, 424, 6: Wrt. Voc. ii. 76, 45. [*O. H. Ger.* rant-pouc.] v. rand.

rand-burh *a town that acts as a shield* (?), *a fortified town, a frontier town* (?):—Rīce gerēfa rondburgum weóld, eard weardade, Exon. Th. 243, 32; Jul. 19. Randbyrig (*the walls formed by the waters of the Red Sea when the Israelites passed through it*) wǽron rofene *were riven* (*when the Egyptians attempted to cross*), Cd. Th. 207, 7; Exod. 463. Or are the walls formed by the water compared to the arrangement of the line of battle when the shields overlapped, called *scild-burh* q. v.? v. next word.

rand-gebeorh *a protection such as that afforded by a shield*:—Se āgend up ārǽrde reáde streámas in randgebeorh *the Lord hath raised the Red Sea's waters as a protecting shield* (cf. the waters were a wall unto them, Ex. 14, 29), Cd. Th. 196, 24; Exod. 296.

rand-hæbbend, es; *m. One who has a shield, a warrior*:—Ōðer nǽnig sēlra nǽre rondhæbbendra, Beo. Th. 1726; B. 861.

rand-wīga, an; *m. A warrior with a shield, a warrior*:—Rīce randwīga (*Æschere*), Beo. Th. 2600; B. 1298. Rōfne randwīgan, 3590; B. 1793. Randwīgena ræst (*the camping of the Israelites on their march*), Cd. Th. 186, 5; Exod. 134. Randwīgum frætwa dǽlan, 171, 14; Gen. 2828.

rand-wīgend, -wīggend (-wiggend?), es; *m. A warrior with a shield, a warrior*:—Rondwīggende (*the men of Holofernes*), Judth. Thw. 21, 9; Jud. 11: 21, 15; Jud. 20. Nū ic gumena gehwæne ðyssa burhleóda biddan wylle randwīggendra (*the people of Bethulia*), 24, 14; Jud. 188: (*the descendants of Abraham*), Cd. Th. 205, 13; Exod. 435.

rāp, es; *m. A rope, cord, cable*:—Rāp *funiculus* vel *funis*, Wrt. Voc. i. 15, 19: 75, 4. Rāp *vel* strenc *funiculus, modicus funis*, ii. 151, 66. Rāp *rudens*, i. 285, 18. Heó lēt hig ūt mid ānum langum rāpe (*per funem*), Jos. 2, 15. Rāpas *funes* vel *restes*, Wrt. Voc. i. 56, 58: *lora*, ii. 51, 40: *restes*, 93, 4: *funes*, Ps. Th. 118, 61. Hig hine gebundon mid twām bæstenum rāpum (*novis funibus*)... Ða rāpas tōburston, Jud. 15, 13–14: 16, 9. Hwæt beóþ ða feówere fǽges rāpas? Gewurdene wyrda, ða beóþ ða feówere fǽges rāpas, Salm. Kmbl. 661–668; Sal. 331–333. Rāpa *nodorum*, Wrt. Voc. ii. 61, 68. Rāpum *rudentibus, funibus*, Hpt. Gl. 529, 27. Ðū gedydest ðæt wē mǽtan ūre land mid rāpum, Ps. Th. 15, 6. Swā swā hē mid gildenum rāpum āhafen wǽre, Bd. 4, 9; S. 576, 36. Ānra gehwilc manna is gewriðen mid rāpum his synna, Homl. Th. i. 208, 4. Hē worhte āne swipe of rāpum (of strengum *of small cords*, Jn. Skt. 2, 15), 406, 7. [*Goth.* raip; *n.*: *Icel.* reip; *n.*: *O. H. Ger.* reif; *m.*] v. ancor-, bealu-, helpend-, mǽrels-, mæst-, met-, net-, scip-, stig-, sund-, wæl-rāp.

rāp-gang (?), es; *m. Rope-dancing*:—Rāpgong (MS. -gon. Cf. l. 33, *where* gegon *is written for* gegong [v. p. 33, 65]) *funambulus*, Wrt. Voc. ii. 38, 36. *The meaning seems to require* rap-gonga (-genga?).

rāp-geweale (?), es; *n. A coil of rope* (?), *a cord*:—Rǽpe gewælc *funiculum*, Ps. Spl. T. 104, 10.

rāpincel, es; *n. A cord, string, rope*:—Rāpincel *funiculus*, Cant. M. ad fil. 9. On rāpincle tōdāles *in funiculo distributionis*, Blickl. Gl.: Ps. Spl. 77, 60. Rāpincel *funiculum*, 104, 10. Mīn rāpincel ðū āsmeádest *funiculum meum investigastis*, Ps. Lamb. 138, 2.

rāp-līc; *adj. Of rope*:—Rāplīc *funale*, Germ. 399, 469.

rāre-dumla, -dumle, an; *m.f. A bittern*:—Rāredumlæ *onocrotalum, avis quae sonitum facit in aqua*, Shrn. 29, 6. Rāradumbla *onocrotalus*, Wrt. Voc. i. 62, 21. Rāredumle, 280, 26: 63, 70: *buban*, 126, 61. [*M. H. Ger.* rōr-tumel *a bittern*: *Ger.* rohr-dommel: *M. Du.* roes-domel. *O. H. Ger. has* horo-tūbil, -tumil.] [Cf. for the second part of the word, *dumble-dore*, the name given in some places to the bee.]

rārian; *p.* ode. I. of human beings, *to wail, lament loudly*:—Seó dreórige mōdor samod mid ðām līcmannum rārigende hī āstrehte æt ðæs apostoles fōtum, Homl. Th. i. 66, 18. II. of other than human beings, *to roar, bellow*:—Hwīlum dióflu him rāredon on swā hrȳðro, Shrn. 141, 10. Rārende ł bellende *rugiens*, Mt. Kmbl. p. 9, 14. Ðære rārigendan *bombosa*, Wrt. Voc. ii. 89, 8.

rárung, e; *f. Roaring, loud cry;* barritus, Wrt. Voc. ii. 10, 68: 79, 29: 125, 18.
rásettan; *p.* te *To move impetuously, to rage* (of fire):—Hé (*Nero*) wolde fandian, gif ðæt fýr (*at the burning of Rome*) meahte swá longe reád rásettan, swá hé secgan gehérde, ðæt Troia burg ofertogen hæfde léga leóhtost, Met. 9, 14. Blác rásetteþ reáda líg, réðe scríþeþ, Exon. Th. 51, 1; Cri. 809. Cf. rǽs.
rásian; *p.* ode *To explore*:—Ðá wæs hord rásod, onboren beága hord, Beo. Th. 4556; B. 2283. v. á-rásian.
raðe (*aspirated and unaspirated forms occur, and each can alliterate; the two forms are given separately.* v. hraðe); *adv. Quickly, soon, at once, directly, without hesitation*:—Raðe *ilico*, Wrt. Voc. ii. 44, 68: *ocius*, 64, 47. Ræðe *ultro*, 90, 8. Heó nam raðe (*cito*) hyre wǽfels, Gen. 24, 65. Cwelle hig man raðe (*statim*), L. Ecg. C. 39; Th. ii. 164, 1. Ðæt hine mon slóge swá raðe swá mon hiora fiénd wolde *that they should kill him as soon* (*with as little compunction*) *as they would their enemies*, Ors. 1, 12; Swt. 52, 35. Ða men wǽron swá raðe deáde swá ðæt yfel him an becom, 4, 5; Swt. 166, 7. Raðe ðæs *directly afterwards*, 3, 10; Swt. 138, 33. Héht lífes brytta leóht forþcuman ofer rúmne grund; raðe wæs gefylled heáhcininges hǽs, Cd. Th. 8, 13; Gen. 123: 95, 26; Gen. 1584: Exon. Th. 93, 15; Cri. 1526: Beo. Th. 1453; B. 724. Ðæs cymþ raðor *iste egredietur prius*, Gen. 38, 28. Ne þincþ eów nó ðý raðor (*none the sooner*) heora genóh, Bt. 13; Fox 38, 31: 30, 1; Fox 108, 9. Nán man hit náh tó geáhnianne raðost þinga (*at the earliest*) ǽr syx mónþum æfter ðam ðe hit forstolen wæs, L. C. S. 24; Th. i. 390, 13. Swá ðæt cild raðost ǽnig þing specan mǽge *as soon as ever the child can speak*, Wulfst. 39, 8. Ðonne mágon wé hí swá raðost (*in the quickest manner possible*) tó ryhte gecierran, Past. 32; Swt. 209, 21.
ráw. v. rǽw.
ráwan (?) *to cut in strips* (?) (v. rǽw.) Cf. Geráwende *infindens*, Wrt. Voc. ii. 91, 24. Geráwende slítende and ceorfende *infindens*, 47, 22. Gerǽwen hrægel *segmentata vestis*, i. 40, 10.
rawe, Wrt. Voc. ii. 128, 39. v. rupe.
reád; *adj. Red*:—Reád deáh *coccus*, Wrt. Voc. i. 40, 40. Reád teafor *minium*, 46, 74. Se reáda telg, Exon. Th. 408, 21; Rä. 27, 15. Reád *ruber*, Wrt. Voc. ii. 119, 35: *flavum, fulvum*, 108, 70: *roseus*, vel *rubeus*, vel *pheniceus*, i. 46, 50: *croceus*, Hpt. Gl. 524, 37. Reádde lǽmene fatu *alsierina*, Wrt. Voc. i. 41, 47. (a) Of plants or fruit:—Reáde wínberige *ceraunis*, 38, 62. Reáde clefre *calta*, 67, 72. Rǽde clæfer, 288, 49. Reád clæfré, Lchdm. ii. 312, 19. Rósena reáde heápas, Dóm. L. 18, 286. Mid reádum rósum *cum purpureis rosis*, Hpt. Gl. 511, 4. (b) of gold:—Reád gold *aurum obrizum*, Wrt. Voc. i. 38, 33: Met. 19, 6: Cd. Th. 219, 24; Dan. 59. (c) of fire, sky:—Reád líg, Dóm. L. 10, 149, 152: Exon. Th. 51, 2; Cri. 810. Ðes heofon ys reád (*rubicundum*), Mt. Kmbl. 16, 2. (d) of blood:—Sió reáde ród *the bloodstained cross*, Exon. 68, 11; Cri. 1102. [*Goth.* rauds: *O. Sax.* ród: *O. Frs.* rád: *O. H. Ger.* rót: *Icel.* rauðr.] v. bleó-, geolu-, weolc-reád; reód.
reáda glosses *tolia* vel *porunula*:—Smæle þearmas *ilia*, reáda *tolia* vel *porunula*, bæcþearm *entales*, Wrt. Voc. i. 44, 46–48.
reádan. v. on-reádan.
reád-basu; *adj. Reddish purple*:—Ðǽr synt ða reádbeswean blóstman gróweñde, L. E. I. prm.; Th. ii. 400, 5.
reádda, an; *m. The robin redbreast*:—Raedda *rubisca*, Wrt. Voc. ii. 119. 38. Cf. rudduc.
reáde; *adv. Redly, in red*:—Hire andwlita biþ reáde wan *livid with a red tinge*, Lchdm. ii. 348, 19. Ðá wearþ beám monig blódigum teárum birunnen reáde and þicce, Exon. Th. 72, 22; Cri. 1176. Ic eom reáde bewǽfed *I am clothed in red*, 484, 2; Rä. 70, 1.
reád-fáh; *adj. Red-stained, having patches of red colour*:—Wág reádfáh, Exon. Th. 476, 19; Ruin. 10.
reádian; *p.* ode *To be* or *become red*:—Ic reádige *rubeo*, Ælfc. Gr. 26, 2; Som. 28, 42. Reádaþ þe heofun *rutilat coelum*, Mt. Kmbl. Rush. 16, 3. Reádode *purpurescit*, Wrt. Voc. ii. 67, 8. Reádede, Hpt. Gl. 503, 51. Reádodon *rubescunt*, Hymn. Surt. 52, 31. Æppel ðe ðonne gyt ne reádige, Lchdm. i. 330, 22. Smire ða ófras ðǽr hit reádige, ii. 108, 20. Reádian *rubescere*, Hymn. Surt. 49, 17. Reádiendum *rubente*, 91, 33. [*O. H. Ger.* róten *rutilare, rubere, erubescere*.] v. reódian.
reád-leáf (?); *adj. Having red leaves*:—On ða hreádleáfan ǽc, Cod. Dip. Kmbl. v. 179, 26.
reádness, e; *f. Redness*:—Reádnyss *rubor*, Ælfc. Gr. 9, 21; Som. 10, 28. Seó reádnes ðære rósan, Blickl. Homl. 7, 29. Seó reádnes ðæs swyles *rubor tumoris*, Bd. 4, 19; S. 589, 31. Reádnysse *ostro, purpura, vermiculo*, Hpt. Gl. 503, 49: 522, 6.
reád-staled; *adj. Having a red stale* or *stalk*:—Reádstalede hárhuna, Lchdm. i. 378, 19.
reád-stán (?), es; *m. Ruddle, red ochre*:—Rédestán *sinopide*, Wrt. Voc. ii. 120, 63. [*O. H. Ger.* rót-stein *sinopis*, Grff. 6, 688.]
reáf, es; *n.* I. *spoil, booty*:—Reáf *exuviae, spolia*, Wrt. Voc. ii. 146, 33: *exuvias*, 31, 56: 93, 1. Weorðlíc reáf *spolia*, Ps. Th. 67, 12. Se ðe beorna reáf manige (*spolia multa*) méteþ, 118, 162. Seó gýtsung hyre reáf (*spolia*) on ðære wynstran sídan scylt, Gl. Prud. 56 a. Hý ðý reáfe rǽdan mótan, Exon. Th. 110, 5; Gú. 103. II. *raiment, a garment, robe, vestment*:—Reáf *vestis* vel *vestimentum* vel *indumentum*, Wrt. Voc. i. 81, 40: *cultus*, 39, 70. Heó æthrán his reáfes (*vestimenti*) fnæd. Heó cwæþ sóðlíce: Ic beó hál gyf ic hys reáfes æthríne, Mt. Kmbl. 9, 20–21. Tó hwí sint gé ymbhýdige be reáfe? 6, 28. Twegen weras on hwítum reáfe *in veste fulgenti*, Lk. Skt. 24, 4. Ne scríde nán wíf hig mid wǽpmannes reáfe ne wǽpman mid wífmannes reáfe, Deut. 22, 5. Hé scrýdde hine mid línenum reáfe *cum stola byssina*, Gen. 41, 42. Hláf tó etenne and reáf tó werigenne, 28, 20. Ðæt hálie reáf ðæt Aaron wereþ, Ex. 29, 29. Johannes hæfde reáf of olfenda hǽrum, Mt. Kmbl. 3, 4. His reáf (*vestimenta*) wǽron swá hwíte swá snáw, 17, 2: Hí sǽton on blacum reáfum weán on wénum, Cd. Th. 191, 10; Exod. 212. Ðá dyde heó of hire wydewan reáf *depositis viduitatis vestibus*, Gen. 38, 14. [*Laym.* reaf, ræf *a robe*: *O. Sax.* nód-róf *rapine*: *O. Frs.* ráf *robbery, booty*; also *a pledge*: *O. Du.* roof: *O. H. Ger.* roub *spolia, praeda*: *Icel.* val-rauf *spoils* taken from the slain.] v. bed-, búr-, deáþ-, gúþ-, heaðo-, here-, lenden-, síd-, wæl-reáf.
reáfere, es; *m. A reaver, robber, spoiler*:—Reáfere *raptor* vel *praedo*, vel *spoliator*, Wrt. Voc. i. 47, 49: *raptor*, 76, 8: *agressor*, 19, 7. Hreáfere *praedo, raptor*, Hpt. Gl. 501, 34. Gif hwilc þeóf oððe reáfere gesóhte ðone cyning, ðæt hé hæbbe nigon nihta fyrst, L. Ath. iv. 4; Th. i. 222, 26. Ueriatus wæs micel þeófmon and on ðære stalunge hé wearð reáfere *Viriathus latro, primum infestando vias, deinde vastando provincias*, Ors. 5, 2; Swt. 216, 8. Gif ðú on hwilcum men ongitst ðæt hé byþ gítsere and reáfere, ne scealt ðú hine ná hátan man, ac wulf, Bt. 37, 4; Fox 192, 15. Ne sǽde ðæt godspel ðæt se ríca (*Dives in the parable*) reáfere wǽre, ac wæs uncystig, Homl. Th. i. 328, 18. Scyld sceal cempan, sceaft reáfere, Exon. Th. 341, 23; Gn. Ex. 130. Ic ne eom swylce óðre men, reáferas (*raptores*), Lk. Skt. 18, 11. Rýperas and reáferas and ðás woruldstrúderas, L. I. P. 2; Th. ii. 304, 19: Wulfst. 165, 35: L. C. S. 7; Th. i. 380, 5. [*O. E. Homl.* reaferes, reveres; *pl.*: *A. R.* reavares: *Laym.* ræveres: *Piers P.* reveres: *O. H. Ger.* roubari *raptor, predo*: *Ger.* räuber: *Icel.* raufari, reyfari.]
reáfian; *p.* ode. I. *to plunder, rifle, spoil, waste, rob* (1) a person:—Úte hí reáfaþ (*vastabit*) swurd, Deut. 32, 25. Se ðe reáfaþ man leóhtan dæge *he who robs a man by daylight*, L. Eth. iii. 15; Th. i. 298, 11. Ǽghwá mec reáfaþ, Exon. Th. 482, 4; Rä. 66, 2. Gé reáfiaþ (*spoliabitis*) Egipte, Ex. 3, 22. Ðenden reáfode rinc óðerne, Beo. Th. 5962; B. 2985. Wígfrecan wæl reáfedon, 2429; B. 1212. Reáfodon (*diripuerunt*) hine ealle oferfarende wæg, Ps. Spl. 88, 40. Reáfa *vastes*, Kent. Gl. 936. Gif hwylc man reáfige (*spoliaverit*) óðerne æt his dehter, L. Ecg. P. iv. 13; Th. ii. 208, 7. Swíðor ðonne hié reáfian earme and unscyldige, Blickl. Homl. 63, 17. (2) a place:—Ic folcsalo bærne, ræced reáfige, Exon. Th. 381, 4; Rä. 2, 6. Ic lond reáfige, 394, 7; Rä. 13, 14. Se snáw gebryceþ burga geatu, reáfaþ swíðor mycle ðonne se swíðra níð, Salm. Kmbl. 65; Sal. 307. Reáfiaþ hine (*the vineyard*) ealle ða farende, Ps. Spl. 79, 13: Blickl. Gl. Hý hergiaþ and heáwaþ, rýpaþ and reáfiaþ and tó scipe lǽdaþ, Wulfst. 163, 12. Rib reáfiaþ réðe wyrmas, Soul. Kmbl. 220; Seel. 113. Ic reáfode beám and ða blǽda æt, Cd. Th. 55, 28; Gen. 901. Ðonne man his hús reáfige (*diripiet*), Mk. Skt. 3, 27. Hord reáfian, Beo. Th. 5540; B. 2773. Helle weallas forbrecan, ðære burge þrym reáfian, Exon. Th. 461, 15; Hö. 36. II. *to seize, take as a robber takes*:—Reáfiaþ *rapiunt*, Kent. Gl. 4. Ic forþ ágef ða ðe ic ne reáfude ǽr *quae non rapui tunc exolvebam*, Ps. Th. 68, 5. [*Goth.* bi-raubon: *Icel.* raufa: *O. Frs.* rávia: *O. Du.* róven: *O. H. Ger.* roubón.] v. á-, be-, ge-reáfian.
reáfigend, es; *m. A spoiler, a plunderer*:—Ic bidde míne æftergengan, ciningas and þeóde wealdendras, ðæt gé ne sýn cyrcean reáfgendras, ac ðæt gé sýn geornfulle bewerigendras Cristes ágenre landáre, Cod. Dip. Kmbl. iii. 350, 26.
reáfigende; *adj. Ravening, rapacious*; rapax, Ælfc. Gr. 9, 60; Som. 13, 42.
reáf-lác, es; *n. m.* I. *rapine, robbery, spoliation, plundering*:—Ðis synt ða ídelnyssa ðysse worlde . . . gýtsung and reáflác (*rapina*) and manslihtas, L. Ecg. P. i. 8; Th. ii. 174, 34. Heáfodleahtras sind . . . reáflác, gítsung . . ., Homl. Th. ii. 592, 6. Ús rýpera reáflác derede swíðe, Wulfst. 159, 11. Gé synt innan fulle reáfláces *pleni rapina*, Mt. Kmbl. 23, 25. Full reáflace and unrihtwísnesse, Lk. Skt. 11, 39. Nellaþ gé tó reáfláce rǽda þencean *in rapinis nolite concupiscere*, Ps. Th. 61, 10. Hé wearð reáfere, and on ðæm reáfláce (*in the course of his plundering*) hé him geteáh tó micelne monfultum, and monege túnas oferhergeade, Ors. 5, 2; Swt. 216, 8. On reáflác *in rapinam*, Wrt. Voc. ii. 45, 20. Be reáfláce. Gif hwá binnan ðám gemǽrum úres ríces reáflác dó, L. In. 10; Th. i. 108, 8 (*where see note*). Gif ciricgrið ábrocen beó, sí hit þurh feohtlác, sí hit þurh reáflác, L. Eth. ix. 4; Th. i. 340, 22: L. C. S. 48; Th. i. 402, 30. Gif hwá reáflác gewyrce, ágife and forgylde, 64; Th. i. 410, 2. Ðæt hé begange nán reáflác, Homl. Th. ii. 46, 4. Þurh rícra reáflác, Wulfst. 166, 23. [Unwrenches, stele oðer refloc oðer drunkenesse, O. E. Homl. ii. 79, 29. Þe vox of giscunge

haued þeos hweolpes . . . þeofþe, reflac . . . , A. R. 202, 19. Þe king his ræflac makede (his lond al forverde, 2nd MS.), Laym. 9939. Ðeft and reflac ðhugte him no same, Gen. and Ex. 436.] II. what is taken, *spoil, booty, plunder*:—Reáflác *preda*, Wrt. Voc. i. 35, 39: ii. 146, 33. Ælc bit ðæs reáfláces ðe him on genumen biþ, oððe eft óðres gítsaþ, Bt. 26, 2; Fox 92, 17. Man wolde biddan ðæs reáfláces ðæt hé hit sciolde ágyfan and forgyldan, Chart. Th. 289, 27. Ágife hé ðone reáflác *he shall restore what has been seized*, L. In. 10; Th. i. 108, 9. Tódǽlan reáflac *dividere spolia*, Ps. Spl. T. 67, 13.

reáfol; *adj. Rapacious*:—Reáfol *captator*, Germ. 397, 19. Cild ácenned þríste reáful ofermód him sylfum gelícigende *a child born on the thirteenth day of the moon will be bold, rapacious, arrogant, pleasing himself*, Lchdm. iii. 190, 14. v. next word.

reáfolness, e; *f. Rapacity*:—Reáfulnesse *rapacitatis*, Hpt. Gl. 508, 44.

reáfung, e; *f. Plundering, spoiling*:—Atheniensum se sige and seó reáfung ðæs Persiscan feós tó máran sconde wurde forðon siððan hié welcgran wǽron hié eác bleáðran gewurdon *castra regiis opibus referta ceperunt, non parvo quidem antiquae industriae damno. Nam post hujus praedae divisionem, aurum Persicum prima Graeciae corruptio fuit*, Ors. 2, 5; Swt. 84, 21.

reám, es; *m. Cream*:—Wið ðon ðe mon blóde hrǽce and spíwe; genim god beren mela and hwít sealt, dó on reám oððe góde fléte, Lchdm. ii. 314, 2. [Cristened we weore In red rem Whon his bodi bledde on þe Beem, H. R. 146, 144. Ream (*subst. and verb*) *cream*, Jamieson. *See also Halliwell's Dict. where instances of* milkes rem *are given under* ream. *Du.* room: *M. H. Ger.* roum: *Icel.* rjómi.]

reáma. v. reóma.

réc, es; *m. Reek, smoke*:—Réc *fumus*, Wrt. Voc. i. 284, 18: 66, 45: ii. 36, 54. Of ðære stówe steám up árás swylce réc, Elen. Kmbl. 1604; El. 804. Réce hí gelícast geteoriaþ *sicut deficit fumus, deficiant*, Ps. Th. 67, 2. Geondfolen fýre, réce and reáde lége, Cd. Th. 3, 31; Gen. 44. In onlícnesse uppástígendra yselena mid réce *instar favillarum cum fumo ascendentium*, Bd. 5, 12; S. 628, 23. Hé geseah ðone líg ðæs fýres and ðone réc ofer ðære burge wallas áhefenne, 3, 16; S. 543, 2: Cd. Th. 155, 26; Gen. 2578. Bráde lígas, swilce eác ða biteran récas, 21, 17; Gen. 325. Ic folcsalo bærne, récas stígaþ haswe ofer hrófum, Exon. Th. 381, 5; Rä. 2, 6. [*O. Frs.* rék: *O. Sax.* wíh-rók: *O. Du.* rook: *O. H. Ger.* rouh: *Icel.* reykr.] v. swefel-, wæl-, wudu-réc.

récan; *p.* réhte *To smoke* (trans.), *steam*:—Réhte (Wrt. reþte: Wülck. reohte) *fumarat*, Wrt. Voc. ii. 151, 55. Ðám mannum ðe fram ðære teóþan tíde ne geseóþ, ðæs ylcan drinces smýc heora eágan onfón and mid ðam broþe récen, and ða lifre wǽten, and gníden and mid smyrgen, Lchdm. i. 346, 22. [*O. H. Ger.* rouhan; *p.* ta *thurificare, sufire, vaporare*: *Icel.* reykja; *p.* ta *to smoke* (trans.).] v. reócan.

récan, réccan (reccan?); *p.* róhte *To care, reck*, (1) with gen.:—Ne can ic eów ne ic eówer récce *I know you not and I care not for you*, L. Ælfc. P. 40; Th. ii. 380, 3. Ðú ǽfre ne récst ǽniges þinges (cf. ðú ne wilnast nánes óðres þinges, Bt. 23; Fox 80, 2) ofer ða áne, Met. 12, 31. Biþ micel rǽd ðam ðe his sylfes récþ, Homl. Skt. i. 12, 122, 132. Se deáþ swelces ne récþ, Bt. 19; Fox 68, 32. Hé wǽpna ne récceþ, Beo. Th. 873; B. 434. Ne réccaþ hí ðara metta, Bt. 25; Fox 88, 19. Hí habbaþ cornes swá fela swá hí mǽst récceaþ (réccaþ, MSS. P. S.) *they have as much corn as ever they care for*, Lchdm. iii. 254, 5: Wulfst. 132, 21. Wé willaþ nú on Englisceum gereorde secgean ðám ðe his (*the book*) récceaþ, Basil prm.; Norm. 32, 14. Hwæt róhte ic hwæðer ic wǽre gyf ic ne lyfde, oððe hwæt róhte ic ðæs lýfes gyf ic náwiht nyste, Shrn. 194, 2. Hé lǽrde ðæt ða þearfan ne wénden ðæt God heora ne róhte, Ps. Th. arg. 48. Ðǽr læig ðæt reáf beæftan, forðon ðe hé ne róhte ðæs eorþlícan reáfes, syððan hé of deáþe árás, Homl. Th. i. 224, 4. Feores hí ne róhton, Byrht. Th. 139, 27; By. 260. Hié ðæs ne róhton, Cd. Th. 79, 31; Gen. 1319: 228, 13; Dan. 201: Exon. Th. 88, 17; Cri. 1441. Gif ðú ðínes feores récce, 119, 30; Gú. 262. Gif ðú aldres récce, Cd. Th. 160, 27; Gen. 2656. Gif hwelc wíf forlǽt hiere ceorl and nimþ hire óðerne wénestú récce hé hire ǽfre má (*numquid revertetur ad eam ultra?*) Past. 52, 3; Swt. 405, 12: L. Alf. 12; Th. i. 46, 15: L. A. G. prm.; Th. i. 152, 6. (1 a) used impersonally, with acc. of person:—Hí ðæs metes ne récþ (cf. above, Bt. 25; Fox 88, 19), Met. 13, 45. [Cf. me ne reccheð (naut I ne recche, MS. C.) *non requiro*, A. R. 104, 21.] (2) with a preposition:—Ðú eart sóðfæst and ðú ne récst be ǽnegum menn (*non curas quemquam*), Mk. Skt. 12, 14. (3) with a clause:—Ne récþ God, ðeáh ic ðus dó *non requiret Deus*, Ps. Th. 9, 33. Hwæt réce wé hwæt wé sprecan *quid curamus quid loquamur?* Coll. Monast. Th. 18, 14. Gé ne réccaþ hwæðer gé áuht tó góde dón, Bt. 18, 4; Fox 66, 20. Hié ne récceaþ hwæðer, Past. 19, 2; Swt. 145, 21. Se cyng ne róhte ná hú swíðe synlíce ða geréfan hit begeátan, ne hú manige unlaga hí dydon, Chr. 1086; Erl. 220, 12. Hí woldon on elþeódignesse beón, hí ne róhton hwǽr, 891; Erl. 88, 8. Men ne róhton hwæt hý worhtan, Wulfst. 163, 16. [*Laym.* rehchen, recchen (*with gen.*): *O. and N.* recche; recþ (*3rd pers.*): *Piers P. Chauc.* recche, rekke: *Havel.* recke: *O. Sax.* rókian: *O. H. Ger.* ruohian: *Icel.* rækja.]

reccan; *p.* reahte, rehte. I. *to stretch, extend*:—Wið hǽrscearde . . . onsníð mid seaxse, seówa mid seolce fæste . . . gif tósomne teó rece mid handa *for harelip . . . cut with a knife, sew fast with silk . . . if there be contraction* (*where the stitches are*) *smooth out with the hand*, Lchdm. ii. 56, 9. II. *to hold out to another, to give*; porrigere:—Hærfest tó honda hérbúendum rípa receþ (cf. hærfest bryngþ rípa bléda, Bt. 39, 13; Fox 234, 15), Met. 29, 63. Eall ðæt ofer biþ tó láfe on heora weoruldspédum árfæstum and gódum is tó recceanne and tó syllanne *omne quod superest, in causis piis ac religiosis erogandum est*, Bd. 1, 27; S. 489, 27. III. *to stretch one's steps, to tend, to go, stray*:—Hé nát hwider hé recþ mid ðám stæpum his weorca *quo gressus operis porrigat, nescit*, Past. 11, 1; Swt. 65, 9. Gif hé (*a close*) biþ untýned, and recþ (receþ, MS. H.) his neáhgebúres ceáp in on his ágen geat, L. In. 40; Th. i. 126, 14. [Swa sone swa heo mihten ut of scipe heo rehten, Laym. 25646.] IV. *to unfold a tale, to narrate, recite, tell, say*:—Recceo *alligeo* (*allego*), Txts. 39, 139. Ic recce (*narrabo*) ealle wundra ðíne, Ps. Spl. 9, 1. Ic ðé má be Gode recce, Bt. 35, 3; Fox 158, 9. Ðonne hé eall ðis recþ and sægþ, Blickl. Homl. 91, 14. Hwæt synt ða spǽca ðe gyt recceaþ (*confertis*) inc betwýnan, Lk. Skt. 24, 17. Hé rehte him óðer bigspel *aliam parabolam proposuit illis*, Mt. Kmbl. 13, 24, 31. Ðá reahte heora ǽgðer his spell *each of them told his tale*, Chart. Th. 170, 14. Hé him his earfoþa rehte, Guthl. 19; Gdwin. 76, 19. Ymb ðæt reahte Paulus swíðe wel *quod bene Paulus exprimit*, Past. 51, 1; Swt. 395, 11. Rehte, 51, 2; Swt. 395, 26. Hé him rehte hú myccle scipbrocu hé gebád, Blickl. Homl. 173, 6. Spell ðæt ús reahte Platon, Met. 22, 53. Rehte, Beo. Th. 4226; B. 2110. Hé Dryhtnes lof reahte, Exon. Th. 111, 23; Gú. 131. Ðam wit rehton (*narravimus*) uncer swefen, Gen. 41, 12. Ne nán ne dyrstlǽce ðæt hé óðrum recce, oððe mid wordum gecýðe, hwæt hé bútan mynstre geseah, R. Ben. 128, 4. Reccan *expedire*, Wrt. Voc. ii. 31, 26. Ic ðé mæg reccan sum spell, Bt. 38, 1; Fox 194, 1. Reccan race, 38, 6; Fox 208, 4. Bigspell reccan *in parabolis loqui*, Mk. Skt. 12, 1. Reccean and secggan, Blickl. Homl. 55, 28. Godes béc reccean and rǽdan, and godspell secggean, 111, 17. Reccean ymbe Dauides dǽda sume, Past. 28; Swt. 196, 10. Sint tó recceanne ða godcundan cwidas *divinae sententiae proferendae sunt*, 37, 2; Swt. 265, 22. Tó lang ys tó reccenne *too long to tell*, Beo. Th. 4192; B. 2093. Hé his intingan wæs reccende *causam dicturus*, Bd. 5, 19; S. 639, 19. Reccendes *loquentis, narrantis*, Hpt. Gl. 460, 68. [Ic þe wulle ræcchen (telle of, 2nd MS.) deorne runen, Laym. 14679.] V. *to unfold the meaning of anything, to explain, interpret, expound*:—Eall hé his leorningcnihtum ásundron rehte (*disserebat*), Mk. Skt. 4, 34. Rehte *interpraetabatur*, Lk. Skt. 24, 27. Ðá wæs ic ungleáw ðæs geþeódes . . . ðá rehte hit mé se bisceop and sægde, Nar. 29, 16. Hú gleáwlíce hé ðæt swefen rehte *quod prudenter somnium dissolvisset*, Gen. 40, 16. Rece, wísworda gleáw, hwæt sió wiht síe, Exon. Th. 415, 19; Rä. 33, 13. Hér begann se deófol tó reccanne hálige gewritu and hé leáh mid ðære race *here the devil began to expound holy writ, and he was false in his exposition*, Homl. Th. i. 170, 4. [Ðe king him bad ben harde and bold, If he can rechen ðis dremes wold; He told him quat him drempte o niht, And Josep rechede his drem wel rigt, Gen. and Ex. 2121–4.] VI. *to unravel a difficult case, give a solution of a difficult question*:—Wé sǽdan hú wé hit reahtan and be hwý wé hit reahtan *we said what decision we had come to in the case, and on what grounds we had come to it*, Chart. Th. 171, 5–7. VII. *to rule, direct, guide*:—Eal ic under heofones hwearfte recce, Exon. Th. 424, 3; Rä. 41, 33. Ðú recest (*reges*) hí, Ps. Spl. 2, 9. Ðú ðe reccest and rǽdest *qui regis*, Ps. Th. 79, 1. Hé rǽt ús and recþ *reget nos*, 47, 12: Mt. Kmbl. 2, 6. Receþ *regit*, Bd. 5, 18; S. 635, 34. Ðes cásere framlíce rehte ða cynewísan *fortissime rempublicam rexit*, 1, 5; S. 476, 7. Hé Ispania heóld and rehte *Hispaniam regebat*, 1, 8; S. 479, 29: 2, 2; S. 500, 10: 4, 27; S. 603, 35. Justus reahte ða gesomnunge æt Hrofes ceastre, 2, 7; S. 509, 10. Steóran and reccan ðone anweald ðe mé befæst wæs, Bt. 17; Fox 58, 27. Sealde hé ðæt mynster tó reccanne his bréðer, Bd. 3, 23; S. 555, 15. Tó healdanne and tó reccanne micelne dǽl ríces, 5, 19; S. 638, 3. Hé ða cyricean wæs reccende and stýrende, S. 639, 12. VII a. *to correct*:—Seó cyrice sum þing þurh wælm receþ (*corrigit*), 1, 27; S. 491, 30. [*Goth.* uf-rakjan *to stretch out*: *O. Sax.* rekkian: *O. H. Ger.* reckian *tendere, extendere, expandere, porrigere, narrare, explicare, disserere*: *Icel.* rekja *to unwind, spread out, unfold.*] v. á-, and-, be-, ge-, ofer-reccan.

-recce. v. earfoþ-recce.

récce-leás. v. réce-leás.

reccend, es; *m. A ruler, governor*. (1) applied to the Deity:—God eálá ðú micele reccend (*rector*), Hymn. Surt. 72, 1: Exon. Th. 2, 12; Cri. 18. Þeóda reccend, Ps. Th. 101, 1. God is ealra þinga reccend, Bt. 35, 5; Fox 166, 9. Dryhten úre reccend is hé ðara læssena ríca reccend is, Ors. 2, 1; Swt. 58, 22–25. God is scyppend and reccend ealra his gesceafta, Blickl. Homl. 185, 27: Met. 4, 30. Ealra gesceafta reccend and stýrend, Wulfst. 255, 17. Án metod, reccend and ríce, Cd. Th. 252, 17; Dan. 580: Exon. Th. 422, 8; Rä. 41, 3. (2) used of earthly rulers:—Ðæt folc biþ gesǽlig þurh snoterne cyning, sigefæst and gesundful þurh gesceádwīsne reccend, Homl. Th. ii. 320, 2. Nis đeós þeód wyrđe đæt hī swylcne reccend and cyning (*as Oswine*) habban, Bd. 3, 14; S. 541, 8.

reccend-dōm, es; *m. Ruling, directing, governance*:—Reccendōm (recen-, other MSS.) *regimen*, Ælfc. Gr. 9, 12; Som. 9, 30. Ūs (*priests*) befæst is seó gȳming Godes folces and se recenddôm heora sāwla, L. E. I. 1; Th. ii. 402, 10. Be đære byrđenne đæs reccenddōmes (reccen-, Cott. MSS.) *de pondere regiminis*, Past. 3, tit.; Swt. 33, 4. Reccendōmes, 17, 7; Swt. 119, 4. Se underfēng sāula reccendōmes *animas suscepit regendas*, R. Ben. 14, 11. *Rex* kyning is gecweden *a regendo*, đæt is, fram reccendōme, Ælfc. Gr. 50; Som. 51, 40. Cyninge is nama gesett of sōđum reccendōme, Homl. Th. ii. 318, 33. v. recedōm.

recceness, e; *f. An interpretation, explanation*:—Sōđ reccenise *vera interpretatio*, Mt. Kmbl. p. 2, 6.

reccere, es; *m.* I. *speaker, rhetorician.* v. racu, III. II. *an interpreter.* v. swefn-reccere. III. *a ruler, director*:—Hū se lāreów (*rector*) sceal bión clǣne on his mōde. Se reccere (*rector*) sceal bión simle clǣne on his geþohte, Past. 13, 1; Swt. 75, 18-19. Se reccere, se ealdormonn, 17, 1; 107, 5, 8. Đone ealdordōm đe se reccere for monigra monna þearfe underfēhþ, 17, 7; Swt. 119, 6. Offa Mercene reccere, Cod. Dip. B. i. 340, 10. Recceras *presbiteri*, Wrt. Voc. ii. 67, 14. [*O. H. Ger.* rechari *executor, doctor, assertor.*] v. freá-reccere.

reced. v. ræced.

rece-dōm, es; *m. Ruling, governance, guiding*:—Recedōm (recendōm?) *regimen, dominium*, Hpt. Gl. 412, 69.

rēce-leás; *adj. Careless, reckless*:—Rēccileás *prefaricator*, Wrt. Voc. ii. 118, 8. Ymb đa gȳmene his ēcre hǣlo hē wæs tō sǣne and tō rēceleás *erga curam perpetuae suae salvationis nihil omnino studii & industriae gerens*, Bd. 3, 13; S. 538, 19. Tō hwam wurde đū swā rēceleás đæra gyfena đe ic đē geaf? Wulfst. 258, 13 note. Hié ne wēndon đætt ǣfre menn sceolden swǣ rēceleáse (rēcce-, Cott. MSS.) weorđan, Past. pref.; Swt. 5, 23. Đū wēndest đæt steórleáse men and rēceleáse wǣron gesǣlige *nequam homines atque nefarios felices arbitraris*, Bt. 5, 3; Fox 14, 1. Se dēmþ stīđne dōm đām rēceleásum æt đam æfterran tōcyme, Homl. Th. i. 320, 18. Gif hē hwīltīdum đām rēceleásum stȳrþ, đonne sceal his steór beón mid lufe gemetegod, ii. 532, 12. [3iff þatt he wære reckelæs to ringenn hise belles, Orm. 932. Đe unwreste herde (*iners pastor*) synegeþ on gemeleste alse he þat is recheles, O. E. Homl. ii. 39, 19. Alle beođ untohene and rechelese hinen, bute 3ef he ham rihte, i. 245, 27. *O. H. Ger.* ruahha-lōs *negligens*: *Ger.* ruch-los.]

rēceleásian; *p.* ode *To be negligent or careless*:—Tō hwon rēceleásedest đū đære gife đe ic đe geaf? Wulfst. 258, 15. [*O. H. Ger.* ruahhalōsōn *negligere.*]

rēceleáslīce; *adv. Negligently, carelessly, without attention*:—Nis ūs nāwht rēcceleáslīce tō gehīranne *neque negligenter audiendum est*, Past. 57, 4; Swt. 439, 31.

rēceleásness, e; *f. Carelessness, negligence*:—*Improvidentia*, đæt is rēceleásnys, Wulfst. 52, 18. Ongeán đam wīslīcan rǣde se wiđerrǣda deófol sǣwþ rēceleásnesse, and eác gemacaþ đæt se man þurh leáse hiwunge dēþ swylce hē rǣdfæst sȳ, 53, 7. Ic andette mīnes mōdes rēceleásnessa Godes beboda, L. Edg. C. 8; Th. ii. 262, 32.

rēceleást, e; *f. Carelessness, negligence, heedlessness*:—Swā hwæs swā his irsung willaþ, đonne gehēt him đæs his rēcceleēst, Bt. 37, 1; Fox 186, 24. Rēcelēst, Met. 25, 53. Hī for heora slǣwþe and for gīmelēste and for rēccelēste forlēton unwriten đara monna þeáwas đe on heora dagum foremǣroste wǣron, Bt. 18, 3; Fox 64, 34. Đæt hē swā stiére đǣm ungeþyldegum irsunga swā hē đone hnescan þafettere on rēccelēste ne gebrenge *sic ab impatientibus extinguatur ira, ut remissis ac lenibus non crescat negligentia*, Past. 60; Swt. 453, 25. [Þurh mannes gēmelēste and þurh mannes recheleste, O. E. Homl. ii. 45, 4.]

rēcels, es; *n. Incense*:—Him lāc brohton đæt wæs gold rēcels (rēcils, Rush.) and myrre (rēcels, Lind.) *obtulerunt ei munera, aurum, tus, et murram*, Mt. Kmbl. 2, 11: Homl. Th. i. 78, 28. Rēcels *thymiama, odoramentum incensi*, Hpt. Gl. 442, 1: *incensum*, Rtl. 88, 30: Bt. 38, 2; Fox 196, 32. Roecels, Lk. Skt. Lind. 1, 9. Ic eom on stence strengre đonne rīcels, Exon. Th. 423, 19; Rä. 41, 24. Rīcels *incensum*, Ps. Th. 140, 2. Rēcilc *balsamum, myrra*, Rtl. 65, 39, 41: 68, 30. Rǣcelc (?) *thuribulum*, 70, 27. Rēcelces *myrrae*, 4, 13. Rēceles, Jn. Skt. Lind. 19, 39. Genim đās ylcan wyrte for rȳcels (rēcels, MS. O.), Lchdm. i. 302, 6. [*O. E. Homl.* recheles: *A. R.* rechles: *Orm.* recless: *Prompt. Parv.* rychellys, richelle *thus, incensum*: *Icel.* reykels.]

rēcels-būc, es; *m. A vessel for holding incense*: — Rȳcelsbūce *acerrā* (cf. fæte ođđe glēdfæte *accerrā*, 5, 66: *hec acerra* a schyp for censse, i. 230, col. 2), Wrt. Voc. ii. 9, 36. [*Perhaps the following should be put here*:—Of đam æscene đe is ōđre namon hrȳgilebūc gecleopad, Chart. Th. 439, 26.]

rēcels-fæt, es; *n. A censer*:—Þriéfēte rīcelsfæt *cythropodes*, Wrt. Voc. ii. 15, 60. Nim đīn rēcelsfæt *tolle thuribulum*, Num. 16, 46. Fȳr ofslōh đa ōđre đe offrodon đone stōr đǣr hig heóldon đa rēcelsfatu, 16, 35. [*O. E. Homl.* rechel-fat: *Orm.* recle-fatt: *Gen. and Ex.* recle-fat.]

rēcelsian; *p.* ode *To cense with incense*:—Rēcelsa hine and sēna gelōme, Lchdm. ii. 344, 18. [Cf. Zacharie gede in þe temple mid his rechelfat to rechelende þe alter, O. E. Homl. ii. 133, 36.]

rēcels-reóce (?), an; *f. Burning incense*:—On đone tīman man offrode on đære ealdan ǣ, and mid rēcelsreócan on đam temple đæt weofod georne weorđode, Btwk. 218, 8.

recen; *adj.* I. *ready, prompt.* v. recenian:—Mæg sige syllan se đe symle byþ recon and rǣdfæst, Wald. 108; Vald. 2, 26. [Cumeđ her forđ, and beđ alle reken, And leređ wel quat he sal speken, Gen. and Ex. 3485. Louerd, ic (*Moses*) am unreken of wurdes, 2817. My rankor refrayne for þy reken (*apt*) wordes, Allit. Pms. 60, 756. (*See the glossary for other instances. See also* rekenli *in the same work, and in Sir Gawayne.*) *O. Frs.* rekon (*of a road which is clear*): *L. Ger.* reken. v. Richthofen. Cf. *O. Sax.* rekōn *to make ready, set in order.*] II. *swift, quick* (cf. recene):—Blāc rāsetteþ recen reáda līg rēđe scrīþeþ geond woruld *bright and swift rushes the red flame, fierce strides through the world*, Exon. Th. 51, 2; Cri. 810. v. full-recen. III. *coming swiftly and so causing terror* (? cf. fǣr *and its compounds*):—God đe on Ægyptum æđele wundur worhte and recene wundar on đam Reádan Sǣ *Deus qui fecit magnalia in Ægypto, terribilia in Mari Rubro*, Ps. Th. 105, 18.

recendōm. v. recend-dōm.

recene; *adv. Quickly, straightway, at once*:—Recene (recone, Lind.) *protinus*, Mk. Skt. Rush. 1, 29. Hēt him recene tō his sunu gangan, Cd. Th. 53, 20; Gen. 864: 134, 41; Gen. 2228. Đū nū recene beheald *intende*, Ps. Th. 29, 1. Recone ł sōna *confestim*, Mk. Skt. Rush. 5, 29: *cito*, 9, 39: *statim*, Lind. 14, 45. Recune (recone, Rush.) *continuo*, Jn. Skt. 4, 27. Yrn ricene forđan đe se streám berþ āweg Placidum, Homl. Th. ii. 160, 7: Cd. Th. 309, 12; Sat. 708. Saga ricene mē hwǣr seó rōd wunige, Elen. Kembl. 1243; El. 623: 1211; El. 607. Ic đonne ricene reste syđđan, Ps. Th. 54, 6. Ricone, Beo. Th. 5958; B. 2983. Rycene, Ps. Th. 108, 11. Ne sceal nǣfre his torn tō rycene beorn of his breóstum ācȳđan, Exon. Th. 293, 7; Wand. 112. Đæt hē recenust tō þrowunge becōme *ad martyrium ocius pervenire*, Bd. 1, 7; S. 478, 11. v. recen, recenlīce.

recenian; *p.* ode *To arrange, dispose, reckon.* [Cristess kinn o modere hallfe be weppmann shollde reccnedd ben, Orm. 2055. Alle sunnen sunderliche ne muhte no mon rikenen, A. R. 210, 7. Him ne poruayþ of his receninge, and wel wot þet rekeni him behoueþ, Ayenb. 19, 6. Reknyn or cowntyn, rekkyn, rekene, *computo*, Prompt. Parv. 428. *O. Frs.* rekenia *to reckon*: *O. H. Ger.* rehhanōn *parare, rationem ponere, disponere*: cf. *Goth.* rahnjan.] v. ge-recenian, recen.

recenlīce; *adv. Quickly, immediately, at once, straightway*:—Eodun hreconlīce (*cito*) from byrgenne, Mt. Kmbl. Lind. 28, 8. Hreconlīce (ricenlīce, Rush.) *protinus*, Mk. Skt. Lind. 1, 18. Reconlīce (ricenlīce, Rush.) *continuo*, 1, 31. Reconlīce (recunlīce, Rush.) *protinus*, 6, 25. v. recen.

recenness, e; *f. A narrative, history*:—Recennysse *historiae*, Hpt. Gl. 474, 30. v. ge-recedness.

recettung, e; *f. Eructation*:—Recetunge *eructantia*, Ps. Spl. C. 143, 16: Ps. Surt. 143, 13. v. rocettan.

recu, e; *f. Guidance, direction, correction* (v. reccan, VII, VII a):—Seó (*Hilda*) gōdre rece and hǣlo intingan þegnade *occasionem salutis et correctionis ministravit*, Bd. 4, 23; S. 594, 42.

(-)rēd(-), rede, rēde-stān. v. (-)rǣd(-), rede, reád-stān.

rēdian (?) *to furnish, provide*:—Noe ongan Nergende lāc rǣdfæst rēdian (MS. redran. *Bouterwek suggests* rēnian. v. regnian), Cd. Th. 90, 20; Gen. 1498. v. ā-rēdian.

rēfa, an; *m. A prefect*:—Đā hēt Ualerianus se rēfa hī ācwellan, Shrn. 121, 26. v. ge-rēfa.

rēf-land. v. sundor-gerēfland.

regen-. v. regn-.

regn, rēn, es; *m. Rain*:—Blōdig regn and fȳren fundiaþ đās eorþan tō forswylgenne and tō forbærnenne, Blickl. Homl. 93, 3: 91, 34. Nǣnig reng on đām stōwum ne com, Bd. 4, 13; S. 582, 28. Rēn *pluvia*, Wrt. Voc. i. 52, 43. Fǣrlīc rēn *imber*, 52, 63. Se rēn wearđ forboden, Gen. 8, 2. Đā com rēn (regn, Lind.: rǣgn, Rush.) *descendit pluvia*, Mt. Kmbl. 7, 25. Nǣnig dǣl regnes ne ungewidres in cuman ne mæg, Blickl. Homl. 125, 33. Hē āriman mæg rægnas scūran dropena gehwelcne, Cd. Th. 265, 22; Sat. 11. Þurh dropunge deáwes and rēnes, Ps. Th. 64, 11. Līget hē tō regne wyrceþ *fulgura in pluviam fecit*, 134, 7. Mid heofonlīcon rēne, Bt. 7, 3; Fox 22, 13: Met. 7, 23. Wilsumne regn wolcen brincgeþ, Ps. Th. 67, 10: 146, 8: Cd. Th. 82, 34; Gen. 1372. Rēn, Gen. 7, 4: Met. 7, 14, 21. Đās windas and đās regnas syndon ealle his, Blickl. Homl. 51, 20. Regna scūr, Cd. Th. 252, 10; Dan. 576. Nalles wolcnu regnas bǣron, 14, 4; Gen. 213. Regnas (rēnas, Ps. Spl.), Ps. Th. 104, 28. Đā ābæd se wītega æt Gode đæt hē sceolde him rēnas forgyfan, Lchdm. iii. 276, 21. [*Goth.* rign; *n.*: *Icel.* regn; *n.*: *O. Sax.* regin, regan: *O. Frs.* rein: *O. H. Ger.* regan.] v. morgen-, wæl-regn.

regn-, *in the compounds* regn-heard, -meld, -þeóf, -weard *has an* *intensive force, implies greatness, might.* The word occurs as part of many proper names, e. g. Rǽdwoldes sunu wæs Regenhere gehâten, Bd. 2, 12; S. 515, 10. Some of these e. g. *Reginald* are still used. [Cf. *Goth.* raginôn *to rule; ragineis a ruler, counsellor;* ragin *ordinance, counsel: Icel.* regin; *pl. n.* (in ancient poems) *the gods, the rulers* of the universe; forming part of compounds, *mighty, great;* ragn-, rögn- *in proper names:* so *O. Sax.* regin-: *O. H. Ger.* ragin-, regin- *in proper names,* v. Grff. ii. 384.]

regnan. v. rignan.

regn-boga, an; *m. A rainbow:*—Rênboga *iris,* Wrt. Voc. i. 52, 42: *yris* vel *arcus,* 76, 33. Hwî wæs se rênboga tô wedde gesette mancynne? God gesette ðone rênbogan tô wedde tô ðam behâte ðæt hê nǽfre eft nolde ealne middanearde mid nânum flôde oferteón . . . Se rênboga cymþ of ðam sunbeáme and of wǽtum wolcne, Boutr. Scrd. 21, 19–26. Ic sette mînne rênbogan (*arcum*) on wolcnum, Gen. 9, 13. [*O. H. Ger.* regan-bogo: *Icel.* regn-bogi.]

regn-dropa, an; *m. A raindrop:*—Hagol cymþ of ðâm rêndropum ðonne hî beóþ gefrorene up on ðære lyfte, Lchdm. iii. 278, 19. [*O. H. Ger.* regan-tropfo.]

regn-heard; *adj. Exceedingly hard, wondrous hard:*—Rondas regnhearde, Beo. Th. 657; B. 326. [Cf. *Icel.* regin-djúpr *very deep;* regin-djúp *the mighty deep: O. H. Ger.* Regin-hart.] v. regn-.

regnian; *p.* ode *To set in order, arrange, dispose, regulate:*—Tungelcræftum *Chaldaeorum,* scincræfta *hierophantorum,* ða ðæt womfreht rêniaþ *ariolorum,* wyrmgalera *marsorum,* Wrt. Voc. ii. 82, 6–9. Gemyne ðû, mucgwyrt, hwæt ðû âmeldodest, hwæt ðû rênadest, Lchdm. iii. 30, 29. Hû geworhte ic ðæt ðæt ðû mê ðus swîðe searo rênodest *how have I deserved that you should lay such a snare for me?* Cd. Th. 162, 9; Gen. 2678. Inwitnet ôðrum bregdan, dyrnum cræfte deáþ rê[nian], Beo. Th. 4343; B. 2168. Sum biþ searocræftig goldes and gimma ðonne him gumena weard hâteþ mâððum rênian *one is a cunning workman in gold and gems, when a prince of men bids him set a jewel,* Exon. Th. 296, 33; Crä. 60. Wrôhtas tô webgenne, ne searo tô rênigenne *to set a trap,* Blickl. Homl. 109, 30. Hê geseh twegen ôðre gebrôðru remigende (rênigende (?): *the later MSS. have* reniende, renigende; *the Lindisfarne MS. glosses* reficientes *by* geboeton ł gestricedon) hyra nett, Mt. Kmbl. 4, 21. [*Goth.* raginôn *to rule.*] v. be-, ge-regnian (-rênian).

regniend, es; *m. One who arranges:*—Rihtes rêniend, Elen. Kmbl. 1756; El. 880. v. preceding word.

regnig; *adj. Rainy:*—Hit wæs rênig weder, Exon. Th. 380, 18; Rä. 1, 10. Rênig sumer, Lchdm. iii. 162, 33.

regn-lîc; *adj. Rainy:*—Rênlîc *pluvialis,* Ælfc. Gr. 9, 28; Som. 11, 36. Rînlîcum (rên-) *pluvio, pluviali,* Germ. 401, 14. Ða regenlîcan weter *pluviales aquas,* Ps. Surt. 77, 44. [*Icel.* regn-ligr.]

regn-meld, e; *f. A mighty, solemn announcement:*—Gemyne ðû, mucgwyrt, hwæt ðû âmeldodest æt regenmelde, Lchdm. iii. 30, 30. v. regn-.

regn-scûr, es; *m. A shower of rain, a shower:*—God sende byrnende rênscûr, Gen. 19, 24. On Ægipta lande ne cymþ nǽfre nân winter ne rênscûras, Lchdm. iii. 252, 20: Homl. Th. i. 64, 30. Ic ofteó mîne rênscûras, ii. 102, 33. God sylþ rênscûras ðâm rihtwîsum and ðâm unrihtwîsum, 216, 19. Rênscûras *imbres,* Ps. Spl. 77, 49. [*Icel.* regn-skûr; *f.*]

regn-þeóf, es; *m. An arch-thief:*—Regnþeóf ne lǽt [mê] on sceade sceððan, Exon. Th. 453, 14; Hy. 4, 14. Swâ nû regnþeófas rîce dǽlaþ (cf. regintheobos farstelad (Mat. vi. 19), Hel. 1646), Cd. Th. 212, 12; Exod. 538. [Cf. *also O. Sax.* regin-skaðo.] v. regn-.

regn-wæter, es; *n. Rain-water:*—Gefulle mid rênwætere, Lchdm. ii. 26, 24. Baþu of rênwætere, 222, 12. [*O. H. Ger.* regan-wazar: *Icel.* regn-vatn.]

regn-weard, es; *m. A mighty guard:*—Yrre wǽron begen rêðe rênweardas (*Beowulf and Grendel*), Beo. Th. 1544; B. 770. [Cf. *O. H. Ger.* Ragin-wart.] v. regn-.

regn-wyrm, es; *m. An earth-worm:*—Regnwyrm *lumbricus,* Wrt. Voc. ii. 113, 26: 71, 13. Rênwyrm, 51, 23. Rênwyrm *vel* angeltwicce, i. 24, 31. [*O. H. Ger.* regan-wurm *lumbricus: Ger.* regenwurm.]

regol, es; *m.* I. *a rule:*—Se gewuna is strængra on ǽlcum worde ðon his regol sŷ, Ælfc. Gr. 30, 4; Som. 34, 67. Sume gâþ of ðam regole, forðan ðe se gewuna is strengra, *eruo* ic nerige, *erutus* generod. Nû wolde se regol ðæs cræftes habban of ðam *eruturus,* ac se gewuna hylt *eruiturus,* 41; Som. 44, 24–26. Ðis is lǽwedra regol æfter bôclîcere gesetnysse, Homl. Th. ii. 94, 8. Se Hǽlend him tǽhte ðone regol, ðæt hî sceoldon yfel mid gôde forgyldan, i. 372, 31. Ðone eásterlîcan regol *the rule for determining Easter,* Lchdm. iii. 264, 16. Ðonne byþ hê geteald tô ðam mônþe and bē his regolum âcunnod, 250, 6. On mynsteres reogolum gelǽred *monasterii regulis erudita,* Bd. 1, 27; S. 489, 10. Hê symle rihte regolas Godes cyricean (*catholicas ecclesiae regulas*) lufode, 5, 19; S. 638, 33. Rûme regulas geongra monna *the lax rules of young men,* Exon. Th. 131, 23; Gû. 460. II. *a rule, pattern, standard, norm:*—Ða leásan wîtegan wǽron gedwolmen, and woldon âwendan ðone sôðan geleáfan of ðam rihtan regole tô heora gedwyldum, Homl. Th. ii. 404, 9. Regol *normam vite,* regol *normam,* Wrt. Voc. ii. 59, 53–54. III. as an ecclesiastical term, (a) *a single rule* or *prescript, a canon:*—Ðæs regles *canonis,* Jn. Skt. p. 1, 12. Reglas *canones,* Mt. Kmbl. p. 2, 18. Bôc ðara reogola *librum canonum,* Bd. 4, 5; S. 572, 25. (b) *the body of rules which guide a particular order of ecclesiastics, a rule,* e. g. the Benedictine *rule:*—Hêr beginþ seó foresprǽc muneca regules, R. Ben. 1, 1. Wite se abbod, eal ðæt hê dô, ðæt hê hit dô mid gehealdsumnesse ðæs regoles, 16, 6. Munecas ðe under regole (*sub regula*) lifigeaþ, Bd. 4, 4; S. 571, 21. Intô Sanctus Benedictus regole, Chart. Th. 548, 4. Ðæt forme muneca cyn is mynstermonna, ðæt is ðara ðe under regule and abbodes tǽcinge wuniaþ, R. Ben. 9, 4. On ǽlcum þingum hié sceolon habban ðone regol tô lâreówe, 15, 20. Benedictus nam ðone hâlgan regol ðe hê mid his handum âwrât, Homl. Skt. i. 6, 66. [*O. H. Ger.* regula *regula, canon: Icel.* regla. From *Lat.* regula.] v. munuc-, riht-regol.

regol-bryce, es; *m. A breach of rule,* v. regol, III:—Þurh gelǽredra regolbryce and þurh lǽwedra lahbryce *through the breach of their rule by clerks and the breach of the law by laymen,* Wulfst. 166, 22.

regol-fæst; *adj. Observing a rule, regular* (of ecclesiastics):—Rincas rægolfæste, Menol. Fox 88; Men. 44.

regol-lagu, e; *f. Monastic law, the law to which the member of a monastic body is subject:*—Mynstermunuc gǽþ of his mǽgþlage ðonne hê gebýhþ tô regollage, L. C. E. 5; Th. i. 362, 28.

regol-lîc; *adj.* As an ecclesiastical term (v. regol, III). I. *regular, in accordance with monastic rules;* regularis:—Regollîces *regularis,* Hpt. Gl. 526, 17. Fram ðâm hê ðæt gemet leornode regollîces þeódscipes *a quibus norman disciplinae regularis didicerat,* Bd. 3, 23; S. 554, 35. On rihtum lîfe and on reogollîcum *recte vivendo et regulariter,* 4, 6; S. 574, 19. Libbaþ regollîcan lîfe, sêcaþ eówre cyrican, and gefyllaþ eówre tîde aa on gesetne tîman, L. I. P. 20; Th. ii. 330, 19. On reogollîcne þeódscipe, Bd. 3, 3; S. 526, 9. II. *in accordance with the canons of the church, canonical:*—Bûtan sealmsange reogollîcre tîde *praeter canonici temporis psalmodiam,* 3, 27; S. 559, 10. Tô reogollîcum þeáwe rihtra Eástrena *ad ritum Paschae canonicum,* 5, 22; S. 643, 38. Æfter regollîcre wîsan, Lchdm. iii. 428, 15. Regulîcra *canonicorum,* Hpt. Gl. 512, 36. Ðǽm regolecum *canonicis,* Wrt. Voc. ii. 24, 19. Ða reogollîcan gesettnysse hâligra fædera *canonica patrum statuta,* Bd. 4, 5; S. 571, 40. [*Icel.* reglu-ligr.]

regollîce; *adv. Regularly, in accordance with rule* (v. preceding word):—Ða þing ðe regollîce gedêmed wǽron *quaeque erant regulariter decreta,* Bd. 2, 4; S. 505, 36. Ðæt biscopas and abbudas, munecas and mynecena, preóstas and nunnan tô rihte gebûgan and regollîce libban, L. Eth. v. 4; Th. i. 304, 27. Sacerd ðe regollîce libbe, L. C. E. 5; Th. i. 362, 8. Riht is ðæt mynecena mynsterlîce macian . . . and â regollîce libban, L. I. P. 15; Th. ii. 322, 35. Ðæt gehâdode menn regollîce libban, and lǽwede lahlîce heora lîf fadian, 18; Th. ii. 324, 26: Wulfst. 160, 1. Ðæt abbodas and munecas regollîcor libban, L. Eth. ix. 31; Th. i. 346, 27.

regol-lîf, es; *m. A life according to ecclesiastical rules:*—Ðâ gestaþelode hê ðǽr mynster and ðæt tô reogollîfe gesette *fundavit ibi monasterium, ac regulari vita instituit,* Bd. 4, 13; S. 583, 12. Gif man folcîscne mæssepreóst mid tihtlan belecge ðe regollîf næbbe, lâdige hine swâ swâ diácon ðe regollîfe libbe, L. Eth. ix. 21; Th. i. 344, 20: L. C. E. 5; Th. i. 362, 17. [*Icel.* reglu-lîf.]

regol-sticca, an; *m. A ruler:*—Reogolsticca *regola,* Wrt. Voc. i. 81, 29. Þwyrnyssa beóþ gerihte ðonne þwyrlîcra manna heortan þurh regolsticcan ðære sôðan rihtwîsnysse beóþ geemnode, Homl. Th. i. 362, 28. [*Icel.* reglu-stika.]

regol-weard, es; *m. The guardian of a rule,* (1) *an authority in the matter of the observance of a rule* (v. regol, I):—Se circul ðe ys gecîged *none aprilis,* hê sceal mid his ealdorscipe ealle ða ôðre gerihtan and gereccan, ðæs ðe ða regolweardas (*those who state with authority what the rule or rules on the point may be*) ûs hêton secgan, Anglia viii. 329, 8. (2) *One who sees that a rule* (v. regol, III) *is observed, a provost,* v. prâfost:—Ðæs mynstres prâfost and reogolweard wæs in ða tîd Boisel . . . Æfter ðon . . . wæs Cûþberht ðæs ylcan mynstres regolweard geworden *cui tempore illo praepositus Boisil fuit . . . Postquam Cudberct eidem monasterio factus praepositus,* Bd. 4, 27; S. 603, 37–43. Se ylca Bosel wæs reogolweard ðæs mynstres on Mailros under Eatan ðam Abbude *idem Boisil praepositus monasterii Mailrosensis sub Abbate Eata,* 5, 9; S. 622, 29. Ond ðâs forecuædenan suǽsenda all âgefe mon ðæm reogolwarde, and hê brytniæ swǽ hîgum mǽst rêd sîe, Chart. Th. 460, 37. Se reogolweord, 460, 16. (3) *a ruler:*—Sum reiglword (regoloword, Rush.) *quidam regulus,* Jn. Skt. Lind. 4, 46. Se reglword *regulus,* 4, 49.

regul, reht. v. regol, riht.

relic-gang, es; *m. A going to visit relics:*—Seó tîd is nemned *laetania majora* . . . on ðæm dæge eall Godes folc mid eáðmôdlîce relicgonge sceal God biddan ðæt hē him forgefe siblīce tīd, Shrn. 74, 10. Letanias, ðæt is ðonne bēne and relicgongas, 79, 29.

reliquias; *pl. m. Relics of saints*:—Ðisra reliquia dǣl hæfde sum mæssepreóst ... Hē ða cyste ontȳnde ðara reliquia, Bd. 4, 32; S. 611, 30–34. Æt his reliquium wæs sum man gehǣled, S. 611, 9. Mon byrþ his heáfod tō reliquium, Shrn. 57, 26: Blickl. Homl. 127, 12, 16. Mid hāligdōme of ðæs Hǣlendes rōde ... and of Martines reliquium, Homl. Skt. i. 6, 74. Ofer his reliquias ðæt heofonleóht wæs scīnende and deófolseóce æt his reliquium wǣron gelācnode, Bd. 3, 11; S. 535, 6–8. Ðæt þurh his reliquias geworden wæs, 4, 32; S. 611, 12. Hē sette ða reliquias on heora cyste, S. 612, 1. Swā hwylc mann swā hrīneþ ðīne reliquias oððe ðīne bān, Nar. 49, 4.

remigende, Mt. Kmbl. 4, 21. v. regnian.

rempan *to go headlong* (like an animal butting with its horns (?), cf. gerumpenu nædre *coluber cerastes*, Wrt. Voc. ii. 15, 68), *be precipitate*:—Oft mon biþ suīðe rempende and rǣsþ suīðe dollīce on ǣlc weorc and hrædlīce and ðeáh wēnaþ men ðæt hit sīe for arodscipe and for hwætscipe *saepe praecipitata actio velocitatis efficacia creditur*, Past. 20, 1; Swt. 149, 12. v. note. [Cf. þei rempede þem to reste, Mand. (quoted by Stratmann).]

rēn. v. regn.

renc, e; *f. Pride, pomp, vanity, bravery, display*:—Bisceopum gebyreþ ðæt hī ne hēdan ne woruldwlence ne īdelre rence, L. I. P. 10; Th. ii. 316, 30. Ǣgwhylce wlence and īdele rence forhogian swā gebyreþ munecum, 14; Th. ii. 322, 9. Ne gerīsaþ biscopum prīta ne īdele rænca ne micele ofermētta, 11; Th. ii. 318, 32. Be īdelum rencum. *Pro eo, quod eleuate sunt filie Sion, etc.* For ofermēttan, hē cwæð, and īdelan rencan eówra leóda, Wulfst. 45, 21–23. [We ne beoð iboren for to habbene nane prudu ne forðe nane oðre rencas, O. E. Homl. i. 7, 27.] v. ofer-renc, ranc.

renge, rynge, ringe (?), an; *f. A spider* or *a spider's web*:—Renge *aranea*, Blickl. Gl. Ūre gǣr swā swā lobbe ł rynge beóþ āsmeáde *anni nostri sicut aranea meditabuntur*, Ps. Lamb. 89, 9. Āȳdlian ðū dydest swā swā ǣtterloppan ł ryngan sāwle his *tabescere fecisti sicut araneam animam ejus*, 38, 13.

reng-wyrm, es; *m. A maw-worm, a worm in the intestines*:—Wið ðæt rængcwyrmas (rengc-, MS. B.; rȳnwyrmas with a gloss *lumbrici*, MS. H.) dergen ymb nafolan, Lchdm. i. 168, 9. Wið ðæt rengwyrmas ymb ðone nafolan wexen, 218, 14. [Cf. *O. H. Ger.* pouh-wurm *lumbricus*.]

rendan; *p.* de *To rend, tear, cut*:—Ōðre ða twigu gibēgdun ł rendun (rindon, Lind.) ða telge of ðǣm trēum *alii frondes caedebant ab arboribus*, Mk. Skt. Rush. 11, 8. Ceorfas ł rendas (hrendas, Lind.) *succidite*, Lk. Skt. Rush. 13, 7. [Scipen gunnen helden bosmes þer rendden, Laym. 7849. Heo haueð bipiled mine figer, irend of al þe rinde *decorticauit ficum meam*, A. R. 148, 23. Þe reue rende his claðes, Jul. 70, 7. *O. Frs.* renda *to tear*; rend *a rent*.] v. tō-rendan.

rendrian. v. Lchdm. ii. Gloss.

rēnian, rēnig, rēn-līc. v. regnian, regnig, regn-līc.

reó. v. reōwe.

reóc; *adj. Fierce, savage*:—[Grendel] grim and grǣdig, reóc and rēðe, Beo. Th. 244; B. 122.

reócan; *p.* reác *To reek, send forth smoke* or *steam*:—Ðonne hē (*helleborus albus*) tōbrocen byþ, hē rȳcþ eal swylce hē smīc of him āsænde, Lchdm. i. 260, 8. Muntas reócaþ *montes fumigant*, Ps. Th. 103, 30: 143, 6. Reác *exalabat*, Wrt. Voc. ii. 32, 46: *fumarat*, 151, 55. Wel on wætere, lǣt reócan on ða eágan ðonne hit hāt sīe, Lchdm. ii. 18, 24: 32, 7. Reócan *fumare*, Germ. 395, 70. Reócende *anhelans*, 400, 92. Rēcende *fumigans*, Mt. Kmbl. Lind. 12, 20. Heó ðæra māðma ne rōhte ðe mā ðe reócendes meoxes, Homl. Skt. i. 7, 20. Būtan rēnscūrum and reócendum deáwe, 18, 57. Ðæs hreóflian līc mid reócendum stence, Homl. Th. i. 336, 33. Æt hreócendum heorðe, Wulfst. 170, 21. Reócendne (reccendne, MS.) weg, Cd. Th. 177, 19; Gen. 2932. Reócende hrǣw, Judth. Thw. 26, 7; Jud. 314. Hreócendum *fumigabundis*, Hpt. Gl. 516, 29. [*O. H. Ger.* riuhhan *fumigare*: *Icel.* rjúka.] v. rēcan.

reóce. v. rēcels-reóce.

reód; *adj. Red*:—Se ðe ǣror com, se wæs reód (*rufus*) and eall rūh, Gen. 25, 25. Ðonne ðū (*the body*) wǣre glæd and reód and gōdes hiwes, ðonne wæs ic (*the soul*) blāc and swȳðe unrōt, Wulfst. 140, 27: L. E. I. prm.; Th. ii. 398, 14. Ðā Moises hæfde gefaren ofer ða Reódan Sǣ, Ex. 15, 1. Hié wǣron sume reóde sume blace sume hwīte *quaedam rubentibus scamis erant quaedam nigri et candidi coloris*, Nar. 13, 17. [*Icel.* rjóðr.] v. bleó-reód, reád.

reód, es; *n. Red, red colouring*:—Reóde gnīdan *fucare*, Wrt. Voc. ii. 37, 49.

reódan; *p.* reád. I. *to redden, stain with blood*:—Deáþwang rudon, Andr. Kmbl. 2006; An. 1005. II. *to redden a person by causing blood to flow from a wound, to wound, kill*:—Næs ðeós eorþe besmiten beornes blōde ðe hine bil rude (cf. ne seó eorþe besmiten mid ofslegenes monnes blōde, Bt. 15; Fox 48, 15), Met. 8, 34. Se eorl wolde sleán eaferan sīnne, ecgum (MS. eagum) reódan magan mid mēce, Cd. Th. 204, 2; Exod. 412. [*Icel.* rjóða *to redden* (*with blood*); rjóða kiðr eins *to slay a person*.] v. on-reódan.

reodian (?):—Ic þragum þreodude and geþanc reodode, Elen. Kmbl. 2476; El. 1239.

reódian; *p.* ode *To be* or *become red*:—Ic reádige (reódige, MS. O.) *rubeo*, Ælfc. Gr. Zup. 154, 7. v. ā-reódian.

reód-mūþa, an; *m. The name of a bird*:—Reódmūþa *faseacus, nomen avis*, Wrt. Voc. ii. 146, 56.

reód-naesc glosses *partica*, Wrt. Voc. ii. 116, 61.

reófan; *p.* reáf, *pl.* rufon; *pp.* rofen. *To break, rend, rive*:—Randbyrig wǣron rofene, Cd. Th. 207, 7; Exod. 463. [*Icel.* rjúfa *to break, rip up*.] v. be-reófan.

reohhe, an; *f. The name of a fish*:—Reohhe *fannus*, Wrt. Voc. i. 56, 5. Reohche, 77, 66. [*Laym.* rehȝe (rohȝe, 2nd MS.): *Du.* rog *a ray*: *Dan.* rokke *a ray*.]

reóma, an; *m. A membrane, ligament*:—Se reóma ðæs brægenes *cartilago*, Wrt. Voc. ii. 22, 58. Biþ ðæt brægen ūtan mid reáman bewefen on ðære syxtan wucan, Lchdm. iii. 146, 4. [A rym (*other* MS. reme) þat es ful wlatsome Es his (a man's) garment when he forth sal com, þat es noght bot a blody skyn þat he byfor was lapped in, Pricke of Conscience, 520. See Nares' Glossary, s. v. *rim*. *O. Sax.* reomo *the latchet of a shoe*: *O. H. Ger.* riumo *corrigia, lorea, balteus, habena*: *Ger.* riemen.]

reomig-mōd. v. reónig-mōd.

reón *mourning, lament*:—Woldan wērigu wīf wōpe bimǣnan æþelinges deáþ, reóne bereótan, Exon. Th. 459. 27; Hö. 6. Cf. rȳn.

reónian; *p.* ode *To whisper, mutter*:—Reónigende *mussitantes*, Hpt. Gl. 472, 5. v. ge-reónian, rūnian.

reónig; *adj. Mournful, sad, gloomy, weary*:—Ā mīn hige sorgaþ reónig reóteþ and geresteþ nō *ever hath my heart care, mournful laments and hath not rest*, Elen. Kmbl. 2163; El. 1083. Hē ðǣr þreó mētte in ðam reónian hofe (*in the hole in which they were buried*) rōda ætsomne greóte begrauene, 1664; El. 834. In ðam reóngan hām *in that gloomy dwelling* (*hell*), Exon. Th. 274, 8; Jul. 530. v. preceding word.

reónig-mōd; *adj. Sad at heart, weary*:—Wæs him ræste neód reónigmōdum *need of rest was there for him weary-hearted*, Exon. Th. 167, 32; Gū. 1069. Ðonne gewīciaþ wērigferðe ... hæleþ beóþ on wynnum reónigmōde ræste geliste *the weary seafarers are eager for rest*, 361, 21; Wal. 23. Fēðan sǣton reónigmōde (reomigmōde, MS. *Grimm suggests a comparison with Gothic* rimis *quiet*) reste gefēgon wērige æfter wæðe, Andr. Kmbl. 1183; An. 592.

reónung, e; *f. Whispering, muttering*:—Nānes mannes stefn oððe reónung gehȳred ne sȳ, būtan ðæs rǣderes ānes *nullius musitatio uel vox audiatur nisi solius legentis*, R. Ben. 62, 14, v. ge-reónung.

reopa, reopan. v. ripa, repan.

reord, e: *f.*: es; *n. Speech, tongue, language, voice*:—Reord ðīn ðæc gecȳðeþ *loquela tua manifestum te facit*, Mt. Kmbl. Rush. 26, 73. Reord wæs eorþbūendum ān gemǣne '*and the whole earth was of one language, and of one speech*,' Cd. Th. 98, 25; Gen. 1635. Reord up āstāg *voices rose high*, Exon. Th. 246, 16; Jul. 62. Æt ealra manna gehwæs mūþes reorde *from the voice of each man's mouth*, Soul Kmbl. 186; Seel. Verc. 93. Herian God hāligum reorde, Hy. 3, 58. Heofonrīces weard spræc hālgan reorde, Cd. Th. 89, 22; Gen. 1484: 248, 10; Dan. 511. Wit scīran reorde song āhōfan, Exon. Th. 324, 32; Vīd. 103. Geác monaþ geómran reorde, 309, 7; Seef. 53. Ðæt him ða swā cūþe wǣron swā his āgene reorde ðe hē on ācenned wæs *ut tam notas ac familiares sibi eas* (Latin and Greek), *quam nativitatis suae loquelam haberet*, Bd. 5, 23; S. 645, 17. Stefn in becom under hārne stān ... hordweard oncneów mannes reorde, Beo. Th. 5103; B. 2555. Hī gehȳrdon hlūde reorde, ðīnes mūþes ða mǣran word, Ps. Th. 137, 5. Hē reorde gesette eorþbūendum ungelīce, Cd. Th. 101, 19; Gen. 1684. Se hālga wer hergende wæs Meotudes miltse, and his mōdsefan rehte þurh reorde, Exon. Th. 188, 25; Az. 51: 111, 24; Gū. 131. Ic glidan reorde mūþe gemǣne, 406, 23; Rä. 25, 5. Se ðe reorda gehwæs ryne gemiclaþ ðara ðe noman Scyppendes hergan willaþ, 4, 3; Cri. 47. Reordana *locutionem*, Jn. Skt. p. 7, 10. Hȳ mislīce mongum reordum wōðe hōfun, Exon. Th. 156, 6; Gū. 870. Fugla cynn songe lofiaþ, mǣraþ mōdigne meaglum reordum, 221, 22; Ph. 338. Hē ūs syleþ missenlīcu mōd, monge reorde, 334, 9; Gn. Ex. 13. [*Orm.* reord, rerd *sound, voice*: *Ps.* rorde *sonus*: *Ayenb.* ecko, þet is þe rearde þet ine þe heȝe helles comþ aȝen. and acordeþ to al þet me him zayþ: *Goth.* razda *speech, tongue*: *O. H. Ger.* rarta *modulatio*: *Icel.* rödd *voice*.] v. ge-reord.

reord, e; *f. A meal, refection, food*:—Reorde mīn *refectio mea*, Mk. Skt. Rush. 14, 14. Fēd feora wōcre ōð ic ðære lāfe lagosīða eft reorde rȳman wille, Cd. Th. 81, 12; Gen. 1344. Hē wæs swā gistlīþe, ðæt hē for Godes lufon eode tō reordum mid ðām tōcumendum mannum, Shrn. 129, 27. v. ge-reord.

-reord. v. el-reord.

reordan; *p.* de *To take food, eat*:—Reordendum *cenantibus* i. *vescentibus*, Wrt. Voc. ii. 130, 72. v. ge-reordan.

reord-berend, es; *m. One gifted with speech, a man*:—Tō midre nihte syððan reordberend reste wunedon, Rood Kmbl. 5; Kr. 3: Cd. Th. 223, 21; Dan. 123. Ealle reordberend, hæleþ geond foldan, Exon. Th. 18, 4; Cri. 278. Reordberende, earme eorþware, 24, 8; Cri. 381: 63, 26; Cri. 1025. Sceall ǽghwylc reordberendra riht gehýran, Elen. Kmbl. 2561; El. 1282. Ðǽr leán cumaþ reordberendum, Exon. Th. 84, 5; Cri. 1369. Hē reordberend lǽrde under lyfte, Andr. Kmbl. 838; An. 419.

reord-hūs, es; *n. A house* or *room where meals are taken*:—Reordhūs *cenaculum*, Mk. Skt. Lind. 14, 15.

reordian; *p. ode.* I. *to speak, say, talk*:—Sleáþ synnigne ofer mūþ, tō feala reordaþ, Andr. Kmbl. 2604; An. 1303. Ðus reordiaþ ryhtfremmende, Exon. Th. 240, 1; Ph. 632. Ðā reordade Waldend and worde cwæþ, Cd. Th. 76, 6; Gen. 1253. Reordode, 161, 30; Gen. 2673. Heáhcyning him tō reordode, 130, 28; Gen. 2166. Sceal se wonna hrefn fela reordian, earne secgan hū him æt ǽte speów, Beo. Th. 6043; B. 3025. Ongan reordigan rǽdum snottor, wordlocan onspeónn, Andr. Kmbl. 637; An. 469. Wolde reordigean rīces hyrde hālgan stefne, Cd. Th. 194, 5; Exod. 256. Him biþ reordiende ēce Drihten, ofer ealle gecwyþ, 304, 7; Sat. 626. Se Hǽlend his gingrum tō spræc ymbe Godes rīce, samod mid him reordigende, Homl. Th. i. 294, 18. II. *to read*:—Ne reordaþ *non legistis?* Mt. Kmbl. Rush. 12, 5. Gē ne reordade *non legistis*, 19, 4. Reordadun, 21, 16. Seó bysen ðæs rihtan geleáfan fram eallum ðe hine gehýrdon oððe reordedon þancwurþlīces wæs onfangen *exemplum catholicae fidei ab omnibus qui audiere vel legere gratantissime susceptum*, Bd. 4, 18; S. 587, 13. [He reordien gan, and þas word sæide, Laym. 22174.]

-reordig. v. el-reordig.

reordung, e; *f. Taking food, refection*:—Riordung mīn *refectio mea*, Mk. Skt. Lind. 14, 14. v. ge-reordung.

reosan glosses *pissli* (in a list of plant names), Wrt. Voc. i. 68, 44.

reóst *a rest* (rest *the wood on which the coulter of a plough is fixed*, Halliw. Dict.):—Sules reóst *dentale*, s. *est aratri pars prima in qua vomer inducitur quasi dens*, Wrt. Voc. ii. 138, 72: *dentalia*, 106, 20: 25, 28. [Cf. *O. H. Ger.* riostar *stiva, dentile.*]

reót (?) (*joyous*) *sound* (?), *gladness* (?):—Gesyhþ sorhcearig on his suna būre wīnsele wēstne, reóte berofene . . . nis ðǽr hearpan swēg, gomen in geardum, Beo. Th. 4905; B. 2457. v. (?) reótan.

reótan; *p.* reát. I. *to make a noise*:—Reótaþ (wreotaþ, MS.) *crepita[n]t*, Wrt. Voc. ii. 21, 44. Reát (hreát?) *desteruit* (*stertuit?*), *somniavit*, 139, 17. II. *to make a noise in grief, to lament, wail*:—Reóteþ meówle, seó ðe hyre bearn gesihþ brondas þeccan, Exon. Th. 330, 5; Vy. 46. Cerge reótaþ fore onsȳne ēces dēman, 52, 20; Cri. 836. Hȳ (*sinners*) reótaþ and beofiaþ fore freán forhte, 75, 32; Cri. 1230. III. *to weep, shed tears*:—Lyft drysmaþ, roderas reótaþ, Beo. Th. 2756; B. 1376. [*O. H. Ger.* riuzan; *p.* rōz *flere, plangere, stridere*: *Icel.* rjóta *to roar, rattle.*] v. be-, wið-reótan.

reótig; *adj. Sad, mournful, tearful*:—Ðonne hit wæs rēnig weder, and ic reótugu sæt, Exon. Th. 380, 19; Rä. 1, 10.

reów; *adj. Fierce, cruel*:—Sume wurdon bisencte under reóne streám, sume ic rōde bifealh, Exon. Th. 271, 12; Jul. 481. Wǽron hȳ reówe tō rǽsanne gīfrum grāpum, 126, 26; Gū. 377: Andr. Kmbl. 2669; An. 1336. v. blōd-, deáþ-, flyge-, gūþ-, wæl-reów.

reówe, an; *f. A rug, mantle, covering*:—Reówu *tapeta*, Wrt. Voc. i. 289, 50. Reówe *lena*, līnen reówe *lena linea*, ii. 53, 71–72. Mon mōt feohtan orwīge gif hē gemēteþ ōðerne æt his ǽwum wīfe betȳnedum durum oððe under ānre reón, L. Alf. pol. 42; Th. i. 90, 27. Reówan and hwītlas wacsan *lenas sive saga lavare*, Bd. 4, 31; S. 610, 11. v. rūwa, rȳhe.

repan (?); *p.* ræp, *pl.* rǽpon *To reap*:—Hié reopaþ *metent*, Ps. Surt. 125, 5. Manig men rǽpon heora corn onbūtan Martines mæssan and gyt lator, Chr. 1089; Erl. 226, 19. [I gaf hem red þat ropen To seise to me with her sykel þat I ne sewe neure, Piers P. 13, 374.] v. wīn-repan, rīpan.

reps, repsan, repsung, rēsele, rēsian. v. ræps, ræpsan, ræpsung, rǽsele, rǽswan.

rest, e; *f.* I. *rest, quiet, freedom from toil*:—Sæterndæges rest (*requies sabbati*) ys Drihtne gehālgod, Ex. 16, 23. Nis nān gesceaft gesceapen ðara ðe ne wilnige ðæt hit ðider cuman mǽge ðonan ðe hit ǽr com, ðæt is tō ræste and tō orsorgnesse. Seó ræst is mid Gode, Bt. 25; Fox 88, 29–32: Met. 13, 71. Ne ðǽr biþ hungor ne þurst . . . ac ðǽr biþ seó ēce ræste, Blickl. Homl. 65, 20. Heó reste stōwe funde, Cd. Th. 88, 17; Gen. 1466. Wæs him ræste neód, Exon. Th. 167, 31; Gū. 1068. Ic sylle ðē reste *requiem dabo tibi*, Ex. 33, 14: Ps. Th. 114, 7. Hē gǽþ sēcende reste, Mt. Kmbl. 12, 43. Wē ræste habbaþ, forðon ðe ðū sylest ūrum leomum ræste, Blickl. Homl. 141, 10–11: 41, 33. Mid gōdum dǽdum man geearnige him ða ēcean ræste, 101, 26. Hwonne him Freá reste āgeáfe, Cd. Th. 86, 9; Gen. 1428. II. *rest, repose, sleep*:—Rest *dormitatio*, Kent. Gl. 894. Hē his limo on reste gesette and onslǽpte *membra dedisset sopori*, Bd. 4, 24; S. 597, 10. Ðā hē ðā tō reste eode *dum iret cubitum*, 3, 2; S. 525, 12. Be muneca reste. Ǽnlȳpige munecas geond ǽnlȳpige bed restan, R. Ben. 47, 2. III. *a place of rest, resting-place*:—Ðū eart seó sēfte ræst sōðfæstra, Bt. 33, 4; Fox 132, 34. Ðæt is sió ān ræst eallra ūrra geswinca, sió ān hȳþ byþ simle smyltu, 34, 8; Fox 144, 27. Ðis is mīn rest ðe ic on worulda woruld wunian þence, Ps. Th. 131, 15. Ðē is ēðelstōl gerȳmed, rest fæger on foldan, Cd. Th. 89, 26; Gen. 1486. Wīc, randwīgena ræst, 186, 5; Exod. 134. IV. *a bed, couch*:—Ðǽr biþ rest of elpenda bāne geworht *lectus eburneus*, Nar. 38, 32. Wæs his seó æþeleste ræst on nacodre eorþan, Blickl. Homl. 227, 10. Salomones reste wæs mid weardum ymbseted.—Hwæt wæs seó Salomones ræste . . . ? Ac hwæt mǽnde ðæt syxtig wera stondende wǽron ymb ða reste? 11, 16–23. Ræst *a sepulchre*, Exon. Th. 459, 28; Hö. 6. On mīnre reste *per stratum meum*, Ps. Th. 62, 6. Mīne cnihtas synt on reste (*in cubili*) mid mē, Lk. Skt. 11, 7. Wæs ān gesittende beforan his reste (*ante lectulum ejus*), Bd. 4, 11; S. 579, 38. Swā swā oferdruncen man wāt ðæt hē sceolde tō his hūse and tō his ræste, Bt. 24, 4; Fox 84, 31. Heó āsette ða hand æt hire heáfdum on hire ræste, Shrn. 60, 1. Hē on his reste gestāhg *lectulum conscendens*, Bd. 3, 27; S. 559, 15: Cd. Th. 134, 22; Gen. 2228. Seó wlitignes heora ræsta and setla, Blickl. Homl. 99, 33. Ræsto *recubitos*, Mt. Kmbl. Lind. 23, 6. [*O. Sax.* resta, rasta *a couch*: *O. H. Ger.* resti *requies, quies, dormitio, pulpitum*; rasta *a stage in a journey*: *Goth.* rasta *a mile*: *Icel.* röst *a stage.*] v. ǽfen-, bed-, flet-, fold-, land-, niht-, sele-, wæl-rest.

restan; *p.* te *To rest.* I. *intrans.* (a) of persons (1) *to cease from toil, be at rest*:—Ic ðonne reste *requiescam*, Ps. Th. 54, 6. Eádige beóþ þearfena gāstas, and hié restaþ on heofena rīce, Blickl. Homl. 159, 29. Hȳ bīdinge mōstun æfter tintergum tīdum brūcan, restan ryneþrāgum, Exon. Th. 115, 3; Gū. 184. Ða restendan *pausantis*, Wrt. Voc. ii. 66, 21. Restendum *fereatis*, i. *quietis, securis*, 147, 59. (2) *to rest on a couch, to sleep*:—Ðonne hié restaþ ðonne restaþ hié būton bedde and bolstre ac on wildeóra fellum heora bedding biþ *homines accubantes et quiescentes sine ullis cervicalibus stratisque, tantum pellibus ferarum*, Nar. 31, 10. On ðære tīde ðe ōðre men slēpon and reston *caeteris quiescentibus et alto sopore pressis*, Bd. 2, 12; S. 513, 37. On niht ǽr hē ræste, Blickl. Homl. 47, 18. Ǽnlȳpige munecas geond ǽnlȳpige bed restan, R. Ben. 47, 3. Ðā bæd hē his þeng on ǽfenne . . . ðæt hē him stōwe gegearwode, ðæt hē restan mihte, Bd. 4, 24; S. 598, 31. Ðā hē gesette his leomu tō restenne *cum ad quiescendum membra sua posuisset*, 2, 6; S. 508, 11. Ðā wæs heo restende on sweostra slǽperne, 4, 23; S. 595, 39. (3) *to rest in death, lie dead, lie in the grave*:—Augustinus on Brytene rest on Cantwarum, Menol. Fox 206; Men. 104. Gerusalem is gereht 'sibbe gesyhþ,' forðon ðe hālige sāula ðǽr restaþ, Blickl. Homl. 81, 2. Reste hē ðǽr *Christ lay in the sepulchre*, Rood Kmbl. 138; Kr. 69. Hæfdon ēðelweardas ealdhettende swyrdum āswefede, hié on swaðe reston (*of the Assyrians slain in battle*), Judth. Thw. 26, 12; Jud. 322. (b) of things, *to remain unmoved* or *undisturbed, be still*:—Flǽsc mīn resteþ (*requiescet*) on hyhte, Ps. Spl. 15, 9. Reste ðǽr eówer sib, Lk. Skt. 10, 6. Ðām folcum sceal sacu restan, Beo. Th. 3719; B. 1857. Se æðeling hēt streámfare stillan, stormas restan, Andr. Kmbl. 3151; An. 1578. Ðīn rīce restende biþ ōþ ðæt ðū eft cymst, Cd. Th. 252, 26; Dan. 584. II. *trans. with reflex. acc. To rest one's self* (1) of cessation from toil:—Ðū rest ðē nū on eorþan, and ic mid sāre tō helle sceal beón lǽded, L. E. I. prm.; Th. ii. 398, 16. Ðǽr hī æðelingas inne restaþ, Runic pm. Kmbl. 340, 22; Rūn. 6. Reste ðæt folc hit *sabbatizavit populus*, Ex. 16, 30. On six dagon God geworhte heofon and eorþan and on ðam seofoþan hē hine reste (*ab opere cessavit*), 31, 17. Ic mē mæg restan on ðissum racentum, Cd. Th. 28, 11; Gen. 434. (2) of rest on a couch or in sleep:—Ðā reste hine se bisceop ðāgiet and mid wildeóra fellum wæs bewrigen . . . Ðā āwehte ic ðone bisceop, Nar. 31, 1. On ðæt hūs ðe heó hié inne reste, Blickl. Homl. 147, 2. Ðonne hē reste hine, ðonne wæs his seó æþeleste ræst on nacodre eorþan, 227, 10. Hū se beorn (*Noah in his drunken sleep*) hine reste on recede, Cd. Th. 95, 25; Gen. 1584. [*O. Sax.* restian: *O. Frs.* resta: *O. H. Ger.* restan *requiescere, dormire, cubare.*] v. ge-restan.

rēstan (?) *to exult*:—Hæfdon beorgas blīðe sǽle and rammum ðā rēstan gelīce *montes exultaverunt ut arietes*, Ps. Th. 113, 4. [Grein compares the word with *O. H. Ger.* hlūt-reisti, -reisig *clamosus, canorus.*]

rest-bedd, es; *n. A bed, couch*:—Ðeáh ic on mīn restbedd gestīge *si ascendero in lectum stratus mei*, Ps. Th. 131, 3.

reste-dæg, es; *m. A day of rest, a day when no work is to be done, a Sabbath*:—Restedæg *feriatus*, Wrt. Voc. i. 22, 20. Restedagas *feriati dies*, ii. 148, 6. Gehālga ðone restedæg . . . Se seofoþa dæg ys Drihtnes restedæg: ne wirc ðū nān weorc on ðam dæge, Ex. 20, 8–10. Mannes sunu ys restedæges hlāfurd, Mt. Kmbl. 12, 8. On ānum ðara restedaga se nū Sunnandæg is nemned, Bd. 3, 17; S. 545, 30.

resten-dæg, es; *m. A day of rest, Sabbath*:—Ðæt þridde bebod is 'Beó ðū gemyndig ðæt ðū ðone restendæg gehālgige' . . . Se Sæternesdæg wæs gehāten restendæg . . . on ðam dæge læg Cristes līc on byrigene, and hē ārās of deáþe on ðam Sunnandæge, and se dæg is cristenra manna restendæg, Homl. Th. ii. 206, 3–33. Se seofoþa dæg is mīn se hālga restendæg . . . healdaþ gē mīnne restendæg, Wulfst. 210, 17-21. Gedafenaþ ǽlcum men tō habbenne restendæg, 227, 22.

resten-geár, es; *n. A year in which work is not done:*—Ne sāw đū đonne (*in the seventh year*) ne rīp ne đīnne wīneard ne wirce, forđam đe hit biþ restengēr, Lev. 25, 4-5.

rest-gemāna, an; *m. Conjugal intercourse;* concubitus :—Hié noldan leng heora hlāforda ne heora wera ræstgemānan sēcean, Blickl. Homl. 173, 16. Restgemanan, Lchdm. i. 350, 10.

rest-hūs, es; *n. A sleeping-chamber:*—Hē đǽr hæfde ān resthūs (*cubiculum*), Bd. 3, 17; S. 543, 23.

rest-leás; *adj. Restless, disturbed:*—Ā biþ ungestillod and restleás đe mid đām unþeáwum belēd biþ, R. Ben. 121, 14.

rēsung. v. rǽswung.

rētan; *p.* te *To cheer, gladden, comfort:*—Geseóþ hū blīþe đa earman beóþ, đonne hī mon mid mete and mid hrægle rētaþ, Blickl. Homl. 41, 29. Ealle đa ōđru gōd ōleccaþ đam mōde and hit rētaþ, Bt. 24, 3; Fox 84, 24 note. Hū se wīsdōm hine eft rēte and rihte mid his andsworum, tit. 5; Fox x, 10. Đæt dolh-rēt mid ferscre buteran, Lchdm. ii. 354, 5. Wudewan and steópcild hȳ (eorlas and heretogan) sculon rētan and þearfena helpan, L. I. P. 11; Th. ii. 318, 26. Se hālga ongann wīgendra þreát wordum rētan, Andr. Kmbl. 3215; An. 1610. Đa wædlan sint tō frēfranne and tō rētanne (*offerre consolationis solatium*), Past. 26, 1; Swt. 181, 6. v. ā-, un-rētan; rōt.

rētend, es; *m. One who cheers or comforts:*—Wǽron wē oft gemyngode đæt wē sceoldan beón wudewena helpend and steópcilda ārigend and earmra rētend and wēpendra frēfriend, Wulfst. 257, 4.

ređe; *adj. Right, just:*—Đū (*God*) eart hālig lǽce, rede and rihtwīs, rūmheort hlāford, Hy. Grn. 7, 63. Mē đīn se gōda gāst lǽdde đæt ic on rihtne wegređne fērde *spiritus tuus bonus deducet me in viam rectam*, Ps. Th. 142, 11. Ic on wīsne weg worda đīnra, ređne rinne, 118, 32. Hī cȳđan đīnes mægenþrymmes mǽre wuldur, riht andređe, rīces đīnes, 144, 11. Ic đæt ongeat dōmas đīne ređe rihtwīse *cognovi quia aequitas judicia tua*, 118, 75. Synd his dōmas ređe mid rǽde rihte gecȳđde *rectum judicium tuum*, 118, 137.

rēđe; *adj. Fierce, cruel, savage.* It glosses the following Latin words, *efferus*, Ælfc. Gr. 14; Som. 16, 57: *ferus*, 38; Som. 41, 45: *trux*, 9, 67; Som. 14, 10: *ferox*, 9, 66; Som. 14, 6: Wrt. Voc. ii. 108, 37: *funestus*, 34, 12: *infestus*, 45, 26: *durus, crudelis, asper*, 142, 19: *severus, immansuetus*, 142, 44: *austerus*, 1, 20: *furibundus, valde iracundus*, Hpt. 450, 1: *truculentus*, 518, 34. Roeđe *asper*, Lk. Skt. Lind. 3, 5. I. applied to persons (a) in a bad sense:—Đes (*Ishmael*) byþ rēđe (*ferus*) man and winþ wiđ ealle and ealle wiđ hyne, Gen. 16, 12. Ealle his ǽhta rīce rēđe mann gedǽle *may a rich and cruel man divide all his possessions;* scrutetur foenerator omnem substantiam ejus (*Grein takes*ređemann *and compares Gothic* raþjo), Ps. Th. 108, 11. Gif hē (*a king*) his folc ofsit, đon biþ hē *tyrannus*, đæt is rēđe, Ælfc. Gr. 50, 20; Som. 51, 47. Grim and grǽdig, reóc and rēđe (*Grendel*), Beo. Th. 244; B. 122. Đā wæs ellenwōd, yrre and rēđe, frēcne and ferþgrim fæder wiđ dehter, Exon. Th. 251, 5; Jul. 140. Sum ārleás hine wolde sleán on his heáfde, ac đæt wǽpen wand āweg of đæs rēđan handum, Homl. Th. ii. 510, 23. Burhrūnan, rēđe *furie*, Wrt. Voc. ii. 151, 77. Twegen đe hæfdon deófolseócnesse wǽron swīđe rēđe (*saevi nimis*), Mt. Bos. 8, 28. Ealle swīđe erre wǽron. Đā wæs heora sum rēđra and hātheortra đonne đā ōđre, Blickl. Homl. 223, 6. (b) of justifiable severity, *severe, stern, austere, zealous:*—Strang wæs and rēđe se đe wætrum weóld (*the Deity at the time of the flood*), Cd. Th. 83, 8; Gen. 1376. Biþ đonne (*at the day of judgment*) rīces weard rēđe and meahtig, yrre and egesful, Exon. Th. 93, 19; 1528. Rēđe biþ Dryhten æt đam dōme, Soul Kmbl. 196; Seel. Verc. 98. Ōđer biscop, rēđes mōdes mon *austerioris animi vir*, Bd. 3, 5; S. 527, 20. Rēđe and stræce for ryhtwīsnesse *justitiae severitate districti*, Past. 5, 1; Swt. 41, 19. Đā wæs se bysceop mycle đig rēđra on gōdum weorcum đe hē ymbe đa cūđlīcan mēde gehȳrde, Shrn. 98, 19. God sylfa đonne ne gȳmeþ nǽnges mannes hreówe . . . ac biþ đonne rēđra and þearlwīsra đonne ǽnig wilde deór, ođđe ǽfre ǽnig mōd gewurde, Blickl. Homl. 95, 30. Wolde heofona helm helle weallas forbrecan . . . rēđust ealra cyninga (*Christ at the harrowing of hell*), Exon. Th. 461, 16; Hō. 36. II. applied to animals, *wild, savage, fierce:*—Rēđe deór *bellua*, Wrt. Voc. i. 22, 40. Rēđe nȳten *feralis bestia*, ii. 147, 53. Rib reáfiaþ rēđe wyrmas, Soul Kmbl. 221; Seel. 113. III. applied to things (punishment, calamity, etc.), *severe, cruel, fierce, dire:*—Rēđe wyrd *fortuna aspera*, Bt. 40, 1; Fox 236, 6-7. Wæs þreālīc þing þeōdum tōweard, rēđe wīte, Cd. Th. 79, 30; Gen. 1319. Weard him on slǽpe gecȳđed đætte rīces gehwæs rēđe sceolde gelimpan eorđan dreámas ende wurđan *on sleep was made known to him that of every kingdom a terrible end should befall, an end be of the joy of earth*, 223, 4; Dan. 114. Līg reád and reáđe, Dōm. L. 152. Rēđe, Exon. Th. 51, 3; Cri. 810. Sprecan rēđe word (*of the judgment passed on the wicked*), 50, 11; Cri. 798. Hē him sylfum rēđne dōm and heardne geearnaþ, Blickl. Homl. 95, 34. Regnas rēđe, hāte of heofenum, Ps. Th. 104, 28: Met. 7, 27. Rēđum wītum *ferocibus cruciatibus*, Hpt. Gl. 487, 10. Mid đȳ hī cwǽdon đæt đæt is wundor đæt đū swā rēđe forhæfednesse and swā hearde habban wylt andswarede hē: 'Heardran and rēđran ic geseah' *cum dicerent: 'Mirum quod tam austeram tenere continentiam velis,' respondebat: 'Austeriora ego vidi,'* Bd. 5, 12; S. 631, 34. v. un-rēđe.

ređe-hygdig; *adj. Right-minded:*—Wel biþ đam eorle đe him oninnan hafaþ ređehygdig wer rūme heortan *well will it be for that man who, being a mortal right-minded, hath a liberal heart within him*, Exon. Th. 467, 15. v. ređe.

rēđe-mōd; *adj.* I. in a bad sense, *of fierce or savage mind:*—Cwǽdon đæt heó (*the rebellious angels*) rīce rēđemōde āgan wolde, Cd. Th. 4, 2; Gen. 47. Ābrecan ne meahton rēđemōde (*the people of Sodom who were trying to break into Lot's house*) reced æfter gistum, 150, 15; Gen. 2492. II. of justifiable severity or anger, *of stern or severe mind, wroth:*—God rēđemōd reorde gesette eorþbūendum ungelīce, 101, 18; Gen. 1684: 218, 2; Dan. 33.

rēđen (?); *adj. Wild:*—Đæt hē hine gereordode mid đām rēđenum (MS. U. rēđum) nȳtenum, Homl. Skt. i. 10, 102.

rēđig; *adj. Fierce, savage, cruel:*—Rēđig *ferox*, Wrt. Voc. ii. 35, 17.

rēđigian; *p.* ode *To rage, be furious:*—Godes yrre ys ofer hig and his wīte rēđegaþ *egressa est ira a Domino, et plaga desaevit*, Num. 16, 46. Rēđegadon *furuerunt, insanierunt*, Wrt. Voc. ii. 151, 71.

rēđig-mōd; *adj. Of fierce or savage mind:*—Hē rēđigmōd rǽst on gehwilcne wēdehunde (rede, MS., *but* cf. wēdende hund, Fox 186, 8) wuhta gelīcost, Met. 25, 17.

rēđ-lic; *adj. Cruel, deadly:*—Rēđlīc scinhiw *ferale monstrum*, Wrt. Voc. ii. 147, 53. Deriendlīcan, rēđlīcan *feralia*, i. *lugubria, tristia, noxia, luctuosa, mortifera, mortalia*, 147, 50. Mid rēđlīcum *feralibus*, 34, 20.

rēđlīce; *adv. Fiercely, furiously:*—Roeđlīce *violenter*, Wrt. Voc. ii. 123, 47.

rēđness, e; *f. Fierceness, rage, cruelty, severity.* It glosses the following Latin words, *ferocitas*, Ælfc. Gr. 9, 25; Som. 10, 65: Wrt. Voc. ii. 34, 11: *austeritas*, 1, 19: *feritas*, i. *crudelitas, inclementia, duritia*, 148, 2: *furor*, 151, 69: *furia, insania*, 151, 73. Rēđnyssa *efferata*, Germ. 399, 380. I. applied to persons, (a) in a bad sense:—Đone lǽddon feówer āwyrgde englas mid mycelre rēđnesse and hine besencton on đa fȳrenan eá, Blickl. Homl. 43, 29. (b) of justifiable severity:—Đæt hē his hiéremonna yfelu tō hneslīce forberan ne sceal ac mid miclum andan and rēđnesse him stiére *subditorum mala, quae tolerare leniter non debent, cum magna zeli asperitate corrigere*, Past. 21, 5; Swt. 16, 1, 1. II. applied to animals, *savageness, fierceness, ferocity:*—Hē ealle mid wildeórlīcre rēđnysse (*ferocitate ferina*) deáþe gesealde, Bd. 2, 20; S. 521, 26. Wiđ hunda rēđnysse and wiđerrǽdnysse: se đe hafaþ hundes heortan mid him, ne beóþ ongeán hine hundas cēne, Lchdm. i. 372, 3. III. applied to things (reproof, calamity, etc.), *harshness, severity:*—Seó rēđnes đæs stormes *saevitia tempestatis*, Bd. 5, 1; S. 614, 9. Rēđnes cyles *frigoris asperitas*, 5, 12; S. 631, 30. Se đe wunde lācnigean wille gióte wīn on đæt sió rēđnes đæs wīnes đa wunde clǽnsige . . . Swā eác đam lāreówe is tō monianne đa liéđnesse wiđ đa rēđnesse *quisquis sanandis vulneribus praeest, in vino morsum doloris adhibeat . . . Miscenda ergo est lenitas, cum severitate*, Past. 17, 11; Swt. 125, 10-13. Sīe đǽr eác rēđnes næs đeáh tō stīþ *sit vigor, sed non exasperans*, Swt. 127, 2. Đonne sió lār wint on rēđnesse suīđur đonne mon niéde scyle *cum sese increpatio, plus quam necesse est in asperitatem pertrahit*, 21, 7; Swt. 167, 8.

rēđra, an; *m. An oarsman, sailor, rower:*—Rēđra *nauta*, Ælfc. Gr. 7; Som. 6, 43. Rēđra *remex*, 9, 61; Som. 13, 47: Wrt. Voc. i. 48, 9: 63, 77. Roeđra, ii. 119, 3. Roedra, Ep. Gl. 22 d, 25. v. ge-rēdra, rōđer.

ređran, -rēđre, -rēđru. v. rēdian, þrī-rēđre, ge-rēđru.

rēđscipe, es; *m. Rage, fierceness, fury:*—Rēđscipas *vel* hātheortnessa *furias, iras*, Wrt. Voc. ii. 151, 77.

rēwet[t], es; *m. n.* (?) I. *rowing:*—Forhwī ne fixast đu on sǽ? Hwīlon ic dō, ac seldon, forđan micel rēwyt mē ys tō sǽ *quia magnum navigium mihi est ad mare*, Coll. Monast. Th. 24, 3. On rēwette swincende *laborantes in remigando*, Mk. Skt. 6, 48. Hī wǽron on rēwute, Homl. Th. i. 162, 10. On đǽre sǽ swuncon on nihtlīcum rēwette, ii. 384, 25. Gif hwā hreóhnysse on rēwytte þolige, Lchdm. i. 302, 5. II. *a ship;* navigium:—Lǽtaþ đæt nett on đa swīđran healfe đæs rēwettes (*nauigii*), Jn. Skt. 21, 6: Homl. Th. ii. 290, 11.

ribb, es; *n. A rib:*—Ribb *costa*, Wrt. Voc. i. 65, 17. Rib, ii. 105, 29. Đā genam hē ān ribb of his sīdan and gefilde mid flǽsce đǽr đǽr đæt ribb wæs. And geworhte đæt ribb tō ānum wīfmen, Gen. 2, 21-22. Hæfde fela ribba, Exon. Th. 415, 9; Rä. 33, 8. Rib reáfiaþ rēđe wyrmas, 373, 21; Seel. 113. Hwīlum cnysseþ đæt sār on đa rib, Lchdm. ii. 258, 4. [*O. H. Ger.* rippa; *f.* rippi; *n.: Icel.* rif; *n.*] v. hrycg-ribb.

ribbe, an; *f. The herb hounds-tongue;* cynoglossum officinale:—Ribbe *cinoglosa*, Wrt. Voc. i. 286, 23: ii. 104, 2: *canes linga*, 102, 51: *quinquenerbia*, i. 68, 33. Ribbe. Đās wyrte đe man cynoglossam and ōðrum naman ribbe nemneþ, and hȳ eác sume men *linguam canis* hāteþ, Lchdm. i. 210, 16–19. Ribban seáw, ii. 40, 29. Genim ribban, 36, 23.

ribb-spâcan; *pl. n.* '*Rib-spokes,' the brisket* (?) [cf. *Icel.* bring-spelir '*breast-rails,' the brisket* or *part where the lower ribs are joined with the cartilago ensiformis*] :—Ribbspâcan *radiolus*, Wrt. i. 283, 47.

Rîc-, -rîc = rîce, q. v. are found in English, as in other dialects, helping to form proper names. For a list of such names see Txts. pp. 629–630, and for *O. H. Ger.* Graff ii. 389.

rîca, an ; *m. A powerful person, ruler* :—Feórðan dǣles rîca *tetrarcha*, Lk. Skt. 3, 1 : 9, 7. Nān ðara cyninga ðe cumaþ æfter mē, oððe ealdorman oððe ōðer rîca, Chart. Th. 243, 13. Wulf biþ se unrihtwîsa rîca ðe bereáfaþ ða eádmōdan, Homl. Th. i. 242, 3. Hē nolde ōlæcan ǣnigum rîcan mid geswǣsum wordum, ii. 514, 13. Ðonne gesihst ðū ða unrihtwîsan cyningas and ða ofermōdan rîcan bión swîðe unmihtige, Bt. 36, 2 ; Fox 174, 27. v. fyðer-, land-rîca, rîce.

rîcceter. v. rîceter.

rîce; *adj.* I. of persons, (a) *powerful, mighty, great, possessed of power* :—Oft gebyreþ ðæm monþwǣran ðonne hē wierð riéce (rîce, Cott. MSS.) ofer ōðre menn *nonnunquam mansueti, cum praesunt*, Past. 40, 1 ; Swt. 287, 23. Freá ælmihtig biþ ā rîce ofer heofonstōlas heágum þrymmum, Cd. Th. 1, 14 ; Gen. 7. Rîce þeóden (*God*), 53, 21 ; Gen. 864 : (*Hygelac*), Beo. Th. 2422 ; B. 1209. Rîce randwîga (*Æschere*), 2600 ; B. 1298. Rîce Drihten *Dominus*, Ps. Th. 96, 1. Wite se rîca man (*vir potens*) ðe him God hæfþ micelne welan and ǣhta ðyses lîfes tō forlǣten, L. Ecg. C. 2 ; Th. ii. 136, 3. Hū mæg ðǣr ānes rîces monnes naman cuman ðonne ðǣr mon furþum ðære burge naman ne geheórþ ðe hē on hāmfæst biþ, Bt. 18, 2 ; Fox 64, 2. Rîccræ wîfe hrægl *regillum* vel *peplum* vel *pella* vel *amiculum*, Wrt. Voc. i. 40, 32. Hē nǣnigum rîcum men ǣfre ǣnig feoh syllan wolde *nullam potentibus saeculi pecuniam umquam dare solebat*, Bd. 3, 5 ; S. 527, 12. Drihten ne wandaþ for rîcum ne for heánum *Dominus personam non accipit*, Deut. 10, 17. Ne dēm nān unriht ne ārwurða ðone rîcan *non injuste judicabis nec honores vultum potentis*, Lev. 19, 15. Āhōf ic rîcne (riicnæ, Ruth. Cross) cyning (*Christ*), Rood Kmbl. 88 ; Kr. 44. Se cyning and se bisceop and monige ōðre ǣfæste weras and rîce *rex cum antistite et aliis religiosis ac potentibus viris*, Bd. 4, 28 ; S. 606, 12. Guman rîce and heáne *men, great and small*, Exon. Th. 415, 18 ; Rä. 33, 13. Rîcera *potentum*, Wülck. 253, 29. Rîccra gesetnes *senatus consultum*, Wrt. Voc. i. 20, 66. Rîccra manna need *vis potestatis*, 21, 28. Him mon þyngode tō ðām rîcum (*the judges*), Bt. 38, 7 ; Fox 208, 29. Hē āwearp ða rîcan (*potentes*) of setle, Lk. Skt. 1, 52. Hē (*God*) hæfþ nǣnne rîcran, ne furþum nǣnne gelîcan, Bt. 42 ; Fox 258, 5. Gyf ðū ðæt gerǣdest ðe hēr rîcost eart *if you decide on this who are here in command*, Byrht. Th. 132, 55 ; By. 36. Wæs Alexandreas ealra rîcost monna cynnes, Exon. Th. 319, 21 ; Vîd. 15. Monege ōðre ðe of Macedonian rîcoste wǣron *multi Macedoniae principes*, Ors. 3, 9 ; Swt. 130, 24. Hē hēt ācwellan ða rîcostan witan and ða æðelestan, Met. 9, 25. (b) *rich, possessed of wealth* :—Eáðere ys olfende tō farenne þurh nǣdle þyrel ðonne se rîca and se welega on Godes rîce gā *facilius est camelum per foramen acus transire quam divitem intrare regnum Dei*, Mk. Skt. 10, 25. Ðā ðā se Hǣlend spræc be ðam rîcan, ðā cwæþ hē : 'Sum rîce man wæs' ... Cūð is eów ðæt se rîca biþ namcūðre on his leóde ðonne se þearfa, Homl. Th. i. 330, 3–6. 'Hē forlēt ða rîcan îdele.' Ðæt sind ða rîcan ða ðe mid mōdignysse ða eorþlîcan welan lufiaþ swîðor ðonne ða heofonlîcan. Fela rîccra manna geþeóþ Gode, ðæra ðe swā dōþ. Swā swā hit āwriten is : 'Ðæs rîcan mannes welan sind his sāwle ālȳsednyss,' 204, 3–7. Be rîccera (rîcra manna, W. F.) and þeárfena (bearna) andfenge. Gif hwylc rîce mon and æþelboren his bearn Gode on mynstre geoffrian wile, R. Ben. 103, 9–11. Rîcra grundleás gîtsung ǣhta, Met. 7, 14. Rîcum mannum *divitibus*, Bd. 3, 5 ; S. 527, 9. II. of things, *strong, powerful, mighty, potent* :—Wǣron hyra rǣdas rîce, siððan hié rodera waldend wið ðone hearm gescylde, Cd. Th. 245, 3 ; Dan. 457. God rîcum mihtum wolde ðæt him eorþe geseted wurde, 6, 34 ; Gen. 98. Gegnîd swefl tō duste ... meng wið ealde sāpan, and sīe swefl rîcra *let the sulphur be the stronger ingredient*, Lchdm. ii. 108, 16. Sió (*jaundice*) biþ ealra ādla rîcust, 106, 20. [*Goth.* reiks *mighty, powerful, having authority, great* : *O. Sax.* rîki : *O. Frs.* rîke : *O. H. Ger.* rîhhe *magnus, potens, magnificus, dives* : *Icel.* rîkr. The word passed into the Romance tongues. *Fr.* riche : *Ital.* ricco : *Span.* rico ; ricos omes *the grandees*.] v. med-, sige-, woruld-rîce.

rîce, es ; *n.* I. *power, authority, dominion, rule, empire, reign*, (a) referring to sovereigns or nations :—Tō become ðîn rîce *adveniat regnum tuum*, Mt. Kmbl. 6, 10. Biornwulfes rîce Mercna cyninges *the reign of Biornwulf king of Mercia*, Chart. Th. 70, 8. Ealle stærwrîteras secgaþ ðæt Asiria rîce æt Ninuse begunne ... From ðæm ǣrestan geáre Ninuses rîces ōþðæt Babylonia burg getimbred wæs wǣron lxiiii wintra ... ðȳ ilcan geáre gefeóll Babylonia and eall Asiria rîce and hiora anwald, Ors. 2, 1 ; Swt. 60, 25–32. Wæs Maximianes rîce brād, Exon. Th. 243, 10 ; Jul. 8. Rîces *imperii*, Wrt. Voc. ii. 44, 42. Wihtrǣde rîxigendum ðē fîftan wintra his rîces, L. Wih. prm. ; Th. i. 36, 5. Under fîftiga cyninga rîce, Ors. 1, 8 ; Swt. 42, 4. Tō rîce fōn *to become king, assume the royal authority*, 4, 6 ; Swt. 178, 19 : Chr. 675 ; Erl. 36, 10 : 754 ; Erl. 48, 17. Hēr Certic and Kynrîc onfēngon West-Seaxna rîce ... and siððan rîxadon West-Seaxna cynebarn of ðam dæge, 519 ; Erl. 15, 24. Hēr Ceadwalla ongan æfter rîce winnan, 685 ; Erl. 40, 16. On ðæs cyninges rîce foreweardum *cujus regni principio*, Bd. 5, 2 ; S. 614, 24. Ðū ealle cyningas ða ðe on Breotene wǣron ǣr ðē in mihte and on rîce (*potestate*) oferstîgest, 2, 12 ; S. 514, 9. Ymb xxxi wintra ðæs ðe hē rîce hæfde *after he had reigned thirty-one years*, Chr. 755 ; Erl. 48, 26. Wē witon ðæt ealle onwealdas from him sindon wē witon eác ðæt ealle rîca sint from him forðon ealle onwealdas of rîce sindon. Nū hē ðara læssena rîca reccend is hū micle swîðor wēne wē ðæt hē ofer ða māran sîe *omnem potestatem a Deo esse* (*omnes*) *recognoscunt. Quod si potestates a Deo sunt, quanto magis regna, a quibus reliquae potestates progrediuntur? Si autem regna diversa, quanto aequius regnum aliquod maximum*, Ors. 2, 1 ; Swt. 58, 23–26. (b) referring to others in authority (bishops, consuls, etc.) :—Biscepes burgbryce mon sceal bētan, ðǣr his rîce biþ *where he has jurisdiction*, L. In. 45 ; Th. i. 130, 8. Brihtwold biscop fēng tō ðam rîce (biscopstōle, MS. F.) on Wiltūnscîre *Brihtwold became bishop of Wiltshire*, Chr. 1006 ; Erl. 140, 2. Ðæt is ðæt hî (*men*) swîðost wilniaþ tō begitanne, wela and weorðscipe and rîce, Bt. 24, 4 ; Fox 86, 28. Nān man for his rîce ne cymþ tō cræftum ac for his cræftum hē cymþ tō rîce and tō anwealde, 16, 1 ; Fox 50, 20–22. Hwî ðū (*Boethius*) swā manigfeald yfel hæfdest on ðam rîce ðe hwîle ðe ðū hit hæfdest, 27, 2 ; Fox 96, 13. Ne forsāwe hē (*Catullus*) nō ðone ōðerne (*Nonium in curuli sedentem*) swā swîðe, gif hē nān rîce ne nǣnne anweald næfde, 27, 1 ; Fox 96, 7. Biþ ǣlc dysig mon ðȳ unweorðra ðe hē māre rîce hæfþ, 27, 2 ; Fox 98, 11. II. *the district in which power is exercised, a kingdom, realm, a diocese* : — Biscop *episcopus* ; bisceopscîr *vel* biscoprîc *dioecesis* ; cyncg *rex* ; rîce *regnum*, Wrt. Voc. i. 42, 2–6. Eal ðæt rîce wiðgeondan Jordanem *omnis regio circum Jordanen*, Mt. Kmbl. 3, 5. Gif him ðæt rîce losaþ *if heaven be lost to them*, Cd. Th. 28, 12 ; Gen. 434. Hū mihtest ðū sittan onmiddum gemǣnum rîce (*intra commune omnibus regnum*) ðæt ðū ne sceoldest ðæt ilce geþolian ðæt ōðre men, Bt. 7, 3 ; Fox 22, 17. Danaus, of his rîce ādrǣfed *regno pulsus*, Ors. 1, 8 ; Swt. 40, 17. Eall Italia rîce ðæt is betwux ðām muntum and Sicilia ðam eálonde, Bt. 1 ; Fox 2, 4. Ðā fērde deós spǣc embe eall ðæt rîce (*regionem*), Lk. Skt. 7, 17. Hē wealdeþ sîdum rîcum, Ps. Th. 71, 8. Of rîcum (*regionibus*) hē gaderode hig, Ps. Spl. 106, 2. Se deófol æteówde him ealle middangeardes rîcu, Mt. Kmbl. 4, 8. Ða heofonlîcan rîco, Bd. 5, 19 ; S. 641, 15. Ða ēcan rîceo, 2, 5 ; S. 507, 7. II a. *the people inhabiting a district, a nation* :—Cumaþ folc feorran tōgædere and rîcu eác, Ps. Th. 101, 20. [*Goth.* reiki *power, authority* : *O. Sax.* rîki : *O. Frs.* rîke : *O. H. Ger.* rîhhi *regnum, imperium, regio* : *Icel.* rîki.] v. abbod-, bisceop-, brego-, bryten-, cyne-, eard-, eást-, eorþ-, ēðel-, fæder-, gum-, heofon-, þrym-, west-, woruld-rîce.

rîce-dōm, es ; *n. Power, rule, dominion* :—Ðîn rîcedōm ofer ūs rîxie '*thy kingdom come*,' Wulfst. 125, 9. [*O. Sax.* rîki-dôm *power* : *O. Frs.* rîke-dôm : *O. H. Ger.* rîhhi-tuom *imperium* ; *divitiae* : *Icel.* rîk-dômr *power* ; *wealth*.]

rîcels, ricene, ricenlîce. v. rēcels, recene, recenlîce.

rîcen[n], e ; *f. A female endowed with power, a goddess* :—Rîcenne *Diane*, Wrt. Voc. ii. 26, 76 : 86, 63.

rîceter[e], es ; *n.* I. *power, dominion, rule, greatness, glory* :—Rîcceter *gloria*, Germ. 389, 41. Wē ne sceolon ða rîcan for heora rîccetere wurðian *we are not to honour the great ones for their greatness*, Homl. Th. i. 128, 22. Ðam lāreówe gedafenaþ ðæt hē hogie hū manegra manna sāwle hē mǣge Gode gestrȳnan ... nā hū micel hē mǣge mid his rîcetere him tō geteón *it behoves the teacher to strive how many men's souls he can gain for God, not how much he can draw to himself by his power*, ii. 532, 30. Gyf kyng mid his rîccetere his folc ofsit, ðon biþ hē *tyrannus*, Ælfc. Gr. 50, 20 ; Som. 51, 47 : Homl. Th. i. 242, 4. Wite se abbod, ðæt hē ða gȳmenne ðara untrumra sāula tō rihtre lācnunge underfēng, and nā for rîcetere ðe hē ofer ða hæbbe ðe hāle syndon, R. Ben. 51, 12. Ne ongyte wē ðæt ðǣr ǣnigra hāda andfencg wǣre, ðæt is ðæt ǣnig be lîues rîcetere, ac ǣlc be his neōde and untrumnesse ancnāwen wǣre *we do not understand that in this case there was any acceptance of persons, that is that recognition was made of any one in proportion to the greatness of his position in life, but of each according to his need and weakness*, 57, 21. Smeáge se abbod hū hē swîðor ðām sāwlum fremian mǣge, ðonne hē hogige embe rîcitere his andwealdes, 118, 21. Hrîceter *monarchium, principatum, regnum*, Hpt. Gl. 414, 17. Rîciter, 422, 26 : 511, 11. Rîcetere ł ealdordōm, 453, 41 : 465, 26. Rîceter *potentiam*, Blickl. Gl. Ðone ealdordōm and ðæt rîceter ðe se reccere for monigra monna þearfe underfēhþ hē hine sceal eówian ūtan, Past. 17, 7 ; Swt. 119, 61. Hē dyde him ðæt rîceter tō sida and tō gewunan *ministerium regiminis vertit in usum dominationis*, 17, 9 ; Swt. 121, 19. II. *power improperly used, violence, force* :—Hē (*Lucifer*) wolde mid rîccetere him rîce gewinnan, Ælfc. T. Grn. 2, 42. Ðæt nān ðara cyninga ðe cumaþ æfter mē oððe eldorman oððe ōðer rîca mid ǣnigum rîccetere oððe unrihte ðiss ne āwende, Chart. Th. 243, 13 :

Homl. Th. i. 82, 21. Hú mæg, oððe hú dear ǽnig lǽwede man him tó geteón þurh rîccetere Cristes wican? ii. 592, 27.

rîcettan (?) *to rule*:—Rirciten (riccetan?) *gubernare*, Hpt. Gl. 414, 20.

rîc-lîc; *adj. Great, splendid, magnificent*:—Ungemetlîce rîclîc lýf *excessively splendid mode of life*, Shrn. 184, 8. [*O. H. Ger.* rîh-lîh *splendidus*: *Icel.* ríku-ligr.] v. next word.

rîclîce; *adv.* I. *powerfully, with power, as one possessing power*:—Gé budon swîðe rîclîce and swîðe ágendlîce *vos cum austeritate imperabatis eis et cum potentia*, Past. 19, 2; Swt. 145, 5. On ðám dagum rîxode Æþelbyrht on Cantwarebyrig rîclîce, and his rîce wæs ástreht fram ðære micclan eá Humbre óð súðsǽ, Homl. Th. ii. 128, 18. Rîclîce *t* stranglîce *t* rîclîcost *potentissime*, Ps. Lamb. 44, 4. II. *splendidly, sumptuously*:—Sum welig man dæghwamlîce rîclîce (*splendide*) gewistfullude, Lk. Skt. 16, 19. [*O. H. Ger.* rîhlîho *splendide, festive, mirifice*: *Icel.* ríkuliga *magnificently; strictly* (of observance).]

rics. v. rysc.

rîcsere, es; *m. A ruler*:—Rîcsares aldormen *dominationes principatum*, Rtl. 113, 12.

rîcsian; *p.* ode. I. *to exercise* or *have power, to rule, govern, reign*:—Eálá ðú scippend heofones and eorþan! ðú ðe on ðam écan setle rîcsast! Bt. 4; Fox 6, 30. Hé rîcsaþ (*regnabit*) on écnesse, and hys rîces ende ne byþ, Lk. Skt. 1, 33. Rîxaþ, Ps. Th. 9, 36. Rîhcsaþ, Ps. Spl. 95, 9. 'Hí rîcsodon (-edon, Hatt. MS.) næs ðeáh mînes þonces'... Ða ðe swǽ rîcsiaþ (-ieaþ, Hatt. MS.) hí rîcsiaþ of hira ágnum dóme *ipsi regnaverunt, et non ex me*'... *Ex se regnant, qui*..., Past. 1, 2; Swt. 26, 14–16. On ðám dagum rîxode Æþelbyrht cyning on Cantwarebyrig, Homl. Th. ii. 128, 17. Circe rîcsode on ðam îglonde, Met. 26, 57. Rîhcsode *regnavit*, Ps. Spl. 92, 1: 96, 1. Gif ðîn willa sîe ðæt rîcsie se ðe on róde wæs, Elen. Kmbl. 1544; El. 774. Se mǽra wyrhta ðe rîhsigende wylt eal ðæt hé geworhte, Lchdm. iii. 432, 15. Wihtrǽde rîxigendum, L. Wih. prm.; Th. i. 36, 4. II. with the idea of supremacy secured by, or exercised with, force or violence, *to domineer, dominate, tyrannize, exercise violence*:—Swá nú rîxiaþ gromhýdge guman, Exon. Th. 445, 26; Dóm. 13. Deáþ rîcsade ofer foldbúend, 154, 16; Gú. 843. Rîxade, 154, 2; Gú. 836. Se þeódsceaða (*famine*) rîcsode, Andr. Kmbl. 2233; An. 1118. Swá rîxode and wið rihte wan ána wið eallum (*of Grendel's successful raids on Hrothgar's hall*), Beo. Th. 290; B. 144. Án ongan deorcum nihtum draca rîcsian, 4429; B. 2211. Gif wé áslaciaþ ðæs weddes ðe wé seald habbaþ, ðonne máge wé wénan ðæt ðás þeófas willaþ rîxian gyta swîðor ðonne hig ǽr dydon *these thieves will get the upper hand yet more than they did before*, L. Ath. v. 8, 9; Th. i. 238, 23. Ðæt hé mǽge rîxian and wealdan ealra his feónda and dón him tó yfele ðæt ðæt hé wylle *omnium inimicorum suorum dominabitur*, Ps. Th. 9, 25. Deáþ him furðor ne biþ rîcsend *mors illi ultra non dominabitur*, Rtl. 26, 33. Drihten rîcsandra *Dominus dominantium*, 101, 10. II a. of things, *to prevail*:—Ða yfelan wǽtan weorþaþ gegaderode on ðone magan, and ðǽr rîxiaþ mid scearfunga innan, Lchdm. ii. 176, 7. On ðisse þeóde rîxode unrihta fela *in this nation many a wrong has prevailed*, Wulfst. 128, 3. Gif preóst forhele hwæt on his scriftscîre betweox mannum tó unrihte rîxigen (rîxige? rîxigende?) gebéte hé *if a priest conceal anything in his district between men that may have force to cause injustice, let him make amends*, L. N. P. L. 42; Th. ii. 296, 14. [*O. H. Ger.* rîhhison *regnare*.] v. ofer-rîcsian.

rîcsiend, es; *m. A ruler*:—Rîcsand *rector*, Rtl. 102, 15.

rîcsung, e; *f. Rule, dominion*:—Rîcsunges *dominationis*, Rtl. 174, 19.

rid *a swinging, swaying*; *in* sand-rid *a quicksand*. v. rîdan. [*Icel.* rið *sway, swing*.]

rîdan; *p.* rád, *pl.* ridon. I. *to ride on horseback*; equitare:—Hwîlum ic on wloncum wicge rîde, Exon. Th. 489, 14; Rä. 78, 7. Hwá rît intó ðam porte *quis equitat in civitatem?* Ælfc. Gr. 5; Som. 3, 52. Ðîn cyning rît uppan tamre assene, Mt. Kmbl. 21, 5. Hú ne wást ðú ðæt nán mon for ðý ne rît ðe hine rîdan lyste, ac rît for ðý ðe hé mid ðǽre ráde earnaþ sume earnunga, Bt. 34, 7; Fox 144, 5–7. Ðonne rîdeþ ǽlc hys weges, Ors. 1, 1; Swt. 21, 4. Sum mon rád be ðære stówe, Bd. 3, 9; S. 533, 30. Him (*the Danes*) Ælfréd and cyninges þegnas oft ráde on ridon, Chr. 871; Erl. 76, 11. Ofer ðý cræte curran, ofer ðý cwéne reodan, Lchdm. iii. 32, 10. Ymbe hlǽw riodan hildedeóre, Beo. Th. 6319; B. 3170. Rîdan ða yldestan men tó ðære byrig, L. Ath. i. 20; Th. i. 208, 29. Ðeáh ðe hé gewuna wǽre ðæt hé má eode ðonne ride, Bd. 3, 14; S. 540, 17. Ne wæs álýfed ðæt hé móste bútan on myran rîdan, 2, 13; S. 517, 7: 4, 3; S. 566, 33. Nalæs rîdende on horse, ac on his fótum gangende, 3, 28; S. 560, 33. Ðes rîdenda here *hic equester exercitus*, Ælfc. Gr. 9, 18; Som. 10, 2. Hé ásent rîdendne here, Wulfst. 200, 21. Rîdende men *equites*, Gen. 50, 9. II. *to ride* (of other modes of transport as a vessel *rides* on the waves):—Wîde rád ðæt scip ofer holmes hringc, Cd. Th. 84, 3; Gen. 1392. Fana up rád *the ensign* (*the fiery pillar*) *moved aloft*, 193, 18; Exod. 248. Ðæt hé (*a vessel*) scyle fǽmig rîdan ýða hrycgum, Exon. Th. 384, 24; Rä. 4, 32. III. without the idea of progress, *to ride* (as in *to ride at anchor*), *to swing, rock*:—Licgaþ mé ymbe îrenbendas rîdeþ racentan sál *the chain swings* (or *presses?*) *on me*, Cd. Th. 24, 3; Gen. 372. Swá biþ geómorlîc gomelum eorle tó gebîdanne ðæt his byre rîde giong on galgan *that his son swing on the gallows*, Beo. Th. 4882; B. 2445. Sum sceal on galgan rîdan, seomian æt swylte, óþðæt báncofa blódig ábrocen weorðeþ, Exon. 329, 13; Vy. 33. [*O. Frs.* rîda: *O. H. Ger.* rîtan *to ride* (*on horseback* or *in a carriage*): *Icel.* ríða *to ride, to swing, sway*.] v. á-, æfter-, be-, for-, ge-, of-, ofer-, óþ-rîdan.

ridda, an; *m.* I. *a horseman, rider*:—Ridda oððe rîdende *eques*, Ælfc. Gr. 9, 26; Som. 11, 8. Ridda *homo equo portatus*, Wrt. Voc. ii. 143, 65. Se ridda (cf. sum wegfarende mann, l. 168) férde forþ on his weg, Swt. A. S. Rdr. 100, 175. II. *a mounted soldier*:—Hors and ðone riddan hé áwearp on sǽ, Cant. Moys. Feówer hund and þúsend cræta hé hæfde and twelf þúsend riddena, Homl. Th. ii. 578, 3. Pharao him filigde mid his crætum and gilplîcum riddum.... Seó sǽ ealle his crætu and riddan oferwreáh, 194, 22–27. Ðá gemétte Martinus ánne nacodne þearfan, and his nán ne gýmde, ðeáh ðe hé ða riddan ðæs bǽde... Ðá hlógon ða cempan sume, 500, 19–28.

rîdel. v. for-rîdel.

rîdend, es; *m. A horseman, knight*:—Rîdend swefaþ, hæleþ *knights and warriors sleep the sleep of death*, Beo. Th. 4906; B. 2457.

[**rîdere**, es; *m. A knight*:—Hé begeat ðone castel æt Albemare and ðárinne hé sette his cnihtas... Æfter ðisum hé begeat má castelas and ðǽrinne his rîderas gelógode, Chr. 1090; Erl. 226, 30. [*M. H. Ger.* rîtare: *Icel.* riðari.]]

ride-soht. v. hrið-suht.

rîdusende (?) *swaying, swinging* (?):—Rîdusende (-aendi, -endi) *pendulus*, Txts. 87, 1562. Cf. rîdan (?).

rîd-wîga, an; *m. A mounted soldier*:—Þrittig rîdwîgena *turma*, Wrt. Voc. i. 18, 24.

rif (?); *adj. Fierce*:—Ic wiste ðæt úre fór wæs þurh ða lond and stówe ðe missenlîcra cynna eardung in wæs rifra wildeóra *ego sciebam per bestiosa loca nobis iter esse*, Nar. 10, 5. Ða rifista *ferociora*, Rtl. 125, 31.

rîfe; *adj. Rife, abundant*:—Ðere .vii. niht gyf wind byoþ, fîr byþ swîðe rýfe ðý geáre, Lchdm. iii. 164, 21. [Baluwe þer wes riue, Laym. 631: 4544: 20079: 20672. Þenne scullen blissen wurðen riue, 32107. Þa hæðene weoren swa riue & auere heo comen, 14542. Alle worldes wele ham is inoh riue, H. M. 29, 22. Lauerd, mi hele so rife, Ps. 26, 1 note. Of him cam kinde mikil and rif, Gen. and Ex. 1252. *Icel.* rífr *munificent, abundant*; ríf-ligr *large, munificent*.]

rifeling, es; *m. A kind of shoe* or *sandal*:—Rifelingas *obstrigilli* (obstrigilli *calcei, qui per plantas consuti, ex superiore parte corrigia constringuntur*, Isidore), Wrt. Voc. i. 26, 25. [Rewelyns, rivlins *shoes* or *sandals of raw hide*, Jamieson's Dict. *See also* riveling in Halliwell's Dict.]

Riffeng *Riphaei montes*:—Of Riffeng ðám beorgum, Ors. 1, 1; Swt. 8, 15.

rift, rifte, es; *n. A veil, curtain, cloak*:—Rift *laena*, Wrt. Voc. ii. 112, 42: *palla*, 116, 35: *biuligo, niger velamen*, 126, 38: *cicla*, 131, 28. Hwîtel *t* ryft *sagum*, i. 284, 62: *pallium*, Ps. Surt. 103, 6. Ðý áwundenan ryfte *plumario*, Wrt. Voc. ii. 77, 15. Hé nywolnessa swá swá ryfte (*pallium*) him tó gewǽde woruhte, Ps. Th. 103, 7. Sprenge se sacerd seofon sîðon on ðæt ryft (*velum*), Lev. 4, 17. [*O. H. Ger.* pein-refta *tibarii*: *Icel.* ript; *f.*; ripti; *n. a kind of cloth* or *linen jerkin*.] v. bán-, cneó-, fleóg-, hálig-, wáh-rift.

rifter, riftr, es; *m. An instrument for reaping, a sickle, scythe*:—Riftr *falx*, Txts. 62, 430. Rifter, Wrt. Voc. ii. 35, 1. Wîngeardseax, rifte[r] *vel* sicul *falx*, 146, 76. Riftre *falce*, 79, 69. Riftras *falcis*, 108, 19.

riftere, es; *m. A reaper*:—Riftre *messor*, Wrt. Voc. ii. 56, 55: 71, 30. Riptere, i. 74, 68. Ðæt gerîp is micel and ða rifteras feáwa, Homl. Th. ii. 520, 16. Riftra[s] *messores*, Mt. Kmbl. Rush. 13, 39. Ic cweþe tó riftrum mînum *dicam messoribus*, 13, 30. Se bær his ryfterum mete tó æcere, Homl. i. 570, 33.

rige, rigen. v. ryge, rygen.

rignan, rînan; *p.* rînde. [*A strong preterite occurs in the Blickling Gloss*, rán *pluit*. Cf. In Elyes tyme heuene was yclosed þat no reyne ne rone (roon, MS. W.: roen, MS. R.: ron, MS. B.: raynade, MS. C.), Piers P. 14, 62.] I. *to rain, to cause rain to fall*, (a) with the agent expressed:—Ic rîne *pluo*, Ælfc. Gr. 28; Som. 30, 53. Hé rýnde ofer synfullan grin, Ps. Spl. 10, 7. Hit ágan rînan xl. daga and xl. nihta tósomne ðæm mǽstan réne, and seó eorþe rînde ealswá swîðe of hire eásprencgum angén ðam heofenlican flóde, Wulfst. 217, 1. Hét hé ða wîdan duru wolcen ontýnan heá of heofenum and hider rignan manna *mandavit nubibus desuper, et januas coeli aperuit; et pluit illis manna manducare*, Ps. Th. 77, 25. (b) with the agent not expressed:—Rînþ *pluit*, Ælfc. Gr. 22; Som. 24, 6. Hit rînde feówertig daga, Gen. 7, 12: Mt. Kmbl. 7, 27. Hyt rînde fýr and swefl of heofone *pluit ignem et sulphur de coelo*, Lk. Skt. 17, 29. Swá gelîc swá... sý fýr onǽled and ðîn heall gewyrmed and hit rîne and snîwe and styrme úte, Bd. 2, 13; S. 516, 17. Drihten lét rînan hagol *pluit Dominus grandinem*, Ex. 9, 24. Hé lǽt rînan (regneþ, and ða unrihtwîsan, Mt. Kmbl. 5, 45. II. *to rain, to fall* (of rain):—Rîneþ blôdig regn æt ǽfen *a bloody rain shall fall at even*, Blickl. Homl. 91, 34. Mon geseah weallan blôd of eorþan and rînan meolc of heofonum *sanguine e terra, lac visum est manare de coelo*, Ors. 4, 3; Swt. 162, 7. [*Goth.* rignjan: *Icel.* rigna, regna: *O. H. Ger.* reganôn.]

riht, es; *n.* I. *that which is straight* or *erect, a plumb line*:—Reht *perpendiculo*, Wrt. Voc. ii. 81, 26. II. that which is straight in a metaphorical sense, *right, law, canon, rule*:—Mennisc riht *jus*; gecynde riht *jus naturale*; ânre burge riht *jus civile*; ealra þeóda riht *jus gentium*; cempena riht *jus militare*; ealdormanna riht *jus publicum*, Wrt. Voc. ii. 49, 5–10. Riht ł Godes riht *fas*, 38, 71. Scipmanna riht *rodia lex*, i. 20, 50. Reht Rômwala *jus Quiritum*, Rtl. 189, 13. Ryhtes wyrðe *entitled to call in the aid of the law*, Chart. Th. 170, 3. Godes rihtes wiðerbreca, Blickl. Homl. 175, 8. Wiþerwearde Godes beboda and ðæs gâstlîcan rihtes *opponents of God's commands and of the spiritual law*, 135, 13. Lufige man Godes riht georne, L. Eth. vi. 30; Th. i. 322, 23. Æfter þeáwe ârwurðra rihta *juxta morem canonum venerabilium*, Bd. 4, 5; S. 572, 5. III. *what is in accordance with law, human or divine, what is just or proper, right, justice, equity*:—Ðâ cwǽdon ealle ða weotan ðæt mon ûðe ðære cyrcan rihtes swâ swel swâ ôðerre ... And Eþelwald cwæð ðæt hê ǽlcre circan aa his dǽla rihtes ûðe, Chart. Th. 140, 7–16. Hî rihtes ne gýmdon, Andr. Kmbl. 278; An. 139. Gif mon ne mihte hî tô rihte gecyrron, ðæt hî heora wôhdǽda geswîcan woldan, Blickl. Homl. 45, 27. Godes lof mid rihte begân, 43, 4. Mid rihte Gode þeówian, 45, 29. Hî mê habbaþ benumen mînes naman ðe ic mid rihte habban sceolde, Bt. 7, 3; Fox 20, 28. On ðînum rihte *in aequitate tua*, Ps. Th. 142, 11. Filige rihtlîce ðam rihte *juste quod justum est persequeris*, Deut. 16, 20. Dêmaþ ǽlcon men riht *quod justum est judicate*, 1, 16. Gif wê sôþ and riht on ûrum lîfe dôn willaþ, Blickl. Homl. 129, 32. Hê â tô ǽghwylcum sôþ and riht sprecende wæs and dônde, 223, 30. On riht *a-right, by rights, according to what is just* or *proper*:—Healdan Godes ǽwe on riht, 45, 9, 22. Ðære cyrican on riht þeówian, 49, 4. Nis eów forboden ðætte ǽhta habban, gif gê ða on riht strênaþ, 53, 28. Hê fêrde mid ðâm þingum ðe his on riht wǽron *quae juris sui erant*, Gen. 31, 21. III a. *what is just in the case of a criminal, just punishment, justice*:—Dô ðam þeófe his riht, swâ hit ǽr Eádmundes cwide wæs, L. Edg. H. 2; Th. i. 258, 9. IV. *what properly belongs to a person, what may justly be claimed, a right, due*:—Ðâ sôna wæs Eþelwald ðæs wordes, ðæt hê nô ðes rihtes (*the right to certain woodland*) wiðsacan wolde, Chart. Th. 140, 12. Nelle ic ða rincas rihte benǽman *I will not deprive the men of what rightly belongs to them*, Cd. Th. 129, 32; Gen. 2152. Hê hafaþ mec bereáfod rihta gehwylces, feohgestreóna, Elen. Kmbl. 1817; El. 910. V. *what is due from a person, duty*:—Ðæt biþ ðæs recceres ryht ðæt hê þurh ða stemne his lâriówdômes ætiéwe ðæt wuldor ðæs uplîcan êðles *debitum rectoris est supernae patriae gloriam per vocem predicationis ostendere*, Past. 21, 5; Swt. 159, 22. Ûs is riht micel ðæt wê rodera weard wordum herigen (cf. nû wê sceolan (*debemus*) herigean heofonrîces weard, Bd. 4, 24; S. 597, 20), Cd. Th. 1, 1; Gen. 1. VI. *what agrees with a proper standard, what is correct or exact, the rights of a case, the truth*:—*h* and *k* geendiaþ on *a* æfter rihte, Ælfc. Gr. 2; Som. 3, 4. Hê ne mæg beón æfter rihte gecweden, bûton ðæt andgit beó ǽr foresǽd, 15; Som. 18, 43. Se ðe secgan wile sôþ æfter rihte, Beo. Th. 2103; B. 1049. Ðæt wîf sǽde him eall ðæt riht *dixit ei omnem veritatem*, Mk. Skt. 5, 33. Ðæt hê be ðære rôde riht getǽhte, Elen. Kmbl. 1199; El. 601. Hê fram Scê Pauline ðæt riht (*rationem*) leornade ðæs hâlgan geleáfan, Bd. 2, 9; S. 512, 9. On riht *a-right, correctly, properly*:—Ne eart ðû fullfremedlîce ne on riht gefullad *non es perfecte baptizatus*, 5, 6; S. 620, 6. Gif ic ðîne unrôtnesse on riht ongiten hæbbe, Bt. 7, 1; Fox 16, 7. VII. *an account, a reckoning*; ratio, *mostly in such phrases as* riht âgildan *to render an account*:—Hió âgeofaþ be ðæm reht *reddent rationem de eo*, Mt. Kmbl. Rush. 12, 36: Lk. Skt. Lind. 16, 2. Hê sceal ealra his dôma riht âgyldan beforan ðæm rihtwîsan dêman on dômesdæge, R. Ben. 16, 7. Hê sceal mid his sâwle ânre Gode riht âgyldan ealles ðæs ðe hê on worlde tô wommum gefremede, Blickl. Homl. 113, 3. Wê sceolan riht âgyldan for ealles ûres lîfes dǽdum, 63, 31. Reht setta *rationem ponere*, Mt. Kmbl. Lind. 18, 23. Hyra lîfes riht, Exon. Th. 84, 18; Cri. 1375. Ǽnige rihte âræfnan *ulla ratione tolerare*, Bd. 5, 12; S. 631, 30. [*O. Sax.* reht: *O. Frs.* riucht: *O. H. Ger.* reht *jus, justitia, judicium, aequitas, rectitudo, ratio*: *Icel.* rêttr; *m. right, law; due, claim.*] v. ǽ-, eald-, êðel-, folc-, ge-, land-, leód-, nîd-, on-, sundor-, swǽn-, un-, word-, woruld-riht; *and* â-riht.

riht; *adj.* I. of direction, (a) literally, *straight, erect, direct*:—Seó heá rôd ryht ârǽred *raised erect*, Exon. Th. 66, 3; Cri. 1066. Rihtes sîþfætes *directi callis*, Wrt. Voc. ii. 140, 55. Rihtre *directo*, 27, 69. Rihtre stîge *recto tramite*, Bd. 1, 12; S. 481, 8. Faran be rihtum wege (*via publica*), Num. 20, 17. Ðeós wyrt hafaþ rihte stelan, Lchdm. i. 316, 8. Wæs ðæt ilce hûs hwemdragen, nalas æfter gewunan mennisces weorces ðæt ða wǽgas wǽron rihte, ac git swîðor on scræfes onlîcnesse ðæt wæs æteówed, and gelômlîce ða stânas swâ of ôðrum clife ût sceoredon, Blickl. Homl. 207, 17–20. Ðâ âxode ic hwylc se weg tô ðære eá ealra rîhtost wǽre, Glostr. Frg. 108, 28. Hê ðan rihtestan wege ðyder tô geferde, Guthl. 3; Gdwin. 20, 12. (b) metaphorically, *right, straight*:—Ða men ðe bearn habban, tǽcean him lîfes weg and rihtne gang tô heofonum, Blickl. Homl. 109, 18. Ic him lîfes weg rihtne gerýmde, Rood Kmbl. 175; Kr. 89. Hî ðâ gelǽdde lîfes ealdor ðǽr hî on rihtne weg (*in viam rectam*) eodan, Ps. Th. 106, 6. Wǽrun Godes mînes gangas rihte, 67, 23. Dôþ hys sîðas rihte (ræhta, Lind.) *rectas facite semitas ejus*, Mt. Kmbl. 3, 3. I a. *right*; dexter. v. riht-hand. II. *agreeable to the spirit of law, human or divine, just, equitable*:—Hwî ne dême gê ðæt riht (*justum*) is? Lk. Skt. 12, 57. Dêmað rihtne dôm *justum judicium judicate*, Jn. Skt. 7, 24. Rihte syndon ðîne dômas, Blickl. Homl. 89, 6. Beóþ rûmmôde ryhtra gestreóna *liberal of gains justly acquired*, Exon. Th. 106, 31; Gû. 49. III. *satisfying the requirements of a law* or *regulation, legitimate, lawful, regular*:—Riht canonicus *a regular canon*, L. Ælfc. C. 5; Th. ii. 344, 12. Heora riht cyning *legitimus rex*, Bd. 4, 26; S. 603, 18. On rihtre ǽwe *in lawful marriage*, Wulfst. 304, 21. Ða ðe on rihtum hǽmede beóþ *qui in legitimo matrimonio sunt*, L. Ecg. C. 25; Th. ii. 150, 22. Ða men ðe bearn habban, lǽran hié ðâm rihtne þeódscipe (*regular discipline*), Blickl. Homl. 109, 17. On rihtne tîman (cf. on gesetne tîman, Th. ii. 296, 3) tîda ringan, L. Edg. C. 45; Th. ii. 254, 5. IV. *satisfying the demands of conduct, right, proper, fitting*:—Ys hit riht ðæt man ðam câsere gafol sylle *licet nobis dare tributum caesari*, Lk. Skt. 20, 22. Riht ðæt is ðæt ealle geleáffulle men ðis feówertig daga on forhæfdnesse lifgean, Blickl. Homl. 35, 8. Hê nǽfre nǽnigum woruldrîcum men swîðor onbûgan nolde, ðonne hit riht wǽre, 223, 29. Mê ðæt riht ne þinceþ, ðæt ic ôleccan âwiht þurfe Gode, Cd. Th. 19, 11; Gen. 289. Reáfode, swâ hit riht ne wæs, beám on bearwe, 55, 29; Gen. 901: Byrht. Th. 137, 23; By. 190. Gif hire forþsîð getîmige ǽr him, ðonne is hit rihtast ðæt hê ðanon forþ bûton ǽlcum wîfe wunige, Wulfst. 304, 23. Sâulscat is rihtast ðæt man gelǽste aa æt openum græfe, 311, 12. V. *satisfying the requirements of a standard, right, correct, true, orthodox*:—Riht gewrit *orthography*, Ælfc. Gr. 50, 16; Som. 51, 22. Hwæt rêce wê hwæt wê sprecan bûton hit riht sprǽc (*recta locutio*) sý, Coll. Monast. Th. 18, 14. Eálâ ðætte ðis moncyn wǽre gesǽlig gif heora môd wǽre swâ riht and swâ geendebyrd swâ swâ ða ôðre gesceafta sindon *O felix hominum genus, si vestros animos amor, quo coelum regitur, regat*, Bt. 21; Fox 76, 1. Hit is swîðe ryht spell ðæt Plato sǽde ... Ða cwæþ ic: 'Ic eom geþafa ðæt ðæt wæs sôþ spell ðæt Plato sǽde,' 35, 1–2; Fox 156, 8–14. Hê wæs riht cyning *he* (*Constantine*) *was a true king*, Elen. Kmbl. 26; El. 13. Ðæt is se rihta geleáfa, Blickl. Homl. 21, 17: Bd. 1, 21; S. 485, 9. Ðonne wile hê onfôn rihtre ondetnesse (*true confession*), Blickl. Homl. 155, 1. Mid rihtum ondgite, 63, 29. Hê ongon hî lǽran ðæt hî rihte sibbe betwih him hæfdon ... Hî ne woldan rihte Eástran healdan on heora tîd *coepit eis suadere ut pace Catholica secum habita ... Non Paschae Dominicum diem suo tempore observabant*, Bd. 2, 2; S. 502, 8–11: 5, 19; S. 638, 33. Sum mæg godcunde reccan ryhte ǽ *one can expound the law divine and true*, Exon. Th. 42, 11; Cri. 671. Hæbbe ǽlc man rihtne anmittan and rihte wǽgan and rihte gemetu ðæt hig nâðer ne sîn ne læssan ne mâran ðonne hit riht sig *pondus habebis justum et verum et modius aequalis et verus erit tibi*, Deut. 25, 15. [*Goth.* raihts: *O. Sax.* reht: *O. Frs.* riucht: *O. H. Ger.* reht *rectus, justus, aequus*: *Icel.* rêttr.] v. forþ-, ge-, on-, un-riht, *and the compounds of which* riht *is the first part.*

rihtæþel-cwên, e; *f. A legitimate wife*:—Ðæt syndon Godes wiðersacan ... unrihthǽmeras ... and ða ðe habbaþ mâ ðonne heora rihtæþelcwêne, Wulfst. 298, 18.

riht-ǽw, e; *f.* I. *legitimate matrimony*:—Gehâdedum mannum is beboden, ðæt hî cýþan sceolan folce hwæt on hâlgum bôcum âwriten is, and hî wîsian, hû hî rihtǽwe healdan sceolan, Wulfst. 304, 18. II. *a legitimate wife*:—Be ðam men ðe hæfþ his rihtǽwe (*legitimam suam uxorem*), L. Ecg. P. ii. tit. x; Th. ii. 180, 16. Se man ðe his rihtǽwe forlǽt and ôðer wîf nimþ, ii. 8; Th. ii. 184, 21. Ðonne hê his rihtǽwe ǽrest hâm bringþ, ii. 21; Th. ii. 190, 11. Gif hwylc man wið ôðres rihtǽwe hǽmþ, ii. 10; Th. ii. 186, 6.

rihtan; *p.* te. I. *to right, to restore to a proper position that which is displaced, erect, direct*:—Hê mid handum eft on heofonrîce rihte rodorstôlas *he* (*God*) *with his hands again in the heavenly kingdom restored the celestial seats* (*after the expulsion of the rebellious angels*), Cd. Th. 46, 24; Gen. 749. Tô rehtanne foet ûsra in woege sibbe *ad dirigendos pedes nostros in uia pacis*, Lk. Skt. Rush. 1, 79. II. *to right* a person, *to replace a person in the rights of which he is wrongfully deprived*:—Heó smeádan hû heó mehton monige men ryhtan, ge godcundra hâda ge weorldcundra, ge on londum ge on mâ ðara þinga ðe heó on forhaldne wêran, Chart. Th. 139, 25. III. *to make right that which is faulty, set right, rectify, correct, amend*:—Ne sêce ic nô ða bêc, ac ðæt ðæt ða bêc forstent, ðæt ic ðîn gewit swîðe rihte *that I may set thy mind thoroughly right*, Bt. 5, 1; Fox 10, 20. Sume dêman myccle swîðor rihtaþ Godes folc ðonne hié reáfian earme. Ða dêman beóþ ǽghwǽr ge ðæt hié him selfum heora synna bebeorgaþ ge eác ôðre syngiende rihtaþ, Blickl. Homl. 63, 16-25. Wē boetas ł wē hrihđ *corrigimus*, Mt. Kmbl. p. 2, 2. Se wīsdōm hine rēte and rihte mid his andsworum, Bt. tit. 5; Fox x, 9. Gemeta and gewihta rihte man georne *let weights and measures be made correct with all diligence*, L. C. S. 9; Th. i. 380, 24. Ælþeódige mæn, gif hió hiora hǣmed rihtan (*amend*) nyllaþ, of lande gewīten, L. Wih. 4; Th. i. 38, 1. Tō rihtanne ł tō boetanne *emendasse*, Mt. Kmbl. p. 2, 12. IV. *to keep right, direct, rule:*—Angelþeóde đe hē rihte *gens Anglorum quam regebat*, Bd. 3, 3; S. 525, 29. Hē đa circan heóld and rihte *rexit ecclesiam*, 3, 20; S. 550, 32: 1, 23; S. 485, 23. Đa sylfan stōwe đe Eata mid abbudes onwalde heóld and rihte (*regebat*), 4, 27; S. 604, 41. Đys eówde stȳran and rihtan, Blickl. Homl. 191, 28. [*Goth.* ga-raihtjan: *O. Sax.* rihtian *to erect, to rule*: *O. Frs.* riuchta: *O. H. Ger.* rihtan *erigere, corrigere, dirigere, ordinare, regere*: *Icel.* rētta *to right.*] v. ge-rihtan.

riht-andswaru, e; *f. An answer that corrects, a reproof, rebuke:*—Se mann đe on his mūþe næfþ nāne rihtandsware *homo non habens in ore suo increpationes*, Ps. Th. 37, 14.

riht-aþelu(o); *pl. True nobility:*—Ealle sint emnæþele, gif wē willaþ đone fruman sceaft geþencan . . . and siđđan eówer ǣlces ācennednesse. Ac đa ryhtæþelo bīþ on đam mōde, næs on đam flǣsce, Bt. 30, 2; Fox 110, 19: Met. 17, 20.

riht-cynn, es; *n. A genuine stock, a race really derived from a particular source:*—Moyses wæs đæs rihtcynnes *Moses was of the true stock of Abraham*, Wulfst. 13, 6.

riht-cynecynn, es; *n. A legitimate royal family:*—Antigones him ondrēd Ercoles đæt đæt folc hiene wolde tō hlāforde geceósan for đon đe hē ryhtcynecynnes wæs *timens ne Herculem Macedones quasi legitimum regem praeoptarent*, Ors. 3, 11; Swt. 150, 10. Dauides cynnes, đæs rihtcynecynnes, Blickl. Homl. 23, 29. [Cf. Se cyng (*Henry*) genam Mahalde him tō wīfe . . . of đan rihtan Ænglalandes kynekynne, Chr. 1100; Erl. 236, 36-39.]

riht-dōnde *right-doing:*—Gif wē beóþ rihtdōnde, Blickl. Homl. 51, 14. Seó duru đæs heofonlīcan rīces biþ ontȳned đǣm rihtgelȳfendum monnum and đǣm rihtdōndum, 61, 10.

rihte; *adv.* I. of direction, *right, due, directly, straight:*—Swā oft ǣspringc ūt āwealleþ of clife hārum, and gereclīce, rihte flōweþ, irneþ wiđ his eardes (*runs straight on in its course*), Met. 5, 14. Ryhte beeástan him *due east of them*, Ors. 1, 1; Swt. 16, 3. [v. eást-, norþ-rihte.] II. of time, *directly, straightway:*—Send nū rihte *mitte jam nunc*, Ex. 9, 19. Nū rihte đū gesihst *jam nunc videbis*, Num. 11, 23. Gif ic on helle gedō hwyrft ǣnigne, đū mē æt byst efne rihte, Ps. Th. 138, 6. [v. đǣr-rihte.] III. *in accordance with justice or equity, justly:*—Hē ymbhwyrft eorþan dēmeþ sōđe and rihte *judicabit orbem terræ in justitia*, Ps. Th. 97, 9: *in aequitate*, 95, 13. IV. *rightly, well, in a manner suited to the circumstances of a case, fittingly, properly, duly:*—Rihte ys hē genemned Jacob; nu hē beswāc mē, Gen. 27, 36: Exon. Th. 9, 7; Cri. 139. Wæs swīđe ryhte (*recte*) tō đæm witgan gecweden, Past. 21; Swt. 153, 16. Ne ǣnig wiđ ōđerne getrȳwlīce ne þohte swā rihte swā hē scolde, Wulfst. 160, 2: Cd. Th. 127, 32; Gen. 2119. Hū gōd is God đām đe mid heortan rihte hycgeaþ *quam bonus Deus his, qui recto sunt corde*, Ps. Th. 72, 1: 62, 6. Scylan eard niman on đīnre ansȳne đa mid rǣde hēr rihte lifigeaþ *habitabunt recti cum vultu tuo*, 139, 13. V. *correctly, in the proper manner, exactly, accurately, truly:*—Wē biddaþ đē, Lāreów, đæt đū tǣce ūs sprecan rihte (*to speak Latin correctly*), Coll. Monast. Th. 18, 8. Bæd đæt hē hyra randan rihte heóldon, Byrht. Th. 132, 23; By. 20. Swā wæs on đǣm scennum þurh rūnstafas rihte (*correctly*) gemearcod, hwam đæt sweord geworht ǣrest wǣre, Beo. Th. 3395; B. 1695. Swylce hȳ wǣron rihte . . . swilce hī nū sindon *they were exactly such then as they are now*, Bt. 7, 2; Fox 18, 1. Heó is swīđe ryhte feówerscȳte *it* (*Babylon*) *is very accurately quadrangular*, Ors. 2, 4; Swt. 74, 13. Ryhtor cweþan *to say with greater accuracy*, 5, 1; Swt. 214, 9.

rihte-bred, es; *n. An instrument for measuring, a square:*—Rihtebred *norma*, Wrt. Voc. ii. 60, 20: 114, 83: *linea*, 54, 16.

rihtend, es; *m. A ruler:*—Eálā đū ælmihtiga scippend and rihtend (*rector*) eallra gesceafta, Bt. 4; Fox 8, 10. Hē gehȳreþ cyning mæđlan, rodera ryhtend sprecan, Exon. Th. 50, 10; Cri. 798.

rihtere, es; *m. A ruler, director:*—Ic wāt đætte God rihtere is his āgnes weorces . . . Gesege mē nū đū cwist đæt đū nāht ne tweóge đætte God đisse worulde rihtere sīe . . . *operi suo conditorem praesidere Deum scio . . . Dic mihi, quoniam a Deo mundum regi non ambigis . . .*, Bt. 5, 3; Fox 12, 5-14. [*O. H. Ger.* rihtari *rector, regulus, rex, judex*: *Icel.* rēttari *a justiciary.*]

rihtes; *adv. Right, straight:*—Foran rehtes in đa rōde *straight on to the cross*, Cod. Dip. Kmbl. iii. 392, 6.

riht-fæderencynn, es; *n. Lineal descent* or *descendants on the father's side:*—Hiera ryhtfæderencyn gǣþ tō Cerdice *they are lineally descended on the father's side from Cerdic*, Chr. 755; Erl. 50, 33: 784; Erl. 56, 5. Gif héó bearn næbbe, feó đonne an hire rehtfæderen[cynnes] sió nēste hond, Chart. Th. 481, 21. v. riht-mēdrencynn.

riht-fæstendæg, es; *m. A regularly appointed fastday:*—Ǣlc đara manna đe yt ođđe drincþ on đam hālgan lenctene ođđe on rihtfæstendagum, Homl. Skt. i. 12, 76: Wulfst. 117, 15.

riht-fremmend, es; *m. One acting rightly:*—Đus reordiaþ ryhtfremmende, Exon. Th. 240, 2; Ph. 632. Geát hǣđen hildfruma hāligra blōd, ryhtfremmendra, 243, 9; Jul. 8. Hǣlu būtan sāre ryhtfremmendum, 101, 9; Cri. 1656.

riht-gefremed; *adj. Rightly constituted, orthodox:*—Forđon đe hē Wilfriþ rihtgefremedne gemētte *quia catholicum Vilfridum comperit*, Bd. 5, 19; S. 638, 34.

riht-gegilda, an; *m. One who is legally a member of a guild:*—Æt ǣlcon rihtgegyldan, Chart. Th. 606, 14.

riht-geleáfful; *adj. Holding a true belief, orthodox:*—Fram đam rihtgeleáffullum bisceope *ab episcopo orthodoxo*, L. Ecg. P. addit. 5; Th. ii. 232, 19. Mid đære hālgan and mid đære rihtgeleáffullan gesomnunge *cum sancta ecclesia*, Bd. 3, 17; S. 545, 31. For rihtgeleáffulra sibbe *pro pace Catholica*, 2, 2; S. 502, 2. Đæt rīce đam unrihtwīsan cyninge āferran and on ryhtgeleáffulra and on rihtwīsra anwald gebringan, Bt. 1; Fox 2, 19. Rihtgeleáffulum *orthodoxis*, Wrt. Voc. ii. 62, 66.

riht-gelīfed; *adj. Possessed of a true belief, orthodox, catholic:*—Eal rihtgelȳfed folc sceal gefeón on đone his tōcyme, Blickl. Homl. 167, 14. Đæs rihtgelȳfdan geleáfan *orthodoxiae*, Wrt. Voc. ii. 65, 13. Đa hālgan gelaþunge rihtgelȳfdan *sanctam aecclesiam catholicam*, Apstls. Crd. Rihtgelēfedan, Blickl. Homl. 111, 9. Of rihtgelēfedum lārum *orthodoxis dogmatibus*, Hpt. Gl. 468, 12. Drihten, đū đe cwǣde on đīnum godspelle tō eallum rihtgelȳfedum mannum *omnibus fidelibus hominibus*, L. Ecg. P. iv. 67; Th. ii. 226, 39. Rihtgelȳfdum, Blickl. Homl. 171, 14. [cf. *Icel.* rētt-trūađr *orthodox.*]

riht-gelīfende *having a true belief, faithful:*—Seó duru đæs heofonlīcan rīces biþ ontȳned đǣm rihtgelȳfendum monnum, Blickl. Homl. 61, 9. Ic beó līfes gāst on eallum rihtgelȳfendum on mē, 185, 34. [Cf. *Icel.* rētt-trūandi *orthodox.*]

riht-geþancod; *adj. Right-minded, having right thoughts:*—Đa rihtgeþancodon *rectos corde*, Ps. Lamb. 7, 10. Rihtgeþancedon, 10, 3.

riht-gewitt, es; *n. Right mind:*—Đā wæs heó of hyre ryhtgewitte *she was out of her mind*, Shrn. 141, 18.

riht-hǣmed, es; *n. Legitimate matrimony:*—Cirraþ tō eówrum ryhthǣmede, Past. 16, 1; Swt. 99, 17. Æfter đon wǣre on rihthǣmed (riht hǣmed?) geþeóded *postea in matrimonio jungatur*, L. Ecg. C. 19; Th. ii. 146, 2. v. unriht-hǣmed.

riht-hand, a; *f. The right hand:*—Se Hǣlend be đære ryhthanda mē genam, Nicod. 21; Thw. 11, 5. Se Hǣlend Adam be đære rihthand genam, 30; Thw. 17, 24.

riht-handdǣda, an; *m. The actual perpetrator of a crime:*—Gif hwā wrace dō on ǣnigum ōđrum būtan on đam rihthanddǣdan, L. Edm. S. 1; Th. i. 248, 12.

riht-heort; *adj. Upright in heart:*—Mid rihtheortum *qui recto sunt corde*, Ps. Th. 93, 14. Đǣm rehtheortum *rectis corde*, Ps. Surt. 111, 4. [*O. H. Ger.* reht-herzi.]

riht-hīwa, an; *m. A legitimate consort:*—Monige beóþ đara đe hié gehealdaþ wiđ unryhthǣmed and swāđeáh his āgenra ryhthīwena ne brȳcþ swā swā hē mid ryhte sceolde *multi sunt, qui scelera quidem carnis deserunt, nec tamen in conjugio positi usus solummodo debiti jura conservant*, Past. 51, 6; Swt. 399, 8.

riht-hlāford, es; *m. A rightful lord:*—Gif wīf ofer hire rihthlāford ōđerne man hæbbe *si mulier, praeter dominum suum legitimum, alium habet virum*, L. Ecg. P. ii. 7; Th. ii. 184, 19.

riht-hlāfordhyldu; *indecl.*: -hyld, e; *f. Fidelity justly due to a lord:*—Uton beón ā ūrum hlāforde holde and getreówe . . . forđam eall đæt wē ǣfre for rihthlāfordhelde dōþ, eal wē hit dōþ ūs sylfum tō mycelre þearfe, Wulfst. 119, 15: 299, 27. v. hlāford-hyldo.

rihting. v. rihtung.

rihtlǣcan; *p.* -lǣhte *To make right, rectify, correct, amend:*—Gif hē đonne (*after punishment*) swā ne bēte and rihtlǣce, hē sȳ of đam ealdorscype āworpen, R. Ben. 46, 19. Se đe ǣr đysum misdyde, đæt hē hit georne gebēte and rihtlǣce hine sylfne, Wulfst. 277, 2. Uton wē nū ǣlces yfeles geswīcan and rihtlǣcan ūs sylfe on eallan þingan, 174, 30. Æfter đam đe hē sylf geriht wearþ hē began georne mynstera wīde geond his cynerīce tō rihtlǣcynne *after his own life was ordered aright, he began to set the monasteries in order*, Lchdm. iii. 440, 2. v. ge-rihtlǣcan.

riht-lǣce, es; *m. A genuine physician, one who is really a doctor:*—Se đe his broces bōte sēcþ būton tō Gode sylfum and tō his hālgum and tō rihtlǣcum hē drȳhþ deófles wyllan *he that seeks a remedy for his malady except from God and from his saints and from regular doctors, he does the devil's will*, Wulfst. 12, 12.

rihtlǣcung, e; *f. Correction, making right:*—Đa underþióddan sint tō maniane đæt hié đara unþeáwas đe him ofergesette bióþ tō swīđe and tō þrisđlīce ne eahtigen . . . đȳ læs hié for đære ryhtlǣcinge weorþen upāhæfene, Past. 28; Swt. 197, 2. Tō đām dōmbōcum đe se heofonlīca Wealdend his folce gesette tō rihtlǣcunge ealra forgǣgednyssa, Homl. Th. ii. 198, 20. Hrihtlǣcinge *ratiocinationis*, Hpt. Gl. 481, 78.

riht-laga, an; *m. Right* or *just law, equity*:—Rihtlaga is, ðæt man óðran gebeóde, ðæt hē wylle ðæt man him gebeóde, Wulfst. 274, 11. v. next word.

riht-lagu, e; *f. Right* or *just law*:—Oferhogan godcundra rihtlaga, Wulfst. 164, 12. Ða ðe godcunde lāre and woruldcunde rihtlage wyrdan on ǣnige wīsan, 168, 8.

riht-líc; *adj.* I. *right, just*:—Rihtlīc *fas, justum*, Hpt. Gl. 460, 16. Ic tōcwȳse eówer deófolgyld, and biþ ðonne rihtlīc geþūht ðæt gē geswȳcon eówres gedwyldes, Homl. Th. i. 70, 33. Gif hiora hwilc swā heardheort wǣre, ðæt hē nāne hreówsunge ne dyde, ðæt hē ðonne hæfde rihtlīc wīte, Bt. 41, 3; Fox 248, 16. II. *right, fitting, adapted to due requirements*:—Hū wolde ðē līcian gif hwylc swīðe rīce cyning wǣre and næfde nǣnne frȳne mon on eallon his rīce, ac wǣron ealle þeówe. Ðā cwæþ ic: 'Ne þūhte hit mē nāuht rihtlīc, ne eác gerisenlīc, gif him sceoldan þeówe men þēnigan,' 41, 2; Fox 244, 26. Rihtlīc ðæt wæs ðæt se blinda be ðæm wege sǣte wædliende; forðon ðe Drihten sylfa cwæþ: 'Ic eom weg sōðfæstnesse,' Blickl. Homl. 17, 30: 29, 17. II a. *adapted, fitted, entitled*:—Ðeáh beóþ ða foremǣrran and rihtlīcran tō herigenne ða ðe beóþ mid cræftum gewyrðode, Bt. 30, 1; Fox 108, 24. III. *right, in accordance with reason*:—Ðæt wǣre rihtlīc tō ongytenne (*merito intelligendum*) ðæt ealle ða ðe Godes willan worhton, fram ðam ðe hī gesceapene wǣron, ðæt hī ðonne wǣron fram him ēce mēde tō onfōnne, Bd. 3, 22; S. 552, 21. IV. *right* as regards conduct, *righteous*:—Ðæt biþ rihtlīc līf, ðæt cniht þurhwunige on his cnihthāde, ōþ ðæt hē on rihtre mǣdenǣwe gewīfige, L. I. P. 22; Th. ii. 332, 28. Ðonne mon hwæt ryhtlīces and gerisenlīces geþencþ *quando et si qua jam justa, si qua honesta cogitantur*, Past. 21, 3; Swt. 155, 24. Ðonne hē ðæm ryhtlīcum inngeþonce his hiéremonna foresægþ ða diéglan sǣtenga ðæs lytegan feóndes *quando rectae intentioni audientium hostis callidi circumspectas insidias praedicit*, 21, 5; Swt. 163, 13. Eahta sweras syndon ðe rihtlīcne cynedōm trumlīce up wegaþ *there are eight pillars that firmly sustain a rightly conducted royal authority*, L. I. P. 3; Th. ii. 306, 19. [*O. H. Ger.* reht-līh *fas, jus, justus, regularis, canonicus*: *O. L. Ger.* reht-, riht-līk: *O. Frs.* riucht-lik: *Icel.* rētt-legr *just, due, meet.*]

rihtlíce; *adv.* I. *rightly, justly, with justice* or *equity*:—Rihtlīce *juste*, rihtlīcor *justius*, rihtlīcost *justissime*, Ælfc. Gr. 38; Som. 40, 50. Him getīmode swīðe rihtlīce ðæt hī mid hiora ārleásan hlāforde ealle forwurdon, Homl. Th. i. 88, 30. Ðū rihtlīce dǣlest mete ðīnum mannum, Hy. 7, 70. II. *rightly, in a manner which suits the circumstances of a case*:—Swīðe ryhtlīce hit wæs āwriten æfter ðǣm nītenum ðæt ða heargas wǣron ātiéfrede *recte post animalia idola describuntur*, Past. 21, 3; Swt. 157, 6: 21, 5; Swt. 163, 21. Æfter ðon wē singaþ rihtlīce on his lof: 'Hǣl ūs on ðǣm hēhstan,' Blickl. Homl. 81, 27. Hū ne belimpþ se weorþscipe tō ðam ðe hine geweorþaþ? ðæt is tō herianne hwēne rihtlīcor, Bt. 14, 3; Fox 46, 13. III. *rightly, in accordance with rules* or *regulations, regularly*:—Gewunelīce ł rihtlīce *rite*, Ælfc. Gr. 38; Som. 41, 44. Rihtlīce gehālgad *canonice ordinatus*, Bd. 3, 28; S. 560, 28. Ða þēnunge hē rihtlīce gefyllan ne mihte *ministerium regulariter implere nequibat*, 5, 6; S. 620, 9. Gif hē rihtlīce (*in such a way as to observe the rules imposed by Christianity*) Cristen beón wille, 4, 5; S. 573, 18. Ða munecas beádon hine (*the abbot*) ðæt hē sceolde healdan hī rihtlīce, Chr. 1083; Erl. 217, 5. Ða witan cwǣdon ðæt him nān leófre hlāford nǣre ðonne heora gecynde hlāford gif hē hī rihtlīcor healdan wolde (*if he would rule with better observance of the laws*) ðonne hē ǣr dyde, 1014; Erl. 150, 7. IV. *rightly* as regards conduct:—Wē sceolan gōd weorc wyricean and rihtlīce libban, Blickl. Homl. 75, 13; 109, 13. Riht is ðæt gehādode men ðām lǣwedum wīsian hū hī heora ǣwe rihtlīcost sculon healdan, L. I. P. 22; Th. i. 332, 28. v. on-rihtlīce.

riht-lícettere, es; *m. A thorough hypocrite*:—Fela manna wyrð þurh deófol forlǣred swā ðæt hȳ eal ōðer specaþ and ōðer hiwiaþ, ōðer hȳ þencaþ; and ða beóþ rihtlīceteras, Wulfst. 54, 14.

riht-líf, es; *n. A right life*:—Wȳf tō onfōnne tō rihtlīfe, Lchdm. iii. 176, 22.

riht-liþlíc; *adj. Articulate*:—Rihtliþlīcu *articulata*, Wrt. Voc. ii. 9, 46.

riht-médrencynn. v. mēdren-cynn, *and* cf. riht-fæderencynn.

riht-meterfers, es; *n. Correct hexameter verse*:—Ðæt rihtmetervers sceal habban feówer and twentig tīman, Anglia viii. 314, 10.

riht-munuc, es; *m. A true monk*:—Beóþ rihtmunecas, gif hȳ libbaþ be ðam geswince heora āgenra handa, R. Ben. 73, 19.

rihtness, e; *f.* I. *rightness, straightness, perpendicularity*:—*Perpendicula* walþrǣd, ðæt is rihtnesse [þrǣd], Wrt. Voc. ii. 91, 67. Cf. rihtung-þrǣd. II. *rightness, justice, equity*:—On rihtnesse *in aequitate*, Ps. Th. 97, 9: 110, 5. Rehtnise, Rtl. 102, 17. III. *in the following passage* rehtnis *glosses* ratio, Rtl. 113, 32: 32, 32: Mt. Kmbl. Lind. 12, 36: 18, 24: 25, 19. [*O. L. Ger.* reht-, riht-nussi *justitia*: *O. H. Ger.* rehtnissa *justitia, aequitas.*]

riht-norþanwind, es; *m. A due north wind*:—Ðā sceolde hē ðǣr bīdan ryhtnorþanwindes, Ors. 1, 1; Swt. 17, 17.

riht-racu, e; *f. A correct account*:—Ðā lȳfde hē ðæt hē mōste beón ryhtes wyrðe for mī[n]re forspǣce and ryhtrace, Chart. Th. 170, 4.

riht-regol, es; *m. A correct rule, a canon*:—Rihtregula *canonum*, Hpt. Gl. 526, 16.

riht-ryne, es; *m. A right course*:—Se brōc ðeáh hē swīðe of his rihtryne ðonne ðǣr micel stān of ðam heáhan munte oninnan fealþ and hine tōdǣlþ and him his rihtrynes wiðstent, Bt. 6; Fox 14, 27-30: Met. 5, 20. Oncerran ðisne swiftan rodor of his rihtryne, 10, 41.

riht-scilling, es; *m. A lawful shilling*:—Se rihtscylling byþ ā be .xii. penegum *legitimus solidus semper est* .xii. *denariorum*, L. Ecg. P. iv. 60; Th. ii. 222, 7.

riht-scrífend, es; *m. One who declares the sentence of the law, a lawyer*:—Rihtscrīfend ł dōmsettend *jurisconsultus, jurisperitus*, Wrt. Voc. ii. 49, 17: i. 20, 69.

riht-scytte; *adj. Sure of aim*:—Sum biþ ryhtscytte, sum leóþa gleáw, sum on londe snel, Exon. Th. 296, 15; Crā. 51.

riht-smeáung, e; *f. Right reasoning, argument*:—Rehtsmeáwung *argumentum*, Mt. Kmbl. p. 11, 10.

riht-tíd, e; *f. A proper time*:—Hē ða Eástran on heora rihttīde ne heóld *Pascha suo tempore non observabat*, Bd. 3, 17; S. 545, 18. v. next word.

riht-tíma, an; *m. A right, proper time*:—Ælc wuht from Gode wiste his rihttīman, Bt. 5, 3; Fox 12, 8.

rihtung, e; *f.* I. *direction, guidance*:—Bisceope gebyreþ ǣlc rihting . . . Hē sceall gehādode men gewissian, ðæt heora ǣlc wite hwæt him gebyrige tō dōnne, L. I. P. 7; Th. ii. 312, 9. Gyrd rihtingce *virga directionis*, Ps. Spl. 44, 8. Him God hālige ǣ sette tō heora līfes rihtinge, Homl. Th. i. 558, 21. Ðonne mann wīsdōm sprecþ manegum tō þearfe and tō rihtinge, Ælfc. T. Grn. 21, 28. Rihtinga *directiones*, Ps. Lamb. 98, 4. II. *correction, setting right*:—Rihtingc *correctio*, 96, 2. Bisceopes dægweorc . . . his gebedu ǣrest, and ðonne his bōcweorc, rǣding oððon rihting (*correcting manuscripts?*), L. I. P. 8; Th. ii. 314, 19. On ða gerād ðæt seó bōc heam sȳ geara, gyf hȳ hyre beþurfan tō ǣnire rihtinge *on the condition that the charter be ready for them, if they need it for any correction*, Chart. Th. 588, 17. III. *correction, reproof*:—For ðære geornfulnesse ðære ryhtinge ne sīe hē tō stīð tō ðære wrace *ne correptionis studia privatus dolor exasperet*, Past. 13, 2; Swt. 79, 11. IV. *a direction, rule*:—Ne scylen hȳ beón būtan regole, ðæt is līfes rihtinge, R. Ben. 61, 14. Ðisne regul, ðæt is līfes rihtunge, wē āwriton tō ðȳ ðæt wē hine on mynstre healden, 132, 14. V. a translation of the technical term *regularis* [*Regulares* apud compotistas, seu computi ecclesiastici conditores, alii sunt *solares*, alii *lunares*. *Regularis solis* est numerus invariabilis datus mensi, qui, adjunctus *concurrenti*, declarat qua feria septimanae quilibet mensis iniret, cujus fuerit regularis. Dicitur regularis a regula quia invariabilis est. *Regularis lunaris* est numerus invariabilis, datus mensi ad inveniendum lunam in kalendis mensium singulorum, Ducange]:—De regularibus feriarum dicamus . . . Januarius and October habbaþ twā rihtinga, and Februarius and Martius and November gladiaþ on fīfum, and Aprilis and Julius habbaþ āne rihtinge, and Maius hæfþ þrȳ, and Agustus mid feówrum glitnaþ, Junius āna hæfþ syx rihtinga, and September and December mid heora seofon gefērum gladiaþ, Anglia viii. 302, 1-4. Cf. Aprilis hǣfþ ānne regularem, 303, 40. De regularibus lunae. Gyf ðū wille witan ðæra rihtinga gesceád ðe geþungene preóstas cweþaþ *lunares*, 305, 8. The word occurs often in the treatise from which these passages are taken. [*O. H. Ger.* rihtunga *regimen, reformatio, emendatio, dispositio.*]

rihtung-þrǽd, es; *m. A directing thread, a plumb-line*:—Wealles rihtungþrēd *perpendiculum*, Wrt. Voc. i. 39, 64.

riht-weg, es; *m. A right way*:—Se ðe secge ðæt hē on Crist gelȳfe fare se ðæs riht-weges ðe Crist sylf fērde *qui se dicit in Cristum credere debet ambulare sicut et ipse ambulavit*, Wulfst. 65, 25. Gebringan on rihtwege ða ðe ǣr dweledan, 75, 2: 49, 19.

riht-wer, es; *m. A legitimate husband*:—Gif wīf hire rihtwer (*virum suum legitimum*) forlǣt, L. Ecg. P. ii. 8; Th. ii. 184, 25.

riht-westende, es; *m. The extreme western limit*:—Hire ryhtwestende *ultimus finis ad occidentem*, Ors. 1, 1; Swt. 8, 32.

riht-willend, es; *m. One whose desires are right*:—Ðū eart ān ðara rihtwillendra, Bt. 15, 1; Fox 10, 6.

riht-wís; *adj. Righteous, just*:—Rihtwīs *justus*, Wrt. Voc. i. 75, 69. Rihtwīs *justus*, rihtwīsre *justior*, ealra rihtwīsost *justissimus*, Ælfc. Gr. 5; Som. 4, 65: 9, 21; Som. 10, 20. Rihtwīs dēma, Hy. 6, 7. Se ðe underfēhþ rihtwīsne on rihtwīses naman, hē onfēhþ rihtwīses mēde, Mt. Kmbl. 10, 41. Unscyldig ic eom fram ðyses rihtwīsan blōde (*a sanguine justi hujus*), 27, 24. Ðē ic geseah rihtwīsne ætforan mē, Gen. 7, 1. Dōmas ðīne rihtwīse *aequitas judicia tua*, Ps. Th. 118, 75, 172. Rihtwīse *non errantes*, Wrt. Voc. ii. 61, 52. Fīftig rihtwīsra manna *quinquaginta justi*, Gen. 18, 24. Heó is rihtwīsre (*justior*) ðonne ic, 38, 26. Boetius wæs on woruldþeáwum se rihtwīsesta, Bt. 1; Fox 2, 4. [*O. H. Ger.* reht-wīs: *Icel.* rētt-vīss.] v. un-rihtwīs.

riht-wís (?), e; -**wíse** (?), an; *f. Righteousness, justice*:—Rihtwīse and sybbe hȳ cyston *justitia et pax osculatae sunt*, Ps. Spl. 84, 11. [Cf. *Icel.* rētt-vīsa, -vīsi.]

riht-wîsend, es; *m. A Sadducee*:—Ðâ hê geseh manega ðæra sunderhâlgena and ðæra rihtwîsendra tô his fulluhte cumende, Mt. Kmbl. 3, 7.

rihtwîsian; *p.* ode *To justify*:—Gê rihtwîsiaþ eów ætforan mannum and God cann eówere heortan *vos justificatis vos coram hominibus, Deus autem novit corda vestra* (Lk. 16, 15), Homl. Th. ii. 404, 15. v. ge-rihtwîsian, riht-wîs.

riht-wîsian; *p.* ode *To direct aright, rule*:—Ðû cwist ðæt ðû nâht ne tweóge ðætte God ðisse worulde rihtere sîe (rihtwîsige, Cott. MS.) *a Deo mundum regi non ambigis*, Bt. 5, 3; Fox 12, 14. v. wîsian.

rihtwîs-lîc; *adj. Righteous, just, rational*:—For ryhtwîslîcum andan *per zelum justitiae*, Past. 17, tit.; Swt. 107, 7: 21, 6; Swt. 163, 20. [*O. H. Ger.* rehtwîs-lîh *rationabilis*.] v. next word.

rihtwîslîce; *adv. Rationally, justly*:—Hû mæg ǽnig man ryhtwîslîce and gesceádwîslîce âcsigan, gif hê nân grot rihtwîsnesse on him næfþ, Bt. 35, 1; Fox 156, 5: Met. 22, 45. v. preceding word.

rihtwîsness, e; *f.* I. *righteousness, justice*:—Óðer mægen (ðære sâwle) is *justitia*, ðæt is rihtwîsnys; þurh ða heó sceal God wurðigan and rihtlîce libban, Homl. Skt. i. 1, 159. On rihtwîsnesse wege *in via justitiae*, Mt. Kmbl. 21, 32. Abram gelîfde Gode and hit wæs him geteald tô rihtwîsnisse (*ad justitiam*), Gen. 15, 6. Ealle rihtwîsnesse gefyllan, Mt. Kmbl. 3, 15. Rihtwîsnysse sprecan, Ps. Spl. 57, 1. Gelǽd mê on rightwîsnysse ðîne, 5, 9. Rechtwîsnisse, Ps. Surt. 44, 5. Gif hî mîne rihtwîsnessa (*justificationes*) gewemmaþ, Ps. Th. 88, 28. II. *rightness, reasonableness, reason*:—Ða sceare onfôn sculon ðe wê gehŷraþ fulle beón ealre rihtwîsnesse *hanc accipere tonsuram quam plenam esse rationis audimus*, Bd. 5, 21; S. 643, 23. Hû mæg ǽnig man ryhtwîslîce and gesceádwîslîce âcsigan, gif hê nân grot rihtwîsnesse on him næfþ? Nis nân swâ swîðe bedǽled ryhtwîsnesse, ðæt hê nân ryht andwyrde nyte, gif men âcsaþ. Plato cwæþ: 'Swâ hwâ swâ ungemyndig sîe rihtwîsnesse, gecerre hine tô his gemynde, ðonne fint hê ðǽr ða ryhtwîsnesse gehŷdde mid ðæs lîchoman hæfignesse, Bt. 35, 1; Fox 156, 5-12: Met. 22, 43-60. v. on-rihtwîsness.

riht-wrîtere, es; *m. One who writes correctly*:—Rihtwrîtera *orthographorum, rectorum scriptorum*, Hpt. Gl. 410, 72. Rihtwrîterum *ortagraphorum*, Wrt. Voc. ii. 64, 22: 75, 41.

riht-wuldriende *orthodox*:—Wê wǽron smeágende rihtne geleáfan and rihtwuldriende. Ðâs wê syndon ârfæstlîce fyligende and rihtwuldriende *tractantes fidem, rectam et orthodoxam . . . Hos sequentes nos pie atque orthodoxe*, Bd. 4, 17; S. 585, 28-34.

rîm, es; *n. Number*:—Rîm miclade monna mǽgþe geond middangeard, Cd. Th. 75, 21; Gen. 1243. His dôgora wæs rîm âurnen, 98, 6; Gen. 1626. Seofon geteled rîmes, 80, 30; Gen. 1336. Ic feówertig folce ðyssum wintra rîmes wunade neáh *forty years in number I dwelt near this folk*, Ps. Th. 94, 10. Æfter rîme fîf Moyses bôca *juxta numerum librorum*, Bd. 1, 1; S. 474, 1. Weaxendum ðam rîme geleáfsumra *crescente numero fidelium*, 4, 5; S. 573, 12. Gecuron hî of heora rîme gemetfæstne man *elegerunt ex suo numero virum modestum*, 5, 11; S. 625, 43. On rîme *in catalogo*, Wrt. Voc. ii. 84, 31. Hundtwelftig geteled rîme wintra, Cd. Th. 76, 27; Gen. 1263. On wera rîme gewurðod, 127, 8; Gen. 2107. Rîm dæga mînra *numerum dierum meorum*, Ps. Surt. 38, 5. Is nû worn wintra sceacen twâ hund oððe mâ geteled rîme, ic ne mæg âreccan nû ic ðæt rîm ne can, Elen. Kmbl. 1267; El. 635. Meotod wolde manna rîm, fela þûsenda, forþ gelǽdan, Cd. Th. 289, 22; Sat. 401. [*O. Sax.* un-rîm: *O. Frs.* rîm: *O. H. Ger.* rîm *numerus*: *Icel.* rîm.] v. cneó-, dæg-, dôgor-, ende-, fæðm-, ge-, geár-, getæl-, mann-, niht-, scilling-, un-, winter-rîm.

rima, an; *m. A rim, border, bank, coast*:—Rima *crepido*, Wrt. Voc. ii. 15, 45. Rimo, Txts. 55, 601. [Cf. *Icel.* rim *a rail*; rimi *a strip of land*.] v. bord-, dæg-, sǽ-, sûþ-, tôþ-rima.

rîman; *p.* de. I. *to count, number*:—*Ducentesimus* se ðe biþ on ðâm twâm hundredum æftemyst, ðon hî man rîmþ, Ælfc. Gr. 49; Som. 50, 5. Næs þeáw ðæt mon ǽnig wæl on ða healfe rîmde ðe ðonne wieldre wæs *mos est, ex ea parte quae viceret occisorum non commemorare numerum*, Ors. 4, 1; Swt. 156, 22. Cyninges þegnas oft râde on ridon ðe mon nâ ne rîmde, Chr. 871; Erl. 76, 12. Gif ic hî rîman onginne *dinumerabo eos*, Ps. Th. 138, 16. Hê mæg rîman steorran *qui numerat multitudinem stellarum*, 146, 4. II. *to enumerate, recount, describe in succession*:—On ðam is godcundnesse wên ðe manna ingehygd wât and can and heora heortena deágol ealle smeáþ and rîmeþ *divinity is to be looked for in him that knows the minds of men, and scrutinizes and tells one by one the secrets of their hearts*, Blickl. Homl. 179, 27. Hû nytt rehton wê and rîmdon ða cǽga bûton wê eác feáwum wordum ætiéwen hwæt hié healden *quid utilitatis est, quod cuncta haec collecta numeratione transcurrimus, si non etiam admonitionis modos per singula pandamus?* Past. 23; Swt. 179, 11. Hwæt sceal ic mâ rîman yfel endeleás? Exon. Th. 272, 27; Jul. 505. Hâligra manna naman rîmende and gebedo singende *laetanias canentes*, Bd. 1, 25; S. 487, 4. III. *to calculate, compute, count up*:—Ða reáferas geþenceaþ swîðe oft hû micel hié sellaþ swelce hié ða mêtsceattas rîmen (*quasi mercedem numerant*), Past. 45, 4; Swt. 343, 16. For ege ðînum graman ðinne tô rîmanne (*dinumerare*), Ps. Spl. 89, 13. [Beón] rîmed *computari, numerari*, Hpt. Gl. 482, 24. IV. *to account, esteem as*:—Gê beóþ mê talade and rîmde on bearna stæl, Exon. Th. 366, 11; Reb. 10. [*O. H. Ger.* ge-rîman.] v. â-, ge-rîman.

rîm-âþ, es; *m. An oath taken by a person and by the number of persons he brings with him as compurgators* (cf. the expressions in Norse law *tylptar-*, *sēttar-eiðr*, oaths in which twelve, six persons respectively took part), L. Ath. i. 9; Th. i. 204, 15. v. cyre-âþ.

rîm-cræft, es; *m. The science of numbers, arithmetic*:—Ða seofon cræftas on ðam beóþ gemêted ealle weoruldwŷsdômas, ðæt ys ǽrest *arythmetica*, ðæt ys rŷmcræft, Shrn. 152, 13. Rîmcræft *arithmetica*, Hpt. Gl. 479, 56: Wrt. Voc. ii. 81, 58: 3, 7. Uton witan hwæt *saltus lunae* sŷ tô sôðe . . . oððe hwâ hine ðæs wurðscipes cûðe ðæt hê sceolde gestandan on ðam rîmcræfte *that he should have a place in the science of computation*, Anglia viii. 308, 22. Ða ðe ǽr wǽran on rîmcræfte rihte getogene *those who were correctly instructed in the art of computing*, Chr. 975; Erl. 126, 1. Hæfdon hié on rîmcræfte âwriten wera endestæf hwænne hié tô môse meteþearfendum weorðan sceoldon *they (the cannibal Mermedonians) had numbered the days of their captives who were to be food to satisfy their hunger*, Andr. Kmbl. 268; An. 134. v. gerîm-cræft.

rîm-cræftig; *adj. Skilful in computation*:—Tô þâm rihtungum ðe rîmcræftige preóstas cweþaþ *lunares*, Anglia viii. 300, 27. On ðâm eahta geárum ðe rîmcræftige weras on Grêcisc hâtaþ *ocdoade*, 315, 23: 327, 34-36. Rŷmcræftige, Menol. Fox 89; Men. 44. v. next word.

rîm-cræftiga, an; *m. One skilful in computation*:—Bêda se ârwurða rîmcræftiga, Anglia viii. 301, 33.

-rîme. v. earfoþ-rîme.

rîmere, es; *m. A computer, reckoner, calculator*:—Betwux ðisre sprǽce sceal se rîmre geþencean, ðæt hê gedô ðæt Februarius mônþ ðŷ geáre hæbbe þrittig nihta ealdne mônan, Anglia viii. 307, 34.

rîm-getæl, es; *n. A number*:—Rîmgetæl daga *the appointed number of days*, Cd. Th. 85, 25; Gen. 1420. Drihten lêt weaxan eft heora rîmgetel, 166, 29; Gen. 2755.

rîmian. v. ge-rîmian.

rimpan (hrimpan?) *to wrinkle, rumple*. [Gerumpenu nædre *coluber cerastis*, Wrt. Voc. ii. 15, 68. Ðære gehrumpnan *rugosa*, 91, 15. Cf. also hry[m]pellum *rugis*, 95, 73. *O. H. Ger.* [h]rimpfan (hrimfit *terit*): rampf *caperrabat*; girumpfan *rugosus, contractus*. v. Grff. ii. 512: cf. *Ger.* rümpfen.]

rimpel (? hrympel. v. preceding word). [*Prompt. Parv.* rympyl *ruga*; rymplyd *rugatus*: *M. H. Ger. O. Du.* rimpel.]

rîm-talu, e; *f. A number, tale*:—Lǽt mec, mihta God, on rîmtale rîces ðînes wunigan, Elen. Kmbl. 1636; El. 820.

Rîn; *m.*; *f. The Rhine*:—Sió eá ðe man hǽt Rîn, Ors. 1, 1; Swt. 22, 23. Neáh Rînes ôfre ðære ié, Swt. 14, 32. Beeástan Rîne, Swt. 14, 36. On ðæm londe beeástan Rîn, Chr. 887; Erl. 86, 7. On cyrican Colonie ðære ceastre bî Rîne, Bd. 5, 10; S. 625, 22. Ðâ wurpon hî heora lîchoman ût on Rîne ða eá, S. 624, 42. [*O. H. Ger.* Rîn; *m.*: *Icel.* Rîn; *f.*]

rînan. v. rignan.

rinc, es; *m. A man* (a poetical term):—Se rinc (*Enoch*) on lîchoman lisse sôhte, Cd. Th. 73, 12; Gen. 1203: (*Abraham*), 107, 17; Gen. 1790. Com ðâ tô recede rinc (*Grendel*) sîðian, Beo. Th. 1445; B. 720. Ârâs ðâ se rîca (*Hrothgar*), ymb hine rinc manig, þegna heáp, 804; B. 399. Ðâ wæs rinc manig, gûðfrec guma, ymb ðæs geongan feorh breóstum onbryrded, Andr. Kmbl. 2234; An. 1118. Ðæt wæs rihtwîs rinc (*Boethius*), Met. 1, 49. Ðæs rinces (*Abraham*) se rîca ongan cyning (*God*) costigan, Cd. Th. 172, 16; Gen. 2845. Junge rince ł hysse *ephebo robusto*, Hpt. Gl. 488, 1. Rôfe rincas (*the fallen angels*), Cd. Th. 19, 4; Gen. 286: (*those who occupied Shinar*), 99, 24; Gen. 1651. [Heo smiten togædere, helmes þere gullen . . . , rinkas feollen (mani m[en] þer fulle, 2nd MS.), Laym. 5188. *Piers P.* renke: *O. Sax.* rink: *Icel.* rekkr (frequent in poetry, but in prose it occurs only in old law phrases).] v. beadu-, fyrd-, gum-, gûþ-, heaðo-, here-, hilde-, magu-, sǽ-rinc.

rinc-getæl, es; *n. A number of men, a host*:—Ðæt wæs wîglîc werod; wâc ne grêtton in ðæt rincgetæl rǽswan herges, Cd. Th. 192, 19; Exod. 234.

rind, e; **rinde**, an; *f. Rind*. I. of a tree, *the bark*:—Rind *cortix*, Wrt. Voc. i. 285, 78. Rinde *cortex*, 79, 68. Sûðerne rind *cinnamonum, resina*, ii. 131, 9. Ofersǽwisc rind, Lchdm. ii. 52, 3. Rômânisc rind, i. 376, 5. Andlang ðæs piþan and andlang ðære rinde ôþ ðone helm, Bt. 34, 10; Fox 150, 3. Of corntreówes rinde *de cortice corni*, Wrt. Voc. ii. 27, 6. Gif hê beget and yt rinde sió ðe cymþ of neorxna wonge ne dereþ him nân âtter; ðonne cwæþ se ðe ðâs bôc wrât ðæt hió wǽre torbegete, Lchdm. ii. 114, 3: 92, 29. Wê ne mâgon geseón on ðam cyrnele nâðor ne wyrtruman, ne rinde, ne leáf, Homl. Th. i. 236, 18. Rinda *cortices* (*codices*, MS.), Wrt. Voc. ii. 135, 60. Rinda *librorum*, Hpt. Gl. 417, 46. Of corntreówes rindum *de cortice corni*,

Wrt. Voc. ii. 138, 7. Rindum *corticibus* (*codicibus*, MS.), 75, 46. Rinde *libros*, 53, 18. Dó of ða rinda, Lchdm. ii. 98, 11. **I a.** metaphorically:—Þeahtigaþ on hiera módes rinde monig gód weorc tó wyrcanne, ac on ðam piþan biþ óðer gehýded, Past. 9, 1; Swt. 55, 22. *The word occurs in combination with names of trees*, e.g. apuldor-, æsc-, ác-, elm-, holen-, sealh-, sláhþorn-, wiþi-grind. **II.** of other things, *crust, rind*:—Rinde *crustula*, Wrt. Voc. ii. 137, 22. Rindan *crustulae*, Hpt. Gl. 462, 77. Wé hédaþ ðæra crumena ðæs hláfes, and ða Judéiscan gnagaþ ða rinde, Homl. Th. ii. 114, 34. Rinda *crusta* (this is omitted from) Wrt. Voc. i. 41, 23. Rindum *crustulis*, Hpt. Gl. 496, 23: 497, 15. [*O. Du.* rinde: *O. H. Ger.* rinta *cortex, liber.*]

-rindan, rinde. v. be-rindan, rind.

rinde-clifer (?) *a wood-pecker* (?), *a bird that sticks to*, or *scratches the bark of trees* (?) [cf. clifer, clifrian, clifian]:—Rindeclifre *ibin*, Wrt. Voc. ii. 48, 34.

rinden; *adj. Of bark*:—Of rindenum *corticeo*, Germ. 390, 43.

rind-leás; *adj. Without bark*; decorticatus, Wrt. Voc. i. 61, 14.

rine, rinel, ring, ringan. v. ryne, rynel, hring, hringan. [*Add under the last*:—Ðæt man on rihtne tíman tída ringe, L. Edg. C. 45; Th. ii. 254, 5: L. N. P. L. 36; Th. ii. 296, 3.]

rinnan; *p.* rann, *pl.* runnon; *pp.* runnen *To run*:—Ic on wísne weg worda ðínra rinne *viam mandatorum tuorum cucurri*, Ps. Th. 118, 32. Satan seolua ran and on susle feóll, Cd. Th. 309, 20; Sat. 712. Wǽn æfter ran, Runic pm. Kmbl. 343, 32; Rún. 22. Gif lioþole út rynne, Lchdm. ii. 12, 24. Blód and wæter út bicwóman rinnan fore rincum, Exon. Th. 69, 3; Cri. 1115. [*Goth.* rinnan: *O. Frs.* rinna: *O. Sax. O. H. Ger.* rinnan: *Icel.* renna, rinna.] v. á-, bi-, ge-, óþ-rinnan, *and* irnan.

rinelle, an; *f. A brook, stream*:—Rinnellan *rivos*, Ps. Surt. 64, 11. Cf. rynel.

rio-. v. reo-.

ríp, es; *n.* **I.** *reaping, harvest*:—Ðæt ríp (*messis*) is worulde endung, Mt. Kmbl. 13, 39. Micel ríp (*messis*) ys, and feáwa wyrhtyna. Biddaþ ðæs rýpes Hláford ðæt hé sende wyrhtan tó his rípe, 9, 37–38: Lk. Skt. 10, 2. Ðæt ríp (rípes tíd, Lind.), Mk. Skt. 4, 29. Ðæt hér wǽre mycel riip, Bd. 1, 29; S. 498, 4. On hærfeste wícode se cyng on neáweste ðare byrig, ða hwíle ðe hié hira corn gerypon, ðæt ða Deniscan him ne mehton ðæs rípes forwiernan, Chr. 896; Erl. 94, 7. Ǽr wintres cyme on rýpes tíman, Exon. Th. 214, 28; Ph. 246. Twuga on geáre ǽne tó mǽþe and óðre tó rípe *twice a-year, once at hay-time and the other at harvest*, Cod. Dip. Kmbl. ii. 400, 30. His men beón gearuwe ge tó rípe ge tó huntoþe, v. 162, 28. Huíto sint tó hrippe (*ad messem*), Jn. Skt. Lind. 4, 35. **II.** *what is reaped* or *gathered in, a sheaf of corn* (cf. Whan thou repist corn in the feeld, and forȝetist and leeuest a repe, Wickl. Deut. 24, 19. See also Halliw. Dict. *reepe* a sheaf):—Rípu gaderian blisse getácnaþ, Lchdm. iii. 208, 15. **II a.** of other products [cf. wín-reopad *vendemiant*, Ps. Surt. 79, 13]:—Wíngeardas (-es, MS.) rípe fulle gesihþ blisse getácnaþ *if he sees vineyards full of fruit ready to gather, it betokens joy*, 210, 32. v. ge-, oht-ríp, *and next word.*

ripa (?), an; *m. A sheaf*:—Berende rypan (Ps. Surt. reopan) heora *portantes manipulos suos*, Ps. Spl. 125, 8: 128, 5. v. ríp, II.

rípan; *p.* ráp, *pl.* ripon *To reap, cut corn*; metaph. *to derive advantage*:—Ic rípe *meto*, Ælfc. Gr. 28, 3; Som. 30, 63. Ðú rípst ðíne æceras *tui agros metis*, 15; Som. 19, 46. Hláford ðú rípst ðǽr ðú ne seówe. . . . Ðú wistest ðæt ic rípe (hrippo, Lind.) ðǽr ic ne sáwe, Mt. Kmbl. 25, 24–26. Hrippes, Lk. Skt. Lind. 19, 21. Hú ne secge gé ðæt nú gyt synt feówur mónþas ǽr man rípan mǽge . . . geseóþ ðás eardas ðæt hig synt scíre tó rípene (rýpanne, MS. A). And se ðe rípþ (hrioppaþ, Lind.) nimþ méde, Jn. Skt. 4, 35–36. Heofonan fuglas ne sáwaþ ne hig ne rípaþ (rioppas, Lind.), Mt. Kmbl. 6, 26. Eal manna bearn sorgum sáwaþ, swá eft rípaþ, Exon. Th. 6, 19; Cri. 86. Ða hié heora corn ripon, Ors. 4, 8; Swt. 188, 27. Gif wé eów ða gástlícan sǽd sáwaþ, hwónlíc biþ ðæt wé eówere flǽslícan þing rípon, Homl. Th. ii. 534, 27. On ðám man ne mæg náðer ne erian ne rípan, Gen. 45, 6. [*O. E. Homl.* repen; *p. pl.* repen: *Jul.* reopen: *Laym.* repen; *p. pl.*: *Ayenb.* ripe: *Wick.* repe: *Piers P.* ropen, repen; *p. pl.*: *Chauc.* ropen; *p. part.*] v. ge-rípan, repan.

rípan, rýpan; *p.* te *To spoil, plunder*:—Ða syndon rýperas ðe scoldan beón hyrdas folces. Hý rýpaþ ða earman bútan ǽlcere scylde, L. I. P. 12; Th. ii. 320, 16. Hý hergiaþ and heáwaþ, rýpaþ and reáfiaþ and tó scipe lǽdaþ, Wulfst. 163, 12. Ðér þeáfas ofdelfes ꝉ hrýpes *ubi fures effodiunt*, Mt. Kmbl. Lind. 6, 19. Hí férdon ǽghweder flocmǽlum and heregodon úre earme folc, and hí rýpton (rǽpton, MS. E.) and slógon, Chr. 1011; Erl. 145, 26. Fram rýpendum ꝉ bereáfiendum *a diripientibus*, Ps. Lamb. 34, 10. v. be-rýpan, *and* cf. reáfian.

rípe; *adj. Ripe, mature*:—Rípe deáþ *matura mors*, Wrt. Voc. i. 39, 19. Swíðe rípe *matura satis*, ii. 58, 36. Swá swá rípe yrþ *quasi maturam segetem*, Bd. 1, 12; S. 480, 35. Se westmbǽra hærfest bringþ rípa bléda, Bt. 39, 13; Fox 234, 15: Met. 29, 63. [*O. Sax.* rípi: *O. H. Ger.* rífi.] v. sǽd-, un-rípe.

rípe (?) es; *n.* or (?) rípu; *indcl.*: ríp, e; *f.* (cf. *O. H. G.* rífi; *f. maturitas*: *Ger.* reife) *Ripeness, maturity*:—On rípe *in maturitate*, Ps. Th. 118, 147.

rípere, es; *m. A reaper*:—Ða ríperas (hrípemenn, Lind.) *messores*, Mt. Kmbl. 13, 39. On ðam ríptíman ic secge ðám ríperum (hrippemornum, Lind.), 13, 30. Cf. riftere.

rípere, es; *m. A robber, plunderer, spoiler*:—Rýperas and reáferas Godes graman habban, búton hig geswícan, L. C. S. 7; Th. i. 380, 5. Má is ðæra rýpera ðonne rihtwísra, and is earmlíc þing, ðæt ða syndon rýperas ðe scoldan beón hyrdas folces, L. I. P. 12; Th. ii. 320, 14–16. Cyning sceal rýperas and reáferas and ðás woruldstrúderas hatian and hýnan, 2; Th. ii. 304, 19: Wulfst. 266, 28: 165, 35. Ús stalu and cwalu . . . and rýpera reáflác derede swíðe þearle, 159, 11. Cf. reáfere.

rípian; *p.* ode *To grow ripe, to mature*:—On hærfest wæstmas rípiaþ, Anglia viii. 312, 23. Dó ðæt sunne scíne ðæt ðíne æceras rípion *cause the sun to shine, that thy fields may ripen*, Homl. Th. ii. 104, 3. Rípian *maturescere*, Wrt. Voc. ii. 3, 27: Hpt. Gl. 419, 64. [*O. Sax.* rípón: *O. H. Ger.* rífón.] v. ge-rípian, ful-rípod, un-gerípod.

ríp-ísern, es; *n. A sickle, an instrument for reaping*:—Rípísern *falcem*, Mk. Skt. Lind. Rush. 4, 29.

ríp-mann. v. rípere.

rípness, e; *f. Ripeness, maturity, season of ripeness, harvest*:—Hrípnes *messis*, Mt. Kmbl. Lind. 13, 29. On rípnysse *in maturitate*, Ps. Lamb. 118, 147. Cf. rípung.

riptere. v. riftere.

ríp-tíma, an; *m. Harvest-time*:—Lǽtaþ ǽgðer weaxan óþ ríptíman, and on ðam ríptíman ic secge ðám ríperum, Mt. Kmbl. 13, 30.

rípu. v. rípe; *n.*

rípung, e; *f.* **I.** *ripening*:—Seó sunne tempraþ ða eorþlícan wæstmas ǽgðer ge on wæstme ge on rípunge, Lchdm. iii. 250, 19. **II.** *ripeness, maturity*:—Tó ðæs mynstres geate sý geatweard geset, eald and wís . . . seó rípung his gestæþþignesse sý swylc, ðæt hine ne worian ne scríðan ne lyste *ad portam monasterii ponatur senex sapiens . . . cujus maturitas non sinat eum vagari*, R. Ben. 126, 17. On rípunga *in maturitate*, Ps. Spl. 118, 147. Se þridda tíma ys *autumnus*. . . . Bóceras getrahtniaþ ðæne naman for ðære rípunge oððe for ðære gaderunge. Hig cweþaþ *autumnus propter autumationem vel propter maturitatem*, Anglia viii. 312, 27.

rípung, e; *f. Spoliation, plundering*:—Fordéminge and rýpincge *proscriptionem, fraudationem*, Hpt. Gl. 480, 38.

-rís. v. ge-rís *rabies*, Wrt. Voc. ii. 118, 67. Cf. rísan *to seize*.

rísan; *p.* rás, *pl.* rison; *pp.* risen. **I.** *to rise*:—Álýs mé from láðum ðe mé lungre on rísan (onrísan?) willaþ *ab insurgentibus in me libera me*, Ps. Th. 58, 1. **II.** *to be fitting, becoming* (*the most usual form is* ge-rísan, q. v. cf. come *and* become, venire *and* convenire, *Ger.* fallen *and* ge-fallen *for similar development of meaning*):—Ne ríseþ *non decent*, Kent. Gl. 681. Ðér ne ríseþ *ubi non debet*, Mk. Skt. Rush. 13, 14. [*Goth.* ur-reisan: *O. Sax.* rísan: *O. Frs. Icel.* rísa: *O. H. Ger.* rísan *cadere* (cf. stígan *which can be used of upward or downward motion*).] v. á-, on-rísan, *and next word.*

rísan; *p.* rás; *pp.* risen (*different word from preceding?*) *To seize, snatch away, carry off*:—Benjamin is rísende wulf *lupus rapax*, Bd. 1, 34; S. 499, 27. Se rísenda *rabula*, Wrt. Voc. ii. 88, 68. Ðære rísendan *rapaci*, 79, 83. Wulfas rísænde ꝉ woedende *lupi rapaces*, Mt. Kmbl. Rush. 7, 15. v. ge-rísan, -rís, rǽs (?).

risc, risel, rísende. v. rysc, rysel, rísan.

risn (?) *a pair of compasses*:—Risn *cercinum* [? risl (hrisel q.v.) κερκις], Wrt. Voc. ii. 130, 30.

risne; *adj. Fitting, becoming, suitable*:—Hé sóna ðám risne andsware (*congrua responsa*) onsende, Bd. 1, 27; S. 488, 35, MS. B. v. ge-risene *and next word.*

risne (?), es; *n. What is fit* or *suitable*; congruum:—Habbaþ eów swylc massereáf and swylce béc and swylce húselfata swylce gé mid risnum (*decently*) eów ða befæstan þénunga þénian mágon, L. E. I. 4; Th. ii. 404, 27. v. ge-risene; *n. and preceding word.*

risoda (?) *rheum*:—Ða yfelan wǽtan on ðam seócum men ðe biþ swá swá horh oððe risoda oððe gillistre, Lchdm. ii. 282, 11.

ríþ, es; *m.* (v. eá-ríþ): e; *f.*: ríþe, an; *f. A rithe* (v. Halliw. Dict. and Leo A. S. Names of Places, p. 86: the word is still to be found in North Frisian in the form *ride, rie*, to denote the bed of running water), *a small stream*:—Ríþ *rivus* . . . lytel ríþ *rivulus*, Wrt. Voc. i. 54, 20–27: *rivus*, 80, 62. Burne ꝉ ríþe *latex*, Hpt. Gl. 447, 4. Norþ tó blacan ríþe, andlang ríþe, Cod. Dip. B. i. 296, 33. On fúlan ríþe, andlang ríþe, Cod. Dip. Kmbl. i. 257, 32. On áne ríþe, andlang ríþes (cf. of ðære ríþe, 24), iii. 385, 28–29: 386, 5. Hinc ad ælrithe, ab ipso rivo ad fraxinum unum, 373, 19. Ðǽr fleów of ðam flinte wæter . . . ðæt hí druncon of ðære ánre ríþe, Num. 20, 11. Ríþe *rivo*, Hpt. Gl. 490, 30. On ða ríþe, Cod. Dip. Kmbl. iii. 10, 25. Óþ ða litlan ríþe, andlang ríþe . . . tó ða ríþe, ðon andlang ríþe, 12, 15–21. Swá swá sum mical ǽwelm, and irnon manige brócas and ríþan (ríþa, Cott. MS.) of, Bt. 34, 1; Fox 134, 10. Ríþa *torrentum, rivulorum*, Hpt. Gl. 499, 54. Ríþum *rivulis*, 448, 61. Hríþum, 477, 37. Eorþan ríþum *terrae rivulis*, Hymn. Surt. 17, 12. Ic geseah ða wlitegan swilce culfran ástígende ofer streámlicum ríþum, Homl. Th. i. 444, 10. Swelce hit eall þytlum ríþum tórinne, Past. 38; Swt. 277, 12: 65; Swt. 469, 5: Met. 5, 20. Tó ðam lande ðe flēwþ on ríþum meolce and hunies, Num. 16, 14. v. wæter-ríþe *and next word.*

ríþig, es; *n.*: e; *f.* (?) *A stream*:—Hit cymeþ on ðæt lytle ríþig, of ðæm ríþige, Cod. Dip. Kmbl. iii. 33, 1. On ðæt ríþig, ondlong ríþiges, 378, 15. Swá on ða ealdan díc, andlang díces on áne ríþige, of ðære ríþe on áne ealde díc, 385, 24. On hweólríþig, 381, 8.

riððа, rixe, ríxian. ryðða, rysc, rícsian.

rocc, es; *m. An upper garment*:—Rocc *callicula*, Wrt. Voc. i. 26, 11. Deórfellen roc *mastruga*, roc *toral*, 82, 3-4. Rooc (rocc?) *toral*, 25, 64. Gǽten vel broccen rooc (rocc?) *melotes* vel *pera*, 40, 27. Mid rocce beón gescríd, orsorhnysse getácnaþ, Lchdm. iii. 200, 12. [*O. Frs.* rok: *O. H. Ger.* rocch *tunica, melotes*: *Ger.* rock: *Du.* rok: *Icel.* rokkr.] v. biscop-, breóst-, pistol-rocc.

rocc *what is chewed* (?), *a cud* (?):—Edreced roc *rumen* (cf. edreceþ, ceóweþ *ruminet*, l. 15), Wrt. Voc. ii. 97, 18. v. ed-roc.

rocc *a rock*. v. stān-rocc.

rocettan, roccettan; *p.* te *To eructate, utter*; eructare:—Roketto ł bilketto forþ ða ðe áhýded wérun *eructabo abscondita*, Mt. Kmbl. Rush. 13, 35. Roccetteþ *eructuat*, Ps. Surt. 18, 3: *eructuavit*, 44, 2. Rocetaþ *eructabunt*, 118, 171. Bylcetteþ, roccetteþ *eructuat*, i. *a corde emittit*, Wrt. Voc. ii. 144, 13. Bleów ł roccette *ructabat*, 96, 1.

rōd, e; *f.* I. *a rod, pole*. v. segl-rōd. II. *a measure of land*:—Se haga is fram ðære eá eástwardes .xxviii. rōda lang and súþwardes .xxiiii. rōda brād and eft ðanon westwardes on sǽferne .xix. rōda long, Cod. Dip. Kmbl. ii. 150, 6-9. III. *a cross, rood* (as in Holy-*rood*):—Ðeós rōd *haec crux*, Ælfc. Gr. 9, 67; Som. 14, 8. Rōd *crux* vel *staurus*, Wrt. Voc. i. 26, 52. Wítestengces, rōde *eculei*, rōde *gabuli*, Hpt. 478, 70-74. Ic bidde ðē for ðære hálegan rōde tácne, Bt. 42; Fox 260, 3. Hē hine gesēnade mid Cristes rōde tácne *signans se signo sanctae crucis*, Bd. 4, 24; S. 599, 6. Hí mearcodon mid blōde Tau, ðæt is rōde tācen, Homl. Th. ii. 266, 8. Se Hǽlend rōde tácen ofer Adam geworhte, Nicod. 32; Thw. 17, 29. Ðæt gē sceolan þurh ðæt treów mýnre rōde oferswýðan ðone deáþ, Thw. 17, 21. Sige forgeaf cyning ælmihtig þurh his rōde treó, Elen. Kmbl. 294; El. 147. Ðá gefæstnodon Judēi hine rōde gealgan . . . Mancynna ealdor ðære rōde gealgan underfēng, Homl. Th. i. 588, 16-19. Hēt Pharao ðē áhōn on rōde (*in cruce*), Gen. 40, 19. Gá nyþer of ðære rōde, Mt. Kmbl. 27, 40. Ðone hig nýddon ðæt hē bǽre hys rōde, 27, 32: Jn. Skt. 19, 17. Hē ðǽr þreó mētte rōde ætsomne, Elen. Kmbl. 1665; El. 834. III. *a crucifix*. v. sweor-rōd. [*O. Sax.* rōda *a cross*: *O. Frs.* rōde *patibulum*: *O. L. Ger.* ruoda *virga*; *rood* (*a measure*): *Icel.* rōða *a rood, crucifix*: *O. H. Ger.* ruota *virga*.] v. wearh-, wyn-rōd.

rōd-begenga, an; *m. One who worships a cross*:—Rōdbigenga *crucicola*, Wrt. Voc. ii. 137, 23. v. rōd-weorðiend.

rōd-bora, an; *m. One who bears a cross*:—Rōdbora *crucifer*, Germ. 389, 1.

rōde-hengen[n], e; *f. A cross, crucifixion*:—Hwæt hæfþ ðes man gefremod, ðæt hē rōdehengene wyrðe sý, Homl. Th. i. 596, 2. Hēt hine áhōn on rōdehencgene, 594, 29. Ðá ðá hē on rōdehengene mancynn álýsde, 58, 20. On rōdehengene genægglod, 82, 25. Hē (*the penitent thief*) geandette his synna on ðære rōdehengene, ii. 78, 22. Úre Hǽlend rōdehengene underbeáh, 600, 6.

rōde-wirðe; *adj. Deserving crucifixion*:—Gangaþ út git godwrecan and gongaþ út git rōdewyrðan, Shrn. 43, 8.

rōd-fæstnian; *p.* ode *To crucify*:—Gerōdfæstnad *crucifixus*, Apstls. Crd.

rodor, rador, es; *m.* I. as a technical term, *the firmament, the heaven of the fixed stars*:—Sunne *sol*, móna *luna*, roder *firmamentum*, Wrt. Voc. i. 41, 55-57: 70, 8. Lyft *aer*, hroder *aether*, 52, 56. Se rodor ymbféhþ útan eall ðás niþerlícan gescæfte, Shrn. 63, 9. Sió eorþe is nioþor ðonne ǽnig óðru gesceaft búton ðam rodore, forðam se rodor hine hæfþ ǽlce dæg útane . . . on ǽlcere stōwe hē is hire emnneáh, Bt. 33, 4; Fox 130, 20, 23. Siððan wæs rodor árǽred and ryne tungla, folde gefæstnad, Exon. Th. 272, 12; Jul. 498. Radores *aethrae* (MS. *uetre*), Wrt. Voc. ii. 92, 43. Hwá unlǽredra ne wundraþ þæs roderes færeldes, hú hē ǽlce dæge úton ymbhwyrfþ ealne ðisne middaneard, Bt. 39, 3; Fox 214, 15. Rodres, Met. 28, 3. Ðú mihtest ðē fleógan ofer ðam fýre ðe is betwux ðam rodore and ðære lyfte, and mihtest ðē féran mid ðære sunnan betwyx ðám tunglum and ðonne weorþan on þam rodore, Bt. 36, 2; Fox 174, 9-12: 33, 4; Fox 130, 15. Ofer rodere ryneswiftum, Met. 24, 28. Micel swég gǽþ of ðam scínendan rodore, ðeáh wē for ðam mycclan fyrlene hit gefrēdan ne mágon, Boutr. Scrd. 18, 43. Se godcunda foreþonc stýreþ ðone rodor and ða tunglu, Bt. 39, 8; Fox 224, 7. Ðás twelf tácna (*the signs of the Zodiac*) synd swá gehiwode on ðám heofenlícum roderum (rodere, MSS. R. L. P.), Lchdm. iii. 246, 6. II. mostly as a poetical term, *the heavens, sky, upper regions*:—Rodores candel *the sun*, Beo. Th. 3148; B. 1572. Hroderes *aetherea*, Hpt. Gl. 521, 23. Roderes *Olimpi*, Wrt. Voc. ii. 64, 61. Ðæs heálícan roderes *celsi Olymphi*, Hymn. Surt. 55, 3. Under radores ryne, Elen. Kmbl. 1586; El. 795. Fram rodere Crist scínþ *ab ethere Christus promicat*, Hymn. Surt. 37, 8. Wunigende on rodore *manens Olimpho*, 91, 19. Sende him of heán rodore God gást ðone hálgan, Cd. Th. 230, 21; Dan. 236. Roderas *aethera*, Kent. Gl. 273. Lyft drysmaþ, roderas reótaþ, Beo. Th. 2756; B. 1376. Dryhten, rodera rǽdend, Andr. Kmbl. 1253; An. 627. Rodra weard, Exon. Th. 394, 23; Rä. 14, 7. Rodera weard *God*, Cd. Th. 1, 2; Gen. 1. Rodora ríce *heaven*, 308, 5; Sat. 688. Under roderum, 7, 21; Gen. 109. Steám up árás swylce rēc under radorum, Elen. Kmbl. 1604; El. 804. Alwalda worhte rúme roderas, Exon. Th. 341, 30; Gen. Ex. 134. [*O. Sax.* radur.] v. beorht-, eást-, gim-, heáh-, norþ-, súþ-, up-, west-rodor.

rodor-beorht; *adj. Heavenly bright*:—Rodorbeorhtan tunglu, Cd. Th. 239, 12; Dan. 369.

rodor-cyning, es; *m. The king of heaven, Christ*:—Þurh ðæs hýhstan meaht, rodorcyninges giefe, se ðe on rōde treó geþrowade, Exon. Th. 269, 8; Jul. 447: 45, 30; Cri. 727: Elen. Kmbl. 1771; El. 887. Radorcyninges rōd, 1245; El. 624.

rodor-líc; *adj.* I. *of the firmament* (v. rodor, I):—Se roderlíca *ethereus*, Wrt. Voc. ii. 144, 25. *Firmamentum* is ðeós roderlíce heofen mid manegum steorrum ámētt, Lchdm. iii. 254, 8. Hí (*Enoch and Elias*) sind genumene tō lyftenre heofenan, ná tō rodorlícere, Homl. Th. i. 308, 3. Godes ríce on rodorlícere heofonan, ii. 330, 27. II. *celestial, heavenly* (v. rodor, II):—Cǽgbora se roderlíca (*aethereus*) mid óðrum apostolum, Hymn. Surt. 118, 11. Cæstergewaran rodorlíce *cives aetherei*, 57, 4. Hí faraþ tō heofonum and rodorlíce wununga underfōþ, Homl. Skt. i. 5, 83.

rodor-líhtung, e; *f. The illumination of the heavens, the dawn*:—Roderlíhtinge *auroram*, Ps. Lamb. 73, 16.

rodor-stōl, es; *m. A celestial throne*:—Hē mid handum his on heofonríce rihte rodorstōlas, Cd. Th. 46, 24; Gen. 749.

rodor-torht; *adj. Heavenly bright*:—(Rodor)torht ryne regen gestilled, Cd. Th. 85, 17; Gen. 1416.

rodor-tungol, es; *n. A star of heaven*:—Torr árǽrde tō rodortunglum, Cd. Th. 100, 21; Gen. 1667.

rōd-weorðiend, es; *m. A worshipper of the cross*:—Rōdwurþiend *crucicola, crucis adorator*, Hpt. Gl. 403, 30. v. rōd-begenga.

rōf; *adj. Valiant, stout, strong* (used only in poetry):—Rōf oretta, heard under helme (*Beowulf*), Beo. Th. 5070; B. 2538. Rōf rúnwita (*Guthlac*), Exon. Th. 167, 30; Gú. 1068. Wís hæleþ, maga mōde rōf, Andr. Kmbl. 1249; An. 625. Ánrǽd oretta, maga mōde rōf, 1967; An. 986. Árás ðá mægene rōf, 2936; An. 1471: 3348; An. 1678. Dǽdum rōf, æþeling ánhýdig, Beo. Th. 5326; B. 2666. Ðeáh hē (*Grendel*) rōf síe níþgeweorca, 1369; B. 682. Rōfne randwígan restan lyste, 3590; B. 1793. Fýrdraca rǽsde on ðone rōfan, 5373; B. 2690. Hæleþas heardmōde, rōfe rincas (*the fallen angels*), Cd. Th. 19, 4; Gen. 286. Ðæt wǽron mǽre men (*the apostles*), frome folctogan and fyrdhwate, rōfe rincas, Andr. Kmbl. 17; An. 9. Rincas wǽron rōfe, randas wǽgon forþ fromlíce, Cd. Th. 19, 4; Gen. 2049. Ic on morgen gefrægn mōdes rōfan hebban herebýman, 183, 28; Exod. 98. [*O. Sax.* rōf (ruob).] v. æsc-, beadu-, cwyld-, cyne-, dǽd-, ellen-, gúþ-, hand-, heaþo-, hete-, hyge-, mægen-, mōd-, mund-, sǽ-, sige-, un-camp-, þræc-rōf.

-rōf. v. secg-rōf.

rogian (?):—Heán sceal gehnígan, ádl gesígan, ryht rogian, Exon. Th. 340, 30; Gn. Ex. 119.

Rōm, e; *f. Rome*:—Ðá wæs ábrocen burga cyst, beadurincum wæs Rōm gerýmed, Met. 1, 19. Hēr onfēng Ecgbriht pallium æt Rōme, Chr. 735; Erl. 47, 19. Petrus gesæt biscepsetl on Rōme, 45; Erl. 6, 20. Hēr sendon Brytwalas tō Rōme, 443; Erl. 10, 21: 721; Erl. 44, 25. Ðæt hē of Rōme cōme, Bd. 1, 25; S. 486, 25. Hē mid ealre his firde wið Rōme weard farende wæs, Ors. 5, 11; Swt. 236, 9. ¶ *The combination* Rōme-, Rōma-burh *is also frequent*:—Wearþ Rōmeburg getimbred fram twám gebrōðrum, Ors. 2, 2; Swt. 64, 21. Swá mildelíce wæs Rōmeburg on fruman gehálgod, Swt. 66, 4. Twám geárum ǽr Rōmaburh ábrocen wǽre . . . wæs Rōmaburh ábrocen fram Gotum, Bd. 1, 11; S. 480, 10-12. On Rōmebyrig, Apstls. Kmbl. 22; Ap. 11. Hēr Gotan ábrǽcon Rōmeburg, Chr. 409; Erl. 10, 7.

Rōmāne (Rōmane?), Rōmānan; *pl. The Romans*:—Nǽfre siþan Rōmāne ne rícsodon on Bretone, Chr. 409; Erl. 10, 9: 418; Erl. 10, 13. Rōmānan gesáwon fíren cleáwen feallan of heofenum, Shrn. 30, 5. Claudius ōðer Rōmāna cyninga, Chr. 47; Erl. 6, 23. Hē onfēng pallium from Rōmāne biscope, 736; Erl. 46, 21. Rōmāna burh, 409; Erl. 11, 10. Rōmāna ríce, Ors. 2, 2; Swt. 66, 7. Ealra ðara Rōmāna wíf, Swt. 66, 29. Wǽron ealle Italie Rōmānum on fultume, 4, 11; Swt. 208, 7.

Rōmānisc; *adj. Roman*:—Se Rōmānisca cásere Octavianus, Homl. Th. i. 30, 1. Se Rōmānisca here, Bd. 1, 12; S. 480, 33. Man Rōmānisces cynnes, 1, 16; S. 484, 18. On ðære hálgan Rōmānisce cyricean, 1, 27; S. 489, 33. Fram ðam Rōmāniscan Pāpan, 2, 20; S. 522, 19. Ealde Rōmānisce weorce geworhte, 1, 33; S. 498, 31. Gúþlác ys on Rōmānisc *belli munus*, Guthl. 2; Gdwin. 10, 24. Ða yfel ðe Þeódríc wið ðam Rōmāniscum witum dyde, Bt. 1; Fox 2, 15. Him leófre wæs ðæt hié Rōmānisce cyningas hæfden ðonne of heora ágnum cynne, Ors. 3, 5; Swt. 106, 25. Ealle ða Rōmāniscan men þe Hannibal gesealð hæfde, 4, 11; Swt. 204, 7.

Rôme-burh, -scot. v. Rôm, Rôm-gesceot.

Rôm-feoh; *gen.* -feós; *n. Peter's pence.* [William of Malmesbury attributes to Ethelwulf the institution of this tax: 'Ethelwulf went to Rome (v. Chron. 855) and there offered to St. Peter that tribute which England pays to this day,' bk. 2, c. 2; but in the earlier and similar payment by Offa, established in 787, may probably be seen the origin of the *Rômfeoh* in England, v. Stubbs, Const. Hist. i. 230. The Chronicle several times during Alfred's reign contains the notice that 'Wesseaxna ælmessan' were sent to Rome, but the first notice in the laws of Rômfeoh occurs in the agreement between English and Danes, to which his son Edward was a party: 'Gif hwâ Rômfeoh forhealde gylde lahslit mid Denum, wîte mid Englum,' Th. i. 170, 2. The penalty, which is not here stated, was a heavy one, as will be seen from the passages given below. There is no mention in these of any being exempted from the contribution on the score of insufficient means, but in the laws of Edward the Confessor, in that which treats 'de denario Sancti Petri qui Anglice dicitur Rômescot,' it is said: 'Omnis qui habuerit .xxx. denariatas vive pecunie de suo proprio in domo suo, lege Anglorum dabit denarium Sancti Petri.' Further with regard to the time of payment it is enacted: 'Iste (denarius) summoniri debet in festivitate sanctorum Apostolorum Petri et Pauli, et ultra festum Sancti Petri ad Vincula non detineatur,' Th. i. 446. So too in the laws of William I: 'Cil ki ad aueir champestre xxx. deñ vaillant deit duner le deñ sein Piere,' Th. i. 474. And see note on p. 170. See too the laws of Henry I: 'Romfech in festo Sancti Petri ad Vincula debet reddi,' Th. i. 520. v. Ducange s.v. Denarius S. Petri.]:—Wê bebeódaþ ǽlcum cristenum men... Rômfeoh... Gif hit hwâ dôn nelle, sý hê âmânsumod, L. Edm. E. 2; Th. i. 244, 17. Rômfeoh gelǽste man ǽghwilce geáre be Petres mæssan; and se đe đæt nelle gelǽstan, sylle đártôeácan .xxx. peninga, and gilde đam cyninge .cxx. scill., L. Eth. ix. 10; Th. i. 342, 24. Rômfeoh gelǽste man be Petres mæssan; and se đe ofer đæne dæg hit healde, âgyfe đam bisceope đæne penig, and đǽrtô .xxx. penega and đam cingce .cxx. scill., L. C. E. 9; Th. i. 366, 15. Rômfeoh gelǽste man ǽghwilce geáre be Peteres mæssan; and se đe đæt ne gelǽste, sylle đǽrtôeácan .xxx. peninga tô Rôme and gylde đam cynge on Engla lage .cxx. scillinga, Wulfst. 272, 9. [Cf. *Icel.* Rôma-skattr.] v. Rôm-pening *and next word.*

Rôm-gescot, es; *n. Peter's pence*:—Man syđđan đæt Rômgesceot be him sende, swâ man manegan geáran ǽror ne dyde, Chr. 1095; Erl. 232, 33. [Hê com æfter þe Rômescot, 1123; Erl. 250, 39.] v. preceding word.

rômian; *p.* ode; *with gen. To strive after*:—Is đes ænga stede (*hell*) ungelîc swîđe đam ôđrum đe wê ǽr cûđon on heofonrîce... deáh wê hine for đam Alwealdan âgan ne môston rômigan ûres rîces *though we are prevented by the Almighty from possessing our former place and from striving after our former power* (cf. Ic eom rîces leás *as marking the inability for further striving on the part of Lucifer,* 24, 3; Gen. 372), Cd. Th. 23, 15; Gen. 350. [*The word seems to be the O. Sax.* rômôn, *to aim at, strive after;* cf. rômôd gi rehtoro things, Hel. 1690. *O. H. Ger.* râmen (*with gen.*) *intendere.*]

rômig (?); *adj. Blackened, sooty*:—Rômei *catabatus* (cf. hrûmig *caccabatus,* 13, 17), Wrt. Voc. ii. 102, 56. [Cf. (?) *O. H. Ger.* raamac, hrâmac *furva.*] v. hrûmig.

Rôm-pening, es; *m. A penny paid to Rome.* v. Rôm-feoh:—Sig ǽlc Rômpenig âgifen be Petres mæssedæge ǽiþer ge uppon lande ge on ǽlcan porte, Shrn. 208, 32. Rômpenegas (cf. seó ǽlc heorþpenig âgifen be Petres mæssedæg, 116, 4), Wulfst. 113, 11. Wê willaþ đæt ǽlc Rômpænig beó gelǽst be Petres mæssan tô đam bisceopstôle, and wê willaþ đæt man namige on ǽlcon wǽpengetæce .ii. trýwe þegnas and ǽnne mæssepreóst, đæt hî hit gegaderian. Gif cyninges þegn ođđe ǽnig landrîca hit forhæbbe, gilde .x. healfmearc, healf Criste, healf cynge. Gif hwilc tûnes-man ǽnigne pænig forhæbbe, gilde se landrîca đone pænig, and nime ǽnne oxan (cf. *the fine of* 30 *pence in the passages given under* Rôm-feoh, *and the value of an ox,* v. oxa) æt đam men, L. N. P. L. 57–59; Th. ii. 298, 29–300, 7.

Rôm-waran, -ware; *pl. The people of Rome, the Romans*:—Hû ungemetlîce gê Rômware bemurciaþ, Ors. 1, 10; Swt. 48, 17. Rômwara sundorriht *jus Quiritum,* Wrt. Voc. ii. 49, 11. Se ǽrra Rômwara câsere Julius, Bd. 1, 2; S. 475, 2. Rômwara rîce, 1, 3; S. 475, 13. Rômwarena hlâford, Elen. Kmbl. 1961; El. 982. Micel sido mid Rômwarum, Bt. 27, 1; Fox 96, 2. [*Icel.* Rôm-, Rûm-verjar.]

Rôm-, Rûm-wealh; *gen.* weales; *m. A Roman* (cf. Bret-walas *the Britons*):—Reht Rômwala *jus Quiritum,* Rtl. 189, 13. Ic wæs mid Rûmwalum, Exon. Th. 322, 27; Vîd. 69. v. wealh.

rop *the colon.* v. ropp.

rop (?) *broth*:—Rop (broþ?) *jus* (*in a list* de suibus), Wrt. Voc. i. 286, 55.

rôp; *adj. Liberal, bountiful*:—Đeós lyft byreþ lytle wihte, đa sind sanges rôpe *they* (*the birds*) *are bountiful of song,* Exon. Th. 439, 2; Rä. 58, 3. v. next word.

rôpness, e; *f. Liberality*:—Roopnis *liberalitas,* Wrt. Voc. ii. 113, 2. Rôpnes, 51, 10.

ropp, es; *m. An intestine, the colon*:—Rop *colum* vel *intestinum,* Wrt. Voc. ii. 134, 60: *extale,* 145, 29. Roop *colus* (in a list of parts of the body), i. 45, 20. Hrop *colum,* 19, 55. Be wambe coþum and tâcnum on roppe and on smælþearmum, Lchdm. ii. 230, 16–18. Tîhþ innan đone rop and on đæt smælþearme, 232, 15. Roppum *extalibus,* Wrt. Voc. ii. 32, 11. [He naȝt ne heþ ine his roppes bote wynd, Ayenb. 62, 32. v. *Halliw. Dict.* ropes: *O. Du.* rop.]

rop-wærc, es; *m. Colic*:—Ropwærc *colica,* Wrt. Voc. ii. 134, 68. Hropwyrc, i. 19, 56.

rôrend. v. rôwend.

rôscian *to dry by fire.* v. ge-rôscian, Wrt. Voc. i. 288, 60: ii. 116, 31. v. rôstian.

rôse, an; *f. A rose*:—Rôse *rosa,* Wrt. Voc. i. 30, 13: 79, 60. Rôsa, 69, 24. Đære rôsan wlite, Bt. 9; Fox, 26, 20. Đæra rôsena blôstman getâcniaþ mid heora reádnysse martyrdôm, Homl. Th. i. 444, 13. [*Icel.* rôs: *O. H. Ger.* rôsa. From Latin.]

rôsen; *adj. Of roses;* roseus, rosatus:—Mid wlite rôsenum *decore roseo,* Hymn. Surt. 105, 20. Mid rôsenan ele gemencged, Lchdm. i. 302, 3. On rôsenne *in rosatum,* Hpt. Gl. 483, 25.

rôsig; *adj. Rosy*:—Mid rôseum hiwe ofergoten, Homl. Th. ii. 334, 30.

rôstian; *p.* ode *To roast, dry by a fire*:—Gerôstode *passos,* Wrt. Voc. ii. 67, 60. [*O. H. Ger.* rôsten *torreri, frigere.*] v. rôscian.

rot *scum,* Lchdm. ii. 204, 1: 286, 4. v. hrot.

rôt; *adj.* I. *glad, cheerful*:—Đǽr moncyn môt for Meotude rôt sôđne God geseón and aa in sibbe gefeón, Exon. 355, 33; Reim. 86. v. un-rôt, rêtan, rôt-hwîl, rôtlîce, rôtness. II. *noble, excellent*:—Se gôda man swâ hê swîđor âfandod biþ, swâ hê rôtra biþ, and neár Gode, ôþ đæt hê mid fulre geþincþe færþ of đisum lîfe tô đam êcan lîfe. Se yfela swâ hê oftor on đære fandunge âbrýđ, swâ hê forcûđra biþ, and deófle neár, ôþ đæt hê færþ of đisum lîfe tô đam êcan wîte, Homl. Th. i. 268, 26–31. Drihten cwæþ, đæt wê sind miccle rôttran đonne đa fugelas (cf. Besceáwiaþ đa hrefnas... gê synt hyra sêlran, Lk. Skt. 12, 24); forđan đe se man is đe Gode geþîhþ ealra gesceafta rôtost, and Gode leófost, buton đâm heofenlîcum englum đe nǽfre ne syngodon, ii. 462, 31–34. On đam ilcan geáre forbarn đæt hâlige mynster on Lundene... and đæt mǽste dǽl and đæt rôtteste ealle đære burh, Chr. 1086; Erl. 220, 20.

rôđer, es; rôđra, an; *m. A rower, sailor*:—Rôđer *nauta,* Wrt. Voc. i. 48, 8. Rôđra, 63, 28. v. rêđra.

rôđer, es; *n. An oar, a rudder* (i. e. an oar for steering):—Rôđr *tonsa,* Wrt. Voc. ii. 122, 48. Rôthor, Ep. Gl. 26 d, 29. Rôđer *remus,* Wrt. Voc. i. 73, 77. Rôđres blæd *palmula,* 48, 15. Ne mæg scip nô stille gestondan, bûton hit ankor gehæbbe, ođđe mon mid rôđrum ongeán tió (*pull against the stream with oars*), Past. 58; Swt. 445, 13. [*O. H. Ger.* ruodar *remus, palmula, clavus, gubernaculum.*] v. scip-, steór-rôđer, ge-rêđru.

rođ-hund, es; *m. A large dog;* molossus. [In later English vocabularies *molossus* is translated by *blood-hound* and *band-dog.* v. Wrt. Voc. i. 177, 15: 187, col. 2.]:—Rođhund *molosus,* Wrt. Voc. ii. 114, 24: 56, 41: i. 288, 27. Rothundas *molosos,* ii. 91, 9. Hrođhund *inutilis canis,* i. 23, 36. [Cf. *O. H. Ger.* rudo *molossus* (v. Grff. ii. 490): *Ger.* rüde.] v. ryđđa.

rôđra. v. rôđer.

rôt-hwîl, e; *f. A time of refreshing*:—Ǽlc rihtwîs man, đonne hê đysne sealm singþ, wilnaþ him sumere rôthwîle on đissere worulde, and êc reste æfter đisum, Ps. Th. 14, arg. Forlǽt mê nû tô sumre rôthwîle on đisse weorulde ǽr ic hire of gewîte *remitte mihi ut refrigerer prius quam eam,* 38, 16.

rotian; *p.* ode *To rot, get corrupt, ulcerate, putrify*:—Đonne se lǽce on untîman lâcnaþ wunde, hió wyrmseþ and rotaþ *secta immature vulnera deterius infervescunt,* Past. 21, 2; Swt. 153, 3. Hit ne rotode *non computruit,* Ex. 16, 24. Mîne wunda rotedan and fûledon *computruerunt et deterioraverunt cicatrices meae,* Ps. Th. 37, 5. Gif sió wund swîđe rotige ôþ đæt hê đæt wursm of mûþe hrǽce, Lchdm. ii. 202, 25. Ǽr se seoloc (*silk thread*) rotige, 56, 8. Mid đam (*myrrh*) man smyraþ rîcra manna lîc đæt hig rotian ne mâgon, Anglia viii. 299, 48. [Cf. *Icel.* rotinn *rotten:* rotna *to putrefy, rot.*] v. for-rotian, rotung.

rôt-lîc. v. un-rôtlîc.

rôt-lîce; *adv. Cheerfully*:—Nû đû đus rôtlîce and đus glædlîce tô us sprecende eart *qui tam hilariter nobiscum velut sospes loqueris,* Bd. 4, 24; S. 598, 37. v. un-rôtlîce.

rôtness, e; *f.* I. *gladness, cheerfulness*:—Of rôtnise (un-r.?) *de merore,* Rtl. 41, 5. From rôtnise *a tristitia,* 69, 34. v. unrôtness. II. *comfort, protection*:—Rôtnys (gebeorh, Ps. Th.: frôfr, Ps. Spl. T.) *refugium,* Blickl. Gl. Rôtnes ł ner (rôtsung, Ps. Spl. T.) đam þearfan *refugium pauperi,* Ps. Lamb. 9, 10. On hûse rôtnysse *in domum refugii,* Ps. Spl. 30, 3.

-rotigendlîc, -rotodness. v. un-forrotigendlîc, for-rotodness.

rôtsian. v. ge-, un-rôtsian, *and next word.*

rôtsung, e; *f. Comfort, protection, cheering*:—Rôtsung *refugium,* Ps. Spl. T. 9, 9.

rotung, e; *f.* I. *corruption, putrefaction* :—Mīn rotung on byrgenne *dum descendo in corruptionem*, Ps. Th. 29, 8. II. *a sore accompanied with putrefaction, an ulcer* :—Rotung *ulcus*, Wrt. Voc. i. 20, 15.

rōw; *adj. Quiet, calm, mild* :—Se cleweþa (*itch*) biþ suīđe rōw, and đeáhhwæđere gif him mon tō longe fylgþ, hē wundaþ and sió wund sāraþ, Past. 11, 6; Swt. 71, 19. [*Icel.* rōr, *quiet, calm.*] v. next word.

rōw, e; *f. Quiet, rest* :—Đǣr hȳ bīdinge mōstun æfter tintergum tīdum brūcan, đonne hȳ of waþum wērge cwōman restan ryneþrāgum, rōwe gefēgon, Exon. Th. 115, 4; Gū. 184. [Biteache mi gast and mi bodi bađen to ro and to reste, Marh. 20, 5. Cristess resste and Cristess ro, Orm. 7042. *O. H. Ger.* ruowa *quies, requies* : *Icel.* rō.]

rōwan; *p.* reów *To go by water, to row* or *sail* :—Ic rōwe *navigo*, Ælfc. Gr. 24; Som. 25, 40. Ic āstīge mīn scyp and rōwe (*navigo*) ofer sǣlīce dǣlas, Coll. Monast. Th. 26, 31. Wērig sceal se wiđ winde rōweþ, Exon. Th. 345, 12; Gn. Ex. 187. Drihten tō đam lande reów, Homl. Th. ii. 378, 31. 'Utun seglian ofer đisne mere.' And hig seglydan đā. Đā hig reówun đā slēp hē (*navigantibus illis obdormivit*), Lk. Skt. 8, 23, 26. Đa ōđre leorningcnihtas reówon *navigio venerunt*, Jn. Skt. 21, 8. Hī gefēngon hine and wurpon hine on đone bāt and reówan tō scipe, Chr. 1046; Erl. 174, 18. Đā git on sund reón, đǣr git eagorstreám earmum þehton, mǣton merestrǣta, mundum brugdon, Beo. Th. 1029; B. 512. Đā wit on sund reón, 1083; B. 539. Đonne mōt hē swā rīdan, swā rōwan, swā swilce færelde faran swylce tō his wege gebyrige, L. E. I. 24; Th. ii. 420, 24. Seó sǣ is hwīltīdum smylte and myrige on tō rōwenne, Homl. Th. i. 182, 32. [*Icel.* rōa *to row.*] v. be-, ofer-, ōþ-rōwan.

rōwan (?) :—On hliór rōuuit *adplaudat*, Wrt. Voc. ii. 99, 37.

rōwend, es; *m. A rower, sailor* :—Nǣfre ic sǣlidan sēlran mētte ... rōwend (rōrend, MS.) rōfran, Andr. Kmbl. 945; An. 473. Đæt scip wile hwīlum stīgan ongeán đone streám, ac hit ne mæg, būton đa rōwend hit teón, Past. 58; Swt. 445, 11. v. scip-rōwend.

rōwet[t] *glosses* remigium :—Rōwette *remigio*, Hpt. Gl. 529, 14. v. rēwet[t].

rōwness, e; *f. Rowing* :—Wē ne mid seglinge ne mid rōwnesse (*neque velo neque remigio*) ōwiht fremian mihte, Bd. 5, 1; S. 613, 25.

rōwung, e; *f. Rowing* :—Winnende in rōwinge *laborantes in remigando*, Mk. Skt. Rush. 6, 48. On scip ꝉ on rōuing *nauigio*, Jn. Skt. Lind. 21, 8.

rudduc *a ruddock* (v. Halliw. Dict.), *a robin red-breast* :—Rudduc *rubisca*, Wrt. Voc. i. 29, 20: 62, 36.

rūde (?) *roughness of the skin, scab* :—Seó rūde *or* se rūda (se rude, MS.) on đam men *scamma in homine*, Wrt. Voc. i. 45, 30. [*O. L. Ger.* rūtha *scabies* : *O. H. Ger.* rūda, rūdo *scabies, impetigo* : *Ger.* räude. Cf. (?) *Icel.* hrūđr *crust* or *scab on a sore.* This form seems to point to *hrūde* as the earlier form in English.]

rūde, an; *f. Rue* :—Rūde *ruta*, Wrt. Voc. i. 30, 40: 69, 1: 79, 18. Wildre rūdan seáw, Lchdm. ii. 26, 10. Mintan and rūdan *mentam et rutam*, Lk. Skt. 11, 42. Rūtan, Wrt. Voc. ii. 73, 46. [*O. H. Ger.* rūta: *Ger.* raute. From Latin?]

rudig; *adj. Ruddy* :—Rudi *purpureus, rubicundus*, Hpt. Gl. 475, 8. [Rudi scheome, A. R. 330, 20. Þi rudi neb schal as gres grenen, H. M. 35, 22.]

rud-molin (?) *redshanks* or *water pepper*; polygonum hydropiper, Lchdm. ii. 342, 12. v. note and glossary.

rudu, e; *f. Red, redness, redness of the cheeks, the countenance* (?) :—Anwlita *vel* rudu *vultus*, Wrt. Voc. i. 42, 52. Mid rude *rubore*, Hpt. Gl. 507, 63. Đā geseah se cyngc đæt Apollonius mid rōsan rude wæs eal oferbrǣded, Ap. Th. 22, 4. Gezabel gehiwode hire eágan and hire neb mid rude, Homl. Skt. i. 18, 342. [The rude of monnes nebbe þet seið ariht his sunnen, A. R. 330, 29. Þe rose mid hire rude, O. and N. 443. Cf. *Icel.* rođi *redness.*]

rūg. v. rūh.

Rug-ern *rye-harvest, the name of a month* :—Sextan dæge Rugernes, L. Wih. proem.; Th. i. 36, 6. [Cf. *O. Frs.* arn: *O. H. Ger.* aran, arn *messis*, and see Grmm. Gesch. D. S. 58.]

rūh; *adj.* I. *rough, hairy, shaggy* :—Rūh *hispidus, hirsutus*, Wrt. Voc. ii. 43, 15–16: 90, 17: i. 51, 20. Rūh hrægel *amphibalum*, 25, 65. Ōxn *vel* rūh ōxn *ascella* vel *subhircos*, 43, 65. Rūh scō *pero*, ii. 68, 6. Se wæs reód and eall rūh *totus in morem pellis hirsutus*, Gen. 25, 25. Mīn brōđer ys rūh and ic eom smēđe, 27, 11. Gif him þince đæt hē habbe rūh līc, Lchdm. iii. 170, 24: Exon. Th. 407, 14; Rä. 26, 5. Rūwes nāt hwæt, 479, 17; Rä. 62, 9. Rūhne wæfels *yrcum tegimen*, Hymn. Surt. 103, 31. Rūhne (rihne, MS.) hine gesihþ gewordenne, Lchdm. iii. 208, 29. Leáf beóþ rūge and brāde, i. 254, 13. Đā gesāwe wē rūge (*pilosos*) wīfmen and wǣpnedmen, wǣron hié swā rūwe and swā gehǣre swā wildeór, Nar. 20, 3–5. Đa rūwan (*pilosae*) handa wǣron swilce đæs yldran brōđur, Gen. 27, 23. Seó clǣne beó blōsman gegrēt swā lange đæt hyre đa rūwan þeóh wurþaþ swȳđe gehefegode, Anglia viii. 324, 13. Rūwe *hirta*, Germ. 398, 258. Hrūhe wulla *hirsutas lanas*, Hpt. 524, 13. II. *rough, untrimmed, uncultivated* :—Rūg *frondosa*, Wrt. Voc. ii. 151, 16. Ne turf ne toft, ne land ne lǣse, ne fersc ne mersc, ne rūh ne rūm, Lchdm. iii. 286, 24. Tō đære rūwan hecgan, Cod. Dip. Kmbl. ii. 172, 32. On đone rūwan hlync; andlang đæs rōwan linces, v. 297, 22. On rūwan beorg; of rūwan beorge, 277, 18. On đa rūgan þyrnan; of đære þyrnan, iii. 419, 12. Đā fērdon begen þurh đa rūgan fennas, Guthl. 3; Gdwin. 20, 25. III. *rough, knotty* :—Rūches *nodosi*, Hpt. Gl. 482, 60. IV. *rough, undressed* :—.xxx. ombra rūes cornes, iv. ambru meolwes, Chart. Th. 40, 9. [Þet ruwe vel, A. R. 120, 23. Nis þet iren acursed þet iwurđed þe swarture and þe ruhure so hit is ofture iviled? 284, 17. Margareet sette hire fot uppon his ruhe necke, Marh. 12, 12. Sharrp and ruhh and gatelæs þurrh þorrness and þurh breress, Orm. 9211. Mid ruȝe felle, O. and N. 1013. Sridde ȝhe Jacob and made him ru, Gen. and Ex. 1539. *O. H. Ger.* rūh *hirtus, hirsutus, hispidus, villosus, scaber, asper* : *O. Du.* rouw, rūgh, rū.]

rūm, es; *m.* I. local, *room, space* :—Under rodera rūm, Cd. Th. 71, 5; Gen. 1166. Hig næfdon rūm on cumena hūse *non erat eis locus in diversorio*, Lk. Skt. 2, 7. II. temporal, *space of time* :—Næhtes rūme *noctis spatio*, Rtl. 36, 35. Þerh alle tīdo rūmo *per omnium horarum spatia*, 171, 41. III. *time which allows unhindered* or *unhurried action, opportunity* :—Rūm wæs tō nimanne londbūendum on hyra ealdfeóndum herereáf *the men of the land had ample opportunity of taking the spoil from their ancient foes*, Judth. Thw. 26, 7; Jud. 314. Hig ne mōston rūm habban đæt hig hit on riht gebōcon (*Aegyptiis nullam facere sinentibus moram*), Ex. 12, 39. Fȳrdraca rǣsde on đone rōfan đa him rūm āgeald (*when the opportunity was given him*), Beo. Th. 5374; B. 2690. Deáþ đæs ne scrīfeþ đonne him rūm forlǣt rodora Waldend, Met. 10, 30. [*Goth.* rūms: *O. Sax.* rūm: *O. H. Ger.* rūm: *Icel.* rūm; *n.*] v. ge-rūm.

rūm; *adj.* I. local, *roomy, spacious, ample, extensive* :—Se weg is swīđe rūm (cf. *Goth.* rūms wigs) đe tō forspillednesse gelǣt *spatiosa via quae ducit ad perditionem*, Mt. Kmbl. 7, 13. Deós sǣ micel and rūm (*spatiosum*), Ps. Spl. 103, 26. Behealde hē hū wīdgille đæs heofones hwealfa biþ, and hū neara đære eorþan stede is, đeáh heó ūs rūm þince, Bt. 19; Fox 68, 23. Rūma rodor *the spacious firmament on high*, Met. 28, 16. Đære sunnan ryne is swīđe rūm, and đæs mōnan ryne is swīđe nearo, Lchdm. iii. 248, 7. Rūme rīce *a realm far-reaching*, Cd. Th. 254, 13; Dan. 611. Rūmes *spatiosae, ampli*, Hpt. Gl. 434, 45: 493, 29. Đū gesettes in stōwe rūmre (*loco spacioso*; in roume stede, E. E. Psalt.) foet mīne, Ps. Surt. 30, 9. On sumne smēđne feld and rūmne (*amplam*), Bd. 5, 6; S. 618, 40. Đis rūme land *the earth*, Cd. Th. 7, 31; Gen. 114. Đa rūman *patula*, Wrt. Voc. ii. 94, 61. Hié ūte wilniaþ đara rūmena wega đisse worulde *causarum secularium foras lata itinera expetunt*, Past. 18, 4; Swt. 135, 6. Sōhton rūmre land, Cd. Th. 99, 25; Gen. 1651. Geseah ic đone rūmestan (*latissimus*) feld, Bd. 5, 12; S. 629, 19. I a. *roomy, open, unencumbered.* v. rūmian :—Ne fersc ne mersc, ne rūh ne rūm *neither uncleared nor cleared* (?) *land*, Lchdm. iii. 286, 24. Þurh đa rūman *per patentes*, Wrt. Voc. ii. 69, 7. II. temporal, *long, extended* :—Būtan him se cyng rūmran fyrstes geunnan wolde, L. Eth. vii. 4; Th. i. 330, 12. III. of mental qualities, *ample, great, liberal* :—Ic mæg þurh rūmne sefan rǣd gelǣran, Beo. Th. 561; B. 278. Rūmran geþeaht, Elen. Kmbl. 2480; El. 1241. IV. *unrestricted, clear, free from conditions* :—Đæt hē hit hæbbe swā rūm tō bōclonde swā hē ǣr hæfde tō lǣnlonde, Cod. Dip. Kmbl. iii. 258, 29. Đē weorđ on đīnum breóstum rūm *your mind will be freed from the trammels hitherto restricting it*, Cd. Th. 33, 13; Gen. 519. V. *not restrained within due limits, lax* :—Rūme regulas, Exon. Th. 131, 23; Gū. 460. VI. *ample, far-reaching* :—Đīne dōmas synd rihte and rūme, Hy. 7, 15. VII. *liberal.* v. rūm-gifa, -gifol, -mōd :—Wel biþ đam eorle đe him oninnan hæfþ rūme heortan (*liberal in giving alms*), Exon. Th. 467, 16. v. rūm-heort. VIII. *great, noble, august* :—Đære rūman *a*[*u*]*guste*, Wrt. Voc. ii. 5, 22. Rūmum *augusto, regali*, Hpt. Gl. 487, 29. Þurh đæt rūme *per augustam*, Wrt. Voc. ii. 65, 59. Đæs æþelan ođđe rūme *fausta*, 33, 76. [He wollde ȝifenn uss heoffness rume riche, Orm. 3689. Mi nest is holȝ and rum, O. and N. 643. He made ys wey roume ynou, R. Glouc. 303, 28. Make this place rom, Chauc. Reeves T. 206. *Goth.* rūms *spatiosus* : *O. Frs.* rūm *spacious, open* : *O. H. Ger.* rūmi *spatiosus, amplus* : *Icel.* rūmr.] v. ge-rūme.

rūma, an; *m. Separation* :—Rūma *discidium*, i. *separatio, divisio*, Wülck. 223, 25. [Cf. He gede on rum *he went apart*, Gen. and Ex. 400. On, a roume *at a distance*, Strat. Dict.]

rūmaþ. v. rȳman.

rūme; *adv.* I. local, *widely, far and wide, so as to extend over a wide space* :—Cyning rūme rīcsaþ *a king* (*the Deity*) *rules far and wide*, Met. 24, 32. Rūme geondwlītan ymb healfa gehwone, Exon. Th. 4, 30; Cri. 60. Heó wīde hire willan sōhte and rūme fleáh, Cd. Th. 87, 29; Gen. 1456: 86, 10; Gen. 1428. Gehȳran mæg ic rūme and swā wīde geseón, 42, 14; Gen. 673: 132, 9; Gen. 2190. Hié ne meahton leng somed blǣdes brūcan ... ac sceoldon đa rincas rūmor sēcan, ellor ēđelseld, 113, 31; Gen. 1895: 115, 1; Gen. 1913. II. *liberally, extensively, amply, abundantly, in a high degree* :—Hyt rūme đa wyrmas forþ gelǣdeþ *it plentifully brings out the worms*, Lchdm. i. 282, 23.

Drihten rûme lêt willeburnan on woruld þringan, Cd. Th. 82, 35; Gen. 1372: 75, 20; Gen. 1243. Ðû meaht his rûme rǽd geþencan *for this in ample measure may'st thou devise means*, 35, 27; Gen. 561. Ne willaþ rûmor unc landriht heora, 114, 27; Gen. 1910. Wes ðissum leódum ârfæst gif ðê Alwalda scirian wille ðæt ðû rûmor (*more liberally than now is in your power* (?)) môte on ðisse folcsceare frætwa dǽlan, 171, 15; Gen. 2828. III. *without restriction* or *encumbrance, without the pressure of care.* v. rûm-heort, II:—Ðâ (*after Judith's prayer was answered*) wearþ hyre rûme (cf. *Ger.* aufgeräumt *of good cheer*) on môde, Judth. Thw. 22, 39; Jud. 97. IV. *without obstruction, plainly, clearly*:—Emmanuhel, ðæt is gereht rûme: Nû is God sylfa mid ûs, Exon. Th. 9, 13; Cri. 134. V. *without contraction, in full*:—Ðê ic âsecgan ne mæg rûme âreccan (*relate at length*), ne gerîm witan heardra heteþonca, 261, 12; Jul. 314. [*O. Sax.* rûmur; *cpve. further*: *O. H. Ger.* rûmo *procul, longe.*]

rûmed (rûm-mêd?)-**lîc**; *adj. Ample, large, liberal*:—Hwæt rûmedlîces oððe micellîces oððe weorðfullîces hæfþ se eówer gilp? Bt. 18, 1; Fox 62, 21. Mid rûmedlîcum ælmessum, Shrn. 80, 10. v. *next word and* rûmmôd-lîc.

rûmedlîce; *adv.* I. *liberally*:—Hê swâ gifol is and swâ rûmedlîce gifþ, Bt. 38, 3; Fox 202, 14. Ða ic rûmodlîce (rûmmôdlîce?) gescarode, Cod. Dip. Kmbl. v. 331, 2. Ne ôðerra monna ne reáfiaþ, ne hiera rûmedlîce dǽlaþ, Past. 23; Swt. 177, 7. Ðonne hwâ ǽgðer ge mete ge hrægl þearfendum rûmedlîce (rûmodlîce, Hatt. MS.) selþ, 44; Swt. 326, 20. II. *at large, fully*:—Ðis ðæt wê nû feám wordum ârîmdon wê willaþ hwêne rûmedlîcor (*paulo latius*) âreccean, 12; Swt. 75, 17. Rûmerlîcor [rûmed-?] *latius, multiplicius*, Hpt. Gl. 420, 30. v. preceding word.

rûm-gâl; *adj. Rejoicing in ample space in which to move* (applied to the dove when sent from the ark):—Seó culufre wîde fleáh ôþ ðæt heó rûmgâl reste stôwe funde *far the dove flew, in flight unconfined rejoicing, until a place of rest she found* (cf. heó rûme fleáh, 87, 29; Gen. 1456), Cd. Th. 88, 16; Gen. 1466.

rûm-gifa, an; *m. A liberal giver*:—Hê wæs eallum rûmgifa *manu omnibus largus*, Bd. 3, 14; S. 540, 8. v. next word.

rûm-gifol; *adj. Liberal, bountiful, munificent*:—Rûmgifol, cystig *prodiga, larga*, Germ. 395, 18. Monig biþ âgiéta his gôda and wilnaþ mid ðý geearnigan ðone hlîsan ðæt hê sîe rûmgiful *se effusio sub appellatione largitatis occultat*, Past. 20; Swt. 149, 7. Ic Ôswald þurh ða rûmgiflan Godes cyste tô biscope gehâdod, Cod. Dip. Kmbl. ii. 400, 25. Hê gewende of Rôme mid ðam rûmgyfolan (-geofolan, MS. V.) þegne, Homl. Skt. i. 5, 330.

rûmgifolness, e; *f. Liberality, bounty, munificence*:—Seó rûmgifolnes (*largitas*) winþ ongeán ða gýtsunge, Gl. Prud. 65. Rûmgyfolnes, 67: 68–70. Hwâ âwent gîtsunge mid rûmgifulnysse bûtan strece? Homl. Th. i. 360, 6.

rûm-heort; *adj.* I. *of liberal heart, liberal, munificent*:—Rûmheort *dapsilis*, Wrt. Voc. ii. 27, 31. Rûmheort hlâford (*the Deity*), Hy. 7, 63. Mê wine Scyldinga fela leánode . . . rûmheort cyning, Beo. Th. 4227; B. 2110: 3602; B. 1799. Rûmheort beón mearum and mâþmum *to be liberal of gifts*, Exon. Th. 3391; Gn. Ex. 87. II. *with mind free from oppression, untroubled.* v. rûme, III:—Se weg ðe tô lîfe lǽt is ûs tô gefarenne mid rûmheortum môde and mid gôdum and glædum geþance *dilatato corde curritur via mandatorum Dei*, R. Ben. 5, 22.

rûmheortness, e; *f. Liberality, munificence*:—Syndon eahta heálîce mægenu . . . ðæt is rûmheortnys (*largitas*) . . . , Wulfst. 68, 19. Eahta sweras syndon ðe rihtlîcne cynedôm trumlîce up wegaþ . . . rûmheortnes (*largitas*), L. I. P. 3; Th. ii. 306, 20. Rûmheortnesse *liberalitatis*, Wrt. Voc. ii. 52, 32: 79, 52. Rûmheortnesse *liberalitatem*, 86, 52.

rûmian; *p.* ode *To get free from encumbrance*:—Ðonne rûmaþ him sôna se innaþ, Lchdm. i. 76, 13. v. rûm, I a.

rûm-lîc; *adj.* I. *gracious, liberal, benign*:—Rûmlîc *benignus* (*Deus*), Rtl. 104, 32. Rûmlîcum helpe *benigno favore*, 17, 35. II. *liberal, abundant, plentiful*:—Nû wille wê ðis âgunnene weorc mid rûmlîcum wæstme begân, Anglia viii. 300, 6. Se ðe mid fôdan ðære upplîcan lufe biþ gefylled, hê biþ swilce hê sý mid rûmlîcum mettum gemæst, Homl. Th. i. 522, 32. v. next word.

rûmlîce; *adv.* I. *largely, fully, at large, at length*:—Ðæt hî rûmlîce roccettaþ swîðe, Ps. Th. 143, 16. Ðâs þing rûmlîce gecýðan, Anglia viii. 303, 48. Ymbe ðâs þing rûmlîcor sprecan, 321, 36. Tôdǽledlîcor *vel* rûm[lîcor?] *differentius*, Wrt. Voc. ii. 140, 15. II. *liberally*:—Gif wê lustlîce and rûmlîce ða welan dǽlaþ earmum monnum ðe God ûs ǽr sealde, Blickl. Homl. 49, 32. III. *graciously, kindly, benignly*:—Rûmlîce *clementer*, Rtl. 89, 38: Mt. Kmbl. p. 16, 7. [Heó rumliche hit (*silver and gold*) ȝef þon kempan, Laym. 2452. *O. H. Ger.* rûmlîho *large.*]

rûm-môd; *adj.* I. *of liberal mind, liberal in giving*:—Hê þearfum rûmmôd (*largus*) wæs, Bd. 3, 6; S. 528, 11. Sýn wê rûmmôde þearfendum mannum and earmum ælmesgeorne, Blickl. Homl. 109, 14. Sellaþ ælmessan, beóþ rûmmôde ryhtra gestreóna, Exon. Th. 106, 30; Gû. 49. I a. *too liberal, profuse*:—Swâ ða rûmmôdan fæsthafolnesse lǽren swâ hî ða uncystegan on yfelre hneáwnesse ne gebrengen *sic prodigis praedicetur parcitas, ut tamen tenacibus periturarum rerum custodia non augeatur*, Past. 60; Swt. 453, 28. II. *benignant, gracious, kind*:—Rûmmôd and mildheart is God *benignus et misericors est Deus*, Rtl. 5, 8: Bt. 42; Fox 258, 22: Lk. Skt. Lind. 6, 35. Rûmmôd *clemens*, Rtl. 74, 10. *The word translates* paracletus, Rtl. 120, 1: Jn. Skt. Lind. 14, 16, 26: 15, 26.

rûmmôdlîc. v. next word.

rûmmôdlîce; *adv.* I. *liberally*:—Gîf wê bliþe and rûmmôdlîce hî (*the tenth part of our goods*) dǽlan willaþ earmum mannum, Blickl. Homl. 51, 10. II. *graciously, favourably*:—Rûmmôdlîce *propitius*, Rtl. 2, 5: 22, 38: *clementer*, 14, 36: *clementissime*, 98, 16.

rûmmôdness, e; *f.* I. *liberality*:—Ðýlæs ða rûmmôdnessa sió unrôtnes gewemme *ne largitatem tristitia corrumpat*, Past. 44, 3; Swt. 323, 10. II. *favour, grace, kindness*:—Snotor rûmmôdnise *sapiens benignitas*, Rtl. 105, 1. Rûmmôdnise *clementiam*, 41, 5: *propitiationem*, 17, 25.

rûmness, e; *f.* I. *breadth, a broad space*:—Ða rûmnisse Jericho feldes *latitudinem campi Jericho*, Deut. 34, 3. II. *breadth, amplitude, abundance*:—Wæs swâ mycel rûmnes on him ðæs hâlgan geleáfan and swâ mycele hê tô ðære Godes lufan hæfde *there was in him so great abundance of the holy belief, and he had besides so great love for God*, Guthl. 20; Gdwin. 82, 8.

rûm-well (= -full?) *spacious*:—Rûmwelle weg *spatiosa via*, Mt. Kmbl. Lind. 7, 13.

rûn, e; *f.* I. *a whisper* (v. rûnian), hence *speech not intended to be overheard, confidence, counsel, consultation* [cf. *Goth.* rûna niman *to take counsel*]:—On hyne nǽnig monna cynnes mihte wlîtan nymþe se môdiga hwæne neár hête rinca tô rûne gegangan (cf. gangan te rûnu, an rûna, Hel. 1273, 5064), Judth. Thw. 22, 7; Jud. 54. Gesittan tô rûne *to sit in consultation*, Beo. Th. 346; B. 172. Gesittan sundor tô rûne, Andr. Kmbl. 2324; An. 1163. Swâ cwæþ snottor on môde gesæt him sundor æt rûne *sat apart communing with himself* (cf. nim thû ina sundar te thî an rûna, Hel. 3227), Exon. Th. 293, 5; Wand. 111. Gefetigan tô rûne (cf. *Icel.* heita einn at rûnum *to consult*), 246, 15; Jul. 61: Elen. Kmbl. 2319; El. 1162. Eodon fram rûne, 821; El. 412. Rûne besittan, Andr. Kmbl. 1254; An. 627. Ic Sîward cinges þegen æt rǽde and æt rûnan (cf. þegno betst (*Peter*) te is herron sprak an rûnun, Hel. 3096), Cod. Dip. Kmbl. iii. 351, 17. Hê (*Christ*) feówertig daga folgeras sîne rûnum (cf. Jesus . . . being seen of them forty days, and speaking of the things pertaining to the kingdom of God, Acts 1, 3) ârêtte, Hy. 10, 36. II. *a mystery*, cf. gerýne:—Rûn biþ gerecenod, Cd. Th. 211, 12; Exod. 525. Bæd him âreccan hwæt seó rûn (*the dream*) bude, 250, 6; Dan. 542. Healdaþ æt heortan hâlge rûne, Exon. Th. 282, 1; Jul. 656: Elen. Kmbl. 666; El. 333. Dryhtnes word, hâlige rûne, 2336; El. 1169. Dêglum rûnum *mystice*, Jn. Skt. p. 4, 4. III. *a secret*:—Rûne healdan *to keep one's counsel*, Exon. Th. 338, 31; Gn. Ex. 87. IV. of that which is written, with the idea of mystery or magic:—Ðæt hê him bôcstafas ârǽdde and ârehte hwæt seó rûn (*the writing on the wall of Belshazzar's palace*) bude, Cd. Th. 262, 9; Dan. 741. Hæfdon hié on rûne and on rîmcræfte âwriten wera endestæf, Andr. Kmbl. 267; An. 134. V. *a rune, a letter.* v. rûn-stæf:—Enge rûne (*referring to* ᚾ = nîd), Elen. Kmbl. 2521; El. 1262. Rǽd sceal mon secgan, rûne wrîtan, leóþ gesingan, Exon. Th. 342, 7; Gn. Ex. 139. Hê hine âcsade hwæðer hê ða âlýsendlîcan rûne cûþe and ða stafas mid hine âwritene hæfde be swylcum menn leásspell secgaþ ðæt hine mon forðon gebindan ne mihte *interrogare coepit, an forte literas solutorias de qualibus fabulae ferunt, apud se haberet, propter quas ligari non posset*, Bd. 4, 22; S. 591, 25. [Ofte heo eoden to ræde ofte heo heolden rune (ȝeode to roune, 2nd MS.), Laym. 25332. Þan kaisere heo radden þat he write runen (writes makede, 2nd MS.), 25340. Godess dærne ræd and run, Orm. 18719. Godes derne runes and his derne domes, A. R. 96, 4. [*Goth.* rûna *counsel, a mystery*: *O. Sax.* rûna *counsel, conference*: *O. H. Ger.* rûna *susurrio, mysterium, litera*, v. Grff. ii. 523: *Icel.* rûn *counsel, mystery, a letter.*] v. beadu-, hete-, hyge-, inwit-, leóþu-, searo-, wæl-rûn.

-rûn *in* burh-rûn:—Burgrûne *Parcas*, Wrt. Voc. ii. 116, 10. [Cf. -rûn *in proper names in Icel.* e. g. Sig-, Öl-rûn: and see Grmm. D. M. 376.] v. -rûne.

-rûna. v. ge-rûna, hell-rûna (-rune?). [Cf. *Icel.* rûni *a counsellor.*] v. -rûne.

rûn-cofa, an; *m. The chamber of secret counsel, the mind, breast*:—Hê mæg on his rûncofan rihtwîsnesse findan on ferhþe fæste gehýdde (cf. ðonne fint hê ðǽr (on his gemynde) ða ryhtwîsnesse gehýdde, Bt. 35, 1; Fox 156, 11), Met. 22, 59.

rûn-cræftig; *adj. Skilled in explaining mysteries*:—Ne mihton ârǽdan rûncræftige men (cf. *the astrologers, Chaldeans, and the soothsayers*, Dan. 5, 7) engles ǽrendbêc (*the writing on the wall of Belshazzar's palace*), Cd. Th. 261, 31; Dan. 734.

-rûne. v. helle-, leód-rûne, burh-rûnan, *and* -rûn. [Cf. *Icel.* rûna *a counsellor.*]

rūnere, es; *m. A whisperer*:—Ðes rūnere *hic susurro*, Ælfc. Gr. 36; Som. 38, 51. [*O. H. Ger.* rūnari *susurro, musitator.*] v. next word.

rūnian; *p.* ode *To talk low, whisper, mutter*:—Ic rūnige *susuro*, Ælfc. Gr. 36; Som. 38, 53. Tōgeánes mē rūnedon (*susurrabant*) ealle fȳnd mīne, Ps. Spl. C. 40, 8. Ðeáh đē mon hwylces hlihge, and đū đē unscyldigne wite, ne rēhst đū hwæt hȳ rǣdon ođđe rūnion, Prov. Kmbl. 12. Ða rūniendan *musitantes*, Wrt. Voc. ii. 54, 72. Rūnigendum stefnum, Guthl. 5; Gdwin. 36, 1 note. [His egen to sen, his muđ to runien, O. E. Homl. ii. 107, 19. Ræden and runan (rouni, 2nd MS.), Laym. 2331. *Chauc. Piers P.* roune *to whisper*: *Prompt. Parv.* rounin *susurrare*: *O. L. Ger.* rūnan *susurrare*: *O. H. Ger.* rūnēn *susurrare, musare, musitare*: *O. Du.* rūnen.] v. reónian, rȳnan.

rūn-líc; *adj. Mystical*:—Færme his rūnlīce ł deóplīce *cenae ejus misticae*, Mk. Skt. p. 5, 11. Cf. rȳne-līc.

runol (*for* hrunol, cf. *Icel.* hrunull *foul-smelling*); *adj. Foul, stinking* (?):—Wiđ đȳ (đa, MS.) runlan āttre, Lchdm. iii. 36, 17.

rūn-stæf, es; *m. A* (*runic*) *letter, a rune.* Cf. rūn, V:—Ðrȳ sind in naman rūnstafas, Exon. Th. 440, 9; Rä. 59, 15. Ic mæg þurh rūnstafas rincum secgan, đam đe bēc witan, 429, 17; Rä. 43, 6. Wæs on đǣm scennum þurh rūnstafas rihte gemearcod, hwam đæt sweord geworht wǣre, Beo. Th. 3394; B. 1695. Ðā āxode se ealdorman đone hæftling hwæđer hē þurh drȳcræft ođđe þurh rūnstafas his bendas tōbrǣce, Homl. Th. ii. 358, 11. On the subject of Runes see Kemble's paper in Archaeologia, vol. xxviii; the Preface to Dr. George Stephens' Handbook of Runic Monuments; Dr. Isaac Taylor's Greeks and Goths, and the same writer's work 'The Alphabet.'

rūnung, e; *f. Whispering, soft speech*:—Seó sōđfæste fǣmne hyre lāca ne rōhte ne hyre rūnunga, Homl. Skt. i. 2, 149.

rūn-wita, an; *m.* I. *a privy councillor, one acquainted with a person's secrets*:—Deád is Æschere mīn rūnwita and mīn rǣdbora, Beo. Th. 2654; B. 1325. II. *one acquainted with mysteries, a sage*:—Rōf rūnwita (*Guthlac*), Exon. Th. 167, 30; Gū. 1068.

rupe (?):—Rupe (rūwe (?), cf. rūh) ođđe drisne *capillamenta* (cf. rawe, drisne *capillamenta*, ii. 128, 39), Wrt. Voc. i. 28, 73.

rusce, an; *f. Rushy ground* (?):—Tō đære wulfruscan, Cod. Dip. Kmbl. iii. 131, 7. v. rysc.

rust, es; *m. n.* (?) *Rust*:—Rust *erugo*, Wrt. Voc. ii. 107, 37: 29, 46. *Erugo* rust, ōm, *vel tinea* .i. *vitium frumenti* vel *ferri*, 144, 3: Mt. Kmbl. Lind. 6, 19. Rost, Txts. 60, 397. Of ruste vel ōme *erugine* .i. *rubigine*, Wrt. Voc. ii. 144, 5. Ðǣr wæs suīđe suīđlīc gesuinc and đeáh ne meahte monn him of āniman đone miclan rust. . . Hē wolde from ūs ādōn đone rust ūrra unþeáwa, Past. 37; Swt. 269, 11-15. Ǣrest ic wille beón gefremed in litlum weorce, đæt ic mǣge sum rust (sinnrust (?) v. syn-rust) on weg ādrīfan of mīnre tungan, Shrn. 35, 20. [*O. Sax.* rost: *O. H. Ger.* rost.] v. syn-rust.

rustig; *adj. Rusty*:—Ðā wurdon Janes dura fæste betȳned and his loca rustega *Jani portas ipse clausit. Quas obseratas otio ipsa etiam rubigo signavit*, Ors. 5, 15; Swt. 251, 21. [*O. H. Ger.* rostag *scabrosus.*]

rūte *rue.* v. rūde.

rūwa, an; *m. A rug, covering, tapestry*:—Hió becwiþ Eádgyfe līnnenne rūwan, Chart. Th. 537, 27. Ðeáh đe đa rīcestan hātan him reste gewyrcan of marmanstāne and mid goldfrætwum and mid gimcynnum eal āstǣned and mid seolfrenum rūwum and godwebbe eall oferwrigen, Wulfst. 263, 4. v. reówe, rȳhe.

ruxlan = hruxlan *to make a noise*:—Ruxlende *tumultuantes*, Mt. Kmbl. Rush. 9, 23. v. ge-hruxl.

rȳan (?), rȳn (cf. *for similar form of infinitive* þȳn); *p.* rȳde *To roar, rage*:—Hwȳ rȳđ (rȳnþ? v. rȳnan) ǣlc folc *quare fremuerunt gentes?* Ps. Th. 2, 1. Seó leó gif heó blōdes onbirigþ heó gemonþ đæs wildan gewunan hire eldrana onginþ đonne rȳn and hire racentan slītan (cf. *the corresponding passage in the Metres*: Onginþ racentan slītan, rȳn, grymetigan, Met. 13, 29) *si cruor horrida tinxerit ora, resides olim redeunt animi, fremituque gravi meminere sui, laxant nodis colla solutis*, Bt. 25; Fox 88, 13. [Cf. *O. H. Ger.* rohōn *rugire*, Grff. ii. 431.] v. rȳung.

rȳcels. v. rēcels.

ryddan (hryddan? v. hryding) *to strip*:—Ārydid *expilatam*, Wrt. Voc. ii. 108, 4.

ryden, es; *n. The name of some plant*:—Wirc beþinge, nim đæt reáde ryden, Lchdm. ii. 340, 5.

rȳe, rȳfe, ryft. v. rȳhe, rīfe, rift.

ryge, es; *m. Rye*:—Ryge *sicalia*, Wrt. Voc. ii. 120, 53: *singula*, i. 287, 18. Riges seofoþa, Lchdm. ii. 48, 20. [*Icel.* rugr; *m.*: cf. *O. L. Ger.* roggo: *O. H. Ger.* rokko.]

rygen; *adj. Rye, of rye*:—Of rigenum melwe, Lchdm. ii. 236, 9. Of sūrre rigenre grūt, 342, 17. Genim rigen healm and beren, 148, 11. Genim rigen mela, 148, 22.

rȳhe, rȳe, an; *f. A rug, rough covering, blanket*:—Rȳhae, rȳe *villosa*, Txts. 106, 1080. Hrȳhae, rȳae, rȳe *tapeta*, 102, 1020. Līnin rȳhae, rȳee *villa*, 106, 1081. Rīhum *tapetibus*, 114, 120. v. reówe, rūwa.

ryht. v. riht.

rȳman; *p.* de. I. *to make roomy, extend, spread, enlarge, amplify*:—Ðū rȳmdest *dilatasti*, Ps. Lamb. 4, 2. Hē ēđelþrym rȳmde and rǣrde, Cd. Th. 98, 24; Gen. 1635. Sōđ metod rȳmde, wīde wǣđde *spread and drove the waters widely*, 208, 7; Exod. 479. Ðæt se gītsere his land mid unryhte rȳme, Past. 44, 8; Swt. 329, 21. Hū feor wolde gē rȳman eówer land *quousque vos extenditis?* Swt. 331, 1. Ic eft reorde under roderum rȳman wille *I will multiply food again under heaven* (*after the deluge*), Cd. Th. 81, 13; Gen. 1344. Hira mearce tō rȳmanne *ad dilatandum terminum suum*, Past. 48, 2; Swt. 367, 15. Heora hūs tō rȳmende, Chart. Th. 436, 18. II. *to make clear by removing obstructions, to clear a way* (lit. and metaph.):—Hē sāwlum rȳmeþ līfwegas, Exon. Th. 148, 4; Gū. 739: 436, 6; Rä. 54, 10. Ðonne rȳmeþ hē đam deádan tō đam āþe đæt hine mōton his mǣgas unsyngian *by such conduct he clears the way for an oath on behalf of the dead man, so that his* (*the dead man's*) *kinsmen may exculpate him*, L. In. 21; Th. i. 116, 7. Gif getrȳwe gewitnes him tō āgenunge rȳmþ *make the way to possession clear for him*, L. Eth. ii. 9; Th. i. 290, 20. Ðæt syndan Antecristes þrǣlas đe his weg rȳmaþ, Wulfst. 55, 9. Ða đe ingang rȳmaþ, Salm. Kmbl. 442; Sal. 221. Se engel āwylte đæt hlid; nā đæt hē Criste ūtganges rȳmde, Homl. Th. i. 222, 9. Se engel rȳmde him weg þurh đæt fȳr, ii. 344, 13. Ic wille rȳman mīnne bertūn and mīne beornu geeácnian (*I will pull down my barns and build greater*, Lk. 12, 18), 104, 1: Wulfst. 286, 19. Seó sealf wile ǣrest đa dolh rȳman, and đæt deáde flǣsc of etan, Lchdm. ii. 332, 24. III. *to make room by removing one's self, yield, give place*:—Ic fare āweg ođđe ic rȳme (rume, MS. W.: hryme, hrime, other MSS.) *caedo* (cf. Wot no mon þe time wanne he sal henne rimen, O. E. Misc. 113, 170), Ælfc. Gr. 28, 4; Zup. 171, 9. Se ōđer rȳmþ him setl, Homl. Th. i. 248, 17. Rūmaþ, steppaþ *cedunt*, Wrt. Voc. ii. 19, 19: 87, 64. Rȳmde *cessit*, 81, 75. Ā man rȳmde (*retreated*) fram đære sǣ, and hī fērdon ǣfre forþ æfter, Chr. 999; Erl. 135, 35. Hī rīmdon heora feóndum *they left the field clear for their foes*, 1015; Erl. 152, 16. Rȳm đysum men setl *da huic locum*, Lk. Skt. 14, 9. Rȳmaþ him (*cease to oppose him*) đæt hē mē leng ne swence, Homl. Th. i. 534, 17. [*Laym.* rumen *to clear* (*a way*), *to yield, give place*: *R. Glouc.* rume *to clear* (*a way*): *Piers P.* roume *to keep clear of*: *O. Sax.* rūmian *to clear*: *O. Frs.* rēma: *O. H. Ger.* rūmman *cedere, abire, laxare*: *Icel.* rȳma *to make room, clear, to quit, leave.*] v. ge-rȳman.

rȳmet[t], es; *n.* I. *space, extent*:—Seó cyrce mid hire portice mihte fīf hund manna eáđelīce befōn on hire rȳmette, Homl. Th. i. 508, 14. Nā swylce on eástdǣle synderlīce sȳ his (*God's*) wunung . . . se đe ǣghwār is andweard nā þurh rȳmyt đære stōwe ac þurh his mægenþrymmes andweardnysse *he who is everywhere present, not through the extent of the place in which he dwells, but through the presence of his glory*, 262, 9. Eall đæt rȳmet đe eówer fōtswaþu on bestæpþ ic eów forgife *omnem locum, quem calcaverit vestigium pedis vestri, vobis tradam*, Jos. 1, 3. II. *clear space, room* (v. rȳmetleást):—Ðǣr næs nān rȳmet on đam gesthūse, Homl. Th. i. 30, 14. Hit is gedōn swā đū hēte, and hēr gyt is rȳmet æmtig, ii. 376, 9. III. *extension, clearance*:—Eádgār mid rȳmette (*by extending the limits of their property and so removing the claims which interfered with the monasteries standing within a ring fence*) gedīhligean hēt đa mynstra on Wintanceastre . . . and đet āsmeágan hēt, đæt nān đera mynstera đǣr binnan þurh þet rȳmet wiđ ōđrum sace næfde, ac gif ōđres mynstres ār on ōđres rȳmette lēge (*if the property of one monastery should lie within the part given by the extension to another*) đæt đes mynstres eáldor, đe tō đam rȳmette fēnge, ofeode đæs ōđres mynstres āre mid swilcum þingum swylce đam hīrēde, đæ đa āre āhte, gecwēme wǣre, Chart. Th. 231, 2-18. v. Lchdm. iii. 417 on this charter. IV. *extension of a person's well-being*:—Ða (*certain property*) ic gescarode mē sylfum and mīnum foregengum and eftyrgengum tō ēcum rȳmete *to the furtherance of the eternal well-being of myself and of my predecessors and successors*, Cod. Dip. Kmbl. v. 331, 3.

rȳmetleást, e; *f. Want of room*:—Maria hire sunu for rȳmetleáste (v. rȳmet, II) on ānre binne gelēde, Homl. Th. i. 34, 22.

rymg. v. rȳung.

rȳmþ, e; *f. Amplitude*; amplitudo (cited by Lye). [Heo bigunnen arumđe (*in large numbers*) ræsen to somne, Laym. 27492. *Prompt. Parv.* rymthe *spacium*; *oportunitas* vel *spacium temporis.*]

rȳn. v. rȳan.

rȳnan; *p.* de *To roar*:—Sume hī sǣdon đæt hió sceolde forsceoppan tō león, and đonne seó sceolde sprecan, đonne rȳnde hió, Bt. 38, 1; Fox 194, 34. Ða đe león wǣron ongunnon lāđlīce yrrenga rȳna (rȳnan (?), rȳan (?)), Met. 26, 84. v. rȳan.

ryne, es; *m. A course, run, running*, both in the sense of *motion* and in that of *the path in which motion takes place.* I. of a ship:—Ānes ceóles ryne on London *free entrance of one ship into the port of London* (cf. ego indico me dedisse unius navis incessum in portu Lundoniae, 220, 18-22), Cod. Dip. B. i. 221, 21. II. of other things, of the heavenly bodies, *an orbit*:—Nǣron nō swā gewīslīce ne swā endebyrdlīce hiora (*the various members of the created world*) stede and hiora ryne funden on hiora stōwum and on hiora tīdum gif ān unāwendendlīc God nǣre *non tam certus naturae ordo procederet, nec tam dispositos motus, locis, temporibus explicaret, nisi unus esset qui has mutationum varietates manens ipse disponeret*, Bt. 35, 2; Fox 158, 3. Roder *firmamentum*, ryne *cursus*, middaneard *mundus*, Wrt. Voc. i. 41, 57–59. Ðære sunnan ryne is swīđe rūm, and đæs mōnan ryne is swīđe nearo, Lchdm. iii. 248, 7–8. Siđđan wæs rodor ārǣred and ryne tungla gefæstnad, Exon. Th. 272, 13; Jul. 198. Ryne *curriculo, cursu*, Hpt. Gl. 457, 18. Ealle gesceafta symle sculon đone ilcan ryne eft gecyrran, Met. 11, 37. Đa mǣran tungl āwđer ōđres rene ā ne gehrīneþ, 29, 10. Tunglu đa đe ryne healdaþ, Cd. Th. 239, 13; Dan. 369. II a. metaph. *course, uninterrupted progress* (cf. that the word of the Lord may have free course, 2 Thes. 3, 1):—Se đe reorda gehwæs ryne gemiclaþ, đara đe noman Scyppendes þurh horscne hād hergan willaþ, Exon. Th. 4, 4; Cri. 47. III. of fluids, *a course, water-course, a flow, flux* of blood:—Đā ætstōd đæs blōdes ryne *fluxus sanguinis*, Lk. Skt. 8, 44: Mk. Skt. 5, 29. Seó eá ætstent on hire ryne, Jos. 3, 13. Hī nāmon twelf stānas on đæs streámes ryne *de medio Iordanis alveo*, 4, 8. Plantud nēh ryne (rynum, Ps. Th.) wetæra *secus decursus aquarum*, Ps. Spl. 1, 3. Wæter đa nū under roderum heora ryne healdaþ, Cd. Th. 10, 20; Gen. 159. Wiđ rynas wætera, Ps. Lamb. 1, 3. IV. of time, *course, cycle, lustre*:—Geár *annus*, tīd *tempus*, ryne *cursus*, Wrt. Voc. i. 52, 38–40. Ryne *cyclus*, rynum *cyclis*, ii. 20, 64–65: 137, 73. Đā se ryne đissa geára gefylled wæs *quo completo annorum curriculo*, Bd. 3, 9; S. 533, 9. Ryne *lustro*, Wrt. Voc. ii. 50, 42. V. *course* of life:—Honorius æfter đon đe hē đa gemǣro his rynes gefyllde of đissum leóhte leórde (*postquam metas sui cursus implevit*), Bd. 3, 20; S. 550, 25. Gif đū hine lufast on đīnes līfes ryne, đe đē is ungewiss, Basil admn. 8; Norm. 52, 8. VI. *currus* is translated by *ryne* in Ps. Spl. T. 67, 18 *and* Cant. Moys. Thw. 29, 10. [Bi his blodi rune þet ron inne monie studen, O. E. Homl. i. 207, 10. Þe stronge rune of þat blodi stream, Marh. 7, 12. Þer is mest neod hold hwon þe tunge is o rune, A. R. 74, 21. *Goth.* runs: *O. Frs.* blōd-rene: *O. H. Ger.* run *meatus*: cf. *Icel.* runi *a flux, stream*.] v. blōd-, eft-, forþ-, gegn-, on-, riht-, streám-, up-, ūt-ryne.

-ryne; *adj.* v. dæg-, hider-, hwider-ryne.

rȳne, es; *n. A mystery, mysterious saying*:—In rȳne *in misterio*, Lk. Skt. p. 3, 3. Tō wuttanne clǣne rȳne ł āsægdnise (*mysterium*) rīces Godes, Lind. 8, 10. Rȳne ongietan reádan goldes guman galdorcwide gleáwe beþuncan *let men understand the mysterious speech of the red gold* (*a ring which is represented as speaking*), *wisely consider its charm*, Exon. Th. 432, 26; Rä. 49, 6. Clǣno rȳno ł gesægdnise ł diópnise *mysteria*, Mt. Kmbl. Lind. 13, 11. v. ge-rȳne.

ryne-gæst, es; *m. A guest* or *foe that comes swiftly* (?), a term used for lightning:—Feá đæt gedȳgaþ đara đe gerǣcaþ rynegiestes wǣpen *few escape whom the lightning strikes*, Exon. Th. 386, 8; Rä. 4, 58.

rȳnegu *in* hel-rȳnegu *pythonissa*, Wrt. Voc. ii. 61, 20.

rynel, es; *m. A runner, messenger, courier*:—Rynel *cursor*, Wrt. Voc. i. 76, 24: Ælfc. Gr. 36; Som. 38, 24. Renel, Kent. Gl. 949. Pilatus hēt geclypian his ǣnne rynel and hym tō cwæþ: Yrn and clypa tō mē đone đe ys Jesus genemned. Se rynel swā dyde and myd mycehm ōfste wæs forþyrnende . . . Hī clypodon tō Pilate: Hēte đū đȳnne bydel and đȳnne rynel hym swā ongeán cuman? Nicod. 3; Thw. 2, 5–16: 4; Thw. 2, 19–36. Renula *cursorum*, Hpt. Gl. 406, 8. Rynela *concurrentium*, Anglia viii. 302, 33 (v. samod-rynel). v. for-rynel.

rynel, es; *m. A stream*:—Rynelas *rivos*, Ps. Spl. 64, 11: Blickl. Gl. cf. rinnelle.

rȳne-līc; *adj. Mystical*; mysticus, Hymn. Surt. 48, 25: 87, 15. v. ge-rȳnelīc, rūn-līc.

rȳnelīce; *adv. Mystically*; mystice, Hymn. Surt. 68, 13. v. ge-rȳnelīce.

rȳne-mann, es; *m. One skilled in explaining mysteries*:—Đa clamme đe đa rǣdellan wiđ rȳnemenn heóld, Exon. Th. 429, 32; Rä. 43, 13.

ryne-strang; *adj. Strong for the course*, Exon. Th. 400, 9; Rä. 20, 7.

ryne-swift; *adj. Swift in its course*:—Ofer uppan rodere ryne-swiftum, Met. 24, 28.

ryne-þrāg, e; *f. A space of time*:—Hȳ bīdinge mōstun tīdum brūcan . . . restan ryneþrāgum, Exon. Th. 115, 3; Gū. 184.

ryne-wægn, -wǣn, es; *m. A swift vehicle, a chariot*:—On ryne-wǣnum *in curribus*, Ps. Th. 19, 7.

rynge. v. renge.

rynig; *adj. Good at running*:—Sum biþ rynig, sum ryhtscytte, Exon. Th. 296, 14; Crä. 51. [Cf. (?) He gon to rusien swa þe runie (wode, 2nd MS.) wulf þenne he cumeđ of holte, Laym. 20123.] v. wīd-rynig.

ryniga (?), an; *m. Liquid that runs off* (?):—Wel mintan on sealtes rynian, Lchdm. ii. 76, 2. Genim rynian sealt[es], gehǣt, þweah mid đȳ, 156, 16.

rynning, e; *f. Rennet*; coagulum, Wrt. Voc. i. 27, 70. [*Gloucestershire* running *rennet*, E. D. S. Gloss. B. 4. '*Earning, yearning*, cheese-rennet, or that which curdles milk,' Brockett. '*Runnet*, called in Derbyshire *erning*; it runs the milk together,' Pegge. E. D. S. Gloss. C. 3.] v. ge-runnen.

rȳpe, rȳpan, rȳpere. v. rīpe, rīpan, rīpere.

ryplen (?); *adj. Made of broom*:—Ryplen (þȳfflen? v. þȳfel) *sparteus*, Germ. 399, 457.

rysć; *m. f.* (?): rysce, an; *f. A rush*:—Risc *juncus*, Wrt. Voc. i. 31, 30: ii. 112, 18. Risce, i. 68, 35. Resce *juncus* vel *scyrpus*, 79, 66. Spyrte biþ of rixum gebrōden. Rixe weaxst gewunelīce on wæter-igum stōwum, Homl. Th. ii. 402, 8–10. Risce *papyro, junco*, Hpt. Gl. 483, 69. Grōwnys hreódes and ricsa *viror calami et junci*, Bd. 3, 23; S. 554, 23. Ricsa wyrttruman, Lchdm. ii. 234, 8. Rixum *juncis*, Wrt. Voc. ii. 97, 21. Đā heó geseah đone windel on đām rixum (*in papyrione*), Ex. 2, 5. [*Ayenb.* resse: *Piers P.* rische, reshe, rusche: *Chauc.* rishe: *Prompt. Parv.* rische, rusche: *M. H. Ger.* rusch; *f. a rush*: *Du.* rusch; *n.* From Latin *ruscus*.] v. eá-(ǣ-, eó-)risc, -rixe.

rysc-bedd, es; *n. A bed of rushes*:—On đæt riscbed, Cod. Dip. Kmbl. iii. 428, 31.

rysce. v. rysc.

ryscen; *adj. Of rushes, rush*:—Riscene weocan *fila scirpea* (*juncea*), Germ. 391, 15.

rysc-leác, es; *n. Rush leek, rush garlick*; allium scharnoprassum:—Riscleác *allans* (*allium?*), Wrt. Voc. ii. 10, 40.

rysc-pytt, es; *m. A pit* or *pool in which rushes grow*:—In hriscpyt; of hriscpytte intō đere dīc, Cod. Dip. Kmbl. iii. 385, 2–3.

rysc-steort, es; *m. A promontory where rushes grow*:—Æt riscsteorte; of đam hriscsteorte, Cod. Dip. Kmbl. v. 217, 12–13.

rysc-þȳfel, es; *m. A rush-bed, bed of rushes*:—Riscþȳfel *juncetum*, Wrt. Voc. i. 63, 73: *juvencibus*, 287, 261. Risc *juncus*; riscþȳfel *jungetum*; riscþȳfel *juvencibus*, ii. 45, 75–77. Risc-, ry[s]c-thȳfel *jungetum*, Txts. 68, 517. Andlang đære dīc on riscþȳfel, Cod. Dip. Kmbl. v. 215, 4.

rysel, rysele, es; *m. Fat*:—Rysel *adeps*, Wrt. Voc. i. 71, 10: *axungia*, ii. 101, 37. Rysle *arvina*, 2, 61: 92, 15. Rysele, 80, 44. Rysle *ilium*, 48, 33. Genim hænne rysele . . . gōse rysele, Lchdm. ii. 40, 10–12. Swīnes rysl, Homl. Th. ii. 144, 29. Đū nimst đone rysel, Ex. 29, 13. Đū nymst đone rysle of đam ramme, 29, 22. Đone risel, Lev. 3, 9. Ryslas ealra eáfisca, Lchdm. ii. 30, 1. [*O. L. Ger.* rusli, hrusli *arvina*.]

ryđđa, an; *m. A large dog, mastiff, blood-hound*:—Ryđđa *molossus*, Wrt. Voc. i. 23, 35: 78, 52. Riđđa, ii. 56, 41. Hē getīgde ǣnne ormǣtne ryđđan innan đam geate đǣr Petrus inn hæfde, đæt hē hine ābītan sceolde, Homl. Th. i. 372, 34. v. rođ-hund.

rytran. v. a-ritrid *expilatam*, Txts. 58, 372.

rȳung (?), e; *f. Roaring, groaning, grunting*:—Ic wiste đæt swīn wǣron đǣm elpendum lāđe and hiora rymg (rȳung? v. rȳan) hié meahte āfyrhton *quorum grunnitas timere bestias noveram*, Nar. 21, 26. Hrīung (?) *suspirium*, Wrt. Voc. i. 19, 34.

S

For the Runic S see Sigel.

sā; *gen.* sān; *m. A tub, pail, vessel*:—Saa *libitorium*, Txts. 35, 17. [*Prompt. Parv.* soo *or* cowl, vessel *tina*. He kam to þe welle, water updrow, And filde þer a michel *so*, Havel. 933. *So, soa* a tub with two ears, to carry on a stang, Ray's North-country words. *Soa, soe* a tub; commonly used for a brewing-tub only, but sometimes for a large tub in which clothes are steeped before washing, E. D. S. Pub. Lincolnshire. 'In Bedfordshire, what we call a *coal* and a *coal-staff*, they call a *sow* and a *sow-staff*,' Kennett. *Icel.* sār *a cask*: *Dan.* saa: *Swed.* så.]

saban, es; *m.* (?) *A sheet*:—On sabanum, *id est* scēte *in sabanis* (cf. on scētum *in sabanis*, 48, 47), Wrt. Voc. ii. 82, 57. [In Mt. 27, 59 the Gothic version translates σινδόνι by *sabana*. *O. H. Ger.* saban, sapon; *m. sabanum, sindon, teristrum, linteum*: Gk. σάβανον: *Mid. Lat.* sabanum: *Span.* sabana *a sheet*. Diefenbach ii. 770 cites an Arabic word *sabaniyat* fine stuff for girdles, veils, etc., with the derivation of it from the name of the town Sabano near Bagdad.]

Sabat, es; *m.* (?) *The Sabbath*:—Sabates *sabbati*, Mt. Kmbl. p. 20, 5. [Cf. *Goth.* Sabbato, Sabbatus.]

Sabīne, a; *pl. The Sabines*:—Hū Rōmāne and Sabīne him betweōnum wunnon, Ors. 2, 4 tit.; Swt. 2, 19. Tō ānwīge gangan wiđ swā fela Sabīna, 2, 4; Swt. 72, 16.

Sabīnisc; *adj. Sabine*:—Đæt Sabīnisce gewinn, Ors. 2, 4; Swt. 68, 32: Swt. 72, 8.

sac. v. sacu.

sac (sæc?); *adj. Accused, charged, guilty*:—Swerian đæt hig nellan nǣnne sacleásan man forsecgean ne nǣnne sacne forhelan *let them swear that they will not bring a charge against an innocent man, nor conceal one who is justly charged*, L. Eth. iii. 3; Th. i. 294, 5. v. un-sac, sæc.

-saca. v. and-, ge-, wiđer-saca. [*O. Sax.* -sako: *O. Frs.* -seka: *O. H. Ger.* -sahho. Cf. *Goth.* ni sakjis ἄμαχος.]

sacan; *p.* sôc, *pl.* sôcon; *pp.* sacen. I. *to fight, strive, contend:*—Þeódscypas winnaþ and sacaþ heom betweónan, Wulfst. 86, 8. Hē geseh twegen Ebrēisce him betwȳnan sacan *conspexit duos Hebraeos rixantes*, Ex. 2, 13. Ic (*Beowulf*) sceal fōn wiđ feónde and ymb feorh sacan, Beo. Th. 883; B. 439. Gōd sceal wiđ yfele, līf sceal wiđ deáþe, leóht sceal wiđ þȳstrum, fyrd wiđ fyrde, feónd wiđ ōđrum, lāđ wiđ lāđe ymb land sacan, Menol. Fox 568; Gn. C. 53. Sceal fǣge sweltan and dōgra gehwam ymb gedāl sacan middangeardes, Exon. Th. 335, 4; Gn. Ex. 28. Đū tælnissum wiđ đa sēlestan sacan ongunne *thou didst attempt to strive with the best* (*the gods*) *with insults*, 254, 23; Jul. 206. Wǣran sacende *emulabantur*, Wrt. Voc. ii. 33, 10. II. *to disagree, act in opposition, not to be*, or *not to act, in unison, to wrangle:*—Đonne se abbod and se prāfost ungerāde beóþ and him betwyx sacaþ *dum contraria sibi inuicem sentiunt*, R. Ben. 124, 19. Ne đa ōđre ongeán đæt ne sacan (wiđcweđon, Wells Frag.) *the others shall offer no opposition to the decision*, 119, 2. Dōm stande đār þegenas sammǣle beón; gif hig sacan (*disagree*), stande đæt hig .viii. secgaþ, L. Eth. iii. 13; Th. i. 289, 3. Đæt hē sōce *altercaretur, sermocinaretur*, Hpt. Gl. 476, 67. III. of litigation, *to bring a suit:*—Đā sōc Wulfstān on sum đæt land *Wulfstan brought a suit laying claim to some of the land*, Chart. Th. 376, 7. IV. *to bring a charge against one, to accuse, blame:*—Hū micla wiđ đec sacas cȳđnessa *quanta adversum te dicant testimonia*, Mt. Kmbl. Lind. 27, 13. Mē mīne āgen word sylfne sōcon *verba mea execrabantur*, Ps. Th. 55, 5. Monige cȳđnisse leóse hiǽ gicwēdun tō sacanne wiđ him *multi testimonium falsum dicebant aduersus eum*, Mk. Skt. Rush. 14, 56. Swā hwæt þwyr and gebolgen mōd... sacendes hātheortnys hit is nā lufu þreáginge *quicquid protervus et indignus animus protulerit, objurgantis furor est, non dilectio correctionis*, Scint. 36. V. *to refuse, deny.* v. on-sacan:—Sæccendum sedlum *negatis sedibus*, Mt. Kmbl. p. 18, 14. [*Goth.* sakan *to strive, rebuke*: *O. Sax.* sakan *to rebuke, blame*: *O. H. Ger.* sahhan *litigare, increpare, objurgare*: *Icel.* saka; *wk. to fight, blame, accuse.*] v. æt-, be-, for-, fore-, ge-, of-, on-, ōþ-, wiđ-, wiđer-sacan; sacian.

sacc, es; *m. A sack, bag:*—Ne bere gē sacc ne codd *sacculum neque peram*, Lk. Skt. 10, 4. Sæc *sacculum*, Kent. Gl. 208. Hig fyldon hira saccas (*saccos*) and lēdon hira ǣlces feoh on his sacc... Đā undyde hira ān his sacc... hē đæt feoh geseah on his facces (*saculi*) mūþe, Gen. 42, 25, 28. Đā guton hig hira hwǣte of hira saccon, 42, 35. Fylle hira saccas and lege hira ǣlces feoh on his āgenne sacc, 44, 1. [*Goth.* sakkus: *O. H. Ger.* sac: *Icel.* sekkr.], Cf. bī-sæc, sæcc.

sacerd, es; *m. A priest* (the term is not confined to the Christian priesthood):—Sacerd *vel* cyrcþingere *sacerdos*, Wrt. Voc. i. 42, 23: Rtl. 125, 1. Hæfde se sacerd (*sacerdos*) on Madian seofon dohtra, Ex. 2, 16. Moises heóld his mǣges sceáp đæs sæcerdes on Madian, 3, 1. Putifares dohtor đæs sacerdes of đære byryg, Gen. 41, 45. Hē slōh đæs sacerdes (hēhsacerdas, Lind. Rush.) þeów, Mk. Skt. 14, 47. Đa word đæs sacerdes *vox praedicatoris*, Past. 21, 5; Swt. 163, 1. Đone clǣnan sacerd (*Christ*), Exon. Th. 9, 19; Cri. 137. Suīđe ryhte đa sacerdas (*sacerdotes*) sint gehātene sacerdas, đæt is on Englisc clǣnseras, forđæm hié sculon lātteówdōm gearwian đām geleáffulum, Past. 18, 7; Swt. 139, 14. Đa sacerdas of Leuies cynne, Deut. 27, 1, 14: Ps. Th. 77, 64. Moyses and Aaron sōđe sacerdas, 98, 6: Andr. Kmbl. 1483; An. 743. Đa mæssepreóstas wǣron đus gehātene... Đā đa gemynegodan sacerdos (-as?) cōman *erant presbyteri... Venientes memorati sacerdotes*, Bd. 3, 21; S. 551, 19. Đæra sacerda ealdor *princeps sacerdotum*, Mt. Kmbl. 26, 51: Blickl. Homl. 77, 8: 239, 28. Hȳrde wē đæt Jacob fore sacerdum swilt þrowode, Apstls. Kmbl. 141; Ap. 71. [From Latin. Anglo-Saxon alone seems to have borrowed this word.] v. ealdor-, heáh-sacerd.

sacerd-bana, an; *m. One who slays a priest:*—Hēr syndan sacerdbanan, Wulfst. 163, 27: 266, 27.

sacerd-gerisne; *adj. Befitting a priest:*—Hē hæfde sacerdgerisene ealdorlīcnysse *auctoritatem sacerdote dignam*, Bd. 3, 17; S. 545, 11.

sacerd-hād, es; *m. Priest-hood:*—Đā Zacharias his sacerdes hādes (sacerdhādes, MSS. A. B. C.) breác *cum sacerdotio fungeretur*, Lk. Skt. 1, 8. Æfter gewunan đæs sacerdhādes hlotes, 1, 9. Đæt hē gesette on sacerdhād Judas đam folce tō bisceope *that he might ordain Judas bishop of the people*, Elen. Kmbl. 2108; El. 1055. Bisceophādas *vel* sacerd-[hādas] *flaminea, i. episcopali gradu*, Wülck. 239, 23.

sacerd-land, es; *n. Land assigned to priests:*—Būtan đam sacerdlande *absque terra sacerdotali*, Gen. 47, 26.

sacerd-līc; *adj. Priestly, sacerdotal:*—Sacerdlīc *sacerdotium*, Rtl. 25, 31: *sacerdotalis*, 195, 4. Sacerdlīce þēnunge dōn *officium sacerdotale agere*, Bd. 4, 5; S. 573, 4. Be sacerdlīcum hræglum *de vestibus sacerdotum*, Bd. 5, 24; S. 647, 38.

sac-full; *adj.* I. *contentious, quarrelsome:*—Hē biþ swīđe sacful and micele ungeþwǣrnesse and mænigfealde saca on đære geferǣdenne wyrcþ *scandala nutriunt et dissensiones in congregatione faciunt*, R. Ben. 124, 8. Ne ǣnig man ne sȳ tō sacfull ne ealles tō geflitgeorn, Wulfst. 70, 19: Lchdm. iii. 428, 34. Sacful wīf *litigosa mulier*, Kent. Gl. 690. Mid secfullan (*rixosa*) wīfe, 790. [Ʒif þe cristene mon biđ sacful, O. E. Homl. i. 109, 1.] II. *given to accusation* (v. sacan, IV):—Ne beó đū sacfull *non eris criminator*, Lev. 19, 16.

sacian; *p.* ode *To strive, brawl:*—Gif men saciaþ *si rixati fuerint viri*, Ex. 21, 22. Fela sind đe wyllaþ fracodlīce him betwȳnan sacian *many there are that will shamefully brawl among themselves*, Homl. Th. ii. 294, 1. v. and-sacian; sacan.

sac-leás; *adj.* I. *free from charge* or *accusation, innocent:*—Swerian hig đæt hig nellan nǣnne sacleásan man forsecgean ne nǣnne sacne forhelan, L. Eth. iii. 3; Th. i. 294, 5. Fiónge mec habbaþ sacleósne (sacleás, Lind., cf. *Icel.* saklaust *without cause*) *odio me habuerunt gratis*, Jn. Skt. Rush. 15, 25. II. *free from charge* or *contention, unmolested, secure:*—On đæt gerād đæt đes cynges men sacleás beón mōston on đām castelan đe hī ǣr þes eorles unþances begiten hæfdon, Chr. 1091; Erl. 227, 9. Eádgār æþeling wæs gefangen; đone lēt se cyng syđđan sacleás faran, 1106; Erl. 241, 20. Sacleáso iwih wē gedōeþ *securos vos faciemus*, Mt. Kmbl. Lind. 28, 14. [Đo þe hadden on þesse liue alle here sunnes forleten and bet... alle he quađ hem saclese, O. E. Homl. ii. 171, 35. Wass Crist sacclæs o rode naȝȝledd, Orm. 1900. Sacles (*without strife, freely*) he let hin welden it so, Gen. and Ex. 916. *Icel.* sak-lauss *innocent, not guilty. Sackless* still remains in Northern dialects, but seems to have got a meaning, with which *innocent* also is used, that of *silly, simple.* v. Jamieson, Halliwell, and E. D. S. Publications.]

sacu, e; *f.* I. *strife, contention, dissension, sedition, dispute:*—Sacu *seditio*, Wrt. Voc. i. 21, 30. Seó sacu (*seditio*) ārās, Num. 16, 42. Wearđ sacu (*rixa*) betwux Abrames hyrdemannum and Lothes... Abram cwæđ tō Lothe: 'Ic bidde đæt nān sacu (*jurgium*) ne sig betwux mē and đē,' Gen. 13, 7, 8. Đanun mæg āspringan seó mǣste sacu and se mǣsta swice ealra ungeþwǣrnessa *exinde grauissima occasio scandalorum oriri potest*, R. Ben. 129, 8. Drihten cwæđ: 'Đonne gē gehȳraþ on middangearde gefeoht and sace ne beó gē āfyrhte.' Gefeoht belimpþ tō feóndum and sacu tō ceastergewarum. Mid đām wordum hē gebīcnode đæt wē sceolon þolian wiđūtan gewinn fram ūrum feóndum and eác wiđinnan fram ūrum nēhgebūrum lāđlīce ungeþwǣrnyssa, Homl. Th. ii. 538, 12–17. Hē (*Caligula*) mǣnde đæt đǣr đā næs swelc sacu swelc đǣr oft ǣr wæs, and hē self fōr oft on ōđra lond, and wolde gewin findan, ac hē ne mehte būton sibbe, Ors. 6, 3; Swt. 256, 28. Sceal Geáta leódum and Gār-Denum sib gemǣnum, and sacu restan, Beo. Th. 3719; B. 1857. Đæne đe wæs for sumere sace (*propter seditionem*) on cwerterne, Lk. Skt. 23, 25. Moises genemde đa stōwe Costung for Israhēla bearna sace *propter jurgium filiorum Israel*, Ex. 17, 7. Đæt hié under đære sibbe tō đære mǣstan sace becōme, Ors. 4, 7; Swt. 182, 28. Sace *militiam*, Hpt. Gl. 494, 70. Grendel wan wiđ Hrōđgār, wæg singale sæce, sibbe ne wolde, Beo. Th. 310; B. 154. Lǣt sace restan, lāđ leódgewin, Exon. Th. 254, 21; Jul. 200. Saca *lites*, Kent. Gl. 575. Of sacum *rixis*, 635. Ne mæg ic āna ācuman eówre saca (*jurgia*), Deut. 1, 12. Mænigfealde saca on đære geferǣdenne wyrcþ *dissensiones in congregatione faciunt*, R. Ben. 124, 9. II. *distress, trouble, affliction, persecution:*—Đǣr eów is sacu būtan ende grim gǣstcwalu *in hell is trouble without end for you devils, fierce torment of spirit*, Exon. Th. 142, 27; Gū. 650. Đǣr biþ ā gearu wrađu wannhālum wīta gehwylces sæce and sorge *there shall be ever ready for the wretched support against every infliction, against distress and care*, Elen. Kmbl. 2059; El. 1031. Ne þearft đū sār nīwigan and sæce rǣran (cf. Gi werđat ōk sō sālige thes iu saka biodat liudī *blessed are ye when men shall persecute you*, Hel. 1336), 1879; El. 941. Đǣr hē hæfþ eal sār and sace, hungor and þurst, wōp and hreám, and weána mā đonne ǣniges mannes gemet sȳ đæt hié āriman mǣge, Blickl. Homl. 61, 36. Seó sunsciéne slege þrowade, sace singrimme, Exon. Th. 256, 11; Jul. 230. III. *crime, guilt:*—Nis đǣr on đam londe synn ne sacu *non huc adit scelus infandum* (cf. O þatt an bukk he leȝȝde All þeȝȝre sake and sinne, Orm. 1335. He alātan mag saka endi sundea *he can forgive sins*, Hel. 1009), 201, 10; Ph. 54. Đā wæs synn and sacu Sweóna and Geáta, wrōht gemǣne, Beo. Th. 4935; B. 2472. IV. *a contention at law, a suit, cause, action:*—Nān sacu đe betweox preóstan sī ne beó gescoten tō world-manna sōme *no suit that there may be between priests shall be referred to the adjustment of secular men*, L. Edg. C. 7; Th. ii. 246, 3. Gif man ōđerne sace tihte *if one man bring a suit against another* (cf. ef man hwemu saka sōkea, Hel. 1522), L. H. E. 8; Th. i. 30, 11. Hit betere wǣre đæt heora seht tōgædere wurde đonne hȳ ǣnige sace hym betweónan heóldan *it would be better that they should come to an agreement than that they should carry on any suit between them*, Chart. Th. 377, 3. V. *jurisdiction in litigious suits.* For the first time apparently in charters of Edward the Confessor the phrase *sac and sōc* or *sōcn* occurs, and in them it is frequent. It is thus explained in the Latin version of an Anglo-Saxon charter where it is found:—Ic an heom ealswā đæt hȳ habben đǣrofer saca and sōcna *iis* (*sanctus Petrus et fratres Westmonasterienses*) *etiam concedens ut insuper habeant priuilegium tenendi curiam ad causas cognoscendas et dirimendas* *lites inter uasallos et colonos suos ortas, cum potestate transgressores et calumniae reos mulctis efficiendi easque leuandi*, Cod. Dip. Kmbl. iv. 202, 7, v. Stubbs, Const. H. i. 184, Cod. Dip. Kmbl. i. xliii sqq., Grmm. R. A. 854 sq. [*Laym*, sake *strife: O. and N.* cheste and sake: *Goth.* sakjō *strife: O. Sax.* saka: *O. L. Ger.* saca *res, causa: O. Frs.* sake, seke *causa, res: O. H. Ger.* sahha *lis, causa, occasio, negotium, res: Icel.* sök *a charge, a crime, a suit, cause, sake.*] v. sæcc.

-sacung. v. wiđ-, wiđer-, yfel-sacung.

sāda, an; *m. A cord, halter, snare*:—Swelce sādo (sāde, Rush.) *tamquam laqueus*, Lk. Skt. Lind. 21, 35. Grin biþ on sādan tōrænded *laqueus contritus est*, Ps. Th. 123, 7. Mid sāde (*laqueo*) hine āwrigde, Mt. Kmbl. Lind. 27, 5. [*O. H. Ger.* seito *laqueus, pedica, tendicula.*] v. wealh-sāda.

Sadducēas; *pl. The Sadducees*:—Eodun tō him Fariseas and Sadducēas, Mt. Kmbl. Rush. 16, 1. Sadducēa *Sadducaeorum*, 16, 6.

Sadducēisc; *adj. Sadducean*:—Hē hēt đa Saducēiscan stylle beón, Mt. Kmbl. 22, 34.

sadian; *p.* ode. I. *to satisfy, satiate.* [*O. H. Ger.* satōn *saturare.* Cf. *Icel.* seđja *to satisfy.*] v. ge-sadian. II. *to become satisfied, to get satiated* or *tired*:—Mē þincþ đæt đū sadige hwæt hwegnunges and đē þincen tō ǣlenge đās langan spell *methinks thou art getting somewhat wearied and these long discourses seem to thee too protracted*, Bt. 39, 4; Fox 218, 5.

sadol (-el, -ul), es; *m. A saddle*:—Sadol *sella*, Wrt. Voc. ii. 120, 33: i. 83, 70. Sadul, 23, 19. Hē hēht eahta mearas on flet teón, đara ānum stōd sadol, đæt wæs hildesetl heáhcyninges, Beo. Th. 2080; B. 1038. [*O. H. Ger.* satal, satul; *m.*: *Icel.* söđull; *m.*] v. seám-sadol.

sadol-beorht; *adj. Having a splendid saddle*:—þrió wicg sadolbeorhte (cf. sadol searwum fāh, since gewurđad, 2080: B. 1038), Beo. Th. 4356; B. 2175.

sadol-boga, an; *m. A saddle-bow*:—Sadolboga *carpella*, Wrt. Voc. i. 291, 16: ii. 128, 71. Sadulboga, 103, 4. Sadelboga, 17, 34: *corbus*, 22, 46. Sadulboga, i. 23, 18. [*Icel.* söđul-bogi: *O. H. Ger.* satalbogo.]

sadol-felg, e; -felge, an; *f. The pommel of a saddle*; pella (cf. Spanish *pella* a ball, anything made in a round form):—Sadulfelgae, -felge *pella*, Txts. 88, 818. Sadolfelg, Wrt. Voc. ii. 68, 9. Sadolfelg (? Wrt. radolfelt), i. 291, 15.

sadolian; *p.* ode *To saddle*:—Ic sadelige hors *sterno*, Ælfc. Gr. 28, 1; Som. 30, 34. [*Icel.* söđla: *O. H. Ger.* satalōn.] v. ge-sadelod.

sǣ; *m. f.*; *gen.* sǣs, sǣes, sǣ, sǣwe, seó; *nom. pl.* sǣs, sǣ; *dat.* sǣm, sǣum, sǣwum. *Sea.* The word is found in the following glosses:—Sǣ *mare* vel *aequor*, Wrt. Voc. i. 41, 62: 70, 13. Brym, sǣ *aequor*, 53, 50. Sǣ *lutex* (*latex?*), ii. 53, 17. Đæs ȳþiendan sǣs *fluctivagi ponti*, 149, 61. And sǣ *et salis*, 32, 28. Mid sǣ *cum pelago*, 21, 27. Ofer sǣ *citra pontum*, 18, 68. Đa hǣwnan sǣs *marmora glauca*, 57, 7. Sǣ *marmora*, 91, 73. I. *sea* (water as opposed to air and earth):—On đæm dæge gewīteþ heofon and eorþe and sǣ, and ealle đa þing đe on đǣm syndon, Blickl. Homl. 91, 21. God gescōp đone rodor betweoh heofone and eorþan and betweoh đǣm twǣm sǣum, đæm uplīcan and đæm niđerlīcan. Se uplīca sǣ . . . cēleþ đære tungla hǣto, and se rodor ymbfēhþ ūtan eall đās niđerlīcan gesceafte, sǣ and eorþan, Shrn. 63, 5–10. On syx dagum Crist geworhte heofenas and eorþan, sǣs and ealle gesceafta, L. Alf. 3; Th. i. 44, 13. II. *sea* (as opposed to land):—Đonne đū wyte đæt sǣ sī ful *at high water*, Lchdm. iii. 176, 18. Ūs drīfaþ đa ællreordan tō sǣ, wiđscūfeþ ūs seó sǣ đām ællreordum, Bd. 1, 13; S. 481, 44. Đæs sǣes flōdes weaxnes, 5, 3; S. 616, 16. On sǣs (sǣes, Lind.: sēæs, Rush.) grund *in profundum maris*, Mt. Kmbl. 18, 6. For gedrēfednesse sǣs swēges, Lk. Skt. 21, 25. Sǣs earm, Ors. 1, 1; Swt. 24, 6, 14. Gang tō đæs sǣs waroþe . . . Hē eode tō đære sǣ, Blickl. Homl. 231, 29–36. Gān ofer sǣs ȳþa, 177, 18. Geswencede of đisse sǣwe hreónesse, 233, 26: 235, 1. Hreónesse đære sǣwe, 235, 5. Monigra ceápstōw of lande and of sǣ cumendra, Bd. 2, 3; S. 504, 19. Bāt on sǣwe, Exon. Th. 458, 12; Hy. 4, 99: Andr. Kmbl. 1029; An. 515. Æt fulre seó, Lchdm. iii. 178, 18. On siewe (?sǣwe), Cant. Moys. Thw. 29, 4. Đā mētte hié micel ȳst on sǣ, Chr. 877; Erl. 78, 18. Hié micel đæs folces ofer sǣ ādrǣfdon, 878; Erl. 78, 30: Bd. 1, 15; S. 484, 7. Ofer đone sǣ, 1, 12; S. 481, 2. Gif hwā his āgenne geleód bebycgge ofer sǣ, L. In. 11; Th. i. 110, 4. God gecīgde đa drīgnesse eorþan and đæra wætera gegaderunga hē hēt sǣs, Gen. 1, 10. Sǣs up stigon, Cd. Th. 83, 6; Gen. 1375. Đæt đās deópan sǣ drī geweorđaþ, Ps. Th. 65, 5. Beūtan eallum sǣwum, 138, 7. III. *sea* (as opposed to water inland):—For hwī ne fixast đū on sǣ? (cf. ic wyrpe max mīne on eá, 23, 9). Hwīlon ic dō, ac seldon, for đam micel rēwyt mē ys tō sǣ, Coll. Monast. Th. 24, 1–5. Sǣs tōslūpan, eal sealt wæter, Lchdm. iii. 36, 27. IV. *a sea*:—Him is be-eástan se sǣ đe man Arfatium hǣt, and westan and be-norþan Creticum se sǣ, Ors. 1, 1; Swt. 26, 32: 28, 1. Nēh đæm clife đære Reádan sǣs, Swt. 12, 20. Be đære reódan sǣ, Ex. 14, 9. Betwih đære sǣ seó is nemned Adriaticus, Blickl. Homl. 197, 21. V. of inland water, *a sea, lake*:—Sume men secgaþ seó eá đǣr wyrcþ micelne sǣ *aliqui auctores ferunt fluvium vastissimo lacu exundare*, Ors. 1, 1; Swt. 12, 24. On đære sǣ *in the sea* (*of Galilee*), Mt. Kmbl. 8, 24. [*Goth.* saiws: *O. Sax.* sēo, sēu: *O. Frs.* sē: *O. H. Ger.* sēo: *Icel.* sær, sjór, sjár; *gen.* sævar; *dat.* sævi, sæ.] v. eást-, heáh-, norþ-, Ost-, Wendel-, west-, wīd-sǣ.

sǣ-æbbung. v. æbbung.

sǣ-ǣl, es; *m. A sea-eel*:—Sǣǣl *murenula* (cf. *hec murenula* a lamprun, i. 222, col. 2), Wrt. Voc. ii. 57, 74.

sǣ-ælfen[n], e; *f. A sea-elf, sea-nymph*:—Sǣælfenne *Naiades*, Wrt. Voc. ii. 62, 32: 59, 12. Sǣelfen, i. 60, 18.

sǣ-bāt, e; *f. A sea-boat*:—On sǣbāte, Andr. Kmbl. 876; An. 438: 980; An. 490. Ic on holm gestāh, sǣbāt gesæt, Beo. Th. 1270; B. 633: 1795; B. 895.

sǣ-beorh *a sea-hill, a hill* or *cliff against the sea*:—Ealle gerīman stānas on eorþan, steorran on heofonum, sǣbeorga sand (MS. sund; but cf. Ic đīnne ofspring gemenigfylde swā swā steorran on heofenum and swā swā sandceosol on sǣ, Gen. 22, 17), Cd. Th. 205, 25; Exod. 441. Hū geweard đē đæt đū sǣbeorgas sēcan woldes, merestreáma gemet, ofer cald cleofu ceóles neósan, Andr. Kmbl. 615; An. 308.

sǣ-burh *a maritime town*:—Hē gewunade in *Capharnaum đæt is sǣburug (-caestrae, Rush.) *habitavit in Capharnaum maritima* (*note on Capharnaum: In đær byrig Capharnaum is genemned and maritimam cuoed, forđon đyú burg is on sǣ), Mt. Kmbl. Lind. 4, 13. [*Icel.* sæborg *a sea-side town.*]

sæc; *adj.* I. *hostile, offensive, hateful*:—Tō āscamelīcum *ad detestabilem, ad odiosum*, sæcum *invisum, exosum*, meltestran hūse *lupanar*, Hpt. Gl. 500, 58–62. v. next word. II. *guilty, charged with guilt.* v. on-sæc, sac; *and* cf. *Icel.* sekr *guilty, convicted.*

-sæc. v. and-, eoful-, wiđer-sæc.

sæcc, es; *m. Sacking, sack-cloth*:—Hē ārās of đam wācan sæcce đe hē lange onuppan dreórig wæs sittende, Homl. Skt. i. 23, 802. Đū slite hǣran (sæcc, MS. C.) mīne *conscidisti saccum meum*, Ps. Spl. 29, 13. v. sacc, sæccing.

sæc[c], e; *f. Strife, contest, conflict*:—Ā wæs sæc, Elen. Kmbl. 2512; El. 1257. Đǣr biþ ceóle wēn slīđre sæcce *there* (*at the rocky shore*) *the vessel may expect fierce conflict*, Exon. Th. 384, 17; Rä. 4, 29. Hē sæcce ne wēneþ tō Gār-Denum, Beo. Th. 1205; B. 600. Se æt sæcce gebād wīghryre wrāđra, 3241; B. 1618: 1910; B. 953. Đam æt sæcce weard Weohstān bana mēces ecgum *Weohstan felled him in fight with the edge of the falchion*, 5218; B. 2612. Nægling geswāc æt sæcce (*in fight with the fire-drake*), 5355; B. 2681. Tīr geslōgon æt sæcce *gained glory in battle*, Chr. 937; Erl. 112, 4: Erl. 114, 8. Æt sæcce forweorþan *to perish in battle*, Judth. Thw. 25, 32; Jud. 289. Æt wīgge spēd, sigor æt sæcce, Elen. Kmbl. 2363; El. 1183. Hē feorg gesealde æt sæcce, Apstls. Kmbl. 117; Ap. 59. Ic ofslōh æt đære sæcce (*the battle with Grendel's mother*) hūses hyrdas, Beo. Th. 3334; B. 1665. Hē tō sæcce bær wǣpen wundrum heard *he to battle bore a weapon wondrous hard*, 5366; B. 2686. Se đe sæcce genæs *he who came safe from conflict* (*Beowulf*), 3959; 1977. Sæcce sēcean, 3982; B. 1989. Nō hē him đam sæcce ondrēd, ne him đæs wyrmes wīg for wiht dyde, 4684; B. 2347. Sæcce fremman *to fight*, 4991; B. 2499: Exon. Th. 496, 28; Rä. 85, 21. Hī hæfdon sæcce gesōhte, sceolde sweordes ecg feorh ācsigan, Andr. Kmbl. 2265; An. 1134. Hē wælfǣhþa dǣl sæcca gesette *he composed many a deadly feud and quarrel*, Beo. Th. 4062; B. 2029. Cf. sacu.

sæccan (?) *to fight, contend*:—Oft ic sceal wiđ wǣge winnan and wiđ winde feohtan, somod wiđ đām sæcce (? sæcce fremman *or* sēcan, v. *preceding word*; *but* cf. *also* sacian, sacan), Exon. 398, 3; Rä. 17, 2.

sæccing, es; *m. Sacking, a bed made of sacking*:—Hī on sæccingum (*in grabatis*) bǣron đa untruman, Mk. Skt. 6, 55. v. sæcc.

sæc-dōm, sǣ-ceaster. v. sceac-dōm, sǣ-burh.

sǣ-ceosol *sand* or *gravel on the sea-shore*:—Sǣceosol *arena maris*, Gen. 32, 12. Sǣcysul *calculus*, Wrt. Voc. i. 38, 23.

sæcg, sæcgan, sæcgen. v. secg, secgan, sægen.

sǣ-cir[r] *the retreat of the sea* (*when the waves drew back and left a passage for the Israelites*), Cd. Th. 196, 13; Exod. 291.

sǣclian. v. sīclian.

sǣ-clif *a cliff by the sea*:—Swā fela welena swā đara sondcorna beóþ be đisum sǣclifum, Bt. 7, 4; Fox 22, 27.

sǣ-cocc, es; *m. A cockle*:—Hwæt fēhst đū on sǣ? Crabban muslan sǣcoccas *cancros, musculos, neptigallos*, Coll. Monast. Th. 24, 11. [Cf. a farthing-worth of muscles were a feste for suche folke, oþer so fele Cockes (cokkys, MS. G.: cokeles, MS. I.), Piers P. C text x. 95. *Welsh* cocs *cockles.*]

sǣ-col, es; *n. Jet*; gagates, Wrt. Voc. ii. 42, 25.

sǣ-cyning, es; *m. A sea-king, a king who was powerful on the sea*:—Helm Scylfinga, đone sēlestan sǣcyninga đara đe in Swióríce sinc brytnade, Beo. Th. 4754; B. 2382. [*Icel.* sæ-konungr.]

sæd; *adj. with gen. Sated, weary, filled, having had one's fill* (the word is not used in the sense of modern *sad*):—Sæd *effetus*, i. *plenus*, Germ. 396, 215. Đǣr læg secg mænig . . . wērig wīges sæd *many a warrior lay dead there* . . .: *of war had had his fill*, Chr. 937; Erl. 112,

20. Beadoweorca sæd, Exon. Th. 388, 4; Rä. 6, 2. Wiste wlonc and wines sæd, 369, 11; Seel. 39. Swiđe ǽtan and sade wurdan *manducaverunt et saturati sunt nimis*, Ps. Th. 77, 29. Hí sæde wǽron *saturavit eos*, 80, 15. [*Goth.* saþs: *O. Sax.* sad: *O. L. Ger.* sad: *O. H. Ger.* sat *satur*: *Icel.* saðr (saddr).] v. hilde-, un-, wín-sæd; sadian.

sǽd, es; *n.* I. *seed, what is sown, that part of a plant which propagates*:—Senepes sǽd *granum sinapis*, Mk. Skt. 4, 31. Đæt treów sceolde sǽde eft onfón *the tree should again bear seed*, Cd. Th. 251, 12; Dan. 562: 252, 24; Dan. 583. Ealle treówu đe habbaþ sǽd on him silfon heora ágenes cynnes *universa ligna quae habent in semetipsis sementem generis sui*, Gen. 1, 29. Đam men đe seów gód sǽd on his æcyre, Mt. Kmbl. 13, 24. Út eode se sǽdere his sǽd tó sáwenne, Mk. Skt. 4, 3. Swylce man wurpe gód sǽd (*sementem*) on his land, 4, 26. I a. fig. *seed, that from which anything springs*:—Đæt háligе sǽd gewát, đæt him ǽr of đæs láreówes múþe bodad wæs, Blickl. Homl. 55, 29. Đeáh biþ sum corn sǽdes gehealden symle on đære sáwle sóđfæstnesse: đæs sǽdes corn biþ simle áweaht mid áscunga, Met. 22, 37–41. Gif wé eów đa gástlícan sǽd sáwaþ, Homl. Th. ii. 534, 26. II. *the ripe fruit, that from which the seed is taken*:—Hí heora sylfra sǽd sníþaþ *they shall reap their crops*, Ps. Th. 125, 5. Se háta sumor giereþ and drígeþ sǽd and blǽda, Met. 29, 61. III. *fruit, growth*:—Of wlite wendaþ wæstma gecyndu, biþ seó síđre tíd sǽda gehwylces mǽtræ in mægne, Exon. Th. 105, 1; Gú. 16. IV. *sowing*, v. sǽd-tima:—Sǽd and geríp sumor and winter ne geswícaþ *sementis et messis, aestas et hiems non requiescent*, Gen. 8, 22. V. applied to animals, *seed, progeny, posterity*:—Sǽd *crementum* (in a list 'de homine et de partibus ejus'), Wrt. Voc. i. 282, 26: ii. 16, 39. Weres sǽd, 44, 55. Mín sǽd him þeówaþ, Ps. Th. 21, 29. Đæt sǽd đara unrihtwísra forwyrđ, 36, 28. Tó Abrahame wæs cweþende đæt his sǽd oferweóxe ealle đás woruld, Blickl. Homl. 159, 26. Swá hé spræc tó Abrahame and hys sǽde, Lk. Skt. 1, 55. Đæt his bróđor nime his wíf and his bróđor sǽd wecce, Mk. Skt. 12, 19. [*Goth.* mana-séþs: *O. H. Ger.* sát: *Icel.* sáđ *seed, crop.*] v. god-, lín-, un-, wád-sǽd.

sǽd-berende *seed-bearing*:—Eorþe swealh sǽdberendes (v. sǽd, V) Sethes líce, Cd. Th. 69, 33; Gen. 1145. Gréwende wirte and sǽdberende *herbam viventem et facientem semen*, Gen. 1, 29.

sǽd-cynn, es; *n.* *A kind of seed*:—Ǽghwilc sǽdcyn *omne genus seminarum*, Wrt. Voc. i. 55, 30. Sǽdere gebyreþ đæt hé hæbbe ǽlces sǽdcynnes ǽnne leáp fulne, đonne hé ǽlc sǽd wel gesáwen hæbbe ofer geáres fyrst, L. R. S. 11; Th. i. 438, 9.

Sǽ-Dene; *pl.* *The sea-Danes, Danes of the islands* (?), or *Danes skilled in sea-faring* (?):—Sigehere lengest Sǽ-Denum weóld, Exon. Th. 320, 13; Víd. 31. Cf. Sǽ-Geátas.

sǽ-deór, es; *m.* *A sea-beast* (cf. Milton's 'that sea-beast Leviathan'):—Hine swencte on sunde sǽdeór monig, Beo. Th. 3025; B. 1510. Hé hét his ágene men hine sǽndan on đone sǽ, and đa sǽdeór hine sóna forswulgon, Shrn. 54, 27. Hý mon wearp in sǽdeóra seáþ, 133, 11. Gif hit on Frigedæig þunrige, đæt tácnaþ sǽdeóra cwealm, Lchdm. iii. 180, 17. [*Icel.* sjó-dýr.]

sǽdere, es; *m.* *A sower*:—Sǽdere *sator, seminator*, Hpt. Gl. 461, 73. Sum sǽdere férde tó sáwenne his sǽd, Homl. Th. ii. 88, 12: Mk. Skt. 4, 3. Be sǽdere, L. R. S. 11; Th. i. 438, 8. v. next word.

sǽdian; *p.* ode *To sow, provide seed for land*:—Folgere gebyreþ đæt hé on twelf mónþum .ii. æceras geearnige, óđerne gesáwene and óđerne unsáwene; sǽdige sylf đæne *he must provide the seed for the latter himself*, L. R. S. 10; Th. i. 438, 5.

sǽd-leáp, es; *m.* *A basket* or *other vessel of wood carried on one arm of the husbandman, to bear the seed which he sows with the other, a seed-leap* (Essex), *seed-lip* (Oxford). v. E. D. S. Pub. B. 18; also *seed-lop*, v. Old Country and Farming words, iii. Hopur or a seed lepe *satorium, saticulum*, Prompt. Parv. 246. A sedlepe *saticulum*, Wülck. Gl. 609, 28: *semilio*, 611, 11:—Sǽdleáp, Anglia ix. 264, 13. [Đæt acersǽd hwǽte, đæt is twegen sédlǽpes, and đæt bærlíc, đæt is þré sédlǽpas, and đæt acersǽd áten, đæt is feówer sédlǽpas, Chr. 1124; Erl. 252, 34–36. In the note on this passage *seed-lip* is said to be still used in Somersetshire.] v. leáp.

sǽd-líc; *adj.* *Seminal*:—Séd sǽdlíc *semen seminalem*, Rtl. 146, 17.

sǽdnaþ, es; *m.* *Sowing*:—Sǽdnaþ *satio, seminatio*, Wrt. Voc. i. 37, 50.

sædness, e; *f.* *Satiety, repletion*:—Óþ sædnesse *ad congeriem, congestionem, nauseam, satietatem*, Germ. 391, 30.

sǽ-draca, an; *m.* *A sea-dragon, sea-serpent*:—Sǽdracan *leviathan* .i. *serpens aquaticus*, Hpt. Gl. 424, 55. Gesáwon æfter wætere wyrmcynnes fela, sellíce sǽdracan, sund cunnian, Beo. Th. 2856; B. 1426.

sǽd-tíma, an; *m.* *Seed-time, time for sowing*:—Sǽdtíma and hærfest, sumor and winter ne geswícaþ nǽfre, Hexam. 7; Norm. 12, 28. [*Icel.* sáđ-tími *the sowing season.*] v. sǽd, IV.

sǽ-earm, es; *m.* *An arm of the sea*:—Scýt se sǽearm up of đæm sǽ westrihte, Ors. 1, 1; Swt. 22, 4.

sǽ-ebbung, -elfen. v. sǽ-æbbung, -ælfenn.

sǽ-færeld *a sea-passage*, used in reference to the attempt made by the Egyptians to pass the Red Sea:—Đá hí (*the Egyptians*) oninnan đæm sǽfærelde wǽron, Ors. 1, 7; Swt. 38, 33.

sǽ-fæsten *the fastness* or *stronghold which the sea constitutes*:—Óþ đæt sǽfæsten landes æt ende leódmægne forstód *the sea was a stronghold which blocked the further passage of the Israelites*, Cd. Th. 185, 24; Exod. 127.

sǽ-faroþ *the sea-shore*:—Ceólas léton æt sǽfearoþe sande bewrecene, Elen. Kmbl. 501; El. 251. Sæfaroþa sand, Cd. Th. 236, 18; Dan. 323. v. sǽ-waroþ.

Sæfern, e; *also indecl. f.* *The river Severn*:—Hié gedydon innan Sæferne múþan, Chr. 918; Erl. 102, 24. On Sæferne staþe, 894; Erl. 92, 23. Hié gedydon æt Sæferne, đá fóron be Sæferne . . . be westan Sæfern, 92, 14–20. Be Sæfern, 896; Erl. 94, 15. Be westan Sæferne, Bd. 5, 23; S. 646, 21. Of Seferne, Cod. Dip. Kmbl. iii. 393, 10. Of Sæfern, 405, 29. Westweardes on Sæferne, ii. 150, 9, 14. *Latin forms in the charters are* Saberna, i. 64, 11: Sabrina, 84, 2: Saebrina, ii. 59, 18.

Sæfern-múþa, an; *m.* *The mouth of the Severn*:—On súþhealfe Sæfernmúþan, Chr. 918; Erl. 104, 4: 997; Erl. 134, 8.

sǽ-fisc, es; *m.* *A sea-fish, fish that lives in the sea*:—Fleógende fuglas and sǽfiscas *volucres coeli et pisces maris*, Ps. Th. 8, 8. Swelaþ sǽfiscas, wǽgdeóra gehwylc swelteþ, Exon. Th. 61, 19; Cri. 987. Óđre sǽfisca cynn, 363, 19; Wal. 56. [Ifulled mid gode sæfisce, Laym. 22550. *Icel.* sæ-fiskr.]

sǽ-flód, es; *m. n.* I. *an incoming tide, flood* (as opposed to *ebb*):—Grécas hátaþ *malina* sǽflód đonne hyt wixst, and *ledon* đonne hyt wanaþ (cf. *ledona* népflód *vel* ebba, *malina* heáhflód, Wrt. Voc. i. 57, 11–12), Anglia viii. 327, 29. Wæs án burg sió wæs néh đæm sǽ óþ án sǽflód com and hié áwéste *civitas repentino maris impetu abscissa, atque desolata est*, Ors. 2, 7; Swt. 90, 20. On đissum geáre com đæt mycele sǽflód, and ærn swá feor up swá nǽfre ǽr ne dyde, and ádrencte feala túna, Chr. 1014; Erl. 151, 14. Đises geáres ásprang up tó đan swíđe sǽflód, and swá mycel tó hearme dyde swá nán man ne gemunnet đæt hit ǽfre ǽror dyde, 1099; Erl. 235, 24. Sǽflóde *indruto*, Wrt. Voc. ii. 48, 27. II. *the sea, the water of the sea*:—Đá fandode forþweard scipes (*Noah*) hwæđer sincende sǽflód wǽre, Cd. Th. 86, 28; Gen. 1437. Heofen and eorþe síde sǽflódas *coeli et terra, mare*, Ps. Th. 68, 35. [He lætte bi sæflode ȝearkien scipen gode, Laym. 2630.]

sǽ-flota, an; *m.* *A ship*:—Næs him cúđ hwá đam sǽflotan sund wísode, Andr. Kmbl. 761; An. 381. [Cf. He makede muchul sæflot, Laym. 4530.]

sǽ-fór, e; *f.* *A journey by sea, a voyage*:—Nis đæs módwlonc mon ofer eorþan . . . đæt hé á his sǽfóre sorge næbbe, Exon. Th. 308, 19; Seef. 42.

sǽ-fugol *a sea-fowl.* Sǽfugl, as a proper name, occurs in the genealogy of Ælle of Northumbria, Chr. 560; Erl. 16, 29. [*Icel.* sjó-fugl.]

sǽgan; *p.* de *To cause to sink*:—Óþ đæt seó sunne on súþrodor sǽged weorđeþ (cf. Só giségid wurđ sedle náhor hédra sunna, Hel. 5715), Exon. 207, 15; Ph. 142. v. on-sǽgan; sígan.

-sǽge. v. on-sǽge.

sǽ-geáp; *adj.* *Roomy enough for sea voyages* (of a ship):—Sǽgeáp naca, Beo. Th. 3797; B. 1896.

Sǽ-Geátas; *pl.* *The seafaring* (?) *Geats*:—Đa Sǽ-Geátas sélran næbben tó geceósenne cyning ǽnigne, Beo. Th. 3704; B. 1850. Sǽ-Geáta (*Beowulf and his companions*) síđas, 3976; B. 1986. Cf. Sǽ-Dene.

sægedness *a sacrifice*, Mk. Skt. Lind. Rush. 12, 33. v. on-sægedness.

sǽ-gemǽre, es; *n.* *A sea-border, coast*:—Sǽgemǽro *maritima*, Lk. Skt. 6, 17. On đám sǽgemǽrum, Mt. Kmbl. 4, 13.

sægen, sæcgen, segen, e; *f.* I. *a saying, statement, assertion*:—Đá sægde se Clitus đæt Philippus máre hæfde gedón đonne hé. Hé đá Alexander áhleóp, and hiene for đære sægene ofslóg, Ors. 3, 9; Swt. 130, 30. Heora biscopas from hiora godum sǽden đæt hié đæt gefeoht forbuden. Ac Papirius đa biscepas for đære sægene swíđe bismrade, 3, 10; Swt. 140, 2. Se Hǽlend cwæđ: 'Ic sittende beó æt mínes Fæder swíđran.' Đá cwæđ se ealdorbiscop: 'Hwæt þincþ eów be đissere segene, Homl. Th. ii. 248, 22: 320, 31: 484, 1. Gyf hé đé segþ đæt hé hwethwugu gesáwe . . . hweđer đé áwuht æt his segene tweóge, Shrn. 196, 17. Đú ne tweódast ymbe Honorius segene, hwí tweóst đú ymbe hera þegena sæcgena, 197, 21–23. Hié sǽdon đæt sió sibb of his mihte wǽre ac hé fleáh đa sægene *he would not admit what they said*, Ors. 3, 5; Swt. 106, 33. Sægenum *assertionibus*, Wrt. Voc. ii. 3, 62. Hié wiston be đæs engles sægenum, ge be heora sige ge be đara hǽđenra manna fleáme, Blickl. Homl. 203, 3. Sæcgenum, Ps. Th. 144, 7. II. *what is said generally, tradition, report, story*:—Đæt is fyrn sægen (fyrn-sægen? cf. fyrn-gewrit, -gid) *it is an old story*, Andr. Kmbl. 2977; An. 1491. Ic wolde gewitan hweđer sió segen sóđ wǽre đe mé mon be đon sægde *I wanted to know whether the story I had been told about it was true*, Nar. 24, 15. Of ealdra manna gewritum ođđe sægene *ex scriptis vel traditione priorum*, Bed. pref.; S. 472, 19. Se hlísa đe þurh yldra manna segene tó ús becom *opinio quae traditione majorum ad nos perlata est*, 2,

1; S. 501, 2. On gewritum oððe on ealdra manna sægenum *munimentis literarum vel seniorum traditione*, pref.; S. 471, 27. Sægenum *scriptis*, 472, 5. III. *a narration, relation* (whether spoken or written):—Ðý læs ðæt eów seó sægen monigfealdlīcor biþ onþūhte tō wrītanne ic ða wille lǣton ðe ðǣr gewurdon *ne sim scribendi multiplex, priora facta praecognita praetereo*, Nar. 3, 29. [*Icel.* sögn *a tale, report.*] v. ge-, sōþ-sægn, eald-gesegen.

sǣ-genga, an; *m.* I. *a sea-goer, a mariner*:—Ða gleáwe sǣgenga (gleáwan sǣgehgan?) wel hig understandaþ ðæt eorþlīce līchamlīce beóþ fulran on weaxendum mōnan ðonne on wanigendum *the skilful mariners well understand that earthly, corporeal things are fuller with a waxing than with a waning moon*, Anglia viii. 327, 21. II. *a vessel, ship*:—Sǣgenga fōr, fleát fāmigheals forþ ofer ȳðe, bundenstefna ofer brimstreámas, Beo. Th. 3821; B. 1908: 3769; B. 1882.

sǣ-geset, es; *n. A maritime district*:—Saegesetu (-seotu) *promaritima*, Txts. 82, 728. Sǣgesetu, Wrt. Voc. ii. 68, 33.

sægl, -sægness, sægnian. v. sigel, on-sægness, segnian.

sǣ-grund (*or* sǣ (*gen.*) grund), es; *m. The depth of the sea, the bottom of the sea*:—Ne mē forswelge sǣgrundes deóp *neque obsorbeat me profundum*, Ps. Th. 68, 15. Paulus āwrāt be him sylfum, ðæt hē ǣnne dæg and āne niht on sǣgrunde ādruge, Homl. Th. ii. 574, 14. Sǣgrunde neáh (cf. ðis fis (*the whale*) wuneð wið ðe se grund, Misc. 16, 517), Beo. Th. 1133; B. 564. Þurh ðone sǣgrund (*profundum maris*, cf. tō sǣs grunde, l. 18, *and* on sǣs grund, Mt. Kmbl. 18, 6) is getācnod hira ende, Past. 2; Swt. 31, 20. Fān Gode besenctun on sǣgrund sigefæstne wer, Menol. Fox 421; Men. 212. Ic styrge wīde sǣgrundas, Exon. Th. 382, 12; Rä. 3, 10: Cd. Th. 196, 9; Exod. 289.

-sægung. v. on-sægung.

sǣ-hengest, es; *m.* I. *a sea-horse, hippopotamus*:—Sǣhengest *ipotamus*, Wrt. Voc. ii. 48, 30. II. *a sea-steed, ship*:—Hū ðū wǣgflotan, sǣhengeste, sund wīsige, Andr. Kmbl. 975; An. 488. Cf. sǣ-mearh.

sǣ-hete (*or* sǣ (*gen.*) hete), es; *m. Raging of the sea*:—Mid ðȳ wē wið ðam winde and wið ðam sǣ (sǣhete, MS. Ca.) campodan *cum vento pelagoque certantes*, Bd. 5, 1; S. 613, 27.

sǣ-holm, es; *m. Sea*:—Sǣholm oncneów, gārsecges begang, ðæt ðū gife hæfdes, Andr. Kmbl. 1058; An. 529.

sæht, sæhtlian. v. seht, sahtlian.

sæl, sel, es; *n. A hall*:—Ic seah rǣplingas in ræced fergan under hrōf sales, Exon. Th. 435, 3; Rä. 53, 2. Gæst yrre cwom, ðǣr wē sæl weardodon, Beo. Th. 4157; B. 2075. Ne gōd hafoc geond sæl swingeþ, 4520; B. 2264. Hȳ sæl timbred (æltimbred, MS., the alliteration requires *s*) ongytan mihton; ðæt wæs foremǣrost receda, 620; B. 307. Heorot (*Hrothgar's hall*), sincfāge sel, 336; B. 167. Geond ðæt sīde sel, Andr. Kmbl. 1523; An. 763. Wuna salu sinchroden *halls splendidly decorated*, 3342; An. 1675. Salo, Cd. Th. 113, 3; Gen. 1881. Gesāwon ofer since salo hlifian, reced ofer reádum golde, 145, 10; Gen. 2403. [Wyn for to schenche, after mete in sale, Horn. 1107. Þyse renkeȝ schal neuer sitte in my sale my soper to fele, Allit. Pms. 41, 107. Such a freke watȝ neuer in þat sale er þat tyme, Gaw. 197. *O. H. Ger.* sal *exsolium, coenaculum*; daz sal *templum*: *Icel.* salr *a hall.*] v. beág-sel, burg-, folc-, horn-sæl; sele, salor.

sǣl, es; *m.*: e; *f.* I. *time, occasion*:—Ðā becom se apostol æt sumum sǣle (*on one occasion*) tō ðære byrig Pergamum, Homl. Th. i. 62, 24: 70, 23. On sumne sǣl *quandoque*, Ælfc. Gr. 38; Som. 40, 66. Heora wīse on nǣnne sǣl wel ne gefōr, Ors. 4, 4; Swt. 164, 13. Ðās wyrte man mæg niman on ǣlcne sǣl *this plant may be gathered at any time*, Lchdm. i. 112, 3. II. *a fit time, season, opportunity, the definite time at which an event should take place*:—Ðēh ðe seel sīe *etiamsi oportuerit*, Mt. Kmbl. Lind. 26, 35. Ðā Godan sǣl þūhte ðā gesōhte hē ðone kynincg *when it appeared to Goda a favourable opportunity, he visited the king*, Chart. Th. 202, 30. Hī wundiaþ, ðonne se sǣl cymeþ, Fragm. Kmbl. 43; Leás. 23. Ðā wæs sǣl and mǣl, ðæt tō healle gang Healfdenes sunu *it was the proper time for Hrothgar to go to the banquet-hall*, Beo. Th. 2021; B. 1008. Ōþ ðæt sǣl ālamp (cf. Ðā seó tīd gelamp, ðæt . . ., Met. 26, 17) ðæt hió Beówulfe medoful ætbær *till the proper time arrived for her to present the mead cup to Beowulf*, 1249; B. 622: 4123; B. 2058. Ic ofslōh æt ðære sæcce ðā mē sǣl āgeald (*when opportunity was offered me*: cf. ðā him rūm āgeald 5374; B. 2690) hūses hyrdas, 3335; B. 1665: Cd. Th. 121, 11; Gen. 2008. Seó sǣl geweard (cf. seó tīd geweard, ðæt se eorl ongan ædele cennan, 74, 25; Gen. 1227), ðæt his wīf sunu on woruld brohte, 72, 14: Gen. 1186. Se sǣl cymeþ, ðæt heó dōmes dæges dyn gehȳre, Salm. Kmbl. 648; Sal. 323. Ne mihte nā lengc manna ǣnig hine sylfne bedyrnan ac gehwā tō sǣles (*at once*) mōste clipian, Homl. Skt. i. 23, 115. Wit þencaþ sǣles bīdan siððan sunne Metod up forlǣt *we intend to wait till after sunrise*, Cd. Th. 147, 10; Gen. 2437. Sǣles bīdeþ hwonne heó cræft hyre cȳþan mōte, Exon. Th. 413, 28; Rä. 32, 12. Hē sōhte ða seel (sēl, Rush.) ðætte hine salde *quaerebat opportunitatem ut eum traderet*, Mt. Kmbl. Lind. 26, 16. III. *time* as in *bad* or *good times, circumstance, condition.* v. IV:—Nū is sǣl (*a time of misery*) cumen, þreá ormǣte, Andr. Kmbl. 2332; An. 1167. Storm oft holm gebringeþ in grimmum sǣlum *storm oft brings ocean into a furious condition*, Exon. Th. 336, 20; Gn. Ex. 52. Jacob byþ on glædum sǣlum *exultabit Jacob*, Ps. Th. 52, 8. Hæfdan beorgas blīðe sǣle *montes exultaverunt*, 113, 14. Sael gewynsumie roeðe *casus secundet asperos*, Ps. Surt. ii. 201, 11. IV. *happiness, good fortune, good time, prosperity* (often in pl.):—On ðære stōwe wē gesunde māgon sǣles bīdan, Cd. Th. 152, 21; Gen. 2523. Mæg snottor guma sǣle brūcan, gōdra tīda, Exon. Th. 104, 12; Gū. 6. Sǣlum geblissad *gladdened with all joys*, 207, 12; Ph. 140. Siteþ sorgcearig, sǣlum bidǣled, 379, 5; Deór. 28. Syngum tō sǣlum (cf. After liked him ful wele for al was turned him to sele, C. M. 4432) *for the happiness of sinners*, 84, 21; Cri. 1377. Ne trīn ðū æfter sǣlum, sorh is genīwod, Beo. Th. 2648; B. 1322. ¶ On sǣlum, sālum *in a state of happiness, happy* [cf. þu ware a sele gief ich was wroð, O. E. Homl. ii. 183, 17. Heora færð wes on sæle *was prosperous*, Laym. 1310. Selden sal he ben on sele (selde wurþ he blyþe and gled, Jes. MS.), Misc. 121, 301]:—Þā wæs þeód on sǣlum (*joyous*), Beo. Th. 1291; B. 643. On sālum, 1218; B. 607. Ðū on sǣlum wes *be fortunate*, 2345; B. 1170. On sǣlum *in times of prosperity*, Met. 2, 2, 7. Folc wæs on sālum, Cd. Th. 184, 13; Exod. 106: 214, 5; Exod. 564: Elen. Kmbl. 387; El. 194. [All middellærdess sceþe and sel, Orm. 14304. For quoso suffer cowþe syt (*trouble*), sele wolde folȝe, Allit. Pms. 92, 5. *Goth.* sēlei *goodness*: *Icel.* sæla *bliss, joy, happiness.*] v. gyte-, heáh-sǣl; sǣlþ.

sǣ-lāc *a gift* or *present* or *offering that comes from the sea* or *from a lake*:—Beówulf maþelode: Hwæt wē ðē ðās sǣlāc (*what B. had brought to Hrothgar from Grendel's lake-dwelling*) brohton tīres tō tācne, Beo. Th. 3308; B. 1652: 3253; B. 1624.

sǣ-lād *a course* or *way on the sea*:—Wē on sǣlāde (*in our course*) brecaþ ofer bæðweg, Andr. Kmbl. 1022; An. 511. Hie on sǣlāde wīf tō Denum feredon *they on the watery way took the woman to Denmark*, Beo. Th. 2319; B. 1157. Hē tō gyrnwræce swīðor þohte ðonne tō sǣlāde *his thoughts were turned rather to vengeance effected by wiles than to taking his way over the sea*, 2283; B. 1139. [Cf. *Icel.* sjó-leiði *a sea-way*; sjó-leiðis *by sea.*]

sǣ-lāf *what is left by the sea*, applied to the spoils of the Egyptians drowned in the Red Sea:—Ongunnon sǣlāfe dǣlan, ealde mādmas, reáf and randas, Cd. Th. 215, 16; Exod. 584.

sǣlan; *p.* de *To happen, betide, fortune* (e. g. in Spenser):—Gif hié ærfeweard ne gestriónen, oððа him sylfum ælles hwæt sǣle . . . Gif him elles hwæt sǣleþ, Chart. Th. 471, 30–472, 1. Sǣlde unc on þām brocum swā unc gesǣlde (sǣlde, Kmbl.) *happen what might to us in those troubles*, 485, 23. Hū ðē sǣle *how it may happen to thee, what your success may be*, Andr. Kmbl. 2710; An. 1357. v. ge-, tō-sǣlan.

sǣlan; *p.* de. I. *to fasten with a cord*:—Hē sǣlde tō sande sīdfæðmed scip oncerbendum fæst, Beo. Th. 3838; B. 1917. Wedera leóde sǣwudu sǣldon, 457; B. 226. Hwǣr wē sǣlan sceolon sǣhengestas ancrum fæste, Exon. Th. 54, 3; Cri. 863. Ymb geofenes stæþ gearwe stōdon sǣlde sǣmearas, Elen. Kmbl. 455; El. 228. II. fig. *to restrain, repress, confine*:—Dōmgeorne dreórigne hyge oft in heora breóstcofan bindaþ fæste. Swā ic mōdsefan mīnne sceolde oft feterum sǣlan, Exon. Th. 287, 29; Wand. 21. Sǣlde sǣgrundas *the bound sea-depths* (in contrast with the relaxing of the bonds which held the sea, when a passage was made through it for the Israelites), Cd. Th. 196, 9; Exod. 289. [*Goth.* in-sailjan.] v. ā-, ge-, on-, un-sǣlan; sāl.

sǣ-land *a maritime district*:—Mīn gafolfisc ðe mē ārīst be sǣlande *maritimos pisces qui mihi contingere debent annualiter per thelonei lucrum*, Chart. Th. 308, 1. [Cf. *Icel.* Sjó-land (*a local name*).]

sæld. v. seld.

sælen; *adj. Of sallow*:—Sælenum *salignis*, Wrt. Voc. ii. 89, 50. [*O. H. Ger.* salahin *salignus.*] v. sealh.

sǣ-leoda. v. sǣ-lida.

sǣ-leóþ *a sea-song, song sung by the sailors in rowing, to keep stroke*:—Sǣleóþes *celeumatis* (κέλευμα), Wrt. Voc. ii. 22, 24.

sǣ-līc; *adj. Of the sea*:—On sǣlīcum strande *on the sea-shore*, Homl. Th. ii. 62, 10. Of sǣlīcum grunde, 138, 11. On sǣlīcere ȳde *in the water of the sea*, 138, 8. Hī fixodon on sǣlīcum ȳðum, i. 576, 21. Gedrēfed on ðām sǣlīcum ȳðum ðyssere worulde, ii. 388, 7. On sǣlīcum *in glarigeris*, Hpt. Gl. 465, 3: *in marinis*, 473, 71. Ðæt hī Seaxna þeóde ofer ðām sǣlīcum (? of ðām ofersǣlīcum) dǣlum him on fultum gecȳgdon *ut Saxonum gentem de transmarinis partibus in auxilium vocarent*, Bd. 1, 14; S. 482, 39. Ic rōwe ofer sǣlīce dǣlas *navigo ultra marinas partes*, Coll. Monast. Th. 26, 33. Drihten gegaderode ða sǣlīcan ȳða fram ðære eorþan brādnysse, Hexam. 6; Norm. 10, 16. Ða sǣlīcan nȳtenu (*two seals*), Homl. Th. ii. 138, 15. v. ofersǣ-līc.

sǣ-lida, -leoda, an; *m. A sea-goer, sailor*:—Snottor sǣleoda (*Noah*), Cd. Th. 201, 18; Exod. 374. Gehȳrst ðū, sǣlida! . . . brimmanna boda! Byrht. Th. 133, 4; By. 45. Ic ǣfre ne geseah ǣnigne mann ðē gelīcne steóran ofer stæfnan . . Ic georne wāt ðæt ic ǣfre ne geseah on sǣleodan syllīcran cræft *I have never seen in a seaman more wondrous skill*, Andr. Kmbl. 999; An. 500. Nǣfre ic sǣlidan sēlran mētte, 941;

An. 471. Offa ðone sǽlidan slôh, Byrht. Th. 140, 10; By. 286. Cf. sǽ-líðend.

sǽlig *blessed, fortunate.* [*O. Sax.* sâlig: *O. L. Ger.* sâlig, sêlig: *O. H. Ger.* sâlig *beatus, felix.*] v. earfoþ-, ge-, gewif-, heard-, ofer-, un-, wan-sǽlig, *and next word.*

sǽliglíce; *adv. Happily*:—Sêliglîce *feliciter*, Rtl. 79, 30. [*O. Sax.* sâliglîko: *O. H. Ger.* sâliglîhho *feliciter.*] v. ge-sǽliglíce.

sǽligness. v. ge-sǽligness.

sǽ-líðend, es; *m. A seaman, sailor, seafarer; also a ship,* cf. sǽ-genga:—Secgaþ sǽlíðend, Beo. Th, 826; B. 411: 3640; B. 1818: 5604; B. 2806. Sægdon sǽlíðende, 760; B. 377. Se ðe bisenceþ sǽlíðende, eorlas and ýðmearas, Exon. 363, 4; Wal. 48. [*O. Sax.* sêo-lîðandi.]

sǽ-líðende; *adj. Seafaring*:—Se mǽra wæs hâten sǽlíðende weallende Wulf, Salm. Kmbl. 422; Sal. 211. [Sæ-liðende men, Laym. 7821.]

sælmerige, an; *f. Brine*:—Sælmerige (sæll-, sel-; -mærige) *salsamentum*, Ælf. Gr. 30; Zup. 192, 18. [Cf. *Span.* salmuera *brine*: *Ital.* salamoja: *Fr.* saumure: *Lat.* sal-muria; cf. *Gk.* ἅλμυρος *briny.*]

sælþ, e; *f. A dwelling, abode*:—Bare hié gesâwon heora lîchaman næfdon on ðam lande ðá giet sælþa gesetena *bare they* (*Adam and Eve after the fall*) *saw their bodies, they had not yet in the land dwellings appointed*, Cd. Th. 48, 33; Gen. 785. [*O. Sax.* seliða; *f. a dwelling*: *O. L. Ger.* salitha, selitha *tabernaculum, habitaculum*: *Goth.* salithwa; *f. a mansion, lodging, guest-chamber*: *O. H. Ger.* salida, selida; *f. mansio, domicilium, habitaculum.*]

sǽlþ, e; *f. Happiness, joy, felicity, good fortune, prosperity* (the word is generally in the plural):—Ic nû hæbbe ongiten ðæt ða mîne sǽlþa and seó orsorgnes ðe ic ǽr wênde ðæt gesǽlþa beón sceoldan nâne sǽlþa ne sint *I have now seen that my prosperity and security, that I supposed were certainly happiness, are none*; non infitiari possum prosperitatis meae velocissimum cursum, Bt. 10; Fox 26, 25-27. Hâtan ðæt sǽlþa ðe nâne ne beóþ, 16, 3; Fox 56, 25. Âfyr fram ðê ða yfelan sǽlþa and unnettan *gaudia pelle*, 6; Fox 14, 32. Ðæm men þincþ ðeáh hê sê godcundlîce gesceádwîs ðæt hê on him selfum næbbe sǽlþa genôge bûton hê mâre gegaderige ðara ungesceádwîsena gescefta ðonne hê beþurfe *divinum merito rationis animal, non aliter sibi splendere, nisi inanimatae supellectilis possessione videatur*, 14, 2; Fox 44, 19. Ys micel niédþearf ðæt mon hiene wið ða ungemetlîcan sǽlþa warenige, Past. 27; Swt. 189, 6. Hý weorðgeornra sǽlþa tôslîtaþ *they destroy the fortunes of the ambitious*, Salm. Kmbl. 697; Sal. 348. Heofenas blissiaþ sealte sǽstreámas sǽlþe habbaþ, Ps. Th. 95, 11. [*O. Sax.* sâlda: *O. L. Ger.* sâlda *salus, salutare*: *O. H. Ger.* sâlida *felicitas, beatitas, bona fortuna*; v. Grmm. D. M. pp. 822 sqq. on Sǽlde=*Fortuna*: *Icel.* sæld *bliss.*] v. ge-, ofer-, un-, woruld-sǽlþ.

sæltna (?) *a bird's name*:—Saeltna, Wrt. Voc. ii. 119, 37: seltra, i. 281, 8: salthaga, 62, 36 gloss *rubisca* which is in the last case also glossed by *rudduc* the robin redbreast. v. rudduc.

sǽl-wang, es; *m. A fertile plain, plain*:—Hê be wealle geseah wundrum fæste under sǽlwange sweras unlytle *by the wall he saw huge pillars with their bases wondrous fast underground*, Andr. Kmbl. 2984; An. 1495. Hwîlum mec mîn freá fæste genearwaþ, sendeþ ðonne under sǽlwonge (MS. sal-), Exon. Th. 382, 27; Rä. 4, 2. Ic geseah hors ofer sǽlwong þrægan, 400, 3; Rä. 20, 3. Hê geseah sîde sǽlwongas synnum gehladene, Cd. Th. 78, 14; Gen. 1293.

sǽ-mann, es; *m.* I. *a seaman, one who journeys by sea*:—Sǽmen æfter fôron flôdwege, Cd. Th. 184, 11; Exod. 105. Sǽmanna sîð, 208, 4; Exod. 478. Gâras, sǽmanna searo, Beo. Th. 663; B. 329. Hê sǽmannum onsacan mihte, 5900; B. 2954. Sigel sǽmannum symble byþ on hihte, Runic pm. Kmbl. 342, 15; Rûn. 16. II. when English affairs are referred to the word is used of the Scandinavians:—Wâlâ ðære woruldscame ðe nû habbaþ Engle. Oft twegen sǽmen oððe þrý drîfaþ ða drâfe cristenra manna fram sǽ tô sǽ, Wulfst. 163, 5. Mê sendon tô ðê sǽmen snelle, Byrht. Th. 132, 41; By. 29. Gif ðû wille syllan sǽmannum feoh, 132, 58; By. 38. Hê his sincgyfan on ðâm sǽmannum wrec, 139, 63; By. 278. [*Icel.* sjó-maðr *a seaman, mariner.*]

sǽ-mearh *a sea-horse, a ship*:—Ûs bær heáhstefn naca, snellîc sǽmearh, Andr. Kmbl. 533; An. 267. Meahte gesión brimwudu myrgan, sǽmearh plegan, Elen. Kmbl. 490; El. 245. Fearoþhengestas, sǽmearas, 455; El. 228. Heáhstefn scipu, sǽmearas, Exon. Th. 361, 5; Wal. 15. [For similar terms in Icelandic v. Corpus Poeticum Boreale, vol. ii. p. 458.] Cf. sǽ-hengest.

sǽmend, sǽmest, sǽmestre. v. sêmend, sǽmra, seámestre.

sǽ-mêðe; *adj. Weary with being on the sea*:—Sǽmêðe (*Beowulf and his companions on their arrival at Hrothgar's palace*), Beo. Th. 655; B. 325.

sǽ-minte, an; *f. Sea-mint*:—Sǽminte *nereta* (cf. sea-minte *nereta*, Lchdm. iii. 304, col, 1), Wrt. Voc. i. 68, 39: *althea*, 68, 79.

sæmninga. v. semninga.

sæmotu (?) glosses *fustrum* (*frustum*?), Wrt. Voc. ii. 152, 10.

sǽmra; *adj.* (without positive) *Inferior, worse*:—Symle wæs ðý sǽmra ðonne ic sweorde drep ferhþgeníðlan *ever was the deadly foe the worse when I struck him with the sword*, Beo. Th. 5752; B. 2880. Hit is sǽmre nû *it is worse now* (*than in the golden age*), Met. 8, 42. Ic lǽre ðæt hê gýme ǽgðer ge ðæs sêlran ge ðæs sǽmran *I advise him to take care both of the more and of the less important matters*, Anglia ix. 260, 10. Hnâhran rince, sǽmran æt sæcce, Beo. Th. 1910; B. 953. Gif ðû sôðne God lufast. . . Gif ðû tô sǽmran gode hǽtsþ hǽðen feoh, Exon. Th. 245, 28; Jul. 51: 264, 9; Jul. 361. Ða sǽmran *deteriora*, Wrt. Voc. ii. 139, 38. Ðû byst se ilca se ðû ǽr wǽre, ne beóþ ðîn winter wiht ðê sǽmran (*anni tui non deficient*), Ps. Th. 101, 24. Hî dweligende sêcaþ ðæt hêhste gôd on ða sâmran (sǽmran, Cott. MS.) gesceafta *id* (good) *error humanus a vero atque perfecto ad falsum imperfectumque traducit*, Bt. 33, 1; Fox 120, 12. Sǽmust *vel* wyrst *pessima*, Blickl. Gl. Ne wǽron ðæt gesîþa ða sǽmestan, Exon. Th. 326, 8; Wîd. 1[illegible] Cf. sâm-.

sæm-tinges. v. sam-tinges.

sǽ-naca, an; *m. A sea-going vessel*, Exon. Th. 474, 7; Bo. 26.

sǽne; *adj. Slow, dull, sluggish, inactive*:—Ymb ða gýmene his êcre hǽlo hê wæs tô sǽne *erga curam perpetuae suae salvationis nihil omnino studii gerens*, Bd. 3, 13; S. 538, 19. Ne sceal se tô sǽne beón, ne ðissa lârna tô læt, Exon. Th. 450, 16; Dôm. 88. Sǽne môd *a sluggish mind*, 122, 32; Gû, 314. Næs ðæt sǽne cyning, 322, 23; Wîd. 67. Eálâ ðæt ðû woldest ðæs sîðfætes sǽne weorðan (*slow to undertake the journey*), Andr. Kmbl. 408; An. 204: 422; An. 211: Elm. Kmbl. 440; El. 220, Næs his brôðor læt, sîðes sǽne, Apstls. Kmbl. 67; Ap. 34. Nǽron ða twegen tohtan sǽne, lindgelâces, 150; Ap. 75. Ðone sǽnan ðe biþ tô slâw ðû scealt hâtan assa mâ ðonne man *segnis ac stupidus torpet? asinum vivit*, Bt. 37, 4; Fox 192, 19. Mægencræft môda gehwilces ofer lîchoman lǽne and sǽnne *might of the mind over the body weak and dull*, Met. 26, 106. Hê (*a sea serpent*) on holme wæs sundes ðê sǽnra (*the slower in swimming*), ðâ hyne swylt fornam, Beo. Th. 2876; B. 1436. Ic sceal sêcan ôðerne ellenleásran cempan sǽnran *I must seek another warrior less courageous and active*, Exon. Th. 266, 9; Jul. 395. [*O. H. Ger.* seine: *Icel.* seinn; *Dan.* seen: *Swed.* sen. Cf. *Goth.* sainjan *to be slow, to tarry.*] v. â-sânian.

sǽ-næss, es; *m. A ness* or *promontory stretching into the sea, a cape*:—Sǽnesse *promontorio*, Hpt. Gl. 420, 7. Ða líðende land gesâwon brimclifu blîcan, beorgas steápe, sîde sǽnæssas, Beo. Th. 451; B. 223. Sǽnæssas geseón, windige weallas, 1146; B. 571.

sǽ-nett *a net for fishing in the sea*:—Sǽnet *sagene*, Wrt. Voc. i. 68, 14.

sæp, es; *n. Sap*:—Sæp *succus*, Hpt. Gl. 450, 12. Cederbeám *cedrus*, his sæp *cedria*, Wrt. Voc. i. 33, 39. Ðâ wearð beám monig blôdigum teárum birunnen, sæp wearð tô swâte, Exon. Th. 72, 23; Cri. 1177. Ðæs swêtestan sæpes *suavissime succi*, Hpt. Gl. 411, 58. Seó drîge gyrd ðe næs mid sæpe âcucod, Homl. Th. ii. 8, 17. Sep *sucum*, Germ. 391, 18. [*Ayenb.* þet zep; *O. H. Ger.* saf: *Icel.* safi; *m.*] v. stôr-sæp.

sæpig; *adj. Full of sap, succulent*:—Sæpig stela *succulentus cauliculus*, Hpt. Gl. 419, 45. [*Prompt. Parv.* sapy or fulle of sap *cariosus.*] v. un-sæpig.

sæppe, an; *f. The spruce fir*:—Sæppe *abies*, Wrt. Voc. i. 285, 40. [Cf. *Lat.* sappinus *from which Fr.* sapin.]

sæp-spôn *a chip* or *shaving with sap in it*:—Genim geongre âcrinde hand fulle . . . sceafe ðæt grêne, wylle ða sæpspône on cûmeolce, Lchdm. ii. 292, 27.

sǽr (=rǽr?), Ps. Th. 7, 6.

sǽ-rima, an; *m. The sea-shore, coast*:—Hî mycel yfel gedydon ǽgðer ge on Defenum ge wel hwǽr be ðæm sǽriman, Chr. 897; Erl. 95, 20: 994; Erl. 133, 19. [Bî ða sǽrime âhwǽr in Engelande *in littore marino alicubi in Anglia*, Chart. Th. 422, 2.] [Bi þisse særime, Laym. 6216.]

sǽ-rinc, es; *m. A sea-man, one who journeys by sea* (used of the Scandinavians, cf. sǽ-mann):—Hine ymb monig snellîc sǽrinc (*of Beowulf and his companions*), Beo. Th. 1384; B. 690. Sende se sǽrinc (*one of the Danes attacking Byrhtnoth*) sûþerne gâr, Byrht. Th. 135, 46; By. 134.

sǽ-rîric *a reed-bed in the sea* (?), *an ait*:—Swylce wôrie bî ôfre sondbeorgum ymbseald sǽrýrica mǽst, swâ ðæt wênaþ wǽglîþende ðæt hý on eálond sum eágum wlîten (*the reference is to the whale, which mariners mistake for an island*), Exon. Th. 360, 24; Wal. 10. [Cf. *O. H. Ger.* rôrahi *arundinetum.*]

sǽ-rôf; *adj. Active on the sea, strong in rowing*:—Ðonne sǽrôfe snelle mægne ârum bregdaþ, Exon. Th. 296, 25; Crä. 56.

sæs *a seat.* v. sess.

sǽ-sceaþa, an; *m. A sea-robber, pirate*:—Sǽsceaþan *piratici*, Wrt. Voc. ii. 68, 12.

sǽ-sîð *a sea-journey, voyage*, Beo. Th. 2302; B. 1149.

sǽ-snægl, es; *m. A sea-snail*:—Sǽsnǽl *chelio, testudo* vel *marina gagalia*, Wrt. Voc. i. 24, 32. Sǽsnæglas *conchae* vel *cochleae*, 56, 7: ii. 136, 14.

sǽ-strand, es; *m. Sea-shore:*—Sǽstrand *litus*, Wrt. Voc. i. 80, 59. Swā mænigfealde swā swā sandceosol on sǽstrande, Jos. 11, 4: Wulfst. 198, 22. Beraþ ða stānas tō sǽstrande, Homl. Th. i. 68, 29. [Heo stepen up a sæstrond, Laym. 9235. *Icel.* sævar-strönd.]

sǽ-streám, es; *m. Sea-stream, water of the sea:*—Ðonne sǽstreámas flōwaþ *elationes maris*, Ps. Th. 92, 5. Sǽstreámas sealte, 79, 11: Andr. Kmbl. 391; An. 196: 1497; An. 750. Swearte sǽstreámas, Cd. Th. 80, 9; Gen. 1326. Sǽstreámum neáh, 193, 22; Exod. 250. Ic his swīðran hand settan þence ðæt hē sǽstreámum syððan wealde *ponam in mari manum ejus, et in fluminibus dexteram ejus*, Ps. Th. 88, 22. Sicilia sǽstreámum in, Met. 1, 15. [He iwende ouer sea-streames, Laym. 326. Þu steorest te sea stream þ hit fleden ne mot fir þan þu markedest, Marh. 9, 34. *O. Sax.* sēo-strōm.]

sǽt, e; *f. An ambush, a place where one lies in wait:*—Hȳ sǽtiaþ mīn and sittaþ swā gearwe swā seó leó dēþ tō ðam ðe hē gefōn wyle and swā swā his hwelp byþ gehȳd æt ðære sǽte *susceperunt me sicut leo paratus ad praedam, et sicut catulus leonis habitans in abditis*, Ps. Th. 16, 11. Deórhege heáwan and sǽte haldan *to maintain the places from which the deer might be shot* (?), L. R. S. 2; Th. i. 432, 15. The Latin version has *stabilitatem observare;* Leo takes *sǽte* = hedges, and Schmid translates 'in ordnung erhalten.' [*Icel.* sāt; *f. ambush.*] v. sǽtian.

sǽta *a resident, inhabitant.* The form occurs only in compounds, and these are for the most part in the plural. There is also beside the weak *-sǽtan* a strong *-sǽte.* v. Dorn- (Dor-), Dūn-, Peác-, Sumor-, Wil-sǽte (-sǽtan). Other instances of the suffix are given in Bd. 4, 12; S. 581, 34, where *Hrypensis ecclesia* is translated *Hrypsǽttna cyrice:* Hiisētena munecas *Hiienses monachi*, 5, 22; S. 644, 24: and in Cod. Dip. B. i. 414. It also forms part of common nouns, v. burh-, ende-, land-sǽta: with which may be compared *O. L. Ger.* land-sētio: *O. H. Ger.* himil-sāzo: *Ger.* land-safs. See too the compounds of sittend[e].

sǽtan, -sǽte; *subst.*, -sǽte; *adj.*, sæten, Sæter-dæg. v. sǽtian, sǽta, and-sǽte, seten, Sætern-dæg.

sǽtere, es; *m. One that lies in wait, one that waylays.* I. *a robber;* latro:—Þeáf and sǽttere *fur et latro*, Jn. Skt. Lind. 10, 1. Þeáfas and sēttera*s fures et latrones*, 10, 8. II. fig. *one who acts insidiously;* insidiator, seductor:—Se sǽtere (*insidiator*), ðæt is se dióful, hē hine spænþ on wōh, Past. 53, 7; Swt. 417, 23. Ðonne cymþ se lytega sǽtere (*seductor*) tō ðæm slāwan mōde, and āteleþ him eall ðæt hē ǽr tō gōde gedyde, 65, 2; Swt. 463, 12. Hī sendon sēteras (*insidiatores*) ðætte genōmo hine on word, Lk. Skt. Lind. 20, 20. v. sǽt, sǽtian.

Sætern-dæg, Sæternes-, Sæter-, Sæteres-dæg, es; *m. Saturday;* dies Saturni:—Sæterndæges rest *requies sabbati*, Ex. 16, 23. On Sæterndæg, Mk. Skt. 9, 2, Rbc. Sæterndæg (sæter-, MS. A.), Lk. Skt. 23, 56. Sæterdæg (sæternes-, MS. A.), 23, 54. Sæternesdæg, Mt. Kmbl. 16, 28, Rbc.: 20, 29, Rbc. On ðone Sæternesdæg, Chr. 1012; Erl. 146, 12: Shrn. 70, 7. Sæternesdæg of Saturno Iovis fæder, Anglia viii. 321, 17. Se seofoþa dæg is se Sæternesdæg, Homl. Th. ii. 206, 6. Ǽghwylce Sæternesdæge *per omne sabbatum*, Bd. 2, 3; S. 504, 40. Seternesdæg *Sabbatum*, Mt. Kmbl. Lind. 12, 8. Sætresdæg (Sæternes-, MS. T.), R. Ben. 37, 23: 38, 8. On ðæm Sæteresdæge, Blickl. Homl. 71, 30. [Saturnus heo (*the forefathers of the English*) ʒiven Sætterdæi (Sateresdai, 2nd MS.), Laym. 13933. *Orm.* Saterrdaʒʒ. High German and Scandinavian take a different form, but Frisian and Dutch agree with English. v. Grmm. D. M. pp. 114–5; 226–7.]

Sætern-, Sæter-niht, e; *f. Friday night, the night between Friday and Saturday:*—His (*Christ*) līc læg on byrgene ða Sæterniht and Sunnanniht *his body lay in the sepulchre on the nights of Friday and Saturday*, Homl. Th. i. 216, 27. [*R. Glouc.* Sater-niʒt.]

sǽ-þeóf, es; *m. A sea-thief, a pirate:*—Heáh-sǽþeóf *archipiratta*, Wrt. Voc. ii. 5, 28.

sæþerige, an; *f. Savory;* satureia hortensis:—Sæþerian sǽd, Lchdm. ii. 314, 19: iii. 72, 8. v. saturege.

sǽtian, sǽtan; *p.* ode *To lie in wait for, waylay* (with gen.):—Forðam hē hine ne meahte mid openlīcum gefeohte ofersuīðan sǽtaþ ðonne diógollīce and sēcþ hū hē hine mǽge gefōn *quia enim publico bello perdidit, ad exercendas occulte insidias exardescit*, Past. 33, 7; Swt. 227, 13. Hē sǽtaþ (*insidiatur*) ðæt hē bereáfige ðone earman, Ps. Th. 9, 30. Se synfulla sǽtaþ ðæs rihtwīsan *observabit peccator justum*, 36, 12. Hȳ sǽtiaþ mīn *susceperunt me*, 16, 11. Ðū scealt fiersna sǽtan, Cd. Th. 56, 18; Gen. 913. Hū ǽghwelc syn biþ sǽtigende ðæs þióndan monnes *quomodo unumquodque peccatum proficientibus insidietur*, Past. 21, 5; Swt. 161, 24. Feóndas and sǽtendan sāwle mīnre *inimici et qui custodiebant animam meam*, Ps. Th. 70, 9. Sētendum *insidiantibus*, Lk. Skt. p. 10, 5. [*Icel.* sæta *to lie in wait for* (with dat.): *M. H. Ger.* sāzen.] v. sǽtnian, sǽt, sǽtere.

sætilcas:—Ne ymbe sciphergas sætilcas ne hērdon ne furþum fira nān ymb gefeoht sprecan, Met. 8, 31. *Grein suggests* scealcas, cf. næs scealca nān *in v.* 21; *the corresponding prose is:*—Ne gehērde nōn mon ðā get nānne sciphere, ne furþon ymbe nān gefeoht sprecan, Bt. 15; Fox 48, 14–16.

sǽtnere, es; *m. One who lies in wait.* v. sǽtnian, sǽtere; but used in the following case to gloss *seditiosus:*—Mid sētnerum *cum seditiosis*, Mk. Skt. Lind. 15, 7. v. sǽtnung.

sǽtnian; *p.* ode *To lie in wait for* (with gen.):—Ðā wǽron ðǽr Sarocine gesamnode, ðæt hig sǽtnodan manna, Shrn. 37, 34. v. sǽtian.

sǽtnung, e; *f.* I. *a lying in wait, plot, snare.* v. sǽtung:—Hē hine bæd ðæt hē his līf gescylde wið swā mycles ēhteres sǽtningum *obsecrans ut vitam suam a tanti persecutoris insidiis tutando servaret*, Bd. 2, 12; S. 513, 5. Hē him ða sǽtnunge (*insidias*) gewearnode ðæs unholdan cyninges, S. 515, 11: 5, 23; S. 646, 37 note. Sētnungum *insidiantes*, Lk. Skt. Lind. Rush. 11, 54. II. in the following passages the word glosses *seditio.* v. sǽtnere:—On sētnuncge (setnong, Lind.) *in seditione*, Mk. Skt. Rush. 15, 7. Fore sētnunge *propter seditionem*, Lk. Skt. Rush. 23, 19, 25.

sǽtung, e; *f. A lying in wait, plot, snare:*—Sǽtunge *aucupatione*, Wrt. Voc. ii. 7, 43. Sētunge, 101, 25. Gif him þince ðæt hē feala earna ætsomne geseó, ðæt biþ yfel nīð and manna sǽtunga and seara, Lchdm. iii. 168, 11. Ðonne hē foresægþ ða diéglan sǽtenga ðæs lytegan feóndes *quando hostis callidi circumspectas et quasi incomprehensibiles insidias praedicit*, Past. 21, 5; Swt. 163, 14. Scottas ne sǽtincge ne gestrodu wið Angelþeóde syrwaþ *Scotti nil contra gentem Anglorum insidiarum moliuntur aut fraudium*, Bd. 5, 23; S. 646, 37.

sǽ-upwearp *what is thrown up on land by the sea, jetsum:*—Ic habbe gegeofen Ǽlfwine abbod ... ða sǽupwearp on eallen þingen æt Bramcæstre, Chart. Th. 421, 33.

sǽ-wǽg *a wave of the sea:*—Sealte sǽwǽgas, Cd. Th. 240, 9; Dan. 384.

sǽ-wæter, es; *n. Sea-water:*—Genim celeþonian seáw and sǽwæter, Lchdm. ii. 28, 12.

sǽ-wang, es; *m. The plain by the sea, the shore:*—Gewāt se hearda æfter sande sǽwong tredan, wīde waroþas, Beo. Th. 3933; B. 1964.

sǽ-wār *sea-weed:*—Sǽwaar *alga*, Wrt. Voc. i. 31, 35. Cf. waar *alga*, ii. 99, 29. See E. D. S. Pub. Plant Names, s. v. *waur.*

sǽ-waroþ *the sea-shore:*—Be sǽwaroþe and be æáōfrum, Bt. 32, 3; Fox 118, 17: Met. 19, 21.

sǽ-weall, es; *m.* I. *a sea-wall, a cliff by the sea:*—Higelāc wunode sǽwealle neáh, Beo. Th. 3853; B. 1924: Exon. Th. 471, 15; Rā. 61, 1. II. *a wall formed by the sea:*—Sǽweall āstāh (cf. Ðæt wæter (*of the Red Sea*) stōd swilce twegen hēge weallas, Ex. 14, 22), Cd. Th. 197, 6; Exod. 302.

sǽ-weard *sea-ward, keeping watch and ward on the sea-coast;* it was a duty that might be required in some cases of the thane and of the 'cotsetla':—Of manegum landum māre landriht ārīst tō cyniges gebanne ... sǽweard (*the section refers to the* 'thegen'), L. R. S. 1; Th. i. 432, 8. Werige his (*the* '*cotsetla*') hlāfordes inland, gif him man beóde, æt sǽwearde, 3; Th. i. 432, 28. Cf. the description of Beowulf's landing:—Ðā of wealle geseah weard Scyldinga, se ðe holmclifu healdan scolde, etc., Beo. Th. 463 sqq.

sǽ-weg *a sea-way, a path through the sea:*—Sǽfiscas ða faraþ geond ða sǽwegas *pisces maris qui perambulant semitas maris*, Ps. Th. 8, 8. [*Icel.* sjó-vegr.]

sǽ-wērig; *adj. Weary with being on the sea:*—Sǽwērige slǽp oferеode, Andr. Kmbl. 1651; An. 817: 1723; An. 864. [We beoþ sæwerie men, Laym. 4619.]

sǽwet, es; *n. Sowing:*—Ofer ða tīd ðæs sǽwetes *ultra tempus serendi*, Bd. 4, 28, tit.; S. 605, 8.

sǽ-wīcing, es; *m. A viking:*—Randas bǽron sǽwīcingas (*the tribe of Reuben*) ofer sealtne mersc, Cd. Th. 199, 3; Exod. 333.

sǽ-wiht, e; *f. A sea-animal:*—Ðeós eorþe is berende missenlīcra fugela and sǽwihta *this land is productive of divers fowls and sea-animals* (*the Latin has* insula ... avium ferax terra marique diversi generis), Bd. 1, 1; S. 473, 15.

sǽ-wilm, es; *m. A billow:*—Gē him syndon ofer sǽwylmas hider wilcuman, Beo. Th. 792; B. 393.

-sǽwisc. v. ofer-sǽwisc.

sǽ-wudu *a ship:*—Hī sǽwudu sǽldon *they fastened their ship to the shore*, Beo. Th. 457; B. 228.

sæx. v. seax.

sǽ-ȳþ, e; *f. A wave of the sea:*—Sǽȳþa *vel* holmas *equomaria*, Wrt. Voc. ii. 143, 74. Hī sǽȳþa swīðe brēgaþ, Runic pm. Kmbl. 343, 23; Rūn. 21. [*O. Sax.* sēo-ūðia.]

safine, an; *f. Savine;* juniperus savina:—Sauine. Genim ðās wyrte, ðe man *sabinam*, and ōðrum naman wel ðam gelīc, *sauinam* hāteþ, Lchdm. i. 190, 13: iii. 16, 8: 58, 20. Safine, 22, 31. Lytel sauinan, 30, 15. Safinan dust, ii. 250, 27. Genim safinan, 100, 10: 294, 24: iii. 44, 5. Safenan, 46, 3: ii. 312, 11. Sauinan, iii. 38, 26.

saftriende *rheumatic:*—Saftriende *reumaticus*, Wrt. Voc. i. 45, 48. Cf. sæp.

sâg (?):—Ic heáfod hæbbe and heáne steort, eágan and eáran and ǽnne foot, hrycg and heard nebb, hneccan steápne and sîdan twâ, sâg on middum, eard ofer ældum, Exon. Th. 490, 3; Rä. 79, 5.

saga, an; *m. A saw:—Saga serula*, Wrt. Voc. i. 16, 17: *serra*, 39, 67. v. sagu.

saga, an; *m. A saying, story, statement:*—Ðîn saga biþ geswutelod, gif ðû ðone sylfan encgel bitst, ðæt hê mînne sunu ansundne ârǽre, Homl. Skt. i. 7, 193. v. sagu.

sagian. v. secgan.

-sagol. v. leás-, sôþ-, unsôþ-, wǽr-sagol.

sâgol (v. sowel *fustis*, Wrt. Voc. i. 94, 22, soþsawel *veridicus*, 90, 19), es; *m. A staff, cudgel, club:*—Sâgol oððe stæf *fustis*, Ælfc. Gr. 9, 28; Som. 11, 44: *fustis*, Wrt. Voc. i. 84, 28. Ða sâglas (*vectes*) sticiaþ inn on ðâm hringum ða earce mid tô beranne . . . Ðæt is ðonne ðæt mon ða earce bere on ðǽm sâglum, Past. 22, 1; Swt. 171, 5–12. Hié Claudium mid sâglum ofbeótan, Ors. 2, 6; Swt. 88, 26. Hêt ða cwelleras mid stearcum sâglum hine beóton, Homl. Th. i. 424, 32. Mid stîðum sâglum beátaþ, 432, 12: 468, 33. Hêt his cwelleras ðone hâlgan beátan mid heardum sâglum. Ðâ bærst sum sâgol intô ânes beáteres eágan, Homl. Skt. i. 4, 142. Mid swurdum and sâhlum *cum gladiis et fustibus*, Mt. Kmbl. 26, 47, 55. Hê stafas ł sâhlas îsenne tôbræc *vectes ferreos confregit*, Ps. Lamb. 106, 16. [Ælc bær an honde ænne saȝel (staf, 2nd MS.) stronge, Laym. 12280.]

sagu, e; *f. A saw:—Sage serram*, Germ. 400, 531. Hê sceal habban æcse, adsan, sage, Anglia ix. 263, 2. [*O. H. Ger.* saga, sega; *f. serra, lima: Icel.* sög; *f. a saw.*] v. saga.

sagu, e; *and indecl.? f.* I. *a saw, say* (to say one's *say*), *saying, statement, story, tale:*—Racu, sagu *sermo*, Hpt. Gl. 433, 12. Nis ðis nân gedwimor ne nân dwollîc sagu, Jud. Thw. p. 159, 27. Ic hâte healdan hî ôþ ðæt heora sagu âfandod sý, Homl. Th. ii. 484, 3. Teónan ðû wyrcst ûs mid ðisse sage *haec dicens nobis contumeliam facis*, Lk. Skt. 11, 45. Sagu *dictu* (cf. gesægene *dictu*, 28, 47), Wrt. Voc. ii. 140, 7. Hî sǽdon ðam kinge ðæt hê hæfde swýðe âgylt wið Crist. . . . Ðâ læg se king and âsweartode eall mid ðare sage, Chart. Th. 340, 1. Gehýr ðû ðâs race nâ swilce leáse sagu ac geworden þing *audi fabulam, non fabulam sed rem gestam*, Ælfc. T. Grn. 16, 12. Geendebrednege ða sago þinga *ordinare narrationem rerum*, Mt. Kmbl. p. 7, 2, 9. *Fabulae* synd ða saga ðe menn secgaþ ongeán gecynde, Ælfc. Gr. 50, 29; Zup. 296, 5. Spellenga, sagena *sermonum*, Hpt. Gl. 505, 77. Ic ðînra bysna ne mæg, worda ne wîsna wuht oncnâwan, sîðes ne sagona, Cd. Th. 34, 9; Gen. 535. Sagum *fabulis*, Lk. Skt. p. 2, 10, 11. II. *saying, narration, telling, report:*—Se hlîsa ðe þurh yldra manna segene (sage, MS. B.) tô ûs becom *opinio quae traditione majorum ad nos perlata est*, Bd. 2, 1; S. 501, 2. III. *statement of a witness, testimony:*—Tô hwî wilnige wê ǽnigre ôðre sage *quid adhuc egemus testibus*, Mt. Kmbl. 26, 65. Ne gehýrst ðû hû fela sagena (*quanta testimonia*) hig ongên ðê secgeaþ, 27, 13. Hî sôhton leáse saga (*falsum testimonium*) ongên ðone Hǽlend, 26, 59. IV. *a saying beforehand, foretelling:*—Of sage *fatidicum*, Wrt. Voc. ii. 147, 22. Saga *presagia*, 67, 46. Sagum *praesagminibus, vaticinationibus, divinationibus*, Hpt. Gl. 448, 64. [Ælc his saȝe sæide, Laym. 26345. Heo wenden þat his sawen (2nd MS. sawes) soðe weren, 749. *A. R.* saȝe, sawe, sahe: *Chauc. Piers P.* sawe: *O. H. Ger.* saga *assertio, narratio, sermo, enuntiatio: Icel.* saga *story, tale.*] v. on-, sôþ-sagu; saga.

saht, sales. v. seht, sæl.

sâl, es; *m.*: e; *f.* (?) I. *a rope, cord, line, bond:*—Licgaþ mê ymbe îrenbendas, rîdeþ racentan sâl, Cd. Th. 24, 3; Gen. 378. Ðâ wæs be mæste segl sâle (cf. *O. H. Ger.* segil-seil *rudens*) fæst, Beo. Th. 3816; B. 1906. Sâlum *nexibus*, Wrt. Voc. ii. 60, 74. II. *a rein:* — Sâlas [*h*]*abenas*, 4, 58: 6, 22. Sâlum ł gewealdleþerum *habenis*, 42, 60. III. *the loop which forms the handle of a vessel* (?):—Sâl *ansa* (cf. hringe *ansa*, 284, 7, *and see* nostle. *The word occurs under the heading* nomina vasorum), Wrt. Voc. i. 25, 11. IV. *the fastening of a door:*—*Repagulum* sâl[-panra?], Wrt. Voc. i. 16, 3. Sâle *repagula*, ii. 119, 4. V. *a necklace, collar:*—Sweorclâþ *vel* [sweor]têg *vel* [sweor?]sâl *collarium*, 134, 49. Sâle *collario*, 18, 17. Saule *callario* (saale *collario*), 78, 71. [Soole, beestys teyynge *ligaculum; restis* a sole to tie beasts, Prompt. Parv. 463. Hi drayeþ myd such sol, Misc. 51, 162. *O. H. Ger.* seil; *n. funis, rudens, lorum, habena, restis: Icel.* seil; *f. a line.*]

sala, an; *m. A sale:*—Ceáp *distractio*, sala *venditio*, Wrt. Voc. i. 55, 55. [*O. H. Ger.* sala; *f. traditio: Icel.* sala; *f. a sale.*]

salf. v. sealf.

salfige, an; *f. Sage:*—Saluige *salvia*, Wrt. Voc. i. 79, 49. Salfige, Lchdm. iii. 22, 31. Saluie. Genim ðâs wyrte ðe man saluian nemneþ. . . . Genim ðâs ylcan wyrte salfian, i. 218, 6–11. Saluian sǽd, iii. 72, 7: ii. 358, 18. Nim saltian, iii. 48, 3. Wyl sealuian, 44, 17. [*O. H. Ger.* salbeia, salveia: *Ger.* salbei. *From Latin.*]

salh *a sallow.* v. sealh.

sallettan *to play on the harp, sing to the harp, sing psalms:*—Singaþ him and salletaþ *cantate ei et psallite ei*, Ps. Th. 104, 2.

salm. v. sealm.

salness, e; *f. Darkness, duskiness:*—*Conticinium*, ðæt ys swîtîma oððe salnyssa tîma, Anglia viii. 319, 29. v. salu.

salor *a hall, palace:*—Eów ðeós cwên laðaþ tô salore (cf. tô hofe, 1111; El. 557), Elen. Kmbl. 1100; El. 552: 764; El. 382. v. sæl, sele.

salo, salowig, salpanra, salt, salt-haga. v. salu, saluwig, sâl IV, sealt, sæltna.

saltere, es; *m.* I. *a stringed musical instrument, a psaltery:*—Saltere *sambucus*, Wrt. Voc. i. 289, 26: *psalterium*, Ps. Spl. 80, 2: 107, 2. On saltere syngaþ him *in psalterio psallite illi*, 32, 2: 91, 3: 143, 11: 150, 3. Cimbalan oððe psalteras oððe strengas ætrînan, Lchdm. iii. 202, 14. II a. *the book of Psalms:*—Se saltere ys ân bôc, ðe hê (*David*) gesette þurh God betwux ôðrum bôcum on ðære bibliothecan, Ælfc. T. Grn. 7, 26. II b. *a psalter, a service-book containing the book of Psalms divided into certain portions for Matins, and the Hours, so as to be gone through in the course of the week:*—Hê (*the mass-priest*) sceal habban ða wǽpna tô ðam gâstlîcum weorce . . . ðæt synd ða hâlgan bêc, saltere and pistolbôc, godspellbôc and mæssebôc, L. Ælf. C. 21; Th. ii. 350, 12: L. Ælfc. P. 44; Th. ii. 384, 1. ii. salteras and se þridda[n] saltere swâ man singþ on Rôme, Chart. Th. 430, 11. ¶ Saltere singan *to sing psalms taken from the psalter:*—Hê gehât gehêt . . . ðæt hê ǽghwylce dæge ealne saltere âsunge *vovit votum quia quotidie psalterium totum decantaret*, Bd. 3, 27; S. 599, 11. Hê âsong ǽlce dæge tuwa his saltere and his mæssan, Shrn. 134, 17. Singe eal geferrǽden ætgædere heora saltere ða þrý dagas, Wulfst. 181, 21. Ælc brôður singe twegen salteras sealma . . . vi. mæssan oððe .vi. salteras sealma *each brother shall sing two portions of psalms from the psalter*, Chart. Th. 614, 7, 11. [*O. H. Ger.* saltari, psaltari *psalterium; salzara sambucus: Icel.* saltari *a psalm-book.*]

saltian; *p.* ode *To dance:*—Gê ne saltudun (sealtedon, MS. A.) *non saltastis*, Lk. Skt. 7, 32. [*O. H. Ger.* salzôn. *From Latin.*]

salu; *adj. Dusky, dark:*—Ic sylfa [eom] salo, Exon. Th. 489, 21; Rä. 48, 11. [*O. H. Ger.* salo *fuscus, furvus, ater, niger: Icel.* sölr *yellow.*] v. following words.

salu-brûn; *adj. Dark-brown:*—Hrefn sweart and sealobrûn, Fins. Th. 70; Fin. 35.

salu-neb; *adj. Dark-faced:*—Se wonna þegn, sweart and saloneb, Exon. Th. 433, 9; Rä. 50, 9.

salu-pâd; *adj. Dark-coated:*—Ða sind blace swîðe, swearte, salopâde, Exon. Th. 439, 1; Rä. 58, 3. Cf. saluwig-pâd.

saluwig-feðera; *adj. Of dusky plumage:*—[Hrefn] salwigfeðera, Cd. Th. 87, 13; Gen. 1448.

saluwig-pâd; *adj. Dark-coated, having dark plumage:*—Hrefn salwigpâd, Exon. Th. 329, 20; Vy. 37. Earn salowigpâda, Judth. 24, 28; Jud. 211. Lêtan hrǽ bryttian saluwigpâdan ðone sweartan hræfn, Chr. 937; Erl. 115, 10.

sâl-wang, sal-warp. v. sǽl-wang, sealt-wearp.

salwian *to make dark, to blacken:*—Heó (*the dove*) nolde ǽfre under salwed bord (*in the ark, which was dark-coloured from the pitch that had been smeared over it*) syððan ætýwan, Cd. Th. 89, 15; Gen. 1481. [Cf. *O. H. Ger.* gi-salwian *decolorare*; salwet *obscuratum*; salawi *fuscatio.* v. Grff. vi. 183.] v. salu.

sam; *conj. Whether, or* (cf. swâ . . . swâ = *whether . . . or*):—Sam hî þyrfon, sam hî ne þurfon, hî willaþ ðeáh, Bt. 26, 2; Fox 92, 29. Sam wê willan, sam wê nyllan, 34, 12; Fox 154, 7: 40, 1; Fox 234, 34. Hý gedôþ ðæt ǽgðer fætels biþ oferfroren sam hit sý sumor, sam winter, Ors. 1, 1; Swt. 21, 17. Sam hý fæsten sam hý ne fæsten *omni tempore siue jejunii siue prandii*, R. Ben. 66, 14. Sam hê hine miclum lufige, sam hê hine lytlum lufige, sam hê hine mydlinga lufige, Shrn. 194, 13. Wið wunda som hý sýn of îserne, som hý sýn of stence, oððe fram nædran, Lchdm. i. 166, 9. [Sam . . . sam *whether . . . or*, O. E. Homl. ii. 107, 8.]

sam- as a prefix denotes *agreement, combination.* v. sam-mǽle, -râd, -winnende, -wist. [*Icel.* sam-.]

sâm- *half-*; the prefix denotes *imperfection.* Cf. sǽmra. [*O. Sax.* sâm-: *O. H. Ger.* sâmi-: *Lat.* semi-: *Gk.* ἡμι-.]

Samaringas, Samaritane, Samaritanisce; *pl. The Samaritans:*—Innan Samaritana ceastre (in burgum ðæra Samaritanesca, Lind.; in cæstra Samaringa, Rush.) *in civitates Samaritanorum*, Mt. Kmbl. 10, 5. Tô Samaritaniscum, Jn. Skt. Rush. Lind. 4, 9. v. next word.

Samaritanisc; *adj. Samaritan, of Samaria:* — Ðâ fêrde sum Samaritanisc man wið hine, Lk. Skt. 10, 33. Ðes wæs Samaritanisc, 17, 16: Jn. Skt. 8, 48. Ðâ cwæþ ðæt Samaritanisce wîf. . . . 'Ic eom Samaritanisc wîf; ne brûcaþ Judêas and Samaritanisce metes ætgædere,' Jn. Skt. 4, 9. [*O. H. Ger.* Samaritanisc.]

sâm-bærned; *adj. Half-burnt:*—Sâmbærnd *semiustus*, Hpt. Gl. 508, 56.

sâm-boren; *adj. Born out of due time:*—Sâmboren *abortus*, Wrt. Voc. ii. 10, 6. Cf. ful-boren.

sâm-bryce *a violation only partially effected:*—Tô hâdbôte, ðâr sâmbryce wurđe, bēte man georne be đam đe seó dǽd sȳ, L. E. B. 9; Th. ii. 242, 9. *The term is in contrast with* ful-bryce *in the preceding sections.* v. sâm-wyrcan.

sâm-cwic, -cucu; *adj. Half-dead:*—Sum mǽden hē gehǽlde, đæt đe læg on legerbedde seóc, sâmcucu geþūht, Homl. Th. ii. 510, 25. Hē sâmcucu læg, Homl. Skt. i. 6, 164: L. Ælfc. C. 31; Th. ii. 354, 10. Hē (*Anthony*) bebeád đæt hiene mon on đa ilcan byrgenne tō hiere (*Cleopatra*) swā sōmcucre ālegde, Ors. 5, 13; Swt. 246, 31. Hī forlēton hine sâmcucene *semiuiuo relicto*, Lk. Skt. 10, 30. Sum mōder bær hire sâmcuce cild, Homl. Th. ii. 150, 16. [*O. Sax.* sâm-quik: *O. H. Ger.* sâmi-quek.]

same (*always in combination with* swā); *adv. Similarly, in the same way.* (1) Swā same:—And eft Lǽdenware swā same wendon ealla on hiora āgen geþeóde *and again the Romans in the same way translated all into their own language*, Past. pref.; Swt. 6, 3. Đeós wyrt is swȳđe scearpnumul wunda tō gehǽlenne, swā đæt đa wunda hrædlīce tōgædere gāþ; and eác swā some hió gedēþ đæt flǽsc tōgædere clifaþ, Lchdm. i. 134, 12: Elen. Kmbl. 2553; El. 1278. Đæt hié lufan Dryhtnes and sybbe swā same sylfra betweónum gelǽston, 2411; El. 1207: 2565; El. 1284. On Adame and on his eafrum swā some, Cd. Th. 25, 24; Gen. 399. Is đæt fȳr swā same on đam wætre and on stānum eác, Met. 20, 150: 24, 33. Deór efne swā some faraþ, Exon. Th. 358, 30; Pa. 53. (2) Swā same swā:—Hū ne forealldodon đa gewritu swā some swā đa wrīteras dydon, Bt. 18, 3; Fox 66, 1. Twā đara gecyndu habbaþ nētenu swā same swā men, 33, 4; Fox 132, 5. Đǽr wīfmenn feohtaþ swā same swā wǽpnedmen, Ors. 2, 4; Swt. 76, 27. [*O. Sax.* sō sama, sō sama sō: *O. H. Ger.* sama, sō sama, sō sama sō.]

samen; *adv. Together:*—Giurnan tuoege somen (*simul*), Jn. Skt. Rush. 20, 4. Wērun somen Simon Petrus and Didimus, 21, 2. [Baþe samenn, Orm. 377. Sitte samen, R. Brun. *Goth.* samana: *O. Sax.* saman: *O. Frs.* samin, semin: *O. L. Ger.* samen, samon: *O. H. Ger.* saman *simul*: *Icel.* saman.]

sâm-grēne; *adj. Half-green, backward* (of a plant):—Spelt sâmgrēne *far serotina*, Wrt. Voc. ii. 36, 41.

sâm-hāl; *adj. Not in perfect health, weak:*—Nū ne beóþ nāht fela manna ætsamne, đæt heora sum ne sī seóc and sâmhāl, Wulfst. 273, 10. [*O. H. Ger.* sâmi-hail *debilis*.]

sam-heort; *adj. Of one heart, of the same disposition*; concors:—Singaþ samheorte sangas Dryhtne, Ps. Th. 149, 1.

sam-hīwan; *pl. Members of the same household* or *family:*—Samhīwna yrfebēc *jus liberorum*, Wrt. Voc. i. 20, 46. Somhīwena yrfebēc, ii. 49, 14.

sam-hwilc; *pron. Some:*—Þeówne .lx. Somhwelcne fīftegum (mid fīftig, MSS. B. H.) *the 'wer' for the 'þeów' is 60 shillings. For one kind it is* 50 (?), L. In. 23; Th. i. 118, 4. Swā hwæt swā ūs God sylle māre đonne wē nēde brūcan sceolan ..., ne sylþ hē hit ūs tō đon đæt wē hit hȳdon, ođđe tō gylpe syllan samhwylcum mannum đe nāht swīđe God ne lufiaþ, Blickl. Homl. 53, 17. Cf. swā hwilc.

sâm-lǽred; *adj. Imperfectly taught:*—Wē lǽraþ đæt ǽnig gelǽred preóst ne scænde đone sâmlǽredan, ac gebēte hine gif hē bet cunne, L. Edg. C. 12; Th. ii. 246, 19. Hieronimus ādwæscte đa dwollīcan gesetnysse đe sâmlǽrede men sǽdon be hire forþsīđe, Homl. Th. ii. 438, 6. *Barbarismus* and *solocismus* bēcumaþ of đam sâmlǽredum leáslīce geclypode ođđe āwritene, Ælfc. Gr. 50, 22; Som. 51, 52.

sam-mǽle; *adj. Agreed, come to an agreement:*—Gif hȳ đonne ǽlces þinges sammǽle beón *if they then be agreed in everything*, L. Edm. B. 6; Th. i. 254, 19. Đæt dōm stande đār þegenas sammǽle beón, L. Eth. iii. 13; Th. i. 298, 3. Hēr swutelaþ on đisum gewrite hū Wulfrīc and Ealdrēd wǽron sammǽle ymbe đæt land at Clife, Cod. Dip. Kmbl. ii. 300, 5. Dene and Engle wurdon sammǽle æt Oxnaforda, Chr. 1018; Erl. 161, 16. [Cf. *Icel.* sam-mæli *an agreement*; sam-mælask á eitt *to agree in a thing*.] Cf. mǽlan, mǽl.

sâm-milt, -melt; *adj. Half-digested:*—Se geþigeda mete hefegaþ đone magan, and hē đone sâmmeltan (*the half-digested food*) þurh đa wambe ūt sent, Lchdm. ii. 186, 22. v. miltan.

-samne. v. æt-, tō-samne.

samnian; *p.* ode. I. *v. trans.* (1) *to collect, assemble, bring together, gather:*—Đa swētestan somnaþ and gædraþ wyrta wynsume and wudublēda *colligit succos et odores divite silva*, Exon. Th. 211, 6; Ph. 193. Somnas his huǽte *congregabit triticum suum*, Mt. Kmbl. Lind. 3, 12. Nāt hwam hit gaderaþ ł somnaþ đa, Ps. Spl. 38, 10. Hē đyder folc samnode, Cd. Th. 230, 5; Dan. 228. Hié here samnodon, Andr. Kmbl. 2250; An. 1126. Wē somnadon ł geadredon đa *colligimus ea*, Mt. Kmbl. Lind. 13, 28. Sommas (somnigas, Rush.) đa đe hiá gelǽfdon, Jn. Skt. Lind. 6, 12. Swylce man fyrde trymme and samnige, Blickl. Homl. 91, 32. Fyrde somnian, Chr. 1016; Erl. 154, 2. Folc somnigean, Cd. Th. 191, 19; Exod. 217. (2) *to draw together, join, unite:*—Đonne samnaþ hió đa wunde and hǽlþ, Lchdm. ii. 22, 11. (3) *to get materials together for a poem to compose:*—Ic đysne sang fand samnode wīde *I was author of this poem, gathered its matter far and wide*, Apstls. Kmbl. 4; Ap. 2. Ne wēne đæs ǽnig ælda cynnes, đæt ic lygewordum leóþ somnige (*that I compose my lay of lying words*), wrīte wōđcræfte, Exon. Th. 234, 29; Ph. 547. II. *intrans.* (1) *to collect, assemble, come together:*—Sellendum đē him hī somniaþ *dante te illis, colligent*, Ps. Spl. 103, 29. Somnode *conglobatur*, Wrt. Voc. ii. 19, 34: 91, 20. Duguþ samnade, Andr. Kmbl. 250; An. 125. Mægen samnode, Elen. Kmbl. 110; El. 55: 120; El. 60. Hī gederedon ł somnodon tōgeánes mē *convenirent adversum me*, Ps. Spl. 30, 17. (2) *to draw together, join, unite:*—Đā weóxon đa fȳr swȳđe and hī tōgædere þeóddon and samnedon ōþ đæt đe hī wǽron on ǽnne unmǽtne lēge geānede and gesomnade *crescentes vero ignes usque ad invicem sese extenderunt, atque in inmensam adunati sunt flammam*, Bd. 3, 19; S. 548, 21. (3) *to glean:*—Hē mid his sceáfe ne mæg sceát āfyllan đeáh đe hē samnige swīđe georne *non implevit sinum suum qui manipulos colligit*, Ps. Th. 128, 5. [*Laym.* somnien, sumnien: *Orm.* sammnenn: *O. Sax.* samnōn: *O. Frs.* samena, somnia: *O. H. Ger.* samanōn: *Icel.* samna.] v. ge-samnian.

samnung, e; *f. An assembly, council:*—Somnung *synagoga*, Mk. Skt. Lind. Rush. 1, 23: Lk. Skt. Lind. Rush. 4, 15, 16: *concilium*, Mk. Skt. Lind. Rush. 14, 55: Lind. 15, 1: Mt. Kmbl. Lind. 26, 59: *congregatio*, Rtl. 173, 3. v. ge-samnung.

samnunga, sæmninga, semninga; *adv. All at once, on a sudden, suddenly, forthwith, immediately*; continuo, subito, repente:—And đā hig đæt sprǽcon samninga (samnunga, MSS. A. B.) se hana creów *et continuo athuc illo loquente cantauit gallus*, Lk. Skt. 22, 60. Hī hine samnuncga (*subito*) scearpum strēlum on scotiaþ, Ps. Th. 63, 4. Đā āsceán samninga mycel leóht, Blickl. Homl. 145, 12. Somnunga, 239, 31. Hié sume somnunga sweltaþ, Lchdm. ii. 176, 9. Sæmninga, Blickl. Homl. 141, 27. Đis is feáwra manna dǽd, đæt hī ealle eorþlīce þing sæmninga forlǽtan māgon, Homl. Th. ii. 398, 33. Hī semninga sneóme forwurdon *subito defecerunt et perierunt*, Ps. Th. 72, 15: Bd. 1, 7; S. 477, 1. Đā āstōd hē semninga *exsurrexit repente*, 2, 9; S. 511, 20. Đā geseah hē semninga (*subito*) mon wiđ his gangan, 2, 12; S. 513, 34. Hit semninga (*subito*) on ūs rǽsde, Nar. 15, 19, 11. Đā cōmon semninga twegen englas, Blickl. Homl. 221, 27: Exon. Th. 257, 5; Jul. 242: Beo. Th. 3284; B. 1640. Ōþ đæt semninga sunu Healfdenes sēcean wolde ǽfenreste, 1293; B. 644. Hē (*the whale*) semninga on sealtne wǽg niþer gewīteþ, Exon. Th. 361, 29; Wal. 27. Đā wæs semninga geworden mycel þunorrād, Blickl. Homl. 145, 28: Exon. Th. 31, 5; Cri. 491. Mec semninga slǽp ofergongeþ, 422, 22; Rä. 41, 10: Andr. Kmbl. 927; An. 464: 1639; An. 821.

samnung-cwide. es; *m. A collect:*—Somnungcwido *collecta*, Rtl. 2, 1.

samod; *adv. Together.* I. marking association in joint action:—Ealle hī āhyldon samod onnitte gewordene sint *omnes declinaverunt, simul inutiles facti sunt*, Ps. Spl. 13, 4. Đa unrihtwīsan forweorđaþ samod (*simul*), 36, 40. Cumaþ ūt samod Ilfing and Wisle (*the two rivers have a common channel*), Ors. 1, 1; Swt. 20, 10. Stōd his handgeweorc (*Adam and Eve*) somod on sande, nyston sorga wiht tō begnornianne, Cd. Th. 16, 12; Gen. 242. Ne beóþ wē leng somed, 168, 20; Gen. 2785. Somod eardedon Meotudes bearn and se monnes sunu, Exon. Th. 8, 30; Cri. 125. Tō gebede feóllon sinhīwan somed, Cd. Th. 48, 19; Gen. 778. Samed sīþian, Exon. Th. 434, 17; Rä. 52, 2. I a. of mutual or reciprocal action:—Hié fela sprǽcon sorhworda somed, Cd. Th. 49, 8; Gen. 789. Cf. samod-geflit. I b. marking union or junction. v. samod-cumende. II. with numerals or with *eall*:—Him wæs bām samod lond gecynde, Beo. Th. 4399; B. 2196. Đendan bū somod, līc and sāwle, lifgan mōte, Exon. Th. 81, 20; Cri. 1326. Þreó tācen somod, 76, 7; Cri. 1236. Seofon winter samod *seven years in unbroken succession*, Cd. Th. 256, 11; Dan. 639. Ic eów bidde đæt gē mē secgan hwylce gemete gē cōman ealle samod tō mē, Blickl. Homl. 143, 20. Hē eal innan samod forswǽled wæs *within he was one mass of inflammation*, Homl. Th. i. 86, 5. III. marking association of similar objects or circumstances, with nearly the force of *and, both . . . and, also, too:*—Somod *jamque*, Wrt. Voc. ii. 45, 31. Weras wīf samod *men and women*, Andr. Kmbl. 3330; An. 1668. Weras, heora wīf somed, Cd. Th. 146, 7; Gen. 2418. Hē đone healsbeáh gesealde, þrió wicg somod, Beo. Th. 4355; B. 2174. Đū geworhtest heofon and eorþan, sǽs sīdne fæđm, samod ealle gesceaft, Elen. Kmbl. 1455; El. 729. Ongan his feax teran and his hrægl somod, Judth. Thw. 25, 28; Jud. 282. Somod for his hǽlo đæs cyninges and đære þeóde đe hē fore wæs *pro salute illius, simul et gentis cui praeerat*, Bd. 2, 12; S. 512, 29. Niht somod and dæg, Cd. Th. 239, 25; Dan. 375. Swylce ic his willan wylle sēcean, samed (*also, likewise, at the same time*) andettan . . ., Ps. Th. 110, 2. Đū đīnra bearna bearn sceáwige; geseó samed gangan sibb ofer Israhēl, 127, 7: Exon. Th. 69, 16; Cri. 1122. IV. in combination with *ætgædere, mid*:—Sende mihtig God his milde gehigd and his sōđfæst mōd samod ætgædere, Ps. Th. 56, 4: 88, 21. Đǽr wæs sang and swēg samod ætgedere, Beo. Th. 2131; B. 1063. Gāras stōdon samod ætgædere, 662; B. 329. Đū đe samod mid mē swēte gripe metas *qui simul mecum dulces capiebas cibos*,

Ps. Spl. 54, 15. Graton samod mid đâm cnihtum feóll tô Johannes fôtum, Homl. Th. i. 62, 17. Cwom samod mid đâm swylce Assur *etenim Assur simul venit cum illis*, Ps. Th. 82, 7. Đa đe someđ miđ hine âstigun *quae simul cum eo ascenderant*, Mk. Skt. Rush. 15, 41. Hê gesette đone mônan fulne on eástdǣle mid scînendum steorrum samod, Lchdm. iii. 238, 28. **IV a.** with *anlîce*:—Hî me ymbsealdon samod anlîce swâ beón *circumdederunt me sicut apes*, Ps. Th. 117, 12: 142, 4: 147, 5. Samod anlîce . . . swâ swâ *sicut*, 123, 6. Samod anlîcast swâ *velut*, 78, 2: *ut*, 91, 11: *sicut*, 127, 4. **V.** translating the prefix *con-* in Latin words:—Ic samod awende *converto*, Ælfc. Gr. 37; Som. 39, 14. Ic samod cume *convenio*, Som. 39, 5. Ic samod fealde *complico*, 24; Som. 25, 52. Ic samod fealle *concido*, 28; Som. 32, 62. Ic samod fleó *confugio*, Som. 32, 49. Ic samod wurpe *conicio*, Som. 32, 40. Somud mengaþ wê *comminiscimur*, Wrt. Voc. ii. 18, 7. Somod geþwǣrende *concordantes*, 24, 8. [*Laym. A. R.* somed: *Goth.* samath: *O. Sax.* samad, samod.] v. next word.

samod; *prep. with dat. With, at*:—Samod ǣrdæge (*with the coming of the dawn*) eode æþele cempa self mid gesîđum, Beo. Th. 2627; B. 1311. Frôfor eft gelamp sârigmôdum somod ǣrdæge *with day came comfort to the sadhearted*, 5877; B. 2942. Cf. mid ǣrdæge.

samod-cumende *flocking together*: — Samadcumendum folcum *populis confluentibus*, Hpt. Gl. 455, 71: 518, 45.

samode (?):—Tala . . . swylce ic nǣfre on eallum đâm fyrngewritum findan ne mihte sôđe samode [samnode (?) *collected* or (?) *composed*, v. samnian, I. 3. Or cf. (?) *Icel.* semja (kvæđi, bôk) *to compose* (*a poem, book*)], Salm. Kmbl. 17; Sal. 9.

samod-eard, es; *m. A common country*:—Git (*Guthlac and his sister*) â môsten in đam êcan gefeán mid đa sibgedryht somudeard niman, Exon. Th. 184, 19; Gû. 1346.

samod-fæst; *adj. Fast joined together*:—Sceal onettan, se đe âgan wile lîf æt Meotude, đenden him leóht and gǣst somodfæst seón, Exon. Th. 96, 28; Cri. 1581.

samod-geflit, es; *n. Strife, conflict*:—Somodgeflit *concertatio*, Wrt. Voc. ii. 24, 18.

samod-gesîþ, es; *m. A companion, comrade*:—Samodgesîþ *coheres*, Germ. 400, 575.

samod-herung, e; *f. A praising*: — Samodhering *conlaudatio*, Blickl. Gl.

[**samodlîce**; *adv. Together, unitedly in a body*:—Iedon ealle samodlîce tô đone kyng, Chr. 1123; Erl. 250, 10.]

samod-rynelas; *pl. translates the technical term* concurrentes:—Đa *concurrentes* synt samodrynelas genemned, Anglia viii. 302, 10.

samod-swêgende *translates the Latin* consonantes:—Đa ôđre stafas syndon gehâtene *consonantes*, đæt is, samodswêgende, forđan đe hî swêgaþ mid đâm fîf clypiendlîcum, Ælfc. Gr. 2; Som. 2, 49.

samod-þyrlîc; *adj. Concordant*:—Somodđyrlîce *concordi*, Wrt. Voc. ii. 22, 13. Cf. (?) ge-þweran.

samod-willung, e; *f. A boiling together, condensing*:—Somodwellunge *concretione*, Wrt. Voc. ii. 23, 19.

samod-wunung, e, *f. A living together*:—Him is tô forbeódenne ǣghwilc gemâna . . ge ǣt, ge drinc, ge samodwunung on hûsum, L. E. I. 26; Th. ii. 422, 31.

samod-wyrcende *co-operating*:—Somodwyrcendum *cooperante*, Wrt. Voc. ii. 24, 76.

sam-râd; *adj. Harmonious, united*:—Se cræftga geferscipas fæste gesamnaþ đæt hî hiora freóndscipe forþ on symbel untweófealde treówa gehealdaþ sibbe samrâde *the mighty one unites societies firmly, so that for ever they continue to maintain their friendship, faith sincere, peace unbroken*, Met. 11, 96. Cf. ge-râd.

sâmran, Bt. 33, 1; Fox 120, 12. v. sǣmra.

sâm-soden; *adj. Half-cooked*:—Gif man âwiht blôdiges þicge on healfsodenum (sâmsodenum, MSS. X. Y.) mete *si quis cruentum quid comederit in semicocto cibo*, L. Ecg. C. 40; Th. ii. 166, 2.

sâm-swǣled; *adj. Half-burnt*:—Sâmswǣlede *semiustos*, sâmswǣled *semiustus*, Hpt. Gl. 508, 55-57.

sam-tinges (sæm-, sem-); *adv. In close connection* (as regards time), *immediately, forthwith*, continuo:—Meahtest đê full recen on đæm rodere upan siđđan weorþan, and đonne samtenges æt đæm ælcealdan steorran, Met. 24, 18. Swâ hrađe swâ đæt wolcn styrode, swâ sîđode samtinges eal seó fyrd after đam wolcne, Homl. Th. ii. 196, 11. Đâ nolde hê hî sæmtinges âcwellan ac lêt him fyrst *he would not kill them immediately, but allowed them time*, 424, 14. Đâ âwurpon đa hǣđenan sôna heora gedwyld, and tô heora Scyppende sæmtinges gebugon, 510, 3: 230, 18. Đæt man hî ofslôge sæmtinges ealle, Anglia ix. 32, 165. Snâw cymþ of đam þynnum wǣtan đe byþ gefroren ǣr đan hê tô dropum geurnen sŷ, and swâ semtinges (sæm-, MS. P.) fylþ, Lchdm. iii. 278, 25. [Cf. *Icel.* sam-tengja *to join, consent*; sam-tenging *a connection*.] v. tengan, ge-tenge.

sam-winnende *struggling together*:—Đa samwinnendan *conluctantia, depugnantia*, Wrt. Voc. ii. 134, 62. [Cf. *Icel.* sam-vinnandi *working together*.]

sâm-wîs; *adj. Dull, foolish*:—Wênaþ sâmwîse (cf. đa dysegan men, Bt. 32, 3; Fox 118, 22) đæt hî on đîs lǣnan mǣgen lîfe findan sôþa gesǣlþa, Met. 19, 34. Đa sâmwîsan (*hebetes*) sint tô manianne đæt hié wilnien tô wiotonne đæt đæt hié nyton, Past. 30, 1; Swt. 201, 7. Cf. med-wîs.

sam-wist, e; *f. A living together, cohabitation, matrimony*:—Samwist *jugalitas*, Hpt. Gl. 438, 63. Samwiste *matrimonii*, 481, 36: *copulae, connubii*, 485, 57: *copulae*, 508, 75. Samwiste *contubernium*, 511, 76. Ne ceara đû (*Hagar*) fleáme dǣlan somwist incre, Cd. Th. 137, 27; Gen. 2280. Þeáh his lîc and gǣst hyra somwiste, sinhîwan tû, gedǣled (-de?), Exon. Th. 160, 9; Gû. 941. Somwist, 172, 28; Gû. 1150. Samwista *contubernia*, Hpt. Gl. 416, 27: 520, 54. [*O. H. Ger.* samwist: *Icel.* sam-vist.]

sâm-worht. v. sâm-wyrcan.

sam-wrǣdness, e; *f. Combination, union*:—Eall đæt đætte ânnesse hæfþ þæt wê secgaþ đætte sîe đa hwîle đe hit ætsomne biþ and đa samwrǣdnesse wê hâtaþ gôd *everything that has unity, that, we say, exists, while it maintains its unity, and the union of its parts we call good*; omne, quod est, unum esse, ipsumque unum bonum esse didicisti, Bt. 37, 3; Fox 190, 23. Cf. wrǣd, wrǣd-mǣlum.

sâm-wyrcan *to do a thing incompletely*:—Gif hwâ on fyrde griđbryce fulwyrce . . . Gif hê sâmwyrce . . ., L. C. S. 62; Th. i. 408, 23. [Cf. sâm-bryce.] Fæsten wæs sâmworht *the fort was not finished*, Chr. 892; Erl. 88, 34. Stântorr (*the tower of Babel*) sâmworht stôd, Cd. Th. 102, 16; Gen. 1701.

sanct, es; *m. A saint*:—Hê wæs on lîfe eorþlîc cing, hê is nû æfter deáþe heofonlîc sanct, Chr. 979; Erl. 129, 10. Đa mynstermenn noldon đone sanct underfôn, Swt. A. S. Rdr. 100, 149. Hê gesôhte đone sanct, Glostr. Frag. 6, 8: 8, 10. Đǣr habbaþ englas eádigne dreám, sanctas singaþ, Cd. Th. 286, 20; Sat. 355: 279, 18; Sat. 240. Đŷ ylcan dæge ealra wê healdaþ sancta symbel, Menol. Fox 367; Men. 200. *The Latin forms* sanctus, sancta (*also* sancte) *are used before proper names*:—Sanctus Johannes, se mon Sancte Johannes, Sanctus Johannes lîf, Blickl. Homl. 163. Sancta Maria, 5, 30. Sancta Marian (*gen.*), 165, 27.

sand, es; *m.* [? *or should the passages that follow be put under* sand; *f.*? cf. *the later application of* witness *to a person*] *A messenger, envoy*:—Đâ wæs Lŷfing b. mid đam kincge . . . Đâ com Xpes cyrc sand tô đam b. and hê forđ (fôr?) đâ tô đam kincge *bishop Lyfing was then with the king . . . Then came a messenger* (or *message*?) *from Christchurch to the bishop, and he* (*the bishop*) *went then to the king*, Chart. Th. 339, 26. Dæg byþ Drihtnes sond deóre mannum mǣre Metodes leóht *day is the Lord's messenger* (or *message*?) *dear to men, God's glorious light*, Runic pm. Kmbl. 344, 9; Rûn. 24. On đîs ylcan geáre com đæs Pâpan sande (sand?) hider tô lande; đæt wæs Waltear bisceop *in the same year came the Pope's legate to this country; that was bishop Walter*, Chr. 1095; Erl. 232, 28. [Here sandes feórden betwyx heom and hî togædere cômen and wurđe sæhte *their envoys went between them, and they came together and were reconciled*, 1135; Erl. 261, 20. Sonden commen betwenen đe sođe word me seiden, Laym. 4651. Euerich wo is Godes sonde. Heie monnes messager, me schal heiliche underuongen, A. R. 190, 15. In alle our neoden sendeđ þeos sonden (*prayers*) touward heouene, 246, 22.]

sand, e; *f.* I. *a sending, mission, message*:—Paulus cwæđ: 'Đâ đâ đæra tîda gefyllednys com, đâ sende God Fæder his sunu tô mancynnes âlŷsednysse.' Seó wurđfulle sand wearđ on đisum dæge gefylled, Homl. Th. i. 194, 17. Gregorius is rihtlîce Engliscre þeóde apostol, forđan đe hê þurh his rǣd and sande ûs fram deófles biggengum ætbrǣd, ii. 116, 28. Nû com ic tô eów þurh đæs Almihtigan sande, 296, 20. Đes ylca apostol becom þurh Godes sande tô Ethiopian, 472, 11. [*Laym.* sande, sonde *a message*; sondes mon *a messenger*: Orm. sanderr-man: sandermen, Chr. 1135; Erl. 249, 28: *C. M.* sandir-men: sander-bodes, O. E. Homl. ii. 89, 22: *Prompt. Parv.* sond or sendynge *missio*: sond or ȝyfte sent *eccenium*: *O. H. Ger.* -santa, santi- *missio*, Grff. vi. 239.] v. onsand. II. *a mess* (from Latin *mitto*), *a dish of food, victuals*:—Wista *vel* sand *dapes* vel *fercula*, Wrt. Voc. i. 26, 63. Sand *daps*, 82, 64: Ælfc. Gr. 9, 54; Som. 13, 20. Godes engel cwæđ: 'Abacuc, bær đone mete tô Babilone' . . . Đâ clypode se Abacuc: 'Đû Godes þeówa, nim đâs lâc đe đê God sende' . . . And hê đâ đære sande breác, Homl. Th. i. 572, 8. Đâ genemnode se hâlga wer đæt wîf đe hî gelađode, and đa sanda tealde đe heó him gebær, ii. 168, 5. Sanda *obsonia*, Germ. 394, 297. Sandae, sondae *commeatos*, Txts. 46, 188. Sanda *ferculorum, epularum*, Hpt. Gl. 444, 57. [Of everilc sonde . . . most and best he gaf Benjamin, Gen. and Ex. 2295.] v. preceding word.

sand, es; *n.* I. *sand, gravel*:—Sand *glarea, glitis*, vel *samia*, Wrt. Voc. i. 22, 8: *arena*, 37, 32. Sande *sablo*, ii. 89, 36. Hê behîdde hyne on đam sande (*sabulo*), Ex. 2, 12. Sume men secgen đæt seó eá sîe eást irnende on đæt sond, and đonne besince eft on đæt sand, and đǣr nêh sîe eft flôwende up of đam sande, Ors. 1, 1; Swt. 12, 20-23. Đa tôdǣlaþ đæt wæsmbǣre land and đæt deádwylle sand đe syđđan hîþ sūþ on ðone gārsecg *qui dividit inter vivam terram et arenas jacentes usque ad oceanum*, Swt. 26, 19. II. *sand by the sea, sands, sea-shore*:—Sand sǣ *arena maris*, Ps. Spl. 77, 31. Sǣfaroþa sand, Cd. Th. 236, 18; Dan. 323. On sande *on the shore of the Red Sea*, 315, 5; Exod. 302. Nacan on sande, Beo. Th. 596; B. 295: 3796; B. 1896. Gewāt him se hearda æfter sande sǣwong tredan, 3932; B. 1964. Ic wæs be sande sǣwealle neáh, Exon. Th. 471, 14; Rä. 61, 1. Swā swā hradu ȳst windes scip tōbrycþ on ðām sandum neáh ðære byrig ðe Tarsit hātte, Ps. Th. 47, 6. [*O. Sax. O. Frs.* sand: *O. H. Ger.* sant *arena, sabulum*: *Icel.* sandr.] v. eolh-sand.

sand-beorh *a sand-hill, sand-bank*:—Ondlong weges tō sondbeorge, Cod. Dip. Kmbl. iii. 402, 11. Sondbeorgum ymbseald, Exon. Th. 360, 23; Wal. 10. Se ðe wille fæst hūs timbrian ne sceall hē hit nō settan up on ðone hēhstan cnol and eft se ðe wille fæst hūs timbrian ne sette hē hit on sondbeorhas *quisquis volet perennem cautus ponere sedem, montis cacumen alti, bibulas vitet arenas*, Bt. 12; Fox 36, 11. Sondbeorgas, Met. 7, 10.

sand-ceosol, es; *m. Sand, gravel*:—Sandceosel *arena*, Wrt. Voc. i. 80, 64. Sandcesel, 54, 32. Sandceosol on sǣ *arenam in litore maris*, Gen. 22, 17. Sandceosol on sǣstrande, Jos. 11, 4. Sandceosol on sǣlīcum strande, Homl. Th. ii. 62, 9. Sandcysel, Wulfst. 198, 22. Hē getimbrode hys hūs ofer sandceosel *supra arenam*, Mt. Kmbl. 7, 26. Hī beóþ gemenigfylde ofer ðære sǣ sandceosol *they shall be multiplied above the sand of the sea*, Homl. Th. ii. 524, 21. [Cf. *Ger.* kiesel-sand *gravel*.]

sand-corn *a grain of sand*:—Gif mīne synna and mīn yrmþ wǣron āwegene on ānre wǣgan, ðonne wǣron hī swǣrran gesewene ðonne sandcorn on sǣ, Homl. Th. ii. 454, 24. Swā fela welena swā ðara sondcorna beóþ be ðisum sǣclifum *quantas pontus versat arenas*, Bt. 7, 4; Fox 22, 27. Hī beóþ ofer sandcorn manige *super arenam multiplicabuntur*, Ps. Th. 138, 16. [*Icel.* sand-korn.]

sand-geweorp, es; *n. A sand-bank, quicksand*:—Sandgewurp *syrtis*, Wrt. Voc. i. 63, 72. On sandgeweorp *in sirtim*, ii. 45, 66. [Cf. *O. H. Ger.* sant-wurfi *syrtis*.] v. *next word and* sand-hrycg.

sand-gewyrpe, es; *n. A sand-heap*:—Tō sandgewyrpe, of sandgewyrpe ūt an Temese, Cod. Dip. Kmbl. vi. 228, 25.

sand-grot *a grain of sand*:—Gerīman sǣs sondgrotu, Exon. Th. 466, 6; Hö. 117.

sand-hliþ *a sand-hill by the sea*:—Gewāt him ofer sandhleoþu tō sǣs faruþe, Andr. Kmbl. 471; An. 236.

sand-hof *a house in the sand, the grave*:—Līc orsāwle sceal in sondhofe wunian, Exon. Th. 173, 31; Gū. 1169.

sand-hrycg *a sand-bank*:—Ðes sandhrycg *haec syrtis*, Ælfc. Gr. 9, 78; Som. 14, 34.

sand-hyll *a sand-hill*:—Sondhyllas *alga* (cf. waar *alga*, 99, 69, wāra *sablonum*, strand *sablo*, Hpt. Gl. 502, 76), Wrt. Voc. ii. 99, 73.

sandig; *adj. Sandy*:—Sandig *arenosa*, sandegum *arenosis*, Hpt. Gl. 502, 73, 75. Sandigum, 449, 25. Ðeós wyrt wihst on sandigum landum, Lchdm. i. 94, 7: 100, 16.

sandiht; *adj. Sandy, dusty*:—Hiora gemitting wæs on sondihtre dūne, ðæt hié for duste ne mehton geseón, hū hī hī behealdan sceolden, Ors. 5, 7; Swt. 230, 15. Of ðam stāne on ðone sandihtan hærepoþ, Cod. Dip. Kmbl. iii. 453, 22.

sand-land *the sea-shore*:—Se hærnflota (*the ship*) æfter sundplegan sondlond gespearn, grond wið greóte, Exon. 182, 11; Gū. 1308.

sand-rid *a quick-sand*:—Sandrid *syrtes*, Wrt. Voc. i. 57, 19. v. rid, *and* cf. sand-geweorp.

sand-seáþ *a sand-pit*:—Ofer ðene hǣþ inn on ðam sandseáþe; of ðam sandseáþe, Cod. Dip. Kmbl. iii. 384, 26. Of ðære ǣc on ða sandseáþas, 80, 2: 169, 4.

sang, es; *m.* I. *song, singing*, (*a*) of human or angelic beings:—Sārlīc sang *trenos* (θρῆνος), Wrt. Voc. i. 28, 18. Twegra sang *bicinium*, 25. Ungeswēge sang *diaphonia*, 34. Geþwǣre sang *armonia*, 39. Ānswēge sang *simphonia*, 40. Wuldres weard wordum herigaþ þegnas ... þǣr is sang æt selde, Cd. Th. 306, 12; Sat. 663. Ðǣr wæs sang and swēg samod ætgædere ... gomenwudu grēted, gid oft wrecen, Beo. Th. 2130; B. 1063: 180; B. 90. Ðǣr wæs singal sang and swegles gong, wlitig weoroda heáp, Andr. Kmbl. 1737; An. 871. Ðǣr is engla song, eádigra blis, Exon. Th. 100, 31; Cri. 1650. Magister cyriclīces sanges *magister ecclesiasticae cantionis*, Bd. 2, 20; S. 522, 27. Songes magister *cantandi magister*, 4, 2; S. 565, 38. Ðā hē ðā ðis leóþ āsungen hæfde, ðā forlēt hē ðone sang, Bt. 24, 1; Fox 80, 5. Ðǣr (*in heaven*) wē hālgan Gode sang ymb seld secgan sceoldon, Cd. Th. 279, 9; Sat. 235. Gesǣton sigerōfe sang āhōfon *lifted up their voices in song*, Elen. Kmbl. 1733; El. 868. (*b*) of birds or animals:—Winsum sanc (*of birds*), Met. 13, 50. Fugla cynn songe lofiaþ mōdigne, Exon. Th. 221, 20; Ph. 337. Mǣwes song, 406, 25; Rä. 25, 6. Earn sang āhōf, Elen. Kmbl. 58; El. 29. Wulf sang āhōf, 224; El. 112. (*c*) of sound caused by inanimate things; v. bȳme-sangere, sang-cræft, singan:—Ealle hearpan strengas se hearpere grēt mid ānre honda, ðȳ hē wile ðæt hī ānne song singen, ðeáh hē hié ungelīce styrige *idcirco chordae consonam modulationem reddunt; quia uno quidem plectro, sed non uno impulsu feriuntur*, Past. 23; Swt. 175, 9. II. *a singing, chanting*:—Se biscop and se mæssepreóst sceolan mæssan gesingan ... and ða ðe on heofenum syndon, hī þingiaþ for ða ðe ðyssum sange fylgeaþ, Blickl. Homl. 45, 36. III. *song, poetry*. v. sang-cræft. IV. *a song, a poem to be sung* or *recited*:—Se hālga song gehȳred wæs, Exon. Th. 181, 23; Gū. 1297. Ðā hæfde hē mē gebunden mid ðære wynnsumnesse his sanges *me carminis mulcedo defixerat*, Bt. 22, 1; Fox 76, 6. Mē Gūðhere forgeaf māþþum songes tō leáne, Exon. Th. 322, 22; Vīd. 67. Galan sigeleásne sang, Beo. Th. 1578; B. 787. Ðonne hē gyd wrece, sārigne sang, 4885; B. 2447. Ic ðysne sang (*the poem which follows*) fand, Apstls. Kmbl. 1; Ap. 1. Word sanga *verba cantionum*, Ps. Spl. 136, 3. Singaþ ūs ymnum ealdra sanga ðe gē on Sione sungan *hymnum cantate nobis de canticis Sion*, Ps. Th. 136, 4. Sangum *carminibus*, Hpt. Gl. 519, 50. Singaþ sangas Drihtne and him neówne sang singaþ *cantate Domino canticum novum*, Ps. Th. 149, 1: 95, 1. [*Goth.* saggws: *O. Sax.* sang: *O. Frs.* song: *O. H. Ger.* sang: *Icel.* söngr. v. ǣfen-, brȳd-, byrig-, cyric-, dæg-, dægrēd-, forannih t-, galdor-, heáf-, hearp-, līc-, lof-, mæsse-, middæg-, niht-, nōn-, offrung-, prīm-, sealm-, tīd-, ūht-, undern-, wōþ-, yfel-sang.

sang, song *a bed*:—Song ɫ bedd *stratum*, Mk. Skt. Lind. 14, 15: Lk. Skt. Lind. 22, 12. [*Icel.* sæing, sæng: *Dan.* sæng: *Swed.* säng *a bed*.]

sang-bōc; *f.* I. *a music-book, a book with the notes marked for singing*:—*Nota* ðæt is mearcung. Ðæra mearcunga sind manega and mislīce gesceapene, ǣgðer ge on sangbōcum ge on leóþcræfte, Ælfc. Gr. 50, 15; Som. 51, 20. II. *one of the service books, containing 'besides the canticles, the hymns which were used in the Anglo-Saxon churches.'* v. Maskell's Monumenta Ritualia, i. cii:—Ðæt synd ða hālgan bēc ... sangbōc ..., L. Ælfc. C. 21; Th. ii. 350, 13. Mæssepreóst sceal habban ... sang-bēc ..., L. Ælfc. P. 44; Th. ii. 384, 1. Nū sindon ðǣr (*in the church at Exeter*) ii. fulle sangbēc, Chart. Th. 430, 8. [*Icel.* söng-bōk.]

sang-cræft, es; *m.* I. *the art of singing, music* (*vocal or instrumental*):—Sangcræft *musica* (in a list of the arts), Hpt. Gl. 479, 46. Wæs hē swȳðest on cyricean sangcræft getȳd Rōmānisce þeáwe *maxime modulandi in ecclesia more Romanorum peritum*, Bd. 4, 2; S. 566, 19. On sangcræft gelǣred *cantandi sonos edoctus*, 5, 20; S. 646, 6. I a. *an art of singing*:—Biþ ðæs hleóþres swēg (*the voice of the Phenix when singing*) eallum songcræftum swētra and wlitigra, and wynsumra wrenca gehwylcum, Exon. Th. 206, 25; Ph. 132. II. *the art of composing poetry*:—Hē (*Cædmon*) þurh Godes gife ðone sangcræft onfēng *gratis canendi donum accepit*, Bd. 4, 24; S. 596, 41.

sangere, es; *m.* I. *a singer*:—Sangere *cantor*, Wrt. Voc. i. 28, 17: 72, 6. Īdel sangere *temelici* (θυμελικός *a musician, singer*), 39, 40. Wē witan ðæt þurh Godes gyfe ceorl wearþ tō eorle, sangere tō sacerde, and bōcere tō biscope, L. Eth. vii. 11; Th. i. 334, 8. Būtan Jacobe ðam sangere, Bd. 4, 2; S. 565, 37. Se bisceop ðǣr gesette gōde sangeras and mæssepreóstas and manigfealdlīce circicean þegnas, Blickl. Homl. 207, 31. II. *a poet*:—David wæs sangere sōðfæstest, swīðe geþancol tō þingienne þeódum sīnum wið ðane Sceppend, Ps. C. 50, 6. [Alse þe holi songere seið on his loft songe, O. E. Homl. ii. 117, 22. *O. H. Ger.* sangari *cantor, psalmista*: *Icel.* söngvari.] v. bȳme-, cyric-sangere.

sangestre, an; *f. A female singer, songstress*:—Sangestre (-ystre) *cantrix*, Ælfc. Gr. 9, 64; Som. 13, 63. Sangystre, Wrt. Voc. i. 72, 5.

sang-pīpe, an; *f. A musical pipe*:—Sangpīpe *camena*, Germ. 389, 26.

-sānian. v. ā-sānian, sǣne.

sāp, e; *f.* (?) *Amber, resin, pomade*:—Sāp, smelting (cf. smulting *electrum*, 94, 61) *succinum* vel *electrum*, Wrt. Voc. i. 38, 31. Reádre deáge (*in margin*, sāpe) *rubro stibio* (*the word occurs in a passage treating of dressing the hair*, cf. *the passage in Pliny describing the use and invention of* 'sapo:' Gallorum hoc inventum rutilandis capillis; fit ex sebo et cinere optimus fagino et caprino, duobus modis, spissus ac liquidus: uterque apud Germanos majore in usu viris quam feminis), Hpt. Gl. 435, 17. v. sāpe *and next word*.

sāp-box *a box for resin*:—Man sceal habban leóhtfæt, blācern, cyllan, sāpbox, Anglia ix. 264, 22.

sāpe, an; *f. Soap, salve* (? v. sāp):—Sāpe *sapo* (*sopo*, MS.), Wrt. Voc. i. 86, 12: *lumentum*, ii. 54, 4. Hē biþ ðonne āþwogen fram his synnum þurh ða untrumnysse, swā swā horig hrægl þurh sāpan, Homl. Th. i. 472, 6. [Monie of þas wimmen smurieð heom mid blanchet, þet is þes deofles sāpe (*unguent?*), O. E. Homl. i. 53, 24. Þe wreche peoddare more noise he makeð to ȝeien his sope, þen a riche mercer al his deorewurðe ware, A. R. 66, 18. *O. H. Ger.* seifa *sabona, smigma*; also *resina*.] v. ār-, pill-sāpe.

sār, es; *n.* I. referring to the body, (1) *pain, suffering, soreness*:—Mē sār gehrān, wærc in gewōd, Exon. Th. 163, 28; Gū. 1000. Sār gewōd ymb ðæs beornes breóst, Andr. Kmbl. 2494; An. 1245. Mid sāre geswenced, mid mislīcum ecum and tyddernessum, Blickl. Homl. 59, 7. On sāre his līchoma sceal hēr wunian, 61, 1. Hǣlu būtan sāre,

Exon. Th. 101, 8; Cri. 1655. Ða ðe on sâre seóce lāgun, 83, 14; Cri. 1356. Hē sār ne wiste *he did not feel pain*, Cd. Th. 12, 3; Gen. 179. (2) *a pain, pang, sore, wound*:—Nis ðǣr ǣnig sār gemēted, ne ādl, ne ece, Blickl. Homl. 25, 30. Hē byð ðæs sāres hāl, Lchdm. i. 352, 2. Wið eágena, eárena, sīdan, wambe, &c. sāre, i. 2, sqq. On his mōdor sāre hē biþ ācenned, Blickl. Homl. 57, 35. Ðȳlæs hwelc ðara niéhstena ðæs ofslægenan for ðæm sāre (*the mortal wound caused by the slipping of an axe*) hine ofsleá, Past. 21; Swt. 167, 3. Mugcwyrt ðæt sār ðara fōta of genimþ, Lchdm. i. 102, 16. Gif sió wamb biþ windes full, ðonne cymþ ðæt of wlacre wǣtan; sió cealde wǣte wyrcþ sār an . . . ðonne dēþ ðæt ðæt sār āweg, Lchdm. ii. 224, 24. Nǣfre ðū ðæs suīðlīc sār gegearwast heardra wīta, ðæt ðū mec onwende worda ðissa, Exon. Th. 246, 2; Jul. 55. Ðū ðæt sār (*stripes and blows*) āber, Andr. Kmbl. 1912; An. 958. Ðæt gē him sāra gehwylc gehǣlde *that you should heal every wound for him*, Exon. Th. 144, 11; Gū. 676. Leomu hefegodon sārum gesōhte *his limbs waxed heavy, visited by pains*, 159, 21; Gū. 930. Ādle gebysgad, sārum geswenced, 170, 11; Gū. 1110. Ðā wæs heó eft hefigod mid ðǣm ǣrran sārum *prioribus adgravata doloribus*, Bd. 4, 19; S. 589, 5. Se Hǣlend his þegnum sǣde ða sār ðe hē ādreógan wolde, Blickl. Homl. 15, 33. Hié ealle līchomlīcu sār oforhogodan, 119, 20. II. of the mind, (1) *grief, pain, trouble, sorrow*:—Ne biþ ðǣr sār ne gewinn, ne nǣnig unēþnes, Blickl. Homl. 103, 35. Wēpende sār, Exon. Th. 79, 14; Cri. 1290. Is sāwl mīn sāres and yfeles gefylled *repleta est malis anima mea*, Ps. Th. 87, 3. Tō tācnunge sorges and ānfealdes sāres, Bt. 7, 2; Fox 18, 21. Hī hī forlǣtaþ on ðam mǣstan sāre, 7, 1; Fox 16, 13. Hē heora helpend wæs on heora sāre, Bd. 3, 9; S. 533, 26. (2) *a grief, sorrow, pain, wound*:—Hit wæs swā gewunelīc on ealdum dagum, ðæt gif hwam sum fǣrlīc sār (*affliction*) becōme, ðæt hē his reáf tōtǣre, Homl. Th. ii. 454, 14. Ðeáh him mon hwæt wiðerweardes doo, oððe hē hwelce scande gehiére be him selfum, hē æt ðæm cierre ne biþ onstyred . . . ac æfter lytlum fæce hē biþ onǣled mid ðȳ fȳre ðæs sāres, Past. 33; Swt. 225, 20. Ðā ðæt mōd ðillīc sār cweþende wæs, Bt. 5, 1; Fox 8, 24. Lufu him sāra gehwylc symle forswīðede, Exon. Th. 160, 4; Gū. 938: 176, 31; Gū. 1218. Æfter ðære menigeo mīnra sāra ðe mē on ferhþe gestōdan *secundum multitudinem dolorum meorum in corde meo*, Ps. Th. 93, 18. Ða angunnenan sār *conceptos dolores*, Wrt. Voc. ii. 136, 12. [*Goth.* sair: *O. Sax. O. L. Ger. O. Frs. O. H. Ger.* sēr *dolor, supplicium, amaritudo, ulcus*: *Icel.* sār *a sore; a wound.*] v. līc-sār, *and next word.*

sār; *adj. Sore, painful, grievous, distressing*, (1) of physical pain:—Se lǣca ðe sceal sāre (yfela, MS. Y.) wunda wel gehǣlan, hē mōt habban gōde sealfe ðǣrtō, L. Pen. 4; Th. ii. 278, 15. Ne wæs hyra ǣnigum sīde ðȳ sārra, ðeáh hȳ swā sceoldan reáfe birofene slītan haswe blēde, Exon. Th. 394, 20; Rä. 14, 6. Wē wieton ðæt sió diégle wund biþ sārre ðonne sió opene, Past. 38; Swt. 273, 22. (2) of mental pain:—Ðā hē ðæs mannes deáþ swā earmlīcne gehȳrde ðā wæs him ðæt swīðe sār *when he heard the man's death was so miserable, it was very grievous to him*, Blickl. Homl. 219, 14. Ne wæs hyre brōðra deáþ on sefan swā sār, Exon. 377, 25; Deór. 9. Ðæt ðam hālgan wæs sār on mōde, Cd. Th. 96, 11; Gen. 1593: 27, 30; Gen. 425. Ðæt wæs Satane sār tō geþolienne, Andr. Kmbl. 3375; An. 1691. Ðonne hī sāres hwæt siófian scioldon (cf. ðonne hī sceoldan heora sār sióflan, Bt. 38, 1; Fox 194, 35), Met. 26, 82. Bīdan sāran sorge, Cd. Th. 266, 26; Sat. 28. Forlǣt sāre sorgceare, Exon. Th. 13, 27; Cri. 209. Hearm, sāre swyltcwale, Andr. Kmbl. 2735; An. 1370. Morþra, sārra sorga, Judth. Thw. 24, 10; Jud. 182: Rood Kmbl. 157; Kr. 80. Manaþ sārum wordum *prompts with words that wound*, Beo. Th. 4122; B. 2058. Ealle ða sāran edwīta ðe hē ādreág, Blickl. Homl. 97, 15. Uncūðne eard cunnian, sāre sīþas *to make trial of a land unknown, of travails sore*, Exon. Th. 87, 2; Cri. 1419. Cwæð ðæt him wǣre weorce on mōde, sorga sārost, Cd. Th. 122, 19; Gen. 2029. [*O. Sax. O. L. Ger. O. Frs. O. H. Ger.* sēr *tristis*: *Icel.* sārr *sore; wounded.*] v. un-sār.

Saracene, Sarocine, Sarcine; *pl. Saracens*:—Sarracene *Sarasene*, Ors. 1, 1; Swt. 12, 5. Wǣron ðǣr Sarocine gesamnode ðæt hig sǣtnodan manna, Shrn. 37, 34. Wit urnon for Sarcina hergunge, 42, 9. Se hefegosta wōl Sarcina þeóde Gallia rīce forhergedon *gravissima Sarracenorum lues Gallias vastabat*, Bd. 5, 23; S. 645, 31. On India Saracena *in India Saracenorum*, Rtl. 196, 35. [Cf. *Icel.* Serkir: *O. H. Ger.* Sarci, Serzi *Arabes.*]

Saracenisc; *adj. Saracen*:—Hē gegaderode of ðām Saraceniscum swīðe micele fyrde, Jud. Thw. p. 162, 25. [Cf. *Icel.* Serkneskr: *O. H. Ger.* Sarcisc, Sarzisc *Arabicus.*]

Saracen-, Sarcin-ware; *pl. The Saracens*:—Ðā hergodon ða hǣþnan Sarcinware on þa stōwe (*Sardinia*), Shrn. 122, 25.

sār-benn, e; *f. A painful wound*:—Wæs ðæs hālgan līc sārbennum soden, swāte bestēmed, bānhūs ābrocen, blōd ȳþum weóll, Andr. Kmbl. 2479; An. 1241. Sārbennum gesōht, Exon. Th. 163, 11; Gū. 992.

sār-bōt, e; *f. Compensation paid for inflicting a wound*, L. W. I.; Th. i. 470, 21. [*Icel.* sār-bætr; *pl.*]

Sarcine, Sarcin-ware. v. Saracene, Saracen-ware.

sār-clāþ, es; *m. A bandage for a wound*:—Sārclāþ *ligatura*, Wrt. Voc. i. 20, 18: ii. 53, 77: *fasciola*, i. 40, 62: ii. 39, 75.

sārcren (?) *disposed to soreness*:—On ðām monnum ðe habbaþ swīðe gefēlne and sārcrenne magan *a very sensitive stomach and one easily made sore*, Lchdm. ii. 176, 9.

sār-cwide, es; *m.* I. *a speech that is intended to give pain, injurious* or *affronting speech, reproach, bitter words*:—Ne gedafenaþ ðē ðæt ðū andsware mid oferhygdum sēce sārcwide *it befits thee not to seek an answer with arrogance and bitter words*, Andr. Kmbl. 693; An. 320. Synnige ne mihton þurh sārcwide sōð gecȳðan, 1929; An. 967. Ðū ūs āsettest on sārcwide ūrum neáhmannum *posuisti nos in contradictionem vicinis nostris*, Ps. Th. 79, 6. Hē ðæt eal þolaþ, sārcwide secga, Exon. Th. 458, 2; Hy. 4, 94. Ic worn for ðē hæbbe sīdra sorga and sārcwida, hearmes gehȳred, and mē hosp sprecaþ, tornworda fela, 11, 14; Cri. 170. II. *a speech in which grief is expressed, a lament*:—Ic nyste ǣr ðū ðē self hit mē gerehtest mid ðīnum sārcwidum *I did not know until you yourself told it me with your lamentations*, Bt. 5, 1; Fox 8, 34. Nū sceal ic siófigende wreccea giómor singan sārcwidas *flebilis moestos cogor inire modos*, Met. 2, 4.

Sardinie; *pl. The Sardinians, the people* or *the island of Sardinia*:—Hū Sardinie wunnon on Rōmāne, Ors. 4, 7, tit.; Swt. 4, 16. On Sicilium and on Sardinium ðǣm īglondum, 4, 7; Swt. 164, 23.

sāre; *adv. Sorely, grievously, bitterly*:—Wǣron earme men sāre beswicene (*sorely deceived*) and hreówlīce besyrwde, Wulfst. 158, 11 note. Hrinon hearmtānas hearde and sāre drihta bearnum, Cd. Th. 61, 5; Gen. 992. Mē ðæt cynn hafaþ sāre ābolgen *that race hath angered me sore*, 76, 14; Gen. 1257. Forgrīpan gumcynne grimme and sāre heardum mihtum, 77, 15; Gen. 1275. Sum sāre angeald ǣfenreste *one paid a heavy price for his night's rest*, Beo. Th. 2507; B. 1251. Hē cenþ unriht and hit cymþ him sāre *it shall trouble him sorely*, Ps. Th. 7, 14. Hī sāre sprecaþ *they speak bitterly*, 63, 4. Wē sittaþ and sāre wēpaþ (cf. *Icel.* grāta sāran: *Scot.* to greet sair), 136, 1. Wæs se hālga wer sāre geswungen, Andr. Kmbl. 2791; An. 1398. [*O. Frs.* sēre: *O. Sax. O. H. Ger.* sēro *dolenter*: *Ger.* sehr.] v. emn-sāre.

sārettan; *p.* te *To lament, complain*:—Hē sārette ðætte ða synfullan sceoldan bytlan onuppan his hrycge *supra dorsum suum fabricasse peccatores queritur*, Past. 21, 2; Swt. 153, 9. Ðæt ilce sārette se wītga *contra hos propheta conqueritur*, 37, 2; Swt. 267, 2. [*O. H. Ger.* sērazzan *dolere.*]

sār-ferhþ; *adj. Sore at heart, wounded in spirit*:—Ðæt wīf (*Sarah complaining to Abraham about Hagar*) mōdes sorge, sārferhþ sægde: 'Ne fremest ðū riht wið mē,' Cd. Th. 135, 17; Gen. 2244. Cf. sārig-ferhþ.

sārga, an; *m. Some kind of trumpet*:—Trūðhorn oððe sārga *lituus*, Wrt. Voc. i. 73, 67. Sārgana *salpicum, tubarum*, Hpt. Gl. 445, 11.

sārgian; *p.* ode. I. *to make sad* (sārig), *to grieve* (trans.), *afflict, wound*:—Hī sārgiaþ fremdne flǣschoman, Salm. Kmbl. 220; Sal. 109. II. *to be* or *become sad, to grieve* (intrans.), *languish*:—Hē sārgaþ ðæs *he is grieved at it*, Past. 33; Swt. 227, 21. Se bisceop hefiglīce sārgode be ðam fylle and mīnre forwyrde *episcopus gravissime de casu et interitu meo dolebat*, Bd. 5, 6; S. 619, 32. Eágan mīne sārgodon *oculi mei languerunt*, Ps. Spl. 87, 9. Ðā ongan hē forhtian and sārgian *et coepit pauere et taedere*, Mk. Skt. 14, 33. Sārgiende ł sorhful *dolens*, Ps. Lamb. 68, 30. Sārgiendne frēfrian *dolentem consolari*, R. Ben. 17, 3 MS. O. [*O. H. Ger.* sēragōn *to sadden, pain, wound.*] v. be-, ge-sārgian.

sārgung, e; *f. Lamentation, grief*:—Ðǣr is sorgung and sārgung and ā singal heóf, Wulfst. 114, 5. Beó ðū forþloten tō sārgungum *esto pronus ad lamenta*, Scint. 6. v. be-sārgung.

sārian; *p.* ode. I. *to feel pain for, feel sorry for*:—Heó is mā tō sārianne *magis dolendum*, Bd. 1, 27; S. 496, 40. II. *to be sore* (v. sār; *adj.*), (1) of physical pain:—Hē (*the disease*) wundaþ and sió wund sāraþ *the wound gets painful*, Past. 11; Swt. 71, 20. Ða liran ðara lendena sāriaþ, Lchdm. ii. 216, 24. (2) of mental pain, *to grieve, be sad*:—Ic sārige on mīnum wītum *I grow sad in my punishments*, Nar. 43, 7. Wē sāriaþ ealle, forðon þe wē seóþ ðīnne līchaman beón cwylmed, 42, 2. Ðīn fæder and ic sārigende (*dolentes*) ðē sōhton, Lk. Skt. 2, 48. Sāriendne (sāriende, MS. T.) frēfrian, R. Ben. 17, 3. [*O. Sax.* gi-sērid *afflicted*: *O. Frs.* sērd: *O. H. Ger.* sēren, sērōn *vulnerare, dolere.*]

sārig; *adj.* I. *feeling grief, sorry, sorrowful, sad*:—Ðā wæs Petrus sārig *contristatus est Petrus*, Jn. Skt. 21, 17: Homl. Th. ii. 248, 11. Ic mē sylfa eam sārig þearfa *pauper et dolens ego sum*, Ps. Th. 68, 30. Ðā sceolde se hearpere weorþan swā sārig ðæt hē ne mihte on gemong ōðrum monnum beón *the harper* (*Orpheus*) *is said to have become so afflicted with grief, that he could not live among other men*, Bt. 35, 6; Fox 168, 6. Se is swīðe sārig for ðīnum earfoþum and for ðīnum wræcsīþe, 10; Fox 28, 18. Ðæs ðe hē swā geómor wearð, sārig for his synnum, Exon. Th. 450, 15; Dōm. 88. Hē wearð swīðe sāri *graviter accepit*, Gen. 48, 17. Ne forseoh sāriges bēne, Ps. Th. 54, 1. On salig wē sārige ūre organan āhēngan, 136, 2. Ðā wurdon hiora wīf swā sârige on hiora mōde, and swā swīðlīce gedrēfed, Ors. 1, 10; Swt. 44, 29. Hig wæron sârie (*dolentes*) for hira geswince, Num. 11, 1. Monge ðe hine sârge gesōhtun, freórigmōde, Exon. Th. 155, 12; Gū. 859. Sōhton sârigu tū (*the two women at the sepulchre*) sigebearn Godes, 460, 2; Hö. 11. Sârge gē ne sōhton, ne him swǣslīc word frōfre gesprǣcon, 92, 19; Cri. 1511. II. *expressing grief, mournful, sad, bitter*:—Hē ðā wēpende wēregum teárum his sigedryhten sârgan reorde grētte, Andr. Kmbl. 120; An. 60. Ðonne hē wrece sârigne sang, Beo. Th. 4885; B. 2447. Sârige teáras, Ps. Th. 55, 7. [*O. Sax. O. H. Ger.* sêrag *dolens, amarus.*] v. efen- (em-) sârig.

sârig-ferhþ; *adj. Sad in soul*:—Geseóþ sorga mǣste synfā men sârigferþe, Exon. Th. 67, 4; Cri. 1083. Cf. sâr-ferhþ.

sârig-mōd; *adj. Sad-hearted, of mournful mood*:—Ðonne fēhþ seó weálāf sorhful and sârigmōd geómrigendum mōde synne bemǣnan, Wulfst. 133, 13. Geneósige ða ðe beóþ sârigmōde and seóce, L. Pen: 16; Th. ii. 282, 28. Frōfor eft gelamp sârigmōdum, Beo. Th. 5876; B. 2942. [Þa wes he sarimod and sorhful an heorten, Laym. 29791. Sorimod and wroþ, O. and N. 1218. Forfrigted folc and sorimod, Gen. and Ex. 3520. *O. Sax.* sêrag-mōd.]

sârigness, e; *f. Sadness*:—Hwæt mæg beón wōp oððe sârignys, gyf ðæt næs se mǣsta ǣgðres, Homl. Skt. i. 23, 102. [Hē hig funde slǣpende for unrōtnesse (*later MS.* sârignesse) *dormientes prae tristitiam*, Lk. Skt. 22, 45. Tristicia þet is þissere worlde sarinesse, O. E. Homl. i. 103, 22. Þer wes sarinesse (wowe, 2nd MS.), sorreȝen inoȝe, Laym. 27560. In eche sorinesse, O. E. Misc. 76, 125. Wiþ muchel sorinesse, Horn. 922]

sâr-līc; *adj.* I. *giving occasion for sorrow, sad, mournful, lamentable, grievous*:—Wā lā wā! ðæt is sârlīc ðæt swā leóhtes andwlitan men sceolan āgan þȳstra ealdor *heu, proh dolor! quod tam lucidi vultus homines tenebrarum auctor possidet*, Bd. 2, 1; S. 501, 15. Sârlīc tō cweðene *dolendum dictu*, Hpt. Gl. 447, 25. Nō his līfgedāl sârlīc þūhte secga ǣnigum *to no man did his death seem occasion for sorrow*, Beo. Th. 1688; B. 842. Sârlīc symbel (*the eating of the forbidden fruit*), Exon. Th. 226, 15; Ph. 406. Sârlīc sīþfæt (*the journey to hell*), 446, 20; Dōm. 25. Se sârlīca cwide: 'Terra es et in terram ibis' *that sad sentence, 'Dust thou art and to dust thou shalt return,'* Blickl. Homl. 123, 7. Mid sârlīcre sceame *confusione*, Ps. Th. 88, 38. I a. *causing pain, grievous*:—Ēþung biþ sârlīc *the breathing is painful*, Lchdm. ii. 258, 17. Wē witon unrīm ðara monna ðe ða ēcan gesǣlþa sōhtan nallas þurh ðæt ān ðæt hī wilnodon ðæs līchomlīcan deáþes ac eác manegra sârlīcra wīta hié gewilnodon *multos scimus beatitudinis fructum non morte solum, verum etiam doloribus suppliciisque quaesisse*, Bt. 11, 2; Fox 36, 4. II. *expressing sorrow* or *grief, sad, mournful*:—Sârlīc sang *trenos*, Wrt. Voc. i. 28, 18. Sârlīc blis *cantilena*, ii. 128, 13. Hē sit mid sârlīcum andwlitan, nāt ic hwæt hē besorgaþ, Ap. Th. 15, 10. Hē cwæð mid sârlīcre stemne, Swt. A. S. Rdr. 101, 205. Sârlīc leóþ *tragoediam*, Wrt. Voc. ii. 82, 37. Hwīlum gyd āwræc sârlīc, Beo. Th. 4224; B. 2109. [Næs heo næuere swa sarlic, þ wes Wenhauer þa quene, sarȝest wimmone, Laym. 28457. *O. H. Ger.* sêr-līh *grievous.*]

sârlīce; *adv.* I. *in a manner that causes* or *is attended by physical pain, sorely, painfully*:—Job sæt sârlīce eal on ānre wunde, Homl. Th. ii. 452, 27. Blōd ðæt wæs sârlīce āgoten, Ps. Th. 78, 11. Ðē sculon slītan sârlīce swearte wihta, Soul Kmbl. 145; Seel. 73. Hē sōhte hū hē sârlīcast, þurh ða wyrrestan wītu, meahte feorhcwale findan, Exon. Th. 276, 25; Jul. 571. II. *in a manner that causes mental pain, sorely, grievously, lamentably*:—Ðæt mīn fōt ful sârlīce āsliden wǣre, Ps. Th. 93, 17. Hī mē on dīgle deorce stōwe settan sârlīce, 142, 4. Hit oft swīðe sârlīce gebyrede ðæt wrīteras forlēton unwritene ðara monna dǣda ðe on hiora dagum foremǣroste wǣron *it has often happened most lamentably, that writers have left unwritten those men's deeds that in their days were most distinguished*, Bt. 18, 3; Fox 64, 32. III. *in a manner that expresses sorrow* or *grief, sorely, bitterly, heavily*:—Apollonius sârlīce sæt, Ap. Th. 14, 21. Sârlīce wēpende *weeping bitterly*, Gen. 21, 16. Ðā onsāc se Wisdōm *then Wisdom sighed heavily*, Bt. 26, 2; Fox 92, 24: 40, 3; Fox 238, 7: Wulfst. 133, 14. Ðā wǣron hié ealle sōna unrōte, and sârlīce gebǣrdon, Blickl. Homl. 225, 14. [*O. Frs.* sêrlīke.]

Sarmondisc; *adj. Sarmatian*:—Nēh ðæm gārsecge ðe mon hāteþ Sarmondisc *Sarmatico aversi oceano*, Ors. 1, 1; Swt. 8, 16.

sârness, e; *f.* I. *bodily pain*:—On sârnysse ðū ācenst cild *in dolore paries filios*, Gen. 3, 16. Freoh fram deáþes sârnysse, Homl. Th. i. 76, 14. II. *mental pain, affliction, grief*:—Geopenige ūre sârnys (*the trouble arising from a pestilence*) ūs infær sōðre gecyrrednysse, ii. 124, 7. Gehrepod mid heortan sârnisse *tactus dolore cordis*, Gen. 6, 6. Hē ðis eal mid sârnesse beheóld, Ap. Th. 14, 19. Āfirsa fram him his sârnesse, 16, 14. *Heu* geswutelaþ mōdes sârnesse, Ælfc. Gr. 5; Som. 4, 1. Helle sârnyssa mē beeodon, and ic on mīnre gedrēfednysse Drihten clypode, Homl. Th. ii. 86, 17. Ðæt beóþ ða angin, hē cwæð, ðara sârnessa . . . ða sorga and ða sârnessa de on woruld becumaþ, Wulfst. 89, 11–14.

Sarocine, Sarracene. v. Saracene.

sâr-seófung, e; *f. Complaint*:—Sârseófunge *querulosis* quiðungum *questibus*, Wrt. Voc. ii. 76, 18–19.

sâr-slege, es; *m. A painful blow, a blow that wounds* or *pains*:—Wē ða heardestan wītu geþoliaþ þurh sârslege, Exon. Th. 262, 31; Jul. 341: 275, 8; Jul. 547. Ne mōstun hȳ Gūþlāces gǣste sceþþan, ne þurh sârslege sāwle gedǣlan wið līchoman, 115, 31; Gū. 198. Ðā wæs hē swungen sârslegum, swāt ȳðum weóll, Andr. Kmbl. 2551; Ann. 1277.

sâr-spell, es; *n. A sorrowful speech, a lament*:—Ic secge ðis sârspell and ymb sīþ spræce, Exon. Th. 458, 6; Hy. 4, 96.

sâr-stæf, es; *m. A term intended to pain, an insult, a reproach*:—Godes andsacan sægdon sârstafum swīðe gehēton ðæt hē deáþa gedāl dreógan sceolde *God's adversaries said with bitter words, vehemently vowed, that he should suffer death*, Exon. Th. 116, 10; Gū. 205.

sârung, e; *f. Mourning, lamentation*:—Ðǣr is sorgung and sârgung (sâruncg, MS. K.) and ā singal heóf, Wulfst. 114, 5.

sâr-wilm, es; *m. A painful burning, a feverish heat*:—Soden sârwylmum (cf. ādle gebysgad, sârum geswenced, 170, 10–11), Exon. Th. 171, 7; Gū. 1123.

sâr-wīs (?) *dull*:—Ða sârwīsan (Cott. MS. sāmwīsan), Past. 30, 1; Swt. 203, 7. v. sām-wīs.

sâr-wracu; *gen.* -wræce; *f. Sore tribulation*:—Nis ðǣr synn ne sacu ne sârwracu (sâr wracu ?), Exon. Th. 201, 11; Ph. 54. Swā ðæt ēce līf eádigra gehwylc æfter sârwræce sylf geceóseþ, 224, 27; Ph. 382: 274, 2; Jul. 527.

Satan, es; *m. Satan*:—God cwæð ðæt se hēhsta hātan sceolde Satan, Cd. Th. 22, 23; Gen. 345: 22, 27; Gen. 347. Hē wæs fram Satane gecostnod, Mk. Skt. 1, 13: Exon. Th. 93, 6; Cri. 1522: Andr. Kmbl. 3374; An. 1691. *The Greek form* Satanas *with acc.* Satanan *also occurs*, Mk. Skt. 3, 23: Lk. Skt. 10, 18; *and* Satanus, Cd. Th. 287, 22; Sat. 371: 292, 27; Sat. 447.

saturege, an; *f. Savory*; satureia hortensis, Lchdm. iii. 24, 4. [*M. H. Ger.* satereie: *Ger.* saturei.] v. sæþerige.

Saturnus; *gen.* Saturnes; *m.* I. *Saturn the god*:—Ðæs (*Jove's father*) nama wæs Saturnus, Bt. 38, 1; Fox 194, 17: Met. 26, 48. Tō ðam cealdan stiorran ðe wē hātaþ Saturnes steorra (cf. Met. 24, 31, *where the star is called Saturn*: ðone steorran Saturnus loudbūende hātaþ), Bt. 36, 2; Fox 174, 13. II. the name occurs often in the Dialogue of Salomon and Saturn.

sauine. v. safine.

sâwan; *p.* seów, sēw; *pp.* sāwen. I. lit. (a) *to sow* (seed in a field):—Tūncersan ðe mon ne sǣwþ, Lchdm. ii. 22, 13. Weard sāweþ on swæð mīn, Exon. Th. 403, 11; Rä. 22, 6. Hig ne sāwaþ *non seminant*, Lk. Skt. 12, 24. Hlāford hū ne seów (seówe, MS. A.) ðū gōd sǣd on ðīnum æcere *Domine, nonne bonum semen seminasti in agro tuo?* Mt. Kmbl. 13, 27. Ūt eode se sǣdere hys sǣd tō sāwenne [sēde ł sēdege, Lind.]. And ðā ðā hē seów, 13, 3–4. Ðā hē sēw (seów, MS. A.) Mk. Skt. 4, 4. Hē wīngeard sette, seów sǣda fela, Cd. Th. 94, 9; Gen. 1559. Be ðæm āworpnan engle is āwriten ðæt hē sēwe ðæt weód on ða gōdan æceras *cum bonae messi inserta fuissent zizania*, Past. 47, 1; Swt. 357, 17. Gehȳre gē ðæs sāwendan (*seminantis*) bigspell, Mt. Kmbl. 13, 18. Sāwondum *seminanti*, Kent. Gl. 370. (b) *to sow* (a field with seed):—Hī seówon æceras *seminaverunt agros*, Ps. Spl. 106, 37. Ne sāw ðū ðīnne æcyr mid gemengedum sǣde *agrum tuum non seres diverso semine*, Lev. 19, 19. Six geár ðū scealt sāwan *sex annis seres agrum tuum*, 25, 3. II. fig. *to sow the seeds of anything, to originate, do an action which produces a result, implant*:—Se eorþlīca anweald ne sǣwþ (*inserit*) ða cræftas ac lisþ unþeáwas, Bt. 27, 1; Fox 94, 25. Āworpen man on ǣlce tīd sāweþ wrōhte *homo apostata omni tempore jurgia seminat*, Past. 47, 1; Swt. 357, 22. Se ealda inwit sāweþ, Fragm. Kmbl. 67; Leás. 35. Ða hēr on teárum sāwaþ hī eft fægerum gefeán snīðaþ *qui seminant in lacrymis, in gaudio metent*, Ps. Th. 125, 5: Exon. Th. 6, 18; Cri. 86. Hē monigfealde mōdes snyttru seów and sette geond sefan monna, 41, 29; Cri. 663. Sibbe sāwaþ on sefan manna, 30, 31; Cri. 487. [*Goth.* saian; *p.* saisō: *O. Sax.* sāian; *p.* sāida, sēu: *O. Frs.* sēa: *O. H. Ger.* sājan; *p.* sāta: *Icel.* sā; *p.* seri, *later* sāði.] v. ā-, be-, ge-, geond-, ofer-, on-, tō-sāwan.

sâwel (ol, ul), sāwl, sāul, sōwhul, e; *f. The soul*:—Sāwul *anima*, Wrt. Voc. i. 76, 30. Sāwl, 42, 32. Sāul, 282, 23: ii. 7, 75. I. *the soul, the animal life*:—Ic secge mīnre sāwle: 'Eálā sāwel, ðū hæfst mycele gōd . . . gerest ðē, et, drinc, and gewista.' Ðā cwæð God tō him: 'Lā dysega, on ðisse nihte hig feccaþ ðīne sāwle fram ðē' . . . Ic eów secge: 'Ne beó gē ymbehȳdige eówre sāwle, hwæt gē etan . . . Seó sāwul ys mā ðonne se līchama, Lk. Skt. 12, 16–23. Mannes Sunu com ðæt hē sealde his sāwle līf (ferh, Rush.) tō ālȳsednesse for manegum, Mt. Kmbl. 20, 28. Gif hwā eácniend wīf gewerde . . . gif hió deád sīe, selle sāwle wið sāwle, L. Alf. 18; Th. i. 48, 19. Se ðe gemēt hys sāwle (sāule ł ferh, Rush.), se forspilþ hig; and se ðe forspilþ his sāwle for mē, hē gemēt hī, Mt. Kmbl. 10, 39: 16, 25: Jn. Skt. 12, 25. Genera sāwle mīne fram ārleásum, Ps. Spl. 16, 14. Sāwle sēcan *to try to kill*, Beo. Th. 1606; B. 801. Ðæt hē gefriðie heora sāwla fram deáþe, and hī fēde on hungres tīde, Ps. Th. 32, 16. II. *the soul, the intellectual and immortal principle in man*:—Hwæt gelȳfeþ se līchoma būtan þurh ða sāwle? Geþencean ða men ðæt hié heora sylfra sāwla geseón ne māgon; ac eal swâ hwæt swâ se gesênelîca lîchama dēþ, eal ðæt dēþ seó ungesŷnelîce sâwl þurh ðone lîchoman; and ðonne seó sâwl hié gedǽleþ wið ðone lîchoman, hwylc biþ hē ðonne bûton swylce stân, oððe treów? Ne hē hine nâ né onstyreþ, siððan seó ungesŷnelîce sâwl him of biþ, Blickl. Homl. 21, 21–28. Se ēcea dǽl, ðæt is seó sâwl, 111, 32. Seó sâul mid gâstlîcum þingum on ēcnesse leofaþ, 57, 15. Ealle men lîchomlîce sweltaþ, and ðeáh seó sâwl biþ libbende. Ac seó sâwl færþ swîðe freólîce tō heofonum, siððan heó of ðam carcerne ðæs lîchoman onliésed biþ, Bt. 18, 4; Fox 68, 13. Sâwl and lîcchoma wyrcaþ ânne mon .. tō ðære sâwle and tō ðam lîchoman belimpaþ ealle ðâs ðæs monnes good, ge gâstlîce ge lîchomlîce ... Ðonne is ðære sâwle gōd wærscipe and gemetgung and geþyld and rihtwîsnes and wîsdōm and manege swelce cræftas, 34, 6; Fox 140, 28–35: 34, 10; Fox 148, 3–4. Nū tō ðam sōþan gefeán sâwel fundaþ, Exon. Th. 178, 3; Gū. 1238: 233, 12; Ph. 523. Gewât sâwol sēcean sōðfæstra dōm, Beo. Th. 5633; B. 2820. Sâwul, Byrht. Th. 136, 64; By. 177. Seó ŷdelnes is ðære sâwle feónd, L. E. I. 3; Th. ii. 404, 11. Hwæt is ðæt ðæm men sŷ mâre þearf tō þencenne ðonne embe his sâuwle þearfe? Blickl. Homl. 97, 20. Nŷtenu and deór, fixas and fugelas hē gesceóp on flǽsce bûtan sâwle, Homl. Th. i. 276, 4. On hwilcum dǽle hætþ se man Godes anlîcnysse on him? on ðære sâwle ... Ðæs mannes sâwl hæfþ on hire þreó þing, ðæt is, gemynd and andgit and willa ... Ân sâwul is, and ân lîf and ân edwist seó ðe hæfþ ðâs þreó þing ... Deáhhwæðere nis nân ðæra þreora seó sâwul, ac seó sâwul þurh ðæt gemynd gemanþ, þurh ðæt andgit heó understent, þurh ðone willan heó wile swâ hwæt swâ hire lîcaþ, 288, 15–30. Se man is ēce on ânum dǽle, ðæt is, on ðære sâwle; heó ne geendaþ nǽfre, 16, 16. Ne mâgon hig ða sâwle ofsleán, Mt. Kmbl. 10, 28. Sâuwle, Blickl. Homl. 43, 23. Monna sâwla sint undeáþlîce and ēce, Bt. 11, 2; Fox 34, 33. Gebid heó sînna sōwhula, Txts. 124, 5. Gemyndige ûre sâula þearfe, Blickl. Homl. 101, 16. Ðæt hē ûre sâula gelǽde on gefeán, 211, 8. III. *a soul, a human creature* (*after death*):—Ða hâlgan sâwla cleopodan tō Drihtne: 'Âstîg nū ðū hafast helle bereáfod,' 87, 20. Hâlige sâula ðǽr (*in Jerusalem*) restaþ, 81, 2. Hē geseah ðæt on ðæm clife hangodan manige swearta sâula be heora handum gebundne ... Ðis wǽron ða sâula ða ðe hēr on worlde mid unrihte gefyrenode wǽron, and ðæs noldan geswîcan ǽr heora lîfes ende, 209, 34–211, 7. Seó menigo hâligra sâula ðe ǽr gehæftnede wǽron (*those who were released when Christ descended to Hell*), 87, 7. Heora (*the angels'*) ēþel sceolde geseted weorþan mid hâlgum sâwlum ... mid ðære menniscan gecynde, 121, 34. Mid eallum ðǽm sâulum ðe hēr on worlde mid rihte tō Gode gecyrraþ, 57, 25: 89, 29: 95, 22. Drihten ða hâlgan sâuwla ðonon (*from Hell*) âlǽdde, 67, 19. [*Goth.* saiwala: *O. Sax.* sēola: *O. Frs.* sēle: *O. L. Ger.* sēla, sîla: *O. H. Ger.* sēla, sēula: *Icel.* sâla.] v. or-sâwle.

sâwel-berend *a being with a soul*:—Sâwlberendra, niðða bearna, grundbûendra, Beo. Th. 2013; B. 1004.

sâwel-cund; *adj. Spiritual*:—Sâwelcund hyrde, Exon. Th. 121, 14; Gū. 288.

sâwel-dreór *life-blood*:—Hē geblōdegod wearð sâwuldrióre, Beo. Th. 5379; B. 2693. Besmiten mid sâwldreóre, Cd. Th. 91, 31; Gen. 1520.

sâwel-gedâl *the parting of soul and body, death*:—Ne biþ ðæs lengra swice sâwelgedâles ðonne seofon niht fyrstgemearces, ðæt mîn feorh heonan on ðisse eahteþan ende gesēceþ, Exon. Th. 164, 7; Gū. 1008. Cf. lîf-gedâl.

sâwel-gescot *soul-scot*:—Ðat sâwulgesceot sceulon ða canonicas habban, Chart. Th. 609, 14, 29. v. sâwel-sceatt.

sâwel-hord *the treasure of life, life guarded as a treasure in the body, the body full of life*:—Ōþ ðæt sâwlhord, bâncofa blōdig, âbrocen weorþeþ, Exon. Th. 329, 15; Vy. 34. Ōþ sâwlhord *to the very soul*, Ps. Th. 77, 49.

sâwel-hûs *the body*:—Ðis sâwelhûs, fǽge flǽschoma, Exon. Th. 163, 34; Gū. 1003. Deáþ sōhte sâwelhûs, 170, 19; Gū. 1114.

sâwel-leás; *adj.* I. *without life* (v. sâwel, I):—Sâwulleás (sâwl-, MS. F.) *exanimis*, Ælfc. Gl. 9, 28; Zup. 56, 16. Hē feóll geswōgen swylce hē sâwleás wǽre, Homl. Skt. i. 21, 299. Hî þwōgon ðone sâwlleásan lîchaman, 20, 97. Magoþegna bær ðone sēlestan sâwolleásne, Beo. Th. 2817; B. 1406. Sâwulleásne, 6059; B. 3033. Sâwelleásne, Exon. Th. 329, 21; Vy. 37. Hēht ðâ âsettan sâwlleásne, lîfe belidenes lîc on eorþan, Elen. Kmbl. 1751; El. 877. II. *without soul* (v. sâwel, II):—On ðæs mannes sâwle is Godes anlîcnyss, for ðam is se mann sēlra ðonne ða sâwulleásan nŷtenu, ðe nân andgit nabbaþ embe heora âgenne Scyppend, Hexam. 11; Norm. 18, 22.

sâwel-sceatt, es; *m. An ecclesiastical due, to be paid for every deceased person to the clergy of the church to which he belonged, in consideration of the services performed by them in his behalf.* It was to be paid before the funeral rites were completed, though the regulation would hardly be carried out in cases where grants of land were made. It appears to have been one of the objects of the early gilds, to provide for the payment of this fee:—Sâwlsceat *vel* syndrig Godes lâc *dano* (*dona?*), Wrt. Voc. i. 28, 44. The passages dealing with the subject in the Laws are the following:—Ic wille ðæt mîne gerēfan gedōn ðæt man âgife ða ciricsceattas and ða sâwlsceattas tō ðâm stōwum ðe hit mid riht tō gebirige, L. Ath. 1. prm.; Th. i. 196, 9. Gelǽste man sâwlsceat (sâul-, MS. A.) æt ǽlcan cristenan men tō ðam mynstre ðe hit tō gebyrige, L. Edg. 1, 5; Th. i. 264, 24. And sâulsceat is rihtast ðæt man symle gelǽste æt openum græfe; and gif man ǽnig lîc of rihtscriftscîre elles hwâr lecge, gelǽste man sâulsceat swâ ðēh intō ðam mynstre ðe hit tō hŷrde, L. Eth. v. 12; Th. i. 308, 4–7: vi. 20–21; Th. i. 320, 4–8: ix. 13; Th. i. 342, 33: L. C. E. 13; Th. i. 368, 5–8. To the same effect it is said in Wulfstan's Homilies:—Eác wē lǽraþ ðæt cristenra manna gehwylc understande, ðæt hē æfter forþsîðe bûtan sâwulsceatte ne licge on mynstre, ac gelǽste man â ðone sâwelsceat æt openum pytte, 118, 4–7. Sâulscat is rihtast ðæt man gelǽste aa æt openum græfe, 311, 12. The *sâwelsceat* is sometimes determined in amount by the will of the deceased:—Ic gean intō Êlig ... ðēr mînes hlâfordes lîchoma rest, ðara þreó landa ðe wit geheótan Gode ... and ðes beáhges gemacan, ðe man sæalde mînum hlâforde, tō sâwlescæatte, Chart. Th. 524, 14–30. See too Shrn. 159, and Turner's Anglo-Saxons, bk. vii. c. xiv. Kemble, Cod. Dip. i. lxii, remarks that in lands leased by the Church, and exclusively in such, there is frequently a stipulation for the payment of sâwelsceat. For the practice in the case of gilds, see Chart. Th. 609, 10–18:—Æt ǽlcum forðfarenum gildan æt ǽlcum heorþe ǽnne penig tō sâwulsceote, sē hit bonda, sē hit wîf, ðe on ðam gildscipe sindon; and ðat sâwulgesceot sceulon ða canonicas habban, and swilce þēnisce dōn for hig swilce hig âgon tō dōne.

sâwel-scot. v. preceding word (the last passage).

sâwel-þearf, e; *f. What is necessary* or *beneficial for the soul*:—Ic wes smeágende ymb mîne sâulþearfe, Chart. Th. 474, 18.

sâwend, es; *m. A sower*:—Ðe sēdere ł sâwend *seminans*, Mk. Skt. Rush. 4, 3. Se sâwena (sâwend?) *qui seminat*, Mt. Kmbl. Rush. 13, 3. Gehēraþ gelîcnisse ðæs sâwendes *audite parabolam seminantis*, 13, 18. Cf. leóhtsâwend *lucisator*, Germ. 389, 2.

sâwere, es; *m. A sower*:—Ūt eode se sâwere his sǽd tō sâwenne, Mt. Kmbl. A. 13, 3. v. word-, wrōht-sâwere.

sâwlian; *p.* ode *To give up the ghost, expire*:—Hē ne geswâc his gebeda ōþ ðæt hē sâwlode, Homl. Th. ii. 518, 1. Flaccus hēt ðone preóst beswingan ōþ ðæt hē sâwlode, Homl. Skt. i. 10, 291. Sōna swâ hē ðyder com swâ sâwlode ðæt mǽden, 22, 101: Homl. As. 59, 202. v. next word.

sâwlung, e; *f. The giving up the ghost, expiring*:—Cwæð sum hâlig biscop ðâ hē wæs on sâwlenga be ðeossum fæder: Arsenius ðū wǽre eádig forðon ðū hæfdest â ðâs tîd beforan ðînum eágum *a certain holy bishop, when he was expiring, said of this father: 'Arsenius, blessed wert thou, for ever hadst thou this hour* (*the hour of death*) *before thine eyes*,' Shrn. 106, 26.

sca-; scâ-, scǽ-; scæ-. v. scea-; sceá-; scea-, sce-.

scaed, Wrt. ii. 120, 8. v. sceabb.

scǽnan; *p.* de *To break*:—Ðâ cōmon ða cempan, and sōna ðæra sceaðena sceancan tōbrǽcon. Hî gemētton Crist deádne, and his hâlgan sceancan scǽnan ne dorston, Homl. Th. ii. 260, 10. Ða gemettan ne mōston ðæs lambes bân scǽnan, ne ða cempan ne mōston tōbrecan his (*Christ's*) hâlgan sceancan, 282, 7. [Helmes gullen ... sceldes gunnen scenen, Laym. 31234. Breken brade sperren, bordes scænden, 5186. Cf. (?) *Icel.* skeina *to scratch, wound slightly*.] v. ge-, tō-scǽnan.

-scǽre. v. ǽ-scǽre.

Scald *the Schelde*:—Hēr fōr se here up on Scald, Chr. 883; Erl. 82, 15.

Scariothisc; *adj. Of Scariot*:—Judas se Scariothisca; forðon hē com of ðæm tûne ðe Scariot hâtte, Blickl. Homl. 69, 5: Mk. Skt. Lind. Rush. 14, 43.

scaþel, Dōm. L. 30, 58. v. staþel.

sceáb, sceaba. v. sceáf, sceafa.

sceabb, scæb, sceb, es; *m. Scab, a scab*:—Scaed (scaeb?) *scara* (*scara* vulneris crusta, Du Cange. Cf. *Span.* escara *the scurf* or *scar of a sore*), Wrt. Voc. ii. 120, 8. Ðone leahtor ðe Grēcas achoras (ἀχῶρας) nemnaþ, ðæt ys sceb (scæb, MS. B.), Lchdm. i. 322, 17. Wið sceb (scæb, MSS. H. B.), 150, 5: 316, 22. Wið sceab, 66, 21. Se hæfþ singalne sceabb se ðe nǽfre ne bliþ ungestæððignesse. Ðonne bî ðæm sceabbe swîðe ryhte sió hreófl getâcnaþ ðæt wōhhǽmed *jugem habet scabiem, cui carnis petulantia sine cessatione dominatur. Per scabiem recte luxuria designatur*, Past. 11, 5; Swt. 70, 3–4. Gif hē hæfde singale sceabbas *si jugem scabiem habens fuerit*, 11, 1; Swt. 65, 6. [*Ger.* schabe *scab, itch*: *Dan.* skab: *Swed.* skabb.]

sceabbed; *adj. Having scabs* or *sores*:—Sceabbede, ǽttren *purulentus*, Hpt. Gl. 519, 32.

sceacan, scacan; *p.* sceóc, scōc; *pp.* sceacen, scacen, scæcen. I. *to shake* (intrans.), *quiver*:—Gerd from uinde styrende ł sceæcende, Mt. Kmbl. Lind. 11, 7. II. but generally used of rapid movement, (1) of living creatures, *to flee, hurry off, go forth* (cf. (?) colloquial *shack* to rove about):—Ðâ sceóc hē on niht fram ðære fyrde him sylfum tō myclum bysmore *he fled at night from the English army to his great disgrace*, Chr. 992; Erl. 130, 32. Hē sceóc dîgellîce of ðære byrig *he hurried off secretly from the town*, Homl. Th. ii. 154, 12. Sceócon mōdige maguþegnas morþres on luste *they hurried on lusting for murder*, Andr. Kmbl. 2280; An. 1141. Hē behēt ðæt hē nǽfre siððan of ðam mynstre sceacan nolde *he promised that he would not leave the monastery in a hurry again*, Homl. Th. ii. 176, 28. Hwī woldest đū sceacan būtan mīnre gewitnisse *cur ignorante me fugere voluisti?* Gen. 31, 27. Deófol ongon on fleám sceacan, Exon. Th. 280, 17; Jul. 630: Judth. Thw. 25, 34; Jud. 292. Hī gewiton in forwyrd sceacan *they hurried to perdition*, Andr. Kmbl. 3187; An. 1596. On gerūm sceacan, Exon. Th. 401, 20; Rä. 21, 14. On lyft scacan, fleógan ofer foldan, Cd. Th. 280, 32; Sat. 263: Beo. Th. 3610; B. 1803. [Nes þer nan biscop ꝥ ford on his wæi ne scoc, na munec ne nan abbed ꝥ he an his wæi ne rad, Laym. 13246.] (2) of material things, *to move quickly, to be flung, be displaced by shaking*:—Hwīlum hāra scōc forst of feaxe *at times the hoar frost was thrown from my hair*, Exon. 498, 26; Rä. 88, 7. Strǣla storm, strengum gebǣded, scōc ofer scyldweall, Beo. Th. 6227; B. 3118. (3) of immaterial things (time, life, thought, etc.), *to pass, proceed, depart*:—Đonne mīn sceaceþ līf of līce *when my life takes flight from the flesh*, Beo. Th. 5478; B. 2742: Exon. Th. 327, 4; Wīd. 141. Swǣ giémeleáslīce oft sceacaþ ūre geþohtas from ūs đæt wē his furđum ne gefrēdaþ *curae vitae ex sensu negligenti quasi nobis non sentientibus procedunt*, Past. 18, 7; Swt. 138, 20. Seó tīd gewāt sceacan *time passed on*, Cd. Th. 9, 2; Gen. 135. Is nū worn wintra sceacen, Elen. Kmbl. 1263; El. 633. Đā wæs dæg sceacen, Beo. Th. 4602; B. 2306: 5448; B. 2727. Đā wæs winter scacen, 2277; B. 1136. Wæs hira blǣd scacen *their glory had departed*, 2253; B. 1124. Biþ se wēn scæcen, Exon. Th. 50, 23; Cri. 805. Biþ his līf scæcen, 329, 25; Vy. 39. Biþ tȳr scecen, 447, 27; Dōm. 45. III. *to shake* (trans.):—Ic sceace (scace, scæce) *concutio*, Ælfc. Gr. 28, 4; Zup. 169, 7. Gūđweard gumena wælhlencan sceóc, Cd. Th. 188, 31; Exod. 176. Sceacas (scæcas, Rush.) đæt asca of fōtum iúrum *excubite te pulverem de pedibus vestris*, Mk. Skt. Lind. 6, 11. Wæs sceacen *vibratur*, Germ. 401, 47. IV. *to weave* (cf. bregdan):—Scecen wē *plumemus* (cf. windan *plumemus*, 83, 78: *plumarium opus* dicitur quod ad modum plumarum texitur, Du Cange), Wrt. Voc. ii. 66, 80. [*O. Sax.* skakan *to depart*; ellior skōk *he died*: cf. *O. H. Ger.* untscachondes *flutivagi*, Grff. vi. 412: *Icel.* skaka *to shake* (trans.).] v. ā-, of-, on-, ōþ-, tō-sceacan.

sceacdōm (?), es; *m. Flight, hurried departure*:—Nolde nā Iacob cȳđan his scæcdōm (sæcdōm, Thw.) his sweore *noluit Jacob confiteri socero suo, quod fugeret*, Gen. 31, 20. v. preceding word.

sceacel, es; *m.* I. *a shackle*:—Sceacul *vel* bend *columbar*, Wrt. Voc. i. 16, 44. II. the word also glosses *plectrum*:—Scecele ođđe slegele scecen wē *plectro plumemus*, ii. 66, 78–80. Sceacelas *plectra*, 89, 10. [*Prompt. Parv.* schakkyl *numella*. Ancren schulen ine so wide scheakeles pleien ine hevuene . . . Þet tet bódi schal beon hwar so euer þe gost wule in one hondhwule, A. R. 94, 25. *O. Du.* schakel *the link or ring of a chain*: *Icel.* skökull *the pole of a carriage*: *Swed.* skakel *the loose shaft of a carriage*: *Dan.* skagle *a trace for a carriage*.] v. sweor-sceacel; sceacan.

sceácere, es; *m. A robber*:—Þeáf and sceácere *fur et latro*, Jn. Skt. Lind. 10, 1. Þeáfas and sceácaras *fures et latrones*, Mt. Kmbl. p. 8, 1. Miđ sceácerum (sceácrum, Rush.) ł miđ sētnerun *cum seditiosis*, Mk. Skt. Lind. 15, 7. [*O. H. Ger.* scāhhāre *latro*; scāh *latrocinium, praeda*: *O. Frs.* skāk *booty*; skēka *to rob*: *Du.* schaak *abduction*.] v. next word.

sceácerian. v. tō-sceácerian.

sceacga, an; *m. The hair of the head*; cf. shaggy:—Feax, sceacga *coma*, Wrt. Voc. ii. 22, 56. [Cf. *Icel.* skegg *the beard*: *Dan.* skæg: *Swed.* skägg.] v. next word.

sceacged; *adj. Having hair on the head, shagged*:—Sceacgede *comosus*, Wrt. Voc. ii. 22, 71. Sceagode, 132, 7. [Cf. *Icel.* skeggjaðr *bearded*.] v. preceding word.

sceac-līne, sceacness, sceacul. v. sceát-līne, on-sceacness, sceacel.

scead, es; *m. ?*:—Siblingchyrst and Trowincsceadas and Rocisfald, Cod. Dip. Kmbl. iii. 123, 8.

scead, scæd, scad, sced, es; *n. Shade*; fig. *shelter, protection*:—Æfter sceades sciman, Salm. Kmbl. 233; Sal. 116. Scedes, Cd. Th. 271, 15; Sat. 106. On sceade (scade, MS. B.) āhōn, Lchdm. i. 284, 21. On đam sceade his geteldes *in abscondito tabernaculi sui*, Ps. Th. 26, 6. Manna bearn hopiaþ tō đæm sceade đīnra fiđera *filii hominum in protectione alarum tuarum sperabunt*, 35, 8. Đonne on sceade weaxeþ, Exon. Th. 214, 5; Ph. 234. Hē in scade weardaþ, on wudubearwe, wēste stōwe, 209, 10; Ph. 168. Đæt gē mec mid searocræftum under scæd scūfan mōtan, 142, 20; Gū. 647. Sceadu beóþ bidyrned, đǣr se leóhta beám leódum byrhteþ, 67, 16; Cri. 1089. Sceadu sweđerodon, Andr. Kmbl. 1672; An. 838. Sceado (sceađo, MS.), Cd. Th. 184, 27; Exod. 113. Scadu, Exon. Th. 179, 16; Gū. 1262. Deorc deáþes sceadu dreógan, 8, 15; Cri. 118. Sunne ofer sceadu scīneþ, 212, 14; Ph. 210. Under sceadu bregdan *to kill*, Beo. Th. 1419; B. 707. Dæg ǣresta geseah deorc sceado sweart swiđrian, Cd. Th. 8, 33; Gen. 133. v. leáf-scead, sceadu.

sceád, scād, es; *n. Shed* (in water-*shed*), *a division, distinction, reason, reckoning*:—Đū scealt gyldan scād wordum *thou shalt give an account* (*of thine actions*) *in words*, Dōm. L. 73. [Haueđ wit and schad bituhhe god and uel, O. E. Homl. i. 255, 30. Shæd and skill, Orm. 5534. Niss bitwenen ȝunnc and hemm nan shæd i manness kinde, 6229. Schead ba of god and of uvel, Kath. 240. *O. L. Ger.* scēth *discrimen*: *O. H. Ger.* sceit *discissio*.] v. ge-, tō-, unge-sceád.

sceáda (sceáde; *f.* (?)), an; *m. The top of the head, parting of the hair*:—Hē tōfylleþ feaxes scādan *conquassabit verticem capilli*, Ps. Th. 67, 21. [Crulle was his heer, and as the gold it schon . . . Ful streyt and evene lay his joly schood, Miller's Tale, 130. The nayl y-dryven in the schode a-nyght, Knight's Tale, 1149. v. *Halliwell's Dict.* shed, *and E. D. S. Pub. Lincolnshire*, shed *the parting of the hair*. Cf. *Prompt. Parv.* schodynge of the heede *discrimen*: *O. L. Ger.* scēthlo, sceithlo *vertex* (*capilli*): *O. H. Ger.* sceitila *vertex*; fahs-sceitila *cervix capilli*.] v. preceding word.

sceada. v. niht-scada.

sceádan, scādan; *p.* scēd, sceád (v. tō-sceádan); *pp.* sceáden. I. *trans.* (1) *to separate, divide, make a line of separation between*:—Eádmund Myrce geeode swā Dor scādeþ, hwītan wylles geat and Humbra eá brāda brimstreám *Edmund conquered Mercia, which Dor, Whitewell's gate, the river Humber, the broad estuary, divides* (*from Northumbria*), Chr. 942; Erl. 116, 9. From Egypta ēđelmearce swā Nilus sceádeþ, Cd. Th. 133, 10; Gen. 2208. Đonne sceádene beóþ đa synfullan and đa sōđfæstan on đam mǣran dæge, Exon. Th. 375, 33; Seel. 147. (2) *to distinguish, decide*:—Scādeþ *discriminet*, Wrt. Voc. ii. 27, 20. Scādet, 93, 34. Đonne biþ gǣsta dōm sceáden swā hī geworhtun ǣr *then shall the spirits' doom be decided, according to their deserts*, Exon. Th. 76, 2; Cri. 1233. Sceáden mǣl *the appointed time* (?), Beo. Th. 3882; B. 1939. (3) *to scatter, shed*:—Nim beolonan sǣd sceád on glēda *take seed of henbane, scatter it on gledes*, Lchdm. ii 38, 1: 52, 2. Sceád (scād, MS. B.), i. 82, 7. Gnīd tōgædere and scād on, ii. 134, 3. Đæt mela biþ gōd on tō sceádenne, 94, 3. [*See also the compounds* (*omitted in their proper places*):—Besceád, 54, 21. Ofersceáde, 182, 2.] Tō scēdende blōd *ad effundendum sanguinem*, Ps. Spl. T. 13, 6. II. *intrans.* (1) *to separate, divide, part*:—Tigelum sceádeþ hrōstbeáges hrōf (rōf, MS.) *the woodwork of the roof parts from the tiles*, Exon. Th. 477, 29; Ruin. 31. Đonne dæg and niht scāde *when day and night separate* (*at morning twilight*), Lchdm. ii. 116, 19. Đonne dæg and niht furþum scāde, 346, 14: 356, 6: iii. 6, 7. Đonne dæg scāde and niht, ii. 138, 16. (2) *to be distinguished, to differ*:—Scādaþ *discrepent*, Wrt. Voc. ii. 27, 1: 88, 39. (3) *to scatter, shed*:—Đonne sceádaþ đa wyrmas on đæt wæter, Lchdm. ii. 38, 4. [He shodeđ þe gode fro þe iuele, O. E. Homl. ii. 67, 24. Eiđer of þisse teres schedde þe apostel, i. 157, 33. Þe halwe men schedden teres, 157, 15. Redde blod scede (sadde, 2nd MS), Laym. 5187. He shadde him fra menn, Orm. 3200. Shædenn hemm fra Criste, 1209. Tobrekeđ hore uetles and schedeđ hore clennesse, A. R. 166, 7. His blode þet he shedde for us, 312, 19. Scheaden þet chef urom þe clene cornes, 270, 27. Blod isched, 402, 21. So wurđ ligt fro đisternesse o sunder sad, Gen. and Ex. 58. On sunder shad, 148. *Goth.* skaidan *to divide, separate*: *O. Sax.* skēdan, skēthan *trans.* and *intrans.*) *to separate*: *O. L. Ger.* scēthan, sceithan: *O. Frs.* skēda, skētha *to separate, to decide*: *O. H. Ger.* sceidan *separare, segregare, discernere, distinguere, discriminare, judicare*.] v. ā-, for-, ge-, tō-(be-, ofer-, v. I. 3 above) sceádan.

sceadd *a shad*:—Ic geann Ælfhelme and Wulfāge đæra landa betwux Ribbel and Mærse and on Wirhalum . . . on đæt gerād đonne sceaddgenge sȳ đæt heora ǣgđer sylle .iii. þūsend sceadda intō đære stōwe æt Byrtūne *I grant to Ælfhelm and Wulfeah the lands between the Ribble and the Mersey, and in Wirral . . . on the condition that, when shad are in season, each of them give .iii. thousand shad to the convent at Burton*, Chart. Th. 544, 21–31.

sceadd-genge; *adj. Seasonable for shad.* v. preceding word.

sceádend. v. tō-sceádend.

sceáde-sealf, e; *f. A salve that may be shed on a place* (? v. sceádan, I. 3), *a medicinal powder*:—Sceádesealf tō eágum, Lchdm. ii. 300, 6. Wyrc gōde drīge scādesealfe: nim gebærned sealt and piper and hwītewudu, gegnīd tō duste āsift þurh clāđ, dō lytlum on, 308, 22.

sceadiht; *adj. Shady*:—Of munte scedehtum *de monte umbroso*, Ps. Surt. ii. p. 189, 16.

sceádlīce; *adv. Reasonably, rationally*:—Gif hē gesceádlīce (sceádelice, Wells Frag.) mid eáđmōdnesse and mid sōþre lufe hwilcu þing on mynstre tǣle *si qua rationabiliter et cum humilitate caritatis reprehenderit*, R. Ben. 109, 8. v. ge-, un-sceádlīce.

sceadu; *gen.* sceaduwe, sceadwe, sceade; *f. Shadow, shade*:—Sceadu *umbra*, Wrt. Voc. i. 77, 8. I. *a shadow* (cast by an object):—Seó sceadu byþ tō underne seofon and twentigoþan healfes fōtes *the shadow* (*of the dial-gnomon*) *will be twenty-six and a half foot long at nine o'clock* (*on Christmas day*), Lchdm. iii. 218, 4 (and often on this and following pages). Nis đeós woruldlīce niht nān þing būton đære eorþan sceadu betweox đære sunnan and mankynne . . . Seó sceadu āstīhþ up ōþ đæt heó becymþ tō đære lyfte ufeweardan, and đonne beyrnþ se mōna hwīltīdum, đonne hē full byþ, on đære sceade ufeweardre and fāggeteþ ođđe mid ealle āsweartaþ, 240, 18–24. On India lande wendaþ heora scada (sceada, MSS. R. P.) on sumera sūđweard and on wintra norđweard. Eft on Alexandria on đam sumerlīcan sunnstede on middæge ne byþ nān sceadu on nānre healfe, 258, 12-16. His sceadu gehǽlde ða untruman, Homl. Skt. i. 10, 19. Dagas mīne swā swā scadu āhyldon, Ps. Spl. 101, 12: 143, 5. Swā ðū on scimiendre sceade lōcige *sicut umbra*, Ps. Th. 143, 5. Dagas mīne swā swā sceaduwa āhyldon, Ps. Lamb. 101, 12. **II.** *shade* as opposed to light, *shadow* (lit. and fig.), *darkness*:—Ða ðe nān sceadu (scadu, Cott. MSS.) ne geþiéstraþ ðære twiéfealdnesse *quos nulla umbra duplicitatis obscurat*, Past. 35, 4; Swt. 243, 23. Þȳstro hæfdon bewrigen mid wolcnum wealdendes hrǽw, sceadu forþeode wann under wolcnum, Rood Kmbl. 108; Kr. 54. Oferwreáh ūs scadu deáþes, Ps. Spl. 43, 22. On midlunge sceaduwe dǽþes, 22, 4. On scade (sceaduwe, Ps. Lamb.) deáþes, 106, 10. Ðis andwearde līf is swīðe anlīc sceade, and on ðære sceade nān mon ne mæg begitan ða sōðan gesǽlþa, Bt. 27, 3; Fox 98, 19. On midde ða sceade deáþes, Ps. Th. 22, 4. Ðā gesundrode sigora Waldend leóht wið þeóstrum, sceade wið scīman, Cd. Th. 8, 22; Gen. 128. For hwon sēcest ðū sceade, 54, 8; Gen. 874. **III.** *shadow, protection*:—Under scaduwe fiðera ðīnra gescyld mē, Ps. Spl. 16, 10. Hī slēpon ūte on triówa sceadum *umbras dabat altissima pinus*, Bt. 15; Fox 48, 12. **IV.** *a shady place, shade, arbour*:—Scadu *scena* (cf. geteld *scena* vel *tabernaculum*, i. 37, 15), Wrt. Voc. ii. 119, 80. Sceadwe *scenam*, 80, 1. **V.** *shadow* as opposed to substance, *an obscure image*:—Seó ealde ǽ wæs swilce sceadu, and seó nīwe gecȳðnys is sōðfæstnys, Homl. Th. i. 356, 1. Genōg ic ðē hæbbe nū gereht ymbe ða anlīcnessa and ymbe ða sceadwa ðære sōðan gesǽlþe *hactenus mendacis formam felicitatis ostendisse suffecerit*, Bt. 33, 1; Fox 118, 34. [*O. E. Homl.* sceadewe, shadewe: *A. R.* scheadewe: *Goth.* skadus: *O. Sax.* skado: *O. H. Ger.* scato.] v. beám-, heolstor-, niht-, scūr-sceadu; scead.

sceadu-geard, es; *m.* *A shady enclosure*:—Sceadugeardas *Tempe*, Wrt. Voc. ii. 122, 17.

sceadu-genga, an; *m.* *One who walks in darkness* (v. sceadu, II):—Com on wanre niht scrīðan sceadugenga (*Grendel*), Beo. Th. 1410; B. 703. Cf. niht-genga.

sceadu-helm, es; *m.* *The cover of night, darkness*:—Niht, scaduhelma gesceapu, Beo. Th. 1304; B. 650.

sceadwian, sceadewian; *p.* ode *To cover with shadow*:—Hē scadewode (scaduaþ, Ps. Lamb.: sceadewede, Blickl. Gl.) *obumbrabit*, Ps. Spl. 90, 4. [*Goth.* ufar-skadwjan: *O. Sax.* skadowan, scadoian: *O. L. Ger.* scedeuuan: *O. H. Ger.* scatewen.] v. ofer-sceadwian; sceadwung.

sceádwīslic. v. ge-, un-sceádwīslīc, *and next word.*

sceádwīslīce; *adv.* *With discretion, rationally*:—Gif ðū him sceádwīslīce æfter spyrast, Bt. 13; Fox 38, 3. v. ge-sceádwīslīce.

sceádwīsness, e; *f.* *Reason*:—Ðā cwæþ seó Gesceádwīsnes (Sceádwīsnes, Cott. MS.), Bt. 5, 3; Fox 12, 1. Ic wēne ðæt hyt mīn sceádwīsnes (*reason*) wēre, Shrn. 164, 29. Sceádwīsnyssum *ratiociniis*, R. Ben. Interl. 17, 6.

sceadwung, e; *f.* *An overshadowing*:—On sumum earde dagas beóþ lengran, on sumon scyrtran for ðære eorþan sceadewunge (sceadwunge, MS. R.) *in one land days are longer, in another shorter, because of the way in which the shadow falls on the earth*, Lchdm. iii. 258, 4. Se fulla mōna fǽrlīce fāgettaþ ðonne hē ðæs sunlīcan leóhtes bedǽled biþ þurh ðære eorþan sceadwunge (*by the casting of the earth's shadow*), Homl. Th. i. 610, 1. v. be-sceadwung.

sceáf, es; *m.* *A sheaf, bundle.* **I.** in the following glosses:—Sceáfes *fascis*, sceáfe *fasculo* (*fasciculo*), Wrt. Voc. ii. 34, 62-63. Sceáfas *areoli*, 7, 16: *garbas*, 40, 60: *garbas, manipulas*, 89, 19. Sceabas, scēbas *areoli*, Txts. 38, 30: *garbas*, 66, 468. Sceáfum *fasciculis*, Hpt. Gl. 520, 19. **II.** *a sheaf* (*of corn*):—Mē þūhte ðæt wē bundon sceáfas (*manipulos*) on æcere and ðæt mīn sceáf ārise ōmiddan eówrum sceáfum and eówre gilmas ābugon tō mīnum sceáfe, Gen. 37, 7. Gȳme hē ðæt nāðor ne misfare ne corn ne sceáf, Anglia ix. 260, 12. Mid his sceáfe sceát āfyllan, Ps. Th. 128, 5. Hē nǽnne sceáf (*manipulum*) ne rīpþ, Past. 39, 2; Swt. 287, 3. Heora sceáfas (*manipulos*) beraþ, Ps. Th. 125, 6. **II a.** *a bundle* (*of herbs*):—Dippaþ ysopan sceáf (sceaft, Thw.) on ðam blōde *fasciculum hyssopi tingite in sanguine*, Ex. 12, 22. Syndrige sceáfas *separate bundles* (*of rue, dill, mint, and marche*), Lchdm. ii. 188, 24. Rūdan sceáfas þrȳ, 216, 2. [*O. H. Ger.* scoub: *Ger.* schaub: *Du.* schoof: *Icel.* skauf *a fox's brush.*]

sceafa, an; *m.* *A plane*:—Sceaba *runcina*, Txts. 92, 853. Scafa *olatrum*, Wrt. Voc. i. 287, 11: ii. 64, 13. Hē sceal habban æcse, adsan, scafan, sage, Anglia ix. 263, 2. [*Prompt. Parv.* schave or schavynge knyfe *scalpellum, scalprum*: *O. H. Ger.* scaba *plana, asperella*: *Ger.* schabe: *Du.* schaaf *a plane*: *Icel.* skafa *a scraper.*] v. mǽl-sceafa, sceafan.

Sceáfa, an; *m.* *The name of a king of the Lombards*:—Sceáfa weóld Longbeardum, Exon. Th. 320, 21; Vīd. 33. *See also* Scyld Scēfing, Beo. Th. 7; B. 4.

sceafan, scafan; *p.* scōf; *pp.* sceafen, scafen *To shave, scrape, shred, polish*:—Scaebe *poleo*, Wrt. Voc. ii. 117, 63. Gif hē ðæt ōmige fæt mid ungemete scæfþ *dum nimis cupit eradere eruginem*, R. Ben. 121, 4. Hē scōf on halig wæter of ðam hālgan treówe, Swt. A. S. Rdr. 102, 216. Man scōf ðæra bōca leáf and ða sceafþan dyde on wæter *rasa folia codicum, et ipsam rasuram aquae immissam*, Bd. 1, 1; S. 474, 37. Monige men sprytlan ācurfon and on wæter scōfan, 3, 17; S. 544, 45, col. 1. Sceaf (scaf, MS. B.) gāte horn on þrȳ scenceas, Lchdm. i. 352, 11: 344, 13. Sceafe ðæt grēne, ii. 292, 26. Ðū scealt hine scafan on wæter . . . and ðære reádan eorþan dǽl scafe ðǽrtō, ii. 290, 11-13. [*Goth.* skaban: *O. L. Ger.* scavan *scalpere*: *O. H. Ger.* scaban, scapan *scabere, scalpere, radere*: *Icel.* skafa.] v. ā-, be-, ge-sceafan (-scafan).

sceáf-fōt; *adj.* *Splay-footed*:—Scābfoot, scaabfōt, scāffo[o]t *pansa*, Txts. 90, 832. Scāffōt, Wrt. Voc. i. 288, 78. [Cf. *Icel.* skeifr *askew, oblique*; skeifa *a horse-shoe.*]

sceáf-mǽlum; *adv.* *In sheaves* or *bundles*:—Gadriaþ ǽrest ðone coccel, and bindaþ sceáfmǽlum, Mt. Kmbl. 13, 30.

sceafoþa, sceafþa, scæfþa, an; *m.* (*or* -e; *f.* ?) *A shaving, chip, what is shaved, scraped,* or *rubbed off*:—Ðā gehālgode ic wæter and scæfþan dyde on ðæs forespreceenan treówes *tunc benedixi aquam, et astulam roboris praefati inmittens*, Bd. 2, 13; S. 539, 5. Ða scæfþan ðe ðǽron genumene wǽron lǽcedōm bǽron *astulae de illo abscissae solent adferre medelam*, 4, 6; S. 574, 9. Man scōf ðara bōca leáf and ða sceafþan (*ipsam rasuram*) dyde on wæter, 1, 1; S. 474, 38. Monige spōnas and sceafþan (*astulas*) nimaþ, 3, 2; S. 524, 31: 3, 17; S. 544, 44, col. 2. Genim heorotes sceafoþan of ðam horne, Lchdm. ii. 72, 13. Genim heorotes sceafoþan of felle āscafen mid pumice, 100, 14.

sceaft, es; *m.* *A smooth, round, straight stick* or *pole, a shaft.* **I.** generally (1) *the shaft of a spear* (cf. *Icel.* skaft *the shaft*, spjót *the point*):—Spereleás sceaft *contus*, Wrt. Voc. i. 35, 42. Gif se ord sié þreó fingre ufor ðonne hindeweard sceaft, L. Alf. pol. 36; Th. i. 84, 17, 18. His sceaft ætstōd ætforan him, and ðæt hors hine bær forþ, swā ðæt ðæt spere him eode þurh ūt, Homl. Skt. i. 12, 53. Hē sceáf mid his scylde, ðæt se sceaft tōbærst, and ðæt spere sprengde, Byrht. Th. 135, 52; By. 136. Gār sceal on sceafte, ecg on sweorde, Exon. Th. 346, 12; Gn. Ex. 202. [He igrap his spere stronge . . . þe scæft al tobrac, Laym. 6494.] Or (2) *a spear*:—Sceaft *asta, quiris*, Wrt. Voc. i. 35, 18: 84, 24. Ðes sceft (scæft, sceaft) *cuspis*, Ælfc. Gr. 9, 28; Zup. 56, 4. Scyld sceal cempan, sceaft reáfere, Exon. Th. 341, 23; Gn. Ex. 130. Scæftes ł speres ðīnes *hastae tuae*, Cant. Ab. 11. Ðæt yrre ðæt geþyld mid ðam sceafte (mid his spere, B.) slihþ *ira patientiam conto percutit*, Glos. Prud. A. 18. Scyld sceft oncwyð, Fins. Th. 12; Fin. 7. Hlyn wearð on wīcum scylda and sceafta, Cd. Th. 124, 13; Gen. 2062. Deáwig sceaftum, 199, 25; Exod. 344. Hig bǽron lange sceaftas, and ne cōman hig nā tō feohtanne, ac ðæt hig woldan mid hlōþe geniman, Shrn. 38, 9. **II.** *the shaft of an arrow*:—Sceaft federgearwum fūs, Beo. Th. 6228; B. 3118. [Þe ssaft (*the arrow that killed William Rufus*), þat was wyþoute, gryslych he tobrec, R. Glouc. 419, 2.] **III.** *a pole*:—Fana hwearfode scīr on sceafte, Met. 1, 11. Ic gegaderode mē stuþan sceaftas . . . Ic lǽre ǽlcne ðara ðe manigne wǽn hæbbe, ðæt hē menige tō ðam ilcan wuda ðār ic ðās stuþan sceaftas cearf, Shrn. 163, 5-14. [Moyses made a wirme of bras, And henget hege up on a saft, Gen. and Ex. 3899.] **III a.** *something shaped like a shaft, a taper*:—Swā swā eles gecynd biþ ðæt hē beorhtor scīneþ ðonne wex on sceafte (*wax in the form of a taper* or (?) *a wax candle in a candlestick*, cf. candelstæf), Blickl. Homl. 129, 1. **IV.** The word occurs in the passage that defines the distance to which the king's 'grið' extended, but the origin of the phrase, of which it forms part, is not evident:—Ðus feor sceal beón ðæs cinges grið fram his burhgeate ðǽr hē is sittende on feówer healfe his, ðæt is, .iii. mīla, and .iii. furlang, and .iii. æcera brǽde, and ix. fōta, and .ix. scæfta munda, and .ix. berecorna, L. Ath. iv. 5; Th. i. 224, 7-10. Cf. Tria miliaria, et .iii. quarantene, et .ix. acre latitudine, et .ix. pedes, et .ix. palme, et .ix. grana hordei, L. H. i. 16; Th. i. 526, 15. As the name of a measure of about six inches the phrase continued to exist. Stratmann gives *schaftmonde*, Nares cites a passage from Harrington's Ariosto in which *shaftman* occurs; in Ray's Collection (1691) *shafman, shafmet, shaftment* is explained 'the measure of the fist with the thumb set up.' v. also Halliwell's Dict., and Jamieson's, s. v. *schaftmon, shathmont.* For the latter form see Sir W. Scott's Antiquary, c. 8 (at the end). [*O. Sax.* skaft *a spear*: *O. H. Ger.* scaft *hastile, hasta, jaculum, telum, arundo*: *Icel.* skapt, skaft *a shaft, haft* (*of an axe*).] v. deoreþ-, here-, lōh, wæl-sceaft.

sceaft, es; *m.*: e, *f.* **I.** *creation, origin*:—Ealle sint emnǽðele gif wē willaþ þone fruman sceaft geþencan and ðone Scippend . . . Ac ǽlc mon ðe allunga underþeóded biþ unþeáwum forlǽt his Sceppend and his fruman sceaft *si primordia vestra auctoremque Deum spectes, nullis degener exstat, ni vitiis pejora favens proprium deserat ortum*, Bt. 30, 2; Fox 110, 17-21. **II.** *a creation, what is created, a creature*:—Ealre sceafte fæder *omniparens*, Germ. 389, 2. Fram fruman gesceafte (scæftes, Lind.) *ab initio creaturae*, Mk. Skt. 10, 6. Of frymmðe ðære gesceafte (ðæs sceæftes, Lind.) ðe God gesceóp *ab initio creaturae quam condidit Deus*, 13, 19. Bodiaþ godspell ealre gesceafte (ēghwelcum sceafte, Lind.) *praedicate euangelium omni creaturae*, 16, 15. Gif God næfde on eallum his rīce nāne frige sceaft (gesceaft, Cott. MS.), Bt. 41, 2; Fox 244, 29. Forðæm sint ðās sceafta (gesceafta, Cott. MS.), 41, 5; Fox 252, 30. Alra þinga ł sceafta *omnium rerum*, Mt. Kmbl. p. 12, 16. [Our schaft wele knawes he *ipse scit figmentum nostrum*, Ps. 102, 14. Godd þatt alle shaffte wrohhte, Orm. pref. 58. Swilc safte (*the tabernacle*) was ęar neuere on werlde brogt, Gen. and Ex. 3628. For be a man faire or foule it falleth nouȝte for to lakke þe shappe ne þe shafte · þat God shope hymselue, Piers P. B. 11, 387. *O. Sax.* -skaft: *O. H. Ger.* -scaft.] v. ǽr-, ed-, frum-, ge-, geó-, hyge-, meotud-, nafel-, orleg-, self-, un-, wan-sceaft.

-sceaft; *adj.* v. feá-sceaft.

Sceaftes-burh *Shaftesbury* in Dorset:—Æt Sceaftesbyrig, Chr. 1036; Erl. 164, 9. Tō Scæftesbyrig, 980; Erl. 129, 34. See also Cod. Dip. Kmbl. vi. 329, col. 1.

sceaft-lōha, an; *m.* (*or* -e; *f.*?) *The strap attached to the shaft of a missile*:—Sceaptlōan *hastilia telorum*, Txts. 66, 489. Sceptlōum *amentis*, 42, 106. v. lōh-sceaft, mæst-lōn, sceaft-tog.

sceafþa. v. sceafoþa.

sceaft-tog (?) *the strap attached to the shaft of a missile*:—Sceptog *ammentum*, Wrt. Voc. ii. 100, 11. v. sceaft-lōha.

sceaga, an; *m. A shaw, small wood, copse, thicket.* The word is found in many local names, and was preserved in various dialects, e.g. *shaw* a small shady wood in a valley, E. D. S. Pub. B. 7 (West Riding): a wood that encompasses a close, B. 16 (Sussex). *Shaws* broad belts of underwood, two, three, and even four rods wide, around every field, Farming words, 4 (Sussex). *Shaw* a natural copse of wood, Cumberland. The word occurs in the following passages of charters:—Juxta silvam quam dicunt Toccansceaga, Cod. Dip. Kmbl. i. 121, 24. Mariscum uocabulo Scaga, quam etiam circumfluit Iaegnlaad, 190, 6: 160, 28. On brēmeles sceagan eásteweardne, ii. 172, 28. On ðone langan sceagan westeweardne; of langan sceagan on ðæt hǽðene byrgils, iii. 85, 19-20. Onbūtan færsscagan, 229, 29. Rihte ūt þurh ðone sceagan ōþ ða lēge, 406, 27. Of ðære byrig þwyres ofer ðane sceagan, 460, 2. Þurh Beaddes scagan, v. 166, 10. [At a schaȝe syde, Gaw. 2161. In a schaȝe (*the reference is to the gourd under which Jonah sat*) þat schade ful cole, Allit. Pms. 105, 452. Wodschaweȝ, 9, 284. For love of hym thou lovedst in the shawe, I mene Adon, Tr. and Cr. 3, 671. Thane schotte owtte of þe schawe schiltrounis many, Mort. A. 1765. In ȝone dyme schawes, 1723. See also Halliwell's Dict. and Nares' Glossary. Cf. (?) *Icel.* skaga *to project.*]

sceagod. v. sceacged.

sceal *shall.* v. sculan.

sceál, scāl (?) *a shoal, troop, band*:—Ic be hondum mōt hǽðenre (-ra ?) sceál grīpan tō grunde, Godes andsacan, Cd. Th. 281, 8; Sat. 268. Cf. Mid his handscále, Beo. Th. 2638; B. 1317.

scealc, es; *m.* I. *a servant*:—Eálā ic eom ðīn āgen esne Dryhten and ðīn swylce eom scealc ombehte (cf. ambeht-scealc) and ðīnre þeówan suna *O Domine, quia ego servus tuus, ego servus tuus, et filius ancillae tuae*, Ps. Th. 115, 6. Ic eom ðīn hold scealc *tuus sum ego*, 118, 94. Dō ðīnes scealces (*servi*) sāwle blīðe, 85, 3. Tō scealce *in servum*, 104, 15. Hǽl ðīnne scealc *salvum fac servum tuum*, 85, 2: 88, 17. Hē Moyses sende his sylfes scealc *misit Moysen servum suum*, 104, 22. Beseoh on ðīne scealcas *respice in servos tuos*, 89, 18. Babilone weard hēt his scealcas scūfan ða hyssas in bǽlblyse, Cd. Th. 230, 10; Dan. 231. II. as a term of reproach:—Ðā hine heówon hǽðene scealcas, Byrht. Th. 137, 5; By. 181. Hwīlum ic gehēre helle scealcas, gnorniende cynn, Cd. Th. 273, 8; Sat. 133. III. *a man, soldier, sailor*:—Scealc (*Beowulf*) hafaþ dǽde gefremede, ðe wē ealle ǽr ne meahton, Beo. Th. 1883; B. 939. Eode scealc monig swīðnicgende tō sele searowundor seón, 1841; B. 918. Hū mæg ðæt gesceádwīs scealc (cf. gesceádwīs mon, Bt. 28; Fox 100, 30) gereccan, ðæt hē him ðȳ sēlra þince, Met. 15, 14. Brugdon scealcas (*the Jews who defeated the Assyrians*) of sceáðum scīrmǽled swyrd, Judth. Thw. 24, 38; Jud. 230. Næs scealca nān *there was no one*, Met. 8, 21. Scipu mid scealcum *ships with their crews*, Exon. Th. 362, 3; Wal. 31. [Þer wes moni bald scalc (cniht, 2nd MS.), Laym. 19126. Heo wenden bi þen scelden þat hit heore scalkes (men, 2nd MS.) weoren, 4219. Schalk *a knight*, Gaw. 160. *Goth.* skalks δοῦλος: *O. Sax.* skalk *servus*: *O. Frs.* skalk *a servant, slave*: *O. H. Ger.* scalch *servus, famulus, manceps*: *Icel.* skálkr *a rogue.* v. Grmm. R. A. 302, and Grff. vi. 480 sqq. for compounds.] v. ambeht-, beór-, freoðo-scealc.

sceald. v. dæg-sceald.

sceald-hūlas glosses *paupilius*, Wrt. Voc. ii. 116, 21. v. next word.

sceald-þȳfel (-hȳfel), es; *m. A thicket*:—Scaldthȳflas, scald[t]hȳblas *alga, alge*; scaldhȳflas *vel* sondhyllas *alga*, Txts. 38, 58. 'Scaldhȳflas *alga*, scaldhūlas *paupilius*, are errors. Scealdþȳfelas, *fruteta, thickets*, occurs in Greg. Dial.' Lchdm. iii. 343, col. 2. [Cf. (?) *O. H. Ger.* scald *sacer*; scald-eiche *ilex*: and see Grmm. D. M. 615.]

scealfor, e; *f.*: scealfra, an; *m. A diver* (bird):—Scalfr, scalfur *mergulus*, Txts. 78, 647. Scealfr *mergus*, Wrt. Voc. i. 29, 13. Scealfor *turdella, mergula*, 63, 15, 16: *mergulus*, 280, 11: ii. 56, 18: 89, 54. Scealfra *mergus* vel *mergulus*, i. 77, 27. Grǽdigre scelfre *voracis mergulae*, Hpt. Gl. 418, 70. Ðā geseah hē swymman scealfran on flōde, and gelōme doppettan ādūne tō grunde ēhtende þearle ðære eá fixa . . . Ðā hēt Martinus ða fugelas ðæs fixnoðes geswīcan, and tō wēstene sīðian; and ða scealfran gewiton āweg tō holte, Homl. Th. ii. 516, 6-12.

scealga, scylga, an; *m. The name of a fish*:—Scealga *rocea*, Wrt. Voc. i. 77, 67. Scylga, 55, 77.

scealian. v. ā-scealian.

sceallan, scallan; *pl. Testiculi*, Lchdm. i. 330, 13: 336, 15: 358, 21.

scealu, e; *f.* I. *a shell, husk*:—Scealu *glumula*, Wrt. Voc. ii. 40, 23. Scalu, scala, Txts. 66, 462. Scale ꝉ hule *glumula*, Hpt. Gl. 439, 50. v. æpel-, beán-, stān-scealu. II. *a platter, dish, cup*:—.VI. mæsene sceala, Chart. Th. 429, 30. III. *the scale of a balance*:—Ðeós wǽge ꝉ scalu *haec lanx*, Ælfc. Gr. 9, 73; Som. 14, 18. Scale *lanx*, twā scale *balances*, Wrt. Voc. i. 38, 39-40. v. wǽg-scealu. [*O. Sax.* skala *a drinking-vessel*: *O. L. Ger.* scala *concha*: *O. H. Ger.* scala *patera, cratera, concha, gluma*: *Icel.* skāl *a bowl, a scale* (of a balance).]

sceám, es; *m. A white horse* (?):—Etsomne cwom .LX. monna wicgum rīdan, hæfdon .XI. eoredmacgas frīdhengestas, IIII. sceámas (cf. (?) hyra bloncan, 405, 5; Rä. 23, 18), Exon. Th. 404, 8; Rä. 23, 4.

sceamel. v. sceamol.

sceam-fæst; *adj. Shamefast* (corrupted later into *shamefaced.* v. 1 Tim. 2, 9 where Wicklif has *schamefastnesse*, the modern copies of the A. V. *shamefacedness*; the Revised Version has restored *shamefastness*), *modest, bashful*:—Scamfæst *verecundus* vel *pudens*, Wrt. Voc. i. 51, 31. Sceamfæst *verecundus*, 86, 56. Seó scamfæste næcednys *pudibunda* (*pudica* .i. *erubescens*) *nuditas*, Hpt. Gl. 492, 53. Mǽden is sceamfæst, Lchdm. iii. 188, 6. Scamfæst, 192, 2. On ōðre wīsan sint tō lǽranne ða scamleásan, on ōðre ða scamfæstan (*verecundi*), Past. 31; Swt. 205, 21. [Sannte Marȝe wass shammfæst, Orm. 2175. Wyfmen þet byeþ ssamuest, Ayenb. 222, 20. Schamefast chastite, Chauc. Kn. T. 1197. Schamefast *verecundus, pudorosus*, Prompt. Parv. 443.] v. un-sceamfæst.

sceam-full; *adj. Modest, chaste*:—Sceomfull *pudica*, Rtl. 108, 25. Sceomfullre *verecundia*, 110, 3. [Schrift schal beon . . . edmod, scheomeful, dredful, A. R. 302, 23. *Dan.* skam-fuld *shamefaced, ashamed.* Chaucer uses the word in its modern sense *ignominious*, As shamful deeth as herte may deusye Come to these Juges, C. T. Group C. 290.]

sceamfullness, e; *f. Modesty*; pudicitia. v. un-sceamfullness.

sceamian; *p.* ode. I. *to feel shame, be ashamed* (with gen. of cause):—Ic ðæs nǽfre ne sceamige *non erubescam*, Ps. Th. 24, 1. Ne ic ne scamige *nec confundar*, Ps. Spl. 30, 20. Gif wē scomiaþ ðæt wē tō uncūðum monnum suelc sprecen *si homo apud hominem, de quo minime praesumit, fieri intercessor erubescit*, Past. 10, 2; Swt. 63, 5. Weorðaþ gescende and hiora scamiaþ ða tō Sione hete hæfdon *confundantur et revereantur, qui oderunt Sion*, Ps. Th. 128, 3. Nā ic ne scamode *non confundebar*, Ps. Spl. 118, 46. Ðiós sǽ cwið ðæt ðū ðīn scamige Sidon *erubesce Sidon, ait mare*, Past. 52, 8; Swt. 409, 33. Hit is cyn ðæt wē ūre scomigen, 52, 4; Swt. 407, 15. Sceamian heora ealle mīne fȳnd *erubescant omnes inimici mei*, Ps. Th. 6, 8. Scamien, 69, 3. Scamien (*confundantur*) heora ealle ða unrihtwīsan, 24, 3. Heora æfstu ealle sceamien, 69, 4. For hwī hī ne māgan heora mā sceamigan ðonne fægnian? Bt. 30, 1; Fox 108, 7. Nō hē ðære feohgyfte scamigan þorfte, Beo. Th. 2057; B. 1026. Ðū ne þearft sceamian, Soul Kmbl. 286; Seel. 147. For hwon sēcest ðū sceade sceomiende? Cd. Th. 54, 8; Gen. 874. Sceomiande man sceal in sceade hweorfan, Exon. Th. 337, 19; Gn. Ex. 67. Ða deóflu wendon sceamigende āweg, Wulfst. 236, 26. Hȳ (*Beowulf's followers who had failed him in his need*) scamiende scyldas bǽron, ðǽr se gomela læg, Beo. Th. 5692; B. 2850. II. *to cause shame* (used impersonally with dat. or acc. of person, gen. of cause, or with *for*, or the cause given in a clause):—Mē sceamaþ *pudet*, Ælfc. Gr. 33; Som. 37, 22. Oft ðone geþyldegestan scamaþ ðæs siges ðe hī ofer ðone dióful hæfde, Past. 33, 7; Swt. 227, 19. Menn scamaþ for gōdan dǽdan swȳðor ðonne for misdǽdan, Wulfst. 164, 16. Ðæs ūs ne scamaþ nā, ac ðæs ūs scamaþ swȳðe, ðæt wē bōte āginnan, 165, 39. Hȳ scamaþ, ðæt hȳ bētan heora misdǽda, 165, 8. Ða woroldlecan lǽcas scomaþ, ðæt . . ., Past. 1, 1; Swt. 25, 20. Mē sceamaþ ðæt ic wædlige *mendicare erubesco*, Lk. Skt. 16, 3. Gehwam sceamaþ, ðæt hē wāclīce gescrȳd cume, Homl. Th. i. 528, 21. Him ðæs sceamode, 18, 12: Gen. 2, 25. Ðā sceamode ealle his wiðerwinnan, Lk. Skt. 13, 17. Hwā biþ gescended, ðæt mē for ðæm ne scamige? Past. 21, 6; Swt. 165, 5. Forgif ūs ūre synna, ðæt ūs ne scamige eft, Hy. 7, 84. Ne sceamige nānum men, ðæt hē ānum lāreow his gyltas cȳðe . . . him sceal sceamian ætforan Gode, Homl. Th. ii. 602, 30. Ðæt mē ne sceamie *non erubescam*, Ps. Th. 24, 18. Hū ne scolde hire sceamian *nonne debuerat rubore suffundi?* Num. 12, 14. Ðonne fægniaþ hī ðæs ðe hī sceamian sceolde, Bt. 30, tit.; Fox xvi, 6. Ðonne mæg hine scamian ðære brǽdinge his hlīsan, 19; Fox 68, 24: Met. 10, 13. Ne þearf ðē ðæs eaforan sceomigan, Cd. Th. 140, 14; Gen. 2327. [*Goth.* skaman (*reflex. with gen.*): *O. L. Ger.* scamōn: *O. H. Ger.* scamōn, scamēn: *Icel.* skamma *to shame*; skammask *to be ashamed.*] v. ā-, for-, e-, of-, on-sceamian.

sceamig. v. un-sceamig.

sceamisc; *adj. Of which one is to be ashamed*; pudendus:—Scamescan lim *veretrum*, Wrt. Voc. ii. 96, 54.

sceam-leás; *adj. Shameless, bold, impudent, wanton* :—Scamleás *impudens*, Wrt. Voc. i. 47, 45. Scamleás *frontosa*, Hpt. Gl. 506, 77. Scamleáse *procax*, 525, 57. Scomleás *impudens*, Wrt. Voc. ii. 44, 38. Se lǽce biþ micles tō beald and tō scomleás (*praesumtione percussus*) ðe gǽþ lǽcnigende, and hæfþ on his āgnum nebbe opene wunde unlācnode, Past. 9, 2; Swt. 61, 3. Of ðysse scamleásan scylde geclǽnsa mē *a delicto meo munda me*, Ps. Th. 50, 3. On ōðre wīsan sint tō lǽranne ða scamleásan (*impudentes*), on ōðre ða scamfæstan . . . Ðone scamleásan mon mæg ðȳ bet gebētan ðe hine mon suīður þreáþ, Past. 31, 1; Swt. 205, 21–207, 5. Ðū hine ongeáte swīðe sceamleásne būton ǽlcum gōdum þeáwe, Bt. 27, 2; Fox 96, 18. God ða sceamleásan (*the people of Sodom*) fordyde, Gen. 19, 24. [*O. H. Ger.* scama-lōs *impudens, procax*: *Icel.* skammlauss *without disgrace*.]

sceamleás-lic; *adj. Shameless, wanton* :—Dauit wæs mid ofermēttum gewundad, and ðæt gecȳðde on Urias slæge, for ðære scamleáslecan gewilnunge his wīfes, Past. 3, 2; Swt. 35, 24.

sceamleáslīce; *adv. Shamelessly, impudently*:—Be ðām Sodomitiscum ðe ongeán gecynd sceamleáslīce syngodon, Boutr. Scrd. 22, 38. Hī swīðe grǽdilīce eorþcundum lustum filigaþ and oft swīðe sceamleáslīce on manna gesyhþe, R. Ben. 139, 28. Hié scamleáslīce gielpaþ ðisses hwīlendlīcan onwaldes *improbe de temporali potestate gloriantur*, Past. 19, 2; Swt. 145, 9. Swā hē scamleáslīcor his yfel cȳð (*impudenter innotescit*), 55, 1; Swt. 427, 25.

sceamleást, e; *f. Shamelessness, want of modesty, impudence, lasciviousness*:—Sceamleást *impudicitia*, Mk. Skt. 7, 22. Scamlēstan (-lēste?) *impudentiam*, Hpt. Gl. 526, 7.

sceam-līc; *adj.* I. *shamefast, bashful*:—Scæmlīc, seó scamfæste *pudibunda, pudica, erubescens*, Hpt. Gl. 492, 53. II. *shameful, base, disgraceful, ignominious*:—Ðā ongan hē him secgan hū lytel and hū scomlīc ðæs monnes līf biþ hēr on worolde . . . and hū wuldorlīc seó ēce eádignes biþ, Shrn. 92, 16. Sceomlīc *corruptibilis*, Rtl. 6, 1. Scildige scamlīcre forgǽgednysse *praevaricationis rei*, Jos. 6, 18. Nys ūs nā tō secgenne ðone sceamlīcan morþ (*the disgraceful events at the siege of Jerusalem*) ðe ðǽr gedōn wæs, Ælfc. T. Grn. 21, 15. Ðæt hē ða sceamlīcan þing and ða mānfullan begǽþ *se res turpes et scelestas committere*, L. Ecg. P. ii. 6; Th. ii. 184, 11. Wæs ðæt feórþe wīte ðæt ealra scamlīcost wæs ðæt hundes fleógan cōmon *post muscas caninas inferentes tam gravia tormenta quam turpia*, Ors. 1, 7; Swt. 38, 1. [Þenne were his cun iscend mid scomeliche witen, Laym. 20462. Eni velunge bitweone mon and ancre is so scheomelich and so naked sunne, A. R. 116, 3. *O. H. Ger.* scama-līh *verecundus, pudibundus*; *turpis, foedus*.] v. ā-, un-sceamlīc.

sceamlīce; *adv. Shamefully, disgracefully*:—Ða ðē ǽwbryce ne wyrceaþ wōlīce and sceamlīce, Homl. As. 19, 140. Hē sceandlīce (scamelīce, MS. N.) sāwlode, 59, 202.

sceam-lim, es; *n. The private member*:—Sceamlim, gecyndlim *dedecus*, Germ. 390, 120.

sceamol, es; *m. A bench, stool.* The word remains in the form *shambles*, properly stalls or benches on which butchers expose meat for sale:—Sceamul *scabellum*, Wrt. Voc. i. 81, 24. Scamol *subsellium*, 289, 24. Scamel, sceamul, sceamol *scabellum*, Ælfc. Gr. 8; Zup. 31, 7. Scamul, scæmol, Ps. Spl. 98, 5. Ðara mynetera sceamelas *mensas nummulariorum*, Mt. Kmbl. 21, 12. Sceomolas, Blickl. Homl. 71, 18. Swā forþ be efise tō lippan hamme; ðæt tō ðām scamelan; swā forþ tō stapole, Cod. Dip. Kmbl. v. 184, 14. [Þe halewen makeden of al þe worlde ase ane stol (scheomel, MS. C.: schamel, MS. T.) to here uet, A. R. 166, 16. I sal set þe faas of þe schamel of þi fete to be, Ps. 109, 1. *O. Sax.* fōtskamel: *O. H. Ger.* scamal *scabellum, subsellium*: *Ger.* schemel *a stool*: *Dan.* skammel. *From Lat.* scamellum.] v. fōt-, rǽde-, rǽding-sceamol.

sceamu, e; *f.* I. *the emotion caused by consciousness of unworthiness* or *of disgrace*, in a good sense (v. sceam-fæst, -full, -leás, -līc), *modesty, bashfulness*; in a bad sense, *shame, confusion*:—Sceamu *pudor* . . . reádnyss oððe sceamu *rubor*, Ælfc. Gr. 9, 21; Som. 10, 17–18. Scamu, scoma, scomo *pudor*, Txts. 84, 732. Scame *pallor*, Hpt. Gl. 474, 77. Scamu *rubor*, 475, 9. Se ðe nū ne mæg his gyltas for sceame ānum men geandettan, him sceal sceamian ðonne ætforan heofenwarum, and seó sceamu him biþ endeleás, Homl. Th. ii. 604, 3–6. Ðū mid sceame (sceoma, Lind.: scomo, Rush.) nyme ðæt ȳtemeste setl *incipias cum rubore nouissimum locum tenere*, Lk. Skt. 14, 9. Ðonne biþ hē self gelādod wið hine selfne mid his āgenre scame and mid his geþylde, Past. 21, 1; Swt. 151, 18. Ðonne ārās hē for sceome *he got up because he was ashamed of his inability to play the harp*, Bd. 4, 24; S. 597, 7. II. *what causes a feeling of shame, disgrace, shame*:—Scoma *obprobrium*, Rtl. 190, 29. Micel hȳnþ and sceamu (*verecundia*) hyt ys men nelle wesan ðæt ðæt hē ys, and ðæt ðe hē wesan sceal, Coll. Monast. Th. 32, 3. Ælce dæge byþ mīn sceamu (*verecundia*) beforan mē, Ps. Th. 43, 17. Byþ ðām scand and sceamu *operiantur confusione et pudore*, 70, 12. Hū mæg māre scamu mannum gelimpan, ðonne ūs dēþ gelōme? Wulfst. 162, 3. Sceome gihēnedo *confusione contempnata*, Rtl. 27, 31. Sceame, Ps. Th. 88, 38. Ic his feóndas gegyrwe mid scame *inimicos ejus induam confusione*, 131, 19. Ðeós woruld scyldwyrcende in scome byrneþ, Exon. Th. 232, 6; Ph. 502. Ne scomu dōaþ *neque calumniam faciatis*, Lk. Skt. Rush. 3, 14: *contumiliam*. 11, 45. Sceame dreógan, habban, þrowian *to be put to shame, be disgraced*:—Beóþ gescende and scame dreógaþ mīne fȳnd *confundantur et revereantur inimici mei*, Ps. Th. 69, 2. Habban sceame *confundantur*, 85, 16. Ne sceolon æt mē ǽnige habban sceame *non erubescant in me*, 68, 7. Sume mǽgon habban ælles woruldwelan genōg ac hī habbaþ ðeáh sceame ðæs welan gif hī ne beóþ swā æðele on gebyrdum swā hī woldon *huic census exuberat, sed est pudori degener sanguis*, Bt. 11, 1; Fox 30, 31. Ðæs ealdfeóndes scyldigra scolu scome þrowedon, Exon. Th. 114, 20; Gū. 175: 269, 5; Jul. 445: 369, 31; Seel. 49. Hī scoma mǽste dreógaþ, 78, 15; Cri. 1274. Mid scomum (sceofmum, Lind.) miclum tō giworhtun *contumeliis affecerunt*, Mk. Skt. Rush. 12, 4: Exon. Th. 153, 19; Gū. 828. III. *the private part* (v. sceam-lim):—Him sī ābrogden swā of brēchrægle hiora sylfra sceamu, Ps. Th. 108, 28. Forhwon wrīhst ðū sceome? Cd. Th. 54, 13; Gen. 876: 58, 7; Gen. 942: 95, 3; Gen. 1573. Scama, ða wǽpenlīcan limo *preputia*, Wrt. Voc. ii. 69, 16. Scamu, 68, 60. [*O. Sax.* skama *shame, disgrace*: *O. L. Ger.* scama *confusio, reverentia*: *O. H. Ger.* scama *verecundia, reverentia, pudor, rubor, confusio, ignominia, turpitudo*: *Icel.* skömm *a shame, outrage*.] v. ār-, hleór-, woruld-sceamu.

sceamung, e; *f. Shaming, disgrace*:—Ðū canst gescændnysse ł sceamunga mīne *tu scis confusionem meam*, Ps. Lamb. 68, 20. v. forsceamung.

sceanca, an; *m.* I. *a shank, shin, the leg from the knee to the foot*:—Sceanca *crus*, Ælfc. Gr. 9, 33; Som. 12, 22: Wrt. Voc. ii. 137, 21: i. 71, 56. Scance(-a?) *crus*, sceanca[n] *crura*, 44, 68. Gif se sconca biþ þyrel beneoðan cneówe, L. Alf. pol. 63; Th. i. 96, 16. Gif monnes sconca biþ of āslagen wið ðæt cneóu, 72; Th. i. 98, 19. Nim blæces hundes deádes ðone swȳðran fōtes sceancan (fōtscancan, MS. B.), Lchdm. i. 362, 27. Sconcan *crura*, Wrt. Voc. i. 65, 41. Scancan, ii. 17, 43. Sceancan *crura*, scancan *tibiae*, i. 283, 69–70. Lǽcedōmas wið scancena sāre, and gif scancan forade synd, Lchdm. ii. 6, 10. Sindon ða scancan (*of the Phenix*) scyllum biweaxen *crura tegunt squamae*, Exon. Th. 219, 20; Ph. 310. Sceancan *tibias*, Hpt. Gl. 482, 64: Kent. Gl. 982. Sconca[n?] *suras*, Wrt. Voc. ii. 93, 5. Ðæt man forbrǽce hyra sceancan (*crura*), Jn. Skt. 19, 31, 32, 33. Se sceocca gewrāð his sceancan, Homl. Skt. i. 11, 223. Sconcan, Salm. Kmbl. 203; Sal. 101. II. *the upper part of the leg* (= þeóhsceanca):—Ic wille ðæt gē fēdaþ ān earm Engliscmon . . . Āgyfe mon hine . . . ān sconc spices oððe ān ram weorðe iiii. peningas, L. Ath. i. prm.; Th. i. 198, 7. [*Dan. Swed.* skank *a shank*: cf. *Germ.* schenkel.] v. earm-, fōt-, hōh-, þeóh-sceanca.

sceanc-bend, es; *m. A band for the leg, a garter*:—Scangbendas *periscelides*, Wrt. Voc. i. 40, 55.

sceanc-forod; *adj. Broken-legged*:—Ðæt sceáp ðæt sceoncforad (scanc-, Cott. MSS.) wæs, Past. 17, 9; Swt. 123, 9. Scancforedum men, Lchdm. ii. 66, 21.

sceanc-gebeorg, es; *n. A protection for the leg, a greave*:—Bānberge, scan[c]gebeorg *ocreas*, Wrt. Voc. ii. 97, 35.

sceanc-gegirela, an; *m. Clothing for the leg, a garter*:—Scancgegirelan *periscelides*, Wrt. Voc. ii. 67, 38.

sceanc-lira, an; *m. The fleshy, brawny part of the shank, the calf of the leg*:—Scanclira *surra*, Wrt. Voc. i. 283, 71.

sceand, es; *m. An infamous person, a buffoon, charlatan*:—Scond *scurra*, Wrt. Voc. ii. 120, 5. Ðonne sægde Petrus, ðæt hē wǽre leás drȳ and sceand and scyldig ǽswica *then Peter said that he* (*Simon the sorcerer*) *was a false sorcerer and a shameless impostor and a guilty deceiver*, Blickl. Homl. 175, 7. Sume hī wyrcaþ heora wōgerum drencas, ðæt hī hī tō wīfe habbon; ac ðyllīce sceandas sceolan sīðian tō helle, Homl. Skt. i. 17, 159.

sceand, e; *f.* I. *shame, disgrace, infamy, ignominy*:—Byþ ðām scand and sceamu *operiantur confusione et pudore*, Ps. Th. 70, 12. *Ignominium* sconde hlēwung (cf. (?) ge-lēwan) *sive* fraceþu, *idem et infamium*, Wrt. Voc. ii. 49, 30. Sume wurdon getawod tō scande *some were shamefully entreated*, Chr. 1076; Erl. 214, 39. Is him ōðer earfeþu scyldgum tō sconde, Exon. Th. 78, 14; Cri. 1274. Sylfum tō sconde *to thine own disgrace*, 90, 27; Cri. 1480. Ðū sceonde æt mē [ne] anfenge ac gefeán eallum *thou gottest not disgrace from me, but gladness ever*, Cd. Th. 54, 9; Gen. 874. Ne þurfun gē wēnan ðæt gē mec mid searocræftum under scæd scōnde (*with ignominy*) scūfan mōtan, Exon. Th. 142, 20; Gū. 647. Unwlite oððe sconde *dedecus*, Wrt. Voc. ii. 27, 35. Hī sceande āgon *confundantur*, Ps. Th. 108, 27. Sceonde fremman ylda bearnum *to bring disgrace on men*, Cd. Th. 149, 3; Gen. 2469. II. *a shameful, infamous, or abominable thing, what brings disgrace*:—Ðonne is suīðe micel scand *ignominiosum valde est*, Past. 22, 2; Swt. 173, 1. Hē ne wolde ða sceonde (*the drunkenness of Noah*) hleómāgum helan, Cd. Th. 95, 20; Gen. 1581. Scande *ignominia* (v. second passage in I), Wrt. Voc. i. 21, 19. Flǽsc scandum þurhwaden, Exon. Th. 78, 32; Cri. 1283. Ðū ðone līchoman scondum gewemdest, 91, 5; Cri. 1487. Āscamode, scondum gedreahte, 79, 32; Cri. 1299. Geseoh ða scande and ða wierrestan þing ðe ðās menn hēr dōþ *vide abominationes pessimas, quas isti* *faciunt hic*, Past. 21, 3; Swt. 153, 20: Swt. 155, 9. Sconde, Swt. 155, 8. [Þatt wass hiss aȝhenn shame ⁊ shande, Orm. 11956. He makede to sconde *he disgraced*, Laym. 7032. Unk schal itide harm and schonde, O. and N. 1733. Þu schalt haue schonde, Horn. 714. To spouse þe emperoures doȝter yt ner hym no schonde, R. Glouc. 65, 12. *Goth.* skanda αἰσχύνη: *O. H. Ger.* scanta *ignominia, confusio.*]

sceand-full; *adj. Shameful, infamous, vile*:—Hē (*John the Baptist*) wæs heáfde becorfen for scandfulra wīfa bēne, and for scondfulles gebeórscypes hleahtre, Shrn. 123, 6-8. [Him wule þunche swiðe strong and swiðe scondful þet he scal al aȝeuen and seoððan bisechen milce et þan ilke monne þe he haueð er istolen, O. E. Homl. i. 31, 2.]

sceand-hūs, es; *m. A house of ill fame, a brothel*:—Đā heó ðæt nolde, ðā hēt hē hī nacode lǣdan tō sumum scandhūse . . . Đæs burhgerēfan sunu wolde rǣsan on hī on ðæm scandhūse, Shrn. 56, 7-11.

sceand-līc; *adj.* I. of persons, *that acts in a disgraceful way, infamous, base, vile*:—On ānre tīde twā mǣdencild cumaþ, and biþ ðæt ān sydefull and ðæt ōðer sceandlīc, Homl. Skt. i. 5, 280. Hierusalem winþ for rihtwīsnysse, and Babilonia winþ ongeán for unrihtwīsnysse . . . Đære heofonlīcan Hierusalem cyning is Crist, ðære scandlīcan Babilonian cyning is deófol, Homl. Th. ii. 66, 32. Đā com ðæs gerēfan suna mid his sceandlīcum gegadum, Homl. Skt. i. 7, 164. God sende tō ðām sceandlīcum mannum (*the people of Sodom*) twegen englas, 13, 207. II. of things, (a) *that is vile in its nature* or *circumstances, disgraceful, foul, shameful, obscene*:—Scandlīc hosp *ridiculosum opprobrium*, Hpt. Gl. 524, 73. Gif hit ǣr sceondlīc wæs, ne biþ hit nō ðȳ fægerre, Bt. 14, 3; Fox 46, 16. Seó gesceádwīsnes; nis ðæt scandlīc cræft, forðæm hit nǣnig hafaþ neát būton monnum, Met. 20, 188. Scandlīcre fūlnesse *spurcae obscoenitatis*, Hpt. Gl. 447, 19. Of scondlīcum geþohte *ex turpi cogitatione*, Bd. 1, 27; S. 497, 5. Mid sceandlīcum willan *with foul lust*, Homl. Skt. i. 7, 170. Đīn mōdor gewīteþ of weorulde þurh scondlīcne deáð and unārlīcne *miserando turpissimoque exitu*, Nar. 31, 29. Ælc ōðerne æftan heáweþ mid scandlīcan onscytan, Wulfst. 160, 5. Hē sang scandlīcu leóþ, and plegode scandlīce plegan, Shrn. 121, 10. Sceondlīcum *corruptibilibus*, Rtl. 24, 36. Ic wille geswigian Tontolis and Pilopes ðara scondlīcestena spella *nec mihi nunc enumerare opus est Tantali et Pelopis facta turpia, fabulas turpiores*, Ors. 1, 8; Swt. 42, 8. (b) *that causes shame, disgraceful*:—Hit is scondlīc ymb swelc tō sprecanne hwelc hit ðā wæs *pudet erroris humani*, 1, 10; Swt. 48, 4. [Wið scondliche deaðe, Laym. 2274. *O. H. Ger.* scant-līh *turpis, probrosus, ignominiosus, teter, lugubris.*]

sceandlīce; *adv.* I. *in a disgraceful manner, disgracefully, shamefully, infamously*:—Heó lyfde sceandlīce, swā swīn on meoxe, Homl. Skt. i. 3, 528. Nān cristen man ne sceal sceandlīce flītan, 13, 122. Him wand ūt his innoþ æt his setle, and hē sceandlīce sāwlode, Homl. As. 59, 202. II. *opprobriously, reproachfully, insultingly*:—Hiera wīf [sægdon] ðæt hié ōðer gener næfden, būton hié on heora wīfa hrif gewiton. Hī ðā, æfter ðæm ðe ða wīf hié swā scondlīce gerǣht hæfdon, gewendan eft ongeán ðone cyning, Ors. 1, 12; Swt. 54, 5. Gif man mannan bismærwordum scandlīce grēte *if one man insult another by abusive words*, L. H. E. 11; Th. i. 32, 5. Ne sceolon æt mē ǣnige habban sceame sceandlīce ðe ðīnes sīðes biddaþ (bīdaþ?) *non erubescant in me, qui expectant te*, Ps. Th. 68, 7.

sceandlīcness, e; *f. Shame, disgrace, dishonour*:—Seó hālige ǣ forbeódeþ ða sceondlīcnysse (*turpitudinem*) onwreón mǣgsibba, Bd. 1, 27; S. 491, 6, 12. Hē [ne] mæg mid weorce begān ða sceondlīcnesse (scond-, MS. Hatt.) *qui turpitudinem non exercet opere*, Past. 11, 7; Swt. 72, 5.

sceandness. v. ge-sceandness.

sceand-word, es; *n. A vile, foul word*, or *an opprobrious, abusive word*:—Đæt ic (*the devil*) wolde, ðæt hȳ (*wicked men*) ðē (*God*) āfremdedon and ðīne circean forgeáton and æt mē leornedan sceandword, Wulfst. 255, 15.

sceán-feld. v. scīn-feld.

sceap, es; *n. A private part*:—Hē getǣlde his fæder Noe, ðǣr hē on his sceape lōcode, Anglia xi. 2, 53. Wið gicþan ðæra sceapa, Lchdm. i. 38, 15. v. for-, ge-, land-sceap.

sceáp, scēp, scīp, es; *n. A sheep*:—Scēp *ovis*, Wrt. Voc. i. 23, 54. Đæt dysige scēp, Ps. Th. 118, 176. Sceáp sceal gongan mid his flíese ōþ midne sumor, L. In. 69; Th. i. 146, 10. Emban ceápgild . . . sceáp tō scill., L. Ath. v. 6, 2; Th. i. 234, 2. Man healde .iii. niht hȳde and heáfod (*of a slain ox*), and sceápes eall swā, L. Eth. iii. 9; Th. i. 296, 19. Nān scyldwyrhta ne lecge nān scēpes fell on scyld, L. Ath. i. 15; Th. i. 208, 10. Eówu biþ mid hire giunge sceápe scill. weorð ōþ ðæt .xiii. niht ofer Eástron, L. In. 55; Th. i. 138, 7. Sceáp mon sceal gildan mid scill., L. O. D. 7; Th. i. 356, 6. Hwylc man ys ðe hæbbe ān sceáp (scēp, Rush.: scīp, Lind.), Mt. Kmbl. 12, 11. Sceáp (scēp, Rush.: scīp, Lind.) ðe hyrde nabbaþ, 9, 36. Scīpo *oves*, Rtl. 19, 37. Sceápa hūs *ovile*, Wrt. Voc. i. 15, 21. Sceápa locu *caule*, 16, 6: ii. 23, 11. Lambra sceápa *agni ovium*, Ps. Spl. 113, 6. Þreó heorda sceápa *tres greges ovium*, Gen. 29, 2. Heald mīne sceáp (scīp, Rush.: scīpo, Lind.) *pasce oves meas*, Jn. Skt. 21, 17. Ic drīfe sceáp mīne tō heora lǽse, Coll. Monast. Th. 20, 11. [*O. Frs.* skēp, schēp: *O. L. Ger.* skāp: *O. H. Ger.* scāf.] v. snǣding-sceáp. The word occurs in local names, v. Cod. Dip. Kmbl. vi. 328, 329.

sceáp-ǣtere, es; *m. The carcase of a sheep* (?):—Ānan esne gebyreþ tō metsunge .xii. pund gōdes cornes, and .ii. scīpǣteras, and i. gōd metecū, L. R. S. 8; Th. i. 436, 27.

sceapen. v. earm-sceapen.

sceápen; *adj. Of a sheep*:—Sceápen smera (cf. on sceápes smerwe, l. 9), Lchdm. ii. 128, 16. Ete sceápen flǣsc and nān ōþer, 358, 22. [*O. H. Ger.* scāfīn *ovinus.*]

sceáp-heord, e; *f. A flock of sheep*:—Nimaþ eówre hrȳðerheorda and eówer sceápheorda and eówer orf *oves vestras et armenta assumite*, Ex. 12, 32.

sceáp-heorden, es; *n. A hovel, shed*:—Bȳre *vel* sceápheorden *magalia* vel *mappalia* vel *capanna*, Wrt. Voc. i. 58, 31.

sceáp-hirde, es; *m. A shepherd*:—Abel wæs sceáphyrde *fuit Abel pastor ovium*, Gen. 4, 2. Hwīlum wearð geworden sceáphyrde tō cynge, L. Eth. vii. 22; Th. i. 334, 10. Scēphyrde *oppilius*, Wrt. Voc. ii. 65, 10. Scȳphyred (-hyrde? cf. gāta hierde *titurus*, 288, 21) *titirus*, Wrt. Voc. i. 18, 57. Swā swā sceáphyrde tōsceát sceáp fram gātum, Wulfst. 288, 2. Scēphyrdas *opiliones*, Coll. Monast. Th. 19, 3. Godes engel ætīwde sceáphirdon, Shrn. 29, 31. Be sceáphyrdan. Sceáphyrdes riht is . . ., L. R. S. 14; Th. i. 438, 21.

Sceáp-īg, e; *f. Sheppy* (= *Sheep-island*, cf. Far-oe, *Icel.* fær *a sheep*):—Hēr hǣþne men ǣrest on Sceápīge (-ēge, MS. E.) ofer winter sǣtun, Chr. 855; Erl. 68, 23. Hēr hǣþne men oferhergeadon Sceápīge, 832; Erl. 64, 18.

sceáp-scearu, e; *f. Sheep-shearing*:—Đā fōr hē tō his scēpscere, Gen. 38, 12.

sceapung. v. for-sceapung.

sceáp-wæsce, an; *f. A place for washing sheep*, the word remains as a place-name in *Sheepwash*, in Worcestershire:—Of ðam stāne on sceápwæscan; andlang sceápwæscan, Cod. Dip. v. 48, 6. Andlang sceápwæscan tō sceápwæscan forda, 174, 11. Tō ðære sceápwæscan, 298, 4. Juxta fluvium qui dicitur Stūr, ad uadum nomine Scēpesuuasce, i. 155, 23.

sceáp-wīc, es; *n. A sheep-fold*:—Tō sceápwīcan, Cod. Dip. Kmbl. iii. 405, 5.

scear, es; *m.* (?) *A plough-share*:—Scer, scær, scear *uomis*, Ælfc. Gr. 9, 28; Zup. 55, 16. Scaer *vomer*, Txts. 35, 32. Scear *vomer* vel *vomis*, Wrt. Voc. i. 15, 1: 74, 72. Scer, 287, 6. Hwanon ðam yrþlinge sylan scear oððe culter, Coll. Monast. Th. 30, 29. Gefæstnodon sceare and cultre mid ðære syl *confirmato vomere et cultro aratro*, 19, 19. Hē sceal habban scear, culter and eác gādīren, Anglia ix. 263, 4. [*Chauc. Piers P. Prompt. Parv.* schare: *O. Frs.* skere, schere: *O. H. Ger.* scar, scaro *vomer.*]

sceár, e; *f. A pair of shears* or *scissors*; but the word is generally used in the plural (dual?) as the modern *shears, scissors*:—Scēr *forfex*, Wrt. Voc. ii. 36, 65. Scēroro, scērero *forfices*, Txts. 60, 401. Īsernscēruru *forfex*, 65, 903. Sceára *forfex*, Wrt. Voc. i. 86, 21. Sceára *forficis*, ii. 1, 15. Tange *forcipis*, tang *forceps*, sceára *forficis*, 33, 35-37. Tangan, tange *forcipis*, sceáre[n] *forficis*, Hpt. Gl. 417, 75. Hī ne scoldon hira loccas lǣtan weaxan ac hié scoldon hié efsigean mid sceárum *non comam nutrient, sed tondentes attondent capita sua*, Past. 18, 7; Swt. 139, 14. Ne hē his loccas mid sceárum wanode, Shrn. 93, 9. Hē sceal habban horscamb and sceára (*shears*) . . . sceárra (*scissors*), nǣdle, Anglia ix. 263, 8-15. Cf. Rægl sceára *forfices*, fexsceára *forpices*, Wrt. Voc. ii. 150, 21, 22. [My berd, myn heer . . . That nevere yit ne felte offensioun of rasour ne of schere, Chauc. Kn. T. 1559. A shepster (*sutrix*) shere, Piers P. 13, 331. Schere (scherys) to clyppe wythe *forfex*, Prompt. Parv. 445, col. 2. *O. Frs.* skēre, schēre; *f.*: *O. H. Ger.* scāri; *pl. forpices*; scāra *forfex*: *M. H. Ger.* schære: *Ger.* schere: *Icel.* skæri; *n. pl. shears.*] v. secg-gescēre.

sceára. v. secg-sceára.

scear-beám, es; *m. The wood to which the ploughshare is fixed* (?):—Scearbeám *brigacus*, Wrt. Voc. ii. 127, 21.

sceard, es; *n. A shard, sherd, pot-sherd, tile*:—Scearda *testarum*, Germ. 398, 257. [Gower uses *sherd* for the scale of a dragon, 'a dragon whose scherdes schinen as the sonne,' iii. 68, 5: and in Shakspere *shard* denotes a beetle's hard wing-case, v. Nares' Glossary. *M. H. Ger.* scharte *a sherd*: *Ger.* scharte.] v. croc-sceard; scirden.

sceard, es; *n. A gap, notch*:—Dō of ðam feórþan deále eall ðæt seó sǣ his ofseten hæfþ and eall ða sceard ðe heó him on genumen hæfþ *subtract from this fourth part* (*of the earth*) *all of it that the sea has covered, and all the gaps* (*bays and creeks*) *it has taken*; huic quartae, si quantum maria premunt subtraxeris, Bt. 18, 1; Fox 62, 13. [*Shard* a gap remains long in some dialects. v. E. D. S. Pub. Gloss. B. 15, 19 (Wiltshire). *O. Frs.* skerd *a notch, cut, gash*: *M. H. Ger. Ger.* scharte: *Icel.* skarð *a notch, chink, gap.*] v. dīc-, hær-sceard, *and next word.*

sceard; *adj.* I. *notched, hacked, having gaps* or *rifts*:—Ic geann Ælmǣre ðæs sceardan swurdes *the hacked sword* (cf. *Icel.* með skarða skjöldu *with hacked shields*), Chart. Th. 561, 1, 23. Tō ðam sceardan beorge (cf. ðone tōbrocenan beorg ðe is tōclofen, Cod. Dip. Kmbl. ii. 251, 5), of ðam sceardan beorge tō ðam rūgan hlǣwe, Cod.

Dip. B. iii. 170, 2. On sceard hweogl (?), Cod. Dip. Kmbl. iii. 419, 11. Hrôfas sind gehrorene . . . scearde scûrbeorge, Exon. Th. 476, 9; Ruin. 5. II. *gashed, mutilated*:—Gif eáre sceard weorðe, L. Eth. 42; Th. i. 14, 7: 48; Th. i. 14, 13. III. *deprived*:—Hê wæs his mǽga sceard, freónda gefylled on folcstede, beslagen æt sæcce, and his sunu forlêt on wælstôwe, Chr. 937; Erl. 114, 6. (Cf. *Icel.* hafa, bera skarðan hlut *to get worsted.*) [*O. Sax.* skard: *O. Frs.* skerde *cut, gashed*: *O. H. Ger.* scart; lid-scart *murcus*; lid-scartî *mutilation*; scartsam *scabrosus*: *M. H. Ger.* schart: *Ger.* schartig: *Icel.* skarðr.] v. scirdan, *and previous word.*

scearfian; *p.* ode *To scrape, cut into shreds*:—Genim ða ylcan wyrte, scearfa hý̆ ðonne, and gnîd swýðe smale tô duste, Lchdm. i. 70, 14: 80, 16: 344, 13 note. Scearfa smæle, ii. 322, 25. Scearfaþ *succidite* . . . gescearfa ðû *succides*, Lk. Skt. Lind. 13, 7, 9. Scearfige ealle ðâs rinda tôgædere, Lchdm. iii. 14, 4. [*O. H. Ger.* scarbôn *concidere.*] v. sceorfan, *and next two words.*

scearflian; *p.* ode *To scrape*:—Scearfla on wæter, Lchdm. i. 184, 18.

scearfung, e; *f. Scraping, scarifying*:—Ða wǽtan ða yfelan weorðaþ gegaderode on ðone magan, and ðǽr rîxiaþ mid scearfunga innan, Lchdm. ii. 176, 7. Âberan ða strangan scearfunga ðæra wǽtena, 176, 10.

scearian *to grant.* v. ge-scearian.

scearn, es; *n. Sharn* (v. E. D. S. Pub. Gloss. B. 17), *dung, filth*:—Scearn, scern *fimus*, Ælfc. Gr. 13; Zup. 83, 13. Gor, scear[n] *letamen*, Wrt. Voc. ii. 50, 38. Swê swê scearn (*stercus*) eorþan, Ps. Surt. 82, 11. Gôse scearn, ðonne hió ne ete, Lchdm. ii. 92, 15. Scearnes *fimi*, Wrt. Voc. ii. 95, 75. Scearn (oxena) *fimum*, Coll. Monast. Th. 20, 1. [*O. Frs.* skern: *Icel.* skarn; *n. dung*: *Dan.* skarn *dung, muck, filth.*]

scearn-fifel. v. scearn-wifel.

scearn-wibba, an; *m. A dung-beetle*:—Scærnwibba *scarabeus*, Wrt. Voc. i. 77, 52. v. next word.

scearn-wifel, es; *m. A dung-beetle*:—Scearnwifel (-fifel, MS.) *scarabeus*, Wrt. Voc. i. 23, 69. [Halliwell gives *sharn-bug*, a cockchafer, as a Sussex word. Cf. Ssarnboddes (*beetles*) þet louieþ þet dong, Ayenb. 61, 32. *Icel.* tord-yfill *a beetle.*]

scearp; *adj.* I. *sharp, having a fine edge* or *point*:—Seaxes ecg scearp, Exon. Th. 70, 21; Cri. 1142. Ic eom heard and scearp, ingonges strong, 479, 19; Rä. 63, 1. Genim ðæs scearpan þistles moran, Lchdm. ii. 314, 11. Scearpe gâras, Cd. Th. 124, 18; Gen. 2064. Ða Walas âdrifon sumre eá ford ealne mid scearpum pîlum, Chr. Erl. 5, 10. Scearpre ðonne ǽni sweord, Ps. Th. 44, 4. Nǽdle scearpran, Exon. Th. 373, 33; Seel. 119. Scearpeste stânas *cautes* vel *murices*, Wrt. Voc. i. 38, 22. II. *sharp* to the taste, *pungent, acid*:—Sió scearpe docce *oxylapatium*, Wrt. Voc. ii. 65, 50: Lchdm. iii. 304, col. 2. Meng wið scearpum ecede, i. 354, 22: ii. 72, 16. On wîne wel scearpum, 180, 16. Mettas ge drincan ða ðe habban hât mægen and scearp, 184, 10. Ðæs scearpestan wînes .v. sestras, 252, 8. II a. *acrid*:—Ða yfelan wǽtan sceorfendan and scearpan, Lchdm. ii. 176, 20. III. *sharp* of speech (cf. *sharp*-tongued):—Hê biþ scarp and biter and swîðe wær on his wordum, Lchdm. iii. 162, 13. Wǽron hyra tungan tô yfele gehwam ungemet scearpe, Ps. Th. 56, 5. IV. *sharp, keen, severe*, of pain or of that which causes pain:—Syððan com se scearpa hungor and âdyde hî mid ealle, Chr. 1086; Erl. 219, 37. Biþ ðæt sâr scearpre ðonne ðæs welmes sâr, Lchdm. ii. 206, 3. V. *sharp, rough* (v. scearpness, III):—Ðǽr sint swîðe scearpe wegas and stânihte *situ terrarum montoso et aspero*, Ors. 1, 1; Swt. 10, 25. VI. *sharp, keen, active, strenuous*:—Ðâ âsende hê him tô ðone scearpan here of Rômâna rîce mid rêdum wǽpnum, Homl. Th. ii. 302, 18: Homl. As. 61, 244. Ðâ geceás hê him gefêran ða ðe ǽgðer ge on heora dǽdum ge on heora gelǽrednesse frome and scearpe wǽron Godes word tô bodienne and tô lǽranne *electis sociis strenuissimis et ad praedicandum verbum idoneis, utpote actione simul et eruditione praeclaris*, Bd. 5, 9; S. 622, 25. VI a. of things, *effectual, penetrating*, cf. scearplîce:—Hyre (*black horehound*) miht ys scearp, Lchdm. i. 310, 7. Seó sunne scînþ mid hyre scearpan leóman, Homl. As. 43, 484. VII. *sharp, keen*, of sight:—Scearp gesihþ *acies*, Ælfc. Gr. 5; Som. 4, 14. Sió sýn biþ ðý scearpre, Lchdm. ii. 30, 21. VIII. *sharp, keen, acute*, of understanding:—Scearp angyte *acre ingenium*, Ælfc. Gr. 9, 18; Som. 9, 66. Bûton hê hæbbe swâ scearp andget swâ ðæt fýr, Bt. 39, 4; Fox 216, 28. Hû ðû eart gleáw and scearp, Exon. Th. 463, 27; Hö. 76. Sceal scearp scyldwîga gescâd witan worda and worca, se ðe wel þenceþ, Beo. Th. 581; B. 288. Scearpe *arguto*, Wrt. Voc. ii. 9, 64. Tôsceád simle scearpe môde in sefan ðînum, Exon. Th. 303, 1; Fä. 46. Ðâ ongeat hê mid scearpre gleáwnysse *ille, ut vir sagacis ingenii, intellexit*, Bd. 3, 9; S. 533, 42. [*O. Sax.* skarp: *O. Frs.* skerp: *O. H. Ger.* scarf: *Icel.* skarpr.] v. beadu-, efen-, heoru-, mylen-, un-scearp.

scearpe; *adv. Sharply, keenly.* I. literal:—Ða fugelas ðe be flǽsce lybbaþ syndon scearpe gebilode *the birds that live on flesh are sharp-billed*, Hexam. 8; Norm. 14, 19. II. referring to seeing, observing:—Scearpe gesceáwian, Ps. Th. 93, 9. Se ðe ealra scearpost lôcianne mæg, Shrn. 187, 1.

scearpe, an; *f. A scarification*:—Âsleah âne scearpan on ðam dolge, Lchdm. ii. 142, 21: 144, 6. Stande on heáfde, âsleá him mon fela scearpena on ðâm scancan, ðonne gewît ût ðæt âtter þurh ða scearpan, 154, 2–4. Wið onfealle: genim hæslenne sticcan oððe ellenne, wrît ðînne naman on, âsleah þrý scearpan on, gefylle mid ðý blôde ðone naman, weorp ofer eaxle oððe betweoh þeóh on yrnende wæter . . . Ða scearpan âsleá, and ðæt eall swîgende gedô, 104, 6–11: 84, 4: 100, 4: 126, 21: 130, 10.

scearp-ecged; *adj. Sharp-edged*:—God hêt ðæt hê nâme scearpecgedne flint, Homl. Th. i. 92, 33.

scearpian; *p.* ode *To scarify, make an incision in the skin*:—Scearpa him ða scancan, Lchdm. ii. 46, 24: 76, 13: 126, 20. Scearpige and smire mid hâtan ele, 130, 7: 284, 8. Ðû scealt ymb .iii. niht scearpian, 264, 1. Scearpigean, iii. 132, 31.

scearp-lîc; *adj. Sharp, keen, searching, effectual*:—Hwæt is sió þyrelung ðæs wâges bûton scearplîcu and smeálîcu fandung ðæs môdes ðæt mon onlûce ða heardan heortan *quid est parietem fodere, nisi acutis inquisitionibus duritiam cordis aperire?* Past. 21, 3; Swt. 155, 1. Ðonne hê him gecýð mid hû scearplîcum costungum wê sint ǽghwonon ûtan behringde *cum tentationum aculeos nos undique circumdantes innotescit*, 21, 5; Swt. 163, 16. Hû ne gesceóp ðê se scaþa scearplîce bysne *nonne exempla tibi dabat latro?* Dôm. L. 53.

scearplîce; *adv.* I. *sharply, keenly, smartly, effectually, quickly*:—Scearplîce *efficaciter, velociter*, Wrt. Voc. ii. 142, 56. Hyt ys gelýfed ðæt heó scearplîce gehǽle, Lchdm. i. 154, 9. Heó gehǽlþ ðæt sâr tô ðam scearplîce, ðæt hê eác gân dyrre *it heals the pain* (*gout*) *so smartly, that he may even venture to walk*, 176, 8: 210, 9: Exon. Th. 209, 9; Ph. 168. II. *sharply, keenly* (of the mind):—Ða ðe meahton smeálîce and scearplîce mid hiera andgite ryht geseón *qui videre recta subtiliter per ingenium poterant*, Past. 11, 4; Swt. 69, 6. III. *sharply, painfully*:—Scearplîce *acerbatim*, Txts. 181, 47. Stingaþ hine scearplîce on ðone mûð, Wulfst. 141, 7.

scearpness, e; *f. Sharpness.* I. referring to the sight:—Scearpnes *acies*, Wrt. Voc. ii. 2, 19. Sió scearpnes ðæs æpples *acies pupillae*, Past. 11, 4; Swt. 69, 3. Seó scearpnes mînra eágena nis nû mid mê *lumen oculorum meorum non est mecum*, Ps. Th. 37, 10. Heó (*betony*) gegôdaþ ðæra eágena scearpnesse, Lchdm. i. 72, 16. Hî ðæs môdes eágena scearpnesse nâuht gebêtaþ tô ðære sceáwunga ðære sôðan gesǽlþe, Bt. 34, 8; Fox 144, 32: Met. 21, 24. II. referring to the mind:—On his môdes scearpnesse *aciem mentis*, Past. 16, 1; Swt. 99, 9. Wæs hê nâwiht hefig . . . ne hê cnihtlîce gâlnysse næs begangende . . . ac on his scearpnysse hê weóx, Guthl. 2; Gdwin. 12, 13–20. III. *roughness* of surface (v. scearp, V):—Ealle wôhnyssa beóþ gerihte and scearpnyssa gesmêðode, Homl. Th. i. 360, 34. IV. *acidity, pungency*:—Sió scearpnes *the acidity of the humours*, Lchdm. ii. 28, 1. Ðæs ecedes afre scearpnes, 224, 22. Sê lîchama gefêlþ ðæs sealtes scearpnesse, Wulfst. 35, 6. V. *efficacy*:—For ðære sealfe scearpnesse (*to make the salve effectual*) genim wîfes meoluc, ii. 28, 7. v. unscearpness.

scearp-numol; *adj. Efficacious*:—Ðeós wyrt ys swýðe scearpnumul (-el, MS. B.) nîwe wunda and wîde tô gehǽlenne, swâ ðæt ða wunda hrædlîce tôgædere gâþ, Lchdm. i. 134, 10. Ðeós wyrt is swîðe scearpnumul wið ðæt âttor, 152, 3. Swâ se lǽcedôm yldra byþ, swâ hê scearpnumulra and hâlwendra byþ, 242, 5.

scearp-sîne, -siéne, -sýne; *adj. Sharp-sighted*:—Gif hwâ biþ swâ scearpsêne (-siéne, Cott. MS.) . . . swâ swâ Aristoteles sǽde ðæt deór wǽre, ðæt mihte stânas þurhseón . . . gif ðonne hwâ wǽre swâ scearpsiéne, Bt. 32, 2; Fox 116, 19–23. v. un-scearpsîne.

scearp-smeáung, e; *f. A sharp, strict examination, argument*:—Scearpsmêung *argumentum*, Mt. Kmbl. p. 12, 7. Scearpsmeáwunges *argumenti*, 13, 9.

scearpþanclîce; *adv. Acutely, effectually*:—Scearpþanclîce *efficaciter*, Scint. 32.

scearp-þancol; *adj. Acute, subtle*:—Ða scearpþanclan witan ðe ðone twýdǽledan wîsdôm tôcnâwaþ, Lchdm. iii. 440, 28.

scearpung, e; *f. Scarifying*:—Lâcna mid scearpinge, Lchdm. iii. 82, 23. Mid gelômlîcre scearpunge, hwîlum mid miclum, hwîlum mid feáwum, 84, 2. Lǽcedômas and scearpunga wið sîdan sâre, 262, 24.

scear-seax, es; *n. A razor*:—Scearsex *rasorium*, Wrt. Voc. i. 35, 21. Scersaex *novacula*, Ps. Surt. 51, 4. Scirseax, Wrt. Voc. ii. 70, 17. Scyrseax, 60, 44: *culter*, 15, 58. Scyrseax scearp *machera acuta*, Blickl. Gl. Ða sacerdas ne sceoldon nô hiera heáfdu scieran mid scearseaxum (scier-, Cott. MS.) *sacerdotes caput suum non radent*, Past. 18, 7; Swt. 138, 14. [*O. L. Ger.* scar-, scer-sahs *novacula*: *O. H. Ger.* scar-, schersahs *novacula, rasorium*: cf. *Icel.* skar-öx *a carpenter's adze.*]

scearu, scyru, e; *f.* I. *a cutting, shaving*:—Scaro *tonsura*, Wrt. Voc. ii. 70, 18. Gif preóst sceare misgýme beardes oððe feaxes, L. N. P. L. 34; Th. ii. 294, 27. II. *a shearing* of sheep:—Fêrde Laban tô his sceápa sceare *ad tondendas oves*, Gen. 31, 19. III. *the ecclesiastical tonsure.* v. L. Ecg. E. 152–154; Th. ii. 124, 9–24:—Tô sceares gefe *ad tondendi gratiam* (in 'oratio ad capilaturam'), Rtl. 97, 4: 95, 31. Ðâ wǽron scorene ealle munecas and sacerdas on ðone bêh Scē

Petres sceare, Bd. 5, 21; S. 643, 29. Tō reogollīcum þeáwe rihtra Eástrena and scyre *ad ritum Paschae ac tonsurae canonicum*, 5, 22; S. 643, 38. Tō scare, 5, 22; S. 643, 38, note. Hēr Eádberht Norþhymbra cining fēng tō scære, Chr. 757; Erl. 53, 6. Ðæt hié heóldon ða ciriclecan scare, 716; Erl. 44, 19. Hē sceare onfēng, Bd. 3, 18; S. 546, 10: 5, 19; S. 636, 26. Ða sceare onfōn, 5, 21; S. 643, 22. Hē onfēng preósthādes scare, Shrn. 50, 27. Ða ðe beóþ gehādode fram Scyttiscum bisceopum oððe fram Bryttiscum, ða ðe sceare nabbaþ swā ōðre cyriclīce preóstas, L. Ecg. P. Addit. 5; Th. ii. 232, 17. Wē lǣraþ ðæt ǣnig gehādod man his sceare ne helige, L. Edg. C. 47; Th. ii. 254, 12. IV. *a share.* v. folc-, hearm-, land-, leód-, sceáp-scearu.

scearu, e; *f. The share;* pubes:—Mannes scaru *alvus*, Wrt. Voc. ii. 10, 26. Scare *ilium*, i. 44, 45. Biþ ðæt sār on ða swīðran healfe on ða scare, Lchdm. ii. 232, 4: 232, 23. [Heo þuruh stihten Isboset adun into schere. Her seið seint Gregorie: 'In inguinem ferire est etc.' Þe ueond þuruh stihð þet scher, A. R. 272, 12-14. Schare *pubes*, Wrt. Voc. i. 183, 29. The shore *le penul*, 148, 17. Schere *pubes*, 246, col. 2. Schore, privy part of a man *pubes*, Prompt. Parv. 448. v. Lchdm. ii. Glossary.]

sceat. v. sceatt.

sceát, es; *m.* I. *a corner, an angle* (v. -scīte); applied to the earth or heaven, *corner, quarter* (cf. the Edda: Þeir görðu þar af himinn ok settu hann yfir jörðina með fjórum skautum. Hence himin-skaut *the four quarters of the heavens;* heims-skaut *the poles*):—Ðā wæs heora lār sāwen and strogden betuh feówer sceátum middangeardes, Blickl. Homl. 133, 33. From feówerum foldan sceátum ðām ȳtemestum eorþan rīces englas blāwaþ bȳman, Exon. Th. 55, 6; Cri. 879. Lege on ða feówer sceáttas ðæs ærnes *lay at the four corners of the house*, Lchdm. ii. 142, 11. II. *a projection, promontory* (cf. sceáta):—Bætweónæ ða twægen brōmfeldas andlang ðæs alarsceátæs (*along the alder-covered piece of land which thrusts itself out into the fields*) on ðonæ fūlan brōc, Cod. Dip. Kmbl. v. 84, 12. III. *a nook, corner, region* (*in the phrases* eorþan, foldan sceát):—Is feor heonan eástdǣlum on æþelast londa ... nis se foldan sceát mongum gefēre *est locus in primo felix oriente remotus*, Exon. Th. 198, 1; Ph. 3. Sceal fromcynne folde ðīne sīd land manig geseted wurðan eorþan sceátas *with thine offspring shall earth be settled, many a wide land, earth's regions*, Cd. Th. 133, 5; Gen. 2206. Foldan sceátas (sceattas, MS.), 204, 33; Exod. 428. Ic ne wāt hwǣr mīn brōþor on wera ǣhtum eorþan sceáta eardian sceal *I know not in what corner of earth my brother must dwell*, Exon. Th. 496, 23; Rä. 85, 19. Hē ne mētte middangeardes, eorþan sceáta (sceatta, MS.) mundgripe māran, Beo. Th. 1508; B. 752. Fyllaþ eówre fromcynne foldan sceátas, Cd. Th. 92, 26; Gen. 1534: 247, 25; Dan. 502. Drihten hāteþ hēhenglas bēman blāwan ofer burga geseotu geond foldan sceátas, 302, 21; Sat. 603: Exon. Th. 445, 20; Dōm. 10. Faraþ geond ealle eorþan sceátas, Andr. Kmbl. 664; An. 332: Exon. Th. 309, 22; Seef. 61. Hē ne mæg ðone (hlīsan) tōbrēdan ofer ðās nearowan eorþan sceátas (cf. tōbrǣdan ofer ða nearwan eorþan āne, Bt. 19; Fox 68, 25), Met. 10, 17. IV. *a lap, bosom:*—Gif ðæs mōdes forhæfdnes mid ungeþylðe ne āscōke ða sibbe of ðæm sceáte ðære smyltnesse *nisi mentes abstinentium impatientia a sinu tranquillitatis excuteret*, Past. 43, 3; Swt. 311, 15. Of midum sceáte (*sinu*) ðīnum, Ps. Surt. 73, 11. Of his ðæm fæderlīcan sceáte, Blickl. Homl. 5, 15. Gyld gramhȳdigum on sceát hiora (*in sinu eorum*), Ps. Th. 78, 13. Ne mæg hē sceát āfyllan *non implevit sinum suum*, 128, 5. Gripon unfægre under sceát werum scearpe gāras *sharp spears fixed cruel fangs within the breasts of men*, Cd. Th. 124, 17; Gen. 2064. In sceát ālegd ł bewedded ł befest *desponsata* (cf. gesceátwyrpe *despondi*, Wrt. Voc. ii. 25, 72, *and Icel.* bera, leiða ā skaut *of the ceremony which was a recognition of a child's legitimacy or of a person's adoption.* v. Cl. and Vig. Dict. skaut, 3, and Grmm. R. A. p. 160), Mt. Kmbl. Rush. 1, 18. Gif hió ōðrum mæn in sceát bewyddod sī *if she be betrothed to another man*, L. Ethb. 83; Th. i. 24, 5. IV a. *the bosom, surface* of the earth:—On ðone sēlestan foldan sceátes (*Thorpe would read* sceáta, cf. III) ðone fira bearn nemnaþ neorxna wong *in the fairest part of earth's surface, which the children of men call Paradise*, Exon. Th. 225, 28; Ph. 396. Geond eorþan sceát *over earth's surface*, 331, 8; Vy. 65. Ic wāt ðætte wile woruldmen tweógan geond foldan sceát būton feá āne (cf. went fulneáh eall moncyn on tweónunga, Bt. 4; Fox 8, 18), Met. 4, 52. Sió forme eld geónd eorþan sceát (cf. seó forme eld ðises middangeardes, Bt. 15; Fox 48, 3), 8, 5. Ofer foldan sceát, Exon. Th. 428, 22; Rä. 42, 5. Ofer ealne foldan sceát, 5, 21; Cri. 72. Deófol gefeallaþ in sweartne lēg under foldan sceát, 94, 2; Cri. 1534. V. *a bay;* sinus:—Wæs hē besenced on sunne sǣs sceát *demersus est in sinu maris*, Bd. 1, 33; S. 499, 6. VI. *a garment:*—Sceát *vel* heortes hȳd *nebris*, Wrt. Voc. i. 26, 26. Ðā āstōd hē semninga and getogene ðȳ wǣpne under his sceáte rǣsde on ðone cyning (cf. *Icel.* hann hafði und skauti sēr leyniliga handöxi) *exsurrexit repente, et evaginata sub veste sica, impetum fecit in regem*, Bd. 2, 9; S. 511, 21: Exon. Th. 431, 3; Rä. 45, 2: 391, 18; Rä. 10, 7. VII. *a cloth, napkin:*—Sceát *manuterium* vel *mantele*, Wrt. Voc. i. 82, 38: *ma[n]tile*, 290, 72: ii. 56, 48: *gausape*, 41, 13. Ealle neádbehēfe þing, ðæt is ... nǣdl sceát weaxbreda *omnia necessaria, id est ... acus, mappula, tabule*, R. Ben. 92, 3. Ðæt hē Godes gifa ne becnytte on ðæm sceáte his slǣwþe, Past. 9; Swt. 59, 16. Nam ðære moldan sumne dǣl, gebond on his sceáte (*inligans in linteo*) ... Āhēng hē ðone sceát (*linteolum*) on āne studu, Bd. 3, 10; S. 534, 24-29. Seóþ eft mid sceáte ōðres godwebbes, Lchdm. i. 332, 5. VII a. with the idea of concealment, *cloak, fold:*—Ne māgon gē ða word geseðan ðe gē hwīle nū on unriht wrigon under womma sceátum, Elen. Kmbl. 1162; El. 583. [*Goth.* skauts; *m. the hem of a garment, skirt: O. Frs.* skāt, *skirt: O. H. Ger.* scōz; *m. f. gremium, sinus;* scōza; *f. gremium, sinus, lacinia: Icel.* skaut; *n.*] v. beód-, feder-, grund-, weofod-sceát, sceáta, scīte.

sceáta, an; *m.* I. *a corner, angle:*—Sicilia is þrȳscȳte (*tria habet promontoria*) on ǣlces sceátan ende sindon beorgas. Ðone norþsceátan man hǣt Polores ... and se sūþsceáta hātte Bachinum ... and ðone westsceátan man hǣt Libeum ... se þridda sceáta is ān hund and syfan and hund syfantig mīla westlang, Ors. 1, 1; Swt. 28, 2-9. II. *the lower corner of a sail* (cf. sheet *the rope fastened to the lower corner of a sail: Icel.* skaut, skaut-reip *the sheet of a sail*):—Sceáta *pes veli*, Wrt. Voc. i. 63, 59. III. *bosom, lap:*—Geond ealne ymbhwyrft eorþan sceátan, Exon. Th. 359, 26; Pa. 68. IV. *a cloth, napkin:*—Hē geseah Godes engel drȳgan mid sceátan sc̄i Laurentius limu, Shrn. 115, 23. [*O. H. Ger.* scōzo; *m. gremium, sinus: Icel.* skauti *a kerchief* used as a purse by knitting all four corners together so as to make a bag.] v. preceding word.

sceát-codd, es; *m. A bag, wallet, sack:*—Metefætels vel sceátcod *sitarchia*, Wrt. Voc. i. 16, 39. [Cf. *Icel.* skauti (*given under the preceding word*).]

sceáþ, scǣþ, e; *f. A sheath:*—Sceáþ *vagina*, Wrt. Voc. i. 35, 19: 84, 25. Sweord of sceáþe ātugon ða synfullan *gladium evaginaverunt peccatores*, Ps. Spl. 36, 14: Judth. Thw. 22, 26; Jud. 79. Of scēþe, Byrht. Th. 136, 37; By. 162. Ða sweord on heora sceáðum behȳdde wǣron *gladii reconduntur in vaginas*, Prud. 72 a. Brugdon scealcas of sceáþum scīrmǣled swyrd, Judth. Thw. 24, 38; Jud. 230. Scǣþum, Cd. Th. 120, 9; Gen. 1992. Hē āwende his swurd intō ðære sceáþe, Homl. Th. i. 482, 32. On scǣáþe (scǣþe, MSS. A. B. C.), Jn. Skt. 18, 11. On hys scǣþe, Mt. Kmbl. 26, 52. [*O. Sax.* skēðia: *O. H. Ger.* sceida *theca, vagina: Icel.* skeiðir; *pl. a sheath.*]

sceaþa, an; *m.* I. *one who does harm, a criminal, wretch, miscreant, an enemy:*—Sceaþa, deógol dǣdhata (*Grendel*), Beo. Th. 554; B. 274. Nū earttū (*Satan*) earm sceaþa in fȳrlocan feste gebunden, Cd. Th. 268, 19; Sat. 57. His feónd āfyllan ðe ðone sceaþan (*the assassin Eomer*) sende, Chr. 626; Erl. 23, 34. Fȳnd ł sceaþan *inimici*, Ps. Lamb. 9, 7. Gewītaþ, āwirgede woruldsorga, of mīnes þegenes mōde, forðam gē sind ða mǣstan sceaþan, Bt. 3; Fox 4, 24. Scyppend sceaþan onfēngon syngum hondum, Exon. Th. 70, 2; Cri. 1132. Beraþ linde forþ in sceaþena gemong *bear the linden shields forth into the press of the foe*, Judth. Thw. 24, 17; Jud. 193. Wælstreámas (*the waters of the Deluge*) werodum swelgaþ, sceaþum scyldfullum, Cd. Th. 78, 32; Gen. 1302. I a. *a spiritual enemy, fiend, devil:*—Se sceaþa (*the devil who tempted Eve*), 38, 14; Gen. 606. Sceaþa, Satanes þegn, Salm. Kmbl. 234; Sal. 116. Ðæt hē ūs gescilde wið sceaþan wǣpnum, lāþra lygesearwum, Exon. Th. 48, 22; Cri. 775: Andr. Kmbl. 2584; An. 1293. Fǣcnum feónde hȳrdes, sceþþendum sceaþan, Exon. Th. 85, 24; Cri. 1396. Helle hæftling, scyldigne sceaþan, Salm. Kmbl. 257; Sal. 128. Sceaþan (*the fallen angels*) hwearfdon earme æglēcan geond ðæt atole scref, Cd. Th. 269, 13; Sat. 72. In ðæt sceaþena scræf *hell*, 304, 20; Sat. 633. Scyldwyrcende sceaþan (*the fallen angels*), Elen. Kmbl. 1521; El. 762. II. *a spoiler, robber:*—Sceaþa *predo*, Wrt. Voc. ii. 88, 66. Hē is þeóf and sceaþa *ille fur est et latro*, Jn. Skt. 10, 1: Exon. Th. 54, 20; Cri. 871. Se sceaþa *the thief* (*on the cross*), Homl. Th. ii. 78, 18. 'Hwæt eart ðū ðe ðȳn ansȳn ys swylce ānes sceaþan.' Hē (*the penitent thief*) hym andswarode: 'Sōð gē secgaþ ðæt ic sceaþa wæs and ealle yfelu on eorþan wyrcende,' Nicod. 32; Thw. 18, 19-22. Hē (*Judas*) wæs gītsere and se wyresta sceaþa, Blickl. Homl. 69, 11. Swā swā tō ānum sceaþan (*ad latronem*) gē fērdon, Mk. Skt. 14, 48: Lk. Skt. 22, 52. Sceaþena scip *paro*, Wrt. Voc. i. 56, 27. Hī habbaþ dēmena and sceaþena dǣda, Blickl. Homl. 63, 9. Ōðer hine scyhte ðæt hē sceaþena gemōt nihtes sōhte (cf. hē (*Guthlac*) menigfeald wæl felde and slōh and of mannum heora ǣhta nam, Guthl. 2; Gdwin. 14, 5-6), Exon. Th. 109, 31; Gū. 98. Gē hit dōþ sceaþum tō scrafum '*ye have mad it a den of thieves*,' Blickl. Homl. 71, 20. Hē wæs on mycelre frecednysse on wēstene betwux sceaþum, Homl. Th. i. 392, 7. Sum man becom on ða sceaþan ða hine bereáfodon *homo quidam incidit in latrones qui etiam despoliauerunt*, Lk. Skt. 10, 30. III. with a favourable meaning, *a warrior:*—Scaþan onetton, wǣron æþelingas eft tō leódum fūse tō farenne, Beo. Th. 3610; B. 1803. Scaþan scīrhame tō scipe fōron, 3794; B. 1895. [*O. Sax.* skaðo *a robber, evildoer.*] v. ātor-, dol-, fǣr-, feónd-, folc-, fyrn-, gilp-, gūþ-, hell-, helle-, hearm-, leód-, lyft-, mān-, mōr-, nīþ-, sǣ-, syn-, þeód-, þeóf-, ūht-, wam-, wīcingsceaþa, *and next word.*

sceaþa, an; *m. Scathe, harm, injury:*—Cwæð ðæt sceaþena mǣst eallum heora eaforum æfter siððan wurde on woruld, Cd. Th. 85, 4; Gen. 549. [*O. H. Ger.* scado *damnum, noxia, detrimentum: Icel.* skaði *scathe, harm, damage.* Cf. *Goth.* skaþis *wrong.*] v. sceþþ[u].

sceaþa (?), sceáþ (?) *a nail*:—Tācon ðara sceaðana (sceoðona, Rush.) . . . styd ðara scæððana *figuram clauorum . . . locum clauorum*, Jn. Skt. Lind. 20, 25. v. horn-sceaþa.

sceaþan; *p.* scōd, sceód; *pp.* sceaþen. [*This strong form seems almost confined to the poetry, the prose making use of* sceþþan, q. v.] *To scathe, hurt, harm, injure*, (a) with dat.:—Ðē ne sceaþeþ ǣnig, Ps. Th. 90, 7. Oft ic ōðrum scōd, Exon. Th. 401, 22; Rä. 21, 15. Hē tōswengde līges leóman, swā hyra līce ne scōd, 189, 16; Az. 60: 197, 9; Az. 187. Se ðe nǣngum scōd, 90, 1; Cri. 1467. Ðæt ēce nīþ ældum scōd, 346, 5; Gn. Ex. 200. Ūs hearde sceód freólecu fǣmne (*Eve*), Cd. Th. 61, 15; Gen. 997: 245, 17; Dan. 464. Sió hæleþum sceód (*punished?*), Elen. Kmbl. 1415; El. 709. Him ða cwyðe frēcne scōdon, Cd. Th. 96, 20; Gen. 1597. Scōdun, Exon. Th. 134, 30; Gū. 516. Ðæt him feóndes hond æt ðam ȳtemestan ende ne scōde, 129, 1; Gū. 414. Sceaþen is mē sāre, frēcne on ferhþe, Cd. Th. 53, 31; Gen. 869. (b) with acc.:—Oft mec īsern scōd sāre on sīdan, Exon. Th. 485, 14; Rä. 71, 13. (c) without a case:—Ne ic ne scaþe (scaþeð, MS.) *neque nocebo*, Ps. Spl. 88, 33. Ðȳ læs scyldhatan sceaþan mihton, Andr. Kmbl. 2296; An. 1149. [*Goth.* skaþjan; *p.* skōþ.] v. sceþþan, sceaþian.

sceaþ-dǣd, e; *f.* *A misdeed, crime*:—Scæþdǣd *facinus*, Wrt. Voc. i. 21, 27. Sceþdǣd, ii. 39, 33. [Þat he hine awreke a þan awarriede uolke, þa hine isend hafden mid heore scaðededen, Laym. 29578.]

sceaþel, e; *f.* *A shuttle* (?):—Hē sceal habban fela tōwtōla . . . cranc-stæf, sceaþele, seámsticcan, Anglia ix. 263, 14.

sceaþenness, e; *f.* *Injury, damage*:—Ān wīf mihte gegān būtan ǣlcere sceaþenysse fram sǣ tō sǣ ofer eall ðis eálond *ut etiam si mulier vellet totam perambulare insulam a mari ad mare, nullo se laedente valeret*, Bd. 2, 16; S. 520, 2. Hē oft stormas fram his sylfes sceþenisse and his gefērena scylde and wiðsceáf *tempestates a sua suorumque laesione repellere consueverat*, 2, 7; S. 509, 32.

sceaþfullīce, sceaþfulness. v. un-sceaþfullīce, un-sceaþfulness.

sceaþian; *p.* ode *To hurt, harm, spoil, rob*:—Ne sceaþa ðū *thou shalt not steal*, Wulfst. 66, 18. Ðæt deófol tō swȳðe ne sceaþige, L. I. P. 7; Th. ii. 312, 26. Gif hwylc þeódsceaþa sceaþian onginneþ, Th. ii. 310, 24: L. C, E. 26; Th. i. 374, 29. Scaðian, Wulfst. 191, 19. Se ðe wǣre sceaþigende (scaþiende), weorðe se tiligende on rihtlīcre tilþe, 72, 12. [*O. L. Ger.* scathan; *pp.* ge-scathot: *O. Frs.* skathia: *O. H. Ger.* scadōn *nocere*: *Icel.* skaða; *p.* skaðaði.] v. ge-sceaþian; sceaþan, sceþþan.

sceaþung, e; *f.* *Injury, damage*:—Ge landfeoh ge fihtewīte ge stale ge wōhceápung ge burhwealles sceatinge (sceaþinge?) ge ǣlc ðæra wō-nessa ðe tō ǣnigre bōte gebyrie, ðæt hit āge healf ðære cyrcean hlāford, Chart. Th. 138, 18.

sceát-līne, an; *f.* *The sheet of a sail, the rope fastened to the lower end of a sail*:—Sceátlīne (sceac-, MS.) *propes*, Wrt. Voc. i. 56, 62: 63, 58. Cf. fōtrāp *propes*, 48, 25, *and Icel.* skaut-reip.

sceatt, es; *m.* I. *property, goods, wealth, treasure*:—Scaet *bona*, Txts. 44, 157. Scet *bona*, scettas *bon[i]*, Wrt. Voc. ii. 11, 22–23. Scættas *bo[n]i*, 126, 45. Hē cwæð ðæt ðē ǣniges sceates þearf ne wurde on worulde, Cd. Th. 32, 15; Gen. 503. Nys unc sceattes wiht tō mete gemearcod, 50, 24; Gen. 813. Nǣron hī bescyrede sceattes willan *non sunt fraudati a desiderio suo*, Ps. Th. 77, 29. [Swā manega gersumas on sceat and on scrūd and on bōkes swā nān man ne mæi tællen, Chr. 1070; Erl. 209, 14.] Hī nāmon ealle his wēpna and gold and seolfor and ealle his sceattas ðe hī mihton geāxian, 1064; Erl. 194, 17: 1069; Erl. 207, 14: 1071; Erl. 210, 23. On geweald woroldcyninga ðæm sēlestan ðara ðe sceattas dǣlde, Beo. Th. 3377; B. 1686. I a. of property which is paid as a price or contribution, *price, gift, bribe, tax, tribute, money, goods*:—Anweald on sibbe smyltnesse gehealdan mid gefeohte oððe mid scette (*by fighting or by paying tribute*), Lchdm. iii. 436, 15. Ne wanda ðū for nānum scette for ðam mēdsceattas āblendaþ wīsra manna geþancas *non accipies munera, quia munera excoecant oculos sapientum*, Deut. 16, 19. Æt ðam lande ðe arcebisceop gebohte mid his āgenan sceatte (*with his own money*), Cod. Dip. Kmbl. iv. 86, 10. God-wine geann Leófwine ðæs dænnes . . . æt ðon sceatte (*at the price*) ðe Leófsunu him geldan scolde, ðæt is, feówertig penega and twā pund and eahta āmbra cornes, vi. 178, 11: Cod. Dip. B. i. 544, 4. Hē begeat swīðe mycelne sceatt of his mannan . . . fērde syððan intō Normandīge *he* (*William*) *levied a large sum of money from his men . . . and after-wards went into Normandy*, Chr. 1085; Erl. 219, 10. Mænige gefōþ hwælas and micelne sceat ðanon begytaþ *multi capiunt cetos, et magnum pretium inde acquirunt*, Coll. Monast. Th. 25, 3: Ps. Spl. 61, 4. Mænig welig man is ðe wolde mycelne scet and ungerīm feós syllan, gif hē hit gebicgan mihte, Homl. Skt. i. 12, 101. Gif hit fācne is him man his scæt āgefe *if the marriage-contract be fraudulent, what he has paid shall be returned to him*, L. Eth. 77; Th. i. 22, 3: 78; Th. i. 22, 4. Gif man mannan ofsleá, āgene scætte and unfācne feó gehwilce gelde, 30; Th. i. 10, 4: 31; Th. i. 10, 7. Abram underfēng fela sceatta for hire hē hæfde ðā on orfe and on þeówum on olfendum and on assum micele ǣhte *Abram bene usi sunt propter illam, fueruntque ei oves et boves et asini et servi et cameli*, Gen. 12, 16. Ða bodan cōmon mid sceattum *habentes divinationis pretium in manibus*, Num. 22, 7. Gif ðū ðæt ge-rǣdest, ðæt ðū wille syllan sǣmannum feoh . . . wē willaþ mid ðām sceattum ūs tō scype gangan, Byrht. Th. 132, 62; By. 40. Hēr fōr se cyng ofer sǣ and hæfde mid him gīslas and sceattas (*the contributions he had levied*), Chr. 1067; Erl. 203, 34. ¶ Teóþa sceatt *a tithe*:—Ðæs hereteámes ealles teóþan sceat sealde '*he gave him tithes of all*' (Gen. 14, 20), Cd. Th. 128, 5; Gen. 2122. Bringaþ gē on mīn beren eówerne teóþan sceat (Malachi 3, 10), Blickl. Homl. 39, 26: 53, 11. Ðonne lǣre ic eów, ðæt gē syllon eówre teóþan sceattas earmum mannum, 49, 19: 43, 3. Abram his teóþan sceattas (*decimas*) offrede, Prud. 5 a: L. Alf. 38; Th. i. 52, 31. II. *a piece of money, a coin*:—Sceat *obulum*, Wrt. Voc. ii. 64, 78. Nis woruldfeoh ðe ic mē āgan wille, sceat ne scilling (cf. *O. Frs.* mit schat ende mit schillinge: *O. H. Ger.* scaz unde schilli[n]ch), Cd. Th. 129, 13; Gen. 2143. Ne þearf ic N. sceatt ne scilling, ne pænig ne pæniges weorð, L. O. 11; Th. i. 182, 9. Se mē beág forgeaf on ðam siex hund wæs smǣtes goldes gescyred sceatta scillingrīme, Exon. Th. 324, 9; Vīd. 92. Hī behēton hire sceattas *dabimus tibi singuli mille et centum argenteos*, Jud. 16, 5. Wē ðē mid ūs willaþ ferigan . . . siððan gē eówre gafulrǣdenne āgifen habbaþ, sceattas gescrifene, Andr. Kmbl. 593; An. 297. II a. as the name of an English coin the word is found in the form *scætt* in the laws of Ethelbert of Kent. It is inferred from a comparison of passages in these that the value of the *scætt* in Kent was one-twentieth of a shilling, v. Thorpe's Glossary. The *sceatt* is also mentioned in the Mercian law, Th. i. 190, 5, where '30,000 sceatta' is equivalent to '120 punda.' This would give 250 sceatts to the pound. In the Northern Gospels *dragmas decem* is glossed by 'fīf sceattas teásīðum,' while the West-Saxon version has 'tȳn scyllingas.' If the sums here given may be regarded as equal, the *sceatt* would be worth a West-Saxon penny, the value which it appears to have in the Mercian law. The coin then seems to be of different values in Kent and in the more northern parts of England. [*Goth.* skatts ἀργύριον, δηνάριον, μνᾶ: *O. Sax.* skatt *money, property, piece of money*: *O. Frs.* skett: *O. H. Ger.* scaz *substantia, mobilia, pretium, lucrum, pecunia, aes, denarius, quadrans, obolus*: *Icel.* skattr *tribute*.] v. feoh-, fere-, freó-, geþing-, gif-, mān-, mēd-, ofer-, teóþing-, wæstm-sceatt; scīr-gesceatt.

-sceatte, -sceattinga, sceát-weorpan. v. twī-sceatte, or-sceattinga, sceát, IV.

sceáwend-sprǣc, e; *f.* *Buffoonery, the speech of the theatre*:—Sceáw-endsprǣc *scurrilitas* (*scarilitas*, MS.), Wrt. Voc. ii. 96, 65. v. sceáw-ere, V.

sceáwend-wīse, an; *f.* *A jesting song, song of a jester*:—Ic sceáw-endwīsan hlūde onhyrge, Exon. Th. 391, 1; Rä. 9, 9. v. preceding word.

sceáwere, es; *m.* I. *an observer, one who examines into a matter*:—Wē willaþ ðæt se sceáwre wite mid fullum gerāde, ðe ðis gewrit āspyraþ, Anglia viii. 331, 1. Ðone dōm ðæs sceáweres *spec-tatoris judicium*, Past. 15, 3; Swt. 93, 6. II. *a spy*:—Hē sende sceáwere (scēware, Lind.) *misso speculatore*, Mk. Skt. Rush. 6, 27. Gē synd sceáweras *exploratores estis*, Gen. 42, 9, 14. Leáse sceáweras, Beo. Th. 511; B. 253. Moises sende twelf sceáweras, Num. 13, 4: Jos. 2, 1. III. *a watch-tower* (?):—Sceáwere *speculia* (the word occurs in a list of military terms), Wrt. Voc. i. 36, 4. IV. *a mirror*:—Sceáwere *speculea* (in a list of words connected with dress. Cf. Alse hit bi þe wimman and bi sheawere . hie bihalt hire sheawere . and cumeð hire shadewe þaronne, O. E. Homl. ii. 29, 10. Godes word is ase a uayr ssewere, ine huam me yzi3t alle þe lakkes of þe herte, Ayenb. 202, 21. Sheweres *glasses* (A. V.), Wick. Isaiah 3, 23), 40, 54. V. *a buffoon, an actor* (v. sceáwend-sprǣc):—Sceáwera *scurra-rum*, ii. 90, 13. [*O. H. Ger.* scouwari *spectator, contemplator, scrutator*.] v. be-, fore-, steór-sceáwere.

sceáwian; *p.* ode. I. *to look*:—Ic sceáwode tō swīðran *con-siderabam ad dexteram*, Ps. Spl. 141, 5: Ps. Th. 141, 4. II. *to look at, observe, behold, see*:—Ðonne hē ðæs fācnes fintan sceáwaþ, Exon. Th. 315, 17; Mōd. 32. Dryhten sceáwaþ hwǣr ða eardien ðe his ǣ healden, 105, 19; Gū. 25. Ðǣr hī sceáwiaþ Scyppendes giefe, 220, 28; Ph. 327. Ðǣr hit eágum folc eall sceáwiaþ *in conspectu omnis populi*, Ps. Th. 115, 8. Ðū ðæs eágan eall sceáwadest gesēge fyrenfulra wīte *oculis tuis considerabis, et retributionem peccatorum videbis*, 90, 8. Sceáwode *conspicatur*, Wrt. Voc. ii. 18, 26: 80, 71. Ðā sceáwode Scyppend ūre his weorca wlite, Cd. Th. 13, 21; Gen. 206. Hī sceáw-odon Scyppend engla, 298, 18; Sat. 535. Ðē wæter sceáwedon *viderunt te aquae*, Ps. Th. 76, 13: Beo. Th. 265; B. 132: 1971; B. 983. Sceáwa heofon, Cd. Th. 132, 6; Gen. 2189. Ðæt ic ðīn wuldur sceáwige *ut viderem gloriam tuam*, Ps. Th. 62, 2. Ðū ðīnra bearna bearn sceáwige (*videas*), 127, 7. Ða mon mæg sceáwian gehealdene on Cantwara cyricean *quae in ecclesiae Cantiae conservata monstrantur*, Bd. 2, 20; S. 522, 10: Beo. Th. 1685; B. 840. Onwreóh ðū mīne eágan, ðæt ic wel mǣge on ðīnre ǣ sceáwian wundur, Ps. Th. 118, 18. Ðæt hē mōste God sceáwian, Cd. Th. 297, 29; Sat. 524. Andgiettācen (*the rainbow*) sceáwigan, 93, 4; Gen. 1540. Ðæt mæg mon on bócum sceáwigean, hú monega gewin hē dreógende wæs, Ors. 1, 11; Swt. 50, 25. Hwylce ða nū synd tō sceáwigenne *quales illi nunc appareant*, L. Ecg. P. iv. 66; Th. ii. 226, 21. Tō sceáwianne, Exon. Th. 57, 7; Cri. 915. Sceáwiendum *contemplantibus, intuentibus*, Wrt. Voc. ii. 134, 83. III. *to look at, look on with favour, to regard, have respect to*:—Ic sceáwiu wegas ðīne '*I will have respect unto thy ways*' (A. V.), Ps. Surt. 118, 15. Hē hyra dǣde sceáwaþ *God will regard the deeds of the charitable*, Exon. Th. 106, 35; Gū. 51. Hē sceáwode ða eáþmōdnesse his þeówene *respexit humilitatem ancillae suae*, Blickl. Homl. 7, 3. Sceáwa (*respice*) ðis folc, Ex. 33, 13. Cyning eallwihta Caines ne wolde tiber sceáwian '*to Cain and to his offering the Lord had not respect*' (A.V. Gen. 4, 5), Cd. Th. 60, 9; Gen. 979. IV. *to look at with care, consider, inspect, examine, scrutinize, reconnoitre*:—Sceáwaþ *speculatur*, Wülck. Gl. 250, 8. Ðā ðæt eall gedōn wæs swā se geótere ðæm æðelinge ǣr behēt se æðeling ðæt ðā sceáwode *when all that was done as the founder* (*Perillus*) *promised the prince* (*Phalaris*), *the prince then inspected it*, Ors. 1, 12; Swt. 54, 29. Se cyng sceáwode ðæt mādmehūs and ða gersuman ðe his fæder ǣr gegaderode, Chr. 1086; Erl. 223, 27. Ðonne seó ādl cume ǣrest on ðone mannan, ðonne sceáwa his tungan, Lchdm. ii. 280, 8. Sceáwiaþ ða lilian hū hī wexaþ *considerate lilia quomodo crescunt*, Lk. Skt. 12, 27. Ic eów bidde ðæt ānra manna gehwylc sceáwige hine sylfne on his heortan, Blickl. Homl. 57, 33: 107, 13. Moyses sende and hēt sceáwian Azer *misit Moyses, qui explorarent Jazer*, Num. 21, 32. Iosue āsende twegen sceáweras dīgellīce and hēt sceáwian ðæt land, Jos. 2, 1. Him ðā fēran gewāt land sceáwian, Cd. Th. 106, 33; Gen. 1780: Beo. Th. 2831; B. 1413. Hord sceáwian, 5481; B. 2744. Land sceáwigan, Cd. Th. 115, 16; Gen. 1920. Ðā ongon ic geornlīcor ða stōwe sceáwigan and geond ða bearwas gongan *igitur perambulare totum nemus incipio*, Nar. 27, 20. Ceós ðē menn ðæt māgon sceáwigean ðone eard *mitte viros, qui considerent terram*, Num. 13, 3. Gē cōmon ðis land tō sceáwienne, Gen. 42, 12. V. *to look out, seek for, select, choose, provide*:—Ðā sceáwode man þreó þegnas of ðam gemōte *three thanes were chosen from the moot* (*to go on a certain business*), Chart. Th. 337, 12. Gyf ðū ēnigne gōdne heorde hæbbe . . . sceáwa hyne mē; gyf ðū ðonne nānne swā gerādne næbbe, sēc hyne ōð ðū hyne finde, Shrn. 164, 31. Se ðe ðās gemōt forbūge, ðonne sceáwige (scifte, MS. D.) man of ðam gemōte ða ðe him tō rīdan, L. Edg. ii. 7; Th. i. 268, 15: L. C. S. 25; Th. i. 390, 18. Him Loth gewāt wīc sceáwian ōþ ðæt hié eorþscræf fundon *Lot went seeking a dwelling, until they found a cave*, Cd. Th. 156, 24; Gen. 2593. Drihtnes earc fōr beforan him þrī dagas sceáwiende ða wīcstōwa *providens castrorum locum*, Num. 10, 33. VI. *to shew* (*favour, respect*, etc.), *to grant*, v. ge-sceáwian, I:—Ðā geornde se eorl griðes and gīsla . . . Ðā wyrnde him mann ðera gīsla and sceáwede him mann .v. nihta grið ūt of lande tō farenne *then the earl asked for safe-conduct and hostages. . . . The hostages were refused him, and safe-conduct during five days was granted him to go out of the country*, Chr. 1048; Erl. 180, 11–14. [*O. Sax.* skawōn *to see, observe*: *O. L. Ger.* scauwōn, scouwōn *respicere, despicere*: *O. Frs.* skawia, skowia *to see, inspect*: *O. H. Ger.* scawōn, scauwōn, scouwōn *videre, conspicere, intendere, considerare, contemplari, scrutari, speculari, perpensare, censere.*] v. be-, ge-, geond-, ofer-sceáwian.

sceáwigend. v. leóht-, ofer-sceáwigend.

sceáwung, e; *f.* I. *a looking at, contemplation, consideration*:—Embeþonc *vel* sceáwung *circumspectio*, Wrt. Voc. ii. 131, 27. Tō dīgolnesse and tō stilnesse becom ðære godcundan sceáwunge ancorlīfes *ad anachoreticae contemplationis silentia secreta pervenit*, Bd. 4, 28; S. 605, 11. Se biþ eallenga blind se ðe nōht ne ongiet be ðam leóhte ðære uplecan sceáwunge *caecus quippe est, qui supernae contemplationis lumen ignorat*, Past. 11, 1; Swt. 65, 7. Sceáwunga, 16, 1; Swt. 99, 2. For ðære sceáwungge ðara ungesewenlīcra þinga *invisibilium contemplatione*, Swt. 99, 8. Tō ðære sceáwunga ðære sōþan gesǣlþe, Bt. 34, 8; Fox 144, 33: Met. 21, 24. Sceáwunge *intuitu*, Wülck. Gl. 250, 7. Sceáunge *aspectu*, Rtl. 74, 7. Ǣrest ic hyt leornode myd ðām eágum, syððan myd ðam ingeþance . . . ac syððan ic hyt ongyten hæfde ðā forlǣt ic ða sceáwunga mid ðām eágum, Shrn. 175, 8. II. *respect, regard*:—Nis scāwung heora deáþes *non est respectus morti eorum*, Ps. Lamb. 72, 4. III. *reconnoitring, surveying, examination*:—Swīðost hē fōr ðider, tōeácan ðæs landes sceáwunge, for ðǣm horschwælum, Ors. 1, 1; Swt. 17, 35. IV. *a spectacle, show*:—Al ðe here hiora ða ðe tōgedre cōmun tō sceáwunga ðæt *ad spectaculum istud*, Lk. Skt. Rush. 23, 48. Ðā hēt Neron gewyrcean mycelne tor, and beád ðæt eall ðæt folc cōme tō ðisse sceáwunga (*the spectacle of Simon flying from the tower*), Blickl. Homl. 187, 13. V. *a show, appearance, pretence*:—Under sceáwunge longes gibedes *sub obtentu prolixae orationis*, Mk. Skt. Rush. 12, 40. VI. as a technical term, the same as *ostensio*, which occurs L. Eth. iv. 2; Th. i. 300, 20, and is explained in Du Cange: Tributum a mercatoribus exigi solitum pro facultate ostendendi et exponendi merces in nundinis. *Seáwing*, *scheáwing* is mentioned as being granted to the church at Westminster by Edward the Confessor in English charters, Cod. Dip. Kmbl. iv. 213, 11: 215, 7: and the form *sceáwing* occurs in Latin charters, Chart. Th. 359, 4: 411, 29. [*O. H. Ger.* scouwunga *consideratio, contemplatio, tuitio, providentia, spectaculum, speculum.*] v. blōd-, for-, fore-sceáwung.

sceb, scecel. v. sceabb, sceacel.

scecgan (?); *p.* scægde *To jut out, project, be distinguished.* [Cf. *Icel.* skaga; *p.* skagði *to project.*] v. tō-scecgan.

sced, scēdan, scedeht, scefe, Scēfing. v. scead, sceádan, sceadiht, scyfe, Sceáfa.

Scede-land, Sceden-īg. *The latter, occurring* Beo. 3376; B. 1686, *is the same as the Icel.* Skān-ey, *in Wulfstan's narrative*, Scōn-ēg (q. v.): *the former* (in pl.) *seems to denote all the Danish or Scandinavian lands*:—Blæd wīde sprang Scyldes eaferan Scedelandum in, Beo. 38; B. 19.

scegð, scǣð, es; *m.*: e; *f. A light, swift vessel*:—Scægð *trieris*, Wrt. Voc. i. 64, 1. Sceið, 56, 13. Lītel scip *vel* sceigð *scapha* vel *trieris*, 47, 61. Ic gean mīnre scǣðe for mīnre sāwle intō Hramsēge healfe ðam abbode and healfe ðam hīrēde, Chart. Th. 598, 9. Syððan hē tō lande cymþ, ðonne forlǣt hē ðæt scyp standan; for ðam him þincþ syððan ðæt hē mǣge ǣð būtan faran ðonne mid. Eáðre mē þincþ ðeáh myd scēðþe on lande tō farande, ðonne mē þynce mid ðām eágum būtan ðære gesceádwīsnesse ǣnigne creft tō geleornianne, Shrn. 175, 11–15. Scehð *liburnam, navim*, Hpt. Gl. 406, 51. Hēr bebeád se cyng ðæt man sceolde ofer eall Angelcynn scipu wircean; ðæt is ðonne of þrȳm hund hīdum and of x hīdon ǣnne scegð (scægð, MS. D.), Chr. 1008; Erl. 141, 18. See note. Scēthas *curuanas* (?), Wrt. Voc. ii. 137, 52. [A word taken from the Danes. *Icel.* skeið; *f. a swift-sailing ship of war.*] v. next word.

scegð-mann, es; *m. A member of the crew of a* scegð, *a Dane, a pirate* (cf. wīcing, sǣ-man, flot-man, scip-here *and similar terms applied to the Danes*):—Wīcing *vel* scegðman *pirata* vel *piraticus* vel *cilix*, Wrt. Voc. i. 18, 59. Wīcing oððe scegðman (scægð-, scǣð-, sceigð-) *pirata*, Ælfc. Gr. 7; Zup. 24, 9. Gif man secge on landes mann ðæt hē orf stǣle oððon man slōge, and hit secge ān sceiðman and ān landes mann (*a Dane and a native Englishman*), L. Eth. ii. 7; Th. i. 288, 8. Ægelsig þe Reáda and Winsig Scægðman, Chart. Th. 337, 17. v. preceding word.

scehdun, Exon. Th. 61, 6; Cri. 980. v. scildan.

-scel. v. wæl-scel.

scel, sceld (*a shield*), sceld (*a fault*), sceldig, scel-ēge. v. scill, scild, scyld, scyldig, sceolh-īge.

scelfan; *p.* sceałf, *pl.* sculfon *To shake, quiver, totter*:—On ðyssum stapelum sceall ǣlc cynestōl standan mid rihte on cristenre þeóde, and āwācie heora ǣnig, sōna se stōl scylfþ . . . āwācie se cristendōm, sōna scylfþ se cynedōm, L. I. P. 4; Th. ii. 308, 1–7: Wulfst. 267, 18. Ne hrisil scelfaeð, Txts. 151, 7. [*Icel.* skjálfa; *p.* skalf *to shiver, shake, quiver.*]

scell. v. scill.

scellan; *p.* sceall; *pl.* scullon *To sound, make a noise*:—Scylþ, cirmþ *crepitat, resonat*, Wrt. Voc. ii. 136, 72. [Cum qð þe culure wið schillinde stefne, Marh. 19, 19. *O. L. Ger.* ir-scal *increpuit*: *O. H. Ger.* scellan; *p.* scal, *pl.* scullun *sonare, clangere, tinnire, crepitare*: *Icel.* skjalla; *p.* skall, *pl.* skullu *to clash, clatter.*] v. scillan.

scelle glosses *concisium*, Wrt. Voc. ii. 105, 10: 15, 15: Wülck. Gl. 214, 7. [Cf. *M. H. Ger.* zer-schellen *to shatter*: *Icel.* skellr *a loud splash; a smiting, beating. Or* (?) cf. *Goth.* skilja *a butcher*: *Icel.* skilja *to divide.*] v. scellan, wæl-scel.

scelliht. v. scilliht.

Sceltifēre (?); *pl. The Celtiberians*:—Se mǣsta ege from Sceltiuērin *ingens Celtiberorum metus*, Ors. 4, 12; Swt. 208, 24.

scenc, es; *m. A draught, cup*:—Scenc ðū sylst ūs *potum dabis nobis*, Ps. Spl. C. 79, 6. Cælc ł scenc wætres caldes *calicem aquae frigidae*, Mt. Kmbl. Lind. 10, 42. Drince scenc fulne, Lchdm. ii. 116, 21. Genim ðysse ylcan wyrte seáw ānne scenc (scænc, MS. H.), i. 110, 21. Nim þrȳ scenceas (scæncas, MS. B.) gōdes wīnes, 90, 19: 110, 10. [He lette heom bringen schenches of feole cunne drenches, Laym. 13461. *M. H. Ger.* shanc *a cup.*] v. medu-scenc.

scencan; *p.* te *To skink* (v. Nares' Glossary for instances of the use of this word), *to pour out liquor for drinking, to give to drink* (lit. and fig.):—Ðū scæncst *potabis*, Ps. Lamb. 35, 9. Ðæt gōde wīn ðæt hē scencþ nū geond his gelaðunge, Homl. Th. ii. 70, 11. Ðonne scencþ hē ða scylde mid ðære bisene ǣlcum ðæra ðe him ǣnges yfles tō wēnþ *cunctis mala credentibus per exemplum culpa propinatur*, Past. 59, 5; Swt. 451, 24. Heó bær drincan and ūs eallum þēnade and scencte ōð ðæt ðæt gereorde gefylled wæs *obtulit poculum, coeptumque ministerium nobis omnibus propinandi usque ad prandium completum non omisit*, Bd. 5, 4; S. 617, 26. Þegn, se ðe on handa bær hroden ealowǣge, scencte scīr wered, Beo. Th. 996; B. 496. Feónd byrlade ðære idese, and heó (*Eve*) hyre were scencte, Exon. Th. 161, 12; Gū. 957. Mē þyrste, and gē mē scencton (cf. drincan sealdon, l. 21) . . . Hwænne gesāwe wē ðē þurstigne, and wē ðē scencton? Homl. Th. ii. 108, 4–11: i. 336, 3:

Wulfst. 288, 15. Ðá hí him betwih beadowíg scencton ðæs heofonlíces lífes *dum sese alterutrum coelestis vitae poculis debriarent*, Bd. 4, 29; S. 607, 17. Scencean *propinare*, Engl. Stud. ix. 40. Deáþes scencende drenc *mortis propinans poculum*, Hymn. Surt. 31, 15. [Nom heo (*Rowena*) ane bolle of ræde golde & heo gon scenchen, Laym. 14962. And tu . . . ne shennkesst nohht tatt wise, ne birrlesst tu þin hird, Orm. 15403. Þe drynke for to schenche, R. Glouc. 118, 12. Schenkyn drynke *propino*, Prompt. Parv. 445 (v. note). *O. Frs.* skenka: *O. H. Ger.* scenchen *fundere, propinare, ministrare, porrigere*: *Icel.* skenkja *to serve drink, fill one's cup*: cf. *O. Sax.* skenkio *a skinker, cupbearer*: *O. L. Ger.* skenki-vaz *cyathus*.] v. bi-, forþ-scencan.

scencel, scencen, gloss *acrum*, Wrt. Voc, ii. 10, 44: i. 16, 4.

scencing-cuppe, an; *f. A cup in which drink is served*:—Heó bit ðæt hí findon betweox him twá smicere scencingcuppan intó beódern for hí, Chart. Th. 536, 7. [Cf. *O. L. Ger.* skenki-vaz *cyathus*: *O. H. Ger.* scenche-bechar *calix*; scenche-uaz *poculum*.]

scendan; *p.* de *To put to shame, to abuse, insult, harm*:—Ic scendo *confundam*, Rtl. 1, 25. Ðone scamleásan mon mæg ðý bet gebétan ðe hine mon suíður þreáþ and sciend (scent, Cott. MSS.) *impudentes melius corrigit, qui invehendo reprehendit*, Past. 31, 1; Swt. 207, 6. Grendel nænegum áraþ leóde Deniga ac swefeþ ond scendeþ (? MS. sendeþ. Leo, Heyne, Grein refer to *sand*, q. v., and would translate by *feasts*) *Grendel spares no man of the Danes, but slays and puts to shame*, Beo. Th. 1204; B. 600. Ealne ðæne bysmor wé gyldaþ mid weorðscype ðám ðe ús scendaþ *all the disgrace we repay with honour to those who bring shame on us*, Wulfst. 163, 10. Hwilcan geþance mæg ǽnig man ǽfre geþencan on his móde ðæt hé tó sacerdan heáfod áhylde . . . and sóna ðǽræfter hí scyrde oððe scynde mid worde oððe weorce *injure or abuse them with word or deed*, L. Eth. vii. 27; Th. i. 334, 36. Wé lǽraþ, ðæt ǽnig gelǽred preóst ne scænde ðone sámlǽredan, ac gebéte hine, gif hé bet cunne, L. Edg. C. 12; Th. ii. 246, 18. Biscopas þá sceótan ná tó lǽwedum mannum ne ne scendan ná hý sylfe *bishops shall not refer (their disputes) to laymen, nor bring disgrace upon themselves*, L. I. P. 10; Th. ii. 316, 36. Giþyll scendende *aura corrumpens*, Rtl. 121, 40. Scend ł forhogod *confunditur, spernitur*, Hpt. Gl. 419, 4. Scende (*confusi*) wǽron ealle ðe mé yfel tó ǽr gesóhton, Ps. Th. 70, 22. ¶ *With dat.*:—Se deópa seáþ mid wíta fela folcum scendeþ, Exon. Th. 94, 33; Cri. 1549. [Also ase þu wult schenden þene schucke, A. R. 316, 11. Men me wolden scenden, Laym. 14167. Shennd and shamedd, Orm. 1985. Uor to ssende and to destrue, Ayenb. 28, 22. Schendyn *confundo, culpo*; schent *culpatus, vituperatus, confusus, destructus*, Prompt. Parv. 445, col. 1. *O. L. Ger.* scendan *confundere*: *O. H. Ger.* scenten.] v. ge-scendan.

-scende. v. un-scende.

scendele (?), an; *f. Abuse, reproach*:—Fore scendla ł scending *propter improbitatem*, Lk. Skt. Lind. Rush. 11, 8.

scendness, scendþ(u). v. ge-scendness, ge-scendþ(u) (Ps. Surt. 108, 29).

scendung, e; *f. Abuse, harm*:—Scendung *afflictio*, Rtl. 86, 16. Fore scending *propter improbitatem*, Lk. Skt. Lind. 11, 8. v. for-scendung.

scéne, scén-feld. v. scíne, scín-feld.

scenn, e; *f.* (?) *A plate of metal on the handle of a sword* (?) (Worsaae, Primeval Antiquities, pp. 29, 49, notes that the handles of some of the early swords were covered with plates of gold. v. hilt):—Wæs on ðǽm scennum scíran goldes þurh rúnstafas rihte gemearcod, hwam ðæt sweord geworht ǽrest wǽre, Beo. Th. 3392; B. 1694.

sceó *a cloud* (?):—Scearp cymeþ sceó wið óðrum, ecg wið ecge (*of the coming together of clouds charged with electricity*), Exon. Th. 385, 8; Rä. 4, 41. [*O. Sax.* skio: *Icel.* ský *a cloud*.]

sceó *a shoe*, sceocca, -sceód, sceófan, sceofl, sceógan, sceóh. v. scóh, scucca, scógan, scúfan, scofl, scógan, scóh.

sceóh; *adj.* I. *shy, timid, fearful*:—Nú mín hreðer is hreóh, heówsíþum sceóh, Exon. Th. 354, 10; Reim. 43. II. *wanton* (?):—Ðæs scíon *petulantis* (*peculantis*, Wrt.), Wrt. Voc. ii. 89, 24. [Lokeð þet ȝe ne beon nout iliche þe horse þet is scheouh, and blencheð uor one scheadewe . . . To scheowe heo beoð mid alle, þet fleoð uor ane peinture, þet þuncheð ham grislich uorto biholden, A. R. 242, 8-12. Schey or skey as hors, Prompt. Parv. 444, col. 2. *M. H. Ger.* schiech *fugax, pavidus*. Cf. *O. H. Ger.* sciuhen *expavescere, terrere*: *Ger.* scheuchen *to scare*: scheuche *a bugbear*: *Dan.* sky *fear*.] v. next word.

sceóh-mód; *adj. Fearful* (*wanton?*) *of heart*:—Se synsceaþa tó scipe sceóhmód éhstreám sóhte, Exon. Th. 282, 32; Jul. 672. v. preceding word.

sceolh, sceol; *adj. Oblique, wry*:—Of ðæm sceolan *de scevo*, Wrt. Voc. ii. 26, 67: 85, 10. Sceolan *scevi*, 91, 47. [*O. H. Ger.* scelah *strabo, strabus, obliquus*: *Ger.* scheel: *Icel.* skjálgr *oblique, squinting*. Cf. skelly *to squint* (Yorks.).] v. next word.

sceolh-eágede; *adj. Cross-eyed, squinting*:—Scelgégede *strabo*, Wrt. Voc. i. 75, 42. Sceolégede (scyl-, MSS. D. H. J.: -eágede, MS. J.) *strabo*, Ælfc. Gr. 9, 3; Zup. 36, 12. Scyleágede *strabus*, Wrt. Voc. i. 45, 56. Scylégede *luscus*, 43, 8. [Sculeiȝede, 89, 64. *Dan.* skel-öjed.] v. preceding and following words.

sceolh-íge; *adj. Cross-eyed, squinting*:—Sceolhégi, sceolégi, scelége *scevus, strabus, torbus*, Txts. 98, 981. Sceolíge *strabos*, Wrt. Voc. ii. 92, 64. [*Icel.* skjól-eygr *squinting*.] v. preceding word.

sceolu, sceom-, sceón *to shoe*. v. scolu, sceam-, scógan.

sceón, scýan (?), scýn (?); *p.* de *To go quickly, fly*:—Ðonne ic forþ sció *when I depart* (*die*), Cd. Th. 67, 20; Gen. 1103. Ðæt fýr scýde (scynde?) tó ðám ðe ða scylde worhton, 232, 26; Dan. 266. [Cf. (?) *Goth.* skéwjan *to go*: *O. H. Ger.* scehanto *vagendo*, Grff. vi. 417; skihtig *fugax*, 418.] v. sceóh, *and next word*.

sceón; *p.* de *To fall to a person's lot*:—Gif unc bán fordsíð scéet on Rómeweȝe *if death be the lot of both of us on the journey to Rome*, Chart. Th. 583, 29. Heom (heo, MS.) on riht sceóde (sceo, MS.) gold and godweb Iosepes gestreón *gold and purple, Joseph's treasure rightly fell to the share of the Israelites* (*after the destruction of the Egyptians in the Red Sea*), Cd. Th. 215, 21; Exod. 586. v. ge-sceón, *and preceding word*.

sceonca, sceond, sceóne. v. sceanca, sceand, scíne.

sceóness, sciéness, scinness, scýness, scynness, e; *f. Suggestion, persuasion, incitement*:—Seó scynnes biþ þurh deófol *suggestio fit per diabolum*, Bd. 1, 27; S. 497, 13. On scynnesse, S. 497, 24. Mid scýnesse, S. 497, 10. Deófol mid hire (*the serpent's*) ðære yfelan sceónesse and fácne beswác ðone ǽrestan wífmon, Blickl. Homl. 5, 1. Sió scyld ðe hiene þurh sciénesse (scinnesse, Cott. MSS.) costaþ *vitium, quod per suggestionem tentat*, Past. 13, 2; Swt. 79, 22. Þurh scynnysse, Bd. 1, 27; S. 497, 12, 17. Hié swíðor fylgaþ deófles lárum and his sceónessum, Blickl. Homl. 25, 11. Uncysta cumaþ oft þurh deófles sceónessa, 19, 7. v. scýan.

sceop, sceoppa, sceoppend, sceór, sceorf. v. scop, scoppa, scippend, scúr, scorf.

sceorfan; *p.* scearf, *pl.* scurfon; *pp.* scorfen *To gnaw, bite, scarify*:—Se (*hiccup*) cymþ of yfelum wǽtan slítendum and sceorfendum ðone magan. Gif se seóca man áspíwþ ðone yfelan bítendan wǽtan on weg, ðonne forstent se geohsa. Spíwe ðá deah ðám monnum ðe gihsa hié innan scyrfþ, Lchdm. ii. 60, 18-25: 176, 20. Gif hé geféle ðæt se geohsa hine innan sceorfe on ðone magan, 62, 10. Gærstapan fréton ealle ða gærscíðas ðe bufan ðære eorþan wǽron ge furðon ða wyrttruman sceorfende wǽron *locustarum nubes, exhaustis omnibus, ipsas quoque radices seminum persequentes*, Ors. 1, 7; Swt. 38, 12. v. for-sceorfan; scearfian; ge-sceorf.

sceorian. v. scorian.

sceorp, es; *n. Dress, apparel*:—Gemétte Macheus his ágenne sunu mid purpurum gegieredne. Hé hiene ðá for ðæm girelan gebealg . . . and wénde ðæt hé for his forsewennesse swelc sceorp werede, Ors. 4, 4; Swt. 164, 33. Somnite áwendan on óðre wísan heora sceorp *Samnites novum habitum sumentes*, 3, 10; Swt. 138, 30. Of manegum landum máre landriht áríst tó cyniges gebanne . . . scorp tó friðscipe (*apparel for those on board?*), L. R. S. 1; Th. i. 432, 8. v. fyrd-, gúþ-, heoru-, hilde-, hleó-, sige-sceorp; ge-scirpla, scirpan.

sceorpan; *p.* scearp *To scrape, to irritate*:—Gif man [hwæt?] sceorpe on ðone innaþ *if anything irritate a man in the insides*, Lchdm. iii. 44, 27. v. ge-sceorpan, *and* cf. sceorfan.

sceort, sceot. v. scort, scot.

sceót; *adj. Quick, ready*:—Hweðer hé carful sý and sceót (gesceót, W. F.) tó godcundum weorce and tó hýrsumnesse *si sollicitus est ad opus Dei, ad obedientiam*, R. Ben. 97, 16. [*Icel.* skjótr *swift*.]

sceóta, an; *m. A kind of trout, a shoate, shot* ['Carew makes a distinction between the trout and *shot*. "The latter," he says, "is in a manner peculiar to Devon and Cornwall. In shape and colour he resembleth the Trowts: howbeit in biggnesse commeth farre behind him." The *shoates* with which is Tavy fraught.—Browne's Brit. Past.,' E. D. S. Pub. E. Cornwall Gloss. *Shote*, a small kind of trout, W. Cornwall]:—Hwilce fixas geféhst ðú? . . . sceótan (*tructos*), Coll. Monast. Th. 23, 33.

sceótan; *p.* sceát, *pl.* scuton, sceoton; *pp.* scoten. I. *to shoot*, (a) *cast a missile*, with acc. of missile:—Ðæt yrre scýt his spere ongeán ðæt geþyld *ira lanceam suam jacit contra patientiam*, Gl. Prud. 20 b. Ða wǽpna ðe ðæt yrre scét (*miserat*), 21 b. Hig sceoton hyra strǽlas tó ðære hynde, Shrn. 148, 6. (b) *to shoot* (intrans.):—Ic torfige oððe sceóte *jacio*, Ælfc. Gr. 28, 6; Som. 32, 38. Se ðe of flánbogan fyrenum sceóteþ, Beo. Th. 3493; B. 1744. Hé hygegár léteþ, scúrum sceóteþ, Exon. Th. 315, 22; Mód. 35. Hé on bord sceát, Byrht. Th. 139, 46; By. 270. Hé mid geǽttredum strǽle ongan sceótan wið ðæs ðe hé geseah ðæt hrýþer stondan, Blickl. Homl. 199, 19. II. *to shoot* an object, *hit* an object with a missile:—Wyrd gást scýt, heó gár bireþ, Salm. Kmbl. 875; Sal. 437. Ðonne hié (*the serpent*) mon slóg oððe sceát, Ors. 4, 6; Swt. 174, 7. Hé óðerne sceát, Byrht. Th. 135, 67; By. 143. Tó ðam ðæt hí mágon sceótan ða unscyldigheortan *ut sagittent rectos corde*, Ps. Th. 10, 2. Ðǽr læg secg mænig ofer scild scoten, Chr. 937; Erl. 112, 19. Gif ðú wǽre on fell scoten, Lchdm. iii. 54, 4-7. II a. where the weapon is the subject:—Ðā ðone ilcan welegan mon se strǣl sceát, ðæt hē sōna deád wæs, Blickl. Homl. 199, 23. III. *to shoot, make an object move rapidly, push* (cf. *to shoot* a bolt):—Ðonne man ða sulh forþ drīfe, and ða forman furh on sceóte, Lchdm. i. 404, 2. Belūcaþ ða ǣrenan gatu and tōforan on sceótaþ ða ȳsenan scyttelsas, Nicod. 27; Thw. 15, 15. Hē lēt dragan up ðæne deádan Harald and hine on fen sceótan, Chr. 1040; Erl. 166, 24. III a. *to give a person help* in escaping (cf. *Icel.* skjóta einum brott, undan *to let a person escape*):—Gyf hine man teó ðæt hē hine (*the criminal*) ūt sceóte, L. Edg. H. 6; Th. i. 260, 9. IV. *to shoot, move rapidly, dart, run, plunge, rush,* (a) of living things:—Swā swā dēþ se ðe his feóndum ofer sumne weall ætfleón wile, ðonne cēpþ hē hwǣr se weall unhēhst sȳ, and ðǣr ofer scȳt, Homl. Th. i. 484, 11. Hē scēt innan sǣ *misit se in mare*, Jn. Skt. 21, 7. Hē unscrȳdde hine sylfne and scǣt intō ðam mere, Homl. Skt. i. 11, 211. Ān culfre scǣt (sceát, MS. V.) of ðam fȳre intō ðære eá, 3, 73. Hī ānmōdlīce him tō scuton *they ran upon him with one accord* (Acts vii. 57), Homl. Th. i. 46, 34: 404, 4: ii. 496, 19. Seó dene wæs āfylled mid manna sāwlum ða scuton of ðam fȳre intō ðam cyle (*utrumque latus erat animabus hominum plenum, quae vicissim hinc inde videbantur quasi tempestatis impetu jactari*, Bd. 5, 12), 350, 10. Gif ðū Godes sunu sȳ, sceót ādūn (*mitte te deorsum*, Mt. 4, 6) . . . Ðæt wǣre swīðe gilplīc dǣd, gif Crist scute ðā ādūn, i. 170, 1, 21. (b) of inanimate things:—On ða burnan ðe of ðam munt scȳtt *in torrentem, qui de monte descendit*, Deut. 9, 21. Ðǣr sciét se Wendelsǣ up of ðæm gārsecge *Tyrrheni maris faucibus oceani aestus immittitur*, Ors. 1, 1; Swt. 8, 25. Scȳt, Swt. 8, 32. Seó eá scȳt ūt on ðone gārsecg, Swt. 14, 14. Ðǣr ocærburna ūtt scȳt on sǣ, Cod. Dip. Kmbl. iii. 175, 31: 424, 4. Seó lacu ūt scyt, 422, 14, 26. Ðonne ða wolcnan sceótaþ betweón hyre (*the sun*) and ðē, Shrn. 201, 25. Him on gafol forlēt feówer wellan scīre sceótan, Exon. Th. 420, 1; Rä. 39, 4. (c) of speech:—Hē ðæs geanwyrde wes ætforan eallum ðām mannum ðe ðǣr gegaderode wǣron, ðeáh him ðæt word of scute his unnþances *though the remark burst from him involuntarily*, Chr. 1055; Erl. 189, 6. V. *to run* (of a road, etc.):—On ðam wege ðe scȳtt tō ðam pytte *per viam, quae ducit ad puteum*, Gen. 24, 62. Tō ðere fyrh ðe scȳt sūþrihte tō ðære miclan strǣt . . . Ōþ ðone weg ðe scȳt tō fealuwes leá . . . tō ðam wege ðe scȳt tō ðam hricgge, Cod. Dip. Kmbl. iii. 422, 4–19, 20, 25. Ōþ ðæt se weall eást sciát, ii. 86, 20. VI. *to refer* a case to a person or court:—Ðus wrāt Hieronimus. Gif hwā elles secge, wē sceótaþ tō him, Homl. Th. ii. 306, 19. Ðā nolde hē, būtan hit man sceóte tō scīregemōte, Chart. Th. 288, 19. Gif preóst dōm tō lǣwedum sceóte, ðe hē tō gehādedum scolde, L. N. P. L. 5; Th. ii. 290, 22. Wē lǣraþ, ðæt nān sacu ðe betweox preóstan sī ne beó gescoten tō woruldmanna sōme, ac sēman heora āgene gefēran, oððe sceótan tō ðam biscope, L. Edg. C. 7; Th. ii. 246, 5: L. I. P. 10; Th. ii. 316, 36. Se engel andwyrde: Uton sceótan tō Godes dōme, Homl. Th. ii. 338, 33. VII. *to advance* money, *contribute, pay* (cf. scot):—Hē forgeaf Middel-Sexon ðæt feoh ðæt hē heom fore sceát, Chart. Th. 551, 12. Sceóte ǣlc gegylda ǣnne gyldsester fulne clǣnes hwǣtes, 606, 6. Sceóte man ælmessan, Wulfst. 170, 18. Sceóte man æt ǣghwilcre hīde pænig oððe pæniges weorð, 181, 4. Wē cwǣdon ðæt ūre ǣlc scute .iiii. pæng tō ūre gemǣne þearfe . . . and forgyldon ðæt yrfe ðe syððan genumen wǣre ðe wē ðæt feoh scuton, L. Ath. V. 2; Th. i. 230, 15–17. VIII. *to shoot* (of sharp pain):—Wið sceótendum wenne, Lchdm. ii. 324, 25: iii. 30, 3. [*O. Frs.* skiata *to shoot*: *O. H. Ger.* sciozan *jaculari, sagittare, ferire*: *Icel.* skjóta *to shoot* with a weapon (dat.); *to push quickly; to refer a case to* (til) *another; to pay*.] v. ā-, be-, for-, ge-, of-, ōþ-, þurh-, un-, under-sceótan; scotian.

sceótend, es; *m. One who shoots, a warrior*:—Sceótend wǣron gūþe gegremede, Judth. Thw. 26, 2; Jud. 305: Beo. Th. 1411; B. 703: Met. 1, 11. Sceótend sendaþ flāngeweorc, Exon. Th. 42, 20; Cri. 675. Hlyn scylda and sceafta, sceótendra fyll, Cd. Th. 124, 14; Gen. 2062. Ofer sceótendum, 184, 24; Exod. 112: 129, 14; Gen. 2143.

sceoþa, sceó-þwang, sceotian, Sceottas, sceotung, sceóung, sceó-wyrhta. v. sceaþa, scōh-þwang, scotian, Scottas, scotung, scōung, scōh-wyrhta.

scēp, scepen, sceppan, scer, scēr. v. sceáp, scypen, scippan, scear, sceár.

sceran, sciran, sceoran; *p.* scær, scear; *pl.* scǣron, sceáron; *pp.* scoren. I. *to cut, shear*:—Ðonne sweord swīn ofer helme scireþ, Beo. Th. 2579; B. 1287. Hæleþ higerōfe linde heówon, scildburh scǣron, Judth. Thw. 26, 2; Jud. 305. Lǣtaþ īren ecgheard ealdorgeard sceoran, Andr. Kmbl. 2364; An. 1183. Ðæt hi hlīpen unwillende on ðæt scorene clif unþeáwa *quia per multa etiam, quae non appetunt, iniquitatum abrupta rapiuntur*, Past. 33, 1; Swt. 215, 8. Scearde scūrbeorge, scorene, gedrorene, Exon. Th. 476, 10; Ruin. 5. Scorenum *rassis*, Wrt. Voc. ii. 84, 77. II. *to shave* hair:—Ic scere *tondeo*, Ælfc. Gr. 26, 6; Som. 29, 9: *rado*, 28, 4; Som. 31, 24. Ǣghwā mīn heáfod scireþ, Exon. Th. 482, 6; Rä. 66, 3. Ne hē his loccas mid sceárum wanode, ne his beard mid seaxe scear, Shrn. 93, 9. Ne gē eów ne efesion ne beard ne sciron *neque in rotundum attondebitis comam, nec radetis barbam*, Lev. 19, 27. Ne eówre hǣr ne sciron *nec facietes calvitium super mortuos*, Deut. 14, 1. Swīðe ryhte wæs ðæm sacerde forboden ðæt hē his heáfod sceáre (*caput radere*), Past. 18, 7; Swt. 139, 25. Heáfdu scieran mid scierseaxum *caput radere*, Swt. 139, 12. Se ylca preóst com tō Gūðlāce, ðæt hē hine wolde scyran, Guthl. 7; Gdwin. 44, 20. Tō sceáranne (beard) *ad tondendum*, Rtl. 97, 16. III. *to cut* the hair of the head:—Heó scear hyre feax swā swā weras, and gegyrede hȳ mid weres hrægle, Shrn. 133, 13. IV. *to shear* sheep:—Hī sculan waxan sceáp and sciran on hiora āgenre hwīle *they shall wash and shear sheep in their own time*, Chart. Th. 145, 13. Sceáp scyran, Anglia ix. 261, 10. Hē fōr scēp tō sciranne *ad tondendas oves*, Gen. 38, 13. [*O. Frs.* skera: *O. H. Ger.* sceran *tondere*: *Icel.* skera *to cut*.] v. ā-, be-, ge-sceran.

scerden, scerian. v. scirden, scirian.

scericge, an; *f. An actress*:—Sc̄a Pilagia wæs ǣryst mima in Antiochia ðære ceastre, ðæt is scericge (scēwicge (?) cf. sceáwere *scurra; or* scernicge (?), cf. *O. H. Ger.* scern *scurrilitas, spectaculum*; scernari *scurra, histrio*) on ūrum geþeóde, Shrn. 140, 11.

scern, scerpan. v. scearn, scirpan.

scerran (?) *to harness* an animal to something [:—Se yrþlingc unscenþ (-scerþ?) ða oxan *arator disjungit boves*, Coll. Monast. Th. 20, 27. Cf. *Ger.* an-, aus-schirren *to harness, un-harness*.]

scerwen, scerpen (?) *a scattering* (?), *sharing* (?), *giving* (?) (cf. besceran *to deprive*):—Denum eallum wearð cēnra gehwylcum eorlum ealuscerwen *there was a fine feast for all the Danes* (?) (the reference is to the disturbance caused by the fight between Beowulf and Grendel), Beo. Th. 1542; B. 769. Myclade mereflōd meoduscerwen (scerpen, MSS.) wearð æfter symbeldæge *the flood increased; a fine feast was there after the banquet* (the reference is to the flood which came from the stone pillar, and swept away some of the Mermedonians. Cf. Ðæt wæs biter beórþegu: byrlas ne gǣldon . . . ðǣr wæs ǣlcum genōg drync sōna gearu, 3063–3069; An. 1534–1537), Andr. Kmbl. 3051; An. 1528. v. Grmm. A. and E. pp. xxxvi, 133, and note to Wülcker's ed. of Grein.

scēte, scēþ, sceþ-dǣd, sceþeness. v. scīte, sceáþ, sceaþ-dǣd, sceaþenness.

sceþness, e; *f. Hurt, harm*:—Hē eft fērde būtan sceþnysse ǣniges sāres, Guthl. 16; Gdwin. 68, 27.

sceþþan; *p.* sceþede *To scathe, hurt, harm, injure* (a) with dat.:—Ic nǣngum sceþþe, Exon. Th. 407, 9; Rä. 26, 2. Nǣfre him deáþ sceþeþ, 203, 23; Ph. 88. Ðonne þunorrād biþ, ne sceþeþ ðam men ðe ðone stān (*agate*) mid him hæfþ, Lchdm. ii. 296, 30: 162, 19. Ne sceþ ðē nān wiht, iii. 178, 25. Eów seó wergþu sceþþeþ scyldfullum, Elen. Kmbl. 619; El. 310. Ūs seó wyrd scyþeþ, Andr. Kmbl. 3121; An. 1563. Nǣnig geweald deáþes him sceþþaþ *leti nil jura nocebunt*, Bd. 2, 1; S. 500, 21. Ðās þing sceþþaþ ðām eágum, Lchdm. ii. 26, 21. Him ðæt ne sceþede, Shrn. 84, 29: 131, 1: Beo. Th. 3033; B. 1514: Blickl. Homl. 161, 32: 169, 6. Ða sǣdeór hyre ne sceþedon, Shrn. 133, 11. Hū ðū sōðfæstum swīðast sceþþe, 263, 14; Jul. 349. Ðȳ læs him gielp sceþþe, Exon. Th. 43, 6; Cri. 684: 299, 11; Crä. 100. Ðam mon sceal sellan ða mettas ða ðe wambe nearwian and ðam magan ne sceþþan, Lchdm. ii. 278, 18. Ðȳ læs hī him and his freóndum sceþeden *ne sibi suisque nocerent*, Bd. 2, 7; S. 509, 35. Se līg ne mæg nā sceþþan ðisse fǣmnan, Shrn. 130, 32: Blickl. Homl. 129, 15: 221, 17: Ps. Surt. 104, 14: Cd. Th. 273, 33; Sat. 146. Scyþþan, Andr. Kmbl. 2096; An. 1049. Ðæt Scottas him nōht sceþþende ne āfuhton, Bd. 4, 26; S. 602, 25. (b) with acc.:—Se lēg ða stuþo sceþþan ne meahte *flamma destinam laedere nullatenus sinebatur*, 3, 17; S. 544, 33. Ne mæg him bryne sceþþan wlitigne wuldorhoman, Exon. Th. 196, 23; Az. 178. (c) without a case:—Ic sceþþu *nocebo*, Ps. Surt. 88, 34. Regnþeóf ne lǣt on sceade sceþþan, Exon. Th. 453, 15; Hy. 4, 15: Beo. Th. 492; B. 243. Sceþþende *nocens*, Wrt. Voc. ii. 130, 12. Seó scæþþende wǣta, Bd. 4, 19; S. 589, 1. Ðū hȳrdes sceþþendum sceaþan, Exon. Th. 85, 24; Cri. 1396. [*Icel.* skeðja; *p.* skaddi.] v. ge-sceþþan; sceaþan, sceaþian.

sceþþend, es; *m. One who harms, a foe, adversary*:—His āras ūs gescildaþ wið sceþþendra earhfarum, Exon. 47, 27; Cri. 761: 126, 23; Gū. 375. Sceþþendum *adversaris*, Rtl. 113, 40.

sceþþig, scæþþig; *adj. Hurtful, noxious*:—Scyldig oððe scæððig (sceaþþig, MS. U.) *sons*, Ælfc. Gr. 9, 29; Zup. 63, 15. v. un-sceþþig.

sceþþigness. v. un-sceþþigness.

sceþþ[u], e; *f. Hurt, injury*:—Wið fōtswylum and sceþþum (scæþþum, MS. H. B.), Lchdm. i. 342, 18. v. sceaþa.

sceþwræc; *adj. Hurtful, noxious, hostile*:—Ðæm (*St. John*) ne sceþede nǣnig scyld ðisse sceþwracan worlde, Blickl. Homl. 161, 33.

sceucca. v. scucca.

scia, an; *m. The shin*; crus:—Scīa *crus*, Txts. 54, 299. Scīu (scīa, scīæ, Rush.) *crura*, Jn. Skt. Lind. 19, 31–33.

sciccels, sciccel, es; *m. A cloak, mantle*:—Scicilse *melote, mantile, veste*, Hpt. Gl. 440, 72. Hē hine unscrīdde ðam healfan scicelse ðe hē on hæfde, Th. Ap. 12, 22. Hē wæs mid horhgum scicelse bewǣfed, 13, 26. Hī scrȳddon hyne mid weolcenreádum scyccelse (*clamys*), Mt. Kmbl. 27, 28, 31. Geteáh his seax and genam his sciccels ðe hē him on hæfde, tōsnād hine on twā, Blickl. Homl. 215, 6. Ðā tōcearf hē his scyccel on twâ, and hyne gesealde healfne đam þearfendum men, Shrn. 146, 36. [Cf. *Icel.* skikkja *a cloak.*] v. next word.

sciccing *a cloak, cape*:—Scicing, scinccing, scicging *cappa*, Txts. 50, 245. Sciccing, Wrt. Voc. i. 284, 64: ii. 13, 24. v. preceding word.

scîd (?) *a course* (?):—Scîd (ryne, MS. T.) *currus* (*cursus?*), Ps. Spl. C. 67, 18. [Cf. (?) *Icel.* skeið *a race, course.*]

scîd, es; *n. A shide* (v. Halliwell's Dict.), *shingle, a piece of wood split thin, a billet*:—Scîd *scindula* (in a list *de igne*), Wrt. Voc. i. 284, 15: 66, 41. Scîdum *scindulis*, ii. 120, 12: 80, 21. [Stickes kan ich breken . . . and kindlen ful wel a fyr . . . ful wel kan ich cleuen shides, Havel. 917. Schyyd or astelle *teda, asula, astula*, Prompt. Parv. 446, col. 1. Go shape a shippe of shides and of bordes, Piers P. 9, 131. *O. Frs.* skîd: *O. H. Ger.* scît: *M. H. Ger.* schît: *Ger.* scheit; *n.*: *Icel.* skíð; *n.*: *a billet, firewood.*]

scîd-hreác, es; *m. A heap of shingles* or *billets*:—.iiii. foðera âclofenas gauolwyda tô scîdhræce on hiora âgenre hwîle, Chart. Th. 145, 6. [Cf. *Icel.* skíða-hlaði *a pile of firewood*: *Ger.* scheiter-haufen *a funeral pile.*]

scîd-weall, es; *m. A wooden fence, palings*:—Scîdwealles eorþbyri *vallum*, Wrt. Voc. i. 37, 34. [From sæ to sæ eode þæ dich (*the wall of Severus*) . . . þer ufenen he makede scidwal, Laym. 10354. Cf. *Icel.* skíđ-garđr *wooden palings, a wooden fence.*]

sciell, sciéne, sciéness, scieppend, scier-, scierpan, scife. v. scill, scîne, sceóness, scippend, scear-, scirpan, scyfe.

sciftan; *p.* te. I. *to divide, separate into shares*:—Fôn đa yrfenuman tô lande and tô æ̂htan, and scyftan hit swîđe rihte *the heirs shall succeed to the land and property, and shall divide it with perfect justice*, L. C. S. 79; Th. i. 420, 17. [*Shift* to divide, *Sussex.* A division of land among co-heirs is called a *shifting*, Halliwell Dict. Cf. *Icel.* skipta arfi, landi.] II. *to appoint, ordain, arrange.* Cf. *shift* used of a set of men which succeeds another in work that is carried on continuously, e.g. in a mine:—Đâ scyfte man Beorn (Harold, MS., but cf. l. 21: Đâ læg Godwine eorl and Beorn eorl on Pefensǽ) up đæs cynges scipe đe Harold eorl ǽr steórde, Chr. 1046; Erl. 174, 4. Moyses be Godes âgenum dihte rihte lage scyfte, Wulfst. 176, 8. Scifte man of đam gemôte đa đe him tô rîdan *those who may go to him shall be appointed from the meeting*, L. Edg. ii. 7; Th. i. 268, 15. [Schyftyñ or part a-sundyr *sepero, disgrego*; Schyftyñ or partyñ or delyñ *divido, partior*, Prompt. Parv. 446, col. 1. Eter gate me his scyft, and þer me hi togesceodeđ, O. E. Homl. i. 237, 30. Prestess and dæcness shifftedenn (*arranged*) hemm betwenenn whillc here shollde serrfenn first, Orm. 470.] v. ge-, tô-sciftan (-scyftan).

-scîgan *in* ge-scîgan:—Heora ǽlc sceal ân .c. þearfendra manna fêdan and ealle đa gescŷgean (*provide them all with shoes*), Chart. Th. 616, 26.

scilbrong. v. scilfrung.

scilcen[n], e; *f. A female servant* or *slave, a woman of bad character*:—Hê gemacode đæt seofon nacode wîmmen urnon plegende on heora gesihþum, đæt heora môd wurde ontend tô gâlnysse þurh đæra scylcena plegan, Hom. Th. ii. 162, 33. [Al nis bute ase a schelchine to seruien þe leafdi, A. R. 12, 24. *M. H. Ger.* schelkin *serva.*] v. scealc.

scild, sceld, scyld, es; *m.* I. *a shield, a piece of defensive armour*:—Scyld *scutum* vel *clipeus* vel *parma*, lytel scyld *pelta* . . . scyld *clipeus, testudo*, lytel scyld *ancile*, đa læssan scyldas *peltae* vel *parmae*, Wrt. Voc. i. 35, 27–28, 57–59. Scyld *cetra*, ii. 20, 9: *pelta*, 68, 4. Sceld *scutum*, i. 289, 30: Ps. Th. 75, 3. Scyld sceal gebunden, leóht linden bord, Exon. Th. 339, 15; Gn. Ex. 94. Scyld sceal cempan, 341, 22; Gn. Ex. 130. Rand sceal on scylde, Menol. Fox 534; Gn. C. 37. Næfde hê scyld (*scutum*) æt handa, đæt hê đone cyning mid gescyldan mihte, Bd. 2, 9; S. 511, 22. Nân scyldwyrhta ne lecge nân scêpes fell on scyld, L. Ath. i. 15; Th. i. 208, 11. Đǽr læg secg mænig ofer scild scoten, Chr. 937; Erl. 112, 19. Dynedan scildas, Judth. Thw. 24, 24; Jud. 204. Scylda *parmarum*, Wrt. Voc. ii. 96, 30. Eorles heregeata . . . ehta spera and eall swâ feala scylda, L. C. S. 72; Th. i. 414, 7. Hlyn wearđ on wîcum scylda and sceafta, Cd. Th. 124, 13; Gen. 2062. Síde scyldas, randas regnhearde, Beo. Th. 656; B. 325. II. fig. *a shield, protection*:—Scild mîn beó đû *refugium meum es tu*, Ps. Spl. T. 70, 4. Đam biþ Dryhten scyld, Exon. Th. 229, 31; Ph. 463. III. *scyld* in the following passage is used of a bird's back (as being shield-shaped? or can *scyld* here be connected with *sculdor?* cf. (?) *shield-bone* = shoulder-blade quoted by Halliwell. *Icel. skjöldr* is used of shield-shaped things):—Is se scyld ufan frætwum gefêged ofer đæs fugles bæc, 219, 17; Ph. 308. [*Goth.* skildus: *O. Sax.* skild: *O. Frs.* skeld: *O. H. Ger.* scilt: *Icel.* skjöldr.] v. bôc-, ge-, pleg-scild.

Scild, es; *m. The name of the ancestor of the Danish kings.* His story is given in the opening canto of Beowulf. According to the Ynglinga Saga, c. 5, one of Odin's sons is Skjöldr. v. Scildingas.

scildan, scyldan, sceldan, sceoldan; *p.* de. I. *to shield, protect, guard, defend*:—Ic hine scylde *protegam eum*, Ps. Th. 90, 14. Hwâ forstandeþ hié, gif đû hié ne scyldest? Blickl. Homl. 225, 19. Ne þearf him ondrǽdan ǽnig, gif hine God scildeþ, Exon. Th. 49, 6; Cri. 781. Se godcunda anweald hî scilde, Bt. 39, 10; Fox 228, 12: Exon. Th. 195, 33; Az. 165. Mê nama Dryhtnes scylde, Ps. Th. 117, 12: Cd. Th. 247, 31; Dan. 505. Đara gâsta đe hine scildon *defensiones spirituum bonorum*, Bd. 3, 19; S. 548, 36. Scild ûsig *tuere nos*, Rtl. 79, 16: 84, 15. Him wæs lŷfnesse seald, đæt hê him môste scyldan and besecgan, Bd. 5, 19; S. 640, 11. Scildende *protegente*, Rtl. 103, 34. Đætte wê sîe scildad *defendi*, 75, 5. Scylded beón *tueri*, Wrt. Voc. ii. 88, 59. ¶ Scyldan wiđ *to shield from, guard against*:—Ic đê wiđ weána gehwam scylde, Cd. Th. 131, 3; Gen. 2170. Wiđ đa speru hié hié scildaþ, Past. 35, 4; Swt. 245, 10. Mê sôđfæstnes mîn scylde wiđ feóndum *scuto circumdabit te veritas ejus*, Ps. Th. 90, 5. Scilde, Lchdm. ii. 238, 5: Exon. Th. 126, 22; Gû. 375. Đa englas hine scildon wiđ đæs fŷres frêcennesse, Bd. 3, 19; S. 548, 32: Exon. Th. 496, 4; Rä. 85, 9. Wê ûs wiđ him sceldan đæs đe wê mihton, Nar. 14, 29. Đa wiđ flôdum foldan sceldun (scehdun, MS.), 61, 6; Cri. 980. Hû hî hî sylfe scyldan sceolan wiđ deóflu, Blickl. Homl. 47, 22. Utan scyldan ûs wiđ đone hâtan bryne đe wealleþ on helle, L. C. S. 85; Th. i. 424, 15. *Without an object*:—God, se đe wiđ ofermægnes egsan sceolde, Cd. Th. 127, 28; Gen. 2117. Wê lǽraþ đæt man wiđ heálîce synna scylde georne, L. C. E. 23; Th. i. 374, 7. II. *to make a defence*:—Siđđan hê his hyspinge gehêred hæfde đâ scylde hê ongeán swîđe ungeþyldelîce *after he had heard his abuse then he made a defence in reply very impatiently*, Bt. 18, 4; Fox 66, 35. v. ge-scildan.

scild-burh; *f.* I. *a battle-array in which men stood shield to shield* [cf. the account of the battle of Stamford-bridge: 'Siđan fylkti Haraldr Konungr liđi sînu, lêt fylkingina langa ok ekki þykka; þâ teygđi hann armana aptr â bak, svâ at saman tôku, var þat þâ vîđr hringr, ok þykkr ok jafn öllum megin ûtan, skjöldr viđ skjöld.' Saga Haralds Harđrâđa, c. 92. When this arrangement is abandoned, they are said 'bregđa skjaldborginni,' c. 95]:—Wearđ scyldburh tôbrocen, Byrht. Th. 138, 56; By. 242. Hæleþ higerôfe scildburh scǽron, Judth. Thw. 26, 2; Jud. 305. II. *a city which affords protection, a city of refuge.* v. scild, II:—Sôđfæste men in heora fæder rîce scînaþ in sceldbyrig (*heaven*), Cd. Th. 283, 23; Sat. 309. Grimm would translate the word here by 'aula clypeis tecta,' and compares it with the description of Valhalla in the Edda, 'skjöldum þökt, lagt gyltum skjöldum, svâ sem spânþak,' D. M. 662. [*O. H. Ger.* scilt-burg *testudo.*]

scildend, es; *m. A protector, guardian, defender*:—Scyldend *protector*, Ps. Spl. T. 17, 21: Ps. Spl. 58, 12: Ps. Th. 26, 2: 83, 9: Blickl. Homl. 141, 14. v. ge-scildend.

scilden[n], e; *f. Protection*:—Scildenne, scildinnae *tutellam*, Txts. 103, 2073.

scildere, es; *m. A shielder, protector*:—Đû eart mîn scyldere *protector meus*, Ps. Th. 17, 3.

scild-freca, an; *m. A warrior with a shield*:—Đonne scyldfreca ongeán gramum gangan scolde, Beo. Th. 2071; B. 1033.

scild-hreáda. v. next word.

scild-hreóđa, -hrêđa, an; *m. Shield-covering*, (1) *a shield, buckler*:—Scinon scyldhreóđan, Cd. Th. 184, 26; Exod. 113. (2) *the arrangement of shields as in the* scild-burh, q. v.:—Scyldrêđan *testudine*, Wrt. Voc. ii. 96, 31. Sumum wîges spêd giefeþ æt gûþe, đonne gârgetrum ofer scildhreádan (-hreóđan?) sceótend sendaþ (cf. *the passage under* scild-weall), Exon. Th. 42, 19; Cri. 675. v. bord-hreóđa, *and* cf. hrêđan *melote*, Wrt. Voc. ii. 56, 63.

scildig. v. scyldig.

Scildingas; *pl. The descendants of Scild*, or more generally *the Danes.* The word occurs often in Beowulf, and is also found in the compounds Âr-, Here-, Sige-, Þeód-Scildingas. [*Icel.* Skjöldungar.]

scildness, e; *f. A protection, defence*:—Scildnisse *defensionis*, Rtl. 41, 13: *protectionis*, 97, 18. v. ge-scildness.

scild-rêđa. v. scild-hreóđa.

scild-rîda (= hreóđa?), an; *m. A phalanx*:—Đeáh hî wyrcen getruman and scyldrîdan wiđ mê *si consistant adversum me castra*, Ps. Th. 26, 4.

scild-truma, an; *m. A phalanx*; testudo:—Under þiccum scyldtruman *subter densa testudine*, Ælfc. Gr. 47; Som. 48, 29. Of sceltruman *testudine*, Hpt. Gl. 475, 66. [He makede his sceldtrume swulc hit weoren an hær wude, Laym. 16371. A scheltrone *hec acies*, Wrt. Voc. i. 240, 9.]

scildung, e; *f. Shielding, protection*:—Đa deófellîcan flân wurdon ealle âdwæscte þurh đæs gewǽpnodan engles scyldunge, Homl. Th. ii. 336, 10. Scilding *tutum*, Rtl. 100, 3.

scild-weall, es; *m. A shield-wall, the shields held by a line of soldiers*:—Đonne strǽla storm scôc ofer scyldweall, Beo. Th. 6227; B. 3118. Cf. scild-burh.

scild-wîga, an; *m. A warrior who bears a shield*:—Scearp scyldwîga, Beo. Th. 581; B. 288.

scild-wyrhta, an; *m. A shield-maker*:—Sceldwyrhta *scutarius*, Wrt. Voc. i. 289, 31. Be scyldwyrhtum. Nân scyldwyrhta ne lecge nân scêpes fell on scyld; and gif hê hit dô, gilde .xxx. scill., L. Ath. i. 15; Th. i. 208, 9–11. Andlang flǽscmangara strǽte đet it cymþ tô scyldwyrhtana strǽte; andlang scyldwyrhtana strǽte eást eft ðæt hit cymþ tō Leófan hagan, Cod. Dip. Kmbl. vi. 135, 18–20.

scilfe, an; *f. A shelf, ledge, floor:*—Gescype scylfan on scipes bōsme (cf. With lower, second, and third stories shalt thou make the ark, Gen. 6, 16), Cd. Th. 79, 4; Gen. 1306. [Cf. *Icel.* Hlið-skjálf; *f. Odin's seat whence he looked out on all the world.*]

Scilfingas; *pl. A Swedish royal family, the Swedes:*—Helm Scylfinga ðone sēlestan sǽcyninga ðara ðe in Swióríce sinc brytnade, Beo. Th. 4752; B. 2381: 5200; B. 2603. *The compounds* Gūþ-, Heaðo-Scilfingas *also occur, and the singular* Scylfing, Beo. Th. 4968; B. 2487. Scilfing, 5928; B. 2968. [*Icel.* Skilfingar; *pl. the name of a mythical royal family;* skilfingr *a prince* (poet.). v. Grmm. D. M. 343.]

scil-fisc, es; *m. A shell-fish:*—Monige sint cwucera gesceafta unstyriende, swā swā scylfiscas sint, Bt. 41, 5; Fox 252, 21. Mettas ðe gōd blōd wyrceaþ, swā swā sint scilfixas, Lchdm. ii. 244, 24. [*Icel.* skel-fiskr.]

scilfor; *adj. Yellow, of the colour of gold:*—Of scylfrum hiwe *flava specie*, Wrt. Voc. ii. 149, 21. Of scilfrum *flava auri specie*, Hpt. Gl. 419, 23.

scilfrung, e; *f. Shaking, balancing, swinging:*—Hwǽr com seó wlitignes heora ræsta and setla . . . and seó scylfring heora leóhtfata ðe him beforan burnon *the swinging* (?) *of the lamps that burnt before them*, Blickl. Homl. 99, 34. Scilbronge *libramine*, Wrt. Voc. ii. 88, 72. Cf. skelfan, *and Icel.* skjálfra *to shake.*

scilian; *p.* ode *To separate, part, remove:*—Eádwerd cing scylode ix scypa of māle and hī fōron mid scypon mid eallon anweg *King Edward put nine ships out of commission, and they went away ships and all*, Chr. 1049; Erl. 174, 38. Cf. (?) āscelede (-scerede?) *dividuntur*, Hpt. Gl. 438, 50. [He wass skiledd ut fra þe follc þurrh halig lif, Orm. 16860. Our king, That wic men fra god sal schille, Met. Homl. 152, 9. Schyllyn owte *segrego*, Prompt. Parv. 446. *Icel.* skilja *to separate, part, divide.*] v. ā-scilian.

scilig; *adj. Shaly.* v. stān-scilig.

scill, scell, scyll, e; *f.* I. *a shell, shell-fish:*—Musclan scil *conca*, Wrt. Voc. ii. 15, 35. Scel, 105, 37. Scel *echinus*, i. *piscis, cancer*, 142, 24: 106, 75. Musclan ł scille *de concha*, Hpt. Gl. 417, 10. Scille *vel* sǽsnæglas *conchae* vel *cochleae*, Wrt. Voc. i. 56, 7. Scellum *concis*, ii. 15, 18. II. *the shell* of an egg:—Se rodor ymbfēhþ ūtan eall þās niðerlīcan gescæfte, swā seó scell ymbfēhþ ðæt ǽg, Shrn. 63, 10: Met. 20, 174. Fæger swylce hē of ǽgerum ūt ālǽde, scīr of scylle, Exon. Th. 214, 4; Ph. 234. III. *a scale* of a fish, serpent, etc.:—Hió dyde sciella tō bisene his heor neohtum and ðus cwæð: Ǽlces fisces sciell biþ tō ōðerre gefēgeð *sub squamarum specie de ejus satellitibus perhibetur: Una uni conjungitur*, Past. 47, 3; Swt. 361, 17. Sumum (*serpents*) scinan ða scilla swylce hié wǽron gyldene, Nar. 13, 19. Ðonne hió (*the serpent*) mon slōg oððe sceát, ðonne glād hit on ðǽm scyllum, swelce hit wǽre smēðe īsen, Ors. 4, 6; Swt. 174, 8. Sindon ða scancan scyllum biweaxen *crura tegunt squamae*, Exon. Th. 219, 21; Ph. 310. Ne ete gē nānne fisc būton ða ðe habbaþ finnas and scilla, Lev. 11, 9. IV. *a shell-shaped dish* (?) or simply a *shell:*—Nim león gelynde, mylt on scylle (*a dish* or *a shell?*), Lchdm. i. 364, 24. Wyrme on scille, ii. 42, 16: 310, 6. [*Goth.* skalja *a tile: Icel.* skel *a shell.*] v. ǽg-, oster-, sǽ-, weolc-scill.

scill; *adj. Sonorous, sounding:*—Scyl wæs hearpe, Exon. Th. 353, 44; Reim. 27. [Cf. Heo song so lude and so scharpe Riht so me grulde schille harpe, O. and N. 142. With a shil vois, Parten. 1997. Schylle and sharpe *acutus, sonorus.* Schylly and scharply *acute, aspere, sonore*, Prompt. Parv. 446. Cf. *O. H. Ger.* scall *sonus, sonitus;* scella *tintinnabulum: Icel.* skillr *a loud splash;* skella *a rattle.*] v. next word.

scillan *to cause to sound:*—Scyllendre *concrepante*, scyllende *concrepans*, Hpt. Gl. 518, 48. [*O. H. Ger.* scellan; *p.* scalta *to cause to sound: Icel.* skella.] v. scellan.

scilliht; *adj. Shell* (of fish):—Ðū scealt sellan scellihte fiscas, Lchdm. ii. 196, 21: 254, 19. Scellehte, 227, 17.

scilling, es; *m.* I. as a denomination of English money (uncoined), *a shilling.* The shilling appears to have been of different values in different parts of the country; in Wessex five pennies make a shilling: Fīf penegas gemacigaþ ǽnne scillingc, Ælfc. Gr. 50; Som. 52, 8: and with this statement agree several passages of Henry I.'s Laws, e.g. c. 93, §§ 3, 19, where unus solidus = v denarii, duo solidi = x denarii. In Mercia four pennies go to the shilling. According to Mercian law (Th. i. 190) the ceorl's wergild is 200*s.*, the thane's six times as much, 1200*s.*, the king's, which is six times the thane's, is £120; so that 7200*s.* = 120 × 240*d.*, i.e. the shilling is four pennies. With this agrees L. W. i. 11; Th. i. 473, where it is said: Solidum Anglicum quatuor denarii constituunt. In the Norman time the shilling is twelve pennies. This reckoning seems to be taken in earlier times. v. riht-scilling and Ex. 21, 10. The word is of constant occurrence in the Laws and Charters; from the latter the following passage may illustrate the point that the shilling was a denomination of value, not a coin: Biscop gesalde six hund scillinga on golde, Chart. Th. 90, 21. It also occurs as a weight: Genim of ðysse wyrte petroselini swȳðe smæl dust ānes scillinges gewihte, Lchdm. i. 240, 11. II. as denoting foreign money the word is used to translate various words:—Scylling *numisma*, Wrt. Voc. i. 57, 30. Scilling *obelus*, ii. 63, 68: *stater*, Mt. Kmbl. Rush. 17, 27. Scylling (scilling, Lind., Rush.) *dragmam*, Lk. Skt. 15, 9. Nis woruldfeoh ðe ic mē āgan wille, sceat ne scilling, Cd. Th. 129, 13; Gen. 2143. Hundraþ scillinga *centum denarios*, Mt. Kmbl. Lind. 18, 18. Þriim peninga ł scillinga, Jn. Skt. Lind. 12, 5. Þrītig scillinga *triginta argenteos*, Mt. Kmbl. 26, 15. Þūsend scyllinga on seolfre *mille argenteos*, Gen. 20, 16. Feówerhund scillinga (*siclos*), 23, 16. Hē hēt heora ǽlcum fīftig scyllinga tō sceatte syllan, Homl. Th. i. 88, 4. [*Goth.* skilliggs: *O. Frs.* skilling: *O. L. Ger., O. H. Ger.* scilling *solidus, aureus: Icel.* skillingr.] v. mene-, riht-, wægn-scilling.

Scilling, es; *m. The name of a poet:*—Wit Scilling for uncrum sigedryhtne song āhōfan, Exon. Th. 324, 31; Vīd. 103.

scilling-rīm, es; *n. A reckoning by shillings:*—Se mē beág forgeaf, on ðam siex hund wæs smǽtes goldes sceatta scillingrīme *a ring containing gold to the value of six hundred shillings*, Exon. Th. 324, 10; Vīd. 92.

scima, an; *m. Shadow, gloom:*—Ne hēr (*in hell*) dæg lȳhteþ for scedes sciman, Cd. Th. 271, 15; Sat. 106. Hȳdeþ hine ǽghwylc æfter sceades sciman, Salm. Kmbl. 233; Sal. 116. [Cf. Ualdandes craft scal thi scadouuan mid skimon *virtus altissimi obumbrabit te*, Hel. 279. *M. H. Ger.* scheme *a shadow, mask;* larva: *Ger.* schemen.] v. scimian.

scīma, an; *m. Splendour, brightness, light:*—Ðonne ðære sunnan scīma hātast scīnþ, Bt. 5, 2; Fox 10, 28: Cd. Th. 232, 23; Dan. 264. Ðæs leóhtes scīma wæs swā mycel *cujus radius lucis tantus exstitit*, Bd. 4, 7; S. 575, 17: 5, 10; S. 625, 9. Se scīma gāstlīcre beorhtnysse, Guthl. 2; Gdwin. 12, 22: Exon. Th. 44, 4; Cri. 697. Wuldres scīma scān, 179, 12; Gū. 1260. Mīn se swētesta sunnan scīma, Iuliana, 252, 21; Jul. 166. Heó nǽnig dǽl leóhtes scīman geseón mihte *ne minimam quidem lucis alicujus posset particulam videre*, Bd. 4, 10; S. 578, 20. Sió beorhtnes ðære sunnan scīman, Bt. 34, 8; Fox 146, 4: 39, 3; Fox 216, 1: 4; Fox 6, 33. Metod æfter sceáf scīrum scīman ǽfen, Cd. Th. 9, 5; Gen. 137. Ðā gesundrode Waldend sceade wið scīman, 8, 22; Gen. 128. Se mōna gehrān mid his scīman (*splendore*) ðǽm treówum ufeweardum, Nar. 30, 7. God hira mōd onliéht mid ðæm scīman (*radio*) his giefe, Past. 35, 4; Swt. 243, 21: 48; Swt. 369, 16. Fore scīman *prae fulgure*, Ps. Surt. 17, 13. Seó sunne scīman ne hæfde *the sun was eclipsed*, Bd. 3, 27; S. 558, 11. Swā ðæt ic mihte geseón swīðe lytellne scīman leóhtes, Bt. 35, 3; Fox 158, 29. Niht ne genīpþ ðæs heofenlīcan leóhtes scīman *nox nulla rapit splendorem lucis amoenae*, Dōm. L. 16, 254. Þȳstro hæfdon bewrigen Wealdendes hrǽw, scīrne scīman, Rood Kmbl. 107; Kr. 54. [*Goth.* skeima *φανή*: *O. L. Ger.* scīmo *splendor, fulgor, nitor: O. Sax.* dag-skīmo: *O. H. Ger.* scīmo *splendor, fulgor, effulgentia, radius, fax: Icel.* skīmi *a gleam of light.*] v. ǽfen-scīma.

scimian; *p.* ode *To grow dark*, (of the eyes) *to be dazzled, bleared:*—Mīne eágan scimiaþ *lippio*, Ælfc. Gr. 30, 5; Som. 34, 59. Swā ðæt nān man ne mihte for ðam mycclum leóhte hire on beseón . . . and swā hī hī geornlīcor sceáwodon, swā scimodon heora eágon swīðor, Homl. Skt. i. 7, 153. Beóþ his dagas dēmde gelīce swā ðū on scimiendre sceade lōcige, Ps. Th. 143, 5. v. scima.

scīmian; *p.* ode *To shine, glisten:*—Ic scīmige (scīne, MS. W.) *mico*, Ælfc. Gr. 24; Zup. 138, 1. Scīmande (scīnende, Rush.) *coruscans*, Lk. Skt. Lind. 17, 24. Cf. Be hiora hiwe . . . beóþ ǽblǽce and eal se līchoma āscīmod (*shiny*), Lchdm. ii. 232, 2. [Þat hus schineð ant schimmeð, O. E. Homl. i. 257, 35. Schan (schimede ant schan, MS. B.), Marh. 2, 34. Wið schimmende sweord, 19, 30. Schiminde (schininde, other MS.) hire nebscheaft, Jul. 55, 4. *O. H. Ger.* scīmit *micat.*] v. scīma.

scimrian *to shine, glisten:*—Scymriendes wǽtes *cerulei gurgitis*, Germ. 401, 10. [Þat hus schineð ond schimmeð (schimereð, MS. T.), O. E. Homl. i. 257, 35. Hit schemered and schon, Gaw. 772. Þat eadi trume of schimerinde meidenes, H. M. 21, 34. *Du.* schemeren: *Ger.* schimmern: *Swed.* skimra. Cf. scimeringe *crepusculum*, Grff. vi. 512.]

scin, scinn, es; *n. An extraordinary appearance, a deceptive appearance, a spectre, evil spirit, phantom:*—Scīn *portentum*, Txts. 87, 1611. Scīn *fantasma*, i. *nebulum* (-*am?*), Wrt. Voc. ii. 37, 43: 95, 65: *prestigiis*, 79, 5. Bōcstafa brego bregdeþ sōna feónd be ðam feaxe, lǽteþ flint brecan scīnes sconcan, Salm. Kmbl. 203; Sal. 101. Egsa āstīgeþ monna cynne ðonne blāce (blace?) scotiaþ scrīþende scīn (*the spirits of the storm*) scearpum wǽpnum, Exon. Th. 385, 29; Rä. 4, 52. Swā biþ scinna þeáw, deófla wīse, 362, 4; Wal. 31. Scinnum *scenis* (cf. *scina* grīma, 94, 904), Txts. 97, 1831. Ðam deófle wiðstandan ðonne hē his wōd scinn (wōde scīn, MS. H.) tōbrædeþ *to oppose the devil, when he spreads abroad his mad spirits* (?), Wulfst. 80, 4. Cf. Ða hǽþenan deófle offrodon . . . and ða brǽdas ðæs flǽsces stigon upp on ǽlce healfe eall swilc hit mist wǽre . . . ða hǽþenan on swilcon deófolscīne (*altered to* -scinne) blissedon, Homl. Skt. i. 23, 39. Deófulscinnu þurh gebed beóþ oferswȳþede *demonia per orationem uincuntur*, Scint. 7. [Cf. *O. H. Ger.* gi-scīn *fantasma*. v. Grmm. D. M. 450, 867.] v. scinna *and the compounds with* scīn-.

scīn (?) *brightness, shine.* [*O. Sax.* (sunnon) skīn: *O. Frs.* (sunna) skīn: *O. H. Ger.* scīn *jubar: M. H. Ger.* schīn: *Ger.* schein: *Icel.* sól-, tungl-skin.] v. sun-scīn.

scīnan; *p.* scān, sceán *To shine.* I. lit.:—Ic scīne *splendeo*, Ælfc. Gr. 26, 2; Som. 28, 42. Sciénþ *candescit*, Past. 14, 6; Swt. 89, 1. Swā se līgræsc scīnþ (*fulget*), Lk. Skt. 17, 24: Bt. 5, 2; Fox 10, 29. Ðonne seó sunne on heofone beorhtost scīneþ. 9; Fox 26, 15. Scȳneþ des mōna, Fins. Th. 13; Fin. 7. Ða steorran scīnaþ beforan ðam mōnan, and ne scīnaþ beforan ðære sunnan, Bt. 39, 3; Fox 214, 30. Scaan *ardebat*, Wrt. Voc. ii. 101, 3. Scān, 7, 29. Se steorra (*comet*) scān .iii. mōnþas, Chr. 678; Erl. 41, 4. His ansȳn sceán (*resplenduit*) swā swā sunne, Mt. Kmbl. 17, 2: Bd. 5, 12; S. 628, 13: Cd. Th. 185, 19; Exod. 125. Seó rōd sceán swā heofenes tungol, Shrn. 149, 11. His ansȳn eal sceán swā swā sunne, and his gewǣda scinon on snāwes hwītnysse, Homl. Th. ii. 242, 7. Hwǣr is seó eorðe ðe nǣfre sunne on ne sceán? In ðære reádan sǣ, Salm. Kmbl. 198, 14. Wīgbord scinon, Cd. Th. 207, 14; Exod. 466. Eoforlīc scionon, Beo. Th. 612; B. 303. Ān cyn ys *olocryseis*, ðæt is on ūre geþeóde gecweden, ðæt heó eall golde scīne, Lchdm. i. 242, 13. Hig scīnon (*luceant*) on ðære heofenan fæstnysse, Gen. 1, 15. Sunnan leóma cymeþ scȳnan, Exon. Th. 56, 18; Cri. 902. Scīnende *refulgens*, Lk. Skt. 9, 29. Beorhtnes scīnendes steorran *fulgor stellae*, Bd. 5, 12; S. 629, 5. Scīnendes lēges, 4, 13; S. 581, 15. Scīnendum *limpidis*, Wrt. Voc. ii. 50, 34. II. fig.:—Ðonne scīnaþ ða rihtwīsan, Mt. Kmbl. 13, 43. Se nama se ðe mid him swā lange sceán and bryhte *nomen quod apud eos tam diu claruerat*, Bd. 1, 12; S. 480, 39: 3, 13; S. 538, 39. Seó stōw on ðære ðe ðu ðæt fægereste weorud on geóguþhādnesse gesāwe scīnan and wynsumian *locus iste in quo pulcherrimam hanc juventutem jocundari ac fulgere conspicis*, 5, 12; S. 630, 15. Ðæt mōd swā beorhte ne mōt blīcan and scīnan, Met. 22, 35: Bt. 35, 1; Fox 156, 2. Ðæt ðū mōste hālig scīnan, eádig on ðam ēcan līfe, Exon. Th. 87, 19; Cri. 1427. On wordum and on dǣdum beorht and scīnende *verbo et actibus clarus*, Bd. 3. 19; S. 547, 4. On scīnendre *praepollenti*, Hpt. Gl. 491, 1. [*Goth.* skeinan: *O. Sax.* skīnan: *O. Frs.* skīna: *O. H. Ger.* scīnan: *Icel.* skīna.] v. ā-, be-, ge-, geond-, ofer-, ymb-scīnan.

scin-bān, es; *n. A shin, shin-bone*:—Scina *vel* scinbān *tibiae*, Wrt. Voc. i. 44, 72: 71, 58. [A schynbone *sura*, 247, col. 2. Oc (*cervus*) leigeþ his skinbon on oðres lendbon, Misc. 12, 359. *M. H. Ger.* schine-bein: *Ger.* schien-bein: *Du.* sheen-been.]

scīn-, scinn-cræft, es; *m.* I. *the art by which deceptive appearances are produced, magic*:—Ðis synt ða īdelnyssa ðisse worlde . . . scīncræft *hae sunt vanitates hujus mundi . . . ars magica*, L. Ecg. P. 1, 8; Th. ii. 174, 34. Hié ne angeátan mid hwelcum scinncræfte and mid hwelcum lotwrence hit deófla dydon, Ors. 3, 3; Swt. 102, 17. Hē behēt ānum drȳmen sceattes, gif hē mid his scȳncræfte (scīn-, MS. O.) him ðæt mǣden mihte gemacian tō wīfe, Homl. Skt. i. 3, 365. Beó ic scyldig, gif ic his scȳncræft ne mæg ādwæscan mid mīnum drȳcræfte, 14, 57. Hȳ wǣron tō sāre beswicene þurh ðæs sweartan deófles scīncræft, Wulfst. 198, 18. II. *a magic art* or *trick*:—Scīncræfte *praestigia*, Wrt. Voc. ii. 66, 59. Wiccan beóþ tō helle bescofene for heora scīncræftum, Homl. Th. ii. 330, 29. Hī mid mislīcum scȳncræfton ðæt folc dwelodon, 482, 4. Hē wolde ðære fǣmnan mōd on his scīncræftum onwendan tō hǣðendōme, Shrn. 135, 1. Ðā cwǣdon hī, ðæt hī scinncræftas ne cūþan, 90, 10. Se sceocca eów lǣrþ ðyllīce scīncræftas, Homl. Skt. i. 17, 106. ¶ *In the following the word is glossed as if it were* scīncræftiga:—Scīncræfta *hierophantorum*, Wrt. Voc. ii. 43, 25: 82, 7: Hpt. Gl. 483, 7.

scīn-cræftiga, an; *m. A magician, sorcerer*:—Gif wiccan oððe wigleras, scīncræftigan oððe hōrcwenan on earde wurðan āgitene, fȳse hī man georne ūt of ðysan earde, L. Eth. vi. 7; Th. i. 316, 20.

scīne, sciéne, scēne, sceóne, scióne, scȳne; *adj. Beautiful, fair, bright*:—Is se forrynel fæger and sciéne, Met. 29, 25: Cd. Th. 41, 14; Gen. 656. Cwæð ðæt his līc wǣre leóht and scēne, 17, 26; Gen. 265. Wæstm wlitig and scēne, 30, 16; Gen. 467. Deór wundrum scȳne (*the panther*), Exon. Th. 356, 30; Pa. 19. Is seó womb wundrum fæger, scīr and scȳne, 219, 16; Ph. 308. Mægþ scȳne, Beo. Th. 6025; B. 3016. Se scȳna stān, Andr. Kmbl. 1532; An. 767. On stede scȳnum, Exon. Th. 70, 33; Cri. 1148. Ic ðē swā sciénne gesceapen hæfde, 85, 6; Cri. 1387. Hē forlǣrde idese sciéne, Cd. Th. 43, 34; Gen. 700. Hē geseah Euan stondan sceóne gesceapene, 35, 3; Gen. 549. Tō sceáwianne ðone scȳnan wlite, Exon. Th. 57, 8; Cri. 915. Forhwon forlēte ðū līf ðæt scȳne, 90, 7; Cri. 1470. Sceóne lambru, Ps. Th. 113, 4, 6. Gimmas swā scȳne, Exon. Th. 43, 27; Cri. 695: 219, 1; Ph. 300. Fuglas scȳne, 237, 17; Ph. 591. Þurh ða scēnan scīnendan rīcu ðæs Fæder *per Patris fulgenti regna paratu*, Dōm. L. 18, 294. Him wīf curon scȳne and fægere, Cd. Th. 76, 5; Gen. 1252. Hyrsta scȳne, Judth. Thw. 26, 9; Jud. 317. Hiwbeorhtra and scȳnra, Exon. Th. 357, 10; Pa. 26. Wurdon ðīn gesceapu scēnran, Cd. Th. 32, 14; Gen. 503. Eue idesa sciénost, 51, 4; Gen. 821. Scēnost, 39, 17; Gen. 626. Sceónost, 44, 5; Gen. 704. Engla scȳnost, 22, 10; Gen. 338. [Feier and sceone (scene, 2nd MS.), Laym. 2299. Regan ꝥ scone (scene, 2nd MS.), 3098. A steorrne . . . brihht and shene, Orm. 3431. Scone and faȝȝerr, 15665. A þusent fold schenre þen þe sunne, A. R. 100, 4. Heo as schene as schininde sunne wende up aloft, Marh. 19, 14. Emelye hire yonge suster schene, Chauc. Kn. T. 114. Æfter sharpe shoures moste shene is þe sonne, Piers P. 18, 409. *Goth* skauns: *O. Sax.* skōni: *O. Frs.* skēne: *O. L. Ger.* scōni *lucidus*: *O. H. Ger.* scōni *splendidus, splendens, formosus, venustus, pulcher, speciosus*: *Ger.* schön.] v. ælf-, sun-, þurh-, wlite-scīne.

scīnefrian *to glitter*:—And scīnefrian *ac micare*, Wrt. Voc. ii. 6, 33.

scīnendlīc; *adj. Clear, bright*:—Beorht ł scīnendlīc ł leóht *lucidum*, Ps. Lamb. 18, 9. v. þurh-scīnendlīc.

scīnere, scinnere, es; *m. One who produces deceptive appearances* (v. scīn), *a magician*:—Scinneras *emaones*, Txts. 59, 746. Scīneras, scinneras *scienicis*, 98, 952.

scīn-feld; *dat.* a; *m. The beautiful, Elysian field*, applied to Tempe:—Hwæt synt ða twegen men on neorxna wange? Enoch and Helias. Hwǣr wuniaþ hȳ? Malifica and Intimphonis (in Tempis?), ðæt is on sunfelda and on sceánfelda (sceón-?), Salm. Kmbl. 202, 2. On scēnfeldum *in Tempis*, Wrt. Voc. ii. 47, 16: 89, 72.

scīn-gedwola, an; *m. A delusion produced by magic, delusive appearance, phantom*:—Scīngedwolan *nebulam*, Wrt. Voc. ii. 61, 30.

scīn-gelāc, es; *n. A magical practice*:—Hī ongunnon secgan ðæt hit drȳcræftum gedōn wǣre scīngelācum ðæt se stān mǣlde *they said that it was done by the sorcerer's arts, by magical practices, that the stone spoke*, Andr. Kmbl. 1531; An. 767.

scīn-, **scinn-hiw**, es; *n. A form produced by magic, phantom, spectre*:—Scīnhiw *prestigium*, Wrt. Voc. i. 21, 61: *fantasma*, ii. 33, 82. Scīnlāc *vel* [scīn]hiw *fantasia*, i. *imaginatio, delusio mentis*, 147, 42. Reþlīc scīnhiw *ferale monstrum*, 147, 53: Hymn. Surt. 142, 12. Ne eom ic nā scinnhiw (*phantasma*), swā swā gē wēnaþ, Homl. Th. ii. 388, 26. Scīnhiowes *fantasiae*, Ps. Surt. ii. p. 190, 11. Scīnhiwe[s] *phantasmate*, Wrt. Voc. ii. 67, 5. Scīnhiwe, 34, 1. Wiccecræftas, scīnhiw *prestigias*, 66, 25.

scin-hosu, e; *f. A shin-hose, a covering for the lower part of the leg, a greave*:—Scinhose *ocreis*, Hpt. Gl. 521, 5.

scīn-lāc, es; *n.* I. *magic, necromancy, sorcery*:—Scȳnlāce *necromantia*, Hpt. Gl. 482, 74. Se mec gescyldeþ wið ðīnum scīnlāce, Exon. Th. 255, 15; Jul. 214. Hī sǣdon ðæt hió sceolde mid hire scīnlāce (cf. mid hire drȳcræft, Bt. 38, 1; Fox 194, 30) beornas forbrēdan and mid balocræftum weorpan on wildra līc, Met. 26, 74. Twegen drȳas ða worhton micel scīnlāc mid twām dracum, Shrn. 131, 29. II. *a particular act of magic, a sorcery, delusion produced by magic*:—Hī ðæt hæfdon gedōn mid yflum scīnlācum, Shrn. 90, 10: 75, 18. Ða ðe galdorcræftas begangaþ, and mid ðǣm unwære men beswīcaþ, and hī āweniaþ from Godes gemynde mid heora scīnlācum, Blickl. Homl. 61, 25. Scīndlācum, Shrn. 141, 27. III. *delusion, superstition, frenzy, rage*:—Scīnlāc *fantasia*, i. *imaginatio, delusio mentis*, Wrt. Voc. ii. 147, 42. Ðætte gifearria from ðære stōwe ǣlc scīnilāc and ymbcerro diúbles fācnes *ut discedat ab eo loco omnis fantasia vel versutia diabolicae fraudis*, Rtl. 120, 33. Næs his scīnlāc ne his hergiung on ða fremdan āne ac hē gelīce slōg and hiénde ða ðe him wǣron mid farende *nec minor ejus* (Alexander) *in suos crudelitas, quam in hostem rabies fuit*, Ors. 3, 9; Swt. 130, 19. Mānfulles scīnlāces *fanaticae superstitionis*, Hpt. Gl. 488, 41: 509, 39. Scīnlāc[e] *superstitione*, 500, 70. Sume Rōmāna wīf on swelcum scīnlāce wurdon and on swelcum wōdan dreáme *incredibili rabie et amore scelerum Romanae matronae exarserunt*, Ors. 3, 6; Swt. 108, 25. IV. *a delusive appearance, a spectre, apparition, phantom*:—Hī cwǣdon: Hyt ys scīnlāc *dicentes*: *Quia phantasma est*, Mt. Kmbl. 14, 26. Scīnlāc *nebulo*, Hpt. Gl. 501, 16. Scȳnlāce *praestigia*, 482, 74. Tō fleánne ǣlc scīnelāc ðiuoles *ad effugandum omne fantasma diaboli*, Rtl. 100, 33. Ðeós wyrt (ἀστέριον) scīneþ on nihte swilce steorra on heofone, and se ðe hȳ nytende gesihþ, hē sægþ ðæt hē scīnlāc geseó, Lchdm. i. 164, 6. Scīnlāc *monstra*, Wrt. Voc. ii. 56, 15: *nebulones*, Hpt. Gl. 501, 73. Wið deófulseócnysse and wið yfelre gesihþe, wulfes flǣsc gesoden . . . ða scīnlāc ðe him ǣr ætȳwdon ne geunstillaþ hȳ hine, Lchdm. i. 360, 13–16. Ðȳ læs cild sȳ hreósende, oððe scīnlāc mēte, 350, 13. Ða ðe scīnlāc þrowien etan león flǣsc; ne þrowiaþ hȳ ofer ðæt ǣnig scīnlāc, 364, 22. Scīnlāca *praestigiarum*, Hpt. Gl. 501, 68. Galdras *praestigias*, scīnlāc *fantasias*, 459, 16. Scīnlācu gesihþ, gestreón of ungewēndum hit getācnaþ, Lchdm. iii. 204, 18. [*O. H. Ger.* scīn-leih *monstrum*.] v. Grmm. D. M. 450.

scīn-lǣca, -lāca, an; *m. A magician, necromancer, sorcerer*:—Scīnlǣcan (-lǣcean, -lēcan) *nebulonis*, Txts. 81, 1372: *nebulis* (*nebulonis?*), Wrt. Voc. ii. 60, 60: 79. 4. Ðæs leásan scīnlǣcan *falsi nebulo*, 147, 2. Sabastianus ongon hine (*St. Victor*) nēdan tō deófolgelde; ðā hē ðæt ne geþafede, ðā hēt hē summe scīnlǣcan him sellan etan ðæt flǣsc ðæt wæs geǣttred, Shrn. 84, 27. Hī gefetton Escolafius ðone scīnlǣcan mid ðære ungemetlīcan nædran ðe mon Epithaurus hēt *horrendum illum Epidaurium colubrum, cum ipso Aesculapii lapide advenerint*, Ors. 3, 10; Swt. 140,

9: 3, 10, tit.; Swt. 3, 19. Scínlǣcan *magi*, Wrt. Voc. ii. 39, 11. On helle beóþ ða scínlǣcan, ða ðe galdorcræftas begangaþ, Blickl. Homl. 61, 23. Ða fǣmnan ðe gewuniaþ onfón gealdorcræftigan and scínlǣcan (-lácan, MS. H.) and wiccan, ne lǣt ðú ða libban, L. Alf. 30; Th. i. 50, 10. v. two following words.

scín-lǣce, an; *f. A woman who practises magic, a sorceress*:—Ðá cwǣdon Rómware ðæt heó wǣre drýegge and scínlǣce, Shrn. 56, 13.

scín-lǣc[e], -lác; *adj. Magical, phantasmal*:—Hí him héton gefeccean tó Escolapius ðone scínlácan mid ðære scínlǣcan (-lácan, MS. L.) nædran, Ors. 3, 10, tit.; Swt. 3, 19. Álésedo from ǣlcum ongifeht scínelácum *libera ab omni inpugnatione fantasmatica*, Rtl. 98, 26. v. preceding words.

scín-líc; *adj. Of the nature of an apparition, phantasmal*:—Suoefno and næhta scínelíco *sompnia et noxia fantasmata* (the glosser seems to have read *noctes fantasmaticae?*), Rtl. 180, 16.

scinn, scinnere. v. scín, scínere.

scinna, an; *m. An evil spirit, spectre*:—Blace hworfon scinnan (*the fallen angels*) forscepene, sceaþan hwearfdon geond ðæt atole scref (*hell*), Cd. Th. 269, 12; Sat. 72. Ðæt hié leóda landgeweorc láþum beweredon scuccum and scinnum, Beo. Th. 1882; B. 939. v. scín.

scínness, e; *f. Brightness, splendour*:—Ðe móna ne seleþ scínisse (*splendorem*) his, Mk. Skt. Lind. 13, 24.

scín-seóc; *adj. Haunted by apparitions*:—Scínseócum men wyrc drenc of hwítes hundes þoste, Lchdm. i. 364, 4.

scinu, e; *f. A shin*:—Scinu *cruscula*, Wrt. Voc. ii. 137, 20. Scina *vel* scinbán *tibiae*, i. 44, 72. Scyne oððe scinbán *tibia* (*ae?*), 71, 58. Scina, 65, 42. Scancan, scina *tibias*, Hpt. Gl. 482, 64. [*O. H. Ger.* scina *tibia*.] v. scin-bán.

scio, scioppa. v. sceón, scoppa.

scip, es; *m. A patch, clout*:—Ne ásend nán man scyp (scep *altered to* scyp, MS. A.: ðæt ésceapa *commisuram*, Lind.) of níwum reáfe on eald reáf; elles ðæt níwe slít, and se níwa scyp (*as before in* MS. A. *and* Lind.) ne hylpþ ðam ealdan, Lk. Skt. 5, 36: Mt. Kmbl. 9, 16. Scyp (*also* scep, MS. A.: later MSS. scep, scyp) *assumentum*, Mk. Skt. 2, 21.

scip, es; *n. A ship*:—Scip *navis* vel *faselus*, scipu *rates*, sceort scip *naviscella* vel *cimba*, vel *campolus* vel *musculus*, litel scip *scapha*, Wrt. Voc. i. 47, 55–61. Scip *ratis*, horsa scip *ypogavus*, swift scip *archiromacus*, sceaþena scip *paro*, ánbýme scip *trabaria*, 56, 11–28. Scip *barca*, ii. 12, 19: *caraba*, 22, 34. Foreweard scip *prorostris*, 68, 48. Scipes botm *carina*, scipes hláford *nauclerus*, i. 48, 3–4. Scipes flór *fori* vel *tabulata navium*, 63, 40. Lytlum scipe *cimbula*, ii. 22, 34. Scipe *cercilo*, 17, 72: 76, 30 (cf. aesc *cercilus*, 103, 56). Ðá wende hé on scype (scipp, Lind.) *ascendens nauem*, Lk. Skt. 8, 37. Scyp ástígan, Lchdm. iii. 184, 13. Swá eode hé on scyp, Bd. 4, 1; S. 564, 47. Scipu *classes*, Wrt. Voc. ii. 14, 46. Scypu (sciopu, Rush.: scioppu, Lind.) *naues*, Jn. Skt. 6, 23. Scipu (sciopo, Lind.), Lk. Skt. 5, 2: *nauiculas*, 5, 7. Scypo (scioppo, Lind.) *naues*, 5, 11. Sceopu, Ps. Surt. 47, 8: 103, 26. [*Goth. O. Sax. O. L. Ger. O. Frs. Icel.* skip: *O. H. Ger.* scif.] v. ǣrend-, ceáp-, fird-, flot-, for-, horn-, hýð-, lang-, pleg-, troh-, unfriþ-scip.

scip-býme, an; *f. A ship-trumpet*:—Scypbýman *classicam tubam*, Germ. 391, 48.

scip-broc, es; *n. Trouble, hardship*, or *labour when journeying in a ship*:—Paulus him rehte hú myccle scipbrocu hé gebád on ðæm síþe *St. Paul related to them the hardships he had undergone on his voyage to Rome*, Blickl. Homl. 173, 6.

scip-brucol; *adj. Causing shipwreck*:—Scypbrucules wæles *naufragi gurgitis*, Germ. 401, 9.

scip-bryce, es; *m. Ship-wreck, what comes ashore from wrecks*:—Ic habbe gegeofen Ælfwine abbod intó Ramesége . . . scipbryce and ða sǣupwarp on eallen þingen swá wel swá ic hit mé seolf betst habbe bí ða sǣrime áhwǣr in Engelande, Chart. Th. 421, 33. (Cf. L. H. i. 10, 1; Th. i. 519, 4 *where among the rights* (jura) *belonging to the king* naufragium *is mentioned*.) [Cf. *Icel.* skip-brot *wreck drifted ashore*.]

scip-cræft, es; *m. Naval power, strength in ships*:—Swegen sende hider and bæd him fylstes ongeán Magnus, ðæt man sceolde sendan .L. scypa him tó fultume. Ac hit þúhte unrǣd eallum folce, and hit wearð gelet þurh ðæt ðe Magnus hæfde micelne scypcræft, Chr. 1048; Erl. 173, 7.

scip-drincende (-drencende? *see* uére gidruncen *mergeretur*, l. 31) *making shipwreck*:—Paulum scipdrincende gifriáde *Paulum naufragantem liberavit*, Rtl. 61, 33.

scipe, es; *m.* I. *pay, stipend*:—Scipe *vel* bigleofa *stipendium*, Wrt. Voc. i. 20, 33. [Hi nolleþ paye þet hi ssolle, and hi ofhealdeþ þe ssepes of ham þet doþ hare niedes, Ayenb. 39, 5 (the word occurs several times in this work). Withholdyng or abrigging of the schipe or the hyre or the wages of servauntes, Chauc. Persones T. (De Ira). And cf. Ne mihte ic of þan kinge habben scipinge; ich spende mine ahte þa wile þa heo ilaste, Laym. 13656.] II. *state, condition, dignity, office*:—Hæbbe ic mínes cynescipes gerihta swá mín fæder hæfde, and míne þegnas hæbben heora scipe (cf. se déma ðe óðrum wóh déme . . . þolige á his þegenscipes, L. Edg. ii. 3; Th. i. 266, 15–18) on mínum tíman swá hý hæfdon on mínes fæder, L. Edg. S. 2; Th. i. 272, 28. ¶ -scipe *-ship*, helps to form many nouns. [*O. Frs.* -skipe, -skip: *O. Sax.* -skepi.]

scipen. v. scypen.

scipere, es; *m. A sailor*:—Hé tealde ðæt his sciperes woldon wændon fram him, búton hé ðé raðor cóme . . . His sciperes geféngon hine and wurpon hine on ðone bát, Chr. 1046; Erl. 174, 13–18. [From Scandinavian (?). *Icel.* skipari *a mariner*.]

scip-fæt, es; *n. A vessel in the form of a ship*:—Húseldisc *patena*, scipfæt *cimbia* (the word occurs under the heading *nomina vasorum*), Wrt. Voc. i. 25, 32. Cf. *Hec acerra* a schyp for censse, 230, col. 2. Wright has the following note on this entry: The *nef*, a vessel in the form of a ship, used in the church from an early period to hold the incense, as well as other articles.

scip-farend, es; *m. A ship-farer, sailor*:—Aidan ðám scypfarendum (*nautis*) ðone storm tówardne foresægde, Bd. 3, 15; S. 541, 16. v. next word.

scip-férend, es; *m. A sailor*:—Wǣron hié on gescirplan scipférendum onlíce, eálíðendum, Andr. Kmbl. 500; An. 250. v. preceding word.

scip-fird, e; *f. A naval force* or *expedition, a fleet*:—Ðá ðeós scipfyrd (*the naval expedition described in the preceding paragraph*) ðus geendod wæs, Chr. 1009; Erl. 142, 15. Wé næfdon ða gesélþa ðæt seó scipfyrd nytt wǣre ðisum earde, 1009; Erl. 141, 26. Ðá cýdde man in tó ðære scipfyrde, ðet hí mann eáðe befaran mihte, Erl. 141, 33. *See* land-fird *for other passages*. [Humber King & al his fleote & his muchele scipferde comen on Albanaces londe, Laym. 2156.]

scip-firdung, e; *f. A naval force* or *armament*:—Æt ðam ende ne beheóld hit nánþing seó scypfyrding ne seó landfyrding, Chr. 999; Erl. 134, 36. Burhbóta and bricbóta áginne man georne on ǣghwilcon ende, and fyrdunga eác, and scipfyrdunga ealswá, L. Eth. vi. 32; Th. i. 322, 32.

scip-flota, an; *m. A sailor*:—Hettend crungun Sceotta leóda and scipflotan (*the Danes*), Chr. 937; Erl. 112, 11.

scip-forðung, -fyrðung, e; *f. Preparation of ships*:—Burhbóta and bricgbóta and scipforðunga (-fyrðunga, MS. B.) áginne man georne (cf. wærlíc biþ ðæt man ǣghwilce geáre sóna æfter Eástron fyrdscipa gearwige, L. Eth. vi. 33; Th. i. 324, 3), L. C. S. 10; Th. i. 380, 27 v. scip-fyrðrung.

scip-fylleþ *the private jurisdiction exercised over a group of three hundreds*. The word occurs in a charter of Edgar granting to Bishop Oswald certain privileges connected with three hundreds, where in reciting the request that had been made to the king it is said: 'quatinus posset ipse (Oswald) cum monachis suis unam naucupletionem, quod Anglice scypfylleð dicitur, per se habere.' The grant of the request is then stated: 'Ego Eadgarus Oswaldo episcopo annuo et dono huius libertatis priuilegium . . . ut ipse episcopus cum monachis suis de istis tribus centuriatibus . . . construant (constituant, Chart. Th. 214) unam naucupletionem, quod Anglice dicitur scypfylleð oððe scypsócne, in loco quem ob eius memoriam Oswaldeslaw deinceps appellari placuit, ubi querelarum causae secundum morem patriae et legum iura iure discernantur; habeatque ipse episcopus debita transgressionum . . . et omnia quaecunque rex in suis hundredis habet,' Cod. Dip. Kmbl. vi. 240. The connection between the sense in which the word seems to be used in the charter and the meanings of the two parts of the compound may perhaps be found in the entry under the year 1008 in the Chronicle. It there apparently states, that from every three hundred hides one ship should be furnished to the national fleet. v. Stubbs' Const. Hist. i. 105, and cf. Kemble's Saxons in England, i. 255. The word *fylleþ* occurs in the compound *winter-fylleþ*, q. v.; cf. also *Icel.* skip-sókn *a ship's crew*.

scip-fyrðrung, e; *f. Fitting out of ships*:—Ymbe scypfyrðrunga, ðæt ǣghwylc geset sý sóna ofer Eástran, L. Eth. v. 27; Th. i. 310, 26. v. scip-forðung.

scip-gebroc, es; *n. Shipwreck*:—Ðæt hié æfter ðæm scipgebroce him ða sǣ ondrǣden *ut mare post naufragium metuant*, Past. 52, 1; Swt. 403, 12. Ic ðé bidde ðæt ðú mé on ðæm scipgebroce ðisses andweardan lifes sum bred gerǣce ðínra gebeda *in hujus quaeso vitae naufragio orationis tuae me tabula sustine*, 65, 7; Swt. 467, 24. Hwelce tibernessa hié dreógende wǣron on hungre ge on scipgebroce, Ors. 1, 11; Swt. 50, 19.

scip-gefeoht, es; *n. A naval battle* or *war*:—Scypgefeoht *bellum classicum*, Germ. 389, 42.

scip-gefére (?), es; *n. A going by ship, navigation, sailing*:—Hé on his scipgefére hwearf eft tó Cent *rediit Cantiam navigio*, Bd. 2, 20; S. 521, 41.

scip-getawu *furniture of a ship*:—Geréþru *vel* scipgetawu *aplustre*, Wrt. Voc. i. 56, 19.

scip-gild, es; *n. A ship-tax, a tax to supply funds for the maintenance of a fleet*:—Swá fela sýðe swá menn gyldaþ heregyld oððe tó scipgylde *quotiens populus universus persolvit censum Danis, vel ad naves seu ad arma*, Chart. Th. 307, 24.

scip-hamer, es; *m. A hammer carried in the hand, by which a signal is given to the rowers*:—Sciphamor *portisculus* vel *hortator remigum*, Wrt. Voc. i. 48, 20. v. hamer.

scip-here, es; *m.* I. *a collection of ships of war, a naval force, a fleet of war*:—Sciphere *classis*, Ælfc. Gr. 9, 28; Som. 11, 56: Wrt. Voc. i. 73, 75: *classica*, ii. 131, 62. Flota, sciphere *classis*, 14, 45. Sciphere eów nymþ *reducet te Dominus classibus in Aegyptum*, Deut. 28, 68. On ðæs sǽs waroþe tō sūþdǽle ðanon ðe hī sciphere on becom *in litore oceani ad meridiem quo naves eorum habebantur*, Bd. 1, 12; S. 481, 11. Ðȳ ilcan geáre gegadrode micel sciphere on Ald-Seaxum, and ðǽr wearð micel gefeoht, Chr. 885; Erl. 84, 6. Gif ǽnig sciphere on Engla lande hergie, L. Eth. ii. 1; Th. i. 284, 15. Ðȳ sumera fōr Ælfrēd cyning ūt on sǽ mid sciphere and gefeaht wið .vii. sciphlæstas, 875; Erl. 78, 6. Persa cyning sende Conon mid scipehere (scip-, MS. C.), Ors. 3, 1; Swt. 96, 25. Ðā cōman hī sōna mid sciphere *mox advecti navibus*, Bd. 1, 12; S. 480, 34. Ðæt on land Dena lāðra nǽnig mid scipherge sceðþan ne meahte, Beo. Th. 491; B. 243. Ne gehērde nōn mon ðǽget nānne sciphere, ne furþon ymbe nān gefeoht sprecan, Bt. 15; Fox 48, 14. Se cyng wæs west on Defnum wið ðone sciphere (*acting against the Danish fleet*), Chr. 894; Erl. 92, 26. On ðysum geáre wæs micel unfriþ on Angelcynnes londe þurh sciphere, 1001; Erl. 136, 2. Sciphergas, Met. 8, 31. II. *the men of a ship of war*:—Ælfrēd cyning gefeaht wið feówer sciphlæstas Deniscra monna and ðara scipa tū genam . . . and tuegen scipheras him on hond eodon, and ða wǽron miclum forslægene, ǽr hié on hond eodon (cf. ðara scipa twā genāmon . . . and twā him on hand eodon, and ða men wǽron myclum ofslagene, ǽr hī on hand eodan, MS. E.), Chr. 882; Erl. 82, 12.

sciphere-līc; *adj. Relating to a fleet, naval*:—Scipherelīcum *classicis*, Hpt. Gl. 406, 40.

scip-hlǽder, e; *f. A ship's ladder, a ladder for passing from a ship to the shore*:—Sciphlǽder *pons*, Wrt. Voc. i. 63, 53. Sciphlædder *ponsis*, 56, 47.

scip-hlæst, es; *m.* I. *the body of (fighting) men on a ship*:—Claudius se consul fōr an Pūnice and him Hannibal ūt on sǽ ongeán com and ealle ofslōg būton .xxx. sciphlæsta ða ōþflugon tō Libeum ðæm īglande *Claudius consul contra hostem profectus superatus est. Et ipse quidem cum triginta navibus Lilybaeum confugit*, Ors. 4, 6; Swt. 178, 32. Hēr gefeaht Ecgbryht cyning wið .xxxv. sciphlæsta, Chr. 833; Erl. 64, 19: 837; Erl. 66, 5: 840; Erl. 66, 19. Ælfrēd cyning gefeaht wið .vii. sciphlæstas and hiera ān gefēng and ða ōðru gefliémde, 875; Erl. 78, 6. Ælfrēd cyning gefeaht wið feówer sciphlæstas Deniscra monna, and ðara scipa tū genam, 882; Erl. 82, 10. II. *a ship of burden, a transport*:—Sciplæst *oneraria*, Wrt. Voc. i. 63, 71. Scyphlæst *honeraria*, ii. 43, 10 (cf. hlaestscip *honeraria*, 110, 46).

scip-hlāford, es; *m. A ship-master*:—Sciphlāford *nauclerus*, Wrt. Voc. i. 56, 16.

scipian *to take shape*:—Ðonne gelimpþ ðæræ (*the mother*) manigfeald sār ðonne ðæs byrþres līc on hire innoþe scypigende biþ, Lchdm. iii. 146, 15. v. scippan.

scipian; *p.* ode *To put in order, equip, man* a ship:—Ðā lǽt Eádweard cyng scypian XL snacca, Chr. 1052; Erl. 183, 33. [From (?) *Icel.* skipa *to give order* or *arrangement to things, to man* a ship.]

scipian; *p.* ode *To take ship*:—Se eorl on Wiht scipode and intō Normandīg fōr, Chr. 1091; Erl. 228, 12. v. ge-scipian.

scipincel, es; *n. A small ship*:—Scipincel *carabus*, Wrt. Voc. i. 48, 1: 64, 3. Scipincel *navicula*, 56, 12.

scip-lād, e; *f. Sailing, navigating*:—Hē wolde on scyplāde mid ða fǽmnan hām hweorfan *navigio cum virgine redire disponebat*, Bd. 3, 15; S. 541, 27.

scip-līc; *adj. Relating to a fleet, naval*:—Ða men ða ðe beóþ winnende in sciplīcum gewinne, Shrn. 35, 12. Ðǽm sciplīcum *classicis*, Wrt. Voc. ii. 75, 7. Flotlīcum, sciplīcum *classicis*, 131, 63. Sciplīcum herium *classicis cohortibus*, Hpt. Gl. 406, 39. [*O. H. Ger.* scef-līh *nauticus, navalis.*]

scip-līðend, es; *m. One who goes in a ship*:—Hē cwæð tō ðǽm sciplīðendum . . . ða sciplīðende ðæt gehērende mearcedon ðone dæg, Shrn. 85, 30–86, 2. Ealla ða þing ða ðe scyplīðendum (*navigantibus*) nydþearflicu gesewen wǽron, Bd. 5, 9; S. 622, 26. v. next word.

scip-līðende; *adj. Going in a ship, sailing*:—Hē sǽde sciplīðendum monnum, Shrn. 85, 28: Homl. As. 117, 17. Ða sciplīðendan *navigeros*, Wrt. Voc. ii. 61, 35.

scip-mǽrels *a ship-rope*:—Scipmǽrls *tonsilla*, Wrt. Voc. i. 57, 4. v. mǽrels.

scip-mann, es; *m. A mariner, sailor*; nauta, navarchus:—Scypman *nauta*, Hymn. Surt. 6, 26. Scipmen *navarcas*, Wrt. Voc. ii. 62, 15. (1) *a sailor, one of a ship's crew*:—Ðā ongunnon ða nȳdlingas and ða scypmen ða ancras on ðone sǽ sendan woldon ðæt scyp mid gefæstnian *tentabant nautae anchoris in mare missis navem retinere*, Bd. 3, 15; S. 541, 40. Volosianus hēt hys scypmen swīðe forþ rōwan, St. And. 44, 4. (2) *one who goes on trading voyages*:—Scipmanna (-e, MS.) myrt *teloneum*, Wrt. Voc. i. 37, 10. Ðǽm scipmannum is beboden gelīce and ðǽm landbūendum, ðæt ealles ðæs ðe him on heora ceápe geweaxe hig Gode ðone teóþan dǽl āgyfen, L. E. I. 35; Th. ii. 432, 27. [Arður him ot scipe fusde and hehte þat his scipmen brohten hine to Romerel, Laym. 28308. Agrayþed ase byeþ þe ssipmen ine ssipe, þet ase zone ase he yhyerþ þane smite of þe lodesmanne hi yerneþ, Ayenb. 140, 22. See Chaucer's Prologue, vv. 388–410. *Icel.* skip-maðr *one of a crew.*]

scippan, scieppan, sceppan; *p.* scōp, sceóp; *pp.* sceapen, scepen. I. *to shape, form*:—Ic hiwige oððe scyppe *fingo*. Ælfc. Gr. 28, 5; Som. 31, 61. II. *to create* (of the act of the Deity):—Ðū scyppest eorþan ansȳne *renovabis faciem terrae*, Ps. Th. 103, 28. Ælmihtig fæder ðe ða scīran gesceaft sceópe and worhtest, Hy. 10, 2. Waldend scōp wudige mōras, Exon. Th. 193, 11; Az. 120: 132, 1; Gū. 466. Ðā hē Adam sceóp, Cd. Th. 77, 21; Gen. 1278. Swā gōd Sceoppend rihtlīce sceóp eall ðæt hē sceóp, Bt. 39, 2; Fox 214, 12. Heortan clǽne scyp (*crea*) on mē, Ps. Lamb. 50, 12. God gesceóp ealle gesceafta, and deófol nāne gesceafta scyppan ne mæg, Homl. Th. i. 102, 1. Hē (*God*) selcūðe syððan scyppan nolde, Hexam. 12; Norm. 20, 15. Ic scyppendum wuldorcyninge hȳrde, rīcum dryhtne, Exon. Th. 453, 16; Hy. 4, 15. Hē bebeád and sceapene synd *ipse mandavit, et creata sunt*, Ps. Spl. 32, 9. III. *to shape* for one (*dat.*) as his fate (*acc.*), *to assign* as a person's lot. v. ge-sceap:—Scōp *censebat*, Wrt. Voc. ii. 19, 28: 91, 1. Unc Dryhten scōp sīþ ætsomne, Exon. Th. 494, 3; Rä. 82, 2. God monna cræftas sceóp and scyrede ǽghwylcum on eorþan eormencynnes, 332, 34; Vy. 95. Ðā sceóp freá ælmihtig fāgum wyrme wīde sīþas, Cd. Th. 55, 32; Gen. 903: 110, 21; Gen. 1841. Hū him weorðe geond woruld wīdsīþ sceapen, Salm. Kmbl. 744; Sal. 371. Ðǽr eów is hām sceapen, Exon. Th. 142, 25; Cri. 649. Wæs sió wrōht scepen wið Hugas, Beo. Th. 5819; B. 2913. III a. *to destine, adjudge* a person (*acc.*) to anything:—Sceóp and scyrede Scyppend ūre oferhīdig cyn engla of heofnum *our Creator adjudged the presumptuous race of angels to banishment from heaven*, Cd. Th. 5, 1; Gen. 65. Ic eom wiht on gewin sceapen *I am a creature destined to strife*, Exon. Th. 400, 15; Rä. 21, 1: 405, 14: Rä. 24, 2. III b. *in the phrases* naman *or* tō naman scippan *to give a name*:—Him se pāpa Petrus tō noman scōp *cui papa Petri nomen imposuerat*, Bd. 5, 7; S. 620, 43. Scōp him Heort naman, Beo. Th. 157; B. 78. Se apostol sceóp ðære cyrcan naman 'resurrectio,' Homl. Th. ii. 474, 33. Rīce menn sceópon heora bearnum naman be him sylfum, i. 478, 9. Sceópan, Shrn. 47, 26. Gē fægniaþ ðæt gē mōton sceppan ðone naman, Bt. 16, 3; Fox 56, 24. [*Goth.* skapjan: *O. Sax.* skeppian: *O. Frs.* skeppa: *O. H. Ger.* scepfen, skeffen: *Icel.* skepja. Cf. also *O. H. Ger.* scaffan: *Icel.* skapa.] v. ā-, for-, ge-scippan, -sceppan.

Scippend, es; *m. The Creator*:—Ðū Scippend heofones and eorþan, Bt. 4; Fox 6, 30: Past. 7; Swt. 49, 17: Cd. Th. 234, 15; Dan. 292: Andr. Kmbl. 556; An. 278. Scieppend *Creator*, Rtl. 145, 24. Scæppend, 166, 29. Scæpend, 180, 8. Sceppend, Bt. 34, 10; Fox 150, 12: Cd. Th. 283, 24; Sat. 309. Sceoppend, Bt. 39, 13; Fox 234, 21: 14, 2; Fox 44, 27: 33, 4; Fox 132, 13. Scyppend, Hexam. 13; Norm. 22, 2: Cd. Th. 5, 2; Gen. 65. [*O. E. Homl.* sceppende, scuppend: *A. R.* schuppinde: *Orm.* shippennd.]

scip-rāp, es; *m. A cable*:—Sciprāpas *rudentes*, Wrt. Voc. i. 48, 24: 57, 1. Hiora (*walruses*) hȳd biþ swīðe gōd tō sciprāpum . . . Ðæt gafol biþ on ðǽm sciprāpum, ðe beóþ of hwæles hȳde geworht and of seoles . . . Se byrdesta sceall gyldan . . . twegen sciprāpas; ǽgðer sȳ syxtig elna lang, ōðer sȳ of hwæles hȳde geworht, ōðer of sioles, Ors. 1, 1; Swt. 18, 1–23.

scip-rēðra, an; *m. A sailor*:—Scyprēðra *nauita*, Germ. 389, 39. Hē on scyp eode, and myd hys scyprēðrum hys segl up āhōf, and forþ seglode, St. And. 38, 32.

scip-rōðer, es; *n. An oar* or *a rudder for a ship*:—Sciprōðor *navalia*, Wrt. Voc. ii. 61, 37.

scip-rōwend, es; *m. One who rows in a ship, a sailor, one of a crew*:—Sciprōwend *nauta*, Wrt. Voc. ii. 61, 33.

scip-ryne, es; *m. A course* or *channel for ships*:—Hē lēt delfon ān mycel gedelf and wolde ðæt scipryne sceolde ðǽrinne licgean eall swā hig dydon on Sandwīc *he had a great trench dug and intended that in it ships could run, just as they did at Sandwich*, Chart. Th. 341, 16.

scip-setl, es; *n. A seat* or *bench for rowers*:—Scipsetl *transtra*, Wrt. Voc. i. 48, 14: 64, 8.

scip-sōcn v. scip-fylleþ.

scip-steall, es; *m. A place for a ship*:—Andlang streámes on scypsteal, God. Dip. B. iii. 316, 16.

scip-steóra, -stȳra, an; *m. A steersman, pilot*:—Swīðe eáðe mæg on smyltre sǽ ungelǽred scipstiéra (-stióra, Cott. MSS.) genōh ryhte stiéran *quieto mari recte navem imperitus nauta dirigit*, Past. 9, 2; Swt. 59, 1. Swā swā gōd scipstȳra (-stioera, Cott. MS.) ongit micelne wind ǽr hit weorþe, Bt. 41, 3; Fox 250, 13. [*Icel.* skip-stjóri *a skipper.*]

scip-steorra, an; *m. The Pole-star*:—Twegen steorran standaþ stille . . . ðone norðran wē geseóþ; ðone hātaþ menn scipsteorra, Lchdm. iii. 270, 20.

scip-teora, -teara, -tara, -tera, an; *m.*: -ter, -teoro (u), -tearo; *gen.* -tearos; *n. Pitch*:—Scipter *bitumen*, Wrt. Voc. ii. 126, 36. Sciptearo, Lchdm. ii. 66, 8. Sciptearos læst, 126, 8. Sciptaran *bituminis*, Wrt. Voc. ii. 11, 77. Scipteran, 82, 40. Scipteran *bitumine*, 84, 41. Dō gôdne sciptaran tô, Lchdm. ii. 326, 14. Ðá hêt se câsere meltan on hwere leád and scipteoran and pic, Shm. 91, 7. Dô scipteаro tô, Lchdm. ii. 122, 17: 124, 10.

scip-toll, es; *m. Passage money:*—Sciptol *naulum* (cf. a schyppes tolle *hoc naulum*, 274, col. 2), Wrt. Voc. i. 56, 49. [*Icel.* skip-tollr.]

scip-wealh; *gen.* -weales; *m. A servant whose service is connected with ships:*—Ðæt land is sum inland, sum hit is ðân scipwealan tô gafole gesett (*the land in question lies by the Severn*), Cod. Dip. Kmbl. iii. 450, 19.

scip-weard, es; *m. One who has charge of a ship:*—Scipweardas, Andr. Kmbl. 596; An. 297.

scip-weorod, es; *n. The crew of a vessel:*—Scipweredes (-weardes?) *naucleri*, Wrt. Voc. ii. 59, 48.

scip-wîse, an; *f. The fashion* or *form of a ship:*—On scipwîsan geworht *made in the fashion of a ship*, Nar. 11, 20. Ðá nam heó ânne iiscenne windel on scipwîsan gesceapenne *sumpsit fiscellam scirpeam*, Ex. 2, 3.

scip-wyrhta, an; *m. A shipwright:*—Scipwyrhta *navicularius*, Wrt. Voc. i. 19, 13.

scîr, e; *f.* I. *office, charge, business, administration, government:*—Scîr *procuratio*, Wrt. Voc. i. 57, 36: 288, 58. Sciir, ii. 117, 71. Scîr *dispensatio*, 106, 51: 25, 55: 140, 65: *negotium*, 59, 65. Ðonne se môna biþ .xx. niht, and .i. and .xx. niht, ðæt biþ scîr oððe ceáp in ðem swefne tôweard, Lchdm. iii. 160, 8. Scîre *prefecturae*, Wrt. Voc. ii. 66, 2. Ne gewanige se reccere nâ ðone ymbhogan ðære inneran scîre for ðære âbisgunge ðære ûterran *sit rector internorum curam in exteriorum occupatione non minuens*, Past. 18, 1; Swt. 127, 13. Persa cyning benom ðone ealdormon his scîre, Ors. 3, 1; Swt. 96, 22. Scîre *negotio*, Ps. Surt. 90, 6. Hê wið ða scîre (*the office of bishop*) ne winne, Past. 10, 1; Swt. 61, 11. Hû dear se grîpan on ða scîre ðæt hê ǽrendige ôðrum monnum tô Gode *qua mente apud Deum intercessionis locum pro populo arripit?* 10, 2; Swt. 63, 7. Se ðe ðone sacerdhâd onfêhþ, hê onfêhþ friccan scîre *praeconis officium suscipit, quisquis ad sacerdotium accedit*, 15, 2; Swt. 91, 21: 45, 1; Swt. 337, 15. Âgyf ðîne scîre *give up thine office* (*of steward*), Lk. Skt. 16, 2. Paulinus ðære cyrican scîre (*curam*) onfêng, Bd. 2, 20; S. 522, 15. Hê forlêt ða scîre ðæs mynstres his brêðer *reliquit monasterii et animarum curam fratri suo*, 3, 19; S. 549, 39. For intingan ðære cynelîcra scýra *negotiorum regalium causa*, 3, 23; S. 551, 1. Him leófre wæs se cristendôm tô begânne ðonne his scîra tô habbanne *omnes officium quam fidem deserere maluerunt*, Ors. 6, 31; Swt. 286, 8. Ic ne oncneów scîre *non cognovi negotiationes*, Ps. Surt. 70, 15. **I a.** where the term refers to an English official:—Se ðe þeóf gefêhþ . . . and hê hine ðonne âlǽte . . . gif hê ealdormon sié, þolie his scîre, L. In. 36; Th. i. 124, 19. **II.** *a district, province*, as an ecclesiastical term *diocese, parish:*—Scîr *provincia*, Wrt. Voc. i. 54, 3. Sió scîr hâtte Hâlgoland ðe hê (*Ohthere*) on bûde, Ors. 1, 1; Swt. 19, 9. Hê âxode hû ðære þeóde nama wǽre ðe hî of cômon . . . Gyt ðâ Gregorius befrân hû ðære scîre nama wǽre ðe ða cnapan of âlǽdde wǽron, Homl. Th. ii. 120, 27-33. Scîre biscopas *vicari episcopi*, Rtl. 194, 33. Hî feórdon fram ðære scîre bisceope, and God him foresceáwode on sumere ôðre scîre on Francena rîce fulgôde wununge, Homl. Skt. i. 6, 122. On Alexandiscre scýre, 2, 29. Tô Cappadoniscre scýre, 3, 88. Ðâ gemunde se ealdorman (*Pilate*) ðæt Herodes wæs on ðære scîre, Homl. Th. ii. 250, 31. Ðæt mynster gesett on Angel-seaxna scîre and eác ôðer mynster on ðære ylcan scîre *monasterium situm in provintia Saxonia, atque aliud monasterium in eadem provintia*, Cod. Dip. B. i. 154, 25: Swt. A. S. Rdr. 100, 154. Scîre *parochiam*, Hpt. Gl. 427, 38. Liódbiscopas, in scîrum and londum gesettedo, Rtl. 194, 35. Scîre *provincias, regiones*, Hpt. Gl. 451, 17. Scîra *provincias*, 512, 12. Ðis wundor âsprang geond ða gehendan scîra, Homl. Th. i. 562, 20. **II a.** *the people of a district, a tribe:*—Hê is swýðe rihtwýs wer, ðæt wât eall ðeós scýr, Homl. Skt. i. 10, 120. Twâ scîra, ðæt ys, Iude and Benjamin, Ps. Th. 45, arg. Ðis sind ðe wǽron ða æðelestan ealdras geond ða scîra *hi nobilissimi principes multitudinis per tribus et cognationes suas*, Num. 1, 16. **III.** as a technical English term, *a shire:*—Hæbbe man scîrgemôt, and ðǽr beó on ðære scîre bisceop and se ealdorman, L. Edg. ii. 5; Th. i. 268, 4: ii. 3; Th. i. 266, 19. Ðære scîre bisceop *episcopus provinciae*, L. Ecg. P. iii. 11; Th. ii. 200, 4. Him man sealde gîslas of ǽlcere scîre, Chr. 1013; Erl. 148, 1. Gif man wille of boldgetale in ôðer boldgetæl hlâford sêcan, dô ðæt mid ðæs ealdormannes gewitnesse ðe hê ǽr in his scîre folgode, L. Alf. pol. 37; Th. i. 86, 4. Gif man spor gespirige of scýre in ôðre . . . drîfan hî ðæt spor ôþ hit man ðam gerêfan gecýðe, fô hê syððan tô and âdrîfe ðæt spor ût of his scîre, L. Ath. v. 8, 4; Th. i. 236, 20-23. Ðæt ǽlc gerêfa nâme ðæt wedd on his âgenre scîre, v. 10; Th. i. 240, 1. Ne nime nân man nâne nâme ne innan scîre ne ûtan scîre, L. C. S. 19; Th. i. 386, 12. Gif hwâ fare unâliéfed fram his hlâforde oððe on ôðre scîre hine bestele, L. In. 39; Th. i. 126, 10. Hêde se ðe scîre healde, L. R. S. 4; Th. i. 434, 33. **III a.** *The people of a shire, the community inhabiting a shire:*—Nân scîr nolde ôðre gelǽstan æt nýxtan *at last no shire would help another*, Chr. 1010; Erl. 144, 11. Ðâ sealde Leófwine ealdorman . . . and eal seó scîr his land clǽne, Chart. Th. 376, 14: L. C. S. 19; Th. i. 386, 15. Se ðe land gewerod hæbbe be scîre gewitnesse, 80; Th. i. 420, 20. Wæs se cyng ðâ ðiderweardes mid ðære scîre ðe mid him fierdedon, Chr. 894; Erl. 90, 32. Hî lifedon of Eást-Seaxum and of ðâm scîrum ðe ðǽr nýxt wǽron, 1002; Erl. 143, 5. **IV.** as an ecclesiastical term, the district in charge of an ecclesiastic (bishop, etc.), *a diocese, parish:*—Swâ biscop him tǽce ðe hit on his scýre sý, L. Edm. S. 4; Th. i. 250, 2. Gif man ǽnig lîc of rihtscîre lecge, L. Eth. vi. 21; Th. i. 320, 6. Gif preóst on unriht ût of scîre hâd begite, gilde .xii. ôr, and þolie his hâdes, bûton scîre biscop him hâdes geunne, L. N. P. L. 12; Th. ii. 292, 13. Ðises ys ealles wana .xxxiii. hîda of ðâm hîdun ðe ôðre bisceopas ǽr hæfdon intô hyra scýre, Cod. Dip. Kmbl. iii. 327, 12. Nǽnigum heora âlýfed sî ǽnige sacerdlîce þênunge dôn bûton ðæs bisceopes leáfe ðe hî on his scîre (*parochia*) gefeormade sîn, Bd. 4, 5; S. 573, 5. [*O. H. Ger.* scîra *procuratio, negotium.*] v. biscop-, burh-, gerêf-, hâm-, mæssepreóst-, mynster-, prâfost-, preóst-, riht-, scrift-, toll-, tûn-scîr; and see Stubbs' Const. Hist. i. 109 sqq.; Kemble's Saxons in England, bk. i. c. 3.

scîr; *adj. Clear, bright:*—Scîr *limpidus*, Wrt. Voc. i. 46, 54. Sciir *sublustris*, Txts. 96, 941. I. of living creatures, *bright, brilliant, splendid, resplendent:*—Scîr Metod (*God*), Beo. Th. 1962; B. 979. Scîr cyning (*Christ*), Exon. Th. 71, 9; Cri. 1153. Is seó womb (*of the phenix*) wundrum fæger, scîr and scýne, 219, 16; Ph. 308: 214, 4; Ph. 234. Ic eom âsceáden from ðære scîran driht (*the heavenly host*), Cd. Th. 275, 26; Sat. 177. Ðone scîran Scippend, Elen. Kmbl. 740; El. 370. **I a.** of a quality:—Gê ða scîran miht (*the power of Christ*) dêman ongunnon, Elen. Kmbl. 620; El. 310. **II.** of inanimate things, (a) of vegetation, *bright, brilliant, white:*—Ofer hine scîr cymeþ mînre segnunga sôðfæst blôstma *super ipsum florebit sanctificatio mea*, Ps. Th. 131, 19. Geseóþ ðâs eardas ðæt hig synt scîre (*albae*) tô rîpene, Jn. Skt. 4, 35. (b) of metals, stones, etc., *bright, lustrous, glittering, brilliant:*—Sceán scîr werod (*the band with glittering armour*), Cd. Th. 185, 19; Exod. 125. Hringîren scîr, Beo. Th. 650; B. 322. Scîran goldes, 3393; B. 1694. Hê gewyrceþ scîrne mêce, Exon. Th. 297, 8; Crä. 65. Hyrste beorhte, reáde and scîre, 392, 25; Rä. 12, 2. Scîre burstan mûras and stânas, 70, 22; Cri. 1142. Scîre helmas, Judth. Thw. 24, 17; Jud. 193. (c) of glass, *clear, transparent:*—Swâ ðæt scîre glæs ðæt mon ýþæst mæg eall þurhwlîtan, Exon. Th. 78, 33. (d) of water, *clear, limpid:*—Ofter Pantan, ofer scîr wæter, Byrht. Th. 134, 42; By. 98. Ða hlûtran and ða scîran wæter *liquidas lymphas*, Wrt. Voc. ii. 50, 10. [Þurh ân scýr wæter Brâdan ǽ hâtte, Chr. 656; Erl. 31, 16.] (e) of wine, *bright, clear, pure, neat:*—Wînes scîres *vini meri*, Ps. Surt. 74, 9. Syle drincan on scîrum wîne, Lchdm. i. 342, 23. Nalles scîr wîn hî ne druncan, Bt. 15; Fox 48, 9: Met. 8, 21. Scîr wered, Beo. Th. 996; B. 496. (f) of light and light-giving things, *bright, clear, brilliant:*—Heofontorht swegl (*the sun*) scîr, Exon. Th. 351, 2; Sch. 74: 486, 18; Rä. 72, 17. Sunne scîr and beorht, Met. 30, 9. Sió scîre scell (*the firmament*), 20, 174. Metod æfter sceáf scîrum scîman ǽfen ǽrest, Cd. Th. 9, 5; Gen. 137. Scîrne scîman, Rood Kmbl. 107; Kr. 54. Fleógan þurh scîrne dæg, Exon. Th. 439, 15: Rä. 59, 4. Þurh ða scîran neaht, Met. 20, 229. Blâce stôdon ofer sceótendum scîre leóman, Cd. Th. 184, 25; Exod. 112. On sumera ðonne ða hâtostan weder synd and ða scîran dagas hwîtan, Lchdm. iii. 252, 10. Scippend scîrra tungla, Met. 4, 1: 20, 8. Hwî hî (*stars*) ne scînen scîrum wederum, 28, 45. (g) of the world:—Þurh ða scîran gesceaft, Exon. Th. 286, 7; Jul. 728. (h) of a banner:—Fana hwearfode scîr on sceafte *the flag fluttered gleaming bright on its staff*, Met. 1, 11. (i) of the voice, *clear:*—Wit Scilling scîran reorde song âhôfan, Exon. Th. 324, 32; Vîd. 103. [Iss all þeȝȝre spell shir atter and shir galle, Orm. 15383. Clene off grediȝnesse and off galnesse skir and fre, 8015: *Prompt. Parv.* schyre, as water and oþer lycure *perspicuus, clarus.* Þe mihte of schir and of clene bone, A. R. 246, 26. Ðat skie scir, Gen. and Ex. 3848. *Goth.* skeirs *clear, evident: O. Sax.* skîr, skîri (wîn, watar): *O. L. Ger.* scîri: *O. Frs.* skîre: *M. H. Ger.* schîr: *Icel.* skírr *clear, bright, pure.*]

sciran *to cut.* v. sceran.

scîran *to discharge an office.* v. ge-scîran.

scîran; *p.* de. I. *to make clear* what is hidden or obscure, *declare, tell, make known:*—Drihten ðæt ongeat and geseah, ðæt se deófol ðone Iudas lǽrde, ðæt hê hine belǽwde. Ac ðæt hê ðeáhhwæðere geðyldelîce âbær and gemetfæstlîce scîrde (*did not declare it in terms of strong reprobation*), Homl. As. 154, 68. Gif hié eallunga forberan ne mǽgen ðæt hié hit ne scîren, ðonne sprecen hié ymbe his unþeáwas, Past. 28; Swt. 198, 9. Ðæt hit sceáden mǽl scýran môste, cwealmbealu cýðan, Beo. Th. 3883; B. 1939. [God ðe soðe shire, Gen. and Ex. 2036.] **II.** *to make clear* by distinguishing between things, *to distinguish, decide:*—Scîro *disceptavero*, Txts. 57, 688. Is gehâten ðæt hê wille cueðan, 'Gewîtaþ from mê âwiergde.' Ne scîrþ hê nô hwæðer hié reáfoden oððe hwelc ôðer yfel fremeden (*no distinction is made in the sentence between various kinds of evil*), Past. 44; Swt. 329, 7. Ðæt gê ne scîraþ *you do not bring out that* (*the difference between a man in his youth and in mature age*) *clearly*, Exon. Th. 132, 21; Gû. 476. Hê hêt wurpan ac hê ne scýrde on hwæðere healfe hî ðæt net wurpan sceoldon *he bade throw, but he did not decide on which side they were to throw the net*, Homl. Th. ii. 290, 9. III. *to bring a charge* against a person:—Scírde *actionabatur* [*or is the verb here connected with* scír *an office?* cf. gescíra *uilicare*, Lk. Skt. Lind. 16, 2, folcgeréfa *actionator*, Wrt. Voc. i. 17, 30], Wrt. Voc. ii. 99, 11: 3, 55. Ealdormenn swýðe sprǽcon and wið mē wráðum wordum scírdan *principes adversum me loquebantur*, Ps. Th. 118, 23. [Cf. Nes nan mon þat durste word sciren, Laym. 16822.] IV. *to get clear* of obligation, trouble, etc., *get exemption*:—Gif hwylc man ðone ándagan forgēmeleásige, æt forman cyrre .iii. messan, æt óðerum cyrre .v., æt þriddan cyrre ne scíre his nān man (*no man shall be exempt from the obligation*), būtun hit sié for mettrumnesse oððe for hlāfordes neóde, Chart. Th. 614, 18. Ðæm folce wæs ǽgðres waa ge ðæt hié ðæt mǽste yfel forberan sceoldon ge eác ðæt hié his scīran ne dorstan *there was trouble to the people on both accounts, that they had to bear a very great evil, and that they durst not get rid of it*, Ors. 3, 7; Swt. 114, 32. [*A. R.* schiren *to make pure*: *Goth.* ga-skeirjan *to interpret*: *Icel.* skíra *to purify, clear* from a charge; skýra *to explain, solve, decide.*]

scír-basu; *adj. Bright purple*:—Scírbasu *benetum* (venetus *caeruleus*, Ducange), Wrt. Voc. ii. 125, 30.

scír-biscop, es; *m. The bishop of a shire* or *diocese* (v. scír, III. 2):—Bēte ðæt, swā se scírbisceop and eal scírwitan dēman, Wulfst. 173, 30. [Ðe scýrbiscop *episcopus dioceseos*, Cod. Dip. Kmbl. v. 28, 32.]

scirdan; *p.* de *To hurt, injure*:—Hwilcan geþance mæg ǽnig man geþencan on his móde, ðæt hē tō sacerdan heáfod āhylde, . . . and hī hrædlīce siððan scyrde oððe scynde mid worde oððe weorce, L. Eth. vii. 27; Th. i. 334, 35. Ða ðe godcunde lāre and woruldcunde rihtlage wyrdan and scyrdan on ǽnige wīsan, Wulfst. 168, 9. [*Icel.* skerða *to diminish*: *O. H. Ger.* giscartit uuerd *dolet.*] v. sceard; *adj.*.

scirden; *adj. Of tiles* or *sherds*:—Scerden *testeum*, Germ. 400, 553. v. sceard *a sherd.*

scíre (?), an; *f. An enclosure, precinct*:—Portic *porticus*, scíre *peribolum*, heall *aula*, Wrt. Voc. i. 58, 3. [Cf. (?) Andlang scíre on hweðels heal, Cod. Dip. Kmbl. v. 358, 15.]

scíre; *adv.* I. of light, *clearly, brightly*:—Scíre scīnan, Exon. Th. 67, 15; Cri. 1089: Andr. Kmbl. 1671; An. 838: Salm. Kmbl. 679; Sal. 339. II. of the voice, *clearly*:—Saga hwætt ic hātte ða (ðe?) swā scíre nige (cíge?), sceáwendwīsan hlūde onhyrge, hæleþum bodige wilcumena fela wōþe mīnre, Exon. Th. 390, 29; Rä. 9, 9.

scír- (scir-?)ecg; *adj. Having a bright* (*cutting?* cf. sceran) *edge*:—Swurd scearp and scírecg, Lchdm. i. 390, 7. Cf. brūn-ecg.

scirfe-mūs. v. scyrfe-mūs.

scír-gemōt, es; *n. A shire-mote, a meeting of the duly qualified men of a shire*:—Hēr swutelaþ on þissum gewrite ðæt ān scírgemōt sæt æt Ægelnōþes stāne be Cnutes dæge cinges. Ðǽr sǽton Æðelstān biscop and Ranig ealdorman . . . and ðǽr wæs Bryning scírgerēfa . . . and ealle ða þegnas on Herefordscíre, Chart. Th. 336, 22. Gif hē æt ðam þriddan cyrre nān riht næbbe, ðonne fare hē feórþan síðe tō scírgemōte, L. C. S. 19; Th. i. 386, 14. Hǽbbe man tuwa on geáre scírgemōt, L. Edg. ii. 5; Th. i. 268, 3. Habbe man twā scírgemōt on geáre, L. C. S. 18; Th. i. 386, 5. See Stubbs' Const. Hist. s. v. shiremoot.

scír-gerēfa, an; *m. A shire-reeve, sheriff*, '*the judicial president of a shire.*' v. Stubbs' Const. Hist. i. 113; Kemble's Saxons in England, bk. ii. c. v. The word glosses *preses* in Wrt. Voc. i. 18, 11. (1) of a secular official, v. scír, III:—Ælfnōþ scírgerēfa, Chr. 1056; Erl. 190, 29. Ān scíregemōt sæt æt Ægelnōþes stāne . . . ðǽr wæs Bryning scírgerēfa, Cod. Dip. Kmbl. iv. 54, 14. On Æðelwines scíregerēfan gewitnesse, 10, 27. (2) of an ecclesiastic, v. scír, IV:—Ðonne sceall Cristes scírgerēfan (*the bishop*) ðæt witan, and ymbe ðæt dihtan and dēman, swā swā bēc tǽcan, L. I. P. 25; Th. ii. 340, 8.

scír-gesceatt, es; *n. The property of a see*:—Æðelrīc bisceop grēt freóndlīce Æðelmǽr: and ic cȳðe ðæt mē is wana æt ðam scȳrgesceatte ðus micelys ðe mīne foregengan hæfdon . . . Ðises ys ealles wana .xxxiii. hīda of ðām hīdun ðe ōðre bisceopas ǽr hæfdon intō hyra scȳre, Cod. Dip. Kmbl. iii. 327, 4.

scír-ham; *adj. Having bright armour*:—Scacan scírhame (*Beowulf and his followers*) tō scipe fōron, Beo. Th. 3794; B. 1895.

scirian; *p.* ede; *pp.* scired, scirred (v. ā-scirred) *To separate, divide* (v. scirung, ā-, tō-scirian), but used only metaphorically of setting apart something as a person's lot, *to ordain, assign, allot, dispense*:—Swā missenlīce meahtig Dryhten geond eorþan sceát eallum dǽleþ, scyreþ and scrīfeþ, Exon. Th. 331, 10; Vy. 66. God geond middangeard monna cræftas sceóp and scyrede, 332, 34; Vy. 95. Ðara gifena ðe him tō duguþe Drihten scyrede, Cd. Th. 221, 13; Dan. 87. Sceóp ðā and scyrede Scyppend ūre oferhīdig cyn engla of heofnum *then did our Creator adjudge and ordain the presumptuous race of angels to banishment from heaven*, Cd. Th. 5, 1; Gen. 65. Gif ðē Alwalda scirian wille ðæt ðū mōte *if the All-ruler be pleased to grant thee opportunity*, 171, 12; Gen. 2827. Sceolde him beón deáþ scyred *should death be the lot doomed him*, 31, 15; Gen. 485. Sié hira dǽl scired mid Marian *may their part be assigned with Mary*, Elen. Kmbl. 2462; El. 1232. Ðǽr womsceaþan on ðone wyrsan dǽl scyrede weorþaþ, hāteþ Scyppend him gewītan on ða winstran hond, Exon. Th. 75, 26; Cri. 1227. [*O. Sax.* skerian: *O. H. Ger.* scerian.] v. ā-, be-, ge-scerian, -scirian.

sciriendlíc; *adj. Derivative*:—Scyriendlīc *dirivativum, deductum*, Wrt. Voc. ii. 140, 44. v. ā-scirigendlīc.

scírig-mann, es; *m. Apparently the same as* scír-mann, q. v. The form occurs only in one (Kentish) charter, where 'Wulfsige preóst se scírigmann' is twice mentioned, Cod. Dip. Kmbl. vi. 127, 128. In a later Latin version of this charter the term is rendered *scírman* and explained by *judex comitatus, judex provinciae*, Chart. Th. 275, 276, and in this sense it is taken by Kemble, v. Saxons in England, ii. 168 sq. In another charter the same person is mentioned, but without the title: a grant of land is made by Ethelred to Winchester 'ofer Wulfsiges dæg preóstes,' Cod. Dip. Kmbl. vi. 135. This document is dated 996; somewhat later, in the time of Cnut, Wulfsige preóst is mentioned in connection with Kent, but then Æðelwine is scíregerēfa, Cod. Dip. Kmbl. iv. 10. In another charter (before 1011) Leófrīc is scíresman in Kent. For the form scírig-, cf. (?) hȳrig-mann.

scír-mǽled; *adj. Brightly marked, bright with inlaid ornaments*:—Scírmǽled swyrd, Judth. Thw. 24, 38; Jud. 230. v. māl-sweord.

scír-mann (scíre-, scíres-), es; *m.* I. *an official, officer, ruler, one who discharges the duties of a* scír (v. scír, I):—Scírman *procurator*, Wrt. Voc. i. 57, 37. Wæs scíremonn (Pontius Pilatus) *procurante Pontio Pilato*, Lk. Skt. Lind. 3, 1. Scíremon (sgiiremonn, Lind.) *dispensator*, Lk. Skt. Rush. 12, 42. Swā sceal gōd scȳrman (*a reeve* or *bailiff*) his hlāfordes healdan, dō ymbe his āgen swā swā hē wylle, Anglia ix. 260, 16. Ne ofermōdgiaþ ða scírmenn nā for ðȳ *nequaquam praepositi ex hoc superbiunt*, Past. 17, 2; Swt. 109, 18. Hwæt elles meahte beón getācnod þurh Ezechiel būton ða scírmenn *per Ezechielem praepositorum persona signatur*, 21, 3; Swt. 153, 24. II. an inhabitant of a district (v. scír, II):—Gregorius befrān, hū þære scíre nama wǽre, ðe ða cnapan of ālǽdde wǽron. Him man sǽde, ðæt ða scírmen wǽron Dere gehātene, Homl. Th. ii. 120, 33. III. as a technical English term = scír-gerēfa. v. Stubbs' Const. Hist. i. 113, Kemble's Saxons in England, ii. 158:—Æðelwine scírman (*in the next charter he is called* scíregerēfa, iv. 10, 27), Cod. Dip. Kmbl. iv. 9, 29. Ufegeat scíreman, 304, 17. Ðā com ðider se scȳresman Leófrīc, 266, 24: 267, 11. Gif hwā him ryhtes bidde beforan hwelcum scírmen oððe ōðrum dēman, L. In. 8; Th. i. 106, 21. v. scírig-mann.

scírness, e; *f. An explanation, declaration* (?):—Scírnis *ypoteseo bassio*, Wrt. Voc. i. 289, 73.

scirpan; *p.* te. I. *to sharpen, whet*:—Scyrpþ *acuit*, Engl. Stud. ix. 40. Hī hwetton (scyrptun, MS. C.) tungan heora *acuerunt linguam suam*, Ps. Spl. 139, 3. Scerptun, Ps. Surt. 139, 4. II. metaph. *to make active, arouse*:—Symle hē sceal his hȳrmen scyrpan mid manunge tō hlāfordes neóde and him eác leánian be ðam ðe hȳ earnian, Anglia ix. 260, 23. v. ā-, ge-scirpan.

scirpan; *p.* te; *pp.* ed *To clothe*:—Engel hine scirpeþ (scierpeþ) on cwicum wǽdum, Salm. Kmbl. 278; Sal. 138. v. ge-scerpan, sceorp.

-scirpla, scir-seax. v. ge-scirpla, scear-seax.

scír-þegen, es; *m. The thane of a shire*:—Ðises is tō gewitnesse . . . Godwine eorl . . . Ælfwine abbod . . . and ealle scírþegenas on Hāmtūnscíre, Cod. Dip. B. i. 544, 8.

scirung, e; *f. Separation, dismission, rejection*:—Gif hē swā biþ ðæt hē ne sȳ wyrðe ðære scyrunge (scirunge, MS. T.: ðæt hē wurðe ne beó, ðæt hē beó ðanon āscyred, Wells Frag.) *si non fuerit talis qui mereatur proici*, R. Ben. 109, 21.

scír-wered; *adj. Bright, clear*:—Wuldres scíma æðele ymb æðelne andlonge niht scān scírwered, Exon. Th. 179, 15; Gū. 1262. Cf. swegl-wered.

scír-wita, an; *m. A chief man* (wita, q.v.) *of a shire*:—Bēte ðæt, swā se scírbisceop and eal scírwitan dēman, Wulfst. 173, 30. Gebēte ðæt, swā scírewitan geceósan, 172, 4.

scítan, scȳtan (?) *to shoot* (of a plant), *flourish*:—Nǽfre on his weorþige weá āspringe mearce mā scȳte (sprȳte?) mān inwides *may ill never fail in his place, rather may guile flourish in his borders*; non defecit de plateis ejus usura et dolus, Ps. Th. 54, 10. [*Or does* scȳte *belong to* sceótan? cf. *for change of vowel in subjunctive* hlīpen, Past. Swt. 215, 7.]

scītan; *p.* scāt, *pl.* sciton; *pp.* sciten *Cacare.* [He sched out his bowels and his lyf wiþ þe dritt þat he schoote (shote) *effudit viscera et vitam cum ipsis stercoribus*, Trev. 5, 153. *Prompt. Parv.* schytyn *merdo, stercoro*: *O. H. Ger.* scīzan: *Icel.* skíta.] v. be-scītan.

scíte, scēte, scȳte, an; *f. A sheet, piece of linen cloth*:—Scēte, loða *sandalium*, Wrt. Voc. ii. 119, 55. Scȳte *sindo*, i. 25, 47: 81, 61: 284, 58. Wǽfelses ł scȳtan *sindonis*, Hpt. Gl. 494, 13. Mid scītan begird, Ap. Th. 12, 17. Heó hire feax gerǽdde and hī mid scȳtan besweóp *crines composuit, caput linteo cooperuit*, Bd. 3, 9; S. 534, 13. Sum iungling mid ānre scȳtan bewǽfed (*amictus sindone*), Mt. Skt. 14, 51, 52. Josep bewand ðone līchoman mid clǽnre scȳtan (scētan, Rush.), Mt. Kmbl. 27, 59: Nicod. 11; Thw. 6, 11: 13; Thw. 6, 31: Guthl.

20; Gdwin. 84, 8. Hí bewundon his líc mid línenre scýtan, Homl. Th. ii. 260, 35. Hé ðone andwlytan (*the face on S. Veronica's handkerchief*) genam, and hyne on pællenre scýtan befeóld, and eác heó wæs gewefen myd golde. And ða scýtan hé dyde ðá on án gylden fæt, St. And. 42, 11–15. Scétan *sindonem*, Kent. Gl. 1148. On scétum *in sabanis*, Wrt. Voc. ii. 48, 47. v. beód-, hop-, -scíte (-scýte).

-scíte -*cornered*. v. feówer-, feðer-, þrí-scíte (-scýte).

scitel, scytel *dung* (?) :—Nim heortes scytel and cnuca tó duste, Lchdm. i. 336, 18. Nim fearres scytel, cnuca and gníd swíðe smale, 368, 12. v. scítan.

Sciððeas, Sciððie, Sciððige, a; *pl. The Scythians* or (using the name of the people where now the name of the country would be used) *Scythia* :—Ða Sciððeas, Bt. 18, 2; Fox 64, 10. Uesoges wolde him tó geteón . . . ðone norþdǽl, ðæt sint Sciþþie; and hú ii ædelingas wurdon áfliémed of Sciððium, Ors. 1, 10, tit.; Swt. 1, 25. Hé wonn on Sciððie . . . His heres wæs seofon hund þúsenda, ðá hé on Sciððie fór. Huæðere ða Sciððie noldon hiene gesécan tó folcgefeohte, 2, 5; Swt. 78, 8–11. Eall Sciððia lond, 1, 1; Swt. 14, 22. Hé wæs mid firde farende on Sciððie on ða norþdǽlas, 1, 10; Swt. 44, 7: 2, 4; Swt. 76, 4. On Sciððie (Sciððige, Bos. 43, 42), Swt. 72, 24.

Sciððia, Sciððiu; *indecl.*: Sciððie, an; *f. Scythia* :—Gotan of Sciððiu mǽgþe, Bt. 1; Fox 1, 1. Of Sciððia, Met. 1, 2. Wurdon twegen ædelingas áfliémde of Sciððian, Ors. 1, 10; Swt. 44, 25. Ðæt lond mon hǽtt þa ealdan Sciððian, 1, 1; Swt. 14, 17. v. preceding word.

scitol; *adj. Purgative* :—Mettas ðe late melten and swá ðeáh ne synd scitole, Lchdm. ii. 178, 1.

scittan. v. scyttan.

scitte, an; *f. Looseness of the bowels, diarrhœa* :—Wið ðon ðe men mete untela melte and gecirre on yfele wǽtan and scittan, Lchdm. ii. 226, 6. [*Prompt. Parv.* skytte or flux *fluxus, lienteria, dissenteria, dyaria* : *Icel.* skita *diarrhœa*.]

Scittisc. v. Scyttisc.

scl-. v. sl-.

scó, scobl, scocca. v. scóh, scofl, scucca.

scocere? :—Innan scocera wege, Cod. Dip. Kmbl. v. 107, 9.

-scód. v. drýg-, ge-, un-scód; scógan.

scóere. v. scóhere.

scofettan; *p.* te *To drive* hither and thither :—For ðam hit is openlíce cúð ðætte sió úterre ábisgung ðissa woruldþinga ðæs monnes mód gedréfþ and hine scofett (scofeð, Cott. MSS.: cf. sciéð, *3rd pers. sing. of* sceótan, Swt. 70, 7) hidres ðædres óþ þæt hé áfielþ of his ágnum willan *cum indubitanter constet, quod cor externis occupationum tumultibus impulsum a semetipso corruat*, Past. 22, 1; Swt. 169, 13. Cf. scúfan.

scofl, e; *f. A shovel* :—Scofl *trulla*, Wrt. Voc. i. 289, 19: ii. 122, 67. Ísern scobl *vatilla*, 123, 12. Scofle, spadu *capella, tuba*, 128, 36. Scoble *palas*, 116, 13. Hé sceal habban spade, scofle, Anglia ix. 263, 6. [*Du.* schoffel; *f.* Cf. *O. H. Ger.* scúvala *pala, vanga* : *Ger.* schaufel.] v. fýr-, gléd-, meox-, steór-, wind-scofl.

scógan, scógean, sceógan, scóan (? v. scóung), sceón; *p.* scóde; *pp.* scód. sceód *To shoe, put on* (*one's*) *shoes, furnish with shoes* :—Ic scóge (sceóge) mé *calceo* vel *calcio*, Ælfc. Gr. 26, 6; Zup. 158, 8. Se engel cwæð: Begyrd ðé, and sceó (gisceó ðec, Rtl. 58, 11) ðé, and fylig mé, Homl. Th. ii. 382, 9. Sceógiaþ *calciate*, Engl. Stud. ix. 40. Sceógeaþ eówre fétt, Past. 5, 2; Swt. 44, 10. Cf. His mǽgas hine anscógen óðre fét ðæt mon mǽge siððan hátan his tún ðæs anscódan tún *unum ei pedem propinquus discalciet, ejusque habitaculum domum discalceati vocet*, Swt. 43, 16. Se biþ mid ryhte óðre fét anscód (on-, Cott. MSS.), and hine mon scyle on bismer hátan se anscóda (*discalceatus*), Swt. 45, 8. [Scheoinde ou & cloðinde *putting on your shoes and clothes*, A. R. 16, 4. Heo scoiden (soide hire stedes, 2nd MS.), Laym. 22291. Ræftres mid irene iscod, 7831. *O. H. Ger.* scuohón; *p.* scuohta : *Icel.* skóa, skúa *to shoe*.] v. -scígan, -scód.

scóh, scó, sceó: *gen.* scós, sceós; *n. pl.* scós, sceós; *gen.* sceóna; *dat.* scón, scóum; *the Ancren Riwle has the weak plural* scheon; *m. A shoe* :—Scóh *caliga*, Wrt. Voc. ii. 103, 11: 127, 67: 13, 43: *calcarium*, i. 291, 29. Scó *fico*, 26, 17. Rúh scó *pero*, ii. 78, 6. Tríwen sceó *coturnus*, i. 26, 21. Gif se innera dǽl ðæs sceós (scós, MS. B.) byþ fixen hýd, Lchdm. i. 342, 11. Þuong scóes (giscóes, Rush.) *corrigiam calciamenti*, Jn. Skt. Lind. 1, 27. Dó on ðínne winstran scó, Lchdm. i. 396, 3. Scóe *calciamentum*, Ps. Spl. T. 59, 9. Scós *gallicula*e, Wrt. Voc. ii. 41, 53. Wífes sceós *baxeae*, unhége sceós *talares*, i. 26, 20–23. Nǽron his scós forwerode, Homl. Th. i. 456, 21. Wíde sceós hangodan on hira (*the Saracens*) fótum, Shrn. 38, 8. His sceóna þwanga, Mk. Skt. 1, 7. Sceóea, Lk. Skt. Lind. 3, 16. Hí brohton swínes rysl his scón tó gedreóge, Homl. Th. ii. 144, 29. On ðínum sceón (scón, MS. B.), Lchdm. i. 330, 5. Scóum (scóeum, Lind.) *calciamentis*, Lk. Skt Rush. 22, 35. Sceówum, p. 4, 7. Ic wyrce sceós *facio ficones*, Coll. Monast. Th. 27, 33. N lt ðú habban yfele sceós, and wylt swá ðeáh habban yfel líf. Ic bidde ðé ðæt ðú lǽte ðé ðín líf deórre ðonne ðíne sceós, Homl. Th. ii. 410, 15–18. Habbaþ eówre scós on eówrum fótum, Anglia viii. 322, 19. Scóas (Lind. scóea), Mt. Kmbl. Rush. 10, 10. Scóeas, Lk. Skt. Lind. 15, 22. [*Goth.* skóhs: *O. Sax.* skóh: *O. Frs. O. L. Ger.* scó: *O. H. Ger.* scuoh: *Icel.* skór.] v. slífe-, slýpe-, steppe-scóh; hand-sció; ge-scý.

scóhere, scóere, es; *m. A shoemaker* :—Scoehere *sutrinator*, Txts. 115, 122. Scóere, 101, 1962. [*Icel.* skóari.]

scóh-nægel, es; *m. A shoe-nail* :—Scóhnegl *clavus caligaris*, Wrt. Voc. ii. 104, 15. Scóhnægl *clavus calicularis*, 131, 54.

scóh-þegn, es; *m. A servant who attends to shoes* :—Be sceóhþénum *de calciariis*, R. Ben. Interl. 91, 9.

scóh-þwang, es; *m. The thong* or *latchet of a shoe* :—Ic ne eom wyrðe ðæt ic hys sceóþwancg (shoþuong. O. E. Homl. ii. 137, 33. Shoþwang, Orm. 10387) uncnytte *non sum dignus soluere corrigiam calciamentorum ejus*, Lk. Skt. 3, 16. Sceóþwang, Jn. Skt. 1, 27. Gisceó ðec sceóhþongum ðínum *calcia te caligas tuas*, Rtl. 58, 11. [*Icel.* skóþvengr.]

scóh-wyrhta, an; *m. A shoemaker.* From the description of his work given by the sceówyrhta (*sutor*) in Ælfric's Colloquy, Thorpe, p. 27, he seems to have been a general worker-in leather. Besides boots and shoes he makes harness, leather bags and bottles :—Facio calceamenta diversi generis, subtalares et ficones, caligas et utres, frenos et phaleras et flascones et calidilia, calcaria et chamos, peras et marsupia. [*M. H. Ger.* schuoch-wurhte.] v. sútere.

scól. v. scolu.

scola *a debtor* :—Gescolan *condebitores*, Wrt. Voc. ii. 105, 23. [*Goth.* skula: *O. Sax.* skolo: *O. H. Ger.* scolo *debitor*.]

scola (scóla? v. scolu) *a learner* :—Gescola *condiscipulus, conscolaris*, Hpt. Gl. 459, 66.

scolere (scólere?), es; *m. A scholar, learner* :—Nim ðú lá geornfulla scoliere, Anglia viii. 304, 16. Seó rǽding pingþ ðæne scoliere, 308, 1. Ða scolieras witon ðe synt getýdde on bóclícum cræfte, 314, 9: 335, 42. Ðám scolierum ðás þing gecýðan, 303, 48. Ðæt ǽnig preóst ne underfó óðres scolere, L. Edg. C. 10; Th. ii. 246, 14. [*O. H. Ger.* scuolari *scholaris, discipulus*.] v. emn-sceólere.

scol-(scól-)mann, es; *m.* I. *one who attends a school, a scholar* :—Scól *scola*, scólman *scolasticus*, Wrt. Voc. i. 75, 27–28: 46, 62. II. *one who belongs to a band* (v. scolu, II), *a follower, client* :—Scolman *cliens*, 46, 62.

scolu, scól (*these two forms may give the later* shoal, school *as* col, cól *give* coal, cool), e; *f.* I. *a school* :—Scól *scola*, Wrt. Voc. i. 75, 27. Scól *scola*, se ðe on scóle (sceóle, MS. U.) ys *scolasticus*, Ælfc. Gr. 5; Zup. 11, 13–15. Ðý ilcan geáre forborn Ongolcynnes scolu, Chr. 816; Erl. 62, 7. Constantinus hiene benǽmde ðære scole ðe hé on leornode, Ors. 6, 31; Swt. 284, 24. His líc líþ on Angelcynnes scole, Chr. 874; Erl. 76, 26. Of scole *ex scole*, Wrt. Voc. ii. 31, 64: 95, 14. Hú ne eart ðú se mon ðe on mínre scole wǽre áféd and gelǽred, Bt. 3, 1; Fox 4, 19. Eubolus underféng ðone cnapan tó lárlícre scole . . . On ðære ylcan scole wæs Iulianus, Homl. Skt. i. 3, 14–16. Ic becom tó Cristes scole, 2, 244. Maria wunode on ealra ðæra apostola gýmene on ðære heofonlícan scole embe Godes ǽ smeágende, Homl. Th. i. 440, 8. Sum leorningman on scole *scholasticus quidam*, Bd. 3, 13; S. 538, 18. Ic (*Ethelwulf*) on Róme Englisce scole gesette, Chart. Th. 116, 33. Se (*Marinus*) gefreóde Ongelcynnes scole be Ælfrédes béne West-Seaxna cyninges, Chr. 885; Erl. 84, 19. Cildru on scole betǽcan, Lchdm. iii. 184, 27: 188, 18. II. *a band* or *troop of people, a shoal, school* (in *school* of fishes) :—Him on healfa gehwone heofonengla þreát ymbútan faraþ, ælbeorhtra scolu, Exon. Th. 58, 2; Cri. 929. Synfulra here, womfulra scolu, 94, 5; Cri. 1535: 98, 15; Cri. 1608: 114, 19; Gú. 175. Seó deóre scolu *the heavenly host*, 235, 21; Ph. 235. Árleásra sceolu, Elen. Kmbl. 2600; El. 1301: 1523; El. 763. Éce fýr wæs Satane and his gesíðum mid, deófle, gegearwad, and ðære deorcan scole, Exon. Th. 93, 9; Cri. 1523. Ðæt gesǽlige weorud gesihþ ðæt fordóne, . . . byrnendra scole, 77, 6; Cri. 1252. Hé gesomnode miccle scole and wereð his geþoftena, Guthl. 2; Gdwin. 14, 2. Ðá weard stearc storma gelác . . . út feor ádráf on Wendelsǽ wígendra scola, Met. 26, 31. [*O. Sax.* skola *a band, troop* : *O. H. Ger.* scuola *schola* : *Icel.* skóli *a school*. From Latin.] v. geneát-, hand-, þegn-, þeóf-scolu.

scom-. v. sceam-.

scóm-hylt, e; *f. A shady wood, thicket, shrubbery* :—Scoomhylti *frutices*, Wrt. Voc. ii. 39, 60. [Cf. (?) *Icel.* skúmi *shade, dusk*.] Cf. holt.

scon-. v. scean-.

Scón-ég *Skaane, a district forming the southernmost part of the Scandinavian peninsula, formerly belonging to Denmark, but since* 1658 *to Sweden: the Icelandic form is* Skáney. The name occurs in Ors. 1, 1; Swt. 19, 35.

scop, sceop, es; *m. A poet* :—Scop *liricus*, unwurð scop *tragicus* vel *comicus*, Wrt. Voc. i. 60, 5, 9. Scop *comicus*, 291, 25: ii. 17, 38. *Comicus, s. est qui comedia scribit, cantator, vel artifex canticorum seculorum, idem satyricus, i.* scop, *joculator, poeta*, 132, 16. Se hǽðena scop *Pompeius historicus*, Ors. 1, 5; Swt. 32, 28. Terrentius se mǽra

Cartaina scop *Terentius comicus*, 4, 10; Swt. 202, 26. Gerîseþ gôd scop gumum, Exon. Th. 341, 18; Gn. Ex. 128. Scop hwîlum sang hâdor on Heorote, Beo. Th. 997; B. 496. Hrôðgares scop, 2137; B. 1066: Exon. Th. 379, 21; Deór. 36. Sceop oððe leóðwyrhta *poeta*, Wrt. Voc. i. 73, 68. Ðes sceop *hic poeta*, ðises sceopes *huius poetae*, Ælfc. Gr. 7; Zup. 24, 6: 36; Zup. 215, 8. Wîtega oððe sceop *vates*, 10; Zup. 77, 3. Be ðam wæs singende sum sceop *unde tragicus exclamat*, Bt. 30, 1; Fox 106, 31. Swâ Parmenides se sceop geddode, 35, 5; Fox 166, 8. Omerus se gôda sceop on his leóþum swîðe herede ðære sunnan gecynd, 41, 1; Fox 244, 4. Ðǽr wæs hearpan swêg, swutol sang scopes, Beo. Th. 180; B. 90. Omerus wæs ðæm mǽran sceope (*Virgil*) magistra betst, Met. 30, 4. Gecuron him ânne scop tô cyninge . . . se heora cyning ongan singan and giddian, Ors. 1, 14; Swt. 56, 29. Unweorþe scopas *tragedi* vel *comedi*, Wrt. Voc. i. 39, 39. Scopas *lyrici*, ii. 54, 9: *vates*, Hymn. Surt. 119, 18. Fram ðisum sceopum ic gehýrde leóþ, Ælfc. Gr. 7; Zup. 24, 2. [Scopes þer sungen, Laym. 30615. *O. H. Ger.* scof *poeta, vates.* Cf. (?) *Icel.* skop *railing, mocking.*] v. ǽfen-, ealu-, sealm-scop.

-scop, -sceop. v. wîd-scop.

scop-cræft, es; *m. The poet's art, poetry*:—Sceop *poeta*, ic leornige sceopcræft (scop-) *poetor*, Ælfc. Gr. 36; Zup. 215, 9.

scop-gereord, es; *n. Poetic diction, the language of poetry*:—Swâ hwæt swâ hê of godcundum stafum þurh bôceras geleornode, ðæt hê in sceopgereorde (*verbis poeticis*) geglencde, Bd. 4, 24; S. 594, 34.

scop-leóþ, es; *n. A poem*:—Se heora cyning ongan singan and giddian and mid ðæm scopleóþe heora môd swîðe getrymede *Tyrtaei ducis composito carmine et pro concione recitato accensi*, Ors. 1, 14; Swt. 56, 32. Hê (*Nero*) ongon wyrcan scopleóþ be ðæm bryne *Iliadem decantabat*, 6, 5; Swt. 262, 1. Swâ hit an scopleóþum sungen is *quod poeta descripsit*, 2, 4; Swt. 72, 20. [*O. H. Ger.* scof-leod.]

scop-lîc; *adj. Poetic*:—Mid meterlîcum fôtum ł scoplîcum *pedibus poeticis*, Hpt. Gl. 411, 4. [*O. H. Ger.* scof-lîh *poeticus*: cf. *O. L. Ger.* scop-lîco *poetice.*]

scoppa, an; *m. A shop, a booth* or *shed* for trade or work (cf. work-*shop*):—Hê geseh ða welegan hyra lâc sendan on ðone sceoppan (*in gazophilacium*), Lk. Skt. 21, 1. [The bowiares ssope hii breke, & the bowes nome echon, R. Glouc. 541, 16. Euerych soutere þ[t] halt shoppe, English Gilds, 358, 22. Marchantz beshetten hym in here shope, Piers P. 2, 213. Schoppe *opella, propala*, Prompt. Parv. A shoppe or a werkehous *operarium*, Wülck. Gl. 599, 10. A schope *opella*, a hordhows *gazafilacium*, 730, 3–6. A schoppe *opella*, a treserhouse *gazafilacium*, 804, 28, 29. Cf. *O. H. Ger.* schof *a building without walls*; also *a vestibule*: *Ger.* schuppen *a shed.*] v. scypen.

scora, an; *m. A hairy garment*:—Bânrift *tibialis*, scora *tricilo*, Wrt. Voc. i. 289, 16.

scorf, sceorf, scurf, scruf, es? *m.* (?) *Scurf*:—Hyt âfeormaþ ðone leahtor ðe Grêcas hostopyturas hâtaþ, ðæt ys scurf ðæs heáfdes, Lchdm. i. 322, 16. Wið scurfe and nebcorne, 68, 10. Wið heáfodsâr, ðæt ys wið scurf, 116, 23. Wið scruf (scurf, MSS. H. B.) and wið sceb, 316, 22. Wið scurfum, 356, 23. Swâ mycel hreófla and sceorfa on his heáfde hæfde ðæt him nǽfre nǽnig feax on ðam uferan dǽle ðæs heáfdes âcenned beón mihte *scabiem tantam ac furfures habebat in capite, ut nil unquam capillorum ei in superiore parte capitis nasci valeret*, Bd. 5, 2; S. 614, 44. [Scrofe or scalle *glabra*, Wrt. Voc. 179, 9, Scurf of scabbys *squama*, scurfe of metel *scorium*, Prompt. Parv. 451. *O. H. Ger.* scorf *scabies*: *Ger.* schorf; *m.*: *Icel.* skurfur; *f. pl.*]

scorfed, sceorfed, scurfed; *adj. Rough, scabbed*:—Wið scurfedum nægle (*unguium scabritiem*); nim gecyrnadne sticcan, sete on ðone nægl wið ða wearta, Lchdm. ii. 150, 4. [Þé ssoruede (*leprous*), þe scallede, Ayenb. 224, 6.] v. next word.

scorfende, sceorfende, scurfende; *part. Getting rough* or *scabby*:—Wið scurfendum næglum *ad scabiem unguium*, Lchdm. i. 370, 9. v. preceding word.

scorian; *p.* ode *To refuse, reject* an offer, *repudiate*:—Ða ðe ne gelýfaþ þurh âgenne cyre hî scoriaþ nâ þurh gewyrd *those who do not believe refuse by their own choice, not by fate*, Homl. Th. i. 114, 12. Ðâ sceorede ðâ gyt se yldesta hǽðengylda mid mycelre þwyrnysse *the chief idolater still refused* (*Christianity*) *with much perversity*, 72, 9. [Cf. *O. L. Ger.* scurgan *avertere, expellere*: *O. H. Ger.* scurgan *trudere, impellere, propellere*; fer-scurgan *repellere.*] v. wið-scorian *and next word.*

scorian; *p.* ode *To project, jut*:—Ða stânas swâ of ôðrum clife ût sceoredon, Blickl. Homl. 207, 20. [Cf. *O. H. Ger.* scorrên *prodire*, fram-, furi-scorrên *pro-, e-minere*, Grff. vi. 539.] v. preceding word.

scort; *adj. Short.* I. marking the length of an object:—Scort sinewealt stân *cilindrus*, Wrt. Voc. i. 41, 35. Sceort bed wið eorþan *cama*, 41, 31. Sceort scip *naviscella*, 47, 60: 56, 33. Ðæt ic ðê môste getǽcan swâ sceortne (scortne, Cott. MS.) weg swâ ic scyrtestne findan meahte, Bt. 40, 5; Fox 240, 17. Hê hæfþ scyrtran (sceortran, MS. R.) sceade ðonne seó sunne, Lchdm. iii. 252, 13. On lxv and þreó hundræd scy[r]tran and lengran ða ǽdron beóþ tôdǽlede, 146, 6. II. marking height, *not tall*:—Hê (*Zacchaeus*) wæs scort on wæstme, Homl. Th. i. 580, 30. III. of time, (1) of a period of time:—Tô scortre hwîle *for a short time*, Past. 36, 6; Swt. 255, 11. Ðæt wê sceolan on ðisse sceortan tîde gearnian êce ræste, Blickl. Homl. 83, 2. Ðû ðâm winterdagum selest scorte tîda, Bt. 4; Fox 8, 4. Sceorta, Met. 4, 20. Nis nǽnig mon ðe wite hwæðer ðis þûsend sceole beón scyrtre ðe lengre, Blickl. Homl. 119, 6. Dagas ne synd nâðor ne længran ne scyrtran ðonne hî æt fruman wǽran, Lchdm iii. 252, 19. Se mônaþ (*February*) is ealra scyrtost (scyrtst, MSS. P. M.: scirtst, MS. L.), 264, 8. Scyrtest, Anglia viii. 306, 8. (2) marking duration, (a) *short-lived, brief*:—Ðeáh se hlîsa ðara foremǽrena monna hwîlum lang sié, hê biþ ðeáh swîðe scort tô metanne wið ðone ðe nǽfre ne geendaþ, Bt. 18, 3; Fox 66, 18. Hû ne biþ simle ðæt lange yfel wyrse ðonne ðæt scorte, 38, 2; Fox 198, 12. Ðæt wuldor ðysses middangeardes is sceort and gewîtende, Blickl. Homl. 65, 15. (b) *not occupying much time*:—Hwâ ne wundraþ ðætte sume tunglu habbaþ scyrtran hwyrft (*an orbit that requires less time to complete*) ðonne sume habban, Bt. 39, 3; Fox 214, 18. Wê hit sæcgaþ eów on ða scortostan wîsan *we will tell it you in the briefest fashion*, Homl. Skt. i. 4, 140. (c) as a grammatical term:—Seó forme geendung is on scortne *a*, Ælfc. Gr. 9, 1; Zup. 32, 17. Mid fîffêtedum ł scertrum *brachycatalectico*, Hpt. Gl. 409, 27. [*O. H. Ger.* scurz. Cf. *Icel.* skortr *want.*] v. next word.

scortian; *p.* ode. I. *to get short, shorten* (intrans.):—Se dæg ðonne sceortaþ, Lchdm. iii. 250, 23. Se sceortigenda (scort-, MS. L.) dæg . . . se langienda dæg, 252, 8. II. *to make short* (? cf. þenne cumeð þe deofel and him scorteð his daȝes, O. E. Homl. i. 25, 14. To schorte oure weie, Chauc. Prol. 791). III. *to run short, fail*:—Ðætte ne scortige (sceortiga, Lind.) gileófa ðîn *ut non deficiat fides tua*, Lk. Skt. Rush. 22, 32. [Cf. *Icel.* skorta *to run short.*] v. a-, ge-, on-sceortian; scyrtan.

scortlîc; *adj. Short*, of time, *not lasting*:—Sceortlîc ł hwîlendlîc *momentaneum*, Scint. 214, 16.

scortlîce; *adv.* I. of time, *shortly, before long, soon*:—Nû gyt scortlîce ł lytel fæc and ne byþ se synfulla *adhuc pusillum et non erit peccator*, Ps. Lamb. 36, 10. Scortlîcor *maturius, citius, velocius*, Hpt. Gl. 527, 14. II. of speech, narrative, etc., *shortly, briefly, compendiously*:—Scortlîce *strictim, breviter*, 492, 27. Scortlîce (*breviter*) ic hæbbe nû gesǽd ymbe ða þrié dǽlas, Ors. 1, 1; Swt. 10, 3: 1, 14; Swt. 58, 7: Ælfc. Gr. 10; Zup. 76, 3. Nû wylle wê sum þing scortlîce eów be him gereccan, Homl. Th. ii. 118, 3. Sceortlîce *summatim, breviter*, vel *commatice*, Wrt. Voc. i. 55, 15: *strictim*, ii. 82, 74. Nû is ôðer cwyde be gôdum mannum sceortlîce gecweden, Homl. Th. i. 484, 20. Wê willaþ furðor swîðor sprecan, and wê secgaþ nû sceortlîce, Lchdm. iii. 240, 2.

scortness, e; *f.* I. *shortness* (of time):—Ðonne byrneþ on scortnisse gramen hys *cum exarsent in brevi ira ejus*, Ps. Spl. 2, 13. Ða scortnesse ðysse woruldе and ða êcnesse ðæs tôweardan lîfes, Homl. As. 168, 117. II. *a short account, an epitome* (cf. a brief, *and* v. scortlîce, II):—Manega synd gyt *coniunctiones*, ðe wê ne mâgon nû secgan on ðissere sceortnysse, Ælfc. Gr. 44; Zup. 266, 8. Wê habbaþ gesǽd on ðisre sceortnysse, hû God geswutelode ða sôðfæstan godspelleras, Homl. Skt. i. 15, 219.

scort-wyrplîc; *adj. Of early fulfilment, coming to pass shortly*:—On .xv. nihta sceortwyrplîc ðæt bid. On .xvi. nihta æfter langre tîde hit âgǽþ *a dream on the fifteenth night of the month will be of early fulfilment. On the sixteenth it will come to pass after a long time*, Lchdm. iii. 156, 2.

scot, es; *n.* I. *a shot, a shooting*:—Hié his siððan wǽran swîðe êhtende ge mid scotum (gesceotum, MS. C.) ge mid stâna torfungum ge mid eallum heora wîgcræftum, Ors. 3, 9; Swt. 134, 15. [II. *a shot, missile.* v. ge-sceot, *and* cf. No man . . . No maner schot, ne pollax, ne schort knyf Into the listes sende, Ch. K. T. 1686. See also the cognate words.] III. *a rapid movement* (v. sceótan, IV, III, ge-sceót (*read* -sceot), II), *a rush, dart*:—Leax sceal on wǽle mid sceóte scrîðan, Menol. Fox 539; Gn. C. 40. IV. *a scot* (as in *scot* and lot, *scot*-free), *a shot* (as in to pay one's *shot*), *a contribution, tax.* v. sâwel-scot, sceótan, VII. V. *a building.* v. sele-scot, ge-sceot, III. [*O. Frs.* scot *a missile; a contribution, tribute*: *O. H. Ger.* scoz; *n. telum, jaculum*: *M. H. Ger.* schoz; *m. tribute, tax*: *Icel.* skot; *n. a shot, shooting; a missile; a contribution.*] v. ge-sceot (-scot); scyte.

scota, an; *m. One who shoots* or *hurls, a soldier*:—Gescota *commanipularius*, Wrt. Voc. ii. 104, 82: 132, 49. [*Icel.* and-skoti *an adversary.*] Cf. scytta.

scotere (?) *one who shoots* or *hurls, a warrior*:—Nô hê ðære feohgyfte for scoterum (? scotenum, MS.) scamigan þorfte, Beo. Th. 2056; B. 1026.

scot-freó; *adj. Scot-free, exempt from imposts*:—Scotfrê and gafolfrê, Cod. Dip. Kmbl. iv. 215, 32: 191, 18.

scotian, sceotian; *p.* ode. I. (1) *to shoot* a person with a weapon:—Hwâ sceotaþ ðæt deófol mid weallendum strǽlum? Se Pater Noster sceotaþ ðæt deófol, Salm. Kmbl. p. 148, 1–3. Hî scotiaþ hine *sagittabunt eum*, Ps. Lamb. 63, 6. Wē mid strǣlum hié scotodon, Nar. 22, 18. Ðæt hȳ scotien rihtheortan, Ps. Spl. 10, 2. Hī unscyldige mid bogan scotian þenceaþ *ut sagittent immaculatum*, Ps. Th. 63, 3. Ðū scealt mid hālgum Godes wordum ðīnne feónd sceotian, Basil admn. 2; Norm. 36, 7. Hȳ wǣron mid strǣlum scotode, Shrn. 135, 29. (2) *to shoot* a weapon at a person, *to hurl*:—Ðæt yrre hys spere scotaþ ongeán ðæt geþyld *ira lanceam suam iacit contra patientiam*, Gl. Prud. 20 a. Drihten līgetas sceotaþ *Dominus jaculatur fulgura*, Bd. 4, 3; S. 569, 22. Hē sceotaþ his flān and his scearpe spere ongeán his wiðerwinnan, Basil admn. 2; Norm. 36, 5. Of heofene dōm scotad is, Ps. Surt. 75, 9. (3) *to shoot* (intrans.):—Hī hine scearpum strēlum on scotiaþ, Ps. Th. 63, 4. Gif ðē man scotaþ tō, Homl. Th. ii. 538, 10. Scotiaþ scrīðende scīn scearpum wǣpnum, Exon. Th. 385, 28; Rä. 4, 51. Mid ðām strǣlum ðæs hālgan sealmsanges hē wið ðām āwerigedum gāstum sceotode, Guthl. 3; Gdwin. 24, 12. Sume scotedon mid arewan tōweard ðam hāligdōme. . . . Hī scotedon swīðe, Chr. 1083; Erl. 217, 19–25. **II.** *to shoot, move rapidly*:—Steorran fōran swȳðe scotienda [cf. *O. H. Ger.* diu scozonten fiur (*a shooting star*)], 744; Erl. 49, 2. [*Laym.* scotien (mid flan).] v. of-scotian.

Scot-land, es; *n.* **I.** *Ireland*, where the Scottas lived before migrating to the country now called Scotland:—On westende (*of Europe*) is Scotland, Ors. 1, 1; Swt. 8, 27. Ān diácon wearð forþfēred on Sceotlande (cf. an Scotta eálonde, 215, 21), and ðæs diácones nama wæs Njál hāten, Wulfst. 205, 16. Hī cōmon on Scotland (*Hiberniam*) upp, Bd. 1, 1; S. 474, 10. **II.** *Scotland*:—Hēr fōr Æþelstān cyning on Scotland (tō Scotlande *in Scotiam*, MS. F.), Chr. 934; Erl. 111, 9. Hē (*Cnut*) fōr tō Scotlande, and Scotta cyng him tō beáh, Mælcolm, 1031; Erl. 163, 20. Hē (*Furseus*) fērde geond eal Ȳrrland and Scotland, Homl. Th. ii. 346, 29. v. Scottas.

scot-lira, an; *m. The fleshy part of the leg, the calf of the leg*:—Scotliran *suras*, Lchdm. i. lxxiv, 19. Cf. spear-lira.

scot-spere, es; *n. A spear for hurling, a javelin*:—Scotsper[a], gāra *jaculorum*, Hpt. Gl. 405, 52.

Scottas; *pl. The Scots*, a race found first in Ireland, whence a part migrated to North Britain, which from them got the name Scotland. (1) *Scots of Ireland*:—Þrié Scottas cuōmon tō Ælfrēde cyninge on ānum bāte būtan ǣlcum gerēþrum of Hibernia, Chr. 891; Erl. 88, 5. Ðā forþgongenre tīde æfter Bryttum and Peohtum þridde cynn Scotta Breotone onfēng . . . Ða wǣron cumene of Hibernia Scotta ealonde . . . Hibernia is āgendlīce Scotta ēþel, heonan cōman seó þeód Scotta, Bd. 1, 1; S. 474, 24–42. Com of Hibernia Scotta eálande Fursius . . . Wæs Furseus of ðam æþelestan cynne Scotta, 3, 19; S. 547, 2–25. In Hibernia mǣgþe, ðæt is on Scotta lande, Shrn. 51, 30. On Sceotta land, Wulfst. 205, 7. Scotta land, eálond, 215, 17, 21. Gif næddre sleá man, ðone blacan snegl āwæsc on hāligwætre, sele drincan oððe hwæthwega ðæs ðe fram Scottum cōme *a little water that has come from Ireland* (because of its peculiar efficacy (?). Cf. Bede's statement of the cures worked on those who were bitten by snakes through the application of water in which scrapings from the leaves of Irish books were put, Bd. 1, 1; S. 474, 36–39), Lchdm. ii. 110, 15. (2) *Scots of Scotland*:—Eádrēd gerād eal Norþhymbra land him tō gewealde, and Scottas him āþas sealdan, Chr. 946; Erl. 118, 1. Hine gecēs tō hlāforde Scotta cyning and eall Scotta þeód, 924; Erl. 110, 14. Crungun Sceotta leóda, 937; Erl. 112, 11, 32. Fērde bodiende betwux Ȳrum and Scottum and siððan ofer eal Angelcynn, Homl. Th. ii. 346, 35. Mid Scottum ic wæs and mid Peohtum (*or under* (1) Cf. Scotta cynn Breotone onfēng on Pehta dǣle, Bd. 1, 1; S. 474, 24), Exon. Th. 323, 15; Vīd. 79.

scottettan (?) *to move about quickly* (? cf. sceotan, III, IV; scotian, II). *to dance, leap*:—Sceottet (or = (?) sceóteþ: t *for* þ *occurs in verb inflexions in the same glossary*, e.g. geþwǣrat, 397, 439) *saltat*, Germ. 394, 222.

scotung, e; *f.* **I.** *shooting*:—Wunda ðe ða wælhreówan hǣðenan mid gelōmre scotunge on his līce macodon, Th. An. 123, 33. **II.** *what is shot, a missile*:—Hī synt scotunga oððe flāna *ipsi sunt jacula*, Ps. Lamb. 54, 22. Sceotunga, Ps. Spl. C. 54, 24. Scotunge ðīne *jacula tua*, Ps. Surt. ii. p. 190, 15. Hē wæs biset mid heora scotungum swylce ȳles byrsta, Th. An. 122, 17. Wið ðām scotungum ðara werigra gāsta hē hine mid gāstlīcum wǣpnum gescylde, Guthl. 3; Gdwin. 24, 5. For ðæs fȳres sceotungum *on account of the flashes of lightning*, Lchdm. iii. 280, 15. v. scotian.

scōung, e; *f. A provision of shoes*:—Hīs mete and scōung and glōfung him gebyreþ *he is to have his food and shoes and gloves provided for him*, L. R. S. 10; Th. i. 438, 6.

scrād, *a moving body* (? v. scrīðan), *a vessel* (?), *a body of travellers* (? cf. *Icel.* skreið *a shoal, flock*):—Scrifen scrād glād þurh gescād in brād, wæs on lagustreáme lād, Exon. Th. 353, 15; Reim. 13.

scrādung. v. screádung.

scræf, es; *m. Some kind of bird, a cormorant* (?):—Scraeb *merga*, Wrt. Voc. ii. 114, 6. Screb *ibinem* (ἶβιν, cf. ibin avis in Affrica habens longum rostrum, 4), Shrn. 29, 19. [Cf. (?) *Icel.* skarfr *the green cormorant.*]

scræf, screaf, scref, es; *n.* **I.** *a cave, cavern, hollow place in the earth*:—Scræf *spelunca*, Wrt. Voc. i. 38, 21. Ðǣr (*hell*) biþ fȳr and wyrm, open ēce scræf, Cd. Th. 212, 10; Exod. 537. Cirice on scræfes onlīcnesse, Blickl. Homl. 197, 18. Hē fērde tō ðam munte and on ānum scræfe (*in spelunca*) wunode, Gen. 19, 30: 23, 11. Hē hēt wilian tō ðam scræfe (*ad os speluncae*) micele weorcstānas, Jos. 10, 18. Scræfe *crypta*, Wrt. Voc. ii. 24, 59. Scrafe *antro*, Hpt. Gl. 483, 76. Tō ānum micclum screafe under ānre dūne, Homl. Th. ii. 424, 21. Tō screfe ɫ scrife *ad cloacum*, Hpt. Gl. 515, 72. Hī ne mihton ofer ðæt scræf, Blickl. Homl. 201, 16. Cwōman wyrmas of ðǣm neáhdūnum and scrafum *ex vicinis montium speluncis*, Nar. 14, 6. On wēstenum and on scræfum, Bd. 1, 8; S. 479, 21. Scræfu *speluncas, concavas petras*, Wrt. Voc. ii. 129, 66. Screafu *cavernas*, 21, 64. **II.** *a miserable dwelling, a den*:—Neara scræf *gurgustulum* vel *gurgustium*, i. 58, 29. Nihthrefne gelīc ðe on scræfe eardaþ *sicut nycticorax in domicilio*, Ps. Th. 101, 5. Gē mīn hūs habbaþ gedōn sceaðum tō screafe (cf. gē worhtun ðæt tō þeófa cote, Mt. Kmbl. 21, 13), Homl. Th. i. 406, 3. Se hæfde on byrgenum scræf (*domicilium*), Mk. Skt. 5, 3. Geond ðæt atole scræf (*hell*), Cd. Th. 272, 33; Sat. 129: 290, 22; Sat. 419. Scref, 266, 23; Sat. 26: 269, 15; Sat. 73. Gē mīn hūs dōþ sceaþum tō scrafum, Blickl. Homl. 71, 20. Ðē is leófre on ðisum wācum scræfum ðonne ðū on healle heālic biscop sitte (cf. ðā wolde se hālga sum hūs timbrian, 144, 31), Homl. Th. ii. 146, 28. On wāclīcum screafum oððe hulcum lutigende, i. 544, 30. v. dūn-, eorþ-, wīte-, wrāþ-scræf.

scrætte, an; *f. An adulteress, a harlot*:—Scrættena *moecharum, meretricum*, Hpt. Gl. 507, 2. Scrættena (scræftena, MS.) *scortarum*, 524, 1. In fifteenth century vocabularies *skratt, skrate* translates *armifrodita*, Wrt. Voc. i. 217, 23: 268, 64; see also Cath. Angl. 325; and in this sense Halliwell gives *scrat* as a word in dialects of the North. *Scritta* is the form glossing *hermaphroditus* in Ælfric's Glossary, Wrt. Voc. i. 45, 28. Corresponding forms but with different meanings are found in *O. H. Ger.* scraz; *pl.* scrazza *pilosi, incubi*; screzza *larvae*; scratun; *pl. pilosi, larvae*: *Icel.* skratti; *m. a wizard, warlock; goblin, monster.* Cf. Old Scratch. v. Grmm. D. M. 447 sqq.

scrallettan *to make a loud sound*:—Ðonne wīn hweteþ beornes breóstsefan stīgeþ cirm on corþre cwide scralletaþ missenlīce *when wine excites a man's mind, clamour arises in the company, they cry out with speech diverse*, Exon. Th. 314, 27; Mōd. 20. Sum sceal mid hearpan æt his hlāfordes fōtum sittan snere wrǣstan lǣtan scralletan *one shall sit with a harp at his lord's feet, bend the strings, make them send forth loud sound*, 332, 10; Vy. 83. [Cf. *Dan.* skralde *to sound loud*; and see *shrill* in Skeat's Etym. Dict.]

screáde, an; screád, e; *f. A piece cut off, a shred, a screed, paring*:—Screáde *sceda*, Wrt. Voc. i. 46, 70. Screádan *praesegmina, praecisiones*, 40, 9. Æppelscreáda *quisquiliae*, 22, 13. [Gif heo mei sparien eni poure schreaden (schiue, MS. T.: schraden, MS. C.), A. R. 416, 2. Hauede he non so god brede, Ne on his bord non so god shrede, þat he ne wolde þorwit fede Poure, Havel. 99. Schrede or clyppynge of clothe or oþer thynge *scissura, presegmen*, Prompt. Parv. 448. *O. Du.* schroode: *O. H. Ger.* scrōt: *Ger.* schrot. Cf. *Icel.* skrjóðr *a shred, strip.*]

screádian; *p.* ode *To shred, cut up* or *off, pare*, (of trees) *to prune*:—Būton ða lāreówas screádian ða leahtras þurh heora lāre āweg, ne biþ ðæt lǣwede folc wæstmbǣre, Homl. Th. ii. 74, 16. Ðā hēt hē (*Herod*) him his seax ārǣcan tō screádigenne (cf. æppelscreáda *quisquiliae*) ǣnne æppel, i. 88, 9. [He (*Herod*) badd himm brinngenn ænne cnif An appell forr to shrædenn, Orm. 8118. Scradieð eower sceldes al of þe smal enden, Laym. 5866. Wortes or othere herbes . . . she shredde and seeth, Chauc. Cl. T. 227. Cf. He shred (*concidit*) the wild gourds into the pot of pottage, 2 Kings iv. 39. Schredyñ or schragge trees *sarculo, sarmento*; schredyñ wortys or oþer herbys *detirso*, Prompt. Parv. 448. *O. Du.* schrooden: *O. H. Ger.* scrōtan; *p.* screot *demere, tondere*: *Ger.* schroten *to cut, gnaw.*] v. ā-, ge-screádian, *and next word.*

screádung, e; *f.* **I.** *pruning, trimming*:—Screádung *putatio*, Wrt. Voc. i. 39, 3. [Schredynge of trees and oþer lyke *sarmentacio, sarculacio*, Prompt. Parv. 448.] v. next word. **II.** *what is cut off, a shred, cutting, fragment, paring, leaving* of food:—Screádunga *fragmentorum*, Mt. Kmbl. Lind. 14, 20: Jn. Skt. Lind. Rush. 6, 12, 13: Mk. Skt. Lind. 6, 43. Scrādunga, Rush. 6, 43. Of screádungum *de micis*, 7, 28. Screádungo *reliquias*, Lk. Skt. Lind. Rush. 24, 43.

screádung-īsen, es; *n. An instrument for pruning* or *trimming*:—Wīngeardes screádungīsen *sarculus*, Wrt. Voc. i. 16, 11.

screaf. v. scræf.

screáwa, an; *m. A shrew-mouse*:—Screáwa *mus araneus*, Wrt. Voc. i. 24, 29: *musiranus*, ii. 55, 80: *massiranus*, 71, 24. Screuua, screáuua, scraeua *musiranus*, Txts. 78, 649. [Cf. *Chauc. Piers P. Prompt. Parv.* schrewe, shrewe *pravus.*]

screb, scrēc, scref. v. scræf; *m.* scrīc, scræf.

scremman; *p.* de *To make a person stumble, put a stumbling-block in a person's way*:—Ne wirige ðū deáfe ne scremme ðū blinde *non maledices surdo, nec coram coeco pones offendiculum*, Lev. 19, 14. [*The word, like* scrimman, q. v., *seems to suggest comparison with forms in* mp. Cf. *Icel.* skreppa; *p.* skrapp *to slip; the causative of this verb might appear in English as* scrempan, *whose meaning would be that given to* scremman. Scrincan, screncan *are parallel, as regards meaning, to* scrimman, scremman.]

screncan; *p.* te *To lay a stumbling-block in a person's way, trip up, ensnare*:—Eft hē cwæđ: 'Ne screnc đū đone blindan' . . . Se screncþ đone blindan đe đone ungesceádwīsan mirþ *protinus adjunxit: 'Nec coram coeco pones offendiculum' . . . Coram coeco offendiculum ponere est . . . ei, qui lumen discretionis non habet, scandali occasionem praebere* Past. 59, 6; Swt. 453, 1–4. Cf. Hē þurh ealle uncysta đa mōd gescrencþ *per universa vitia animum supplantat,* 11, 6; Swt. 73, 2. Healden hié đæt hié đa ne screncen đa đe gāþ on ryhtne weg tōweard đæs hefonrīces *ne ad ingressum regni tendentibus obstaculum fiunt,* 9; Swt. 59, 19. [Ute we bidden God đæt he us shilde þerwiđ þat he (*the devil*) us ne shrenche and seien: *Custodi me a laqueo,* O. E. Homl. ii. 209, 18. Þe deouel þat weneđ me to schrenchen ant schunchen of þe weie þat leadeþ to eche lif, Jul. 34, 1. He wile screnkenn hemm Full hefig fall to fallenn, Orm. 11861. To screnkenn ure sawless, 2618.] v. ā-, for-, ge-screncan.

scrence, screncedness, screncend. v. ge-, mis-screnсe, ge-screncedness, for-screncend.

screón (?); *p.* scrāh *To cry out, proclaim;* dicare:—Forscrāh *abdicavit* (in Lye). [*O. H. Ger.* scrīan *clamare.*]

screpan; *p.* scræp, *pl.* scrǣpon; *pp.* screpen *To scrape, scratch*:—Scriopu *scalpio,* Txts. 97, 1828. Scripiđ, scripith, scribid *scarpinat,* 95, 1805. Screpes *scratches* (? the word glosses *arescit.* v. scrīpan), Mk. Skt. Rush. 9, 18. Screp đæt blōd of, Lchdm. ii. 262, 6: 38, 20. [Þet he screpe zennes of al of oure herten, Ayenb. 98, 19. *But generally later English forms seem to represent a verb* scrapian. Cf. *Icel.* skrapa: *O. Du.* schrapen:—Heo schulden schreapien þe eorđe up of hore putte, A. R. 116, 15. Al þet scrift ne schreapeđ nout of, 344, 13. Shame shrapeth his clothes, Piers P. 11, 423. Scrapyn̄ (shrapyn) awey *abrado;* scrapyn̄ (schrapyn) *scalpo, scalpito,* Prompt. Parv. 450.] v. ā-, be-screpan.

screpe, scroepe; *adj. Suitable, adapted, convenient*:—Hit (*Britain*) is gescrǣpe (scroepe, MS. C.) on lǣswe sceápa and neáta *alendis apta pecoribus ac jumentis,* Bd. 1, 1; S. 473, 13. v. ge-scrǣpe.

screpu (?), e; *f. A curry-comb*:—Ǣren screop[u ?] *strigillus,* Txts. 99, 1935. Screope *strigillum,* 99, 1906.

scric, scrēc *a kind of thrush, screech, skrike* [v. E. D. S. Pub. Provincial names of birds, where *screech, skrike* are given as names of the missel-thrush, p. 1, and *screech bird, screech thrush* as those of the fieldfare (*turdus pilaris*), p. 6]:—Scrīc, scrēc, scruc (scriic ?) *turdus,* Txts. 103, 2069. Scrīc *turdus,* Wrt. Voc. i. 29, 30: 281, 20.

scrid, es; *n. A carriage, chariot, litter*:—Scrid *basterna,* Wrt. Voc. ii. 101, 49: *carracutium, vehiculum,* 121, 81. Scrid (*currus*) Godes, Ps. Surt. 67, 18: ii. p. 187, 14. Scrides *basterne,* Wrt. Voc. ii. 11, 80. Scrides, Hpt. Gl. 504, 15. On scride ł on cræte *in carruca,* Wrt. Voc. ii. 47, 42. Đā hēht se cāsere gesponnan fiówer wildo hors tō scride and hine gebundenne in đæt scrid āsetton . . . Hió gelǣddon đæt scrid on heá dūne, Shrn. 71, 34. Heó wæs on gyldenum scryd, 156, 11. Screoda siex hun[dred]a *six hundred chariots* (cf. Exod. 14, 7), Exon. Th. 468, 9; Phar. 5. Līgbǣrum scridum *vel* crætum *flammigeris quadrigis,* Wrt. Voc. ii. 149, 14. v. scriđa.

-scrid *in* ful-scrid. v. scrȳdan, IV.

Scride-finnas; *pl. m. A people who, according to Jornandes and Procopius, seem to have inhabited the present Russian Lapland and other tracts thereabouts, and even to have extended into the present Swedish Finnland.* [Procopius, σκριθίφινοι; Adam of Bremen, *Scritefinni;* Paulus Diaconus, *Scritobini;* Saxo Grammaticus, *Scricfinni.*]:—Scridefinnas, Ors. 1, 1; Swt. 16, 36. Ic wæs mid Scridefinnum, Exon. Th. 323, 16; Vīd. 79. The distinguishing prefix seems to refer to the use of snowshoes or skates, cf. *Icel.* skriðr *a sliding motion,* skrīða *to glide, slide* in snow-shoes.

scrid-wægn, -wǣn, es; *m.* I. *a chariot*:—Hū seó gesceádwīsnes bæd đæt mōd đæt hit sǣte on hire scridwǣne (cf. on hrædwǣne, 36, 1; Fox 174, 1), Bt. 36, tit.; Fox xviii, 4. II. *sella curulis*:—Sittan on gerēnedum scridwǣne *in curuli sedere,* 27, 1; Fox 96, 1: 27, tit.; Fox xiv, 22.

scrid-wīsa, an; *m. A charioteer*:—Scridwīsa *auriga,* Wrt. Voc. i. 39, 38.

scrif. v. scræf, ge-scrif.

scrīfan; *p.* scrāf, *pl.* scrifon; *pp.* scrifen *To decree, appoint* (cf. ge-scrif):—Scribun *promulgarunt,* Wrt. Voc. ii. 117, 74. Scriben *decerni,* 106, 22. I. *to decree* to a person as his lot, *to allot, assign*:—Swā missenlīce Dryhten eallum dǣleþ, scyreþ and scrīfeþ, Exon. Th. 331, 10, Vy. 66. Him (*God*) þonc ǣghwā secge đæs đe hē for his miltsum monnum scrīfeþ, 333, 7; Vy. 98. II. *to fix as his lot* for a person:—Ic sceal sēcan đa hāmas đe đū mē ǣr scrife *I must visit the abodes that you (the body) have made my (the soul's) portion,* 371, 4; Seel. 70. Brūcan swylcra yrmþa swā đū unc ǣr scrife, 373, 2; Seel. 102. Đæt wyt gesāwon heofona wuldor swylc swā đū mē ǣr scrife, 375, 25; Seel. 143. III. *to decree after judgment, to adjudge, doom, inflict, impose, pass as a sentence* upon a person:—Folca gehwylcum Scyppend scrīfeþ bī gewyrhtum eall æfter ryhte, 75, 12; Cri. 1220. Scrīfeþ bī gewyrhtum meorde monna gehwam, 286, 8; Jul. 728. Gif hē bētan mōte sylle wiđ his līfe swā hwæt swā man him scrīfe *si pretium ei fuerit impositum, dabit pro anima sua, quidquid fuerit postulatus,* Ex. 21, 30. Þrowige hē (*a pledgebreaker*) swā biscep him scrīfe, L. Alf. pol. 1; Th. i. 60, 10. Þolige hē (*a criminal priest*) ǣgđres ge hādes ge eardes, and wræcnige swā wīde swā pāpa him scrīfe, L. Eth. ix. 26; Th. i. 346, 6. Đǣr ābidan sceal maga māne fāh, hū him Metod scrīfan wille, Beo. Th. 1963; B. 979. Heó woldan đīne dōmas gehȳran, and hū đū đām forworhtum scrīfan woldest, Wulfst. 254, 17. IV. as an ecclesiastical term, *to shrive, to impose penance after confession, to hear confession and then impose penance*:—Đonne sacerd mannum fæsten scrīfeþ *quum sacerdos jejunium hominibus injungit,* L. Ecg. C. 1; Th. ii. 132, 25. Đæt hē hit swā gebētt hæbbe, swā him his scrift scrīfe, L. Ath. i. 25; Th. i. 212, 22. Wē lǣraþ đæt ǣlc preósta scrīfe and dǣdbōte tǣce đam đe him andette, L. Edg. C. 65; Th. ii. 258, 9. Ofer ealle đa scīre đe hē (scrift) on scrīfe, L. I. P. 7; Th. ii. 314, 5. Man sceal đam unstrangan men līđelīcor dēman and scrīfan đonne đam strangan . . . Man sceal on godcundan scriftan ge on woruldcundan dōman đās þingc tōsceádan, L. C. S. 69; Th. i. 412, 5. Hire nān preóst scrīfan ne mōt *neque ulli presbytero confessionem ejus accipere licebit,* L. Ecg. P. ii. 16; Th. ii. 188, 6. His scrift him sceal swā scrīfan, swā hē on his dǣdum gehȳreþ, đæt him tō dōnne biþ . . . Gyf hwā tō đam (*making peace*) cyrran nylle, đonne ne mæg hē đam scrīfan, L. E. I. 36; Th. ii. 432, 37–434, 4. V. *to care for, regard* [cf. *O. Sax.* bi-skrīban (*with gen.* or *prep.*) *to care about*], (a) with gen.:—Deáþ đæs ne scrīfeþ (cf. se deáþ swelces ne rēcþ *mors spernit altam gloriam,* Bt. 19; Fox 68, 32), Met. 10, 29. Rihtes ne scrīfeþ, 25, 53. Ne scrīfe hē đæs hlīsan būton hū hē ryhtosđ wyrce *opus rectitudinis appetitio ignoret favoris,* Past. 44, 3; Swt. 323, 16. (b) with dat.:—Se hlāford ne scrīfþ, se đam here waldeþ, freónde ne feónde, feore ne ǣhtum (cf. se đe hiora welt ne murnþ nāuđer ne friénd ne fiénd, Bt. 37, 1; Fox 186, 7), Met. 25, 15. (c) with a clause:—Hī (*the people of Sodom*) forlēton eallinga đone brīdele đæs eges, đā hī ne scrifon hwæđer hit wǣre đe dæg đe niht, đonne đonne hī syngodon, Past. 55, 1; Swt. 427, 31. [He (*the pope*) þe scal scriuen of þine weorldlifen, þat þine sunen alle scullen þe from falle, Laym. 32074. Þe preost shall shrifenn þe and huslenn, Orm. 6128. Him for to hoslon au for to shriue, Havel. 361. Schryvyn̄ or here schryftys *audire confessiones,* Prompt. Parv. 449. *Also* schriven (*reflex.*) means *to confess*:—Ich chulle schriuen me *confitebor,* A. R. 344, 6. Mede shroue (shrof, shroof) hire of hire shrewednesse . . . Thanne he assoilled hir sone, Piers P. 3, 44. Schryvyn̄ or ben aknowe synnys yn schryfte *confiteor,* Prompt. Parv. 449. *O. Frs.* scrīva *to impose a punishment.*] v. for-, ge-scrīfan; riht-scrīfend; scrift.

scrifen *painted* (?):—Scrifen scrād glād, Exon. Th. 353, 15; Reim. 13. [Cf. (?) *Icel.* skrifa *to paint;* scrifan *a picture.*]

scrīfend. v. riht-scrīfend.

scrift, es; *m.* I. *what is prescribed as a punishment, a penalty* (cf. scrīfan, III):—Ic (*bishop Werferth*) him (*Eadnoth*) sealde đæt lond and đa bēc . . . and ūre āgen rǣdengewrit đæt wǣre him tō đam gerāde đæt land tōlǣten đe mon ǣlce gēre gesylle fīftēne scillingas clǣnes feós đam bisceope and him eác đone ne scrift (scrift ne?) healde *our agreement that the land was resigned to him on the condition that fifteen shillings a year be paid to the bishop, and also that the penalty* (the land had before been subject to the condition that if it were not held by a person in orders it must pass to the church at Worcester; this condition was now removed) *be not maintained in respect to him (Eadnoth),* Chart. Th. 168, 18. I a. as an ecclesiastical term, (1) *penance* imposed after confession:—Gif feorhlyre wurþe, tōeácan đam rihtwere, twā pund tō bōte mid godcundan scrifte, L. E. B. 2; Th. ii. 240, 16; also in five following paragraphs. Ǣgđer man sceal ge on godcundan scriftan ge on woruldcundan dōman đās þingc tōsceádan *these things (the various circumstances of persons) are to be discriminated in the penances of the church and in the sentences of the law,* L. C. S. 69; Th. i. 412, 11. (2) *confession* which is followed by penance, *shrift*:—Đæt hē scriftes gyrnde and hūsles *quod confessionem et eucharistiam desideravisset,* L. Ecg. P. i. 3; Th. ii. 172, 19: 9; Th. ii. 176, 7. Gif preóst fulluhtes ođđe scriftes forwyrne, L. N. P. L. 8; Th. ii. 292, 1. Ǣghwylc cristen man . . . gewunige gelōmlīce tō scrifte; and unforwandodlīce his synna gecȳþe, L. Eth. v. 22; Th. i. 310, 5. Gā man tō scrifte (*ad confessionem*), Wulfst. 181, 3. [Scrift ihalden *to carry out the penance imposed,* O. E. Homl. i. 9, 31. Nimen scrift *to accept penance,* Laym. 18395. Takenn shriffte, Orm. 6613. Schrift (*confession*) and penitence, A. R. 8, 6. Þe holy ssrifte (*confession, one of the seven sacraments*), Ayenb. 14, 8. Schryfte *confessio,* Prompt. Parv. 449. *Icel.* skript, skrift, *confession, penance.*] II. *one who passes sentence, inflicts punishment, a judge* (v. scrīfan, III):—Wā is worulde scriftum, būtan heó mid rihte dōmas reccan, Wulfst. 263, 18. II a. as an ecclesiastical term, *one* *who hears confession and imposes penance, a confessor*:—Ða bôte âberan đe his scrift (*confessarius*) him tæcþ, L. Ecg. P. i. 4; Th. ii. 172, 24. Ðonne sceal se scrift hine âhsian be đǽm đe hē him andettaþ, hū đa þing gedōn wǽron, L. E. I. 31; Th. ii. 428, 10. His scrift him sceal swā scrîfan, swā hē đonne on his dǽdum gehȳreþ, đæt him tō dōnne biþ, 36; Th. ii. 432, 37: Homl. Th. ii. 94, 9. Libban đam līfe, đe scrift ūs wîsige, Wulfst. 112, 18. Ne mæg þurh đæt flǽsc se scrift geseón on đære sâwle, Exon. Th. 80, 13; Cri. 1307. Bēte hē be his scriftes geþeahte, L. C. E. 23; Th. i. 374, 8: L. P. M. 1; Th. ii. 286, 15. Hē ondette ǽlce costunge đam mōde his scriftes *tentationes suas menti pastoris indicet*, Past. 16, 5; Swt. 105, 16. Cweđe his andetnessa tō his scrifte, and đus cweđe: Ic andette Ælmihtigum Gode and mînum scrifte đam gāstlîcan lǽce ealle synna, L. de Cf. 6; Th. ii. 262, 18–21: Blickl. Homl. 43, 20. Gif him þince đæt hē wiđ his scrift sprece, đæt tâcnaþ his synna forgyfennysse, Lchdm. iii. 174, 14. Ūre mîsdǽde bētan, swā ūre scriftas ūs tǽcon, Wulfst. 142, 12. Andettan ūre synna ūrum scriftan, 115, 12: Blickl. Homl. 193, 22. [Hit ibeten swa þin scrifte þe techet, O. E. Homl. i. 19, 3. Wiđuten schriftes leaue, A. R. 418, 24.]

scrift-bóc; *f.* I. *a penitential, a book stating the penances to be enjoined after confession for various sins*:—i. scriftbōc on Englisc, Chart. Th. 430, 20; cf. L. Ælfc. P. 44; Th. ii. 384, 2. Swā hwylc swā đās scriftbōc tilige tō âbrecanne *quicunque Confessionale hoc violare conatus fuerit*, L. Ecg. P. Addit.; Th. ii. 238, 8. Ða mæssepreóstas sceolan heora scriftbēc mid rihte tǽcan and lǽran, swā swā hié ūre fæderas ǽr dēmdon, Blickl. Homl. 43, 8. II. *a discourse referring to penance*:—Lârspel and scriftbōc (*the title of the homily*), Wulfst. 242, 22.

scrift-scír, e; *f.* *The district in which a confessor exercises his functions*:—Gif preóst on his scriftscîre ǽnigne man wite Gode oferhȳre, L. Edg. C. 6; Th. ii. 244, 22: 9; Th. ii. 246, 12: 15; Th. ii. 246, 26. Sacerda gehwylc on his scriftscîre, Wulfst. 79, 17. Sacerdum gebyreþ on heora scriftscîrum, L. I. P. 7; Th. ii. 312, 38: 19; Th. ii. 326, 2. v. riht-scriftscîr.

scrift-sprǽc, e; *f.* *Confession*:—Gif deáþscyldig man scriftsprǽce gyrne, ne him man nǽfre ne wyrne, L. E. G. 5; Th. i. 168, 24: L. C. S. 44; Th. i. 402, 4.

scrimman; *p.* scramm *To shrink, draw up, contract*:—Gif monnes fōt tō hommum scrimme and scrince (cf. monegum men gescrincaþ his fēt tō his homme, 68, 3), Lchdm. ii. 6, 15. [Cf. scram *distorted; benumbed with cold*: scrambed *deprived of the use of a limb by a nervous contraction of the muscles*: scrimed *shrivelled up*: shrammed, shrimmid *benumbed with cold*: scrimp *to spare, pinch*: shrump-shouldered *humpbacked*, all from Halliwell's Dictionary: scrimp, scrimpit *scanty, contracted*, Jamieson's Dict. *M. H. Ger.* schrimpfen: *Ger.* schrumpfen *to wrinkle*: *Dan.* skrumpe *to shrink, shrivel*; skrumpen *shrunk, shrivelled*. See also Skeat's Dictionary s. v. *shrimp*.] v. scremman.

scrín, es; *n.* I. *a chest, coffer, casket, box in which precious things are kept*:—Scrîn *arca* vel *scrinium*, Wrt. Voc. i. 26, 49: *capsella*, 33, 62: *arca*, 80, 79. Ðæt hālige scrîn *the ark of the covenant*, Homl. Th. ii. 214, 35: Jos. 4, 7. Godes scrîn, 7, 6: Num. 14, 10. Ðæt scrîn, Jos. 3, 8, 13. Hē (*Judas*) hæfde scrîn (*loculos*) and bær đa þing đe man sende, Jn. Skt. 12, 6: 13, 29. Hire scrîn mid hiræ hāligdōmæ, Chart. Th. 553, 12. II. *a receptacle for the relics of a saint, a shrine*:—Se earm wearđ gelēd on scrîne of seolfre âsmiđod on Sancte Petres mynstre, Swt. A. S. Rdr. 99, 143. Đā þwōh man đa hālgan bān, and bær intō đære cyrcan on scrîne, 100, 158. Ic genam đa reliquias đære hālgan fǽmnan and hî gesætte on scrîn đæt ic sylf ǽr of stâne geworhte *ego tuli reliquias beatae Margaretae et reposui in scrinio, quod feci de lapide*, Nar. 49, 7. Đā gebrohte se bisceop ealle đa hālgan bān on gelimplîcum scrȳnum, and gelōgodon hî up on cyrcan, Homl. Skt. i. 11, 275. Đā wolde se cāsere wyrcan him eallum (*the seven sleepers*) gyldene scrȳn, Homl. Th. ii. 426, 22. [Hî nāmen đǽre (*in the minster*) twā gildene scrînes and .lx. seolferne, Chr. 1070; Erl. 209, 11.] III. *a cage* in which a criminal is confined:—Hig Pilatum on ânum ȳsenum scrȳne gebrohton on đære byrig Damascum, and hyne myd scrȳne myd eallum on feastum cweartерne beclȳsdon, St. And. 38, 8: 44, 19. [*O. H. Ger.* scrîni *scrinium, loculus*: *Icel.* skrín *a shrine*. From Latin.]

scrincan; *p.* scranc, *pl.* scruncon; *pp.* scruncen. I. of a plant, *to wither away, dry up, shrivel*:—Mid đam mǽstan bleó hȳ (*the male and female pennyroyal*) blōwaþ đonne neálîce ōđre wyrta scrincaþ and weorniaþ, Lchdm. i. 204, 13. Scrincan *marcescere*, Hpt. Gl. 419, 74. II. of a living being, *to pine away, become weak*:—Hē scrinceþ *arescit*; he pineth away (A. V.), Mk. Skt. Lind. 9, 18. Đā wearđ se cyning (*Belshazzar*) tō đan swîđe âfyrht, đæt hē eal scranc (cf. Then the king's countenance was changed, and his thoughts troubled him, so that the joints of his loins were loosed, and his knees smote one against another, Dan. 5, 6), Homl. Th. ii. 436, 2. [Þu scalt scrinchin (deȝe, 2nd MS.), Laym. 2278. Heo scrynketh for shome, P. S. 158, 7.] III. *to contract, shrink*:—Ða tān scrincaþ (-ed, MS.) up, Lchdm. iii. 48, 28. Gif sino scrince . . . ođđe gif monnes fōt tō hommum scrimme and scrince, ii. 6, 13–15. v. â-, for-, ge-scrincan.

scrind *swiftness* (?):—Ofer đæne (sǽ) mægene oft scipu scrîþende scrinde fleótaþ *over the sea oft sail the ships strongly and swiftly*, Ps. Th. 103, 24. [*Grein compares Lith.* skrindus *flying, running swiftly*.]

scrípan (?); *p.* te *To waste away, wither*:—Screpes *arescit*, Mk. Skt. Rush. 9, 18. [Cf. *Icel.* skrjupr *frail*: *Norweg.* skrypa *to waste*: *Swed. dial.* skryyp *to shorten*; skryp *weak*.]

scripel. v. eár-scrypel.

scripen, scripende gloss *austerus*, Lk. Skt. Lind. Rush. 19, 21.

scripp, es; *n.* (?) *A scrip, bag*:—Petrus forlēt lytle þing, scripp and net, ac hē forlēt ealle þing, đā đā hē for Godes lufon nān þing habban nolde, Homl. Th. i 394, 7. [Horn tok burdon and scrippe, Horn. 1061. Palmere with pike ne with scrippe, Piers P. 5, 542. Scrippe *pera*, Prompt. Parv. 450. *Icel.* skreppa.]

scrippa, an; *m.*?:—Of đære dîc on đone midmestan scrippan, Cod. Dip. Kmbl. v. 78, 27.

scriptor *occurs in the compound* tîd-scriptor *chronographus*, Wrt. Voc. ii. 131, 8. [Cf. *O. H. Ger.* scriptora; *n. pl. scriptores*.]

scrida *or* **scridu**, an; *m.* or *f.* *A chariot*:—Scriđena ł cræta *bigarum, curruum*, Hpt. Gl. 457, 77. v. scrid.

scrídan; *p.* scrâd, *pl.* scridon; *pp.* scriden, scriđen. I. *to go, take one's way* to a place:—Drihten gecwyđ: 'Âstîgaþ nū âwyrgde in đæt wîtehūs.' Sōna æfter đǽm wordum werige gâstas hwyrftum scrîđaþ in đæt sceađena scræf, Cd. Th. 304, 17; Sat. 631. Men ne cunnon hwyder helrūnan hwyrftum scrîđaþ, Beo. Th. 329; B. 163. Com on wanre niht scrîđan sceadugenga, 1410; B. 703. II. *to go hither and thither, go about, wander*:—Lîg scrîđeþ geond woruld wîde *fire shall spread itself far and wide through the world*, Exon. Th. 51, 3; Cri. 810. Fîfte cyn is wîdscriþelra hleápera, đe under muneces gegyrlan ǽghwider scrîđaþ, R. Ben. 135, 21. Bana wîde scrâd (*of the destroying angel that smote the firstborn of Egypt*), Cd. Th. 180, 3; Exod. 39. Ðæt hine ne worian ne scrîđan (*uagari*) ne lyste, R. Ben. 126, 18. Swā scrîđende hweorfaþ gleómen, Exon. Th. 326, 27; Vîd. 135. III. of the gliding motion of a ship, cloud, etc., or of the motion of a heavenly body in its orbit:—Ne æt mē hrisil scrîđeþ, Exon. Th. 417, 20; Rä. 36, 7. Sió scîre scell scrîđeþ ymbūtan dōgora gehwylce *the heavens make one revolution each day*, Met. 20, 174: 28, 16. Sume tungl scrîđaþ leng ūtan ymb eall đis, 28, 8. Wolcnu scrîđaþ *clouds sail along*, Menol. Fox 486; Gn. C. 13. Leax sceal on wǽle mid sceote scrîđan, 539; Gn. C. 40. Sægl (*the sun*) gewât under scrîđan, Andr. Kmbl. 2913; An. 1459. Lēton scrîđan bronte brimþisan, Elen. Kmbl. 474; El. 237. Scrîđende (*revolving*) færþ hweóle gelîcost, Met. 20, 216. Scrîđende scîn (*the storm-clouds*), Exon. Th. 385, 29; Rä. 4, 52. Ofer đæne (sǽ) oft scipu scrîđende fleótaþ, Ps. Th. 103, 24. IV. of the increase or decrease of light:—Heó đæt leóht geseah ellor scrîđan, Cd. Th. 48, 9; Gen. 773. Niht ofer ealle scrîđan cwōme, Beo. Th. 1305; B. 650. V. of the coming of times or seasons, of the passage of time:—Ðæs scrîđ ymb seofon niht Weódmōnaþ on tūn, Menol. Fox 270; Men. 136. Dagas forþ scridun, Exon. Th. 160, 12; Gū. 942. Ofer niđđa bearn nihtrîm scridon, 167, 35; Gū. 1070. Cymeþ wlitig scrîđan on tūn Maius, Menol. Fox 152; Men. 77. Ðenden him đeós woruld scrîđende scînan mōte, Exon. Th. 97, 3; Cri. 1585. Mîn feorh ende gesēceþ dæg scrîđende, đonne dōgor beóþ mîn forþ scriđen, 164, 10–16; Gū. 1011. [Þa com Scottene king scriđen to hirede, Laym. 10799. He scrađ (com, 2nd MS.) to þisse londe, 4109. Tweien scalkes scriđen under bordes & skirmden, 8405. None of þe Normandes fro þam might skrith, Min. v. 68. To scrythe *labi*, Cath. Angl. 326. *O. Sax.* scrîđan, scrîdan *to go, pass* (of time, light): *O. H. Ger.* scrîtan *gradi*: *Icel.* skríđa *to creep, crawl; to glide, slide*.] v. geond-, tō-, þurh-, ymb-scrîđan.

scride, es; *m.* *A course*:—Ða habbaþ scyrtran scriđe and færeld, ymbhwerft læssan đonne ōđru tungl, Met. 28, 11. [*O. H. Ger.* scrit *gradus, passus*: *Icel.* skriđr *a creeping* or *sliding motion*.]

scridol, scritta. v. wîd-scriđol, scrætte.

Scrobbes-burh; *f.* *Shrewsbury*:—Đā fērdon hî intō Stæffordscîre and intō Scrobbesbyrig, Chr. 1016; Erl. 154, 4. Cf. Civitas Scrobbensis, Cod. Dip. Kmbl. ii. 137, 24.

Scrobbesbyrig-scír, *and later* Scrob-scîr; *f.* *Shropshire*:—Đā wæs se cyng gewend ofer Temese intō Scrobbesbyrigscîre, Chr. 1006; Erl. 140, 29. Hugo eorl of Scrobscîre, 1094; Erl. 230, 37.

Scrob-sǽte, -sǽtan; *pl.* *The men of Shropshire*; also used where now the name of their district would be used, *Shropshire*:—Đā fyrdedon hî intō Stæffordscîre and intō Scrobsǽton, Chr. 1016; Erl. 154, 22.

scroepe. v. screpe.

scrofell, es; *n.* (?) *Scrofula*:—Cyrneles and scrofelles and ǽghwylces ȳfles, Lchdm. iii. 62, 22.

scrúd, es; *n.* I. *dress, clothing, attire*:—Hrægłung *vestitus*, scruud *habitus*, Wrt. Voc. i. 39, 69. Hwæt begytst đū of đînum cræfte? Bigleofan and scrūd (*vestitum*) and feoh, Coll. Monast. Th. 23, 5. Hē sylþ him andlyfene and scrūd *dat ei victum et vestitum*, Deut. 10, 18: L. Pen. 15; Th. ii. 282, 26. II. *an article of dress, a garment*:—Scrūd *vestis, clamis*, Wrt. Voc. i. 25, 50. Cildes scrūd *praetexta*, 25, 56. Slēfleás scrūd *colobium*, slēfleás ancra scrūd *levitonarium*, 40, 20, 21.

Scrūde *melote, veste*, Hpt. Gl. 492, 52. Hē sealde hira ǽlcum twā scrūd (*stolas*), and hē sealde Beniamine fīf scrūd, Gen. 45, 22. [*Laym.* scrud: *Orm.* shrud: *A.R.* schrud: *Ayenb.* ssroud: *Piers P.* shroud *dress, garment*: *Icel.* skrūð *shrouds of a ship, tackle.*] v. beadu-, byrdu-, gūþ-, munuc-, nun-, ofer-, wīf-scrūd.

scrūd-fultum, es; *m. Assistance in providing clothing;* the word occurs in grants made to religious houses of funds for the provision of clothing:—Ealle ða sōcna ofer ðæt fennland him (*the monks of Ely*) tō scrūdfultume (cf. stent causas seculares emendandae fratrum loco manentium victui vel vestitui necessaria ministrantes, p. 238), Chart. Th. 242, 18. Twelf hīda tō scrūdfultume ðam hīrēde (*Winchester*), 499, 13. Ic habbe gifen ðæt land intō Sanctes Petres mynstre intō Baðan ðām munecan tō scrūdfultume, Cod. Dip. Kmbl. iv. 171, 15. v. next word.

scrūd-land, es; *n. Land given to provide means for buying clothing, land given as* scrūdfultum, q. v.:—Hē geunn(-ann?) ðæs landes æt Orpedingtūne for his sāwle intō Cristes cyrican ðām Godes þeówum tō scrūdland, Chart. Th. 329, 19.

scrudnian, scrutnian; *p.* ode *To examine carefully, consider, investigate*:—Ic scrudnige ł ic smeáge bebodu Godes mīnes *scrutabor mandata Dei mei*, Ps. Lamb. 118, 115. And Drihten on micelre folces menige smeáþ and scrutnoþ (scrudnaþ, MS. T.) hwæt ða feáwa syndan ðe his willan wyrcean willen *et querens Dominus in multitudine populi*, R. Ben. 2, 16. Mīne gebrōðra, scrutniaþ mid hū wāclīcum wurðe Godes rīce biþ geboht, Homl. Th. i. 582, 25. Twā þing sind ðe wē sceolon carfullīce scrutnian, ii. 82, 25. Scrutniende *scrutando, investigando*, Hpt. Gl. 410, 12. Tō āsmeáganne mid scrutniendre scrutnunge, Anglia viii. 302, 36. Scrudinend (scrudniend?) *scrutantes*, Ps. Spl. 63, 6. [Cf. *O. H. Ger.* scrodōn, scrutōn *scrutari.*] v. ā-scrudnian.

scrudnung, scrutnung, e; *f. Examination, investigation, enquiry*:—Hē began mid geornfulre scrudnunge smeágan and āhsian be ðām gebodum ðæs hālgan regules, Lchdm. iii. 440, 20. Tō āsmeáganne mid scrutniendre scrutnunge. Anglia viii. 302, 36.

scrūd-waru, e; *f. Habit, dress*:—Ðæt hē (*a monk*) healdan wille his clǽnnisse and munuclīce scrūdware, L. Eth. v. 6; Th. i. 306, 9: vi. 3; Th. i. 314, 27.

scruf, scrutnian, scrutnung. v. scorf, scrudnian, scrudnung.

scrybb, e; *f. Scrub, underwood, shrubbery*:—Of ðare stānstrǽte andlang scrybbe, Chart. Th. 525, 21.

scrȳdan; *p.* de. I. *to put clothes on* a person, *to clothe* a person with (*mid*) a garment, *to dress*:—Ic mē scrȳde *induo*, Ælfc. Gr. 28, 2; Zup. 167, 2. Ic [mē] scrȳdde mid hǽran *induebar cilicio*, Ps. Spl. 34, 15. Heó scrȳdde Iacob mid ðam deórwurðustan reáfe *vestibus valde bonis induit eum*, Gen. 27, 15. Hine man efosode and scrȳdde hine and brohte hine tō ðam cynge *Joseph totonderunt, ac veste mutata obtulerunt ei*, 41, 14. Hē scrīdde (*vestivit*) ðone bisceop mid līnenum reáfe, Lev. 8, 7. Ic wæs nacud and gē mē scrȳddon (*operuistis*), Mt. Kmbl. 25, 36, 38. Mōdor, scrȳd (*vesti*) ðīnne sunu, Ælfc. Gr. 18; Zup. 111, 3 Ne scrīde nān wīf hig mid wǽpmannes reáfe, Deut. 22, 5. II. *to clothe, to furnish with clothes, provide with clothes*:—Hē scrȳt mē wel and fētt, Coll. Monast. Th. 22, 33. Gif æcyres weód God scrȳt, Mt. Kmbl. 6, 30. Scrȳtt, Lk. Skt. 12, 28. Hē hī fēdan scolde and scrȳdan, Chr. 1012; Erl. 147, 11. Hingrigendum mete syllan and nacode scrȳdan, Blickl. Homl. 213, 18. III. *to put on* a garment:—Wlite ðū scrȳddest *decorem induisti*, Ps. Spl. 103, 2. Līnen reáf scrēdan sume seócnysse ge'ācnaþ (*in a dream*) *to put on a linen garment betokens some sickness*, Lchdm. iii. 206, 30. IV. *to rig* a ship (? cf. *shrouds* of a ship: *Icel.* skrūð *the shrouds of a ship, standing rigging; tackle, gear*):—Is ðeós bāt fulscrīd, Andr. Kmbl. 992; An. 496. [He hine lette ueden, he hine lette scruden, Laym. 8945. Nolde þe neodfule ueden ne schruden, A. R. 214, 17. He wollde shridenn uss wiþþ heofennlike wæde, Orm. 3676. He ne hauede nouth to shride but a kowel, Havel. 963. Ssrede þe poure, Ayenb. 90, 25. *Icel.* skrȳða *to clothe, dress.*] v. ge-, mis-, un-, ymb-scrȳdan; wan-scrȳd.

scrynce; *adj. Withered*:—Menigo ðara unhālra blindena haltra scryngcara (giscrungenra, Rush.: forscruncenra, W. S.) *multitudo languentium, caecorum, claudorum, aridorum*, Jn. Skt. Lind. 5, 3. Cf. scrence, *and for the inflexion* tuoegara, 8, 17.

scūa. v. scūwa.

scucca, sceucca, sceocca, scocca, an; *m. A devil, demon;* in sing. generally *the devil, Satan, Beelzebub*:—Wæs se scucca (*Satan*) him betwux. Tō ðæm cwæð Drihten: 'Hwanon cōme ðū?' Se sceocca andwyrde: 'Ic fērde geond ðās eorþan,' Homl. Th. ii. 446, 25–27. Se scucca, 452, 13, 17. Se sceocca, 448, 4. Gang ðū sceocca (sceucca, MS. A.) on bæc *vade Satanas*, Mt. Kmbl. 4, 10. Æfter ðæs sceoccan (scoccan, Thw.) ēhtnysse, Homl. Th. ii. 450, 3. Sceoccan *Belzebulis*, Germ. 399, 267. Sceoccan betǽht tō flǽsces forwyrde, R. Ben. 50, 1. Deóful ł scuccan *Zabulun*, Hymn. Surt. 115, 15. Ða āwyrigedan sceoccan (scuccan), Homl. Th. i. 68, 1: Wulfst. 249, 1. Þurh ðara scuccena lotwrencas, Bt. 39, 6; Fox 220, 14. Scucna englas, Blickl. Homl. 189, 7. Ðæt hié leóda landgeweorc lāþum beweredon scuccum and scinnum, Beo. Th. 1882; B. 939. Ongunnan heora bearn blōtan feóndum, sceuccum onsæcgean *immolaverunt filios suos et filias suas daemoniis*, Ps. Th. 105, 27. *The word is found in the name of a place,* Scuccanhlāu, Cod. Dip. Kmbl. i. 196, 1. [Þu scheomelese schucke (*the reeve that condemned St. Margaret*), Marh. 7, 26. Þe laðe unwiht, þe hellene schucke, H. M. 41, 35. Schenden þene sckucke (schucke), A. R. 316, 11. Þe scucke wes bitweonen, Laym. 276. Þu (*the reeve before whom Juliana was brought*) þat schucke art schucken (shuken, Bod. MS.) herien, Jul. 56, 2.]

scucc-gild, es; *n. An idol*:—Hī sceuccgyldum guldan *servierunt sculptilibus eorum*, Ps. Th. 105, 26.

scūdan *to shake, tremble, shiver, shudder*:—Hȳ (*Adam and Eve*) on uncȳððu scomum scūdende scofene wurdon on gewinworuld *they shivering with shame into a strange land were thrust, into a world of struggle*, Exon. Th. 153, 19; Gū. 828. [Cf. *O. Sax.* skuddian: *O. Frs.* skedda: *O. H. Ger.* scuten, scutten *to shake* (trans.): *O. L. Ger.* scuddinga *excussus.*]

scūfan, sceūfan, sceófan; *p.* sceáf, *pl.* scufon, sceufon, sceofon; *pp.* scofen, sceofen *To shove, push, thrust;* trudere, praecipitare:—Ic sceūfe (sceófe, scūfe) *praecipito*, Ælfc. Gr. 24; Zup. 137, 11: *trudo*, 28, 4; Zup. 171, 1. Scīfþ *trudit*, Hpt. Gl. 406, 71. Scūfaþ *praecipitate*, Wrt. Voc. ii. 68, 78. I. *to shove, push, try to move something*:—Hē sceáf mid ðam scylde, ðæt se sceaft tōbærst, Byrht. Th. 135, 50; By. 136. Sume sceufon, sume tugon, and seó Godes fǽmne hwæðre stōd, Shrn. 154, 26. II. *to shove, thrust, cause to move with violence.* (1) literal:—Ðā ne gelīfde Apollonius ðæt heó his gemæcca wǽre ac sceáf hī fram him, Ap. Th. 25, 6. Hē sceáf reáf of līce, Cd. Th. 94, 20; Gen. 1564. Hī dracan scufon, wyrm ofer weallclif, Beo. Th. 6254; B 3131. 'Uton hine underbæc sceófan' . . . Hī ðā hine underbæc scufon . . . ac hē næs āceweald þurh ðam heálīcan fylle, Homl. Th. ii. 300, 14–20. Hēt his scealcas scūfan ða hyssas in bǽlblȳse, Cd. Th. 230, 11; Dan. 231: Exon. Th. 142, 21; Gū. 647. Leahtra leáse in ðæs leádes wylm scūfan, 277, 21; Jul. 584. Scūfan scyldigne in seáþ, Elen. Kmbl. 1380; El. 692. Ūs ys miht geseald ðē tō sceófanne on ðās wītu ðisse deópnysse, Guthl. 5; Gdwin. 38, 17. (2) of proceedings which imply violence, *to thrust* into prison, out of a place, etc.:—Drihten heó (*the fallen angels*) furðor sceáf in ðæt neowle genip, Cd. Th. 292, 24; Sat. 445. Hig scufon (*ejecerunt*) hine of ðære ceastre, Lk. Skt. 4, 29. Sume scufon heora māgas forþ tō heofenan rīce, and fērdon him sylfe tō helle wīte, Homl. Th. ii. 542, 22. Būton man āgeáfe Eustatsius and his men heom tō hand sceofe *unless Eustace were given up and his men were handed over to them*, Chr. 1052; Erl. 179, 22. Se cyning wæs yrre wið mē and hēt sceófan mē on cweartern *me retrudi jussit in carcerem*, Gen. 41, 10. Gē (*devils*) scofene wurdon fore oferhygdum in ēce fȳr, Exon. Th. 140, 5; Gū. 605. Hȳ (*Adam and Eve*) scofene wurdon on gewinworuld, 153, 20; Gū. 828. III. *to shove, push, cause to move* (without notion of violence):—Hī scufon ūt heora scipu and gewendon heom begeondan sǽ, Chr. 1048; Erl. 180, 15: Beo. Th. 436; B. 215. IV. of the production of natural phenomena:—Metod æfter sceáf ǽfen, Cd. Th. 9, 4; Gen. 136. Ðā wæs morgenleóht scofen and scynded, Beo. Th. 1840; B. 918. [Cf. Grmm. D. M. 706.] V. *to push* a person's cause, *advance, forward*, cf. scyfe, II:—Scūfeþ Freá forþwegas folmum sīnum, willan ðīnne, Cd. Th. 170, 13; Gen. 2812. VI. *to urge, prompt* a thought or action, cf. scyfe, III:—Mid ðȳ se weriga gāst ða synne scȳfþ on mōde *cum malignus spiritus peccatum suggerit in mente*, Bd. 1, 27; S. 497, 19 note. VII. *to push on* or *forward, to move* (intrans.):—Merecondel (*the sun*) scȳft on ofdæle, Met. 13, 58. Werige gāstas scūfaþ tō grunde in ðæt nearwe nīþ, Cd. Th. 304, 21; Sat. 633. [*Goth.* skiuban: *O Frs.* skūva: *O. H. Ger.* sciuban: *Icel.* skȳfa (*wk.*) *to shove, drive, push.*] v. ā-, æt-, be-, for-, ōþ-, tō-, wið-scūfan.

[sculan, sceolan]; ic, hē sceal, scal, ðū scealt, *pl.* wē sculon, sceolon; *p.* sceolde, scolde, scealde, scalde; *subj. prs.* scyle, scile, sciele, scule. I. *to owe; debere*:—Ān him sceolde (scalde, Rush.: āhte tō geldanne, Lind.) tȳn þūsend punda. Se hlāford forgeaf him ðone gylt. Se þeówa gemētte hys efenþeówan, se him sceolde (sculde, Rush.) ān hund penega, and hē cwæð; 'Āgyf ðæt ðū mē scealt,' Mt. Kmbl. 18, 24. 28. Hū mycel scealt ðū (āht ðū tō geldanne, Lind.) mīnum hlāforde? Lk. Skt. 16, 5, 7. Gif hwā ōðrum scyle (scule) borh oððon bōte, gelǽste hit georne, L. Eth. v. 20; Th. i. 308, 31. [Cf. Uoryef me þet ich þe ssel, Ayenb. 115, 29. By the feith I shal Priam, Tr. and Cr. iii. 472.] II. denoting obligation or constraint of various kinds, *shall, must, ought,* (*I*) *have* or *am* (with infin.), *am bound*, with an infinitive expressed or that may be inferred from a preceding clause. (1) denoting a duty, moral obligation:—Ðū scealt on ǽghwylce tīd Godes willan wercan, Blickl. Homl. 67, 33. Nǽnig mon ne sceal lufian ne ne gēman his gesibbes, gif . . . (*it is a man's duty not to love*), 23, 16. Swā sceal oretta ā in his mōde Gode compian, Exon. Th. 122, 33; Gū. 315. God sceal mon ǽrest hergan, 333, 15; Gn. Ex. 4. Swā hire eaforan sculon æfter lybban, ðonne hié lād gedōþ, hié sculon lufe wyrcean, Cd. Th. 39, 12; Gen. 624. Næs fela manna, ðe hogade ymbe ða bōte swā georne, swā man scolde (sceolde, MS. B.), Wulfst. 156, 12. Hē (*the bishop*) ne cūðe dōn his gerihte swā wel swā hē sceolde, Chr. 1047; Erl. 177, 9. Đā andswarede se cyning đæt hē ǽgđer ge wolde ge scolde đam geleáfan onfōn *rex suscipere se fidem et velle et debere respondebat*, Bd. 2, 13; S. 515, 35. Hwider hyra gehwylc faran scolde, Blickl. Homl. 229, 5. Seó lufu đe wē tō ūrum Hǽlende habban sceoldan, 109, 4. Forđæm ne scyle nān wīs man nǽnne mannan hatian, Bt. 38, 7; Fox 210, 15. (2) *shall, ought* as being fit, right, proper, in accordance with reason:—Ic mid grāpe sceal fōn wiđ feónde, Beo. Th. 881; B. 438. Hwȳ sceal ic æfter his hyldo þeówian ... ic mæg wesan god swā hē, Cd. Th. 18, 33; Gen. 282. Se đe tō reccenddōme cuman sceal *qui ad regimen venire debeat*, Past. 11; Swt. 61, 5. Forđan sceal gehycgan hæleđa ǽghwylc, đæt hē ne ābælige bearn Waldendes, Cd. Th. 276, 25; Sat. 194. Đonne gē geseóþ đære tōworpednysse āsceonunge standan đǽr heó ne sceal (rīseþ, Rush.), Mk. Skt. 13, 14. Be ūre ǽ hē sceal (gedaefnaþ, Lind.) sweltan *debet mori*, Jn. Skt. 19, 7. Seó cyrice sceal fēdan đa đe æt hire eardiaþ, Blickl. Homl. 41, 27: 47, 21. Hwæt sculon wē nū dōn tō đam đæt wē mǽgon cumon tō đām sōþum gesǽlþum *quid nunc faciendum, ut illius summi boni sedem reperire mereamur?* Bt. 33, 3; Fox 126, 32. Dēmaþ ūs hwylcum deáđe wē sweltan sceulon, for đam đe wē đone Hǽlend tō deáđe gesealden, St. And. 36, 16. Oncnāwan hwǽr wē sǽlan sceolon sundhengestas, Exon. Th. 54, 3; Cri. 863. Ne sceole gē swā sōfte sinc gegangan, Byrht. Th. 133, 32; By. 59. Ne sceolon unc betweónan teónan weaxan, Cd. Th. 114, 10; Gen. 1902. His weorc sceolon beón đæs weorđe, đæt him ōđre menn onhyrien, Past. 11, 1; Swt. 61, 17. Ic worda gespræc mā đonne ic sceolde, Andr. Kmbl. 1848; An. 926: Hy. 3, 43. Đone māđđum đe đū mid rihte rǽdan sceoldest, Beo. Th. 4119; B. 2056. Swylc sceolde secg wesan æt þearfe, 5410; B. 2708. Gūþbill geswāc, swā hit nō sceolde, 5164; B. 2585. Oft mon forlǽt đone ege đe hē mid ryhte on him innan habban scolde, Past. 4, 1; Swt. 37, 18. Hē ūs lǽrde, hū wē ūs gebiddan sceoldan, Blickl. Homl. 19, 36. Hī cuǽdon, đæt hié đæt tō his honda healdan sceoldon, forđæm hira nān næs on fædrenhealfe tō geboren, Chr. 887; Erl. 86, 4. Hū hié libban sceoldon, Cd. Th. 52, 30; Gen. 851. Hié nīþ āhōfon, swā hié nō sceoldon, Elen. Kmbl. 1673; El. 838. Gif ic scile *etsi oportuerit me*, Mk. Skt. Lind. 14, 31. Hū hē scyle (scile, Cott. MSS.) eall earfođu forsión *quod adversa quaeque despicienda sunt*, Past. 3; Swt. 33, 4. Ne scyle nān mon blǽcern ǽlan under mittan, 5, 1; Swt. 43, 2. Hū gehiérsum đǽm đe hē mid ryhte hiéran sciele, 9; Swt. 56, 14: 10; Swt. 60, 6. (3) denoting obligation to perform an engagement, to do appointed work, to carry out the terms of an agreement:—Wīsdōmes beþearf se đære æđelan sceal andwyrde āgifan *he will need wisdom to whom the task of giving an answer is assigned*, Elen. Kmbl. 1085; El. 545. Sume sceolon (*it will be the task of some*) hweorfan geond hæleþa land, Cd. Th. 281, 11; Sat. 270. Næs đæt forma sīđ đæt hit (*the sword*) ellenweorc æfnan scolde, Beo. Th. 2933; B. 1464. Đonne scyldfreca ongeán gramum gangan scolde, 2073; B. 1034. Đone ende đe Æđerēd healdan sceolde, Chr. 894; Erl. 92, 2. Hī woldon đisne eard healdan, and hē hī fēdan scolde and scrȳdan, 1012; Erl. 147, 10. Būtan đǽm monnum đe đa burga healdan scolden, Erl. 90, 19. Sceótend swǽfon, đa đæt hornreced healdan scoldon, Beo. Th. 1413; B. 704. His scipu sceoldan cumon ongeán, ac hī ne mihton, Chr. 1000; Erl. 137, 3. Gnornian hū oft hē feohtan scule (scyle, Cott. MS.), Bt. 40, 3; Fox 238, 10. (4) denoting bidding, commanding:—'Hwæt sceal ic singan?' Cwæđ hē: 'Sing mē frumsceaft,' Bd. 4, 24; S. 597, 16. Hǽlend him cwæđ: 'Đū scealt fylgean mē,' Blickl. Homl. 23, 14: Cd. Th. 139, 15; Gen. 2310: 172, 29; Gen. 2851. Scealtū mid ǽrdæge ceól gestīgan, Andr. Kmbl. 439; An. 220. Ic secge đæt hē sceal wesan Ismahel hāten, Cd. Th. 138, 2; Gen. 2285. Ne sceolon gē mīne đa hālgan hrīnan, Ps. Th. 104, 13. Ne scule gē hit þurhteón, 4, 5. Sægþ on đissum bōcum, đæt Drihten cwǽde, đæt đis mennisce cyn ne sceolde āgīmeleásian, đæt hié sealdon heora wæstma fruman for Gode, Blickl. Homl. 41, 4: Exon. Th. 15, 9; Cri. 233. Se (*God*) ūs đās lāde sceóp, đæt wē on Egiptum sceolde ūs fremu sēcan, Cd. Th. 110, 23; Gen. 1842. Hē ūs gesette đæt wē hine biddan sceoldan *he made this ordinance for us, that we should pray to him*, Blickl. Homl. 21, 3. Đa þing đe ic eów foresægde, đæt gē dōn sceoldon, 131, 34. Landfranc bebéad đan munecan, đæt hī scoldan hī unscrȳdan, Chr. 1070; Erl. 208, 8. Hē oncwæđ, đæt hié gyldan sceolde, Cd. Th. 229, 5; Dan. 212. 'On đæt fȳr gē (*the wicked at the day of judgment*) hreósan sceolan.' Ne māgon hī gehȳnan heofoncyninges bibod, Exon. Th. 93, 11; Cri. 1524. (5) where the obligation results from a law, statute, regulation:—Se byrdesta sceall gyldan fīftȳne mearđes fell, Ors. 1, 1; Swt. 18, 19. Nū sceal beón ǽfre on Ii abbod, and nā biscop, and đan sculon beón underþeódde ealle Scotta biscopas, Chr. 565; Erl. 18, 6. Sceolde sweordes ecg feorh ācsigan, Andr. Kmbl. 2266; An. 1134. Se đe scyle (*since the regulations of the Penitential require it*) āne wucan dǽdbōte dōn, L. Ecg. C. 2; Th. ii. 134, 13. (6) denoting the necessity of fate, of the order of providence, *shall, must* as being decreed by fate or providence:—Đū scealt greót etan đīne līfdagas, Cd. Th. 56, 9; Gen. 909. Đū eart eorþe, and þū scealt eft tō eorþan weorđan, Blickl. Homl. 123, 9. Gyt scyl (sceal, MS. A.) beón gefylled đæt be mē āwriten is, Lk. 22, 37. Sceal hine wulf etan *his fate will be to be eaten by a wolf* (cf. swā missenlīce Dryhten eallum dǽleþ, 331, 6; Vy. 64), Exon. Th. 328, 5; Vy. 12 (*and often*). Mon sceal on eorþan geong ealdian, 333, 21; Gn. Ex. 7. Gǽþ ā wyrd swā hió scel, Beo. Th. 915; B. 455. Hié (*the Jews*) God sylfne āhēngon; đæs hié sculon wergđu dreógan, Elen. Kmbl. 420; El. 210: Exon. Th. 455, 28; Hy. 4, 56. Hī đǽr geferdon māran hearm đonne hī ǽfre wēndon đæt him ǽnig burhwaru gedōn sceolde *more than they ever expected it would be the fate of any citizens to do them*, Chr. 994; Erl. 132, 22. Đā hē from sceolde niþþum hweorfan, Cd. Th. 74, 15; Gen. 1222. Nǽnig heora þohte đæt hē đanon scolde eft gesēcean folc *every one of them thought himself fated not to visit his people again*, Beo. Th. 1387; B. 691. Đonne đū forþ scyle metodsceaft seón, 2363; B. 1179: Cd. Th. 63, 27; Gen. 1038. Se dæg đe hē sceole wiđ đæm līchomon hine gedǽlon, Blickl. Homl. 97, 20. Hwæđer đis þūsend sceole beón scyrtre þe lengre, 119, 6. Scile, Beo. Th. 6335; B. 3177. Đeáh gē wēnen đæt gē lange libban scylan, Bt. 19; Fox 70, 15. Nele se Waldend đæt forweorđan scylen sāula ūsse *it is not God's will, that our souls be destined to destruction* (*but* cf. hē nyle đæt đa sāula forweorđan, Bt. 34, 8; Fox 144, 37), Met. 21, 34. (7) *to be forced, must* because there is no possible alternative, because one cannot help one's self:—Nū sceal ic (*Hagar*) on wēstenne witodes bīdan, Cd. Th. 137, 16; Gen. 2274. Ic (*Satan*) sceal bīdan in bendum, 268, 1; Sat. 48. Ic teáras sceal geótan, Exon. Th. 11, 18; Cri. 172. Ne sceal ic mīne onsȳn fore eówere mengu mīþan, 144, 16; Gū. 679. Đū scealt furþor sīþfæt secgan, 261, 18; Jul. 317. Blind sceal his eágna þolian, 335, 27; Gn. Ex. 39. On đǽm gesuincum hē sceal hine selfne geþencean đeáh hē nylle *in adversis ad sui memoriam nolens etiam coactusque revocatur*, Past. 3, 1; Swt. 35, 7. Sculon hié đās helle sēcan, Cd. Th. 26, 14; Gen. 406. Đū neorxna wonges wlite nȳde sceoldes āgiefan, Exon. Th. 86, 11; Cri. 1406. Ordfruma earmre lāfe đære đe đǽm hǽđenan hȳran sceolde, Cd. Th. 225, 13; Dan. 153. Scolde, Beo. Th. 20; B. 10: 1935; B. 965. Hyne Hetware gehnǽgdon mid ofermægene, đæt se byrnwīga būgan sceolde, 5829; B. 2918. Sceoldon wræcmæcgas ofgiefan grēne beorgas, Exon. Th. 116, 5; Gū. 202. Đonne hī siófian scioldon *when they could not help sighing*, Met. 26, 82. Đȳ læs ic scyle leng þrowian, Andr. Kmbl. 154; An. 77. Hē tō foo gif hē niéde sciele *coactus ad regimen veniat*, Past. 9; Swt. 59, 9. (8) *to be obliged, must, shall* because from the conditions or nature of a case no alternative is admissible, because a conclusion is inevitable:—Gif đæt wīf nele hider tō lande mid mē, sceal ic lǽdan đīnne sunu eft tō đam lande đe đū of fērdest? Gen. 24, 5. Nū ic eówer sceal frumcyn witan, ǽr gē furþur fēran, Beo. Th. 508; B. 251. Ic forworht hæbbe hyldo đīne, forđon ic lāstas sceal weán on wēnum wīde lecgan, Cd. Th. 63, 3; Gen. 1026. Đū meaht be sumum tācnum ongietan, hwæs đū wēnan scealt *what with certainty you may expect*, Past. 21, 3; Swt. 157, 20. Se đe wille Drihtne bringan gecwēme lācfæsten, đonne sceal hē đæt mid ælmessan fullian, Blickl. Homl. 37, 18. Nū sceal hē sylf faran, ne mæg his ǽrende his boda beódan, Cd. Th. 35, 18; Gen. 556. Đonne hē æt hilde sceall līfes tiligan, Salm. Kmbl. 320; Sal. 159. Eart đū đe tō cumenne eart, hwæđer đe wē ōđres scylon (sceolon, MS. A.: sculon, MSS. B. C.) onbȳdan (*expectamus*), Lk. Skt. 7, 19, 20. Sceolon, Mt. Kmbl. 11, 3. Forđon wit sculon unc stađolwangas rūmor sēcan, Cd. Th. 114, 29; Gen. 1911. Đǽr hig ǽnne sculan eard weardian, Ps. Th. 132, 1. Sculun, Runic pm. Kmbl. 343, 21; Rūn. 21. Đȳ sceolon gelȳfan eorlas, hwæt mīn æđelo sién, Andr. Kmbl. 1466; An. 734. Ne sceolon mē þegenas ætwītan *men shall not reproach me* (*because there will not be the slightest grounds for reproach*), Byrht. Th. 138, 14; By. 220. Wēnde ic đæt đū đȳ wærra weorđan sceolde *I expected that you must have got more cautious*, Exon. Th. 268, 1; Jul. 425. Đā sceolde hē đǽr bīdan ryhtnorþanwindes, Ors. 1, 1; Swt. 17, 17. Scolde herebyrne sund cunnian, Beo. Th. 2890; B. 1443. Hit ofetes noman āgan sceolde, Cd. Th. 44, 35; Gen. 719. Ne meahton leng somed heora begra đǽr ǽhte habban, ac sceoldon đa rincas đȳ sēcan ellor ēđelseld, 113, 29; Gen. 1894. Mē þincþ wundor tō hwon đū sceole for ōwiht đysne man habban ungelǽredne fiscere *what reason obliges you to hold this man, an ignorant fisherman, as of any account?* Blickl. Homl. 179, 13. Gif hine mon tō genēdan scyle, and hē elles nylle *if there is no other course open but to compel him*, L. Alf. pol. 1; Th. i. 60, 13. Seó orsorge wyrd simle līhþ, đæt mon scyle wēnan, đæt heó seó sió sōþe gesǽlþ, Bt. 20; Fox 70, 30. (9) denoting need, *shall, must*, where an end is to be attained or a task to be completed or a purpose to be served:—Hwæt sceal ic mā secgean fram Sancte Iohanne *what more need I say of St. John?* Blickl. Homl. 169, 24. Đæt scell ǽgleáwra mann đonne ic mē tælige findan on ferđe *a more learned man than I reckon myself is necessary to perform the task*, Andr. Kmbl. 2965; An. 1485. Sculan wē gyt martira gemynd mā āreccan, Menol. Fox 136; Men. 68. 'Satan ic đǽr (*in hell*) sēcan wille.' ... Sceolde hē đa brādan līgas sēcan, Cd. Th. 47, 20; 763. Nihtweard (*the fiery pillar*) sceolde wīcian ofer weredum, 185, 2; Exod. 116. Tō hwon sceolde đeós smyrenes đus beón tō lore gedōn *what end was to be served by thus wasting this ointment?* Blickl. Homl. 69, 6. Hwȳ gē ǽfre scylen unrihtfióungum eówer mōd drēfan *quid tantos juvat excitare motus?* Met. 27, 1. (10) denoting the certainty of a future event, that results from a settled purpose or decision:—Ic gefremman sceal eorlīc ellen odde endedæg mīnne gebīdan *I am determined to do or die*, Beo. Th. 1277; B. 636. Mid eárum ne sceal ic (*it is settled that I shall not*) gehēran dære bēman stefne, Cd. Th. 275, 13; Sat. 171. Đū scealt deáde sweltan *thou shalt surely die*, Gen. 2, 17: Ps. Th. 118, 39. Đæt dū sunu Dryhtnes cennan sceolde, Exon. Th. 19, 10; Cri. 298. Hē (*Christ*) wiste, dæt seó burh (*Jerusalem*) sceolde ābrocen weorþan, Blickl. Homl. 77, 29. On dære nihte de hȳ on done dæig tōgædere fōn sceoldan, Chr. 992; Erl. 130, 32. Hæfdon hié on rūne āwriten wera endestæf, hwænne hié tō mōse weordan sceoldon, Andr. Kmbl. 274; An. 137. (10 a) denoting the certainty of a result under proper conditions:—Đū him fæste hel sōdan sprǣce, swā dū mīnum scealt feore gebeorgan *you are then certain to save my life*, Cd. Th. 110, 113; Gen. 1837. Fordan de (*on account of his previous conduct*) hē sceal ēce wīte þrowian, Homl. Th. i. 66, 14: Blickl. Homl. 41, 32. Hū sceal mīn cuman gǣst tō geóce? Exon. Th. 124, 10; Gū. 337. Se hlǣw sceal tō gemyndum mīnum leódum heáh hlifian on Hronesnæsse, Beo. Th. 5600; B. 2804. Wē cwǣdon ǣr, dæt se sceolde lytel sāwan, se de him done wind ondrēde, Past. 39; Swt. 285, 23. Wēndun gē dæt gē Scyppende sceoldan gelīce wesan, Exon. Th. 141, 33; Gū. 636. Đā hēht se cāsere gesponnan fiówer wildo hors . . . dæt da wildan hors scealden iornan on hearde wegas and him da limo all tōbrecan, Shrn. 72, 1. Hē fægenaþ dæs, hū hiene mon sciele (scyle, Hatt. MS.) herigean, Past. 8; Swt. 54, 7. Scile (sciele, Hatt. MS.), 9; Swt. 54, 19. Hē wēneþ dæt hē sceole tō heofenum āhafen weorþan, Blickl. Homl. 185, 5. Gif wē ǣnige bōte gebīdan sculan (scylen, MS. B.) *if improvement in our condition is certainly to take place*, Wulfst. 157, 2. (11) denoting probability:—Neron cwæd tō Paule: 'Forhwon ne sprecst dū, Paulus?' Đā andswarede him Sanctus Paulus: 'Wēnstū dæt ic sceole sprecan tō dissum treówleásan men' *do you think it likely that I shall speak to this false man?* Blickl. Homl. 183, 32. (12) as an auxiliary:—Ic sceal rǣdan tō merigen *lecturus sum cras*, dū scealt rǣdan *lecturus es*, hī sceolon (sceolan, sculon) rǣdan *lecturi sunt*, Ælfc. Gr. 24; Zup. 136, 10–12. Ōder *participium* is tōwerdre tīde se de rǣdan sceal *lecturus* . . . dæt de sceal beón gerǣd *legendus*, 41; Zup. 246, 10–15. Se de wyle odde sceal sprecan *loquuturus*, Zup. 247, 15, 11: 248, 6. Se de sceal beón gecyssed *osculandus*, 248, 7. Sceal habba ł hæfis *habebit*, Mt. Kmbl. Lind. 1, 23. Hæfeþ ł hē scile habba, 6, 24. Wē stīges ł wē scilon stīge *ascendimus*, 20, 18. Gē sciolon geseá ł gē geseás *videbitis*, 13, 14. Ne hēras hiá ł ne sciolon gehēra *non audiunt*, 13, 13. Đonne dū ǣfre on moldan man gewurde odde ǣfre fulwihte onfōn sceolde, Soul Kmbl. 172; Seel. 86. On dæs engles wordum wæs gehȳred, dæt þurh hire beorþor sceolde beón gehǣled eall wīfa cynn and wera, Blickl. Homl. 5, 23. Đā bæd Swegen hine det hē sceolde faran mid him, Chr. 1046; Erl. 174, 12. Wēndon dæt hig sceoldon māre onfōn *plus essent accepturi*, Mt. Kmbl. 20, 10. Đa donne de sió godcundde stefn þreáde and cuæd dæt hié scolden leásunga wītgian *quos divinus sermo falsa videre redarguit*, Past. 15, 2; Swt. 91, 8. Hyra þeáw wæs dæt hī da untruman in lǣdan sceoldan, Bd. 4, 24; S. 598, 28. Đeáh hē micel āge, and him mon erigan scyle ǣghwelce dæg æcera þūsend, Met. 14, 4. (13) denoting an assertion not made by the speaker, when a statement is matter of report [cf. *Ger.* sollen, and the use of *should* in the following passage:—There was something said about ane Campbell, that suld hae been concerned in the robbery, and that he suld hae had a warrant frae the Duke of Argyle, Rob Roy 1, 219]:—Be dære frēcnan coþe de se mon his ūtgang þurh done mūþ sceal (*is said*) āspīwan. Hē sceal oft bealcettan, Lchdm. ii. 236, 13. Ys sǣd, dæt Diana dās wyrta findan scolde, i. 106, 5, 23: 120, 4. Đū gehērdest reccan on ealdum leásum spellum, dætte Iob sceolde beón se hēhsta god, Bt. 35, 4; Fox 162, 6. Đā sǣdon hī, dæt dæs hearperes wīf sceolde ācwelan, and hire sāwle mon sceolde lǣdon tō helle. Đā sceolde se hearpere weordan swā sārig. . . Đā hē dider com, da sceolde cuman dære helle hund ongeán hine . . . se sceolde habban þrió heáfdu, 35, 6; Fox 168, 3–17: 38, 1; Fox 194, 30–34. Đeáh hē Cristen beón sceolde *though he was said to be a Christian*, Bd. 2, 20; S. 521, 29. Fundon dā leáse gewitan de forlugon Nabod dæt hē sceolde wyrigan God (*they brought reports of his blasphemy*), Homl. Skt. i. 18, 197. Ulf biscop com and forneáh man sceolde tōbrecan his stef *the report was that they were very near breaking his staff*, Chr. 1047; Erl. 177, 7. Swā swā manige men sǣdon þe hit geseón sceoldan *who were said to have seen it*, 1098; Erl. 235, 5: 1100; Erl. 235, 33. III. without an infinite (1) denoting constraint, necessity, need, fixed purpose:—Ealle wyrd forsweóp mīne māgas, ic him æfter sceal *I must after them*, Beo. Th. 5625; B. 2816. Hē sceal nēde tō dara hlāforda dōme de hē hine ǣr underþeódde *non facit, quod optat, ipse dominis pressus iniquis*, Bt. 37, 1; Fox 186, 28. Sió manbōt de dam hlāforde sceal *the fine that must go to the lord*, L. In. 76; Th. i. 150, 16. Tō myclan bryce sceal micel bōt nȳde, and tō miclum bryne wæter unlytel, Wulfst. 157, 8. Earc sceal dȳ māre *the ark must be the bigger*, Cd. Th. 79, 19; Gen. 1313. Hié tō helle sculon, Cd. Th. 45, 26; Gen. 732. Xersis āscade hwæt sceolde æt swā lytlum weorode māra fultum būton da āne de him ǣr ābolgen wæs *Xerxes demanded what a greater force was needed for in dealing with so small a band, than those only with whom he had before been angry*, Ors. 2, 5; Swt. 80, 16. Eall swā hī sceoldon tō Sandwīc *as if they had* or *purposed to go to Sandwich*, Chr. 1049; Erl. 174, 26. Đæt hē of disse worlde sceolde, Blickl. Homl. 225, 5. Đonne seó eorþe him on ufan scealde *when the earth came to be put upon them*, Shrn. 81, 2. Ǣr hē onweg scyle *before he die*, Exon. Th. 310, 14; Seef. 74. (2) denoting obligation, fitness, propriety, use (cf. *Ger.* wozu soll dies?):—Đys sceal on twelftan dæg *this is the proper gospel for twelfth-day* (cf. dys godspel gebyraþ, Rubc. 1, 18), Mt. Kmbl. Rubc. 2, 1 (*and often*). Hwæt scal dē swā lādlīc strīd *what good will the strife do you?* Cd. Th. 41, 28; Gen. 663. Rǣd sceal mid snyttro . . . til sceal mid tilum, Exon. Th. 334, 26; Gn. Ex. 22. Wita sceal geþyldig, ne sceal nō tō hātheort, 290, 15; Wand. 65. Hige sceal þe heardra, mōd sceal de māre, de ūre mægen lytlaþ, Byrht. Th. 140, 62; By. 312. Hī gecnāwan ne cunnan ne da medtrymnesse ne eác da wyrta de dǣrwid sculon *the herbs that are proper for the disease*, Past. 1, 1; Swt. 25, 22. Ōdre wyrtdrencas sculon (*are proper*), Lchdm. ii. 208, 3. Đās wyrte sculon tō lungensealfe, iii. 16, 6. Hwæt sceolon (sculon, MS. H.) hī gesǣde nū wē swerian ne mōton *what good would they (adverbia jurativa) do stated, now we may not swear?* Ælfc. Gr. 38; Zup. 227, 10. Hē āxode done cāsere hū hē embe hī sceolde *how he was to deal with them*, Homl. Skt. i. 5, 370. Ne meahte geþencan hū ymb dæt sceolde *what ought to be done about it, how the matter ought to be dealt with*, Exon. Th. 378, 7; Deor. 12. Hwæt sceoldon (*deberent*) hig mē būton ic cūþe temian hig *what good would they (hawks) be to me unless I knew how to tame them?* Coll. Monast. Th. 25, 23. Hié be dǣm wiston hwider hié sceoldon *they knew by that in which direction they had to go*, Ors. 3, 5; Swt. 106, 15. Hié wiston hū hié tō dǣm elpendon sceoldon *they knew the proper way of attacking the elephants*, 4, 1; Swt. 156, 17. Warnige man done stīwerd tō hwylcere stōwe dæt līc sceole, Chart. Th. 607, 15. Hwæt sceoldon dē ūre ælmessan? Wulfst. 240, 15. [*Goth.* [skulan]; *prs.* skal, *pl.* skulum; *p.* skulda: *O. Sax.* [skulan]; *prs.* skal, *pl.* skulun; *p.* skolda: *O. Frs.* skila; *prs.* skal, skel, skil, *pl.* skilun; *p.* skolde: *O. H. Ger.* scolan; *prs.* scal, *pl.* sculumes; *p.* scolta: *Icel.* skulu; *prs.* skal, *pl.* skulum; *p.* skyldi.]

sculdor; *pl.* (*dual?*) sculdru (-o), sculdra; *m. A shoulder*:—Sculdur *scalpula*, Wrt. Voc. ii. 120, 18: *scapulus*, i. 64, 68. Sculdor, 283, 6. Sculder *scapula*, 44, 27. His sculdor and his hleór wurdon ontende mid dam fȳre, Homl. Th. ii. 344, 16. Wæs dæt bærnet on his sculdre ǣfre gesewen, 346, 26. On his sculdre *in humero*, Bd. 3, 19; S. 549, 15. Ōþ done swīdran sculdor, Lchdm. ii. 198, 19. Duru dæt mannes heáfod ge da sculdro māgan in, Blickl. Homl. 127, 9. Sculdra *scapula* (*-ae?*), Wrt. Voc. i. 71, 19. On bǣm sculdrum *in utroque humero*, Past. 14, 3; Swt. 83, 9, 21. Hē onfeóld hys hrægl æt hys sceoldrum, Shrn. 98, 17. In scyldrum ł bæccum *in humeros*, Mt. Kmbl. Lind. 23, 4: Lk. Skt. Lind. Rush. 15, 5. Hī dydon ānne hwītel on hira sculdra *pallium imposuerunt humeris suis*, Gen. 9, 23: Bd. 3, 19; S. 549, 1. Sculdru (sculdra, MS. X.), L. Ecg. C. 9; Th. ii. 140, 10. Gif mon ōdrum da sculdru forsleá, L. Alf. pol. 73; Th. i. 98, 21. Se sacerd smyreþ breóst and sculdru (sculdran, MS. E.), Wulfst. 35, 16: Lchdm. ii. 260, 17. [Schuldren; *pl.* Jul. 49, 18. He let smyte of ys hede by þe ssoldren, R. Glouc. 313, 7. *O. Frs.* sculder: *O. H. Ger.* scultarra *humerus, scapula, spadula.*]

sculdor-hrægel, es; *n. A garment to cover the shoulders*:—Sculdorhrægl *superhumerale*, Wrt. Voc. i. 81, 44.

sculdor-wærc, es; *m. Pain in the shoulders*:—Wid sculdorwærce and earma, Lchdm. ii. 340, 12: 6, 2.

scult-hēta. v. scyld-hǣta.

scunian, sceonian; *p.* ode. I. *to shun, fear, avoid a thing from fear*:—Hē his hatunge fleáh and scunode, Guthl. 19; Gdwin. 76, 16. II. *to be afraid*:—Scunian *revereantur*, Ps. Spl. T. 69, 2. III. *to detest, abhor*:—Mid āne mōde wurd hē gescunned *uni animo detestetur*, Chart. Th. 318, 37. [Mi uader scunede (sonede, 2nd MS.) þene cristindom & þa hædene laȝen luuede to swide, þa we sculled sceonien (hatie, 2nd MS.), Laym. 14868. Birrþ þe shunenn (*avoid from fear*) to follȝhenn ohht tærinne, Orm. 4502. Ancren owen to hatien ham, and schunien, þ heo ham ne iheren, A. R. 82, 23. Þu ahtest þis werc ouer alle þing to schunien (*avoid with abhorrence, abhor*), H. M. 35, 11. Al hit him uleh and scunede, þet him er luuede, O. E. Homl. i. 79, 29. Ȝif him wrattheth, be ywar and his weye shonye (*avoid from fear*), Piers P. prol. 174.] v. ā-, on-scunian.

scunung, e; *f. An abomination*:—On scunungum *in abominationibus*, Cant. M. ad fil. 16. v. a-, on-scunung.

scūr, sceór, scyūr, es; *m.*: e; *f.* (?) I. *a shower, storm of rain, snow, hail, etc.*:—Scūr *nimbus*, Wrt. Voc. i. 52, 60: 76, 42. Scyūr (scūr, Rush.), Lk. Skt. Lind. 12, 54. Đes scūr *hic imber*, Ælfc. Gr. 9, 18; Zup. 43, 7. Swylce scūr ofer gærs *quasi imber super herbam*, Cant. M. ad fil. 2. Rēnes scūr, Exon. Th. 215, 1; Ph. 246. Regna scūr, Cd. Th. 252, 10; Dan. 576. Hægles scūr, 50, 13; Gen. 808. Syddan (*after the overflow of the Nile*) tō twelf mōndum ne cymþ dǣr nān ōder scūr, ōd dæt seó eá eft up ābrece, Lchdm. iii. 254, 2. Đonne sceór cymeþ, Andr. Kmbl. 1024; An. 512. Đá wæs geblissod seó Godes burh for đam cyme đæs scūres đe hý geclǣnsode *fluminis impetus laetificat civitatem Dei*, Ps. Th. 45, 4. Scūre *nimbo*, Wrt. Voc. ii. 61, 54: *inserenae*, Hpt. Gl. 514, 15. Scūras *imbres*, Ps. Lamb. 77, 44. Geþēnsume scūras *coloni nimbi*, Wrt. Voc. ii. 134, 28. Wealcaþ hit (*hail*) windes scūras (? MS. scūra), Runic pm. Kmbl. 341, 6; Rūn. 9. Scūra *procellarum*, Hpt. Gl. 509, 20 [H]reósendlīcum scūrum *ruituris imbribus*, 499, 64: 501, 6: Wrt. Voc. ii. 47, 15. Seó lyft liccaþ đone wǣtan of ealre eorþan and of đære sǣ and gegaderaþ tō scūrum, Lchdm. iii. 276, 13. Weal sceal wiđstondan storma scūrum, Exon. Th. 281, 25; Jul. 651. **I a.** metaph. *a shower* of missiles:—Flāna scūras, Judth. Thw. 24, 34; Jud. 221: Elen. Kmbl. 234; El. 117. Hygegār lēteþ, scūrum sceóteþ, Exon. Th. 315, 22; Mōd. 35. **I b.** *a shower* of blows of a hammer falling on a weapon (?):—Scearpne mēce scūrum heardne, Judth. Thw. 22, 26; Jud. 79. Cf. scūr-heard. **II.** metaph. *a storm, trouble, disquiet*:—Swā đeós woruld fareþ scūrum (cf. scȳr-mǣlum) scyndeþ *hurries on stormily*, Exon. Th. 469, 24; Hy. 11, 7. [*Goth.* skūra (windis) λαῖλαψ, *procella*: *O. Sax.* skūr *a missile, weapon*: —That man ina wītnōdi wāpnes eggiun, skarpun skūrun, Hel. 5138. *O. H. Ger.* scūr *tempestas, grando*; also of weapons: —Dō lēttun sē askim scrītan, scarpēn scūrim, Hildebrandslied 66. *Icel.* skūr *a shower; a shower* of missiles; vāpna, hjálma skūr *id.*] v. hægl-, hagal-, hilde-, regn-, winter-scūr; scȳr-mǣlum, *and next word.*

scūra (-e; *f.* ?), an; *m. A shower*:—Hē ārīman mæg rægnas scūran dropena gehwelcne, Cd. Th. 265, 22; Sat. 11.

scūr-beorh, *gen.* -beorge; *f. A shelter against storm*:—Hrōfas sind gehrorene . . . scearde scūrbeorge, Exon. Th. 476, 9; Ruin. 5.

scūr-boga, an; *m. A rain-bow*:—Đonne ic scūrbogan mīnne iéwe, Cd. Th. 93, 5; Gen 1541.

scurf, scurfed, scurfende. v. scorf, scorfed, scorfende.

scūr-heard; *adj. Made hard by blows* (v. scūr, **I b**; *and* cf. heoru hamere geþuren, Beo. Th. 2575; B. 1285):—Sweordes ecg, scerp and scūrheard, Andr. Kmbl. 2267; An. 1135. Đæt him fēla lāf (*the sword*) ne meahte scūrheard sceþþan, Beo. Th. 2070; B. 1033.

scūr-sceadu (*or* -scead; *n.*); *f. A protection against storms* (cf. *umbrella*):—Nys unc wuht beforan tō scūrsceade, Cd. Th. 50, 23; Gen. 813.

-scuta *in* an-scuta *falarica*, Hpt. Gl. 425, 14. [Cf. (?) He þa fla lette gliden bi Corineus siden Corineus bleinte & þene scute biberh, Laym. 1461.]

scutel *a dish*:—Scutel *catinus*, Wrt. Voc. i. 290, 21: ii. 17, 17. [Scotylle *scutella*, 257, 15. *O. H. Ger.* scuzzilà *scutula, scutella, discus, catinus, lanx*: *Icel.* skutill *a dish.* From Latin (?) *scutella.*]

scutel *and* scytel, es; *m.* **I.** *a dart, missile, arrow*:—Sciutil *jaculum, sagitta*, Txts. 110, 1177, 1179. Scytelum cilda *sagittis parvulorum*, Ps. Th. 63, 7. [*Icel.* skutill *an instrument shot forth, a harpoon.* Cf. scytyl *a shuttle;* schytle, chyldys game *sagitella*, Prompt. Parv. 447. Schetylle *navecula*, Wrt. Voc. i. 235, 3.] **II.** *the tongue of a balance* (?):—Scytel *momentum*, 76, 632. Scutil, Wrt. Voc. ii. 71, 20. Scutel, 56, 52. [*M. Lat.* momentum *languette de bilance.* Cf. schytylle, schityl, onstabyl *preceps*, Prompt. Parv. 447.]

scūwa, scūa, an; *m.* **I.** *the shadow* thrown by an object:—Oferwrāh muntas scūa his *operuit montes umbra ejus*, Ps. Surt. 79, 11. Dægas mīne swē swē scūa (*umbra*) onhældun, 101, 12: 143, 4. Ic eom scūan gelīc swȳþe āhylded *sicut umbra cum declinat*, Ps. Th. 108, 23. **II.** *shade, darkness*:—Mid đȳ wit forþgongende wǣron under đam scūwan đære þȳstran nihte *cum progrederemur sola sub nocte per umbras*, Bd. 5, 12; S. 628, 14. **II a.** fig. *shadow*:—Scūa deáþes *umbra mortis*, Ps. Surt. 43, 20. In midle scūan deáþes, 22, 4. Ālǣd mē ūt of đyses carcernes hūse and of deáþes scūan, Blickl. Homl. 87, 35. Scūia (scūa, Rush.), Mt. Kmbl. Lind. 4, 16. In scȳa, Rtl. 168, 9. Sealde him deorcne deáþes scūwan, Ch. Th. 293, 15; Sat. 455. **III.** *shadow, protection*:—Ic on fægerum scūan fiđera đīnra gewīcie *in umbra alarum tuarum spero*, Ps. Th. 56, 1. Under scūan fiđra đīnra gesild mē *sub umbra alarum tuarum protege me*, Ps. Surt. 16, 8. **IV.** *shadow* as opposed to substance:—Scūan ł leásunge *fallacis*, Hpt. Gl. 459, 14. [Screne *or* scu *or* spere *scrinium, ventifuga*, Prompt. Parv. 450. Spere *or* scuw (schuu), 468. Þe skuues of the scowtes, Gaw. 2167. Cf. *Goth.* thairh skuggwan δι' ἐσόπτρου, 1 Cor. 13, 12. *O. H. Ger.* scūwo *umbra*: *Icel.* skuggi *a shadow; a spectre.*] v. dǣd-, deáþ-, dim-, heolstor-, hlīn-, niht-scūwa (-scūa).

scūwan, scūan (?) *to shade.* [*O. H. Ger.* scūit *adumbrdt*: *Icel.* skyggva *to overshadow.*] v. ofer-scūwan.

scȳan (*for* scȳhan), scȳn (?); *p.* de *To prompt, urge, persuade, suggest*:—Đa ǣrestan synne se weriga gāst scȳde . . . Forđon mid đȳ se weriga gāst đa synne scȳſþ (scȳþ, MS. C.: scȳeþ, MS. T.) on mōde *primam culpam serpens suggessit . . . Cum enim malignus spiritus peccatum suggerit in mente*, Bd. 1, 27; S. 497, 14–20. Wē getǣceþ ł scȳaþ him *nos suadebimus ei*, Mt. Kmbl. Rush. 28, 14. Cf. scȳhend, scȳend *maulistis*, Txts. 78, 654. Scȳhend *malistis*, Wrt. Voc. ii. 55, 52. [Cf. *O. H. Ger.* scūhenti *exhortans*, Grff. vi. 417.] v. sceóness, scyhtan.

scyccels. v. sciccels.

scydd, es; *m. Alluvial ground* (?):—Đis synt đa denbæra . . . hudelinga scydd, Cod. Dip Kmbl. ii. 195, 19. On timberslǣd in stǣpa cnolles scydd on hanslǣdes heáfdan, iii. 380, 26. Haec sunt pascua porcorum . . . in communi silua pascuale quod dicitur Palinga Schittas (scyddas ?), ii. 303, 19. [Cf. *M. H. Ger.* schüt: *Ger.* schutt.]

scȳde, Cd. Th. 232, 26; Dan. 266. v. sceón.

scȳend. v. scȳan.

scȳe-uange:—Scōe ł scȳeuange (-þwange ?) *calciamentum*, Ps. Spl. T. 59, 9.

scyfe, es; *m.* **I.** of rapid motion caused by a push (metaph.), *precipitation*, v. scūfan:—Word scyfes *verba praecipitationis*, Ps. Lamb. 51, 6. Hié weorđaþ oft āscrencte on đæm scyfe đære styringe hira mōdes đæt hī hira selfra ne āgon đȳ māre geweald đe ōđerra monna *motionis impulsu praecipites quaedam velut alienati peragunt*, Past. 33, 1; Swt. 215, 12, 17. **I a.** glossing *preceps*:—Seó ūs on scefe gedwelde teáh mid wegleásum *quae nos in preceps errore traxit devio*, Hymn. Surt. 24, 11. **II.** *furtherance* of a project, *the pushing* of a matter, *prompting, instigation* in a good sense, cf. scūfan, **V**:—Ǣlc burhgemet beó be his dihte ge scife swīđe rihte, L. I. P. 7; Th. ii. 312, 21. **III.** *prompting, instigation* in a bad sense, cf. scūfan, **VI**:—Se đe þurh deófles scyfe on synna befealle, L. C. E. 23; Th. i. 374, 9. Befeallen þurh deófles scyfe on heálīce misdǣde, Wulfst. 103, 21. v. niđer-scyfe.

scyfel, e: scyfele, an; *f.* [*Shovel* in *shovel*-hat ?] *A covering for a woman's head;* mafors (*mafors* operimentum capitis maxime feminarum, Ducange):—Hacele *capsula*, cōp *ependiten*, scyfele *mafors*, nunne *sanctimonialis*, Wrt. Voc. i. 284, 67. Scyfla, scybla *maforte* (*-ae*), Txts. 77, 1267: Wrt. Voc ii. 55, 38. Scyfelum *mafortibus*, 55, 39: 87, 63. [Cf. (?) *scuffle*, a linen garment worn by children to keep their clothes clean, a pinafore, an apron (Sussex). *Icel.* skupla; *f.*; skypill; *m. a woman's hood hiding* or *shading her face.*]

scyftan, -scȳgean, scȳhend. v. sciftan, -scīgan, scȳan.

scyhtan; *p.* te *To instigate, prompt, urge*:—Mē nædre beswāc and mē neódlīce tō forsceape scyhte and tō scyldfrece, Cd. Th. 55, 22; Gen. 898. Ōđer him đās eorþan ealle sægde lǣne . . . Ōđer hine scyhte đæt hē sceađena gemōt nihtes sōhte, Exon. Th. 109, 30; Gū. 98. [We schuchted hine ueor awei hwon we dođ deadliche sunne, A. R. 312, 10, MS. C.] v. scȳan.

scyl, scylcen, scyld *a shield.* v. scill, scilcen, scild.

scyld, e: scyldu (o); *indecl. f.* **I.** *guilt, sin, crime, fault*:—Hē sume māndǣde gefremede đā seó scyld đā tō his heortan hwearf đā onscunode hē hī hefelīce *sceleris aliquid commiserat, quod commissum, ubi ad cor suum rediit, gravissime exhorruit*, Bd. 4, 25; S. 599, 34. Sitte sió scyld (*the killing of a slave*) on him, L. Alf. 17; Th. i. 48, 15. On eów scyld siteþ, Exon. Th. 131, 2; Gū. 449. Is Euan scyld eal forpynded, 7, 6; Cri. 97. Hē his scylde forgyfenysse bæd *veniam reatus postulans*, Bd. 3, 22; S. 553, 33. Đa byrđenne suā micelre scylde *tanti reatus pondera*, Past. 2, 2; Swt. 31, 14. Būtan scylde *sine culpa*, 3, 1; Swt. 33, 16: L. H. E. 12; Th. i. 32, 9. Hī būton ǣlcere scylde (*without being guilty of any crime*) wurdon fordōne, Bt. 29, 2; Fox 104, 30. Ǣt openre scylde *flagrante delicto*, L. In. 37; Th. i. 124, 23. Hafaþ đæt mōd hwylcehugu scyldo *habet animus aliquem reatum*, Bd. 1, 27; S. 496, 42. Synna, scylda *piacula*, Wrt. Voc. ii. 66, 78. Mīne scylde *delicta mea*, Ps. Th. 68, 6: Ps. Surt. 58, 13. Scylđa, Past. 32, 2; Swt. 211, 20. Scelda, Ps. C. 45. Brōđres schyldo *fratris vitia*, Mt. Kmbl. p. 15, 5. Āscyred scylda gehwylcre, deópra firena, Elen. Kmbl. 2624; El. 1313: 937; El. 470. Hwīlum biþ gōd wærlīce tō mīđanne his hiéremonna scylda (*vitia*), Past. 21, 1; Swt. 151, 9. **II.** *a debt, due*:—Ryhtlīcor cweđan đæt wē him gielden scylde đonne wē him mildheortnesse dōn *justitiae debitum potius solvimus, quam misericordiae opera implemus*, 45, 1; Swt. 335, 19. Āgefnæ beón đa scylde *reddi debitum*, Mt. Kmbl. Rush. 28, 25. Hē đa scyld forlēt wiđ hine *debitum dimisit ei*, 27: 30. [Sculd *scelus*, Wrt. Voc. i. 95, 74. *O. Sax.* skuld *a crime; a due*: *O. L. Ger.* sculd: *O. Frs.* skelde, schuld, schild: *O. H. Ger.* sculd, sculda *causa, facinus, noxa, injuria, crimen, debitum, meritum*: *Icel.* skuld, skyld *a due, tax; sake.*] v. deáþ-, frum-, ge-, god-, mān-, nīd-scyld.

scyldan, scyldend. v. scildan, scildend.

scyldan, scyldian *to charge, accuse*:—Hȳ gān .xii. sume and gescyldigen (gescylden, *other MS.*) hine, L. Ath. i. 11; Th. i. 206, 3.

scyld-frecu, e; *f Guilty greed*:—Mē (*Eve*) scyhte tō scyldfrece fāh wyrm þurh fægir word, Cd. Th. 55, 23; Gen. 898.

scyld-full; *adj. Guilty, criminal, sinful, wicked*:—Ic (*Adam*) wreó mē scyldfull, Cd. Th. 53, 30; Gen. 869. Bearn Godes on wergum folce wīf curon, scyldfulra mægđ, scȳne and fægere, 76, 4; Gen. 1252. Đonne sweart wæter swelgaþ sceađum scyldfullum *when the deluge swallows the wicked*, 78, 32; Gen. 1302: Elen. Kmbl. 619; El. 310.

scyldgian, scyldgung. v. scyldigian, scyldigung.

scyld-hǣta, an; *m. One who demands a due* or *debt, a bailiff*:—

Scultheta *exactor*, Wrt. Voc. ii. 107, 70. Scyldlǣta (-hǣta?) *exactor*, i. *postulator*, 144, 54. [*O. Frs.* skeltata, skelta (der stellvertreter des grafen, v. Richthofen, pp. 1023 sqq.): *O. L. Ger.* sculd-hēto (quicunque villicus est abbatis quod nos vulgo dicimus *sculthētho*): *O. H. Ger.* scult-heizo *vilicare, tribunus, procurator, exactor populi*: *Ger.* schult-heisz. Cf. *Goth.* dulga-haitja *a creditor.*]

scyld-hata, an; *m. One who hates wrongfully, an enemy*:—Scyld-hatan, ealdgenīðlan, Andr. Kmbl. 2095; An. 1049. Scyldhatan, egle ondsacan, 2295; An. 1149. v. next word.

scyld-hete, es; *m. An enemy, a foe*:—Mid scyldhetum, werigum wrōhtsmiðum, Andr. Kmbl. 170; An. 85. v. preceding word.

scyldian *to commit a fault*:—Gesette God ǣ scyldiendum *legem statuit delinquentibus*, Ps. Th. 24, 7. v. scyldigian, scyldan.

scyldig; *adj.* I. *guilty, sinful, criminal*:—Scyldig *reus*, Wrt. Voc. i. 49, 1: 86, 61: *sons*, Ælfc. Gr. 9, 39; Zup. 63, 14. Gif man wāt, ðæt ōðer mān swerað, hē biþ scildig (*portabit iniquitatem suam*), gif hē hit forhilþ, Lev. 5, 1. Wæs gecueden tō ðæm scyldegan folce *delinquenti populo dicitur*, Past. 15, 1; Swt. 91, 2. Ðæt hē hine scyldigne ongete *reum se cognoscat*, Bd. 1, 27; S. 496, 33: Elen. Kmbl. 1380; El. 692. Hū hē ðæt scyldige werud forscrifen hefde, Cd. Th. 267, 4; Sat. 33. Scyldge men, Exon. Th. 71, 10; Cri. 1153. Scyldigra scolu, 98, 15; Cri. 1608: 132, 22; Gū. 476. Hendum scyldigra *manibus nocentium*, Rtl. 24, 11. Heó nāuht ne þreáþ ðām scildigum, Bt. 4; Fox 8, 13. Earfeþu scyldgum tō sconde, Exon. Th. 78, 14; Cri. 1274. Hié ða scyldigan þearlwīslīce dēmaþ, Blickl. Homl. 63, 20. Stræc wið ða unryhtwīsan and wið ða scyldgan, Past. 17, 5; Swt. 113, 23. I a. *guilty* of committing a crime, (1) with gen. of crime:—Se biþ ēces gyltes scyldig *reus erit aeterni delicti*, Mk. Skt. 3, 29. Morðres scyldig, Beo. Th. 3370; B. 1683. Deáðes scyldig *guilty of causing death*, L. In. 5; Th. i. 104, 13. Mansleges scyldig, Blickl. Homl. 189, 34. Morðres scyldige ... deáþes scyldige, 65, 10–11: H. R. 107, 1. (2) with inst. of crime:—Synnum scyldig, Beo. Th. 6135; B. 3071. Dǣdum scyldige, Cd. Th. 76, 35; Gen. 1267. Lehtrum scyldige, Andr. Kmbl. 2434; An. 1218. I b. *guilty* against (*wið*) a person:—Ǣlc man ðe yfel dēþ mid yfelum willan is scyldig wið God, H. R. 105, 33: Cd. Th. 250, 20; Dan. 549. Menn wǣron deádlīce and wið heora Drihten scyldige, Hexam. 17; Norm. 24, 26: Blickl. Homl. 47, 21. II. *responsible* for, *liable* for, *chargeable* with an ill result, (1) with gen.:—Gif hwylc mæssepreóst untruman men sprǣce forwyrne, and hē on ðære tyddernesse swelte, sȳ hē on dōmes dæg ðære sāwle scyldig (*ejus animae reus*), L. Ecg. P. i. 2; Th. ii. 172, 29. Hē sceal mid rēðnesse him stiére ðȳlæs hē sié scyldig ealra hira scylda *ne culparum omnium reus ipse teneatur*, Past. 21, 5; Swt. 161, 1. Gif hwelc gōd lǣce gesihþ, ðæt his hwam þearf biþ, and ðonne for his slǣwþe āgiémeleásaþ ðæt hē his helpe, ðonne wille wē cweðan ðæt hē sié genōg ryhtlīce his brōðor deáþes scyldig, 49, 1; Swt. 377, 21. Swā feala earmra manna swā on ðæs rīcan neáweste sweltaþ, and hē him nele syllan his teóþungsceatta dǣl, ðonne biþ hē ealra ðara manna deáþes sceldig, Blickl. Homl. 53, 7. (2) with inst.:—Gif God him ne āraþ, ðonne beóþ hié suā monegum scyldum scyldige suā hié manegra unþeáwa gestīran meahton mid hiora lārum, gif hī ongemong monnum beón wolden *ex tantis rei sunt, quantis venientes ad publicum prodesse potuerunt*, Past. 5, 3; Swt. 45, 22. III. *liable* for a debt, *bound* by an obligation:—Swā hwā swā swereþ on ðæs temples golde se ys scyldig *qui juraverit in auro templi, debet*, Mt. Kmbl. 23, 16. Suǣ uoe forgefon scyldgum ūsum (*debitoribus nostris*), Mt. Kmbl. Lind. 6, 12. Syndrigum scyldgum *singulis debitoribus*, Lk. Skt. Lind. 16, 5. IV. *liable* to forfeiture, *forfeiting* (1) with gen. of forfeit:—Gif hwā ymb cyninges feorh sierwie, sié hē his feores scyldig and ealles ðæs ðe hē āge, L. Alf. pol. 4; Th. i. 64, 1: L. Ath. v. 1, 4; Th. i. 230, 6, 12. Hē æt wīge gecrang, ealdres scyldig, Beo. Th. 2680; B. 1338: 4128; B. 2061. Feores sceldig, Ps. C. 20. Sȳ hē scyldig his sylfes and ealles ðæs ðe hē āge, L. Ath. iv. prm.; Th. i. 220, 12. Beó hē .cxx. scill. scildig wið ðone cing, L. Ath. v. 1, 5; Th. i. 230, 11: L. In. 4; Th. i. 104, 10. Beó hē wið ðone cyninge scyldig ealles ðæs ðe hē āge, Wulfst. 271, 26. Se ðe ðæt gecwēme ne dēþ, beó hē his inganges scyldig, Ch. Th. 606, 21. Sȳ hē his tungan scyldig, L. Edg. ii. 4; Th. i. 266, 25. (2) with inst.:—Ðū, ealdre scyldig, deáþe sweltest, Exon. Th. 250, 9; Jul. 124. Gebeád ðæt se wǣre aldre scyldig, se ðæs onsōce, Cd. Th. 244, 19; Dan. 450. V. *liable* to punishment, *deserving* of punishment:—Scyldig *obnoxius*, Wrt. Voc. ii. 115, 31. (1) with gen. of punishment:—Hē is deáþes scyldig *reus est mortis*, Mt. Kmbl. 26, 66: Mk. Skt. 14, 64. Ðū eart wið mē deáþes scyldig *dignus es morte*, Bd. 4, 22; S. 591, 41. (2) with dat. (?):—Se ðe ofslihþ se byþ dōme (dōmes, MS. A.) scyldig *qui occiderit, reus erit judicio*, Mt. Kmbl. 5, 21. [Þe bið al swa sculdig þe þet uuel iþeuað swa þe þe hit deð, O. E. Homl. i. 113, 2. *A. R.* schuldi: *O. Sax.* skuldig *guilty, liable* to a payment or penalty: *O. Frs.* skeldech: *O. H. Ger.* sculdig *reus, culpabilis, meritus, debitus, debitor, obnoxius.*] v. feorh-, for-, god-, hand-, mān-, morþor-, þeóf-, þurh-, twī-, un-, wam-scyldig.

scyldigian, scyldgian; *p.* ode *To sin*:—Wið ða scyldgiendan (scyldgigendan, Hatt. MSS.) *contra peccantem*, Past. 21, 1; Swt. 151, 23. v. for-, ge-scyldigian; scyldian.

scyldiglīc. v. un-scyldiglīc.

scyldigness, e; *f. Guiltiness*:—Synnignise ł scyldignise *reatum*, Rtl. 42, 33: 103, 17.

scyldigung, scyldgung, e; *f. A criminal charge*:—Be ðon ðe scyldgunge bǣde æt ofslegenum. Wē cwǣdon, se ðe scyldunga (be ðon ðe scyldgunga, *other* MS.) bǣde æt ofslagenum þeófe ðæt hē eode þreora sum tō ... and ðone āþ syllen ðæt hȳ on heora mǣge nāne þȳfþe nyston ... and hȳ gān siþþan .xii. sume and gescyldigen hine *of him who asks for the charge* (*in order to refute it*) *in the case of a slain thief. We ordained, he that should ask for the charge in the case of a slain thief, that he should go with two others ... and they shall make oath that they knew of no theft on the part of their kinsman ... and afterwards twelve on the other side shall go and bring the charge against him* (*the thief*) (cf. Qui culpam exigit de fure occiso, L. H. i. 74, 2; Th. i. 578), L. Ath. i. 11; Th. i. 204, 26.

scyld-lǣta, scyldung. v. scyld-hǣta, scyldigung.

scyld-leás; *adj. Guiltless*:—Scyldlǣs *insons*, Lchdm. i. lxiii, 2.

scyld-wreccende *punishing guilt*:—Hell scyldwreccende, Exon. Th. 71, 25; Cri. 1161.

scyld-wyrcende *committing sin* or *guilt*:—Ðū (*the soul*) ðone līchoman scyldwyrcende gewemdest, Exon. Th. 91, 4; Cri. 1487. Ðonne ðeós woruld scyldwyrcende byrneþ, 232, 5; Ph. 502: 269, 4; Jul. 445. Ðū womfulle, scyldwyrcende sceaþan āwurpe, Elen. Kmbl. 1520; El. 762.

scyl-ēgede. v. sceolh-eágede.

scylf, scylp, es; *m.* I. *a peak, crag, tor* (in local names):—Ðonon ofer ealne ðone hǣþfeld tō Hnæfes scylfe, Cod. Dip. Kmbl. iii. 130, 37. Tō byrnan scylfe, 38, 36. Sticule scylpas *scabri murices*, Germ. 399, 446. Scylfa *scopulorum*, Hpt. Gl. 421, 43. II. *a turret, tower, pinnacle*:—Se deófol gesette hine uppan ðam scylfe ðæs heágan temples, Homl. Th. i. 166, 17: 170, 1. Wē biddaþ ðæt ðū āstīge tō ðam sticelan scylfe ... Hwæt ða bōceras hine gebrohton tō ðæs temples scylfe, ii. 300, 1–3. Hē hine āsette ofer ðæs temples scylf, Blickl. Homl. 27, 11. Scylfas *maciones*, Wrt. Voc. ii. 59, 29: *pinnas*, Blickl. Gl. Ða torras and ða scylfas on him bǣron ða elpendas *elephanti superpositas turres gestaverunt*, Nar. 4, 16. [Cf. (?) *O. H. Ger.* sculpa *gleba.*] v. stān-scylf; scylfig.

scylfe. v. scilfe.

scylfig, scylpig; *adj. Craggy, rocky*:—Scylpige *scopulosas*, Hpt. Gl. 529, 29. v. scylf.

Scylfingas, scylfor, scylfring, scylga, scylian, scylig, scyll, scylp, scylpig, scymrian. v. Skilfingas, scilfor, scilfrung, scealga, scilian, scilig, scill, scylf, scylfig, scimrian.

scyltumend (? fultumend), es; *m. A helper*:—Drihten is mīn scyltumend and mīn gescyldend *Dominus adjutor meus et protector meus*, Ps. Th. 27, 8.

scyndan, scendan; *p.* de. I. *intrans. To hurry, hasten*:—Swā ðeós woruld fareþ, scūrum scyndeþ, Exon. Th. 469, 24; Hy. 11, 7. Brimwudu scynde, 182, 5; Gū. 1305. Scynde Gregorius in Godes wære, Menol. Fox 77; Men. 38. Scynde beaduþreáta mǣst tō hilde, Elen. Kmbl. 60; El. 30. Fǣge scyndan (*of death by violence*), Exon. Th. 271, 29; Jul. 489. Hī ǣghwonon tō him ēfston and scyndon, Guthl. 15; Gdwin. 66, 10: Bd. 4, 27; S. 604, 8. Ðā ongunnan monige ēfstan and scyndan tō gehȳranne Godes word *coepere plures ad audiendum verbum confluere*, 1, 26; S. 488, 11: Guthl. 2; Gdwin. 14, 25. Hē gewāt scrīðan, tō gesceape scyndan, Beo. Th. 5133; B. 2570. Manna freóndscipe biþ swīðe hwīlwendlīc and swīðe scendende (cf. gnorn-scendende), Blickl. Homl. 195, 26. II. *trans.* (1) *To cause to hasten, to hurry*:—Ðā wæs morgenleóht scofen and scynded, Beo. Th. 1840; B. 918. (2) *to urge, incite, exhort*:—Se feónd his (*Judas*) heortan tō ðan lǣrde and scynde, ðæt hē Drihten tō deáðe belǣwde, Homl. As. 153, 55. Hū mon monige scyndan scyle (*de exhortatione multis exhibenda*) tō ðæm ðætte his gōdan dǣda ne weorðen tō yflum dǣdum, Past. 60; Swt. 453, 6. [*O. Sax.* far-skundian *to incite, egg on*: *O. H. Ger.* scuntan *sollicitare, suggerere, urgere*: *Icel.* skynda *to hasten*: *Dan.* skynde.] v. ā-, ge-scyndan.

-scynde. v. un-scende.

scyndel?: — Tīwesdæges nama wæs of Martie, Iovis sunu ðæs scyndles (cf. (?) scyndan, II. (1); scyndel *one who causes swift movement*, referring to the lightning (?). Or cf. (?) scendan, scendele; scyndel, scendel *a shameful person* (?)), Anglia viii. 321, 16.

scyndendlīce; *adv. Hurriedly, hastily*; consummatim, Wrt. Voc. ii. 18, 41: 82, 75.

scȳne, scȳ-nes, scyp. v. scīne, sceó-ness, scip.

scypen, e; *f. A shippen* [in some northern dialects; also pronounced *shup'm* (Cumberland)], *a cow-house, stall*:—Scypen *bovile*, Wrt. Voc. ii. 12, 72. Scipen, 126, 59: *bostar* vel *boviale*, i. 58, 25. Scepen, steal, *vel* fald *bovile, stabulum*, 15, 23. Ða þing tō begānne ðe tō scipene belimpaþ, Anglia ix. 260, 4. Ūt wæs gongende tō neáta scypene (*ad* *stabula jumentorum*), Bd. 4, 24; S. 597, 9. Nǽnig mann scypene his neátum ne timbreþ, 1, 1; S. 474, 32. Andlang díces on ðæs cinges scypena; of ðan scypenum on ðæt riscbed, Cod. Dip. Kmbl. vi. 62, 27. Scipena behweorfan, Anglia ix. 261, 18. [Schepyn *boscar* (*-tar?*), Wrt. Voc. i. 178, 10. Schyppune *boster*, 204. col. 2. The schepne brennyng with the blake smoke, Chauc. Kn. T. 1142.] Cf. scoppa.

scyppan, scyppend, scȳr, scyran, scȳran, scyrdan. v. scippan, scippend, scīr, sceran, scīran, scirdan.

scyrfe-mūs, e; *f. A shrew-mouse:*—Scirfemūs *sorex*, Wrt. Voc. ii. 71, 27. Cf. sceorfan.

scyrft *a scraping* (?); scansio, Wrt. Voc. ii. 119, 78. Cf. sceorfan.

scyrian, scyriendlīc. v. scirian, sciriendlīc.

scȳr-mǽlum; *adv. Stormily:*—Seó orsorhnes gǽþ scȳrmǽlum swā ðæs windes þys *prosperam fortunam videas ventosam*, Bt. 20: Fox 72, 4. v. scūr.

scyrpan, scyr-seax. v. scirpan, scear-seax.

scyrtan; *p.* te *To make short, to shorten:*—Gif God his hwīle ne scyrte (gescyrte, MSS. B. C.), Wulfst. 19, 9. v. ge-scyrtan; scortian.

scyrte (-a; *m.?*), an; *f. A short garment, skirt, kirtle:*—Scyrtan *pretexta*, tunecan *togae*, Germ. 393, 143. [He ches stiue here to shurte and gret sac to curtle, O. E. Homl. ii. 139, 16. Arður warp an his rugge a ræf swiðe deore, ænne cheisil scurte & ænne pallene curtel, Laym. 23761. He broucte bred in his shirte or in his couel, Havel. 768. He yaf ofte his kertel and his sserte to þe poure, Ayenb. 191, 9. *M. H. Ger.* schurz: *Ger.* schurz *an apron: Icel.* skyrta *a kind of kirtle.*]

scyrting, e; *f. A shortening, an abridgement:*—Gif hwilc gelǽred man ðās race (*the homily on Job*) oferrǽde, ðonne bidde ic ðæt hē ðās scyrtinge ne tǽle, Homl. Th. ii. 460, 6.

scyrtra, scyrtest, scyru, scȳtan. v. scort, scearu, scītan.

scyte, es; *m.* I. *shooting:*—Hié fortendun ðæt swīðre breóst foran ðæt hit weaxan ne sceolde ðæt hie hæfden ðȳ strengran scyte (*ne sagittarum jactus inpedirentur*), Ors. 1, 10; Swt. 46, 13. Dryhten dǽleþ sumum wyrp oððe scyte, Exon. Th. 331, 17; Vy. 69. II. *a shot, blow:*—Scytum *ictibus*, Hpt. Gl. 478, 76. III. *what is shot or thrown, a javelin, dart:*—Scytas *iacula*, Lchdm. i. lxix, 9. [He þene scute biberh, Laym. 1461. Mid scute of eien, A. R. 60, 16. Wið þe schute wite heo hire, 62, 1. An carpenter that sset the ssute, R. Glouc. 537, 4. *O. Frs.* sket: *O. H. Ger.* scuz *jactus.*] v. on-, under-, ūt-, wæter-scyte.

scȳte. v. scīte.

scyte-finger, es; *m. The forefinger;* digitus secundus quo sagittatur:—Scytefinger *index* vel *salutaris*, Wrt. Voc. i. 44. 5. Bēcnend, scytefinger *index*, ii. 46, 35. Gif se scytefinger biþ ofāslegen, sió bōt biþ .xv. scilł., L. Alf. pol. 57; Th. i. 96, 1. *In Ethelbert's Laws the fine is only eight shillings*, L. Eth. 54; Th. i. 16, 10. Scytefingres, Anglia viii. 326, 28. Euenmicel swā ðū mǽge mid ðīnan scitefingre tō ðīnum þuman befōn, Lchdm. iii. 6, 21. Mid scetefingre ðū gebēcnest *indice prodis*, Hymn. Surt. 104, 5. [Cf. *O. Frs.* skot-finger.] v. scytel-finger.

scyte-heald, -healden; *adj.* I. *bent so as to shoot downwards* (cf. scyte-rǽs), *sloping steeply:*—Scyteheald *preceps*, Wrt. Voc. ii. 68, 77. II. *oblique, inclined:*—Scytehald *obliquum*, 115, 13. Sió scytehealde onbēgnes *obliqua curvatura*, 64, 24. Sió scythealde *obliqua*, 79, 1. Scytehealden, 62, 61.

scytel *dung.* v. scitel.

scytel *a dart.* v. scutel: *a bolt*, v. scyttel.

scytel-finger *the arrow-finger, the forefinger:*—Scytelfinger (scyte- ? v. scyte-finger) *index*, Wrt. Voc. i. 71, 31.

scytels. v. scyttels.

scyte-rǽs, es; *m. A headlong rush:*—On scyterǽs oððe on fǽrfyll, unforesceáwadlīc *in preceps*, Wrt. Voc. ii. 47, 43.

scytere, es; *m.* I. *a shooter, an archer.* v. scyteres (sciteres) clif, flōde, streám, Cod. Dip. Kmbl. vi. 330. [*Icel.* skytari *a shooter.*] II. *one that moves swiftly* (?):—Ad rivulum qui scitere dicitur, Cod. Dip. Kmbl. v. 102, 29. Cf. scytta.

scytling. v. ūt-scytling.

scytta, an; *m. A shooter, an archer:*—*Sagittarius* ðæt is scytta, Lchdm. iii. 246, 2. Strǽlbora and scytta *arcister*, Wrt. Voc. ii. 7, 32. Ðā gebende ān scytta his bogan, Homl. Skt. i. 18, 219. On scyttan fæn, Cod. Dip. Kmbl. iii. 132, 22. On scyttan mere; ðæt on scyttan dūne, 381, 11. Wulfsiges mōdor scyttan, vi. 212, 5. Ðā gegaderade Regulus ealle ða scyttan ðe on ðæm færelte wǽron, ðæt hié (*the serpent*) mon mid flānum ofercōme, Ors. 4, 6; Swt. 174, 5. Wǽron on his fyrdinge twelf þūsenda scyttena, Homl. As. 104, 55. [Alle þe scutten, Laym. 27046. *O. H. Ger.* scuzzo *sagittarius: Icel.* skyti *one who shoots or hurls.*]

scyttan; *p.* te. I. *to cause rapid movement, to shoot* a bolt, *to shut:*—Ic scytte sum loc *sero*, Ælfc. Gr. 37; Zup. 220, 2. II. *to discharge* a debt:—Ic wille ðæt man selle ðæt land et Fersafeld . . . and recna man iungere Brūn ān marc gol and mid ðan lāue scytte man mīna borgas (*my loans shall be paid off*), Chart. Th. 568, 19. [Schutteð þet þurl to, A. R. 96, 10. *Ayenb.* ssette: *Piers P.* shutte, shette: *Wick.* schitte: *O. Frs.* sketta *to stop, close.*] v. for-scyttan.

-scytte. v. riht-scytte.

scyttel, scytel, es; *m. A bar, bolt:*—Ealle ða īsenan scyttelas helle loca wurdan tōbrocene, Blickl. Homl. 87, 5: 85, 7: Nicod. 27: Thw. 15, 24. Scyttelas *vectes*, Ps. Spl. 106, 16. Scetelas, Kent. Gl. 658. [A gardin besset myd tuo ssetteles, Ayenb. 94, 30. Schyttyl *pessulum* vel *pessellum*, Prompt. Parv. 447: ondoynge of schettel!ys *apercio*, 365.] v. scutel *and next word.*

scyttels, scytels, es; *m. A bar, bolt:*—Ða scytelses (scittelsas, MS. O.) tōburston, Homl. Skt. i. 3, 348. Openiaþ ðās gatu and ða fæstan scytelsas, Wulfst. 230, 31. Scytelsas *seras*, Ps. Spl. 147, 2. Scettelsas, Hymn. Surt. 122, 28. Scyttylsum *vectibus*, Germ. 399, 349. [Þet (*the cross*) is þet scutles þe ðe deofel ne mei nefre tocysan, O. E. Homl. i. 127, 35.] v. fore-scytteis, *and preceding word.*

Scyttisc; *adj. Scottish, Scotch* (v. Scottas):—Ðǽr læg secg mænig . . . guma norþerna . . . swilce Scittisc eác, Chr. 937; Erl. 112, 19. Scyttisc gecost gealdor wið ǽlcum ātre, Lchdm. ii. 10, 23. Scyttysces cynnes *natione Scottus*, Bd. 3, 21; S. 551, 16. Gif hē hæfþ Scyttisc weax, Lchdm. ii. 114, 11: iii. 46, 17. Scittisc, ii. 156, 26. ¶ Of speech:—Sind on ðis īglande fīf geþeóde . . . Scyttisc, Chr. Erl. 3, 3. Se cyning Scyttysc (*linguam Scottorum*) geleornad hæfde, Bd. 3, 3; S. 525, 39. On ðam mynstre ðe on Scyttisc is nemned Rathmelsigi, 3, 27; S. 558, 35.

se, sió, Lchdm. ii. 260, 1; *m.*: seó, ðeó, Blickl. Homl. 65, 13; se, Lchdm. ii. 228, 8; *f.*: ðæt; *n.* I. a demonstrative adjective, *the, that.* (1) marking an object as before-mentioned or already well-known (a) with substantives:—Se Hǽlend, Mt. Kmbl. 3, 13. Se steorra stōd ofer ðǽr ðæt cild wæs, 2, 9. Wæs se engel sprecende tō ūres Drihtnes mēder, Blickl. Homl. 5, 2. Seó heofon biþ gefeallen æt ðǽm feówer endum middangeardes, 93, 4. Seó eorþe, Lchdm. iii. 254, 15. Seó sǽ and se mōna geþwǽrlǽcaþ him betweónan, 268, 12. Seó lyft *the air*, 272, 20. On ðone gemānan ðæs brȳdguman and ðære brȳde, Blickl. Homl. 11, 5. Hē fægnode ðæs miclan weorces ðærre ceastre, Past. 4; Swt. 39, 15. Ðæt mon ða earce bere on ðǽm saglum, 22; Swt. 171, 12. Mid ðȳ selflīce se Dēma biþ geniéded tō ðæm ierre, 4; Swt. 39, 10. Ðȳ þearlan dōme (*by the severe sentence just mentioned*) hē forleás his mennisce, Swt. 39, 23. Ðæt mæsten is gemǽne tō ðām (*those mentioned in the charter*) ān and twentigum hīdum, Cod. Dip. Kmbl. v. 319, 29. On hāte ða ahsan, Lchdm. ii. 32, 13. (b) with adjectives:—Se dumba spræc, Mt. Kmbl. 9, 33. Ðā æthrān hē ðæs blindan hand, Mk. Skt. 8, 23. (c) with numerals:—Ða þrȳ cōmon, Cd. Th. 221, 24; Dan. 93. Ðīna āgna treówa and seó godcunde lufu and se tōhopa, ða þreó ðē ne lǽtaþ geortrēwan be ðam ēcan līfe, Bt. 10; Fox 32, 8. (d) with proper names:—Se Iohannes *the same John* (A.V.), Mt Kmbl. 3, 4. Se (*the one in question*) Cynewulf oft feaht wið Bretwalum . . . Hē wolde ādrǽfan ǽnne æþeling, se wæs Cyneheard hāten, and se Cyneheard wæs ðæs (*the one previously mentioned*) Sigebryhtes brōður, Chr. 755; Erl. 48, 24–28. Fēng Carl tō ðam westrīce . . . se Carl wæs Hlōþwīges sunu, se Hlōþwīg wæs Carles brōður, se wæs Iuþyttan fæder, . . . and hié wǽron Hlōþwīges suna. Se Hlōþwīg wæs ðæs aldan Carles sunu; se Carl wæs Pippenes sunu, 885; Erl. 84, 10–17. Seó Asia (*Asia Minor*), Ors. 1, 1; Swt. 12, 11. Him Iosep gehealp. From ðæm Iosepe . . ., 1, 5; Swt. 32, 28. (2) marking an object which is further described (a) by an adjective:—Se heofonlīca cyning, Blickl. Homl. 5, 18. Mīn se heofonlīca Fæder, Mt. Kmbl. 18, 35. Se earma upāhafena, Past. 26; Swt. 183, 13. Se dysega ungeþyldega, 33; Swt. 220, 9. Ðeó deáþberende uncyst, Blickl. Homl. 65, 13. Mid hire ðære yfelan sceónesse beswāc ðone ǽrestan wīfmon, 5, 1. Ðone yfelan fæsðrǽdan willan fulneáh nān wind ne mæg āwecgan, Past. 33; Swt. 225, 6. ¶ The weak declension usually occurs with the demonstrative, but in the following instances strong forms are found:—On ðam seócum men, Lchdm. ii. 282, 11. Snāw cymþ of ðam þynnum wǽtan, iii. 278, 23. Of ðam hātum bæðe, Homl. Th. i. 58, 29. Ða gleáwe sǽgenga[n] hig understandaþ, Anglia viii. 327, 21. Ða anbestungne saglas, Past. 22; Swt. 171, 11. For ðære sceáwungge ðara ungesewenlīcra þinga, 16; Swt. 99, 8. Ðara eádigra apostola, Bd. 5, 19; S. 637, 31. Orhlyte ðæra hāligra mihta, Homl. Th. i. 346, 26. (b) by a pronoun:—Mon sceal suā manian ðæt se hiera folgoþ hine ne ōþhebbe, Past. 28, 1; Swt. 189, 17. Ða mīne sǽlþa and se mīn weorðscipe, Bt. 10; Fox 30, 14–15. Ǽnigne dǽl ðara ðīnra gesǽlþa, 11, 1; Fox 32, 26. (c) by a numeral:—Ðæt þridde gebed, Homl. i. 264, 16. Hyt eall āléd biþ on ðære ānre mīle, Ors. 1, 1; Swt. 20, 32. Ðā āxode se cāsere ðone ǽnne preóst, Homl. Th. ii. 310, 14. Ðis synt ðæra twelf Apostola naman, Mt. Kmbl. 10, 2. Hū mon scule blōdlǽse on ðara six fīfa ǽlcum on mōnþe forgān, Lchdm. ii. 146, 19: 148, 2. (d) by a genitive:—Ðā wæs gesended ðæt goldhord ðæs mægenþrymmes on ðone bend ðæs clǽnan innoþes, Blickl. Homl. 9, 28. Se emnihtes dæg, Lchdm. iii. 256, 26. Nēh ðæm clife ðære Reádan Sǽs, Ors. 1, 1; Swt. 12, 19. Ða diógolnesse ðæs þriddan hefones, Past. 16; Swt. 99, 8. (e) by a phrase:—Ðara twentiges hīda landgemǽra tō

Burhtûne. . . . Ðara .vii. hîda landgemǽra æt mæðelgâres byrig, Cod. Dip. Kmbl. iii. 429, 25–32. (f) by an appositive:—Saul se cyning, Past. 3; Swt. 35, 14. Membrað se ent . . . Ninus se cyning, Ors. 2, 4; Swt. 74, 9–10. Ðæt land Cilia . . . seó sǽ Euxinus . . . se hêhsta beorg Olimpus . . . Nilus seó eá; . . . neh ðam beorge Athlans, 1, 1; Swt. 12, 11–21. (g) by a clause, v. IV:—Eart ðû se Beowulf, se ðe wið Brecan wunne, Beo. Th. 1016; B. 506. Seó Ægyptus ðe ûs neár is, Ors. 1, 1; Swt. 12, 16. Seó menigo ðe beforan fêrde, Blickl. Homl. 71, 9. Sŷ ðæs cynnes orf ðe hit sŷ, L. Ff.; Th. i. 226, 3. Gif esne eorlcundne mannan ofslæhþ ðane ðe sió (*whoever it be*), L. H. E. 1; Th. i. 26, 8: 3; Th. i. 28, 4. Ða hwîle ðe hié tô nânre ôðerre note ne mǽgen, Past. pref.; Swt. 7, 12. Oft mon forlǽt ðone ege and ða fæsðrǽdnesse ðe hê mid ryhte on him innan habban scolde, 4, 1; Swt. 37, 17. Ða twelfe ðe mid him wǽron, Mk. Skt. 4, 10. Ða fîf hlâfas ðe se cnapa bær getâcniaþ ða fîf bec ðe Moyses sette, Homl. Th. i. 186, 13. Hwæt ða sume dreógaþ, ðe ða wræclâstas wîdost legcaþ, Exon. Th. 309, 13; Seef. 56. (h) by a clause in apposition:—Ne sceal hê ðæt ân dôn, ðæt hê âna wacie, Past. 28; Swt. 193, 21. (i) by relation to other objects mentioned:—Se ðe ne gǽþ æt ðam gete intô sceápa falde, Jn. Skt. 10, 1. Hig gefyldon ða[fatu] ôþ ðone brerde, 2, 7. Irnende on ðæt sond, and ðonne besince eft on ðæt sand, Ors. 1, 1; Swt. 12, 22. (3) with adjectives used as epithets:—Salomonn se snottra, Past. 4, 1; Swt. 37, 16. Hit is Hǽlend se Nazarenisca, Blickl. Homl. 15, 19. Sidroc eorl se alda and Sidroc eorl se gioncga, Chr. 871; Erl. 74, 22. Eádweard se langa, Byrht. Th. 139, 53; By. 273. (4) marking an object as the representative of a class:—Ys seó æx tô ðæra treówa wyrtruman âsett, Mt. Kmbl. 3, 10. Hû nys seó sâwl sêlre ðonne mete, 6, 25. Ða lîchamlîcan gôd bióþ forcûþran ðonne ðære sâwle cræftas . . . Seó fægernes ðæs lîchoman geblissaþ ðone mon, Bt. 24, 3; Fox 84, 5–8. Ǽr ðan ðe ðæs dæges lenge oferstîge ða niht, Lchdm. iii. 256, 13. Bere is swîðe earfoþe tô gearcigenne, and ðeáhhwæðere fêt ðone mann, ðonne hê gearo biþ, Homl. Th. i. 188, 5. (4 a) marking genus:—Se mon *homo*, Bd. 1, 27; S. 497, 40. Se mann âna gǽþ uprihte, Bt. 41, 6; Fox 254, 29. (5) marking a definite whole or a class of objects:—Hié hâtaþ ða landmen (*the natives*) Nuchul, Ors. 1, 1; Swt. 12, 24. On ôðre wîsan mon sceal manian ða blîðan, on ôðre ða unrôtan . . . ða underþiéddan . . . ða ofer ôðre gesettan . . . ða woroldwîsan . . . ða dysegan, Past. 23; Swt. 175, 14–17. Ðæra Persiscra cyning . . . gegaderode of ðâm Saraceniscum micele fyrde, Jud. Thw. 162, 23. Hê clypode ða gelaðodan tô ðam gyftum. . . . Hê sǽde ðâm gelaðedon, Mt. Kmbl. 22, 3–4. (6) with abstract nouns where modern English would not use the article:—Sió hǽlu ðone mon gedêþ lûstbǽrne, Bt. 24, 3; Fox 84, 9. Gif se weorðscipe and se anweald gôd wǽre, 16, 3; Fox 54, 8. Hê ða geþyld ðe is môdur ealra mægena for ðæm unwrence ðære ungeþylde forlêt, Past. 33, 1; Swt. 215, 20. Þurh ða wilnunga ðære woroldâre, 3; Swt. 33, 8. On ðǽm gesundfulnessum ðæt môd wierð upâhafen; and on ðǽm earfeðum hit biþ geeáðmêdd. On ðære gesundfulnesse mon forgiett his selfes; on ðǽm gesuincum hê sceal hine selfne geþencean. On ðære orsorgnesse . . . on ðǽm earfoðum. . . . Suîðe oft monn biþ ðære earfoðnesse lâreówdôme underþiéded, Swt. 35, 4–10. (6 a) where an abstraction is personified:—Se Wîsdôm and seó Gesceádwîsnes, Bt. 3; Fox 6, 13 (and often). **II.** as a demonstrative pronoun, *he, she, it, that*, (1) referring to a person or thing:—Se wæs betera ðonne ic, Beo. Th. 943; B. 469. On ðâm ys sǽd, and ðæt sweart, Lchdm. i. 278, 1. Heó hafaþ leáf sinewealte and ða bitere, 290, 18. Ðonne hî eów êhtaþ on ðysse byrig, fleóþ on ôðre; and ðonne hî on ðære eów êhtaþ, fleóþ on ða þryddan, Mt. Kmbl. 10, 23. Hêt se câsere hine lǽdan tô his deófolgelde, ðæt hê ðæm gulde, Shrn. 88, 22. Heó hafaþ stelan and ðone on bôgum geþûfne, Lchdm. i. 298, 20. Ðâ swungon hî ðæne, Mk. Skt. 12, 3. Hê sorgaþ ymb ða and biþ ðara suîðe gemyndig, Past. 4, 1; Swt. 37, 19. Ðâ wǽron ealle ða wîf geladede; ðara wæs iii hund and hundeahtatig, Ors. 3, 6; Swt. 108, 32. Ðæt hê nânes þinges bûton ðǽm þurfe, Bt. 24, 4; Fox 86, 6. Gesyllan .xv. leaxas and ða gôde, Cod. Dip. Kmbl. iii. 296, 1. (2) referring to the subject dealt with in a clause *that, it*:—Gif gê gesâwen hwelce mûs ðæt wǽre hlâford ofer ôðre mŷs . . . hû wunderlîc wolde eów ðæt þincan, hwelce cehhettunge gê woldon ðæs habban, Bt. 16, 2; Fox 52, 1–4. Hwylc ðæs cyninges geleáfa wǽre, ðæt æfter his deáþe mid wundrum wæs gecŷþed, Bd. 3, 19; S. 533, 15. Ðæt hê ðæs (*for praying in a certain place*) hæfde mêde wið God, Shrn. 88, 32. Hê ðæs (*for beheading a saint*) dyde hreówsunga, 89, 18: Ps. Th. 28, 7: 30, 1. Ic hit scortlîce secgan scyle, hwâ ðæs (*the stirring up of strife*) ordfruman wǽron, Ors. 5, 9; Swt. 232, 18. Hû his gesceafta weaxaþ and eft waniaþ, ðonne ðæs tîma cymþ, Bt. 34, 10; Fox 150, 13. Heora æfterfyligendas wǽron deófolgylde folgiende, for ðam Mellitus and Iustus of Breotene gewiton, Bd. 2, 5; S. 506, 3. Nis hit lang (feor) tô ðon, 4, 24; S. 599, 5. Gif eáran sŷn innan sâre, and ðǽr wyrms sŷ, on dô ða ylcan sealfe, heó ys swŷðe gôd tô ðam, Lchdm. i. 358, 17. Se hearpere suîðe ungelîce ða strengas styreþ, and mid ðŷ gedêþ ðæt . . ., Past. 23; Swt. 175, 7. (2 a) in apposition with a clause: see also V:—Wê nyston ðæt hê ðæs girnan wolde, ðæt wê ûrne brôður ðyder lǽddon, Gen. 43, 7. Hié wǽron gebrocede mid ceápes cwilde, ealles swîðost mid ðæm, ðæt manige ðara sêlestena cynges þêna forþfêrdon, Chr. 897; Erl. 94, 32. Ðâ næs long tô ðon, ðæt wê tô sumre eá cwôman, Nar. 8, 19. Næs lang tô ðŷ ðæt his brôðor ðyses lǽnan lîfes tîman geendode, Lchdm. iii. 434, 25. Se scamfæsta hæfþ genôh on ðæm tô his bettrunge, ðæt his lâreów hine suîðe lythwôn gemyndgige his unþeáwa, Past. 31; Swt. 207, 3. Wê leornedon æt him ðæt wê flugen ða ôliccunga ðisses middangeardes, and eác ðæt, ðæt wê his ege ûs ne ondrêden, 3; Swt. 33, 23. (3) *ðæt* referring to an object of any gender or number:—Ðæt (se ǽwelm ealra gôda) eart ðû, Bt. 33, 4; Fox 132, 30. Hê ðæt is, se ða gebundenan ût âlǽdde, St. And. 14, 33. Ðæt is mid Estum þeáw, ðæt . . ., Ors. 1, 1; Swt. 21, 11. Ðæt is Iohannes gewitnes, Jn. Skt. 1, 19. Godes bearn, ðæt wǽron gôde men, Gen. 6, 2. Ða eágan, ðæt beóþ ða lâreówas, and se hrycg, ðæt sint ða hiéremenn, Past. 1; Swt. 29, 12: Nar. 34, 2, 7. Ðæt wǽron eall Finnas, Ors. 1, 1; Swt. 17, 26. Ðæt wǽron fiéftiéne hund þûsend monna, 3, 9; Swt. 128, 22. (3 a) ðæt is = *there is*:—Ðæt nis nân man ðætte sumes eácan ne þurfe, Bt. 24, 4; Fox 86, 6. (4) *one* in contrast with *another*:—For hwî se gôda lǽce selle ðam hâlum men sêftne drenc, and ôðrum hâlum strangne, Bt. 39, 9; Fox 226, 10. Ðonne lufaþ sum ðæt sum elles hwæt *one man likes one thing, another something else*, Bt. 33, 2; Fox 122, 24. **III.** as a relative:—Sum hîrêdes ealdor wæs, se (*qui*) plantode wîngerd, Mt. Kmbl. 21, 33. Nys nân þing dŷhle, ðæt ne wurðe geswutelod, 10, 26. Ðonne tôdǽlaþ hî his feoh, ðæt tô lâfe biþ, Ors. 1, 1; Swt. 20, 28. Gif ðû sŷ his discipul, se is cweden Crist, St. And. 8, 13. Ondrǽd ðê Drihten and his rôdtâcn, beforan ðæm forhtigaþ heofon and eorþe, 20, 25. Ðæt ic eów secge on þŷstrum, secgaþ hyt on leóhte, Mt. Kmbl. 10, 27. Manige synt on ðisse ceastre, ða sculon geleófan on mînne naman, St. And. 12, 7. **III a.** where relative and antecedent are included in the same word:—Môste on êcnisse æfter lybban se ðæs wæstmes onbât, Cd. Th. 30, 21; Gen. 470: 63, 8; Gen. 1029. Ðæt gê on eáre gehŷraþ bodiaþ uppan hrôfum, Mt. Kmbl. 10, 27. Ðonne ðû hæfdest ðæt ðû noldest, oððe næfdest ðæt ðû woldest, Bt. 26, 1; Fox 90, 31. Ðæt hî tôweorpen ðæt God geteohhad hæfþ tô wyrcanne, Ps. Th. 10, 3. Cum and geseoh ðæt hié mê dôþ, St. And. 16, 34. ¶ where the construction is incomplete:—Eác sculon wiotan ða ofergesettan ðæt ðæt hié unâliéfedes þurhteóþ, swǽ manigra wîta hié beóþ wyrðe, swǽ swǽ hié manna on wôn gebrohten, Past. 28; Swt. 190, 6. **IV.** (see also **I.** 2 g) in correlative sentences where antecedent and relative are represented (1) by *se . . . ðe*:—Gif him gebyrige ðæt hê on ðæs hwæt befoo ðe wið his willan sié, Past. 28; Swt. 198, 23. Ne þearf hê nânes þinges bûton ðæs ðe hê on him selfum hæfþ, Bt. 24, 4; Fox 86, 8. Ða gife ic wylle tô ðon dôn ðe ic heóld *I will put the gift to the use for which I kept it*, Guthl. 20; Gdwin. 84, 12. (1 a) by *se . . . ðe hê*:—Forðon mæg gehycgan se ðe his heorte deáh, Cd. Th. 282, 8; Sat. 283. Ðæs bihofaþ se ðe him hâlig gǽst wîsaþ, Exon. Th. 123, 34; Gû. 332. (2) by *se . . . se*:—Se ilca se monegum yfelum geârode, Past. 3; Swt. 35, 24. Ðonne cymeþ se man se ðæt swiftoste hors hafaþ, Ors. 1, 1; Swt. 20, 36. Se þurhwunaþ ôþ ende, se byþ hâl, Mt. Kmbl. 10, 22. Gif ðæt wæs, ðæt seldon gelomp, Bd. 3, 5; S. 527, 2. Beó ðæt þinga, ðæt hit beó, ðæt se man tô note wyrcean wille, Btwk. 222, 8. Hê for Godes ege dêþ ðæt ðæt hê dêþ, Past. 22; Swt. 169, 4. Herigan ðæt ðæt hê fæsðrǽdes wiste, 32, 2; Swt. 213, 7. (2 a) by *se . . . se hê*:—Ðæt is se Abraham, se him (= ðe him *to whom*) engla God naman âsceóp, Cd. Th. 201, 30; Exod. 380. (3) by *se . . . se ðe*:—Ðys ys se be ðam ðe gecweden ys, Mt. Kmbl. 3, 3. Se ðe brŷde hæfþ, se is brŷdguma, Jn. Skt. 3, 29. Seó ilce burg, seó ðe mǽst wæs, seó is nû læst, Ors. 2, 4; Swt. 74, 22. Ðæt mon ne wæs, se ðe him ætŷwde, Bd. 2, 12; S. 514, 25. Ðæt ðe âcenned is of flǽsce, ðæt is flǽsc; and ðæt ðe of gâste âcenned is, ðæt is gâst, Jn. Skt. 3, 6. Ða, ða ðe *hi, qui*, Rtl. 5, 33. Ðæs monnes nama wæs, se ðe hî beheáfdade, Dorotheos, Shrn. 89, 17. Ða eallreordan þeóde, ðara ðe hî ða gereorde ne cûþan, gesêcan, Bd. 1, 23; S. 485, 33. Ðætte tǽlwyrðes sié, ðæt hié ðæt tǽlen, Past. 28; Swt. 195, 24. Hî nâmon him wîf of eallum ðâm, ða ðe hig gecuron, Gen. 6, 2. (3 a) irregular constructions:—Se, seðe ǽr worolde rîcsode on hefenum, hit is âwriten, Iudêas woldon hine dôn tô cyninge, Past. 3; Swt. 33, 12. Se ilca, seðe wênde ðæt hê wǽre ofer ealle ôðere menn, him gebyrede . . ., 4; Swt. 39, 24. Se hondwyrm, se ðe secgas seaxe delfaþ, Exon. Th. 427, 24; Rä. 41, 96. Se biþ leófast, se ðe hym God syleþ gumena rîce tô gehealdenne, 326, 21; Vîd. 132. Cf. Hê weorðeþ eádig se ðe hine God geceóseþ *beatus quem elegisti*, Ps. Th. 64, 4. (4) by *se . . . se se*:—Swâ þyncþ him, ðæt se hié him niédscylde sceolde, se se hié him sealde, Past. 9; Swt. 57, 6. Ðæt ðæt lator biþ, ðæt hæfþ angin, Homl. Th. i. 284, 7. Ǽlc mon tiohhaþ him ðæt tô sêlestum goode ðæt ðæt hê swîðost lufaþ, Bt. 33, 2; Fox 122, 23. (4 a) irregular:—Se Drihten, se ðæs (= ðe his) setl ys on heofenum, Ps. Th. 10, 4. **V.** in adverbial or conjunctional forms. In phrases such as *for ðam ðe* the pronominal element was represented later by *that*, as in Shakspere, and is now usually omitted altogether. (1) Nô (nalæs, nallas nô) ðæt ân ðæt . . . ac *not only . . . but also*, Bt. 21; Fox 74, 17: 22, 1; Fox 76, 13: 37, 3; Fox 190, 18: Guthl. 5; Gdwin. 30, 23. (2) *Ðæs* (a) in reference to time, or sequence of events, marking the point from which measurement is made, *after* :—Sume men secgen đæt hire ǽwielme sié on westende Affrica, and đonne folrađe đæs (*very soon after*) sié eást irnende on đæt sond, Ors. 1, 1; Swt. 12, 21. Fulrađe đæs ic clipode tō him, Bt. 22, 1; Fox 76, 8. Đæs on morgen *the next morning*, Ors. 3, 4; Swt. 104, 5. Đæs on đæm æfterran geáre *anno ab hoc proximo*, 4, 6; Swt. 172, 17. Đæs ymb iii geár *tertio anno*, Swt. 176, 24. Đæs ymb iii niht, Chr. 871; Erl. 74, 6, 14, 25. Wífes wer gif hē forþfærþ ymbe .xii mōnaþ đæs heó mōt niman ōđerne *mortuo viro, post annum licet mulieri alium accipere*, L. Ecg. C. 19; Th. ii. 146, 10. ¶ Đæs đe:—Đæs đe đā seó costung gestilled wæs, đā wǽron forþgongende đa geleáfsuman, Bd. 1, 8; S. 479, 19: 3, 22; S. 552, 39. Sōna đæs đe hī on đis eálond cōmon, đā compedon hī, 1, 12; S. 480, 29. Đæs đe . . . đā sōna, 5, 6; S. 620, 11. Æfter siextegum daga đæs đe đæt timber ācorfen wæs *intra sexagesimum diem quam arbores caesae erant*, Ors. 4, 6; Swt. 172, 4. Hē đā gyt lifde æfter ændlefan geárum đæs đe [hē] wæs bebyrged, Shrn. 82, 15. Đæt wæs ymb twelf mōnaþ đæs đe hié ǽr hider cōmon, Chr. 894; Erl. 93, 14: 895; Erl. 93, 32: 896; Erl. 94, 23. (b) marking degree, proportion, *so* (cf. colloquial use of *that* = *so*, with adjectives):—Nǽre flōd đæs deóp, merestreám đæs micel, đæt his mīn mōd getweóde, Cd. Th. 51, 26, 27; Gen. 832, 833. Nō đæs frōd leofaþ gumena bearna đæt đone grund wite (*so wise as to know*), Beo. Th. 2737; B. 1366. Wurde đū đæs gewitleás, đæt đū þonc ne wisses, Exon. Th. 90, 12; Cri. 1473. Nis ǽnig đæs horsc ne đæs hygecræftig đe đīn fromcyn mǽge gesēþan, 15, 24; Cri. 241. Wē ūs wiđ him seldan đæs đe wē mihton *we protected ourselves against them as far as we could*, Nar. 14, 29: Ps. Th. 10, 3: Homl. Th. ii. 550, 20: L. Eth. v. 23; Th. i. 310, 11: vi. 1; Th. i. 314, 6: Lchdm. ii. 86, 23. Næs ic nǽfre git nāne hwīle swā emnes mōdes, đæs đe ic gemunan mǽge (*from what*, or *as far as, I can remember*), Bt. 26, 1; Fox 90, 25. ¶ with comparatives:—Đā clypodon hig đæs đe mā (*so much the more*), Mt. Kmbl. 20, 31: Mk. Skt. 10, 26. Sió wund biþ đæs đe wierse and đȳ māre, Past. 17; Swt. 123, 18: 18; Swt. 131, 16. Đæt hié wēnden đæt hié đæs đe (*tanto*) untǽlwyrđran wǽren đe (*quanto*) hié wēndon đæt hē nyste hira leóhtmōdnesse, 32, 2; Swt. 215, 1. (b 1) with *tō* :—Tō đæs mycel đæt . . . *so great that* . . ., Bd. 1, 1; S. 474, 13. Wæs seó eorþe tō đæs heard and tō đæs stānihte đæt . . ., 4, 28; S. 605, 27. Nis nān tō đæs lytel ǽwelm, đæt hē đa sǽ ne gesēce, Bt. 24, 1; Fox 80, 24. Hē him đæs leán forgeald tō đæs đe hē in ræste geseah Grendel līcgan *he gave him reward for that so*, or *to such a degree, that he saw Grendel lie dead*, Beo. Th. 3175; B. 1585. (c) marking agreement, *according to what, as* :—Wē him andswaredon đæs đe hē ūs āxode *respondimus juxta id quod fuerat sciscitatus*, Gen. 43, 7. Hū hē him ondwyrdan sceolde đæs hē hiene āscade *quid sibi tamquam consulenti responderi velit*, Ors. 3, 9; Swt. 126, 30. Đæs đe (*ut*) mē gesawen is, Bd. 1, 25; S. 487, 12: Bt. 24, 3; Fox 84, 10. Swā efne đæs đe *ita ut*, Bd. 1, 34; S. 499, 20. And se mon biþ đæs đe swā tō cweþanne sī ǽghwæđer ge gehæfted ge freó *itaque homo est, ut ita dixerim, captivus et liber*, 1, 27; S. 497, 40. Đæs đe bēc secgaþ *as books say*, St. And. 26, 6. (d) *because, since* :—Waa mē đæs ic swigode *vae mihi quia tacui*, Past. 49, 2; Swt. 379, 24. (3) Đæm, đam, đan, đon (đe). (a) with a comparative:—Gif hē ne biþ đon raþor gelācnod, Lchdm. ii. 200, 20. (b) *with prepositions* :—Æfter đæm đe Rōmeburg getimbred wæs *urbe condita*, Ors. 4, 6; Swt. 170, 19 (*and often*). Æfter đæm đe Cartainiense gefliémde wǽron hié wilnedon friþes *Carthaginenses, fracti bellis, pacem poposcerunt*, Swt. 174, 23. Ǽr đæm đe Rōmeburh getimbred wǽre, 1, 3; Swt. 32, 1 (*and often*). Ǽr đam đe *donec*, Mt. Kmbl. 12, 20. Ǽr đon, Past. 33, 1; Swt. 215, 15. Wurdon viiii folcgefeoht gefohten . . . and būtan đam đe him cyninges þegnas oft rāde onridon đe mon nā ne rīmde *there were nine pitched battles . . . and besides king's thanes often made raids upon them, that were not counted*, Chr. 871; Erl. 76, 10. For đæm đe (1) *for, because* :—Eádige synt đa līđan; for đam đe (*quoniam*) hī eorþan āgun, Mt. Kmbl. 5, 4. For đam, 5, 3. For đon đe *quia*, 7, 13. Đa Deniscan sǽton đǽr behindan, for đæm hiora cyning wæs gewundod, Chr. 894; Erl. 91, 2. For đæm đe, 91, 28. For đam, Ps. Th. 9, 13. Đȳ . . . for đam *therefore . . . because*, Bt. 36, 7; Fox 184, 15. (2) *therefore* :—Hē for đæm nolde, đȳ hē mid his folce getrūwode đæt hē hiene beswīcan mehte, Ors. 2, 4; Swt. 76, 8: Bt. 38, 2; Fox 188, 16. For đon (*therefore*) ic đē bebióde, Past. pref.; Swt. 5, 1. (3) *for the purpose, in order* :—Geþence gē hwæt gē sién; for đæm đæt gē eówer mōd gemetgien *pensa, quod es; ut se spiritus temperet*, Past. 21, 4; Swt. 159, 14. Mid đæm đe *whilst, when, as*, of simultaneous events:—Mid đæm đe đa burgware swā geómorlīc angin hæfdon đā com se cyning self mid his scipe *inter haec procedit ipse de navi sua imperator*, Ors. 4, 5; Swt. 166, 14. Mid đam đe se apostol stōp intō đære byrig, đā bær man him tōgeánes ānre wydewan līc, Homl. Th. i. 60, 11. Ongemang, onmang đam (đe) *whilst, meanwhile* :—Ongemang đæm đe hié wilnaþ đæt hié gifule þyncen, Past. 45, 3; Swt. 339, 24. Seó sunne sāh tō setle onmang đam đe hī on wōpe wæron, Homl. Skt. i. 23, 246: Chr. 1105; Erl. 240, 4. Ongemang đam (*interea*) his leorningcnihtas hine bǽdon, Jn. Skt. 4, 31. Tō đam (1) marking degree *so, to such a degree* :—Đā wǽron hié tō đæm gesārgode, đæt hié ne mehton Sūđ-Seaxna lond ūtan berōwan, Chr. 897; Erl. 96, 8. Men tō đam dyrstige đæt hī đæt gold nimen *men so bold as to take the gold*, Nar. 35, 9: Bt. 11, 1; Fox 32, 32. Nis nān tō đam ungelȳfedlīc spel . . . đæt ic hym ne gelīfe, Shrn. 196, 18. Tō đam đū mē hæfst gerētne đæt . . ., Bt. 22, 1; Fox 76, 11. (2) marking purpose, *to the end* (*that*):—Tō đæm đæt (*ut*) hē forleóse heora gemynd, Ps. Th. 33, 16: 10, 2. Ne com hē nā tō đam on eorþan đæt him mon þēnade, Past. 17; Swt. 121, 8. Tō đæm đæt, pref.; Swt. 5, 3. Đa cwōman tō đon đæt hié woldan ūs wundigan *nos adlacessere temptabant*, Nar. 22, 17. Wiđ đam đe *in return for, on condition* (*that*), connecting two clauses containing mutual concessions, v. wiđ :—Se cyng and his witan him (*the Danes*) gafol and metsunga behētan wiđ đam đe hī heora hergunga geswicon, Chr. 1011; Erl. 144, 22: Past. 36, 6; Swt. 255, 3, 9. (4) Đæt *in* ōþ đæt. v. ōþ, II. 2. (5) Đȳ, đī, đig (1) *therefore, so* :—Đȳ him is micel þearf, đonne hē tela lǽrþ, đæt hē eác tela doo, Past. 28; Swt. 193, 12; Bt. 36, 7; Fox 184, 14. Đȳ *ideo*, L. Ecg. P. i. 15; Th. ii. 178, 29. Đig *itaque*, Th. ii. 176, 15. (2) *because* :—Wēnst đū, đæt ealle đa þing đe gōde sint, for đȳ gōde sint, đȳ hī habbaþ hwæthwegu gōdes on him, 34, 9: Fox 146, 30: Ors. 2, 4; Swt. 76, 8. (3) with comparatives, *the, any* :—Būton đū mē đȳ gesceádlīcor ōđer gerecce, Bt. 39, 2; Fox 214, 7. Hió ne biþ đȳ neár đære sǽ đe hió biþ on midne dæg, 39, 3; Fox 214, 28. Đæt hié hira selfra ne āgon đȳ māre geweald đe ōđerra monna, Past. 33, 1; Swt. 215, 13. Hié woldon đæt hēr đȳ māra wīsdōm on londe wǽre đȳ wē mā geþeóda cūđon, Past. pref.; Swt. 5, 24. (2) *with prepositions*. For đȳ (đe), (a) *therefore* :—For đȳ . . . đȳ *therefore . . . because*, Bt. 34, 9; Fox 146, 30. For đȳ . . . for đæm *therefore . . . because*, Past. 21; Swt. 157, 10. (b) *because* :—Đæt wæs for đȳ đe hié wǽron benumene đæs ceápes, Chr. 895; Erl. 93, 17. Mid đȳ (đe) (a) of time, *when, as* :—Mid đȳ đe hē đis gebed gecweden hæfde, Blickl. Homl. 229, 27: 231, 7. Sumre tīde mid đȳ đe wē wǽron mid ūrum Drihtne, 235, 2. Mid đī đe, 237, 17. Mid đī hē đis cwæđ, hē āstāh on heofonas, 237, 15. Mid đȳ *cum*, Bd. 4, 24; S. 598, 33. Mid đȳ *cum*, Mt. Kmbl. Lind. 24, 15 (*and often*). (b) denoting a cause or consequence, *when, as, since* :—Mid đȳ Peohtas wīf næfdon, hī bǽdon him wīfa fram Scottum, Bd. 1, 1; S. 474, 19. (c) *though* :—Gif hē eów forhogige and eów ne wylle ārīsan tōgeánes mid đȳ eówer mā is *sin autem vos spreverit, nec coram vobis adsurgere voluerit, cum sitis numero plures*, 2, 2; S. 503, 13. Tō đȳ . . . đæt *to the end that* :—Ne com hē for đȳ đæt hē wolde his eorþlīce rīce mid riccetere him tō geteōn; ac tō đī hē com đæt hē wolde his heofenlīce rīce geleáffullum mannum gyfan, Homl. Th. i. 82, 20–24: ii. 226, 9. Ne dō nā se Godes þeówa Godes þēnunge for sceattum, ac tō đȳ đæt hē geearnige đæt ēce wuldor þurh đæt, L. Ælf. C. 27; Th. ii. 352, 23. [Gothic and Icelandic have forms corresponding with the *nom. m. f. se, seó*, and O. Sax. also has a masculine *se*; in other dialects the dental forms prevail throughout. In the Lindisfarne Gospels *đe* (= ipse, Mt. Kmbl. 15, 24), *điú* (= quae, 24, 15) are used, but also *se đe* (= qui, 6, 4). In later English *þe, þeo* replace *se, seó*.]

se so :—Se đeáh *yet, still*, Exon. Th. 13, 31; Cri. 211: 159, 30; Gū. 934: 328, 24; Vy. 22: 454, 6; Hy. 4, 28: 455, 12, 18; Hy. 4, 48, 51: 495, 13; Rā. 84, 7. Hwæđre se đeáh, 417, 27; Rā. 36, 11. Efne se đeáh, 421, 33; Rā. 40, 27: 482, 2; Rā. 66, 1. Se đeána, 127, 3; Gū. 380. Sete hī samod anlīce swā se wægnes hweól *pone illos ut rotam*, Ps. Th. 82, 10. [Hi rihtleceden þat folc swa se hi mihten, O. E. Homl. i. 235, 32. *Se* in combinations *hwat se, alse* is frequent in later English.] v. swā, nese (?).

seád, seáda, seáfian, seaht, seal, sealcan, seald. v. seód, seáđa, seófian, seht, sealh, ā-sealcan, solcen, sellan.

sealdness, e; *f. Giving* :—Sealdnesse *dandi*, Wrt. Voc. ii. 28, 7. v. ge-saldniss.

sealf, e: sealfe, an (?); *f. Salve, ointment* :—Salf, salb *malagma*, Txts. 77, 127. Sealf, Wrt. Voc. i. 68, 6. Smyrels *vel* sealf *unguina* vel *unguenta*, 49, 29. *Fota*, i. *confortata vel* sealf, ii. 149, 76. Smyrels odđe sealfe *unguentum*, i. 74, 8. Sealfe *nardi*, Hpt. Gl. 517, 28. For hwī wæs đisse sealfe forspillednes? Đeós sealf mihte beón geseald, Mk. Skt. 14, 4, 5: Jn. Skt. 12, 3, 5. Wyrc tō salfe (sealfe, MSS. H. B.), Lchdm. i. 110, 18. Sealfe *fotu*, Wrt. Voc. ii. 90, 74. Lǽcedōmnessa odđe sealfe *cataplasma*, 18, 31. [*O. Sax.* salƀa: *O. H. Ger.* salb *and* salba (*gen.* -a *and* -un) *unctio, unguentum, malagma, cataplasma*.] v. bæþ-, bān-, ciper-, cū-, dolh-, eág-, eár-, ele-, mūþ-, sceáde-, smeoru-, tōþ-, weax-, weaxhlāf-, wen-sealf.

sealf-box, es; *m.? n.? A box for ointment* :—Ān wīf hæfde hyre sealfbox deórwyrþes nardes, and tōbrocenum sealfboxe ofer his heáfod āgēt, Mk. Skt. 14, 3: Lk. Skt. 7, 37.

sealf-cynn, es; *n. An ointment* :—Sealfcyn (seals-, Wrt.) *amaracium* (cf. *Span.* unguento amaracino *a sort of ointment made of marjoram*), Wrt. Voc. ii. 7, 74.

sealfian; *p.* ode *To salve, anoint* :—Sealfode *fotam*, Wrt. Voc. ii. 37, 16: 85, 22. Gisalbot *delibutus*, Txts. 56, 325. [Salue me mine wunden, Marh. 5, 30. Eȝhesallfe to sallfenn þe follkes herrtess eȝhe, Orm. 9427. Þatt mann þatt smeredd iss and sallfedd, 13243. Buten ȝif heorte wunden beon isalued, A. R. 274, 30. *Goth.* salbōn *to anoint*: *O. Sax.* salƀōn: *O. H. Ger.* salbōn *ungere, fovere, impinguare*.]

sealf-lǽcnung, e; *f. Curing by means of salves* or *ointments*:—*Farmacida in Latinum medicamina sonat, id est* sealflǽcnung, Wrt. Voc. ii. 39, 19. v. next word.

sealf-lǽcung, e; *f. Pharmacy*; pharmacia, Wrt. Voc. i. 20, 27. v. preceding word.

sealh, salig, es; *m. A sallow, sally, selly* (v. E. D. S. Pub. Plant Names, p. 607):—Salch, salh *salix*, Txts. 94, 892. Sealh *amera*, Wrt. Voc. i. 285, 61. Seal, ii. 8, 41. Seales rinde, Lchdm. iii. 14, 2. Reádes seales leáf (*red sally* lythrum salicaria, Plant Names, p. 413), 58, 28. Genim sealh, ii. 18, 26: 86, 7. On salig (saligum, Ps. Lamb.: salum, Ps. Surt.: sealum, Ps. Spl.) wē ūre organan up āhēngan *in salicibus suspendimus organa nostra*, Ps. Th. 136, 2. Salhas *salices*, Txts. 113, 58. Selas *saliunculas*, Hpt. Gl. 408, 56. [In selihes (salyhes, MS. H.), Ps. 136, 2. *Chauc.* salwes: *Prompt. Parv.* salwhe: *O. H. Ger.* salaha; *gen.* -un; *f. salix, saliuncula*: *Ger.* sahl-weide: *Icel.* selga (cf. selly, *Yorks.*); *f.*] v. following words.

sealh-beorh *a hill where sallows grow*:—Tō sahlbeorge, Cod. Dip. Kmbl. iii. 451, 17.

sealh-hangra *a meadow where sallows grow*:—On sealhangran, Cod. Dip. Kmbl. vi. 234, 18.

sealh-hyrst *a sallow-copse*:—Tō sealhyrstæ foreweardræ, Cod. Dip. Kmbl. v. 256, 1.

sealh-rind *the bark of sallow*:—Nim sealhrinde, Lchdm. ii. 98, 9. Grēne sealhrinde, 318, 9.

Sealh-wudu *Selwood*:—Be eástan Sealwyda, Chr. 878; Erl. 80, 9. Sealwuda, 894; Erl. 92, 19.

sealm, psealm, psalm, es; *m. A psalm, song* (a) in a general sense:—*Psalmus, propie* hearpsang; *canticum* psalm, æfter hearpan sang; *psalmus* ǽr hearpan sang, Wrt. Voc. i. 28, 36–38. On fatum sealmes *in vasis psalmi*, Ps. Spl. 70, 24. Syngaþ Gode sealm, 67, 4. Salma *psalmorum*, Ps. Surt. 70, 21. On sealmum wē drȳman him *in psalmis jubilemus ei*, Ps. Spl. 94, 2. Ðæt ic Gode sealmas singe, Ps. Th. 56, 9, 11. (b) the psalms of David:—David wītegode fela ymbe Crist, swā swā ūs cȳđaþ đa sealmas đe hē gesang, Ælfc. T. Grn. 7, 25. On Moyses ǽ, on wītegum and on sealmum, Lk. Skt. 24, 44. On psalmum (salmum, Cott. MSS.) Past. 48; Swt. 375, 1. (c) with special reference to the services of the church:—Hū fela psealma on nihtlīcum tīdum tō singenne synt, R. Ben. 6, 15. Sealma, 33, 5: 6, 22. Nǽnig mon ne dorste for hine sæalmas ne mæssan singan, Bd. 5, 14; S. 634, 35. Seofon seolmas, Coll. Monast. Th. 33, 29. [*O. L. Ger.* salm: *O. H. Ger.* salmo, psalmo: *Icel.* sālm.] v. bletsing-, gebed-, lof-sealm.

sealma, selma, an; *m. A couch*:—Selma, benc *sponda*, Txts. 98, 955. Gewīteþ đonne on sealman, Beo. Th. 4911; B. 2460. (Cf. Lazarus answebit ist an selmon, Hel. 4008.) [*O. Frs.* bed-selma *bedstead.*]

sealm-cwide, es; *m. A psalm*:—On stefne sealmcwides *uoce psalmi*, Ps. Lamb. 97, 5.

sealm-fæt:—On sealmfatum *translates* in vasis psalmorum, Ps. Th. 70, 20.

sealm-getæl, es; *n. A tale* or *number of psalms*:—Ðæs sealmgetæles is elles tō lyt, R. Ben. 43, 19.

sealm-glig, -gliw, es; *n. Psalmody*:—On sealmglige *in psalterio*, Blickl. Gl. Sealmglywe, Ps. Lamb. 143, 9.

sealmian; *p.* ode *To play on the harp (and sing)*:—Ic singe and sealmige *cantabo et psallam* (I sal sing and salme, Ps.), Ps. Spl. M. 107, 1.

sealm-leóþ, es; *n. A psalm*:—Sealmleóþ and hearpswēg *psalterium et cythara*, Blickl. Gl.

sealm-lof, es; *n. A psalm*:—Sealmlof *psalmus*, Ps. Lamb. 146, 1: 17, 50: *psalterium*, 107, 3. Sealmlof cweđaþ *psallite*, 97, 4.

sealm-lofian *to sing psalms*:—Singaþ him and sealmlofiaþ him *cantate ei et psallite ei*, Ps. Lamb. 104, 2.

sealm-sang, es; *m.* I. *a psalm*:—Sealmsang *psalmus*, Ps. Lamb. 146, 1. Salmsang, 60, 9. On sealmsangum *in psalmis*, Hymn. Surt. 7, 34. II. *psalm singing, psalmody*:—Ðā đā se sealmsang gefylled wæs *expletis psalmodiis*, Bd. 4, 7; S. 575, 2. Ðæs dæglīcan sealmsanges *diurne psalmodie*, Wrt. Voc. ii. 141, 61: R. Ben. 34, 9. On fæstenne and on sealmsange, Blickl. Homl. 199, 34. Gif se man sealmsang ne cunne *si homo psalmos cantare nesciat*, L. Ecg. P. iv. 61; Th. ii. 222, 16. Sealmsang *melodiam*, Wrt. Voc. ii. 56, 77. III. *the making and reciting of psalms*:—Ða twegen fixas getācnodon sealmsang and đæra wītegena cwydas. Ān đæra bodode Cristes tōcyme mid sealmsange and ōđer mid wītegunge. Nū sind đa twā gesetnyssa, đæt is sealmsang and wītegung, Homl. Th. i. 188, 16–19. [*O. H. Ger.* salm-sang *psalmus, psalterium, psalmodia.*]

sealm-scop, es; *m. A writer* or *maker of psalms, a psalmist* (generally *the psalmist* David):—Se sealmscop (salm-, Cott. MSS.), Past. 1; Swt. 29, 8. Salmscop, 14; Swt. 85, 23. Psalmsceop (-scop, Cott. MSS.), 37; Swt. 273, 13: 275, 21. Se sealmsceop, Blickl. Homl. 55, 12: 57, 1: L. Ecg. P. i. 9; Th. ii. 176, 14: Homl. Th. ii. 82, 30. Sealmscopes *psalmigraphi*, Hpt. Gl. 430, 40. Heáhfæderas, wītigan, sealmsceopas, Blickl. Homl. 105, 10: Wulfst. 250, 18.

sealm-traht, es; *m. A commentary on the psalms* or *on a psalm*:—Swā swā Hieronimus se wīsa trahtnere āwrāt on sumum sealmtrahte, Homl. As. 36, 297.

sealm-wyrhta, an; *m. A psalmist*:—Se psalmwyrhta (*David*), Homl. Th. ii. 82, 32. Sealmwyrhta, Ælfc. T. Grn. 1, 24.

sealo-brūn. v. salu-brūn.

sealt, es; *n. Salt* (lit. and fig.):—Sealt *sal*, Wrt. Voc. i. 82. 89. Gē synt eorþan sealt (salt, Lind., Rush.): gyf đæt sealt āwyrþ, Mt. Kmbl. 5, 13: Mk. Skt. 9, 49, 50. Hwylc manna werodum þurhbrȳcþ mettum būton swæcce sealtes *quis hominum dulcibus perfruitur cibis sine sapore salis?* Coll. Monast. Th. 28, 17. Nim ācorfenes sealtes (*rock salt*) đæt wæter đe đǽrof gǽþ, Lchdm. ii. 246, 18. Hwītes sealtes, iii. 20, 26. Greát sealt *rock salt*, 40, 20, 10: i. 158, 34. [*Goth.* salt: *O. Sax. O. L. Ger.* salt: *O. H. Ger.* salz: *Icel.* salt.] See following words, Cod. Dip. Kmbl. vi. 331, col. 2, and Leo on Anglo-Saxon Names, p. 27.

sealt, salt; *adj. Salt*, (1) of that which is naturally salt:—For hwam wæs seó sǽ sealt geworden? Moises āwearp đa .x. word in đa sǽ, and his teáras āgeát in đa sǽ; for đam weard seó sǽ sealt, Salm. Kmbl. 188, 15–19. Sealt wæter *the sea*, Ps. Th. 68, 2: Cd. Th. 13, 6; Gen. 198. Brim sceal sealt weallan, Menol. Fox 552; Gn. C. 45. On sealtum mersce *in salsuginem*, Ps. Spl. 106, 34. Ōþ đone sealtan mere *usque ad lacum Salinarum*, Ors. 1, 1; Swt. 26, 8. Ofer sealtne (saltne, Cott. MSS.) sǽ, Past. pref.; Swt. 9, 8. Sió onlīcnes sendde mycel wæter þurh hiora mūþ swā sealt (*very salt*), Blickl. Homl. 245, 25. Eahtođe wæs sealtes pund, đanon him wǽron đa teáras sealte, Salm. Kmbl. 180, 16. Sealte ȳđa, Cd. Th. 205, 26; Exod. 441. Sealte sǽwēgas, 240, 9; Dan. 384. Sealte streámas, Exon. Th. 206, 2; Ph. 120. Sealte flōdas, Ps. Th. 68, 14. Swēg sealtera wætera, 76, 13. Salte sǽstreámas, Andr. Kmbl. 1497; An. 750. (2) of that which is artificially salt, *salt* (meat):—Tū hriéđeru, ōđer sealt, ōđer fersc, Ch. Th. 158, 27. Forgā sealtes gehwæt, Lchdm. ii. 56, 23. Ete sealtne mete and nōwiht fersces, iii. 28, 24. Sele đū him sealte mettas, 182, 13: 184, 8. [*O. Frs.* salt: *Icel.* saltr.] v. un-sealt.

sealt-ærn, -ern, es; *n. A salt-house, a place where salt is prepared*:—.i. sealtern, Cod. Dip. Kmbl. ii. 64, 28. Būtan đem sealtern and būtan đem wioda đe tō đem sealtern limpþ, 66, 22. Sealtearn, iii. 426, 19.

sealt-brōc, es; *m. A brook that runs from salt works* (?):—Of salterewellan eástriht on saltbrōc; and swā ondlong saltbrōces, Cod. Dip. Kmbl. iii. 206, 32.

sealten; *adj. Salt, salted*:—In đæm đe biþ salten *in quo salietur*, Mt. Kmbl. Rush. 5, 13.

sealtere, es; *m. A salt-worker*:—Sealtere *salinator*, Wrt. Voc. i. 74, 10. Sealtere, saltere, Ælfc. Gr. 9, 21; Zup. 47, 2. Sealtere, hwæt ūs fremaþ cræft đīn? . . . Nān eówer blisse brȳcþ on gereorduncge ođđe mete, būton cræft mīn gistlīþe him beó, Coll. Monast. Th. 28, 5–11. On đone saltherpaþ; and swā ondlong đæs herpaþes đæt on salteredene . . . on salterewellan; of salterewellan eástriht on saltbrōc, Cod. Dip. Kmbl. iii. 206, 28–32. Sealtera cumb, 412, 24. In saltera weg; of sealtera wege, 80, 16. [*Prompt. Parv.* saltare or wellare of salt *salinator.*]

sealt-fæt, es; *n. A vessel for salt, a salt-cellar*:—Sealtfæt *salinare* vel *salinum*, Wrt. Voc. i. 26, 59: *vas salis*, 290, 23: Anglia ix. 264, 18. Se Hǽlend bestang đone hlāf on đæt sealtfæt đe him beforan stōd, Homl. As. 163, 254. [*O. H. Ger.* salz-faz *salinum*: *Icel.* salt-fat.]

sealt-hālgung, e; *f. Salt-hallowing*; benedictio salis:—Salthālguncge tō acrum ł in hūsum, Rtl. 117, 33.

sealt-herepaþ *a road to salt-works*. v. sealtere, *and cf.* sealt-strǽt.

sealt-hūs, es; *n. A house where salt is prepared* (?) or *sold* (?); salinarium, Wrt. Voc. i. 56, 49. [*O. H. Ger.* salz-hūs *salsamentarium.*]

sealtian *to dance*. v. saltian *and next word*.

sealticge, an; *f. A dancer*:—Hēt Herodes đæt heáfod beran on disce and sellan ānre sealticgan (*the daughter of Herodias who danced before Herod*) hire plegan tō mēde, Shrn. 123, 2.

sealt-leáf *glosses* mozicia, Wrt. Voc. ii. 59, 35.

sealt-leáh; *gen.* -leáge; *f. A salt lea*; hence *Saltley*:—Of đan swīnhagan đæt on sealtleáge; and of sealtleáge in đone hyrstgeard, Cod. Dip. Kmbl. iii. 400, 1.

sealt-mere, es; *m*: *A salt mere* or *marsh*; hence *Saltmere.*—Tō sealtmere; of sealtmere, Cod. Dip. Kmbl. iii. 82, 3.

sealtness, e; *f. Saltness*:—Eorþan wæstmbēre sealtsæleđan ł tō sealtnesse *terram fructiferam in salsuginem*, Ps. Lamb. 106, 34. In saltnisse *in salsilaginem*, Ps. Surt. 106, 34.

sealt-sæleđa. v. preceding word.

sealt-seáþ, es; *m. A salt-pit, salt-spring*:—Hafaþ eác đis land sealtseáþas *habet fontes salinarum*, Bd. 1, 1; S. 473, 22. [Cf. *O. H. Ger.* salz-suti *salina.*]

sealt-stān, es; *m.* I. *rock salt*:—Ðis mæg tō eáhsalfe: genim geoluwne stān (*ochre*) and saltstān, Lchdm. i. 374, 14. II. *a stone formed of salt, a pillar of salt*:—Heó on sealtstānes sōna wurde anlīcnesse ǽfre siđđan, Cd. Th. 154, 31; Gen. 2564. Lothes wīf wearđ āwende tō ānum sealtstāne (*in statuam salis*), Gen. 19, 26: Anglia vii. 48, 472. [*O. H. Ger.* salz-stein: *Icel.* salt-steinn. In English *salt-stone* somewhat later means a rock in the sea, translating *cautes*, Wrt. Voc. i. 256, col. 1.]

sealt-strǣt, e; *f. A road to salt-works* (?); hence *Saltstreet*:—Andlang sealtstrǣte, Cod. Dip. Kmbl. iii. 38, 20. Ondlong ðære sealtstrǣt, 160, 13. Tō ðære sealtstræte, 263, 24. Cf. sealt-herepaþ.

sealt-wíc, es; *n. A place where salt is sold;* hence *Saltwych*:—In unico emptorio salis quem nos Saltuuic uocamus, Cod. Dip. Kmbl. i. 81, 9. Æt Saltwíc, v. 143, 21.

sealt-wille, -welle, an; *f. A salt spring* or *well;* hence *Saltwell*:—In saltwyllan; of saltwyllan, Cod. Dip. Kmbl. iv. 70, 24. Ða saltwælla ł of sæltwælla *a saliua* (translator seems to have read *salina*), Mt. Kmbl. p. 1, 5.

sealt-ȳþ, e; *f. A salt wave, sea-wave*:—Ðæt ic sealtȳþa gelāc cunnige, Exon. Th. 308, 5; Seef. 35. Sealtȳþa geswing, 356, 7; Pa. 8.

seám, es; *m. A seam*:—Heáfodpanne *capitale*, heánnes ðære heáfodpannan *cacumen capitalis*, seám ðære heáfodpannan *cerebrum*, brægen *cervellum*, Wrt. Voc. ii. 22, 51–55. Seám *panicenū*, 116, 8. His tunece wæs eal būton seáme (*inconsutilis*, Jn. 19, 23), Homl. Th. ii. 254, 32. Geclǣm ealle ða seámas mid tyrwan, i. 20, 33. [*O. Frs.* sām: *O. H. Ger.* saum *ora, lacinia, limbus*: *Icel.* saumr.]

seám, es; *m.* I. *a seam, a load, burden* [a *seam* of corn is a quarter, eight bushels; a *seam* of wood is a horse-load; a *seam* of dung 3 cwts. (Devon), v. E. D. S. Pub. Reprinted Glossaries, and Farming Words 1, 3, 7. Bailey gives a *seam* of glass as 120 lbs.]:—Seám *vel* berþen *sarcina*, Wrt. Voc. i. 16, 27: Ælfc. Gr. 9, 32; Zup. 59, 3. Seáme *sarcina*, Hpt. Gl. 528, 35. Gē sȳmaþ men mid byrþenum (seámum, Lind.: seómum, Rush.) . . . and gē ne āhrīnaþ ða seámas mid eówrum ānum fingre, Lk. Skt. 11, 46. Wæs þridde healf þūsend mūla ðe ða seámas (*sarcinas*) wǣgon, Nar. 9, 10: 23, 1–2. II. *the furniture of a beast of burden*:—Rachel hig hæfde gehȳdd under ānes olfendes seáme (*subter stramenta cameli*), Gen. 31, 34. III. *that in which a burden may be carried, a bag*:—Būta seáme (seóme, Rush.) *sine sacculo*, Lk. Skt. Lind. 22, 35. Nællaþ gié gebeara seám (seóm, Rush.) *nolite portare sacculum*, 10, 4. IV. as a technical term, *a service which consisted in supplying the lord with beasts of burden*; summagium, sagmegium:—Hē sceal beón gehorsad, ðæt hē mǣge tō hlāfordes seáme ðæt (*the horse*) syllan oððe sylf lǣdan, swæðer him man tǣce, L. R. S. 5; Th. i. 436, 6. [I shal assoille þe myselue for a seme of whete, Piers P. 3, 40. Seem of corne *quarterium*, Prompt. Parv. 452. *O. H. Ger.* soum *sagma, sella, sarcina.* From *Lat.* (*Gk.*) *sagma*, later *salma*; cf. *Ital.* salma; *Fr.* somme.] v. ofer-seám; sīman.

seámere, es; *m. A tailor*:—Seámere *sartor*, Wrt. Voc. i. 74, 12. Seámere, seamyre, Ælfc. Gr. 30, 2; Zup. 190, 6 note. Seámere *burdus* (burdus *sutor vestiarius*), Wrt. Voc. i. 21, 47. Se smiþ secgþ . . . Hwanon seámere (*sartori*) nǣdl? nis hit of mīnon geweorce? Coll. Monast. Th. 30, 33.

seámere, es; *m. A beast of burden, a mule*:—Hors *equus*, hengest *caballus*, seámere *burdus* (= *burdo*; hic burdo, i. genitum inter equum et asinam, 219, col. 1), Wrt. Voc. i. 287, 42–44. Seámere *burdus*, oxa *bova*, ii. 11, 61–62. [*O. H. Ger.* soumari *burdo, saumarius, dromedarius*: *Ger.* säumer.]

seámestre, an; *f. One who sews, a tailor, sempstress* (though the noun is feminine it seems not confined to females, cf. bæcestre):—Seámestre *sartrix*, Wrt. Voc. i. 74, 13. *Sarcio* . . . of ðam is *sartor* seámystre (-estre, *other MSS.* seámere) *sartrix* heó, Ælfc. Gr. 30, 2; Zup. 190, 6. Hió becweð Eádgyfe āne crencestræn and āne sēmestran, ōðer hātte Eádgyfu, ōðer hātte Æðelyfu, Cod. Dip. Kmbl. vi. 131, 32. Fīf pund Ælffǣhe mīn sǣmestres, Chart. Th. 568, 10. [Sadlers, souters, semsteris fyn, Destr. Tr. 1585. Good semsters be sowing . . . good huswifes be mending, Tusser 176, 7.]

seám-hors, es; *n. A pack-horse*; sagmarius equus, Wrt. Voc. i. 23, 13. [*Ger.* saum-ross.]

seám-penig, -pending, es; *m. A toll of a penny on a load* (of salt):—Se wægnscilling and se seámpending gonge tō ðæs cyninges handa swā hē ealning dyde æt Saltwīc, Cod. Dip. Kmbl. v. 143, 20. Cf. *statio sive inoneratio plaustrorum* mentioned in connection with *salis coctiones*, 125, 31. v. Kemble's Saxons in England, ii. 329.

seám-sadol, es; *m. A pack-saddle*; sagma, Wrt. Voc. i. 23, 12. [*O. H. Ger.* soum-satol *sagma*: *Ger.* saum-sattel.]

seám-sticca, an; *m. Some part of a weaver's apparatus*:—Hē sceal fela tōwtōla habban . . . seámsticcan, scearra, nǣdle, Anglia ix. 263, 14.

seár *and* siére; *adj. Sear, dry, withered, barren*:—Hit stent on ðam siéran bōchagan; andlang ðes siéran bōchagan, Cod. Dip. Kmbl. v. 70, 32. Seáre *steriles*, Germ. 402, 69. [His body wex alle seere, R. Brun. 18, 25. With seere braunches, blossoms ungrene, Chauc. R. R. 4752. Seere or dry, as treys or herbys *aridus*, Prompt. Parv. 453. *O. Du.* sore *dry*; zoor *dry, withered*, or seare (Hexham): *L. Ger.* soor *dry.*] v. seárian.

Sear-burh. v. Searo-burh.

seárian; *p.* ode *To grow sear, wither, pine away*:—Eorþan indryhto ealdaþ and searaþ, Exon. Th. 311, 9; Seef. 89. His leáf and his blǣda ne fealwiaþ ne ne seáriaþ *folium ejus non decidet*, Ps. Th. 1, 4. Grēnu leáf wexaþ . . . hȳ eft onginnaþ seárian, Shrn. 168, 22. Hē (*Regulus*) slāpan ne mehte, ōþ hē swā seárigende his līf forlēt, Ors. 4, 6; Swt. 178, 24. [*Prompt. Parv.* seeryn̄ or dryyn̄ or welkyn̄, dryyn up *areo, aresco*: *O. H. Ger.* ar-sōrēn *emarcescere*; un-saorentlīh *immarcescibilis.*] v. ā-, for-seárian.

searo. v. searu.

Searo-burh *Salisbury*:—In ðære stōwe ðe is genemned [æt] Searobyrg (-byrig, Searoburh, Sælesberi), Chr. 552; Th. pp. 28, 29. Tō Searebyrig, 1086; Th. 353, 18. Tō Searbyrig, 1003; Th. pp. 252, 253. [Seresbyrig (Særes-), 1123; Th. 374, 5, 20, 24, 34.]

searu, searo, [w]e; *f.*: [w]es; *n. Device, design, contrivance, art.* I. in the following glosses it is uncertain whether the word is used with a good or with a bad meaning:—Sarwo *adventio*, Wrt. Voc. ii. 99, 38. Searo *molimen*, 54, 29. Searwe *molimine*, 89, 64. Searwe *argumenta*, 84, 69. Searwum *commentis*, 14, 82: 80, 76. Seorwum, 104, 75. Seara *machinas*, Hpt. Gl. 510, 21. II. in a bad sense, *craft, artifice, wile, deceit, stratagem, ambush, treachery, plot*:—Searu *factio* (cf. fācn *factiones*, 64; bepǣcunga *factione*, Hpt. Gl. 474, 26), Wrt. Voc. ii. 33, 81. Gleáwnisse and seare (sceare, Wrt.) *astu*, Wrt. Voc. ii. 9, 27. Mid searwe on gewald gedōn *per proditionem tradere*, Ors. 1, 12; Swt. 52, 27. Swīðor beswicen for Alexandres searewe ðonne for his gefeohte *non minus arte Alexandri superata, quam virtute Macedonum*, 3, 9; Swt. 124, 19. Mid searuwe ācwellan *morti tradere*, Ps. Th. 108, 16. Ðara feónda searo beswīcan and ofercuman, Blickl. Homl. 201, 29. Searo rēnian *to lay a snare*, 109, 30: Cd. Th. 162, 9; Gen. 2678. Þurh ðæs deófles searo dōm forlǣtan, 39, 27; Gen. 632: Exon. Th. 153, 7; Gū. 822: 227, 6; Ph. 419. Þurh īdel searu, Ps. Th. 138, 17: Elen. Kmbl. 1438; El. 721. Swilt þurh searwe *death by treachery*, Andr. Kmbl. 2695; An. 1350. Searwa *molimina* (*magorum*), Hpt. Gl. 502, 53. Sarwa *mendacia*, Wrt. Vōc. ii. 132, 41. Full fācnes and searuwa *plenum dolo*, Ps. Th. 9, 27: Met. 9, 27. In searwum *in insidiis*, Ps. Surt. 9, 29. Searwum *factionibus*, Wrt. Voc. ii. 34, 9. Mid sibbe wē cōmon næs mid searwum *pacifice venimus nec quidquam machinamur mali*, Gen. 42, 11. Beswicen mid deófles searwum *daemonica fraude seductus*, Bd. 5, 13; S. 632, 26. Mid searewan (his searum, MS. C.) *consiliis*, Ors. 3, 7; Swt. 112, 18. Searowum beswicene, Andr. Kmbl. 1489; An. 745. Hié þurh seara (*per insidias*) ofslægene wurdon, Ors. 1, 10; Swt. 44, 28. Ðā funde hē swīðe yfel geþeaht and searwa ymb hira līf *contra eorum vitam consilium praebuit*, Past. 54, 4; Swt. 423, 15. Gif hwā ofsleá his ðone nēhstan þurh searwa, L. Alf. 13; Th. i. 48, 1: Blickl. Homl. 83, 33. Hwylce searwa se drȳ ārefnde *what artifices the sorcerer practised*, 173, 8. Nyston ða searwe ðe him sǣton bæftan *ignorans quod post tergum laterent insidiae*, Jos. 8, 14. III. in a good sense, *art, skill, contrivance*, (*in the adverbial inst.* searwum *skilfully, ingeniously, with art*):—Searwum āsǣled, Cd. Th. 207, 21; Exod. 470. Salem stōd searwum (*or* IV?) āfæstnod, weallum geweorðod, 218, 17; Dan. 40. Sadol searwum fāh (cf. searu-fāh), Beo. Th. 2080; B. 1038. Earmbeága fela searwum gesǣled (cf. searu-sǣled), 5521; B. 2764: Exon. Th. 438, 10; Rä. 57, 5 (cf. searu-bunden): 216, 17; Ph. 269. Būr ātimbran, searwum āsettan, 411, 27; Rä. 30, 6. IV. *that which is contrived with art, a machine, engine, fabric*:—Stæfliðere oððe searu *ballista, machina belli*, Wrt. Voc. ii. 10, 62. Searu *ballista, catapulta*, vel *machina belli*, 125, 9. Middaneardes wyrhta seares *mundi factor machinae*, Hymn. Surt. 29, 9. Ic seah searo hweorfan, grindan wið greóte, giellende faran, Exon. Th. 414, 29; Rä. 33, 3. IV a. *armour, equipment, arms*:—Byrnan, gūðsearo gumena, gāras . . . sǣmanna searo, Beo. Th. 663; B. 329. Beran beorht searo, Cd. Th. 191, 23; Exod. 219. Licgeþ lonnum fæst . . . swīðe swingeþ and his searo hringeþ, Salm. Kmbl. 534; Sal. 266. Hringīren song in searwum (*coats of mail*), Beo. Th. 651; B. 323: 5053; B. 2530. Secg on searwum, 503; B. 249: 5392; B. 2700. Geseah on searwum (*among the arms*) sigeeádig bil, 3118; B. 1557. Searwum gearwe *equipped*, 3631; B. 1813. [*Goth.* sarwa; *n. pl.* τὰ ὅπλα, πανοπλία: *O. H. Ger.* saro; gi-sarwi, -sarwa *lorica, armatura, arma*: *Icel.* sörvi *a necklace; armour.*] v. beadu-, bealu-, fācen-, fǣr-, fyrd-, gūþ-, hlāford-, inwit-, lāþ-, lyge-, nearu-searu; siru; *and cf.* or-þanc.

searu-bend; *m. f. A cunning, curious clasp* or *fastening*:—Glōf searobendum fæst, sió wæs orþoncum eall gegyrwed diófles cræftum, Beo. Th. 4179; B. 2086. Cf. orþanc-bend.

searu-bunden; *adj. Cunningly fastened, bound with art*:—Wunden gold, sinc searobunden, Exon. Th. 437, 7; Rä. 56, 4.

searu-cǣg, e; *f. An insidious key*:—Flānþracu feorh onleác searocǣgum gesōht (*of the insidious attacks of disease*), Exon. Th. 170, 27; Gū. 1118.

searu-ceáp, es; *n. An ingenious piece of goods, a curious implement*:—Næfde sellīcu wiht folme, exle ne earmas, sceal on ānum fēt searoceáp (cf. searo, IV) swīfan, Exon. Th. 415, 6; Rä. 33, 7.

searu-céne; *adj. Bold in arms* or *skilfully daring*:—Wæs Dauid æt wīge sōð sigecempa, searocȳne man, cāsere creaftig, Ps. C. 10. Cf. searu-grim.

searu-cræft, es; *m.* I. *a treacherous art, wile, stratagem, an artifice, a machination, plot*:—Searecræft *molimen*, Hpt. Gl. 502, 56. Searocræft *machinam*, Wrt. Voc. ii. 54, 28. Þurh diófles searucræft, Cod. Dip. Kmbl. ii. 304, 26. Þurh searocræft, Andr. Kmbl. 217; An. 109. Searecræftum *argumentis*, Hpt. Gl. 471, 27: *machinamentis*, 478, 54. Bepǽht mid ðæs deófles searocræftum, Homl. Th. i. 192, 17: Exon. Th. 136, 13; Gū. 540: 142, 19; Gū. 646. Ealdfeónda nīþ searocræftum swīð, 110, 25; Gū. 113. Searecræftas *machinas* (*fraudulentas*), Hpt. Gl. 474, 15. Ðe hē ne beswīce þurh his searucræftas (searo-, searæ-), Wulfst. 97, 8. Uton forfleón mān and morþor and searacræftas, 115, 9. Swīðe forsyngod þurh swicdōmas and þurh searacræftas, 164, 3. II. *art, skill, cunning, a cunning art* (in a good sense, v. next word):—Wuldres ealdor gesweotula þurh searocræft ðīn sylfes weorc, Exon. Th. 1, 16; Cri. 9. Ða rōde mid ðām æðelestum eorcnanstānum besetton searocræftum (*cunningly, skilfully*, cf. searu, III), Elen. Kmbl. 2049; El. 1026. Ne hī searocræftum godweb giredon, Met. 8, 24. III. *an engine, machine* (cf. searo, IV):—Stæfliðera *ballista*, searecræftes *machinae*, Hpt. Gl. 487, 22.

searu-cræftig; *adj.* I. *skilful, skilled in* (with gen.), *cunning* (in a good sense):—Snottor, searocræftig sāwle rǽdes, Frag. Kmbl. 80; Leás. 42. Sum biþ searocræftig goldes and gimma, Exon. Th. 296, 29; Crä. 58. II. *wily, cunning* (in a bad sense), 416, 7; Rä. 34, 7.

searu-fāh; *adj. Curiously, cunningly coloured* (cf. gold-fāh):—Herebyrne sīd and searofāh, Beo. Th. 2892; B. 1444.

searu-geþræc, es; *n. A store of things in which art is displayed*:—Seón and sēcean searogeþræc (*the dragon's hoard*), wundur under wealle, Beo. Th. 6196; B. 3102 [cf. geþræce *apparatu*, Wrt. Voc. ii. 85, 72].

searu-gim[m], es; *m. A curious gem, precious stone*:—Seærogim *topazion*, Ps. Spl. T. 118, 127. His ēgan scinan swā searagym, Nar. 43, 15. Searogemme *unio*, Wrt. Voc. ii. 89, 34. Meregrota oððe gymmas (saragimmas, MS. V.) *margaritae*, Nar. 37, 29. Stān, searogimma nān (ǽlces cynnes gimmas ne ..., Bt. 34, 8; Fox 144. 31), Met. 21, 21: Beo. Th. 2318; B. 1157. Ðæt ic ǽrwelan, goldǽht ongite, gearo sceáwige sigel, searogimmas (*the dragon's hoard*), 5491; B. 2749: Exon. Th. 478, 5; Ruin. 36.

searu-grim; *adj. Fierce in arms* or *skilfully fierce, having fierceness accompanied by skill*:—Gif ðīn hige wǽre swā searogrim swā ðū self talast *if thy spirit had been as cunningly fierce* (?) *as thyself reckons*, Beo. Th. 1192; B. 594. Cf. searu-cēne.

searu-hæbbend[e] [*one*] *having armour, armed*:—Slǽpe tōbrugdon searuhæbbende *the warriors started from sleep*, Andr. Kmbl. 3054; An. 1350. Searohæbbendra, 2934; An. 1470: Beo. Th. 480; B. 237: Exon. Th. 468, 12; Phar. 6.

searu-lic; *adj. Ingenious, cunning, clever, displaying art* or *skill*:—Ðæt (*writing being able to convey a message*) is wundres dǽl, on sefan searolīc ðam ðe swylc ne conn, Exon. Th. 472, 4; Rā. 61, 11. Sum hafaþ searolīc gomen gleódǽda, 298, 9; Crä. 82. v. next word.

searulīce; *adv. Ingeniously, cunningly, cleverly, with art* or *skill*:—Sum mæg searolīce wordcwide wrītan, Exon. Th. 42, 14; Cri. 672. Is se finta sum splottum searolīce beseted, 218, 19; Ph. 297. Ne hī gimreced setton searolīce, Met. 8, 26.

searu-net[t], es; *n.* I. *an armour-net*, or *a net ingeniously wrought, a coat of mail*:—On him byrne scān, searonet seowed smiþes orþancum, Beo. Th. 816; B. 406. II. *a net of treachery* or *guile, a net* (metaph.), *a snare, wile*:—Mē elþeódige inwitwrāsne, searonet seóþaþ, Andr. Kmbl. 127; An. 64. Searonettum beseted *beset with snares*, 1885; An. 945.

searu-nīþ, es; *m.* I. *hostility to which effect is given by treachery, crafty enmity*:—Ic ne sōhte searonīþas ne ne swōr fela āþa on unriht *I had not recourse to the arts of the treacherous foe, nor swore many oaths wrongfully*, Beo. Th. 5469; B. 2738: 2405; B. 1200. Swā wæs Biówulfe, ðā hē biorges weard sōhte, searonīþas (*the wily hostilities of the dragon, who used poison to destroy his foe*, cf. āttorsceaþa, 5670, *and is called* inwitgest, 5333. Cf. *too* inwit-nīþ), 6126; B. 3067. II. *armour-hate* (v. searu, IV a), *martial strife, the strife of armed men, battle*:—Nō ic wiht fram ðē swylcra searunīþa secgan hȳrde, billa brōgan, 1168; B. 582.

searu-pīl, es; *m. An implement with a point*:—Mīn heáfod is homere geþuren, searopīla wund, sworfen feóle, Exon. Th. 497, 17; Rä. 87, 2.

searu-rūn, e; *f. A cunning mystery*:—Searorūna gespon, Exon. Th. 347, 20; Sch. 15.

searu-sǽled; *adj. Cunningly tied*:—Nelle ic unbunden ǽnigum hȳran, nymþe searosǽled (cf. searu, III, *and* searu-bunden), Exon. Th. 406, 12; Rä. 24, 16.

searu-þanc, es; *m.* I. *a cunning* (in a bad sense) *thought, device, artifice, wile*:—Geþeóddum searaþancum *adhibitis argumentis*, Hpt. Gl. 502, 16. Eác ic gelǽrde Simon searoþoncum, ðæt hē sacan ongon, Exon. Th. 260, 16; Jul. 298. Sume ic mīnum hondum searoþoncum (*cunningly, craftily*) slōg, 272, 4; Jul. 494. Searoþancum beseted *beset with snares* (v. searu-net), Andr. Kmbl. 2511; An. 1257. II. *a cunning* (in a good sense) *thought, skilful device*:—Þurh sefan snyttro, searoþonca hord, Past. pref.; Swt. 9, 10. Saga sōðcwidum, searoþoncum, gleáwwordum wīsfæst, hwæt ðis gewǽdu sȳ, Exon. Th. 418, 3; Rä. 36, 13. Se wītga, snottor searuþancum, Elen. Kmbl. 2377; El. 1190. Georne smeádon, sōhton searoþancum (*sagaciously, shrewdly*), hwæt sió syn wǽre, 827; El. 414. Se wīnsele fæste wæs īrenbendum searoþoncum (*skilfully, cunningly*) besmiþod, Beo. Th. 1554; B. 775. Cf. or-þanc.

searu-þancol; *adj. Of cunning thought, cunning, sagacious, wise*:—Searoþoncol mægþ (*Judith*), Judth. Thw. 23, 28; Jud. 145. Nis ǽnig secg searoþoncol tō ðæs swīðe gleáw, Exon. Th. 14, 16; Cri. 220. Ðe (*which*) secgas searoþoncle seaxe delfaþ, 427, 26; Rä. 41, 97. Gesǽton searuþancle sundor tō rūne, Andr. Kmbl. 2323; An. 1163. Mon ǽnig searoþoncelra, Judth. Thw. 26, 17; Jud. 331.

searu-wrenc, es; *m. A crafty trick, treacherous device*:—Hē hié biddende wæs ðæt hié mid sume searawrence from Xerse āwende, Ors. 2, 5; Swt. 82, 21. v. siru-wrenc.

searu-wundor, es; *n. A wonderful thing in implements* or *engines* (v. searu, IV, *and* cf. searu-pīl. The term is applied to Grendel's arm, which had been torn away by Beowulf):—Eode scealc monig searowundor seón, Beo. Th. 1844; B. 920.

searwaþ, L. N. P. L. 40; Th. ii. 296, 10. v. next word.

searwian; *p.* ode *To act with craft* or *treachery, to feign*:—Hē sarwaþ *fingitur*, Wrt. Voc. ii. 132, 13. Hió searwaþ *insidiatur*, Kent. Gl. 191. Gif preóst ordāl misfadige, gebēte ðæt. Gif preóst searwaþ be winde, gebēte ðæt *if a priest do not conduct an ordeal rightly, let him make 'bōt.' If a priest uses deceit in respect to the wrapping up of the hand or arm exposed to the ordeal, let him make 'bōt,'* L. N. P. L. 39, 40; Th. ii. 296, 9–10. Sinc searwade *treasure played the traitor* (left its possessor (?)), Exon. Th. 353, 62; Reim. 37. Searw[a] ð[ū] *insidieris*, Kent. Gl. 935. Searwiende *machinans*, 151. Hē cwæð him tō særwigendum mōde (*insidiously*), Homl. Th. ii. 308, 6. v. sirwan *and next word*.

searwung, e; *f. Treachery, artifice, plot, snare*:—Hē sit mid searwungum *sedet in insidiis*, Ps. Lamb. 9 second, 8. v. sirwung.

seáþ, es; *m. A pit, hole, well, reservoir, lake*:—Seáþ *lacus*, Ælfc. Gr. 11; Zup. 79, 10: Ps. Spl. 7, 16: 27, 1: Mk. Skt. 12, 1: *lacus, lacuna*, Wrt. Voc. i. 54, 31: *fovea*, ii. 150, 10: Ps. Spl. 7, 16: 56, 9: *puteus*, Bd. 5, 12; S. 628, 16: *cisterna*, Wrt. Voc. ii. 24, 4: Kent. Gl. 102: *barathrum*, Hpt. Gl. 422, 50: *cloaca*, 484, 19: 508, 70. Ðǽr is se seáþ ðæs singalan susles ... Æfter ðam ðe ðū deád bist, ðonne cymst ðū tō helle ... and ðīn seáþ biþ twegea cubita wīd and feówra lang, Nar. 50, 23–29. On hū grundleásum seáþe *on how bottomless a pit*, Bt. 3, 2; Fox 6, 8. Ðā wæs ðǽr on ōðre sīdan ðæs hlāwes gedolfen swylce mycel wæterseáþ wǽre. On ðam seáþe ufan Gūþlāc him hūs getimbrode, Guthl. 4; Gdwin. 26, 8. Danihel læg betwux seofan leónum on ānum seáþe, Homl. Th. i. 488, 5. Hēht scūfan scyldigne in drīgan seáþ, Elen. Kmbl. 1382; El. 693. In synna seáþ, Exon. Th. 267, 10; Jul. 413. Ðǽr syndon twegen seáþas (*lakes*) ... heora wīde is .cc. mīla ðæs læssan mīlgetales, Nar. 36, 25. [Inne deope seaðen setten þa deade, Laym. 841. *O. Frs.* sāth: *M. H. Ger.* sōt *puteus*.] v. adel-, cealc-, fǽr-, helle-, horu-, lām-, sand-, sealt-, wæter-, wulf-seáþ.

seáða, an; *m.* '*A feeling as if the cavity of the body were full of water swaying about*,' Cockayne. The word glosses *tendiculum*, Wrt. Voc. ii. 77, 3:—Wið seáðan (seádan, 4, 18), Lchdm. ii. 56, 10.

seáw, es; *n. Juice, moisture, humour*:—Genim tūncersan ... dō in ða nosu ðæt se stenc mǽge on ðæt heáfod and ðæt seáw, Lchdm. ii. 22, 14. Genim cileþoniam seáwes cucler fulne, 28, 2. Ys sǽd ðæt se earn wylle mid ðam seáwe (*of wood lettuce*) his eágan hreppan and wǽtan, i. 128, 12. Seáw *ius*, 80, 13: 128, 18. Ðæt seáw sele on cuclere sūpan, ii. 120, 19. Gemeng wið huniges seáw *mix with pure honey*, 30, 7. Feallan lǽtaþ seáw of bōsme, wǽtan of wombe, Exon. Th. 385, 20; Rä. 4, 47. Seá *sucum*, Txts. 182, 83. Cumaþ ða ādla on [of?] yflum seáwum, Lchdm. ii. 176, 5. [*Used later of food.* With diverse spieces The flesh ... She taketh and maketh thereof a sewe, Gow. ii. 325, 4. Seew, Wick. Gen. 27, 4. I wol nat tellen of her strange sewes, Chauc. Sq. T. 67. Sew *cepulatum*, Wülck. Gl. 572, 9: Prompt. Parv. 454. *O. H. Ger.* sou; *n. succus, venenum, alimentum*: cf. *Icel.* söggr *dank, wet*: saggi; *m. moistness.*] v. liþ-, plūm-seáw; ge-seáw; *adj.*

seax, es; *n.* I. *a knife, an instrument for cutting*:—Seax *cultellus*, Wrt. Voc. i. 287, 3. Seax oððe scyrseax *culter*, ii. 15, 58. Saex, 105, 69. Ðæt stǽnene sex ðe ðæt cild ymbsnāþ, Homl. Th. i. 98, 10. Seaxes ord, Exon. Th. 472, 6; Rä. 61, 12. Seaxes ecg, 70, 20; Cri. 1141. Snīþ mid seaxse, Lchdm. ii. 56, 7. Ða hēt hē him his seax ārǽcan tō screádigenne ǽnne æppel, Homl. Th. i. 88, 9. Nim ðæt seax ðe ðæt hæfte sié fealo hrȳðeres horn and sién .III. ǽrene næglas on, Lchdm. ii. 290, 22. Sting ðīn seax on ða wyrte, 346, 12. Hȳ begyrde resten and nāne sex (seax, MSS. T. F.) be heora sīdan næbben *cultellos ad latus non habeant*, R. Ben. 47, 10. Wirc ðē stǽnene sex *fac tibi cultros lapideos*, Jos. 5, 2. II. as a weapon, *a short sword, dagger*:—Ðǽr gebrægd ðara hǽðenra manna sum his seaxe; ðā hē hine đā stingan mynte, đā nyste hē fǣringa hwǣr đæt seax com, Blickl. Homl. 223, 16. Heó hyre seaxe geteáh, brād, brūnecg, Beo. Th. 3095; B. 1545. Hē (*St. Martin*) tōcearf his basing on emtwā mid sexe, Homl. Th. ii. 500, 26. Geteáh his seax, Blickl. Homl. 215, 6. [*O. L. Ger.* sahs: *O. Frs.* sax: *O. H. Ger.* sahs *cultrum, semispathium*: *Icel.* sax *a short sword.*] v. blōd-, ceorf-, hand-, hup-, lǣce-, nægel-, scear-, þeóh-, wæl-seax; *and* cf. sagu.

Seax- *in proper names*:—Sigeferþ Seaxing, Seaxa Sledding (*in a list of East Saxon kings*), Txts. 179, 23. Cf. *Icel.* Járn-Saxa = *iron-chopper*, the name of an ogress in the Edda. Đā fēng tō Eást-Seaxna rīce Swīþhelm Seaxbaldes suna, Bd. 3, 22; S. 553, 42. Đæs cyninges (*Anna of East Anglia*) dohter Sexburh, 3, 8; S. 531, 24: Chr. 639; Erl. 27, 6. Hēr forþfērde Cēnwalh (*of Wessex*), and Seaxburg ān geár rīcsode his cuēn æfter him, 672; Erl. 34, 34. Gesecg Seaxnēting (*East Saxon*), Txts. 179, 16. Cf. Saxnōt *in the formula of renunciation.* v. Grmm. D. M. 184. Seaxrēd (*East Saxon*), 179, 19. Seaxulf biscop (*of Lichfield*), Bd. 4, 6; S. 573, 40. Saxulf (Sæx-), Chr. 656; Erl. 30, 2, 10.

seax-ben[n]. v. six-ben[n].

Seaxe, Seaxan; *pl. The Saxons*, (1) in connection with England:—Cōmon hī of þrīm folcum đām strangestan Germanie, đæt [is] of Seaxum and of Angle and of Geátum ... Of Seaxum, đæt is of đam lande đe mon hāteþ Eald-Seaxan, cōman Eást-Seaxan (-Seaxa, -Sexa, Chron. 449) and Sūþ-Seaxan (-Sexa, Chron.) and West-Seaxan (-Sexa, Chron.), Bd. 1, 15; S. 483, 20–24. Đā wǣron Seaxan sēcende intingan, S. 483, 36. On Germanie đanon Engle and Seaxan cumene wǣron, 5, 9; S. 622, 14. Engle and Seaxe, Chr. 937; Erl. 115, 19: Menol. Fox 368; Men. 185. Sexna kyning, 459; Men. 231. Æt Seaxena handa forwurþan, Chr. 605; Erl. 21, 28. Englum and Sexum (Sæxum), 1065; Erl. 196, 30. Đæt spell đæt ic āwrāt be Angelþeóde and Seaxum, Bd. pref.; S. 471, 10. (2) continental Saxons:—Đȳ ilcan geáre gegadrode micel sciphere on Ald-Seaxum, and đǣr wearþ micel gefeoht ... and đa Seaxan hæfdun sige, Chr. 885; Erl. 84, 8. Ic wæs mid Seaxum, Exon. Th. 322, 12; Vīd. 62. [*O. H. Ger.* Sahsun: *Icel.* Saxar. For the connection of Seaxe(-an) with Seax, v. Grmm. Gesch. D. S. c. xxiii.] v. Eald- (Ald-), Eást-, Sūþ-, West-Seaxe.

Seax-land, es; *n. England*:—Com Gūđrum on eástdǣle Sexlandes, Shrn. 16, 4.

sēcan, sēcean; *p.* sōhte; *pp.* sōht *To seek.* I. (1) *to try to find, to look for, make search for*:—Ic sēce mīne gebrōđru *fratres meos quaero*, Gen. 37, 16. Hwæne sēcst đū? Jn. Skt. 20, 15. Se đe sēcþ, hē hyt fint, Mt. Kmbl. 7, 8. Hwæđer gē willen on wuda sēcan gold đæt reáde? ... Hit witena nān đider nē sēceþ (cf. gē hit đǣr ne sēcaþ, ne finde gē hit nō, Bt. 32, 3; Fox 118, 9), Met. 19, 8. Đonne gē Drihten sēcaþ, đonne gemēte gē hine, gif gē hine mid inweardre heortan sēceaþ, Deut. 4, 29. Gē sēceaþ (soecas, Lind.) đone Hǣlynd, Mt. Kmbl. 28, 5. Hē āxode hine, hwæt hē sōhte, Gen. 37, 15. Đīn fæder and ic sārigende đē sōhton, Lk. Skt. 2, 48. Hī sōhton hyne, Mt. Kmbl. 21, 46: Blickl. Homl. 241, 12. Mannes sunu com sēcean (tō soecanne, Lind.) and hāl dōn đæt forwearđ, Lk. Skt. 19, 10. Sēcende God *requirens Deum*, Ps. Spl. 13, 3. (2) *to try to get* (the source from which a thing is sought marked by *tō*):—Ic monnes feorh tō slagan sēce (MS. seđe) *I will require man's life of the slayer*, Cd. Th. 92, 7; Gen. 1525. Ic tō Drihtne sēce đæt ic gōd æt him begitan mōte *quaesivi bona tibi*, Ps. Th. 121, 9. Gif đū đē tō swā mildum mundbyrd sēcest, Exon. Th. 252, 29; Jul. 170. Heó ūrne fultum sēhþ, Homl. Th. ii. 112, 18. Gumena gehwylcum đara đe geóce tō him sēceþ, Andr. Kmbl. 2307; An. 1155. Đǣr is help gearu manna gehwylcum đam đe sēceþ tō him, 1818; An. 911. Gē hī sēcaþ tō fremdum gesceaftum, Bt. 14, 2; Fox 44, 17, 29. Sūþ-Seaxna mǣgþ him biscopþēninge sēceaþ tō West-Seaxna biscope, Bd. 5, 23; S. 646, 24. Đæt se ān ne ætburste đe hē sōhte, Homl. Th. i. 82, 13. Hwīlum man ceás đa men đe noldan swician ... and syđđan hit man sōhte be đām đe nearwlīcast cūđan swician *at one time the men were chosen that would not deceive ... and since they have been looked for among those that could most oppressively deceive*, L. I. P. 12; Th. ii. 320, 24. Ūs is nēdþearf đæt wē sēcan đone lǣcedōm ūre sāuwle, Blickl. Homl. 97, 31. Biddon wē Drihten đæs leóhtes đe nǣfre ne geendaþ ... đæt leóht wē sceolan sēcan, đæt wē mōtan habban mid englum gemǣne, 21, 14. Bearn Godes brȳda ongunnon on Caines cynne sēcan, Cd. Th. 75, 33; Gen. 1249. Woldon tō dūnscræfum drohtoþ sēcan, Andr. Kmbl. 3077; An. 1541. Uton sibbe tō him sēcan, Exon. Th. 365, 11; Wal. 87. Seócan, Ps. C. 109. Hwæt elles is tō sēcanne wiđ đam hungre nymþe andlyfen, Bd. 1, 27; S. 494, 16. Hē gǣþ sēcende reste, Mt. Kmbl. 12, 43. Sió ǣ sceal beón sōht on đæs sacerdes mūþe, Past. 15; Swt. 91, 17. (3) *to try to attain an end, strive to effect a purpose, aim at, strive after, make something the object of endeavour*:—Ic ne sēce mīnne willan ac đæs đe mē sende, Jn. Skt. 5, 30: 8, 50. Hwæt sēcst đū? 4, 27. León hwelpas sēcaþ, đæt him ǣt God gedēme, Ps. Th. 103, 20. Gif hē đone dōm ofer hine sōhte *if the other tried to get judgment upon him*, L. Alf. 49; Th. i. 56, 33. Đā hālgan đe on đyssum līfe nāht ne sōhton ne ne gyrndon tō hæbbene, Blickl. Homl. 53, 25. Hī sōhton hine him tō hlāforde and tō mundboran *they tried to get him to be their lord and protector*, Chr. 921; Erl. 107, 29: 922; Erl. 108, 20, 28. Gif đæt riht tō hefig sȳ, sēce siþþan đa lāhtinge tō đam cynge, L. Edg. ii. 2; Th. i. 266, 11. (4) *to try to find out* by investigation or examination:—Hwylc sēceþ đæt đe sōđfæst byþ *veritatem quis requiret?* Ps. Th. 60, 6. Sōhte synnum fāh, hū hē sārlīcast meahte feorhcwale findan ... Feónd hine gelǣrde, Exon. Th. 276, 24; Jul. 571. Georne smeádon, sōhton searoþancum, hwæt sió syn wǣre, Elen. Kmbl. 827; El. 414. Ongan on sefan sēcean sōđfæstnesse weg tō wuldre, 2295; El. 1149. Ic đīne gewitnesse wylle sēcan *testimonia tua exquisivi*, Ps. Th. 118, 22. Lǣcedōm sǣcan *medicamentum explorare*, Bd. 1, 27; S. 494, 18. Hwīlum beóþ đa wǣtan on đære wambe filmenum, đonne sceal mon đæt wīslīce sēcean, Lchdm. ii. 222, 24. (5) *to try to learn* by asking, *to ask*:—Đa mē cunnon andsware cȳđan tācna gehwylces đe ic him tō sēce, Elen. Kmbl. 638; El. 319. Đā cwæđ Maria tō đæm engle: Hwæt is đīn nama? Đā cwæđ se engel tō hire: Hwæt sēcestū mīnne naman? Blickl. Homl. 137, 29. Hē đā Drihtnes willan sōhte *he tried to learn what was the will of the Lord*, 225, 30. Wīslīce gē dyde, đætte mannum bedīgled wæs on eorþan, đæt gē đæt on heofenas tō Gode sōhtan, 201, 2. Tō sēcenne, 205, 27. Ic wāt đæt hió wile sēcan (*ask*. Cf. Đā seó cwēn ongan fricggan, 1116; El. 560) be đam sigebeáme, Elen. Kmbl. 840; El. 420. II. *to go* or *come to*:—Oft sēcende *frequentantem*, Wrt. Voc. ii. 34, 18. (1) *to seek* a person, *to visit* (cf. *Ger.* be-suchen):—Đǣr beóþ gegearwoda Godes mildheortnessa đǣm mannum đe đa līchoman sēceaþ þurh heora gebedo, Blickl. Homl. 193, 21. Đa đe æfter deáþe Dryhten sēcaþ, Andr. Kmbl. 1200; An. 600. Đā hē đone cyningc sōhte *when he visited the king*, Ors. 1, 1; Swt. 18, 10. Sārge gē ne sōhton *ye did not visit the afflicted*, Exon. Th. 92, 19; Cri. 1511. Hig đæs wyrđe wǣron đæt Godes englas hig sōhton, L. E. I. 25; Th. ii. 422, 15. Sēc nū đīnne þeów, Blickl. Homl. 87, 31. Hider ic wille đæt wē sēcan Sće Petre, Chr. 656; Erl. 31, 32. Satan ic sēcan wille, Cd. Th. 47, 15; Gen. 761. Gewīt đū đīnne eft waldend sēcan *go back again to your master*, 138, 17; Gen. 2293: Andr. Kmbl. 1886; An. 945. (1 a) *to seek* a person for protection, *to take refuge with* a person. v. sōcn, VI. 2:—Gif hwilc þeóf ođđe reáfere gesōhte đone cing ... hē hæbbe nigon nihta fyrst. And gif hē ealderman ođđe abbud ođđe þegen sēce, hæbbe þreora nihta fyrst, L. Ath. iv. 4; Th. i. 222, 28. (2) *to seek* a place, *to visit, resort to*:—Hē (*the phenix*) sunbeorht gesetu sēceþ, Exon. Th. 217, 11; Ph. 278. Đa men đe đyder cōman and đa hālgan stōwe sōhton, Blickl. Homl. 125, 28: 201, 11. Hī syđđan gewunelīce đider sōhton *they afterwards resorted thither*, Homl. Th. i. 504, 6. Sēce man hundredgemōt, L. Edg. ii. 5; Th. i. 268, 2. Đæt đeós onlīcnes eorþan sēce *fall to earth*, Andr. Kmbl. 1462; An. 731. Đeáh heorot holtwudu sēce, Beo. Th. 2743; B. 1369. Đæt hī secggan đæm folce đæt hī sunnandagum Godes cyrican georne sēcan, Blickl. Homl. 47, 28: L. C. E. 2; Th. i. 358, 14. Gif hié ǣnigne feld sēcan wolden *if they should attempt to come into the open country*, Chr. 894; Erl. 90, 11. Gewitan him Norþmen Difelin sēcan, 937; Erl. 115, 4. Đonne sculon hié đās helle sēcan, Cd. Th. 26, 14; Gen. 406: 136, 30; Gen. 2266. Ōđerne ēđel sēcan, Blickl. Homl. 23, 6. Mere sēcan *to go to sea*, Exon. Th. 474, 5; Bo. 25. (3) *to seek* immaterial things, *to go to* war, *resort to* artifice, etc.:—Ic ne sōhte searonīþas, ne ne swōr fela āþa on unriht, Beo. Th. 5469; B. 2738. Se wuldres dǣl sigorleán sōhte *the soul has gone to its reward*, Exon. Th. 184, 14; Gū. 1344. Se rinc sōhte ōđer līf, Cd. Th. 98, 9; Gen. 1627. Hī clǣnsunge bæþes sōhton, Bd. 1, 27; S. 495, 16. Hié noldan leng heora hlāforda ne heora wera ræstgemānan sēcean, Blickl. Homl. 173, 16. Đā đū gehogodest sæcce sēcean, Beo. Th. 3982; B. 1989: 5117; B. 2562. Fǣhþe sēcan, 5020; B. 2513. III. *to seek with hostile intent* (as in *to seek* a person's life), *to try to get at, to go to attack*:—Mē fyrenfulle fǣcne sēceaþ, wyllaþ mē līfes āsēcean *me expectaverunt peccatores, ut perderent me*, Ps. Th. 118, 95. Him (hié, hī *other MSS.*) mon mid ōđrum floccum sōhte, Chr. 894; Erl. 90, 14. Hié micle fierd gegadrodon and đone here sōhton æt Eoforwīcceastre, 867; Erl. 72, 13. Đa đe mīne fȳnd wǣron, and mīne sāwle sōhton mid nīđe, Ps. Th. 69, 2: 85, 13: Mt. Kmbl. 2, 20. Hié alle from him ondrēdon, đæt hī hié mid gefeohte sōhte, Ors. 1, 10; Swt. 48, 17. Sēcan mīne fȳnd mīne sāwle *persequatur inimicus animam meam*, Ps. Th. 7, 5. Đā hié gewin drugon, and on healfa gehwone heáwan þohton, sāwle sēcan, Beo. Th. 1606; B. 801. Sēcean sāwle hord, sundur gedǣlan līf wiđ līce, 4835; B. 2422. [*Goth.* sōkjan: *O. Frs.* sēka: *O. Sax.* sōkian: *O. L. Ger.* suocan: *O. H. Ger.* suohhan *quaerere, petere, exquirere, arcessire, appetere, invisere*: *Icel.* sœkja *to seek, fetch*; *to visit, frequent*; *to prosecute* (*a suit*); *to attack.*] v. ā-, for-, ge-, geond-, ofer-, on-, under-sēcan.

secg, es; *m. n. Sedge*; carex, gladiolum, lisca:—Đis secg (segc) *haec carex*, Ælfc. Gr. 9, 61; Zup. 69, 16. Segg, secg, saecg *gladiolum*, Txts. 66, 463. Sech *carex*, 50, 251. Seic, 115, 151. Secg, Wrt. Voc. ii. 13, 28. Segc, i. 79, 65. Segg, 67, 3. Segc *gladiolum*, ii. 40, 70. Segc, 70, 29. Secgg, i. 67, 55. Secg *lisca*, ii. 53, 45: *carex* vel *sabium* vel *lisca*, i. 31, 28. Endlefan snǣda reádes secges, Lchdm. ii. 102, 17. Handfulle secges, 356, 1. Wyl neoþoweardne secg, 52, 16: 66, 5.

[Eolug-secg *papyrus*, Wrt. Voc. ii. 67, 58. Ilug-segg, Txts. 86, 781. *See also* eolhx, hamer-, mōr-secg. Grein cites risc-seccas *carices*.] Cf. secg *a sword*.

secg, es; *m. A man* (used only in poetry):—Secg oððe meówle *man or maid*, Exon. Th. 387, 15; Rä. 5, 5. Nis ǣnig eorl under lyfte, secg searoþoncol, 14, 16; Cri. 220. Se beorn, sēfteádig secg, 309, 12; Seef. 56. Secg, lagucræftig mon, Beo. Th. 422; B. 208. Swylc sceolde secg wesan, þegen æt þearfe, 5410; B. 2708. Beówulf, sigoreádig secg, 2626; B. 1311. Ðǣr læg secg mænig, guma norþerna, Chr. 937; Erl. 112, 17. Secgas and gesīþas fōron tō gefeohte, Judth. Thw. 24, 22; Jud. 201. Seccas, Cd. Th. 124, 23; Gen. 2067. Wǣron æscwȳgan, secggas ymb sigecwēn sīðes gefȳsde, Elen. Kmbl. 519; El. 260. Rōmware, secgas sigerōfe, 93; El. 47. Ðā ic sǣbāt gesæt mid mīnra secga gedriht, Beo. Th. 1271; B. 633. [*Laym.* seg, sæg; *pl.* segges: *Piers P.* segge: *O. Sax.* segg: *Icel.* seggr (*poet.*).] v. ambyht-, ǣrend-, sele-secg.

secg, es; *m. The sea*:—*Salum* seeg (secg?) *vel mare*, Txts. 95, 1786. Segg, seg *salum*, 98, 966. Segc, Wrt. Voc. i. 289, 37. v. gār-secg.

secg, e; *f. A sword*:—Wit sculon secge ofersettan, gif hē gesēcean dear wīg ofer wǣpen, Beo. Th. 1372; B. 684. Secgum ofslegene, Cd. Th. 120, 27; Gen. 2001. [Cf. *Icel.* ben-sægr *as a name for the sword.*] Cf. secg *sedge, and* sagu; *and see* secg-hwæt, -plega.

secga, an; *m. One who says* or *tells, an informant*:—Ne ic nān sōðre wāt, būte swā mīn secga mē sǣde, L. O. 4; Th. i. 180, 12. [Þer weore segge (*or from* seg *a man* (?). *The other MS. has* gleomenne) songe, Laym. 5109. Cf. *O. Sax. O. H. Ger.* sago: *O. Frs.* sega, *in compounds*.]

secgan, secgean, secggan, secggean, sæcgan; *p.* sægde, sǣde; *pp.* sægd, sǣd. [*Forms as from an infin.* sagian—sagast, sagaþ; *p.* sagode; *imp.* saga, *are given here.*] *To say* (of written or spoken words). I. *to say* certain words, the words used being given:—Hē segþ: Gē ne māgon cuman ðyder ic fare, Jn. Skt. 8, 22. Gif hwā segþ, corban, Mk. Skt. 7, 11. Sege folce: Ðis sind ða dagas, Lev. 23, 2. Secgaþ ðæs hūses hlāforde: Ūre lāreów secgþ: Hwār is mīn gysthūs, Mk. Skt. 14, 14. Hwæðer is ēðre tō secgenne tō ðam laman: 'Ðē synd ðīne synna forgyfene,' hwæðer ðe cweðan: 'Ārīs, nim ðīn bed, and gā, Mk. Skt. 2, 9. Wē gehȳrdon hine secgan: Ic tōwurpe ðis tempel, 14, 58. I a. of words, *to mean*:—*Cantica canticorum*, ðæt segþ on Englisc ealra sanga fyrmest, Ælfc. T. Grn. 7, 42. II. with acc. (1) where the object denotes a collection of words, a story, poem, regulation, etc., *to tell* a tale, *recite* a poem, *pronounce, deliver*:—Ic bī mē secge ðis sārspell, Exon. Th. 458, 6; Hy. 4, 96. Ðonne ic ðē ǣfenlāc secge, Ps. Th. 140, 3. Ðās word ðe ðū mē sagast, Exon. Th. 247, 26; Jul. 84. Ðū worn fela ymb Brecan sprǣce, sægdest from his sīðe, Beo. Th. 1068; B. 532. Ðā sǣde hē him sum bigspel, Lk. Skt. 12, 16. Se magorǣswa mǣgþe sīnre dōmas sægde (cf. *O. Sax.* ēo-sago: *O. Frs.* ā-sega: *Icel.* segja lög; lögsögu-maðr), Cd. Th. 98, 4; Gen. 1625. Ēce rǣdas Moyses sægde, 210, 17; Exod. 516. Sægde eorlum Abimeleh waldendes word, 161, 19; Gen. 2667. Wordum sægde Lameh unārlic spel, 66, 27; Gen. 1090. Wē lofsonga word sǣdon, 274, 18; Sat. 156. Ābeód eft ongeán, sege ðīnum leódum miccle lāþre spell, Byrht. Th. 133, 14; By. 50. Nāne gewitnesse æfter him ne saga ðū, L. Alf. 40; Th. i. 54, 5. His naman secgeaþ mid sealmum, Ps. Th. 65, 1. Secgan spell, Bt. 13; Fox 36, 31: 30, 1; Fox 106, 30. Andsware secgan *to return answer*, Elen. Kmbl. 752; El. 376: 1131; El. 567. Sang secgan *to sing a song*, Cd. Th. 279, 10; Sat. 235. Naman sæcgean, Ps. Th. 141, 8. Ðonne wē gehȳron Godes bēc reccean and rǣdan, and godspell seccgean, Blickl. Homl. 111, 17. Hié forgytaþ ðæt hié hwēne ǣr gehȳrdon reccean and secggan, 55, 28. Hwæt sceal ic mā secgean fram Sancte Iohanne? 169, 24. Ðæt him ǣr of ðæs lāreówes mūþe wæs bodad and sægd, 55, 31: 69, 19. Byþ sægd nama Drihtnes *ut annuntient nomen Domini*, Ps. Th. 101, 19. ¶ where the object is included in a genitive:—Ðæs ðū mē wylle wordum secgean *from what you tell me*, Cd. Th. 162, 2; Gen. 2675. (1 a) where the written form of a word is referred to:—Ic mæg þurh rūnstafas secgan naman ðara wihta, Exon. Th. 429, 18; Rä. 43, 6. (2) where the object denotes that which is spoken about, *to speak of, tell, relate, narrate, declare, announce, give an account of* something:—Ic ðē orlæg secge *I will tell thee thy fate*, Cd. Th. 262, 19; Dan. 746. Ic Gode līf mīn secge *vitam meam nuntiavi tibi*, Ps. Th. 55, 7. Ic mīne earfeþu sæcge *tribulationem meam pronuntio*, 141, 2: 54, 17. Ðū sagast līfceare, Cd. Th. 54, 17; Gen. 878. Ðis gewrit oððe hit gōd sagaþ be gōdum mannum, oððe hit yfel sagaþ be yfelum mannum *sive historia de bonis bona referat ... seu mala commemoret de pravis*, Bd. pref.; S. 471, 14. Mīn mūþ sægeþ (*pronuntiabit*) ðīne mægenspēde, Ps. Th. 70, 14. Hī secgeaþ (*narrabunt*) eall ðīn wundur, 144, 5. Gē scyldigra synne secgaþ, Exon. Th. 132, 23; Gū. 477. Nēh ðæm clife ðe ic ǣr sǣde *that I spoke of before*, Ors. 1, 1; Swt. 12, 30. Heó sǣde him eall ðæt riht, Mk. Skt. 5, 33. Hǣlend his þegnum sǣde his þrowunga, Blickl. Homl. 15, 33. Sagode *refert*, Germ. 396, 10. Hē sīðfæt sægde, Cd. Th. 256, 31; Dan. 649. Hit forhæfed geweard, ðætte hié sǣdon swefn cyninges, 225, 2; Dan. 148. Bodan þurh hleóþorcwide hyrdum cȳððon, sægdon sōðne gefeán, Exon. Th. 28, 23; Cri. 451. Ic ðē hāte, ðæt ðū ðās gesyhþe secge mannum, Rood Kmbl. 190; Kr. 96. Ne wē wītegan habbaþ, ðæt ūs andgytes mā secgen, Ps. Th. 73, 9. Hī ðīne mihte sæcgeon *potentiam tuam pronuntiabunt*, 144, 4. Ic ðē secgan wille or and ende, Andr. Kmbl. 1296; An. 648. Hē secgan ongan swefnes wōman, Cd. Th. 249, 32; Dan. 539. Ðæt ðū hellwarum hyht ne ābeóde, ah ðū him secgan miht sorga mǣste, 308, 21; Sat. 696. Nō ic wiht fram ðē swylcra searunīþa secgan hȳrde, billa brōgan, Beo. Th. 1169; B. 582. Ðara ārfæstra dǣda sume gehȳran sæcgan, Blickl. Homl. 213, 26. Wē gehȳraþ oft secggan worldrīcra manna deáþ, 107, 29. Ne his snytru mæg secgean ǣnig, Ps. Th. 146, 5. Hī sculon his weorc sæcgean *annuntient opera ejus*, 106, 21. (3) *to express in words* feelings of gratitude, admiration, etc., *to give* thanks, glory, etc., to a person (cf. *Ger.* Dank sagen):—Ic ðara frætwa þanc wuldurcyninge wordum secge, Beo. Th. 5583; B. 2795. Wē ðē wuldur sæcgeaþ, Ps. Th. 78, 14. Hē sægde him ðæs leánes þanc, Beo. Th. 3623; B. 1809. Secggan wē him þanc ealra his miltsa, Blickl. Homl. 103, 25. Þancas secggan, 115, 22. Ðæm Scyppende lof and wuldor secgean ðara āra, 123, 4. Lof secgan Dryhtne, Andr. Kmbl. 2011; An. 1008: Exon. Th. 138, 34; Gū. 586. Ðæs wē ealles sculon secgan þonc and lof, 38, 25; Cri. 612. Hē for his hǣlo Drihtne þanc secgende wæs *pro sua sanitate Domino gratias referens*, Bd. 4, 31; S. 610, 38. (4) where the object is a pronoun referring to a clause:—'Eart ðū Iudēa cining?' Ðā andswarude hē: 'Ðū hit segst,' Lk. Skt. 23, 3. Saga mē ðæt, for hwon sēcest ðū sceade, Cd. Th. 54, 6; Gen. 873. Gif ðū wille mildheortnesse ūs dōn, sæge ūs ðæt hrædlīce, Blickl. Homl. 233, 19. Dryhten micellīce dyde; seggaþ ðis in alre eorþan, Ps. Surt. ii. p. 184, 15. Ic ðæt londbūend secgan hȳrde, ðæt hié gesāwon ..., Beo. Th. 2697; B. 1346. Ðæt (*all that had been seen and heard*) mancynne bodian and secgan, Blickl. Homl. 121, 4. Is ðæt sægd, ðæt ..., Bd. 3, 2; S. 524, 16. (5) where the verb is of incomplete predication, *to declare* a person or thing so and so:—Ic secge hine māran ðonne ǣnigne wītgan, Blickl. Homl. 165, 3. Se hæfde mægen ofer ealle gesceafta ðe hē tōwearde sægde, 9, 16. Ōðer him ðās eorþan ealle sægde lǣne, Exon. Th. 109, 15; Gū. 90. Hī ðone clǣnan sacerd sægdon tōweard, 9, 20; Cri. 137. Ða hālgan hine tōweardne sægdon, Blickl. Homl. 81, 31. Hié hine scyldigne sægdon, 173, 33. Hié sægdon hine sundorwisne, Elen. Kmbl. 1172; El. 588. III. with gen.:—Swā se secghwata secggende wæs lāðra spella, Beo. Th. 6049; B. 3028. IV. where the object is a clause, *to say, tell*:—Ic secge ðē, ðæt ðū eart Petrus, Mt. Kmbl. 16, 18. Nū segþ ūs seó bōc, ðæt God āfēdde ðone here, Ælfc. T. Grn. 5, 32. Seó bōc segþ, hū hē fērde, 6, 5. Heó mē sagaþ, ðæt ..., Exon. Th. 246, 30; Jul. 69. Swā Arculfus sagaþ, ðæt hē gesāwe ..., Shrn. 95, 31. Ðæs is tō tācne, sæcgeaþ men, ðæt oft .XL. manna ... ðæt hī hī be handum nōman and of sǣs ōfre ūt feóllan, Bd. 4, 13; S. 582, 30. Ic wordum sægde, ðæt Sarra mīn sweostor wǣre, Cd. Th. 163, 25; Gen. 2703. Sæge Adame, hwilce ðū gesihþe hæfst, 38, 35; Gen. 617. Saga mē, hwylces cynnes ðū sī, Bd. 1, 7; S. 477, 26. Secgaþ mē, hwæt git gesāwon, Gen. 40, 8. Secgge Petrus, hwæt ic þence, Blickl. Homl. 181, 8. Ic eów bidde, ðæt gē mē secgan, hwylce gemete gē cōman ealle samod tō mē, 143, 20. Ðæt hī secggan, ðæt ... 47, 26. Secgan, hū him æt ǣte speów, Beo. Th. 6044; B. 3026: Exon. Th. 437, 31; Rä. 56, 16. Be songe secgan, hwǣr ic sēlast wisse goldhrodene cwēn, 324, 26; Vīd. 100. Seggan, ðæt ic gesǣlig mon wǣre, Bt. 2; Fox 4, 13. Secgian hwæðer wǣre twegra strengra, Salm. Kmbl. 851. Micel is tō secgan, ðæt hē ādreág, Exon. Th. 134, 4; Gū. 502. Long is tō secganne, hū ..., 421, 23; Rä. 40, 22: Andr. Kmbl. 2961; An. 1483. Swā hit is nū hrædost tō secganne be eallum ðǣm woruldgesǣlþum ... ðæt ðǣr nān wuht on nis ðæs tō wilnianne seó *postremo idem de tota concludere fortuna licet, in qua nihil expetendum*, Bt. 16, 3; Fox 56, 29. Ðæt is nū hraðost tō secganne, ðæt ic wilnode weorþfullīce tō libbanne ða hwīle ðe ic lifede, 17; Fox 60, 14. Sægd is, ðæt ..., Blickl. Homl. 61, 16. Se wæs sǣd ðæt his brōðor wǣre Oswīes sunu *qui frater ejus et filius Oswiu esse dicebatur*, Bd. 4, 26; S. 603, 7. V. where the verb is used impersonally (cf. *Icel.* segir *it is told*):—Hit segþ on bōcum, ðæt ..., Wulfst. 146, 16. Swā hit hȳrefter segeþ, L. Wih. pref.; Th. i. 36, 13. Hī ēcton ða ǣ ðyssum dōmum ðe hȳrefter sægeþ, L. H. E. pref.; Th. i. 26, 7. Hēr segþ, hū se æþela wæs sprecende, Blickl. Homl. 55, 3. Gehȳraþ hwæt hēr segþ on ðissum bōcum be Sancta Marian, 137, 20. Segeþ ðǣron, ðæt sum rīce man wǣre on ðære burh, 197, 27. Sægþ on ðissum bōcum, ðæt ..., 41, 3. Hēr sægþ be ðisse tīde ārwyrþnesse, hū Drihten hine selfne geeáþmēdde, 65, 29. [Hēr] sagaþ, ðæt Idpartus ðam cāsere hǣlo bodade, Lchdm. i. 326, 1. VI. where the verb is used absolutely (secgan be, fram, ymbe *to speak of*):—Swā swā ic nū æt feáwum wordum secge, Bd. 3, 17; S. 545, 14. Swā swā seó bōc sagaþ, 3, 19; S. 547, 32. Swā wē eft secgeaþ, 3, 21; S. 551, 31. Tō ðǣm gesǣlþum, ðe wē secgaþ ymb, Met. 21, 4. Swā ic ǣr sǣde, Chr. 894; Erl. 92, 6. Mē lyste bet, ðæt ðū mē sǣdest sume hwīle ymbe ðæt, Bt. 34, 6; Fox 142, 12. Gehēraþ hū Lucas sægde be ðisse tīde, Blickl. Homl. 15, 4. Heáhfæderas sægdon and cȳððon, sealmsceopas sungon and sægdon, 105, 9–10. 'Ic hæbbe ðē tō secgenne sum þing.' Ðā cwæð hē: 'Lāreów sege ðænne,' Lk. Skt. 7,

40. Saga mē from đam lande, Salm. Kmbl. 418; Sal. 209. Đū đone māngengan mē helan woldest, swȳđor đonne mīnum þegnum secgean, Bd. 1, 7; S. 477, 20. Hwylcumhwego wordum secgan be đære ārwyrþnesse đisse hālgan tīde, Blickl. Homl. 115, 29. Secggean, 211, 12. Wē nū gehȳrdon of hwylcumhugu dǣle secggan be đǣm eádmōdnessum, 103, 18. VII. secgan on (*with acc., dat.*) *to ascribe to* a person, *lay to the charge of, accuse of, attribute to*:—Ne mæg se scrift geseón on đære sāwle, hwæđer him mon sōđ đe lyge sagaþ on hine sylfne, Exon. Th. 80, 16; Cri. 1308. Đæs hē sceal fægnian, đæt hī him sōđ on secggaþ, Bt. 30, 1; Fox 108, 10. Ne andwyrtst đū nān þing ongēn đa đe điss đē on secgeaþ *nihil respondes ad ea, quae isti adversum te testificantur?* Mt. Kmbl. 26, 62. Hī wrōhta and yfel on sægdon, Bd. 3, 19; S. 548, 35. Wæs kȳđed đæt his wrēgend leáse wiđ hine syredon and on sægdon *probatum est accusatores ejus falsas contra eum machinasse calumnias*, 5, 19; S. 640, 14. Gif ǣnig mann ōđerne wrēge and him hwilcne gilt on secge *si steterit testis mendax contra hominem, accusans eum praevaricationis*, Deut. 19, 16. Gif đē mon sōđ on secge, Prov. Kmbl. 70. Gif man secge on landesmann, đæt hē orf stǣle, L. Eth. ii. 7; Th. i. 288, 7. Đæm gielpnan biþ leófre đæt hē secge on hine selfne gif hē hwæt gōdes wāt ge þeáh hē nyte hwæt hē sōđes secge him is leófre đæt hē leóge *eligit arrogans bona de se vel falsa jactari*, Past. 33, 2; Swt. 217, 14. Hwæt gōdes māgan wē secgan on đa flǣsclīcan unþeáwas *quid de corporis voluptatibus loquar?* Bt. 31, 1; Fox 110, 24. Geunsōđian đæt him man on secgan wolde *to disprove what a man would charge him with*, L. Edg. ii. 4; Th. i. 266, 4. Ne mōt nān mann secgan on hine sylfne đæs đe hē wyrcende næs, Homl. Skt. i. 12, 177. Ic nelle secgan unsōđ on mē sylfe, 195. [*O. Frs.* sega, sedsa: *O. Sax.* seggian: *O. H. Ger.* sagēn: *Icel.* segja, seggja.] v. ā-, be-, for-, ge-, on-, sōþ-secgan.

secge, an; *f. Speaking, speech*:—Mē nāwđer deág secge ne swīge *neither speech nor silence will avail me*, Exon. Th. 12, 23; Cri. 190. Cf. secga.

secgend, es; *m. A speaker, relater, narrator*:—Nǣnig tweógende secgend mē đis sǣde *non quilibet dubius relator hoc mihi narravit*, Bd. 3, 15; S. 542, 7. Sió leásung simle deret đǣm secggendum, Past. 35, 1; Swt. 237, 10. [*Icel.* segendr, seggendr; *pl. sayers, reporters.*]

secg-gescēre (?) *sedge-shears* (?), a name of the grasshopper:—Secggescēre *vel* hāman *cicad[ae]*, Txts. 51, 464. v. sceár.

secg-hwæt; *adj. Vigorous* or *bold in using the sword*:—Se secghwata, Beo. Th. 6048; B. 3028.

secgihtig; *adj. Sedgy, full of sedge* or *reeds*:—Secgihtig *vel* hreódihtig *carecta, loca caricis plena, spinacurium*, Wrt. Voc. ii. 129, 14.

secg-leác, es; *n. Chive garlic, rush garlic, rush leek* (v. E. D. S. Pub. Plant Names); allium schoenoprasum, Lchdm. ii. 128, 11: iii. 28, 11.

secg-plega, an; *m. Sword-play, battle*:—Æt đam secgplegan, Andr. Kmbl. 2705; An. 1355. Cf. sweord-plega.

secg-rōf *a host of men* (?):—Cwōman wōldagas swylt eall fornom secgrōf wera *death carried off the host of men*, Exon. Th. 477, 20; Ruin. 27. [Cf. *O. H. Ger.* ruaba; *f. numerus*: *Icel.* segg-fjöld *a host of men; and* rinc-getæl, folc-getæl.]

secg-sceára, -scāra (-scara?), an; *m. A corn-crake* or *a quail*:—Secgscāra *ortigometra* (cf. erschen *ortigomera*, ii. 63, 53: edischen, 115, 67), Wrt. Voc. i. 63, 21. v. E. D. S. Pub. Names of Birds, p. 177, where *bean crake, grass drake, meadow drake, gorse duck* are given as names of the corn-crake. [Cf. (?) *Icel.* skāri *a sea-mew.*]

sēcness, e; *f. Seeking, visiting, visitation*:—Tīde soecnisse (sōcnises, Lind.) *tempus visitationis*, Lk. Skt. Rush. 19, 44.

sēdan *to satisfy* [:—Āsoedan *satiare*, Wrt. Voc. ii. 119, 68. Gesēdeþ (-sedeþ? v. next word: but cf. *Goth.* ga-sōþjan) *satiavit*, Ps. Th. 106, 4.]

seddan *to satisfy*. v. un-āsedd; sadian.

sēde, sēdege *to sow*, Mt. Kmbl. Lind. 13, 3. v. sǣdian.

seding-līne, sedl. v. steding-līne, setl.

Sedlingas (?) *Ethiopians*:—Sedlingum (Rēdlingum?) *Aethiopia*, Ps. Spl. T. 67, 34.

see, seeg. v. seón, secg *the sea.*

sefa, an; *m. Understanding, mind, heart*:—Sefa *sensus* (cf. gewit *sensus*, 42, 35), Wrt. Voc. i. 64, 17: 282, 27. Sefa nearwode (*of Noah when drunk*), Cd. Th. 94, 32; Gen. 1570. Him (*Nebuchadnezzar on recovery from his madness*) in gāst becwom rǣdfæst sefa, 257, 2; Dan. 652. Næs him hreó sefa, Beo. Th. 4367; B. 2180. Gif đīn hige wǣre, sefa swā searogrim, swā đū self talast, 1192; B. 594. Him wæs leóht sefa, hyge untyddre, Andr. Kmbl. 2504; An. 1253: Exon. Th. 164, 33; Gū. 1021. Geómor sefa, mōd morgenseóc, 458, 3; Hy. 4, 94: Beo. Th. 98; B. 49. Leóht sefa, ferhþ gefeónde, Elen. Kmbl. 346; El. 173. Weá biþ in mōde, siofa synnum fāh, Frag. Kmbl. 28; Leás. 16. Mōdcræfte sēc þurh sefan snyttro, Exon. Th. 28, 5; Cri. 442. Sēcan sefan gehygdum, Cd. Th. 219, 4; Dan. 49. Sefan sīdne geþanc, 249, 26; Dan. 536. Sefan (seofan, MS. A.) snytro, Salm. Kmbl. 133; Sal. 66. On sefan (ondgete, Ps. Surt. 77, 72) *in sensu*, Blickl. Gl. Hié đam Hālgan Gāste onfēngon on heora sefan, Blickl. Homl. 137, 6. On wērigum sefan, Exon. Th. 74, 18; Cri. 1208. On mildum sefan, 83, 6; Cri. 1352. On sīdum sefan, 169, 17; Gū. 1096. On sārgum sefan, 183, 20; Gū. 1330. Tō ontȳnenne mīne sefan, Nar. 40, 30. Ic heom āblende hera sefan, 45, 7. Þurh rūmne sefan rǣd gelǣran, Beo. Th. 561; B. 278. Begēm ūrum sefum *intende nostris sensibus*, Hymn. Surt. 22, 3. Ūrum sefum leóht gearce *nostris sensibus lumen prebe*, 53, 22. v. breóst-, ferhþ- (firhþ-, fyrhþ-), mōd-, wīs-sefa.

sēferlīce, sēfian, sēfre. v. sȳferlīce, seófian, sȳfre.

sēfte; *adj. Soft*:—*Delicatus*, i. *tenerus, querulus, amoenus* unbrocheard *vel* sēfta, Wrt. Voc. ii. 139, 40. I. of persons, *gentle, mild, not stern*:—Drihten is swȳđe sēfte *suavis est Dominus*, Ps. Th. 33, 8. Weorđ ūrum synnum sēfte and milde *propitius esto peccatis nostris*, 78, 9. II. of medicine, *mild, not strong*:—Đæt is, for hwī se gōda lǣce selle đam hālum men sēftne drenc and swētne, and ōđrum hālum biterne and strangne, Bt. 39, 9; Fox 226, 11. III. of rest, sleep, *undisturbed, untroubled*:—Đū eart seó sēfte ræst sōđfæstra, Bt. 33, 4; Fox 132, 34. IV. *easy, comfortable, pleasant, without pain* or *discomfort*:—Rād byþ on recyde rinca gehwylcum sēfte, Runic pm. Kmbl. 340, 13; Rūn. 5. Dōþ sīđfæt sēftne and rihtne, Ps. Th. 67, 4. Ful sēfte seld, đæt hī sǣton on, 88, 3. Hē his līchoman forwyrnde sēftra setla and symbeldaga, Exon. Th. 111, 33; Gū. 136. Sēlre mē wæs and sēftre, Ps. Th. 118, 71. Đone deáþ hē him gedēþ sēftran đonne ōđrum monnum, Bt. 39, 10; Fox 228, 10. IV a. in a bad sense, *luxurious, voluptuous, effeminate*:—Đȳ ne sceolde nān wīs man wilnian sēftes līfes gif hē ǣnigra cræfta rēcþ *neque enim vos in provectu positi virtutis, diffluere deliciis, et emarcescere voluptate venistis*, Bt. 40, 3; Fox 238, 13. [*O. H. Ger.* semfti.] v. ge-sēfte; sōfte.

sēft-eádig (?); *adj. In easy circumstances, free from hardships*:—Se beorn ne wāt, eft eádig (sēfteádig, Grein) secg, hwæt đa sume dreógaþ, đe đa wræclāstas wīdost lecgaþ, Exon. Th. 309, 12; Seef. 56.

sēftness, e; *f. Quiet, repose, freedom from disturbance*:—Hié woldon hiera dagas on sēftnesse geendian *ut in privato otio consenescerent*, Ors. 6, 30; Swt. 280, 22. Hī gewurdon on đære sēftnysse (*of the seven sleepers*), Homl. Skt. i. 23, 261.

sege, segel, -segel *a seal*, segen *a saying*, segen *a sign*, segl *sun.* v. secg, segl, in-segel, sægen, segn, sigel.

segl, swegel, segel, es; *m. n.* I. *a sail*:—Segl *artemon*, Wrt. Voc. ii. 7, 24. Segl *velum*, se mǣsta segl *acateon*, se medemesta segl *epidromas*, se lesta segl *dalum*, i. 56, 48-53. Segel *velum*, lytel segel *dalum*, 48, 22, 23. Đes segl *hic carbasus*, đās seglu *haec carbasa*, Ælfc. Gr. 13; Zup. 86, 3. Đā wæs be mæste merehrægla sum, segl sāle fæst, Beo. Th. 3816; B. 1906. Đæt scip wæs ealne weg yrnende under segle, Ors. 1, 1; Swt. 19, 34. Nefne hē under segle yrne, Exon. Th. 345, 11; Gn. Ex. 186: Andr. Kmbl. 1009; An. 505. Be đæs scipes segele, Bt. tit. 7; Fox x. 16. Gif đū đīnes scipes segl ongeán đone wind tōbrǣdst, đū lǣtst eal eówer fǣreld tō đæs windes dōme, 7, 2; Fox 18, 32. Fealdan đæt segl *to furl the sail*, 41, 3; Fox 250, 15. Eówre seglas sendon geseted *your sails are set*, Shrn. 60, 11. Seglu *vela*, Wrt. Voc. i. 63, 54. I a. used metaphorically of the fiery and cloudy pillars:—Swegl sīđe weóld *the pillar governed their journey*, Cd. Th. 184, 10; Exod. 105. Hæfde God sunnan sīđfæt swegle ofertolden, swā đa mæstrāpas men ne cūđon, ne đa seglrōde geseón meahton, 182, 26; Exod. 81. Fyrd geseah, hū đǣr hlifedon hālige seglas, 183, 10; Exod. 89. II. *a veil, curtain*:—Đæs temples segl, Exon. Th. 70, 16; Cri. 1139. III. *a flag, banner* (?):—Segl *larbanum* (*labarum* (?). *Labarum* signum militare Romanorum, pensile, ex panno aut serico contectum, et transversario antennae specie ligno affixum, a suprema conti parte pendens. v. segl-gird, II), Wrt. Voc. ii. 52, 8. [*O. Sax.* segel: *O. H. Ger.* segal *velum, artemon, carbasus*: *Icel.* segl; *n.*] v. ofer-segl.

seglan, siglan, seglian; *p.* de, ede, ode *To sail*:—Đā hē hāmweard seglde, Ors. 4, 10; Swt. 202, 1. Hē siglde đā eāst be lande, 1, 1; Swt. 17, 16. Se sciphere sigelede (seglode, MS. E.) west ymbūtan, Chr. 877; Erl. 78, 17. Hē hys segl up āhōf, and swȳđe forđ seglode, St. And. 38, 33. Ūt on sǣ tō seglanne, Prov. Kmbl. 64. [*O. H. Ger.* segelen: *Icel.* sigla.] v. ge-seglian.

segl-bōsm, es; *m. The swelling out of a sail, sail swelled out by the wind*:—Seglbōsm *carbasus*, Wrt. Voc. ii. 13, 57: 103, 28: *carbasus, tumor veli*, 128, 53. Seglbōsmas *carbasa, vela navium*, 54: *carbasa*, 88, 24.

segl-gerǣde, es; *n. Sail-furniture, tackle*:—Hē becwæđ his lāford his beste scip and đa segelgerǣda đārtō *domino suo meliorem suarum navium unam cum sibi pertinentibus armamentis contulit*, Chart. Th. 549, 18. [Cf. *Icel.* segl-reiđi *sail-rigging.*]

segl-gird, es; *m.*: e; *f.* I. *a sail-yard, yard* of a ship:—Seglgærd *antenna*, Wrt. Voc. ii. 100, 30. Segelgyrd *antenna*, i. 48, 17: *antenna* vel *temo*, 56, 39. Mæst sceal on ceóle, segelgyrd (*Grein takes this = sail-girt, and as applying to the mast*) seomian, Menol. Fox 509; Gn. C. 25. Đa twegen endas đære seglgyrde *cornua*, Wrt. Voc. i. 56, 40: 48, 18. Segelgyrda *antennarum*, ii. 5, 41: 88, 25. Segelgyrdena, mæsta *antennarum*, Hpt. Gl. 529, 18. Segelgyrdas *antemnas*, 97, 29. II. *the cross rod from which a banner hangs* (? v. segel, III):—Segelgyrd *labara*, Wrt. Voc. ii. 78, 24. [*Prompt. Parv.* seylȝerd *antenna*. Cf. *O. H. Ger.* segal-poum *antenna; also malus: Icel.* segl-viðr *a yard*.] Cf. segl-rōd.

seglian. v. seglan.

segling, e; *f. Sailing*:—Ðæt wē ne mid seglinge ne mid rōwnesse ōwiht fremian mihte *ut neque velo neque remigio quicquam proficere valeremus*, Bd. 5, 1; S. 613, 25. Hē mid seglunge binnon ānum dæge com tō Antiochian, Ap. Th. 6, 27.

segl-rād, e; *f. The sail-road, the sea*:—Sīđ on seglrāde, Beo. Th. 2863; B. 1429.

segl-rōd, e; *f. A sail-yard*, Cd. Th. 182, 29; Exod. 83. (v. segl, I a.) [*O. H. Ger.* segal-ruota *antenna*.] Cf. segel-gird.

segn, segen, es; *m. n. A sign*:—Segn *signum*, Wrt. Voc. ii. 120, 61. I. *a sign, mark, token*:—Abraham sette friđotācn (*circumcision*) on his selfes sunu, hēht đæt segn wesan (wegan?) heáh gehwilcne, đe his hīna wæs wǣpnedcynnes, Cd. Th. 142, 32; Gen. 2370. II. *a military standard, banner, an ensign*:—Segn *ban[dum]*, Txts. 45, 278. Segn, seng, segin *labarum* (v. segl, III), *vixilla*, 73, 1167. Seign (segin?) *vexilla*, 105, 2093. His segen se wæs mid golde and mid godewæbbe gefrætewod and ofer his byrigenne geseted *vexillum ejus super tumbam auro et purpura compositum adposuerunt*, Bd. 3, 11; S. 535, 31. Segn, Beo. Th. 5909; B. 2958. Đā wæs þūf hafen, segen for sweótum, Elen. Kmbl. 247; El. 124. Sió bȳman stefen and se beorhta segn, Exon. Th. 65, 30; Cri. 1062. Segnes gūþfana *labara*, Wrt. Voc. ii. 49, 74. Segne *pendiculo* (cf. labarum, signum *pensile*), 66, 48. Hæfdon him tō segne beácen ārǣred, gyldenne león *the tribe of Judah had a golden lion for their standard*, Cd. Th. 198, 7; Exod. 319. Hē under segne sinc ealgode *fighting under his flag he defended his treasure*, Beo. Th. 2412; B. 1204. Hié him āsetton segen gyldenne heáh ofer heáfod, 94; B. 47: 2046; B. 1021. Hē siomian geseah segn eallgylden, gelocen leóþocræftum, 5528; B. 2767: 5546; B. 2776. Đæt nalæs đæt ān đæt hī segen fore him bǣron æt gefeohte ac swylce eác on sibbe tīde ... him mon symble đæt tācen beforan weg *ut non solum in pugna ante illum vexilla gestarentur, sed et tempore pacis ... semper antecedere signifer consuesset*, Bd. 2, 16; S. 520, 9. Segn and sīde byrnan, Salm. Kmbl. 907; Sal. 453. Wiđ đone segn foran þengel rād, Cd. Th. 188, 23; Exod. 172. Segnas stōdon *standards were stationary*, 214, 7; Exod. 565: 197, 4; Exod. 302. Eall mīn weorod ... herebeácen and segnas beforan mē lǣddon *totum agmen me ... sequebatur cum signis et uexillis*, Nar. 7, 16. II a. used metaphorically:—Wynrōd segn sōđfæstra *the cross, the standard of the righteous*, Salm. Kmbl. 471; Sal. 236. Gesāwon randwīgan segn (*the pillar of fire*) ofer sweóton, Cd. Th. 185, 23; Exod. 127. [From Latin.] v. eafor-heáfod-segn; segnian.

segn-berend, es; *m. One bearing a standard* (or *crest?*), *a warrior*:—Ne mæg mec oferswīđan segnberendra ǣnig ofer eorþan, nymþe se āna God, Exon. Th. 423, 13; Rā. 41, 20. v. next word.

segn-bora, an; *m. A standard-bearer*:—Hē (*John*) wæs segnbora đæs ufancundan Kyninges, Blickl. Homl. 163, 22. Segnbora *draconarius* (draconarius *vexillifer, qui fert vexillum ubi est draco depictus*), i. *vexillarius, signifer*, Wrt. Voc. ii. 142, 5. Segnboran, tācnboran *draconarii* vel *vexillarii* vel *signiferi*, i. 21, 66.

segn-cyning, es; *m. A king before whom a banner is borne*:—Him đǣr segncyning (*Grein would read* sigecyning; *but cf.* (?) *the passages from Bede under* segn) wiđ đone segn foran rād, Cd. Th. 188, 22; Exod. 172.

segne, an; *f. A seine, sean, a drag-net*:—Næs điú segni tōsliten *non est scissum rete*, Jn. Skt. Lind. 21, 11. Of suegna fiscum *de saginae piscibus*, Mt. Kmbl. p. 17, 6. Ongelīc segne *simile saginae*, Lind. 13, 47. Sendas đæt nett ł segna *mittite rete*, Jn. Skt. Lind. 21, 6. Segni, 8. Hī ongunnon sǣlāfe segnum dǣlan, Cd. Th. 215, 17; Exod. 584. [(Pecher) de nase *wit a seyne*, Wrt. Voc. i. 159, 7. *O. Sax.* segina: *O. Frs.* seine: *O. H. Ger.* segina *sagena*. From Latin; cf. *Fr.* seine.]

segnian, sēnian; *p.* ode. I. *to make the sign of the cross upon* anything in token of blessing or consecration, *to bless, consecrate*:—Se biscop nam hlāf and sēnode *essent manus ad panem benedicendum missuri*, Bd. 3, 6; S. 528, 15 note. Đā sang hē orationem ofer hine and hine bletsode and sēnode *dixit orationem, ac benedixit eum*, 5, 5; S. 618, 8. Sēnade, 5, 6; S. 619, 42. Hē mid his handum hūsel sēnode, Homl. Skt. i. 3, 114. Đā hē sēnade đæt fæt đe đæt āttor on wæs, đā tōbærst hit, Shrn. 65, 11. Sǣnade, 52, 32. Đonne đū hlāf brece, sǣna đū đa cruman, 53, 18. Đeáh đe man wafige wundorlīce mid handa, ne biþ hit đeáh bletsung, būta hē wyrce tācn đære hālgan rōde ... Mid þrȳm fingrum man sceall sēnian and bletsian, H. R. 105, 22. Hine sylfne sēniende *signando sese*, Bd. 4, 24; S. 599, 13. II. without reference to the sign of the cross:—Segnade earce innan āgenum spēdum Nergend, Cd. Th. 82, 21; Gen. 1365: 83, 35; Gen. 1390. III. of speech (?):—Uē sægnade *bene dicimus*, Jn. Skt. Lind. 8, 48. [We sculen ure forheafod mid þere halie rode tacne seinian, O. E. Homl. i. 127, 25. Godd feder ant his sune iseinet (*blessed*), Marh. 23, 18. Þanne sat sleuthe up and seyned hym swithe, Piers P. 5, 456. Swa sal I saine þe, Ps. 62, 5. *O. Sax.* seginōn: *O. H. Ger.* seganōn *benedicere*: *Icel.* signa *to sign, consecrate*, in heathen times, with Thor's hammer, in Christian times, with the cross; *to bless*.] v. ge-segnian.

segnung, sēnung, e; *f. Blessing, consecration*:—Ofer hine cymeþ mīnre segnunga blōstma *super ipsum florebit sanctificatio mea*, Ps. Th. 131, 19. Wæs hē lǣded tō Brytta biscopum and hē nǣnige hǣle ne frōfre þurh heora segnunge (þegnunge?) onfēng *qui cum oblatus Brittonum sacerdotibus, nil curationis vel sanationis horum ministerio perciperet*, Bd. 2, 2; S. 502, 26. v. hlāf-sēnung.

seht, es; *m.*: e; *f.* I. *a settlement, an agreement, terms arranged between two parties by an umpire, a peace between two powers*:—Se seht đe Godwine eorl worhte betweónan đam arcebisceop and đam hīrēde æt Sc̄e Augustine, and Leófwine preóste, Chart. Th. 349, 19. Spǣcon đā Leófrīces freónd and Wulfstānes freónd, đæt hit betere wǣre, đæt heora seht tōgædere wurde, đonne hȳ ǣnige sace hym betweónan heóldan; sōhtan đā hyra seht. (*The terms are then given.*) Đis wæs ūre ealra seht, 377, 1–13. Syđđan đæs cāseres seht wæs and Baldwines, Chr. 1050; Erl. 173, 33. Hī tōhwurfon mid đisum sehte (*the agreement between Edmund and Cnut*), 1016; Erl. 159, 6. Đā fērdon betwux Rōdbeard eorl and Eádgār æđeling and þæra cinga sehte swā gemacedon. (*The terms are then given.*) On đisum sehte wearđ Eádgār eþeling wiđ đone cyng gesæhtlad, 1091; Erl. 228, 1–8. [Fērden þe ærcebiscop and te wīse men betwux heom and makede đæt sahte đæt ..., 1140; Erl. 265, 30.] II. *peace, friendship*:—Syđđan seaht and sib mycelre tīde betwyh đa ylcan cyningas and heora rīce āwunode, Bd. 4, 21; S. 590, 25 note. Đæt đa cyningas seht nāmon (cf. friþ niman) heom betweónan, Chr. 1016; Erl. 159, 1. Hī mōston mid ealle đæs cynges wille folgian, gif hī woldon land habban ođđe wel his sehta, 1086; Erl. 222, 35. [Sib and sæhte sculde bēn betwyx heom and on al Engleland, 1140; Erl. 265, 32. Betere weore sæhte þene swilc unisibbe, Laym. 9844. God lihte to eorđe uorte makien þreouold seihte, A. R. 250, 2. *Taken from the Danes* (?) cf. *Icel.* sātt *a settlement, agreement; peace.*] v. un-seht *and following words.*

seht; *adj. In agreement* about the terms of a settlement, *agreed*:—Hī wurdon sehte đæt đa gebrōđra ealle geeodon of đam lande būtan ānum, Cod. Dip. Kmbl. vi. 195, 25. Hī him đæs gætīđodon wiđ swylcon gersumen swylce hī đā sehtæ wǣron *such as they were then agreed upon*, 198, 16. Hī wurdon sehte on đa gerād đæt ..., Chr. 1093; Erl. 229, 25. Wearđ se cyng and his brōđor sehte ... and eall Normandīg æt him mid feó ālīsde, swā swā hī đā sehte wǣron, 1096; Erl. 233, 17. Sæhte, 1077; Erl. 215, 10. [Sehte, 1120; Erl. 248, 1. Sæhte, 1135; Erl. 261, 21. Þus iwerađ Brennes sæht (isehte, 2nd MS.) whit his brođer, Laym. 5114. Hiss bodiȝ wiþþ hiss gast sammtale & sahhte wurrþe, Orm. 5731. Cf. *Icel.* sāttr verđa ā eitt *to agree on.*] v. un-seht *and next word.*

sehtan; *p.* te *To bring about agreement between* people, *to settle* a dispute:—Cristenum cyninge gebyreþ đæt hē eall cristen folc sibbie and sehte mid rihtre lage, L. I. P. 2; Th. ii. 304, 12: Wulfst. 266, 17. Đæt wē habban ūs gemǣne sibbe and sōme, and ǣlce sace sehtan, 272, 23. Bisceop sceal beón symle ymbe sōme and ymbe sibbe ... Hē sceal georne saca sehtan and friþ wyrcan, L. I. P. 7; Th. ii. 312, 14. [A porueance ... thut lond uor to seyte, R. Glouc. 533, 15. We schul saughte sone (cf. we schulle ben at oon, 156), Chauc. Tale of Gamelyn, 150. Ȝe schulle sauȝte (*agree*), Piers P. A-Text, MS. T. 4, 2. *Icel.* sætta *to bring about agreement.*] v. ge-sehtian.

sehtlian (?); *p.* ode. I. *to settle, bring to an agreement, settle a dispute between* people (the word seems to occur only in the later part of the Chronicle) [:—Đā eodon gōde men heom betwēnen and sahtloden heom, Chr. 1066; Erl. 203, 27. Đa twegen kyngas wurđon sæhtlod, 1070; Erl. 209, 26. II. *to come to an agreement*:—Đā feórden đe wīse men betwyx þe kinges freónd & te eorles freónd & sahtlede suā đæt ... Sithen sahtleden þe king and Randolf eorl, 1140; Erl. 264, 31–35. Þe eorles sæhtleden wyd þemperice, Erl. 265, 6.] [Forr to sahhtlenn hemm towarrd hiss Faderr, Orm. 351. When a sawele is saȝtled to dryȝtyn, Allit. Pms. 72, 1139. Ȝe schulle saghtlyn, Piers P. A-Text, MS. U. 4, 2.] v. ge-sæhtlian.

sehtness, e; *f. Agreement, accord, concord, peace*:—Đām dōmbōcum đe se heofonlīca Wealdend his folce gesette tō sōme and tō sehtnesse, Homl. Th. ii. 198, 19. [Geaf đone cyng .xl. marc goldes tō sahtnysse, Chr. 1066; Erl. 203, 29.] [Crist wass borenn her sahhtnesse & griþþ to settenn, Orm. 3515. He sahtnesse wrohte, Laym. 2809. Sæhtnesse underfon *to accept terms*, 8262. Næfde þa sehtnesse ilast buten seouen ȝere urist, 30137. 'Pax vobis.' Seihtnesse beo bitweonen ou, A. R. 250, 5.] v. ge-sehtness.

[**seim** [*from earlier* segem (?)] *fat, lard*:—Seime ł fetnesse *adipe*, Ps. Spl. T. 62, 6. [Ge ne schulen eten ulesche ne seim, A. R. 412, 26. *See Halliw. Dict.* saim, seam, *and cf. Fr.* sain: *Ital.* saime. *From late Lat.* sagimen.]]

sel *a hall*, **sēl** *a season*. v. sæl, sǣl.

sēl (*the positive form does not occur, but is found in Layamon*); *cpve.* sēlra, sēlla; *spve.* sēlest, sēlost; *adj. Good.* I. of health:—Sōna seó blǣdder tō sēlran (*to a healthier condition*) gehwyrfeþ, Lchdm. i,

206, 15. II. *good, worthy, having excellent qualities* or *properties*:—Sancte Iohannes wæs māra and sēlra eallum ōðrum mannum, Blickl. Homl. 163, 20. Sȳlra, 161, 24. Ðeáh hine se dysiga dō tō cyninge, hū mæg gesceádwīs scealc gereccan, ðæt hē him ðȳ sēlra sié oððe þince, Met. 15, 15. Nǣnig sēlra nǣre rondhæbbendra rīces wyrðra *no warrior was worthier, more deserving of rule*, Beo. Th. 1725; B. 860. Næs mid Rōmwarum sincgeofa sēlla *among the Romans was not a prince of nobler character*, Met. 1, 50. Bōþ his sylfes swīðor micle ðonne se sēlla mon, Exon. Th. 315, 11; Mōd. 29. Him wearþ sēlle līf bihȳded, 227, 3; Ph. 417. Wē sculon īdle lustas forseón and ðæs sēllran gefeón, 47, 19; Cri. 757. Ðæt hē fēre him tō ðam sēlran rīce (*heaven*), 352, 24; Sch. 102. On sȳllan mon, 377, 20; Deór. 6. Uton wē georne teolian ðæt wē ðe beteran sȳn & ðe sēlran for ðære lāre ðe wē gehȳrdon, Blickl. Homl. 111, 19. Gē sōhtun ða sǣmran and ða sēllan nō dēmdan æfter dǣdum, Exon. Th. 131, 30; Gū. 463. Ðū se sēlusta Theophilus *optime Theophile*, Lk. Skt. 1, 3. Hlāford mīn and brōðor ðīn se sēlesta, Exon. Th. 183, 26; Gū. 1333. On gōdre and on sēlestre heortan *in corde bono et optimo*, Lk. Skt. 8, 15. Nymaþ of eówrum sēlustan wæstmum, Gen. 43, 11. III. *good of its kind*, (a) of persons, *possessing the excellences of a class, excellent, well-qualified, skilful, efficient*:—Hē ðæs wǣpnes onlāh sēlran sweordfrecan, Beo. Th. 2940; B. 1468. Nǣfre ic sǣlidan sēlran mētte, Andr. Kmbl. 942; An. 471. Ic fæste binde swearte wealas, hwilum sēllan men, Exon. Th. 393, 23; Rä. 13, 4. Omerus se gōda sceop ðe mid Crēcum sēlest wæs . . . Firgilius wæs mid Lǣdenwarum sēlest, Bt. 41, 1; Fox 244, 4–6. Cwēna sēlost, Drihtnes mōdor, Menol. Fox 334; Men. 168. Ealra sigebearna ðæt sēleste and æþeleste, Exon. Th. 33, 4; Cri. 520. Twegen wǣron biscopas and twegen mæssepreóstas ealle ða sēlestan *omnes sacerdotes fuere praeclari*, Bd. 3, 23; S. 555, 19. Manige ðara sēlestena cynges þēna forþfērdon, Chr. 897; Erl. 94, 32. (b) of things:—Næs sincmāðþum sēlra on sweordes hād *there was no greater treasure in the shape of a sword*, Beo. Th. 4392; B. 2193. Hī nǣfre song sēllan ne hȳrdon, Exon. Th. 325, 8; Vīd. 108. Īdel stōd hūsa sēlest, Beo. Th. 294; B. 146. Hof sēleste (*the ark*), Cd. Th. 84, 6; Gen. 1393. Ēce līf, sēlust sigeleána, Elen. Kmbl. 1051; El. 527. Blīcan swā ðæt sēloste gold, H. R. 15, 35. Seó sēleste gesǣlþ, Bt. 24, 2; Fox 82, 3. Biþ Drihten ūre se sēlosta scyld *the Lord will be our most effectual shield*, Blickl. Homl. 13, 10. Heó hié gegyrede mid ðon sēlestan hrægle, 139, 7. III a. marking the rank or class of a person:—Ðone sēlestan (*of the highest class*) . . . ðane ōðerne . . . ðane þriddan, L. Ethb. 26; Th. i. 8, 12. IV. *good, advantageous, to one's interest, advisable*:—Is hit micle sēlre ðæt wē hine ālȳsan, Andr. Kmbl. 3124; An. 1565. Sēlle, Exon. Th. 371, 15; Seel. 76. Him sylfum sēlle þynceþ leahtras tō fremman, 266, 33; Jul. 407. Ne mæg ðec sēllan rǣd mon gelǣran, 119, 4; Gū. 249. Wē ðē māgon sēlre gelǣran, Andr. Kmbl. 2706; An. 1355. Ðā forlēton wē ða frēcnan wegas and ðǣm sēlran wē fērdon, Nar. 17, 13. Ðæt him soelest wǣre ðæt hié friþes wilnaden *nullam esse residuam spem, nisi in petenda pace*, Ors. 4, 10; Swt. 202, 18. Hē brytniæ swǣ hīgum maest rēd sié and ðaem sāwlum soelest, Chart. Th. 461, 2: 465, 33. Ōfest is sēlost, Cd. Th. 196, 18; Exod. 293: Andr. Kmbl. 3129; An. 1567: Beo. Th. 518; B. 256. Hwæt sēlest wǣre tō gefremmanne, 351; B. 173: Elen. Kmbl. 2328; El. 1165. Ellen biþ sēlast ðam ðe sceal dreógan dryhtenbealu, Exon. Th. 183, 4; Gū. 1322. Biþ andgit ǣghwǣr sēlest, Beo. Th. 2123; B. 1059. Is hit ealles sēlest tō sēcenne hwæt ðæs willa sié, Blickl. Homl. 205, 27. V. *good, honourable, noble, proper*:—Deáþ biþ sēlla eorla gehwylcum ðonne edwītlīf, Beo. Th. 5773; B. 2890. Sēlre biþ ǣghwæm ðæt hē his freónd wrece, ðonne hē fela murne, 2773; B. 1384: Andr. Kmbl. 640; An. 320. Ðē ðæt sēlre geceós, ēce rǣdas, Beo. Th. 3523; B. 1759. Hē smeáde hwæt him sēlest (or under III) tō dōnne wǣre *quid sibi esset faciendum tractabat*, Bd. 2, 9; S. 512, 15. Maria geceás ðone sēlestan dǣl, Lk. Skt. 10, 42. VI. *of value, precious*:—Ðū golde eart, sincgife sȳlla, Andr. Kmbl. 3016; An. 1511. Hū nys seó sāwl sēlre ðonne mete *nonne anima plus est quam esca?* Mt. Kmbl. 6, 25. Ne hȳrde ic guman ǣnigne bringan ofer sealtne mere sēlran lāre, Menol. Fox 204; Men. 103. Gē synt sēlran ðonne manega spearuan, Mt. Kmbl. 10, 31. Gif hē nele ðone sēlestan dǣl Gode gedǣlan, Blickl. Homl. 195, 7. VII. *good, happy, pleasant*:—On ðǣm sēlran þingum *in secundis rebus*, Nar. 7, 26. Wē dreámas hefdon sēlrum tīdum, Cd. Th. 267, 29; Sat. 45. [Þu scalt uurþan sæl *thou shalt prosper*, Laym. 1234. Cloten hauede enne sune þe sel (bold, 2nd MS.) wes, 4071. Mid selere strengðe *with great strength*, 21654. Seoue þusend selere (boldere, 2nd MS.) þeinen, 18011. Ich wulle sende to selen mine þeinen, 25162. Ne isæh na man selere cniht nenne, 21166. Þat us is selest (best, 2nd MS.) to don, 918. In al þat sel is, H. M. 47, 34. *Goth.* sēls *good, kind*: *Icel.* sæll *blest, happy*.] v. next word.

sēl, soel; *also* sēlor; *adv.* (*cpve.*) *Better.* I. of health:—Cwæð ðæt heó gelȳfde ðæt hire sōna sēl wǣre *quia crederet eam mox melius habituram*, Bd. 5, 3; S. 616, 11. Sōna ic wæs wyrpende and mē sēl wæs *statim melius habere incipio*, S. 616, 34: 5, 5; S. 618, 4. Sōna him biþ sēl, Lchdm. iii. 288, 19. Him biþ soel *bene habebunt*, Mk. Skt. Lind. 16, 18. I a. of moral or spiritual well-being:—Ne mæg ic gehycgan, hwȳ him on hige þorfte ā ðȳ sǣl wesan, Met. 15, 10. II. of knowledge:—Gē sind searowum beswicene oððe sēl nyton, mōde gemyrde, Andr. Kmbl. 1490; An. 746. Findaþ ða ðe fyrngewritu sēlost cunnen, Elen. Kmbl. 748; El. 374. III. of the operation of the senses:—Hē biþ suā micle sēl gehiéred, suā hē ufor gestent, Past. 14, 1; Swt. 81, 17. IV. denoting excellence in act or in conduct:—Nō ðȳ sēl dyde, ac ðam æðelinge oferhygd gesceód, Cd. Th. 246, 35; Dan. 489. Ne gefrægn ic nǣfre wurðlīcor æt hilde sixtig sigebeorna sēl gebǣran, Fins. Th. 77; Fins. 38: Beo. Th. 2029; B. 1012. Hwylc hira sēlast simle gelǣste hlāforde æt hilde, Andr. Kmbl. 821; An. 411. Bet gē rǣdaþ *melius legitis*, sēlost (sǣlost, MS. T.) hī rǣdaþ *optime legunt*, Ælfc. Gr. 5; Zup. 9, 17. Hwǣr ic sēlast wisse cwēn giefe bryttian, Exon. Th. 324, 28; Vīd. 101. V. denoting advantage or profit:—Hwæt byþ ūs tō mēde (ūs ðȳ soel, Lind.), Mt. Kmbl. 19, 27. Tō hwan hió ða næglas sēlost and deórlīcost gedōn meahte, Elen. Kmbl. 2315; El. 1158. VI. denoting success or good result, *with* (*more*) *success*, (*more*) *effectually, to* (*more*) *purpose*:—Ic gelȳfe ðe sēl and ðȳ fæstlīcor ferhþ staþelige, Elen. Kmbl. 1589; El. 796. Ne gefrægn ic nǣfre sixtig sigebeorna medu sēl forgyldan, Fins. Th. 79; Fins. 39. For ðȳ ðe mon ðās feorme ðȳ soel gelǣste, Chart. Th. 474, 12. Næs him wihte ðe sēl *he did not succeed any the better*, Beo. Th. 5368; B. 2687. Sēl æfter wælrǣse wunde gedȳgan *to be more successful in escaping wounds*, 5054; B. 2530. Se æcer syððan gegreów .c. sīða sēlor ðonne hē ǣr dyde, Shrn. 137, 25. Hū man sēlost mæg synna forbūgan *how sins may most effectually be avoided*, Ælfc. T. Grn. 7, 38. Hū ic ðīne sōðfæstnesse sēlest heólde, Ps. Th. 118, 54, 26. Hié hīgon gefeormien swǣ hié soelest þurhtión mēgen, Chart. Th. 476, 31. VII. with verbs of liking or pleasing:—Hē nānum menn sēl ne ūðe ðonne mē *there was no one he would sooner give it to than to me*, Chart. Th. 485, 17. Ða men ðe ic mīnes erfes seólest onn, 480, 20. Se getreówa man sceal syllan his gōd on ða tīd ðe hine sylfne sēlest lyste his brūcan, Blickl. Homl. 101, 20. Hī genāman ðæs folces ðe ðǣr tō lāfe wæs and him sēlost līcodan, 79, 21.

seld, es; *n.* I. *a seat, that on which one sits, a throne*; sedes:—In heofene seld his *his throne is in heaven* (A. V.), Ps. Surt. 10, 5: 44, 7. Dōm gegearwung seldes ðīnes, 88, 15: 96, 2. Of dūne sette maehtge of selde, ii. p. 200, 20: Cd. Th. 275, 17; Sat. 173: 276, 12; Sat. 187. Ðǣr is sang æt selde (*the throne of God*), 306, 12; Sat. 662. Sang ymb seld secgan, 279, 9; Sat. 235. Siteþ him on heofnum, hafaþ wuldres bearn his seolfes seld, 301, 27; Sat. 588. God siteþ ofer seld hālig his, Ps. Surt. 46, 9: 9, 8. Ealdormenn sǣton on seldum, Ps. Th. 118, 23. Hī on seldon sǣton æt dōmum, 121, 5. II. *a seat, residence, mansion, hall*:—Scyppendes seld, Salm. Kmbl. 160; Sal. 79. Ðā hē ða mænego (*the rebellious angels*) ādrāf of ðæm heán selde (*heaven*), Cd. Th. 277, 10; Sat. 202. Cwom Daniel in ðæt seld gangan, 225, 9; Dan. 151: 262, 1; Dan. 737. Engel lēt his hand cuman in ðæt heá seld (*Belshazzar's hall*), 261, 7; Dan. 722. Hié tempel strudon, Salomanes seld, 260, 19; Dan. 712. Com tō Heorot, ðǣr Hring-Dene geond ðæt sæld swǣfon, Beo. Th. 2564; B. 1280. Wǣron on ðyssum felda unrīme gesomnunge manna and monig seld (*or to* I?) gefeóndra weorada *erant in hoc campo innumera hominum conventicula, sedesque plurimae agminum laetantium*, Bd. 5, 12; S. 629, 25. Ða heallīcan seld *palatias zetas*, Wrt. Voc. ii. 81, 23. Hū hē eft gesette swegeltorhtan seld, Cd. Th. 6, 27; Gen. 95. Heáhgetimbru, seld on swegle, Exon. Th. 137, 10; Gū. 557. [Ær he arise of selde, Laym. 25988. Cf. *Goth.* salithwa; *f. a mansion, chamber*: *O. Sax.* seliða, selda: *O. H. Ger.* selida; *f. domicilium, mansio, habitaculum, tabernaculum.*] v. ān-, biscop-, cear-, ēðel-, heáh-, medu-, pāp-, sundor-, þrym-, weard-seld; selde.

-selda. v. ge-selda.

seldan (-on, -un, -um); *cpve.* seldnor; *adv. Seldom, rarely*:—Seldan (-on) *raro*, Ælfc. Gr. 38; Zup. 240, 12: Bt. 16, 1; Fox 50, 14. Oft nalæs seldan, Ps. Th. 74, 4. Tō seldan hit biþ, beó hit seldor on dæg ðonne seofon sīðum, Btwk. 194, 11. Oft (of? cf. *Icel.* of- *too, and* v. of-) seldan hwǣr æfter leódhryre lytle hwīle bongār būgeþ *too rare are the cases in which after the fall of men the deadly weapon retires*, or *often after slaughter the spear is seldom at rest*, i. e. in most cases frequent strife follows (cf. the first passage under *seld-hwanne, and* seldum hwonne), Beo. Th. 4063; B. 2029. Him seldon teola gespeów, Ors. 4, 5; Swt. 168, 19: Bd. 1, 1; S. 474, 31: Met. 28, 71. Seldon wē ǣnig seolfor fundon, Nar. 5, 15. Hwīlon ic dō ac seldon *aliquando facio, sed raro*, Coll. Monast. Th. 24, 3. Se ðe him ealneg wind ondrǣt, hē sǣwþ tō seldon, Past. 39, 2; Swt. 285, 18. Seldun, 9; Swt. 57, 16. Seldum ǣfre, Salm. Kmbl. 540; Sal. 269. Ac ðeáh hī seldum hwonne (cf. seldhwanne) beswemde weorþon ðonne sleáþ hē eft on ða solu *but though on rare occasions they* (*swine*) *get washed, at such times they return to the mire*, Bt. 37, 4; Fox 192, 28. Ðæt dysie folc ðæs hit seldnor gesihþ swīðor wundriaþ, Met. 28, 66. [*O. Frs.* sielden: *O. H. Ger.* seltan; *cpve.* seltanor: *Icel.* sjaldan; *cpve.* sjaldnor; *spve.* sjaldnast.] v. unseldan, seldor.

seld-, sel-cūþ; *adj. Little known, strange, wonderful, unfamiliar*:—Se seldcūþa tungel gebīcnode ðæs sōðan cyninges ācennednysse, Homl,

Th. i. 106, 27. Hē wæs oflyst đæs seldcūþan sōnes (*the sound of Orpheus' harp*), Bt. 35, 6; Fox 168, 23. Hī willaþ simle hwæthwegu nīwes and seldcūþes eówian, 34, 4; Fox 138, 29. Đū hwerfest ymbūton sume wunderlīce and seldcūþe sprǣce, 35, 5; Fox 164, 17. Dīglu þing tǣcan and seldcūþe, 39, 4; Fox 216, 13. Selcūþe reáf *varias vestes*, Coll. Monast. Th. 27, 9. [Þeo wimon was mid ane sune þat wes a selcuđ bearn (wonderfol to telle, 2nd MS.), Laym. 280. Þatt wass sellcuþ mecleȝȝc, Orm. 19217. Gif him þunched wunder & selkuđ of swuch onswere, A. R. 8, 26. Gret outrage we se ... in selcouthe maners, Pr. C. 1518.]

seld-cyme, es; *m. A rare visit*:—Wēna mē đīne seóce gedydon, đīne seldcymas, Exon. Th. 380, 27; Rä. 1, 14. [Cf. *Icel.* sjald-kvæmr *seldom coming*.]

selde, an; *f. A porch*:—Selde *proaula* (*porticus* a porche, *proaula idem est*, 204, col. 2), i. *domus coram aula*, Wrt. Voc. i. 57, 46. v. sumor-, winter-selde; seld.

seld-guma, an; *m. A hall-man, one who has a place in a lord's hall, a retainer*:—Nǣfre ic māran geseah eorl ofer eorþan đonne is eówer sum ... nis đæt seldguma (*he is no mere retainer*. Grein translates 'vir qui semper in domo manet.' Heyne says '*seldguma* ist hier offenbar der gemeine Mann, der nur ein *seld* besitzt, im Gegensatz zu dem edeln, der einen *hof* zu eigen hat.' But *seld* is used of royal residences, so that Bugge's explanation seems better, 'en mand som holder til en hövdings sal, en mand som er traadt i en hövdings tjeneste'), Beo. Th. 504; B. 249. Cf. sele-secg.

seld-hwanne; *adv. Seldom, rarely*:—Oft đonne đæt mōd đæs fæstendan biþ mid đȳ irre ofseten, đonne cymþ sió blis seldhwanne, swelce hió sié elþeódig, Past. 43, 6; Swt. 313, 24. Đeáh seldhwænne leáf geseald sié tō sprecenne *quamvis rara loquendi concedatur licentia*, R. Ben. 21, 16. Heó wolde seldhwænne hire līc bađian, Homl. Skt. i. 20, 44. Seldhwonne biþ đætte āuht manegum monnum ānes hwæt līcige, Bt. 18, 3; Fox 64, 29. [Swuch ouh wummone lore to beon liđe and seldhwonne sturne, A. R. 428, 25. Cf. *Icel.* sjald-stundum *rarely*.]

seld-, sel-, syl-līc; *adj.* I. *strange, extraordinary, wonderful*:—Đis godspel þincþ dysegum mannum sellīc, Homl. Th. ii. 466, 9. Nū þincþ eów đis syllīc tō gehȳrenne, L. Ælfc. C. 6; Th. ii. 344, 16: Wulfst. 269, 26. Is đæt sellīc þincg, đæt hī ne wundriaþ hū ..., Met. 28, 53. Næfde sellīcu wiht sȳne ne folme, Exon. Th. 415, 2; Rä. 33, 5. Glōf sīd and syllīc searobendum fæst, Beo. Th. 4178; B. 2086. Ic seah sellīc þing singan, Exon. Th. 413, 9; Rä. 32, 3. Đa rēđan león and đa sellīcan (syl-) pardes and đa egeslīcan beran, Hexam. 9; Norm. 14, 33. Sellīce sǣdracan, Beo. Th. 2856; B. 1426. Syllīce tācn, Blickl. Homl. 91, 29. Syllīce stānas *monstrous stones*, 189, 15. Seldlīcra fela *many wonderful creatures*, Exon. Th. 193, 34; Az. 131. Hit is sellīcre đæt hiora ǣnig ne mæg būtan ōđrum bión, Met. 11, 50. Hī đǣr gesēgon syllīcran wiht, Beo. Th. 6069; B. 3038. II. *having unusual good qualities, excellent, admirable*:—Þeódnes cynegold sōđfæstra gehwone sellīc glengeþ, Exon. Th. 238, 19; Ph. 606: 341, 16; Gn. Ex. 127. Is đes middangeard missenlīcum wīsum gewlitegad, wrættum gefrætwad, sīþum sellīc, 414, 28; Rä. 33, 3. Freólīc, sellīc, 492, 29; Rä. 81, 23. Wundor syllīc (*the pillar of fire*), Cd. Th. 184, 17; Exod. 109: Rood Kmbl. 25; Kr. 13. Hē wundur worhte seldlīc, Ps. Th. 125, 3. Ǣnlīcra and fægerra, symle sellīcra, Exon. Th. 357, 17; Pa. 30. Him (*the phenix*) sette sōđ cyning sellīcran gecynd ofer fugla cyn, 221, 4; Ph. 329. Ic ǣfre ne geseah syllīcran cræft, Andr. Kmbl. 1000; An. 500: Rood Kmbl. 8; Kr. 4. [*Laym.* sel-, sil-, seol-, sul-lich: *O. E. Homl.* sullic: *Jul.* sul-lich: *O. and N.* sel-, seol-lich: *Goth.* silda-leiks: *O. Sax.* seld-līk.]

seld-, sel-, syl-līce; *adv.* I. *strangely, wonderfully*:—Nǣfre hié đæs sellīce bleóum bregdaþ, Salm. Kmbl. 300; Sal. 149. Singeþ syllīce, 539; Sal. 269. II. *wonderfully well, excellently, admirably*:—Iericho wæs sellīce getimbrod, mid seofon weallas beworht and wel wiđinnan geset, Homl. Th. ii. 212, 25. Syllīce hyt đæt āttor tōsceádeþ, Lchdm. i. 352, 13.

seldnor, seldon. v. seldan.

seldor; *cpve.*: seldost; *spve.* (*the positive seems expressed by* seldan, *which however has a comparative* seldnor); *adv. More seldom, less frequently*:—Seldan *raro*, seldor *rarius*, ealra seldost (-ast, MS. H.) *rarissime*, Ælfc. Gr. 38; Zup. 240, 13. Tō seldan hit biþ, beó hit seldor on dæg đæt wē God herian đonne seofon sīđum, Btwk. 194, 11. Bæþ đām untrumum, swā oft swā hit framige, sȳ geboden; hālum sȳ seldor getīđod, R. Ben. 61, 1. Đæt ungestæđđige folc wundraþ đæs đe hit seldost gesihþ, Bt. 39, 3; Fox 216, 2. [Gon seldere þene he sholde to his chirche, O. E. Homl. ii. 207, 26. *Icel.* sjaldar.]

seld-sīne, -sȳnde; *adj. Seldom seen, uncommon, unfamiliar*:—Cirus geāhsade đæt đæm folce seldsiéne and uncūđe wǣron wīnes dryncas, Ors. 2, 4; Swt. 76, 12. Ǣlc seldsȳnde fisc đe weorđlīc biþ, Cod. Dip. Kmbl. iii. 450, 27. [Hit is seltsene on eorđe, H. M. 27, 22. Our speche schal beon seldcene, A. R. 80, 19. *Icel.* sjald-sēnn.]

sele, es; *m. A hall, house, dwelling*:—Cwom bytla (*Guthlac*) tō đam beorge ... wæs sele (*his hermitage*) nīwe, Exon. Th. 146, 24; Gū. 714. Sele sceal stondan, sylf ealdian, 343, 16; Gn. Ex. 158. Sele (*Heorot, Hrothgar's hall*) hlifade, heáh and horngeáp, Beo. Th. 163; B. 81. Đes sele, receda sēlest, 827; B. 411. Đes windiga sele (*hell*), Cd. Th. 273, 14; Sat. 136. Hē on temple gestōd... Hē anlīcnesse geseh on seles (*or from* sæl, cf. 1523; An. 763) wāge, Andr. Kmbl. 1428; An. 714: Exon. Th. 394, 17; Rä. 14, 4. Þegen đe on cinges sele his hlāforde þēnode, L. R. 3; Th. i. 192, 1. Hē (*Pharaoh*) lǣdan hēht wīf tō his selfes sele, Cd. Th. 111, 17; Gen. 1857. Geseah hē engles hand in sele (*Belshazzar's hall*) wrītan, 261, 16; Dan. 727. Hié tō sele (*the Danish king's hall*), gangan cwōmon, Beo. Th. 652; B. 323. In sele đam heán, 1431; B. 713: (*Hygelac's hall*), 3973; B. 1984. On sele *in the dragon's cave*, 6248; B. 3128. Tō sele *to the prison*, Andr. Kmbl. 2624; An. 1313. Cyning mec on sele weorþaþ, Exon. Th. 401, 12; Rä. 21, 10. Ic sōhte sele sinces bryttan, hwǣr ic findan meahte đone đe in meoduhealle mec frēfran wolde, 288, 2; Wand. 25: Beo. Th. 1657; B. 826: 4694; B. 2352. Sele āsettan, sīdne ræced fæste gefēgan, Exon. Th. 296, 6; Crä. 47. Brūcan đæs boldes đe ūs gearwaþ gǣsta ealdor; đæt is sigedryhten đe đone sele frætweþ, 450, 24; Dōm. 92. Innan on đone ealdan sele, Cod. Dip. Kmbl. iii. 406, 13. Đone werigan sele (*hell*), Cd. Th. 285, 4; Sat. 332. Ongunnon heora burh rǣran and sele settan, salo nīwian, 113, 2; Gen. 1881. [*O. Sax.* seli; *m.*: *Icel.* salr; *pl.* salir: cf. *O. H. Ger.* seli-hūs: *Goth.* saljan *to dwell, abide*.] v. bān-, beág-, beór-, burg-, burn-, deáþ-, dreór-, dryht-, eorþ-, gæst-, gold-, grund-, gūþ-, heáh-, horn-, hring-, hrōf-, nīþ-, will-, wīn-, wind-, wyrm-sele; sæl.

sele?:—Winter ȳþe beleác īsgebinde ōþ đæt ōđer com geár in geardas swā nū gyt dēþ đa đe sele (=sǣle?) bewitiaþ wuldortorhtan weder *winter shut up the waves with bonds of ice, until another year came to men's dwellings; so still the new year comes, and brilliant weather* (*as is apparent to those*) *who keep constant watch on the seasons*, Beo. Th. 2275; B. 1135. But see Heyne's Beowulf, or Paul and Braune, Beiträge, 12, 31.

sele-dreám, es; *m. Mirth of the hall, joyous life of the hall, festive pleasure*:—Beorgas wǣron blīđe gebǣrdon swā rammas wurdan gesweoru swā on seledreám swā on sceápum beóþ sceóne lambru *montes, quare exultastis ut arietes, et colles velut agni ovium*, Ps. Th. 113, 6. Oft ic secga seledreám sceal onþeón, Exon. Th. 480, 13; Rä. 64. 1. Goldburg ofgifan, secga seledreám, beorht beágselu, Andr. Kmbl. 3310; An. 1658: Beo. Th. 4496; B. 2252. Swǣfon seledreámas, Cd. Th. 179, 29; Exod. 36: Exon. Th. 292, 3; Wand. 93.

sele-ful[1], es; *n. A cup used in a hall*:—Hē geþah symbel and seleful Beo. Th. 1242; B. 619.

sele-gescot, -gesceot, es; *n. A tabernacle*:—In selegescote đīnum *in tabernaculo tuo*, Ps. Surt. 14, 1. Selegesceote, Ps. Th. 60, 3. Đeáh đe ic on mīnes hūses hyld gegange ođđe selegesceot *si introiero in tabernaculum domus meae*, 131, 3, 5, 7. Đæt selegescot, hūs tō wynne (*the body*), Exon. Th. 90, 28; Cri. 1481. Selegescotu *tabernacula*, Ps. Th. 77, 28. Selegesceotu, 82, 6: 107, 6. On đīnum selegescotum, 146, 11. v. sele-scot, ge-sceot.

sele-gist, es; *m. A guest in a hall*:—Heó ofsæt đone selegyst (*Beowulf who was in Hrothgar's hall*), Beo. Th. 3094; B. 1545.

selen, sellen, sylen, e; *f.* I. *a gift*:—Ic đē nū āfyrre fram mīnre selene đe ic đē forgeaf, Wulfst. 258, 14. Seó gōde antswaru sȳ ouer đa sēlestan selene *sermo bonus super datum optimum*, R. Ben. 55, 9. Sylena *donaria*, Germ. 394, 343. Gāstlīcra sellena ł gifa *sanctorum donorum*, Hpt. Gl. 414, 37. Syllena, 473, 50. Mid selenum hē gewelgie *donis maneret*, Hymn. Surt. 4, 32. Đū onfēnge selena *accepisti dona*, Ps. Spl. 67, 19. Gōde sylena syllan, Mt. Kmbl. 7, 11. Sylene, Lk. Skt. 11, 13. II. *a giving, donation, grant*:—His handseten and sælen, Cod. Dip. Kmbl. ii. 89, 12. Ic geeácnode tō đare ǣrran sylene tȳn þūsenda ǣlfixa, Chart. Th. 242, 11. Ic đās ūre selene trymme, 106, 10. Þurh his sylene and gyfe *ipso largiente*, Bd. 2, 12; S. 515, 24. Þurh ælmyssan sylene *per erogationem eleemosynae*, L. Ecg. P. iv. 63; Th. ii. 222, 32. Mid gebedum and mid wæccum and mid ælmessa sylenum, Wulfst. 228, 20. III. *the habit of giving, liberality, munificence*:—Sylen *liberalitas*, mid sylene *munificentia*, Hpt. Gl. 466, 52, 49. Cystigre sylene *prodiga liberalitate*, 517, 36. v. ælmes-, hand-, mann-selen, -silen.

seleness, selnes *tradition*; traditio, Mt. Kmbl. Lind. 15, 2, 3: Mk. Skt. Lind. Rush. 7, 3, 9.

sele-rǣdend, es; *m. One who takes part in the councils held in a hall, a counsellor of a prince*:—Manige cōmon snottere selerǣdend, symble gefēgon beornas burhweardes cyme, Andr. Kmbl. 1317; An. 659. Men ne cunnon secgan tō sōđe, selerǣdende (-rǣdenne, MS.), hæleþ under heofenum, hwā đæm hlæste onfēng, Beo. Th. 102; B. 51. Ic đæt leóde mīne, selerǣdende, secgan hȳrde, 2696; B. 1346.

sele-rest, e; *f. A bed in a hall*:—Hine ymb monig sǣrinc selereste gebeáh (*of Beowulf and his men when sleeping in Hrothgar's hall*), Beo. Th. 1384; B. 690.

sele-scot, es; *n. A tabernacle, dwelling*:—Gewyrce wē þreó selescotu (*tabernacula*), Mt. Kmbl. Rush. 17, 4. Fuglas heofunas habbaþ selescota (*nidos*), 8, 20. v. sele-gescot.

sele-secg, es; *m. A hall-man, a retainer who has a place in his lord's hall*:—Gemon hē selesecgas and sincþege, hū hine his goldwine wenede tō wiste, Exon. Th. 288, 20; Wand. 34. Cf. seld-guma.

sele-þegn, es; *m. A hall-thane, chamberlain*:—Him (*Beowulf*) sele-þegn sīðes wērgum forþ wīsade, se ealle beweotede þegnes þearfe (*the chamberlain who saw after everything Beowulf needed*), Beo. Th. 3592; B. 1794.

sele-weard, es; *m. A hall-warder, guard of a hall*:—Hæfde hē Grendle tōgeánes seleweard āseted, Beo. Th. 1338; B. 667.

self, seolf, silf, sylf; *pron.* A. *self, very, own.* I. with a noun (*α*) which it immediately follows:—Ðam ðe se þeóden self sceóp nihte naman, Cd. Th. 9, 10; Gen. 139. Drihten sylf, Blickl. Homl. 41, 4: 51, 6. God selfa cuman wille, 163, 31. Hē, Drihten selfa, cwæð, 165, 2. Drihten sylfa, 39, 25. God seolfa, Cd. Th. 286, 11; Sat. 350. Nǣniges gebyrd círicean ne mǣrsiaþ nemþe Cristes sylfes and ðyses Iohannes, Blickl. Homl. 161, 11. From ðære dura selfre ðisse bēc *ab ipso libri hujus exordio*, Past. proem.; Swt. 25, 11. Gode sylfum underþeódde, Blickl. Homl. 109, 22: 73, 12. Gearo mōd ge eác swylce deáþ sylfne tō þrowienne *paratum vel etiam ad moriendum animum*, Bd. 1, 26; S. 487, 38. On ðæt dægrēd sylf, Judth. Thw. 24, 24; Jud. 204. Rōmāne selfe sǣdon, Ors. 5, 3; Swt. 220, 20. Nǣnig man ða lǣstas sylfe ufan oferwyrcean ne mihte, Blickl. Homl. 125, 35. Hē ða deádan sylfe āwehte, 173, 29. (*β*) which it follows, but not immediately:—Nergend com nihtes self, Cd. Th. 159, 12; Gen. 2633. Ðeáh ðe ðæt hūs ufan open sȳ sylf, Blickl. Hom. 125, 30. Mē sægde ǣr ðæt wīf hire wordum selfa, Cd. Th. 160, 11; Gen. 2648. Hē mid hondum Hǣlend genom sylfne be sīdan, 299, 5; Sat. 545. (*γ*) along with a personal pronoun in the dative:—Pilatus on hys dōmerne hym sylf āwrāt ealle ða þyng, Nicod. 34; Thw. 19, 33. Ōðra gesceafta weorðaþ him selfe tō nāuhte, Met. 11, 87. (*δ*) which it immediately precedes:—On ðē sylf cyning wrāt, wuldres God, Andr. Kmbl. 3017; An. 1511. Hēht sylf cyning him Abraham tō, Cd. Th. 161, 27; Gen. 2671. Hit is se seolfa sunu Waldendes, 289, 11; Sat. 396. Se sylfa cyning lȳsde (hié) of firenum, Exon. Th. 74, 20; Cri. 1209. Sylfes ðæs folces, 481, 20; Rä. 65, 6. Under ðam sylfum norþdǣle middangeardes *sub ipso septentrionali vertice mundi*, Bd. 1, 1; S. 473, 29. Ic tō sylfum Drihtne cleopode, Ps. Th. 54, 16. Ðæt ða sylfan ȳþa wǣron āhofene ofer ðæt scip, Blickl. Homl. 235, 6. Ðæt ða sylfan his lāreówas æt his mūþe leornodan *that his very teachers learned from his mouth*, Bd. 4, 24; S. 598, 8. (*ε*) which it precedes, but not immediately:—Bidon þegnas . . . swā him sylf bebeád swegles āgend, Exon. Th. 34, 16; Cri. 543. Bīdan selfes gesceapu heofoncyninges, Cd. Th. 52, 12; Gen. 842: 36, 4; Gen. 566. Wearð sylfum ætȳwed ðam cāsere swefnes wōma, Elen. Kmbl. 138; El. 69. II. with a pronoun. (1) in agreement with a personal pronoun denoting the subject of the sentence and (*α*) following it immediately:—Ic sylf (seolf, Lind.: solfa, Rush.) hit eom *ipse ego sum*, Lk. Skt. 24, 39. Heó sylf hié þeówen nemde, Blickl. Homl. 13, 13. Ðæt hē sylfa cwæð, 13, 26: 95, 5. Beó hē sylfa syxta, L. C. S. 30; Th. i. 394, 5, MS. G. Sȳ hē scyldig his sylfes, L. Ath. iv. prm.; Th. i. 220, 12. Hē swīðor mīnes feores wilnade ðonne his selfes, Nar. 8, 6. Mid his sylfes willum, willan *ultro*, Bd. 1, 7; S. 477, 15, 22. Gif þeów ete his sylfes rǣde, L. Wih. 15; Th. i. 40, 11. Hwæt segst ðū be ðē sylfum (seolfum, Lind.: fore ðec solfne, Rush.), Jn. Skt. 1, 22. Heó hæfde hire sylfre geworht ðæt mǣste wīte, Blickl. Homl. 5, 26. Gif his rīce on him sylfum biþ tōdǣled . . . Gif ðæt hūs ofer hit sylf ys tōdǣled . . . Gif Satanas winþ ongēn hine sylfne, Mk. Skt. 3, 24–26. Mē siolfne, Chart. Th. 476, 19. Ic swerige þurh mē sylfne *per memetipsum juravi*, Gen. 22, 16. Heó hié sylfe tō þeówene genemde, Blickl. Homl. 9, 23. Nū mæg sōð hit sylf gecȳðan, 187, 16. Ðone anwald ūre selfra, Past. 33; Swt. 220, 7. Suā micle giéman ūrra niéhstena suā suā ūre selfra, 5; Swt. 45, 12. Hī hiora selfra nānne anweald nabbaþ, Bt. 16, 3; Fox 54, 18. Hiora seolfra hǣlo, Nar. 30, 18. Heó hié selfe āweredon . . . him leófre wæs ðæt hié hié seolfe fornēðdon, Ors. 5, 3; Swt. 220, 23–26. Eáþmōdgiaþ eów sylfe, Blickl. Homl. 99, 3. (*α* 1) with irregular construction:—Ðeáh ðe hī synd of miclum dǣle heora sylfes anwealdes *quamvis ex parte sui sint juris*, Bd. 5, 23; S. 647, 3. (*β*) following the pronoun, but not immediately:—Hē eác self biþ gecostod, Past. 16; Swt. 104, 20. Hwæt hē mē self bebeád *what he himself bade me*, Cd. Th. 34, 10; Gen. 535. Hē his brȳde ofslōh self mid sweorde, Met. 9, 31. Gif hē wille sylf Godes dōmas gedēgan, Blickl. Homl. 43, 11. Hē wæs þridda sylf, Elen. Kmbl. 1707; El. 855: Andr. Kmbl. 1330; An. 665. Ne wēn ðū ðæt ic tō ānwillīce winne wið ða wyrd, forðam ic hit nō selfe ne ondrǣde, Bt. 20; Fox 70, 21. Ðā ðā wē hit nōhwæðer ne selfe ne lufodon, Past. pref.; Swt. 5, 6. Sylfe, Blickl. Homl. 53, 1: 223, 20. Hié wēnaþ ðæt hié wīsran sién selfe ðonne ōðre, Past. 48, 1; Swt. 365, 20. (*γ*) along with a pronoun in the dative:—Ðū meaht nū ðē self geseón, Cd. Th. 38, 23; Gen. 611. Hē feóll him silf *quem percussit Josue ad internecionem*, Jos. 10, 33. Hī weorþaþ him selfe tō nāuhte, Bt. 21; Fox 74, 36. (*δ*) preceding the pronoun:—Ðǣr syndon dǣlas on sylfre hire *cujus participatio ejus in idipsum*, Ps. Th. 121, 3. (2) in agreement with a demonstrative:—Þurh ðæs sylfes hand ðe ic ǣr onsended wæs, Soul Kmbl. 111; Seel. 56. (3) with a possessive:—Be mīnre seolfre nīdþearfe *de propio meo periculo*, Nar. 9, 24. On ðīnes silfes hand, Hy. 7, 83. Ðīn rīce and ðīnes sylfes feorh, Blickl. Homl. 185, 1. Mīnes sylfes mūþ *os meum*, Ps. Th. 77, 2. Ðīnre sylfre sunu, Exon. Th. 21, 23; Cri. 339. Wē sceoldon ūrra selfra waldan, Past. 33; Swt. 220, 5. II a. where the pronoun with which *self* agrees is not the subject of the sentence:—Hē (*Claudius Marcellus*) fōr on ðone ende Hannibales folces ðe hē self (*Hannibal*) on wæs, and hiene selfne (*Hannibal*) gefliémde, Ors. 4, 9; Swt. 192, 11–13. Antonius forlēt Octauianuses swostor and him selfum onbeád gewin, 5, 13; Swt. 244, 32. Ðæt man tō ōðrum lǣþþe hæbbe and hine hatige and tǣle behindan him sylfum, Blickl. Homl. 65, 1. Neoptolomus com tō Antigone . . . Ðā sende Antigones hiene selfne (*Neoptolomus*), Ors. 3, 11; Swt. 146, 9. Æðelstān wið Anlāf gefeaht and his firde ofslōh and āflīmde hine sylfne, Jud. Thw. p. 163, 10. Ðā gelȳfde ic him . . . beswang hine and tō heora sylfra dōme āgeaf, Blickl. Homl. 177, 24. III. standing alone:—Oft gebyreþ, ðonne se scrift ongit ðæs costunga ðe hē him ondetteþ, ðæt eác self biþ mid ðǣm ilcum gecostod, Past. 16; Swt. 105, 20. Hit Scipia hām onbeád, . . . and eác self sǣde, ðā hē hām com, Ors. 4, 12; Swt. 208, 34. Seolf, Cd. Th. 143, 5; Gen. 2374. Nime fīf and beó sylf sixta, L. C. S. 44; Th. i. 402, 7, MSS. A. G. For hwon wrīhst ðū sceome, and ðīn sylf þecest līc, Cd. Th. 54, 15; Gen. 877. Is ðīn āgen sprǣc innan fȳren, sylf swīðe hāt *ignitum eloquium tuum vehementer*, Ps. Th. 118, 140. Ðǣr habbaþ englas dreám, sanctas singaþ, ðæt is seolfa for God, Cd. Th. 286, 21; Sat. 355. Ðā onfēng hē gāste . . . and sylfa his wunda āwrāþ, Bd. 4, 22; S. 590, 36. Hē his torn gewræc selfes mihtum, Cd. Th. 4, 26; Gen. 59: Beo. Th. 1404; B. 700. Hē beáhhordes brūcan mōste selfes dōme, 1794; B. 895. Sleáþ synnigne ofer seolfes mūþ, Andr. Kmbl. 2602; An. 1302: Cd. Th. 248, 17; Dan. 514. Gest hine clænsie sylfes āþe, L. Wih. 20; Th. i. 40, 19. Sylfæs, 18; Th. i. 40, 14. Sylfum tō sconde *to thine own shame*, Exon. Th. 90, 27; Cri. 1480. Se swōre for sylfne æfter his rihte, L. R. 4; Th. i. 192, 6. Se cāsere hēht eft gearwian sylfe tō sīðe, Elen. Kmbl. 1998; El. 1001. III a. along with a pronoun in dative:—Biþ him self sunu and fæder *ipsa sibi proles, suus est pater*, Exon. Th. 224, 12; Ph. 374. Ðæt ðū ūs sunnan onsende, and ðē sylf cyme, 8, 8; Cri. 114. Nime fīf and beó him sylf sixta, L. C. S. 44; Th. i. 402, 7. Him sylfa, 30; Th. i. 394, 5. Eall ðis māgon him sylfe geseón, Exon. Th. 69, 6; Cri. 1116. IV. denoting voluntary or independent action (not inflected?). Cf. *Goth.* Silbō airtha akran bairith αὐτομάτη ἡ γῆ καρποφορεῖ, Mk. 4, 28; *and see* self-dēma, -līc, -sceaft, -will, -wille, -willende:—Genim tūncersan, sió ðe self weaxeþ, and mon ne sǣwþ, Lchdm. ii. 22, 12. Gif hē wīf self hæbbe gange hió ūt mid him. Gif se hlāford him wīf sealde sié hió ðæs hlāfordes *if he have a wife that he got himself, let her go out with him. If the lord gave him a wife, she shall be the lord's*, L. Alf. 11; Th. i. 46, 4. Gif hit cucu feoh wǣre and hē secgge ðæt hit self ācwǣle *died a natural death*, L. Alf. 28; Th. i. 52, 2. Marius and Silla gefōran him self, and Cinna wæs ofslagen, Ors. 5, 11; Swt. 236, 24. Hié woldon of ǣlcerre byrig him self anwald habban *imperare singulae cupiunt*, 3, 7; Swt. 112, 20. Hē ne mihte hine handum self mid hrægle wryón, Cd. Th. 95, 1; Gen. 1572. Ðonne wearp seó eorþe hit sōna sylf (*of its own accord*) of hire, Blickl. Homl. 127, 2. Ðone sylf ne mæg man āspyrigean *man left to himself cannot investigate it*, Elen. Kmbl. 930; El. 466. B. (*the*) *same*, (*α*) with a demonstrative:—Ðū eart se sylfa God ðe ūs ādrife fram dōme, Ps. Th. 107, 10. Ðæt ilce geþanc and seó sylfe carfulnyss ðe heom amang ðam nihtslǣpe wæs on heora heortan, eall ðā hī āwacodon hī ðæt sylfe geþohton, Homl. Skt. i. 23, 441. Ðæt selfe wæter þegnunge gearwode beforan his fōtum, Blickl. Homl. 247, 10. Weorðeþ sunne sweart gewended . . . Mōna ðæt sylfe, Exon. Th. 58, 19; Cri. 938: 387, 25; Rä. 5, 10. Ic ðē sǣde ǣr on ðisse selfan bēc (cf. on ðisse ilcan bēc, Bt. 37, 1; Fox 186, 25), Met. 25, 54. On ðære sylfan nihte . . . On ðam sylfan mynstre, Bd. 4, 23; S. 595, 33, 36. On ðam sylfan leóhte, S. 596, 3. On ðam sylfan stede ðe ðū him settest, Ps. Th. 83, 6. Ðȳ sylfan dæge, Exon. Th. 71, 12; Cri. 1154: Menol. Fox 94; Men. 47. Dōn ðæt selfe, Past. 44, 3; Swt. 323, 21. Ðæt seolfe, L. E. G. proem.; Th. i. 166, 9. Hī cumaþ tōgeánes Antecriste . . . and beóþ ofslegen þurh ðone sylfan feónd, Ælfc. T. Grn. 3, 45. On ða sylfan tīde, Blickl. Homl. 171, 19. Heó tōfereþ ðæt sār; ðæt sylfe heó dēþ mid wīne gecnucud, Lchdm. i. 190, 18: Ps. Th. 81, 3: 83, 6: 128, 1. His freónda forspǣc forstent him eal ðæt sylfe, swylce hit sylf spǣce, Wulfst. 38, 17. (*β*) alone:—Ic mē on mūþe mægene hæbbe, and ic sōðfæst word on sylfan healde, Ps. Th. 118, 43. On selfe wīsan *in the same fashion*, Lchdm. ii. 72, 17. [*Goth.* silba: *O. Frs. O. Sax. O. L. Ger.* self: *O. H. Ger.* selp: *Icel.* sjálfr.] v. selfe.

self-ǣta, an; *m. An eater of those belonging to its own species*, (applied to man) *a cannibal, anthropophagus*:—Ðū scealt fēran . . . ðǣr sylfǣtan eard weardigaþ . . . swā is ðære menigo þeáw, ðæt hié uncūðra ǣngum ne willaþ feores geunnan, Andr. Kmbl. 350; An. 175.

self-ǣte, an; *f.* A plant name, *wild oat* (?):—Selfǣte, eoforþrote, Lchdm. ii. 312, 15. Wyl on buteran selfǣtan, 80, 13. [Cockayne cites *O. H. Ger.* selbēza *senecion*, iii. 344, col. 1.]

self-bana, an; *m. One who kills himself, a suicide*:—Selfbona *bictonatus* (l. *biothanatus*, qui mortem sibi ipsi consciscit aut qui violenta morte perit), Wrt. Voc. ii. 126, 10. Selfbonan *biothanatas*, 11, 69. Seolfbonan (-boran, MS.), 101, 74. Selfbanan *biothanatos*, Hpt. Gl. 469, 26.

self-cwalu, e; *f. Self-slaughter, suicide*:—Sum sceal ful earmlíce ealdre linnan . . . and hine tō sylfcwale secgas nemnaþ *speak of him as committing suicide*, Exon. Th. 330, 24; Vy. 56. [Cf. We scole witan, þet nan seolfcwale, þet is aȝenslaȝa, ne cumeð to godes riche, O. E. Homl. i. 103, 3.]

self-, selfe-dēma, an; *m. One who depends upon his own judgment* [cf. ǣlc ídel mon liofaþ æfter his āgenum dōme, Past. 39; Swt. 283, 21], used of a certain kind of monks called *sarabaitae*, monachi qui nulla regula approbati . . . proprio arbitratu vivunt:—Þridde cyn is muneca ealra atelucost, sylfdēmena (*sarabaitarum*), ðe nō on regules and lāreówa tǣcinge ne beóþ āfandode, swā swā gold on heorðe . . . Ðæt feórþe muneca cyn ðe is wīdscriþul genæmned . . . hié synt wyrsan ðænne ða sylfedēman (sylf-, MS. T.), R. Ben. 9, 10–10, 2. Hȳ āscyriaþ hȳ sylfe fram mynsterlīcum þeáwum and heora āgenum lustum filiaþ, hȳ sint Egyptiscan gereorde genemnede *sarabagite* oððe *renuite*, ðæt ys sylfedēman and wiðersacan, 136, 12. [Cf. *Icel.* sjálf-dæmi *judgment given in a case by one of the parties themselves*.]

selfe; *adv. In the same way*, in combination with swā: cf. gelīce, same:—Hē forlǣt līfes frumsceaft and his āgene æðelo swā selfe, Met. 17, 25. Hæfþ ða wilnunga welhwilc nēten and ða yrsunga eác swā selfe, 20, 192, 199. [Cf. *O. Sax.* sō self *also, likewise*: *O. H. Ger.* sō selp (sō), selp sō *sic, sicut*.]

self-līc; *adj. Of one's own accord, spontaneous, voluntary*:—Selflīces *spontaneae, ultroneae, voluntariae*, Hpt. Gl. 436, 75.

self-līce, es; *n. Self-love, self-complacency, self-satisfaction, conceit, arrogance*:—Ðonne ðæt selflīce gegriépþ ðæt mōd þæs recceres *amor proprius cum rectoris mentem ceperit*, Past. 19, 1; Swt. 143, 5. Ðonne āhefþ hē hine on his mōde . . . mid ðȳ selflīce se Dēma biþ geniéded tō ðæm ierre, 4, 2; Swt. 39, 10. Ðǣm lytegan is ǣresð tō beleánne hiera selflīce ðæt hié ne wēnen ðæt hié sién wiése . . . hē biþ ǣr ūpāhæfen on selflīce for his lotwrencium *in sapientibus hoc primum destruendum est, quod se sapientes arbitrantur*, 30, 1; Swt. 203, 9, 18. Ðȳlæs hē sié āhafen on his mōde and on ofermēttum āþunden and þurh ðæt selflīce his gōdan weorc forleóse *ne perfecta opera tumor elationis extinguat*, proem.; Swt. 25, 7. Hē hiene up āhefeþ on his mōde on suelc gielp and on suelc selflīce *se apud se per arrogantiam exaltat*, 11, 4; Swt. 71, 1. Ðæt freódōm ne gewende on selflīce and on ofermētto *ut libertas in superbiam non erumpat*, 19, 3; Swt. 147, 3. Upāhafene þurh selflīce, Bt. 3, 4; Fox 6, 25.

self-līce; *adj. Self-satisfied, self-complacent, conceited, arrogant*:—Oft se welega and se wædla habbaþ suā gehweorfed hira þeáwum ðæt se welega biþ eáðmōd and sorgfull and se wædla biþ upāhæfen and selflīce *plerumque personarum ordinem permutat qualitas morum, ut sit dives humilis, sit pauper elatus*, Past. 26, 2; Swt. 183, 11. Selflīcne secg *the self-satisfied man*, Met. Introd. 7.

self-myrþe (?); *adj. Self-destructive*:—Betweónan sylfmyrþe *inter biothonatas*, Wrt. Voc. ii. 80, 2. v. next word.

self-myrþere (?), es; *m. One who destroys himself, a suicide*:—Betweónan selfmyrþras (-an? *but* cf. *Icel.* myrða *to murder*: *O. H. Ger.* murdit *jugulat*: *Ger.* morden) *inter biothanatas*, Wrt. Voc. ii. 46, 61. Cf. self-bana.

self-sceaft, es; *m. Self-shaping, spontaneous generation*, applied to Adam, who had not father and mother:—Adam maþelode ðǣr hē on eorþan stōd selfsceafte guma *a man by spontaneous generation*, Cd. Th. 33, 20; Gen. 523.

self-will, es; *n.* (?) *Self-will, one's own will, free-will*:—Be ðām ðe beóþ hyra sylfwilles (*sua sponte*) gefullode, L. Ecg. C. 17, tit.; Th. ii. 128, 30. Be selfwille *ultro*, Wrt. Voc. ii. 73, 27. Getǣc mē sumne mann ðara ðe ðē gesǣlegost þince and on his selfwille sȳ swīðost gewiten *who most has had things his own way*, Bt. 11, 1; Fox 32, 16. Gif ðū ne wilt wirde steóran ac on selfwille sīgan lǣtest *if thou wilt not guide fate, but lettest her go at her own will*, Met. 4, 50. [Cf. *O. H. Ger.* (pī) selpwillin *sponte, ultro*; *Icel.* með, at sjálfvilja *of one's own will*.] v. self-willes.

self-wille; *adj. Voluntary, spontaneous*:—Mid selfwilre *spontanea*, Hpt. Gl. 415, 11: *spontaneo, voluntario*, 439, 11. For ðan selfwillan *propter spontaneum*, 413, 33. [*Goth.* silba-wiljōs *voluntarii*, 2 Cor. 8, 3.]

self-willende; *adj. Voluntary*:—Rēn sylfwillendne *pluviam voluntariam*, Ps. Lamb. 67, 10. [*Goth.* silba-wiljandi galaith *sua sponte profectus est*, 2 Cor. 8, 17: *Icel.* sjálf-viljandi.]

self-willes; *adv. Voluntarily, of one's own accord*:—Selfwilles *ultro*, Wrt. Voc. ii. 92, 74. Sylfwilles *sponte*, Ælfc. Gr. 38; Zup. 234, 19: *ultro*, Zup. 237, 2. (1) of persons:—Drihten ðe on rōde selfwilles þrowode, H. R. 17, 21. Ealle hyra unlustas hī sceolon gebētan sylfwylles on ðyssum līfe, oððe unþances æfter ðyssum līfe, Homl. Th. i. 148, 27. Wrȳt nū sylfwylles ðæt ðū wiðsace Criste, Homl. Skt. i. 3, 379. Hē sylfwilles menniscnesse underfēng, Wulfst. 15, 12. Hē gǣþ sylfwilles twā mīla tō ānre geneádod, R. Ben. 28, 6. (2) of things:—Ðonne his wæstmas weaxaþ sylfwilles *quae sponte gignet humus*, Lev. 25, 5. Sylfwilles (*ultro*) seó eorþe wæstm beraþ, Mk. Skt. 4, 28. v. self-will.

selian, sēlla. v. sylian, sēl.

sella, an; *m. A giver*:—Ðone glædan syllan *hilarem datorem*, R. Ben. Interl. 25, 6.

sellan, sillan, syllan; *p.* salde, sealde; *pp.* sald, seald *To give* something (*acc.*) to somebody (*dat.*). I. of voluntary giving, *to put into the possession* of a person, *transfer ownership* from one to another:—Ic sello Werburge ðās lond, Chart. Th. 480, 30: 481, 5. Ðæt land ic sylle eów tō āgenne, Ex. 6, 8. Ealle ðās rīcu ic sylle (sello, Lind.: selle, Rush.) ðē, Mt. Kmbl. 4, 9. Ðū sāwlum selest ginfæsta gifa, Met. 20, 226. Eówer Fæder syleþ (selleþ, Rush.) gōd ðām ðe hyne biddaþ, Mt. Kmbl. 7, 11. Hig wǣron ðīne, and ðū hȳ sealdest mē, Jn. Skt. 17, 6. Salde *inpendebat* (cf. geben wæs *inpendebatur*, 21), Wrt. Voc. ii. 111, 24. Ecgbryht salde Basse mæsseprióste Reculf mynster on tō tymbranne, Chr. 669; Erl. 34, 25. Hié saldon hiera nefum Wiehte eálond, 534; Erl. 14, 33. Ðeáh Balac mē sille goldes ān hūs full, Num. 22, 18. Hī ne māgon sellan ðæt hī gehātaþ, Bt. 16, 1; Fox 90, 16. Nelle gē syllan (sella, Lind.) ðæt hālige hundum, Mt. Kmbl. 7, 6. Gē cunnun gōde sylena eówrum bearnum syllan (sellan, Rush.), 7, 11. Biþ sald *dabitur*, Kent. Gl. 338. II. *to give* what one is bound to give, *to pay* tribute, *offer*, *dedicate* to God:—Sylle mē ðīn forme bearn. Dō eall swā of hrīðerum . . . syle (*reddas*) hit mē on ðam ehtuþan dæge, Ex. 22, 29, 30. Norþmonnum niéde sceoldon gombon gieldan and gafol sellan, Cd. Th. 119, 12; Gen. 1978. Gafol syllan, Chr. 1006; Erl. 141, 10. Hī willaþ eów tō gafole gāras syllan, Byrht. Th. 133, 7; By. 46. Hié næfdan for him lamb tō syllenne, Blickl. Homl. 23, 26. III. *to give, furnish* or *supply with* food, medicine, poison, etc.—Hwā sylþ ūs flǣsc? . . . Drihten eów silþ flǣsc and gē etaþ, Num. 11, 18. Byrelas sealdon wīn of wunderfatum, Beo. Th. 2327; B. 1161. Hié him sealdon āttor drinccan, Blickl. Homl. 229, 16: Ealle ða mettas ge drincan ða ðe habban hāt mægen and scearp sele þicgean, Lchdm. ii. 184, 10 (often in Leechdoms). Him man metsunge syllan sceolde, Chr. 1006; Erl. 141, 10. Hē wolde syllan his assan fōddur, Gen. 42, 27. III a. with infin. instead of acc.:—Hwīlum ic deórum drincan selle, Exon. Th. 393, 25; Rä. 13, 5. Gehwylc mē drincan sealde, 484, 24; Rä. 71, 6. IV. *to give* one thing for another. (a) *to sell* for (*wið*) a price:—Ic sylle wið wirðe *vendo*, Ælfc. Gr. 28, 8; Zup. 181, 17. Hwī ne sealde heó ðās sealfe wið þrīm hundred penegon, Jn. Skt. 12, 5. Sume man wið feó sealde, Chr. 1036; Erl. 164, 34: Blickl. Homl. 79, 22. (b) *to sell* at (*tō*) a price:—Sēlre ys ðæt wē hine syllon tō ceápe Ysmahēlitum, Gen. 37, 27. (c) *to sell*:—Hē sylþ (*vendit*) eall ðæt hē āh, Mt. Kmbl. 13, 44. Hē worhte his weorc tō seofon nihtum, and sealde on ðone Sæternesdæg, Homl. Th. ii. 356, 6. Hī sealdon heora gymstānas, i. 62, 21. Ne eów ne ofþince ðæt gē mē sealdon (*vendidistis*) on ðis rīce, Gen. 45, 5. Syllaþ (*vendite*) ðæt gē āgon, Lk. Skt. 12, 33. Nān man hig nā undeóror ne sylle (sille, MS. D.); and gif hwā hī undeóror sylle, gilde ǣgðer .xl. scillinga, ge se ðe hī sylle ge se ðe hī bycge, L. Edg. ii. 8; Th. i. 270, 3–6. Mōna se ōðer on eallum þingum tō dōndum nytlīc ys, bicgan, syllan, scip āstīgan, Lchdm. iii. 184, 13. Ða syllendan *vendentes*, Lk. Skt. 19, 45. (d) *to give* in payment:—Hē sealde his ðone reádan gim, ðæt wæs his ðæt hālige blōd, mid ðon hē ūs gedyde dǣlnimende ðæs heofonlīcan rīces, Blickl. Homl. 9, 36. Eall ðæt feoh ðe hié wið ðæm weorce sellan woldon, Ors. 4, 12; Swt. 210, 4. Syllan feoh wið freóde, Byrht. Th. 132, 58; By. 39. V. (a) *to give* into the keeping of, *hand over, deliver, commit, entrust*:—Gif ðū mē sylst underwedd, Gen. 38, 17. Ic befæste ðē ðæt eówde ðæt ðū mē sealdest, Blickl. Homl. 191, 27. Hē hire sāule sealde Sancte Michahele, 147, 13. Hē sealde his sweord ombihtþegne, Beo. Th. 1349; B. 672. Hié sealdon ānum unwīsum þegne Miercna rīce tō haldanne, and hē him gīslas salde, Chr. 874; Erl. 76, 26–28. Hié sealdon hiera suna tō gīslum *they gave their sons as hostages*, Ors. 4, 11; Swt. 204, 4. Hī on wedde sealdon, hwæt hȳ hyre syllan woldon, Homl. As. 196, 24. Ðā wæs ic mid gȳmenne mīnra māga seald tō fēdanne and tō lǣranne Abbude Benedicte, Bd. 5, 23; S. 647, 22. (b) *to give* a woman to be a man's wife:—Ðā wolde se fæder hī sellan sumum æþelon men tō brȳde, Shrn. 31, 6. Nyme hē hig tō rihtwīfe. Gif se fæder hig him syllan nelle, Ex. 22, 17. (c) *to give over* to a hostile power, *deliver up* to. (1) with dat.:—Ne syle (*tradas*) ðū unscyldigra sāwla deórum, Ps. Th. 73, 18. Ðȳ læs ðe ðīn wiðerwinna ðē sylle ðam dēman, and se dēma ðē sylle ðam þēne, Mt. Kmbl. 5, 25. (2) without dat.:—Ne syle mē ne ne send mē mid ðām synfullan *ne tradas me cum peccatoribus*, Ps. Th. 27, 3. (3) with prepositions:—Hē sealde on edwīt ðe mē ǣr trǣdan, Ps. Th. 56, 3. Hē sealde his folc sweordes under ecge, 77, 62. Ne syle mē tō ðara mōdes willan, 26, 14. Ne ðū mē ne syle on ðone biterestan deáþ, Blickl. Homl. 229, 26. Ne syle ðū mē in wīta forwyrd, Frag. Kmbl. 14; Leás. 9. Mannes sunu ys tō syllenne on manna handa, Mt. Kmbl. 17, 22. (4) with dat. and prep.:—Drihten him sealde ða burh on his handa, Jos. 10, 32. (d) with a bad sense, *to deliver wrongfully, to betray*; cf. colloquial *to sell* a person. Mannes sunu þū mid cosse sylst (seles, Rush.: selles, Lind.), Lk. Skt. 22, 48. Nū is gehende se đe mē sylþ (seleþ, Rush.: selleþ, Lind.), Mk. Skt. 14, 42. Đæt mon ne selle his weorđscipe fremdum menn, Past. 36; Swt. 249, 21. **VI.** *to give up, yield up*:—Hē feorh seleþ *he dies*, Beo. Th. 2745; B. 1370. **VII.** *to give forth, produce, be the source of*:—Ne seleþ đē wæstmas eorþe, Cd. Th. 62, 17; Gen. 1015. Sume sealdon (saldun, Rush.: saldon, Lind.) wæstm, Mt. Kmbl. 13, 8. God lǣteþ hrusan syllan blǣda beornum, Runic pm. Kmbl. 341, 23; Rūn. 12. **VII a.** *to give* light, *emit* sound:—Sylle se friccea his stefne, Blickl. Homl. 163, 31. Leóht sellan, Bt. 6; Fox 14, 23. **VIII.** where the object is immaterial, (a) *to give* an answer, a pledge, a promise, etc.:—Ic eów treówa mīne selle, Cd. Th. 92, 29; Gen. 1536. Ic đē wǣre mīne selle, 132, 35; Gen. 2203. For đīnum gebode đe đū mē sealdest, Blickl. Homl. 241, 33. Se Hǣlend him ne sealde nāne andsware, Jn. Skt. 19, 9. Hī sealdon āþas, Met. 1, 24. Him lof syllaþ, Ps. Th. 65, 1. Heora ǣlc sylle đone āþ, đæt . . . , L. Edg. S. 6; Th. i. 274, 15. ¶ where the object is expressed by a clause:—Ic eów behāta and on hand selle, đæt gē sculon finden reste eowre sāwlen, Homl. As. 171, 29. Đæt hȳ ealle đam sēmende syllan, đæt cyninges mund stande, L. E. G. 12; Th. i. 174, 22. Slaga sceal his forspecan on hand syllan, and se forspeca māgum, đæt se slaga wille bētan wiđ mǣgþe. Đonne gebyreþ đæt man sylle đæs slagan forspecan on hand, đæt se slaga mōte mid griþe weddian, L. Edm. S. 7; Th. i. 250, 14–17. (b) *to give* leave, consent, forgiveness, etc.:—Đyssum wordum ōđer ealdormann geþafunge sealde (*tribuens assensum*), Bd. 2, 13; S. 516, 13. Hē him ne sealde leáfe, Homl. Th. ii. 380, 5. Nis nān tweó đæt hē forgifnesse syllan nelle đām đe hié geearnian willaþ, Blickl. Homl. 65, 8. (c) *to give* help, pain, peace, victory, etc.:—Ic đē mīne sylle sibbe, Andr. Kmbl. 194; An. 97. Đū sylest ūrum leomum ræste, Blickl. Homl. 141, 11. Se đe sigor seleþ, Cd. Th. 170, 5; Gen. 2808. Sile đīne āre đīnum earminge, Hy. 2, 3. Ūs fultum sile, 7, 80. Gif Drihten him sige syllan wolde, Bd. 3, 24; S. 556, 18. Ne biþ đæm seald Drihtnes mildheortnes, Blickl. Homl. 49, 24. ¶ where the object is expressed by a clause:—Ne syleþ hē sōđfæstum, đæt him ȳþende mōd innan hređre, Ps. Th. 54, 22. Gūþlāce engel sealde, đæt him swedraden synna lustas, Exon. Th. 109, 1; Gū. 83. Syle mē, đæt đū mē generige nīđa gehwylces, Ps. Th. 118, 169. (d) *to give* punishment, reward:—Sealde him wītes clom, Cd. Th. 193, 11; Sat. 453. Leán sellende eallum, 240, 34; Dan. 396. (e) *to give, endow with* a capacity, life, sight, understanding, etc.:—Đū sylest andgit eallum eorþbūendum, Ps. Th. 118, 130. Đū man geworhtest and him sealdest word and gewitt and wæstma gecynd, Hy. 9, 56. Đū sealdest ǣlcre gecynde āgene wīsan, 7, 66. Sealde hē dumbum gesprec, Andr. Kmbl. 1153; An. 577. Syle mē heortan clǣne, Ps. Grn. 50, 11. Ǣghwylc đe him eágna gesihþ cyning syllan wolde, Exon. 350, 22; Sch. 67. Đē biþ ēce līf seald, Elen. Kmbl. 1052; El. 527. ¶ with the gerund:—Heáh geweorc furþor āspyrgen đonne him freá sylle tō ongietanne, Exon. Th. 348, 17; Sch. 29. (f) *to give* one's heart to a person:—Nemne ic Gode sylle hȳrsumne hige, Exon. Th. 124, 12; Gū. 338. [*Goth.* saljan *to offer*: *O. Frs.* sella *to give, sell, pay*: *O. Sax.* sellian *to give*: *O. H. Ger.* sellan *tradere*: *Icel.* selja *to hand over, to sell.*] v. ā-, be-, for-, ge-, ymb-sellan; un-seald.

sellend, es; *m.* I. *a giver*:—God gōdra mægna sellend (*dator*), Rtl. 103, 36. Sigora sellend (*the Deity*), Exon. Th. 282, 24; Jul. 668: 359, 10; Pa. 64. Syllend, 284, 30; Jul. 705. Drihten se is ordfruma and syllend (*largitor*) ealra eádignesse, Bd. 4, 30; S. 609, 17. Hihton hī on God, đæra gōda syllend, Homl. Th. ii. 328, 1. Hē lufaþ đone glædan syllend, 212, 9. II. *a betrayer*:—Se sellend his *traditor ejus*, Mk. Skt. Lind. Rush. 14, 44. v. ǣ-sellend.

sel-līc, selma, selmerige, selnes, sēlost, sēlra, seltra. v. seld-līc, sealma, sælmerige, seleness, sēl, sæltna.

sēma, an; *m. An arbitrator, umpire*:—Sēma (sȳma, sīma) *sequester*, Ælfc. Gr. 9, 18; Zup. 43, 16. v. sēman.

sēman *to load.* v. sīman.

sēman; *p.* de; *pp.* ed. I. with acc. of person, (1) *to bring to an agreement* those who have a dispute:—Đā hēt hē hié sēman. Đā wæs ic đara monna sum đe đǣrtō genemned wǣran . . . Đā wē hié sēmdan *then bade the king to bring them* (the parties in a dispute about some land) *to an agreement. Then was I one of the men who were nominated for the purpose* . . . *When we had brought them to an agreement*, Chart. Th. 170, 6–35. (2) *to satisfy* a person in a matter of doubt or difficulty:—Sēme ic đē recene ymb đa wrætlīcan wiht, Salm. Kmbl. 504; Sal. 252. II. with acc. of thing, *to settle* a dispute:—Hī sace sēmaþ, sibbe gelǣraþ, Exon. Th. 334, 22; Gn. Ex. 20. III. used intransitively, *to arbitrate, bring about agreement*:—Nān sacu đe betweox preóstan sī ne beó gescoten tō worldmanna sōme, ac sēman and sibbian heora āgene geferan, L. Edg. C. 7; Th. ii. 246, 6. Gif hē healt weorđ, đǣr mōtan freónd sēman, L. Ethb. 65; Th. i. 18, 14. v. ge-sēman; sōm.

sēmend, sǣmend, es; *m. One who brings about agreement between parties in a dispute, an arbitrator, umpire*:—Đæt hȳ ealle gemǣnum handum of ǣgđere mǣgþe on ānum wǣpne đam sēmende syllan, đæt cyninges munde stande, L. E. G. 12; Th. i. 174, 22. Ymb .iii. niht gesēcæn hiom sǣmend, L. H. E. 10; Th. i. 30, 18. v. preceding word.

sēmestre, semian, semle. v. seámestre, seomian, symble.

semnendlīce; *adv. By chance, fortuitously*:—Semnendlīce *fortuito*, Wrt. Voc. ii. 37, 10: 80, 40: *fortuis*, 84, 78.

semninga, senap. v. samnunga, senep.

senatus *the senate, senators.* The treatment of this word in the translation of Orosius is somewhat exceptional. The Latin form *senatus* occurs in the nom. and acc., but in the former *senatas, senatum*, and in the latter *senatum, senatos* are also used; in the gen. *senatuses, senatusa* are found, and in the dat. *senatum*; in every case but one (?) the word is plural. The Latin *senator* is also used, though the word *witan* is generally employed to denote the senators:—Sceoldon ealle hiera senatus (senatas, Bos. 43, 5) cuman . . . sceoldon hiera senatus (-as) rīdan, Ors. 2, 4; Swt. 70, 24, 28. Ealle heora senatus *senatores*, 4, 9; Swt. 190, 19. Ealle đa senatus *omnis senatus*, 5, 12; Swt. 240, 13. Đā wolde ān (woldan, Bos. 70, 36) senatus hiene āweorpan . . . Đā bæd his fæder đæt đa senatum (*altered to* senatus *in other MSS.*) forgeáfen đæm suna đone gylt, 3, 10; Swt. 140, 14–16. Se consul bæd đætte senatus him fultum sealdon, 4, 9; Swt. 192, 22. Đa senatus him hæfden đa dǣd forboden . . . Ne mehten đa senatus nǣnne consul under him findan, 4, 10; Swt. 196, 7–10. Būton his āgnum fultume and būton đara senatuses, 5, 12; Swt. 242, 1. Hē forneáh nānne đara senatusa ne lēt cucne *plurimos senatorum ad mortem coegit*, 6, 2; Swt. 256, 1. (Cf. Đara senatorum xxxv *triginta quinque senatores*, 6, 4; Swt. 260, 23: 6, 14; Swt. 268, 28.) Hē sende tō đǣm senatum đæt hē đæt irre gesette wiđ hié, 4, 11; Swt. 206, 26: 2, 6; Swt. 88, 12. Hē hit sǣde đǣm senatum, đa wurdon hié alle wiđ hiene wiđerwearde *senatus indignatione motus*, 6, 2; Swt. 254, 25: 5, 12; Swt. 244, 16. Romulus gesette senatum, 2, 4; Swt. 70, 36. Đēh hē hit wiđ đa senatus hǣle, 4, 10; Swt. 196, 16. Hē sette senatus, 5, 12; Swt. 242, 28. Đæt hē sprǣce wiđ đa senatos (-us *other MSS.*), 4, 11; Swt. 206, 29: 4, 13; Swt. 210, 16: 5, 5; Swt. 226, 16.

sencan; *p.* te; *pp.* ed. I. *to sink* (trans.), *plunge, immerse*:—Wæs his gewuna đæt hē hine on đam streáme sencte *solebat in flumine supermeantibus undis immergi*, Bd. 5, 12; S. 631, 22. II. *to submerge, flood* with water:—Abraham wolde his sunu cwellan folmum sīnum fȳre(?)sencan mǣges dreóre (*flood the pile with his son's blood*), Cd. Th. 176, 4; Gen. 2906. Ne biþ flōd tō sencende (tō stencende (?) *dissipans*) đa eorþan, Gen. 9, 11. [Forte reauin hire bodi and i þea sea senchen, Jul. 79, 1. *Goth.* saggkwjan: *O. Sax.* be-senkian: *O. H. Ger.* sencan *mergere*: *Icel.* sökkva.] v. ā-, be-, ge-sencan.

sendan; *p.* sende; *pp.* sended, send *To send, cause to go.* I. where the object is a living thing, (1) *to send* after (*æfter*), on an errand, for a purpose, *despatch*:—Ic sende ǣrendracan tō mīnum hlāforde, Gen. 32, 5. Ic eów sende swā swā sceáp gemang wulfas, Mt. Kmbl. 10, 16. Hē sent ǣrendracan, Lk. Skt. 14, 32. God sendeþ his engla gāstas tō ǣrendwrecum, Blickl. Homl. 203, 14. Hē ūsic sendeþ đæt wē sōđfæstra mōd oncyrren, Exon. Th. 261, 34; Jul. 325. Đa twegen leorningcnihtas đe Crist sende æfter đam assan, Homl. Th. i. 206, 23. Đā sendon hī him hyra leorningcnihtas tō, Mt. Kmbl. 22, 16. Gif đū wylt hine mid ūs sendan, Gen. 43, 4. Hē mē on đisne sīđ sendan wolde, Exon. Th. 460, 35; Hö. 27. Se đe englas gehēt wiđ mē tō sendenne, Blickl. Homl. 181, 26. Fram Gode hē is send, 247, 19. Ōþ đæt đū gefylle đīne þegnunge tō đære đe đū sended eart, 233, 28. Hē senden (?) wæs tō hādianne, and Wilfreþ on Gallia rīce tō hādianne sended wæs, Bd. 4, 2; S. 566, 12, 13. Đā wæs culufre sended, Cd. Th. 88, 13; Gen. 1464. Ealle Drihtnes apostolas beóþ sende đē tō bebyrgenne, Blickl. Homl. 137, 27. (2) with a sense of compulsion or violence, *to send* to prison, into exile, etc.:—Se đec on wræc sendeþ, Cd. Th. 251, 26; Dan. 569. Se đec sendeþ in đa sweartestan wītebrōgan, Elen. Kmbl. 1858; El. 931. Hē hine on fȳr and on wæter sende, Mk. Skt. 9, 22. Wē iii hæfdon cniehtas gebunden in fȳres leóman, nū ic đǣr iiii men sende tō sīđe (cf. gesеó tō sōđe *in the version given*, Cd. Th. 242, 8; Dan. 416), Exon. Th. 196, 16; Az. 175. Đara đe hē of hleó sende, Cd. Th. 7, 7; Gen. 102. Hié mē sendon on đis carcern, Blickl. Homl. 237, 31. Hē wile đa sāula sendan on ēce wītu, 95, 4: 125, 2. Wē wǣron on đysne wræcsīþ sende, 23, 6. II. where the object is not a living creature, *to send* a message, present, help, etc.:—Đū senst ūrne hlāf dæghwamlīce, Hy. 7, 68. Dryhten sendeþ þurh monnes hond mīne þearfe, Exon. Th. 121, 22; Gū. 292. Meotud monnum dǣleþ, syleþ sundorgiefe, sendeþ wīde āgne spēde, 293, 23; Crä. 5. Sende ic Wylfingum ealde mādmas, Beo. Th. 946; B. 471. Đē sende God đās helpe, Cd. Th. 33, 15; Gen. 520. Sende đā his bēne fore bearn Godes, Andr. Kmbl. 3224; An. 1615. Sendon hira bēne fore bearn Godes, 2055; An. 1030. Þinga gehwylces đara đe đū mē sendan wylle tō cunnunge, Exon. Th. 453, 32; Hy. 4, 23. Ǣrendgewrit suelce hit from ūs send sié, Past. 32; Swt. 213, 18. III. *to send, move* to a place of rest, *put, lay*:—Ic sende mīne hond on đās fǣmnan *I will lay my hand on this woman*, Shrn. 130, 27. Đū sāwle sendest intō đam flǣsce, Hy. 7, 4. Đonne se wæstm hine forþbringþ, sōna hē sent his sicol, Mk. Skt. 4, 29. Sumum wordlaþe sendeþ on his mōdes gemynd Exon. Th. 41, 32; Cri. 664. In eorþan fæþm sendaþ līchoman, 231, 12; Ph. 488. Ælmihtig eácenne gāst in sefan sende, Cd. Th. 246, 28; Dan. 486: Beo. Th. 3688; B. 1842. Hié sendon rāp on his sweoran, Blickl. Homl. 241, 24. Ðæt on ðone hālgan handa sendan fæderas ūsse, Elen. Kmbl. 912; El. 457. Uton sendon rāp on his swyran, Blickl. Homl. 241, 10. **IV.** with a stronger sense of motion, *to send* a missile, *cast* lots, *throw, hurl*:—(a) Ðonne sceótend sendaþ flāngeweorc, Exon. Th. 42, 20; Cri. 675. 'Nū, anlīcnes, sænd mycel wæter þurh þīnne mūþ.' Sió onlīcnes sendde mycel wæter þurh hiora mūþ, Blickl. Homl. 245, 20–24. Gūþfrecan gātas sendon in heardra gemang, Judth. Thw. 24, 35; Jud. 224. Hié sendon hlot him betweónum, Blickl. Homl. 229, 5. Send ðē nyþer of ðisse heánesse, 27, 12. Ðā hēt ic feá strǣla sendan in ða burh innan, Nar. 10, 22. Hē geseh ða welegan hyra lāc sendan on ðone sceoppan, Lk. Skt. 21, 1. Sendende hyra nett on ða sǣ, Mt. Kmbl. 4, 18. Seó strǣl wæs sended, Blickl. Homl. 199, 22. (b) of the operations of Nature, *to send* rain, *fire*, etc.:—Drihten sende regn, Cd. Th. 82, 33; Gen. 1371. Him brego engla wylmhātne līg tō wræce sende, 156, 6; Gen. 2584. God eástan sende leóhtne leóman, Judth. Thw. 24, 16; Jud. 190. Sceolde hē sendan þunras and lȳgetu, Bt. 35, 4; Fox 162, 13. Ic sendan gefrægn swegles aldor swefl of heofonum, Cd. Th. 153, 17; Gen. 2540. (c) *to send* punishment, pestilence, etc.:—Drihten sende on hié māran wræce, Blickl. Homl. 79, 9. Ðæt God wolde sendan hungor and ādla on manna ceáp, Wulfst. 209, 28. **V.** *to send forth, emit* a sound:—Heofenfuglas sendaþ stefne mycle *dabunt voces suas*, Ps. Th. 103, 11. **VI.** where the object is not expressed, *to send a message* or *a messenger*. (1) to or after (*tō, æfter*) a person or thing, *to send for* (æfter):—Hēr sende se cyng tō ðam here, Chr. 1011; Erl. 144, 20: 1048; Erl. 180, 9. Ðā sende se cing æfter ðām scypon, 1049; Erl. 172, 39. Ðā sende se cyng æfter eallon his witan, 1048; Erl. 178, 13. Hī sendon on Perse æfter Conone, Ors. 3, 1; Swt. 98, 19. Ðā sendon hié on Affrice tō Cartaginenses æfter fultume, 4, 1; Swt. 160, 2. Ðæt hié tō Rōme sendon tō ðæm pāpan, Blickl. Homl. 205, 19. (2) where the person or thing sent to or for is not stated:—Hī sendon geond eall ðæt land, and brohton tō him ealle untrume, Mt. Kmbl. 14, 35. [*Goth.* sandjan: *O. Frs.* senda: *O. Sax.* sendian: *O. H. Ger.* sentan: *Icel.* senda.] v. ā-, āgēn-, for-, fore-, geond-, in-, of-, ofer-, on-, tō-sendan.

sendeþ, Beo. Th. 1204; B. 600. v. scendan.

sendlīc; *adj. To be sent*:—Ða sendlīcan gebrōðra on wege *dirigendi fratres in viam*, R. Ben. Interl. 113, 4.

sendness, e; *f. A sending, dismission*:—Sendnessa *missarum* (*Low Latin* missa *dimissio*), Wrt. Voc. ii. 56, 71: 80, 70.

senep (-ap, -op), es; *m. Mustard*:—Senep *sinapis*, Wrt. Voc. i. 31, 47. Senap, 69, 20. On ða gelīcnesse geworht ðe senop biþ getemprod tō inwīsan, Lchdm. ii. 184, 22. Gelīc senepes corne, Mt. Kmbl. 13, 31: Lk. Skt. 13, 19. Senepes sǣd, Mk. Skt. 4, 31: Lchdm. ii. 20, 11. Mid sinope gnīde, 186, 6. Gerēnodne senep, 184, 9: 20, 22. [*Goth.* sinapis (*gen.*): *O. H. Ger.* senaf: *Ger.* senf.]

senep-sǣd, es; *n. Mustard-seed*:—Nim senepsǣd, Lchdm. iii. 88, 15.

sengan; *p.* de; *p.* ed *To singe, scorch*:—Gȳme eác swān ðæt hē æfter sticunge his slyhtswȳn wel behweorfe, sæncge, L. R. S. 6; Th. i. 436, 16. [*Chauc.* senge; *pp.* seind: *Prompt. Parv.* sengin *ustulare*: *O. Frs.* senga: *M. H. Ger.* sengen: *Du.* zengen: cf. *Icel.* sangr *burnt, scorched; sengja a singed taste.*] v. be-sengan, unbesenged; singan.

sēnian, senn, senoþ, seó (*pron.*), seó (*verb*). v. segnian, synn, seonoþ, se, sī.

seó; *gen.* seón, seó; *acc.* seón, seó; *f. m.* (?) *The pupil, apple of the eye*:—Seó *pupilla* vel *pupula*, Wrt. Voc. i. 43, 1: 64, 40: *papilla, papula*, 282, 53, 54. Seó sceal in eágan, Exon. Th. 341, 8; Gn. Ex. 123. Ðæs (ðære?) seó hringc *circulus*, Wrt. Voc. i. 42, 72. Hē heóld hig swā his eágan seón (*quasi pupillam oculi sui*), Deut. 32, 10: Ps. Spl. 16, 9. Seán, Ps. Surt. 16, 8. Sión, Kent. Gl. 177. Swylce hē hreppe ða seó mīnes eágan, Homl. Th. i. 390, 15: 516, 23. Seón *pupillae*, Wrt. Voc. i. 65, 8. Seóna *pupillarum*, Hpt. Gl. 404, 28. Sión *pupillis*, Lchdm. i. lxx, 6. Seóum, lxxiv, 7. [*O. H. Ger.* seha (*acc.* sehun, sehe, *n. pl.* seha, sehun, v. Grff. vi. 123) *pupilla, acies*.]

seóbgende. v. seófian.

seóc; *adj. Sick, ill.* **I.** of bodily infirmity or disease:—Sum seóc man *quidam languens*, Jn. Skt. 11, 1. Se is seóc *infirmatur*, 3. Hē seóc wæs *infirmabatur*, 6. Seóc hē biþ ðe tō seldan ieteþ, Exon. Th. 340, 16; Gn. Ex. 111. Seonobennum seóc, 328, 17; Vy. 19: Beo. Th. 5473; B. 2740: 5800; B. 2904. Gif mon sȳ ðære healfdǣdan ādle seóc, Lchdm. ii. 284, 31. Seó lange mettrumnes ðæs seócan mannes, Blickl. Homl. 59, 28. Swā swā lǣca gewuna is ðonne hió seócne (siócne, Cott. MS.) mon gesióþ, Bt. 36, 4; Fox 178, 26. Ða ðe on sāre seóce lāgun, Exon. Th. 83, 15; Cri. 1356. Feóllon wergend bennum seóce, Cd. Th. 118, 29; Gen. 1972. Seócra manna hūs *nosocomium*, Wrt. Voc. i. 58, 52. Ofer seóce (*aegrotos*) hī hyra handa settaþ and hī beóþ hāle, Mk. Skt. 16, 18. ¶ used as a noun:—Þurh his hrepunge beóþ gestrangode ða unstrangan seócan, Homl. Skt. i. 7, 54. **II.** of moral disease:—Hǣðne wǣron begen, synnum seóce, Exon. Th. 246, 21; Jul. 65. Gif hē his seócum ðæt is synfullum dǣdum ealle lācnunge gegearwade *si morbidis eorum actionibus universa fuerit cura exibita*, R. Ben. 11, 5. **III.** of mental disquiet, *sick* at heart, *ill* at ease, *sad*:—Ne beó ðū on sefan tō seóc, Exon. Th. 166, 29; Gū. 1050. Seóc and sorhful, Cd. Th. 281, 20; Sat. 275. Ic ðysne sang sīðgeómor fand on seócum sefan, Apstls. Kmbl. 3; Ap. 2. Wēna mē ðīne seóce gedydon, Exon. Th. 380, 26; Rä. 1, 14. [*Laym.* seoc, seac, sec, sæc: *Orm.* seoc, sec: *A. R.* sec, sic: *Chauc.* sek, sik: Wick. seek, siik: *Ayenb.* zik: *Prompt. Parv.* seek: *Goth.* siuks: *O. Sax.* seok, siok, siak: *O. Frs.* siak, siek: *O. H. Ger.* sioh, siuh, sieh: *Ger.* siech: *Icel.* sjúkr.] v. bræc-, brægen-, deófol-, ellen-, fefer-, feónd-, feorh-, fylle-, gebræc-, gewit-, heaðu-, lifer-, lim-, milte-, mōd-, mōn-, mōnaþ-, morgen-, scīn-, wæter-, wamb-, wan-, wit-seóc.

seócan *to seek*. v. sēcan.

seócen (?); *adj. Troubled with sickness*:—On ðās seócnan (seócan?) tīd *in this time of sickness*, Exon. Th. 166, 11; Gū. 1041.

seóclian. v. sīclian.

seócness, e; *f. Sickness, illness, disease*:—Ðæt God wolde sendan ǣrest hungor and ādla on manna ceáp, ǣr ðæt fȳr cōme on heó, and heó mid mislīcre seócnesse æt mannum genyman, Wulfst. 209, 30. v. deóful-, fylle-, lifer-, mōd-, mōnaþ-, ofer-, wæter-seócness.

seód, es; *m. A money-bag, purse, pouch*:—Seód *marsupium* vel *marsippa* (cf. *marsupium* a purse, 197, 16), Wrt. Voc. i. 40, 65: 83, 12. Kyninga seód *fiscus*, ii. 39, 80. Ðā ic eów sende būtan seóde (*sacculo*) and codde ... Se ðe hæfþ seód gelīce nime codd, Lk. Skt. 22, 35, 36. Seódas *marsupia*, Hpt. Gl. 500, 40: Wrt. Voc. ii. 55, 9. Siódas, 84, 37. Ðæt feoh ðæt hī hæfdon on heora seódum, Homl. Skt. i. 23, 262. Seódas *loculos*, Wrt. Voc. ii. 52, 22: 74, 18. Wyrcaþ seódas (seádas, Rush.: seádo, Lind. *sacculos*) ða ðe ne forealdigeaþ, Lk. Skt. 12, 33. Seádo *loculos*, Jn. Skt. Lind. 12, 6. Seódas, Blickl. Homl. 69, 11. [*Icel.* sjóðr *a money-bag*: cf. *O. H. Ger.* siut *sutura*.]

-seódan. v. ā-seódan.

seód-cist, e; *f. A coffer*:—Seódcist (seód, cist?) *loculum*, Wrt. Voc. ii. 74, 46. Seódcyst, 52, 23.

seodu, seofa, seofan, seofen. v. sidu, sefa, seofon.

seófian, sēfian, sȳfian; *p.* ode. **I.** *trans. To lament, complain of*:—His sylfes earfoþu hē seófaþ tō Drihtne, Ps. Th. 3, arg. Gilleþ geómorlīce and his gyrn sēfaþ, Salm. Kmbl. 536; Sal. 267. Hē seófode his ungelimp tō Drihtne, Ps. Th. 7, arg.: 3, arg. Hleahtor ālegdon sorge seófedon *laughter they laid aside, woes they bewailed*, Exon. Th. 116, 2; Gū. 201. Ne forlǣt hē nō ða seófunga ðæt hē ne seófige his eormþa *humanum miseras haud ideo genus cesset flere querelas*, Bt. 7, 4; Bt. 22, 29. Sege mē hwæðer ðū mid rihte mǣge seófian (siófian, Cott. MS.) ðīna unsǣlþa *poterisne de infortunio jure caussari?* 10; Fox 28, 8. Ðonne hī sceoldan hiora sār siófian, ðonne grymetodan hī, 38, 1; Fox 194, 35: Met. 26, 82. Ongan sīðfæt seófian, sār cwānian, Exon. Th. 274, 22; Jul. 537. Synna bemǣnan and sārlīce sȳfian (sīf-, seóf-), Wulfst. 133, 14. Hū Boetius his sār seófiende wæs, Bt. tit. 2; Fox x, 4. ¶ with cognate accusative:—Seó seófung ðe ðū siófodost *the complaint you made*, 41, 3; Fox 246, 26. **II.** *intrans. To lament, complain of* (*be, ymbe*):—Hwæt (*why*) seófast ðū wið mē *quid igitur ingemiscis?* Bt. 7, 3; Fox 20, 14. Hī seófiaþ be heora feóndum, Ps. Th. 10, arg. Be Iudan Scarioth hē seófode tō Drihtne, 3, arg. Seófade, seáfade ł (ge)mǣnde *ingemescens*, Mk. Skt. Lind. Rush. 8, 12. Ceare seófedun ymb heortan, Exon. Th. 306, 20; Seef. 10. Ðā ongunnon ða hīwan seófian be ðære untrumnysse *cum familiares de infirmitate quererentur*, Bd. 3, 9; S. 534, 6. Ne sceal hē sȳfian (seófian, MS. T.) ne mǣnan ymb woruldspēda *ne causetur de minore substantia*, R. Ben. 14, 13. Seófende wæs *maerens erat*, Mk. Skt. Lind. Rush. 10, 22. Be ðæm Dryhten siófigende cwæð *unde Dominus queritur dicens*, Past. 48, 3; Swt. 369, 4. Sceal ic siófigende wōpe gewǣged wreccea giómor singan sārcwidas *flebilis moestos cogor inire modos*, Met. 2, 2. **III.** uncertain:—Sȳfaþ *causatur*, i. *querelatur, causam dicit*, Wrt. Voc. ii. 130, 10. Seófade *causavit*, 130, 11. Sȳfiende *cupide*, i. *avare*, 137, 36, 64. Seóbgendum *querulis*, 106, 9. [Cf. *O. H. Ger.* sūftōn *gemere, ingemiscere, suspirare*: *Ger.* seufzen.]

seofon, syfon; *when used without a following noun it is declined, nom., acc.* seofone; *g.* seofona; *d.* seofonum. *Seven*, (1) as adjective:—Mid ūs wǣron seofun (-on, MS. A.) gebrōðru, Mt. Kmbl. 22, 25. Ða seofon gōdan geár, Gen. 41, 53. His heres wæs seofon hund þūsenda, Ors. 2, 5; Swt. 78, 10. Seofon nihta fyrst, Elen. Kmbl. 1385; El. 694. On ðām seofon wæstmbǣron geárum, Gen. 41, 47. Hē ābād ōðre seofon dagas, 8, 10. Hē him tō genymþ seofun (-en, MS. A.: seofona, Lind.: siofun, Rush.) ōðre gāstas, Mt. Kmbl. 12, 45. (2) without a following noun:—Ðā nam se þridda hig, and swā ealle seofone (-ene, MS. A.: seofono, Lind.: ða siofune, Rush.), Lk. Skt. 20, 31. Ealle seofon (-en, MS. A.: -an, MS. B.: ða seofona, Lind.: ða siofune, Rush.) hī hæfdon, Mk. Skt. 12, 22. Hwylces ðara seofona biþ ðæt wīf, 12, 23. Hwylces ðæra sufona (seofena, MS. A.: of ðǣm seofonum, Lind.: ðara siofuna, Rush.), Mt. Kmbl. 22, 28. Ðā com seofona sum, Andr. Kmbl. 2623; An. 1313. Mid feáwum brōðrum, ðæt is seofonum oððe eahtum, Bd. 4, 3; S. 567,

4. Ðú seofone genim tudra gehwilces, Cd. Th. 80, 27; Gen. 1335. Geseh hē hyrdas standan seofone ætsomne, Andr. Kmbl. 1987; An. 996. Syfone, Beo. Th. 6235; B. 3122. [*Goth.* sibun: *O. Sax.* sibun: *O. Frs.* saven, sigun: *O. H. Ger.* sibun: *Icel.* sjau.]

seofon-feald; *adj. Sevenfold:*—Seofonfeald wracu biþ sealde for Cain and hundseofontig seofonfeald for Lamech, Gen. 4, 24. Hē onbryrt ūre mōd mid seofonfealdre gife, Homl. Th. i. 326, 12. Gyld seofonfealde wrace, Ps. Th. 78, 13: Gen. 4, 15. Him ofer wacedon syfanfealde weardes, Homl. Skt. i. 3, 271.

seofonfealdlīçe; *adv. Sevenfold, seven times:*—Geclǣsnad seofenfaldlīce *purgatum septuplum*, Ps. Surt. 11, 7: 78, 12.

seofon-leáfe, an; *f. Seven-leaves, setfoil;* potentilla tormentilla:—Seofenleáfe. Ðeós wyrt ðe man *eptafilon* and ōðrum naman *septifolium* nemneþ and eác sume men seofenleáfe, Lchdm. i. 232, 1-3. [Cf. *O. H. Ger.* sibun-blat *heptaphyllon.*]

seofon-nihte; *adj. Seven days old:*—Se .vii. nihta mōna is gōd on tō fixiane, Lchdm. iii. 178, 13. On .vii. nihtne mōnan, 178, 9.

seofon-stirre, es; *n. The Pleiades:*—Sifunsterre (sibun-) *pliadas*, Txts. 86, 762. [Cf. *O. H. Ger.* sibun-stirni, -stirri, es; *n. pliades, orion: Ger.* sieben-gestirn: *Icel.* sjau-stirni; *n. the Pleiades.*]

seofonteóþa, -teogoþa *seventeenth:*—Se wæs seofonteogeþa fram Agusto, Bd. 1, 5; S. 476, 6. Ðȳ seofonteóþan dæge, 3, 24; S. 557, 12. On ðone seofenteóþan dæge ðæs mōnþes, Gen. 7, 11. Seofontegðan, Shrn. 91, 32.

-seofontig. v. hund-seofontig.

seofon-tīne *seventeen:*—Æfter seofentȳnum nihtgerīmes, Menol. Fox 50; Men. 25. Hē lyfode seofentȳne gēr, Gen. 47, 28. Seofontȳne, Bd. 1, 5; S. 476, 7: 2, 15; S. 519, 13.

seofontīne-nihte; *adj. Seventeen days old:*—On .xvii. nihte mōne, Lchdm. iii. 180, 7.

seofon-wintre; *adj. Seven years old:*—Mid ðȳ ic wæs seofonwintre *cum essem annorum septem*, Bd. 5, 23; S. 647, 21. Ic wæs syfanwintre, Beo. Th. 4847; B. 2428. Ðā ðā hē syfonwintre wæs, Homl. Skt. i. 3, 5. [*Icel.* sjau-vetra *seven years old.*]

seofoþa *seventh:*—Tō ðære seofoþan (ðió seofunda, Lind.: ðȳ siofunda, Rush.) tīde, Jn. Skt. 4, 52. Ōþ ðone seofoþan (tō ðæm seofunda, Lind.: siofund, Rush.), Mt. Kmbl. 22, 26. On ðone seofeþan dæg, Gen. 2, 2.

seofoþa *bran.* v. sifeþu.

seófung, e; *f. Lamenting, complaining, complaint:*—Hwī biþ elles swelc seófung and swelce dōmas *unde forenses querimoniae?* Bt. 26, 2; Fox 92, 16. Ðis is seó ealde siófung ðe ðū longe siófodost (siófodes, Cott. MS.) *vetus haec est querela*, 41, 3; Fox 246, 25. Ne beó ðū tō ceástful; of irsunge wyxt seófung, Prov. Kmbl. 23. Ic ne mæg ādreóhan ðīne seófunga for ðam lytlan ðe ðū forlure, Bt. 11, 1; Fox 30, 20. Forlǣtan ða seófunga his eormþa *miseras fugare querelas*, 29, 3; Fox 106, 20: Met. 16, 7. v. sār-seófung; seófian.

seohhe, an; *f. A strainer:*—Seohhe *colatorium*, Wrt. Voc. i. 24, 52. Man sceal habban seohhan, Anglia ix. 264, 18. [A mylke syhe *colum*, Prompt. Parv. 79, note 1. A sigh-clout, Halliwell Dict. (*under* sie). Sye-dish *a milk-strainer*, E. D. S. Pub. country words, 6. Cf. *O. H. Ger.* sīha *colum, colatorium: Ger.* seche: *Icel.* sīa *a strainer.*] v. seón *to strain*, seohtre.

seoh-tor[r] (?), es; *m. A look-out place* (?):—Ofer ðone cnol tō ðæn seohtore (-torre?), Cod. Dip. Kmbl. iii. 451, 14.

seohtre, sihtre, an; *f. A pipe through which a small stream is directed, a drain:*—Andlang seohtran, Cod. Dip. B. i. 295, 11. Tō ðare reádan sihtran, 296, 28. In wǣtan sihtran (cf. sīce, 382, 7); of ðam wǣtan sīce, Cod. Dip. Kmbl. iii. 386, 10. Ad locum qui dicitur hylsan seohtra, 373, 12.

seol, seolc, seolcan, seolcen, seolc-wyrm, seolf. v. seolh, seoluc, ā-seolcan, seolucen, seoluc-wyrm, self.

seolfor, siolufr, silofr, sylfor (-er, -ur), es; *n. Silver:*—Seolfor *argentum*, Wrt. Voc. ii. 8, 52. Seolfer, i. 85, 7. Seolfur, Ps. Th. 134, 15. Feówer hund scillinga seolfres, Gen. 23, 16. Fīftig yntsena seolfres, Deut. 22, 29. Hwītes seolfres, Jos. 7, 21. Silofres, Salm. Kmbl. 62, MS. B.; Sal. 31. Siolufres (siolofres, Cott. MSS.), Past. 37; Swt. 269, 4. Tō siolofre, Swt. 266, 20. Ic sealde siolfor (sylofr, Cott. MSS.), 48; Swt. 369, 6. Silofr, Swt. 368, 20. Hwītan seolfre bētan, Cd. Th. 165, 14; Gen. 2731. Sylfore, Exon. Th. 395, 4; Rä. 15, 2. Næbbe gē seolfer (sulfer, Lind.: sylfur, Rush.), Mt. Kmbl. 10, 9. Wēnst ðū ðæt wē ðīnes hlāfordes seolfor stǣlon, Gen. 44, 8. Sealde him tō bōte gangende feoh and glæd seolfor, Cd. Th. 164, 24; Gen. 2719. [*Goth.* silubr: *O. Frs.* selover, selver, silver: *O. Sax.* silubar, silobar: *O. H. Ger.* silabar, silbar: *Icel.* silfr.] v. cwic-seolfor.

seolfor-fæt, es; *n. A vessel of silver:*—Seolforfatum *argenteis vasis*, Bd. 4, 1; S. 563, 21. [*O. H. Ger.* silbar-faz. Cf. *Icel.* silfr-bolli, *and many similar cpds.*]

seolfor-gewiht, es; *m. Silver-weight, the scale of weight by which silver is weighed*, where the pound is of sixteen ounces:—Se sester sceal wegan twā pund be sylfyrgewyht, Lchdm. iii. 92, 14. v. sester, II.

seolfor-hammen; *adj. Silver-coated:*—Ǣnne seolforhammenne blǣdhorn, Chart. Th. 559, 24.

seolfor-hilt; *adj. Silver-hilted:*—Ic geann mīnon brēðer ānes seolferhiltes swurdes, Chart. Th. 560, 10. Ðæs sealferhiltan swurdes ðe Ulfcytel āhte, 559, 13.

seolfor-hilted; *adj. Silver-hilted:*—Twā seolforhilted sweord, Chart. Th. 544, 4.

seolfor-smiþ, es; *m. A silver-smith, worker in silver:*—Seolforsmiþ *argentarius*, Wrt. Voc. i. 73, 31. Seolfersmiþ, 47, 13. Ic hæbbe smiþas ... seolforsmiþ *habeo fabros ... argentarium*, Coll. Monast. Th. 29, 35. [*O. H. Ger.* silbar-smid: *Icel.* silfr-smiðr.]

seolfor-stycce, es; *m. A piece of silver, a coin:*—Ðæt þrītig seolforsticca *the thirty pieces of silver* (*given to Judas*), Anglia xi. 8, 3.

seolfren, seolofren, seolfern, silfren, sylofren, sylfren; *adj. Silvern, of silver:*—Sylofren sinc, Met. 21, 21. Glæsen fæt on seolfrenre racenteáge, Blickl. Homl. 209, 4. In seolfren fæt belūcan, Elen. Kmbl. 2050; El. 1026. Hafaþ silfren (seolofren, MS. B.) leáf, Salm. Kmbl. 129; Sal. 64. Nim mīnne sylfrenan læfyl, Gen. 44, 2: Bd. 1, 25; S. 487, 3. Seolferne *silver coins*, Mt. Kmbl. p. 20, 2. Sylfrenu (selfrenu, Cott. MS.) fatu, Bt. 36, 1; Fox 172, 19. Ða seolfrenan stānas, 34, 8; Fox 144, 31. Sweopum seolfrynum, Salm. Kmbl. 287; Sal. 143. Sylfrenum, Homl. Th. ii. 212, 30. Ne wyrce gē sylfrene godas, Ex. 20, 23: 3, 22. [*Goth.* silubreins: *O. Frs.* selvirn: *O. Sax.* silubrin: *O. H. Ger.* silbarīn.]

seolfrian. v. be-, ofer-seolfrian.

seolh; *gen.* seoles; *m. A seal, sealgh, selcht* (v. Jamieson's Dict.), *sea-calf:*—Seolh *focca*, Wrt. Voc. ii. 149, 81: *bromus marinus*, i. 22, 54: *focus*, 281, 58. Seol *foca*, 55, 79: *focus*, ii. 38, 48. Ðās wyrt onsænde seolh ofer sǣs hrygc, Lchdm. iii. 34, 15. Of seoles hȳde, Ors. 1, 1; Swt. 18, 18. Sioles, 18, 23. Seolas *vituli marini*, Bd. 1, 1; S. 473, 16. [*O. H. Ger.* selah: *Icel.* selr.]

seolh-bæþ, es; *n. The seal's bath, the sea* (cf. fisces, ganotes bæþ):—Mec wind wīde bær ofer seolhbaþo, Exon. 392, 21; Rä. 11, 11.

seolh-wæd (?), -pæð (?), es; *n. The seal's ford, path, the sea:*—Hié on ȳðum æðelinga wunn ofer seolhwaðu (-wadu ?, -paðu ?) geseón mihton, Andr. Kmbl. 3424; An. 1716. Cf. *preceding word and* mearc-pæð, -wæd.

seolh-ȳða (?); *pl. The waves where the seal swims:*—Oferswam ðā sioleða (siolȳða? cf. flōda, holma begang. *Or* (?) sioleþ *still water.* Cf. *Goth.* ana-silan: *Swed. dial.* sil *still water.* v. Heyne's note) bigong sunu Ecgþeówes, Beo. Th. 4723; B. 2367.

seolofren. v. seolfren.

seoluc (-oc), seolc, es; *m. Silk:*—Seolc *sericum*, Wrt. Voc. i. 40, 2. Gōd geolo seoluc, Lchdm. ii. 10, 16: 106, 22. Seowa mid seolce fæste, smire mid ðære sealfe ǣr se seoloc rotige, 56, 7-8: 358, 25. Heora wǣda sioloce siowian, Met. 8, 24. Gyf man mǣte ðæt hē seoluc oððe godweb hæbbe, Lchdm. iii. 174, 29. [*Icel.* silki. *From Latin* sericum (?). But see Kluge, Etymol. Wörterb. under *seide.*]

seolucen, seolcen; *adj. Silken, of silk:*—Seolcen *bombicinum*, Wrt. Voc. i. 39, 72. Siolcen, ii. 11, 67: 75, 74. Seolcen gegerla *bombicinium*, 126, 50. Seolcen āb *tramasericum*, i. 40, 4. Seolce[n] hnygele *platum*, 40, 38. Silcen *serica*, Hpt. Gl. 417, 37. Seolocenra hrægla, Bt. 15; Fox 48, 11. v. eal-seolcen.

seoluc-wyrm, es; *m. A silk-worm:*—Siolucwyrm *bombix*, Wrt. Voc. ii. 12, 22. Seolcwyrm, i. 24, 6: 40, 1.

seomian, siomian, semian; *p.* ode *To rest.* (1) *to remain suspended, to hang, to lower* as a cloud:—Hit bærneþ boldgetimbru, seomaþ steáp, Salm. Kmbl. 827; Sal. 413. Deorc deáþscūa seomade *the dark shadow of death hung over them*, Beo. Th. 324; B. 161. Sum sceal on galgan rīdan, seomian æt swylte, Exon. 329, 14; Vy. 34. Mæst sceal on ceóle segelgyrd seomian *the mast shall be fixed in a boat and the yard hang from it*, Menol. Fox 509; Gn. C. 25. Hē siomian geseah segn, Beo. Th. 5527; B. 2767. Geseah deorc gesweorc semian, Cd. Th. 7, 20; Gen. 109. (2) *to remain supported, to lie* so as to press, *lie heavily, lie securely:*—Se wong seomaþ eádig and onsund, Exon. Th. 199, 2; Ph. 19. Seomaþ (-ad, MS.) wīr ymbe ðone wælgim, 400, 19; Rä. 21, 3. Seomaþ sorgcearig *lies troubled*, 285, 4; Jul. 709. Hē siomode in sorgum seofon nihta fyrst, Elen. Kmbl. 1384; El. 694. Flota stille bād, seomode on sole scip, Beo. Th. 609; B. 302. Heó on wrace seomodon, Cd. Th. 5, 15; Gen. 72. Him on healfa gehwam hettend seomedon mægen oððe merestreám *on each side of them lay foes pressing, the Egyptian force or the Red Sea*, 191, 4; Exod. 209. Ðǣr ic seomian wāt ðinne sigebrōðor *I know thy brother lies in prison there*, Andr. Kmbl. 365; An. 183.

seó-mint, *plant name*, altea *vel* eviscus, Wrt. Voc. i. 32, 12. v. sǣminte.

seón *to be:*—See *esse*, Mt. Kmbl. p. 1, 11. v. eom, sī.

seón; *p.* seah, *pl.* sāwon, sǣgon, sēgon; *pp.* sewen, sawen. I. *to see* with the eyes, (1) *with acc.:*—Oft ic wīg seó, Exon. Th. 388, 6; Rä. 6, 3. Ic seah wundorlīce wiht, 495, 1; Rä. 84, 1. Ne seah ic medudreám māran, Beo. Th. 4033; B. 2014. Hī wuldres þegn eágum sâwon, Andr. Kmbl. 3355; An. 1681. Ðæs ðe (hió) ælda bearn eágum sâwe, Exon. Th. 493, 7; Rä. 81, 26. Eode scealc monig searowundor seón, Beo. Th. 1844; B. 920: 2735; B. 1365: Cd. Th. 125, 25; Gen. 2084. (2) *with acc. and infin.*:—Ic seah turf tredan .vi. gebrōðor, Exon. Th. 394, 10; Rä. 14, 1: 400, 1; Rä. 20, 1: 414, 29; Rä. 33, 3: 434, 15; Rä. 52, 1. (3) *with acc. and predicative adj. or participle*:—Hȳ grim helle fȳr gearo tō wīte andweard seóþ, Exon. Th. 78, 8; Cri. 1271. Ne seah ic elþeódige mōdiglīcran, Beo. Th. 678; B. 336. Hȳ God upstīgende eágum sēgun, Exon. Th. 34, 3; Cri. 536. (4) *with clause*:—Hȳ on ða clǣnan seóþ, hū hī blissiaþ, Exon. 79, 6; Cri. 1286: Beo. Th. 5428; B. 2717. II. *to see, to visit*:—Nǣnig cēpa ne seah (geseah, Bt. 15; Fox 48, 13) ellendne wearod *nondum nova litora viderat hospes*, Met. 8, 29. Hāt in gān seón sibbegedriht, Beo. Th. 779; B. 387. Uton ēfstan seón and sēcean searogeþræc, 6195; B. 3102. II a. metaph.:—Hē heán gewāt deáþwīc seón, Beo. Th. 2555; B. 1275. III. *to see, perceive, discern, understand*:—Ic seó ðē, ðæt is, ðæt ic ongite ðīnne willan būtan tweón, Ps. Th. 5, 3. Sōðfæst blissaþ, ðonne hē sīþ hū ða ārleásan ealle forweorðaþ, 57, 9. Sioh nū sylfa ðē, hū ðec heofones cyning gesēceþ, Exon. Th. 4, 27; Cri. 59. Seh ðē *ecce*, Ps. Surt. 32, 18: 38, 6. Sih ðē, Mt. Kmbl. Rush. 19, 16, 27: 24, 25, 26. Wēnaþ ða dysgan, ðæt ǣlc mon sié blind swā hī sint, and ðæt nān mon ne mǣge seón (gesión, Cott. MS.) ðæt hī gesión ne māgon, Bt. 38, 5; Fox 206, 21. IV. *to see* (as in *to see* death), *to experience*:—Mec ongan hreówan ðæt moncynnes tuddor sceolde māncwealm seón, Exon. Th. 86, 33; Cri. 1417. Morðorleán seón, 98, 24; Cri. 1612. Hē forþ gewāt metodsceaft seón *he died*, Cd. Th. 104, 31; Gen. 1743: B. 2364; B. 1180. V. with prepositions, *to look* at, on:—On ðæt ða folc seóþ, Exon. Th. 80, 2; Cri. 1301. Seóþ on ēce gewyrht, 448, 29; Dōm. 61. Ealle synd gedrēfede ðe hī on sióþ *conturbati sunt omnes qui videbant eos*, Ps. Th. 63, 8. Secg seah on unleófe, Beo. Th. 5719; B. 2863. Folc tō sǣgon, 2849; B. 1422: Elen. Kmbl. 2208; El. 1105. Ðǣr hī tō sēgon, Andr. Kmbl. 1422; An. 711: Exon. Th. 260, 3; Jul. 291. Sēgun, 31, 14; Cri. 495. Hī cōmon on ðæt wundor seón, Cd. Th. 261, 25; Dan. 731. Fægre leomu on tō seónne, Blickl. Homl. 113, 22. [*Goth.* saihwan: *O. Sax.* sehan: *O. Frs.* sīa: *O. H. Ger.* sehan: *Icel.* sjá.] v. be- (bi-), for-, fore-, ge-, geond-, of-, ofer-, on-, þurh-, ymb-seón.

seón (*from* sīhan); *p.* sāh, *pl.* sigon; *pp.* sigen (cf. león), seowen (v. ā-seowen, Lchdm. ii. 26, 11), siwen (v. ā-siwen, Lchdm. ii. 124, 14), seón (v. bi-seón, Exon. Th. 67, 13; Cri. 1088). I. *trans. To strain, filter*:—Siid *excolat*, Wrt. Voc. ii. 107, 71. Seóh þurh clāþ, Lchdm. ii. 24, 1: iii. 14, 18. II. *intrans. To run* as a sore, *ooze, trickle*:—Manegum men liþseáu sȳhþ, Lchdm. ii. 132, 10. Ðæt se lǣce sceolde āsceótan ðæt geswell; ðā dyde hē swā, and ðǣr sāh ūt wyrms, Homl. Skt. i. 20, 64. Wið seóndre exe, Lchdm. iii. 70, 20. Wið seóndum geallan, Lchdm. ii. 314, 7, 10. Wið seóndum ōmum, 102, 9. Eal ðæt folc wæs on blǣdran and ða wǣron berstende and ða worms ūt sióndе (*ulcera manantia*), Ors. 1, 7; Swt. 38, 7. [Mid þornene crune his heaued was icruned, swa þet þet rede blod seh ut on iwulche half, O. E. Homl. i. 121, 12. Syynge or clensynge *colacio, colatura*, Prompt. Parv. 455. I sye mylke, Cath. Ang. 339, n. 3. Halliwell gives *sie* as a word still in use in Derbyshire. *O. H. Ger.* sīhan *colare, excolare, liquare*: *Ger.* seihen: *Icel.* sía *to strain.*] v. ā-, ge-seón; seohhe, sīgan.

seón; seondon, -seonod. v. sīn, wlite-, wundor-seón; sind, ā-seonod.

seonoþ, sionoþ, senoþ, sinoþ, synoþ (-aþ, -od), es; *m. A synod, council, meeting*:—Sinoþ *sinodus*, Wrt. Voc. i. 72, 76. I. mostly used of the councils of the Christian Church:—Seonod (sinoþ) wæs æt Ācleá, Chr. 782; Erl. 57, 6. Wæs senoþ (sinoþ, MS. E.) æt Heorotforda, 673; Erl. 56, 2: 822; Erl. 62, 13. Hēr wæs geflitfullīc senoþ æt Cealchȳþe, 785; Erl. 56, 7. Se hālga sinoþ, Bd. 4, 17; S. 585, 41. Ǣfter ealles sinoþes dōme, 3, 7; S. 530, 35. Be ðæm sinoþe se wæs geworden on ðam felda se wæs genemned Hǣþfeld, 4, 17; S. 585, 7. On ðam miclan synoþ æt Greátanleáge, L. Ath. i. 26; Th. i. 214, 7. Eádmund cyning gesomnode micelne sinoþ tō Lundenbyrig ǣgðer ge godcundra hāda ge woruldcunda, L. Edm. E. proem.; Th. i. 244, 2. Gif preóst sinoþ forbūge, gebēte ðæt, L. N. P. L. 44; Th. ii. 296, 16. Monega þeóda Cristes geleáfan onfēngon; ðā wurdon monega seonoþas gegaderode, L. Alf. 49; Th. i. 58, 2. Ðās feówer sinoþas (*the councils of Nice, Ephesus, Constantinople, and Chalcedon*), Wulfst. 270, 15. II. in other senses:—Bǣdon ðæt eft ōðer seonaþ wǣre (*of the meeting between Augustine and the British Christians*), Bd. 2, 2; S. 502, 36. Tō sionoþe (*the Council called by Constantine to enquire about the cross*), Elen. Kmbl. 307; El. 154. Hig tō ðæra Iudēa synoþe cōmon, Nicod. 18; Thw. 8. 31. Wile fæder engla seonoþ gehēgan Exon. Th. 231, 23; Ph. 493. [The word is borrowed also by *O. Frs.* and *O. H. Ger.*] v. bisceop-seonoþ, *and following words.*

seonoþ-bóc; *f. A book containing the decrees of a synod*:—Hié on monegum senoþum monegra menniscra misdǣda bōte gesetton, and on monega senoþbēc hȳ writon, hwǣr ānne dōm, hwǣr ōðerne, L. Alf. 49; Th. i. 58, 15.

seonoþ-dóm, es; *m. The decree of a synod*:—Seonoþdōmas reccan, Elen. Kembl. 1101; El. 552.

seonoþlīc; *adj. Synodal, of a synod* or *meeting*:—Ðā wæs sionoþlīc gemōt, Chart. Th. 70, 10. Ðære sinoþlīcan dǣde *synodicae actionis*, Bd. 4, 5; S. 572, 1. Mid sinoþlīcum stafum *synodalibus literis*, 4, 17; S. 585, 15.

seonoþ-stów, e; *f. A place for a synod* or *meeting, a place of assembly*:—Sinaþstōw *conciliabulum, locus sinodalis*, Wrt. Voc. ii. 136, 19. Geseóþ gē ðæt hē ǣrest tō ðære sinoþstōwe (*ad locum synodi*) cymeþ, Bd. 2, 2; S. 503, 9.

seonu, sionu, senu, sinu, synu; *gen.* seonwe, sine; *weak forms also occur*; *f. A sinew, nerve, tendon*:—Sionu *nervus*, Wrt. Voc. ii. 114, 67. Sinu, i. 71, 42. Gif sin[o] scrince . . . and gif sino clæppette, Lchdm. ii. 6, 13–15. Ðā æthrān hē his sine on his þeó *tetigit nervum femoris ejus*, Gen. 32, 25. Healt for ðære sinwe (synewe, MS. B.) wunde, L. Alf. pol. 75; Th. i. 100, 5. Gif man on sinwe besleá æt blōdlǣtan, Lchdm. ii. 16, 8. Gif mon ða greátan sinwe (synewe, MS. B.) forsleá, L. Alf. pol. 75; Th. i. 100, 3. Gif ða smalan sinwe (synewan, MS. B.) mon forsleá, 76; Th. i. 100, 8. Nellaþ folc etan sine (*nervum*), Gen. 32, 32. Seonuwa [beóþ] fortogene, Lchdm. iii. 48, 28: 50, 5. Seonowe onsprungon, Beo. Th. 1639; B. 817. Seonwe (sina, Soul Kmbl. 217), Exon. Th. 373, 19; Seel. 111. Sionwe, Andr. Kmbl. 2849; An. 1427. Senwe *nerve*, Wrt. Voc. i. 283, 37. Sena, 65, 15. Sinu (-a ?), 44, 23. Gif sinwe sȳn forcorfene, Lchdm. ii. 328, 5. Wið sina sāre, i. 84, 10. Wið ðara sina bifunge, 104, 27. Sina togung, 136, 9. Syna, 136, 19. Sina getog, 356, 3. Seonowum beslītan, Exon. Th. 371, 9; Seel. 73. Seonwum (synum, Soul Kmbl. 123), 370, 20; Seel. 62. Mid rāpum of sinum geworhte *nerviceis funibus*, Jud. 16, 7. Se līchama wæs geboren mid blōde and mid bānum, mid felle and mid sinum, Homl. Th. ii. 270, 19. Ārǣran of duste flǣsc and bān, sina and fex, i. 236, 21. On ða sāran sinua, Lchdm. ii. 282, 6. For flǣsc and for bān and for sinuwan, L. Edg. C. 9; Th. ii. 264, 4. Sinuwa, Anglia xi. 101, 47. [*C. Frs.* sini(-e), sene, sin: *O. H. Ger.* senawa: *Icel.* sin; *pl.* sinar and sinur.] v. hōh-sinu.

seonu-ben[n], e; *f. A wound* or *injury of a sinew*:—Seonobennum seóc *crippled*, Exon. Th. 328, 17; Vy. 19. v. next word.

seonu-bend (?), e; *f. A bond made of sinews* (?):—Siððan hine Nīðhād on nēde legde swoncre seonobende (Grein would read *-benne*, which is more in accordance with the story in the Edda, that Völund had the sinews of the knees cut: v. Thorpe's note on this passage, and his Northern Mythology, i. 86. For confusion of *benne* and *bende* see *ben*), Exon. Th. 377, 19; Deór. 6. v. preceding word.

seonu-dolh, es; *n. A wound of a sinew*:—Benna weallaþ, seonodolg swātige, Andr. Kmbl. 2811; An. 1408.

seonu-wealt (sionu-, sinu-, sino-, sine-, sin-, syne-); *adj. That may be always rolled, round*:—Sinewealt gesceap *volubile scema*, Wrt. Voc. i. 55, 18. Sionuualt *torosa* (*teres?*), ii. 122, 54. Sionewaltum *conteriti* (*cum teriti?*), 21, 56. I. *round, circular, cylindrical*:—Sinewealt cleofa *absida*, Wrt. Voc. i. 58, 34. Syneweald wafungstede *amphitheatrum*, 37, 1. Sineweald trendel *circulus*, Hpt. Gl. 418, 16. Se mōna went his hrigc tō ðære sunnan, ðæt is, se sinewealta ende ðe ðǣr onlȳht biþ, Lchdm. iii. 242, 14. Ðæs sinewealtan hringes *teretes*(*-is?*) *cycli*, Wrt. Voc. ii. 89, 60. Timbredon men seonewalte (cf. cyrice is sinhwyrfel . . . seó is unoferhrēfed, Blickl. Homl. 125, 21) cirican, Shrn. 80, 37. Hæfde ðæt deór seonowealt heáfod swelce mōna, Nar. 20, 27. Heó is leáfun sinewealton, Lchdm. i. 290, 8, 18. II. *round, spherical, globular*, of a building, *having a concave roof* or *dome*:—Seó heofon is sinewealt, Lchdm. iii. 232, 20: Boutr. Scrd. 18, 24. Sineweald cliuen *rotundus, teres globus*, Hpt. Gl. 446, 67. Corn sonuuald (*the manna eaten in the desert*), Jn. Skt. Lind. 6, 31, rubc. Hyre wyrttruma ys syneweald *the root is a bulb*, Lchdm. i. 152, 16. Seó byrgen (*Christ's tomb*) is sinowalt hūs ācorfen of ānum stāne, Shrn. 68, 35. Of sinuwealtum cliwene *ex teriti glomere*, Wrt. Voc. ii. 31, 20: 83, 19. Sinewæltum, Hpt. Gl. 494, 17. Wyrc hit sinewealt *make it into a ball*, Lchdm. i. 72, 21. Sinwealte swammas *volvi*, Wrt. Voc. i. 30, 28. Heó hafaþ berian synewealte, Lchdm. i. 276, 24. v. sin-, sin-hweorfol.

seonuwealtian *to reel, not to stand firmly*:—Sinewealtigan (wine-, Wrt.) *vacillare*, Wrt. Voc. ii. 88, 48.

seonuwealtness, e; *f. Roundness, circularity, sphericity*:—Sinewealtnes *globositas*, Wrt. Voc. i. 55, 19. Ðære eorþan sinewealtnes *the sphericity of the earth*, Lchdm. iii. 258, 10. For ðære eorþan sinewealtynysse, 260, 11.

seonu-wind *an artery*:—Sinewind *arteriae*, Wrt. Voc. ii. 8, 29. [Cf. (?) *O. H. Ger.* sen-ādra *arteria, nervus.*] Cf. wind-ǣdre, sin-.

seorðan, seordan (?); *p.* searð *To violate*:—Ne serð ðū ōðres monnes wīf *non moechaberis*, Mt. Kmbl. Lind. 5, 27. [From (?) Scandinavian. Cf. *Icel.* serða *stuprare*: *M. H. Ger.* serte. See Altdeutsche Gespräche. Nachtrag vom W. Grimm, p. 18.]

seóslig; *adj. Afflicted, troubled, vexed*:—Se hālga wer ælda gehwylces ðe hine seóslige sōhtun hǣlde līc and sāwle *the holy man healed body and soul of all that in affliction sought him*, Exon. Th. 157, 29; Gū. 899. Cf. sūsl.

-seóþa. v. newe-seóþa.

seóđan (? cf. seód, â-seódan?) *to put in a bag, wrap up*:—Bewind đone æppel on weolcreádum godwebbe, and seóđ eft mid sceáte ôđres godwebbes, and beheald đæt đes lǽcedôm ne hrîne ne wæteres ne eorþan, Lchdm. i. 332, 5.

seóþan; *p.* seáþ, *pl.* sudon; *pp.* soden. I. *to seethe, boil, cook in a liquid*:—Ic seóþe *coquo*, Ælfc. Gr. 28, 5; Zup. 175, 16. Gif đû seóþest rûdan on ele, Lchdm. ii. 206, 23. Gif mon sýþ gârleác on henne broþe, Lchdm. ii. 276, 15. Seóþ on wætere tô þriddan dǽle, i. 72, 2. Seóþ on wîne, 134, 4. Seóþaþ (*coquite*) eówerne mete beforan đæs temples dura, Lev. 8, 31. Seóþe on strangum wîne, Lchdm. i. 142, 2. Seóþan đa þingc đe tô seóþenne synd *coquere quae coquenda sunt*, Coll. Monast. Th. 29, 19. II. metaph. (1) with the idea of purification, *to subject to a fiery ordeal, to try as with fire*:—Seóþeþ swearta lêg synne on fordônum . . . ôþ đæt hafaþ ældes leóma woruldwidles wom forbærned, Exon. Th. 62, 1; Cri. 995. Đû mê sude mid đam fýre monegra earfoþa swâ swâ gold *igne me examinasti*, Ps. Th. 16, 3. (2) *to subject to great pain, to afflict grievously*:—Mê elþeódige searonet seóþaþ *me barbarian snares afflict* (?), Andr. Kmbl. 127; An. 64. Mid đý hê đâ lange mid swîgendum nearonessum his môdes and mid đý blindan fýre soden wæs *cum diu tacitis mentes angoribus et caeco carperetur igni*, Bd. 2, 13; S. 513, 34. Herebryht wæs mid singale untrumnesse soden and swenced, 4, 29; S. 607, 41. Sorgwylmum soden, Exon. Th. 166, 21; Gû. 1046: 171, 7; Gû. 1123: 177, 32; Gû. 1236. Sârbennum soden, Andr. Kmbl. 2479; An. 1241. (2 a) *to reduce* by pain or disease:—Heó swâ swýđe mid đa untrumnysse soden wæs đæt đa bân ân tô lâfe wǽron *in tantum ea infirmitate decocta est, ut vix ossibus haereret*, Bd. 4, 9; S. 577, 15. (3) *to prepare food for the mind, to make fear, hope*, etc., *subjects with which the mind may be occupied*; cf. to feed a person with hopes:—Ic đæs môdceare sorhwylmum seáþ *on account of your dangerous journey anxiety was the food I prepared for my mind*, Beo. Th. 3990; 1993. Swâ đa mǽlceare maga Healfdenes singala seáþ *Hrothgar had that care ever ready to feed his mind with*, 382; B. 190. [*O. Frs.* siatha: *O. H. Ger.* siodan: *Icel.* sjóða: cf. Goth. sauths *a burnt-offering*.] v. â-, be-, for-, ofer-, tô-seóþan; ge-, healf-, sâm-, un-soden.

seođđan, seotl, seotol, seotu, seóung. v. siđđan, setl, sweotol, set, eág-seóung.

seowian, seówan, siwian; *p.* ode; *pp.* od, ed, id *To sew*:—Sióuu *sarcio*, Wrt. Voc. ii. 119, 52. Ic siwige *sarcio*, Ælfc. Gr. 30, 2; Zup. 190, 6. Ic sywige (siwige, MS. R.), 28, 3; Zup. 167, 6. Heó siwaþ (seowaþ, MS. U.) *illa suit*, 15; Zup. 97, 6. Siwaþ (siuieþ, Lind.: siowes, Rush.) *assuit*, Mk. Skt. 2, 21. Sum sûtere siwode (seowode, MS. C.) đæs hâlgan weres sceós, Homl. Skt. i. 15, 23. Hig siwodon fîcleáf and worhton him wǽdbrêc, Gen. 3, 7. Seowa mid seolce fæste, Lchdm. ii. 56, 7. Wǽda sioloce siowian, Met. 8, 24. Byrne, searonet seowed smiþes orþancum, Beo. Th. 816; B. 406. Golde siowode *segmentata*, Wrt. Voc. ii. 95, 49. [*Goth.* siujan: *O. Frs.* sia: *O. H. Ger.* siuwan: *Icel.* sýja: *Lat.* suere.] v. â-, be-seowian (-siwian); ge-seówan; ge-siwed.

sêpan (seppan?); *p.* te *To cause to perceive, to teach*:—Se stân sêpte sacerdas sweotolum tâcnum, Andr. Kmbl. 1483; An. 743. Đus mê fæder mîn unweaxenne wordum lǽrde, sêpte sôđcwidum, Elen. Kmbl. 1057; El. 530. Hyssas heredon Drihten for đam hǽđenan folce, sêpton (MS. stepton) hié sôđcwidum, and him sǽdon fela sôđra tâcna, Cd. Th. 244, 10; Dan. 446. [Cf. (?) *O. Sax.* af-sebbian; *p.* -sôf *to perceive*: *O. H. Ger.* int-suab; *p.*: *M. H. Ger.* en-seben *to perceive, understand*. v. Grff. vi. 168.]

serc, syrc, syric, es; *m.*: serce, syrce, an; *f. A shirt, shift, smock, tunic, sark* (Scott.):—Lođa, serc *colobium*, Hpt. Gl. 493, 76. Smoc *vel* syrc, Wrt. Voc. i. 25, 60. Syric *colobium* vel *interula*, 81, 69. Syrc *suppar, interula*, 59, 24. Serc *armilausia*, 284, 61: ii. 8, 16. Serce, 100, 77: 7, 4. Swâtfâh syrce, Beo. Th. 2226; B. 1111. Đæt hê hæbbe syric (*tunicam*), R. Ben. 89, 10. Genôh is munuce đæt hê hæbbe twegen syricas (*tunicas*), for đære nihtware and for đæs reáfes þweále, 91, 3. Syrcan, gûþgewǽdo *shirts of mail*, Beo. Th. 458; B. 226: 673; B. 334. [*Icel.* serkr *a shirt*; hring-, járn-serkr *a shirt of mail*.] v. beadu-, heoru-, here-, hilde-, leoþu-, lîc-, under-serc (-serce).

serede, serđ, serwan. v. sirwan, seorđan, sirwan.

sess, es; *m. A seat, bench*:—Ses, sæs *transtrum*, Txts. 103, 2050. Hê gesæt on sesse, Beo. Th. 5427; B. 2717: 5506; B. 2756. [*Icel.* sess; *m.*]

sessian; *p.* ode *To subside*:—Sǽ sessade (sǽs essade, MS.), smylte wurdon merestreáma gemeotu, Andr. Kmbl. 905; An. 453.

sester, seoxter, es; *m.* I. *a vessel, jar, pitcher*:—Sester *amfora*, Wrt. Voc. i. 24, 36: 83, 23. Hê hêt heora ǽlcne geniman ânne æmtigne sester . . . Hig slôgon tôgædere đa sestras (*lagenas*), Jud. 7, 16–19. Cristallisce drynciatu and gyldne sestras wǽron forþborenne *crystallina vasa potatoria et sextariola aurea invenimus*, Nar. 5, 14. II. *a measure* for liquids or for dry things; its capacity is uncertain. (a) as an English measure:—Twegen sestres sâpan and twege[n] hunies and þrê ecedes, and se sester sceal wegan twâ pund be sylfyrgewyht, Lchdm. iii. 92, 14. Cf. Unum sextarium mellis triginta duarum unciarum, Cod. Dip. Kmbl. iv. 285, 1. Wæs swýđe mycel hungor, and corn swâ dýre, swâ nân mann ǽr ne gemunde, swâ đæt se sester (*Henry of Huntingdon renders this*: '*sextarius frumenti, qui equo uni solet esse oneri*') hwǽtes eode tô .lx. penega and eác furđor, Chr. 1043; Erl. 169, 31. xv pund (yntsan? cf. 'sextarius medicinalis habet uncias decem,' note on this passage) wætres gâþ tô sestre, Lchdm. ii. 298, 26. Fîftêne sestras lîđes aloþ, Chart. Th. 105, 12. Twelf seoxtres beóras, 158, 22. (b) as a foreign measure:—Under sestre *sub modio*, Mt. Kmbl. Lind. 5, 15. Hund sestra (*cados*) eles, Lk. Skt. 16, 6. Ǽlc wæterfæt wæs on twegra sestra gemete ođđe on þreora *capientes singuli metretas binas uel ternas*, Jn. Skt. 2, 6. Gecned þrî sestras (*sata*) smedeman, Gen. 18, 6. Habbaþ emne gemetu and sestras *sint justus modius aequusque sextarius*, Lev. 19, 36. [*O. H. Ger.* sehstâri, sehtâri: *Ger.* sester, sechter *a measure of grain, twelve bushels; measure of liquids, sixteen quarts. From Lat.* sextarius. Cf. *Fr.* sêtier (*for grain*) *twelve bushels; for liquids, two gallons*: *Ital.* sestiere *a pint-measure*.] v. wîn-sester.

set, es; *n. A seat.* I. of the sun, *the place where the sun sets*:—Miđđý tô sete eode sunne *cum occidisset sol*, Mk. Skt. Rush. 1, 32. Gewât sunne tô sete glîdan, Andr. Kmbl. 2498; An. 1250: 2610; An. 1306. Tô sete sîgeþ, Menol. Fox 221; Men. 112. Cf. set-gang, setl. II. of men, *a place where people remain*, of an army, *a camp, entrenchment*, cf. to *sit* down before a place:—Ne com se here oftor eall ûte of đǽm setum đonne tuwwa, ôđre sîþe đâ hié ǽrest tô londe cômon . . . ôđre sîþe đâ hié of đǽm setum faran woldon (cf. Đa Deniscan sǽton đǽr behindan, 91, 1), Chr. 894; Erl. 90, 19–22. III. of animals, *a place where animals are kept, a stall, fold*, or *where they feed, pastures*:—Seotu *bucitum* (cf. hrýđra fald *bucetum*, Wrt. Voc. i. 15, 22), Txts. 47, 339. Seto *stabula*, 99, 1903. Siota, Wrt. Voc. i. 289, 11. ['In sedibus quies imperturbata.' I þe sette is reste & eise bitocned, A. R. 358, 23. Þat folc hafden alle iȝeten and arisen from heore seten, Laym. 30841. *O. H. Ger.* sez *sedes, suggestus*: *Icel.* set *the sitting-room*, v. Cl. & Vig. Dict.] v. ge-set, -sete (*read* -set), ymb-set.

sêta (seta?), setel. v. sǽta, setl.

seten, [n]e; *f.* I. *a set, shoot, branch*:—Setene *propagines*, Ps. Surt. 79, 12. v. ymb-seten. II. *a nursery, plantation*:—Setin *pla[n]taria*, Wrt. Voc. ii. 117, 49. Plantunga seten *plantaria*, 65, 76. Ǽghwilc wæstma seten đa đe ne sette fæder mîn *omnis plantatio quam non plantavit Pater meus*, Mt. Kmbl. Lind. 15, 13. III. *what is planted* or *set*:—Gif mon gesîđcundne monnan âdrîfe, fordrîfe đý botle næs đære setene (*the ejected tenant was not to be deprived of what he had planted* (?); *or* seten, V, *he was to be compensated for the cultivation of the land* (?)), L. In. 68; Th. i. 146, 8. IV. *a cultivated place.* v. land-seten, I, *and* feldsætennum *campo*, Ps. Lamb. 77, 12. V. *planting, cultivation.* v. land-seten, II. VI. *a setting, putting.* v. hand-seten. VII. *a stopping.* v. blôd-seten. *See also* in-seten.

-setenness, sêtere. v. ge-setenes, on-setenness, sǽtere.

set-gang, es; *m. Setting* of the sun:—Ofer setgong *super occasum*, Ps. Surt. 67, 5: 49, 2: 103, 19. v. set, setl-gang.

sêđan; *p.* de *To declare true, affirm, attest, prove*:—Ic sêđe *testificor*, Ælfc. Gr. 25; Zup. 146, 3. Ealle hâlige gewritu sôđlîce sêđaþ, đæt se is Hǽlend Crist, Homl. Th. ii. 414, 9. Hê ârâs on đam þriddan dæge, swâ swâ gewritu sêđaþ, 598, 4. Sum ôđer sêđde and cwæþ *alius quidam affirmabat dicens*, Lk. Skt. 22, 59. Is sêđende and cweđende *adstipulatur*, Wrt. Voc. ii. 2, 17. Sume (*adverbs*) syndon *con- vel adfirmativa*, đæt synd fæstnigende ođđe sêđende, Ælfc. Gr. 38; Zup. 226, 11. Sêđende đæt Crist is Godes Sunu '*proving that this is very Christ*' (Acts 9, 22), Homl. Th. i. 388, 4. v. â-, ge-sêđan; sôđian, sêđend, sêđung.

seđe, Cd. Th. 92, 7; Gen. 1525: sedel. v. sêcan, I (2), setl.

sêđend, es; *m. One who affirms* or *asserts*:—Sêđend *stipulatorem* (cf. trymmend *stipulatorem*, Wrt. Voc. ii. 88, 2), Hpt Gl. 527, 34. v. ge-sêđend.

set-hrægl, es; *n. A cloth for covering a seat*:—Setrægl *tapeta*, Wrt. Voc. i. 82, 19. Ic gean tô Cristes weofede ânre lytlere goldenre rôde and ânes sethrægles (*an altar-cloth?*), Chart. Th. 564, 10, 18. Ân lang healwâhrift and þrió sethrægl, 538, 4. [Cf. *Icel.* set-klæđi.] v. setl-hrægl.

sêđung, e; *f. Attestation, affirmation, proof*:—Sêđunge *adstipulatione, adsertione, adfirmatione*, Hpt. Gl. 444, 41. Hwæne mǽrsiaþ đâs wundra mid heora sêđunge, Homl. Th. ii. 34, 5. Hê đæs ârleásan eáre gehǽlde tô sêđunge sôđre godcundnysse (*in proof of true divinity*), 248, 2. Hê heora goda geendunge mid swutelum sêđungum gewissode, i. 558, 16. Sêđingum *assertionibus*, Hpt. Gl. 525, 35. Sêđincgum, 409, 53. v. ge-sêđung; sêđan.

setin. v. seten.

setl, sedl, sedl, seotl, sotl, seatl, sitl (-el, -ol, -ul), es; *pl.* setl, setlu, sotelas, setlas (*North.*); *n. m.* (?) I. *that on which one sits, a settle, seat, place to sit*:—Setl *sella*, Wrt. Voc. i. 83, 70. Sotol, 289, 23. Gâ nû tô setle, symbelwynne dreóh' . . . Geât geóng sôna setles neósan, swâ se snottra hêht, Beo. Th. 3576; B. 1786. Se wæs setles yldest (on setle yldost, MS. B.) *he had the chief seat,* Bd. 5, 13; S. 633, 4. Sæt Agustinus on sotole, 2, 2; S. 503, 15. Hē hēt him ūte setl gewyrcean, 1, 25; S. 486, 38. Mē hē wiđ his sylfes sunu setl getǣhte, Beo. Th. 4031; B. 2013. Ofer setol *super sellam,* Kent. Gl. 304. Sotelas *sella,* Germ. 393, 143. Seó wlitignes heora ræsta and setla, Blickl. Homl. 99, 33. Hē his līchoman forwyrnde sēftra setla and symbeldaga, Exon. Th. 111, 33; Gū. 136. On đæm forþmestum seatlum (seotlum, Rush.) sitta in somnungum and đa forþmesto setla æt farmum *in primis cathedris sedere in sinagogis et primos discubitos in cenis,* Mt. Skt. Lind. 12, 39. Hē ūt āwearp đa setl đara mynetera, Blickl. Homl. 71, 19. Hyra setlu (ceatlas, Lind.: settlas, Rush. *cathedras*) đara đe culfran sealdon hē tōbræc, Mt. Kmbl. 21, 12. Lufigaþ đæt ǣreste sætil (*recubitos*) æt ēfengereordum and forþmestu setulas (seatlas, Lind. *cathedras*) on heora somnungum, Rush. 23, 6. Seotlas, Mk. Skt. Rush. 11, 15. Đa yldstan setl (seatlas, Lind., Rush.), Lk. Skt. 20, 46. **I a.** *an official seat* of a king, judge, etc., *a throne, judgment-seat:*—On swīđre sedles Godes, Rtl. 27, 33. Fore sedle *before the throne,* 47, 26. Đū Scippend heofones đū đe on đam ēcan setle rīcsast, Bt. 4; Fox 6, 30. Setle *solio,* Wrt. Voc. ii. 142, 13. Đonne sitt hē ofer his mægenþrymme setl (seđel, Lind.: on sedle, Rush.), Mt. Kmbl. 25, 31. Hit is swīđe gewunelīc đætte dōmeras & rīce menn on setelum sitten, Past. 56; Swt. 435, 21. Gē sittaþ ofer twelf setl (seatla tuelfa, Lind.: on sedlum twelfe, Rush.) dēmende, Mt. Kmbl. 19, 28. **I b.** metaph. *seat, place, position:*—Hē āwearp đa rīcan of setle (sedle, Lind., Rush.), Lk. Skt. 1, 52. Se sit on wōles setle, se đe yfel wyrcþ mid geþeahte, Past. 56; Swt. 435, 19–22: Ps. Th. 1, 1. Đū setst ūs on đæt setl đīnes Sceoppendes, Bt. 7, 5; Fox 24, 2. Ofer seatul (on setule, Rush.) Moyses, Mt. Kmbl. Lind. 23, 2. Him sylþ God his fæder Dauides setl (sedle, Lind.: seđel, Rush.), Lk. Skt. 1, 32. On sotelum sōđfæstra *in cathedra seniorum,* Ps. Th. 106, 31. **I c.** *in reference to the heavenly bodies,* tō setle gān, etc. (cf. *Fr.* le coucher du soleil, le soleil se couche) *to set:*—Syđđan sunne beó on setle *after sunset,* Lchdm. iii. 8, 19. Đonne heó (*the sun*) tō setle gǣþ, Bt. 39, 3; Fox 214, 27: Salm. Kmbl. 186, 6. Đā đā sunne eode tō setl *cum occubuisset sol,* Gen. 15, 17. Ǣr sunne tō setle eode *usque ad occasum solis,* Ex. 17, 12. Đā sunne tō setle eode *cum occidisset sol,* Mk. Skt. 1, 32. Sunne sāh tō setle, Chr. 937; Erl. 112, 17. Đonne heó (*the sun*) on setl eode, Bt. 5, 23; S. 645, 26. Đonne hió on setl glīdeþ, Met. 28, 39. Se ǣfenstiorra on setl glīdeþ, 29, 27, 31. On setel, Salm. Kmbl. 202, 34. v. setl-gang. **II.** *a seat, place where one abides, an abode, a residence, dwelling:*—Him wæs geseald setl on swegle đǣr hē symle mōt eardfæst wesan, blīđe bīdan, Exon. Th. 149, 5; Gū. 757: 125, 15; Gū. 354. Geswīc đisses setles, 119, 3; Gū. 249. Đa stōwe his seþles *locum sedis illius solitariae,* Bd. 3, 16; S. 542, 36. Hē eft tō đæm fæderlīcan setle eode, Blickl. Homl. 115, 33: 129, 12. Đā næfde hē nān setl hwǣr hē sittan mihte, for đan đe nān heofon nolde hine āberan, Ælfc. T. Grn. 2, 45: Ps. Th. 88, 37: Exon. Th. 116, 31; Gū. 215. On prēstes setel (*a hermitage?*), Cod. Dip. Kmbl. iii. 416, 29. Đa hālgan setl sceoldon weorþan gefylde mid đære menniscan gecynde, Blickl. Homl. 121, 34: Cd. Th. 6, 10; Gen. 86. Gumena rīce, secga sitlu, Met. 9, 42. ¶ *a stall* for animals:—On đam (*in the ark*) đū scealt gerȳman rihte setl ǣlcum eorþan tudre, Cd. Th. 79, 1; Gen. 1304. **II a.** as an ecclesiastical term, *a see:*—Sanctus Gregorius đæs Rōmāniscan setles bisceop, Lchdm. iii. 432, 24. Đæs Apostolīcan setles, Bd. 1, 23; S. 485, 23: 4, 1; S. 563, 23. Hēr Rōmāne đone pāpan of his setle āfliémde, Chr. 797; Erl. 58, 14. On setl biscopstōles *in sedem pontificatus,* 5, 23; S. 646, 32. **II b.** metaph. *seat* of a disorder, etc., *dwelling-place* of non-material things:—Đȳ læs ingǣ se fiónd in sāuelo hiora & seđel habba ne mǣgi, Rtl. 117, 31. **III.** *the part of the body on which one sits, the seat:*—Wiđ gicþan đæs setles, Lchdm. i. 218, 10. Gif se uīc weorđe on mannes setle geseten, iii. 30, 16. Wrīđ under đæt setl neoþan, i. 366, 17. Him wand ūt his innoþ æt his setle, Homl. As. 59, 201. **IV.** *a sitting, the being in,* or *assuming, a sitting position;* sessio:—Hē frægn for hwon hē āna swā unrōt on stāne wæccende sǣte . . . 'Ne tala đū đæt ic ne cunne đone intingan đīnre unrōtnesse and đīnre wacone and ānlēpnesse đīnes setles' *ne me aestimes tuae moestitiae & insomniorum & solitariae sessionis causam nescire,* Bd. 2, 12; S. 513, 41 note. Đū mīn setl (*sessionem*) oncneówe and mīnne ǣrist æfter gecȳđdest, Ps. Th. 138, 1. **IV a.** *stay, residence:*—On đæm setle đe hē đǣr sæt *during the stay he made there,* Chr. 922; Erl. 108, 22. **IV b.** as a military term, *a siege:*—Him (*the besiegers*) đæt setl (*obsidio*) swīđor derede đonne đām đe đǣrinne (*in Veii*) wǣron, Ors. 2, 8; Swt. 90, 24. Porsenna đæt setl forlēt *Porsenna raised the siege,* 2, 3; Swt. 68, 30. Đā forlēt hē đæt setl *ab obsidione discessit,* 3, 11; Swt. 146, 20. [Heo isetten Iacob on Cristes selt, O. E. Homl. i. 93, 9. Adam set on the setle of unhele, ii. 59, 25: Ps. 1, 1. Ich mai þe finde at þe rumhuse . . . þu sittest and singst behinde þe setle, O. and N. 594. Our loverd sal sitt . . . opon þe setil of his mageste, Pr. C. 6122. *Goth.* sitls; *m. a seat, throne, nest: O. H. Ger.* sez[z]al *cathedra, sponda, solium, tribunal;* sedal, sethal, sedhal *sedes, thronus, triclinium, occasus* (*solis*): *O. Frs. O. Sax.* sedel.] v. ān-, ancer-, ancor-, beór-, bisceop-, burhgeat-, cyne-, dōm-, ēđel-, ge-, heáh-, hilde-, lāreów-, medu-, pāp-, scip-, sunder-, þrym-, ūt-, weard-, wræc-setl; beorg-seđel; set.

setla. v. ān-, cot-, ge-, wēsten-setla.

setlan; *p.* [e]de. **I.** *trans. To settle, seat, put in a position of rest:*—Wǣglīđende setlaþ sǣmearas, and đonne in đæt ēglond up gewītaþ, Exon. Th. 361, 5; Wal. 15. **II.** *intrans. To settle, take a position of rest,* of the sun, *to set.* v. setlung *and the Mid. E. forms.* [Þatt allderrmann þatt heȝhesst wass Att tatt bridale settledd (ἀρχιτρίκλινος), Orm. 15285. Til þe sunne was setled to reste, Will. 2452. Him thoughte a goshauk . . . Setlith on his beryng, Alis. 484.]

setl-gang, es; *m. Setting* of the heavenly bodies, generally of the sun, (1) marking time:—Đā bād se sacerd sunnan setlgonges, forđon sunnan trió āgefeþ ondsware æt đæm upgonge & eft æt setlgonge, Nar. 27, 15–18. Sunne, setlgonges fūs, Exon. Th. 174, 34; Gū. 1187. Æfter sunnan setlgonge, Chr. 773; Erl. 52, 24. Ǣr sunnan setlgange, Bd. 1, 27; S. 495, 7. Æt sunnan setlgange, Blickl. Homl. 93, 16. Sunne hire setlgang healdeþ *sol cognovit occasum suum,* Ps. Th. 103, 18. Đā se æþela glǣm setlgong sōhte, Exon Th. 178, 32; Gū. 1253. (2) marking place, *the west:*—Be đam wege đe līþ tō sunnan setlgange *by the road that runs to the west,* Deut. 11, 30. Fram sunnan upgange ōþ hire setlgang *from the east unto the west,* Ps. Th. 49, 2. [*Ps.* setl-gang. Cf. *O. H. Ger.* sedal-gang: *O. Sax.* gangan, sīgan te sedle, werđan an sedle (*of the sun*). v. Grmm. D. M. 700, R. A. 817.] v. setl, **I c,** set-gang, *and next word.*

setl-gangende; *adj.* (*ptcp.*) *Setting:*—Setlgangendre sunnan *occidenti,* Bd. 5, 23; S. 645, 27.

setl-hrægl, es; *n. A covering for a seat:*—vii. setlhrægel, Chart. Th. 429, 28. v. set-hrægl.

setl-rād, e; *f. Setting* of the sun:—Æfter sunnan setlrāde, Cd. Th. 184, 19; Exod. 109. Cf. setl-gang.

setlung, e; *f.* **I.** *a taking of a seat, a sitting down:*—Đū understōde setlunge mīne and ǣriste mīne *tu cognovisti sessionem meam et resurrectionem meam,* Ps. Lamb. 138, 2. **II.** *setting* of the sun; occasus:—Seó niht hæfþ seofon dǣlas fram đære sunnan settlunge (setlunge, MS. P.), Lchdm. iii. 242, 26. Æfter sunnan setlunge, 266, 5. Fram sunnan uprine ōþ setlunge, Ps. Spl. 112, 3. Setellung, 49, 2. v. setlan.

sētnere, sētnung. v. sǣtnere, sǣtnung.

setness, e; *f.* **I.** *an ordinance, a regulation, an institution:*—Đis is seó gerǣdnes đe Eádulf hæfþ gerād tō setnesse, Cod. Dip. Kmbl. iii. 295, 32. Gē forlǣtaþ Godes bebod and healdaþ manna laga (setnesse, Lind.: setnisse, Rush. *traditionem*), Mk. Skt. 7, 8, 3, 13. Setnesa, Mt. Kmbl. Lind. 15, 2. The word glosses also *testimonium,* Mt. Kmbl. p. 1, 11: *testamentum,* p. 2, 5. **II.** *constitution, arrangement:*—From setnisse middangeardes *a constitutione mundi,* Mt. Kmbl. Rush. 25, 34. [Heo makeden ane sætnesse . . . þe ælc cheorl eæt his sulche hæfde griđ, Laym. 4258. Godess laȝhe & hiss hallȝhe settnesse þeȝȝ didenn fallen dun, & hofenn affterr þeȝȝre wille settnessess, hu mann birrde Godess laȝhe follȝhenn, Orm. 16836–43.] v. ā-, fore-, ge-, in-, on-, wiđ-setness.

setnung. [*Icel.* setning.] v. frum-setnung.

settan; *p.* sette; *pp.* seted, set[t] (*generally transitive, but see* XII). **I.** *to set, place, put, cause to take a certain position:*—Ic sette mīnne rēnbogan on wolcnum, Gen. 9, 13. Ic sette max on stōwe gehæppre, Coll. Monast. Th. 21, 13. Hwæđer gē settan eówer nett on đa hēhstan dūne, đonne gē fiscian willaþ? Ic wāt đæt gē hit đǣr ne settaþ. Hwæđer gē eówer net ūt on đa sǣ lǣdon, đonne gē huntian willaþ? Ic wēne đæt gē hī đonne setton up on dūnum, Bt. 33, 3; Fox 118, 11–15. Ne hī ne ǣlaþ hyra leóhtfæt and hit under cȳfe settaþ, Mt. Kmbl. 5, 15. Heó (*the fallen angels*) God sette on đa sweartan helle, Cd. Th. 20, 20; Gen. 312. Hē sette his đa swīđran hand (cf. mid đa swīđran hand, 514, 21) him on đæt heáfod, Bd. 2, 12; S. 515, 19. Hī đā nō đa studu ūton tō đam wāge tō fultume ne setton, ac hī heó on đa cyricean setton, 3, 17; S. 544, 37. Hié setton hié æt đære byrgenne dura, Blickl. Homl. 155, 8. Đā hē bebyrged wæs, hié settan him hyrdas tō, 177, 26. Setton scyldas wiđ weal *they set their shields against the wall,* Beo. Th. 655; B. 325. Sete đīn hand under mīn þeóh, Gen. 24, 2: 48, 18. Se đe wille fæst hūs timbrian ne sceall hē hit nō settan up on đone hēhstan cnol (*must not take the top of a hill as a site for his house*) . . . and eft se đe wille fæst hūs timbrian, ne sette hē hit on sondbeorhas, Bt. 12; Fox 36, 7–11. Đā lēt hē hine on hæft settan *he had him put into prison,* Chr. 1036; Erl. 164, note 3. Hē gearwe hæfde reliquias in tō settenne, Bd. 5, 11; S. 625, 37. **I a.** *to set down:*—Đā hēt se apostol đa bǣre settan, Homl. Th. i. 60, 16. **II.** figurative, *to set* to work, *set* before one a choice, *set* a mark, a name, one's mind, *lay* a charge, a curse, etc., upon one, *put* one in a position, *put* into one's power, etc.:—Ic sette beforan eów bletsunga and wirignissa, Deut. 11, 26. Ic hine wergþo on mīne sette, Cd. Th. 105, 20; Gen. 1756. Swā hit mē sealde se đe ic hit nū on hande sette, L. O. 3; Th. i. 180, 4. Đū setst (settes, Cott. MSS.) ūs on đæt setl đīnes Sceoppendes, Bt. 7, 5; Fox 24, 2. Swā hwæt swā đū mē on settest and bebeódest tō dōnne, Bd. 4, 25; S.

600, 4. God him sette naman, Homl. Th. i. 12, 31. Hē him naman on sette, Mk. Skt. 3, 17. Abraham sette friþotācn on his selfes sunu, Cd. Th. 142, 29; Gen. 2369. Hine Abraham on beácen sette, 167, 19; Gen. 2768. Gē setton mē in edwīt ðæt . . . *you laid to my reproach, that* . . . , Exon. Th. 131, 21; Gū. 459: Cd. Th. 165, 8; Gen. 2728. Gē ða wintergerīm on gewritu setton, Elen. Kmbl. 1305; El. 654. Sete heora ealdormenn, swā ðū Oreb dydest *make their nobles like Oreb* (A.V.), Ps. Th. 82, 9. Sete on Drihten ðīn gehygd, 54, 22. Setton hī hine on borh *they shall make him give security*, L. Ath. i. 20; Th. i. 208, 30: 210, 7. Deáþ settan *to kill*, Elen. Kmbl. 955; El. 479. Wīte settan *to impose punishment*, Cd. Th. 76, 33; Gen. 1266. On gewrit settan *to put into writing*, L. Alf. 49; Th. i. 58, 22. Wutan ūs tō symbeldæge settan, Ps. Th. 117, 25. II a. of travelling, cf. lecgan *and Ger.* zurücklegen:—On weg setteþ wīse gangas, Ps. Th. 84, 12. Sceal ic nū wreclāstas settan, sīðas wīde, Cd. Th. 276, 15; Sat. 189. Gesundne sīð settan *to make a safe journey*, Elen. Kmbl. 2008; El. 1005. III. *to set, plant*:—Sette *pastinat*, Wrt. Voc. ii. 96, 52. Hē leác sette *he set vegetables*, Shrn. 61, 20. Hē wīngeard sette, seów sǣda fela, Cd. Th. 94, 8; Gen. 1558: 172, 7; Gen. 2840. Settan *pastinare*, Wrt. Voc. ii. 116, 6. Settende *pastinantem*, 66, 18. Settum beámum anlīce *sicut novellae plantationes*, Ps. Th. 143, 14. IV. *to set, fix, implant*:—Hē mōdes snyttru seów and sette geond sefan monna, Exon. Th. 41, 29; Cri. 663. Settaþ on eówerum heortum, ðæt gē ne þurfon āsmeágan, hū gē andwyrdan sceolon, Homl. Th. ii. 542, 3. Uton wē ðæs dæges fyrhto on ūre mōd settan, Blickl. Homl. 125, 6. V. *to set, fix, appoint* a limit, time, place (cf. *set* day, time in A.V.):—In ðam frumstōle ðe him freá sette, Exon. Th. 349, 25; Sch. 51. Hī settan dæg tō ðæt man tō ðam lande scolde faran *they appointed a day for going to the land*, Chart. Th. 376, 16. Ðæt ic ðē symbledæg sette, Ps. Th. 75, 7. Settan gemǣro, Ex. 19, 23. Mearce settan, Cd. Th. 171, 19; Gen. 2830. VI. *to set* a task, *ordain, establish* a law, regulation, *appoint* a condition:—Wē settaþ ǣghwelcere cirican ðis frið, L. Alf. pol. 5; Th. i. 64, 8. Hē sette gecamp geleáffullum sāwlum, Homl. Th. i. 64, 18. Se ðe ða ealdan ǣ sette, 94, 4. Sylfa sette, ðæt ðū sunu wǣre efeneardigende, Exon. Th. 15, 14; Cri. 236. Ǣ ðū mē sete, Ps. Th. 118, 33. Gif gē nū gesāwen hwelce mūs, ðæt wǣre hlāford ofer ōðre mȳs and sette him dōmas, Bt. 16, 2; Fox 52. 2. VII. *to build, erect*:—Hūs settan and tūn timbrian, Shrn. 163, 16. Ongunnon heora burh rǣran and sele settan . . . weras on wonge wībed setton, Cd. Th. 113, 2–5; Gen. 1881–2. VIII. *to set up, institute, found, establish*:—Hwā ǣrost bōcstafas sette? Salm. Kmbl, p. 192, 6. Hē sette scole *instituit scholam*, Bd. 3, 18; S. 545, 44. Ǣgðer ge cyninga rīcu settan ge ceastra timbredon, Ors. 1, 10; Swt. 48, 9: Met. 1, 4. Ðæt wæs weallfæstenna ǣrest ealra ðara ðe æðelingas settan hēton, Cd. Th. 65, 3; Gen. 1060. VIII a. of the operations of the Deity:—Ðū dæg settest and deorce niht, Ps. Th. 73, 16: 138, 11: Exon. Th. 258, 33; Jul. 274. Ðā hē ðisne ymbhwyrft ǣrest sette, 422, 17; Rā. 41, 7: Cd. Th. 265, 29; Sat. 15. Ðā ðū wǣre settende ðās sīdan gesceaft, Exon. Th. 22, 23; Cri. 356. IX. *to set, base, found*:—Gif ðū wīsdōm timbrian wille, ne sete ðū hine uppan ða gītsunga, Bt. 12; Fox 36, 11. X. *to appoint* an officer or a person to an office or duty:—Hine tō ealdormenn sette, Ps. Th. 104, 16. Hē sette hine on his hūse tō hlāfwearde *constituit eum dominus domus suae*, 104, 17. Sette hē getreówe borgas, L. Eth. i. 1; Th. i. 280, 19: L. C. S. 30; Th. i. 394, 8. X a. *to appoint* something for a purpose:—Bæd þrymcyning, ðæt hē him ða weádǣd tō wræce ne sette, Elen. Kmbl. 988; El. 495. XI. *to settle* a quarrel, *allay* animosity, *compose* a difference:—Witan scylon fǣhþe settan, L. Edm. S. 7; Th. i. 250, 13. XII. *intrans. To settle, abate, subside*:—Lege uppa þat geswollene and hyt sceal sōna settan, Lchdm. iii. 86, 19. Ðonne biþ ðæs innoþes sār settende, i. 74, 9. XIII. *to compose* a book, etc.:—Ic ðās bōc wrāt and sette . . . ic sette feówer bēc, Bd. 5, 23; S. 647, 32–37. For ðisum þingum ic ðās bōc sette, Guthl. prol.; Gdwin. 4, 26. Sēe Isidorus ðe ðās bōc sette *qui hunc librum instituit*, L. Ecg. P. i. 6; Th. ii. 174, 16. Dauid ða sealmas sette, ðe wē æt Godes lofsangum singaþ, Homl. Th. ii. 576, 5. Se cyng hēt ðone arcebisceop bōc settan *the king ordered the archbishop to draw up a charter*, Chart. Th. 376, 3. [*Goth.* satjan: *O. Sax.* settian: *O. Frs.* setta: *O. H. Ger.* sezzan: *Icel.* setja.] v. ā-, an-, be- (bi-), for-, fore-, ge-, in-, of-, on-, tō-, un-, wið-, ymb-settan.

settaþ, Ps. Th. 9, 29 *for* sǣtaþ (?).

settend, es; *m. An ordainer, appointer*:—Ðæt ðū āna eart ēce Drihten, weroda Waldend, sigora settend (sigerōf settend, Exon. Th. 188, 17; Az. 47), Cd. Th. 237, 5; Dan. 333. v. dōm-settend.

set-þorn *some kind of tree*:—Andlang fura on setþorn; of setþorne on fūlan rīþig, Cod. Dip. Kmbl. iii. 436, 14.

sētung. v. sǣtung.

sewte, Andr. Kmbl. 1483; An. 743. v. sēpan.

sex. v. seax, six.

sī *be*:—Him sī ābrogden hiora sceamu, Ps. Th. 108, 28. Hwæt hēr sī gedōn, Blickl. Homl. 179, 34. Hwæðer hit sig ðe sōð ðe leás, Gen. 42, 16. Ðæs sig Metode þanc, Beo. Th. 3561; B. 1778. Ðæt gē witen hwæt hit sié, Past. 8; Swt. 53, 13. Gif ðū sié Godes sunu, Blickl. Homl. 27, 7. Him sió wuldor, Hy. 8, 4. Ðæt ðæt betst sȳ, ðæt mon seó foremǣre, Bt. 34, 2; Fox 82, 10. Gif heó leng sȳ ðonne hē *if she live longer than he*, L. Edm. B. 3; Th. i. 254, 13. Ðeáh ðe heora hundred seó, Ps. Th. 89, 10. Hē cwyð ðæt ic seó teónum georn, Cd. Th. 36, 34; Gen. 581: 309, 4; Sat. 704. Gyf ðū Godes sunu sȳ (sig, MS. A.: sié, Rush.), Mt. Kmbl. 4, 3. Sib sȳ (sig, MS. A.) eów, Lk. Skt. 24, 36. Ðæt gē ne sīn (sié, Lind.) ymbhȳdige, Mt. Kmbl. 6, 25. Sīn (sién, Hatt. MS.) hira eágan āþīstrode, Past. 1; Swt. 28, 9. Ðæt sién gewemmede ealle, Blickl. Homl. 245, 22. Ðæt mē æfter sié eaforan sīne yrfeweardas, Cd. Th. 131, 28; Gen. 2183. Seón, Exon. Th. 96, 28; Cri. 1581. Sīn (sē, Lind.: sié, Rush.), Mt. Kmbl. 6, 1. Ðæt hī sȳn (sié, Lind.: siǣ, Rush.) ān, Jn. Skt. 17, 11, 21, 22, 23. v. eom.

sib[b], e; *f.* I. *relationship*:—Sybbe *propinquitatis*, Hpt. Gl. 469, 55. Gif hwā sibleger gewyrce, gebēte ðæt be sibbe mǣðe (*according to the degree of relationship*), L. C. S. 52; Th. i. 404, 25. Sameramis gesette ðæt nān forbyrd nǣre æt geligere betwuh nānre sibbe, Ors. 1, 2; Swt. 30, 35. On ðæs lāfe ðe swā neáh wǣre on woruldcundre sibbe, L. Eth. vi. 12; Th. i. 318, 16. For ðære mǣglīcan sibbe (*of Christ and John*), Homl. Th. i. 58, 6. Ðā com Swein eorl and bæd Beorn eorl, ðe wæs his eámes sunu, ðæt hē his gefēra wǣre tō ðam cynge. Hē wende ðā for ðære sibbe mid him, Chr. 1050; Erl. 175, 18. Hrēðel (*the grandfather of Beowulf*) sibbe gemunde, næs ic (*Beowulf*) him lāðra beorn ðonne his bearna hwylc, Beo. Th. 4854; B. 2431. Hē biþ his mōder twām sibbum (*in two relationships, in double relationship*) getǣht, ðæt hē biþ ǣgðer ge sunu ge brōðer, Wulfst. 193, 7. I a. in a spiritual sense, cf. *gossip*:—Se cyning him tō godsuna onfēng and tō tācne ðære sibbe him twā mǣgþe forgeaf (*in signum adoptionis, duas illi provincias donavit*), Bd. 4, 13; S. 582, 9. II. *friendliness, kindness*, the opposite of hostility:—Sibbe cos *pacis osculum*, R. Ben. 82, 6. Ne gehȳrde nǣnig man on his heortan ōht elles būton mildheortnesse and sibbe, Blickl. Homl. 225, 2. Ne mihte hē mid ðone cyning sibbe habban, ac mycel ungeþwǣrnys betwih him ārās, Bd. 3, 14; S. 539, 35. Feóndscype dwæscaþ, sibbe sāwaþ, Exon. Th. 30, 31; Cri. 487. Ā ic sibbe wið ðē healdan wille *I will ever maintain my friendliness to thee*, 177, 33; Gū. 1236. Gē hȳ mid sibbum sōhtun *ye visited the sick with kind attentions*, 83, 22; Cri. 1360. III. *peace*, the opposite of war:—Ǣgðer ge on sibbe ge on gewinne, Bt. 24, 2; Fox 82, 11. Hē him gebeád wið his sibbe (*in pretium pacis*) unrīm māþma, Bd. 3, 24; S. 556, 8. Gif hī sibbe mid Godes mannum onfōn ne woldan ðæt hī wǣron gefeoht fram heora feóndum onfōnde *si pacem cum fratribus accipere nollent, bellum ab hostibus forent accepturi*, 2, 2; S. 503, 29: Chr. 605; Erl. 21, 28. Se bisceop betweox ðām cyningum sibbe geworhte, Bd. 4, 21; S. 590, 11. Eall ðeós worold geceás Agustuses frið and his sibbe, Ors. 5, 15; Swt. 250, 17. On ða tīd (*in the golden age*) wæs sibba genihtsumnes (*an utter absence of wars*), Blickl. Homl. 115, 9. IV. *peace, concord, unity, absence of dissension* or *variance*:—Suā ðætte ān sibb (sib, Cott. MSS.) Godes lufe būtan ǣlcum ungerāde ūs gefēge tōsomne, Past. 36; Swt. 253, 22. Ongeán ðæt sint tō manienne ða ðe ða sibbe sāwaþ ðæt hié swā micel weorc tō unwærlīce ne dōn and hūru ðǣr ðǣr hié nyton hwæðer sió sibb (sib, Cott. MSS.) betre betwux gefæstnod biþ ðe ne biþ forðæm swā swīðe swā hit dereþ ðætte ǣnig wana sié ðære sibbe betwux ðǣm goodum swā swīðe hit eác dereþ ðæt hió ne sié gewanod betwux ðǣm yfelum. Forðæm gif ða unryhtwīsan hiera yfel mid sibbe gefæstnigaþ and tōsomne gemengaþ ðonne biþ geīced hiera mægen *at contra admonendi sunt pacifici, ne tantae actionis pondus levigent, si, inter quos fundare pacem debeant, ignorent. Nam sicut multum nocet, si unitas desit bonis, ita valde est noxium, si non desit malis. Si ergo perversorum nequitia in pace jungitur, profecto eorum malis actibus robur augetur*, 47, 3; Swt. 361, 5–12. Beó mannum sib and sōm gemǣne, and ǣlc sacu getwǣmed, L. Eth. v. 19; Th. i. 308, 29. Sibb, vi. 25; Th. i. 320, 28. Crist ðe ys ðære sibbe ealdor, Ǣlfc. T. Grn. 8, 1. Sibbe (sibbes, Lind., Rush.) bearn, Lk. Skt. 10, 6. Mid sibbe *cum consensu*, Ps. Spl. 54, 15. Ðā wiste hē sumne hīrēd ðe ungeþwǣre him betwēónum wǣron . . . hē wolde ðæt hié ealle on sibbe wǣron, Blickl. Homl. 225, 9. God sylfa bebeád ðæt wē sōðe sibbe heóldan and geþwǣrnesse ūs betweónon habban, 109, 15: Ps. Th. 33, 14. Ne wēne gē ðæt ic cōme sybbe on eorþan tō sendanne; ne com ic sybbe tō sendanne, ac swurd, Mt. Kmbl. 10, 34. Sybbe . . . tōdāl, Lk. Skt. 12, 51. Habbaþ sibbe betwux eów, Mk. Skt. 9, 50. Ðonne forlǣtaþ hī ða sibbe ðe hī nū healdaþ, and winþ heora ǣlc on ōðer, and forlǣtaþ heora geferrǣdenne, Bt. 21; Fox 74, 34: Elen. Kmbl. 2411; El. 1207. V. *peace, freedom from disturbance* or *molestation, tranquillity*:—Gerusalem is gereht sibbe gesyhþ (cf. sib-gesihþ), forðon ðe hālige sāula ðǣr restaþ, Blickl. Homl. 81, 1. Nū is ǣghwonon hreám and wōp and sibbe tōlēsnes, 115, 16. Iethro cwæþ: 'Gā on sybbe,' Ex. 4, 18. Hī ðā feówertig wintra wunodon on sibbe *quievit terra per quadraginta annos*, Jud. 5, 32. Beóþ on sibbe ða þing ðe hē āh, Lk. Skt. 11, 21. Hū wēne gē hwelce sibbe ða weras hæfden, ðonne heora wīf swā monigfeald yfel dōnde wǣron? Ors. 1, 10; Swt. 50, 2. V a. *the peace* of a country, the king's *peace*:—Ða kyningas ǽgðer ge hiora sibbe ge hiora onweald innanbordes gehióldon, Past. pref.; Swt. 3, 6. Hē (*Augustus*) bebeád ðæt eall moncynn âne sibbe hæfde, Ors. 5, 14; Swt. 248, 20. **VI.** *peace* of mind, *freedom from agitation, fear*, etc.:—Sib sī mid eów, ne ondrǽde gē eów, Gen. 43, 23. Sȳ sibb betwux eów; ic hit eom, ne beó gē nâ âfyrhte, Homl. Th. i. 220, 13: Jn. Skt. 20, 19. Ūs biþ gearu sōna sibb æfter sorge, Andr. Kmbl. 3134; An. 1570. Lēton ðone hâlgan swefan on sibbe, blīðne bīdan, 1663; An. 834. Wē mōtan his ða wuldorfæstan onsȳne mid sibbe sceáwian, Blickl. Homl. 103, 29. [Sæhte and sibbe, Laym. 6096. Off Daviþess kin and sibbe, Orm. 3315. We ne muȝe grið ne sibbe macie, O. E. Homl. i. 243, 14: O. and N. 1005. *Goth.* sibja *relationship, adoption*: *O. Sax.* sibbia *relationship*: *O. Frs.* sibbe: *O. H. Ger.* sippa, sibba *adfinitas, propinquitas, pax, foedus*: *Icel.* sifjar; *pl. affinity;* Sif *the wife of Thor;* she was the goddess of the sanctity of the family and wedlock. v. Grmm. D. M. 286 and R. A. 467.] v. brōðor-, cneów-, dryht-, friðu-, mǽg-, mǽgþ-, neáh-, nīd-, un-sib[b], *and next word.*

sib[b]; *adj. Sib* (dial. e. g. Lancashire, Scottish), *related;* also absolute, *one related, a relation* (In *god-sibbas* the word is inflected as a noun, cf. *Icel.* sifr *a near relation.* In the passage below, Lk. 14, 12, the form may be taken as a weak noun, cf. *Icel.* sifi *a relation by marriage*, guð-sifi *a god-sib*: *O. L. Ger.* sibbeo: *O. H. Ger.* sibbo *consanguineus*):—Ne biþ nâ gelīc ðæt man wið swustor gehǽme and hit wǽre feor sibb (*or*? feorsibb; cf. neáh-sibb), L. C. S. 52; Th. i. 404, 28. Ðǽr ne byþ sybbes lufu tō ōðrum, Wulfst. 146, 13. Ðære sibban *ob cognate*, Wrt. Voc. ii. 64, 26. Hē biþ his mōder on twâm wīsum tō sibbum getǽht, ðæt hē biþ ǽgðer ge sunu ge brōðer, Wulfst. 193, 7. Hât in gân seón sibbe gedriht samod ætgædere, Beo. Th. 779; B. 387: 1462; B. 729. (*Grein takes* sibbe *as gen. of* sibb, *Thorpe and Heyne make it the first part of a compound.* Cf. sib-gedryht.) Ðonne se deáþ cymeþ âsundraþ ðâ sibbe ða ðe ǽr somud wǽron līc and sâwle *when death comes, it separates then relations, who before were together, body and soul*, Exon. Th. 367, 7; Seel. 4. Hē (*Augustus*) bebeád ðæt ǽlc mǽgþ tōgædere cōme, ðæt ǽlc man ðȳ gearor wiste hwǽr hē gesibbe (sibbe, MS. C.) hæfde, Ors. 5, 14; Swt. 248, 17. Sibbo ł cūðo menn (gisibbe, Rush.) *cognatos*, Lk. Skt. Lind. 14, 12. [Hiss follc, þatt wass himm sibb o moderr hallfe, Orm. 19144. Sohhtenn himm betwenenn sibbe and cuþe (v. Lk. 2, 44), 8922. Bitwhwe sibbe, vlesliche oðer gostliche, A. R. 204, 20. Iosep bad sibbe (*his kinsmen*) cumen him biforen, Gen. and Ex. 2503. Who is sibbe to þis seuene . . . he is wonderliche welcome, Piers P. 5, 634. Sybbe or of kynne *consanguineus*, Prompt. Parv. 455. *Goth.* un-sibis *impious*: *O. Frs.* sibbe *related*: *O. H. Ger.* sippe.] v. ge-, neáh-sib[b].

sibaed *sifted* (?); arbatae, Txts. 43, 216. v. sife, sifeþa.

sib-æðeling, es; *m. A prince and kinsman*:—Sibæðelingas (*Beowulf and Wiglaf;* a few lines before the former is spoken of as the *mǽg* of the latter), Beo. Th. 5409; B. 2708.

sibban (?); *p.* sifde (?) *To rejoice*:—Sifeþ *gaudet*, Bd. 5, 23; S. 646, 35 note. [*Goth.* sifan; *p.* sifaida *to rejoice.*]

sibbian; *p.* ode *To make people friends, make peace between* disputants, *reconcile*:—Se seðe ða unryhtwīsan tōsomne sibbaþ (*pace sociat*), hē seleþ ðære unryhtwīsnesse fultom, Past. 47, 3; Swt. 361, 22. Sipbade *paciscitur*, Lk. Skt. p. 11, 2. On .iiii. nyhta mōnan sibba ða cīdenda[n] men, and ðū hié gesibbast, Lchdm. iii. 176, 25. Cyninge gebyreþ, ðæt hē eall cristen folc sibbie and sehte, L. I. P. 2; Th. ii. 304, 12. Sybbie, Wulfst. 266, 17. Wē lǽraþ, ðæt nân sacu, ðe betweox preóstan sī, ne beó gescoten tō worldmanna sōme, ac sēman and sibbian heora âgene gefēran, L. Edg. C. 7; Th. ii. 246, 4. Ðâ wǽron on ðam tīman ungeþwǽre preóstas, ða hē wolde sibbian, Homl. Th. ii. 516, 5. v. ge-, unsibbian.

sib-cwide, es; *m. A speech professing peace and friendliness, fair words*:—Ða leásan men, ða ðe mid tungan treówa gehâtaþ fægerum wordum . . . hafaþ on gehâtum hunigsmæccas, smēðne sybcwide, Fragm. Kmbl. 54; Leás. 29.

sib-fæc, es; *n. A degree of relationship*:—Ǽfre ne geweorðe, ðæt cristen man gewīfige in .vi. manna sibfæce on his âgenum cynne, ðæt is binnan ðam feórþan cneówe, L. Eth. vi. 12; Th. i. 318, 14: L. C. E. 7; Th. i. 364, 22. Cf. Christiani ex propinquitate sui sanguinis usque ad septimum gradum connubia non ducunt, Th. i. 257, note b, and ii. 19, note 1. v. Grmm. R. A. 468.

sib-gebyrda; *pl. f. Relationship*:—Ic (*Abraham*) eom fædera ðīn (*Lot*) sibgebyrdum, Cd. Th. 114, 8; Gen. 1901.

sib-gedryht, e; *f.* **I.** *a band of kinsmen*:—Bâd eall seó sibgedriht (*the Israelites*) somod ætgædere, Cd. Th. 191, 13; Exod. 214. **II.** *a peaceful band*:—Swinsaþ sibgedryht (*the host of spirits who live in the peace and tranquillity of heaven*), Exon. Th. 239, 8; Ph. 618. In ðam ēcean gefeán mid ða sibgedryht somud eard niman, 184, 18; Gū. 1346.

sib-gemâgas; *pl. m. Kinsmen*:—Heáhlond stigon sibgemâgas (*Abraham and Isaac*), Cd. Th. 202, 10; Exod. 386.

sib-geornness, e; *f. Eagerness for peace and kindness, love*:—Sybgeornes *caritas Dei et proximi*, Wulfst. 69, 2. Sibgeornes, 189, 21.

sib-gesihþ, e; *f. A vision of peace*:—Sibgesyhþe *Hierosolymae* (v. sib, V), Hpt. Gl. 447, 56.

sibi. v. sife.

sib-lâc, es; *n. A peace-offering*:—Ic ðē wille gesyllan mīne siblâc (*hostias pacificas*), L. Ath. i. prm.; Th. i. 196, 21.

sib-leger, es; *m. An incestuous person*:—Be siblegerum. And æt siblegerum ða witan gerǽddan, ðæt cyng âh ðone uferan and bisceop ðone nyðeran, L. E. G. 4; Th. i. 168, 13–15. Cf. for-liger; *m.*

sib-leger, es; *n. Incest*:—Be siblegere. Gif hwâ sibleger gewyrce gebēte ðæt be sibbe mǽðe, L. C. S. 52; Th. i. 404, 24. Wearþ ðes þeódscype swȳðe forsyngod þurh sibblegeru and þurh mistlīce forligru, Wulfst. 164, 5: 165, 31.

sib-lîc; *adj. Of peace*:—Mid siblīcum cosse, Homl. Skt. i. 22, 31. God biddan ðæt hē forgefe siblīce tīd and smyltelīco gewidra, Shrn. 74, 11. Wē sceolan ūs geearnian ða siblecan wǽra Godes and manna, Blickl. Homl. 111, 3.

sibling, es; *m. A relation, kinsman*:—Sibling *affinis* vel *consanguineus*, Wrt. Voc. i. 72, 46: Homl. Th. i. 516, 14. Hæfst ðū suna oððe dohtra oððe âðum oððe ǽnigne sibling? Gen. 19, 12. Gebrōðru *vel* siblingas *fratres*, Wrt. Voc. i. 52, 3. Ofsleáþ ðâs ealdras, ðonne beóþ heora siblingas tō heófunge geneádode, Homl. Th. i. 88, 1. Fæder and mōder and flǽsclīce siblingas, 398, 8. Ūre frȳnd geseón and ūre siblingas gegrētan, ii. 526, 33. Siblingum *contribulibus, propinquis, parentibus*, Hpt. Gl. 472, 23. v. ge-sibling.

sib-lufu, an; *f. Kindly affection, kindness, love such as exists between kinsmen*:—Ic (God) tō eów mid siblufan gecyrre þurh milde mōd, Exon. Th. 366, 6; Reb. 8: 40, 7; Cri. 635. Hié (*the fallen angels*) of siblufan Godes âhwurfon, Cd. Th. 2, 25; Gen. 24. Git mē sibblufan and freóndscipe cȳðaþ, 152, 3; Gen. 2514.

[**sib-rǽden[n]**, e; *f. Affinity, relationship*:—Þes ilce Willelm hæfde ǽror numen ðes eorles dohter of Angeow tō wīfe oc hī wǽron siððen tōtweamde for sibrēden, Chr. 1127; Erl. 255, 21. The king him let uor sibrede todele fram is wif, R. Glouc. 492, 9. A sybredyn̄ *consanguinitas*, Cath. Ang. 338, where see note. See also *sib-rit, sibbe-ridge, -red* banns of marriage, E. D. S. Pub. B. 16.]

sib-sum; *adj. Peaceable, pacific, friendly*:—Sibsum *pacificus*, Rtl. 39, 9. Eálâ ðū sōða and ðū sibsuma, Crist ælmihtig, Exon. Th. 14, 5; Cri. 214. Ða Gotan lustlīce sibbsumes friðes æt eów biddende sindon *the Goths willingly ask for a friendly peace at your hands;* Gothi societatem Romani foederis precibus sperant, Ors. 1, 10; Swt. 48, 22. Sibsume ł friðgeorne (ł friðsume, Rush.) *pacifici*, Mt. Kmbl. Lind. 5, 9. [*O. H. Ger.* sippi-sam *pacificus.*] v. ge-sibsum.

sibsumian. v. ge-sibsumian.

sibsumlîce; *adv. Peaceably, in peace*:—Sibsumlīce gebunden mid ðīnum bebode, Bt. 33, 4; Fox 128, 31. v. ge-sibsumlīce.

sibsumness, e; *f. Peaceableness, peace, tranquillity*:—Hē ðæt rīce heóld on gōdre geþuǽrnesse and on micelre sibsumnesse, Chr. 860; Erl. 70, 24. Lufa sibsumnysse and geþwǽrnysse, Wulfst. 247, 1. [Þa weren alle mid sibsumnesse, O. E. Homl. i. 91, 17. Sibsumnesse eu beo among *pax vobiscum*, Misc. 54, 599.] v. ge-sibsumness.

sibsumung, sibun. v. ge-sibsumung, seofon.

sîc, es; *n.*: *but* sīce, es; *m. seems also to occur. A sike.* '*Sike* a watercourse; applied to a natural as well as to an artificial stream; the latter usually constructed to receive the contents of field gutters, for discharge into the river.' Mid-Yorks. Gloss. See also E. D. S. Pub. 13, 15, and Old Farming Words, III:—*Sike* a quillet or furrow. Jamieson gives *sike* a rill. Cuddie Headrigg says 'I took up the syke a wee bit.':—Of ðam mere west . . . ðonne innan ânne sīce, ðonne andlange sīces ðæt cymþ tō ðæm horpytte, Cod. Dip. Kmbl. iii. 37, 20–22. Of ðæm beorge on ðæt sīc; ondlong sīces ofer ðone brōc, 38, 28: 35, 7. In wǽtan sīce; of ðæm wǽtan sīce in ða bakas, 382, 7: 386, 11. In ðæt wǽte sicc; of ðam sīce, 386, 16. On ðæt eástre sīc, 438, 28. In ðæt sīc, 31, 12. [Syke *rivus*, Wrt. Voc. i. 195, col. 2. *Icel.* sīk *a ditch, trench*: *O. H. Ger.* gi-sīch *stagnum, lacus, palus* (cf. *Scott.* sike *a marshy bottom with a small stream running through it*), Grff. vi. 58.] Cf. seohtra.

sîcan, sȳcan; *p.* te *To cause to suck, to suckle, give suck*:—Ðū sȳcst hâlgum breóste *lactas sacrato ubere*, Hymn. Surt. 75, 43. Ða breóst ðe ne sīctun (sȳctun, MS. A.) *ubera quae non lactauerunt*, Lk. Skt. 23, 29. v. ge-sīcan, â-sīcyd; sūcan.

sîcan; *p.* sâc. **I.** *to sike* (still in dial. e. g. Lancashire), *sigh, groan*:—On mīnum bedde ic sīce and wēpe, Ps. Th. 6, 5. **II.** *to sigh* for, *long* for:—Ðæt wǽron ða tīda ðe Rōmâne nū ǽfter sīcaþ *en tempora . . . quibus recordatio suspirat*, Ors. 2, 8; Swt. 92, 35. [Seoruhfulnesse made him siken sore, A. R. 110, 13. Wepenn & sikenn sare & suhhȝhenn, Orm. 7924. Þe king gon siche (sike, 2nd MS.) sare, Laym. 12772. He sikede, Jul. 20, 9. Sike, Horn. 426: Havel. 291. She neither weep ne syked, Clerkes Tale 545. Thanne syked Sathan, Piers P. 18, 263.] v. â-, on-sīcan, *and following words.*

siccettan. v. sicettan.

sîce, es; *m. A sigh, groan;* gemitus:—Ic mē on Godes helde bebeóde wiđđ đane sâra[n] sice, wiđ đane sâra[n] slege, wiđ đane grymma[n] gryre . . . and wiđ eal đæt lâđ đe intô land fare, Lchdm. i. 388, 12. [He weorp a sic as a wiht þat sare were iwundet, Jul. 21, 12. He ne feched noht þe sore siches on neđerward his heorte, O. E. Homl. ii. 83, 26. Mid seoruhfule sikes, A. R. 284, 3. Đor sat his moder in sik and sor, Gen. and Ex. 1239. With a sik she seyde, Tr. and Cr. 3, 207. Amang his sobbes and his sikes sore, 4, 50.]

sicel. v. sicol.

sicerian; *p.* ode *To ooze*, of a fluid, *to make way through a small opening:*—Swīđe lytlum siceraþ đæt wæter and swīđe dēgellīce on đæt hlece scip and đeáh hit wilnaþ đæs ilcan đe sió hlūde ӯđ dēþ on đære hreón sǣ būton hit mon ǣr ūt āweorpe *by very small quantities and with very great secrecy does the water make its way into the leaky ship, and yet it has the same intention as the loud wave in the rough sea, unless it be cast out beforehand;* hoc agit sentina latenter excrescens, quod patenter procella saeviens, Past. 57, 1; Swt. 437, 14. [*Ger.* sickern *to ooze, trickle.*]

sicet[t], es; *n. A sigh, groan:*—On siccetum *in gemitibus*, Ps. Lamb. 30, 10.

sicet[t]an, siccet[t]an; *p.* te. I. *to sigh, groan:*—Sicetit *singultat*, Wrt. Voc. ii. 120, 50. Đā begann se ealda siccetan and mid wōpe wearþ ofergoten, Ælfc. T. Grn. 18, 1. II. as opposed to expressing grief by speech (?):—Đa unryhtwīsan sicettaþ (siccettaþ, Cott. MSS.) on đǣm þiéstrum *impii in tenebris conticescent*, Past. 11, 1; Swt. 65, 12. Siccitan *conticiscent, silebant*, Wrt. Voc. ii. 135, 15.

sicet[t]ung, siccet[t]ung, e; *f. A sigh, sob, heavy* or *short breathing, sighing:*—Siccetung *suspirium*, Wrt. Voc. i. 19, 34. Siccitung *singultus*, 46, 19. Mē điós siccetung hafaþ āgǣled, đes geocsa, Met. 2, 4. Mīn geár wǣron on sicetunga and on gestæne (*in gemitibus*), Ps. Th. 30, 11. Sicetunge *singultu*, Hpt. Gl. 514, 66. In sicettunge and geoxunge *in singultum*, Wrt. Voc. ii. 46, 8. Getogene sicetunge *ducta suspiria*, Hpt. Gl. 511, 41. Heófunga sicetungum *lamentorum singultibus*, 472, 57. Siccitungum, 504, 63. Hē angsumlīce siccetunga teáh swā đæt hē earfoþlīce orđian mihte *he drew his breath painfully and heavily, so that he could hardly breathe*, Homl. Th. i. 86, 8. Hē wearþ đā gesīcelod and siccetunga teáh of niwellīcum breóste on bedde licgende *he fell ill and drew sighs from the bottom of his heart, as he lay in his bed*, Homl. Skt. i. 7, 65.

Sicilie; *pl. The Sicilians, the people of Sicily*, or (as in the older stage of the language the name of a people was used where now that of their country is put) *Sicily*. [In this sense the Latin form also occurs:—Sicilia, ēglond micel, Met. 1, 15. Sicilia đæt īgland is þrȳscȳte, Ors. 1, 1; Swt. 28, 2. On Sicilia đæm londe, 2, 6; Swt. 88, 31. Betwux đām muntum and Sicilia đam eálonde, Bt. 1; Fox 2, 4]:—Sicilie ungerāde wǣron him betweónum, Ors. 2, 7; Swt. 90, 6. Hit Sicilia fela ofslōg, 2, 6; Swt. 88, 32. Sicilia folc, burh, 4, 6; Swt. 170, 20, 30. Sicilia īglond *insulas Siciliae*, Swt. 172, 30. On Sicilium *in Sicilia*, 4, 4; Swt. 164, 23: 5, 3; Swt. 222, 27. Of Sicilium *ex Sicilia*, 4, 6; Swt. 174, 20. Hī wunnon on Sicilie (*adversus Siculos*), 4, 5; Swt. 168, 19. Hē gefōr mid firde an Sicilie *cum in Sicilia bellum gereret*, Swt. 166, 6: 4, 10; Swt. 194, 3.

Sicilisc; *adj. Sicilian:* — Sicili[s]c, Sicul inberdli(n)c ꝉ burhleód, Sicilisc inbyrdlincg *siculus indigena, Sici[li]ensis incivis*, Hpt. Gl. 499, 35–39. Se Sicilisca *Siculus*, Wrt. Voc. ii. 84, 26.

siclian, sīcelian; *p.* ode *To sicken, be* or *fall sick:*—Lange hē sīclaþ *diu egrotat*, Lchdm. iii. 151, 8. Sīcclaþ (sīclaþ, MS. T.), 13. [Đā wæs Leófrīc abbot of Burh æt ꝥ ilca feord, and sǣclode đǣr, and com hām, and wæs dǣd sōne đǣr æfter, Chr. 1066; Erl. 203, 12. Þat ilce đæi þat Martin abbot of Burch sculde þider faren, þa sǣclede hē & ward dēd .iv. no. Jañ., 1154; Erl. 266, 10.] [Leste oure soule secli, A. R. 50, 20. *O. H. Ger.* siechelōn *languere.*] v. ge-sīclian.

sicol (-el, -ul), es; *m. A sickle:*—Đes sicol *haec falx*, Ælfc. Gr. 9, 72; Zup. 73, 6: Wrt. Voc. i. 85, 2: *falciola* vel *falcicula*, 34, 63. Sicul *falx*, ii. 146, 77. Sicel *baxus*, 12, 53: Wülck. Gl. 193, 9. Ne rīp đū nā mid sicele (*falce*), Deut. 23, 25. Hē sent his sicol *mittit falcem*, Mt. Skt. 4, 29. Hē sceal sicol habban, Anglia ix. 263, 5. [*O. H. Ger.* sihhila; *f. falx, falcicula: Ger.* sichel. *Probably from Latin* secula.]

sicor; *adj.* with *gen. Secure* from, *free* from guilt and the punishment it brings, *safe, free* from danger or harm, *sure, certain, free* from doubt:—Swā ūs biþ æt Gode đonne wē wiđ hine gesyngiaþ; đeáh wē nǣfre eft swā ne dōn, gif wē đæt gedōne mid nānum þingum ne bētaþ ne ne hreówsiaþ, ne bió wē nō đæs sicore; gif ūs đæt ne mislīcaþ đæt ūs ǣr līcode, đonne ne biþ hit nō ūs færgiefen. Đeáh wē nū nāuht yfeles ne dōn on đisse worulde, ne sculon wē đeáh forđȳ bión tō orsorge, gif wē nāuht tō gōde ne dōþ; forđæmđe swīđe fela unālēfedes wē oft geþenceaþ. Hū mæg se đonne bión orsorg, se đe him self wāt, đæt hē gesyngaþ *ita et cum Deo delinquimus, nequaquam satisfacimus, si ab iniquitate cessamus, nisi voluptates quoque, quas dileximus, e contrario appositis lamentis insequamur. Si enim nulla nos in hac vita operum culpa maculasset, nequaquam nobis hic adhuc degentibus ipsa ad securitatem innocentia nostra sufficeret; quia illicita animum multa pulsarent. Qua ergo mente securus est, qui perpetratis iniquitatibus ipse sibi testis est, quia innocens non est?* Past. 54, 5; Swt. 425, 3, 10. [Hi harm hadde, hii wende þat hii siker were, Laym. 9401 (2nd MS.). Dead is þe king, & siker þu miht hider comen, 15092. Wā wes Brutten þere, þenne heo wenden beon sikere, 29289. Be þu sikerr þatt he shall þe ȝifenn eche blisse, Orm. 4844. Beođ ancren wise, þet habbeđ wel bitined ham aȝein þe helle leun, uorte beon þe sikerure, A. R. 164, 12. Ne migten he siker ben, for magnie of đo woren ouertaken, Gen. and Ex. 876. Þat ich mowe a siker bold arere, R. Glouc. 116, 1. Syker þou be Engelond ys nou þyn, 359, 9. Hit is sikerest in þi heeued (*safest to sprinkle water on the head at baptism*), Shoreham. Þai salle be þare syker and certayne To have endeless joy, Pr. C. 8559. A man hath most honour To deyen . . . whan he is siker of his goode name, Chauc. Kn. T. 2191. Her none sikerer þan other, Piers P. 12, 162 note. *O. Frs.* sikur (-er) *free* from guilt; *sure, trustworthy: O. Sax.* (sundiono) sikur (-or): *O. H. Ger.* sihhur *securus, immunis, liber, tutus. From Latin* securus.]

sīd; *adj.* I. *wide, broad, spacious, ample, extensive.* (a) applied to the world, universe, ocean, etc.:—Điós sīde gesceaft þēnaþ and þiówaþ *the wide world ministers and serves*, Met. 29, 76. Eorþe and sīd wæter *earth and ocean broad*, Cd. Th. 7, 2; Gen. 100. Geseah sceado swīđrian geond sīdne grund, 8, 35; Gen. 134. Sǣs sīdne grund, Exon. Th. 349, 2; Sch. 40. Geond sīdne sǣ, 53, 19; Cri. 853. Sǣs sīdne fæđm, Elen. Kmbl. 1454; El. 729. Is đæs fȳres frumstōl ofer eallum ōđrum gesceaftum geond đisne sīdne grund, Met. 20, 127. (b) applied to a tract of land, to a kingdom, etc., v. sīd-land:—Sīde rīce *a broad realm*, Beo. Th. 4404; B. 2199. Nyttade Noe mid sunum sīnum sīdan rīces, Cd. Th. 96, 24; Gen. 1599. Unlytel dǣl sīdre foldan (*the district of Sodom and Gomorrah*), 154, 5; Gen. 2551. Sennar sīdne and wīdne *Shinar's plain broad and wide*, 99, 33; Gen. 1655. Sīde sǣlwongas, 78, 14; Gen. 1293. Sīde sǣnæssas, Beo. Th. 451; B. 223. Hē wealdeþ sīdum rīcum *he shall rule broad realms*, Ps. Th. 71, 8. (c) applied to a comparatively small surface:—Ic bere sīdne scyld, Beo. Th. 879; B. 437. Setton sīde scyldas wiđ weal, 656; B. 325. Sīde weallas, Exon. Th. 1, 9; Cri. 5. (d) applied to a number of people who cover a wide space, v. sīd-folc:—Sēcan sīde herge, Exon. Th. 33, 12; Cri. 524. Weorode, sīde herge, Beo. Th. 4683; B. 2347. Sīde worude (? worulde, MS.), Cd. Th. 118, 11; Gen. 1963. Ofer sīd weorod, Elen. Kmbl. 316; El. 158. Sīde þeóde, Ps. Th. 117, 10. Sīde hergas, Cd. Th. 194, 14; Exod. 260: Andr. Kmbl. 1304; An. 652. (e) figuratively, *far-reaching, large:*—Geþolode wine Scyldinga weána gehwylcne, sīdra sorga, Beo. Th. 300; B. 149. Ic worn hæbbe sīdra sorga gehȳred, Exon. Th. 11, 13; Cri. 170. Ne behwylfan mæg heofon and eorþe his wuldres word wīddra and sīddra đonne befæđman mǣge foldan sceátas (*stretching too far and wide to be embraced*), Cd. Th. 204, 31; Exod. 427. II. *capacious, ample, spacious, large:*—Glōf sīd, Beo. Th. 4178; B. 2086. In sīdum ceóle, Exon. Th. 345, 10; Gn. Ex. 186. On đyssum sīdan sele, Cd. Th. 273, 3; Sat. 131. Geond đæt sīde sel, Andr. Kmbl. 1523; An. 763. Con hē sīdne ræced fæste gefēgan, Exon. Th. 296, 7; Crā. 47. II a. figuratively of the capacity of the mind:—On sīdum sefan, Exon. Th. 169, 17; Gū. 1096. Þurh sīdne sefan, Beo. Th. 3456; B. 1726. Sefan sīdne geþanc and snytro cræft, Cd. Th. 249, 26; Dan. 536. III. *long, hanging, of ample length*, of clothes, hair, etc., v. sīd-feax:—Sīd reáf swilce mēteras wyrceþ on anlīcnesse *toga*, Wrt. Voc. i. 41, 3. Iohannes geseah ūrne Drihten mid alban gescrīdne, and seó wæs sīd niđer ōþ đa andcleówa (*it reached down to the ancles*, cf. *Icel.* kné-, skō-sīđr *reaching to the knee, the shoes* (of dress)), L. Ælfc. P. 15; Th. ii. 370, 3. Herebyrne sīd (cf. *Icel.* brynja rūm ok sīđ), Beo. Th. 2892; B. 1444. Mid sīdum bearde (cf. *Icel.* sītt skegg), Homl. Th. i. 466, 24. Sīde beardas, 456, 18. Se beard and đæt feax him wǣron ōþ đa fēt sīde (cf. *Icel.* lokkar sīđir til jarđar), Shrn. 120, 25. Hī habbaþ beardas ōþ cneów sīde and feax ōþ helan *barbas habentes usque ad genua, comas usque ad talos*, Nar. 35, 2: 38, 8. Wīf habbaþ beardas swā sīde ōþ heora breóst, 38, 2. [Now wers men short and now syde, Pr. C. 1534. Syyd, as clothys *talaris*, Prompt. Parv. 455 where see note. See also Halliwell Dict. *side. Icel.* sīđr *long, hanging.*]

sīd-ādl, e; *f. Pleurisy:*—On sīdan lama *vel* sīdādl *pleuriticus*, Wrt. Voc. i. 19, 31. Cf. sīd-wærc.

sīdan; *adv. From a wide area:*—Of gehwilcum stōwum wȳdan and sȳdan gegaderod, Cod. Dip. B. ii. 389, 23. Cf. next word.

sīde; *adv. Widely, extensively, amply:*—Sīde *prolixius*, Hpt. Gl. 526, 60. ¶ *The word generally occurs along with* wīde, *far* and wide:—Sīde and wīde *longe lateque*, Wrt. Voc. ii. 53, 59: Cd. Th. 8, 3; Gen. 118: El. 554; El. 277. Hē Godes lof rǣrde wīde and sīde, Chr. 959; Erl. 119, 26: Cd. Th. 1, 20: Gen. 101. Is wuldur đīn wīde and sīde ofer đās eorþan ealle *in omnem terram gloria tua*, Ps. Th. 56, 6, 13. Gesamnadon weras wīde and sīde, Andr. Kmbl. 3273; An. 1639. Cyningas hine wīde wordodon sīde, Chr. 975; Erl. 125, 23. Ealra lǣca đæra đe gewurde wīde ođđe sīde, Hy. 1, 7. [Þis wes itald wide and side, Laym. 29902. Wide and side spelledd iss, Orm. 5900. Sidder (*hanging*) *lower*, Piers P. 5, 193.] Cf. preceding word.

sīde, an; *f.* I. *a side, flank*, of living things:—Sīde *latus*, Wrt.

Voc. i. 44, 24: ii. 51, 72: *lumbus*, 113, 29. Wiđ đære swīđran sīdan sāre and đære winestran, Lchdm. ii. 6, 3. On sīdan lama *pleuriticus*, Wrt. Voc. i. 19, 31. Hē Hǽlend genom be sīdan, Cd. Th. 299, 5; Sat. 545. Hit (*the horse*) ongan walwian and on gehwæđere sīdan hit oferweorpan (*in diversum latus vicissim sese volvere*), Bd. 3, 9; S. 533, 40. Ān đæra cempena geopenode his sīdan (sīdu, Lind.: sīdo, Rush.) mid spere, Jn. Skt. 19, 34. Sīdan (đa sīdu ł đæt sīdu, Lind.: đa sīdo, Rush.) *latus*, 20, 20. **II.** *side* of a house, ship, etc.:—Duru đū setst be đære sīdan (*the side of the ark*), Gen. 6, 16: Past. 22; Swt. 169, 24. Đæt scyp on sīdan licgende, Bd. 5, 9; S. 623, 21. **III.** marking direction on this or that *side*:—Đeós þridde India hæfþ on ānre sīdan þeóstru, on ōđere gārsecg, Homl. Th. i. 454, 14. Ǽfre byþ on sumre sīdan đære eorþan dæg, and ǽfre on sumre sīdan niht, Lchdm. iii. 234, 27: Anglia viii. 319, 39. **IV.** of descent, cf. on the father's, mother's *side*:—Hig wǽron ācennede of Constantines sīdan, đæt ys of gestreónde, Shrn. 97, 6. [*O. Sax.* sīda: *O. Frs.* sīde: *O. H. Ger.* sīta: *Icel.* síða.]

sīde, an; *f. Silk*:—Sīdan *sericum*, Coll. Monast. Th. 27, 7. [*O. H. Ger.* sīda *sericum*: *Ger.* seide. From *Mid. Lat.* seta. Cf. *Span.* seda: *Ital.* seta: *Fr.* soie.] v. sīd-wyrm, sīden.

sīd-ece, es; *m. Side-ache*:—Drenc wiđ sīdece, Lchdm. iii. 48, 9, 18.

side-ful[l]; *adj.* **I.** *of good behaviour* or *manners, honest, modest, virtuous, sober*:—Sideful *pudicus*, Wrt. Voc. i. 51, 33. Se ārfæst snoter eádmod sidefull sǣfre clǣne wæs *qui pius, prudens, humilis, pudicus, sobrius, castus fuit*, Hymn. Surt. 137, 1. Sidefull mann and mid þeáwum gefrætwod, Homl. Th. i. 596, 31. Sideful *pudica, casta*, Hpt. Gl. 439, 16. On ānre tīde twā mǽdencild cumaþ, and biþ đæt ān sydefull and đæt ōđer sceandlīc, Homl. Skt. i. 5, 280. Sidefulre *pudicae, castae*, Hpt. Gl. 428, 48. Đa heáhfæderas wǽron sidefulle on þeáwum and sȳferlīce lybbende, Homl. As. 37, 327. Wē witon đæt manega sydefulle clericas (*many honest clerks*) nyton hwæt byþ *quadrans*, Anglia viii. 306, 27. **II.** of dress, *sober, modest, decorous*:—Mid hāligre drohtnunge and sidefullum gyrlan, Homl. Th. i. 546, 25. [Sannte Marȝe wass shammfasst & daffte & sedefull, Orm. 2175.] v. un-sidefull.

sidefullīce; *adv. Virtuously, decorously*:—Sidefullīce *honeste*, Germ. 389, 33.

sidefulness, e; *f. Honesty, modesty, sobriety*:—Clǣnnyss and sidefulnys eówres līchaman and sāule *castitas atque sobrietas corporis simul et spiritus vestri*, Cod. Dip. B. i. 155, 13. Sidefulnysse *pudicitiae*, Hpt. Gl. 433, 56. Mæg[þ]hādlīcere sidefulnysse *pudicitiae* (*castitatis*) *virginalis*, 440, 65: 447, 9. Wīfmen ne beón būtan sidefulnysse, Homl. Skt. i. 13, 120. v. un-sidefulness.

side-līc; *adj. Sober, sedate, modest*:—Of sidelīcre ansȳne *serio*, Germ. 389, 36. [*O. H. Ger.* situ-līh *moralis, deliberatus*: *Ger.* sitt-lich: *Icel.* sið-ligr *well-bred*.]

sidelīce; *adv. In a proper manner, suitably*:—Monige scylda openlīce witene beóþ tō forberanne đonne đæs þinges tīma ne biþ đæt hit mon sidelīce gebētan mǽge . . . Ac đonne se lāreów ieldende sēcþ đone tīman đe hē his hiéremenn sidelīce on þreátigean mǽge . . . *nonnulla aperte cognita mature toleranda sunt, cum rerum minime opportunitas congruit, ut aperte corrigantur . . . Sed cum tempus subditis ad correptionem quaeritur* . . . , Past. 21, 2; Swt. 153, 1–6. [*O. H. Ger.* situlīho *rite*: *Icel.* siðliga *nicely*.]

sīden; *adj. Silken, of silk*:—Sīden *sericum*, Hpt. Gl. 417, 34. [*O. H. Ger.* sēdīn *sericeus*: *Ger.* seiden.]

-siden[n]. v. ælf-siden.

sidesa (?), sidsa, an; *m. A charm* (?), *magical influence* (?):—Wiđ ælfe and wiđ uncūþum sidsan, Lchdm. ii. 296, 10. [Cf. (?) *Icel.* síða *to work a charm*; seiðr *a spell, charm, enchantment*.] Cf. ælf-siden.

sideware, an; *f. Zedoary*:—Nim sidewaran, Lchdm. iii. 10, 30. [*O. H. Ger.* citawar, zitwar: *Ger.* zitwer: *Low Lat.* zedoaria, zeduarium (v. hoc zeduarium *zeduarye*, Wrt. Voc. i. 227, col. 1) *from Arabic* zedwār. *From a French form* citoual *comes Mid. E.* zeduale, A. R. 370, 11, cetewale, Chauc. Group B 1951, see Skeat's note on the passage.]

sīd-fæđme; *adj. Broad of bosom*, of a ship, *broad in the beam*:—Hē sǽlde tō sande sīdfæđme scip, Beo. Th. 3839; B. 1917. Cf. wīd-fæđme.

sīd-fæđmed; *adj. Broad-bosomed, broad-beamed*:—Seomode on sole sīdfæđmed scip, Beo. Th. 610; B. 302.

sīd-feax, -feaxe, -fexe; *adj. With long hair*:—Absalon wæs sīdfeaxe, Homl. Skt. i. 19, 221 MS. U. Sīdfexe *capillatus*, Ælfc. Gr. 43; Zup. 256, 10 note. Hī lange tīd eodon ealle unscorene and sīdfeaxe, Th. Ap. 6, 12. Sume gāþ sīdfeaxe, đæt hȳ þurh đæt wiđmetene sȳn Samuele and Elian and ōđerum hālgum đe sīdfeaxe wǽron, R. Ben. 135, 27–30. v. sīd, III, *and next word.*

sīd-feaxode, -fexede; *adj. Long-haired*:—Absalon wæs sīdfæxede (-feaxode, MS. D.), Homl. Skt. i. 19, 221. Sīdfexede *capillatus*, Ælfc. Gr. 43; Zup. 256, 10. v. preceding word.

sīd-folc, es; *n. A people occupying an extensive space*, (1) *a multitude*:—Sīdfolc micel (*the multitude that accompanied St. Juliana's body*), Exon. Th. 284, 4; Jul. 692. (2) *a great people, great nation*:—God hī of sīdfolcum gesamnade *Dominus de regionibus congregavit eos*, Ps. Th. 106, 2. v. sīd, **I d**; wīd-folc.

sīdian; *p.* ode *To make* or *to become wide, ample* (sīd):—Sīdaþ, Exon. Th. 354, 53; Reim. 65. v. be-sīdian; sīdung.

sīd-land, es; *n. A broad, spacious land*:—Sceal fromcynne folde đīne, sīdland manig, geseted wurđan, Cd. Th. 133, 3; Gen. 2205. Sǽs and sīdland, 148, 3; Gen. 2451. Cf. wīd-land.

sīdling-weg, es; *m. A road that runs obliquely* (?):—Ofer feld on đa rihtlandgemǽre on đone sīdlingweg tō wuda, Cod. Dip. Kmbl. iii. 446, 19. Cf. Halliwell Dict. *sidelings* aslant, sideways: Jamieson *sideling*, oblique; *sydlingis* obliquely, not directly.

sido. v. sidu.

sīd-rand, es; *m. A broad shield*:—Đā wæs on healle heardecg togen sweord ofer setlum, sīdrand manig hafen, Beo. Th. 2583; B. 1289.

sidsan, Lchdm. ii. 296, 10. v. sidesa.

sidu, seodu, siodu (o); *gen. dat.* a; *m.* **I.** *a custom, use, manner, habit, practice*:—Đæt heó cōme tō him mid hire cynehelme, swā swā heora seodu wæs, Anglia ix. 28, 31. Micel sido mid Rōmwarum wæs, Bt. 27, 1; Fox 96, 2. Se sido đe sume men secgaþ đæt [hē] sié mēde wyrđe, sume men secgaþ đæt hē sié wȳtes wyrđe, 39, 9; Fox 226, 4. Hē dyde him đæt rīceter tō sida (sioda, Cott. MSS.) and tō gewunan *ministerium regiminis vertit in usum dominationis*, Past. 121, 9; Swt. 121, 19. Đū ne meaht hiora sidu and heora gecynd onwendan, Bt. 7, 2; Fox 18, 30. God gesette unāwendendlīcne sido and þeáwas his gesceaftum, 21; Fox 74, 1: Met. 11, 12. Þeóda swīđe ungelīca ǽgđer ge on sprǽce ge on þeáwum ge on eallum sīdum *nationes lingua, moribus, totius vitae ratione distantes*, Bt. 18, 2; Fox 62, 30. **I a.** *a religious practice, a rite* (cf. *Icel.* siðr *religion, faith*, Kristinn, heiðinn siðr *Christianity, heathenism*):—Moyses wolde Obab ob đæs hǽđendōmes siđum ālǽdan *cum Hobab a gentilitatis conversatione vellet educere*, Past. 41, 5; Swt. 304, 9. **II.** *good conduct, morality, modesty*:—Hādlīcere side (fǽmnhādlīcere sidefulnysse (?) *v.* sidefulness) *virginalis pudicitiae* (*castitatis*), Hpt. Gl. 449, 4. Side (? -fulnysse) *pudicitia, castitate*, 454, 53. Đa kyningas (*of England*) ǽgđer ge hiora sibbe ge hiora siodo (sido, Cott. MSS.) ge hiora onweald gehióldon *the kings maintained peace, morality, and power*, Past. pref.; Swt. 3, 7. Gif hē þurh cūscne siodo lǽst mīna lāra *if by modest conduct he carry out my instructions*, Cd. Th. 39, 2; Gen. 618. [*Goth.* sidus gōds *boni mores*: *O. Sax.* sidu *a custom*: *O. Frs.* side: *O. H. Ger.* situ *mos, consuetudo, habitus, usus, ritus, indoles, moralitas*: *Icel.* siðr.] v. land-, un-sidu.

sīdung, e; *f. An extension, augmentation*:—Ymbe đises bissextus gefyllednysse wē wyllaþ rūmlīcor iungum cnihtum geopenian . . . đæt hig syđđan his sȳdunge ōđrum gecȳđon . . . De augmentatione bissexti, (*then follows the promised account*), Anglia viii. 306, 16.

sīd-wærc, es; *m. A pain in the side*:—Wiđ sīdwærce, Lchdm. ii. 62, 24: 256, 12: iii. 20, 20.

sīd-weg, es; *m. A road that stretches far*; in the plural *distant parts*:—Đā wæs gesamnod of sīdwegum mægen unlytel, Elen. Kmbl. 564; El. 282. Fugla cynn on healfa gehwone heápum þringaþ sīgaþ sīdwegum *contrahit in coetum sese genus omne volantum*, Exon. Th. 221, 19; Ph. 337. Cf. wīd-weg.

sīd-wyrm, es; *m. A silk-worm*:—Siolucwyrm ođđe sīdwyrm *bombix*, Wrt. Voc. ii. 12, 22. Sȳdwyrm, i. 24, 6. [*O. H. Ger.* sīda-wurm.]

sié, siemle, sién (*be*), sién (*vision*), siendon, sient, siére, sierede, siex. v. sī, simle, sī, sīn, sind, seár, sirwan, six.

sife, es; *n. A sieve*:—Sibi *crebrum*, Wrt. Voc. ii. 105, 41. Sife *crebrum, cribellum*, 136, 62: *cribrum*, i. 34, 41: *cribra* vel *cribellum*, 83, 20. Lytel sife *cribellum*, 34, 42. Āsift smale þurh smæl sife *sift fine through a fine sieve*, Lchdm. ii. 94, 2: 72, 28. Man sceal habban . . . syfa . . . hǣrsyfe, Anglia ix. 264, 13. [*O. H. Ger.* sib; *n. cribrum, cribellum*.] v. hǽr-, windwig-sife.

sifer, sifeþ. v. sȳfer, sibban.

sifeþa, seofoþa; *pl. f.*: *but also* sifeþa, an; *m.* **I.** *siftings, bran, chaff*:—Sifeþa *furfur*, Wrt. Voc. i. 67, 49: *acus*, 83, 19. Sifiþan, siuida *furfures*, Txts. 65, 940. Syfeþa, Wrt. Voc. ii. 38, 75. Swā swā mon melo sift; đæt melo þurhcrȳpþ ǣlc þyrel and đa siofoþa (syfeþa, Cott. MS.) weorþaþ āsyndred, Bt. 34, 11; Fox 152, 3. Genim đysse wyrte sǣd on ele gesodene and mid syfeþon gemencged, Lchdm. i. 282, 1. Dō seofoþa on sealt wæter, ii. 262, 13. Riges seofoþa, 48, 20. Oferwylle on đam selfan ecede sifeþan, 250, 23. **II.** *useless seeds, tares*:—Āta ł sifþa ł unwæstm *zizania*, Mt. Kmbl. Lind. 13, 38. Sifþe, 13, 25. Sifþena *zizaniorum*, p. 17, 5. [Syvedys or brynne or palyys *furfur*, Prompt. Parv. 457.]

sīfre. v. sȳfre.

siftan; *p.* te *To sift, pass through a sieve*:—Ic syfte *cribro*, Ælfc. Gr. 24; Zup. 137, 10. Siftiþ (-it, -id) *crebrat*, Txts. 55, 596. Syfteþ, Wrt. Voc. ii. 15, 44. Sift, 136, 61. Swā swā mon melo sift (seft, Cott. MS.), Bt. 34, 11; Fox 152, 2. Sifte, *cribraret*, Wrt. Voc. ii. 74, 3. Syfte, 15, 57. v. ā-, be-, ge-siftan.

sifþa(e), sig. v. sifeþa, sī.

sig (?) *himself*:—Se ðe gebysmreþ sig *qui se polluerit*, L. Ecg. iv. 68, 16; Th. ii. 230, 14.

sígan; *p.* sáh, *pl.* sigon; *pp.* sigen. **I.** *to pass from a higher to a lower position, to sink, descend, decline, fall down*:—Hé (*a man hung on a tree*) on wyrtruman sígeþ, fealleþ on foldan, Exon. Th. 328, 29; Vy. 25. Ðá hé on eorþan sáh *cadens in terram*, Bd. 3, 12; S. 537, 31. Hí áheówon ðæt treów ðæt hit brastliende sáh tó ðam hálgan were. Ðá worhte hé ongeán ðam hreósendum treówe róde tácn, Homl. Th. ii. 508, 33. Him sáh (*here, or from* seón (?), *but* cf. *Icel.* höfðu út sigit iðrin í þat sárit) se innoþ eall út, L. Ælfc. C. 3; Th. ii. 344, 6. Sitte gé sigewíf, sígaþ tó eorþan (*in a charm for bees*), Lchdm. i. 384, 24. Ðú gestaþoladest eorþan swíðe wundorlíce . . . nánwuht eorþlíces hí ne healt, ðæt hió ne síge, and nis hire éðre tó feallanne ofdúne ðonne up, Bt. 33, 4; Fox 130, 37. Ne mæg hió hider ne ðider sígan, Met. 20, 165. Hit hreósan wile, sígan sond æfter réne, 7, 23. Ic sígan lǽte wællregn ufan *I will cause to descend destructive rain from above*, Cd. Th. 81, 23; Gen. 1349. Gewát se wilda fugel earce sécan, wérig sígan tó handa hálgum rince, 88, 9; Gen. 1462. Sígende *preceps*, Germ. 399, 460. [Þe kinge sah to grunde (deide, 2nd MS.), Laym. 10255. Scal þi saule siȝen to helle 14589.] **I a.** *to sink* as the sun to its setting:—Heó (*the sun*) síhþ tó ðam tácne (*Aries*) óþ ǽfen, Anglia viii. 307, 20. Tungla torhtast tó sete sígeþ, Menol. Fox 221; Men. 112. Ealle stiorran sígaþ æfter sunnan under eorþan grund, Met. 29, 15. Sió æþele gesceaft (*the sun*) sáh tó setle, Chr. 937; Erl. 112, 17. [The sunne arist anes a dai and eft sigeð, O. E. Homl. ii. 109, 22.] **I b.** in a figurative sense:—Ða men ðe sígaþ on ðisses middangeardes lufan óþ ðæt hié áfeallaþ of hiera ryhtwísnessum *cadentes a sua rectitudine animas, atque in hujus mundi se delectatione reclinantes*, Past. 19, 1; Swt. 143, 16. Mé on sáh unrihtes feala *declinaverunt in me iniquitates*, Ps. Th. 54, 3. Swá swá wé sigon ǽr on ðæt unáliéfede óþ ðæt wé áfeóllon *qui per illicita defluendo cecidimus*, Past. 54, 5; Swt. 425, 15. Ðonne áginþ hé sylf sígan oððe áfylþ *inclinavit se et cadet*, Ps. Th. 9, 30. Forlǽte heteníþa gehwone sígan, Exon. Th. 352, 23; Sch. 101. **II.** *to move* towards a point (cf. to make a *descent* upon a place):—Fugla cynn on healfa gehwone heápum þringaþ sígaþ sídwegum *contrahit in coetum sese genus omne volantum*, Exon. Th. 221, 19; Ph. 337. Godwine sáh him ǽfre tóweard Lundenes mid his liþe ðæt hé com tó Súþgeweorce *Godwin kept moving towards London with his force until he came to Southwark*, Chr. 1052; Erl. 184, 19. Ðæt folc him sáh eall onbútan *the people pressed upon him on all sides*, Homl. Skt. i. 23, 650. Eall seó burhwaru sáh út ætgædere ongeán ðæs cáseres tócyme *the whole town moved out together in the direction of the emperor's approach*, 814. Guman sigon ætsomne, Beo. Th. 619; B. 307. Gif ðú ne wilt wirde steóran ac on selfwille sígan lǽtest (cf. gif seó wyrd swá hweorfan mót on yfelra manna gewill, and ðú heore nelt stýran, Bt. 4; Fox 8, 18), Met. 4, 50. Him englas tógeánes heápum cwóman sígan, Exon. Th. 34, 30; Cri. 550. [Engles sihen in to heouene, Jul. 77, 7. Heo siȝen to his hærme, Laym. 8682. Forð heo gunnen siȝen, 29071.] **II a.** of the movement of time:—Iunius síhþ tó mancynne . . . Agustus síhþ tó mannum, Anglia viii. 311, 6–17. Solmónaþ sígeþ tó túne, Menol. Fox 32; Men. 16. **II b.** figurative:—Sigon tó slǽpe *they sank to sleep*, Beo. Th. 2506; B. 1251. Hine man þreáge mid teartran steóre ðæt is him síge on swingella wracu (*verberum vindicta in eum procedat*), R. Ben. 52, 7. [Wið þene sele brudgume þat siheð alle selhðe of *from whom proceeds all happiness*, H. M. 47, 35.] **III.** *to ooze, run* as matter. v. seón:—Gif ðæt brægen út síge *if the brain protrude*, Lchdm. ii. 22, 19. Lǽt sígan út on sum fæt *let it drain out into a vessel*, iii. 48, 6. **IV.** *to strain, filter, act as a filter*, cf. (?) sígere:—Sígende sond rén swylgþ *bibulae arenae*, Bt. 12; Fox 36, 12, 16. [*O. Sax.* sígan *to sink* (of the sun); *to proceed*: *O. Frs.* síga: *O. H. Ger.* sígan *declinare, ruere*: *Icel.* síga *to sink down, slide*.] v. á-, ge-, on-sígan; sígend, *and* seón.

sigdi. v. síðe.

sige, es; *m. A fall, setting* of the sun:—Sió sunne ðonne hió on sige weorðeþ (cf. Bt. 25; Fox 88, 25), Met. 13, 111. v. niðer-sige.

sige, es; *m. Victory, triumph.* **I.** *success in war*:—Sige *victoria*, Wrt. Voc. i. 84, 19. Ic siges mihte eów sille, ðæt gé eów tó gamene feónda áfillaþ, Wulfst. 132, 19. Se cyng áhte siges geweald *victory remained with the king*, Chr. 1066; Erl. 201, 12. Hí mid mycele sige (*triumpho magno*) hám fóran, Bd. 1, 12; S. 480, 32. Palm getácnaþ syge, Homl. Th. i. 218, 11. Sige forgifan *to grant victory*, Bd. 2, 9; S. 511, 36: Elen. Kmbl. 288; El. 144. Sige syllan, Val. 2, 25. Sige habban *to conquer, be victorious*, Num. 31, 18. Hæfde sige *vincebat, superabat*, Ex. 17, 11. Ða Cretense hæfdon ðone grimlecan sige *cruentiorem victoriam Cretenses exercuerunt*, Ors. 1, 9; Swt. 42, 28. Sige geræ̌can, gesleán, gewinnan *to gain the victory*, 3, 1; Swt. 96, 33: Bd. 1, 16; S. 484, 22: Num. 21, 1. Sige niman, onfón *to obtain the victory*, Chr. 800; Erl. 60, 9: 845; Erl. 66, 24: Bd. 1, 16; S. 484, 21. Hié ðæt an missenlícum sigum dreógende wǽron, Ors. 4, 7; Swt. 182, 3. Ðæt hié mec mid heán sigum (*cum sublimibus tropheis*) geweorðedon, Nar. 24, 24. **II.** *success in conflict*:—Siges *triumphi*, Hpt. Gl. 447, 76. Mid sigerlícum sige *triumphali tropheo*, 473, 41: Hymn. Surt. 44, 27. Sige onsendan *to make victorious*, Salm. Kmbl. 487; Sal. 244. Heó bád ðone écan sige, Bd. 4, 23; S. 593, 14. Sigas *triumphos*, Hymn. Surt. 47, 20: *victorias*, 129, 24: *trophea*, 131, 22. **II a.** *success* in commerce:—Oxan grasiende gesihþ sige ceápas (-es? *or* sigeceápas?) getácnaþ, oxan slápende gesihþ yfelnysse ceápes getácnaþ, Lchdm. iii. 200, 9. [The word occurs often as one of the components of proper names: e.g. see Txts. 512–513. Siȝe (syȝe, siȝen) habben, Laym. 23896: 17409: 16199. Siȝe winnenn, Orm. 5461. Sy *triumph*, Jul. 11, 16. *Goth.* sigis: *O. Sax.* sigi: *O. H. Ger.* sigi, sigu: *Icel.* sig.] v. weorc-, word-sige, *and* sigor.

sige-beác[e]n, es; *n.* **I.** *a sign* or *monument of victory gained, a trophy*:—Se palm is sigebeácen, Homl. Th. ii. 402, 10. Ðǽr ðæt heofonlíce sigebeácen (*trophaeum*) árǽred beón sceolde, Bd. 3, 2; S. 524, 35. Æþelinges (*Christ*) ród, sigebeácen (cf. sige-beám, -bearn) sóð, Elen. Kmbl. 1772; El. 888. Be ðam sigebeácne (*the cross*), 336; El. 168. Sélest sigebeácna (*the cross*), 1946; El. 975. Sigebécn, sigbeácn *tropea, signa*, Txts. 103, 2043. Ðis sigbécn, 124, 2. **II.** *an ensign that is to lead to victory, a banner*:—Mid sigebeácne *vexillo, signo*, Hpt. Gl. 450, 35. Árǽraþ eówer sigebécn, and onginnaþ eówer gefeoht, Homl. Skt. i. 5, 59. v. sigor-beác[e]n.

sige-beáh; *g.* -beáges; *m. That which encircles the head of the victor, a crown*:—Hé onféng sigebeáh (*coronam*) éces lífes, Bd. 1, 7; S. 478, 34. Sigbég, Jn. Skt. Lind. 19, 2: Rtl. 1, 15. Sigbéh, 6, 1.

sige-beám, es; *m. A tree on which a victory is gained*, generally *the cross*:—Se sigebeám *the cross*, Rood Kmbl. 25; Kr. 13: 251; Kr. 127: Elen. Kmbl. 1927; El. 965. Be ðam sigebeáme, on ðam þrowode þeóda Waldend, 840; El. 420: 885; El. 444. Sélest sigebeáma, 2053; El. 1028. Sigebeámas þrý (*the three crosses at the crucifixion*), 1691; El. 847. v. sige-beácen, -bearn.

sige-bearn, es; *n. A victorious child*, applied to Christ:—His gást onsende sigebearn Godes, Elen. Kmbl. 959; El. 481: Exon. Th. 460, 3; Hö. 11. Ðæt sygebearn, 461, 29; Hö. 43. Ealra sigebearna ðæt séleste, 33, 3; Cri. 520.

sige-beorht; *adj. Rendered illustrious by victory, triumphant*:—Hié swá sigebeorhte and swá gebégde mid mycelre blisse tó hám fóran, Blickl. Homl. 203, 30. Cf. *the proper name* Sigebryht, -berht, Chr. 755; Erl. 48, 18: Txts. 512. v. sigor-beorht.

sige-beorn, es; *m. A victorious warrior*:—Ne gefrægn ic æt wera hilde sixtig sigebeorna sél gebǽran . . . Hig fuhton fíf dagas, swá hyra nán ne feól, Fins. Th. 76; Fin. 38. [Cf. *Icel.* Sig-björn (*proper name*).]

sige-bíme, an; *f. A trumpet which is sounded after victory*:—Sungon sigebýman (*after the Israelites had escaped from the Egyptians*), Cd. Th. 214, 6; Exod. 565. [Cf. *Icel.* sigr-lúðr.]

sige-bróðor; *m. A victorious brother*, used in speaking to St. Andrew of St. Matthew, who was not daunted by his heathen captors, Andr. Kmbl. 366; An. 183.

sige-cempa, an; *m. A victorious warrior*:—Wæs Dauid æt wíge sóð sigecempa, Ps. C. 50, 10.

sige-cwén, e; *f. A victorious queen*, applied to Elene, Elen. Kmbl. 519; El. 260: 1992; El. 998.

sige-déma, an; *m. A victorious, triumphant judge, the irresistible judge of the day of judgment*:—Se sigedéma, freá mihtig (*Christ*) Andr. Kmbl. 1322; An. 661. Ne beóþ ðǽr (*at the last judgment*) forþ borene sigele tó ðam sigedéman, Wulfst. 254, 1: Exon. Th. 65, 28; Cri. 1061.

sige-dryhten, es; *m. A victorious lord*, (1) as a complimentary epithet of an earthly chief:—Sigedrihten mín, aldor Eást-Dena, Beo. Th. 788; B. 391. Sigedryhten mín (*the departed Guthlac*), Exon. Th. 184, 24; Gú. 1349. Wit for uncrum sigedryhtne song áhófan, 324, 33; Víd. 104. (2) as an epithet of the Deity:—Þeóda Waldend, sigedryhten mín, Andr. Kmbl. 2905; An. 1455: Exon. Th. 176, 19; Gú. 1212: Ps. C. 50, 119. Þeóden engla, sóð sigedrihten, Hy. 6, 34. Ðú eart selfa sigedrihten God, Met. 20, 260. Ðonc secgan sigedryhtne, ðæs ðe hé hine sylfne ús sendan wolde, Exon. Th. 9, 1; Cri. 128: Andr. Kmbl. 1753; An. 879. Sigedrihten, mihtigne God, Cd. Th. 33, 21; Gen. 523: 48, 20; Gen. 778. [*O. Sax.* sigi-drohtin (*applied to the Deity*).]

sige-eádig; *adj. Blessed with victory, victorious*:—Sigeeádig bil, Beo. Th. 3119; B. 1557. [Cf. *Icel.* sigr-sæll.] v. sigor-eádig.

sige-fæst; *adj. With victory secured, victorious, triumphant.* (1) applied to persons:—Sigefæst *victor*, Wrt. Voc. i. 84, 18. Sigfæst *triumphator*, Rtl. 122, 12. And hé sigefæst swá eft hám férde *sicque victor in patriam reversus*, Bd. 2, 9; S. 512, 5: Exon. Th. 460, 26; Hö. 23. Þurh cyningces wísdóm folc wyrð gesǽlig, gesundful and sigefæst, L. I. P. 2; Th. ii. 306, 5. Hé ofslóh mid ðam sigefæstan here eall ðæt mennisc, Jos. 10, 40. Hí sigefæste ofer sǽ férdon, Bd. 1, 12; S. 481, 15. Sigefæste *triumphabiles, triumpho plenos*, Hpt. Gl. 489, 33. Hý beóþ ðý gesundran and ðý sigefæstran, Exon. Th. 408, 29; Rä. 27, 19. Se sigefæstesta cyning *victoriosissimus rex*, Bd. 3, 7; S. 529, 16. (2) applied to things:—Sigefest wuldor, Hy. 8, 4. Sigefæstne hâm, Menol. Fox 298; Men. 150. Sigefæst tâcon *victricia signa*, Bd. 1, 8; S. 479, 24: H. R. 105, 21. Sigefæstan gûþfanan *victricia, victoriosa*, Hpt. Gl. 447, 54. v. sigor-fæst.

sigefæstan; *p.* te *To triumph*:—Sigefeston *triumphant*, Txts. 182, 77. v. ge-sigefæstan.

sigefæstness, e; *f. Victoriousness, triumph*:—Hē wîtgode be Cristes sigefæstnesse, ðā ðā hē on heofonas âstâh, Ps. Th. 23, arg. Ðeáh ânra gehwylc wind hæbbe twelf sigefæstnissa, Salm. Kmbl. 152, 3. Sigefæstnissum *triumphis*, Rtl. 93, 7: 75, 19. v. sigorfæstness.

sige-folc, es; *n. A victorious* or *triumphant people*:—Heó (*Judith*) ðæt word âcwæþ tō ðam sigefolce (*the Jews who were about to destroy the Assyrians*), Judth. Thw. 23, 32; Jud. 152. Ðā wæs þeód on sǣlum, sigefolca swēg, Beo. Th. 1292; B. 644: Menol. Fox 593; Gn. C. 66.

sige-gealdor, es; *n. A charm that gives victory*:—Ic mē on ðisse gyrde belûce . . . wið eal ðæt lāð ðe intō land fare; sygegealdor ic begale, sigegyrd ic mē wege, Lchdm. i. 388, 14.

sige-gefeoht, es; *n. A victorious battle, a victory*:—On sigegefeohtum ellreordra cynna *in victories over foreign races*; in expugnandis barbaris, Bd. 3, 3; S. 525, 25.

sige-gird, e; *f. A rod that brings victory*. v. sige-gealdor.

sige-hrēmig; *adj. Exultant with victory, triumphant*:—Gesæt sigehrēmig on ða swîðran hand ēce eádfruma (*Christ*) âgnum Fæder, Exon. Th. 33, 25; Cri. 531: Hy. 8, 30.

sige-hrēð *fame gained by victory*:—Onsǣl sigehrēð secgum *tell men of the fame you have won* (cf. the account of his deeds which Beowulf had given to Hrothgar), Beo. Th. 984; B. 490. Cf. gûþ-hrēð.

sige-hrēðig; *adj. Triumphant*. (1) applied to men:—Dômeádig cempa . . . sigehrēðig (*Guthlac*), Exon. Th. 146, 4; Gû. 704. Hig ne wēndon ðæt hē sigehrēðig sēcean cōme þeóden *they did not expect that Beowulf would come triumphant* (*from his fight with Grendel's mother*) *and visit Hrothgar*, Beo. Th. 3198; B. 1597: 5505; B. 2756. (2) applied to the Deity:—Se Ælmihtiga . . . gesette sigehrēðig sunnan and mônan, 188; B. 94.

sige-hwîl, e; *f. A time of victory, the hour of victory*:—Wedra helm feónd gefylde . . . Ðæt ðam þeódne wæs sîðes sigehwîl, Beo. Th. 5413; B. 2710.

sigel, sægl, segl; *n.* (?) *The sun*; also *the name of the rune = S*:— ᛋ sǣmannum symble byþ on hihte (cf. Icelandic Runic poem—Sôl er landa ljómi), Runic pm. Kmbl. 342, 15; Rûn. 16. Woruldcandel scân, sigel sûþan fûs, Beo. Th. 3936; B. 1966. Wuldres tâcen swylce hâdre sægl, Andr. Kmbl. 178; An. 89. Hâdor sægl gewât under scrîðan, 2911; An. 1458. Heáfdes segl *the sun of the head, the eye* (cf. *Icel.* enni-mâni, -tungl = *the eye*), 100; An. 50. [*Goth.* sauil; *n. the sun*: *Icel.* sól; *f.*] v. heáðo-sigel; sigel-beorht, -hearwa, -hweorfa, -torht, -waras.

sigel, sigl; *n.* (?) *A clasp, brooch, jewel*:—Sigl, sigil *bulla*, Txts. 45, 331: *fibula*, 63, 874: *sibba*, 97, 1856. Sigl *bulla, gemma*, Wrt. Voc. ii. 126, 70: *fibula*, 148, 57. Sigil *bulla*, i. 288, 7. Sigel, ii. 11, 34: *fibula*, 35, 42. [Cf. *O. H. Ger.* sigilla; *f. lunula. From Latin* (?) sigillum.] v. sigle.

sigel-beorht; *adj.* I. *sun-bright, bright with the sun, sunny*:—Wintres dæg sigelbeorhtne genimþ hærfest mid herige hrîmes and snâwes *winter's day takes captive sunny autumn with its army of frost and snow*, Menol. Fox 404; Men. 203. Bringþ sigelbeorhte dagas sumor tō tûne, 175; Men. 89. II. *bright as the sun*:—Sitt sigelbeorht swegles brytta on heáhsetle *ille sedens solio fulget sublimis in alto*, Dôm. L. 117. [*Icel.* sól-bjartr.] Cf. sigel-torht.

sige-leán, es; *n. A reward of victory, prize, palm*:—Sigeleán ł edleán *palma*, Hpt. Gl. 482, 5: 432, 75: *triumphus, palma*, 424, 53. Ðæt wē brûcan sigeleáne *ut perfruamur bravio*, Hymn. Surt. 129, 18. Simon and Thaddeus beornas beadorôfe sceoldon þurh wǣpenhete sigeleán sēcan, Apstls. Kmbl. 161; Ap. 81. Ēce lîf, sēlust sigeleána, Elen. Kmbl. 1051; El. 527. [*Goth.* sigis-laun *bravium*.] v. sigor-leán.

sige-leás; *adj.* I. *without victory, unsuccessful in conflict, defeated*:—Engle nû lange [wǣron] eal sigeleáse *the English now for a long time have been deserted by victory*, Wulfst. 162, 15. Hȳ sigeleáse (*defeated*) ðone grēnan wong ofgiefan sceoldan, Exon. Th. 130, 33; Gû. 447: 141, 6; Gû. 623: Cd. Th. 20, 20; Gen. 312. I a. of an expedition, *unattended by victory*:—Sigeleásne sîð, Exon. Th. 120, 17; Gû. 273. I b. of a song, *that tells of defeat*:—Gehȳrdon galan Godes andsacan sigeleásne sang, Beo. Th. 1578; B. 787. [*O. H. Ger.* sigu-lôs.]

sige-leóþ, es; *n. A song of triumph*:—Ðā wæs sigeleóþ (cf. *Icel.* sigr-óp) galen on herefelda, Elen. Kmbl. 248; El. 124. Engla þreátas sigeleóþ sungon (*when Guthlac came to Heaven*), Exon. Th. 181, 6; Gû. 1289.

Sigel-hearwa (Sîl-), an; *m. An Ethiopian*:—Se deófol wearþ ætеówod swylce ormǣte Sîlhearwa, Homl. Th. i. 466, 24. Hē him ætȳwde micelne Sigelhearwan, ðæm wæs seó onsȳn sweartre ðonne hrûm, Shrn. 120, 24. Twegen blace Sîlhearwan, Homl. Th. ii. 496, 17: Homl. Skt. i. 4, 285. Sigylhearwan (Sielhearwæn, MS. T.) *Aethiopes*, Ps. Spl. 71, 9. Sigelhearwena (Sȳl-, Ps. Spl.) folc, Ps. Surt. 73, 14: ii. p. 189, 36. Ethiopia, ðæt is ðæra Sîlhearwena rîce, Homl. Th. ii. 472, 13: i. 454, 12. Ðæra Sîlhearwena land *terra Aethiopiae*, Gen. 2, 13. Sîllhearewena (Sîlhearwena, MSS. R. P.) land, Lchdm. iii. 258, 18. Ðû sealdest Sigelhearwan (-as, MS.) tō môse *dedisti in escam populo Aethiopum*, Ps. Th. 73, 14. Cf. Sigel-waras.

Sigelhearwen; *adj. Ethiopian*:—For his Sigelhearwenan wîfe *propter uxorem ejus Aethiopissam*, Num. 12, 1. Sȳlhearwenre, *Aethiopica*, Hpt. Gl. 514, 49.

sigel-hweorfa, an; *m.* A plant-name, a word equivalent in meaning to the Greek *heliotrope*. It is found as the representative of foreign words in the following:—Sigelhweorfa *heliotropus*, Wrt. Voc. i. 68, 5, 80: Lchdm. iii. 302, col. 1. Sigelhuerpha *eliotropia*, id. Sigelhueorua *nimphea*, 304, col. 1: *solsequia*, 305, col. 1. Sigelwearfa. Ðeós wyrt ðe Grēcas *heliotropus*, and Rômâne *uertamnum* nemnaþ, and eác Angle sigelhweorfa hâtaþ, Lchdm. i. 152, 21. Sigilhweorfa *eliotropus*, 254, 11. In the following no foreign equivalent is given:—Sigelhweorfa, ii. 94, 25: iii. 24, 4. Nim nioþoweardne sigelhweorfan, 326, 17. See Lchdm. ii. 404, col. 2.

sigel-hweorfe, an; *f.* A plant name:—Sigelhwerfe *solsequium* vel *heliotropium*, Wrt. Voc. i. 30, 30. *Eleotropam*, Grece; Latine, *solsequium, idem* sigelhweorfe, ii. 32, 26. Nim sigelhweorfan ða smalan unwæscene, Lchdm. ii. 108, 23. v. preceding word.

sige-lîc; *adj. Victorious*:—Ða sigelîcan *victricia*, Wrt. Voc. ii. 78, 21: *victoria*, 92, 4. v. sigor-lîc.

sigel-torht; *adj. Bright with sunshine* or *bright as the sun*, cf. sigelbeorht:—Swā wæs ealne dæg ôððæt ǣfen com sigeltorht (*epithet of* ǣfen *or of* Andrew?) swungen, Andr. Kmbl. 2493; An. 1248.

Sigel-waras, -ware; *pl. The Ethiopians*:—Mannkynn sweartes hiwes . . . ða man hâteþ Sîlhearwan (Sigilwara, MS. V.), Nar. 38, 30. Hine Sigelwearas (*Aethiopes*) sēceaþ, Ps. Th. 71, 9. Folc Sigelwara *populus Aethiopum*, 86, 3. Sigelwara land, Cd. Th. 182, 2; Exod. 69. Hē (*St. Matthew*) gelǣrde Sigelwara mǣgþe, and of Sigelwarum hē flȳmde twegan drȳas, Shrn. 131, 27: Apstls. Kmbl. 127; Ap. 64. Cf. Sigelhearwa.

sige-mēce, es; *m. A victorious sword, a sword wielded by a victor's hand*, Exon. Th. 93, 24; Cri. 1531.

Sigen, e; *f. The Seine*; Sequana:—Andlang Sigene, Chr. 887; Erl. 84, 31. Be Sigene (Signe, MS. A.), 660; Erl. 35, 8: 897; Erl. 94, 28. [*O. H. Ger.* Sigana.]

sîgend, es; *m. Movement of the sea, wave*:—Sîgend *flustra*, i. *undae*, Wrt. Voc. ii. 35, 62. Flôd *flustra*, sîgendum *flustris*, 33, 33: 76, 63. v. sîgan.

sîgere (?), es; *m. A glutton*:—Sîgiras (siras, Corpus Gl.) *lurcones, avidi*, Txts. 72, 568. v. sîgerian, *and* cf. (?) sîgan, IV.

sige-reáf, es; *n. A triumphal robe*; toga palmata, Wrt. Voc. i. 41, 4.

sigerian. v. sigorian.

sîgerian (?) *to act as a glutton*:—Sîgergendum *lurconibus*, Wrt. Voc. ii. 76, 34. v. sîgere.

sige-rîce; *adj. Victorious, triumphant*. (1) applied to the Deity:—Witig Drihten . . . sigerîce, Cd. Th. 179, 11; Exod. 27. (2) applied to men, cf. *prop. name* Sigerîc:—Gif gē (*the Israelites*) gehealdaþ hâlige lâre, gē gesittaþ sigerîce beórselas beorna, Cd. Th. 213, 34; Exod. 562. [*Ger.* sieg-reich.]

sige-rôf; *adj. Of victorious energy, triumphantly active*. (1) applied to a warrior or to a king:—Sigerôf kyning (*Hrothgar*), Beo. Th. 1243; B. 619: (*Constantine*), Elen. Kmbl. 315; El. 158: 141; El. 70. Wǣron Rômware secgas sigerôfe, 93; El. 47: Judth. Thw. 24, 8; Jud. 177. (2) without reference to battle:—Mîn yldra fæder sigerôf sægde, frôd fyrnwiota, Elen. Kmbl. 873; El. 437. Sigerôfne (*St. Andrew*), Andr. Kmbl. 2451; An. 1227. Gesǣton sigerôfe . . . rǣdþeahtende, Elen. Kmbl. 1732; El. 868. Sigerôfra (*the saints in glory*), Lchdm. i. 390, 4. (3) applied to the Deity:—Ēce Dryhten, sigerôf settend, Exon. Th. 188, 17; Az. 47.

sige-sceorp, es; *n. Triumphal apparel*, Exon. Th. 341, 16; Gn. Ex. 127.

sige-sîþ, es; *m. A victorious expedition* or *journey*:—Oft dǣdlata dôme foreldit sigisîtha gahuem *generally the dilatory man is too late for glory, for every successful undertaking*, Txts. 152, 9.

sige-spēd, e; *f. Triumphant faculty, ability that gains its ends*:—Ðē God sealde sâwle sigespēd and snyttro cræft *God hath given thee effectual power of soul and wisdom's art*, Elen. Kmbl. 2341; El. 1172. Ic on ðē oncnâwe wîsdômes gewit, sigespēd geseald, Andr. Kmbl. 1291; An. 646. v. sigor-spēd.

sige-tâc[e]n, es; *n. A sign of victory*:—Ðæt hâlige sigetâcen (*the cross*), Blickl. Homl. 97, 13. Hē sigetâcen sende *misit signa*, Ps. Th. 134, 9. v. sigor-tâc[e]n, sige-beác[e]n.

sige-þeód, e; *f. A victorious people, a powerful people*:—Hyne gesôhton on sigeþeóde hearde hildefrecan, Beo. Th. 4415; B. 2204: Exon. 473, 23; Bo. 19. Sigeþeóda (*the victorious Goths*), Met. 1, 4. Secgeaþ his wuldor geond sigeþeóde (*inter gentes*), Ps. Th. 95, 3.

sige-þreát, es; *m. A triumphant band*, Exon. Th. 53, 2; Cri. 844.

sige-þúf (?), es; *m. A banner that conducts to victory, a victorious banner*:—Stôpon secgas and gesíþas, bǽron þúfas (sigeþúfas?), Judth. Thw. 24, 22; Jud. 201. Cf. sige-beác[e]n.

sige-tiber, es; *n. A sacrifice for victory* (? cf. *Icel.* sigr-blót):—Wolde líge gesyllan his swǽsne sunu tó sigetibre, Cd. Th. 203, 12; Exod. 402. v. sigor-tiber.

sige-torht; *adj. Splendid with victory, triumphant*:—Sigetorht árás éce Drihten, Cd. Th. 279, 19; Sat. 240. Cf. sige-beorht.

sige-tudor, es; *n. A victorious, triumphant progeny*, applied to the human race, Exon. Th. 154, 5; Gú. 838.

sige-wǽpen, es; *n. A weapon with which victory is won*, Beo. Th. 1612; B. 804.

sige-wang, es; *m. A plain where victory is won, a glorious plain.* (1) where actual fighting has taken place:—Se mǽsta dǽl ðæs heriges læg on ðam sigewonge, Judth. Thw. 25, 36. (2) where actual fighting is not referred to, *a place in which evil is overcome*:—Smeolt wæs se sigewang (*the place where St. Andrew's heathen enemies had been overwhelmed*), Andr. Kmbl. 3160; An. 1583. Smylte is se sigewong (cf. ðæt torhte lond, l. 19, wlitig is se wong eall, 198, 8, *the dwelling-place of the Phenix*), Exon. Th. 199, 29; Ph. 33: 146, 23; Gú. 714. Mennisce áras on ðam sigewonge (*Guthlac's dwelling-place*) helpe gemétton, 157, 18; Gú. 893.

sige-wíf, es; *n. Grimm supposes this word may be a general denomination of wise women*, D. M. 402; *the passage in which it occurs is a charm, where it is addressed to bees when swarming*:—Sittaþ gé, sigewíf, sígaþ tó eorþan, Lchdm. i. 384, 24.

sigle, es; *n. A necklace, collar, band for the neck*:—Ne beóþ ðǽr forþ borene sigele ne beágas ne heora heáfodgold, Wulfst. 253, 23. Ðá gemétte heó under hrægele gylden sigele (*monile*), Bd. 4, 23; S. 595, 5. Háma ætwæg Brósinga mene, sigle and sincfæt, Beo. Th. 2404; B. 1200. In mínum sweoran ic mé gemon beran ða ýdlan byrþenne gyldenra sigla *in collo me memini supervacua monitium pondera portare*, Bd. 4, 19; S. 589, 27: Beo. Th. 2318; B. 1157. Hí on beorg dydon bég and siglu . . . hyrsta, 6308; B. 3164. [*Icel.* sigli *a necklace.*] v. máðum-sigle; sigel, in-sigle.

sigle, an; *f. Rye*:—Siglan dust, Lchdm. ii. 126, 7. [*Lat.* secale; *later* segale, sigalum, sigla: cf. *Ital.* segale: *Fr.* seigle.]

sigor, es; *m. Victory, triumph*:—Mé oferswíðde se wyrresta sigor, Shrn. 37, 24. Sigor eft áhwearf of norþmonna nídgeteóne, æsctír wera, Cd. Th. 124, 24; Gen. 2067. Sigores *palmam*, Wrt. Voc. ii. 67, 32. Mid sigores wuldre tó heofonum ástígan, Wulfst. 199, 13. Swegles ealdor hyre (*Judith*) sigores onleáh, Judth. Thw. 23, 16; Jud. 124. Sigere *tropheo*, Hpt. Gl. 508, 64. Elne gewurðod, dóme and sigore, Cd. Th. 129, 3; Gen. 2138. Hlísfulne sigor, *famosum tropheum*, Wrt. Voc. ii. 147, 29. Ic sceal his róde sigor (*the triumph of Christ's cross*) swíðor wíscan ðonne ondrǽdan, Homl. Th. i. 594, 20. Sigor æt sæcce, Elen. Kmbl. 2363; B. 1183. Folc ðe hé on deóflum genom þurh his sylfes sygor, Exon. Th. 36, 24; Cri. 581. Sigera *triumphorum*, Hpt. Gl. 425, 33. Ðyssum sigorum ðú Godes biscop blissian miht *hisque Dei consul factus laetare triumphis*, Bd. 2, 1; S. 500, 31. Mid ðǽm siogorum geweorðad *triumphans*, Nar. 28, 4. ¶ *The word occurs often in reference to the Deity* (cf. *in Icel.* Sig-föður *one of Odin's names*, sig-tívar *the gods of victory*, sigr-goð *a god of victory*):—Swegles aldor se ðe sigor seleþ, Cd. Th. 170, 5; Gen. 2808. Ðæt hé sigora gehwæs ána weólde (cf. Hans (*Odin's*) menn trúðu því, at hann ætti heimilan sigr í hverri orrostu, Ynglinga Saga, c. 2), Exon. Th. 276, 5; Jul. 561. Sigores ágend, ealdor, freá, fruma, God, weard, Cd. Th. 307, 11; Sat. 678: Hy. 3, 20: Exon. Th. 25, 21; Cri. 404: 19, 2; Cri. 294: Andr. Kmbl. 1519; An. 761: Exon. Th. 15, 29; Cri. 243. Sigora dryhten, freá, God, sellend, settend, sóðcyning, waldend, weard, Cd. Th. 63, 23; Gen. 1036: Exon. Th. 242, 18; Ph. 675: Elen. Kmbl. 2613; El. 1308: Exon. Th. 359, 17; Pa. 64: Cd. Th. 237, 5; Dan. 333: Exon. Th. 75, 29; Cri. 1229: Cd. Th. 8, 19; Gen. 126: 106, 13; 1770. Bidde ic sigere (-a?, -es?) Godes miltse, Lchdm. i. 390, 10. [*Icel.* sigr.] v. hréð-, wíg-sigor; sige, *and following words.*

sigor-beác[e]n, es; *n. A symbol of victory*, applied to the cross, Elen. Kmbl. 1967; El. 985. v. sige-beác[e]n.

sigor-beorht; *adj. Triumphant*, epithet of Christ, Exon. Th. 1, 18; Cri. 10. v. sige-beorht.

sigor-cynn, es; *n. A triumphant, glorious race*, epithet of the Seraphim, Elen. Kmbl. 1506; El. 755.

sigor-eádig; *adj. Blessed with victory, victorious*, Beo. Th. 2626; B. 1311: 4693; B. 2352. v. sige-eádig.

sigor-fæst; *adj. Victorious, triumphant.* (1) as an epithet of the Deity:—Se Sunu (*Christ*) wæs sigorfæst on ðam síðfate, Rood Kmbl. 297; Kr. 150. God sigorfæst, Exon. Th. 217, 18; Ph. 282. (2) of an angel:—Meahtig Meotudes þegn, sigorfæst, 176, 30; Gú. 1218. (3) of a passion:—Brondhát lufu, sigorfæst in sefan, 160, 3; Gú. 938. v sige-fæst.

sigorfæstness, e; *f. Victoriousness*:—Be sigerfestnisse and swíðmódnisse úses Drihtnes mid ðǽm hé ða hǽþnan ofercom, Anglia xi. 173, 12. v. sigefæstness.

sigorian, sigerian, sigrian; *p.* ode *To vanquish, triumph over, triumph*:—Ic sigerie (sigerige, sigrige, sigrie) *triumpho*, Ælfc. Gr. 24; Zup. 137, 5. Ic sigrige be Cristes mádmum, and ic ðíne tintregu ne gefréde, Homl. Th. i. 424, 33. Fullfremed sóðlufu middaneardes sigoraþ ealdor *perfecta caritas mundi triumphat principem*, Hymn. Surt. 123, 38. Sigerode *triumphat*, 105, 32. Sigoriende *triumphans*, 85, 9. Sigriende, Germ. 395, 4. Sigirendes *triumphantis*, Hpt. Gl. 455, 64. [*O. H. Ger.* ubarsigirôn *triumphare*: *Icel.* sigra: *Dan.* seire.]

sigoriend, sigriend, es; *m. A victor*:—Sigriend *victor*, Hymn. Surt. 38, 7.

sigor-leán, es; *n. A reward of victory, prize*:—Dryhten hyre (*Judith*) geaf sigorleán in swegles wuldre, Judth. Thw. 26, 26; Jud. 345. Sigorleán sécan, Exon. Th. 154, 29; Gú. 850: 184, 14; Gú. 1344. Sigorleán habban, Elen. Kmbl. 1246; El. 623. Sigorleánum onfón, Cd. Th. 176, 27; Gen. 2918. Tó sigorleánum sellan, Exon. Th. 97, 14; Cri. 1590. v. sige-leán.

sigor-líc; *adj. Triumphal*:—Ðæt sigorlíce leóþ *carmen triumphale*, Wrt. Voc. ii. 23, 48: Hpt. 438, 16. Mid sigerlícum sige *triumphali tropheo* (*victoria*), 473, 40. v. sige-líc.

sigor-spéd, e; *f. Abundant success*:—Is help gearu æt mǽrum, manna gehwylcum sigorspéd geseald, Andr. Kmbl. 1817; An. 911. Mé is miht ofer eall, sigorspéd geseald, 2868; An. 1437. v. sige-spéd.

sigor-tác[e]n, es; *n. A sign of victory, a convincing sign*:—Godspel bodian, secgan sigortácnum *to preach the gospel, tell it with convincing proofs* or *with marks shewing how it had prevailed*, Exon. Th. 169, 3; Gú. 1089. v. sige-tác[e]n.

sigor-tiber, es; *n. A sacrifice for victory* or *deliverance*:—Wes ðú on ófeste . . . ðæt ðú lác onsecge sigortifre *hasten to offer with a sacrifice, that may deliver you from your peril*, Exon. Th. 257, 30; Jul. 255. v. sige-tiber.

sigor-weorc, es; *A victorious work, a victory*:—Sigorworca hréð, Cd. Th. 198, 2; Exod. 316. [*Icel.* sigr-verk *a victory.*]

sigor-wuldor, es; *n. Triumphant glory, the glory of the victor*:—Háligra sáula gesittaþ in sigorwuldre Dryhtnes dreámas, Exon. Th. 109, 21; Gú. 93.

sigrian. v. sigorian.

sigsonte? *a plant name*, Lchdm. i. 74, 11: 102, 24.

-siht, -sihte. v. ge-, in-, út-siht, blód-, út-sihte.

sihþ, e; *f. A vision*:—Bóc ðæra sighðana *apocalypsis*, Jn. Skt. p. 1, 11. Ða sihðo (gisihðe, Rush.) *quae vidissent*, Mk. Skt. Lind. 9, 9. v. æt-, ge-sihþ.

sihtre, silcen. v. seohtre, seolucen.

silf, silfren, Síl-hearwa, sillan. v. self, seolfren, Sigel-hearwa, sellan.

Sillende *Zealand*, Ors. 1, 1; Swt. 19, 20, 23.

sil-líc, silofor. v. seld-líc, seolfor.

siltan; *p.* te *To salt, season*:—Ic sylte *condio*, Ælfc. Gr. 30; Zup. 192, 13. Selt *condit*, Wrt. Voc. ii. 135, 55. On ðæm ðe gé hit syltaþ (*condistis*), Mk. Skt. 9, 50. Selte mon hiora mettas, Lchdm. ii. 234, 14. Láreówum gedafenaþ ðæt hí mid wísdómes sealte geleáffulra manna mód sylton, Homl. Th. ii. 536, 17. ge-, un-silt (-sylt).

síma, an; *m. A cord, rope*:—Satan læg símon gesǽled (cf. *Icel.* sím-bundinn), Cd. Th. 47, 23; Gen. 765. [*O. Sax.* símo *a cord*: *O. Frs.* sím: *Icel.* síma; *n.*; *cf. also* seimr *a string*: *Dan.* sime *a seton.*]

síman; *p.* de *To load, put a burden* (seám) *on*:—Gé sýmaþ (sémaþ, Lind.) men mid ðám byrþenum . . . and gé ne áhrínaþ ða seámas mid eówrum ánum fingre *oneratis homines oneribus . . . et ipsi uno digito uestro non tangitis sarcinas*, Lk. Skt. 11, 46. Sýmaþ *onerant*, Engl. Stud. ix. 40. Hig sýmdon hira assan *oneratis asinis*, Gen. 44, 13. Sýmaþ eówre assan, 45, 17. v. ge-, ofer-síman (-sýman).

simbel, symbel, simel; *adj. Continual, perpetual.* [*The word occurs only in the adverbial forms* simbles, simble, on simbel (cf. on ídel), *and the compounds* simbel-farende, -geféra; *similarly O. H. Ger.* simpal *for the most part appears in adverbial forms, but Graff vi. 26 gives one instance of its adjective use*, simplêm *assiduis. Icel.* simul *ever, is preserved in only one or two passages*]:—On simbel *ever, always, continually*:—Hí hiora freóndscipe forþ on symbel gehealdaþ *they continue ever to maintain their friendship*, Met. 11, 94. Hió þyrstende wæs on symbel mannes blódes *she was continually thirsting for human blood*; haec, sanguinem sitiens, inter incessablia homicidia, Ors. 1, 2; Swt. 30, 27. Ðǽr se ríca hyne reste on symbel nihtes *where the ruler ever rested at night*, Judth. Thw. 22, 2; Jud. 44. v. following words.

simbel-farende; *adj.* (*ptcp.*) *Always travelling, wandering, roving*:—Ða simbelfarendan Æthiopes *Aethiopum gentes pervagantes*, Ors. 1, 1; Swt. 26, 16. v. next word.

simbel-geféra, an; *m. One who continually goes with another, a constant companion*:—Nis hit nó ðæt án ðæt swá eáðe mæg wiðerweard gesceaft wesan ætgædere symbelgeféran, ac hit is sellícre ðæt hiora ǽnig ne mæg bûtan ôðrum bión *it is not only that it is so easy for opposites to be able to be constant companions, but it is more extraordinary that no one can exist without another,* Met. 11, 50. v. preceding word.

simble, symble, simle, siemle, semle, symle; *adv. Ever, always.* I. *continually, continuously, without intermission.* (1) alone:—Symble mid ðê *semper tecum,* Ps. Th. 72, 18. Symble fŷr oððe gâr *ever fire or piercing cold,* Cd. Th. 20, 29; Gen. 316. Simle *diuturne,* Wrt. Voc. ii. 139, 23. Hié simle lôcigeaþ tô ðære eorþan *ad terram semper inclinantur,* Past. 21, 3; Swt. 155, 20. Hié wǽron simle healfe æt hâm, healfe ûte, Chr. 894; Erl. 90, 17. In ðê sâule sôðfæstra simle gerestaþ, Exon. Th. 4, 16; Cri. 53: Met. 20, 238. Semle, 20, 198. Ic siemle mid ðê beó, Bt. 7, 3; Fox 22, 23. Hê symle Drihtne folgode, Homl. Th. i. 58, 17. Symle wesan on lustum, Cd. Th. 30, 26; Gen. 472. Ne swylteþ hê symle ac him eft cymeþ bôt *he does not die for ever, does not remain dead, but remedy comes again to him,* Exon. Th. 419, 13; Rä. 38, 5. ¶ in clauses with a comparative:—Symle biþ ðŷ heardra ðe hit sǽstreámas swîðor beátaþ *it keeps getting harder the more the waves beat it,* Cd. Th. 80, 7; Gen. 1325: Beo. Th. 5752; B. 2880: Salm. Kmbl. 485; Sal. 243. (2) with words of similar meaning:—His sôðfæstnyss wunaþ symble êce *justitia ejus manet in seculum seculi,* Ps. Th. 110, 2. Symble on êcnesse *in aeternum,* 118, 142. Simle singales beclŷsed, Exon. Th. 20, 25; Cri. 323. Singallîce simle, Met. 7, 46. Forþ simle, Exon. Th. 23, 30; Cri. 376. Symle âwo tô ealdre, 149, 6; Gû. 757. Â symle, 459, 10; Hy. 4, 114. ¶ with comparative:—Ðê biþ â symble of dæge on dæg drohtaþ strengra, Andr. Kmbl. 2768; An. 1386. II. *on every occasion* or *opportunity, without missing, in unbroken succession:*—Faraþ six dagas simble (*without missing a day*) ymb ða burh, Jos. 6, 3. Symble biþ gemyndgad morna gehwylce, Beo. Th. 4891; B. 2450. Symble gefêgon burhweardes cyme *they rejoiced whenever he came,* Andr. Kmbl. 1318; An. 659. Ðû simle mǽnst, gif ðê ǽnies willan wana biþ, Bt. 11, 1; Fox 30, 21. Ðæt môd siemle biþ gebunden ðǽr ðissa twega yfela âuðer rîcsaþ *whenever either of these two evils prevails, the mind is bound,* 6; Fox 16, 2. Nǽfre ic ða geþeahte sêcan wolde, ac ic symle mec âscêd ðara scylda, Elen. Kmbl. 936; El. 469. Ðæt hê symle oftost God weorþige, Exon. Th. 27, 17; Cri. 432: 243, 34; Jul. 20. Symle hŷ Gûðlâc fromne fundon, ðonne hŷ neósan cwôman, 123, 7; Gû. 319: 205, 6; Ph. 108. ¶ where a series of times is mentioned:—Symble (symle, Exon. Th. 367, 19) ymbe seofon niht *every seven days,* Soul Kmbl. 19; Seel. 10: Andr. Kmbl. 313; An. 157. Simle ymb .xii. mônaþ, Chart. Th. 461, 9: 474, 5: 475, 3. [*O. Sax.* simbla, simla: *O. H. Ger.* simple *semper.*] v. simbel.

simbles, simles; *adv. Ever, always:*—Â ic simles wæs on wega gehwam willan ðînes georn on môde, Andr. Kmbl. 128; An. 64. [*O. H. Ger.* simles, simples *semper.*] v. simbel.

simblian, simlian *to frequent:*—Symligaþ ł oftginiósaþ *frequentant,* Rtl. 15, 17.

simblunga, simlunga; *adv. Always, continually:*—Symlinga *jugiter,* Rtl. 33, 17. Symlunge *continuo,* 59, 33. Symlinga *continua* (-o?), 17, 5.

simel, simering-wyrt. v. symbel, symering-wyrt.

sîn, seón, sién, sŷn, e; *f.* I. *power of seeing, sight, vision:*—Smire on ða eágan, sió sŷn biþ ðŷ scearpre, Lchdm. ii. 30, 21. Se hwæl se ðe gârsecges grund bihealdeþ sweartan sŷne *the whale that beholds the depths of ocean with darkened sight,* Exon. Th. 427, 20; Rä. 41, 94. Ne wyrt ðæt ða seón *it does not injure the sight,* Lchdm. ii. 26, 14. Se ðe hire ða siéne onlâh, ðæt heó swâ wîde wlîtan meahte, Cd. Th. 38, 16; Gen. 607. Oft ic sŷne ofteáh, âblende beorna unrîm, Exon. Th. 270, 21; Jul. 468. Næfde sellîcu wiht sŷne ne folme, 415, 3; Rä. 33, 5. II. *the instrument of sight, the eye:*—Sŷne *pupillam,* Hpt. Gl. 487, 54. [He feide þe sene to þe egen, þe hlust to þe earen, O. E. Hom. ii. 25, 12. ȝiff þatt tin eȝhe iss unnhal o þe sêne, Orm. 9394. Ich (*the owl*) habbe gode sene, O. and N. 368. *Goth.* siuns *sight: O. Sax.* siun *sight; eye: Icel.* sjón, sŷn *sight; eye.*] v. an-, heáfod-sŷn (-sién).

sîn; *possess. pron. His, her, its, their;* suus. This pronoun, which is regularly used in the cognate dialects, rarely occurs in English prose, where its place seems to have been early taken by the genitive of *hê, heó, hit.* I. referring to a sing. masc.:—Gif hæleþa hwilc eágum môdes sînes (cf. his môdes, Bt. 34, 8; Fox 146, 3), Met. 21, 38. Him Hrôðgâr gewât tô hofe sînum, Beo. Th. 2477; B. 1236. Harold hŷrde holdlîce hærran sînum, Chr. 1065; Erl. 198, 13. Man æt ðam âgende sînne willan æt gebicge, L. Ethb. 82; Th. i. 24, 4. Esne wið dryhten gebête sîne hŷd, L. Wih. 10; Th. i. 38, 22. II. referring to a sing. fem.:—Bær seó brimwylf hringa þengel tô hofe sînum, Beo. Th. 3019; B. 1507. Heáfod on hand âgeaf Iudith gingran sînre, Judth. Thw. 23, 21; Jud. 132. Ðæt wîf (wîf *though neuter is represented by a fem. pron.*) ðîn heáfod tredeþ mid fôtum sînum, Cd. Th. 56, 16; Gen. 913. III. referring to a plural:—Ðec Israêla herigaþ, herran sînne (þînne, MS.), 240, 28; Dan. 393. Gebid sînna sôwhula, Txts. 124, 5. Âhealtedon fram stîgum sŷnum ł fram heora paðum *claudicaverunt a semitis suis,* Ps. Lamb. 17, 46. [*Goth.* seins: *O. Sax. O. Frs. O. H. Ger.* sîn: *Icel.* sînn (sinn).]

sîn *be.* v. sî.

sin- (sine-, seonu-, v. *cpds.*). The form does not occur as an independent word; as a prefix it has usually the force *ever, everlasting;* but in some cases it seems to denote *magnitude,* e. g. sin-here; cf. *O. H. Ger.* sin-vluot *the deluge.* [*O. Sax. O. Frs. O. H. Ger.* sin-: *Icel.* sí- (*but in the phrase* sî ok æ *the independent word is found*): cf. *Goth.* sinteins *continual, daily.*]

sin-birnende *ever burning, continually burning:*—Hit (*the fire of Etna*) simle biþ sinbyrnende, Met. 8, 52.

sinc, es; *n.* (*used only in poetry*) *Treasure, gold, silver, jewels:*—Gold gerîseþ on guman sweorde, sinc on cwêne, Exon. Th. 341, 17; Gn. Ex. 127. Sinc, gold on grunde, Beo. Th. 5522; B. 2764. Ða ðe seolfres beóþ since gecoste *qui probati sunt argento,* Ps. 67, 27. Gesâwon ofer since salo hlifian, reced ofer reádum golde, Cd. Th. 145, 9; Gen. 2403. Bereáfodon receda wuldor (*the temple*) reádan golde, since and seolfre, 219, 25; Dan. 60. Sadol searwum fâh, since gewurþad, Beo. Th. 2081; B. 1038: 3234; B. 1615. Se wyrm ligeþ since (*the hoard which it guarded*) bereáfod, 5486; B. 2746. Cyning mec gyrweþ since and seolfre, Exon. Th. 401, 11; Rä. 21, 10. Seah on sync, on sylfor, on searogimmas, 478, 4; Ruin. 36. Tô heánlîc mê þinceþ, ðæt gê mid ûrum sceattum tô scype gangon unbefohtene . . . ne sceole gê swâ sôfte sinc gegangan, Byrht. Th. 133, 33; By. 59. Leóda gôd, sûðmonna sinc, Cd. Th. 121, 28; Gen. 2017. Hê bebohte bearn Wealdendes on seolfres sinc, 301, 7; Sat. 578. Hê beágas dǽlde, sinc æt symle, Beo. Th. 162; B. 81. Ðone hring hæfde Higelâc nŷhstan sîðe, siððan hê under segne sinc ealgode, Beo. Th. 2413; B. 1204. Ðû ða mâdmas Higelâce onsend; mæg ðonne on ðæm golde ongitan, ðonne hê on ðæt sinc stariaþ . . ., 2975; B. 1485. ¶ Sinces brytta, hyrde *a dispenser, guardian of treasure, a prince,* cf. sinc-gifa, *and* Sinca baldor . . . Hrêðel cyning geaf mê sinc and symbel, 4853; B. 2431. Ðone sêlestan sǽcyninga ðara ðe sinc brytnade, 4756; B. 2383:—Sinces brytta, goldwine gumena (*Hrothgar*), 2344; B. 1170. Sinces brytta, folces hyrde, 1219; B. 607: Exon. Th. 288, 3; Wand. 25: (*Holofernes*), Judth. Thw. 21, 22; Jud. 30. Sinces brytta, aðelinga helm (*Pharaoh*), Cd. Th. 111, 18; Gen. 1857. Sinces hyrde, Melchisedec, 126, 27; Gen. 2101. [*O. Sax.* sink.] v. fæted-sinc.

sincan; *p.* sanc, *pl.* suncon; *pp.* suncen. I. *to sink:*—Ðâ ingon sincan *cum coepisset mergi,* Mt. Kmbl. Rush. 14, 30. Hwæðer sincende sǽflôd wǽre, Cd. Th. 86, 27; Gen. 1437. II. *to act as an aperient:*—Gif ðæt sié ômihte wǽte innan, tyhte hié mon ût mid lîþum mettum sincendum, and ne lǽt inne gesittan on ðam lîchoman, Lchdm. ii. 218, 14. [*Goth.* siggkwan: *O. Sax.* sinkan: *O. H. Ger.* sinchan: *Icel.* sökkva.] v. â-, be-, ge-sincan.

sin-ceald; *adj. Ever-cold:*—Sincalda sǽ, Cd. Th. 207, 25; Exod. 472.

sin-cealdu; *indecl. f. Continual cold:*—Ne mæg ðǽr rên ne snâw, ne sunnan hǽtu, ne sincaldu wihte gewyrdan, Exon. Th. 198, 29; Ph. 17.

sinc-fæt, es; *n.* I. *a costly vessel, a vessel of gold* or *of silver,* cf. mâðum-fæt:—Hordweard (*the dragon*) sincfæt (cf. fǽted wǽge, 4553; B. 2282, dryncfæt dŷre, 4601; B. 2306) sôhte, Beo. Th. 4589; B. 2300: B. 2231. Ides sincfato sealde . . . hió Beówulfe medoful ætbær, 1248; B. 622. Forsôc hê ðâm syncfatum, beága mænigo, Vald. 1, 28. II. *a receptacle for treasure, a casket,* cf. hord-fæt:—Hê ætwæg Brôsinga mene, sigle and sincfæt, Beo. Th. 2404; B. 1200.

sinc-fâg, -fâh; *adj. Variegated with costly ornament:*—Ic winde sceal sincfâg swelgan, Exon. Th. 395, 29; Rä. 15, 15. Heorot, sincfâge (cf. goldfâh *applied to Heorot,* 621; B. 308) sel, Beo. Th. 336; B. 167.

sinc-gestreón, es; *n. Treasure:*—Hê wolde ofgifan secga seledreám and sincgestreón, beorht beágselu, Andr. Kmbl. 3311; An. 1658. Ic ðê an tela sincgestreóna, Beo. Th. 2456; B. 1226. Hringum þênede, sincgestreónum fǽttan goldes, 2189; B. 1093.

sinc-gewǽge, es; *n. A weight of treasure, abundance of treasure:*—Oft rinc gebâd ðæt hê in sele sǽge sincgewǽge *it was a frequent experience to see abundance of treasure in the hall,* Exon. Th. 353, 24; Reim. 17.

sinc-gifa, an; *m. A treasure-giver, a prince, chief* who was expected to be liberal in his gifts. Cf. other compounds of *gifa:*—Næs mid Rômwarum sincgeofa sêlla (*of Boethius*), Met. 1, 50. Hŷ (*the disciples*) word ne gehyrwdon hyra sincgiefan (*Christ*), Exon. Th. 29, 9; Cri. 460. On hyra sincgifan (*Beowulf*), Beo. Th. 4611; B. 2311. Sincgyfan, 2688; B. 1342. Se ðe wât his sincgiefan holdne beheledne hê sceal heán hweorfan *he who knows his gracious lord buried shall wander downcast,* Exon. Th. 183, 13; Gû. 1326. Hê his sincgyfan (*Byrhtnoth*) wrec, Byrht. Th. 139, 62; By 278. Cf. sinc-gim, -þegu.

sinc-gifu, e; *f. A gift of treasure, costly gift:*—Ðû golde eart, sincgife sŷlla, Andr. Kmbl. 3016; An. 1511.

sinc-gimm, es; *m. A precious gem, jewel:*—Fyrdrincas fôron . . . hyrstum gewerede. Ðǽr wæs gesŷne sincgim locen, hlâfordes gifu, Elen. Kmbl. 528; El. 264.

sinc-hroden; *adj.* (*ptcp.*) *Treasure-laden, adorned with costly ornaments:*—Ðec biddan hêt se ðisne beám âgrôf, ðæt ðû sinchroden gemunde

. . . , Exon. Th. 473, 11; Bo. 13. Salu sinchroden *halls richly adorned*, Andr. Kmbl. 3342; An. 1675.

sinc-māðum, es; *m. A treasure*:—Næs sincmāððum sēlra on sweordes hād *there was no greater treasure in the shape of a sword*, Beo. Th. 4392; B. 2193.

sinc-stān, es; *m. A jewel*:—Gylden māðm, sylofren sincstān (cf. ða gyldenan stānas and ða seolfrenan, Bt. 34, 8; Fox 144, 30), Met. 21, 21.

sinc-þegu(o), e *or indecl.*; *f. Acceptance of treasure* the gift of a lord: —Sceal sincþego and sweordgifu eówrum cynne ālicgean . . . syððan æðelingas gefricgean eówerne dōmleásne dǣd *for your kin shall receiving a lord's costly present and gift of sword be no more . . . after men learn your inglorious deed* (*the desertion of their lord, Beowulf, at his need*), Beo. Th. 5760; B. 2884. Gemon hē sincþege *he remembers receiving costly presents from his lord*, Exon. Th. 288, 21; Wand. 34. Cf. sinc-gifa, *and see other cpds. of* þegu.

sinc-weorðung, e; *f. A costly decoration, jewel*:—Ic ðē beága lyt, sincweorðunga, syllan meahte, Andr. Kmbl. 543; An. 272: 953; An. 477. Him Elene forgeaf sincweorðunga, Elen. Kmbl. 2435; El. 1212.

sind, synd, sint, sient, siont, synt, sindon, seondon, siendon, syndon *are*:—Hig sind strengran ðonne wē, Num. 13, 32: Met. 10, 33. Synd, Ps. Th. 21, 26: Cd. Th. 19, 7; Gen. 287. Sint, Num. 13, 17: Andr. Kmbl. 696; An. 348: Elen. Kmbl. 1484; El. 744. Sient (sint, Cott. MSS.), Past. 28; Swt. 197, 4: Bt. 11, 1; Fox 32, 32: 16, 3; Fox 54, 18. Siont, Kent. Gl. 232. Synt (synd, MS. A.), Mt. Kmbl. 6, 26, 28: Cd. Th. 114, 14; Gen. 1904. Sindon, Bt. 42; Fox 256, 10, 14. Sindan, 5, 3; Fox 14, 19: Met. 20, 149. Seondon, Cd. Th. 271, 12; Sat. 104: 309, 13; Sat. 709. Seondan (siendon, Cott. MS.), Bt. 3, 4; Fox 6, 24. Siendon (sindon, Cott. MSS.), Past. 6; Swt. 47, 8: Cd. Th. 235, 4; Dan. 301. Syndun, Ps. Th. 58, 10. v. eom.

sind (=sīð?):—Yfla ðara ðe ic gefremede nalæs feám sindon (cf. gylta ðara ðe ic gefremede nales feám sīðum, Elen. Kmbl. 1633; El. 818; *also* Andr. Kmbl. 1210; An. 605: Hy. 4, 65), Exon. Th. 263, 24; Jul. 354.

sinder, es; *n.*: sindra (-e?), an; *m.* (*f.?*) *Dross, impurity of metal*:—Sinder *scoria*, Wrt. Voc. ii. 120, 4. Sindor *caries, putredo lignorum* vel *ferri*, 129, 11. Synder *scorium*, i. 86, 18. Syndran blæccan *scoriae atramento*, Hpt. Gl. 421, 59. Nim seolferun syndrun, Lchdm. iii. 112, 24. Ðiss folc is geworden nū mē tō sindrum *versa est mihi domus Israel in scoriam*, Past. 37, 3; Swt. 267, 17. Seaxes ecg sindrum begrunden (*with all impurities ground off*), Exon. Th. 408, 3; Rä. 27, 6. [*O. H. Ger.* sintar *scoria, purgamen*: *Icel.* sindr; *n. dross.*]

sinder-ōm *rust*:—Sinderōme *ferrugine*, Wrt. Voc. ii. 35, 35.

sin-dolh *a lasting, very great wound*:—Him on eaxle wearð syndolh sweotol, Beo. Th. 1638; B. 817.

sindon. v. sind.

sin-dreám, es; *m. Everlasting joy, joy of heaven*:—Wuldres āras . . . in sindreáme, Elen. Kmbl. 1478; El. 741. Tō heofonrīces gefeán hweorfan mōstan and ðǣr siððan ā in sindreámum tō wīdan feore wunian mōstun, Exon. Th. 154, 20; Gū. 811: 164, 23; Gū. 1016: 225, 6; Ph. 385.

-sīne. v. eág-, ge-, on-, scearp-sīne, -sȳne.

sineht; *adj. Sinewy*:—Mid sinehtum limum gehæfd, Lchdm. ii. 242, 19.

sin-ēðe, sine-wealt, sine-wind. v. sin-īðe, seonu-wealt, seonu-wind.

sin-freá, an; *m. A perpetual lord, a husband*:—Nǣnig nefne sinfreá *none but her wedded lord*, Beo. Th. 3873; B. 1934. Cf. sin-hīwan.

sin-fulle, an; *f. House-leek*; sempervivum tectorum:—Sinfulle *sempervivum*, Wrt. Voc. i. 68, 64; but the word also glosses *eptafolium*, ii. 106, 83: 107, 31: 30, 50: i. 286, 30: *parulus*, 286, 37: *pariulus*, ii. 67, 64: *paliurus*, 116, 38. Genim ðās wyrte ðe man *sempervivum* and ōðrum naman sinfulle nemneþ, Lchdm. i. 236, 20. Genim sinfullan, ii. 190, 2. Nim ða miclan sinfullan, 240, 8. See Lchdm. iii. 305, col. 1: ii. 405, col. 1.

sin-gal; *adj.* I. referring to things of the next life, *everlasting, perpetual*:—Dreám ys singal *canor est jugis*, Hymn. Surt. 58, 4. On ðam heofenlīcum ēðele is singal leóht, Lchdm. iii. 240, 12: Homl. Th. i. 238, 5: Rood Kmbl. 280; Kr. 141. Ðǣr (*in hell*) is ā singal sorh, Wulfst. 26, 8. II. referring to things of time, *continual, constant, without intermission*:—Swā singal gebiórscipe *quasi juge convivium*, Kent. Gl. 521. Hine gedreht singal slǣpleást, Homl. Th. i. 86, 16. Singal oferdrenc, ii. 592, 6. Ðis is singal sacu, Elen. Kmbl. 1808; El. 906. Singal gesīþ *a constant companion*, Exon. Th. 257, 4; Jul. 242. Se singala ege ne lǣt nǣnne mon gesǣligne beón *continuus timor non sinit esse felicem*, Bt. 11, 2; Fox 34, 28: 12; Fox 36, 28. Mid ðæm singalum geþohte *ab hac cogitatione continua*, Past. 11, 7; Swt. 72, 6. Geleáfan singalum *fides jugis*, Hymn. Surt. 44, 39. Mid singalre ēstfulnysse *sedula devotione*, 88, 15. Singalre *assidua*, Hpt. Gl. 407, 65. Men habbaþ singalne andan betwuh him, Bt. 39, 3; Fox 214, 33. Mid singalum bēnum *sedulis questibus*, Hymn. Surt. 127, 14. Mid singalum gebedum *orationibus adsiduis*, Bd. 4, 28; S. 606, 29. II a. of the regular succession of time, *daily* (cf. *Goth.* sinteins *daily* (*bread*)):—Syle ūs hlāf ūserne ðone singalan, Exon. Th. 469, 4; Hy. 5, 8. Singal tīdo *diurna tempora*, Rtl. 164, 36. II b. of an unbroken series, *in succession, continuous*:—Þurh syx singal geár *per sex continuos annos*, Bd. 4, 23; S. 595, 17: 5, 9; S. 623, 27. III. *of long continuance, lasting*:—Wæs seó ēhtnys[se] singalre (*diuturnior*) eallum ðām ǣrgedōnum, 1, 6; S. 476, 24. v. following words.

singale, singala; *adv. Ever, continually, constantly*:—Singale *olim*, Wrt. Voc. ii. 115, 48. Ðeáh hine se wind . . . swence, and hine singale (seó singale? cf. seó singale gēmen, Bt. 12; Fox 36, 28) gēmen gǣle, Met. 7, 50. Singala, Beo. Th. 382; B. 190. v. next word.

singales; *adv. Ever, continually*:—Ic singales wæg mōdceare micle, Beo. Th. 3559; B. 1777: Exon. Th. 115, 15; Gū. 190. Simle singales, 20, 25; Cri. 323: 24, 31; Cri. 393. Syngales, Beo. Th. 2274; B. 1135.

singal-flōwende; *adj.* (*ptcpl.*) *Continually flowing*:—Singalflōwende eá *fluvius*, Wrt. Voc. i. 54, 18.

singallīce; *adv. Perpetually, continually, constantly*:—Hieremias wilnode singallīce (*sedulo*) hine geþiédan tō ðære lufan his Scippendes, Past. 7, 1; Swt. 49, 16: Blickl. Homl. 101, 27. Wē him gyldaþ singallīce, and hȳ ūs hȳnaþ dæghwamlīce, Wulfst. 163, 10. Swīðe singallīce beswīcþ monna mōd, Bt. 18, 1; Fox 60, 20. Hī (*Cherubim*) singallīce singaþ '*they continually do cry*,' Elen. Kmbl. 1490; El. 747. Syle drincan singallīce nigon dagas, Lchdm. i. 230, 22. Hine ǣghwonan God singallīce simle gehealdeþ, Met. 7, 46: Bt. 12; Fox 36, 27. [*O. H. Ger.* sincalīhho *jugiter.*]

singalness, e; *f. Constancy, perseverance, assiduity*:—Ānrǣdnys ł singalnys *perseverantia, assiduitas*, Hpt. Gl. 434, 18.

singal-ryne, es; *m. A continual running* of water:—Singalrenes ł swift[renes] *decursus*, Hpt. Gl. 418, 51.

singan; *p.* sang, song, *pl.* sungon; *pp.* sungen *To sing*. I. *used absolutely*; (1) of persons, (a) *to sing, recite, relate musically* or *in verse*:—Singan *modulare*, singe *modulabor*, Wrt. Voc. ii. 57, 2, 3. Ic Gode singe *gaudebo Deo*, Ps. Th. 74, 8. Ic Drihtne singe *cantabo Domino*, 103, 31. Hwæt is ðis folc ðe ðus hlūde singeþ? Blickl. Homl. 149, 30. Ðǣr habbaþ englas eádigne dreám, sanctas singaþ, Cd. Th. 286, 20; Sat. 355. Scop hwīlum sang on Heorote, Beo. Th. 997; B. 496. Singende heáp *chorus*, Wrt. Voc. i. 28, 27. Hē geseah Matheus ǣnne sitton singende, Blickl. Homl. 237, 23. (b) *to compose verse, narrate*:—On ðē ic singge *in te decantatio mea*, Ps. Th. 70, 5. Song hē be middangeardes gesceape and be fruman moncynnes, Bd. 4, 24; S. 598, 9: Exon. Th. 44, 33; Cri. 712. Be ðam Moyses sang, Elen. Kmbl. 674; El. 337. Swā se wītega sang, Menol. Fox 119; Men. 59. Wītgan sungon be Godes bearne, Elen. Kmbl. 1119; El. 561. (2) of other living creatures:—Se fugel singeþ, Exon. Th. 206, 9; Ph. 124: Salm. Kmbl. 539; Sal. 269. Fugelas singaþ, gylleþ grǣghama, Fins. Th. 9; Fin. 5. Se hana sōna hlūdswēge sang *immediately the cock crew*, Homl. Th. ii. 248, 33: Shrn. 30, 29. Sang se wanna fugel, Cd. Th. 119, 22; Gen. 1983. Mǣw singende, Exon. Th. 307, 11; Seef. 22. (3) of inanimate resonant objects:—Ic þurh mūþ sprece, wrencum singe, Exon. Th. 390, 15; Rä. 9, 2. Wiht is wrætlīc, singeþ þurh sīdan, 483, 13; Rä. 69, 2. Se hearpere gedēþ, ðæt hearpan strengas nāwuht ungelīce ðæm sone ne singaþ ðe hē wilnaþ, Past. 23; Swt. 175, 8. In ðæm dæge singaþ ða bȳman, Wulfst. 183, 10. Syngaþ, L. E. I. prm.; Th. ii. 396, 8. Hringīren scīr song in searwum, Beo. Th. 651; B. 323. Ic seah sellīc þing singan, Exon. Th. 413, 10; Rä. 32, 3. II. with a cognate accusative, or followed by the words used or by a clause; (1) of persons (a) *to sing* a song, *recite* a poem, prayer, formula, etc., *read* aloud:—Wē singaþ on his lof: 'Hǣl ūs on ðǣm hēhstan,' Blickl. Homl. 81, 27. Heáhgealdor ðæt snotre men singaþ *a charm that wise men recite*, Ps. Th. 57, 4. Hī singaþ Metude lof, Exon. Th. 239, 7; Ph. 617. Ðegnas singaþ, ðæt ðū sié hlǣfdige, 18, 14; Cri. 283. Ða lióþ ðe ic song, Bt. 2; Fox 4, 7. Heó 'Magnificaþ' sang, Blickl. Homl. 159, 1. Crist sylf sang Pater Noster ǣrest, L. C. E. 22; Th. i. 372, 26. Engla þreátas sigeleóþ sungon, Exon. Th. 181, 6; Gū. 1289. 'Sing mē hwæthwegu.' Ðā andswarede hē: 'Ne con ic nāu þing singan,' Bd. 4, 24; S. 597, 12. Sing ðās gebedsealmas, Lchdm. iii. 12, 6. Singan sangas *cantare canticum*, Ps. Th. 136, 4. Ðā ongan hē singan ða fers and ða word ðe hē nǣfre ne gehȳrde, Bd. 4, 24; S. 597, 17. Leóþ singan *dicere carmen*, 597, 31. Cwide singan, Salm. Kmbl. 171; Sal. 85. Singan Pater Noster, 333; Sal. 166. Hē wæs ymen singende, Blickl. Homl. 147, 3. On ðære hālgan cyricean biþ sungen ðæt hālige gerȳne, 77, 15. Wæs se wītedōm beforan sungen, Elen. Kmbl. 2306; El. 1154. (b) *to narrate in verse, write*:—Se scop sang, ðæt mā manna fægnodon . . . , Bt. 30, tit.; Fox xvi. 4. Sealmsceopas sungon and sægdon, ðæt se wolde cuman, Blickl. Homl. 105, 10. For hwam wolde gē secgan oððe singan, ðæt ic gesǣllīc mon wǣre, Met. 2, 17. (2) of other living creatures:—Earn sang hildeleóþ, Judth. Thw. 24, 28; Jud. 211. Wulfas sungon ǣfenleóþ, Cd. Th. 188, 7; Exod. 164. (3) of inanimate things:—Seó byrne sang gryreleóþa sum, Byrht. Th. 140, 7; By. 284. Horn song fūslīc leóþ, Beo. Th. 2851; B. 1423. Ealle hearpan strengas hē grēt mid ânre honda, đȳ đe hē wile đæt hī ânne song singen, Past. 23; Swt. 175, 9. **III.** where the subject of the song is the object of the verb, *to sing about, recite* or *compose a poem about* something:—Ic đíne strengđu singe, Ps. Th. 58, 16. Ic mildheortnesse and dōm Drihtnes singe and secge, 100, 1. Cwæþ hē: 'Hwæt sceal ic singan?' Cwæþ hē: 'Sing mē frumsceaft,' Bd. 4, 24; S. 597, 16. [*Goth.* siggwan *to sing, read aloud: O. Sax.* singan: *O. Frs.* singa: *O. H. Ger.* singan *canere, cantare, decantare, psallere, modulari, edere, jubilare: Icel.* syngva (-ja) *to sing; to ring* (of metals, etc.), *whistle* (of the wind).] v. â-, be-, ge-singan.

-singe, -singend. v. ge-singe, æfter-, fore-, mid-singend.

singend-líc; *adj. That may be sung:*—Singendlíce *cantabiles*, Ps. Spl. 118, 54.

singian *to sin.* v. syngian.

sin-grēne, an; *f.* A plant name (lit. *ever-green*), *sin-green* (*sen-, sim-*), *house-leek;* sempervivum tectorum: see E. D. S. Pub. Plant Names, s. v. sen-green (sin-, sim-), and Lchdm. ii. 405, col. 1. Besides *semperviνum* the word glosses several other names:—Singrēne *titemallos*, Wrt. Voc. i. 68, 33: *temolus* ł *titemallos*, Lchdm. iii. 305, col. 1. Syngrēne. Đeós wyrt đe man *temolum* and ōđrum naman singrēne nemneþ, i. 152, 12. Singrēne *colatidis*, iii. 301, col. 2: Wrt. Voc. i. 69, 4. Nim singrēnan, Lchdm. ii. 56, 22. Đa smalan singrēnan, 54, 2. [*Iovis barba* jubarbe, singreue, Rel. Ant. i. 37, col. 2. Howsleke or sengrene *barba Jovis, semperviva*, Prompt. Parv. 251, where see note. *Ger.* sin-grün *and Dan.* sin-grøn *is periwinkle.* Cf. *Icel.* sí-grænn; *adj. evergreen.*]

sin-grim; *adj. Ever-fierce, of unceasing fierceness:*—Sace singrimme, Exon. Th. 256, 11; Jul. 230.

sin-here; *gen.* -her(i)ges; *m. An immense army:*—Besæt sinherge sweorda lāfe *he besieged the fugitives with an immense army*, Beo. Th. 5864; B. 2936.

sin-hīgscipe. v. sin-hīwscipe.

sin-hīwan, -hīgan; *pl. Members of a family united by the lasting bond of marriage, a married pair:*—Sinhīwan (*Adam and Eve*), Cd. Th. 48, 19; Gen. 778: 49, 9; Gen. 789: Exon. Th. 153, 9; Gū. 823. Hyra somwist sinhīwan (*body and soul*) gedǣlden, 160, 10; Gū. 941: 284, 17; Jul. 698. [*O. Sax.* sin-hīwun (-iun): *O. Frs.* sin-hīgen, sinnane, senne: *O. H. Ger.* sin-hīun *conjuges.*] v. ge-sinhīwan, *and following words.*

sin-hīwian *to marry:*—Ne sinīgaþ (synnīgaþ, Rush.) *neque nubunt*, Lk. Skt. Lind. 20, 35. v. ge-sinīgan.

sin-hīwscipe, es; *m. The lasting family relation of marriage:*—God sinhīgscipas gesamnaþ mid clǣnlícre lufe *conjugii sacrum castis nectit amoribus*, Bt. 21; Fox 74, 38. v. ge-sinīgscipe, *and* cf. sin-scipe.

sin-hweorfende, -hwurfende *ever-turning, round:*—Sintredende (-trendende?) ł sinhwurfende *teretes, rotundos*, Hpt. Gl. 408, 73. v. *next word, and* cf. seonu-wealt.

sin-hwurfol, -hwyrfel; *adj. Round, cylindrical:*—Sinuurbul, sinuulfur, siunhuurful (sinu-?) *teres*, Txts. 104, 1047. Đonne is swíđe mycel cyrice getimbred, and is sinhwyrfel on wilewīsan geworht (cf. *under* seonu-wealt *passage from* Shrn. 80, 37), Blickl. Homl. 125, 21. [Cf. *O. H. Ger.* sin-, sina-[h]werbal *teres, rotundus: Icel.* sí-valr.]

sinīgaþ. v. sin-hīwian.

sin-íđe, -ēđe; *adj. Very gentle:*—Mid sinēđre ondōunge wyrtdrences þurh horn ođđe pīpan sió wamb biþ tō clǣnsianne, Lchdm. ii. 260, 11.

sinlíce. v. ge-sinlíce.

sinnan; *p.* sann, *pl.* sunnon; *pp.* sunnen; *with gen. To care for, mind, heed:*—Ne ic mē eorþwelan ōwiht sinne, ne mē mid mōde micles gyrne, Exon. Th. 121, 18; Gū. 290. Hē wæs swungen sārslegum . . . hrā weorces ne sann (*the body cared not for pain*), Andr. Kmbl. 2556; An. 1279. Hié fægerra (-o, MS.) lyt for ædelinge idesa (-e, MS.) sunnun ac hié Sarran swíđor micle wynsumne wlite heredon *they* (*Pharaoh's nobles*) *heeded little fair women before the prince, but much more did they praise the winsome beauty of Sarah*, Cd. Th. 111, 10; Gen. 1853. [Cf. *Icel.* sinna (*wk.*) *to care for, mind, give heed to.*]

sin-niht, e *and* es (v. niht); *f. Continual night, perpetual darkness:*—Đa đe in þeóstrum sǣton sinneahtes *those who sat in the shades of perpetual darkness*, Exon. Th. 8, 13; Cri. 117. Hām sweart sinnehte (*hell*), Exon. Th. 142, 26; Gū. 650. Hȳ ābīdan sceolon in sinnehte, 99, 29; Cri. 1632. Sinnihte, 94, 20; Cri. 1543: Cd. Th. 3, 27; Gen. 42: Salm. Kmbl. 138; Sal. 68. Grendel sinnihte heóld mistige mōras, Beo. Th. 325; B. 161: (*of the darkness of chaos*), Cd. Th. 7, 20; Gen. 109. Synnihte, 8, 2; Gen. 118. [Cf. *O. Sax.* sin-nahti *the darkness of hell.*]

sin-nīþ, es; *m. Continued enmity* or *trouble*, Exon. Th. 354, 27; Reim. 52.

sinoþ, sino-walt. v. seonoþ, seonu-wealt.

sin-rǣden[n], e; *f. A perpetual, lasting condition, wedlock:*—On ōđre wīsan sint tō manienne đa đe mid synnrǣdenne bióþ gebundene *aliter admonendi sunt conjugiis obligati*, Past. 51, 1; Swt. 393, 22. Đa đe beóþ gebundne mid synrǣdenne *conjugati*, Swt. 393, 21. Cf. sinhīwan, -hīwscipe, -scipe.

sinscipe, es; *m. Marriage, wedlock:*—Sinscipe *conjungium* vel *matrimonium*, Wrt. Voc. i. 72, 11. Senscipe *consortium, matrimonium*, Hpt. Gl. 469, 44: *jugalitas*, 416, 25: 417, 5. Đrȳ hādas . . . mægđhād, wudewan hād, and riht sinscype, Homl. Th. i. 148, 7. Sinscipe, 604, 30. Mē nū ne lyst nānes synscipes ac đæs Hǣlendes geþeódnysse mid gehealdenre clǣnnisse, Homl. Skt. i. 4, 37. Heó wunode twelf geár on đæs cynincges synscype, 20, 16. Hū miht đū đam Ælmihtigan his brȳde beniman and đīnum sinscipe geþeódan, Homl. Th. ii. 476, 33. Đa đe on sinscipe wuniaþ *married people*, i. 448, 2. Đa đe beóþ mid sinscipe (syn-, Hatt. MS.) gebundene *conjugati*, Past. 23; Swt. 176, 21. Gif hwā on swilcum mānfullum sinscipe (*conjugio*) þurhwunaþ, L. M. I. P. 20; Th. ii. 270, 20. Tō senscipum *ad commercia, connubia*, Hpt. Gl. 490, 54. Gesamnaþ sinscipas, clǣnelíce lufe *conjugii sacrum castis nectit amoribus*, Met. 11, 91. v. ge-, on-sinscipe, *and preceding word.*

sin-snǣd, e; *f. A huge bit:*—Grendel slǣpendne rinc slāt . . . synsnǣdum swealh (*swallowed by huge bits*, or *by bits that followed each other continuously?*), Beo. Th. 1490; B. 743.

sin-sorh(g), e; *f. Continual trouble:*—Habban breostceare, sinsorgna gedreag, Exon. Th. 444, 10; Kl. 45.

sint. v. sind.

sin-þyrstende *ever thirsting:*—Alexander tōēcan đæm đe hē hiénende wæs ǣgđer ge his folc ge ōđerra cyninga hē wæs sinþyrstende monnes blōdes *Alexander humani sanguinis insaturabilis, sive hostium sive etiam sociorum, recentem tamen semper sitiebat cruorem*, Ors. 3, 9; Swt. 130, 31.

sin-tredende. v. sin-hweorfende.

sin-trendel, -tryndel; *adj. Round, circular,* or *globular:*—Dō hyt syntrændel (sinetrundæl, MS. V.: sinetrum del, MS. H.) *make a ball of it*, Lchdm. i. 106, 17. Sintryndel lytel scyld *ancile*, Wrt. Voc. i. 35, 58. v. *next word, and* cf. sin-hwurfol, seonu-wealt.

sin-trendende (?) *ever-turning, round:*—Sintredende (-trendende?) *teretes, rotundos*, Hpt. Gl. 408, 73. v. preceding word.

sinu, sin-wealt. v. seonu, seonu-wealt.

sin-wrǣnness, e; *f. Continual wantonness:*—Synwrǣnnys *vel* gālscipe *saturiasis*, Wrt. Voc. i. 19, 51.

sio-, sió-. *See generally* seo-, seó-.

sió (*be*), siodo, siofa, siofoþa, sioleđa, siolf, siota. v. sī, sidu, sefa, sifeþa, seolh-ȳđa, self, set.

sipian, Siras(-e), sīras. v. sypian, Syras, sīgere.

siru; *gen.* sirwe; *f. An artifice, a snare, wile, crafty device;* as a military term, *an ambush:*—Gif hwā gewealdes ofsleá his đone nēhstan þurh syrwa (*with guile*, Exod. 21, 14), L. Alf. 13; Th. i. 48, 1, note. Sette syrwa *pone insidias*, Jos. 8, 2. v. searu, sirwe.

siru-tūn (?) *a place for an ambush, lurking-place:*—Syretum (-tūn?) *latibulum*, Wrt. Voc. ii. 54, 27. v. preceding word.

siru-wrenc, es; *m. An artifice, crafty trick, wile:*—Hī ymbsǣton Cantwareburuh and hī in tō cōman þuruh syruwrencas (syre-, MS. E.), Chr. 1011; Erl. 145, 29. v. searu-wrenc.

sirwan, sirwian, sirewan; *p.* sirwde, sirwede, sirede, sirewede, sirwode. **I.** in a good sense, *to plan, devise, use art in doing* something:—Hē (*the Creator*) serede and sette eorþan dǣlas, Cd. Th. 265, 29; Sat. 15. **II.** in a bad sense, (1) *trans. To plan, contrive, devise, plot, attempt with craft:*—Hī ne sǣtincge ne gestrodu wiđ Angelþeóde syrwaþ *nil contra gentem Anglorum insidiarum moliuntur aut fraudium*, Bd. 5, 23; S. 646, 37. Syrwiaþ *concinnant* (*iniquitatem*), Blickl. Gl. Đām đe mē syrwedan yfel *qui quaerunt mala mihi*, Ps. Th. 70, 12. Hī fācen geswipere syredan *astute cogitaverunt consilium*, 82, 3: Andr. Kmbl. 1220; An. 610. Beó serewede *moliretur, machinaretur*, Hpt. Gl. 487, 23. (2) with a clause:—Hē angan sierwan hū hē hiene beswīcan mehte, Ors. 1, 12; Swt. 52, 3. (3) without a case (a) in the following glosses:—Syrwaþ *moliuntur*, Wrt. Voc. ii. 54, 30. Serwede *machinaretur*, Hpt. Gl. 509, 73. Serwedon *machinabantur*, 520, 4. Serewedan, 506, 5. Seredon *concinnabant*, Wrt. Voc. ii. 20, 26. Seruuende *convenientes*, 105, 26. Syrwende, 15, 28. (b) *to lie in wait, plot:*—Hē syrwþ (Ps. Lamb. syrwaþ) swā swā leó *insidiatur quasi leo*, Ps. Spl. second 9, 10. Se đe nānþing ne syrwde *qui non est insidiatus*, Ex. 21, 13. Syrede, Beo. Th. 324; B. 161. Se syrwienda deóful, Wulfst. 107, 22. (c) with prep. *to lie in wait* for, *plot* against:—Đū syrwst ongeán hyre hō, Gen. 3, 15. Deófol syrwþ ymbe Godes gelađunge, Homl. Th. i. 240, 1. Mē manige ymb mægene syrewaþ, Ps. Th. 54, 18. Đā syrwde Herodias ymbe hine *Herodias insidiabatur illi*, Mk. Skt. 6, 19: Homl. Th. i. 82, 20. Đa đe ymbe đæs cildes feorh syrwdon *those who sought the child's life*, 88, 18: ii. 112, 33. Đa đe emb his feorh syredon *quos in necem suam conspirasse didicerat*, Bd. 2, 9; S. 512, 4. Mē seredon ymb secgas monige, hū heó mē deáþes cwealm hrefnan mihten, Cd. Th. 296, 6; Sat. 498. Gif hwā ymb cyninges feorh sierwie (syrwie, MSS. B. H.), L. Alf. pol. 4; Th. i. 62, 15. Seó næddre wolde syrwan ongeán hire hó, Boutr. Scrd. 20, 12. v. be-, ge-sirwan (-serian, -syrewian, -syrian, -syrwan).

sirwe, an; *f. An artifice, device, plot, wile:*—Syrwan (serwan) *insidiae*, Ælfc. Gr. 13; Zup. 84, 14. v. siru.

sirwian. v. sirwan.

sirwung, e; *f. Plotting, machination, contrivance*:—Beó âídlod Amanes sirwung ongeán ðám Judéiscum, Homl. As. 101, 308. Be hláfordes syrwunge. Gif hwá embe cynincg oððe hláford syrwie *of plotting against a lord. If any man plot against king or lord*, L. C. S. 58; Th. i. 408, 1. Gif hwá ofsleá his ðone néhstan þurh syrwunge (*with guile*, Exod. 21, 14), L. Alf. 13; Th. i. 48, 1, note. Hé cýdde his fácenfulle syrewunge, Homl. Th. i. 82, 18. Mid syrewungum hé becom tó ðære cynelícan geþincþe, 80, 34. God heóld hine wið ðæs deófles syrwungum, ii. 454, 3. Serewungum *machinamentis*, Hpt. Gl. 478, 54. Syrwunga *insidias*, Hymn. Surt. 47, 26. Samson heora syrwunga undergeat, Jud. 16, 3. v. searwung.

sise-mús *a dormouse*:—Sisemús *glis*, Wrt. Voc. i. 22, 56: 78, 22. [*O. H. Ger.* sise-, zise-mús: cf. (?) sise-sang *carmen lugubre*, sisegomio *pelicanus*.]

síþ, es; *m.* I. *going, journeying, travel*:—Síþes ámyrred *hindered from going*, Cd. Th. 24, 16; Gen. 378. Síþes wérig *weary of swimming*, Beo. Th. 1162; B. 579. Síþes sǽne *slow in travelling*, Apstls. Kmbl. 67; Ap. 34. Ne æt hám ne on síþe ne on ǽnigre stówe *neither at home, nor when travelling, nor in any place*, L. I. P. 9; Th. ii. 314, 33: Exon. Th. 339, 34; Gn. Ex. 104. Se ðe of síþe cwom feorran geféred, Salm. Kmbl. 356; Sal. 177. I a. *going* from this world:—Is nú fús ðider gǽst síþes georn, Exon. Th. 164, 27; Gú. 1018. Ic eom síþes fús, 166, 30; Gú. 1050: 212, 10; Ph. 208. Líf biþ on síþe, 213, 6; Ph. 220: 328, 32; Vy. 26. Beó ðú on síþ gearu, 172, 24; Gú. 1148. II. *a journey, voyage, course, expedition*:—Síþ wæs gedǽled *the course of the Israelites and Egyptians was no longer a common one*, Cd. Th. 190, 31; Exod. 297. Lust leófes síþes (*the journey out of Egypt*), 180, 31; Exod. 53: Andr. Kmbl. 2084; An. 1043. Cwén síþes (*her voyage to Palestine*) gefeah, Elen. Kmbl. 494; El. 247. Ne lǽt ðú ðec síþes getwǽfan, láde gelettan, lifgendne mon ongin mere sécan, Exon. Th. 474, 2; Bo. 23. Nó wǽgflotan wind síþes getwǽfde, sǽgenga fór forþ ofer ýþe, Beo. Th. 3820; B. 1908. Flówan môt ýþ ofer eal lond, ne wile heó áwa ðæs síþes geswícan, Salm. Kmbl. 647; Sal. 323. Hú myccle scipbrocu hé gebád on ðæm síþe ðe hé (*St. Paul*) wæs ðyder rǽpling gelǽded, Blickl. Homl. 173, 7. Ǽghwelc mon ðe on ðæm síþe wǽre *every man that was on the expedition*, L. Alf. pol. 29; Th. i. 80, 8: Ps. Th. 76, 2: Andr. Kmbl. 1590; An. 796: Exon. Th. 451, 13; Dóm. 103. Ne gǽle gé mínne síþ, nú míne fét gongaþ on heofenlícne weg, Blickl. Homl. 191, 21. Waldend sende here on langne síþ, Cd. Th. 5, 8; Gen. 68. Hét mé on ðysne síþ faran, 32, 7; Gen. 499. Heó on síþ gewát wésten sécan, 136, 29; Gen. 2265. Hí tugon longne síþ in hearmra hond, Exon. Th. 228, 19; Ph. 440. Gif ðú hafast mid ðé wulfes hrycghǽr on síþfæte, bútan fyrhtu ðú ðone síþ gefremest, ac se wulf sorgiaþ ymbe his síþ, Lchdm. i. 360, 22. Gegán sorhfulne síþ, Beo. Th. 2560; B. 1278. Síþ ásettan, Elen. Kmbl. 1990; El. 997. Hwílum ús earfoþlíce gesǽleþ on sǽwe ðéh wé síþ nesan frécne geféran *at times we have hard hap at sea, though we come safe from and perform our dangerous voyage*, Andr. Kmbl. 1030; An. 515. Ðære sunnan síþ behealdan, Exon. Th. 203, 27; Ph. 90. Hwylce Sǽ-Geátas síþas wǽron: 'Hú lomp eów on láde?' Beo. Th. 3977; B. 1986. Síþa rest *rest from journeys*, Cd. Th. 86, 8; Gen. 1427. Wíde síþas, 55, 36; Gen. 905: 276, 16; Sat. 189. II a. *the journey* of the spirit from this world, cf. forþ-síþ:—Ne mæg mon foryldan ðone deóran síþ, Salm. Kmbl. 723; Sal. 361. Mín dohtor is on ýtemestum síþe (*in extremis*), Mk. Skt. 5, 23. III. *coming, arrival*:—Hió rícsode on ðæm íglonde ðe Aulixes com tó líþan; cúð wæs sóna æðelinges síþ, Met. 26, 62: Andr. Kmbl. 88; An. 44. Geseah Iohannes sigebearn cuman tó helle, ongeat Godes sylfes síþ, Exon. Th. 462, 15; Hö. 52: Beo. Th. 1007; B. 501: 3946; B. 1971. Sorgian for his síþe, Cd. Th. 49, 30; Gen. 800. IV. *a proceeding, course* of action, *way* of doing, *conduct*:—Hí deófle offredon, swá him ǽfre se síþ hreówan mihte, Homl. Skt. i. 23, 64: Beo. Th. 6109; B. 3058. Hé hafaþ mec bereáfod rihta gehwylces; nis ðæt fæger síþ, Elen. Kmbl. 1819; El. 911. Ne biþ swylc earges síþ *such is not a coward's way*, Beo. Th. 5076; B. 2541: 5058; B. 2532: 5166; B. 2586. Ic ne mæg ðínra worda ne wísna wuht oncnáwan síþes ne sagona *I cannot understand aught of thy words or of thy ways, of thy proceeding or of thy sayings*, Cd. Th. 34, 9; Gen. 535. Ne can ic Abeles fóre, hleómǽges síþ, 61, 34; Gen. 1007. Nú ðú seolfa miht síþ úserne (*our course of action*, as described in the command of Christ given in the preceding lines, or *our journey*, cf. faraþ l. 663, fóre, 673) gehýran, Andr. Kmbl. 680; An. 340. [Þat te schal bireowe þat sið, þat tu euer dides te into swuch þeowdom, H. M. 9, 2. A nyð ðat weldeþ al his sið, Gen. and Ex. 274.] V. denoting that which occurs to a person, how a person fares, *the course of events* in the case of a person, *lot, condition, fate, experience*:—Secgan hwelc siððan wearþ herewulfa síþ *to say what happened afterwards to the war-wolves*, Cd. Th. 121, 25; Gen. 2015. Hú ðæs gǽstes síþ æfter swyltcwale geseted wurde *how it might be appointed that the spirit should fare after the death-pang*, Andr. Kmbl. 310; An. 155. Tó hwon ðínre sáwle síþ (þing, Vercel.) wurde *what the lot of thy soul would come to be*, Exon. Th. 368, 11; Seel. 20. Ðæt wæs hreówlíc síþ eallre ðissere þeóde, ðæt hé swá raðe his líf geendade, Chr. 1057; Erl. 192, 20. Wá heom ðæs síðes ðe hí men wurdon *alas for them that it was their lot to be born men*, Wulfst. 27, 3. Hú lange wilt ðú bewépan Saules síþ, ðonne ic hine áwearp, ðæt hé leng ne ríxige? Homl. Th. ii. 64, 4: Cd. Th. 49, 14; Gen. 792. Wé ðé gecýðaþ síþ úserne *we will tell thee what happened to us* (the incidents are then related), Andr. Kmbl. 1719; An. 862. [Iob minegede alle his wrecche siðes (*all the miseries he had experienced*), O. E. Homl. ii. 169, 9. Mi muchel unseli sið (unselhðe, Bod. MS.), Jul. 46, 8.] VI. *a path, way*:—Brim, sǽmanna síþ, Cd. Th. 208, 4; Exod. 478. Hié tó helle sculon on ðone sweartan síþ (cf. the account of Hermóðr going to Hell: Hann reið dökkva dala ok diúpa), 45, 27; Gen. 733. Dóþ hys síþas (*semitas*) rihte, Mt. Kmbl. 3, 3: Mk. Skt. 1, 3. VII. *a time* (cf. colloquial *go, and Dan.* gang), (1) with ordinals:—Eft óðre síþe hé férde *iterum secundo abiit*, Mt. Kmbl. 26, 42: Gen. 27, 36. Ðæt deófol hine genam þriddan síþe, Blickl. Homl. 27, 16. (2) with cardinals:—Se hét forbærnan ealle Rómeburh on ǽnne síþ (*all at once*), Bt. 16, 4; Fox 58, 4. Oftor ðonne on ǽnne síþ *oftener than once*, Beo. Th. 3163; B. 1579. On þrý síþas drince *let him drink it at three times*, Lchdm. i. 352, 13. Ǽne síþa (síþe, MS. C.) *once*, Bd. 4, 5; S. 572, 44. Hig férdon seofon síþon embe þa buruh, Jos. 6, 15: Gen. 33, 3: Lk. Skt. 17, 4. (2 a) used in multiplying numbers:—Feówer síþon seofon beóþ eahta and twentig &c., Anglia viii. 302, 47 sqq. Cweþ .xii. síþum twelf, 298, 22. Endleofan síþon hund þúsenda . . . eahtatýne sýþum hundteóntig þúsenda, Blickl. Homl. 79, 19, 22. (2 b) marking degree:—Heó hæfde seofon síþum beorhtran sáule, 147, 16. [Spenser uses *sithe* in the sense of *time. Goth.* sinþ[s] *time: O. Sax.* sīð; *m. way, journey; a time: O. H. Ger.* sind; *m. iter, trames; vicis: Icel.* sinn; *n.* (in adverbial phrases) *a time: Dan.* sind (in numeral forms, e. g. tre-*sinds*-tyve *three times twenty, sixty*).] v. bealu-, cear-, earfoþ-, eft-, ellor-, forþ-, from-, gryre-, hám-, heonan-, hin-, lagu-, láþ-, neó-, oft-, sǽ-, sige-, spild-, un-, unrǽd-, út-, wíd-, wíg-, wil-, wræc-síþ; sind; manig-síþes; ge-síþ.

[**síþ**]; *cpve.* síþra; *spve.* síþest, síþ[e]mest; *adj. Late*:—Biþ seó síþre tíd sǽda gehwylces mǽtræ in mægne, Exon. Th. 104, 31; Gú. 16. Se síþemesta dóm (síþemesða demm, Hatt. MS.) *extrema damnatio*, Past. 2; Swt. 30, 21. Sardanopolus wæs se síþmesta cyning ðe on ðæm londe rícsade *novissimus apud Assyrios regnavit Sardanapalus*, Ors. 1, 12; Swt. 50, 29. Ðæt ǽreste . . . ðæt síþmeste ríce *primum . . . novissimum regnum*, 2, 1; Swt. 60, 5. Him lásta wearþ síþast gesýne *the last trace of them was seen*, Exon. Th. 270, 34; Jul. 475. Ðæt ðæm þeódne wæs síþas[t] sigehwíl (*his last hour of victory*), Beo. Th. 5413; B. 2710. On ðæm ǽrestan and on ðæm síþmestan (onwealdum), Ors. 2, 5; Swt. 86, 17. Síþmestan, 6, 1; Swt. 254, 1. Gesæt tó symble síþestan (síð-, MS.) dæge cyning, Cd. Th. 259, 34; Dan. 701. Mæssige man swá fela mæssan . . . and æt ðare síþmæstan dó man absolutionem, L. P. M. 3; Th. ii. 288, 10. ¶ *In the adverbial phrase* æt síþestan, síþ[e]mestan *at last, in the end*:—Gif hé æt síþestan (síþmestan, MS. H.) sié gefongen, L. In. 18; Th. i. 114, 7: Beo. Th. 6018; B. 3013: Cd. Th. 217, 31; Dan. 31. Ǽt síþemestan *novissime*, Mt. Kmbl. 22, 27. [*Icel.* síðari; *cpve. later;* síðastr; *spve. last.*] v. next word.

síþ. I. *adv.* (1) *Late, after some time*:—Síþ *sero*, Wrt. Voc. ii. 88, 22. Him ðá síþ oncwæþ, sóna ne meahte oroþ up geteón, Exon. Th. 163, 19; Gú. 996. Síþ and late, Judth. Thw. 25, 24; Jud. 275. Tó síþ, Exon. Th. 96, 3; Cri. 1568. ¶ *In phrases with* ǽr (cf. *O. Sax.* ni sīð noh ēr: *O. H. Ger.* ēr enti sīd: *Icel.* ár ok síð, síð ok snemma):—Ǽr and síþ *early and late, always*, Beo. Th. 4993; B. 2500. Síþ and ǽr, Cd. Th. 177, 24; Gen. 2934: Exon. Th. 38, 5; Cri. 602. Ǽr oððe síþ, ǽfre *ever, at any time*, 56, 1; Cri. 894: 65, 12; Cri. 1053: 471, 28; Rä. 61, 8. Míne gyltas ðe ic síþ oððe ǽr ǽfre gefremode, L. de Cf. 11; Th. ii. 264, 24: Elen. Kmbl. 1947; Elen. 975. Sýþ oððe ǽr, Menol. Fox 398; Men. 200. Ne síþ ne ǽr *never*, Elen. Kmbl. 480; El. 240. Ne ǽr ne síþ, 1140; El. 572. Sume ǽr, sume síþ, Exon. Th. 154, 25; Gú. 848. Hé síþor fór on leófes lást, Cd. Th. 199, 10; Exod. 336. (2) *later, afterwards*; postmodum:—Ǽrest hí sculon ongietan ðæt hí fleón ðæt ðæt hí lufiaþ ðonne mágon hí síþ íeðelíce ongietan ðæt ðæt is tó lufianne ðæt hí ǽr flugon *prius videant fugienda, quae amant, et sine difficultate postmodum cognoscant amanda esse, quae fugiunt*, Past. 58, 1; Swt. 441, 14. II. *prep.* cf. siððan, *After*:—Síþ ðam *after that*, Exon. Th. 110, 14; Gú. 107. III. *conj. After*:—Síþ heora tuuege dæg ágán sié, Cod. Dip. Kmbl. ii. 47, 2. [*Goth.* seithu *sero;* ni thanaseiths *no longer: O. Sax.* sīð; *cpve.* sīðor: *O. H. Ger.* sīd (*adv., prep. with dat., conj.*); *cpve.* sīdor: *Ger.* seit: *Icel.* síð; *cpve.* síðarr; *spve.* síðast.]

síþ-berend, es; *m. A scythe-bearer, a mower*:—Síþberend *vel* mǽþre *falcarius* i. *falciferens*, Wrt. Voc. ii. 146, 80.

síþ-bóc; *f. An itinerary*:—Síþbóc *itinerarium*, Hpt. Gl. 454, 19.

síþ-boda, an; *m. One who announces that a journey or march is to begin*, applied to the pillar of cloud, Cd. Th. 193, 21; Exod. 250.

síþ-boren *late-born*:—Of ðǽm síþborenum *de post fetantes*, Ps. Surt. 77, 70: Wrt. Voc. ii. 138, 84.

síþ-dagas; *pl. Latter days, later times*:—On síþdagum ácenned *born in the latter days*, Elen. Kmbl. 1274; El. 639. Cf. ǽr-dagas.

síþe (*from* sigþe), es; *m. A scythe, implement for mowing*:—Sigdi, síþe *falcis*, Txts. 62, 430. Síþe, Wrt. Voc. ii. 35, 1: *falx*, 38, 51: i. 34, 64: *falcastrum*, 16, 16: 85, 3: ii. 33, 74. Befeóll án síþe of ðam snǽde intō ānum deópan seáþe, Homl. Th. ii. 162, 10. Hē sceal habban . . . síþe, Anglia ix. 263, 5. [*Icel.* sigðr; *m.*: sigd (*in Norway*) *a sickle*.]

síþemest. v. síþ.

síþ-fær, es; *n. A way, journey*:—Wið sȳðfære *juxta iter*, Ps. Spl. 139, 6.

síþ-fæt, es; *in sing. generally masc., in pl. neut.* I. *a journey, expedition*:—'Se síþfæt is ðyder tō lang, and ðone weg ic ne con.' Drihten him tō cwæþ: 'Andreas ic ðīnne síþfæt gestaþelode,' Blickl. Homl. 231, 26-8: Andr. Kmbl. 840; An. 420: Elen. Kmbl. 458; El. 229. Ðæt gewin ðæs síþfætes *labor itineris*, Bd. 1, 23; S. 486, 1. Ðone intingan his síþfætes *itineris sui causam*, 4, 1; S. 563, 24: Andr. Kmbl. 407; An. 204. Síþfates, Elen. Kmbl. 439; El. 220. Ðæt folc wearþ þrít mid ðam síþfæte *taedere coepit populum itineris*, Num. 21, 4. Ðū mē hafast on ðissum síþfæte sibbe gecȳðed, Andr. Kmbl. 715; An. 358. Hē byþ on sȳþfæte and gysthūses beþearf, L. E. I. 32; Th. ii. 430, 25. Ðȳ ongunnenan síþfate, Bd. 5, 19; S. 641, 2: Kent. Gl. 307: Cd. Th. 211, 4; Exod. 521: Judth. Thw. 26, 19; Jud. 336. Ðonne hwā síþfæt onginnan wille, ðonne genime hē ðās wyrte artemisiam, and hæbbe mid him, ðonne ne ongyt hē nā mycel tō geswynce ðæs síþes, Lchdm. i. 102, 4. Ðone síþfæt him ceorlas lythwōn lōgon, Beo. Th. 406; B. 202: Exon. Th. 274, 3; Jul. 527. Ongan síþfæt (*his journey* or (?) *his fate*, cf. síþ, V) seófian, wyrd wānian, 274, 22; Jul. 537. II. *a path, course, way, road*:—Weg *via*, síþfæt *iter*, Wrt. Voc. i. 53, 59. Rihtes síþfætes *directi callis*, ii. 140, 55. Síþfæte *tramite*, Hpt. Gl. 513, 26. Sunnan síþfæt *the sun's path*, Cd. Th. 182, 25; Exod. 81. Ealne gōdne síþfet *omnem semitam bonam*, Kent. Gl. 20. Ðā oncierde ðæt scip on wōnne síðfæt *the ship took a wrong course*, Shrn. 60, 8. Síþfatu *calles*, 27. Síþfata *semitas, vias*, Hpt. Gl. 457, 9. Ðā forlēton wē ða frēcnan wegas and síþfato, Nar. 17, 13. III. fig. *a way, path, course*:—Síþfæt ārleásra losaþ *iter impiorum peribit*, Ps. Spl. 1, 7. Gerece mē on síþfæte (*semita*) rihtum, 26, 17. Gesundfull (gesundne, Ps. Th. 67, 20) síþfæt dō ūs, 67, 21. Síþfæt sægde ðe hē mid wilddeórum āteáh *told of his life with the wild beasts*, Cd. Th. 256, 31; Dan. 649. Nū ðū ædre const síþfæt mīnne. Ic sceal sārigferþ hweorfan . . . *now thou shalt speedily know my course. Mournful must I wander* . . ., Exon. Th. 184, 30; Gū. 1352. Hine geheald ōþ ðæt hē his síþfæt secge ealne from orde (*the devil is then made to give an account of his proceedings*), 259, 20; Jul. 285: 261, 20; Jul. 318. Síþfatu *semitas*, Ps. Spl. 24, 4. IV. *course* of time (?):—Ðā wæs æfter síþfate ðæt mægen on him weóx *in course of time it came to pass that strength grew in him*, Guthl. 2; Gdwin. 12, 25.

síþ-from; *adj. Good at travelling, bold in journeying*:—Síþfrome, searwum gearwe, wīgend (*Beowulf and his men when ready for their homeward voyage*), Beo. Th. 3630; B. 1813: Andr. Kmbl. 493; An. 247. Land Perséa sōhton síþfrome Simon and Thaddeus, Apstls. Kmbl. 153; Ap. 77: Andr. Kmbl. 1281; An. 641: Exon. Th. 157, 17; Gū. 893.

síþ-geómor; *adj. Sad and weary with travel*:—Ic ðysne sang síþgeómor fand, on seócum sefan samnode wīde, hū ða æþelingas ellen cȳðdon, Apstls. Kmbl. 2; Ap. 1.

síðian; *p.* ode *To journey, go, travel*:—Hwider síðast ðū būtan ðīnum bearne? Homl. Th. i. 416, 33. Ðǣr ic síðade *juxta iter*, Ps. Th. 139, 5. Hē ðider síðode, Homl. Th. ii. 516, 6. Sum undercyning hine bæd ðæt hē hām mid him síðode, i. 128, 6. Ðā ðā se Hǣlend síðode, sum man him cwæþ tō: 'Ic wille síðian mid ðē and ðē folgian,' Homl. Skt. i. 16, 154. Nǣnig wæs ðæt hē eft síðade hyhta leás, Exon. Th. 157, 24; Gū. 896. Þurh ðē Freá on ðās eorþan ūt síðade, 21, 4; Cri. 329. Hig intō helle cuce síðodon *descenderunt vivi in infernum*, Num. 16, 33. Hig síðodon ealle tō Egipta lande, Ælfc. T. Grn. 5, 3. Síðedon, Cd. Th. 121, 13; Gen. 2009. Hine cneówmǣgas mid síðedon, 104, 13; Gen. 1734. Ðæt ic hlāfordleás hām síðie, wende fram wīge, Byrht. Th. 139, 9; By. 251. Ðǣr gē síðien, Cd. Th. 195, 6; Exod. 272. Síðien and fǣren *comitentur*, Wrt. Voc. ii. 22, 14. For ðē sceal ǣlc flǣsc forþ síðian *ad te omnis caro veniet*, Ps. Th. 64, 2. Ðā com eorl síðian on Egypte, Cd. Th. 110, 27; Gen. 1844. Gewāt him hām síðian, 130, 18; Gen. 2161. Hēht hine twegen men mid síðian, 173, 28; Gen. 2868. Samed síðian, Exon. Th. 434, 17; Rā. 52, 2. Up síðian, Hy. 3, 56. Síðigean, Andr. Kmbl. 1657; An. 831. Ic eom engel Godes ufan síðende, Exon. Th. 258, 7; Jul. 261. ¶ of the spirit's journey to another world:—Æfter deáþe somod síðiaþ sāwla mid līce, 237, 2; Ph. 584. Scolde se ellorgāst on feónda geweald feor síðian, Beo. Th. 1621; B. 808. Ðæt mīn sāwul tō ðē síðian mōte, Byrht. Th. 136, 65. [*O. E. Homl.* siðian: *Laym.* siðen: *O. Sax.* síðōn: *O. H. Ger.* sindōn: *Icel.* sinna.] v. for-, gemid-, mid-, wræc-síðian.

síþ-lǣdness, e; *f. A leading* or *taking away*:—Síþlǣdnisse *abductione*, Ps. Surt. ii. p. 195, 39. Cf. onwegalǣdness.

síþlice; *adv. Late* (?), *after some time, at last, in the end, lately*:—Eft ðā siððan ōðre twegen swearte hremmas síþlīce cōmon and his hūs tǣron mid heardum bile *again afterwards two other black ravens came after some time, and tore his house with hard bill*, Homl. Th. ii. 144, 21. Næs Petrus gewunod tō nānre wǣpnunge ac ðǣr wǣron twā swurd síþlīce gebrohte *Peter was not accustomed to arms, but two swords had lately* (?) *been brought there*, 248, 4.

síþmæst, síþor. v. síþ.

síþ-stap[p]el *a track, footstep*:—Ðæt ne sȳn āstyrode síþstapla mīne ł wegas ł fōtswaþu *ut non moueantur uestigia mea*, Ps. Lamb. 16, 5. v. under-stapplian.

síþ[þ], e; *f. Travel, journey*:—Bǣm wæs on síþþe hæbbendes hyht *to both when journeying was the possessor's joy*, Exon. Th. 481, 12; Rā. 65, 2. v. gesíþ[þ].

siððа; *adv. Afterwards*:—Ðonne meaht ðū siðða sōðes leóhtes habban ðīnne dǣl, Bt. Met. Fox 24, 59. v. next word.

siððan, siððon, syððan, seoððan. [*From* síþ ðam; cf. *Ger.* seitdem.] I. *adv. Afterwards, since*:—Gē faraþ siððan *postea transibitis*, Gen. 18, 5. Siððon, Exon. Th. 131, 33; Gū. 465. Sioððan, Elen. Kmbl. 2292; El. 1147. Syððan (*exinde*) ongan se Hǣlend bodian, Mt. Kmbl. 4, 17. Ðā ongan hyne syððan hingrian *postea esuriit*, 4, 2. Hē biþ ðonne seoððan ðǣm englum gelīc, Blickl. Homl. 49, 7. Siððon, 59, 7. Ða ðe seoððan after Cristes cyme wǣron tō Gode gecyrrede, 81, 15. Ðā æfter ðisse dǣde his noma wæs ā seoððan mǣre geworden, 219, 4. Ā syððan ðenden wunaþ hūsa sēlest, Beo. Th. 571; B. 283. Siððan ā, Andr. Kmbl. 2387; An. 1195: 2757; An. 1381. Seoððan ā, Cd. Th. 289, 16; Sat. 398. Siððan ǣfre, Elen. Kmbl. 1012; El. 507. Hī sunnan ne geseóþ syððan ǣfre, Ps. Th. 57, 7. Ā forþ sioððan, Ps. C. 103. Hraðe seoððan, Beo. Th. 3879; B. 1937. Nǣnig efenlīc ðam ǣr ne siððan, Exon. Th. 3, 21; Cri. 39. II. *conj.* (1) where the tense of the verb in the clause introduced by *siððan* is past, in the other clause present, *since*:—Ðē is ungelīc wlite, siððan ðū lǣstes mīne lāre, Cd. Th. 38, 28; Gen. 613: Exon. Th. 44, 13; Cri. 702. Wē ælþeódige wǣron, siððon se ǣresta ealdor Godes bebodu ābræc *we have been exiles, since Adam broke God's commands*, Blickl. Homl. 23, 4. Hū lang tīd is, syððan him ðis gebyrede? Mk. Skt. 9, 21. Ðeós syððan ic ineode ne geswāc ðæt heó mīne fēt ne cyste, Lk. Skt. 7, 45. Manige geár syndon āgān nū seoððan ūre bisceopas tō mē gewreoto sende, Blickl. Homl. 187, 3. (2) where the tense is the same in each clause, *after*:—Ðonne biþ his wela for nāuht, siððan hī ongitaþ . . ., Bt. 27, 3; Fox 100, 2. Ðū scealt Isaac onsecgan, siððan ðū gestīgest dūne, Cd. Th. 172, 32; Gen. 2853: 174, 22; Gen. 2882. Him eorla mōd ortrȳwe wearþ, siððan hié gesāwon fyrd Faraonis, 187, 22; Exod. 155. Wǣron Adames dagas, siððan (*postquam*) hē gestrīnde Seth, Gen. 5, 4. Syððan, 18, 12. Syððan Iohannes geseald wæs, com se Hǣland, Mk. Skt. 1, 14. Hwæt biþ hit būton flǣsc, seoððan se ēcea dǣl of biþ? Blickl. Homl. iii. 31: Cd. Th. 309, 7; Sat. 706. [Later forms are *sithenes*, which gives modern *since, sin*, still used in dialects, and *sithe, sith*, which latter is common in Elizabethan writers.]

síþ-weg, es; *m. A road to travel on, high-road* (?):—Hē gehǣlde hygegeómre ðe hine gesōhtun of sīðwegum (síð-? v. síd-weg) *he* (*Guthlac, who lived in the wilderness*) *healed the sad in heart that from the travelled ways sought him*, Exon. Th. 155, 13; Gū. 859.

síþ-weorod, es; *n. A band out on an expedition*:—Ne meahton síþwerod gūþe spōwan, Cd. Th. 127, 22; Gen. 2114.

síþ-wíf, es; *n. A noble lady*:—On sumes síþwīfes (gōdes wifes, 2nd MS.) hūse *in domum inclytae matronae*, Nar. 49, 9. v. gesíþ-wīf.

sitl. v. setl.

sittan; *p.* sæt, *pl.* sǣton; *pp.* seten. I. *to sit, be seated*:—Ðū sitst on ðam heán setle, Ps. Th. 9, 4. Sitest, Hy. 8, 30. Ðū ðe sittest ofer cherubin, Ps. Th. 79, 2. On ðam ðe ofer ðæt [þrymsetl] sitt, Mt. Kmbl. 23, 22. God sitt ofer setle his, Ps. Spl. 46, 8. Ðe sit on his cynesetle, Ex. 11, 5. Siteþ, Cd. Th. 17, 16; Gen. 260. Se ðe sitteþ ofer cherubim, Ps. Spl. 98, 1. Hē on bolcan sæt, Andr. Kmbl. 610; An. 305. Weard on wicge sæt, Beo. Th. 578; B. 286. Hē æt fōtum sæt freán Scyldinga, 1004; B. 500. Maria sæt be Hǣlendes fōtum, Blickl. Homl. 73, 30. Wē on geflitum sǣton *we sat engaged in discussions*, Salm. Kmbl. 862; Sal. 430. Hié æt swǣsendum sǣton, Cd. Th. 1688; Gen. 2779. Hæleþ in sǣton, Andr. Kmbl. 724; An. 362. Site nū tō symle, Beo. Th. 982; B. 489. Geseah twegen englas sittan, ānne æt ðām heáfdon, ōðerne æt ðām fōtum, Jn. Skt. 20, 12. Sittan ofer ða eorþan, Mk. Skt. 8, 6. Sittan on scridwǣne, Bt. 27, 1; Fox 96, 1. Tō sittanne on mīne swīðran healfe, Mt. Kmbl. 20, 23. Sittende, Lk. Skt. 22, 69. Uppan assan folan sittende, Jn. Skt. 12, 15. Sittendum wīfe under gelēd, Lchdm. i. 266, 6. I a. with reflexive dative:—Ða him sǣton sundor on portum, Ps. Th. 68, 12. Sǣton him æt wīne, Cd. Th. 259, 23; Dan. 696. I b. of kneeling:—Hié for ðam cumble on cneówum sǣton, 227, 2; Dan. 180. I c. applied to the position of a bird at rest:—Ic (*picus*) glado sitte, Exon. Th. 406, 26; Rā. 25, 7. Hē (*the phenix*) siteþ síþes fūs, 212, 10; Ph. 208. Nēfuglas under beorhhleoþum sittaþ, Cd. Th. 130, 14; Gen. 2159. II. *to stay, dwell, sojourn, abide, reside, remain in a place*, (a) of persons:—Wē in carcerne sittaþ sorgende,

Exon. Th. 2, 28; Cri. 26. Ða ðe on þȳstrum sittaþ, Lk. Skt. 1, 79. Ealle ða ðe sittaþ ofer eorþan ansȳne, 21, 35. Unc mōdige ymb mearce sittaþ *dwell on our borders*, Cd. Th. 114, 21; Gen. 1907. On ðam setle ðe hē ðǣr sæt *during the stay he made there*, Chr. 922; Erl. 108, 22. Inne on ðæm fæstenne sǣton feáwa cirlisce men *a few common men were living in the fort*, 893; Erl. 88, 33. Wē on ðam gōdan rīce sǣton, Cd. Th. 27, 1; Gen. 411. Hæleþ lāgon, on swaþe sǣton (*were left behind dead*), 125, 10; Gen. 2077. Gang tō ciricean and site ðǣr and stille wuna and geseoh ðæt ðū ūt ðanon ne gonge ǣr seó ādl from ðē gewiten sȳ *ingredere ecclesiam & ibi reside, quietus manens; vide ne exeas inde, nec de loco movearis, donec hora recessionis febris transierit*, Bd. 3, 12; S. 537, 9. Sitte gē on ceastre ōþ gē sȳn ufene gescrȳdde, Lk. Skt. 24, 49. Se ðe sitte uncwydd on his āre on līfe, L. Eth. iii. 14; Th. i. 298, 9. (a 1) referring to warlike or hostile operations, as in *to sit* down before a place (cf. *siege*), *to encamp*:—Ðū sǣte ongeán ðīnne brōþor (cf. *Icel.* sitja á svikum við einn *to plot against one*), Ps. Th. 49, 21. Hē him æfter rād ōþ ðæt geweorc and ðǣr sæt .xiiii. niht, Chr. 878; Erl. 80, 15. (Often in the Chronicle.) (b) of things:—Sió hefige eorþe sit ðǣr niþere be ðæs cyninges gebode, Bt. 39, 13; Fox 234, 13. Flōd mycel on sæt *there was a great flood in the river*, Bd. 3, 24; S. 556, 35. **II a.** *to continue* in a state or condition, *live* (in hope, fear, etc.), *remain* (silent, etc.):—Ic ā on wēnum sæt *I lived in constant expectation*, Cd. Th. 163, 18; Gen. 2700. Mǣre þeóden unblīðe sæt, Beo. Th. 261; B. 130. Sæt secg monig sorgum gebunden, weán on wēnan, Exon. Th. 378, 30; Deór. 24. Sitte ǣlc wuduwe werleás twelf mōnaþ, L. C. S. 74; Th. i. 416, 6. **III.** with the idea of oppression (cf. colloquial *to sit* on a person, *Icel.* sitja á sēr *to restrain one's self*), *to sit* or *bear heavy* on, *weigh, press, rest*:—Ne mē wiht an siteþ egesan āwiht ǣniges mannes *non timebo quid faciat mihi homo*, Ps. Th. 55, 9. Seó hefige byrþen siteþ on ðæm deádan līchoman ðære byrgenne *the heavy burden of the tomb presses on the dead body*, Blickl. Homl. 75, 7: Lchdm. iii. 110, 23, 26. On eów scyld siteþ, Exon. Th. 131, 2; Gū. 449. Ūs Godes yrre hetelīce on sit, Wulfst. 162, 2. Ða yrmþa ðe ūs on sittaþ, 157, 5. Swā sæt seó byrþen synna on ðissum cynne, Blickl. Homl. 75, 9. For ðǣm earfoþum ðe him on sǣton *for the miseries that sat heavy on them*, Met. 26, 97. Sitte sió scyld on him, L. Alf. 17; Th. i. 48, 15. Ǣr ðon ðe him se egesa onufan sǣte, Judth. Thw. 25, 10; Jud. 252. **IV.** *to sit* in authority, *preside*:—Ðæt mōd ðe ofer ðæm flǣsce sitt *mens carni praesidens*, Past. 36, 7; Swt. 256, 3. **V.** *trans. To occupy* a seat:—Sæt hē ðæt biscopsetl .xxxvii. wintra, Bd. 5, 23; S. 646, 9. [*Goth.* sitan: *O. Sax.* sittian: *O. Frs.* sitta: *O. H. Ger.* sizzan: *Icel.* sitja.] v. ā-, æt-, be-, eft-, for-, fore-, ge-, of-, ofer-, on-, tō-, under-, ymb-sittan; *and next word.*

-sittende *-sitting, -occupying, -inhabiting.* v. benc-, burh-, flet-, hām-, heal-, in-, land-, þrym-, ymb-sittende.

siun-huurful. v. sin-hwurfol.

siwen-īge, -ēge; *adj. Blear-eyed*:—Se biþ siwenīge (-igge, Cot. MSS.) se ðe his andgit biþ tō ðon beorhte scīnende ðæt hē mæge ongietan sōðfæstnesse, gif hit ðonne āþīstriaþ ða flǣsclīcan weorc. On ðæs siwenīgean (-iggean, Cott. MSS.) eágum beóþ ða æpplas hāle . . . Se biþ eallinga siwenīge (-igge, Cott. MSS.) ðonne his mōd and his andgit ðæt gecynd āscirpþ and hē hit ðonne self gescint mid his ungewunan *lippus vero est, cujus quidem ingenium ad cognitionem veritatis emicat, sed tamen carnalia opera obscurant. In lippis quippe oculis pupillae sanae sunt . . . Lippus itaque est, cujus sensum natura exacuit, sed conversationis pravitas confundit*, Past. 11, 4; Swt. 67, 24-69, 9. Siwenēge *lippos*, Germ. 396, 284.

siwian *to sew.* v. seowian.

six, siex, syx *six.* I. *as adj. indecl.*:—Wirc six dagas, Ex. 20, 9. On six dagum God geworhte ealle þing, 20, 11. Æfter six (sex, Lind., Rush.) dagum, Mt. Kmbl. 17, 1. Betweox ðara sex fīfa ǣlcum, Lchdm. ii. 148, 2. Sex *bis terna*, Wrt. Voc. ii. 12, 10. On siex dagum, Exon. Th. 105, 13; Gū. 22. Ða siex stafas sweotule bēcnaþ, 407, 4; Rā. 25, 10. Syx (sex, Lind., Rush.) dagon ǣr, Jn. Skt. 12, 1. **I a.** in multiplication:—Ceorles wergild is .cc. scill. Ðegnes wergild is syx swā micel, L. M. L.; Th. i. 190, 3. **II.** *as subst. declined*:—Ðā hyra syxe wǣron ācwealde, Shrn. 111, 10. On ðam mynstre wǣron fīf brōþra oððe syxe, Bd. 4, 13; S. 582, 22. Hē sǣde ðæt hē syxa sum ofslōge syxtig, Ors. 1, 1; Swt. 18, 7. Ymbsealde sint mid sixum, Elen. Kmbl. 1481; El. 472. [*Goth.* saihs: *O. Sax.* sehs: *O. Frs.* sex: *O. H. Ger.* sehs: *Icel.* sex.]

six-benn, e; *f. A wound made by a* 'seax':—Ealdorgewinna (*the fire-drake*) siexbennum seóc (cf. cyning wælseaxe gebrǣd . . . forwrāt Wedra helm wyrm on middan, 5400; B. 2703), Beo. Th. 5800; B. 2904.

six-ecge; *adj. Hexagonal*:—Sixecge *exagonum*, Wrt. Voc. i. 55, 3. Sixecge bere *exaticum*, ii. 144, 58.

six-feald; *adj. Six-fold*:—Sixfeald *exagonum*, sixfealdum leóþcræfte *exametro heroico*, Wrt. Voc. ii. 144, 46, 47. Siexfealdre anlīcnesse *sena paradigmata*, 89, 39.

six-fēte; *adj. Having six feet* (of verse):—Ðæt syxfēte vers, Anglia viii. 335, 13. Mid getelferse ł sixfētum *catalectico versu*, Hpt. Gl. 409, 21.

six-gilde; *adj. Requiring six-fold payment* or *fine*:—Diácones feoh .vi. gylde *a deacon's property* (*when stolen*) *shall be paid for with a six-fold fine*, L. Ethb. 1; Th. i. 2, 5. v. -gilde.

six-hynde; *adj. Of a class whose wergild is six hundred shillings*:—Gif wealh hafaþ fīf hȳda hē biþ sixhynde, L. In. 24; Th. i. 118, 10. Be syxhyndum men. Gif hit sié syxhynde mon, [gielde] ǣlc mon .lx. scill., L. Alf. pol. 30; Th. i. 80, 11. Gif hió sié syxhyndu, 18; Th. i. 72, 14. Syxhyndes monnes burhbryce .xv. scill., 40; Th. i. 88, 10. Gif syxhyndum ðissa hwæðer gelimpe, gebēte be ðæs syxhyndan bōte, 39; Th. i. 88, 2-5. Syxhyndum men .c. scill. gebēte, 10; Th. i. 68, 10. ¶ applied to the wergild:—Æt twȳhyndum were mon sceal sellan tō monbōte .xxx. scill., æt syxhyndum .lxxx. scill., L. In. 70; Th. i. 146, 14. v. twelf-hynde, and see Stubbs' Const. Hist. i. 161, note 3.

six-hyrnede; *adj. Having six corners* or *angles*:—Sixhernede *sexangulatum*, Wrt. Voc. i. 55, 4.

six-nihte; *adj. Six days old*:—Se ðe biþ ācenned on .vi. nihtne mōnan, Lchdm. iii. 160, 23: 178, 6.

sixta; *ord. num. Sixth*:—Se sixta (sexta) *sextus*, Ælfc. Gr. 49; Zup. 282, 17. Siexta wæs Ōswald, Chr. 827; Erl. 64, 4. Ðā wæs syxte geár, Elen. Kmbl. 14; El. 7. Wæs ðā sihste tīd, Exon. Th. 171, 8; Gū. 1123. Seista (sesta, Rush.), Mk. Skt. Lind. 15, 33.

sixteóþa; *ord. num. Sixteenth*:—Se syxteóþa (six-) *sextus decimus*, Ælfc. Gr. 49; Zup. 283, 3. Sextegða, Shrn. 91, 20.

sixtig; *used as subs.* or *adj. Sixty*:—Syxtig *sexaginta*, Ælfc. Gr. 49; Zup. 281, 18. Salomones reste wæs ymbseted mid syxtigum werum . . . Hwæt mǣnde ðæt syxtig wera strongera? Blickl. Homl. 11, 16-22. Æfter siextegum daga *intra sexagesimum diem*, Ors. 4, 6; Swt. 172, 4. Mid iii hund scipa and LXgum, Swt. 176, 25. Sexdig (sextig, Rush.), Mk. Skt. Lind. 4, 8. Sexdig ł sextih, Mt. Kmbl. Lind. 13, 23. Sexdeih, 13, 8.

sixtigoþa *sixtieth*:—Se sixteogoþa *sexagesimus*, Ælfc. Gr. 49; Zup. 283, 12.

sixtig-feald *sixty-fold*, Mt. Kmbl. 13, 8, 23.

sixtig-wintre *sixty years old*:—Hē wæs fīf and sixtigwintre, Gen. 5, 15, 18, 20, 21, 23.

sixtīne *sixteen*:—Syxtȳne *sedecim*, Ælfc. Gr. 49; Zup. 281, 13.

sixtīne-nihte; *adj. Sixteen days old*:—On .xvi. nihte mōnan, Lchdm. iii. 180, 3.

sixtīne-wintre; *adj. Sixteen years old*:—Ðǣr georn .xvi. wintre mǣden, Shrn. 140, 1: 141, 9.

slā (*from* slāhe); *gen.* slān: *but also* slāh, slāg, e; *f. A sloe*:—Slā *brumela, bellicum*, Wrt. Voc. ii. 127, 26. Slāg *bellicum*, Txts. 45, 289. Genim onwǣre slāh ðæt seáw . . . gif sió slāh biþ grēne, Lchdm. ii. 32, 18-20. Gewring tōsomne swilce sié ān slāh, 54, 6. Slān *moros*, Wrt. Voc. i. 285, 33: ii. 56, 32. [Cockayne quotes from a late MS.: 'Acasia est succus prunellarum [im]maturarum, grene slane wose:' and *pl. slon* occurs Alis. 4983. In Baker's Northants. Gloss. *slacen-, slaun*-bush are given as used of the blackthorn. *O. H. Ger.* slēha, slēa *prunella, agacia*: *Ger.* schlehe: *Dan.* slaaen.] v. plūm-slā: slāh-þorn.

slacian, slæcian, sleacian; *p.* ode *To slacken, relax an effort*:—Gif hē lithwōn slacode . . . his handa ne slacedon *sin autem paulalum remisisset . . . factum est, ut manus illius non lassarentur*, Ex. 17, 11, 12. Ðæt ne ða sleacgiendan (*pigritantes*) hē ofhreóse, Hymn. Surt. 18, 15. [Nullich neuer slakien to drien herd wiðuten, A. R. 134, 22. Ne schaltu seon me slakien to leuen, Jul. 26, 1. He mot slakie his bendes, Laym. 23345 (2nd MS.). Cf. *Icel.* slakna *to get slack*.] v. ā-, tō-slacian; slæccan.

slacigendlīc, slǣ. v. ā-slacigendlīc, sleahe.

slæc, sleac, slec (v. slæcness); *adj. Slack.* I. of persons (1) *inactive, slothful, lazy, not willing to make an effort*:—Slæc *reses*, Wrt. Voc. ii. 118, 77. Sleac *piger*, i. 74, 33: *lentus* vel *piger*, 49, 35. Sleac *vel* slāw *pigrus* vel *lentus*, 16, 48. Ðū yfela þeówa and sleac *thou wicked and slothful servant*, Homl. Th. ii. 554, 7. Sægdon ðæt hē sleac wǣre, æðeling unfrom, Beo. Th. 4381; B. 2187. Ðæt ðæm sleacan preóste ne þince tō mycel geswinc, ðæt hē undō his eágan, Anglia viii. 317, 4. Tō swilcum sleacum cweð se hīrēdes ealdor: 'Tō hwī stande gē hēr ealne dæg ȳdele?' Homl. Th. ii. 78, 10. (2) *careless, negligent, remiss, not strict in the performance of duty*:—Ne tō stræc on ðære lāre ne tō slæc on ðære mildheortnesse *ne aut districtio rigida, aut pietas remissa*, Past. 17, 10; Swt. 125, 1. Se ðe sleac wǣre tō gōdnesse, Homl. Th. ii. 100, 22. Se biþ wacigende . . . se biþ sleac and slǣpende, Btwk. 220, 32. Sleaces *socordis*, Germ. 388, 34. Ne beón gē tō slāpole ne tō sleace, ac scyldaþ eów georne wið deófles dare, Wulfst. 40, 21. Sleace tō ǣnig wyrcenne gōd *pigre ad aliquod operandum bonum*, Anglia xi. 117, 36. (3) *languid, ill*:—Slæce *egra*, Wrt. Voc. ii. 107, 8: 29, 18. **II.** of things, (1) of physical movement, *slow, gentle*:—Sum munuc mid sleaccre stalcunge his fōtswaðum filigde, Homl. Th. ii. 138, 6. (2) *that makes inactive, sluggish*:—Wē sceolon āsceacan ðone sleacan slǣp ūs fram, i. 602, 15. (3) *not attended with effort*:—Hit is ealles tō sleac munuca þeówdōm (*nimis iners seruitium*), gif hié læsse singaþ, R. Ben. 44, 18.

(4) *lax of conduct*:—Gemetgie ðæt fȳr ða bilewitnysse, ðæt heó tō sleac ne sȳ, Homl. Th. ii. 46, 8. Þeówode hē druncennesse and monigum ōðrum unālȳfednessum ðæs sleacran līfes (*vitae remissioris*), Bd. 5, 14; S. 634, 15. [*O. Sax.* slak: *O. H. Ger.* slah: *Icel.* slakr.] v. un-slæc.

slæccan, sleccan (?); *p.* slæcte, slæhte *To make slack* or *slow, to delay*:—'Ðū ūs oftrædlīce mid elcunge geswænctest.' . . . Ðā cwæþ se cyngc, 'Ðe læs ðe ic eów ā leng slæce (slæcce?),' Th. Ap. 20, 6. v. ā-slæccan, ge-sleccan; slacian.

slæcfull; *adj. Slothful*:—Slacfulran for belādunge *propter somnolentorum excusationes*, R. Ben. Interl. 55, 8.

slæcian. v. slacian.

slæclīc; *adj. Slow*:—Mid sleacilera (sleaclīcere?) *sera, tarda*, Hpt. Gl. 472, 49. v. next word.

slæclīce; *adv. Lazily, slothfully, languidly*:—Sleaclīce *enervatius*, i. *debilius*, Wrt. Voc. ii. 143, 54. Sume sleaclīce (scleac-, MS. F.) lāgon and slēpon, R. Ben. 68, 21. v. un-slæclīce.

slæcness, e; *f. Sloth, inertness, laziness*:—Slecnes *accidia*, Wrt. Voc. ii. 5, 73: 97, 5. Scleacnes *pigredo*, Kent. Gl. 694. I. *slowness* of physical movement:—Swā swā ðære sunnan sleacnys ācenþ ǣnne dæg and āne niht . . . swā eác ðæs mōnan swiftnys āwyrpþ ūt ǣnne dæg and āne niht, Lchdm. iii. 264, 19. II. *slowness* in action:—Ðæs þeówes sleacnys (*he seemed long in doing his errand*), Shrn. 43, 15. Wæs beboden ðæt hī sceoldon caflīce etan, forðan ðe God onscunaþ ða sleacnysse on his þegnum, Homl. Th. ii. 282, 3. III. *mental inertness*:—Nū wolde ic ðæt ða æðela[n] clericas āsceócon fram heora andgites orþance ǣlce sleacnysse, Anglia viii. 301, 4. IV. *remissness, slowness* in performance of duty:—Oft eác sió gōdnes ðære monþwǣrnesse biþ diégellīce gemenged wið sleacnesse . . . Wē sculon manian ða manþwǣran ðæt hié fleón ðæt ðǣr suíðe neáh liegeþ ðære monnþwǣrnesse, ðæt is sleacnes, Past. 40; Swt. 289, 18–22.

slæcorness, e; *f. Slackness, laziness, remissness*:—Ic ondette sleacornesse and slāpornesse, Anglia xi. 98, 40.

slǣd, slēd, es; *n. A slade* (in local names, e.g. Water*slade*, v. W. Somerset Words, E. D. S. Pub., and in some dialects. '*Slade* a breadth of greensward in ploughed land; a flat piece of grass; but now most commonly applied to a broad strip of greensward between two woods, generally in a valley,' Baker's Northampt. Gloss. 'Narrow strips of boggy ground running into the hard land at Rockland are called "The Slades,"' E. Anglian Gloss. *Slade* a breadth of greensward in ploughed land, or in plantations, E. D. S. Publ. Gloss. B. 7 (West Riding). In Levin's Manip. Vocab. (1570) a slade, valley = *vallis*, and Drayton uses the word in this sense, v. Nares; see also Halliwell's Dict.), *low, flat, marshy ground, with a broad bottom, a valley*. (1) The word occurs not unfrequently in the charters, e.g.:—On slēdes heáfad, Cod. Dip. Kmbl. v. 148, 3. Andlang slǣdes on pyt, iii. 48, 24: 407, 12. Tō brocces slǣde, 233, 34. On ðæt slǣd, 385, 28. Ōþ ðæt niéhste slǣd, 416, 21. On slǣd, 25, 24. *It occurs also in composition*:—Tō wulfslǣde, 456, 6. On Fugelslēd; of ðam slēde, 48, 21. In barfodslǣd; and swā on timberslǣd . . . on hamslǣdes heáfdan, 380, 25–6. On fearnslǣd, 385, 30. On ðæt riscslǣd, 437, 15. Ondlong slǣdbrōces, 405, 17. (2) In other connections it is not common, but occurs in the following passage:—Dameris beforan ðæm cyninge farende wæs swelce heó fleónde wǣre ōþ hió hiene gelǣdde on ān micel slǣd . . . Ðǣr wearþ Cirus ofslægen and twā þūsend monna mid him *Tomyris simulat diffidentiam, paulatimque cedendo, hostem in insidias vocat. Ibi quippe, compositis inter montes insidiis, ducenta millia Persarum cum ipso rege delevit*, Ors. 2, 4; Swt. 76, 29. Cf. Iulius ferde ut of Doure in to ane muchele slæde & his folc hudde, Laym. 8585. Heo talden whar me heom kepen mihte in ane slade deopen, 26887. Geond slades & geon dunen, 28365. By slente oþer slade, Allit. Pms. 5, 141. Loke a littel on þe launde on þi lyfte honde & þou schal se in þat slade þe self chapel, Gaw. 2147.

slæge. v. slege.

slægu, e; *f. Slag, dross*.—Slaegu, slægu, slegu *lihargum* (= *lithargyrum*), Txts. 75, 1230. Slægu *liliagrum*, Wrt. Voc. ii. 51, 6.

slæht, slæhtan. v. sliht, slihtan.

slǣp, slēp, sleáp, slāp, es; *m. Sleep*:—Befeóll slǣp (*sopor*) on Abram, Gen. 15, 12. Hrædlīce se slǣp becymeþ, Lchdm. i. 246, 17. Slǣp biþ deáþe gelīcost, Salm. Kmbl. 624; Sal. 611. Hine slǣp ofereode, Andr. Kmbl. 1640; An. 821. Mec slǣp ofergongeþ, Exon. Th. 422, 23; Rä. 41, 10. Slēp, Prov. Kmbl. 1. Gif ic mīnum eágum unne slǣpes, Ps. Th. 131, 4. Slēpes *soporis*, Ps. Surt. ii. p. 201, 38: *somni*, 202, 15. Hī wēndon ðæt hē hyt sǣde be swefnes slǣpe (slēpe, Lind., Rush. *de dormitione somnii*), Jn. Skt. 11, 13. Mid ðȳ heó ðȳ slǣpe tōbrǣd *somno excussa*, Bd. 4, 23; S. 596, 5: Andr. Kmbl. 3053; An. 1529: Cd. Th. 161, 15; Gen. 2655. Of slǣpe onwōc æþeling, 249, 2; Dan. 524. Tō slǣpe; gāte horn under heáfod gelǣd weccan hē on slǣpe gecyrreþ, Lchdm. i. 350, 21–2. Sigon tō slǣpe, Beo. Th. 2506; B. 1251. Se ðe for sleápe āwēd *freneticus* (cf. slǣpleást), Wrt. Voc. i. 45, 72. Mid slǣpe (slēpe, Lind., Rush.) gehefegude, Lk. Skt. 9, 32. Ealle hefige slǣpe swundon *omnes somno torpent inerti*, Bd. 4, 25; S. 601, 11. Ic sōftum slǣpe mē reste, Homl. Th. i. 566, 22. Gif hē ðære hnappunge ne swīcþ ðonne hnappaþ hē ōþ hē wierþ on fæstum slǣpe *dormitando oculus ad plenissimum somnum ducitur*, Past. 28, 4; Swt. 195, 12. Ðȳ swīðan slǣpe, Blickl. Homl. 205, 4. Slāpe *somno*, Eng. Stud. ix. 40, col. 1. Ðæt dust ðysse wyrte ðone slǣp on gelǣdeþ, Lchdm. i. 286, 6: 158, 2. Næfþ hē nānne slǣp, ii. 198, 25. Slēp, i. 158, 2. Sió slǣwþ him giét on ðone slǣp, Past. 39; Swt. 283, 8. Āsceacan ðone sleacan slǣp, Homl. Th. i. 602, 15. Slǣpa sluman, Exon. Th. 122, 31; Gū. 314. ¶ *The sleep of death*:—'Ic wille āwreccan hyne of slǣpe' . . . Se Hǣlend hit cwæþ be his deáþe, Jn. Skt. 11, 11. Up āstandan of slǣpe ðæm fæstan, Andr. Kmbl. 1589; An. 796: Exon. Th. 55, 27; Cri. 890. [*Goth.* slēps: *O. Sax.* slāp: *O. Frs.* slēp: *O. H. Ger.* slāf.] v. frum-, niht-, ofer-slǣp.

slǣp, es; *m.* (?) *A slippery, miry place* (?):—Ðis sind ða landgemǣro . . . Ǣrest of ðan ealdan slǣpe . . . tō ðan ealdan slǣpe ðǣr hit ǣr ongan, Cod. Dip. Kmbl. vi. 112, 30–113, 3. On occan slǣw (slǣp?), iii. 48, 19. [Cf. *O. H. Ger.* sleifa *labina* (labina *a myre*, Wulck. Gl. 591, 11: *a fenne*, 797, 10): *Icel.* sleipr *slippery*. Slape *soft, slippery* is given in Halliwell as a North-country word. See also E. D. S. Pub. Gloss. B. 2 (E. Yorks.), 'slape *slippery* as a dirty path,' and Gloss. B. 7 (W. Yorks.), B. 15 (Ray's North-country Words).] Cf. slipor.

slǣp-ærn, -ern, es; *n. A dormitory*:—Slǣpern *dormitorium*, Wrt. Voc. i. 58, 10. Hwǣr slǣpst (ðū)? On slǣperne (*dormitorio*) mid gebrōþrum, Coll. Monast. Th. 35, 25: Bd. 4, 23; S. 595, 39. Canonicas, ðǣr seó ār sī, ðæt hī beóddern and slǣpern habban māgan, healdan heora mynster mid rihte, L. Eth. v. 7; Th. i. 306, 12. Ic begeat ðæt stǣinene slāpern and ðǣrtō ðæs landes be sūþan ðæn slēpern .xxiiii. gerda on lange, Chart. Th. 156, 20–27.

slǣpan, slēpan; *p.* te. [*The Northern Gospels also shew forms from* slēpian:—Gif hē slēpaþ, Jn. Skt. Lind. 11, 12. Slēpiaþ ł slēpeþ ⁊ ārīsaþ (slēpiaþ ⁊ ārīsas, Rush.), Mk. Skt. Lind. 4, 27. Slēpade (geslēpedon, Lind.) *dormitaverunt*, Mt. Kmbl. Rush. 25, 5.] I. *to sleep*:—Ðū slēpes, Mk. Skt. Lind., Rush. 14, 37. Slēpes *dormit*, Mt. Kmbl. Lind., Rush. 9, 24. Hwǣr resteþ (-aþ, MS.) ðæs mannes sāwul ðonne se līchama slēpþ? Salm. Kmbl. 188, 12. Slǣpeþ *dormitet*, Ps. Lamb. 120, 3. Slǣpeþ (slēpeþ, Ps. Surt.) *obdormiet*, Ps. Th. 120, 4. Tō slǣpe; wulfes heáfod lege under pyle; se unhāla slǣpeþ, Lchdm. i. 360, 18. Gif gē slǣpaþ (slēpaþ, Ps. Surt.), Ps. Th. 67, 13. Slēpes, Lk. Skt. Lind. 22, 46. Hē æt ðæm stāne slǣpte, Past. 16; Swt. 101, 18. Hwæðer hē wacode ðe slēpte, Bd. 2, 12; S. 513, 39. Ðā hié slēptun (geslēpdon, Lind.) *cum dormirent*, Mt. Kmbl. 13, 25. Slēptun (slēpdon, Lind.) *dormierant*, 27, 52. Hneapedun ł slȳpton (in a later hand, v. Txts. p. 293) *dormierunt*, Ps. Surt. 75, 6. Ðeáh ðæt mōd slǣpe gōdra weorca, Past. 56; Swt. 431, 25. Mē lyste slǣpan *dormiturio*, Ælfc. Gr. 34; Zup. 211, 12 note. Ongunnon slēpan *dormitaverunt*, Ps. Th. 75, 5. Wæs ic slǣpende, 56, 4: 77, 65. Ðā gemētte hē his geþoftan slǣpendne, Bd. 3, 27; S. 559, 15: Beo. Th. 1486; B. 741. Hē hig funde slǣpende (slēpende, Lind., Rush.), Lk. Skt. 22, 45. II. *to sleep, lie* with a person:—Gif hwā fǣmnan beswīce unbeweddode, and hire mid slǣpe (slēpe, MS. G.), L. Alf. 29; Th. i. 52, 6. [*Laym. p.* slæpte, slepte: *A. R. p.* slepte: *Orm.* sleppte.] v. ge-, on-slǣpan; healf-slǣpende; slāpan, slāpian.

slǣp-bǣre; *adj. Somniferous, soporific*:—Hys gecynde is swīðe hāt and slǣpbǣre, Lchdm. i. 284, 22.

slǣpere, es; *m. A sleeper*:—Ðæra eádigra seofon slǣpera þrowung, Homl. Skt. i. 23, 1. v. slāpere.

slǣpig; *adj. Sleepy*. [*O. H. Ger.* slāfag.] v. un-slǣpig.

slǣp-leás; *adj. Sleepless*:—Slǣpleás *insomne*, Germ. 399, 263. [*O. H. Ger.* slāf-lōs.]

slǣp-leást, e; *f. Sleeplessness*:—Hine gedrehte singal slǣpleást, Homl. Th. i. 86, 16. Wið slǣpleáste, genym ðysse ylcan wyrte (*poppy*) wōs, smyre ðone man mid; sōna ðū him ðone slēp on senst, Lchdm. i. 158, 1. [Þe þet þuruh slōplēste āwēt *frenetus*, Wrt. Voc. i. 89, 81.]

slǣpness, e; *f. Sleepiness, drowsiness*:—Deófol ūs lǣreþ slǣpnesse and sent ūs on slǣwðe, Homl. As. 168, 106.

slǣpor; *adj. Addicted to sleep*:—Ne beó ðū tō slǣpor, forðan ðe slēp fēt unhǣlo ðæs līchoman, Prov. Kmbl. i. v. slāporness.

slǣp-wērig; *adj. Weary and sleepy, sleepily weary, so tired as to sleep*, cf. deáþ-wērig; or (?) *weary of sleep*, cf. symbel-wērig:—Oft mec (*a mill-stone*) slǣpwērigne secg oððe meówle grētan eode, Exon. Th. 387, 14; Rä. 5, 5.

slǣtan; *p.* te [*causative of* slītan; cf. *bait* an animal, and *bite*] *To slate* [Halliwell quotes from a book of 1697 'to *slate* a beast is to hound a dog at him;' and in Ray's North-country Words (1691), E. D. S. Pub. Gloss. B. 15, 'to *slete* a dog,' is to set him at anything, as swine, sheep, etc. In Gloss. B. 17 the form is *sleat*. Jamieson also gives 'to *slate* to let loose, applied to dogs in hunting'], *bait, set dogs on, hunt with dogs*:—Man slǣtte ǣnne fearr, and se fear arn him tōgeánes, Homl. Skt. i. 12, 72. [Heo leiden to him, sum wið stan, sum wið ban, and sleatten on him hundes (sletten him wið hundes), Jul. 53, 16. To slætenn affter sawless, Orm. 13485. Tho hede the wrecche (*the wolf*) fomen inowe, That weren egre him to slete Mid grete houndes, and to bete, Rel. Ant. ii. 278, 23. Cf. *O. H. Ger.* sleizan *scindere, vellicare*.] v. next word.

slǣting, e; *f. Hunting*:—Hē (*William Rufus*) geátte mannan heora wudas and slǣtinge (cf. William of Malmesbury's statement that he gave the English free leave to hunt), Chr. 1087; Erl. 225, 7. [Toward þan kinge heo weoren beien þær he wes an slæting (an hontyng, 2nd MS.), Laym. 12304. Bole slating, Alis. 200.] v. preceding word.

slǣw; slǣwan. v. slāw; ā-, for-slǣwan, slāwian.

slǣwþ, e; *f. Sloth, laziness, inertness, torpor*; accidia, inertia, pigredo, torpor:—Se sixta leahter is *accidia* gehāten, ðæt is āsolcennyss oððe slǣwþ on Englisc, Homl. Skt. i. 16, 296. Sió slǣwþ giétt slǣp on ðone monnan *pigredo immittit soporem*, Past. 39, 1; Swt. 283, 6. Slǣwþ *torpor*, Hymn. Surt. 26, 28. Slēuþ *pigredo*, Kent. Gl. 694. On ðæm sceáte his slǣwþe *in sudario lenti torporis*, Past. 9; Swt. 59, 16. From ðære slǣwþe his synna *a peccati torpore*, 28, 4; Swt. 193, 23. Slǣwþe *inertia*, Engl. Stud. ix. 40, col. 1. Hī for heora slǣwþe and for gīmelēste forlēton unwriten ðara monna dǣda, Bt. 18, 3; Fox 64, 33. Ic wāt ðæt swongornes hī mid slǣwþe ofercymþ, 36, 6; Fox 180, 34. Gyf hē for slǣwþe his hlāfordes forgȳmþ, ne biþ his āgnum wel geborgen, L. R. S. 20; Th. i. 440, 16. Slǣwþum *torporibus*, Hymn. Surt. 4, 10. v. un-slǣwþ.

slāg *a sloe*. v. slā.

slaga, an; *m. A slayer, homicide*; interfector, percussor, lanio:—Slaga *lanio*, Wrt. Voc. ii. 53, 36. Hū ne biþ hē swelce hē sié his slaga (*mortis auctor*), ðonne hē hine mæg gehǣlan and nyle? Past. 38, 4; Swt. 275, 9. Gif man þeóf gemēte, and hē hūs brece, and hine man gewundie, se slaga biþ unscildig, Ex. 22, 2. Se slaga (cf. ðæs sleges andetta, 29; Th. i. 80, 7), L. Alf. 30; Th. i. 80, 12. The procedure in cases of homicide is given L. E. G. 13; Th. i. 174, 15 sqq., and L. Edm. S. 7; Th. i. 250, 12 sqq. Ic monnes feorh tō slagan sēce, Cd. Th. 92, 7; Gen. 1525. Slagum *interfectoribus*, Engl. Stud. ix. 40, col. 1. Se Hǣlend miltsian wolde his āgenum slagum, H. R. 107, 5. [*O. H. Ger.* (man-)slago.] v. āgen-, brōðor-, fæder-, mǣg-, mann-, mōdor-, morþ-, morþor-slaga.

slāgian, slāg(h)-þorn, slagu (?), slāh, slahae. v. slāwian, slāh-þorn, mān-, morþor-slagu, slā, sleahe.

slāh-hyll *a hill where sloes grow*:—On slāhhyll, Cod. Dip. Kmbl. iii. 367, 3.

slāh-þorn, es; *m. A sloe-thorn, blackthorn*:—Slāghþorn, slāchthorn, -dorn *nigra spina*, Txts. 81, 1380. Slāhþorn, slāgh-, salach-thorn, 99, 1898. Slāhþorn, Wrt. Voc. ii. 60, 39. Slāgþorn, i. 285, 32. Ādelf niþeweardne slāhþorn, Lchdm. ii. 92, 30. [Le fourder (*slothorne*) que la fourdine (*slon*) porte, Wrt. Voc. i. 163, 1. *Dan.* slaaentorn.]

slāhþorn-ragu *lichen from a blackthorn*, Lchdm. ii. 144, 1.

slāhþorn-rind *bark of a blackthorn*, Lchdm. ii. 98, 7: 108, 11: 132, 9: iii. 58, 8.

slāhþorn-weg *a road along which blackthorns grow*, Cod. Dip. Kmbl. iii. 130, 27.

slāp. v. slǣp.

slāpan; *p.* slēp, sleáp; *pp.* slāpen *To sleep*. I. of natural sleep:—Slǣpst ðū? Mk. Skt. 14, 37. Heó slǣpþ, Mt. Kmbl. 9, 24: Jn. Skt. 11, 12. Simle hē biþ lōciende, ne slǣpþ hē nǣfre, Bt. 42; Fox 258, 8. Ðonne wē slāpaþ, 34, 11; Fox 152, 5. Hwī slāpe gē? Lk. Skt. 22, 46. Ic slēp (sleáp, Ps. Spl.), Ps. Lamb. 56, 5. Hē slēp, Gen. 2, 21: 28, 11: Bd. 3, 9; S. 534, 11. Ōðre men slēpon, 2, 12; S. 513, 37: Bt. 15; Fox 48, 12. Ealle slēpun, Mt. Kmbl. 25, 5. Slāpaþ *dormite*, Mk. Skt. 14, 41. Ðeáh hē slāpe, Ps. Th. 40, 9: Lchdm. ii. 36, 9. Swelce se stióra slēpe, Past. 56; Swt. 431, 30. Mē lyste slāpan *dormiturio*, Ælfc. Gr. 34; Zup. 211, 12: Ps. Th. 3, 4: Ors. 4, 6; Swt. 178, 24: Bd. 3, 11; S. 536, 30: Shrn. 106, 23. Ðonne mon wile slāpan gān, Lchdm. ii. 228, 5. Hē wæs slāpende, Mk. Skt. 4, 38: Homl. Th. i. 566, 17. Ia. figurative, *to sleep, be inactive, be motionless*:—For hwī slǣpst ðū, Drihten? Ps. Th. 43, 24. Ðæt mōd slǣpþ ðæs ðe hit wacian sceolde, and wacaþ ðæs ðe hit slāpan sceolde, Past. 56; Swt. 431, 27. Ðonne wē slāpaþ fæste, ðonne wē nōhwæðer ne hit witan nyllaþ, ne hit bētan nyllaþ . . . ne slǣpþ hē nō fæsðe, ac hnappaþ . . . , 28; Swt. 195, 5–8. Ðæt ic (*the creation*) ne slēpe siððan ǣfre, Exon. Th. 422, 20; Rä. 41, 9. Ib. of death:—Ic slāpe on deáþe, Ps. Spl. 12, 4. Lazarus slǣpþ . . . Se Hǣlend hit cwæþ be his deáþe, Jn. Skt. 11, 11. Ðæt mīne eágan nǣfre ne slāpan on swylcum deáþe, Ps. Th. 12, 4. Be ðām slāpendum, ðæt is, be ðām deádum. Hwī sind ða deádan slāpende gecwedene? . . . Ealle mōton slāpan on ðam gemǣnelīcum deáþe, Homl. Th. ii. 566, 30–34. Ic. of numbness in the limbs, *to sleep, be paralyzed*:—Gif wē tō lange sittaþ ūs slāpaþ ða lima, i. 490, 1. Gif þeóh slāpan . . . lǣt reócan on ðæt lim ðætte slāpe, Lchdm. ii. 66, 5–6. Wið slāpende (*paralyzed*) līce, i. 380, 18. Cf. Wið āslāpenum līce, ii. 12, 17. II. *to sleep, lie* with a person:—His hlǣfdige cwæþ tō him: 'Slāp mid mē,' Gen. 39, 7. [Strong preterites, as well as weak, are found in Chaucer and Langland. *Goth.* slēpan: *O. Sax.* slāpan: *O. Frs.* slēpa: *O. H. Ger.* slāfan.] v. ā-, on-slāpan, be-slǣpan (-slāpan); slǣpan, slāpian.

slāpere, es; *m. A sleeper*:—Ðæra seofon slāpera gemynd, Homl. Th. ii. 424, 8. v. slǣpere.

slāp-ern. v. slǣp-ærn.

slāpfulness, e; *f. Sleepiness, drowsiness*:—Ungelimplīce slāpfulnys [slāpful (? cf. slāpor)] *lethargus*, Wrt. Voc. i. 46, 1.

slāpian; *p.* ode *To cause to sleep*, used impersonally with acc.; cf. *O. H. Ger.* mih slāphōta *dormitavit anima mea*:—Ne geþafa ðū ðīnum eágum ðæt hié slāpige ne ne hnappigen ðīne brǣwas . . . Ne slāpige nō ðīn eáge (eágan, Cott. MSS.) . . . Ðæt is ðæt mon his eáge lǣte slāpian (slāpan, slāpigen, Cott. MSS.) *ne dederis somnum oculis tuis, ne dormitent palpebrae tuae . . . Ne dederis somnum oculis tuis . . . Somnum oculis dare, est* . . . , Past. 28, 4; Swt. 193, 18–25. v. slāpan, slǣpan.

slāpol; *adj. Addicted to sleep, somnolent*:—Ne sceal mon beón tō slāpol (*somnolentus*), R. Ben. 17, 16. Se ðe wǣre slāpol, weorðe se ful wacor, Wulfst. 72, 13. Ne beón gē tō slāpole ne ealles tō sleace, 40, 21. Tō ðam Godes weorce ārīsende, heora ǣlc ōðerne myngige, ðæt ða slāpule (-an, MS. F.) nāne lāde næbben, R. Ben. 47, 17. Hana ða slāpolan þreáþ, Hymn. Surt. 7, 1. [Unilimpliche slāpel *letargicus*, Wrt. Voc. i. 90, 1.]

slāpolness, e; *f. Somnolence, sleepiness*:—Seó slāpolnys byþ gescrȳdd mid wācum tætticum *dormitatio vestietur pannis*, Homl. As. 9, 237. Ādrǣf slāpolnyssa *expelle sompnolentiam*, Hymn. Surt. 18, 13. Āsolcennys ācenþ īdelnysse and slāpolnysse, Homl. Th. ii. 220, 25. Ic syngede þurh slǣwþe and þurh slāpelnesse *per accidiam et somnolentiam*, Confess. Peccat.

slāporness, e; *f. Somnolence*:—Ic ondette slāpornesse, Anglia xi. 98, 40. v. *preceding word, and* slǣpor.

slarige, an; *f. Clary*; salvia sclarea:—Slarege *sclaregia*, Wrt. Voc. i. 79, 16. Slarige, Lchdm. iii. 6, 10. Slarian sǣd, 72, 8. Slarian gōdne dǣl, ii. 58, 11. [From Latin.]

slāw, slǣw, sleáw; *adj. Slow, inert, sluggish, slothful, torpid*:—Sleac *vel* slāw *pigrus* vel *lentus*, Wrt. Voc. i. 16, 48. Slāw *reses* vel *deses* vel *piger*, 49, 30. Se ðe wǣre full slāw, weorðe se unslāw, Wulfst. 72, 14. Ðone sǣnan ðe biþ tō slāw ðū scealt hātan assa mā ðonne man *segnis ac stupidus torpet? asinum vivit*, Bt. 38, 4; Fox 192, 20. Sió slāwe *torpens*, Wrt. Voc. ii. 60, 2. Mōd ðæt slāwe *mens torpida*, Hymn. Surt. 37, 10. Ðū yfela þeów and slāwa (*piger*), Mt. Kmbl. 25, 26. Ðū slāwa gā ðē tō æmethylle *vade ad formican, o piger*, Past. 28, 3; Swt. 191, 25. On ōðre wīsan sceal man manian ða slāwan (cf. late, Swt. 281, 16), on ōðre ða ðe beóþ tō hrade, Past. 23; Swt. 175, 25. Ðā slāwan (*pigri*) sint tō manianne ðæt hié ne forielden ðone tīman ðe hié tiola on dōn mǣgen, 39, 1; Swt. 281, 19. Slāwera *desidiosorum*, Wrt. Voc. ii. 28, 12. [Slak (slēu, MS. C.) an mōde, Hel. 4962. *O. H. Ger.* sléo *hebes*: *Icel.* slær, sljór *blunt, dull*: *Dan.* sløv.] v. un-slāw.

slāwian; *p.* ode *To be or become slow, sluggish, inactive*:—Hwæs wilnast ðū ðæt ðū ne slāwedest swā micel geswinc tō gefremmanne *what dost thou desire, that thou hast not been slow to perform so great a labour*, Homl. Skt. ii. 23 b, 224. Wacige and swince ðār ongeán ðæt hē oft ǣr beslēp and slāwode, L. Pen. 16; Th. ii. 284, 3. Slāgige (slacige?) ł slāwige *pigeat*, Hpt. Gl. 479, 5. [*O. H. Ger.* slēwēn *hebere, torpere*: cf. *Icel.* sljófa *to blunt*.] v. ā-, for-slāwian.

slāwlīce; *adv. Slowly, sluggishly*; pigre:—Ðæt hié tō slāwlīce ðara ne giémen ðe him befæste sién *ut a commissorum custodia minime torpescant*, Past. 28, 3; Swt. 191, 23. Ic wēne ðæt hē hiene snide slāwlīcor (slāulīcor, Hatt. MS.) *pigrius fortasse incideret*, 26, 3; Swt. 186, 3. [Ne dyde hē ꝥ nāht slāulīce, Anglia x. 143, 87. Man slawliche arised, and late to chireche goð, O. E. Homl. ii. 11, 35. *Icel.* slæ-, sljó-liga *slowly, dully, carelessly*.] v. un-slāwlīce.

slā-wyrm, es; *m. A slow-worm, blind-worm* (cf. a slaworme *cecula*, Cath. Angl. 343), *a kind of snake*:—Slāwyrm *stellio*, Wrt. Voc. i. 24, 25: 78, 60: *spalangius*, 24, 27: Hpt. Gl. 450, 26: *regulus* (cf. regulus est serpens, avis, et rex parvulus omnis, Wrt. Voc. i. 221, 9), Kent. Gl. 913: Engl. Stud. x. 40. Efete ł slāwyrm *stellio*, Ælfc. Gr. 9, 3; Zup. 35, 7 note. [Cf. *Norweg.* slo, orm-slo *a blindworm*: *Swed.* slå, orm-slå.] Cf. sleán *to strike*.

sleac, sleacian. v. slæc, slacian.

sleahe, slǣ; *f. A slay* (or *sley*), *a weaver's reed, an instrument of a weaver's loom that has teeth like a comb*:—Slahae *pectica*, Wrt. Voc. ii. 117, 23. Slǣ *pe[c]tica*, i. 282, 6. [Purvu de une lame (*slay*), Wrt. Voc. i. 157, 26. Sley *lamia*, *pecten*, 217, col. 2. Slaye *lanea*, 234, col. 2. Slay *pecten*, *lania*, Cath. Angl. 342, col. 2, and see note. Slay, webstarys loome *lanarium*, *radius*, Prompt. Parv. 458, col. 1.]

sleán; *p.* slōh, slōg, slōgh, *pl.* slōgon; *pp.* slagen, slægen, slegen. A. *trans.* I. *to strike* an object, smite:—Gif ðū slehst *si percusseris*, Kent. Gl. 880. Gif man ōðerne mid fyste in naso slæhþ, L. Ethb. 57; Th. i. 16, 17. Ðæt fell hlȳt, ðonne hit mon sliehþ, Past. 46; Swt. 347, 5. Ðæt ār ðonne hit mon slihþ, 37; Swt. 267, 24. Ðam ðe ðē slihþ (slyhþ, MS. A.: slǣþ, Lind.) on ðīn gewenge, Lk. Skt. 6, 29. Ic sylfa slōh grēne tācne gārsecges deóp, Cd. Th. 195, 21; Exod. 280. Ðonne hié (*the serpent*) mon slōg oððe sceát, Ors. 4, 6; Swt. 174, 7. Hē ðone nīðgæst slōh, ðæt ðæt sweord gedeáf, Beo. Th. 5392; B. 2699. Slōh ðā wundenlocc ðone feóndsceaþan fāgum mēce, Judth. Thw. 23, 3; Jud. 103. Sume hyne slōgon (slōgan, Lind., Rush.) on his ansȳne mid hyra handum, and cwǣdon: 'Sege hwæt is se ðe ðē slōh (slōg, Rush.),' Mt. Kmbl. 26, 67. Mē weras slōgon and swungon, Andr. Kmbl. 1927; An. 966. Hī mē mid sweopum slōgun, Exon. Th. 88, 18; Cri. 142.

Ne sleá gē nānne *neminem concutiatis*, Lk. Skt. 3, 14. Sleáþ synnigne ofer seolfes mūþ, Andr. Kmbl. 2601; An. 1302. Se đe sleá (*percusserit*) his fæder ođđe his mōder swelte hē deáþe, Ex. 21, 15. Gehȳrde ic đæt Eádweard ānne slōge swīđe mid his swurde, Byrht. Th. 135, 13; By. 117. Đā beáh hē sleánde his breóst, H. R. 107, 11. Āhsa hwæđer hē ǽfre wǽre slegen on đa sīdan, Lchdm. ii. 258, 23. Biþ slaegen *percellitur*, Wrt. Voc. ii. 117, 3. An slægenre *in pacte*, 48, 77. **II.** of special kinds of striking, (a) *to strike* coin, *to stamp* money (cf. similar use in *O. Frs.* and *Icel.*), cf. mynet-slege:—Wæs đæs feós ofergewrit đæs ylcan mynetsleges đe man đæt feoh on slōh, sōna đæs forman geáres đā Decius fēng tō rīce, Homl. Skt. i. 23, 476. Ǽlc mynetere đe man tīhþ đæt fals feoh slōge, L. Eth. iii. 8; Th. i. 296, 12. Godes feoh biþ befæst myneterum tō sleánne, Homl. Th. ii. 554, 14. (b) *to forge* a weapon (cf. *Icel.*), cf. slecg-hamer:—Sæt smiþ, slōh seax, Lchdm. iii. 52, 27. **III.** of a serpent, *to sting*:—Gif næddre sleá man, Lchdm. ii. 110, 14. **IV.** *to strike so as to kill, to slay*:—Slēs đū *occideris*, Ps. Surt. 138, 19. Hē slēþ *occideret*, 77, 34. Mann slihþ đīnne oxan *bos tuus immoletur*, Deut. 28, 31. Ic slōg niceras, Beo. Th. 847; B. 421: Exon. Th. 272, 4; Jul. 494. Đonne God hié slōg (*occideret*), đonne sōhton hié hine, Past. 36, 3; Swt. 251, 20: Beo. Th. 217; B. 108. Slōgh, Bd. 3, 9; S. 533, 14. Hē slōh and fylde feónd, Cd. Th. 124, 32; Gen. 2071. Se hagol slōh ealle đa þing đe ūte wǽron, ǽgđer ge men ge nȳtenu, Ex. 9, 25. Slōgon *obruerunt*, Wrt. Voc. ii. 65, 20. Abraham ne sleah đīn bearn, Cd. Th. 176, 18; Gen. 2913. Sleh, 204, 12; Exod. 418. Sleá man đone leásan wītegan *propheta ille interficietur*, Deut. 13, 5. Đās folc sleán mid cwealmþreá, Cd. Th. 151, 10; Gen. 2506. Se eorl wolde sleán eaferan sīnne, 203, 30; Exod. 411. On deáþ sleán (cf. *Dan.* at slaa ihjel) scyldige, 76, 34; Gen. 1267. Hē biþ . . . tō sleánne ođđe tō ālȳsenne, L. Wih. 28; Th. i. 42, 25. Hié wǽron đa wǽpnedmen sleánde, Ors. 1, 10; Swt. 48, 6. Wæs Fin slægen, Beo. Th. 2309; B. 1152. Sacerdas wǽron slægene, Bd. 1, 15; S. 484, 1. Đa hǽþenan wǽron slægne, 3, 24; S. 556, 29. **V.** *to make by striking, to strike* fire, *to make* a mark, sound, signal *by a stroke*:—Đā arn sum þeng and slōh tācen æt đam gæte *cucurrit minister, et pulsans ad ostium*, Bd. 3, 11; S. 536, 17. Hē tācen mid his handa slōh *sonitum manu faciens*, 4, 3; S. 568, 6. Men tācen slōgon, Guthl. 11; Gdwin. 54, 24: 12; Gdwin. 58, 23. Sleah feówer scearpan, Lchdm. ii. 100, 3: 142, 18. Sleá him ānne spearcan, 290, 17. **V a.** *to strike* a bargain (cf. *Icel.* slā kaupi):—Hig slōgon heora wedd ǽgđer tō ōđrum, Gen. 21, 27. **VI.** *to strike, drive so as to cause impact*:—Hē slōh fȳr on feóndas *he drove the fire on to the foes*, Cd. Th. 237, 28; Dan. 344. **VI a.** metaph.:—Ic wēne gif wit uncre word tōsomne sleáþ, đæt đǽr āsprunge sum spearca sōþfæstnesse, Bt. 35, 5; Fox 164, 2. **VI b.** *to pitch* a tent, *drive* a stake into the ground (cf. *Icel.* slā landtjöldum; *Ger.* ein Lager schlagen):—Iacob slōh his geteld on đære dūne, Gen. 31, 25. Sleah ǽnne stacan onmiddan đam ymbhagan, Lchdm. i. 395, 4. Đā hēt Moises sleán ān geteld būtan hira wīcstōwe, Ex. 33, 7: Homl. Th. ii. 242, 8. Đa stōwa đe gē eówre geteld on sleán sceoldon, Deut. 1, 33. **VI c.** *to cast* into chains (cf. *O. Frs.* on tha helda slein):—Hió sceolde đa men weorpan an wildedeóra līc and siđđan sleán on đa raccentan and on copsas, Bt. 38, 1; Fox 194, 32. **VII.** *to move by a stroke, to strike* off a limb, etc.:—Hī slōgon him of đæt heáfod, Th. An. 122, 23. Sleá mon hond of ođđe fōt, L. In. 18; Th. i. 114, 7: 37; Th. i. 124, 23. **VIII.** metaph. *to strike* with disease, punishment, etc., cf. a paralytic, apoplectic *stroke*:—Ic āstrecce mīne hand and sleá Egipta land on eallum mīnum wundrum, Ex. 3, 20. Sliét *concidet* (*cervices peccatorum*), Blickl. Gl. Hī mid đȳ wīte đæs foresprecenan wræces slægene wǽron *praefatae ultionis sunt poena multati*, Bd. 4, 25; S. 601, 31. **B.** *intrans.* **I.** *to strike, make a stroke*:—Hē yrringa slōh *in anger he struck*, Beo. Th. 3135; B. 1565: 5350; B. 2679. On đone eádgan andwlitan men hondum slōgun, Exon. Th. 69, 22; Cri. 1124. Đæt hē mē ongeán sleá, Beo. Th. 1367; B. 681. **I a.** *to strike* as a smith does:—Hē sulh heóld and on īren slōh and corn đærsc and windwode, Shrn. 61, 18. **II.** *to kill* (the object not being expressed):—Ne sleah đū, L. Alf. 5; Th. i. 44, 17. Slyh (sleh, MS. A.), Mk. Skt. 10, 19. Þeóf ne cymþ būton đæt hē stele and sleá, Jn. Skt. 10, 10. Hié wǽron đa burg hergende and sleánde, Ors. 2, 8; Swt. 92, 16. **III.** *to move rapidly* (v. **A. VI.**), *rush, dash, break, take* a certain direction; cf. *to strike* into a path, across a country (cf. *Icel.* slāsk *to betake one's self*):—Gesca slǽt *singultat* (cf. *Icel. impersonal use* slō ā hann hlātri *he was seized with a fit of laughter*), Wrt. Voc. ii. 120, 50. Đǽr seolesburna sliht on meóne, Cod. Dip. Kmbl. iii. 13, 31. Deáh swīn beswemde weorþon, đonne sleáþ hē eft on đa solu, Bt. 37, 4; Fox 192, 28. Hē on scip āstāh and slōh ūt on đa sǽ *put to sea*, Ap. Th. 6, 6. Se lēg slōh tō leofonum, Shrn. 73, 36. Đā slōh đǽr micel mist *a great mist came on suddenly*, Gen. 15, 17. Seó sǽ slōh tōgædere *occurrerunt aquae*, Ex. 14, 27. Hē ofdrǽd slōh ādūn đǽrrihte *terrified he straightway fell down as if struck* (cf. *Icel.* slā sēr niđr *to throw one's self down* on a bed), Homl. Skt. i. 23, 718. Đā slōh đǽr micel leóht ūt æfter đām englum (cf. *Icel. impers. use*, e. g. loganum slō ūt), Homl. Th. ii. 342, 7; 350, 24.

On slōgan *incursere*, Wrt. Voc. ii. 48, 1. Drenc wiđ deádum swile đæt hē ūt sleá, Lchdm. ii. 74, 18: 102, 20. Đȳ læs hit in sleá, 324, 3. Gif hié ūt sleán *if they* (*pocks*) *break out*, 106, 4. [*Goth.* slahan: *O. Sax.* slahan: *O. Frs.* slā: *O. H. Ger.* slahan: *Icel.* slā.] v. ā-, be-, for-, ful-, ge-, of-, ofer-, tō-, wiđ-sleán; fȳst-slægen.

sleáw, slēbe-scōh, sleccan. v. slāw, slīfe-scōh, slæccan.

slecg, e; *f. A sledge-hammer, mallet*; malleus:—Slecg, hamur *malleus*, Wrt. Voc. ii. 57, 78. Slegc, i. 86, 16. Hwæt sylst đū ūs on smiþþan đīnre būton īsene fȳrspearcan and swēgincga beátendra slecgea (*malleorum*), Coll. Monast. Th. 31, 7. Wē hit uneáþe mid īsernum hamerum and slecgum gefyldon *quam ferreis uix comminuimus malleis*, Nar. 21, 5. [The gret slegges, Parten. 3000. *Icel.* sleggja *a sledge-hammer*: *O. H. Ger.* slaga *malleus*.]

slecgettan; *p.* te *To palpitate, beat, throb*:—Seó wamb cloccet, swā swā hit slecgete, Lchdm. ii. 220, 18. [*O. H. Ger.* slagazen *palpitare, tremere*.]

slēd, slēf, slēfan, slēfe. v. slǽd, slīf, slīfan, slīfe.

slege, slæge, es; *m.* **I.** *a stroke, blow*:—Mē and mīne gefēran mid ānum slege (*ictu*) hē (*the whale*) mæg besencan, Coll. Monast. Th. 24, 33. Gif hine mon geyflige mid slege ođđe mid bende, L. Alf. pol. 2; Th. i. 62, 3. Geswell đe wyrđ of fylle ođđe of slege, Lchdm. ii. 6, 28. His eáge wand ūt mid đam slæge, Homl. Skt. i. 4, 143. Slægum *ictibus*, Wrt. Voc. ii. 47, 54. Of wundum ođđe of snīþingum ođđe of slegum, Lchdm. ii. 82, 23. **II.** of a serpent's sting, cf. sleán, **III**:—Wiđ nædran slege, Lchdm. ii. 10, 21: 110, 22. **III.** *a striking, beating*, (a) *scourging*:—Seó sunsciéne slege þrowade, Exon. Th. 256, 10; Jul. 229. Þēh đū þolie synnigra slege *though thou suffer scourging at the hands of sinners*, Andr. Kmbl. 1911; An. 958. (b) *stamping, coining*, v. mynet-slege, sleán, **II a.** (c) *clashing, collision*, v. sleán, **VI a**:—Slæge *conlisio*, Wrt. Voc. ii. 105, 27. Slege, 15, 29. Slægum *contunsionibus*, 24, 43. Slegum, 20, 32. **IV.** *a crash, clap* of thunder, cf. *Ger.* donner-schlag:—Đǽr com swylce þunres slege, Nicod. 24; Thw. 13, 4. Hreám swā hlūd swā þunres slege, 27; Thw. 15, 5. [Wæs swyđe mycel lihtinge and ungemetlice slæge đæræfter, Chr. 1118; Erl. 246, 40.] **V.** *a fatal stroke, slaying, slaughter, death* (by violence. On the difference between *slege* and *morþor* see Grmm. R. A. 625):—Đæra cildra slege (*the murder of the innocents*), Homl. Th. i. 80, 28. Hū nyt is đē mīn slæge *quae utilitas in sanguine meo*, Ps. Th. 29, 8. Nū is ǽghwonon yfel and slege, Blickl. Homl. 115, 16. Gif mon twȳhyndne mon mid hlōđe ofsleá, gielde se đæs sleges andetta sié . . . , L. Alf. pol. 29; Th. i. 80, 7. For geclǽnsunge his unrihtes slæges *ob castigationem necis ejus injustae*, Bd. 3, 24; S. 557, 25. Ǽfter Pendan slæge *post occisionem Pendan*, S. 557, 30. Ǽfter his slæge (*interfectionem*), 3, 9; S. 533, 30. On Urias slege (slæge, Hatt. MS.), Past. 3; Swt. 34, 23. Be elþiódies monnes slege. Gif mon elþeódigne ofsleá, L. In. 23; Th. i. 116, 13. Mid his brōđor slege *parricidio*, Ors. 2, 2; Swt. 64, 23. Hē tihte đæt folc tō đæs Hǽlendes slege, Homl. Th. i. 292, 6: 216, 15. Hē is gelǽd tō slege swā swā scēp, ii. 16, 20. Hī heora swuran gearcodon sylfwylles tō slege *they voluntarily preferred their necks for the fatal stroke*, Homl. Skt. i. 5, 47. Mid micelre gnornunge ymb đæs cyninges slege, Ors. 2, 4; Swt. 76, 23. Þurh đæs hyrdes slege byþ seó heord tōdrǽfed, Mt. Kmbl. 26, 31. **VI.** *a defeat, loss* inflicted on an army; clades:—Đæt tācen nūgiet cūþ is on đære eá noman đæs consules sleges Fauiuses *testatur hanc Fabii cladem Allia, sicut Cremera Fabiorum*, Ors. 2, 8; Swt. 92, 17. Crist him gefylste tō his feónda slege (cf. hī ālēdon heora fȳnd, 96, 22), A. S. Rdr. 95, 13. **VII.** metaph. *a stroke* of affliction, punishment, disease, etc. v. sleán, **VIII**:—Ǽr đan đe se fǽrlīca slege (*the pestilence*) ūs āstrecce, Homl. Th. ii. 124, 21. **VIII.** *an instrument for striking* (or to be put with the next word?). (a) *a slay*:—Slege *percussorium* (the word occurs among terms connected with weaving), Wrt. Voc. i. 59, 44. v. sleahe. (b) *a plectrum* [v. Hearp-slege *plectro*, Engl. Stud. xi. 64]. [*Goth.* slahs *a stroke, blow*: *O. Sax.* slegi *slaying*: *O. Frs.* slei: *O. H. Ger.* slag *plaga, ictus, tusio, percussio*: *Icel.* slagr *a blow, defeat*; cf. *also* slag; *n. a blow*; *a defeat, slaughter, loss*; *a stroke* of apoplexy.] v. brōđor-, deáþ-, dolg-, eár-, gegn-, hearm-, hearp-, hleór-, morþor-, mynet-, on-, sār-, sweord-, þeóf-slege(-slæge).

slege, es; *n. A beam, bar.* v. heáfod-, ofer-slege (-slæge). [Cf. *Icel.* slā; *f. a cross-beam.*]

slege-bītel, es; *m. A beetle, hammer, mallet*:—Sleah đonne on mid slegebȳtle, Lchdm. ii. 342, 7.

slege-fǽge; *adj. Doomed to slaughter, doomed to death by the sword*:—Slegefǽge hæleþ (*the Assyrians before their defeat*), Judth. Thw. 25, 7; Jud. 247.

slegel, es; *m. An instrument for striking a harp*:—Slegele *plectro*, Wrt. Voc. ii. 66, 79. [*O. H. Ger.* slegil *percussorium, maza*: *Ger.* schlägel: *Du.* slegel *a hammer, mallet*.]

sleg-neát, es; *n. A beast to be slaughtered*:—Hē geselle ēghwelce gēre tuā slegneát (slægnǽt, Chr. 852; Erl. 67, 39), Ch. Th. 105, 4. [Cf. *Icel.* slag-ā *a ewe to be slaughtered*.] Cf. sliht-swīn.

sleht, sleów, slēpan (*to sleep*), slēpan (*to drag*), slī. v. sliht, slīw, slǽpan, slīpan, slīw.

slíc (?); *adj.* I. *sleek, smooth.* v. slícian. II. *cunning, crafty, using smooth words* (v. *words given under* slícian):—Ic wæs ána slícera ðonne ealle óðre drýas *sapientior eram omnium sapientium magorum*, Nar. 50, 19. [*Prompt. Parv.* slyke or smothe *lenis*. With browis smothe and slyke (*rimes with chike*), Chauc. R. R. 542. Thowe make hem slyke and fatte ynough, Pall. 1, 689. *Icel.* slíkr *sleek*.]

slic[c] (?), es; *n. A hammer*:—Sleánde slicc (slicc *for* slecg?) *mallei percutientes*, Kent. Gl. 723, see the note. Hé sceal habban . . . slic (*in a list of weaver's implements*; slíc (?) *an implement for smoothing what is woven, a sleek-stone*, cf. slykston *amethon*, Wülck. Gl. 563, 26: *letatorium*, 593, 19. Slekstone *lacinatorium*, Wrt. Voc. i. 218, 2. A slikestone *lucchier*, 172, 15. See also Prompt. Parv. 458, note 2), Anglia ix. 263, 15. v. sliccan *and* slícian.

sliccan (?) *to strike, slap* (cf. (?) colloquial *lick* = to beat. Halliwell gives *slick* as an Oxfordshire word for *a blow, slap*):—Se ðe his wiel sliceþ (slieþ (?), slihþ (?)) mid girde *qui percusserit servum suum virga*, Ex. 21, 20. Gif men cídaþ and hira óðer his néxtan mid fýste slicþ (?), and hé deád ne biþ . . . hé biþ unscildig, ðe hine slóh, 21, 18–19. Gif hwilc slicþ eacniende wíf, 21, 22. v. slic[c].

slícian; *p.* ode *To make sleek, smooth*, or *glossy*:—Heó glytenode swá scýnende sunne oððe nígslýcod hrægel, Shrn. 149, 8. [v. Prompt. Parv. 458, note 2, where 'to sleek clothes' is quoted from Kennett, and a passage from Walter de Bibelesworth is given (v. also Wrt. Voc. i. 172, 13): la dame ge ta koyf luche (*slike*). Til sleuth and slepe slyken his sides, Piers P. 2, 98. The word is also applied to making a fair show in speech:—Alle þine wordes beoþ isliked, And so bisemed and biliked, O. and N. 841. Wordes afaited and ysliked, Ayenb. 212, 2. He can so well his wordes slike, Gower ii. 365, 22. See, too, Jamieson's Dictionary, *sleekie* fawning and deceitful; *sleekit* smooth, shining (of the face); but also, deceitful; *sleekit-gabbit* smooth-tongued.] v. slíc.

slídan; *p.* slád; *pp.* sliden *To slide, slip, fall.* I. of actual movement, *to slide, glide*:—Ðá cómon twegen deóflu tó him of ðære lyfte slídan, Guthl. 5; Gdwin. 30, 16. II. fig. *to make a mistake, to fail, err*:—Ðonne hé geong fareþ, hafaþ wilde mód, slídeþ geneahhe (*makes many a slip*), Salm. Kmbl. 758; Sal. 378. III. *to fall* into an unhappy condition:—Gif seó sáwl slídan sceal in ða écan wíte, Wulfst. 187, 16. IV. *to pass away, be transitory* or *perishable*:—Ðeós mennisce tyddernes biþ swá slídende swá glæs, ðonne hit scínþ and ðonne tóbersteþ; ac Godes wuldor nafaþ nǽnigne ende, Shrn. 119, 23. Fleóg ðú wesan ealdor slídendes plegan (*labentis ludi*), Lchdm. i. lviii, 2. [Þer on geð him one in one sliddrie weie, he slit & falleþ sone; and ter monie goð togederes, . . . ȝif eni uoð on uorte sliden, þe oðer breideð hine up er þen he allunge ualle, A. R. 252, 10–12. Mony folk slod to helle, H. R. 136, 157. Huanne þe on uot slyt, þe oþer him helpþ, Ayenb. 149, 2. *M. H. Ger.* slíten.] v. á-, æt-slídan; útásliden.

slide, es; *m. A slip, fall*; lapsus, Ælfc. Gr. 11; Zup. 79, 9. I. of an actual slip:—Ðá wearþ mé slide and ic him (*the horse*) of áfeóll *lapsus decidi*, Bd. 5, 6; S. 619, 18. II. fig. *a slip* into misfortune or error:—Forðæm hit ǽr hit nolde behealdan wið unnyt word, hit sceal ðonne niédinga áfeallan for ðæm slide, Past. 38; Swt. 279, 5. Ðú generedest fét míne fram slide (*de lapsu*), Ps. Spl. 55, 13: 114, 8. Forwyrd ł slide *lapsum, ruinam*, Hpt. Gl. 440, 61. Þurh synna slide *through falling into sin*, Exon. Th. 263, 13; Jul. 349. Slidas *lapsus*, Hymn. Surt. 7, 17. v. fǽr-slide.

sliding. v. á-sliding.

slidor; *adj. Slippery*:—Ýs byþ ungemetum slidor, Runic pm. Kmbl. 341, 15; Rún. 11. Slideres *lubrici*, Hpt. Gl. 405, 46. Sýn heora wegas þýstre and slidore *fiant viae eorum tenebrae et lubricum*, Ps. Th. 34, 7. [*Prompt. Parv.* slydyr *lubricus*. Þu schalt falle, þe wei is slider, O. and N. 956. To a dronke man the wey is slider, Chauc. Kn. T. 406: Gower iii. 14, 8.]

slidor, es; *n.* (?) I. *a slippery, miry place*; lubricum:—Turf *gleba*, sliddor *labina* (cf. labina *a myre*, Wülck. Gl. 591, 11: *a fenne*, 797, 10), sol *volutabrum*, moor *uligo*, Wrt. Voc. i. 37, 20–24. Cf. slǽp. II. *In a list giving names of things connected with ships*, slidor *glosses* pulvini (*pulvini* machinae quibus naves *deducuntur* et subducuntur in portum, Du Cange), 56, 54.

slidorian, slidrian; *p.* ede *To slither* (in various dialects; Dryden uses *sliddering*), *to slide, slip*:—Ðonne hié on monigfealdum wordum slidrigaþ *dum per multiplicia verba dilabuntur*, Past. 38, 6; Swt. 277, 5. Míne fét ne slideredon *non sunt infirmata vestigia mea*, Ps. Th. 17, 35. Gif hý geseón ðæt míne fét slidrien *dum commoverentur pedes mei*, 37, 16. [*Prompt. Parv.* slyderyn̄ *labo* vel *labor*: *O. Du.* slideren. Cf. Vondunge is sliddrunge, A. R. 252, 14.]

slidorness, e; *f. Slipperiness, a slippery place*:—Slidornis *lubricum*, Blickl. Gl. (Ps. 34, 6): Ps. Spl. T. 34, 8. [*Prompt. Parv.* slydyrnesse *labilitas*.]

slíf, sléf, slýf, e: slífe, an; *f. A sleeve*:—Slýf *manica*, Wrt. Voc. i. 81, 70. Be slífan gebunden *submanicatus*, 21, 64. Slýfa *manicae* vel *brachila*, 25, 63. Slýfan *manice*, ii. 55, 23: 87, 58: *bracile*, 127, 14: *manicas*, 87, 43. Ǽghwelcere wunde beforan feaxe and beforan sliéfan (sléfan, MS. B.: slýfan, MS. H.) and beneoðan cneowe sió bót biþ twýsceatte máre (cf. 45; Th. i. 92, 20 for this double compensation when a wound was not concealed by the hair), L. Alf. pol. 66; Th. i. 96, 30. Synd gesealde from ðam abbode ealle neádbehéfe þing, ðæt is cugele . . . slýfa (slýfan, MSS. O. T.), gyrdel, R. Ben. 92, 3. Hé one hláf tóbræc and bewand on his twám slýfum, Homl. Th. i. 376, 30. Hé ðone hláf gedyde on his twá sléfan, Blickl. Homl. 181, 17. v. earm-slífe.

slífan; *p.* sláf; *pp.* slifen *To slive* ('*Slive* to cut, slip, or slice off . . . Palsgrave, "I *slyve* a gylowfloure or any other floure from his branche or stalke."' Baker, Northants Gloss.) [Slyvyn̄ a-sundyr *findo, effisso*. Cf. also slyvynge, cuttynge a-wey *avulsio, abscissio*; slyvynge of a tre or oþer lyke *fissula*. He al hool or of hym slyvere (*a slice, cutting*), Chauc. T. and C. iii. 138. Sliver = *slice* still used in Scotland. v. Jamieson's Dict.] v. tó-slífan.

slífan, sléfan; *p.* de *To slip* or *put* a garment on a person:—Hé hine sylfne ungyrede, and ðæt reáf ðe hé on hine hæfde hé sléfde on ðone forespreecenan man . . . Sóna swá hé mid ðan hrægle swá miccles weres gegyred wæs, Guthl. 16; Gdwin. 68, 18. [*Slive* to dress carelessly, *Cumb.* A garment rumpled up about any part of the person is said to be *slived*. *Sliver* a short slop worn by bankers or navigators, *Linc.* It was formerly called a *sliving*. The *sliving* was exceedingly capacious and wide. Halliwell's Dict.] Cf. slípan, slíf (?), slífe-scóh.

slífe. v. slíf.

slífe-scóh *a loose shoe easily drawn on, a slipper*:—Socc, slébescóh *soccus*, Wrt. Voc. ii. 120, 69. Cf. slífan, slípe-scóh.

slíf-leás; *adj. Sleeveless*:—Sléfleás scrúd *colobium*, sléfleás ancra scrúd *levitonarium*, Wrt. Voc. i. 40, 20, 21. Hæbban hý scapulare, ðæt is gehwǽde cugelan and slýfleáse, R. Ben. 89, 13.

slifor; *adj. Slippery, deceitful* (?):—Slideres ł sliferes *lubrici*, Hpt. Gl. 405, 46. [Cf. *sliverly* cunning, deceitful, *Linc.* Halliwell's Dict.] Cf. slipor.

sliht, sleaht, sleht, slieht, sliét, slyht (*see the cpds.*), es; *m.* I. *a striking* of coin. v. pening-sliht. II. *a stroke, flash* of lightning. v. líget-sliht. III. *slaughter, death* by violence:—Ðes sliht *haec caedes*, Ælfc. Gr. 9, 27; Zup. 53, 4. Æt eallum slyht[e?] and æt ealre ðære hergunge ðe ǽr ðam gedón wǽre, ǽr ðæt frið geset wǽre . . . nán man ðæt ne wræce ne bóte ne bidde, L. Eth. ii. 6; Th. i. 288, 1. Hú hé mid forhergiunge and mid heora mǽga slihtum on his geweald geniédde, Ors. 2, 5; Swt. 82, 17: 5, 11; Swt. 238, 5. III a. *the deadly stroke* of disease:—Ðis folc is mid swurde ðæs heofonlícan graman ofslegen, and gehwilce sind mid fǽrlícum slihte áwéste, Homl. Th. ii. 124. 10. IV. *what is to be killed, animals for slaughter.* v. sliht-swín (cf. *Icel.* slátr *butcher's meat*; slátra *to slaughter cattle*):—Gafolswáne gebyreþ ðæt hé sylle his slyht be ðam ðe on lande stent. On manegum landum stent ðæt hé sylle ǽlce geáre .xv. swýn tó sticunge, L. R. S. 6; Th. i. 436, 11. [*Kath.* slaht · *Laym.* slaht, slæht, sclæht, sleȝht: *R. Glouc.* slaȝt. Cf. *O. Sax.* man-slahta; *f.*: *O. Frs.* slachte *a blow, mortal blow; stamp, coining*: *O. H. Ger.* slahta *strages, occisio*: *Icel.* sláttr; *m. mowing; striking of an instrument.*] v. fiðer(-el?)-, for-, hand-, hlóþ-, líget-, mǽg-, mann-, morþ-, morþor-, pening-, þeóf-, wæl-sliht; *cf.* slege.

sliht (?); *adj. Level, smooth*; in the cpd. eorþ-slihtes *level with the ground* (?):—Swá swá oxa gewunaþ tó áwéstenne gærs óþ ða wirttruman eorþslihtes mid tóþum (*eats the grass to the root, to the level of the ground*), Num. 22, 4. [*Goth.* slaihts wigs *a level road*: *O. H. Ger.* sleht *planus*: *Icel.* sléttr *plain, level.*]

slihtan; *p.* te *To smite, slay*:—Gif ðú fallas ł slæhtas *cadens* (translator seems to have read *caedens* in the second case), Mt. Kmbl. Lind. 4, 9. [Cf. *O. H. Ger.* slahtón *mactare*: *Ger.* schlachten.]

sliht-swín, es; *A swine to be killed*:—Gýme eác swán ðæt hé æfter sticunge his slyhtswýn wel sæncge, L. R. S. 6; Th. i. 436, 16. [Cf. *Ger.* schlacht-vieh *cattle to be killed.*] Cf. sleg-neát.

slím, es; *m.* (?) *n.* (?) *Slime, mud, mire*:—Slím *limus*, Wrt. Voc. ii. 54, 14: *borbus, cena*, 126, 53. Áfæstnod ic eom on líme (slíme? cf. Ps. 68, 3: I am festened in slime depenesse) grundes *infixus sum in limo profundi*, Ps. Spl. 68, 2. [*M. H. Ger.* slím; *m.*: *Ger.* schleim: *Du.* slijm: *Icel.* slím; *n.*]

slincan; *p.* slanc, *pl.* sluncon. I. *to crawl*:—Eodon ða wyrmas and scluncon wundorlíce; wǽron him ða breóst up gewende, Nar. 14, 8. Slincendes *reptantis*, Hymn. Surt. 28, 17. Hé gescóp eall wyrmcynn and creópende and fleógende and swymmende and slincgende, Anglia viii. 310, 17. II. fig. *to slink away*:—Se earma flýhþ uncræftiga slǽp slincan on hinder, Dóm. L. 240. [Cf. *O. H. Ger.* slíhhan *repere, reptare.*] v. next word.

slincend, es; *m. n. A crawling thing, a reptile*:—Ealle slincendu (Ps. Spl. slincende) *omnia reptilia*, Ps. Lamb. 68, 35: 103, 25. Fram ðám slincendum óþ ða fugelas, Gen. 6, 7.

slingan; *p.* slang, *pl.* slungon *To wind, twist, worm, move as a serpent.* Cf. *sling* to move quickly, Var. dial. It also has the same meaning as *slinch* (slink). Halliwell's Dict.:—Gif heó (*the adder*) ðæt heáfod innan ðone man bestingþ ðonne slingþ (= slincþ?) heó mid ealle inn *if it strikes its head into the man, then it winds itself quite in*, Boutr. Scrd. 20, 15. [*O. H. Ger.* slingan: *Ger.* schlingen *to wind*: *Icel.* slyngva *to wind.*]

slipa (slypa?), an; *m. A viscous, slimy substance*:—Genim sealh and ele dó ahsan (tō?) gewyrc ðonne tō slypan . . . dō ðonne on ðone slipan, Lchdm. ii. 18, 26-28. Wyrc slypan of wætere and of axsan, iii. 38, 1. v. slipig, slipor, *and* slyppe.

slīpan (?); *p.* slāp, *pl.* slipon *To slip, glide.* [He with feigned chere him slipeth (rimes with wipeth) *he slips off*, Gower ii. 347, 30. *Slype* to move freely, as any weighty body which is dragged through a mire, Jamieson's Dict. *O. H. Ger.* slīfan *labi.*] Cf. slipor, *and see* slūpan.

slīpan, slēpan; *p.* te *To slip, put* something on or off. Cf. *slipe* to take away the outside covering from anything, Halliwell's Dict. *Slype* to strip off the skin or bark of anything, Jamieson's Dict.:—Se hlāford hefig gioc slēpte on ða swyran sīnra þegena, Me. 9, 55. Se cyning slȳpte his beáh of *the king slipped his ring off*; tulit rex annulum de manu sua, Anglia ix. 32, 158. [*Goth.* af-slaupjan thana fairnjan mannan *to put off the old man*: *O. Sax.* slōpian *to slip* one's self from a bond: *M. H. Ger.* sloufen, ana-sloufen *induere.*] v. be-slēpan; un-slīped, slīpe-scōh, slūpan; *and* cf. slīfan.

slīpe-scōh *a slip-shoe* (Halliwell gives the word from a work dated 1615. Cf. *slip-shod*), *a shoe easily slipped on, a slipper*:—Slȳpescōs *soccus*, Wrt. Voc. i. 289, 7. v. slīpan; slīfe-scōh.

slipig; *adj. Slippy, slimy, viscid*:—Mid slipigre and þiccere wǣtan, Lchdm. ii. 280, 4. Ða þiccan and ða slipigan (slipinga, MS.) wǣtan on ðam magan and ðæt þicce slipige horh ðū scealt mid ðām lǣcedōmum wyrman and þynnian, 194, 20-22. Wǣtan þicce and slipegran, 178, 15. Of þiccum wǣtum slipegrum . . . Wið slipegrum wǣtum ðæs miltes, 246, 17. [*M. H. Ger.* slipfic.] v. next word.

slipor; *adj.* I. *slippery, not easy to hold, moving easily*:—Deófol næddre ys slipor ðæs gif heáfde nā byþ wiðstanden eall on innemystum heortan ðænne nā byþ ongyten byþ āsliden *diabolus serpens est lubricus, cuius si capiti non resistitur, totus in interna cordis, dum non sentitur, inlabitur*, Scint. 210, 9. II. *slipping easily, easily moved*:—Ymhīdignyssa ofþriccaþ ðæt mōd, and unlustas tōlȳsaþ; þwyrlīce þing ðe heora hlāfordas dōþ geswencte fram carum, and slipere þurh unstæððignysse, Homl. Th. ii. 92, 16. III. *foul*:—Fūl ne sȳ oððe slipor *nec feda sit nec lubrica*, Hymn. Surt. 5, 9. Ǣlc þing slipores ł fūles *omne lubricum*, 30, 9. Bedǣled andgite sliporum ł fūlum *excita sensu lubrico*, 3, 17. Gilt sliporne ł fūlne *culpam lubricam*, 15, 38. Ne tunge leás ne eágan syngian slipere *ne lingua mendax occulive peccent lubrici*, 24, 27. [Sliper *lubricum*, Ps. 34, 6. Nares gives several instances of *slipper* in sixteenth century, and Shakspere uses the form: A *slipper* and a subtle knave, Oth. ii. 1. *O. H. Ger.* slefar, Grff. vi. 506: *M. H. Ger.* slepfer.] Cf. slifor; slǣpe, slīpan (?).

sliporness, e; *f. Foulness*:—Beón ūt ānȳdde slipornesse *sint pulsa lubrica*, Hymn. Surt. 36, 16.

slip-ræsn *a sliding beam* (?):—Slypræsn *ferna*, Wrt. Voc. ii. 147, 75.

slipung (?), e; *f. Viscidity*:—Wið slipunge (slipigre? *the text has* sliþegrum wǣtum. v. slipig) wǣtan ðæs miltes, Lchdm. ii. 166, 24.

slit. v. ge-, lah-slit.

slītan; *p.* slāt, *pl.* sliton; *pp.* sliten *To slit, tear, rend.* I. in the following glosses:—Sclāt *carpebat*, Wrt. Voc. ii. 103, 51. Bītende and slītende *mordax*, 57, 52. Slītende *mordens*, Kent. Gl. 580: *corrumpens*, Hpt. Gl. 454, 68. Ic beó sliten *carpor*, Wrt. Voc. ii. 21, 40. Wǣran slitene *carpebantur*, 22, 22. II. *to tear* a garment, *rend*:—Ðæra sacerda ealdor slāt (*scidit*) hys āgyn reáf, Mt. Kmbl. 26, 65. Ne slīte wē hȳ *non scindamus eam*, Jn. Skt. 19, 24. Se heáhsacerd his reáf slītende, Mk. Skt. 14, 63. III. *to tear, split, rend, cleave, divide*:—Hē slāt sǣ *interrupit mare*, Ps. Spl. 77, 16. Hē slāt stān *interrupit petram*, 77, 18. IV. *to tear, rend*, as an animal does with the teeth or feet, a bird with its beak, etc. v. slite II, slītung:—Fōtum ic fēre, foldan slīte, Exon. Th. 393, 17; Rä. 13, 1. Hrefn hine slīteþ, 329, 20; Vy. 37. Hine se wulf slīteþ, 342, 27; Gn. Ex. 148. Hē (*the evil spirit*) bītes and slītes hine, Mk. Skt. Rush. 9, 18. Heora heortan wyrmas ceorfaþ and slītaþ, Dōm. L. 12, 168: 14, 210: Exon. 497, 5; Rä. 85, 24. Hē (*Grendel*) slǣpendne rinc slāt, Beo. Th. 1487; B. 741. Ða wyrmas mid ðæm scillum gelīce mid ðē mūþe eorþan sliton and tǣron *oribus scamisque humum atterentes*, Nar. 14, 12. Gif hund slīte, Lchdm. ii. 92, 10. Hié (*lions and bears*) noldon slītan hȳ (*St. Tecla*), Shrn. 133, 10. Gesāwon fuglas slītan, Cd. Th. 126, 1; Gen. 2088. Ðē sculon moldwyrmas slītan, Soul Kmbl. 145; Seel. 73. Hió (*the lioness*) onginþ racentan slītan (cf. brecan, Bt. 25; Fox 88, 13), Met. 13, 29. Se unclǣna gāst hine slītende (*discerpens*), Mk. Skt. 1, 26. Slītende wulfas *ravening wolves*, Blickl. Homl. 63, 10. Slītendum ł terendum tōþreómum *rabidis* (*voracibus*) *gingivis*, Hpt. Gl. 423, 42. IV a. fig. applied to inanimate subjects:—Nū slīt mē hunger and þurst, Cd. Th. 50, 2; Gen. 302. Hungor innan slāt merewērges mōd, Exon. Th. 306, 22; Seef. 11. Hī beóþ mec slītende (*of the waves tearing at an anchor*), 398, 11; Rä. 17, 6. V. *to tear, bite* (of pungent things, cf. slitol), *irritate* (of physical or mental irritation):—Slīto (suto, Wrt., cf. slītung) *lacesso*, Wrt. Voc. ii. 112, 29. Slīteþ *lacessat*, 95, 32. Ðæt wīn slīt ða wunda *per vinum mordentur vulnera*, Past. 17, 10; Swt. 125, 9. Sliten oððe gremeden *lacessant*, Wrt. Voc. ii. 52, 54. Of yfelre wǣtan slītendre, Lchdm. ii. 4, 30. Of yfelum wǣtan slītendum and sceorfendum, 60, 21. VI. *to tear* (fig.), *to destroy, waste, consume.* v. slītendlīc, slītere, slītness II:—Nān cræft nis Gode deórwyrðra ðonne sió lufu ne eft ðæm deófle nān cræft leóftǣlra ðonne hié mon slīte *nihil pretiosius est Deo virtute dilectionis, nil est desiderabilius diabolo extinctione caritatis*, Past. 47, 2; Swt. 359, 24. Tō slītenne (breccanne, Rush.) ae *solvere legem*, Mt. Kmbl. Lind. 5, 17. VII. *to carp at, back-bite.* v. bæc-slitol:—Ǣt ǣrestum lyst ðone monn unnyt sprecan be ōðrum monnum & ðonne æfter firste hine lyst tǣlan and slītan ðara līf būtan scylde *ut prius loqui aliena libeat, postmodum detractionibus eorum vitam mordeat*, Past. 38, 7; Swt. 279, 7. VIII. *to tear* (intrans.):—Godwebba cyst (*the veil of the temple*) eall forbærst . . . ðæs temples segl . . . sylf slāt on tū, swylce hit seaxes ecg þurhwōde, Exon. Th. 70, 19; Cri. 1141. [*Prompt. Parv.* slytyn *attero*: *O. Sax.* slītan *to tear, split*: *O. Frs.* slīta *to tear, break*: *O. H. Ger.* slīzan *scindere, lacerare, laniare, lacessere, saevire, delere*: *Icel.* slīta *to slit, tear, break.*] v. ā-, be-, for-, ge-, of-, tō-slītan; wæl-slītende, sliten, un-sliten.

slit-cwealm *death by the tearing of animals*:—Neát ðe slitcwealm begēte *animalia quae lacerationem mortiferam nacta sunt*, L. Ecg. C. 40; Th. ii. 166, 24.

slite, es; *m.* I. *a slit, tear, rent* in cloth, etc.:—Se slite byþ wyrsa *pejor scissura fit*, Mt. Kmbl. 9, 16: Mk. Skt. 2, 21. II. *a rent, tear* made by an animal, *a bite.* v. slītan, IV:—Wið hundes slite, Lchdm. i. 148, 7. Īces slite oððe hundes, ii. 86, 2. Be hundes slite. Gif hund mon tōslīte oððe ābīte, L. Alf. pol. 23; Th. i. 78, 1. Wið nædran slite, Lchdm. ii. 10, 21. Wyrma slite, Exon. Th. 77, 4; Cri. 1251. Slita *morsuum*, Germ. 392, 30. III. *a coil* of a snake (?):—Nædre sprotum slitas (?) līces clyniende *vipera sarmentis laqueos corporis inplicans*, Germ. 401, 24. IV. *a breach, infraction* of a law. v. lah-slit. [*O. H. Ger.* sliz: *Ger.* schlisz; *m.*: cf. *Icel.* slit; *n.*] v. folc-, lah-, wyrm-slite.

slite, an (?); *f.* A plant name, *cyclamen, sowbread*:—Slite. Ðeós wyrt ðe man *orbicularis* and ōðrum naman slite nemneþ, Lchdm. i. 110, 11. Slite *cyclaminos*, iii. 301, col. 2: *cyclamen*, Wrt. Voc. i. 67, 53: *ciclamina*, ii. 131, 37.

sliten *schismatic, heretic*:—Slītenum *haereticis*, Mt. Kmbl. p. 10, 9. *Lye gives* sliterum (slitenum?) sagum *haereticis fabulis*, Josc. (?). v. slītan.

slītend-līc; *adj. Consuming, devouring, wasting.* v. slītan, VI:—Slītendlīcum *lurconibus*, Wrt. Voc. ii. 52, 71.

slitenness (?), e; *f. Tearing, laceration*:—Sliten[nesse] *morsum, lacerationem*, Hpt. Gl. 490, 62.

slītere, es; *m.* I. *a waster, destroyer*:—'Hwæt is seó ungesǣlige sāwel?' Ðā sǣde hē him, ðæt hē wǣre cyrican slītere, Wulfst. 235, 24. II. *a consumer* of food, *a glutton*:—Slīteras *lurcones*, Wrt. Voc. ii. 52, 26. v. slītan, VI.

slīþan *to harm, hurt, damage, destroy*:—Heoro slīþendne, Exon. Th. 346, 10; Gn. Ex. 202. [Cf. *Goth.* ga-sleithjan *to injure.*] v. next word.

slīþe; *adj. Dire, hard, cruel, hurtful, dangerous*:—Biþ ceóle wēn slīþre sæcce *the ship may expect dire strife*, Exon. Th. 384, 17; Rä. 4, 29. On ða slīþan tīd (*the crucifixion*), Elen. Kmbl. 1710; El. 857. Þurh slīþne nīþ sāwle bescūfan in fȳres fæþm, Beo. Th. 370; B. 184. Hē nīþa gehwane genesen hæfde, slīþra geslyhta, 4787; B. 2398. [*Goth.* sleithis *dangerous, perilous, fierce*: *O. Sax.* slīði *dangerous, destructive, cruel*: cf. *O. H. Ger.* slīdic, *saevus, malus*: *Icel.* slīðr *fearful, dire*; slīðr-hugaðr *atrocious*; slīðr-liga *savagely.*] v. slīþen.

slīþe; *adv. Cruelly*:—Bearn ðara ðe ofslegene slīþe wǣran *filios interemtorum*, Ps. Th. 101, 18.

slīþe (?); *adj. Formed, moulded*; fictus. I. *graven* (of images):—Ealle ðe gebiddaþ ða slīþan *omnes qui adorant sculptilia*, Ps. Spl. T. 96, 7. Hī offrodon ðæ sliððan *sacrificaverunt sculptilibus*, 105, 35. II. *feigned, false*:—Hē oncneów slīþe mōd ūre *cognovit figmentum* (taken by the translator = *fictam mentem?*) *nostrum*, Ps. Spl. T. 102, 13. v. slīþness, *and next word.*

slīþelic; *adj. Graven*:—Gebǣdon ða slīþelecæn *adoraverunt sculptile*, Ps. Spl. T. 105, 19.

slīþen; *adj. Cruel, hard, evil*:—Slīden *infastum*, Wrt. Voc. ii. 111, 66. Ðū wēndest ðæt ðiós slīþne wyrd ðās worulde wende būtan Godes þeahte, Bt. 5, 3; Fox 14, 4. Fin eft begeát sweordbealo slīþen *dire harm from the sword overwhelmed Fin*, Beo. Th. 2298; B. 1147. Hū slīþen biþ sorg tō gefēran *how cruel is care as a comrade*, Exon. Th. 288, 12; Wand. 30. Hē him feorgbona þurh slīþen searo weorþeþ *a destroyer of life through cruel craft to him he becomes*, 362, 25; Wal. 42. On ða slīþnan tīd *at that dread hour* (*of death*), 161, 27; Gū. 965. In ða slīþnan tīd *in the evil days of the present life*, 316, 22; Mōd. 52.

slīþ-heard; *adj. Excessively hard.* I. of living things, *very fierce, savage*:—Slīþherde deór (*the boar and the bear*), Exon. Th. 344, 22; Gn. Ex. 177. II. of inanimate things, *very hard, cruel*:—Mē habbaþ hringa gespong slīþhearda sāl sīþes āmyrred *the cruel chain has hindered me from going*, Cd. Th. 24, 15; Gen. 378.

slīþness, e; *f. A formation* (?), *a graven image*:—Hī þeówedon slīþnesse *servierunt sculptilibus*, Ps. Spl. T. 105, 33. v. slīþe (?).

slītness (slit-?), e; *f.* I. *a tearing, rending, laceration.* v.

slītan, IV:—Ða slītnysse gedīgean *a laceratione* (by wolves or dogs) *convalescere*, L. Ecg. C. 40; Th. ii. 166, 25. II. *a wasting, destroying, desolation.* v. slītan, VI:—Slītnese *desolationis*, Mt. Kmbl. Lind. 24, 15. v. from-, tō-slītness.

slitol; *adj.* I. *pungent, biting.* v. slītan, V:—Slitul lēc *mordax allium*, Germ. 394, 260. II. *carping, backbiting.* v. bæc-slitol, slītan, VII.

-slitt. v. lah-þrī-slitt.

slītung, e; *f.* I. *tearing, rending, biting.* v. slītan, IV:—Slītinc ł geter *dilaceratio*, Hpt. Gl. 499, 21. Fugelas hig fretaþ mid ðære biterustan slītunge *devorabunt eos aves morsu amarissimo*, Deut. 32, 24. Sume men fram ðara wyrma slītunge sweltaþ, Lchdm. ii. 176, 14. II. *wasting, spoiling.* v. slītan, VI:—Slītunge *arpagine* (or under I?), Wrt. Voc. ii. 5, 38: 87, 72 (*Wright has* sutunge). [*Prompt. Parv.* slytynge *consumpcio*: *O. H. Ger.* slīzunga *saevitia.*]

slīw, sleów, sliú, slī, es; *m.* The name of a fish, *a tench* or *a mullet*:—Slīw *tinca*, Wrt. Voc. i. 55, 73: *tinctus*, 281, 52. Sliú *tincus*, 66, 1. Sleów *mugilis*, ii. 57, 75. Slī *tincti*, Txts. 101, 2020. Slii, 116, 221. [*O. H. Ger.* slīo; *m. tinca, tincus*: *Ger.* schleie *a tench.*]

sloca. v. slota.

slōh, slōg; *gen.* slōges, slōs; *dat.* slōh, slō; *acc.* slōg, slōh, slō; *m. n.* *A slough, hollow place filled with mire, a pathless, miry place*:—Slōh *devium*, orwegnes *devia*, s. *loca secreta, quasi invia, sine via*, Wrt. Voc. ii. 139, 53–56. Tō ðam ealdan slō; of ðam slō tō ðam lytlan beorhe, Cod. Dip. Kmbl. iii. 38, 27. In reádan slōe, 391, 31. On ðæt reáde slóh; of ðam slōh, 376, 5. On ðæt fūle slōh; of ðam slō, 406, 32. In ðone fūlan slō, 381, 5. On horgan slōh, Cod. Dip. B. ii. 394, 30. On reádan slōh, 398, 38. Ðæt hors sum slōg on ðam wege oferhleóp *equus quoddam itineris concavum transiliret*, Bd. 5, 6; S. 619, 17. Ðeáh se man nime ǣnne stān and lecge on fūl slōh, Wulfst. 239, 10. [Heo arist up of þe slo, O. and N. 1394. He hath also to do more than ynough To kepe him and his capel out of slough, Chauc. Mancip. Prol. 64. Skeat takes this to be a word borrowed from Celtic. v. Etym. Dict.]

slop *a loose, upper garment.* '*Slop* a smock-frock; any kind of outer garment made of linen,' Halliwell's Dict. [These cuttid sloppis or anslets, that thurgh her schortness ne covereth not the schamful membres of men, Chauc. Pers. T. Sloppe, garment *mutatorium*, Prompt. Parv. 460, col. 1. *Icel.* sloppr *a gown, a loose garment*, esp. *a priest's gown.*] v. ofer-slop, *and cf.* slīpan, slype.

-sloppe. v. cū-slyppe.

slota, an; *m. A bit, morsel*:—Betere ys slota (cf. bite, Kent. Gl. 587) drȳge mid blisse ðænne hūs full mettum mid sace *melior est bucella sicca cum gaudio quam domus plena uictimis cum iurgio*, Scint. 153, 12. [Lye gives sloca *bucella*, with a reference to Past. 47, an error probably for Scint. 47. If this were the form the word might be compared with *Ger.* schlucken: but Halliwell gives *slot* a small piece.]

sluma, an; *m. Slumber*:—Sleac mid sluman, Dōm. L. 240. Ðæt hine elne binōman slǣpa sluman oððe sǣne mōd, Exon. Th. 122, 31; Gū. 314. [Upon a sloumbe, A. P. 97, 186. Cf. *Laym.* slumen *to slumber.*]

slūpan; *p.* sleáp; *pl.* slupon; *pp.* slopen *To slip, glide*:—Sōna swā ūs seó sāwl of ðam līchaman slȳpþ *simul atque anima de corpore se subduxerit*, L. Ecg. P. iv. 66; Th. ii. 226, 23. Gārsecg wēdde on sleáp (*of the Red Sea coming upon the Egyptians*), Cd. Th. 208, 28; Exod. 490. Hwīlum ic wǣgfatu wīde tōþringe ... hwīlum lǣte eft slūpan tōsomne *sometimes I* (*the storm*) *drive apart the clouds, sometimes make them again glide together*, Exon. Th. 385, 3; Rä. 4, 39. [*Goth.* Thaiei sliupand in gardins *they which creep into houses*, 2 Tim. 3, 6. *O. H. Ger.* sliufan *to slip, creep.*] v. ā-, tō-slūpan.

slūping, slȳcod, slȳf, slypa, slȳpan. v. tō-slūping, slīcian, slīf, slipa, slīpan.

slype *a garment, slip.* [Slyp or skyrte *lascinia*, Prompt. Parv. 459, col. 2. *Slip* a child's pinafore; an outside covering, as a pillow-*slip* (= -case): in earlier times, a sheath, Halliwell's Dict. *Slip* an upper petticoat, Jamieson.] v. ofer-slype, slop.

slȳpe-scōh. v. slīpe-scōh.

slyppe, an; *f. A viscous, slimy substance*:—Wyrc slypan of wætere and of axsan, genim finol, wyl on ðære slyppan, Lchdm. iii. 38, 2. [Cf. slyp, slype, slypp *limus*, Prompt. Parv. 459, col. 2.] v. cū-, oxan-slyppe, *and* slipa.

slyp-ræsn. v. slip-ræsn.

smacian; *p.* ode *To smack, pat, caress*:—Ic smacige *demulceo*, Hpt. Gl. 476, 72. [Cf. *Du.* smak *a loud noise*: *Dan.* smække *to smack, slap*: *Swed.* smacka.] v. ge-smacian.

smæc[c], es; *m. Smack, taste, savour*:—*Dulcis sapor* swēte smæc, i. *dulcis odor*, Wrt. Voc. ii. 142, 6. Ðone swētan smæc *nectar*, 61, 31. [Witt iss þurrh salltes smacc bitacnedd, Orm. 1653. Smech muðes & neoses smel, A. R. 276, 15. Smeorðrinde smoke smecche forcuðest, Marh. 9, 6. More he uynt smak in ane zoure epple þanne in ane huetene lhoue, Ayenb. 82, 21. Smak or taste *gustus*, Prompt. Parv. 460. *O. Frs.* smek[k]: *O. H. Ger.* smac (*dat.* smacche) *gustus, sapor.* v. hunig-smæc.

smæccan, smecgan; smæhte *To taste*:—Ic smæcce (smæcge, MS. J.) *sapio*, Ælfc. Gr. 28; Zup. 166, 6. ['Cum gustasset acetum noluit bibere;' þet is, he smeihte þet bittre drunch & wiðdrouh him anon, A. R. 238, 21. Summe þinge ꝥ me haueð ismeiht oðer smelled, 92, 4. Al þet ich abbe mid muþ ismaht, O. E. Homl. i. 189, 5. Unlouely þei smauȝte, Piers P. 5, 363. *O. Frs.* smekka: *O. H. Ger.* smecchen *sapere.*] v. ge-smæccan, -smecgan, *and preceding word.*

smæl; *adj. Small.* I. in the following glosses:—Smæl *gracilis*, smælre *gracilior*, ealra smælst *gracillimus*, Ælfc. Gr. 5; Zup. 16, 8. Smel, smael, smal, Txts. 67, 992. Smæl *gracilis* vel *exilis* vel *subtilis*, Wrt. Voc. i. 51, 18. Greát and smæl *grossas et graciles*, ii. 41, 68. II. *small, little, not great*:—Smæl þistle *carduus*, Wrt. Voc. i. 66, 66. Smæl ǣl *anguilla*, 281, 69. Se smala ciið ... se greáta beám, Past. 33; Swt. 224, 3. Æt ǣlcon smalon orfe penig, L. Ft.; Th. i. 224, 22. Dō tō smale netelan, Lchdm. ii. 68, 4. Smæle þearmas *the small guts*; ilia, Wrt. Voc. i. 44, 46. Ða gnættas and ða smalan wyrmas ... ge þeós lyttle loppe, Bt. 16, 2; Fox 52, 11. Flǣsc smælra fugla, Lchdm. ii. 180, 13. Smealum bryt (brycum?) *minutatim*, Hpt. Gl. 443, 1. Hæfaþ seó læsse smæle (smale, MSS. H. B.) leáf and gehwǣde ... seó ōðer hafaþ māran leáf and fǣtte, Lchdm. i. 264, 18. III. *narrow, not broad*:—Hē sǣde ðæt Norðmanna land wǣre swȳðe lang and swȳðe smæl ... ðæt bȳne land is eásteweard brādost, and symle swā norðor swā smælre ... and norðeweard, hē cwæð, ðǣr hit smalost wǣre, ðæt hit mihte beón þreora mīla brād tō ðæm mōre, Ors. 1, 1; Swt. 18, 24–33. Andlangan ðes smalan paðes, Cod. Dip. B. ii. 600, 9. IV. *slender, thin, not thick*:—Swiora smæl *a slender neck*, Exon. Th. 486, 15; Rä. 72, 15. Him ne hangaþ nacod sweord ofer ðam heáfde be smalan þrǣde, Bt. 29, 1; Fox 102, 28. Wið ðam smalan wyrme *for hair worm*, Lchdm. ii. 122, 18. V. *fine* (of a powder, texture, etc.), *not coarse*:—Smæl hlāf *artocobus* [*artocopa* (also -*us*) quaevis placenta, panis quidem dulciarius et arte confectus], Wrt. Voc. ii. 10, 47. Tū hund greátes hlāfes (*coarse bread*) and þridde smales (*fine*), Chart. Th. 158, 26. Swīðe lytle beóþ ða dropan ðæs smalan rēnes, Past. 57; Swt. 437, 12. Cnuca tō swīðe smalan duste, Lchdm. i. 240, 4. Genim swȳðe smæl dust, 240, 11. Smæl beren mela, ii. 86, 24. Āsifte smale þurh smæl sife *sift through a fine sieve*, 94, 1: 72, 28. Hī smalo hrægel wefaþ and wyrceaþ *texendis subtilioribus indumentis operam dant*, Bd. 4, 25; S. 601, 16. Heortes hornes ðæs smælestan dustes, Lchdm. i. 334, 19. Gnīd swīðe ðæt hit sȳ ðæt smælste, iii. 18, 15. VI. of the voice, *not loud.* v. smale, II. [*Goth.* smals: *O. Sax.* smal: *O. Frs.* smel: *O. H. Ger.* smal *gracilis, exilis, subtilis, minutus, strictus*: *Icel.* smār; cf. *also* smali *a sheep, small cattle.*] v. ǣ-smæl.

smæle *finely.* v. smale.

smæll, es; *m. A smack, blow with the open hand*:—Dynt ł smæll mid honde uutearde *alapam*, Jn. Skt. Lind. 18, 22. [Cf. At þan uorme smællen Romanisce veollen, Laym. 27052. *Icel.* smellr *a smacking* or *cracking sound*: *Dan.* smæld *a crack, smack*: *Swed.* smäll.] v. hand-smæll, smellan.

smæl-þearmas, -þyrmas; *pl. m. The small guts, intestines*:—Smælþearmas *intestina*, Wrt. Voc. i. 44, 44: *inguina*, ii. 44, 4: *jejuna*, 49, 51. Wið smælþearma sāre, Lchdm. ii. 236, 18. Smælþearmum *ilibus*, Wrt. Voc. ii. 44, 1. Be wambe coþum and tācnum on roppe and on smælþearmum, Lchdm. ii. 230, 16. Hē clǣnsaþ ðone magan and ða smælþyrmas, i. 80, 21. [*Icel.* smā-þarmar *the small gut*, also *the lower abdomen.*] v. next word.

smæl-þearme, es; *n. The small gut, lower abdomen*:—Wyrð gegaderodu ōmig wǣte on ðære wambe oððe on ðam smælþearme, Lchdm. ii. 218, 17. Sīhþ innan ðone rop and on ðæt smælþearme, 232, 15: 246, 21. Ðā þȳdde Æfner hine mid hindewerde sceafte on ðæt smælþearme *percussit eum Abner aversa hasta in inguine*, Past. 40, 5; Swt. 295, 18. v. preceding word.

smǣr[e?], es; *m. A lip*:—Smǣras (?*printed* sinæres) *labra*, Hpt. Gl. 457, 39. Reádum smǣrum *roseis labris*, 481, 25. Smǣrum *buccis*, 422, 72. Smērum, Lchdm. i. lxx, 6. [Cf. For hire speche he smere loh, Laym. 14981. Tho he (*the fox*) wes inne, smere he lou, Rel. Ant. ii. 272, 23.] v. gāl-smere (*where read* gāl-smǣre), *and next word.*

smǣran (?); *p.* de *To laugh at, deride*:—Gehlōgun ł smērdon (besmerdon? cf. besmeradun *in Rush.*) hine *deridebant eum*, Mt. Kmbl. Lind. 9, 24. v. preceding word.

smǣte; *adj. Refined, pure* (of gold):—Smaete gold *obrizum*, Wrt. Voc. ii. 115, 11. Smǣte *obrizum*, 75, 72. Hié wurdan sōna tō ðam golde ðe man hāteþ *obritsum*, ðæt is smǣte gold, Shrn. 32, 21. Smǣte gold ðæt in wylme biþ þurh ofnes fȳr eall geclǣnsod, Elen. Kmbl. 2616; El. 1309. Beág on ðam siex hund wæs smǣtes goldes gescyred sceatta, Exon. Th. 324, 8; Vīd. 91: Salm. Kmbl. 29; Sal. 15. On smǣtum *in obrizum*, Hpt. Gl. 449, 10. Hē hēt smiðian of smǣtum golde āne lytle rōde, Homl. Th. ii. 304, 16: Homl. Skt. i. 2, 113. [Kynehelm of smeate gold, Chr. 1070; Erl. 209, 7. Guldene ȝerde alre gold smeatest, Marh. 11, 24.]

smǣte-gylden; *adj. Of refined gold*:—Smǣtegyldne *obridzum*, Wrt. Voc. ii. 89, 25. Ða smǣtegyldenan clāþas *auri obriza lammina*, 2, 7.

smale, smæle; *adv.* I. *finely* (v. smæl, V):—Hundes tux gebærned and smale gegniden, Lchdm. i. 372, 1. Gegníd tō duste swȳðe smale, 196, 12: 198, 1, 15. Genim wæterhæfern gebærnedne and ðonne gegniden smale, ii. 44, 20. Genim swefl, gebeát swíðe smale, 88, 17: i. 358, 9. Āsift smale þurh smæl sife, ii. 94, 1. Getrifula smale, 90, 27. Ðeáh ðū hié smale tōdǣle swā dust, Bt. 13; Fox 38, 33. Ic hī tōdǣlde swā smæle and swā swā dust beforan winde *comminuam eos ut pulverem ante faciem venti*, Ps. Th. 17, 40. Ðæs dustes smæle gecnucudes, Lchdm. i. 286, 2. Gegníd smæle on mortere, ii. 60, 1. Gebeát smæle, 88, 5. Gegníd tō duste swā ðū smalost mǣge, 108, 15. II. of the voice, *not loudly*:—Ðæs cocces þeáw is ðæt hē micle hlūdor singþ on ūhtan ðonne on dægrēd ac ðonne hit neálǣcþ dæge ðonne singþ hē smælor and smicror *gallus profundioribus horis noctis altos edere cantus solet; cum vero matutinum jam tempus in proximo est, minutas ac tenues voces format*, Past. 63; Swt. 461, 3.

smalian; *p.* ode *To become small, slender*, etc.:—Fram mettum smaligan *to get slender by diet*, Lchdm. ii. 282, 29. [*Prompt. Parv.* smaliñ *minoro*.] v. next word.

smalung, e; *f. Diminishing, lessening*:—Lǣcedōmas ða ðe þynnunge mægen habben and smalunge *medecines that have the power of thinning and reducing*, Lchdm. ii. 260, 23.

smeágan, smeán; *p.* smeáde; *ppr.* smeágende, smeánde; *pp.* smeád. I. in the following glosses:—Ic smeáge *scrutor*, Ælfc. Gr. 25; Zup. 145, 3: *meditor*, Wrt. Voc. i. 50, 3. Smeáþ *investigabit*, Kent. Gl. 652. Smeáde *disputavit*, Wrt. Voc. ii. 25, 61. Smēgan *investigare*, Kent. Gl. 953. Tō smyágenne *tractanda*, 749. II. used absolutely, or with prepositions (be, on, ymbe), *to consider, meditate, inquire, deliberate*:—Ic smēgu *meditabor*, Ps. Surt. ii. p. 185, 3. Hē smeáþ on his mōde ymb ðis eorþlīce līf, Bt. 39, 7; Fox 224, 4. Be ðam gē smeágeaþ *de hoc quaeritis*, Jn. Skt. 16, 19. Ða senatores dæghwamlīce smeádon on ānum sindrian hūse embe ealles folces þearfe, Thw. p. 161, 33: Nicod. 19; Thw. 9, 10: Homl. Skt. i. 3, 44. Ðā hig mid him smeádon *dum secum quaererent*, Lk. Skt. 24, 15. Smeá (smeáge, Lind.: smeóge, Rush.) and geseoh ðæt . . . *scrutare et vide quia*, Jn. Skt. 7, 52. Ðeáh wē ofer ūre mǣþ þencen and smeágean, Past. 16; Swt. 101, 11. Ic mid eallum mīnum ealdormonnum wæs smeágende be ðære hǣlo ūrra sāwla, L. In. prm.; Th. i. 102, 7. Smeágende ymbe heora sāwla ārǣd, L. Edm. S. prm.; Th. i. 244, 5. Ymb his ǣ hē byþ smeágende *in lege ejus meditabitur*, Ps. Th. 1, 2. On eallum ðīnum weorcum ic wæs smeágende, 76, 10. III. *to consider, ponder, examine, inquire into, discuss, search*, (1) with acc.:—Ðenden ic Godes bebodu smeáge *scrutabor mandata Dei*, Ps. Th. 118, 115. Ne sēcþ hē nānwuht, ne ne smeáþ, for ðam ðe hē hit wāt eall, Bt. 42; Fox 258, 1. Hwī smeágaþ hī unnytt *quare populi meditati sunt inania*, Ps. Th. 2, 1. Hwæt smeáde gē be wege *quid in via tractabatis*, Mk. Skt. 9, 33. Drihten, smeá mīne geþohtas, Ps. Th. 25, 2. Smeágeaþ (smeás gié, Lind.: smeógas gē, Rush.) hālige gewritu *scrutamini scribturas*, Jn. Skt. 5, 39. Ðæt hē his āgene dǣda georne smeáge, Blickl. Homl. 109, 12. Ðeáh wē fela smeán (smeágen, Cott. MS.), wē habbaþ litellne gearowitan būton tweón, Bt. 41, 5; Fox 254, 9. Ðæt ic smeáde (*meditarer*) sprǣce ðīne, Ps. Spl. 118, 148. Ðū woldest mīne lāre smeágean, 22, 1; Fox 76, 25. Ic ðē sende ðæt spell tō rǣdanne and tō smeágeanne (*ad legendum ac probandum*), Bd. pref.; S. 471, 10. Com Mellitus tō Rōme be ðām nȳdþearflīcum intingum Angelcyricean and hē ða wæs smeágende mid ðone pāpan *venit Mellitus Romam de necessariis ecclesiae Anglorum cum papa tractaturus*, 2, 4; S. 505, 30. Godes mǣrþa smeágende, H. R. 105, 8. Scmegende wes *scrutata est*, Ps. Surt. 118, 129. Smēgende (smeánde, Ps. Spl.), 118, 70. Biþ smeád *meditabitur*, 36, 30. (2) with a clause introduced by ðæt, hū, hwilc, hwæt, etc.:—Smeádon men oft, and gyt gelōme smeágaþ, hū se hlāf māge beón āwend, Homl. Th. ii. 268, 7: L. Ed. 4; Th. i. 162, 1. Ic smeáde mid mīnra witena geþeahte, hū ic mæhte cristendōmes mǣst ārǣran, L. Edm. S. prm.; Th. i. 246, 19. Hē sōhte and smeáde (*tractavit*), hwæt tō dōnne wǣre, Bd. 2, 5; S. 507, 29: Elen. Kmbl. 826; El. 413. Maria smeáde and þohte, hwæt seó hālettung wǣre, Blickl. Homl. 7, 16. Smeáge man geornlīce, hwæðer hit sōþ sī, Deut. 19, 18. Hī āgunnon smeágan, hwilc of him ðæt tō dōnne wǣre, Lk. Skt. 22, 23. Dauid ongan smeágan and þencan, hwilce ðæs gōdan mannes dǣda wǣron, Blickl. Homl. 55, 12. Ðonne mōt man smeágan and geornlīce spyrian hwār ða mānfullan wununge habban, L. Eth. ix. 40; Th. i. 348, 26. Mid wæccere mōde is tō smeágeanne and tō geþencenne (*pensandum est*), ðæt Drihten bebeád, ðæt hī heora hrægel clǣnsodon, Bd. 1, 27; S. 496, 3. Ūs is tō smeágenne, ðæt Drihten on ðære costunge nolde his ða myclan miht gecȳþan, Blickl. Homl. 33, 17. III a. *to seek an opportunity*:—Ðā smeáde hē ðæt hē hine gesāwe *querebat videre eum*, Lk. Skt. 9, 9. Hē smeáde geornlīce ðæt hē hyne wolde belǣwan *quaerebat opportunitatem ut eum traderet*, Mt. Kmbl. 26, 16. IV. *to accept as the result of inquiry, to suppose*:—Be ðisum þingum ne cunne wē smeágean nān ōðer þing būton hīt sig on Godes dōme gelang *de his rebus nihil aliud conjicere possumus, nisi quod ad judicium Dei pertineat*, L. Ecg. P. i. 13; Th. ii. 178, 16. v. ā-, fore-, tō-, þurh-smeágan; smeáh *and cpds. with* smeá-; cf. smūgan.

smeágelegen, e; *f. A syllogism*:—Smeágelegena *syllogismos*, Hpt. Gl. 503, 57. Cf. riht-smeáung, *and preceding word*.

smeágend-līc; *adj. Meditative*:—Smeágendlīc *meditativa*, Ælfc. Gr. 34; Zup. 211, 6.

smeágung, smeáwung, smeáung, smēung, smeáng, e; *f.* I. *search, inquiry, investigation* where something is lost:—On swylcere smeágunge (*the search for stolen cattle*), L. Edg. S. 12; Th. i. 276, 21. Habban ðās ylcan smeágunge on mīnum cucum orfe and on mīnra þegena, 13; Th. i. 276, 24: 14; Th. i. 276, 32. II. *inquiry carried on by the mind, inquiry, consideration, meditation, discussion, deliberation*:—Smeágung *studium*, Wrt. Voc. i. 51, 27. Sió smeáung and sió gesceádwīsnes *ratiocinatio*, Bt. 39, 8; Fox 224, 4. Smeáung (Ps. Surt. smeáng) *meditatio*, Ps. Spl. 118, 24, 97, 99. Smeágunge *scrutinio*, 63, 6. On smeáwunge and on leornunge hāligra gewrita *meditationi scripturarum*, Bd. 4, 3; S. 567, 29. Smeáunge, 1, 1; S. 474, 5: Past. 11; Swt. 67, 5. Smeánge, Ps. Surt. 38, 4. Hī hæfdon on ðam gemōte micle smeáunge and geþeaht hwæt him tō dōnne wǣre *illi tractatum magnum in concilio quid esset agendum habere coeperunt*, Bd. 3, 5; S. 527, 26. Ðā geseah se ārleása āīdlian his smeágunge *then the impious king saw all his deliberation was of no avail*, Homl. Skt. i. 4, 399. Smeáunga yfle *cogitationes malae*, Mt. Kmbl. Lind. 15, 19. Smeáwunga, 9, 4. Smeáwungas (smeóunge, Rush.), Lk. Skt. Lind. 11, 17. Smeáungas (smēunges, Rush.), 2, 35. v. ā-, ofer-, riht-, scearp-smeágung, -smeáung.

smeáh, smeóh; *adj.* I. *creeping in, penetrating*:—Wið smeógan wyrme, Lchdm. iii. 10, 17. v. smeá-wyrm. II. *subtle, crafty*. [Ðe man is ȝiep toȝenes him seluen! þat is smegh oðer man to bicharren and to biswiken, O. E. Homl. ii. 195, 5. Cf. Two þing ben in þe manne, on his þat clene kinde þat God haueþ þeron broht þureh his smehnesse (*wisdom, skill*), 205, 19. Smeihliche bicharede, 71, 28. Cf. *Icel.* í-smeyg-iligr *insinuating*.] *See* smeá-wrenc *and other compounds with* smeá-, *and* smeágan, ge-smeáh.

smeá-līc; *adj.* I. *searching, penetrating* (of inquiry, trial, etc.):—Hwæt is sió þyrelung ðæs wǣges būton scearplīcu and smeálīcu fandung ðæs mōdes ðæt mon mid ðære . . . onlūce ða heardan heortan *quid est parietem fodere, nisi acutis inquisitionibus duritiam cordis aperire?* Past. 21, 3; Swt. 155, 1. II. *that goes to the root* or *heart of a matter, profound*:—Hū ðū mē hæfst āfrēfrodne ǣgðer ge mid ðīnre smeálīcan sprǣce ge mid ðære wynsumnesse ðīnes sanges *quantum me vel sententiarum pondere vel canendi jucunditate refovisti*, Bt. 22, 1; Fox 76, 10: tit.; Fox xiv, 6. III. *exquisite, choice* (?):—Smeálīcran *exquisitiores*, Wrt. Voc. ii. 145, 15.

smeálīce; *adv.* I. of inquiry, investigation, etc., *searchingly, carefully, narrowly, closely*:—Hī smeálīce sōhtan *perquirentes subtilius*, Bd. 3, 10; S. 534, 37. Hī smeálīce sōhton ðone behȳddan mete, Ælfc. T. Grn. 21, 12. Hit is smeálīce and geornlīce tō sēceanne *subtiliter perscrutanda*, Past. 21, 1; Swt. 150, 11. Wē sculon swīðe smeálīce ðissa ǣgðer underþencean *hoc in utrisque est subtiliter intuendum*, 7, 1; Swt. 49, 23. Gesceád ða wē smeálīce geþencan sculan *discretio, quae subtiliter pensari debeat*, Bd. 1, 27; S. 496, 35. Smeálīcor, Past. 11, 2; Swt. 67, 6. II. of reasoning, thinking, etc., *closely, deeply, acutely, with penetration*:—Hē ongann smeálīce þencan on his mōdes ingeþance *velut in augustam suae mentis sedem recepta*, Bt. 24, 1; Fox 80, 5. Mē þincþ ðæt wit mǣgen smeálīcor sprecan and diógolran wordum *validioribus rationibus utendum puto*, 13; Fox 36, 32: 13, tit.; Fox xii, 16. Ðonne ic ymbe swelc smeálīcost þence *when I think most deeply about such a matter*, 10; Fox 26, 29. III. of knowing, seeing, etc., *clearly, accurately, exactly*:—Ða ðe meahton smeálīce and scearplīce mid hiera andgite ryht geseón *qui videre recta subtiliter per ingenium poterant*, Past. 11, 4; Swt. 69, 5. Ðeáh se lāreów ðis eall smeálīce and openlīce gecȳðe *cuncta haec licet subtiliter rector insinuet*, 21, 6; Swt. 163, 18. Se ðe wile geornlīce ðone Godes cwide singan sōðlīce (smeálīce, MS. B.), Salm. Kmbl. 171; Sal. 85. IV. *closely*:—Ān cliwen suīðe nearwe and suīðe smeálīce gefealden, Past. 35; Swt. 241, 24. v. smeáh.

smeá-mete, es; *pl.* -mettas; *m. A delicacy*:—On ðās tīd (*Lent*) sceal beón forhæfednes gehwylcra smeámetta, L. E. I. 40; Th. ii. 438, 9. Disc mid cynelīcum mettum (smeámettum, MS. B.) gefylled *discus, regalibus epulis refertus*, Bd. 3, 6; S. 528, 15.

smeán. v. smeágan.

smearcian, smercian; *p.* ode *To smirk, smile*:—Ic smercige *subrideo*, Ælfc. Gr. 47; Zup. 268, 8. Ðonne ðū smercodest and hlōge, ðonne weóp ic biterlīce, Wulfst. 140, 28. Ðā smearcode hē, Bt. 34, 10; Fox 148, 17. Smercode (smearcode, Cott. MS.), 34, 12; Fox 154, 8: 35, 4; Fox 160, 31: 40, 2; Fox 236, 22. Smercode, Blickl. Homl. 189, 4: Homl. Skt. i. 14, 126: Ap. Th. 19, 23. Ðā ongan hē smearcian, Bt. 39, 4; Fox 216, 14. Smercigende *subridendo*, Scint. 172, 17. Gūþlāc tō smerciende fēng *Guthlac received it smiling*, Guthl. 11; Gdwin. 56, 6. Mid smercigendum mūþe, Homl. Th. i. 430, 34.

smeart; *adj. Smart, painful*:—Ic wylle swingan eów mid ðam smeartestum swipum, ðæt is, ðæt ic wītnige eów mid ðam wyrstan wīte, Wulfst. 295, 10. [Gif þi sulf one smerte discepline & drauh þet swete likunge into smeortunge, A. R. 294, 12. Stede and twei sporen and ane smearte ȝerd, O. E. Homl. i. 243, 23. Mid smerte smiten of smale longe ȝerden, ii. 207, 6. Me him smæt mid smærte ȝerden, Laym. 20318. If men smot it with a yerde smerte (*adv.*), Chauc. Prol. 149.] v. smeortan.

smeáþ, e; *f. Meditation:*—Æ ðín smeáþ (*meditatio*) mín is, Ps. Spl. 118, 77. Cf. smeágung.

smeáþanclíce; *adv. Exactly, at large; subtiliter:*—Swá wé hér bufan smeáþanclíce áwriten habbaþ, Anglia viii. 309, 22.

smeá-þancol; *adj. Acute, subtle:*—Mid smeáþancelre trahtnunge *tenaci memoriae textu*, Hpt. Gl. 410, 64.

smeáþancol-líc; *adj. Subtle, crafty:*—Smeáþancollíce wriþan ꝉ cnottan cræftelícum *sertaque mystica dactylico*, Germ. 389, 28.

smeáþancollíce; *adv. Exactly, in a searching manner, thoroughly; subtiliter:*—Smeáþancelíce *subtiliter, eleganter*, Hpt. Gl. 431, 49. Hí smeádon swíðe smeáþancollíce ymbe ðæt éce líf *they went into the question of eternal life in the most searching manner*, Homl. Skt. i. 3, 44. Hé hí gewissode swíðe smeáþancellíce ymbe ðæs mynstres gebytlungum *he gave them most exact directions about the buildings of the monastery*, Homl. Th. ii. 172, 16. Hé lǽrþ manna mód mid godcundre láre smeáþancellíce, i. 412, 32.

smeáþancolness, e; *f. Exactness, strictness:*—Ðeáh wé witon hú fela gód oððe hú micele wé gefremodon nyte wé ðeáh mid hwylcere smeáþancelnysse se upplíca Déma ða áfandaþ, Homl. Th. ii. 80, 34.

smeáung. v. smeágung.

smeá-wrenc, es; *m. A crafty device, sharp trick:*—Hé begeat mid his sméhwrencan and mid his golde and seolfre eall dyrnunga, ðæt him geweard se þridda pænig of ðære tolne on Sandwíc, Chart. Th. 339, 8. v. smeáh.

smeá-wyrhta, an; *m. A skilled workman, an artisan:*—Gif hé smeáwyrhtan hæfþ ðám hé sceal tó tólan fylstan, Anglia ix. 263, 16.

smeá-wyrm, es; *m. A penetrating worm, worm that makes its way into the flesh:*—Wið smeáwyrme (cf. wið smégea-wyrme, 302, 12) smiring . . . seó sealf ðone wyrm deádne gedéþ oððe cwicne of drífþ, Lchdm. ii. 332, 3-26. Wið sméga-wyrme, 126, 1. Wið smoega-wyrmum, 12, 14. v. smeáh.

sméc, smécan, smecgan. v. smíc, smícan, smæccan.

smedema, smeodema, smidema, smedma, an; *m. Fine flour, meal:*—Smeoduma *polenta*, Wrt. Voc. ii. 117, 51. Melewes smedma *simila*, 83, 65. Smedma of melwe *pollis*, Ælfc. Gr. 9, 28; Zup. 55, 15. Smedma *simila* vel *pollis*, Wrt. Voc. i. 41, 24. Hwǽtes smedma, Lchdm. ii. 108, 10. Gecned þrí sestras smedeman (*similae*), Gen. 18, 6: Ex. 29, 40. Smideman, Lev. 2, 2. Genim smedman six yntsena gewihte, Lchdm. i. 150, 17. Mid hwǽtes smedeman *with the fat of kidneys of wheat* (A.V.); cum medulla tritici: cf. óþ smedeman *ad medullam*, Hpt. Gl. 410, 28. Ðá hláfas wǽron berene. Bere is swíðe earfoþe tó gearcigenne, and ðeáhhwæðere fét ðone mann, ðonne hé gearo biþ. Swá wæs seó ealde ǽ swíðe earfoþe tó understandenne, ac ðeáhhwæðere ðonne wé cumaþ tó ðam smedman, ðæt is tó ðære getácnunge, ðonne gereordaþ heó úre mód, Homl. Th. i. 188, 7. Genim ácrinde, wirc tó smedman, Lchdm. ii. 132, 19. Of mealtes smedman geworht, 332, 20. Genim hwǽtenes meluwes smedman, 134, 4. v. hwǽte-smedeme (*read* -a; *m.*).

smedemen, smedmen; *adj. Of fine flour:*—Smedmen hláf *similagineus panis*, Scint. 154, 1.

sméga-wyrm, sméh-wrenc. v. smeá-wyrm, -wrenc.

smellan (?); *p.* smeall *To crack, make a noise.* [*Mod. Icel.* smella; *p.* small *to crack* as a whip.] v. smillan, smæll.

smelt, smylt, es; *m. A smelt:*—Smelt *sardina*, Wrt. Voc. i. 281, 71. Smylt *sartate*, 66, 7. Smeltas *sardas*, ii. 119, 63.

smelt (?). v. dolh-smeltas; smelte *serene*. v. smylte.

smelting, smilting, e; *f. Amber:*—Smelting *electrum*, Wrt. Voc. i. 38, 31. Smilting, 34, 66. Smyltinc, 85, 14. Anlícnyssa gyldena and sylfrena, sume of smyltinga, sume of crystallan, Homl. Skt. i. 4, 165. [Smulting, Wrt. Voc. i. 94, 61. Cf. *O.H.Ger.* smelzi *electrum*, smelzida *electrum*: *Icel.* smeltr *enamelled.*]

smeócan; *p.* smeác, *pl.* smucon; *pp.* smocen. I. *intrans. To smoke, emit smoke:*—Smeógoþ *fumigant*, Ps. Spl. 103, 33. Muntas smeócaþ *montes fumigabunt*, 143, 6: Wülck. Gl. 244, 35. Eall Sinai munt smeác (*fumabat*), Ex. 19, 18. Smeóce *fumet*, Germ. 393, 187. Heortes mearh gebærned óþ ðæt hyt smeóce, Lchdm. i. 338, 13. Eall folc gesáwon ðone munt smeócan, Ex. 20, 18: Engl. Stud. ix. 40. Smeócende (smécende, Lind.: smíkende, Rush.) flex *linum fumigans*, Mt. Kmbl. 12, 20. II. *trans. To smoke, fumigate:*—Smeóc ðone man mid gáte hǽrum, Lchdm. i. 352, 1. Smeóce mid hǽþe, 354, 23. Heortes hǽr beóþ swíðe góde mid tó smeócanne, 338, 4. [*Prompt. Parv.* smekyn *fumo, fumigo.*] v smícan, smocian, smíc.

smeodoma, smeóh, smeolt. v. smedema, smeáh, smolt.

smeortan; *p.* smeart, *pl.* smurton; *pp.* smorten *To smart:*—Gnættas cómon mid fýrsmeortendum bitum *ignitos ciniphes*, Ors. 1, 7; Swt. 36, 30. [Þenne akeþ his heorte and smerteð, O. E. Homl. ii. 207, 21. Hire ne oc, ne ne smeart, 21, 27. Ðenne wile his heorte aken and smerten, 207, 34. Me iveleð hit bitterliche smeorten, A. R. 238, 29. Smertyn *uro*, Prompt. Parv. 460. *O. H. Ger.* smerzan; *p.* smarz *dolere.*]

smeoru, smeru (o, a), wes; *n. Fat, grease, suet, tallow.* I. in the following glosses:—Smeoru *unguentum*, Wrt. Voc. ii. 124, 9. Unsilt smeoro *saevo*, 119, 45. Smero *sevo* (in a list 'de igne'), i. 284, 27. Unámaelte smeoruwe *pice, saevo*, ii. 117, 28. Smerwe *sevo*, 80, 45. Smeruwe, Hpt. Gl. 503, 18. Smerewe *arvina*, 471, 4. II. in the following passages:—Wið útsihte, hunig and unsylt smeoru and wex, Lchdm. iii. 18, 5. Heortes smeoro (smeru, smero), i. 338, 15: 354, 4. Sceápes smeru, ii. 66, 7. Foxes smero, iii. 2, 25. Heorotes smera oððe gáte oððe góse, 68, 26: 80, 18. Ðæt smeru wand út, Jud. 3, 22. Smeoruwes, Ps. Th. 62, 5. Beran smeruwes (smerwes, MS. B.), Lchdm. i. 216, 15. Mid gáte smeorwe (smerwe, MS. B.), 354, 1. Mid smeorwe *adipe*, Ps. Surt. 62, 6. Of swínes smerwe, Lchdm. ii. 66, 7. Ofer smere (*unguento*), Rtl. 115, 34. Cnucige wið eald smeoru (smera, MS. B.: smeru, MS. O.), Lchdm. i. 74, 21: 86, 7. Genim heortes smeoruw (smeruw, MS. H.: smeru, MS. B.). Genim góse smero, 76, 9. Sceápen smera, ii. 128, 16: 148, 20. Eal ðæt smeru hig forbærndon, Lev. 8, 25. [Smeredd ꝧ sallfedd þurrh nan eorþliȝ smere, Orm. 13244. *O. H. Ger.* smero *adeps, arvina, unctura*: *Icel.* smjör *grease, fat; butter.*] v. flot-, heorot-smeoru.

smeoru-mangestre, an; *f. A butter-woman, woman who deals in butter and cheese:*—Smeremangestre, que mangonant in caseo et butiro, L. Eth. iv. 2; Th. i. 301, 5.

smeoru-sealf, e; *f. A grease-salve:*—Gif ðú wǽtan dést tó oððe smerusealfe, ne meaht ðú hit gelácnian, Lchdm. ii. 148, 23.

smeoru-þearm, es; *m. An entrail:*—Smeruþearm *extale*, Wrt. Voc. ii. 145, 29. Smæreþerm *julium* (in a list 'de suibus'), i. 286, 61.

smeoruwig; *adj. Fatty, greasy, unctuous:*—Eal ða wǽtan þing and ða smerewigan sint tó forbeódanne, Lchdm. ii. 210, 27. [*Icel.* smjörugr *greasy.*] v. un-smeoruwig.

smeoru-wyrt, e; *f. Smer-wort.* '*Aristolochia rotunda*, in allusion to its use in ointments.' E. D. S. Plant Names. Halliwell gives '*smereworth* the round birthwort, or the herb mercury.' It is found in the following glosses:—Smeoruwyrt *veneria*, Wrt. Voc. ii. 123, 33. Smerowyrt *nam* (*nap?*) *silvatica*, 62, 39. Smerewyrt *aristolochia*, i. 67, 17: Lchdm. iii. 300, col. 1. It occurs also in the Leechdoms:—Smerowyrt. Ðeós wyrt ðe man aristolochiam and óðrum naman smerowyrt nemneþ, Lchdm. i. 114, 9-11. Smeruwyrt, ii. 338, 13. Smerewyrt, 128, 15.

smér[e], smera, smercian, smereness, smerewig, smerian, smering, smeru, smerwan. v. smǽr[e], smeoru, smearcian, smireness, smeoruwig, smirwan, smiring, smeoru, smirwan.

smédan; *p.* de *To make smooth, to soothe:*—Him is tó sellanne ðæt ðone innoþ stille and sméðe, Lchdm. ii. 210, 20. v. ge-sméðan, sméðian.

sméðe; *adj. Smooth.* I. in glosses:—Sméðe *lenis*, Wrt. Voc. ii. 51, 48. Smoeðum *politis*, 117, 55. Ðæs sméðestan *politissimis*, 66, 27. II. *smooth, without roughness* or *inequalities* of surface:—Sméðe ringce *tinius*, Wrt. Voc. i. 40, 56. Mín bróður ys rúh and ic eom sméðe, Gen. 27, 11. Ðonne glád hit on ðǽm scyllum swelce hit wǽre sméðe ísen, Ors. 4, 6; Swt. 174, 8. Wæs cyrtil unrúh ꝉ smoeðe, Jn. Skt. Lind. 19, 23. Án dún ful sméðe, Homl. Skt. i. 19, 109. On sméðum felda *on a plain*, Ors. 3, 11; Swt. 142, 14. Wé becóman on sumne sméðne feld (*in viam planam*), Bd. 5, 6; S. 618, 40. Ðeós wyrt biþ cenned on sméðum landum, Lchdm. i. 90, 3: 298, 3. On sméðe (smoeðum, Lind., Rush.) wegas *in vias planas*, Lk. Skt. 3, 5. Hé hæfþ ðe sméþran líchoman, Lchdm. ii. 298, 13. III. *smooth, without discomfort* or *annoyance:*—Wǽron hyra gongas under Godes egsan sméðe and geséfte, Exon. Th. 146, 3; Gú. 704. IV. *smooth, suave, avoiding offence:*—Hé biþ hwílum tó ungemetlíce sméðe, hwílum tó ungemetlíce réðe *amor proprius mentem aliquando inordinate ad mollitiem, aliquando ad asperitatem rapit*, Past. 19, 1; Swt. 143, 7. V. *smooth, not irritating* (of food, medicine, etc.):—Ne se mete ne sié tó scearp ne tó súr, ac sméðe and fǽt, Lchdm. ii. 196, 8. Eáðmylte mettas and scír wín and sméðe, 220, 13. Ða wambe man sceal clǽsnian mid sméþe wyrtdrence, 262, 17. Wyrc sméþe eágsealfe, 308, 27. VI. *smooth* (of words):—Sméðne sybcwide, Frag. Kmbl. 54; Leás. 29. Ðám ðe ful sméðe sprǽce habbaþ, 20; Leás. 12. Ðone ele, ðæt wǽron ða sméðan lyffetunga, Homl. Th. ii. 572, 1. Bepǽcean mid sméðan wordan, Homl. Skt. i. 23, 602. Se Hǽlend lufaþ swíðor ða dǽde ðonne ða sméðan word, Ælfc. T. Grn. 14, 34. VII. of the voice, *not harsh, melodious, harmonious:*—Stefen smoeðu *vox canora*, Ps. Surt. ii. p. 202, 5. v. unsméþe; smóþ.

sméðian; *p.* ode; *pp.* od. I. *to become smooth:*—Ðonne sméðaþ ðæt neb and hálaþ, Lchdm. i. 86, 8. II. *to make smooth:*—Ic sméðie *polio*, Wrt. Voc. i. 28, 74. [He wile foxliche smeþien mid worde, O. E. Homl. i. 31, 8. Rihteð and smeðeð þe heorte, A. R. 4, 23.] v. ge-sméðian; sméðan.

sméðness, e; *f.* I. *smoothness:*—Hé forgeaf hreóflium sméðnysse, Homl. Th. i. 26, 11. II. *a smooth, level surface:*—Feld *campus*, sméðnys *planities*, Wrt. Voc. i. 53, 49.

smíc, sméc, smýc, es; *m. Smoke, vapour, steam:*—Swelce se bitresta smíc, Ors. 3, 11; Swt. 142, 20. Smíc *fumus*, Ælfc. Gr. 8; Zup. 28, 12: Ex. 19, 18: Homl. Th. ii. 68, 20. Hí losiaþ swá swá sméc, Bt. 27, 3; Fox 98, 31: Ps. Th. 36, 19. Smýc, Hpt. Gl. 501, 78: Shrn. 52, 33

Ða þicnyssa smîçes stigon upp on ǽlce healfe, Homl. Skt. i. 23, 36. Ða ýsla up flugon mid ðam smîce, Gen. 19, 18: Homl. Th. i. 530, 34. Se wǽta gǽþ up swylce mid smîce oððe miste, Lchdm. iii. 278, 9. Smēce gelîce *sicut fumus*, Ps. Th. 101, 3. On ðam fýre and on ðam smýce, Homl. Th. ii. 202, 32. Se wind ðæt fýr and ðone smîc ofer ða wallas drāf, Bd. 3, 16; S. 543, 1. Genim spices snǽd, lege on hâtne stān, drince ðonne smîc, Lchdm. ii. 58, 17. Ðonne hē (*the root*) tôbrocen byþ, hē rýcþ eal swylce hē smîc of him āsænde, i. 260, 9. Ðæs drinces smýc heora eágan onfōn, 348, 22. Smēc *vaporem*, Ps. Surt. ii. p. 202, 15. [Ne michte ut seon for smike, O. E. Homl. i. 161, 16. Smeche, ii. 220, 18. Smiche, 258, 20. Smec off recless, Orm. 1088. Smeke or smoke, Prompt. Parv. 460. *M. H. Ger.* smouch: *Ger.* schmauch.] v. smoca.

smîcan, smēcan; *p.* te. I. *to smoke, emit smoke*:—Muntas smîcaþ *montes fumigabunt*, Ps. Surt. 103, 32: 143, 5. II. *to smoke, fumigate*:—Sume mid pice smîcaþ, Lchdm. ii. 236, 9. Nim gāte hǽr, smēc under ða brēc wið ðæs rægereósan, 146, 3. Smîce mid fearne swîðe ða þeóh, 64, 26. [*Wicklif has a wk. past* smekide.] v. smeócan, smocian.

smicer; *adj. Fair, fine, beautiful, elegant*:—Smicre *elegans, loquax*, Txts. 59, 737: *elegans*, Wrt. Voc. ii. 29, 22. Smicerre ansîne *eleganti forma*, 30, 26. Smicere leóþe *carmine rithmico*, 23, 24. Windan manigne smicerne wǽn and manig ǽnlîc hūs settan and fegerne tūn timbrian, Shrn. 163, 16. Hió bit ðæt hî findon twā smicere scencingcuppan intō beódern *she asks them to provide two fair goblets for the refectory*, Ch. Th. 536, 7. Ðæs smicerestan *politissimis*, Wrt. Voc. ii. 66, 26. [He warrþ till atell defell off shene smikerr enngell, Orm. 13679. *O. H. Ger.* smechar *elegans, delicatus*.]

smicere; *adv. Finely, fairly, elegantly*:—Cræftlîce *vel* smicere *affabre*, ic smicere geglengce *orno*, Wrt. Voc. i. 54, 55-58. Smicere geworhte *fabrefactum*, ii. 33, 68: Shrn. 165, 27: Ps. Th. 118, 164, 84. Sió lufu scînþ suîðe smicere (*fulgescit*), Past. 14, 6; Swt. 87, 9. In burh raðe smicere cymeþ wlitig scrîðan þrymlîce on tūn Maius, Menol. Fox 150; Men. 76. Ðonne singþ hē smælor and smicror *minutas ac tenues voces format*, Past. 63; Swt. 461, 3.

smicerness, e; *f. Elegance, neatness*:—Þurh smicernesse and hiwunge *hironiam* (=per ironiam; irony is explained as combining elegance and dissimulation), Wrt. Voc. ii. 42, 53.

smidema. v. smedema.

smillan; *p.* de. I. *to cause to crack* as a whip, etc. II. *intrans. To crack* as a whip:—Under smyllendum gyrdum weóp *crepantibus flevit sub ferulis*, Germ. 388, 7. [*Icel.* smella; *p.* small *to crack*, as a whip; smella (*wk.*) *to cause to crack.*] v. smæll, *and cf. trans. and intrans. forms of* miltan.

smilt, smilting. v. smylt, smelting.

smirels, es; *m. An unguent, ointment, unction, salve*:—Smyrels *vel* sealf *unguina* vel *unguenta*, Wrt. Voc. i. 49, 29: *unguentum*. Hē gehǽlde ān mǽden mid hālwendum smyrelse gehālgodes eles, Homl. Th. ii. 508, 14. Wē lǽraþ ðæt preósta gehwilc ǽgðer hæbbe ge fulluhtele ge seócum smyrels, L. Edg. C. 66; Th. ii. 258, 15. [Nicodemus brouhte smuriles uorte smurien mide ure Louerd, A. R. 372, 18. Þat swote smirles þat is icleopet basme, H. M. 13, 21. Kepen ðe lich wiðuten smerles, Gen. and Ex. 2454. Þe Magdalene smerede Cristes uet mid þe precious smerieles, Ayenb. 187, 32. *Dan.* smörelse *grease*.]

smireness, e; *f. Ointment, unguent*:—Cwæþ se wrîtere ðæt Maria genāme ān pund deórwyrðre smyrenesse (smerenesse, 69, 1). . . . Ðeós smerenes wæs geworht of ehtatēne cynna wyrtum, Blickl. Homl. 73, 17-20. Smirinis (smerenisse, Rush.) *unguentum*, Mt. Kmbl. Lind. 26, 12. Smirenisse *unguenti*, Rtl. 115, 41. Smyrenisse, Lchdm. i. 346, 9. Mið smiriniss *unguento*, Lk. Skt. Lind. 7, 38: *oleo*, 46. Smyrenesse *unctum*, Wrt. Voc. ii. 91, 35. Smerenessa and sealf, Lchdm. ii. 10, 19: 158, 9. Hié selfe mid smirenissum hié smerwan, 224, 1.

smirian, smiring. v. smirwan, smirwung.

smirwan, smerwan, smiirewan, smeruwan, smirian, smerian, smyrian; *p.* smirede, ode *To smear, anoint*:—Ic smirie mîne flān on blōde, Deut. 32, 42. Ðū smirest *unges*, Ex. 29, 36. Ðū smyrest *linies*, Wrt. Voc. ii. 51, 46. On ðam dæge ðe hig man smiraþ *in die unctionis suae*, Lev. 6, 20. 'Smirewaþ (smiriaþ, Hatt. MS.) eówre eágan mid sealfe.' Ðonne wē smirewaþ (smierewaþ, Hatt. MS.) ūre heortan eáge mid sealfe, Past. 11; Swt. 68, 10-12. Smiriaþ, Ps. Surt. 140, 6. Smirede *linivit*, Wrt. Voc. ii. 74, 15. Smyrede, 51, 47. Smerede *unxit*, Ps. Spl. 44, 9: Blickl. Homl. 69, 2. Smyrede, 73, 18. Hē worhte fenn and smyrede (smiride, Lind., Rush.) mîne eágan, Jn. Skt. 9, 11. Mîn heáfod ðū mid ele ne smyredest, ðeós smyrede mid sealfe mîne fēt, Lk. Skt. 7, 46. Smyredon (smiredon, Lind.), Mk. Skt. 6, 13. Smire mid, Lchdm. ii. 132, 1 (and often). Smyre, i. 216, 5 (and often). Smyra ðîn heáfod *unge caput tuum*, Mt. Kmbl. 6, 17. Þweah ǽr ðū hit smeruwe, Lchdm. ii. 156, 2. Gnîde and smerwe, 186, 7. Hý hine smyrigon . . . ǽr hē hyne smyrige . . . hine ne mōt nān mann smyrigan, L. Ælfc. C. 32; Th. ii. 354, 21-31. Hié selfe mid smirenessum hié smerwan, Lchdm. ii. 224, 1. Ða menn ðū scealt smerwan mid ðý ele, 194, 18: 156, 4. Smirewan, 184, 2: 238, 26. Smyrian, 118, 16. Smerian, Blickl. Homl. 73, 24: 75, 17. Tō smirwanne, Lchdm. ii. 244, 19. Tō smerwanne, 288, 16. Tō smergenne, iii. 4, 14. Heó com tō smyrianne (smiriane, Lind.: smiranne, Rush.) mînne lîchaman, Mk. Skt. 14, 8. [*O. H. Ger.* pi-smeruit *unctus*: *Icel.* smyrja, smyrwa *to anoint.*] v. ā-, be-, ge-, geā-smirwan, -smirian.

smirwung, smiring (-ung), e; *f.* I. *anointing, unction*:—Ðus cwæð se apostol be ðǽre smyrunge seócra manna, L. Ælfc. C. 32; Th. ii. 354, 27. Gif se seóca man girnþ ðæt man hine smerige, hē dō ðonne his andetnesse ǽr ðare smerunge, and gif hē æfter ðare smyrunge hāl wurð, hē mōt flǽsces brūcan. On ðare smyrunge biþ lǽcedōm, L. Ælfc. P. 47, 48; Th. ii. 384, 27-32. II. *an ointment*:—Smiring *cassia*, Ps. Surt. 32, 9. Smyring *unguentum*, Ps. Spl. 132, 2. Balzaman smiring wið eallum untrumnessum, Lchdm. ii. 174, 7. Smyring, 288, 12. Gif ðū myhtest ǽnig þing fyndan on smyrunge oððe on wyrtum, ðæt ðu myhtest mýne wunde myd gehǽlan, St. And. 28, 17. Smerwunga wyrce of ele and of wermōde, Lchdm. ii. 182, 16.

smirwung-, smiring-ele, es; *m. Oil for anointing*:—Of ðam smiring-ele *de oleo unctionis*, Ex. 29, 21.

smîtan; *p.* smāt, *pl.* smiton; *pp.* smiten. I. *to daub, smear, smudge*:—Ðū nymst his blōd and smîtst ofer ūteweard Aarones swýðré eáre, Ex. 29, 20. Smāt, gemaercode *inpingit* (*cf. inpingit* gemearcode *vel signat*, 45, 59), Wrt. Voc. ii. 111, 57. Genim gāte tord, gemeng wið eced, smît on, Lchdm. ii. 68, 2. Genim ðæs hornes melo, meng wið wætere, smît on, 72, 14. Mid feðere smît on, 102, 8. Smîte mon ða sealfe ǽrest on ðæt heáfod, iii. 14, 29. Smîte of ðam sylfan blōde on ðæs weofodes hyrnan, Lev. 4, 18. Nymon of his blōde and smîton on ǽgðer gedyre, Ex. 12, 7. Ðissa (*oil, grease, and tar*) ealra emfela and ðara dusta ealra emfela, gemeng eal ceald tōsomne, ðæt hit fram ðām wōsum eal wel smîtende [sî] (*may be adapted for smearing*), smire mid, Lchdm. ii. 126, 11. [Ofersmît mid ele, 180, 28.] II. *to defile, pollute*:—Wīāþ āþ smîteþ, Exon. Th. 354, 52; Reim. 64. Smiton *funestavere*, Wrt. Voc. ii. 109, 43. [*Goth.* be-, ga-smeitan *to smear, anoint*: *O. Frs.* smîta *to cast*: *O. H. Ger.* smîzan *linere*. Later English takes the word in the sense of *strike*. In Mt. 26, 68 the later MS. has Hwæt ys se þe ðe *smat*, where the earlier has *slōh*. Brutus heom smat on, Laym. 534. He hoff þe swerd to smitenn, Orm. 14677. Ase ofte ase eni hund binimeð þe þine mete, nultu aþe ofte smiten? A. R. 324, 23. So in later works.] v. be-, ge-smîtan; smittian.

smite (?), es; *m. Pollution*:—Mustfleógan *vel* wurma smite *bibiones vel mustiones*, Wrt. Voc. i. 23, 75. v. must-fleóge.

smîte, an; *f. A foul, miry place* (?):—Ego mansam in loco qui celebri a solicolis nuncupatur æt Smitan uocabulo ministro meo largitus sum . . . Ðis is ðǽre ānre hîde landgemǽru tō Smîtan . . . of ðæm slō tō Smîtan; of ðære Smîtan tō berge, Cod. Dip. Kmbl. iii. 166, 2-20. Of smîtan on ðone stān . . . of ðære apoldran innan smîtan, v. 105, 13-36.

smitenness. v. be-smitenness.

smiþ, es; *m. A smith, a worker in metals* or *in wood*:—*Cudo* ic smiðige; eft gyf ðū cweðst *hic cudo*, ðonne byþ hit nama, smiþ, Ælfc. Gr. 36; Zup. 216, 10. Se smiþ *ferrarius* . . . se treówyrhta *lignarius*, Coll. Monast. Th. 30, 29. Smiþ *faber* vel *cudo*, Wrt. Voc. i. 73, 26: *faber*, 286, 74. Fýres god, heile smiþ *Vulcanus*, ii. 95, 7. Wæs sum brōðor syndrilîce on smiþcræfte well gelǽred; þeówode hē swýðe druncennesse and monigum ōðrum unālýfednessum ðæs sleacran lîfes, and hē mā gewunode on his smiþþan dæges and nihtes sittan and licgean, ðonne hē wolde on cyricean singan and gebiddan . . . wið ðon ðe smiþ ðæs þýstran modes and dǽde his deáþe neálǽhte . . . , Bd. 5, 14; S. 634, 13-42. Gif smiþ monnes andweorc onfō, hē hit gesund āgife swā hē hit ǽr onfēnge, L. Alf. pol. 19; Th. i. 74, 9. Mōdcræftig smiþ, ðonne hē gewyrceþ helm oððe hupseax, Exon. Th. 297, 2; Cri. 62. Wǽpna smiþ, Beo. Th. 2908; B. 1452. Hū nys se smiþ (smiþ ł wyrihte *faber*, Lind.) Marian sunu, Mk. Skt. 6, 3. Ðes ys smiþes sunu *hic est fabri filius*, Mt. Kmbl. 13, 55. Byrne, searonet seowed smiþes orþancum, Beo. Th. 817; B. 406. Gif gesîþcund man fare, ðonne mōt hē habban his smiþ mid him, L. In. 63; Th. i. 144, 3. Weorc, handweorc smiþa, Exon. Th. 408, 18; Rä. 27, 14: 388, 16; Rä. 6, 8: 401, 6: Rä. 21, 7. Ic hæbbe smiþas, îsene smiþas, goldsmiþ, seolforsmiþ, ārsmiþ, treówwyrhtan, Coll. Monast. Th. 29, 35. ¶ In poetical compounds the word is used figuratively. v. gryn-, hleahtor-, lār-, wig-, wîg-, wrōht-smiþ. [*Goth.* aiza-smiþa: *O. Frs.* smeth, smid: *O. H. Ger.* smid *faber, cudo*: *Icel.* smiðr.] v. ambiht-, ār-, gold-, îsen-, seolfor-, wundor-smiþ.

smiþ-cræft, es; *m. Smithcraft, the craft* or *art of the worker in metal* or *wood*:—Wæs sum brōðor syndrilîce on smiþcræfte well gelǽred *erat fabrili arte singularis*, Bd. 5, 14; S. 634, 14.

smiþ-cræftig; *adj. Skilled as a smith*. v. next word.

smiþ-cræftiga, an; *m. One skilled in the smith's art*:—Tubal Cain smiþcræftega wæs, Cd. Th. 66, 15; Gen. 1084.

smiðian; *p.* ode To *make* out of metal *or* wood, *to fashion, forge*:—Ic smiðige *cudo*, ðū smiðast *cudis*, Ælfc. Gr. 36; Zup. 216, 8: 28, 6; Zup. 178, 10. Smiðode oððe gescōp *cuderet*, Wrt Voc. ii. 19, 36. Hē hēt smiðian of smǽtum golde āne lytle rōde, Homl. Th. ii. 304, 16. Smiðian on smǽtum golde ānre culfran anlîcnysse, Homl. Skt. i. 3, 126. Smeoðed *fabricata*, Hpt. Gl. 418, 3.

[Brien enne smiđ funde þe wel cuđe smiđie . . . þe smiđ gon to smiđeȝe ane pic, Laym. 30742–9. Ofte a ful hawur smiđ smeođiđ a ful woc knif, A. R. 52, 8. A smith that in his forge smithed plowharneis, Chauc. C. T. 3760. To smythye wepne into sikul or to sithe, Piers P. 3, 305. *Goth.* ga-smiþôn: *O. H. Ger.* smidôn *fabricare, cudere: Icel.* smiða.] v. â-, be-, ge-smiđian.

smiþlíce; *adv. After the manner of a smith, with skill*:—Smiþlíce *fabrile*, Wrt. Voc. ii. 108, 33: 35, 14: 146, 59. [*O. H. Ger.* smidilîho *fabriliter.*]

smiþþe, an; *f. A smithy, a smith's workshop*:—Smiđđe *officina*, Wrt. Voc. ii. 64, 12: i. 34, 55: 73, 27. Smiþþe, 286, 75. Smiđþe *vel* weorchûs, 58, 23. On smiđđan *in conflatorio*, Kent. Gl. 1033. Hwæt sylst đû (*the smith*) ûs on smiþþan đînre bûton îsene fýrspearcan, Coll. Monast. Th. 31, 5. Hê mâ gewunode on his smiþþan dæges and nihtes sittan and licgean, đonne hê wolde on cyricean singan and gebiddan, Bd. 5, 14; S. 634, 16. Gâþ tô smiđđan and fandiaþ đises goldes and đissera gymstâna, Homl. Th. i. 64, 6. Đæt wîde geat be-eástan Welandes smiđđan, Cod. Dip. Kmbl. v. 332, 23. [*O. Frs.* smithe: *O. H. Ger.* smitta, smidda *officina, fabrica: Icel.* smiðja.]

smiþu. v. gold-smiþu.

smitta (-e; *f.*?), an; *m. A smear, blot, mark, spot*:—Bûtan smittan *sine macula*, R. Ben. Interl. 4, 3. Smyttena *naevorum, notarum*, Hpt. Gl. 421, 56. v. next word.

smittian; *p.* ode *To smear, pollute, defile*:—Smittodan *funestavere, maculavere*, Wrt. Voc. ii. 151, 60. Smittud *cacabatus*, Hpt. Gl. 514, 47. [Smitted *contaminata*, Ps. 105, 39. As reignes shall ben flitted Fro folk to folk, or whan they shal ben smitted, Chauc. T. and C. v. 1544. Ismittet (*smeared*) wiđ smirles, H. M. 13, 23. Bismitted (-smuddet, MS. T.) and bismeoruwed, A. R. 214, 22. Besmetted ine herte mid kueade þoȝtes, Ayenb. 229, 20. *O. H. Ger.* pi-smizzit *illitus, unctus.*] v. be-smittian; smîtan.

smoc[c], es; *m. A smock, shift*:—Smoc *vel* syrc *colobium*, Wrt. Voc. i. 25, 60. Loþa, hom *vel* smoc *colobium, dictum quia longum est et sine manicis*, ii. 134, 37. [Smokke *interula*, 182, 1. Smok, schyrt *camisia, interula*, Prompt. Parv. 461. *O.H. Ger.* smoccho *interula: Icel.* smokkr.]

smoca, an; *m. Smoke*:—Âstâh smoca on yrre his *ascendit fumus in ira ejus*, Ps. Lamb. 17, 9. Ût æt his nosu eode micel smocca, Nar. 43, 16. Hê nele đone wlacan smocan wâces flǣsces wætere gedwæscan *nec vult lini tepidos undis exstinguere fumos*, Dôm. L. 51. v. smíc.

smocian; *p.* ode. I. *intrans. To smoke, emit smoke*:—Muntas smociaþ, Ps. Lamb. 103, 32. Smeócaþ ł smociaþ *fumigabunt*, 143, 5. Swilce ân ofen eall smociende, Gen. 15, 17. Smocigende, Homl. Th. ii. 202, 24. II. *trans. To smoke*:—Genim đû đâs ylcan wyrte and smoca đæt cild mid, Lchdm. i. 116, 9. Smeóce (smoca, MS. R.) mid hǣþe, 354, 23. [Þa iseȝen heo a fur smokien, Laym. 25734. Smekyñ or smokyñ *fumo, fumigo*, Prompt. Parv. 460.] v. smeócan, smîcan.

smoega-wyrm, smoh. v. smeá-wyrm, ǣ-, in-smoh.

smolt, smeolt; *adj. Serene, quiet, peaceful*:—Smolt wæs se sigewong, Exon. Th. 146, 23; Gû. 714. Smeolt, Andr. Kmbl. 3160; An. 1583. Smolt regn *imbres*, Rtl. 85, 9: *torrens*, Blickl. Gl. (Ps. 125, 4). Smolt biþ *serenum erit*, Mt. Kmbl. Lind. 16, 2. Smolt dæg ł restdæg (smolte dæge, Rush.) *sero die*, Jn. Skt. Lind. 20, 19. Êfern ł smolt (efern ⁊ smolt, Rush.) *sero*, Mk. Skt. Lind. 6, 47. Wê hæfdon smolte niht *nox serena reddita est nobis*, Nar. 23, 52. [With smeþe smylyng and smolt, Gaw. 1763.] v. smylte, *and next word.*

smolte; *adv. Quietly, mildly*:—Đonne smolte (cf. smylte, Bt. 9; Fox 26, 17) blǣwþ sûþan and westan wind under wolcnum, Met. 6, 8. [Cf. *O. Sax.* smultro gibârean (*of the wind and waves*).]

smoltlíce; *adv. Gently, quietly*:—Flôwæþ seó welle swâ fægere and swâ smoltlíce swâ hunig, Engl. Stud. viii. 477, 10. v. smylt-líc.

smorian; *p.* ode *To choke, suffocate*:—Wyrgeþ *vel* smoraþ *st[r]angulat*, Wrt. Voc. ii. 121, 32. Se esne genimende smorede hine (*suffocabat eum*), Mt. Kmbl. Rush. 18, 28. Đa þornas smoradun (*suffocaverunt*) hiǽ, 13, 7. [Wend he smore þat sede, C. M. 5573. All suld be smored, Pr. C. 7601. Smore wythe smeke *fumigo*, smoryd *fumigatus*, smorynge *fumigacio*, Prompt. Parv. 461. Halliwell gives *smore* as a word in northern dialects, and quotes Hall's Chronicles; and *smoor* is given as a Lincolnshire word, E. D. S. Pub.] v. â-, for-, of-smorian.

smôþ; *adj. Smooth, unruffled*:—Mid smôđestum andwlite *serenissimo vultu*, Engl. Stud. ix. 40. v. un-smôþ, *and* smêđe.

smûgan; *p.* smeág, *pl.* smugon; *pp.* smogen *To creep, crawl, move gradually*:—Ic smûge *serpo*, Ælfc. Gr. 28, 4; Zup. 170, 15: *crepo* (*serpo*?), Wrt. Voc. ii. 136, 84. Smûgaþ *serpunt*, Wülck. Gl. 248, 19. Smûgen(-an?) *serpere*, Hpt. Gl. 527, 49. Hê (ǽwelm) biþ smûgende geond đa eorþan, Bt. 24, 1; Fox 80, 26. [Nedre smuȝeđ derneliche, O. E. Homl. i. 153, 22, 32. Smuȝđ, smuhgđ digeliche, ii. 191, 7, 15, 17. *M. H. Ger.* smiegen: *Icel.* smjúga *to creep through* a hole, narrow space, etc.] v. â-, under-smûgan; smeágan, *and next word.*

smûgendlíc; *adj. Creeping, reptile*:—Ealle slincendu ł smûendlícu *omnia reptilia*, Ps. Lamb. 68, 35.

smygel, smygels, es; *m. A burrow, place to creep into*:—Smygels *cuniculus*, Wrt. Voc. ii. 137, 34. Smygelas *cuniculos*, 15, 51. Smygilas, smigilas, smyglas, Txts. 48, 199. [Cf. *Icel.* smuga *a narrow cleft to creep through, a hole*; smogall, smugall *penetrating.*] v. smûgan.

smyllende, smyltan. v. smillan, ge-smyltan.

smylte; *adj. Quiet, tranquil, calm, serene.* I. of physical calmness:—Se mônaþ (*June*) is nemned on ûre geþeóde se ǣrra lîđa, for đon seó lyft biþ þonne smylte, Shrn. 87, 34. Swilce seó heofone đonne heó smylte (*serenum*) byþ, Ex. 24, 10. Hyt byþ smylte weder, Mt. Kmbl. 16, 2. Smylte weder biþ đý þancwyrþre, gif hit hwêne ǣr biþ stearce stormas and micle rênas and snâwas, Bt. 23; Fox 78, 26. Smylte reng *pluvia serena*, Bd. 4, 13; S. 582, 34. Smelt hagol *imber serotinus* (v. smolt), Kent. Gl. 560. Swâ biþ sǣ smilte, Exon. Th. 336, 26; Gn. Ex. 55. Sió ân hýþ byþ simle smyltu æfter eallum ýstum *that haven is ever calm after all the storms*, Bt. 34, 8; Fox 144, 28. Smylte is se sigewong, Exon. Th. 199, 29; Ph. 23. Smeltre *intempestae, tranquillae, serenae*, Hpt. Gl. 495, 4. Swiđe eáđe mæg on smyltre sǣ ungelǣred scipstiéra genôh ryhte stiéran, Past. 9; Swt. 59, 1. Đonne heó bađaþ hî on smyltum wætre, Shrn. 85, 21. Smylte wedere *aure tenuis*, Wrt. Voc. ii. 4, 56. Seó sǣ môt brûcan smyltra ýþa, Bt. 7, 3; Fox 20, 23. Ic becume tô đære smyltestan hýđe, Guthl. prol.; Gdwin. 4, 20. I a. *gentle, mild*, of the wind:—Þurh đone smyltan sûþan-westernan wind, Bt. 4; Fox 8, 8. Hê ýste mæg oncyrran đæt him windes hweođu weorđeþ smylte *statuit procellam in auram*, Ps. Th. 106, 28. I b. fig. *favourable, prosperous*:—Smyltum belimpum *successibus*, Anglia xiii. 32, 132. II. of mental calm, *placid, serene, tranquil, unruffled*:—Cild âcenned smylte *a child born on the ninth day of the moon will be placid*, Lchdm. iii. 188, 12. Hê smylte môde and blîþe (*placida mente*) him eall forlêt, Bd. 3, 22; S. 553, 20. Đâ frægn hê hwæđer hî ealle smylte môd (*placidum animum*) tô him hæfdon, 4, 24; S. 598, 40. Mid smyltre willsumesse *tranquilla devotione*, S. 599, 9, 10. Smylte ł blîđelíce ârfæstnisse *sinceram pietatem*, Rtl. 48, 28. Smyltum þohtum *sinceris mentibus*, 7, 21: 16, 37. v. mere-smylte; smolt, smyltness.

smylte; *adv. Quietly, mildly, gently*:—Đonne smylte blâweþ sûþan-westan wind, Bt. 9; Fox 26, 17. v. smolte.

smylte-líc, smylting. v. smylt-líc, smelting.

smylt-líc; *adj. Tranquil, serene*:—Smyltelíco gewidra, Shrn. 74, 11. Smyltlîcum *tranquilla*, Rtl. 39, 9. Smyltlîcum *seneris* (*serenis*?), 98, 8.

smyltness, e; *f. Quiet, calm, serenity, tranquillity.* I. of physical calm:—Đâ bebeád hê đam winde and đære sǣ, and đǣr wearđ geworden mycel smyltness, Mt. Kmbl. 8, 26. Smyltnes, Mk. Skt. 4, 39: Blickl. Homl. 235, 9. On smyltnysse lyfta *serenitate aerum*, Bd. 1, 1; S. 474, 30. I a. *the quiet of evening, evening*:—Middý êfern ł smyltnis, (*sero*) wêre âwordæn, Mk. Skt. Lind. 4, 35. Smyltnise, Jn. Skt. Lind. 6, 16. Næhtes smyltnisse *noctis quiete*, Rtl. 37, 35. I b. *gentleness, quietness* in action:—Hig hine mid ealre smyltnesse swâ gelǣddon and on heora fiđerum bǣron, đæt hê ne mihte ne on scipe fægeror gefered beón, Guthl. 5; Gdwin. 40, 16, 14. II. *quiet, silence*:—Smyltnisse gesette *silentium inposuisset*, Mt. Kmbl. Lind. 22, 34. III. *placidity, calmness*:—Cara *cura*, oferfǣt *obesus*, smyltnys *pinguedo* (placidity?), Wrt. Voc. i. 51, 11. IV. *peace, tranquillity, quiet*:—Smyltnes wæs ofor eorþan and sibba genihtsumnes, Blickl. Homl. 115, 9. Þurh đæt wierđ tôslieten sió stilnes hiera hiéremonna môdes and biþ gedrêfed sió smyltnes hiera lîfes *eo subditorum vitam dissipata quietis tranquillitate confundunt*, Past. 40, 1; Swt. 289, 8. Anweald on sibbe smyltnesse gehealdan, Lchdm. iii. 436, 13. Swefn smyltnysse and glædnysse gehâtaþ, 156, 14. Tîdlîc smyltnisse girǣce and lîf gibrenga êce *temporalem tranquilitatem tribuat et vitam conferat sempiternam*, Rtl. 31, 28. V. *calmness, composure*:—Đý læs đa smyltnesse đæs dômes gewemme tô hræd ierre, Past. 13; Swt. 79, 13.

smyréls, smyrian, smyring, smytta. v. smirels, smirwan, smirwung, smitta.

snaca, an; *m.*: snacu (?), e; *f. A reptile, a snake*:—Snaca *coluber*, Wrt. Voc. i. 78, 56: 287, 30: ii. 16, 75: Ælfc. Gr. 8; Zup. 27, 7. Sý Dan snaca on wege *fiat Dan coluber in via*, Wulfst. 192, 20. Snace *colubro*, Hpt. Gl. 409, 72. Gif đû gesihst snacan ongeán đê cuman, ongeán yfele wýfmen đê bewerian mynegaþ, Lchdm. iii. 214, 9. Snacan *colubros*, Wrt. Voc. ii. 21, 37: *scorpiones*, Lk. Skt. 10, 19. [*O. Du.* snake: *Icel.* snâkr (*only in poetry*).] v. ban-snaca.

snacc, e; *f.* (?) *A swift-sailing vessel*:—Đâ lêt Eádweard cyng scypian xl snacca, Chr. 1052; Erl. 182, 36. Hê fôr tô Scotlande mid xii snaccum, 1066; Erl. 201, 8. [(Borrowed from?) *Icel.* snekkja *a swift-sailing vessel*, belonging to the kind of 'lang-skip:' *Dan.* snekke *a bark, sailing vessel.*]

snǣd, es; *m.* '*A piece of land within defined limits, but without enclosures, a limited circumscribed woodland or pasturage*,' Leo, Anglo-Saxon Names of Places, pp. 68–9. Or (?) *a clearing* in a wood. Cf. snǣdan, II:—Ic hire lête tô đæt ceorla grâf tôsundran . . . and se alhmunding snǣd hêre intô preosda byrig, Cod. Dip. Kmbl. ii. 100, 16. Be đam grâue đæt hit cymþ intô đam snǣde; and of đam snǣde, iii. 399, 34. Đet firhde bituihu longanleág and đem sudtûne and đa snâdas illuc pertinentia, i. 261, 10. Tô Ôswaldingtûne hiérþ holenhyrst . . . cyrþringhyrst, triphyrst, and insnādis(-as?) intō Ōswaldingtūne, ii. 228, 4. *Also* snǣdfeld occurs iii. 399, 20:—On ðone lytlan snǣdfeld; *and* snādhyrst, i. 273, 6.

snǣd, es; *m. The handle of a scythe.* Under the forms *snathe, sneath, snead, sned* the word occurs in the glossaries of many dialects, e. g. Wilts, Somerset, Northamptonshire. Jamieson also gives it. v. E. D. S. Pub. Gloss. B. 15, 16, 19, C. 4:—Hwīlon befeóll ān sīðe of ðam snǣde intō ānum deópan seáðe. Benedictus heóld ðone snǣd bufon ðam wætere ðǣr ðæt īsen āsanc, and ðǣrrihte hit becom swymmende tō ðam snǣde, Homl. Th. ii. 162, 10–14.

snǣd, e; *f. A cut, slice, morsel, bit:*—Snǣd *offa*, Wrt. Voc. i. 82, 73: *morsus*, ii. 58, 12. Spices snǣd *offella* vel *particula*, i. 27, 19. Seó snǣd ðæs hūsles ðe heó þicgan sceolde, Homl. Th. ii. 272, 26: Salm. Kmbl. 809; Sal. 404. Hē began tō etenne; hē feóll ðā æt ðære forman snǣde, Homl. Skt. i. 12, 62. Ða sweartan snǣd *atram offam*, Wrt. Voc. ii. 90, 23: 63, 14. Genim spices snǣde þynne, lege on hātne stān, Lchdm. ii. 58, 16. Heorotes horn gebærned tō ahsan ... and mid hunige gewealcen tō snǣdum, 238, 2. Genim þreó snǣda, 52, 23. Genim fǣttes flǣsces, sele twā snǣda, 268, 31. Nim of ðam gehālgedan hlāfe feówer snǣda, iii. 290, 27. Ðās sweartan snǣda *atras offulas*, Wrt. Voc. ii. 84, 40. Swā swā snǣda *sicut buccellas*, Ps. Spl. 147, 6. Snǣda *offulas, partes*, Hpt. Gl. 500, 78. [*Icel.* sneið *a slice.*] v. sin-snǣd.

snǣdan; *p.* de. I. *to slice, cut into slices:*—On hunig gesnǣd, Lchdm. ii. 294, 9. II. *to snathe* [given by Halliwell as a northern word = *to prune trees*, and occurs in Ray's collection, E. D. S. Pub. Gloss. B. 15. Jamieson gives *sned* to prune, lop off, *sned* a branch pruned off.] *to lop, prune, cut* branches off trees:—Snēdit *putat*, Txts. 117, 249. Sume snēddun telgran of treówum *alii caedebant ramos de arboribus*, Mt. Kmbl. Rush. 21, 8. Hit biþ unnyt ðæt mon hwelces yfles bōgas snǣde būton mon wille ða wyrtruman forceorfan ðæs staðoles *incassum foras nequitia ex ramis inciditur, si surrectura multiplicius intus in radice servatur*, Past. 33, 5; Swt. 222, 15. III. *to hew* or *trim* stones. [In this sense Jamieson gives *sned* as a word of northern Scotland.]:—Ðara werhtena ðe ðanæ stān sneóddon and fēgdon, Anglia xi. 5, 7. [Þe moder mid sexe hine tosnæde & al todælde, Laym. 4015. Þa quene ich al tosnaðde mid mine sweorede, 28050. *O. H. Ger.* gi-sneitōn *putare: Icel.* sneiða *to cut into slices.*] v. be-snǣdan; snīðan.

snǣdan; *p.* de *To take food, take a meal:*—Ðā hē com to Cantwarbyrig, ðā snǣdde hē ðǣr and his menn, and tō Dofran gewende, Chr. 1048; Erl. 177, 31. [*Icel.* snæða *to take a meal;* snæði *a meal;* snāð *food, meat.*] v. snǣding.

snǣdel, (*more generally*) snǣdelþearm, es; *m. The great gut:*—Snaedil *vel* þearm, snaedilþearm, snēdildaerm *extale*, Txts. 58, 381. Snǣdel, Wrt. Voc. i. 286, 59. Snǣdel(-?) *vel* bæc-þearm *extales*, 44, 48. Snǣdelþearm *extale*, ii. 29, 74: 145, 29: *fither*, 149, 1: *fiber*, 38, 54. Snǣdelþearm *fithrem*, Lchdm. i. lxxii, 5.

snǣding, e; *f. A (slight?) meal:*—Seó wucaþēn nime snǣdinge (*mixtum*, = déjeûner, consistant en un verre de vin et un peu de pain, Migne. Cf. the translation of the passage, R. Ben. 63, 1:—Ðære wucan rǣdere gange tō hlāfe and drince) ǣr ðan ðe hē āginne rǣdan, R. Ben. Interl. 70, 4. [*Icel.* snæðing *a meal.*] v. snǣdan *to take food, and next two words.*

snǣding-hūs, es; *n. An eating-house, a place where cooked meat is sold:*—Snǣdinghūs *popina*, Wrt. Voc. i. 58, 21.

snǣding-sceáp, es; *n. A sheep to be killed for eating:*—Hȳ teohhiaþ ūs him tō snǣdincgsceápum *aestimati sumus ut oves occisionis*, Ps. Th. 43, 23.

snǣd-mǣlum; *adv. By bits, a bit at a time:*—Pusla snǣdmǣlum *pick them out by a bit at a time*, Lchdm. ii. 356, 13.

snæegel, snǣs. v. snegel, snās.

snǣsan; *p.* de *To spit, run through with a pointed implement* or *weapon:*—Gif mon hafaþ spere ofer eaxle and hine mon on āsnāseþ (āsnǣseþ, MS. H., snǣseþ, MS. B.), gielde ðone wer būtan wīte; gif beforan eágum āsnāse (āsnǣse, MS. H.) gielde ðone wer, L. Alf. pol. 36; Th. i. 84, 13. [Þe deoflen schulen mid helle sweordes al snesien (snesen, MS. C.: sneasin, MS. T.) ham þuruhut, A. R. 212, 22. *Icel.* sneisa *to spit.*] v. snās.

snǣd-feld. v. snǣd; *m.*

snās, snǣs, e; *f. A spit, skewer:*—Snaas *veru*, Txts. 115, 144. Ān snǣs fisca oððe ōðra þinga *una serta;* a number of fish or other things run on to a stick, Wrt. Voc. i. 64, 9. Snāsum *veribus*, ii. 91, 37: *feribus*, 148, 7. [*Icel.* sneis; *f. a skewer: Dan.* snes *a score.*] v. snǣsan.

snāð, es; *m.* (?) *A killing:*—Snāðes *occisionis*, Hpt. Gl. 478, 45.

snāw, es; *m. Snow:*—Snāw *nix*, Wrt. Voc. i. 52, 47. Swā hwīte swā snāw (snā, Lind.: snāu, Rush.), Mt. Kmbl. 28, 3. Snāuw, Shrn. 50, 15. Snāua *nix*, Mk. Skt. Lind. 9, 3. Snāw cymþ of ðam þynnum wǣtan ðe byþ up ātogen mid ðære lyfte, and byþ gefroren ǣr ðan hē tō dropum geurnen sȳ, and swā semtinges fylþ, Lchdm. iii. 278, 23. Ðǣr (*in Ireland*) seldon snāu leng ligeþ ðonne þrȳ dagas, Bd. 1, 1; S. 474, 31. Micle rēnas and snāwas, Bt. 23; Fox 78, 28. Hæglas and snāwas, 39, 13; Fox 234, 16. Forstas and snāwas, Cd. Th. 239, 31; Dan. 378. Snāwum *nivibus*, Wrt. Voc. ii. 61, 45. [*Goth.* snaiws: *O. Sax.* snēu: *O. H. Ger.* snēo: *Icel.* snjór.]

snāw-ceald; *adj. Cold as snow:*—Ðæt sió fȳrene (ne) mōt sunne gesēcan snāwcealdes weg monna (*but read* (?) mōnan. Cf. Bt. 39, 13; Fox 232, 28) gemǣro, Met. 29, 8.

snāw-gebland, es; *n. A snow-storm:*—Fōr Hannibal ofer Bardan ðone beorg, þēh ðe ymb ðone tiéman wǣren swā micel snāwgebland swā ðætte ǣgðer ge ðara horsa fela forwurdon ge ða elpendas ealle būton ānum ge ða men selfe uneáðe ðone ciele genǣson *Annibal, cum in Etruriam transiret, in summo Apennino tempestate correptus, nivibus conclusus obriguit; ubi magnus hominum numerus, jumenta complurima, elephanti pene omnes frigoris acerbitate perierunt*, Ors. 4, 8; Swt. 186, 34.

snāw-hwīt; *adj. Snow-white:*—Snāwhwīt *niveus*, Wrt. Voc. i. 52, 48. Snāwītre clǣnnysse *nivei pudoris*, Hymn. Surt. 104, 17. Mid snāwhwītum hreóflan beslagen, Homl. Th. i. 400, 29. Sittende on snāwhwītum horse, ii. 134, 27. Snāwhwītne hlāf, Homl. Skt. i. 2, 405: 18, 164. [*Icel.* snjó-hwītr.]

snāwig; *adj. Snowy.* v. next word.

snāwlīc; *adj. Snowy:*—Snāwlīc *nivalis*, Wrt. Voc. i. 52, 49. Se feórða heáfodwind hātte *septemtrio:* se blǣwþ norðan and cealde and snāwlīc (snāwig, MS. L.), Lchdm. iii. 274, 23. [*O. H. Ger.* snē-līh *ninguidus: Icel.* snjó-ligr.]

snearu, an; *f. A snare, noose:*—Snearan *tendiculam, decipulam, laqueum quod tenditur leporibus* ɫ *avibus*, Hpt. Gl. 429, 17. [*Icel.* snara *a snare:* cf. *O. L. Ger.* snari; *n. fidis, fidicula.*] v. snēr.

snegel, snægel, snegl, snēl, snǣl, es; *m. A snail:*—Snegl, snēl *limax*, Txts. 75, 1220. Snegel, Wrt. Voc. i. 78, 63. Snægl, 24, 4: ii. 51, 4. Snegel se ðe hæfþ hūs *testudo*, i. 78, 64. Snegl, snægl, snægel, Ælfc. Gr. 9, 3; Zup. 37, 8. Gehūsed snægl, Wrt. Voc. i. 24, 5. Snegl, snægl *marruca*, Txts. 77, 1283: Wrt. Voc. ii. 55, 50: *coclea*, 22, 3. Snægl *cuniculus*, 137, 34. Lytle sneglas *cocleae*, 104, 61. Snæglas, 135, 45. Mē is snægl swiftra, Exon. Th. 426, 7; Rä. 41, 70. Ðone blacan snegl āwæsc on hāligwætre, sele drincan, Lchdm. ii. 110, 14. Blace sneglas on pannan gehyrste, 144, 2. [*Icel.* snigill: *Dan.* snegl.] v. sǣ-snægl.

snell, snel; *adj. Quick, active, strong.* I. in following glosses:—Snel *alacris*, Wrt. Voc. ii. 99, 75: 6, 50: *expeditus, velox, fortis*, 30, 17: *explicitus, liber, efficatus*, 145, 35. Snellne *adultum*, Hpt. Gl. 485, 25. II. of rapid movement, *quick, rapid, swift:*—Sum biþ on londe snel, fēþe spēdig, Exon. Th. 296, 17; Crä. 52. Fareþ feþrum snell, 206, 7; Ph. 123. Snel, 208, 29; Ph. 163. Hē is snel and swift and swīðe leóht *est levis et velox*, 220, 8; Ph. 317. Wæterþissa snel, 182, 2; Gū. 1304: Andr. Kmbl. 1009; An. 505. Snelle *veloces*, Ps. Spl. T. 13, 6. Fērend snelle *swift emissaries*, Exon. Th. 246, 12; Jul. 60. Se wæs mid his dǣdum snelra ðonne hē mægnes hæfde *celeritate magis quam virtute fretus*, Ors. 2, 5; Swt. 78, 27. Mē is snægl swiftra, snelra regnwyrm, Exon. Th. 426, 8; Rä. 41, 70. III. *active, prompt, ready, quick in action, bold.* [*Snell* is given in Jamieson's Dictionary with the meanings, *keen, severe; sharp* (of the air); *acute* (of the mind); *firm, determined.* Also in Cumberland it is used of the wind]:—Se snella sunu Wonrēdes, Beo. Th. 5934; B. 2971. Mē sendon tō ðē sǣmen snelle, Byrht. Th. 132, 41; By. 29: Cd. Th. 191, 26; Exod. 220: Exon. Th. 296, 25; Crä. 56. Snellra werod, cēnra *the band of the bold and the brave*, Judth. Thw. 24, 21; Jud. 199. [Snel (strong, 2nd MS.) cniht wes Carric, Laym. 28860. *O. Sax.* snell *bold, active: O. H. Ger.* snell *alacer, acer, agilis, strenuus, robustus, pernix: Icel.* snjallr *valiant, brave; ready of speech, eloquent.*] v. swīð-snell.

snel-līc; *adj.* I. *moving rapidly, swift:*—Snellīc sǣmearh, Andr. Kmbl. 533; An. 267. II. *quick in action, ready, bold:*—Monig snellīc sǣrinc, Beo. Th. 1384; B. 690. [*M. H. Ger.* snellec *strenuus.*]

snellīce; *adv. Rapidly, quickly, with activity:*—Sum sceal snellīce snēre wrǣstan *one rapidly bends the harpstrings*, Exon. Th. 332, 9; Vy. 82. [*O. H. Ger.* snellīcho *strenue.*]

snelness, e; *f. Quickness, readiness, activity, agility:*—Hē slōh swā hē hine (*the ball*) nǣfre feallan ne lēt. Se cyngc ðā oncneów ðæs iungan snelnesse, ðæt hē wiste ðæt hē næfde his gelīcan on ðam plegan, Ap. Th. 13, 7.

sneóme, snióme; *adv.* I. *swiftly, rapidly:*—His word yrneþ wundrum snióme *velociter currit sermo ejus*, Ps. Th. 147, 4. II. *quickly, immediately, at once:*—Hēt ōfstlīce up āstandan ... sneóme of slǣpe ðæm fæstan, Andr. Kmbl. 1589; An. 796: Exon. Th. 55, 27; Cri. 890. Hī semninga sneóme forwurdon *subito defecerunt*, Ps. Th. 72, 15: 106, 13. Snióme, 74, 7: 103, 33; 123, 2. Swā heó sǣ geseah, hē hió snióme fleáh, 113, 3. Sniómor, Cd. Th. 51, 21; Gen. 830. [*O. Sax.* sniumo: *O. H. Ger.* sniumo *velociter, cito, subito, statim;* sniumor, *citius:* cf. *Goth.* sniumundō *quickly;* sniumjan *to hasten.*]

sneorcan; *p.* snearc *To shrivel:*—Ic gesnerc swē swē deád from heortan *excidi tamquam mortuus a corde*, Ps. Surt. 30, 13. [Cf. Þte hude swartete as hit snarchte (*shrivelled with the heat*), Marh. 18, 14. Cf. (?) *Icel.* snerkja *to wrinkle the face in displeasure* (?): *Scott.* snirk *to draw up the nose in contempt* or *displeasure.*]

sneówan; *p.* sneáw (?), sneówde (?) *To proceed, go, come, hasten:*—On brim sneóweþ snel under segle, Andr. Kmbl. 1008; An. 504. Mid ǣrdæge eástan sneóweþ (snoweþ, MS.) wlitig and wynsum (*of the sun*), Exon. Th. 350, 12; Sch. 62. Ðā com beácna beorhtost (*the sun*) ofer breomo sneówan, Andr. Kmbl. 484; An. 242: 3333; An. 1670. [*Goth.* sniwan; *p.* snau, *pl.* snêwun *to go, come:* cf. (?) *Icel.* snöggr *sudden.*]

snér, e; *f. The string of a musical instrument:*—Snēr *fidis,* Txts. 115, 148. Gellende snēr, Exon. Th. 353, 40; Reim. 25. Snellīce snēre wrǽstan, 332, 9; Vy. 82. [*O.H.Ger.* snuor; *f. filum, lineolus:* cf. *Icel.* snœri; *n. a twisted rope: Goth.* snōrjō *a (twisted) basket.*] v. snearu.

snerian. v. snirian.

snícan; *p.* snāc, *pl.* snicon *To crawl, creep* (1) of the motion of a reptile:—[Sume wuhta] creópaþ and snīcaþ, eall līchoma eorþan getenge (cf. sume licgaþ mid eallon līchaman on eorþan and snīcende faraþ, Bt. 41, 6; Fox 254, 26), Met. 31, 6. Wyrm com snīcan, Lchdm. iii. 34, 21. On đīnum wambe and on đīnum breóstum đū scealt snīcan *pectore et ventre repes,* Past. 43, 2; Swt. 311, 1. Snīcan *serpere,* Txts. 180, 5. Đǽr (*in Ireland*) monn ǽnigne snīcendne wyrm ne gesihþ *nullum ibi reptile videri soleat,* Bd. 1, 1; S. 474, 33. Snīcende *reptilia,* Ps. Surt. 103, 25. Đa creópendan and đa snīcendan (scnīcendan, Hatt. MS.), Past. 21, 3; Swt. 154, 18. (2) fig. of imperceptible movement:—Đa wunde snīcaþ (*irrepunt*) in đa innođas mīnes līchoman, Bd. 5, 13; S. 633, 18. [Sniked in and ut neddren, O. E. Homl. i. 251, 16. *Dan.* snige *to sneak:* cf. *Icel.* snīkja (*wk.*) *to hanker after.*]

snid, snide, es; *m. A saw:*—Saga *vel* snide *serula,* Wrt. Voc. i. 16, 17. Snid *serra,* 85, 1. Hié wǽron snidene mid snide *secti sunt,* Past. 30; Swt. 205, 13.

snid, es; *n. A slice, cut:*—Đæt snid *copus,* Wrt. Voc. ii. 21, 59. [*Icel.* sniđ; *n. a slice:* cf. *O. H. Ger.* snita; *f. buccella.*] v. ge-snid.

snide, es; *m.* I. *a cut, incision:*—Đa wunde đæs snides *vulnus incisurae,* Bd. 4, 19; S. 589, 17. Gif đū wille on snide blōd forlǽtan *if you wish to let blood at an incision,* Lchdm. ii. 148, 10: 16, 5. II. *slaying.* v. snīđan, IV;—Swā swā scēp tō snide *tamquam ouis ad occisionem,* Engl. Stud. xiii. 27, 9. [*O.H.Ger.* snit *concisio, laceratio.*]

snid-ísen, es; *n. A lancet:*—Đonne đū ongite đæt geswel hnescige and swiþrige, đonne hrīn đū him mid snidīsene and snīđ listum, Lchdm. ii. 208, 16.

snirian, (snerian?), snyrian; *p.* ede *To go quickly, hasten:*—Brimwudu scynde, lagumearg snyrede tō hȳđe, Exon. Th. 182, 7; Gū. 1306. Snyredon ætsomne, Beo. Th. 809; B. 402. Gesión brecan ofer bæđweg brimwudu snyrgan, sǽmearh plegan, wadan wǽgflotan, Elen. Kmbl. 488; El. 244. [Cf. *Icel.* snarr *swift;* snara *to make a quick turn, step out quickly.*]

sniring *a sharp rock;*—Stānum ođđe snyringum *cautibus,* Wrt. Voc. ii. 18, 15.

snite, an; *f. A snite, snipe.* [Halliwell quotes: 'A snipe or snite, a bird lesse than a woodcocke,' Baret, 1580, and gives *snite* as a word still in use. See also E. D. S. Pub. Bird Names, p. 192.]:—Snīte *vel* wudecocc *aceta,* Wrt. Voc. i. 29, 52. Snīte *acegia,* 62, 23: ii. 4, 36: 99, 14. [In later glossaries *snyte* glosses *ibis,* i. 177, 29: 253, 1. *Prompt. Parv.* snype or snyte *ibex.*]

sníđan; *p.* snāđ, *pl.* snidon; *pp.* sniden. I. *to cut, make an incision in* anything:—Snāđ đæt īs đara hāligra līchoman, Shrn. 62, 1. Mec snāđ seaxes ecg, Exon. Th. 408, 2; Rä. 27, 6. II. *to cut* as a surgeon does, *to lance* or *to amputate:*—Mon snīđ đa bearneácnan wīf *secuerunt praegnantes,* Past. 48, 2; Swt. 367, 14. Gif đonne đæt worms up stīhþ tō đon đæt đē þince đæt hit mon snīþan mǽge and ūt forlǽtan . . . đonne hrīn đū him mid đȳ snidīsene and snīđ listum . . . đonne đū hit tōstinge ođđe snīþe, Lchdm. ii. 208, 11–21. Snīđ ođđe ceorf on đæt hāle and đæt cwice līc, 84, 28: 52, 2. Gōd lǽce đe wel cann wunda snīđan, Past. 49; Swt. 377, 18. Ic wēne đæt hē hiene snide slāwlīcor, gif hē him ǽr sǽde đæt hē hiene snīđan wolde . . . se lǽce, đonne hē cymþ đone untruman tō snīđanne, 26; Swt. 186, 2–7. II a. metaphorically:—Đæt mon mǽge snīþan and bærnan his unþeáwas *ut culpae morbos supplicio resecarent,* Bt. 38, 7; Fox 210, 3. III. *to cut* up or to pieces:—Đone ramm đū snīđst tō sticcon, Ex. 29, 17. Hié wǽron snidene mid snide *secti sunt,* Past. 30; Swt. 205, 13. IV. *to cut* so as to kill, *to slay* an animal (v. of-snīđan, snīđung, II):—Đæra ēwena meolc gē brucon and đa đe fǽtte wǽron gē snidon (*mactavistis*), L. Ecg. P. iii. 16; Th. ii. 202, 24. Đa ealdan sacerdas cealf snidon, Homl. Th. ii. 210, 19. God hēt niman ānes geáres lamb and snīđan on Eástertīde, 40, 11: 262, 29. V. *to cut* stone, *to hew:*—Đæra wyrhtena đe đæne stān snidon and fēgdon, Anglia xi. 4, 12. VI. *to cut* hair:—Wiđ heáfodece, hundes heáfod gebærn tō ahsan and snīđ đæt heáfod; lege on, Lchdm. ii. 20, 2. VII. *to cut* corn, *to reap:*—Đa on teárum sāwaþ, hī eft gefeán snīđaþ *in gaudio metent,* Ps. Th. 125, 5. [Tacc Ysaac þiŋ wennchell & sniþ itt alls itt wære an shep, Orm. 14666. *Goth.* sneiþan *to reap: O. Sax.* snīđan to *cut: O. Frs.* snītha: *O. H. Ger.* snīdan *secare, resecare, caedere, putare, dolere, attondere: Icel.* snīđa; *p.* sneiđ (*but* sniddi *also occurs*) *to cut, prune.*] v. ā-, be-, ge-, of-, tō-, ymb-snīđan; snǽdan.

sniđing. v. snīđung.

snid-streó[w] *carline thistle* (?):—Snīthstreó *gacila,* Txts. 35, 13. Snīđstreó, snīdstreó, snīdstreú *sisca, sista,* 97, 1868. Cf. Eoforþrote *scisca,* 35, 27: *scasa* ł *scapa* ł *sisca,* Lchdm. iii. 305, col. 1. In Spanish *sisca* is the cylindrical sugar-cane.

sniđung, e; *f.* I. *a cutting, cut* (v. snīđan, I):—Gif đa ōmihtan þing sȳn ūtan cumen of wundum ođđe of snīþingum ođđe of slegum, Lchdm. ii. 82, 22. II. *slaying, slaughtering* (v. snīđan, IV):—Offrung *sacrificium,* snīþung *mactatio,* Wrt. Voc. i. 28, 50. Snīđing, ii. 59, 10.

sníwan; *p.* de *To snow:*—Ic snīwe *ninguo,* Ælfc. Gr. 28, 5; Zup. 174, 8. Hit snīwþ *ningit,* 22; Zup. 128, 17. Snīuuith, snīuidh *ninguit,* Txts. 78, 669. Snīweþ, Wrt. Voc. ii. 60, 14. Đā cwom đǽr micel snāw and swā miclum snīwde swelce micel flȳs feoll, Nar. 23, 13. Norþan snīwde, Exon. Th. 307, 30; Seef. 31. Swā swā hit rīne and snīwe and styrme ūte, Bd. 2, 13; S. 516, 17. [*Chauc.* snewede; *p.: Mand.* snew; *p.,* and a similar form remains in dialects. *O. H. Ger.* snīwan: *Icel. has a strong form* snivinn; *pp.*] v. be-snīwod.

snóca, an; *m. A bend, bay* (?):—Of đære dīc on færscmærus westsnōcan; of đam snōcan on fūlan mære eástweardnæ *from the dike to the western bay of fresh mere; from the bay to the east side of the foul mere,* Cod. Dip. Kmbl. v. 344, 33. With some variations the same boundaries are given in a later charter:—De Elmede dych usque ad solemeres westsnok; de solemeres westnok usque ad Horehyrne, iii. 119, 29. [Cf. (?) *O. H. Ger.* snōh; *forestum, nomine* bracten snōh, Grff. vi. 839.]

snód, e; *f. A snood, fillet, head-dress:*—Snōd *cappa,* Wrt. Voc. ii. 103, 8: 13, 42: *capsa* (*cappa?*), 128, 34: *cinthium, mitra,* 131, 10: *vitta,* i, 16, 65: 26, 5. Đā lǽrde hī sum man, đæt heó nāme ǽnne wernægel of sumes oxan hricge, and becnytte tō ānum hringe mid hire snōde . . . Đā geseah heó licgan đone hring on đam wege mid snōde mid ealle . . . Đā wēnde heó đæt se hring tōburste, ođđe seó snōd tōslupe, ac đā đā heó āfunde . . . đa snōde mid eallum cnottum fæste gewriđen . . ., Homl. Th. ii. 28, 16–26. Snōda *vittarum,* Hpt. Gl. 526, 57. Wæs đæm deóre se hrycg ācæglod swelce snōda (snide?) *belua serrato tergo,* Nar. 20, 27.

snofl *mucus, snivel:*—Wiđ langum sāre đæs heáfdes þurh horh ođđe þurh snofl, Lchdm. ii. 24, 4. v. next word.

snoflig; *adj. Full of snivel, having a cold in the head:*—Hiemps ys winter, hē byþ ceald and wǽt . . . Swā byþ se ealda man ceald and snoflig; *flegmata,* đæt byþ hraca ođđe geposu, deriaþ đam ealdan and đam unhālan, Anglia viii. 299, 36.

snoru, e; *f. A daughter-in-law:*—Snorp *nurus,* Wrt. Voc. ii. 115, 3: 83, 83. Snoru, 73, 52: 60, 49: i. 52, 10. Snoru, snora, Ælfc. Gr. 11; Zup. 79, 18. Swegr on hyre snore and snoru on hyre swegere, Lk. Skt. 12, 53. Sca Maria is Godfæder snoru and Godes suna mōdur and hāligra sāuwla sweger, Shrn. 118, 6. Hió genom hiere snore, Alexandres lāfe, Ors. 3, 11; Swt. 148, 18. [*O. Frs.* snore: *O. H. Ger.* snura: *Icel.* snor.]

snot *mucus from the nose, snot* [*found in the compound* ge-snot:—Wiđ gesnote and geposum, Lchdm. ii. 54, 17. *O. Frs.* snotte: *M. H. Ger.* snuz: *Dan.* snot]. v. snȳtan.

Snotinga-hám *Nottingham:*—Hēr fōr se ilca here innan Mierce tō Snotengahām (Snotinghām, MS. E.), Chr. 868; Erl. 72, 21. Fōr hē tō Snotingahām and gefōr đa burg and hēt hié gebētan and gesettan ǽgđer ge mid Engliscum mannum ge mid Deniscum, 922; Erl. 108, 30. Hēr Eádmund cyning Myrce geeode, burga fīfe, . . . Snotingahām . . ., 942; Erl. 116, 13.

Snotingaham-scír, e; *f. Nottinghamshire,* Chr. 1016; Erl. 154, 8.

snotor, snottor (-er, -ur); *adj. Prudent, wise, sagacious:*—Snotor *prudens,* Wrt. Voc. i. 47, 35. Snoter, 76, 12. Cwom Daniel tō dōme, se wæs snotor, Cd. Th. 225, 8; Dan. 151. Nis nǽnig swā snotor . . . ne đæs swā gleáw, nymþe God seolfa, 286, 8; Sat. 349. Ā sceal snotor hycgean ymb đysse woruld gewinn, Menol. Fox 570; Gn. C. 54: Beo. Th. 1656; B. 826. Snotur, Ps. Th. 118, 23. Đæs snottor in sefan đæt hē āna mǽge ealle gerīman stānas on eorđan, Cd. Th. 205, 19; Exod. 438. Frōd wita, snottor ār, Exon. Th. 313, 18; Mōd. 2. Swā cwæđ snottor on mōde, gesæt him sundor æt rūne, 293, 4; Wand. 111. Rǽdum snottor, wīs on gewitte, Andr. Kmbl. 938; An. 469. Se wītga snottor searuþancum, Elen. Kmbl. 2377; El. 1190. Se snotera, Beo. Th. 2631; B. 1313. Snotra, 6231; B. 3120. Snottra, 3577; B. 1786. Salomon se snottra, Past. 4; Swt. 37, 16. Seó snotere mægđ, Judth. Thw. 23, 17; Jud. 125. Snottrum men snǽd ōđglīdeþ, Salm. Kmbl. 803; Sal. 401. Hāligne wer and snotorne *virum sanctum et sapientem,* Bd. 3, 23; S. 554, 9. Đū mē snoterne gedydest *prudentem me fecisti,* Ps. Th. 118, 98. Đone snoteran Salomon, Ælfc. T. Grn. 7, 28. Mīn sōđfæste snotere bīdaþ *me expectaverunt justi,* Ps. Th. 141, 9. Snotre men, 57, 4. Snotre *urbana,* Hpt. Gl. 481, 40. Snottere selerǽdend, Andr. Kmbl. 1317; An. 659. Snottre and unwīse, Blickl. Homl. 107, 11. Snottre ceorlas, Beo. Th. 3187; B. 1591. Hwylc is wīsra, wel snotera, Ps. Th. 106, 42. Engla werod snotra, Hy. 3, 16. Snoterra mon, Salm. Kmbl. 502; Sal. 251. Gomol snoterost, fyrngeárum frōd, Menol. Fox 482; Gn. C. 11. Đū oferswīþdest đone snotrestan helwerena cyning, Exon. Th. 275, 1; Jul. 543. Burgsittendum đām snoterestum, Elen. Kmbl. 553; El. 277. Đa đe hē wīseste and snotereste wiste *quos sapientiores noverat,* Bd. 2, 9; S. 512, 11. [Þet folc biđ iseli þurh snoterne biscop, O. E. Homl. i. 117, 19. Uþwitess unndersstodenn þurrh snoterr gyn, Orm. 7087. *Goth.* snutrs: *O. H. Ger.* snot[t]ar *prudens: Icel.* snotr.] v. fore-, forþ-, gearo-, hyge-, mōd-, rǽd-, þanc-, un-, word-, woruld-snotor; snytre.

snotor-líc; *adj. Wise, prudent, philosophical:*—On snoterlīcum lārum *in philosophicis dogmatibus,* Hpt. Gl. 459, 63. [*Icel.* snotr-ligr.]

snotorlîce; *adv. Wisely, prudently, philosophically*:—Snotorlîce *sapienter*, Ps. Lamb. 46, 8. Snotorlîce (snotur-, Rush.) ł wîslîce *sapienter*, Mk. Skt. Lind. 12, 34. Uton ðâs þing geþencean swîþe snotorlîce & wîslîce, Blickl. Homl. 97, 1. Snotorlîce *academice*, Wrt. Voc. i. 61, 27. Ne hŷrde ic snotorlîcor guman þingian, Beo. Th. 3689; B. 1842. [*O.H.Ger.* snotarlîhho: *Icel.* snotr-liga.] v. un-snotorlîce.

snotorness, e; *f. Prudence, wisdom, sagacity*:—*Prudentia*, ðæt ys snoternys, Wulfst. 247, 15: Homl. Skt. i. 1, 157. Hî (*the innocents*) wǽron gehwǽde and ungewittige âcwealde, ac hî ârîsaþ on ðam gemǽnelîcum dôme mid fullum wæstme and heofenlîcere snoternysse, Homl. Th. i. 84, 23. Snotornesse ł wîsdôm *sapientiam*, Ps. Lamb. 48, 4. Salomon gesette þreó bêc þurh his snoternesse, Ælfc. T. Grn. 7, 36.

snotorung. v. word-snotorung.

snotor-wyrde; *adj. Prudent* or *wise of speech*:—Herodes wearð gewrêged tô ðam câsere . . . hê wæs snotorwyrde tô ðan swîðe, ðæt se câsere hine mid mâran wurðmynte ongeán âsende, Homl. Th. i. 80, 9. Sum man wæs gehâten Mercurius on lîfe, se wæs swŷðe fâcenfull and ðeáh full snotorwyrde, Wulfst. 107, 1.

snûd *swiftness, quickness*:—Ûs bær naca, snellîc sǽmearh, snûde bewunden (*possessed by swiftness*), Andr. Kmbl. 534; An. 267.

snûd; *adj. Coming at once, coming soon* or *suddenly*:—Biþ ǽghwylcum synwyrcendra on ða snûdan tîd (*the day of judgment, which was to come suddenly*, cf. Matt. 24, 39; or *to come soon?*), Exon. Th. 52, 32; Cri. 842. v. next word.

snûde; *adv. At once, quickly, directly*:—Snûde *denuo*, Jn. Skt. Lind. Rush. 3, 3. Gangaþ snûde *go directly*, Elen. Kmbl. 625; El. 313: 307; El. 154. Hêt hine snûde eft cuman *bade him quickly return*, Beo. Th. 3743; B. 1869. Se wyrm gebeáh snûde tôsomne, 5129; B. 2568. Snûde forsended, 1812; B. 904: Exon. 231, 12; Ph. 488: Judth. Thw. 22, 8; Jud. 55: 23, 17; Jud. 125. Wearþ snellra werod snûde gegearewod, 24, 21; Jud. 199. Mec Dryhten hêt snûde gesecgan, Exon. Th. 144, 10; Gû. 676. Snûde cŷðan, 19, 7; Cri. 297: Elen. Kmbl. 890; El. 446: 3947; B. 1971: 4639; B. 2325. Ic snûde gefrægn, 5497; B. 2752. [Cf. *Icel.* ganga snúðigt *to walk fast*.]

snyrian, snyring. v. snirian, sniring.

[**snŷtan** *to clear the nose*. (*Prompt. Parv.* snytyn a nese or a candyl *emungo, mungo*. *Snite, snyte* in this sense remains in several dialects. *O.H.Ger.* snûzan *emungere, nasum purgare*: *Icel.* snýta.) v. snŷting, snot.]

snyðian *to go* as a dog with its nose to the ground (?):—Neb is mîn niþerweard . . . ic snyþige forð (*it is a plough that speaks*), Exon. Th. 403, 12; Rä. 22, 6. [*Icel.* snyðja *to go sniffing like a dog*, but applied also to the going of ships, and other things.]

-snyðian. v. be-snyðian.

snŷting, e; *f. A clearing of the nose, sneezing*:—Snŷtingc *vel* fneósung *sternutatio* vel *sternutamentum*, Wrt. Voc. i. 46, 20. [*Prompt. Parv.* snytynge of a nose or candyl *munctura, emunctura*.] v. snŷtan.

snytre; *adj. Wise*:—Se ðe sigor seleþ snytrum mihtum, and ðîn môd trymeþ godcundum gifum, Cd. Th. 170, 6; Gen. 2808. v. snotor.

snytrian; *p.* ode *To be* or *to become wise*:—Hwæt is se dumba, se ðe swîðe snyttraþ, hafaþ seofon tungan, hafaþ tungena gehwylc .xx. orda, hafaþ orda gehwylc engles snytro, Salm. Kmbl. 459; Sal. 230. Snytrian *philosophari*, Hpt. Gl. 527, 63.

snytro, snyttro, snytero(u); *indecl. in sing.; pl. is used with the same force as sing.; f. Prudence, wisdom, sagacity*:—Snytru *sapientia*, Mk. Skt. Lind. Rush. 6, 2. Hwǽr com heora snyttro *what has become of their wisdom?* Blickl. Homl. 99, 31. Wera snytero, Cd. Th. 295, 25; Sat. 492. Se þurh snytro spêd smiðcræftega wæs, 66, 14; Gen. 1084. Ic eom gewis ðînra mægena and snytro, Lchdm. i. 326, 4. Snyttro, Elen. Kmbl. 586; El. 293. Hié ðære snytro gelŷfdon, Cd. Th. 217, 25; Dan. 28. Full mid snyttro (snytrum, Rush.) *plenus sapientia*, Lk. Skt. Lind. 2, 40. Ealle ðû mid snyteru worhtest *omnia in sapientia fecisti*, Ps. Th. 103, 23. Wîsdôm ł snytro *sapientiam*, Ps. Spl. 18, 8. Ic ðê gelǽrde swelce snytro swylce manegum ieldran gewittum oftogen is, Bt. 8; Fox 24, 28. Snyttro, 7, 3; Fox 20, 11. Þurh his godcunde meht and þurh his êcean snyttro, Blickl. Homl. 121, 16. Tô hêraune snytro (snyttro, Rush.) Salomones, Mt. Kmbl. 12, 42. Þurh sefan snyttro, Past. pref.; Swt. 9, 10: Exon. Th. 28, 5; Cri. 442. Beoran on breóstum sibbe and snytero, Cd. Th. 277, 19; Sat. 207. Ealle heora snytru beóþ forglendred *omnis sapientia eorum devorata est*, Ps. Th. 106, 26. Spræc sunu Arones snytra gemyndig, Cd. Th. 148, 28; Gen. 2463. Snyttra, Exon. Th. 304, 30; Fä. 78. Þurh snyttra cræft, Andr. Kmbl. 1261; An. 631. Ðara ðe geóce tô him sêceþ mid snytrum, 2307; An. 1155. On snytrum *in sapientia*, Ps. Th. 89, 14. Mid môdes snyttrum, Beo. Th. 3416; B. 1706. Snyttrum *wisely, prudently*, Andr. Kmbl. 1292; An. 646. Ðeáh ânra gehwylc hæbbe ða .xii. snyttro Habrahames and Isaces and Iacobes, Salm. Kmbl. 150, 2. Þurh ða snyttra (snyttro, MS. O.) ðe ic fram ðam sôþan Gode onfêng *per sapientiam mihi a Deo vero donatam*, Bd. 2, 13; S. 517, 3. Paulus ðæt lof Gode betǽhte ðe him snytera (snytra, MS. F.) and wîsdôm sealde, R. Ben. 4, 6. [*Goth.* snutrei.] v. ge-, un-snytro.

snytro-cræft (*or* snytro (*gen.*) cræft, cf. þurh snyttra cræft, Andr. Kmbl. 1261; An. 631), es; *m. Prudent skill, prudence, wisdom*:—Wundra mǽst, ðæt swylc snyttrocræft ǽnges hæleþa hreþer weardade, Exon. Th. 169, 28; Gû. 1101. Se mæg eal secgan, ðam biþ snyttrucræft bifolen on ferhðe, 42, 4; Cri. 667: 239, 18; Ph. 622. Sefan sîdne geþanc and snytrocræft, Cd. Th. 249, 27; Dan. 536. Daniel gespræc þurh snyttrocræft, 253, 14; Dan. 595. Ða ðe fyrngewritu þurh snyttrocræft sêlest cunnen, Elen. Kmbl. 747; El. 374. Ða ðe snyttrocræft þurh fyrngewrito gefrigen hæfdon, 308; El. 154. Ðê God sealde sigespêd and snyttrocræft, 2342; El. 1172. Snyttrucræft, Exon. Th. 113, 10; Gû. 155. Nǽnig ðæs swîþe þurh snyttrucræft, 294, 21; Crä. 18. Ælmihtig eácenne gâst in sefan sende, snyttrocræftas, Cd. Th. 246, 29; Dan. 486.

snytro-hûs, es; *n. The house of wisdom*:—Hê ðâ swâ gelôme wiðsôc snytruhûse *repulit tabernaculum Silon*, Ps. Th. 77, 60.

soc, es; *n. Suck, sucking* at the breast:—On ðone dæg ðe man ðæt cild fram soce âteáh *in die ablactationis ejus*, Gen. 21, 8. [Seseȝ childer of her sok, A. P. 103, 391. Taken awei fro sok, or wenyd, Wick. (Isaiah 11, 8).] v. ge-soc.

socc, es; *m. A sock, kind of shoe*:—Socc *soccus*, Wrt. Voc. ii. 120, 70. Soccas *pedules* (cf. meó), R. Ben. Interl. 92, 1. [*O. H. Ger.* soc *soccus, caliga, calicula*: *Icel.* sokkr a *sock*. From Latin.]

sôchtha. v. sôhþa.

socian; *p.* ode I. *to soak* (trans.), *to steep in a liquid*:—Socodon *coquebant*, Germ. 399, 378. II. *to soak* (intrans.), *to lie in a liquid*:—Glædenan rinde lytelra gedô þreó pund on glæsfæt, gedô ðonne ðæs scearpestan wînes tô .v. sestras, âsete ðonne on hâte sunnan . . . ðæt hit socige .iiii. dagas oþþe mâ, Lchdm. ii. 252, 11. Dweorge dwostlan weorp on weallende wæter, lǽt socian on lange, 240, 7: iii. 14, 17. v. sûcan.

sôcn, e; *f.* I. *a seeking, search, exploring*. v. land-sôcn, sêcan, I. i. II. *a seeking, desiring, trying to get*. v. mete-sôcn, sêcan, I. 2. III. *a seeking* to obtain an end. v. hlâford-sôcn, sêcan, I. 3. IV. *a seeking* for information, *question, inquiry*. v. sêcan, I. 5:—Be monigum sôcnum and frignyssum ða ðe him nŷdþearflîce gesewen wǽron *de eis quae necessariae videbantur quaestionibus*, Bd. 1, 27; S. 488, 33. V. *a seeking, visiting* of a place, *attendance* at a place, *resort*. v. cyric-sôcn, sêcan, II. 2:—Wê ûre synna georne bêtan mid fæstene and mid ælmessan and mid ciriclîcere sôcne (*with going to church*), Wulfst. 134, 17. Ðâ tôwende se biscop ðæt weofod and ða dwollîcan sôcne mid ealle âdwæscte (*put an end to the resorting to the place, which had been supposed erroneously to be holy*), Homl. Th. ii. 508, 5. Ic cŷþe ðæt ic nelle sôcne habban tô mînum hîrêde ðone ðe mannes blôd geóte ǽr hê hæbbe godcunde bôte underfangen . . . *I declare that I will not that he who sheds man's blood have resort to my court before he have undertaken ecclesiastical 'bôt'* . . . , L. Edm. S. 4; Th. i. 248, 22. [Cf. From sôcne þes folkes *free from the resort of the people*, Laym. 2365. Sookne or custom of hauntynge *frequentacio, concursus*, Prompt. Parv. 463, col. 2. Gret soken hadde this meller With whete and malt of al the londe aboute, Chauc. Reeve's T. 67.] VI. *a seeking for protection* or *a place so sought, refuge, sanctuary, asylum*, (1) in a general sense:—Ic sêce sôcne *refugio*, of ðam is *refugium* sôcn, Ælfc. Gr. 28, 6; Zup. 179, 13–14. Ðǽr se freónd wunaþ on ðære sôcne ðe ic ða sibbe wið hine healdan wille, Exon. Th. 145, 1; Gû. 688. (2) as a technical term in reference to the protection afforded by a church or by the king's court, etc. v. ciric-, friþ-sôcn:—Gif hwilc þeóf oþþe reáfere gesôhte ðone cing oþþe hwylce cyrican and ðone biscop, hê hæbbe nigon nihta fyrst. And gif hê ealderman oþþe abbud oþþe þegen sêce, hæbbe þreora nihta fyrst. And gif hine hwâ lecge binnan ðæm fyrste, ðonne gebête hê ðæs mundbyrde ðe hê ǽr sôhte, oþþe hê hine twelfa sum lâdige, ðæt hê ða sôcne nyste. And sêce hê swylce sôcne swylce hê sêce, ðæt hê ne sŷ his feores wyrðe bûtan swâ feola nihta swâ wê hêr cwǽdon, L. Ath. iv. 4; Th. i. 224, 2. Be ciricena sôcnum. Gif hwâ ðara mynsterhâma hwelcne for hwelcre scylde gesêce ðe cyninges feorm tô belimpe oþþe ôðerne frióne hiérêd ðe ârwyrðe sié, âge hê þreora nihta fierst him tô gebeorganne, L. Alf. pol. 2; Th. i. 60, 22. Cf. Si fur qui furatus est postquam concilium fuit apud Ðunresfeld, vel furetur, nullo modo vita dignus habeatur, non per socnam, non per pecuniam, si per verum reveletur in eo, L. Ath. iii. 6; Th. i. 218, 30. VII. *a seeking* with hostile intent, *an attack*. v. hâm-sôcn, sêcan, III:—Ic ðære sôcne (*the hostility of Grendel*) singales wæg môdceare micle, Beo. Th. 3558; B. 1777. VIII. as a legal term, frequently in connection with *sacu*. Kemble says: 'Sôcn is *inquisitio*, the preliminary and initiative in Sacu, in other words the right of investigating, necessary to and a part of power of holding plea,' Cod. Dip. Kmbl. i. xlv. But from a Latin version of a charter it would seem that *sôcn* was the power of *seeking* or levying fines; the English 'Ic an heom ðæt hŷ habben saca and sôcna' is rendered by 'cedens ut habeant privilegium tenendi curiam ad causas cognoscendas et dirimendas lites inter vasallos et colonos suos ortas, cum potestate transgressores et calumniae reos mulctis afficiendi easque levandi,' iv. 202, 7. Other instances of the occurrence of the word, whose Latin form is often *soca*, are the following:—Ic habbe gegeofen . . . Ælfwine abbod saca and sôcna (*sacam et socam*, Lat.) . . . And ic wylle ðæt seó sôcne (*soca*, Lat.) wiðinnen Bichâmdîc licge intô Ramesêge on eallen þingen swâ full swâ ic heó mêseolf âhte . . . and se abbod and ða gebrôðra intô Ramsêge habben ða sôcne (*socam*) ofer heom

. . . And in ǽlcer[e] scíre ðǽr sanctus Benedictus hafþ land inne [habbe hē] his saca and his sōcne . . . swā hwylc man swā ða sōcne āhe, Sanctus Benedictus habbe his freódōm on eallen þingen, 208, 19–209, 14. Mōrtūn and eal seó sōcna ðe ðǽrtō hēreþ, vi. 148, 36. Ne gyrne ic ðīnes ne sace ne sōcne *I desire nothing of yours, neither your privileges nor your rights*, L. O. 14; Th. i. 184, 16. Cyninges þegenes heregeata ðe his sōcne hæbbe, L. C. S. 72; Th. i. 414, 16. Nān man nāge nāne sōcne ofer cynges þegen būton cyng sylf, L. Eth. iii. 11; Th. i. 296, 23. [Þe reue of Rotland sokene, Piers P. 2, 110. *Goth.* sōkns *quaestio*: *O. H. Ger.* sōhni *inquisitio*: *Icel.* sōkn *an attack;* as a law-term, *an action, prosecution; an assemblage of people* at church, etc.; *a parish* (*Dan.* sogn).] v. cyric-, friþ-, hām-, hlāford-, land-, mete-, scip-sōcn.

sod. v. ge-sod.

Sodoma, Sodome, an; *or indecl. The town of Sodom*:—Ða cininingas of Sodoman and Gomorran . . . on ðām burgum Sodoma and Gomorra, Gen. 14, 10, 11. Hē eardode on ðære byrig Sodoma, 13, 12. Hig eodon tō Sodoman weard, 18, 22. On ðære byrig Sodoman, 18, 26. On Sodoman weallsteápe burg, Cd. Th. 145, 6; Gen. 2401. Woldon Sodome burh werian, 119, 6; Gen. 1975.

Sodome; *pl. The people of Sodom*:—Hī lǽrdon hira synna swā swā Sodome dydon . . . Gif Sodome hira synna hǽlen, Past. 55; Swt. 427, 28. Sodoma lande (eorðe Sodominga, Rush.), Mt. Kmbl. 10, 15. On Sodomum (Sodomingum, Rush.), 11, 23.

Sodomingas. v. preceding word.

Sodomisc; *adj. Of Sodom*:—Sodomisc cynn, Cd. Th. 116, 12; Gen. 1935. *Used as a noun*, sodomita:—Sodomisce .vii. geár fæston *sodomitae .vii. annos jejunent*, L. Ecg. P. iv. 68, 5; Th. ii. 228, 16.

Sodomitisc; *adj. Of Sodom*:—Ða Sodomitiscan menn, Gen. 13, 13. Sodomitiscra cining, 14, 17: 18, 20.

Sodom-ware; *pl. The people of Sodom*:—Cōmon Sodomware, Cd. Th. 148, 4; Gen. 2451: 120, 18; Gen. 1996. Būton Sodomwarum ānum, Blickl. Homl. 79, 10.

sōfte (sōft?); *adj. Soft*:—Sōfte *suavis*, Ælfc. Gr. 9, 28; Zup. 54, 5. I. *soft* (of sleep), *quiet, undisturbed*:—Ic sōftum slǽpe mē gereste, Homl. Th. i. 566, 22. II. *soft, luxurious*:—Ne hē ne cume on wearmum bæðe ne on sōftum bedde, L. Ælfc. C. 11; Th. ii. 280, 22. On ðam sōftum baðe, Homl. Skt. i. 11, 231. III. *gentle, not harsh, not stern.* v. sōfte, III [:—He wæs swīðe gōd and sōfte man and dyde mycel tō gōde, Chr. 1114; Erl. 244, 38. Hē milde man was and sōfte and gōd, 1137; Erl. 261, 31.] v. sēfte.

sōfte; *cpve.* sōftor, sēft; *adv. Softly, gently*:—Sōfte *suaviter*, Ælfc. Gr. 38; Zup. 228, 6: *gradatim*, Wrt. Voc. ii. 41, 37: *pedetemtim*, 81, 39: *sensim*, 120, 41. Ðone sōfte langan *morosam*, 32, 6. I. of sleep, rest, etc., *softly, quietly, without disturbance*:—Hē sōfte swæf, Cd. Th. 12, 2; Gen. 179. Reste hē hine sōfte, Lchdm. ii. 292, 7: Ps. Th. 77, 65. II. *calmly, at ease, without trouble*:—Ðǽr mē sōfte byþ, ðǽr ic beó fægere beþeaht fiðerum ðīnum, Ps. Th. 60, 3. Hié sōfte ðæs bidon, Exon. Th. 10, 3; Cri. 146. Hī willniaþ manifeald earfoþe tō þrowianne, for ðam ðe hī willniaþ mǽran āre mid Gode tō habbanne, ðonne ða habbaþ ðe sōftor libbaþ, Bt. 39, 10; Fox 228, 17: Shrn. 163, 20. Ðæt ic ðȳ sēft mǽge mīn ālǽtan līf and leódscipe *that with mind the more at ease I may relinquish life and people*, Beo. Th. 5492; B. 2749. III. *gently, not harshly*:—Ðū sōfte wealdest gesceafta, Met. 20, 7. Ðū sōfte gedēst, ðæt hī ðē selfne gesión mōten, 20, 272. IV. *without discord*:—Gebunden gesiblīce sōfte tōgædere, Met. 20, 68. V. *easily, without opposition*:—Ne sceole gē swā sōfte sinc gegangan, ūs sceal ord and ecg ǽr gesēman, Byrht. Th. 133, 32; By. 59. [*O. Sax.* sāfto: *O. H. Ger.* samfto *facile.*] v. un-sōfte.

sōftness, e; *f. Softness, ease;* in a bad sense, *luxury, effeminacy*:—Heora fela wǽron mid olfendes hǽrum tō līce gescrȳdde, and ðǽr lāðode sōftnys, Homl. Th. ii. 506, 24. Mid sōftnysse and mid yfelum lustum, i. 270, 5: Homl. As. 15, 59. Ða ðe ðǽr (*in heaven*) singaþ ne swincaþ on ðam sange, ac mid sōftnysse būtan geswince hī heriaþ ðone Hǽlend, 43, 470. Sōftnysse *luxuriam*, Germ. 401, 19.

sogoþa, an; *m.* I. *hiccough, heartburn* (?):—Gyf men sȳ sogoþa getenge oððe hwylc innan-gundbryne . . . ðonne wēne ic ðæt hyt him wel fremie ge wið sogoðan ge wið ǽghwylcum incundum earfoðnyssum Lchdm. i. 196, 16–21. Of hōmena stieme and of wlætan cymþ eágna mist and sió scearpnes and sogoþa ðæt dēþ wið ðon is ðis tō dōnne *the acidity and heartburn* (?) *cause that against which this is to be done*, ii. 28, 1. Wið sogoþan and geohsan ðe of milte cymþ, 248, 1. Ne yrne he ðe læs hē mid ðæs rynes ēðgunge hwylcne wleattan and sogeðan on his heortan ne āstyrige *lest the running cause nausea or give him heartburn* (?): the Latin version has 'ut non scurilitas inveniat fomitem,' R. Ben. 68, 3. II. *gastric juice* (?):—Lǽcedōmas ðe gefōge sind ge heáfde ge heortan and wambe and blǽdran and sogeþan, Lchdm. ii. 166, 3. v. ælf-sogoþa, sūgan.

soht. v. suht.

sōhþa? Sochtha glosses *iota*, Wrt. Voc. ii. 112, 4. *The word is written* sohctha, 45, 72. *Somner suggests* ioctha.

sol *a sole* (?), 'a collar of wood, put round the neck of cattle to confine them to the stelch. "A bow about a beestes necke." Palsgrave.' Halliwell. '*Sole*, a rope or halter to tie cattle in the stall,' Kennett's Parochial Antiquities. Among 'husbandlie furniture' Tusser gives '*soles*, fetters, and shackles [cf. *however* sāl.]:—Sol *orbita*, Wrt. Voc. ii. 65, 6.

sol, es; *n.*: solu, we, e; *f. Mire* or *a miry place* [Halliwell gives *soul*, *sole* = a dirty pond, as a Kentish word]:—Sol *volutabrum*, Wrt. Voc. i. 37, 22. On grǽgsole burnan; andlang burnan on grǽgsole hagan, Cod. Dip. Kmbl. v. 336, 24. Wið Heortsolwe, iii. 391, 32. Of ðam wylle on ðæt heorotsol; of ðam heorotsole, ii. 249, 37. In ða heortsole; of ðære sole, iii. 380, 6. On ðæt sol; of ðan sole on ða ealdan strǽte, Cod. Dip. B. i. 518, 40. Sole *volutabro*, Wrt. Voc. ii. 97, 17. Tō sole ł fȳlþe *ad volutabrum*, Hpt. Gl. 477, 70. Seomode on sole sīdfæðmed scip, Beo. Th. 609; B. 302. Sió sugu hī wile sylian on hire sole æfter ðæm ðe hió āþwægen biþ, Past. 54; Swt. 419, 27. Gif swīn eft filþ on ðæt sol, Swt. 421, 3. Þonon ðæt cume in ða reádan sole, Cod. Dip. Kmbl. iii. 375, 8. In reádan solo, Txts. 431, 6. Ad stagnum quendam cujus vocabulum est Ceabban solo, Cod. Dip. Kmbl. iii. 388, 2. Tō Higsolon; of Higsolon, 219, 3. Swīn simle willnaþ licgan on fūlum solum . . . ðeáh hī beswemde weorþon, ðonne sleáþ hē eft on ða solu and bewealwiaþ þǽron, Bt. 37, 4; Fox 192, 26–29. [Cf. sol; *adj. filthy*:—Wule a sol cloð et one cherre beon hwit iwaschen? A. R. 324, 1. His (the priest's) alter cloð great and sole, and hire (the priest's concubine's) chemise smal and hwit; and te albe sol, and hire smoc hwit, Rel. Ant. i. 129. Solwy *dirty*, Wrt. Voc. i. 171, 41. *O. H. Ger.* sol *volutabrum.*] v. Sol-mōnaþ, solian, sylu, sylian.

sōl, e; *f.* (?) *The sun*:—Ne ðē sunne on dæge sōl ne gebærne *per diem sol non uret te*, Ps. Th. 120, 6. [*Goth.* sauil; *n.*: *Icel.* sōl; *f.*] v. sunne.

solate, solcen, solen, solere. v. sōlsece, a-, be-solcen, solu, solor.

solian; *p.* ode *To make* or *to become foul*:—Searo hwīt solaþ sumur hāt cōlaþ eorðmægen ealdaþ ellen cōlaþ *the armour* or *implement that was bright grows rusty, summer that was hot grows cool, earthly might grows old, strength grows chill*, Exon. Th. 354, 57; Reim. 67. [Cf. Nis noht so hot þat hit na coleþ, ne noht so hwit þat hit ne soleþ, O. and N. 1276. *O. H. Ger.* bi-, gi-solōt *made filthy.*] v. sol, sylian.

Sol-mōnaþ, es; *m. The old name for February*:—Ðonne se Solmōnaþ biþ geendod, ðonne biþ seó niht feówertȳne tīda lang and se dæg tȳn tīda, Shrn. 59, 2. Solmōnaþ sīgeþ tō tūne, Februarius, Menol. Fox 31; Men. 16. [The first part of the compound is of doubtful meaning. Bede says, 'Solmōnaþ dici potest mensis placentarum, quas in eo diis suis [Angli] offerebant;' but there is no word *sol* = placenta, unless it be found in the gloss *panibus sol*, Epinal Glossary, ed. Sweet, p. 21 a, 11. Kluge takes the word to be *sōl* = sun, and observes 'die form des kuchens war für die benennung massgebend,' Engl. Stud. viii. 479. *Sol* = mire would give a name that suggests the later February fill-dyke, and would not be inappropriate. The form *sille, selle* is found in some L. G. dialects, and also *sporkel*, which may be connected with *spurcalia*. See Grimm, Gesch. D. S. c. vi.]

solor, soler[e?], es; *m. An upper chamber, a soler.* v. Halliwell's Dict.:—Ic wilnige ðætte ðeós sprǽc stigge on ðæt ingeþonc ðæs leorneres suǽ suǽ on sume hlǽdre ōððæt hió fæstlīce gestonde on ðæm solore ðæs mōdes *until it stand firmly in the upper chamber of the mind*, Past. proem.; Swt. 23, 18. Se fugel ofer heánne beám hūs getimbreþ, and gewīcaþ ðǽr sylf in ðam solere *in that upper chamber* (*its nest*), Exon. Th. 212, 2; Ph. 204. [Soler *solarium*, Wrt. Voc. i. 178, 12. Solere, 273, col. 2. Solere or lofte *solarium, hectheca*, Prompt. Parv. 464 (see note). Garytte, hey solere *specula*, 187. Wicklif (Jos. 2, 6) uses the word for the flat roof of a house. *O. Sax.* soleri *an upper room* (Mk. 14, 14). *O. H. Ger.* soleri, solær *solarium, coenaculum*: *Ger.* söller. *From Lat.* solarium.]

sōlsece, sōlosece, an; *f. Heliotrope*:—Sōlsece vel sigelhwerfe *solsequium* vel *heliotropium*, Wrt. Voc. i. 30, 30. Sōlsæce *solsequium*, 79, 15. Ðās wyrte ðe man solate and ōðrum naman sōlosece nemneþ, Lchdm. i. 178, 21. Cf. sōlesege *solata*, iii. 305, col. 1. Halliwell gives solsekille.

solu, an, e (?); *f. A sole, a sandal*:—Solen *soleae*, Wrt. Voc. i. 26, 18. [*Goth.* sulja *a sandal*: *O. H. Ger.* sola, *pl.* solun, sola *solea, sandallo, planta. From Lat.* solea.]

solu *mire.* v. sol.

som, som-. v. sam, sam-.

sōm, e; *f.* I. *agreement, concord*:—Beó eallum mannum sibb and sōm gemǽne, and ǽlc sacu tōtwǽmed, L. Eth. vi. 25; Th. i. 320, 28: L. C. E. 17; Th. i. 370, 10: Wulfst. 118, 3. Ðām dōmbōcum ðe se heofonlīca Wealdend his folce gesette tō sōme and tō sehtnesse, Homl. Th. ii. 198, 19. Tō sibbe and tō sōme, Chart. Th. 231, 35. Hē sceal beón symle ymbe sōme and ymbe sibbe *he shall ever be engaged in promoting concord and peace*, L. I. P. 7; Th. ii. 312, 13. Sibbe and sōme lufie man georne, Wulfst. 73, 16. II. *the bringing about of concord, reconciliation, adjustment of differences*:—Nān sacu ðe betweox preóstan sī ne beó gescoten tō woroldmanna sōme *no dispute between priests shall be referred to the adjustment of secular men*, L. Edg. C. 7; Th. ii. 246, 4. Bisceopum gebyraþ, gyf ǽnig ōðrum ābelge, ðæt man geþyldige ōð geférena sōme, L. I. P. 10; Th. ii. 316, 35. III. *an agreement, arrangement* of a matter in dispute:—Ūs eallan ðe æt ðære sōme wǽran, Chart. Th. 171, 1. v. un-sōm; sēman, ge-sōm.

sôn, es; *m. A musical sound, music* vocal or instrumental:—Nân neát nyste nǽnne andan tô ôþrum for ðære mergþe ðæs sônes ... Hê wæs oflyst ðæs seldcúþan sônes (*the music of Orpheus' harp*), Bt. 35, 6; Fox 168, 11, 23. Ða hearpan strengas se hearpere suíðe ungelíce tiéhþ and styreþ and mid ðý gedêþ ðæt hí nâwuht ungelíce ðæm sône ne singaþ ðe hê wilnaþ *chordas tangendi artifex, ut non sibimetipsi dissimile canticum faciat, dissimiliter pulsat*, Past. 23; Swt. 175, 8. Gif hit mycel geférǽden is sýn hý (*the psalms*) mid antefene gesungene, gif seó geférǽden lytel is, sýn hý forðrihte bûtan sône gesungene *si major congregatio fuerit cum antiphonis, si vero minor in directum psallantur*, R. Ben. 41, 9. In efnum sônum *in consonantibus*, Mk. Skt. p. 1, 13. Sônas tô singanne on cyricean *sonos cantandi in ecclesia*, Bd. 4, 2; S. 565, 35. [*Icel.* sónn. From Latin.]

sôna; *adv. Soon, immediately, directly, at once*:—Sôna *actutum*, Wrt. Voc. ii. 5, 2: 82, 70: *extemplo*, 31, 45. Hí wǽron sôna deáde *they died at once*, Bd. 1, 12; S. 481, 22. Lege ðǽrtô, ðonne biþ hit sôna gebêt, Lchdm. i. 116, 13: 118, 11. Ǽlc cræft biþ sôna forealdod, Bt. 17; Fox 60, 10. And sôna (*statim*) gâst hine on wêsten genýdde, Mk. Skt. 1, 12, 10. Hí ðâ sôna forlêton hyra nett, Mt. Kmbl. 4, 22. Ðâ sôna (*continuo*) forscranc ðæt fictreów, 21, 19: Cd. Th. 53, 16; Gen. 862. Ðâ sôna and hræðe *ac[t]utum*, Wrt. Voc. ii. 9, 17. Forhwon ne woldest ðû sôna hraþe ða dígolnesse mê cýþan *quare non citius hoc compertum mihi revelare voluisti?* Bd. 4, 25; S. 601, 21. Se ðe wille wyrcan wæstmbǽre lond, âtió of ðæm æcere ǽrest sôna (*first of all*; cf. ǽrest, Bt. Fox 78, 22) fearn and þornas, Met. 12, 2, 25. Eft sôna *again*, Soul Kmbl. 134; Seel. 67. Sôna æfter ðæra daga gedrêfednesse *statim post tribulationem dierum illorum*, Mt. Kmbl. 24, 29: Cd. Th. 304, 14; Sat. 630. Sôna ðæs forman geáres ðâ Decius fêng tô ríce, Homl. Skt. i. 23, 476. Sôna ðæs ðe hê ðam biscopsetle onfêng *ubi sedem episcopalem accepit*, Bd. 1, 33; S. 498, 29. Ðâ sôna ðæs ðe ðis fæsten geworht wæs *quo mox condito*, 1, 12; S. 481, 12. Sôna hraþe ðæs ðe hê biscop geworden wæs *mox ut ipse pontificatus officio functus est*, 2, 1; S. 501, 34. Sôna ðæt him bet wæs *nec mora, melius habere coepit*, 3, 13; S. 539, 6. Sôna swâ seó sunne sealte streámas oferhlífaþ, swâ se fugel of beáme gewíteþ, Exon. Th. 206, 1; Ph. 120. Sôna swâ ..., ðâ, Met. 8, 1. [*O. Sax.* sân, sâno: *O. Frs.* sôn, sân: cf. *Goth.* suns.]

sôn-cræft, es; *m. Music*:—Sôncræft *musicam*, Anglia xiii. 38, 306.

sond, song. v. sand, sang.

sopa, an; *m. A sup, draught*:—On wearmum wætre drince betonican týn sopan, Lchdm. ii. 134, 22. Sûpe cû buteran .viii. morgnas .iii. sopan, 294, 1. [Þer (in hell) is o wateres flod ... a þusen saulen beoþ bi sore ofþurst ... ne moten heo biden neuer o sope, Misc. 152, 169. Þyse renkeȝ schul neuer suppe on sope of my seve, Allit. Pms. 41, 108. *Icel.* sopi *a sup, mouthful.*] v. sûpan.

sopp-cuppe, an; *f. A sop-cup, a cup into which sops were put*:—Ic ann mînæn cinæhlâfordæ ânræ sopcuppan, Chart. Th. 553, 31: 554, 4. Ic ann Ælfwerdæ ânræ sopcuppan and Æþelwerde ânæs drincæhornæs, 555, 4. Ânæ soppcuppan an þrým pundum, 527, 7. Twâ sopcuppan, 522, 22. See Brand's Popular Antiquities, on Nuptial Usages, ii. 84-6, and next word.

soppe (?) *a sop*. [Soppe *offa*, soppe in wyne *vipa*, Prompt. Parv. 465. Cf. *vipa* a wynsope, *offa* a ale sope, Wrt. Voc. i. 242, col. 1. Ase is a zop of hot bryead huanne me hit poteþ into wyn, Ayenb. 107, 5. Wel loved he by the morwe a sop in wyn, Chauc. Prol. 334. If he soupeth, he ete but a soppe of *spera-in-deo*, Piers P. 15, 175. *Icel.* soppa.] v. preceding word.

soppian *to sop*:—Genim hlâf, geseóð on gâte meolce, soppige on súþerne [drenc], Lchdm. ii. 228, 31.

sorg. v. sorh.

sorgian, sorhgian (*and* sorgan, v. *pres. part.* sorgende); *p.* ode. I. *to care, be anxious, feel anxiety* or *care*, (a) with a clause:—Hê nalles sorgode hwæðer siððan â Drihten âmetan wolde wrece be gewyrhtum *he felt no anxiety as to whether the Lord would ever mete out vengeance according to deserts*, Met. 9, 34. Hí lyt sorgodon hwylc him ðæt edleán æfter wurde, Andr. Kmbl. 2456; An. 1229. (b) *with preps.* ymbe, for:—Hê sorgaþ ymb ða (*useless works*) and biþ ðara suíðe gemyndig and forgiett his selfes *mens fit in exteriorum dispositione sollicita, et sui ignara*, Past. 4, 1; Swt. 37, 19. Geþenceaþ ðæt gê winnaþ and â embe ðæt sorgiaþ, ðæt wê úrne líchoman gefyllan, Blickl. Homl. 99, 6. Ða ðe for his life lyt sorgedon, Exon. Th. 116, 19; Gû. 209. Nô ðû ymb mînes ne þearft líces feorme leng sorgian, Beo. Th. 907; B. 451. (c) absolute:—Hê sceal winnan and sorgian, ðonne se dæg cume ðæt hê sceole ðæs ealles ídel hweorfan, Blickl. Homl. 97, 25. Sorgiende *anxius*, Wrt. Voc. i. 287, 67. Sorgende, ii. 6, 66. Hû him woruldmanna seó unclǽne gecyrd cearum sorgende hearde ondrêde, Exon. Th. 63, 10; Cri. 1017. Sume dæge ðæt hê sorgiende (*sollicitus*) bâd hwonne seó âdl tô him côme, Bd. 3, 12; S. 537, 6. Ac hwæðere sorhgiende môde geornlíce þohte *sed multum sollicitus ac sedula mente cogitans*, 2, 12; S. 514, 28. II. *to sorrow, grieve, be sorry*, (a) *with preps.* ymbe, for, on:—Gif ðû hafast mid ðê wulfes hrycghǽr ... on síðfæte, bûtan fyrhtu ðû ðone síð gefremest, ac se wulf sorgaþ ymbe his síð *the wolf will be sorry for his journey*, Lchdm. i. 360, 22. Swíþe on ðon sorhgedon ðæt hí ðam lâreówe onfôn ne woldon ðe hí him tô sendon *de non recepto quem miserant predicatore dolentes*, Bd. 3, 5; S. 527, 29. Wit hreówige mâgon sorgian for his síðe, Cd. Th. 49, 30; Gen. 800. Sorgiende for ðâm ermþum, Bt. 38, 1; Fox 196, 7. (b) absolute:—Sorgedon Adam and Eve, and him oft betuh gnornword gengdon, Cd. Th. 47, 24; Gen. 765. Ne sorga, snotor guma, sêlre biþ ǽghwæm ðæt hê his freónd wrece, ðonne hê fela murne, Beo. Th. 2772; B. 1384. Ða woruldâre ðe ðû nû sorgiende ânforlête, Bt. 7, 3; Fox 20, 12: Cd. Th. 22, 28; Gen. 347. Ðǽr mon mæg sorgende folc gehýran hygegeómor, Exon. Th. 55, 28; Cri. 890. Sume ofer sǽ sorgiende (*dolentes*) gewiton, Bd. 1, 15; S. 484, 7. Him sorgendum sâr ôðclífeþ, Exon. Th. 77, 35; Cri. 1267. [*Goth.* saurgan *to be anxious; to sorrow*: *O. Sax.* sorgôn: *O. H. Ger.* sorgên: *Icel.* sorga.] v. be-, for-sorgian.

sorgung, e; *f. Sorrowing, grieving, sorrow, grief*:—Ðǽr (*in hell*) is sorgung and sârgung and â singal heóf, Wulfst. 114, 4.

sorh, sorg, sorhg, e; *f.* I. *care, anxiety*:—Sorg *accidia, tedium* vel *anxietas*, Wrt. Voc. ii. 99, 17: *cura*, 19, 62. Mec sorg dreceþ on sefan, ic ne mæg rǽd âhycgan, Cd. Th. 131, 21; Gen. 2179. Nis mê ðæs deáþes sorg *death causes me no anxiety*, Exon. Th. 125, 7; Gû. 350. Frêfrigende gesihþe seó him ealle ða nearonesse ðære gemyngedan sorhge âfyrde *visionem consolatoriam, quae omnem ei anxietatem memoratae sollicitudinis auferret*, Bd. 4, 11; S. 579, 34. Ða ðe nǽfre nânne mon buton sorge (*securum*) ne forlǽtaþ, Bt. 7, 2; Fox 18, 14. Ðæt gê lybbon eówre líf bûtan ǽlcre sorge *absque ullo pavore*, Lev. 25, 18. Ûs biþ sibb æfter sorge, Andr. Kmbl. 3134; An. 1570. Ne biþ him on ðâm wícum wiht tô sorge *there shall be nothing in heaven to cause them anxiety*, Exon. Th. 238, 29; Ph. 211. Gê mê lyt sorge sealdun *ye caused me little care*, 121, 13; Gû. 288. Ne ic ðæs deáðes hafu sorge on môde, 166, 12; Gû. 1041: 308, 20; Seef. 42: 376, 33; Seel. 164. Sorgum *curis*, Wrt. Voc. ii. 19, 63. Heorte mid sorgum gedrêfed, Judth. Thw. 22, 31; Jud. 88. Ferhð sorgum âsǽled, Cd. Th. 132, 18; Gen. 2195. II. *sorrow, grief, affliction, trouble*:—Ne biþ ðǽr sorg ne wôp, Blickl. Homl. 103, 36. Wât se ðe cunnaþ, hû slíþen biþ sorg tô geféran, Exon. Th. 288, 13; Wand. 30: 288, 30; Wand. 39. Mec sorg bicwom ... ic bihlyhhan ne þearf síðfæt ðisne, 273, 33; Jul. 525. Ðæt wæs Satane sâr tô geþolienne, micel môdes sorg, Andr. Kmbl. 3376; An. 1692. Ne frín ðû æfter sǽlum, sorh is geníwod, Beo. Th. 2649; B. 1322: Ps. Th. 118, 28. Sorh is mê tô secganne, hwæt ... *it is a grief to me to tell, what* ..., Beo. Th. 950; B. 473. Se Hǽlend wiste ðæt his gingran wolde unrôte beón ... Wǽron swâ manigfealdlíce sorga Cristes þegnum ... Wæs him micel langung and sorh on heora heortan, ðâ hié ðæt ongeáton, ðæt hê leng mid him líchomlíce wunian nolde; hê hié ... frêfrede for ðære gelômlícan sorge, Blickl. Homl. 135, 14-23. Nû hý ðê willaþ on murnunga gebringan ðonne hié ðê fram hweorfaþ tô hwæm cumaþ hí ðonne elles bûtan tô tâcnunge sorge[s] and anfealdes sâres *si calamitosos fugiens facit, quid est aliud fugax, quam futurae quoddam calamitatis indicium*, Bt. 7, 2; Fox 18, 21. Ne hié sorge wiht, weorces wiston; ac hié wel meahton libban, Cd. Th. 49, 1; Gen. 785. Wraðu wíta gehwylces, sæce and sorge, Elen. Kmbl. 2059; El. 1031. Seó hreówsung ne beoþ nâ bûtan sorge, Bt. 31, 1; Fox 110, 29. Wedera helm æfter Herebealde heortan sorge weallende wæg ... mid ðære sorge, ðâ him sió sâr belamp, gumdreám ofgeaf, Beo. Th. 4937; B. 2468. Sægde him tô sorge, ðæt hý ðone grênan wong ofgiefan sceoldan, Exon. Th. 130, 32; Gû. 447: 39, 11; Cri. 620. Gê ðæs næfdon nâne sorge (*luctum*), Past. 32, 1; Swt. 211, 10. Weán cúðon, sâr and sorge, Cd. Th. 5, 21; Gen. 75: Beo. Th. 239; B. 119. Ðû his (*for it*) sorge ne þearft beran on ðínum breóstum, Cd. Th. 45, 28; Gen. 733. Ic ða sorge gemon, hû ic bendum fæst bisga unrím dreág, Exon. Th. 280, 5; Jul. 624. Hyge wearð mongum blissad sáwlum, sorge tôglidene, 71, 31; Cri. 1164. Sorga sârost, 122, 19; Gen. 2029. Sorga mǽst, 308, 22; Sat. 696. Weána gehwylcne, sídra sorga, Beo. Th. 300; B. 149. Holofernus ðe ûs monna mǽst morþra gefremede, sârra sorga, Judth. Thw. 24, 10. Sorgna hâtost, Exon. Th. 163, 12; Gû. 992. Manna bearn sorgum sáwaþ, 6, 18; Cri. 86. Ne biþ him hyra yrmðu ân tô wíte, ac ðara ôþerra eád tô sorgum, 79, 22; Cri. 1294. On wíte mid swâte and mid sorgum libban, Cd. Th. 31, 8; Gen. 482. Mid sorgum geswenced, Andr. Kmbl. 231; An. 116. Ǽghwilc man sceolde mid sâre on ðâs world cuman, ond hêr on sorhgum beón and mid sâre of gewítan, Blickl. Homl. 5, 29. [*Goth.* saurga *sorrow, care*: *O. Sax.* sorga: *O. H. Ger.* sorga *cura, solicitudo, angor, moeror, labor*: *Icel.* sorg *care, sorrow*.] v. bealo-, cear-, gnorn-, hyge-, inwit-, môd-, nearu-, sin-, torn-, þegn-sorh (-sorg); be-, or-, unbe-sorh; *adj.*

sorh-byrðen *a burden of sorrow, a grievous trouble*:—Ðæt (*the drowning of a number of people*) wæs sorgbyrðen, Andr. Kmbl. 3063; An. 1534.

sorh-cearig; *adj. Having grievous care, oppressed with anxiety* or *sorrow, anxious, sorrowful*:—Siteþ sorgcearig sǽlum bidǽled, Exon. Th. 379, 4; Deór. 28: 278, 25; Jul. 603: 285, 4; Jul. 709: Beo. Th. 6294; B. 3152. Gesyhþ sorhcearig wínsele wêstne, 4901; B. 2455. Wreclâstas settan sorhgcearig, Cd. Th. 276, 15; Sat. 189.

sorh-cearu *grievous care, painful anxiety*:—Næs him sorgcearu ðeáh his líc and gǽst hyra somwiste gedǽled(-de ?), Exon. Th. 160, 6; Gû. 939.

sorheriunge *infestatione*, Wrt. Voc. ii. 45, 43. *Read* forheriunge. v. for-hergung.

sorh-full; *adj.* I. *full of care* or *anxiety*, *careful*, *anxious*, (a) *feeling anxiety*:—Seldan snottor guma sorgleás blissaþ swylce dol seldon drýmeþ sorgful ymbe his forðgesceaft nefne hē fǣhþe wite *seldom does the prudent man rejoice without anxiety about his future, just as the fool seldom rejoices with trembling, unless he know that hostility* (or *death?* fǣhþe *from* fǣge?) *is near*, Exon. Th. 303, 19; Fä. 55. Symble beó gē sorhfulle for eówre sāwle hǣlo *ever be ye solicitous for your soul's salvation*, L. E. I. prm.; Th. ii. 394, 14. Ðæt hē sorgfulra sié ymb hine selfne *ut circa se solicitius vivant*, Past. 28, 2; Swt. 191, 19. (b) *attended with anxiety*, *causing anxiety*:—Ðeós woruld is sorhful *the present time is full of anxieties*, Wulfst. 189, 6. Ne inc ǣnig mon beleán mihte sorhfulne sīð (*the perilous swimming match of Beowulf and Breca*), Beo. Th. 1028; B. 512. II. *sorrowful*, *mournful*, *sad*, (a) *feeling sorrow* or *grief*:—Oft se welega and se wædla habbaþ suā gehweorfed hira þeáwum ðæt se welega biþ eáðmōd and sorgfull, and se wædla biþ upāhæfen and selflīce, Past. 26, 2; Swt. 183, 11. Ic eom þearfa and sorhful *ego sum pauper et dolens*, Ps. Lamb. 68, 30. Sorhfull, Ps. Th. 85, 1. Ic sceal gnornian seóc and sorhful, Cd. Th. 281, 20; Sat. 275. Mōdor sīðode sorhfull, sunu deáþ fornam, Beo. Th. 4244; B. 2119. Hig heora synna andetton mid sorhfullum mōde, Jud. 10, 10. Hē hafaþ wērige heortan, sefan sorhfulne, Salm. Kmbl. 757; Sal. 378. Ða sorgfullan *illi quos caminus paupertatis excoquit*, Past. 26, 1; Swt. 183, 4. (b) *attended with* or *causing sorrow*, *grievous*:—Mōdor gegān wolde sorhfulne sīð, sunu wrecan, Beo Th. 2560; B. 1278. Ða sorhfullan sāule wunde, Ps. C. 50, 141. Adam and Eve in ðās deáðdene drohtað sōhton, sorgfulran gesetu, Exon. Th. 227, 2; Ph. 417. [*O. H. Ger.* sorg-fol *sollicitus*: *Icel.* sorg-fullr.]

sorh-leás; *adj.* I. *free from anxiety* or *care*, *secure*:—Sorgleás *secura*, Rtl. 63, 10: 8, 23: 40, 15. Ic hit ðē gehāte, ðæt ðū mōst sorhleás swefan, ðæt ðū ondrǣdan ne þearft aldorbealu eorlum, Beo. Th. 3348; B. 1672. Ne sculon wē nǣfre sorhleáse beón, ac symble ūrne deáðes dæg beforan ūres līchoman eágum settan, L. E. I. prm.; Th. ii. 396, 22. Wē gedōþ eów sorhleáse *securos vos faciemus*, Mt. Kmbl. 28, 14. Þeóf, ðe on þýstre fæ̂reþ, sorgleáse hæleð forfēhþ, Exon. Th. 54, 24; Cri. 873. Cyning wæs þe sorgleásra (cf. mōdsorge wæg cyning, 122; El. 61), Elen. Kmbl. 193; El. 97. II. *free from sorrow*:—Wē sorgleáse mōtan wunigan in wuldre, Exon. Th. 22, 3; Cri. 346. [*Icel.* sorg-lauss.]

sorhleást, e; *f.* *Security*:—Gif ðū gesihst ðæt ðū on wætere fægere in gā oððe ofer gā, sorhleáste getācnaþ. Gif ðū gesihst ðæt ðū mid swurde bist begyrd, sorhleáste hit getācnaþ, Lchdm. iii. 212, 30–33.

sorh-leóþ, es; *n.* *A sorrowful song*, *a lay of grief*:—Gesyhþ sorhcearig on his suna būre wīnsele wēstne . . . nis ðǣr hearpan swēg, gomen in geardum swylce ðǣr iú wǣron. Gewīteþ ðonne, sorhleóð gæleþ, Beo. Th. 4912; B. 2460. Ongunnon ðā (*after putting Jesus in the grave*) sorhleóð galan, Rood Kmbl. 134; Kr. 67.

sorh-līc; *adj.* *Sorrowful*, *causing sorrow*, *grievous*, *sorry*, *miserable*:—Hit is earmlīc and sorhlīc mannum tō gehýranne, eall ðæt man ūs foresægþ, Wulfst. 241, 21. Ðonne biþ sorhlīc sār and earmlīc gedāl līces and sāwle, 187, 14. Ðonne wyrð ehtnes grimlīc and sorhlīc *there shall be persecution cruel and grievous*, 89, 16. Stingaþ hine mid sorhlīcum sāre on his heortan, 141, 9. Setl his ðū gesettest sorglīc on eorðan *sedem ejus in terra collisisti*, Ps. Th. 88, 37. [*O. H. Ger.* sorg-līh: *Icel.* sorg-ligr.] v. next word.

sorhlīce; *adv.* *Miserably*, *grievously*:—Herodes hys spere genam, and hyne sylfne ofstang; and hē swā sorhlīce hys lýf geendode, St. And. 34, 7. Ðǣr synd sorhlīce (cf. tō sorge, Dōm. L. 190) tōsomne gemencged se þrosmiga lig and se þrece gycela, Wulfst. 138, 25. [Þonne biþ ꝥ soule hus seoruhliche bereaued, Fragm. Phlps. 5, 39. Sorhliche heo gunnen clupien (hii gonne grede, 2nd MS.), Laym. 21883. *O. H. Ger.* sorglīcho: *Icel.* sorgliga.]

sorh-lufu, e, an; *f.* *Love that is attended with anxiety* or *sorrow*, *hapless love*:—Him seó sorglufu slǣp ealle binom, Exon. Th. 378, 14; Deór. 16.

sorh-stæf, es; *m.* *Trouble*, *care*, *affliction*:—Æfter sorgstafum, Exon. Th. 282, 8; Jul. 660. Cf. sār-, hearm-stæf.

sorh-wilm, es; *m.* *Violent emotion of anxiety* or *sorrow*:—Soden sorgwælmum, Exon. Th. 177, 32; Gū. 1236. Sorgwylmum, 166, 21; Gū. 1046. Ic ðæs mōdceare sorhwylmum seáð, Beo. Th. 3990; B. 1993.

sorh-wīte, es; *n.* *A grievous punishment*, *torment*:—Ðara sorhwīta mǣst, Wulfst. 187, 2.

sorh-word, es; *m.* *A word expressive of care* or *sorrow*:—Hié (*Adam and Eve*) fela sprǣcon sorhworda, Cd. Th. 49, 8; Gen. 789.

sorig; *adj.* *Sorry*, *grieved*:—Hē biþ suīðe sorig (sārig, Cott. MSS.) *dolet*, Past. 33; Swt. 227, 8.

soru (?), e; *f.* *A particle of dust*, *bit of straw*:—Sore (strēu, Rush.) *festucam*, Mt. Kmbl. Lind. 7, 3, 4. v. seár, *and* cf. (?) *Icel.* sori *dross*.

sot. v. sott.

sōt, es; *n.* *Soot*:—Sōt *fuligo*, Ælfc. Gr. 9, 3; Zup. 37, 4. Sōt *fuligo*, deorces sōtes *furvae fuliginis*, Hpt. Gl. 504, 6–8. Soote *fuligine*, Wrt. Voc. ii. 36, 28. Sooth, 109, 46. Meng wið sōte, Lchdm. ii. 76, 8. Meng ðǣrtō sōt and sealt and sand, i. 356, 24. [*Icel.* sót; *n.*]

sotel. v. sotol.

sōþ, es; *n.* *Sooth.* I. *truth* in a general sense, *conformity with an absolute standard*:—Ðæt is fruma worda ðīnra ðæt ðǣr byþ sōð symble mēted *principium verborum tuorum veritas*, Ps. Th. 118, 160. Ðæt his sōð fore ūs genge weorðe, Exon. 147, 33; Gū. 736. Swā ic geornlīcor ðæt sylfe sōþ sōhte swā ic hit læs mētte. Nū ðonne ic ondette ðæt on ðysse lāre ðæt sylfe sōþ scīneþ, ðæt ūs mæg syllan ēces līfes hǣlo, Bd. 2, 13; S. 516, 29–32. Ic on ðīnum sōðe gancge *ambulabo in veritate tua*, Ps. Th. 85, 10. I a. *truth*, *that which conforms to an absolute standard*:—Mid Sigelwarum sōð yppe wearð, dryhtlīc dōm Godes, Apstls. Kmbl. 128; Ap. 64. Ða ðe Godes lage healdaþ and sōþes gelýfaþ, Wulfst. 4, 8. Of eorðan cwom æþelast sōða, Ps. Th. 84, 10. I b. *truth*, *what is true* in general:—Se ðe lýhþ oððe ðæs sōðes ansaceþ, Salm. Kmbl. 365; Sal. 182. Hē can him gesceád betweox sōðe and unsōðe, Wulfst. 51, 29. Ic tō sōðe (*as a general truth*) wāt ðæt biþ in eorle indryhten þeáw, ðæt hē his ferðlocan fæste binde, Exon. Th. 287, 9; Wand. 11. II. *truth* in regard to a particular circumstance, *exact conformity with the facts of a case*:—Ðære gesyhþe sōþ (*its agreement with what actually occurred*) wæs hraþe gecýþed on ðære fǣmnan deáþe, Bd. 4, 8; S. 576, 10. Ðæs gehātes and ðæs wītedōmes sōþ se æfterfyligenda becyme ðara wīsena gesēþde, 4, 29; S. 607, 35. Ne meaht ðū nō mid sōþe getǣlan ðīne wyrd . . . hit is leásung ðæt ðū wēnst ðæt ðū seó ungesǣlig, Bt. 10; Fox 28, 1. Is tō ðære tīde tælmet hwīle emne mid sōðe seofon and twentig, Andr. Kmbl. 227; An. 114. II a. *truth*, *fidelity to a promise*:—Hē him gehēt his ǣriste, swā hē mid sōðe (*in exact accordance with his promise*) gefylde, Blickl. Homl. 17, 4. Deópne āð Drihten āswōr and ðone mid sōðe getrymede, Ps. Th. 131, 11. Gif hē on sōþe tōweard cynerīce gehāteþ, Bd. 2, 12; S. 514, 7. II b *truth*, *reality*, *certainty*, *real condition of things*, *what really is*:—Nū mæg sōð hit sylf gecýþan *now can the truth declare itself*, Blickl. Homl. 187, 16. Tō lytel andgyt biþ on ðæs mannes heortan ðe nele sōðes gelýfan, ðēh hē sylf his āgenum eágum eal ne gesāwe, Wulfst. 3, 20: 93, 22. Gē mengan ongunnon lyge wið sōðe, Elen. Kmbl. 613; El. 307. Gē widsōcon sōðe, ðæt in Bethleme bearn cenned wǣre, 780; El. 390. Gif hit man tō sōðe ongite *if it is known as a fact*, Deut. 17, 4. Ic tō sōþe wāt, Exon. Th. 275, 9; Jul. 547. Men ne cunnon secgan tō sōðe *men cannot certainly say*, Beo. Th. 101; B. 51. Secge ic ðē tō sōðe, ðæt . . . , 1184; B. 590. Gif ðū him tō sōðe sægst *if you tell him it as a fact*, Cd. Th. 36, 11; Gen. 570. Ic feówer men geseó tō sōðe *I really see four men*, 242, 8; Dan. 416. Syle mē ða tō sōðe *give me it really*, Ps. Th. 118, 144. Ic wāt ðæt ðū sōþ segst, Bt. 26, 1; Fox 92, 8: Jn. Skt. 19, 15. Hē ā tō ǣghwylcum sōð sprecende wæs, Blickl. Homl. 223, 29. Ðeáh gē ða ǣ cūðon, gē ne woldon sōð oncnāwan, Elen. Kmbl. 790; El. 395. Būtan ðū forlǣte ða leásunga and mē sweotollīce sōð gecýðe, 1377; El. 690. Ðeáh ic ðæt sōð tō late gecneówe, 1412; El. 708. Hwæðer mon sōð ðe lyge sagaþ, Exon. Th. 80, 15; Cri. 1307. Wite ðū for sōð *be certain of this*, Bt. 7, 3; Fox 20, 17. Nǣni eft cymeþ ðe ðæt for sōð mannum secge, hwylc sý Meotodes gesceaft, Menol. Fox 590; Gn. C. 64. Ic eów fela wille sōða gesecgan, Exon. Th. 116, 30; Gū. 215. II c. *affirmation of truth*, *asseveration*:—Preóst hine clǣnsie sylfæs sōðe ðus cweðende: Veritatem dico in Xpo, non mentior, L. Wih. 18; Th. i. 40, 14. III. *truth*, *conformity with right*, *righteousness*, *equity*, *justice*:—Hū ic mīne heortan heólde mid sōðe *justificavi cor meum*, Ps. Th. 72, 11. Ic sōð dēme *ego justitiam judicabo*, 74, 2. Ðæt mǣre sōð *justitiam tuam*, 70, 18. Suna cyningces syle ðæt hē sōð healde *justitiam tuam da filio regis*, 71, 1. Se ðe his sōþ and riht symble healdeþ *justus*, 111, 6. Gif wē sōþ and riht on ūrum līfe dōn willaþ, Blickl. Homl. 129, 32. Se ðe sōð and riht fremeþ on folce, Beo. Th. 3405; B. 1700. Snyttra brūceþ ðe warnaþ him wommas worda and dǣda and sōþ fremeþ, Exon. Th. 304, 35; Fä. 80. Hié firendǣda tō frece wurdon sōð ofergeáton, Drihtnes dōmas, Cd. Th. 155, 32; Gen. 2581. [*O. Sax.* sōð.] v. un-sōþ, *and next word.*

sōþ; *adj.* *Sooth*, *very*, *true.* I. *the opposite of that which is false*, or *merely pretends*, or *has the appearance of*, *genuine*, *real*:—Ðæt hī oncnāwon ðæt ðū eart ān sōþ God *ut cognoscant te solum Deum verum*, Jn. Skt. 17, 3. Hē wæs sōþ man, ðý hine dorste deófol costian, swylce hē wæs sōþ God, ðý him englas þegnedon, Blickl. Homl. 33, 33. Ðes is sōð wītega, Jn. Skt. 7, 40. Sōð leóht wæs *erat lux vera*, 1, 9: 15, 1. Ælc sōþ wela and sōþ weorþscipe sindon mīne āgne þeówas, Bt. 7, 3; Fox 20, 15. Ðis is sōð lǣcæcræft, Lchdm. i. 376, 8. Se sōþa boda ðæs heán leóhtes Agustinus, Bd. 2, 2; S. 502, 31. Ðæt hig geleornigen in ðæs gewinnes onlīcnesse ðæt hig hiom eft nānwiht ondrǣdon in ðæs sōðan gewinnes gefiohte, Shrn. 35, 17. Ðæt wē ūre synna bēton mid sōþre hreówe, Blickl. Homl. 25, 17: 171, 12. Tō ðon sōþan andgite gecyrran, 107, 15. Ðæt wē sōþe sibbe heóldan, 109, 15. Se ðe his godcundnesse mid sōþum wīsum gerýmeþ, 179, 24. II. *true*, *in conformity with the actual state of things*:—Mīn gewitnes is sōþ, Jn. Skt. 8, 14: 19, 35. Ic eom geþafa ðæt ðæt is sōþ ðæt ðū ǣr sǣdest, Bt. 38, 2; Fox 196, 16. Sōþ is ðæt ic eów secgge, Blickl. Homl. 53, 2. Hē þohte on him sylfum hwæt his sōðes wǣre *he thought in himself what there was of it true*, Homl. Skt. i. 23, 545. Fela spella him sǣdon ða

Beormas . . . ac hē nyste hwæt ðæs sōþes wæs, Ors. 1, 1; Swt. 17, 33. Ealle ða word sind sōþe ðe Paulus sægþ, Blickl. Homl. 187, 2. Wite gē tō sōðum þingum *scito ergo*, Deut. 9, 6. Ic secge eów tō sōðum, 8, 19: Mt. Kmbl. 5, 32. Nis nān þing sōþre ðonne ðæt ðū segst, Bt. 26, 1; Fox 92, 12: 34, 4; Fox 138, 25. Hig biddan God ðæt hē ðæt sōðeste geswytelie, L. Ath. iv. 7; Th. i. 226, 30. III. *true, righteous, just*:—Ðæt ic sōðne dōm healde *custodire judicia justitiae tuae*, Ps. Th. 118, 106. Sī ðīn seó swīðre hand ofer sōðne wer *fiat manus tua super virum dexterae tuae*, 79, 16. Ða ðe wyllaþ sōðe dōmas efnan *qui custodiunt judicium*, 105, 3. [*O. Sax.* sōð: *Icel.* sannr, saðr. Cf. Lat. -sent in prae-sent-.] v. un-sōþ, *and preceding word.*

sōþ *occurs in the Northern specimens apparently corresponding to Latin* pro *in compounds*:—Sōð wē cliopiaþ *provocamus*, Rtl. 42, 15. In sōð (sōðe, Rush.) cneóreso *in progenies*, Lk. Skt. Lind. 1, 50. Sōð cymes *procedit*, Jn. Skt. Lind. Rush. 15, 26. Sōðcuom *processit*, Rtl. 2, 37: *procedit*, 57, 6. Sōðfylga *prosequere*, 29, 36. Sōð gistrȳnd *progeniem*, 29, 28. Sōðlǣde *producere*, 108, 36. *Also* (?) sōð-cwide *proverbium*; sōþ-secgan *pronuntiare*; sōþ-tācen *prodigium*, q.v.

sōþ-bora (?), an; *m. A truth-bearer, one who has exact knowledge*:—Ðone hæleð higegleáwe hātaþ wīde comēta be naman, cræftgleáwe men, wīse sōðboran (*other MSS. have* wōþboran, *which suits better the alliteration*), Chr. 975; Erl. 126, 27. v. wōþ-, rǣd-bora.

sōþ-cwǣde (?); *adj. Veracious*:—Sōðcuoed (sōðcweden, Rush.) *verax*, Jn. Skt. Lind. 7, 18: 8, 26. Sōðcuēd, 3, 33.

sōþ-cweden; *adj. True-spoken* (cf. fair-*spoken*), *speaking truly, veracious.* v. preceding word.

sōþ-cwide, es; *m.* I. *a true saying, a truth*:—Ic fela sette sōðcwida, Met. 2, 7: 7, 3. Ðæt ðeós onlīcnes word sprece, secge sōðcwidum; ðȳ sceolon gelȳfan eorlas, hwæt mīn æðelo sién, Andr. Kmbl. 1465; An. 733: Cd. Th. 294, 14; Sat. 471: 244, 10; Dan. 446: Elen. Kmbl. 1057; El. 530: Exon. Th. 418, 2; Rä. 36, 13. Hit is ǣlces mōdes wīse ðæt sōna swā hit forlǣt sōþcwidas swā folgaþ hit leásspellunga *eam mentium constat esse naturam, ut quoties abjecerint veras, falsis opinionibus induantur*, Bt. 5, 3; Fox 14, 16: Met. 6, 2: 8, 3. I a. *a proverb*:—Ðās sōðcwide (-cuido, Lind.) ł gedd cwæð him ðe Hǣlend *hoc proverbium dixit illis Jesus*, Jn. Skt. Rush. 10, 6. In sōðcwidum *in proverbis*, 16, 25. II. *a righteous saying.* v. sōþ, III:—On ðīne sōðcwidas *in tuis justificationibus*, Ps. Th. 118, 48.

sōþ-cyning, es; *m. The king of truth* or *justice, the Deity*:—Ic wāt geare, ðæt ðam līchryre (*the murder of Cain*) on lāst cymeþ sōðcyninges seofonfeald wracu, Cd. Th. 67, 13; Gen. 1100. [Sōþ *and* cyning often occur together in the nominative, but it is doubtful whether they form a compound.] Cf. sōþ-fæder.

sōþe; *adv.* I. *truly, genuinely, really*:—Ic mē sōðe sāwle mīne tō Gode hæfde georne geþeóded, Ps. Th. 61, 5. Mīn sāwl on ðē sōðe getreóweþ, 62, 7: 118, 15. Is on sibbe his stōw sōþe behealden, 75, 2. II. *truly, in accordance with the facts of a case*:—Ic eów sōðe secgan wille, ðæt . . ., Andr. Kmbl. 915; An. 458. Word sōðe gebunden (*the facts were truly told in the poem*), Beo. Th. 1746; B. 871. Hī sōðe ne ongeáton *they did not rightly understand*, Ps. Th. 73, 5. III. *truly, in accordance with a promise, agreement*, or *forecast*:—Ic ða wǣre forð sōðe gelǣste, ðe ic ðē sealde, Cd. Th. 139, 11; Gen. 2308: 142, 22; Gen. 2365. Beót eal wið ðē hē sōðe gelǣste, Beo. Th. 1053; B. 524. Sceolde wītedōm in him sylfum beón sōðe gefylled, Exon. Th. 14, 3; Cri. 213.

sōþes; *adv. Of a truth, verily, indeed, really*:—Sōþes ic secge ðē *amen dico tibi*, Mt. Kmbl. 5, 26. Sōðes ðū eart Godes sunu, Lk. Skt. 4, 41. Ðēh hē sylf his āgenum eágum eal ne gesāwe, ðæt sōðes is geworden, Wulfst. 3, 21.

sōþ-fæder *the father of truth* or *justice, the Deity*:—Ā tō worulde forð in engla dreáme mid sōðfæder symble wunian, Exon. Th. 7, 18; Cri. 103. Cf. sōþ-cyning.

sōþ-fæst; *adj.* I. *true, without deception*:—Ðes man is sōþfæst, ac git sindon bigswicon, Blickl. Homl. 187, 29. II. *true in deed, just, righteous, pious, without wickedness*:—Sōðfæst *justus*, Ps. Th. 114, 5: 57, 9: Mt. Kmbl. Lind. 1, 19: Rtl. 102, 15. Sōðfæst sunu, ðam wæs Seth noma, Cd. Th. 67, 25; Gen. 1106. Sōþfæst eart ðū, Drihten, and rihte syndon ðīne dōmas, Blickl. Homl. 89, 6. Ānra gehwylc, sōðfæst ge synnig, Exon. Th. 233, 11; Ph. 523. Hwylc sēceþ ðæt ðe sōðfæst biþ *misericordiam et veritatem quis requiret?* Ps. Th. 60, 6. Se ðe onfōes ðone sōðfæst (*justum*) in noma sōðfæstes (*justi*), Mt. Kmbl. Lind. 10, 41. Hī on ðīn sōðfæst weorc (*in justitiam tuam*) ne gangan, Ps. Th. 68, 28: 70, 14, 20, 22. Ðīn sōðfæst word *justificationes tuas*, 118, 20. Hē gecȳþde ðæt sōþfæste men habbaþ mid him þeófas and synfulle men, Blickl. Homl. 75, 27. Hit (*the law*) sōðfæste siððan heóldon godfyrhte guman, Andr. Kmbl. 3026; An. 1516. Ðū eart seó sēfte ræst sōþfæstra *tu requies tranquilla piis*, Bt. 33, 4; Fox 132, 34: Blickl. Homl. 131, 23. Yfele gerēfan ða ðe rihte dōmas sōþfæstra manna onwendaþ, 61, 27. On ða swīþran healfe Drihtnes mid sōþfæstum sāwlum, 95, 22. Mon mid gōdum and sōþfæstum dǣdum geearnige him ða ēcean ræste, 101, 26. Þurh sōþfæste dǣda and þurh mildheortnesse weorc, 97, 2. Ne cwom ic tō ceigenne sōðfæsto (*justos*) ah synfullo, Mk. Skt. Lind. 2, 17. III. *true in speech, veracious*:—Sōðfæst *verax*, Wrt. Voc. i. 76, 17: Mt. Kmbl. 22, 16: Mk. Skt. 12, 14: Jn. Skt. Lind. 3, 33: Ps. Th. 85, 14. Gefyrn sōðfæst sægde sum wōðbora, Esaias, Exon. Th. 19, 17; Cri. 302. Cwom Daniel snotor and sōðfæst, Cd. Th. 225, 8; Dan. 151. Sōðfæst word *verbum veritatis*, Ps. Th. 118, 43. Sangere hē (*David*) wæs sōðfæstest, Ps. C. 50, 6. [*O. Sax.* sōð-fast.] v. un-sōþfæst.

sōþfæstian *to justify*:—Gié sōðfæstigeþ *justificatis*, Lk. Skt. Lind. 16, 15.

sōþfæst-līc; *adj. True, sincere*:—Hī (*patriarchs and martyrs*) sungon sigedryhtne sōðfæstlīc lof *praise unfeigned*, Andr. Kmbl. 1754; An. 879. [Cf. uss birrþ soþfasstlike trowwenn þatt Godess Gast iss soþfasst Godd, Orm. 2995.]

sōþfæstness, e; *f.* I. *truth, faithfulness, good faith, sincerity*:—On worulda woruld wunaþ ðīn sōðfæstnes *thy faithfulness is unto all generations* (A. V.), Ps. Th. 118, 90: 56, 12. Ūs is wyrse ðæt wē ūrne ceáp teóþian gif wē willaþ syllan ūre ðæt wyrste Gode. Cwæþ se æþela lāreów: 'Onsecggaþ gē Drihtne mid sōþfæstnesse wæstmum,' Blickl. Homl. 41, 10. Ongan ðā geornlīce gāstgerȳnum on sefan sēcean sōðfæstnesse (*in sincerity*; or (?) gen. with *weg*) weg tō wuldre, Elen. Kmbl. 2296; El. 1149. Sete ðīne hand under mīn þeóh and cȳð mē ðīne sōðfæstnysse, and swera mē, ðæt ðū mē nǣfre ne bebirge on Egipta lande, Gen. 47, 29. II. *truth, righteousness, justice*:—Beseah sōðfæstnes (*justitia*) of heofonum, Ps. Th. 84, 10, 12: 71, 7. His sōðfæstnyss wunaþ symble, 111, 8. Ǣ wæs geseald þurh Moysen, and gyfu and sōþfæstnes is geworden þurh Hǣlend Crist, Jn. 1, 17. Cwæþ Pilatus: 'Nys nān sōþfæstnys on eorþan.' Se Hǣlend hym andswarode and cwæþ: 'Begȳm hū ryhte dōmas ða dēmon ðe on eorðan syndon and anweald habbaþ, Nicod. 9; Thw. 5, 5. Se ðe wæs sōþfæstnesse bysen and cining ealre clǣnnesse forlēt mid him beón ðone godwracan þeóf, Blickl. Homl. 75, 25. Ic eom weg sōðfæstnesse, 17, 32. For sōðfæstnesse ðæt wē lufigen gesuinc, Past. 3; Swt. 35, 1. Se ðe hylt sōðfæstnysse on worulde, hē dēþ dōm on teónan þoliendum, Ps. Spl. 145, 5. III. *truth* of speech or thought:—Deófol ne wunode on sōðfæstnesse, forðam ðe sōðfæstnes nis on him. Ðonne hē sprcyþ leásunga, hē sprycþ of him sylfum, forðam ðe hē is leás. Gē ne gelȳfaþ mē forðam ðe ic secge eów sōðfæstnysse, Jn. Skt. 8, 44, 45. Ðū settest on mīnum mūðe ðīnre sōðfæstnysse word, Homl. Th. i. 74, 33. Hē mid ðære sōþfæstnesse stefne geweorþod wæs, Blickl. Homl. 165, 1. Se mon se ða sōþfæstnesse mid his mūþe sprecþ and hié on his heortan geþencþ, 55, 14. Ðonne ðære sōþfæstnysse gāst cymþ hē lǣrþ eów ealle sōþfæstnysse; ne sprycþ hē of him sylfum, ac hē sprycþ ða þing ðe hē gehȳrþ, and cȳð eów ða þing ðe tōwearde synt, Jn. Skt. 16, 13. v. un-sōþfæstness.

sōþ-gid *a true tale*:—Sōðgied wrecan, Exon. Th. 306, 2; Seef. 1: 314, 17; Mōd. 15.

sōþ-hwæðere; *conj. However, yet, nevertheless*:—Sōðhueðre ic cueðo *verumtamen dico*, Mt. Kmbl. Lind. 26, 64: Jn. Skt. Lind. Rush. 12, 42.

sōðian; *p.* ode *To prove true*:—Sōðeþ *probat*, Mt. Kmbl. p. 9, 9. Sōðadon *probarunt*, Jn. Skt. p. 7, 2. [Ich hit wulle soðien, Laym. 8491. *Icel.* sanna *to prove, make good.*] v. ge-, un-sōðian; sēðan.

sōþ-līc; *adj.* I. *true, genuine, unfeigned*:—Nǣnig ōðerne freóþ in fyrhðe, ðæt hē sōðlīce (*or adv.?*) sybbe healde, gāstlīce lufe, Fragm. Kmbl. 72; Leás. 38. II. *true, right*:—Ne þincþ mē nǣfre nānwuht swā sōþlīc swā mē þincþ ðīn spell ðǣm tīmum ðe ic ða gehiére *cum tuas rationes considero, nihil dici verius puto*, Bt. 38, 5; Fox 204, 22. [*O. Sax.* sōð-līk: *Icel.* sann-ligr *probable; just; fit.*] v. next word.

sōþlīce. I. *as adv. Truly, really, certainly, verily*:—Sōðlīce ðū eart Godes sunu *vere filius Dei es*, Mt. Kmbl. 14, 33: 27, 54. Sōðlīce ic secge eów *amen dico vobis*, 6, 16 (and often). Ðām ðe sōðlīce sēcaþ Dryhten, Ps. Th. 104, 3. Ðis wæs sōðlīce eádig wer *vere beatus vir*, Blickl. Homl. 223, 31. Ðū bist sōþlīce ǣr þrīm dagum genumen of ðīnum līchoman *certainly before three days thou wilt be taken from the body*, 137, 25. Is sōðlīce se cwide gefylled, 139, 27. Swȳþe sōþlīce (*with great truth*) wē māgon geþencan, ðæt hit biþ deáþes ylding swīðor ðonne līfes, 59, 31. Ic sōðlīce meahte ongitan, Exon. Th. 313, 24; Mōd. 5. Se ðe ðē ðyslīce gife and swā mycle sōþlīce (-re, MS.) ðē tōwearde forecwyþ *is qui tanta taliaque dona veraciter adventura praedixerit*, Bd. 2, 12; S. 514, 13: Exon. Th. 9, 19; Cri. 137. Weras ða ðe eówre ǣ on ferhðsefan fyrmest hæbben, ða mē sōðlīce secgan cunnon, Elen. Kmbl. 633; El. 317: Beo. Th. 284; B. 141. Hī ðȳ sōðlīcor ongeáton ðæt hit wæs sōðlīce his āgen līchoma, Shrn. 68, 33. Ic sōðlīcost wēne, 164, 28. II. *as conj. Now, then, for*; representing Latin autem, ecce, enim, ergo, nam, vero:—Sōðlīce Iosep hyre wer *Joseph autem vir ejus*, Mt. Kmbl. 1, 19 (and often). Sōðlīce seó fǣmne hæfþ on innoðe *ecce virgo in utero habebit*, 1, 23: 2, 9: 3, 17. Sōðlīce wē gesāwon hys steorran, *vidimus enim stellam ejus*, 2, 2: 3, 1: 4, 18 (and often). Gehȳre gē sōðlīce ðæs sāwendan bigspell *vos ergo audite parabolam seminantis*, 13, 18. Sōðlīce ic eom man under anwealde gesett *nam et ego homo sum sub potestate*, 8, 9. Sōðlīce ðæt ðe āsāwen wæs on ðæt gōde land *qui vero in terra bona seminatus est*, 13, 23, 29. [*O. Sax.* sōðlīko: *Icel.* sannliga.]

sōþ-sægen, -segen, e; *f. A true statement, statement of the truth,* *statement of the facts of a case*:—Se Hǽlend nolde hine betellan mid nânre sôðsegene ðeáh ðe hê unscyldig wǽre *the Saviour would not clear himself by any statement of the truth, though he was innocent*, Homl. Th. ii. 250, 11. Hî sceolon forsuwian heora geférena unþeáwas, ðý læs ðe hî þurh heora sôðsegene ungeðyldige beón, 230, 17.

sôþ-sagol; *adj. Veracious*:—Sôðsagol *veridicus*, Wrt. Voc. i. 76, 18: *verax*, Ps. Lamb. 85, 13. Swâ swâ sôþsagol stǽrwrîtere *quasi verax historicus*, Bd. 3, 17; S. 545, 4. Se ðe wǽre leássagol, weorðe se sôþ-sagol, Wulfst. 72, 16. [*Icel.* sann-sögull.] v. un-sôþsagol.

sôþ-sagu, e; *f.* I. *true speech, truth*:—On manna gehwylces môde and mûðe sôðsagu stande, Wulfst. 74, 16. II. *a true saying, a history*:—Sôðsaga *historia*, Mt. Kmbl. p. 9, 4: *historiae*, 7, 9. [Þilke soþsaȝe (*saw*), þat man schal erien and sowe þar he wenþ after sum god mowe, O. and N. 1038. *Icel.* sann-saga *a true tale.*]

sôþ-secgan *to say truly, declare*:—Sôðsæges *pronuntiat*, Jn. Skt. p. 4, 11: 6, 15 (*see* sôþ=*pro*). Ðes man is sôþsecgende, Blickl. Homl. 187, 29.

sôþ-spell *a true story, history*:—Sôðspell *historia*, Mt. Kmbl. p. 9, 4. [*O. Sax.* sôð-spell.]

sôþ-sprǽc *a true saying*:—Sôðsprǽco *eloquia*, Rtl. 171, 35.

sôþ-tâcen *a true sign, prodigy*:—Sôðtâceno *prodigia*, Rtl. 43, 35 (*see* sôþ=*pro*).

sôþ-word *a true word*:—Ic Gode sealmas singe, sôðword sprece, Ps. Th. 56, 9: 118, 93.

sotol *a seat.* v. setl.

sotscipe, es; *m. Folly, stupidity*:—Sotscipe *hebetudo*, Wrt. Voc. i. 50, 60. [Sæide se abbot of Clunni, ꝥ hi heafdon foloron S. Iohes mynstre þurh hi and þurh his mycele sotscipe, Chr. 1131; Erl. 260, 8. Nolde þe leodking his sothscipe (folie, 2nd MS.) bilæuen, Laym. 3024. Muchel sotschipe hit is uorto uorleosen uor one deie tene oðer tweolue, A. R. 422, 24.]

sott; *adj. Foolish, stupid*; substantively, *a fool*:—Sot *sottus*, Wrt. Voc. i. 76, 16. Sott *hebes*, 50, 59. Se ðe his âgene sprǽce âwyrt, hê wyrcþ *barbarismus*. Swylce hê cweðe ðû sôt ðǽr hê sceolde cweðan ðû sott, Anglia viii. 313, 21. Ne biþ se nâ wita, ðe unwîslîce leofaþ, ac biþ open sott, ðeáh ðe him swâ ne þince, Homl. Skt. i. 13, 132. [Þu ebure sot (fol, 2nd MS.), Laym. 2271. Þa weoren Scottes ihalden for sottes, 21806. Seide ꝥ heo weoren sotten iueren, 17309. Nout to ȝunge preostes, ne to sot olde, A. R. 336, 12. Lat sottes chide, O. and N. 297. The word is of doubtful origin, v. Skeat's Etym. Dict. *sot.*]

spâca, an; *m.* I. *the spoke* of a wheel:—Ða sêlestan men faran nêhst Gode, swâ swâ sió nafu férþ nêhst ðære eaxe, and ða midmestan swâ swâ spâcan; for ðam ðe ǽlces spâcan biþ ôþer ende fæst on ðære nafe, ôþer on ðære felge . . . Ða felga hangiaþ on ðâm spâcan, Bt. 39, 7; Fox 222, 1–13. Spâcan *radii*, Wrt. Voc. i. 16, 23: 284, 47: 66, 54. II. part of the body [=ribb-spâcan]:—Spâcan *radioli*, 65, 21. [*O. L. Ger.* spêca *radius*: *O. H. Ger.* speicha *radius, lignum in rota*: *Ger.* speiche.]

spad, spada. v. spadu.

spade *eunuchus*:—*Eviratus*, i. *effeminatus, eunuchus, enervus* spade, Wrt. Voc. ii. 144, 37.

spâdl. v. spâtl.

spadu, an, e; *f.*: spada (?); *m. A spade*:—Spadu *fossorium*; spada *vanga*; spad[u?] *scudicia* vel *fossorium*, Wrt. Voc. i. 16, 14, 8, 29. Spadu, spædu *uanga* vel *fossorium*, Ælfc. Gl. Zup. 318, 17. Ic nât mid hwî ic delfe, nû mê wana is ǽgðer ge spadu ge mattuc, Homl. Skt. ii. 23 b, 765. Sum underdealf ða duru mid spade, Swt. A. S. Prim. 87, 174. Ðâ genam hê âne spada[n?] and dealf ða eorþan, H. R. 13, 13. Spadan *vangas*, Wrt. Voc. ii. 123, 10. [*O. L. Ger.* spado *sarculum, rastrum*: *Gk.* σπάθη.]

spæc, es; *m.* (?) *n.* (?) *A thin twig, tendril, runner*:—Twig *ramus*, spæc *framen* (cf. *framen* streáberie-wîsan, 31, 70), Wrt. Voc. i. 285, 81: ii. 36, 57: *cremium* (*cremia* ligna tenuia et arida), 151, 2. Ðara spaca speldra *malleoli* (*malleolus* manipulus sparteus pice contectus quem incensum in muros jaciebant), 54, 57. [*O. H. Ger.* spah, spahha(o) *sarmentum, cremium, fasciculus ex siccis lignis, malleolus, ramus.*] v. spræc.

spǽc, spædu. v. sprǽc, spadu.

spær; *adj. Spare, frugal*:—Spær mete *parcus cibus*, Scint. 52, 6. [*O. H. Ger.* spar *parcus*: *Icel.* sparr.] v. spær-hende, -lîc, -ness.

spærca. v. spearca.

spæren; *adj. Of plaster, of mortar*:—Spaeren, sparaen, sparen *gipsus*, Txts. 67, 968. Spæren, Wrt. Voc. ii. 40, 67. v. spær-stân.

spær-habuc. v. spear-hafoc.

spær-hende; *adj. Of sparing hand, frugal, sparing*:—Spærhende *frugi* vel *parcus*, Wrt. Voc. i. 76, 6. Uncystig oþþe spærhynde (-hende) *frugi*, Ælfc. Gr. 9, 78; Zup. 74, 12. Spærhynde *parcus*, Germ. 392, 66. [*O. H. Ger.* un-sparahenti *prodigus.*]

spær-lîc; *adj. Sparing, frugal*:—Swâ sperlîc *tam frugalis*, Hpt. Gl. 494, 43.

spærlîce; *adv. Sparingly, sparely*:—Spærlîce *parce*, Scint. 156, 9. Ðý mon dǽlþ spærlîce ðe mon nele hit forberste *sparingly people spend, because they do not want to run short*, Prov. Kmbl. 19. Ic sperlîcor mid wordum sægde ðonne hié dǽdum gedôn wǽrun *solere me parcius loqui quam gesta sint omnia*, Nar. 2, 24. [*O. H. Ger.* sparalîhho *parce, frugaliter*: *Icel.* sparliga *sparingly.*]

spær-lira. v. spear-lira.

spærness, e; *f. Sparingness, frugality, parsimony*:—Spærnes *frugalitas*, i. *temperantia, parcitas*, Wrt. Voc. ii. 151, 29. Drences and metes spearness *potus cibique parcitas*, Hymn. Surt. 9, 24. Spærnisse, Rtl. 163, 7. Spærnesse *frugalitatis*, Hpt. Gl. 456, 56: *frugalitatis, temperantiae, moderationis*, 425, 64: *frugalitatis, abstinentiae*, 496, 22: 513, 61: *parsimonia, penuria, temperantia*, 454, 59.

spær-stân, es; *m. Gypsum, chalk*:—Spærstân *gipsum*, Wrt. Voc. i. 85, 22: *creta argentea*, 37, 30.

spǽtan; *p.* te. I. *to spit* (a) intrans.:—Ic hrǽce oððe spǽte *screo*, Ælfc. Gr. 26, 6; Zup. 158, 6. Ic spǽte *spuo*, 28, 3; Zup. 167, 10. Hê spǽtte on his eágan *expuens in oculos ejus*, Mk. Skt. 8, 23: Jn. Skt. 9, 6. Hî spǽtton on hine, Mt. Kmbl. 17, 30: 26, 67. Hig spǽtton him on *conspuebant eum*, Mk. Skt. 15, 19. Spǽte ðæt wîf on his nebb, Deut. 25, 9. Suelce hié him on ðæt nebb spǽten, Past. 5; Swt. 45, 4. Sume âgunnon him on spǽtan (*conspuere eum*), Mk. Skt. 14, 65. Hê spǽtende (*expuens*) his tungan onhrân, 7, 33. Spâtende *expuentes*, Mt. Kmbl. Lind. 27, 30. Hê byþ on spǽt *conspuetur*, Lk. Skt, 18, 32. (b) trans.:—Ic spǽte âttor, Exon. Th. 405, 26; Rä. 24, 8: 398, 27; Rä. 18, 4. II. *to syringe, squirt*[:—Gespǽt ða wunde, Lchdm. ii. 22, 22. v. geond-spǽtan.] v. be-spǽtan.

spǽtl. v. spâtl.

spǽtlan, spǽtlian; *p.* ede. I. *to emit saliva, to foam*:—Spǽtleþ *spumat*, Wrt. Voc. ii. 73, 37. II. *to spit* on anything:—Hié hine bindaþ and spǽtliaþ on his onsýne, Blickl. Homl. 15, 11. Hié spǽtledon on his onsýne, 23, 32. Spǽtlædon, 237, 11. Spǽtledon (-odon), Anglia xii. 505, 14. v. spâtlian.

spǽtung, e; *f. Spitting, expectoration*:—Gelôme spǽtunga oððe hrǽcunga, Lchdm. ii. 174, 20.

spala, an; *m. A representative, substitute*:—Gif hê untrum byþ, begyte him lahlîcne spalan, L. Wil. ii. 2; Th. i. 489, 16. Cf. ge-spelia.

Spaldas *a tribe name left in Spalding* (?). In a list giving the extent of territory belonging to various districts in England it is said:—Spalda syx hund hýda, Cod. Dip. B. i. 414, 20. Cf. Spaldyng, Cod. Dip. Kmbl. vi. 333, col. 2.

spaldur *asphalt*; aspaltum, Txts. 43, 228.

-span *allurement.* v. ge-span.

spanan; *p.* spôn, speón; *pp.* spanen *To allure, entice, lure, decoy, attract, urge*:—Spenst *illicias*, Hpt. Gl. 524, 9. Spones *inlicias*, Wrt. Voc. ii. 47, 7: 87, 26. I. in a good sense, (a) with a preposition marking the direction of aim:—Ðû spenst (spænst, Cott. MS.) mê on ða mǽstan sprǽce and on ða earfoþestan tô gereccenne *ad rem me omnium quaesitu maximam vocas*, Bt. 39, 4; Fox 216, 14. Swâ earn his briddas spænþ tô flihte *sicut aquila provocans ad volandum pullos suos*, Deut. 32, 11. Ðâ hê spôn his hiéremen tô ðære geðylde *cum patientiam discipulis suaderet*, Past. 33, 5; Swt. 222, 8. Ðâ ðâ hê his apostolas spôn of ðissum andweardan tô ðæm êcan *cum ad venturam discipulos ex praesenti provocaret*, 46, 5; Swt. 351, 11. Speón (spôn, Cott. MSS.), 17, 8; Swt. 121, 2. Speón, Andr. Kmbl. 1194; An. 597. Ælcne man spane hê of synnum *let him draw every man from sins*, L. Edg. C. 16; Th. ii. 284, 14. Ða spone (spane, Cott. MSS.) ðe his ðeáwa giémaþ tô ryhte *spectatores suos ad sublimia invitet*, Past. 14, 2; Swt. 83, 2. Hê sende his englas ûs hâm tô spananne tô him *exhortantes angelos misit*, 52, 4; Swt. 405, 34. (b) with a clause:—God hine spænþ ðæt hê tô him gecierre *Deus ad se redire persuadet*, Swt. 407, 10. Hî hine speónnan and lǽrdon ðæt hê ða fôre ðurhtuge *eum id perficere suadebant*, Bd. 5, 19; S. 637, 26. Span ðû hine georne ðæt hê ðîne lâre lǽste, Cd. Th. 36, 22; Gen. 575. Cwæð, ðæt hine his hige speóne, ðæt hê trymede getimbro, 18, 17; Gen. 274. II. in a bad sense, (a) with a preposition:—Hine spænþ his môd tô unnyttum weorce, Past. 4; Swt. 37, 18. Deófol hine on wôh spaneþ, Salm. Kmbl. 1002; Sal. 502: 990; Sal. 496. Hî spanaþ ðê tô ðînre unþearefe, Bt. 7, 2; Fox 18, 9. On ðæm weorce ðe hine ǽr nân willa tô ne spôn *quo non trahit desiderium*, Past. 33, 1; Swt. 215, 10. Hió speón hine on ða dimman dǽd, Cd. Th. 43, 2; Gen. 684. Hê mid listum speón idese on ðæt unriht, 37, 12; Gen. 588. Hî (*the conspirators against William*) speónan ða Bryttas heom tô, Chr. 1075; Erl. 213, 14. (b) with a clause:—Hê hiene spôn ðæt hê on Umenis unmyndlenga mid here becôme *quem, ut Eumenem de insperato opprimat, perurget*, Ors. 3, 11; Swt. 146, 7. [*O. Sax.* spanan; *p.* spôn: *O. Frs.* spona: *O. H. Ger.* spanan; *p.* spuon *suggerere, suadere, persuadere*: cf. *Icel.* spenja; *p.* spandi *to allure.*] v. â-, be-, for-, ge-spanan.

Spâneas; *pl. The Spaniards* or *Spain*:—Betux Galleum and Spâneum, Ors. 4, 8; Swt. 186, 15. [Cf. *Icel.* Spâna-land *Spain.*] v. Spêne.

spanere, es; *m. One who entices*:—Sponera *lenonum*, Wrt. Voc. ii. 52, 42: 84, 39. [*O. H. Ger.* spanari *hortator, suasor, persuasor, illex.*]

spang, e; *f. A clasp, fastening*:—Hæleðhelm on heáfod âsette and ðone full hearde geband spênn mid spangum *drew the helmet firmly on with its clasps*, Cd. Th. 29, 4; Gen. 445. [*O. H. Ger.* spanga; *f. seracula, prena*: *Ger.* spange *a clasp*: *Icel.* spöng; *f. a clasp.*]

spann, e; *f. A span:*—Span *vel* handbred *palmus*, Wrt. Voc. i. 43, 52. Wæs se līchoma sponne lengra đære đrȳh *invenerunt corpus mensura palmi longius esse sarcofago*, Bd. 4, 11; S. 580, 5. [*O. H. Ger.* spanna; *f. cubitus: Icel.* spönn; *f. a span.*] Cf. ge-spann.

spannan; *p.* spēnn, speónn; *pp.* spannen. I. *to join* one thing to another, *to attach, fasten, clasp*, (a) literal:—Hē helm spēnn mid spangum (cf. *Dan.* spænde ved spænder, *Swed.* spänna med spänne *to buckle*) *he buckled on his helmet*, Cd. Th. 29, 4; Gen. 445. (b) figurative:—Wā eów đe gadriaþ hūs tō hūse and spannaþ æcer tō đæm ōđrum *vae, qui conjungitis domum ad domum, et agrum agro copulatis*, Past. 44, 8; Swt. 329, 23. II. *to span, clasp.* v. ymb-spannan, spanning. [*O. H. Ger.* spannan; *p.* spien *nectere; intendere, contendere*: cf. *Icel.* spenna; *p.* ta *to clasp; to span.*] v. ge-, on-, ymb-spannan.

spanning, e; *f. Spanning, bend, span:*—Eln *vel* spanning betwiox þuman and scitefingre *ulna*, Wrt. Voc. i. 43, 53.

spanu, e, an; *f. A teat:*—Tittas *mammille*, spana *ubera*, Wrt. Voc. i. 283, 30. Tittas ođđe sponan *mammillas*, Lchdm. i. lxxiv, 24. [Speen, spene *a cow's pap*, E. D. S. Gloss. B. 16: C. 3. Speans *the teats of a cow*, C. 4. *Icel.* speni; *m. a teat, dug: Norweg.* spæne: *Swed.* spene.]

spanung. v. for-, leás-spanung(-ing).

sparian; *p.* ode. I. *to spare, to show mercy to, to refrain from injuring* or *destroying:*—Ic sparige ođđe ārige *parco*, Ælfc. Gr. 28, 7; Zup. 180, 12. Đætte hē spærio *parcere*, Rtl. 40, 19. (a) with acc.:—Ic geswerge đæt ic hī ne sparige, ac on spild giefe, Exon. Th. 247, 27; Jul. 85. Hē āraþ (sparaþ, MS. C.: spearaþ, Ps. Surt.) *parcet*, Ps. Spl. 71, 13. Hié ne sparodan đa synfullan, ac slōgon, Past. 46; Swt. 353, 16. Hī nānne ne sparedon đæs herefolces, Jud. Thw. 24, 40; Jud. 233. Spara mē đīnne đeów *parce servo tuo*, Ps. Th. 18, 11. (b) with dat.:—[Ne spareþ se fæder đan sune ne nān mann ōđren; ac ǽlc man winþ ongeán ōđren, Shrn. 17, 27.] Swā đæt ne cyricum ne mynstrum seó herehand ne sparode ne ārode *ita ut ne ecclesiis quidem aut monasteriis manus parcerit hostilis*, Bd. 4, 26; S. 602, 8. God ne sparode his āgenum bearne, Homl. Th. ii. 62, 20. Nā hē sparode (spearede, Ps. Surt. v. 50) sāulum heora *non pepercit animabus eorum*, Ps. Spl. C. 77, 55. Spær esne đīnum *parce servo tuo*, Rtl. 168, 19: 39, 38. II. *to spare, preserve, not to use, to leave alone, abstain from:*—Hē sparode đæt gōde wīn ōđ his āgenum tōcyme, Homl. Th. ii. 70, 10. Fēđe ne sparode eorl, Cd. Th. 153, 6; Gen. 2534. Sindon đa loccas tō sparianne (-enne, Hatt. MS.) đæm sacerde đæt hī đa hȳd behelien *capilli in capite sacerdotis servantur, ut cutem cooperiant*, Past. 18, 7; Swt. 141, 9. [*O. H. Ger.* sparōn *parcere, fovere: Icel.* spara *to spare.*] v. ge-sparian.

sparrian *to bar, shut.* [Sparren, sperren is not uncommon in later English. v. Stratmann's Dict. Cf. *O. H. Ger.* sperren *claudere.*] v. be-, ge-sparrad.

spātl, es; *n. Spittle, saliva:*—Spātl *sputum*, Wrt. Voc, ii. 70, 21. Hē worhte fenn of his spātle *he made clay of the spotle* (Wick), Jn. Skt. 9, 6. Đīn spātl spīw on, Lchdm. ii. 322, 7: 24, 8: 36, 17. Se nā ne forbeág mid his nebbe đara triówleásena monna spātl, Past. 36; Swt. 261, 9: Exon. Th. 88, 7; Cri. 1436. Spādl, Elen. Kmbl. 600; El. 300. Spādl, Mt. Kmbl. Rush. 27, 30. Đa spǽtlu āþwōgon ūre sweartan gyltas, Homl. Th. ii. 248, 26. Spātlum *salivis*, Germ. 396, 283. Đæne đe hȳ heora spātlum on spiwon, Wulfst. 183, 21. Spātlu *sputa*, Hymn. Surt. 80, 1. [Heo bispeted hire mid hire blake spotle, A. R. 288, 10. Spotle *sputum, screa, saliva*, Prompt. Parv. 469, col. 2.]

spātlian; *p.* ode *To spit out:*—Ic spātlige *pitisso*, Wrt. Voc. i. 46, 16. [I (*the old man*) spitte, I spatle, Rel. Ant. ii. 211, 34.] v. *next word, and* spǽtlan.

spātlung, e; *f. Spitting out, spittle:*—*Pituita*, i. *minuta saliva* horas *vel* hrǽcunga *vel* spātlung, Wrt. Voc. i. 46, 15. [I (*Christ*) þolede schomeliche spateling of unwurđi ribauz, O. E. Homl. i. 279, 34. Þenched þet te worldes weldinde wolde þolien buffetes, spotlunge, blindfellunge, A. R. 188, 10.]

spearca, an; *m. A spark.* I. literal:—Spærca *scintella*, Wrt. Voc. ii. 120, 21. Spearca *scintilla*, i. 66, 39: 284, 14. Ne biþ đǽr leóhtes ān lytel spearca, Wulfst. 139, 11. Sleá hē him ānne spearcan, Lchdm. ii. 290, 17. Hī āsprungan up swā swā spearcan, Homl. Th. ii. 350, 23: Bd. 3, 10; S. 534, 31. Đæt manega menn geseóþ feallan of đære heofene, swylce hit sȳn steorran, hit beóþ spearcan of đam rodere, Anglia viii. 320, 33. His eágan wǽron fȳrene spearcan sprengende, Homl. Th. i. 466, 26. II. metaphorical:—Se spearca đara gōdra weorca, Past. 14; Swt. 87, 6. Sum spearca sōþfæstnesse, Bt. 35, 5; Fox 164, 2. Ne furđum ān spearca mīnes cynrenes nis mē forlǽtan, Homl. Skt. ii. 30, 206. Gif đa scyldigan ǽnigne spearcan wīsdōmes hæfdon, 38, 7; Fox 210, 9. Word spearcum fleáh āttre gelīcost, Cd. Th. 274, 32; Sat. 162. v. fȳr-spearca.

spearcian, spearcan (?) *To sparkle, emit sparks:*—Hē sweartade (spearcade?) đonne hē spreocan ongan fȳre and āttre, Cd. Th. 269, 24; Sat. 78. Sparcendum *scintillante*, Hpt. Gl. 501, 5. [*Prompt. Parv.* sparkyn *scintillo.* It sparkede and full brith shon, Havel. 2144.] v. spircan.

spear-hafoc, es; *m. A sparrow-hawk:*—Spaerhabuc *alietum* (*alietus* an hobey, Wülck. Gl. 562, 48), Wrt. Voc. ii. 99, 67. Spearhafuc, 7, 65: i. 280, 20. Spearhafoc *hetum*, 62, 16: *accipiter* vel *raptor*, 29, 58: *ismarus* (= *ismerlus?* cf. *French* émerillon *a merlin*), 63, 25. [Sparowhawke *nisus*, Wrt. Voc. i. 177, 14. *Icel.* sparr-haukr. Cf. *O. H. Ger.* sparwāri *nisus: Ger.* sperber; and the borrowed Romance forms, *Fr.* épervier; *Ital.* sparviere.]

spear-lira, an; *m. The calf of the leg:*—Spærlira *sura*, Wrt. Voc. i. 44, 71: 71, 55. Sperlira, 65, 43. Spærlirena *surarum*, Hpt. Gl. 478, 56. Spærlirum *suris*, 483, 37. Spærliran *suras*, 482, 65. On spearlirum *in suris*, Deut. 28, 35. Speoruliran *suras*, Lchdm. i. lxxi, 10. [Hose . . . þat spenet on his sparlyr & clene spures under, Gaw. 158. Sparluris, Wick. Deut. 28, 35.] v. spearwa.

spearlirede *having a large calf:*—Spærlirede *surosus*, Wrt. Voc. i. 45, 42.

spearnlian; *p.* ode *To spurn, strike out with the feet, kick:*—Đæt đū ne spear[n]last *ut non calcitres*, Hpt. Gl. 463, 77. Se sticca him eode ūt þurh đæt heáfod in tō đære eorđan and hē ætforan hire spearnlode mid fōtum *the nail went through his head into the earth, and he* (Sisera) *struck out with his feet before her*, Jud. 4, 21. Cf. spurnan.

spearwa, an; *m. A sparrow:*—Spearuua, spearua, sperua *fenus*, Txts. 62, 435. Spearwa, Wrt. Voc. ii. 35, 22: *passer*, i. 77, 29: 281, 27: Bd. 2, 13; S. 516, 17: Ps. Spl. 83, 3. Spearewa, Wrt. Voc. i. 63, 7. Spearuwa, Ps. Th. 10, arg.: 83, 3. Speara, Ps. Surt. 83, 4. Đā geseah heó spearwan nest, Homl. As. 120, 116. Ic spearuwan gelīce geweard, Ps. Th. 101, 5. Spearwan nystlaþ *passeres nidificabunt*, 103, 16. Spearwan (hrond-sparuas, Lind.: spearwas, Rush.), Mt. Kmbl. 10, 29, 31: Lk. Skt. 12, 6. Beteran manegum spearwum, 12, 7. [*Goth.* sparwa: *O. H. Ger.* sparo: *Icel.* spörr.] v. neód-spearuwa.

spearwa, an; *m. The calf of the leg:*—Sparuua, sparua, spearua *surum*, Txts. 94, 897. v. spear-lira.

spec, spēc, speca, specan. v. spic, sprǽc, spreca, sprecan.

specca, an; *m. A speck, spot, blot:*—Đone sweartan speccan *maculam pullam*, Wrt. Voc. ii. 57, 11: 92, 84. Speccan *notae*, 114, 80: 60, 18: *scoriae*, Hpt. Gl. 421, 59. Smire đa speccan (*in a case of shingles*) mid đære sealfe, Lchdm. ii. 88, 19. v. next two words.

specel (?); *adj. Speckled.* v. haran-specel, *and see* Lchdm. ii. 390, col. 2.

spec-fāh; *adj. Speckled, spotted, full of spots:*—Specfaag *maculosus*, Wrt. Voc. ii. 98, 25.

specol. v. sprecol.

sped *phlegm, rheum:*—Sped *petuita*, Wrt. Voc. ii. 117, 22: 68, 18. Sped *glaucoma* (cf. *spade* the congealed gum of the eye, Halliwell's Dict.), Hpt. Gl. 447, 22. v. spediende.

spēd, e; *f. Speed, success, means.* The word is found in the following glosses:—Spoed *proventus, praeventus*, Txts. 88, 815: *successus*, 96, 940: *praesidium*, 89, 1648. Spēd *proventus*, Wrt. Voc. i. 61, 25: ii. 68, 44. Đeós spēd *haec ops*, Ælfc. Gr. 9, 56; Zup. 67, 18. Spēde *facultatem*, Hpt. Gl. 437, 40. Spēdum *successibus*, Wrt. Voc. ii. 76, 56. I. *speed, quickness;* spēdum *speedily, quickly:*—Gewiton him ædre æfter đære sprǽce spēdum fēran, Cd. Th. 144, 32; Gen. 2398. Spēdum sægde eorlum Abimeleh egesan geđreád Waldendes word, 161, 19; Gen. 2667. Him đa brōđor þrȳ spēdum miclum (*very speedily*) hǽldon hygesorge heardum wordum, 122, 30; Gen. 2034. [Waterrstræm erneþþ towarrd te sæ wiþþ mikell sped ȝiff þatt itt nohht ne letteþþ, Orm. 18094.] II. *speed* (as in good *speed*), *success, prosperous issue:*—Đæt mīnre sprǽce spēd folgie *that success may attend my speech*, Ps. Th. 55, 4. Heó (*Sarah*) ne gelȳfde đæt đære sprǽce spēd folgode *she did not believe that any happy result would follow those words, did not believe that she should have a son*, Cd. Th. 144, 4; Gen. 2384. Hit ne becymþ eów nā tō nānre spēde *vobis non cedet in prosperum*, Num. 14, 41. Đǽr rīcxaþ sib mid spēde *peace and happiness reign there*, Dōm. L. 267. On spēd *successfully, to purpose, with effect*, Beo. Th. 1750; B. 873: Exon. Th. 387, 28; Rä. 5, 12. Swā wit him an spēd sprecaþ *we shall speak so as to convince him*, Cd. Th. 36, 21; Gen. 575. Ic on đīnre hǽlo hyldo sōhte and on đīnre sprǽce spēd sōđfæste *in salutari tuo, et in eloquio justitiae tuae*, Ps. Th. 118, 123. Wīges spēd *success in war*, Exon. Th. 42, 16; Cri. 673. Æt wigge spēd, sigor æt sæcce, Elen. Kmbl. 2362; El. 1182. Hié đære spǽce spēd ne āhton *the people at Babel had no advantage from speech*, Cd. Th. 101, 23; Gen. 1686. Se đe him dōm forgeaf, spōwende spēd (*good speed*), 246, 14; Dan. 479. Æt đam sperenīde spēde lǽnan, 124, 8; Gen. 2059: 187, 19; Exod. 153. III. *means, substance, abundance, wealth:*—Spēd ł dǽl mīn đū eart *portio mea es*, Ps. Lamb. 118, 57: 141, 6. Spēd *substantia*, Ps. Spl. 38, 7, 11: 68, 2: Ps. Th. 88, 40. His meahta spēd *the abundance of his powers*, Exon. Th. 240, 18; Ph. 640. Hē is mægna spēd, Cd. Th. 1, 6; Gen. 3. Wilna gehwilces weaxende spēd *a growing abundance of every thing to be desired*, 100, 7; Gen. 1660. Ic on mīnre heortan hȳdde georne đæt ic đīnre sprǽce spēd gehealde *in corde meo abscondi eloquia tua*, Ps. Th. 118, 11: 38. Tubal Cain þurh snytro spēd smiđcræftega wæs *Tubal Cain was a workman cunning through wealth of wisdom*, Cd. Th. 66, 14; Gen. 1084. Metod tōbrǽd þurh his mihta spēd monna sprǽce, 102, 6; Gen. 1696: 306, 23; Sat. 668: Exon. Th. 225, 25; Ph. 394. Hē ūs giefeþ ǽhta spēd, welan ofer wīd lond, 38, 10; Cri. 604. Hwǽr sind spēda rīcera *ubi sunt opes potentum*, Wülck. Gl. 253, 38: Ors. 1, 1; Swt. 18, 8. Eorđan spēda, Soul Kmbl. 154; Seel. 77. Đīnre sprǣce spēde *eloquia tua*, Ps. Th. 118, 172. Đa đe đære mycelnesse hiora spēda gylpaþ *qui multitudine abundantiarum suarum gloriabuntur*, 48, 6. Đū on đīnes mægenes mihte spēdum sǣ gesettest *tu confirmasti in virtute tua mare*, 73, 13. Ōđre him of hyra spēdum (*de facultatibus suis*) þēnedon, Lk. Skt. 8, 3. Mid eallum hira spēdum đe hig hæfdon *cum universa substantia eorum quam habebant*, Deut. 11, 6. 'Redemptio animae propriae divitiae' . . . wē sceoldon mid ūrum spēdum ūrum sāulum đa ēcan gesǣlinesse begitan, Chart. Th. 124, 27. Mē đīn sprǣc spēdum (*richly, abundantly*) cwycade *eloquium tuum vivificavit me*, Ps. Th. 118, 50. Ealle mynstres fata and spēde hē sceal beseón *omnia uasa monasterii cunctamque substantiam conspitiat*, R. Ben. 55, 1. Đīn sunu đe hys spēde (*substantiam*) āmyrde, Lk. Skt. 15, 30. Gemicla đū heora wīn and heora worldlīce spēde, Shrn. 104, 26: Ps. Th. 51, 6. Hē næfþ rihtwīsnysse spēda and wīsdōmes goldhordas đe sind sōđe welan, Homl. Th. ii. 88, 28. IV. *power, faculty*:—Đǣr wæs gesȳne his seó sōđe spēd *videbitur in majestate sua*, Ps. Th. 101, 14. Þurh đīnra dǣda spēd dagas hēr gewuniaþ *ordinatione tua perseverat dies*, 118, 91. Hafast đū heáh mægen đīnes earmes spēd wiđ ealle fȳnd *in virtute brachii tui dispersisti inimicos tuos*, 88, 9. Þurh his ǣgne spēd witan, Exon. Th. 351, 9; Sch. 77. Syndon on đissum Simone twā spēda, mannes and deófles, Blickl. Homl. 179, 10. Đū eart mægena God, nis đē gelīc on spēdum, Ps. Th. 88, 7. Wæs heofonweardes gāst ofer holm boren miclum spēdum, Cd. Th. 8, 8; Gen. 121. Meotud monnum syleþ sundorgiefe, sendeþ wīde āgne spēde (*faculties peculiar to each*), Exon. Th. 293, 24; Crä. 6. V. *opportunity*, or *means* of doing anything:—Đæt hē him spēde and lȳfnysse sealde đæt hē đǣr wunian mōste for intingan his gebeda *ut sibi facultatem et licentiam ibidem orationis causa demorandi concederet*, Bd. 3, 23; S. 554, 29. Se ealdormon him spēde and lȳfnesse sealde tō farene swā hwider swā hī woldan *major domus regiae copiam pergendi quoquo vellent, tribuit eis*, 4, 1; S. 564, 34. VI. *progeny* (?):—On cederbeámum mid heora spēdum spearwan nystlaþ, Ps. Th. 103, 16. [Huand iu thiu spōt cumid, helpe fon himile (cf. thurgh helpe and spede of prayer, Pr. C. 2882), Hel. 1901. *O. H. Ger.* spuot *celeritas, successus, provectus, prosperitas, substantia*.] v. ǣht-, freónd-, freoþo-, here-, land-, mægen-, sige-, sigor-, tuddor-, un-, wīg-, woruld-, wuldor-spēd.

spēdan; *p*. de *To speed, have success, succeed* in doing something:—Eów betere is đæt gē đisne gārrǣs mid gafole forgyldon . . . ne þurfe wē ūs spillan gif gē spēdaþ tō đam (cf. Gif hē ne geþeó būton tō healfre hīde *if he succeeds in obtaining no more than a half hide*, Ll. Th. i. 188, 1) *for you is it better to buy off this attack . . . We need not destroy one another, if you succeed in doing this*, Byrht. Th. 132, 51; By. 34. [Swā hē spēdde, swā him Crist hūđe, swā þet in fēuna geáre wæs ꝥ mynstre gare, Chr. 656; Erl. 30, 18. Hē spēdde litel, and be gode rihte, for hē wæs ān yuel man, 1140; Erl. 265, 17. His broþer heo him wolde binimen, ah he ne mihte speden, Laym. 403. He wollde winnenn Crist alls he wann Eve and Adam ȝiff þatt he mihhte spedenn, Orm. 12317. *O. H. Ger.* gi-spuotōn *accelerare*.] v. ā-, ge-spēdan.

sped-dropa (spēd-?), an; *m. A rheumy* (?) *drop*:—Mec (*a book*) fugles wyn (*a pen*) geond speddropum (*ink*) spyrede, Exon. Th. 408, 6; Rä. 27, 8. v. sped.

spediende *suffering from rheum* or *phlegm* (?):—Spediende (swed-, Wrt.) *molaricus* (the preceding words are *podagricus, flegmaticus, reumaticus*), Wrt. Voc. i. 45, 49: ii. 58, 2. v. sped.

spēdig; *adj*. I. *having good speed, prosperous*:—Him fēran gewāt Abraham wīde ođ đæt hē tō Siem com sīđe spēdig (*prosperous in travel*), Cd. Th. 107, 3; Gen. 1783. II. *having means, wealthy, opulent, rich in material wealth*:—Hē wæs swȳđe spēdig man on đǣm ǣhtum đe heora spēda on beóþ, đæt is, on wildrum, Ors. 1, 1; Swt. 18, 8. Ic ne eom swā spēdig (*dives*) đæt ic mǣge bicgean mē wīn, Coll. Monast. Th. 35, 17. Of spē[digre], of gestreónfulre *sumptuosa, copiosa*, Hpt. Gl. 491, 4. III. *rich in, abounding in, abundant, copious*:—Mundbora meahtum spēdig *a protector abundant in power* (*God*), Exon. Th. 143, 27; Gū. 667: 198, 14; Ph. 10: 305, 2; Fä. 82. Wæstmum spēdig, Cd. Th. 169, 19; Gen. 2802. Mihtum spēdge, 101, 25; Gen. 1687. Spēdige, Ps. Th. 59, 5. IV. *powerful* (cf. rīce):—Spēdig *potens*, Ps. Lamb. 77, 65. Hē on eorđan byþ eádig and spēdig *potens in terra erit*, Ps. Th. 111, 2. Se sunu wæs sigorfæst, mihtig and spēdig, Rood Kmbl. 299; Kr. 151. Mægena God, milde and spēdig *Deus virtutum*, Ps. Th. 79, 14. Dǣdum spēdig, 67, 18: 104, 7. [*O. H. Ger.* spuotig *uber, efficax, brevis*.] v. ǣht-, fēđe-, freónd-, gōd-, gold-, heán-, land-, med-, þurh-, un-, wan-, wuldor-spēdig.

spēdiglīce. v. ge-spēdiglīce.

spēdigness, e; *f. Wealth, opulence*:—Welan, spēdignesse *opulentia*, Hpt. Gl. 491, 9.

spēdlīce; *adv. Successfully, efficaciously, powerfully, in a manner which produces a result*:—Him spēdlīce spearuwa hūs begyteþ *the sparrow succeeds in finding a house for itself*, Ps. Th. 83, 3: 105, 2. Dō mē spēdlīce cuicne *quicken me effectually*, 118, 154. Syle mē spēdlīce đæt đū mē nerige *grant me effectual release*, 169: 170. Đonne ic him spēdlīce tō spræc and hī lǣrde *when I spoke to them with power and taught them*, 119, 6. [Cf. *O. H. Ger.* spuot-līh *prosper*.]

spēdsumian, spel. v. ge-spēdsumian, spell.

spelc, spilc *a splint*:—Monegum men gescrincaþ his fēt tō his homme . . . dō spelc tō, Lchdm. ii. 68, 7. Wiđ foredum lime . . . dō spilc tō *apply a splint*, 66, 23. [Spelke *fissula*, Prompt. Parv. 468, col. 1. *Spelk* a splinter or narrow strip of wood. 'To spelk in Yorkshire, to set a broken bone; whence the splints used in binding up of broken bones are called spelks,' Kennett MS., Halliwell's Dict. *Icel.* spelkur, spjalkir; *pl. f. splints* for binding up broken bones.] v. spilcan.

spelcean. v. spilcan.

speld, es; *n.*; *pl.* speld *and* speldru (? *or* speldra (*see below*) *from* speldr. Cf. 'Spelder of woode *esclat*, Palsgrave. The schafte to *spildurs* spronge, Avow. of Arthur,' Halliwell's Dict.): speld, e; *f. A splinter, a thin piece of wood used as a torch, a torch*:—On spelde *in favillam*, Anglia xiii. 35, 213. Speldum *favillis*, 36, 234. Đara spaca speldra *malleoli* (v. spæc), Wrt. Voc. ii. 54, 56. Biernende speld *tedas*, 95, 26. Spelde *tedas*, 82, 29. [*Will.* speldes (*splinters*) of a broken spear. *Mod. E.* spell, spill. *M. H. Ger.* spelte *splinter of a lance*: *Icel.* speld, spjald; *n. a tablet*; spilda *a flake*: *Goth.* spilda *a tablet*.]

spelian; *p*. ode *To act as the representative of* another, *to represent, to take*, or *stand in, the place of* another:—*Pronomen* spelaþ đone naman . . . Gif đū cwest: 'Hwā lǣrde đē?' đonne cweđe ic: 'Dūnstān.' 'Hwā hādode đē?' 'Hē mē hādode:' đonne stent se hē on his naman stede and spelaþ hine, Ælfc. Gr. 5; Zup. 8, 11–16. Se abbod, for đig đe hē Godes gespelia is (*quia uices Christi in monasterio creditur agere*), sig hlāford gehāten . . . for đæs lufe đe hē spelaþ *for the love of him whom he represents*, R. Ben. 114, 24. Næs Isaac ofslegen ac se ramm hine spelode, Homl. Th. ii. 62, 25. Hē God spellode (spelode?) *he* (*Nebuchadnezzar*) *put himself in the place of God*, Cd. Th. 257, 16; Dan. 658. Gif hē wrītan ne cunne bidde ōđerne đe cunne đæt hine spelige *si non scit literas, alter ab eo rogatus scribat*, R. Ben. 100, 5. Nān gehādod man ne sceal him tō geteón, đæt hē Crist spelige ofer his hālgan hīrēd, būton him seó notu fram Godes lāreówum betǣht sȳ, Homl. Th. ii. 592, 29. v. ā-spelian; ge-spelia, *and next two words*.

speliend, speligend, es; *m. A representative, vicar*:—*Pronomen* is đæs naman speliend, se spelaþ đone naman, Ælfc. Gr. 5; Zup. 8, 12. Se cyning is Cristes sylfes speligend under him sylfum, Bd. Whelc. 151, 39. v. preceding word.

speling, e; *f. The taking the place* of another, *the acting as the representative* of another:—Cristes gespelia hē (*the abbot*) is and his note and spelinge on mynstre healt *Christi uices agere in monasterio creditur*, R. Ben. 10, 12.

spell, es; *n*. I. *a story, narrative, account, relation*:—Đæt is mǣre spell (*the story of Lot's wife*), Cd. Th. 155, 2; Gen. 2566. Spelli *relatu*, Txts. 93, 1720. Đā rehton hī him sum hālig spel *exponebant illi quendam sacrae historiae sermonem*, Bd. 4, 24; S. 597, 34. Se man sǣde fram helle sīđfæte swylc sār spell (sārspell?) swylce nǣfre ǣr on men ne becom ne nāht oft siđđan *the man told such a dismal story of the journey to hell as never before had come to men, and not often since*, Shrn. 49, 10: Cd. Th. 66, 31; Gen. 1092. Spel wrecan *to tell the story* (*of Beowulf's exploit*), Beo. Th. 1751; B. 873. Hwīlum gyd āwræc, hwīlum spell rehte, 4225; B. 2109. Lyt swigode nīwra spella ac hē sōđlīce sægde *little of the story of what had just happened did he leave unsaid, but told truly*, 5788; B. 2898: 6050; B. 3029. Fela spella him sǣdon đa Beormas of hiera āgnum lande, Ors. 1, 1; Swt. 17, 31. Đās nīwan spel ic đē ealle in cartan āwrīte *has nouas explicaturas historias omnia cartis commendabo*, Nar. 3, 17. Ic mæg singan and secgan spell in meoduhealle, hū mē cynegōde cystum dohten, Exon. Th. 321, 31; Vid. 54. I a. *a historical narrative, history*:—Ic sette be hāligra spelle (*de historiis sanctorum*) āne bōc . . . Đara abbuda stǣr and spell đysses mynstres on twām bōcum ic āwrāt *historiam abbatum monasterii hujus in libellis duobus descripsi*, Bd. 5, 24; S. 648, 20, 28. Ic đē sende đæt spell đæt ic āwrāt be Angeldeóde and Seaxum *historiam gentis Anglorum quam edideram tibi transmisi*, Bd. pref.; S. 471, 9. Ic cȳþe hwanan mē đās spell (*the narratives contained in the history*) cōman, S. 471, 20. Hē spell martyra đrowunge gesomnade *historias passionis martyrum congregans*, 5, 20; S. 641, 43. Ic longe spell hæbbe tō secgenne *uber dicendi materia est*, Ors. 2, 8; Swt. 94, 16. I b. *a false* or *foolish story, a fable*:—Ealdra cwēna spell *anilis fabula*, Wrt. Voc. i. 55, 24. Spel *vel* unnyt sprǣc *fabula*, i. *bella*, ii. 146, 64. Mē mānwyrhtan manige on spellum sægdon *narraverunt mihi iniqui fabulationes*, Ps. Th. 118, 85. Đū gehērdest reccan on ealdum leásum spellum, đætte Iob sceolde beón se hēhsta god, Bt. 35, 4; Fox 162, 5: Met. 26, 2. Đā ongunnon leáse men wyrcan spell, and sǣdon đæt hió sceolde mid hire drȳcræft men forbrēdan, Bt. 38, 1; Fox 194, 30. II. *an instructive talk, discourse, a philosophical argument*, as a theological term *a sermon, homily* (v. spell-bōc):—Sunnandæges spell . . . Se diácon sǣde fram đysum fȳre emne swā wē rǣdaþ on Sunnandæges spelle, Wulfst. 205, 4–206, 1. Đæt nis tō spelle ac elles tō rǣdenne *it is not to be taken as a sermon, but to be read otherwise*, Lchdm. iii. 232, 6. Se wīsdōm ēcte đǣt spell mid leoþe *wisdom, added verse to his argument*,

Bt. 12; Fox 36, 7. Secgan spell *to discourse*, 13; Fox 36, 31. Geher nú ân spell be ðám ofermôdum cyningum, 37, 1; Fox 186, 1: Met. 25, 1. Ongan Waldend wið Abraham sprecan sægde him unlytel spell *held with him long discourse*, Cd. Th. 145, 14; Gen. 2405. Spella and lára rǽd-hycgende, Exon. Th. 301, 27; Fä. 25. Ða twá béc on hundeahtatigum spellum (*homilies*), Ælfc. Gr. pref.; Zup. 2, 15. Bæd ðæt [hé] him on spellum gecýðde, onwrige worda gongum, hú . . . , Exon. Th. 171, 28; Gú. 1133: Cd. Th. 33, 7; Gen. 516. Gif ðú gesihst gimmas deórwyrða findan, spellu (*parabolas*) getácnaþ, Lchdm. iii. 214, 1. III. *a saying, remark, sentence, statement of a single point, dictum*, cf. the later *spell*:—Hit is swíþe ryht spell ðæt Plato sǽde (*the saying is then given*). Ðá cwæþ ic: 'Ic eom geþafa ðæt ðæt was sóð spell, ðæt Plato sǽde, Bt. 35, 1, 2; Fox 156, 8–14: 38, 3; Fox 202, 19. Ic ðé mæg eáþe geandwyrdan ðæs spelles *I can easily give you an answer on the point you have mentioned*, 41, 2; Fox 244, 24. III a. *a saying* that is to be repeated to another, *a message, an announcement.* v. spell-boda, I, god-spell:—Brimmanna boda ábeód eft ongeán, sege ðínum leódum miccle láþre spell *give them a much less pleasant message*, Byrht. Th. 133, 15; By. 50. Drihten dóm forgeaf ðám ðe his spel beraþ *the Lord gave glory to those that bear his messages*, Cd. Th. 246, 15; Dan. 479. IV. *speech, language* of prose:—Ðá hé ðás bóc of Lǽdenum tó Engliscum spelle hæfde gewende, ðá geworhte hé hí eft tó leóþe, Bt. pref.; Fox viii, 9. [*Goth.* spill *a fable, tale*: *O. Sax.* spell: *O. L. Ger.* spell *fabulatio, parabola*: *O. H. Ger.* spell *sermo, narratio, parabola, fabula, mythus*: *Icel.* spjall *a saying.*] v. bealu-, bí-, eald-, fǽr-, forþ-, god-, gúþ-, hilde-, inwit-, lár-, láþ-, leás-, leóf-, lyge-, morgen-, riht-, sár-, sóþ-, weá-, wil-spell.

spell-bóc *a book of homilies*:—.i. full spelbóc wintres and sumeres, Chart. Th. 430, 21.

spell-boda, an; *m.* I. *one who delivers a message*, or *brings intelligence, a messenger, an ambassador*:—Sancte Iohannes wæs gelíc Godes englum & hé wæs béme, Cristes fricca on ðysne middangeard, & wæs Godes Suna spellboda, Blickl. Homl. 163, 22. Hú ðæt wæs weallende spelboda, se ðe ðone Hǽlend on ðysne middangeard cumendne gesecgean wolde, 165, 33. Heora feóndas flód ádrencte ðæt ðæra ǽfre ne com ân spelboda *there was never a one left to tell the tale*, Ps. Th. 105, 10. Him andswarode Godes spelboda (*the prophet Daniel*): 'Nó ic wið feohsceattum ofer folc bere Drihtnes dómas,' Cd. Th. 262, 12; Dan. 743: 249, 20; Dan. 533: *the angel Gabriel*, Exon. Th. 21, 17; Cri. 336. Ðus gieddade Godes spelboda (*Job*), 236, 9; Ph. 571. Godes spelbodan *the prophets*, 104, 22; Gú. 11. Godes spellbodan (*the angels who came to Lot*), Cd. Th. 150, 19; Gen. 2494. Spelbodan (*those who should have brought the news of Pharaoh's overthrow*), 210, 10; Exod. 513. Spelbodan *oratores*, Wrt. Voc. ii. 115, 68. II. *one who delivers a discourse, a public speaker*:—Spelboda *causidicus*, Wrt. Voc. ii. 130, 14.

spell-cwide, es; *m. Historical narrative*:—Ic wolde gesecgan and mid spellcwidum gemearcian, Ors. 3, 1; Swt. 100, 12.

spellian; *p.* ode. I. *intrans. To talk, converse, discourse*:—Ic spellige *fabulor*, Ælfc. Gr. 25; Zup. 145, 13. Hí ealne dæg fleardiaþ and spelliaþ, L. I. P. 14; Th. ii. 322, 25. Ðá hig spelledon (woeron spellendo, Lind.: spellende, Rush.) *dum fabularentur*, Lk. Skt. 24, 15. Mid deádum spellian, gestrión hit getácnaþ, Lchdm. iii. 202, 5. Man ne mót spellian ne sprǽce drífan binnan Godes cyrcan, Homl. Skt. i. 13, 69: L. Ælfc. C. 35; Th. ii. 356, 28. Ðá se Wísdóm ðis leóþ ásungen hæfde, ðá ongan hé spellian, Bt. 37, 2; Fox 186, 34. Spelligan, 32, 1; Fox 114, 2. Spellien (spillian, Cott. MS.), 20; Fox 70, 20. II. *trans. To announce, proclaim, tell, utter*:—Hig spelliaþ ł tógǽnaþ and spræcaþ unrihtwísnesse *effabuntur et loquentur iniquitatem*, Ps. Lamb. 93, 4. Him wæs lust ðæt hé ðiossum leódum leóð spellode, Met. Introd. 4. Hié (*the prophets*) ðære sóþfæstnesse tácen spellodan and secgende wæron, Blickl. Homl. 161, 20. [Þat folc gan to spelien (vsi, 2nd MS.) Irlondes speche, Laym. 10068. Speken heom togadere & speleden, 4051. Þe posstless forenn . . . till hæþenn follc to spellenn, Orm. 8528. Mardocheus speleð *amare conterens impudentem*, A. R. 170, 19. *Goth.* spillôn *to tell, announce*: *Icel.* spjalla *to talk.*] v. ge-spellian.

spell-stów, e; *f. A place where announcements are made* (?):—Andlang dene tó ðære spelstówe, Cd. Dip. Kmbl. iii. 429, 28.

spellung, e; *f.* I. *talking, conversation, discourse, narration*:—Ðý læs on mé mǽge ídel spellung oþþe scondlíc leásung beón gestǽled *ne aut fabulae aut turpi mendacio dignus efficiar*, Nar. 2, 20. Forbúgaþ ídele spellunge and dyslíce blissa *avoid idle conversation and foolish pleasures*, Homl. Th. i. 180, 13: 148, 2: ii. 336, 19: Cd. Th. 304, 31; Sat. 638. Spellung *fabulositas*, Wrt. Voc. i. 55, 23. II. *a tale, conversation, discourse, narrative*:—*Fabulae*, ðæt synd ídele spellunga, Ælfc. Gr. 50, 29; Zup. 296, 5. Spellenga *sermonum*, Hpt. Gl. 505, 77. Spellunga ł saga *fabulas*, 410, 54. Ídele spellunga *otiosas fabulas*, Confess. Peccat. Hí cýð[d]on mé spellunga *narraverunt mihi fabulationes*, Ps. Spl. 118, 85. [Spellunge and smecchunge (*talking and tasting*) beoð ine muðe boðe . . . we schulen speken nu of spellunge, and ter efter of herrunge, A. R. 64, 11. *O. L. Ger.* spellunga *tragoediae.*] v. eft-, leás-spellung.

spelt, es; *m.* (?) *spelt, corn*:—Spelt *planta*, Wrt. Voc. i. 75, 11: 46, 66: *faar*, 287, 19: ii. 34, 38. Spelt sámgréne *far serotina*, 36, 39. Hwǽtes, speltes *farris*, 34, 37. [*O. H. Ger.* spelza *spelta, far.* From Latin *spelta.*]

spén (?), es; *m. A fibre*:—Spénas *fibras*, Wrt. Voc. ii. 35, 52. Cf. spón.

spendan *to spend.* [*O. H. Ger.* spentón *consumere, impendere, expendere.* From Latin.] v. á-, for-spendan, *and next word.*

spendung, e; *f. Spending*:—Sum underféhþ eorðlíce ǽhta and se sceal ðæs pundes spendunge Gode ágifan of his ǽhtum *one receives earthly possessions, and he must repay the spending of the pound to God out of his possessions*, Homl. Th. ii. 556, 29. [*O. H. Ger.* spentunga *dispensatio, impensa.*]

Spéne (Spene?); *pl. The Spaniards*:—Amilcor wearð from Spénum ofslagen, Ors. 4, 7; Swt. 182, 31. v. Spáneas.

spennan *to allure.* v. for-spennen, -spennend[e], -spennestre, -spennung. [*O. H. Ger.* spennen *allicere, illicere, sollicitare, seducere*: *Icel.* spenja.] Cf. spanan.

spennels, es; *m. A clasp*:—*Fibula* .s. *dicta quod ligat* cnæp, sigl, spennels, Wrt. Voc. ii. 148, 58. [Cf. *O. H. Ger.* spenula *fibula*: *Icel.* spennill *a clasp.*] v. spannan.

speoftan (?); *p.* speaft *To spit*:—Speaft (speoft, Rush.; cf. á-speaft, -speoft, Jn. Skt. Lind, Rush. 9, 6), Mk. Skt. Lind. 8, 23. Speufton *expuerunt*, Mt. Kmbl. Lind. 26, 67. Speofton, 27, 30. Speafton (speoftun, Rush.), Mk. Skt. 15, 19. [Gespeoftad biþ *conspuetur*, Lk. Skt. Lind. 18, 32.]

speówan; *p.* de *To spit*:—Hí on his hleór hyra spátl speówdon, Exon. Th. 69, 17; Cri. 1122. Gé mid horu speówdon on ðæs andwlitan, Elen. Kmbl. 594; El. 297. Hí áttre spiówdon, Exon. Th. 156, 34; Gú. 884. [Cf. *Icel.* spýja (*strong*).] Cf. spiwian, spíwan.

speówung, e; *f. Spewing, vomiting*:—Speówung *evomatio*, Wrt. Voc. ii. 144, 40. v. spíwing.

speowþa. v. spiweþa.

spere, es; *n. A spear, lance, pike, javelin*:—Spere *lancea, falarica*, Wrt. Voc. i. 35, 11: 84, 17: *falarica*, ii. 86, 82: *hasta*, i. 287, 4: ii. 43, 19. Getridwet spere *hasta*, i. 35, 40. His sceaft ætstód ætforan him, swá ðæt ðæt spere him eode þurh út, Homl. Skt. i. 12, 55: Byrht. Th. 135, 53; By. 137. Nægle oððe spere *cuspide*, Wrt. Voc. ii. 21, 24. Ecg sceal on sweorde, ord spere, Exon. Th. 346, 14; Gn. Ex. 204. Mid spere *lancea*, Jn. Skt. 19, 34. Hé nam him spere on hand *accepit lanceam in manu*, Bd. 2, 13; S. 517, 8. Ða speru sóðfæsðnesse *veritatis jacula*, Past. 35, 5; Swt. 245, 9: 38, 6; Swt. 277, 22. Spera *sparorum*, Wrt. Voc. ii. 96, 33. Mid sperum tósticad *confossum vulneribus*, Ors. 3, 9; Swt. 128, 14. Spiorum (swiorum, Wrt.) *contis*, Wrt. Voc. ii. 21, 57. Speoru *contos*, 104, 58. Speru, 14, 72: 20, 15: *ansatas* (cf. *ansatas* ætgáras, 3, 68), 5, 44: 88, 16. Speru, boltas *catapultas*, 18, 58: 85, 16. Hí léton of folman feólhearde speru fleógan, Byrht. Th. 134, 63; By. 108. ¶ In the following the word refers to a shooting pain or stitch:—Út lytel spere gif hér inne sié, Lchdm. iii. 52, 18. [*O. Sax.* sper; *n.*: *O. Frs. O. H. Ger.* sper; *m. hasta, lancea, sparus, catapulta*: *Icel.* spjör; *n. pl.* (poetical).] v. átor-, bár-, deáþ-, huntig-, pull-, scot-, wæl-, wíg-spere.

spere-bróga, an; *m. Terror caused by the casting of spears* or *darts*:—Ic spǽte sperebrógan . . . mé of hrife fleógaþ hyldepílas, Exon. Th. 398, 27; Rä. 18, 4.

spere-healf, e; *The male side* or *line* (in speaking of inheritance. Cf. swert-, gér-mâge, Grmm. R. A. 470):—Mín yldra fæder hæfde gecweden his land on ða sperehealfe, næs on ða spinlhealfe, Chart. Th. 491, 20. [Cf. spera-hand *in Richthofen O. Frs. Dict.*] Cf. wǽpned-healf, -hand.

spere-leás; *adj. Without a point* or *head*:—Spereleás sceaft *contus*, Wrt. Voc. i. 35, 42.

spere-mann. v. spyre-mann.

spere-níþ, es; *m. Spear-strife, battle*:—Him Drihten mihte æt ðam spereníðe spéde lǽnan, Cd. Th. 124, 7; Gen. 2059.

spere-wyrt, e; *f. A plant name*; the word translates *innule(-a) campane(-a)*, Wrt. Voc. i. 68, 17: Lchdm. i. 210, 7: *nap silvatica*, Wrt. Voc. i. 31, 27.

speriend, sper-lira, sperlíce. v. spyriend, spear-lira, spærlíce.

sperran, spirran, spyrran; *p.* de *To strike, spar*:—Ðǽr eác cwóman hreáþemýs . . . and ða on úre ondwlitan sperdon and ús pulledon *et uespertilionum uis ingens . . . in ora uultusque nostros ferebantur* (the translator has read *feriebant?*), Nar. 15, 6. Spyrrynde *verberans*, Germ. 399, 411. [Cf. *Icel.* sperrask *to struggle*: *Ger.* sich sperren *to struggle, resist.*] v. next word.

sperring, spirring, spyrring, e; *f. Striking*:—Clifra spyrringe *ungularum arpagine* (cf. slítunge *arpagine*, Wrt. Voc. ii. 5, 38), Hpt. Gl. 526, 67. Spyrrince *arpagine*, Anglia xiii. 37, 297.

sperte. v. spyrte.

spic, es; *n. Bacon, lard, the fat flesh of swine*:—*Hi lares* ðás hús; ðanon ys gecweden *lardum* spic, forðan ðe hit on húsum hangaþ lange, Ælfc. Gr. 9, 17; Zup. 42, 17. Spic *lardum*, Wrt. Voc. i. 82, 25: *larda*, 286, 52: ii. 52, 1: *tanea*, i. 26, 47. Spices snǽd *offella* vel *particula*, 27, 19: ii. 65, 7: Homl. Skt. ii. 25, 87. Man nime áne cuppan huniges and healfe cuppan clǽnes gemyltes spices, and mænge on gemang ðæt hunig and ðæt spic tógædere, Lchdm. iii. 76, 5. Án sconc spices *a ham*,

L. Ath. i, prm.; Th. i. 198, 7. Hē ǽlce gēre āgefe đēm hīgum .iii. wēga spices, Chart. Th. 471, 14: 473, 28. Speces, 468, 24. Mid ealdan spice oþþe mid ferscre buteran, Lchdm. ii. 354, 5. Gemelte eald spic, 52, 20. Nim clǽne spic, iii. 40, 26. Đonne hē spic behworfen hæfþ *when he has attended to the bacon*, L. R. S. 7; Th. i. 436, 23. Etan spicc, Homl. Skt. ii. 25, 111. ¶ *Spic* occurs in names of places where swine were fed, e. g. Holan-spic, Cod. Dip. Kmbl. i. pp. 115, 137, 184, but its meaning here is not evident. Kemble suggests that it may refer to the mast on which the swine were fed. [Þer com spic (fleas, 2nd MS.), Laym. 24437. Spyk or fet flesche *popa*, Prompt. Parv. 469, col. 1. *O. L. Ger.* spec[-suīn]: *O. H. Ger.* spech *lardum*: *Ger.* speck: *Icel.* spik *fat of seals, whales, etc., blubber*: *Dan.* spek *blubber, lard*: *Swed.* späk *lard.*] v. offrung-spic.

spīca, an; *m. Spikenard; any aromatic herb* (?):—Đeós smerenes wæs geworht of ehtatēne cynna wyrtum; đǽr wǽron þreó đa betstan—ele, & nardus, & spīca (*or is this merely the Latin word?*), Blickl. Homl. 73, 21. Lǽcedōm . . . spīcan wiþ ūtsihtan, and dracontjan wiþ fūle horas, . . . and balzaman smiring wiþ eallum untrumnessum, Lchdm. ii. 174, 4.

spic-hūs, es; *n. A larder*:—Spichūs *lardarium*, Wrt. Voc. i. 58, 16: *lar* (kitchen?), Lchdm. i. lxiii. 3. [*O. H. Ger.* spech-hūs *lardarium.*]

spīcing, es; *m. A spike* (? Halliwell gives *spiking* a large nail, as a northern word):—Spīcyngas gadirian ođđe wyrcean, geswinc hit getācnaþ, Lchdm. iii. 200, 24.

spic-māse, an; *f. A titmouse*:—Spicmāse (*Wright prints* swic-) *parrula*, Wrt. Voc. i. 62, 40. [In E. D. S. Pub. Bird Names, p. 33, *blue spick* is given as the name of the blue titmouse in North Devon. Cf. *Icel.* spiki *a tit.*]

spīder *a spider* (?):—Hēr com in gangan in spīder wiht, hæfde him his haman on handa, Lchdm. iii. 42, 11. The passage is the beginning of a charm.

spigettan; *p.* te *To spit*:—Gif hire fæder spigette (*spuisset*) on hire nebb, Num. 12, 14. Đā ongan se Catulus him spigettan on, Bt. 27, 1; Fox 96, 5.

spilæg:—Spilæg se ǽtterne *spilagius*, Rtl. 125, 29.

spilc. v. spelc.

spilcan, spelcean; *p.* te *To bind with splints*:—Đæt sceáp đæt sceoncforad wæs ne spilcte gē đæt *quod fractum est, non alligastis*, Past. 17, 9; Swt. 123, 10. Gif scancan forade synd . . . hū mon spelcean scyle, Lchdm. ii. 6, 12. v. spelc.

spild, es; *m. Destruction, ruin*:—Spildes *internicionis*, Wrt. Voc. ii. 76, 65. Spilde geblonden, Exon. Th. 405, 27; Rä. 24, 8. Ic hī ne sparige, ac on spild giefe, 247, 28; Jul. 85. Spilth *pessum*, Wrt. Voc. ii. 116, 75. Đætte hié đone spild đæs hryres him ondrǽden *ut praecipitem ruinam metuant*, Past. 52, 5; Swt. 407, 20. Đæt mōd . . . ongit hine selfne on swelcne spild forlǽd *mens . . . sese in praecipitium pervenisse deprehendit*, 58, 2; Swt. 441, 27. Đurh deófles spild *through the ruin caused by the devil*, Elen. Kmbl. 2235; El. 1119. [Cf. *O. H. Ger.* spildi; *f. desperatio, effusio.*] v. for-spild.

spildan; *p.* de *To waste, destroy, make away* with:—Đeáf ne cymes būta đætte [hē] spildeþ (*perdat*), Jn. Skt. Lind. 10, 10. Seđe lufaþ sāuel his spildeþ (*perdet*) hiá, 12, 25. Đū wilnast, đæt đū đīne feore spilde, Andr. Kmbl. 568; An. 284. [*O. H. Ger.* spildan *effundere, expendere.*] v. for-spildan, *and* spillan.

spilde. v. an-spilde.

spild-sīþ, es; *m. A journey undertaken with the object of causing destruction*, Cd. Th. 187, 18; Exod. 153.

spilian; *p.* ode *To play, sport, wanton*:—Hī lufiaþ īdele blisse . . . and ealne dæg fleardiaþ, spelliaþ and spiliaþ, and nǽnige note dreógaþ, L. I. P. 14; Th. ii. 322, 25. Eówra leóda đe spiliaþ and plegaþ and rǽdes ne hēdaþ, Wulfst. 45, 24. [Uortigerne mid his hirede hæhliche spilede, Laym. 13816. In blisse spilen, Gen. and Ex. 2532. *O. Sax.* spilōn *to play, dance*: *O. H. Ger.* spilōn *ludere, ludificare, lascivire.*]

spillan; *p.* de *To destroy*:—Suā huelc soecaþ sāuel his hāl gewyrca spilleþ hiá (*perdet illam*), Lk. Skt. Lind. Rush. 17, 33: Jn. Skt. Rush. 12, 25. Đeóf ne cymeþ būta đætte [hē] spilleþ (*perdat*), 10, 10. Ne spildic ł ne losade *non perdidi*, Lind. 18, 9. Eal đæt God spilde *God destroyed it all*, Cd. Th. 154, 22; Gen. 2559. Sumne man tō Lundene lǽdde, and đǽr spilde, Chr. 1096; Erl. 233, 9. Đætte ne ic losige ł ic ne spillo *ut non perdam*, Jn. Skt. Lind. 6, 39. Đætte đū spilla *ut dissipes*, Rtl. 55, 22. Ne þurfe wē ūs spillan *we need not destroy one another*, Byrht. Th. 132, 50; By. 34. Sōhton hine tō spillanne *quaerebant eum perdere*, Jn. Skt. Lind. Rush. 10, 39. Swil[g]ra, gliw[e]ra [*in margin* spillendra (spiliendra?); *but see* onspillendra *parasitorum*, Anglia xiii. 28, 29] *parasitorum*, Hpt. Gl. 422, 37. [Wæron six men spilde of here ægon, Chr. 1124; Erl. 253, 14. ȝif ȝe hit willed ich hine uulle spillen, Laym. 880. Unleoden spilden al his þeoden, 28863. Speche þu maht spillen, ant ne speden nawiht, Jul. 24, 14. Late ye nouth mi bodi spille, Havel. 2422. To spille hem þat ben gulty, Piers P. 19, 298. Spyllyn̄ or destroyyn̄ *confundo*, Prompt. Parv. 469. *Icel.* spilla *to destroy, spoil.*] v. for-, ge-spillan; spildan.

spilling, e; *f. Destruction, waste*:—Nān þing . . . būton folces geswinc and feós spylling and heora feónda forđbylding, Chr. 999; Erl. 134, 37. [*Prompt. Parv.* spyllinge or lesynge or schendynge *confusio, deperdicio.*] v. feoh-spilling.

spind *fat*:—Spind *arbina*, Wrt. Voc. ii. 5, 54. Hrysel *vel* gelend *vel* spind (swind, Wrt.) *vel* swīnes smere *arvina* vel *adeps*, i. 44, 20. [*O. L. Ger.* spind *arvina*: *O. H. Ger.* spint *adeps, arvina, pinguedo.*] v. hago-spind.

spindel. v. sprindel.

spinel, spinl, e; *f. A spindle*:—Spinil (spinel), *stilium* vel *fusa*, Txts. 98, 967: *nitorium*, 81, 1377. Spinel *fusum*, 65, 933. Spinl, Wrt. Voc. ii. 34, 30: *fusu*, 152, 12: *nitorium*, 60, 12: *fusus*, i. 26, 15: 82, 10: *fussum*, 281, 74. Spinle *fusi*, Wülck. Gl. 245, 23. Spinele *fuso*, Wrt. Voc. ii. 83, 21. Spinle, 34, 29: Hpt. 494, 20. Spinle *fussum*, Kent. Gl. 1142. Hē sceal . . . spinle habban, Anglia ix. 263, 10. [*O. L. Ger.* spinnila: *O. H. Ger.* spinnala, spinala *fusus.*] v. eár-, þrāwing-, wealc-spinel(-spinl).

spinel-healf, e; *f. The female side* or *line*:—Mīn yldra fæder hæfde gecweden his land on đa sperehealfe, næs on đa spinlhealfe, Chart. Th. 491, 21. [Cf. *O. Frs.* spindel-sīda. v. Richthofen, O. Frs. Dict.] Cf. wīf-hand, *and see* spere-healf.

spinnan; *p.* spann, *pl.* spunnon; *pp.* spunnen. I. *to spin*:—*Neo* ic spinne, *neui* ic spann, *neuisti* vel *nesti* đū spunne, *neuistis* vel *nestis* gē spunnon, *neuerunt* vel *nerunt* hī spunnon, Ælfc. Gr. 25; Zup. 147, 2-4. Ic spinne *neo*, Wrt. Voc. ii. 60, 13. Spinnaþ *neunt*, 19: Mt. Kmbl. 6, 28: Lk. Skt. 12, 27. Hig spinnaþ wulle *illae nent lanam*, Ælfc. Gr. 15; Zup. 97, 9. Nim đone hweorfan đe wīf mid spinnaþ, Lchdm. ii. 310, 22. Spunnun *neverant*, Wrt. Voc. ii. 119, 10. Đa of his leáfum and of his flȳse đæs treówes spunnon and swā eác tō godewebbe wǽfon and worhtan *foliis arborum ex siluestri uellere uestes detexunt*, Nar. 6, 18. II. of the action of the tide on the sand:—Sand sǽcir span (*Grein would read* spān) *the ebb hath knit the sand together* (?), Cd. Th. 196, 13; Exod. 291. III. of convulsive movement (?), *to writhe, twist*:—Sum ungesceádwīs man hine sylfne āhēng đæt hē fōtum span (*for* sparn? v. spornan) and his feorh forlēt *a certain foolish man hung himself, so that he moved his feet convulsively* (*could not rest them on the ground?*), *and gave up the ghost*, Homl. Th. ii. 504, 34. Heó hī sylfe on grine āhēng, đæt heó fōtum span, 30, 23. [*Goth. O. H. Ger.* spinnan: *Icel.* spinna.] v. ā-, ge-spinnan; twī-spunnen.

spiówan, spiowian. v. speówan, spiwian.

spīr *a spire* [v. E. D. S. Pub. Plant Names, where *spire* is given as the name of the reed and of various spiked grasses. The word is also used of tapering trees, v. Baker's Northampt. Gl.]:—Hreódes spīr, Lchdm. ii. 266, 10. [*Prompt. Parv.* spyre of corne or herbe *hastula*, spyryn̄ as corne and oþer lyke *spico*. Imeind mid spire and grene segge, O. and N. 18. The word occurs in Chaucer and Piers Plowman. v. Skeat's note on the latter, 13, 180 (C text). Cf. *Icel.* spīra *a spar*: *Dan.* spire *a sprout*; spir *a spar*: *Swed.* spira *a spar; a sceptre; a pistil.*]

spircan. I. *to sparkle*:—Spircendre *scintillante*, Hpt. Gl. 429, 42. Spyrcendum *scintillantibus*, 499, 43. II. *to fall in drops*. v. spircing:—Hē hēt mycel ād ontendan on ymbhwyrfte đæs mǽdenes and mid pice hī besprencgan and mid spyrcendum ele (*with oil that bespattered her*), Homl. Skt. i. 9, 118. v. for-spyrcan; spearcian.

spircing, e; *f. A sprinkling, dropping*:—Spyrcinge *aspergine*, Germ. 398, 225. v. previous word.

spirian, spirte. v. spyrian, spyrte.

spitel *a kind of spade, a spud, a spittle* ['*spittle* a spade, used for light digging, which is *spittling*. The square board, with a short flat handle, used in putting cakes into an oven, is a baking-*spittle*,' Mid-York. Gl. '*Spittle* a spade with a curved edge, used for grip-digging.' Holderness Gl. See also E. D. S. Pub. Gl. B, 2, 12, and Halliwell's Dict. In A. R. 384, 18, where one MS. has *spade*, another has *spitelstaf.*] v. hand-, wād-spitel, *and* spittan.

-spitel. v. wrōht-spitel.

spittan; *p.* te *To dig with a spittle*:—In Agusto and Septembri and Octobri man mæg māwan, wād spittan, fela tilđa hām gæderian, Anglia ix. 261, 16. Cf. '*Spittle* to cut weeds with a spittle-staff,' E. D. S. Pub. Linc. Gl. '*Spittle ower* to dig over a piece of ground with a spade,' Holderness Gl. '*Spitter* a small tool with a long handle for cutting up weeds,' Halliwell's Dict. v. spitel.

spittan *to spit*. v. spyttan.

spitu, e; *f. A spit*:—Spitu *veru*, Wrt. Voc. i. 27, 9: 82, 66: Ælfc. Gr. 11; Zup. 80, 10. *Ueru* spitu, *ueribus* spitum, 14; Zup. 89, 13. [*O. H. Ger.* spiz *veru.*]

spīwan; *p.* spāw, *pl.* spiwon. I. *to spew, vomit, spit up* (a) with acc.:—Đonne spīwaþ hié đæt horh, Lchdm. ii. 194, 16. Hē spāw blōd, Homl. Skt. i. 12, 63. Hē spāw his innođ ūt þurh his mūđ, Shrn. 66, 33. Đonne man đa cild cwalde, đonne spiwon hī đa meoloc, 33, 1. Hit eft spīwende, Blickl. Homl. 57, 7. (b) with dat.:—On đa ādle đe mon wormse spīweþ (cf. worms spīwende, 208, 9), Lchdm. ii. 200, 22. Ic blōde spāu *vomebam sanguinem*, Bd. 5, 6; S. 619, 30. Holm heolfre spâw, Cd. Th. 206, 9; Exod. 249. (c) without a case:—Stinge him gelôme on ða hracan, ðæt hē māge spîwan, Lchdm. ii. 62, 12. Gelôme tô spîwanne, 174, 21: 286, 20. Ðā gebrǣd hē hine seócne, and ongan hine brecan tô spîwenne, Chr. 1003; Erl. 139, 9. II. *to spit*:—Geót ðæt blôd on yrnende wæter, spîw þrîwa æfter, Lchdm. ii. 76, 15. Ðonne is cynn, ðæt him spîwe ðæt wîf on ðæt nebb, Past. 5; Swt. 45, 2. [*Goth.* speiwan *to spit*: *O. Sax.* spîwan: *O. Frs.* spîga, spîa: *O. H. Ger.* spîwan *vomere, spuere*: *Icel.* spýja.] v. ā-spîwan.

spiw-drenc, -drinc (spiwe-), es; *m. An emetic*:—Spiwedrenc, Lchdm. ii. 136, 25: 270, 19: 272, 4, 6. Se ðe hæfþ þearfe spiwdrinces, 60, 26. Tô spiwdrence, 268, 21. Wyrc spiwdrenc, 270, 27: 302, 17. Se man þurh spiwedrenc āspîwþ ðone wǣtan, 60, 22: 336, 1. Spiwedrencas, 170, 6.

spiwe, es; *m. A vomiting, vomit*:—Spiwe deah ðām monnum ðe for fylle gihsa slihþ, Lchdm. ii. 60, 23.

spiwe-drenc, spiwel. v. spiw-drenc, spiwol.

spîwere, es; *m. One who vomits*:—Spîwere *vomex* vel *vomens*, Wrt. Voc. i. 17, 6.

spiweþa, an; *m.* I. *vomiting*:—Gif hié (*diseases*) cumen of oferfyllo, mid spiweþan hȳ mon sceal lytlian, Lchdm. ii. 178, 11. Wið miclan spiweþan, and hē ne māge nānne mete gehabban, 190, 8. Wið spiwþan, 190, 1. Ðurh spiwðan, i. 274, 21. Spiweþan dôn *to vomit*, iii. 214, 23. Hî beóþ oferfyllede ôþ spiweþan, R. Ben. 136, 25. Drincan ôð speowðan, Homl. Th. ii. 292, 35. II. *vomit, what is vomited*:—Lǣt spîwan . . . gesceáwa hwæðer ðe spiwða sȳ swā micel swā hē ǣr gedranc, Lchdm. ii. 286, 22. Gif hund ðone spiweðan frete *si canis vomitum illum devoraverit*, L. Ecg. P. iv. 47; Th. ii. 218, 5. Hund eft hwyrfde tô his spiwðan, Shrn. 37, 16.

spiwian; *p.* ode *To spit up, vomit* (with dat.):—Him bānlocan blôde spiowedan *their carcases spouted forth blood*, Exon. Th. 271, 3; Jul. 476. v. spîwan, speówan.

spîwing, e; *f. Spewing, vomiting*:—Spîwingc *evomitio*, Wrt. Voc. i. 46, 17. Spîwing, ii. 32, 57. v. blôd-spîwing; speówung.

spiwol; *adj. Emetic, causing vomiting*:—Drince hē spiwles drences, Lchdm. ii. 264, 24. Drince se man spiwolne drenc, 216, 11. Speowolne drenc, 216, 16. Mid wyrtdrencum ūtyrnendum oþþe spiwlum oþþe migolum, 82, 17. v. lîg-, un-spiwol.

spjungean. v. sponge.

splott, es; *m.* I. *a plot of land*:—Mann ðe āhte geweald ealles ðæs splottes æt Celian dūne, ðār ðæt scræf wæs tômiddes, ðe ða seofon hālgan lāgon inne slāpan, Homl. Skt. i. 23, 415. On clǣnan splott sūðeweardne, Cod. Dip. B. iii. 336, 23. II. *a spot*:—Is se finta fægre gedǣled sum brūn sum basu sum blācum splottum searolîce beseted *cauda porrigitur fulvo distenta metallo, in cujus maculis purpura mista rubet*, Exon. Th. 218, 18; Ph. 296. [Cf. Hyre treówenan gesplottude cuppan, Chart. Th. 537, 33. Wicklif uses *splotti*=spotted in Gen. 30, 35; and Halliwell gives *splotch* as an East-country word for a splash of dirt.] v. æcer-, friþ-, land-, mǣd-splott.

splottian *to spot, blot*. v. preceding word.

spôn, es; *m.*: e; *f.* (? v. sæp-spôn) *A chip, shaving*:—Spôn *astula*, Wrt. Voc. ii. 5, 63: *gingria*, 109, 71. *Fomes* spoon; idem *astula*, 39, 70. Geswǣled spoon *vel* tynder *fomes*, i. 39, 21. Monige of ðam treówe ðæs hālgan Cristes mǣles spônas and sceafþan nimaþ *multi de ipso ligno sacrosanctae crucis astulas excidere solent*, Bd. 3, 2; S. 524, 31: 3, 17; S. 544, 44. Genim ðone wyrttruman . . . þwît nigon spônas, Lchdm. ii. 292, 2. [*O. Frs.* spôn: *O. H. Ger.* spān *hastula, carpenta*: *Icel.* spánn, spônn *a chip, splinter*.]

sponan *teats*, sponere. v. spanu, spanere.

spong, e; *f. A spongy excrescence* (?):—Gif on eágan weaxen reáde sponge drȳpe on hāt culfran blôd . . . ôþ ðæt ða sponge āweg synd, Lchdm. ii. 308, 17: 300, 5. v. next word.

sponge, an; *f. A sponge*:—Ān heora genam āne spongean, Mt. Kmbl. 27, 48. Genim spjungean, gedô on scearp eced, Lchdm. ii. 192, 18. [*O. Sax.* spunsia: *O. H. Ger.* spunga.] v. spynge.

sponn, spoon. v. spann, spôn.

spor, es; *n.* I. *a trace, track, spoor*:—Ne biþ ðǣr ēþe ðîn spor on tô findanne *vestigia tua non cognoscentur*, Ps. Th. 76, 16. Stande ðæt spor for ðone foreāð, L. Ath. iv. 2; Th. i. 222, 16. Wē noldon tô ðæm spore onlūtan, Past. pref.; Swt. 5, 18: Exon. Th. 497, 8; Rä. 85, 26. Hwæt mæg bión dyslîcre ðonne hwā lufige hwelcre wuhte spor on ðæm duste and ne lufige ðæt ðætte ðæt spor worhte *quid esse dementius potest, quam vestigia in pulvere impressa diligere, sed ipsum, a quo impressa sunt, non amare?* Past. 46, 5; Swt. 351, 1-2. Gif man spor gespirige of scȳre on ôðre, fôn ða menn tô ðe ðǣr nȳcst syndon, and drîfan ðæt spor ôð hit man ðam gerēfan gecȳðe; fô hē syþþan tô and ādrîfe ðæt spor ūt of his scîre, L. Ath. v. 8, 4; Th. i. 236, 20-23. Hē ūs spor tǣce, v. 8, 7; Th. i. 238, 3. Gif ðū gesyxt wulfes spor, Lchdm. i. 360, 19. II. *a trace, vestige, mark left by anything* (of the marks made by weapons; cf. *Icel.* sverða, eggja spor, dôlg-spor *a wound*):—Lǣtaþ hȳ lāþra leána hleótan þurh wǣpnes spor (*by a wound*), Exon. Th. 280, 2; Jul. 623: Andr. Kmbl. 2362; An. 1182. Bealubenne, lîcwunde spor, Cd. Th. 193, 1; Exod. 239. III. *tracing, tracking*:—Ðū teohhast ðæt ðū spyrige æfter mē, and swîþor swincst on ðam spore ðonne hî dôn, Bt. 38, 5; Fox 206, 14. Ðæt ǣlc man wǣre ôðrum gelāstfull ge æt spore ge æt midrāde, L. Ath. v. 4; Th. i. 232, 11. Befæste mon ðæt spor landes mannum, L. O. D. 1; Th. i. 352, 5. [*O. H. Ger.* spor *vestigium, indago*; *Icel.* spor.] v. fôt-, hôh-spor.

spora, spura, an; *m. A spur*:—Spora *calcar*, Txts. 47, 361: 110, 1164. Spura, Wrt. Voc. ii. 17, 3, 63: i. 84, 3: 288, 22: Hpt. Gl. 505, 70: Ælfc. Gr. 9, 16; Zup. 42, 10. *Calcaria* spuran *dicta, quia in calce hominis ligantur*, Wrt. Voc. ii. 127, 44. Spurum *calcaribus*, 17, 62. Hē heów ðæt hors mid ðam spuran (cf. *Icel.* höggva hest sporum), Ælfc. T. Grn. 18, 22. .ii. spuran on .iii. pundan, Chart. Th. 503, 8. [*O. H. Ger.* sporo: *Icel.* spori.] v. hūn-, tāh-spora, -spura; hand-spor(a?); sporu.

sporettan (?); *p.* te *To kick*:—Sporetteþ (spornetteþ?) *recalcitravit*, Ps. Surt. ii. p. 193, 7. *next word.*

sporettung (?), e; *f. Kicking*:—Sportengæ *calcaneum*, Ps. Spl. T. 55, 6. v. *previous word.*

spor-leþer, es; *n. A spur-leather*:—Spurleþera *calcaria* (amongst things made by the shoemaker), Coll. Monast. Th. 27, 35. [*O. H. Ger.* spor-leder *calcarium*.]

spornan, spurnan; *p.* spearn, *pl.* spurnon; *pp.* spornen. I. *to strike with the foot, spurn*:—Ðe læs ðū on stān fôte spurne *ne offendas ad lapidem pedem tuam*, Ps. Th. 90, 12. On spurnan *inpingere*, Wrt. Voc. ii. 44, 72. On spornendum fēt *in offenso pede*, Scint. 187, 8. (See (?) *passages under* spinnan, III.) II. *to spurn, reject*:—Æfter ðæs mǣdenes sprǣce, ðe hine spearn mid wordum, Homl. Skt. i. 7, 64. [Makede he þe spurnen (*stumble*) ine wreððe, A. R. 188, 2. *O. Sax.* spurnan *to strike with the feet, tread*: *O. H. Ger.* spurnan (*also wk.*): *Icel.* sperna.] v. æt-, ge-, ôþ-spornan, -spurnan.

spornere, es; *m. One who treads* or *strikes with the feet, a fuller*:—Spornere, spurnere *fullo*, Ælfc. Gr. 9, 3; Zup. 35, 2.

spornettan; *p.* te *To strike with the feet, kick*:—Ne spornette ðū *non calcitres*, Wrt. Voc. ii. 60, 61: 80, 10.

sporning, e; *f. A stumbling, stumbling-block*:—Þurh sporningce *per offendiculum*, Scint. 134, 5. [Cf. *O. H. Ger.* spurnida *offensio, scandalum*.] Cf. spyrning.

spor-plætt, es; *m. A kick* (?):—Spātlu spurplættas (eárplættas?) bendas ðū þrowodest *tu sputa, colaphos, vincula passus*, Hymn. Surt. 80, 1. v. plætt, *and next word.*

sporu (?), an; *f. A heel*:—Spuran mîne *calcanei mei*, Ps. Spl. T. 48, 5. v. hēl-spure.

spor-wrecel (?), es; *m. What is tracked after being driven off* (?):—Ðā forstæl hē ða unlǣdan oxan æt Funtial, and drāf tô cytlid, and hine mon ðǣræt āparade, and his speremon āhredde ða sporwreclas *the man who tracked him rescued the cattle that had been driven off* (?), Chart. Th. 172, 26.

spôwan; *p.* speów *To succeed.* I. used personally with instrumental of that in which the person succeeds, *to be successful*:—Hū mæg hē ǣnige gewinne wið mē spôwan *how can he succeed in any struggle with me?* Nar. 16, 20. Ne môt ic ǣnige rihte spôwan, Elen. Kmbl. 1830; El. 917: Andr. Kmbl. 3087; An. 1546: Cd. Th. 127, 23; Gen. 2115: Exon. 35, 27; Cri. 564. Spôwende spēd, 117, 16; Gū. 225: 139, 14: Gū. 593: Cd. Th. 246, 14; Dan. 479. II. used impersonally, *it succeeds* with a person (dat.) (1) absolute:—Him spēwþ ðe bet, Btwk. 222, 9. Ðā hié ongeáton, ðæt him ne speów, L. Alf. 49; Th. i. 56, 8. Him wiht ne speów, Judth. Thw. 25, 23; Jud. 274: Beo. Th. 5701; B. 2854. Gesæh Pilatus ðæt him nāuwiht speóu (spēua, Lind.) *videns Pilatus quia nihil proficeret*, Mt. Kmbl. Rush. 27, 24. Him speów hwônlîce, Homl. Skt. i. 7, 94. Hū swȳþe him speówe *quantum profecerit*, Bd. 2, 4; S. 505, 27. (2) with gen. of that in which a person succeeds:—Ðā ðā him ðæs (*the attempt to raise the dead*) ne speów, Homl. Th. ii. 474, 11. Ðē speów ðæs ðū wið freónd oððe feónd fremman ongunne, Cd. Th. 170, 9; Gen. 2810. (3) the object of success governed by a preposition:—Ða ðe on eorðlîcum weorcum hwônlîce speówþ, Homl. Th. i. 526, 16. Hū him speów ǣgðer ge mid wîge ge mid wîsdôme, Past. pref.; Swt. 3, 8. Hū him æt ǣte speów, Beo. Th. 6045; B. 3026. [*O. H. Ger.* spuon, spuoan (*wk.*).] v. ge-, mis-spôwan.

spôwendlîce; *adv. Thrivingly, prosperously, abundantly*:—Mē ofer cume hǣlu æfter ðînre sprǣce spôwendlîce *veniat super me salutare tuum secundum eloquium tuum*, Ps. Th. 118, 41, 58: 147, 4.

spôwness. v. forþ-spôwness.

spracen, es; *n.* '*The berry-bearing alder*; rhamnus frangula. *Germ.* Spreckenholz: *Dan.* spregner: *Swed. dial.* sprakved,' Lchdm. ii. 406. The word glosses *apeletum* in Wrt. Voc. i. 285, 83: ii. 8, 43, for *alnetum* (Cockayne):—Genim spracen berindred, Lchdm. ii. 58, 8: 66, 3.

spræc *a shoot*:—Spraec *sarmentum*, Wrt. Voc. ii. 119, 48. [*Icel.* sprek *a stick*. Cf. *O. H. Ger.* sprachila *siliqua*. *Graff also cites* spraioh *sarmenta*, vi. 391.] v. spæc; sprǣte (?).

sprǣc, spǣc, sprēc, e; *f. Speech.* I. in the following glosses:—Sprǣce *disputationis*, Wrt. Voc. ii. 28, 49. Godcundra sprēca *divinorum eloquiorum*, Hpt. Gl. 442, 37. Sprǣce *faminem*, Wrt. Voc. ii. 37, 28: 95, 38. Sprǣce *fatu*, 38, 6. Spēce wîse *scema locutionis*, i. 55, 22.

Sprǣc *loquela*, 88, 7. Sprǣce *omelias*, 288, 53: ii. 64, 16. Spǣc *oraculum*, sprēca *oraculorum*, 62, 59, 60: Hpt. Gl. 503, 10. Spǣcum *oraculis*, 518, 33. Sprēce *procacitate*, 506, 2. Sprǣc *sermo*, Wrt. Voc. ii. 120, 45. Gesmeád sprǣc *sermo commentitius*, i. 55, 25. **II.** *speech, talking*:—Ne sȳ đǣr nān ōđer spǣc inne, būton đæt hig biddan God . . ., L. Ath. iv. 7; Th. i. 226, 29. Đæt hī sīn gehȳrede on hyra menigfealdan spǣce (sprǣce, MS. A.: sprēc, Lind. Rush.) *in multiloquio suo*, Mt. Kmbl. 6, 7. **III.** *speech, the faculty of speaking*:—Gif sprǣc āwyrd weorđ, L. Ethb. 52; Th. i. 16, 5. Be đam đe him his sprǣc ofnimþ *de eo cui sermo deficit*, L. Ecg. P. I, tit. 3; Th. ii. 170, 6. Gif hwam seó sprǣc ōþfylþ, Lchdm. ii. 288, 18. Strong on sprǣce, Exon. Th. 410, 9; Rä. 28, 13. **IV.** *skilful speech, speaking with art, eloquence*:—Sprǣc *eloquentia*, Hpt. Gl. 529, 57. Sumum men hē forgifþ wīsdōm and sprǣce, Homl. Th. i. 322, 25. **V.** *what is said, a speech, saying, collection of words*:—Heard is đeós sprǣc *durus est hic sermo*, Jn. Skt. 6, 60. Spēc, Kent. Gl. 503. Ic āhsige eów āne sprǣce, gif gē mē đa sprǣce secgeaþ *interrogabo vos ego unum sermonem, quem si dixeritis mihi*, Mt. Kmbl. 21, 24. God geopenude Abrahame, hwæt hē mid đære sprǣce mǣnde, Gen. 18, 20. For đære sprǣce đe ic tō eów spræc, Jn. Skt. 15, 3. 'Đīn sunu leofaþ.' Đā gelȳfde hē đære sprǣce, 4, 50: Lk. Skt. 1, 29. Hē āsende hī, đus cweđende: 'Faraþ . . .' Hī fērdon æfter đæs cyninges sprǣce, Homl. Th. i. 78, 22: Cd. Th. 144, 3; Gen. 2384. Iudas him andwyrde and cwæđ . . . Æfter đyssere sprǣce, Homl. Skt. ii. 86, 317. Engla sum Abraham cȳgde, hē stille gebād āres sprǣce, Cd. Th. 176, 11; Gen. 2910. Wiste sprǣca fela, wōra worda, 29, 5; Gen. 445. Đā se Hǣlend geendode đās sprǣca, Mt. Kmbl. 19, 1: 26, 1. Spēcce, Kent. Gl. 873. **VI.** *speech, language, talk, discourse, words*:—Þreó þing syndon đe gebringaþ đone gesǣligan tō heofenan rīce; đæt is, hālig geþanc and gōd spǣc (cf. īdele word, 9) and fullfremed worc, Wulfst. 299, 12. Mē đīn sprǣc cwycade *eloquium tuum vivificavit me*, Ps. Th. 118, 50; 140. Ne gelȳfe wē nā for đīnre sprǣce (sprēc, Lind.: sprēce, Rush.) *propter tuam loquelam*, Jn. Skt. 4, 42. Þeáwlīcre spǣce *tropologium*, Hpt. Gl. 410, 44. Đū him hel sōđan sprǣce *conceal the truth from him*, Cd. Th. 110, 12; Gen. 1837. Ic on đisse byrig (*Sodom*) gehȳre yfele sprǣce werod habban, 145, 20; Gen. 2408. Hī habbaþ on mūđe milde sprǣce, Ps. Th. 58, 7. Īdele sprǣce, Hy. 7, 108. **VI a.** of written words:—For đære gelīcnisse his gelōgodan sprǣce *from the likeness to his style*, Ælfc. T. Grn. 8, 43. **VII.** *a speech, language*:—Đeóda ungelīca ǣgþer ge on sprǣce ge on đeáwum . . . heora sprǣc is tōdǣled on twā and hundseofontig, and ǣlc đara sprǣca is tōdǣled on manega đeóda, Bt. 18, 2; Fox 62, 28–34. Hē reorde gesette eorđbūendum ungelīce, đæt hié đære spǣce spēd ne āhton, Cd. Th. 101, 22; Gen. 1686. On Engliscre sprǣce, Ælfc. T. Grn. 1, 26. Hē sealde heora ǣlcum synderlīce sprǣce, đæt heora ǣlcum wæs uncūđ, hwæt ōđer sǣde, 4, 11. Ealle men sprǣcon āne sprǣce, Gen. 11, 1. Đa apostolas cūđan ealle đa sprǣca đe syndon swā wīde swā middaneard is, Wulfst. 294, 8: 296, 1. Mid sprēcum hiá sprecas nīuum *linguis loquentur nouis*, Mk. Skt. Lind. 16, 17. **VIII.** *speech*, e. g. to have *speech* of or with a person, *conversation, consultation, conference, discussion*:—Nis đæt lytulu sprǣc tō gehēganne (*of the day of judgment*), Exon. Th. 445, 17; Dōm. 8. Folc biþ gebonnen tō sprǣce, 451, 10; Dōm. 101. Se dēma æfter langsumre sprǣce lēt đa mōdor tō đam suna. . . . 'Bǣde đū forđī đīnre mōdor sprǣce, đæt đū hī gebīgdest fram mē,' Homl. Skt. i. 4, 341–357. Hē hēt Agustinum tō his sprǣce cuman *jussit Augustinum ad suum advenire colloquium*, Bd. 1, 25; S. 486, 39: Guthl. 9; Gdwin. 48, 21: 11; Gdwin. 54, 4: Cd. Th. 33, 6; Gen. 516. Æt sprǣce đære *at that consultation*, 122, 29; Gen. 2034: Bd. 2, 13; S. 516, 13. Æfter heora sprǣce, Jud. 3, 19. Gisomnadun đa biscopas tō sprēce *colligerunt pontifices concilium*, Jn. Skt. Rush. 11, 47. Sprǣce and geþeahte habban *to treat, consult*; agere, Bd. 1, 27; S. 492, 16. Cwæþ đæt hē wolde mid his freóndum sprǣce and geþæht habban *cum amicis suis sese de hoc collaturum esse dicebat*, 2, 13; S. 515, 37. Hæfdon betwih him sprǣce and geþeahte *habito inter se consilio*, 3, 29; S. 561, 6. Đā hī hæfdon lange sprǣce and geflit *longa disputatione habita*, 2, 2; S. 502, 13. Gif hwylc mæssepreóst untruman men sprǣce forwyrne (*colloquium denegaverit*), L. Ecg. P. i. 2; Th. ii. 172, 27. **VIII a.** *a question, case that requires explanation*:—Ungelīc đære sprǣce đe wē æfter spyriaþ, Bt. 38, 2; Fox 198, 25. Đæt folc đe hæfde ǣnige sprǣce eode ūt tō đam getelde *omnis populus, qui habebat aliquam quaestionem, egrediebatur ad tabernaculum*, Ex. 33, 7. Đū spenst mē on đa mǣstan sprǣce and on đa earfoþestan tō gereccenne . . . and uneáþe ǣnig com tō ende đære sprǣce; fordam hit is þeáw đære sprǣce and đære āscunge, đætte simle đonne đǣr ān tweó of ādōn biþ, đonne biþ đǣr unrīm āstyred . . . Swā is đisse sprǣce đe đū mē æfter ācsast *ad rem me omnium quaesitu maximam vocas, cui vix exhausti quidquam satis sit; talis namque materia est, ut una dubitatione succisa innumerabiles aliae succrescant*, Bt. 39, 4; Fox 216, 14–26. **IX.** *a sentence, decision, agreement, terms*:—Đā com Putrael tō Bora and bed his forespēce tō Ælfrīce. Đā sette Bora đās spēce wiđ Ælfrīce: đæt wes, đæt Putrael sealde Ælfrīce .viii. oxan, and gef Bora sixtig penga for đere forespǣce, and dide hine sylfne sacclēs wiđ Ælfrīce, Chart. Th. 628, 17. **X.** *a case, cause, suit, claim*, (a) in a general sense:—Wiđ đon đe heó his spǣce underfēnge *in consideration of her receiving his suit* (Godwine asked for the lady in marriage), Chart. Th. 312, 14. Đeáh hié ryhte sprǣce hæbban hiera yfel on him tō tǣlanne *mala recte redarguunt*, Past. 28, 5; Swt. 197, 2. Đū dēmst mīne sprǣce *fecisti causam meam*, Ps. Th. 9, 4. (b) as a legal term:—Đæt đis ǣfre gesett sprǣc wǣre *that this for ever should be a settled suit*, Chart. Th. 203, 4: 172, 2. Ongan đā tō specenne on đat land . . . ōđ đæt seó sprǣc wearđ đam cynge cūđ, 302, 15. Be dōme and sprǣce. . . . Gehwilc sprǣc hæbbe āndagan hwænne heó gelǣst sȳ, L. Ed. proem.; Th. i. 158, 3–7: 11; Th. i. 164, 22. Ǣgehwilcre sprǣce đe māre sȳ đonne .iiii. mancussas, L. A. G. 3; Th. i. 154, 9. Gif man mæssepreóst tihtlige ānfealdre sprǣce . . . æt þrīmfealdre sprǣce, L. Eth. ix. 19; Th. i. 344, 11–13, 15–17. Fultum æt swā micelere sprǣce, L. Ath. v. 8, 3; Th. i. 236, 16. Gif ūs feoh ārīse æt ūrum gemǣnum sprǣce, v. 3; Th. i. 232, 5. Æt cynges spǣce, lecge man .vi. healfmarc wedd, L. Eth. iii. 12; Th. i. 296, 25. Clǣne ǣlcere spǣce, L. C. S. 28; Th. i. 392, 12. Swā fela manna . . . tō gewitnesse gehwylcere sprǣce, L. Ath. iv. 1; Th. i. 222, 11. Ǣlcne wītefæstne man đe ic on sprǣce āhte (*gained at law, as the result of a suit*), Chart. Th. 557, 22. Hē drāf his sprǣce *he prosecuted his suit*, 376, 11. Ic spǣce drīfe mid fullan folcrihte, L. O. 2; Th. i. 178, 13. Habban đa gerēfscypas begen đa fullan spǣce gemǣne, L. Ath. v. 8, 4; Th. i. 236, 25. Man ne mōt sprǣca drīfan binnan Godes cyrican, L. Ælf. C. 35; Th. ii. 356, 29. **XI.** *talk* about a person or thing, *report, fame*:—Đæs đe mā seó sprǣc be him fērde, Lk. Skt. 5, 15. Đā fērde đeós sprǣc be him, 7, 17. Hē ongan bodian and wīdmǣrsian đa spǣce, Mk. Skt. 1, 45. **XII.** *in the Northern Gospels* sprēc *translates words denoting places where there is speaking*:—In sprēce (sprēc, Lind.) *in synagoga*, Mk. Skt. Rush. 6, 2. On sprēce (sprēc, Lind.) *in foro*, 12, 38: Lk. Skt. Rush. 20, 46: Lind. 7, 32. [*O. Sax.* sprāka: *O. Frs.* sprēke: *O. H. Ger.* sprāhha *lingua, loquela, sermo, sermocinatio, colloquium, eloquium, ratio, judicium, consilium, senatus.*] v. ǣfen-, æfter-, ǣrend-, burh-, bysmor-, dol-, eald-, edwīt-, ellen-, for-, fore-, frēcnen-, frum-, gedwol-, gegaf-, gilp-, hete-, Lǣden-, morgen-, of-, ofer-, on-, sceáwend-, scrift-, sōđ-, stunt-, teosu-, tō-, twī-, untīd-, wiđer-, woruld-, ymbe-sprǣc (-spǣc); -sprǣce, -sprec.

sprǣc-ærn, -ern, es; *n. A place for speaking, court-house*:—In sprēcern *in praetorium*, Jn. Skt. Lind. Rush. 18, 28: 19, 9. Cf. sprǣc-hūs.

sprǣc-cynn, es; *n. A mode of speaking*:—Bōc be gesetnessum and gemetum sprǣccynna *libellum de figuris modisque locutionum*, Bd. 5, 24; S. 648, 42.

-sprǣce. [*O. L. Ger.* bi-sprāki: *O. H. Ger.* ga-sprāhhi.] v. ge-, god-sprǣce.

-sprǣce, -spǣce; *adj.* [*O. Sax.* -sprāki: *O. H. Ger.* -sprāhhi.] v. ān-, fela-, ge-, gegaf-, īdel-, ofer-, stunt-, twī-, yfel-, ymb-sprǣce.

sprǣcelic. v. ge-sprǣcelic.

sprǣcful; *adj. Talkative, loquacious*:—Wer sprǣcful *vir linguosus*, Ps. Lamb. 139, 12.

sprǣc-hūs, es; *n. A house for speaking*:—Sprǣchūs *auditorium*, Wrt. Voc. i. 58, 11. Ūþwitena sprǣchūs *curia* vel *senatus*, 13. [*O. L. Ger.* sprāc-hūs *curia*: *O. H. Ger.* sprāh-hūs *curia, consistorium, praetorium.*] Cf. sprǣc-ærn.

sprǣcleás; *adj. Speechless, without the power of speech*:—Spǣcleáse ł dume *elinguia*, Germ. 398, 72. [*O. H. Ger.* sprāhhalōs *elinguis.*]

-sprǣcness. v. twī-sprǣcness.

sprǣdan; *p.* de *To spread, expand.* [*O. L. Ger.* te-spreidan *dispergere*: *O. H. Ger.* spreiten *pandere, expandere, diffundere.*] v. ge-, ofer-, tō-sprǣdan, ā-spreádan; sprǣdung.

sprǣdung, e; *f. Spreading, diffusion, propagation*:—Sprǣdung mennisces cynnes *propagatio humani generis*, Rtl. 109, 4.

sprængan. v. sprengan.

sprǣte (?), spræt (?), es; *n. A sprout, shoot*:—Sprǣtu (spræcu? v. spræc) *labruscas*, Hpt. Gl. 454, 16. [Cf. (?) spreat, sprat, sprett *the jointed-leaved rush*, Jamieson's Dict. Sprat-barley *barley with very long beards*; sprats *small wood*, Halliwell's Dict.]

spranc (?), es: spranca, an; *m. A shoot, twig, sprig*:—Spranca (sprauta, Wrt.) *sirculus* vel *virgultum*, Wrt. Voc. i. 32, 44. Styb *vel* spranca (sprauta, Wrt.) *stirps*, 33, 57. Treówes sprancan *plante*, 39, 14. Deáđbǣre sprancan *letiferas labruscas*, Hpt. Gl. 454, 17. Spranca *sarmentorum*, 468, 22.

sprauta. v. preceding word.

spreáwlian; *p.* ode *To sprawl, move convulsively*:—Spreáwlige *palpitet*, Germ. 392, 10. [Sprawlyn *palpito*; sprawlynge *palpitacio*, Prompt. Parv. 470 (and see note). Leyen and sprauleden in the blod, Havel. 475. Spraulend with her winges twey, Gow. ii. 5, 11.]

-sprec, sprēc. v. ge-, god-sprec, sprǣc.

spreca, speca, an; *m. A speaker, one who speaks in council* (cf. sprǣc, VIII), *a councillor*:—Forht folces weard hēht him fetigean sprecan sīne, Cd. Th. 161, 18; Gen. 2667. [*O. Frs.* for-spreka: *O. H. Ger.* sprehho.] v. edwīt-, for-, fore-, ge-, mid-, on-spreca (-speca).

sprecan, specan; *p.* spræc, spæc; *pl.* sprǣcon, spǣcon; *pp.* sprecen, specen *To speak.* **I.** *to exercise the faculty of speech*:—Se dumba spræc,

Mt. Kmbl. 9, 33. Dumbe sprǣcon, Mk. Skt. 7, 37. Ðū byst suwiende, and ðū sprecan ne miht, Lk. Skt. 1, 20. Ǣnne līcþrowere . . . unsprecende forneán. . . . Basilius gelǣdde hine forð wel sprecande, Homl. Skt. i. 3, 489. Wæs eall weoruld sprecende on ān gereord, Wulfst. 211, 19. Geseónde dumbe specende (sprecende, MS. A.), Mt. Kmbl. 15, 31. II. *to use words* in conversation, discourse, etc. :—Ic ne sprece tō ðǣm, ac ic sprece tō ðē, Bt. 38, 5; Fox 206, 12. Ic secge ðis sārspell and ymb sīþ spræce, Exon. Th. 458, 7; Hy. 4, 96. Hwæþer ic be mē sylfum spece. Se ðe be him sylfum sprycþ, Jn. Skt. 7, 17, 18. Nū ðū sprycst openlīce, 16, 29. Eorl ōðerne tǣleþ behindan, spreceþ fægere beforan, Frag. Kmbl. 8; Leás. 5. Ðā spræc se ofermōda cyning, Cd. Th. 22, 9; Gen. 338. Hió spræc him þicce tō, 43, 1: Gen. 684. Drihten wið Abrahame spræc, 139, 2; Gen. 2303. Hig spǣcon (sprǣcon, MS. A.) him betwȳnan, Lk. Skt. 24, 14. Ðæt ðū ne belge wið mē, gif ic spræce. . . . Nū ic ǣne begann tō sprecanne tō mīnum drihtne, ic wylle sprecan git, Gen. 18, 30–31. Ic eom āsend wið ðē sprecan, Lk. Skt. 1, 19. Ðonne hē spreocan ongan, Cd. Th. 269, 25; Sat. 78. III. with acc. (a) *where the object of the verb is* word *or a similar form*:—Ic ðās word spræce, Exon. Th. 457, 12; Hy. 4, 82. Ðū ða word spricest, 12, 2; Cri. 179. Se ðe God sende sprycþ Godes word, Jn. Skt. 3, 34. Ðū worn fela ymb Brecan sprǣce, Beo. Th. 1067; B. 531. Him ellenrōf andswarode, word æfter spræc, 688; B. 341. Ðæt gē on eárum sprǣcon, Lk. Skt. 12, 3. Hié fela sprǣcon sorhworda somed, Cd. Th. 49, 7; Gen. 788. Spǣcon, Ps. Th. 57, 3. Gilde ǣlc ðe hit (*the exculpation on oath*) ǣr sprece .cxx. scill., L. Ath. i. 13; Th. i. 206, 6. Warna ðæt ðū nān þing elles ne sprece, būton ðæt ic ðē bebeóde, Num. 22, 35. Ðis synd ða word ðe ðū scealt sprecan tō folce, Ex. 19, 6. Ongan hospword sprecan, Andr. Kmbl. 2632; An. 1317. Ðæt ǣrende wæs sprecen, 3242; An. 1623: Beo. Th. 1290; B. 643. (b) where the object of the verb is a word denoting the matter expressed in the words spoken:—Ic rǣd sprece *I give counsel in my words*, Cd. Th. 115, 2; Gen. 1913. Ðū bysmor spycst *blasphemas*, Jn. Skt. 10, 36. Tunga his sprecþ dōm, Ps. Spl. 36, 32. Se ðe sōð spriceþ, Exon. Th. 3, 9; Cri. 33. Hē beót spriceþ, 290, 25; Wand. 70. Heó mē wom spreceþ, 402, 22; Rä. 21, 23. Ða ðe sprecaþ sybbe, Ps. Spl. 27, 4. Hié sprecaþ fācen and inwit, Cd. Th. 145, 30; Gen. 2413. Fela hē mē lāðes spræc, 39, 9; Gen. 622. Ðam ðe sār sprece sāwle mīnre, Ps. Th. 108, 20. (c) where the object is that which is spoken about, *to mention*:—On swelcum cræftum swelce wē ǣr sprǣcon, Past. 9; Swt. 59, 12. Of ðǣm beorgum ðe wē ǣr sprǣcon (sǣdon, MS. L.), Ors. 1, 1; Bos. 17, 44. Wē gehȳrdon hī sprecan Godes mǣrða mid ūrum gereordum, Homl. Th. i. 314, 19. III a. with a clause, *to say*:—Hié sprǣcon, ðæt hit betere wǣre, Ors. 2, 3; Swt. 68, 8. Ðā gehȳrde hē sumne ðara brōþra sprecan, ðæt hē wolde fēran, Bd. 3, 2; S. 525, 5. III b. with the words that are spoken:—Hī sāre sprecaþ: 'Hwā gesyhþ ūsic?' *dixerunt, Quis videbit eos?* Ps. Th. 63, 4. IV. with a gen.:—Mīne fȳnd sprǣcon mē yfeles, Ps. Th. 40, 8. V. with inst., *to speak* in a language, with words:—Ic sprece mongum reordum, Exon. Th. 390, 13; Rä. 9, 1. Beówulf beótwordum spræc, Beo. Th. 5014; B. 2510: Exon. Th. 253, 24; Jul. 185. Hē spræc him wordum tō, Ps. Th. 98, 7. Hē wordum wið his Waldend spræc, Cd. Th. 155, 22; Gen. 2576. Hē tō Noe spræc hālgan reorde, 89, 19; Gen. 1483. Hī sprǣcon ūrum gereordum, Homl. Th. i. 314, 18. Tō Geátum spræc mildum wordum, Beo. Th. 2347; B. 1171. VI. with prep.:—Hē mid heardre ðreá hī on spræc and hī gebētte *aspera illos invectione corrigebat*, Bd. 3, 5; S. 527, 11. Wē sind an specende *dicturi*, Wrt. Voc. ii. 28, 66. On specende *inspirans*, 93, 40. On spæcende (swætende, Wrt.), 47, 31. Ongeán sprecendes *obloquentis*, Ps. Spl. 43, 18. ¶ *In technical terms*, v. sprǣc, X, sprecan æfter, on, ymb *to sue for, make a claim against, lay claim to*:—Ðæt orf ðæt ic on spece *the cattle that I lay claim to*, L. O. 2; Th. i. 178, 15. Āgnung biþ nēr ðam ðe hæfþ ðonne ðam ðe æfter sprecþ, L. Eth. ii. 9; Th. i. 290, 21. Ða fīf hīda ðe Æðelm Hīga ymb spycþ. . . . Ongon Hīga him specan on mid ōðran onspecendan and wolde him ōðflītan ðæt lond *the five hides about which Æthelm Higa has a suit . . . Higa along with other claimants began to make a claim against him (Helmstan), and wanted to get the land from him by litigation*, Chart. Th. 169, 17–24. Ðā spræc ic on ða māgas *then I made a claim against the kinsmen*, 167, 18. Hē spæc on his āgene mōdor æfter sumon dǣle landes, 337, 4. Ðā gemǣtæ hē ða swutelunga and ðǣrmid on ðæt land spæc, ongan ðā tō specenne on ðat land, 302, 12. Hine man tō rihte gelǣde ðām ðe him on sprǣcon (*those that bring charges against him*), L. Eth. i. 4; Th. i. 284, 1. Ðone āð ðe se gelȳfan mihte ðe on sprece, L. Ed. 1; Th. i. 158, 18. Ðæt nān man on his yrfenuman ne spece *that no man bring an action against his heir*, L. Eth. iii. 14; Th. i. 298, 10. Ðone āð syllan, ðæt hē mid folcrihte on ðæt land sprece, L. O. D. 1; Th. i. 352, 13. [*O. Frs.* spreka: *O. Sax.* sprekan: *O. H. Ger.* sprehhan.] v. ā-, be-, for-, forþ-, ge-, mis-, ofer-sprecan; un-sprecende, for-, fore-sprecen.

spreccan. v. on-spreccan.

sprecel *a spot* (?). v. haran-specel. [Cf. Spreckled *speckled*, Halliwell's Dict.: spreckly, spreckled, Jamieson's Dict. *O. H. Ger.* sprehhiloht *maculosus*: *Icel.* spreklōttr *speckled*.]

sprecend, sprecende. v. on-sprecend, un-sprecende.

sprecol, specol; *adj. Talkative, loquacious*:—Wer sprecul *vir linguosus*, Ps. Spl. 139, 12. v. fela-, ofer-, swīð-sprecol.

sprecolness, e; *f. Talkativeness, loquacity*:—Genihtsumian on gebeórscypum sprecolnyss gewunaþ *abundare in conuiuiis loquacitas solet*, Scint. 170, 15. v. ofer-sprecolness.

sprengan; *p.* de *To cause to spring*. I. *to scatter*:—Ðū gaderast ðǣr ðū ne sprengdest (*sparsisti*), Mt. Kmbl. 25, 24. His eágan wǣron spearcan sprengende, Homl. Th. i. 466, 26. II. *to sprinkle*, (a) an object with something:—Ðū spren[g]st Aaron and his reáf, Ex. 29, 21. Hē nam ðæt blōd and sprengde ðæt folc, 28, 8. (b) something on to an object:—Spræng̃e se mæssepreóst hāligwæter ofer hig ealle, L. Ath. iv. 7; Th. i. 226, 23. Genim ðās ylcan wyrte gesodene, sprenge intō ðam hūse, Lchdm. i. 264, 15. Nime se sacerd his blōd and dyppe his finger ðǣron and sprenge on ðæt ryft, Lev. 4, 17, 6. (c) government uncertain:—Ðā ðā hē sprencde *dum rorat*, Germ. 402, 43. III. *to burst, crack* (cf. *to spring* a leak, *sprung*, applied to a bat):—Hē sceáf mid ðam scylde, ðæt se sceaft tōbærst, and ðæt spere sprengde (*shivered the spear-head*), ðæt hit sprang ongeán, Byrht. Th. 135, 52; By. 137. IV. as a medical term, *to apply a clyster*. v. spring, IV (3):—Ðæt mon on morgen on sprenge, Lchdm. ii. 48, 24. [Sprengeð on mid hali water, A. R. 16, 9. *O. H. Ger.* sprengen *quassare, rorare*: *Ger.* sprengen *to burst, scatter, sprinkle*: *Icel.* sprengja *to burst*: *Dan.* sprænge: *Swed.* spränga.] v. ā-, be-, ge-, geond-sprengan.

spreót, es; *m. A pole, sprit* (in bow-*sprit*):—Spreót *contus*, Wrt. Voc. i. 33, 61. Ānes mannes lenge ðe healt ānne spreót on his hand and strecþ hine swā feor swā hē mæg ārǣcan intō ðere sǣ *statura unius hominis tenentis lignum quod Angle nominant* spreot, *et tendentis ante se quantum potest*, Chart. Th. 318, 10. Spreótas *trudes* vel *amites*, Wrt. Voc. i. 35, 43: *trudes* (in a list of things connected with ships), 48, 13: 57, 16: 64, 7: *ansatas*, ii. 3, 68: *contos*, 14, 72. Spreótum, spreútum *contis*, Txts. 48, 211. [*Prompt. Parv.* sprete *contus*: *Du.* spriet *sprit*: *Dan.* sprød: *Swed.* spröt.] v. eofor-spreót.

spreótan. v. sprūtan.

sprinca *glosses* circopythicos, Wrt. Voc. ii. 131, 29.

sprincan. v. springan.

sprincel, es; *m. A wicker-basket*:—Sprinclum *fiscillis*, Wrt. Voc. ii. 108, 58: 35, 43. [Cf. *Dan.* sprinkel, sprinkel-værk *trellis, lattice*.] Cf. tǣnel, windel.

sprincting, sprind. v. springung, springd.

sprindel *a tenter-hook*:—Sprindel (-il) *tenticum*, Txts. 101, 2003. Spindel, Wrt. Voc. i. 289, 18. v. next word.

-sprindlian. v. ā-sprindlad.

spring, spryng, es; *m.* (*but* eá-spring; *n.*) I. *a source* of water:—Spring *casta* (*castalia*?), Wrt. Voc. ii. 129, 31. Æt ðæs wæteres sprynge, Cod. Dip. Kmbl. iii. 389, 7. [*Prompt. Parv.* sprynge *scaturigo, scatebra*: *O. L. Ger.* gi-spring *fons*: *O. Sax.* aho-spring: *O. H. Ger.* ur-spring *fons*.] v. ǣ-, eá-, ge-, will-spring. II. *a springing, rising, spring* in day-*spring*. v. up-spring III. *what springs* up *or* from. [Sprynge of a tre or plante, springe or yonge tre *planta, plantula*, Prompt. Parv. 470.] v. of-spring. IV. as a medical term, (1) *an ulcer, a sore, pustule*:—Spryng *carbunculus*, Wrt. Voc. ii. 102, 46: 13, 11: *papula*, 116, 22. *Carbunculus* spring *vel* angset *vel pustula*, i. 19, 19. Tō sealfe wið springe, Lchdm. ii. 80, 8. Wið ðæt man wille spring on gesittan, i. 2, 19. Lāðlīc biþ ðæs hreóflian līc mid menigfealdum springum and geswelle, Homl. Th. i. 122, 22: 336, 33. Wið uncūðe springas ðe on līchoman ācennede beóþ, Lchdm. i. 150, 14. Springas (sprincas, MS. B.), 262, 10. [Cf. *O. H. Ger.* gesprinc *pustula*.] v. fǣr-, wen-, wund-spring. (2) *a flux*:—Wið ðæs magan springe, ii. 190, 16 (where see note): 192, 12. (3) *a squirting, sprinkling*:—Mon sceal ǣr mid wearmum springum and hāte wætre beþian and þweán ða stōwe, 202, 21. Mid spryngum, 206, 17: 208, 14.

springan; *p.* sprang, *pl.* sprungon; *pp.* sprungen *To spring*. I. *to leap, bound*:—Ðæt cild on sprang *the babe leaped in her womb* (Lk. 1, 41), Blickl. Homl. 165, 29. Hrā wīde sprong, syþðan hē drepe þrowade, Beo. Th. 3181; B. 1588. II. *to burst forth*, of a fluid *to spirt*, of sparks, etc., *to fly*:—Ðæt spere sprang ongeán *the spear-head sprang out again* (*under the pressure of the shield*), Byrht. Th. 135, 53; By. 137. Leád wīde sprong *the drops of boiling lead flew far*, Exon. Th. 277, 24; Jul. 585. Swāt ǣdrum sprong *the blood spirted from the veins*, Beo. Th. 5925; B. 2966. Wīde sprungon hildeleóman, 5158; B. 2582. Sprungon spearcan of ðam mūðe, Shrn. 120, 26. III. *to grow* as a plant:—Swā swā of ānum treówe springaþ manega bogas, swā gāþ of ānre lufe manega ōðre mihta, Homl. Th. ii. 314, 22. Hig hrædlīce up sprungon, for ðam ðe hig næfdon ðære eorðan dȳpan, Mt. Kmbl. 13, 5. IV. *to rise* as the sun, cf. spring, II:—Up sprungenre sunnan *sole orto*, Mt. Kmbl. 13, 6. V. *to move as a spring moves*:—Þeáh ðū teó hweicne boh ofdūne tō ðære eorþan, swā ðū hine ālǣtst, swā sprincþ hē up, Bt. 25; Fox 88, 24. VI. *to spread, be diffused*:—Ða wīde springaþ *crebrescunt*, Hpt. Gl. 517, 4. Wīde springaþ, wīdmǣrsiaþ, 471, 16. Ðes hlīsa sprang (spranc, Lind.)

ofer eall ðæt land *exiit fama haec in universam terram illam*, Mt. Kmbl. 9, 26. Sprang ꝉ foerde *processit*, Mk. Skt. Rush. 1, 28: Beo. Th. 36; B. 18: Apstls. Kmbl. 12; Ap. 6. Ðā sprang ðæt word *the report spread*, Homl. Th. i. 384, 8: Ap. Th. 25, 13. Wīde springende *crebrescens*, Hpt. Gl. 519, 37: 513, 21. [*O. Sax.* springan *to spring* as blood from a wound: *O. Frs.* springa: *O. H. Ger.* springan *to spring* as water: *Icel.* springa *to burst, crack.*] v. ā-, æt-, ge-, geond-, on-, tō-springan.

springd, sprind; *adj. Active, vigorous*:—Snellne, sprindne *adultum, juvenem*, Hpt. Gl. 485, 26. Geþogenne ꝉ sprindne *adultum, maturum*, 491, 13. Sprindne *adultum*, Anglia xiii. 34, 186. His geðoht is springdra and swiftra. ðonne xii. ðūsendu hāligra gāsta, Salm. Kmbl. p. 150, 34. v. next word.

springdlīce, sprindlīce; *adv. Actively, vigorously*:—Sprindlīce ꝉ cāflīce *naviter, alacriter, agiliter, velociter*, Hpt. Gl. 405, 22. Fromlīce ꝉ sprinlīce *naviter, velociter, viriliter* ꝉ *fortiter*, 423, 71.

springe. v. ǣ-springe.

springung (?), e; *f. Growth*:—Mǣda ꝉ sprinctinge (sprincunge?) ꝉ grēnnessa *prata, viriditates*, Hpt. Gl. 409, 38. v. ā-springung.

spring-wyrt, e; *f. Wild caper, caper-bush, -plant, -spurge;* Euphorbia lathyris, Lchdm. ii. 104, 2: 106, 1. [*O. H. Ger.* spring-wurz *actureda, lactaridia;* springa *actureda, lactarida.*]

sprot, es; *n. A sprout, shoot, twig, small branch*:—Sprote *with a rod* (?), Coll. Monast. Th. 23, 35. Sprota *sarmentorum, ramorum, qui de vinea exciduntur*, Hpt. Gl. 445, 32: 489, 10: *palmitum*, Germ. 401, 16. Sprotum *sarmentis*, 401, 24. [Halliwell gives *sprote*-wood as a word still in use for small wood or sticks for firing. Jamieson gives *sprŏt* (1) the withered stump of any plant, broken and lying on the ground; (2) the end of a branch blown off a growing tree; (3) a chip of wood, flying from the tool of a carpenter. *O. L. Ger.* gi-sprot *surculum*: *Du.* sprot *a sprout, twig* (Hexham).] v. sprūtan, *and next word.*

sprota, an; *m.* I. *a sprout, shoot*:—Sprotena *sarmentorum*, Hpt. Gl. 478, 64. II. *a peg*:—Nægl oððe sprota *clavus*, Wrt. Voc. ii. 22, 10. [I ne have stikke, i ne have sprote, Havel. 1142. *O. H. Ger.* sprozzo *rung of a ladder*: *Ger.* sprosse: *Icel.* sproti *a shoot, twig; a rod.*] v. preceding word.

sprott, es; *m. A sprat*:—Ða myclan hwælas and ða lytlan sprottas and eall fisckynn, Anglia viii. 310, 18. [A sprott *hec epimera*, Wrt. Voc. i. 222, col. 2. *Du.* sprot: *Ger.* sprotte.]

-sprungenness. v. ā-, on-sprungenness.

sprūtan; *p.* spreát, *pl.* spruton; *pp.* sproten *To sprout.* [Blosme, þat beo ha eanes fulliche forcoruen, ne spruteð ha neauer eft, H. M. 11, 20. *Egredietur uirga de radice iesse* an gerd sal spruten of iesse more, O. E. Homl. ii. 217, 25. In a night sua did it sprute, C. M. 11216. Sproutyn̄ *pululo*, Prompt. Parv. 471. Faine sal he sproutand ai *laetabitur germinans*, Ps. 64, 11. *O. Frs.* sprūta; *pp.* spruten.] v. ā-spreótan (*read* -sprūtan), geond-spreót.

sprȳtan, sprītan (?); *p.* te *To sprout, spring* as a plant:—Of ðam blado bealwa gehwilces sprȳtan (spryttan?) ongunnon, Cd. Th. 61, 10; Gen. 995. v. spryttan.

sprytele, sprītele (?), an; *f. A twig, chip.* (v. quotation from Jamieson's Dict. under *sprot*):—Men of ðære ylcan styde sprytlan ācurfon *astulis ex ipsa destina excisis*, Bd. 3, 17; S. 544, 43. [Halliwell gives *sprittel* a sprout or twig. Cf. *O. H. Ger.* spruzil: *M. H. Ger.* sprüzzel *rung of a ladder.* Or (?) cf. *M. H. Ger.* sprīzel *a splinter.*] v. sprot *and* spreót.

spryttan; *p.* te I. *intrans. To sprout, spring, germinate*:—Ðonne sprit his gird *germinabit virga ejus*, Num. 17, 5. Up spryt rihtwīsnys *orietur justitia*, Ps. Lamb. 71, 7. Tō ðȳ hē sprytt, ðæt hē mid cwyldum fornyme swā hwæt swā hē ǣr sprytte, Homl. Th. i. 614, 9. Ðonne treówa spryttaþ, ðonne wite gē ðæt hit sumorlǣhþ, 614, 4. Ðonne treów and wyrta ǣrest up spryttaþ, Lchdm. ii. 148, 6: Met. 29, 68. Up spryttende *pululantes*, Wrt. Voc. ii. 66, 4. Folc weóx swilce hig of eorðan spryttende wǣron *creverunt et quasi germinantes multiplicati sunt*, Ex. 1, 7. Ealle spryttende þingc *universa germinantia*, Hymn. T. P. 76. Eft spryttendum ðām twigum *renascentibus virgultis*, Bd. 1, 21; S. 485, 5. [He is ase þe wiði þet sprutted ut þe betere ꝥ me hine ofte croppeð, A. R. 86, 15.] II. *trans.* (a) *To put forth* a shoot, *bring forth* fruit:—Seó eorðe spryt hyre wæstmas eów, Homl. Skt. i. 13, 159. Ðes wīngeard sprytte Godes gecorenan, Homl. Th. ii. 74, 4: i. 614, 10. Spritte seó eorðe grōwende gærs *germinet terra herbam virentem*, Gen. 1, 11. God hēt ða eorðan spryttan grōwende gærs, Hexam. 6; Norm. 10, 33. Nǣnne wæstm tō spryttanne, Homl. Th. ii. 90, 18. (b) *to incite* (cf. þurh þes (*Ranulf's*) macunge and tōspryttinge se eorl þis land mid unfriðe gesōhte, Chr. 1101; Erl. 238, 1):—Sprytte *instigavit*, Anglia xiii. 36, 245. Ðā sprytte se deófol ðæt folc tō his (*Christ's*) slege, Homl. Th. i. 216, 14. Ðæt hē ðisne freóls ǣfre gefyrðrian wolde, and his bearn tō ðam ylcan sprittan wolde, Chart. Th. 116, 22. v. ā-spryttan.

sprytting, e; *f.* (*but pl. in* -as in Ps. Lamb. 79, 12) *A sprig, shoot, sprout, plant*:—Ne biþ spryttinge on wīngeardum *non erit germen in uineis*, Cant. Abac. 17. Spryttinc *incrementum*, spryttincgum ꝉ eácnungum *incrementis, fructibus*, Hpt. Gl. 491, 56–59. Hāligre spryttinge *almo germine*, Hymn. Surt. 76, 3. Sprettinge forð bringende *germen proferens*, 19, 35. Sprittincga *plantaria, plantationes*, Hpt. Gl. 433, 34. Gescōp se ælmihtiga God eorðan and ealle eorðlīce spryttinga, Lchdm. iii. 234, 3. Hē āstrehte ōþ flōd his spryttingas *extendit usque ad flumen propagines ejus*, Ps. Lamb. 79, 12.

spura, spurnan, spurnere. v. spora, spornan, spornere.

spurul *glosses calcatiosus*, Txts. 110, 1162.

spynge, an; *f. A sponge*:—Elpendes hȳd wile drincan wǣtan gelīce and spynge dēþ (*tanquam spongia*), Ors. 5, 7; Swt. 230, 27. Hī bewundon āne spyngan (spingan, MS. B.) mid ysopo, Jn. Skt. 19, 29 MS. A. Spingan, Mk. Skt. 15, 36. Spincgan, Homl. Th. ii. 256, 32. Spync ꝉ spynga, Lind.: spynge, Rush. Mt. Kmbl. 27, 46. v. sponge.

spyrcan, spyrcing. v. spircan, spircing.

spyrd, es; *m.* The word glosses *stadium* (1) with the meaning *a course*:—Ða ðe in spyrde iornaþ *qui in stadio currunt*, Rtl. 5, 33. (2) with the meaning *a measure of distance*:—Swelce spyrdas fīftēne (spyrdum fīftēnum, Lind.) *quasi stadiis quindecim*, Jn. Skt. Rush. 11, 18. Swelce spyrdo fīfe and twoegentig *quasi stadia .xxv.*, 6, 19. Ðara spyrda *stadiorum*, Lk. Skt. Lind. Rush. 24, 13. *In all these passages the West-Saxon uses* furlang. [*Goth.* spaurds (1) *a course;* (2) *a distance*: *O. H. Ger.* spurt *stadium.*]

spyre-mann, es; *m. One who tracks*:—His speremon *the man who tracked him*, Chart. Th. 172, 25. v. spor-wrecel.

spyrian; *p.* ede, ode I. *to track, go in a track* (v. spor, spyremann), *follow, make a journey in search of something*:—Deáð spyraþ (spyreþ, Met. 27, 9) ǣlce dæge æfter fuglum and æfter diórum and æfter monnum, and ne forlǣt nān swæþ, ǣr hē gefēhþ ðæt, ðæt hē æfter spyreþ, Bt. 39, 1; Fox 210, 28–212, 1. Nyle deáð ǣnig swæð forlǣtan, ǣr hē gehende ðæt hē hwīle ǣr æfter spyrede, Met. 27, 16. Mon mæg giet gesión hiora swæð ac wē him ne cunnon æfter spyrigean *we can still see their track, but we do not know how to follow the track after them*, Past. pref.; Swt. 5, 16. II. *to make a track, go*:—Mec fugles wyn geond speddropum spyrede geneahhe . . . beámtelge swealg stōp eft on mec sīþade sweartlāst *me* (*a book*) *throughout the bird's joy* (*the pen*) *with drops made frequent tracks, . . . swallowed the tree's dye* (*ink*), *stepped on to me, journeyed with footprints black*, Exon. Th. 408, 7; Rä. 27, 8. Syndan onhrērede anlīcast hū druncen hwylc spyrige *as any drunken man makes his way*, Ps. Th. 106, 26. III. *to enquire, investigate, examine*:—Ðā cwæþ se wīsdōm: 'Hwī . . .?' Ðā andswarode ic: 'Genōh ryhte ðū spyrast, swā hit is swā ðū segst, Bt. 26, 2; Fox 92, 18. Hī spyredan hwæt and hwonan hē wæs *investigantes unde vel quis esset*, Bd. 1, 33; S. 499, 11. Gelēfe hē ðæt wit on riht spirien (spyrigen, Cott. MS.) *let him believe that we conduct the enquiry aright*, Bt. 38, 2; Fox 198, 27. Uton spirian (spyrian, MSS. G. I.) be bōcan, hwæt ða gefōran, ða ðe God lufedon, Wulfst. 130, 11. Ic ongann ðīne sprǣce spyrian georne *ut meditarer eloquia tua*, Ps. Th. 118, 148. Spirian *enucleare*, Hpt. Gl. 498, 16. Spiriende *indagando, inquirendo*, 410, 52: *scrutando, investigando, meditando*, 479, 20. III a. *with* æfter, (1) *to enquire after* or *into, seek to know about*:—Ðære sprǣce ðe wit æfter spyriaþ *the subject into which we are enquiring*, Bt. 38, 2; Fox 198, 26. Se ðe wile wīslīce æfter ðam hlīsan spyrian, ðonne ongit hē, hū lytel hē biþ, 18, 1; Fox 60, 28. Wē sceoldon eallon mægne spirian æfter Gode, 42; Fox 256, 1. (2) *to search after, seek to attain*:—Ealle men spyriaþ æfter ðam hēhstan gōde. Ac ne māgon ða yfelan cuman tō ðam hrōfe eallra gōda, forðam hī ne spyriaþ on riht æfter, 39, 9; Fox 224, 24–27. Hwȳ nyllaþ hī spyrigan æfter cræftum and æfter wīsdōme, 36, 6; Fox 180, 32. Spirigan, 35, 1; Fox 154, 19. Hī ǣfre ne lyst æfter spyrian, sēcan ða gesǣlþa, Met. 19, 33. [Speer, speir *to ask* in Scot. and North-E.: *O. H. Ger.* spuren, spurien *investigare, indagare, sciscitari*: *Icel.* spyrja *to track; to investigate; to ask.*] v. ā-, ge-, of-spyrian.

spyrigend, spyrgend, spyriend, es; *m. An enquirer, investigator*:—Speriend *investigator*, Kent. Gl. 384. Godes spyrigendes *of an enquirer after God*, Salm. Kmbl. 281; Sal. 140. v. ā-spyrigend.

spyrigness. v. ā-spyrigness.

spyrigung, spyrgung, spyriung, e; *f. Enquiry, investigation*:—Spiriungum ꝉ āxungum *argumentis*, Hpt. Gl. 524, 50. [*O. H. Ger.* spurunga *indagatio, investigatio.*] v. ā-spyrgung.

spyrnung, e; *f. Spurning.* v. æt-, ōþ-spyrning.

spyrran, spyrring. v. sperran, sperring.

spyrte, an; *f. A basket*:—Spyrte *fiscella*, Germ. 400, 492. Spirte *cistula*, Wrt. Voc. i. 288, 33: ii. 17, 7. Of ðære lāfe wǣron gefyllede seofon spyrtan. . . . Spyrte biþ, swā swā gē sylfe witon, of rixum gebroden, oððe of palmtwygum, Homl. Th. ii. 402, 6–9: 396, 8. Siofun sperta *septem sportas*, Mt. Kmbl. Rush. 15, 37: 16, 10. [*Lat.* sporta.]

spyttan *to spit*:—Spittas (-es, Lind.) *conspuent*, Mk. Skt. Rush. 10, 34. Spittadun *expuerunt*, Mt. Kmbl. Rush. 26, 67. Spittende *expuentes*, 27, 30. [Blod to spitten ant te speowen, Jul. 48, 18. Þenne spit leccherie meidenhad oþe nebbe, H. M. 17, 13. Spit him amidde þe bearde, A. R. 290, 20. Cf. *Ger.* speutzen, spützen: *Icel.* spȳta.] v. ge-spittan.

staca, an; *m. A stake*:—Nygon fēt of ðam stacan tō ðære mearce, L. Ath. iv. 7; Th. i. 226, 12. Ðǣr his brōðor heáfod stōd on stacan gefæstnod, Homl. Skt. ii. 26, 166. Wrít ðysne circul on ánum mealan stáne and sleah ǽnne stacan on middan ðam ymbhagan, and lege ðone stán on uppan ðam stacan, Lchdm. i. 395, 3-5. Mon hæfde ða burg mid stacum gemearcod, wulfas átugan ða stacan up, Ors. 5, 5; Swt. 226, 17-19. Álege ðone man upweard, drīf .ii. stacan æt ðám eaxlum, Lchdm. ii. 342, 5. ¶ In the following passages there seems to be a reference to the method of witchcraft, that consisted in thrusting a pin or the like into the figure of a person, whom it was desired to injure. On this practice, see, *inter alia*, Brand's Antiquities, ed. Hazlitt, vol. iii. p. 65, Grmm. D. M. 1045, and the Glossary to Thorpe's edition of the Early Laws, s. v. stacung:—Gif hwá drīfe stacan on ǽnigne man. . . . And gif se man for ðære stacunge deád biþ *si quis acus in homine aliquo defixerit. . . . Et si homo ex illa punctura mortuus sit*, L. Ecg. P. iv. 17; Th. ii. 208, 26-29: L. Edg. C. 38; Th. ii. 274, 26-28. (In each case the section occurs amongst regulations dealing with witchcraft.) Án wyduwe and hire sune drifon íserne stacan on Alsie, Wulfstánes feder . . . Man téh ðæt morð forð of hire inclifan. Ða nam man ðæt wíf and ádrencte hí æt Lundenebrigce, Chart. Th. 230, 12-19. [*O. Frs.* stac[e].]

stacga (?), an; *m. A stag*:—Regalem feram, quam Angli staggon appellant, L. C. F. 24; Th. i. 429, 5. [Cf. *Icel.* steggi, steggr *a he-bird; in* modern usage also *a tom-cat.*]

stacung, e; *f. Staking, piercing with a stake.* v. *passages under* staca.

stæf, es; *m.* I. *a staff, stick*:—Staeb *olastrum*, Wrt. Voc. ii. 115, 49. Stæf, 63, 41: *baculus*, i. 80, 2: *fustis*, Ælfc. Gr. 9, 28; Zup. 55, 9. Ðín gyrd and ðín stæf (*baculus*) mé áfréfredon, Ps. Th. 22, 5. Mid gierde mon biþ beswungen, and mid stæfe hé biþ áwreðed. Gif ðǽr ðonne sié gierd mid tó ðreágeanne, sié ðǽr eác stæf mid tó wreðianne, Past. 17; Swt. 126, 2. Gangan bí stafe *to walk with the aid of a staff*, L. Alf. 16; Th. i. 48, 10: Ex. 21, 19. Mid ylpenbánenon stæfe ða eorðan delfan, Lchdm. i. 244, 24. 'Hafa ðé mínne stæf on handa.' Se drý ðá nam ðone stæf, Homl. Th. ii. 418, 1-2. Ða cild rídaþ on heora stafum, and manigfealdne plegan plegiaþ, Bt. 36, 5; Fox 180, 9. Stafas *vectes*, Ps. Lamb. 106, 16. II. *a written character, a letter*, the old letters having been carved on staves. Cf. *Germ.* buch-stabe:—*Littera* is stæf on Englisc, and is se læsta dǽl on bócum . . . Wé tódǽlaþ ða bóc tó cwydum, and syððan ða cwydas tó dǽlum, eft ða dǽlas tó stæfgefégum, and syððan ða stæfgefégu tó stafum; ðonne beóþ ða stafas untódǽledlíce; forðan ðe nán stæf ne byþ náht, gif hé gǽþ on twá. Ǽlc stæf hæfþ þreó ðing, *nomen, figura, potestas*, Ælfc. Gr. 2; Zup. 4, 18-5, 5. S, wuldres stæf, Salm. Kmbl. 225; Sal. 112: 250; Sal. 124. Ic háten eom, swá ða siex stafas sweotule becnaþ, Exon. Th. 407, 4; Rä. 25, 10. Áwriten Gréciscum stafum, Lk. Skt. 23, 38. Gemétte ic sweartum stafum áwritene eall ða mán ðe ic ǽfre gefremede, Bd. 5, 13; S. 633, 8. Oft gehwá gesihþ fægre stafas áwritene, ðonne heraþ hé ðone wrítere and ða stafas, and nát hwæt hí mǽnaþ, Homl. Th. i. 186, 1-3: Lchdm. iii. 290, 13. Ne cúðe hé bóclíce stafas . . . hé nǽnne stæf ne cúðe, Homl. Th. ii. 96, 24-30. II a. *a mark in writing*:—Stafum *apicibus*, Wrt. Voc. ii. 5, 29. II b. *a letter* as representing a minute detail:—Án strica oððe án stæf ðære ealdan ǽ ne biþ forgǽged, Homl. Th. ii. 200, 1. III. in pl. *a collection of written symbols, a letter, writing*:—Hé mé ealle on stafum áwrát, Bd. pref.; S. 472, 3. Ðysne geleáfan hé gýmde gefæstnian sinoþlícum stafum . . . Ðara stafa is ðes fruma, 4, 17; S. 585, 14-17: 41. Swá hwæt swá hé of godcundum stafum geleornode *whatever he learnt from the sacred writings*, 4, 24; S. 596, 33. Bæd hé ðone Abbud ðæt hé him sende trymmendlíce stafas and gewrito (*exhortatorias litteras*), 5, 21; S. 642, 38: Chr. 167; Erl. 8, 15. Nim ðíne stafas and wrít hundeahtatig, Lk. Skt. 16, 7. IV. *letters, book-learning, literature*:—Bóclícum stafum *litteris liberalibus*, Hpt. Gl. 503, 55. Húmeta cann ðes stafas, ðonne hé ne leornode? Jn. Skt. 7, 15. Hé ðá wæs in stafas and on leornunge getogen, Guthl. 2; Gdwin. 18, 6. [*Goth.* stabs *an element, a rudiment*: *O. Sax. O. L. Ger.* [bók-]staf: *O. Frs.* stef: *O. H. Ger.* stap *baculus, virga, regula*: *Icel.* stafr *a staff, post; a letter*; in pl. *learning.*] v. ár-, bóc-, candel-, cranc-, di[s]-, ende-, fácen-, gebregd-, gleó-, gyrn-, hearm-, heg-, inwit-, leád-, píl-, rún-, sár-, sorh-, wróht-, wyrd-stæf (-stafas); stafa.

stæf-cræft, es; *m.* I. *the art of letters, grammar*:—Ic Ælfríc wolde ðás lytlan bóc áwendan tó Engliscum gereorde of ðam stæfcræfte, ðe is geháten *grammatica* . . . forðan ðe stæfcræft is seó cǽg ðe ðæra bóca andgit unlícþ, Ælfc. Gr. pref.; Zup. 2, 13-17. *Gramma* is on Englisc stæf, and *grammatica* is stæfcræft, 50; Zup. 289, 10. *Litteratus* se ðe can stæfcræft, 43; Zup. 257, 7. II. *skill in letters* (v. stæf, IV), *learning, study*:—Ðeodorus mid hálgum gewritum and stæfcræftum hí (*the English*) georne hét beón lǽrende *literarum sanctarum coeperint* (*Angli*) *studiis imbui*, Bd. 4, 2; S. 565, 12. [Crist sceolde don us mid his mihte þat stefcreft ne mihte, O. E. Homl. i. 235, 35.] v. next two words.

stæfcræftig; *adj. Skilled in letters*:—Stæfcræftigra *grammaticorum*, Hpt. Gl. 410, 69. Stæfcræftira, 473, 16. Stæfcræftigera, 529, 34. Stæfcræftiera *grammaticorum, litteratorum*, 459, 58.

stæf-cyst, e; *f. Excellence in letters* or *learning, book-learning*:—'Leornodest ðú ǽfre sealmas oþþe óþre hálige gewritu?' 'Ic stæfcyste ne leornode ne ðæra manna nánum ne hlyste ðe ða smeádon and rǽddon' '*didst thou ever learn psalms, or other holy writings?*' '*I never learned anything from books, nor have I listened to any of those men that have studied and read them*,' Homl. Skt. ii. 23 b, 593. Cf. stæf-cræft, II.

Stæf-ford *Stafford*:—Æt Stæfforda, Chr. 913; Th. i. 186, col. 2.

Stæfford-scír *Staffordshire*:—Ðá férdon hí intó Stæffordscíre, Chr. 1016; Erl. 154, 3.

stæf-gefég, es; *n.* I. *a combination of letters* (a) that forms a syllable:—*Syllaba* is stæfgefég on ánre orðunge geendod. *A domo* fram húse; hér is se *a* for ánum stæfgefége; *ab homine*; hér is se *ab* án stæfgefég. Hwílon byþ ðæt stæfgefég on ánum stæfe, hwílon on twám, etc., Ælfc. Gr. 3; Zup. 7, 4-11. Wé tódǽlaþ . . . ða dǽlas tó stæfgefégum and syððan ða stæfgefégu tó stafum, 2; Zup. 5, 1-2. (b) that forms a diphthong:—*Dyptongus* is twýfeald swég oððe twýfeald stæfgefég, 4; Zup. 7, 13. *Diptongon*, ðæt ys twýfeald stæfgefég, Anglia viii. 326, 4. II. *a forming of letters in writing*:—Stæfgefég *literaturam*, Ps. Spl. 70, 17.

-stæf-lǽred. v. ge-stæflǽred.

stæf-leornere, es; *m. A learner of letters, a scholar*:—Stæfleornera *stoicorum*, Hpt. Gl. 479, 64. v. stǽr-leornere.

stæflíc; *adj.* I. *literal*:—Wé understandaþ ðæt gástlíce andgit ðæra bóca, and hí rǽdaþ ða stæflícan gereccednesse, Homl. Th. ii. 114, 35. Hí nellaþ understandan bútan ðæt steaflíce (stæf-, MSS. C. D.) andgit *the literal meaning*, Homl. Skt. ii. 25, 73. II. *literate*:—Stæflecum *liberalitatis* (*literatis*?), Wrt. Voc. ii. 53, 55. [*Icel.* stafligr *pertaining to letters.*]

stæf-liðere, an; *f.*: -liðera, an; *m. An engine for casting stones, a kind of sling*:—Staeblidrae, steblidrae, staefliðre *ballista*, Txts. 44, 136. Stæfliðere, Wrt. Voc. ii. 10, 62: *fundabulum*, i. 35, 31: *fundibalum*, 84, 36: *balista*, Hpt. Gl. 423, 63. Stæfliðera *ballista*, 487, 21. Stæfliðera[n] *fundibulo*, 521, 12.

stæfn, stæfnan. v. stefn, stefnan.

stæf-plega, an; *m. A letter-game* or *a literary game*:—Staebplegan, staefplagan *ludi litterari, ludi litterali*, Txts. 72, 577. Stæfplegan, Wrt. Voc. ii. 51, 17.

stæf-rǽw, e; *f. A letter-row, an alphabet*:—Mid stæfrǽwe endebyrdnesse tósceádene *alphabeti ordine distinctum*, Bd. 5, 24; S. 648, 40. [Cf. *Icel.* staf-róf *an alphabet.*]

stæf-róf glosses *elimentum*, Wrt. Voc. ii. 32, 24.

stæf-sweord, es; *n. A sword-stick*:—Stæfsweord *dolones*, Wrt. Voc. i. 35, 55. [*O. H. Ger.* stapa-swert *framea.*]

stæf-wís; *adj. Skilled in letters, literate*:—Gelǽred, stefwís, Lchdm. iii. 186, 24. v. un-stæfwís.

stæf-wrítere, es; *m. A writer about letters* or *grammar*:—Stæfwríterum *grammaticorum*, Wrt. Voc. ii. 41, 33: 75, 40. The word glosses *historiographus*, 42, 45, but perhaps *stær-* should be read for *stæf-*: and 18, 67 stæfwríterum glosses *caracteribus*, which seems an error.

stæg, es; *n. A stay, a rope supporting a mast*:—Stæg *safo* (in a list of nautical words), Wrt. Voc. i. 63, 60. [*Icel.* stag; *n. a stay*: *Dan.* stag. Cf. *O. French* estay (from German).] v. stæþ.

stǽgel; *adj. Steep, abrupt*:—Staegilrae, stégelræ, staegilre *praerupta*, Txts. 84, 747. Heánne beám stǽlgne (=stǽglne?) gestígan, Exon. Th. 42, 27; Cri. 679. [Jamieson gives *stell* steep. *O. H. Ger.* steigal *abruptus*. Cf. *O. L. Ger.* stégil *crepido.*]

stǽger, e; *f. A staircase*:—Stǽger *ascensorium*, Wrt. Voc. i. 26, 37. Hé ástáh up tó ðære stǽgre ðe stód wið ðæs cáseres botl, Homl. Skt. i. 5, 438. Hé feóll of ánre stǽgere, 18, 232. [On þe steire of fiftene stoples, O. E. Homl. ii. 165, 34. Þolemodnesse haueð þreo steiren, A. R. 282, 7.]

stǽger; *adj. Steep.* [Þise twelue degres wern brode & stayre, A. P. 31, 1021. A cliffe so staire and so stepe, ib. 196, col. 1.] v. wiðer-stǽger; stǽgel.

stæl, es; *n.* I. *a place*:—Stalu tó fuglum *umbrellas*, Txts. 107, 2153. II. *place, stead*:—Cristenum cyninge gebyraþ ðæt hé sý on fæder stæle cristenre þeóde, L. I. P. 2; Th. ii. 304, 23: Beo. Th. 2963; B. 1479. Ic eom gesceádwísnes and ic eom ǽlcum manniscum móde on ðam stale ðe seó háwung byþ ðam eágum, Shrn. 178, 9. Gé beóþ mé talade on bearna stæl, Exon. Th. 366, 13; Reb. 11: Cd. Th. 68, 7; Gen. 1113. III. *stead* (as in the phrase to stand a person in good *stead*. Cf. stælwirðe):—Hié ðæm ádrǽfdan on nánum stale beón ne mehton *they could not be of any assistance to the exile*, Ors. 5, 9; Swt. 232, 23. IV. *situation, condition*;—Mé lyste witan be ðam gewitte, hweðer hyt æfter ðæs líchaman gedále and ðare sáwle weóxe ðe wanede, ðe hyt swá on stæle stóde, ðe hyt swá dyde, swá hyt ǽr dæð on ðisse weorulde, óðre hwíle weóxe óðre hwíle wanode (cf. 200, 17-19), Shrn. 199, 26-30. v. æt-, on-stæl; steall.

stǽlan; *p.* de *To impute* a crime to (*on, ongeán*) a person, *to charge, declare* something against a person:—Ic ðé þreáge and stǽle beforan ðé and ðé cýðe eal ðás yflu *arguam te, et statuam contra faciem tuam*, Ps. Th. 49, 23. Se deófol ða syndǽda stǽleþ on ða gástas *the devil charges* *the spirits with their sinful deeds*, Wulfst. 256, 7: Exon. Th. 84, 16; Cri. 1374. Stǽleþ fǽhđe *declares enmity*, Cd. Th. 305, 2; Sat. 640. Hē būtan leahtrum wæs clǽne gemēted đara đinga đe hine mon forewrēgde and on stǽlde *absque crimine accusatus fuisse inventus est*, Bd. 5, 19; S. 639, 31. Wē đec sōđ on stǽldun *we brought a true charge against thee*, Exon. Th. 130, 17; Gū. 439. Wiđ mē ārison leáse gewitan and stǽldon on mē đæt īc nāwþer ne nyste ne ne worhte *exurgentes testes iniqui quae ignorabam interrogabant me*, Ps. Th. 34, 12. Ic wolde andettan and stǽlan ongeán mē sylfne mīne scylda *pronuntiabo adversum me injustitias meas*, 31, 6. Synne stǽlan, Menol. Fox 569; Gn. C. 54. Fǽhđe ic wille on weras stǽlan (*of the threatened deluge*), Cd. Th. 81, 27; Gen. 1352. Ic gefrægn mǽg ōđerne billes ecgum on bonan stǽlan *I heard that one kinsman with the edge of the sword brought home to the slayer the death of the other* (? Eofor killed Ongentheow, who had slain his brother), Beo. Th. 4964; B. 2485. v. be-, ge-, ofer-stǽlan; -stāl.

stæl-giest, es; *m. A thievish guest* (of an insect eating a book):—Þeóf in þȳstro . . . stælgiest ne wæs wihte đȳ gleáwra đe hē đām wordum swealg, Exon. Th. 432, 13; Rä. 48, 5.

stǽlgne. v. stǽgel.

stæl-here; *g.* -her(i)ges; *m. A marauding band, predatory army*:—Hié fōron ūt mid stælherge nihtes . . . and genōmon unlytel ǽgđer ge on mannum ge on ierfe, Chr. 921; Erl. 106, 13. Drehton đa hergas West-Seaxna lond mid stælhergum, 897; Erl. 95, 9. Đæt hié đa burga hira mōdes wiđ stælherigas behealden, Past. 33; Swt. 229, 5.

stæl-hrān, es; *m. A decoy-reindeer*:—Đa deór hī hātaþ hrānas; đara wǽron syx stælhrānas; đa beóþ swȳđe dȳre mid Finnum, for đæm hȳ fōþ đa wildan hrānas mid, Ors. 1, 1; Swt. 18, 11.

staeli *steel*, stællan *to put in a stall*, stællo. v. stēle, ge-stællan, steall.

stæl-tihtle, an; *f. A charge of theft*:—Be stæltyhtlan (staltihtlan, MS. B.). Đonne mon monnan betȳhþ đæt hē ceáp forstele, L. In. 46; Th. i. 130, 11: L. O. D. 4; Th. i. 354, 14. Gif hwā þurh stæltihtlan freót forwyrce, L. Ed. 9; Th. i. 164, 10.

stæl-wirđe; *adj. Able to stand a person in good stead* (v. stæl, II), *serviceable*:—Se đe geornlīce conn ongietan đæt hē gadrige đæt him stælwierđe sié *qui sollicite noverit sumere, quod adjuvat*, Past. 17, 5; Swt. 115, 3. Đa scipu đe stælwyrđe wǽron binnan Lundenbyrig gebrohton *the ships that could be of service they brought into London*, Chr. 896; Erl. 94, 19. Hē gyfþ gooda gifa on đissa wurlda; þeáh hī ēca ne sién, hī beóþ þeáh stælwyrđa đa hwīle đe wē on đisse wurlde beóþ, Shrn. 192, 6. [In later English the word seems used more in the sense of the modern *stalwart* = strong:—Ic em hal and fere and strong and stelewurđe, ȝet ic mei longe libben, O. E. Homl. i. 25, 12. Þeo þat beođ stalewurđe and warpeđ mid strencđe ut of hare heorte hare unwreste wil, Jul. 44, 7. Þeo þ stalewurđe beođ ant starke to ȝein me, Marh. 15, 32. Þou hart on staleworþe (hende, 1st MS.) gome, Laym. 3812. Gurguont, stalworþe mon and hardy, R. Glouc. 39, 4. A man þat es yhung and light, Be he never swa stalworth and wyght, Pr. C. 689. Cf. stanndenn stallwurrþlig ȝæn þe deofless wille, Orm. 1194. Louerd mi stalwurnesse (stalworthhede, other MSS.) *Domine, virtus mea*, Ps. 17, 2.] Cf. nyt-wirđe.

stæl-wyrt, e; *f. Water starwort*:—Stælwyrt *callitriche* (cf. wæterwyrt *callitriche*, 67, 18), Wrt. Voc. i. 68, 15.

stǽna (*or* -e; *f.*), an; *m. A stean, a pot of stone* or *earth*:—Stǽnan *gillone* (gillo *lagena, vas vinarium*), Wrt. Voc. ii. 42, 3. [Sete adun þine stene (*waterpot*, Jn. 4, 28), Misc. 85, 29. Stene (*cruse*, 1 Kings 17, 12), Wick. Into a stene lette hem be pressed, Pall. 4, 666. See Halliwell's Dict., and Spenser's F. Q. vii, stanza 42: Upon an huge great earth-pot steane he stood. *O. H. Ger.* steinna *olla, cacabus*.]

stǽnan; *p.* de I. *to stone, cast stones at*:—Đū stǽnæst (stǽnas, Lind.) đa đe tō đē sende wēran, Mt. Kmbl. Rush. 23, 37. Ne stǽnas uē đec *non lapidamus te*, Jn. Skt. Lind. 10, 32. Heó wæs stǽned ōþ đæt heó hire gāst onsænde; đā com þunerrād and ofslōh đone mǽstan dǽl đæs folces đe hī stǽnde, Shrn. 57, 34-36. Hig hine stǽndon, Jos. 7, 25. Stǽne hine man mid stānum, Lev. 20, 2. Đā hēt se dēma hine stǽnan, Shrn. 48, 28. Tō stǽnenna, Jn. Skt. Rush. 11, 8. Hī hine gelǽddon tō stǽnenne, Homl. Th. i. 46, 35. Hē for đǽm stǽnendum gebæd, 52, 19. Hȳ wǽron stǽned, and đa stānas wǽron on bæc gecyrred, Shrn. 135, 27. [*Goth.* stainjan: *O. H. Ger.* steinōn.] v. ge-, of-stǽnan. II. *to adorn with* (*precious*) *stones*. [*O. H. Ger.* gi-steinen.] v. ā-stǽned.

stǽnen (*in the oblique cases the* -en *is sometimes contracted or absorbed; see below, and for other instances see under* stapol); *adj.* I. *stony*. v. next word:—Se āfeól of his horse ofer stǽnene eorþan, and him wǽron đa limo gecnyssed, Shrn. 126, 18. Of sandigum ł stǽnenum *de arenosis*, Hpt. Gl. 449, 26. II. metaph. *of stone, stony, hard as stone*, (1) in a good sense:—Ic đē secge, đæt đū (*Peter*) eart stǽnen, and ofer đysne stān ic timbrige mīne cyrcan, Homl. Th. i. 364, 23. (2) in a bad sense:—Hié wǽron stǽnenre heortan' and blindre, Blickl. Homl. 105, 27. Hī hæfdon stǽnene heardnysse on heora heortan, Homl. Th. ii. 236, 21. Hæfdon heortan stǽn[e]ne, Exon. Th. 40, 20; Cri. 641. III. *stone, made of stone, built of stone*:—Stǽnen elefæt *alabastrum*, Wrt. Voc. i. 24, 40. Stǽnen cyrice *ecclesia de lapide facta*, Bd. 3, 23; S. 555, 12. Stǽnen bedd, Shrn. 69, 4. Đæt stǽnna fæt *alabastrum*, Mk. Skt. Rush. Lind. 14, 3. Be đære stǽnenan strǽte *the paved way*, Blickl. Homl. 189, 13. Stǽnen weofod *altare lapideum*, Ex. 20, 25. Weall stǽnenne, Cd. Th. 101, 33; Gen. 1691. Wīf hæbbende stǽnna (stǽna, Rush.) fulle smirinisse *mulier habens alabastrum unguenti*, Mt. Kmbl. Lind. 26, 7. Đa stǽnenan bredu *the tables of stone*, Past. 17; Swt. 125, 18: Ex. 31, 18. Stǽnene (stǽnine, Lind.) wæterfatu, Jn. Skt. 2, 6. Geond ealle đās strǽt and stǽnene wegas, Homl. Skt. i. 14, 156. [*Goth.* staineins: *O. Frs.* stēnen: *O. H. Ger.* steinīn.]

stǽner (? v. stǽnen, I) *stony ground*:—In stǽrer (stǽnen?) *in petrosa*, Mt. Kmbl. Lind. 13, 5. Stǽner, 20. Ofer stǽnere *super petrosa*, Mt. Skt. Rush. 4, 5, 16. Stǽnero, Lind. 4, 16.

stæng, stǽnig. v. steng, stānig.

stǽniglīc; *adj. Stony*:—On stǽnilīcum stōwum, Lchdm. i. 216, 20.

stǽniht. v. stāniht.

stǽning, e; *f.* I. *stoning, casting of stones*:—Saulus heora mōd tō đære stǽninge geornlīce tihte, Homl. Th. i. 50, 30: ii. 236, 29: Shrn. 32, 1. II. *ornamenting with stones*. v. bleó-stǽning.

stæpe, stepe, es; *pl.* stæpas, stapas, stæpe; *m.* I. *a step, pace* (lit. and fig.):—Stæpe, stepe *passus*, Ælfc. Gr. 11; Zup. 79, 8. Ne māgon becuman đa stæpas đæs weorces đieder đe hē wilnaþ, Past. 11; Swt. 65, 17. Āgotene synt mīne stapas (stæpas, Spl.), Ps. Lamb. 72, 2. Ǽlc đæra stæpa and fōtlǽsta đe wē tō cyricean weard gestæppaþ, Wulfst. 302, 26. Mid heora þeáwa stæpum Drihtne filiaþ, Homl. Th. i. 120, 28. Se đe beforan đǽm stæpum his weorca ne lōcaþ, Past. 39; Swt. 287, 18. His weg and his stæpas tō sceáwianne, 18; Swt. 131, 21. Geriht mīne stæpas on đīne wegas, Ps. Th. 16, 5. Stapas, Ps. Lamb. 84, 14: 118, 133: Wulfst. 247, 2. Gelǽd mē on stige đǽr ic stæpe mīne on đīnum bebodum brȳce hæbbe *deduc me in semitam mandatorum tuorum*, Ps. Th. 118, 33. I a. *a step, pace* as a measure of distance:—Stæpe *passus*, furlang *stadium*, Wrt. Voc. i. 38, 8. Nis ān stæpe đæt seó eá wille oferyrnan, Wulfst. 211, 14. Ne gang đū, mōna, ānne stæpe furđor, Jos. 10, 12. Swā hwā swā đe genȳt þūsend stapa, Mt. Kmbl. 5, 41. II. *stepping, going*:—Germanus đam healtan geongan his stæpe geednīwode and đam Godes folce geednīwode đone stæpe rihtes geleáfan *Germanus claudo juveni incessum et populo Dei gressum recuperarit fidei*, Bd. i. 21; S. 485, 5-9. Strong on stæpe, Exon. Th. 498, 23; Rä. 88, 6. III. *a step, that on which the foot may be placed*:—Đā āstāh Isachar up on đone ȳtemestan stæpe *the topmost of the steps leading to the temple*, Homl. Ass. 129, 431. Stapas *vel* stīrāpas *scansilia*, Wrt. Voc. i. 41, 34. On đære hlǽddra is twā and sixti stapa, Anglia xi. 5, 22. Stæpena, 4, 11. Ne gā đū on stapum tō mīnum weofode, Ex. 20, 26. Hē stīhþ be đære hlǽddre stapum, Homl. Skt. i. 1, 22. III a. that on which the lower part of any thing rests, *the step* of a mast, *a pedestal*:—Stepe *bassis*, Wrt. Voc. ii. 12, 50. Hig fæstniaþ đone stepe þurh đa þilinge, Shrn. 35, 14. Tredelas *vel* stæpas *bases*, Wrt. Voc. i. 21, 48. Hearpan stapas *cerimingius* (? v. stalu), Wrt. Voc. ii. 130, 40. IV. *a degree*:—Hād ođđe stæpe (stepe) *gradus*, Ælfc. Gr. 11; Zup. 79, 9. *Positivus* is se forma stæpe (stepe), *comparativus* is se ōđer stæpe (stepe), *superlativus* is se đridda stæpe (stepe), 5; Zup. 15, 20. Synd þrȳ stæpas gecorenra manna. Se nyđemysta stæpe . . . Se ōđer stæpe is on wydewan hāde . . . Se hēhsta stæpe is on mægđhādes mannum, Homl. Th. ii. 70, 17-23: 94, 15. Be đām twelf stæpum eáđmōdnesse. Đære forman eáđmōdnysse stæpe is, R. Ben. 23, 16. Seofon stapas sindon hāligra hāda . . . Đone forman stæpe bēte man mid āne punde . . . Ǽt đam ōđrum stæpe twā pund tō bōte . . . Ǽt đam þriddan stæpe, etc., L. E. B. 1-8; Th. ii. 240, 242. [*O. Frs.* stap: *O. H. Ger.* stapfo *passus, gradus, incessus, vestigium*.] v. in-, on-stæpe; ord-stapu (*read* -stæpe); in-stæpe, -stæpes.

stæpe-gang, es; *m. A step*:—Ic stepegongum weóld *I had control of my steps*, Exon. Th. 353, 34; Reim. 22.

stæp-mǽlum; *adv.* I. *step by step*:—Wæs gesewen micel cyrce tō đære hī stæpmǽlum āstigon (cf. Blickl. Homl. 207, 11), Homl. Th. i. 508, 12. II. *step by step* (fig.), *gradually, by degrees*:—Stæpmǽlum *gradatim, per singulos gradus*, Hpt. Gl. 497, 54: Scint. 101, 13. Đæt mōd glīt niđor and niđor stæpmǽlum, Past. 38; Swt. 279, 3. Suǽ suǽ on sume hlǽdre, stæpmǽlum, proem.; Swt. 23, 17: Shrn. 188, 12. [*O. H. Ger.* stapf-mālum *gradatim*.]

stæppa (*or* -e), an; *m.* (*or f.*) *A step*:—Þūsend stæppan *mille passus*, Mt. Kmbl. Rush. 5, 41.

stæppan, steppan; *p.* stōp; *pp.* stapen *To step, go, proceed*:—Ic stæppe *gradior*, Ælfc. Gr. 29; Zup. 185, 18. Gange se wīfman tō birgenne, and stæppe ofer đa byrgenne . . . Đonne heó tō hyre hlāforde on reste gā, đonne cweþe heó: 'Up ic gange, ofer đē stæppe,' Lchdm. iii. 66, 18-26. Ic steppe on grēne græs, Exon. Th. 396, 16; Rä. 16, 5. Đonne stæpþ se sacerd tǽlleáslīce on đone weg *tunc sacerdos irreprehensibiliter graditur*, Past. 13, 1; Swt. 77, 18: Homl. Th. i. 374, 21. Hē stæpþ beforan đison folce *praecedet populum istum*, Deut. 3, 28. Stepeþ, Exon. Th. 264, 34; Jul. 374. Steppeþ, 499, 33; Rä. 88, 25. Rūmaþ, steppaþ *cedunt*, Wrt. Voc. ii. 19, 19: 87, 64. Stōp forđ (*prodiit*) se đe deád wæs, Jn. Skt. 11, 44. Deáđ neálǽcte, stōp stalgongum, sōhte sāwelhūs, Exon. Th. 170, 17; Gū. 1113. Se cyning stōp tōforan đam biscope, Bd. 3, 14; S. 540, 36. Seó wīfman stōp inn *ingressa*, Jud. 4, 21: Cd

Th. 69, 16; Gen. 1136. Se apostol stōp intō ðære byrig, Homl. Th. i. 60, 11: Byrht. Th. 134, 3; By. 78. Hē wið ðǣs beornes stōp, 135, 41; By. 131. Hié stōpon tō ðam gysterne, Judth. Thw. 21, 29; Jud. 39: 24, 36; Jud. 227: Cd. Th. 95, 26; Gen. 1584. Stæppaþ ryhte, ne healtigeaþ leng, Past. 11; Swt. 65, 18. Ðȳlæs hē ofer ðone ðerscold stæppe, 13; Swt. 77, 22: Lchdm. ii. 124, 6. Ðæt hié stæppen on ryhtne weg, Past. 18; Swt. 131, 25. Ðǣr ic stæppan scyle, Ps. Th. 16, 5: Cd. Th. 86, 22; Gen. 1434: Wulfst. 303, 10: Homl. Th. i. 118, 32. Steppan, Ps. Th. 31, 9: Wulfst. 239, 11: Cd. Th. 88, 2; Gen. 1459: 279, 35; Sat. 248. Com stæppende sum cempa, Homl. Th. i. 452, 14. [*O. Sax.* stōp; *p.*: *O. Frs.* steppa; *p.* stōp; *pp.* stapen: cf. *O. H. Ger.* stepfen, stapfōn.] v. æt-, be-, for-, fore-, forþ-, ge-, in-, of-, ofer-, on-, wið-stæppan (-steppan, -stapan. *In the compounds, instead of* stapan *read* stæppan).

stæppend. v. fore-stæppend.

stæppe-scōh *a slipper*:—Stæppescōs *subtalaris*, Wrt. Voc. i. 289, 8. Steppescōh, ii. 121, 73.

stæppung. v. fore-stæppung.

stær, es; *m. A starling, a stare* (the latter is the name used in some dialects. v. E. D. S. Pub. Bird Names, and Halliwell's Dict.):—Staer *sturnus*, Wrt. Voc. ii. 121, 17. Stær, i. 63, 6: *turdus*, 77, 30. Stær *turdus*, se māre stær *turdella*, 29, 40, 41. Etan gebrǣdne stær, Lchdm. ii. 320, 4. Staras ł hrondsparuas *passeres*, Mt. Kmbl. Lind. 10, 29. Staras (stearas, Rush.), Lk. Skt. Lind. 12, 6. [*O. H. Ger.* stara *sturnus, turdus*: *Ger.* staar: *Icel.* stari: *Dan.* stær *a starling*: *Swed.* stare.]

stǣr, stēr, steór, es; *n. A history*; historia:—Tō eallum ðe ðis ylce stǣr becyme ūres cynnes tō rǣdanne *omnes ad quos haec eadem historia pervenire poterit nostrae nationis legentes*, Bd. pref.; S. 472, 33. Ðæt getæl ðæs hālgan stǣres and spelles ... Song hē eall ðæt stǣr Genesis *illum seriem sacrae historiae ... Canebat de tota Genesis historia*, 4, 24; S. 598, 5-10. In ðyssum ūrum stǣre, 4, 30; S. 609, 33. Be stǣre Angelþeódes cyricean, 5, 24; S. 647, 16: 4, 22; S. 592, 31. On Ongelcynnes steóre, ðæt is, on *historia Anglorum*, Shrn. 87, 7. Ðara Abbuda stǣr and spell ðysses mynstres on twām bōcum ic āwrāt, Bd. 5, 24; S. 648, 28. On ðis ūre cyriclīce stēr, 4, 7; S. 574, 28.

stær-blind; *adj. Blind from giddiness, purblind, quite blind*:—Stæ[r]-blind *scotomaticus* (cf. scotomaticorum, cecorum, 78, 20), Wrt. Voc. ii. 119, 81. Næfþ nān man tō ðæs unhāle æágan, ðæt hē ne māge lybban be ðare sunnan and hire nyttian, gyf hē ēnyg wiht geseón mæg, būton hē stareblind sī, Shrn. 187, 5. Sume unæáðe āwiht geseóþ; sume beóþ stæreblinde and nyttiaþ þeáh ðare sunnan, 27. Stærbli[nde] *scotomaticos*, Hpt. Gl. 478, 20. [Bi daie þu (the owl) art stareblind, O. and N. 241. *O. Frs.* staru-, stare-, star-blind: *O. H. Ger.* stara-plint: *Ger.* staar-blind *suffering from cataract*: *Dan.* stær-blind *purblind*: *Swed.* starr-blind *quite blind*: cf. *Icel.* star-blinda *blindness*.]

stærced-, sterced-ferhþ; *adj.* I. *having the mind strengthened, stouthearted, courageous*:—Deareðlācende (*the Huns*) on Danūbie stærcedfyrhðe stæðe wīcedon, Elen. Kmbl. 75; El. 38. Stercedferhþe hæleþ, Judth. Thw. 22, 9; Jud. 55. II. *of hard* or *cruel mind*:—Drōgon hine (*St. Andrew*) ymb stānhleoðo stærcedferðe *cruelhearted ones dragged him about the stony slopes*, Andr. Kmbl. 2468; An. 1235.

stǣr-leornere (?), es; *m. One who learns history, a historical scholar*:—Stǣrleornera (? stæf-, v. stæf-leornere), leornera *stoicorum* (*storicorum*?), Hpt. Gl. 503, 64.

stærn. v. stearn.

stǣr-trahtere, -tractere, es; *m. One who treats of history*:—Stǣrtractere *commentarius*, Wrt. Voc. ii. 132, 42.

stǣr-wrītere, es; *m. A writer of history, a historian*:—Swā swā sōþsagol stǣrwrītere (*verax historicus*) ða þing ðe be him oþþe ðurh hine gewordene wǣron ic āwrāt, Bd. 3, 17; S. 545, 5. Stæfwrītere (stǣr-?) *historiographus*, Wrt. Voc. ii. 42, 45. Swā swā Trogus and Iustinianus sēdon heora stǣrwrīteras, Ors. 4, 4; Swt. 164, 12: 2, 1; Swt. 60, 25.

stæþ (?) *a stay*:—Stæð *safon* (in a list of nautical words. In a similar list *stæg*, q. v., occurs as the gloss), Wrt. Voc. i. 56, 63. Cf. stæððan, stæððig.

stæþ, es; *n. A bank, shore, the land bordering on water*:—Stæð *ripa*, Wrt. Voc. i. 54, 19. Stæð *vel* brerd *labrum*, *margo*, vel *crepido*, 57, 25. Of ðæm mere ðe Truso standeþ in staðe, Ors. 1, 1; Swt. 20, 9. On ðam staþe ðe is genemned Ypwines fleót, 449; Erl. 12, 2. Treówlīcre hit is be staðe tō [swim]manne, ðonne ūt on sǣ tō seglanne, Prov. Kmbl. 64. On geofones staðe, Cd. Th. 215, 8; Exod. 580: Exon. Th. 361, 11; Wal. 18. On Sæferne staþe, Chr. 894; Erl. 92, 23. Hē befeól ofer ðam stæðe intō ðam streáme, Homl. Th. ii. 160, 5: Elen. Kmbl. 76; El. 38. Of stæðe on ōðer *from one bank of the boundary stream to the other*, L. O. D. 1; Th. i. 352, 4, 11: 2; Th. i. 354, 3: 6; Th. i. 354, 25. Sume cuce tō ðam stæðe cōmon, and ða man sōna ofslōh æt ðære eá mūðan, Chr. 794; Erl. 59, 23: Byrht. Th. 132, 32; By. 32. Æt Wendelsǣ on stæðe, Elen. Kmbl. 463; El. 232. Stæð *marginem*, Hpt. Gl. 492, 72. Be wætera staðum, Ps. Th. 22, 2. Stæðum *marginis*, Wrt. Voc. ii. 58, 25. Betweox stæðum *between those living on the two sides of the boundary stream*, L. O. D. 2; Th. i. 352, 16. Oft stille wæter staðo brecaþ, Prov. Kmbl. 63. Streámas staþu beátaþ, Exon. Th. 382, 4; Rä. 3, 6: Met. 6, 15. Staþu āstīgan geswinc getācnaþ. Of staþe niþer stīgan gōdne tīman getācnaþ, Lchdm. iii. 210, 16. ¶ In the following passage the word seems to be masculine:—Wægn brohte beornas ofer burnan from stæðe heáum, ðæt hȳ stōpan up on ōðerne of wǣge, Exon. Th. 405, 6; Rä. 23, 19. [Uppen Seuarne staþe, Laym. 7. Stathe *a wharf*, Halliwell's Dict. *Goth.* staths *a shore*: *O. Sax.* stað *a bank, shore*: *O. H. Ger.* stad, stado *ripa, litus, margo*.] v. bord-, eá-, streám-, sūþ-, wǣg-stæþ.

stæþ-fæst; *adj. Firm on the shore* (? epithet of sea-cliffs), *stable*:—Heáhcleofu stīð and stæðfæst, staþelas wið wēge, Exon. Th. 61, 7; Cri. 981.

stæþ-hlīþe; *adj. Running to the shore* (?), *steeply sloping, precipitous*:—Stæþhlēpe *divexum*, i. *inclinatum*, *pronum*, Wrt. Voc. ii. 141, 52. Hī ne mihton ofer ðæt scræf swā swæðhlȳpe (stæþ-?) [wæs] ðǣr hī gongan [sceoldon] ǣr ðon hié gerȳmdon ðone upgang and geworhtan *they could not pass the cave, so steep was it where they had to go, before they had cleared and constructed the ascent*, Blickl. Homl. 201, 16. v. next word.

stæþhlīplīce; *adv. At a steep inclination*:—Wæs ðæt hūs ... on scræfes onlīcnesse ...; and gelōmlīce ða stānas swā of ōðrum clife stæðhlȳplīce ūt sceoredon, Blickl. Homl. 207, 20. v. preceding word.

stæðig. v. stæððig.

stæþ-swealwe, an; *f. A sand-martin*:—Staeðsuualwe *ripariolus*, Wrt. Voc. ii. 119, 22. Gif mon fundige wið his feónd tō gefeohtanne, stæþswealwan briddas geseóþe on wīne, ete ðonne ǣr, Lchdm. ii. 154, 5.

stæððan *to make staid, to stay*:—Saga hwā mec rǣre, ðonne ic restan ne mōt, oþþe hwā mec stæðþe, ðonne ic stille beóm, Exon. Th. 387, 4; Rä. 4, 74.

stæððig; *adj. Staid, sober, sedate, grave*:—Ðæt cild Cūðberhtes dyslīcan plegan mid stæððigum wordum þreáde, Homl. Th. ii. 134, 7. v. ge-, un-stæððig, *and next word*.

stæððigness, e; *f. Staidness, sedateness, gravity, seriousness*:—Ðǣr is stæðignyss iógūðe, Wulfst. 265, 8. Mōderlīcere stæððinysse *materna gravitate*, Hpt. Gl. 469, 37. Hē on heálīcere stæððignysse symle þurhwunode *he ever continued deeply serious*, Homl. Th. ii. 134, 22. Gif wē ða ungesceádwīslīcan styrunga on stæððignysse āwendaþ, 210, 31. Fore stilnesse stæððinesse *propter taciturnitatis gravitatem*, R. Ben. Inter. 26, 6.

stæþ-weall, es; *m. The wall formed by the shore*:—Sǣs up stigon ofer stæðweallas, Cd. Th. 83, 7; Gen. 1376.

stæþ-wyrt, e; *f. A plant name*, Cockayne suggests *statice*, Lchdm. ii. 78, 3.

stafa (?), an; *m. A letter*:—Stafana *litterarum*, Hpt. Gl. 460, 54. v. stæf.

stafian; *p.* ode *To direct, dictate*:—Se gerēfa ðone āð him swōr swā hē hyne sylf stafode *the steward swore the oath to Abraham, as Abraham himself dictated it*, Gen. 24, 9. Abraham ðurh wītegunge stafode ðone āð, Homl. Th. ii. 234, 34. [*O. H. Ger.* stabēn *dirigere*: *Icel.* stafa eið *to dictate an oath* to a person.]

staggon. v. stacga.

-stāl. v. ge-, on-, wiðer-stāl; stǣlan.

stala *one who steals*. v. ge-stala.

stāl-ærn, es; *n. A place where charges are heard* (? v. stǣlan. *Or* stāl = staþel; cf. stālian = staþelian):—Stālern *consistorium*, Wrt. Voc. ii. 133, 70.

stalaþ(-eþ), stalcung, staled. v. staþel, stealcung, reád-staled.

stal-gang, es; *m. A stealthy step*:—Deád neálǣcte, stōp stalgongum, sōhte sāwelhūs, Exon. Th. 170, 17; Gū. 1113. v. stalian, II.

stalian; *p.* ode I. *to steal*:—Se ðe stalaþ on Sunnanniht, L. Alf. pol. 5; Th. i. 64, 22. Ðæra þeófa ðe staledon, L. Ath. i. 3; Th. i. 200, 24. Ne stala ðū, L. Alf. 7; Th. i. 44, 19: Homl. Th. ii. 208, 24. Be stale. Gif hwā stalie (stalige) ... Gif hē stalie (stalige) on gewitnesse ealles his hīrēdes, gongen hié ealle on þeówot, L. In. 7; Th. i. 106, 14-17: 22; Th. i. 116, 9-10. Be þeófum. Gif þeóf ofer ðæt stalige, L. Ath. i. 1; Th. i. 198, 25. II. *to proceed stealthily, steal* upon a person:—Hē oftrædlīce on Rōmāne stalade *Marianum exercitum creberrimis incursionibus fatigavit*, Ors. 5, 7; Swt. 230, 9. Læcedemonie hæfdon māran unstillnessa ðonne hié mægenes hæfden and hlōðum on hié (*the Thebans*) staledon *Lacedaemonii, inquieti magis quam strenui, tentant furta bellorum*, Ors. 3, 1; Swt. 100, 2. v. for-, ge-stalian.

stālian (= staþelian) *to confirm*:—Stālige (staþelige, L. I. P. 4; Th. ii. 308, 3) man and strangie and trymme hī georne mid wīslīcre Godes lage, Wulfst. 267, 21. Cf. (?) efenstāledan *conficiebantur*, Wrt. Voc. ii. 133, 31.

stalla, stallere, stal-tihtle. v. stealla, steallere, stæl-tihtle.

stalu, e; *f.* I. *theft, stealing*:—Stalu ne lufaþ nāne yldinge *stealing loves not any delay*, Homl. Th. i. 220, 9. Be stale. Gif hwā stalie, L. In. 7; Th. i. 106, 14. Gif hwā Godes cyricean brece for stale, L. Ecg. P. iv. 24; Th. ii. 210, 30: Blickl. Homl. 75, 31. Sum wer wæs betogen ðæt hē wǣre on stale, Homl. Skt. i. 21, 265. Se ðe cyricean ǣhte mid stale āfyrde, Bd. 2, 5; S. 506, 30. Sume stale fremmaþ, 1, 27; S. 490 9, 5. Of ðære heortan cumaþ stale (stala, MS. A.), Mt. Kmbl. 15, 19: Mk. Skt. 7, 22. Ða heáfodleahtras sind ... leásgewitnyssa, stala, Homl. Th. ii. 592, 5. Stala *furtum*, Wrt.

Voc. ii. 38, 31. Mōna se syxteóða nānum þingum nytlīc nymþe stalum, Lchdm. iii. 192, 7. II. *what is stolen*:—Stalu biþ funden, 186, 14: 188, 2. Gif hē næbbe, hwæt hē wið ðære stale sylle, sylle man hine wið feó, Ex. 22, 3. Gif preóst mycele stale forstele, L. Ecg. C. 11; Th. ii. 140, 14. Gif hwylc man medeme þing stele, āgyfe ða stale ðam ðe hig āhte, L. Ecg. P. ii. 25; Th. ii. 192, 20: iv. 24; Th. ii. 212, 1. III. *a fine payable for theft*, Chart. Th. 138, 17. See Kemble's Saxons in England, ii. 329. IV. *anything done by stealth*:—Ðæt sc̄s Petrus on dæge folce be Criste sǣde, ðonne wrāt sc̄s Marcus ðæt on niht, and hē ðæt hæl sc̄e Petre; for ðon his godspell is swā cweden, *furtum laudabile*, hergendlīco stalo, Shrn. 74, 22. [To cumen bi stale ferliche, O. E. Homl. i. 249, 20. *O. H. Ger.* stala *furtum*.] v. ge-stalu.

stalu, e; *f. A stale*:—Hearpan stala *the pieces of wood into which the strings are fixed* (?): ceminigi, Wrt. Voc. ii. 130, 66 (cf. 40). [Scheome and pine beoð þe two leddre stalen þet beoð upriht to þe heouene, and bitweonen þeos stalen beoð þe tindes ivestned, A. R. 354, 18–20.]

stalung, e; *f. Stealing, robbery*:—Ān hirde, se wæs Veriatus hāten, wæs micel þeófmon and on ðære stalunge hē wearð reáfere *Viriathus, homo pastoralis et latro, primum infestando vias, deinde vastando provincias*, Ors. 5, 2; Swt. 216, 7.

stam, stamm; *adj. Stammering*:—Stom, wlisp *balbutus*, Txts. 45, 277: *blessus*, 308. Stam *battulus* (*balbutus*?), 109, 1150. Stomm *blessus*, stom, wlisp *balbutus*, Wrt. Voc. ii. 10, 72, 75. [*Goth.* stamms: *O. H. Ger.* stam, stamm: *Icel.* stamr, stammr.]

stamer (-or, -ur), *adj. Stammering*:—Stomer *balbutus*, Wrt. Voc. ii. 125, 12. Stamer *balbus*, i. 45, 51. Stamur, 75, 37. Stamor *blessus*, 288, 9. Stamerum *balbis*, ii. 81, 41: Hpt. Gl. 478, 14: 507, 45. [Cf. *O. H. Ger.* stamel *balbus*.]

stamerian; *p.* ode *To stammer*:—Stamaraþ *balbutit*, Germ. 392, 12. Mē þinceþ ðæt mē sió tunge stomrige, Shrn. 42, 33. [Cf. *O. H. Ger.* stam[m]elōn *balbutire*.]

stammettan; *p.* te *To stammer*:—Stommeteþ *mutulat*, Wrt. Voc. ii. 57, 68.

stampe *a pestle*. [*O. H. Ger.* stampf *pilum*.] v. pīl-stampe; stempan.

stān, es; *m.* I. *stone* as a material:—Hig hæfdon tygelan for stān, Gen. 11, 3. Genim geoluwne stān *take ochre*, Lchdm. i. 374, 14. Se ðe ofer ðone stān (*supra petrosa*) āsāwen is, Mt. Kmbl. 13, 20. II. *a stone, a piece of stone*:—Se pitt wæs geheled mid ānum stāne . . . Hig āwylton ðone stān of ðam pitte, Gen. 29, 2–3. Hē nam stānas and lēde under his heáfod, 28, 11. II a. *a stone* for building, *wrought stone*:—Ne biþ lǣfed stān uppan stāne, Mt. Kmbl. 24, 2. Lōca hwylce stānas hēr synt, Mk. Skt. 13, 1. Holum stānum *fornicibus*, Wrt. Voc. ii. 40, 5. Ne tymbra ðū ðæt of gesnidenum stānum, Ex. 20, 25. II b. *a stone* (in its natural state or wrought) that serves as a mark:—Andlang herepaðes west on ðone þyrla[n] stān; of ðam stāne on ðone hāran stān, Cod. Dip. Kmbl. iii. 406, 12 (*and often*). Hē nam ðone stān and ārǣrde hine tō mearce, Gen. 28, 18. II c. *an image of stone*:—Se stān mǣlde for mannum (cf. ic bebeóde ðæt ðeós onlīcnes word sprece, 1460; An. 731), Andr. Kmbl. 1532; An. 767. II d. *a stone* to which worship is paid. v. stān-weorþung:—Gehātaþ hȳ ælmessan þurh deófles lāre oðþon tō wylle oððon tō stāne, Wulfst. 12, 3. Gif hwylc man his ælmessan gehāte oððe bringe tō hwylcon wylle oððe tō stāne, L. Ecg. P. ii. 22; Th. ii. 190, 24. Gif friðgeard sī on hwæs lande ābūton stān oððe wille, L. N. P. L. 54; Th. ii. 298, 16. Ða gemearr ðe man drīfþ . . . on stānum, L. Edg. C. 16; Th. ii. 248, 6. Cf. Si quis ad fontes vel ad lapides votum voverit, L. Th. P. 27, 18; Th. ii. 34, 6–8. Gē þeówiaþ fremdum godum, stoccum and stānum, Deut. 28, 36. Hǣðenscipe biþ ðæt man weorðige wæterwyllas oððe stānas, L. C. S. 5; Th. i. 378, 20. II e. *a stone* that contains metal:—Ða gyldenan stānas and ða seolfrenan *aureae arenae*, Bt. 34, 8; Fox 144, 30. II f. *a precious stone*:—Gerēnod mid golde and mid ðæm stāne iacinta, Past. 14; Swt. 83, 24. Stāne gelīcast gladum gimme, Exon. Th. 219, 5; Ph. 302. II g. *a stone* in the bladder:—On ðære blǣdran stānas weaxaþ, Lchdm. ii. 238, 18: i. 212, 22. III. *rock, a rock* (lit. and fig.):—Ðæt hig sucon hunig of stāne and ele of ðam heardustan stāne, Deut. 32, 13. Hē lǣdde wæter of stāne (*de petra*), Ps. Spl. 77, 19. Gē tō ðam lifgendan stāne staþol fæstniaþ, Exon. Th. 281, 30; Jul. 654. Ic stande beforan ðē uppan Oreb stāne (*supra petram Horeb*), Ex. 17, 6. Ðū eart Petrus and ofer ðisne stān (*petram*) ic timbrige mīne cyricean, Mt. Kmbl. 16, 18: 7, 24. Stearcheort styrmde, stefn in becom under hārne stān, Beo. Th. 5100; B. 2553. Stānum *cautibus*, Wrt. Voc. ii. 18, 15. [*Goth.* stains: *O. Sax. O. Frs.* stēn: *O. H. Ger.* stein: *Icel.* steinn.] v. beácen-, ceosel-, clif-, cweorn- (cwyrn-), eá-, earcnan- (eorcnan-, eorcan-, eorclan-), flōr-, gefōg-, gim-, grund-, hiéwe-, hwet-, hyrn-, loc-, mægen-, mǣr-, marm-, marman-, marmor-, mylen-, nume-, papol-, pumic-, sealt-, tæfl-, tigel-, weall-, weorc-stān.

stān-æx, e; *f. A stone axe*; or (?) *an implement for working stone* [Halliwell gives *stone-ax* a stone-worker's axe]:—Stānæx *bipennis*, Wrt. Voc. i. 34, 60. Stānex, 84, 68. For an account of stone axes found in England, see Wright's The Celt, the Roman, and the Saxon, pp. 69 sqq.: see also Nilsson's Stone Age, pp. 60 sqq. v. stān-bill.

stān-bæþ, es; *n. A vapour bath made by the help of heated stones on to which water was poured*:—Dō on troh hāte stānas wel gehǣtte, gebeþe ða hamma mid ðam stānbaðe; ðonne hié sién geswāte, recce hē ða bān, Lchdm. ii. 68, 4–7. Stānbæþ, 10, 13: 60, 9. Tō stānbæþe, 106, 16. Sele him stānbaðu gelōme, 106, 25.

stān-beorh, -beorges; *m. A stony elevation, rocky hill*:—On gerihte wið ðæs lytlan stānbeorges up on hæslhille; of ðam stānbeorge ofer ða dene . . . tō ðon lytlan stānbeorge; of ðam stānbeorge tō ðon ōðerum lytlan stānbeorge, Cod. Dip. Kmbl. v. 194, 15–18. Of riscmere on stānbeorg, iii. 453, 23. Stānbeorh, 381, 1. Stānbeorh steápne, Beo. Th. 4432; B. 2213. Sunt termini ab occasu stānbergas, Cod. Dip. Kmbl. i. 159, 14.

stān-berende *stone-bearing, stony*:—In ðǣm stānberendum *in glanigeris* (*glarigeris*?), Wrt. Voc. ii. 48, 51.

stān-bill, es; *n. An implement of stone*, or *one used in working stone*:—Bill *marra*, stānbill *mastellas*, Wrt. Voc. ii. 57, 71. v. stān-æx.

stān-boga, an; *m. A natural stone arch*:—Hē geseah stondan stānbogan, streám ūt ðonan brecan of beorge, Beo. Th. 5083; B. 2545. Seah on enta geweorc hū ða stānbogan (*of the cave within the rock*) stapulum fæste ēce eorðreced innan healde, 5429; B. 2718. [*Icel.* steinbogi, steina-brū *a stone arch* or *bridge* (a natural one).]

stān-brycg, e; *f. A stone bridge*:—Andlang brōces ōð stānbrycge, sūð from stānbrycge, Cod. Dip. Kmbl. iii. 429, 9–10. Andlang burnan ōð hit cymþ ðēr Blīðe ūt scȳt; ðæt andlang Blīðan ōð ða stānbriccge; ðæt eást of ðære bricgge, 421, 34. Ðis sint ða landgemǣre . . . Ǣrest on stānbriccge; of stānbriccge eást onlang Temese, v. 395, 29–31. Stānbricge (?) *lithostratos*, Wrt. Voc. i. 22, 6.

stān-bucca, an; *m. A mountain goat*:—Ðes stānbucca *hic cynyps*, Ælfc. Gr. 9, 57; Zup. 68, 5. [*O. H. Ger.* stein-boch *caper, Capricornus*.]

stān-burh *a town built with stone, a walled town* (?):—Steápe stānbyrig, Cd. Th. 133, 17; Gen. 2212.

stanc *a sprinkling*:—Stanc *pluvicinatio*, Wrt. Voc. i. 46, 25. v. stancrian, stencan.

stān-carr *rock, stone*:—Stāncarr heard *petram durissimam*, Rtl. 19, 21.

stān-ceastel, -cistel, es; *m. A chestnut-tree*:—Ðonon sūðrihte wið ðara stānceastla, and ðonne of ðǣm stānceastlum, Cod. Dip. Kmbl. ii. 172, 16. On ðane stāncistel, iii. 434, 33. v. cystel, stān-cist.

stān-ceosel, es; *m. Sand*:—Hē getimbrode hys hūs ofer stānceosel, Mt. Kmbl. 7, 24 MS. A. Stāncislas *glareas*, Hpt. Gl. 449, 16.

stān-cist, -cisten *a chestnut-tree*:—Of ðane þorne on ðo stāncysten on holencumbe; of ðane stāncyste on blacmanne bergh, Cod. Dip. Kmbl. iv. 8, 22. v. cisten-, cyst-beám, stān-ceastel.

stān-clif, es; *n. A rocky cliff, a rock*:—Hē of stānclife burnan lǣdde *qui eduxit aquam de petra rupis*, Ps. Th. 135, 17. Beorgas ðǣr ne muntas steápe ne stondaþ, ne stānclifu heáh hlifiaþ, Exon. Th. 199, 8; Ph. 22. Sume flugon æfter stānclifum, Elen. Kmbl. 269; El. 135. Stormas stānclifu beótan, Exon. Th. 307, 13; Seef. 23. Stāncleofu, Beo. Th. 5073; B. 2540.

stān-clūd, es; *m. A rock*:—*Haec Caribdis* ān stānclūd on sǣ, Ælfc. Gr. 9, 78; Zup. 75, 7. Ðā āhēng se munuc āne lytle bellan on ðam stānclūde, Homl. Th. ii. 156, 5. God him (*the Israelites*) forgeaf wæter of heardum stānclūde, 264, 22: Homl. Skt. i. 6, 279. Stānclūd *rupem*, Ps. Lamb. 113, 8. Swelce hit sié ungemong miclum and monigum stānclūdum tōbrocen *quasi per obviantia saxa frangatur*, Past. 9; Swt. 59, 7.

stān-cræftiga, an; *m. A skilled worker in stone*:—Ðæt wǣron .iiii. stāncræftigan . . . and nǣron nāne ōðre him gelīce; hȳ gesēnodon ǣlce morgen heora īsernġelōman, and ðonne nǣron hȳ nā tōbrocene, Shrn. 146, 13.

stancrian *to sprinkle*:—Ic stancrige *pluvicino*, Wrt. Voc. i. 46, 26. Cf. stanc.

stān-cropp, es; *m. Stone-crop; sedum acre*:—Nim stāncroppes sǣd, Lchdm. iii. 72, 10.

stān-crundel *a tumulus of stones* (?):—Tō ðam stāncrundle, Cod. Dip. Kmbl. iii. 408, 33.

stand, es; *m. A stand, stay, pause, delay*:—Miððȳ stondas (stando, Lind.) monige wērun *cum mora multa fieret*, Mk. Skt. Rush. 6, 35.

standan; *p.* stōd, *pl.* stōdon; *pp.* standen *To stand*. I. of attitude, (1) of persons:—Ðonne gē standaþ eów tō gebiddenne, Mk. Skt. 11, 25. Stand ofer ðone man, Lchdm. ii. 104, 10. Stande on heáfde, 154, 2. Ða ðe beóþ mid hiora āgnum byrðennum ofðrycte, ðæt hié ne māgon standan, Past. 7; S. 50, 25. (2) of things:—Segnas stōdon *the banners were raised*, Cd. Th. 214, 7; Exod. 565. Hē ðǣr geseah swer standan *there was an upright column*, Blickl. Homl. 239, 21. II. of situation or position, (1) of persons:—Ic stande beforan ðē uppan Oreb stāne, Ex. 17, 6. Ic niste, ðæt ðū stōde ongeán mē, Num. 22, 34. Ǣðelm self stōd ðǣrinne mid, Chart. Th. 171, 8. Ðā stōdan him twegen weras big, Blickl. Homl. 121, 23. Lǣde hig tō ðære eardungstōwe dura, ðæt hig standon ðǣr mid ðē, Num. 11, 16. Pharao mǣtte, ðæt hē stōde be ānre eá, Gen. 41, 1. Geseah hē deófol ðǣr unfeor standan, Blickl. Homl. 227, 24. (2) of things:—Se port stent betuh Winedum and Seaxum and

Anglum, Ors. 1, 1; Swt. 19, 23. Se steorra âna stent, Met. 29, 16. Nis ðæt feor heonon, ðæt se mere standeþ, Beo. Th. 2729; B. 1362. Se tôð se ðe bî ðam standeþ, L. Ethb. 51; Th. i. 16, 4. Ða wîc ðe beforan inc stondeþ, Blickl. Homl. 77, 22. Sió burg stôd bî ðære sǽ, Past. 52; Swt. 409, 33. Ðâ com genip and stôd æt ðære dura, Ex. 33, 9. Him æt heortan stôd ord, Byrht. Th. 136, 3; By. 145: Beo. Th. 5352; B. 2679. Gemearca hû ða tyrf ǽr stôdon, Lchdm. i. 398, 5. Ða stânas on ðæm mǽran temple . . . ǽr hié mon tô ðæm stede brohte ðe hié on standan sceolde, Past. 36; Swt. 253, 15. (3) of time:—Ðæt se dæg swîðe neáh stôde his forþfôre, Bd. 4, 3; S. 568, 16. II a. of situation or position in a figurative sense, denoting resistance, assistance, representation, degree, etc.:—Stande ðæs cyreâð ofer .xx. peninga *let his oath be valid in matters above xx pence*, L. Ath. i. 15; Th. i. 204, 15. Stande ðæt spor for ðone forâð, iv. 2; Th. i. 222, 16. Gif hwâ on leásre gewitnesse stande, and hê oferstǽled weorðe, ne stande his gewitnesse syþþan for âht, L. C. S. 37; Th. i. 398, 12. Hû hê sceal swerigean ðe mid ôðre on gewitnesse standaþ (-eþ?), L. O. 8; Th. i. 180, 26: 6; Th. i. 180, 17. Ǽlc man ðara ðe ðǽr mid stande, L. Ath. 1, 1; Th. i. 200, 3. Ðone wîsdôm ðe on hâlgum bôcum stent, Homl. Th. i. 258, 14: L. Ath. v. 3; Th. i. 232, 9. On Gode standeþ mîn hǽle, Ps. Th. 61, 7. Stande hit on his âgenan gewealde, Chart. Th. 329, 35. Se ðe unriht gestreón on his handa stôde, L. Eth. ii. 9; Th. i. 290, 5. Wulfgeat wæs se forma man and Wulfmǽr is ðe ôðer ðe hit nû on honda stant, Cod. Dip. Kmbl. iii. 260, 28. For ðare neóde, ðe ûs nû on handa stent *that we now have on our hands*, Wulfst. 181, 25. Gyf neód on handa stande *if the need present itself*, L. Edg. H. 2; Th. i. 258, 7. Ðonne stent se hê on his naman stede and spelaþ hine, Ælfc. Gr. 5; Zup. 8, 15. Ða ðe stôdon ongeán ûs *insurgentes in nos*, Ps. Th. 43, 7. Ne manna getrŷwða tô âhte ne standaþ, Wulfst. 82, 11. Godu ðe ðissum folce tô freme stondaþ, Exon. Th. 250, 7; Jul. 123. Swâ hî ufor stondaþ ðonne ða ôðre, Past. 52; Swt. 407, 21. Stond heó wið âttre, Lchdm. iii. 32, 21: 36, 6. Se wið mongum stôd, wuldres cempa, Exon. Th. 121, 26; Gû. 294. III. of condition:—Heó grôwende standeþ, Blickl. Homl. 197, 25: 109, 22. Be ðam cûþ standeþ ðæt hê fram deáþe gescylded wæs *quem a morte constat esse servatum*, Bd. 3, 23; S. 555, 27. Hê gearu standeþ, Ps. Th. 117, 2. Heó gewuldrad stondeþ, Blickl. Homl. 197, 10. Hê stent þeófscyldig, L. Eth. ii. 9; Th. i. 290, 16. Ðǽr geworht stondaþ Adam and Eue, Cd. Th. 27, 16; Gen. 418. Ðus hit stôd on ðâm dagum mid Englum *such was the condition of things among the English*, L. Eth. vii. 3; Th. i. 330, 9. Stôd bewrigen folde mid flôde, Cd. Th. 10, 14; Gen. 156. Ða ciricean giond eall Angelcynn stôdon mâðma and bôca gefyldæ, Past. pref.; Swt. 5, 10. Hié môston stondan on frióum anwalde *they might be in a condition of freedom*, 52; Swt. 405, 28. IV. of constitution:—Ic ongite ðæt sió sôþe gesǽlþ stent on gôdra monna geearnunga and sió unsǽlþ stent on yfelra monna geearnungum *video quae sit vel felicitas, vel miseria in ipsis proborum atque improborum meritis constituta*, Bt. 39, 2; Fox 212, 12. Seó gelaðung ðe stent on mǽdenum and on cnapum, Homl. Th. ii. 566, 11. V. of occupation or action:—Petrus stôd on gebedum *Peter was praying*, Blickl. Homl. 181, 21. Gif mæssepreóst stande on leásre gewitnesse, L. Eth. ix. 27; Th. i. 346, 8: L. C. S. 37; Th. i. 398, 11. VI. *to be fixed* as a law or regulation:—Griðlagu ðus stent *the regulations are as follows*, L. Eth. vii. 9; Th. i. 330, 22. Ne stent nân ôðer lâd, L. O. D. 2; Th. i. 354, 1. Geneátriht is mistlîc be ðam ðe on lande stænt, L. R. S. 2; Th. i. 432, 12. Hwîlon stôd ðæt . . . *at one time the law was that* . . ., L. Ff.; Th. i. 226, 1: L. Eth. ii. 9; Th. i. 288, 29. Ðæt his grið stande swâ forð swâ hit fyrmest stôd on his yldrena dagum *that the regulations be as full as ever they were*, iii. 1; Th. i. 292, 3. Stande betwux burgum ân lagu æt lâdunge, L. C. S. 34; Th. i. 396, 22. VII. *to remain undisturbed*:—Hit fela wintra siþþan on ðæm stôd *regnum Assyriorum diu inconcussa potentia stetit*, Ors. 2, 1; Swt. 60, 15. Stande þridda[n] dǽl ðære bôte inne *let a third part of the fine remain unpaid*, L. Alf. pol. 47; Th. i. 94, 6. Lǽt standan neáhterne, Lchdm. ii. 24, 21: 32, 11. Ða ðe unne ðæt ðeós gerǽdnis stondon môte, Chart. Th. 168, 28. VIII. *to stand still, cease to move, remain without motion, stop*:—Gedôn ðæt se Hǽlend stent, se ðe ǽr eode, Homl. Th. i. 156, 26. Hê clypode: 'Hǽlend, gemiltsa mîn.' Ðâ stôd se Hǽlend, 152, 19. Hê fêrde ðurh his menniscnysse, and hê stôd þurh ða godcundnysse, 156, 34. Hwæt stondaþ gê hêr? Blickl. Homl. 123, 21. Ða eá stôdon, Bt. 35, 6; Fox 168, 8. IX. *to reside, abide*:—Ða standendan munecas ðǽr *consistentes ibi monachi*, Bd. 4, 4; S. 571, 12. X. *to continue, remain*:—Ðenden standeþ woruld, Cd. Th. 56, 21; Gen. 915. Stande hê on þeówete, L. Ath. v. 12, 2; Th. i. 242, 5. Ðes middangeard eów ne mæg ealneg standan, Past. 51; Swt. 395, 29. XI. *to stand, not to fall, to be upheld*:—Ic getrymed fæste stande, Blickl. Homl. 225, 34. Seó godcunde meht staþolfæstlîce stondeþ, 19, 21. Hî on ðam geleáfan fæstlîce stôdan, Bd. 2, 17; S. 520, 21. Ðæt dôm stande ðâr þegenas sammǽle beón; gif hig sacan, stande ðæt hig .viii. secgaþ, L. Eth. iii. 13; Th. i. 298, 2-4. Hû mæg his rîce standan, Mt. Kmbl. 12, 26. Stondan, Blickl. Homl. 175, 15. XII. of direction (lit. and fig.):—Him stent ege of ðê *timebunt te*, Deut. 28, 10. Ðǽron stent ðam bisceope eahta marca goldes *eight marks are due to the bishop*, Chart. Th. 595, 2. Swâ micel ege stôd deóflum fram eów *the devils stood in such awe of you*, Homl. Th. i. 64, 25: Ps. Th. 104, 33: Cd. Th. 249, 5; Dan. 525. Him stôd stincende steám of ðam mûðe, Homl. Th. i. 86, 13. Him of eágum stôd leóht unfæger, Beo. Th. 1457; B. 726. Fŷrleóma stôd geond ðæt atole scræf, Cd. Th. 272, 32; Sat. 128. Ic wille ðat se freóls stonde intô ðat minstre, Cod. Dip. Kmbl. iv. 219, 19. [*Goth.* standan: *O. Sax.* standan: *O. Frs.* standa: *O. H. Ger.* stantan: *Icel.* standa.] v. â-, æt-, âgên-, and-, be-, for-, fore-, ge-, of-, ôþ-, tô-, under-, wiþ-, ymb-standan; ân-standende.

standend, es; *m. One who stands*:—Ðrîfaldo stondendo *ternos statores*, Rtl. 193, 35.

standendness. v. â-standendness.

stân-fæt, es; *n. A stone vessel*:—On stânfate gehîded, Wald. 62. Com wîf hæbbende stânfæt (*alabastrum*), Mk. Skt. Rush. 14, 3. Miððŷ gebrocen wæs ðæt stânfæt, Lind. 14, 3. [*O. Sax.* stên-fat.]

stân-fâh; *adj. Many-coloured with stones*, epithet of a road, Beo. Th. 645; B. 320: Andr. Kmbl. 2473; An. 1238.

stân-gaderung, e; *f. A collection of stones, a wall*:—Stângaderunge *maceriae*, Ps. Spl. T. 61, 3. Cf. stân-lesung.

stân-geat, es; *n. An opening to pass through between stones*:—On stângeat; of stângeate, Cod. Dip. Kmbl. iii. 81, 16.

stân-gedelf, es; *n. A stone quarry*:—Tô ðan stângedelfe; of ðam stângedelfe, Cod. Dip. Kmbl. iii. 77, 23. Æt ðæm stângedelfe, 366, 18. On ðæt stângedelf, v. 304, 21: vi. 144, 9.

stân-gefeall, es; *n. A mass of fallen stones*:—Twâ wîf âhŷddon ðone lŷchaman under myclum stângefealle, Shrn. 152, 4.

stân-gefôg, es; *n. A joining of stones* in building:—Ða ðe wyrcan cûðon stângefôgum *those that could work at putting stones together*, Elen. Kmbl. 2039; El. 1021. v. gefôg-stân.

stân-gella, -gilla, an; *m. A stone-yeller, a bird whose cry is heard among the rocks* (gellan *is used of the cry of the hawk*, Rä. 25, 3), *a pelican*:—Stângella *pellicanus*, Wrt. Voc. i. 63, 20. Gelîc geworden ic eom ðam stângillan (-gyllan, MS. C.: stânegellan, Ps. Surt.) wêstene *similis factus sum pellicano solitudinis*, Ps. Spl. T. 101, 7.

stân-getimbre, es; *n. A stone building*:—Stângetimbru *moenia*, Wrt. Voc. ii. 54, 67.

stân-geweorc, es; *n. Working in stone, stone-work*:—Bæd hê ðæt hê him onsende sumne heáhcræftigan stângeweorces *architectos sibi mitti petiit*, Bd. 5, 21; S. 643, 1. On hire wurðmynte is ârǽred mǽre cyrce mid wundorlîcum stângeweorce, Homl. Th. i. 440, 18. Cf. stân-weorc.

stân-gripe, es; *m. A seizing of stones, stones seized*:—Deáh hê stângreopum (-greótum, Kmbl.) worpod wǽre *though he was stoned with the stones that they seized*, Elen. Kmbl. 1645; El. 824.

stân-hege, es; *m. A stone fence, a wall*:—Tô hwŷ tôwurpe ðû his stânhege *quid destruxisti maceriam ejus*, Ps. Lamb. 79, 13.

stân-hifete. v. stân-hîwet.

stân-hîpe, an; *f. A stone-heap*:—Andlang burhweges tô ðære stânhŷpan, Cod. Dip. Kmbl. iii. 431, 10.

stân-hîwet, es; *n. A stone-quarry*:—Stânhŷwet *lapidicina* vel *lapidicedum*, Wrt. Voc. i. 19, 17. Tô ðam stânhifete (-hîwete?); of ðam stânhifete (-hîwete?) tô ðam hêðe, Cod. Dip. Kmbl. vi. 60, 24.

stân-hliþ, es; *n. A rocky slope, a rock*:—Mîn freónd siteþ under stânhliðe, Exon. Th. 444, 16; Kl. 48. Bîdaþ stânhleoþu streámgewinnes, 384, 11; Rä. 4, 26. Under stânhliðum, Cd. Th. 219, 28; Dan. 61. Stânhleoðum, Elen. Kmbl. 1302; El. 653. Ðâs stânhleoþu stormas cnyssaþ, Exon. Th. 292, 18; Wand. 101. Se æðeling hêt stormas restan ymb stânhleoðu, Andr. Kmbl. 3152; An. 1579. Æfter dûnscræfum ymb stânhleoðo, 2467; An. 1235. Ofereode æþelinga bearn steáp stânhliðo, stige nearwe, Beo. Th. 2822; B. 1409.

stân-hof, es; *n. A house of stone*:—Stânhofu stôdan, Exon. Th. 478, 10; Ruin. 39.

stân-hol, es; *n. A hole in rocks*:—Hié (*serpents and wild beasts*) in stânholum hié selfe dîgliaþ *saxorum latebris occulta*, Nar. 6, 1. Ðâ flugon hié in ða wæter and hié ðǽr in ðâm stânholum hŷddon, 22, 13. [*O. H. Ger.* stein-hol *spelunca*.]

stân-hrycg, es; *m. A ridge of rock*:—Swilce betwux stânhricgum *quasi inter Scyllam*, Hpt. Gl. 529, 22.

stân-hŷwet. v. stân-hîwet.

stânig, stǽnig; *adj. Stony, rocky*:—Of ðan hǽðenan byrgelse on ðone stânigan beorh; of ðan stânigan beorge ôð ða heáfda, Cod. Dip. Kmbl. iii. 454, 2-4. On ðone stânigan weg, vi. 186, 19. On stǽnig lond *in petrosa* . . . on ða stânige lond *supra petrosa*, Mt. Kmbl. Rush. 13, 5, 20. Ðǽr synd swŷðe scearpe wegas and stânige (stânihte, Laud. MS.), Ors. 1, 1; Bos. 16, 32. Ðeós wyrt biþ cenned on stânigum stôwum, Lchdm. i. 102, 3. Stǽnigum, 212, 9 note: 216, 20 note: 256, 22. [*O. H. Ger.* steinag(-ig) *saxosus, petrosus*.]

stâniht, stǽniht, *adj. Stony, rocky*:—Wæs seó eorþe tô ðæs heard and tô ðæs stânihte *erat tellus durissima et saxosa*, Bd. 4, 28; S. 605, 27. Tô ðære stânehtan dæne, Cod. Dip. Kmbl. v. 179, 24. On stânehtan ford, iii. 389, 1. On ðone stânihtan ford, 168, 31. On ðone stânihtan weg, 409, 11. On stǽnihtum stôwum, Lchdm. i. 212, 9. Sume feóllon on stǽnihte *alia ceciderunt in petrosa*, Mt. Kmbl. 13, 5. [*O. H. Ger.* steinaht: *Ger.* steinicht.]

stânincel, es; *n. A little stone:*—Stâninclu *lapillulos*, Anglia xiii. 31, 86.

stân-lesung, e; *f. A gathering of stones, building with stones and without cement:*—Stânlesung *lithologia* (λιθολογέω *to gather stones; to build with stones and without cement*), Wrt. Voc. i. 22, 5. Cf. stân-gaderung.

stân-lîm, es; *m. Mortar:*—Stânlîm *cimentum*, Wrt. Voc. ii. 131, 45.

stân-merece, -merce *parsley:*—Stânmerce *sigsonte*, Wrt. Voc. i. 68, 36. [*Prompt. Parv.* stanmarche, herbe Macedonia, *Alexandria.*]

stân-rocc, es; *m. A high rock, a peak; an obelisk:*—Stânrocces *obolisci* (cf. *obolisci*, genus lapidis, 78, 17. *Obolisci* ðæs stânes, 82, 43), Wrt. Voc. ii. 62, 57. Stânrocca, torra *scopulorum*, Hpt. Gl. 449, 15. Stânrocca ł torra *scopulorum, saxorum eminentium*, 454, 47. Cf. scylf.

stân-scealu, -scalu, e; *f. Shale:*—Of Stûre on ða stânscale, Cod. Dip. Kmbl. iii. 378, 12. v. next word.

stân-scilig; *adj. Shaly, stony:*—Sum feóll ofer stânscyligean . . . ofer ða stânscylian *super petrosa*, Mk. Skt. 4, 5, 16. v. preceding word.

stân-scræf, es; *n. A cave in the rocks:*—Sča Maria hine âcende on ânum holum stânscræfe, Shrn. 29, 28: 107, 28. Gongaþ on ðis stânscræf, and git ðǽr mētaþ weal, se is mid ifige bewrigen, 139, 26.

stân-scylf, es; *m. A peak, rock:*—Stânscylfa *scrupearum* (*scrupea*, i. *aspera saxa*). . . . Of sandigum stânscilfum *de arenosis sablonibus*, Hpt. Gl. 449, 20, 25.

stân-strǽt, e; *f. A road made with stones, a paved road:*—Ðonne forð ðæt hit cymþ tô ðare stânstrǽte; of ðare stânstrǽte, Chart. Th. 525, 20. Cf. stân-weg.

stân-stycce, es; *n. A bit of stone:*—Stânsticcum *crustis* (*frustis?*), Wrt. Voc. ii. 20, 61.

stân-torr, es; *m.* I. *a stone tower:*—Stântorr *the tower of Babel*, Cd. Th. 102, 14; Gen. 1700. II. *a rock, crag, tor* (cf. stân-rocc, -scylf):—Ad locum qui stântor dicitur, Cod. Dip. Kmbl. v. 104, 2.

stân-wang, es; *m. A stony plain:*—Stânwongas grôf, Exon. Th. 498, 24; Rä. 88, 6.

stân-weall, es; *m. A wall of stone:*—Stânweal[les] *maceriae, muri*, Hpt. Gl. 409, 77. Stânwealle (-walle, Ps. Surt.) *maceriae*, Ps. Spl. T. 61, 3. Ða hwîle ðe mon worhte ða burg mid stânwealle, Chr. 921; Erl. 107, 27. Ðæt wæter (*of the Red Sea*) him stôd swilce stânweallas bufan heora heáfdum, Ælfc. T. Grn. 5, 27: Homl. Ass. 105, 104. Stânweallas tôfeóllan, Shrn. 67, 19.

stân-weg, es; *m. A road made with stones:*—On ealdan stânwege; of stânwege, Cod. Dip. B. i. 417, 15. [*O. Sax.* stên-weg.] Cf. stân-strǽt.

stân-weorc, es; *n. Stone-work, stone-building:*—Hē worhte of seolfre ǽnne heáhne stýpel on stânweorces gelîcnysse, Homl. Skt. ii. 27, 29. [*O. Sax.* stên-werk.] Cf. stân-geweorc.

stân-weorþung, e; *f. Worship of stones:*—Wē lǽraþ ðæt preósta gehwilc forbeóde stânwurþunga, L. Edg. C. 16; Th. ii. 248, note 2. v. stân, II d, and Grmm. D. M. 611.

stân-wurma, an; *m. Colour got from a stone:*—Stânwurman *vermiculo, tinctura*, Hpt. Gl. 431, 34.

stân-wyrht (?), e; *f. A stone building:*—Stânwyrhte *mationes* (cf. scylfas *maciones*, Wrt. Voc. ii. 59, 29), Wrt. Voc. i. 39, 55.

stân-wyrhta, an; *m. A stone-wright, worker in stone, a mason:*—Stânwyrhta *latomi*, Wrt. Voc. i. 19, 16. Stânwyrhtan *cementario*, Hpt. Gl. 459, 38. From ðǽm stânwyrhtum *a cimentario*, Wrt. Voc. ii. 2, 40.

stapa, an; *m. One who steps.* I. a name given to the *grass-hopper* or *locust:*—Stapan *locuste*, Wrt. Voc. ii. 52, 20: 71, 62. v. gærs-stapa. [*O. H. Ger.* houui-staffo *locusta.*] II. in cpds. ân-, eard-, hǽþ-, hild-, mearc-, môr-stapa.

stapol (-el, -ul), es; *m.* I. *a post, pillar, column:*—Stapul *batis* (*basis?*), Wrt. Voc. ii. 12, 49: *patronus* (in a list giving parts of a house), i. 26, 36. Stapole *cione* (κίων *a column, pillar*), ii. 131, 41. Of ðam beorge on ðone stapol; of ðam stapole, Cod. Dip. Kmbl. iii. 14, 11: 378, 15. Tô ðam stǽnenan stapole; ðonne andlang ðæs weges ôð ðone stǽnan stapol; of ðam stapole, 418, 28. Æt stēnan steaple, Txts. 436, no. 25. Stapul ǽrenne, Andr. Kmbl. 2126; An. 1064. Ælc riht cynestôl stent on þrým stapelum, L. I. P. 4; Th. ii. 306, 31: Wulfst. 267, 9. Stânbogan stapulum fæste, Beo. Th. 5430; B. 2718. Hē hēt stapulas âsettan *erectis stipitibus*, Bd. 2, 16; S. 520, 6. Sweras unlytle, stapulas, Andr. Kmbl. 2986; An. 1496. Staplas *columbas* (*l. columnas*), Mt. Kmbl. Lind. 21, 12. II. *a step, threshold* (?):—Hē tô healle gong, stôd on stapole, geseah Grendles hond (*the hand had been laid in the hall*), Beo. Th. 1856; B. 926. [*O. Frs.* stapul (-el) *a block*: *O. H. Ger.* stafol (-el) *basis*: *Icel.* stöpull *a pillar*: *Dan.* stabel *a boundary-stone, post.*] v. stapola.

stapol; *adj.* v. fore-stapol.

stapola, an; *m. A post, stock, piece of wood standing upright in the ground:*—Licge ðæt îren uppan ðām glēdan . . . lecge hit man syþþan uppan ðam stapelan (cf. stacan, l. 12), L. Ath. iv. 7; Th. i. 226, 28.

stapol-weg, es; *m. A road marked out by posts* (?):—Fram tûnweges ende forð be efise tô stapolwege ufeweardan, Cod. Dip. Kmbl. v. 281, 23.

stappa, stapplian. v. stoppa, under-stapplian.

stappel (?) *a step.* [*O. H. Ger.* staffalun *passibus*: *Ger.* staffel *step, degree.*] v. sîþ-stap[p]el.

stare-blind. v. stær-blind.

starian; *p.* ode *To stare, look fixedly, gaze* (*with* on, tô):—Ðæt ic on ðone hafelan eágum starige, Beo. Th. 3567; B. 1781. Starie, 5585; B. 2796. Secga gehwylcum ðara ðe on swylc staraþ, 1997; B. 996: 2975; B. 1485. Wē on ðæt bearn foran breóstum stariaþ, Exon. Th. 21, 28; Cri. 341. Ðe gē hēr on stariaþ, 33, 6; Cri. 521: 36, 3; Cri. 570. Him ðæt tâcen wearð, ðǽr hē tô starude, Cd. Th. 260, 32; Dan. 718. Ðe hire an eágum starede, Beo. Th. 3875; B. 1935. Hî on mere staredon, 3211; B. 1603. On ða beorhtan gescæft ne môt ic ǽfre mā eágum starian, Cd. Th. 273. 22; Sat. 140: Judth. Thw. 24, 9; Jud. 179. Se earn mæg starian on ðære sunnan leóman, Homl. Skt. i. 15, 199. Hî stôden æt ðæra dura stariende on ðæt leóht, 3, 133. [Staryñ wythe brode eyne *patentibus oculis respicere*, Prompt. Parv. 472. *O. H. Ger.* starēn: *Ger.* starren: *Icel.* stara.] v. ge-starian.

staþol (-el, -ul), es; *m.* I. *a foundation* (lit. or fig.) (cf. *staddle* the bottom of a hay-stack, E. D. S. Pub. Gloss. 15, 19):—Staþol *fundamen*, Wrt. Voc. ii. 152, 15. Se fruma and se staþol eallra gôda ðe of him cumaþ, Bt. 34, 5; Fox 140, 4. Biþ Drihten ûre se trumesta staþol, Blickl. Homl. 13, 10. On ðissum cwydum is se staðol ealles geleáfan, L. E. I. 22; Th. ii. 418, 29: 29; Th. ii. 426, 1. Hié oft gebidon on lytlum staþole and on unwēnlîcum, Ors. 4, 9; Swt. 192, 34. Wera gied sumes, þrymfæstne cwide and ðæs strangan staþol *a glorious saying and the strong man's firm support*, Exon. Th. 432, 12; Rä. 48, 5. Staðol *fundum*, Hpt. Gl. 488, 6. Dûna staðelas *montium fundamenta*, Deut. 32, 22. Eorðan staþelas, Ps. Th. 81, 5: 103, 6. Steaðelas, Ps. Surt. 17, 8: ii. p. 194, 9. Staðulas, Cd. Th. 207, 28; Exod. 473. Ða staþolas ðære cyrican, Bd. 2, 4; S. 505, 16. Hē ða staþelas gesette ðæs mynstres, 3, 23; S. 554, 28. On staþelum healdan, Exon. Th. 312, 14; Seef. 109. I a. *the lower, firmer part, base* of a pillar, *trunk* of a tree:—Se is stemn and staðol ealra gôda and of ðæm cumaþ eall gôd, Bt. 34, 5; Fox 140, 2. Hit biþ unnyt ðæt mon hwelces yfles bōgas snǽde, bûton mon wille ða wyrtruman forceorfan ðæs staðoles, Past. 33; Swt. 222, 16. Gehēr ðû marmanstân . . . Lǽt nû of ðînum staðole streámas weallan, Andr. Kmbl. 3004; An. 1505. Genim feówer tyrf on feówer healfa ðæs landes . . . Nim ele etc., and dô hâligwæter ðǽron, and drýpe on ðone staðol ðara turfa (*the lower side of the sods*), Lchdm. i. 398, 11. I b. that on which a thing depends:—Staðul *cardo*, Wrt. Voc. ii. 20, 60. II. *fixed condition, state, position:*—Hwylc se staþol is Angelcynnes ðeóde *qui sit status gentis Anglorum*, Bd. 5, 23; S. 645, 4. Ic wæs smeágende be ðære hǽlo ûrra sâwla and be ðam staðole ûres rîces, L. In. pref.; Th. i. 102, 8. Hē hit nyle up ârǽran tô ðam staðole fulfremedes weorces *ad virtutis statum consuetudo non erigitur*, Past. 11; Swt. 65, 16. Hiera geðohtes staðol *cogitationis statum*, Swt. 67, 17. Stede ł stalað (*l.* staðal) *statum, stabilitatem*, Hpt. Gl. 469, 12. Hē geþyld lufige and ne âwâcige nā ne his staþel ne lǽtende fram Gode bûge, R. Ben. 27, 2. Sette heora staðol sceápum anlîce *posuit sicut oves familias*, Ps. Th. 106, 40. III. *a fixed position, station, place, site:*—Staþol wæs wyrta wlitetorhtra (*the plain*) *was the site of beauteous plants*, Exon. Th. 484, 4; Rä. 72, 2. Be ðære stôwe staðole *secundum positionem loci*, R. Ben. 59, 1. Staðele, 88, 4. Se wyrtruma stille wæs on staðole, Cd. Th. 252, 21; Dan. 582: 251, 9; Dan. 561. Wē stôdon on staðole, Rood Kmbl. 141; Kr. 71. Æsc byþ stîð staðule, stede rihte hylt, Runic pm. Kmbl. 344, 25; Rûn. 26. Ic sceal bordes on ende staþol weardian (*keep my station*; cf. Wulches cunnes þinges under þissen stane staðel habbeoð inumen (under þis ston unnieþ, 2nd MSS.), Laym. 15911), sto[n]dan fæste, Exon. Th. 496, 19; Rä. 85, 17. Hē ûs sealde mid englum ēce staþelas, 41, 26; Cri. 661. Ðû âlǽtan scealt lǽne staþelas, eard and ēþel, Dôm. L. 30, 58. IV. *the firmament, the heavens:*—Wearð ætýwed steorra on staðole, Chr. 975; Erl. 126, 24; Edg. 50. [*O. H. Ger.* stadal *scuria, horreum*: *Ger.* stadel: *Icel.* stöðull *a milking shed.*] v. burh-, ēðel-, frum-, môd-, wēsten-staþol.

staþol-ǽht, e; *f. An estate, landed possession*, Exon. Th. 353, 33; Reim. 22.

staþol-fæst; *adj. Steadfast, stable, firm;* stabilis, Ælfc. Gr. 9, 28; Zup. 55, 3. I. in a physical sense:—On ðam feórþan mônþe hē (*the foetus*) biþ on limum staþolfæst, Lchdm. iii. 146, 11. Staðolfæst stân (*glosses* Petrus), Mt. Kmbl. Lind. 16, 18. Beðearf seó sâwel staðolfæstre brycge ofer ðone glideran weg hellewîtes, Wulfst. 239, 14. Staleðfæste (*l.* staðel-) tremmincge *firmo fulcimento*, Hpt. Gl. 439, 63. II. *stationary, keeping in one place:*—Staþolfæst ne mæg gewunian in gebedstôwe, Exon. Th. 265, 1; Jul. 374. Faraþ hý geond missenlîce þeóda, nǽfre staþolfeste, nǽfre wuniende, nâhwâr sittende, R. Ben. 135, 23. III. *firm* in a moral sense, *unwavering, unyielding, constant:*—God is âna staþolfæst wealdend, Bt. 35, 3; Fox 158, 24: Andr. Kmbl. 241; An. 121. Staðulfæst, 2673; An. 1338. Swîðe geþungen on his ðeáwum and staðolfæst on his wordum *not to be moved from what he had said*,

Blickl. Homl. 217, 7. Staðolfæst on hire heortan wið deófles costnungum, Wulfst. 237, 12. Beó strang and staðulfæst *confortare et esto robustus* Deut. 31, 7. Ic eów friðe healde strengðu staþolfæstre, Exon. Th. 31, 3; Cri. 490. Mid steaðulfestum aldum *cum stabilito sene*, Ps. Surt. ii. p. 194, 27. Sele mē staðolfæste heortan, Anglia xi. 114, 71. Staðolfæstne geðoht, Salm. Kmbl. 478; Sal. 239. 70 manna of folces ealdrum ðe ðū wite ðæt sīn staðulfæste and lāreówas, Num. 11, 16. Onginnaþ esnlīce and beóþ staðulfæste *viriliter agite et confortamini*, Deut. 31, 6. v. un-, under-staþolfæst.

staþolfæstan. v. ge-staþolfæstan.

staþolfæst-līc; *adj. Steadfast, firm*:—Mē sum staþolfæstlīc smyltnyss tō becom, Homl. Skt. ii. 23 b, 551.

staþolfæstlīce; *adv.* I. in a physical sense, *firmly*:—On ðam eahtoþan mōnþe hē (*the foetus*) biþ eall staþolfæstlīce geseted, Lchdm. iii. 146, 19. II. *steadfastly, constantly, firmly*:—Seó godcunde meht ā staþolfæstlīce stondeþ, Blickl. Homl. 19, 21. Symble in Godes lofe wē sceolon staþolfæstlīce gewunigan, L. E. I. 42; Th. ii. 438, 32. Ðæt ðiós ūre sylene staðulfæstlīce ðurhwunian mōte, Cod. Dip. Kmbl. v. 186, 12.

staþolfæstness, e; *f. Steadfastness, stability*:—Staðolfæstnys *stabilitas*, R. Ben. Interl. 23, 3: Ps. Lamb. 103, 5: *firmamentum*, 18, 2: *status*, Rtl. 108, 38. Steaðulfestnisse *stabilitatem*, Ps. Surt. 103, 5. v. ge-, un-staþolfæstness.

staþolfæstnian. v. ge-staþolfæstnian.

staþolfæstnung, e; *f. A foundation*:—Tō staðolfæstnunga *ad fundamentum*, Ps. Lamb. 136, 7.

staþolian; *p.* ode. I. *to establish, found, settle, fix*:—Ic tō ānum ðē mōd staðolige *to thee alone do I keep my mind constant*, Andr. Kmbl. 164; An. 82. Staþelige, Exon. Th. 255, 30; Jul. 222. Ðū in God getreówdes ic in mīnne fæder hyht staþelie *thou didst trust in God, I found my hope on my father*, 268, 25; Jul. 437. Ic ðȳ fæstlīcor ferhð staðelige, hyht untweóndne, on Crist, Elen. Kmbl. 1591; El. 797. Ðe ðæs hūses hrōf staðeliaþ *qui aedificant domum*, Ps. Th. 126, 1. Ic on heofonum hām staðelode, Cd. Th. 281, 23; Sat. 276. Staðelodest *fundasti*, Ps. Spl. 101, 26: 103, 6, 9. Se steaðelade eorðan ofer steaðulfestnisse his. Ps. Surt. 103, 5. Hē woruld staþelode, Exon. Th. 206, 22; Ph. 130. Ðǣr hē hungrium hām staðelude *collocavit illic esurientes*, Ps. Th. 106, 35. Ðā hē æt Rōme Cristes cyricean staþelode *fundata Romae ecclesia Christi*, Bd. 2, 4; S. 505, 13. Se wealdend ðe ðæt weorc staðolade, Andr. Kmbl. 1598; An. 800: Met. 29, 87. Ðā heó in helle hām staðeledon, Cd. Th. 266, 21; Sat. 25. Staðelodon, 286, 1; Sat. 345. Staðola ðū ða ōðra on hira hāmon, Gen. 48, 6. Geleáfan fæste staðelian on ūrum heortum, Blickl. Homl. 111, 4. Staþelian, 115, 1. II. *to make steadfast, confirm, endow with steadfastness*:—Ne mīð ðū for menigo, ah ðinne mōdsefan staðola wið strangum . . . herd hyge ðinne, heortan staðola, Andr. Kmbl. 2419–2428; An. 1212–1215. Staþelige man and strangie hī georne, L. I. P. 4; Th. ii. 308, 3. Se hālga ongan hyge staðolian, Elen. Kmbl. 2186; El. 1094. Mōd staþelian geleáfan, Exon. Th. 168, 26; Gū. 1083: 264, 15; Jul. 364. Ūre heortan rihtan and staðelion, Wulfst. 253, 18. v. ge-, gegrund-staðolian (-elian).

staþoliend, es; *m. A founder*; fundator, Ps. Lamb. 47, 2.

staþolness. v. mōd-staþolness.

staþolung, e; *f. Founding, foundation, settling*:—Steaðelinge *plantationis*, Ps. Surt. 143, 12. Tō staþolungæ *ad fundamentum*, Ps. Spl. T. 136, 10. Staleðunga (*l.* staðelunga) *fundamina*, Hpt. Gl. 502, 71.

staþol-wang, es; *m. A plain to establish one's self in.* v. staþol, III:—Lǣteþ hió ða wlitigan wyrtum fæste stille stondan on staþolwonge (*in the field they occupy*), Exon. Th. 417, 4; Rä. 35, 8. Teón wē of ðisse stōwe and unc staþolwangas (*places where we may establish ourselves*) sēcan, Cd. Th. 114, 31; Gen. 1912.

stealc; *adj. Steep*:—Bīdaþ stille stealc stānhleoþu streámgewinnes, Exon. Th. 384, 11; Rä. 4, 26. On stealc hleoþa, 382, 6; Rä. 3, 7. Stealc hliþo stīgan, 498, 17; Rä. 88, 3.

stealcian, v. be-stealcian, *and next word.*

stealcung, e; *f. Stalking* (cf. deer-*stalking*), *cautious walking*:—On sumere nihte hlosnode sum ōðer munuc his færeldes and mid sleaccre stealcunge his fōtswaðum filigde, Homl. Th. ii. 138, 6. [Cf. stalkyn or gon softe *serpo*, Prompt. Parv. 472. Though I wolde stalke and crepe, Gow. ii. 351, 18. With dredful fot than stalketh Palamon . . . in that grove he wolde him hyde, Chauc. Kn. T. 621.]

-steald. v. ge-, hæg-, hago-steald.

stealdan; *p.* steóld *To possess*:—Ic staðolǣhtum steóld, Exon. Th. 353, 33; Reim. 22. [*Goth.* ga-staldan *to possess, gain.*]

steall, es; *m.* I. *a standing position*:—Setl gedafenaþ dēman, and steall fylstendum . . . Stephanus hine (*Christ*) geseah standende, forðan ðe hē wæs his gefylsta, Homl. Th. i. 48, 29. Syle hāt drincan in stalle stonde gōde hwīle *give him the medicine hot to drink in a standing position; let him stand a good while*, Lchdm. iii. 28, 5. II. *the way matters stand, position of affairs, state, condition*:—Se steall cyricean *status ecclesiae*, Bd. 2, 4; S. 505, 10. On frǣcenesse heora stealles *in periculum sui status*, 4, 25; S. 601, 18. Be ðisses biscopes līfes stealle *de cujus statu vitae*, 5, 19; S. 637, 2. Be ðam stalle cyrican, 3, 19; S. 561, 7. On ðone ǣrran steall *priscum in statum*, 5, 20; S. 642, 10: 5, 24; S. 646, 38. Ðone stal ðæs rīces *regni statum*, 4, 26; S. 603, 8. III. *position, place*:—Horsa steal *carceres* (the starting-place in the circus), scridwīsa *auriga*, Wrt. Voc. i. 39, 37. On brǣdo his stealles *latitudine sui status*, Bd. 1, 1; S. 474, 29. Ðæt se sȳ furþor forlǣten on stealle and on setle (cf. on stede and on setle, 13, 1), se ðe furðor on gearnunge sȳ, R. Ben. 12, 19. Stande hē ealra ȳtemest, oððe on ðam stede ðe se abbod swā gēmeleásum monnum tō stealle on sundrum betǣht hæfþ *ultimus omnium stet aut in loco quem talibus negligentibus seorsum constituerit abbas*, 68, 11. Ðæt hī nǣfre ne beón on stede ne on stealle, ðǣr ǣfre undōn worde ðæt ūre forgengles geūðen, Chart. Th. 348, 30. IV. *place, stead*:—Brihtwald gehālgode Tobian on his steall, Chr. 693; Erl. 43, 19. Steal, 780; Erl. 57, 1: 803; Erl. 61, 23. Stall, 779; Erl. 55, 38. Stal, 678; Erl. 41, 7: 727; Erl. 47, 2: 796; Erl. 59, 39. V. *a place for cattle, a stall*:—Stal *stabulum*, Wrt. Voc. ii. 121, 11. Steal, i. 15, 23. Ðæra tamra nȳtena steall, Boutr. Scrd. 21, 9. VI. *a place for catching fish*:—Lēt ða netto on stællo *laxa retia in capturam* (captura *locus piscosus, ubi capiuntur pisces*), Lk. Skt. Lind. 5, 4. (Cf. *stell*, a deep pool, in a river, where nets for catching salmon are placed, Jamieson.) [*O. Frs.* stall *standing; place; stall*: *O. H. Ger.* stall *stabulum, caula, praesepe; locus, statio, status*: *Icel.* stallr *a stall; shelf on which another thing is placed.*] v. æt-, bīd-, burg-, fore-, ge-, geard-, hege-, mylen-, ofer-, on-, scip-, treów-, wæter-, weal-, weard-, weofod-, weoh-, wīc-, wīg-, wið-, wiðer-steall (-steal); fæst-steall; *adj.* Cf. stæl, stede.

stealla, an; *m. A crab* (?):—Stalla *cancer* (*carcer?* cf. steall, III), Wrt. Voc. i. 291, 30.

-stealla. v. ge-, ofer-stealla.

steallere, stallere, es; *m. A marshall.* [The word occurs only in late documents; the passages given belong to Edward the Confessor's reign]:—On Esgēres stealres and on Roulfes steallres and on Lifinges steallres gewitnesse, Cod. Dip. Kmbl. iv. 291, 13–14. Esgār stallere and Roberd stallere, 191, 11–12: 221, 13: Chr. 1047; Erl. 171, 31. [*Icel.* stallari.]

steallet. v. ān-steallet.

steallian *to take place.* v. forþ-steallian.

steám, stēm, stiém, es; *m.* I. *steam, hot exhalation, hot breath*:—Him (*Herod*) stōd stincende steám of ðam mūðe, Homl. Th. i. 86, 14. Forlǣt wynsumne rēc āstīgan . . . Ðā of ðære stōwe steám up ārās swylce rēc, Elen. Kmbl. 1603; El. 803. Stenc ūt cymeþ of ðam wongstede, wynsumra steám swæcca gehwylcum, Exon. Th. 358, 14; Pa. 45. Man pintreów bærne tō glēdum . . . wende his neb tō and onfō ðam stēme (*the heat proceeding from the embers*), Lchdm. ii. 284, 16. Of hōmena æþme and stiéme cymþ eágna mist; 26, 26. Fleó ða mettas ða ðe him stiém on innan wyrcen, 226, 10. II. *that which emits hot vapour, blood*:—Forlēton mē standan steáme bedrifenne *they left me* (*the cross*) *standing bespattered with blood*, Rood Kmbl. 123; Kr. 62. [A stem als it were a sunnebem, Havel. 591. Steem or lowe of fyre *flamma*, steem of hothe lycure *vapor*, Prompt. Parv. 473.]

steáp, es; *m. A stoup, drinking vessel, cup, flagon*:—Steáp *ciatum*, Wrt. Voc. i. 290, 78: ii. 17, 28. Micel steáp ful, Lchdm. ii. 294, 19. Se wīnes steáp fægere gefylled is *calix vini meri plenus est*, Ps. Th. 74, 7. Steápes *poculi*, Hpt. Gl. 450, 6. Nalles wīn druncon scīr of steápe, Met. 8, 21. Dō steáp fulne wīnes tō wōse, Lchdm. ii. 18, 4. Gif man ōðrum steóp āsette ðǣr mæn drincen āgelde .vi. scill. ðam ðe man ðone steáp āset *if a man remove* (?) *a cup from another where men are drinking, let .vi. s. be paid to the man from whom the cup was taken*, L. H. E. 12; Th. i. 32, 8–10. Steápas *fialas*, Wrt. Voc. ii. 149, 4. [A stope *hec cupa*, Wrt. Voc. 235, 16. *O. H. Ger.* stouf *calix, cyathus*: *Icel.* staup; *n. a cup, beaker.*]

steáp; *adj.* I. *lofty, high, towering*, of buildings, hills, etc.:—Se streám ætstōd swā steáp swā munt *the stream* (*Jordan*) *stood as high as a hill*, Homl. Th. ii. 212, 23. Wāg steáp gedreás, Exon. Th. 476, 22; Ruin. 11. Seó steápe burh on Sennar stōd, Cd. Th. 102, 15; Gen. 1700. Fȳr steápes and geápes swōgende forswealh eall *fire everything lofty and spacious devoured roaring*, Cd. Th. 154, 16; Gen. 2556. On ðisum steápum munte, Homl. Skt. i. 13, 9. Worhton mid stānum ānne steápne beorh him ofer *congregaverunt super eum acervum magnum lapidum*, Jos. 7, 26. Steápne hrōf, Beo. Th. 1857; B. 926. Þurh steápne beorg strǣte wyrcan, Exon. Th. 397, 11; Rä. 16, 18. Steápe dūne, Cd. Th. 172, 33; Gen. 2853. Steápe stānbyrig, 133, 17; Gen. 2212. Weallas steápe, Exon. Th. 383, 13; Rä. 4, 10. Beorgas ðǣr ne muntas steápe ne stondaþ, 199, 7; Ph. 22: Beo. Th. 450; B. 222: Andr. Kmbl. 1680; An. 842. I a. of smaller objects:—Heard and steáp (*the pillar into which Lot's wife was turned*), Cd. Th. 155, 8; Gen. 2569. Wið steápne rond *by the tall shield*, Beo. Th. 5126; B. 2566. Ic hæbbe hneccan steápne, Exon. Th. 490, 1; Rä. 79, 4. Bollan steápe *tall flagons*, Judth. Thw. 142, 6; Jud. 17. Hī habbaþ on heáfde helmas steápe (cf. *O. Frs.* with thene stāpa helm. *Icel.* steypðir hjálmar), Wulfst. 200, 12. I b. of fire, *mounting high* (see also I c):—Hit ðurh hrōf wadeþ, bærneþ boldgetimbru, seomaþ steáp and geáp, Salm. Kmbl. 827; Sal. 413. I c. *standing out*, or *up*, *prominent* [or *bright?* In later English *steap* applied to the eyes or to gems seems to have this meaning. 'Twa ehnen steappre þene steorren ant þene ȝimstanes,' Marh.

9, 4. In the note on this passage Cockayne gives other instances of this use, e. g. Schinende and schenre þen eni ȝimstanes, steapre þen is steorre. In Chaucer's line, Prol. 201, the meaning might be *prominent*. In the passage quoted below from Ælfric the Latin from which the description is taken has *oculi grandes*.] Gim sceal on hringe standan steáp and geáp, Menol. Fox 505; Gn. C. 23. Se steápa gim, Salm. Kmbl. 570; Sal. 284. Hé hæfþ steápe eágan, Homl. Th. i. 456, 17. **II.** *lofty, high, placed high*:—Óđ đa steápan heofenan *to high heaven*, Homl. Th. i. 3, 500. [Þer wes moni steap (bold, 2nd MS.) mon, Laym. 1532. An lawe swiþe stæp and heh, Orm. 11379. *O. Frs.* stāp. v. **I a** above.] v. heađu-, weall-steáp; stípel, stípan.

steápan. v. á-steápan, stípan.

stearc; *adj.* **I.** *stiff, rigid, not soft, not bending*:—Is seó eág-gebyrd stearc and hiwe stáne gelícast, Exon. Th. 219, 4; Ph. 302. Hláf and stán, streac and hnesce, Elen. Kmbl. 1226; El. 615. Stánas and đæt starce ísen, Homl. Skt. i. 8, 29. Beátan mid stearcum stengum, Homl. Th. i. 428, 6. **I a.** fig. *unyielding, stiff-necked, obstinate*:—Heó wǽron stearce, stáne heardran, Elen. Kmbl. 1126; El. 565. **II.** *hard, rough, strong*, of wind or weather:—Stearc winter *aspera hyems*, Coll. Monast. Th. 19, 17. Se stearca wind norþan-eástan, Bt. 9; Fox 26, 18. Se stearca storm, Met. 6, 11. Stearc storma gelác, 26, 29. Þurh đone stearcan wind norþan and eástan, Bt. 4; Fox 8, 5. Stearce stormas, 23; Fox 78, 27. Gescyrped mid rinde wiđ đa stearcan stormas, 150, 8. **III.** *rough, attended with hardship, hard*, of living, discipline, etc.:—Hé đa stíđnyssa his stearcan bigleofan betwux lǽwedum folce geheóld, Homl. Th. ii. 148, 31. Se đe mec lǽreþ from đé on stearcne weg, Exon. Th. 259, 14; Jul. 282. Hú hé mihte swá stearce forhæfednysse (*rigid abstinence*) healdan, Homl. Th. ii. 354, 23. **IV.** *stern, severe*:—Hé (*William*) wæs milde đám gódum mannum and ofer eall gemett stearc đám mannum đe wiđcwǽdon his willan . . . Hé wæs swýđe stearc man swá đæt man ne dorste nán þing ongeán his willan dón, Chr. 1086; Erl. 221, 17, 32: Erl. 222, 21. Hé đa heardheortan đeóde mid stearcre đreále and stíđre myngunge tó lífes wege gebígde, Homl. Th. i. 362, 34. **V.** *strong, impetuous, violent, vehement*, (a) lit.:—Hé of stánclife stearce burnan lǽdde, Ps. Th. 135, 17. (b) fig. v. stearc-heard:—Nán stefn búton stearc and heard wóp for wóhdǽdum, Wulfst. 139, 3. [*O. Sax.* stark: *O. Frs.* sterk: *O. H. Ger.* starc, starah *fortis, validus*: *Icel.* sterkr *strong*.]

stearc-ferhþ; *adj. Of harsh* or *stern soul*:—Hí stearcferþe cwellan þohtun, Exon. Th. 280, 29; Jul. 636.

stearc-heard; *adj. Violent, unrestrained*:—Stearcheard wóp *durus fletus*, Dóm. L. 200. v. stearc, **V b.**

stearc-heort; *adj. Stout-hearted*:—Stearcheort (*the fire-drake*), Beo. Th. 4566; B. 2288: (*Beowulf*), 5097; B. 2552. [Cf. *O. Sax.* stark-mód *valiant*.]

stearcian; *p.* ode *To grow stiff* or *hard*:—Stearcode *riget, durescit*, Germ. 402, 56. [His skyn shall starken, Rel. Ant. i. 65, 3. *O. H. Ger.* starcēn *solidari*.]

stearclíce; *adv. Strongly, vigorously, vehemently, fiercely*:—Đá gewende se here tó Lundene and đa buruh útan embsæt and hyre stearclíce (cf. stranglíce, MS. E.) on feaht ǽgđer ge be wætere ge be lande *made a vigorous assault upon it by land and water*, Chr. 1016; Erl. 156, 32.

stearn, es; *m. Some kind of bird.* [*Starn* is a name for the starling in the Shetland Isles; the same bird is called a *starnel* in Northants. v. E. D. S. Pub., Bird Names, p. 73. *Starn* is used in Norfolk for the common tern: and *stern* is a name for the black tern, ib. pp. 202, 204]:—Stearn, stearno, stern *beacita* (according to Migne *beacita* is a woodcock or snipe), Txts. 45, 284. Stearn, Wrt. Voc. i. 281, 3: ii. 11, 1: *beatica*, i. 62, 32: *beacita* vel *sturnus*, 29, 6: *fida*, ii. 108, 52. Stern, 35, 28. Stern *avis qui dicitur gavia*, Txts. 108, 1116. Stærn *stronus* (=*sturnus*), Wrt. Voc. i. 29, 39. Him stearn (*the tern*) oncwæđ ísigfeþera, Exon. Th. 307, 14; Seef. 23.

steartlian; *p.* ede *To kick with the foot, stumble*:—Đæt đú ne spear[n]-last ł steartlest, stærtlige *ut non calcitres*, Hpt. Gl. 464, 1. [In later English *startle* is used of quick movement:—A courser, startling as the fyr, Chauc. Leg. G. W. 1204. Thouȝ ne havest frend that ne wolde fle, come thouȝ stertlinde in the strete, Mapes 335, 24. See also Halliwell's Dict. *stertle*.]

steb. v. stybb.

stéda, an; *m. A stallion, an entire horse*; the word is also used of a *camel*:—Hors *equus*, stéda *emisarius*, Wrt. Voc. ii. 30, 55: *misarius*, 56, 39: i. 287, 40. Stéda *faussarius*, hengst *canterius*, 23, 9. Hé hleóp on đæs cyninges stédan *ascendens emissarium regis*, Bd. 2, 13; S. 517, 9: Chart. Th. 501, 12. Ne hét Crist him tó lǽdan módigne stédan, Homl. Th. i. 210, 14: Homl. Skt. ii. 27, 97. Đonne lǽdaþ hý mid him olfenda myran mid hyra folan and stédan . . . đa stédan hý forlǽtaþ . . . đa æmettan ymbe đa stédan ábisgode beóþ *tollent camelos masculos et feminas illas quae habent foetas . . . masculi remanent . . . formicae masculos comedunt*, Nar. 35, 10–15.

stede, es; *m.* **I.** *a place, spot, locality*:—Mid wæter ymbtyrnd stede *circumlutus locus*, Wrt. Voc. i. 59, 15. Se stede ys hálig đe đú on stenst *locus, in quo stas, sanctus est*, Jos. 5, 16. Đes ænga stede (*Hell*), Cd. Th. 23, 9; Gen. 356. Hí cóman tó Brytene on đam stede Heopwines fleót, Chr. 449; Erl. 13, 4. In đone stede đe is gecueden Cerdices óra, 495; Erl. 14, 10. Đone stede healdan, Byrht. Th. 132, 21; By. 19. Tó hwí hremþ hit đisne stede (*quid terram occupat?* Lk. 13, 7), Homl. Th. ii. 408, 5. Eode on woestigum styd (steyde, Rush.) *abiit in desertum locum*, Mk. Skt. Lind. 1, 35. Stydd, Lk. Skt. Lind. 10, 1. Hí sǽton tú winter on đám twám stedum, Chr. 887; Erl. 84, 33. **II.** of fixed position, *a place which a person or thing occupies, an appointed place, station, site*:—Hú neara đære eorþan stede is *arctum terrarum situm*, Bt. 19; Fox 68, 23. Đæs fýres ágen stede is ofer eallum woruldgesceaftum gesewenlícum, 33, 4; Fox 130, 16. Heáfudponnes styd *calvariae locus*, Mt. Kmbl. 27, 33. Ǽr mon đa stánas tó đæm stede brohte đe hié on standan scoldon, Past. 36; Swt. 253, 15. Of hiora stede styrede, Met. 7, 25. On his ágenum stede, Ps. Th. 102, 21. Ne stande hé on his stede and endebyrdnesse, ac stande hé ealra ýtemest, R. Ben. 68, 10. Sig him geþafod, đæt hé stede æfter đam abbode healde, 106, 2. Æsc stede rihte hylt, Runic pm. Kmbl. 344, 26; Rún. 26. Næfþ náđer ne sǽ ne eá nǽnne stede búton on eorđan, Lchdm. iii. 256, 2. Gecerr suord đín in styd his, Mt. Kmbl. Lind. 26, 52. **II a.** *place, standing, position, status*:—Đes dǽl (*the participle*) næfþ nán angin ne nǽnne stede of him sylfum, ac byþ of worde ácenned and becymþ syþþan tó his ágenre geþingđe, Ælfc. Gr. 41; Zup. 244, 17. **II b.** *place, sphere of action*:—Gif ealle men on worulde ríce wǽron, đonne næfde seó mildheortnys nǽnne stede, Wulfst. 287, 9. **III.** of position in the case of a moving body:—Ne stira đú, sunne, of đam stede furđor ongeán Gabaon . . . Đá stód seó sunne on đam stede, Jos. 10, 12, 13. **IV.** *standing* as opposed to moving, *stopping, standing still*. v. sunn-stede:—Hwæt is đæs Hǽlendes stede ođđe hwæt is his fær? Homl. Th. i. 156, 33. **IV a.** fig. *stability, unchanging condition, fixity*:—Nán stede nis úres líchaman; cildhád gewít tó cnihthádе and cnihthád tó geđungenum wæstme, 490, 2. Stede ł staþal *statum, stabilitatem*, Hpt. Gl. 469, 12. **IV b.** *state, condition*:—Stede *status*, Wülck. 254, 31. On stede *statu*, Hpt. Gl. 458, 10. Swá hwæt swá stede (*statum*) módes áhwyrfþ, Scint. 106, 7. **IV c.** as a technical medical term *strangury*:—Wiđ stede and wiđ blǽddran sáre, Lchdm. i. 360, 4: 338, 3. [*Goth.* staþs: *O. Sax.* stedi: *O. Frs.* sted, stid, steith: *O. H. Ger.* stat; *f. locus*: *Icel.* staðr.] v. æsc-, ǽl-, bæþ-, beorg-, burg-, camp-, deáþ-, ealh-, eard-, eolh-, eorþ-, folc-, gemót-, gener-, gléd-, heáfod-, heáh-, hleóđor-, hús-, land-, mearc-, međel-, mylen-, sunn-, þing-, wang-, wíc-stede; cf. steall.

stede-fæst; *adj. Steadfast, constant, holding one's ground*:—Wíslíc wærscipe and stedefæst (styde-, MS. G.) módstađol biþ witena gehwilcum weorđlícre micle, đonne hé his wísan for ǽnigum þingum fágige tó swíđe, L. I. P. 10; Th. ii. 318, 38. Stódon stædefæste *they stood unyielding*, Byrht. Th. 135, 33; By. 127. Ne þurfon mé stedefæste hæleđ wordum ætwítan, 139, 5; By. 249. [*Icel.* stað-fastr.]

stedefæstness, e; *f. Steadfastness, constancy*:—Stydfæstnise *constantiae*, Rtl. 50, 4.

stedefulness. v. on-stedefulness.

stede-heard; *adj. Of enduring hardness* (?), *very hard*:—Strǽlas stedehearde, Judth. Thw. 24, 34; Jud. 223.

stede-leás; *adj. Without stability, unsteady, without power to retain one's place*:—Đonne biþ hé đam men gelíc, đe árǽrþ sume heáge hlǽddre and stíhþ be đære hlǽddre stapum, ođ đæt hé tó đæm ænde become, and wylle đonne git stígan ufor; ástíhþ đonne búton stapum, ođ đæt hé stedeleás fylþ, Homl. Skt. i. 1, 24. Stedeleáse steorran hreósaþ, Dóm. L. 107. [*Icel.* stað-lauss *unsteady*.]

stede-wang, es; *m. A plain, open place*:—On đam stedewange, Elen. Kmbl. 2040; El. 1021: 1346; El. 675: Andr. Kmbl. 1548; An. 775. Stedewangas, 667; An. 334. Ǽfter stedewonga stówum, Exon. Th. 154, 23; Gú. 847.

stede-wist, e; *f. Stability, steadiness, constancy*:—Stedewist *subsistentia, perseverantia*, Hpt. Gl. 530, 4.

stedig; *adj. Sterile, barren*:—Se đe eardian déþ stedigne *qui habitare facit sterilem*, Ps. Lamb. 112, 9. Nǽron đíne heorda stedige (*steriles*), Gen. 31, 38. Cf. (?) stede, **IV c**, *and see next word.*

stedigness, e; *f. Sterility, barrenness*:—Stedignysse sáwle mínre *sterilitatem animae meae*, Ps. Spl. 34, 14.

steding-líne, an; *f. A rope that supports a mast, a stay*:—Stedinglíne *opisfera*, Wrt. Voc. i. 63, 61. S[t]edinglíne, 57, 2.

stefn, stemn, es; *m.* **I.** *a stem* of a tree:—Hwæt wénst đú for hwí ǽlc sǽd gréwe innon đa eorþan and tó wyrtrumum weorþe on đære eorþan, búton for đý đe hí tiohhiaþ đæt se stemn and se helm móte đý fæstor standon . . . Eal se dǽl, se đe đæs treówes on twelf mónþum geweaxeþ, hé onginþ of đám wyrtrumum and swá upweardes gréwþ óþ đone stemn, Bt. 34, 10; Fox 148, 31–150, 2. Ic (*the cross*) wæs áheáwen holtes on ende, ástyred of stefne (swefne, Kemble) mínum, Rood Kmbl. 59; Kr. 30. Beám yldo ábreóteþ and bebriceþ telgum, ástyreþ stefn on síđe, áfylleþ hine on foldan, Salm. Kmbl. 594; Sal. 296. **I a.** fig.:—God is se stemn and stađol ealra góda, Bt. 34, 5; Fox 140, 2. Se đorn ðære gîtsunga ne wyrð forsearod on ðæm helme gif se wyrttruma ne biþ færcorfen oððe forbærned æt ðæm stemne *si radix culpae non exuritur, nunquam per ramos avaritiae spina siccatur*, Past. 45, 3; Swt. 341, 11. I b. *a stem, stock, race.* v. leód-, þeód-stefn. II. *prow* or *stern* of a vessel:—Se æftera stemn *puppis*, Wrt. Voc. i. 63, 37. Tô lides stefne, Chr. 937; Erl. 112, 34. Of nacan stefne, Andr. Kmbl. 582; An. 291. Beornas on stefn stigon, Beo. Th. 429; B. 212. [*O. Sax.* stamn (*of a vessel*): *O. Frs.* stevne: *O. H. Ger.* stamm *stips, truncus, caudex*: *Icel.* stafn, stamn *prow* or *stern* of a vessel.] v. forþ-, frum-, steór-stefn; stefna, *and next word.*

-stefn, -stæfn; *adj.* v. brond-, heáh-stefn (-stæfn).

stefn, stemn, es; *m.* I. *a turn, time*:—Ðâ besæt sió fierd hié (*the Danes*) ðǽr ða hwîle ðe hié ðǽr lengest mete hæfdon, ac hié hæfdon heora stemn gesetenne *the English force had sat out its turn of service*, Chr. 894; Erl. 90, 31. But the word occurs mostly in phrases:—Ðâ Noe ongan nîwan stefne (*anew, a second time*) hâm staðelian, Cd. Th. 94, 2; Gen. 1555: Beo. Th. 5181; B. 2594. Eft ... niówan stefne, 3582; B. 1789: Andr. Kmbl. 2607; An. 1305: Cd. Th. 113, 12; Gen. 1886. Hê hine Cyriacus syððan nemde nîwan stefne *he afterwards named him afresh Cyriacus*, Elen. Kmbl. 2119; El. 1061. Emb stemn *uicissim*, Germ. 388, 77. Emb stem, Scint. 140, 17. II. *a body of persons who take their turn at any work* (v. fird-stemn), *the English military force* (?):—On stemnes peð (cf. here-paþ), Cod. Dip. Kmbl. v. 121, 33. v. stefnan, stefning.

stefn, stæfn, stemn, e; *f.* I. *a voice, sound uttered by the mouth* (lit. or fig.):—Stemn is geslagen lyft gefrêdendlîc on hlyste ... Ǽlc stemn byþ geworden of ðæs mûðes clypunge and of ðære lyfte cnyssunge; se mûð drîfþ ût ða clypunge, and seó lyft byþ geslagen mid ðære clypunge and gewyrð tô stemne. Ǽlc stemn is oððe andgytfullîc oððe gemenged; andgytfullîc stemn is, ðe mid andgyte biþ geclypod ...; gemenged stemn is, ðe biþ bûtan andgyte, swylc swâ is hrýðera gehlôw and horsa hnǽgung, hunda gebeorc, treówa brastlung *et cetera*, Ælfc. Gr. 1; Zup. 4, 5–16. Stebn *vox*, Wrt. Voc. ii. 124, 18. Stefn of heofenum ðus cwæð, Mt. Kmbl. 3, 17: Mk. Skt. 1, 11. Seó ârleáse helwarena stefn wæs gehýred and heora gnornung, Blickl. Homl. 87, 3. Seó stemn ðære heortan biþ gedrêfed, 19, 9. Seó stemn ys Iacobes stefn, Gen. 27, 22. Seó stefen heom andswarode, Nicod. 24; Thw. 13, 5. Swâ him seó stefen beád, Gl. Prud. 1 a. Sió býman stefen, Exon. Th. 65, 29; Cri. 1062. Heó clypode micelre stefne, Lk. Skt. 1, 42. Hê cûþre stæfne wæs tô mê sprecende, Bd. 4, 25; S. 600, 43. Gif ðû sanges stæfne gehýrdest, 4, 3; S. 568, 30. Hig gecnâwaþ his stefne, Jn. Skt. 10, 4. Hig mycelre stefne bǽdon ðæt hê wǽre âhangen; and hyra stefna swîðredon, Lk. Skt. 23, 23. Stæfna, Ps. Spl. 18, 3. Lâðe cyrmdon fǽgum stæfnum, Cd. Th. 207, 5; Exod. 462. II. as a grammatical term, *form to mark relation*:—Se forma hâd and se ôðer hâd habbaþ ǽnlîpige stemna, forðan ðe hî beóþ ǽfre ætgædere and him betwýnan sprecaþ. Ðonne ic cweþe *ego* ic, and ðû cwest tô mê *tu* ðû, ðonne beó wyt ætgædere and for ðî ne behôfaþ nâðor ðissera *pronomina* nâ mâ stemna bûton twegra. Se ðridda hâd hæfþ syx clypunga, forðan ðe hê ys hwîlon mid, hwîlon on ôðre stôwe, Ælfc. Gr. 15; Zup. 93, 2–8. [*Chauc.* steven: the word is used by Gawin Douglas. *Goth.* stibna: *O. Sax.* stemna: *O. Frs.* stemme: *O. H. Ger.* stimna, stimma, stemna, stemma.] v. þunorrâd-, wæter-stefn.

stefn, e; *f. A summons, citation* (*in* râd-stefn *a summons carried by a mounted person.* v. râd-stefn, where this meaning may be substituted for the one there given). [*Icel.* stefna *a summons, citation.*] v. stefnian.

stefna, an; *m. The prow* or *stern* of a vessel:—Æt lides stefnan, Andr. Kmbl. 806; An. 403: 3411; An. 1709. Æt nacan stefnan, Exon. 306, 14; Seef. 7. Sum wǽg stefnan steóreþ, 296, 20; Crä. 54. Steóran ofer stæfnan, Andr. Kmbl. 989; An. 495. v. -stefn, *and next word.*

stefnan; *p.* de. I. *to regulate, direct, fix, institute*:—Hê stefnde Godes cyrican and Godes gesomnunga on ðære byrig eahta and twentig geára *he had the direction of God's church and God's congregations in that town eight-and-twenty years*, Shrn. 108, 6. Ongann timbrian ða stôwe ðæs mynstres ðe hê from ðam cyninge onfêng and mid regollîcum ðeódscipum stæfnde *curavit locum monasterii, quem a rege acceperat, construere ac regularibus instituere disciplinis*, Bd. 3, 19; S. 547, 21 note. II. *to alternate*:—Staefnendra *alternantium*, Wrt. Voc. ii. 99, 74. Stefnendra, 6, 49. v. ge-stefnan; stefn; *m. a turn.*

stefnan, stefnian *to provide with a hem* or *border, to fringe* [:—Bebyrde (cf. gebyrded *clabatum*, 104, 18. *Clavatum, sutum vel* gebyrd, 131, 57) oððe bestefnde *clavatae*, Wrt. Voc. ii. 20, 42. Gestefnode *clavate*, Anglia xiii. 37, 288.] v. stefning, II.

stefn-byrd, e; *f. Regulation, direction*:—Sceoldon eal beran stîþe stefnbyrd swâ him se steóra bibeád missenlîce gemetu *all creatures had to submit to firm direction, as the guide ordered them, various modes*, Exon. Th. 349, 12; Sch. 45. v. stefnan *to regulate.*

-stefne; *adj. -voiced.* v. hlûd-stefne.

stefnettan, stemnettan; *p.* te *To stand firm* (?):—Swâ stemnetton stîðhugende hysas æt hilde, Byrht. Th. 135, 22; By. 122. [Hwi studgi ȝe nu and steuentið se stille, Kath. 59, 1265.]

stefnian; *p.* ode *To cite, summon* (with dat.):—Stefnode man Godwine eorle and Harolde eorle tô ðon gemôte ... Ðâ hî ðider cômon, ðâ stefnede heom man tô gemôte, Chr. 1048; Erl. 180, 3–6. Se cing him steofnode tô Glôweceastre, 1093; Erl. 228, 33. [Taken from Scandinavian (?); cf. *Icel.* stefna *to cite, summon* a person (*dat.*).]

stefnian. v. stefnan.

stefning, stemning, e; *f.* I. *a turn*, used of service where one set of persons replaces another. (In E. Cornwall Glossary *stemming* is given as 'a turn in succession, as when in dry seasons people have to take their regular turn for water at the common pump'):—Hié (seó fyrd) hæfdan heora stemninge (steminge, *another MS.*) gesetene, Chr. 894; Th. i. 166, col. 2, l. 14. v. stefn; *m.*; stefnan, II. II. *a border, hem*:—Stemning *vel* hem *limbus*, Wrt. Voc. i. 26, 6. v. limb-stefning; stefnan *to fringe.*

stela, steola, stæla; *m.* I. *the stalk* of a plant:—Steola *caulem*, Wrt. Voc. ii. 102, 53: *cauliculus*, 103, 50: 129, 84. Stela *caulem*, 13, 14: *cauliculus*, 76, 11: i. 33, 10. Healm *vel* stela *culmus*, i. *stramen spicarum*, ii. 137, 58. Sæpig stela *succulentus cauliculus* (*ramusculus*), Hpt. Gl. 419, 45. Hyre (*leechwort*) stela byþ mid geþûfum bôgum, Lchdm. i. 248, 18. Genim ðysse wyrte wôs oððe ðone stelan mid ðam wæstme, 156, 21: 160, 11: 184, 20. Eleleáfes stelan, ii. 272, 23. Heó hafaþ nigon wyrttruman and swâ fela stelena, i. 238, 17. Mid feówer reádum stælum (stelum, MS. B.), 154, 15. Genim nigon stelan, 230, 20. II. fig.:—Witan sceoldon smeágan hwilc ðæra stelenna ðæs cinestôles wǽre tôbrocen, and bêtan ðone sôna. Se cinestôl stynt on ðisum þrîm stelum: *laboratores, bellatores, oratores*, Ælfc. T. Grn. 20, 15–19. [*O. H. Ger.* stil *thyrsus herbae*: *Ger.* stiel.] v. cawel-stela; -steled.

stelan; *p.* stæl, *pl.* stǽlon; *pp.* stolen *To steal* (with dat. of person from whom):—Stilith *conpilat*, Wrt. Voc. ii. 105, 33. Stiled, 15, 32. Gif frigman frêum stelþ, L. Ethb. 9; Th. i. 6, 2. Se ðeo stelaþ on ðone dæg, ne geâhsaþ hit manna, Lchdm. iii. 178, 5. Stæl *conpilabat*, Wrt. Voc. ii. 22, 32. Wênst ðû, ðæt wê ðines hlâfordes gold stǽlon, Gen. 44, 8. Ne stel ðû, Ex. 20, 15: Mt. Kmbl. 19, 18. Ic stele *furer*, Kent. Gl. 1081. Þeóf ne cymþ bûton ðæt hê stele *fur non uenit nisi ut furetur*, Jn. Skt. 10, 10. Gif frigman cyninge stele, L. Ethb. 4; Th. i. 4, 3. [*Goth.* stilan: *O. Sax. O. H. Ger.* stelan: *O. Frs. Icel.* stela.] v. be-, for-, ge-stelan; þeóf-stolen; stalian.

stêle *steel*, -steled. v. stîle, ân-steled, staled.

stellan, stillan; *p.* stealde; *pp.* steald. I. *to give a place to, set, place*:—Hê ôðrum yfele bisene steleþ, Past. 28; Swt. 191, 12. Hwelce bisena hê ðǽr stellende wæs, Ors. 2, 2; Swt. 64, 24. II. *to take a place* (?), *to stand*:—Ðonne cumaþ upplîce eoredheápas stîþmægen âstyred styllaþ embûtan eal engla werod êcne behlǽnaþ ðone mǽran Metod (cf. ðonne cumaþ ealle engla þreátas stîðe âstyrode standaþ âbûtan eall engla werod êcne ymbtrymmaþ ðone mǽran kyning, Wulfst. 137, 14) *tum superum subito veniet commota potestas, coetibus angelicis regem stipata supernum*, Dôm. L. 114. [*Laym.* stalde; *p.*: *A. R.* stolde; *p.*: *O. Sax.* stellian: *O. H. Ger.* stellen.] v. â-, on-stellan.

stellan; *p.* stealde, *and* stillan, styllan, stiellan; *p.* de *To leap, rush*:—Ðus hêr on grundum Godes êce bearn ofer heáh hleoþu hlýpum stylde; swâ wê men sculon heortan gehygdum hlýpum styllan of mægne in mægen, Exon. Th. 46, 28–36; Cri. 744–748. Ðonne hî ðæt mægen ðære unmǽtan hǽto âræfnan ne mihton ðonne stealdon hî eft on middan ðæs unmǽtan cyles and mid ðý hî ðǽr nǽnige reste gemêtan mihton stelldon (stældon, MS. T.) hî eft on middel ðæs unâdwæscendlîcan lîges *cum vim fervoris immensi tolerare non possent, prosiliebant in medium frigoris infesti; et cum neque ibi requiei invenire valerent, resiliebant rursus in medium flammarum inextinguibilium*, Bd. 5, 12; S. 627, 40–628, 1. Seó ofermôdnes stellan wile ofer eáðmôdnesse *superbia inruere vult super humilitatem*, Gl. Prud. 32 a. v. â-, ge-, ofer-stellan (-styllan); still.

stel-mêle, es; *m. A vessel with a stem* or *handle*:—Stelmêlas, Anglia ix. 264, 11.

stel-scofl (?), e; *f.* The word apparently should mean *a shovel with a long handle* (v. stela), but it glosses *faselus*:—Steolscofle *faselo*, Germ. 400, 498.

stêm, stêman, stêming, steming, stemn, stemnettan, stemning. v. steám, stîman, stîming, stefning, stefn, stefnettan, stefning.

stempan; *p.* te; *pp.* ed *To stamp, bray*:—Nim ysopo and stemp, Lchdm. i. 378, 20. [Cf. *O. H. Ger.* stampfôn *comminuere*: *Icel.* stappa *to stamp, bray.*] v. â-stempan, *and next word.*

stemping-îsern, es; *n. A stamping-iron*:—Âgrafen, âstemped *celatum*, i. *pictum*; stempingîsern *celon*; stempingîsern *cilion, celox*, Wrt. Voc. ii. 130, 57–61.

stênan; *p.* de. I. *to groan*:—Ic grymetige and stêne mid ealle môde *rugiebam a gemitu cordis mei*, Ps. Th. 37, 8. [*Du.* stenen *to groan.*] II. *to cause to sound* (?):—Com ðâ wîgena hleó þegna þreáte þryðbord stênan beadurôf cyning burga neósan (*came with clang of shields*), Elen. Kmbl. 302; El. 151. v. stinan.

stenc, es; *m.* I. *a smell, scent, odour*:—Ic eom on stence strengre ðonne rîcels, Exon. Th. 423, 18; Rä. 41, 23. Stencas *sapores*, Kent. Gl. 1178. Mid ðære nose wê tôsceádaþ ða stencas, Past. 11, 2;

Swt. 65, 21. Góde stencas and yfele, 56; Swt. 433, 22. I a. *a pleasant smell, fragrance, perfume*:—Ys mínes suna stenc swilce ðæs landes stenc, ðe Drihten bletsode, Gen. 27, 27. Swētnys swā ðæra wynsumestra blōstmena stenc, Guthl. 20; Gdwin. 86, 19: Exon. Th. 363, 16; Wal. 54. Swīðe swēte stenc, Blickl. Homl. 145, 29. Mycel swētnysse stencg, Bd. 3, 8; S. 532, 18. Balzamum ðæs betstan stences, Nar. 27, 22. Tō wynsumum stence, Lev. 1, 9. Ða swētan stencas ðara wuduwyrta, Blickl. Homl. 59, 3. Mid ðām fægrestum foldan stencum, Exon. Th. 198, 11; Ph. 8. I b. *an unpleasant smell, stench, stink*:—Se wōlberenda stenc ðære lyfte, Bd. 1, 13; S. 482, 8. Ðǣr slōh ūt of ðære niwelnysse ormǣte stenc, Homl. Th. ii. 350, 25. Eall forweard for ðæm stence, Ors. 5, 4; Swt. 226, 13. Stænce, 2, 6; Swt. 90, 1. Se līchoma on ðone heardestan stenc and on ðone fūlostan biþ gecyrred, Blickl. Homl. 59, 12. Micgan stencgum *urinae foetoribus*, Hpt. Gl. 483, 3. Stencum, 516, 32: Homl. Th. i. 68, 7: ii. 374, 6. II. *the sense of smell*:—Stengc *odor, odoratus, olfactus*, Wrt. Voc. i. 42, 57, 61: Hpt. Gl. 488, 23. Ða fīf andgitu ūses līchaman . . . stenc, Homl. Th. ii. 372, 26: i. 138, 27. [*O. Sax.* stank: *O. H. Ger.* stanc *odor, odoratus, foetor.*] v. æðel-, un-, wyrt-stenc; ge-, swōt-stence; *adj.*

stencan; *p.* te *To pant, emit breath with effort*:—Stenecendra renula *anhelantium cursorum*, Hpt. Gl. 406, 8. [Jamieson gives *stank* to gasp for breath. Cf. *Swed.* stånka *to pant.*]

stencan; *p.* te *To scatter*:—Se ðe ne somnaþ se stenceþ *qui non congregat, spargit*, Mt. Kmbl. Rush. 12, 30. Ðū somnast ðǣr ðū ne strenctæs (stenctæs?, sprenctæs?) *congregas ubi non sparsisti*, 25, 24. Ðū stenctest (swenctest?) ða elðeódgan folc and hȳ āwurpe *afflixisti populos et expulisti eos*, Ps. Th. 43, 3. [*Goth.* ga-staggkwan *to dash*: *Icel.* stökkva *to cause to spring, sprinkle*: *Dan.* stænke *to sprinkle*: *Swed.* stänka *to sprinkle, scatter.*] v. tō-stencan; stincan *to spring.*

stenc-brengende; *adj.* (*ptcpl.*). *Odoriferous*:—Stengcbrengendra blōstmana sigbēgo *odoriferas florum coronas*, Rtl. 77, 39.

stencedness, stencend, stencness, stencende. v. tō-stencedness, -stencend, -stencness, swōt-stencende.

stencness, e; *f. Scent, odour*:—Salde stencgnisse *dedit odorem*, Rtl. 4, 13.

steng, es; *m. A stang* (v. Halliwell's Dict.), *pole, stake, staff, cudgel, bar*:—Steng (stencg, stengc) *vectis*, Ælfc. Gr. 9, 28; Zup. 55, 10: Wrt. Voc. i. 26, 44. Stengc, 81, 29. Steng *clava*, ii. 104, 11: 14, 41: *claumentia*, 131, 55. Styng *clava*, i. 33, 60. Wið slege īsernes oððe stenges (stænges, MS. H.), Lchdm. i. 132, 4. Wið wunda som hȳ sȳn of īserne, som hȳ sȳn of stence (stæncge, MS. H.), 166, 10. Ðā hēt se dēma hī nacode gebindan tō ānum stænge, Shrn. 115, 13. Heáfod on steng (*stipitem*) āsettan, Bd. 3, 12; S. 537, 34. Stengcum *fustibus*, Hpt. Gl. 487, 48. Stencgum (stængum, Rush.), Mt. Kmbl. Lind. 26, 47. Stengum *sudibus*, Wrt. Voc. ii. 85, 53. Mid stengum ðyrscan, Shrn. 55, 10. Mid stearcum stengum beátan, Homl. Th. i. 428, 6. Hāt wyrcean twegen stengeas (stengas, Hatt. MS.) of ðæm treówe ðe is haten sethim *facies vectes de lignis sethim*, Past. 22, 1; Swt. 168, 22. [*O. H. Ger.* stanga; *f. fustis, vectis, contus*: *Icel.* stöng; *f. a pole.*] v. wīte-steng.

steola, steol-scofl. v. stela, stel-scofl.

steóp *a cup.* v. steáp.

steóp- *deprived of* a relative. The form seems to have been used in the first instance in combination with words denoting children, to mark loss of parents, and then to have been combined with father, mother to express the relation of one who married the mother or father of an orphan. It is a common Teutonic word. [*O. Frs.* stiap-, stiep-: *Du.* stief-: *O. H. Ger.* stiuf-: *Ger.* stief-: *Icel.* stjúp-: *Dan.* stif-: *Swed.* stjuf-, styf-.] v. stīpan, *and following words.*

steóp-bearn, es; *n. An orphan*:—Steópbearn *pupillus*, Ps. Vos. 81, 3. Ðam steópbearne ic geheólp, Homl. Th. ii. 448, 14, 20. Ðæt mann wydewan geneósige and steópbearnum gehelpe, Homl. Skt. i. 9, 63. [He scal biwerian widewan and steopbern, O. E. Homl. i. 115, 20. *Icel.* stjúp-barn.]

steóp-cild, es; *n.* I. *an orphan, one who has lost a parent*:—Steópcild *privignus*, Wrt. Voc. i. 50, 47: *pupillus*, 285, 1. Steópcilde *orphano*, Ps. Spl. 9 second, 17. Eówer bearn beóþ steópcild (*pupilli*), Ex. 22, 24. Steópcild *orphani*, Ps. Th. 108, 9. Heó wæs wuduwena and steópcilda ārigend, Lchdm. iii. 430, 1. Stēpcilda, Ps. Surt. 67, 6. Ne deriaþ wudewum and steópcildum, Ex. 22, 22: Blickl. Homl. 45, 1: Ps. Th. 108, 12. Ðæt hī widuwan and steópcild gladian, L. Eth. vi. 47; Th. i. 326, 25. Steápcildo *pupillos*, Rtl. 29, 13. II. fig. *one deprived of protection*:—Wē wǣron steópcild gewordene, forðan ðe wē wǣron āstȳpede ðæs heofenlīcan rīces, Wulfst. 252, 10. Ne lǣte ic eów steópcild, Jn. Skt. 14, 18.

steóp-dohtor; *f. A step-daughter*:—Steópdohter *filiaster*, Wrt. Voc. i. 72, 34. Stēpdohter, 51, 69. [Ic and Algif mīn stēpdouter, Chart. Th. 583, 23.] [*O. H. Ger.* stief-tohter *filiastra*: *Icel.* stjúp-dóttir.]

steóp-fæder; *m. A step-father*:—Steópfaeder *bitricius*, Txts. 45, 300. Steópfaeder, steúpfaedaer, staupfotar, steúffeder *vitricius*, 107, 2124. Steópfæder *vitricus* vel *patraster*, Wrt. i. 52, 11: 72, 31: 284, 75: ii. 11, 10. Hē ofslōh ge his āgenne fæder ge his steópfæder (*vitricum suum*), Ors. 1, 8; Swt. 42, 22. [*O. Frs.* stiap-fader: *O. H. Ger.* stiuf-fater *vitricus*: *Icel.* stjúp-faðir.]

steóp-mōdor; *f. A step-mother*:—Steópmōder *noverca*, Wrt. Voc. i. 72, 32: 284, 76. Steópmōdur, ii. 60, 33. Heó wæs Philippuses steópmōdor, Ors. 3, 7; Swt. 110, 26. Ðæt mon hine menge mid his steópmēder, Bd. 1, 27; S. 491, 11. Steópmōdrum, S. 490, 35. Gē sume hæfdon eówre steópmōdur, Past. 32; Swt. 211 9. [*O. Frs.* stiap-mōder: *O. H. Ger.* stiaf-mōter: *Icel.* stiup-mōðir.]

steóp-sunu, a; *m. A step-son*:—Steópsunu *filiaster*, Wrt. Voc. ii. 108, 69: 35, 61: *privignus*, i. 52, 12: 72, 33. Hē ofslōh his steópsunu, Ors. i. 8; Swt. 42, 22. [*O. H. Ger.* stiuf-sun *privignus*: *Icel.* stjúp-sonr.]

steór, es; *m. A steer, young bull*, or *cow*:—Ðrīuuintri steór, steúr *prifeta*, Txts. 89, 1655: Wrt. Voc. ii. 68, 42. Steór *anniculus*, 10, 41: *juvencus*, vel *vitula*, i. 23, 43: *laudaris*, 287, 61: *ludares*, ii. 51, 22: *ludarius*, 113, 24. [*Goth.* stiurs *a calf*: *O. L. Ger.* stier *taurus*: *O. H. Ger.* stior *juvencus*: *Icel.* stjórr.] v. steór-oxa.

steór *and* stȳr, e; *f.* I. *guidance, direction*:—Lār *vel* steór *disciplina*, Wrt. Voc. i. 46, 57: 75, 31. Gyrd steóre *virga directionis*, Ps. Lamb. 44, 7. Ðæt hē ðoncfull sī stȳre him ðæs bebodenan folces *contentus sit gubernatione creditae sibi plebis*, Bd. 4, 5; S. 572, 33. God sette ǣ ðam folce tō steóre, Ælfc. T. Grn. 5, 36: L. Eth. ix. 36; Th. i. 348, 14: L. Ælfc. P. 8; Th. ii. 366, 18: Boutr. Scrd. 18, 4. Gegrīpaþ stȳre *adprehendite disciplinam*, Ps. Surt. 2, 12. II. *that which guides, a rule, regulation*:—Seó ǣ, ðæt is se[ó] rihtwīse steór, ne gegrēt ðone rihtwīsan mid nānum yfele, Homl. Skt. i. 17, 19. Ǣlc mīnra þegna ðe ða steóre swā healdan nelle swā ic beboden habbe, L. Ath. v. 11; Th. i. 240, 21. III. *correction, discipline, reproof*:—Gif hē ðām rēceleásum stȳrþ, ðonne sceal his steór beón mid lufe gemetegod, Homl. Th. ii. 532, 12. Eallum him sceal beón ān steór and ān lār æfter heora gearnunga anddyfene *una prebeatur in omnibus secundum merita disciplina*, R. Ben. 13, 7. Steór *correptio*, Scint. 117, 8. Ðæt man cȳde būton steóre intingan, Homl. Th. ii. 590, 23. Wrǣnnes mid stīðre steóre lāre sī geweld *lascivia duro disciplinae paedagogio refrenetur*, Hpt. Gl. 432, 34: Homl. Th. i. 360, 18. Ðæt wise men sceolon settan steóre dysigum mannum, swā ðæt hī ðæt dysig and ða unðeáwas ālecgan, 268, 2. On steórum *in increpationibus*, Ps. Spl. 38, 14. [See O. E. Homl. i. 117, 21–35.] IV. *restraint, check*:—Ðæt mōd hæfþ fulfremedne willan tō ðære wrǣnnesse būtan ǣlcre steóre and wearne *animus voluptate luxuriae sine ullo repugnationis obstaculo delectatur*, Past. 11, 7; Swt. 73, 8. Ðæs unrǣdes stīðferhð cyning steóre gefremede (*checked that evil plan* (building the tower of Babel)), ðā hē reorde gesette eorðbūendum ungelīce, Cd. Th. 101, 17; Gen. 1683. V. *punishment, penalty*:—Ic hæbbe gecoren hwæt seó steór beón mǣge gif ǣnig man andbyrdnysse beginþ, L. Edg. S. 14; Th. i. 276, 31. Oft gē in gestalum stondaþ, ðæs cymeþ steór of heofonum, Exon. Th. 132, 32; Gū. 481. Ǣgðer wǣre unnyt ge mildheortnes ge steór, gif hié ānlīpe wǣron . . . Fordæm scel bión on ðæm reccere ðæt hē sié mildheortlīce wītniende, Past. 17; Swt. 125, 3. Ǣfter ðæs gyltes gemete sceal beón gelengen ðære steóre gemet (*disciplinae mensura*), R. Ben. 48, 16. Ðæt hī stȳran (*punish*) ǣlcum ðara ðe ðis ne gelǣste . . . and on ðære steóre ne sȳ nān forgifnes, L. Edg. S. 1; Th. i. 272, 8. Mid woruldcundre steóre *with punishment inflicted by the secular power*, L. Eth. vi. 50; Th. i. 328, 3. Mid worldlīcre steóre, ix. 15; Th. i. 344, 4: L. I. P. 2; Th. ii. 304, 18: Wulfst. 169, 8: 311, 16. Gif feohbōt ārīseþ swā swā woroldwitan tō steóre gesettan (*fixed as penalty*), L. Eth. vi. 51; Th. i. 328, 5. Ðæt gehwilc man his teóðunge rihtlīce gelǣste be ðære steóre ðe Eádgār gelagede *under pain of the punishment that Edgar fixed by law*, Wulfst. 272, 8. Ceóse Dene be lagum hwylce steóre hȳ be ðan healdan willaþ, L. Edg. S. 13; Th. i. 276, 28. Ðā āsende him God tō swȳðlīce steóre (*he was carried away captive*), Homl. Skt. i. 18, 437. Tōscādan ge on godcundan scriftan ge on woroldcundan steóran, L. Eth. vi. 52; Th. i. 328, 19. Hig gesetton woruldlīce steóra . . . and ða woruldbōte hig gesetton gemǣne Criste and cyngé, L. E. G. prm.; Th. i. 166, 13. Gerǣde man friðlīce steóra and ne forspille for lytlum Godes handgeweorc, L. Eth. v. 3; Th. i. 304, 20: vi. 10; Th. i. 318, 3. Ðonne wurð ȝeó heardnes stīðmōdre heortan gehnexad þurh grimlīce steóra and heardlīce ðreála, Wulfst. 133, 19. Se rihtwīsa ne þearf him ondrǣdan ða stīðan steóra ðe Godes ǣ tǣcþ, Homl. Skt. i. 17, 22. V a. where the punishment is stated to be a money one, *a fine, penalty*:—Ðone feórðan pening on folclīcre steóre, Chart. Th. 242, 30. Gif se landrīca nelle tō steóre filstan *will not assist to levy the fine*, L. N. P. L. 54; Th. ii. 298, 19. [*O. H. Ger.* stiura *gubernaculum, clavus, stipendium.* v. Grmm. R. A. 298.] v. woruld-steór; steóran.

steór, es; *n. A rudder, helm.* [Itt iss sett att te ster to sterenn, Orm. 15258. Hys sterisman . . . the stere smote overe borde, Chauc. H. of F. i. 437. ȝif he ne rauȝte to þe stiere (steere, stere) þe wynde wolde þe bote ouerthrowe, Piers P. 8, 35. *Du.* stuur; *n. helm, rudder*: *O. Frs.* stiure: *M. H. Ger.* stiure; *n.*: *Ger.* steuer; *n.*: *Icel.* stýri; *n.*] v. steór-, steóres-mann.

steóra, stiéra, styra, an; *m. One who directs the course of a ship*, (a) lit.:—Steóra *gubernio*, Wrt. Voc. i. 48, 7: *gubernator*, 56, 17: *proreta*, ii. 69, 5: 75, 10. Swelce se stióra slēpe on midre sǣ and forlure ðæt stiórrōður . . . Se biþ swīðe onlīc ðæm stióran ðe his stiórrōðor forliést on sǣ *quasi dormiens in medio mari et quasi sopitus gubernator amisso* *clavo . . . Quasi clavum gubernator amittit*, Past. 56, 3; Swt. 431, 30–36. Gelīc ðam scipe būton ǣlcum steóran, Basil admn. 6; Norm. 46, 21. (b) fig.:—God is steóra and steórrōþer, forðæm hē reht and rǣt eallum gesceaftum, swā swā gōd steóra (stióra, Cott. MS.) ānum scipe, Bt. 35, 3; Fox 158, 25. [Ilc ðhusent adde a meister wold, and under ðis tʒen steres ben, Gen. and Ex. 3413. *O. H. Ger.* stiuro *gubernator, nauclerus*: *Icel.* stjóri *a ruler* (poet.).] v. fore-, scip-steóra.

steóran, stióran, (*and with umlaut*) stiéran, stēran, stīran, stȳran; *p.* de. I. *to steer, guide a vessel*:—Sum [on] fealone wǣg stefnan steóreþ, Exon. Th. 296, 20; Crä. 54. Ic ǣfre ne geseah ǣnigne mann ðē gelīcne steóran ofer stæfnan, Andr. Kmbl. 989; An. 495. Swīðe eáðe mæg on smyltre sǣ ungelǣred scipstiéra genōh ryhte stiéran, Past. 9; Swt. 59, 2. Ia. fig. *to steer, guide, rule, direct*:—Se stiórþ ðam hrædwǣne eallra gesceafta *volucrem currum regit*, Bt. 36, 2; Fox 174, 20. Swā dēþ ðæt mōd, ðonne hit wacorlīce stiéreþ ðære sāwle *cum mens vigilanter animam regit*, Past. 56, 3; Swt. 433, 4. Stȳrþ *regit*, Wülck. Gl. 254, 29. Steórdes *gubernasti*, Ps. Surt. ii. p. 188, 5. Se stȳrde Dǣre mǣgþe *qui Deirorum provinciam gubernaret*, Bd. 4, 12; S. 581, 19: 5, 23; S. 645, 38. Steóran and reccan ðone anweald ðe mē befæst wæs, Bt. 17; Fox 58, 27. Ða geornfulnesse ðe hē mid stióran scolde ðære sāwle and ðæm līchoman, Past. 56, 3; Swt. 431, 34. Þurh ðē ic ðys eówde stȳran and rihtan [mihte], Blickl. Homl. 191, 28. Hē ða cyricean wæs reccende and stȳrende *ecclesiam regens*, Bd. 5, 19; S. 639, 13. II. *to correct, restrain* a person (*dat.*) from wrong, (*gen.* or *prep.*) *give a right direction* to what is wrong:—Ic bēte sume leáse bōc oððe ic stȳre (steóre, MS. H.) sumum stuntum menn *corrigo*, Ælfc. Gr. 28, 5; Zup. 173, 10. Se micla cræftiga hiertende tōscȳfþ and egesiende stiérþ ofermētta mid ðære tǣlinge his hiéremonnum ðæt hē hié gebringe on līfe *magnus regendi artifex favoribus impellit, terroribus retrahit, ut auditores suos et descripto irreprehensibilitatis culmine restringat a superbia, et officium laudando, quod quaeritur componat ad vitam*, Past. 8, 1; Swt. 53, 16. Gif hē ðām rēceleásum stȳrþ, ðonne sceal his steór beón mid lufe gemetegod. . . Wel dēþ se ðe ungewittigum stȳrþ mid swinglum, gif hē mid wordum ne mæg. Hit is āwriten: 'Ne biþ se stunta mid wordum gerihtlǣced,' Homl. Th. ii. 532, 11–15. Gif hē him sylfum stȳrþ fram eallum stuntnyssum, Homl. Skt. i, 17, 22. Ðæt stȳrþ (*checks*) ðam þurste, Lchdm. ii. 192, 11. Hē missenlīce monna cynne gielpes stȳreþ, Exon. Th. 299, 20; Crä. 105. Swā biþ geóguðe ðeáw, ðǣr ðæs ealdres egsa ne stȳreþ, 127, 25; Gū. 391. Gif bisceopas forgȳmaþ, þæt hī synna ne stȳraþ ne unriht forbeódaþ *if bishops neglect to restrain from sins and to forbid wrong*, Wulfst. 176, 29. Gif hē hit herede and on tyhte eft hē stiérde ðære gewilnunge *qui tamen laudans desiderium in pavorem vertit protinus*, Past. 8, 1; Swt. 53, 9. Iacobus his stīrde *Jacobus prohibet*, 3, 1; Swt. 33, 10. Ðæt hē fram synnan gecyrre and ōðrum mannum unrihtes stȳre, L. Eth. vi. 42; Th. i. 326, 9: Wulfst. 308, 19. Mānfulra dǣda on ǣghwilcan ende stȳre man swȳðe, 309, 27. Gif seó wyrd swā hweorfan mōt and ðū heore nelt stīran (steóran, Met. 4, 49), Bt. 4; Fox 8, 19. Stiéran sceal mon strongum mōde, Exon. Th. 312, 13; Seef. 109. Stȳran, 336, 18; Gn. Ex. 51. Ðæm sacerde nāht ne fremaþ ðæt hē rihtwīs beó gif hē ðām unrihtwīsan nele hyra unrihtes stȳran (cf. preósta nān ne wandige, ðæt hig ne bodigan ǣlcum men, hwæt him sig tō dōnne and hwæt tō forgānne, Th. ii. 202, 11–13) *sacerdoti nihil prodest, quod ipse justus sit, si injustos pro injustitia eorum corrigere nolit*, L. Ecg. P. iii. 15 tit.; Th. ii. 196, 10. Se ðe wylle eard clǣnsian, ðonne mōt hē georne ðyllīces stȳran (steóran, MS. B.) *restrain such crimes*, L. C. S. 7; Th. i. 380, 9. Hē wolde ūs mid līðnysse stȳran, Homl. Th. i. 320, 10: Blickl. Homl. 63, 22. Him stȳran cwom stefn *a voice came restraining Abraham from sacrificing Isaac*, Cd. Th. 204, 8; Exod. 416. Stȳran his mōdes styrunge mid singalre gemetfæstnesse, Homl. Th. i. 360, 15. IIa. *to keep back* from what is good:—Ic dysge dwelle and ōðrum stȳre nyttre fōre *I (night) lead the foolish astray and keep back others from a useful course*, Exon. Th. 393, 3; Rä. 12, 4. III. *to reprove, chide, rebuke*:—Se ðe steórþ þeóda *qui corripit gentes*, Ps. Lamb. 93, 10. Stiórde ł stiórend wæs him *comminatus est eis*, Mk. Skt. Lind. Rush. 8, 30. Seó menigo stȳrde ðæm blindan ðæt hē cleopode *the multitude rebuked him for calling out*, Blickl. Homl. 19, 5: 191, 12. Se hālga wer wordum stȳrde unryhtre ǣ (cf. Herod being reproved by John for Herodias his brother Philip's wife, Lk. 3, 19), Exon. Th. 260, 13; Jul. 296. Steórdon *increpabant*, Mt. Kmbl. Rush. 19, 13. Stiórdun *comminabantur*, Mk. Skt. Rush. 10, 13, 48. Swā hié him swȳðor stȳrdon, swā hē hlūdor cleopode, Blickl. Homl. 15, 21. Nā on ðīnum yrre stȳr ðū mē *neque in ira tua corripias me*, Ps. Lamb. 6, 2: Mt. Kmbl. 18, 15. God wolde stȳran ðære nytennysse Cūðberhtes, and āsende ān cild, ðæt hit his dyslīcan plegan wīslīce ðreáde, Homl. Th. ii. 134, 5. IV. *to punish*:—Ðonne hȳ āgyltaþ him man stȳre odþe mid swīðlīcum fæstenum odþe mid teartum swingellum hȳ wylde *dum delinquunt, aut nimiis jejuniis affligantur, aut acribus verberibus coherceantur*, R. Ben. 54, 3. Ðonne beóde ic mīnum gerēfan ðæt hī stȳran ǣlcum ðara ðe ðis ne gelǣste . . . and on ðære steóre ne sȳ nān forgifnes, L. Edg. S. 1; Th. i. 272, 6. Swā hwilc ðissa (*various punishments*) swā man gerǣde; swā man mæg stȳran, and eác ðære sāwle gebeorgan, L. C. S. 30; Th. i. 394, 16. Hī sceoldan ðǣm unrihtdōndum mid grimnesse stēran; þeófum and mānswarum . . . sceolan ða dēman grimlīce stȳran, Blickl. Homl. 63, 12–15. [Iesu Crist shall ben hæfedd to steorenn hemm, Orm. 1559. In yherde irened salt þou stere (*reges*) þa, Ps. 2, 9. Þu steorest te sea stream ꝥ hit fleden ne mot fir þan þu markedest, Marh. 9, 34. *Goth.* stiurjan *to establish*: *O. Frs.* stiora, stiura *to steer; to hinder*: *O. H. Ger.* stiuren *gubernare, fulcire*: *Icel.* stȳra, *to steer; to direct, govern.*] v. ge-, on-steóran (-stīran, -stȳran); steór, steórend.

steór-bord, es; *n.* *Star-board, the right side of a ship looking forward*:—Hē lēt him ealne weg ðæt wēste land on ðæt steórbord and ða wīdsǣ on ðæt bæcbord, Ors. 1, 1; Swt. 17, 10, 25. [Cf. *Icel.* stjórnborði: *Da. Swed.* styr-bord: *Du.* stuur-boord.]

steóre, an: *f.* *A regulation*:—Gif eówer hwilc forgȳmeleásaþ and mē hȳran nelle and emban ða steóran (steóra?) swā beón nelle swā ic beboden hæbbe and on ūrum gewritum stent, L. Ath. v. 11; Th. i. 240, 17. v. steór.

steórend, stȳrend, es; *m.* I. *a ruler, governor*:—God, staðulfæst steórend, Andr. Kmbl. 2673; An. 1338. Stȳrend, 241; An. 121. Drihten, ealra sceafta reccend and stȳrend, Wulfst. 255, 18. II. *one who corrects, one who reproves*:—Stȳrend *corrector, increpator*, Wrt. Voc. ii. 135, 82. v. steóran.

steórere, es; *m.* *A steerer*:—Hit wǣre swelce se stióra slēpe on midre sǣ . . . Ðæm stiórere biþ gelīcost se mon ðe ongemong ðisses middangeardes costungum hine āgīmeleásaþ, Past. 56, 3; Swt. 431, 31. [*O. H. Ger.* stiurari *gubernator, recuperator.*] v. steóra.

steóres-mann, es; *m.* *A steersman, one who guides a vessel, the captain of a vessel*:—Be ðon ðe mon on scipe bereáfod sȳ. Gif man beó æt his ǣhtan bereáfod, and hē wite of hwilcum scipe, āgyfe steóresman ða ǣhta, L. Eth. ii. 4; Th. i. 286, 17. [Steres-men *rulers of ten men*, Gen. and Ex. 3417. Twelue scipen weoren forloren, þa oðere weoren al todriuen, nes þer na steoresmon þat æuere aht cuðe þer on, Laym. 11985. Þe steoressmann aʒʒ lokeþþ till an steorrne, Orm. 2135. *Swed.* styresman *a chief, ruler.*] v. steór-mann.

steorfa, an; *m.* I. *mortality, pestilence*:—Sceal āspringan wīde and sīde stric and steorfa and fela ungelimpa, Wulfst. 86, 12: 159, 10. Gif hit geweorðe ðæt folce mislimpe þurh here odþon hungor, þurh stric oððe steorfan, L. I. P. 18; Th. ii. 324, 29. II. *flesh of animals that have died a natural death*:—Se ðe steorfan ete *qui morticinam ederit*, L. Ecg. P. iv. 27; Th. i. 212, 3. III. *a place where death has taken place* (?):—Andlang mōres tō sīferþingcsteorfan, Cod. Dip. B. i. 296, 34. [Stala and steorfa swiðe eow scal hene, O. E. Homl. i. 13, 29. *O. Sax.* man-sterbo: *O. H. Ger.* sterbo *pestis, cladis, pestilentia.*] v. fǣr-steorfa.

steorfan; *p.* stearf, *pl.* sturfon; *pp.* storfen *To die*:—Se ðe gelīð raðe hē styrfþ oððe gēnunge hē ārīseþ *he that takes to his bed (on the tenth day of the moon), soon will he die or he will be up again directly*, Lchdm. iii. 188, 21. Gif hrȳðera steorfan, 54, 30. Annanias and Saphira mid fǣrlīcum deáðe ætforan ðām apostolum steorfende āfeóllon, Homl. Th. i. 398, 34. [Se man þe nān gōd ne heafde stærf of hungor, Chr. 1124; Erl. 253, 22. Wrecce men sturuen of hungær, 1137; Erl. 262, 27. Hi sturfe hungre, O. E. Homl. i. 233, 5. Caim starf (*died*), Gen. and Ex. 481. Summe storuen, 2975. Ilc was storuen, 3162. Steruyn̄, *idem quod* deyyn̄, Prompt. Parv. 474, col. 2. *O. Sax.* sterban: *O. L. Ger.* steruan: *O. Frs.* sterva: *O. H. Ger.* sterban.] v. ā-steorfan.

steor-gleáw; *adj.* *Skilled in a knowledge of the stars*:—Steorgleáwra, tuncgelwītegana *mathematicorum*, Hpt. Gl. 467, 75.

steór-leás; *adj.* I. *without restraint, ungovernable, fierce*:—Sió rēþe oððe sió steórleáse *efferra*, Wrt. Voc. ii. 31, 16. II. *without regulation, profligate*:—Ðū cȳþdest ðæt ðū nestest hwelces endes ǣlc angin wilnode ðā ðū wēndest ðæt steórleáse men and rēceleáse wǣron gesǣlige and wealdendas ðisse worulde *quis sit rerum finis, ignoras, nequam homines atque nefarios, potentes felicesque arbitraris*, Bt. 5, 3; Fox 12, 35. III. *without instruction, foolish, ignorant*:—Þeáh hió (*the earth*) unwīsum wīdgel þince, on stede stronglīc steórleásum men, Met. 10, 11. IV. *without rule, not living under rule*:—Gif bescoren man steórleás (*not living under the rule of any religious house*) gange him on gestlīðnesse, L. Wih. 7; Th. i. 38, 12. [Gif þu unel were, iwend þe from uuele, þi les þe ðū steorles losie on ende, O. E. Homl. i. 117, 35. Cf. *Goth.* libands usstiuriba ζῶν ἀσώτως, Lk. 15, 13. *Icel.* stjórn-lauss *unruly.*]

steór-mann, es; *m.* *A steersman, pilot, captain*:—Steórman *gubernio*, Wrt. Voc. i. 56, 18: *gubernator* vel *nauclerus*, 73, 79. Hera ðone steórman ac nā ǣrðan ðe hē become gesundful tō ðære hȳðe, Homl. Th. ii. 560, 22. [Stereman *proreta*, Wrt. Voc. i. 274, col. 2. He nom alle þa scipen and þa steormen alle, Laym. 28436. *Du.* stuur-man: *Icel.* stȳri-maðr *a skipper, captain*: *Dan.* styr-mand *a mate*: *Swed.* styr-man.] v. steóres-mann, steór-rēþra.

steorn (?), e; *f.* *The forehead.* [*O. H. Ger.* stirna *frons.*] v. steornede.

steór-nægl (?), es; *m.* *The handle of a helm*:—Steórsceofol oððe [steór-?]nægl *clavus*, Wrt. Voc. i. 74, 3. [*O. H. Ger.* stiur-nagal *clavus.*]

steornede; *adj. Having a big forehead;* fig. *bold, active*:—Steornede (*the word occurs in a list of adjectives denoting the possession of physical characteristics*) *frontalis* vel *calidus*, Wrt. Voc. i. 45, 36. Steorrede (steornede?) *frontialis*, ii. 38, 55: 151, 25.

Steórnes-healh. v. Streónes-healh.

steór-, stiér-, stȳr-ness, e; *f. Correction, discipline*:—Hine sylfne đreágian mid stȳrnysse đære gāstlīcan steóre, Homl. Th. i. 360, 17. Hwīlon hē gewītnaþ đæs mannes gewitleáste mid stȳrnysse ōđrum tō steóre, Homl. Ass. 62, 259. Stiérnesse *disciplinam*, Ps. Spl. T. 2, 12. [Cf. *O. H. Ger.* stiurida *gubernatio*.]

steór-oxa, an; *m. A steer*:—Steóroxa *anniculus* vel *trio*, Wrt. Voc. i. 23, 41. [*Ger.* stier-ochs *a bull*.]

steorra, an; *m. A star*:—Steorra *stella*, tungel *sidus*, Wrt. Voc. i. 41, 53. Swāna steorra *hesperius*, ii. 43, 39. Se hāra (hāta?) steorra *canis* vel *canicula*, *stella quae Sirius vocatur*, 128, 25. Se steorra đe wē hātaþ Ursa ne cymþ nǽfre on đam westdǽle, þeáh ealle ōþre steorran faren æfter đære sunnan, Bt. 39, 13; Fox 232, 29–32. Se steorra (stearra, Lind.) đe hī on eástdǽle gesāwon, Mt. Kmbl. 2, 9. Steorra, se is cweden *commeta*, Bd. 4, 12; S. 581, 13. Beorhtnes scīnendes steorran, 5, 12; S. 629, 5. Stiorran, Met. 28, 44. Đone beorhtan steorran đe wē hātaþ morgensteorra; đone ilcan wē hātaþ ōþre naman ǽfensteorra, Bt. 4; Fox 8, 2–4. Tācna on steorrum, Lk. Skt. 21, 25. [*O. Frs.* stera: *O. Sax. O. H. Ger.* sterro: *Goth.* stairnō; *f.*: *O. H. Ger.* sterno: *Icel.* stjarna; *f.*] v. ǽfen-, dæg-, heofon-, morgen-, sǽ-, scip-, swān-steorra.

steór-rēđra, an; *m. A steersman, skipper, captain*:—Crist wæs on đæm scipe swā se steórrēþra ... Andreas āstāg on đæt scip and gesæt be đæm steórrēþran, Blickl. Homl. 233, 4, 24: 235, 23. v. steór-mann.

steór-rōđor (-er, -ur), es; *n. A rudder*, lit. and fig.:—Steórrōþer *remus* (an oar used for steering), Wrt. Voc. i. 48, 11. Steórrōđer *palmula*, ii. 67, 68. Steórrōđor, 116, 52. Steórrōþur *gubernaculum*, i. 63, 52. God is steórrōþer and helma *clavus atque gubernaculum*, Bt. 35, 3; Fox 158, 25. God ǽghwæs wealt mid đæm helman and mid đæm stiórrōþre his gōdnesse *Deus omnia bonitatis clavo gubernare credatur*, 35, 4; Fox 160, 15. Steórrōđre (stiór-, Cott. MS.), 35, 5; Fox 164, 28. Swelce se stióra slēpe and forlure đæt stiórrōđur (*clavum*) ... Se dēþ swā se stióra đe đæt stiórrōđor forliésþ, Past. 56, 3; Swt. 431, 30–33. [*O. H. Ger.* stiur-ruodar *gubernaculum, clavus, artemo*.]

steor-sceáwere, es; *m.* I. *an observer of the stars, an astronomer, astrologer*:—Up on đæm rodore đara steorsceáwera *Epicurii*, Wrt. Voc. ii. 32, 4. [Cf. *O. H. Ger.* himil-scouwari *mathematicus*; sterrowartal *magus*.] II. *a constellation* (?):—Steorrscēwere (sceorr-, Wrt.) *constellationem*, Wrt. Voc. ii. 79, 66. v. steor-wigle.

steór-scofl, e; *f. A rudder*:—Steórsceofl *gubernaculum*, Wrt. Voc. i. 56, 46. Steórsceofol *clavus*, 74, 3.

steór-setl, es; *n. The steering-seat, the stern*:—Steórsetl *puppis*, Wrt. Voc. i. 48, 10: 56, 55: 64, 5: Ælfc. Gr. 9, 78; Zup. 75, 12. Scip ođđe steórsetl *puppis*, 9, 28; Zup. 56, 10. Se Hǽlend wearđ on slǽpe on đam steórsetle *erat in puppi dormiens* (Mk. 4, 37), Homl. Th. ii. 378, 17.

steór-stefn, es; *m. The stern, poop*:—Steórstefn *puppis*, Wrt. Voc. ii. 73, 28.

steort, es; *m.* I. *a tail, start* (as in rēd-*start*, one of the names for *ruticilla phoenicurus*, also called fire-tail. *Start*, plough-*start* = plough-*tail*, v. Halliwell's Dict. *Stark*-naked is a corruption of *start*-naked):—Steort *cauda*, Wrt. Voc. ii. 103, 20: 129, 75. Se hālga stert *sacra spina*, i. 283, 50. Đære helle hund ongan fægenian mid his steorte, Bt. 35, 6; Fox 168, 17. Nym hyre (*the adder's*) steort (*caudam*), Ex. 4, 4. Sume wyrmas wǽren and sume fiscas đe hæfden ān heáfod and monigne steort. Đa steortas, hē sǽde, đæt hulpan ealle đæs heáfdes, Shrn. 162, 14–16. II. *a promontory, tongue of land* (cf. *Start* Point in Devon, *Start* Island in the Orkneys):—Andlang weges đæt hit sticaþ on norđeweardum cynges steorte, Cod. Dip. Kmbl. iii. 48, 9. Of đæm weall tō steorte, 464, 25. Be gemǽre đæt on đone steort; of đam steort on đa strǽt, 438, 22. Ōđ đone steort; fram đam steorte andlang đæs fūlan brōces, ii. 250, 22. Cf. Penwiht-steort *the Land's End*, Chr. 997; Erl. 135, 10. [Đe leun drageđ dust wiđ his stert đer he steppeđ, Misc. 1, 9. Stert of an appull, of a handle of a vessel, of a plow, Prompt. Parv. 474, col. 2. See also Cath. Angl. 363, nn. 2, 3. *O. Frs.* stert *tail*: *Du.* staart: *O. H. Ger.* sterz *stiva*: *Ger.* sterz *tail; plough-tail*: *Icel.* stertr *tail*: *Dan.* stjert: *Swed.* stjert *tail; plough-tail*.] v. rysc-steort.

steor-wigle, -wigl (?), es; *n. Prognostication by the stars, astrology*:—Stiorwigle ł mearcunge *constellationem* (cf. *constellatio* leáses spelles talu, Wrt. Voc. ii. 20, 68; and *Span.* constelacion *prognostication of the stars*), stiorwiglu *constellationes*, Hpt. Gl. 467, 78. Stiorwigl (-wiglunge?) *astrologiam*, 528, 64. v. steor-wiglung, wigle.

steor-wiglung, e; *f. Astrology*:—Æfter steorwiglunge *juxta constellationem*, Anglia xiii. 33, 141. v. steor-wigle.

steór-wirđe; *adj. Deserving reprobation*:—Đonne wē hwæthwugu stiórwierđes ongietaþ on đa đe ūs underđiédde bióþ *cum ea quae in subditis arguenda cognoscunt*, Past. 28, 4; Swt. 194, 3.

stēpan; *p.* te *To cause to take a step, to initiate*:—Gistoepid *initiatum*, Wrt. Voc. ii. 112, 2. Gestēped, gehālgodne *initiatum*, 45, 70. Cf. stæppan; *p.* stōp. v. (?) on-stēpan.

stēpan *to bereave*, stēpan *to exalt*, stepe, -stēped, stēpel, stēpness, steppan, steppe-scōh, stēr. v. stīpan *to bereave*, stīpan *to exalt*, stæpe, stēpan, stīpel, stīpness, stæppan, stæppe-scōh, stǽr.

stēran; *p.* de. I. *to cense, burn incense as a sacrifice*:—Aaron stērde mid thimiama, Num. 16, 47. Ozias wolde offrian and stērde æt đam weofode (*Uzziah went into the temple to burn incense upon the altar of incense*, 2 Chron. 26, 16), Homl. Ass. 58, 185. Nim ǽlc his stōrcillan and stēre ætforan Gode, Num. 16, 7. Stþērde (= stērde) *adoleret, sacrificaret*, Hpt. Gl. 509, 59. Stērden *thurificarent*, 513, 69. Tō stȳrenne *ad thurificandum, ad sacrificandum*, 477, 66. II. *to perfume* a person as with incense:—Stēr (stȳr, MS. B.) hyne mid đære wyrte, Lchdm. i. 98, 19: 206, 2. [Þer ne schulen heo helle stenches stinken, þer me schal ham steoren mid guldene chelle, O. E. Homl. i. 193, 45.] v. stōr, stēring.

sterced-ferhþ. v. stærced-ferhþ.

stēring, e; *f. Incense*:—Stēmendre stēringce *fragrantis incensi*, Hpt. Gl. 441, 73. v. stēran.

ster-melda, an; *m.* The word occurs in the following apparently corrupt passage:—Gif frigman mannan forstele gif hē eft cuma stermelda secge an andweardne gecænne hine gif hē mǽge *if a freeman steal a man; if he* (*the man who has been stolen*) *come back to give information of the theft, let him make his charge against the thief when the latter is present; let him* (*the thief*) *clear himself if he can*, L. H. E. 5; Th. i. 28, 10. In the note on this passage *stermelda* is taken as *steórmelda* = delator fiscalis; Schmid, on the other hand, gives the meaning 'delator qui rem, factum (stær) prodit.' Perhaps for *stermelda* might be written *stelmelda*, a sense which has been given in the translation above.

stern, stert, stete, stēþa. v. stearn, steort, stīle, stēda.

stic[c] (?); *adj. Sticky, viscous*:—Wiđ ōmena geberste.... Sleah feówer scearpan ymb đa poccas and lǽt yrnan đæt sticce (*the sticky matter*) đe hit wille, Lchdm. ii. 100, 4.

stic-ādl, e; *f. Stitch, pain in the side*:—Sticwærc, sticādl *telum, i. dolor lateris*, Wrt. Voc. i. 19, 23. v. stice.

sticca, an; *m.* I. *a stick, peg*:—Sticca *gergenna* (*gergenna* lignum teres, quo per duas ansas transmisso operculum firmatur ne excidat, Migne), Wrt. Voc. i. 287, 38: ii. 41, 32. Se sticca (*the tent-peg*) him eode ūt þurh đæt heáfod in tō đære eorþan, Jud. 4, 21. Styre mid sticcan, Lchdm. ii. 76, 26. Genim twegen sticcan feđerecgede and wrīt on ǽgđerne sticcan be hwælcere ecge, i. 386, 4–6. Nim ǽnne sticcan and gnīd tō sumum þinge, iii. 274, 3. I a. *the pointer of a dial*:—Se sticca on đæm dægmǽle, Anglia viii. 317, 20. II. *a spoon* (cf. spōn):—Lǽt yrnan đæt blōd on grēnne sticcan hæslenne, weorp đonne ofer weg āweg, Lchdm. ii. 142, 20: 144, 7: 104, 7. Genim fīf sticcan fulle ecedes, i. 110, 21: iii. 4, 18. Wring đæt wōs of, ānne sticcan fulne, and huniges þrȳ sticcan fulle, 102, 14. Nim wīfes meolce þrȳ sticcæs fulla and cyleþena ānne sticce fulne, 96, 27. [*O. H. Ger.* steccho *palus, paxillus, fustis, clavus*: *Icel.* stika; *f. a stick*.] v. candel-, clader-, geoc-, plant-, regol-, seám-, stōr-, tōþ-sticca.

sticce *sticky matter*. v. stic[c]. Sticce *a piece*. v. stycce.

stice, es; *m.* I. *a prick, puncture, stab, thrust with a pointed implement*:—Se đe ūs gehǽleþ from đæm stice ūrra synna hē geđafode đæt him mon sette đyrnenne beág on đæt heáfud *a peccatorum nos punctionibus salvans spinis caput supponere non recusavit*, Past. 36, 9; Swt. 261, 13. Gif man þeóh þurhstingþ, stice gehwilce .vi. scillingas, L. Ethb. 67; Th. i. 18, 16. II. *a pricking sensation, a stitch*:—Gif stice būtan innođe sié, Lchdm. ii. 274, 28. Wiđ miltewærce and stice, 174, 4. Se hwīta stān mæg wiþ stice, 290, 10. Wiđ eágena hǽtan and stice, i. 352, 5. [Wiđ gestice, 393, 20.] [In his soule he hefde þe stiche of sore pine.... Þeos stiche was þreouold, þet, ase þreo speres smiten him tō þer heorte, A. R. 110, 12–14. Stiches iþi lonke, H. M. 35, 26. Styche, peyne on þe syde *telum*, Prompt. Parv. 475, col. 1. *Goth.* stiks *a point of time*: *O. Frs.* steke *a prick, stab*: *O. H. Ger.* stih[h] *ictus*: *Ger.* stich *a prick, stitch, puncture*: *Dan.* stik *a stab*: *Swed.* stick *a prick, stitch, stab*.] v. fǽr-, in-stice; stic-ādl, *and next word*.

sticel, es; *m. That with which a prick may be given*, (*stickle* in stickle-back; cf. *stickly* prickly, Halliwell's Dict.) *a sting, goad*:—Ōđerne hē drāf mid sticele, ōđrum hē wiđteáh mid bridle *illum stimulo impellere nititur, hunc freno moderatur*, Past. 40, 3; Swt. 293, 1. Hē sǽwþ đone sticel đæs andan *seminantur stimuli*, 38, 7; Swt. 279, 9. Þē mid stīđum āstyrest sticelum gǽlsan *luxuriae stimulis te agitabis acutis*, Dōm. L. 179. Đa gnættas mid swīþe lytelum sticelum hine deriaþ, Bt. 16, 2; Fox 52, 11. Sticelas *ramnos*, Blickl. Gl. [*O. H. Ger.* stihhil *aculeus*: *Icel.* stikill *the pointed end of a horn*.] v. sticels.

sticel; *adj.* v. sticol.

sticels, es; *m. A goad, stimulus, thorn* (lit. and fig.):—Sticels *aculeus*, Wrt. Voc. i. 75, 2. Sticels (*not* sticel) *vel* gādīsen, 15, 15. Mē is geseald sticels mīnes līchaman.... Ic bæd mīnne Drihten đæt hē āfyrrode đæs sceoccan sticels fram mē (*there was given to me a thorn in the *flesh. . . . I besought the Lord, that it might depart from me*, 2 Cor. 12, 7-8), Homl. Th. i. 474, 12-15. Sticelse *stimulo, monitione*, Hpt. Gl. 420, 45. Se yfela gāst hine drehte mid deófollīcum sticelsum, Homl. Skt. i. 18, 10. Sticelsas *rhamnos*, Ps. Spl. 57, 9. v. sticel.

stic-fōd[d]er *a case for pegs* (? v. sticca, I), *a case for spoons* (? v. sticca, II), *a case made of twigs* (? cf. stic-tǣnel):—Man sceal habban . . . sealtfæt, sticfōdder, piperhorn, Anglia ix. 264, 19.

stician; *p.* ode. I. *trans. To stick, stab, pierce, prick*:—Oxa spæc and cwæð: 'Tō hwon sticast ðū mē,' Shrn. 30, 12. Mē on fæðme sticaþ hygegālan hond, Exon. Th. 394, 1; Rä. 13, 11. Hē (*the wounded elephant*) ða ōþre elpendas sticade, Ors. 4, 1; Swt. 156, 13. Gē hyne (*Christ*) myd spere sticodon, Nicod. 13; Thw. 6, 35. Sticedon, Cd. Th. 297, 1; Sat. 510. Stycodon, Shrn. 147, 36. Hī ne mihte þorn stician, 66, 17. Stycigende *stimulosa*, Scint. 104, 6. I a. *to kill* (*to stick* is still used of killing pigs. Cf. sticung, II):—Wē oþþe sticode beóþ oþþe on sǣ ādruncene *aut jugulamur aut mergimur*, Bd. 1, 13; S. 482, 1. Monige fanggene wǣron and heápmǣlum sticode *nonnulli comprehensi acervatim jugulabantur*, 1, 15; S. 484, 5. I b. *to thrust* out (cf. stingan):—Sticode him mon ða eágan ūt *effossis oculis*, Ors. 4, 5; Swt. 168, 4. I c. *intrans.*:—Ðæt mē ongeán sticaþ, Exon. Th. 497, 20; Rä. 87, 3. II. *intrans.* (1) *To stick, remain fixed*:—Ðæs spācan sticaþ ōþer ende on ðære felge, ōþer on ðære nafe, Bt. 39, 7; Fox 222, 7. Lǣt ða sāglas stician ðǣron . . . Ða sāglas sticiaþ eallne weg inn on ðām hringum . . . Simle ða ofergyldan sāglas sceolden stician on ðǣm gyldnum hringum, Past. 22; Swt. 171, 1-22. Mē on hreðre heáfod sticade, Exon. Th. 479, 10; Rä. 62, 5. On ðære rōde sticodon mænige arewan, Chr. 1083; Erl. 217, 21. Sting ðīn seax on ða wyrte, lǣt stician ðǣron, Lchdm. ii. 346, 12, 20: Jud. 3, 22. (2) fig. *to be involved, be prevented from free action, lie encumbered*:—On hū ðióstrum hora seáþe ðara unþeáwa ða yfelwillendan sticiaþ *quanto in coeno probra volvantur*, 37, 2; Fox 188, 2. Sticiaþ gehȳdde beorhte cræftas *latet obscuris condita virtus clara tenebris*, 4; Fox 8, 15. Ðæt ða synfullan sāwla sticien helle tōmiddes, Salm. Kmbl. 344; Sal. 171. (3) *to be inherent*:—Seó godcundnys ðe on ðam men sticode, Homl. Th. ii. 386, 19. (4) *to be in possession* of (of demoniacal possession), *to lurk*:—Deófol ðē sticaþ on *daemonium habes*, Jn. Skt. 7, 20. 'Ðonne gesihst ðū hwæt ðǣron sticaþ' . . . Ðǣr gewende ūt of ðam fæte ān næddre, Homl. Th. ii. 170, 19. Wē bebeódaþ ðām deóflum ðe on ðisum anlīcnyssum sticiaþ, ðæt hī ūt faron, 496, 8. Se apostol cwæð tō ðam āwyrgedan gāste ðe hire on sticode, i. 464, 22. Ða deóflu ðe on ðām anlīcnyssum sticodon, ii. 482, 8. III. of direction, *to run, lie* (cf. sceótan):—Ūt æt ðæs croftes heáfod ðæt sticaþ on ðære lace, Cod. Dip. Kmbl. iii. 37, 24. Andlang weges ðæt hit sticaþ on norðeweardum cynges steorte . . . andlang weges ðæt hit sticaþ æt wīchām, 48, 8-11. Ðonne swā forð ðæt hit sticaþ on miclancumb; and of miclancumbe ðæt hit sticaþ on litlancumb, 405, 30. Ðonne tō ðam wuduwege ðæt hit sticaþ innan Nodre; ðonne andlang Noddre ðæt hit sticaþ on Eatstānes landscare; ðæt hit sticaþ up tō herpoðe, 446, 8-11. Wið sūðan ða mēde ðæt it sticaþ tōemnes ðam wiðigðyfelum, v. 194, 32. [*M. H. Ger. Ger.* stecken *to remain fixed.* Cf. *O. Sax.* stekan; *p.* stak *to pierce, stab*: *O. Frs.* steka: *O. H. Ger.* stehhan; *p.* stah *pungere.*] v. of-, tō-, þurh-stician.

sticol; *adj.* I. *lofty, reaching to a great height*, of a mountain:—'Ic wille standan on ðisum steápum munte' . . . Moyses ðā āstāh tō ðam sticolan munte, Homl. Skt. i. 13, 9-12. Wæs ān myrige dūn . . . fūl smēðe . . . se streám arn of ðære sticolan dūne, 19, 108-115. Hēt hī āstīgan tō ānre sticolre dūne, 3, 235. II. *lofty, placed high, situated at a great height*:—Wē biddaþ ðæt ðū āstīge tō ðam sticelan scylfe, Homl. Th. ii. 300, 1. Martinus āstāh on ðam sticelan hrōfe, 510, 7. Eraclius āstāh tō ðære sticolan upflōra, Homl. Skt. ii. 27, 67. Āstāh heofonan sticole *conscendit caelos arduos*, Hymn. Surt. 89, 8. III. *rough, rugged, difficult, steep* (Halliwell gives *stickle* as a Devonshire word = steep):—Sticol *asper*, Wülck. Gl. 256, 32. Se weig is swīðe nearu and sticol, se ðe lǣt tō heofonan rīce . . . Ðonne māge wē ðurh Godes fultum āstīgan ðone sticolan weg, ðe ūs gelǣt tō ðam ēcan līfe, Homl. Th. i. 162, 23-35. Se weg is rūm and forðheald, ðe tō deáðe lǣt; se is neara and sticol, ðe tō līfe lǣt, R. Ben. 5, 21: Shrn. 12, 19. On wyrmes līc sticoles (*rough, scaly*), Salm. Kmbl. 307; Sal. 153. Be westan rōde ōð sticelan stīg, Cod. Dip. Kmbl. iii. 406, 29. Sticule scylpas *scabri murices*, Germ. 399, 446. III a. *difficult, arduous*:—Sticol *arduam* (*rem*), R. Ben. Interl. 16, 1. [*O. L. Ger.* stecul *confragosus, fragosus, preruptus*: *O. H. Ger.* stechal *arduus, asper, fragosus, praeceps, praeruptus, abruptus.*]

stic-tǣnel *a wicker basket*:—Stictēnel *fiscillus*, Wrt. Voc. ii. 108, 55. Stictǣnel *fiscilus*, 35, 37.

sticung, e; *f.* I. *a pricking, piercing*:—Hié (*the elephants*) fōran wēdende ǣgðer ge for ðæs flexes bryne ge for ðara nægla sticunge, Ors. 4, 1; Swt. 158, 8. II. *sticking* (pigs), *killing*; cf. stician, I a:—On manegum stent ðæt se gafolswān sylle ǣlce geáre .xv. swȳn tō sticunge . . . Gȳme eác swān ðæt hē æfter sticunge his slyhtswȳn wel behweorfe, L. R. S. 6; Th. i. 436, 12-16.

stic-wærc. v. stic-ādl.

stic-wyrt, e; *f. Stitch-wort*; stellaria holostea; but the word glosses *agrimonia*, Wrt. Voc. i. 32, 2.

stiell, stiém, stiép, stiéra, stiéran, stiérness, stiernlīce. v. still, steám, stīþ, steóra, steóran, steórness, stirnlīce.

stīf; *adj. Stiff, unbending, rigid*:—Stīfne *rigentem*, Germ. 394, 272. [He ches stiue here to shurte, O. E. Homl. ii. 139, 16. He (*the dead man*) biþ sone stif, Fragm. Phlps. 5, 45. Stif he wes on þonke, Laym. 2110. Sa strang and stijf in fight, C. M. 18140. Þat plaid (*plea*) was stif and starc and strong, O. and N. 5. *Du.* stijf: *M. H. Ger.* stīf: *Ger.* steif: *Dan.* stiv: *Swed.* styf.] v. stīfian.

stī-ferh. v. stig-fearh.

stīfian; *p.* ode *To be* or *to become stiff*:—Ic stīfige *rigeo*, Ælfc. Gr. 26, 2; Zup. 154, 15. Ic stīfie *obrigesco*, Wrt. Voc. i. 22, 32. Stīfodan *rigebant, durescebant*, Hpt. Gl. 483, 68. v. ā-stīfian.

stīfician. v. stȳfician.

stīg, e; *f. A path* (lit. and fig.), *footpath*, (*narrow*) *way*:—Orweg stīg (*given already as a compound*, orweg-stīg, *but* orweg *should be taken as adjective*) *devia callis*, Wrt. Voc. ii. 139, 57. Horweg stīg, 25, 25. Horuaeg stiig, Txts. 56, 340. Strǣt wæs stānfāh, stīg wīsode gumum ætgædere, Beo. Th. 646; B. 320: 4433; B. 2213: Andr. Kmbl. 1970; An. 987. Eástewearde andlang weges on hemlēclēge; eástewearde andlang stīge on Ulfan treów, Cod. Dip. Kmbl. iii. 437, 4. Of Heortwyllan on ða ealdan stīge; ðæt andlang stīge, 438, 34. Leóht stīge mīnre *lumen semitis meis*, Ps. Th. 118, 105. Stīge *calce* (*calle?*), Wrt. Voc. ii. 15, 66: 95, 74. Gebīgdre stīge *flexo tramite*, 149, 46: Hpt. Gl. 493, 18. Fram stīge *tramite, via*, 486, 68. Tō rihtre stīge geteón *ad rectum tramitem revocare*, Bd. 5, 9; S. 623, 13: 1, 12; S. 481, 8. Ðū nā forfleó [weg] hǣle se ðe nis būton mid stīge tō onginnenne *non refugias viam salutis que non est nisi angusto initio incipienda*, R. Ben. Interl. 6, 8. Be westan rōde ōð sticelan stīg; ðonne be ðære stīge ōð ða eáldan dīc, Cod. Dip. Kmbl. iii. 406, 29. Of ðam stāne tō ðære grēnan stīge, 38, 23. Ðȳlæs ða gongen on suā frēcne stīge ða ðe ne māgon uncwaciende gestondan on emnum felda *ne, qui in planis stantes titubant, in praecipiti pedem ponant*, Past. 4, 2; Swt. 41, 7. Geseoh nū seolfes swæðe, swā ðīn swāt āgeát, blōdige stīge, Andr. Kmbl. 2883; An. 1444. Stīga ðīne *semitae tuae*, Ps. Spl. 76, 19. Stīge (*semitas*) ðīne lǣr mē, Ps. Surt. 24, 4. Gif se nīðsceaþa nearwe stīge mē on swaþe sēceþ *if the foe seek narrow paths in my track*, Exon. Th. 397, 24; Rä. 16, 24. Steáp stānhliðo, stīge nearwe, enge ānpaðas, Beo. Th. 2823; B. 1409. [We sculde makien his stiȝes, O. E. Homl. i. 7, 1. He sende bi stiȝen (weies, 2nd MS.) and by straten, Laym. 16366. Þiss Lamb iss þatt rihhte stih, Orm. 12916. Rihhteþþ Drihhtiness narrwe stiȝhess, 9202. Sty, by pathe *semita, callis*, Prompt. Parv. 475. v. in Halliwell's Dict. *stie*, and cf. *Stye*-head, the pass from Borrowdale to Wastdale. *O. H. Ger.* stīga *semita, trames, callis*: *Icel.* stīgr; *m. a path, footway.* Cf. *Goth.* staiga *a path.*] v. medu-, mylen-stīg; stīga.

stig (?), es; *n. A wooden enclosure, a sty*; but also part of a house, *a hall* (?) cf. stig-weard:—Gif cniht binnan stig sitte *if a servant sit within the hall* (?), Chart. Th. 612, 32. Stigo *vistrina* (*suestrina?* the word occurs at the head of a list 'de suibus'), Wrt. Voc. i. 286, 41. Stigu *auriola* (*oriola?* oriolum *porticus, atrium*, Migne), Txts. 38, 45. Cf. (?) forestige *vestibulum, introitum*, Hpt. Gl. 514, 59. Ondlong herpoðes on burghardes ānstigo; ðonne forð tō bāres ānstigon, Cod. Dip. Kmbl. ii. 172, 18. [Ase swin ipund ine sti, A. R. 128, 1. Stye *ara*, Wrt. Voc. i. 178, 14. Sty, swynys howus *ara, porcarium*, Prompt. Parv. 475. Þenk on helle stynkyng stye, H. R. 215, 3. Cf. *O. H. Ger.* stīga; *f. cancelli, ara, ovile*: *Ger.* steige; *f. hen-coop*: *Icel.* stía; *f. a kennel*; svína-stí pig-*sty*: *Dan.* stī *enclosure for swine, sheep, hens, etc.*: *Swed.* stia; *f. sty for pigs, geese, etc.*] v. stigian.

stīga (?), an; *m.*: stīge (?), an; *f. A path*:—Faestin *vel* ānstīgan, festin (-s, MS.) *vel* ānstīga *termofilas*, Txts. 104, 1042. v. stīg.

stīgan; *p.* stāh, *pl.* stigon; *pp.* stigen. I. *intrans. To go* (1) without implying ascent or descent:—Seó sunne stīgþ on ða dæglan wegas wið hire uprynæs, *Phoebus secreto tramite currum solitos vertit ad ortus*, Bt. 25; Fox 88, 26. Of stīges *discedite*, Mt. Kmbl. Lind. 25, 41. Alle stīgende (*discedentes*) from rehtwīsnissum, Ps. Surt. 118, 118. (2) implying ascent, *to go* from a lower to a higher level, *to ascend, mount*:—Sió sunne ofer moncyn stīhþ ā upweardes, Met. 13, 69. Bryne stīgeþ heáh tō heofonum, Exon. Th. 233, 6; Ph. 520. Hālge gǣstas stīgaþ tō wuldre, 234, 19; Ph. 542. Rēcas stīgaþ ofer hrōfum, 381, 5; Rä. 2, 6: Ps. Th. 73, 22. Stigon ða þornas *ascenderunt spinae*, Mk. Skt. 4, 7. Sǣs up stigon ofer stæðweallas, Cd. Th. 83, 6; Gen. 1375. Ic wilnige ðæt ðeós sprǣc stigge on ðæt ingeðonc ðæs leorneres suǣ suǣ on sume hlǣdre, Past. proem.; Swt. 23, 16. Ǣrðon up stige āncenned sunu, Exon. Th. 29, 17; Cri. 464. Sweart racu stīgan onginneþ, Cd. Th. 82, 1; Gen. 1355. Gesēgon hī on heáhþu hlāford stīgan, Exon. Th. 31, 20; Cri. 498: Shrn. 50, 15. Ðæt scip wile hwīlum stīgan ongeán ðone streám (*contra ictum fluminis conscendere*), Past. 58, 7; Swt. 445, 10. Gē geseóþ Godes englas up stīgende (*ascendentes*), Jn. Skt. 1, 51. (2 a) of getting into a vessel, etc., climbing a tree, etc.:—Hē stāh up on ān treów *ascendit in arborem*, Lk. Skt. 19, 4.

Ðā stāh hē on scip *ascendit navem*, Bd. 5, 9; S. 623, 27. Beornas on stefn stigon, Beo. Th. 429; B. 212. In ceól stigon, Andr. Kmbl. 697; An. 349. Ðā gē on holm stigon, 858; An. 429. Leóde on wang stigon *they landed*, Beo. Th. 456; B. 225. Ǣr hē on bed stige, 1357; B. 676. Stīgan on wægn, Exon. Th. 404, 16; Rä. 23, 8. Hēt hē ǣnne mon stīgan on ðone mæst (*adscendere in arborem navis*), Ors. 4, 10; Swt. 202, 2. (3) Where the movement is downwards, *to descend*:—Ne stīhþ hē nyðer *ne descendat*, Lk. Skt. 17, 31. Ða stīgaþ on helle *in infernum descenderent*, Past. 55, 2; Swt. 429, 26. Ðā stāh and com smylte reng, Bd. 4, 13; S. 582, 34. Hié on sund stigon *they went down into the bed of the Red Sea*, Cd. Th. 198, 8; Exod. 319. Stīh ādūn *descend*, Homl. Th. i. 580, 33. Ne stīge hē on his hūs *non descendat in domum*, Mk. Skt. 13, 15. Ðæt engel ufan of roderum stīgan cwōme, Cd. Th. 248, 8; Dan. 510. Niþer stīgende, of dūne stīgende *descendentem*, Mt. Kmbl. 3, 16: Jn. Skt. 1, 51. II. *trans. To ascend, mount*:—Heáhlond stigon sibgemāgas, Cd. Th. 202, 9; Exod. 385. Stealc hliþo stīgan, Exon. Th. 498, 18; Rä. 88, 3. [The verb remained long in English and is used by Spenser: 'Ambition, rash desire to *sty*,' F. Q. ii. 7, 46. *Goth.* steigan: *O. Sax. O. L. Ger. O. H. Ger.* stīgan: *Du.* stijgen: *Ger.* steigen: *O. Frs.* stīga: *Icel.* stīga: *Dan.* stige: *Swed.* stiga.] v. ā-, fore-, ge-, ofer-stīgan.

stige, es; *m. A going up* or *down*:—Drihtnes stige on heofonas up, Menol. Fox 129; Men. 64. v. niþer-, up-stige.

stigel, e; *f. A stile, set of steps for getting over a fence*:—Fram ðam wōn stocce tō cinta stiogole; ðanne fram cinta stiogole tō earnes beáme, Cod. Dip. Kmbl. ii. 73, 24. Stigole, iii. 227, 19. Stigele, 236, 25: v. 40, 6, 7, 10: 148, 1. Tō ðære stigelæ tō ðæs bisceopæs mearcæ, 84, 13, 16. Of ðam seáðe in ða eáldan stihle; of ðære stihle, iii. 386, 17–18. The word occurs also in compounds:—Ðanon on ðone bōchagan wið ðere bōcstigele, v. 70, 27. [Ryght as they wolde han troden ouer a style, Chauc. Pard. T. 712. Style, where men gon over *scansillum, scansile*, Prompt. Parv. 475, col. 2. *O. H. Ger.* stiglia *a postern*; posticium.]

stigel-hamm, es; *m. An enclosure reached by a stile* (?):—On stigelhammas; of stigealhammum on wīgferðes leáge, Cod. Dip. Kmbl. v. 289, 2.

stīgend, es; *m. A sty, a small tumour on the edge of the eyelid*:—Stīgend *ordeolus* (= *hordeolus*), Wrt. Voc. i. 20, 11. [Cf. *Norweg.* stig, sti, stigje.]

stīgend, stīgendlīc, stigenness. v. ā-, on-stīgend, ofer-stīgendlīc, ofer-, upā-stigenness.

stig-fearh *a young pig to keep in a sty*:—Ǣhteswāne gebyreþ stīfearh, L. R. S. 7; Th. i. 436, 22.

stigian *to shut up in a sty* or *pen*:—Oððe ic stigie, nyttes bicge, Salm. Kmbl. 402; Sal. 202. Swȳn stigian, Anglia ix. 262, 2. [*Icel.* stīa *to pen* sheep.] v. stig.

stīgness, e; *f. A going down, a descent*:—Tō stīgnisso *ad descensum*, Lk. Skt. Lind. 19, 37.

stigo. v. stig.

stig-rāp, es; *m. A stirrup*:—Stigrāp *scansile*, Wrt. Voc. i. 84, 1. Stīrāp, 23, 17. (In each case the word occurs in a list of words connected with riding.) Stīrāpas *scansilia*, 41, 34. [*O. H. Ger.* stega-reif: *Ger.* steg-reif: *Icel.* stig-reip.]

stigu. v. stig.

stigul, Wrt. Voc. i. 26, 45, *read* sāgul.

stig-weard, es; *m.* I. *a steward* (v. stig), *one who has the superintendence of household affairs; especially matters connected with the table.* [The word, which is found generally with the form *stī-ward* and in late documents, occurs in Eadred's will, and in a connection which seems to shew the relative importance of the officer denoted by it. The king leaves to the archbishop 240 mancuses, to bishops and aldermen 120, to every *discðegn, hræglðegn*, and *biriele* 80, to every *stigweard* 30: Ðænne an ic ǣlcan gesettan stigweard þritig mancusa goldes, Cod. Dip. B. iii. 75, 34.]:—Stīward *economus*, Wrt. Voc. i. 28, 13. Stīweard *discoforus, discifer*, ii. 140, 74. Ðat lond ðat Godrīc mīne stīward haueþ . . . Ælfwȳ mīn stīward . . . Ælfnōð mīn stīward, Cod. Dip. Kmbl. iv. 268, 28–31. Se wæs ðæs eorles stīward, Chr. 1093; Erl. 229, 6: 1096; Erl. 233, 6. Se ðe mā manne in lǣde ðonne hē sceolde būton ðæs stīwerdes leáfe and ðæra feormera, Cod. Dip. Kmbl. iv. 278, 20. Mīna cnihtas ða mīna stīwardas witan, 59, 1. II. fig. *a steward, guardian*:—Mē þincþ betere ðæt ic forlēte ða gyfe and folgyge ðam gyfan ðe mē ēgðer ys stīward ge ðas welan ge eác hys freónscypes, Shrn. 176, 20. [Numbert, kinges stiward (*he is called* aldermon, l. 1420), Laym. 1451. Luue is heouene stiward, uor hire muchele ureoschipe, uor heo ne ethalt no þing, auh heo giueð al þet heo haueð, A. R. 386, 26. He (*the king*) called Aþelbrus, þat was stiward of his hus, Havel. 666. Putifar ðe kinges stiward, Gen. and Ex. 1991. *Icel.* stī-varðr (*from English*).] v. next word.

stig-wita, an; *m. An officer of a household* (v. stig):—Ða ðe Sodoma and Gomorra golde berōfan bestrudon stigwitum *those who robbed Sodom and Gomorrah of gold, despoiled their houses of officers*, Cd. Th. 125, 14; Gen. 2079. Weallas beofiaþ ofer stīwitum *the walls tremble above the household*, Exon. Th. 383, 13; Rä. 4, 10. v. preceding word.

stihtan; *p.* te. I. *to dispose, arrange, regulate, direct, rule*:—Ic stihte (*disposui*) gekȳþnysse mīnum gecorenum, Ps. Lamb. 88, 4. Stapas on his heortan hē stihte *ascensiones in corde suo disposuit*, 83, 6. On ðam ān and twentigan geáre ðæs ðe Willelm weólde and stihte Engleland, Chr. 1086; Erl. 219, 27. II. *to instigate, incite*:—Stihte hī Byrhtnōð, bæd ðæt hyssa gehwylc hogode tō wīge, Byrht. Th. 135, 34; By. 127. Ic heó tō þeófendum and tō geflitum stihte, Wulfst. 255, 12. [*Du.* stichten: *O. H. Ger.* stiften *componere, concinnare*: *Icel.* stētta *to found, establish*.] v. ā-, fore-, ge-stihtan; stihtian.

stihtend, es; *m. A disposer, ruler*:—Þȳstra stihtend (*the devil*), Exon. Th. 267, 23; Jul. 419. v. next word.

stihtere, es; *m. A disposer, director*:—Ðæt hié geornlīce geðencen mid hū micelre giefe ofer him wacaþ se Scippend and se stihtere ealra gesceafta ðonne hē hī nyle lǣtan tō hiera āgnum wilnungum *ut sollicita consideratione perpendant, Creator dispositorque cunctorum quanta super eos gratia vigilat, quos in sua desideria non relaxat*, Past. 50, 4; Swt. 391, 22.

stihtian; *p.* ode *To dispose, arrange, order, ordain, rule*:—Stihtaþ word his in dōme *disponet sermones suos in judicio*, Ps. Surt. 111, 5. Suīðe ryhte stihtaþ ðone anwald se ðe geornlīce conn ongietan ðæt hē of him gadrige ðæt him stælwierðe sié *potentiam bene regit, qui tenere illam noverit*, Past. 17, 5; Swt. 115, 2. Hē ealle gesceafta þurh his godcunde meht and þurh his ēcean snyttro æfter his willan receþ and stihtaþ, Blickl. Homl. 121, 16. Settaþ ða tō dōmerum, ðæt hié stihtien ymb ða eorðlican ðing (*ut dispensationibus terrenis inserviant*), Past. 18, 2; Swt. 131, 8. Ðȳ upplīcan dōme stihtigende *superno dispensante judicio*, Bd. 4, 3; S. 567, 7. v. fore-, ge-stihtian; stihtan.

stihtung, e; *f. A disposition, arrangement, dispensation*:—Wæs ðæt wunderlīco stihtungc ðære godcundan foreseónesse *mira divinae dispensatio provisionis erat*, Bd. 5, 22; S. 644, 36. Hit wæs sweotole gesiéne, ðæt hit wæs Godes stihtung, Ors. 6, 1; Swt. 252, 29. Eal seó stihtung wæs gefremed on ðære sōþan onflǣscnesse for gefyllnesse ðæs heofonlīcan ēþles, Blickl. Homl. 81, 28. Wæs ðæs deóplīc eall word and wīsdōm and ðæs weres stihtung, Exon. Th. 169, 34; Gū. 1104. Mid wunderlīcre stihtunge (*dispensatione*) ðære godcundan ārfæstnesse, Bd. 5, 22; S. 644, 11: 4, 29; S. 607, 42: Guthl. 2; Gdwin. 10, 20. Þurh godcunde stihtunge ðære ēcan eádignysse him wǣre seó gifu forestihtod, 1; Gdwin. 10, 11: Bd. 5, 13; S. 633, 26. v. ā-, fore-, ge-stihtung.

stīlan; *p.* de; *pp.* ed *To steel, temper, harden*:—Sum mæg stȳled sweord, wǣpen gewyrcan, Exon. Th. 42, 28; Cri. 679. [Þat istelet (istelede, Bodl. MS.) irn tolimede hire, Jul. 58, 8. *Icel.* stæla *to steel, temper*; sverð stælt mēð eitri *a sword tempered with poison*; cf. eitri herðr: *Germ.* stählen.]

stīle, es; *n. Steel*:—Stēli, steeli, stēl *accearium*, Txts. 37, 55. Staeli *ocearium*, 81, 1431. Stete *acerra* (? stēle *acearium*), Wrt. Voc. ii. 95, 56. Stȳle *accearium*, 4, 29: 63, 34. Þeáh mec heard bīte stīðecg stȳle, Exon. Th. 499, 11; Rä. 88, 14. Flinte ic eom heardra, ðe ðis fȳr drīfeþ of ðissum strongan stȳle heardan, 426, 26; Rä. 41, 79. Stȳle gelīcost, Beo. Th. 1975; B. 985. Heó oferbīdeþ stānas, heó oferstīgeþ stȳle, Salm. Kmbl. 600; Sal. 299. [*Laym. A. R.* stel: *O. H. Ger.* stahal: *Icel.* stāl.]

stīl-ecg; *adj. Steel-edged*:—Stīð and stȳlecg (*a sword*), Beo. Th. 3070; B. 1533.

stīlen; *adj. Of steel, hard as steel*:—Ðære stȳlenan helle, Salm. Kmbl. 978; Sal. 490. Ne mihte ic of ðære heortan heardne āðringan stȳlenne stān, 1009; Sal. 506. [Wæs þe stelene brond swiðe brad and swiðe long, Laym. 7634. The stilen swerde, Parten. 256. *O. Frs.* stēlen: *O. H. Ger.* stēlin *ex calibe*.].

still, stiell, es; *m. A leap, spring*:—Cyning engla munt gestylleþ, gehleápeþ hyllas . . . woruld ālȳseþ þurh þone æþelan styll. Wæs se forma hlȳp . . . wæs se ōðer stiell . . . se þridda hlȳp . . . se feórða stiell, Exon. Th. 45, 7–33; Cri. 715–728. v. stellan *to leap*.

stillan *to leap*. v. stellan.

stillan *to stall* [:—Hrȳðer anstyllan, swīn stigian, Anglia ix. 262, 1].

stillan; *p.* de. I. *to become still* or *calm*:—Ðā stylde se storm sōna, and seó sǣ wearð eft smylte, Shrn. 147, 9. Se æðeling hēt streámfare stillan, stormas restan, Andr. Kmbl. 3150; An. 1578: Salm. Kmbl. 796; Sal. 397. II. *to make still* or *calm, to still, pacify, appease, assuage* (with dat. or acc.):—Ðæt stilþ ðam sāre, Lchdm. ii. 60, 5. Ðæt swēte word gemanigfealdaþ mannes freóndscipe and stilleþ mannes feónd, Salm. Kmbl. p. 206, 2: Salm. Kmbl. 268; Sal. 133. Cyning (*Christ*) ȳðum stilde, wæteres wælmum, Andr. Kmbl. 902; An. 451. Ðæt se ðām ōmum stille, Lchdm. ii. 182, 6. Beóþ ða elcran tō stillanne, 178, 14. [*O. Sax.* stillōn *to become quiet*; stillian *to make quiet*: *O. H. Ger.* stillēn *stupere, silere*: stillen *compescere, mitigare, mederi*: *Icel.* stilla *to still, calm, soothe, moderate*.] v. æt-, ge-, un-stillan; stillian.

stille; *adj. Still, quiet.* I. in a physical sense, (1) of motion, (a) *without motion, at rest, not moving from a place, not disturbed*:—Seó sunne stōd stille ānes dæges lencge, Lchdm. iii. 262, 8. Swā hē stille stande, ðǣr hine storm ne mæg āwecgan, Andr. Kmbl. 1003; An. 502. Stille on wīcum siteþ, Exon. Th. 390, 26; Rä. 9, 7. Stille þynceþ lyft, 383, 14; Rä. 4, 10: 387, 5; Rä. 4, 74. Se monlīca (*the* *pillar of salt*) stille wunode, Cd. Th. 155, 3; Gen. 2567. Wundum stille *motionless from wounds*, Beo. Th. 5653; B. 2830. Stānas sint stilre gecynde and heardre, Bt. 34, 11; Fox 150, 24. Seó sǣ ne mōt heore mearce gebrǣdan ofer ða stillan eorþan, 21; Fox 74, 28. Twegen steorran standaþ stille, Lchdm. iii. 270, 17. Wit be ðisse strǣte stille þencaþ bīdan, Cd. Th. 147, 9; Gen. 2436. Hī nȳdde se tōwarda winter ðæt hī stille wunodon swā hwǣr swā hī mihton *coegerat eos imminens hiems ut ubicumque potuissent quieti manerent*, Bd. 4, 1; S. 564, 39. Ðȳ læs fyrhtu stille (*quietos*) āwecce, Ps. Surt. ii. p. 202, 19. His wyrtruman wesan stille on staðole, Cd. Th. 251, 9; Dan. 561. *And fig.*:—Gif hē ne wolde lǣtan wræce stille, Exon. Th. 114, 10; Gū. 170. (b) *moving little* or *gently*:—Se man sceal swīþe stille beón *the patient must move about as little as possible*, Lchdm. ii. 148, 25. Oft stille wæter staðo brecaþ (cf. *still waters run deep*), Prov. Kmbl. 63. (c) *not easily moved* (?), *that will not run freely* (?):—Wǣte þicce and stille, Lchdm. ii. 138, 13. (2) of sound, (a) *silent*:—Deáh ðū stille sȳ and unrōt *though thou be silent and sad*, Ap. Th. 15, 17. Se fæder hit gemǣnde stille *pater rem tacitus considerabat*, Gen. 37, 11. Hē hēt ða Saducēiscan stylle beón *silentium inposuisset Sadducaeis*, Mt. Kmbl. 22, 34. *And fig.*:—Mid heortan stilre *corde tacito*, Hymn. Surt. 132, 30. Wēn is ðæt eówer sum cweðe tō him sylfum on stillum geðohtum . . ., Homl. Th. i. 580, 5. (b) *not loud*:—Mid stylre stemne, Homl. Th. ii. 410, 20. II. *quiet, unchanging, undisturbed, stable*:—Ðū ðe unstilla āgna gesceafta tō ðīnum willan wīslīce āstyrest and ðē self wunast swīðe stille unāwendendlīc ā forð simle *stabilis manens das cuncta moveri*, Met. 20, 16. III. *quiet, not vehement, gentle*:—Heó wæs on eallum þingum eáðmōd and stille, Lchdm. iii. 430, 3. Ne āstyrige gē ðone stillan Drihten tō ǣnigre yrsunge, Homl. Th. i. 592, 3. Tō hwæm lōcige ic būton tō ðǣm eáðmōdum and tō ðǣm stillum *ad quem respiciam, nisi ad humilem et quietum?* Past. 41, 1; Swt. 299, 20. IV. *abstaining* from, *quit* of. v. stillness, IV:—Sió hē stille his þegnungæ ōð biscopes dōm, L. Wih. 6; Th. i. 38, 11. [*O. Frs.* stille: *O. Sax.* stilli: *O. H. Ger.* stilli *quietus, tranquillus, serenus, immobilis, mitis, placidus.*] v. un-stille.

stillian. v. un-stillian; stillan.

stillness, e; *f. Stillness, quiet*; quies, Ælfc. Gr. 9, 27; Zup. 53, 9. I. in a physical sense, *absence of noise* or *disturbance*:—On ðisse tīde nihtlīcre stillnesse *tempore isto nocturno quietis*, Bd. 4, 25; S. 601, 1. Windum stilnesse bebeódan, Blickl. Homl. 177, 17. Ðonne (*in church*) lǣrþ ūs Godes engel stilnesse and gemetlīce sprǣce . . . lǣrþ ūs se deófol unstilnesse and ungemetlīce hleahtras and unnytte sprǣce, Wulfst. 233, 13–18. II. *quiet, silence*:—Stilnysse *taciturnitatis*, Hpt. Gl. 455, 54. Swīgan ł stilnysse *taciturnitatem*, 503, 63. Hē mid stilnesse (*cum silentio*) his līf geendode, Bd. 4, 24; S. 599, 7. III. *absence of disturbance* or *molestation, tranquillity, peace, security*:—Stilnys *securitas, requies* ł *quietudo*, Hpt. Gl. 451, 43. Hē on ðære gewunelīcan stilnesse Drihtne lifde *solito in silentio vacare Domino coepit*, Bd. 5, 9; S. 623, 31. Ðā hæfde Hannibal and Rōmāne ān geár stilnesse (*quies a tumultu bellorum*) him betweónum . . . On ðære stilnesse Scipia geeode ealle Ispanie, Ors. 4, 10; Swt. 198, 34. Ðū eart nū of ðīnre stilnesse āhworfen, Bt. 7, 1; Fox 16, 24. Gif wē ða stilnesse habbaþ, Past. pref.; Swt. 7, 9. Habbaþ eów stilnysse and sibbe, Homl. Th. i. 592, 6. Ða stylnysse middaneardlīcere sibbe wē āwendaþ tō ȳdelre orsorhnysse, ii. 540, 7. IV. *abstinence* from, *exemption* from. v. stille, IV:—Ðā ðā hē lǣrde ðæt ðære ciricean ðegnas sceoldon stilnesse ðæra ðēnunga habban (*be exempt from secular services*, cf. 129, 10), Past. 18; Swt. 130, 4. V. *that which appeases* (? cf. *O. Frs.* stilnese *nursing*: *Ger.* still-amme *wet-nurse*: *Swed.* stilla *to give fodder to cattle; to suckle a child*):—Stilnesse, gefylnesse *supplemento* (*supplementum* viaticum, subsidium ad vitae necessaria, Migne), Wrt. Voc. ii. 77, 9. [*O. H. Ger.* stilnissi *tranquillitas, silentium.*] v. un-stillness.

stīman, stēman, stȳman; *p.* de *To emit a scent* or *vapour, exhale*:—Ic stēme *oleo*, Ælfc. Gr. 26, 1; Zup. 153, 2. Stēmþ *exalet*, i. *redolet, spiret, fetet*, Wrt. Voc. ii. 144, 42: *fragrat, odorat, odorem dat*, 150, 34. Willsele stȳmeþ swētum swæccum, Exon. Th. 212, 21; Ph. 213. Stēmde *redolet*, Hpt. Gl. 516, 41. Unāsecgendlīc brǣð stēmde of hire gyrlum, Homl. Th. i. 444, 11: Homl. Skt. ii. 27, 110. Ne mihte nān wyrtbrǣð swā wynsumlīce stēman, 27, 113. Ðū stēmenda *redolens*, Hymn. Surt. 47, 22. Stēmendre *fragrantis, odorantis*, Hpt. Gl. 441, 72. Stēmendes swæcces *nardi pistici*, 516, 38. Stēmende *fragrantia*, 419, 52. Stēmendum *fumigabundis*, 516, 30. Stēmende *olentes, odorantes*, Wrt. Voc. ii. 150, 35. v. be-stēman, -stȳman.

stīme (?) *a name given to a plant in* Lchdm. iii. 32, 19:—Stīme hǣtte ðeós wyrt, heó on stāne geweóx. Cockayne says *water-cress*, in the note to the passage, but *nettle* in his glossary. Perhaps the alternative reading *stune* is the better, as it is said of the plant: stunaþ heó wærce . . . wiðstunaþ heó āttre.

stīming, e; *f. Fragrance*:—Stēmincge *fragrantia*, Hpt. Gl. 516, 40. Stēmingce *fragrantiam, odorem*, 488, 28.

stinan (?); *p.* stan, *pl.* stānon; *pp.* stunen *To make a loud noise* [:—Grānode *vel* āsten (āstēnde? v. stēnan) *rugiebam* (Ps. 37, 9), Blickl. Gl.]. v. stunian.

stincan; *p.* stanc, *pl.* stuncon; *pp.* stuncen *To emit a smell* or *vapour, exhale*, (1) where the kind of smell is not marked:—Stincþ *fragrat*, i. *odorat*, i. *odorem dat*, Wrt. Voc. ii. 150, 34. Stanc *exalavit*, 29, 62. Stonc, 107, 54. Swā hȳ swȳþost stincen *give out the strongest smell*, Lchdm. i. 206, 8. Ðæs stincendan *fumigabundi*[s], Wrt. Voc. ii. 37, 20: 86, 40. Ðære stincendan *spirantis*, 75, 51. Stincende *fragrans*, 35, 73: 74, 65. Stincendi, 108, 76. (2) where the smell is a pleasant one:—Ic stince swōte *oleo*, Ælfc. Gr. 37; Zup. 220, 13. Swecca swētast, swylce on sumeres tīd stincaþ wyrta geblōwene, Exon. Th. 178, 22; Gū. 1248. Stanc *redolet*, Hpt. Gl. 516, 41. Se līchoma stanc swā swōte, Shrn. 143, 28: 140, 13: Homl. Skt. i. 4, 347. (3) where the smell is an unpleasant one:—Hē stingð (stincð, MSS. B. C.) *faetet*, Jn. Skt. 11, 39. Ðæt oreð stincþ and āfūlaþ ðe ǣr wæs swēte on stence, Wulfst. 148, 7. Se līchoma stincþ fūle, Lchdm. ii. 236, 14: 220, 6. Stinceþ, Exon. Th. 424, 1; Rä. 41, 32. Ongan se cealc mid ungemete stincan; ðā wearð hē mid ðæm brǣþe ofsmorod, Ors. 6, 32; Swt. 288, 1. Him stōd stincende steám of ðam mūðe, Homl. Th. i. 86, 13, 10. Stingendum *putenti*, Hpt. Gl. 487, 64. [*O. H. Ger.* stinchan *odorem dare, odorare, fragrare, putere.*] v. ge-, tō-stincan; fūl-, swīð-, wel-stincende; swōt-stencende; cf. stīman.

stincan; *p.* stanc, *pl.* stuncon *To spring, leap, move rapidly*:—Dust stonc tō heofonum, deáw feól on eorþan, Exon. Th. 412, 10; Rä. 30, 12. Se wyrm stonc æfter stāne, Beo. Th. 4565; B. 2288. [*Goth.* stigkwan withra *to proceed against*: *Icel.* stökkva *to spring, leap, take to flight.*] v. stencan.

sting, es; *m.* I. *a sting, stab, thrust made with a pointed instrument; the wound made by a stab* or *sting*:—Beslōh se þorn on ðone fōt and swā strang wæs se sting ðæs þornes ðæt hē eode þurh ðone fōt *the prick of the thorn was so hard, that the thorn went through the foot*, Guthl. 16; Gdwin. 68, 3. Lilla sette his līchoman beforan ðam stynge (*ante ictum pungentis*), Bd. 2, 9; S. 511, 24. Wið scorpiones stincg, Lchdm. i. 168, 3: 248, 21. Wið scorpiones stincg, genim ðās ylcan wyrte . . . lege tō ðam stinge (cf. lege tō ðære wunde, 168, 7), 272, 22–24. II. v. in-, on-sting; stingan, I a.

stingan; *p.* stang, *pl.* stungon; *pp.* stungen. I. *to thrust* something into:—Sting ðīn seax on ða wyrte, Lchdm. ii. 346, 12. Stingaþ stranglīc sār on his eágan, Wulfst. 141, 4. Nim ān feðere, and stynge on hys mūðe, Lchdm. iii. 130, 17. Wæs on slǣpe ætȳwed ðæt hyre man stunge āne sȳle on ðone bōsum, Shrn. 149, 1. Crist hēt stingan sweord in scǣðe, Charter quoted by Lye. I a. fig. *to thrust* one's self into the affairs of another, *to exercise authority*. v. in-, on-sting:—Nā stinge nān mann on ðæt land, būton se hȳred æt Xp̄es cyrcean, Chart. Th. 578, 6. Ic habbe ðæt geleornod, ðæt nān lǣwede man nāh mid rihte tō stingan hine on ānre ciricean, nā an ān ðara ðinga ðe tō cyrcan belimpþ. And for ðī wē forbeódaþ eallan lǣwedan mannum ǣure ǣnne hlāuordscipe ouer cyrcan, Cod. Dip. B. i. 137, 24. (Cf. *Icel.* þū hefir mjök stungizk til þessa māls *thou hast meddled much with this case.*) II. *to prick* with something, *to sting, stab, pierce*:—Swā swā seó beó sceal losian, ðonne heó hwæt yrringa stingþ, Bt. 31, 2; Fox 112, 26. Stingeþ, Met. 18, 7. [Wyrm] stingeþ niéten, Salm. Kmbl. 308; Sal. 153. Hē mid gāre stang wlancne wīcing, Byrht. Th. 135, 55; By. 138. Stincge *transfigat*, Anglia xiii. 37, 276. Gif þorn stinge man on fōt, Lchdm. ii. 336, 20. Gif hine beón stingen, iii. 168, 13. Se lǣce his seax hwæt, ǣrðonðe hē stingan wille, Past. 26; Swt. 187, 6. Se cāsere hine hēt stingan mid īrenum gyrdum, Shrn. 115, 24. Stingaþ hyne mid sāre on his eágan, L. E. I. prm.; Th. ii. 398, 19. [*Goth.* us-stiggan *to thrust out*: *Icel.* stinga *to sting, stick, stab.*] v. ā-, be-, ge-, of-, on-, tō-, þurh-, under-stingan.

stintan, stiōp, stiór, stiorc. v. styntan, steóp, steór, stirc.

stīp, stiép, es; *m. Deprivation* (?), *overthrow* (?):—Hē his torn gewræc on gesacum swīðe strengum stiépe, Cd. Th. 4, 27; Gen. 60. The passage refers to the expulsion of the angels from heaven. Cf. steóp-, ā-stēpness *orbitatio*, ā-stȳpan *in* Wulfst. 252, 11: Wē wǣron āstȳpede (bedǣled, MS. D.: āstȳpte, Blickl. Homl. 107, 4) ðæs heofenlīcan rīces. Grein suggests *overthrow* (cf. Milton's 'the dire event, That with sad overthrow and foul defeat Hath lost us Heaven'), *fall* as the meaning, and compares with *Icel.* steypa *to cast down, overthrow*; steyping *an overthrow*. Cf. also *Norweg.* stup *a precipice*, and see stūpian.

stīpan *to deprive*. [*O. H. Ger.* stiufen *orbare.*] v. ā-stīpan; steóp-.

stīpan; *p.* te. I. *to raise, build high, erect*:—Tō heofonum up hlǣdræ rǣrdon, strengum stēpton stǣnenne weall ofer monna gemet, Cd. Th. 101, 2; Gen. 1676. II. fig. *to exalt, elevate, dignify, ennoble*:—Ic ðē on tīda gehwone duguðum stēpe, Cd. Th. 139, 7; Gen. 2306. Hē him frēmum stēpeþ, Exon. Th. 434, 10; Rä. 51, 8. Deáh ðe hine mihtig God mægenes wynnum stēpte ofer ealle men, Beo. Th. 3438; B. 1717. Se feónd (*Nero*) his diórlingas duguþum stēpte (cf. hē weorþode his deorlingas mid miclum welum, Bt. 28; Fox 100, 29) *dabat improbus verendis patribus indecores curules*, Met. 15, 8. Sinces brytta (*the king of Egypt*) hēht Abrahame duguðum stēpan, Cd. Th. 111, 21; Gen. 1859: 142, 21; Gen. 2365. v. ge-, on-stēpan; stīpere, steáp.

stīpel, es; *m. A tower*:—Stȳpel *turris*, Wrt. Voc. i. 36, 39: 83, 32: Lk. Skt. 13, 4. Ðū ðencst tō gewyrcenne wundorlīcne stȳpel and swīðe heálīcne; hoga ymbe ða gāstlīcan gestreón tō ðæs stȳpeles getimbrunge

. . . Ne biþ ðes stȳpol getimbrod mid ǣnigum weorcstāne, Basil admn. 2; Norm. 38, 6–14. Stēpel stræncðe *turris fortitudinis*, Ps. Lamb. 60, 4. Stēpeles *turris*, Hpt. Gl. 499, 60. Hine man byrigde æt ðam westende ðam stȳple (stȳpele, MS. D.) ful gehende *he was buried at the west end* (*of the minster at Ely*) *quite close to the tower*, Chr. 1036; Erl. 165, 38. Ðæt hē gesāwe ða burh and ðone stīpel (*the tower of Babel*), Gen. 11, 5. Stȳpel, Homl. Th. i. 22, 19: ii. 472, 25. Timbrian ānne stȳpel *turrem aedificare*, Lk. Skt. 14, 28. Hē worhte of seolfre ǣnne heáhne stȳpel and mid scīnendum gymmum besette eall ðæt hūs, and on ðære upflōra his cynestōl geworhte, Homl. Skt. ii. 27, 29. On stȳpelum *in turribus*, Ps. Spl. 47, 11: 121, 7. [Hī clumben upp tō þe stēpel, Chr. 1070; Erl. 209, 9. Þā com se fīr on ufenweard þone stēpel, and forbearnde ealle þe minstre, 1122; Erl. 249, 6.]

stīpere, es; *m. A support, prop, pillar*:—Stīpere *destina* vel *postis* vel *fulcimen*, Wrt. Voc. i. 26, 38. [Þe stipre þat is vnder þe vyne set May not bringe forþ þe grape, H. R. 135, 135. Cf. Heo wuneð under þe chirche, ase uorte understipren hire, ȝif heo wolde uallen, A. R. 142, 16. Cf. *O. Frs.* stīpe *a post.*] v. stīpan.

stīpness, stīran, stī-rāp. v. ā-stēpness, steóran, stig-rāp.

stirc, stiorc, styric, es; *n. A stirk, calf, a young bullock* or *a heifer*:—Stirc *bucula, juvenca, vitula*, Wrt. Voc. ii. 126, 63. Styrc *juvencus*, i. 78, 44. Ðæt þridde stōd ānum styrce (cealfe, MS. C.: cf. ðæs celfes gelīcnyss belimpþ tō Lucan, 192) gelīc, Homl. Skt. i. 15, 183. Tō fēttum stiorce *ad vitulum saginatum*, Kent. Gl. 525. Stirc *buculam*, Wrt. Voc. ii. 12, 11: 93, 12. Bringaþ ān fǣtt styric *adducite vitulum saginatum*, Lk. Skt. 15, 23. [Styrk *boviculus*, Wrt. Voc. i. 204, 5. Styrk, neet, or heifer *juvenca*, Prompt. Parv. 476. *Ger.* stärke, sterke *a young cow that has not calved*: *M. H. Ger.* stirke, sterke.]

stirfan *to kill*. [*O. H. Ger.* ir-sterben *interficere, necare.*] v. ā-styrfan.

stirfig; *adj. Pertaining to an animal that has died*:—Gif hwā ete styrfig flǣsc *si quis carnem morticinam ederit*, L. Ecg. P. iv. 27; Th. ii. 212, 17. [*O. H. Ger.* stirbig *mortalis, morticinus, moribundus.*]

stiria, stirian, stirigend-līc. v. styria, styrian, styrigend-līc.

stirnan (?); *p.* de *To be severe*:—Gistmægen (*the two angels with Lot*) styrnde (stȳrde? v. steóran) werode mid wīte, Cd. Th. 150, 22; Gen. 2495.

stirne; *adj. Stern, hard, austere, rigorous, severe*:—Ic wāt ðæt ðū eart swīðe styrne mann *scio quia homo durus es* (Mt. 25, 24), Homl. Th. ii. 552, 31. Cyning sceal beón milde ðām gōdum and styrne ðām yfelum, L. I. P. 2; Th. ii. 306, 1: Wulfst. 267, 3. [God] hæfde styrne mōd, gegremed grymme, Cd. Th. 4, 28; Gen. 60. [Se cyng heafde gifen ꝥ abbotrīce ān Frencisce abbot . . . hē wæs swīðe styrne man, Chr. 1070; Erl. 207, 32. *Laym. A. R.* sturne: *Orm.* stirne.]

stirninga; *adv. Sternly, inexorably*:—Ðæt wundor ðæt geond ðās woruld fareþ, styrnenga gǣþ, staðolas beáteþ, Salm. Kmbl. 565; Sal. 282.

stirn-līc; *adj.* I. *hard, harsh*:—Warna ðæt ðū nān þing styrnlīces ne sprece ongēn Iacob *cave, ne loquaris contra Jacob quidquam durius*, Gen. 31, 29. II. *hard, unpleasant, severe* (of weather):—Hwīltīdum ðeós woruld is gesundful and myrige on tō wunigenne, hwīlon heó is eác swīðe styrnlīc and mid mislīcum þingum gemenged, swā ðæt heó biþ swīðe unwynsum on tō eardigenne, Homl. Th. i. 182, 35. Sceal āspringan here and hunger, bryne and blōdgyte and styrnlīce styrunga, Wulfst. 86, 11. Seó heofone ūs winþ wið, ðonne heó ūs sendeþ styrnlīce stormas, 92, 17.

stirnlīce; *adv.* I. *sternly, hardly, harshly*:—Hē him ondwyrde and him suīðe stiernlīce stiērde *fregit eos responsionibus*, Past. 28, 6; Swt. 197, 19. Welig spycþ styrnlīce *dives affabitur rigide*, Scint. 78, 18. II. *inflexibly, rigorously*:—Cyning sceal eallum Godes feóndum styrnlīce wiðstandan, L. I. P. 2; Th. ii. 304, 20.

stirn-mōd; *adj. Stern of mind*:—Stōpon styrnmōde (*the Hebrews proceeding against the Assyrians*), stercedferhðe, Judth. Thw. 24, 37; Jud. 227.

-stirre, -stirred, stirung. v. seofon-stirre, ā-stirred (-styrred), styrung.

stīþ; *adj. Stiff, hard.* I. in the following glosses:—Stīþ, rēþe *durus, crudelis, asper*, Wrt. Voc. ii. 142, 19. Stīð *inmitis*, Germ. 392, 33: *rigens*, 393, 172. Stīðes *ardui, stricti*, Hpt. Gl. 416, 18: *violentis, validis* ł *turbidis*, 440, 34. Stīðre *torridae*, 515, 46. On stīðum *in arto, duro, constricto*, 444, 15. II. of material, *stiff, firm*, (1) *strong, not bending easily, unyielding*:—Hit (*the sword*) on eorðan læg stīð and stȳlecg, Beo. Th. 3070; B. 1533. Æsc byþ stīð stadule, ðeáh him feohtan on firas monige, Runic pm. Kmbl. 344, 25; Rūn. 26. Stranga tor stīð wið feóndum *turris fortitudinis a facie inimici*, Ps. Th. 60, 2. Mec stīþne (*an anchor*), Exon. Th. 398, 17; Rä. 17, 9. Stīðe and rūge breóstroccas *renones*, Wrt. Voc. i. 40, 24. Hine mid stīðum sāglum beátaþ, Homl. Th. i. 432, 11: 468, 32. Mid stīðum sticelum *stimulis acutis*, Dōm. L. 179. Se gestaþelade stīþe grundas *he fixed the firm foundations*, Exon. Th. 312, 4; Seef. 104. Ðeós wyrt hafaþ lange leáf and stīþe, Lchdm. i. 288, 15. Heó hafaþ māran leáf and stīðeran, 274, 7. (2) *of a thick consistency*:—Gif tō stīð sié *if the mixture be too stiff*, Lchdm. ii. 108, 17. Ðæt hit sȳ swā stīð ðæt hit wille wel clyfian, iii. 40, 13. II a. fig. (1) in a good sense:—Mē wæs strengðu strang stīþ on Dryhtne *fortitudo mea Dominus*, Ps. Th. 117, 14. Standan stīðe mōde *to stand with unshaken soul*, 147, 6. Ic ðīnes earmes āsecge stīþe strencðe, 70, 17. Ðone stīðan swioran fortredan *rigida colla victorum calcare*, Past. 33; Swt. 228, 8. (2) in a bad sense, *stiff* (as in *stiff*-necked):—Gē wiðstandaþ ðam Hālgan Gāste mid stīðum swuran, Homl. Th. i. 46, 23. III. of persons, *hard, stern, inexorable, severe, austere*:—Ðū eart stīð man *homo austerus es*, Lk. Skt. 19, 21, 22. Heard ł stīð *durus*, Mt. Kmbl. Lind. 25, 24: Past. proem.; Swt. 23, 24. Hē wæs swā stīð, ðæt hē ne rōhte heora eallra nīð, ac hī mōston ðes cynges wille folgian, gif hī woldon libban, Chr. 1086; Erl. 222, 31. Se man ðe tō ðon stīð biþ ðæt hē āðas sylþ ðæt hē tō nānre sybbe fōn nelle *homo qui adeo durus sit ut juramenta praestet, se nullam pacem admittere velle*, L. Ecg. P. ii. 29; Th. ii. 194, 9. IV. of things that cause discomfort or require effort, e. g. weather, conflict, illness, punishment, *hard, severe, unrelenting, stubborn*:—Ðǣr wæs stīð gemōt, Byrht. Th. 140, 40; By. 301. Gif seó untrumnes swā stīð beó, Lchdm. i. 260, 22. Sié ðǣr eác lufu, næs ðeáh tō hnesce; sié ðǣr eác rēðnes, næs ðeáh tō stīð, Past. 17; Swt. 127, 3. Hēr wæs se stīþa winter, Chr. 1048; Erl. 171, 33. Beóþ ymbgyrde stranglīce tō ðysum stīðan gewinne, Homl. Skt. ii. 25, 341. Se dēmþ stīðne dōm ðām rēceleásum *he will pass severe sentence on the careless*, Homl. Th. i. 320, 18. Gelācnian myd līðum lǣcedōmum ðe mȳd stīðum *to cure with gentle remedies or severe*, Shrn. 189, 24. Wiþ ða stīþustan feferas, Lchdm. i. 114, 16. V. where conformity to a standard or rule is imposed, of discipline, mode of life, etc., *strict, rigid, severe, austere, hard*:—Se[ó] ealde ǣ næs swā stīð on ðām þingum swā swā Cristes godspel is, Boutr. Scrd. 22, 24. Ða on wēstenum wunigende woruldlīce ēstas and gǣlsan mid stīðum līfe fortrǣdon, Homl. Th. i. 544, 28. Ðæt gāte hǣr getācnode ða stīþan dǣdbōte ðæra manna ðe heora sinna behreówsiaþ, Ælfc. Thw. 3, 36. Ðā ðā hī āxodon hū hē mihte swā stearce forhæfednysse healdan, hē andwyrde: 'Stīðran and wyrsan ic geseah,' Homl. Th. ii. 354, 24. VI. of speech whose subject-matter is unpleasing, *hard*:—Stīð is ðis word, hwā mæg hine gihēra, Jn. Skt. Rush. Lind. 6, 60. Cyning cunnode hwilc ðæs æðelinges ellen wǣre stīðum wordum: 'Ðū scealt mē onsecgan sunu ðīnne,' Cd. Th. 172, 22; Gen. 2848. VII. *harsh* to the taste:—Ðeós wyrt biþ ðam gōman stīð and wiðerrǣde for mete geþiged, Lchdm. i. 300, 10. Gemencged mid stīþum ecede, 156, 15. [*O. Frs.* stīth (*opposite of* teddre): *Icel.* stinnr *stiff, unbending, strong.*]

stīþe; *adv.* I. *strongly, very much, effectively*:—Cumaþ ealle engla þreátas stīðe āstyrode (*commoti*; v. stīþ-mægen), Wulfst. 137, 14. Ðæt ðū mīne stefne stīðe gehȳre *exaudiet vocem meam*, Ps. Th. 54, 17. [Hou thai mai stithe stand igain the fend, Met. Homl. 4, 11.] II. *hardly, harshly, sternly, severely*:—Hū stīðe (*dure*) se landhlāford spræc wið hig, Gen. 42, 30. Him ðæt stīðe geald fædera Lothes, Cd. Th. 125, 15; Gen. 2079. III. *austerely, strictly*, Homl. Th. ii. 146, 7.

stīþe, an (?); *f. A name given to lamb's cress, or to nettle* (cf. the lists of plants given in sections 45, 46, Lchdm. iii. pp. 30–36):—Stīðe ðeós wyrt hātte, Lchdm. iii. 32, 23. v. stīþ.

stīþ-ecg; *adj. Of stiff* or *strong edge*:—Stīðecg stȳle, Exon. Th. 499, 11; Rä. 88, 14.

stīþ-ferhþ, -frihþ; *adj.* I. *of firm, strong mind*:—Hālig Drihten, stīðferhð cyning, Cd. Th. 16, 10; Gen. 241. Stīðfrihþ, 7, 16; Gen. 107. Standaþ stīðferhðe (*Cherubim and Seraphim*), Andr. Kmbl. 1443; An. 722. Stīðferhþe hæleð higegleáwe, Chr. 975; Erl. 126, 24. II. *of stern mind*:—Stīðferhð cyning (*the Deity at the time of the deluge*), Cd. Th. 84, 32; Gen. 1406. Stīðferhð cyning steóre gefremede, ðā hē rēðemōd reorde gesette eorðbūendum ungelīce, 101, 16; Gen. 1683.

stīþ-hugende; *adj. Of purpose stern*:—Stīðhugende hysas æt hilde, Byrht. Th. 135, 23; By. 122.

stīþ-hycgende; *adj.* I. in a good sense, *of firm, inflexible purpose, resolute*:—Stōpon tō ðære stōwe stīðhycgende, Elen. Kmbl. 1429; El. 716. II. in a bad sense, *obstinate, stubborn*:—Hire Iudas oncwæð stīðhycgende: 'Ic ða stōwe ne can,' 1362; El. 683. Stīðhycgendum (*the multitude of unbelievers*), Andr. Kmbl. 1481; An. 742. III. *having hard, unpleasant thoughts*:—'Is mē feorhgedāl leófre micle ðonne ðeós līfcearo.' Him ðā stefn oncwæð stīðhycgendum, 2858; An. 1431.

stīþ-hygd; *adj. Resolute, constant*:—Gē tō ðam lifgendan stāne stīðhygde staþol fæstniaþ, Exon. Th. 281, 30; Jul. 654.

stīþ-hygdig, -hȳdig; *adj. Of stern purpose*:—Gestāh stīðhȳdig (*Abraham when about to offer Isaac*) steápe dūne, Cd. Th. 175, 16; Gen. 2896. Stōpon stīðhȳdige . . . þrungon þræchearde, Elen. Kmbl. 241; El. 121.

stīþian. v. ā-, ge-, on-stīþian.

stīþ-līc; *adj.* I. *firm, strong*:—Stīðlīc stāntorr (*the tower of Babel*), Cd. Th. 102, 14; Gen. 1700. II. of immaterial things, weather, conflict, discipline, penance, *hard, severe*:—Stīðlīc hreóhnys *a severe storm*, Homl. Th. ii. 18, 5. Wæs ðæra deófla gefeoht swīðe stīðlīc ongeán ða sāwle, 340, 30. Mōt tō bōte stīðlīc dǣdbōt, L. Pen. 3; Th. ii. 278, 8. Hī begunnon tō sleánne ǣlc heora ōðerne mid stīðlīcum gefeohte, Jud. 7, 22. Swā swā hē strengest beón mihte ongeán ða stīðlīcan scūras, Boutr. Scrd. 21, 6. III. of speech, *hard*, *harsh, severe*:—Ne sceal nān mon geþrīstlǣcan ðæt hē āht stīþlīces spræce ongeán his abbod, R. Ben. 16, 2. Sió æcs wient of ðæm hielfe ðonne of ðære ðreátunga gāþ tō stīðlīco word *ferrum de manubrio prosilit, cum de correptione sermo durior excedit*, Past. 21, 7; Swt. 167, 10. Sege ūs for hwī ðū ūs ðus stīþlīce word tō sprece, H. R. 7, 35. IV. of persons, *stern, hard, fierce*:—Ðā Ælfrēd ðæt ofāxode, ðæt se here swā stīðlīc wæs, Shrn. 16, 8.

stīþlīce; *adv. Hardly, severely*; violenter, Hpt. Gl. 435, 60: 514, 22: rigide, Kent. Gl. 660. Stīðlīcor *restrictius*, R. Ben. Interl. 6, 5. Stīþlīcor *districtior*, i. *rigidior*, Wrt. Voc. ii. 141, 49. I. *firmly, without giving way*:—Ðās geweorc standaþ stīðlīce, Exon. Th. 351, 28; Sch. 87. II. *strongly, effectually*:—Mē com stīðlīce tō mōde *it was strongly impressed on my mind*, Anglia viii. 313, 3. Ðū stīðlīce eallum miltsadest, Ps. Th. 101, 12. III. *sternly, hardly, severely*:—Hwīlon lāreów mīn āwecþ mē stīþlīce (*duriter*) mid gyrde, Coll. Monast. Th. 35, 31. Stīðlīce clypode wīcinga ār, Byrht. Th. 132, 33; By. 25. Hē stīðlīce þrowode for ūre ealra neóde, Wulfst. 126, 10. Hȳ fuhton stīðlīce ymbe ða hālgan sāwle, 236, 23. Hē hit sceal swīðe stīðlīce gebētan, L. E. I. 14; Th. ii. 412, 2. Hē wæs gescrȳd wāclīce and stīðlīce, Homl. Th. i. 330, 2. Hē swīðe stīðlīce leofode, ii. 38, 6. Stīðlīce drohtnigende, 354, 16. Hē stīðlīcor mid untrumnyssum ofsett wæs, 120, 7. IV. *strictly*:—Ðæt līf stīðlīce healdan *to observe a course of life strictly*, R. Ben. 76, 4. [Hū hē stīðlucest hēr on līfe libben mihte, Shrn. 12, 18.] [*Icel.* stinn-liga *strongly*.]

stīþ-mægen, es; *n. A strong force*:—Ðonne cumaþ upplīce eored-heápas stīþmægen āstyred *tum superum subito veniet commota potestas*, Dōm. L. 114. [Cf. Stið-imainede eorl, Laym. 25820.]

stīþ-mōd; *adj.* I. *of constant mind, resolute*:—Strang and stīðmōd gestāh hē on gealgan, Rood Kmbl. 79; Kr. 40. II. *of stern mind, stern*:—Stīðmōd gestōd wið steápne rond bealdor (*Beowulf*), Beo. Th. 5125; B. 2566. Him (*the people of Sodom*) tō sende stīðmōd cyning (*God*) āras sīne, Cd. Th. 146, 16; Gen. 2423. Se þeóden wæs strang and stīðmōd, 279, 34; Sat. 248. Cyning stīðmōd sȳ wið yfele, L. I. P. 3; Th. ii. 306, 26. Se stīðmōda cyning, Drihten ælmihtig, āwearp of ðam setle ðone mōdigan feónd, Wulfst. 145, 27. III. *of violent* or *fierce mind*:—Se stīþmōda (*Holofernes*) styrmde and gylede, mōdig and medugāl, Judth. Thw. 21, 19; Jud. 25. IV. *of stubborn mind, stubborn, obstinate*:—Ðonne wurð seó heardnes stīð-mōdre heortan swīðe gehnexad þurh grimlīce steóra, Wulfst. 133, 17. [Cf. Arður stīðimoded kempe . . . Æuere wes Arður ærhðe bideled, Laym. 26022.]

stīþness, e; *f. Hardness, severity, force*; violentia, Hpt. Gl. 435, 76: 516, 23: duritia, 482, 66. I. *hardness, stiffness* in a physical sense:—Gif hwylc stīðnes on līchoman becume, genim ðās wyrte . . . lege tō ðam sāre, Lchdm. i. 132, 16. Wiþ ǣghwylce gegaderunga þe on ðam līchoman ācenned beóþ, genim ðās wyrte . . . lege tō ðam sāre, hit tōfereþ ealle ða stīðnyssa, 140, 14: 150, 10. I a. fig. *hardness* of heart:—Stīðnise heartes *duritiam cordis*, Mt. Kmbl. Lind. 19, 8. II. *firmness, constancy*:—Ða hnescan *vel* wācmōd, ðæt synd ða ðe nāne stīðnysse nabbaþ ongeán leahtras, Homl. Skt. i. 17, 40. III. *severity, strictness, hardness, rigour*:—Mid micelre car-fulnysse stīðnyss seó sȳ gemetegud *magna sollicitudine districtio ipsa moderetur*, Scint. 123, 9. Beó him gesǣd eall seó stīðnys and earfoðnys ðe tō Gode lǣt *predicentur ei omnia dura et aspera per que itur ad Deum*, R. Ben. 96, 19. Ne hȳ mid weorces stīðnesse ofsette sȳn *ut . . . ne violentia laboris opprimantur*, 75, 9. Ðæt wē mid sumere stīðnysse tō ðam gāstlīcum gefeohte ūs gegearcian, Homl. Th. ii. 86, 12, 26: 374, 15. Gif hwā ða stīðnysse āberan ne mæg ðe his scrift him tǣcþ *si quis austeritatem perferre nequeat, quam confessarius ejus ei prae-scripserit*, L. Ecg. P. iv. 60; Th. ii. 220, 25.

stīþ-weg, es; *m. A hard, rough way*:—Strong on stīðweg, Exon. Th. 384, 29; Rä. 4, 35.

stī-weard, -wita. v. stig-weard, -wita.

stōc (stoc ?). A word occurring mostly in local names, either alone or in compounds. The meaning seems, like that of *stōw*, to be *place* (in the first instance perhaps a place fenced in, cf. (?) staca), and both words remain now only as names of places, *Stoke, Stowe*, or as parts of such names, Basing*stoke*, Tavi*stock*, Walthams*tow*. As may be seen from the Index to the Charters, Stōc occurs frequently, some of the references are here given:—Ðis is ðara þreora hīda and .xxx. æcera bōc æt Stōce, Cod. Dip. Kmbl. iii. 190, 9: 34, 12. Tō Stōce, 203, 21. Intō Stōce, 123, 8. In loco, qui celebri a soliculis nuncupatur æt Stōce uocabulo, 19, 32: 33, 27. (With these two passages may be compared the fol-lowing:—Apud locum ubi uulgari dicitur nomine æt Stōwe, 323, 32.) In Stōce . . . in Sūthstōce, 75, 25, 33. As an instance of a compound in which the word occurs may be given the following:—Sihtrīc abbud on Tæfingstōce, vi. 196, 1. Hī Ordulfes mynster æt Tæfingstōc (Tefingstōce, MS. E.) forbærndon, Chr. 997; Erl. 134, 14. [Crist inn oþre stokess nemmneþþ þa þosstless hise breþre, Orm. 15694.] v. stōc-līf, -weard, -wīc.

stocc, es; *m.* I. *a stock, trunk, log*:—Stoc *truncus*, Wrt. Voc. i. 32, 42: 80, 32: *axima*, 287, 32. On ðone lytlan beorg ðǣr se stoc stōd . . . on geribte tō ðam stocce on eásteweardan ðam leá, of ðam stocce sūðrihte on ðære strǣt, Cod. Dip. Kmbl. ii. 250, 9-17. Tō ðam wōn stocce, ðanne fram ðam wōn stocce, 73, 22. Tō paðe stocce *to the sign-post* (?), v. 401, 37. Hē gehæfte hī on ānum micclum stocce and mid īsenum pīlum heora īlas gefæstnode . . . Hī stōdon stille on ðam stocce gefæstnode, Homl. Skt. i. 5, 386-402. Ic hæbbe of ðam stocce ðe his (*Oswald's*) heáfod on stōd, ii. 26, 260. Ōþ ðone calewan stoc, Cod. Dip. Kmbl. ii. 216, 1. Hē gefeól on ðone stocc be ðære stǣnenan strǣte ðe is gehāten sacra uia, and tōbærst on feówer dǣlas. Ðā ge-nāman men eft ðone stoc on weg and feówer syllīce stānas on ðære ilcan stōwe ālegdon, Blickl. Homl. 189, 12-15. Gē þeówiaþ fremdum godum, stoccum and stānum (*ligno et lapidi*), Deut. 28, 36. Stoccon *lignis*, 64. Tō stoccum, Cod. Dip. Kmbl. iii. 429, 7. II. *a wooden trumpet* (?):—Bēma ł stocc *tuba*, Mt. Kmbl. Lind. 6, 2. [*O. Frs.* stokk *a stock; stocks*: *O. L. Ger.* stokk *stipes*: *O. H. Ger.* stocch *truncus, stipes, lignum, cippus*: *Icel.* stokkr.] v. hand-, heáfod-, pīl-stocc.

stoccen; *adj. Made of logs*:—Andlang Teóburnan tō ðære wīde herestrǣt; æfter ðære herestrǣt tō ðære ealde stoccene sancte Andreas cyricean *to the old wooden St. Andrew's church*, Cod. Dip. Kmbl. iii. 73, 20. Cf. *Stoken*church in Oxfordshire, *Stoken*ham in Devonshire.

stōc-līf, es; *n. A town, habitation*:—Stōcclīf *oppidum, civitas*, Hpt. Gl. 500, 18. Se mæg gedōn ðæt ic sōftor eardian ǣgðer ge on ðisum lǣnan stōclīfe (cf. Here have we no continuing city, Heb. 13, 14) ða whīle ðe ic on ðisse weorulde beó ge eác on ðam hēcan hāme ðe hē ūs gehāten hefþ *he can make me dwell more at ease both in this transitory habitation, while I am in this world, and also in that eternal home that he hath promised us*, Shrn. 163, 20. Se ðe ēgðer wilt ge ðissa lǣnena stōclīfe ge ðara ēcena hāma, 164, 9. Cf. cot-, mynster-līf *for words in which* līf *is similarly used; and see* stōc.

stōc-weard, es; *m. A townsman*:—Stōcweardum *oppidanis*, Hpt. Gl. 525, 49. v. stōc.

stōc-wīc, es; *n. A habitation, residence*:—On Casino ðam stōcwīc *in the monastery at Monte Casino*, Earle, A. S. Lit. 200, 34. v. stōc.

stod *a post*:—Stod *propolim* vel *pertica*, Wrt. Voc. i. 16, 28. [A stake or a stode *palus*, Wülck. Gl. 600, 4. Stothe or post *posticulus*, Prompt. Parv. 478, col. 2.] v. duru-stod; studu.

stōd, es; *n. A stud, a herd of horses*:—Stood *equartium*, Wrt. Voc. i. 23, 10. Ic geann mīnon heáhdeórhunton ðæs stōdes ðe is on Colinga-hrycge, Cod. Dip. Kmbl. iii. 363, 25. Ic gean mīnum wīfe healfes ðæs stōdes æt Trostingtūne and mīnum gefēran healfes ðe mē mid rīdaþ, and fō mīn wīf tō healfum ðe on wealde is, and mīn dohter tō healfum, iv. 300, 28. Ðat stōd ðe ic ðēr habbe, Chart. Th. 574, 20. [Asse . . . thou come of lither stode, P. S. 201, 2. Þe sulve stottes in þe stode, O. and N. 495. The hors of thilke stood Devoureden the mannes blood, Gow. 3, 204, 19. *O. H. Ger.* stuot *equaritia, grex equarum*: *Icel.* stōð; *n.*: *Dan.* stod.]

stōd-fald, es; *m. An enclosure for a stud of horses*:—Tō ðam aldan stōdfalde; and ðonne fram ðam stōdfalde, Cod. Dip. Kmbl. iii. 393, 21. Of ðam wylle on ðone stōdfald; of ðam stōdfalde, vi. 213, 21. Be norðan stōdfaldan, iv. 66, 8. [*Dan.* stod-fold *an enclosure for horses*.]

stōd-hors, es; *n. A stud-horse*:—Gyf mon mǣte ðæt hē feola stōd-horsa habbe, Lchdm. iii. 176, 5. [*Icel.* stōð-hross.]

stodl *a post*. v. dur-stodl [*O. H. Ger.* turi-studil, -stuodil, -stodal *limen, postis*: *Icel.* stuðill *a prop, stay*]. v. stod, studu, *and next word*.

stodle (-a; *m.*?), an; *f. A stay, part of a loom*:—Hē sceal fela tōwtōla habban . . . stodlan, Anglia ix. 263, 11. [Stodul or stedulle of wevynge *telarium* (cf. *Span.* telar *a loom*), Prompt. Parv. 476. Stodyll a toole for a wever, *lame* (cf. *lama* sleybrede, Wülck. Gl. 591, 28) *de tisserant*, Palsgrave (Halliwell's Dict.). Cf. *M. H. Ger.* stodel *pidonius* (*textoris*); in a gloss the word is further explained by *warfsteche*. v. Grff. vi. 654.] v. preceding word.

stōd-mere, an; *f. A brood-mare, mare with a foal*:—Gif mon cū oþþe stōdmyran forstele, and folan oþþe cealf of ādrīfe, L. Alf. pol. 16; Th. i. 70, 24. [Ich am a ful stodmere, a stinckinde hore, A. R. 316, 15. Stodemere, Perceval 367 (Halliwell's Dict.). *Icel.* stōð-merr.]

stōd-þeóf, es; *m. One who steals from a stud, a horse-stealer*, L. Alf. pol. 9; Th. i. 68, 5.

stofa, an; *m. A room for a warm bath*:—Stofa *balneum*, Wrt. Voc. ii. 101, 60. [*O. H. Ger.* stuba *a chamber that may be warmed*: *Icel.* stofa, stufa *a bathing-room that has a fire; a room*. The Romance languages borrowed from Teutonic, hence *Fr.* étuve: *Ital.* stufa: *Span.* estufa *a hot-house, bath-room*.] v. stuf-bæþ.

stofn, e; *f.* I. *a stem*:—Stoc *truncus*, stofn *stipes*, Wrt. Voc. i. 32, 43. [Þai thre stod on a stouen (stalke, stocke, other MSS.), C. M. 8036. *Stovin* a stump or stake; the part of a hawthorn left in a hedge after 'splashing' it, E. D. S. Pub. Leicestershire. *Icel.* stofn *a stem, stump of a tree*.] II. *a shoot of a tree*:—Stofna ł telgena *surcu-lorum, virgultorum*, Hpt. Gl. 419, 65. Stofnes (stofne ?), ōwæstmas *surculos, ramusculos*, 409, 1. II a. fig. *offspring, progeny*:—Mid gestrēnendlīcere stofne *progenie propaganda*, 445, 64. [*Stoven* a sapling shoot from the stump of a fallen tree, E. D. S. Pub. B. 22, and Whitby

Gloss.] III. *a foundation*:—Swā gē āwurpon wāh of stofne *tamquam parieti inclinato*, Ps. Th. 61, 3. [*Icel.* stofn *a foundation*; stofna *to establish, lay the foundation of.*]

stōl, es; *m.* I. *a stool, seat*:—Stool *tripes*, Wrt. Voc. ii. 122, 75. Gewyrc stōl of þrīm treówum . . . geót under đone stōl, Lchdm. ii. 76, 21–24. Man sceal habban . . . sceamelas, stōlas, Anglia ix. 264, 21. II. *the seat* (lit. and fig.) of one in authority, *the throne* of a king, *see* of a bishop:—Sōna se stōl (*the throne*) scylfþ, L. I. P. 4; Th. ii. 308, 1. Stōles *cathedrae* (*pontificalis*), Hpt. Gl. 454, 33. Se sit swelce hē sitte on đæm stōle đæs forhwierfdan gemōtes . . . Se biþ beforan đe on đæm stōle sitt đǣm ōđrum đe đǣr ymb stondaþ, Past. 56; Swt. 435, 24–28. Heofnes Wealdend đe siteþ on đam hālgan stōle, Cd. Th. 17, 16; Gen. 260: 19, 33; Gen. 300. Hū hē him strenglīcran stōl geworhte, 18, 15; Gen. 273. Geseón selfes stōl herran đīnes, 36, 4; Gen. 566. Ofer stōl *super cathedram* (*Mosi*), Mt. Kmbl. Lind. 23, 2. [*Goth.* stōls *a seat, throne*: *O. Sax. O. Frs.* stōl: *O. H. Ger.* stōl, stuol *sedes, sella, thronus*: *Icel.* stōll *a seat, throne, see.*] v. arce- (erce-), arcebiscop-, biscop-, brego-, cyne-, ealdor-, Eoforwīc-, ēđel-, fealde-, friþ-, frum-, gang-, gebed-, gif-, gleow-, gum-, heáfod-, heofon-, hleów-, rodor-, þeóden-, yrfe-stōl.

stole, an; *f.*: stol, es; *n.* (in Northern specimens) *A stole, long outer garment*:—Stole *stola*, Wrt. Voc. i. 81, 43. Stol wuldres gigeride hine *stola glorie induit eum*, Rtl. 45, 29. Đæt stol ǣriste *stolam primam*, Lk. Skt. Lind. 15, 22. Geonga in stolum (stollum, Rush.) ł on oferslopum *ambulare in stolis*, 20, 46: Mk. Skt. Lind. Rush. 12, 38. [*Icel.* stola; *f. a stole.* From Latin.]

stom[m], stomer, stommettan, stomrian, stondan, stood. v. stam, stamer, stammettan, stamerian, standan, stōd.

stōpel, es; *m. A foot-step, mark left by the foot*:—Man dæghwamlīce đa moldan nimeþ on đǣm lāstum . . . and nǣfre man đære moldan tō đæs feale ne nimeþ, đæt mon ǣfre þurh đæt mǣge ā đȳ māran dǣl on đǣm stōplum gewercean (*make the footprints larger*) . . . Forlēt ūre Drihten his đa hālgan fēt đǣr on đa eorþan besincan . . . and swā nūget on đære eorþan đa stōplas onāþrycte syndon, Blickl. Homl. 127, 14–26. [Cf. *O. Sax.* stōpo *foot-print.*]

stoppa, an; *m. A stop, a bucket, pail.* Halliwell gives *stop* a small well-bucket, and also *stoppe* a bucket, or milking-pail, as Norfolk words; the latter being still in use. 'The holy-water *stoppe* was a vessel containing holy-water placed near the entrance of a church, and was sometimes made of lead':—Stoppa *situla*, Wrt. Voc. i. 25, 10: *bona* (?), 288, 2: *botholicula*, ii. 126, 55: *bothonicla*, 11, 20: *bothonicula*, Txts. 42, 122. [Prompt. Parv. stoppe, boket *situla, haustrum*, stoppe, vessel for mylkynge *multra, multrale, multrum.*] v. buter-stoppa.

stoppian *to stop, close* an aperture. v. for-stoppian, Lchdm. ii. 42, 12. [From Latin (?).]

stōr, es; *m. Frankincense, storax*:—Đes stōr *hoc thus*, Ælfc. Gr. 9, 33; Zup. 59, 14: Wrt. Voc. i. 81, 25. Stōr đe biþ of gewringe *stacten*, 20, 28. Hī him geoffrodon gold and rēcels and myrran . . . se stōr getācnode đæt hē is sōđ God, Homl. Th. i. 116, 9. Āne hand fulle stōres, Lev. 2, 2. Nymeþ stōr *sumite modicum storacis*, Gen. 43, 11. Đa đe offrodon đone stōr *qui offerebant incensum*, Num. 16, 35. Brimne stōr and hwītne rȳcels, Lchdm. iii. 14, 21. [Encens, stor *olibanus*, Wrt. Voc. i. 140, 24 (13th cent.) 'Mj bene bi ydi3t beuore þe ase þet stor.' þet stor huanne hit is ope þe uere smelþ zuete, Ayenb. 211, 17.] v. stēran.

stōr; *adj. Great, strong, violent*:—Swā stōr þunring wes, Chr. 1085; Erl. 219, 22. [Of þan fehte þe was feondliche stor, Laym. 85. Onkumen was Cadalamor . . . wiđ ferding stor, Gen. and Ex. 842. Wunder wel starc and stor, O. and N. 1473. Stoor (store) or hard or boystows *austerus, rigidus*, Prompt. Parv. 477. See also *store* in Halliwell's Dict. *O. Frs.* stōr: *O. L. Ger.* stōri *inclytus*: *Icel.* stórr: *Dan. Swed.* stor. Borrowed (?) from Scandinavian.]

storc, es; *m. A stork*:—Storc *ciconia*, Wrt. Voc. ii. 103, 81: 14, 33: i. 29, 19: 77, 18: 280, 24: Ælfc. Gr. 7; Zup. 25, 6. Storc and swalewe heóldon đone tīman heora tōcymes, Homl. Th. i. 404, 25. [*O. H. Ger.* storah, storc *ciconia, ophimachus, ibis*: *Icel.* storkr.]

stōr-cyll, e: -cylle, an; *f. A censer*:—Stōrcyl *turibulum*, Wrt. Voc. i. 81, 27. .i. silfren stōrcylle, Chart. Th. 429, 35. Se đe bær đa stōrcyllan tō đære offrunge, Homl. Th. ii. 294, 20: Homl. Ass. 58, 185. Nime eówer ǣlc his stōrcillan, Num. 16, 6. Đās stōrcyllan *haec turibula*, Ælfc. Gr. 14; Zup. 90, 4. Stōrcillan, Lev. 10, 1.

storm, es; *m.* I. *a storm, tempest*:—Storm *nymbus*, Wrt. Voc. ii. 114, 70: *procella*, i. 52, 62: 76, 45: *grando*, Blickl. Gl. Se swearta storm norđan and eástan, Met. 4, 22. Se stearca storm, 6, 11. Seó rēþnes đæs stormes *saevitia tempestatis*, Bd. 5, 1; S. 614, 9. Hē ofslōh on storme (*grandine*) wīngeardas heora, Ps. Spl. 77, 52. Mid đȳ storme đæs wintres *hiemis tempestate*, Bd. 2, 13; S. 516, 19. Đās stānhleoþu stormas cnyssaþ, Exon. Th. 292, 19; Wand. 101: 307, 13; Seef. 23. Storma *nimborum*, Hpt. Gl. 439, 71. Stormum *nimbis*, Wrt. Voc. ii. 61, 36. On đære hreón sǣ and on đǣm miclan stormum, Past. 9; Swt. 59, 3. Gescyrped mid đære rinde wiđ đa stearcan stormas, Bt. 34, 10; Fox 150, 8. Seó lyft ābyrþ ealle wolcna and stormas, Lchdm. iii. 274, 10. I a. fig. *a storm* of arrows:—Strǣla storm scōc ofer scyldweall, Beo. Th. 6225; B. 3118. I b. *storm, disturbance, disquiet*:—Hwæt is đonne đæt rīce and se ealdordoom būtan đæs mōdes storm, se biþ simle cnyssende đæt scip đære heortan, Past. 9; Swt. 59, 4. Swelce eác tōætēcte đisse gedrēfnisse storm Sǣberhtes deáþ, Bd. 2, 5; S. 507, 6. Đa strongan stormas weoruldbisgunga, Met. 3, 3. II. *uproar, tumult*:—Storm up ārās æfter ceasterhofum, cirm unlytel hǣđnes heriges, Andr. Kmbl. 2474; An. 1238. Storm up gewāt heáh tō heofonum, herewōpa mǣst, Cd. Th. 206, 30; Exod. 459. III. *violent attack*, cf. to *storm* a place:—Đis is stronglīc, nū đes storm becom, þegen mid þreáte (*of the harrying of hell*), Cd. Th. 288, 26; Sat. 387. Forstond đū mec and gestȳr him (*the devils*), đonne storm cyme mīnum gǣste ongegn, Exon. Th. 455, 32; Hy. 4, 58. [*O. Sax.* storm: *O. H. Ger.* sturm *procella, tempestas*; *strepitus, agitatio, motus, seditio, tumultus*: *Icel.* stormr *a tempest; tumult, uproar.*] v. styrman.

stōr-sæp, es; *n. Resin*:—Stōrsæpes *resinae*, Hpt. Gl. 501, 1.

stōr-sticca, an; *m. An incense-stick, rod for stirring the incense in the censer* (?):—.i. silfren stōrcylle mid silfrenum stōrsticcan, Chart. Th. 429, 35.

stōw, e; *f. A place.* The word remains either alone or in composition in place-names, e.g. *Stow* in Huntingdonshire, *Stowe* in Northamptonshire, Chep*stow* old *ceáp-stōw* q. v.:—Stōw *locus*, Wrt. Voc. i. 85, 31. I. *a place, spot, locality, site*:—Đeó stōw (*Calvary*) wæs gehende đære ceastre, đǣr se Hǣlend wæs āhangen, Jn. Skt. 19, 20: Elen. Kmbl. 1347; El. 675. Nis đæt heóru stōw, Beo. Th. 2749; B. 1372. Wæs seó londes stōw bimiþen fore monnum, ōþþæt Meotod onwrāh beorg on bearwe, Exon. Th. 110, 32; Gū. 117. Đā hwearf hē eft tō đære leófan stōwe his ellþeódignesse *tunc reversus ad dilectae locum peregrinationis*, Bd. 5, 9; S. 623, 30. Teón wit of đisse stōwe, Cd. Th. 114, 30; Gen. 1912. Stōpon tō đære stōwe đe Dryhten ǣr āhangen wæs, Elen. Kmbl. 1428; El. 716. Tō đam stōwe (-um?) *ad loca*, Ex. 3, 8. Geseóþ đa stōwe đe se Hǣlynd wæs on āled, Mt. Kmbl. 28, 6. Đæt hē đǣr forgeáfe stōwe mynster on tō timbrianne, Bd. 3, 24; S. 557, 26. On wēstum stōwum *in desertis locis*, Mk. Skt. 1, 45. Hē gǣþ þurh unwæterie stōwa, Lk. Skt. 11, 24. Muntas and mōras and eác monige wēste stōwa, Salm. Kmbl. 683; Sal. 341. II. *a place* on the body:—Gif đū wille lim āceorfan . . . gesceáwa đū hwilc sió stōw sié and đære stōwe mægen, fordon đe đara stōwa sum raþe rotaþ, gif hire mon gīmeleáslīce tilaþ, Lchdm. ii. 84, 22–25. Wiđ wīfa earfođnyssum đe on heora inwerdlīcum stōwum earfeþu þrowiaþ . . . wyrc tō sealfe, dō on wīfa stōwe, i. 338, 19–22. Lācnian đa sāran stōwa, ii. 22, 3: 70, 8: 150, 16. III. *a place* which is built, *a house* or *collection of houses, a habitation, dwelling*:—Seó stōw (*Ely*) wæs gehālgod đam hālgan Petre, Chart. Th. 241, 2. On đære stōwe dura *in introitu tabernaculi*, Num. 12, 5. Ne onscunige ic nō đæs neoþeran and đæs unclǣnan stōwe (*the prison of Boethius*), Bt. 5, 1; Fox 10, 15. Gange seó sōcn intō đære stōwe (*the monastery at Ely*), Chart. Th. 243, 1. On đære stōwe (*the town of Zoar*) wē gesunde māgon bīdan, Cd. Th. 152, 19; Gen. 2522. Đā sealde se cyning him wununesse and stōwe on Cantwarabyrig *dedit eis mansionem in civitate Doruvernensi*, Bd. 1, 25; S. 487, 18. Hē āna gesæt dȳgle stōwe (*a hermitage*), Exon. Th. 111, 21; Gū. 130. Folc of eallum tūnum and stōwum, Bd. 2, 14; S. 518, 10. IV. *a place, position, station*:—Sió wyrd dǣlþ eallum gesceaftum stōwa and tīda, Bt. 39, 5; Fox 218, 33. Đa nū ryne healdaþ, stōwe gestefnde, Cd. Th. 10, 21; Gen. 160. V. *a place* in a series:—Onfēngon hī đa teóþan stōwe on ehtnysse Godes cyrcena æfter Nerone, Bd. 1, 6; S. 476, 22. VI. *place, room, stead*:—Se đe lifigende wǣre đæs hādes hæfde mihte ōþerne biscop his stōwe tō hālgianne đēr se ōđer forþfērde *is qui superest consors ejusdem gradus, habeat potestatem alterum ordinandi, in loco ejus qui transierat, sacerdotem*, 2, 18; S. 520, 35. VII. *a place, passage* in a book:—Ic đē sende đæt spell đē sylfum tō rǣdanne and on emtan tō smeágeanne and eác on mā stōwa tō wrītanne and tō lǣranne, Bd. pref.; S. 471, 11. [*O. Frs.* stō *a place*: *Icel.* eld-stō *a fire-place.*] v. ancor-, byrgen-, ceáp-, cot-, cwealm-, dōm-, eardung-, ēđel-, folc-, freóls-, friþ-, fulwiht-, gemōt-, gewin-, heáfod-, heg-, leger-, mold-, munuc-, mynster-, neáh-, onbīd-, oret-, pleg-, seonoþ-, spell-, sundor-, tintreg-, wæl-, wāfung-, weall-, wīc-, win-, wītnung-, wītung-, wræc-stōw.

stōwian; *p.* ode *To hold back, restrain*:—Stōuuigan *retentare*, Wrt. Voc. ii. 118, 72. [He sette stronge lawen to steowien (stewe, 2nd MS.) his folke, Laym. 6266. Stew þine unwittie wordes, Marh. 6, 2 (and see note, p. 109). Læte me steowe (cf. steowe = A. S. stōw, 145, 5) mi flesc, Misc. 193, 34. Beo stiward in oure stude til 3e be stouwet (stowed, C-text MS. I.; ruled, B-text) betere, Piers P. A-text 5, 39. 3iff any man stow me this nyth I xal hym 3eve a dedly wownde, Cov. Myst. (Halliwell's Dict.). Stowyn or with stond idem quod stoppyn, stowynge, stowwynge *obsistencia, resistencia*, Prompt. Parv. 478, col. 1.]

stōw-līc; *adj. Local, relating to place*, (1) *occupying a place*:—God is ǣghwǣr, þeáh đe se engel stōwlīc sȳ. Nis se ælmihtiga Wealdend stōwlīc, forđan đe hē is on ǣlcere stōwe, and swā hwider swā se stōwlīca engel flīhþ, hē biþ befangen mid his andwerdnysse, Homl. Th. i. 348, 12–15. Stōwlīcere moldan *situ*, Germ. 391, 195. (2) *expressing* *relations of place*:—Sume naman syndon *localia* ðæt synd stówlíce; ða geswuteliaþ gehendnysse oððe ungehendnysse, Ælfc. Gr. 5; Zup. 14, 18. Sume (*adverbs*) synd stówlíce, forðan ðe hí getácniaþ stówa, 38; Zup. 224, 12.

stówlíce; *adv. Locally, in respect of place*:—Ða Iudéiscan ðe on Crist gelýfdon wǽron him gehendor stówlíce and eác ðurh cýððe ðære ealdan ǽ: wé wǽron swíðe fyrlyne ǽgðer ge stówlíce ge ðurh uncýððe, Homl. Th. i. 106, 19–21.

strácian; *p.* ode *To stroke*:—Se lǽce grápaþ and strácaþ, ǽrðonðe hé stingan wille, Past. 26; Swt. 187, 5. Wildu hors, ðonne wé hié ǽresð gefangnu habbaþ, wé hié ðacciaþ and strácíad mid brádre handa *equos indomitos blanda prius manu tangimus*, 41, 4; Swt. 303, 10. Myd swýþe drígeon handum stráca geornlíce ðane innoþ, Lchdm. iii. 134, 17. [*O. H. Ger.* streichōn *demulcere*.]

strácung, e; *f. Stroking, caressing*:—Strácung *vel* ólæcung *delinimentum*, Wrt. Voc. i. 54, 69.

stræc, strec; *adj.* I. *strict, severe, rigorous, stern, hard*:—Hú se reccere sceal bión wið ðara yfelena unðeáwas stræc for ryhtwíslícum andan *ut sit rector contra delinquentium vitia per zelum justitiae erectus*, Past. 17; Swt. 107, 6. Stræc (strec, Cott. MSS.), 12; Swt. 75, 12. Ðæt se streca Déma ús geárige, Homl. Th. ii. 126, 13. Ætforan ðæs gesihðe ðæs strecan Déman, 124, 15. Streccere *rigidae, durae*, Hpt. Gl. 416, 16. Ðære stræcan *asperrima*, Wrt. Voc. ii. 2, 24. Wé scoldon mid strecum móde stíðlícor libban and winnan wið leahtras, L. Ælfc. P. 12; Th. ii. 368, 18. Réðe and stræce for ryhtwísnesse *justitiae severitate districti*, Past. 5, 1; Swt. 41, 19. Déde strece *actus strenuos*, Ps. Surt. ii. p. 201, 11. Tó ðæm stræcstum (strecestum, MS. T.: strænestum, MS. A.) mynstermonna cynne *ad cenobitarum fortissimum genus*, R. Ben. 10, 4. II. *rigid, unyielding, obstinate, persistent.* v. stræcness:—On óðre wísan sint tó manianne ða ánfealdan stræcan on óðre ða unbealdan. Ðǽm anfealdan stræcum is tó cýðanne ðæt hié bet [ne] truwien him selfum ðonne hié ðyrfen ðonne hí nyllaþ geðafan beón óðerra monna geðeahtes *aliter admonendi sunt pertinaces, atque aliter inconstantes. Illis dicendum est, quod plus de se, quam sunt, sentiunt, et idcirco alienis consiliis non acquiescunt*, Past. 42, 1; Swt. 305, 12–15. III. *violent, using force, uncompromising, vehement*:—Manig strec (stræc, MS. B.) man wyle werian his man swá hwæðer him þincþ ðæt hé hine eáð áwerian mǽge. Ac wé nellaþ geþafian ðæt unriht, L. C. S. 20; Th. i. 388, 1. Heofena ríce þolaþ neád, and strece (*violenti*) nimaþ ðæt, Mt. Kmbl. 11, 12. Godes ríce ðolaþ neádunge, and ða strecan mód hit gegrípaþ . . . Eal cristen folc sceal mid neádunge and strecum móde ðæt heofonlíce ríce geearnian, Homl. Th. i. 358, 25–35. Ða hǽþenan féngon tó wurðienne entas and strece woruldmen ðe mihtige wurdan on woruldafelum and egesfulle wǽran ða hwýle ðe hý leofedon, Wulfst. 105, 34. [Cf. strek *straightway*: He sal noght wend strek til purgatory bot even til helle, Pr. C. 3378. *M. H. Ger.* strac.] v. ánstræc, *and next word.*

stræc, es; *n.* (?) I. *strictness, rigour*:—Stræc *districtio, rigor*, Wrt. Voc. ii. 141, 48. Sý nátóðæshwón regoles stræc gehealden *nullatenus districtio regule teneatur*, R. Ben. 61, 15. II. *violence, force*:—Hú mæg beón bútan strece and neádunge ðæt gehwá mid clǽnnysse ðæt gále gecynd þurh Godes gife gewylde? Homl. Th. i. 360, 1, 10. Hér man ýtte út Ælfgár eorl, ac hé com sóna inn ongeán mid strece þurh Gryffines fultum, Chr. 1058; Erl. 192, 36.

stræc-líc; *adj. Rigorous, strict, severe*:—Gif hié ne beóþ gebundne mid stræclíce láreówdóme *si hanc districtionis severitas non coarctat*, Past. 17, 9; Swt. 123, 17. Streclícere hǽse *rigid oimperio*, Hpt. Gl. 437, 4.

stræclíce; *adv.* I. *strictly, sternly, vehemently*:—Gif him God ryhtlíce and stræclíce (streclíce, Cott. MSS.) déman wile *si districte judicentur*, Past. 5, 3; Swt. 45, 20. Hwílum líðelíce tó ðreátigenne hwílum suíðlíce and stræclíce tó ðráfianne *aliquando leniter arguenda, aliquando autem vehementer increpanda*, 21, 1; Swt. 151, 12. II. *violently, forcibly*:—Swá swá deáð streclíce ásyndraþ sáwle fram líchamann ealswá lufu Godes streclíce ásyndraþ mann fram middaneardenre lufe *sicut mors uiolenter separat animam a corpore, ita dilectio Dei uiolenter segregat hominem a mundano amore*, Scint. 16, 14–16.

stræcness, e; *f. Persistence, perseverance, pertinacity*:—Mid unáteriendlíc[r]e strecnysse *indefessa instantia* (*perseverantia*), Hpt. Gl. 434, 24. Hí mid ánrǽdnesse and mid strecnesse geearnodon heofona ríce, L. Ælfc. P. 13; Th. ii. 368, 29.

strǽd[a, -e?] *a pace, stride*:—Míle straedena *mille passus*, Mt. Kmbl. Lind. 5, 41.

strægdness. v. stregdness.

strǽgl (*from Latin* stragula?), strǽl, strél, e; *f. A covering for beds, a rug, a mattress, bed*:—Strégl (g *over* a), strél *aulea*, Txts. 43, 249. Strél *stragua*, 99, 1907. Strǽl *vel* bedding *mataxa* vel *conductum* vel *stramentum*, Wrt. Voc. i. 59, 29. Strǽle mínum (-e?) ic wǽte *stratum meum rigabo*, Ps. Spl. 6, 6. Strǽla *stragularum*, Hpt. Gl. 430, 67. Ealle strǽla his ðú ácyrdest *universum stratum ejus versasti*, Ps. Spl. 40, 3. [*Prompt. Parv.* strayle, bed clothe *stragula*.]

strǽl, strél, streál, es; *m.*: e; *f.*: strǽle, an; *f. An arrow, shaft, dart* (lit. and fig.):—Ðá genam hé his bogan and hine gebende and ðá mid geǽttredum strǽle ongan sceótan . . . Ðá sóna mid ðan ðe se strǽl on flyge wæs, ðá com swíðe mycel windes blǽd, ðæt seó strǽl wearð eft gecyrred, and ðá ðone ilcan mon, ðe heó ǽr from sended wæs, hé sceát, Blickl. Homl. 199, 17–23. Hé cwæð tó ðam deófle: 'Ðú heardeste strǽl tó ǽghwilcre unrihtnesse, 241, 3: Andr. Kmbl. 2380; An. 1191. Hé his costunge streále on ðam móde gefæstnode ðæs cempan. Hé mid ðære geǽttredan streále gewundod wæs . . . Ðá hæfde hine seó deófollíce strǽl mid ormódnysse gewundodne, Guthl. 4; Gdwin. 28, 2–14. Swá seó strǽle byþ strangum on handa *sicut sagittae in manu potentis*, Ps. Th. 126, 5. Leóhtes strǽle ł leóma *lucis spiculum*, Hymn. Surt. 30, 6. Se mon wæs ofscoten mid his ágenre strǽle mid ðý ðe hé wolde ðone fearr sceótan, Shrn. 83, 6. Hé forð onsendeþ biterne strǽl, Exon. Th. 48, 2; Cri. 765. Strǽlas *sagittae*, Ps. Spl. 63, 8: Blickl. Homl. 203, 9. Strélas, Ps. Surt. 56, 5. Stréle beóþ scearpe *sagittae acutae*, Ps. Th. 119, 4: 143, 7. Scearpum strélum, 63, 4. Hé sende his strǽlas, 17, 14: Judth. Thw. 24, 34; Jud. 223. Ðá hét ic feá strǽla (*paucas sagittas*) sendan in ða burh innan, Nar. 10, 22. Hé sendeþ his strǽlo, Bd. 4, 3; S. 569, 20. Lǽteþ strǽle fleógan, farende flán, Exon. Th. 386, 4; Rä. 4, 56. Hé ða strǽle ðara áwerigdra gásta him fram ásceáf, Guthl. 6; Gdwin. 42, 24. Strǽle bitere sendan, Ps. Th. 77, 11: 76, 14. [Strales hate, Laym. 5695. *O. L. Ger. O. H. Ger.* strála; *f. sagitta, jaculum*: *M. H. Ger.* strál, stråle; *m. f.*: *Ger.* strahl; *m.*] v. here-, wæl-, wǽpen-strǽl.

strǽl-bora, an; *m. An archer*:—Strélbora *arcister*, Wrt. Voc. ii. 101, 8. Strǽlbora and scytta, 7, 32. Strǽlbora, 55.

strǽlian; *p.* ode *To shoot*:—Hí strǽliaþ hine *sagittabunt eum*, Ps. Spl. 63, 4.

strǽl-wyrt, e; *f. Club-moss* (?). Somner gives the word as glossing *callitrichon*:—Gif dolh fúlige, ceów strǽlwyrt on and gearwan, Lchdm. ii. 96, 9.

strǽt, e (*but uninflected forms occur*); *f.* I. *a road*:—Læg án dríe strǽt þurh ða sǽ. And ðæt wæter stód an twá healfa ðære strǽte, Ex. 14, 21–22. Him þurh streámræce strǽt wæs gerýmed, Andr. Kmbl. 3159; An. 1582. Tó ðære ealdan strǽt; ondlong ðære strǽt, Cod. Dip. Kmbl. iii. 79, 30. On ða sealtstrǽt; andlang strǽt, 82, 26. Foldweg, cúþe strǽte, Beo. Th. 3272; B. 1634. Ceastre and torras and stréta and brycge geworhte wǽron *civitates, farus, pontes, et stratae factae*, Bd. 1, 11; S. 480, 16. II. *a road in a town, a street, a paved road*:—Strǽt wæs stánfáh . . . hié tó sele gangan cwómon, Beo. Th. 645; B. 320. Ða stánas ðæs temples licggeaþ æt ǽlcre strǽte ende *in capite omnium platearum*, Past. 18, 3; Swt. 133, 12. Loth sæt on ðære strǽt (*in foribus civitatis*) . . . Hig cwǽdon: 'Wé willaþ wunian on ðære strǽt (*in platea*), Gen. 19, 1–2. Be ðisse strǽte, Cd. Th. 147, 8; Gen. 2436. Eode se apostol be ðære strǽt, Homl. Th. i. 60, 21: ii. 120, 16. Hé eode in burh, stóp on strǽte, Andr. Kmbl. 1969; An. 987. Enta ǽrgeweorc innan burgum strǽte stánfáge, 2473; An. 1238. Fenn strǽta *lutum platearum*, Ps. Spl. 17, 44. On strǽta hyrnum, Mt. Kmbl. 6, 5. On strǽton *in plateis*, Mk. Skt. 6, 56. Hí synd stǽnene mid ðám ðe man strǽta wyrcþ, Homl. Skt. i. 7, 134. Ðá arn se ceorl geond ealle ða strǽt, Homl. Th. ii. 302, 8. [*O. Sax. O. L. Ger.* stráta: *O. Frs.* stréte: *O. H. Ger.* stráza. *From Latin* strata.] v. cyne-, faroþ-, fird-, heáh-, here-, lagu-, mere-, port-, ranc-, sealt-, stán-strǽt.

strǽt, e; *f. A couch, bed*:—On beddinge strǽte mínre *in lectum strati mei*, Ps. Spl. C. 131, 3. Ofer strǽte *super lectum*, 62, 7: 6, 6. [From Latin.]

strand, es; *n. A strand, shore*:—Strand *litus*, Wrt. Voc. i. 54, 24: *sablo*, Hpt. Gl. 502, 77. Se Hǽlend stód on ðam strande . . . Ðæt strand getácnode ða écan staðolfæstnysse ðæs tóweardan lífes, Homl. Th. ii. 288, 30. Wudes ne feldes, sandes ne strandes, Lchdm. iii. 288, 1. Hí sǽton be ðam strande *secus littus sedentes*, Mt. Kmbl. 13, 48: Jn. Skt. 21, 4. Ðá eode hé be strande, Ap. Th. 7, 19. Gáþ tó ðære sǽ strande, Homl. Th. i. 64, 3. Urk mín húskarl habbe his strand eall forne gén hys ágen land, Cod. Dip. Kmbl. iv. 221, 6. Stranda *litorum*, Hpt. Gl. 449, 28. Strandum *litoribus*, 465, 9. [*O. Du.* strande; *n.*: *M. H. Ger.* strant; *m.*: *Icel.* strönd; *f.*] v. sǽ-strand.

strang; *adj. Strong*; fortis, Wrt. Voc. i. 83, 56: acer, vehemens, 17, 28: strenuus, ii. 74, 60. I. of living beings, (1) *strong, powerful, mighty*:—Hé wæs strang foreþingere *he was a powerful intercessor*, Homl. Skt. i. 5, 6. Fugel meahtum strang, Exon. Th. 40, 31; Cri. 647. Ðú eart mægenes strang, Beo. Th. 3692; B. 1844. Hú mæg man ingán on stranges (*fortis*) hús and hys fata hyne bereáfian, búton hé gebinde ǽrest ðone strangan (*fortem*)? Mt. Kmbl. 12, 29. Paminunde ðæm strongan cyninge *apud Epaminondam, strenuissimum imperatorem*, Ors. 3, 7; Swt. 110, 21. Wǽron hér strange cyningas (*fortissimi reges*), Bd. 4, 2; S. 565, 30. Hé ys strengra (strængra, Rush.: strongra, Lind.) ðonne ic *est fortior me*, Mt. Kmbl. 3, 11: Lk. Skt. 11, 22. Wé wénaþ ðæt mon beó ðý strængra (strencra, Cott. MS.) ðe hé biþ micel on his líchoman, Bt. 24, 3; Fox 84, 7. Ic eom se strengesta (*fortissimus*) God ðínes fæder, Gen. 46, 3. Se strangesta cyning Æþelfriþ *rex fortissimus Ædilfrid*, Bd. 1, 34; S. 499, 18. Ætýwan ðíne mǽrðe and ðíne strengestan hand, Deut. 3, 24. Feówer ða strengestan him betweónum gesprǽcon, Ors, 3, 10; Swt. 138, 3. Of ðrím folcum ðám strangestan Germanie *de tribus Germaniae populis fortioribus*, Bd. 1, 15; S. 483, 20. Of mínum strengestum feóndum, Ps. Th. 17, 18. (2) *strong, firm, resolute, hardy*:—Beó strang and staðulfæst *confortare et esto robustus*, Deut. 31, 7, 23. Ic wénde ðæt ic wǽre swíðe strong on manegum cræftum ac ic ongeat siððan ðú mé forléte hú untrum ic wæs *fortem me inter virtutes credidi, sed, quantae infirmitatis sim, derelictus agnovi*, Past. 65, 5; Swt. 465, 21. Ðætte úre mód ðý fæstre and ðý strengre beforan Gode sié on ðæm cræftum *ut cor robustius in virtute solidetur*, 65, 6; Swt. 467, 9. Ðǽr wæs heáfde beslagen se strengesta martyr Scs Albanus, Bd. 1, 7; S. 478, 33. (3) *hard, severe, fierce, stern*:—Strang wæs and reðe se ðe wætrum weóld, Cd. Th. 83, 8; Gen. 1376. Se þeóden wæs strang and stíðmód, 279, 34; Sat. 248. Petrus gecýðde ðæt hé wæs strengesð wið scylda, Past. 17, 6; Swt. 115, 17. Seó strengeste þeód *gens ferocissima*, Ors. 4, 11; Swt. 206, 34. II. of things, (1) *strong, able to resist force, firm*:—Ðú wǽre mé stranga tor, Ps. Th. 60, 2. Gé nánuht mid eów nabbaþ fæstes ne stronges ðætte þurhwunigean mǽge, Ors. 2, 4; Swt. 74, 28. Æt strangum stáne, Ps. Th. 140, 8. Of ðissum strongan stýle, Exon. Th. 426, 25; Rä. 41, 79. Ðeós wyrt biþ cenned on fæstum landum and on strangum, Lchdm. i. 134, 19. Ðeós wyrt on Illyrico swíðost and strengost wexeþ, 284, 17. (2) *firm, valid, assured*:—Mé ðynceþ wíslíc, gif ðú geseó ða þing beteran and strengran ðe ús bodade syndon, ðæt wé ðám onfón, Bd. 2, 13; S. 516, 10. (3) *strong in operation, effective, producing a great effect, potent*:—Ongeán swelce mettrymnesse mon beðorfte stronges lǽcedómes . . . Is ðæm lǽce tó giémanne ðæt hé strangne lǽcedóm selle ðæm seócan, Past. 61, 2; Swt. 455, 26–29. Ða leáf syndon stranges swæcces, Lchdm. i. 310, 7. Gif ðú ðás wyrte sylst þicgean on strangon wíne, 172, 12. Strangre stemne, Cd. Th. 33, 24; Gen. 525. Ða recceras ætiéwaþ strangne andan *fortem zelum rectores exhibent*, Past. 21, 6; Swt. 164, 11. Ðæt is for hwí se góda lǽce selle ðam hálum men séftne drenc and swétne, and óðrum hálum biterne and strangne, Bt. 39, 9; Fox 226, 12. Gelácnian mid ðǽm drencum strangra wyrta gemanges, Past. 37; Swt. 269, 24. Se gewuna is strengra on ǽlcum worde, ðonne his regol sý, Ælfc. Gr. 30; Zup. 193, 2. Ðæt hié hæfden ðý strengran scyte *ne sagittarum jactus inpedirentur*, Ors. 1, 10; Swt. 46, 13. Strongrum helpum *validioribus auxiliis*, Rtl. 61, 11. (4) *strong, earnest*:—Ðá sealdon hí him strange manunge, Bd. 1, 12; S. 481, 13. (5) of that which is hard to bear, *hard, severe*:—Godes bebod, þéh hit strong wǽre, Ors. 6, 1; Swt. 252, 2. Hú strang hit biþ an helle tó biónne, Wulfst. 225, 12. Is se drohtað strang ðam ðe lagoláde lange cunnaþ, Andr. Kmbl. 626; An. 313. Strang wíte, Cd. Th. 155, 4; Gen. 2567. Ðæt sár biþ tó ðon strang, and hé næfþ nánne slǽp ðonne hit strangost biþ. Lchdm. ii. 198, 25. Strang fefer, 226, 16. Com se stranga winter mid forste and mid snáwe and mid eallon ungewederon, ðæt næs nán man ðá on líue, ðæt mihte gemunan swá strangne winter swá se wæs, Chr. 1046; Erl. 170, 32: Chart. Th. 163, 1. Hé ástealde swíðe strang gyld, Chr. 1040; Erl. 166, 20. Ealle ða gesetnessa ðe tó stronge wǽron and tó hearde, Ors. 5, 12; Swt. 244, 15. Wæs ðis gefeoht wælgrimre and strengre eallum ðám ǽrgedónum, Bd. 1, 12; S. 481, 25. Manig broc byþ mycle strengre ðonne tóðæce, ðeáh ic nǽfre nán strengre ne geðolode, Shrn. 185, 15. Ðonne biþ Drihtnes word réðe gehýred, ðám synfullum stefna strangast, Wulfst. 256, 16. (6) of violent motion or action, *fierce, violent*:—Strong wind, Met. 7, 25. Strang storm, Lchdm. i. 326, 19. His tógán biþ ðearle strang, 364, 17. Se stranga rén, Ps. Th. 71, 6. Ðá gemunde hé ða strangan dǽda ðara unmanna and ðæra woruldfrumena, Guthl. 2; Gdwin. 12, 27. Gif strongra storm and genip swýðor ðreáde, Bd. 4, 3; S. 569, 12. [*O. Sax.* strang: *Icel.* strangr: *O. H. Ger.* strengi.] v. byrðen-, for-, hyge-, lang-, mægen-, med-, ryne-, swíþ-, un-strang; strenge.

strange; *adv.* I. *severely*:—Rícum mannum man sceal strangor (*severius*) déman ðonne ðám heánum, L. Ecg. C. 1; Th. ii. 132, 30. Ðeáh ðe ðæt wíte heardor and strangor dón sý *cum districtius agitur*, Bd. 1, 27; S. 490, 12. II. *strongly, violently*:—Seó sǽ strange geondstyred on staþu beáteþ, Met. 6, 15: Soul Kmbl. 89; Seel. 45.

strang-hende, -hynde; *adj. Strong of hand*:—Dauid is gecweden *fortis manum*, ðæt ys stranghynde, Ælfc. T. Grn. 7, 14.

strangian; *p.* ode. I. *to grow strong, be strong, prevail, flourish*:—Ic strangige oððe geðeó *uigeo*, Ælfc. Gr. 26, 2; Zup. 154, 14. Strongaþ *praevaluit*, Ps. Surt. 51, 9. Ic strongade wið him *praevalui adversus eum*, 12, 5. Word unrehtwísra strongadun (*praevaluerunt*) ofer ús, 64, 4. Strangadan, swíðodon *invalescebant*, Wrt. Voc. ii. 74, 6. Strangedon, 46, 49. [Þet eower heorte erȝian and eower feond strongian, O. E. Homl. i. 13, 28. *O. H. Ger.* strangên *confortari*.] II. *to make strong, confirm, comfort*:—Staþelige man and strangie and trumme hí georne, L. I. P. 4; Th. ii. 308, 3. Hé ðǽr wunode strangende hira heortan on geleáfan, Blickl. Homl. 249, 17. [Heo strangede þe walles, Laym. 4461.] v. ge-strangian; strangung.

strang-líc; *adj.* I. of persons, *strong, robust*:—Cniht, stranglíc on wæstme and wénlíc on nebbe, Ælfc. T. Grn. 16, 41. Hwæðer ðæt landfolc sí tó gefeohte stranglíc oððe untrumlíc *populum, utrum fortis sit an infirmus*, Num. 13, 20. II. of things, (1) *strong, firm, solid, able to resist force*:—Næs nán ðæs stronglíc stán gefæstnod, ðæt mihte ðam miclan mægne wiðhabban, Cd. Th. 297, 14; Sat. 517. Ðeáh ðeós eorðe þince on stede stronglíc, Met. 10, 11. Mínne stronglícan stól, Cd. Th. 23, 27; Gen. 366. Sume bióþ beforan monna eágum gesewen swelce hié fæstlícu and stronglícu weorc wyrce *quidam quaedam ante humanos oculos robusta exerceant*, Past. 34, 6; Swt. 234, 19. (2) *requiring strength, laborious, hard*:—Nánne mon ðæs ne tweóþ ðæt se seó strong on his mægene ðe mon gesihþ ðæt stronglíc weorc wyrcþ *nemo dubitat esse fortem cui fortitudinem inesse conspexerit*, Bt. 16, 3; Fox 54, 29. (3) *hard to bear, severe*:—Ðis is stronglíc, nú ðes storm becom, Cd. Th. 288, 25; Sat. 387. Stingaþ stranglíc sár on his eágan, Wulfst. 141, 5. [*O. H. Ger.* strang-lîh *robustus*.]

stranglíce; *adj. Strongly*:—Stranglíce *roborabiliter*, Wrt. Voc. ii. 84, 63. Stranglíce *fortiter*, stranglícor *fortius*, stranglícost *fortissime*, Ælfc. Gr. 38; Zup. 230, 15. I. *with power, with energy, strenuously, vigorously*:—Hé stranglíce ríxode and bewerode ðæt folc wið ða hǽðenan leóda, Ælfc. T. Grn. 7, 7. Hé galdorcræftum wiðstód stranglíce, Andr. Kmbl. 333; An. 167: Exon. Th. 156, 15; Gú. 875. Hwæt getácnaþ ða bán búton stronglíce geworht weorc *quid per ossa nisi fortia acta signantur?* Past. 34, 6; Swt. 235, 16. II. *with violence, fiercely, vehemently*:—Hé byrnende from gebede swíceþ, stepeþ stronglíce, Exon. Th. 264, 34; Jul. 374. Se here ða burh besǽton and hire stranglíce wið feaht, Chr. 1016; Erl. 156, 15. Hire mǽtte ðæt heó hæfde sweord on handa and ðæt heó stranglíce fuhte mid ðý, Shrn. 60, 30. Ðæt se wind swá stronglíce hrure on ða circan, ðæt ðǽr ne mihte nǽnig mon gestandan oððe gesittan, 81, 22. III. *boldly, bravely, hardily*:—Hí heora land stronglíce geeodan and freódóm onféngon, Bd. 3, 24; S. 557, 46. Him gesewen wæs ðæt hé heardlíce and stranglíce sprǽce, 5, 13; S. 632, 25. IV. *firmly, in a manner to resist force*:—Hé biþ stranglíce wið ða getrymed, Past. 21; Swt. 165, 7. Tó ðon ðæt hé swá micle stranglícor árise swá hé hefiglícor áfeóll *tanto post solidius surgeret quanto prius cecidisset*, 58, 5; Swt. 443, 32. V. *severely, sternly*:—On ðám is stronglíce tó ehtanne ða ðe him ne ondrǽdaþ wítende syngian *in his fortiter insequenda, qui non metuunt sciendo peccare*, Bd. 1, 27; S. 491, 37. Se man wæs stranglíce gewítnad, Shrn. 73, 12. Se ðe swá stronglíce ða Iudéas þreáde, Blickl. Homl. 169, 7.

strang-mód; *adj. Of strong mind, confident, resolute*:—God ða unstrangan ðyses middangeardes geceás, ðæt ða strangmódan, ðe on ágenum mihtum truwiaþ, gescende wǽron, R. Ben. 138, 28.

strangness, e; *f.* I. *strength*:—Strangnysse míne *fortitudinem meam*, Ps. Spl. 58, 10. II. *force, violence*:—Of him is bodud Godes ríce and ealle on ðæt strangnysse wyrcaþ *ex eo regnum Dei euangelizatur, et omnis in illud uim facit*, Lk. Skt. 16, 16.

strangung, e; *f.* I. *strengthening, invigorating*:—Hé (*Christ*) ne behófode nánes wæstmes ne nánre strangunge on ðære godcundnysse, Homl. Th. i. 150, 5. Mettas ðe célunge and strangunge úres mægen hæbben, Lchdm. ii. 176, 16. Ðæt lyft hé gesceóp tó úres lífes strangunge, Hexam. 4; Norm. 8, 17. II. *vigor*:—Helias lyfaþ git on líchaman mid langsumre strangunge, Homl. Skt. i. 18, 275. v. ge-strangung; strangian.

strapul, es; *m. A covering for the leg, kind of trouser*:—Strapulas *tubroces* (*tubrucus* lanea ocrea, ocreis aut calceis coriaceis superimponi solita, Migne) vel *brace*, Wrt. Voc. i. 25, 61. [A strapylle *tibiale*, Wrt. Voc. i. 259, col. 2 (15th cent.). Straple of a breche, strappyl *femorale, feminale*, Prompt. Parv. 478. Þe strapils of breke *tribraca, femoralia*, Cath. Ang. 367. Sum wummon wereð þe brech of heare and þe strapeles adun to hire uet ilaced ful ueste, A. R. 420, 5. Seide þat þey were liche to mares wiþ white legges up to þe þiȝes, for þat tyme þe Longobardes usede strapeles wiþ brode laces doun to þe sparlyver *asserens eos fore similes equabus, quarum cruretenus pedes sunt albi, eo quod Longobardi tunc temporis usque ad suras candidis fasceolis uterentur*, Trev. v. 355, 4.]

stré, streá-berige, streac, streál. v. streáw, streáw-berige, stearc, strǽl.

streám, es; *m. A stream, current, flowing water*; in the plural used of the sea in poetry:—Streám *vel* wǽto *irriguum*, Wrt. Voc. i. 28, 9. Streám *fluens*, ii. 149, 68: *alveus*, i. 54, 26. Streám, streúm *rema, reuma*, Txts. 92, 855. Streámum, streaumum, streúm *torrentibus*, 103, 2036. Hí on ðæs streámes brycge ábysgade wǽron . . . Scs Albanus eode tó ðære burnan . . . ðá sóna ádrúgode se streám *fluminis ipsius occupabat pontem . . . Sanctus Albanus accessit ad torrentem . . . illico siccato alveo*, Bd. 1, 7; S. 478, 8–13. Hé wolde ða eá mid sunde oferfaran, ac hiene se streám fordráf, Ors. 2, 4; Swt. 72, 30. Ymbútan ðone weall is se mǽsta díc, on ðæm is iernende se ungefóglecesta streám *fossa extrinsecus late patens, vice amnis circumfluit*, Swt. 74, 18. Ealle ða gewítaþ swá swá wæteres streám, Blickl. Homl. 59, 20. Forðon seó stów on ófre ðæs streámes (*super ripam fluminis*) wæs geseted, wæs his gewuna ðæt hé on ðone streám eode and hine on ðam streáme sencte, Bd. 5, 12; S. 631, 18–22. Humbre streámes *Humbrae fluminis*, 1, 25; S. 486, 17. On Trenton streáme *in fluvio Treenta*, 2, 16; S. 519, 31. Temese streáme *Tamense fluvio*, 2, 3; S. 504, 16: 2, 14; S. 518, 15. Gehlade áne cuppan fulle ford mid ðam streáme, Lchdm. iii. 74, 14. Hát gefeccean ongean streáme healfne sester yrnendes wæteres, 12, 1. Sing ðis on yrnendum wætere, and wend ðæt heáfod ongeán streám, 70, 8. Ondlang ðæs streámes . . . ondlang ðæs Doferdæles ongeán streám tō Wīcforda, Cod. Dip. Kmbl. vi. 218, 29. Streámas stōdon, Cd. Th. 206, 29; Exod. 459. Streámas wundon, Beo. Th. 430; B. 212. Wǣgas grundon, streámas styredon, Andr. Kmbl. 747; An. 374. Reáde streámas *the waters of the Red Sea*, Cd. Th. 196, 23; Ex. 296. Sealte streámas, Exon. Th. 206, 2; Ph. 120. Streámas, sealtȳþa gelāc, 308, 4; Seef. 34. [*O. Frs.* strâm: *O. Sax.* strōm: *O. H. Ger.* stroum, strūm *alveus, amnis, torrens*: *Icel.* straumr.] v. brim-, eá-, ēg-, ēgor-, fīfel-, firgen-, fyrn-, lagu-, mere-, sǣ-, wǣg-, wæl-, wæter-, wille-streám.

streám-faru, e; *f. The going* or *flowing of a stream of water, a current*:—Se æðeling hēt streámfare stillan *the prince bade the rush of waters cease*, Andr. Kmbl. 3150; An. 1578.

streám-gewinn, es; *n. The strife of waters*:—Bīdaþ stille stealc stānhleoþu streámgewinnes, Exon. Th. 384, 12; Rä. 4, 26.

streám-līc; *adj. Of water*:—Ofer streámlīcum rīðum *over rivers of waters*, Homl. Th. i. 444, 10.

streám-racu, e; *f. The bed* or *channel of a stream, a water-course*:—Streámracu *alveus*, Wrt. Voc. i. 54, 26. Streámrace *alveum*, ii. 4, 59. Him þurh streámræce strǣt wæs gerȳmed, Andr. Kmbl. 3158; An. 1582. Fram streámracum ōþ ðysse eorðan ūtgemǣru *a flumine usque ad terminos orbis terrae*, Ps. Th. 71, 8.

streám-rād, e; *f.* I. *the bed, course of a stream*:—Streám-raad, -rād, streúmrād *alveus*, Txts. 39, 129. II. *a watery road, the way across the sea*:—Sum streámrāde con, weorudes wīsa ofer wīdne holm, Exon. Th. 296, 21; Crä. 54.

streám-ryne, es; *m. The running of a stream*:—Ðæt wæter swā genihtsumlīce ūt fleów ðæt hit arn streámrynes of ðam munte *the water flowed out so abundantly, that it ran streaming from the mountain*, Homl. Th. ii. 162, 8.

streám-stæþ, es; *n. A shore*:—Ofer streámstaðe stæppan *to land*, Cd. Th. 86, 21; Gen. 1434.

streám-weall, es; *m. A shore*:—Stāh ofer streámweall *he landed*, Cd. Th. 90, 12; Gen. 1494.

streám-wilm, es; *m. The boiling of the waters, surge*; aestus:—Streámwelm hwīleþ, Andr. Kmbl. 990; An. 495.

streáw, streów, strēu, strēw, es; *n. Straw, hay*:—Gærs oððe streów *foenum*, Ælfc. Gr. 4; Zup. 8, 3. Strēw, streów, streáw, 13; Zup. 83, 17. Strēwu, eglan *fistucam*, Wrt. Voc. ii. 36, 69: 72, 25. Ðæt strēu (strē (*printed* sore, *but* cf. lytles strēes *festucae*, Mt. Kmbl. p. 15, 4), Lind.), Mt. Kmbl. Rush. 7, 4, 5. Sume hī cuwon hoora gescȳ, sume streáw, Homl. Th. i. 404, 6. Bærne streúw, Lchdm. iii. 114, 7. [Þe cwene þet mid one strea brouhte o brune alle hire houses, A. R. 296, 12. *Havel.* stra: *Chauc.* stre, stree: *Piers P.* strawe: *O. Frs.* strē: *O. L. Ger.* strō; *gen.* strōs: *O. H. Ger.* strō, strao: *Icel.* strā.] v. snīð-, windel-streáw (-streów).

streáw-berige (streá-, streów-, strēu-), an; *f. A strawberry* (*plant* or *fruit*):—Streáwberige *fraga*, Wrt. Voc. i. 67, 71. Streáberige, 31, 69. Streówberian wīse (streáwberge, MS. H.). Ðeós wyrt ðe man *fraga* and ōðrum naman streáwbergean nemneþ, Lchdm. i. 138, 20. Streówberge *fraga*, Wrt. Voc. i. 286, 4: ii. 36, 59. Strēuberie *fascinium*, strēuberian *fraga*, 38, 65, 66. Streáwberian wīsan *fraga*, i. 79, 37. Streáwbergean leáf, Lchdm. ii. 350, 27. Streáwbergean wīse, 36, 11. Streáwberian wīsan nioþowearde, 34, 24: 334, 11. Genim streáwberian nyþeweardan, iii. 2, 18. Streábergan *vel* eorþbergan *fragium* i. *pumorum*, Wrt. Voc. ii. 150, 30.

streáwberige-wīse, an; *f. A strawberry-plant* or *runner*:—Streáberiewīsan *framen*, Wrt. Voc. i. 31, 70. [A strebery-wyse *hec fragus*, a strebery *hoc fragum*, Wrt. Voc. i. 247, col. 1.]

streáwian, streówian; *p.* ode: strēwian; *p.* ede *To straw, strew*:—Ic strewige (streáwige, streówige) *sterno*, Ælfc. Gr. 28, 1; Zup. 165, 9. Wē streówiaþ (strewiaþ) axan uppan ūre heáfda, Homl. Skt. i. 12, 38. Streáwiaþ *evernenent* (*sternerent?*), Wrt. Voc. ii. 144, 30. Mid ðǣm hē strewede ðone weg, Past. 16; Swt. 103, 13. Sume of ðām treówum heówon and streówodon (streówedon, MS. A.: strewedon, MS. B.) on ðone weg, Mk. Skt. 11, 8. Strewodun (streówedon, MS. A.), Mt. Kmbl. 21, 8. Streówodan, Blickl. Homl. 71, 8, 9. Ða hǣþenan byrnende glēda streáwodon, Homl. Skt. i. 23, 35. Hē hēt streówian geond ða flōr fela byrnende glēda, 8, 168. [*Orm.* strawwenn: *Chauc.* strawe: *Prompt. Parv.* strowiñ: *Goth.* straujan; *p.* strawida: *O. Frs.* strewa: *O. Sax.* strōedun, streidun, *p. pl.*: *O. L. Ger.* streidin *sternerent*: *O. H. Ger.* strewen, strouwen: *Icel.* strā.] v. be-, ge-streáwian, -streówian; strēgan.

streáwung, strec. v. strewung, stræc.

streccan; *p.* strehte, streahte; *pp.* streht, streaht, streced (v. strecedness) *To stretch.* I. *to hold out, extend*:—Ðū strecst (*extendes*) ðīne handa, and ōðer ðē gyrt, Jn. Skt. 21, 18. Strece ðǣrtō ðīnne hiht, Homl. Th. i. 252, 7. II. *to spread out*:—Ðæt folc strehton (*straverunt*) hyra reáf on ðone weg, Mt. Kmbl. 21, 8: Mk. Skt. 11, 8: Lk. Skt. 19, 36. III. *to prostrate*:—Hē hine wæs on gebed streccende æt līchoman ðæs Godes weres *prosternens se ad corpus viri Dei pia intentione*, Bd. 4, 31; S. 610, 29. [*O. H. Ger.* strecchen *extendere, porrigere, prosternere*.] v. ā-, ge-streccan.

strecedness, e; *f. A couch*; stratum:—Strecednes *stratum*, Ps. Lamb. 40, 4. Strecednysse mīne ic beþweá, 6, 7.

strec-līc, -līce, -ness. v. stræc-līc, -līce, -ness.

strēdan. v. stregdan.

strēgan *to strew*:—Græf golde strēgan (stregdan?), Exon. Th. 311, 25; Seef. 97. [*Goth.* straujan.] v. stregdan.

stregdan. [There are two verbs of this form, a strong and a weak. The conjugation is further complicated by the frequent loss of g, so that forms of the strong verb are found (?) belonging to two classes (cf. *bregdan*): while in the Northern Gospels strong and weak inflections are combined in the same word. The two verbs are here put together]; ic stregde, strigde, strēde, hē stregdeþ, strigdeþ, strēt; *p.* (*strong*) strægd, *pl.* strugdon *and* strǣdon (v. strēdun, Mk. 11, 8: *but the form may be weak* = strægdon): (*weak*) stregde, strēdde, strugde (*North.*); *pp.* (*strong*) strogden: (*weak*) stregd, strēded, strēd *To strew, spread, scatter, sprinkle.* I. *to strew* something:—Se ðe ne somnigas streigdæs *qui non congregat, spargit*, Mt. Kmbl. 12, 30. Geswerc swē swē eascan strigdeþ (*spargit*), Ps. Surt. 147, 16. Monige ðæt wæter on ādlige men strēdaþ, Bd. 3, 2; S. 524, 32. Se wind se ðe ða bærnnisse in ða burg strægd *ventus qui urbi incendia sparserat*, 2, 7; S. 509, 28. Ōðre ða telge strēdun (*sternebant*) on ðone woeg, Mk. Skt. Rush. 11, 8. Ðū somnas ðēr ðū ne strugdes (*sparsisti*) . . . Ic somnigo ðǣr ic ne strugde (strægde, Rush.: strēdde, W. S. *sparsi*), Mt. Kmbl. Lind. 25, 24, 26. Ðæt āttor on eallum cyricum hē stregde (*aspersit*), Bd. 1, 8; S. 479, 35. Sió mængu strægdun hrægl heora on ðæm wege, sume telgran strægdun on ðæm wege, Mt. Kmbl. Rush. 21, 8. Nim ðæs hornes acxan and strēd, Lchdm. i. 334, 17. Strēd on hālig wæter *sprinkle holy water on*, iii. 56, 11, 18. On ðæs feóndes feax flāna stregdan, Salm. Kmbl. 262; Sal. 130. Stregdende weter *aspargens aquas*, Ps. Surt. ii. p. 190, 9. Wæs heora lār sāwen and strogden betuh feówer sceátum middangeardes, Blickl. Homl. 133, 33. Wæs him morþorbed strēd, Beo. Th. 4864; B. 2436. II. *to sprinkle* a place with something:—Ðū strēdest (āstregdest, MS. T.) mē mid hysopon *asperges me hysopo*, Ps. Spl. 50, 8. Strēde man hit mid hāligwætere *aspergatur aqua benedicta*, L. Ecg. P. iv. 38; Th. ii. 216, 1. III. *intrans. To scatter, disperse*:—Steorran strēdaþ of heofone, stormum ābeátne, Exon. Th. 58, 24; Cri. 940. Stregdaþ tōðas, Salm. Kmbl. 230; Sal. 114. Hī tō scipon strēddon *they dispersed to their ships*, Chr. 1010; Erl. 144, 3. IV. *to lay in order* (?):—Streide *struere* (*struerem?*), strīdae, streide *struere*, Txts. 99, 1910. v. ā-, be-, ge-, geond-, on-, under-stregdan, -strēdan.

stregdness, e; *f. Scattering, sprinkling*:—Mid strægdnesse (*aspersione*) ðæs wæteres, Bd. 5, 18; S. 635, 29.

strēl *a couch*, strēl *an arrow*, strēme, strencan, strēn. v. strǣgl, strǣl, strīme, strencan, streówen.

streng, es; *m.* I. *a string, cord, rope*:—Rāp *vel* strenc *funiculus, modicus funus*, Wrt. Voc. ii. 151, 67. Strengas *vel* bendas *lora*, 136, 77. Hē worhte swipan of strengon (*de funiculis*), Jn. Skt. 2, 15. (1) *a string* of a musical instrument:—Streng *fidis*, Wrt. Voc. i. 73, 54. On saltere tȳn strenga (*chordarum*), Ps. Spl. 32, 2. Strengum *fidibus*, Wrt. Voc. ii. 37, 22: 148, 71: Hpt. Gl. 520, 61. Mid tȳn strengum getogen hearpe, Ps. Th. 143, 10. (2) *a bow-string*:—Boga *arcus*, bogen (-an?) streng *anquina* (*ar-?*), Wrt. Voc. i. 35, 26. Strǣla storm strengum gebǣded, Beo. Th. 6226; B. 3117. (3) in a ship, *part of the rigging*; also *a cable*. v. ancer-streng *and cf. Icel.* strengr *in this sense*:—Ðæt scyp ūte on ðære sǣ byþ gesund, gyf se streng (v. ancerstreng, l. 18) āþolaþ, for ðam hys byþ se ōðer ende fast on ðære eorðan and se ōðer on ðam scype . . . Ðū scealt gefastnian ðone streng on Gode, ðæt ðæt scyp healdan sceal ðīnes mōdes, Shrn. 175, 21–31. Windas weóxon, strengas gurron, Andr. Kmbl. 748; An. 374. (4) *a ligament, string* (of the tongue):—Wið ðam ðe se streng under ðare tunga tōswollen byþ, Lchdm. iii. 102, 2, 4, 5, 8. Strengce *nervo*, Hpt. Gl. 405, 73. Strenga *nervorum*, 475, 13. II. fig. *a line, lineage* (cf. *Icel.* strengr, used of a narrow water-channel):—Of ðam strenge com Noe and his wīf, Ælfc. T. Grn. 3, 28. [*O. H. Ger.* strang *funus, funiculus*: *Icel.* strengr.] v. ancer-streng.

strengan; *p.* de *To make strong.* [Þild birrþ ben wiþþ ihwillc mahht to beoldenn it and strengenn, Orm. 2614. Þe wepnen þ strenged ham stalewurdlukest aȝein me, Marh. 14, 19.] v. æt-strengan, ā-strenged; strangian.

streng *strength*. v. strengu.

strenge; *adj. Severe, hard* (v. strang, II. 5):—Hē his torn gewræc on gesacum swīðe strengum stiépe, Cd. Th. 4, 27; Gen. 60. v. strang.

-strenge, -strenged. v. tīn-strenge, -strenged.

strengel, es; *m. One who strengthens* or *emboldens, a gallant leader*:—Nū sceal glēd fretan wīgena strengel (*Beowulf*), Beo. Th. 6222; B. 3115.

strengest. v. strang.

streng-līc; *adj. Strong, firm*:—Hū hē him strenglīcran stōl geworhte, heáhran on heofonum, Cd. Th. 18, 14; Gen. 273. Cf. strang-līc.

strengra. v. strang.

strengđu (o); *indecl.*: strengđ, e; *f. Strength*:—Strengđ *acha*, i. *virtus*, Wrt. Voc. i. 17, 27. Seó strengđ *vis*, Gl. Prud. 71. I. referring to living beings, (1) *strength, power to do, fortitude, power to bear, firmness, vigour*:—Strengþu heáfdes mínes *fortitudo capitis mei*, Ps. Th. 59, 6: 117, 14. Mægnes strengđu, Exon. Th. 239, 23; Ph. 625. Módes strengđ *fortitudo*, Wulfst. 51, 7. *Fortitudo*, đæt is strængđ ođđe ánrǽdnyss, þurh đa sceal seó sáwul forbæran earfođnysse mid ánrǽdum móde, Homl. Skt. i. 1, 165. Strængþ *vigor*, Hymn. Surt. 10, 10. Strengcþ mín *fortitudo mea*, Ps. Spl. 17, 1. Strenđ *robur*, Kent. Gl. 795. Ic eów healde strengđu staþolfæstre, Exon. Th. 31, 3; Cri. 490. In đære gǽstes strengđu, 40, 14; Cri. 638. Beón wiđmeten đínre strengđe *comparari fortitudini tuae*, Deut. 3, 24: Ps. Spl. 38, 14. On strengđe horses, 146, 11. Mid strencgđe *cum potentia*, Ps. Th. 88, 11. Mid micelre strencđe áfylled hé worhte micele tácna, Homl. Th. i. 44, 23. Swá se fulfremeda wæstm biþ on fulre strencđe þeónde, ii. 76, 19. Se weard (*the angel at the gate of Eden*) hafaþ miht and strengđo, Cd. Th. 58, 22; Gen. 950. Ic đíne strengþu (*virtutem*) singe, Ps. Th. 58, 16. Strengđe *fortitudinem*, Ps. Spl. 58, 18. Hí lǽrdon đæt hí módes strengþo náman, Bd. 1, 12; S. 481, 5. (1 a) *the time when a man is strong, mature years*:—On mínum cildháde ođđe on mínre geógođe ođđe on mínre strengđe ođđe on mínre ylde, Anglia xi. 102, 2. (2) *violence, force*:—Hé đa ongeánwinnendan fǽmnan mid micelre strengđe earfođlíce ofercom, Ap. Th. 2, 5. Strenđe *violentiam*, Kent. Gl. 842. Hié ongunnon mid sweordum and mid strengþum þyder gán; þohton đæt hié woldan ofsleán đa apostolas, Blickl. Homl. 151, 1. II. referring to things, (1) *strength, efficacy, virtue, beneficial power*:—Hæfþ hit đa strængđe hyne tó gewyrmenne, Lchdm. i. 116, 1. Đás sylfan strengþe heó hafaþ gewylled wiđ đæs migþan earfođlícnyssa, 284, 3. Hæfþ đeós wyrt ealle heora strengđa, 244, 1. (2) of that which is hard to bear, *strength, violence, severity, force*:—Đí læs seó strengđ đære wyrte đa góman bærne, Lchdm. i. 316, 20. Wiđ áttres strenđe (strengđe, MS. B.), genim đás wyrte . . . heó oferswíđ ealle strenđe đæs áttres, 114, 13–15. Ne mæg man ǽfre for his strengđe đysne wyrttruman syllan þicgean on sundrum, 260, 18. Hé sceal upweard licgean, đý læs hé đa strengþe đyssæ lácnunge ongite, 300, 21. v. mægen-strengđu.

strengu (o); *indecl.*: streng, e; *f. Strength.* I. referring to living beings, *strength, power, vigour, fortitude*:—Đæs líchoman fæger and his strengo mæg bión áfyrred mid þreora daga fefre, Bt. 32, 2; Fox 116, 31 note. Dryhten strengo (*fortitudo*) folces his, Ps. Surt. 27, 8. Tor strengu, 60, 4. Đa medomnesse đære strengio (-eo, Cott. MSS.) *dignitatem fortitudinis*, Past. 14, 5; Swt. 85, 23. Đære gástlícan strenge hyht, Blickl. Homl. 135, 27, 34. Of ælre strengu (-o, Lind.), Mk. Skt. Rush. 12, 33. Strengo bistolen, mægene binumen, Exon. Th. 410, 8; Rä. 28, 13. Strengo getrúwode ánes mannes, Beo. Th. 5074; B. 2540. Strenge, 3071; B. 1533. Full strenge *plenus fortitudine*, Rtl. 43, 34. Mid míne ágne mægene and strengo (-eo, Cott. MSS.), Past. 4; Swt. 39, 18: Cd. Th. 98, 19; Gen. 1632. Strengeo, 150, 21; Gen. 2495. Hé gemunde mægenes strenge, Beo. Th. 2545; B. 1270. Strengum *vigorously*, Cd. Th. 101, 2; Gen. 1676. II. of things, (1) *strength, power*:—Mec wolcna strengu byreþ, Exon. Th. 390, 4; Rä. 8, 5. (2) *vigour, firmness*:—On strengo þeódscipes wlæc *in disciplinae vigore tepidus*, Bd. 1, 27; S. 492, 18. On færhæfdnesse strenge (strengeo, Cott. MSS.) strange *abstinentiae robore validi*, Past. 5, 1; Swt. 41, 14. (3) *virtue*:—Sint tó manianne đa mettruman tó đæm đæt hié gehealden đa strenge đære geđylde *admonendi sunt aegri, quatenus patientiae virtutem servent*, 36, 9; Swt. 261, 2. [The word occurs often in a later MS., where *strengđ(u)* is found in the earlier in the passages given under that word from Lchdm. i. Deades strenge warp him dun, Gen. and Ex. 714. Edmond uor ys strenge was ycluped Yrensyde, R. Glouc. 302, 7. *O. Sax. O. H. Ger.* strengî *robur, fortitudo.*] v. hilde-, mægen-, mere-, woruld-strengu(o).

streón, es; *n.* I. *gain, acquisition, treasure*:—Đér is strión đín *ubi est thesaurus tuus*, Mt. Kmbl. Lind. 6, 21: 12, 35: Lk. Skt. Lind. 6, 45. Striónes *thesauri*, p. 17, 5. Tilđa ł stre (= streóna *or* streón) *quaestuum, lucrum*, Hpt. Gl. 452, 7. Đa đe geléfeþ in striónum (on gistrión, Rush.) *confidentes in pecuniis*, Mk. Skt. Lind. 10, 24. Of striónum hiora *de facultatibus suis*, Lk. Skt. Lind. 8, 3. Strióna *thesauros*, Mt. Kmbl. Lind. 6, 20. [Gif þu hauest welþe . . . ahte nis non eldere stren (ayhte nys non ildre istreon, Jes. MS.), O. E. Misc. 113, 184.] II. *begetting* (?), *generating*:—Swá hwylc monn swá his wíf for intingan ánum brúceþ tó streónne (streónenne ?; *other text has* bearna tó strýnenne) *si quis suam conjugem creandorum liberorum gratia utitur*, Bd. 1, 27; S. 495, 33 MS. T. [Crist is his sune, Noht after chesunge ac after strene; for þan he him strende, alse þe sunne streneđ liht, O. E. Homl. ii. 19, 24. The word is used also in the sense of *what is begotten, progeny, lineage, strain*:—Of hire owene streone (*race*), Laym. 2737. Streon (*offspring*) of a swuch strunde, Jul. 55, 16. Ne not ich none sunne þet ne mei beon iled to one of ham seouene ođer to hore streones, A. R. 208, 15. All follc wass þatt illke streon þatt Adam haffde strenedd, Orm. 27. Hiss stren shollde ben todrifenn, 16396. Þat holy streon, O. E. Misc. 153, 217. Of God, nat of the streen of which they been engendered, Chauc. Cl. T. 157. Spenser uses the form *strene* in this sense.] III. *power* (?):—Geþencaþ hwelc đǽs flǽsclícan gód sién and đa gesǽlþa đe gé ungemetlíce wilniaþ đonne mágon gé ongeotan đæt đæs líchoman fæger and his streón mágon (strengo mæg, Cott. MS.) beón áfeorred mid þreora daga fefre *aestimate, quam vultis nimio corporis bona, dum sciatis hoc, quodcumque miramini, triduanae febris igniculo posse dissolvi*, Bt. 32, 2; Fox 116, 31. v. ge-streón; streónan.

streón *a couch.* v. streówen.

streónan, (*but more often with umlaut*) striénan, strénan, strínan, strýnan; *p.* de (*with gen. acc.*). I. *to gain, acquire*:—On đæm hiewe đe hé sceolde his gielpes stiéran, on đæm hé his striénþ. Mid đý đe hé sceolde his gestreón tóweorpan, mid đý hé hié gadraþ, Past. 8; Swt. 55, 10. Strýneþ *foeneratur*, Wrt. Voc. ii. 38, 45. Se đe him sylfum strýnþ *qui sibi thesaurizat*, Lk. Skt. 12, 21. Gif hé strióneþ allne middangeard *si lucretur universum mundum*, Lk. Skt. Lind. Rush. 9, 25. Nis eów forboden ǽhta habban, gif gé đa on riht strénaþ, Blickl. Homl. 53, 28. Guman gylpe strýnaþ *men proudly lay up treasure*, Exon. Th. 445, 28; Dóm. 14. Hé hié gemyndgaþ đara welegra đe longe stríndon (striéndon, Hatt. MS.), and lytle hwíle brucon; hú hrædlíce se fǽrlíca deáđ hié on lytelre hwíle bereáfode đæs đe hié on longre hwíle mid unryhte striéndon (stríndon, Hatt. MS.), Past. 44; Swt. 332, 15–17. Hí dugeþa strýndon, welan and wiste, Cd. Th. 59, 28; Gen. 970. Striónas *thesaurizate*, Mt. Kmbl. Lind. 6, 20. Riht is đæt geréfan geornlíce tylian and symle heora hláfordan strýnan mid rihte, L. I. P. 12; Th. ii. 320, 13. Hé ús féran hét gásta streónan, Andr. Kmbl. 662; An. 331. Se đe his feore nyle hǽlo strýnan, Exon. Th. 96, 16; Cri. 1575. Tó striónanne *thesaurizandum*, Mt. Kmbl. p. 15, 1. Đú đe wǽre welena strýnende, L. E. I. prm.; Th. ii. 398, 12. II. *to beget, generate, create*:—Gé strínaþ suna and dohtra *filios generabis et filias*, Deut. 28, 41. Of đysum þrím mannum, Noes sunum, eall đes middangeard wearđ eft onwæcnod, þéh hyé Drihten on þreó streónde (*created them of three conditions*), Anglia xi. 3, 60. Seth strýnde suna and dohtra, Cd. Th. 69, 20; Gen. 1138: 70, 13; Gen. 1152. Hé be wífe bearna strýnde, 70, 5; Gen. 1148: 73, 8; Gen. 1201. Hié tósomne férdon and bearna striéndon, Ors. 1, 10; Swt. 46, 10. Đæt his bróđor nyme hys wíf and strýne him bearn, Mt. Kmbl. 22, 24. Hié sculon bearna striénan, Past. 51; Swt. 397, 10: Ors. 4, 1; Swt. 154, 17: Cd. Th. 59, 19; Gen. 966. Hé ongan óđres striénan bearnes be brýde, 68, 17; Gen. 1118. Strýnan, 71, 15; Gen. 1171. For intingan bearna tó strýnenne *creandorum liberorum gratia*, Bd. 1, 27; S. 495, 33. Ic wille đæt hit gange on đa nýhstan hand mé, bútan hyra hwylc bearn hæbbe; đonne is mé leófast đæt hit gange on đæt strýned on đa wǽpnedhealfe (*to the child born on the male side*), Cod. Dip. Kmbl. ii. 116, 15. [On hir he scal streonen (streni, 2nd MS.) þat scal wide sturien, he scal streonien (streoni, 2nd MS.) hire on ænne swiđe sellichne mon, Laym. 18844. Sikernesse streoneđ ȝemeleaste, A. R. 234, 3. All þatt streonedd wass þurrh Adam, Orm. 33. Behinden he (*elephants*) hem sampnen đanne he sulen ođre strenen, O. E. Misc. 19, 609. Strenen *fornicantur*, Ps. 72, 27. See also Halliwell's Dict. *strain, strene. O. H. Ger.* striunen *lucrari.*] v. ge-streónan.

Streónes-halh *Whitby*:—On đære stówe seó is gecweden Streóneshalh, Bd. 3, 24; S. 557, 2: 4, 23; S. 592, 37. Hild abbodesse on Streónesheale, Chr. 680; Erl. 40, 13. Tymbrend đæs mynstres đe ys nemned Steórneshealh, Shrn. 148, 40. For the forms streanæs, streunaes, strenes, found in Bede's History, v. Txts. 489. In Bd. 3, 25 the word is explained by *sinus fari.*

streón-ful, streów. v. gestreón-ful, streáw.

streówen, streón, strén, e; *f.* I. *a couch, bed*:—In bed stréne mínre *in lectum stratus mei*, Ps. Surt. 131, 3. Stréne míne *stratum meum*, 6, 7: 40, 4: 62, 7. Đá héht hé him streówne gegearwian (bedd gewyrcian, MS. B.) *jussit sibi stratum parari*, Bd. 2, 6; S. 508, 8. II. *a place where anything rests*:—Hord sceal in streónum bídan . . . hwonne hine guman gedǽlen *treasure shall remain in its places of rest . . . until men distribute it*, Exon. Th. 337, 22; Gn. Ex. 68.

streówian, streówung. v. streáwian, strewung.

streówness, e; *f. Bedding, what is spread to lie on*:—Đá bǽdon hine his discipulos đæt hié móstan húru sume streównesse him under gedón for his untrumnesse; đa cwæđ hé: 'Bearn, ne bidde gé đæs; ne gedafenaþ cristenan men đæt hé elles dó, bútan swá hé efne on axan and on duste licge,' Blickl. Homl. 227, 12.

strét, stređđan, stréu, strewian. v. strǽt, be-stređđan, streáw, streáwian.

strewung, e; *f. What is spread to lie on, a couch*:—On bedde mínre strewunge *in lectum strati mei*, Ps. Lamb. 131, 3. [*O. L. Ger.* strewunga *stramentum.*]

stric, es; *m.* (?) *Plague* (?):—Eác sceal áspringan wíde and síde . . . stric and steorfa and fela ungelimpa, Wulfst. 86, 12. Stric and steorfa, orfcwealm and uncođu, 159, 10. Gif hit geweorđe đæt folce mislimpe þurh stric ođđe steorfan, þurh unwæstm ođđe unweder, L. I. P. 18; Th. ii. 324, 29. v. ge-stric.

strica, an; *m.* I. *a stroke* of a pen, *a tittle, a mark, line*:—Án strica oððe ān stæf ðære ealdan ǣ ne biþ forgǣged *iota unum aut unus apex non praeteribit* (Mt. 5, 18), Homl. Th. ii. 200, 1: Jud. 15. Strican ł mærcunge *characteres*, Hpt. Gl. 473, 13. Stricena *apicum*, stricum *characteribus, notis*, 512, 23, 52. Stricum *apicibus literarum*, 501, 56. II. *a streak, tract:*—Hit getīmaþ hwīltīdum ðonne se mōna beyrnþ on ðæm ylcan strican ðe seó sunne yrnþ, ðæt his trendel underscȳt ðære sunnan tō ðam swīðe ðæt heó eall āþeóstraþ, Lchdm. iii. 242, 19. [Longe, croked strykes, Chauc. Astrolabe. Strek or ·poynt betwyx ij clausys yn a boke *liminiscus*, Prompt. Parv. 479. *Goth.* striks *κεραία*: *O. H. Ger.* strich *linea, nota, zona.* Cf. *Icel.* stryk *a stroke, dash.*]

strīcan; *p.* strāc, *pl.* stricon; *pp.* stricen. I. *to stroke, smooth, rub, wipe:*—Ne delfe hȳ nān man mid īsene and mid wætere ne þweá, ac strīce hȳ mid clāðe clǣne, Lchdm. iii. 30, 24. [Baldulf lette striken to þan bare lichen his bærd and his chinne *had his beard shaved off quite smoothly*, Laym. 20303. To make murrour bryȝt. Stryke theron blak sope, Rel. Ant. i. 108, 23 (15th cent.). Strekyn̄ or make pleyne *complano*, strekyn̄ or make playne by mesure *hostio*, strekyn̄, as menn do cattys *palmito*, Prompt. Parv. 479, col. 2. To stryke a buschelle *hostiare*, Cath. Ang. 369. This pecke to conteyne stryken with a strykell as mutche as our standerd pecke holdeth upheaped, ib. note 1. To stryke a bed = to make it smooth, is quoted by Halliwell, who gives *strike* as a Devonshire word for to rub gently. *O. H. Ger.* strīhhan *linere, fovere.* Cf. *Icel.* strjúka *to stroke, rub, wipe*: *Dan.* stryge.] v. ymb-strīcan. II. *to make a stroke.* v. be-strīcan; strica. III. *to go, move, run:*—Būton ðæm rodere ðe ðās rūman gesceaft ǣghwylce dæge ūtan ymbhwyrfeþ, strīceþ ymbūtan, Met. 20, 140. [Strikeð a stream ut of þ stanene þruh, Kath. 122, 2479. Comen alle strikinde of eauer euch strete *fit ex omni civitate concursus*, 35, 732. Hamun him to strac (wende to, 2nd MS.), Laym. 9318. Faraon strac inn affterr Godes follc, Orm. 14810. þ blod strac adun of hire bodí, Marh. 5, 34: 11, 7. Striken men þiderward, 17, 31. Þe strunden þe striken (*ran*) adun of þine fet, O. E. Homl. i. 187, 28. A mous . . . stroke forth sternly and stode biforn hem alle, Piers P. prol. 183. See also Halliwell, *streke, strike* (2). The word is still used of motion as in *to strike* across a country. *O. H. Ger.* strīhhan *ire, meare*: *Ger.* streichen *to move, rush, rove.* Cf. *Icel.* strjúka *to go, rush*: *Dan.* stryge *to go*, stryge Landet om *to stroll about the country.*]

stricel, es; *m.* I. *a strickle, an implement for smoothing corn in a measure*, v. strīcan, I:—Stricilum *trocleis, rotis modicis*, Txts. 100, 994. [*Hic modius* a buschylle, *hic corus* a mesur, *hoc os[t]orium* a strikylle, Wrt. Voc. i. 233, col. 2 (15th cent.). Strykylle *hostorium*, Cath. Ang. 369. In note 1 on this page are given the following: '*Rouleau* the round pin, stritchell, or strickle used in the measuring of corn, etc. *Lorgaulté* the strickle used in the measuring of corne.' Cotgrave. 'When wee goe to take up corne for the mill, the first thinge wee doe is to looke out poakes, then the bushell and strickle.' Farming Books of H. Best, 1641. II. *that from which liquid flows* (? v. strīcan, II), *a breast that gives milk, a fount:*—Of stricele *ubere*, Germ. 390, 67. Of feówer stricelum *bis binis de fontibus*, Wrt. Voc. ii. 12, 39. v. tit-stricel.

strician *to knit, net.* [*O. H. Ger.* stricchen *nectere*: *Ger.* stricken.] v. ge-strician.

strīdan; *p.* strād, *pl.* stridon. I. *to stride:*—Strīdit *varicat*, Txts. 105, 2078. II. *to get by force* (?), *pillage, rob:*—Strād (streád? *from* strūdan) *conpilat*, Wrt. Voc. ii. 20, 14: 96, 74. [Cf. *O. Sax.* strīdian *to dispute, contend*; strīd *contest, strife*: *O. Frs.* strīda (*wk.*) *to contend*; strīd *strife*: *O. H. Ger.* strītan; *p.* streit *pugnare, contendere, obtinere*; strīt *pugna, certamen.*] v. be-strīdan, *and next word.*

stride, es; *m. A stride, pace:*—Faeðm *vel* tuegen stridi *passus*, Txts. 85, 1510. [Stryde *clunicatus*, strydyn̄ or steppyn̄ ovyr a thynge *clunico*, Prompt. Parv. 480.]

striénan. v. streónan.

strīman *to resist, oppose:*—Strīmendi *innixus*, Txts. 71, 1132: *obnixus*, 81, 1404. [In some dialects, e.g. Northants, *to strime* = to stride. Could the verb have existed with the same double meaning as *strīdan*, q.v.?]

strīme, strēme; *adj. Having a current.* [*Icel.* streymr *having a current, running.*] v. swīþ-strīme.

strīnan. v. streónan.

strīnd, strȳnd, e; *f. A generation, stock, race, kin, tribe:*—Hē ne wæs of ðearfendum folce ac wæs æþelre strȳnde *non erat de paupere vulgo, sed de nobilibus*, Bd. 4, 22; S. 591, 34. Wæs hē of æþelre strȳnde Angelðeóde *de nobilibus Anglorum*, 5, 19; S. 637, 40. Of ðære cynelīcan strȳnde *de stirpe regia*, 5, 7; S. 621, 8. Of Wōdenes strȳnde (*stirpe*) monigra mǣgþa cyningcynn fruman lǣdde, 1, 15; S. 483, 30. Hié wǣron of Dauides cynnes strȳnde, Blickl. Homl. 23, 28. His cynnes lātwuā from ðon ðæt fore biþ his strȳnde *tribunus, ab eo quod praessit tribui*, Rtl. 193, 15. In strȳnd twoelfa *in tribus duodecim*, 78, 26. Doemende twoelf strȳnda, Mt. Kmbl. Lind. 19, 28. Strȳndum, Lk. Skt. Lind. 22, 30. [Of heore strund (owene streone, 2nd MS.), Laym. 2736. Strend toward *generatio futura*, Ps. 21, 32. Streon of a swuch strunde, Jul. 55, 17. Þet tu wite me wið ham (*deadly sins*) and alle heore strunden, A. R. 28, 7.] v. eormen-strȳnd; streónan, streón.

strīpan; *p.* te *To strip.* [Erest he (*the devil*) strepte of him (*Job*) his shep, O. E. Homl. ii. 195, 28. Heo haueð istruped mine figer sterc naked, A. R. 148, 24. Þu struptest and herhedest helle, Jul. 63, 16. Het strupen hire steortnaket, Kath. 1537. *O. H. Ger.* stroufen *stringere.*] v. be-strīpan (-strȳpan).

strīð, es; *m.* I. *struggle, fight, contest:*—Strange geneátas ða ne willaþ mē æt ðam strīðe geswīcan, Cd. Th. 19, 1; Gen. 284. II. *contention, dispute, strife of words:*—Hwæt scal ðē swā lāðlīc strīð wið ðīnes hearran bodan? 41, 28; Gen. 663. Ðone lāðan strīð, yfel andwyrde, 36, 16; Gen. 572. [The word seems to occur only in that part of the Genesis which is supposed to be derived from an Old Saxon original, and to be a form borrowed from Old Saxon *strīd.* In the Liber Scintillarum *strīþlīce* glosses *districte*, 132, 9, and *strīðnysse* glosses *districtionis*, 123, 18; but these may be explained as errors for *stīþlīce*, *stīðnysse*: the nominative of the latter glossing *districtio* occurs 123, 9.]

strīþ-līce, -ness. v. preceding word.

strōd (strod?), es; *n.*?:—Andlang dīces on ðæt strōd; eást andlang strōdes; of ðam strōde on scagan, Cod. Dip. Kmbl. v. 230, 4. Ūtt þurh Wynnawudu on strōd norðweard (*the reference is to the same place in both charters*), 334, 32. On secglāges strōd; of secglāhes strōde, iii. 79, 17. *The word occurs in local names*, Strōdwīc *Strudwick* (Northants), ii. 318, 30. Ðæt land æt Strōðistūne, iv. 288, 18. Perhaps it is left in *Strood* (Kent). [*O. H. Ger.* struot *silva*, Grff. vi. 751, Grmm. R. A. 635.]

-strod. v. ge-strod.

strogdness, e; *f. Scattering*; aspersio, Rtl. 122, 3. v. ge-strogdness.

strong. v. strang.

strop[p] *a strap, strop:*—Strop *vel* ārwiððe *struppus*, Wrt. Voc. i. 56, 37. [From Latin.]

-strowenness. v. ā-strowenness.

strūdan; *p.* streád, *pl.* struden; *pp.* stroden *To spoil, ravage, plunder, pillage, defraud:*—Hwæt is ðis manna ðe mīnne folgaþ wyrdeþ, ǣhta strūdeþ, Elen. Kmbl. 1807; El. 905. Ðonne wē ūs for nōwiht dōþ ðæt wē earme menn reáfiaþ and strūdaþ in heora ǣhtum and heora gōdum *cum infirmiores spoliare et eis fraudem facere pro nihilo ducimus*, Bd. 3, 19; S. 548, 19. Fȳnd gold strudon, Cd. Th. 121, 7; Gen. 2006: Exon. Th. 436, 7; Rä. 54, 10. Hié tempel strudon, Cd. Th. 260, 18; Dan. 711. Hwā ðæt hord strude, Beo. Th. 6244; B. 3126. Se ðone wong strude (MS. strade), 6139; B. 3073. Iudas hæfde onlīcnesse ðara manna ðe willaþ Godes cyricean yfelian and strūdan, Blickl. Homl. 75, 24. Strūdende fȳr, Cd. Th. 154, 15; Gen. 2556. [Cf. *O. H. Ger.* strutit *fraudat*, zi-strudida *destruxit.*] v. be-, ge-strūdan; strȳdan, *and following words.*

strude, Wrt. Voc. ii. 148, 26. v. next word.

strūdend, es; *m. A spoiler, robber, usurer:*—Strūdend oððe grīpend *raptor*, Wrt. Voc. ii. 88, 69. Lǣnend *vel* strūde[nd] *fenerator*, 148, 26.

strūdere, es; *m. A spoiler, robber:*—Strūdere *vel* reáfere *agressor*, Wrt. Voc. i. 19, 7. Strūderes *grassatoris*, Hpt. Gl. 513, 54. Strūderum *praedonibus, raptoribus*, 469, 74. [*M. H. Ger.* strudære.] v. woruldstrūdere; strȳdere.

strūdung, e; *f. Spoliation, robbery, pillage:*—Deóflīce dǣda on stalan and on strūdungan, L. Eth. v. 25; Th. i. 310, 16: vi. 28; Th. i. 322, 16. Utan forfleón stala and strūdunga (strūtunga, MS. C.), Wulfst. 115, 9: 164, 1: 129, 18.

strūta. v. strȳta.

strūtian; *p.* ode *To stand out stiffly* or *projectingly:*—Se hālga wer hié (*the robbers who were trying to break into the church*) wundorlīce geband, ǣlcne, swā hē stōd, strūtiendne mid tōle, ðæt hiera nān ne mihte ðæt morþ gefremman . . . Menn ðæs wundrodon, hū ða weargas hangodon, sum on hlǣddre, sum leát tō gedelfe, and ǣlc on his weorce wæs fæste gebunden, Swt. A. S. Prim. 87, 177. [Ne be þi winpil nevere so ȝelu ne so stroutende, Rel. Ant. ii. 15, 8 (13th cent.). His here strouted as a fanne, Chauc. C. T. 3315. Strowtyn̄ or bocyn̄ owte *turgeo*, Prompt. Parv. 480. *M. H. Ger.* striuzen. Cf. a-strout. 'A-strout. This word is still used in Somersetshire, explained by Mr. Norris, MS. Glossary, "in a stiff, projecting posture, as when the fingers are kept out stiff." The word occurs in Wright's Political Songs: The knif stant astrout, 336, 3. Further instances are: Hys yen stode owte astrote, Le Bone Florence of Rome, 2029. Bothe his eghne stode one strowte, Sir Isumbras.' Halliwell's Dict. The word *strut* is also used in the sense of *strife*: þair strut (*other* MSS. strife) it was unstern stith, C. M. 3461. *M. H. Ger.* strūz: *Ger.* strauss *strife, struggle.*]

strūtung, strycel. v. strūdung, stricel.

strȳdan *to spoil, waste:*—Ðæs strȳdendan (stryndedan, Wrt.) *prodiga* (cf. *O. H. Ger.* strutenti *prodigus*), Wrt. Voc. ii. 86, 51. v. ge-strȳdan; strȳdere.

strȳdere, es; *m. A waster, prodigal:*—Strȳdere *prodigus*, Wrt. Voc. ii. 68, 49. Stryndere (strȳdere?), 118, 28. v. preceding word.

strȳnan, strȳnd, stryndan, stryndere, strȳpan. v. streónan, strīnd, strȳdan, strȳdere, strīpan.

strýta, strúta, an; *m. An ostrich:*—Strýta *strutio*, Wrt. Voc. ii. 121, 38. Strúta, i. 280, 4. [*O. H. Ger.* strûz *struthio.* From Latin.]

stryððan, stubb. v. be-streððan, stybb.

studu, studu; *gen.* stude, studu; *dat.* stude(-u), styde, styðe; *acc.* studu, studu(-o); *pl.* styde, styðe(-a); *gen.* studa; *f. A post, pillar, prop, stud* (v. Halliwell's Dict. '*Stud* the upright in a lath and plaster wall, *Oxon.*'):—Áhēng hē ðone sceát on āne studu ðæs wǽges (*in una posta parietis*). . . . Ðæt hūs forbarn nemþe seó studu ān (būtan ðære ānre stýðe, MS. B.), Bd. 3, 10; S. 534, 28-35. Se lēg ðære studu (ða ilcan studu, col. 2) gehrīnan ne mihte. . . . Ðæt fȳr eode andlang ðara nægla ðe seó studu (*destina*) mid gefæstned wæs and ðære stude nō ne onhrān (ða stuþo sceþþan ne meahte, col. 2). . . . Hī ðā ða studu on ða cyricean setton. . . . Monige men of ðære ylcan styde (styþe, styðe, MS. B., col. 2) sprytlan ācurfon, 3, 17; S. 544, 28-43. Hē hine onhylde tō ānre ðære studa ðe ūtan tō ðære cyrican geseted wæs ðære cyricean tō wraþe and ðǽr his gāst āgæf (hē genom ða studu ðe seó cirice mid āwreþed wæs and on ðære styde stondende forðfērde) *adclinis destinae quae extrinsecus ecclesiae pro munimine erat adposita, spiritum vitae exhalaret ultimum*, S. 543, 37-41. Cypressus styde hié ūtan wreþedon and gyldne styþa hié ūton wreþedon, Nar. 5, 7, 8. Begēmþ stuðe (*or* stoðe) mīnre dure *observat postes ostii mei*, Kent. Gl. 281. [*Icel.* stoð; *f., pl.* stöðr, steðr, *later* stoðir, stuðir.] v. feor-, wræð-studu (-stuðu); stod, stuðan-sceaft.

stuf-bæþ, es; *n. A hot-air bath, vapour bath:*—Sile him drincan on stufbaþe, Lchdm. iii. 132, 13. Man machiæ stufbæþ and baþege hine ðāron, 92, 21. v. stofa.

stulor; *adj. Furtive:*—Stulor *furtiva, clandestina, secreta*, Wülck. Gl. 245, 42: *furtiva*, Wrt. Voc. ii. 38, 30. I. *acting with stealth, stealthy:*—Seó hreóhnys is open costung, and seó smyltnys is stulor and dīgele swica, Homl. Th. ii. 392, 24. II. *stolen:*—Wæteru stulre swēttran synd *aque furtiuae dulciores sunt*, Scint. 110, 11. [Cf. *O. Sax.* stulina *theft*: *O. H. Ger.* stulingun *clam*: *Icel.* stuldr *theft.*] v. next word.

stulorlice; *adv. Furtively, stealthily;* furtim, Ælfc. Gr. 38; Zup. 238, 4.

-stun. v. ge-stun.

stund, e; *f.* I. *a stound* (used by Spenser and Fairfax, v. Nares, and still later in dialects, v. Halliwell), *a while, time, hour:*—Nis seó stund latu ðæt (*the hour will not be long in coming when*) ðē wælreówe wītum belecgaþ, Andr. Kmbl. 2422; An. 1212: Exon. Th. 156, 16; Gū. 875. Nō ic ða stunde bemearn, ne for wunde weóp *that* (*hard*) *time I bewailed not, nor wept for the wound*, Exon. Th. 499, 12; Rä. 88, 14. Æt stunda gehwam, 436, 30; Rä. 55, 9. II. *the hour appointed for a particular act, the signal which marks the hour:*—Geendedum gebedum sī swēged ōþer tācn ɫ stund *finitis orationibus sonetur secundum signum*, Anglia xiii. 380, 215. On ðam fæce ðe stunda beón gehringede *in interuallo quo signa pulsantur*, 406, 952. Gecnyllendum ōþrum stundum *pulsatis reliquis signis*, 380, 219. Cf. tīd, I c. ¶ *adverbial use of cases or adverbial phrases*, cf. hwīl:—Hē word stunde āhōf *he spoke at once* (cf. *Ger.* zur Stunde), Andr. Kmbl. 832; An. 416: 2993; An. 1499: Elen. Kmbl. 1445; El. 724: Ps. Th. 55, 11. Hē winnan nyle ǽnige stunde, Met. 25, 68. Ðū þolades mægenearfeþu micle stunde, Exon. Th. 86, 21; Cri. 1411. Hwīlon hē on bord sceát, hwīlon beorn tǽsde, ǽfre embe stunde (*every now and again, from time to time*) hē sealde sume wunde, Byrht. Th. 139, 48; By. 271. Stundum (1) *at times, from time to time* [*Icel.* stundum: *Dan. Swed.* stundom *sometimes, now and then*]:—Stundum *punctis*, Germ. 398, 227. Ic ðīne strengþu stundum singe and ðīn milde mōd morgena gehwylce, Ps. Th. 58, 16. Horn stundum song fūslīc leóð, Beo. Th. 2851; B. 1423. Ða ic sylf stundum gerād, stundum gereów (cf. *Icel.* stundum . . . stundum *sometimes . . . sometimes, now . . . now*), Cod. Dip. Kmbl. v. 331, 1. (2) *with exertions* or *pains* (v. ā-stundian, *and* cf. *Icel.* stund *in the sense of* care, pains, exertion; stundar *very, exceedingly;* stunda *to strive, take pains;* stundan *pains-taking;* stundliga *eagerly*):—Hē oroð stundum teáh *he* (*the dying Guthlac*) *drew his breath laboriously*, Exon. Th. 178, 17; Gū. 1245. (2 a) *with effort, earnestly, eagerly, fiercely:*—Stundum wrǽcon mægen æfter ōðrum, Elen. Kmbl. 464; El. 232: 242; El. 121. Strong, stundum rēþe *exceedingly fierce*, Exon. Th. 380, 41; Rä. 2, 3. Streámas staþu beátaþ, stundum weorpaþ on stealc hleoþa stāne and sonde, 382, 5; Rä. 3, 6. Mē strange stundum ongunnon *irruerunt in me fortes*, Ps. Th. 58, 3: 93, 6. Ic stefne tō ðē stundum (*earnestly*) cleopige, 85, 5: 97, 8. [*O. Sax. O. L. Ger.* stunda: *O. Frs.* stunde: *O. H. Ger.* stunta: *Icel.* stund.] v. orleg-, winter-, woruld-stund; stund-mǽlum.

stundian. v. ā-stundian.

stund-mǽlum; *adv.* I. *at intervals, gradually, little by little:*—Stundmǽlum *sensim*, Ælfc. Gr. 38; Zup. 228, 6: Zup. 236, 13: *sensim, paulatim*, Hpt. Gl. 451, 6: 469, 72: 482, 51. II. *at different times, alternately, now at one time now at another:*—Stundmǽlum *alternatim, singulatim, separatim*, 438, 53: *vicissim*, Ælfc. Gr. 38; Zup. 238, 4. Stuntmælum, R. Ben. Interl. 38, 10. [See *stoundmele* in Halliwell.]

stune, Lchdm. iii. 32, 19. v. stīme, *and next word.*

stunian; *p.* ode. I. *to crash, make a loud sound:*—Sum biþ wīges heard, beadocræftig man ðǽr bord stunaþ *where the shield resounds*, Exon. Th. 295, 29; Crā. 40. Stunaþ eal geador winsum sanc *a pleasant song sounds all together* (*from the union of many voices*), Met. 13, 49. II. *to strike with a loud sound, crash, dash:*—Stīme (stune?) hǽtte ðeós wyrt . . . stond heó wið āttre stunaþ heó wærce stīðe heó hātte wiðstunaþ heó āttre *it resists poison, dashes on pain, stiff is it called, dashes against poison*, Lchdm. iii. 32, 22. Ðā wearð stearc storma gelāc; stunede sió brūne ȳð wið ōðre *one dark wave dashed against the other*, Met. 26, 29. [Later the word means *to confound, astonish, stupefy:*—If he hem stowned vpon fyrst, stiller were þanne alle þe heredmen, Gaw. 301. Stonyn̄ *stupefacio, percello*, Prompt. Parv. 476. Stonyd *attonitus*, Cath. Ang 365. Stoned ne basshed of no thyng be ye, Parten. 2940. Halliwell gives *stound* as a Northern word = to beat a drum. Cf. *Icel.* stynja *to groan;* stynr *a groan.*] v. stinan, ge-stun.

stunt; *adj. Foolish, stupid:*—Stunt *stultus*, Wrt. Voc. i. 47, 53. Stunt folc and unwīs *popule stulte et insipiens*, Deut. 32, 6. Ic wæs stunt, and ic eom nū wīs, Homl. Th. i. 432, 6. Ðū sprǽce swā swā ān stunt wīf, ii. 452, 31. Ðū stunta *fatue*, Mt. Kmbl. 5, 22. For eówer stuntan lage *per traditionem vestram*, Mk. Skt. 7, 13. Swā stunte nȳtenu *sicut bruta animalia*, Coll. Monast. Th. 32, 19. Cweþaþ ða ðe syndan stunte, ðæt mycel forhæfedness lytel behealde, Wulfst. 55, 23. [Mannkinn þatt wass stunnt and dill and skilllæs swa summ asse, Orm. 3714. *M. H. Ger.* stunz *dull*: *Icel.* stuntr *short, scant, stunted.*] v. styntan.

stunt-līc; *adj. Foolish:*—Stuntlīc ys ǽnig þing swȳþor lufian ðænne God *stultum est aliquid plus amare quam Deum*, Scint. 17, 16. Hē nān þing stuntlīces ongeán God spræc *Job charged not God foolishly* (A. V.), Homl. Th. i. 472, 33. [Hwet is eure swa dusi and swa stuntlic swa is þet þe olde mon nule his mod to Gode awendan mid gode huhte, O. E. Homl. i. 109, 12.]

stuntlīce; *adv. Foolishly, stupidly:*—Stuntlīce fæst se ðe hine sylfne mid gālnysse befȳlþ, Homl. Th. ii. 100, 16. Hī nellaþ understandan hū stuntlīce hī dōþ, Homl. Skt. i. 17, 132. Hwæt is stuntlīcor *quid est stultius?* Ælfc. Gr. 48; Zup. 279, 11.

stuntness, e; *f. Foolishness, folly, stupidity:*—*Stultitia*, ðæt is stuntnys, Wulfst. 52, 17. Ðysses middaneardes wȳsdōm is stuntnis ætforan Gode, Homl. Skt. i. 1, 228. Nelle ðū beón eádmōd on wīsdōm ðīnum ne geeádmētt on stuntnesse (*stultitia*), Scint. 19, 13. Ðā āwende Crist ūre stuntnysse tō gerāde, Homl. Th. i. 208, 19. Nū ðingþ ðam dysegan menn . . . ac hē ne understent nā his āgene stuntnysse, Hexam. 20; Norm. 28, 20. Gif hē him sylfum stȳrþ fram eallum stuntnyssum, Homl. Skt. i. 17, 23. [Fela stuntnesse beoð þer nan steore ne bið, O. E. Homl. i. 117, 22.]

stuntscipe, es; *m. Foolishness;* stultitia, Mk. Skt. 7, 22.

stunt-sprǽc, e; *f. Foolish speech:*—Þurh stuntspǽce *per stultiloquium*, Confess. Pecc.

stunt-sprǽce; *adj. Talking foolishly, foolish in speech:*—Stuntspǽcne *stultiloquum*, Scint. 97, 10.

stunt-wyrde; *adj. Using foolish words, foolish in speech:*—Se ðe wǽre stuntwyrde, weorðe se wīswyrde, Wulfst. 72, 17.

stūpian; *p.* ode *To stoop, bend the back:*—Gyf seó sunne hine (*the moon*) onǽlþ ufan þonne stūpaþ hē (*it has the light part curving downwards*) . . . for ðan ðe hē went ǽfre ðone hricg tō ðære sunnan weard, Lchdm. iii. 266, 20. Ðæt hē swā oft sceolde stūpian swā se cyning tō his horse wolde and ðonne se cyning hæfde his hrycg him tō hliépan *ut ipse acclinis humi regem superadscensurum in equum dorso adtolleret*, Ors. 6, 24; Swt. 274, 24. [Ha schulde stupin and strecche forð þat swire, Jul. 73, 11. Marie adun stupede, Misc. 53, 559: Fl. a. Bl. 697. He nimþ hede þet his tour ne hongi ne stoupi, Ayenb. 151, 6. To stoupe *nutare*, Rel. Ant. i. 6, col. 1 (14th cent.). Over þe table he gon stoupe, Alis. 1103. Layamon uses the verb transitively: Mon mæi mid strenðe stupen (stoupe, 2nd MS.) hine to grunde, 25950. [*O. Du.* stuypen *to bow*. Cf. *Icel.* stūpa (*st.*); steypa *to cause to stoop*: *Dan.* stupe *to fall*: *Swed.* stupa *to fall, tilt, lean forward;* stupande *sloping.*] v. stīp.

sturtan (? *vowel as in* murnan?); steart *To start, jump up:*—Sturtende (styrtende (*wk.*)? v. *examples from Middle English*) se halta gistōd *exiliens claudus stetit*, Rtl. 57, 27. [Arður up sturte (storte, 2nd MS.), Laym. 23951. Pharaon stirte up, Gen. and Ex. 2931. Stirte forth, Havel. 873. Þe Romeyns sturte to anon her prince up to rere, R. Glouc. 212, 1.]

stūt *a gnat, midge;* culex, Wrt. Voc. i. 23, 76: 77, 55. [His hors eren were so ful of gnattes and stoutes and of great flyes *aures equorum culicibus et ciniphibus ita sunt repletae*, Trev. v. 159, 9. Halliwell gives *stout* as a West Country word with an instance of its use. Perhaps some local names keep traces of the word, v. Cod. Dip. Kmbl. vi. 336, col. 2.]

stūtere, es, *m.?*:—On stūteres hylle, Cod. Dip. Kmbl. v. 48, 10: 182, 10: 328, 10.

stuðan-sceaft, es; *m. A prop, stay:*—Ic gaderode stuþansceaftas, Shrn. 163, 5. Tō ðam ilcan wuda ðǽr ic ðās stuðansceaftas cearf, 14. [Cf. *Icel.* stoði (*wk.*) *a post;* styðja *a post.*] v. studu.

stuþu. v. studu.

stybb, stubb, stebb, es; *m. A stub, stump of a tree*:—Stybb *stirps*, Ælfc. Gr. 3; Zup. 7, 10. Ðes stybb *hic stirps*, 9, 58; Zup. 68, 8. Styb, Wrt. Voc. i. 33, 57; 80, 33. Treówwes steb *stipes*, 17, 7. Mid stybbe mid ealle *stirpitus*, Ælfc. Gr. 38; Zup. 239, 8. Æt ðæne ellenstyb; of ðam stybbe, Cod. Dip. Kmbl. iii. 24, 4. Andlang dîces on ðone stubb, 10, 21. [*Icel.* stubbi, stubbr *a stump.*] v. ellen-, þorn-stybb (-stubb).

stycce, es; *n.* I. *a piece, bit*:—Stycce *frustrum*, Wrt. Voc. i. 82, 72. Sticce *offa*, 290, 47: *offa* vel *frustum*, 27, 18. Cnuca ân sticce ðære wyrt, Lchdm. iii. 4, 21. Swê swê stycce hlâfes *sic ut frusta panis*, Ps. Surt. 147, 17. Sticcum *frustris, partibus*, Wrt. Voc. ii. 151, 39. On lytlum sticcum leóðworda dǽl reccan, Andr. Kmbl. 2974; An. 1490. Hit (*the veil of the temple*) on eorþan læg on twâm styccum, Exon. Th. 70, 15; Cri. 1139. Hig curfon ðone ram eall tô sticceon (*in frusta*), Lev. 8, 20. Tô sticcon, 1, 6: Ex. 29, 17. Tô sticcum, Jud. 14, 6. Ðæt mon ðone disc tôbrǽce tô styccum, Bd. 3, 6; S. 528, 21. Hê feallende tôbærst on feówer sticca. Ða feówer sticca clifodon tô feówer stânum, Homl. Th. i. 380, 24. Hî tôcurfon ðone lîchaman on manugu sticceo. . . . Ðâ gesomnodon hî ða sticceo, Shrn. 125, 10, 12. Þurh sticceo *per cola*, Wrt. Voc. ii. 69, 8. In sticco *frusta*, in sticce *frustatim*, 34, 32, 33. In sticce *frustatim*, 86, 78. On sticca *in frusta, in partes*, Hpt. Gl. 495, 30. Hê genam ða sticcu, Homl. Th. ii. 154, 19. II. *a small piece of money*:—Twâ stycgce (stycas, Lind.) *duo minuta*, Mk. Skt. Rush. 12, 42. III. *a short space of time*:—Ðû â embe sticce (*after a bit*) fêhst eft on ða ilcan sprǽce ðe ðû ǽr spǽce, Bt. 35, 5; Fox 164, 14. [Stucchen (sticches, 2nd MS.), Laym. 16703. To stucchen, Kath. 99, 1992. Smalliche be little stechches, Ayenb. 111, 14. *O. L. Ger.* stukki: *O. H. Ger.* stucchi *frustum, pars; obolum; spatium, tempus*: *Icel.* stykki *a piece.*] v. fell-, land-, molegn-, seolfor-stycce.

stycce-mǽlum (sticce-, stic-); *adv. In pieces, bit by bit, piecemeal*:—Styccimêlum *particulatim*, Wrt. Voc. ii. 115, 81. Styccemǽlum *minutatim*, 54, 55. Sticcemǽlum, 77, 70. Sticmǽlum *frustratim, particulatim, minutatim*, 151, 37: *membratim, per singula membra*, Hpt. Gl. 407, 19. I. *to pieces, to bits*:—Þrié wulfas ânes deádes monnes lîchoman styccemǽlum tôbrudon, Ors. 4, 2; Swt. 160, 21. Stânas sticmǽlum tôburston, Homl. Th. i. 108, 19. Hê sticmǽlum tôbræc ða anlîcnysse, 464, 26. Ðæt hûsel biþ sticmǽlum tôdǽled, ii. 270, 33. II. *here and there, in different places*:—Styccimêlum *passim*, Wrt. Voc. ii. 116, 60. On feáwum stôwum styccemǽlum wîciaþ Finnas, Ors. 1, 1; Swt. 17, 5. Se cnoll is styccemǽlum mid wuda oferwexen, Blickl. Homl. 207, 27. Ðæs muntes cnoll is sticmǽlum mid wuda oferwexen, and eft sticmǽlum mid grênum felda oferbrǽded, Homl. Th. i. 508, 23. III. *little by little, by degrees, gradually*:—Ða ðýstru styccemǽlum swâ ðicce wǽron *tenebrae in tantum paulisper condensatae sunt*, Bd. 5, 12; S. 628, 12. Men dydon styccemǽlum ðæt hî ða moldan nômon *paulatim ablata terra*, 3, 9; S. 533, 22. Óþþæt ðû hî styccemǽlum âfêdde mid ðý Godes worde *donec paulatim enutriti verbo Dei*, 3, 5; S. 527, 34. Sticcemǽlum, 1, 7; S. 477, 3: 1, 16; S. 484, 15: 5, 10; S. 624, 37. Ðone song hê gehýrde sticcemǽlum tô him neálǽcan, 4, 3; S. 567, 43. Ðâ bleówan wit ða hylla and âstigon ðǽron and scufon hig ût on ða eá and wit reówan sticcmǽlum mid uncrum fôtum ôð ðæt hig unc âsetton on ôðre healfe ðære eá *then we inflated the bags, and mounted on them, and pushed them out into the river, and little by little we rowed with our feet, until they landed us on the other side of the river*, Homl. Ass. 205, 346.

stýfician; *p.* ode *To root up*:—Môna se ðridda weorca onginnan nâ gedafanaþ bûtan ðæt biþ geedcenned stîfician *the third day of the moon is not good to attempt works, except to root up what has grown up again*, Lchdm. iii. 184, 18. [Cf. (?) *Icel.* stýfa *to chop off, curtail*; stúfr *a stump.*] v. â-stýfician, *and next word; and see* swetecian.

stýficung, e; *f. A clearing* (?):—Of ðære stýfycunge, Chart. Earle 248, 11. In ðone norðran stýfecing, Cod. Dip. Kmbl. iii. 399, 35. Stýfecinc, 18, 33.

stýle, stýl-ecg, stýled, stýlen, styll, styllan *to take a place*, styllan *to leap*, styllan *to stall*. v. stîle, stîl-ecg, stîlan, stîlen, still, stellan *to place*, stellan *to leap*, stillan.

styltan; *prs. subj.* (wið-)stylte; *p.* stylte, stylde, (for-)styldte; *pp.* stylted *To be amazed, confounded, be at a loss, be doubtful*:—Stylton *stupebant*, Mk. Skt. Lind. 6, 51. Styldon (stylton, Rush.), 1, 22. Hiá stylton *haesitantes*, Jn. Skt. Lind. Rush. 13, 22. [Cf. *O. H. Ger.* stullen; *p.* stulta:—*Jumenta in partem alterum haeserunt* (stultun) *pavefacta*, v. Graff. vi. 676.] v. â-, for-, ge-, wið-styltan.

stýman. v. stîman.

styntan; *p.* te *To make* or *to become dull*; hence *to stint*:—Styntid *hebetat*, Wrt. Voc. ii. 110, 36. [In later English the verb is found transitive and intransitive:—Þe qual gon to stunte, Laym. 31891. Menn sholldenn stinntenn to þewwtenn, Orm. 12844. Þe uorðe hweolp is Idelnesse, þet is, hwo se stunt mid alle (*is utterly inactive*), A. R. 202, 10. Ystunt (*dulled*) is al my syht; This day me thuncheth nyht . . . Stunt is all my plawe, Rel. Ant. i. 123, 18, 39 (14th cent.). God gan stable and stynte, Piers P. 1, 120. Of this cry they nolde neuere stenten, Chauc. Kn. T. 45. The preyere stynte, 1563. Styntyn̄ of werkynge or mevynge *pauso, desisto*; styntyn̄ or make a thynge to secyn̄ of hys werke or mevynge *obsto*, Prompt. Parv. 475–6. *Icel.* stytta *to shorten.*] v. â-, for-styntan; stunt.

stýpel, styr *a stir*, stýr, stýran, styrc, stýrend. v. stîpel, ge-styr, steór, steóran, stirc, steórend.

styreness, e; *f.* I. *motion, movement*:—Mid his ôðra lima styrenessa *aliorum motu membrorum*, Bd. 4, 11; S. 579, 27. Ic ealle mîne styrenesse forleás *motum omnem perdidi*, 5, 6; S. 619, 19. Ðæt hors blon fram ðâm unhâlum styrenessum ðara [h]leoma *equus cessabat ab insanis membrorum motibus*, 3, 9; S. 533, 39. II. *a commotion, agitation, disturbance, perturbation*, (1) in a physical sense:—Styrnise michelo (*motus magnus*) geworden wæs in sae, Mt. Kmbl. Lind. 8, 24. Æfter styrenisse wætres *post motum aquae*, Jn. Skt. Rush. 5, 4. (2) figuratively:—Styrenise *tumultus*, Mk. Skt. Lind. 14, 2. Swâ monigum and swâ myclum styrenesse (-um?) wiþerweardra ðinga *tot ac tantis rerum adversantium motibus*, Bd. 5, 23; S. 646, 4. Styrenissum *perturbationibus*, Rtl. 59, 5. v. eorþ-, ge-, on-styreness.

styrfan, styrfig. v. stirfan, stirfig.

styria, styriga, styrga, styra, an; *m. A sturgeon*; but the word is used as the equivalent of several Latin names of fishes:—Styria *cragacus*, Wrt. Voc. ii. 105, 50: 15, 48. Styrga, styria, styra *porcopiscis*, Txts. 87, 1614. Styria, Wrt. Voc. ii. 68, 29. Styriga, i. 281, 59. Stiriga, 65, 63. Styria *rombus*, 55, 61. Ælc seldsýnde fisc ðe weorðlîc byþ, styria and mereswýn, Cod. Dip. Kmbl. iii. 450, 27. Andlang strǽte ût on styrian pôl, vi. 9, 6. Mereswýn and stirian *delphinos et sturias*, Coll. Monast. Th. 24, 9. [*O. H. Ger.* sturo, sturjo *sturio, rombus, purro*: *Ger.* stör: *Du.* steur: *Icel.* styrja: *Dan.* stør: *Norweg.* størje. The Teutonic word was adopted in Romance speeches, and the French form is seen in English *sturgeon.*]

styrian; *p.* ede, ode *To stir, move*:—Ic styrige *moveo*, Ælfc. Gr. 26, 5; Zup. 156, 9. I. *intrans. To be in motion*:—Hê sig ofer ða deó and ofer ealle ða creópende ðe stiraþ on eorþan *praesit bestiis omnique reptili, quod movetur in terra*, Gen. 1, 26. Ealle ða þing ðe on eorðan stiriaþ . . . Eall ðæt ðe styraþ and leofaþ, 9, 2, 3. Eall flǽsc ðe ofer eorðan styrode, 7, 21. Streámas styredon, Andr. Kmbl. 747; An. 374. Ne stira ðû, sunne, of ðam stede, Jos. 10, 12. Hî ne môton swîþo styrian, Bt. 21; Fox 74, 8. Ða styriendan nêtenu, 41, 5; Fox 252, 24. Hý wǽron styriende *commoti sunt*, Ps. Th. 47, 5. Styrendum *mobilibus*, Mt. Kmbl. p. 8, 7. II. *trans. To put in motion*:—Styrede *agitabat*, Wrt. Voc. ii. 10, 53: *exagitabat*, Txts. 180, 2. (1) of physical movement:—Hê styreþ ðone rodor and ða tunglu *coelum ac sidera movet*, Bt. 39, 8; Fox 224, 6: Exon. Th. 422, 29; Rä. 41, 13. Hî heora âgene stefne styriaþ, Met. 13, 49. Hê dyde ðæt ân ǽren nædre hý styrede, Wulfst. 98, 22. Ða stânas hî styredon for ðam swêge, Bt. 35, 6; Fox 168, 1. Hê sceal gân and hyne styrian *he must walk and move about*, Lchdm. i. 316, 17. (1 a) *to move* the strings of an instrument:—Ealle strengas se hearpere grêt mid ânre honda, ðeáh hê hié ungelîce styrige, Past. 23; Swt. 175, 10. Ic mîne hearpan genam and mîne strenga styrian ongan, Wulfst. 255, 9. Hearpan stirgan, Exon. Th. 42, 8; Cri. 669. (1 b) *to put in violent motion, to stir up, disturb, agitate*:—I (*the storm*) streámas styrge, Exon. Th. 386, 31; Rä. 4, 70: 382, 11; Rä. 3, 9. Ðonne wind styreþ lâð gewidru, Beo. Th. 2753; B. 1374. Hê hringsele hondum styrede, 5673; B. 2840. Styre mid sticcan, Lchdm. ii. 76, 25. [Streámas] styrgan, Exon. Th. 383, 29; Rä. 4, 18. Sel him styrgendne drenc, Lchdm. ii. 106, 25. Duruþegnum wearð hildbed styred (*disturbed*; referring to the only course that seemed left to the cannibals, when the prison was found without their intended victims, viz. to feed on the bodies of the dead prison-guards), Andr. Kmbl. 2186; An. 1094. (2) figuratively, *to stir up, to excite, incite, rouse, move*:—Ô sædnysse stirgit *ad congeriem* (*satietatem*) *coartet*, Germ. 391, 30. Nâ ðæra wǽtena ðe druncennysse styriaþ, Homl. Th. ii. 298, 19. Saca and wraca hê styrede gelôme, Wulfst. 106, 26. Gârulf Gûðere styrode, Fin. Th. 37; Fin. 18. Swâ sceal ǽghwelc lâreów tô ânre lufan mid mislîcum manungum his hiéremonna môd styrigean, Past. 23; Swt. 175, 12. (2 a) *to handle, treat, deal with*:—Secg ongan sîð Beówulfes snyttrum styrian, Beo. Th. 1749; B. 872. (2 b) *to move, disturb, trouble, agitate*:—Mid ðǽm bisgum ðe on breóstum styreþ mon on môde, Met. 22, 64. Ðara synfullena handa mê nâ ne styrien, Ps. Th. 35, 11. Ða ð mê mid unryhte ǽnige styrian *qui insurgunt in me*, 108, 27. Swâ bió môdsefan of hiora stede styrede, Met. 7, 25. [*Laym. A. R.* sturien: *Orm.* stirenn: *Ayenb.* sterie. Cf. *Icel.* styrr *stir, tumult, disturbance.*] v. â-, be-, ge-, geond-, on-, ymb-styrian.

styric, styrigend. v. stirc, â-styrigend.

styrigend-lîc; *adj. Moving*:—Hê styrigendlîces nân þincg findan n mihte, Homl. Skt. ii. 23 b, 735. Of styrigendlîcum *mobilibus*, Germ. 391, 26. God gesceóp eall libbende fisccinn and stirigendlîce *omnem animam viventem atque motabilem*, Gen. 1, 21.

styring. v. styrung.

styrman; *p.* de. I. of weather, *to storm, rage*:—Hit rîne and snîwe and styrme ûte *furentibus foris turbinibus hiemalium pluviarum vel nivium*, Bd. 2, 13; S. 516, 17. Styrmendum wederum, Bt. 7, 3

Fox 22, 5. II. of persons, *to storm, make a great noise, cry aloud, shout*:—Ic (*the wood pigeon*) būgendre stefne styrme (cf. ic hlūde cirme, l. 18), Exon. Th. 390, 25; Rä. 9, 7. Gehȳr mīn gebed nū ic stefne tō đē styrme hlūde *exaudi vocem orationis meae*, Ps. Th. 139, 6. Mīn stefn tō đē styrmeþ Drihten *voce mea ad Dominum clamavi*, 141, 1. Stearcheort styrmde, stefn in becom heađotorht hlynnan under hārne stān, Beo. Th. 5097; B. 2552. Holofernus hlōh and hlȳdde, hlynede and dynede, đæt mihten fira bearn feorran gehȳran, hū se stīþmōda styrmde and gylede, Judth. Thw. 21, 19; Jud. 25. Styrmdon hlūde grame gūþfrecan, 24, 35; Jud. 223. Ic mid stefne ongann styrman tō Drihtne *voce mea ad Dominum clamavi*, Ps. Th. 76, 1. [Þe trouble wynde þat hyȝt auster stormynge and walwyng þe see, Chauc. Boet. 29, 712. *O.H. Ger.* sturmen *tumultuari, perstrepere*: *Ger.* stürmen *to roar, rage; to take by storm*: *Icel.* styrma *to be stormy* (of weather); *to make a great noise, make much ado.* Layamon uses the verb in the sense *to attack violently*:—þat hæđene uolc mid muchelere strengđe sturmden (sweinde, 2nd MS.) þa Bruttes and driuen heom to ane munte, 18327. Þa Freinsce weoren isturmede & nođelas heo stal makeden, 1670.] v. be-styrman.

styrnan, styrne, styrnenga, stȳr-ness, styrn-līc, styrnlīce, styrn-mōd, -styrred, styrtan. v. stirnan, stirne, stirninga, steór-ness, stirn-līc, stirnlīce, -stirred, sturtan.

styrung, e; *f.* I. *motion*:—Sterung *gestus, motus corporis*, Hpt. Gl. 455, 44. Đara unstillena gesceafta styring ne mæg nō weorþan gestilled, Bt. 21; Fox 74, 4. Monige beóþ blīđe and eác unblīđe . . . for đæs blōdes styringe and for līchoman medtrymnesse, Past. 27; Swt. 187, 24. Đonne hī (*prepositions*) getācniaþ styrunge, đonne beóþ hī geþeódde *accusativo*, Ælfc. Gr. 47; Zup. 274, 7. I a. *exercise, practice*:—Sió wiþerweardnes biþ wæru āscerred mid đære styringe hire āgenre frēcennesse *adversam fortunam videas ipsius adversitatis exercitatione prudentem*, Bt. 20; Fox 72, 6. II. of violent movement, (1) literal, *disturbance, agitation, commotion*:—Weard mycel styrung (*motus*) geworden on đære sǣ, Mt. Kmbl. 8, 24. Ārās micel styrung and hreóhnys on đære sǣ, Homl. Th. ii. 378, 14. Seó burh Naim is gereht ȳđung ođđe styrung, i. 492, 1. Æfter đæs wæteres styrunge *after the troubling of the water* (A.V.), Jn. Skt. 5, 4. (2) fig. (a) *a disturbance, tumult*:—Đe læs tō mycel styrung (*tumultus*) wurde on đam folce, Mt. Kmbl. 26, 5. Blon sié styring *cessavit quassatio*, Ps. Surt. 105, 30. Đæt wīf đurh đa fǣrlīcan styrunge ne gȳmde hire cildes, Homl. Th. i. 566, 8. Sceal āspringan bryne and blōdgyte and styrnlīce styrunga, Wulfst. 88, 11. (b) *trouble*:—Wē sceolan on ǣlcne tīman and on ǣlcere styrunge mid rōdetācne đa rēđan āflīan, Homl. Skt. i. 17, 143. (c) of the mind, *perturbation, agitation, emotion*:—Stȳrau his mōdes styrunge mid singalre gemetfæstnysse, Homl. Th. i. 360, 16. *Interjectio* geopenaþ đæs mōdes styrunge mid behȳddre stefne, Ælfc. Gr. 48; Zup. 278, 3. Gif wē đa unsceádwīslīcan styrunga on stæđđignysse āwendaþ, Homl. Th. ii. 210, 30. v. ā-, eorþ-styrung.

styđe. v. studu.

sū. v. sugu.

su-. For words beginning with *su-* followed by a vowel see *sw-*.

sub-diácon, es; *m. A sub-deacon*:—Hit is beboden subdiáconum and munecum, Blickl. Homl. 109, 25. v. under-diácon.

sūcan; *p.* seác, *pl.* sucon; *pp.* socen *To suck*:—Ic sūce *sugo*, Ælfc. Gr. 28, 5; Zup. 175, 4. Heó (*the air*) sȳcþ ǣlcne wǣtan up tō hire, Lchdm. iii. 278, 7. Of đæra cilda mūđe đe meolc sūcaþ, Ps. Th. 8, 2. Đa breóst đe đū suce (*suxisti*), Lk. Skt. 11, 27: Homl. Skt. i. 8, 125. Sucun (*suxerunt*) hunig of stāne, Ps. Surt. ii. p. 192, 43. Đæt hig sucon, Deut. 32, 13. Ongunnon ealle đa nǣddran heora blōd sūcan, Homl. Th. ii. 488, 35. Sūcende mid ealdum men *lactentem cum homine sene*, Deut. 32, 25. Ǣgđer ge men ge đa sūcendan cild, Homl. Th. i. 246, 21. Of mūđe sūkendra (*lactantium*), Mt. Kmbl. Rush. 21, 16. [He moste suken, Laym. 13194. Vther þa ȝæt sæc (soc, 2nd MS.) his moder, 12981. Þa tittes þ þu suke, 5026. Bi þeo tittes þet he sec, A. R. 330, 6.] v. ā-, for-sūcan, meolc-sūcend; sūgan, sīcan.

sūce. v. hunig-sūce.

sūcengra for sūcendra, Ps. Spl. 8, 3.

sucga, an; *m. The name of a bird.* [In later times the word seems to apply to the *whitethroat*, which is called *hazeck* (Worcest.) and *hay sucker* (Devon), and to the *hedge-sparrow*, *isaac* or *hazock* (Worcest.), *segge* (Devon), E. D. S. Pub., Bird Names, pp. 23, 29. Chaucer uses *heysugge* (-*sogge*, -*soke*) of the sparrow: Thou (*the cuckoo*) mordrer of the heysugge, Parl. of F. 612. *Heges-sugge* (q. v.) is used to gloss the same word, *vicetula*, as *sucga* does.]:—Sucga, sugga, suca *ficetula*, Txts. 62, 422. Sucga, Wrt. Voc. ii. 35, 53. Sugga, i. 62, 43. Tō sucgan grǣf, Cod. Dip. Kmbl. iii. 437, 27. [Sugge, bryd *curuca, linosa*, Prompt. Parv. 483, col. 2. Halliwell quotes *sugge* from Palsgrave.]

suchtyrga, suctyria. v. suhteriga.

sufel, es; *n. Anything, whether flesh, fish, or vegetable, eaten with bread, sowl* [‘Anything used to flavour bread, such as butter, cheese, etc., is called *sowl* in Pembrokeshire,’ Halliwell]; pulmentarium:—Sile him fōrmete on hlāfe and on sufle and on wīne *dabis viaticum de gregibus et de area et torculari tuo* (*the* sufle *corresponds to the* gregibus, v. winter-sufel), Deut. 15, 14. Hæbbe gē sufol (*numquid pulmentarium habetis?*) . . . Hē cwæđ tō him: Lǣtaþ đæt nett on đa swīđran healfe đæs rēwettes and gē gemētaþ, Jn. Skt. 21, 5–6. Wē gelȳfaþ, đæt genōh sȳ tō dæghwamlīcum gereorde twā gesodene sufel (*cocta duo pulmentaria*). . . Gif mon æppla hæbbe ođþe hwylces ōþres cynnes eorđwæstmas, sȳ đæt tō þriddum sufle. Sȳ ānes pundes gewihte hlāf tō eallum dæge, R. Ben. 63, 10–15. Đæt hiae simle ymb xii mōnaþ gegeorwien tēn hund hlāfa and swǣ feola sufla, and đæt mon gedēle tō ælmessan for mīne sāwle, Chart. Th. 461, 11. [Ne þerf þet meiden sechen nouđer bread ne suuel, A. R. 192, 18. Kam he neuere hom handbare, Þat he ne broucte bred and sowel In his shirte, or in his couel, Havel. 767. I ne haue neyþer bred ne sowel, 1143. Þes two fishes ben souel to þes loves, Wicklif, Select Wks. i. 63. Sowvel, þat is mete to make potage and to medle among potage, ii. 137. Sowil, as thow knowe me to wiln (savoury meat, such as I love, A. V.), Gen. 27, 4. Alle that greden at thy gate . . . after fode, Parte with hem of thy payn of potage other of souel, Piers P. C. 9, 286. Forto haue my fylle of that frute I wolde forsake al other saulee (glossed by *edulium*), B. 16, 11. *Hoc potagium* a^{e} potage, *hoc edulium* a^{e} sówle, Wrt. Voc. i. 199, col. 2 (15th cent.). Sowylle, 266, col. 1 (15th cent.). *Edulia* sowell, Wülck. Gl. 579, 41 (15th cent.). Sowle *edulium, pulmentarium*, Cath. Ang. 349, col. 2. See the note there (from which the Wicklif passages have been taken), where from Andrew Boorde's Introd. to Knowledge is quoted, ‘A gryce is gewd sole;’ and from Turner's Herbal, ‘The most part vse Basil for a sowle or kitchen;’ and ‘The fyrste grene leaues of elm tre are sodden for kichin or sowell as other eatable herbes be.’ *Icel.* sufl *whatever is eaten with bread*: *Swed.* sofwel: *Dan.* sul *meat.* Cf. *O. H. Ger.* pi-sufili *pulmentum, polentum.*] v. lencten-, winter-sufel; gesufel; *adj.*, syflig.

sūgan; *p.* seáh, *pl.* sugon; *pp.* sogen. I. *to suck*:—Đū suge *suxisti*, Wrt. Voc. ii. 74, 49. Đæt sió rēđnes đæs wīnes đa forrotedan wunde sūge and clǣnsige, Past. 17, 10; Swt. 125, 12. [In Txts. 64, 455 the entry *fellitat suggit* is perhaps all Latin, as the same form occurs again in a later glossary, where the termination of the verb is never *-it*, *fellitat*, i. decepit, suggit, beswīcþ, Wrt. Voc. ii. 148, 29] II. *to fall in as the cheeks do when sucking* (?):—Đonne him on đam magan sūgeþ *when it is in his stomach as if it were sucked in*, Lchdm. ii. 192, 13: 160, 1. [*O. H. Ger.* sūgan: *Icel.* sūga, sjúga.] v. ā-, for-sūgan; sūcan, sīgan (sȳgan) *to soak*, Lchdm. i. 134, 14.

sūge, sugga, sugian. v. hunig-sūge, sucga, swigian.

sugu, e: sū, e; *f. A sow*:—Sugu *scroffa*, Ælfc. Gr. 7; Zup. 25, 7: *scrofa*, Wrt. Voc. i. 22, 73: 286, 46: ii. 120, 7. Sió sugu hī wille sylian on hire sole, Past. 54, 1; Swt. 419, 27. Suge *scrofe*, Wrt. Voc. ii. 92, 14. Suge sweard *vistula*, 124, 1. Mē (*a badger*) on bæce standaþ her swylce sweon leorum (= hǣr swilce sūe on hleórum, Grein) hlifiaþ tū eáran ofer eágum, Exon. Th. 396, 13; Rä. 16, 4. [*A. R.* suwe: *Ayenb.* zoȝe: *Chauc. Piers P. Wick.* sowe: *Du.* zog: *Swed.* sugga: *O. H. Ger.* sū: *Ger.* sau: *Icel.* sȳr; *acc.* sū: *Dan.* so.] v. gefearh-sugu.

suht, e; *f. Sickness*:—Him yldo ne derede ne suht swāre, Cd. Th. 30, 24; Gen. 472. [This, the only instance of the use of the word, may be due to Old Saxon influence; see the Hēliand where the word occurs many times, in two of them with the same adjective as in the passage. The word is however widely spread: *Goth.* sauhts: *O. L. Ger.* suht *morbus*: *O. H. Ger.* suht *morbus, tabes*: *Ger.* sucht: *Icel.* sótt *sickness*: sūt *affliction*: *Dan. Swed.* sot. It is found in the Cursor Mundi: Þai troud þat he moght þair broþer (*Lazarus*) hale of all his soght (miȝte make him hool to be, Trin. MS.), 14157; and Halliwell quotes a passage in which jaundice is called *ȝalow souȝt*, Dict. 950.]

suhter-fæderan, -gefæderan; *pl. m. Uncle and nephew*:—Hrōþwulf and Hrōđgār suhtorfædran, Exon. Th. 321, 15; Vīd. 46. Đa gōdan twegen (Hrōþgar and Hrōþulf) sǣton suhtergefæderan, Beo. Th. 2332; B. 1164. [Cf. the double meaning in *M. H. Ger. veter*, father's brother, brother's son.] v. next word.

suhter[i]ga, suhtriga, suhtria, an; *m. A brother's son, a nephew*; or, expressing the relation of those whose fathers were brothers, *a cousin*:—Suhterga *fratuelis*, Wrt. Voc. ii. 109, 16. Suchtyrga *fratuelis* i. *filius fratris*, 36, 4. Suctyrian *fratres patrueles, sic dictus est ad patres eorum, si fratres inter se fuerunt*, 39, 49. Ic (*Abraham*) eom fædera đīn sibgebyrdum, đū (*Lot*) mīn suhterga, Cd. Th. 114, 9; Gen. 1901. His (*Abraham's*) suhtriga *Lot*, 122, 20; Gen. 2029. His suhtrian wīf, 106, 23; Gen. 1775. v. sweór.

sulh, suluh, sul[l]; *gen.* sule, *but also* sules; *dat.* sylg, sylh, syl; *acc.* sulh, sul; *n. pl.* sylh, syll; *gen.* sula; *dat.* sulum: *a weak genitive seems also to occur in* sylan scear; *generally feminine, but see the genitive.* I. *a plough*:—Sulh *aratrum*, Wrt. Voc. i. 15, 2: 289, 76. Sul, ii. 6, 19: Ælfc. Gr. 17; Zup. 109, 18. Swā seó sulh đone teóđan æcer gegā, L. Eth. ix. 7; Th. i. 342, 11: L. Edg. i. 1; Th. i. 262, 9: L. C. E. 8; Th. i. 366, 7. Ā be đan wuda swā sulh and sīđe hit gegān mǣge, Cod. Dip. Kmbl. iii. 458, 20. Sule reóst *vomes*, Wrt. Voc. ii. 138, 72. Sules reóst, 25, 28: 106, 20. Đæs sules bodig, Lchdm. i. 402, 2. Sylan scear *vomer*, Coll. Monast. Th. 30, 29. Đæt nān mon ne scyle dōn his hond tō đære sylg, Past. 51; Swt. 403, 2. Ǣlc man hæbbe æt ðære sylh (syhl, MS.) .ii. wel gehorsede men, L. Ath. i. 16; Th. i. 208, 12. Tō syl . . . mid ðære syl *ad aratrum . . . aratro*, Coll. Monast. Th. 19, 15, 21. Man ða sulh forð drīfe, Lchdm. i. 404, 1. Mann ðe hys hand āsett on his sulh (suluh, Rush.), Lk. Skt. 9, 62. Hē his sulh on handa hæfde, Ors. 2, 6; Swt. 88, 8. Hē sulh heóld, Shrn. 61, 18. Mid sul tō erianne, Salm. Kmbl. p. 186, 28. Heora sylh unrihte gangaþ *aratra eorum non recte incedunt*, Bd. 5, 9; S. 623, 12. Ðīne syll eodon, Homl. Th. ii. 450, 6. Þeáh hē erige his land mid ðūsend sula, Bt. 26, 3; Fox 94, 14. Sulum *aratris*, Wülck. Gl. 254, 6. II. In the following passage perhaps the word is used to denote *the quantity of land which could be cultivated with one plough*; v. sulincel and cf. plōg. *Caruca*, which occurs in the passage quoted below from the Laws, seems to have been used in this sense; e. g. in Florence of Worcester's description of the compilation of Domesday Book *quot carrucas* seems to represent *hū mycel landes* in the Chronicle; and later *sulh* is certainly so used, e. g. Ich þe ȝiue þritte solh of londe, Laym. 18779. Seouen sulȝene lond, 18789. Twenti sulhene lond, 13176. But the unit of assessment may have been *the plough with its team of oxen*. v. Seebohm, Vill. Comm., pp. 112-3. Sceóte man ælmessan . . . swā æt heáfde peninc, swā æt sylh (*one MS. has* æt sulhgange. v. sulh-gang) peninc (cf. detur de omni caruca denarius vel denarium valens, et omnis, qui familiam habet, efficiat, ut omnis hirmannus suus det unum denarium, L. Eth. viii. 1; Th. i. 336, 24; *and see* sulh-ælmesse), Wulfst. 170, 20. [Gif þe suluh (ploh, MS. T.) ne erede, A. R. 384, 18. Þer cheorl draf his sulȝe ioxned swiðe fæire, Laym. 31811. Þe ilke þet zet þe hand aþe zuolȝ, Ayenb. 242, 31. The word is still used in Somerset, *zool*, v. E. D. S. Pub., W. Somerset Glossary.]

sulh-æcer, es; *m. A strip of land for ploughing*. v. Seebohm, Vill. Comm. s. v. æcer:—Eallum ǣhtemannum gebyreþ . . . sulhæcer, L. R. S. 9; Th. i. 438, 1.

sulh-ælmesse, an; *f. Plough-alms, a contribution of one penny to be paid for every* sulh, v. sulh, II. It is first mentioned in the laws of Edward and Guthrum, and its payment is enjoined in those of succeeding kings. It was to be paid within fifteen days after Easter, or a penalty was incurred:—Sulhælmesse hūru fīfiēne niht ofer Eástran, L. C. E. 8; Th. i. 366, 3. Gif hwā sulhælmyssan ne sylle, gylde lahslit mid Denum, wīte mid Englum, L. E. G. 6; Th. i. 170, 5: L. Ath. i. prm.; Th. i. 196, 10. Wē bebeódaþ . . . sulhælmessan, and gif hit hwā dōn nelle, sȳ hē āmānsumod, L. Edm. E. 2; Th. i. 244, 17. Gelǣste man sulhælmessan ðonne .xv. niht beón onufan Eástran, L. Edg. i. 2; Th. i. 262, 17: L. Eth. v. 11; Th. i. 306, 31: vi. 16; Th. i. 318, 30. Sulhælmessan gebyreþ ðæt man gelǣste be wīte ǣghwylce geáre ðonne .xv. niht beóþ āgān ofer Eástertīd, ix. 12; Th. i. 342, 31. Suluhælmessan, Shrn. 208, 29.

sulh-beám, es; *m. The curved hinder part of a plough, plough-tail*:—Sulhbeám *burris, curvamentum aratri*, Wrt. Voc. ii. 126, 79: *buris*, 12, 54: i. 15, 4. [Solowbeme *buris*, Wrt. Voc. i. 180, 29 (14th cent.?). Cf. plughbeme *buris*, 232, col. 2.]

sulh-gang, es; *m. A plough-gang* (*pleuch-, plough-gang* as much land as can be properly tilled by one plough, Jamieson's Dict. See too *pleuch-gate*, ib. Cf. for a similar use of *gang* in measurements *Icel.* sōlar-gangr = *a day*):—Æt heáfde peninc, æt sulhgange peninc, Wulfst. 170, 37. v. sulh II, sulung.

sulh-gesīde, es; *n. An appurtenance of a plough*:—Man sceal habban wǣngewǣdu, sulhgesīdu, Anglia ix. 264, 5. Cf. next word.

sulh-geteóh; *gen.* -teóges; *n. An implement belonging to a plough*:—Gegaderie hē ealle his sulhgeteógo tōgædere *let him collect together all the apparatus of his plough*, Lchdm. i. 400, 19.

sulh-geweorc, es; *n. Plough-work, making of ploughs*:—Tubal Cain smiðcræftega wæs and monna ǣrest sulhgeweorces fruma wæs ofer foldan (*Tubal Cain an instructor of every artificer in brass and iron*, A. V.), Cd. Th. 66, 19; Gen. 1086.

sulh-hæbbere, es; *m. One who holds a plough* (cf. hē his sulh on handa hæfde, Ors. 2, 6; Swt. 88, 8), *a ploughman*:—Sulhhæbbere *stibarius*, Wrt. Voc. ii. 79, 24. v. next word.

sulh-handla, an; *m. One who holds the handle of a plough, a ploughman*:—Sulhandla *stivarius, arator*, Hpt. Gl. 461, 71.

sulh-handle (-a; *m.?*), an; *f. A plough-handle, plough-tail*:—Sulhhandla (-e? v. handle *stiba*, Wrt. Voc. ii. 121, 10) *stiba*, Wrt. Voc. i. 15, 8. Sulhandlan *stivam*, Hpt. Gl. 470, 33.

sulian (?); *p.* ode *To sully* [:—Besutod (-sulod?) *obsoletum, sordidum*, Germ. 403, 26.] v. sylian.

sulincel, es; *n. A small portion of arable land*:—Sulincela *aratiuncula*, Wrt. Voc. ii. 6, 18. v. sulh, II.

sulung, e; *f.* A Kentish word for a certain quantity of land, derived, like *carrucata*, from a name of the plough; from its origin it might mean *so much land as could be cultivated by one plough*. From the first two passages given below it would seem that the *sulung* was equivalent to two hides (*manentes*), and later a *solanda*, which is probably the same word, is said 'per se habere duas hidas.' v. Seebohm, Vill. Comm., p. 54. But perhaps it may be inferred that both hide and *sulung* were considered as on the same footing as regards the plough. Thus to the *gebūr* with his *gyrd landes*, i. e. one quarter of a hide, are to be given two oxen, L. R. S. 4; Th. i. 434, 23, while a gift of half a *sulung* is accompanied by the further gift of four oxen, Chart. Th. 470, 9-14. v. Seebohm, pp. 138-9, and generally. In the Domesday Survey of Kent the assessment was given by *solins*, and the word remained in use. v. Pegge's Kenticisms, s.v. *sulling*:—Aliquam terrae partiunculam, hoc est duarum manentium . . . ritu Cantiae *ān sulung* dictum, Cod. Dip. Kmbl. i. 249, 19. Terrae particula duarum manentium, id est, *ān sulung*, 250, 8. Yc gean intō Cristes cyrican on Cantwarabyrig ðæs landes æt Holungaburnan . . . būton ðære ānre sulunge ðe ic Sīferðe geunnen hæbbe, Chart. Th. 558, 27. Him man sælle ān half swulung . . . and mon selle him tō ðem londe .iiii. oxan, and .ii. cȳ, and l. scǣpa, 470, 8-14. Ðisses londes aran thrié sulong æt hægethe thorne, Cod. Dip. Kmbl. i. 235, 7. Siendan feówer swulung ðæs londes ðe gebyreþ inntō Raculfe on Tænett . . .; ðonne is ealles ðæs londes .xxv. swulunga and ān swulung on Ceólulfingtūne, iii. 429, 14-18. Ðæt lond æt Stānhāmstede (*Stanstead, in Kent*) .xx. swuluncga, i. 292, 23. Se cyning (*Ethelbert of Kent*) sealde Wullāfe fīf sulung landes et Wassingwellan (*Washingwell, in Kent*) wið ðēm fīf sulungum et Mersahām (*Mersham, in Kent*), ii. 66, 17-19. Twā sulung æt Denetūne (*Denton, in Kent*), 380, 32.

sum; *indef. prn. Some.* I. *one* of many, *part* of a whole, used substantively and (1) governing in the genitive (a) a noun or pronoun, cf. the Gothic use of *sums*:—Wæs ic ðara monna sum *I was one of the men*, Chart. Th. 170, 7. Mē tō aldorbanan weorðeþ wrāðra sum, Cd. Th. 63, 18; Gen. 1034. Ðē wile beorna sum him geāgnian, 109, 26; Gen. 1828. Ðæt is wundra sum ðara ðe geworhte wuldres aldor, 155, 14; Gen. 2572: 199, 28; Exod. 345: 200, 15; Exod. 357. Wæs Seón sum ðara kynincga, Ps. Th. 134, 11. Swā swā ūre sum *quasi unus ex nobis*, Gen. 3, 22. Wæs hira Matheus sum, Andr. Kmbl. 22; An. 11. Hē cȳþde on sumre his bōca, Bt. 18, 2; Fox 64, 9. Hī woldon cuman tō sumere ðara stōwa, 34, 7; Fox 144, 9. Anlīc ðara his þegna sumum, 37, 1; Fox 186, 12. Fȳr cymþ sume ðissa hærfesta (cf. the phrase *some* or *one of these days*), Wulfst. 205, 6. Manna cynnes sumne besyrwan, Beo. Th. 1430; B. 713. (b) a cardinal numeral, (*a*) *one* of a company containing the number:—Iacob fērde hundseofontigra sum *omnes animae domus Jacob fuere septuaginta*, Gen. 46, 27. Hē ācīgde syfone . . . eode eahta sum, Beo. Th. 6237; B. 3123. Hē twelfa sum hire āð sealde (*secum acceptis undecim comparibus suis*, p. 205), Chart. Th. 203, 2: L. Ath. i. 11; Th. i. 206, 3 note. (*β*) *one* with a company containing the number:—Hannibal oþfleáh feówera sum *Annibal cum quatuor equitibus confugit*, Ors. 4, 10; Swt. 202, 16. Gange hē feówra sum tō and beó him fīfta, L. Eth. ii. 4; Th. i. 286, 18. Hē com twelfa sum *cum duodecim lectis militibus venientem*, Bd. 3, 1; S. 523, 31. Wæs Agustinus feówertigra sum *socii ejus viri ut ferunt ferme quadraginta*, 1, 25; S. 486, 23. Com seofona sum (cf. ðæt deófol genam mid him ōþre seofon deóflo, St. And. 18, 7), Andr. Kmbl. 2623; An. 1313. Gewāt xii-a sum . . . se wæs on ðam ðreáte þreotteóða secg, Beo. Th. 4793; B. 2401. Fīfēna sum (cf. 3287; B. 1641, where Beowulf's companions, after one has been slain, are said to be fourteen), Beo. Th. 420; B. 207. (*γ*) uncertain:—Ðæt hē syxa sum ofslōge syxtig, Ors. 1, 1; Swt. 18, 7. (2) followed by *of*:—Sumne of ðām wītegum *unum de prophetis*, Mk. Skt. 8, 28. Ðā geneálǣhton sume of Saducēum, Lk. Skt. 20, 27. (3) where the whole, of which the object denoted by *sum* is part, is to be inferred from the context:—Sigon ðā tō slǣpe: sum (*one* of the sleepers) sāre angeald ǣfenreste, Beo. Th. 2507; B. 1251. Habbaþ wē micel ǣrende ne sceal ðǣr dyrne sum (*any* of the errands) wesan, 548; B. 271. Sumne (*one* of the creatures on the mere) Geáta leód feores getwǣfde, 2869; B. 1432. Sume (*some* of the thanes) ðǣr bidon, 806; B. 400. (4) where the word is quite indefinite, *some one*:—Sum tō lyt hafaþ, Salm. Kmbl. 688; Sal. 343. Ic sceal swelgan of sumes bōsme, Exon. Th. 395, 30; Rä. 15, 15. (5) where two members or two classes of the same group, or two parts of the same whole, are contrasted, *one . . . another, some . . . some*:—Ðonne lufaþ sum ðæt sum elles hwæt *one loves that, another something else*, Bt. 33, 2; Fox 122, 24. Hī gaderodon sum māre sum læsse *alius plus, alius minus*, Ex. 16, 17. Eorle monigum Dryhten āre gesceáwaþ, sumum weána dǣl, Exon. Th. 379, 17; Deór. 34. Sum heó hire on handum bær, sum hire æt heortan læg, Cd. Th. 40, 8-9; Gen. 636. Ānra gehwylc hæfþ syndrige gyfe fram Gode sume furðor ðonne sume *alius sic, alius vero sic*, R. Ben. 64, 10. Sume hī beóton sume hī ofslōgon *quosdam caedentes, alios uero occidentes*, Mk. Skt. 12, 5. Sió ungelīcnes hira gearnunga hié tiéhþ sume behindan sume, Past. 17; Swt. 107, 20. (6) where a series of individuals or of groups or of parts is enumerated:—Sum feóll wið ðone weg . . . sum feóll ofer stānscyligean . . . sum feóll on þornas . . . sum feóll on gōd land; ān brohte þrītigfealdne, sum syxtigfealdne, sum hundfealdne, Mk. Skt. 4, 4-8: Exon. Th. 42, 6-30; Cri. 668-680. Is se finta . . . sum brūn, sum basu, sum splottum beseted, 218, 17; Ph. 296. Ānum hē sealde fīf pund, sumum twā, sumum ān, Mt. Kmbl. 25, 15. Ðā sende hē his þeów . . . hē sende ōðerne . . . eft hē sumne sende, Mk. Skt. 12, 2-5. Sume hī sǣdon ðæt hió sceolde forsceoppan tō león . . . sume sceoldan bión eforas . . . sume wurdon tō wulfan . . . sume wurdon tō ðam deórcynne ðe mon hātte tigris, Bt. 38, 1; Fox 194, 32 sqq.: 34, 7;

Fox 144, 7–9: Mt. Kmbl. 16, 14. II. as an adjective (1) with a noun with or without a qualifying adjective, *a certain, some*, see also (5):—Sum man (*homo quidam*) hæfde twegen suna, Lk. Skt. 15, 11. Sum ǽgleáw man *quidam legis peritus*, 10, 25. Sum wîtega of đám ealdum, 9, 19: Bd. 3, 2; S. 524, 39. Đeáh sum broc and sumu wiđerweardnes hiera forwiernþ, Past. 50; Swt. 391, 35. Wæs him gegearwod sum heard harmscearu, Cd. Th. 28, 7; Gen. 432. Sum wæs ǽhtwelig æþeles cynnes rîce gerêfa, Exon. Th. 243, 29; Jul. 18. On his heortan cwæđ unhýdig sum *dixit insipiens in corde suo*, Ps. Th. 52, 1. Sumes hundredmannes þeówa, Lk. Skt. 7, 2. Sumes þinges wana, Bt. 34, 9; Fox 146, 18. Weorđ forhwerfed ǽlc tô sumum dióre, 38, 1; Fox 196, 3. Hê com tô sumre stôwe, Gen. 28, 11. For sumere twýrǽdnesse on cwertern âsend, Lk. Skt. 23, 19. (1 a) where two members of the same group are contrasted (*some . . . other*):—Sume tunglu habbaþ scyrtran hwyrft, đonne sume habban, Bt. 39, 3; Fox 214, 17. Sume lâreówas sindon beteran đonne sume, Homl. Th. ii. 48, 16. (2) with a pronoun where later English would use *some of*:—Hê gebâd mid sumum đæm fultume, Ors 3, 10; Swt. 140, 20. Lǽfdon hig hit sume *quidam ex eis*, Ex. 16, 20. Sume hî gelýfdon on deáde entas, Homl. Th. i. 366, 21. Sume gê (*quidam ex vobis*) ne gelýfaþ, Jn. Skt. 6, 64. Sume đa bôceras *quidam de scribis*, Mt. Kmbl. 12, 38. Đa têđ hié brohton sume, Ors. 1, 1; Swt. 18, 1. Đa sume wê nû gýmdon, Bd. 4, 7; S. 574, 27. (3) with *ođer*:—Sum ôđer wîtega, Homl. Th. i. 364, 18. Hê nales tô îdelnysse swâ sume ôþre ac tô gewinne on đæt mynster eode, Bd. 4, 3; S. 567, 27. (4) with words denoting measure, *some* as still used with numerals, *one*; the use of *ân*, and in later English of the indefinite article with numerals, may be compared with this use of *sum*:—'Âsend him twâ scrûd and sum pund.' Se đegen him andwyrde: 'Genim feówer scrûd and twâ pund, Homl. Th. i. 400, 19. Genim đysse wyrte sumne (*one*) gripan, Lchdm. i. 184, 18. Đâ gegaderedon hî sum hund scipa, and fôron sûđ ymbûtan and sum feówertig scipa norþ ymbûtan, Chr. 894; Erl. 91, 4–6. Hié besǽton đæt weorc ûtan sume twegen dagas, Erl. 93, 9. Đâ wǽron hî sume tên geár on đam gewinne, Bt. 38, 1; Fox 194, 7. Hý gân .xii. sume (twelfa sum, MS. B.), L. Ath. i. 11; Th. i. 206, 3. (4 a) where the number is indefinite, *some*:—Đâ se Aulixes tô đam gefiohte fôr, đâ hæfde hê sume hundred scipa, Bt. 38, 1; Fox 194, 7. (5) adverbially or in adverbial phrases:—Se biscop is þeáh geset sumes (*in some degree*) tô mâran bletsunge đonne se mæssepreóst sý, L. Ælfc. P. 36; Th. ii. 378, 20. Sumes onlîce swâ *velut*, Exon. Th. 214, 21; Ph. 242: Met. 8, 47. Swîđe gelîce, sumes hwæđre þeáh ungelîce (cf. *the corresponding prose* on sumum þingum ungelîce, Bt. 33, 4; Fox 128, 26), 20, 54. Sió eorđe hit helt and be sumum dǽle swilgþ, Bt. 33, 4; Fox 130, 5: Met. 20, 96. Seó hæfþ sume dǽle (cf. *som del* in Chaucer) læssan leáf, Lchdm. i. 144, 13. Æt sumum cyrre *once, on one occasion*, Ors. 1, 1; Swt. 17, 7: Cd. Th. 298, 25; Sat. 538. Sume sîþe, Exon. Th. 20, 16; Cri. 318. Sumera đinga eáđelîcor *in some respects easier*, Homl. Th. i. 236, 11. [*Goth.* sums: *O. Sax. O. Frs. O. H. Ger.* sum: *Icel.* sumr.]

-sum *an adjective suffix* as in glad-*some*, win-*some*. [*Goth.* lustu-sams: *O. Sax. O. H. Ger.* lang-sam: *Icel.* friđ-samr: *O. Frs.* hâr-sum.] v. ang-, frem-, gehýr-, genyht-, lang-, lof-, luf-, sib-, wyn-sum *as examples*.

sumer (-or, -ur), es; *dat.* a, e; *m. Summer*:—Feówer tîda synd getealde on ânum geáre . . . *Aestas* is sumor, Lchdm. iii. 250, 10. On đone nygeþan dæg đæs mônđes (*May*) biþ sumeres fruma. Se sumor hafaþ hundnygontig daga, Shrn. 83, 33. Sumor biþ sunwlitegost, Menol. Fox 473; Gn. C. 7. Beorht sumor, Cd. Th. 239, 23; Dan. 374. Sumer and winter; on sumera hit biþ wearm and on wintra ceald, Bt. 21; Fox 74, 23. Swâ hâttra sumor, swâ mâra đunor and lîget on geáre, Lchdm. iii. 280, 9. Gê witun đæt sumor (-er, MSS. A. B. Lind. Rush.) ys gehende, Mt. Kmbl. 24, 32. Ǽr sumor on tûn gâ *before summer come*, Lchdm. iii. 6, 1. Yldum bringþ sigelbeorhte dagas sumor tô tûne, Menol. Fox 176; Men. 89. Sumur, Exon. Th. 354, 58; Reim. 67. Đonne on sumeres tîd sunne hâtost scîneþ, 212, 12; Ph. 209. Đû đe đâm winterdagum selest scorte tîda, and đæs sumeres dahum langran, Bt. 4; Fox 8, 5. Swâ hê in swoloþan middes sumeres wǽre *quasi in mediae aestatis caumate*, Bd. 3, 19; S. 549, 30. Wintres and sumeres *in winter and in summer*, Exon. Th. 200, 7; Ph. 37. Ic (*the fowler*) nelle fêdan hig (*the hawks*) on sumera, forđamđe hig þearle etaþ, Coll. Monast. Th. 26, 9. Wiþ đære sunnan hǽto on sumere, Bt. 34, 10; Fox 150, 9. Đý sumera fôr Ælfrêd cyning ût on sǽ, Chr. 875; Erl. 78, 5. Đæs on sumera, 896; Erl. 94, 1. Đý ilcan sumera, 897; Erl. 96, 14. Sumere, 885; Erl. 82, 25. Ofer đone midne sumor (midne-sumor? cf. midne-dæg), 1006; Erl. 140, 5. Heó sý geworht ofer midne sumor, Lchdm. iii. 74, 11: Menol. Fox 235; Men. 119. [*O. Sax. O. H. Ger.* sumar: *O. Frs.* sumur: *Icel.* sumar; *n.* (but earlier *m.*).] v. mid-, midde-, middan-sumer. See Grmm. D. M. c. 24.

sumer-hǽte, an; -hætu (o); *indecl.* or *gen.* e; *f. Summer heat*:—Gif đære stôwe neód oþþe gedeorf odþe sumerhǽte hwylces eácan behôfige *si loci necessitas uel labor aut ardor aestatis amplius poposcerit*, R. Ben. 64, 17. For đære sumorhǽte, Ors. 3, 9; Swt. 132, 31. [Cf. *Icel.* sumar-hiti.]

sumer-lǽcan; *p.* -lǽhte *To draw near to summer*:—Wite gê đæt hit sumorlǽhþ, Homl. Th. i. 614, 5.

sumer-lang; *adj. Long as in summer*, epithet of a day (cf. *live-long*):—Ic âsecgan ne mæg, þeáh ic gesitte sumerlongne dæg, eal þa earfeþu, Exon. Th. 272, 7; Jul. 495. Sumorlangne dæg, 443, 29; Kl. 37. Đû wercest sumurlange dagas swîđe hâte, Met. 4, 19. [*O. Sax.* thiu niguđa tîd sumarlanges dages, Hel. 3422. *M. H. Ger.* sumer-lanc.]

sumer-lîc; *adj. Summer*:—Sumorlîc dæg *aestivus dies*, Wrt. Voc. i. 53, 28. Se sumerlîca sunnstede, Lchdm. iii. 250, 21. Mid đære sumerlîcan hǽtan, 252, 10. On sumerlîcum tîman, Anglia xiii. 431, 939. [Eauer iliche sumerlich, Kath. 1663. *O. H. Ger.* sumar-lîh *aestivus*: *Icel.* sumar-ligr.]

sumer-lida, an; *m.* [*Lida*, like the equivalent Icel. *liđi* in *sumar-liđi*, elsewhere refers to a single object, man or ship (v. lida, sǽ-, ýđ-lida), but in the passage given below from the Chronicle seems to mean a fleet. Later in the same work *liþ* (q. v.), which seems taken from the Scandinavians, is used in this sense, e. g. đæt liđ đæt on Sandwîc læg, 1052; Erl. 183, 40, can *sumer-lida* be intended to represent Norse *sumar-liđ*? In one other place *sumer-lida* occurs, in company with words relating to the sea, and it there glosses *malleolus*; but here perhaps *sumer-loda* should be read, and *malleolus* be taken in the sense *shoot, twig* (see *spæc*); cf. *O. H. Ger.* sumar-lota, -lata *virgultum, palmes*. v. Anglia xiii. 330.] *A summer fleet, one that sets forth in summer and returns in autumn*:—Æfter đissum gefeohte cuom micel sumorlida (tô Reádingum, MS. E.), Chr. 871; Erl. 74, 35. [Steenstrup takes the word to mean a force moving from its quarters in England, and leaving women, children, and goods behind there; but if Asser may be trusted, the reinforcement was from abroad. He says: 'quo praelio peracto, de *ultramarinis* partibus alius paganorum exercitus societati se adjunxit.'] Sumerlida *malleolus*, hýdscip *mioparo*, mæstcyst *modius*, Wrt. Voc. ii. 59, 25–27.

sumer-rǽdingbôc; *f. A lectionary for the summer*:—.ii. sumerrǽdingbêc, Chart. Th. 430, 16. [Cf. *Icel.* sumar-bôk.] v. rǽding-bôc.

Sumer-sǽte, -sǽtan; *pl. The people* or *district of Somerset*:—Sumursǽtna se dǽl se đǽr niéhst wæs . . . Sumorsǽte alle and Wilsǽtan, Chr. 878; Erl. 80, 6–10. Mid Sumursǽtum, 845; Erl. 66, 21. On Dorsǽtum and on Sumærsǽton (Sumersǽtum, MS. C.), 1015; Erl. 152, 12. Ofer Sumersǽton and ofer Wealas, 1048; Erl. 180, 27. [He nom Sumersete, Laym. 21013. Dorsete and Wiltschire and Somersete also, R. Glouc. 3, 23.]

Sumersǽtisc; *adj. Of Somerset*:—Defenisces folces and Sumorsǽtisces, Chr. 1001; Erl. 137, 11.

sumer-selde, an; *f. A summer-house*:—Selde *proaula*, i. *domus coram aula*, sumerselde *zetas aestivales*, Wrt. Voc. i. 57, 47. [Cf. *Icel.* sumar-setr *a summer abode*.]

sûmness, e; *f. Delay*:—Æfter monige ɫ longsum ɫ monigful sûmnise (æfter micclum fæce, Rush.: fyrste, W. S.) *post multum*, Mt. Kmbl. Lind. 25, 19. [Cf. *O. H. Ger.* sûmig *negligens*; sûmheit *tardatio, negligentia*: *Ger.* säumniss *delay, stay*; säumen *to stay*; säumig *tardy*.]

sumor. v. sumer.

sumsende *humming, sounding* (of falling rain):—Hî (*the storm-clouds*) feallan lǽtaþ sweart sumsendu (suinsendu? v. swinsian) seáw of bôsme, wǽtan of wombe, Exon. Th. 385, 19; Rä. 4, 47. [*Ger.* summen, sumsen *to hum, buzz*.]

sumur, sun-, suna. v. sumer, sunn-, sunu.

sund *sound*. v. an-, on-, ge-sund. [Sund, Ps. Th. 67, 20, *is an error for* ge-sund.]

sund, es; *n.* I. *power of swimming*:—Hê sealde đâm fixum sund and đâm fugelum fliht, Homl. Th. i. 16, 7: Hexam. 8; Norm. 14, 10. Dol biþ se đe gǽþ on deóp wæter, se đe sund nafaþ, ne gesegled scip, Salm. Kmbl. 449; Sal. 225. [Heore (*fishes*) sund is awemmed, Laym. 21326.] II. *the act of swimming*:—Hê on holme wæs sundes đe sǽnra, Beo. Th. 2876; B. 1436. Hê đê æt sunde oferflât *he beat you at swimming*, 1039; B. 517. Hê mid sunde (cf. *Icel.* međ sundi) đa eá oferfaran wolde, Ors. 2, 4; Swt. 72, 29. Apollonius becom mid sunde tô Pentapolim, Ap. Th. 11, 6. Hié on sunde (cf. *Icel.* á sundi) tô đære byrig fôron, Nar. 10, 28: Beo. Th. 3240; B. 1618. Đû đe wiđ Brecan wunne on sîdne sǽ ymb sund flite *thou that didst strive with Brecan on the wide sea, didst contend in the matter of swimming*, 1019; B. 507. Flôd on sund (cf. *Icel.* á sund) âhôf earce from eorđan, Cd. Th. 83, 32; Gen. 1388. III. *sea, water*:—Streámas wundon, sund wiđ sande, Beo. Th. 431; B. 213. Đâ wæs sund liden *then was the sea passed*, 452; B. 223. Se stân tôgân, streám ût âweóll . . . sund grunde onfêng, Andr. Kmbl. 3055; An. 1530. Sund unstille, Exon. Th. 338, 14; Gn. Ex. 78. Swelaþ sǽfiscas sundes getwǽfde (*the ocean having been dried up by the heat*), 61, 20; Cri. 987. Wǽglîþende setlaþ sǽmearas sundes æt ende *by the shore* (or *at the end of their swimming* (?)), 361, 6; Wal. 15. Ic on sunde âwôx ufan ýþum þeaht, 392, 6; Rä. 11, 3. Sǽmearas sunde getenge, Elen. Kmbl. 456; El. 228. Of nihtes sunde, Salm. Kmbl. 675; Sal. 337. Hié on sund (*the Red Sea*) stigon, Cd. Th. 198, 8; Exod. 319: Beo. Th. 1029; B. 512. Đone đe grund and sund, eorđan and hreó wǽgas, salte sǽstreámas âmearcode, Andr. Kmbl. 1494; An. 748. Hwâ đam sǽflotan sund wîsode *who* *acted as pilot for the vessel*, 762; An. 381: 976; An. 488. [Fiss on sund (watir, Trin. MS.), C. M. 621. *Icel.* sund *swimming; a sound: Dan. Swed.* sund *a sound, strait.*] v. syndig.

sund-bûend, es; *m. A sea-dweller*, but the word, which occurs only in the plural, is used for *men, mankind;* cf. fold-bûend:—Saturnus đone sundbûende hêton, hæleþa bearn, Met. 26, 48. Đone Saturnus sundbûende hâtaþ (cf. stiorran đe wê hâtaþ Saturnes steorra, Bt. 36, 2; Fox 174, 12), 24, 21. Hí (*acc.*) ne gesâwon sundbûende (cf. Hí (*the people of the golden age*) hió (*acc.*) nânwuht ne gesâwon, Bt. 15; Fox 48, 5), 8, 13. Đæs đe ǽfre sundbûend (*men*) secgan hýrdon, Exon. Th. 5, 22; Cri. 73. Đæt âsecgan sundbûendum, 14, 19; Cri. 221.

sund-corn, es; *n. Saxifrage;* saxifraga granulata:—Sundcorn *saxifraga*, Wrt. Voc. i. 30, 55: 79, 25. Sundcorn. Đeós wyrt đe man *saxifragam* and ôþrum naman sundcorn nemneþ. . . . Wiđ đæt stânas on blǽdran wexen, genim đâs wyrte, Lchdm. i. 212, 7–11 (see the plate at the beginning of the volume). Sundcornes leáf, ii. 342, 9. Gif men weaxan stânas on đære blǽdran, wyl sundcorn on ealaþ, 320, 6. Genim neogon piporcorna, fîftêne sundcorn (*saxifragia*), iii. 18, 13.

sund-deáw (?), a plant name, *rosemary:*—Sundeáw (=sund-deáw? v. sund, **II**) *rosmarinus*, Wrt. Voc. i. 68, 77. *Sundew* remains as a name for *drosera rotundifolia*, v. E. D. S. Pub., Plant Names.

sund-flite, Beo. Th. 1019; B. 507. v. sund, **II.**

sund-gebland, es; *n. The water's mingling*, used of the mere into which Beowulf plunged:—Se đe meregrundas mengan scolde, sêcan sundgebland, Beo. Th. 2904; B. 1450. Cf. ýđ-gebland.

sund-gird, e; *f. A rod to measure the depth of water, a sounding-pole:*—Sundgyrd *bolis* (βολίς *sounding-lead*), Wrt. Voc. i. 63, 67: *bolidis*, 57, 7. Sundgerd in scipe *vel* metrâp *bolides*, ii. 102, 14. Sundgyrd on scipe *vel* metrâp *bolidis*, 126, 46: 11, 17. Cf. sund-lîne, -râp.

sund-helm, es; *m. A water-covering, the sea which covers:*—Mec sundhelm þeahte and mec ýþa wrugon, Exon. Th. 488, 4; Rä. 76, 1. Ic sundhelme ne mæg losian, 382, 13; Rä. 3, 10.

sund-hengest, es; *m. A sea-horse, a ship:*—Ceólum lîdan, sundhengestum, Exon. Th. 53, 20; Cri. 853. Sǽlan sundhengestas, ealde ýđmearas, 54, 4; Cri. 863.

sund-hwæt; *adj. Active in swimming:*—Sǽfisca cynn swimmaþ sundhwate, đǽr se swêta stenc ût gewîtaþ (-eþ?), Exon. Th. 363, 21; Wal. 57.

sund-lida (Th.), -liden (Grn.), Beo. Th. 452; B. 223. v. sund, **III.**

sund-lîne, an; *f. A sounding-line:*—Sundlîne *cataprorates* (*cataprorates* linea cum massa plumbea qua maris altitudo tentatur, Migne), Wrt. Voc. i. 53, 8: 63, 66. Cf. sund-gird, -râp.

sund-mere, es; *m. A place for swimming:*—On sundmere *in natatario*, Wrt. Voc. ii. 46, 50.

sundness. v. on- (an-) sundness.

sund-nytt, e; *f. The employment of swimming:*—Beówulf sundnytte dreáh *Beowulf swam*, Beo. Th. 4710; B. 2360.

sundor (-er, -ur); *adv.* **I.** *apart, aloof, by one's self, separately:*—Ne scealt đû sunder beón from đînum gefêrum on Ongelcyricean *tua fraternitas seorsum fieri non debet a clericis suis in ecclesia Anglorum*, Bd. 1, 27; S. 489, 11. Geseah se cyning heora sacerdas sundor stondon (*seorsum consistere*), 2, 2; S. 503, 38. Hê gesæt him sundor æt rûne, Exon. Th. 293, 3; Wand. 111: Andr. Kmbl. 2324; An. 1163. Gebærne wulfes ceácan and đa têþ sundor *burn the teeth by themselves*, Lchdm. ii, 102, 13. Se Hǽlend genam his twelf þegnas sundor of đæm weorode, Blickl. Homl. 15, 7. Sundor âcîgan *to call aside*, Elen. Kmbl. 1203; El. 603. **II.** *severally, each by himself:*—Sundor ânra gehwilc herige đec *let each one severally praise thee*, Cd. Th. 239, 15; Dan. 370. Fêran sceal sundor ânra gehwæs sâwl of lîce, Exon. Th. 191, 24; Az. 93. Swâ monig beóþ men ofer eorþan, swâ beóþ môdgeþoncas; ǽlc him hafaþ sundor sefan (sundor-sefan?), 344, 5; Gn. Ex. 169. Heó wile gesêcan sundor ǽghwylcne feorhberendra, 420, 18; Rä. 40, 5: Salm. Kmbl. 130; Sal. 64. **III.** *in a manner different from others:*—Ilco đoht ôđer suindir âurât *eundem sensum alius aliter expressit*, Mt. Kmbl. p. 3, 5. **IV.** *in a way that separates, asunder:*—Sundur gedǽlan lîf wiđ lîce *to part asunder life from body*, Beo. Th. 4836; B. 2422. Seó cwên bebeád cræftum getýde sundor âsêcean đa sêlestan (*to pick out the best workmen*), Elen. Kmbl. 2035; El. 1019: 813; El. 407. [*Goth.* sundrô: *O. Sax.* sundar (-or): *O. H. Ger.* suntar: *Icel.* sundr.] v. on-sundrum.

sundor-anweald, es; *m. Single authority, monarchy:*—Sunderanweald *monarchia*, Engl. Stud. xi. 66, 54. [*O. H. Ger.* suntar-walt *monarchia.*]

sundor-cræft, es; *m. A special power* or *art, one possessed* or *exercised by an individual* or *a class:*—Đa rîcan on đam woruldwelan nabbaþ nǽnne sundorcræft, Bt. 27, 2; Fox 98, 7. Seó wiht sundorcræft hafaþ, Exon. Th. 420, 14; Rä. 40, 3. Đæt hý sundorcræfta sumne eác cunne *that each have some craft of his own that he knows*, L. I. P. 9; Th. ii. 314, 29. Sió gesceádwîsnes is se sêlesta sundorcræfta *reason is the best of distinguishing faculties* (*as being the faculty peculiar to man;* cf. hió is synderlîc cræft đære sâwle, Bt. 33, 4; Fox 132, 10), Met. 20, 203.

sundor-cýþþ[u]; *f. Special, private knowledge* or *acquaintance, intimacy:*—Riht is đæt mynecena ǽnige sundorcýþþe tô woruldmannum nabban, L. I. P. 15; Th. ii. 322, 34.

sundor-feoh; *n. Private property, private estate:*—Mîn sundorfeoh on đam neoþeran Hysseburnan, Chart. Th. 488, 10.

sundor-freódôm, es; *m. A special immunity, a privilege:*—Mid andweardum apostolîcum sunderfreódômum *cum praesentibus apostolicis privilegiis* (153, 10), Cod. Dip. B. i. 155, 17: 154, 22. v. next word.

sundor-freóls, es; *m. A special immunity, a privilege:*—On đissum sunderfreólse *priuilegio*, Cod. Dip. Kmbl. iii. 349, 26. Đysne mînne sunderfreóls *hoc nostrum priuilegium*, 350, 12, 16, 32. v. preceding word.

sundor-gecynd *a peculiar nature:*—Hê hafaþ sundorgecynd, Exon. Th. 357, 18; Pa. 30.

sundor-genga, an; *m. One who goes by himself:*—Sum fearhrýþer đæs ôþræs ceápes gefêrscipe oferhogode, and him gewunode đæt hê wæs geond đæt wêsten sundorgenga, Blickl. Homl. 199, 5. Cf. ân-genga.

sundor-gerêfland, es; *n. Land reserved to the jurisdiction of a gerêfa* (?):—On đæm sundorgerêflande *in tribulano* (in the same glossary *in tribulanam* is rendered *in þa burh*) *territorio*, Wrt. Voc. ii. 45, 4. Cf.:—Æylmer habbe þat lond at Stonham þe ic hym er to hande let to reflande. And ic an Godric mine reue at Waldingfeld þa þritti acre đe ic hym er to hande let, Chart. Th. 570, 34. *See also* gerêf-mǽd.

sundor-gifu, e; *f. A special gift* or *grace, prerogative, privilege:*—For đære sundorgife đe him God sealde gumena rîce, Cd. Th. 254, 4; Dan. 606. Wê swylc ne gefrugnan ǽfre gelimpan, đæt đû in sundorgiefe swylce befênge, Exon. Th. 6, 6; Cri. 80. God monnum syleþ sundorgiefe *God gives to each man a special gift*, 293, 22; Crä. 5. Sindergife *privilegium*, Hpt. Gl. 466, 76. Ǽlc cræft hæfþ his sundorgife and đa gife and đone weorþscipe đe hê hæfþ hê forgifþ ǽlcum đara đe hine lufaþ *inest dignitas propria virtuti, quam in eos, quibus fuerit adjuncta, transfundit*, Bt. 27, 2; Fox 96, 30. Sundorgife *prerogativa*, Wrt. Voc. ii. 66, 37. Syndergyfa, Hpt. Gl. 468, 53. [*O. H. Ger.* suntar-gepa.]

sundor-hâlga, an; *m. A Pharisee*, (but in one passage it seems to mean) *a scribe:*—Twegen men . . . ân wæs sunderhâlga, and ôđer wæs openlîce synful, Homl. Th. ii. 428, 3: 420, 34: 422, 3. Bôceras and sunderhâlgan, Scint. 203, 3. Đa Farisêiscan and sundorhâlgan (*scribes*) hine tô deáđe fordêmdon, H. R. 9, 28. Manega đæra sunderhâlgena (*Pharisaeorum*), Mt. Kmbl. 3, 7. Đæra wrîtera and sundorhâlgena, 5, 20. Sunderhâlgena, Homl. Th. ii. 216, 26. Đa wǽron of sundorhâlgon, Jn. Skt. 1, 24. [Þa sunderhalȝe and þa bocere, O. E. Homl. i. 245, 3. Cf. *O. H. Ger.* sundir-lebin *pharisaei.*]

sundor-irfe, es; *n. A private inheritance:*—Eal đæt se rinca baldor sinces âhte ođđe sundoryrfes, Judth. Thw. 26, 22; Jud. 340. Wilsumne regn wolcen brincgeþ and đonne âscâdeþ God sundoryrfe *pluviam voluntariam segregabis, Deus, haereditati tuae*, Ps. Th. 67, 10.

sundor-land, es; *n. Separate land, an estate belonging to particular persons* (?):—Tô hira sundorlande *ad prediolum*, Wrt. Voc. ii. 3, 51. Sundorland *predia*, 66, 75. The word occurs in an enumeration of boundaries, and Kemble explains it there as 'land set apart for special purposes':—Æfter đære strǽte be đære wællan on Sunderlond, Cod. Dip. Kmbl. iii. 118, 20.

sundor-lîc; *adj. Special, peculiar:*—Đâm is sundorlîc sang tô singanne *singulariter canticum cantare*, Past. 52, 7; Swt. 409, 10. [*O. H. Ger.* suntar-lîh *singularis.*] v. synder-lîc.

sundorlîce; *adv. Apart, separately:*—Sundurlîce *seorsum*, Mk. Skt. Lind. 7, 33. v. synderlîce.

sundor-lîf, es; *n. A private life:*—Hê sundorlîf (*vitam privatam*) and munuclîf wæs foreberende eallum đâm weolum đæs eorþlîcan rîces, Bd. 4, 11; S. 579, 7.

sundor-lîpe. v. synder-lîpe, *and next word.*

sundor-lîpes; *adv. Separately, severally, specially:*—Sunderlîpes *sequestratim, diverse, alternatim*, Hpt. Gl. 411, 18. Sunderlîpas *separatim, singulariter*, 438, 40. [Weren þas þreo laȝe gewriten inne þa ođre tablebreode sunderlipes *written separately on the one table* (*of stone*), O. E. Homl. i. 11, 32. Þu hauest iseiđ of euch a setnesse sunderlepes *of each order separately*, 261, 33. He cumeđ to elch man sunderlupes, ii. 5, 15. Ich habbe sunderliche (sunderlepes, MS. C.) ispeken of þeos þreo limes, A. R. 90, 5. Cf. Đe almisse þe mon đeđ sunderlîpe (*specially*) for to quemen ure drihten, O. E. Homl. i. 137, 18. *O. Frs.* sunder-lêpis *specially.*] v. synder-lîpes.

sundor-mǽd; *f. A separate, private meadow:*—Seó mêd đe đærtô gebyreþ wiđ Hummingtûn seó his sundermêd, Cod. Dip. Kmbl. v. 354, 30.

sundor-mǽlum; *adv. Singly, separately;* singillatim, Anglia xiii. 380, 217.

sundor-notu, e; *f. A special office:*—Gif ceorl geþeáh đæt hê hæfde sundornote on cynges healle, L. R. 2; Th. i. 190, 17. v. next word.

sundor-nytt, e; *f. A special office, employment*, or *use:*—Ǽlc hæfþ sundornytte (sunder-, Hatt. MS.) *per officium diversa sunt*, Past. 34, 3; Swt. 232, 4. Hæfde Hrôđgâr seleweard âseted; sundernytte beheóld ymb aldor Dena, eóten weard âbeád, Beo. Th. 1339; B. 667. v. preceding word.

sundor-riht, es; *n. A special right, right peculiar to a class:*—Rômwara sundorriht *jus Quiritum*, Wrt. Voc. ii. 49, 11. Weala sunderriht, i. 20, 64.

sundor-seld, es; *n. A special seat, a seat that stands apart, a throne:*—Ðæt hē sundurseld wuldres nimeþ *ut solium gloriae teneat*, Ps. Surt. ii. p. 186, 27.

sundor-setl, es; *n. A residence apart, a hermitage:*—Hē ongan wilnian wēstenes and sundersetle[s ?]. . . Hē leornode be ðām anceıum ðe on wēstene and on sundorsettlum heora līf leofodon, Guthl. 2; Gdwin. 18, 20–24. Hē his fultum tō ðam sundorsetle sōhte, 3; Gdwin. 24, 2.

sundor-sprǣc, e; *f.* I. where a single person speaks privately with one or more, *private speech, a private conversation:*—Nero cwæð: 'Sege mē, Petrus, on sundorsprǣce, hwæt ðū ðence,' Homl. Th. i. 376, 27. Swā swā him (*Moses*) God silf dihte on heora sundersprǣce, Ælfc. T. Grn. 3, 14. Cornelius Asina gefōr tō Hannibale tō sundorsprǣce *ad colloquium*, Ors. 4, 6; Swt. 172, 7. Ðā nam Eugenia hī on sundorsprǣce, Homl. Skt. i. 2, 48. Ðā clypode Herodes ða ðrȳ tungelwītegan on sundersprǣce, Homl. Th. i. 78, 17. Ðætte hē hæbbe his sundorsprǣce mid ðǣm bilwitum *cum simplicibus sermocinatio ejus*, Past. 35, 4; Swt. 243, 16. Hȳ (*Hannibal and Scipio*) hiera sundorsprǣce (*colloquium*) tō unsibbe brohton, Ors. 4, 10; Swt. 202, 12. II. where many speak in private, *a private conference, council:*—Hī cōmon ealle tōsomne tō heora sundersprǣce, Homl. Th. ii. 250, 9.

sundor-stōw, e; *f. A separate place, a place set apart for a particular object:*—Ǣlcum ðara ðū gesettest his āgene sunderstōwe, Bt. 33, 4; Fox 128, 30.

sundor-weorþung, e; *f. Special honour, prerogative, privilege:*—Heó (*St. Michael's church*) nalles on goldes wlite and on seolfres ne scīneþ, ac on sundorweorþunge þurh godcundra mægen heó gewuldrad stondeþ, Blickl. Homl. 197, 9. Sundorweorðunge *prerogativam*, Wrt. Voc. ii. 65, 75. v. synder-weorþmynt.

sundor-wine, es; *m. A special friend, an intimate friend:*—Ne āswīc sundorwine, ac ā symle geheald rihtum gerisnum, Exon. Th. 301, 34; Fä. 29.

sundor-wīs; *adj. Specially, singularly wise:*—Ǣnne giddum gearusnottorne . . . ðone hié ðære cwēne āgēfon, sægdon hine sundorwīsne, Elen. Kmbl. 1172; El. 588.

sundor-wundor, es; *n. A special wonder, that which especially excites wonder:*—Mē frōd wita sægde sundorwundra fela, Exon. Th. 313, 19; Mōd. 2.

sund-plega, an; *m. Play in the water:*—Se tīreádga (*the Phenix*) twelf sīþum hine bibaþaþ . . . siþþan hine sylfne æfter sundplegan hefeþ on heánne beám, Exon. Th. 205, 12; Ph. 111. Se hærnflota (*the ship*) æfter sundplegan (*its journey across the sea*) sondlond gespearn, 182, 10; Gū. 1308.

sund-rāp, es; *m. A sounding line:*—Sundgyrd in scipe oððe [sund-] rāp, i. metrāp *bolidis*, Wrt. Voc. ii. 11, 17. v. sund-gird.

sund-reced, es; *n. A sea-house*, a term for the ark:—Ðū (*Noah*) seofone genim on ðæt sundreced tūdra gehwylces, Cd. Th. 80, 28; Gen. 1335.

sundrian; *p.* ode *To sunder, separate.* [Scheaden þe eilen urom þe clene cornes, þet is, sundren god from vuele, A. R. 270, 28. Marie and Marthe weren sustren, auh hore lif sundrede, 414, 12. Nan ne mei sundrin from oðere, Kath. 1776. To sundren and mengen, Gen. and Ex. 468. *O. H. Ger.* suntarōn: *Icel.* sundra.] v. ā-, ge-, on-, tō-sundrian; syndrian.

sund-wudu, a; *m. A ship:*—Sum mæg fromlīce ofer sealtne sǣ sundwudu drīfan, Exon. Th. 42, 24; Cri. 677: Beo. Th. 421; B. 208: 3817; B. 1906.

suner *a herd.* v. sunor.

sunna, an; *m. The sun:*—Sōna eode sunna up, Gen. 32, 31: Ps. Th. 148, 3. Sunne (-a, MS. J.), Ælfc. Gl. Zup. 297, 7. Sunna and mōne, Nar. 28, 20. Ðæs sunnan āsprungnis oððe ðære mōnan, 28, 10. [The word is usually feminine in the Teutonic dialects, but masculine forms are found in *Goth.* sunna: *O. Sax. O. H. Ger.* sunno.] v. sunne.

Sunnan-ǣfen, es; *m. The evening before Sunday:*—On Sunnan-ǣfen *dominica uespera*, Anglia xiii. 396, 447. Gif esne ofer dryhtnes hǣse wyrce an Sunnan-ǣfen efter hire setlgange oð Mōnan-ǣfenes setlgang, L. Wih. 9; Th. i. 38, 19. Hī lǣddon hine tō hiora hūstinge on ðone Sunnan-ǣfen, Chr. 1012; Erl. 146, 34. [Giester sunneue, Chart. Th. 437, 18.] [*O. H. Ger.* sunnūn āband *vesper sabbati*: *Ger.* Sonnabend.]

sunnan-corn *gromel*; lithospermon officinale, Lchdm. i. 314, 18; see the remark in Lchdm. ii. 407, col. 1.

Sunnan-dæg, es; *m. Sunday:*—Iúdagum Romani and eác Angli gehālgedon on ðisra tungla gemynde heora dagas, and ðæne forman dæg hig hēton Sunnandæg, forðan heó ys ealra tungla wlitegost, and se dæg wæs ealra daga fyrmest on heora dagum, and nū ys on ūrum tīman, Gode lof ealles, Anglia viii. 321, 4–7. On ānum ðara restedaga se nū Sunnandæg is nemned *una Sabbati quae nunc Dominica dies dicitur*, Bd. 3, 17; S. 545, 30. Dōmes dæg . . . se hālgesta Sunnandæg . . . ðȳ dæge blissiaþ ða ðe Sunnandæges freóls heóldan, Wulfst. 244, 14–19. Ǣghwelce Sæternes dæg and Sunnan, Shrn. 88, 33: Lchdm. iii. 228, 4. Crist ārās of deáðe on ðone Eásterlīcan Sunnandæg, Homl. Th. i. 216, 33. Men ne mōton baðian Sunnandagum, L. Ecg. C. 35; Th. ii. 160, 27. Gif wē ða six Sunnandagas of ādōþ, Wulfst. 284, 4. ¶ The observance of the Sunday was enjoined by the laws. The time that had to be so observed was according to Wihtræd's Laws from sunset on Saturday to sunset on Sunday:—Gif esne wyrce an Sunnanǣfen efter hire setlgange oð Mōnanǣfenes setlgang, 9; Th. i. 38, 19; but later the time seems to have been extended, and to be from 3 on Saturday until dawn on Monday:—Healde man ǣlces Sunnandæges freólsunga fram nōntīde ðæs Sæternes-dæges ōþ ðæs Mōnandæges līhtinge, L. Edg. i. 5; Th. i. 264, 18: L. Ælfc. C. 36; Th. ii. 362, 1: Wulfst. 231, 9. During this time servile and free were forbidden to work under various penalties, the latter being liable even to a loss of freedom, L. In. 3; Th. i. 104, 6: L. E. G. 7; Th. i. 170, 15; the servile to a fine or to corporal punishment, *ib.*; and see L. Wih. 9–11; Th. i. 38, 18: L. C. S. 45; Th. i. 402, 13; in general terms it is said:—[Ealra] Woroldlīcra weorca on ðam hālgan dæge geswīce man georne, L. Eth. vi. 22; Th. i. 320, 12: L. C. E. 15; Th. i. 368, 18. The only exception is the preparation of food:—Nān weoruldweorc, būton mon his mete gearwige, L. E. I. 24; Th. ii. 420, 22. In case of necessity, however, and under certain conditions, travelling was allowed:—Gif hwam gebyrige ðæt hē nȳde faran scyle, ðonne mōt hē swā rīdan, swā rōwan, swā swilce færelde faran swylce tō his wege gebyrige, on ða gerād ðæt hē his mæssan gehȳre and his gebedu ne forlǣte, *ib.* More specifically there are prohibitions of Sunday trading:—Sunnandæges cȳpinge gif hwā āgynne, þolie ðæs ceápes and twelf ōrena mid Denum and .xxx. scill. mid Englum, L. E. G. 7; Th. i. 170, 15: L. Ath. i. 24; Th. i. 212, 15: L. Eth. v. 13; Th. i. 308, 11: of assemblies, except in case of extreme need:—Wē forbeódaþ ǣlc folcgemōt, būton hit for mycelre neódþearfe sī, L. C. E. 15; Th. i. 368, 17: L. Eth. v. 13; Th. i. 308, 10: vi. 44; Th. i. 326, 21: of hunting:—Huntaðfara geswīce man georne, L. Eth. vi. 22; Th. i. 320, 12: L. C. E. 15; Th. i. 368, 18; and compare the answer of the hunter in Ælfric's Colloquy:—Ic næs tōdæg on huntnoðe, forðam Sunnandæg ys, Coll. Monast. Th. 22, 1: of legal proceedings, L. E. G. 9; Th. i. 172, 10–15. Theft on Sunday incurred a double fine, L. Ælf. pol. 5; Th. i. 64, 22–25. As to the religious observances connected with the day it is said:—Hit gedafenaþ ðæt gehwylce cristene men, ða þurhteón māgon, on Sæternesdæg cume tō cyrcean, and him leóht mid bringe, and ðǣr ǣfensang gehȳran and on ūhtan ðone ūhtsang, and on morgenne mid heora offrungum cuman tō ðære mæssan symbelnysse. And ðonne hig ðyder cumen, ne sȳ ðǣr nān fācn, ne nǣnig geflytu, ne nǣnig ungeþwǣrnes gehȳred, ac smylte mōde, æt ðære hālgan þēnunge, ǣgðer ge for hig sylfe ge for eal Godes folc þingien, ǣgðer ge mid heora gebedum ge mid heora ælmessan; and æfter ðære hālgan þēnunge him gehwā hām hwyrfe, and mid his freóndum and his nȳhstum and mid ældeódigum hine gāstlīce gereordige, and hine wið oferǣt and druncennysse beorge, L. E. I. 24; Th. ii. 420, 32 sqq. [*O. L. Ger.* Sunnun-dag: *Du.* Zon-dag: *O. H. Ger.* Sunnūn-tag: *Ger.* Sonn-tag: *Icel.* Sunnu-dagr.] v. Eáster-, Palm-Sunnandæg.

Sunnan-niht, e; *f. The night between Saturday and Sunday:*—Ǣlcum gesinhīwum gebyreþ ðæt hig hyra clǣnnysse healdon ǣfre Sunnannihte (*nocte diei Dominici*), L. Ecg. P. ii. 21; Th. ii. 190, 18. His līc læg on byrgene ða Sæterniht and Sunnanniht . . . and hē ārās of deáðe on ðone Eásterlīcan Sunnandæg, Homl. Th. i. 216, 27–33. Se ðe stalaþ on Sunnanniht . . . oððe on ðone Hālgan Ðunresdæg, L. Alf. pol. 5; Th. i. 64, 22. Hū on Sunnannihtum nihtlīc wæcce tō healdenne sȳ. On Sunnandæge mon sceal hraðor ārīsan tō ūhtsange, R. Ben. 35, 2: 42, 15: Wulfst. 305, 23.

Sunnan-ūhta, an; *m. The time before day-break on Sunday;* as an ecclesiastical term *the hour of matins on Sunday*, or *the service then held:*—'On Sunnandæg ðū cymst tō mē' . . . Se apostol on ðam Sunnanūhtan ǣrwacol tō ðære cyrcan com, Homl. Th. i. 74, 20. Gē sculon singan Sunnanūhtan, L. Ælfc. P. 44; Th. ii. 384, 4.

sunn-beám, es; *m. A sun-beam:*—Ealle ða niht stōd swylce beorht sunnbeám *tota ea nocte columna lucis stabat*, Bd. 3, 11; S. 535, 24: Homl. Skt. ii. 26, 184. Him gǣþ of se leóma swylce ōðer sunnbeám, Lchdm. iii. 272, 5. Hwæt fremaþ ðam blindan seó beorhta sunbeám? Homl. Skt. i. 4, 275. Se rēnboga cymþ of ðam sunbeáme and of wǣtum wolcne, Boutr. Scrd. 21, 26. v. sunne-beám.

sunn-bearu (-o), wes; *m. A sunny grove:*—Sunbearo līxeþ, wuduholt wynlīc, Exon. Th. 199, 30; Ph. 33.

sunn-beorht; *adj. Bright with the sunshine:*—Hē his cȳþþu eft, sunbeorht gesetu sēceþ *contendit solis ad ortus*, Exon. Th. 217, 10; Ph. 278: 228, 10; Ph. 436.

sunn-bryne, es; *m. Sun-burn:*—Wiþ sunbryne, Lchdm. ii. 324, 16: 300, 30.

sunn-deáw (?). v. sund-deáw.

sunne, an (sunnu, Cd. Th. 286, 14; Sat. 352, *and acc.* sunne, 147, 11; Gen. 2437: *O. Sax. O. L. Ger.* have acc. *sunna*); *f.* I. *the sun:*—On ðam feórðan dæge gesceóp God twā miccle leóht, ðæt is sunne and mōna, and betǣhte ðæt māre leóht, ðæt is seó sunne, tō ðam dæge,

Lchdm. iii. 234, 6-8. Seó sunne is micle ufor đonne se mōna sȳ, 242, 10. Seó sunne is swīđe mycel; eall swā brād heó is, đæs đe bēc secgaþ, swā eall eorđan ymbhwyrft, 236, 6. Đā (*at the creation*) wæs seó sunne seofon sīđum beorhtre đonne heó nū is, Shrn. 64, 19. Seó sunne (sunna, Lind.) byþ forsworcen, Mt. Kmbl. 24, 29. On sumera sunne scīneþ, Cd. Th. 233, 16; Dan. 276. Dæge sunnan *die sabbati*, Lk. Skt. Lind. 4, 16. I a. epithets or metaphors applied to the sun:—Hāte scīneþ, blīcþ đeós beorhte sunne, Cd. Th. 50, 19; Gen. 811. Swegles gim, sunne, Exon. Th. 212, 13; Ph. 209. Goldtorht sunne, 351, 11; Sch. 78. Heofones gim, wyncondel wera, sweglbeorht sunne, 174, 33; Gū. 1187. Sunne swegeltorht, Andr. Kmbl. 2497; An. 1250. Æđele sunne, Ps. Th. 103, 21. Sunne, mǣre tungol, sió æþele gesceaft, Chr. 937; Erl. 13, 16. *See also* candel, tapor. I b. forms used of the sun's course:—Seó sunne gǣþ be Godes dihte betweox heofenan and eorđan, on dæg bufon eorđan and on niht under đysse eorđan, eall swā feorr ādūne on nihtlīcre tīde under đære eorþan swā heó on dæg bufon up āstīhþ, Lchdm. iii. 234, 18-22. Đonne sunne on setle sié, ii. 346, 10. Ǣr sunne tō setle eode, Ex. 17, 12. Sunne setlgonges fūs, Exon. Th. 174, 33; Gū. 1187. Sōna swā seó sunne sealte streámas heá oferhlifaþ, 206, 1; Ph. 120. Sunne gewāt tō sete glīdan, Andr. Kmbl. 2609; An. 1306. Sunne up on morgentīd glād ofer grundas . . . sió æþele gesceaft sāh tō setle, Chr. 937; Erl. 112, 13-17. Wē hātaþ ǣnne dæg fram sunnan upgang ōđ ǣfen; ac swā þeáh is on bōcum geteald tō ānum dæge fram đære sunnan upgange ōđ đæt heó eft becume đǣr heó ǣr upstāh, Lchdm. iii. 236, 1-5. Æfter sunnan setlgange, Gen. 28, 11: Ex. 22, 26. Æfter sunnan setlrāde, Cd. Th. 184, 19; Exod. 109. II. used in phrases expressing exposure to the sun's heat or light, e. g. *in* or *out of the sun*:—Gelicge upweard wiđ hātre sunnan *let him lie on his back with his face turned towards a hot sun*, Lchdm. iii. 2, 10. Drīge on hātre sunnan, ii. 30, 19. Ryslas eáfisca on sunnan gemylte, 30, 1. Hē sæt ūt on sunnan, Shrn. 61, 24. Āsete on hāte sunnan, Lchdm. ii. 252, 9: Exon. Th. 407, 34; Rä. 27, 4. Þeáh hine (*the sick man*) mon on sunnan lǣde, 340, 17; Gn. Ex. 112. II a. in the phrase *under sunnan* = in this world, cf. *sublunary*:—Hié ǣfre geseón under sunnan, Andr. Kmbl. 2025; An. 1015. Đæt hit wurde, đæt on eorđan geond đās wīdan weoruld wǣren swelce under sunnan, Met. 8, 42. III. used metaphorically:—Seó sōþfæste sunne, Exon. Th. 237, 9; Ph. 587. Mīn se swētesta sunnan scīma, Juliana, 252, 21; Jul. 166. [*Goth.* sunnō: *O. Sax. O. L. Ger. O. H. Ger. Icel.* sunna. In the Scandinavian languages the ordinary word is *sōl*, *sunna* is poetical: Sōl heitir með mönnum, en sunna með goðum.] v. sunna; swegel, II.

sunne-beám, es; *m. A sun-beam*:—Hēr æteówede cometa se steorra, and scān iii mōnđas swilce sunnebeám, Chr. 678; Erl. 41, 5. v. sunn-beám.

sunn-feld, es *or* a; *m. Elysium*:—Sunfeld *Eliseum*, Wrt. Voc. ii. 32, 8. Hwǣr wuniaþ Enoc und Helias? Ic đē secge, Malifica and Intimphonis (in tempis?), đæt is, on sunfelda and on sceánfelda, Salm. Kmbl. p. 202, 1. (v. scīn-feld.) [*O. H. Ger.* sunna-velt *Elysium*.]

sunn-folgend a plant-name (rendering the Latin *solisequia*), *heliotrope*, Wrt. Voc. ii. 120, 71. v. sōlsece.

sunn-gang, es; *m. The course of the sun.* v. next word.

sunn-ganges; *adv. In the direction of the sun's movement, with the sun*:—Wende đē đonne iii sunganges, Lchdm. i. 400, 10. Bebeóde hē hine Gode geornlīce and hine gesēnige, cyrre hine sungonges ymb, ii. 116, 9. To move with the sun was considered lucky, to move in the reverse direction unlucky; the latter method is consequently taken by witches in their ceremonies. So Spenser, 'She turned her contrary to the sunne . . . for she the right did shunne.' Cf. *Icel.* sōlar-sinnis *with the sun*:—Þeir höfðu gengit sōlarsinniss um goðahūs, Droplaugarsona Saga 11, 4. At sōlu *prosperously; and*-sælis *against the course of the sun;* mostly used of witches or uncanny appearances:—Sā sauðamaðr Grō at hon gēkk ūt, ok gēkk andsælis um hus sīn ok mælti erfitt mun verða at standa ī mōt giptu Ingimundarsona, Vatnsdæla Saga 59, 4. Cf. also Scotch *withershins*, see the examples in Jamieson's Dictionary.

sunn-gihte, es; *n.* (?) *A solstice*:—On đone ylcan dæg (*June* 24) byþ *solstitia*, đæt ys on ūre geþeóde, sungihte, forđon đe seó sunne standeþ on mydre lyfte. . . . Đonne gelympeþ đæt wundorlīce on đæs sumeres sungihte on mydne dæg, đonne seó sunne byþ on đæs heofones mydle, đonne nafaþ seó sȳl (*at Jerusalem*) nǣnige sceade; đonne đæs sungihtes beóþ þrȳ dagas forđ āurnen, đonne hafaþ seó sȳl ǣrest lytle sceade, Shrn. 95, 29-96, 3. Cf. gebed-giht; *and see* sunn-stede.

sunn-līc; *adj. Solar*:—Đæt sunlīce leóhtfæt *lampas Titanea*, Wrt. Voc. ii. 53, 24. On swā hwilcum sunlīcum mōnđe swā se mōna geendaþ, Lchdm. iii. 250, 3. [*O. H. Ger.* sunna-līh.]

sunn-sceadu, we *or* e; *f. A sun-shade, veil, covering to keep off the sun*:—Sunsceadu *flammeolum* (*flameolum* curchyfe, Wrt. Voc. i. 238, col. 2), Wrt. Voc. ii. 149, 6.

sunn-scin *sun-shine* (? the word glosses *speculum*, Wrt. Voc. ii. 90, 14). v. scīn.

sunn-scīne; *adj. Beautiful* or *splendid as the sun*:—Seó sunsciéne fǣmne, Exon. Th. 256, 9; Jul. 229.

sunn-set, es; *n. The place where the sun sets, the west*:—From sunsete (sunnsett, Lind.) *ab occasu*, Lk. Skt. Rush. 12, 54. Sunset *occidentem*, Mt. Kmbl. Lind. 24, 27. [Cf. *Icel.* sōlar-seta, -setr *sunset;* sōl-setr; *n. pl. sunrise and sunset.*]

sunn-stede, es; *m. A solstice*:—Sumor hæfþ sunnstede . . . winter hæfþ ōþerne sunnstede . . . Gǣþ seó sunne norđweard ōđ đæt heó becymþ tō đam tācne đe is gehāten *Cancer*, đǣr is se sumerlīca sunnstede . . . seó sunne cymþ eft sūđ tō đam winterlīcan sunnstede, Lchdm. iii. 250, 10-24. Đa Grēciscan onginnaþ hyra geár æt đam sunnstede, 246, 19. God sette twegen sunnstedas, đæne ǣnne on .xii. kl. Ian. and đone ōđerne on .xii. kl. Iulii, Anglia viii. 299, 16. v. sunn-gihte.

sunn-treów (?). In Wrt. Voc. i. 291, 3 *origia* is glossed by *suntreów*. Cockayne suggests, *oryza* sum treów, Lchdm. iii. 346, col. 1.

sunnu. v. sunne.

sunn-wlitig; *adj. Beautiful with the sun*:—Winter biþ cealdost, lencten hrīmigost, sumor sunwlitigost, Menol. Fox 473; Gn. C. 7.

sunor (-er), e; *f. A herd of swine, a sounder* ('That men calleth a trip of a tame swyn is called of wylde swyn a *soundre;* that is to say, ȝif ther be passyd v. or vi. togedres.'—Halliwell's Dict.):—Wæs unfeor suner swīna (suner berga, Lind. *grex porcorum*) etende. Đa deóful bēdun hinae: 'send ūsic in đās sunrae (suner, Lind. *gregem*) swīna.' . . . Eode all siu suner niþerweardes in sae, Mt. Kmbl. Rush. 8, 30-32. Sunor . . . đæt sunor, Lk. Skt. Lind. 8, 32, 33. [The word seems to be found in the Lombard sonar-pair, sonor-pahir *verres qui omnes alios verres in grege batuit et vincit;* see Grmm. Gesch. D. S. 483; Graff. 3, 202: and in the Frankish sonesti = *duodecim equas cum admissario, aut sex scrovas cum verre, vel duodecim vaccas cum tauro*, Grmm. Gesch. D. S. 383.]

sun-sunu; *m. A grandson*:—Gif his sunu and đæs sunsunu, L. Wg. 11; Th. i. 188, 23.

sunu; *gen.* a, u; *dat.* a, u; *n. pl.* a, u, o: there are also weak forms *sing.* suna; *n. pl.* sunan; *gen.* sunena; *m.* I. *a son*:—Mīn se gecorena sunu (sune, Rush.), Mt. Kmbl. 3, 17. Sum man hæfde twegen suna (suno, Lind. Rush.) . . . ealle his þing gegaderude se gingra sunu (suno, Rush.), Lk. Skt. 15, 11, 13. Sunu Healfdenes, Beo. Th 1294; B. 645. Fēng tō Beornica rīce Æþelfriþes suna, Bd. 3, 1; S. 523, 13. Swīþhelm, Seaxbaldes suna, 3, 22; S. 553, 42: 3, 24; S. 556, 26. Hwæđer hit sig đīnes suna, Gen. 37, 32. Word hiere suna, Elen. Kmbl. 443; El. 222: Exon. Th. 6, 34; Cri. 94. Heó ne gehȳrde nā hyre leófan sunu stemne (*but* suna ll. 20, 24), Wulfst. 152, 16. Gif his sunu and his sunu sunu geþeóþ, L. Wg. 11; Th. i. 188, 10. Cyning đe macode hys suna (sune, Lind.: sunu, Rush. *filio*) gyfta, Mt. Kmbl. 22, 2. Ān mann hæfde twegen suna (sunu, Lind.: sunes, Rush.); đā cwæđ hē tō đam yldran suna, 21, 28: Beo. Th. 4055; B. 2025. Ic fare tō mīnum sunu, Gen. 37, 35: Exon. Th. 40, 8; Cri. 635. Wille ic āsecgan sunu Healfdenes, mǣrum þeódne, mīn ǣrende, Beo. Th. 694; B. 344. Ic đē forgife sunu, Gen. 17, 16. Heó sunu (suno, Rush.) cende, Lk. Skt. 1, 57. Sege đæt đās mīne twegen suna (suno, Lind.: sunæ, Rush.) sittan . . ., Mt. Kmbl. 20, 21: Cd. Th. 93, 24; Gen. 1551. Suno, 97, 19; Gen. 1615. Sunu, 199, 1; Exod. 332: 199, 19; Exod. 341. Hē worn gestrȳnde suna and dohtra, Cd. Th. 74, 13; Gen. 1221. Hwæt suna hæfde Adam? .xxx. sunena and .xxx. dohtra, Salm. Kmbl. p. 184, 31-32. Hwī sceal ic beón bedǣled ǣgđer mīnra sunena on ānum dæge? Gen. 27, 45: Lev. 7, 32. Zebedēis sunena (suna, MS. A., Lind.: sunena, Rush.) mōdor *mater filiorum Zebedaei*, Mt. Kmbl. 27, 56. Sunana, p. 18, 14. Beód Aarone and his sunum, Lev. 6, 20. Mid sunum đīnum, Cd. Th. 78, 28; Gen. 1300. Heora bearn blōtan feóndum, sceuccum onsæcgean suna and dohter, Ps. Th. 105, 27. Hire selfre sunu sweolođe befæstan, bānfatu bærnan, Beo. Th. 2234; B. 1115. ¶ In expressions denoting degrees of descent:—Suna sunu *nepos, neptis*, þridda sunu *pronepus, proneptis*, Wrt. Voc. ii. 62, 35. Feórþa sunu *abnepos*, 4, 73: 8, 22. Fīfta sunu *adnepos*, 8, 23. Suna sune *vel* brōđer sune *nepos*, feówerþe sune *abnepos*, fīfte sune *adnepos*, sixte sune *trinepos*, i. 51, 71-77. Fæderan sunan *patrueles*, mōddrian sunan *matrueles*, fæderon sunan *fratres patrueles*, 52, 1-4. II. used of animals:—Đære myran sunu *equae filius*, Bd. 3, 14; S. 540, 30. Đæs gores sunu *the beetle*, Exon. Th. 426, 11; Rä. 41, 72. [*Goth.* sunus: *O. Sax.* sunu (-o), *pl.* suni: *O. L. Ger.* sunu (-o), sun: *O. Frs.* sunu, sun, son; *pl. acc.* suna, sunar, sonen: *O. H. Ger.* sunu, sun; *pl.* suni: *Icel.* sonr; *pl.* sønir, synir, *acc.* sonu.] v. bisceop-, gāst-, god-, hornung-, steóp-, sun-sunu.

sunu-cennicge (?) *one who bears a son, a mother*:—Sunucenn *genetrix*, sunucennices *genetricis*, sunucennic *genetricis*, Rtl. 66, 23, 17, 11.

sūpan; *p.* seáp, *pl.* supon; *pp.* sopen. I. *to sup, to take* [*fluid*] *into the mouth*:—Gif hē đæt brođ sȳpþ, Lchdm. ii. 336, 16. Hē sǣp (seáp, MSS. O. V.) of đæm calice blōd, Homl. Skt. i. 3, 162. Sūp đæt wōs, Lchdm. i. 86, 17. Hrefnes fōt wel on wīne, sūp swā đū hātost mǣge, ii. 50, 25: 56, 2: iii. 48, 2. Seóđ on wīne, sūpe hit swā wearm and healde on his mūđe, i. 94, 20. Wyl on gāte meolce and sūpe, ii. 100, 24. Þeáh đū mid cuclere đæt sūpe, đæt hylpþ, 184, 25. Genim fīfleáfan seáw . . . syle him sūpan, i. 86, 25, 28: 82, 23. Dō on swȳþe gōd beór, syle hyt him đonne wlacu sūpan, 196, 19. Hē gelæhte ǣnne calic and sealde his gingrum of tō sūpenne, Homl. Th. ii. 244, 14. Hē scōf on hālig wæter of ðam hālgan treówe, sealde ðam ādligan of tō sūpenne, Homl. Skt. ii. 26, 264. II. used figuratively:—Ðeáh ic hine sūpe, ic hine wille eft ūt āspīwan of mīnum mūðe, Past. 58; Swt. 447, 1. Ða ðe ne suppas deáð *qui non gustabunt mortem*, Mt. Kmbl. Lind. 16, 28. Ne mē se seáð sūpe mid mūðe *neque urgeat super me puteus os suum*, Ps. Th. 68, 15. [To frete ar ful tyme were and þanne to sitten and soupen, Piers P. 2, 96. Soupe the lene broth, P. S. 324, 239. Soop up *absorbuit*, Wick. Apoc. 12, 16; sopen, *pp.*, Ps. 123, 4. Me þoȝte Kaym tok Abelles blod and sop it op, Anglia i. 314, 473. Sowpone or sowpe *sorbeo, absorbeo;* sowpynge *sorbicio*, Prompt. Parv. 466, col. 2. [*Du.* zuipen *to drink, quaff: O. H. Ger.* sūfan *sorbere: Ger.* saufen: *Icel.* sūpa.] v. be-, ge-sūpan; sopa, *and next word.*

sūpe, an; *f.* (?) *A sup, draught:*—Sūpe nigon sūpan, Lchdm. ii. 102, 16. v. sopa.

supe *in* ic supe *sarcio*, Wrt. Voc. i. 288, 50, *read* (?) sūwe, v. seowian.

sur glosses *lurco*, Wrt. Voc. ii. 70, 41, *read* (?) siir. v. sīgere, sȳr.

sūr; *adj. Sour:*—Sūr meolc *oxygala, acidum lac*, Wrt. Voc. i. 28, 2. Āwyl on sūrum ealaþ, Lchdm. ii. 34, 15: 134, 10. Genim sūrne æppel, 132, 15. Dō on sūre flētan, 130, 12. Forgā sūr and sealtes gehwæt, 56, 23. Genim sūre cruman berenes hlāfes, 134, 8. Wīnberian sūre geseón, iii. 212, 24. [*O. H. Ger.* sūr: *Icel.* sūrr.]

sūre, an; *f. Sorrel;* rumex acetosa (v. E. D. S. Pub., Plant Names, for terms in which *sour* is used to denote this plant):—Sūrae *salsa*, Txts. 98, 974. Sūre, Wrt. Voc. i. 68, 54: *saliunca*, ii. 119, 64. Wiþ canceiādle, sūre, sealt . . ., Lchdm. ii. 108, 9: 266, 16. Wensealf, cersan, sūran, 128, 14. Genim monnes sūran, 124, 19. *See also* geáces sūre *under* geác. [*Icel.* sūra: *Dan.* syre. Cf. *Ger.* sauer-ampfer.] v. wudu-sūre.

sūr-eágede, -ēgede; *adj. Blear-eyed:*—Sūreágede *lippus*, Wrt. Voc. i. 45, 57. Sūrēgede, 75, 43. Sūreágede (-egede, MS. H.), Ælfc. Gr. 30; Zup. 192, 10. v. sūr-īge.

Surfe, Surpe; *pl. A Slavonic race inhabiting northern Germany;* Latin forms are *Sorabi, Soravi, Sorbi:*—Be norþaneástan Maroara (*Moravia*) sindon Dalamentsan . . . and be norþan Dalamentsan sindon Surpe, Ors. 1, 1; Swt. 16, 20. Surfe, Swt. 16, 33.

sūrian *to sour.* [*O. H. Ger.* sūrēn.] v. ā-sūrian.

sūr-īge, -ēge; *adj. Blear-eyed:*—Gif mon sūrēge sié, Lchdm. ii. 2, 9: 36, 21. Ða sūrīgan eágan *lippos oculos*, Wrt. Voc. ii. 52, 55: 92, 22. [*O. H. Ger.* sūr-ouger *lippus*, Grff. i. 123: *Icel.* sūr-eygr; sūrnar ī augum *the eyes smart* from smoke; sūr (applied to the eyes) *bleared.*] v. sūr-eágede.

sūr-milisc, -melsc; *adj. Having a mixture of sour and sweet in taste:*—Apulder *malus*, sūrmilsc apulder *malus matranus*, swēte apulder *malomellus*, Wrt. Voc. i. 32, 48. Ða mettas ðe strangunge mægen hæbben swā swā beóþ æppla nales tō swēte ac sūrmelsce, Lchdm. ii. 176, 18.

sūrness, e; *f. Sourness:*—Sūrnesse *acredinis*, Wrt. Voc. ii. 6, 1.

sūsl, es; *n.: e; f. Torment*, (1) where the word is certainly neuter:—Se seáð ðæs sing[alan] sūsles, Nar. 50, 23. Sūsles þegnum, Exon. Th. 275, 30: Jul. 558: 304, 18; Fä. 72. Hié ðæt sūsl þrowiende wǣron, Ors. 1, 12; Swt. 54, 26. In ðæt swearte sūsl (*hell*), Exon. Th. 142, 4; Gū. 639. Ða ungeendodan sūslo ðū byst þrowigende, Nicod. 29; Thw. 17, 12. Helle sūslu *inferni supplicia*, Scint. 27, 8. (2) where the word is feminine:—Ðeós hellīce sūsl *hic tartarus*, Ælfc. Gr. 13; Zup. 86, 4. Fram ðam ēcan hungre helle sūsle, Ælfc. Gen. Thw. 3, 26. Gefērlǣhte on ānre sūsle, Homl. Th. i. 132, 20. Faraþ hig on ēce sūsle, and ða rihtwīsan on ðæt ēce līf *ibunt hi in supplicium aeternum, justi autem in vitam aeternam*, Mt. Kmbl. 25, 46. Hū hē synfullum sūsle gefremme, Wulfst. 138, 9: Dōm. L. 153. (3) where the gender is uncertain:—Ðē is sūsl weotod, Cd. Th. 308, 14; Sat. 692: 257, 8; Dan. 654. Satan on sūsle (*dat.* or *acc.*) gefeól, 309, 20; Sat. 712. Sūsle geinnod, 3, 28; Gen. 42. Swingan, sūsle þreágan, Exon. Th. 251, 9; Jul. 142. Sūsl þrowian, Cd. Th. 5, 22; Gen. 75: 255, 9; Dan. 621. Sūsel, 267, 21; Sat. 41. Hafastū māre sūsel, 268, 33; Sat. 64. In sūsla grund, Elen. Kmbl. 1885; El. 944: Exon. Th. 98, 8; Cri. 1604. On hwilcum sūslum hē mōste ēcelīce cwylmian, Homl. Th. i. 86, 2. Sūslum beþrungen, Elen. Kmbl. 1896; El. 950: Exon. Th. 10, 8; Cri. 149. [*Grein compares the word with Icelandic forms*, sȳsl, sȳsla *business*, sȳsl *painstaking*, sȳsla *to do business*, sȳsliga *busily.*] v. cwic-sūsl; seóslig.

sūsl-bana, an; *m. A torturing destroyer, one who tortures while he destroys:*—Swarte sūslbonan (*devils*), Cd. Th. 305, 1; Sat. 640.

sūsl-cwalu, e; *f. A destruction* or *death accompanied by torment:*—Ða ārleásan geseóþ heora wīte and heora sūselcwale hym tōweard, Wulfst. 238, 23. Ðū scealt habban sūselcwale ā on ēcnysse, 241, 13.

sūslen. v. cwic-sūslen.

sūsl-hof, es; *n. A place of torment, hell:*—Of helle, of ðam sūslhofe, Hy. 10, 31.

suster *a sister*, sustras, L. R. S. 5; Th. i. 436, 2, sutel. v. sweostor, sester, sweotol.

sūtere, es; *m. A shoemaker, souter* (Scotch):—Sūtere *sutor*, Wrt. Voc. i. 74, 11. Sum sūtere siwode ðæs hālgan weres sceós . . . Anianus wæs gehāten se ylca sūtere, Homl. Skt. i. 15, 23, 27. Eówer sūtere hē is *uester sutor est*, eówer sūteres tōl *uestri sutoris instrumenta*, Ælfc. Gr. 15; Zup. 105, 14. Gif hē smeáwyrhtan hæfþ, ðām hē sceal tō tōlan fylstan; sūtere and ōðran wyrhtan ǣlc weorc sylf wīsaþ hwæt him tō gebyreþ, Anglia ix. 263, 18. Sūtera hūs *sutrina domus*, Wrt. Voc. i. 59, 3. [A sutare þet haueð forloren his el, he secheð hit anonriht, A. R. 324, 17. Euerych soutere þ[t] wonyeþ in þe citee [of Wynchestre] þ[t] halt shoppe, E. G. 358, 22. Euerych sowtere þ[t] makeþ shon of newe roþes leþer, 359, 14 (14th cent.). More borynde þanne zouteres eles, Ayenb. 66, 12. Sowtare or cordewaner *sutor*, Prompt. Parv. 466, col. 2. *O. H. Ger.* sūtāri: *M. H. Ger.* sūtære; schuoch-sūtære (*from which Ger.* schuster): *Icel.* sūtari *a tanner. From Latin* sutor.] Cf. scōh-wyrhta.

[**sūþ**;] *cpve.* sūþra; *spve.* sūþmest; *adj. South, southern:*—Andlang ðæs sūðeran weges, Cod. Dip. Kmbl. iii. 408, 32. On ðone sȳðeran steð . . . on ðone norðere steð, v. 148, 20. Ðone sūðran sunnstede, Lchdm. iii. 252, 15. Ðone sūðran steorran, 270, 18. On ðæm sūðmestan onwalde, Ors. 6, 1; Swt. 252, 15. Ða sūðmestan Æthiopian hæfdon bryne for ðære hǣte, 1, 7; Swt. 40, 5. ¶ Sūþan *in combination with prepositions:*—Be-sūðan sǣ *south of the sea*, Shrn. 145, 17. Him be-sūðan, Cd. Th. 182, 1; Exod. 69. Nāðer ne be-norðan mearce ne be-sūðan, L. Ath. v. 5; Th. i. 232, 19. Be-sūþan ðæm mūþan, Ors. 1, 1; Swt. 10, 8. Wið-sūðan ðone Sciringes-heal, Swt. 19, 18. Be ðam wigbede sūþan *juxta altare ad austrum*, Bd. 5, 19; S. 641, 19. [*O. H. Ger.* sund- *and Icel.* sunn- *point to the* n *that has been lost from the English word.*] See the compounds which follow, and Cod. Dip. Kmbl. vi. 337, 338, for names of places in which *sūþ* forms the first part.

sūþ; *adv. In a southerly direction* or *position:*—Twelf mīla brād sūð and norð *ab austro in boream duodecim milia passuum*, Bd. 1, 3; S. 475, 19. Him is ðæt heáfod sūð gewend and ða fēt norð, Shrn. 66, 23. Syndon ōðere eálond sūð fram Brixonte, Nar. 36, 7. Seó eá sūþ ðonan ligeþ, Ors. 1, 1; Swt. 8, 21: Salm. Kmbl. 382; Sal. 190. Fōron ðā sūþ ofer Temese, Chr. 851; Erl. 68, 1. Sūð ofer sǣ fōron, 897; Erl. 94, 28. Fōron sūð ymbūtan, 894; Erl. 91, 5. Seó sunne cymþ eft sūð tō ðam winterlīcan sunnstede, Lchdm. iii. 250, 24: 260, 10: Cd. Th. 118, 16; Gen. 1966. Sūð ne norð ofer eormengrund ōþer nǣnig sēlra nǣre, Beo. Th. 1720; B. 858: Met. 10, 24. Sūð eást and west, 9, 42: 10, 5. Sūð west and eást, 14, 7. Swā heó (*the sun*) sūðor biþ, swā hit swīþor winterlǣcþ, Lchdm. iii. 252, 2.

sūþan; *adv.* I. *from the south:*—On ðysum geare com micel sciphere hider sūþan of Lidwiccum, Chr. 918; Erl. 102, 22. Gefaren tōsomne sūðan and norðan, Cd. Th. 120, 2; Gen. 1988. Gif hēr wind cymþ westan oððe eástan, sūðan oððe norðan, 50, 11; Gen. 807. Sūþan, Exon. Th. 55, 18; Cri. 885: 220, 23; Ph. 324. II. marking position, *to* or *in the south:*—Asia is befangen mid ðæm gārsecge sūþan and norþan and eástan, Ors. 1, 1; Swt. 8, 7. Ne dohte nāðer ðisse leóde ne sūðan ne norðan, Chr. 1013; Erl. 149, 27. Healdaþ hine norðan and sūðan on twā healfa twā hund wearda, Salm. Kmbl. 520; Sal. 259. [*O. L. Ger.* sūthon *ab austro: O. H. Ger.* sundan: *Icel.* sunnan.]

sūþan-eástan. I. *adv. From the south-east:*—Sūþaneástan sunnan leóma cymeþ, Exon. Th. 56, 15; Cri. 901. II. in phrases marking position, *to the south-east:*—Be-sūþaneástan (*ad Eurum*) ðæm porte, Ors. 1, 1; Swt. 10, 9. On-suðaneástan ðissum lande, Chr. 449; Erl. 13, 5. [*O. H. Ger.* sundan-ōstan.]

sūþaneástan-wind, es; *m. A south-east wind;* euroafricus, Wrt. Voc. i. 36, 14.

sūþan-eásterne; *adj. South-eastern:*—Hē ferade sūþaneásterne wind of heofenan *transtulit austrum de coelo*, Ps. Lamb. 77, 26. v. sūþ-eásterne.

Sūþan-hymbre, -humbre; *pl. The Southumbrians, the Mercians:*—Hēr Sūþanhymbre (-humbre, Laud. MS.) ofslōgon Æþelrēdes cwēne (cf. Æþelrēd Myrcna cyning, Bd. 4, 21; S. 590, 14), Chr. 697; Th. 67, cols. 1, 3. Hēr Cēnrēd fēng tō Sūþanhymbre rīce (cf. Cēnrēd Myrcna rīce fore wæs. Bd. 5, 19; S. 636, 24), 702; Th. 67, col. 1. Ūre cynecynn and Sūðanhymbra eác, 449; Erl. 13, 21. v. Sūþ-hymbre.

sūþan-westan; *adv. From the south-west:*—Sūðanwestan *ab affrico*, Wrt. Voc. ii. 98, 35: 4, 15: *a fafonio*, 99, 50.

sūþanwestan-wind, es; *m. A south-west wind;* africus, Wrt. Voc. i. 36, 15.

sūþan-wind, es; *m. A south wind:*—Sūþanwind *auster* vel *nothus*, Wrt. Voc. i. 36, 9. Se ðe hit mid sūðanwinde onginne, ðonne hæfþ hē sige, Lchdm. iii. 182, 3. Sūþanwind (southenwind, Ps.) *austrum*, Ps. Surt. 77, 26. [A suðenwind blew ðat day, Gen. and Ex. 3084. *Icel.* sunnan-vindr.]

sūþ-dǣl, es; *m. A south part, the south:*—Sūþdǣl *auster*, Ælfc. Gr. 8; Zup. 27, 7. Sūðdǣles cwēn *regina austri*, Mt. Kmbl. 12, 42. Hig cōmon tō sūðdǣle *ad australem plagam*, Gen. 13, 1. Tō sūðdǣle *ad meridiem*, 14. Of sūðdǣle Asiam, Ors. 1, 10; Swt. 44, 5. Hī on ðam sūþdǣle inn eodon, Homl. Th. i. 508, 9. Fram sūþdǣle *a meridie*, Bd. 1, 1; S. 473, 12. Ðære Asian sūþdǣl *meridianam partem Asiae*, Ors.

1, 1; Swt. 14, 5. Ða sūþdǽlas middangeardes, Bd. 1, 1; S. 473, 33. Ða sūþdǽlas ðysses eálondes *australes partes Britanniae*, S. 474, 8. [Suþdale off þiss werelld is Mysimmbrion ȝehatenn, Orm. 16418. Cf. *O.H. Ger.* sunder-teil *dextera pars (templi).*]

sūþ-duru, a; *f. A south door*:—Wæs seó sūðduru hwæthwega hāde māre, Blickl. Homl. 201, 15. [Cf. *Icel.* sūðr-dyrr; *pl. south doors.*]

sūþ-eást; *adv. South-east*:—Donua mūða ðære eá scȳt sūðeást ūt, Ors. 1, 1; Swt. 22, 5: Cd. Th. 42, 1; Gen. 667.

sūþ-eástende, es; *m. The south-east end*:—Ðæt (*India*) is se sūþeástende ðisses middangeardes, Bt. 29, 3; Fox 106, 22.

sūþ-eásterne; *adj. South-eastern*:—Sūðeásterne wind *eurus*, Ælfc. Gr. 4; Zup. 8, 2.

Sūþ-Engle; *pl. The people of the south of England*:—On Sūð-Engla lage griðlagu ðus stent, L. Eth. vii. 9; Th. i. 330, 22.

suþerige. A plant nàme glossing *satirion*, Wrt. Voc. i. 32, 18. Cockayne takes the word to be the same as sæþerige (q.v.), and the gloss to be a mistake, Lchdm. ii. 403, col. 1; but cf. *satirion* sanycle, Wülck. Gl. 613, 33, *saniculum* sanicle i. wudemerch, 554, 8.

sūþerne; *adj. Southern, coming from the south*:—Se ōðer heáfodwind is sūðerne, *auster* gehāten, Lchdm. iii. 274, 16: Met. 5, 7. Se sūðerna wind, Lchdm. iii. 276, 7: Bt. 6; Fox 14, 23. Cwoen sūðerne (sūðernæs ł sūðdǽles, Lind.) *regina austri*, Lk. Skt. Rush. 11, 31: Exon. Th. 480, 10: Rä. 63, 9. Fram deófle sūðernum *ab demonio meridiano*, Ps. Spl. 90, 6. Sūþerne wind *austrum*. 77, 30: *austrum, affricum*, Blickl. Gl. Sende se sǽrinc sūþerne gār, Byrht. Th. 135, 47; By. 134. Hire (*the queen of Sheba*) olfendas bǽron sūðerne wyrta, Homl. Th. ii. 584, 10. ¶ The word is often used in reference to things coming to England from the south of Europe, plants or medicine:—Genim sūþerne cymen, Lchdm. ii. 184, 15. Ða sūþernan finuglan, 142, 2. Sūþerne popig, 212, 8. Sūþerne rind *cinamonium*, iii. 301, col. 2: *cinnamomum*, Wrt. Voc. ii. 131, 9. Dō ðone sūþernan wermōd, ðæt is *prutene*, Lchdm. ii. 236, 19. Sūðerne wudu *aprotanum*, Wrt. Voc. i. 79, 6. Sūþerne wuda. Ðeós wyrt ðe man *abrotanum* and ōðrum naman sūðerne wuda nemneþ, Lchdm. i. 250, 16–18: iii. 12, 15: 40, 5. Næglæs (cunæglæsse) hātte wyrt sūþerno, ii. 106, 9. Ōþer swilc *ameos* hātte sūþerne wyrt, 192, 7. *Oxumellis* . . . drenc sūþerne, 212, 6: 254, 16. On ðam sūðrenan *oxumelle*, 152, 1. Ðæt is sūþerne lǽcedōm, 224, 14. On ðam sūþernan lǽcedōme ðe hātte *oxumelle*, 248, 10. [*O. Frs.* suthern: *O. H. Ger.* sundirin *australis*: *Icel.* suðrænn.]

sūþe-weard; *adj. Southward, south*:—Tōemnes ðæm lande sūðeweardum, Ors. 1, 1; Swt. 19, 1. From sūþeweardum ōð norþeweardne, Bt. 16, 4; Fox 58, 12: 18, 1; Fox 62, 1. On splott sūðeweardne, Cod. Dip. B. iii. 336, 23. Ða gesǽtan sūðewearde Bryttene, Chr. Erl. 3, 5. v. sūþ-weard.

sūþ-folc, es; *n. A southern people, a people living south in relation to some other*:—Rōmāne and eall sūþfolc (ealle sūþfolc, 146, 15), Lchdm. ii. 16, 1. Humbre streám tōsceádeþ sūþfolc Angelþeóde and norþfolc, Bd. 1, 25; S. 486, 17. Eorldōm on Norðfolc and Sūðfolc (*Suffolk*), Chr. 1075; Erl. 213, 5. Norðmen wǽron sūðfolcum swice, Cd. Th. 120, 17; Gen. 1996. [Cf. *O. Sax.* sūðar-liudi.]

sūþ-gārsecg, es; *m. A southern ocean*; meridianus oceanus, Ors. 1, 1; Swt. 8, 30.

sūþ-gemǽre, es; *n. A southern boundary*:—Hiera sūþgemǽro licgeaþ tō ðam Reádan Sǽ, Ors. 1, 1; Swt. 10, 34.

Sūþ-geweorc, es; *n. Southwark*:—Ðā cōmon hȳ tō Sūþgeweorce, Chr. 1052; Erl. 181, 3. [*Icel.* Sūðr-virki.]

Sūþ-Gyrwas (-e, -an); *pl. The southern division of the Gyrwas*:—Sūþ-Gyrwa syx hund hȳda, Cod. Dip. B. i. 414, 18. Sūþ-Gyrwa ealdormon *princeps Australium Gyruiorum*, Bd. 4, 19; S. 587, 21. Sūð-Gerwa, Shrn. 94, 20. Sūð-Gyrwena, Lchdm. iii. 430, 14.

Sūþ-hāmtūn *Southampton*:—Æt Sūðhāmtūne, Cod. Dip. Kmbl. vi. 49, 20. v. Hām-tūn.

Sūþhāmtūn-scīr *Hampshire*, Cod. Dip. Kmbl. iv. 204, 16. [Þe nywe forest þat ys in Souþhamtescyre, R. Glouc. 375, 9.]

sūþ-heald; *adj. Sloping or tending to the south*:—Rodor sūðheald swīfeþ swift, Met. 28, 17. Swā sūðhealde swīþe hlimman *sicut torrens in austro*, Ps. Th. 125, 4. [*Icel.* sūðr-hallr (*applied to the sun*).]

sūþ-healf, e; *f. The south side*, mostly, if not exclusively, in the phrase *on (ða) sūþhealfe*:—On sūðhealfe *ad meridianam plagam*, Num. 3, 29: *contra meridiem*, Deut. 1, 7. On sūþhealfe *a meridie*, Ors. 1, 1; Swt. 10, 26: 14, 2. On sūðhealfe ðære eás, Chr. 921; Erl. 108, 18: 913; Erl. 102, 10. On sūðhalfe Humbre streámes *ad meridianam Humbrae fluminis ripam*, Bd. 2, 16; S. 519, 19. Hī wendon ābūtan Penwihtsteort on ða sūðhealfe, Chr. 997; Erl. 135, 10. Hī wendon tō Lundene and dulfon āne mycele dīc on ða sūðhealfe (on sūðhealfe, MS. D.), 1016; Erl. 155, 9. On ða sūðhealfe fram Babilonia *in dextera parte ab Babilonia*, Nar. 34, 17. On ða sūðhealfe (*dexteriore parte*) landes Egiptna, 34. On ða sūðhealfe gārsecges *oceano dexteriore parte*, 36, 15. (Cf. *O. H. Ger.* sunder-teil *under* sūþ-dǽl.) [Þe an is a norðhalf, þe oðer a suðhalf, Laym. 15937. *O. H. Ger.* sund-, sundar-halpa *auster, meridies*: *Icel.* sūðr-hālfa *the southern region.*]

Sūþ-hymbre; *pl. The Mercians*:—Sūðhymbra (-humbra, Laud. MS.) rīce, Chr. 702; Th. 67, col. 3. Hēr wæs Ōsuuald ofslagen fram Pendan (and) Sūþhymbrum (cf. fram ðam ylcan hǽþenan cyninge and ðære hǽþenan ðeóde Myrcna, Bd. 3, 9; S. 533, 11), 641; Erl. 27, 8. v. Sūþan-hymbre.

sūþ-land, es; *n. A land lying to the south*:—Hē eardode on ðām sūðlandum *in terra australi*, Gen. 24, 62. [He hæfde to dæle þat suðlond þat Locres wes icleped, Laym. 2111. *Icel.* sūðr-land (*hence* Suther-land).]

sūþ-mǽgþ, e; *f. A southern tribe* or *province*:—Ōðrum folcum ðara sūþmǽgþa *caeteris australium provinciarum populis*, Bd. 3, 24; S. 557, 31. Hē eallum sūþmǽgþum weóld and rīce hæfde ōþ Humbre streám, 2, 5; S. 506, 10.

sūþ-mann, es; *m. A man living in the south*:—Sūðmonna sinc (*those who carry off the treasure are said* sēcan sūð, 118, 16; Gen. 1966, *and are called* norðmen, 120, 16; Gen. 1995), Cd. Th. 121, 28; Gen. 2017: 126, 4; Gen. 2096. [*Icel.* sūðr-maðr.]

sūþmest. v. sūþ; *adj.*

Sūþ-Mirce; *pl. The South Mercians*:—Sūþ-Myrcna rīce, Bd. 3, 24; S. 557, 36.

Sūþ-Peohtas, -Pihtas; *pl. The South Picts*:—Sūð-Pihtas (-Pyhtas, MS. E.), Chr. 565; Erl. 18, 4.

sūþ-portic, es; *m. A south porch*:—On ðam sūðportice, Chr. 1036; Erl. 165, 39.

sūþ-rador, -rodor, es; *m. The south of the heavens*:—Sūþrador *australis*, Blickl. Gl. Ōþþæt seó sunne on sūðrodor sǽged weorþeþ *postquam Phoebus equos in aperta refudit Olympi*, Exon. Th. 207, 14; Ph. 141.

Sūþr-īg *the people* or *the district of Surrey*:—Cantwara him tō cyrdon and Sūðrīg and Sūð-Seaxe, Chr. 823; Erl. 63, 20. Hī heafdon ofergān ealle Ceutingas and Sūð-Seaxe and Sūðrīg and Bearrucscīre, 1011; Erl. 144, 28. v. next word.

Sūþr-īge; *gen.* [e]a, ena; *pl. The people* or *district of Surrey*:—Cantware him tō cirdon and Sūþrīge and Sūþ-Seaxe, Chr. 823; Erl. 62, 22. Cantwara rīce and Sūþrīgea and Sūþ-Seaxna, 836; Erl. 66, 3. Sūþrīgea, 855; Erl. 70, 19. On Sūþrīgena lande be Temese streáme *in regione Sudergeona juxta fluvium Tamensem*, Bd. 4, 6; S. 574, 14. Ealhere mid Cantwarum and Huda mid Sūþrīgium (Sūþrīgum, MS. E.) gefuhton wiþ herige, Chr. 853; Erl. 68, 17. Of Cent ge of Sūþrīgum, 921; Erl. 107, 7. Fēngon tō West-Seaxna rīce and tō Sūðrīgean, 855; Erl. 71, 2. Tō Sūðrīgan, 836; Erl. 67, 3. Tō Godes ciricum in Sūðrēgum and in Cent, Cod. Dip. Kmbl. ii. 121, 8. Hē gewāt on Sūþrīge (Sūðrēge, MS. E.) and on Sūþ-Seaxe, Chr. 722; Erl. 44, 28. Fōron sūþ ofer Temese on Sūþrīge (Sūðrīge, MS. E.), 851; Erl. 68, 2. *The word occurs in a Latin charter* . . . In loco que appellatur *Cyningestūn* in regione Sūðrēgie, Cod. Dip. Kmbl. i. 318, 5. [Souþsex and Soþerei, Kent and Estsex, R. Glouc. 3, 21. Soþerey, 5, 23.]

sūþ-rihte; *adv. Due south*:—Seó eá irnþ ðonan sūðryhte, Ors. 1, 1; Swt. 8, 17: 17, 18, 19. Sūðrihte, Cod. Dip. Kmbl. ii. 250, 17.

sūþ-rima, an; *m. A south coast*:—Ðȳ ilcan sumera forweard nō læs ðonne xx scipa mid monnum mid ealle be ðam sūðriman, Chr. 897; Erl. 96, 15: 1009; Erl. 141, 32. v. sūþ-stæþ.

sūþ-rodor, -sceáta. v. sūþ-rador, sceáta, I.

Sūþ-Seaxe, -Seaxan; *pl. The people* or *district of Sussex*:—Him tō cirdon Sūþ-Seaxe, Chr. 823; Erl. 62, 22. Of Eald-Seaxon cōmon Sūð-Sexa, 449; Erl. 12, 10. Sūþ-Seaxan *meridiani Saxones*, Bd. 1, 15; S. 483, 24. Sūþ-Seaxan āgen[n]e biscopas onfēngon, 5, 18; S. 635, 14. Sūþ-Seaxena landes is syufan þūsend hȳda, Cod. Dip. B. i. 415, 1. Ælle Sūþ-Seaxna cyning, Chr. 827; Erl. 62, 35. Sūþ-Seaxna (Sūð-, MS. E.) rīce, 836; Erl. 66, 3. Sūð-Seaxna (Sūð-Seaxena, MS. E.) cyning, 661; Erl. 34, 15. Hē gewāt on Sūþ-Seaxe and Ine gefeaht wiþ Sūþ-Seaxum, 722; Erl. 44, 29. Eádulf cynges þegn on Sūð-Seaxum, 897; Erl. 95, 3. Se here on Sūð-Seaxum and on Bearrucscīre hergodon, 1009; Erl. 142, 22: 998; Erl. 135, 21. Hēr Ceólwulf gefeaht wið Sūð-Seaxe, 607; Erl. 20, 27. Hī heafdon ofergān Sūð-Seaxe and Sūðrīg and Bearrucscīre, 1011; Erl. 144, 27. [Folc læi inne Suð-sæxe, Laym. 15368. Souþsex (*a shire*), R. Glouc. 3, 21.]

Sūþ-Seaxisc; *adj. South-Saxon, of Sussex*:—Wulnōð cild ðone Sūð-Sexiscān (-Seaxscian, col. 1: -Seaxcisan, 260, col. 2), Chr. 1009; Th. 261, col. 2.

sūþ-stæþ, es; *n. A south shore, coast*, or *bank*:—West-Seaxna lond be ðæm sūþstæðe, Chr. 897; Erl. 95, 9. v. sūþ-rima.

sūþ-wāg, es; *m. A south wall*:—Wið middan ðæs sūðwāges, Homl. Th. i. 508, 15. Wið ðone sūðwāg tōmiddes ðæs wāges, Blickl. Homl. 207, 15. [*Icel.* suðr-veggr.]

sūþ-weard; *adv. Southward, in a southerly direction, towards the south*:—Wilþ seó eá sūþweard Eufrates *fluvius Euphrates tendens in meridiem*, Ors. 1, 1; Swt. 14, 10. Heó (*the sun*) cyrþ eft sūðweard, Lchdm. iii. 250, 22: 258, 13: 252, 1.

sūþ-weardes; *adv. Southwards, in the south*, Met. 1, 4.

sūþ-weg, es; *m. A road lying to the south*; in pl. *southern countries*, *the south*:—Hié gesāwon of sūđwegum fyrd Faraonis, Cd. Th. 187, 23; Exod. 155. [*Icel.* sūðr-vegr; in pl. *southern countries*.]

sūþ-west; *adv. South-west*:—Ān đæra gārena līþ sūđwest (*in africum*), Ors. 1, 1; Swt. 24, 3.

sūþ-westerne; *adj. South-western*:—Se sūđwesterna wind him ongeán stōd, Apol. Th. 11, 3.

sūþ-wind, es; *m. A south wind*, Cd. Th. 196, 10; Exod. 289.

suto, -sutod, sutol, sutung, suwian. v. slītan, sulian, sweotol, slītung, swigian.

swā, swǣ, swē (swē is the form in Ps. Surt.; see also Txts. 600, col. 1. The form also occurs in Blickl. Homl. 23, 7). I. *rel. pron. As, that*:—Forgylde đæt āngylde and đæt wīte swā tō đam āngylde belimpan wille, L. Alf. pol. 6; Th. i. 66, 3. Đon gelīc swā lǣcas cunnon *such as doctors know*, Lchdm. ii. 192, 23. Brūcan swylcra yrmþa swā đū unc ǣr scrife, Exon. Th. 373, 2; Seel. 102: Homl. Th. ii. 162, 18. Yrfan hī swā hī wyrđe witan *let such inherit as they know to be entitled*, Chart. Th. 578, 9. Ne wīte hē ūs swā neóde and hǣse gehȳrsumodon, Guthl. prol.; Gdwin. 4, 5. Ealne đisne ymbhwyrft đises middangeardes swā swā Oceanus ūtan ymbligeþ, Ors. 1, 1; Swt. 8, 2. I a. in combination with the *hw-* pronominal forms, *so*, as in whosoever, etc.:—Tō syllenne swā hwæt swā (suǣ huæt *quodcumque*, Lind.) heó hyne bǣde, Mt. Kmbl. 14, 7. Swā hwylc swā (suā huā, Lind.: swā hwā swā, Rush.) sylþ ānne drinc, 10, 41. Fram swā hwylcere untrymnesse swā hē on wæs, Jn. Skt. 5, 4. Swā hwylc man swā mildheortnesse nafaþ, Blickl. Homl. 13, 22. Swā hweđer swā hē wylle, L. Eth. i. 1; Th. i. 280, 16. Đæt git ne lǣstan welhwilc ǣrende swā hē sendeþ, Cd. Th. 35, 15; Gen. 555. Folcrihta gehwylc swā his fæder āhte, Beo. Th. 5210; B. 2608: Elen. Kmbl. 1287; El. 645. Swā hū swā hē mǣge *howsoever he can*, L. P. M. 2; Th. ii. 286, 25. Swā hwæder (hwyder, MS. A.) swā (suā huider, Lind.: hwider swā, Rush.) đū færst *quocunque ieris*, Mt. Kmbl. 8, 19: Lk. 9, 57: Blickl. Homl. 233, 33. *See other instances under the pronominal forms.* II. *demonst. pron.*:—Æt men fīftēne peningas, and æt horse healf swā, L. Ff.; Th. i. 224, 26. III. representing an adjective, generally one used with a verb of incomplete predication, *so, the same, such*—Hē gemētte ǣnne blindne mann, se wæs geboren swā, Homl. Skt. ii. 29, 52: Cd. Th. 44, 33; Gen. 7, 8. Bebycggen đone oxan and hæbben him đæt weorđ gemǣne, and eác đæt flǣsc swā (i. e. *in common*), L. Alf. 23; Th. i. 50, 11. Đæt hē wǣre heora munuc æt fruman and hī woldon hine habban swā deádne *that he had been their monk at first, and they would have him so* (*their monk*) *when dead*, Homl. Th. ii. 518, 23. Cild điónde on eallum cræftum on cnihthāde and swā forþ eallne giógoþhād (*going on thriving all its youth*), Bt. 38, 5; Fox 206, 24. Gē wiþerwearde wǣron ūrum gewunan and ealre Godes cyricean swā (i. e. wiþerwearde), Bd. 2, 2; S. 503, 19. III a. swā swā *such as*:—Onlegena strengran swā swā is ārōm *stronger applications such as is copperas*, Lchdm. ii. 192, 22. IV. *adv.* (1) defined by that which precedes (a) of manner or condition (α) *so, in this or that way, thus*:—'Beón gegaderode đa wæteru' . . . Hit wæs đā swā gedōn, Gen. 1, 9, 15. Nis hit nā swā *it is not so* (*as you have said*), 18, 15. Hit ne mæg nā swā beón, Ex. 10, 11. Đeáh hī his nǣfre ne gelēfan, đeáh it is swā, Bt. 36, 6; Fox 182, 17. Hē ārās āblendum eágum, and his gefēran hine swā (*in the manner mentioned*) blindne tō đære byrig gelǣddon, Homl. Th. i. 386, 14: 432, 11: L. In. 21; Th. i. 116, 3. Hē hine dyde ōđrum monnum suā (swǣ, Cott. MSS.) ungelīcne, Past. 17; Swt. 113, 14. (β) *so, in the same way, in like manner*:—And swā forđ (cf. *Germ.* und so weiter) *and so on, et caetera*, Ælfc. Gr. 18; Zup. 114, 5, and often. Se ealdor dyde hand swā gelīce *similiter fecit*, Th. An. 74, 4. *See* eal-swā. (b) of degree or extent, (α) where a high degree is implied, *so* (*exceedingly*):—Ne gemētte ic swā mycelne geleáfan, Mt. Kmbl. 8, 10. Nān fullere ne mæg swā hwīte gedōn, Mk. Skt. 9, 3. For hwon sǣdest đū swā gēmeleáslīce and swā wlætlīce đa đing, Bd. 5, 9; S. 623, 9. Đā đū swā lustlīce gehērdest mīne lāre, Bt. 22, 1; Fox 76, 23: 35, 3; Fox 158, 7. Đonne hī heora gōd on swā manige dǣlas tōdǣlaþ, 33, 2; Fox 122, 25. (β) where the degree is definitely marked:—Se consul fōr mid þrīm hunde scipa . . . him cōmon ongeán Punice mid swā fela scipa (*cum pari classe*), Ors. 4, 6; Swt. 176, 11. Se twelf sīþum hine bibaþaþ . . . and swā oft of wyllgespryngum beorgeþ, Exon. Th. 205, 6; Ph. 108. Syx swā micel *to the same extent much six times, six times as much*, L. M. L.; Th. i. 190, 3. (c) of cause (v. V. 6), *so, therefore, on that account*:—Hē him đet land forbeád . . . and hē hit swā ālēt *he forbade him the land . . . and so he gave it up*, Chart. Th. 202, 12. (2) defined by that which follows, (a) of manner, *so, in such a manner* that:—Far mid him swā đæt đū dō đæt ic đē bebeóde *vade cum eis, ita duntaxat, ut, quod tibi praecepero, facias*, Num. 22, 20. Ælc wīf sceolde gebīdan swā đæt heó ne cōme intō Godes temple, Homl. Th. i. 134, 16. Crist is Godes Sunu swā đæt (*in such sort that*) se Fæder hine gestrȳnde of him sylfum, 258, 26. Swā beclȳsed đæt nǣnig ōþer hȳ onlūceþ, Exon. Th. 20, 26; Cri. 323. Wearþ đæt geat belocen swā đæt đa stānas feóllon tōgædere, H. R. 103, 7. Gif eów swā līce þuhte utan gangan on đissum carcerne, Blickl. Homl. 247, 1. Swā đon gelīcost đe tōbrocen fæt, Lchdm. ii. 230, 25. Se mon biþ, đæs đe swā tō cweþanne sī, ǣghwæđer ge gehæfted ge freó, Bd. 1, 27; S. 497, 40. (b) of degree:—Swā ealde swā hié đā wǣron hié gefuhton *as old as they then were, they fought*, Ors. 3, 11; Swt. 152, 16. Nys hyt swā stearc winter, đæt ic durre lutian æt hām, Coll. Monast. Th. 19, 17. Swǣ opene scylde đæt hē his brōđor ofslōge, Past. 34; Swt. 234, 2. Đīn mægen is swā mǣre, swā đæt ǣnig ne wāt đa deópnesse Drihtnes mihta, Hy. 3, 31: Ors. 4, 10; Swt. 198, 15. Swā fullīce điónde . . . ōþ đe hē wyrþ ǣlces cræftes medeme, Bt. 38, 5; Fox 206, 22. Đa habbaþ beardas swā sīde ōđ heora breóst, Nar. 38, 1. Sūþ swā đū hātost mǣge, Lchdm. ii. 50, 25. (3) used indefinitely, *so and so*:—Đeáh đū nyte for hwī hē swā and swā dō *though thou know not why he act in this or that manner*, Bt. 39, 2; Fox 214, 13. (4) used emphatically, *so, exceedingly, as much as possible*:—Ongan hē hine bađian swā swātigne (*when perspiring profusely*), Ors. 3, 9; Swt. 124, 30: Jud. Thw. 22, 19; Jud. 67. Đū meaht swā wīde geseón, Cd. Th. 36, 1; Gen. 565: 25, 30; Gen. 425. Sió onlīcnes sendde mycel wæter swā sealt (*exceedingly salt*), Blickl. Homl. 245, 25. Genim đās wyrte swā mearwe (*as tender as possible*), Lchdm. i. 192, 8: 194, 2. Wel on swā hātum, ii. 50, 15. (5) with comparatives, *the*, (1) singly:—Oft wē māgon beón suā (swǣ, Cott. MSS.) nyttran æt him gif wē hié myndgiaþ hira gōdna weorca *plerumque utilius apud illos proficimus, si eorum bene gesta memoramus*, Past. 32, 2; Swt. 211, 20. Beþe đa eágan, betere swā oftor *the oftener the better*, Lchdm. ii. 34, 16. Leng swā swīđor, Cd. Th. 60, 30; Gen. 985: Beo. Th. 3712; B. 1854. (2) correlatives *the . . . the*:—Swā norđor swā smælre *the further north one goes, the narrower the land becomes*, Ors. 1, 1; Swt. 18, 29. Swā betere swā fǣtran and ferscran, Lchdm. ii. 196, 22. Swā hāttra sumor, swā māra đunor and līget, iii. 280, 9. Efne swā hē ūs mǣrlīcor gifeþ, swā wē him mǣrlīcor þancian scylon; swā þrymlīcre ār, swā māre eádmōdnes, Wulfst. 261, 19–21. Swā swā leng swā bet, Bt. 35, 3; Fox 160, 8. Swā swā hē lengra biþ, swā hī bióþ ungesǣligran, 38, 4; Fox 204, 15. Swā mycele swā đū hēr on worulde swȳþor swincst, swā đū eft bist on ēcnysse fæstlīcor getrymed; and swā myccle swā đū ōn đisum andweardan līfe mā earfođa drīgast, swā myccle đū eft on tōweardnesse gefēhst, Guthl. 5; Gdwin. 32, 10–14. (2a) with a comparative and a positive:—Đæt hē suā micle wærlīcor hine healde wiđ scylda swā hē gere witan mæg đæt hē nō āna forwierđ, Past. 28; Swt. 191, 10. V. *adverbial conjunction*, (1) with indic. (a) with a clause of comparison, *as*:—Ne biþ hē eall swā hē ǣr wæs, Bt. 34, 9; Fox 148, 8. Beóþ mildheorte, swā eówer fæder is mildheort, Lk. Skt. 6, 36. Hē gedreósan sceal, swā đeós eorđe eall, Exon. Th. 124, 27: Elen. Kmbl. 1761; El. 882. Hī mē ymbsealdon samod anlīce swā beón, Ps. Th. 117, 12. Hēht onlīce, swā hē đæt beácen geseah, tācen gewyrcan, Elen. Kmbl. 200; El. 100. (1 a) swā swā:—Eall đæt đe leofaþ beóþ eów tō mete, swā swā grōwende wyrta ic betǣhte ealle eów, Gen. 9, 3. Gewurđe đīn willa on eorđan, swā swā on heofenum, Mt. Kmbl. 6, 10. Dōn swā swā hȳ git dōþ, Bt. 16, 1; Fox 50, 2. (2) with indic. or subjunct. expressing an actual or possible result, *so that*:—Se consul fōr tō Tarentan, swā Hannibal nyste, and đa burg ābræc, swā đa nyston đe đǣrinne wǣron, Ors. 4, 10; Swt. 198, 7–9: 4, 11; Swt. 206, 3. Gif hwā stalie, swā his wīf nyte, L. In. 7; Th. i. 106, 15. Wesan swā him yldo ne derede, Cd. Th. 30, 22; Gen. 471: 256, 12; Dan. 639. Bær hine seó brimwylf, swā hē ne mihte wǣpna gewealdan, Beo. Th. 3020; B. 1508. Se mā eallum Angelcyningum Brytta đeóde fornom, swā efne đæs đe hē mihte wiþmeten beón Saule, Bd. 1, 34; S. 499, 20. (3) with subjunctive, *as* (*if*):—Iosue fleáh, swā hē āfyrht wǣre, Jos. 8, 15. Đū hī betweónum wætera weallas lǣddest, swā hī wǣron on drīgum, Ps. Th. 105, 9. Cweđan swā hē tō āuum sprece, Exon. Th. 84, 23; Cri. 1378. Nū is đon gelīcost swā wē ceólum līđan, 53, 16; Cri. 851. (4) with optative, *so*:—Swā đyós dǣd for monnum mǣre gewurþe, Lchdm. iii. 60, 14. Ic đæt geswerige þurh sōþ godu, swā ic āre æt him ǣfre finde, Exon. Th. 247, 19; Jul. 81: Beo. Th. 875; B. 435. (5) with a conditional force, *provided that, if so be that, so* (as in Shakspere: *So* it be new, there's no respect how vile; v. Abbott, Shak. Gram. § 133):—Nim, swā hit đē ne mislīcyge, Ap. Th. 20, 12. Hē him đet land forbeád, swā hē ǣniges brūcan wolde, Chart. Th. 202, 10. (6) marking a consequence, *so, therefore, on that account*:—Ic mæg rǣdan on his rīce; swā mē đæt riht ne þinceþ . . ., Cd. Th. 19, 11; Gen. 289: 24, 22; Gen. 381: Andr. Kmbl. 2657; An. 1330. (7) local, *where*:—On eallum Norþan-hymbrum ge eác on Pehtum swā Ōswīes rīce wæs đæs cyninges *quousque rex Osuin imperium protendere poterat*, Bd. 4, 3; S. 566, 30. Geseh hē bearwas standan, swā hē ǣr his blōd āgeát, Andr. Kmbl. 2897; An. 1451: 3163; An. 1584. (8) temporal, *as, when*:—Swā heó sǣ geseah, hē hió snióme fleáh, Ps. Th. 113, 3. Ic wāt God ābolgen wyrđ, swā ic him đisne bodscipe secge, Cd. Th. 35, 10; Gen. 552. (9) marking the grounds of action, *as, since*:—Wē đē lofiaþ, swā đū hǣlend eart, Hy. 7, 116. (10) *although, yet*:—Swā hē þurh feóndscipe tō cwale monige dēmde, swā þeáh him Dryhten eft miltse gefremede, Elen. Kmbl. 994; El. 498: Cd. Th. 25, 10; Gen. 391. (11) in contracted clauses, *as, as* (*being*):—Hwone hē lǣran scyle suā earmne, and hwane suā eádigne, Past. 26; Swt. 183, 9. Heora hlāford weorđodon swā swā wuldres cyning (cf. hiora cyningas hī weorþodon for Godas, Bt. 38, 1; Fox 194, 16), Met. 26, 45. VI. swā . . . swā, (1)—where *swā* occurs once with a demonstrative, once with a relative force, *so . . . as, so . . . that, as . . . as*:—Swá forð swá uncre wordgecwydu fyrmest wǽron *as far as ever our agreements went*, L. O. 11; Th. i. 182, 11. Swá gelíc swá ðú æt swǽsendum sitte, Bd. 2, 13; S. 516, 15. Suá suíðe suá hé of ðære ǽwe ne cerre *so as he turn not from the law*, Past. 23; Swt. 175, 4. Búton hé suá monige gecierre suá hé mǽsð mǽge, 28; Swt. 191, 9. Hafa on múþe swá hát swá ðú hátost mǽge, Lchdm. ii. 50, 15. Swá forð swá ða óðre, Ælfc. Gr. 18; Zup. 114, 3. Ða unrótnessa swá ilce ofergǽþ, swá ðú cwist ðæt ða blissa ǽr dydon, Bt. 8; Fox 24, 33. Swá wíde swá wegas tólǽgon, Andr. Kmbl. 2469; An. 1236. Hé hine wolde swá weligne gedón swá hé his sunu wǽre, Shrn. 84, 14. Sóna swá seó sunne sealte streámas oferhlifaþ, swá se fugel gewíteþ, Exon. Th. 206, 1–6; Ph. 120. (1 a) swá swá:—Dó rysle tó swá swá sýn twá pund *add lard so as there may be two pounds*, Lchdm. ii. 74, 1: 250, 26. (2) correlative, (a) *either . . . or, as well . . . as*:—Onfón swá ǽcum lífe swá ǽcum deáðe swá ðú ǽr geworhtest swá ǽcum lífe swá ungeendodon wíte *accipere sive vitam aeternam, sive mortem aeternam, prout antea fecisti; sive vitam aeternam, sive infinitum supplicium*, L. Ecg. P. iv. 65; Th. ii. 226, 13. Ðæt heó gecure óðer ðæra, swá heó forférde, swá heó ðám godum geoffrode, Homl. Skt. i. 8, 63: 11, 33. Nim swá wuda swá wyrt swá hweðer swá ðú wille, Bt. 34, 10; Fox 148, 25: Wulfst. 108, 10. Smire mid ðære sealfe swá niht swá twá swá þearf sié *smear with the salve one night or two, as need be*, Lchdm. ii. 128, 1. Sié ðæt on cyninges dóme swá deáð swá líf swá hé him forgifan wille *be it in the judgement of the king, as well death as life, as he will grant him*, L. Alf. pol. 7; Th. i. 66, 10. Hit biþ gewrecen swá ǽr, swá lator, Homl. Ass. 62, 253. Gilde swá wer, swá wíte, swá lahslite, aa be ðam ðe seó dǽd sý, L. Eth. v. 31; Th. i. 312, 10. Ðonne mót hé swá rídan, swá rówan, swá swilce færelde faran swylce tó his wege gebyrige, L. E. I. 24; Th. ii. 420, 24. (b) *whether . . . or*:—Saga him, swá hé wille swá hé nelle, hé sceal cuman, Bd. 5, 9; S. 623, 11. Wé be him náþor nyton, swá hí libban, swá hí deáde licgon, Homl. Skt. i. 23, 306. God lét hí habban ágenne cyre, swá hí heora Scyppend lufedon, swá hí hine forléton, Homl. Th. i. 10, 19: 18, 30. Syle etán ǽr ðære tíde his tócymes, swá on dæge swá on nihte, swæþer hyt sý, Lchdm. i. 364, 16. On swelce healfe swelce hié winnende beón woldan, swá súþ, swá norþ, swá eást, swá west, Ors. 3, 5; Swt. 106, 13. (c) swá hwæðer swá . . . swá *whether . . . or*:—Sete man ofer ðæne þriddan dæg, swá hwæðer swá heó beó fúl swá clǽne, L. Ath. iv. 7; Th. i. 226, 31. (2 a) with the first *swá* omitted, *or*:—Dém ðú hí tó deáþe, swá tó lífe lǽt, Exon. Th. 247, 33; Jul. 88. VII. *in combination with the particles* git, same, þeáh, þeána, *see those words*. [*Goth.* swé, swa: *O. Frs.* sá: *O. Sax. O. H. Ger.* só: *Icel.* svá (*later* svó): *Dan.* saa: Swed. så.] v. eal-swá.

swǽ, swæc[c]. v. swá, swecc.

swǽfan (?):—Sió gítsung ðe nǽnne grund hafaþ swearte swǽfeþ (swǽleþ? v. swǽlan) sumes onlíce efne ðam munte ðe nú monna bearn Etne hátaþ se swefle byrneþ, Met. 8, 46–50. The Latin original has: Saevior ignibus Aetnae fervens amor ardet habendi, which is rendered in the prose version: Manna gítsung is swá byrnende swá ðæt fýr on ðære helle seó is on ðam munte ðe Ætne hátte, Bt. 15; Fox 48, 29. From comparison of these three passages, it seems that *swǽfeþ* should mean *burns*, while the form of the word suggests comparison with *O L. Ger.* suëvón *in* berg suëvót *mons coagulatus*, with *O. H. Ger.* sweibón *volvere, ferri*, and later English *swayue* in:—He (*the whale that swallowed Jonah*) swenges and swayues to þe se boþem, Allit. Pm. 99, 253. All these verbs denote movement, a meaning which does not seem to suit *swǽfan* in the passage where it occurs.

Swǽfas, Swǽfe; *pl. A Germanic people, the Suevi* or *Alamanni* ('um diese zeit (4th cent.) pflegt an die stelle des alten Suevennamens die benennung Alamannen einzutreten,' Grmm. D. S. 348), *the Swabians*:—Swǽfas forhergodon ealle Galliam *Alamanni Gallias pervagantes*, Ors. 6, 24; Swt. 276, 3. Wið norþan Donua ǽwielme and be eástan Ríne sindon Eást-Francan; and be súþan him sindon Swǽfas, on óþre healfe ðære ié Donua; and be súþan him and be eástan sindon Bægware, se dǽl ðe mon Regnesburg hǽtt . . . Tó ðǽm beorgan ðe mon Alpis hǽtt licgaþ Begwara landgemǽro and Swǽfa, 1, 1; Swt. 16, 1–14. Engle and Swǽfe, Exon. Th. 321, 10; Wíd. 44. Mid Englum ic wæs and mid Swǽfum. 322, 10; Wíd. 61. Witta weóld Swǽfum, 319, 34; Wíd. 22. [*O. H. Ger.* Suáb *Alamannus*, Suába, Suápa *Suevi.*]

swǽlan; *p.* de *To burn* (trans.):—Onǽl ł swǽl ł bærn lændenu *ure renes*, Ps. Lamb. 25, 2. Hé sende of heofonum swǽlende lég, Wulfst. 213, 6. [Heo heom letten swalen inne swærte fure (þe mahunes mid fure hii forswelde. 2nd MS.), Laym. 10188. Berned heore halles & swaleð heore bures, 6147. A bernene drake borwes swelde, 25594. Halliwell gives *sweal, swale* to burn.] v. be-, for-, ge-swælan (*read* -swǽlan); sám-, unfor-swǽled, swelan.

swǽm, es; *m. A trifler, vain, foolish person*:—Swǽm *nugator, inutilis, vanus*, Germ. 389, 32. Ic wylle ðæt Latona móder Apollinis and Diane fram mé gewíten, ðe Delo ákende, ðæs ðe ealde swǽmas gecýddon (*as the foolish triflers of old declared*), Anglia viii. 325, 29. Nú mæg hér manna gehwilc gehýran hwet ðás swǽmas wǽron ðe úre yldra[n] him tó gebǽdon *now may every one hear in this account* (*of the gods*) *what these vain creatures were, that our forefathers prayed to*, H. Z. xii. 408, 15.

swǽman; *p.* de *To trouble, afflict, grieve*. The verb occurs in this sense in later English:—Ofte hit timeð þat tat leoueste bearn sorheð and sweameð meast his ealdren, H. M. 35, 5. Þe engles beoð isweamed, þat seoð hare suster swa sorhfulliche afallet, 17, 20. Ure Louerd ne mei uor reouðe wernen hire, ne sweamen hire heorte mid wernunge, A. R. 330, 11. Þe swemande sorȝe soȝt to his hert, Allit. Pms. 54, 563. Cf. also: His hert began to melt For veray sweme of this swemeful tale, Lydgate (cited ib. *p.* 199). Swemyn *molestor, mereo*; sweem, swemynge or mornynge *tristicia, molestia, meror*, Prompt. Parv. 482, col. 1. In A. S. only the compound *á-swǽman* (q. v.) is found, apparently with the meaning *to become troubled* or *grieved*. To the instance given under *á-swǽman* may be added the following:—Swá Sanctus Paulus cwæþ ðætte God héte ealle ða áswǽman æt heofona ríces dura, ða ðe heora cyrican forlǽtaþ *God would bid all those grieve . . .*, Blickl. Homl. 41, 34. Sceolde se mín þearfa áswǽman (*have cause to grieve*) æt ðínre·handa, Wulfst. 258, 2. Se sceocca sceall áswǽman æt ús, gif wé ánrǽde beóþ on úrum geleáfan, Homl. Skt. i. 17, 203. v. swámian.

swǽpa, swépa (-e, -o); *pl. Sweepings*, in compounds (not inserted in proper place):—Ǽswǽpe (beánscalu) *quisquiliarum, surculi minuti*, Hpt. Gl. 420, 59. Áswépa *peripsema*, 504, 3. Geswǽpa *peripsema*, Wrt. Voc. ii. 65, 68. Geswépa, geswǽpa (gen., MS.), 95, 18. Geswépo, 76, 17. Bió hé gehealden for æscegeswǽp *pro purgamento favillae deputetur*, Chart. Th. 318, 33. [*O. H. Ger.* á-sueipha *purgamenta, quisquilias.*]

-swǽpe, -swápe. v. hád-, heorþ-, ymb-swǽpe.

swǽpels (*m.?*); swǽpelse, an; *f. A wrap, garment*:—Swǽpels *amictus*, Ps. Surt. 106, 3. Ða swǽpelsan *amicula*, Wrt. Voc. ii. 3, 49. [Cf. *Icel.* sveipa *to wrap, swaddle*; sveipa *a kerchief, hood*: *Dan.* svøbelse-barn *child in swaddling-clothes.*] v. swápan.

swǽpig; *adj. Fraudulent, deceitful*:—Swǽpige ł swicfulle *fraudulentas*, Hpt. Gl. 474, 17. v. ge-swip, swipor.

swǽr, swǽre, *and* swár; *adj.* [Halliwell gives *sweer* unwilling as a Northumbrian word, and *swere* dull, heavy, as a Durham one. In Jamieson's Dictionary the forms *sweir, swere, sweer, swear* are given with meanings lazy, indolent; unwilling; unwilling to give.] I. *heavy* as a burden, *of great weight* (lit. or fig.), *oppressive*:—Swǽr is seó byrðen ðe Godes bydel beran sceall, gif hé nele georne unriht forbeódan, L. I. P. 5; Th. ii. 308, 35: Wulfst. 178, 8. Hé bið deófles tempel, and byrð swíðe swǽre byrðene on his bæce, Homl. Th. i. 212, 4. Ðæt swǽre gioc underlútan, Met. 10, 20. His wǽpna syndon swǽre tó berenne, ac Cristes geoc is wynsum, Basil admn. 2; Norm. 36, 14. Sorh biþ swǽrost byrðen, Salm. Kmbl. 623; Sal. 311. Gif míne synna wǽron áwegene on ánre wǽgan, ðonne wǽron hí swǽrran gesewene ðonne sandcorn on sǽ, Homl. Th. ii. 454, 24. II. *heavy, grievous, painful, unpleasant*:—Him yldo ne derede, ne suht swáre, Cd. Th. 30, 24; Gen. 472. Swár leger, Exon. Th. 101, 21; Cri. 1662: 201, 15; Ph. 56. Gebrec swár and swíðlíc *a crash grievous and great*, 59, 19; Cri. 955. Ðæt hé swǽre áhweorfe hæftnéd hefige, Ps. Th. 125, 1. Ðú þolades swár gewin, Exon. Th. 86, 22; Cri. 1412. Geswencean mid swárum wítum, Homl. Skt. i. 4, 181. Ða swáran (swǽran, *other MSS.*) wíta onfón, 19, 46. Is swǽrra ðínra synna ród, ðonne seó óþer wæs, ðe ic ǽr ástág, Exon. Th. 91, 10; Cri. 1490. Nis ðys eall geswinc? and gyt mycele swǽrran ealle ða ungelimp ðe on ðysum lífe becumaþ, Hexam. 20; Norm. 28, 26. III. *heavy, sad, feeling* or *expressing grief*:—Ðæt swǽre *triste*, Wrt. Voc. ii. 88, 49. Mé is swǽre stefn, hefig, gnorniende *vox gemitus mei*, Ps. Th. 101, 4. IV. of sin or evil, *grave, grievous*:—Be hefigtýmum gyltum. Se bróðor se ðe mid swǽrra gylta hæfene bið gedered *de gravioribus culpis. Frater qui gravioris culpe noxa tenetur*, R. Ben. 49, 13. On scyldum swǽrum *in delictis*, Ps. Th. 67, 21. Gebundene swárum (*var.* swǽrum) gyltum, Anglia xi. 113, 38. Ða swǽran gyltas ðe hí ádrugon, Homl. Th. i. 340, 27. Ðú micele swǽrran synna gefremodest, 54, 33. V. of physical or mental inactivity, *heavy, slow, dull, sluggish, slothful, indolent*:—Suuǽr *desis*, Wrt. Voc. ii. 105, 79. Swǽr *deses*, 25, 12. Ðú yfle esne and swǽr (swér, Lind.) *serve male et piger*, Mt. Kmbl. Rush. 25, 26. Sum welig man wæs swangor and swǽr, and him wæs láð þearfendum mannum mete tó syllenne, Wulfst. 257, 12. Nis hé swár ne swongor *non est tarda*, Exon. Th. 220, 4; Ph. 315. On swárran ðisum líchoman *in gravi isto corpore*, Hymn. Surt. 13, 15. V a. *inactive from weakness, enfeebled, weak*:—Mé is mín gást swǽr geworden *defecit spiritus meus*, Ps. Th. 142, 7. V b. of sleep, *heavy*:—Swá fram slǽpe hwylc swǽrum áríse, Ps. Th. 72, 15. Gehefegod mid ðam swǽran slǽpe, Basil admn. 1; Norm. 34, 3. [Forr hefig & forr sware unngriþþ, Orm. 16280. *Goth.* swérs *grave, honoured*: *O. Sax.* swári *grievous* (*sin, sickness*): *O. Frs.* swére: *O. H. Ger.* swár, swári *gravis, onerosus*: *Ger.* schwer: *Icel.* svárr (a poetic word) *heavy, grave.*] v. ge-swǽre.

swǽran; *p.* de *To make heavy, to oppress*[:—Eall se líchama geswǽred byþ and gehefegud, Lchdm. iii. 120, 22.] [*O. H. Ger.* swáren *gravare, praegravare, opprimere*; gi-swáren *gravare.*]

swǽre, swáre; *adv. Grievously, oppressively*:—Eam ic swǽre geseald ðǽr ic út swícan ne mæg *traditus sum, et non egrediebar*, Ps. Th. 87, 8. Se hláford hefig gioc slépte swáre on ða swyran sínra þegena, Met. 9, 56.

[Ne set me neuer naþing swa swere (sare, Bodl. MS.), Jul. 46, 10. *O. Sax. O. H. Ger.* swâro *graviter.*]

swǽr-líc; *adj. Grievous*:—Benedictus mid swǽrlícum heófungum bemǽnde, ðæt his leorningcild ðæs óðres deáðes fægnian sceolde, Homl. Th. ii. 164, 9. [*O. H. Ger.* swâr-lîh *gravis.*]

swǽrlíce (swâr-); *adv.* I. of doing or bearing what is painful, *heavily, grievously*:—Nán man ne sceal his wífe geneálǽcan, siððan heó mid bearne swǽrlíce gebunden gǽþ, Homl. Th. ii. 324, 21. Hé sceolde hit mid fæstene swárlíce gebétan, Homl. Skt. i. 21, 261. II. of sleeping, *heavily.* v. swǽr, V b:—Wé feóllon on slǽpe swárlíce, swylce wé on deáðe lágon, Homl. Skt. i. 11, 239. [*O. H. Ger.* swârlîhho *graviter.*]

swǽr-mód (swâr-); *adj. Of an indolent, sluggish disposition*:—Sum welig man wæs prútswongor and swǽrmód, and him wæs láð þearfendum mannum mete tó syllenne, Wulfst. 257, 12 MS. D. v. swǽr, V, *and next word.*

swǽrmódness (swâr-), e; *f. Sluggishness of disposition, slowness, dullness*:—Oft mon biþ suíðe wandigende æt ǽlcum weorce and suíðe lætrǽde, and wénaþ menn ðæt hit sié for suármódnesse and for unarodscipe, and biþ ðeáh for wisdóme and for wærscipe (*but the Latin is*: Saepe agendi tarditas gravitatis consilium putatur), Past. 20; Swt. 149, 15.

swǽrness (swâr-), e; *f.* I. *heaviness* of a burden (lit. or fig.), *weight.* v. swǽr, I:—Hwí settest ðú ðises folces swárnysse (*pondus*) uppan mé? Num. 11, 11. Ne mæg ic ána eówre swárnissa (*pondus*) and eówre saca ácuman, Deut. 1, 12. II. *heaviness, want of readiness in moving, sluggishness,* v. swǽr, V:—Nán hæfignes ðæs líchoman ne nán unþeáw ne mæg eallunga átión of his móde ða rihtwísnesse . . . ðeáh sió swǽrnes ðæs líchoman and ða unþeáwas oft ábisegien ðæt mód mid ofergiotolnesse *non omne mente depulit lumen obliviosam corpus invehens molem,* Bt. 35, 1; Fox 154, 31.

swǽrnung, swarnung. v. swornian.

swǽs; *adj.* I. (*one's*) *own*; proprius. v. swǽslíce, I:—Ðæt selegescot ðæt ic mé swǽs on ðé gehálgode *the tabernacle that I hallowed me as my own in thee,* Exon. Th. 90, 29; Cri. 1481. II. the word, which occurs rarely in prose (see, however, the first passage cited), is used mostly in reference to the connection that belongs to relationship by blood or by marriage, or to dear companionship, and so often has the force of (*one's*) *own dear,* (*one's*) *dear*:—Ælþeódige mæn . . . swǽse mæn *foreigners . . . men of one's own race, natives,* L. Wih. 4; Th. i. 38, 2. Biþ him self sunu and swǽs fæder and eác yrfeweard *ipsa sibi proles, suus est pater et suus haeres,* Exon. Th. 224, 13; Ph. 375. Ic and mín swǽs fæder, Elen. Kmbl. 1032; El. 517. Mín ðæt swǽse bearn! (cf. mín ðæt leófe bearn! 166, 28; Gú. 1049), Exon. Th. 167, 1; Gú. 1053. Swǽs eft ongon (cf. fæder eft ongon etc., 7) his bearn lǽran, 302, 29; Fä. 43. Cwæð brýd tó beorne: 'Mín swǽs freá,' Cd. Th. 168, 15; Gen. 2783. Heó Adame hyre swǽsum were scencte, Exon. Th. 161, 11; Gú. 975. Wið fæder swǽsne, 39, 4; Cri. 617. Gif ðú sunu áge, oððe swǽsne mǽg, oððe freónd ǽnigne, Cd. Th. 150, 28; Gen. 2498: 203, 11; Exod. 402. Heora swǽs cynn, Ps. Th. 105, 21. Geseh swǽsne geféran *he saw his own dear comrade,* Andr. Kmbl. 2018; An. 1011. Æfter swǽsne (*one's own dear lord*), Exon. Th. 289, 18; Wand. 50. Swǽse gesíþas *his own familiar comrades,* Beo. Th. 57; B. 29. Nǽnig swǽsra gesíða, 3872; B. 1934. Freónda má swǽsra and gesibbra *more of friends dear and near,* Exon. Th. 408, 34; Rä. 27, 22. Freóndum swǽsum and gesibbum, Cd. Th. 97, 13; Gen. 1612. Hé hét hine (*Beowulf*) leóde swǽse sécean, Beo. Th. 3741; B. 1868. Mǽgburge swǽse and gesibbe *my kindred, dear and near ones* (or *dear and near kindred*), Exon. Th. 397, 19; Rä. 16, 22. Twá dohtor, swáse gesweostor, 431, 29; Rä. 47, 3. III. with a development of meaning similar to that in *kind* or *gentle*; *gracious, kind, agreeable, pleasant* (used of persons or things). v. swǽs-líc:—Swǽs *vel* wynsum *eucharis,* Wrt. Voc. i. 61, 17. Líþe, swǽs *blanda,* ii. 127, 2. Tunge swǽse tóbrycþ heardnysse *lingua mollis confringit duritiam,* Scint. 8, 17. Drihten is niðum swǽs *suavis est Dominus,* Ps. Th. 99, 4. Ðú swǽs tó mé ðín eáre onhyld, 101, 2. Þeáh ðe ic on hyld gegange, ðænne swǽs wese *when it may be agreeable,* 131, 3. On sóðfæstra swǽsum múðe *in the gracious mouth of the just,* 117, 15. Weredum beóbreáde *vel* swǽsum *dulci favo,* Wrt. Voc. ii. 142, 9. Fram swésere tungan *a blanda lingua,* Kent. Gl. 159. Steorran forléton hyra swǽsne wlite *the stars resigned their sweet beauty,* Exon. Th. 71, 1; Cri. 1149. Sete swǽse geheald múðe mínum *set pleasant guard for my mouth,* Ps. Th. 140, 4. Beseoh on ðíne scealcas swǽsum eágum (*with gracious eyes*), 89, 18. Swǽsum wordum *dulcibus verbis,* Coll. Monast. Th. 32, 31: *blandimentis,* Gl. Prud. 43 a. Swáse swegldreámas, Exon. Th. 82, 35; Cri. 1349. [*Goth.* swês ἴδιος; swês; *subst. property*: *O. Sax.* swâs (man): *O. Frs.* swês *near, related*: *O. H. Ger.* swâs *familiaris, domesticus*: *Icel.* svâss *beloved, dear; pleasant.*] v. ge-, un-swǽs; swǽs-líc.

swǽse; *adv. Agreeably, pleasantly* [:—Geswǽse *blandide,* Wrt. Voc. ii. 127, 5].

swǽsend-dagas (swǽsing-); *pl. The ides*; the Latin term seems to be so rendered from supposing it to be connected with the verb *edere*; v. next word:—Swǽsingdagas *idus, ab edendo dicuntur,* Wrt. Voc. i. 53, 37. Swǽsenddagas *idus, ab edendo,* ii. 62, 27: 48, 55.

swǽsende, es; *but occurring almost always in pl.* swǽsendu (-a, -o); *n.* I. *food, victuals, refection*:—Swǽsende *fercula,* Wrt. Voc. ii. 35, 19. Swǽsendo *fercula, cibaria,* 147, 83. Hé þanc gesægde ðá hé gereordod wæs: 'Ðé ðissa swǽsenda Meotud leán forgilde,' Andr. Kmbl. 771; An. 386. Ðæt hí on his hús ne eodon ne of his swǽsendum mete ðygedon *ne domum ejus intrarent neque de cibis illius acciperent,* Bd. 3, 22; S. 553, 28. Mid hígna suésendum (*the articles of food are then given*). Ond ðás forecuedenan suésenda all ágefe mon ðem reogolwarde, Txts. 444, 14–26. Ða ilcan wísan on swǽsendum tó mínre tíde léstan (cf. hígon gefeormian tó mínre tíde, 449, 9), 450, 1. Suoesendo *agapem,* 39, 108. Swǽsendo, Wrt. Voc. ii. 2, 22. Ælmessum swǽsendo, 5, 35. Ða six Sunnandagas ðe wé swǽsendo on habbaþ *the six Sundays in Lent when we may take meat* (cf. nán dæg (*in Lent*) ne sý bútan Sunnandagum ánum, ðæt ǽnig mon ǽniges metes brúce ǽr ðære teóðan tíde oððe ðære twelfte, L. E. I. 37; Th. ii. 436, 6–8), Wulfst. 284, 5. Ðone mete and ða swǽsendo *dapes,* Bd. 3, 6; S. 528, 20. ¶ In phrases:—Gán tó swǽsendum *to go to dinner*; ire ad reficiendum, 5, 4; S. 617, 18. Sittan æt *or* tó swǽsendum *to sit at meat, take a meal*:—Hí æt beóde and æt swǽsendum sǽton *sederunt ad mensam,* 5, 5; S. 617, 10: Cd. Th. 168, 7; Gen. 2779. Sittan tó his swǽsendum *residens ad epulas,* Bd. 3, 14; S. 540, 42: 5, 5; S. 618, 17. Woldon wé tó úrum swǽsendum sittan *ceperamus uelle epulari,* Nar. 21, 12. Ðá hét ic eallne ðone here ðæt hé tó swǽsendum sǽte and mete þigde *cenare militem jussi,* 23, 8. Swǽsende, swǽsenda þicgan *to take food*:—Sæt hé and swǽsende ðeah and dranc (sæt hé on swǽsendum and æt and dranc, MS. B.) *residebat, vescebatur, bibebat,* Bd. 5, 5; S. 618, 18. Hé on his hús eode and his swǽsendo ðeah *intravit epulaturus domum ejus,* Bd. 3, 22; S. 553, 30. Swá ðæt hé nǽfre mete onféng ne swǽsendo ðeah *ita ut nihil unquam cibi vel potus perciperet,* 4, 25; S. 599, 29. Swǽsendo þicgean *jejunium solvere, prandere,* 5, 4; S. 617, 13, 16. Swǽsenda (up) girwan *to prepare a feast,* Judth. Thw. 21, 7; Jud. 9. Symbel ł swoese (swoesende?) mín ic gearuade *prandium meum paravi,* Mt. Kmbl. Lind. 22, 4. II. *flatteries, blandishments, fair speech.* v. swǽs, III, ge-swǽsness, swǽslǽcan:—Swésendum *blanditiis,* Kent. Gl. 212. v. dæg-, undern-swǽsendu (-o).

swǽslǽcan; *p.* -lǽhte *To flatter, cajole, speak fair*:—Hió swéslécþ *blanditur,* Kent. Gl. 194. v. ge-swǽslǽcan.

swǽs-líc; *adj. Kindly, pleasant, agreeable*:—Sárge gé ne sóhton, ne him swǽslíc word frófre gé sprǽcon, Exon. Th. 92, 20; Cri. 1511. Hé (*Antecrist*) winþ ongeán Godes gecorenan mid swǽslícum gifum. Hé sylþ ðam, ðe on hine gelýfaþ, goldes and seolfres genyhða, Wulfst. 196, 21. [*O. Frs.* swês-lîk *familiaris*: *O. H. Ger.* swâs-lîh *privatus, civilis, familiaris.*] v. un-swǽslíc, *and next word.*

swǽslíce; *adv.* I. *properly.* v. swǽs, I:—Wé andettaþ swǽslíce and sóþlíce Fæder and Sunu and Hálige Gást *confitemur proprie et veraciter Patrem et Filium et Spiritum Sanctum,* Bd. 4, 17; S. 585, 36. II. of persons, *kindly, in a gracious, friendly manner, blandly*; of things, *agreeably, pleasantly.* v. swǽs, III:—Ða nán lust yfel swǽslíce gewemþ *eos nulla voluptas mala blande corrumpit,* Scint. 3, 10. Him (*the good*) swǽslíce (cf. on ðæt fræte folc (*the evil*) hé firene stǽleþ láþum wordum, 84, 17; Cri. 1375) sibbe gehāteþ heáhcyning, Exon. Th. 82, 15; Cri. 1339. Nealles swǽslíce mé wæs síð álýfed *the way was not made easy for me,* Beo. Th. 6169; B. 3089. Cóman him tó and hine swǽslíce grétton, Homl. Skt. i. 5, 210. Busiris wolde ǽlcne cuman swíþe árlíce underfón and swíþe swǽslíce wiþ gebǽran (*behave in a very friendly manner to him*), ær hé (*the guest*) sceolde beón ofslegen, Bt. 16, 2; Fox 52, 32. Tó fela manna is ðe þurh hiwunge eal óðer specaþ, óþer hý þencaþ . . . and swá geráde mánswican on ða wísan swǽslíce swiciaþ (*deceive under an appearance of friendliness.* v. swǽslǽcan, swǽsness), Wulfst. 55, 6. Swǽslíce swicole *deceiving with fair words,* 79, 4: 82, 2. [*O. Sax.* swâslîko *friendlily*: *O. H. Ger.* swâslîhho *familiariter.*]

swǽsness, e; *f. Blandishment, fair speech*:—Swǽsnyssum *blandimentis, lenociniis,* Hpt. Gl. 481, 10. Gé Godes cempan, gé áwurpaþ eówerne cynehelm for ðám earmlícan swǽsnyssum (*the appeals made to your feelings*) ðissera heófiendra. Ne áwurpe gé eówerne sige for wífa swǽsnyssum, Homl. Skt. i. 5, 54–58. Ðæt hé ðissere worulde swǽsnyssa (*blanditias*) warnige, Scint. 216, 12. v. ge-swǽsness.

swǽsung, e; *f. A making pleasant, an alleviation, a mitigation*:—Swǽsunga *fomenta,* Wrt. Voc. ii. 150, 7.

swǽs-wyrde; *adj. Of pleasant speech, pleasant in speech*; facetus, Wrt. Voc. i. 61, 18.

swǽtan; *p.* te *To sweat.* I. of the natural moisture of the skin:—Ðætte hé swa swíþe swǽtte swá hé in swoloþan middes sumeres wǽre *quia ita, quasi in media aestatis caumate, sudaverit,* Bd. 3, 19; S. 549, 29. Sitte hé on bæþe óð ðæt hé swǽte . . . óþ hé wel swǽte, Lchdm. ii. 290, 1–6. Ðæt se mon swǽte swíþe, 332, 2: iii. 8, 11. Hé ongan blácian and ungefóhlíce swǽtan, Homl. Th. i. 414, 12: Wulfst. 141, 3. I a. *to sweat* with hard labour, so *to toil*:—Ðæm ðe nú on gódum weorcum ne swǽt and suíðe ne suincеþ *qui nunc in bonis operibus non exsudat,* Past. 39, 2; Swt. 285, 13. Sume sceufon, sume tugon and swýðe swǽtton, óð ðæt hig geteorode wǽron, Shrn. 154, 27. Winnende *vel* swǽtende *desudans, i. laborans,* Wrt. Voc. ii. 139, 37. II. *to* *sweat, send forth like sweat, to exude* (of persons or things):—Hī fleóþ and blōde hī swǣtaþ, Nar. 35, 33. Fȳre swǣtaþ blācan līge *they sweat fire and flame*, Exon. Th. 385, 12; Rä. 4, 43. Mon geseah twegen sceldas blōde swǣtan (*sanguine sudare*), Ors. 4, 8; Swt. 188, 25. Hī gemētton ðone clūd swǣtende, Homl. Th. ii. 162, 6. **II a.** *to send forth blood, to bleed.* v. swāt, II. 2:—Hit ǣrest ongan swǣtan on ða swīðran healfe, Rood Kmbl. 39; Kr. 20. [*Icel.* sveita *to sweat.*] v. ā-, be-, ge-swǣtan; swītan.

swæþ, es; *n.* **I.** *a track, the mark left by a moving body, a single footprint* or *a series of footprints* (lit. or fig.):—Mē (*the plough*) biþ gongendre mīn swæð sweotol, Exon. Th. 403, 19; Rä. 22, 10. Ðonne fylge wē Drihtnes swæþe, Blickl. Homl. 75, 14: Rtl. 26, 5. Ðonne stæpþ se sacerd on ðone weg, ðonne hē on ðæt swæð ðara hāligra winnaþ tō spyriganne, Past. 13; Swt. 77, 20: pref.; Swt. 5, 16. Deáþ ne forlǣt nān swæþ ǣr hē gefēhþ ðæt ðæt hē æfter spyreþ, Bt. 39, 1; Fox 212, 1: Met. 27, 14. Weard sāweþ on swæð mīn (*the plough's*), Exon. Th. 403, 11; Rä. 22, 6. Swearte wǣran lāstas, swaþu swīþe blacu, 434, 19; Rä. 52, 3. Ða swaðo wǣron ūtwearde ongunnen ðe on ðæm marmanstāne gemēted wǣron, Blickl. Homl. 207, 11. Swylce mannes swaðu, ðon gelīcost ðe ðǣr sum mon gestōde; and ða fōtlāstas wǣron swutole, 203, 35. Alle suæðo *omnes semite*, Rtl. 81, 20. Forlēt ūre Drihten his fēt on ða eorþan besincan ... leóhtfæt biþ ā byrnende for ðara swaþa weorþunga, Blickl. Homl. 127, 31. Suoeðum, suæðum *semitis*, Rtl. 167, 1, 13. **II.** *a vestige, trace*:—Hwæt is elles ðiós gewītendlīce sibb būton swelce hit sié sum swæð ðære ēcean sibbe *quod est enim pax transitoria, nisi quoddam vestigium pacis aeternae?* Past. 46, 5; Swt. 351, 25. v. bil-, dolh-, fōt-swæþ; swaþu.

swæþ(?), swaþu(?) *a bandage, swathe*:—In swaþum *institis* (v. Jn. 11, 44 to which the gloss refers), Wrt. Voc. ii. 74, 17: 46, 51. v. sweþel, sweþian.

swæþel. v. sweþel.

swæðer, swaðer (= swā hwæðer, cf. *O. H. Ger.* sueder). **I.** *pronoun, Whichever of two*:—Swaðer uncer leng wǣre, Cod. Dip. Kmbl. ii. 113, 20, 25. Hwæðres ðara yfela is betere ǣr tō tilianne būton swæðres swæðer frēcenlīcre is *quae pestis ardentius insequenda est, nisi quae periculosius premit?* Past. 62; Swt. 457, 22. Dō swæþer ðū wille *do whichever you like*, Bt. 39, 4; Fox 218, 10. **II.** *in combination with* swā ... swā ... *either ... or ... whichever, whether ... or*:—Hē mōste swā geceósan swā āweorpan swaþer (swæðer, *other MSS.*) hē wolde *licuit ei excusare aut suscipere*, R. Ben. 99, 15. Beón swæðer hig beón, swā (þe, *other MSS.*) sacerdhādes swā clerichādes, 110, 7. Gewylde man hine swaðor man mǣge, swā cucenne swā deádne, L. Edg. ii. 7; Th. i. 268, 17. Hī gefeallaþ on ða heortan suā nytt suā unnyt suæðer hié beóþ (*whether they be profitable or unprofitable*), Past. 15; Swt. 97, 2: 14; Swt. 85, 15. Biþ ǣlc gōd weorc gōd, sié swā open swā dēgle, swæðer hit sié, 59; Swt. 451, 14. Wyl wermōd swā drīgne swā grēnne swaþer hē hæbbe *boil wormwood, either dry or green, whichever he have*, Lchdm. ii. 296, 14. Ðeáh wē spirian swā mid læs worda swā mid mā swæþer wē hit gereccan māgon *though we use more or less words in our enquiry, according as we can explain the matter*, Bt. 35, 5; Fox 166, 12: 36, 7; Fox 184, 16. Hī mōston dōn swā gōd swā yfel, swæþor swā hī woldon, 41, 2; Fox 246, 2.

swæð-hlȳpe, swæþian, swæðorian, swæðrung, swagoþ, swalewe, swaloð. v. stæþ-hlīpe, ge-swæþian, swaðrian, ge-swæðrung, swēgan, swealwe, sweoloþ.

swāmian; *p.* ode *To become dark*:—Rodor swāmode ofer niððа bearn *heaven grew dark above the children of men*, i. e. *night came*, Exon. Th. 167, 33; Gū. 1069. v. ā-swāmian; swǣman.

swamm, es; *m. A fungus, mushroom*; also *a sponge*:—Suom, suamm *fungus*, Txts. 65, 938. Swamm oððe feldswam *fungus*, Wrt. Voc. ii. 36, 22. Swom *fungus, spongus, dicta ab uligine*, 152, 21. Ðes swam *hoc tuber* (cf. *tubera* taddechese (= toadstool), Wülck. Gl. 618, 4), Ælfc. Gr. 9, 18; Zup. 44, 1. Nym hlāf and sealt and swamm, and cnuca hit eal tōgadere, Lchdm. iii. 94, 21. Syle etan gebrǣdne swam, 142, 11. Sinwealte swammas *volvi*, Wrt. Voc. i. 30, 28. For mete heó sceal sume hwīle swamma brūcan; wundorlīce heó geeácnaþ, Lchdm. i. 346, 8. [*Goth.* swamms *a sponge*: *O. H. Ger.* swamm, swamp *fungus, tuber*: *Ger.* schwamm *sponge, fungus, excrescence*: *Du.* zwam: *Icel.* svöppr *a sponge*: *Dan.* svamp *sponge, fungus*: *Swed.* swamp.] v. feld-, mete-swamm.

swan, swon, es; *m. A swan*:—Suan *holor*, Wrt. Voc. ii. 110, 42. Swan, 43, 7. Suon *olor*, 115, 45. Swon, ilfetu, 63, 40: *alvor*, 6, 55. Swann *olor*, i. 62, 12. Swan *diomedia*, 63, 14. Swanes feðre, Exon. Th. 207, 6; Ph. 137. *For instances of the word in local names, see* swonleáh, swonweg, Cod. Dip. Kmbl. iii. 48, 78. [*O. L. Ger.* swan: *O. H. Ger.* swan; *m.*, swana; *f. cygnus*: *Icel.* svanr.]

swān, es; *m.* **I.** *a herd*, particularly *a swineherd*; the herds of swine formed a very important item in the live-stock of the Anglo-Saxons. v. swīn. For some account of the duties and rights of different kinds of *swānas*, see L. R. S. 6, 7; Th. i. 436:—Suān *subulcus*, Wrt. Voc. ii. 121, 59: *flabanus*, 108, 72. Swān, 35, 66: *bubullus* (*-cus?*), in a list *de suibus*, i. 286, 58: ii. 11, 59. Hiene ān swān (*subulcus*, Flor. Wig.) ofstang, Chr. 755; Erl. 48, 23. Hē (*Alfred*) on sumes swānes (the *swān* is called *vaccarius* in the Latin Vita S. Neoti, but in other forms of the story, e. g. Matthew of Westminster's, he is *subulcus* and drives 'porcos ad solita pascua') hūse his hleów gernde ... Hit gelamp ðæt ðæs swānes wīf hǣtte hire ofen ... and cwæþ tō ðan kinge: 'Wænd ðū ða hlāfes ðæt heó ne forbeornen, for ðam ic geseó dæighwamlīce ðæt ðū micelǣte eart, Shrn. 16, 13–20. Swāna steorra (cf. swān-steorra) *hesperius*, Wrt. Voc. ii. 43, 39. Oxena hierdas *bobulcos*, swānas *subulcos*, 80, 18. Cūhyrdas *bubulcos*, swānas *subulcos*, Hpt. Gl. 464, 23. **II.** *a man, warrior* (? cf. *Icel.* sveinn):—Ne gefrægn ic nǣfre wurðlīcor æt wera hilde sixtig sigebeorna sēl gebǣran, ne nǣfre swānas swētne medu (swa noc hwitne, Hickes) sēl forgyldan, Fins. Th. 78; Fin. 39. [The form which in later English should be taken by the word is *swon*, and this is found in Palladius on Husbandry: Thy *swon* may se thaire (the pigs') nombr and up save The oppressed pigge, 3, 1086. It has not, however, come into modern English; the corresponding Scandinavian form, *Icel.* sveinn = *boy, lad, man, servant*, on the other hand, remains in *swain*. Early instances of its occurrence are: His sweyn (*also* swain) Leir forþ sende þat was hiredman hende, Laym. 3512. Þreo cnihtes and heore sweines, 18128. Erl ne barun, knict ne sweyn, Havel. 273. Cf. too *Dan.* svend *boy, lad, journeyman*: *Swed.* swen. *O. H. Ger.* swēn, *like* swān, = *subulcus*.] v. ǣhte-, gafol-, in-swān.

swancor; *adj. Bending easily.* **I.** of a horse (cf. *Icel.* svangr used in the same connection), *slender, slim, active and graceful in movement*:—Þrió wicg swancor and sadolbeorhte, Beo. Th. 4356; B. 2175. [Jamieson gives *swank* slender; limber, agile: *swanking* supple, active: *swanky* tall and lank: *swanky* a strapping young countryman.] **II.** *pliant, supple*:—Hine Nīðhād on nēde legde swoncre seonobende *supple sinew-bands* (? *see* seonu-bend), Exon. Th. 377, 19; Deór. 6. [Cf. *M. H. Ger.* swankel: *Ger.* schwank *flexible, slim*: *Swed.* swank *a bend*; swank; *adj. pliable, flexible*; swank-rem *girth-leather*.] **III.** *without firmness, feeble, weak*:—Mīn sāul geweard swancur on mōde ðǣr ic on ðīnre hǣlu hogode *defecit in salutari tuo anima mea*, Ps. Th. 118, 81.

swane-wyrt (?), Lchdm. ii. 74, 20.

swān-gerēfa, an; *m. An officer whose duties were connected with the management of forests in respect to the pasturing of swine in them and to the use of wood. He seems to have been under the direct control of the alderman*:—Ðā (*at a gemōt in* 825) wæs tiolo micel sprēc ymb wudulēswe tō sūðtūne ongægum west on scȳrhylte waldon ða swāngerēfan ða lǣswe forður gedrīfan ond ðone wudu geþiogan (-cgan, Thorpe) ðon hit aldgeryhto wēron ðon cuæð se biscop and ðara hīna wiotan ðet hió him nēren māran ondeta ðon hit ārǣded wæs on Aeðelbaldes dæge ðrīm hunde swīna mæst ond se biscop (and) ða hīgen (tugen, Kemble) āhten twǣde ðæs wuda ond ðæs mæstes ... In ða tiid wæs hama suāngerēfa tō sūðtūne and hē rād ðæt hē wæs et ceastre and ðone aað gesceáwade suā hine his aldormon hēht Eádwulf *there was then a very great case about pasture in the wood at Sutton* (in Worcestershire). *The swain-reeves wanted to push the pasture and take the wood beyond the old rightful limits. The bishop and the counsellors of the brethren said, that they would never make further admission to them than was contained in the terms settled in Ethelbald's time*:—*mast for three hundred swine, and the bishop and brethren should have two-thirds of the wood and of the mast* ... *At that time Hama was swainreeve at Sutton, and he rode to Worcester and watched the oath* (*taken by the bishop in support of his case*), *as his alderman Eadwulf* (Eadwulf dux is a witness to the charter) *bade him*, Cod. Dip. Kmbl. i. 278–279. See Kemble's Saxons in England, ii. 177; 81: and cf. the later *swain*-mote, which is a court touching matters of the forest.

swangor; *adj. Heavy* in movement of the body or mind, *slow, slothful, sluggish, indolent*, (a) physically:—Nis hē (*the Phenix*) swār ne swongor swā sume fuglas ða ðe late þurh lyft lācaþ fiþrum ac hē is snel and swift *non est tarda, ut volucres quae corpore magno incessus pigros per grave pondus habent, sed levis et velox*, Exon. Th. 220, 4; Ph. 315. (b) metaphorically:—Hē wæs swangor (prūtswangor, MS. D.) and swǣr, and him wæs lāð þearfendum mannum mete tō syllenne, Wulfst. 257, 12. Nalæs eallum monnum swongrium (swengum, MS. B.: suongrum, Bd. M.) and heora līfes ungemyndum *non omnibus desidiosis et vitae suae incuriosis*, Bd. 5, 12; S. 630, 38. [*O. H. Ger.* swangar *gravidus, praegnans*: *Du.* zwanger: *Dan.* swanger.]

swangorness, e; *f. Heaviness, torpor, sloth, indolence, sluggishness*:—Ic wāt ðæt swongorness hī ofsit and hī mid slǣwþe ofercymþ, Bt. 36, 6; Fox 180, 33. Ðæt is ðæt hē ða Godes gifa becnytte on ðæm sceáte his slǣwðe and hē for his swongornesse hié gehȳde *pecuniam quippe in sudario ligare est percepta dona sub otio lenti torporis abscondere*, Past. 9; Swt. 59, 16. Ðæt is ðonne ðæt mon his eáge lǣte slāpian ðæt mon for his unwīsdōme and for his suongornesse ne mǣge ongietan ða unðeáwas ðara ðe him underðiédde beóþ. Ne slǣpþ se nō fæsðe ac hnappaþ se ðe gecnāwan mæg hwæt tǣlwierðe biþ and suāðeáh for his mōdes swongornesse oððe rēceliéste forwandaþ ðæt hē bēte his hiéremenn *somnum quippe oculis dare est intentione cessante subditorum curam negligere ... Non autem dormire, sed dormitare, est quae quidem reprehenda sunt cognoscere, sed tamen propter mentis taedium dignis ea increpationibus non emendare*, 28; Swt. 195, 1–10.

swân-riht, es; *n. Law concerning the* swân (q. v.):—On manegum landum gebyreþ deópre swânriht, L. R. S. 6; Th. i. 436, 15.

swân-steorra, an; *m. The herd's star, the evening star*:—Suânsteorra *vesper*, Wrt. Voc. ii. 123, 42. Cf. swâna steorra *under* swân.

swâpan; *p.* sweóp; *pp.* swâpen *To sweep.* I. *trans.* (a) *To sweep* with a brush (lit. or metaph.):—Ic swâpe *uerro*, Ælfc. Gr. 28, 4; Zup. 169, 14. Ic sweóp gâst mînne *scopebam spiritum meum*, Ps. Spl. 76, 6. (b) *to sweep, move* (*something*) *with the action of one sweeping*:—Swâpeþ sigemêce mid ðære swîðran hond ðæt deófol gefeallaþ in sweartne lêg *he shall sweep the victorious blade with the right hand, so that devils shall fall into dark flame*, Exon. Th. 93, 24; Cri. 1531. [Mid beseme clene swopen *scopis mundatam*, O. E. Homl. ii. 87, 10. Me wule swopen þin hus, Misc. 176, 151: Fragm. Phlps. 7, 6. Heó swoped þe duste awei, A. R. 314, 6. Clensi and zuope þe herte, Ayenb. 109, 5. Chaucer has swope, swoope.] II. *intrans. To sweep, have a sweeping motion, drive*; the form and much of the sense belong to *swoop*:—Hûse on munte on swift wind swâpeþ (cf. hûs on munte full ungemetlîc wind gestent, Bt. 12; Fox 36, 16) *montis cacumen protervus auster totis viribus urget*, Met. 7, 20. Cf. answeóp, -suaep *afflarat* (*at-, ad-*), Txts. 38, 32. Onsweóp, 43, 235. Brim wîde wǽdde, wælfæðmum sweóp, Cd. 208, 9; Exod. 480. Hê geseah swâpendum (or under I. b) windum ðone lêg ðæs fŷres ofer ðære burge wallas âhefenne (se wind ðæt fŷr ofer ða wallas drâf, MS. B.) *cum ventis ferentibus globos ignis supra muros urbis exaltari conspiceret*, Bd. 3, 16; S. 542, 37. Cf. onsuâpen *instincta*, Wrt. Voc. ii. 111, 79. Inswâpen, 44, 35. [Swyfte swaynes ful swyþe swepen þertylle, Allit. Pms. 83, 1509.] III. *to wrap.* v. be-, ymb-swâpan. [*O. H. Ger.* sweifan *to swing.* Cf. *Icel.* sveipa (*wk.*) *to sweep, stroke; make a sweeping stroke* with a weapon; *wrap, swaddle.*] v. â-, for-, tô-, ymb-swâpan.

swâr, swâr-. v. swǽr, swǽr-.

swara *in* âþ-swara:—Ðes âðswara *hoc jus jurandum*, Ælfc. Gr. 14; Zup. 88, 6.

swarcan, swarcian, swâre. v. swearcan, swearcian, swǽre.

swarian. v. and-swarian. [*Icel.* svara *to answer*: *Dan.* svare. He wass wis to swarenn and to fraȝȝnenn, Orm. 8938. He called to his chamberlayn, þat cofly hym swared, Gaw. 2011.]

swaring (-ung), swarnian, swarnung, swart. v. âþ-swaring, swornian, swornung, sweart.

swaru (1) *swer* in an-*swer*. v. and-swaru. [Cf. *Icel.* svar; *n. answer*: *Dan.* svar. Forrhwi ȝho ȝaff swillc sware onnȝæn, Orm. 2422.] (2) *swearing, oath.* v. âþ-, mân-, mânâþ- (be mânâþsware *de perjurio*, L. Ecg. C. tit. 34; Th. ii. 130, 24) swaru. [Mid false sware, O. E. Homl. ii. 259, 35. Of alle sunnen . . . of sum uals word, of sware, A. R. 344, 3. He sahtnesse mid sware (treoðe, 1st MS.) hadde ifastned, Laym. 10893.]

swâse. v. swǽs.

swât, es; *n.* [The passages in which the gender is marked are doubtful. Ðæt swôt, Lchdm. iii. 98, 17, occurs in a late MS.; îsen swât, ii. 296, 18, may be a compound; ða swât, iii. 72, 28, may be a mistake for spâtl, v. ii. 56, 15. Dutch has a neuter, German and Scandinavian have masculines.] I. *sweat, perspiration*:—Seofoðe (*the seventh of the constituents from which Adam was made*) wæs deáwes pund, ðanon him (*Adam*) becom swât, Salm. Kmbl. 180. 15. Suât, Rtl. 192, 17. His swât (*sudor*) wæs swylce blôdes dropan, Lk. Skt. 22, 44. Of ealdum clâðum ðe beóþ eal on swâte, Homl. Ass. 35, 280. Swâ ða swât (*but* ii. 56, 15 *has* spâtl), beóþ missenlîcu, Lchdm. iii. 72, 28. I a. *that which exudes like sweat*:—Ðanne þeó brǽde geswâte nim ðæt swôt *when the roast meat sweats, take that which exudes*, Lchdm. iii. 98, 17. I b. *that which lies on anything as sweat lies on the skin* (?):—Wiþ gongelwæfran bite, smît on îsen swât (isen-swât?), ii. 296, 18. II. used of other moisture that comes from the body, (1) *foam*:—Mid swâte *cum spuma*, Lk. Skt. Rush. 9, 39. (2) *blood*:—Saga mê hwæt ðæs lifigendan mannes gleng sŷ. Ic ðê secge ðæs deádan swât, Salm. Kmbl. 200, 10. Geseoh seolfes swæðe, swâ ðîn swât âgeát, blôdige stîge, Andr. Kmbl. 2881; An. 1443: 2552; An. 1277: Beo. Th. 5380; B. 2693. Him for swenge swât ǽdrum sprong forð under fexe, 5925; B. 2966. Beswyled mid swâtes gange, Rood Kmbl. 45; Kr. 23. On rôde ðû ðîn blôd âgute for heó and [hŷ] mid ðînum ðam æþelan swâte gebohtest, Wulfst. 255, 23. Cwealmdreóre, monnes swâte, Cd. Th. 60, 24; Gen. 986. Be sîdan ðǽr Hǽlend his swât forlêt, 299, 6; Sat. 545: Andr. Kmbl. 1935; An. 970: Exon. Th. 88, 33; Cri. 1449. III. *sweat* that comes from labour, hence *labour, toil*:—Ðǽr wæs suîðe suîdlîc gesuinc and ðǽr wæs micel swât âgoten and ðeáh ne meahte monn him of âniman ðone miclan rust *multo labore sudatum est, et non exivit de ea nimia rubigo ejus*, Past. 37, 3; Swt. 269, 12. On swâte ðînes andwlitan ðû brîcst ðînes hlâfes, Gen. 3, 19. Se man on gewinne and on swâte hê leofaþ, Blickl. Homl. 59, 36: Cd. Th. 33, 8; Gen. 482. [*O. Sax. O. Frs.* swêt: *Du.* zweet; *n.*: *O. H. Ger.* sweiz: *M. H. Ger.* sweiz *sweat; blood*: *Ger.* schweiss; *m.*: *Icel.* sweiti *wk. m.*: *Dan.* sved; *m.*: *Swed.* swett; *m.*] v. heaðu-, hilde-swât; swǽtan, *and next word.*

-swât; *adj. in* ge-swât *sweaty, sweating*:—Ðara breósta biþ deáwig wǽtung, swâ swâ sié geswât, Lchdm. ii. 258, 18. Gebeþe ða hamma mid ðam stânbaðe; ðonne hié sién geswâte, ðonne recce hê ða bân, 68, 6.

swâtan (swatan? v. Engl. Stud. viii. 479); *pl. Beer*:—Swâtan *cervisia*, Wrt. Voc. i. 290, 62: ii. 17, 25. Âwyl on sûrum swâtum oþþe on sûrum ealað, Lchdm. ii. 34, 15. [Jamieson gives *swaits* new ale or wort; but also *swats* new ale; the thin part of flummery.]

swât-clâþ, es; *m. A handkerchief, towel, napkin*; sudarium:—Se apostol him âsende his swâtclâð . . . Hê wearð âlŷsed swâ hraðe swâ se swâtclâð hine hrepode, Homl. Th. ii. 414, 21–25. [Cf. *O. H. Ger.* sweiz-tûh *sudarium, orarium*: *Ger.* schweiss-tuch *handkerchief*: *Icel.* sveita-dûkr *a napkin*: *Dan.* svede-dug *a handkerchief.*] v. swât-lîn.

swât-fâh; *adj. Blood-stained*:—Oft æt hilde gedreás swâtfâg and sweordwund sec[g] æfter ôðrum, Vald. 1, 5. Swâtfâh syrce, Beo. Th. 2226; B. 1111.

Swa-ðeód, swaðor. v. Sweó-þeód, swæðer.

swaðrian, swæðorian; *p* ode *To retreat, withdraw, subside*:—Geofon swaðrode . . . geótende gegrind grund eall forswealg, Andr. Kmbl. 3169; An. 1587. Hærn eft onwand . . . wædu swæðorodon, 1066; An. 533. Brimu swaþredon, ðæt ic sǽnæssas geseón mihte, Beo. Th. 1145; B. 570. v. sweðrian.

swaþu, e; *f. A track, trace, footstep, vestige*; left in *swathe* a row of mown grass:—On Oliuetes dûne syndon nû gyt ða swæþe Drihtnes fôtlâsta . . . ne mihte seó his swaðu beón ðǽm ôðrum flôrum geonlîcod . . . ða his swaða syndon monnum tô êcre lâre . . . men mihton sceáwian Drihtnes fôta swaðe, Shrn. 80, 35–81, 15. Næs bûtan seó swaðu (*the trace of a wound, scar*) on, 95, 3. Wê sôðfæstes swaðe folgodon, Andr. Kmbl. 1346; An. 673. Him on swaðe fylgeþ *follows in his track, pursues him*, Salm. Kmbl. 186; Sal. 92: Exon. Th. 397, 25; Rä. 16, 25: 487, 23; Rä. 74. Hæleð lâgon, on swaðe sǽton *sat in the track, were left dead in the track of the retreating force*, Cd. Th. 125, 10; Gen. 2077: 127, 21; Gen. 2114: Andr. Kmbl. 2844; An. 1424. Hié (*the defeated Assyrians*) on swaðe reston, Judth. Thw. 26, 11; Jud. 322. On swaðe feóllon æðelinga bearn, Cd. Th. 120, 28; Gen. 2001. Hig unc âsetton on ôðre healfe ðære eá, ðæt ða ne mihton uncre swaðe findon, Shrn. 42, 3. Nǽnige swaðe his *nullum ejus vestigium*, Bd. 4, 23; S. 595, 3. Þeáh ælda bearn lâstas mîne sêcaþ, ic swaþe mîne bemîþe, Exon. Th. 500, 26; Rä. 89, 12. Swæðe, Andr. Kmbl. 2880; An. 1443. Ða swaþe âwuniaþ reogollîces lîfes *regularis vitae vestigia permanent*, Bd. 4, 3; S. 566, 43. Sweðe mîne *vestigia mea*, Ps. Surt. 16, 5: 17, 37. v. dolh-, fôt-, swât-, weald-, wund-swaþu; swæþ.

swaþu?:—Swîna swaþu *suesta*, Wrt. Voc. i. 286, 56. Suîna suadu (sceadu, Corp. Gloss.) *suesta, sivesta*, Txts. 98, 972.

swaþul, es; *m. That which swathes* or *wraps* (? v. sweþel):—Ðæs ne wêndon witan Scyldinga ðæt hit (*the hall*) manna ǽnig tôbrecan meahte nymþe lîges fæðm swulge on swaþule *unless the flame's embrace swallowed up the house in its swathing fire*, i. e. *unless the house were completely wrapt in flames* (Thorpe would read *swaloðe* = heat, v. sweoloþ: Grein translates the word by *rauchqualm*; compare *Ger.* schwaden *vapour*: *M. H. Ger.* swadem: *O. H. Ger.* swedan *cremare*), Beo. Th. 1568; B. 782.

swâtig; *adj.* I. *sweaty*:—Ðâ ongan hê hine baðian swâ swâtigne *cum sudans in amnem descendisset*, Ors. 3, 9; Swt. 124, 31. Godes engel mid handclâðe wîpaþ ðîne swâtigan limu, Homl. Th. i. 426, 31. II. *bloody*:—Sweord wæs swâtig, Beo. Th. 3143; B. 1569. Sweord and swâtigne helm, Judth. Thw. 26, 20; Jud. 338. Ðû meaht geseón on mînre sîdan swâtge wunde, Exon. Th. 89, 19; Cri. 1459. [*M. H. Ger.* sweizec: *Ger.* schweissig: *Icel.* sveitugr.]

swâtig-hleór; *adj. Having a sweaty face*:—Ðû scealt swâtighleór ðînne hlâf etan (*in the sweat of thy brow shalt thou eat bread*, Gen. 3, 19), Cd. Th. 57, 27; Gen. 934.

swât-lîn, es; *n. A napkin, handkerchief*:—Swâtlîn *sudorium*, Wrt. Voc. ii. 73, 68. On ðæm swâtlîne (*in sudarium*) ðe Xrist ymbe spræc on his godspelle, Past. 9; Swt. 59, 13. Ðîn pund ðe ic hæfde on swâtlîn (*in sudario*) âléd, Lk. Skt. 19, 20. v. swât-clâþ.

swât-swaþu, e; *f. A bloody track*:—Wæs sió swâtswaþu Sweóna and Geáta, wælrǽs wera, wîde gesŷne, Beo. Th. 5884; B. 2946.

swât-þyrel, es; *n. A pore*:—Swâtþyrlu *pori* i. *spiramenta unde sudor emanat*, Wrt. Voc. i. 44, 25. [Cf. Swete-holle *porus*, Wrt. Voc. i. 209, 9. Swet-hole, Cath. Ang. 373, col. 2. *O. H. Ger.* sweiz-loh: *Ger.* schweissloch *a pore*: *Icel.* sweita-bora: *Dan.* svede-hul.]

swealwe, swealewe, an; *f. A swallow*:—Suualuae, suualuuae, suualuue *progna*, Txts. 90, 828. Sualuuae, sualuae, sualuue *hirundo*, 68, 498. Swealwe, Wrt. Voc. ii. 43, 5. Swalowe, swaluwe, swalewe, Ælfc. Gr. 9, 3; Zup. 37, 7. Storc and swalewe, Homl. Th. i. 404, 25. Genim swealwan nest, Lchdm. ii. 100, 18. Swolwan, iii. 44, 13. Genim swealwan, gebærn tô ahsan, ii. 156, 8. Hû ða swalawan on him sǽton and sungon . . . . Twâ swalewan heora sang up âhôfon and hî setton on ða sculdra ðæs hâlgan weres Gûðlâces, Guthl. 10; Gdwin. 52, 3–10. For instances of the word in local names, see Cod. Dip. Kmbl. vi. 338. [*O. H. Ger.* swalawa: *Icel.* swala.] v. hae-, heoru-, stæþ-swealwe.

swearc (?); *adj. Weak, feeble, faint.* v. *next word, and* swearcan.

swearc-môdness, e; *f. Faintheartedness, pusillanimity*:—Fram swearcmôdnesse gâstes *a pusillanimitate spiritus*, Ps. Lamb. 54, 9. v. next word.

swearcan (?) *to grow dark* (?); metaph. *to grow faint, languish.* v. ā-swarćan, *the preceding and following words, and* sweorcan.

swearcian; *p.* ode. I. *to make* or *to become dark*:—Seó swearcigende sunne and ða gesceafta samod ealne middaneard ādeóstrodon mid sweartre nihte for heora Scyppendes ðrowunge, Homl. Th. ii. 258, 15. II. *to make* or *to become troubled, to dismay.* v. ā-swarcian, *and preceding words.*

sweard, es; *m.* (?) *Sward* (=rind of bacon; cf. too green-*sward* the turf-covering of the earth), *skin, hide*:—Sweard *cutis*, fel *pellis*, Wrt. Voc. i. 283, 32-3. Sweard *cutis*, rib *costa*, heorte *cor*, ii. 16, 54-6. Swearth *cater*, 103, 22. Suge sweard *vistula*, 124, 1. Swearð *catrum*, 13, 52. [Swarde or sworde of flesche *coriana*, Prompt. Parv. 482. Turfe, swarde of þe erþe *cespes*, 506. *O. Frs.* swarde *skin* (*of the head*): *Du.* zwoord; *n. skin*: *M. H. Ger.* swarte, swart; *f. skin with hair on*: *Ger.* schwarte; *f. skin, rind*: *Icel.* svörðr; *m. the skin* (especially of the head); *hide* of walrus; gras-, jarðar-svörðr *green-sward.*]

swearm, es; *m. A swarm, crowd*:—Sue[a]rm *examen*, Wrt. Voc. ii. 107, 82. Swearm, 32, 17: 144, 43 (*examen* has been omitted here by Wright, see Wülck. Gl. 230, 6): Ælfc. Gr. 9, 12; Zup. 40, 14: *examen, multitudo*, Hpt. Gl. 457, 37: 496, 14. [*O. H. Ger.* swaram, swarm; *m. examen*: *Icel.* svarmr; *m. tumult*: *Swed.* swärm; *m. a swarm*: *Dan.* sværm *a swarm; rioting*: *Du.* zwerm; *m. a swarm, crowd.*]

sweart; *adj.* I. of colour, *swart, swarthy, black, dark*:—Sweart *ater, teter; ceruleus*, Wrt. Voc. i. 46, 32, 53 (in a list of colours): *furvus*, ii. 34, 39, 40: *fuscus*, 38, 27: *luridus*, 53, 15: *pullus*, 57, 10: *niger*, Ælfc. Gr. 8; Zup. 27, 9: *caeruleus*, Hpt. Gl. 516, 14. Wudurēc sweart, Beo. Th. 6281; B. 3145. Hræfn sweart and sealobrūn, Fins. Th. 70; Fin. 35. On ðæm clife hangodan manige swearte sāula . . . and ðæt wæter wæs sweart under ðæm clife neoðan, Blickl. Homl. 209, 34-211, 1. Ðonne sweartan wolcnu (*nubes atrae*) him beforan gāþ, Bt. 6; Fox 14, 22. Engla and deófla, hwītra and sweartra, Exon. Th. 56, 9; Cri. 898. Mænigeo sweartra gāsta *spirituum deformium multitudo*, Bd. 5, 12; S. 628, 4. On sweartum stafum and atollīcum āwritene *tetricis descripta litteris*, 5, 13; S. 633, 8. Sweartran *furviores*, Wrt. Voc. ii. 37, 51. Hī āsettan ofer hyre ða sweartestan fyðra, L. E. I. prm.; Th. ii. 398, 27. II. of absence of light or brightness, *dark, black, gloomy*:—Ōðer (beám) wæs swā wynlīc, wlitig and scēne . . . wæs se ōðer eallenga sweart, dim and þȳstre, Cd. Th. 30, 35; Gen. 477. Eów is hām sceapen sweart sinnehte, Exon. Th. 142, 26; Gū. 650. Ða þeóstre ðære sweartan nihte, Bt. 4; Fox 6, 34. Ðære sweartan helle grund, Cd. Th. 22, 24; Gen. 345. Se ðe on þȳstre færeþ, on sweartre niht, Exon. Th. 54, 23; Cri. 873. Deorc gesweorc sinnihte sweart, Cd. Th. 7, 21; Gen. 109. Tō helle on ðone sweartan sīð, 45, 27; Gen. 733. On dīglum ꝉ on sweartum dymnyssum *latibulis*, Hpt. Gl. 480, 28. Landa sweartost *hell*, Cd. Th. 31, 19; Gen. 487. III. of absence of good, *black* (crime), *dark, dismal*:—Gāstas twegen, ōðer biþ golde glædra, ōðer biþ grundum sweartra, Salm. Kmbl. 976; Sal. 488. Sweartes hǣðendōmes *tetrae gentilitatis*, Hpt. Gl. 523, 41. Micel yfelnyss wæs on Iudēiscum mannum, ðā ðā hī syrwdon mid sweartum geþance (*with dark design*), hū hī Crist ācwealdon, Homl. Skt. i. 11, 318. Swā lange swā hē hylt ðone sweartan nīð on his heortan, Homl. Th. i. 54, 13. Mānfulra heáp sweartne *the devils*, Salm. Kmbl. 299; Sal. 149. Ic fela gefremede sweartra synna, Exon. Th. 261, 10; Jul. 313: 270, 20; Jul. 468. Gē hellfirena sweartra geswīcaþ, 366, 4; Reb. 7. In ða sweartestan and ða wyrrestan wītebrōgan, Elen. Kmbl. 1859; El. 931. [*Goth.* swarts: *O. Sax. O. Frs.* swart: *O. H. Ger.* swarz: *Icel.* svartr.] v. fȳr-, swefel-sweart.

swearte; *adv. Darkly, dismally, evilly*:—Sió gītsung swearte swǣfeþ onlīce ðam munte ðe monna bearn Etne hātaþ, Met. 8, 47 (v. swǣfan). Satanus swearte geþohte (cf. Milton's 'dark designs,' and v. sweart, III), ðæt hē wolde on heofonum hēhseld wyrcan, Cd. Th. 287, 22; Sat. 371. Satanus swearte (*miserably*) þingaþ and ða atolan mid him wītum wērige, 292, 28; Sat. 447. Him ðæt swearte forgeald (*made grievous compensation*) Iudas innon helle, 301, 8; Sat. 578.

sweart-hǣwen; *adj. Dark purple, violet-coloured*:—Ða sweart-hǣwenan *cerula*, Wrt. Voc. ii. 20, 67.

sweartian; *p.* ode *To make* or *to become black*:—Ðanne sweartigaþ (sweratiged, MS.) hȳ (*the teeth*) and feallaþ (-eð, MS.), Lchdm. iii. 104, 17. Hē sweartade (*but see* spearcian), Cd. Th. 269, 24; Sat. 78. Ðā ārās se wind, and ða wolcnu sweartodon, Homl. Skt. i. 18, 151. Gesweartode *denigratos*, Hpt. Gl. 514, 32. [Þ te hude snawhwit swartete as hit snarchte, Marh. 18, 14. *O. H. Ger.* swarzen *to become black*: *Icel.* svarta *to dye black.*] v. ā-sweartian.

sweart-lāst; *adj. Leaving a black track*:—Fugles wyn (*a pen*) stōp eft on mec (*a book*), sīþade sweartlāst, Exon. Th. 408, 12; Rä. 27, 11.

sweartness, e; *f.* I. *blackness*:—Sweartnysse *nigredine*, Hpt. Gl. 514, 50. II. *a black material*:—Sweartnesse *atramentum*, Wrt. Voc. ii. 84, 72: 5, 31.

swebban; *p.* swefde, swefede; *pp.* swefed. I. *to send to sleep, lull*:—Suebbo *sopio*, Wrt. Voc. ii. 120, 72. Ne hȳ lyft swefeþ, Exon. Th. 115, 19; Gū. 192. Swefed *sopitus*, Kent. Gl. 917. Wæs hē sæmninga mid leóhte slǣpe swefed, Guthl. 6; Gdwin. 42, 13. II. of the sleep of death, *to put to death, kill*:—Hē swefeþ ond scendeþ, Beo. Th. 1204; B. 600. Ic hine sweorde swebban nelle, aldre beneótan, 1363; B. 679. Ne mōton wyt wrecan torn Godes, swebban synnig cynn, Cd. Th. 152, 35; Gen. 2531. [God sweueð hus mid þiestre nicht, O. E. Homl. i. 233, 33. He swefede þe mid þen sweiȝe, swote þu sleptest, Fragm. Phlps. 7, 42. *O. Sax.* an-swebian *to send to sleep, to cause to die*: *O. H. Ger.* int-swebben *sopire*: *Icel.* svefja *to lull, assuage.*] v. ā-, on-swebban; swefian, swefan.

swecc, swæcc, es; *m.* I. *a taste, flavour, savour*:—Ðæs (*the manna's*) swæc (*gustus*) wæs swilce smedema mid hunige, Ex. 16, 31: Bt. 34, 11; Fox 152, 1. Swæcces *nectaris, saporis*, Hpt. Gl. 488, 26. Būton swæcce (*sapore*) sealtes, Coll. Monast. Th. 28, 15. On swæce swylce grēne cystel, Lchdm. i. 108, 2. On swæcce swēttran ðonne beóna hunig, Homl. Th. ii. 136, 30: 144, 4. Ia. *the sense of taste*:—Mid ūrum fīf andgitum . . . swæc and stenç, Homl. Th. i. 138, 27. Swæcc, ii. 550, 11: Wrt. Voc. i. 42, 60. II. *an odour, a scent, smell*:—Wundorlīces brǣðes swæc, Homl. Th. ii. 352, 15. Seó wundriende swētnes ðæs swæcces (*odoris*), Bd. 5, 12; S. 629, 20. Stēmendes swæcces *nardi pistici*, Hpt. Gl. 516, 38. Ðæt hūs wæs gefylled of ðære sealfe swæcce (*odore*), Jn. Skt. 12, 3. Gif ðū hyre blōsðman brȳtest, hē hæfþ swæc swylce ellen, Lchdm. i. 104, 20. Swecca swētast swylce stincaþ wyrta geblōwene, Exon. Th. 178, 20; Gū. 1247. Swæcca, 358, 16; Pa. 46. Swētum swæccum (*odoribus*), 212, 22; Ph. 214. Sweccum, Kent. Gl. 1016. IIa. *the sense of smell*:—Swæc *odoratus* (in a list 'de homine et de partibus ejus'), Wrt. Voc. i. 282, 31: 64, 19. Stenc, swæc *olfactum*, swæc *odoratus*, ii. 62, 45, 46. [*O. Sax.* swek *an odour*: *O. H. Ger.* swehhi *odor.*]

sweccan *to smell.* [*O. H. Ger.* swehhen *olere, adolere, fragrare.*] v. ge-sweccan.

swediende. v. spediende.

swefan; *p.* swæf, *pl.* swǣfon; *pp.* swefen *To sleep.* I. of natural sleep:—Se ne slǣpeþ ne swefeþ (*or* III a) swȳðe *non dormitavit neque obdormiet*, Ps. Th. 120, 4. Hē swifeþ slǣpe gebiesgad, Exon. Th. 358, 1; Pa. 39. Hē sōfte swæf, Cd. Th. 12, 2; Gen. 179: 94, 19; Gen. 1564. Sceótend swǣfon, ða ðæt hornreced healdan scoldon, Beo. Th. 1411; B. 703: 2564; B. 1280. Ðū mōst sorhleás swefan, 3348; B. 1672: 238; B. 119. Geseah hē in recede swefan sibbegedriht samod ætgædere, 1462; B. 729: Exon. Th. 344, 25; Gn. Ex. 179. Swefan under swegles hleó, Andr. Kmbl. 1663; An. 834. Swefan on slǣpe, 1695; An. 851. II. of the sleep of death:—Se fǣge þegn æfter billes bite swefeþ, Beo. Th. 4127; B. 2060. Se wyrm ligeþ, swefeþ sāre wund, 5485; B. 2746. Swefaþ ða ðe beadogrīman bȳwan sceoldon, 4505; B. 2256. Hȳ deáðdrepe drihte swǣfon, synfullra sweót sāwlum lunnon, Cd. Th. 209, 7; Exod. 495. Hǣðene swǣfon, deáðwang ridon, Andr. Kmbl. 2004; An. 1004. Hlāfurd sēcan oððe hēr swefan, Vald. 1, 31. III. metaphorically, (a) to denote lack of watchfulness:—Ðonne se weard swefeþ, sāwele hyrde, Beo. Th. 3487; B. 1741. (b) to denote cessation of activity:—Swǣfon seledreámas, Cd. Th. 179, 29; Exod. 36. [Cf. Þa sæ sweuede, Laym. 25548. *Icel.* sofa; *p.* svaf *to sleep*: *Dan.* sove: *Swed.* sofwa.] v. swebban.

swefecian. v. ā-swefecian, Wrt. Voc. ii. 31, 5: 77, 32. Cf. stȳfecian.

swefel, swefl, es; *m. Sulphur, brimstone*:—Swefl, swefel, swæfl *sulfur*, Ælfc. Gr. 9, 22; Zup. 49, 3. Swefel, Wrt. Voc. i. 37, 27. Ðæt sceal wrecan swefyl and sweart līg, Cd. Th. 145, 33; Gen. 2415. Se byrnenda swefl ðone munt (*Etna*) bærnþ, Bt. 16, 1; Fox 50, 4. Swefles *sulphuris*, Hpt. Gl. 489, 1. Nīwes swefles fīf cuclermǣl, Lchdm. ii. 252, 21. Eallbyrnende rēnscūr mid swefle gemencged, Gen. 19, 24: Met. 8, 50. Swæfle, Boutr. Scrd. 22, 29, 32. Hit rīnde fȳr and swefl, Lk. Skt. 17, 29: Cd. Th. 153, 19; Gen. 2541. Hwylce þinc gelǣdest ðū (*the merchant*) ūs? . . . mæstlingc, ǣr and tin, swefel and glæs, Coll. Monast. Th. 27, 11: Lchdm. i. 200, 2. Swefl, ii. 56, 10. [*Goth.* swibls: *Du.* zwavel: *O. H. Ger.* swebal(-el, -il, -ul), sweval *sulphur*: *Ger.* schwefel: *Dan.* svovl: *Swed.* swafwel.]

swefel-rēc, es; *m. Sulphur-smoke, the smoke from burning sulphur*:—Rīneþ ofer ða synfullan swefelrēc *pluet super peccatores sulphur*, Ps. Surt. 10, 7. Cf. swefel-þrosm.

swefel-sweart (?); *adj. Dark with the smoke of sulphur* (?):—Sueflsweart *sulforia*, Wrt. Voc. ii. 121, 61.

swefel-þrosm, es; *m. The vapour* or *smoke of sulphur*:—Hē rȳnde ofer synfullan swefiðrosm *pluit super peccatores sulphur*, Ps. Spl. 10, 7. Cf. swefel-rēc.

swefen, swefn, es; *n.* I. *sleep*:—Hit wæs deáðes swefn . . . menniscra morð, Cd. Th. 45, 1; Gen. 720. Hī slēpon swæfnum *dormierunt somnum*, Ps. Spl. 75, 5. Gif ic selle swefnu ꝉ slǣp eágum mīnum *si dedero somnum oculis meis*, Ps. Lamb. 131, 4. II. *a dream*:—Hē rehte him his swefen (*somnium*) and bæd, ðæt hig him sǣdon, hwæt ðæt swefen beheóld, Gen. 41, 8. Him wearð on slǣpe swefen ætȳwed, Cd. Th. 247, 13; Dan. 496. Swefn, 257, 7; Dan. 654. Hē ne wisse word swefnes sīnes, 223, 27; Dan. 126. Com on sefan hwurfan swefnes wōma, 222, 25; Dan. 110: Elen. Kmbl. 142; El. 71. Ōðer swefen hine mǣtte and hē rehte ðæt his brōðrum: 'Ic geseah on swefne (*per somnium*),' Gen. 37, 9. For ðære gesihðe ðe hē on ðæm swefne geseah, Past. 16;

Swt. 101, 18. Đā stōd him sum mon æt đurh swefen (*per somnium*) . . . Đā hēt heó secgan đæt swefen, Bd. 4, 24; S. 597, 11–31. Swefn, Cd. Th. 159, 16; Gen. 2635. Tō āsecganne swefen, 224, 1; Dan. 129. Swefnu gefremminge habbaþ *dreams will have accomplishment*, Lchdm. iii. 186, 12. Swefenu, 196, 11. Swefna ȳdele sint, 188, 21. Swefne (swæfna) gewisse synt, 186, 19, 27. Feor āweg gewītan swefna and nihta gedwymeru *procul recedant somnia et noctium fantasmata*, Hymn. Surt. 11, 29. Ic swefna cyst secgan wylle, Rood Kmbl. 1; Kr. 1. Hī āfēngon andsware on swefnum, Mt. Kmbl. 2, 12. On swefnum (soefnum, Lind.) gemynegod, 22: Homl. Th. i. 88, 15. Heó ādrǣfe swefnu *pellat sompnia*, Hymn. Surt. 37, 6. [Now God my swevene rede aright, Chauc. Nonne Pr. T. 76. Thanne gan I to meten a merueilouse sweuene, Piers P. prol. 11. Swevene or dreme *sompnium*, sweuene or slepe *sompnus*, Prompt. Parv. 483. *O. Sax.* sweƀan *a dream*: *Icel.* svefn, sǫfn *sleep*: *a dream*: *Dan.* sǫvn *sleep*: *Swed.* sömn *sleep*.] v. un-swefen.

swefen-racu, e; *f. The interpretation of a dream*:—Galdorcræftas and swefenraca *incantationes et somniorum interpretationes*, L. Ecg. C. 29; Th. ii. 154, 29. v. next word.

swefen-reccere, es; *m. An interpreter of dreams, a diviner, soothsayer*:—Swefnreccere *conjectorem*, Wrt. Voc. ii. 15, 40. [Cf. *O. H. Ger.* troum-rechare *conjector*.] v. preceding word.

swefet, swefian *to lull*. v. sweofot, ge-swefian.

swefian (?) *to move*. v. *passage given under* forþ-swebban (-swefian?) [cf. *O. H. Ger.* swebēn: *Ger.* schweben]. Cf. swīfan.

sweflen; *adj. Sulphurous, of brimstone*:—Him stōd swæflen līg of đam mūđe, Homl. Th. i. 466, 26. Eđna đæt sweflene fȳr, Ors. 2, 6; Swt. 88, 30. Hē eal đæt land mid sweflenum fȳre forbærnde *Deus pluit super hanc terram ignem et sulphur, totamque regionem exustam aeterna perditione damnavit*, 1, 3; Swt. 32, 10: Ælfc. T. Grn. 4, 17. Swæflenum, Boutr. Scrd. 22, 32. Sweflenum þicnyssum *sulphureis flammarum globis*, Hpt. Gl. 499, 49.

swefn. v. swefen.

swefnian; *p.* ode. I. *with acc. of person*, cf. mǣtan, *To appear in a dream to* a person:—Swā hwæt swā hine swefnaþ *whatever he dreams*, Lchdm. iii. 184, 9. Swā hwæt swā đē geswefnaþ, 154, 24. Āhicgan on sefan đīnne hū đē swefnede, Cd. Th. 224, 5; Dan. 131. Đē heortan deópnyssa swefnian *te cordis alta somnient*, Hymn. Surt. 3, 19. II. *with nom. of person, To dream*:—Gif đū swefnast đē twege[n] mōnan geseón *if you dream that you see two moons*, Lchdm. iii. 212, 25. [As sweveneth the hungrende and eteth (Isaiah 29, 8), Wick. Cf. *Dan.* sǫvne *to fall asleep*.]

swefnigend, es; *m. A dreamer*:—Hēr gǣþ se swefnigend *ecce somniator venit*, Gen. 37, 19.

swēg, es; *m.* I. *unregulated, confused sound, noise, din, crash*:—Suoeg, cirm *fragor*, Wrt. Voc. ii. 109, 27. Swǣg *clangor, sonitus*, Hpt. Gl. 451, 44. Ne wind ne wætres swēg, Blickl. Homl. 65, 19. Swēg on windes onlīcnesse, 133, 15. Swēg innan đan heáfedan, Lchdm. iii. 92, 25. Wæs đeód on sǣlum sigefolca swēg, Beo. Th. 1292; B. 644: Cd. Th. 289, 26; Sat. 403. For gedrēfednesse sǣs swēges (*sonitus*), Lk. Skt. 21, 25. Swoeges, Ps. Surt. 76, 18. Gebrece, swoege *fragore*, Wrt. Voc. ii. 33, 79. Mid micle swēge *cum maximo fragore*, Ors. 5, 10; Swt. 234, 3. Wiđ eárena swēge *for singing in the ears*, Lchdm. i. 350, 1. Nān monn ne gehiérde ne æxe hlem ne biétles suēg, Past. 36; Swt. 253, 17. Hig fleóþ leáfes swēg (*sonitus folii volantis*), Lev. 26, 36. Micelne swēg unmǣtes wōpes, Bd. 5, 12; S. 628, 29. Swēgas (-es, MS.) *tonitrua*, Hpt. Gl. 452, 60. Swoegum *bombis*, Wrt. Voc. ii. 12, 8. II. *regulated, modulated* or *articulate sound*, (a) *sound* made by living creatures, *voice, cry* or *note of a bird, song*:—Dyptongus is twȳfeald swēg, Ælfc. Gr. 4; Zup. 7, 13. *Accentus*, đæt is swēg, on hwylcum stæfgefēge ǣlc word swēgan sceal, 50, 13; Zup. 290, 16. Swēg *tenor*, Hpt. Gl. 528, 21. Heofoncyninges stefn, wordhleóđres swēg, Andr. Kmbl. 186; An. 93. Swēg (*the voice of Moses*) swīđrode, Cd. Th. 197, 18; Exod. 309. Engla þreátas sigeleóđ sungon, swēg wæs on lyfte gehȳred, Exon. Th. 181, 7; Gū. 1289. Biþ đæs hleóđres swēg (*the song of the phenix*) eallum songcræftum swētra, 206, 24; Ph. 131. Sume synd geworhte æfter gelīcnysse āgenes swēges, *turtur* turtle, Ælfc. Gr. 5; Zup. 14, 2. Ganetes hleóþor and hūilpan swēg, Exon. Th. 307, 9; Seef. 21. Swēga mǣste, 239, 9; Ph. 618. Tyrnende swēgas *rotatiles trocheos*, Germ. 403, 8. (b) *sound* made by means of an instrument. v. swēg-cræft. *voice*; also *the instrument*:—Đære bȳman swēg, Ex. 19, 19. Hearpan swēg, Beo. Th. 179; B. 89. Sume syndon geworhte æfter gelīcnysse āgenes swēges. *titinnabulum* belle, Ælfc. Gr. 5; Zup. 14, 2. Swēge *classica*, Wrt. Voc. ii. 19, 67. On swēge (swōge, Ps. Surt.) bȳman *in sono tubae*, Ps. Spl. 150, 3. On swēge *in tympano*, 149, 3, MS. T. For đam swēge (*of the harp*), Bt. 35, 6; Fox 168, 1. Hearpan swinsigende swēg, Cd. Th. 66, 8; Gen. 1081. Heó gehȳrde bellan swēg, Shrn. 149, 9: Homl. Th. ii. 156, 6. Swēgas *classica*, Wrt. Voc. ii. 131, 62. Dreámas (swēgas, MS. T.) *organa*, Ps. Spl. 136, 2. ¶ In Wrt. Voc. ii. 110, 43: 43, 7, *swēg* glosses *hora*, because of the striking of a bell at the hours? III. *a person*:—Be onfangenysse swēgea *de acceptione personarum*, Scint. 183, 17 (swēg *is used several times in the section under this heading to gloss* persona). v. benc-, hearp-, here-, hilde-, morgen-swēg.

swēgan; *p.* de *To sound*. I. *to make a noise*, (a) with the idea of movement, *to move violently with noise, to roar, rush, crash*:—Đonne swēiþ *cum insonuerit*, Kent. Gl. 12. Heora fyđera swēgaþ swā swā wæteres dyne, Wulfst. 200, 15. Æt đam forman gedelfe swēgde ūt ormǣte wyllspring, Homl. Th. i. 562, 14. Swēgde swīđlīc wind of đam wēstene, ii. 450, 18. Đa wæterburnan swēgdon and urnon, Dōm. L. 3: Ps. Spl. 45, 3. Ærđan đe đæt scearpe swurd swēge tō his hneccan *descend with a crash upon his neck*, Homl. Skt. i. 19, 185. Swēgende *tumultuans*, Hpt. Gl. 528, 43. Com seó sǣ fǣrlīce swēgende, Homl. Th. i. 566, 7. Hē sette hine sylfne ongeán đam swēgendan līge, ii. 510, 8. Hē āsende swǣgende fȳr of heofonum, Homl. Skt. i. 2, 260. (b) without the idea of movement:—Swēgþ *tinnit*, Ælfc. Gr. 22; Zup. 128, 16. Swagoþ (swēgaþ? v. swēg, I) đa eáran, Lchdm. iii. 88, 5. Se heáf swēgde geond ealle đa ceastre, Ap. Th. 6, 10. Đæt ne sace ōga on swēge *ne litis horror insonet*, Hymn. Surt. 9, 12. (b 1) with a personal subject:—Drihten swēgþ *Dominus tonabit*, Cant. An. 10. God swēgde *Deus intonuit*, Ps. Spl. 28, 3: Ps. Lamb. 17, 14. II. of regulated, modulated sound, of speech, tone, music:—Swēgþ eádmōdnys on his stemne, Homl. Th. ii. 374, 11. *Consonantes*, đæt is samodswēgende, forđan đe hī swēgaþ mid đām fīf clypiendlīcum, Ælfc. Gr. 2; Zup. 5, 17. Fæder stemn swēgde đus cweđende, Homl. Th. i. 104, 24: ii. 242, 8. Seó stefn đīnre grētinge swēgde on mīnum eárum, 202, 17. Heora bodunge swēg swēgde geond eall, Homl. Ass. 56, 144. Swēgde *increpuerit* (*musica*), Hpt. Gl. 445, 17. Ōþ đæt đæt forme tācn undernes swēge, Anglia xiii. 432, 953. Hwylc bōc is đæt đæt ne clypige and swēge, R. Ben. 133, 6. Đē ūre stefn ǣrest swēge (*sonet*), Hymn. Surt. 7, 25. *Accentus*, đæt is swēg, on hwilcum stæfgefēge ǣlc word swēgan sceal, Ælfc. Gr. 50, 13; Zup. 290, 17. Sī swēged ōþer tācn, Anglia xiii. 380, 215. III. *to signify*:—Gregorius is Grēcisc nama, se swēigþ on Lēdenum gereorde Uigilantius, Homl. Th. ii. 118, 12. Biscop sceal beón ealle ofersceáwigende, swā swā his nama swēgþ, ii. 320, 7, 12. Swēgeþ, L. Ælfc. P. 37; Th. ii. 378, 28. [*Goth.* swōgjan *to groan*.] v. swōgan.

swēg-cræft, es; *m. The art of playing on a musical instrument*. v. swēg, II b:—Đā ongunnon ealle đa men hī herian on hyre swēgcræft . . . Apollonius cwæđ. 'Ic ongite đæt đīn dohtor gefeól on swēgcræft, ac heó næfþ hine nā wel geleornod,' Ap. Th. 16, 17–24.

swēg-dyne, -dynn, es; *m. A resounding din, crash*:—Heard gebrec, hlūd, unmǣte, swēgdynna mǣst (*the crack of doom*), Exon. Th. 59, 20; 955.

swēge; *adj. Sounding*:—Ungeswēge sang *diaphonia*, sum swēge (samswēge?) sang *canticum*, Wrt. Voc. i. 28, 35. v. ān-, ge-swēge [:—Geswēge *consona*, Wrt. Voc. ii. 134, 23. Of geswēgum *consona*, geswēgre *canora*, Anglia xiii. 132, 135, 137], swēt-, swīþ-swēge; hlūd-swēge; *adv.*

swegel, swegl, es; *n.* I. in a physical sense, *heaven, sky*:—Đætte sūđ ne norđ, be sǣm tweónum, ofer eormengrund, ōþer nǣnig, under swegles begong, sēlra nǣre, Beo. Th. 1724; B. 860: 3550; B. 1773. Under swegles gang, Andr. Kmbl. 415; An. 208: 910; An. 455. Swefan under swegles hleó, 1664; An. 834: Elen. Kmbl. 1011; El. 507: Exon. Th. 38, 13; Cri. 606: 224, 11; Ph. 374. Swegles gim, heofontungol (cf. seó sunne, Bt. 35, 1; Fox 154, 29), Met. 22, 23. Swegles gim, sunne, Exon. Th. 212, 11; Ph. 208. Swegles leóht, gimma gladost, 218, 2; Ph. 288. Swegles leóma, 204, 26; Ph. 103. Swegles tapur, 205, 18; Ph. 114. On swegle *in the sky*, 34, 30; Cri. 550. Fareþ feþrum snell swegle tōgeánes, 206, 10: Ph. 124. Under swegle *under heaven*, 31, 27; Cri. 502: 210, 15; Ph. 186: Cd. Th. 85, 13; Gen. 1414: 105, 36; Gen. 1764: Beo. Th. 2160; B. 1078. Weorđeþ his (*the phenix*) hūs onhǣted þurh hādor swegel (*cloudless sky*, cf. hādrum heofone, Met. 28, 48; or *bright sun*, v. III, and cf. hādor sægl, Andr. Kmbl. 2911; An. 1458), Exon. Th. 212, 19; Ph. 212. II. *heaven*, (a) as the abode of the Deity:—Swegles āgend, Exon. Th. 34, 17; Cri. 543. Swegles aldor, Cd. Th. 53, 17; Gen. 862: 153, 18; Gen. 2540: 170, 4; Gen. 2807: Judth. Thw. 22, 31; Jud. 88. Swegles brytan, wuldres waldend, Cd. Th. 266, 17; Sat. 23. Swægles brytta, wihta wealdend, 272, 24; Sat. 124. Swegles gǣst *the Holy Ghost*, Exon. Th. 13, 16; Cri. 203. Swegles weard, Judth. Thw. 22, 27; Jud. 80. (b) as the abode of the blessed:—Nō đæs gilpan þearf synfull sāwel đæt hyre sié swegl ongeán, Exon. Th. 449, 11; Dōm. 69. Gāstas sōhton swegles dreámas, engla ēđel, Andr. Kmbl. 1282; An. 641. Ic mæg swegles (*or under* IV?) gamen gehȳran on heofonum, Cd. Th. 42, 18; Gen. 675. Swegles leóman, Cd. Th. 286, 13; Sat. 351. Swegles leóht, 266, 27; Sat. 28. Englas feredon sōþfæste sāwle innan swegles leóht, Chr. 1065; Erl. 198, 9. In swegles wuldre, Judth. Thw. 26, 26; Jud. 345. Gesǣlgum on swegle, Exon. Th. 101, 17; Cri. 1660: 137, 10; Gū. 557. Swegle benumene, 139, 23; Gū. 597. Sigorleán in swegle, Elen. Kmbl. 1242; El. 623. Đa đe swegl būan, Cd. Th. 6, 2; Gen. 82. On swegl faran, Exon. Th. 32, 15; Cri. 513. III. *the sun* (but can *swegel* here = *segel*, *sigel* (q. v.)? cf. swegl = segl *a sail*, Cd. Th. 184, 10; Exod. 105: 182, 26; Exod. 81):—Heofontorht swegl gescyndeþ under foldan fæþm, farende tungol, Exon. Th. 351, 1; Sch. 73. Swegl hāte scān blāc ofer burgsalo,

182, 3; Gû. 1304. Swegel byþ hâtost (on sumera), Menol. Fox 474; Gn. C. 7. IV. *music* (?). v. swegel-horn:—Ðǽr (*in heaven*) wæs singal sang and swegles gong . . . Englas heredon hâlgan stefne Dryhten, dreám wæs on hyhte, Andr. Kmbl. 1738; An. 871. Eádige ðǽr sittaþ mid swegle, Cd. Th. 305, 17; Sat. 648. v. Grmm. D. M. 708.

swegel-befealden; *adj. Heaven-surrounded, with heaven around*:—Háfaþ wuldres bearn his seolfes seld sweglbefalden (-healden, Th.), laðaþ ûs ðider tô leóhte, Cd. Th. 301, 28; Sat. 588.

swegel-beorht; *adj. Heaven-bright*:—Sweglbeorht sunne, Exon. Th. 174, 33; Gû. 1187. Cf. swegel-torht, heofon-beorht.

swegel-bôsm, es; *m. The interior of heaven, heaven*:—Hê biþ â rîce ofer heofenstôlas . . . sweglbôsmas heóld; ða wǽron gesette wuldres bearnum, Cd. Th. 1, 18; Gen. 9.

swegel-candel[l], e; *f. The candle of the sky, the sun*:—Ǽr ðæs beácnes cyme, sweglcondelle, Exon. Th. 205, 5; Ph. 108. Cf. heofon-candel.

swegel-cyning, es; *m. The king of heaven*:—Ðæt ic wuldres God sêce, swegelcyning, Exon. Th. 167, 4; Gû. 1055. Sweglcyning, Cd. Th. 160, 30; Gen. 2658. Cf. heofon-cyning.

swegel-dreám, es; *m. Heavenly joy*:—Ufancundes engles of swegldreámum word, Exon. Th. 169, 21; Gû. 1098. Cheruphim and Seraphim on swegeldreámum, Andr. Kmbl. 1439; An. 720. Swâse swegldreámas gê (*the good at the day of judgment*) geseón môsten, Exon. Th. 82, 35; Cri. 1349. Cf. heofon-dreám.

swegel-horn, es; *m. Some kind of musical instrument*:—Sueglhorn *sambucus*, Wrt. Voc. ii. 119, 56. Swegelhorna *sambucorum, simphoniarum* (cf. simfonia, lignum concavum, Wrt. Voc. ii. 73, 60) i. *citharistarum*, Hpt. Gl. 445, 19. [Cf. *Goth.* swigljôn *to pipe, play* the flute; swiglja *a piper, flute-player*: *O. H. Ger.* swegala *fistula, tibia, barbita, chelys, sistrum, calamus*; swegalari *tibicen, fidicen*; swegil-bein *cornus tibia* (*a wind instrument*, Grff. 3, 129).] v. swegel IV, *and next word*.

swegel-râd, e; *f. Music* (?):—Scyl wæs hearpe, hlûde hlynede, hleóþor dynede, sweglrâd swinsade, Exon. Th. 353, 47; Reim. 29. [Cf. *O. H. Ger.* swegal-sang *music of the flute*.] v. preceding word.

swegel-torht; *adj. Heaven-bright*:—Swegeltorht sunne, Met. 29, 24. Beorht gewât sunne swegeltorht tô sete glîdan, Andr. Kmbl. 2497; An. 1250. Tunglu sweglforht, Exon. Th. 335, 31; Gn. Ex. 41. Wuldorfæstan wîc, sîd and sweglforht, Cd. Th. 2, 32; Gen. 28. Swegeltorhtan seld, 6, 27; Gen. 95. Cf. heofon-torht.

swegel-wered; *adj. Clothed with heavenly brightness*:—Siððan morgenleóht, sunne swegelwered sûþan scîneþ, Beo. Th. 1216; B. 606. Cf. scîr-wered.

swegel-wuldor, es; *n. The glory of heaven*:—Ðæt wit unc in ðam êcan gefeán on sweglwuldre geseón môstun, Exon. Th. 173, 13; Gû. 1160. Cf. heofon-wuldor.

swegel-wundor, es; *n. A heavenly wonder*, or *a wondrous sound* (?). v. swegel, IV:—Se burgstede wæs gefylled swêtum stencum and sweglwundrum, eádges yrfestôl engla hleóðres *the dwelling-place was filled with sweet odours and with wondrous music* (?), *the blessed one's home with the voice of angels*, Exon. Th. 181, 13; Gû. 1292.

swêgend-lîc; *adj. Vocal, vowel*:—*I* and *u* beóþ âwende tô *consonantes*, gif hî beóþ tôgædere gesette oððe mid ôðrum swêgendlîcum, Ælfc. Gr. 2; Zup. 6, 15.

sweger, swegr, e; *f. A mother-in-law*:—Sueger *socrus*, Wrt. Voc. ii. 120, 68. Sweger, i. 52, 8. Sweger, swegr, Ælfc. Gr. 11; Zup. 79, 18. Swegr (suegir, Lind.) on hyre snore, and snoru on hyre swegere (swegre, MS. A., Rush.: suoegir, Lind.), Lk. Skt. 12, 53. Sca Maria is Godfæder snoru and Godes suna môdur and hâligra sâuwla sweger, Shrn. 118, 7. Sweger *socrum*, Wrt. Voc. ii. 72, 51. Ðâ geseah hê Petres swegre (swægre, Rush.: suêr ł his wîfes môdor, Lind.) licgende, Mt. Kmbl. 8, 14. Snore ongên hyre swegre (swegran, MS. A.: swêr, Lind.), 10, 35. Swegere, Deut. 27, 23. [*O. H. Ger.* swigar: *Ger.* schwieger-mutter. Cf. *Goth.* swaihrô.]

swêg-hleóþor, es; *m. Sound, voice*:—Swêghleóþor (*rugitus magnus*, v. Anglia vi. 243) cymeþ, wôþa wynsumast, þurh ðæs wildres mûð; æfter ðære stefne stenc ût cymeþ of ðam wongstede, Exon. Th. 358, 8; Pa. 42. Swêg[h]leóþres geswin *the melody of vocal music*, 207, 5; Ph. 137.

swêging, e; *f. A sounding, sound, noise, roaring* (of the sea, etc.), *clanging* (of implements, etc.):—Sûeguingisso (swêgung ł swêgnisso ?) sǽs *sonitus maris*, Lk. Skt. 21, 25. Swêgincga beátendra slecgea *sonitus tundentium malleorum*, Coll. Monast. Th. 31, 7. v. swêgan.

swegl. v. swegel.

swegle; *adj. Bright as the sun, splendid, brilliant*, (1) in a physical sense:—Ðæt ic sceáwige swegle searogimmas, Beo. Th. 5491; B. 2749. (2) metaphorical, *celestial*:—Hê lîfes weg gesôhte swegle dreámas (cf. swegel-dreám), beorhtne boldwelan, Apostls. Kmbl. 64; Ap. 32. [*O. Sax.* swigli (sunnun lioht).]

swegle; *adv. Brightly, brilliantly, splendidly*, (1) in a physical sense:—Ðonne sió reáde rôd ofer ealle swegle scîneþ on ðære sunnan gyld, Exon. Th. 68, 13; Cri. 1103. Scîneþ sunna swegle hât, sôna gecerreþ îsmere ǽnlîc on his âgen gecynd (cf. ðæt îs for ðære sunna[n] scîman tô his âgnum gecynde weorþe, Bt. 39, 3; Fox 216, 1), Met. 28, 61. Sumor swegle hât, Exon. Th. 338, 13; Gn. Ex. 78. (2) metaphorical:—Hý môtan his (*Christ's*) ætwiste brûcan, swegle gehyrste weorðian Waldend (cf. ðonne scînaþ ða rihtwîsan swâ swâ sunne on hyra Fæder rîce, Mt. 13, 43), Exon. 24, 32; Cri. 393.

swegles æppel. Cockayne suggests *beetle nut*, Lchdm. ii. 32, 2: 36, 5: 56, 10: 66, 8: 308, 9, 22; and see glossaries to vols. ii, iii.

swêg-lîc; *adj. Sonorous*:—Mid swêglîcre stefne *sonora voce*, Anglia xiii. 412, 675.

swegl-siðe, Cd. Th. 184, 10; Exod. 105. v. segl, I a.

swegne *a net*. v. segne.

swegran *in* ge-swegran *cousins*; consobrimi i. ex sorore et fratre, vel ex duabus sororibus, Wrt. Voc. ii. 134, 18.

-swêgsumlîce. v. ge-swêgsumlîce.

swelan; *p.* swæl, *pl.* swǽlon. I. *to burn* (intrans.), *perish with heat*:—On fýrbaðe swelaþ sǽfiscas sundes getwǽfde, wǽgdeóra gehwylc wêrig swelteþ, Exon. Th. 61, 19; Cri. 987. II. *to burn* (of a hot sensation):—Sió wund ongon, ðe him se eorðdraca ǽr geworhte, swelan and swellan, Beo. Th. 5419; B. 2713. [Cf. *O. H. Ger.* suilizo *calor*; suilizôn *calere, arere*.] v. for-swelan; swǽlan.

swelc. v. swilc.

swelca, an; *m. A pustule, blister*:—Swelca *pustula*, Wrt. Voc. i. 19, 19. Cf. swellan.

swelgan; *p.* swealh, *pl.* swulgon; *pp.* swolgen (*with acc.* or *inst.* (*dat.*)) *To swallow*. I. in a physical sense, (a) of taking food, etc., by living creatures:—Se draca hig swealh, and hig eft âspâw, L. E. I. prm.; Th. ii. 398, 40. Hê gefêng slǽpendne rinc, bât bânlocan, synsnǽdum swealh, Beo. Th. 1490; B. 743. Hê (*a book-moth*) ðâm wordum swealg, Exon. Th. 432, 15; Rä. 48, 6. Laures ceówe and ðæt seáw swelge, Lchdm. ii. 230, 4. Syle ðam cilde swelgan, i. 350, 14. Swylgende (-fende, Wrt.) drenc *a potion to be gulped down*; catapodia (= καταπότιον), Wrt. Voc. i. 20, 22. (b) of absorption or reception by inanimate things, *to swallow, take in, drink, absorb*:—Swâ sond rên swylgþ, Bt. 12; Fox 36, 13. Seó eorþe ðæt wæter swilgþ, 33, 4; Fox 130, 6. Swelgeþ, Exon. Th. 439, 27; Rä. 59, 10. Eorðe wældreóre swealh hâlge of handum dînum, Cd. Th. 62, 19; Gen. 1016: 60, 22; Gen. 985. Eorðe swealh Sethes lîce *the earth closed over Seth's body*, 69, 32; Gen. 1144. Heofon rêce swealg (sealg, MS.) *the smoke mounted into the air*, Beo. Th. 6292; B. 3156. Fugles wyn (*the pen*) beámtelge (*ink*) swealg, Exon. Th. 408, 9; Rä. 27, 9. Ic (*a horn*) windesceal swelgan of sumes bôsme, 395, 29; Rä. 15, 15. Hwîlum ic (*a fortress*) swelgan onginne beadowǽpnum, 399, 7; Rä. 18, 7. (b 1) figuratively:—Ðonne lîf and deáð sâwlum swelgaþ (cf. ðonne heofon and hel fira feorum fylde weorþeþ, 97, 17–20; Cri. 1592), 98, 7; Cri. 1604. II. figuratively, *to take in to the mind, accept, imbibe* (wisdom):—Swelhþ *affluit* (the passage to which the gloss belongs is Prov. 3, 13, where the Vulgate has: Beatus homo . . . qui affluit prudentia), Kent. Gl. 41. Ðâ ðâm wordum swealg brego *when the prince had heard those words*, Exon. Th. 196, 25; Az. 179. Hâliges lâre synnige ne swulgon, ðeáh hê sôðra swâ feala tâcna gecýðde, Andr. Kmbl. 1419; An. 710. Wile se Waldend, ðæt wê wîsdôm â snyttrum swelgen, Exon. Th. 147, 32; Gû. 736. III. with the idea of violence or destruction, *to devour* (lit. or fig.), *to consume, engulf*:—Ic swelge wuda and wætre, Exon. Th. 499, 20; Rä. 88, 18. Lîg eal þigeþ eorþan ǽhtgestreón, grǽdig swelgeþ londes frætwe, 232, 16; Ph. 507. Swâ swylgþ seó gîtsung ða dreósendan welan ðisses middangeardes, Bt. 12; Fox 36, 13. Ða ðe swelgaþ folc mîn *qui devorant plebem meam*, Ps. Spl. 52, 5. Wælstreámas werodum swelgaþ, Cd. Th. 78, 31; Gen. 1301. Grundas swelgaþ Godes andsacan, Exon. Th. 97, 21; Cri. 1594. Nymþe lîges fæðm swulge, Beo. Th. 1568; B. 782. [*O. L. Ger.* far-swelgan *absorbere*: *O. H. Ger.* swelgan *glutire*: *Icel.* svelgja *to swallow*.] v. for-, ge-, of-swelgan.

-swelge *in* ge-swelge[:—Geswelge *barathrum*, Hpt. Gl. 421, 30. Geswelgum *charybdibus, voraginibus*, 513, 29. Cf. swelwhe of a water or of a grownde *vorago*, Prompt. Parv. 482. *Icel.* svelgr; *m. a whirlpool*.]

-swelge. v. grund-swelge.

swelgend, es; *m. A voracious person, a glutton, debauchee*:—Ðes man is swelgend *ecce homo devorator*, Lk. Skt. 7, 34. Se swelgend, Alexander, Ors. 3, 7; Swt. 120, 16. v. swelgere.

swelgend, e; *f.*, *but also* es; *m. n. A place which swallows up* (lit. or fig.), *a very deep place, an abyss, a gulf, whirlpool*:—Ðýlæs hî forswelge sió swelgend ðære upâhæfenesse *ipso elationis suae barathro devorantur*, Past. 57, 3; Swt. 439, 3. Seó grundleáse swelgend (gîtsunge) *vorans rapacitas*, Bt. 7, 4; Fox 22, 32. Swelgend *vorago*, Wrt. Voc. i. 54, 37: Kent. Gl. 449: Scint. 117, 9. Sweliend *barathrum*, Hpt. Gl. 529, 26. Swyliendes *voraginis*, 421, 31. Swelgendes, Anglia xiii. 28, 23. Swelgendi *voragine*, Wrt. Voc. ii. 124, 14. West tô ðære swelgende; ðonne fram ðære swelgende, Cod. Dip. Kmbl. v. 281, 29. Tô swelgenc ; ðanne fram swelgende, ii. 73, 27. Andlang brôces on ðæt swelgend, iii. 460, 5. Andlang streámes on ðone sweliende, of ðæm sweliende, 464, 27. v. ge-swelgend.

swelgendness, e; *f. A gulf, whirlpool*:—Swelgendnessum *carybdibus*, Wrt. Voc. ii. 18, 69. v. swelgness.

swelgere, es; *m. A glutton*:—Ic ne eom swâ micel swelgere ðæt ic ealle cynn metta on ânre gereordinge etan mǽge *non sum tam vorax, ut omnia genera ciborum in una refectione edere possim*, Coll. Monast. Th. 34, 35. [*O. H. Ger.* swelgari *glutto*: *Ger.* schwelger.] v. swelgend.

swelgness, e; *f. A whirlpool, gulf*:—Swelgnessum *carybdibus*, Wrt. Voc. ii. 86, 11. v. swelgendness.

sweliend, swell. v. swelgend, ge-swel.

swellan; *p.* sweall, *pl.* swullon; *p.* swollen *To swell*:—Wiđ wunda đe swellaþ, Lchdm. iii. 86, 16. Gif sino gescrince and æfter đon swelle, ii. 68, 1. Gif fôt ođđe scancan swellan, iii. 38, 21. Sió wund ongon swelan and swellan, Beo. Th. 5419; B. 2713. Swellende blæddran *vesicae turgentes*, Ex. 9, 9, 10. Wiþ ǽlcre yfelre swellendre wǽtan, Lchdm. ii. 6, 26. Swellende yfele swilas, 264, 12. [*O. L. Ger. O. H. Ger.* swellan *tumere, turgere, obturgescere*: *Icel.* svella. Cf. *Goth.* uf-swalleins *inflatio*.] v. â-, ge- (Lchdm. ii. 46, 9: 200, 22: 202, 5), tô-swellan.

swelling, e; *f. A swelling*, used of a sail swelled out by the wind:—Gesión brecan ofer bæđweg brimwudu, snyrgan under swellingum (cf. snel under segle, Andr. Kmbl. 1009; An. 505), Elen. Kmbl. 489; El. 245.

sweltan, swyltan, swiltan; *p.* swealt, *pl.* swulton; *pp.* swolten *To die* a natural or a violent death:—Swelte ic (*morior*) hēr on lande, Deut. 4, 22. Wǽgdeóra gehwylc swelteþ, Exon. Th. 61, 22; Cri. 988. Swylteþ, 385, 33; Rä. 4, 54: 419, 13; Rä. 38, 5. Ne swylteþ *non obierit*, Wrt. Voc. ii. 88, 35. Swylt *moritur*, Jn. Skt. 21, 23. Hē swelt, Blickl. Homl. 245, 11. Gē sweltaþ, 8, 21. Ealle men sweltaþ, Bt. 18, 4; Fox 68, 13. Hí ne swyltaþ, Blickl. Homl. 47, 1. Hē swealt, Cd. Th. 70, 15; Gen. 1153. Swealt (sweolt, Thw.), Num. 20, 1. Hí swulton, Homl. Th. i. 84, 6: Cd. Th. 207, 10; Exod. 464. Đæt ân man swelte for folce, Jn. Skt. 11, 50. Đæt hyt wǽre beteré, đæt ân man swulte, 18, 14. Đæt hē swungen wǽre ôþþæt hē swylte, Blickl. Homl. 193, 4. Hwí lǽddest đū ūs đæt wē swulton on đisum wēstene, Num. 21, 5. Ic mæg sweltan blíđelíce *laetus moriar*, Gen. 46, 30: Mt. Kmbl. 26, 35: Ex. 10, 28. Sceal fǽge sweltan, Exon. Th. 335, 2; Gn. Ex. 27. Swyltan, Blickl. Homl. 59, 30. Se man scyle deádlíce swyltan (swiltan, MS. C.), Wulfst. 5, 9. Sweltende *obeuntem*, Wrt. Voc. ii. 64, 54. Beón swyltende, Blickl. Homl. 75, 33. ¶ *to die* by or of something, where the cause of death is expressed by a case or by a preposition with a noun:—Ne swelte ic mid sâre, Ps. Th. 117, 17. Đū þurh deóra gripe deáþe sweltest, Exon. Th. 250, 11; Jul. 125. Gē sweltaþ deáđe, Cd. Th. 224, 28; Dan. 143. Draca morđre swealt, Beo. Th. 1789; B. 892: 5558; B. 2782. Hē forneáh hungre swealt, Ors. 4, 6; Swt. 170, 30. Hié hungre swultan, Blickl. Homl. 79, 15. Monige for hiora wundum swultan, Nar. 16, 9. Heora mænige mâne swultan, Ps. Th. 77, 30. Tō đam đe hē deáđe swelte, L. Alf. 13; Th. i. 48, 2. Đū scealt deáđe sweltan *morte morieris*, Gen. 2, 17: L. Alf. 14; Th. i. 48, 4. Ic sceal æt đē sweltan deáđe, Homl. Th. ii. 308, 27. Wundum sweltan, Byrht. Th. 140, 25; By. 293. Hí ondrǽdaþ him đæt hí sceolan swyltan for đam hūsle, L. Ælf. E.; Th. ii. 392, 3. ¶ *to die* to anything, *become dead to, have no further concern* with:—Đū scealt sweltan synna and Criste lybban, Homl. Skt. i. 3, 592. [*Laym. O. E. Homl.* swelten: *Orm.* swelltenn: *Chauc. Piers P.* swelte: *Goth.* swiltan: *O. Sax.* sweltan: *Icel.* svelta *to die*; svelta hungri *to starve*: *Dan.* sulte *to starve*; sulten *hungry*.] v. â-, for-, ge-sweltan.

sweltend-líc; *adj. Ready to die, about to die*:—Se wæs sweltendlíc *erat moriturus* (*ready to die*, A.V.), Lk. Skt. 7, 2. Wambe sweltendlíces flǽsces *uentrem moriture carnis*, Scint. 53, 2.

swemman; *p.* de *To cause to swim, to bathe, wash.* [*Ger.* schwemmen *to water, wash, float*: *Dan.* svømme (heste) *to take* (*horses*) *into the water*.] v. be-swemman; swimman.

swenc, es; *m. Trial, tribulation, affliction*:—In niđrung ł in suoenc deáđes *in damnationem mortis*, Lk. Skt. Lind. 24, 20. On swencum (suoenccum, Lind.: geswincum, W. S.) ł costungum mínum *in temtationibus meis*, Rush. 22, 28. In suoencum *in tribulationibus*, Rtl. 184, 4. v. ge-swenc.

swencan; *p.* te; *pp.* swenced, swenct (cf. *swinkt* = wearied, Comus v. 293) *To cause* a person *to labour, to cause trouble to* a person (a) where no good is implied, *to harass, vex, afflict, distress*:—Ic swencu hió *adfligam illos*, Ps. Surt. 17, 39. Hwí swencst đū đis folc . . . Pharaon swencþ đín folc *cur afflixisti populum istum?* . . . *Pharao afflixit populum tuum*, Ex. 5, 22-23. Ælc deáþlíc man swencþ hine selfne mid manigfealdum ymbhogum *omnis mortalium cura, quam multiplicium studiorum labor exercet*, Bt. 24, 1; Fox 80, 6. Eów nǽnig wiht ne deraþ ne ne swenceþ, Blickl. Homl. 239, 12. Suenceth *defatiget*, Wrt. Voc. ii. 106, 3. *Defatiget, lassat*, swenceþ, *flagellat*, 138, 16. Đa đe mē swencaþ *qui tribulant me*, Ps. Th. 12, 5. Hwí swenctest đū (*afflixisti*) đínne þeów? Num. 11, 11. Man swencte đæt earme folc đe on đâm scipon lâgon, Chr. 999; Erl. 135, 32. Hine wundra fela swe[n]cte on sunde, Beo. Th. 3024; B. 1510. Đa werigan gâstas đe mē swenctan and drycton *qui me premebant spiritus maligni*, Bd. 3, 11; S. 536, 37. On đínre hâtheortnesse ne swenc mē *ne in furore tuo corripias me*, Ps. Th. 6, 1. Beorge hē đæt hē âwōh ne befō, đý læs đe hine mon swence swâ hē ōđerne man þohte, L. Eth. ii. 9; Th. i. 290, 8. Þeáh hine se wind woruldearfoþa swíđe swence, Met. 7, 50. Đý læs đe mon unmihtigne man tō feor and tō lange for his âgenan swencte *lest a man of small means should be made to toil too far and too long for his own*, L. Eth. ii. 9; Th. i. 290, 4. Ne sceal nân mon siócne monnan gesârgodne swencan, ac hine mon sceolde lǽdan tō đam lǽce, Bt. 38, 7; Fox 210, 20. Hē (*William I*) lēt castelas wyrcean and earme men swíđe swencean, Chr. 1086; Erl. 222, 21. Đū đec sylfne ne þearft swíþor swencan *you need not trouble yourself any more*, Exon. Th. 245, 19; Jul. 47. Wítebendum swencan, Andr. Kmbl. 218; An. 109. Perseus wæs ealne đone geár Rōmâne swíþe swencende, Ors. 4, 11; Swt. 208, 13. Forhwon sindun gē swæncende (*molesti*) đam wífe? Mt. Kmbl. Rush. 26, 10. Fram unclǽnum gâste swenced beón *ab immundo spiritu vexari*, Bd. 3, 11; S. 536, 11. Mid đa âdle swenced *affectus incommodo*, 4, 31; S. 610, 21. Swâ gewinnfullícum fyrdum swencte beón *tam laboriosis expeditionibus fatigari*, 1, 12; S. 481, 4: 2, 18; S. 520, 36. (b) where a good result is intended, *to mortify, chasten*:—Đa sylfan, đe hí mid đâm wítum đreágeaþ and swenceaþ (*adfligunt*), lufiaþ eác, Bd. 1, 27; S. 490, 18. Hí firenlustas forberaþ . . . swencaþ hí sylfe, sâwle frætwaþ, Exon. Th. 150, 13; Gū. 778. Đa lâreówas sceolan heora âgenne líchoman swencean on forhæfdnesse, Blickl. Homl. 81, 6. [*O. E. Homl. A. R. Laym.* swenchen: *Orm.* swennkenn, swennchenn: *O. H. Ger.* swenchen *verberare*]. v. ge-swencan; swincan.

swencedness. v. ge-swencedness.

sweng, es; *m. A blow, stroke*:—Sweng *ictus*, Ælfc. Gr. 11; Zup. 79, 6. Sweng ođđe cnyssung *ictus*, 43; Zup. 255, 3. Eádweard ânne slōg swíþe mid his swurde, swenges ne wyrnde, Byrht. Th. 135, 15; By. 118. Hē hond swenge ne ofteáh, Beo. Th. 3045; B. 1520. Him for swenge swât ǽdrum sprong, 5924; B. 2966: 5365; B. 2686. Ic mē gūđbordes sweng gebearh, Cd. Th. 163, 5; Gen. 2693. Weras him ondrēdon for đære dǽde Drihtnes handa, sweng (*the stroke*, i. e. *the punishment threatened if Sara were not returned to Abraham*), 161, 26; Gen. 2671. Iacob swilt þrowode đurg stenges sweng, Apostls. Kmbl. 143; Ap. 72. Hē feorhwunde hleát sweordes swengum, Beo. Th. 4761; B. 2386. Bord oft onfēng ýđa swengas *oft the vessel's side received the billows' blows*, Elen. Kmbl. 478; El. 239. [In later English the word is used in a metaphorical sense similar to that of *stroke* in modern English, and may be compared with *M. H. Ger.* swanc, swang *a trick*: *Ger.* schwank: cf. also *Ger.* streich = *trick*. To wrastlen ȝein þes deofles swenges, A. R. 80, 8. Ȝef ha etstonden wulleđ mine unwreste wrenches ant mine swikele swenges, wrestlin ha moten wiđ ham seoluen, Marh. 14, 12. Ȝif tweie men goþ to wrastlinge . . . and þe on can swenges swiþe fele . . . and þe oþer ne can sweng bute ane, O. and N. 795. Cf. *O. H. Ger.* swanch *swinging, stroke*: *M. H. Ger.* swanc, swang: *Ger.* schwang.] v. feorh-, heađu-, heoru-, hete-, wæl-sweng.

swengan; *p.* de *To cause to swing, to cause rapid movement, to swing, fling, dash, strike*:—Đâ âhleóp ân leó of đæs eorđscræfes þýstrum and hió swengde on hine . . . Đâ eode uncer hlâford sylf in đæt scræf đa swengde sió lió sōna forđ and forswealh hine *then a lion ran out from the darkness of the cavern and dashed on to him . . . Then our lord himself went into the cave; then the lion dashed out at once and swallowed him up*, Shrn. 43, 9-18. Swengende *discutiens*, Wrt. Voc. ii. 141, 43. [He smat hine sare . . . æft he him to (to him, 2nd MS.) sweinde . . . dunt he him ȝef þane þridde, Laym. 8183. His sweord he sweinde bi his side, 21138. Swengeđ of þa hafden, 22839. He sweinde ham adun into helle grunde, A. R. 280, 13. Breid up þene rode stef and sweng him aȝean (*strike at him*), 290, 18. Þe drake rahte ut his tunge and swende hire in (*swung her into his mouth*) ant forswalh into his wide wombe, Marh. 10, 19. Swengyn or schakyn as menne done clothys *excucio*, Prompt. Parv. 482. *Goth.* af-swaggwjan *to cause to waver, to shake one's confidence, make desperate*.] v. â-, fram-, tô-swengan; swingan.

swenge (?); *adj. Heavy, slothful.* v. swangor (b).

sweocol. v. swicol.

sweofot, es; *n. Sleep*:—Hē Hrōđgâres heorđgeneátas slōh on sweofote, slǽpende frǽt, Beo. Th. 3166; B. 1581: 4579; B. 2295. Hē (*the panther*) þreó nihta fæc swefeþ on sweofote, slǽpe gebiesgad, Exon. Th. 358, 1; Pa. 39. Đonne hē selþ gecorenum his swefetu (cf. *the use of* swefen *in pl.*) ł slǽp *cum dederit dilectis suis somnum*, Ps. Lamb. 126, 3. [Þe king læi on sweuete, Laym. 17773. On sweouete, 17802. Ne þuhte hit ꝥ ha weren deade, ah ꝥ ha slepten a sweouete *dormientes potius quam extinctos putares*, Kath. 1427.] v. swefan.

sweogian. v. swigian.

sweogode glosses *praevaluit*, Ps. Spl. 51, 7, *a mistake* (?) *for* strongode.

Sweó-land, es; *n. The land of the Swedes, Sweden*, Ors. 1, 1; Swt. 19, 2. v. Sweó-ríce, -þeód.

sweoloþ, swoloþ (swōloþ?), es; *m. Heat, burning*:—Swolođ *aestus* vel *cauma*, Wrt. Voc. i. 53, 41. Swolođ (swalođ, MS. J.: sweoli, MS. W.) *cauma*, Ælfc. Gl. Zup. 306, 15. Đes swolaþ (swoli, MS. W.) *hoc cauma*, Ælfc. Gr. 9, 1; Zup. 33, 12 note. Swoleđe *caumate*, Hpt. Gl. 482, 48: 495, 22. Hēt Hildeburh æt Hnæfes âde hire selfre suna sweolođe befæstan, bânfatu bærnan and on bǽl dōn, Beo. Th. 2235; B. 1115. v. swelan, *and next word.*

sweoloþa, an; *m. Heat, burning*:—Hē swâ swíþe swǽtte swâ hē in swoloþan middes sumeres wǽre *quasi in media aestatis caumate sudaverit*, Bd. 3, 19; S. 549, 30. Mid hǽtan and mid swoluđan *ardore et aestu*, Deut. 28, 22. v. preceding word.

sweolung (?), e; *f. Burning, inflammation:*—Biþ micel āþundenes and fefer mid sweolunga (sweopunga, MS. v. note on passage) ōmena *with inflammation from corrupt humours*, Lchdm. ii. 204, 25.

Sweón; *pl. The Swedes:*—Burgendan habbaþ Sweón be norþan him ... Sweón habbaþ be súþan him đone sǽs earm, Ors. 1, 1; Swt. 16, 31–34. Đā Sweón heafdon weallstōwe geweald, Chr. 1025; Erl. 163, 11. Sacu Sweóna and Geáta, Beo. Th. 4936; B. 2472: (Swona, MS.), 5885; B. 2946: 5908; B. 2958. Ic wæs mid Sweóm, Exon. Th. 322, 4; Víd. 58: 320, 19; Víd. 31. Đās land hȳraþ tō Sweón, Ors. 1, 1; Swt. 20, 4. [*Icel.* Svíar. *The Latin form is* Suiones *in Tacitus, later* Sueones.] v. Sweó-land, -rīce, -þeód.

sweopung. v. sweolung.

sweór, swehor, es; *m.* I. *a father-in-law:*—Sueór *vetellus*, Txts. 106, 1099. Su[eó]r *socer*, 97, 1878. Sweór, Wrt. Voc. i. 52, 7: 72, 51: Ælfc. Gr. 8; Zup. 27, 13. Se wæs Caiphas sweór (sueór, Lind.), Jn. Skt. 18, 13: Gen. 38, 13. Sweór, swiór, Bt. 10; Fox 28, 13. Hǽđne wǽron begen, sweór and āþum, Exon. Th. 246, 22; Jul. 65. Đā sende heó tō hire sweóre (*ad socerum suum*), Gen. 38, 25: 30, 25. Obab his sweór (*cognatum*), Past. 41, 5; Swt. 304, 9. Suehoras, sueóras *vitelli*, Txts. 104, 1062. Wæs Rōmeburg on fruman gehālgod mid brōđor blōde and mid sweóra (*the fathers of the Sabine women who were taken as wives by the Romans*), Ors. 2, 2; Swt. 66, 5. II. the word is also used to translate *consobrinus; a cousin:*—Sueór *consobrinus*, Wrt. Voc. ii. 104, 83. Gesweóras *consobrini*, sweór *consobrinus, filius patruelis*, 134, 17–20. Sw[e]ór *consobrinus*, 15, 2. [*Goth.* swaihra *father-in-law: O. H. Ger.* sweher, swēr *socer, levir: Ger.* schwäher.] v. sweger, suhtriga.

sweor, swer, swyr, es; *m. f. A column, pillar* (lit. or fig.), *that which is shaped like a pillar:*—Swer *columna*, Wrt. Voc. i. 26, 32: 81, 15. Ufeweard swer *epistilia*, ii. 30, 29. Đū eart leóhtes swer, Blickl. Homl. 141, 1. Drihten swutelode him đone weg on dæg þurh swert tācn on sweres gelīcnysse, and on niht swilce ān byrnende swer him fōr beforan, Ex. 13, 21: Homl. Th. ii. 196, 8. Mid đȳ fȳrenan sweore on nieht and on dæg mid đȳ sweore đæs wolcnes, Past. 41, 5; Swt. 304, 7. On swere (swiorum, MS. T.) *in columna* (*nubis*), Ps. Spl. 98, 7. Þurh wolcnes swyr, Ps. Th. 98, 7. Hē geseah swer standan, and ofer đone swer ǽrne onlīcnesse, Blickl. Homl. 239, 21. Greáte swā stǽnene sweras *uastitudine columnarum*, Nar. 36, 13. Hī hēton hine standan betwux twām stǽnenum swerum: on đām twām swerum stōd đæt hūs geworht. And Samson ... gelǽhte đa sweras, Jud. 16, 25–29. Đæt gēr is underwyrđed mid þrīm swerum, đa synd đus gecīged, id.' and non. and kl.', Anglia viii. 301, 37. Swyras (swioras, MS. T.: sweras, MS. C.) *columnas*, Ps. Spl. 74, 3. Sweoras gata *seras portarum*, Ps. Spl. T. 147, 2. Hire swyre *columnas ejus*, Ps. Th. 74, 3. Sweras unlytle, stapulas, Andr. Kmbl. 2985; An. 1495. [Sweor *columna*, Wrt. Voc. i. 92, 55.] [Grimm, R.A. 370, gives from a Swiss source 'an ein *schwiren* binden.']

sweora, swira, swyra, swura, an; *m.* I. *a neck:*—Sweora *collum*, Wrt. Voc. ii. 16, 51: *cervix*, 52. Foreweard sweora *capitium*, 45. Sweora *vel* swura *collum*, i. 43, 36. Swira *collum*, 283, 2: *cervex*, 3. Swyra *collum*, 64, 65: Soul Kmbl. 218; Seel. 111. Swiora smæl, Exon. Th. 486, 15; Rä. 72, 15. Đā heó đrycced wæs mid sāre hire sweoran đæt heó oft cwǽde: 'Ic wāt đæt ic be gewyrhtum on mīnum sweoran bere đa byrþenne đysse ādle' *quia cum praefato dolore maxillae sive colli premeretur solita sit dicere: 'scio, quia merito in collo pondus languoris porto*, Bd. 4, 19; S. 589, 22–26. Swile on hire sweoran *tumorem sub maxilla*, S. 588, 43. Tō his suiran getīged, Past. 2; Swt. 31, 18. Tō hys swyran (sweoran, MS. A.: suire, Lind.: swira, Rush.) gecnytt, Mt. Kmbl. 18, 6. Swuran (sweoran, MS. A.: suiro, Lind.: swira, Rush.), Mk. Skt. 9, 42. Swioran *ceruice*, Lchdm. i. lxx, 9. Swiran *ceutro* (cf. *cervellum*, i. *ceutrum* brægen, Wrt. Voc. ii. 130, 31. *Ceutrum* þrotbolla, 131, 1), lxxi, 1. Underlūtan mid eówrum swiran đæt deáþlīcne geoc, Bt. 19; Fox 68, 26: Met. 10, 19. Đeáh hē him đone stīđan swioran (swiran, Hatt. MS.) fortrǽde, Past. 33; Swt. 228, 9. Hē wȳscte đæt ealle Rōmāne hæfden ǽnne sweoran (*unam cervicem*), Ors. 6, 3; Swt. 256, 27: Judth. Thw. 23, 5; Jud. 106. Hié sendon rāp on his sweoran (swyran, 20), Blickl. Homl. 241, 24. Is ymb đone sweoran (*the neck of the phenix*) beága beorhtast, Exon. Th. 219, 10; Ph. 305. Ōþ mannes swuran, Blickl. Homl. 245, 33: Gen. 41, 42: Deut. 28, 48. Swiran (swioran) *cladam*, Lchdm. i. lxx, 1 (see note). On đa swyran sīnra þegena, Met. 9, 56. II. of land, *a hause* (as in Esk *Hause*), *a col;* cf. ge-sweoru:—Dūna swioran *juga*, Wrt. Voc. ii. 48, 18. [*Sware, swire*, the neck, the declination of a mountain near the summit; the most level spot between two hills, Jamieson. Cf. *Icel.* Swīri, the local name of a neck-shaped ridge in western Iceland.] III. of water, *the part where the distance between opposite shores is least:*—Ofer swira sǽs (cf. ofer đære sǽs mūđan, W. S.) *trans fretum maris*, Mk. Skt. Lind. Rush. 5, 1. On pūles sweran, Cod. Dip. Kmbl. iii. 97, 5. [Swiere (*rimes with* (wilde) diere), O. E. Homl. ii. 224, 146. Swore (*rimes with* (wilde) dore), i. 169, 144. Sweore, 49, 28: A. R. 394, 19. Swire, 58, 7: Marh. 9, 8. Swure (swere, 2nd MS.), Laym. 4012. Sweore (swere, 2nd MS.), 26565. Sweore, swore (*rimes with* deore, dore *beast*), O. and N. 1125. Sweore, swore, suere, 73. Suere (*rimes with* ouerdere), R. Glouc. 389, 22. Swire (*rimes with* sire), Havel. 311. Swere (*rimes with* there), Gow. ii. 30, 17. *Icel.* svíri.] v. belced-sweora.

sweor-bān, es; *n. The neck-bone, the neck:*—Mīn Drihten, đū đīn hālige sweorbān geeádmēddest, Anglia xii. 505, 22. Ōđ swirbān *usque ad cervices*, Ps. Surt. ii. p. 190, 27: Ps. Spl. C. 128, 4. Onheldon eówerra feónda swyrbān, Shrn. 86, 22. [The swyrebane he swappes in sondyre, Morte Arthure (Halliwell).]

sweor-beáh; *gen.* -beáges; *m. A collar, band* or *chain for the neck, necklace:*—Myne *vel* sweorbēh *monile* vel *serpentinum*, Wrt. Voc. i. 40, 50. Swurbeáh *monile*, 74, 58. Swurbēh *murenula* vel *torques*, 16, 57. Ic ann đære hlǽfdigan ānes swyrbeáges on hundtwelftigum mancussum and ānæs beáges on þrītegum mancussum, Chart. Th. 554, 1. Ǽnne sweorbeáh (on XL mancysan, on LXXX mancys), 501, 20, 31. Ic đē forgife gyldenne swurbeáh *thou shalt have a chain of gold about thy neck* (A. V.), Homl. Th. ii. 436, 4, 16. Swurbeágas *crepundia* (cf. *crepundium*, i. *monile gutturis* myne, *crepundia* frætwunga, Wrt. Voc. ii. 136, 68–70), Ælfc. Gr. 13; Zup. 85, 9. Suirbēg[as] *monilia*, Rtl. 4, 3. Sweorbeágum ł halsmenum *monilibus, lunulis*, Hpt. Gl. 434, 63. Ic frætwode mīnne swuran mid mænigfealdum swurbeágum, Homl. Skt. i. 20, 57.

-sweorc. v. ge-sweorc.

sweorcan; *p.* swearc, *pl.* swurcon; *pp.* sworcen. I. in a physical sense, *to become dark, be obscured:*—Wedercandel swearc windas weóxon *the sun was darkened, the winds rose*, Andr. Kmbl. 744; An. 372. Swearc norđrodor won under wolcnum, woruld miste oferteáh, Exon. Th. 178, 33; Gū. 1253. II. figuratively of mental gloom, (a) of that which feels sadness, *to become troubled, gloomy, sad:*—Siteþ sorgcearig, on sefan sweorceþ, sylfum þinceþ, đæt sȳ endeleás earfođa dǽl, Exon. Th. 379, 6; Deór. 29. Hē mōdsorge wæg, hreþer innan swearc, 165, 8; Gū. 1025. On hū grundleásum seáđe swinceþ đæt sweorcende mōd *quam praecipiti mersa profundo mens hebet*, Met. 3, 2. (b) of that which causes sadness, *to become grievous, troublesome, saddening:*—Ne hine wiht dereþ, ādl ne yldo, ne him inwitsorh on sefan sweorceþ *nor in his mind springs gloomy care*, Beo. Th. 3478; B. 1737. [Swelleđ þe mære and swærkeđ þa uđen, Laym. 22030. Swurken (þirkede (dirkede?), 2nd MS.) under sunnen sweorte weolcnen, 11973. *O. Sax.* swerkan: Ni lāt thū thīnan sebon swerkan *do not be sad*, Hēl. 4042. *O. H. Ger.* swercan.] v. ā-, for-, ge-, tō-sweorcan.

sweorcend-ferhþ; *adj. With the mind growing gloomy:*—Beornas (*the Assyrians after Holofernes' death*) stōdon ymbe hyra þeódnes træf sweorcendferhþe ... Đā wæs hyra tīres æt ende, Judth. Thw. 25, 19; Jud. 269.

sweor-clāþ, es; *m. A cloth for the neck, a collar:*—Sweorclāþ *collarium*, Wrt. Voc. ii. 134, 48.

sweorcness. v. ge-sweorcness.

sweor-cops, es; *m. A neck-bond, pillory:*—Iuc ođđe swurcops (sweor-) *bogia*, (*bogia* torques damnatorum quasi jugum bovis, Migne), Ælfc. Gl. Zup. 321, 2. Sweorcopsas *vel* handcopsas *boias, catenas*, Wrt. Voc. ii. 126, 43.

sweor-coþu, e; *f. A disease of the neck* or *throat, quinsy:*—Sweorcoþu *arteriasis*, Wrt. Voc. i. 19, 33. Wiđ sweorcoþe, Lchdm. ii. 2, 20: 44, 9. Various methods of treatment are given, 48, 4–28.

sweord, swurd, swyrd, es; *n. A sword:*—Sweord *framea*, Wrt. Voc. ii. 36, 11. Sweorde *mucrone*, sweordum *mucronibus*, sweord *macheram*, 54, 33–36. Sweord *gladius* vel *machera* vel *spata* vel *framea* vel *pugio*, i. 35, 7. Litel sweord *sica*, 13. Hiltleás sweord *ensis*, 33. Swordes ord *mucro*, 15. Sweordes sceáđ *classendis*, 34, 29. Swyrdes gyrdei *baltheus*, 40, 58. Đæt ūs cwealm on ne become ne swurdes ecg *ne occidat nos pestis aut gladius*, Ex. 5, 4. Blōtan mid sweordes ecge, Cd. Th. 173, 6; Gen. 2857. Đurh sweordes bite gedǽlan feorh wiđ flǽsce, Apstls. Kmbl. 68; Ap. 34. Hig feallaþ on swurdes (sweordes, MS. A.: suordes, Lind.: swordana, Rush.) ecge *cadent in ore gladii*, Lk. Skt. 21, 24. Standan mid ātogenum swurde, Jos. 5, 13. Hēr synt twā swurd (sweord, MS. A.: suordas, Lind.: sworde, Rush.) *ecce gladii duo*, Lk. Skt. 22, 38. Sweorda gelāc *the play of swords, battle*, Beo. Th. 2084; B. 1040. Sweorda lāfe *those whom the sword had spared*, 5865; B. 2936. ¶ The high esteem in which good swords were held in old times is marked in many ways. Their forging is in many legends said to be the work of other than human hands; so the sword which Beowulf seizes in Grendel's home is 'eald sweord eotenisc (cf. eald sweord eácen, 3330; B. 1663), ecgum dyhtig, ... giganta geweorc,' Beo. Th. 3120–9; B. 1558–62; and twice besides occurs the phrase 'eald sweord eotonisc,' 5225; B. 2616: 5950; B. 2979; see also 'enta ǽrgeweorc' applied to the workmanship of a sword, 3362; B. 1679. Cf. too the forging of Sigurd's sword in the Völsunga Saga. They are precious heirlooms, handed down through many years (v. epithet *eald* above); so Beowulf speaks of his sword as 'eald lāf,' Beo. Th. 2981; B. 1488, and the same phrase is used of the sword wielded by one of his followers in the chief's defence, 1595; B. 795. In reference to the sword given by Beowulf to the Dane who had guarded his ship, it is said that the recipient 'syððan wæs on meodobence mādme ðȳ weorðra, yrfelāfe,' 3810; B. 1903; another sword is called 'Hreðles lāf,' and of it is said 'næs mid Geátum sincmāðþum sēlra on sweordes hād,' 4389–93; B. 2191–3; and later on mention is made of 'gomel swyrd, Eánmundes lāf,' 5216; B. 2611; Hrunting, the sword which is lent to Beowulf, is 'ān ealdgestreóna,' 2921; B. 1458. So, too, Byrhtnoth tells the Danes who demand tribute of him, that the tribute will take the form of 'ealde swurd,' used with unpleasant effect upon the invaders. The same point may be illustrated from other than poetical sources. Thus in Alfred's will it is said that he leaves 'Æþerēde ealdormenn ān sweord on hundteóntigum mancusum,' Chart. Th. 489, 32; in another will is the passage 'Freoðomunde fōe tō mīnum sweorde, and āgefe ðǣræt feówer ðūsenda,' 471, 23; another testator bequeathes his sword 'mid ðam sylfrenan hylte and ðone gyldenan fetels,' 558, 10; and another mentions the sword 'ðat Eádmund king mē selde on hund-tuelftian mancusas goldes and fōur pund silueres on ðan fetelse,' 505, 28. Indeed the sword is often mentioned in wills. The importance of the sword is further marked by its receiving a name. The sword with which Beowulf is armed for his attack on Grendel's mother is named Hrunting, and to the praise of this weapon the poet devotes several lines, Beo. Th. 2914–33; B. 1455–64; at a later period it is with 'Nægling . . . gomol and grǣgmǣl' that he fights, 5354; B. 2680. See, too, Wald. 4; Vald. 1, 3. And elsewhere the same point may be noted, e.g. in the Nibelungenlied. 'daz Nibelunges swert . . . Palmunc was genant;' and this weapon plays a part in the drama to the last scene. In Scandinavian story there is Hākon's sword 'kvernbītr,' which king Athelstan gave him, and Egill has his sword that he called 'Naðr.' See, too, the story of the Cid and the two swords, Colada and Tizona, which he gave to his sons-in-law, the Infantes of Carrion, and which he claimed from them after their unworthy treatment of their wives, Chronica del Cid, c. cclii. Of the value of the sword and of the decoration bestowed upon it, of the shape or colouring, of the make, many epithets and phrases speak. In the Gnomic verses it is said, 'Gold gerīseþ on guman sweorde,' Exon. Th. 341, 15; Gn. Ex. 126; and 'māðm in healle, goldhilted sweord' is mentioned, 437, 27; Rä. 56, 14. See, too, the passages quoted under *seolfor-hilt, -hilted.* In the dragon's hoard are 'dȳre swyrd,' Beo. Th. 6089; B. 3048: the sword which Beowulf seized in Grendel's retreat was golden-hilted, 3358; B. 1677, and 'wæs on ðǣm scennum scīran goldes þurh rūnstafas gesǣd, hwam ðæt sweord geworht, īrena cyst, ǣrest wǣre, wreoþenhilt and wyrmfāh,' 3390–3400; B. 1694–8. Beowulf lays aside his 'hyrsted sweord, īrena cyst,' Beo. Th. 1349; B. 672: he gives a sword 'bunden golde,' 3805; B. 1901: his own sword is 'fāh and fǣted,' 5395; B. 2700. Byrhtnoth's sword is 'fealohilte,' Byrht. Th. 136, 45; By. 166; and 'gerēnod,' 35; By. 161. Beowulf's Nægling is 'grǣgmǣl,' Beo. Th. 5357; B. 2681: the swords of the Hebrews are 'scīrmǣled,' Judth. Thw. 24, 38; Jud. 230: other swords are 'hringmǣled,' Cd. Th. 120, 10; Gen. 1992: Abraham girds himself 'grǣgan sweorde,' 173, 22; Gen. 2865: the Hebrews fight 'fāgum sweordum,' Judth. Thw. 24, 18; Jud. 194: 25, 17; Jud. 264. The sword is 'brād,' 26, 9; Jud. 318: Byrht. Th. 132, 12; By. 15: brād and brūnecg, 136, 38; By. 163: it is 'gōd,' 138, 58; By. 237; 'heard,' Beo. Th. 5966; B. 2987: 5269; B. 2638: Exon. Th. 325, 32; Vīd. 120: 'heardecg,' Beo. Th. 2581; B. 1288: 'ecgum dyhtig,' 2578; B. 1287: Cd. Th. 120, 11; Gen. 1993: 'ecgum gecost,' Judth. Thw. 24, 39; Jud. 231: stȳled, Exon. Th. 42, 28; Cri. 679. For some account of old swords, see Wright's The Celt, The Roman, and the Saxon, pp. 404–6, and Worsaae's Antiquities: see also Grmm. Gesch. D. S. p. 12. [*O. Sax. O. Frs.* swerd: *O. H. Ger.* swert: *Icel.* sverð.] v. gūð-, māl-, māðum-, stæf-, wǣg-sweord.

sweord (*or* sweorð) *swearing.* [*O. H. Ger.* swert, swart *juramentum.*] v. āþ-sweord.

sweord-bealu (-o), wes; *n. Bale* or *hurt caused by the sword,* Beo. Th. 2298; B. 1147.

sweord-berende; *adj.* (*ptcp.*) *Sword-bearing:*—Æðelingas sweordberende, Cd. Th. 65, 2; Gen. 1060.

sweord-bite, es; *m. The bite of a sword, wounding with a sword:*—Āswebban þurh sweordbite *to kill with the sword,* Exon. Th. 278, 26; Jul. 603.

sweord-bora, an; *m.* I. *one who bears a sword for his own use, a swordsman:*—Sweord *spata* vel *pugio,* swyrdbora *spatarius,* Wrt. Voc. i. 35, 8. Swurdbora, 84, 13. Swurdboran (*gladiatorem*) hine gewordene gesihþ *if* (*in a dream*) *he sees himself become a gladiator,* Lchdm. iii. 204, 25. Sweordboran *pugiles,* Wrt. Voc. ii. 76, 46. II. *one who bears his lord's sword, a swordbearer:*—Swā swā Eádmundes sweordbora hit reahte Æþelstāne cyninge, Swt. A. S. Prim. 83, 7. Totila āsende his swurdboran, Riggo gehāten, gescrȳdne mid his cynelīcum gyrelum, Homl. Th. ii. 168, 12. [Cf. *Icel.* sverð-berari (*translating* lictor).]

sweord-fetels, -fætels, es; *m. A sword-belt:*—Se cāsere heora ǣlces sweordfætelsas hēt forceorfan *the emperor ordered the sword-belts of each of them to be cut,* Homl. Skt. i. 23, 178. Cf. Ðat swerd on hundtwelftian mancusas and fōur pund silueres on þan fetelse, Chart. Th. 505, 32. Ðæs swurdes mid ðam sylfrenan hylte ðe Wulfrīc worhte and ðone gyldenan fetels, 558, 12. [Cf. *O. H. Ger.* swert-fezzil *faidilus, vagidilus: Icel.* sverð-fetill *a sword-belt.*] v. fetel.

sweord-freca, an; *m. A warrior who uses a sword:*—Hē ðæs wǣpnes (*the sword Hrunting*) onlāh sēlran sweordfrecan, Beo. Th. 2940; B. 1468.

sweord-genīðla, an; *m. A foe armed with a sword:*—Ðonne fyrdhwate on twā healfe tohtan sēcaþ sweordgenīðlan, Elen. Kmbl. 2359; El. 1181.

sweord-geswing, es; *n. Striking with swords, an attack with swords:*—Swyrdgeswing swīþlīc eówan *to make a fierce attack,* Judth. Thw. 25, 3; Jud. 240.

sweord-gifu, e; *f. Gift of a sword:*—Sceal sincþego and sweordgifu eówrum cynne ālicgean *taking of treasure and gift of sword shall fail for your race,* Beo. Th. 5761; B. 2884.

sweord-gripe, es; *m. Sword-grasp, seizing of swords:*—Ðæt hī in wīnsele þurh sweordgripe sāwle forlētan *so that in the banquet hall through seizing their swords they lost their lives,* Exon. Th. 271, 26; Jul. 488.

sweord-hwīta, an; *m. One who polishes a sword:*—Gif sweordhwīta ōðres mannes wǣpn tō feormunge onfō (cf. Si quelibet arma politori vel emundatori commissa sunt, L. H. I. 87, 3; Th. i. 593, 15), L. Alf. pol. 19; Th. i. 74, 8. Ic geann mīnon swurdhwītan ðæs sceardan mālswurdes, Chart. Th. 561, 22.

sweord-leóma, an; *m. The glitter of swords:*—Swurdleóma stōd swylce eal Finnsburuh fȳrenu wǣre *there was flashing of swords, as if all Finnsburg were on fire,* Fins. Th. 71; Fin. 35.

-sweordod. v. ge-swurdod.

Sweordoras (?); *pl. m. A people of Mercia occupying a district of three hundred hides:*—Sweordora þryú hund hȳda (*the name occurs in a list of districts in the land of the Mercians*), Cod. Dip. B. i. 414, 21. [Mr. Birch suggests a connection with Swerford in Oxfordshire, and with the river Swere. Could the word contain as its second part the Celtic *dwr* = water, seen in many river names, v. Taylor's Names and Places, p. 133, and mean the dwellers by the river Swere?]

sweord-plega; an, *m. Sword-play, battle:*—Æt ðam sweordplegan wīg forbūgan, Wald. 22; Vald. 1, 13.

sweord-rǣs, es; *m. A sword-rush, an attack with swords:*—Sweordrǣs fornam, ðǣr se hālga gecrang wund for weorudum, Apstls. Kmbl. 118; Ap. 59.

sweord-slege, es; *m. A sword-stroke, stroke with a sword:*—Hyre sāwl wearð ālǣded of līce þurh sweordslege, Exon. Th. 282, 30; Jul. 671.

sweord-wegende *sword-bearing:*—Swurdwege[n]de anbidian gehende saca mǣste getācnaþ (*in a dream*) *to await men carrying swords betokens strifes at hand and very great ones,* Lchdm. iii. 204, 28.

sweord-weras; *pl. The name of a people* (cf. the *Suardones* of Tacitus. v. Grmm. Gesch. D. S. 329):—Mid Seaxum ic wæs and mid Sweordwerum, Exon. Th. 322, 13; Vīd. 62.

sweord-wīgend, -wīgende *one who fights with a sword:*—Sweordwīgendra sīde hergas, Cd. Th. 194, 13; Exod. 260.

sweord-wund; *adj. Wounded with the sword:*—Oft æt hilde gedreás swātfāg and sweordwund sec[g] æfter ōðrum, Wald. 7; Vald. 1, 5.

sweord-wyrhta, an; *m. A sword-wright, maker of swords, armourer:*—Mōna se ān and twentigoða unnytlīce tō wyrcenne būtan swurdwyrhtan (but the word glosses *gladiatoribus*), Lchdm. iii. 194, 10.

-sweorf *in* ge-sweorf *rasura ferri, ferrugo,* Wrt. Voc. ii. 147, 65: 35, 32. [Cf. *Icel.* svarf *filings.*] v. ge-sweorf.

sweorfan; *p.* swearf, *pl.* swurfon; *pp.* sworfen *To rub, scour, file:*—Swyrfþ *limat,* Germ. 394, 274. Corfen sworfen *cut and scoured* (of the preparation of a wine-vat), Exon. Th. 410, 24; Rä. 29, 4. Mīn heáfod is homere geþuren sworfen feóle, 497, 18; Rä. 87, 2. *Cpds. with* for, *omitted in their place, are added here:*—Forsweorfeþ *elimat,* i. *mundat,* Wrt. Voc. ii. 143, 1. Biþ forsworfen *vel* forgniden *demolitur, exterminatur,* 138, 63. [In later English the verb has the sense of *swerve* = to turn (aside):—Swerve to no side, Gow. 3, 92. Þe dint swarf, Arth. and Merl. 9369. Heo swarf to Criste *migravit ad Christum,* Kath. 2181. Cf. *Du.* zwerven *to wander, rove: O. Frs.* swerva *to move, go.* For the old English verb, cf. *Goth.* af-swairban *to wipe out;* delere; bi-swairban *to wipe: O. Sax.* swerban *to wipe: O. H. Ger.* swerban *tergere, extergere, siccare: Icel.* sverfa *to file.*] v. ā-, ge-sweorfan.

sweor-hnitu, e; *f. A neck-nit, a nit that breeds at the back of the neck:*—Sweorhnitu *ursie,* Wrt. Voc. i. 287, 48. Suernit (= sweorhnitu?) *usia* (cf. swīnes lūs *usia,* 122, 26), Wülck. Gl. 54, 34.

Sweó-rīce, es; *n. Sweden:*—Ðone sēlestan sǣcyninga ðara ðe in Swiórīce sinc brytnade, Beo. Th. 4755; B. 2383: 4983; B. 2495. [*Icel.* Svía-ríki: *Swed.* Sverige.]

sweor-racenteáh; *g.* -teáge; *f. A chain for the neck:*—Swurracentēh *catelle,* Wrt. Voc. i. 16, 64.

sweor-rōd, e; *f. A cross suspended from the neck:*—Hē becwæð Wulfstāne ærcebiscope āne sweorrōde (*the Latin version has* philacterium; cf. *the use of this word for chains and medals worn by gladiators round* *their necks as tokens of victory*), Chart. Th. 551, 5. Óðrum litlum silfrenum swurródum, 429, 15.

sweor-sál *a collar.* v. sál, V.

sweor-sceacel, es; *m. A neck-shackle, pillory*:—Fótcopsa[s] *vel* sweorscacul *nerui, boia*, Wrt. Voc. i. 21, 15. v. sweor-cops.

sweor-teáh, -téh; *g.* -teáge, -tége; *f. A collar*:—Sweortéh *millus* vel *collarium*, Wrt. Voc. i. 23, 34. Sweorcláþ *vel* [sweor]tég *collarium*, ii. 134, 48. Swiortégum *collaribus, vinculis*, Hpt. Gl. 501, 38.

-sweoru. v. ge-sweoru, sweora, II.

sweor-wærc, es; *m. A pain in the neck*:—Lege on ðone sweorwærc, Lchdm. ii. 44, 22. Cf. sweor-coþu.

sweostor, swistor, swystor, swustor (-er, -ur); *indecl. in sing.*; *pl.* sweostor, sweostra, sweostru (u, y); *f. A sister.* I. of blood relationship:—Saga ðæt ðú sié sweostor mín, líces mǽge, Cd. Th. 110, 3, Gen. 1832. Ðære swustur (suoester, Lind.: swester, Rush.) wæs Maria *huic erat soror nomine Maria*, Lk. Skt. 10, 39. Soester, Lind. 10, 40. Swuster, Gen. 12, 13. Seó yldre swyster, 19, 33. Sweostor bearna *nepotum*, Wrt. Voc. ii. 59, 70. Se wæs his sweostor sunu, Bd. 4, 16; S. 584, 16. Sweoster sunu, 2, 3; S. 504, 20. Swuster sunu, Byrht. Th. 135, 8; By. 115. Ðæt ðú gesecge sweostor mínre, Exon. Th. 172, 32; Gú. 1152. Óþer him sylfum, óþer his sweoster, Bd. 4, 6; S. 574, 13: Homl. Th. ii. 546, 35. Gif hé gemēteþ óðerne æt his swister, L. Alf. pol. 42; Th. i. 90, 28. Hé betǽhte hý his swyster, Chr. 1048; Erl. 180, 23. Tó hyre gingran swuster, Gen. 19, 31. Forlēt hé Pendan sweoster, Bd. 3, 7; S. 529, 29. Swustor (suoester, Lind.: swester, Rush.) *sororem*, Jn. Skt. 11, 5. Swuster, Gen. 25, 20. Hiera swostur (sweostor, swystor (-er), swustra) wǽrun Cuēnburg and Cúþburh, Chr. 718; Th. pp. 70, 71. Neogone wǽran Noðþæs sweoster, Lchdm. iii. 62, 18. Ealle his swustra (suoester, Lind.: swæster, Rush.), Mt. Kmbl. 13, 56. Swustra (suoestro, Lind.: swester, Rush.), Mk. Skt. 6, 3. Swestro, Jn. Skt. Rush. 11, 3. Ic seah vi. gebróþor and hyra sweostor mid, Exon. Th. 394, 13; Rä. 14, 2. Ðe ne onfó swustru (swustra, MS. A.: suoestro, Lind.: swester, Rush.). Mk. Skt. 10, 30. II. of membership in a religious house: —Ætýwde sumre gódre swuster wundorlíc gesyhþ . . . Ðeós sweoster . . ., Bd. 4, 9; S. 576, 18–30. Seó gesomnung bróþra and sweostra, 4, 19; S. 589, 9. Ðá ongan heó on gesomnunge ðare sweostra sēcan . . . Heó nǽnige andsware findan mihte, ðeáh ðe heó georne sóhte æt ðám swustrum, 4, 7; S. 574, 35, 40. Ðá geseah heó óþre sweoster (*sorores*) ymb hí restende . . . ðá áwæhte heó ealle ða sweostera, 4, 23; S. 596, 5–14. [*Goth.* swistar: *O. Sax.* swestar: *O. Frs.* swester, suster: *O. H. Ger.* swestar: *Icel.* systir.] v. ge-sweostor; ge-sweosternu.

sweót, es; *n. A troop, band, squadron*:—Him on láste fór sweót Ebréa sigore geweorþod, Judth. Thw. 25, 38; Jud. 299: Ðý deáððrepe drihte swǽfon, synfullra sweót sáwlum lunnon, Cd. Th. 209, 8; Exod. 496. Segn ofer sweóton, 185, 23; Exod. 127. Segen for sweótum, Elen. Kmbl. 247; El. 124. Sweótum *in crowds, in shoals*, Beo. Th. 1138; B. 567. Sunu Simeonis sweótum cómon (*came in bands*), Cd. Th. 199, 20; Exod. 341. Fífe fóran folc cyningas sweótum (*marched with their squadrons*), 119, 5; Gen. 1975. Moyses bebeád cígean sweót (*summon the bands*), 119, 25; Exod. 220.

sweóta (?), an; *m. The scrotum*:—Sweótan *marsem* (=*marsupium*, v. Cockayne's remark, Lchdm. iii. 371, col. 1), Lchdm. i. lxxiv, 27.

Sweó-þeód, e; *f. The Swedish people*:—Ne ic tó Sweóðeóde sibbe oððe treówe wihte ne wēne, Beo. Th. 5836; B. 2922. Swíðe mycel here ǽgðer ge landhere ge sciphere of Swaðeóde (Sweóðode, MS. F.), Chr. 1025; Erl. 163, 9. [*Icel.* Sví-þjóð.]

sweoþol. v. sweþel.

sweotol, swutol, switol, swytol, sutol (-ul, -al, -el); *adj. Plain, manifest, evident, clear, patent*:—Sweotul, gewis *evidens*, i. *manifestus, patens, perspicuus, certum*, Wrt. Voc. ii. 144, 35. Sweotol *evidens*, 29, 51. Seotol, 107, 42. I. of what may be clearly perceived by the senses, (a) by sight:—Biþ mín swæð sweotol, sweart on óþre healfe, Exon. Th. 403, 19; Rä. 22, 10. Wiht sweotol and gesýne, 420, 13; Rä. 40, 3. Him on eaxle wearð syndolh sweotol, Beo. Th. 1638; B. 817. Ða fótlástas wǽron swutole and gesýne, Blickl. Homl. 203, 36. Fell hongedon sweotol and gesýne, Exon. Th. 394, 16; Rä. 14, 4. (b) by hearing:—Ðǽr wæs hearpan swēg, swutol sang, Beo. Th. 180; B. 90. (c) by taste:—Ne sié on bergnesse tó sweotol ðæs ecedes scearpnes, Lchdm. ii. 224, 22. II. *manifest* to observation, *that may be noticed by all, public, open, patent*:—His nama wæs swutol geworden, Mk. Skt. 6, 14. Hit is on ús eallum swutol and gesýne, ðæt wē oftor brǽcan, ðonne wē bēttan, Wulfst. 159, 5. Sweotol and gesēne, Cd. Th. 170, 1; Gen. 2806. Hē wundra fela weorodum gecýðde sweotulra and gesýnra, Andr. Kmbl. 1129; An. 565. Swutelra, Menol. Fox 255; Men. 129. Sutelum *publicis*, Hpt. Gl. 525, 20. III. *clear* to the understanding, *free from obscurity, plain*, of proof, argument, indication, etc.: —Swutol is *constat*, Ælfc. Gr. 33; Zup. 206, 7: *liquet*, Zup. 207, 6. Ðæt is swíþe sweotol tó ongitanne be sumum æðelinge, Bt. 16, 2; Fox 52, 18. Genóh sweotol is, ðætte gód word biþ betera ðonne ǽnig wela, 13; Fox 38, 22: 36, 3; Fox 176, 27: 36, 7; Fox 184, 5. Is on mē sweotul ðæt . . . *it is plain from my case that* . . ., Exon. Th. 275, 17; Jul. 551. Biþ hit sweotol (swutul, Hatt. MS.), Past. 14; Swt. 83, 20. Swutol, 21; Swt. 153, 4. Ðæt wæs tácen sweotol *it was a token that was an evident proof*, Beo. Th. 1671; B. 833. Ðæt is swíþe swital (sweotol, Cott. MS.) on ðære týdrunge, Bt. 34, 12; Fox 152, 25. Wæs swytol, ðæt hē ǽr mihte wið deáð gebeorgan, Wulfst. 23, 15. Ðis eástorlíce gerýno ús æteóweþ ðæs ēcean lífes sweotole bysene, Blickl. Homl. 83, 8: 99, 14. Tácen sutol, Cd. Th. 270, 12; Sat. 89. Orðancum swutulum *argumentis evidentibus* (*apertis, manifestis*), Hpt. Gl. 486, 21. Ðæt him biþ ungewítnode hiora yfel on ðisse worulde, ðæt is ðæt sweotoloste tácn (*the clearest indication*) ðæs mǽstan yfeles on ðisse worulde, Bt. 38, 3; Fox 200, 29. [Sutel (sotel, 2nd MS.) word *a clear message*, Laym. 1519. Bi Moisen is sutel and eðcene, A. R. 154, 22. Wass full sutell and full sene, þatt . . ., Orm. 18862.] v. un-sweotol.

sweotole; *adv.* I. of a physical action, *clearly, without obstruction*:—Steorran geseón swá sutole swá on niht, Blickl. Homl. 93, 20. Gē sweotule geseóþ Dryhten faran, Exon. Th. 32, 13; Cri. 512. Sweotole on ðæs hǽþenes heáfod starian, Judth. Thw. 24, 8; Jud. 177. Ðonne sió sunne sweotolost scíneþ, Met. 6, 3. II. *in a manner open to general observation, evidently, openly, plainly, publicly*:—Wǽron heardingas sweotole gesamnod, Elen. Kmbl. 51; El. 26. Sweotule ða forweorðaþ (*their destruction will be seen by all*), Ps. Th. 101, 23. Sunne hire setlgang sweotule healdeþ, 103, 18. III. *openly, without reserve* or *concealment, plainly*:—Nis nú nán ðe ic him módsefan mínne durre sweotule ásecgan, Exon. Th. 287, 8; Wand. 11. IV. of thinking, knowing, stating, explaining, etc., *clearly*:—Sweotole ongitan, Bt. 33, 2; Fox 124, 34: Met. 26, 107. Sueotole, sweotule, Past. 7; Swt. 49, 2. Sweotule cunnan, Ps. Th. 118, 12. Sweotele gecnáwan, Bt. 3, 1; Fox 4, 29. Sweotole oncnáwan, Met. 12, 29. Swotole, Bd. 2, 12; S. 515, 20: 3, 14; S. 540, 15. Swutele, swutole tócnáwan, Bt. 20; Fox 72, 15, 20. Be ðære sunnan sweotole geþencean, Met. 5, 1. Sweotole secgan, Met. 20, 182: Elen. Kmbl. 335; El. 168. Sweotole gecýðan, 1718; El. 861. Sweotole gereccan, Bt. 35, 3; Fox 160, 5. Swetole, Met. 8, 2. Sweotule gesēþan, Exon. Th. 15, 28; Cri. 243. Ða siex stafas sweotule bēcnaþ, 407, 5: Rä. 25, 10. Sweotolor, Bt. 34, 6; Fox 142, 3: 11, 1; Fox 30, 29: Met. 12, 23: Shrn. 188, 31. Hwæðer ðú hit á sweotolor (*any more clearly*) ongiton mǽge, Bt. 34, 4; Fox 138, 16. Swá hē hit sweotolost and andgitfullícost gereccan mihte, Bt. procem.; Fox viii, 4.

sweotolian, swutelian, swytelian; *p.* ode. I. *to make clear* or *manifest, to shew, declare*:—Ǽlc gesceaft ðæt sweotolaþ, ðæt God ēce is *Deum aeternum esse cunctorum degentium commune judicium est*, Bt. 42; Fox 256, 7. Hēr swutelaþ on ðison cwyde hú Æðelrēd geúðe ðæt Æðeríces cwyde standan móste, Chart. Th. 539, 20: 320, 24: 312, 8. Swytelaþ, 586, 25. Swetelaþ *expremit*, Kent. Gl. 1120. Ðæt ðæt man beháteþ, ðonne man fulluhtes gyrnþ, swytelaþ, ðæt man wile on ǽnne God gelýfan, L. I. P. 24; Th. ii. 338, 12. Hē ongan swutelian (*ostendere*) his leorningcnihtum, ðæt hē wolde faran, Mt. Kmbl. 16, 21. [He schawde and sutelede þ he wes soð godd, Kath. 1037. He schawde him and sutelede him seolf to hire, 1834. Þet hit sutelie in us hwuch was his lif, A. R. 382, 3.] II. *to become manifest*:—Ðín mycele miht manegum swutelaþ, Hy. 9, 32. [Hit schal sutelin (*become manifest*) sone, Jul. 18, 4. Þurh þis suteleð soð al þ ich segge, Kath. 1089.] v. ge-sweotulian.

sweotol-líc; *adj. Clear, plain*:—Gehýraþ hwæt God sylfa sǽde swytellícre (swutel-, MS. C.) segene, Wulfst. 45, 1.

sweotollíce; *adv. Clearly*:—Swutollíce *manifeste* and *manifesto*, Ælfc. Gr. 38; Zup. 235, 12. I. of a physical action, *clearly, plainly, distinctly*:—Hié sweotollíce geseón mihten ðære byrig weallas blícan, Judth. Thw. 23, 23; Jud. 136. Hí swutolíce (*manifeste*) engla sang gehýrdon, Bd. 3, 8; S. 532, 5. Swutollíce hē sprecþ *expresse loquitur*, Ælfc. Gr. 38; Zup. 228, 11. II. *openly, publicly*:—Ðæt heó swutollíce (*palam*) eallum cýdde, Bd. 4, 19; S. 588, 17. III. of perceiving, knowing, shewing, stating, etc., *clearly, plainly*:—Sweotollíce ongitan, Blickl. Homl. 97, 22: 219, 36: Bd. 5, 1; S. 614, 13. Sweotolíce, 4, 28; S. 607, 3. Swutollíce oncnáwan, Hy. 7, 90. Sweotollíce gecýðan, Elen. Kmbl. 1376; El. 690: Blickl. Homl. 27, 26. Swutollíce, 181, 27: Homl. Th. i. 76, 28. Him wæs gesǽd swutelíce, Gen. 15, 13. Sweotolícor gecnáwan, Exon. Th. 263, 26; Jul. 355. Swætolocor getēcan, Shrn. 175, 34. Omarus sweotelícost sægde *Homerus luculentissimo carmine palam fecit*, Ors. 1, 11; Swt. 50, 15.

sweotolung, e; *f.* I. *a manifestation*:—Ðes freólsdæg (*Epiphany*) is Godes swutelung gecweden, Homl. Th. i. 104, 29. II. *an explanation, definition*:—Ásmeáde swutelunge *elucubratam definitionem* (*manifestationem*), Hpt. Gl. 522, 47. III. *a declaration, setting forth, exposition, shewing*:—Hēr onginþ seó bóc peri didaxeon (περὶ διδαξέων), ðæt ys seó swytelung hú fela gēra wæs behúded se lǽcecræft, Lchdm. iii. 82, 1. IV. *evidence, testimony, declaration*; when written, *a testament, title-deed, certificate, prescript*:—Hēr is seó swutelung (*the will, testament*) hú Ælfhelm his áre and his ǽhta gefadod hæfþ, Chart. Th. 596, 5. Ðeós swutelung (*the evidence or testimony which has been recited in the previous part of the charter*) wæs ðǽrrihte gewriten and beforan ðam cincge geræ̌dd, 540, 35. Wē habbaþ gedōn swá swá ús swutelung (*evidence of your wish, mandate*) from eów com æt ðam b. (*in *respect to consecrating the bishop*), 314, 1. Hí ða bóc tó swutelunge sealdan *they gave the charter as evidence* (*of a grant*), 588, 14. Tó swutulunge ðæt man wite ðæt man clǽne bæc hæbbe (tó swutelunge ðæt man mid rihte fare, 9), L. A. G. 5; Th. i. 156, 5. Ic wille, ðæt ðú underfó ðás seofon lamb æt mé, ðæt hig tó swutelunge (*in testimonium*) beón, ðæt ic dealf ðisne pytt, Gen. 21, 30. Gyf ǽnig man sý, ðæt wylle ǽnig ðæra sócna him tó handa drægen, ic wylle ðæt hé cume beforan mé mid his sweotelunge (*with the evidence that substantiates his claim*), Cod. Dip. Kmbl. iv. 222, 32. Bringe hé swutelunge (switelunge, MS. D.), ðæt hé swá micel betǽht hæbbe, L. Edg. i. 4; Th. i. 264, 10. Ðá gemǽtæ hé on ðam mynstre ða ylcan swutelunga (*evidences, title-deeds*) ðe his foregenga hæfde . . . Syððon se bisceop his swutelunge geeówod hæfde, Chart. Th. 302, 8-33. On ðissan þrím cyrografum ðe on ðissun ðrým mynstrum tó swytelungum gesette syndon, 233, 2. Swutelung[um] *adstipulationibus* (cf. *adstipulationibus* trymnessum, cýðnessum, Wrt. Voc. ii. 3, 63), Hpt. Gl. 525, 36. v. ge-swutelung.

Sweotolung-dæg, es; *m. Epiphany*:—Ðes dæg (viii. Idus Ian.) is gehâten on bócum Swetelungdæg, forðan ðe on ðisum dæge wearð Crist mancynne geswutelod, Homl. Th. ii. 36, 20. Epiphania Domini *is translated by* Godes geswutelungdæg, i. 104, 18.

swer *a pillar*, swér *a mother-in-law*, swér *heavy*. v. sweor, sweger, swǽr.

swerian; *p.* swór (*but a weak* swerede *occurs*; cf. *Icel.* svarði *as well as* sór), *pl.* swóron; *pp.* sworen *To swear, make oath.* I. absolute:—Se ðe sweraþ (swereþ, Ps. Th. Surt.) néhstan his *qui jurat proximo suo*, Ps. Spl. 14, 6. Ðæt land ðe ic fore swór heora fæderum *terram pro qua juravi patribus eorum*, Num. 14, 23. Ðæt land ðe ðú hira fæderum fore swóre, 11, 12. Hí wið mé sweórun *adversum me jurabant*, Ps. Surt. 101, 9. Ic secge eów, ðæt gé eallunga ne swerion, Mt. Kmbl. 5, 34. Hí mé hraþe æfter swerigean ongunnon, Ps. Th. 101, 6. Hé mót swerian for syxtig hída, L. In. 19; Th. i. 114, 11. I a. *to swear* by *or* on:—Swá hwylc swá swereþ on temple . . . swá hwá swá swereþ on ðæs temples golde, Mt. Kmbl. 23, 16, 18, 20, 21. Swá swá ðú swóre on sóðfæstnysse ðíne, Ps. Spl. 88, 48. Ic swerige ðurh God *juro per Deum*, Ælfc. Gr. 38; Zup. 227, 4. Ne swerie gé þurh útencymena goda naman, Ex. 23, 13: Mt. Kmbl. 5, 34, 35. Ne swerigen gé nǽfre under hǽðene godas, L. Alf. 48; Th. i. 54, 23. I b. *to swear* to anything:—Ðæt hí hit gegaderian and eft ágifan swá hí durran tó swerian, L. N. P. L. 57; Th. ii. 300, 2. II. with an object, (1) a noun (pronoun):—Ðá swóron hí swíðe, ðæt hit swá wǽre. Ðá cwæð hé tó him: 'Ac tó hwon sweriaþ git mán?' Guthl. 14; Gdwin. 64, 6. Ic ne swór fela áþa on unriht, Beo. Th. 5470; B. 2738. Hé mé áðas swór, 949; B. 472. Hé him ðone áð swór, Gen. 24, 9. Ðone swergendan áð ðone hé swór *jusjurandum quod juravit*, Ps. Surt. ii. p. 199, 20. Wyrgdan, áð sweredan (áðsweredan?) *devotabant*, Wrt. Voc. ii. 26, 48. Se ðe mánáð swerige, L. Ath. i. 25; Th. i. 212, 18. Ðæs deádan mǽgas swerian unceáses áð, L. In. 35; Th. i. 124, 7. (1 a) *to swear* an oath by something:—Ða ðe áðas sweriaþ on hine, Ps. Th. 62, 9. Ic ǽne swór áð on hálgum, 88, 31. Gange ǽlc man ðæs tó gewitnesse ðe hé durre on ðam háligdóme swerian, L. Eth. iii. 2; Th. i. 292, 14. Ic swór mǽne áðas mínra hláforda lífe, L. de Cf. 9; Th. ii. 264, 11. (2) where the object is a clause that contains a statement of that which is confirmed by oath:—Ðá ætsóc hé and swerede ðæt hé nǽfre ðone man ne cúðe *tunc coepit detestari et jurare quia non novisset hominem*, Mt. Kmbl. 26, 74. Hig swóron him betweónan, ðæt hig sibbe heóldon, Gen. 21, 31. Ðá swóran hié swíðe, ðæt hié sóð sægdon, Nar. 25, 27. Swerige hé, ðæt hé him nán fácn on wiste, L. In. 56; Th. i. 138, 12: L. Ath. v. 12, 2; Th. i. 242, 4. Begite hé ðara .v. .i. ðæt him mid swerige, ðæt . . ., i. 9; Th. i. 204, 11. Swerian (cf. gif hí ðone áð syllan ne durren, 394, 3) hí, ðæt him nǽfre áð ne burste, L. C. S. 30; Th. i. 392, 27. (2 a) *to swear* by, on . . . that . . .:—Swerian hí on ðam háligdóme, ðæt hig nellan nǽnne sacleásan man forsecgean, L. Eth. iii. 3; Th. i. 294, 4. Ic swerige þurh mé sylfne . . . ic ðé bletsige, Gen. 22, 16. Sweriaþ þurh Drihten, ðæt gé dón wið mé mildheortnisse, Jos. 2, 12. Ðá áswear todе eall se king and swór under God ælmihtine and under ealle hálgan ðártó, ðæt hit næs ná his rǽd, Chart. Th. 340, 1. (3) where noun and clause both occur:—Swerige hé ðone áð, ðæt hé sý unscyldig, L. Ath. i. 23; Th. i. 210, 31. Ðæt Drihten swóre áð swíðe, ðæt God wolde sendan hungor, Wulfst. 209, 26. (3 a) with adjuration:—Áð swereþ engla þeóden þurh his sylfes líf, ðæt ðínes cynnes rím ne cunnon yldo, Cd. Th. 205, 5; Exod. 431. [*Goth.* swaran: *O. Sax.* swerian: *O. Frs.* sweria, swera, swara: *O. H. Ger.* swerien, sweren: *Icel.* sverja.] v. á-, æt-, for-, ge-, óþ-swerian; swerigend-líc.

swerian; *p.* ede *To speak, talk*:—Oft ic fróde men gehýrde secgan and swerian ymb sume wísan hwæðer wǽre twegra strengra wyrd ðe warnung *I have often heard wise men speak and talk* (or? *swear, support what they said with oath*) *about a certain thing, whether of the twain were stronger, fate or caution*, Salm. Kmbl. 851; Sal. 425. v. and-swerian.

swerigend-líc; *adj. Pertaining to swearing*:—Sume (*adverbia*) synd *jurativa*, ðæt synd swerigendlíce, *per* ðurh . . . Má syndon swergendlíce *adverbia*, ac hwæt sceolon hí gesǽde, nú wé swerian ne móton? Ælfc. Gr. 38; Zup. 227, 3-11.

swertling, es; *m. A tit-lark*:—Swertling *ficedula* (in later glossaries *ficedula* is translated *rooke*, Wülck. Gl. 583, 12: *nuthage = nuthatch*, 702, 32. See also *sucga*), Wrt. Voc. i. 29, 10. v. sweart.

swerum, Wrt. Voc. ii. 56, 44, swerung, swés, swésende. v. swéte, áþswerung, swǽs, swǽsende.

swétan; *p.* te; *pp.* swéted, swét *To sweeten, make sweet.* I. in a physical sense:—Nim hunig and swét ðone drænc, Lchdm. iii. 58, 30: ii. 120, 11. Swéte swíðe mid hunige, 216, 4. Swétedne, 111, 8, 15. II. *to make pleasant*:—Hé (*the devil*) mec féran hét, ðæt ic ðé sceolde synne swétan, Exon. Th. 273, 32; Jul. 525. [Saullt þatt ure mete sweteþþ, Orm. 1649. Swetyñ or make a thynge swete to mannys taste *dulcoro*, Prompt. Parv. 483. *O. H. Ger.* suozen: *Icel.* sœta.] v. ge-swétan; swétian.

swéte; *adj. Sweet.* I. in reference to the senses (lit. or fig.) (1) of taste:—Ðis ofet is swá swéte, Cd. Th. 41, 12; Gen. 655. Ðæt is for hwí se góda lǽce selle ðam hálum men séftne drenc and swétne, and óðrum hálum biterne and strangne, Bt. 39, 9; Fox 226, 11, 13. Swéte ofer hunig *dulcia super mel*, Ps. Spl. 118, 103. Gif hwá biteres hwes onberede, ðæt him þúhte beóbreád ðí swétre, Bt. 23 tit.; Fox xiv, 10. Sweótran ofer hunig, Ps. Surt. 18, 11. ¶ used substantively:—Wá eów ðe taliaþ ungód tó góde, biter ðing tó swéte and swéte belǽþaþ, Wulfst. 47, 7. (1 a) of food, *sweet* in *sweet*-meat, *delicate*:—Swéte mete *dapis*, Wrt. Voc. ii. 28, 29. Se swéta mete ðe hié héton monna, Past. 17; Swt. 125, 19. Wyt ǽton swétne mete (*dulces cibos*), Ps. Th. 54, 13. Fram swéttrum mettum *a cibis luculentioribus*, Wrt. Voc. ii. 6, 25. ¶ used substantively:—Hé forlét eall ðæt ðǽr líðes wæs and swétes *astu instructa vino epulisque deseruit*, Ors. 2, 4; Swt. 76, 14. Ys sáwl mín swétes gefylled *adipe et pinguedine repleatur anima mea*, Ps. Th. 62, 5. Ne mæg se flǽschoma swéte forswelgan, Exon. Th. 311, 20; Seef. 95. (2) of smell, *sweet, fragrant*:—Ðǽr wæs swíþe swéte stenc, Blickl. Homl. 145, 29. Wyrta wearmiaþ, willsele stýmeþ swétum swæccum, Exon. Th. 212, 22; Ph. 214. Swétum wyrtum *with sweet-smelling herbs*, 241, 6; Ph. 652. Wynsumra steám, swéttra and swíþra, 358, 15; Pa. 46. Of múðe cwom swecca swétast, 178, 20; Gú. 1247. Ðara swétestena wyrta, Bd. 3, 8; S. 532, 20. (3) of freedom from unpleasant taste or smell, *sweet, pure, untainted*:—Mere in ðæm wǽre fersc wæter and swéte genóg (*stagnum dulcissime aque*), Nar. 11, 26. Ðá wæs ic gefeónde ðæs swétan wætres and ðæs ferscan *dulci aqua potata gaudio*, 12, 10. *Merum* hlúttor wín oððe swerum, *mero* wíne (l. (?) *mero* swétum wíne), Wrt. Voc. ii. 56, 44. Drince on swétum wætre, Lchdm. ii. 134, 23. Bæþ of swétum ferscum wæterum, 194, 10. (4) of sound, *sweet, harmonious*:—Swég ðæs swétan sanges, Bd. 5, 12; S. 630, 23. Swég eallum songcræftum swétra, Exon. Th. 206, 26; Ph. 132. Ðá gehýrde hé ða swétestan stæfne, Bd. 4, 3; S. 567, 39. II. in reference to the feelings, *sweet, agreeable, pleasant*:—Mé swéte and wynsum wæs ðæt ic oððe leornode oððe lǽrde *aut discere aut docere dulce habui*, Bd. 5, 24; S. 647, 27. Cristes onsýn on sefan swéte sínum folce, biter bealofullum, Exon. Th. 56, 29; Cri. 908. Hwæt déþ ðæt swéte word? Hit gemanigfealdaþ mannes freóndscipe and stilleþ mannes feónd (cf. *a soft answer turneth away wrath*), Salm. Kmbl. 204, 45. Geocc mín suoet ł éðe (wynsum, Rush., W. S.) is *jugum meum suave est*, Mt. Kmbl. Lind. 11, 30. Swoete and reht Dryhten *dulcis et rectus Dominus*, Ps. Surt. 24, 8. Ðú ðín swéte good sealdest þearfum, Ps. Th. 67, 11. Ða geógoðlustas ðe him swéte wǽron tó árǽfnenne, Blickl. Homl. 59, 10. Hí mihton eáþe secgan sóþspell, gif him ða leásunga nǽron swétran, Bt. 35, 4; Fox 162, 16. Se swétesta láreów and se wynsumesta *doctor suavissimus*, Bd. 5, 22; S. 644, 3. Hwæt ðé sý hér on worlde swétast and leófast gesewen ðínra ǽhta, Blickl. Homl. 195, 20. Mín se swétesta sunnan scíma, Iuliana, Exon. Th. 252, 20; Jul. 166. Dóhtor mín seó dýreste and seó swéteste, 248, 11; Jul. 94. [*O. Sax.* swóti: *O. Frs.* swéte: *O. H. Ger.* suozi: *Icel.* sœtr.] v. hunig-, un-swéte; swót, swóte.

sweþel, sweoþol, es; *m. A swathe, wrap, band, bandage*; cf. *swaddling* band, clothes:—Sweþil *fascia*, Wrt. Voc. ii. 34, 74. Sueðelas, suedilas *instites*, Txts. 69, 1060. Sweþelas, Wrt. Voc. ii. 45, 48. Sweoþolas *fascia* [*e?*], 93, 69. Suuoeðles *institis*, Jn. Skt. Lind. 11, 44. Suaeðila *fasciarum*, Wrt. Voc. ii. 108, 18. Sweþila, 34, 76. Sweþela, 82, 36. Sweþelum *fasciarum*, 34, 21. Suithelon *institis*, Txts. 113, 72. ¶ of a funeral pile in whose fire the body is wrapped (?):—Wudurēc ástáh sweart ofer swioðole (swicðole, MS.) *the smoke rose black above the pile where Beowulf's body lay enwrapped*, Beo. Th. 6281; B. 3146, cf. swaþul. [Cf. Bondon wit a sueþelband (suadiling band, swaþeling bonde, other MSS.), C. M. 1343. A child in swethelcloutes, Met. Homl. 91, 14. *O. H. Ger.* swedili *malagma*.] v. sweðian.

sweðerian. v. sweðrian.

sweðian; *p.* swede *To swathe, wrap.* [She swaþed (swetheled, suedeld, other MSS.) him wiþ cloþes, C. M. 11236. Swathyñ chyldyr *fascio*, Prompt. Parv. 482. Sweethed togeder, Pall. 149, 19.] v. beswedian (where add these passages, Lchdm. ii. 46, 32: 182, 19: 250, 18), bi-sweðian.

sweðrian, swiðrian, sweoðerian; *p.* ode (*some instances of the cpd.* geswedrian, *omitted under that word, are given here*) *To retire, withdraw, abate, subside, decrease, fail, come to an end*:—Sweðraþ *facessit, discedit*,

Wrt. Voc. ii. 33, 30. Gesweđeriaþ *fatescunt* (fatiscere *dissolvi*, Migne), 96, 18. Mylt, sweþrede, āswand, āteorade *dissolvitur, desinit, discedit*, 147, 25. Gesuedrade, gesuidradae, gisuderadae *constipuisse*, Txts. 53, 525. Geswiđrade, Wrt. Voc. ii. 14, 71. Gesweþrade *constipuit*, i. *defecit*, 133, 63. Sweþeredan *fatescunt*, 37, 29: *facescunt*, 91, 61. Gesueđradun, -suedradum *exoleverunt*, Txts. 61, 786. *Exoliverunt*, i. *tabuerunt, eruperunt, arripuerunt, vel* gesweþredon, Wrt. Voc. ii. 145, 82. Sweþriendum *facessante*, 33, 29. Sweđriende, 75, 20. I. in reference to concrete things:—Se bryne sweþraþ *the burning ceases*, Exon. Th. 213, 24; Ph. 229. Swēg swiđrode *the sound ceased*, Cd. Th. 197, 18; Exod. 309. Cyre (cyrr?) swiđrode sǣs æt ende (*the sea no longer ebbed* (?), *it rolled back upon the Egyptians*), 207, 12; Exod. 465. Mere sweođerade (*the sea subsided*), ȳđa ongin eft oncyrde, hreóh holmþracu, Andr. Kmbl. 930; An. 465. Dryhten forlēt dægcandelle scīre scīnan, sceadu sweđerodon, 1672; An. 838. Sweþredon, Exon. Th. 179, 16; Gū. 1262. Swiđredon, Cd. Th. 184, 27; Exod. 113. Đonne đū ongite đæt đæt geswel hnescige and swiþrige, Lchdm. ii. 208, 16. Đæt fȳr ongon sweđrian, Beo. Th. 5397; B. 2702. Swiđrian, Cd. Th. 8, 34; Gen. 134. II. in reference to abstract things:—Se longa gefeá ǣfre ne sweþraþ *the long joy never comes to an end*, Exon. Th. 238, 23; Ph. 608. Hwæþere him đæs wonges wyn sweđrade *whether the delight in the plain was abating with him*, 123, 16; Gū. 323. Hild sweđrode, earfođ and ellen, Beo. Th. 1807; B. 901. Gif mægen swiđrade, Cd. Th. 193, 7; Exod. 242. Nō swiđrode rīce, 256, 12; Dan. 639. Him sweđraden synna lustas *sinful joys subsided in him*, Exon. Th. 109, 2; Gū. 84. Metod lēt Babilone blǣd swiđrian, d. Th. 258, 30; Dan. 683. v. gesweđerian; swađrian, *and next word.*

sweđrung, e; *f. Diminution, failure* [:—Đæt tācnaþ wæstma gesweþrunge *that betokens a failure of crops*, Lchdm. iii. 180, 13.]

sweđung, swođung, e; *f. A poultice*:—Sweþing wiþ swile ... gecnuwa đa wyrte, gemeng wiđ ǣges đæt hwīte, beclǣm đæt lim mid đe se swile on sié, Lchdm. ii. 74, 24. Sealfæ and sweþinge wiđ swylum, 6, 30. Gif hē sweđunga (swođunga, R. Ben. Interl. 59, 11) gegearwode *si exibuit fomenta*, R. Ben. 52, 11. [*O. H. Ger.* swedunga *fomentum*.]

swētian; *p.* ede *To be sweet* or *pleasant*:—Đætte ūs biterige sió hreówsung, swā swā ūs ǣr swētedon đa synna *that repentance may prove bitter to us, as before sins were sweet to us*, Past. 54, 5; Swt. 425, 14. v. swētan.

swētlǣcan. v. ge-swētlǣht.

swētlīce; *adv. Sweetly, pleasantly*:—Swētlīce drincan đa word đīnes wīsdōmes *verba tuae scientiae dulciter haurire*, Bd. 5, 24; S. 649, 1.

swēt-mete, es; *m. A sweet-meat, delicacy*:—Of đām swētmettum and of mistlīcum dryncum đæs līþes onwæcnaþ sió wōde þrāg đære wrǣnnesse, Bt. 37, 1; Fox 186, 16: Met. 25, 40. v. swōt-mete.

swētness, e; *f. Sweetness*:—Swētnys *dulcedo*, Ælfc. Gr. 9, 3; Zup. 37, 6. Swētnesse *dulcedinis*, Wrt. Voc. ii. 28, 34. I. in reference to the sense (a) of smell, *fragrance*:—Mycel swētnys wundorlīces stences *fragrantia mirandi odoris*, Bd. 4, 10; S. 578, 13. Swētnes, 5, 12; S. 629, 20. Swētnysse stencg, 3, 8; S. 532, 18. In gistenc suoetnises *in odore suavitatis*, Rtl. 12, 17. Ic nardes stenc oferswīþe mid mīnre swētnesse, Exon. Th. 423, 30; Rä. 41, 30. (b) of taste:—Suoetnis *ambrosea*, Wrt. Voc. ii. 100, 14. Đæs monnan swētnes, Past. 17; Swt. 125, 23. Of bitternise in suoetnisse, Rtl. 114, 36. II. *sweetness, pleasantness, agreeableness*:—Seó swētnes đæs hǣmedþinges đe hē ǣr lufode, Blickl. Homl. 59, 16. Hū micel is seó mycelnes đīnre swētnesse (*dulcedinis tuae*), Ps. Th. 30, 21. Mid đære swētnesse đīnra bletsunga, 20, 3. Ūre heortan gefyllan mid đære swētnesse godcundra beboda, Blickl. Homl. 37, 8. Be swētnesse đæs heofonlīcan rīces, Bd. 4, 24; S. 598, 16. Đa woruldsǣlþa mid swīþe manigre swētnesse ōleccaþ đǣm mōdum, Bt. 7, 1; Fox 16, 10. Beswīcan þurh đa swētnesse đara worda ... þurh đa swētnesse đara synna, Blickl. Homl. 55, 22, 24. Mid đa mǣstan swētnesse *maxima suavitate*, Bd. 4, 24; S. 596, 34.

swetole. v. sweotole.

swēt-swēge; *adj. Of sweet sound, harmonious, melodious*:—Mid swētswēgum leóþum *suavisonis carminibus*, Hymn. Surt. 58, 16.

swēt-wyrde; *adj. Agreeable of speech, bland*:—*Blandis sermonibus, lenis verbis* līþum *vel* swētwyrdum, Wrt. Voc. ii. 127, 4. *Balbus, qui vult loqui et non potest* wlips *vel* swētwyrda (*blandus* seems to have been read?), 125, 11.

swic (swice? *q. v.*), es; *n. Deception, illusion*:—For swicum deóflīcum *propter illusiones diabolicas*, Anglia xiii. 396, 441. [*O. H. Ger.* ā-, bi-swih; *pl.* -swicha; *m.*: *Icel.* svik; *n.*: *Dan.* svig *fraud, deceit.*] v. ǣ-, be-, ge-, lār-swic; swice.

swica, an; *m.* I. *a deceiver*:—Swica *planus* vel *seductor*, Wrt. Voc. i. 47, 51. Se swica (*se ductor ille*) sǣde: 'Æfter þrȳm dagon ic ārīse,' Mt. Kmbl. 27, 63. Seó smyltnys is stulor and dīgele swica, Homl. Th. ii. 392, 25. II. *one who fails in fidelity* or *fealty, a traitor*:—Him man wearp on, đæt hē wæs đes cynges swica and ealra landleóda *that he was a traitor to his king and country*, Chr. 1055; Erl. 189, 4. Swā wurdon Willelmes swican geniđrade, 1075; Erl. 214, 17. [The suikes undergæton đ he (*Stephen*) milde man was, Chr. 1137; Erl. 261, 30. Ueond þet þunched freond is swike ouer alle swike, A. R. 98, 6. Sweoke (*the false fiend*), H. M. 45, 34. Þus speken þeos swiken, ... swa long heo hine lærde, þat he heom ileuede, Laym. 3816. Godard was þe moste swike ... withuten on, þe wike Iudas, Havel. 423. *Icel.* drōttin-sviki.] v. ǣ-, be-, fæder-, hlāford-, mann-swica.

swīcan; *p.* swāc, *pl.* swicon; *pp.* swicen. I. *to move about, wander*:—Ōđer lifaþ lytle hwīle, swīceþ on đisse sīdan gesceafte, and đonne eft mid sorgum gewīteþ, Salm. Kmbl. 737; Sal. 638. [*O. H. Ger.* swīhante *vagus*.] II. *to move away, depart, escape*:—Wiþ đæt beón æt ne fleón, genim veneriam and gehōh hȳ tō đære hȳfe; đonne beóþ hȳ wunigende and nǣfre ne swīcaþ, Lchdm. i. 98, 2. Hē for mundgripe mīnum scolde licgean līfbysig, būtan his līc swice *unless his body had escaped* (*from my grasp*), Beo. Th. 1937; B. 966. Eam ic geseald đǣr ic ūt swīcan ne mæg *traditus sum et non egrediebar*, Ps. Th. 87, 8. Hē biþ on đæt wynstre weorud wyrs gesceáden, đonne hē on đa swīþran hond swīcan mōte, Exon. Th. 449, 25; Dōm. 76. Sceal ānra gehwylc ōđrum swīcan, forđam Dryhten wile đæt earme flǣsc eorđan betǣcan *each one must depart from other, for the Lord will commit frail flesh to earth*, Runic pm. Kmbl. 343, 14; Rūn. 20. II. a. swīcan from *to turn from, to withdraw favour* or *allegiance from, to rebel*:—Đa leóde him from swicon *the people renounced their allegiance to the king of the Elamites* (cf. recesserunt ab eo, Gen. 14, 4), Cd. Th. 119, 18; Gen. 1981. Nōhwæđere ælmihtig ealra wolde Adam and Euan ārna ofteón đeáh đe hē him from swice *although he had withdrawn his favour from them* (perhaps *hē* = *hié* and *swice* is plural *though they had turned from him*, 58, 31; Gen. 954. III. *to desist* from (*dat.* or *prep.*), *cease* from:—Gif hē đære hnappunge ne swīcþ, đonne hnappaþ hē ōđ hē wierđ on fæstum slǣpe, Past. 28; Swt. 195, 11. Hē from gebede swīceþ, Exon. Th. 264, 33; Jul. 373. Ā byþ on færylde, nǣfre swīceþ, Runic pm. Kmbl. 342, 26; Rūn. 17. IV. *to deceive*:—Se đe sweraþ nēhstan his and nā swīcþ (*decipit*), Ps. Spl. 14, 6. Se swīceþ đa mengo *seducit turbas*, Jn. Skt. Rush. 7, 12. Ne nim đū nāne sibbe wiđ đæs landes menn, đe læs đe hira ǣnig đē swīce, Ex. 34, 15. V. *to fail in one's duty* to another, *be a traitor* to, *desert*:—Hwider hweorfaþ wē (*St. Andrew's followers*) hlāfordleáse ... gif wē swīcaþ đē *if we desert thee*, Andr. Kmbl. 814; An. 407. Nǣfre hit (*the sword*) æt hilde ne swāc manna ǣnigum *it never failed any man in fight*, Beo. Th. 2925; B. 1460. Đæt đū Gode swīce *that thou prove traitor to God*, Andr. Kmbl. 1916; An. 960. Hē nele Gode swīcan, Exon. Th. 265, 27; Jul. 387. Đa rīceste Frencisce men wolden swīcan heora hlāforde đam cynge, Chr. 1087; Erl. 224, 3. Drihten mē swīcan ne wile *the Lord will not desert me*, Ps. Th. 53, 4. [His men him suyken (*deserted*) and flugæn, Chr. 1140; Erl. 264, 14. Heo sworen swiken (*deceive*) þat heo nolden, Laym. 4101. Đe hunte him (*the elephant*) wille swiken (*deceive*), O. E. Misc. 20, 637. Þas ilke nefre ne swiken (*ceased*) to brekene þa licome, O. E. Homl. i. 43, 9. Bute ȝef þu swike ham (*cease from such words*), Marh. 5, 4. Hwanne ich swike (*cease*), O. and N. 1459. Hy ne zuykeþ (*cease*) neure niȝt ne day, Ayenb. 157, 21. *O. Sax.* swīkan: *O. Frs.* swīka: *O. H. Ger.* swīchan: *Icel.* svīkja: *Dan.* svige *to deceive, leave in the lurch*: *Swed.* swika.] v. ā-, be-, ge-swīcan; swician.

swicc. v. swice.

swic-cræft, es; *m. Deception, treachery, fraud*:—Se þurh swiccræft (*by treachery*; but the Latin has *in seditione*) manslyht geworhte, Mk. Skt. 15, 7. Deóflīce dǣda on swiccræftan, L. Eth. v. 25; Th. i. 310, 18: vi. 28; Th. i. 322, 18.

swic-dōm, es; *m.* I. *deceit, fraud*:—Wæs swicdōm swīđra đonne wīsdom, and þūhte hwīlum wīsost se đe wæs swicolast, and se đe litelīcost cūđe leáslīce hiwian unsōđ tō sōđe, Wulfst. 128, 7: 243, 13: 52, 31. Swicdōm woruldwelena *deceptio divitiarum*, Mk. Skt. 4, 19. Mid syrewungum and swicdōme hē becom tō đære cynelīcan geđincđe, Homl. Th. i. 80, 34. Hī (*the Romans*) mid swicdōme hié (*the Sabine women*) begeáton, Ors. 2, 2; Swt. 64, 27: Ælfc. T. Grn. 13, 20. Annanias and Saphira wurdon ofslegene for heora swicdōme, Homl. Ass. 59, 194. Hē (*Christ*) synne ne worhte ne nǣnne swicdōm on līfe, 47, 565. Hē hire sǣde þurh hire swicdōm bepǣht, on hwam his strengđ wæs, Jud. 16, 5. Se cyning swīđor micle wēnende wæs đæt hié đonon fleónde wǣren đonne hié ǣnigne swicdōm cȳþan dorsten *the king thought it was far more probable that they were fleeing thence, than that they would venture to practise any ruse*, Ors. 2, 4; Swt. 76, 16. Swicdōma *deceptionum*, Hpt. Gl. 502, 18. II. *treachery, failure in loyalty, treason*:—Đā tugon hiene đære burge witan đæt hē heora swicdōmes wiđ Alexander fremmende wǣre *the chief men of the town accused him of treasonable practices against them in his relations with Alexander*; quasi urbem regi venditasset, Ors. 4, 5; Swt. 168, 17. Be hlāfordsearwe (be cynincges swicdōme, MS. B.) *of treason*, L. Alf. pol. 4; Th. i. 62, 14. Hī sǣdon đæt hī woldan cuman đider for đes cynges swicdōme *for the purpose of acting treacherously towards the king*, Chr. 1048; Erl. 178, 27. Wæs đis land swīđe āstirad and mid mycele swicdōme āfylled *the land was much disturbed and filled with treason*, 1087; Erl. 224, 2. Wiđ đam đe hī ealle ānrǣdlīce būton swicdōme (*without failure of their loyalty*) tō him (*Ethelred*) gecyrdon,

1014; Erl. 150, 13. III. *an offence;* scandalum:—Wā đysum middangearde þurh swicdōmas (*a scandalis*): neód ys đæt swycdōmas (*scandala*) cumon; þeáhhwæđere wā đam menn đe swycdōm (*scandalum*, þurh hyne cymþ, Mt. Kmbl. 18, 7. [Misdon þurh Beelzebubes swikedom, O. E. Homl. i. 55, 10. Þis nis nan swikedom, for þat weord ich hit halde, Laym. 8310. All þatt follȝheþþ swikedom, Orm. 3997. Þu me misraddest . . . Schild þi swikedom from þe lihte, O. and N. 163. *Icel.* svik-dōmr *treason.*]

swice, es; *m.* I. *departure, escape.* v. swīcan, II:—Helle hlinduru nāgon hwyrft ne swice, ūtsīþ ǣfre *the gates of hell allow of no return or escape, of egress ever*, Exon. Th. 364, 30; Wal. 78. I a. *escape* from that which threatens to befall, *evasion:*—Ne biþ đæs lengra swice sāwelgedāles đonne seofon niht fyrstgemearces *there will not be a longer escape from death than a period of seven days*, Exon. Th. 164, 6; Gū. 1007. I b. *outcome, event, issue:*—Hē þenceþ đæt his wīse þince unforcūþ biþ đæs ōþer swice đonne hē đæs fācnes fintan sceáwaþ *he thinks that his ways appear respectable; their event will be different when he observes the result of the fraud*, Exon. Th. 315, 15; Mōd. 31. II. *deceit, fraud, treachery.* v. swīcan, IV, V:—Hē ealle đa cyningas mid biswice (mid his swice, Cott. MS.) ofslōg *captos per dolum reges interfecit*, Ors. 3, 7; Swt. 114, 8. Hī on đīnum folce fācen geswipere syredan and tō swice hogedon *in plebem tuam astute cogitaverunt consilium.* Ps. Th. 82, 3: Exon. Th. 317, 6; Mōd. 61. III. *offence, stumbling-block, snare;* scandalum:—Đanun mæg āspringan seó mǣste sacu and se mǣsta swice ealra ungeþwǣrnessa *exinde grauissima occasio scandalorum oriri potest*, R. Ben. 129, 8. Hī settan mē swyce (swyþe, MS.) đǣr ic sīþade *juxta iter scandalum posuerunt mihi*, Ps. Th. 139, 5. [*O. H. Ger.* -swih; *pl.* -swihhi.] v. be- (*acc.* bigswicae, Lchdm. iii. 208, 12), hlāford-, un-swice; swic.

swice, an; *f. A trap:*—Swican *decipulam*, Hpt. Gl. 520, 30: Anglia xiii. 36, 263. [Þenne þe mon wule tilden his musestoch he bindeđ uppon þa swike chese, O. E. Homl. i. 53, 21. A swyke *discipula*, Wrt. Voc. i. 221, col. 2 (15th cent.).]

swice; *adj.* I. *deceitful, fraudulent:*—Hī wiđstandaþ đam swican (*or subst.?* v. swica) Antecriste, Wulfst. 198, 14. [He minne fader biswak þurh swike his craftes (mid his luþer craftes, 2nd MS.), Laym. 14865.] II. *proving false to what is expected:*—Norđmen wǣron sūđfolcum swice (i. e. *the southern people were deceived in their estimate of the northmen's power* (?); *swice*, as applied to the northmen, cannot mean *rebellious, renouncing allegiance*, for it was the southern peoples who had rebelled against the northern, v. 119, 8–18; Gen. 1976–1981). Cd. Th. 120, 17; Gen. 1996. III. *treacherous, failing in loyalty*, v. swīcan, V. [Feren swike đe sulden him witterlike, Gen. and Ex. 2845.]

swice *and* (?) swicc, es; *m. A scent, smell:*—Suice, suicae *osma* (Gk. ὀσμή; cf. *Span.* husmo *smell, scent;* andar a la husma *to be on the scent;* husmear *to find out by smelling*), Txts. 83, 1468. Swice, Wrt. Voc. ii. 63, 57. Đæt wæs swēte stenc . . . tō đæm swicce men þrungon, Exon. Th. 359, 21; Pa. 66. v. swecc.

swīcend, es; *m. A deceiver, betrayer:*—Se sāula swīcend *the devil*, Homl. Ass. 196, 39: 197, 87. v. be-swīcend.

-swicenness. v. be-, ge-swicenness.

swic-full; *adj. Deceitful, fraudulent, crafty:*—Swicfulles *strophosae, callidae*, Hpt. Gl. 423, 61. Swicfullum *fraudulento*, 517, 45. Swicfulle *frivola, fraudulenta, falsa*, 444, 26. Swicfullum *fraudulentis*, 521, 31.

swician; *p.* ode. I. *to wander:*—Đǣr hī swiciaþ on swīman, firenweorc beraþ, Exon. Th. 79, 33; Cri. 1300. Suicade, suicudae *spatiaretur*, Txts. 99, 1893. Hī đurh cūþe stōwe swicedon and fōron *per nota loca dispersi vagarentur*, Bd. 4, 4; S. 571, 4. Hī swycedan geond wēsten *erraverunt in solitudine*, Ps. Th. 106, 3. Swicedan, 39. Swiciende *pervagatus*, Wrt. Voc. ii. 68, 79. II. *to depart, turn:*—Nā ic fram đīnum dōmum dǣdum swicade *a judiciis tuis non declinavi*, Ps. Th. 118, 102. III. *to deceive:*—Mǣst ǣlc swicode and ōđrum derede wordes and dǣde, Wulfst. 160, 3. Ne ǣnig ne syrwe ne ōđrum ne swicie, 73, 12: 70, 5. Lytelīce swician, 55, 16. Đa men đe ne dorstan for Godes ege swician . . . đa đe cūđan swician and befician and mid leásbregdum earmum mannum derian, L. I. P. 12; Th. ii. 320, 21–26. Swiciende licceteras ārīsaþ and forlǣraþ tō manege, Wulfst. 89, 17. III a. with prep. on, ymb, *to practise deceit* in relation to a matter; cf. *O. Sax.* swīkan umbi:—Se đe on mynstres ǣhtum mid fācne swicaþ *he who fraudulently deceives in the matter of a monastery's possessions*, Homl. Th. i. 398, 26. Annanias and Saphira swicedon on heora āgenum ǣhtum, 33. Se syrwienda deófol ā swicaþ, embe mancyn *is ever practising deceit in respect to man*, Wulfst. 107, 23. Se sceađa georne swicode ymb đa sāwle, Cd. Th. 38, 15; Gen. 607. IV. *to offend;* also *to be offended;* scandalizare, scandalizari:—Gif đīn hand đē swicaþ (*scandalizat*), Mt. Kmbl. 18, 8, 9: Mk. Skt. 9, 43, 45. Þeáh đe ealle swicion ne swicige ic đē nā *etsi omnes scandalizati fuerint sed non ego*, 14, 29. IV a. *to give offence by words, speak injuriously:*—Nā murcna đū nā swica đū *non murmures, non blasphemes*, Scint. 164, 16. [*O. H. Ger.* swichōn *vagari.*] v. ā-, ǣ-, be-swician; swīcan.

swicn, e; *f. Clearance from a criminal charge:*—Se đe hereteáma betygen sié, hē hine be his wergilde āliése, oþþe be his were geswicne. Se āđ sceal bión healf be hūslgengum. Đeóf, siþþan hē biþ on cyninges bende, nāh hē đa swicne *is not allowed the alternative of clearing himself by oath*, L. In. 15; Th. i. 112, 5. [*Goth.* swikns *innocent, clear of wrong-doing;* swiknei, swikniþa *purity;* swikneins *purification: Icel.* sykn *free from guilt, cleared from a criminal charge;* sykn, sykna *clearance from a criminal charge.*] v. ge-swicn; ge-swicnan.

-swicnan, -swicneful. v. ge-swicnan, ge-swicneful.

swicol, sweocol; *adj.* I. *deceitful, false, treacherous, crafty:*—Swicol *fallax* vel *mendax*, Wrt. Voc. i. 47, 50. (1) of persons:—Næs heó swicol nānum đæra đe hyre tō đohte *she never deceived any one who trusted her*, Lchdm. iii. 428, 34. Se swicola Herod . . . cȳdde syđđan his fācenfullan syrewunge, Homl. Th. i. 82, 15. Đæt swicole wīf (*Delilah*), Jud. 16, 8. Đa gescotu đæs sweocolan feóndes *insidiantis hostis jacula*, Past. 56; Swt. 431, 5. Āfandod þurh đone swicolan deófol, Ælfc. T. Grn. 10, 45. Đa swicolan *virum dolosum*, Ps. Th. 5, 6. Se đe wæs swicolast and se đe litelīcost cūđe leáslīce hiwian unsōđ tō sōđe, Wulfst. 128, 9. Swicolost, 268, 17. (2) of things:—Đis līf is swā swicol, đæt hit symble bepǣcþ, Homl. Skt. i. 5, 65. Ne sceole wē nā besettan ūrne hiht on đissum swicelum līfe, Homl. Th. i. 162, 18. Geseoh gif ic on swiculne weg odđe on unrihte eode *vide, si via iniquitatis in me est*, Ps. Th. 138, 21. II. *occasioning offence* (?). v. swice, III, swician, IV, swicol-līc, II:—Sōđ biþ swicolost (switolost?), Menol. Fox 479; Gn. C. 10. [*O. E. Homl. Laym. A. R. Havel.* swikel: *O. H. Ger.* pi-swichal *subdolus: Icel.* svikall *treacherous.*] v. be-(bi-), un-swicol.

swicol-līc; *adj.* I. *deceitful, fraudulent:*—Swicollīce dǣda and lādlīce unlaga āscunige man swȳđe; đæt is, false gewihta and wōge gemeta and leáse gewitnessa, L. Eth. v. 24; Th. i. 310, 12: vi. 28; Th. i. 322, 12. II. *occasioning offence.* v. swice, III;—Ǣnig þing ungeþwǣrlīces and swicollīces (the Latin has *scandalorum spinas*), R. Ben. 38, 18.

swicollīce; *adv. With deceit, with guile, deceitfully, fraudulently, craftily:*—Hē cwæđ đæt hī wære wurdan đæt hȳ ǣnig man tō swicollīce ne bepǣhte mid leáslīcre lāre '*uidete, ne quis uos seducat*,' Wulfst. 88, 26: 55, 3. Đæt wyrse is, đæt hē swicollīce hiwige, swylce hē ārfæstes mōdes sȳ, 53, 26. Aman smeáde swicollīce embe đæt hū hē eall Iudeisc cynn fordyde *Haman plotted how to destroy all the Jewish race*, Homl. Ass. 96, 145.

swicolness, e; *f. Deceit, fraud, treachery:*—Mīne synna đe ic gefremede on mǣnan āđe and swicolnyssæ, Anglia xi. 102, 85. Antecrist lǣrþ unsōđfæstnysse and swicolnesse, Wulfst. 55, 12.

swicđole, Beo. Th. 6281; B. 3146. v. sweþel.

swīcung, e; *f.* I. *deceiving, deluding, deceit, fraud, delusion:*—Mid swīcunge deóflīcre *inlusione diabolica*, Anglia xi. 117, 29. Swīcunge ceápes *fraud in trade*, Lchdm. iii. 198, 31: 202, 13. For swīcuncgum *propter illusiones*, R. Ben. Interl. 88, 5. II. *offence, occasion of stumbling;* scandalum:—Se đe lufaþ brōđer his, swīcung (*scandalum;* v. 1 Jn. 2, 10) on him nys, Scint. 14, 12. Neód hit ys đæt cuman swīcunga (*scandala*), swā þeáh wā đam menn þurh đæne swīcung (*scandalum*) cymþ, 134, 2–3. [He (*false men*) đe swiken, đin agte wiđ swiking, đi soule wiđ lesing, O. E. Misc. 19, 602.] v. ā-, ǣ-, be-, hlāford-swīcung.

-swidung *in* ge-swidung, Lchdm. iii. 168, 2. v. swedring.

swīfan; *p.* swāf, *pl.* swifon; *pp.* swifen. I. *to move* in a course, *wend, sweep:*—Hond hwyrfeþ geneahhe swīfeþ mē geond sweartne *the hand passes over me* (a skin), Exon. Th. 394, 4; Rā. 13, 13. On đære ilcan eaxe hwerfeþ rodor, recene scrīþeþ, sūđheald swīfeþ swift (*sweeps swift*), Mèt. 28, 17. Mọnnum þyncþ đæt sió sunne on mere gange, under sǣ swīfe, đonne hió on setl glīdeþ, 39. Sceal on ānum fēt searoceáp (*a ship*) swīfan, swīþe fēran, faran ofer feldas, Exon. Th. 415, 6; Rā. 33, 7. [*Here are added examples of* ā-swīfan *omitted in their place:*—Āsuāb *exorbitans*, Wrt. Voc. ii. 107, 74. Āswīfende *exorbitans, exorbitantes*, 31, 19, 31: 83, 7: 86, 10: *exorbitantes*, i. *circuientes, declinantes*, 145, 80.] II. of a course of action, *to come* to take part in a matter:—Đā swāf Eánulf on wæs gerēfa đā genom eal đæt yrfe him on đæt hē āhte tō Tyssebyrig *then* (after the commission of a crime) *Eanulf, who was reeve, struck in* or *intervened, and took all the property from him* (the criminal) *that he owned at Tisbury*, Chart. Th. 172, 31. [*O. Frs.* swīva *to be uncertain: Icel.* svīfa *rove, turn, sweep.* Cf. *O. H. Ger.* sweibōn *ferri, volvere, incitari. Gothic has the verb* sweiban; *p.* swaif (Lk. 7, 45) *with the meaning* to cease, leave off.] v. ā-, on-, tō-swīfan.

swift; *adj. Swift, fleet, that does* or *can move quickly:*—Suift *alacer*, Wrt. Voc. ii. 99, 76. Swift, 6, 51: *expeditus*, 145, 36: *celer*, Ælfc. Gr. 9, 18; Zup. 44, 9. Swyft *pernix*, 9, 64; Zup. 71, 2. Swift scip *archiromachus*, Wrt. Voc. i. 63, 30. Hē (*the phenix*) is snel and swift *velox est*, Exon. Th. 220, 8; Ph. 317. Ne se swifta mearh burhstede beáteþ, Beo. Th. 4521; B. 2264. Him on swift wind (cf. ungemetlīc wind, Bt. 12; Fox 36, 15) swāpeþ, Met. 7, 20. Rodor swīfeþ swift, 28, 17. Bufan đam swiftan rodore, Bt. 36, 2; Fox 174, 15. Micel swēg gǣþ of heora (*the stars*) swiftan ryne, Boutr. Scrd. 18, 43. Hors swiftne, Exon. Th. 400, 3; Rā. 20, 3: 487, 22; Rā. 74, 1. Swifte ǽrendracan *veltes* (= *velites*), Wrt. Voc. i. 18, 23. Ic hæbbe swíþe swifte feþera, Bt. 36, 2; Fox 174, 4. Se móna is be sumum dǽle swiftre ðonne seó sunne, Lchdm. iii. 248, 3. Ða (*Alfred's ships*) wǽron ǽgðer ge swiftran ge unwealtran ge eác hiéran ðonne ða óðru, Chr. 897; Erl. 95, 13. Wind byþ on lyfte swiftust, Menol. Fox 464; Gn. C. 3. Gecunnian hwylc heora swiftost hors hæfde, Bd. 5, 6; S. 619, 1. Ealle ða menn ðe swyftoste hors habbaþ... Ðǽr beóþ ða swiftan hors ungefóge dýre, Ors. 1, 1; Swt. 20, 34–21, 6. v. ryne-swift.

swiftlere, es; *m. A slipper, shoe*:—Swiftlere *suptularis* (*suptalaris*), swiftlæras *suptalares*, Ælfc. Gl. Zup. 314, 15. Swyftleras *subtalares*, Coll. Monast. Th. 27, 31. Swifteleares, Wrt. Voc. i. 26, 19. [Cf. *O. H. Ger.* suftelara *talaria*, which Graff derives from Latin *subtalaris*. The English and German words seem to have the same origin.]

swiftlíce; *adv. Swiftly*:—Hredlíce ł swiftlíce *velociter*, Ps. Lamb. 6, 11. Gálful líf swiftlíce (*celeriter*) gelǽt tó ylde, Scint. 88, 19. Ðá férde his gást swyftlíce, Homl. Th. i. 452, 30. Zacheus swyftlíce of ðam treówe álíhte, 580, 34. Hí fleóþ swiftlíce, Wulfst. 200, 17.

swiftness, e; *f. Swiftness, fleetness, celerity*:—Hwá unlǽredra ne wundraþ ðæs roderes færeldes and his swiftnesse, Bt. 39, 3; Fox 214, 16. Dysig se ðe getrúwaþ on his horses swiftnesse, Ps. Th. 32, 15. Hé swang ðone top mid swá micelre swiftnesse, Ap. Th. 13, 13. Da óðre deór ðe mihton hire ætfleón þurh heora fóta swiftnysse, Homl. Ass. 63, 280. Þurh ða swiftnysse (*the rapidity of the moon's motion*), Lchdm. iii. 248, 4. Uton behealdan ða wundorlícan swyftnysse ðære sáwle; heó hæfþ swá mycele swyftnysse, ðæt heó on ánre tíde besceáwaþ heofonan and ofer sǽ flýhþ, Homl. Skt. i. 1, 123.

swift-ryne (?), es; *m. A swift course, rapid running* of water:—Singalrenes ł swift[renes] *decursus*, Hpt. Gl. 418, 51.

swiftu (-o); *indecl. f. Swiftness*:—Hwá unlǽrdra ne wundrige rodres swifto? Met. 28, 3. v. swiftness.

swígan; *p.* de. I. *to be silent*:—God ná swígeþ *Deus non silebit*, Ps. Spl. 49, 3. Stiórdon him menigo ðætte hé suígde (*ut taceret*), Mk. Skt. Lind. 10, 48. Ðú bist suígende (swígende, Rush.), Lk. Skt. Lind. 1, 20. Geót swígende ðæt blód on yrnende wæter, Lchdm. ii. 76, 14: 140, 26: 290, 26: 292, 25. Ðæt eall swígende gedó, 104, 10. Swígende (suígende, Hatt. MS.) hé cwæð on his móde... Ða swígendan (suígendan, Hatt. MS.) stefne se dígla Déma gehírde, Past. 4; Swt. 38, 16–20: Blickl. Homl. 7, 16. Þú ána hí swígende tǽlst *thou alone by thy silence dost blame her*, Ap. Th. 16, 21. Hé oft ána sæt swígende múðe *saepe solus residens ore tacito*, Bd. 2, 9; S. 512, 13. Ðæt ánra manna gehwylc sceáwige hine sylfne swígende móde, Blickl. Homl. 57, 34. II. *to become silent* from astonishment; stupere. v. swígung, III, swíge, III:—Swígdon ł styldon *stupebant*, Mk. Skt. Lind. 1, 22. Stylton ł suígdon, 6, 51. Suígdon (swígdon, Rush.), 10, 32. [*O. H. Ger.* swígén *silere, reticere*: *Ger.* schweigen.] v. for- (Ðeáh hé hit silf forswíge, his gegirla hine geswutelaþ, Ap. Th. 14, 3), ge- (*see* ge-swígde, -on, *given under* geswígian), óþ-swígan; swigian.

swíg-dæg, es; *m. A day on which silence was to be observed*:—Circlíce þeáwas forbeódaþ tó secgenne ǽnig spel on ðám þrým swígdagum, Homl. Th. i. 218, 31: ii. 262, 16. [The three days referred to are the last three days of Passion Week. 'Besides the general injunction of silence in the ordinary business of life, and in various ritual matters, even the bells were to remain silent from the Thursday evening, which commemorated our Lord's betrayal, to the following Sunday morning. Nothing more, probably, was at first meant by this, than to impress a character of unusual solemnity upon the season, but it was eventually said that men were thus to be reminded of the time when the preaching of the Gospel wholly ceased; Jesus Himself being actually dead during most of it, and His disciples all along being dispersed panic-stricken.' Durand, quoted in Soames' Anglo-Saxon Church, p. 263. Cf. the injunction in the Ancren Riwle: Holdeð silence al þe swiðwike (swihende wike, MS. T.: swiwike, MS. C.) uort non of Ester euen, 70, 5–8. In German Good Friday is *der stille Freitag*.]

swíge (*but* swígea *occurs*, Scint. 82, 1), an; *f.* I. *silence, absence of speech*:—Hú se láreów sceal bión gesceádwís on his swígean (swiggean, Cott. MSS.) and nytwyrðe on his wordum... Sió ungemetgode suíge (swigge, Cott. MSS.) ðæs láreówes on gedwolan gebringþ ða ðe hé lǽran meahte, Past. 15; Swt. 89, 3–10. Essaias cwæð, ðætte sió suýge (swigge, Cott. MSS.) wǽre ðære ryhtwísnesse fultum, 38; Swt. 279, 24. Sý heálíc swíge æt ðæm gereorde, ðæt nánes mannes stefn gehýred ne sý bútan ðæs rǽderes ánes, R. Ben. 62, 13. Ðá wearð stilnes and swíge geworden innon ðare healle, Ap. Th. 17, 6. Mé náwðer deág secge ne swíge, Exon. Th. 12, 23; Cri. 190. Náht framaþ, gif on eardungstówe swígea sý, Scint. 82, 1: 213, 14. Be swígan... Hé for swígan mægene clypunge geswác... Leornerum for swígean hefignesse seldhwænne leáf geseald sié tó sprecenne ymbe hálige sprǽca, R. Ben. 21, 8–17. Hí clumiaþ mid ceaflum, ðǽr hí sceoldan clypian; wá heom ðære swígean, L. I. P. 5; Th. ii. 308, 21: Wulfst. 177, 1. Óðer ondréd ðæt hé forlure sprecende ða gestrión ðe hé on ðære swígean (swiggean, Cott. MSS.) geðencan meahte; óðer ondréd ðæt hé ongeáte on his swýgean (swiggean, Cott. MSS.) ðæt hé sumne hearm geswigode, Past. 7; Swt. 49, 19–22. Mid suígean, 35; Swt. 237, 12. Mid swígan forberan *to bear in silence*, Homl. Th. ii. 164, 20. Heó swígan lufode, 546, 28. Wé cweðaþ ðæt sí best æfter Gode, ðæt man gemetigian cunne ge his sprǽce ge his swígan, Prov. Kmbl. 2. II. *silence, quiet, absence of noise*; also *a time of silence*. v. swíg-tíma:—Ne árfæstness ne sib ne hopa ne swíge gegladaþ *nec pax nec pietas immo spes nulla quietis*, Dóm. L. 220. In swígean midre nihte *intempestive*, Wrt. Voc. ii. 46, 74. Swígan *conticinio* (cf. *conticinium*, ðonne ealle þing sweowiaþ on hyra reste, Lchdm. iii. 244, 2), 20, 30. III. *silence* from astonishment, *amazement*; stupor. v. fǽr-swíge, swígan, II, swígung, III. IV. *delay* (?). v. swígung, IV:—Suígo dyde ðe brýdgum *moram faciente sponso*, Mt. Kmbl. Lind. 25, 5. [*Or is this a different word?* cf. (?) *Icel.* svig *a curve, circuit*; sveigja *to bend, sway*.] [*O. H. Ger.* swíga *taciturnitas, silentium*.]

swíge; *adj.* I. *silent, not speaking*:—On óðre wísan mon sceal manigean ða swíðe swígean, on óðre wísan ða felaídelsprǽcean, Past. 23; Swt. 174, 24. Ða ðe tó swíðe swíge (swigge, Cott. MSS.) beóþ... ða suíðe suígean (swiggean, Cott. MSS.) *taciturni... nimis taciti*, 38; Swt. 271, 6–10. Ðá wæs swígra secg (*Hunferth*) on gylpsprǽce (cf. Ðú worn fela, wine mín Húnferð, beóre druncen ymb Brecan sprǽce, 1064; B. 530), Beo. Th. 1964; B. 980. II. *silent, not making a noise, still*:—Wind wédende færeþ, and eft semninga swíge gewyrðeþ, Elen. Kmbl. 2548; El. 1275. Stille þynceþ lyft ofer londe, and lagu swíge, Exon. Th. 383, 16; Rä. 4, 11. Nis mín sele swíge, ne ic sylfa hlúd, 494, 1; Rä. 82, 1. v. swíþ-swíge.

swígen[n], e; *f. Silence, refraining from speech*:—Ðam láreówe sylfum deraþ hwílon his swígen, ac heó deraþ symle his underðeóddum, gif him biþ seó heofenlíce lár oftogen, Homl. Th. ii. 532, 4.

swigene ? :—Ðæs mannes bilcofa is tó besceáwianne: ǽrest him is tó sellanne ðæt ðone innoð stille and sméþe, ne sié scearp ne tó afor ne slítende ne swigene, Lchdm. ii. 210, 21.

swigian, sweogian, sweowian, swugian, swuwian, sugian, suwian; *p.* ode. I. *to be silent*, (a) of that which has voice:—Ic suwige (swugige, swuwie) *taceo*, Ælfc. Gr. 26, 2; Zup. 26, 13. Swigaþ *silet* (*vipera*), Rtl. 125, 27. God ne swugaþ (swigaþ, Surt.) *Deus non silebit*, Ps. Th. 49, 3. Ðonne swíaþ (*silet*) hé (*the phenix*), Exon. Th. 207, 16; Ph. 142. Swigiaþ *conticiscent*, Wrt. Voc. ii. 14, 53. Ða ðe má swigiaþ (swugiaþ, Hatt. MS.) ðonne hié ðyrfen, Past. 38; Swt. 272, 24. Ða ðe swigiaþ (swugiaþ, l. 3), ðæt hié hié ne bodiaþ, 48; Swt. 365, 7. *Conticinium*, ðonne ealle þing sweowiaþ (suwiaþ, MSS. R. P.) on hyra reste, Lchdm. iii. 244, 2. Ic swigode (swygode, Spl.: sugode, Th.) *tacui*, Ps. Surt. 31, 3: Exon. Th. 485, 16: Rä. 71, 14. Ic swugode, swá swá se dumba, Ps. Th. 37, 13: 49, 22. Ðeáh ðe seó tunge swigode, ðæt his líf wæs sprecende, Bd. 5, 12; S. 627, 30: Ap. Th. 16, 19: Cd. Th. 250, 15; Dan. 547. Hé suwode (swygode, MS. A.: swugode, MSS. B.C.: swigade, Rush.) *tacebat*, Mk. Skt. 14, 61: Mt. Kmbl. 26, 63. Ðá swigoden hí ealle and stille wǽron *conticuere omnes*, Bd. 3, 11; S. 536, 31. Hí suwodon (swigedon MS. A.: swigadun, Rush.), Mk. Skt. 3, 4. Ne swiga (swuga, Th.: suwa, Lamb.) ðú *ne sileas*, Ps. Spl. Surt. 38, 17. Ne swiga (swyga, Spl.) ðú *ne taceas*, Ps. Th. Surt. 82, 1. Ne swiga (swyga, Spl.: swuga, Th.)... ne suga *ne sileas... ne taceas*, Ps. Lamb. 27, 1. Ne swuga, Ps. Spl. 34, 25. Ðe læs ðú suwige *ne taceas*, 27, 1. Ic swigiende ealle ða niht áwunode, Bd. 5, 6; S. 619, 29. Ðú byst suwiende (swygende, MS. A.: suwigende, MSS. B. C.), Lk. Skt. 1, 20. (b) of that which has not voice, *not to make a noise*:—Hrægl mín swigaþ, Exon. Th. 389, 21; Rä. 8, 1. Ða ýða swygiaþ (swigadon, Surt.: swigedon, Spl.) *siluerunt fluctus ejus*, Ps. Th. 106, 28. II. *to be silent* from astonishment, *be amazed*:—Swigadun ł stylton ofer lǽre his *stupebant super doctrina ejus*, Mk. Skt. Rush. 1, 22. III. with an object (gen. or acc.) *to be silent about* something, *to refrain from the mention of* something:—Gif ðú suwast hit and nylt folce his þearfe gecýðan, Wulfst. 283, 3. Hié nyllaþ geopenian ðǽm syngiendum hiera unryht ac suigiaþ (swigiaþ, Cott. MSS.) ðara ðreáunga *iniquitatem peccantium nequaquam aperiunt, quia ab increpationis voce conticescunt*, Past. 15; Swt. 91, 11. Lyt swigode níwra spella se ðe næs geràd, Beo. Th. 5787; B. 2897. Hé ne suigige ðæs ðe nyttwyrðe sié tó sprecanne, ne ðæt ne sprece ðæt hé suigigean (swigian, Cott. MSS.) scyle *ne aut tacenda proferat, aut proferenda reticescat*, Past. 15; Swt. 89, 6–7. Hié mon sceal lǽran ðæt hí hwílum suigien (swugien, Cott. MSS.) ðæs sóðes *admonendi sunt, ut noverint nonnunquam vera reticere*, 35; Swt. 237, 9. [*O. Sax.* swigón: *O. Frs.* swigia.] v. for-, ge-swigian; swígan.

swigiendlíce; *adv. Silently, in silence*:—Sæt ic ána in ðam wéstenne... Ðá ongann ic swigiendlíce þencan be manegra munuca lífe, Homl. Ass. 204, 311.

swígness, e; *f. Silence; a time of silence*:—Cwyldtíd, swígnes *conticinium*, Wrt. Voc. ii. 135, 14. v. swíge, II, *and next word*.

swíg-tíma, an; *m. A time of silence*:—Seó niht hafaþ seofon tódǽlednyssa... þridde ys *conticinium*, ðæt ys swítíma, Anglia viii. 319, 29. v. swíge, II, *and the preceding and following words*.

swígung, e; *f.* I. *silence, absence of speech*:—Hé (*John the Baptist*) ðam fæder (*Zacharias*) ða stefne ágeaf, ðá se heáhengel mid ðære swígunge fæstnunga geband ðone fæder, Blickl. Homl. 167, 11.

Hwanne besmât hine seó scyld ðære fealasprecolnesse? . . . oþþe hû sceþede him seó synn ðære swîgunga? 169, 7. Mid suîgunga *cum silentio*, Rtl. 20, 15. Swîgunge, Shrn. 41, 26. II. *silence, absence of noise*:—Martha ceigde Mariam suiugunga (swîunga, Rush.) and cwoeð *Martha vocavit Mariam silentio, dicens*, Jn. Skt. Lind. 11, 28. II a. *a time of silence*. v. swîge, II, and two preceding words:—Ðære swîgunge *conticinio*, Wrt. Voc. ii. 24, 31: 20, 29. Ih swîgunge *in conticinio*, 47, 46. III. *silence* from astonishment, *amazement*. v. swîgan, II, swîge, III:—Forstylton swîgunge micelre *obstupuerunt stupore maximo*, Mk. Skt. Rush. 5, 42. IV. *delay*. v. swîge, IV:—Suîgiunc dóes hlâferd mîn *moram facit dominus meus*, Mt. Kmbl. Lind. 24, 48. [*O. H. Ger.* swîgunga *silentium*.] v. ge-swîgung.

swilc, swelc; *pron.* (the word can take the weak declension). I. where the word points to what has been already described, *such*, (1) used substantively, *that which has been already described, the like, the same*:—Ne biþ swylc (*the practice already described*) cwênlîc þeáw, Beo. Th. 3885; B. 1940. Ne biþ swylc earges sîð, 5076; B. 2541. Ne sceolde ðê nân man swelces tô gelêfan *no one would believe such a thing of you*, Bt. 5, 1; Fox 10, 2: 19; Fox 68, 32. Hê ǽfre swylces geswîce, L. Ath. i. 6; Th. i. 202, 17. Heó âwiht swylces ne hýrdon, Elen. Kmbl. 1139; El. 571. Gif wîfmen hwæt swylces derige, Lchdm. i. 236, 3: Beo. Th. 1764; B. 880. Hæringcas and leaxas . . . and fela swylces (*et similia*), Coll. Monast. Th. 24, 13. Hæleða fela swelces and swelces wundraþ, Met. 28, 49. Be swilcum and swilcum ðû miht ongitan, Bt. 38, 1; Fox 196, 11: Met. 26, 107. Wundorsióna fela secga gehwylcum ðara ðe on swylc staraþ, Beo. Th. 1997; B. 996: 5589; B. 2798: Met. 30, 18. Gif him (*a lunatic*) gelimpe ðæt hê man ofsleá . . . his mâgas hine wið ôðær swylc gescyldan *propinqui ejus eum contra simile quid servent*, L. Ecg. P. addit. 29; Th. ii. 236, 31. Swylcra sîþfæt (*the journey of those just mentioned*), Exon. Th. 400, 12; Rä. 20, 9. Hû hê swylce âcwealde, Ps. Th. 108, 16. Oft ða swelcan (swylcan, Cott. MSS.) monn sceal forsión, Past. 37, 2; Swt. 265, 17. (2) used adjectivally, *like that already described*, (a) agreeing with a noun:—Hine swelces gamenes gilpan lyste, Met. 9, 19. Swylces morðres, 32. Hig worhton ôðer swilc þing *fecerunt quaedam similiter*, Ex. 7, 11. Hê ǽr ne sîð ôðre swylce lâre gehýrde, Exon. Th. 169, 10; Gû. 1092: Blick. Homl. 189, 22. Geþyld and ryhtwîsnes and wîsdôm and manege swelce cræftas, Bt. 34, 6; Fox 142, 1. Se is tô lytel swelcra lâriówa, Met. 10, 55. Manegum swylcum (*talibus*) bigspellum hê spræc tô him, Mk. Skt. 4, 33. Manna sâulum hê gyfþ swilca gyfa. Ða swilcan gifa hî ne þurfon forlǽtan, Shrn. 192, 3. (b) predicatively:—Hió nǽfre siþþan swelc wæs *it* (*Rome*) *was never the same afterwards*, Ors. 6, 1; Swt. 252, 24. Gif hê suelc (swelc, Cott. MSS.) wǽre, Past. 16; Swt. 101, 10. Swelc wæs þeáw hira, Andr. Kmbl. 50; An. 25. Swylc, Beo. Th. 359; B. 178. Ðæt ûre tîda ne mihtan weorðan swilce, Bt. 15; Fox 48, 18. Swelce, Met. 8, 42. II. as an antecedent:—Swælc monn se ðe tô mînum ærfe fôe gedêle hê ǽlcum messepreóste binnan Cent mancus goldes, Cod. Dip. Kmbl. i. 351, 4. Ðâ com leóht swilc swâ hî ǽr ne gesâwon, Homl. Skt. ii. 29, 263. Eal swylce seó mettrumnes biþ ðæs seócan mannes . . . swylc is ðæt lîf ðysses middangeardes, Blickl. Homl. 59, 31. Wǽre se man on swelcum lande swelce hê wǽre, Bt. 27, 3; Fox 98, 27. Ðæt hê ðone hlâf on swilcere stôwe âwurpe, ðǽr hine nân man findan ne mihte, Homl. Th. ii. 162, 25. Wê swylc ne gefrugnan gelimpan, ðæt ðû befênge, Exon. Th. 6, 3; Cri. 78. Ymb swelc tô sprecanne hwelc hit ðâ wæs, Ors. 1, 10; Swt. 48, 4. Swelce burg gewyrcan swelce sió wæs, 2, 4; Swt. 74, 8. Gif ic hæfde swilcne anweald, swylce God hæfþ, Bt. 38, 2; Fox 196, 19. Se wolde habban swilcne hlîsan swâ Benedictus, Homl. Th. ii. 162, 18: Soul Kmbl. 278; Seel. 143. Hî ne þurhwuniaþ swelca, swelce hî ǽr tô côman, Bt. 11, 1; Fox 30, 28. Swylcra yrmða swâ ðû unc scrife, Soul Kmbl. 201; Seel. 102. Bûton hê hæbbe swylce þêningmen ðe þeáwfæstnysse him gebeódon, Homl. Skt. i. pref., 62. III. in correlative clauses, swilc . . . swilc *such* . . . *as*:—Swylc biþ wedera cyst, swylc wæs on ðam fýre, Cd. Th. 238, 6; Dan. 350. Swylc scolde eorl wesan, swylc Æschere wæs, Beo. Th. 2661; B. 1328. Mid swelce hrægle hê in eode, mid swelce gange hê ût, L. Alf. 11; Th. i. 46, 3. Swylce mǽla swylce hira mandryhtne þearf gesǽlde, Beo. Th. 2502; B. 1249. Eahtige hê hine selfne suelcne suelcne hê ondrǽtt ðæt hê sié, Past. 17; Swt. 119, 8. Sêce swylcne hlâford, swylcne hê wille, L. Ath. iv. 1; Th. i. 220, 24. Beóþ swylce (suælce, Lind.) gedrêfednessa swylce (suelco, Lind.) ne gewurdon (*tales quales non fuerunt*), Mk. Skt. 13, 19: Beo. Th. 6309; B. 3165. IV. containing both antecedent and relative, *such as*:—Ðonne ic wæs mid Iudêum, ic wæs swelc hié, Past. 16; Swt. 101, 6. Gestreón swilc ðǽr funden wæs, Cd. Th. 220, 5; Dan. 66. Nâ hýrde wê ðæt ǽnig wurde hûs ârǽred swylic ðæt mǽre wæs, Anglia xi. 9, 30. Gôdfremmendra swylcum gifeðe biþ *to such as it shall be granted*, Beo. Th. 604; B. 299: Met. 26, 87. Swilce wê ðê daga cîgen *on such day as we call to thee*, Ps. Bên. 19, 9. Eahtige hê hiene selfne swelcne hê ondrǽt ðæt hê sié, Past. 17; Swt. 118, 8. Hæfde his ende gebidenne swylcne hê ǽr æfter worhte, Judth. Thw. 22, 17; Jud. 65. Eall gedǽlan swylc him God sealde, Beo. Th. 145; B. 72. Ealle swylce hî habban scoldon, 3599; B. 1797. Cyningas swylce iú wǽron, Exon. Th. 310, 32; Seef. 83. Beaduþreáta mǽst swylce cyning ymbsittendra meahte âbannan tô beadwe, Elen. Kmbl. 64; El. 32. V. in expressions relating to quantity or number, *so* (*as*) *much*, so (*as*) *many*:—Hwîtes sealtes swilc swâ mǽge mid feówer fingrum geniman *as much white salt as may be taken with four fingers*, Lchdm. ii. 130, 2. Swelc swâ biþ þreó beána, 228, 5. Selle him twâ swylc swylce man æt him nime, i. 400, 18. Mealwan seáwes þrý lytle bollan gemengde wiþ swilc tû wæteres (*twice as much water*), 214, 15. Genim wînes and eles swilc healf *take some wine and of oil half as much*, 180, 11. Medmicel pipores and ôþer swilc cymenes *a moderate amount of pepper and an equal quantity of cummin*, 256, 5: 134, 26. Feówertig daga nihta ôðer swilc *forty days and as many nights*, Cd. Th. 83, 21; Gen. 1383: Beo. Th. 3170; B. 1583: Menol. Fox 279; Men. 141. [*Laym.* swilc, swulc, swulch; soch, 2nd MS.: *Orm.* swillc: *A. R. Marh. O. and N.* swuch: *R. Glouc.* such: *Goth.* swa-leiks: *O. Sax.* su-lîk: *O. Frs.* se-lîk, selk, sulk, sulch, suck: *O. H. Ger.* so-lîh, su-lîh, solh: *Icel.* slîkr.]

swilce, swelce; *adv. conj.* I. *in like manner, also, as well, too*:—Se com swylce tô-dæg tô mê *ad me quoque hodie venire dignatus est*, Bd. 4, 3; S. 568, 17. Swylce hê brohte mycel feoh *attulit autem et summam pecuniae non parvam*, 4, 11; S. 599, 20. Hê wæs sôþ man, ðý hine dorste deófol costian; swylce hê wæs sôþ God, ðý him englas þegnedon, Blickl. Homl. 33, 34. Swilce gelamp eft ôðer wundor ðysum onlîc, 221, 18. Swilce ôþre dæge ðæt ilce hié dydon, 241, 30: Cd. Th. 81, 2; Gen. 1339: 247, 24; Dan. 502. Swilce is seó feórðe *there is also the fourth*, 15, 14; Gen. 233. Wǽglîðende swilce wîf heora *the seafarers, their wives too*, 86, 18; Gen. 1432. Swylce, Beo. Th. 226; B. 113. End suelce (suilcae, suilce) *atqueve*, Txts. 37, 75. Ic God herige and on God swylce gelýfe, Ps. Th. 55, 4. Ge swylce, Beo. Th. 4508; B. 2258. Hié hæfdon manige glengas; eác swylce hié hæfdon wîf, Blickl. Homl. 99, 20. On ðære hâlgan Ðrynnesse naman beó ðû hâl, mid mînes lâreówes geearnungum eác swylce gefultumod, Homl. Skt. i. 6, 40. Nâ ðæt ǽnne ac eác swilce manige *non solum unum, sed etiam plures*, Coll. Monast. Th. 26, 19. Næs nô on gesundum þingum ânum, ac eác swylce on wiðerweardum þingum, Blickl. Homl. 13, 8. Eác ic swylce on God gewêne, Ps. Th. 55, 4. Engla cynn and manna cynn and eác swylce werigra gâsta, Blickl. Homl. 83, 12. Swylce eác feówer tîda syndan, 35, 15. Hê helpeþ þearfan swylce eác wædlan *parcet pauperi et inopi*, Ps. Th. 71, 13: Blickl. Homl. 75, 19: Judth. Thw. 21, 14; Jud. 18: 26, 20; Jud. 344. Swylce hê ûs âlêsde, Blickl. Homl. 103, 13. Fîfe cyningas, swilce seofene eác eorlas, Chr. 937; Erl. 112, 30. And ic ðê on hleóðre hearpan swylce eác gecwême, Ps. Th. 107, 2. II. *so, in such manner, in a manner already described*:—Ðîn mildheortnes is mycel wið heofenas, is ðîn sôðfæstnes swylce wið wolcnum, Ps. Th. 56, 12. Lifge Ismael lârum swilce ðînum, Cd. Th. 141, 18: Gen. 2346. Ne wê swylc ne gefrugnan ǽfre gelimpan, ðæt ðû in sundurgiefe swylce (*in such manner*) befênge, Exon. Th. 6, 7; Cri. 80. III. *as, like*:—Ðonne ic wæs mid Iudêum ic wæs swelce hié, Past. 16; Swt. 100, 7. Ne beó gê swylce lîceteras *non eritis sicut hypocritae*, Mt. Kmbl. 6, 5. Genôh byþ ðam leorningcnihte ðæt hê sý swylce (*sicut*) hys lâreów, and þeów swylce hys hlâfurd, 10, 25. Se âwyrgda gâst is heáfod ealra unrihtwîsra dǽda, swylce unrihtwîse syndon deófles leomo, Blickl. Homl. 33, 8. Hyre twigu beóþ swylce swînen byrst, Lchdm. i. 156, 2. Wearð gesewen swilce ânes mannes hand wrîtende on ðære healle wâge, Homl. Th. ii. 434, 33. Steám up ârâs swylce rêc, Elen. Kmbl. 1604; El. 804: Andr. Kmbl. 178; An. 89. Hwylc biþ hê (*the body after death*) ðonne bûton swylce stân, Blickl. Homl. 21, 26: Homl. Th. i. 406, 14. Mê geweorðode wuldres ealdor swylce swâ hê his môdor eác geweorðode, Rood Kmbl. 181; Kr. 92. *See also passages under* swilc, II. IV. *as if*:—Se wearð wið hine forwrêged swylce (suoelce, Lind.) hê his gôd forspilde *quasi dissipasset bona ipsius*, Lk. Skt. 16, 1. Swelce hié cwǽden *as if they had said*, Past. pref.; Swt. 5, 13. Men gehýraþ myccle stefne on heofenum, swylce ðǽr man fyrde trymme and samnige, Blickl. Homl. 91, 31: Ps. Th. 101, 3. Ðæs temples segl sylf slât on tû, swylce hit seaxes ecg þurhwôde, Exon. Th. 70, 20; Cri. 1141. Hié on swîman lâgon, swylce hié wǽron deáðe geslegene, Judth. Thw. 21, 23; Jud. 31. V. with words denoting measure, *about*:—Maria wunude mid hyre swylce (suælce, Lind.: swelce, Rush.) þrý mônþas *quasi mensibus tribus*, Lk. Skt. 1, 56. Se Hǽlend wæs on ylde swylce þrîtigwintre *quasi annorum triginta*, 3, 23. Betuh ðæm clife on (ond?) ðæm wætre wǽron swylce twelf mîla, Blickl. Homl. 211, 3. [Sulch (ase, 2nd MS.) hit an liun were, Laym. 4085. Sulc (alse, 2nd MS.) he walde awede, 6486.]

swilcness, e; *f. Quality*:—Sý gebrôðrum reáf geseald be swilcnesse and staþele ðære stôwe ðe hý on wuniaþ *secundum locorum qualitatem ubi habitant*, R. Ben. 89, 4. Ðysne wyrttruman syllan þicgean mid sumum ôðrum mete gemencgedne be ðære swylcnysse ðe seó untrumnys ðonne byþ, Lchdm. i. 260, 20.

swile. v. swyle.

swilian *and* swillan *to swill*. I. *to wash*:—Ic þweá oððe ic swilige mîn bed mid mînum teárum *lavabo lectum meum lacrimis meis*, Ps. Lamb. 6, 7. II. *to swill the mouth* or *throat, to gargle*:—Iagul swyleþ *gargarizat*, Wrt. Voc. ii. 40, 54. Seóh þurh clâð and swile mid ðæt geagl; after ðam lǽcedôme gelôme mid ele swille ða hracan, Lchdm. ii. 24, 25-27. Swille ðone geagal . . . swille ða ceolan, 48, 19, 21. Gagul suille *gargarizet*, Wrt. Voc. ii. 109, 46. Sceal mon ðone geagl swillan, Lchdm. ii. 48, 15. Ðæt geagl tō swillanne, 24, 12, 28. [Kan ich dishes swillen, Havel, 919.] v. (?) ā-spȳlian (-swylian?), be-swylian = *to wash* (not *to soil*), *and see next word.*

swiling *and* swilling, e; *f. A swilling, washing, gargling, gargle:*—Clǽsnunga and swiling wið hrūm and gillistrum, Lchdm. ii. 2, 3. Wyrc ðus swilinge tō heáfdes clǽnsunge . . . habbe on mūþe lange, ðonne yrnþ ðæt gillister ūt. Eft ōþru swiling . . . sūpe wlæc and ðæt geagl swile and þweá his mūð, 24, 14-23. Swille ða ceolan . . . sȳn ða swillinga hwīlum hāte, 48, 22. v. preceding word.

swillan, swilling, swilt. v. swilian, swiling, swylt.

swīma, an; *m.* I. *swimming in the head, dizziness, giddiness, vertigo:*—Hī āscamode swiciaþ on swīman *ashamed they wander dizzily*, Exon. Th. 79, 33; Cri. 1300. Wið ðone swīman, nim . . . and cnuca . . . wyrta . . . ofgeót mid wætere . . . nim ðone wǽtan and lafa ðīn heáfod, Lchdm. iii. 48, 3. II. *a state of unconsciousness, a swoon:*—Licgan on swīman *to lie unconscious*, Judth. Thw. 21, 22; Jud. 30: 23, 5; Jud. 106. [For to wacken him (*Lazarus in the grave*) of his suime (swyme), C. M. 14201. Halliwell gives three instances of the word, in the following phrases, *to fall in swyme, to lie in swyme, to come as in swyme.* (In these four passages *swyme* rimes with *tyme.*) He also gives *swimy* = giddy in the head, as a Sussex word (v. also E. D. S. Pub. C. 4, where *swimy* or *swimy-headed* = giddy, is given as a Surrey word); and *swimer* a hard blow as used in Devonshire. *O. Frs.* swīma *giddiness, swoon: Du.* zwijm *swoon: Icel.* svimi; liggja í svima *to lie in a swoon,* slā í svima *to stun: Dan.* svime *a swoon;* svime-slag *a stunning blow.*] v. heáfod-swīma.

swimman; *p.* swamm, *pl.* swummon; *pp.* swummen *To swim:*—Swimþ, swam *nat*, swimmende *nantes*, Wrt. Voc. ii. 61, 11, 13. Swam *nat*, 95, 80. I. of living creatures moving in or on water:—Swā swā fixas swimmaþ on wætere, Lchdm. iii. 272, 19: Exon. Th. 363, 21; Wal. 57. Ic on flōde swom, deáf under ȳþe, 487, 17; Rä. 73, 4. Hié swummun ofer tō ðæm ēglande. Ðā hié ðā hæfdon feórðan dǽl ðære eá geswummen, Nar. 10, 29. Com tō lande lidmanna helm swymman, Beo. Th. 3252; B. 1624. Swimman hine geseón hearm getǽcnaþ, Lchdm. iii. 212, 18. Ðā geseah hē swymman scealfran on flōde, Homl. Th. ii. 516, 6. Teón ða wæteru forð swimmende cynn, Gen. 1, 20. II. of a vessel moving on water:—Secga geseldan swimmaþ on weg, Exon. Th. 289, 25; Wand. 53. Hine (*a vehicle*) oxa ne teáh, ne [hē] on flōde swom, 404, 28; Rä. 23, 14. Se swymmenda arc (*Noah's ark*), Homl. Th. ii. 60, 2. III. of lying on the surface of water:—Nim ompran neoþowearde ða ðe swimme, Lchdm. ii. 52, 19: 76, 5. Genim doccan ða ðe swimman wille, 88, 13. [*O. H. Ger.* swimman: *Icel.* svimma.] v. æt-, ge-, ofer-, ōþ-swimman; -swemman.

swimmend-līc; *adj. Able to swim:*—Swymmendlīc *natatilis*, Ælfc. Gr. 9, 28; Zup. 55, 3.

swīn, es; *n.* I. *a swine.* [As may be seen from the charters and the laws, swine were an important item in the livestock of the English. They were owned in large numbers (contrast the number held by the Norwegian Ohthere, *v. infra*), as appears from the passages given below, in which gifts of swine are recorded; references to their pasturage often occur, v. mæst, mæstan, mæsten; to the herd who had charge of them is assigned the second place in the list of those whose employments are defined in the Rectitudines Singularum Personarum, v. Th. i. 436; while the frequent occurrence of the word *swīn* in local names, v. Cod. Dip. Kmbl. vi. 339, may be taken as further evidence. The value of swine, as compared with other domestic animals, is determined by the passages (*v. infra*) in the laws where the various animals are mentioned together.]:—Swīn *porcus* vel *sus*, Wrt. Voc. i. 78, 36. Swīn *sus*, 286, 43. *Suovetaurili* æt ðǽm geldum ðǽr wǽs swīn and sceáp and fear, ii. 31, 33: 86, 33. Māra ic eom and fǽttra ðonne āmæsted swīn, Exon. Th. 428, 9; Rä. 41, 105. Binnan cirictūne ǽnig hund ne cume, ne swīn ðe mā, L. Edg. C. 26; Th. ii. 250, 8. Emban ūrne ceápgild: hors tō healfan pund . . . And oxan tō mancuse, and cū tō .xx., and swȳn tō .x. (*pence*), and sceáp tō sciƚƚ., L. Ath. v. 6, 2; Th. i. 234, 1. Be ǽlces nȳtenes weorðe gif hī losiaþ. Hors mon sceal gyldan mid .xxx. sciƚƚ., myran mid .xx. sciƚƚ., oxan mid .xxx. p̄., cū mid .xxiiii. p̄., swȳn mid .viii. p̄., man mid punde, sceáp mid sciƚƚ., gāt mid .ii. p̄., L. O. D. 7; Th. i. 356, 5. Swīnes smere *arvina* vel *adeps*, Wrt. Voc. i. 44, 20. Ðǽr wæs ān swȳna heord (suner berga, Lind.: suner swīna, Rush. *grex porcorum*) . . . Ða deófla hyne bǽdon . . . 'Āsende ūs on ðās swīna heorde' . . . And hig fērdon on ða swīn, Mt. Kmbl. 8, 30-32. Hē (*Ohthere*) hæfde tamra deóra syx hund . . Hē wæs mid ðǽm fyrstum mannum on ðæm lande (*Norway*); næfde hē þeáh mā ðonne twentig swȳna, Ors. 1, 1; Swt. 18, 14. Ða ȳtemestan leomo swīna beóþ eáðmelte, Lchdm. ii. 196, 23. Mon selle tō Folcanstāne .x. oxan and .x. cȳ and .c. swīna, Cod. Dip. Kmbl. i. 310, 27. Ic sello ðās lond . . . and twā þūsendu swīna ic sello mid ðēm londum ii. 120, 15. Ic sello Berhtsige ān hīde bōclondes and ðǽrtō .c. swīna, and geselle hió .c. swīna tō Cristes cirican for mē and for mīne sāwle and .c. tō Ceortesēge, 121, 3-6. Ðā hēt ic geniman swīna micelne wrǽd (*sues*) . . . forðon ic wiste ðæt swīn wǽron ðæm elpendum lāðe, Nar. 21, 23-26. Gif mon on his mæstene unāliéfed swīn gemēte . . . Gif mon nime æfesne on swȳnum; æt þrȳfingrum (*three fingers thick in fat*), ðæt þridde; æt twȳfingrum, ðæt feórðe; æt þymelum, ðæt fīfte, L. In. 49; Th. i. 132, 12-19. Gafolswān sylle ǽlce geáre .xv. swȳn tō sticunge, L. R. S. 6; Th. i. 436, 13. II. *the image of a boar* as the crest of a helmet. Cf. swīn-līca, eofor-cumbol, -līc:—Swīn ofer helme, Beo. Th. 2577; B. 1286. Æt ðæm āde wæs ēþgesȳne swātfāh syrce, swȳn ealgylden, eofer īrenheard, 2227; B. 1111. [*Goth.* swein: *O. Sax. O. Frs. O. H. Ger.* swīn: *Icel.* svín.] v. gærs-, mere-, sliht-swīn.

swinc, es; *n. Swink* (this form is used in the 16th century. v. Nares' Glossary), *labour, trouble, affliction:*—Erian se ðe hine gesihþ swincu mǽste him ongeán cumaþ *he that in a dream sees himself ploughing, very great troubles are coming upon him*, Lchdm. iii. 198, 28. Suinca *verberum*, Rtl. 40, 29. v. ge-swinc, swinc-full, -leás.

swincan; *p.* swanc, *pl.* swuncon; *pp.* swuncen. I. *to toil, labour, work with effort:*—Hwæt dēst ðū on ðīs folce? hwī swingst ðū āna? Ex. 18, 14. Hē nǽre nā ælmihtig, gyf him ǽnig gefadung earfoðe wǽre. His nama is *omnipotens*, ðæt ys, ælmihtig, for ðan ðe hē mæg eall ðæt hē wile, and his miht nāhwār ne swincþ *his power nowhere works with effort*, Lchdm. iii. 278, 17. Unnytlīce wē swincaþ, ðonne wē ūs gebiddaþ, gif . . . , Bt. 41, 2; Fox 246, 21. Cumaþ tō mē ealle ðe swincaþ (wyrcas ł winnes, Lind.: winnaþ, Rush. *laboratis*), Mt. Kmbl. 11, 28: Met. 4, 56. Būton Drihten timbriende hūs on ȳdel swingaþ (*laboraverunt*) ða ðe timbriaþ, Ps. Spl. 126, 1. Git (*Beowulf and Breca in their match*) seofon niht swuncon, Beo. Th. 1038; B. 517. Ōðre swuncon (*laboraverunt*), and gē eodun on hyra geswinc, Jn. Skt. 4, 38. Swince *laboret*, Wülck. Gl. 250, 31. Swunce māre se ðe unriht gestreón on his handa stōde and læsse se ðe āriht on sprǽce *he in whose hand was unjust gain should take the greater trouble, he who made claim rightfully the less*, L. Eth. ii. 9; Th. i. 290, 4. I a. with prep. marking the end of the labour, *to labour* at, after, etc., anything:—Ne swincþ hē nāuht æfter ðam hū hē foremǽrost seó; ne nān mon ne begit ðæt hē æfter ne swincþ, Bt. 33, 2; Fox 122, 33-35. Hē swanc for heofonan rīce mid singalum gebede, Homl. Skt. ii. 26, 111. Ðe læs ðe unmihtig man feorr for his āgenon swince, L. Ff.; Th. i. 226, 1. Ic wundrige hwī swā manige wīse men swā swīþe swuncen mid ðære sprǽce, Bt. 41, 4; Fox 250, 20. Ðū swīþor swincst on ðam spore, ðonne hī dōn, 38, 5; Fox 206, 13. Suā hwā suā suinceþ (swinceþ, Cott. MSS.) on ðæn ðæt hē leornige unþeáwas, Past. 36; Swt. 251, 4. Æfter ðam unrihte ðe hī an swincaþ, Ps. Th. 27, 5. Hē geseah hī on rēwette swincende, Mk. Skt. 6, 48. Hī swincaþ wið synnum, Exon. Th. 150, 21; Gū. 782. Ða ðe meahton Godes friénd beón būtan gesuince hié suuncon (swuncon, Cott. MSS.) ymb ðæt hū hié meahton gesyngian *qui amici veritatis sine labore poterant, ut peccent laborant*, Past. 35; Swt. 239, 21. Ða race sōhton and ymb swuncon, Bt. 39, 4; Fox 216, 16. Hwȳ gē ymb ðæt unnet swincen, Met. 10, 21. Ne þearfe ic swīþe ymbe ðæt swincan, Bt. 35, 3; Fox 158, 8. II. *to be troubled, travail, be in difficulty* or *distress:*—Ic swince on mīnre grānunge *laboravi in gemitu meo*, Ps. Th. 6, 5. On hū grimmum seáðe swinceþ ðæt sweorcende mōd, Met. 3, 2. Ic swanc (*laboravi*) on mīnre geómrunge, Ps. Lamb, 6, 7. Ðām wīfum ðe æfter beorþre on sumum stōwum swincen, Lchdm. i. 344, 2. [Cf. Ðonne se ufera dǽl ðæs līchoman on ǽnigum sāre oððe on earfeþum geswince, 332, 9.] II a. of inanimate things:—Gif se midwinter byþ on Seternesdæg, ðonne byþ windig lengten and westmas swincaþ and scēp cwellaþ *the fruits of the earth will not thrive, and sheep will die*, Lchdm. iii. 164, 11. [The verb is common in Middle English and is used as late as Spenser's time.] v. be-swincan (*for* ge-swincan, *see under* II above); swencan.

swinc-full; *adj. Full of trouble* or *distress, disastrous:*—Ðæs ilcan geáres wæs swīðe hefelīc geár and swīðe swincfull and sorhfull geár binnan Englelande on orfcwealme, and corn and wæstmas wǽron ætstandene, Chr. 1085; Erl. 219, 19. [Þeos world is swincful, O. E. Homl. i. 7, 20. Ȝho (*the Virgin Mary*) wass swinncfull (*hard-working*) inn alle gode dedes, Orm. 2621.] v. geswinc-full, geswincfulnys.

swincgel. v. swingel.

swinc-leás; *adj. Without labour* or *toil:*—On ð m ēcan līfe wē būtan geswince God heriaþ. Wē sceolon on andwerdum līfe hine herian, ðæt wē mōton becuman tō ðære swincleásan herunge, Homl. Th. ii. 364, 9.

swinc-līc; *adj. Laborious, toilsome*[:—Ðæt gē healdan ðone Sunnandæg fram ǽlcum geswinclīcum worce, Wulfst. 294, 18.]

swincness. v. geswincness, Guthl. 12; Gdwin. 28, 23.

swind, Wrt. Voc. i. 44, 20. v. spind.

-swind. v. ǽ-swind.

swindan; *p.* swand, *pl.* swundon; *pp.* swunden *To waste away, languish, grow languid, be consumed:*—Se synfulla swindeþ *peccator tabescet*, Ps. Spl. 111, 9. Sāwel heora on yfelum swand *anima eorum in malis tabescebat*, 106, 26. Ealle oþþe hefige slǽpe swundon oþþe tō synne wacedon *omnes aut somno torpent inerti, aut ad peccata vigilant*, Bd. 4, 25; S. 601, 11. (v. ǽ-swind.) Swindan (*tabescere*) ðū dydesð sāwle his, Ps. Spl. 38, 15: 118, 139. on ðam frumwylme heora gecyrrednesse hȳ Hī sylfe fulfremede taliaþ, ac hý swíþe recene âwlaciaþ and swindende âcôliaþ, R. Ben. 135, 6. [Nede in swot and in swynk swynde mot the pore. Nede he mot swynde . . . that nath nout en hod his hed for te hude, P. S. 150, 2–4. *O. H. Ger.* swintan *tabescere, tabefieri, deficere, conticescere: Ger.* schwinden *to dwindle, decay, die away.*] v. â-swindan.

swínen; *adj. Of swine*:—Suínin *suellium*, Wrt. Voc. ii. 121, 72. Mid swínenum gore, Lchdm. i. 100, 11. Genim swínen (swýnes, MS. H.) smero, 114, 24. Ðæt hí eton swýnen flǽsc (ða swínnan, Ps. Surt. *porcina*), Ps. Th. 16, 14: Shrn. 111, 7. Hyre twigu beóþ swylce swínen byrst, Lchdm. i. 156, 2. [*O. H. Ger.* swînîn *porcinus, suillus.*]

swing. v. ge-swing; swinge.

swingan; *p.* swang, *pl.* swungon; *pp.* swungen. I. *to swinge, flog, beat, scourge,* (a) literal:—Ðâs cild ic swinge *hos pueros flagello,* Ælfc. Gr. 7; Zup. 23, 21. Ic swinge *verbero,* ic eom beswungen *verberor,* 5; Zup. 9, 4. Gif hwylc wíf hire wífman swingþ (*flagellis verberavit*), L. Ecg. P. ii. 4; Th. ii. 184, 1. Hig swingaþ eów *flagellabunt vos,* Mt. Kmbl. 10, 17: Mk. Skt. 10, 34. Ǽrest hiene mon swong *primo virgis caesus,* Ors. 4, 5; Swt. 168, 4: Bd. 2, 6; S. 508, 13. Ðâ nam Pilatus ðone Hǽlend and swang (*flagellavit*) hyne, Jn. Skt. 19, 1. Hié hine swungon, Blickl. Homl. 23, 31. Mê weras slôgon and swungon, Andr. Kmbl. 1927; An. 966. Ða deóful hine (*St. Anthony*) swungan, ðæt hê ne mihte hine âstyrigean, Shrn. 52, 27. Wiþ ðon ðe mon sié mônaþseóc; nim mereswínes fel, wyrc tô swipan, swing mid ðone man, sôna biþ sêl. Amen, Lchdm. ii. 334, 2. Gyf hit cild sý oððe cniht, swinge hine man (*vapulet*), L. Ecg. P. iv. 52; Th. ii. 218, 31. Swingon *vapulare,* Lchdm. iii. 212, 2. Hê ða fǽmnan hêt nacode mid sweopum swingan, Exon. Th. 253, 30; Jul. 188: 251, 8; Jul. 142. Hê byþ geseald ðeódum tô swingenne (tô swinganne, Rush. *ad flagellandum*), Mt. Kmbl. 20, 19: Exon. Th. 99, 11; Cri. 1623. Hine mid swipum swingende geangsumiaþ, Homl. Th. i. 426, 22. Ðæt hê swâ lange swungen wǽre ôþþæt hê swylte, Blickl. Homl. 193, 4. (b) metaphorical, *to chastise, afflict, plague*:—Ic ðreáge and suinge (swinge, Cott. MSS.) ða ðe ic lufige . . . God suingeþ (swingeþ, Cott. MSS.) ǽlc bearn ðe hê underfôn wile, Past. 36; Swt. 253, 1–4. Ðone heó ǽr mid wítum swong, Exon. Th. 279, 22; Jul. 617. Mid monnum ne biþ swungne *cum hominibus non flagellabuntur;* they are not plagued as other men, A. V., Ps. Surt. 72, 5. II. *to give a blow with the hand*:—Ðæt deófol cwæð: Swingaþ hine (*St. Andrew*) on his múð (cf. Sleáþ synnigne (*St. Andrew*) ofer seolfes múð, Andr. Kmbl. 2601; An. 1302), Blickl. Homl. 243, 2. [Wæs] suungen *exalaparetur* (cf. wæs fýstslægenu *exalaparetur,* 32, 2), Wrt. Voc. ii. 107, 75. III. without the idea of hurting, *to whip* a top, cream, etc., *beat up*:—Mid gelǽredre handa hê swang ðone top, Ap. Th. 13, 13. Genim mærcsâpan and hinde meolc, mæng tôsomme and swinge, Lchdm. iii. 4, 2. Swyng, 14, 32. Nime man sealt and þreora ǽgra geolcan, swinge hit swíðe tôgædere, 40, 22. IV. *to strike, dash*:—Hê swang ðæt fýr on twâ *he drove back the fire on either hand* (cf. that giswerk warð teswungan, bigan sunnun lioht hêdrôn an himile, Hêl. 5634), Cd. Th. 29, 12; Gen. 449. V. *to beat* the wings (?): —Se fugel licgeþ lonnum fæst swíðe swingeþ *beats its wings violently* (?), Salm. Kmbl. 533; Sal. 266. Nis hearpan wyn, ne gôd hafoc geond sæl swingeþ (*flaps its wings* (?) as it sits on the perch; cf. the opening lines of the Poema del Cid, where one mark of the desolation of the Cid's home is that the perches are 'sin falcones e sin adtores:' or swingeþ = *flies* (?), *soars,* v. swengan, and cf. for the idea of movement: Bigan ûst up stîgan, swang geswerk an gemang, Hêl. 2243, and *Ger.* schwingen *to wing, soar,* schwinge *a wing, pinion: Dan.* svinge (*of a bird*) *to soar*) ne se swifta mearh burhstede beáteþ, Beo. Th 4520; B. 2264. [*O. Sax. O. H. Ger.* swingan: *O. Frs.* swinga.] v. be-, ge-, of-swingan; swengan.

swinge, swynge (*both forms occur in the Pastoral*), an; *f. A stripe, stroke.* I. literal, *a stroke with a scourge* or *rod*:—Scs. Petrus hine mid grimmum swingum swong and þreáde (*flagellis artioribus afficiens*) . . . Cwæþ him eác tô: 'Ic bende and swingan (*vincula, verbera*) ðrowade' . . . Ðâ wæs Laurentius mid ðæs Apostoles swingum (*flagellis*) swíþe gebylded; cwom and eáwde mid hû miclum swingum (*verberibus*) hê ðreád wæs, Bd. 2, 6; S. 508, 12–24. Bedrífe hine (*a* wíteþeów, v. Grmm. R. A. 703) tô swingum, L. In. 48; Th. i. 132, 10: 54; Th. i. 138, 4. Ða hâlgan men geðafedon on ðisse worlde monige swyngean and monige bendas and carcernu *sancti verbera experti, insuper et vincula et carceres,* Past. 30; Swt. 205, 12. II. metaphorical, *chastisement, afflicting stroke*:—Geféged tô ðǽm gefôgstânum on ðære Godes ceastre bûtan ðæm hiéwete ǽlcre suingean (swingan, Cott. MSS.) *sine disciplinae percussione,* Past. 36; Swt. 253, 20. Sunu mín ne âgiémeleása ðû Godes suingan (swingan, Cott. MSS.) *fili mi, noli negligere disciplinam Domini,* Swt. 253, 2. Ic neósiu in swingum (*verberibus*) synne heara, Ps. Surt. 88, 33. [With a swinge of his sworde [he] swappit hym in the face, Destr. Tr. 1271. *O. H. Ger.* swinga *flagellum: Ger.* schwinge *a winnow, fan.*] v. sweng, *and next word.*

swingel[l], e; *and* swingel[l]e, an; *f.* I. literal, (a) *a stripe, stroke*:—Hine man þreáge mid teartran steóre, ðæt is, him sîge on swingella wracu (*verberum vindicta*). Gif hê þurh ða swingella ne biþ geriht . . ., R. Ben. 52, 6–8. Mid teartum swingellum *acribus verberibus,* 54, 4. Geswencte on bendum and on swingelum (swinglum, MSS. C. V.) for ðam sôþan geleáfan, Homl. Skt. i. 5, 27. Swinglum, L. In. 48; Th. i. 132, 9, MSS. B. H. Wê witun ðê nellan on belǽdan swincgla ûs *inferre plagas nobis,* Coll. Monast. Th. 18, 24. (b) *a scourging, whipping, flogging*: —Gif hwâ his hýde forwyrce and ciricân geierne sié him sió swingelle (swingle, MS. B.) forgifen *if any one incur the punishment of flogging, and run to a church, let the flogging be remitted to him,* L. In. 5; Th. i. 104, 16. Hyne Drihten þreáde mid þearlwýslîcere swingle. Ðâ eode hê tô ðam bysceope . . . and hym eówde ða lǽla ðæra(-e?) swingellan ðe hê from Dryhtne onfêng, Shrn. 98, 14–18. Hê wênde ðæt hê mid swinglan (*verberibus*) sceolde ða ânrêdnesse his heortan ânescian . . . Hê hine mid tintregum and mid swinglan oferswíþan ne mihte, Bd. 1, 7; S. 477, 43–478, 2. Hié hine swingaþ . . . and æfter ðære swinglan hié hine ofsleáþ, Blickl. Homl. 15, 11. Hê lîchamlîce wrace mid swingelle þolige *vindicte corporali subdatur,* R. Ben. 48, 12. Ðonne âh se teónd âne swingellan (swingelan, MSS. B. H.) æt him (*the* wíteþeów), L. In. 48; Th. i. 132, 9. Gif hwylc wíf hire wífman swingþ and heó þurh ða swingle wyrð deád *si mulier aliqua ancillam suam flagellis verberaverit, et ex illa verberatione moriatur,* L. Ecg. P. ii. 4; Th. ii. 184, 1. Hê hire swingele behêt, Homl. Skt. i. 9, 69. (c) *a scourge, rod, whip*:—Swinela *palmarum,* Hpt. Gl. 510, 40. (d) *a swingle, a stick to beat flax* [cf. a swinglestok *pessel,* the swingle *le pesselin,* to swingle the flax *estonger vostre lyn,* Wrt. Voc. i. 152, 39–44. A swyngelstok *excussorium, excudia,* Wülck. Gl. 581, 30: *studia,* 614, 1. A swyndylstoc *exculidium,* a swyndilland *excudium,* 696, 7, 8. I bete and swyngylle flax, Rel. Ant. ii. 197, 34. See also Cath. Angl. 374–5 and the notes there. Cf. *Du.* zwingelen *to beat flax.* Halliwell gives *swingel* as a name in several dialects for the part of the flail that strikes the corn, and *batillus* is translated by a belle clapere *vel* swyngell, Wülck. 567, 39]: —Ic ða swingle (*but* spinle, MS. O.; and the Latin text is *proiiciens quam gestabam colum*) mê fram âwearp, ðe ic seldon gewunode on handa tô hæbbene, Homl. Skt. ii. 23 b, 367. II. figurative, *chastisement, affliction*:—Wê scylen beón on ðisse ælðeódignesse ûtane beheáwene mid suingellan . . . ðætte suâ hwæt suâ nû on ûs unnytes sié ðætte ðæt âceorfe sió suingelle from ûs *nunc foris per flagella tundimur . . . quatenus quidquid in nobis est superfluum, modo percussio resecet,* Past. 36; Swt. 253, 18–22. Ðæt sâr ðære suingellan (swingellan, Cott. MSS.) ðissa woruldbroca, Swt. 259, 2. Balthasar næs gemyndig his fæder swingle, Homl. Th. ii. 434, 27. Ða ðe him ondrǽdaþ Godes swingellan . . . ða ðe suâ âheardode beóþ ðæt hié mon mid nânre swingellan gebêtan ne mæg, Past. 37; Swt. 263, 1–9. Ic eom nû tô swingellan gearu *ego in flagella paratus sum,* Ps. Th. 37, 17. Manifealde synt synfulra manna swingelan, 31, 12. Swingellan, 34, 15. Swyngla, Ps. Spl. 72, 5. Swinla *flagra,* Hpt. Gl. 527, 24. On swingelum *in verberibus,* Ps. Spl. 88, 32: Homl. Th. i. 578, 25. Swinglum, Ps. Th. 88, 29. God ðurh mislîce swingla his folces synna gehǽlþ, Homl. Th. i. 472, 12. v. wind-swingla, *and preceding word.*

swingere, es; *m. One who scourges*:—Nû ic (*mead*) eom bindere and swingere, sôna weorpere, Exon. Th. 409, 26; Rä. 28, 7.

swinglung, e; *f. Giddiness, dizziness, vertigo* [cf. swingan, though the verb does not seem much used in the sense of modern *swing.* For the idea of *turning round,* seen in *vertigo,* cf. the following: He dude fore of his cnihtes forte turnen þat hweol . . . ant het swingen hit swiftliche abuten ant tidliche turnen, Jul. 58, 5. *See also* swengan, geswing]: —Swinglung *scottomia,* Wrt. Voc. i. 19, 20. Ðâm mannum ðe swinclunge (swinglunge, MS. B.) þrowiaþ, Lchdm. i. 344, 6. [Cf. *Icel.* svingla *to rove: Dan.* svingle *to reel;* svingel *giddy.* Cf. too *O. H. Ger.* swintilunga *vertigo.*]

swín-haga, an; *m. An enclosure for swine*:—In ðone swínhagan; of swínhagan, Cod. Dip. Kmbl. iii. 18, 33: 399, 35.

swín-líca, an; *m. The figure of a swine* or *boar*:—Wǽpna smið (ðone helm) besette swínlîcum, Beo. Th. 2910; B. 1453. v. swín, II.

swin[n], es; *m. Sound, melody*:—Swin, sang *melodia* (*Wright gives* swinsang *melodio; perhaps* swinsung *should be read, but see the following gloss*), Wrt. Voc. ii. 57, 28. Swinne ł sangge *melodia,* Hpt. Gl. 467, 41. Swinn, dreám *melodiam,* 515, 42. [*From the same root as Latin* sonus?] v. ge-swin, *and following words; and* cf. hlyn[n], hlynsian *for similar formation.*

swinsian; *p.* ode *To make a* (*pleasing*) *sound, make melody* or *music*:—Se fugel swinsaþ and singeþ swegle tôgeánes *incipit illa sacri modulamina fundere cantus, et mira lucem voce ciere novam,* Exon. Th. 206, 9; Ph. 124: 207, 11; Ph. 140. Swinsaþ sibgedryht swêga mǽste, 239, 8; Ph. 618. On psalterio ðe him swynsaþ oft *on the psaltery that oft makes music to him,* Ps. Th. 143, 10. Frætwe míne (*the swan's*) swinsiaþ, torhte singaþ, Exon. Th. 390, 8; Rä. 8, 7: 55, 17; Cri. 885. Wit song âhôfan hlûde bi hearpan, hleóþor swinsade, 325, 2; Víd. 105: 353, 47; Reim. 29. Ðǽr wæs hæleþa hleahtor, hlyn swynsode (*a cheerful sound arose*), word wǽron wynsume, Beo. Th. 1227; B. 611. Sǽ swinsade *the sea made its music* (*but see* swinsung, II), Elen. Kmbl. 479; El. 240. Hearpan hlyn, swinsigende swêg, Cd. Th. 66, 8; Gen. 1081.

swinsung, e; *f.* I. *melody, harmony*:—Suinsung *armonia,* Wrt.

Voc. ii. 100, 62: *melodium*, 113, 79. Dreám, swinsunge (-c?) *armonia*, 3, 29: 90, 61. Swinsung, Hpt. Gl. 498, 63. Gedrēmere swinsunge *consona melodia*, 519, 6: *consona vocis harmonia (modulatione)*, 467, 9. Wensumne swinsunge ł dreám *melodiam*, 438, 8. Bebudon him gif hē mihte ðæt hē in swinsunge leóþsanges ðæt gehwyrfde *praecipientes ei, si posset, hunc in modulationem carminis transferre*, Bd. 4, 24; S. 597, 35. Swinsunga *melos*, Wrt. Voc. ii. 57, 27. II. *sound* that is not harmonious:—Swinsunge sǣs *sonitus maris*, Lk. Skt. Rush. 21, 25. Wið eárena swinsunge and ungehýrnesse *for singing in the ears and hardness of hearing*, Lchdm. iii. 70, 23.

swinsung-cræft, es; *m. Music*:—Swinsungcræft *musicam*, Wrt. Voc. ii. 55, 29.

swio-, swió-. v. sweo-, sweó-.

swipa, swipe. v. swipu.

swipian, sweopian; *p.* ode *To scourge, strike, beat, lash*:—Hafaþ hē gyrde lange and ðone feónd sweopaþ, Salm. Kmbl. 185, MS. A.; Sal. 92. Rodor swipode meredeáða mǣst *the destroying sea lashed the skies*, Cd. Th. 207, 8; Exod. 463. [*Icel.* svipa *to whip; to move swiftly*.] v. swippan.

swipor; *adj. Astute, cunning*:—Reáfaþ se snāw swíðor mycle ðonne se swipra (swíðra, Kmbl., *but see* Anglia i. 151) níð, Salm. Kmbl. 616; Sal. 307. [Swypyr or delyvyr *agilis*, swypyr and slydyr *labilis*, Prompt. Parv. 484. Cf. *Icel.* svipall *shifty*.] v. ge-swipor (*misprinted* ge-swip), -swiporness.

swippan; *p.* te *To scourge, beat, strike*:—Hafaþ hē gyrde lange and ðone feónd swipeþ, Salm. Kmbl. 185; Sal. 92. [The verb seems to be not uncommon in later English in the sense *to strike*, and also in that of *to move quickly* (Layamon also uses the noun *swipe* a stroke):—He his sweord up ahof and adun sloh (swipte, 2nd. MS.), Laym. 23962. He braid ut his sweord and him to sweinde (swipte to þan kinge, 2nd MS.), 27627. He hine adun swipte, 16518. He his sweord swipte mid maine, 23978. He swipte þat hæfued of, 21425. Ich wulle his heued of swippen, 878. He lette his sweord adun swippen (hit adun swipte, 2nd MS.), 16510. Ine swifte wateres þe þet is isundred he is sone iswipt forð, A. R. 252, 20. He swipte hire of þ heaued *decollavit eam*, Kath. 2452. Heo swipten of mid sweord hire heaued *gladio percussa*, 2179. When þe saul fra þe body swippes, Pr. C. 2196. See also Halliwell's Dict. *swippe*, and cf. *Dan.* svippe *to smack, crack* a whip: *Ger.* schwippen *to whip*. Cf. also *swingan* and words related to it for connection of the ideas of striking and moving.] v. swipian.

swipu, e; swipu(-e), an; *f.*: swipa (?), an; *m.* I. literal, *a scourge, whip, rod*:—Suibæ *mastigia*, Txts. 78, 641. Swipe, Wrt. Voc. ii. 71, 22. Swipa (-u?) *anguilla* vel *scutica*, i. 21, 16. Sweopan *fla[g]ri*, ii. 37, 64. Āwundenre suipan, suiopan *verbere torto*, Txts. 104, 1051. Nim mereswīnes fel, wyrc tō swipan, swing mid ðone man, Lchdm. ii. 334, 2. Ðām gelīc ðe Crist ādrǣfde mid swipe of ðam temple, L. Ælfc. C. 27; Th. ii. 352, 21. Suiopan, suipan *mastigium*, Txts. 77, 1276. Swipan, Wrt. Voc. ii. 55, 26. Hē worhte swipan (suuopa, Lind.: swiopa, Rush.) of strengon *flagellum de funiculis*, Jn. Skt. 2, 15. Sweopan, Salm. Kmbl. 219; Sal. 109. Hē worhte āne swipe of rāpum, Homl. Th. i. 406, 7. Leádene swipa and ōðre gepīlede swipa wurdon forð āborene, 424, 20. Swipena *flagrorum*, i. *flagellorum*, Wrt. Voc. ii. 149, 30: Hpt. Gl. 487, 58. Swipum *mastigiis, flagris*, 487, 49: *flagris*, Wrt. Voc. ii. 35, 70. Suiopum, 108, 74. Mid sweopum sleán, Exon. Th. 88, 18; Cri. 1442. Mid sweopum swingan, 253, 30; Jul. 188. Sweopum seolfrenum, Salm. Kmbl. 287; Sal. 143. Hī hine swungon mid īsenum swipum, Guthl. 5; Gdwin. 36, 23. Mid swiopum (suuippum, Lind.) giðorscenne *flagellis caesum*, Mk. Skt. Rush. 15, 15. I a. *that with which a stroke is struck, a sword* (?), *a javelin* (?):—Swypu *romphea*, Germ. 398, 189. Frome folctogan faraþ him tōgegnes, habbaþ leóht speru lange sceaftas, swīðmōde sweopan, swenga ne wyrnaþ, deórra dynta, Salm. Kmbl. 243; Sal. 121. II. figurative, *affliction, chastisement*:—Swipu ne geneálǣcþ dīnum getealde *flagellum non appropinquabit tabernaculo tuo*, Ps. Lamb. 90, 10. Ne mæg heard sweopu weorðan hūse dīnum on neáweste, Ps. Th. 90, 10. Ðære uplecan ðreá sweopon *supernae flagella districtionis*, Bd. 2, 5; S. 507, 2. Ic wylle swingan eów mid ðām smeartestum swipum, ðæt is, ic wītnige eów mid ðām wyrstan wīte, Wulfst. 295, 11. Synna suippum, Rtl. 42, 21. Suyppa ðines uraððo, 8, 35. Syuipa, 41, 35. Syppo, 15, 25. Swipa *mastigias*, Hpt. Gl. 527, 27. [Gief he fend were, me sceolden eter gat ȝemete mid gode repples and stiarne swepen, O. E. Homl. i. 231, 21. Crist wrohhte an swepe, Orm. 15562. *Icel.* svipa *a whip*: *Ger.* schwippe *a lash, switch*. Cf. *Prompt. Parv.* sweype for a top, or scoorge *flagellum*.] v. preceding word.

swira, -swiria. v. sweora, ge-swiria *consobrinus*, Wrt. Voc. ii. 14, 73.

swirman; *p.* de *To swarm* (of bees):—Ðonne hī (*bees*) swirman, Lchdm. i. 384, 23.

swital (-el). v. sweotol.

swītan (?); *p.* swāt *in* for-swītan *to exhaust, impair, impoverish* land (?):—Ðe lond æt Moran ic mid mīne wīfe bigat, and ic it siðen nāwer ne forswāt (-swāc?) ne forspilde, Chart. Th. 584, 5. v. swǣtan.

swīþ; *adj.* I. *strong*, (1) of persons or personifications:—Metod mihtum swīð, Cd. Th. 233, 32; Dan. 284: Andr. Kmbl. 2415; An. 1209: Exon. Th. 45, 8; Cri. 716. Ðȳ læs hē for wlence, mon mōde swīð, of gemete hweorfe, 294, 34; Crā. 25. Hwæt wæs ðē, sǣ swīþa? forhwan fluge ðū swā? Ps. Th. 113, 5. Wyrd seó swīþe, 477, 16; Ruin. 25: Salm. Kmbl. 886; Sal. 442. Hē tōswengde þurh swīðes meaht līges leóman, Exon. Th. 189, 14; Az. 59. Ǣnne hæfde hē swā swīðne geworhtne, swā mihtigne on his mōdgeþohte, Cd. Th. 16, 33; Gen. 252. Hī swīðra oferstāg weard, Exon. Th. 116, 3; Gū. 201. Biþ seó mōdor frommast and swīþost, 493, 1; Rā. 81, 23. (2) of things, (*a*) in reference to material things, (α) *producing a powerful effect*:—Swīð drenc wiþ āswollenum milte, Lchdm. ii. 256, 14. Ofgeót ðās wyrte mid swīþe beóre ... wyl on swīþum beóre, 358, 14, 18. Stenc swīþra swæcca gehwylcum, Exon. Th. 358, 15; Pa. 46. Gif ðū wolde ðæt sió sealf swīðre sié, Lchdm. ii. 84, 8. Wylle swīþre medo ... Wyrc swīðran (*the draught*), gif hē wille, 270, 7, 16. (β) *strong, violent* (of wind, stream, etc.):—Swīþe hlimman *torrens*, Ps. Th. 125, 4. Gif swīþra wind ārās *si flatus venti major adsurgeret*, Bd. 4, 3; S. 569, 10. (γ) *strong, not easily broken*:—Swīðne bogan, Ps. Th. 63, 3. (*b*) of immaterial things:—Ealdfeónda nīð, searocræftum swīð, Exon. Th. 110, 25; Gū. 113. Wæs ðæt gewin tō swȳð, tō lāð and longsum, Beo. Th. 385; B. 191: 6163; B. 3085. Mid ðæm swīðan welme hātheortnesse, Met. 25, 46. Intō ðȳ swīðan slǣpe, Blickl. Homl. 205, 4. Þurh ða swīðan miht, Cd. Th. 237, 24; Dan. 342. Se willa biþ ðonne strengra ðonne ðæt gecynd. Hwīlum biþ se willa swīþra ðonne ðæt gecynd, hwīlum ðæt gecynd ofercymþ ðone willan, Bt. 34, 11; Fox 152, 11. Ðæt swȳðre mægen wæteres, Ps. Th. 123, 4. ¶ *Swīþ* occurs often as part of proper names, either as the first or second element, v. Txts. 625, col. 1. II. The comparative is used where later English uses *right* (hand, side, etc.):—Swīðra *dexter*, Ælfc. Gr. 5; Zup. 13, 1. (1) With a noun:—Ðīn swȳðre eáge, ðīn swīðre hand, Mt. Kmbl. 5, 29, 30. Ðū smītst ofer Aarones swȳðre eáre ... and ðæs swȳðran fōtes micclan tān, Ex. 29, 20. Hē sette his ða swīþ[r]an hand him on ðæt heáfod, Bd. 2, 12; S. 515, 19. Hē sette Ephraim on his swīðran hand ... and Mannases on his winstran hand, ðæt wæs on Israhēles swīðran healfe ... Hē hefde ðā his swīðran hand ofer Ephraimes heáfod, Gen. 48, 13, 14. Drihten mē ys on ða swȳþran healfe, Guthl. 5; Gdwin. 36, 20. Ðū nymst ðone swȳðran bōh, Ex. 29, 21. Gif hwā ðē sleá on ðīn swȳðre wenge, Mt. Kmbl. 5, 39. (2) Used without a noun, *the right hand, the right*:—Godes swȳðra(-e?) forbeád Abrahame ðæt hē his sunu ne ofslōge, ac funde him ānne ram, Prud. 1 b. Ðæne ðīn seó swīðre sette *quam plantavit dextera tua*, Ps. Th. 79, 14. Tō swȳðran *a dextris*, Ps. Spl. 15, 8. Hī āsetton hreód on hys swīðran, Mt. Kmbl. 27, 29. Ic sceáwade on ða swȳðran *considerabam ad dexteram*, Ps. Th. 141, 4. Æt swȳþrum þearfan *a dexteris pauperis*, Ps. Spl. 108, 30. Fram swȳðrum ðīnum *a dextris tuis*, 90, 7. [*Goth.* swinþs: *O. Sax.* swīði: *O. Frs.* swīth: *M. H. Ger.* swinde, swint *strong, quick*: *Ger.* ge-schwind: *Icel.* svinnr, sviðr *quick, wise*] v. earm-, for-, mōd-, ofer-, un-swīþ.

swīðan; *p.* de; *but a strong form* swāð *also occurs*. I. *to make strong, give strength to, strengthen, support*:—Leng ne woldon Elamitarna aldor swīðan folcgestreónum, Cd. Th. 119, 16; Gen. 1980. Ongan Abimæleh Abraham swīðan woruldgestreónum, 164, 18; Gen. 2716. Swā reordode manna mildost mihtum swīðed, 213, 9; Exod. 549. II. *to be strong, exercise strength, prevail* (?):—Ic oforswīðrode āgen ł ongēn ł swāð (= oferswāð? v. ofer-swīðan) hine *praevalui adversus eum*, Ps. Lamb. 12, 5. v. for-, ge-, ofer-, þurh-swīðan; swīðian.

swīðe; *adv. Very, much, exceedingly*:—Tō ðam swīðe *in tantum*, Hpt. Gl. 509, 34. Tō ðan swȳðe *adeo*, Ælfc. Gr. 30; Zup. 193, 5. I. with adjectives, (1) of quantity:—Mid swīþe manigre swētnesse, Bt. 7, 1; Fox 16, 11: 11, 1; Fox 32, 34. Swīþe feáwa manna ongit, 19; Fox 70, 12. Swīðe lytle fiorme, Past. pref.; Swt. 5, 11. (2) of quality:—Hē biþ ðæra suīðe gemyndig, Past. 4; Swt. 37, 20. Ða swīðe swīgean *nimis taciti*, 23; Swt. 174, 24. Swīþe heá dūne, Blickl. Homl. 27, 16. Ūs is swīþe uncūþ, 51, 35. Hē wæs swīðe welig *dives erat valde*, Lk. Skt. 18, 23. II. with adverbs or adverbial phrases:—Suīðe oft, Past. 3; Swt. 35, 9. Ðæt his lāreów hine suīðe lythwōn gemyndgige, 31; Swt. 207, 4. Ðā wundrade ic swīðe swīðe, pref.; Swt. 5, 19. Swīðe ðearle *vehementer nimis*, Gen. 17, 2. Drinc swȳþe þearle, Lchdm. i. 78, 10. Swīþe eáþe ... swīþe raþe, Blickl. Homl. 21, 17, 21. Swīþe lytelīce, Bt. 7, 1; Fox 16, 11. II a. in the superlative, *chiefly, especially, mostly*:—Seó bōc (*St. John's gospel*) hrepaþ swȳðost ymbe Cristes godcundnysse, Homl. Th. i. 70, 1. Hwiþer wilt ðū mē swīþost lǣdan *whither especially wilt thou lead me?* Bt. 22, 2; Fox 78, 5. Þurh ofermētto ealra swīðost *most of all through pride*, Cd. Th. 22, 8; Gen. 337. Swīþost hē fōr ðider for ðæm horschwælum *it was chiefly on account of the walruses that he went thither*, Ors. 1, 1; Swt. 17, 35. Swīðost hys spēda hȳ forspendaþ mid ðam langan legere, 21, 8. Ðæs hē wæs ealles swīþost tō hergenne, ðæt ... *he was to be praised most of all for this, that ...*, Blickl. Homl. 223, 27. Smire hine mid hrȳþeres oþþe swīðost mid oxan geallan, Lchdm. ii. 44, 11. III. with verbs, intensifying their force:—Ne ðæt swīþe tō wundrianne is *it is not much to be wondered at*, Bd. 3, 9; S. 533, 24. Ðā arn ðæt wīf swīðe *then the woman ran fast*, Homl. Skt. i. 3, 650. Ælmyssan sylle hē swýðe *eleemosynas reddat largiter*, L. Ecg. C. 3; Th. ii. 136, 34. Þicge hit swýðe, Lchdm. i. 80, 19. Seóð swýþe and ete swýþe *cook thoroughly and eat largely*, 82, 1. Ðæt Drihten swóre ád swíðe *solemnly swore an oath*, Wulfst. 209, 27. Ðæt wē his tō suíðe ne gītseden, Past. 3; Swt. 33, 18. Drihten is þearle swīþe tō herienne, Lchdm. iii. 436, 18. Hē þearle swīþe wearþ gegladod, 438, 27. Swā swýþe swā hē ðam cyninge wæs līciende, swā swýþe hē him sylfum mislīcade, Bd. 5, 13; S. 632, 8. Mē swā swýþe ne lyst, swā . . . , Bt. 5, 1; Fox 10, 18. Hī swīþor clypodon *illi magis clamabant*, Mt. Kmbl. 27, 23. Nis ðē nāuht swīþor *nothing affects you more*, Bt. 7, 1; Fox 16, 8: 7, tit.; Fox x, 13. Wē nellaþ be ðām nā swíðor āwrītan *we will not write further about them*, Homl. Th. ii. 466, 20. Wē willaþ furðor ymbe ðās emnihte swíðor sprecan . . . Embe ðis wē sprecaþ eft swíðor *we will say more about it later on*, Lchdm. iii. 240, 1, 7. Ða brōþra ōþra weorca swýðor gýmdon *paid more attention to other works*, Bd. 3, 8; S. 532, 30. Swā hē him swīþor bebeád swā hī swíðor bodedon *quanto eis praecipiebat, tanto magis plus praedicabant*, Mk. Skt. 7, 36. Wæs hē swā micle swíðor on his mōde gedrēfed, swā his mōd ǣr swíðor tō ðām woruldsǣlþum gewunod wæs, Bt. 1; Fox 2, 27. Biþ ðý heardra ðe hit sǣstreámas swíðor beátaþ, Cd. Th. 80, 10; Gen. 1326. Ðǣm mōdum ðe hī willaþ swīþost beswīcan *the minds that they will most completely deceive*, Bt. 7, 1; Fox 16, 12. Ðā hē hī swíðost forslagen hæfde *when he had inflicted a most severe defeat upon them*, 16, 2; Fox 54, 2. Ðā hī swíðost worhton *when they were working hardest*, Homl. Th. i. 22, 22. Ðonne heó blēwþ swíðust *when it is in fullest blossom*, Lchdm. i. 160, 14. Forlǣtan unnytte ymbhogan swā hē swīþost mihte *as much as ever he could*, Bt. 35, tit.; Fox xvi, 27. Hiora scamiaþ swīþust ealles ða tō Sione hete swíðost hæfdon, Ps. Th. 128, 3. Swýþust ealra, 108, 28. Næfde se here Angelcynn ealles for swíðe gebrocod; ac hié wǣron micle swīþor gebrocede mid ceápes cwilde and monna; ealles swīþost mid ðæm ðæt manige ðara sēlestena cynges þēna forðférdon, Chr. 897; Erl. 94, 29–32. [The word is common in Middle English. *O. Sax.* swīðo: *O. Frs.* swīthe.] v. efen-, for-, ofer-, un-swíðe.

swíðestre. v. ofer-swíðestre.

swīþfæstness, e; *f. Violence, force*:—Þurh swíðfæstnesse his geþohtes *prae violentia cogitationis suae*, L. Ecg. C. 5; Th. ii. 138, 27.

swīþ-feorm; *adj.* I. *abounding in substance*:—Him ðā Abraham gewāt ǣhte lǣdan golde and seolfre swíðfeorm and gesǣlig (cf. gewiton him ǣhta lǣdan, feoh and feorme, 99, 22; Gen. 1650), Cd. Th. 106, 12; Gen. 1770. II. *producing abundant sustenance, very fruitful*:—Beóþ gōde wīngeardas and swīþfeorme mannum, Lchdm. iii. 162, 31. III. *violent*. v. next word:—Ic (*a storm*) wíde fēre swift and swīþfeorm, Exon. Th. 386, 35; Rā. 4, 72. Cf. swīþ-from.

swīþ-feormende *growing violent*:—Ða swīþfeormende *crudescentes*, Wrt. Voc. ii. 92, 23: 19, 42.

swīþ-ferhþ; *adj.* I. *of strong mind* or *soul*:—Snotor and swýðferhð (*Beowulf*), Beo. Th. 1656; B. 826. Swíðferhþe (*Beowulf's companions*), 990; B. 493. Hwæt swíðferhðum (*the Danes*) sēlest wǣre tō gefremmanne, 348; B. 173. II. *of violent mind, violent, impetuous*:—Geswearc ðā swíðferð (*Juliana's father*), Exon. Th. 247, 13; Jul. 78. Oft bemearn swíðferhðes (*Sigemund*) sīð snotor ceorl monig, Beo. Th. 1820; B. 908.

swīþ-ferom. v. next word.

swīþ-from; *adj. Exceedingly strong, of great energy*:—Hē (*the Deity*) biþ ā rīce ofer heofenstōlas heágum þrymmum sōðfæst and swíðfrom (-ferom, MS.; *but see also* swīþ-feorm) sweglbōsmas heóld, Cd. Th. 1, 17; Gen. 9. Cf. Mīn geswīþfroma (*addressing the Deity*), Anglia xii. 508, 1. v. next word.

swīþfromlīce; *adv. Strenuously, with great energy*:—Suíðfromlīce *naviter*, Wrt. Voc. ii. 114, 58.

swīþ-hwæt; *adj. Very strong*, Runic pm. Kmbl. 340, 13; Rūn. 5. v. rād; *f.*

Swīþ-hūn, es; *m. St. Swithin, bishop of Winchester, in which see he succeeded Helmstan, who died* 852. *In one MS. of the A. S. Chronicle, under the year* 861, *is the entry*:—Hēr forðfērde S. Swíðūn biscop, Erl. 71, 20; *but in a charter of* 863, Swíðhūn episcopus *is given as one of the witnesses*, v. Cod. Dip. Kmbl. v. 117, 22. *The name occurs often in the same connection in previous years* [For an account of him see Earle's Gloucester Fragments, and for the complete homily of which a fragment is given in that work, see Homl. Skt. vol. i. No. 21]:—Ðes Swýðūn wæs bisceop on Winceastre, Homl. Skt. i. 21, 14. Se ārwurða Swýðūn (Swíðhūn, Gloucester Frg.), 23. Æt Swýðūnes (Swíðhūnes, G. F.) byrgene, 98. Se smið andwyrde ðam ārwurðan Swýðūne (Swíðhūne, G. F), 29. ¶ *For the name where there is no reference to the saint, cf.* ðæt suíðhūningclond, Cod. Dip. Kmbl. i. 243, 10. Ab aquilone habens terminum suuealuue fluminis, a plaga oriente suíðhūninglond, a parte occidentali ealhfleót, ab austro sighearding mēduue ond eac suíthhūninglond, 250, 9–12.

swīþ-hycgende; *adj.* (*ptcpl.*) *Of strong purpose*:—Scealc monig swíðhicgende, Beo. Th. 1842; B. 919. Māgas ðara swíðhicgendra, 2036; B. 1016.

swíðian; *p.* ode. I. *to be* or *become strong, to prevail*:—Strangadan, swíðodon *invalescebant*, Wrt. Voc. ii. 74, 6. Strangedon, swīþedon, 46, 49. Ne wæs ðæt tō wundrianne ðeáh ðe ðæs cyninges bēne ðā hē mid Drihtne rīcsade mid hine swīþode and genge wǣre *nec mirandum preces regis illius iam cum Domino regnantis, multum valere apud eum*, Bd. 3, 12; S. 537, 19. II. *to make firm, to fix*:—Suíðigaþ *figite*, Wrt. Voc. ii. 108, 68. Swīþiaþ, 35, 60. v. for-swíðan (*under which* for-swíðede *is wrongly put*); swíðan.

swīþ-līc; *adj.* I. *very great, exceedingly great*:—Swíðlīc *grande, magnum*, Hpt. Gl. 434, 41. Samson gelǣhte ða sweras mid swíðlīcre mihte and slōh hī tōgædere *Samson apprehendens ambas columnas concussit fortiter columnas*, Jud. 16, 29. Hig cumaþ mid swíðlīcum ǣhtum (*cum magna substantia*), Gen. 15, 14. II. with the idea of violent disturbance, *violent, strong* (of storm, wind, etc.):—Reóhnys swýðlīc *tempestas valida*, Ps. Lamb. 49, 3. Swēgde swíðlīc wind of ðam wēstene, Homl. Th. ii. 450, 18. Heard gebrec, swār and swíðlīc, swēgdynna mǣst, Exon. Th. 59, 19; Cri. 955. For swīþlīcum rēne, Bt. 12; Fox 36, 17. Wið swíðlīcne flēwsan ðæs sǣdes, Lchdm. i. 220, 3. On wæterum swýðlīcum *in aquis vehementibus*, Cant. Moys. 10. Hī sāwon swíðlīce rēnas, Boutr. Scrd. 21, 22. III. of energetic, violent action, *vehement, violent*:—Wið swíðlīcne bracan, Lchdm. i. 270, 2. Him swyrdgeswing swīþlīc eówdon weras, Judth. Thw. 25, 3; Jud. 240. IV. of that which affects the senses or the feelings, *strong, intense, severe*:—Nǣfre ðū ðæs swíðlīc sār gegearwast, ðæt ðū mec onwende worda ðissa, Exon. Th. 246, 1; Jul. 55. Ða tēð cwaciaþ on swíðlīcum cyle, Homl. Th. i. 132, 27. Ðonne hē on sumura for swíðlīcre hǣtan geteorud byþ, Lchdm. i. 226, 22. Ðeós wyrt is hāttre gecynde and swýðlīcre, 236, 11. Strang tō swíðlīcum drencum, Homl. Th. ii. 322, 15. God him sende swíðlīce ōgan tȳn cinna wīta, Ælfc. T. Grn. 5, 18. V. of feeling, or emotion, *intense, vehement*:—Hē mid swíðlīcum luste his līfes gewilnode, Homl. Th. i. 86, 19. On swíðlīcre blisse *in jubilo*, Ps. Lamb. 46, 6. VI. of discipline or conduct, *stern, severe, strict*:—Cildru behōfiaþ swíðlīcere steóre, Homl. Th. ii. 324, 33. Hē munucregol gesette mid swýðlīcre drohtnunge, Basil prm.; Norm. 32, 6.

swīþlīce; *adv.* I. *very greatly, exceedingly*:—Se dēma wundrode swíðlīce (*vehementer*), Mt. Kmbl. 27, 14. Swā sārige on hiora mōde and swā swíðlīce gedrēfed *permotae*, Ors. 1, 10; Swt. 44, 30. Ic wāt ðæt ðū woldest swīþe swīþlīce beón onǣled *quanto ardore flagrares*, Bt. 22, 2; Fox 78, 3. Ðā wunode se hālga wer on ancerlīfe swíðlīce stíðe, Homl. Th. ii. 146, 7. II. *powerfully, energetically, strongly*:—Mē þincþ ðæt ðīn gecynd and ðīn gewuna flīte swīþe swīþlīce wiþ ðæm dysige, Bt. 26, 4; Fox 178, 28. III. *sternly, strictly, severely*:—Hwīlum līðelīce tō ðreátianne, hwīlum suíðlīce and strǣclīce tō ðrāfianne, Past. 21; Swt. 151, 12. [Þe king him answerede swiðeliche fæire, Laym. 4421. *O. Sax.* swīðlīko (ēð giswerian).]

swīþlīcness, e; *f. Excess*; nimietas, R. Ben. Interl. 73, 7.

swīþ-mihtig; *adj. Exceedingly mighty, of great might*:—Gesamnincga swíðmihtigra *synagoga potentium*, Ps. Th. 85, 13.

swīþ-mōd; *adj.* I. in a good sense, (a) *great-souled, magnanimous, stout-hearted*:—Com ðā tō lande lidmanna helm (*Beowulf*) swíðmōd swymman, Beo. Th. 3252; B. 1624. Swíðmōd cyning, Cd. Th. 222, 5; Dan. 100: 225, 29; Dan. 161: 244, 18; Dan. 450. (b) *stern-minded*:—Ā ðone feónd swíðmōd swipeþ, Salm. Kmbl. 185; Sal. 92. Folctogan faraþ him tōgeánes, habbaþ swíðmōde sweopan, swenga ne wyrnaþ, 243; Sal. 121. II. in a bad sense, *of violent mind, arrogant, haughty, high-minded*:—Dryhtguman sīne drencte mid wīne swīþmōd (cf. stīþmoda, l. 19) sinces brytta (*Holofernes*), Judth. Thw. 21, 21; Jud. 30: 26, 22; Jud. 340. Swíðmōd cyning (*Nebuchadnezzar after putting the three children in the furnace*), Cd. Th. 233, 1; Dan. 269: (*the king at the time of the dream*; cf. hē wæs wið God scyldig, 250, 20; Dan. 549), 249, 12; Dan. 529. Wearð hē swíðmōd in sefan for ðære sundorgife ðe him God sealde, 254, 3; Dan. 606. v. next word.

swīþmōdness, e; *f. Greatness of soul, magnanimity*:—Be sigerfestnisse and swīþmōdnisse ūses Drihtnes mid ðǣm hē ða hǣþnan ofercom, Anglia xi. 173, 12. Ne māgon hȳ ðære tungan gerecnisse ne hire mægnes swíðmōdnisse āspyrian, Salm. Kmbl. 150, 4.

swīþness, e; *f. Strength, violence*:—Cyles swīþness *frigoris nimietas*, Anglia xiii. 397, 458. v. ofer-swīþness.

swíðor, swíðra, swíðrian. v. swíðe, swīþ, II, sweðrian.

swíðrian; *p.* ode. I. *to become* or *be stronger, to prevail*:—Ðæt wæter swíðrode swíðe ofer ða eorðan *aquae praevaluerunt nimis super terram*, Gen. 7, 19. Se hunger þearle swíðrode *praevaluerat fames in terra*, 12, 10. Hē swýðrode on īdelnysse his *praevaluit in vanitate ejus*, Ps. Lamb. 51, 9. Saulus micclum swýðrode *Saul increased the more in strength* (A. V. Acts 9, 22), Homl. Th. i. 388, 3. Hyra stefna swíðredon *invallescebant voces eorum*, Lk. Skt. 23, 23. II. *to avail*:—Seó hālwende onsægedness[e] tō ēcre ālȳsnesse swīþrade and fromade *sacrificium salutare ad redemptionem valeret*, Bd. 4, 22; S. 592, 28. Swīþrian *valere*, swīþrigende *valens*, Hymn. Surt. 70, 3, 5. v. oferswíðrian.

swîþ-snel; *adj. Very quick*:—Sum biþ swîđsnel, hafaþ searolîc gomen gleódǽda, leóht and leoþuwâc, Exon. Th. 298, 8; Crä. 82.
swîþ-sprecol; *adj. Proud in speech, speaking proud things*:—Ða swýđsprecelan tungan *linguam magniloquam*, Ps. Lamb. 11, 4.
swîþ-stincende; *adj.* (*ptcpl.*) *Emitting a strong scent*:—Swîþstincendre *flagrantior*, Wrt. Voc. ii. 38, 29.
swîþ-strang; *adj. Of great strength* or *force*. v. next word.
swîþ-strîme; *adj. Having a strong stream*:—Ðâ com hê tô swîþstrêmre (swîđstrangre, MS. B.) eá *pervenit ad flumen meatu rapidissimo*, Bd. 1, 7; S. 478, 4.
swîþ-swêge; *adj. High-sounding, heroic* (verse):—Swîđswêgum metrum *heroico hexametro*, Hpt. Gl. 440, 12. Mid swîđswîum (=-swêgum?) sangum dreámes *dulcisonis* (*jucundis*) *melodiae*, 416, 1.
swîþ-swîge; *adj. Taciturn, too silent*:—Ða suîđsuîgean (swîđe swîgean, Cott. MSS.) đa felaîdelsprǽcæn *nimis taciti, multiloquio vacantes*, Past. 23; Swt. 175, 24.
swî-tîma, switol. v. swîg-tîma, sweotol.
swîung, e; *f. A spasm*:—Hramma *vel* swîung *spasmos*, Wrt. Voc. i. 19, 21.
swodrian; *p.* ode *To get drowsy, fall asleep*:—Ic hnæppode and ic swodrode *ego dormivi et soporatus sum*, Ps. Spl. 3, 5. [In his chaire he sat longe . . . a lutel he bigan to swoudri as a slep him nome. Þo þoȝte him in his swoudringe þat a whit coluere com, L. S. 439, 268. Cf. A day as he wery was, and a suoddrynge him nome . . . Seyn Cutbert to him com, R. Glouc. 264, 22. Halliwell gives *zwodder* = drowsy, dull, as a West-country word.] v. swađrian, swеđrian.
swôg. v. swêg.
swôgan; *p.* sweóg; *pp.* swôgen. I. *to make a sound, move with noise, rush, roar* (of wind, water, flame):—Swôgaþ windas, blâwaþ brecende bearhtma mǽste, Exon. Th. 59, 10; Cri. 950. Frætwe mîne (*a swan*) swôgaþ hlûde, 390, 7; Rä. 8, 7. Drihten lêt willeburnan on woruld þringan, êgorstreámas swôgan, Cd. Th. 83, 5; Gen. 1375. Fýr swôgende, 154, 17; Gen. 2557. Swôgende lêg, Beo. Th. 6282; B. 3145. Swôgende *strepente*, Wrt. Voc. ii. 74, 72. Ðǽm swôgendum, hleóđregendum *argutis*, 5, 36: 86, 74. II. fig. *to move with violence, enter with force, invade*. v. in-swôgenness:—Ðæt nǽnig bisceop ôþres bisceopscîre on swôge *ut nullus episcoporum parochiam alterius invadat*, Bd. 4, 5; S. 572, 32. [Þe soun of our souerayn þen swey in his ere, Allit. Pms. 104, 429. Cf. the noun in Mid. E. *swoughe, swoghe* = noise, e. g. of the see he herde a swoghe (Halliwell's Dict. q. v.), modern *sough* of the wind. But both verb and noun are used in the sense of swoon; for the verb v. geswôgen, and as later instances swowinde, A. R. 288, 25; he feol iswowen (-swoȝe, 2nd MS.), Laym. 3074: for the noun see Stratmann and Halliwell. *O. Sax.* swôgan:—Swôgan quam engil, faran an feđerhamon, Hêl. 5798.] v. â-, ofer-, þurh-swôgan; swêgan.
swôgenness, swôgung. v. in-swôgenness, ge-swôgung.
swôl, es; *m.* (?), *n.* (?) *Heat, burning*:—Suôl *chaumos*, Wrt. Voc. ii. 103, 75. Swôl *camos*, 17, 8: i. 288, 41. Suôle *caumati*, ii. 103, 31. Swôle *caumate*, 22, 21. I. of the heat of fire:—Hê (*the phenix*) somnaþ swôles lâfe, gegædraþ bân gebrosnad æfter bǽlþræce, Exon. Th. 216, 16; Ph. 269. On swôle byrneþ þurh fýres feng fugel mid neste, 212, 23; Ph. 214. II. of the sun's heat:—Hê swâ swîþe swǽtte swâ hê in swôle (*caumate*) middes sumeres wǽre, Bd. 3, 19; S. 549, 30 MS. T. III. of feverish heat:—Sió ungemetlîce hǽto ðæs miltes cymþ of feferes swôlle, Lchdm. ii. 244, 6. Hû se hâta maga swôl þrowaþ, 160, 5: 194, 12. [Cf. *Du.* zwoel *sultry*.] v. swôlig.
swolgettan; *p.* te *To swallow, take into the throat*:—Ðonne sceal mon ðone geagl swillan gelôme on ðære âdle (*quinsy*), and swolgettan eced wiþ sealt gemenged, Lchdm. ii. 48, 16.
swôlig (cf. dysig *for the form*), es; *n. Burning, heat*:—Swôlig *caumatio*, Wrt. Voc. ii. 130, 8. Hât lyft and swôlga (*sultriness*?) bringaþ âdle on ðam milte, ðonne se mon wyrđ tô swîþe forhǽt, Lchdm. ii. 244, 7. [In a late MS. of Ælfric's Grammar and Vocabulary, *swoli, sweoli* translate *cauma*, Zup. 33, 12 note, 306, 15 note.]
swôlig (?); *adj. Sultry*. v. preceding word.
swoloþ, swon-. v. sweoloþ, swan-.
swoncen-ferhþ; *adj.*?:—Hê (*a man who has been hung*) sîgeþ swoncenferđ (swoncerferđ *life having failed*, (?) v. swancor, I; *or* sworcenferđ *with darkened soul*, i. e. *dead* (?)), sâwle bireáfod, fealleþ on foldan, Exon. Th. 328, 29; Vy. 25.
swôr *consobrinus*, -swora, -sworc, -sworcenness, -sworcenlîc, -sworenness. v. sweór, mân-swara, ge-sworc, for-sworcenness, for-sworcenlîc, for-sworenness.
sworettan; *p.* te *To draw a deep breath, to sigh, pant*:—Sworette *oscitavit*, Wrt. Voc. ii. 63, 64. Hê of inneweardre heortan swîþe sworete *ille intimo ex corde longa trahens suspiria*, Bd. 2, 1; S. 501, 14. Hê sume hwîle sæt and sworette *modicum suspirans*, 5, 19; S. 640, 29. Ða ûs nû bysmriaþ, đa đe ǽr on ûrum bendum sworettan, Blickl. Homl. 85, 25. Ðâ ongan hê sworettan, swâ swâ eallunga gewǽced, on ðam oređe belocen, Homl. Skt. ii. 23 b, 234. v. â-sworettan.
sworettend-lîc; *adj. Panting*:—Sworetendleca *anhela*, Wrt. Voc. ii. 9, 47.
sworettung, e; *f. A deep drawing of the breath*. I. as a sign of trouble, *a sigh*:—From sworetunge mînum *a singultu meo*, Rtl. 20, 27. Heó mid wôpe and mid teárum wæs geondgoten and longe sworetunge wæs teónde (*suspiria longa trahens*), Bd. 4, 23; S. 596, 10. Hê gemænigfealdode đa sworetunga đâm siccetungum, Homl. Skt. ii. 23 b, 201. II. *breathing hard* from illness or labour, *gasping, panting*:—Wiđ nearwre sworetunge, Lchdm. i. 340, 11. Hê mid langre sworetunge đæt ord of đâm breóstum teáh, Guthl. 20; Gdwin. 80, 13. Hê wæs swîđe gewǽced on đam langan geswince, and hê mid sworettungum wæs genyrwed, Homl. Skt. ii. 23 b, 770. Betwih đa[m] untruman sworettunga *inter aegra suspiria*, Bd. 3, 13; S. 538, 23.
swornian, swarnian; *p.* ode *To coalesce*:—Suornodun, suornadur suarnadun *coaluissent*, Txts. 48, 198. Swornodon, Wrt. Voc. ii. 14, 14. v. â-swarnian.
swôt; *adj. Sweet*:—Ðæt hûs gefylled wæs of suôt stenc đæs smirinese *domus impleta est ex odore ungenti*, Jn. Skt. Lind. 12, 3. Mid swôtum wyrtum, Nar. 49, 8. [Þe swote bređ of spices, A. R. 80, 2. His swote sauur, Marh. 4, 33. Þe swote Ihû, swottre þen euer ani þing, 11, 14. Se swiđe swote smeal, Kath. 1588. Swete Iesu, alre smelle swotest, 617. Aprille with his showres swoote, Chauc. C. T. prol. 1.] v. swête, swôtness.
swôte; *adv. Sweetly*:—Ic stince swôte *oleo*, Ælfc. Gr. 37: Zup. 220, 14. Se lîchoma stanc swôte, Shrn. 143, 29. [Þu sleptest swôte, A. R. 238, 5. *O. H. Ger.* sôzo *suaviter*.]
swođung. v. sweđung.
swôt-lîc; *adj. Sweet, savoury*:—Hû sió womb weorđe mid swôtlecustum mettum gefylled *ut venter delectabiliter cibis impleatur*, Past. 43; Swt. 311, 8. [*O. H. Ger.* sôz-lîh.] Cf. swêtlîce, *and next word*.
swôt-mete; es; *m. A sweet-meat, delicacy*:—Nǽron đâ welige hâmas ne mistlîce swôtmettas, Bt. 15; Fox 48, 4. v. swêt-mete *and preceding word*.
swôtness, e; *f. Sweetness*:—Mycel swôtnysse stænc, Shrn. 16, 1. In stencg suôtnisses *in odore suavitatis*, Rtl. 88, 32. Suôtnise stences, 65, 41. v. swêtness.
swotole. v. sweotole.
swôt-stence; *adj. Sweet-scented, odoriferous*:—*Ambrosia* elesealfe, *divino odore* đære swôtstencan, Wrt. Voc. ii. 2, 35.
swôt-stencende (-stincende?) *emitting a sweet odour*:—Suǽ đæt rêcilc suôtstencende stenc ic gisalde *sicut balsamum aromatizans odorem dedi*, Rtl. 65, 39.
swugian, swulung, -swundenness, swur-, swuster, swutol, swyft, swyftlere, swylc. v. swigian, sulung, â-swundenness, sweor-, sweostor, sweotol, swift, swiftlere, swilc.
swyld (?), e; *f. A pang*:—Sâr (þar, MS.) mê ymbsealde swylde (*Grein suggests* swylce) deáđes *trouble encompassed me, the pangs of death*; circumdederunt me dolores mortis, Ps. Th. 114, 3. v. swelan, *and* cf. cwyld, cwelan.
swyle, es; *m. A tumour, swelling, abscess*:—Swyle *apostema*, Wrt. Voc. i. 19, 35: ii. 7, 68. Unwlitig swile . . . đone ungeþwǽran swyle *tumor deformis* . . . *tumorem illum infestum*, Bd. 4, 32; S. 611, 17, 41. Se earm wæs on mycelne swyle gecyrred . . . đeáh đe se swyle đæs earmes gesýne sî *brachium versum est in tumorem . . . tametsi tumor brachii manere videretur*, 5, 3; S. 616, 6, 38. Ðâ âsweóll him se lîchama . . . Ðâ sôna eall se swyle gewât fram him, Guthl. 16: Gdwin. 68, 24. Wiþ innan-gewyrsmedum geswelle . . . lege on gelôme ôþ đætte open sié se swile, Lchdm. ii. 72, 24. Wiþ ceácena swyle and wiþ geagles swyle, 2, 19, 20. Wiþ ǽlcum heardum swile ođđe geswelle, 70, 20. Wiþ deádum swile, 74, 12, 15. Wiþ springe . . . lege on đone swile, 80, 17. Wiđ swylas, gâte tord; smyre mid đa swylas; hyt hý tôdrîfþ, and gedêþ đæt hý eft ne ârîsaþ, i. 354, 27. v. fǽr-, fôt-, geagl-, hand-swyle.
swylfende, Wrt. Voc. i. 20, 22, swylian. v. swelgan, swilian.
swylt, es; *m. Death, destruction*. I. of the death of the body:—Swylt hâligra *mors sanctorum*, Ps. Th. 115, 5. Ende becwom, swylt æfter synnum, Beo. Th. 2514; B. 1255. On galgan rîdan, seomian æt swylte, Exon. Th. 329, 14; Vy. 34. Deáđberende gyfl (*the forbidden fruit*) đa sinhîwan tô swylte geteáh, 153, 10; Gû. 823. Swylt settan đînum esnum *to put thy servants to death*, Ps. Th. 78, 2. Swylt ætfæstan, Andr. Kmbl. 2695; An. 1350. Swilt þrowian, Apstls. Kmbl. 142; Ap. 71. ¶ *The word often occurs with somewhat of a personal sense as the subject of* niman, forniman:—Ǽr đec swylt nime, deáđ for duguđe, Exon. Th. 257, 31; Jul. 255: Elen. Kmbl. 892; El. 447. Ðǽr Seón cyning swylt dreórig fornam, Ps. Th. 135, 20: Beo. Th. 2877; B. 1436. Ealle swylt fornam, druron dômleáse, deáđrǽs forfêng, Andr. Kmbl. 1988; An. 996: Exon. Th. 283, 5; Jul. 675: 477, 19; Ruin. 27. II. of the second death, *the perdition of the soul*:—Hî leahtrum fâ, lêge gebundne, swylt þrowiaþ . . . đæt is êce cwealm, Exon. Th. 94, 14; Cri. 1540. [Cf. *Goth.* swulta-wairþja *lying at the point of death*: *Icel.* sultr *hunger, famine*.]
swylt (?=swylht, cf. swelgan?), es; *m. A whirlpool*:—Swyttes (swyltes?) *gurgitis*, Hpt. Gl. 468, 72.
swylt-cwalu, e; *f. Death-pang, death*, (1) of the death of the body:—

Þæs gāstes sīð æfter swyltcwale, Andr. Kmbl. 311; An. 156. (2) of the death of the soul:—Gif seó sāwl sceal mid deóflum drohtnoð habban . . . on swyltcwale and in sārum sorgum, Wulfst. 188, 4. Cf. deáþ-cwalu.

swylt-dæg, es; *m. Death-day, day of death*:—Ǣr his swyltdæge, Cd. Th. 74. 12; Gen. 1221: Beo. Th. 5588; B. 2798.

swylt-deáþ, es; *m. Death*:—Ðū mīne sāwle of swyltdeáðes lāþum wiðlæddest *eripuisti animam meam de morte*, Ps. Th. 55, 11.

swymman, swȳn, swynge, swyr, swyra, swyrd, swyrige (= *partiat*, R. Ben. Interl. 54, 4), swyster, -swystrenu, swytel, swȳþ, sȳ, syb[b], sȳcan. v. swimman, swīn, swinge, sweor, sweora, sweord, scirian, sweoster, gesweosternu (-swistrenu), sweotol, swīþ, sī, sib[b], sīcan.

-syd *in* ge-syd *a miry place*. [Halliwell gives *suddie* = miry, boggy. Cf. also *sod*. Cf. *O. H. Ger.* salz-suti *salsugo*: *Ger.* sudel *a puddle*.] Cf. seáþ.

syde, es; *m. A decoction, the water in which anything has been seethed* or *boiled*:—Ðysse sylfan wyrte syde ðære tōþa sār geliðigaþ, gyf hyne man swā wearmne on ðam mūþe gehealdeþ, Lchdm. i. 280, 3. [*M. H. Ger.* sut: *Ger.* sud *seething*; ab-sud *a decoction*: cf. *Icel.* soð *the broth* or *water in which meat has been sodden*.] v. seóðan.

sydung (*better* sidung, *under which form the word should be entered*), e; *f. A regulation, rule*:—Sydung *regula*, Germ. 398, 217. Cf. Gesidode *determinabit*, 399, 431: *conserit*, 469. Gesydod *concinna, conveniens, benecomposita*, 396, 321. *Goth.* sidōn *meditari*. *O. Sax.* gi-sidōn sorga *to cause sorrow* to a person: *O. H. Ger.* sitōn *machinari, disponere*; gi-sitōn *instituere, destinare, conglutinare*. (*See* sīdung, *where perhaps* sidung *should be read*.) v. sidu.

syfe. v. sife.

sȳfer-ǣte; *adj. Moderate in eating, sober, temperate*:—Sig se abbod clǣne and sȳferǣte (sȳfre, Wells Frgt.) *oportet eum esse castum, sobrium*, R. Ben. 119, 25. v. sȳferness.

sȳfer-līc (?); *adj. Sober, moderate*:—Sēferlīce *sobriam* (but the termination of the Latin word is doubtful, v. note), Hymn. Surt. 16, 21.

sȳferlīce; *adv.* I. *with cleanliness, without impurity*:—Ðæt gē witen ðæt hit (*the preparation of the wafers for the mass*) clǣnlīce and sȳferlīce gedōn sȳ, L. E. I. 5; Th. ii. 404, 36. II. *soberly, purely, without excess* or *grossness*:—Sidefulle on ðeáwum and sȳferlīce lybbende, Homl. Ass. 37, 327. III. *soberly, prudently, circumspectly*:—Ða cild ðe beóþ sȳferlīce āfēdde (cf. *the contrast in* l. 9, cild rēceleáslīce āfēdd), and wið unðeáwum gestȳrede, Homl. Th. ii. 326, 17. Biddende sēferlīce *precantes sobrie*, Hymn. Surt. 19, 11. [*O. H. Ger.* sūbarlīcho *ad sobrietatem*.]

sȳferness, e; *f. Sobriety, moderation, temperance, abstinence, purity*:—Sȳfernys *abstinentia*, Wrt. Voc. i. 51, 7. Seó sȳfernes þreáde ðæt werod cweðende ðæt hit ne fyligde ðære gālnesse *sobrietas increpat acies dicens ne sequantur luxuriam*, Prud. 46 a: 47 a–49 a. Seó sȳfernes and ōðre mægnu, 54. Rūmheortnys and sȳfernys (*opposed to* gītsung and gīfernes, 68, 15), Wulfst. 69, 1. Sȳfernysse þearf *sinceritatis azima*, Hymn. Surt. 82, 31: Scint. 42, 16. Ðære sȳfernysse (*opposed to drunkenness*, v. l. 54) gōd bodian, Homl. Ass. 146, 60. Mid micelre sȳfernysse and gemetfæstnysse, and nā mid nānre oferfylle ne mid oferdrince, 144, 15. Sȳfernysse (*opposed to* druncenscipe, l. 18), 145, 20: Homl. Th. i. 360, 5. Ic brūce ðisum mettum mid sȳfernysse (*cum sobrietate*), Coll. Monast. Th. 35, 5. Began ðā his geþanc tō sȳfernysse (*opposed to lust*, v. 197, 75) gehwyrfan, Homl. Ass. 198, 96. [*O. H. Ger.* sūbarnessi *purificatio, purgatio*.] v. un-sȳferness.

syfeþa, sȳfian. v. sifeþa, seófian.

syflan; *p.* de; *pp.* ed *To provide with* sufel, q.v. [:—Gesyfledne hlāf, Wulfst. 170, 20. Brādne hlāf well gesyfled, Chart. Th. 606, 3. *Icel.* syfldr brauðhleifr.] v. ge-syflan; syfling.

syflige, an; *f. A dish to be eaten with bread*:—Genihtsumian wē gelȳfaþ twā gesodene syflian (oððe?) sanda . . . twā sanda genihtsumiaþ *sufficere credimus cocta duo pulmentaria* . . . *duo pulmentaria cocta sufficiant*, R. Ben. Interl. 70, 11–15. v. next word.

syfling, e; *f. Food to be eaten with bread*:—Syflyncge *pulmentario* (pulmentarium *quilibet cibus extra panem*, Migne), Hpt. Gl. 494, 57. Ðǣr feóll ādūne wearm hlāf mid his syflinge, Homl. Th. ii. 136, 18. Sind ða twā gesetnyssa, ðæt is sealmsang and wītegung, swylce hī syflinge wǣron tō ðām fīf berenum hlāfum, ðæt is tō ðām fīf ǣlīcum bōcum, i. 188, 19. v. sufel, *and two preceding words*.

sȳfre; *adj. Sober, not giving way to appetite* or *passion, pure, temperate, circumspect*:—Sȳfre (sȳfer, Wrt., *but see* Anglia viii. 451) *abstinens*, Wrt. Voc. i. 51, 8. Gif ðū drincst wīn gemetlīce, sȳfre (*sobrius*) ðū byst, Scint. 105, 17. Se mynstres hordere sī wīs sȳfre and nā oferettol *cellerarius monasterii sit sapiens, sobrius, non multum edax*, R. Ben. 54, 8. Sig se abbod clǣne and sȳfre and mildheort *oportet eum esse castum, sobrium, misericordem*, 118, 26. Sidefull man . . . gesceádwīs and sȳfre, Homl. Th. i. 596, 32. Fæste ðæt mōd sȳfre *jejunet ut mens sobria*, Hymn. Surt. 63, 3. Sēfre, 2, 32: 27, 17. Mid sȳfrum andgyte, Homl. Skt. ii. 23 b, 78. Swā swā Petrus cwæð: 'Beóþ sȳfre and wacole' *be sober, be vigilant* (1 Pet. 5, 8), Homl. Th. ii. 448, 8. Clǣne and rihte and sēfre *castique recti ac sobrii*, Hymn. Surt. 19, 5. Ða clǣnheortan . . . ða ðe heora līchaman geclǣnsiaþ mid sȳfrum þeáwum, Homl. Skt. ii. 23 b, 43. Clǣnust and sȳfrust (*sincera*) gebedes āthtincg, Scint. 35, 14. [*O. Sax.* sūbri: *O. H. Ger.* sūbar, sūbiri *mundus*: *Ger.* sauber: *Du.* zuiver *clean, neat*.] v. un-sȳfre.

syge (*better* (?) sige), es; *m. Sight, aim* (?):—Scyppend hafa ðē tō hyhte and ā sōð tō syge ðonne ðū secge hwæt *have God as your hope, and ever truth as your aim, when you say anything*, Exon. Th. 304, 2; Fä. 64. [Cf. (?) *Icel.* sigta *to aim at*.]

sȳl, e; *f. A pillar, column*:—Scs Arculfus sagaþ ðæt hē gesāwe on Hierusalem āne sȳle . . . ðonne seó sunne byþ on ðæs heofones mydle ðonne nafaþ seó sȳl nǣnige sceade . . . and swā ða dagas forð on sceortiaþ, swā byþ ðære sȳle sceade lengra. Ðeós sȳl cȳþeþ ðæt Hierusalem ys geseted on myddre eorðan, Shrn. 95, 30–96, 5, 8. In sȳle wolcnes *in columna nubis*, Ps. Surt. 98, 7. Ðære mēder wæs on slǣpe ætȳwed . . . ðæt hyre man stunge āne sȳle on ðone bōsum, 149, 2. Ercoles sȳla *Herculis columnae*, Ors. 1, 1; Swt. 8, 26. Ðæt feoh ðe hié wiþ ðām sȳlum sellan woldon, 4, 12; Swt. 210, 4. Ic getrymede sȳle his *confirmavi columnas ejus*, Ps. Surt. 74, 4. [*O. Frs.* sēle: *O. L. Ger. O. H. Ger.* sūl *columna*: *Icel.* sūla *a pillar*. Cf. *Goth.* sauls *a pillar*.] Cf. syll.

syl = **sylh**, syl = syll. v. sulh, syll.

syla (= sylha), an; *m. A ploughman*:—Syla *arator*, Hpt. Gl. 461, 72.

sylan. v. sulh.

syle. v. sylu.

sylen *a gift*, sylf, sylfor, sylfren. v. selen, self, seolfor, seolfren.

Syles eá *Selsey*; insula vituli marini, Bd. 4, 13; S. 583, 8. v. seolh.

sylfring (*should be given under* seolfring), es; *m. A silver coin*:—Þreó hund sylfringa *trecentos argenteos*, Gen. 45, 22.

sylh, Sȳl-hearwa. v. sulh, Sigel-hearwa.

sylian; *p.* ede *To sully, soil, pollute, defile*:—Hē on unscyldgum eorla blōde his sweord selede (cf. besyled, Bt. 16, 4; Fox 58, 18), Met. 9, 60. Sió sugu hī wille sylian on hire sole æfter ðæm ðe hió ādwægen biþ, Past. 54; Swt. 419, 27. [Þis sunne suleð þi sawle, H. M. 35, 15. Blind mon To þare diche his dweole fulieþ (*follows*) And falleþ and þar one sulieþ, O. and N. 1240. Mi sawle mit sunne isulet, Marh. 3, 14. Isuled, A. R. 396, 1. *O. Sax.* sulian: *O. H. Ger.* bi-sullen. Cf. *O. Frs.* sulenge *soiling*: *Goth.* bi-sauljan *to defile*.] v. be-sylian; solian, sulian, sol, syle.

syll, e; sylle, an; *f.* I. *a beam that serves as a foundation* or *support, a sill, a basis, support*:—Grundstānas *cementum*, syll *basis*, fōtstān *fultura*, Wrt. Voc. i. 61, 47–49. Syl *basis*, post *postis*, 86, 28, 29: ii. 10, 74: 101, 54. Syl *taber*, i. 289, 48. *Copsus* syl, *securis* [æx?], ii. 133, 9. *Cobsus* syl, ætx [æcx [*securis*]?], 22, 48. Getimbrung *aedificium*, post *basis*, sylle *postis* vel *fulcimentum*, i. 47, 19–21. Ðā wolde hē hūs timbrian mid his gebrōðra fultume. Ðā bæd hē hī ānre sylle, ðæt hē mihte ðæt hūs on ða sǣhealfe mid ðære underlecgan. Ða gebrōðra him behēton, ðæt hī woldon ðæt treów him gebringan. Ðā cōmon hī and wurdon ðæs treówes ungemyndige; ac God him ðā sylle āsende mid ðam sǣlīcum flōde, Homl. Th. ii. 144, 31–146, 4. Ðǣr fram sylle (*from the plank to which it was fixed*) ābeág medubenc monig, Beo. Th. 1555; B. 775. Ǣrest man āsmeáþ ðæs hūses stede, and eác man ðæt timber beheáwþ, and ða syllan man fægere gefēgþ, and ða beámas gelegþ, and ða ræftras tō ðære fyrste gefæstnaþ, Anglia viii. 324, 8. II. figurative, *a support, foundation*:—Ðonne hī ne beóþ mid nānre sylle underscotene ðæs godcundlīcan mægenes *nullis fulti virtutibus*, Past. 1; Swt. 27, 17. [Sulle *bassis*, Wrt. Voc. i. 95, 38. Sylle of an howse *silla, soliva*, Prompt. Parv. 456. Til he came to the selle, upon the flore, Chauc. C. T. 3820. *Icel.* syll *and* sylla *a sill*: *Dan.* syld: *Swed.* syll. Cf. *Goth.* ga-suljan *to lay a foundation*: *O. H. Ger.* swelli; *n. basis*: *Ger.* schwelle. *Also* (?) *Lat.* solea.]

syll *ploughs*, sylla *a giver*. v. sulh, sella.

sylla (= sella? *borrowed from Latin*?), an; *m. A saddle*:—Sylla *sella*, sadolfelt *pella*, sadolboga *carpella*, Wrt. Voc. i. 291, 14–16.

sȳlla, syllan, syllend, syl-līc, sylofren, syltan. v. sēl, sellan, sellend, seld-līc, seolfren, siltan.

sylu, e, an; *f. A miry place*:—Syle, sylen *volutabra*, Hpt. Gl. 486, 51. Syle, 506, 54. Ðis sint ða denstōwa, brōchyrst and beaddan syla, Cod. Dip. Kmbl. ii. 318, 30. v. sol, sylian, syl-weg.

syl-weg, es; *m. A miry way* (?):—On sylweg; andlang weges on ða hǣðihtan leáge, and swā on ðæt fūle slōh, Cod. Dip. Kmbl. iii. 262, 22. v. syle.

sȳma, sȳman, symbel *continual*. v. sēma, sīman, simbel.

symbel, symel, es; *n.* I. *a feast, banquet, entertainment*:—Him (*Adam and Eve*) . . . and hyra eaferum swā wearð sārlīc symbel, Exon. Th. 226, 15; Ph. 406. Him (*the blessed*) is symbel and dreám, 352, 12; Sch. 96. Se becom tō Prisce, ðǣr hē deófolgeldum geald. Ðā gelaþode hē hine tō his symble. Ðā sǣde Marcellus him ðæt hē wǣre cristen, and him nǣre ālȳfed ðæt hē birgde ðara hǣþenra symbles, Shrn. 125, 28–31. Swefan æfter symble, Beo. Th. 238; B. 119. Symle, 2020; B. 1008. Ðonne ārās hē fram ðam symle *surgebat a media coena*, Bd. 4, 24; S. 597, 7. Ðæt hāmweorud tō symble gesomnod wæs and hē sæt mid him æt ðam symble *vicani coenantes epulabantur, resedit et ipse cum eis ad convivium*, 3, 10; S. 534, 26–28. Sittan æt symble,

Exon. Th. 413, 27; Rä. 32, 12: 314, 16; Mōd. 15. Sittan tō symble, Cd. Th. 259, 33; Dan. 701: Beo. Th. 4214; B. 2104. Symle, 982; B. 489. Tō ðam symle, Judth. Thw. 21, 12; Jud. 15. Ðǽr is Dryhtnes folc geseted tō symle, Rood Kmbl. 279; Kr. 141. Symbel (*prandium*) mín ic gearuade, Mt. Kmbl. Lind. 22, 4. Herodes symbel (*cenam*) worhte, Mk. Skt. Lind. 6, 21. Hē hēt beran on ðæt hūs manegra cynna symbel, Shrn. 152, 25. Hē geaf mē sinc and symbel, Beo. Th. 4853; B. 2431. Symbel (ge)þicgan, 1242; B. 619: 2025; B. 1010. Symbel ymbsittan, 1132; B. 564. Symbel habban *epulari*, Ps. Th. 67, 2. Symbel ne ālēgon *feasts failed not*, Exon. Th. 352, 34; Reim. 5. Hwǽr cwom symbla gesetu? hwǽr sindon seledreámas, 292, 2; Wand. 93. Ðā wæs symbla mǽst geworden, 34, 31; Cri. 550: Beo. Th. 2469; B. 1232. Ðonne gecerres from symblum *quando reuertatur a nuptis*, Lk. Skt. Lind. Rush. 12, 36. II. *a feast, religious festival*:—Ðerh ðone dæg symbles (symbel, Lind.) *per diem festum*, Mk. Skt. Rush. 15, 6. Ðȳ ylcan dæge ealra wē healdaþ sancta symbel, Menol. Fox 397; Men. 200. [*O. Sax.* sumbal *a feast, banquet*: *Icel.* sumbl *a banquet*.]

symbel; *adj. Of a feast* or *festival*:—Simbel onsāh dæg *sollempnis urgebat dies*, Hymn. Surt. 96, 1. Gesettaþ dæg symbelne *constituite diem sollemnem*, Ps. Lamb. 117, 27. Dæg symbelne hȳ dōþ ðē *diem festum agent tibi*, Ps. Spl. 75, 10. Ealle dagas simle *omnes dies festos*, 73, 9. v. symbelness.

symbel-calic, es; *m. A chalice for use at festivals* or *at the solemnity of the Mass.* v. symbelness, II:—Ic an Ðeódrēd mīn wīte massehakele ðe ic on Pauie bouhte and simbelcalice, Chart. Th. 515, 18.

symbel-cenness, e; *f. The festival of a person's birth*:—Of his symbelcenn' *de ejus natalicio*, Rtl. 80, 17. Symbelcen' ðæt uē ðerh brūca *natalicio perfrui*, 78, 21. Symbelcenn' *natalitiis*, 93, 25. Ðaes symbelcennise wē bigōaþ *cujus natalitia colimus*, 65, 8: 79, 18. Symbelcen', 56, 13: 67, 8. [The meaning seems to require that the two parts of the compound should be separated, but the absence of inflexion in *symbel* where datives occur in the Latin seems to require the compound.]

symbel-dæg, es; *m.* I. *a feast-day, a day of a banquet*:—Æfter symbeldæge, Andr. Kmbl. 3052; An. 1529. Hē his līchoman wynna forwyrnde, symbeldaga, Exon. Th. 111, 34; Gū. 136. II. *a festival, day of a religious feast*:—Symbeldæg *dies festus*, Bd. 1, 27; S. 497, 1. Com ðyder mycel menigo for ðon symbeldæge, Blickl. Homl. 99, 29: Homl. Th. ii. 242, 21: Ps. Th. 117, 25. Se biscop sæt sume symbeldæge on ðære cierecan, Shrn. 78, 26. Ðone mǽron symbeldæg Drihtnes upstiges, Blickl. Homl. 131, 10. On symmeldæge (symbel-, MS. A.) *per diem festum*, Mk. Skt. 15, 6. His symbeldæg (*natalitia*) wē mērsiaþ, Rtl. 44, 28. Ic ðē symbledæg (*diem festum*) sette, Ps. Th. 75, 7. Symbeldagas *dies festos*, 73, 8.

symbel-gāl; *adj. Wanton with feasting*:—Se ðe him wīnes glæd wilna brūceþ, siteþ him symbelgāl, Exon. Th. 449, 30; Dōm. 79.

symbel-gefēra. v. simbel-gefēra.

symbel-gereorde, es; *n. A feast, banquet*:—Biþ seó ān snǽd sēlre mycle tō þicganne ðonne him sȳn seofon daga symbelgereordu, Salm. Kmbl. 816; Sal. 407.

symbel-gifa, an; *m. A feast-giver*:—Sāwla symbelgifa (*the Deity*), Andr. Kmbl. 2833; An. 1419.

symbel-hūs, es; *n. A banqueting-hall, dining-room*:—Hē æteóweþ iów symbelhūs (*cenaculum*) micel, Lk. Skt. Rush. Lind. 22, 12.

symbel-līc; *adj. Of a feast* or *festival, solemn*:—Dæge symellīcum *die sollempni*, Anglia xiii. 390, 354. Gebedu symellīce *orationes sollempnes*, 417, 750. Daegas symbellīce *dies festos*, Ps. Surt. 73, 8.

symbellīce; *adv. Solemnly*:—Symbellīce *solempniter*, Rtl. 9, 7: 48, 40: Anglia xiii. 402, 539. Simbollīce, R. Ben. Interl. 98, 10.

symbelmōnaþ-līc; *adj. Pertaining to a month in which a solemnity was celebrated* (?); the word translates *comitiales* in the gloss:—Ða symbelmōnaðlīcan ādla *comitiales*, Wrt. Voc. ii. 20, 39.

symbelness, e; *f. Festivity, solemnity*:—Symmelnysse *festivitate, solemnitate*, Hpt. Gl. 496, 17. Semelnyssa *solemnia, festivitates*, 500, 7. I. *festivity, feasting*:—Ðǽr ðurhwunaþ seó ēce bliss; ne byþ ðǽr hungor ne þurst . . . , ac hāligra symbelnys ðǽr þurhwunaþ ā būtan ende, Wulfst. 143, 2. Symbelnes, Blickl. Homl. 65, 21. Hwǽr beóþ ðonne ða symbelnessa and ða īdelnessa and ða ungemetlīcan hleahtras? 59, 17. II. *a religious festival* or *solemnity*:—Æftersanga symbolnys *matutinorum sollempnitas*, R. Ben. Interl. 43, 2. In dege mērum symbelnisse (*sollemnitatis*) eówerre, Ps. Surt. 80, 3. Symelnysse, Ps. Spl. 80, 3. On ðære Eástorlīcan tīde symbelnysse *in ipso tempore festi Paschalis*, Bd. 3, 24; S. 557, 40. On Iudēa symbelnysse (*festivitate*) wǽron geworden Drihtnes ǽfengereordu, Homl. Ass. 153, 40. Gērlīco symbelnise *annua solemnitate*, Rtl. 49, 25. Cuman tō ðære mæssan symbelnysse, L. E. I. 24; Th. ii. 420, 36: Bd. 1, 27; S. 496, 43: 2, 4; S. 505, 22. Ða symbelnessa mæssena *sollemnia missarum*, 4, 22; S. 592, 20. II a. *festive nature*:—Ðonne ealle dagas āteoriaþ, ðonne þurhwunaþ hē (*Sunday*) aa on his symbelnysse (*it continues ever in its character of festival*), Anglia viii. 310, 28.

symbel-tīd, e; *f. A religious festival* or *solemnity*:—Ārwyrðe symbeltīd *veneranda solemnitas*, Rtl. 65, 1, 8. Eádges apostoles symbeltīde (*festivitate*), 47, 9. Symbbeltīd *solempnitatem*, 2, 27. Heald ða symbeltīde ðæs mōnðes frumsceatta ðīnes weorces, Ex. 23, 16. Ārwyrðo symbeltīdo, Rtl. 49, 4. Symbeltīdum *sollennitatibus*, 80, 31. Symeltīdum, Anglia xiii. 397, 452. Symbeltīdo *solemnia*, Rtl. 49, 13: 50, 15: *natalicia*, 49, 25: 53. 1. Symbeltīde *festa*, 54, 11.

symbel-wērig; *adj. Weary with feasting*:—Wer (*Noah*) wīne druncen swæf symbelwērig, Cd. Th. 94, 19; Gen. 1564. Him symbelwērig (*Abimelech*) synna brytta þurh slǽp oncwæð, 159, 26; Gen. 2640.

symbel-wlanc; *adj. Elate with feasting*:—Siteþ symbelwlonc, lǽteþ wīne gewǽged word ūt faran, Exon. Th. 315, 32; Mōd. 40.

symbel-wynn, e; *f. The pleasure of feasting, the delight of the feast*:—Gā nū tō setle, symbelwynne dreóh, Beo. Th. 3569; B. 1782.

symblan; *p.* ede; *and* symblian; *p.* ode *To feast*:—Hū mǽre ðīn folc is, ǽlce dæge hit symblaþ, Ps. Th. 22, 7. Hió ofer hire suna symblaþ and blissaþ, 112, 8. Se weliga se ðe on ðæm godspelle gesǽd is ðætte ǽlce dæge symblede . . . Ða ðe ǽlce dæg symblaþ *dives ille, qui epulatus quotidie dicitur splendide . . . epulando quotidie*, Past. 43; Swt. 309, 3–9. Rihtwīse symbliaþ *justi epulentur*, Ps. Spl. C. 67, 3. Se weliga ǽlce dæge symblede (simblede, Cott. MSS.) *dives epulabatur quotidie splendide*, Past. 45; Swt. 337, 24. Mid ðȳ hī lange symbledon *cum diutius epulis vacarent*, Bd. 3, 10; S. 534, 30. Utan simblian *epulemur*, Wrt. Voc. ii. 143, 62. Symblendra swēg *sonus epulantis*, Ps. Th. 41, 4.

symble, symblian, symel. v. simble, symblan, symbel.

symering-wyrt, e; *f. The name of some plant*:—Simæringcwyrt (symeringc-, Wrt. Voc. i. 79, 12) *malua crispa*, Ælfc. Gl. Zup. 310, 12. Simeringwyrt *viola*, Wrt. Voc. i. 68, 67.

symle, symlian, symlinga, symmel-dæg, sȳn *be*, sȳn *sight*, syn- *ever-*. v. simble, simblian, simblunga, symbel-dæg, sī, sīn, sin-.

syn[n], e; *f.* I. with reference to human law or obligation, *misdeed, fault, crime, wrong*:—Se cyning his feóndum swīþe ārede . . . Ðyslīc wæs seó syn (*culpa*) ðe se cyning fore ofslegen wæs, Bd. 3, 22; S. 553, 21. Hié georne smeádon hwæt sió syn wǽre ðe hié gefremed hæfdon wið ðam cāsere, Elen. Kmbl. 828; El. 414. Ne synn ne sacu ne sār wracu *nec scelus infandum, . . . aut Mars, aut ardens caedis amore furor*, Ex. Th. 201, 10; Ph. 54. Ðā wæs synn and sacu Sweóna and Geáta *then was there wrongdoing and strife between Swedes and Geats*, Beo. Th. 4935; B. 2472. Senne *facinus*, Hpt. Gl. 519, 22. Synne stǽlan *to charge with crime*, Menol. Fox 569; Gn. C. 54. II. with reference to divine law, *sin*:—Heora synn (*peccatum*) ys swīðe gehefegod, Gen. 18, 20. Hē onfunde Godes ierre . . . ðeáh hē wēnde ðæt hit nān syn nǽre, Past. 4; Swt. 39, 6. Seó geofu wæs broht for ðære synne ðæs ǽrestan wīfes . . . and seó synn wæs ādilegod, Blickl. Homl. 5, 4–6. Syn, 3, 7. Mænige līf būtan leahtre (*crimine*) habban māgon, būtan synne (*peccato*) hī nā māgon, Scint. 230, 12. Ǽlc ðe synne (*peccatum*) wyrcþ is ðære synne (*peccati*) þeów, Jn. Skt. 8, 34. Se ðe dēþ āweg middaneardes synnæ (*peccatum*; synna, MS. A.: synne, MS. B. Lind. Rush.), 1, 29. Se hæfþ māran synne (synn, Lind.), 19, 11. Synne ne āspringaþ *sins cease not*, Exon. Th. 94, 11; Cri. 1538. Beóþ ðæs mannes synna gecwēmran ðonne eal eorþlīc goldhord, Blickl. Homl. 43, 21. Wē fela sinna didon, Hy. 7, 106. On synnum geboren, Jn. Skt. 9, 34. Of synnum mīnum clǽnsa mē, Ps. Spl. 50, 3. Sennum, Ps. C. 38. Andettan synna, Mt. Kmbl. 3, 6. Senna, Blickl. Homl. 43, 14. [*O. Sax.* sundia: *O. Frs.* sende: *O. H. Ger.* sunta *peccatum, culpa, noxa, nefas*: *Icel.* synd.] v. fyrn-, heáh-, nīd-syn[n].

syn-bōt, e; *f. Amends for sin, penance*:—Bisceopum gebyreþ ðæt hī ne beón tō feohgeorne æt synbōte, ne on ǽnige wīsan on unriht ne strȳnan, L. I. P. 10; Th. ii. 316, 32.

syn-byrðen[n], e; *f. The burden of sin*:—Hī synbyrþenne, firenweorc beraþ, Exon. Th. 79, 34; Cri. 1300. Ne þearf ðæs nān man wēnan ðæt his līchama mōte ða synbyrþenna on eorþscrafe gebētan, Blickl. Homl. 109, 31.

syn-bysig; *adj. Troubled in consequence of sin*:—Hē heteswengeas fleáh ond ðǽrinne fealh secg synbysig, Beo. Zup. 2227.

syn-cræft, es; *m. A sinful art*:—Ne syncræftas (scyn-, *other MS.*) wē ne onhyrgen, Wulfst. 253, 10.

syn-dǽd, e; *f. A sinful deed, sin, wicked act*:—For syndǽda ðara eardendra ðe hire on lifdan *a malitia inhabitantium in ea*, Ps. Th. 106, 33. Se deófol ða syndǽda stǽleþ on ða gāstas, Wulfst. 256, 7.

synder-ǽ; *f. A separate, private law, law for an individual*:—Syndurae *privilegium*, Rtl. 190, 19, col. 2. [*O. H. Ger.* suntar-ēwa *privilegium.*]

synder-gifu. v. sundor-gifu.

synder-līc; *adj. Separate, special, private*:—And ðære synderlīc[an] *ac privata*, Wrt. Voc. ii. 9, 10. Ða synderlīcan *privatam*, 75, 56. I. *that is apart, separate, remote*:—On senderlīcum hulce *in remoto* (*separato*) *tugurio*, Hpt. Gl. 465, 43. II. *private, that is done apart, not public*:—Ða heáfodmenn on synderlīcum geþeahte ðone sceat him sealdon, and bǽdon, ðæt hī sǽdon, ðæt ðæs Hǽlendes līc him wurde forstolen . . . Hī nāmon ðone sceatt, and swā þeáh on synderlīcum rūnungum ðæt riht eall rǽddon, Homl. Ass. 79, 156–161. II a. *private, without distinction, ordinary*:—On synderlícum dagum (cf. on weorcdagum *in contrast to* freólstídum, R. Ben. 37, 5; 36, 9) *diebus privatis*, R. Ben. Interl. 43, 2. III. *that belongs to an individual* or *that is adapted to a particular purpose, not in common, special, peculiar, proper*:—Seó gesceádwísnes is synderlíc cræft ðære sáwle, Bt. 33, 4; Fox 132, 10. Synderlíc gifu *praerogativa*, Hpt. Gl. 466, 42. Næfde se Fæder nán ðing synderlíces búton his Suna *the Father had nothing not in common with his Son*, Homl. Th. ii. 366, 12. Heora nán næfde siððan nán þingc sinderlíces, ac didon him eal gemǽne, L. Ælfc. P. 20; Th. ii. 370, 36. For synderlícum wurðmente *privilegium, singularem honorem*, Hpt. Gl. 411, 30. Ðes miccla wurðmynt nis ná ealra manna, ac on synderlícum wurðmynte ðám gesǽligum mǽdenum and ðám clǽnum cnapum, Homl. Ass. 41, 431. Ánra gehwylc ðara apostola biþ geseted tó his synderlícre stówe, Blickl. Homl. 143, 23. Hé ða syx dagas ǽr his þrowunga synderlíc weorc ǽlce dæge cýþde, 71, 30. God sealde heora ǽlcum synderlíce sprǽce, Ælfc. T. Grn. 4, 11. Ðonne wé for synderlecum synnum synderleca hreówsunga dóþ, Past. 53; Swt. 413, 28. Sume naman syndon *specialia*, ðæt synd synderlíce, ða ðe beóþ tódǽlede fram ðam gemǽnelícum, Ælfc. Gr. 5; Zup. 14, 6. IV. *separated by superiority, singular, excellent, specially good*:—Ðys is synderlíc lǽcedóm wið eágena dymnysse, Lchdm. i. 178, 8. Synderlícere *singulari, speciali*, Hpt. Gl. 431, 23. v. sundor-líc.

synderlíce; *adv.* I. *apart, away from all others, in private*:—Synderlíce (*separatim*) hine Petrus and Iacobus and Iohannes and Andreas áhsodon, Mk. Skt. 13, 3. II. where many things are to be distinguished from each other, *separately, severally, apart*:—Se án monn ongitt ðæt ðæt hé on óþrum ongit synderlíce (*in several ways*); hé hine ongit þurh ða eágan synderlíce, þurh ða eáran synderlíce, ðurh his rǽdelsan synderlíce, ðurh gesceádwísnesse synderlíce, Bt. 41, 5; Fox 252, 16–19. Synderlíce ánne gehwylcne hǽd God and hláford andettan wé synt geneádede *singulatim unamquamque personam Deum et dominum confiteri compellimur*, Ath. Crd. 19. Hine synderlíce ǽlc man beheóld, Homl. Skt. i. 23, 625. Ðara is ánra gehwylc synderlíce xxxtigum ðúsendum dǽla lengra ðonne eal middangeard, Salm. Kmbl. p. 150, 13. Heora ǽghwylc be heom sylfum synderlíce ðus cwæð, Homl. Ass. 162, 243. III. where one thing is to be distinguished from others of the same kind, *specially, in particular* (as opposed to generally):—Wé nemnaþ ealle ðing ǽgðer ge synderlíce ge gemǽnelíce; synderlíce be ágenum naman, *Eadgarus*; gemǽnelíce, *rex* cyning, Ælfc. Gr. 5; Zup. 8, 9–11. *Animal* is ǽlc ðing ðe orðaþ; ðonne is synderlíce *homo* man, *equus* hors . . .; gemǽnelíce *arbor* treów; synderlíce *uitis* wíntreów, Zup. 14, 8–10. Þeáh heó synderlíce Iohannes gýmene betǽht wǽre, hwæðere heó drohtnode gemǽnelíce mid ðam apostolícum werode, Homl. Th. i. 438, 31: ii. 112, 18–22. Hwí ne cwæð ðæt hálige gewrit be ðam men synderlíce, ðæt hé gód wǽre, swá swá hit cwæð mænigfealdlíce be ðám óþrum gesceaftum, ðæt hí góde wǽron? Boutr. Scrd. 19, 18. IV. where the reference is to a single person or circumstance, *only, exclusively, solely, to* or *by one's self*:—Ðæt word belimpþ synderlíce tó Gode ánum *that phrase belongs exclusively to God alone*, Homl. Th. ii. 236, 12. Hé him synderlíce (*to himself; or* (?) synderlíce, *adj.*, wíc *being used in plural*) wíc getimbrede *ipse sibi monasterium construxit*, Bd. 3, 19; S. 547, 30. Sume men ðæs wóses synderlíce (*by itself*) brúcaþ, Lchdm. i. 178, 11. Hú mæg ðǽr synderlíce ánes ríces monnes nama cuman *non fama hominum singulorum pervenire queat*, Bt. 18, 2; Fox 64, 1. Ðæt hors ic ðé synderlíce (*specialiter*) tó ǽhte geceás, Bd. 3, 14; S. 540, 28. Mæssige man áne mǽssan sinderlíce for ðare neóde, ðe ús nú on handa stent, Wulfst. 181, 24. Hí hæfdon ǽlce dæge heora wítena gemót, and wǽron gesette synderlíce tó ðam ða senatores, Jud. p. 161, 32. Ná synderlíce for ðære ðeóde *non tantum pro gente*, Jn. Skt. 11, 52. Synderlíce on hyhte ðú gesettest mé *singulariter in spe constituisti me*, Ps. Spl. 4, 10. Ðonne hié synderlíce ðenceaþ hú hié selfe scylen fullfremodeste weorðan . . . mið ðý hí bereáfiaþ hié selfe ðara góda ðe hié wilniaþ synderlíce habban *cum sua lucra cogitant, ipsis se, quae privata habere appetant, bonis privant*, Past. 5; Swt. 41, 22–43, 1: Swt. 45, 14. Nówuht him selfum synderlíce wilnian *nihil proprium quaerere*, 13; Swt. 77, 26. Senderlíce (*a Domino*) *proprie* (*uxor prudens*, Prov. 19, 14), Kent. Gl. 692. V. where degree is marked, *specially, exceedingly, to a greater extent than in any other case, singularly*:—Syndirlíce *excellenter*, Rtl. 47, 1. Nalles ná ðæt án ðæt hé gód doo gemang ódrum monnum ac eác synderlíce suá suǽ hé on ðyncðum biþ furður ðonne óðre ðæt hé eác sié on his weorcum suá micle furður *ut non solum sit ejus operatio utilis, sed etiam singularis . . . sicut honore ordinis superat, ita etiam morum virtute transcendat*, Past. 14; Swt. 81, 22. Sum bróþor synderlíce mid godcunde gyfe gemǽrsod (*specialiter insignis*), Bd. 4, 24; S. 596, 30. Hé him synderlíce wilnade ðæt wuldor, 5, 7; S. 620, 32. Hé hine lufode synderlíce, Homl. Th. i. 58, 6. Is synderlíce eallum Godes folce beboden ðæt hí heora gebeda lufian and ælmessan dǽlan, Homl. Ass. 164, 5. Se ðe synderlíce Cristes dýrling wæs, 151, 11. Ieremias ys úre wítega synderlíce, Ælfc. T. Grn. 9, 35. [Sunderliche, O. E. Homl. i. 11, 21: 13, 1: 261, 3: A. R. 90, 5. *O. H. Ger.* sunderlícho *signanter, singulariter.*] v. sundorlíce.

synderlícness, e; *f. Singularity, peculiarity*:—Forlǽtenre synderlícnysse *omissa specialitate* (*singularitate, peculiaritate*), Hpt. Gl. 413, 62.

synder-lípe; *adj. Special, singular, separate*:—Senderlípes *speciali*, Hpt. Gl. 522, 63. Senderlípum *speciali, singulari*, 450, 66. Synderlýpum *peculiaribus*, Anglia xiii. 369, 62. Cf. án-lípe, *and see next word.*

synder-lípes; *adv. Separately, singly*:—Sindorlípes *singillatim*, R. Ben. Interl. 47, 5. Senderlípes, Hpt. Gl. 484, 7. v. sundor-lípes.

synder-weorðmynt *a special honour, prerogative*:—Synderwurðmynt *praerogativa*, Wrt. Voc. i. 54, 61. Cf. sundor-weorþung.

syndig; *adj. Skilled in swimming* (?):—Sum byþ rynig; . . . sum on londe snel, féðe spédig; sum fealone wǽg stefnan steóreþ . . .; sum biþ syndig, Exon. Th. 296, 28; Crä. 58. v. sund, I, II, *and* cf. *Icel.* syndr *able to swim.*

-synd-líc, syn-dolh, syndon. v. gesynd-líc, sin-dolh, sind.

syndrian; *p.* ode *To sunder, separate*:—Eorþena langnyss ná syndraþ (*separat*), ða ðe sóð lufu geþeód, Scint. 5, 13. Se ðe syndraþ fram leahtre, R. Ben. Interl. 117, 3. Ðæt God gegeadrade, monn ne suindria (*separet*), Mt. Kmbl. Lind. 19, 6. v. á-, ge-, tó-syndrian; sundrian.

syndrig; *adj.* I. *separate, alone, not joined with others*:—Ic mé syndrig eom *singulariter sum ego*, Ps. Th. 140, 12. Wiþ fefre hylpþ syndrigo marubie tó drincanne *to drink marrubium alone*, Lchdm. ii. 134, 27. Heáfdehtes porres [croppan] syndrigne sele þicgan, 230, 11. Nim syndrig sealt oððe wið weaxhláfsealfe gemeng, 246, 9. Áwyl ða wyrte and syndrigea betonican, neftan, etc., 76, 18. I a. *standing apart, not accessible* (?); cf. synder-líc, I:—Hé (*Hannibal*) com tó Alpis ðǽm muntum . . . and ðone weg geworhte ofer munt Iof (munti fór MS. C.). Swá ðonne hé tó ðæm syndrigum stáne com ðonne hét hé hiene mid fýre onhǽtan and siþþan mid mattucan heáwan *ad Alpes pervenit . . . atque invias rupes igni ferroque rescindit*, Ors. 4, 8; Swt. 186, 18. II. *special, set apart for a particular purpose*:—Sáwlsceat *vel* syndrig Godes lác *dano* (*dona*?), Wrt. Voc. i. 28, 44. Ða Senatores dæghwamlíce smeádon on ánum sindrian húse, Jud. p. 161, 33. III. *special, singular, extraordinary, remarkable for an unusual quality* or *for the unusual degree in which some quality exists*:—Ðæt is syndrig cynn, symle biþ ðý heardra ðe hit sǽstreámas swíðor beátaþ, Cd. Th. 80, 6; Gen. 1324. Him ðá wæs syndrig ege ðǽr him ǽr wæs seó mǽste wyn, Ors. 2, 8; Swt. 92, 32. Míne þrié ða getreówestan frýnd ða wǽron míne syndrige treówgeþoftan (*my special confidants*), Nar. 29, 28. IV. of that which concerns a single person, *private, own*; proprius, privatus:—God, ðæm syndrig (*proprium*) is ðætte hé gimilsage, Rtl. 40, 19. Syndriges *propriae*, 33, 30. Be ðam ðæt munecas syndrige ǽhte næbben . . . Nǽnig nán ðing syndries ne áge *si debeant monachi proprium habere . . . Ne quis presumat aliquid habere proprium*, R. Ben. 56, 15–19: L. I. P. 15; Th. ii. 322, 10. Fíf hída syndries landes . . . fíf hída gemǽnes landes, Cod. Dip. B. iii. 395, 28. Æfter syndrig mægn *secundum propriam virtutem*, Mt. Kmbl. Lind. 25, 15: Ps. Th. 97, 2. Syndrige wyrðmenta *privilegia*, Hpt. Gl. 517, 1. Suindrig *propria*, Mt. Kmbl. p. 3, 9. From syndrigum *ex propriis*, Jn. Skt. Lind. 8, 44. Standan on syndrigum gebedum *to be engaged in private devotions*, Homl. Skt. ii. 26, 115. In syndrige *in propria*, Jn. Skt. Lind. 16, 32. V. *separate, several, sundry, each separately*:—Moyses gebletsode ða twelf mǽgða ǽlce mid sindrigre bletsunge, Deut. 33, 5. Hé syndrigne ácsode hwylces geleáfan hí wǽron *cujus essent fidei singuli, inquirebat*, Bd. 4, 17; S. 585, 13. Hwylcne ende syndrigo ðing (*singula*) hæbbende synd, 5, 23; S. 646, 6. Hig eodon and syndrie (*singuli*) férdon on hyra ceastre, Lk. Skt. 2, 3. Ongunnon suindrige (*or adv.?*) ǽghwelc (*singuli*) cwoeða, Mt. Kmbl. Lind. 26, 22. Ic syndrigra (*singulorum*) hús and bedd geseah, Bd. 4, 25; S. 601, 9. Hé syndrigum geárum (*annis singulis*) hine neósode, 4, 29; S. 607, 12. Hig gesamnodon hig be sindrigum mǽgðum, Jos. 7, 16. Hé syndrigum (*singulis*) hys hand on settende hig gehǽlde, Lk. Skt. 4, 40. Scíp ceigeþ syndrigum nomum *oues uocat nominatim*, Jn. Skt. Lind. 10, 3. Suindrigum his suá hwælc ðú eftsettes *singulis sua quaeque restitues*, Mt. Kmbl. p. 3, 11: p. 4, 7. Þurh syndrige ðine andsware ic ongeat, Bd. 4, 22; S. 591, 39. V a. in a distributive sense, *one a-piece, one each*:—Ðá onféngon hig syndrige penegas (cf. ǽlc his pening, v. 9, the Latin in each case being *singulos denarios*), Mt. Kmbl. 20, 10. On septem epistolas canonicas ic sette syndrie béc (*libros singulos*), Bd. 5, 24; S. 648, 13. Dile, mintan and merce, syndrige sceafas geseóð, Lchdm. ii. 188, 24: 228, 26. [*O. H. Ger.* sunderig *separatus, singularis, privatus, peculiaris.*]

syndrige; *adv.* I. *apart, separately, by one's self*:—Hé gefoerde in stówe unbýed syndrige (*seorsum*), Mt. Kmbl. Lind. 14, 13: Mk. Skt. Lind. 4, 34. Syndrige áuunden *separatim involutum*, Jn. Skt. Lind. 20, 7. II. *singly, one at a time*:—Ða ongunnon cuoeða him swyndria (*singillatim*), Mk. Skt. Lind. 14, 19. Ongunnon suindrige (*or adj.?*) ǽghwelc (*singuli*) cwoeða, Mt. Kmbl. Lind. 26, 22. [*O. H. Ger.* sunderigo *separatim, seorsum, specialiter.*]

syndrigend-líc; *adj. Separating*:—*Adverbia discretiva* synd syndrigendlíce, Ælfc. Gr. 38; Zup. 229, 7.

syndrig-líc; *adj. Special, singular, peculiar*:—Twegen cynelíce cnihtas mid syndriglícre (*speciali*) Godes gyfe wǽron gesigefæste, Bd. 4, 16; S. 584, 20. v. next word.

syndriglíce; *adv.* I. *specially, particularly*:—Ðæt hálige gewrit cýþeþ and syndriglíce (*specialiter*) Paules epistola, Bd. 1, 27; S. 489, 2. II. *singly, severally, one by one, of each one*:—Hé syndriglíce (*singillatim*) wæs fram him eallum frignende, Bd. 2, 13; S. 515, 40.

-syndrung. v. á-syndrung *divortium*, Wrt. Voc. ii. 28, 26.

syndur-ae, -sýne, syne-wealt. v. synder-ǽ, -síne, seonu-wealt.

syn-fáh; *adj. Stained with sin*:—Synfá men, Exon. Th. 67, 3; Cri. 1083.

syn-full; *adj. Sinful; used substantively, a sinner*:—Synful *peccator*, Wrt. Voc. i. 86, 63. Ðæt synfull gesyhþ *peccator videbit*, Ps. Th. 111, 9. Ic eom synfull (synn-, Lind.) mann *homo peccator sum*, Lk. Skt. 5, 8. Synful, Jn. Skt. 9, 16. Þeáh ðe se mæssere synfull sý, L. Ecg. C. 7; Th. ii. 140, 1. Ðonne se synfulla his líf geendaþ, Blickl. Homl. 61, 2. Beó ðú milde mé synfullum, Lk. Skt. 18, 13. Ðæt gé gebiddan for mé ðam unwyrðestan synfullan, Anglia xi. 103, 95. On ðisse synfulran (*peccatrice*) cneórisse, Mt. Skt. 8, 38. Ða synfullan (synn-, Cott. MSS.) bytledon uppe on mínum hrygge, Past. 21; Swt. 153, 9: Blickl. Homl. 71, 35. Geseald on synfulra hand, Mt. Kmbl. 26, 45. Synnfullum mannum tǽcan, Blickl. Homl. 43, 15. Þeófas and synfulle men, 75, 28. Gesete him synfulle tó ealdrum *constitue super eum peccatorem*, Ps. Th. 108, 5. [*Icel.* synd-fullr.]

syngian; *p.* ode *To sin*:—Ic syngige *committo, admitto*, Ælfc. Gr. 37; Zup. 221, 8. Ic eom se lyðra man, se syngige swíðe genehhe, Hy. 3, 42. Ic singie nitende *peccavi nesciens*, Num. 22, 34. Gyf ðín bróðor syngaþ wið ðé *si peccaverit in te frater tuus*, Mt. Kmbl. 18, 15, 21. Ic ánum ðé syngode *tibi soli peccavi*, Ps. C. 47. Ðá sǽde him Plenius ðæt hé wóh bude, and miclum on ðǽm syngade, Ors. 6, 10; Swt. 264, 28. Wé singodon on úrum bréðer *peccavimus in fratrem nostrum*, Gen. 42, 21. Ne synga ðú *non moechaberis*, Ex. 20, 14. Ðe læs gé syngien (nelle gé syngian, Ps. Lamb.), Ps. Th. 4, 5. Se unrihtwísa cwyð ðæt hé wylle syngian (*ut delinquat*), 35, 1: Past. 17; Swt. 109, 17. Singian, Homl. Skt. i. 1, 88. Wið God singian *in Deum peccare*, Gen. 39, 9. Geopenian ðǽm syngiendum hiera unryht, Past. 15; Swt. 91, 11. Ðæt hié óþre syngiende rihtaþ, Blickl. Homl. 63, 24. [Hwenne þe muð sunezeð on muchele ete, O. E. Homl. i. 153, 31. Þu sunegest . . . we sunegieð, 17, 20, 36. Heo sunegede . . . heo makede him sunegen, A. R. 56, 1, 4. Þatt mann ne sinnȝheþþ nohht, Orm. 3970. Ine þri maneris me may zeneȝi, Ayenb. 20, 4. Ho so syngeþ (synegeþ, synneþ), Piers P. C-text, 11, 26. *O. Sax.* sundión: *O. H. Ger.* sunteón: *Ger.* sündigen: *Icel.* syndga.] v. for-, ge-syngian.

syngig (?); *adj. Sinful*:—Hwí flihst ðú mé forealdodne syngigan (synnigan ?), Homl. Skt. ii. 23 b, 192.

syn-grin *the toil* or *snare which a sin constitutes*:—Ðæt ús deófol of rihtan wege þurh deriende þýstra belǽdan ne mǽge, ne mid syngrinum tó swíðe gehremman *not hamper us too much with the snares of sin*, Btwk. 196, 19. Ðonne mæg se biscop ðæs mannes syngrina (*the toils of sin in which he is involved*) þurh Godes þafunge ðe swýðor gelíðian, Wulfst. 155, 26.

syngung, e; *f. Sinning*:—Ús is swíðe þearle tó éfstanne ðæt wé bewépan ðæt wé ǽr tó yfele gedydon, and ofer ðis ðære syngunge geswícan, Homl. Ass. 149, 137.

syn-leahter, es; *m. A sinful fault, a sin*:—Forbúgan ða synleahtras ðe ús forbodene synd, ðæt is unrihthǽmed and ǽrǽtas and oferdruncennessa, Wulfst. 134, 24.

syn-leás; *adj. Sinless, without sin*:—Hwylc eówer sí synleás (*sine peccato*), Jn. Skt. 8, 7. Crist þrowade for ús synleás, Wulfst. 121, 14: 151, 5. Ne biþ nǽfre nán man leahterleás ne synleás ealra þinga, 233, 24. Biþ oft synleás yfel geðoht ðǽm gódum *plerumque boni innoxie tentantur ad culpam*, Past. 54; Swt. 423, 3. Úre Drihten gescóp Adam hálgne and clǽnne and synleásne, Wulfst. 153, 13. [*O. Sax.* sundi-lós.]

syn-léw, -leáw, e; *f. A sinful injury*:—Hér syndan þurh synleáwa sáre geléwede tó manege on earde, Wulfst. 165, 25. v. léw, lim-lǽw.

syn-líc; *adj. Sinful*:—Hé sceal scyldan cristenum mannum wið ǽlc ðara þinga ðe synlíc biþ, L. I. P. 7; Th. ii. 312, 24. Anbúgan tó nánum fúllícum and synlícum luste, Past. 14; Swt. 83, 15. Fyrenlusta and synlícra dǽda á má and má, Wulfst. 56, 7. Wé geáxiaþ nǽnig gód áwunigende and ealle worldlícu þing swíþe synlícu, Blickl. Homl. 109, 3. [Wǽron swíðe hefige and sinlíce gewinn betwux ðam Cásere of Sexlande and his sunu, Chr. 1106; Erl. 241, 23.] [*O. H. Ger.* sunt-líh *facinorosus, peccatorius*: *Icel.* synd-ligr.]

synlíce; *adv. Sinfully, wickedly*:—Hí sóhton synlíce sáwle míne, Ps. Th. 62, 8. Ða hǽðnan synlíce heora ða leásan godas mid mislícum deófolgeldum him laþodan on fultum, Blickl. Homl. 201, 30. Ðæs lífes ðe ðú mid leahtrum hafast ofslegen synlíce, Exon. Th. 90, 26; Cri. 1480. Se cyng and ða heáfodmenn lufedon swíðe and oferswíðe gítsunge on golde and on seolfre and ne róhtan hú synlíce hit wǽre begytan, Chr. 1086; Erl. 220, 6, 12. [*O. H. Ger.* suntlícho *impie*.]

syn-lust, es; *m. Sinful pleasure* or *desire, lust*:—Ic wæs swíðe onǽled mid ðære hátheortnysse ðæs synlustes, ðæt ic gewilnode bútan ceápe ðæt hí mé tó geurnon, Homl. Skt. ii. 23 b, 337. Crist lǽrde, ðæt gehwá synnluste fæste wíðstóde; Antecrist lǽrþ, ðæt gehwá his luste georne fulgange, Wulfst. 55, 11. Ða hlíwðe ðe hé ǽr þurh synlust gefremode, L. Edg. C. 16; Th. ii. 284, 5: Exon. Th. 17, 12; Cri. 269. Mancyn ðe nú is in ídelum gylpe and on synnlustum beswicen, Wulfst. 182, 13. Synlustum, Blickl. Homl. 57, 23. Synlustas fremman, Dóm. L. p. 30, 53.

synn. v. syn[n].

synnicge (-ecge), an; *f. A sinner, a sinful woman*; peccatrix:—Seó (*Mary Magdalen*) wæs ǽrest synnecge, Shrn. 107, 10.

synnig; *adj.* I. in a religious sense, *sinful, wicked*:—Ánra gehwylc, sóðfæst ge synnig, Exon. Th. 233, 11; Ph. 523. Se feónd and se freónd . . . synnig and gesǽlig, Elen. Kmbl. 1908; El. 956. Synnig wið sáwla nergend, Andr. Kmbl. 1841; An. 923. Hwí swigast ðú, synnigu tunge, Dóm. L. 67. Ðæs synnigan mód *peccantis mentem*, Past. 46; Swt. 357, 10. Sleáþ synnigne ofer seolfes múð, Andr. Kmbl. 2601; An. 1302. Synnig cynn (*the people of Sodom*), Cd. Th. 152, 35; Gen. 2531. Háliges láre synnige ne swulgon, Andr. Kmbl. 1419; An. 710. Beóþ ða syngan flǽsc scandum þurhwaden, Exon. Th. 78, 31; Cri. 1282. Fyrenfulra ðreát, heáp synnigra *peccatores*, Ps. Th. 91, 6: Cd. Th. 145, 17; Gen. 2407. Hé biþ ðám yflum egeslíc tó geseónne, synnegum monnum, Exon. Th. 57, 18; Cri. 920. Syngum hondum, 70, 3; Cri. 1133: 84, 21; Cri. 1377. Ðú ðe ús synnige ádrife fram dóme, Ps. Th. 107, 10. Hí hyra synnigan breóst beátaþ, Wulfst. 138, 12. Monige æfter ðæs líchoman scylde hí swá micle fæsðlícor gestaðoliaþ on gódum weorcum swá hí hí selfe synnigran ongietaþ, Past. 52; Swt. 411, 3. II. in a legal sense, *guilty, culpable.* v. scyldig:—Scyldig *t* synnig *reus*, Mk. Skt. Lind. 14, 64. Synnig *culpabilis*, Rtl. 102, 7. Gif ceorl ceáp forstelþ . . . biþ se his dǽl synnig (scyldig, MS. H.) bútan ðam wífe ánum, L. In. 57; Th. i. 138, 17. Se ðe þeóf ofslihþ, se mót gecýðan mid áðe ðæt hé hine synnigne (scyldigne, MS. B.) ofslóge, 16; Th. i. 112, 8. Mon synnigne gefón æt openre scylde, 37; Th. i. 124, 22. [*O. Sax.* sundig: *O. H. Ger.* suntig *peccator, damnosus, noxius*: *Icel.* syndigr.] v. bær-, fela-, firen-, lyge-, un-synnig.

synnigness, e; *f. Sinfulness, guilt*[:—Deáðsynnignise *reatum*, Rtl. 42, 33.]

synoþ. v. seonoþ.

syn-rǽs, es; *m. A sinful impulse*:—Þence hé swíðe georne hwæt tó bóte mǽge ongeán ǽlcne synrǽs, ðe þurh deófles sǽd ǽr wearð áweaxen, L. Pen. 16; Th. ii. 284, 9.

syn-rust, es; *m. The foulness of sin*:—Synrust þweán and ðæt wom ǽrran wunde hǽlan *to wash away the foulness of sin and to heal the scar of the former wound*, Exon. Th. 81, 9; Cri. 1321. [Cf. the line in the Cathemerinon of Prudentius, 'quod limat aegram pectoris rubiginem.' v. Mod. Lang. Notes, May, 1889. Cf. *also* synne rust *peccati rubigo*, Scint. 4, 14.] Cf. syn-wund.

syn-sceaþa, an; *m. One who wickedly does harm, a malefactor, criminal, miscreant*:—Se synsceaþa sceaþena þreáte éhstreám sóhte, Exon. Th. 282, 31; Jul. 671. Hié ne móste se synscaþa (*Grendel*) under sceadu bregdan, Beo. Th. 1418; B. 707. Ðone synscaðan gúðbilla nán grétan nolde, 1607; B. 801. Ða synsceaðan (*the heathens*) Godes tempel brǽcan and bærndon, Exon. Th. 44, 21; Cri. 706. Metod beslóh synsceaþan (*the apostate angels*) sigore and gewealde, Cd. Th. 4, 17; Gen. 55. Cf. mán-sceaþa.

syn-scyldig; *adj. Guilty of sin, wicked*:—Heortan wyrmas synscyldigra ceorfaþ and slítaþ *vermes scelerum mordebunt intima cordis*, Dóm. L. 168.

synt, -synto. v. sind, ge-synto.

syn-wracu, e; *f. The punishment of sin*:—Biþ him (*those in hell*) synwracu andweard, ðæt is éce cwealm, Exon. Th. 94, 15; Cri. 1540. Ðære synwræce siþþan sceoldon mægð and mæcgas morþres ongyldon, 153, 27; Gú. 832. Ic ne heóld teala, ðæt mé Hǽlend mín bibeád; ic ðæs sceal geseón synwræce, 50, 2; Cri. 794.

syn-wrǽnness. v. sin-wrǽnness.

syn-wund, e; *f. A wound inflicted by sin*:—Ne syndon náne swá yfele wunda swá syndon synwunda, forðam þurh ða forwyrð se man écan deáðe, L. Pen. 4; Th. ii. 278, 17. Wé á sculon ídle lustas, synwunde, forseón, Exon. Th. 47, 18; Cri. 757.

syn-wyrcende *working sin, sinning, working iniquity*:—Synwyrcende (*the devil*), Elen. Kmbl. 1884; El. 944. Synwyrcende (*operantes iniquitatem*), ða ðe unrihtes ǽghwær þenceaþ, Ps. Th. 140, 11. Ansýna synnwyrcendra *facies peccatorum*, 81, 2.

sype, es; *m. Suction*:—Seó eorþe ðæt wæter helt and be sumum dǽle swilgþ, and for ðam sype heó biþ geleht, Bt. 33, 4; Fox 130, 6: Met. 20, 97. Cf. súpan, *and next word.*

sypian *to take in moisture*:—Glædenan rinde lytelra gedó þreó pund on glæsfæt; gedó ðonne ðæs scearpestan wínes tó .v. sestras, ásete ðonne on háte sunnan . . . ðæt hit sipige and socige .iiii. dagas, Lchdm. ii. 252, 11. Cf. súpan, *and preceding word.*

sypian (?), sipian (?); *p.* ode *To delay, be slow*:—Hé (*a sick person*) sipaþ and árísþ *tricabit et surget*, Lchdm. iii. 151, 2, 19, 28. (The reference is to an illness which begins on the 5th, 17th, or 27th day of the month.) Sypigende *senescens, frigescens*, Germ. 397, 345.

sȳr, *in the gloss* grundswylige, sȳr *senecio*, Wrt. Voc. i. 68, 42, *seems to have a meaning similar to that of* swylige. v. sur.

Syras, syrc, syrede(-on). v. Syre, serc, sirwan.

Syre, Syrie (?); *pl. The Syrians*:—Antiochus Sira cyning, Ors. 4, 11; Swt. 204, 24. Sennacherib Syria cyning, Homl. Th. i. 568, 2, 28. [*Goth.* Saur: *O. H. Ger.* Syr *Syrus*.] v. Syr-ware.

syretum *latibulum* (= (?) syrwetum *latibulis; and see* siru-tūn), Wrt. Voc. ii. 54, 27.

syre-wrenc. v. siru-wrenc.

syrfe, an; *f. A service-tree*; sorbus:—Of caweldene tō ðære syrfan; ðonne of ðære syrfan tō healwīcum, Cod. Dip. Kmbl. v. 262, 13. Ðonon tō ðan wōn stocce; and ðǣr tō wuda; ðonon on ða syrfan, vi. 234, 26. v. next word.

syrf-treów, es; *n. A service-tree*; sorbus:—In ðæt syrftreów; of ðam syrftreów in ðæt rūge mapel-treów, Cod. Dip. Kmbl. iii. 379, 22.

Syria (?) *Syria*:—Godes engel ofslōh ðæs Syrian cyninges here, Homl. Th. i. 570, 2. [*Goth.* Syria, Saura.]

sȳring, e; *f. Butter-milk*:—Hwæg *serum*, sȳring *raptura*, rynning *coagulum*, Wrt. Voc. i. 27, 68–70. Sȳring *baptua*, ii. 12, 64. Sceáphyrdes riht is ðæt hē hæbbe blēde fulle hweges oððe sȳringe ealne sumor, L. R. S. 14; Th. i. 438, 25. Cȳswyrhtan gebyreþ ðæt heó of wringhwæge buteran macige tō hlāfordes beóde, and hæbbe ða sȳringe ealle būton ðæs hyrdes dǣle, 16; Th. i. 438, 33. [Cf. *Icel.* sȳra *sour whey* used as a drink instead of small beer.]

-syringas *in* Exsyringas, Exon. Th. 323, 22; Vīd. 82.

Syrisc; *adj. Syrian*:—Naaman se Sirisca, Lk. Skt. 4, 27. Hī bǣdon Godes gescyldnysse wið ðone Syriscan here, Homl. Ass. 107, 170. [*O. H. Ger.* Sirisc *Arabicus*.]

Syro-fēnisc; *adj. Syro-phoenician*:—Wīf Sirofēnisces cynnes, Mk. Skt. 7, 26. [*Goth.* Saurini-fynikisks.]

syrwa, syrwan. v. siru, sirwan.

Syr-ware; *pl. The people of Syria, Syrians*:—Syrwara lond *Syria* Exon. Th. 209, 6; Ph. 166.

syððan, syx. v. siððan, six.

T

For the Runic T, see Tīr.

tā, (*contracted from*) tāhe, an; *f. A toe*:—Tāhae *allox*, Wrt. Voc. ii. 100, 8. Tā, i. 71, 64. Sió micle tā . . . sió æfterre tā . . . sió midleste tā . . . sió feórðe tā . . . sió lytle tā, L. Alf. pol. 64; Th. i. 96, 19–24. Seó mycle tā . . . ðare mycclan tāan nægl, L. Ethb. 70, 72; Th. i. 20, 2, 5. Hē æthrān his swīðran þūman and ðæs wynstran fōtes miclan tān *tetigit pollicem manus ejus dextrae, similiter et pedis*, Lev. 8, 23. Tān and fingras *decies senos*, Wrt. Voc. ii. 27, 73. Ða miclan tān *alloces*, 5, 18. Ða tān scrincaþ (-eþ, MS.) up (*in gout*) *the toes shrink up*, Lchdm. iii. 48, 28. On ðan seofoþan mōnþe ða tān and ða fingras beóþ weaxende, 146, 17. Gif heó mid ðām tān stæpeþ, 144, 15. Æt ðām ōðrum tāum ealswā æt ðām fingrum, L. Ethb. 71; Th. i. 20, 3. Mid ðǣm tāum *cum mentagris*, Lchdm. i. lxxiv, 21 (cf. lxxi, 13). Ofer hira handa þūman and ðæs swȳðran fōtes micclan tān *super pollices manus eorum ac pedis dextri*, Ex. 29, 20. [*O. H. Ger.* zēha: *Icel.* tā.] v. tān *a toe*.

tā; *gen.* tān; *f.* I. *a twig, shoot*:—Tān *t* twiga *vimina, virgulae*, Hpt. Gl. 428, 34. II. *a lot*:—Ðæt him dēme seó tā, gif hī hwæt dǣlan willaþ, Homl. Skt. i. 17, 86. Ðā dǣldon ða cwelleras Cristes reáf on feówer, heora ǣlcum his dǣl, swā him dēmde seó tā, Homl. Th. ii. 254, 31. Hī wurpon ðā tān betweox him, and bǣdon ðæt God sceolde geswutulian hwanon him ðæt ungelimp becōme. Ðā com ðæs wītegan tā upp, i. 246, 3–5. v. tān, *and cf. for a similar pair of forms* flā *and* flān.

tabule (-ele), an; *f.*: *also* tabula; *m.* I. *a table*:—Hæfdon hī mid him gehālgode fato and gehālgode tabulan on wigbedes wrixle *habentes secum vascula sacra et tabulam altaris vice dedicatam*, Bd. 5, 10; S. 624, 34. II. *a tablet, table on which to inscribe*:—Ðæra eára getæl hæfþ seó tabule ðe wē mearkian willaþ, Anglia viii. 327, 41. On ānum leádenum tabulan (*but* āne leádene tabulan (*acc.*), 766), Homl. Skt. i. 23, 342. Ðās ðreó word stōdon on ānre tabulan. On ðære ōðre tabelan wæs ðæt forme bebod: 'Ne hǣm ðū unrihtlīce,' Homl. Th. ii. 198, 5. Tabelan, 196, 34. Pilatus āwrāt ðæs wītes intingan on ānre tabelan, 254, 24. Tȳn beboda āwrāt se Ælmihtiga on ðām twām tabelum . . . Ða twā tabelan getācnodon ða twā bebodu, 204, 17–20. Twā stǣnene tabulan, Ex. 32, 15: 34, 1. III. *a board which is struck to give a signal*:—Tabule æfter capitule byþ gecnucod *tabula post capitulum pulsatur*, Anglia xiii. 402, 536. Gecnucedre tabulan *pulsata tabula*, 390, 359: 393, 397. [*O. H. Ger.* tavala, tabella *tabula, pugillaris*. From Latin.]

tacan; *p.* tōc *To take*:—Ða menn ealle hē tōc, and dyde of heom ðæt hē wolde (cf. ðamen hē āteáh swā swā hē wolde, MS. E.), Chr. 1072; Erl. 211, 20. Hē tōc swilce gerihta swā hē him gelagade (cf. hē nam swilce gerihta swā se cyng him geūðe, MS. E.), 1075; Erl. 212, 38. [*From Icel.* taka; *p.* tōk.]

taccian (?); *p.* ode *To tame* [:—Getaccodon (-þaccodon? v. þaccian) *edomitis*, Germ. 402, 63].

tācn, tācen, es; *n. A token, sign*:—Tācne *dicimenta*, Wrt. Voc. ii. 106, 53: 25, 57. Tācn *indicia*, 44, 68. I. *a sign, significant form*:—Heofoncyninges tācen *the cross*, Elen. Kmbl. 341; El. 171. Torht tācen Godes *the sun*, Exon. Th. 204, 11; Ph. 96. Būtan Godes tācne (*the cross*), 271, 32; Jul. 491. Þurh tācen ðære hālgan rōde, Homl. Th. i. 62, 12. Tācna torhtost, Elen. Kmbl. 327; El. 164. Ia. *an ensign* (lit. or fig.); cf. tācn-berend, -bora:—Tācon *vexillum*, Rtl. 94, 7. Ic slōh grēne tācne (*Moses' rod; Grein suggests tāne*) gārsecges deóp, Cd. Th. 195, 23; Exod. 281. Swā swā sigefæst tācon *veluti victricia signa*, Bd. 1, 8; S. 479, 24. Eal werod gehwyrfedum tācnum (*versis signis*) fōron, Gl. Prud. 45 a. Hī āsetton tācna heora *posuerunt signa sua*, Ps. Spl. 73, 6. Ib. *a token, a credential*:—Ne hē onfongen sī būtan biscopes tācne oþþe gewrite *ne absque commendatitiis litteris sui praesulis suscipiatur*, Bd. 4, 5; S. 572, 43. Ne ðū mē ōdiéwest ǣnig tācen ðe hē mē tō onsende, Cd. Th. 34, 20; Gen. 540. Ic. *a sign, monument*:—Hē hēt brycge gewyrcan his sige tō tācne ðe hē on ðæm sīþe þurhteón þohte, Ors. 2, 5; Swt. 84, 4. Id. *a sign* of the Zodiac:—Ðonne ðære sunnan ryne beó on ðam tācne ðe man *virgo* nemneþ, Lchdm. i. 164, 12. Ða twelf tunglena tācna, iii. 242, 4. II. *a sign, distinguishing mark* (lit. or fig.):—Tācon *titulus*, Mt. Kmbl. p. 4, 3. Swylc wæs ðæs folces tācen (*a practice which distinguished them, a distinct feature of their manners*), Andr. Kmbl. 58; An. 29. Hē onfēng torhtum tācne (*circumcision*), Cd. Th. 143, 6; Gen. 2375. God him sealde tācen (*posuit Dominus Cain signum*), ðæt nān ðæra ðe hine gemētte hine ne ofslōge, Gen. 4, 15. III. *a sign to attract attention, a signal*:—Ðonne ætȳwþ mannes suna tācn on heofonan, Mt. Kmbl. 24, 30. Cōmon þrȳ men tō ðære hȳðe and ðǣr tācn slōgon (*gave a signal by striking*), Guthl. 11; Gdwin. 54, 24. Tācen, 12; Gdwin. 58, 23. III a. *a sign of anything future, a prognostic*:—Ealle ða tācno and ða forebeácno ða ðe ūre Drihten ǣr tōweard sægde, ðæt ǣr dōmes dæge geweorþan sceoldan, Blickl. Homl. 117, 30. III b. *a sign, an action that conveys a meaning*:—Ðis sindon ða tācna ðe mon on mynstre healdan sceal, ðǣr mon swīgan haldan wile . . . Ðæs abbudes tācen is ðæt mon his twēgen fingras tō his heáfde āsette and his feax mid genime, Techm. ii. 118, 1–5, *and often*. Treófugla tuddor tācnum cȳððon eádges eftcyme, Exon. Th. 146, 10; Gū. 707. IV. *a sign, indication, mark which shews condition* or *state*:—Nān tācen ðære ǣrran tōcwȳsednesse næs gesewen, Homl. Th. i. 62, 16. Nǣfre wommes tācn eáwed weorþeþ, Exon. Th. 4, 18; Cri. 54. Ongietan be sumum tācnum on his hiéremonna mōde eal ðæt ðǣr gehȳddes lutige, Past. 21; Swt. 153, 14. Witan ðæra tīda tācnu, Mt. Kmbl. 16, 3. IV a. as a medical term, *a symptom*:—Tācnu ðære ādle, Lchdm. ii. 20, 26. Be tācnum on roppe, 230, 16. Gif sié ða ceácan āswollen and sió þrotu and ðū ða tācn geseó, 46, 22. V. *a sign, symbol, emblem*:—Hwæt wille wē cweþan be ðam andweardan welan, ðe oft cymþ tō ðǣm gōdum, hwæt hē elles sié būtan tācn ðæs tōweardan welan, Bt. 39, 11; Fox 230, 12. Healdaþ mīnne restedæg, hē ys tācn betwux mē and eów, Ex. 31, 13. Fugles tācen *the symbolical character of the phenix*, Exon. Th. 232, 22; Ph. 510. Ðæt wē ðȳ geornor ongietan meahten tīrfæst tācen, ðæt se fugel þurh bryne beácnaþ, 236, 14; Ph. 574. VI. *a sign which shews the truth* or *reality of anything, proof, demonstration, evidence*:—Ðæt biþ tācn wīsdōmes, ðæt hine mon wilnige gehēran and ongitan, Bt. 38, 2; Fox 198, 22. Ðæt is swīþe sweotol tācn ðam wīsan, ðæt hē ne sceal lufian tō ungemetlīce ðās woruldgesǣlþa, forðæm hī oft cumaþ tō ðǣm wyrstum monnum, 39, 11; Fox 230, 8. Him ðæt (*the writing on the wall*) tācen wearð, ðæt hē ligeword gecwæð, Cd. Th. 260, 31; Dan. 718. Ðæt wæs tācen sweotol, Beo. Th. 1671; B. 833. Hwæt dēst ðū tō tācne, ðæt wē gelȳfon, Jn. Skt. 6, 30. On ða ylcan tiid ðe hē (*David*) genam his (*Saul's*) spere on his getelde on niht, tō tācne ðæt hē inne mid him slǣpendum wæs, Ps. Th. 35, arg.: Bd. 1, 1; S. 474, 36: 2, 6; S. 508, 42: 4, 28; S. 606, 41: Blickl. Homl. 7, 15. Wē ðe ðās sǣlāc brohton tīres tō tācne, Beo. Th. 3312; B. 1654. Ic ðæs tācen wege sweotol on mē selfum, Cd. Th. 54, 31; Gen. 885. Sancte Iohannes mycelnesse se Hǣlend tācn sægde, *the Saviour shewed by his words the greatness of St. John*, Blickl. Homl. 167, 18. Ðǣr biþ on eádgum ēðgesȳne þreó tācen somod, ðæs ðe hī hyra þeódnes wel willan heóldon, Exon. Th. 76, 7; Cri. 1236. Ic wēne ðæt ic ðē hæfde ǣr gereht be manegum tācnum, ðætte monna sāwla sint undeáþlīce *tu idem es, cui persuasum atque insitum permultis demonstrationibus scio, menteis hominum nullo modo esse mortaleis*, Bt. 11, 2; Fox 34, 33: Elen. Kmbl. 1704; El. 854. VII. *a supernatural sign, miracle, prodigy*:—Ðis (*the turning of water into wine*) is ðæt forme tācn ðe hē on his menniscnysse openlīce geworhte, Homl. Th. i. 58, 14. Ðisse fǣmnan monige weorc gāstlīcra mægna and monig tācon heofonlīcra wundra gewuniaþ gesǣde beón *hujus virginis multa solent opera virtutum et signa miraculorum narrari*, Bd. 3, 8; S. 531, 28. Hē (*Christ*) sōðra swā feala tācna gecȳðde, ðǣr hié tō sēgon, Andr. Kmbl. 1421; An. 711. Ic (*St. Michael*) gecȳþe on eallum ðǣm tācnum ðe ðǣr gelimpeþ, ðæt ic eom ðære stōwe hyrde, Blickl. Homl. 201, 8. On eallum tācnum and forebeácnum ðe

God sende þurh hine, Deut. 34, 11. Gif ǽnig wîtega secge tâcnu and forebeácnu, 13, 1. Tâcna, Homl. Th. i. 44, 24. Noldan hî ða torhtan tâcen oncnâwan ðe him beforan fremede freóbearn Godes, Exon. Th. 40, 22; Cri. 642. Gesiáþ werc Dryhtnes ða set[t]e tâcen ofer eorðan *videte opera Domini quae posuit prodigia super terram*, Ps. Surt. 45, 9. **VII a.** *a signal event, remarkable circumstance*:—Andsware cýðan tâcna gehwylces ðe ic him tô sêce *to give me an answer in reference to every remarkable circumstance about which I enquire of them* (cf. mê þinga gehwylc gecýðan, ðe ic him tô sêce, 817; El. 409), Elen. Kmbl. 637; El. 319. Wê on gemynd witon âlra tâcna gehwylc swâ Trôiâna þurh gefeoht fremedon, 1286; El. 645. [*Goth.* taikns; *f.*: *O. Sax.* têkan; *n.*: *O. Frs.* têken: *O. H. Ger.* zeihhan *signum, signaculum, nota, titulus, miraculum*: *Icel.* teikn, tákn *a token, sign, wonder.*] v. andgit-, bell-, fâcen-, fore-, friðo-, luf-, sige-, sigor-, sôþ-, weá-, weder-, wer-, wundor-tâcn.

tâcn-berend, es; *m. A standard-bearer*:—Tâcnberend *signifer*, Ælfc. Gr. 8; Zup. 27, 15.

tâcn-bora, an; *m.* **I.** *a standard-bearer*:—Tâcnbora *signifer, vexillifer*, Wrt. Voc. i. 35, 10: *signifer*, 84, 16. Tâcenbora, Hymn. Surt. 113, 3. Tâcnboran *draconarii* vel *vexillarii* vel *signiferi*, Wrt. Voc. i. 21, 66. **II.** *a leader, guide, director*:—Ðis is mîn tâcenbora ðe mê getǽhte ðæt ic tô ðê becom (*the word is used of the old fisherman who had directed Apollonius to the town*, v. p. 12), Ap. Th. 27, 22.

tâcn-circul, es; *m. A circle* or *cycle which marks the date.* **I.** *the indiction*, a cycle of fifteen years. v. ge-ban:—Ðæm gǽre ðe wæs âgân fram Cristes âcennednesse eahta hund wintra and feówer and sixtig, and in ðam tâcencircole ðæt twelfte geár (*the year of the indiction is the remainder after dividing* 864 + 3 *by* 15; *this remainder is* 12, *which agrees with the passage*), Chart. Th. 126, 3. **II.** *the lunar cycle of nineteen years; the place which any year occupies in the cycle is marked by the golden number of the year*:—Ðis wæs gewriten on ðam geáre ðe wæs âgân fram Cristes âcennednysse ân þusend geára and ân and sixtig geára, and an ðam tâcncircule ðæt seofanteóðe geár (*the golden number of the year* 1061 *is the remainder after dividing* 1061 + 1 *by* 19; *this remainder is* 17, *which agrees with the number given in the passage*), Chart. Th. 390, 19.

tâcnian; *p.* ode. **I.** *to make a mark upon* something, *to mark*:—Seó lîget ðæt deófol bærneþ and tâcnaþ, Salm. Kmbl. p. 148, 4. **II.** *to be a token* or *mark of* something, *to indicate, mark*:—Se steorra ðe wê hâtaþ ǽfensteorra, ðonne hê biþ west gesewen, ðonne tâcnnaþ hê ǽfen, Bt. 39, 13; Fox 232, 34. Ðysne dæg hié nemdon siges dæg; se nama tâcnaþ ðone sige ðe Drihten wiþstôd deófle, Blickl. Homl. 67, 14. Tâcnendi *index*, Wrt. Voc. ii. 111, 40. **III.** *to indicate, point out*:—Hê þurh his lâre êces lîfes wegas sægde and tâcnode, Blickl. Homl. 129, 18. **IV.** *to signify*, (a) *to express a meaning by means of figure* or *symbol, to express figuratively* or *symbolically*:—Hâlige gewreotu ûs tâcniaþ ðâs world þurh ðone mônan, Blickl. Homl. 17, 21. Hê bær him æcse and adesan on handa, tâcnode (*signabat*) on ðâm, ðæt hê tô gewinne on ðæt mynster eode, Bd. 4, 3; S. 567, 27. Tâcnade Leoniða, hwelc moncwealm on Crêca londe wæs, mid ðæm ðe hê sprecende wæs tô his geférum: 'Uton brûcan ðisses undernmetes swâ ða sculon ðe hiora ǽfengifl on helle gefeccean sculon,' Ors. 2, 5; Swt. 84, 31. Ðæt hê sǽde and tâcnode hwylcum deáðe hê wolde sweltan *hoc dicebat significans qua morte esset moriturus*, Jn. Skt. 12, 33: 21, 19. (b) *to be the figurative expression of, be a figure of* something, *to symbolize*:—Huæt tâcnaþ ðæt gold bûton ða heánesse ðæs hâligdômes *quid auro nisi excellentia sanctitatis exprimitur?* Past. 18; Swt. 133, 12. Hwæt tâcnaþ Ezechhiel bûton ða lâreówas *cujus Ezechiel nisi magistrorum speciem tenet?* 21; Swt. 161, 8: Blickl. Homl. 79, 29: 17, 14. Cwæþ se godspellere ðæt leóht cyrde tô ðon blindan. Ðæt tâcnaþ ðæt seó godcundnes onfêng ûre týdran gecynde, 17, 27. Hê cwæþ ðæt his þegnas dydon swâ hê him bebeád. Ðæt tâcnaþ ðæt ðâs lâreówas ne sceolan Godes dômas nâwþer ne nâ wanian ne ne êcan, 81, 3. Ðæt sweflene fŷr tâcnade hwelc gewinn ðâ wǽron be ðǽm ðe nû sindon, Ors. 2, 6; Swt. 88, 30. **V.** *to indicate* what is future, *to portend*:—Hî (*two stars*) wîtegan wǽron grimmes wæles . . . ðæt hî micel yfel mannum tôward tâcnedon (*signarent*), Bd. 5, 23; S. 645, 28. Bêcnende, tâcniende *portendentes*, Wrt. Voc. ii. 66, 11. [Þes fuȝel tacnede faie sið þes kinges, Laym. 2832. Tacnenn *to express symbolically*, Orm. 1639. Ðe blo tokened ðe wateres wo, Gen. and Ex. 638. Toknyñ or make tokene *signo*, Prompt. Parv. 495. *Goth.* taiknjan δεικνύναι: *O. H. Ger.* zeihhanôn, zeihhanen *signare, significare, indicare, monstrare*: *Icel.* tákna, teikna *to betoken, mark, denote.*] v. fore-, ge-tâcnian; tǽcnan, tǽcnian.

tâcnung, e; *f. Signification*:—Tâcnunga *significationem*, Ps. Spl. 59, 4. **I.** *an indication, sign, characteristic mark, symptom*:—Lǽcedômas and tâcnung on ðam roppe (cf. be tâcnum on ðam roppe, 230, 16), Lchdm. ii. 164, 5. Be lyfte tâcnungum *de aeris indiciis*, Nar. 3, 14. Hit nû is bûton swylcum tâcnungum ðæs yfeles ðe hit ǽr dyde *Aetna nunc tantum innoxia specie ad praeteritorum fidem fumat*, Ors. 2, 6; Swt. 90, 3. **II.** *an indication, evidence, proof*:—Wæs ðæs godcundan wundres sweotol tacnung (*indicium*), ðæt ðære fǽmnan lîchoma bebyriged brosnian ne mihte, Bd. 4, 19; S. 587, 35. Ða hê mê in tâcnunge his lufan bebeád *quos mihi in indicium suae dilectionis commendaverat*, 2, 6; S. 508, 18. Gewuniaþ tô tâcnuncge his mægenes gelômlîce wundor hǽlo geworden beón *ad indicium virtutis illius solent crebra sanitatum miracula operari*, 4, 3; S. 570, 9. **III.** *an indication of what is future, a presage, prognostic*:—Is seó stôw nemned Heofenfeld wæs heó geára swâ nemned for tâcnunge ðæra tôweardra wundra *vocatur locus ille Heofenfelth, quod certo utique praesagio futurorum antiquitus nomen accepit*, Bd. 3, 2; S. 524, 34. Tô hwæm cumaþ hî elles bûtan tô tâcnunge sorges and ânfealdes sâres *quid est aliud, quam futurae quoddam calamitatis indicium?* Bt. 7, 2; Fox 18, 21. **IV.** *a figurative representation, an emblem*:—Hwæt syndon ða woruldsǽlþa ôþres bûton deáþes tâcnung? for ðam se deáþ ne cymþ tô nânum ôþrum þingum bûtan ðæt hê ðæt lîf âfyrre; swâ eác ða woruldsǽlþa cumaþ tô ðam môde tô ðam ðæt hî hit beniman ðæs ðe him leófast biþ ðisse worulde, Bt. 8; Fox 26, 6. **V.** *direction, ordering*:—Ðâs feówer heáfodrîcu sindon on feówer endum ðyses middangeardes mid unâsecgendlîcre Godes tâcnunge *eadem ineffabili ordinatione per quatuor mundi cardines quatuor regnorum principatus fuerunt*, Ors. 2, 1; Swt. 60, 1. [Þa wes he awundred, what weore þis tacninge (*portent*), Laym. 15974. He tolde heom þa tacni[n]ge (*prophetic notice given in a dream*), 32126. Sette he up ðat ston for muniging And get on olige for tokning (*sign*; cf. Iacob lapidem erexit in titulum, fundens oleum desuper, Gen. 28, 18), Gen. and Ex. 1624. Ich wat al of þe tacninge (*signification*), O. and N. 1213. *O. H. Ger.* zeihhanunga *significatio, descriptio.*] v. ge-tâcnung; tǽcning.

tâcor (-ur), es; *m. A husband's brother, brother-in-law*:—Tacor (-ur) *levir*, Txts. 74, 598. Tâcor, Ælfc. Gr. 8; Zup. 27, 20: *levir*, i. *frater mariti*, Wrt. Voc. i. 52, 31. Tâcor, ðæt is brýdguma[n] brôðor *levirum*, ii. 84, 16. Tâcor, 50, 30: Hpt. Gl. 498, 75. [*O. H. Ger.* zeihhor (-ir, -ur) *levir, frater mariti.*]

tâdige, tâdie, an; *f. A toad*:—Tâdige *buffo*, Wrt. Voc. i. 24, 21. Tâdie *rubeta*, 78, 57: Ælfc. Gr. 9, 3; Zup. 35, 3. [Tadde [*ru*]*beta*, Wrt. Voc. i. 91, 17. Liggeþ alse þe tadde ded in þere eorðe, O. E. Homl. i. 53, 14.]

tæbere (?) *some implement used in weaving*:—Tæbere *claus* (the word occurs in a list *de arte textoria*; but in an almost identical list, p. 282, the form is *teltre*. v. teld-treów), Wrt. Voc. i. 66, 27. [Cf. (?) syl *taber*, Wrt. Voc. i. 289, 48, and *claus, lignum textorii vel* telde, ii. 131, 56.]

tǽcan; *p.* tǽhte *To shew.* **I.** *to offer to view, present*:—Tǽhte hê ðâ ðam pâpan sumne munuc ðæs nama wæs Andreas *cum monachum quemdam, nomine Andream, pontifici offerret*, Bd. 4, 1; S. 564, 4. Se ðe hæfþ .xx. hîda, se sceal tǽcan .xii. hîda gesettes londes, ðonne hê faran wille. Se ðe hæfþ .x. hîda, se sceal tǽcan, .vi. hîda . . . Se ðe hæbbe þreó hîda tǽce ôðres healfes, L. In. 64–66; Th. i. 144, 5–11 MS. B. **II.** *to shew* an object to a person so that the object may be attained by the person, *to shew* a way, a place, etc. (1) lit.:—Ic tǽce sumum men his weg *dirigo*, Ælfc. Gr. 28, 5; Zup. 173, 8. Tǽceþ ûs se torhta trumlîcne hâm, Cd. Th. 282, 29; Sat. 294. Him mon setl tǽhte and hê sæt æt ðam symble *he was shewn a seat, and sat at the feast*, Bd. 3, 10; S. 534, 28: 5, 19; S. 639, 35. Him freá tǽhte wegas ofer wêsten, Cd. Th. 174, 5; Gen. 2873. Gewât him tô ðæs gemearces ðe him Metod tǽhte, 174, 29; Gen. 2885. Ðæs embe twâ niht ðætte tǽhte God Elenan eádigre æþelust beáma, Menol. Fox 164; Men. 84: Elen. Kmbl. 1259; El. 631. (1 a) without an object, *to shew the way, direct*:—On niht hê tǽhte eów þurh fŷr *nocte ostendens vobis iter per ignem*, Deut. 1, 33. (2) fig.:—Hig bugon raðe of ðam wege ðe ðû him tǽhtest *recesserunt cito de via, quam ostendisti eis*, Ex. 32, 8. Ða men ðe bearn habban him tǽcean hié lîfes weg and rihtne gang tô heofenum, Blickl. Homl. 109, 17. (2 a) without an object, *to direct*:—Hwâ tǽcþ ûs teala and hwâ sylþ ûs ða gôd ðe ûs man gehǽt *quis ostendit nobis bona?* Ps. Th. 4, 7. **III.** *to shew* a person (*dat.* or *acc.*) the direction that must be taken, *to direct, to cause a certain direction to be taken*, the direction being marked by a preposition. (1) lit.:—On ðære stôwe ðe him se stranga tô wordum tǽhte *on the place to which the Lord had directed him to go* (cf. 172, 24–; Gen. 2849–), Cd. Th. 175, 24; Gen. 2900. Nân man ne tǽce his getihtledan man fram him *let no one send his accused man away*, L. Ath. i. 22; Th. i. 210, 23: L. C. S. 28; Th. i. 392, 11. Tǽce him mon siððan tô nigcumenra manna hûse, R. Ben. 97, 11. (2) fig.:—Niman hî ðone teóðan dǽl tô ðam mynstre and tǽcan him tô ðam nigoðan dǽle and tôdǽle man ða eahta dǽlas on twâ *let them take the tithe for the minster, let the next tenth fall to his share* (*let him be directed to take the next tenth*), *and let the remaining eight tenths be divided in two*, L. Edg. 3; Th. i. 264, 2. Ðû, fæder Agustinus, hié hæfst on ðînum bôcum gesǽd, and ic gehwam wille ðǽrtô tǽcan ðe hiene his lyst mâ tô witanne *I will refer every one to the books, who desires to know more*, Ors. 3, 3; Swt. 102, 25. (2 a) where the dat. is omitted:—Seó ealde ǽ næs swâ stîð on ðâm þingum swâ swâ Cristes godspel is and tǽcþ tô ânum wîfe *points to, directs a man to take, one wife*, Scrd. 22, 25. **IV.** *to shew* the course that must be followed, what should be observed, *to direct, appoint, prescribe, enjoin.* v. tǽcend:—Ðû tǽcst folce gemǽro âbûtan ðone munt (*constitues terminos populo in circuitum*) and cwist:

'Warniaþ ðæt gē ne cumon tō nēh ðison munte,' Ex. 19, 12. Symle ðū tǣhtest mildheortnesse, and ðæt man ōðrum miltsode, Homl. Th. i. 68, 23. Crist tǣhte: 'Syllaþ ōðrum būtan ceápe,' Homl. Th. i. 412, 12. Eft hē him tǣhte tō fultome ðæt hē him genāme āne īserne hearstepannan *ei ad munitionem suam protinus subinfertus: 'Et tu sume tibi sartaginem ferream,'* Past. 21; Swt. 161, 6. Hig didon hine on cweartern, ōð hig wiste, hwæt Drihten be him tǣhte (*quid juberet Dominus*), Lev. 24, 12. Hē hine ǣlces þinges geclǣnsode, swā se pāpa him tǣhte *in the manner prescribed by the pope,* Chr. 1022; Erl. 161, 38. Ðā tǣhte man hyre ðæt hió sciolde bringan his fæder gold *the court directed that she was to bring his father's gold,* Chart. Th. 289, 34. Ðæt hē him dǣdbōte tǣce *ut sibi poenitentiam praescribat,* L. Ecg. C. proem.; Th. ii. 130, 35. Ne sig nān ðing forlǣten ðæs ðe se regol tǣce on his fandunge, R. Ben. 104, 17. Bēte hē swā micel swā dēman tǣcan *quantum arbitri judicaverint,* Ex. 21, 22. Ðæt hȳ bētan swā swā bēc tǣcan, Wulfst. 165, 9. V. *to shew* to the mind by way of instruction or of proof, *to teach.* (1) of persons:—Se Hālga Gāst ðe tǣhþ rihtwīsnysse, Homl. Th. i. 322, 5. Ǣfre se ðe āwent oþþe se þe tǣcþ of Lēdene on Englisc ǣfre hē sceal gefadian hit swā ðæt ðæt Englisc hæbbe his āgene wīsan *he that makes a translation from Latin into English, or he that in teaching turns Latin into English must use idiomatic English,* Ælfc. Gen. Thw. 4, 9. Ic ðē bebeóde ðæt ðū ne forgite ðæt ðæt ic ǣr tǣhte . . . Ic ðē tǣhte ðætte ðǣr wǣre ðæt hēhste gōd *maneant quae paullo ante conclusa sunt . . . nonne monstravimus ea vera bona non esse,* Bt. 34, 9; Fox 146, 13–19. Tǣc mē ðīnne willan tō wyrcenne, 42; Fox 260, 11. Ic ðē mæg tǣcan ōþer ðing, 38, 3; Fox 198, 29. Ða mæssepreóstas sceolan heora scriftbēc mid rihte tǣcan and lǣran. Ða lāreówas sceolan synnfullum mannum eádmōdlīce tǣcan and lǣran, ðæt hié heora synna cunnon onrihtlīce geandettan, Blickl. Homl. 43, 7–16. .xii. lahmenn scylon riht tǣcean Wealan and Ænglan . . . Ðolien ealles ðæs hȳ āgon, gif hī wōh tǣcen, L. O. D. 5; Th. i. 354, 9–11. Gif hwylc gōdra wile his lytlingas hiom tō lāre befæstan, hig sceolon him ēstlīce tǣcan, L. E. I. 20; Th. ii. 414, 10. Hē wile mōdum tǣcan, Cd. Th. 211, 17; Exod. 527. Hē wæs tǣcende dæghwomlīce binnan ðam temple, Homl. Th. i. 412, 29. (2) of things:—Seó emniht is swā swā wē ǣr cwǣdon on .xxima. kl. April., swā swā ða geleáfullan rǣderas hit gesetton, and eác gewisse dægmǣl ūs swā tǣcaþ, Lchdm. iii. 256, 22. VI. *to shew, indicate, signify:*—Tāhte *significat,* Jn. Skt. p. 8, 12: 21, 19: *indicaret,* Lk. Skt. p. 2, 14. Gif ðū hwæt be capitelhūse tǣcan wylle, Techm. ii. 122, 4: 118, 8, 17: 129, 3. v. be-, ge-, mis-tǣcan.

tǣcend, es; *m. One who prescribes* or *orders.* v. tǣcan, IV:—Gif hwylcum brēþer hwæt hefelīces beboden sȳ underfō hē ða geboda his tǣcendes *si cui fratri aliqua gravia injunguntur, suscipiat jubentis imperium,* R. Ben. 128, 11.

tǣcing, e; *f.* I. *the pointing out of a course to be followed, direction, teaching.* v. tǣcan, IV, and previous word:—Hēr is seó ǣ, ðe ðū under hire tǣcinge winnan wylt, R. Ben. 96, 23. Sȳ him þreál geboden be regoles tǣcinge, 126, 4. Hē nolde nān ðing dōn be ðæs deófles tǣcunge, Homl. Th. i. 168, 26. Gif hē be bōca tǣcinge his līf gefadige, L. Eth. ix. 28; Th. i. 346, 17. Gif hwā nelle bētan æfter mīnra biscopa tǣcinge, Chart. Erl. 230, 22. Gode þeówian æfter Sanctus Benedictus tǣcinge *according to the rule of St. Benedict,* Chart. Th. 549, 8: 227, 24: Lchdm. iii. 438, 20. Underfō hē ǣlcne regoles þeáw and tǣcinge; sig hē æfter Cristes bōce tǣcinge ðus geáxod, R. Ben. 104, 19. Þurh hāligra bōca tǣcunge ūres Drihtnes willan mid gōdum dǣdum gefyllan, Homl. Ass. 144, 2. II. *teaching, doctrine:*—Swā ðæt wē þurhwunigen on Cristes lāre and tǣcinge, R. Ben. 6, 1. *x* āna ongynþ of ðam stæfe *i* æfter ūðwitena tǣcinge, Ælfc. Gr. 2; Zup. 6, 5. Ðæra sind feówer æfter Priscianes tǣcinge, 24; Zup. 129, 16.

tǣcnan; *p.* [e]de. I. *to shew, present:*—Se ðe hæfþ .xx. hīda se sceal tǣcnan (tǣcan, MS. B.) .xii. hīda gesettes landes ðonne hē faran wille. Se ðe hæfþ .x. hīda se sceal tǣcnan (tǣcan, MS. B.) .vi. hīda gesettes landes. Se ðe hæbbe þreó hīda tǣcne (tǣce, MS. B.) ōðres healfes, L. In. 64–66; Th. i. 144, 5–11. II. *to shew* the road, *point out* an object, *make known:*—Se him wægas tǣcneþ, Exon. Th. 434, 26; Rä. 52, 7. Tǣcne *indicet,* Jn. Skt. Lind. 11, 57. Taecnaendi (-endi) *index,* Txts. 70, 544. III. *to appoint, prescribe:*—Se mec wrǣde on legde, ðæt ic onbūgan ne mōt of ðæs gewealde, ðe mē wegas tǣcneþ, Exon. Th. 383, 26; Rä. 4, 16. v. tācnian, tǣcnian, tǣcan, tǣcnend.

-tǣcne. v. earfoþ-tǣcne.

tǣcnend, es; *m. One that shews* or *points out:*—Tǣcne[n]d *index,* Wrt. Voc. ii. 47, 74.

tǣcnian; *p.* ode *To shew, prove:*—Forðam ūs segþ ǣlc gesceádwīsnes and ealle men ðæt ilce andettaþ ðæt God sié ðæt hēhste gōd forðam ðe hī tǣcniaþ ðæt eall gōd on him sȳ *ita vero bonum esse Deum ratio demonstrat, ut perfectum quoque in eo bonum esse convincat,* Bt. 34, 2; Fox 136, 6. v. tācnian, *and next word.*

tǣcning, e; *f. Shewing, proof:*—Ðā cwæþ hē: 'Ic hit ðē ðonne wille getǣcan; ac ðæt ān ic ðē bebeóde ðæt ðū þeáh for ðære tǣcninge ne forgite ðæt ðæt ic ǣr tǣhte' *atqui hoc verissima, inquit, ratione patefaciam, maneant modo quae paullo ante conclusa sunt,* Bt. 34, 9; Fox 146, 14. v. tācnung.

tæfl, e; *f.:* es; *n.* (?): tæfle, an (?); *f.* Properly *a board for the playing of a game.* But the word seems also used of *a game played on such a board:* cf. the use of the word *tables* at a later time:—Wyþ pleyynge at tables oþer atte chekere, R. Glouc. 192, 3. Kueade gemenes of des and of tables huer me playþ uor pans, Ayenb. 45, 16. Tabulles *tabella* (15th cent.), Wrt. Voc. i. 202, col. 2. See also Strutt's Sports, Bk. iv, c. 2. The word seems to denote also *a die used in playing a game.* What was the precise nature of the games, to which this word and related forms are applied, does not appear; some of the references below would imply that games of chance are meant, and this would be in keeping with the love of gaming which Tacitus, Germ. c. 24, noticed among the Germans. But games of skill like chess may sometimes be meant. In Icelandic *tafl* is used of chess or draughts, as well as of dicing, and the Danes in England seem to have played chess (see Thrupp's Anglo-Saxon Home, c. xvi, sec. 7); and in O. H. Ger. *scah-zabel*=scacarium. Among the Welsh, too, was a game something like draughts, called *tawlbwrdd* (Thrupp, p. 388):—Tefil, tebl, teblae *alea,* Txts. 36, 6. Tæfl, Wrt. Voc. ii. 8, 7. *Incipit de alea.* Tæfl *alea,* ic tæfle tæflum *cotizo tesseris,* i. 284, 28, 31. Tæfel, 66, 47. Tæfel *alea,* cynningstān on tæfle *pirgus* (cf. *O. H. Ger.* zabel-bret *pirgus*), feðerscīte tæfel *tessere* vel *lepusculae,* 39, 45–49. Tæslum *tesellum* (=tæflum *tessellis?* v. Wülck. Gl. 526, 5), ii. 93, 44. Dryhten dǣleþ sumum tæfle cræft, bleóbordes gebregd, Exon. Th. 331, 19; Vy. 70. Sum biþ hræd tæfle, sum biþ gewittig æt wīnþege, 297, 25; Crä. 73. Hȳ twegen sceolon tæfle ymbsittan . . . habban him gomen on borde, 345, 2; Gn. Ex. 182. [Sum men pleoden on tæuelbrede (mid tauel, 2nd MS.), Laym. 8133. *O. H. Ger.* zabel; *n. alea,* wurf-zabel *alea, tessera: Icel.* tafl; *n. a game;* tafla *a piece used in a game.*] See the following words.

tæflan, tæflian; *p.* [e]de, ode *To gamble, game:*—Ic tæfle tæflum *cotizo tesseris,* Wrt. Voc. i. 289, 31. Ic tæfle *cotizo,* Wrt. Voc. ii. 16, 63. Teblíþ, tebleþ *cotizat,* Txts. 46, 178. Tæflaþ, Wrt. Voc. ii. 135, 36. [Þe manne þat taveleþ and forleost þat game, O. and N. 1666. *Elsewhere the word means* to talk, argue:—Ich leote ham talkin and tauelin of godlec, Marh. 13, 31. Nefde hare nan tunge to tauelin (teuelin, MS. C.) a tint wið, Kath. 1247. Teuele he wið me, 820. *Icel.* tefla *to play at draughts, dice,* etc.]

tæfle (?); *adj. Given to play:*—Hond tæfles monnes *the hand of the gamester,* Exon. Th. 345, 8; Gn. Ex. 185.

tæflere, es; *m. A gamester, dicer, gambler:*—Teblere, teblheri *aleator, aleo,* Txts. 36, 7. Tæflere *aleator,* Wrt. Voc. ii. 8, 8: i. 66, 49: 284, 30. Wē lǣraþ, ðæt preóst ne beó hunta, ne hafecere, ne tæflere, ac plege on his bōcum, swā his hāde gebiraþ, L. Edg. C. 64; Th. ii. 258, 8. [*M. H. Ger.* zabelære *aleo.*]

tæfl-stān, es; *m. A die,* or *a piece in a game* (tæfl):—Teblstān (tebel-) *calculus,* Txts. 47, 349. Tæflstān *calculus* (in a list 'de alea'), Wrt. Voc. i. 284, 29. Tæfelstān, 66, 48. Tæfelstānas *aleae,* 39, 46.

-tǣfran, tǣg. v. ā-tǣfran, teáh.

tǣg tǣg *glosses* puppup, Wrt. Voc. ii. 88, 71.

tægl, es; *m. A tail:*—Oxan tægl biþ scill. weorð, L. In. 59; Th. i. 140, 3. Foxes tægles se ȳtemesta dǣl, Lchdm. i. 340, 22. Se ðrowend slihþ mid ðam tægle tō deáðe, Homl. Th. i. 252, 5, 10, 12. Ða beón beraþ ǣtterne tægel, Frag. Kmbl. 37; Leás. 20. Hī habbaþ tæglas ðām wyrmum gelīce ðe men hātaþ þrowend, Wulfst. 200, 14. [*Goth.* tagl; *n. hair: O. H. Ger.* zagel; *m. a tail: Icel.* tagl; *n. a* (*horse's*) *tail: Norweg.* tagl *horse-hair: Swed.* tagel *hair of mane* or *tail.*] v. cū-tægl.

tægl *dye.* v. telg.

tægl-hǣr, es; *n. A hair of an animal's tail:*—Gif ðū hafast mid ðē wulfes hrycghǣr and tæglhǣr ða ȳtemæstan on sīðfæte, būtan fyrhtu ðū ðone sīð gefremest, ac se wulf sorgaþ ymbe his sīð, Lchdm. i. 360, 21.

tæher, tæherende. v. teár, teárian.

tæl, tel, es; *n. A tale, number, series:*—Heora tel biþ swā menigfeald, ðæt hit oferstīhþ sandceosles gerīm, Homl. Th. i. 536, 33. Ðæra etendra tal *manducantium numerus,* Mt. Kmbl. Lind. 14, 21. Of tale *numero,* Jn. Skt. Rush. 6, 10. Tele *laterculo, numero,* Hpt. Gl. 442, 51. In tēnum talum *in decem numeros,* Mt. Kmbl. p. 3, 1. Cf. Forerīm ł (fore-)tal *prologus,* p. 1, 1. [Hundred is ful tel, A. R. 372, 9. *O. Sax.* gēr-tal: *Icel.* tal; *n. a number, series.*] v. ge-, ofer-tæl; tæl-cræft, -mearc, -met; talu.

tǣl, e; *f.* (?) *Evil speaking, calumny, detraction:*—Tǣl *blasphemia, vituperatio,* Wrt. Voc. ii. 127, 9: *detractatio, vituperatio,* 139, 44. 'Ǣlc tǣl sié ānumen fram eów.' . . . Hit biþ unnyt ðæt mon tǣl ūtane forlǣte gif se yfela willa ðone onwald hæfþ ðæs ingeðonces '*omnis blasphemia tollatur a vobis.*' . . . *Frustra blasphemia ab exterioribus tollitur, si in interioribus malitia dominatur,* Past. 33; Swt. 222, 8–14. Ne frīne ic ðē for tǣle ne þurh teóncwide *I do not question you that I may detract or abuse,* Andr. Kmbl. 1265; An. 633. Hē þolaþ sārcwide secga . . . Ic bī mē secge ðis sārspell . . . Ic for tǣle ne mæg ǣnigne moncynnes gelufian, Exon. Th. 458, 1–26; Hy. 4, 93–106. Ðæt heó mec tǣle gerahte (-rǣhte? cf. ðæt hē ða hālgan weras hospe gerahte (-rǣhte?) *he calum-*

niated, 260, 21; Jul. 300) hēt mē fremdne god ofer ða ōþre ðe wē ǣr cūþon weorþian *that she attacked me with blasphemy, bade me honour a strange god above the others that we knew before*, 247, 4; Jul. 73. v. tāl.

-tǣl. v. leóf-tǣl.

tǣlan; *p.* de. I. *to blame, rebuke, reprove, reproach, censure, accuse.* (1) *to blame* a person for what is wrong:—Ne ðreáþ ūs nān monn ne furðum āne worde ne tǣlþ *ne verbi quidem ab aliquo invectione laceramur*, Past. 17; Swt. 117, 22. Tēlaþ ðegnas *accusant (pharisaei) discipulos*, Mk. Skt. p. 3, 14. Ðū mē tǣldesð and ðū mē cīddesð *me reprehendis*, Past. proem.; Swt. 23, 10. Ða scamleásan Galatas suíðe openlīce Paulus tǣlde (*increpat*), 31; Swt. 207, 14. Hē lǣrde and tǣlde ealle men ðe worulde welan gaderiaþ mid unrihte, Ps. Th. 38, arg. Hī tǣldon hī *vituperaverunt*, Mk. Skt. 7, 2. Ðætte hiǽ tēldun (*accusarent*) hine, Mk. Skt. Rush. 3, 2. Ðæt hié ongieten ðæt hié mon tǣle *that they may know that they are censured*, Past. 21; Swt. 151, 14. Se ðe ōðerne tǣlan wile, ðonne gange hē ǣrest on dīgle stōwe and besceáwige hine sylfne, Wulfst. 233, 20. (2) *to blame* what is wrong in a person:—Ne tǣle ic nā micel weorc ne ryhtne onwald ac ic tǣle ðæt hine mon forðȳ up āhebbe on his mōde *non potestatem reprehendimus*, Past. 4; Swt. 41, 2–3. Ðonne gē eów selfum ondrǣdaþ ðæt ðæt gē on ōðrum tǣlaþ *dum sibi, quod increpat, timet*, 21; Swt. 159, 16. Hē tǣlde (*exprobravit*) hyra ungeleáffulnesse, Mk. Skt. 16, 14. Ða bōceras ðæt tǣldon, Homl. Th. i. 338, 20. Gif hē gesceádelīce hwilcu þing tǣle *si qua rationabiliter reprehenderit*, R. Ben. 109, 9. Leahtras tǣlan, 135, 18. Ðæt ðæt him mon on tǣlan wille *quod in eis reprehenditur*, Past. 31; Swt. 206, 6. Unþeáwas tǣlan and gōde herian, Bt. 38, 3; Fox 200, 7: Met. 19, 39. Tō tǣlenne, Bt. 27, 4; Fox 100, 19. II. *to speak evil of, blaspheme, revile, slander, calumniate, backbite:*—Eorl ōðerne mid teónwordum tǣleþ behindan, spreceþ fægere beforan, Fragm. Kmbl. 7; Leás. 4. Tǣleþ *blasvemiat*, Wrt. Voc. ii. 73, 21. Ðis weorc heora ðe tǣlaþ (tēlaþ, Ps. Surt.) mē *þe werke of þa þat bacbite me* (Ps. 108, 20), Ps. Spl. 108, 19. For ðara stemne ðe mē hyspaþ and tǣlaþ *a voce exprobrantis et obloquentis*, Ps. Th. 43, 18. Of ðæm cristendōme ðe hié nū swīþost tǣlaþ, Ors. 2, 1; Swt. 64, 19. Ðū sǣte ongeán ðīnne brōþor and tǣldest (tēldes, Ps. Surt., *detrahebas*) hine, Ps. Th. 49, 21. Hē his godu tǣlde, Exon. Th. 278, 16; Jul. 598. Hī tǣldon (tēldon, Ps. Surt. *detrahebant*) mē *me bakbate þai* (Ps. 108, 4), Ps. Spl. 108, 3. Hī mē tǣldon *exprobaverunt animam meam*, Ps. Th. 34, 8. Hig tǣldon ðæt land mid heora teónwordum *they brought up an evil report of the land* (A. V.), Num. 13, 33. Forðan ðe hig ðæt land tǣldon *by bringing up a slander upon the land* (A. V.), 14, 36. Ne hine ne tǣl, ne ne ter mid wordum, Basil admn. 5; Norm. 46, 11. Ne tǣl ðū ðīnne Dryhten *thou shalt not revile the gods*, L. Alf. 37; Th. i. 52, 29: Ex. 22, 28. Þreora cynna syndon morþras; ðæt is ðæt ǣrest, ðæt man tō ōþrum lǣþþe hæbbe, and hine hatige, and tǣle behindan him sylfum; forðon seó synn biþ swīþe mycel, ðæt man ōþerne hatige and tǣle, Blickl. Homl. 65, 1–2. Tēlan *carpere*, Wrt. Voc. ii. 19, 23: 90, 11. Underfōh mē nū behreówsiendne, ðone ðe ðū ōð ðis audigendne and tǣlendne forbǣre, Homl. Th. ii. 418, 10. Tēlendne wið ðæm nēstan his dēgullīce *dernlike his neghburgh bakbitand* (Ps.), Ps. Surt. 100, 5. Gebiddaþ for eówre ehteras and tǣlendum eów (*calumniantibus vos*), Mt. Kmbl. 5, 44. III. *to treat with contempt, to scorn, despise, insult, mock, deride, jeer at:*—Se stunta tǣlþ (*inridet*) lāre, Scint. 113, 18. Ðæt fæsten tǣlþ God, Homl. Th. i. 180, 10. Se ðe tēleþ (*spernit*) mec, Jn. Skt. Rush. 12, 48. Tēld *deridet*, Kent. Gl. 718. Ða unrihtwīsan tǣlaþ (cf. habbaþ on hospe, Met. 4, 44) ða rihtwīsan, Bt. 4; Fox 8, 15. Tǣlde hē Rōmāne and hié swīþe bismrade mid his wordum *Romam infami satis notavit elogio*, Ors. 5, 7; Swt. 228, 19. Tēlde (*sprevit*) hine Herōdes, Lk. Skt. Lind. Rush. 23, 11. Tǣldon *sugillent*, Wrt. Voc. ii. 92, 18. Ðā tǣldon hī hine *inridebant eum*, Mk. Skt. 5, 40. Tǣldon *deridebant*, Lk. Skt. 8, 53. Hié hine on ðæm tǣldon and bismrodan, ðæt hē his swā ānfealdne gegyrelan tōsnīðan sceolde, Blickl. Homl. 215, 9. Ealle āgynnaþ hine tǣlan (*inludere ei*), Lk. Skt. 14, 29. Sellas hine hǣðnum tō tēlenne (*ad deludendum*), Mt. Kmbl. Lind. 20, 19. Hēhsacerdas tēlende (*ludentes*) cuoedon, Mk. Skt. Lind. Rush. 15, 31. Tǣlende *cavillantes*, Wrt. Voc. ii. 3, 60. Tēled is *calcatur*, 18, 48: 83, 46: *detractatur*, Kent. Gl. 924. Hē biþ tǣled fram swylcum mannum swylce ðære wyrte mihta cunnun *he is laughed at by such men as know the virtues of the plant*, Lchdm. i. 164, 6. [He is cnihtscipe tælden *they blamed his want of manhood*, Laym. 3801. Tælen *to reproach*, 3334. Giff mann wollde tælenn þatt (*reprove the sin*), Orm. 2033. Swuch he may telen of golnesse, O. and N. 1415. *Icel.* tæla *to delude, mock.*] v. be-, ge-tǣlan; tǣlende, un-tǣled.

tæl-cræft, es; *m.* *Arithmetic:*—Mæg geseón ǣlc man ðe telcræftas ǣnig gesceád can (*that knows anything of arithmetic*), ðæt hit māre is ðonne þreó hund geára syððan ðyllīc feoh wæs farende on eorðan, Homl. Skt. i. 23, 699. v. getel-cræft; rīm-cræft.

-tǣle. v. leóf-, un-tǣle.

tǣlend, es; *m.* I. *a reprover:*—Ðǣm tēlendum *reprehensoribus*, Mk. Skt. p. 2, 17. II. *a slanderer, backbiter, detractor:*—Swīþe seldon ǣnig man wile beón andetta, ðæt hē æfēstig sȳ oððe tǣlend, Blickl. Homl. 65, 4. Ðone tǣlend *detrahentem*, Ps. Lamb. 100, 5. Mid tēlendum *cum detractoribus*, Kent. Gl. 938. III. *a scorner, mocker, derider:*—Sēcþ tǣlend (*derisor*) wīsdōm . . . gearwe synd tǣlendum (*derisoribus*) dōmas, Scint. 171, 13–14. Nelle ðū þreágean tǣlend (*derisorem*), 113, 12. Tēlend, Kent. Gl. 289.

tǣlende; *adj.* (*ptcpl.*) I. *prone to blame, censorious:*—Ne beó hē tō tǣlende, L. E. I. 21; Th. ii. 416, 17: Exon. Th. 305, 18; Fä. 90. Cf. Uton beorgan ūs wið tǣlnysse and wið twysprǣcnysse *caveamus nobis a vituperatione et a biloquio*, L. Ecg. P. iv. 66; Th. ii. 226, 31. II. *slanderous, backbiting:*—Ða æfstigan men and ða tǣlendan, Blickl. Homl. 65, 10.

tǣlere, es; *m.* *A scorner, scoffer, mocker:*—Tēlerum *derisoribus*, Kent. Gl. 721.

tælg. v. telg.

tǣl-hleahtor, es; *m.* *Scornful laughter, derision:*—Tǣlhlehter *derisio*, Wrt. Voc. i. 51, 4.

tǣling, e; *f.* I. *reproof, rebuke:*—Hē egesiende stiérþ ofermētta mid ðære tǣlinge, Past. 8; Swt. 53, 16. Petrus anfēng Paules tǣlinge (*increpationem*), 19; Swt. 145, 18. Hié forberaþ ǣghwelce unryhte tǣlinge . . . hié forberaþ ðæt hié mid ðæm sweorde hiera tungna tǣlinge ne sleáþ hira hlāfurdes ðeáwas *piae subditorum mentes ab omni se peste obtrectationis abstinentes praepositorum vitam nullo linguae gladio percutiunt*, 28; Swt. 199, 4. Hiera gefērena tǣlinge *reprehensionem proximorum*, 38; Swt. 273, 8. II. *evil-speaking, slander, calumny:*—Gif ðū gesihst fæla penega tǣlincga oððe wærginga getācnaþ *if you see many pennies, it betokens calumnies or curses*, Lchdm. iii. 214, 16.

tælla (= telga? q. v.):—Tællan *tyrso, vitibus*, Germ. 394, 280.

tǣl-leás; *adj.* *Blameless:*—Biscepe gedafnaþ ðæt hē sié tǣlleás *oportet episcopum irreprehensibilem esse*, Past. 8; Swt. 53, 10.

tǣlleáslīce; *adv.* *Blamelessly:*—Ðonne stæpþ se sacerd suíðe tǣlleáslīce on ðone weg *tunc sacerdos irreprehensibiliter graditur*, Past. 13; Swt. 77, 19.

tǣl-līc; *adj.* *Blasphemous:*—Tǣllīce word *blasphemiae*, Mt. Kmbl. 15, 19, MS. A. v. tāl-līc.

tǣllīce; *adv.* *Blasphemously, calumniously:*—Hē Criste wiðsōc and be ðam sōðan Gode tǣllīce sprecþ, Homl. Skt. i. 3, 249. v. un-tǣllīce; tāllīce.

tæl-mearc, e; *f.* *A date:*—Sume ǣr sume sīð sume in ūrra æfter tælmearce tīda gemyndum *some early, some late, some by the date in the memory of our times*, Exon. Th. 154, 27; Gū. 849.

tæl-met, es; *n.* *A measure expressed by number:*—Is tō ðære tīde tælmet hwīle seofon and twentig nihtgerīmes *there is to that season a space of time expressed by the number twenty-seven if the reckoning be by days*, Andr. Kmbl. 226; An. 113.

tǣlness, e; *f.* *Reproach, slander, calumny, detraction:*—Tēlnesse *sugillationis*, Wrt. Voc. ii. 87, 76. Sceomaes ꝉ tēlnisses *confusionis*, Mt. Kmbl. p. 3, 10. Ða ðe mē tǣlnysse teónan ætfæstan *qui detrahunt mihi*, Ps. Th. 108, 28. Tēlnysse, 108, 3. Uton beorgan ūs wið tǣlnysse (*vituperatione*), L. Ecg. P. iv. 66; Th. ii. 226, 31: Wulfst. 233, 19. Tō niomanne tēlnisse (*opprobrium*) mīne, Lk. Skt. Rush. 1, 25. Tēlnise ꝉ sceoma *calumniam*, Lind. 3, 14. Tǣlnysse *detractio*, L. Ecg. C. proem.; Th. ii. 132, 7. Tēlnisse weorlde *aerumnae saeculi*, Mk. Skt. Rush. 4, 19. Ða ðe tǣlnessa teónan wið heora ðam nēhstan nīð āhōfan *detrahentem adversus proximum suum*, Ps. Th. 100, 4. Ðū tǣlnissum wiþ ða sēlestan sacan ongunne, Exon. Th. 254, 31; Jul. 205. Tǣlnyssa (tēlnisse, Ps. Surt.) *vituperationem*, Ps. Spl. 30, 16.

tælsum; *adj.* *Numerous, harmonious, rhythmic:*—On tælsumum leóðe *carmine rythmico* (*numerali*), Hpt. Gl. 415, 55.

tǣlweorðlīcness, e; *f.* *Blameworthiness:*—Gē sweotolran gedōþ eówre tǣlweorðlīcnesse (-wierð-, Cott. MSS.) *foedior vestra reprehensibilitas appareat*, Past. 8; Swt. 53, 15.

tǣl-wirðe, -wierðe, -wyrðe; *adj.* *Blameworthy, reprehensible:*—Gecnāwan hwæt tǣlwierðe biþ *quae reprehendenda sunt cognoscere*, Past. 28; Swt. 195, 8. Tǣlwyrðes (-wierðes, Cott. MSS.), 195, 24. v. untǣlwirðe.

tǣlwirð-līc; *adj.* *Blameable, reprehensible:*—Ðæt on ōðrum lande betst līcaþ ðæt biþ hwīlum on ðam ōþrum tǣlwyrþlīcost and eác miceles wītes wyrþe *quod apud alios laude, apud alios supplicio dignum judicetur*, Bt. 18, 2; Fox 64, 24. v. un-tǣlwirðlīc.

tǣlwirðlīce; *adv.* *In a way that deserves censure, reprehensibly:*—Tǣlwyrðlīce *notabiliter*, Wrt. Voc. ii. 61, 16.

tǣlwirðlīcness. v. tǣlweorðlīcness.

tǣman, tæmes-pīle. v. tēman, temes-pīle.

tǣnel, es; *m.* *A wicker basket:*—Taenil, tēnil *fiscilla* (-*ella*), Txts. 62, 403. Tǣnel, Wrt. Voc. ii. 35, 36: *canistrum, vas vinetum*, 128, 18: *cistella, capsilla, cartellum*, 131, 20: *corbis* vel *qualus*, i. 24, 57. Litel tǣnel *quasillus*, 25, 6. Hē him on hand genam ǣnne lytelne tǣnel mid caricum gefylledne, Homl. Skt. ii. 23 b, 661, 714. Tǣnelas *fiscellos*, tǣnel *fiscellus*, Hpt. Gl. 497, 42, 43. Tǣnelum *fiscellis*, 468, 25: Wrt. Voc. ii. 34, 4. [Tenel or crele *cartallus*, Prompt. Parv. 489. Cf. *Goth.* tainjō κόφινος: *O. H. Ger.* zeinna *canistrum, calathus, cartallus, fiscella*; zeinnilī *cartallus*: *Icel.* teinur; *pl. f. a basket, creel.*] v. stic-tǣnel; tān; *and* cf. wilige, windel.

tǣnen; *adj. Of twigs*:—Tǣnene *sceptrinae* (sceptrum = *virga* in Aldhelm. v. Migne), Hpt. Gl. 483, 62. v. tân.

tæppa, an; *m. A tap*:—Ðonne ðû wîn habban wille, ðonne dô ðû mid ðînum twâm fingrum swilce ðû tæppan of tunnan onteón wille, Techm. ii. 120, 10. Tæppan teón, 12. [Hit behoueþ þet zuich wyn yerne by þe teppe ase þer is inne þe tonne, Ayenb. 27, 31. *Chauc.* tappe: *O. H. Ger.* zapfo; *m. duciculum, duciolus*: *Ger.* zapfen: Icel. tappi.] v. tæppian.

tæppa *or* tæppe, an; *m.* or *f. A band, ribbon, tape*:—Tæppan *tenia*, Wrt. Voc. i. 16, 63. [The tapes of hire white volupere, Chauc. C. T. 3241. Tappe *tenea*, Wrt. Voc. i. 196, col. 2 (15th cent.). Cf. *O. H. Ger.* teppi *sagum, tapetia*.]

tæpped, tæppet, es; *n. A covering* for a floor, wall, etc., *a carpet, hanging, coverlet*; for a person, *a tippet*:—Ân healf-hrûh tæppet *sipla* (*sipha?* cf. in a list *de lectis et ornamentis eorum*:—Hec amphicapa, est tapeta ex utraque parte villosa. Hec sipha, idem est, 243, col. 1), Wrt. Voc. i. 40, 35. vii. oferbrǣdelsas and .ii. tæppedu, Chart. Th. 429, 26. Gemētum tepedum (*lectulum meum stravi*) *tapetibus pictis* (Prov. 7, 16), Kent. Gl. 200. [Cf. typet, tepet, Chauc. C. T. 233. Typitte *leripipium*, Wrt. Voc. i. 238, col. 2. Typett, Prompt. Parv. 494. *O. H. Ger.* teppid(-th, -t), tepid(-t) *tapetium, saga cilicina*. From Latin.]

tæppel-bred, es; *n. A board covered with a carpet, a foot-stool*:—Fôtscamel ɫ tæppelbred his fôta *scabellum pedum ejus*, Mt. Kmbl. Rush. 5, 35. Tæppilbred, 22, 44. [Cf. *O. H. Ger.* tepul *tapetum*.] v. preceding word.

tæppere, es; *m. One who sells wine, a tavern-keeper*:—Tæppere *caupus*, i. *tabernarius, qui vinum vendit*, Wrt. Voc. ii. 130, 3. Tæppere, wînbrytta *caupo, tabernarius*, i. 28, 10. Tæppere *caupo*, 74, 17: Ælfc. Gr. 9, 3; Zup. 36, 13: Scint. 226, 10. [*O. Frs.* tapper. Cf. *Icel.* tappr *a tapster*.] v. wîn-tæppere; tæppian.

tæppestre, an; *f. A woman who sells wine, a hostess*:—Tæppestre *caupona*, Ælfc. Gr. 9, 3; Zup. 36, 13. [He knew the tavernes . . . and everych hostiler and tappestere, Chauc. C. T. 241.]

tæppet, tæppil-bred. v. tæpped, tæppel-bred.

tæppian; *p.* ode *To tap, put a tap into a cask*:—Gyf ðê gedrȳptes wînes lyste, ðonne dô ðû mid ðînum swȳþran scytefingre on ðîne wynstran hand, swylce ðû tæppian wille, and wænd ðînne scytefinger âdûne and twænge hine mid ðînum twâm fingrum, swylce ðû of sumne dropan strîcan wylle, Techm. ii. 125, 18. [*Icel.* tappa: *Ger.* zapfen.]

tær (?); *adj. Gaping, cleft* (?):—Ða giniendan oððe tara *hiulcas*, Wrt. Voc. ii. 42, 49. Cf. (?) teran.

tǣsan; *p.* de *To tear to pieces, pull to pieces, tease* wool, *tear* a person's flesh with a weapon, *wound*:—Ic tôtere oððe pluccige oððe tǣse (wulle *added in* MS. W.) *carpo*, Ælfc. Gr. 28, 4; Zup. 170, 13. *Carpsit, discerpsit, trahit, evellit, vel* tǣst, Wülck. Gl. 200, 5. (In Wrt. Voc. ii. 128, 76 a line is omitted.) Hwîlon hê on bord sceát, hwîlon beorn tǣsde; ǣfre embe stunde hê sealde sume wunde, ða hwîle ðe hê wǣpna wealdan môste, Byrht. Th. 139, 47; By. 270. Nim wulle, and tǣs hȳ, Lchdm. iii. 112, 8. [Þay (*the does*) were tened at þe hyȝe, and taysed to þe wattreȝ, Gaw. 1169. *But later forms seem also to point to a form* tâsian:—Sheep, that is fulle of wuile upon his backe, they toose and pulle, Gow. i. 17, 8. Tosyn or tose wul *carpo*, Prompt. Parv. 497, and see note. I toose owlle and card het, Rel. Ant. ii. 197, 36 (15th cent.). Cf. *O. H. Ger.* zeisan; *p.* zias *carpere*: *O. Du.* teesen *to tease* wool: *Dan.* tæse.] v. â-, ge-tǣsan; tǣsl.

tǣse (?); *adj. Convenient, for general use* (?):—Andlang herpoðes tô tǣsan mǣde and se hǣðfeld eal gemǣne, Cod. Dip. Kmbl. v. 78, 32. Tô têsan mêde and se hêðfeld eal gemǣne, 138, 19. v. (?) ge-tǣse, tǣs-lîc.

tǣsl, tǣsel, e; *f. Teasel, teazle*:—Ðeós wyrt ðe man *camelleon alba*, and ôþrum naman wulfes tǣsl (tǣsel, MS. B.) (cf. *wolf's-thistle*, E. D. S. Pub. Plant Names) nemneþ, hafaþ leáf wiþerrǣde and þyrnyhte, and heó hafaþ on middan sumne sinewealtne crop and þyrnyhtne, Lchdm. i. 282, 15. [Wilde tesel *virga pastoris*, Wrt. Voc. i. 141, 13 (13th cent.). Tasylle *carduus*, 191, col. 2 (15th cent.). Tasyl *carduus* vel *cardo fullonis*, Prompt. Parv. 487. Cloth . . . with taseles cracched, Piers P. 15,446. *O. H. Ger.* zeisala *carduus*; wolf(es)-zeisala *arnica*.]

tǣs-lîc; *adj. Advantageous, good, convenient*:—Gewelgad ɫ tǣslîcro (-or?) *potius*, Mt. Kmbl. Lind. 25, 9. v. next word.

tǣslîce; *adv. Conveniently*:—Sôhte huu hine teáslîcor gesealla mæhte *querebat quomodo illum opportune traderet*, Mk. Skt. Lind. 14, 11. v. ge-tǣslîce.

tæslum, Wrt. Voc. ii. 93, 44. v. teosol *and* tæfl.

tǣsness, tæso. v. ge-tǣsness, teosu.

tǣtan (?) *to gladden, make cheerful*:—Ful oft ðæt gegongeþ, ðætte wer and wîf in woruld cennaþ bearn, and mid bleóm gyrwaþ, tennaþ and tǣtaþ (*the father and mother try to make the child joyous, to amuse it*; Thorpe suggests *temiaþ and tǣcaþ*), Exon. Th. 327, 15; Vy. 4. [*Icel.* teita *to gladden, cheer*; teiti *gladsomeness, joy*; teitr *glad*.]

tættec (-a, -e?) *a rag, tatter*:—*Dormitatio vestietur pannis* seó slâpolnys byþ gescrȳdd mid wâcum tætticum, Homl. Ass. 9, 238. Nis se loddere mid his tættecon mîn gelîca, Homl. Th. i. 256, 9. Cf. the following passages from charters relating to the same land:—On tættucan stân (*in a later charter it is called* mægenstân, 291, 7), Cod. Dip. Kmbl. v. 112, 35. Tættucæn stân, 340, 35. Tættaces stân, 325, 30. Tæddduces stân, 253, 4. Could the word mean *beggar?* In the first mentioned charters *lodderes sæccing* (*sæxcing*) occurs.

tâgum, tâhae. v. teáh, tâ.

tâh-spora, -spura, an; *m. The point of the toe* (?):—Tâhspura *calcis finis*, Wrt. Voc. ii. 127, 47. v. hand-spora, hêl-spure, sporu.

tal *a number*. v. tæl.

tâl, e; *f.*: es; *n.* (?) I. *evil-speaking, calumny, slander, vituperation, detraction*:—Tâl *denotatio, detractio*, Scint. 83, 6. Tâle *suggilationis* (*vituperationis*, Hpt. Gl. 527, 3), Anglia xiii. 37, 298. Tâle *vituperationem*, Ps. Spl. 30, 16. Þurh tâle *per detractionem*, Confess. Peccat. Ne tâle ne dôþ *neque calumniam faciatis*, Lk. Skt. 3, 14. Ðurh ðis beóþ âwecte saca and tâla *hinc suscitantur rixe, detractiones*, R. Ben. 124, 18. Môdignys âcenþ yfelsacunge, ceorunge, and gelômlîce tâla, Homl. Th. ii. 222, 8. I a. *evil-speaking* in reference to the Deity, *blasphemy*:—Ǣlc synn and tâl biþ forgifen mannum, ac ðæs Hâlgan Gâstes tâl ne bið nǣfre forgifen *omne peccatum et blasphemia remittetur hominibus, Spiritus autem blasphemia non remittetur* (Mt. 12, 31), Homl. Th. i. 498, 22. Se cwyð tâl ongeán ðone Hâlgan Gâst, se ðe mid unbehreówsigendre heortan þurhwunaþ on mândǣdum, 500, 15. Nân man ne beó swâ dyrstig, ðæt hê ǣnig word oððe ǣnig (ǣnige?) tâl cweðe ongeán eówerum Gode, ii. 20, 28. II. *scorn, mock, derision, reproach*:—Tâl and gebismerung *subsannatio et illusio*, Ps. Lamb. 78, 4. Þe læs ðe heó dô ðê on tâle cuman feóndum ðînum *ne faciat te in obprobrium uenire inimicis tuis*, Scint. 177, 4. Ðæt man God tô tâle habbe *that God be mocked*, Wulfst. 299, 14. Ðâs word ðe Sennacherib âsende tô hospe and tô tâle ðê and ðînum folce (*verba Sennacherib, qui misit ut exprobraret nobis Deum viventem*, 2 Kings 19, 16), Homl. Th. i. 568, 19. Tâle *gannniturae, cachinnatione*, Hpt. Gl. 441, 2. Tâle *subsannationem*, Ps. Lamb. 43, 14. III. *blame, censure, reproof*:—Ða bôceras ðæt tǣldon; ac heora tâl næs nâ of rihtwîsnysse, Homl. Th. i. 338, 20. *Adjectiva* getâcniaþ oððe herunge oððe tâl (tâle, MS. V.: tǣl, MS. T.), Ælfc. Gr. 5; Zup. 12, 11. [Cf. *O. H. Ger.* zâla *periculum*: *Icel.* tâl *allurement, device*.] v. tǣl, tǣlan.

talente, an; *f. A talent*:—Hê ǣlce geáre gesealde twâ hund talentana siolfres: on ǣlcre ânre talentan wæs .lxxx. punda, Ors. 4, 6; Swt. 170, 27. III M talentana, Swt. 180, 14. Swâ fela talentena, 4, 10; Swt. 202, 22. [*O. H. Ger.* talenta; *f. strong*.]

talian; *p.* ode. I. *to suppose* a thing (to be) such and such, *consider, reckon, account*, (a) where the object is a noun or pronoun:—Nô ic mê hnâgran talige, ðonne Grendel hine, Beo. Th. 1359; B. 677. Ðæs ðe ic sôð talige, Andr. Kmbl. 3125; An. 1565. Talge, Exon. Th. 50, 3; Cri. 794. Hê hit swîðe unâberendlîc talaþ, Past. 33; Swt. 226, 18. Hê mê ofslægenne talaþ, Bd. 4, 22; S. 591, 29. Hê talaþ hine sylfne wîsne, Wulfst. 52, 29. Ða ðe hî sylfe wâce taliaþ, Homl. Th. ii. 374, 29. Ðæt hié taliaþ hâlig, R. Ben. 9, 19. Talige hê hine sylfne wið God forworhtne, Wulfst. 155, 11. Hwæðer ðæt sié tô talianne wâclîc, Bt. 24, 4; Fox 86, 16. Gê beóþ mê talade and rîmde on bearna stæl, Exon. Th. 366, 11; Reb. 10. (b) where the object is expressed by a clause:—Sôð ic talige, ðæt ic merestrengo mâran âhte, Beo. Th. 1069; B. 532. Wên ic talige . . . ðæt ða Sǣ-Geátas sêlran næbben tô geceósenne cyning ǣnigne, 3695; B. 1845. Wê fremful taliaþ, ðæt eal mynstres fadung on ðæs abbodes dôme stande, R. Bên. 125, 5. (c) where the supposition is expressed by a clause:—Ðû talas (*putas*), ðæt ic ne mǣge gebidda fader mîn, Mt. Kmbl. Lind. 26, 53. Se man talaþ, ðæt hê ðonne hâl sié, Lchdm. ii. 208, 6. Hwylc talge wê, ðæt se ende ðæs heora lîfes wǣre, Blickl. Homl. 163, 5. (d) where the supposition is not expressed:—Nis ðis seó hell swâ ðû talost and wênest, Bd. 5, 12; S. 628, 7. Gif ðîn hige wǣre swâ searogrim swâ ðû talast, Beo. Th. 1193; B. 594. ¶ *with* swylce, tô, *to consider as*:—Ða âteorigendlîcan ðing ðe heó nû tô sibbe and blisse talaþ, Homl. Th. i. 408, 26. Wâ eów ðe taliaþ eów sylfe tô ðeódwitan *ve, qui sapientes estis coram oculis vestris*, Wulfst. 46, 26. Ne talode se ofermôda Phariseus tô suâ micle mægene ða forhæfdnesse suâ hê dyde, Past. 43; Swt. 313, 4. Heora lîf is rihtor tô talianne tô êcan deáðe, Wulfst. 25, 6. Tala ðê ðînne brôðor, swylce hê beó ðîn lim, Basil admn. 5; Norm. 46, 11. Tô for nâht taliende *parvi pendenda, neglegenda, ad nihilum judicanda*, Hpt. Gl. 418, 36. II. *to impute, ascribe, lay to the account of*:—Gif ðû talast tô ðînum geswince ðæt, ðæt ðû hæfst, Homl. Th. ii. 102, 29. Ne talige ic ðê ðæt tô nânre scylde *I do not impute it to you as any fault*, Shrn. 184, 21. Eádig se wer ðam ðe ne talode (*imputavit*) Drihten synne, Ps. Lamb. 31, 2. Ne tala ðû mê, ðæt ic ne cunne ðone intingan ðînre unrôtnesse, Bd. 2, 12; S. 513, 40. Ne talige nân man his yfelan dǣda tô Gode, ac talige ǣrest tô ðam deófle, Homl. Th. i. 114, 18. III. *to reckon, enumerate*:—Tô talanna longsum is *enumerare longissimum est*, Mt. Kmbl. p. 7, 7. [*O. Sax.* talôn: *O. Frs.* talia: *O. H. Ger.* zalôn *considerare, reputare*: *Icel.* tala *to talk*.] v. ge-talian; tellan.

tâl-lîc; *adj.* I. *that conveys reproach, calumny*, etc., *calumnious, blasphemous*:—Þeáh hwâ cweðe tâllîc word ongeán mê, him biþ forgifen,

Homl. Th. i. 498, 24. Of ðære heortan cumaþ . . . tâllíce word (*blasphemiae*), Mt. Kmbl. 15, 19. Hí cwǽdon ðæt hē tâllíce word sprǽce be Moyse and be Gode (*this man ceaseth not to speak blasphemous words against this holy place, and the law*, Acts 6, 13), Homl. Th. i. 44, 29: 46, 1. Se ðe ídele spellunge oððe tâllíce word (*calumnies, backbiting*) lustlíce gehýrþ, 492, 19. II. *that deserves reproof, blameable, reprehensible*:—Gif ǽnig biþ mēt teállíc *si quisque repertus fuerit reprehensibilis*, R. Ben. Interl. 54, 7. Nis ðæt clǽne herigendlíc, ne ðæt gâle tâllíc, gif him steorran forgēfon, ðæt hí swā lyfedon, Homl. Skt. i. 5, 281. v. tǽl-líc, *and next word*.

tallíce; *adv. In a way that deserves blame, reprehensibly*:—Tâllíce *reprehensibiliter*, Wrt. Voc. i. 54, 46. Ne forseó gē Godes ðearfan, ðeáh ðe hí tâllíce hwæt gefremman, Homl. Th. i. 332, 13. v. un-tâllíce; tǽllíce.

talu, e; *and indecl.*; *f.* I. *a tale, talk, story, account*:—Leáses spelles talu *constellatio* (cf. *Span.* constelacion *prognostication of the stars*), Wrt. Voc. ii. 20, 68. Ðā sprǽcon hí betwux him, and seó mōdor sæt hlystende hire tale . . . Ðā se gingra brōðor ðis eall gehýrde fram ðam yldran brōðor hē sǽde: 'Ic eom ðín brōðor be ðí[n]re tale,' Homl. Skt. ii. 30, 319-337. Ðæt se Ælmihtiga God gehýre ða talu ðe Syria cyning āsende tō hospe and tō edwíte his micclan mægenðrymme (*si forte audiat Dominus universa verba Rabsacis, quem misit rex Assyriorum, ut exprobraret Deum viventem*, 2 Kings 19, 4), Homl. Th. i. 568, 27. Mē ða treahteras tala wísedon, Salm. Kmbl. 10; Sal. 5. II. *talk, discussion, dispute*:—Tale(-u?) *disputatio, contentio, litigatio*, Hpt. Gl. 481, 60. Tale *disputationis, dissensionis*, 439, 57: *disputationis, certationis*, 459, 60. III. *a charge, claim*:—Ða heáhsacerdas sōhton tale āgēn ðone Hǽlend *summi sacerdotes quaerebant aduersum Iesum testimonium*, Mk. Skt. 14, 55. Se ðe nānum ne derede, him man dyde talu, and hē wæs beswungen unscyldig for ūs, Basil admn. 4; Norm. 42, 27. Ðæt ǽlcere neóde belādung sý ādilegod ðæt hý þurh neóde nāne tale tō syndrigre ǽhte næbben *that the excuse of necessity may be removed, so that they may not have any claim to private property on the ground of necessity*, R. Ben. 92, 5. Hē begeat swíðe mycelne sceatt of his mannan ðǽr hē mihte ǽnige teale tō habban oððe mid rihte oððe elles *where, rightly or otherwise, he could advance any claim to what he exacted*, Chr. 1085; Erl. 219, 11. IV. *an excuse, a defence*:—Míne gebrōðra, hwilcere tale māge wē brūcan on his dōme, nū wē nellaþ būgan fram woruldlufe? Homl. Th. i. 580, 2: Lchdm. iii. 442, 3. Ðæt hý nāne tale næbben, ðæt hý þurh nytennesse misfōn þurfen, 442, 10. Nabbe wē nāne tale ongēn ðē *we have no excuse to offer you*; quid juste poterimus obtendere? Gen. 44, 16. Hē ne mihte nāne tale findan *he could not devise any defence*, Homl. Skt. i. 23, 624. Gif hē his yfelan dǽda mid leásum talum bewarian wile *si defendere uoluerit opera sua*, R. Ben. 52, 10. V. as a law term, *a case* (as regards either plaintiff or defendant), *an action*, cf. sprǽc:—Ongan tō specenne on ðat land . . . Ðam cynge seó talu cūð wæs, Chart. Th. 302, 16. Ēdwine spæc on his āgene mōdor æfter sumon dǽle landes . . . Ðā ācsode þe bisceop, hwā sceolde andswerian for his mōdor. Ðā sǽde Ðurcil Hwíta, ðæt hē sceolde, gif hē ða talu cūðe. Ðā hē ða talu nā ne cūðe, ðā sceáwode man þreó þegnas ðǽr ðǽr heó wæs . . . Ðā ācsodon heó, hwylce talu heó hæfde ymbe ða land . . . Ðā sǽde heó, ðæt heó nān land hæfde, ðe him āht tō gebyrede, 337, 2-24. Tale wyrðe *entitled to bring an action*, 266, 11. VI. *a tale, list, series*:—Talu *laterculus*, Wrt. Voc. ii. 53, 23. Ða talo *canones*, Mt. Kmbl. p. 2, 18. [*O. Sax.* gēr-tala: *O. Frs.* tale *a (legal) case*: *O. H. Ger.* zala *numerus, series, catalogus, sententia, calculatio, supputatio*: *Icel.* tala *talk; tale, number*.] v. bōc-, folc-, hrægl-, of-, on-, rím-, tō-, wiðer-talu.

tam; *adj. Tame*, the opposite of wild:—Tam *subjugalis*, Wrt. Voc. ii. 73, 6. Wilde bār *aper*, tam bār *verres*, i. 22, 70-71. Seó leó, ðeáh hió wel tam sē, Bt. 25; Fox 88, 9. Tiles and tomes meares, Exon. Th. 342, 13; Gn. Ex. 142. Hē rít uppan tamre assene and hyre folan (sittende on eosule and on folan sunu ðære teoma, Rush.) *sedens super asinam et pullum filium subjugalem*, Mt. Kmbl. 21, 5. Wildu diór woldon stondan swilce hí tamu wǽron, Bt. 35, 6; Fox 168, 2. On ðære feórþan flēringa wæs ðæra tamra nýtena steall, Boutr. Scrd. 21, 9. Hē hæfde tamra deóra (*reindeer*) syx hund, Ors. 1, 1; Swt. 18, 10. Tame (wudufuglas), Bt. 25; Fox 88, 18: Met. 13, 44. [*O. H. Ger.* zam *subjugalis, domitus, mansuetus, mitis*: *Icel.* tamr *tame; ready for, used to*.]

tama, an; *m. Tameness*:—Ne þearf beorna nān wēnan ðære wyrde, ðæt hió (*the lioness*) wel hire taman healde; ac ic tiohhie, ðæt hió ðæs níwan taman nāuht ne gehicgge, ac ðone wildan gewunan wille geþencan hire eldrena, Met. 13, 23-28. Gif heó blōdes onbirigþ, heó forgit sōna hire níwan taman, and gemonþ ðæs wildan gewunan hire eldrana, Bt. 25; Fox 88, 12.

tān, es; *m.* I. *a twig, sprout, shoot, branch*:—Tānas *arbusta*, Ps. Th. 79, 10: *vimina*, Germ. 390, 44: *antes*, Hpt. Gl. 496, 73. Ic on neorxna wonge āsette treów, ðæt ða tānas æpla bǽron, Cd. Th. 295, 7; Sat. 482. Tānum, fingeræpplum *dactylis*, Hpt. Gl. 496, 64. Hē (*the phenix*) getimbreþ tānum and wyrtum nest on bearwe, Exon. Th. 227, 29; Ph. 430. Wudubearwas tānum týdraþ, 191, 6; Az. 84: 435, 17; Rä. 54, 2: 458, 23; Hy. 4, 105. God gibloedsia gimeodomia ðās tānas missenlícra treóna *Deus benedicere dignare has frondes diversarum arborum*, Rtl. 95, 21. Beorc bereþ tānas būtan tuddre, Runic pm. Kmbl. 342, 29; Rūn. 18. I a. *a stake* (? cf. *Icel.* teinn *a stake* to hang things on):—Ðis syndan ða landgemǽre. Of ðam ealdan hornforda . . . ādūn on ealda tān; swā anlang streámes on ealda hornford, Cod. Dip. Kmbl. iv. 45, 25. II. *a twig used in casting lots* ['Augury and divination by lot no people practise more diligently. The use of the lots is simple. A little bough is lopped off a fruit-bearing tree, and cut into small pieces; these are distinguished by certain marks, and thrown carelessly and at random over a white garment,' Tacitus' Germania, c. 10], *a lot*; also *a share that is determined by lot*:—Ða Eald-Seaxan næfdon āgenne cyning, ac monige ealdormen wǽron heora ðeóde foresette; and ðonne seó tíd gewinnes com, ðonne hluton hí mid tānum tō ðam ealdormannum, and swā hwylc heora swā him se tān ætýwde, ðonne gecuron hí ðone him tō heretogan, and ealle ðam fyligdon *non habent regem antiqui Saxones, sed satrapas plurimos suae genti praepositos, qui ingruente belli articulo mittunt aequaliter sortes, et quemcumque sors ostenderit, hunc tempore belli ducem omnes sequuntur*, Bd. 5, 10; S. 624, 22-26. Ðā wæs eall geador tō ðam þingstede þeód gesamnod; lēton him ðā betweónum tān wísian hwylcne hira ǽrest ōðrum sceolde tō foddorþege feores ongildan, hluton hellcræftum . . . Ðā se tān gehwearf ofer ǽnne ealdgesíða, Andr. Kmbl. 2196-2210; An. 1099-1106. Hē sealde him wēste land ðæt hí mid tāne getugan rihte *sorte divisit eis terram in funiculo distributionis*, Ps. Th. 77, 55. Nǽfre forlǽteþ Drihten firenfulra tān furðor gangan ðonne hē sōðfæstra settan wylle *never will the Lord let the lot of sinners go further than he will appoint the lot of the just*; non derelinquet Dominus virgam peccatorum super sortem justorum, 124, 3. Tān sendende *sortem mittentes*, Mt. Kmbl. Lind. Rush. 27, 35: Jn. Skt. Lind. 19, 24. Hié ðysne middangeard on twelf tānum tōhluton and ǽghwylc ānra heora in ðæm dǽle [wunode?] ðe hē mid tān geeode *the apostles divided the world into twelve parts that were to be assigned by lot, and each one of them [remained?] in that part which he got by lot*, Blickl. Homl. 121, 7-9. Sendon tānas *miserunt sortes*, Lk. Skt. Lind. 23, 34. [*Goth.* tains *a twig, branch*: *O. H. Ger.* zein, zain *sarmentum, calamus, regula*: *Du.* teen *twig, osier*: *Icel.* teinn *a twig, sprout; a spit*: *Dan.* ten *a spindle*: *Norweg.* ten *a slender rod*: *Swed.* ten *spindle, rod*.] v. āc-, ātor-, ellen-, hearm-, mistel-, wuldor-tān; tān; *adj.*, tā *a lot*, tǽnel *a basket*.

tān, e; *f. A toe*:—Tān *mentagra*, (seó) micele tān *allox*, Wrt. Voc. i. 45, 24, 25. Mid tānum *cum mentagris*, Lchdm. i. lxxi, 13 (cf. lxxiv, 21). [*O. Frs.* tāne; *f.*: *Du.* teen.] v. tā *a toe*, tānede; *and* cf. *the double forms* tān, tā *a lot*.

tān; *adj. Having branches, spreading*, used metaphorically of the offspring of a parent; cf. the use of *branch* in speaking of the members of a family:—Ic Ismael wille bletsian, swā ðū bēna eart, ðæt feorhdaga on woruldríce worn gebíde tānum tūdre (*with a family that has many branches*. The passage in Genesis is: And as for Ishmael, I have heard thee: Behold, I have blessed him, and will make him fruitful, and will multiply him exceedingly; twelve princes shall he beget, and I will make him a great nation, 17, 20), Cd. Th. 142, 11; Gen. 2360. v. tān *a twig*.

tānages. v. tānian.

tānede; *adj. Having the toes diseased*:—Tānede *mentagricus* (the word occurs in a list of adjectives denoting diseases of the leg), Wrt. Voc. i. 45, 43: ii. 58, 9. v. tān *a toe*.

tang, e; tange, an; *f. A pair of tongs*:—Tang *forceps*, Ælfc. Gr. 9, 55; Zup. 67, 3: Wrt. Voc. i. 286, 78: ii. 33, 36: *delebra*, 138, 62. Tong *forceps*, 109, 6. Tange *forceps*, i. 86, 19. Tange *forcipis*, ii. 33, 35. Tangan, tange, Hpt. Gl. 417, 74. Ic hopige ðæt cherubin mid his gyldenan tange spearcan tō mínre tungan gebringan, Anglia viii. 325, 31. Tangan *forcipes*, Wülck. Gl. 241, 35 (omitted by Wright). Hí woldon mē gelæccan mid heora byrnendum tangum, Homl. Th. ii. 352, 1, 5. Hí fýrene tangan him on handa hæfdon, Bd. 5, 12; S. 628, 42. [*O. L. Ger.* tanga *forceps*: *Du.* tang: *O. H. Ger.* zanga: *Icel.* töng.] v. fýr-tang, Anglia ix. 263, 9, mǽl-tange, ísen-tanga (*read* -tange. v. Ælfc. Gr. Zup. 314, 9).

-tang *touching*. v. gader-, ge-tang; -tenge.

tān-hlyta, an; *m. One who divines by casting lots*:—Tānhlyta *sortilegus*, Wrt. Voc. i. 60, 13. v. tān, II.

tān-hlytere, es; *m. One who divines by casting lots*:—Tānhlytere *sortilegus*, Wrt. Voc. i. 57, 41. v. preceding word.

tānian(?) *to decide by lot*:—Tānages *decimatis*, Mt. Kmbl. Lind. 23, 23.

tannere, es; *m. A tanner* (?):—Be eástan eá and tannera hole, Cod. Dip. Kmbl. ii. 411, 22.

tapor (-er, -ur); *m. A taper*; also *the wick of a lamp*:—Leóhtfæt *lampas*, candel *candela*, taper *papyrus* (cf. leóhtfæt *lucernarium*, weoce *papirus*, 26, 56), Wrt. Voc. i. 284, 35. Tapor *cereus*, 81. 32: *cerastus*, ii. 130, 23. Swegles tapur *the sun*, Exon. Th. 205, 18; Ph. 114. Onfangenum tapere *accepto cereo*, Anglia xiii. 403, 548. Hē hiene onǽlþ mid ðæm tapore (-ure, Hatt. MS.) ðæs godcundan liegges, Past. 36; Swt. 258, 13. *Acolitus* is gecweden se ðe candele oððe tapor byrþ, ðonne mann godspell rǽt, L. Ælfc. C. 14; Th. ii. 348, 4. Se sacerd gehálgodne tapor in ðæt wæter déþ, Wulfst. 36, 5. Taperas *cerei*, Anglia xiii. 402, 529: 403, 541. Ðrítig teapera, Chart. Th. 473, 32. Ðá com ðæs landes menigu mid leóhtfatum and mid taperum, Homl. Th. ii. 474, 24. Taporas *cereos*, Germ. 395, 72. Taperas, Lchdm. iii. 202, 4.

tapor-æx, e; *f. A small axe*:—Swá feorr swá mæg án taperæx beón geworpen út of ðam scipe up on ðæt land *quam longius de nave potest securis parvula, quam Angli vocant* tapereax *super terram projici*, Chart. Th. 317, 30. Habbe hé áne taperæx on his [handa], Chr. 1031; Erl. 162, 8. [*Icel.* tapar-öx (*borrowed from English*).]

tapor-berend, es; *m. An acolyte* (v. tapor):—Taporberend *accolitus*, Anglia xiii. 418, 759. Taporber[n]endum *accolitis*, 424, 840.

tappa, teappa?:—Of rúwan beorge on teappan treów; of tappan treów on westleás hagan, Cod. Dip. Kmbl. v. 277, 21. Teppan hýse, i. 194, 36. On teppen cnolle, iii. 415, 19. Ad Tapan halan, ii. 344, 6.

tara *tar*. v. teoru.

targe, an; *f.*: targa, an; *m. A targe, small shield* [apparently with the same development of meaning as *rand*, q.v. Cf. *O. H. Ger.* zarga *costa* (*aheni*) with the English word]:—Ic geann Ælmére mínen discðéne mínes taregan, Cod. Dip. Kmbl. iii. 363, 12. Targa[n] *parma, scuto*, Hpt. Gl. 423, 50. Twá targan and twegen francan, Cod. Dip. Kmbl. iii. 304, 30. Targena *peltarum*, Hpt. Gl. 475, 64. [*Icel.* targa *a small round shield.* The word seems to have been taken into the Romance languages from Teutonic.] v. ge-targed.

-targed, tasol. v. ge-targed, teosol.

tawa (?) *an implement, a tool, an article for use in an employment.* [That towe (*part of a cart*) is toothed thicke, Pall. 159, 36. Tew of tyschynge *piscalia*, in plurali *reciaria*, Prompt. Parv. 490. Halliwell gives *tow*=tools, apparatus, as a word of the East of England. *O. Du.* touwe *the instrument of a weaver.*] v. ge-, web-tawa; tawian.

tawian; *p.* ode. I. *to taw, dress* or *prepare* material:—Ðá bæd se Godes man ðæt him man ísengelóman mid hwǽte ðyder brohte ðæt land mid tó tawienne. Ðá ðæt land ða getawod wæs and hé on gerisne tíd mid hwǽte hit seów *ferramenta sibi ruralia cum frumento adferri rogavit, quod dum praeparata terra tempore congruo seminaret*, Bd. 4, 28; M. 366, 24. [Birrþ læredd mann þurrh spell mekenn þin herrte, and turrnenn itt and tawwenn itt and nesshenn itt, Orm. 15908. The sotter that tawith ȝure lethir, Rel. Ant. ii. 175, 24 (about 1308). Tewyñ lethyr *frunio, corrodio*, Prompt. Parv. 490. *O. Du.* touwen *to curry leather*: *O. H. Ger.* zauwen, zouwen *exercere* (*ferrum*). Cf. *also* tew or tewynge of lethyr *frunicio*, Prompt. Parv. 489: *O. H. Ger.* zawa *tinctura*: *Goth.* taui *work.* Teware *corridiator*, Prompt. Parv. 490: *O. H. Ger.* zauwari *tinctorius*]. v. tewestre. II. but the word seems to occur in the older time in reference to the ill-treatment of persons or things, *to intreat* shamefully *or* evilly, *treat* badly, *abuse, insult.* Cf. to *tew*=to trouble, vex, E. D. S. Pub. (Linc.), and see Halliwell:—Oft týne oððe twelfe (flotmen) ǽlc æfter óðrum scendaþ and tawiaþ tó bysmore ðæs þegnes cwenan and hwílum his dohtor oððe nýdmágan, ðǽr hé on lócaþ ðe lǽt hine sylfne rancne and rícne, ǽr ðæt gewurde, Wulfst. 162, 20. Se deófol eów tawode þurh his drýmen swá swá hé wolde *the devil hath treated you as he pleased* (the persons addressed had been deprived in turn of the power of speech, motion, and sight) *by his wizards*, Homl. Th. ii. 486, 31. Hé heora burga forbærnde and hí tó bysmore tawode (tucode, MSS. C. V.) *he burnt up their cities and evilly intreated them*, Homl. Skt. ii. 25, 388. Hé Godes templ tawode tó bysmore *he had shamefully abused God's temple* (cf. l. 538), 25, 542. Ðæt folc hine hæfde swá yfele swilce hé sumes þinges scyldig wǽre; and ealle men hine fram stówe tó stówe brudon, and tó wundre tawedon *treated him wondrous ill*, i. 23, 654. Ða ðe gefongne wǽron hié tawedan mid ðære mǽstan uniéðnesse; sume ofslógon, sume ofswungon, sume him wið feó gesealdon. Ðá Rómáne ðæt geácsedan, ðá sendan hié ǽrendracan tó him . . . Ðá tawedan hié eft ða ǽrendracan mid ðæm mǽstan bismere, swá hié ða óþre ǽr dydon, Ors. 4, 1; Swt. 154, 7-13. Ðæt hié hié móston tawian mid ðære mǽstan bismrunge, 3, 3; Swt. 102, 21. v. ge-tawian; teágan.

táxe (tádie? *q.v.*), an; *f. A toad*:—Táxan *rubetae, quae et ranae dicuntur*, Hpt. Gl. 450, 19.

te; *prep. To*:—Ða mægenu weorðaþ te færwyrde (cf. tó færwyrde, 8), Past. 65; Swt. 463, 6. Heom te cwæþ *illis dixit*, Mt. Kmbl. Rush. 26, 21. Áléfed te habbanne, 14, 4. Te fullfremmanne, Past. 58; Swt. 445, 30: 50; Swt. 391, 29. [*O. Sax.* te: *O. Frs.* te, ti: *O. L. Ger.* te, ti: *O. H. Ger.* za, ze, zi.] Cf. tó.

te-. v. te-flówan, -tredan, -weorpan *given under* tó-flówan, -tredan, -weorpan. [*O. Frs.* te-, ti-: *O. H. Ger.* za-, ze-, zi-.] Cf. tó-.

te=þe *in* þætte.

teá *ten.* v. tín.

teáfor, es; *n.* I. *a pigment, material used for colouring, tiver* (red ochre for marking sheep (Suffolk), v. E. D. S. Pub. Old Farming Words, no. vi):—Métingc *pictura*, reád teáfor *minium*, Wrt. Voc. i. 46, 74. Teáfor *minium*, 75, 20. Tfafrf (=teáfre) *minio*, Germ. 400. 130. Meng swá ðú dést teáfor, Lchdm. ii. 56, 6. II. *a material used in making a salve*:—Nim ladsar (*benzoin*) ðæt teáfur (*gum*), and galpani óþres healfes panige whit, and gníd hyt tógadere mid wlacan ecede; and nim ðanne ða sealfe and geót on ðæs seócys mannes éare, iii. 88, 20. [In other dialects the word occurs with a meaning not easily connected with that of the English form. A somewhat similar connection, perhaps, is seen in the case of the different meanings of lybb, q.v. *O. H. Ger.* zoubar; *n. fascinum, fascinatio, divinatio*: *Icel.* taufr; *n. sorcery.* Cf. *O. L. Ger.* toufere *veneficus.* v. Grmm. D. M. 984.] v. tífran.

teáfor?, Exon. Th. 477, 27; Ruin. 31.

teág. v. teáh.

teágan, teán; *p.* teáde; *pp.* teád *To dress, prepare*:—Ísengelóman ðæt land mid tó teágenne. Ðá ðæt land ðá geteád wæs, Bd. 4, 28; S. 605, 33. Wel geteád alwe, Lchdm. ii. 226, 14. v. ge-teágan; tawian.

teagor, es; *n. The water from the eyes, tears*:—Teagor ýðum weól, háte hleórdropan, Exon. Th. 182, 23; Gú. 1314. [*Goth.* tagr *a tear.*] v. teár.

teáh, tǽh, téh, tíh(-g); *gen.* teáge; *f.* I. *a tie, band*:—Teág, taeg *sceda*, Txts. 98, 964. Teáh, Wrt. Voc. i. 289, 36. Lege ðé his teáge an sweoran, Lchdm. iii. 42, 13. Hé cyning gebond fýrnum teágum, Exon. Th. 46, 7; Cri. 733. Liðewácum tagum (teágum?, tánum?, *or* tógum? *as an alternative gloss to* lentis. v. tóh) (*alii*) *lentis viminibus* (*caedentes*), Hpt. Gl. 514, 70. [Teien togadere mid guldene teȝen, Laym. 20998. A teiȝ-dogge þat is in strongue teiȝe (*rimes with* eiȝe (*eye*)), L. S. 308, 301. He huld an hache harde wiþ teis, Jos. 504. *Icel.* taug; *f. a rope, string.*] v. lád-, racent-, sweor-, web-teáh. II. *a case, coffer, casket, box*:—Cest *vel* earc *cistella*, tǽg *mozytia* vel *arcula*, Wrt. Voc. i. 16, 38. Taeg *mantega* (=*mantica*?), Txts. 35, 19: 77, 1300. Tíg, Wrt. Voc. ii. 55, 57. Hí ðás hálgan martyrrace on ánum leádenum tabulan mid stafon ágrófon, and ðæt gewrit mid twám inseglum on ánre teáge geinsegledon, Homl. Skt. i. 23, 344. Gemétton hí áne teáge, seó wæs geinsæglod mid twám insæglum . . . Man bær út ða teáge . . . Ðá féng se portgeréfa tó ðære tége and hí sóna unhlidode, 23, 755-765. Búton hit (*the stolen property*) under ðæs wífes cǽglocan gebroht wǽre . . . ðæt is hire hordern and hire cyste and hire tége, L. C. S. 77; Th. i. 418, 22. Tégum, fódrum *tepis* (=*thecis*), Txts. 101, 2010. [At hom is hire pater noster biloken in hire teye (*rimes with* eye (*eye*)), Misc. 191, 2. A riche tie Made all of gold and of perrie Out of the which she nam a ring, Gow. ii. 246, 19. Teye of a cofyr *teca*, Prompt. Parv. 487.] v. beorm-teáh. III. *an enclosure, a close* (cf. *Icel.* teigr (teygr?) *a close, paddock*):—Hujus telluris termini . . . et aquilone meara-teág (=*horses' close*; cf. horsa croft, iii. 464, 3), Cod. Dip. Kmbl. i. 248, 12. Mansionem et clausulam, quam Angli dicunt *teáge*, que pertinet ad predictam mansionem, Chart. Th. 467, 19. Circumcincta est . . . a meritie brómteágh, ii. 49, 20.

teala, tealgor, teál-líc. v. tela, telgor, tál-líc.

tealt; *adj.* I. in a physical sense, *unsteady*:—Gif hí sculun néðan on nacan tealtum, and se brimhengest brídles ne gýmeþ (cf. The floating vessel . . . Rode tilting o'er the waves, Milton, P. L. xi. 747), Runic pm. Kmbl. 343, 22; Rún. 21. II. in a figurative sense, *unstable, not to be relied on, untrustworthy, precarious*:—Hú lǽne ðis líf is, hú tealt, Wulfst. 273, 7. Tealte syndon eorðan welan, 149, 8. Tealte beóþ eorðan dreámas, 264, 3. Tealte getrýwða sindon mid mannum, 82, 12: 129, 6: 159, 14. v. next word.

tealtian; *p.* ode *To be unsteady, to shake, not to stand firm*:—Mid tealtendum grundwealle *nutabundo* (*titubando*) *fundamento*, Hpt. Gl. 497, 49. [Cf. Þenne schal Niniue tylte to grounde, Allit. Pms. 102, 361. Feole temples tulten to þe eorþe, Jos. 100. *O. H. Ger.* zeltend rosz, zeltari *equus trutinans*: *Ger.* zelt *amble*; zelter *palfrey*: *Icel.* tölta *to amble*; tölt *an ambling pace.*] v. next word.

tealtrian; *p.* ode *To shake, totter, stagger, be unsteady, to be in an uncertain* or *a precarious condition*:—Wé tealtrigaþ týdran móde hwearfiaþ heánlíce *we move with uncertain step and feeble mind, wander abjectly*, Exon. Th. 23, 19; Cri. 371. Ðý læs ðe ðæt eásterlíce gesceád tealtrige *lest the calculation of Easter be untrustworthy*, Anglia viii. 308, 4. Tealtrian mid fótum *to stagger*, Dial. 1, 4 (Lye). Ðý læs se steall cyricean tealtrian (taltrigan, Bd. M.) ongunne *ne status ecclesiae vacillare inciperet*, Bd. 2, 4; S. 505, 11. Tealtrian *vacillare, titubare*, Hpt. Gl. 529, 73. Tealtriendum ł gliddriendum *nutabundis*, 503, 3. Fela óþera gesynto ða ðe him tealtriende (taltriendum, Bd. M.) gelumpon *alia quae periclitanti ei contigissent prospera*, Bd. 4, 22; S. 592, 21. Tealnie̅nde (tealtriende?, tealtiende?) *nutantes*, Ps. Lamb. 108, 10. [v. Skeat's Dict. s.v. *totter.*] v. preceding word.

teám, es; *m. A line*; but the word which is used in the related dialects (v. *infra*) with a physical meaning is used in English figuratively. I. *a line* of descendants, *offspring, progeny, family, children*:—Nán wer ne wífaþ, ne wíf ne ceorlaþ, ne teám ne biþ getýmed *children are not brought forth*, Homl. Th. i. 238, 1. Seó gelaþung is úre ealra módor . . . hire teám nis ná líchamlíc ac gástlíc, 492, 8: Homl. Skt. i. 20, 9. Wuenumon and hire teám, Moruiw and hire teám and Wurgustel and his teám wuárun gefreód . . . Marh gefreóde Leðelt and ealle hire teám, Chart. Th. 626, 22-37. Ðæs teámes wæs tuddor gefylled unlytel dǽl eorðan gesceafta, Cd. Th. 97, 15; Gen. 1613. Berende in teáme *fecunda in sobole*,

Rtl. 110, 7. Hē Noe bearh and his wīfe and his teáme, Gen. 5, 31 note: Homl. Skt. i. 8, 18. Caines ofspring forwearð ādrenced on ðam deópan flōde . . . and of ðam yfelan teáme ne com nān þing siððan, Ælfc. T. Grn. 3, 27. Sēd ł teám *semen*, Mk. Skt. Lind. 12, 21, 22. Ðæt folc tȳmde micelne teám on ðam wēstene, Homl. Th. ii. 212, 17. Teám gestrȳnan, 324, 11. Ðreó wīteþeówe men mē salde bisceop and hire teám, Chart. Th. 152, 22. Fyllaþ eówre fromcynne foldan sceátas, teámum and tūdre, Cd. Th. 92, 27; Gen. 1535. ¶ of animals:—Beón tȳmaþ heora teám mid clǣnnysse, Homl. Th. ii. 10, 17. [Weóx swa Adames team her, ne mahte hit na mon tellen, Jul. 61, 7. Drauh togedere al þene team under þe moder, A. R. 336, 15. Wurrþenn wiþþ childe, and tæmenn hire tæm, Orm. 2415. Ys foure sones . . . þys was a stalwarde tem, R. Glouc. 261, 4.] **I a.** *bringing forth* children, *child-bearing*:—Ðonne wīf byþ teámes ætealdod, Homl. Ass. 20, 159. His wīf wearð mid Esau and Iacob, and heó geswāc ðā teámes, 38, 339. [Weren boðe (*John's parents*) teames ateald, O. E. Homl. ii. 133, 32.] **II.** *a line* of animals harnessed together, *a team*:—Oxa on ðam forman teáme (cf. oxa on frumteáme *imus*, ii. 48, 36) *imus*, on ðam æfteran teáme *binus* (*bimus*), Wrt. Voc. i. 23, 47, 48. On ðæm æftran teáme *bimus*, ii. 12, 70. v. feoþer-tīme, iuc-tīma, ge-tȳme. The old pictures represent the plough as drawn by two pairs of oxen one behind the other. Cf. My plowman . . . a teme (teome, MS. C.) shal he haue. Grace gaue Piers a teme, foure gret oxen, Piers P. B. 19, 256. **III.** as a legal term, (1) *vouching to warranty*. The word denotes one step in the proceedings of a suit for the recovery of property, which was found in one man's possession and claimed by another, who alleged that it had been stolen or had strayed from him. The peculiar character of the process to which it refers was determined by the formalities insisted upon by the law when property changed hands. At such a transaction the presence of witnesses was necessary (L. Ed. 1; Th. i. 158, 11: L. Edg. H. 4; Th. i. 258, 22: L. Edm. C. 5; Th. i. 253, 8: L. C. S. 23; Th. i. 388, 21: 24; Th. i. 390, 4), and one responsible person (*geteáma*), who according to Ine's laws must not be a *þeów man* (L. In. 47; Th. i. 132, 5), was to be fixed upon as representing the party that made the sale or transfer, and to him, if a question subsequently arose as to ownership, the new owner might refer (*tīman*) in support of his right; this referring the property to the party who had sold it was *teám*. In cases of undivided ownership the *geteáma* would be the person making the sale; in cases of joint ownership one of the parties would be taken. The proceedings in a suit in which *teám* was resorted to seem to have been somewhat as follows. The plaintiff, who made claim to property on the plea that it had been stolen from him, had to give security that he would carry on his case: Warige hine, se ðe his āgen befōþ, ðæt hē tō ǣlcan teáme hæbbe getrȳwne borh, L. Eth. ii. 9; Th. i. 290, 6: Wil. I. 21; Th. i. 477, 11; the defendant had to declare how the property came into his hands, and to give security that he would produce his *geteáma* in court: Gif hwā befō ðæt him losod wæs, cenne se ðe hē hit æt befō hwanon hit him cōme, sylle on hand and sette borh (*pledge himself and find security*) ðæt hē bringe his geteáman in ðǣr hit bespreceu biþ, L. Eth. ii. 8; Th. i. 288, 15. On the case being brought into court (which was to be held in *cynges sele*, L. H. E. 7; Th. i. 30, 18: 16; Th. i. 34, 7, or *kyninges burh*: Ælc teám beó on ðæs kyninges byrig, L. Eth. iii. 6; Th. i. 296, 4), the plaintiff made oath, that he prosecuted his suit lawfully and fairly, L. O. 2; Th. i. 178, 10, and without malice, 4; Th. i. 180, 8; the defendant on his side made oath that he had had no part in the alleged robbery, but had acquired the property in a lawful manner, 3; Th. i. 178, 16, and was guiltless, 5; Th. i. 180, 14. He was now bound to produce witnesses of the transaction which resulted in his acquiring the property in dispute, or *teám* was denied him: Būton hē ðara ōðer (*certain witness*) hæbbe, nele him mon nǣnne teám geþafian, L. Edg. H. 4; Th. i. 260, 2. Ne beó ǣnig man ǣniges teámes wyrðe būton hē getrȳwe gewitnysse hæbbe, L. C. S. 23; Th. i. 388, 20. Ne beó ðǣr nān teám, 24; Th. i. 390, 6. If the witness was forthcoming, the *geteáma* had to be produced, and witness or oath again was called for to prove that the defendant's proceedings were correct: Wē cwǣdon, se ðe tȳman scolde, ðæt hē hæfde ungeligene gewitnesse ðæs ðæt hē hit on riht tȳmde, oþþe ðone āð funde ðe se gelȳfan mihte ðe on sprece, L. Ed. 1; Th. i. 158, 16. If the *geteáma*, though living, were not brought, according to one regulation the defendant lost his case, and had to resign the property, L. H. E. 7; Th. i. 30, 9; according to another, if he could bring witness to prove the sale, he received the price of the property he had to give up, 16; Th. i. 34, 8. If the *geteáma* were dead other formalities were prescribed, L. In. 53; Th. i. 134, 17: L. Eth. ii. 9; Th. i. 290, 9. If all the requirements had been satisfied the property in question was handed over to the *geteáma*: Se ðe yrfe bycge on gewitnesse, and hit eft tȳman scyle, ðonne onfō se his ðe hē hit ǣr æt bohte, L. Ath. i. 24; Th. i. 212, 12. Swā ic hit tȳme swā hit mē se sealde ðe ic hit nū on hand sette, L. O. 3; Th. i. 180, 3: L. Eth. ii. 8; Th. i. 288, 20; and the defendant thereupon appealed to the *geteáma* to corroborate his statement of the case, 21. If the latter accepted the property, the former was cleared, and the *geteáma* himself was now in a similar position to that in which the defendant had stood, 22; but if he declined to receive it, and declared that it was not the property he had sold, then the defendant had to prove that it was: Gif se mon (*the geteáma*) onfōn ne wille, and sægþ ðæt hē him nǣfre ðæt (*the property*) ne sealde, ac sealde ōðer, ðonne mōt se gecȳðan, se ðe hit tiémþ, ðæt hē him nān ōðer ne sealde būton ðæt ilce, L. In. 75; Th. i. 150, 7: cf. 35; Th. i. 124, 10. If however the case were not stopped, the process, in earlier times, was repeated until either there was a failure to produce a *geteáma* (v. teám-byrst), or the property was traced to some person whose right to its possession was undoubted: Gange se teám forð ōþþæt man wite hwǣr hē ōðstande, L. Ed. 1; Th. i. 158, 15: L. Eth. ii. 9; Th. i. 290, 3. Betweox teáme gif hwā tō fēhþ, and nā furðor teám ne cenþ, ac āgnian wile, ne mæg mon ðæs wyrnan, gif getrȳwe gewitnes him tō āgenunge rȳmþ, 290, 18. Later *teám* was necessary only three times: Tȳme hit man þrywa, æt ðam feórðan cyrre āgnige hit, odðe āgyfe ðam ðe hit āge, L. C. S. 24; Th. i. 390, 9. At one time also a change was made in the place where *teám* should be made: Be teámum. Hwilon stōd ðæt man sceolde þrywa tȳman ðǣr hit ǣrest befangen wǣre, and syþþan fylgean teáme swā hwǣr swā man tō cende. Ðā gerǣddan witan, ðæt hit betere wǣre, ðæt man ǣure tȳmde ðǣr hit ǣrest befangen wǣre . . . ðȳ læs ðe mon unmihtigne man tō feor and tō lange for his āgenan swencte, L. Eth. ii. 9; Th. i. 288, 28. A case in which a defendant is cleared by his *geteáma*, who, however, cannot get himself cleared, is given Chart. Th. 206, 19 sqq. A woman had been stolen, and was found in the possession of one Wulfstan. Ðā tȳmde Wulfstān hine (*the woman*) tō Æðelstāne; ðā cende hē tēm and lēt ðone forberstan. v. teám-byrst. Another case is mentioned where a bishop was not allowed *teám*: Ne mōste se bisceop beón ðara þreora nānes wyrðe ðe eallum leódscipe geseald wæs on wedde, tale, ne teámes, ne āhnunga, 266, 11. (2) The word also occurs often in charters along with *sac*, *sōc*, *toll*, etc., where according to one definition it refers to the right to the forfeitures which were made in the suits where *teám* was resorted to: Theam, quod si aliquis aliquid interciebatur super aliquem, et ipse non poterat warrantum suum habere, erit forisfactura, et justicia similiter de calumpniatore, si deficiebat, sua erit, L. Ed. C. 22; Th. i. 452, 1. Donavi abbati . . . consuetudinem que dicitur teames, Chart. Th. 405, 1. v. teám-byrst. A different meaning is given elsewhere to the word. In Cod. Dip. Kmbl. iv. 202, 7 *teám* occurs, and in the Latin form of the charter is rendered by 'privilegium habendi totam suorum seruorum propaginem,' 203, 6. [*O. Frs.* tām *a bridle; a line of descendants, progeny, family*: *O. L. Ger.* tōm *frenum*: *Du.* toom: *O. H. Ger.* zoum *funis, habena*: *Icel.* taumr *bridle, rein, cord.*] v. bearn-, frum- (v. II above), here-, leger-teám; tīman.

teáman. v. tīman.

teám-byrst, es; *m. The failure to produce a* geteáma *in a suit.* v. teám, III. 1:—Ðā tȳmde Wulfstān hine (*the stolen slave about whom the case had arisen*) tō Æðelstāne; ða cende hē tēm and lēt ðone forberstan (*he admitted having sold the slave to Wulfstan, but would not declare from whom he had obtained it*) . . . Ðā bæd Byrhferhð ealdormann Æðelstān his wer for ðam tēmbyrste, Chart. Th. 207, 4.

teám-full; *adj. Prolific, productive*:—Tudderfulle, teámfulle *fetose*, Wrt. Voc. ii. 148, 33. Sceáp heora teámfulle ł berende *oues eorum foetosae*, Ps. Lamb. 143, 13: Ps. Spl. 143, 17.

teám-pōl, es; *m. A breeding-pool*:—Up on Exan on ðone neáran teámpōl; ðanon up on Exan; ðonne of Exa[n] on ða smala[n] lace; of ðære lace eft on Exa[n]; ðanon up and lang Exa[n] on ðone uferan teámpōl, Cod. Dip. Kmbl. ii. 205, 8–11: iii. 441, 5–8.

teān (?), tēgan (?); *p.* tēde *To grow tough* or *pliant*:—Tēdan *lentescunt*, Wrt. Voc. ii. 52, 57: 92, 77. v. tōan, tōh; *see also* (?)ge-teágan.

teán-, teaper, teappa. v. teón-, tapor, tappa.

teár (= teahor), teór, tæher, teher, tehher, es; *m. A tear.* **I.** *a drop of water from the eye*, (1) caused by emotion, generally by grief:—Teár *flemen, flentium humor*, Wülck. Gl. 240, 13: *lacryma*, Wrt. Voc. i. 43, 7. Teáras *lacrime*, 282, 55. Sealtes pund, ðanon him (*Adam*) wǣron ða teáras sealte, Salm. Kmbl. 180, 16. Hruron him teáras, Beo. Th. 3749; B. 1872. Nalles for torne teáras feóllon, Elen. Kmbl. 2266; El. 1134. Pund saltes, of ðon sindon salto tehero, Rtl. 192, 15. Mid teára āgotennysse, Lchdm. iii. 428, 10. Mid teára gytum, Blickl. Homl. 61, 20. Eágan gefyllede mid teárum, 189, 1. Wēpende mid teárum, 151, 20: Bd. 3, 14; S. 541, 3. Teárum mǣnan, Exon. Th. 285, 10; Jul. 285. Teárum geótan, 95, 34; Cri. 1567. Heó ongan mid hyre teárum (tæherum ł teárum, Lind.) hys fēt þweán, Lk. Skt. 7, 38. Teárum ł tehrum, Lind. 7, 44. Mið teherum (teórum, Rush.), Mk. Skt. Lind. 9, 24. Wēpende wēregum teárum, Andr. Kmbl. 118; An. 59. Wrāðum teárum, Ps. Th. 59, 11. Tornlīcum teárum, 125, 5. Sārige teáras, 55, 7. Teáras geótan *to shed tears*, Bd. 4, 28; S. 606, 14: Exon. Th. 11, 18; Cri. 173. (1 a) in plural, used for the feeling of which the tears are a sign, *grief, affliction*:—On deópnysse wōpes and teóra *profunditate fletus et lacrimarum*, Scint. 47, 4. Ðū fēdest ūs teára hlāfe, and ūs drincan gifest deorcum teárum, Ps. Th. 79, 5. Heó is fulneáh deád for teárum and for unrōtnesse, Bt. 19; Fox 28, 30. Eua bær teáras on hire innoþe, Maria brohte ðone ēcean gefeán eallum middangearde,

Blickl. Homl. 3, 12. Tehhero, Rtl. 40, 35. (2) caused by weakness. v. tīran:—Ðeós eáhsealf mæg wiþ ǽlces cynnes broc on eágon . . . wiþ tēr, Lchdm. iii. 292, 2. Lǽcedōmas wiđ eallum tiédernessum eágena . . . wiđ eágna teárum, ii. 2, 8. Wiđ eágena teára (-e, -as?), iii. 44, 29. II. *a tearlike drop*:—Ðā wearđ beám monig blōdigum teárum birunnen . . . sæp wearđ tō swāte, Exon. Th. 72, 20; Cri. 1175. IIa. *that which drops* or *exudes*, e. g. honey from a comb:—Balsames teár *opobalsamum*, Wrt. Voc. i. 33, 51. Swā þicce swā huniges teár *of the consistency of honey that has dropped from the comb*, Lchdm. ii. 74, 4. Genim balsami and huniges teáres emmicel, 28, 10, 4: 108, 17. Gegadriende swā swā beón hunigcamb teáres *colligentes uti apes favu[m] nectaris*, Anglia xiii. 368, 46. Þynceþ þegna gehwylcum huniges bībreád healfe đȳ swētre, gif hē hwēne ǽr huniges teáre bitres onbyrgeþ, Met. 12, 10. Meng wiđ huniges teáre, Lchdm. iii. 46, 7. Nim huniges teár and merces sǽd . . . mæng wiđ đone teár, 4, 16. [*O. Frs.* tār: *O. H. Ger.* zaher: *Icel.* tār; *n.*] v. bryne-, hunig-teár; teagor.

-teáren. v. hunig-teáren.

tearflian; *p.* ode *To wallow, roll over*:—On eorđan forgnyden fǽmende hē tearflode (terflede, teorflede, later MSS.) *elisus in terram uolutabatur spumans*, Mk. Skt. 9, 20. [Cf. Þe riȝt schul ryse to ryche reynynge, Truyt and treget to helle schal terve, L. H. R. 207, 311. *O. H. Ger.* zerben (sih) *to turn.*]

teár-geótende; *adj.* (*ptcpl.*) *Tear-shedding, weeping*:—Adam myd teárg[e]ótendre hālsunge and myd mycelre stefne đus cwæþ, Nicod. 30; Thw. 17, 27.

teárian; *p.* ode *To shed tears*:—Tæherende (teherende, Rush.) wæs se Hǽlend *lacrimatus est Jesus*, Jn. Skt. Lind. ii. 35. [*Icel.* tārask *to shed tears.*]

teárig; *adj.* I. *tearful, weeping*:—Teárigum sīcetungum *lacrimosis singultibus*, Hpt. Gl. 421, 3. v. teár, I. 1. II. *watery, watering* (*of the eyes*):—Gif mon biþ on wæterælfādle, đonne beóþ him đa eágan teárige, Lchdm. ii. 350, 22. v. teár, I. 2, tīran.

teárig-hleór; *adj. Having the cheeks wet with tears*:—Ic (*Hagar*) sceal teárighleór on wēstenne witodes bīdan, Cd. Th. 137, 16; Gen. 2274. [Cf. *Icel.* tārug-hlȳra *with tearful cheeks.*]

teár-līc, tearo. v. hunig-teárlīc, teoru.

teart; *adj. Tart, sharp* (of pain, punishment, etc.), *severe*; acer, asper:—Sticol ođđe teart *asper*, Wulck. Gl. 256, 32. Ūs đincþ swīđe teart wīte đæt ān ūre fingra on fȳr becume, Homl. Th. ii. 590, 32. Ðæt hē ne đurfe becuman tō đam teartum bryne, 592, 17. Hē ālȳsþ mē fram teartum worde (*a uerbo aspero*), Ps. Lamb. 90, 3. Beó him gesǽd đa teartan wītu, Homl. Th. ii. 344, 32: Homl. Skt. i. 11, 82. Mid teartum wītum getintregod, 8, 156. Mid teartum swingellum *acribus uerberibus*, R. Ben. 54, 4. Mislimp tearte *casus asperos*, Hymn. Surt. 16, 5. Teartere þrǽiung *acrior correptio*, R. Ben. Interl. 59, 6. Hine man þreáge mid teartran steóre, R. Ben. 52, 6. Hē stīđran and teartran steóre underfō *majori uindicte subjaceat*, 71, 8. [Chaucer uses *tart* = sharp to the taste:—Poudre-marchaunt tart, Prol. 381.]

teart-līc; *adj. Sharp, severe*:—Þeáh hwæt teartlīccs on đisum regule geset sȳ, R. Ben. 5, 11.

teartlīce; *adv. Sharply, severely*:—Teartlīce *acriter*, Hpt. Gl. 477, 13: 507, 53. Hē đē tintregaþ teartlīce on wītum, Homl. Skt. ii. 25, 154. Hē beó teartlīce geswungen, Wulfst. 248, 13. Teartlīcer *acrius*, Hpt. Gl. 515, 47. Teartlīcur, Scint. 210, 12. Wē beóþ forswǽlede teartlīcor *crememur acrius*, Hymn. Surt. 5, 15: Homl. Th. i. 330, 34. Sȳ hē ealra teartlīcost geþreád *acrius coherceatur*, R. Ben. 129, 10.

teartness, e; *f. Sharpness, severity, asperity*:—Drihten herede Iohannem for đære teartnysse his reáfes, forđan đe hē wæs mid olfendes hǽrum gescrȳd wāclīce and stīđlīce, Homl. Th. i. 330, 1. For đæs wyntres teartnysse, Homl. Skt. i. 11, 152. Teartnesse *acerbitatem, crudelitatem*, Hpt. Gl. 480, 56. Mid menigfealdum đeówracena teartnyssum gebrēgede, Homl. Th. i. 578, 27.

teart-numol; *adj. Efficacious*:—Ðeós wyrt is swȳþe scearpnumul (teart-, MS. B.) wiđ đæt āttor, Lchdm. i. 152, 3. v. scearp-numol.

teáslīce, -teáw, tebl, teblere, tebl-stān, tēder-, tēdre, te-flōwan, tēfrung, tēgan, tēge, teging *tinctura*, tegđian, tegđung, teher, teherian, teigđa, teigđian, teissum, tel. v. tǽslīce, æl-, eal-teáw, tæfl, tæflere, tæfl-stān, tīder-, tīdre, tō-flōwan, tīfrung, teán, teáh, telgung, teóþian, teóþung, teár, tīran, teóþa, teóþian, teosu, tæl.

tela, teala, teola, telo, tiolo; *adv. Well.* I. *well, rightly, aright, correctly*:—Hē hine sceal nīde tela lǽran. Ðȳ him is micel đearf đonne hē tela lǽrþ đæt hē eác tela doo *dum commissis sibi cogitur bona dicere, ipsum prius necesse est, quae dixerit, custodire*, Past. 28, 3; Swt. 193, 12. Teala, Blickl. Homl. 75, 14. Ða slāwan sint tō manianne đæt hié ne forielden đone tīman for hiera slǽwđe đe hié tela (tiola, Hatt. MS.) on dōn mǽgen *pigri suadendi sunt, ne agenda bona, dum differunt, amittant*, Past. 39, 1; Swt. 280, 20. Gif hī đone frȳdōm tela gehealdon . . . gif hī đone frȳdōm forheólden, Bt. 41, 3; Fox 208, 10. Hē rīce geheóld tela, Beo. Th. 4423; B. 2208: 5468; B. 2737. Teala, Cd. Th. 74, 35; Gen. 1232. Lǽst eall tela, Beo. Th. 5320; B. 2663. Nū ic wāt tela and ic onfēng gewit mīnes mōdes *modo sanum sapio, recepi enim sensum animi mei*, Bd. 3, 11; S. 536, 33. 'Geseoh đæt đū teala wite.' Cwæþ hē: 'Ne wēde ic' '*vide ut sanum sapias.*' '*Non,*' *inquit*, '*insanio,*' 5, 13; S. 632, 32. Ðæt ic teala cunne đīn weorc healdan, Ps. Th. 118, 68: Exon. Th. 336, 10; Gn. Ex. 46. Is wuldres leóht ontȳned đam đe teala þenceþ, Cd. Th. 299, 29; Sat. 557: Exon. Th. 347, 30; Sch. 20. Gif gē teala hycgaþ, Andr. Kembl. 3223; An. 1614. Beó nū on yfele, noldæs ǽr teala, Cd. Th. 310, 26; Sat. 733. Teala foresecgan, Ps. Th. 118, 172. Tela, Exon. Th. 432, 19; Rä. 49, 2. II. *well, perfectly, completely, thoroughly, certainly*:—Heald forđ tela sibbe *continue without interruption to maintain peace*, Beo. Th. 1901; B. 948. Wudufuglas tela ātemede, Met. 13, 36. Ic đē teala forgulde ealle đa gehāt, Ps. Th. 65, 13. Ðǽr đū mē teala hǽle, 70, 2. Se đe teala cūþe, Exon. Th. 349, 9; Sch. 43. Ic his bīdan ne dear . . . nele đæt rǽd teale *I dare not await him* . . . *good counsel certainly will not require that*, 397, 8; Rä. 16, 16. III. *well, prosperously, happily*:—Geþeóh tela, Beo. Th. 2441; B. 1218. Ðū hulpe mīn đæt ic teala mihte, Ps. Th. 70, 20. Hē hēt đæt teala wunian ēce, 77, 68. Ǽfter đæm Cartainenses wunnon on Sicilie đǽr him seldon teola gespeów *cum adsidua nec umquam satis prospera adversus Siculos bella gererent*, Ors. 4, 5; Swt. 168, 20. IV. *well, in a beneficial* or *pleasant manner*:—Wē wǽron hēr tela willum bewenede, Beo. Th. 3645; B. 1820. Ontȳn đīnne mūđ, and ic hine teala fylle, Ps. Th. 80, 11: 105, 5. Gif wē willaþ ōþrum geleáffullum teala dōn and helpan đæs earman, Blickl. Homl. 75, 18: 69, 17. Tala, Lk. Skt. 6, 27. V. marking degree, *very, to a great extent*:—Ic þigde tela micelne mete, Nar. 30, 25. Drincan tela micel, Lchdm. ii. 290, 12. Tela micel steáp, 294, 19. Teala, i. 374, 9. Teala līciendlīc, Ps. Th. 68, 13. Teala wynsume, 125, 2. Ðā wæs tiolo micel sprēc, Chart. Th. 70, 17. Ic đē an tela sincgestreóna *I give thee treasures in abundance*, Beo. Th. 2455; B. 1225. VI. as an exclamation, *well, good*:—Ðā andswaredon hī: 'Nis hit lang tō đon.' Cwæþ hē: 'Tela, utan wē đære tīde bīdan,' Bd. 4, 24; S. 599, 5. Cwæþ ic: 'Hwī ne sceolde mē swā đincan?' Ðā cwæþ hē: 'Telo; đonne đæt đē swā þincþ, đonne ongit đæt . . ., Bt. 38, 3; Fox 200, 22. v. un-tela; til; *and* cf. wel *for similar uses.*

tēlan. v. tǽlan.

teld, es; *n. A tent, pavilion*; left still in *tilt* of a cart:—On đam telde (*tabernaculo*) heó ys, Gen. 18, 9. Eardungstōwa ł teld his *tabernaculum ejus*, Ps. Spl. 17, 13. Mon teld (geteld, MS. B.) đǽrofer ābrǽdde (*tentorio majore extenso*), Bd. 3, 11; S. 535, 22. [And Alfrīc biscop I biqueđe mīne teld and mīn bedreáf þat ic best hauede ūt on mī fare mid mē, Chart. Th. 566, 32.] [Þer Oswald sette his teld, Laym. 31384. Hengest bilæfde al his teld (hii lete stonde hire teldes, 2nd MS.), 16462. In here teld (on heora geteldum, Num. 16, 27) he (*Dathan and Abiram*) stonden, Gen. and Ex. 3769. Telte or tente *tentorium*, Prompt. Parv. 488. *O. H. Ger.* zelt; *n. papillio*: *Ger.* zelt; *n.*: *Icel.* tjald; *n. a tent*: *Dan.* telt; *n.*] v. ge-teld.

teldan; *p.* teald, *pl.* tuldon; *pp.* tolden *To spread a covering.* v. beofer-teldan; teldian.

telde *a tent-peg*:—*Claus* (= *clavus*) *lignum tentorii vel* telde, Wrt. Voc. ii. 131, 56. v. teld-sticca, -treów.

teldian; *p.* ode, ede *To spread* (a tent, an awning, a net, a snare, etc.):—Teldat *conectit*, Wrt. Voc. ii. 105, 35: 15, 36. Hī teldedon gryne and đa gehȳddon *absconderunt mihi interitum laquei sui*, Ps. Th. 34, 8. [Þenne mon wule tilden his musestoch, O. E. Homl. i. 53, 20. At pleȝe he (*the devil*) telded þe grune of idelnesse . . . on þe grune þe þe werse haued itelded . . . Drinch, þere telded þe werse þe grune of unrihte, ii. 211, 13–27. Tristre is þer me sit, oder tilded þe nettes, A. R. 334, 1. Weoren teldes itælded, Laym. 17489. Fantummes of fendes (*idols*) telded on lofte, Allit. Pms. 78, 1342. Sone watȝ telded up a tapit on treste ȝ ful fayre, Gaw. 884. Þei tildeden Absalon a tabernacle (*they spread Absalom a tent*, 2 Sam. 16, 22), Wick. A green an other hath for hem ytilde, Pall. 110, 164. *Icel.* tjalda *to spread a tent, to cover with an awning, stretch a covering over.*] v. teldan.

teld-sele (?) *a tent*:—Ganggeteld *papilio*, tyldsyle *tenda*, Wrt. Voc. i. 59, 12–13.

teld-sticca, an; *m. A tent-peg*:—Gelǽhte seó wīfman ān đæra teldsticcena geslōh đā . . . đæt se sticca him eode ūt þurh đæt heáfod . . . Hē geseah hwār Sisara læg and se teldsticca sticode þurh his heáfod *tulit Iahel clavum tabernaculi . . . et clavum defixit in cerebrum . . . vidit Sisaram jacentem et clavum infixum in tempore ejus*, Jud. 4, 21, 22. [*O. H. Ger.* zelt-steccho *paxillus.* Cf. *Icel.* tjalds-nagli *a tent-peg.*]

teld-treów (?), es; *n. A tent-peg* (?), *some implement in weaving*:—Teltreó *clus*, Wrt. Voc. ii. 104, 19. Teltrē *claus*, 16, 34: i. 282, 10. In the last instance the word occurs in a list *de textrinalibus.* v. telde, tæbere.

teld-wyrhta, an; *m. A tent-maker*:—Paulus se đe wæs on woruldcræfte teldwyrhta, Homl. Th. i. 392, 21.

tēlend, tēlere. v. tǽlend, tǽlere.

telg, tælg, es; *m. A dye*:—Taelg *faex, fucus*, Wrt. Voc. ii. 109, 36: 39, 3 (the entry is given, *fuscus* tægl ođđe feax). Telg, deág *fucus*, telga *fucorum*, 36, 66, 67: 70, 19: 151, 52. Se weolocreáda tælhg (tægl, MS. C.) *tinctura coccinei coloris*, Bd. 1, 1; S. 473, 20. Se reáda telg, Exon. Th. 408, 21; Rä. 27, 15. Telges *conquilii*, Wrt. Voc. ii. 19, 15. Telge *murice*, 57, 50: *ostro*, 64, 37: 87, 10. Telga *fucorum*, 88, 43. Ðætte Iosephes tunece wǽre telga gehwylces bleóm bregdende, Exon. Th. 357, 2; Pa. 22. v. æt-, beám-, weoloc-telg; telgan.

telga, an; *m. A branch, bough*, (a) literal:—Telge *ramus*, Mt. Kmbl. Lind. 24, 32: Mk. Skt. Lind. 13, 28. Telgan *fronde*, Wrt. Voc. ii. 33, 60. Telgan *virgultum*, i. 39, 17. Unberende telgan *spadones*, 38, 8. Telgan gehladene, Exon. Th. 202, 28; Ph. 76. Telgu *rami*, Mk. Skt. Rush. 13, 28. Telgena *palmitum*, Wrt. Voc. ii. 66, 34. Telgum gescafenum *corticibus*, Hpt. Gl. 412, 41. Balzamum of ðæra treówa telgan (*ramis*) weól, Nar. 26, 21. Blǽda on treówes telgum, Cd. Th. 55, 10; Gen. 892: 88, 24; Gen. 1470: Exon. Th. 210, 19; Ph. 188. Beorc byþ on telgum wlitig, Runic pm. Kmbl. 342, 30; Rūn. 18: Ps. Th. 57, 8: 103, 16. Telgo *frondes*, Mk. Skt. Lind. 11, 8: *ramos*, 4, 32. Genim ðysse wyrte (*yarrow*) telgan, Lchdm. i. 198, 12 note. ¶ In the following passage Kemble and Leo take the word as meaning a strip of land (fallow), but as such a strip of land if fallow one year would not be so the next, its designation as the fallow strip would hardly serve the purpose of marking a boundary. *Telga* might rather refer to a branch distinguishable from the loss of its bark:—Andlang strǽte on ðone calewan telgan, Cod. Dip. Kmbl. i. 258, 7. See iii. xxxix, and Leo, Place Names, p. 66. (b) figurative:—Hē bær ða wǽtan ðære uncyste in ðæm telgan, ðone hē geteáh ǽr of ðan wyrtruman, Bd. 1, 27; M. 82, 14. Wrōhtes telgan, Cd. Th. 61, 3; Gen. 991. Ealle ða telgan ðū gebrǽddest *extendisti palmites ejus*, Ps. Th. 79, 11. Telgo mīno *ramos meos*, Rtl. 68, 32. v. wudu-telga; telgor, telgra.

telgan *to dye* [:—Getelged oððe gedeágod *colerata*, Wrt. Voc. ii. 19, 14. Getelgode *fucate*, getelgod *fucatum*, 33, 58, 59. Getælged *colerata, fucata*, 134, 35.] v. twi-telged; telgung.

telg-berend *that which produces a dye*:—Tæl(g)berend *ostriger*, Wrt. Voc. ii. 64, 72. v. telg.

telge (?):—On xiiii nihte mōnan is gōd ǽlc telge tō anginnanne, Lchdm. iii. 178, 31. Cockayne refers the word to *telg* and translates *dyeing*; but the passage at 190, 21, in which the same date is said to be 'eallum gōd þingum gōd' suggests a different meaning. The forms of the whole piece are corrupt.

telgian; *p.* ode *To put forth shoots, to flourish*:—Treów telgade tīr welgade *good faith flourished, glory abounded*, Exon. Th. 353, 57; Reim. 34.

telgor, tealgor, es; *m.*: e; *f. A plant, shoot, twig*:—On ðam dæge ðe God geworhte ǽlcne telgor on eorðan (*omne virgultum agri*), Gen. 2, 5. Telgre *vimen*, Engl. Stud. xi. 67, 95. Gif hwā mid him ðysse wyrte (*verbascum*) āne tealgre byrþ, ne biþ hē brēged mid ǽnigum ōgan, Lchdm. ii. 176, 3. Tealgras *propagines*, Blickl. Gl. Ðeós wyrt (*wild gourd*) wið ða eorðan hyre telgra tōbrǽdeþ, Lchdm. i. 324, 3 note. [*Icel.* tjálgr; *n. a prong*.] v. next word.

telgra, an; *m. A shoot, branch, twig; sucker of a root*:—Telgra *virgultum*, Wrt. Voc. i. 80, 4. Telgra *ramus* (*fici*), Mt. Kmbl. Rush. 24, 32. Dō on āne telgran (morbeámes), Lchdm. i. 332, 22. Of ānum stelan manega telgran weaxaþ, 276, 22. Ða telgran (ðæs wyrttruman), 318, 10. Telegran *antes, virgultus*, Hpt. Gl. 496, 71. Telgrum *viminibus, virgulis*, 483, 58: *ramis*, Mt. Kmbl. Rush. 13, 32. Telgran *ramos*, 21, 8: *surculos, virgulta*, Hpt. Gl. 433, 47. Genim ðysse wyrte (*yarrow*) telgran, Lchdm. i. 198, 12. Ðeós wyrt (*polium*) of ānum wyrttruman manega telgran āsendeþ, 276, 8. Ðeós wyrt (*wild gourd*) wið ða eorðan hyre telgran tōbrǽdeþ, 324, 3.

telgung, e; *f. Dyeing*, or *a dye*:—Te[l]ging *tinctura* (cf. deáh *tinctura*, 40, 39), Wrt. Voc. i. 32, 8. Telgung *tinctorium*, 289, 13. Telgunge *tinctura*, ii. 89, 28.

tellan; *p.* tealde; pp. teald: *also forms as from* telian *occur*: ic telge, hī teliaþ; *p.* telede; *p.* teled. I. *to tell, narrate, recount, state* a case:—Þeáh ic hit lengre telle *though I make my story longer*, Chr. 1085; Erl. 218, 31. Dō ðæs leán tō ðām foresprecenan gōdum ðe ic ðē ǽr tealde on ðriddan bēc, Bt. 37, 2; Fox 190, 2. Se sunderhālga tealde his gōdan dǽda, swilce God hī nyste, Homl. Th. ii. 428, 18. Swegen tealde ðæt his sciperes woldon wændon fram him *Swegen told* (*Beorn*) *that his* (*Swegen's*) *men would desert him* (*Swegen*), Chr. 1046; Erl. 174, 13. Dauid tealde his ungelimp, and hū hē hine gebæd tō Gode, Ps. Th. 34, arg. Ða ungewiderunge ðe cōmon swā wē beforan tealdon, Chr. 1086; Erl. 219, 33. Hī tealdon him (*Constantine*) ða þrowunga ðe ūre Hǽlend ðrowode, H. R. 5, 21. Telle (*narrės*) dīnum suna hū oft ic hæbbe fordōn ða Egiptiscan, Ex. 10, 2. Ute nū tellan (*let us state the case*) beforan swilcum dēman swilce ðū wille *quovis judice contende*, Bt. 7, 3; Fox 20, 6. Ūs sceamaþ hit nū māre tō tellanne *we are ashamed to tell any more of the matter*, Chr. 1050; Erl. 175, 39: 1085; Erl. 218, 35. II. *to tell, count, reckon, compute, calculate*:—Hē teleþ (*computat*) ða andfengas ðe hine behēfe synt, Lk. Skt. 14, 28. Hē ne telþ hū miccle spēda wē āspendon, Homl. Th. i. 580, 17. Se lāreów Bēda telþ mid micclum gesceáde ðæt se dæg is xii. KL. Aprilis, 100, 13. 'Telle (*numera*) ǽlcne wēpnedman' . . . Moises tealde (*numeravit*), Num. 3, 15, 16. Eallum ðe ðara cyninga tiide teledon *cunctis regum tempora computantibus*, Bd. 3; 1; M. 154, 10. Hī hluton, teledon *they cast lots and counted*, Andr. Kmbl. 2207; An. 1105. Tele nū ða lenge ðære hwīle, Bt. 18, 3; Fox 66, 6. Tele nū ða gesǽlþa wiþ ðām sorgum *strike a balance between the happiness and cares*, 8, tit.; Fox x, 22. Tele ðū ðæs mōnan elde kl. Ian. ōð ðæt ðū cume tō þrittiga; fōh eft on ðone nīwan, tele ōð tȳne *starting from Jan.* 1 *with the number that marks the age of the moon on that day, count up to thirty; begin then with the new moon, and count up to ten* (*the next Sunday after the date so reached will be Septuagesima Sunday*), Lchdm. iii. 226, 30–228, 2. Telle ðǽs steorran *numera stellas*, Gen. 15, 5: Num. 1, 2, 3. III. *to reckon, account, consider*, (a) with an object having a noun, adjective, or phrase in apposition, *to consider* a thing such and such:—Hwam telle ic (*aestimabo*) ðās cneórysse gelīce? Mt. Kmbl. 11, 16: Lk. Skt. 7, 31. Ic Heaþobeardna hyldo ne telge Denum unfǽcne, Beo. Th. 4141; B. 2067. Ǽgleáwra mann ðonne ic mē tælige, Andr. Kmbl. 2967; An. 1486. Cyn ðara ðe hȳ ānsetlan teliaþ, R. Ben. 135, 4. Ic ðæt wēnde and witod tealde, ðæt . . ., Exon. Th. 264, 1; Jul. 357. Ðone ic on firenum fæstne talde, Elen. Kmbl. 1815; El. 909. Ic mē ǽnigne . . . gesacan ne tealde, Beo. Th. 3551; B. 1773. Suā suā Saul ǽresð fleáh ðæt rīce and tealde hine selfne his suīðe unwierðne *sic Saul, qui indignum se prius considerans fugerat*, Past. 3; Swt. 35, 14: Bd. 3, 14; S. 539, 42: Beo. Th. 1592; B. 794: 3625; B. 1810. Gif se sacerd hine hreófligne tealde, Homl. Th. i. 124, 9. Hī hine oferhȳdigne tealdon *eum notantes superbiae*, Bd. 2, 2; S. 503, 16. Hine Geáta bearn gōdne ne tealdon, Beo. Th. 4375; B. 2184. Forcūþre is ðæt hē telle hine wīsne, Wulfst. 59, 5. Ne mæg heó ūs leáse tellan *mendacii arguere nos non potest*, Gen. 38, 23. Hine sylf ofer ealle men tellan, Chr. 1086; Erl. 222, 37. (b) with an object and prepositional phrase, *to consider* as (*tō, for, on*):—Ne telle ic eów tō ðeówan *non dico vos servos*, Jn. Skt. 15, 15. Wē ðæt sylfe sār and wīte hyre on synne tellaþ *ipsam ei poenam suam in culpam deputamus*, Bd. 1, 27; S. 493, 25. Hig tellaþ mīn wedd for nāht *irritum facient pactum meum*, Deut. 31, 20. Ic ðā geþeóde tō micclan gesceáde telede, Lchdm. iii. 442, 5. For nāhte hē tealde ǽnig ðing tō biddenne būton gesihðe, Homl. Th. i. 158, 21. On bōcum ðe ungelǽrede men þurh heora bilewitnysse tō micclum wīsdōme tealdon *in books which unlearned men in their simplicity have considered as great wisdom*, 2, 22. Ðonne on ūrum mōde biþ ācenned sum ðing gōdes, and wē ðæt tō weorce āwendaþ, ðonne sceole wē ðæt tellan tō Godes gyfe, and ðæt Gode betǽcan *consider it as God's grace, and attribute it to God*, 138, 23. Nis nū anweald tō tellanne tō sumum ðara hēhstēna gōda? . . . hwæðer nū gōd hlīsa sié for nāuht tō tellenne? Nis hit nān cyn, ðæt mon ðæt for nāuht telle, Bt. 24, 4; Fox 86, 14–19. Se untweofealda biþ tō tellenne for fullfremod weorc, 36, 7; Fox 184, 24. (c) with a clause:—Hē tealde and wēnde ðæt hē sceolde ða byldo his heortan ānescian *autumans se cordis ejus emollere constantiam*, Bd. 1, 7; S. 477, 43. Mid ðȳ hē tealde and hē wēnde ðæt hē sweltan sceolde *cum se aestimasset esse moriturum*, 3, 27; S. 558, 41: Cd. Th. 87, 3; Gen. 1443. Hū ne tealdan wit ðætte genyht wǽre gesǽlþa *nonne in beatitudine sufficientiam numeravimus?* Bt. 35, 3; Fox 158, 12. Swā ðætte monige tealdon (*putarent*), ðæt heó gehǽled beón mihte, Bd. 4, 19; S. 589, 3: Blickl. Homl. 117, 16. IV. *to impute* to (*dat.* or *prep.*), *ascribe, assign, put* a thing to a person's account:—Telle ic ða weorþmynd ðæm wyrhtan næs nā ðē *ingenium mirabor artificis*, Bt. 14, 1; Fox 42, 18. Crist tealde ealne his wurðmynt tō his Fæder, Homl. Th. ii. 366, 16. Se wer ðam ðe ne tealde (*imputavit*) Drihten synne, Ps. Lamb. 31, 2. Ðæt ilce gēr tō ðæs æfterfylgendan cyninges rīce teledon *idem annus sequentis regis regno adsignaretur*, Bd. 3, 1; M. 154, 12. Hī ealne ðone bryce uppon ðone cyng tealdon (cf. *O. Sax.* tellian an *to charge*; *Icel.* telja á: *see also* on-talu) *they put all the breach of faith upon the king*, Chr. 1094; Erl. 230, 4. Ne tele ðū him ðis synn *ne statuas illis hoc peccatum*, Rtl. 44, 15. Telle hē ðæt Gode, næs him sylfum, L. E. I. 21; Th. ii. 416, 18. His niéhstena gōd hē sceal tellan him selfum *he is to reckon as an item in the account of his own prosperity that of his neighbour*; sua commoda propinquorum bona deputare debet, Past. 13; Swt. 79, 1. Se fulla anweald is tō tellanne tō ðām hēhstum gōdum *complete power is to be assigned to the class of highest goods*, Bt. 36, 7; Fox 184, 9. [*O. Sax.* tellian: *O. Frs.* tella: *O. H. Ger.* zellen; *p.* zalta, zelita *numerare, computare, reputare, dicere, referre, narrare, notare, tribuere*: *Icel.* telja.] v. ā-, be-, ge-, tō-tellan; talian.

tēlnis, telo, teltrē, tēm, -tēma, tēman, -tēme, tēmen. v. tǽlness, tela, teld-treów, teám, -tīma, tīman, -tīme, tīmen.

Temes, Temese *the Thames*. In the declension both weak and strong forms are found. [In Latin, *nom.* Temis, Cod. Dip. Kmbl. i. 30, 12, Temes, ii. 23, 12: *gen.* Tamisae, i. 98, 1: *dat.* Taemise, 216, 25: *acc.* Tamesim Bd. 1, 2; S. 42, 34 may be cited]:—Neáh ðære ié ðe mon hǽt Temes (Temese, MS. C.) *ad flumen Tamesim*, Ors. 5, 12; Swt. 238, 22. Sȳ eá hātte Temese, Chr. Erl. 5, 11. Ymbe heora landgemǽra: andlang Temese (on Temese, 8), L. A. G. 1; Th. i. 152, 18. Ūt on Temese; ðonne ondlong Temese, Cod. Dip. Kmbl. iii. 438, 3–4. Fōron be Temese . . . be norþan Temese, Chr. 894; Erl. 92, 14, 20. Hī tugon hira scipu up on Temese, 895; Erl. 93, 31. Hī nāmon him wintersetl on Temesan and lifedon of Eást-Seaxum, 1009; Erl. 143, 4.

temes(-is), es; *m.* (? cf. lynis *for form and gender*) *A sieve.* [Temse *taratantarum*, Wrt. Voc. i. 200, col. 2 (15th cent.). Temze, temeze, temse, sive *setarium*, Prompt. Parv. 488. See also Halliwell, who quotes: 'Marcolphus toke a lytyll cyve or temse.' He gives, besides, '*temzer* a range or coarse searche' as an early Wiltshire word. Wright, in the note to the word in his Vocabulary, says that *temse* is still in use in the North of England. *O. Du.* tems. (The word seems to have been borrowed from a Teutonic source by French, which has *tamis* a sieve, *tamiser* to sift.) Cf. *O. H. Ger.* zemisa *furfures.*] v. next two words.

temesian, temsian *to sift*:—Hlāfo foregegearwad ł temised *panes propositionis* (cf. Tusser's Husbandry, 39, 10: 'Some mixeth the rie with the wheat *Temmes* lofe on his table to haue for to eate.' In such a loaf the coarse bran only is removed. v. Glossary. *Temse-bread* is given in Ray's South and East-Country Words, E. D. S. Pub. B. 16), Mk. Skt. Lind. 2, 26. [Temzyn wythe a tymze, temsyn with a tenze *attamino, setario.* To tempse or syfte *taratantariso*, Prompt. Parv. 488. Cf. *temsing*-chamber, the sifting-room, Halliwell. *O. Du.* temsen *to sift.*] v. ge-temesed, *and preceding word.*

temes-pīle, an; *f. A stake to support a sieve* [A 'temsynge staff' = *cervida*, lignum quod portat cribrum, Prompt. Parv. 488, note 3]:—Man sceal habban syfa, hriddel, hērsyfe, tæmespīlan, fanna, Anglia ix. 264, 14. v. preceding words.

temian; *p.* ede, ode *To tame*:—Ic temige *domo*, Ælfc. Gr. 24; Zup. 138, 2. Ic gewylde odde temige, 36; Zup. 213, 14. Ic genyme mē briddas on hærfæste and temige hig, Coll. Monast. Th. 26, 5. Mon temeþ his unāliéfde lustas mid ðǽm wordum ðære hālgan lāre, Past. 56; Swt. 433, 12. Gewylt, temaþ *domat, superat*, Wrt. Voc. ii. 141, 73. Hē ðone ealdan līchoman swencte and temede (*domabat*), Bd. 5, 12; S. 631, 36. Heora lāreówas ðe hī (wudufuglas) temedon, Met. 13, 39. Canst ðū temian (*domitare*) hig (*hawks*)? Coll. Monast. Th. 25, 21, 25. Wilde deór temian, Lchdm. iii. 200, 1: 186, 21. Nȳtenu tymian, 184, 18. Temma *domare*, Mk. Skt. Lind. Rush. 5, 4. [*Goth.* ga-tamjan: *O. Frs.* tema: *O. H. Ger.* zemmen: *Icel.* temja.] v. ā-, ge-temian.

temised. v. temesian.

templ, tempel, es; *n. A temple*:—Se wītga spræc suelce ðæt templ wǽre eal tōworpen; hē cuæð . . . 'Tōworpne sint ða stānas ðæs temples,' Past. 18; Swt. 133, 10. 'Ðis tempel wæs getimbrod on six and feówertigon wintron' . . . Hē hyt cwæð be hys līchaman temple, Jn. Skt. 2, 20, 21. Ðæt templ ealre clǽnnesse (*the Virgin's womb*), Blickl. Homl. 5, 19. Ofer ðæs temples heáhnesse, Mt. Kmbl. 4, 5: 24, 1. On hālierne ł hergan, temple *sacello*, Hpt. Gl. 482, 37. Se Hǽlend com tō ðam temple, Jn. Skt. 8, 2. Wē wunedon wið Phogores templ *mansimus contra fanum Phogor*, Deut. 3, 29. Ðes tōwyrpþ Godes templ, Mt. Kmbl. 27, 40. On ðæt hālige Salemannes templ, Blickl. Homl. 71, 18. Ic lǽre ðæt ðæt tempel wē forleósan, Bd. 2, 13; S. 516, 33. Ōdre þeóda fela templa āræ̅rdon, Homl. Th. ii. 574, 27. In Godes templum, Exon. Th. 131, 26; Gū. 461. Hī Godes tempel brǽcon and bærndon, 44, 24; Cri. 707. Templu ūre wē gehealdan, Scint. 16, 9. [*O. H. Ger.* tempal. For native words used before the Latin form was borrowed, v. hearh, ealh; and cf. *Goth.* alhs: *O. Sax.* alah: *Icel.* hof, for similar terms in other dialects.]

templ-geat, es; *n. The gate* or *door of a temple*:—Hē æt sumum sǽle stōd æt ðam tempelgeate, Wulfst. 49, 25.

templ-geweorc, es; *n. A temple-building, temple*:—His þegnas āgunnon specan wið hine ymbe ðæt mǽre tempelgeweorc ðe ðǽr geworht wæs Gode tō wyrðmynte, Wulfst. 88, 17. Salomon wes se forma man ðe Gode tō lofe ǽrest on eorðan templgeweorc ārǽrde, 277, 25.

templ-hālgung, e; *f. A consecration-festival*:—Ðā wǽron templhālgunga (*encenia*), Jn. Skt. 10, 22: *schenofegias*, Engl. Stud. xiii. 27, 14.

templ-līc; *adj. Pertaining to a temple;* the word translates *fanaticus*:—Hearhlīcre, ðæs hǽþenan, *vel* templīcre *fanatice*, i. *profani*, Wrt. Voc. ii. 147, 38. Templīcre ł dióflīcre *fanatica*, Hpt. Gl. 482, 25: Anglia xiii. 34, 176.

temprian; *p.* ode, ede. I. *to mix in due proportion, to mingle*:—Ic temprede (*potum meum cum fletu*) *temperabam*, Blickl. Gl. II. *to temper, regulate, moderate*:—Seó sunne gǽþ geond stōwa and tempraþ ða eorðlīcan wæstmas ǽgðer ge on wæstme ge on rīpunge, Lchdm. iii. 250, 17. Hī nā tempredon gȳfernysse hǽtan *non temperauerunt gulae ardorem*, Scint. 107, 12. Bryne līchamena mid cealdrum ēstum tō temprigenne (*temperandus est*), 52, 2. [*O. H. Ger.* temp[a]rōn *obtemperare, temperare, medicare*: *Icel.* tempra. From Latin.] v. ge-temprian.

temprung, e; *f. Tempering, moderation*:—Swā hwæt on temprunge byþ hālwende hit ys *quicquid temperamento fit salutare est*, Scint. 55, 1. Hafa ðū temprunge (*temperamentum*, i. *mediocritatem*), 172, 13. [*O. H. Ger.* temp[a]runga *temperantia, compositio.*]

temsian, tēn. v. temesian, tīn.

[**tendan**; *p.* de *To kindle.*] [A gnast wule al þe brond tenden, O. E. Homl. i. 81, 7. Cwench hit er þen hit waxe and tende þe, A. R. 296, 21. It bigynnez forto tiende, L. S. 314, 523. Itend of wreððe, Kath. 154. Teenden *incendere*, Wick. *Goth.* tandjan; *Da.* tænde: *Swed.* tända.] v. ā-, on-tendan; tennan.

-tendend, -tending, -tendness. v. ā-tendend, ā-tending, on-tendness.

tender *fuel*:—Tender *fomes*, Ælfc. Gr. 9, 26; Zup. 52, 11. Ðæt ne gehigeleás[t] mēte tender *ut non scurilitas inveniat fomitem*, R. Ben. Interl. 75, 17. v. tynder.

Tenet, Tænet[t]; *also* Tenet-land *the isle of Thanet*:—Augustinus wæs cumende on Bretone ǽrest on Tenet ðam eálonde (Tenet-land, MS. B.) (*in insula Tanato*) . . . Is on eásteweardre Cent mycel eálond Tenet (*Tanatos insula*), ðæt is syx hund hīda micel . . . Ðæt eálond tōsceádeþ Wantsumo streám fram ðam tōgeþeódden lande, Bd. 1, 25; S. 486, 10–20. Hēr hǽðene men on Tenet ofer winter sǽton, Chr. 851; Erl. 67, 20: 865; Erl. 70, 31. On ðyssum geáre Eádgār cyng hét oferhergian eall Tenetland, 969; Erl. 125, 5. Tænet, Cod. Dip. Kmbl. iv. 232, 22. Inntō Raculfe on Tænett, iii. 429, 16. The following forms occur in Latin charters:—Tenid, i. 21, 1. Tenaet, 129, 18. Tanet, 118, 1. Tanat, vi. 189, 31. Tanatos insulam, iv. 237, 20. Insula Tanatorum, iii. 347, 15. Thanet, i. 13, 30: 18, 15. Ðanet, v. 21, 19. Insula Thaeneti, i. 42, 16. Insula Thaenet, 116, 27.

tengan; *p.* de *To press, hasten, hurry, proceed with haste* or *violence*:—Ðā tengde se Pharao æfter mid mycelre fyrde *then Pharaoh hastened after with a great army*, Homl. Th. i. 312, 3: ii. 194, 16. Hē ðā þearle āblicged āweg tengde, 182, 2. Hē ontende ða burh and tencgde him forð syððan, Homl. Skt. ii. 25, 416. Se cāsere tengde tō ðam botle, Homl. Th. i. 430, 23. Se fugol tō wuda tengde, ii. 162, 27. Æt suman cyrre tengde hē tō fyrde ongeán Persiscne leódscipe *on one occasion he was hastening to march against Persia*, i. 448, 32. Tengdon ða hǽþenan mid wǽpnum tō ðam ǽwfæstum heápe, and slōgon ða cristenan, Homl. Skt. ii. 28, 66. Teng recene tō ðam fæstenne (*haste thee, escape thither*, Gen. 19, 22), Cd. Th. 152, 29; Gen. 2527. Hié hæfdon gecweden ðæt hié ealle emlīce on Latine tengden *they had agreed that they all in unbroken order would proceed to the attack of the Latins*, Ors. 3, 6; Swt. 108, 9. v. ge-tengan; ge-tenge.

tennan (?) *to incite, encourage to effort*:—Ful oft ðæt gegongeþ, ðætte wer and wīf in woruld cennaþ beorn, and mid bleóm gyrwaþ, tennaþ and tǽtaþ, ōþþæt seó tīd cymeþ, ðæt ða geongan leomu, liffæstan leoþu, geloden weorþaþ (*the parents try to awaken the child's activity of body and mind, while it is still an infant*), Exon. Th. 327, 15; Vy. 4. [Thorpe would read *temiaþ*. Grein suggests comparison with *O. M. H. Ger.* Cf. Ih zeno sie *provocabo eos*, Grff. v. 685. Could *tendaþ* be read? *Ontendan* and connected words are used figuratively; see also *tendan.*]

tenys, Hpt. Gl. 513, 65. v. tȳnness.

teofonian; *p.* ode *To associate, join*:—Ealswā teofanade se ðe teala cūþe ǽghwylc wiþ ōþrum; sceoldon eal beran stīþe stefnbyrd, swā him se steóra bibeád, missenlīce gemetu (cf. þeáh ānra hwilc (*each of the elements*) wið ōþer sié miclum gemenged . . . fæste gebunden . . . mid bebode ðīne, Met. 20, 65–69). Exon. Th. 349, 8; Sch. 43. Swā teofenede se ðe teala cūþe dæg wiþ nihte . . . fisc wið ȳþum, 351, 18; Sch. 82.

teofrian; *p.* ode *To allot* (?), *appoint*:—Ðone sylfan stān ðe hine wyrhtan āwurpan nū se geworden is hwommona heágost hālig Drihten tō wealles wrade wīs teofrade (*he has appointed it to be the wall's support*) *lapidem quem reprobaverunt aedificantes, hic factus est in caput anguli: a Domino factum est illud*, Ps. Th. 117, 21. v. tiber (tifer).

teogoþa (-eþa), teogoþian. v. teóþa, teóþian.

teoh[h], e; *f.*; but also *m.* or *n. An association, a company, band*:—Besæt hē ðā sinherge sweorda lāfe weán oft gehēt earmre teohhe *with a mighty host he besieged then those whom the sword had spared, to the wretched band woe he oft promised*, Beo. Th. 5868; B. 2938. Ōððæt ic ðīnes earmes āsecge strencðe ðisse cneórisse eallum ðam teohhe ðe nū tōweard ys *donec annuntiem brachium tuum generationi omni, quae ventura est*, Ps. Th. 70, 17. Ðā hié gemitton teoche æt torre (*the people who were building the tower of Babel*), Cd. Th. 101, 26; Gen. 1688. Hēt tuddorteóndra teohha gehwylcre wæstmas fēdan *he bade each productive race bring forth fruits*, 59, 6; Gen. 959. [*M. H. Ger.* zeche; *f. succession, association, company*: *Ger.* zeche.] v. next word.

teohhian, teohchian, teohgian, tihhian, teohian, teochian, tihian; *p.* ode. I. *to suppose, consider, think*, (a) with a clause:—Ic tiohhie, ðæt hió ðæs taman nāuht ne gehicgge, Met. 13, 25. Gif hwā teochaþ (tiohhaþ, Cott. MSS.) ðæt hē ǽfæst sié *si quis putat se religiosum esse*, Past. 38; Swt. 281, 2. Swā hwæt swā hē swīþost lufaþ ðæt hē teohhaþ (tiohhaþ, Cott. MS.) ðæt him sié betst . . . ðonne hē ðæt begiten hæfþ ðonne tihhaþ hē ðæt hē mǽge beón swīðe gesǽlig *quod quisque prae ceteris petit, id summum esse judicat bonum . . . beatum esse judicat statum, quem prae ceteris quisque desiderat*, Bt. 24, 3; Fox 84, 11–14. Tehhaþ, Fox 84, 16. Sume wēnaþ, ðæt . . . Sume teohhiaþ, ðæt . . . Manege tellaþ, ðæt . . . , 24, 2; Fox 82, 7–12: 26, 2; Fox 92, 26: Ps. Th. 11, 4. Hió tiohchiaþ ðæt ðæt (*silence*) scyle bión for eáðmēttum *tacere se aestimant ex humilitate*, Past. 41; Swt. 302, 3. Nān ðara gōda ðīn nis ðe ðū teohhodest (tiohhodes, Cott. MS.) ðæt hī ðīne beón sceoldan *nihil horum, quae in tuis computas bonis, tuum esse bonum monstratur*, Bt. 14, 2; Fox 42, 29. Se leása wēna ðara dysigena monna tiohhie, ðæt . . . *hominum fallax adnectit opinio*, 27, 3: Fox 98, 32. (b) with *tō*, *to consider as*:—Of gromra gripe, ðe ðū tō godum tiohhast *from the clutch* *of cruel ones, whom thou countest as gods*, Exon. Th. 255, 17; Jul. 215. Ælc mon tiohhaþ him ðæt tō sēlestum goode ðæt ðæt hē swīþost lufaþ *every man considers that as his best good, which he most loves*, Bt. 33, 2; Fox 122, 23. Hī teohhiaþ ūs him tō snǣdincgsceápum *aestimati sumus ut oves occisionis*, Ps. Th. 43, 23. Ðam wīsan men com tō lofe and tō wyrðscipe ðæt se unrihtwīsa cyning him teohhode tō wīte *cruciatus, quos putabat tyrannus materiam crudelitatis, vir sapiens fecit esse virtutis*, Bt. 16, 2; Fox 52, 27. Gif hē hit ne tiohchode eall tō anum *si utraque unum esse non decerneret*, Past. 49; Swt. 385, 34. (c) in other ways:—Teohgaþ *decreverit, cogitaverit*, Hpt. Gl. 412, 48. Ne biþ hē swā brād swā hē teohgaþ (tihhaþ, Cott. MS.), Bt. 30, 1; Fox 108, 12. II. *to purpose, determine, intend, appoint*, (a) with an accusative:—Man ūs tyhhaþ twegen eardas *two dwellings are intended for us*, Hy. 7, 97. Oft ic leán teohhode hnāhran rince, Beo. Th. 1907; B. 951. (b) with an accusative and (implied) infinitive:—Swilce hē nā ða sprǣce ne mǣnde and tiohhode hit þeáh þiderweardes (*and yet he intended it to go in that direction*), Bt. 39, 5; Fox 218, 12. (c) with a clause:—Tō ðǣm sōþum gesǣlþum ic tiohhie (tiohige, Cott. MS.) ðæt ic ðē lǣde, Bt. 22, 2; Fox 78, 7. Swā swā hē tiohhaþ, ðæt hit sié, 39, 6; Fox 220, 7. Nis nān gesceaft ðe hē tiohhige (tiohhie, Cott. MS.) ðæt hió scyle winnan wiþ hire Scippendes willan . . . Hwæt wēnst ðū gif ǣnegu gesceaft tiohhode ðæt hió wiþ his willan sceolde winnan hwæt hió mihte wiþ swā mihtine swā wē hine gerehtne habbaþ *nihil est quod Deo contraire conetur . . . quid si conetur, num tandem proficiet quidquam adversus eum, quem potentissimum esse concessimus*, 35, 4; Fox 160, 21–27. Ðæt hē forðȳ reáfige ðȳ hē tiohchie (teohhige, Cott. MSS.) ðæt hē eft scyle mid ðȳ reáflāce ælmessan gewyrcean *pro misericordia facienda peccare*, Past. 45; Swt. 341, 22. (d) with *tō*:—Swā hwæt swā ðū mē tō gyfe tihhie bring ðæt Gode tō onsægednysse *whatever you may intend as a gift to me, bring that as a sacrifice to God*, Homl. Ass. 123, 209. (e) with gerundial infinitive:—Ðǣr ðū ongeáte hwidre ic ðē teohhie (tiohige, Cott. MS.) tō lǣdenne *si, quonam te ducere aggredimur, agnosceres*, Bt. 22, 2; Fox 78, 1. Cildum ðe wē tiochiaþ ūrne eard tō te forlǣtanne, and hié tiochiaþ ūs tō ierfeweardum tō habbanne, Past. 50; Swt. 391, 28. Hȳ teohhiaþ mē tō āfyrranne, Ps. Th. 39, 16. Hē tiohchode him mā tō fultemanne . . . hē teohchode hine tō lǣdanne on līfes weg, Past. 41; Swt. 305, 4, 5. His (*Ulysses'*) þegnas for hiora eardes lufan tihodon hine tō forlǣtanne, Bt. 38, 1; Fox 194, 29. (f) undetermined:—Teohhaþ *distinat*, i. *disponit, contendit*, Wrt. Voc. ii. 141, 35. [Cf. *O. H. Ger.* gi-zehōn *instaurare, resarcire*.] v. ge-teohhian; teón (*wk*.).

-teohhung, teolian. v. fore-teohhung, tilian.

teol-þyrel, es; *n. A window*:—Teolþerla *fenestrarum*, Hpt. Gl. 409, 31. Cf. eág-þyrel.

teolung, teoma. v. tilung, tam.

teón (*from* teóhan); *p*. teáh, *pl*. tugon; *pp*. togen, tigen (v. of-teón) *To draw, pull*:—Ic teó *traho*, ic teó swȳðe *pertraho*, Ælfc. Gr. 28, 5; Zup. 176, 5, 6. Teáþ *trahunt*, Wülck. Gl. 253, 32. I. (1) with the idea of horizontal movement, *to draw* along, *pull, drag*:—Ðū mē gebundenne mid fȳrenum racenteágum tȳhst in ēce fȳr, Shrn. 117, 18. Heó teáh hyne (*Holofernes*) folmum wiþ hyre weard, Judth. Thw. 23, 1; Jud. 99. Ðā geseah ic monige ðara wērigra gāsta fīf monna sāwla teón (*trahere*) on midde ða ðȳstro . . . Tugon hī ða werīgan gāstas, Bd. 5, 12; S. 628, 32–36. Valerianus hēt teón Ypolitum geond ðornas and brēmelas, Homl. Th. i. 432, 34: Blickl. Homl. 241, 21. Se eádiga Andreas wæs togen, 241, 26. (2) where the movement is from within or from without, *to draw* a sword, blood, etc., *to haul* a net, *draw* in *or* out:—Ðū scealt, ðonne ðū on ðām sculdrum tȳhst blōd, teón swīðe on ðære sīdan, Lchdm. ii. 262, 26. Se iil tīhþ his fēt suā hē inmest mæg . . . Hē tiéhþ his heáfod in tō him, Past. 35; Swt. 241, 11–21. Ða synfullan teóþ heora sweord *gladium evaginaverunt peccatores*, Ps. Th. 36, 13. Simon Petrus tēh his nett on land, Jn. Skt. 21, 11. Teóh mid glæse oþþe mid horne, Lchdm. ii. 200, 13: 262, 5. Tæppan teón, Techm. ii. 120, 12. Teón ūt lange, Lchdm. iii. 16, 13. Onlegena ūt teónde ðone heardan swile, ii. 182, 16. Wæs on næs togen wundorlīc wǣgbora, Beo. Th. 2883; B. 1439. (3) where the movement is up or down, *to draw* up *or* down, *to draw* breath, *heave* a sigh, &c., *to hoist* a sail, *pull* a bell:—Mē tō grunde teáh feóndscaða, Beo. Th. 1111; B. 553. Hē oroð stundum teáh (cf. oroð up hlæden, v. 30), Exon. Th. 178, 17; Gū. 1245: Guthl. 20; Gdwin. 86, 16. Godwine eorl teáh up his segl, Chr. 1052; Erl. 183, 12. Hī tugon up heora segel, 1046; Erl. 174, 19. Ða apostolas tugon hié up and hié gesetton on ðæm fægran neorxna wange, Blickl. Homl. 143, 24. Tugon hié heora hrægl bufan cneów, Ors. 3, 5; Swt. 106, 16. Dō mid his handa, swylce hē wille āne hangigende bellan teón, Techm. ii. 118, 16. Heó longe swōretunge wæs teónde, Bd. 4, 23; S. 596, 10. (4) *to draw* to, *to attract*:—Ðære lyfte gecynd is ðæt heó tēhþ tō ða rēnas of ðæm sealtan sǣ, Shrn. 63, 27. (5) *to pull* the string of a bow, *strike* the strings of an instrument:—Ðære hearpan strengas se hearpere suīðe ungelīce tiéhþ and styreþ, Past. 23; Swt. 175, 7. Ða teóþ heora swīðne bogan *intenderunt arcum*, Ps. Th. 63, 3. Togenum strengum, Ps. Th. 67, 24. (6) *to pull* a boat, *to row*:—On ða eá hī tugon up hiora scipu ōþ ðone weald, Chr. 893; Erl. 88, 31: 895; Erl. 93, 31. Ðæt scip wile hwīlum stīgan ongeán ðone streám, ac hit ne mæg, būton ða rōwend hit teón, ac hit sceal fleótan mid ðȳ streáme; ne mæg hit nō stille gestondan, būton hit ankor hæbbe, oððe mon mid rōðrum ongeán tió, Past. 58; Swt. 445, 10–13. Hē āstīgende on ān scyp bæd hyne ðæt hē hit lythwōn fram lande tuge . . . Hē cwæþ tō Simone: 'Teóh hit on dȳpan,' Lk. Skt. 5, 3, 4. (7) *to draw, be of weight*:—Ðonne man sett ða synne and ða sāwle on ða wǣge, and hȳ man wegeþ, swā man dēþ gold wið penegas. And gif ða penegas teóþ swīðor ðonne ðæt gold, ðonne miswyrð ðam men hraðe. Swā biþ ðære sāwle and ðære synne; gif seó synn tīhþ swȳðor ðonne seó sāwel, ðonne faraþ hȳ on forwyrd, Wulfst. 240, 1–6. (8) where there is no movement, *to pull, tug*:—Sume sceufon, sume tugon . . . and seó Godes fǣmne hwæðre stōd. Ðā brudon hig rāpas on hyre handa and on hyre fēt, and hig tugon myd ðām, and hig ne myhton hig ðā git ānne fōtlāst furður āteón, Shrn. 154, 26–30. Se deófol wolde geniman ðone cnapan of Basilius handum, hetolīce teónde, Homl. Skt. i. 3, 443. II. *to bring, lead, put*:—Ðā teáh hine Penda fyrde and here on, Bd. 3, 7; S. 529, 30: 1, 34; S. 499, 29. Penda teáh here wiþ Eást-Engle, 3, 18; S. 546, 14. 'Teóh eft ðīne hand on ðīnne bōsum.' Ðā teáh hē hig ongeán, Ex. 4, 7. Hēht eorla hleó eahta mearas on flet teón, Beo. Th. 2077; B. 1036. II a. with an idea of violence or compulsion:—Ðā cwæð Iosue: 'Teóþ ða cynegas ūt of ðam scræfe,' Jos. 10, 22. Gif fāh mon cirican geierne, hine seofan nihtum mon ūt ne teó, L. Alf. pol. 5; Th. i. 64, 10. Belǣwende eów on gesamnungum and teónde tō cynegum, Homl. Th. ii. 540, 17. III. in various figurative senses, many of which may be rendered by words containing the root of *trahere* or of *ducere*. (1) *to teach, educate, bring up*:—Ic tȳ (teó, MSS. J. W.) oððe lǣre *imbuo*, ic teáh *imbui*, Ælfc. Gr. 28, 3; Zup. 166, 14. Hū lange tȳhst ðū ūs and fēdest teára hlāfe *cibabis nos pane lacrymarum*, Ps. Th. 79, 5. Hwā teáh ðē? . . . Se Hǣlend mē lǣrde mid onwrigenysse, Homl. Th. i. 378, 9. Hē iunge men teáh georne mid lāre, swā ðæt ealle his gefēran sceoldon sealmas leornian, Homl. Skt. ii. 26, 76. Wē lǣraþ ðæt preóstas geóguðe geornlīce lǣran and tō cræftan teón (*bring them up to crafts*), L. Edg. C. 51; Th. ii. 254, 26: L. Pen. 14; Th. ii. 282, 6. (2) *to draw* to or from, *attract, induce, seduce*:—Sió leáse gesǣlþ tīhþ ða ðe hiere tō geþeódaþ from ðǣm sōþum gesǣlþum mid hiere ōlecunge, Bt. 20; Fox 72, 7. Sió gecynd eów tīhþ tō ðam angite, ac eów tīhþ (teóhþ, MS. Bod.) gedwola of ðam angite, 26, 1; Fox 90, 7. Þes middangeard wæs tō ðon fæger, ðæt hē teáh men tō him þurh his fægernesse fram Gode, Blickl. Homl. 115, 11. Ðone mon sciele ealle mægene tō biscephāde teón ðe gāstlīce liofaþ *ille modis omnibus debet ad exemplum vivendi pertrahi, qui spiritaliter vivit*, Past. 10; Swt. 60, 7. (3) *to draw* to one's self, *to take*:—Ic teó (nimo, Lind. Rush.) ealle þing tō mē sylfon, Jn. Skt. 12, 32. Sume hī teóþ *nominativum casum*, Ælfc. Gr. 33; Zup. 2068. Ne teáh Crist him nā tō on ðisum līfe land ne welan, Homl. Th. i. 160, 32: Ors. 5, 11; Swt. 236, 27. Hē æfter ðysum geþance teáh him elnunge tō be dǣle *after this thought he in some measure took courage*, Homl. Skt. i. 23, 524. On ðæt gerād ðæt hié him Siciliam tō ne tugen ne Sardiniam *conditiones erant, ut Sicilia Sardiniaque decederent*, Ors. 4, 6; Swt. 180, 13. Ðæt hē hit on folcryht him tō teó, L. Ath. i. 9; Th. i. 204, 12. Ne teó se hlāford nā māre on his ǣhte būtan his rihtan heregeate, L. C. S. 71; Th. i. 412, 29. Ne teón hié nānwuht ðæs lofes tō him, Past. 44; Swt. 323, 1. (4) *to take* on one's self, *to assume*:—Hié him on teóþ, ðæt hié sién heortan lǣcas, Past. 1; Swt. 27, 1. Ðæt hé tió on hine selfne ōðerra monna scylda, 16; Swt. 99, 1. Sanctus Paulus ðone ōðerne lǣrde, ðæt hē him anwald on tuge, 40; Swt. 291, 20. Se him wæs on teónde ealdordōm ofer ða ōþere, Ors. 2, 6; Swt. 88, 20. (5) *to bring, bring forth, produce, display*:—Meaht forð tīhþ heofoncondelle and holmas mid, Exon. Th. 349, 29; Sch. 53. Ða ðe plegaþ æt deádra manna līce and ǣlce fūlnysse ðǣr forð teóþ mid plegan, Homl. Skt. i. 21, 309. Ðū wið Criste wunne and gewin tuge, 267, 27; Jul. 421. Ðā sceolde se ealdorman Ælfrīc lǣdan ða fyrde, ac hē teáh forð ðā his ealdan wrenceas *he brought out his old tricks*, Chr. 1003; Erl. 139, 7. Hygewælmas (-os, MS.) teáh beorne on breóstum nīð *envy produced fierce passions in the breast of the man*, Cd. Th. 60, 12; Gen. 980. Teón nū ða wæteru forð swimmende cynn . . . eall fisccynn ðe ða wæteru tugon forð (*produxerunt*), Gen. 1, 20, 21. Tō teónne forð ðone wīsdōm ðære ealdan ǣ, Homl. Th. i. 190, 8. (6) *to bring, place*:—Sió ungelīcnes hira geearnunga hié tiéhþ sume behindan sume and hira scylda hī ðǣr gehabbaþ *variante meritorum ordine alios aliis culpa postponit*, Past. 17; Swt. 107, 20. Þisceop sceal scyldan cristenum mannum wið ǣlc ðæra þinga ðe synlīc biþ, and ðȳ hē sceal on ǣghwæt hine ðe swȳðor teón (*he must the rather bring himself to everything, apply himself*), ðæt hē ðe geornor wite hū seó heord fare, L. I. P. 7; Th. ii. 312, 24. IV. *to draw* (ar in *to draw* nigh), *to go, proceed*, (1) intrans.:—Seó tō hām tȳhþ, Exon. Th. 416, 26; Rä. 35, 4. Hē ne mihte ongemong ōþrum mannum bión, ac teáh tō wuda, Bt. 35, 6; Fox 168, 7. Hī tugon forð *they went on their way*, Homl. Th. i. 246, 11: ii. 490, 1. Fela hām tugon, Chr. 1096; Erl. 233, 23. Hira tungan tugon ofer eorðan *lingua eorum transivit super terram*, Ps. Th. 72, 7. Gif tōsomne teó *if (hair-lip) draw together*, Lchdm. ii. 56, 9. (2) *with* acc. *to go* a journey:—Æghwylcum ðara ðe mid Beówulfe brimláde leáh, Beo. Th. 2107; B. 1051: 2669; B. 1332. Yldran ûsse tugon tongne sîð, Exon. Th. 228, 19; Ph. 440: 110, 28; Gû. 115. (3) figuratively:—Nû fandiaþ swelce wræccan and teóþ tô, woldon underfón ðone weorðscipe *such wretches press forward in their wish to receive the honour*, Past. 7; Swt. 51, 22. [*Laym.* teon *to go, march: Kath.* teon *to pull:* Gen. and Ex. ten *to go; to bring up. Goth.* tiuhan: *O. Sax.* tiohan: *O. Frs.* tiá: *O. H. Ger.* ziohan *trahere, ducere, nutrire.*] v. â-, be-, ge-, of-, ofer-, on-, ôþ-, þurh-, wið-teón; for-, íð-togen; teónd.

teón (*from* tîhan; *but the verb seems to have almost entirely given up the conjugation to which this form would belong and to take that of* teón *from* teóhan); *p.* teáh, *pl.* tugon; *pp.* togen, tygen *To accuse* a person of something (acc. of person and gen. of charge, or charge expressed by a clause):—Ðû mê stale týhst *furti me arguis*, Gen. 31, 32. Hwî tîhþ ûre hlâford ûs swâ micles falses? 44, 7. Gif gê scyld on eów witen ðæs ðe eów man tîhþ, Txts. 176, 10; Rtl. 114, 23: Exon. Th. 345, 13; Gn. Ex. 187. Týhþ, Cd. Th. 36, 33; Gen. 581. Ic eom unscyldig æt ðære tihtlan ðe N. mê tîhþ (týhþ, MS. B.), L. O. 5; Th. i. 180, 16. Hý teóþ ðê ðæs ðe hý sylfe habbaþ, Prov. Kmbl. 12. Hê teáh hiene ðæt hê his ungerisno spræ̂ce wið ða senatos *he* (Philip) *charged him* (Demetrius, his son) *that he had spoken disparagingly of him to the senate*, Ors. 4, 11; Swt. 206, 28. Ðâ tugon hié hiene, ðæt hê heora swicdômes wið Alexander fremmende wæ̂re, and hiene for ðære tihtlan ofslôgon, 4, 5; Swt. 168, 16. Gif hine hwâ hwelces teó, L. Alf. pol. 17; Th. i. 72, 6: 11; Th. i. 68, 19: L. In. 30; Th. i. 120, 18. Gif hine man æ̂niges þinges teó, L. C. S. 31; Th. i. 394, 28. Gif hine mon tió gewealdes on ðære dæ̂de, L. Alf. pol. 36; Th. i. 84, 15: 31; Th. i. 80, 16. Gif man ðone hlâford teó, ðæt hê be his ræ̂de ût hleópe, L. C. S. 30; Th. i. 394, 19. Gyf hine þreó men ætgædere teón, Th. i. 392, 23. Se man ðe man tuge *the man who shall have been accused*, L. Ath. iv. 6; Th. i. 224, 15. Gif hwâ óðerne tión wille, ðæt hê hwelcne ne gelæ̂ste ðara ðe hê him gesealde, L. Alf. pol. 33; Th. i. 82, 5. [*Goth.* teihan *to shew: O. Sax.* af-tîhan *to refuse: O. H. Ger.* zîhan *arguere: Ger.* zeihen *to accuse: Icel.* tjá (*wk.*) *to shew*; cf. tiginn *distinguished.*] v. be-teón; teónd; tiht.

teón; *p.* teóde. I. *to make, frame, create, ordain, arrange, contrive, bring about, construct,* (1) referring to material objects:—Ðysne wig ðe ðû ðê tô wundrum teódest, Cd. Th. 228, 25; Dan. 208. Thâ middungeard moncynnæs uard æfter tiáde (teóde, Bd. 4, 24; S. 597, 23) *dehinc terram custos humani generis creavit*, Txts. 149, 8. Helm worhte wæ̂pna smið, wundrum teóde, besette swînlîcum, ðæt hine beadomêcas bîtan ne meahton, Beo. Th. 2909; B. 1452. Tô ðam golde ðe hê him tô gode teóde *the gold that he had shaped for a god to himself*, Cd. Th. 229, 13; Dan. 216. Se ðâs woruld teóde, Exon. Th. 335, 16; Gn. Ex. 34: Andr. Kmbl. 1594; An. 798. (1 a) in a figurative expression:—Ða heora tungan teóþ (*but the word may be from* teón *to draw* (v. teón, I. 2), *as it seems also to govern* bogan *in the following clause*) teónan gehwylce sweorde efenscearpe *exacuerunt ut gladium linguas suas*, Ps. Th. 63, 3. (2) referring to immaterial objects:—Ðæs ðê þanc sié ðæt ðû ûs ðâs wrace teódest *for this be thanks to thee that thou didst order this exile for us*, Cd. Th. 235, 21; Dan. 309. Him heáhcyning fultum tiódе *for him the high king contrived help*, 11, 11; Gen. 173. Se ðe ûs ðis lîf tiódе *he that framed for us this life*, Met. 20, 131. Waldend him ðæt wîte teóde, Exon. Th. 336, 4; Gn. Ex. 43. II. *to furnish* with; instruere:—Mid beorhtnyssa æ̂rnemergen þû tihst and mid fýrum middæg *splendore mane instruis et ignibus meridiem*, Hymn. Surt. 10, 25. Nalæs hî hine læssan lâcum teódan ðonne ða dydon ðe hine æt frumsceafte forð onsendon, Beo. Th. 86; B. 43. [*M. H. Ger.* zechen; *p.* zechte *to arrange, contrive, bring about.*] v. fore-, ge-teón; teohhian.

teón. I. *hurt, damage, vexation*:—Ðone on teón wigeþ feónd his feónde *him* (the dog) *foe brings for the annoyance of his foe*, Exon. Th. 433, 28; Rä. 51, 3. II. *insult, abuse, reproach, calumny*:—Ðâ hine teóne wyrde (teónode and wyrgde? *see note*) Chus, Ps. Th. 7, arg. Teóna *calumniarum*, Hpt. Gl. 506, 22. [*Icel.* tjón; *f. n. damage, loss.*] v. nið-geteón, *and next word.*

teóna, an; *m.* I. *damage, harm, hurt, mischief, annoyance, trouble, vexation, detriment, loss*:—Mid ðý hunige smire . . . ne biþ sôna nân teóna *smear with the honey . . . there will be no hurt* (*from the disease*) *directly*, Lchdm. ii. 104, 23: 156, 30. Ðis weorc biþ deóflum se mæ̂sta teóna *this work will prove the greatest vexation to devils*, Blickl. Homl. 47, 6. Hit him wyrþ tô teónan *it will turn to his hurt*, 51, 9. Ne him wiht gescôd ðæs ðe hý him tô teónan þurhtogen hæfdon, Exon. Th. 127, 36; Gû. 397: 269, 30; Jul. 458. Ðæt behýded wæs tô teónan cristenum folce *the cross had been hidden to the detriment of Christians*, Elen. Kmbl. 1973; El. 988. Þohton ðæt hié sceoldon gewrecan hira teónan *they thought they would avenge the harm that had been done them*, Chr. 921; Erl. 107, 17. Ymb ðone teónan (*mischievous doctrine*) wæs gegaderad III hund biscepa and eahtatiéne hiene tô âmânsumianne *conventus cccxviii episcoporum factus est, per quos Arianum dogma exitiabile reprobatum est*, Ors. 6, 30; Swt. 282, 34. Tiónan *infestationes*, Wrt. Voc. ii. 111, 61. Teónan, 45, 27. Se ðe hine fram swâ monigum yrmðum and teónum (*tot ac tantis calamitatibus*) generede, Bd. 2, 12; S. 514, 19. Mid miclum teónum and wîtum, Ors. 5, 15; Swt. 250, 28: Cd. Th. 36, 34; Gen. 581. Ðæt tô teónum weorþeþ, þeódum tô þreá, Exon. Th. 67, 20; Cri. 1091: 75, 1; Cri. 1215. Synfull tôþum torn þolaþ teónum grimetaþ (*grievously groans*), Ps. Th. 111, 9. Ne mæg hê nô ryhtlîce gedyld læ̂ran bûton hê self gedyldelîce óðerra monna tiónan geðolige *neque potest veraciter bona docendo impendere, si vivendo nescit aequanimiter aliena mala tolerare*, Past. 33; Swt. 217, 4. On his tîman hæfdon men mycel geswinc and swîðe manige teónan, Chr. 1086; Erl. 222, 20. II. *hurt that comes from wrongful action, wrong, injury, wrongful action, iniquity, offence, abuse, ill-usage, violence*:—Wolde hê ðæt gyld âbrecan. Ða hæþenan men hine mid teónan (*violence*) âweg âdrifon . . . Hê hit for manna teónan gebrecan ne môste, Blickl. Homl. 221, 20–27. Ne dô ic ðê næ̂nne teónan (teáne, Rush.) *non facio tibi injuriam*, Mt. Kmbl. 20, 13. Se unrihtwîsa wer wyle niman on teónan his nêxtan dæ̂de deáh ðe hê him teónan ne gedô, Basil admn. 4; Norm. 44, 19. Ðæt hê geþence ðone teónan (*injuriam*), ðe wê him dydon, Gen. 50, 15: Ps. Th. 102, 6. Se ðe ûre ealra teónan wræ̂ce *he that should avenge the wrong done to us all*, L. Ath. v. 7; Th. i. 234, 20: 8, 3; Th. i. 236, 18: Blickl. Homl. 33, 24: Ors. 1, 11; Swt. 50, 12. Gê ne ongitaþ hû micelne teónan gê dôþ Gode eówrum sceppende *nec intelligitis quantam conditori vestro faciatis injuriam*, Bt. 14, 2; Fox 44, 31. Ic (*the devil*) ðæs wealles geat ontýne þurh teónan (*by means of the iniquity which I introduce into the man's mind*), Exon. Th. 266, 22; Jul. 402. Ic fleáh hlæ̂fdigan hete, tregan and teónan, Cd. Th. 137, 15; Gen. 2274: 226, 5; Sat. 497. Se cyning ne gemunde ðæra monigra teónena ðe hiora æ̂gðer ôþrum gedyde *Astyages oblitus sceleris sui*, Ors. 1, 12; Swt. 52, 22. Hê ða gefremedon teónan (*factas injurias*) him eall forlêt, Bd. 3, 22; S. 553, 19. Teónan and unriht *iniquitates nostras*, Ps. Th. 102, 12. III. *reproach, insult, shame, calumny, abuse, contumely*:—Teóna *calumnia*, Hpt. Gl. 514, 64: *contumelia*, Scint. 19, 4. Tióna, Kent. Gl. 345. Ic ehte mid teónan *calumnior*, Ælfc. Gr. 25; Zup. 145, 1. Genimeþ his æ̂hta Drihten mid mycclum teónan on him *the Lord will take from him his possession with great shame to him*, Blickl. Homl. 53, 4. For teónan *for shame*, 179, 12. Ða blæ̂da ðe ic ðê on teónan geþah *the fruit which I insulted you by taking*, Cd. Th. 54, 30; Gen. 885. Teónan ðû wyrcst ûs mid ðisse sage *haec dicens nobis contumiliam facis*, Lk. Skt. 11, 45. Ða ðe tæ̂lnessa teónan wið heora ðam nêhstan âhôfan *detrahentem adversus proximum suum*, Ps. Th. 100, 4. Hî (*two well-born nuns*) wæ̂ron æfter æþelborennysse oferhýdige and hearmcwydole, and ðone wer oft gedrehton. Ðâ cýdde se wer Benedicte, hû micelne teónan hê forðyldegode mid ðâm mynecenum, Homl. Th. ii. 174, 10. Teónan *calumniae*, Wrt. Voc. ii. 24, 49. Mid teónum gewæ̂cende *afficientes contumelia*, Lk. Skt. 20, 11. IV. *strife, discord*:—Eall ðæra Iudêiscra teóna ârâs þurh ðæt hwî Drihten Crist se ðe æfter flæ̂sce sôðlîce is mannes sunu eác swilce wæ̂re gecweden Godes sunu *all the strife of the Jews arose from the question, why the Lord Christ, who according to the flesh is truly son of man, should be called also son of God*, Homl. Th. i. 48, 15. Oft wæ̂ron teónan wæ̂rfæstra wera weredum gemæ̂ne heardum hearmplega. Ðâ ongan Abraham sprecan . . . 'Ne sceolon unc betweónan teónan weaxan wroht wriðian' (*facta est rixa inter pastores gregum Abram et Lot . . . Dixit ergo Abram ad Lot: 'Ne quaeso sit jurgium inter me et te,'* Gen. 13, 7, 8), Cd. Th. 113, 33–114, 12; Gen. 1896–1903. Symle teónan sêcþ yfel *semper jurgia quaerit malus*, Scint. 134, 12. Tiónan, Kent. Gl. 145. [The word remains in use in later English, but gradually restricts the meaning to *pain, vexation. Laym. A.R.* teone. Onn himm wrekenn hire tene, Orm. 19866. Ne do he þe neure swa muchelne teone ne wite, O. E. Homl. i. 15, 30. Wiðute teone and treie, 193, 61. Hi hedden teone and seorewe, Misc. 89, 14. Þu seist me boþe teone and schame, O. and N. 50. Teone ne tintreohe, Kath. 402. Berninde of grome and of teone *furiis agitatus*, 1354. Mi tene and min anger, Will. 552. Anger and tene, sorge and wo, Gen. and Ex. 2992. Tyene *strife*, Ayenb. 66, 1. Nô word of jelousye or any other teene, Chauc. Kn. T. 2248. In pure tene *in sheer vexation*, Piers P. 6, 119. With tranaille and with tene, 135. Tene or angyr or dyshese *angustia, tribulacio*, Prompt. Parv. 488. *O. Sax.* tiono *wrong, evil.*] v. hyge-teóna; teóne, *and preceding word.*

teón-cwide, es; *m. Reproachful, abusive, insulting speech, blasphemy, contumely, calumny, slander*:—Ne frîne ic ðê for tæ̂le ne þurh teóncwide, Andr. Kmbl. 1266; An. 633. Þurh teóncwide *by their blasphemous language* (saying that a miracle was wrought by magic), 1541; An. 772. Godscyld wrecan, teóncwide, Exon. Th. 254, 30; Jul. 205. Tióncwida *conviciorum*, Wrt. Voc. ii. 20, 44. Mið teáncuidum *contumelia*, Lk. Skt. Lind. 20, 11. Hî ermþu geheton tornum teóncwidum, Exon. Th. 129, 10; Gû. 419. Cf. hearm-cwide.

teón-cwidian; *p.* ode, ede *To reproach, abuse, revile, calumniate*:—Teóncwidedon *conviciebant*, Wrt. Voc. ii. 17, 58. Teóncwid[ed]on, 74, 33. Fore teáncuidendum ûs *pro calumpniantibus nobis*, Rtl. 176, 33. Cf. hearm-cwidian.

teónd, es; *m. One who draws*:—Heó behealdende wæs hwylcum teónde hê upp âhafen wæs, Bd. 4, 9; S. 576, 34.

teónd, es; *m. An accuser*:—Gif wîteþeów mon betýhþ . . . ðonne âh se teónd âne swingellan æt him, L. In. 48; Th. i. 132, 9. Eode se man sylf tō ðe man tuge, and hæbbe se teónd (se ðe týhþ, MS. B.) cyre, swā wæterordāl swā ýsenordāl, L. Ath. iv. 6; Th. i. 224, 15. Tiónd, L. Eth. iii. 6; Th. i. 296, 3. Gylde man ðam teónde his ceápgyld, L. Edg. ii. 7; Th. i. 268, 19: L. Eth. i. 1; Th. i. 280, 20: 282, 3.

teóne, an; *f. Calumny, reproach*:—Teóne *calumnia*, Wrt. Voc. i. 21, 29. Wǣron hyra tungan getale teónan gehwylcre and tō yfele gehwam ungemet scearpe, Ps. Th. 56, 6. v. teóna.

teónere, es; *m. A calumniator*:—Hē geeádmē. ðane teónere *humiliabit calumniatorem*, Ps. Lamb. 71, 4.

teón-full; *adj.* I. *grievous, vexatious, troublous, woeful*:—Se teónfulla dæg (*the last day*), Wulfst. 187, 3. Hū geswincful and hū teónful ðis līf is *how full of travail and trouble this life is*, 273, 6. Ða teónfullan *infesta*, Wrt. Voc. ii. 88, 15. II. of persons, (1) *causing hurt* or *injury*:—Teónfullum on teso *so as to hurt the harmful* (those who were attending to the fiery furnace), Cd. Th. 232, 4; Dan. 255. (2) *causing vexation* or *annoyance, exasperating*. v. teónian, I:—Mǣgþ teónful *generatio exasperans*, Ps. Spl. 77, 10. III. *insolent, abusive, contumelious, contemptuous, calumnious*:—Teónful *injuriosus*, geflitful *contentiosus*, Wrt. Voc. i. 49, 32: 74, 32. Se mynstres hordere sī . . . nā drēfend ne teónful (*non turbulentus, non injuriosus*), R. Ben. 54, 9. Ðū ne scealt nānne man wyrigan, ne nǣnne man tǣlan, ne teónful beón, Homl. Skt. i. 21, 359. Ys steór leás on mūþe teónfulles (*contumeliosi*), Scint. 114, 9. Teónfulle wē synd *contumeliosi sumus*, 155, 14. Wǣron hī æfter æþelborennesse oferhýdige and hearmcwydole . . . Hī ðurhwunedon on heora teónfullum wordum *they persisted in their insolent language*, Homl. Th. ii. 174, 14. [In þa teonfulle (*destructive*) sæ, Laym. 4585.]

teón-hete, es; *m. Harmful* or *wrongful hate, dire hostility*:—Wið ðam teónhete (*the hostility of the Egyptians in pursuit of the Israelites*), Cd. Th. 191, 34; Exod. 224. Wið teónhete, Ps. Th. 147, 2.

teónian; *p.* ode. I. *to vex, irritate.* v. teón-full, II. 2:—Hý teónedon ꝉ hig gremedon *irritaverunt* (*Moysen*), Ps. Lamb. 105, 16. II. *to reproach, revile, abuse, calumniate*:—Se ðe teónaþ þearfan tǣlþ Scyppende his *qui calumniatur pauperem, exprobat factori ejus*, Scint. 156, 14: 178, 18. Ðā hine (*David*) teóne wyrde (teónode and wyrgde? see note) Chus, Ps. Th. 7, arg. Ne teónian mē ða mōdigan *non calumnientur me superbi*, Ps. Lamb. 118, 122. Teóniendum mē *calumniantibus me*, 121. [Hwon his briddes teoneð him *when its young ones vex it* (*the pelican*), A. R. 118, 10. Me teoneð mare þ . . . *quod altius me urit*, Kath. 550. I tene (*trouble*) hem no more, Allit. Pms. 60, 759. Þe naked to tene, Gaw. 2002. Alle wordes him tyeneþ and greueþ, bote yef hi ne by to god, Ayenb. 142, 28. Tyrauntz þat teneþ trewe men, Piers P. 15, 412. Tenyn̄ or urethyn̄ *irrito*, Prompt. Parv. 489. *O. Frs.* tiona, tiuna *to injure*: *O. Sax.* gi-tiunean *to harm*.] v. tīnan.

teónlīce; *adv.* I. *in a manner that causes harm* or *trouble, grievously, miserably*:—Hī gedrēfde deópe weorðaþ . . . swylce teónlīce geteoriaþ, Ps. Th. 103, 27: Exon. Th. 226, 17; Ph. 407. II. *in a way that brings shame* or *affront, with insult* or *ignominy*:—Man sceal ða geóguðe lǣdan gehæft heánlīce and swā bysmorlīce bringan of heora ēðle and betǣcan eów teónlīce on hǣðenra hand, Wulfst. 295, 19. Sende on heora eorþan toscean teónlīce *he brought shame on them by sending frogs into their land*, Ps. Th. 104, 26. Ðencan hū hig hyne teónlýcost āteón myhton *to devise how they might treat him with most ignominy*, Nicod. 14; Thw. 7, 7.

teón-līg, es; *m. Hurtful, destructive flame*, of the conflagration at the last day:—Eall þreó nimeþ fýres wælm . . . teónlēg somod bærneþ þreó (*earth, sea, and sky*) eal on ān, Exon. Th. 60, 14; Cri. 969. Tiónlēg, Elen. Kmbl. 2556; El. 1279.

teón-rǣden[n], e; *f. Wrong, injury*:—Ðæt hig wrecan mihton heora teónrǣdenne mid tintergum on him (*ut reddamus ei* (Samson), *quae in nos operatus est*) . . . Hig woldon hine tintregian for heora teónrǣdene, Jud. 15, 10, 14. Nicanores heáfod hī setton tō tācne for his teónrǣdene (*the wrong he had done to them*), Homl. Skt. ii. 25, 640: Ælfc. T. Grn. 5, 18. Gif hē on gehwylcum teónrǣdennum (*injuriis*) geþyld lufige . . . Gē eác earfeþa and teónrǣdena (*injurias*) forberaþ, R. Ben. 27, 1, 21.

teón-smiþ, es; *m. A worker of hurt* or *wrong, an evil-doer*:—Wǣron teónsmiðas (*the evil spirits that persecuted Guthlac*) tornes fulle, . . . earme andsacan, Exon. Th. 114, 21; Gū. 176.

teóntig. v. hund-teóntig.

teón-word, es; *n. A word that conveys reproach, insult, abuse, calumny; a word that does wrong*:—Hig tǣldon ðæt land mid heora teónwordum *they slandered the land with their calumnies*, Num. 13, 33. Eorl ōðerne mid teónwordum tǣleþ behindan, spreceþ fægere beforan, Frag. Kmbl. 6; Leás. 4. Næs heó swā nū æðelborene men synt mid ofermēttum āfylled . . . ne mid teónwordum *she was not, as nobly born men now are, filled with haughtiness* . . . *or with insolent words*, Lchdm. iii. 428, 33.

teorian; *p.* ode. I. *to tire* (intrans.), *faint, fail, cease*:—Treówgeþofta teoraþ hwīlum wāciaþ wordbeót *faithful comrade fails at times, feeble prove promises*, Exon. Th. 469, 21; Hy. 11, 5. Tiorade *desisse*, Txts. 57, 668. Teorode, Wrt. Voc. ii. 25, 37: Exon. Th. 436, 29; Rä. 55, 8. Eágan mē teoredon *defecerunt oculi mei*, Ps. Th. 118, 82. Gif mon on langum wege teorige *if a man tire on a long journey*, Lchdm. ii. 16, 16. Lǣcedōm wiþ miclum gange ofer land ðý læs hē teorige, 16, 26. Be ðone ðe lād teorie (*fail*). Ðeáh æt stæltyhtlan lād teorie Ængliscan, L. O. D. 4; Th. i. 354, 13-14. Gif ðeós lād teorie, 6; Th. i. 354, 31. II. *to tire* (trans.), *to cause to fail* or *faint*:—Gif mīne grame þenceaþ gāst teorian *if foes think to make my spirit faint*, Ps. Th. 141, 3. [Him trukeþ his iwit, him teoreþ (*fails*) his miht, Fragm. Phlps. 5, 38. *O. Sax.* far-terian *to destroy*.] v. ā-, ge-teorian; teran.

teorig, teorigend-līc, teorodness, teorung. v. un-teorig, ā-teorigendlīc, ge-teorodness, ā-, ge-teorung.

teors, es; *m. A tarse* (v. Halliwell's Dict.); membrum virile:—Teors *calamus*, herþan *testiculi*, Wrt. Voc. i. 65, 30. Teors *veretrum*, teors, ðæt wǣpen *vel* lim *calamus*, 283, 55, 56. Wið hærþena sāre and teorses, Lchdm. i. 358, 4. Smyre ðone teors and ða hærþan, ðonne hafaþ hē mycelne lust, 358, 19: 350, 9. [*O. H. Ger.* zers *veretrum*.]

teoru(-o), teru(-o), tearo, taru; *gen.* teorwes, *also* tearos; *n.*: teora, tara, an; *m. Tar, resin, gum*; also *the wax of the ear*:—Teoru *gluten*, Txts. 67, 985. Teoru, teru *cummi*, 55, 616: *resina*, 93, 1716. Blaec teoru (teru) *napta*, 79, 1360. Teru *bapis*, Wrt. Voc. ii. 125, 17: *cummi*, 137, 44. Blæc teru *napta*, 60, 5. Tero *gluten*, 40, 25: *napta*, 71, 35. Taru, Lchdm. ii. 312, 20. Wiþ teorwe, 132, 5. Meng wiþ sōte sealt, teoro, hunig, 76, 8: 134, 11. Dō of ðīnum eáran ðæt teoro, 112, 3. Meng wiþ pipor and wiþ teoran, 76, 7. [To maken a tur of tigel and ter, Gen. and Ex. 662. The tarre that to thyne sheep bylongeth, Piers P. C-text, x. 262. Terre *butumen*, Wrt. Voc. i. 227, col. 2 (15th cent.). Tere, 279, col. 2. Terre or pyk, Prompt. Parv. 489. *Icel.* tjara.] v. ifig-, scip-, treów-teoru (-tearo, -teora); tirwa.

teorung, e; *f. Fainting, failing, exhaustion*:—Sum gemyndleás wīf fērde wōrigende geond wudas and feldas and ðǣr gelæg ðǣr hī seó teorung gelette *a certain witless woman went wandering about the woods and fields, and lay down where exhaustion prevented her going further*, Homl. Th. ii. 188, 15. v. ā-, ge-teorung.

teosol(ul, -el), es; *m. A small squared piece of stone, a die*:—Tasul(-ol) *tessera*, Txts. 101, 2000. Tæslum *tesellum* (*tessellis* in text, v. tæfl), Wrt. Voc. ii. 93, 44. Tæfles monnes, ðonne teoselum weorpeþ, Exon. Th. 345, 9; Gn. Ex. 185. Tesulas *tesseras*, Txts. 114, 84. [From Latin.]

teosu, tesu, tæsu(-o), wes; *m*(?). *n*(?). I. *hurt, injury*:—Ālet gehwearf teónfullum on teso *the fire turned to the hurt of the harmful*, Cd. Th. 232, 4; Dan. 255. Lēcnade monigo of teissum ꝉ cualmum *curavit multos a plagis*, Lk. Skt. Lind. 7, 21. II. *wrong, fraud*:—Ālýs mīne sāwle from ðære tungan ðe teosu wylle *libera animam meam a lingua dolosa*, Ps. Th. 119, 2. Biþ deófla wīse ðæt hī duguðe beswīcaþ and on teosu tyhtaþ *the devils' way is to seduce from virtue and to incite to wrong*, Exon. Th. 362, 9; Wal. 34. Ōðer hine lǣreþ ðæt hē healde Metodes miltse, ōðer hine tyhteþ and on tæso lǣreþ, Salm. Kmbl. 984; Sal. 493. v. next two words.

teosu-sprǣc, e; *f. Hurtful, deceitful speech*:—Se getynga wer on teosusprǣce *vir linguosus*, Ps. Th. 139, 11.

teoswian, teswian; *p.* ode *To hurt, injure, annoy*:—A hine ofslyhþ, T hine teswaþ, and hine on ða tungan sticaþ, Salm. Kmbl. 189; Sal. 94.

teóða, teogeða; *ord. num. Tenth*, (1) marking order:—Seó teóðe (teigða, Lind.) tīd *hora decima*, Jn. Skt. 1, 39. Ða wæteru wanedon ōð ðæne teóðan mōnð, and on ðam teóðan mōnðe æteówdon ðæra munta cnollas, Gen. 8, 5. Wite cristenra manna gehwilc, ðæt hē his Drihtene his teóðunge, ā swā seó sulh ðone teóðan æcer gegā, rihtlīce gelǣste, L. Eth. ix. 7; Th. i. 342, 11. See Seebohm's Village Community, p. 114. Ðý teogeþan dæge mōnþes, Bd. 5, 23; S. 646, 15. In regula ða teiða *in canone decimo*, Mt. Kmbl. p. 3, 17. On ðone teogeþan dæg ðæs mōnðes, Shrn. 102, 22. Teogþan, 84, 1. (2) marking division:—Syle ðone teóðan dǣl ealra ðīnra wæsma, Deut. 14, 22. Ðý ilcan geáre gebōcude Æþelwulf cyning teóþan dǣl his londes ofer al his rīce Gode tō lofe and him selfum tō ēcere hǣlo, Chr. 855; Erl. 68, 25: Ex. 29, 40. Ðæs hereteámes ealles teóðan sceat Abraham sealde Godes bisceope, Cd. Th. 128, 5; Gen. 2122. Ðone tēþan (teóþan, Bd. M.) dǣl, Bd. 4, 29; S. 608, 18. Ðīne teóðan sceattas āgyf ðū Gode, L. Alf. 38; Th. i. 52, 31. (2 a) used substantively, *a tithe*:—'Ic ðē wille gesyllan mīne teóðan (*decimas*)' . . . Gif wē ūre teóðan gesyllan nyllaþ, ūs ða nygon dǣlas biþ ætbrǣdene, and se teóða ān ūs biþ tō lāf[e], L. Ath. i. prm.; Th. i. 196, 20-26, cf. L. Edg. i. 3; Th. i. 264, 1-5.

teóðian, teogoðian; *p.* ode. I. *to take out a tenth part of anything*:—On eallum geáre sind getealde ðreó hund daga and fīf and sixtig daga; ðonne gif wē teóðiaþ ðās geárlīcan dagas (*if we take a tenth of the days of the year*), ðonne beóþ ðǣr six and ðrītig teóðingdagas, Homl. Th. i. 178, 21. II. *to take a tenth part and give it, to pay tithe of* anything:—Ic teóðie ealle mīne ǣhta, Homl. Th. ii. 428, 25. Gē ðe teóðiaþ (teóðigaþ, MS. B.: tægþigaþ, Rush.) mintan and dile, Mt. Kmbl. 23, 23. Gē ðe teóþiaþ (teigðas, Lind.: tegðigas, Rush.)

ǽlce wyrte, Lk. Skt. 11, 42. Gē teogođiaþ eowrne kymen, Past. 57; Swt. 439, 28. Teóđige hē eal đæt hē āge, L. Pen. 15; Th. ii. 282, 22. Ūs is wyrse đæt wē ūrne ceáp teóþian, gif wē willaþ syllan ūre đæt wyrste Gode, Blickl. Homl. 41, 7. Heáfodmen teóđian, Wulfst. 181, 18. Gif gē nellaþ teóđian ǽlc đæra þinga đe eów God lǽnþ. 297, 2: Homl. Th. i. 178, 30: ii. 608, 21. II a. *to grant* a tenth:—Đā đā hē teóđode gynd eall his cynerīce đone teóđan dǣl ealra his lande *quando decimam partem terrarum per omne regnum meum dare decreui*, Cod. Dip. Kmbl. v. 106, 21. v. ge-teóđian; un-teóđod.

teóđung(-ing), e; *f.* I. *tithe, a tenth part*, (a) in passages not relating to the Christian church:—Hē sealde him đa teóđunge (*decimam*) of eallum đām þingum, Gen. 14, 20. Of eallum þingum, đe đu mē sylst, ic bringe đē teóđunga (*decimas*), 28, 22. Ic sylle teóþunga (teg-đunge, Rush.: teigđuncgas, Lind. *decimas*) ealles đæs đe ic hæbbe, Lk. Skt. 18, 12. Abraham geaf đam kincge Melchisedech đa teóđunga (*decimas*) of đām đingon đe hē gewunnen hæfde, Prud. 56. (b) with special reference to the English church. 'In A.D. 787 tithe was made imperative by the legatine councils held in England, which being attended and confirmed by the kings and ealdormen had the authority of witenagemots,' Stubbs' Const. Hist. i. 228. See also Kemble's Saxons in England, vol. ii, c. x. Accordingly laws of a later date and ecclesiastical writings contain injunctions for the payment of tithe:—Ic Ǽđelstān cyningc . . . eów bidde . . . đæt gē of mīnum āgenum gōde āgifan đa teóđunga, ǽgđer ge on cwicum ceápe ge on đæs geáres eorđwæstmum; . . . and đa biscopas đæt ilce dōn on heora āgenum gōde, and mīne ealdormen and mīne gerēfan đæt silfe. And ic wille đæt bisceop and đa gerēfan hit beódan eallum đām đe him hīran sculon, đæt hit tō đam rihtan āndagan gelǽst sȳ . . . Gif wē đa teóđunga Gode gelǽstan nellaþ, hē ūs benimeþ đara nigon dǽla đonne wē læst wēnaþ, L. Ath. i. prm.; Th. i. 194, 1–196, 7: L. Edm. S. 2; Th. i. 244, 15. Đæt neádgafol ūres Drihtnes, đæt sȳn ūre teóđunga and cyricsceattas . . . Ǽgđer ge earm ge eádig, đe ǽnige teolunga habbe, gelǽste Gode his teóđunga mid ealre blisse, L. Edg. S. 1; Th. i. 270, 25–272, 2. Wile cristenra manna gehwilc, đæt hē his Drihtene his teóđunge, ā swā seó sulh đone teóđan æcer gegā, rihtlīce gelǽste, L. Eth. ix. 7; Th. i. 342, 11. Godes ǽ ūs bebȳt, đæt wē sceolon ealle đa đing đe ūs gesceótaþ of ūres geáres teolunge Gode đa teóđunge syllan, Homl. Th. i. 178, 28: Wulfst. 102, 20. Further, the time of payment and the penalties for neglect to pay were fixed:—Gif hwā teóđunge forhealde, gylde lahslit mid Denum, wīte mid Englum, L. E. G. 6; Th. i. 170, 1. Gif hwā teóđinge forhealde, and hē sī cyninges þegn, gilde .x. healfmearc, landāgende .v. healfmearc, ceorl .xii. ōr, L. N. P. L. 60; Th. ii. 300, 9. Be teóđungum. Sȳ ǽlcere geóguđe teóđung gelǽst be Pentecosten, and đara eorđwæstma be emnnihte . . . and gif hwā đonne đa teóđunge gelǽstan nelle, swā wē gecweden habbaþ, fare đæs cynges gerēfa tō and đæs bisceopes and đæs mynstres mæssepreóst and niman unþances đone teóđan dǽl tō đam mynstre đe hit tō gebyrige and tǽcan him tō đam nigođan dǽle; and tōdǽle man đa eahta dǽlas on twā, and fō se landhlāford tō healfum, tō healfum se bisceop, L. Edg. i. 3; Th. i. 262, 19–264, 4: L. Eth. v. 11; Th. i. 308, 1: ix. 8; Th. i. 342, 14–23. Some information as to the destination of tithe is contained in the following:—Man āgife ǽlce teóđunge tō đam ealdan mynstre đe seó hȳrnes tō hȳrþ, L. Edg. i. 1; Th. i. 262, 6. Gif hwā þegena sȳ đe on his bōclande cyricean hæbbe đe legerstōw on sȳ, gesylle hē đone þriddan dǽl his āgenre teóđunge into his cyricean, i. 2; Th. i. 262, 13: L. C. E. 11; Th. i. 366, 25. Be teóđunge se cyng and his witan habbaþ gecoren and gecweden, đæt þridda dǽl đare teóđunge þe tō circan gebyrige gā tō ciricbōte, and ōđer dǽl đām Godes þeówum, þridde Godes þearfum and earman (v. teođung-sceatt) þeówetlingan, L. Eth. ix. 6; Th. i. 342, 6–9. Gange ǽgđer ge cyricsceat ge teóđunge intō đam hālgan mynstre, Chart. Erl. 236, 2. In a charter, which speaks of Edward as dead, a tithe of eight pennies from each hide is mentioned as due to Taunton:—Hēr swutulaþ on đisum gewrite hwylce gerihta langon intō Tāntūne. Đæt is . . . teóđung of ǽlcere hīde eahta penegas, Cod. Dip. Kmbl. iv. 233, 8. v. æcer-, corn-teóđung. II. *a tithing, an association of ten men* (ten such associations formed a *hynden*, q. v.). The word remains as the name of a local division in many of the southern counties, v. Stubbs' Const. Hist. i. 86, n. 2, but in the earlier time it seems to be personal. v. teóđung-ealdor, -mann:—Đæt man funde ǽnne man đǽr māre folc sig swā of ānre teóđunge đǽr læsse folc sȳ *that one man should be provided alike where the population was large, as where it was so small that there was only one tithing to draw upon*, L. Ath. v. 4; Th. i. 232, 14. Đæt wē ūs gegaderian ā emban ǽnne mōnađ đa hyndenmenn and đa đe đa teóđunge bewitan, v. 8, 1; Th. i. 236, 3. Đæt ǽlc mon beó on teóđunge. Wē wyllaþ, đæt ǽlc freó man beó on hundrede and on teóđunge gebroht, đe lāde wyrđe beón wylle ođđe weres wyrđe, L. C. S. 20; Th. i. 386, 18–22. See Stubbs' Const. Hist. i. 85; Kemble's Saxons in England, vol. i, c. 9.

teóđung-ceáp, es; *m. Tithe-stock, stock paid as tithe*:—Gehēraþ hwæt se æþela lāreów sægde be manna teóþungceápe. Hē cwæþ: Nū neálǽceþ đæt wē sceolan ūre ǽhta and ūre wæstmas gesamnian. Dōn wē đonne Drihtne þancas đe ūs đa wæstmas sealde, and sȳn wē gemyndige đæs đe ūs Crist sylfa bebeád. Hē cwæþ, đæt wē symble emb twelf mōnaþ āgeáfon đone teóþan dǽl đæs đe wē on ceápe habban . . . Ūre Drihten bebeád, đæt wē symle emb twelf mōnaþ gedǽlan đone teóþan dǽl on ūrum wæstmum and on cwicum ceápe, Blickl. Homl. 39, 10–20.

teóđung-dagas; *pl. Tithing-days, days amounting to a tithe of the year*, a term applied to the thirty-six week days in the six weeks of Lent from the first Sunday in Lent until Easter-day:—Gif wē teóđiaþ đās geárlīcan dagas, đonne beóþ đǽr six and đrītig teóđingdagas; and fram đisum dæge (*the first Sunday in Lent*) ōđ đone hālgan Eásterdæg sind twā and feówertig daga; dō đonne đa six Sunnandagas of đam getele, đonne beóþ đa six and đrītig đæs geáres teóđingdagas ūs tō forhæfednysse getealde . . . Wē sceolon on đisum teóđingdagum ūrne līchaman mid forhæfednysse teóđian, Homl. Th. i. 178, 21–30: ii. 608, 20: L. E. I. 37; Th. ii. 436, 10. Ūs gebyreþ, đæt wē ǽlces þinges ūre teóđunge rihtlīce Gode betǽcan; đonne syndan đās dagas (*fast days of Lent*) getealde for teóđingdagas innan geáres fæce, and wē sculan eác đa teóđunge wyrđlīce Gode gelǽstan, Wulfst. 102, 21.

teóđung-ealdor, es; *m. A chief of ten monks, a dean*:—Hwylce mynstres teóđingealdras (*decani*) beón sceolon. Gif seó geferrǽden tō đam micel sȳ, sȳn gecorene of đām sylfum gebrōđrum đa đe gōdes gewittes sȳn, and syn gesette tō teóđingealdrum (*constituantur decani*), R. Ben. 46, 6–10: 137, 17–20. Cf. teóđung, II.

teóđung-georn; *adj. Sedulous in paying tithes*:—Ǽlmysgeorn and cyricgeorn and teóþunggeorn tō Godes cyricean and earmum mannum *eleemosynas libenter erogans, et ad ecclesiam libenter frequens, et sedulo decimas erogans ecclesiae Dei ac pauperibus*, L. Ecg. C. prm.; Th. ii. 132, 15: Anglia xii. 518, 26.

teóđung-land, es; *n. Land that was subject to the payment of tithe* (?):—Ic fēng tō mīnan londe and sealde hit đon biscope đa fīf hīda wiđ đon londe æt Lidgeard wiđ fīf hīdan and biscop and eal hīwan forgeáfan mē đa feówer and ān wæs teóđinglond *I resumed my land and sold it, the five hides to wit, to the bishop* (*of Winchester*) *for the land at Liddiard, for five hides, and the bishop and brethren granted me the four* (*free of tithe?*) *and one was subject to tithe*, Cod. Dip. Kmbl. ii. 135, 2–6. As may be seen from another charter, the land at Liddiard was in the hands of the bishop of Winchester, v. 144; and several names besides will be found common to the two charters. For the *teóđung* of a hide, see the last passage given under teóđung, I b.

teóđung-mann, es; *m.* I. *one set over ten persons, a ruler of ten*:—Ic sette hig tō teóđingmannum *constitui eos decanos*, Deut. 1, 15. Geceós wīse men and sōđfæste . . . and gesete of him . . . teóđingmen (*decanos*), Ex. 18, 21. II. as a technical English term, *the head of a tithing*, v. teóđung, II:—Wē cwǽdon be uncūđum yrfe, đæt nān man næfde būton hē hæfde đæs hundredes manna gewitnyssa ođđe đæs teóđingmannes, L. Edg. ii. 4; Th. i. 260, 1. Gyf neód on handa stande, cȳđe hit man đam hundredes men, and hē syđđan đām teóđingmannum, 2; Th. i. 258, 8.

teóđung-sceatt, es; *m. A tax of a tenth, a tithe*:—Teóþingsceat *decimatis*, Wrt. Voc. ii. 26, 36: 73, 44. Swā feala earmra manna swā on đæs rīcan neáweste sweltaþ, and hē him nele syllan his teóþungsceatta dǽl, đonne biþ hē ealra đara manna deáþes sceldig, Blickl. Homl. 53, 6. Mid đam oftige đæs neádgafoles đe cristene men Gode gelǽstan scoldon on heora teóđingsceattum, L. Edg. S. 1; Th. i. 270, 14.

teped, ter. v. tæpped, ge-ter.

teran; *p.* tær, *pl.* tǽron; *pp.* toren *To tear, rend, bite, lacerate*, (1) literal:—Feallcþ on sīdan đæt ic (*a plough*) tōþum tere, Exon. Th. 403, 27; Rä. 22, 14. Hit tyrþ (*mordebit*) eal swā snaca, Scint. 105, 8. Teraþ *carpunt*, Germ. 395, 403. Gif swīn deáde men teraþ (*laceraverint*), L. Ecg. C. 40; Th. ii. 164, 38. Đā tær hē his clāđas *scissis vestibus*, Gen. 37, 29, 34. Wyrmas gelīce mid đǽm scillum gelīce mid đē mūþe đa eorđan sliton and tǽron *oribus scamisque suis humum atterentes*, Nar. 14, 12. Hæfdon hié tēđ and hié mid đǽm đa men wundodon and tǽron *habentes dentes quibus artus militum violabant*, 15, 9. Đa fuglas mid hiora clēum đa fixas tǽron, 16, 21. Hē ongon his hrægl teran, Exon. Th. 278, 10; Jul. 595. Feax teran *to tear the hair*, Judth. Thw. 25, 28. Ne sceal hē teran ne bītan swā swā wulf, Homl. Th. ii. 532, 9. Tō teorenne *lacerandum*, Txts. 172, 2. Terende weleras *mordens labia*, Scint. 78, 14. Teorende hine *discerpens eum*, Mk. Skt. Rush. 9, 26. Mid slītendum ł terendum tōđreómum *validis* (*voracibus*) *gingivis*, Hpt. Gl. 423, 43. (1 a) *to bite*, of pungent food, etc.:—Hē is swīđe biter on mūþe and hē đē tiiþ on đa þrotan đonne đū his ǽrest fandast *talia sunt, ut degustata mordeant*, Bt. 22, 1; Fox 76, 29. (2) figurative:—Ne đū hine ne tǽl ne ne ter mid wordum *do not backbite*, Basil admn. 5; Norm. 46, 11. [*Goth.* dis-, ga-tairan: *O. H. Ger.* zeran.] v. ā-, ge-, tō-teran.

Ter-finnas; *pl. Finns occupying country west of the White Sea*:—Đa Beormas hæfdon swīþe wel gebūd hira land . . . Ac đara Terfinna land wæs eal wēste . . . Finnas, him þūhte, and đa Beormas sprǽcon neáh ān geþeóde, Ors. 1, 1; Swt. 17, 29.

tergan. v. tirgan.

termen, es; *m. A term, fixed date*:—Gif đū wille witan đæt gemǽre *terminum septuagesimalis*, đonne tele đū . . . đonne on đam teóđan stent se termen, đæt gemǣre, Lchdm. iii. 228, 3. On noñ Aprilis byđ se forma termen on đam circule đe ys *decennovenalis*, odđe *pascalis* gehāten, Anglia viii. 310, 42: 323, 3. Đæt gemǣre đæs termenes pasche, 322, 34. On đam termine đære eásterlīcan tīde, 315, 19. Ymbe đæne termen, 324, 29. [*Icel.* termin. From Latin.]

tero(-u), teso, tesulas, teswian. v. teoru, teosu, teosol, teoswian.

teter, tetr, es; *m. Tetter, a cutaneous disease*:—Teter *balsis*, Txts. 43, 262: Wrt. Voc. ii. 10, 61: 125, 13: *briensis*, i. 288, 5. Teter, tetr *inpetigo*, Txts. 69, 1047: *petigo*, 85, 1550. Teter, Wrt. Voc. ii. 68, 3. Spryng *vel* tetr *papula* vel *pustula*, Txts. 88, 791. Se hæfþ teter (*impetiginem*) on his līchoman, se hæfþ on his mōde gītsunga . . . Būtan tweón se teter būtan sāre hē ofergǣþ đone līchoman, and suā đeáh đæt lim geunwlitegaþ, Past. 11; Swt. 71, 15–17: Scint. 99, 10. On tetere *inpetigine*, Wrt. Voc. ii. 46, 27. Wiđ sceb and wiđ teter, Lchdm. i. 150, 5: 234, 10. Wiđ teter, of andwlitan tō dōnne, 336, 3. *The form* tetra, *perhaps influenced by* lepra *which precedes it, also occurs*:—Đonne becymþ of đām yflum wǣtum odđe sió hwīte riéfþo þe mon on sūþerne *lepra* hǣt, oþđe tetra, oþþe heáfodhriéfđo, odđe ōman, Lchdm. ii. 228, 13. [A tetere *serpedo*, Wrt. Voc. i. 267, col. 2 (15th cent.). Cf. *O. H. Ger.* zitaroh *impetigo, scabies*: *Ger.* zitteroch; zittermal *tetter, ring-worm.*]

tēþa, tēđed, te-treþ, te-tridit, te-weorpan, tewestre. v. teóđa, ge-tēđed, tō-tredan, tō-weorpan, wull-tewestre.

tiber, tifer, es; *n. A sacrifice, offering, victim*:—Wit fȳr and sweord habbaþ, hwǣr is đæt tiber đæt đū torht Gode tō đam brynegielde bringan þencest (cf. ic āxige hwǣr seó offrung sig; hēr ys wudu and fȳr *ecce ignis et ligna; ubi est victima?* Gen. 22, 7), Cd. Th. 175, 4; Gen. 2890. Đū scealt mē onsecgan sunu đīnne tō tibre *offeres filium tuum in holocaustum* (Gen. 22, 2), 172, 31; Gen. 2852. Se đe on tifre gesalde Drihten Hǣlend, 301, 1; Sat. 575. Hié Drihtne lāc begen brohton; brego engla beseah on Abeles gield, cyning eallwihta, Caines ne wolde tiber sceáwian (*ad munera illius (Cain) non respexit Dominus*, Gen. 4, 5), 60, 9; Gen. 979. Noe tiber onsægde (*obtulit holocausta*, Gen. 8, 20), 90, 29; Gen. 1502: 108, 17; Gen. 1807. Hālig tiber (*Isaac*), 204, 6; Exod. 415. Ic on đīn hūs gange and đǣr tīdum đē tifer onsecge . . . Đās ic mid mūđe āspræc . . . đæt ic đē on tifrum forgulde ealle đa gehāt đe ic mid mīnum welerum tōdǣlde *introibo in domum tuam in holocaustis . . . Haec locutum est os meum . . . : Holocausta offeram tibi*, Ps. Th. 65, 12–13. Tiber, Cd. Th. 9, 2; Gen. 135. v. timber. [*O. H. Ger.* zepar, zebar *hostia, sacrificium, holocaustum*: *Ger.* ziefer *in* ungeziefer. Cf. *Icel.* tafn *a sacrifice, victim.* See Grmm. D. M. p. 36.] v. fyrd- (?), sige-, sigor-, wīn-tiber (-tifer).

tiberness, e; *f. Sacrifice, destruction, immolation*:—Rǣde on his bōcum hwelce tibernessa ǣgđer ge on monslihtum ge on hungre ge on scipgebroce *let him read in his books what sacrifices of life there were by slaughter, famine, and shipwreck* (the Latin, which is not closely followed, has *qui caedem didicerunt*), Ors. 1, 11; Swt. 50, 18.

tican, Lchdm. ii. 60, 18, *read* tilian.

ticcen, es; *n. A kid*:—Ticcen *hedus*, Wrt. Voc. i. 23, 1: 78, 34: *edum*, 288, 18: ii. 30, 56. Ticcenes geallan, Lchdm. ii. 28, 21. Đā nāmon hig ān ticcen and ofsnidon hit, Gen. 37, 31. Ic sende đē ān ticcen (*hoedum*) of mīnre heorde, 38, 17, 20. Buccan wē offriaþ odđe ticcen, Homl. Th. ii. 210, 32. Ne sealdest đū mē nǣfre ān ticcen (ticgen, Lind.: tycchen, *later MS.*), Lk. Skt. 15, 29. Ticcenu beóþ eáđmelte, Lchdm. ii. 196, 24. Bring mē twā đa betstan tyccenu (*hoedos*) . . . Heó befeóld his handa mid đæra tyccena fellum, Gen. 27, 9, 16. Swā swā se hyrde āsyndraþ đa scēp fram tyccenum (ticgenum, Lind.: ticnum, Rush.: ticchenan, *later MS.*), Mt. 25, 32. The word occurs in local names, e. g. Ticcenes-, Ticnes-feld. v. Cod. Dip. Kmbl. vi. 342. [*O. H. Ger.* zicchīn, zicchī *hoedus*: *Ger.* zicke *a kid.*]

ticgende. v. tycgan.

ticia, an; *n. A tick* (an insect infesting animals):—Ticia *ricinus*, Txts. 109, 1130. [A teke *ascarida*, Wrt. Voc. i. 255, col. 1 (15th cent.). A tyke, Wülck. Gl. 566, 18. Tyke, wyrm, Prompt. Parv. 493. To fles ant to fleye, to tyke ant to tadde, P. S. 238, 4. *O. Du.* teke: *M. H. Ger.* zeche, zecke: *Ger.* zecke. Cf. *the borrowed Romance forms, Fr.* tique: *Ital.* zecca.]

ticlum, Exon. Th. 420, 12; Rä. 40, 2. v. til.

tictator, es; *m. The Anglicized form of Latin* dictator:—Hié him gesetton hīr[r]an lādteów đonne hiera consul wǣre, đone đe hié tictatores hēton, and hié mid đæm tictatore micelne sige hæfdon, Ors. 2, 4; Swt. 70, 3.

tīd, e; *f. Tide* (as in Shrove-*tide*, etc.), *time, hour*; tempus, Wrt. Voc. i. 52, 39: hora, 53, 17. I. marking time when, *time* at which anything happens, *time* or *date* of an event, *time, hour*:—Be đam dæge and đære tīde nān mann nāt . . . Gē nyton hwænne seó tīd ys, Mk. Skt. 13, 32, 33. Đā com his tīd đæt hē sceolde of middangearde tō Drihtne fēran, Bd. 4, 3; S. 567, 13: 4. 9; S. 577, 16. Tō morgen on đisse ylcan tīde ic sende micelne hagol, Ex. 9, 18. Đæt sylþ his wæstmas tō rihtre tīde, Ps. Th. 1, 4. Hē on gerisene tīd mid hwǣte seów, Bd. 4, 28; S. 605, 34. On eallum tīdum secggan wē him þanc, Blickl. Homl. 103, 25. I a. *a proper time, time at which a thing can* or *ought to be done, time* (as in to be in *time*), *season, opportunity*:—Đæt tīd wǣre stānas tō sendanne and tīd tō somnienne, Bd. 4, 3; S. 567, 9. Tīd is đæt đū fēre, Exon. Th. 179, 30; Gū. 1269. Hwīlum sié sprǣce tiid, Past. 38; Swt. 275, 17. Hē bīt đære tīde, hwonne hē đæs wierđe sié, đæt hē hine besuīcan mōte, 33; Swt. 227, 11. On tīde hē sende hys þeów *at the season he sent a servant* (A. V.), Lk. Skt. 20, 10. Đæt hē him on tīde mete sylle *to give them meat in due season* (A. V.), Mt. Kmbl. 24, 45. Tō tīde, Past. 63; Swt. 459, 12. Se đe his ǣr tīde ne tiolaþ, đonne biþ his on tīd untilad, Bt. 29, 2; Fox 106, 3. Ic ondette gīfernesse metes ǣr tīdum, and in tīde, ge eác ofer rihttīde, Anglia xi. 98, 24. Bi đon hérǣfter in heora tiid is tō secgenne *de quibus in sequentibus suo tempore dicendum est*, Bd. 3, 18; S. 546, 40. Ofer đa tīd đæs sǣwetes, 4, 28; S. 605, 8. I b. marking a definite time in the day, *an hour*:—Hit wæs đā seó teóđe tīd *hora erat quasi decima*, Jn. Skt. 1, 39. Đā wæs neán seó syxte tīd, and þȳstro wǣron ofer ealle eorþan ōđ đa nigoþan tīde, Lk. Skt. 23, 44. Fram đære sixtan tīde ōđ đa nigođan tīd, Mt. Kmbl. 27, 45. Hē ūt eode embe đa sixtan and nigođan tīde . . . embe đa endlyftan tīde, 20, 5–6. Ymbe đa nygođan tīd clypode se Hǣlend, 27, 46. Ymb đa teóđan tīd dæges, Bd. 3, 27; S. 558, 12. Sele drincan on þreó tīda, on undern, on middæg, on nōn, Lchdm. ii. 140, 1. I c. as an ecclesiastical term, *a canonical hour, hour for a service, the service at such an hour*:—Ic sincge ǣlce dæg seofon tīda *psallo omni die septem synaxes*, Coll. Monast. Th. 18, 30. Wē lǣraþ đæt man on rihtne tīman tīda ringe, L. Edg. C. 45; Th. ii. 254, 5. Gif preóst on gesetne tīman tīda ne ringe, oþþe tīda ne singe, L. N. P. L. 36; Th. ii. 296, 3–4. I d. *a time at which a commemoration takes place, a tide, festival, anniversary*:—On đone þriddan dæge đæs mōnđes biþ đæs hālgan pāpan tīd đe is nemned Scē Antheri, Shrn. 47, 31: 48, 5, *and often*. Tȳd, 150, 11: 151, 17. Đæs heáhengles (*St. Michael*) tīd, Blickl. Homl. 197, 4. Seó tīd (*the anniversary of a victory*), 205, 28. Cristes tīd *Christmas*, Lchdm. ii. 294, 27. Tō Scē Michaeles tīde *at Michaelmas*, Chr. 759; Erl. 54, 14. Se cyng nam đǣr his feorme in đære middewintres tīde, 1006; Erl. 140, 30. Ic bebeóde đæt mon hiora tīd boega geuueorđiæ tō ānes dæges tō Ōsuulfes tīde *I enjoin that the anniversary of them both be kept on one day, on Oswulf's anniversary*, Chart. Th. 460, 1–7. Is đeós tīd (*Easter*) ealra tīda hēhst and hālgost, Blickl. Homl. 83, 19. Beó đām hālgum tīdan eallum cristenum mannum sib and sōm gemǣne, L. Eth. v. 19; Th. i. 308, 28. II. marking duration, (1) where the length of time is indefinite, *time, a period of time*; in pl. *times* (as in *our times*, etc.):—Uncūþ biþ ǣghwylcum ānum men his līfes tīd, Blickl. Homl. 125, 7. Wē sceolan on đisse sceortan tīde geearnian ēce ræste, 83, 2. Hē langre tīde ealle heora mǣgþe wæs geondfarende, Bd. 2, 20; S. 521, 26. On sibbe tīde *in time of peace*, 2, 16; S. 520, 10. Đū ne oncneówe đa tīde đīnre geneósunge, Lk. Skt. 19, 44. On đa tiid suā huelc suā biscephād underfēng, hē underfēng martyrdōm. On đa tiid wæs tō herigeanne đæt mon wilnode biscephādes, Past. 8; Swt. 53, 18. Ic sume tīd fram đē gewāt, Bd. 5, 12; S. 630, 29. Twelf wintra tīd *for the space of twelve years*, Beo. Th. 296; B. 147. Eálā đæt wolde God đæt ūssa tīda wǣren swelce, Met. 8, 40. Hē wæs him feor manegum tīdum (*for a long time*, A. V.), Lk. Skt. 20, 9. Ǣr eallum tīdum ācenned, Blickl. Homl. 31, 24. Đa đe on mē gelȳfaþ eallum tīdum on ēcnesse, 231, 4. Đæt wæs geworden on Wulfheres tīdum, Bd. 3, 21; S. 551, 42. On đām tīdum ārās Pelaies gedwild, Chr. 380; Erl. 11, 6. Sió wyrd dǣlþ eallum gesceaftum stōwa and tīda, Bt. 39, 5; Fox 218, 33. (1 a) *time, condition of things*:—On đam endenȳhstan dagum đissere worulde beóþ frēcenlīce tīda, Wulfst. 81, 12. (2) where the period is a definite one:—Đā (*after the first act of creation*) eodon þrȳ dagas forđ būton tīda gemetum (*without measurement of hours and days*); for đan đe tunglan nǣron gesceapene, Homl. Th. i. 100, 7. (2 a) *an hour* of the day:—Æfter lytlum fæce swylce ānre tīde, Lk. Skt. 22, 59. Healfre tīde fæc, Bd. 4, 3; S. 568, 1. On ānre tīde dæges *in the course of one hour*, Blickl. Homl. 31, 2. Steorran hié ætiéwdon ful neáh healfe tīd ofer undern, Chr. 540; Erl. 16, 4. Āne tīd dæges, 879; Erl. 80, 30. Hū ne synt twelf tīda đæs dæges? Jn. Skt. 11, 9. Feówer and twentig tīda . . . đæt is ān dæg and ān niht, Lchdm. iii. 254, 13: 260, 13–15. Æfter þrīm tīdum gelǣd hyne tō bæþe, Lchdm. i. 302, 17. Ān wæcce hæfþ þreó tīda, Homl. Th. ii. 388, 14. (2 b) *one of the four seasons of the year*:—Hærfestlīcre tīde *autumnali (tempore)*, Hpt. Gl. 496, 48. Ōþ sumeres tīd, Bd. 4, 28; S. 605, 35. Feówer tīda syndan on đæm geáre, Blickl. Homl. 35, 15. On lenctenlīcere emnihte wurdon geárlīce tīda gesette, Homl. Th. i. 100 3. Þurh đæt gewrixle đara feówer tȳda, đæt ys lencten and sumer and herfest and winter, Shrn. 168, 12. Nihte and dæg đū đe gewissast and tīdena đū selst tīda *noctem diemque qui regis et temporum das tempora*, Hymn. Surt. 6, 6. On wintregum tīdum, Ors. 1, 1; Swt. 12, 34. (2 b 1) *a season* of the year:—Se cyng gewende tō đam middan wintra tō Wihtlande and wæs đǣr đa tīd, and æfter đære tīde gewende ofer sǣ, Chr. 1013; Erl. 149, 11–13. Gehealdaþ đās tīd (*Lent*), Homl. Th. i. 180, 2. (2 c) *an age*:—Þreó tīda sind on đysre worulde; ān is seó đe wæs būtan ǣ, ōđer is seó đe wæs under ǣ, seó đridde is nū æfter Cristes tōcyme, Homl. Th. i. 312,

29. III. as a grammatical term, *tense:—Verbum* ys word mid tíde and háde bútan case ... Him gelimpþ ... *tempus* tíd, Ælfc. Gr. 19; Zup. 119, 8–14. Tíd gelimpþ worde for getácnunge mislícra dǽda. Æfter gecynde synd þreó tída ... andwerd tíd ... forðgewiten tíd ... tówerd tíd, 20; Zup. 123, 12–17. [*O. Sax. O. Frs.* tíd: *O. H. Ger.* zît *tempus, hora, aevum, saeculum: Icel.* tíð.] v. ǽfen-, án-, bed-, behreówsung-, bén-, blódlǽs-, cwyld-, cyric-, Eáster-, fæsten-, freóls-, fulwiht-, gebed-, gebyrd-, gefylling-, hærfest-, hancréd-, heáh-, heáhfreóls-, heófung-, hláfmæsse-, lencten-, merigen-, mete-, middæg-, morgen-, neáh-, nón-, riht-, symbel-, þrowung-, úht-, undern-, winter-tíd; hwíltídum; tíma.

tídan; *p.* de *To betide, befall, happen:*—Bisceopum gebyreþ ðæt symle mid heom wunian wel geþungene witan, ... ðæt heora gewitan beón on ǽghwylcne tíman, weald hwæt heom tíde, L. I. P. 10; Th. ii. 316, 25. Gif ðan biscop[e] hwæt tíde, Cod. Dip. B. iii. 75, 6, 10, 13. [Þa tidde hit on an Wodnesdei, þet se king rad in his derfald, Chr. 1123; Erl. 249, 30. Ne tyt þe no part wiþ me, Marg. 308. What shulde us tyden? Chauc. M. of L. 337. Som tymes hym tit (bitit, B-text) to folwen hus kynde, Piers P. 14, 213, C-text. A merueillouse meteles me tydde to dreme, 11, 5, B-text. Tydyn̄ idem quod happyn̄, Prompt. Parv. 493.] v. ge-, mis-tídan; tídung.

tíd-dæg, es; *m. The period of a person's life* (cf. the use of *dæg* = time, e. g. Gif ðú wistest on ðysum ðínum dæge, Lk. Skt. 19, 42):—Enoses sunu ealra nigon hund wintra hæfde, ðá hé woruld ofgeaf, and týne eác, ðá his tíddæge rím wæs gefylled *when for his lifetime the number of years was completed,* Cd. Th. 71, 4; Gen. 1165.

tidder-. v. tíder-.

tíd-ege (?), es; *m. Fear of a time, fear of the time of death.* v. tíd, I:—Simle þreora sum þinga gehwylce ǽr his tídege (tide ge, MS.) tó tweón weorþeþ ádl oþþe yldo oþþe ecghete fǽgum fromweardum feorh óðþringeþ *ever in every case, before the fear of his end becomes doubtful* (*before his fear of death has lost any of its certainty?*), *one of three things, disease or age or violence, crushes the life out of the fey man, outward bound from this world,* Exon. Th. 310, 3; Seef. 69.

tíder-líc; *adj. Weak, frail:*—Se ðe gehielt his unsceadfulnesse and his gódan willan ðeáh hé hwæt tiéderlíces oððe yfelra weorca útan doo hé mæg ðæt æt sumum cierre bétan *si mentis innocentia custoditur, etiam si qua foris infirma sunt, quandoque roborantur,* Past. 34; Swt. 235, 23. In giscæf[te] téderlícum *in sexu fragili,* Rtl. 51, 7. Tydderlícne líchoman hád *fragilem corporis sexum,* Hymn. Surt. 139, 13. Ic eom þurh míne tydderlíce gecynd líchamlíc man, Homl. Ass. 156, 123. Ðætte suǽ fealo téderlícro wé sindon suǽ suíðe strongrum helpum wé sié áholpen *ut quanto fragiliores sumus, tanto validioribus auxiliis foveamur,* Rtl. 61, 9. v. tídre.

tíderness, e; *f.* I. *weakness, frailty,* (a) *weakness* in a general sense, physical, mental, or moral:—Ne mæg úre tyddernes ðyder (*to heaven*) ástígan, Homl. Th. i. 138, 12: ii. 6, 29: 88, 18. Ðeós mennisce tyddernes biþ swá slídende swá glæs, ðonne hit scínþ and ðonne tóbersteþ, Shrn. 119, 22. Sió niht getácnaþ ða ðístro ðære blindnesse úrre tídernesse *per noctem caecitas nostrae infirmitatis exprimitur,* Past. 56; Swt. 433, 13. Tiddernysse *fragilitatis* (*humanae*), Hpt. Gl. 437, 31. Tédernise, Rtl. 45, 16: 46, 32. For líchoman tídernesse (tiéder-, Hatt. MS.) *per imbecillitatem corporis,* Past. 10; Swt. 60, 10. Ðære tídernesse úres flǽsces wé beóþ underðiédde, 21; Swt. 159, 5. For ðæs módes týdernesse, Bt. 3, 2; Fox 6, 7: Blickl. Homl. 31, 30. Swá hwæt swá ic for unwísnesse and for tyddernesse (*fragilitate*) ágylte, Bd. 4, 29; S. 607, 29: Boutr. Scrd. 21, 17. Ðú wást, Drihten, ða menniscan tyddernysse, Blickl. Homl. 243, 30. (b) *the weakness* of ill-health, *infirmity:*—Gif hwylc mæssepreóst untruman men sprǽce forwyrne, and hé ðonne on ðære tyddernesse (*infirmitate*) swelte, L. Ecg. P. i. 2; Th. ii. 172, 28. Wiþ ǽlces dæges mannes tyddernysse inneweardes, Lchdm. i. 86, 16: ii. 196, 9. Lǽcedómas wið eallum tiédernessum eágena, 2, 6. Mid sáre geswenced, mid mislícum ecum and tyddernessum, Blickl. Homl. 59, 8. (c) *spiritual infirmity, sinfulness:*—Ægylt, mislimp *vel* tyddernes *excessus,* i. *culpa, delicta,* Wrt. Voc. ii. 145, 68. Ic eom andetta ealra synna ðara ðe ic ǽfre tó tiédernesse gefremede wið mínre sáwle þearfe, Anglia xi. 99, 89. Swá neár ende ðyssere worulde swá biþ unstrengre mennisc ðurh máran tyddernysse, Homl. Th. ii. 370, 17. v. innan-, innoþ-tíderness.

tíd-fara, an; *m. A traveller the time of whose journey is come* (?), or *one who journeys for a* (*short*) *time* (?):—Nú ðú (*the blessed soul immediately after death*) móst féran ðider ðú fundadest ... eart nú tídfara tó ðam hálgan hám, Exon. Th. 102, 18; Cri. 1674.

tíd-genge; *adj. Current* or *lasting for a time:*—Tídgenge *menstruam,* Germ. 392, 10.

tíding. v. tídung.

tíd-líc; *adj.* I. *lasting for a time, temporary, not eternal, of this world:*—Tyddre ys tídlíc miht *fragilis est temporalis potentia,* Scint. 215, 8. For tídlícre geswencednysse *pro temporali afflictione,* 149, 1. Þing tídlíc *rem temporalem,* 17, 9: Rtl. 31, 28. Fram tídlícra þinga geþance, Scint. 34, 8. Tídlícum *temporalibus,* Rtl. 8, 9: 18, 23: Anglia xiii. 381, 230. II. *seasonable, opportune:*—Seó tídlíce *oportunus,* Wrt. Voc. ii. 64, 27: 80, 41. Ðú him mete sylest mǽla gehwylce and ðæs tídlíce tíd gemearcast *tu das escam illis in tempore opportuno,* Ps. Th. 144, 16. III. *expressing relations of time, of time:*—Hwílon hé (*the word* ut) getácnaþ tíde ... on ðissere stówe hé is *temporale adverbium,* ðæt is tídlíc, Ælfc. Gr. 44; Zup. 265, 19. Sume naman syndon *temporalia,* ðæt synd tídlíce, ða æteówiaþ tíman, 5; Zup. 14, 16. [*O. H. Ger.* zît-líh *temporalis, momentaneus: Icel.* tíð-ligr *temporal.*] v. un-tídlíc.

tídlíce; *adv.* I. *for a time, temporarily:*—Yrsunge tídelíce (*but* tíde ne, MSS. O.T.) sceal mon gehealdan *iracundie tempus non reseruare,* R. Ben. 17, 6, I a. *for time, in this world:*—Se ðe on ðisse worulde wel tídlíce (*temporaliter*) wealdt, bútan ende on écnysse ríxaþ, Scint. 182, 1. II. *conveniently, at a suitable time:*—Hé sóhte ðætte tídlíce ðætte mæhte sellan hine (cf. hé sóhte hú hé eáðelícust hine gesealde, W. S.) *quaerebat oportunitatem ut traderet illum,* Lk. Skt. Rush. 22, 6. II a. *seasonably, in a manner appropriate to a season:*—Seó dún wæs tídlíce gréne *the hill, as was natural to the season* (the date was June 22), *was green;* mons opportune laetus, Bd. 1, 7; S. 478, 21. III. *in time, in good time, betimes, early, soon, quickly:*—Ic tídlíce tó mínre reste eode, for ðon ic wolde beón gearo æt sunnan upgonge, Nar. 30, 27. Ðæt gefremede Diulius hiora consul ðæt ðæt angin wearð tídlíce þurhtogen *quod Duilius consul celeriter implevit,* Ors. 4, 6; Swt. 172, 3: 3, 1; Swt. 98, 14. Gif hió mon tídlíce tó bringþ *if it be brought in time,* 5, 13; Swt. 246, 34. Him spédlíce spearuwa hús begyteþ, and tídlíce turtle nistlaþ, Ps. Th. 83, 3: 105, 5. Ædre cymþ, tídlíce, ús Iulius mónað, Menol. Fox 260; Men. 131. Tídlícor, hrædlícor *maturius,* Wrt. Voc. ii. 55, 24. [Tidlike (*soon*) hem gan ðat water laken, Gen. and Ex. 1231. Let turnen hit tidliche (swiftliche, MS. C.), Kath. 1932: Jul. 58, 6. *O. H. Ger.* zîtlîhho *temporaliter, in tempore, mature.*] Cf. tímlíce.

tídlícness, e; *f. Opportunity:*—Tídlícnisse *opportunitatem,* Lk. Skt. Lind. 22, 6.

tídran. v. týdran.

tídre, tiédre, tédre, týdre, tiddre, tyddre, *and* tíder (? v. tidder, Hpt. Gl. 436, 59); *adj.* I. *weak, fragile, easily broken:*—Tédre swá swá gangewifran nett, Ps. Th. 38, 12. Se wyrttruma byþ breáþ and tídre, ðonne hé gedríged byþ, Lchdm. i. 260, 7. II. *weak, frail,* of physical, mental, or moral weakness in persons:—Ðæt hiw úre tyddran gecynde, Blickl. Homl. 29, 4. Seó godcundnes onféng úre týdran gecynde, 17, 27. Wé tealtrigaþ týdran móde, Exon. Th. 23, 20; Cri. 371. For úre eágena tyddernysse, Lchdm. iii. 232, 16. Ðæt týdre gewitt, Exon. Th. 2, 34; Cri. 29. Ða týdran mód, 147, 19; Gú. 729. Ða hildlatan holt ofgeáfon, týdre treówlogan, Beo. Th. 5686; B. 2847. Hwæt sind ða ðe ús biddaþ? Earme men, and tiddre, and deádlíce, Homl. Th. i. 256, 2. Tyddre, Boutr. Scrd. 22, 37. Nánre wuhte líchoma ne beoþ téderra ðonne ðæs monnes, Bt. 16, 2; Fox 52, 9. Ða hwítan líchoman beóþ mearuwran and tédran ðonne ða blacan and ða reádan, Lchdm. ii. 84, 21. II a. *weak, having bad health, infirm:*—Gif wíf on ðon tédre sié *if a woman have that infirmity,* Lchdm. ii. 8, 25. Is ðæm lǽce tó giémanne ðæt hé swá líðne lǽcedóm selle ðæm seócan swá se týdra líchoma (*corpus debile*) mǽge ástandan, Past. 61; Swt. 455, 30. Gewǽht, tidder *fessa, fatigata,* Hpt. Gl. 436, 59. III. of immaterial things, *frail, not lasting, fleeting:*—Hú lytel hé (*fame*) biþ, hú lǽne, hú tédre and hú bedǽled ǽlces gódes *quam sit exilis et totius vacua ponderis,* Bt. 18, 1; Fox 60, 29. Se wlite ðæs líchoman is swíþe flíonde and swíþe tédre and swíþe anlíc eorþan blóstmum *formae nitor ut rapidus est, ut velox, et vernalium florum mutabilitate fugacior,* 32, 2; Fox 116, 17. Ðis líf is lǽnlíc and tyddre and feallende and earm, L. E. I. prm.; Th. ii. 400, 16. Ðissere worulde wuldor gewítendlíc ys tyddre tídlíc miht *hujus saeculi gloria caduca est, fragilis temporalis potentia,* Scint. 215, 8. Týdrum *lubrico,* Germ. 401, 45. Sint swíþe tédre and swíþe hreósende ðás gesǽlþa *caduca felicitas,* Bt. 11, 2; Fox 34, 22. Tiédre (tédra, Cott. MS.), 20; Fox 72, 3. Tyddre weorþmyntas *fragiles honores,* tyddrum gefeohte *fragili bello* vel *inbecilla,* Wrt. Voc. ii. 150, 38–40. [*O. Frs.* teddre: *Du.* teeder.] v. un-tídre.

tíd-regn, es; *m. A seasonable rain:*—Drihten geopenaþ heofunan his sélustan goldhord and sent tídrénas on ðín land (*to give the rain unto thy land in his season;* ut tribuat pluviam terrae tuae in tempore suo), Deut. 28, 12.

tídrian; *p.* ode. I. of persons, *to get weak* or *infirm* from illness or weariness:—Týdraþ ðis bánfæt *this body grows weak,* Exon. Th. 178, 5; Gú. 1239. Gif mannes fét on síþe týdrien *if a man get footsore while travelling,* Lchdm. i. 84, 23. II. of things, *to get* or *be frail, perishable:*—Ðæt sind ða getimbru ðe nó týdriaþ *those are the buildings that decay not,* Exon. Th. 103, 5; Cri. 1683. v. ge-tídrian.

tíd-sang, es; *m. A song used at a particular time, the service held at one of the canonical hours:*—Seofon tídsangas hí gesetton ús tó singenne dæghwamlíce ... Se forma tídsang is úhtsang mid ðam æftersange ðe ðártó gebiraþ, prímsang, undernsang, middægsang, nónsang, ǽfensang, nihtsang. Ðás seofon tídsangas gé sculon singan, L. Ælfc. P. 31; Th.

ii. 376, 1–8: L. Ælfc. C. 19; Th. ii. 350, 3–7. Wē syngaþ on đone Đunresdæg ūre tīdsangas tōgædere . . . On đone Frigedæg wē singaþ ealle đa tīdsangas on sundor būton đam ūhtsange ānum, 36; Th. ii. 358, 30–33. Wē lǽraþ đæt man on rihtne tīman tīda ringe, and preósta gehwilc đonne his tīdsang on circan gesēce, L. Edg. C. 45; Th. ii. 254, 6: R. Ben. 67, 18: Homl. Th. ii. 160, 19–24. Æt ǽlcan tīdsange eal hīréd āþenedum limum ætforan Godes weófode singe đone sealm: *Domine, quid multiplicati sunt*, and *preces*, and *collecta*, Wulfst. 181, 26: 171, 14. Đonne bid hic hīwan tō tīdsongum mīn gemund dōn, Chart. Th. 159, 9, 19. Tīdsangas *canonica*, Wrt. Voc. ii. 128, 26. Se tīdsang *matins*, R. Ben. 33, 1: *complines*, 67, 10. v. tīd-þegnung.

tīd-sceáwere, es; *m. An observer of times and seasons, an astrologer:*—Tīdsceáwere *horoscopus* (horoscopus *astrologus, qui horas, maxime natales, inquirit vel considerat*, Migne), Wrt. Voc. i. 53, 18. v. tīd-ymbwlātend.

tīd-scriptor *a chronographer;* chronographus, Wrt. Voc. ii. 131, 8. v. tīd-wrītere.

tīd-þegnung, e; *f. Service performed at one of the seven canonical hours:*—Nū ic hæbbe be suman dǽle āhrepod be đam dæghwamlīcan tīdþēnungum (*the services at the several hours are described in what precedes this remark*), Btwk. 220, 40. v. tīd-sang.

tīdung, e; *f. Tidings:*—Hī cȳddan đam cinge eall. Đā wearđ se cing swȳþe blīđe [đis]sere tīdunge, Chr. 995; Th. 244, 38. [Ich þonkie mine drihte þissere tidinge, Laym. 24907. Gabriel brohte hire þe tidinge of Godes akenesse, H. M. 45, 7. Swilc tiding đhugte Adam god, Gen. and Ex. 407. Ich mai bringe tidinge (tiþinge, Cot. MS.), O. and N. 1035. Tydyng, R. Glouc. 172, 1. Tyþing, 79, 11. No tale ne tiđinge of þe worlde, A. R. 70, 19. *M. H. Ger.* zītunge: *Du.* tijding. Cf. *the forms* in -ende, -inde:—Þa come þe tidende (tidinge, 2nd MS.) þat Aganippus was dead, Laym. 3734. Tiđinde (tidinge, 2nd MS.), 5153. Neowe tidinde (tidinge, 2nd MS.) *fresh events*, 2052. Goddspell on Ennglissh nemmnedd iss . . . god tiþennde, Orm. D. 158. *Icel.* tīðindi *tidings; an event: Dan.* tidende. The use of the word, even if its form be not borrowed from Scandinavian, seems to shew Scandinavian influence.] v. tīdan.

tīd-weorþung, e; *f. Worship at a particular time, service at one of the canonical hours:*—Hit nis nā tō gelȳfanne, đæt hȳ fæstende synd rihtlīce, būtan hȳ æfter hyra mæssan đæs ǽfenes tīdwurđunga gebīden, Homl. Ass. 140, 67.

tīd-wrītere, es; *m. A chronicler, annalist;*—Tīdwrītera *cronographorum*, Wrt. Voc. ii. 17, 68: 75, 39. Tȳdwrītera *chronographorum, temporum scriptorum*, Hpt. Gl. 410, 58. v. tīd-scriptor.]

tīd-ymbwlātend, es; *m. An astrologer:*—Tīdembwlātent *oroscopus*, Lchdm. i. lxi, 2. v. tīd-sceáwere.

tiéder-, tiédran, tiédre, -tiéfran, tiegle, tién. v. tīder-, tȳdran-, tīdre, ā-tiéfran, tigele, tīn.

tiér *distillation* (? cf. teár); *ornament, splendour* (? cf. *O. H. Ger.* ziarī, zierī, ceerī *ornamentum, venustas, decus*); *treasure* (? cf. *Icel.* taurar; *pl. treasures*); *glory* (? v. tīr):—Nis nān wundor đæt sió lyft sié wearm and ceald wǽt wolcnes tiér winde geblonden (cf. sió lyft is ǽgđer ge ceald ge wǽt ge wearm; nis hit nān wunder, Bt. 33, 4; Fox 128, 35), Met. 20, 81.

tife, an; *f. A bitch:*—Gif đū wille đæt wīf cild hæbbe oþþe tife hwelp, Lchdm. ii. 172, 21. [*Icel.* tefja *a bitch;* tefja *to call a person a bitch: Dan.* tæve *a bitch: Swed.* tüfwa.]

tifer, -tīfran. v. tiber, ā-tiéfran.

tifrung, e; *f. Painting:*—Đū leornodest onn ānum þōđere . . . ātēfred, đađ đū meahtest beo đære tēfrunge ongytan đises rođores ymbehwirft, Shrn. 174, 18.

tīg (?), es; *m. An open place* (?); *a form occurring in composition with* fore, forþ. *For the former see* fore-tīge (*read* -tīg); *the instances of the latter are as follows:*—Forđtīges *vestibuli, atrii*, Hpt. Gl. 496, 28. On đam forđtēge *in ipsis foribus*, Kent. Gl. 228. *Graff gives* zieh *forum, and Grimm*, R. A. 748, *cites* tie *a meeting-place, as a term of lower Saxony.*

Tīg, tīg *a case.* v. Tīw, teáh.

-tig *-ty, a numeral suffix in words denoting the decades;* up to 60 such words are formed with a suffix only, from 60 to 120 *hund* is prefixed and *tig* suffixed, *hund-seofon-tig, hund-twelf-tig.* Other dialects make a distinction in the numerals at the same point. Gothic uses *tigus* (*pl. tigjus*) in the earlier, *-têhund* in the later, O. Saxon *-tig* in the earlier, while 70 is given by *ant-sibunta; in O. H. Ger.* the two forms are *-zug* and *-zō*. In *O. Frs.* and *Icel.* the same forms are used throughout. *Tig* is another form of the root seen in *ten* (*tehan, g* for *h* according to Verner's Law).

tīgan; *p.* de *To tie*, (a) literal:—Valerianus hēt beheáfdian on Ypolitus gesihđe ealle his hīwan, and hine sylfne hēt tīgan be đām fōtum tō ungetemedra horsa swuran, Homl. Th. i. 432, 33. (b) figurative:—Nū đū miht gehȳran, hū đes dǽl (*the conjunction*) tīgþ đa word tōgædere, Ælfc. Gr. 44; Zup. 258, 10. [Heo wolden þa ban alle teien (tiȝe, 2nd MS.) togadere, Laym. 20997. Iteied (-tiȝed, 2nd MS.) tosomne, 25972. He teide ane clot to hire, A. R. 140, 7. Is þe latere dole euer iteied (-teiȝet) to đe vorme, 14, 2. Tached oþer tyȝed, Allit. Pms. 14, 464. Kynges shulde taken transgressores and tyen hem faste, Piers P. 1, 96.] v. ge-, on-, un-tīgan.

tige, tigel *a tile*, tigel *a trace.* v. tyge, hrōf-tigel, tygel.

tigel-ærne(-a?), an; *f.* (*m.*?) *A building made of brick* (?), *a building for making bricks* (?), *brick-kiln* (?):—Forđ on đa mearce in on đa tigelærnan, Cod. Dip. Kmbl. iii. 130, 29.

tigele, tigle, tiegle, an; *f. A tile, brick:*—Tigule *tegula*, Txts. 101, 1992. Tigele *figulum*, Wrt. Voc. ii. 148, 79. Tigle *testula*, Germ. 391, 17: *testa*, Ps. Spl. 21, 16. Mid weorcum clāmes and tigelan *operibus luti et lateris*, Ex. 1, 14. Se weall is geworht of tigelan and eorđtyrewan *murus coctili latere atque interfuso bitumine compactus*, Ors. 2, 4; Swt. 74, 17. Genim swealwan, gebærn under tigelan tō ahsan, Lchdm. ii. 156, 9. Đa reádan tigelan gecnuwa tō duste, 114, 24. Nim sume tigelan (tiglan, Cott. MSS.) and wrīt on hiere đa burg Hierusalem *sume tibi laterem, et describes in eo civitatem Jerusalem*, Past. 21; Swt. 161, 3, 9, 11. Tieglan (tiglan, Cott. MSS.), Swt. 161, 12, 20. Se đe lǽrþ stuntne swylce se đe belīme tigelan (*testam*) *whoso teacheth a fool is as one that glueth a potsherd together* (Eccl. 22, 7), Scint. 96, 19. Tigelan *lateres*, Wrt. Voc. ii. 51, 41. Tigelena gemet *a tale of bricks*, Ex. 5, 14. Tiglena *testularum*, Hpt. Gl. 499, 28. Tighelana *tegularum*, 459, 40. Tigelum, Exon. Th. 477, 28; Ruin. 31. Hig hæfdon tygelan (*lateres*) for stān, Gen. 11, 3. [*O. H. Ger.* ziagel, ziagalo *later, testa, imbrex: Icel.* tigl; *n. a tile, brick.* From Latin.] v. þæc-tigele; hrōf-tigel (-tigele ?; *perhaps for pl.* -tigla, -tiglan *should be read*).

tigelen; *adj. Of pot:*—Fæt tigelen (-an?; lāmys, MS. C.) *vas figuli*, Ps. Spl. 2, 9. [*O. H. Ger.* ziagalin *laterinus, latericius.*]

tigel-fāh; *adj. Many-coloured with tiles* or *bricks:*—Tigelfāgan trafu, Andr. Kmbl. 1683; An. 844.

tigel-getæl, es; *n. A tale of bricks; laterum numerus:*—Gē sceolon āgifan đæt ilce tigolgetel, Ex. 5, 18.

tigel-geweorc, es; *n.* I. *brickmaking:*—Ne sylle gē nān cef tō tigelgeweorce (*ad conficiendos lateres*), Ex. 5, 7. II. *work at making bricks:*—Āsettaþ him đæt ilce tigelgeweorc đe hig ǽr worhton *mensuram laterum, quam prius faciebant, imponetis super eos*, Ex. 5, 8. Tigulgeweorc, 16.

tigel-leáh; *f. A brick-field:*—On tigelleáge, Cod. Dip. Kmbl. v. 267, 21.

tigel-stān; es; *m. A tile, pan-tile:*—Tigelstān *imbrex*, Engl. Stud. xi. 66, 50. [Cover hit wele with a teghellstane, Rel. Ant. i. 54, 30. Tielstoon, Wick. (Is. 16, 11). Tilston *tegula*, Wrt. Voc. i. 256, col. 1.]

tigel-wyrhta, an; *m. A brickmaker, a potter:*—Fæt tygelwirhtan *vas figuli*, Ps. Lamb. 2, 9. Ǽcyr tigylwyrhtena *agrum figuli*, Mt. Kmbl. 27, 7. Tigelwyrhtena, 10.

tiger (?) *a tiger; pl.* tigras, Nar. 38, 4; tigris, 12, 13; 15, 3. Deór đe sind tigres gehātene . . . Đās rēđan tigres, Homl. Th. ii. 492, 10–21. v. tigrisc.

tīgere (?). v. bufan-tīgere.

tīging, e; *f. Tying, connection:*—Sume naman syndon *absolutivae*, đæt synd ungebundene, đa ne behōfiaþ nānre tīginge ōđres naman, Ælfc. Gr. 5; Zup. 14, 14.

tigl *a trace*, tigle *a lamprey*, tigole. v. tygel, tygele, tigele.

tigrisc; *adj. Of a tiger:*—Mid tigriscum fellum *tygridum pellibus*, Nar. 26, 14.

tigþian, tih(h)ian. v. tīþian, teohhian.

tiht, es; *m. A charge, an offence with which one is charged;* crimen:—Legerteám ođđe tiht *flagitium*, Wrt. Voc. ii. 39, 34. Gif hwā cyninges borg ābrece, gebēte đone tyht (tihtlan, MS. H.) swā him ryht wīsie, L. Alf. pol. 3; Th. i. 62, 8. [*O. Frs.* tichta *accusation: O. H. Ger.* biziht *nota;* in-ziht *crimen.*] v. teón *to accuse*, and next word.

tihtan; *p.* te *To charge* a person (*acc.*) with an offence:—Tyhte *intentabat*, Hpt. Gl. 519, 76. Hē hæfþ gelǽd fulle lāde æt đan unrihtwīfe đe Leófgār bisceop hyne tihte *he has completely cleared himself of the offence with which the bishop charged him*, Chart. Th. 373, 33. Gif man ōđerne sace tihte, L. H. E. 8; Th. i. 30, 11: 10; Th. i. 30, 17: L. Wih. 22; Th. i. 42, 3: 23; Th. i. 42, 6: 24; Th. i. 42, 10, 11. [Cf. *O. H. Ger.* in-zihtōn *criminari: Ger.* be-zichten, -zichtigen *to accuse.*] v. preceding word.

tihtan *to exhort.* v. tyhtan.

tiht-bisig; *adj. Labouring under frequent accusations, often accused, and so of bad repute;* infamatus et accusationibus ingravatus, L. Edm. C. 7; Th. i. 253, 23: accusacionibus infamatus, L. H. I.; Th. i. 567, 18. Cf., *too, the phrase* oft betygen, L. In. 18; Th. i. 114, 6: 37; Th. i. 124, 21. One to whom the epithet applied was in an unfavourable position when brought into court, for he was forced to go to the three-fold ordeal, and if he failed to clear himself was subject to a heavier penalty than others:—Gif hē tyhtbysig sȳ, gange tō đæm þryfealand ordāle . . . Gif hē fūl wurđe, æt đam forman cyrre bēte đam teónde twygylde . . . And æt đam ōđran cyrre ne sȳ đǽr nān ōđer bōt būtan đæt heáfod, L. Eth. i. 1; Th. i. 280, 9–282, 2. Niman đa tihtbysian men . . . and ǽlc tihtbysig man gange tô þryfealdan ordâle, odđe gilde feówergilde, iii. 3; Th. i. 294, 6–11. Gif hwylc man sý swâ tihtbysig and hine đonne þreó men ætgædere teón, đonne ne beó đâr nân ôđer bûton đæt hê gange tô đam þryfealdan ordâle, L. C. S. 30; Th. i. 392, 22 (*and see the whole section for the penalties*). Be tihtbysigum. Se đe tihtbysig sý, L. Edg. ii. 7; Th. i. 268, 13: L. C. S. 25; Th. i. 390, 17. Sý ǽlc man đe tihtbysig nǽre . . . ânfealdre lâde wyrđe, 22; Th. i. 388, 9.

tihte, tihten, tihtend, tihtend-lîc, tihtere, tihting, tihtness. v. hôl-tihte, tyhten, tyhtend, tyhtend-lîc, tyhtere, tyhting, tyhtness.

tihtle, an; *f. A charge, accusation:*—Gif hit ânfeald tyh[t]le sý, dûfe seó hand æfter đam stâne ôđ đa wriste, and gif hit þryfeald sý, ôđ đæne elbogan, L. Ath. iv. 7; Th. i. 226, 16. Gif hit tihtle (tihtla, MS. B.) sî and lâd forberste *if a charge be brought, and the attempt to refute the charge fail*, L. C. S. 54; Th. i. 406, 10: 57; Th. i. 406, 26. Swerige hê đane âđ (cf. *next passage*), đæt hê sý unscyldig đære tihtlan (tyhtelan) . . . And ofgâ ǽlc man his tihtlan mid foreâđe (cf. L. O. 2; Th. i. 178, 10: L. O. D. 6; Th. i. 354, 30), L. Ath. i. 23; Th. i. 212, 1–5. Ic eom unscyldig æt đære tihtlan đe N. mê tîhþ, L. O. 5; Th. i. 180, 16. Gif man folciscne mæssepreóst mid tihtlan belecge lâdige hine swâ swâ diácon đe regollîf libbe *if a charge be brought against a secular priest, let him clear himself as a regular deacon would*, L. Eth. ix. 21; Th. i. 344, 19: 22; Th. i. 344, 22. Tyhtlan (tihlan, MS. A.), L. C. E. 5; Th. i. 362, 7. Ne stent nân ôđer lâd æt tihtlan bûte ordâl betweox Wealan and Englan, L. O. D. 2; Th. i. 354, 1. Đâ tugon hié hiene đæt hê heora swicdomes wiđ Alexander fremmende wǽre and hiene for đære tihtlan ofslôgon *they accused him of betraying them to Alexander, and on that charge slew him;* hunc, quasi urbem Alexandro venditasset, necaverunt, Ors. 4, 5; Swt. 168, 18. Se đe đa tihtlan âge *the plaintiff, prosecutor*, L. H. E. 10; Th. i. 30, 19. v. frum-, stæl-, wiđer-tihtle; tiht, *and next word.*

tihtlian; *p.* ode *To charge* with an offence, *to accuse:*—Gif man mæssepreóst tihtlige ânfealdre sprǽce, L. Eth. ix. 19; Th. i. 344, 11: 20; Th. i. 344, 15. Tihtlige (tihlige, MS. A.), L. C. E. 5; Th. i. 362, 12. v. be-tihtlian, ge-tihtlod.

Tiig. v. **Tîw.**

til; *adj.* I. *good* at anything, *apt, capable, competent:*—Hê wæs selfa til, heóld â rîce êđeldreámas, Cd. Th. 97, 2; Gen. 1606: Beo. Th. 122; B. 61. Til sceal on êđle dômes wyrcean, Menol. Fox 500; Gn. C. 20. Sum biþ beórhyrde gôd, sum biþ bylda til hâm tô habbanne, Exon. Th. 297, 29; Crä. 75. Till, Beo. Th. 5436; B. 2721. Hié wǽron an wîg gearwe . . . efne swylce mǽla swylce hira mandryhtne þearf gesǽlde; wæs seó þeód tilu, 2505; B. 1250. Wǽron men tile, Cd. Th. 99, 11; Gen. 1644. Dióre gecêpte drihten Crêca Trôia burh tilum gesîđum, Met. 26, 20. [Cf. *Goth.* manna gatils (εὔθετος, *aptus*) in thiudangardja Guths *a man fit for the kingdom of God*, Lk. 9, 62.] II. *good* for anything, *that serves a purpose, beneficial, serviceable, convenient, opportune:*—His mildheortnyss is til mancynne, Ps. Th. 116, 2. Ys mîn (*a town's*) innađ til, wombhord wlitig, Exon. Th. 399, 11; Rä. 18, 9. Ne wæs đæt gewrixle til, đæt hié on bâ healfa bicgan scoldon freónda feorum, Beo. Th. 2613; B. 1304. Âhte ic folgađ tilne (*a service that benefited me*), Exon. Th. 379, 25; Deór. 38. Đû mê þeódscipe lǽr đînne tilne *bonitatem et disciplinam doce me*, Ps. Th. 118, 66. Gebiddaþ ealle hâlige tô đê on tilne tîman (*in tempore opportuno*), 31, 7. [Cf. *Goth.* dags gatils (εὐκαίρος, *opportunus*) *a convenient day*, Mk. 6, 21. Ei bigêteina til du wrôhjan ina, Lk. 6, 7.] III. *good, kind, gentle* [cf. till = *tame* in Pegge's Kenticisms, E. D. S. Pub. Reprinted Gloss. C. 3]:—Til mon tiles and tomes meares *a kind man is mindful of a gentle and tame horse*, Exon. Th. 342, 12; Gn. Ex. 142. Him đæs leán âgeaf Metend gumcystum til (*liberally kind*), Cd. Th. 108, 23; Gen. 1810. IV. *good, excellent*, (a) of moral good:—Til biþ se đe his treówe gehealdeþ, Exon. Th. 293, 6; Wand. 112. Til sceal mid tilum *the good shall be associated with the good*, 334, 28; Gn. Ex. 23. Đæt hió đære cwêne oncweđan meahton swâ tiles swâ trâges, swâ hió him tô sôhte, Elen. Kmbl. 649; El. 325. Tile and yfle *the good and the evil* (*at the day of judgment*), Cd. Th. 303, 10; Sat. 610. Hî (*devils*) duguđe beswîcaþ and on teosu tyhtaþ tilra dǽda, Exon. Th. 362, 10; Wal. 34. Habbaþ freónda đý mâ sôþra and gôdra, tilra and getreówra, 409, 2; Rä. 27, 23. (b) of physical excellence:—Toscean teolum hûsum on, cyninga cofum, eardedan, Ps. Th. 104, 26. V. til *is found in proper names*, see for examples Txts. 497. [Cf. *O. H. Ger.* zil: *Ger.* ziel *aim, purpose.*] v. tela, *and next word.*

til, es; *n.* I. *use, service, convenience.* v. til, II:—Gewritu secgaþ đæt seó wiht (*day*) sý mid moncynne miclum ticlum (tielum? tilum?) sweotol and gesýne, sundorcræft hafaþ, Exon. Th. 420, 12; Rä. 40, 2. II. *goodness, kindness.* v. til, III:—Mê on đînum tile gelǽr đæt ic teala cunne đîn sôđfæst weorc healdan *in bonitate tua doce me justificationes tuas*, Ps. Th. 118, 68. v. til-fremmende.

til; *prep.* (*used only in the North*) *To:*—Fûsæ fearran kwômu æþþilæ til ânum (cf. fûse feorran cwômon tô đam æđelinge, Rood Kmbl. 115; Kr. 58), Txts. 126, 13. Hê scôp ælda barnum heben til hrôfe (cf. tô hrôfe, Bd. 4, 24; M. 344, 11), 149, 6. Đâ cueđ til (tô, Rush.) him đe Hǽlend *tunc dicit illis Jesus*, Mt. Kmbl. Lind. 26, 31. Huér wiltû đæt wê gearuiga đê til eottanne (tô etanne, Rush.) Eástro *ubi vis paremus tibi comedere Pascha?* 26, 17. [The word retains its meaning in the Northern dialects, but otherwise it is used in reference only to time. *O. Frs.* til: *Icel.* til.]

tila *well*, Tile *Thule.* v. tela, Tyle.

til-fremmende *doing good:*—Tillfremmendra, Exon. Th. 440, 23; Rä. 60, 7. Cf. gôd-fremmende.

tilia, tiliga, an; *m. A husbandman, cultivator of land:*—Tilia *colonus*, Wrt. Voc. i. 74, 66. Bigenga, tilia, inbûend *colonus*, i. *incola, cultor, inquilinus*, ii. 134, 25. Tilia *colonus, habitator*, Hpt. Gl. 422, 60. Se merigenlîça tilia *the labourer who came in the morning*, Homl. Th. ii. 74, 30. Đâ sende hê tô đâm tiligum (tilium, MS. A. *ad agricolas*) his þeów . . . Đâ cwǽdon đa tilian (*coloni*) . . . Đæs wîngeardes hlâford fordêþ đa tiligean (tylian, MS. A. *colonos*), Mk. Skt. 12, 2, 7, 9. [Þe wise teolie *prudens sator*, O. E. Homl. i. 133, 10.] v. eorþ-, irþ- (yrþ-) tilia.

tilian, tiligan, tilgan, teolian, tiolian, tielian; *p.* ode *To strive* after *or* for some object. I. where the construction is not determined:—Hê higode odđe tilode *nititur*, Wrt. Voc. ii. 59, 69. Tioludun *perstant*, 117, 15. Tilege *nitatur*, 61, 56. Teolige *decrevit*, Hpt. Gl. 469, 50. Tilgende *nisus*, Wrt. Voc. ii. 60, 28. Tilgendum *adnitentibus*, 99, 32. Tillgendum, 6, 23. II. where the object of effort is not expressed, *to strive to obtain, to labour, toil, procure with effort, provide, acquire*, (1) where the person for whom the action takes place is not expressed:—Ic bebeóde eallum mînan gerêfan đæt hî on mînan âgenan rihtlîce tilian and mê mid đam feormian *I command all my reeves, that they obtain revenue rightfully from my own property and maintain me therewith*, L. C. S. 70; Th. i. 412, 21. Se đe wǽre scađiende, weorđe se tiligende on rihtlîcre tilđe, Wulfst. 72, 13. (2) with dat. of person for whom the effort is made:—Oxa teolaþ his hlâforde, Homl. Th. i. 412, 3. Se đe him sylfum teolaþ, 14. Se đe him sylfum teolaþ, nâ Gode, ne com se nâ gyt binnon Godes wîngearde. Đa tyliaþ Gode, đa đe ne sêcaþ heora âgen gestreón đurh gýtsunge, ii. 76, 32–34. Đæt hê đa eorđan worhte and him đêron tilode (*he should provide for himself from it*), Gen. 3, 23. Hit mâre is đonne ccc geára and lxxii wintra syđđan đyllîc feoh wæs farende on eorđan and ealle men heom mid tiledon (*procured for themselves what they wanted with that money;* cf. Amang đam feó đe wê ûre neóde mide bicgaþ, 706), Homl. Skt. i. 23, 703. Hê is wyrđe đæt đû him tilige *he deserves that you exert yourself for him;* dignus est ut hoc illi praestes, Lk. Skt. 7, 4. Preósta gehwilc tilige him rihtlîce and ne beó ǽnig mangere mid unrihte *let every priest provide for himself honestly, and let none be a trader dishonestly*, L. Edg. C. 14; Th. ii. 246, 23. Swâ hwâ swâ ǽnige cýpinge on đam dæge begǽþ . . . odđe ǽnig cræftig man him on his cræfte tylige (*gets gain for himself by working at his craft*), Wulfst. 296, 8. III. with gen. (1) of an object to be obtained by effort, (a) without reference to person for whom, *to seek after, get after seeking, procure, make provision* of:—Đû wyfst and wǽda tylast *you weave and make provision of garments*, Homl. Th. i. 488, 26. Tilaþ ânra gehwilc âgnes willan (cf. winþ heora ǽlc on ôþer æfter his âgenum willan, Bt. 21; Fox 74, 34), Met. 11, 83. Ǽlc man đæs tiolaþ, hû hê on êcnesse swincan mǽge, Ps. Th. 48, 7. Đa đe on đam beóþ âbisgode đæt hié sibbe tiligaþ (tiliaþ, Cott. MSS.) *qui faciendae pacis studiis occupantur*, Past. 47; Swt. 363, 9. Đæt hî unrihtes tiligeaþ, Ps. Th. 143, 9. Tilgaþ, Exon. Th. 230, 14; Ph. 472. Sume tiliaþ wîfa for đam đæt hî þurh đæt mǽge mǽst bearna begitan and eác wynsumlîce libban *uxor ac liberi, qui jucunditatis gratia petantur*, Bt. 24, 3; Fox 82, 25. Man tilode tô his hergeatwæn đæs đe man habban sceolde *what was necessary for his heriots should be provided*, Cod. Dip. Kmbl. iii. 352, 16. Mid his handcræfte hê teolode his and his gefêrena forđdǽda, Homl. Th. i. 392, 16. Hî wunnon æfter wyrþscipe and tiledon (tiolodon, Cott. MS.) gôdes hlîsan mid gôdum weorcum, Bt. 40, 4; Fox 240, 5. Đæt hê suâ tilige đære orsorgnesse mid đære ânfealdnesse đætte hê đone ymbeđonc đæs wærscipes ne forlǽte *ut sic securitatem de simplicitate possideant, ut circumspectionem prudentiae non amittant*, Past. 35; Swt. 237, 16. Ic an đæs landes Ǽffan, and heó tilige uncer begea sâwla þearfe đǽron *I grant the land to Ǽffe, and let her provide what is necessary for both our souls therefrom*, Chart. Th. 495, 34: 497, 18. *Laboratores* syndon weorcmen đe tilian sculon đæs đe eall þeódscype big sceall libban laboratores *are workmen, that have to obtain by their efforts that by which all the nation has to live*, L. I. P. 4; Th. ii. 306, 35: Beo. Th. 3651; B. 1823. Hê sceal fela tôla tilian *he must procure many tools*, Anglia ix. 262, 27: 261, 10. Seó lufu tuddres tô tilianne *amor ortandi sobolis*, Bd. 1, 27; S. 495, 38. (b) with dat. of person:—Paulus him sylfan nânes lofes ne tilade *Paul took no praise to himself;* nec Paulus sibi aliquid imputavit, R. Ben. 4, 5. Se here tilode him đæs đe hî behôfdan *the Danes provided themselves with what they needed*, Chr. 1006; Erl. 140, 16. Hî heom metes tilodon, 1016; Erl. 157, 3: Hexam. 17; Norm. 26, 9. Ic lǽre đæt đû [ne?] fægenige ôþerra manna gôdes and heora æþelo tô đon swîþe đæt đû ne tilige đê selfum âgnes *I advise you [not] to rejoice so much in other men's goodness and nobility, that you do not provide yourself with your own*, Bt. 30, 1; Fox

108, 31. Ðæt man him ðurh fixnoðe bigleofan tilige, Homl. Th. ii. 208, 19. Tiliaþ eów freónda *get friends for yourselves*, i. 334, 27. Ðū scealt mid earfoðnyssum ðē metes tilian, 18, 15: Homl. Skt. i. 23, 219. Noe ongan tō eorðan him ǽtes tilian *Noe began to provide himself with food from the earth*, Cd. Th. 94, 6; Gen. 1557. Him tilian fylle on fǽgum, Jūdth. Thw. 24, 26; Jud. 208. Him metes tō tylienne, Chr. 1052; Erl. 183, 20. (2) of an object to which care, attention, is directed, (a) in a general sense, *to care for, attend to, work for, provide for*:—Ðonne ðū tilast ðīn on eorðan ne sylþ heó ðē nāne wæstmas *when you try to get subsistence for yourself from the ground, it will give you no fruit*, Gen. 4, 12. Ðonne se sacerd his on ða ilcan wīsan tielaþ (tiolaþ, Cott. MSS.) ðe ðæt folc dōþ *when the priest provides for himself in the same way that the people do*, Past. 18; Swt. 133, 8. Se ðe ne gȳmþ ðæra sceápa ac tylaþ his sylfes *he that heeds not the sheep, but takes care of himself*, Homl. Th. i. 242, 1. Se ðe his ǽr tīde ne tiolaþ ðonne biþ his on tīd untilad *he that makes no provision for himself beforehand will be without provision when the time comes*, Bt. 29, 2; Fox 106, 3. Hē wæs fiscere and mid ðam cræfte his teolode, Homl. Th. i. 394, 2. Hē þearfendra þinga teolode *he attended to the concerns of the needy*, Ps. Th. 108, 30. Huntigan and fuglian and fiscian and his on gehwilce wīsan tō ðære lǽnan tilian, Shrn. 164, 6. Līfes tiligan *to care for life*, Exon. Th. 81, 6; Cri. 1319: Salm. Kmbl. 322; Sal. 160. Hié Norðanhymbra lond ergende wǽron and hiera tilgende (*providing for themselves*), Chr. 876; Erl. 78, 15. (b) in a special sense of medical care, *to cure, treat, tend, attend to*:—Sceal ðæs mōdes lǽce ǽr tilian ðæs ðe hē wēnþ ðæt ðone mon ǽr mǽge gebrengan on færwyrde. Hwīlum, ðeáh, ðǽr ðǽr mon ōðres tiolaþ, ðǽr weaxð se ōðer. Forðæm sceal se lǽce . . . tilian ðæs māran . . . Hwæðres ðara yfela is betere ǽr tō tilianne? Past. 62; Swt. 457, 10–22. Ðara stōwa sum raþe rotaþ, gif hire mon gīmeleáslīce tilaþ, Lchdm. ii. 84, 25. Tiloden (*curabant*) his lǽcas, Bd. 4, 32; S. 611, 19. Būtan his man tilige hē biþ ymb þreó niht gefaren *unless the patient be attended to, he will be dead in three days*, Lchdm. ii. 46, 18. Hū mon scyle gebrocenes heáfdes tiligean, 2, 4. Tilian, 56, 14. Hira man sceal tilian mid wyrtdrencum, 82, 16. Hwonan ic ðīn tilian scyle *qui modo sit tuae curationis*, Bt. 5, 3; Fox 10, 35. **IV.** with a dative, *to cure, treat*:—Wīfman gif heó tilaþ (*curet*) hīre cilde mid ǽnigum wiccecræfte, L. Ecg. P. iv. 20; Th. ii. 210, 17. **V.** with an accusative, (1) *to gain, obtain*:—Se āsolcena ðeówa ðe nolde tilian nān ðing his hlāforde mid ðam befæstum punde, Homl. Th. ii. 552, 29. (2) *to attend to, bestow care on, care for*, (a) in a general sense:—Se ðe ymbe ða eorðlīcan spēda singallīce hogaþ, and ða ēcan gestreón ne teolaþ *he that is continually anxious about earthly wealth, and cares not for the eternal treasures*, Homl. Th. ii. 372, 23. (b) of medical attention, *to treat, attend to*:—His lǽcas hine mid sealfum lange teolodon, Guthl. 22; Gdwin. 96, 15. (c) *to till*:—Ðæt land tō tilianne, Chr. 1091; Erl. 228, 20. (c 1) without object:—Ðā man oððe tilian sceolde oððe eft tilða gegaderian, 1097; Erl. 234, 24. **VI.** where the object for the sake of which an effort is made is pointed out by a preposition:—Tō ðisum swicolum līfe wē swincaþ and tiliaþ and tō ðam tōwerdan līfe wē tiliaþ hwōnlīce *we labour and toil for this deceitful life, and for the future life we toil little*, Homl. Skt. ii. 28, 168. **VII.** where the object of effort is expressed by an infinitive (simple or gerund), or a clause, *to strive, attempt, endeavour, intend*, (1) with infin.:—Ðæt ðe wē bēcnan tiliaþ, Met. 11, 79. Ic nǽfre ne teolade sittan on ānum willan mid ðām ārleásum *cum impiis non sedebo*, Ps. Th. 25, 5. Ðā tilode hē ða stōwe geclǽnsian *studens locum purgare*, Bd. 3, 23; S. 554, 26. Hē hine monnum gēcyþan teolode, Blickl. Homl. 165, 31. (2) with gerund:—Ðū tilast (tiolast, Cott. MS.) wædle tō fliónne, Bt. 14, 2; Fox 44, 7: 10; Fox 30, 1. Manege tiligaþ (tiliaþ, Cott. MS.) Gode tō cwēmanne, 39, 10; Fox 228, 13. Ic tilode ðē tō līcianne, Ps. Th. 25, 3. Tylode, Bd. 5, 24; S. 649, 11. Hē tiolode (tilode, Cott. MSS.) hié betwux him tō tōscādanne, Past. 47; Swt. 363, 1. Hē teolode tō ārīsenne, Blickl. Homl. 219, 18. Hié ða londliōde tiolode mā ūssa feónda willan tō gefremmanne ðonne ūrne *illi maiorem hosti quam mihi fauorem accomodantes efficere pergebant*, Nar. 6, 19. Swā hwylc man swā ðās scriftbōc tilige tō ābrecanne *quicunque confessionale hoc violare conatus fuerit*, L. Ecg. P. Addit.; Th. ii. 238, 8. Ðæt hié tilgen (tiligen, Cott. MSS.) tō kȳðanne, Past. 47; Swt. 363, 10. Hē sceal tilian suā tō libbanne *sic studet vivere*, 10; Swt. 61, 18. (3) with a clause:—Ða bilewitan sint tō herigenne forðæmðe hié simle suincaþ on ðæm ðæt hī tieligeaþ (tiliaþ, Cott. MSS.) ðæt hié ne sculen leásunga secgan *laudandi sunt simplices, quod studeant numquam falsa dicere*, Past. 35; Swt. 237, 8. Ðīn esne teolode ðæt hē ðīne sōðe word beeode *servus tuus exercebatur in tuis justificationibus*, Ps. Th. 118, 23. Ðæt wē teolian, ðæt wē sȳn gearwe, Blickl. Homl. 125, 11. Uton teolian ðæt ūs ðās tīda īdle ne gewītan, 129, 36: 111, 18. Hē sceal tilian ðæt hē līcige *debet studere se diligi*, Past. 19; Swt. 147, 14: L. E. I. 28; Th. ii. 424, 26: Bt. 29, 3; Fox 106, 18: Met. 16, 1. Tiligean, Ps. Th. 138, 17. Hē ne onginþ tō tilianne, ðæt hē ðæt weorð āgife, 48, 7. [Sculdest thu neure finden land tiled . . . War sæ me tilede, þe erthe ne bar nan corn, Chr. 1137; Erl. 262, 25, 39. To teoliende efter istreone, O. E. Homl. i. 133, 13. Tulien after strene, ii. 155, 4. Heo tileden on eorðen, Laym. 1940. þat lond heo lette tilien, 2618. Ure Louerd tiled efter hore luue, A. R. 404, 14. Silence tilcð hire, and heo itiled bringeð forð uode, 78, 15. Ase lomen uorte tilien mide þe heorte, 384, 17. In swinc ðu salt tilen ði mete, Gen. and Ex. 363. Lond to tilie, R. Glouc. 21, 9. Heo swonke and tilede here lyflode, 41, 22. To taken his teme and tulyen (tilien, tilie) þe erthe, Piers P. 7, 2. Many wyntres men lyveden and no mete ne tulyeden (tylied, tiliden, tilieden, teleden), 14, 67. Ichave tyled him for that sore, Beves of Hamtoun (Halliwell's Dict.). *Goth.* ga-tilōn *to obtain*: *O. Sax.* tilian (*with gen.*) *to obtain*: *O. L. Ger.* tilōn *festinare, exercitari*: *O. Frs.* tilia *to till, to beget*: *O. H. Ger.* zilēn *studere, conari, niti, contendere, moliri, adniti*; zilōn (*with gen.*).]

tiliga. v. tilia.

till *a fixed point, station*:—Swā stent eal weoruld stille on tille, Met. 20, 172. On ðam gim āstīhþ on heofenas up hȳhst on geáre and of tille āgrynt *in it (June) the sun mounts up into the skies highest in the year and declines from that point*, Menol. Fox 220; Men. 111. [Cf. *O. H. Ger.* zil *destinatum*: *Ger.* ziel.]

tillan; *p.* tilde *To touch, reach. In compounds* ā-, ge-tillan; *instances omitted under those words are given here*:—Ðeáh ðe hē stæpe fulfremednysse ātilþ (*adtingit*), Scint. 100, 15. Getilþ *contingat*, getilde *contigit*, Wrt. Voc. ii. 135, 9–13. Gif wē ðone hrōf ðære heálīcan eáðmōdnesse getillan willaþ (*adtingere*), R. Ben. 23, 2. [Þe niþer end tilde to his chinne, Brand. 24. He hadde a long berd þat tilled (tylde) to his wombe *habuit barbam prolixam usque ad ventrem*, Trev. v. 193. 8. Alle þat he miȝt tille, Fer. 59. *O. H. Ger.* [zillen]; *p.* zilta *tangit*.]

til-līc; *adj. Good, capable, able.* v. til, **I**:—Þegn . . . tillīc esne . . . strong, Exon. Th. 436, 28; Rä. 55, 8: 480, 20; Rä. 64, 5.

tillīce; *adv. Kindly, graciously.* v. til, **III**, Exon. Th. 352, 28; Reim. 2.

til-mōdig; *adj. Noble-minded*:—Se eádga (*Abraham*) Drihtnes noman weorðade, tilmōdig eorl tiber onsægde, Cd. Th. 113, 14; Gen. 1887. Ic ðē (*Abraham*) bidde ðæt ðū tilmōdig treówa selle, ðæt ðū wille mē wesan freónd fremena tō leáne ðara ðe ic ðē gedōn hæbbe, 170, 22; Gen. 2817. Heofona heáhcyning trymede tilmōdigne (*Abraham*): 'Ne lǽt ðū ðē ðīn mōd āsealcan,' 130, 27; Gen. 2166. Ða ædelingas . . . .xii. tilmōdige (*the twelve apostles*), Apstls. Kmbl. 171; Ap. 86.

tilþ, e; *also* tilþe, an; *f.* **I.** *labour which brings gain, by which acquisition is made, an employment*, (1) in a general sense:—Se ðe wǽre scaðiende weorðe se tiligende on rihtlīcre tilðe *he that has been accustomed to steal, let him support himself by an honest employment*, Wulfst. 72, 13. (2) with special reference to agriculture, *tillage, cultivation, work on land*:—Se scādwīs gerēfa sceal witan ǽlcre tilðan tīman ðe tō tūne belimpþ; for ðam on manegum landum tilð biþ redre ðonne on ōðrum ge yrðe tīma hrædra, ge mǽda rædran . . . ge gehwilc ōðer tilð, Anglia ix. 259, 3–12. **II.** *gain from labour, produce of labour, acquisition*, (1) in a general sense:—Tilða ɫ stre[óna] *quaestuum*, Hpt. Gl. 452, 7. (2) with reference to agriculture, *crop, produce, fruit*:—Þurh mycele rēnas, ðe ealles geáres ne āblunnon, forneáh ǽlc tilð on mersclande forfērde, Chr. 1098; Erl. 235, 12. Ðæt land mid ðære tilðe ðe ðār ðænne on sȳ, Chart. Th. 329, 12. Ic geann ðæs landes mid mete and mid mannum and mid ealre tylðe swā ðǽrtō getilod biþ, 529, 18, *and often in the same will.* Fela tilða hām gæderian, Anglia ix. 261, 16. Ðā man oððe tilian sceolde oððe eft tilða gegaderian, Chr. 1097; Erl. 234, 25. Ealle eówre wæstmas and eorþlīce tilþa, Wulfst. 132, 14. [Þe tilðe of rihtwisnesse, þæt is silence *cultus justiciae silencium*, A. R. 78, 15: Wick. Is. 32, 17. God sent þe sonne to saue a cursed mannes tilthe, Piers P. 19, 430. To sowe cockel with the corn So that the tilthe is nigh forlorn, Gow. ii. 190, 12. *O. Frs.* tilath *cultivation*.] v. ge-tilþ.

tilþe, an; *f.* v. preceding word.

tilung, teolung, tiolung, tielung, e; *f.* **I.** *striving, endeavour, effort, labour*:—On swelcum lǽnum weorþscipum ǽlces mennisces mōdes ingeþanc biþ geswenced mid ðære geornfulnesse and mid ðære tiolunga (tiluncga, Cott. MS.) *with the desire and striving for them*, Bt. 24, 3; Fox 82, 22. Hī swuncon on wīngeardes biggencge mid gecneordlīcere teolunge, Homl. Th. ii. 74, 33. Hī forgȳmeleásodon ðæs ēcan līfes teolunge *they neglected striving after the life eternal*, 76, 2. Æfter nīðum teolunge heara *secundum nequitias studiorum ipsorum*, Ps. Surt. 27, 4. **II.** *a pursuit, occupation, employment, business*:—Gestreón of ðære teolunge ðe hē him befæste *gain from the occupation he committed to them*, Homl. Th. ii. 552, 1. Sume teolunga sind ðe man begān mæg būton synnum . . . Petrus hæfde unpleólīce teolunge ǽr his gecyrrednysse, and hē for ðī eft būton pleó tō his fixnoðe gecyrde, 288, 20–26. Se rīca man geswīcþ his gebeórscipes, gif ða ðeówan geswīcaþ ðæra teolunga, i. 274, 1. Gif se biscep self drohtaþ on ðam eorðlīcum tielongum (tielengum, Cott. MSS.) *si presul ipse in terrenis negotiis versatur*, Past. 18; Swt. 133, 4. Getīgede tō eorðlīcum tielengum (tiolengum, Cott. MSS.) *deditae terrenis negotiis*, Swt. 135, 15. Gecorene tō Godes teolungum, Homl. Th. ii. 96, 1. Sēcan ða gāstlīcan tylunga, 552, 10. Hē begǽþ his hlāfordes teolunga, i. 412, 4. Wē willaþ sprecan ymbe manna tilunga *ad hominum studia revertor*, Bt. 24,

4; Fox 84, 27. III. *care, attention, treatment, cure.* v. tilian, III. 2 b, IV:—Ðonne man tó wiccan tilunge sēce æt ǽnigre neóde, Wulfst. 171, 11. Hē his hǽlde sēcan wyle æt unālȳfedum tilungum, Homl. Th. i. 474, 21. Hē lǽrde đurh đa tielunga (tiolunga, Cott. MSS.) đæs Samaritaniscan (*per Samaritani studium*) ymb đone gewundedan, Past. 17; Swt. 125, 7. IV. *gain that comes from labour, acquisition, fruit* got by tilling the earth:—Tilunge *quaestu, lucro*, Hpt. Gl. 419, 63. Swā hwæt swā hȳ gespariaþ on heora forhæfednessæ, and swā hwæt swā tōforan neádbehēfum belifen byþ on heora mægenes tilunge *whatever they save by their abstinence, and whatever over and above necessaries remains of acquisition by their ability*, R. Ben. 138, 17. Se gȳtsere gȳmþ grǽdelīce his teolunge, Homl. Th. i. 66, 10. Ða đe ne sēcaþ heora āgen gestreón ac smeágaþ ymbe Godes teolunge (*gain to be made for God*), ii. 76, 35: 558, 16. Ðū stunta, tō niht đū scealt đīn līf ālǽtan; hwæs beóþ đonne đīne teolunga *whose shall thy gains be then?* Wulfst. 286, 24. Hī sceolon heora geáres teolunga Gode đone teóđan dǽl syllan, Homl. Th. ii. 608, 22. Lāc of eorđan tilingum *de fructibus terrae munera*, Gen. 4, 3. Ete ælþeódig folc đīne tilinga *fructus terrae et omnes labores tuos comedat populus quem ignoras*, Deut. 28, 33. Ǽgđer ge earm ge eádig, đe ǽnige teolunga (tylunge, MS. F.) hæbbe, gelǽste Gode his teóđunga, L. Edg. S. 1; Th. i. 272, 1. [False teolunges, A. R. 208, 17. Þe wingeardes þet mot muche tilunge to uorte beren winberies, 296, 1. Fourty wynter folke lyued withouten tulyinge (tiliyng, tilynge), Piers P. 14, 63.]

tīma, an; *m. Time, hour*; tempus, Wrt. Voc. i. 76, 66: hora, ii. 132, 67. I. *time* when, *time* at which an event takes place:—Hit wæs đā se tīma đæt wīnberian rīpodon *erat tempus, quando jam praecoquae uvae vesci possunt*, Num. 13, 21. Swā mon eorđan wæstmas hām gelǽdeþ on rȳpes tīman, Exon. Th. 214, 28; Ph. 246. Ðā geweard hit on đisum ilcan tīman ođđe litle ǽr, đæt . . ., Chr. 1009; Erl. 141, 28: 1015; Erl. 152, 9. Thomas tō đam tīman āgeán fērde būton bletsunga, 1070; Erl. 208, 9. Tȳman on āsettum tȳman, Homl. Th. i. 18, 26. On unālȳfedum tīman, ii. 94, 3. Gebiddaþ ealle hālige tō đē on tilne tīman (*in tempore opportuno*), Ps. Th. 31, 7. Ðonne hē nytwyrđne tīman ongiet tō sprecenne *cum opportunum considerat*, Past. 38; Swt. 275, 14. Ymbe đone tīman đe điss wæs *at the time when this was happening*, Ors. 4, 5; Swt. 168, 36. Tiéman, 4, 8; Swt. 186, 34. Ðæt hié đoligen earfeđu đǽm tīmum đe hié đyrfen, Past. 36; Swt. 253, 10. Ne đincþ mē nǽfre nāuwuht swā sōþlīc swā mē þincþ đīn spell đǽm tīmum (tīdum, Cott. MS.) đe ic đa gehēre *cum tuas rationes considero, nihil dici verius puto*, Bt. 38, 5; Fox 204, 23. I a. *a time when a thing can* or *ought to be done, a proper time, opportunity*:—Ðonne đæs đinges tīma ne biþ đæt hit mon sidelīce gebētan mǽge . . . ac đonne se lāreów ieldende sēcþ đone tīman đe hē his hiéremenn sidelīce on đreátigean mǽge *cum rerum minime opportunitas congruit, ut aperte corrigantur . . . Sed cum tempus subditis ad correptionem quaeritur*, Past. 21; Swt. 153, 1-6. Ūs is tīma đæt wē onwæcnen of slǽpe *hora est nos de somno surgere*, 63; Swt. 459, 33. Hwænne wylle gē singan? Þonne hyt tīma byþ, Coll. Monast. Th. 34, 5. Se wīsa hit ieldcaþ and bītt tīman, Past. 33; Swt. 220, 10. Nis hit nān wundur, đeáh se wīsa bīde his tīman, 38; Swt. 275, 13. Hē đencþ đæs tīman hwonne hē hit wyrs geleánian mǽge *deteriora rependere, si occasio praebeatur, quaerat*, 33; Swt. 227, 23. I b. *time* as in the phrases, in *time*, in good *time*, *be-times; proper time* because soon enough:—Ealle đās ungesǽlđa ūs gelumpon þurh unrǽdas, đæt mann nolde him tō tīman (ā tīman, MS. C.) gafol bēdan; ac đonne hī mǽst tō yfele gedōn hæfdon, đonne nam man grid and frid wid hī, Chr. 1011; Erl. 145, 2. Þeófas tō tīman (*forthwith*) forwurđan, būton hig geswīcan, L. C. S. 4; Th. i. 378, 13. I c. *an appointed time*:—Mīn tīma ys gehende, Mt. Kmbl. 26, 18. Drihtenes engel com tō his tīman on đone mere, and đæt wæter wæs āstyred, Jn. Skt. 5, 4. II. *a period of time*:—His tīma ne biþ nā langsum, Homl. Th. i. 4, 18. Hire tīma wæs gefylled, đæt heó cennan sceolde, i. 30, 11. Ǽlces mannes tīma *the time that each man lives*, Anglia viii. 336, 27. II a. marking date or limit, *time* during which certain events are happening, during which a particular person is living, etc.:—On đet gerād đet hē hæbbe đone bryce đes landes swā lange swā his tȳma sȳ *so long as he live*, Cod. Dip. B. iii. 106, 39. Hit wæs gewunelīc on đam tīman, Homl. Th. i. 60, 26. On mīnum tīman swā on mīnes fæder, L. Edg. S. 2; Th. i. 272, 28. On ūrum tīman, Chart. Th. 240, 11. On đara heáhfædera tīman . . . on Moyses and on đara wītegena tīman, L. Ælfc. P. 6; Th. ii. 366, 7-8. Eall đās geeodon in ūssera tīda tīman, Exon. Th. 147, 12; Gū. 726. II b. *a season of the year*:—Feówer tīman beóþ . . . *Uer* ys lengtentīma, and hē gǽþ tō tūne on .vii. id. Febr. . . . Se ōđer tīma hātte *aestas* . . . Se þridda tīma ys *autumnus* . . . Se feórđa tīma ys genemned *hiemps*, Anglia viii. 312, 14-31. On wintres tīman, đæt is fram đan anginne đæs mōnđes, đe is Nouember gehāten, ōþ Eástran, R. Ben. 32, 10. On ǽlcne tīman, ge on wintra ge on sumera, 33, 20. II c. *an age of the world*:—Þrȳ tīman sind on đyssere worulde; Ante legem, Sub lege, Sub gratia, Homl. Th. ii. 190, 1. Ðrȳ tīman synd getealde on đissere worulde. Ān tīma wæs ǽr Godes ǽ . . . Ōđer under Godes lage . . . Ðridde under Cristes āgenre gife, L. Ælfc. P. 6; Th. ii. 366, 6. III. as a grammatical term, *time of pronouncing a syllable, quantity*:—Ðæt rihtmetervers sceal habban feówer and twēntig tīman . . . Dactilus stent on ānum langum tīman and twām sceortum, and spondeus stent of feówrum langum, Anglia viii. 314, 10-15: 335, 14. IV. *time, condition of things*:—Ǽfter đisum fæce gewurđan sceall swā egeslīc tīma, swā ǽfre ǽr ne wæs, Wulfst. 19, 3. Wā đām wīfum đe on đam earmlīcan tīman heora cild fēdaþ, 81, 7. [*Icel.* tími.] v. ǽfen-, ende-, gebyrd-, hærfest-, lencten-, mǽrsung-, nōn-, riht-, rīp-, sǽd-, swig-, þrowung-, un-tīma; tīd.

-tīma. v. here-tēma, ge-tȳma.

tīman; *p.* de. I. *to teem, be productive.* v. teám, I. (1) referring to a female, *to be with child, bear, bring forth* young:—Wā đām wīfum, đe đonne tȳmaþ and heora cild fēdaþ (*vae praegnantibus et nutrientibus*, Mt. 24, 19), Wulfst. 81, 6. Sindon sume gesceafta đe tȳmaþ būton hǽmede, and biþ ǽgđer ge seó mōder mǽden ge seó dohtor; đæt sind beón: hī tȳmaþ heora teám mid clǽnnysse, Homl. Th. ii. 10, 14-17. Lia underget đæt heó leng ne tȳmde (*quod parere desiisset*), Gen. 30, 9. Ðonne heó (*the wife*) leng tȳman ne mæg, geswīcan hī hǽmedes, Homl. Th. ii. 94, 5. Heó tȳmende nā leng beón ne mæg, Wulfst. 305, 29. (2) referring to a male, *to beget, have intercourse* with (*wiđ*) a woman:—Godes bearn tȳmdon wiđ manna dohtra and hig cendon *ingressi sunt filii Dei ad filias hominum illaeque genuerunt*, Gen. 6, 4. Ðā bæd heó hire wer đæt hē wiđ hire wylne tȳman sceolde (*ingredere ad ancillam meam*, Gen. 16, 2), Boutr. Scrd. 22, 23. Mōste se bisceop niman him ān clǽne mǽden and wiđ hȳ tȳman on āsettum tīman, L. Ælfc. C. 7; Th. ii. 346, 2: Homl. Th. i. 18, 26. (3) where neither male nor female is specified, *to have offspring, bring forth*:—Fugelas ne tȳmaþ swā swā ōđre nȳtenu, Homl. Th. i. 250, 22. Ðæt folc tȳmde micelne teám on đam wēstene, Homl. Th. ii. 212, 17. Þeóda tȳmdon, Cd. Th. 75, 19; Gen. 1242. Tēmaþ and wexaþ, 13, 1; Gen. 196. Tȳmaþ and tiédraþ, 91, 14; Gen. 1512. Feoh sceal on eorđan tȳdran and tȳman, Menol. Fox 557; Gn. C. 48. [Þe two tentaciuns þet temeđ alle þe ođre, A. R. 220, 15. Elysabæþ ne mihhte tæmenn, Orm. 130. Ȝif ha ne mei nawt teamen . . . ha cleopeđ ham weolefulle þat teamen hare teames, H. M. 33, 22-25. Ghe sulde sunen and timen, and clepen it Smael, Gen. and Ex. 982. Aȝen þat þu (*the nightingale*) wilt teme, O. and N. 499.] II. as a technical term. v. teám, III, *to vouch to warranty* (acc. of that which is to be warranted and person vouched governed by *tō*), *to refer* property (*acc.*) to (*tō*) the person from whom it was obtained in support of the right of possession:—Gif sió hond tiémþ, sió đone ceáp mon æt befēhþ, tō ōđrum men, L. In. 75; Th. i. 150, 6. Swā hē hit āgnode, swā hē hit tȳmde, L. Ed. 1; Th. i. 160, 8. Ðā tȳmde Wulfstān đone mann tō Æđelstāne, Chart. Th. 206, 25. Tǽme hē tō đam mæn đe him sealde, L. H. E. 16; Th. i. 34, 6. Ne mōt forstolenne ceáp mon tiéman tō þeówum men, L. In. 47; Th. i. 132, 5. Se đe yrfe bycge on gewitnesse and hit eft tȳman (mon teáman, *var. lect.*) scyle, L. Ath. i. 24; Th. i. 212, 13: L. Ed. 1; Th. i. 158, 16. II a. in a general sense, *to refer* an opinion to the source from which it is derived in its support:—Benedictus ūs bōc āwrāt leóhtre be dǽle đonne Basilius, ac hē tȳmde swā đeáh tō Basilies tǽcinge for his trumnysse *for confirmation he referred to the teaching of Basil as the source from which he had drawn*, Basil prm.; Norm. 32, 9. Benedictus tȳmde tō đam regole đe Basilius gesette, Homl. Skt. i. 3, 152. [*In later English* temen to = (1) *to betake one's self to* a place, *go to*:—To Albion þu scalt teman (wende, 2nd MS.), Laym. 1245: 7174. (2) *to resort to, appeal to* in reverence or for help:—To hire he wolde teman (hire wolde he louie, 2nd MS.), Laym. 1265. Al hit trukeđ us an hond þat we to temden, 16800. Gif þu temest (*appealest*) to þan rihten, and þu wult of Rome þolien æi dome, 24816. He temed him to þe king, Trist. 431. To witnesse temen, P. L. S. viii. 54. I hope to trede on þy temple & teme to þy seluen, Allit. Pms. 101, 316. (3) *to lead to* (?):—Ic wolde iwiten to whan þis tocne wule ten, to wulche þinge temen, Laym. 9135.] v. ge-tēman; un-tīmende.

timber, es; *n.* I. *material* for constructing a house, ship, etc., *timber*:—Ǽfter siextegum daga đæs đe đæt timber (*arbores*) ācorfen wæs, đǽr wǽron xxx and c scipa gearora, Ors. 4, 6; Swt. 172, 4. Ne sceal cyrcean timber (*ligna ecclesiae*) tō ǽnigum ōđrum weorce, L. Ecg. P. Addit. 16; Th. ii. 234, 16. Ðætte ne meahten godo beón đa đe monna hondum geworhte wǽron of eorđlīcum timbre ođþe of treóm ođþe of stānum *deos esse non posse, qui hominum manibus facti essent; dei creandi materiam lignum vel lapidem esse non posse*, Bd. 3, 22; M. 224, 15. Ǽrest man āsmeáþ đæs hūses stede, and eác man đæt timber beheáwþ, Anglia viii. 324, 8: Lchdm. iii. 180, 8. I a. *material* of which anything is formed:—Sió lifer is blōdes timber and blodes hūs and fōstor, Lchdm. ii. 198, 2: 160, 13. II. *a structure, building, edifice*:—Heó mid đǽm tō đǽm timbre (*aedificio*) gefæstnad wæs, Bd. 3, 17; S. 544, 31. Tō đam heofonlīcum timbre, 4, 3; S. 567, 12. In timbre *in aedificio*, Ps. Surt. 101, 8. Seó tīd gewāt ofer timber (? tiber, MS.) sceacan middangeardes, Cd. Th. 9, 2; Gen. 135. Huulig timber *quales structurae*, Mk. Skt. Lind. Rush. 13, 1. Timbra *aedificiorum*, Ps. Surt. 128, 6. Ða burh manige menn mid heán timbrum frættewodon (*augustioribus aedificiis adornarunt*), Bd. 3, 19; S. 547, 24. III. *the building* of a house, ship, etc.:—Hē (*the sixth day of the moon*) is gōd circan on tō timbrane, and eác scipes timber on tō anginnanne, Lchdm. iii. 178, 9. [*O. L. Ger.* timbar: *O. Frs.* timber: *O. H. Ger.* zimbar *materia, fabrica, structura, aedificium*: *Ger.* zimmer a *chamber, timber*: *Icel.* timbr. Cf. *Goth.* timreins *a building*, ga-timrjō *a building*.] v. an-, and-, boh-, bolt-, fugol-, fyrd- (?), heáh-, heofon-, hrōf-, magu-timber; ge-timbru.

timber-geweorc, es; *n.* *Timber-work, preparation* or *cutting of timber for building* (?):—In bōcholte timbergeweorc and widigunge *in beechholt the right to get timber for building and to cut wood for fuel*, Cod. Dip. B. i. 344, 12. v. timbran, III.

timber-hrycg, es; *m.* *A wooded ridge* (?); as a local name *Timber-ridge*:—On timberhricges snād, Cod. Dip. Kmbl. v. 71, 1. Ofer fild-burnan on timberhrycg, iii. 463, 31. Timberrycg, 393, 27.

timberness, tim-bor. v. ge-, on-timberness, tym-bor.

timbran, timbrian; *p.* ede, ode. I. *to build* (lit. or fig.), *construct*:—Ic timbrige *struo, construo*, Ælfc. Gr. 28, 5; Zup. 175, 11. Tōweorp hié, ne ðū timbres (*aedificabis*) hié, Ps. Surt. 27, 5. Timbreþ Dryhten Sion, 101, 17: Ps. Th. 146, 2: Exon. Th. 450, 25; Dōm. 93. Gē timbriaþ (timbraþ, Rush.) wītegena byrgene, Mt. Kmbl. 23, 29: Lk. Skt. 11, 47, 48. Ic timbrode setl ðīn, Ps. Spl. 88, 5. Ða gōdan weorc ðe hē ǣr timbrede, Past. 33; Swt. 215, 18. Hē burh timbrede, Cd. Th. 172, 6; Gen. 2840: Chr. 722; Erl. 44, 28. Timbrade, Ps. Th. 101, 14. Hié ceastra timbredon, Ors. 1, 10; Swt. 48, 10. Drehton ða hergas mid ðǣm æscum ðe hié ǣr timbredon. Ðā hēt Alfrēd cyng timbran langscipu ongēn ða æscas, Chr. 897; Erl. 95, 7–11. Æfter ðæm hryre ðære upāhæfennesse hē ongan timbran eáðmōdnesse, Past. 58; Swt. 443, 30. Wē ceorfaþ treówu on holte, ðæt wē hī eft up ārǣren on ðæm botle, ðǣr ðǣr wē timbran willen, Swt. 445, 1: Cd. Th. 64, 29; Gen. 1057. Weall stǣnenne timbran, 101, 34; Gen. 1692. On ðām telgum timbran nest, Exon. Th. 210, 20; Ph. 188. Ne mæg fira nān wīsdōm timbran (timbrian, Bt. 12; Fox 36, 11, 8, 10), ðǣr ðǣr woruldgītsung beorg oferbrǣdeþ, Met. 7, 12. Uton timbrian ūs ceastre *faciamus nobis civitatem*, Gen. 11, 4: Ps. Th. 128, 2. Ecgbryht salde Reculf mynster on tō tymbranne (-ianne, MS. E.), Chr. 669; Erl. 34, 26. Timbriende *aedificans*, Ps. Surt. 146, 2. Timbrende *aedificantes*, 117, 22. Ðǣr wæs timbred templ, Nar. 37, 22: Beo. Th. 620; B. 307. Bióþ timbrede cestre, Ps. Surt. 68, 36. II. *to instruct, edify*:—Hē nōwiht elles dyde ðonne ðæt folc mid godcundre lāre timbrede *nil aliud ageret quam plebem Christi verbo salutis instruere*, Bd. 2, 14; S. 518, 10. III. *to cut timber* (?). v. timber-geweorc, *and* cf. wudian:—Me mæig on sumera . . . bytlian . . . tymbrian, wudian, Anglia ix. 261, 11. [Letten þa kinges timbrien þa hallen, Laym. 5940. To timbren me mine crune, A. R. 124, 8. To timmbrenn himm an hus, Orm. 13368. Who tauȝte hem (*peacocks*) on trees to tymbre so heighe, Piers P. 11, 352. *Goth.* timrjan: *O. Sax.* ge-timbrōn (-ian): *O. L. Ger.* ge-timbran: *O. Frs.* timbra, timmera: *Du.* timmeren: *O. H. Ger.* zimbaren, zimbarōn *aedificare, struere, instruere*: *Ger.* zimmern: *Icel.* timbra: *Dan.* tømre.] v. ā-, be-, for-, ge-, in-, on-timbran (-ian), *and next word.*

timbrend, es; *m. f.* *A builder, constructor*:—Se wæs timbrend (*constructor*) ðæs mynstres ðe gecweden is Mēdeshāmstyde, Bd. 4, 6; S. 573, 40. Heó wæs seó ǣryste tymbrend ðæs mynstres ðe ys nemned Steórneshealh, Shrn. 148, 39.

timbrian. v. timbran.

timbrung, e; *f.* *Building, a building*:—Ealdere timbrunga bōte *instructio*, nīwe timbrung *constructio*, Wrt. Voc. i. 39, 58, 59. Timbrunga *domum exstructam*, Kent. Gl. 472. [Bileafden heo (*the builders of the tower of Babel*) heore timbrunge, O. E. Homl. i. 93, 23. Timbringe, 227, 4. Al is to his behefe and timbrunge toward his blisse, A. R. 124, 1.] v. ge-timbrung.

-tīme (v. teám, I, tīman, I, *and* cf. -bǣre). v. luf-, þweorh-tīme; wrōht-getīme.

-tīme (v. teám, II). v. feoþer-, ge-tīme (-tȳme).

tīme (v. tīma). v. un-tīme.

tīmen (?); *adj.* *Belonging to a team.* v. teám, II:—Tēmen *bibina* (=*bis bina?*), Wrt. Voc. ii. 126, 8.

tīmian. v. ge-, mis-tīmian.

tīmlīce; *adv.* *In good time, soon*:—Ðū bǣde mē foroft Engliscra gewritena and ic ðē ne getīðode ealles swā tīmlīce ǣr ðam ðe ðū mid geweorcum ðæs gewilnodest æt mē *you very often asked me for English writings, but I did not grant your request so very soon, not before you desired it from me with works*, Ælfc. T. Grn. 1, 16. [Ic mei longe libben and alle mine sunne timliche ibeten *repent of all my sins time enough*, O. E. Homl. i. 25, 13. Ase timliche as he hefde iherd þis (sone so he iherde þis, *other MS.*), Jul. 9, 5. He wolde timliche him speken wið, Laym. 31369. Bute ȝef þu þe timluker (*nisi maturius*) ure godes grete, Kath. 2086. *Icel.* tīmaliga *timely, early*.] Cf. tīdlīce.

tīmness. v. un-tīmness.

timpana, an; *m.* *A tabret, timbrel*:—Hergaþ hine in timpanan *laudate eum in tympano*, Ps. Surt. 150, 4. Sellaþ timpanan, 80, 3. Plægiendra timpanan *tympanistriarum*, 67, 26. Ic filigde ðē mid timpanum and mid hearpum, Gen. 31, 27. [*O. H. Ger.* timpana: *Icel.* timpan. From Latin.]

timpestere, es; *m.* *A player on the timbrel*:—Timpestera (timpanestera?) *tympanistriarum*, Ps. Lamb. 67, 26. [Cf. *O. L. Ger.* timparinna: *O. H. Ger.* tympinara; *pl.*]

timple, an; *f.* *Some implement used in weaving*:—Hē sceal habban fela tōwtōla . . . flexlīnan, spinle . . . presse, pihten, timplean, wifte, Anglia ix. 263, 12.

tīn, tién, tēn, tȳn teá (*North.*) *ten.* I. as an adjective with a noun uninflected, except in the Northern specimens:—Tīn dagas, Bd. 1, 23; S. 485, 24. Ðis is ðara tȳn hīda bōc, Cod. Dip. Kmbl. v. 316, 33. Mid tién bebodum, Past. 17; Swt. 125, 18. Tién ceastro *Decapoleas*, Wrt. Voc. ii. 26, 14. Sume tēn geár, Bt. 38, 1; Fox 194, 7. Tȳn þūsend (tēno ł teá ðūsendo, Lind.: tēn þūsende, Rush.) punda, Mt. Kmbl. 18, 24. Gelīc ðām tȳn fǣmnum (tēwm hehstaldum, Lind.: tēn fēmnan, Rush.), 25, 1. Mid tȳn (tēum ł tēnum, Lind.: tēn, Rush.) þūsendum, Lk. Skt. 14, 31. Tȳn (teá, Lind. Rush.) hreófe weras, 17, 12. Teá sīðum, Lind. 15, 8. Fram wintrum tēnum, p. 8, 4. Teá ł tēno hreáfo, p. 9, 8. Of tēum hehstaldum, Mt. Kmbl. p. 19, 16. Teá monna lātwu *decanus*, Rtl. 193, 19. II. used as a substantive and declined, *nom.* -e, *gen.* -a, *dat.* -um. (1) alone:—Ðā gebulgon ða tȳne (tēno, Lind.: tēnu, Rush.) hī, Mk. Skt. 10, 41. Ða hildlatan, tȳne ætsomne, Beo. Th. 5687; B. 2847. Tȳna ealdor *decanus*, Wrt. Voc. ii. 138, 4. Næs tō ānum dæge, ne tō fīfon, ne tō tȳnum, ne tō twēntigum, Num. 11, 19. Aldormonn ofer tēno *decanus*, Rtl. 193, 21, 19. (2) governing a genitive:—Gif ðǣr beóþ tȳn rihtwīsra, Gen. 18, 32. Hæfde se ealwalda engelcynna tȳne getrymede, Cd. Th. 16, 24; Gen. 248. Nigon hund wintra hæfde and tȳne, 71, 3; Gen. 1165. IIa. *a set of ten*:—Tȳnum and twēntigum on ānum inne ætgædere restan *let them sleep by tens and twenties in one house*, R. Ben. 47, 7. IIb. *the number ten*:—Ðis tal under him hæfis ōðer tal ðe tō tēnum wið forecyme (*a number that goes up to ten*), Mt. Kmbl. p. 3, 20. Tele ðū ōð ðæt ðū cume tō þrittiga, eft . . . tele ōð tȳne (*count up to ten*), Lchdm. iii. 228, 2. [*Goth.* taihun: *O. Sax.* tehan: *O. Frs.* tian, tien: *O. L. Ger.* tēn, tein, tian: *O. H. Ger.* zehan: *Icel.* tíu.]

tin, es; *n.* *Tin*:—Tin *stagnum*, Wrt. Voc. i. 85, 10: 286, 71: Ælfc. Gr. 5; Zup. 15, 11. Ðæt tin, ðonne hit mon mid sumum cræfte gemengþ and tō tine gewyrcþ, ðonne biþ hit swiðe leáslīce on siolufres hiewe. Suā hwā ðonne suā līcet on ðære swingellan, hē biþ ðæm tine gelīc inne on ðæm ofne, Past. 37; Swt. 269, 2–5. Tinnes *stagni*, Hpt. Gl. 431, 69. Ðiss folc is geworden mē tō āre and tō tine and tō īserne and tō leáde, Past. 37; Swt. 267, 17. Tin *stannum*, Coll. Monast. Th. 27, 11. [*O. H. Ger.* zin: *Icel.* tin.]

tin *a beam.* v. tinn.

Tīna(-e?), an *the river Tyne*:—Be Tīnan ðære eá *juxta amnem Tinam*, Bd. 5, 21; S. 642, 36: Chr. 875; Erl. 76, 35.

tīn-āmbre; *adj.* *Containing ten* '*āmbras*':—Genim tȳnāmberne cetel, Lchdm. ii. 86, 12.

tīnan; *p.* de *To vex, annoy, irritate, provoke*:—Se wellwillenda man wyle forberan gif hine man āhwǣr tȳnþ, oððe him tale gecwyð, Basil admn. 4; Norm. 44, 18. Ðā ðā se ān (sunu) ðē tȳnde (cf. tirigde, l. 9), Homl. Th. ii. 30, 12. Hī yrsodon ł tȳndon Moyses *irritaverunt Moysen*, Ps. Spl. 105, 16, 8: Blickl. Gl.: Cd. Th. 153, 24; Gen. 2543. Ne tȳn ðū ðīne neáhgebūras *non memor eris injuriae civium tuorum*, Lev. 19, 18. Ne ǣnig man ōðerne ne tyrie ne ne tȳne ealles tō swȳðe, Wulfst. 70, 9. Ne āblinnan wē, ðæt wē Gode cwēmon and deófol tȳnan, Blickl. Homl. 47, 11. Ðæt hī ælþeódige men ne tyrian ne ne tȳnan, L. Eth. vi. 48; Th. i. 326, 28: Wulfst. 309, 5. Gebiddaþ for eówerum ehterum and eów tȳnendum *orate pro persequentibus et calumniantibus vos* (Mt. 5, 44), Homl. Th. ii. 216, 17. v. teónian.

tinclian; *p.* ode *To tickle*:—Nāht swā onǣlþ and tinclaþ gecyndlima ðænne gemylt mete *nihil sic inflammat et titillat membra genitalia quam indigestus cibus*, Scint. 52, 5. Hē wiðstynt weorce se ðe tincligendre nā geþwǣrlǣcþ lustfullunge *resistit operi qui titillanti non accomodat delectationi*, 88, 9. [In Wycklif *tynclen* translates *tinnire*, 1 Sam. 3, 11: 1 Cor. 13, 1.]

tind, es; *m.* *A tine, prong, tooth* of an implement:—Tindas *rostri*, tindum *rostris*, Wrt. Voc. ii. 119, 30, 28. Ðeáh ānra gehwylc horn hæbbe .xii. tindas īrene, and ānra gehwylc tind hæbbe synderlīce .xii. ordas, Salm. Kmbl. p. 150, 25. [Tindes *the rungs of a ladder*, A. R. 354, 20. Tynde *branch of a tree*, Allit. Pms. 3, 78. Tindes of harowis, Alex. 3908. A tynde *cremale* (a hook); a tynde of a beste, Cath. Angl. 389 (*where see several instances*). Tyynde, prekyl, tynde, pryke *carnica*; tyndyt with tyndys *carnicatus*, Prompt. Parv. 494. Cf. *tine* stocks, the short crooked handles on the pole of a scythe, Halliw. Dict. *M. H. Ger.* zint *a spike, tooth*: *Icel.* tindr *a spike*; also, *a peak*.] v. following words.

tindect. v. tindiht.

tindig; *adj.* *Having spikes* or *prongs*:—Ôstig gyrd *vel* tindig *scorpio* (scorpio *genus flagelli, ex virgis nodosis confecti, vel scutica in modum scorpionis aculeata*, Migne), Wrt. Voc. i. 20, 17. v. next word.

tindiht; *adj.* *Having spikes* or *teeth, beaked*:—Tindicti (-ecte) *ros-*

tratum, Txts. 92, 868. Se cāsere hine (St. Romanus) hēt stingan mid īrenum gyrdum tyndehtum, Shrn. 115, 25. v. preceding words.

tindting (tending?, tihting?) :—Tindtingce *suasionis, exhortationis*, Hpt. Gl. 485, 66.

Tīne. v. Tīna.

tinen; *adj. Of tin* :—Tinen *stagneus*, Ælfc. Gr. 5; Zup. 15, 11. Ælc calic gegoten beó, gylden odde seolfren (odde) tinen, de man hūsl on hālgige, L. Edg. C. 41; Th. ii. 252, 21 note. Tynen, L. Ælfc. C. 36; Th. ii. 360, note 2. On tinum (= tinenum) fæte, Lchdm. ii. 236, 5. [With tynnen tonges, Pall. 152, 99. *O. H. Ger.* zinīn *stanneus*.]

tīnend, es; *m. One who vexes, annoys*, etc. v. tīnan :—Gebiddaþ for eówerum ēhterum and tȳnendum, Homl. Th. ii. 36, 16.

tīn-feald; *adj. Tenfold* :—Tȳnfealde *deni*, Ælfc. Gr. 5; Zup. 13, 15. Tȳnfealdum odde twēntifealdum *deni aut viceni*, R. Ben. Interl. 54, 15. Þreowa on teónfealdum *ter denis*, Hymn. Surt. 104, 23. Feówer sīdo teáfald tal *quater denario numero*, Mt. Kmbl. p. 12, 12.

tinga, tingan, tingce. v. in-tinga, ge-tingan, tynge.

tinn, e; *f.* (?) *A beam, rafter* :—Tin *tignum*, Txts. 101, 2023. [Cf. (?) *O. H. Ger.* zinna *pinna*.]

tinnan *to stretch, extend* :—Blǣd his blinniþ . . . lustum ne tinneþ *does not joyously extend* (?), Exon. Th. 354, 32; Reim. 54. Tinde bogan *tetendit arcum*, Blickl. Gl.

tīn-nihte; *adj. Ten days old* :—On .x. nihtne mōnan bidde swā hwas swa dū wylle, hyt de byoþ gere. Se .x. nihta mōna hē ys gōd tō standanne mid ædelum monnum, Lchdm. iii. 178, 19–21. Se de biþ ācenned on .x. nihtne ealdne mōnan, se biþ drowere, 160, 28.

tīn-strenge; *adj. Having ten strings* :—On tȳnstrengum saltere *in decacordo psalterio*, Ps. Spl. 91, 3: 143, 11. v. next word.

tīn-strenged; *adj. Provided with ten strings* :—On tȳnstrengedum saltere, Blickl. Gl. Tȳnstrængedum, Ps. Lamb. 91, 4. Tȳnstrængdom, 143, 9. v. preceding word.

tinterg. v. tin-treg.

tin-treg, -terg, es; *n.*: tin-trega, an; *m. Torment* :—Dǣr (*in heaven*) ne biþ nān besārgung dæra mānfulra yrmde, ac heora tintrega becymþ dam gecorenum tō māran blisse, Homl. Th. i. 334, 11. Nis dǣr ne caru ne hreóh tintrega (cf. hreóge tintrega, Wulfst. 139, 30), Dōm. L. 261. Dæt wæs helle tintreges mūþ *ipsum est os gehennae*, Bd. 5, 12; S. 630, 13. On dām grundum helle tintreges *in profundis tartari*, 5, 14; S. 634, 25. Ic on eorþan gebād tintregan fela, Cd. Th. 296, 4; Sat. 497. Mē genihtsumiaþ dās tintrega, Blickl. Homl. 243, 26. Dē sȳn helle tinterga ontȳned, Shrn. 79, 11. On dissa tintrega stōwe *in locum hunc tormentorum*, Lk. Skt. 16, 28. For dara tintregena mænigfyldnesse, Wulfst. 199, 6. Tintegrena *tormentorum*, Hpt. Gl. 415, 72. On tintregum gegripene *tormentis comprehensos*, Mt. Kmbl. 4, 24. Tintregum (tintergum, Lind.), Lk. Skt. 16, 23. Būton tintregum þeáh on hellewīte, Homl. Th. i. 94, 6. Wrecan heora teónrǣdenne mid tintergum on him, Jud. 15, 10: Exon. Th. 114, 33; Gū. 182. Donne hē dara manna tintrego oferhiérde, Ors. 1, 12; Swt. 54, 27: Bd. 5, 14; S. 635, 1: Blickl. Homl. 243, 20. On da wyrstan tintregu, 239, 10. In da ēcan tintregu, Wulfst. 185, 11. Tintergu, Exon. Th. 141, 3; Gū. 621. In tintergo *in gehennam*, Mt. Kmbl. Lind. 10, 28. Hié ealle worldlīce tintrega and ealle līchomlīcu sār oforhogodan, Blickl. Homl. 119, 19. Dȳ læs de dū þurh tintrega forwurde, Homl. Th. i. 432, 9. Ic geseó, dæt dū dās tintregan gebȳsmerast, 426, 5. Ān deófol ārehte ānum ancran dara synfulra sāwla tintregan and sūsla, Wulfst. 146, 19. [Eordliche tintreohen, O. E. Homl. i. 261, 16. Ne schal þe na teone ne tintreohe trukien, Kath. 403. Þu biþenche teonen and tintreohen, 1888. Cf. *Goth.* us trigōm ἐκ λύπης, 2 Cor. 9, 7. *Icel.* tregi *grief, woe.*]

tintregend, es; *m. A torturer* :—Fram dǣm tintergendum (*or ptcpl.?*) *a tortoribus*, Wrt. Voc. ii. 2, 49.

tin-tregian, -tergian; *p.* ode *To torment, torture, afflict* :—Da de hē ne mæg fram rihtan geleáfan tō him gebīgan, donne tintregaþ hē da on mænigfealde wīsan, Wulfst. 197, 7: Blickl. Homl. 59, 31. Philippus hī miclum tintrade (tintergade, MS. C.) and bismrade, Ors. 3, 7; Swt. 118, 25. Se kāsere hine tintregode mid unāsecgendlīcum wītum, Shrn. 116, 1. Da de tintergedon done hālgan wer, 73, 1. Hī tintregodon hine and forlēton hine sāmcucene *plagis impositis abierunt semivivo relicto*, Lk. Skt. 10, 30. Da wīfmen hié swā tintredon, Ors. 1, 10; Swt. 48, 13. Deáh de dæt fȳr tintregige da unrihtwīsan, Homl. Th. ii. 590, 3. Hēt swingan and tintregian done Godes andettere *caedi Dei confessorem a tortoribus praecepit*, Bd. 1, 7; S. 477, 42. Tintergian, Shrn. 76, 33. Tinterga *torquere*, Mt. Kmbl. Rush. 8, 29. Decius gewende tō tintregienne da cristenan, Homl. Th. ii. 424, 19. Tō tintreinne *torquendus, cruciandus*, Hpt. Gl. 482, 35. Dǣr hē tintregad weard; ǣrest hiene mon swong, da sticode him mon da eágan ūt, and siþþan him mon slōg da handa of, dā dæt heáfod, Ors. 4, 5; Swt. 168, 3. [Heo eow tintraȝed and heow iswenchet, O. E. Homl. i. 13, 30. Cf. *O. Sax.* tregan *to trouble*: *Icel.* trega.] v. ge-tintregian; tregian.

tintreg-līc; *adj. Tormenting, torturing, of hell* :—Be fyrhto dæs tintreglīcan (tintreganlīces, MS. B.) wītes *de horrore poenae gehennalis*, Bd. 4, 24; S. 598, 16.

tintreg-stōw, e; *f. A place of torment* :—Hī (*the devils*) done hālgan wer gelǣddon tō dām sweartum tintrehstōwum, Guthl. 5; Gdwin. 38, 4.

tintreg-þegn, es; *m. An officer who torments, an executioner* :—Tinter[g]degnum *lictoribus*, Wrt. Voc. ii. 3, 47. His dryhten hine salde tintergaþægnum (*tortoribus*), Mt. Kmbl. Rush. 18, 34.

tintregung, e; *f. Torment, punishment* :—Tintregung *vel* wīte *tormentum*, Wülck. Gl. 178, 20. Hī ne mihton fram Gode þurh nāne tintregunga beón gebīgede, Homl. Th. i. 544, 2.

tīn-wintre; *adj. Ten years old* :—.x. wintre cniht mæg bión þiéfde gewita *a ten year old boy can be accessory to a theft*, L. In. 7; Th. i. 106, 18. Dā dā hē tȳnwintre on ylde wæs, Homl. Th. ii. 498, 28.

tīr, es; *m. Glory, honour* :—Eów ys wuldorblǣd torhtlīc tōweard and tīr gifeþe, Judth. Thw. 23, 35; Jud. 157. Tīr æt getohte, Byrht. Th. 134, 54; By. 104. Nis hēr (*in hell*) eádiges tīr ne worulde dreám, Cd. Th. 270, 20; Sat. 93. Ne biþ hira (*two twins*) tīr gelīc, Salm. Kmbl. 730; Sal. 364: Exon. Th. 448, 11; Dōm. 52. Biþ tȳr scæcen, eorþan blǣdas, 447, 27; Dōm. 45. Tīres Wealdend (cf. wuldres Waldend, Cd. Th. 216, 27; Dan. 13) *the Deity*, Ps. Th. 79, 14. Tīres brytta, Judth. Thw. 22, 36; Jud. 93. Dæt hȳ mōstun tīres blǣd ēcne āgan, Exon. Th. 74, 27; Cri. 1212: Andr. Kmbl. 210; An. 105. Tīres eádige *abounding in glory*; reges, Ps. Th. 71, 10: Cd. Th. 91, 15; Gen. 1512: Judth. Thw. 25, 22; Jud. 272. Tīres tō tācne *in token of glory gained*, Beo. Th. 3312; B. 1654. Hē benam his feónd torhte tīre, Cd. Th. 4, 23; Gen. 58. Is dæs wuldres ful heofun and eorde, and eall heáhmægen tīre getācnod, Elen. Kmbl. 1504; El. 754. Hwonne ūs līffreá dæt tȳdre gewitt tīre bewinde, Exon. Th. 3, 1; Cri. 29. Dryhten dǣleþ sumum gūþe blǣd, sumum wyrp odde scyte, torhtlīcne tiir, 331, 18; Vy. 70. Dē tīr cyning and miht forgef, Andr. Kmbl. 970; An. 485. Hēr Æþelstān cyning and his brōþor ealdorlangne tīr (tȳr, *one MS.*) geslōgon æt sæcce, Chr. 937; Erl. 112, 3. Gē dōm āgon, tīr æt tohtan, Judth. Thw. 24, 19; Jud. 197. Æsca tīr æt gūde, Cd. Th. 127, 10; Gen. 2108. Hē mē tīr forgeaf, wīgspēd wid wrādum, Elen. Kmbl. 328; El. 164. Da (*friends*) hyra tȳr and eád ȳcaþ, Exon. Th. 409, 3; Rä. 27, 23. Dū tīrum fæst nida Nergend *thou Saviour of men, gloriously firm*, Cd. Th. 235, 27; Dan. 312: Exon. Th. 354, 7; Reim. 42. [Þa kingges weoren deædde, heore duȝede todealde, here tir wes atfallen, Laym. 4237. *O. Sax.* tīr; *see too* tīrlīce *gloriously*: *Icel.* tīrr. Cf. (?) *O. H. Ger.* ziarī *decus.*] v. æsc-tīr, *and words in which* tīr *is the first component*.

Tīr, es; *n. One form of the name of the Runic T; it is also the name of the god corresponding to the Latin Mars, and apparently used also of the planet bearing his name; as Grimm notices, the Runic symbol* ↑ *resembles that used for the planet* ♂ :—Tīr byþ tācna sum, healdaþ trȳwa wel wid ædelingas, ā byþ on færylde ofer nihta genipu, nǣfre swīceþ, Runic pm. Kmbl. 342, 21–26; Rūn. 17. *The other name of the rune is* Tī, v. Tīw, *the two forms* Tīr, Tīw *may be compared with Icelandic* Tȳrr; *gen.* Tȳrs (cf. *Dan.* Tirs-dag), Tȳr; *gen.* Tȳs.

tīran; *p.* de *To run with tears, to water* (of the eyes) :—Mē tȳraþ mīne eágan *lippio*, Ælfc. Gr. 30, 5; Zup. 192, 9. Dǣr biþ wōp and tōda gebitt, for dan de da eágan tȳraþ on dam micclum bryne, and da tēd cwaciaþ on swīdlīcum cyle, Homl. Th. i. 132, 26. Wiþ don de eágan tȳren (cf. wid eallum tiédernessum eágena, 2, 6), Lchdm. ii. 32, 28. Gif eágan tȳren, 34, 1: 308, 19: iii. 4, 23. Wid tȳrendum eágan, 4, 6: i. 374, 3. Wid tȳrende eágan, i. 72, 14. v. teár, I. 2, tearig, II.

tīr-eádig; *adj. Glorious* :—Tīreádig cyning (*the Deity*), Hy. 3, 2, 55: (*Constantine*), Elen. Kmbl. 207; El. 104. Elene, tīreádig cwēn, 1206; El. 605. Tīreádig and trāg (*Judas and the devil*), 1906; El. 955. Tȳreádig cyning (*the Deity*), Hy. 7, 56, 82. Se tīreádga (*the Phenix*), Exon. Th. 205, 1; Ph. 106. Tīreádigum men (*Hygelac*), Beo. Th. 4384; B. 2189. Torhte and tīreádige (*the twelv eapostles*), Apstls. Kmbl. 7; Ap. 4: Andr. Kmbl. 4; An. 2: 1329; An. 665. Tīreádige, hæleþ headurōfe on Brytene, Menol. Fox 26; Men. 13. Tīreádge, Exon. Th. 366, 10; Reb. 10. Þeóden hæfde him ālesen leóda dugede, tīreádigra twā þūsendo; dæt wǣron cyningas, Cd. Th. 189, 13; Exod. 184. Gārberendra, gūdfremmendra, tīreádigra, 192, 16; Exod. 232. [Cf. *Icel.* tīr-gōfugr-, -sæll (*poetical epithets of a hero*).]

tīr-fæst; *adj. Of assured glory, glorious* :—From treówe becwom tīrfæst rīce Drihten ūre *Dominus regnavit a ligno*, Ps. Th. 95, 9. Cyning tīrfæst cystum gecȳþed, Beo. Th. 1848; B. 922. Tīrfæst Metod, Cd. Th. 64, 2; Gen. 1044. Tīrfæst hæled, bisceop se gōda . . . dam wæs Cyneweard nama, Chr. 975; Erl. 126, 7. Tīrfæstne hæled (*Moses*), Cd. Th. 181, 19; Exod. 63. Hwǣr ic tīrfæste treówe funde *ambulans in via immaculata*, Ps. Th. 100, 6: Exon. Th. 473, 7; Bo. 11. Dæt tīrfæste lond, 202, 14; Ph. 69. Ongietan tīrfæst tācen dæt se torhta fugel þurh bryne beácnaþ, 236, 14; Ph. 574. Fyrd, tīrfæstra getrum, Menol. Fox 523; Gn. C. 32. Cf. blǣd-, þrym-, wuldor-fæst.

tīr-fruma, an; *m. The source of glory* or *the prince of glory, the Deity*, Exon. Th. 13, 21; Cri. 206.

tirgan, tirwian, tirigan, tirian; *p.* tirgde, tirwede, tirigde *To vex, irritate, provoke, exasperate* :—Ic tyrige *lacesso*, Ælfc. Gr. 28, 1; Zup. 165, 12. Tirhþ *inridet*, Kent. Gl. 508. Tyrweþ *improperabit*, Ps. Lamb. 73, 10. Da tredaþ dec and tergaþ, and hyra torn wrecaþ, Exon.

Th. 119, 23; Gū. 259. Ða ðe tyrwiaþ *qui exasperant*, Ps. Lamb. 65, 7: 67, 7. Hē tyride *exacerbavit*, i. *provocavit*, *adflixit*, Wrt. Voc. ii. 144, 56. Tyrgide *exacerbavit*, Hpt. Gl. 527, 51. Ðæt wīf cwæð, ðæt heó wolde ðone sunu ðe hī tirigde awyrian, Homl. Th. ii. 30, 9. Hȳ tyrgdon (tyrigdon, Ps. Spl. 104, 26) *exacerbaverunt*, Blickl. Gl. Mē weras wordum tyrgdon, Andr. Kmbl. 1926; An. 965. Hī tyrgdon God mid gramlīcum weorcum, Homl. Skt. i. 18, 52. Tyrwedon, tyrwadon ł gremedon, tyrwodan *exacerbaverunt*, Ps. Lamb. 77, 40, 41, 56. Hig mē tirigdon *ipsi me provocaverunt*, Deut. 32, 21. Hī hine mid heora wordum tirigdon, Homl. Th. ii. 454, 17. Earme ne tyrewiaþ *vex not the poor*, Wulfst. 50, 2. Ǣnig man ōðerne ne tyrie ne ne tȳne, 70, 8. Ðæt hī elðeódige menn ne tyrian ne ne tȳnan, 309, 4. Hē ðās leóde mid here and mid ungylde tyrwigende wæs, Chr. 1100; Erl. 236, 2, Mǣgþ tyrwiende *generatio exasperans*, Ps. Lamb. 77, 8. [Tirgen *to get weary*, Misc. 12, 362. Tarien *to fatigue*, Chauc. Terren to wraþþe *provocare ad iram*, Wick. Deut. 4, 25. Terwyn̄ or make wery *lasso*, *fatigo*, terwyd *lassatus*, *fatigatus*, Prompt. Parv. 489. *O. Du.* tergen *to vex*: *Dan.* tærge *to exasperate*, *irritate*: *Ger.* zergen.] v. ge-tirgan.

tirging, tirwing, tiring, e; *f. Vexation, provocation, harassing emotion*:—Tyrging, tyring *zelus*, Blickl. Gl. [Terwynge *lassitudo*, *fatigacio*, Prompt. Parv. 489. *Du.* terging *provocation*.]

tiriaca, an; *m. A medicine*, properly *an antidote for poison*, cf. *tiriaca* drenc wyð āttre, Wrt. Voc. i. 20, 20:—Tyriaca is gōd drenc wiþ eallum innoðtȳdernessum, and se man se ðe hine swā begǣþ swā hit hēr on segþ, ðonne mæg hē him miclum gehelpan . . . Nime āne lylte snǣd ðæs tyriacan, Lchdm. ii. 288, 23–290, 3. [Low Latin *tiriaca* from Latin *theriaca*. In Mid. E. *triacle* = a sovereign remedy is common, see Skeat's note on Piers P. C. ii. 147.]

tirian, tirigan. v. tirgan.

tīr-leás; *adj. Inglorious*:—Ðara ðe tīrleáses (*Grendel's*) trode sceáwode, Beo. Th. 1690; B. 843. [Cf. *Icel.* tīrar-lauss *inglorious*.]

tīr-meahtig; *adj. Gloriously mighty*:—Tīrmeahtig cyning (*the Deity*), Exon. Th. 72, 1; Cri. 1166: 209, 24; Ph. 175. [Cf. *Icel.* tīrar-sterkr.]

tirwa, tirwe, an; *m. f. Tar, resin, gum*:—Tyrwa *bitumen*, tyrwan *bituminis*, Hpt. Gl. 488, 78, 77. On swæce swylce tyrwe *smelling of resin*, Lchdm. i. 278, 2. Tirwan *resinae*, Hpt. Gl. 501, 4. Sumne dǣl tyrwan *modicum resinae*, Gen. 43, 11. Ðū clǣmst mid tyrwan *bitumine linies*, 6, 14: Homl. Th. i. 20, 33: Ex. 2, 3. Croppas mid tyrwan gesodene, Lchdm. i. 224, 10. Hig hæfdon tyrwan (*bitumen*) for weallīm, Gen. 11, 3. Teorwena, tyrwena *naptarum*, Hpt. Gl. 445, 29. Dō ðonne ða tyrwan on *put the gums in*, Lchdm. iii. 14, 24. v. eorþ-tyrewa; teoru.

tirwan. v. ge-tirwan.

tirwen (?); *adj. Of resin*:—Tyrwene, stōrsæpes, hryseles *resinae*, Hpt. Gl. 501, 1.

tirwian. v. tirgan.

tīr-wine, es; *m. A glorious friend*, an epithet of the follower of a successful chief:—Se hlāford biþ tō upāhæfen inne on mōde for ðæm anwalde ðe him ānra gehwilc his tīrwina tō fultemaþ, Met. 25, 21.

tiscge = disce:—In tiscge *in cateno*, Wrt. Voc. ii. 46, 53. Cf. in disce *in cateno*, 74, 29.

tit[t], es; *m. A teat, pap, breast*:—Tit *mamilla*, Wrt. Voc. i. 44, 13. Titt *uber*, Ælfc. Gr. 9, 18; Zup. 44, 2. Lege ofer ðone wynstran tit, Lchdm. i. 192, 17. Tittas *mamillas*, lxxiv, 24: Wrt. Voc i. 65, 7: 283, 29: ii. 56, 28. Wið tittia sār wīfa, Lchdm. i. 112, 16. Titto (tito, Rush.) ł breósto *ubera*, Lk. Skt. 11, 27: Rtl. 4, 17. [Þa tittes ðæt þu suke, Laym. 5025. Bi þan titten (tyttes, 2nd MS.) anhon, 11936. Bi þeo tittes þet he sec, A. R. 330, 5. Teon þe tittes awei of þine breosten, Kath. 2098. A fostre wimman on was tette he sone aueð lagt, Gen. and Ex. 2621. Tete *rimes with* swete (*I sweat*), Chauc. C. T. 3704; *with* lete, *pp.* of leten, Gow. i. 268, 3. Tete *uber*, Prompt. Parv. 489. *O. Du.* titte: *M. H. Ger.* zitze: *Ger.* zitze. The Teutonic form seems to have been borrowed by Romance languages, *Ital.* tetta, zizza: *Fr.* tette: *Span.* teta.]

tite-gār *read* (?) ategār:—Titegārum *phalarica*, *lanceis magnis* (cf. ategāra *falarica*, *hasta*, 521, 6), Hpt. Gl. 425, 14. v. æt-gār.

-titelian. v. ge-titelian, *and next word*.

titelung, e; *f. A giving of the titles* or *headings*:—Titelung *recapitulatio*, Hpt. Gl. 433, 72.

tīþ, e; *f. Grant, cession, concession*:—Tȳþ *cessio*, Wrt. Voc. ii. 131, 6: *concessio*, 136, 11. Hȳ wǣron ðē biddende mīnra gōda and ðū him symble tīðe forwyrndest *they were asking thee for my goods and thou didst ever refuse them the grant thereof*, Wulfst. 259, 11. Ne hæfde wit monig ōðer hors ðæt wē mihton ðearfum tō tȳþe syllan *numquid non habuimus equos plurimos quae ad pauperum dona sufficerent?* Bd. 3, 14; S. 540, 27. Mid tȳþe and mid geþafunge Eádgāres cynenges, Cod. Dip. Kmbl. ii. 400, 23. Fela wundra gelumpon æt ðæra apostola byrgenum ðurh ðæs Hǣlendes tīðe, Homl. Th. i. 384, 19. Hyre ðæs Fæder on roderum tīðe gefremede, Judth. Thw. 21, 5; Jud. 6. v. next two words.

tīþe, tīþa (-e, -a; *masc.*: -u, -a, -e; *fem.*: -a; *pl.*) *in the phrases* tīþe(-a) beón, weorþan *to obtain* one's request, *to have granted the request* for something (*gen.*):—Sōna wæs gelǣred ðætte hē wæs from Drihtne tȳþe ðære bēne ðe hē bæd *statim edoctus impetrasse se quod petebat a Domino*, Bd. 4, 29; S. 607, 32. Myceles ðū (*masc.*) bǣde, ac ðū bist tīða, Homl. Skt. i. 18, 284. Tȳða, 3, 513. Ðū (*Abraham*) ðæs tīða beó, Cd. Th. 142, 12; Gen. 2360. Hē ongann tō Gode wīsdōmes wylnian, and hē eác ðæs tīða wearð, Wulfst. 277, 19. Ðū (*Lot*) scealt ðære bēne tīða weorðan, Cd. Th. 152, 28; Gen. 2527. Þeáh ðū (*Esther*) biddan wille healfne ðone anweald . . . ðū scealt beón tīþu ðæs, Anglia ix. 33, 185. Heó ābæd æt Gode Godes willan tō ðām ðæt heó sunu hæfde, and heó sōna wæs tīðu (*other MSS.* tīða), Homl. Ass. 38, 357. For swā hwæne swā heó bit, heó biþ tīða simle, Homl. Skt. ii. 29, 274. Ðæt ic (*a widow*) beó ðæs tīðe ðe ic bidde, Homl. Th. i. 566, 15. Ealles ðæs ðe gē biddaþ gē beóþ tīða *omnia quaecunque petieritis in oratione accipietis*, Mt. Kmbl. 21, 22. v. bēn-tīðe; tīþ, tīþian.

tīþian, tigþian; *p.* ode *To grant, concede*, (a) with gen. of that which is granted:—Bed Beorn ðæt hē sceolde faran mid him tō ðam cynge . . . and hē ðæs tīðode, Chr. 1046; Erl. 174, 10. Treówe and hyldo tīðiaþ mē, Cd. Th. 152, 7; Gen. 2516. Ðæt preósta gehwilc fulluhtes tīðige, sōna swā man his girne, L. Edg. C. 15; Th. ii. 246, 25. Nolde gē mē wǣda tīþian, Wulfst. 288, 33. Hit is swīðe geleáflīc, ðæt hē hyre myceles ðinges tīðian wylle, Homl. Th. i. 454, 2: Gen. 18, 3. Hē nāteshwōn hire ðæs tīðian nolde *qui nequaquam acquiescens operi nefario*, 39, 8. Ne hine mon on ōðre wīsan his bēne tȳþigean (tygþian, M. 220, 26) wolde *neque aliter quod petebat impetrare potuit*, Bd. 3, 21; S. 550, 43. (b) with acc. (?) the case is probably determined by the Latin:—Se him fultum tīþaþ *qui eis adjutorium prestitit*, Anglia xiii. 391, 366. Wīsdōm lǣnende ł tīðiende litlingum *sapientiam praestans parvulis*, Ps. Lamb. 18, 8. (c) with a clause:—Nolde se cyning him tīðian ðæt Israēl fērde forð ofer his gemǣru *qui concedere noluit*, *ut transiret Israel per fines suos*, Num. 21, 23. (d) used absolutely:—Ðonne ðū him tīðast, Hy. 7, 56. Drihten mē gehīrde and tīðode mē *exaudivit me Dominus*, Deut. 9, 19. Ðā oferhogode hē ðæt hē him āðer dyde oþþe wiernde oþþe tigþade, Ors. 6, 34; Swt. 290, 22. Ic gelȳfe ðæt hē wille ðē tīðian, Homl. Skt. i. 21, 218: Homl. Th. i. 250, 2. Tō tīþienne is *praestanda est*, Wülck. Gl. 251, 6. [Leafdi, tuðe me mine bone, O. E. Homl. i. 207, 31. God haueð herd þine bede and tiðed te bene *exaudita est oratio tua*, ii. 135, 7. Drightin has þe tid (tidd, MS. G.) þi bon, C. M. 10966. All þatt ned uss iss Godess Gast uss tiþeþþ, Orm. 5365. O þing ich wolde bidde þe, þat þou me woldest tyþe (*rimes with* bliþe), R. Glouc. 114, 18.] v. ge-tīþian; tīþ, tīþe.

tit-stricel, es; *m. A nipple of the breast*:—Tit *mamilla*, meolce breóst *ubera*, tittstrycel *papilla*, Wrt. Voc. i. 44, 13–15. v. stricel, II.

titt. v. tit[t].

titul *a title, superscription*:—Titul ł merca *titulus*, Mk. Skt. Lind. 15, 26. [*O. H. Ger. also borrows* titul *in the same connection*:—Screib titul Pilatus sīneru sahhu.]

Tīw, Tīg, Tī, es; *m.* I. *the god Tiw*, a Teutonic deity to whom amongst the Latin gods Mars most nearly corresponded:—Tiig *Mars*, *Martis*, Txts. 77, 1293. Tīg, Wrt. Voc. ii. 55, 56. Tuu (Tīw?), 58, 40. Ðone Syxtum nēdde Decius se cāsere Tīges (*Martis*) deófolgylde, Shrn. 114, 9. ¶ The word occurs oftenest in the connection in which it remains—in the name of one of the days:—On Tīwes-dæg *tertia feria*, R. Ben. 38, 6; R. Ben. Interl. 49, 14: Wulfst. 180, 25. On Tīwes-niht, Lchdm. iii. 146, 23. II. *one form of the name of the Runic T*; *Ti* is given as the name of the symbol ᛏ in some alphabets, see Kemble on Anglo-Saxon Runes in Archæologia, vol. 28, pp. 338, 339. The word is probably to be recognized in the form *tyz*, which is given as the name of the Gothic T in the Vienna MS. containing a Gothic alphabet, and from it a Gothic Tius may be inferred. *O. H. Ger.* Ziu(-o) *the name of a god* (preserved in *M. H. Ger.* Zies-tag), *the name of a letter*: *Icel.* Tȳr *the name of a god* (*kept in* Tȳs-dagr), *name of a rune*. See Grmm. D. M. c. ix.] v. Tīr.

tō; *prep. adv.* I. with dat. (1) with words expressing motion. (a) with verbs of coming, going, falling, etc., marking the end reached by that which moves, *to*, *at*:—Cōmon twēgen englas tō ðære birig, Gen. 19, 1. God him com tō, 20, 3: Mk. Skt. 5, 21. Hē fērde tō ðam munte, Gen. 19, 30. Fēran tō ðissum dimman hām, Cd. Th. 271, 27; Sat. 111. Bryne stīgeþ tō heofonum, Exon. Th. 233, 7; Ph. 521. Conon gelende tō ðære byrig, Ors. 3, 1; Swt. 98, 23. Nēðan tō hilde, Cd. Th. 124, 11; Gen. 2061. Ðā feóll hē tō ðæs Hǣlendes fōtum, Lk. Skt. 8, 41: 5, 8. Hē feóll tō foldan, Andr. Kmbl. 1835; An. 920. Būgan tō eorðan, Rood Kmbl. 84, Kr. 43. Nū sceal hē faran tō incre andsware, Cd. Th. 35, 19; Gen. 557. (b) with verbs of bringing, bearing, drawing, sending, taking, etc., marking the end reached by that which is moved:—Mēce ðone ðīn fæder tō gefeohte bær, Beo. Th. 4103; B. 2048. Hī him tō nimaþ mægeð tō gemæccum, Cd. Th. 76, 17; Gen. 1258. Him fetigean tō sprecan sīne, 161, 17; Gen. 2666. Hē hine lǣdde tō ðam hālgan hām, 300, 19; Sat. 567. Hē him tō sende āras sīne, 146, 15; Gen. 2422. Hē his gingran sent tō ðīnre sprǣce, 33, 6; Gen. 516. Sende se Fæder his sunu tō cwāle, Homl. Th. ii. 6, 17. Hē tō āwylte stān tō hlide ðære byrgene, Mt. Kmbl. 27, 60. (c) where the motion is directed to, but does not reach the object:—Hī tō ðam hǣðengilde bugon, Num. 25, 2. Ealle ābūgaþ tō ðē, Hy. 7, 10. Hié onhnigon tō đam herige, Cd. Th. 227, 3; Dan. 181. Âhyld mē đīn eáre tō *inclina ad me aurem tuam*, Ps. Th. 70, 2. (1 a) with words implying motion:—Hig woldon tō Basan *ascenderunt per viam Basan*, Num. 21, 33: Chr. 1036; Erl. 164, 26. Hē hēht him Abraham tō *he summoned Abraham to him*, Cd. Th. 112, 3; Gen. 1865: 249, 18; Dan. 532: Elen. Kmbl. 307; El. 154. (2) where the motion is figurative, (a) with words denoting change of condition, marking that to which a thing is changed, what a thing becomes, to what a thing is brought:—Hē heora wæter wende tō blōde, Ps. Th. 104, 25: Cd. Th. 17, 13; Gen. 259. Heó alle forsceóp Drihten tō deóflum, 20, 14; Gen. 309: Bt. 38, 1; Fox 194, 33. His gebed hweorfe tō fyrenum, Ps. Th. 108, 6. Forhwerfde tō sumum dióre, Met. 26, 87. Đā weard hē tō deófle, Homl. Th. i. 12, 22: Cd. Th. 20, 9; Gen. 305. Weorđan tō duste, Ps. Th. 89, 6. Đū scealt tō frōfre weorþan leódum đīnum, Beo. Th. 3419; B. 1707. Weorđan tō wræce, Elen. Kmbl. 33; El. 17. Hī weorþaþ tō nāuhte, Bt. 21; Fox 74, 36. Tō hwon sculon wit weorđan? Cd. Th. 50, 28; Gen. 815. Ic tō nāwihte eom gebīged *ad nihilum redactus sum*, Ps. Th. 72, 17, 16. Paulus hine āwende of wōge tō rihte, Homl. Skt. ii. 29, 8. Swā is lār and ār tō spōwendre sprǣce gelǣded, Exon. Th. 139, 14; Gū. 593. Đam yfelan men ne becymþ tō nānum gōde, gif hē đæs hālgan hūsles unwurde onbyrigþ, Homl. Th. ii. 278, 4. (b) with words denoting attainment, reaching to an object:—Fōn tō rīce *to come to the throne*, Chr. 871; Erl. 76, 3, and often. Đē tō heortan grīpeþ ādl, Cd. Th. 57, 30; Gen. 936. (c) with verbs of attracting, alluring, drawing, forcing, etc.:—On đæm weorce đe hine nān willa tō ne spōn, Past. 33; Swt. 215, 10. Đone fultum đe hē him tō āspanan mehte, Ors. 3, 9; Swt. 126, 10. Þurh lāre spanan tō gefeán, Andr. Kmbl. 1195; An. 598. Đæt đa sinhīwan tō swylte geteáh, Exon. Th. 153, 10; Gū. 823. Tō đam gebede gebǣdon, Cd. Th. 228, 15; Dan. 202. v. ge-nȳdan. (3) marking the end of extent, (a) marking the object reached:—Hī woldon witon hū heáh hit wǣre tō đæm hefone, Bt. 35, 4; Fox 162, 22. Đanon wǣre tō helle duru hund þūsenda mīla, Cd. Th. 310, 8; Sat. 723. Sió stōw đe se weg tō ligþ, Bt. 33, 4; Fox 132, 37. Weg tō wuldre, Elen. Kmbl. 2297; El. 1150. Strǣte tō englum, Cd. Th. 282, 17; Sat. 228. (b) marking degree:—Gē etaþ tō fylle, Lev. 26, 5. Seóđ tō feórđan dǣle, Lchdm. i. 188, 22. Seó sunne āþȳstrode tō sweartre nihte, Homl. Skt. ii. 29, 11. Hē weard tō feore āfyrht *he was mortally afraid*, Homl. Th. i. 384, 7: Homl. Skt. i. 7, 242. Fæsten tō berenan hlāfe *a fast when nothing better than barley bread should be eaten*, Wulfst. 173, 10. Tō ānum mǣle fæstende *fasting to the point of taking but one meal in the day*, Homl. Skt. i. 20, 42. Gif man đæt fȳr sceal tō āhte ācwæncan, Wulfst. 157, 9. Tō nāhte *not at all*, 190, 18: 191, 3. Wǣron hié tō đæm gesārgode, đæt hié ne mehton Sūđ-Seaxna lond ūtan berōwan, Chr. 897; Erl. 96, 8. Wæter-seócnyss hine ofereode tō đan swīđe, đæt . . ., Homl. Th. i. 86, 10. Wela ne mæg his hlāford gehealdan tō đon đæt hē ne þurfe māran fultumes, Bt. 29, 1; Fox 102, 16. (c) marking result attained, effect produced, *so as to produce* or *become, to* (the satisfaction, etc.). (1) where the object is concrete:—Tōbrecan tō styccum, Bd. 3, 6; S. 528, 21. Ceorfan tō sticcon, Lev. 1, 6. (2) where the object is abstract:—Đa đe ealle gewītendlīce đing tō đæra apostola efenlǣcunge (*and so imitate the apostles*) forseóđ for intingan đæs ēcan līfes, Homl. Th. i. 398, 23. Hannibal æt đære ié gewīcade eallum Rōmānum tō đæm mǣstan ege (*which was the cause of very great terror to all the Romans*), Ors. 4, 9; Swt. 194, 8. Geweóx hē him tō wælfylle *he grew up to be a cause of destruction to them*, Beo. Th. 3427; B. 1711: Salm. Kmbl. 747; Sal. 373. Gif hē hwæt tō gōde gefremode, Homl. Th. i. 332, 5: 8, 9: Exon. Th. 297, 1; Crä. 61. Dryhtne tō willan *to please the Lord*, Andr. Kmbl. 3280; An. 1643. Đæs đe gē him tō dare gedōn mōtan, Exon. Th. 144, 2; Gū. 672: 127, 36; Gū. 397. Tō wundre *so as to produce wonder, wondrously*, Homl. Skt. i. 23, 654. Tō þance, Andr. Kmbl. 2225; An. 1114: Cd. Th. 32, 20; Gen. 506: Beo. Th. 762; B. 379. Eal đa earfeþu đe ic gefremede tō fācne, Exon. Th. 272, 10; Jul. 497. (4) marking the end towards which an action or object is directed, (a) with verbs of looking, listening (lit. and fig.):—Beseoh tō mē *respice me*, Ps. Th. 12, 3. Tō heofenum beseoh, Elen. Kmbl. 166; El. 83. Đā lōcode Petrus tō Paule, Blickl. Homl. 187, 34: Beo. Th. 3313; B. 1654. Hī đē tō hēraþ, Met. 4, 5. v. lōcian, hȳran. (b) with verbs of pointing, directing:—Se Dryhtnes dōm wīsade tō nȳdgedāle, Exon. Th. 129, 4; Gū. 415. Tǣcan tō, Cd. Th. 175, 22; Gen. 2899. (c) with verbs of urging, prompting, inciting, etc.:—Onbryrde tō godcundre lāre, Blickl. Homl. 33, 23: Andr. Kmbl. 2237; An. 1120. Ūsic lust hwæteþ tō đærre mǣran byrig, 574; An. 287. (d) with words denoting destination, intention, etc.:—Hē monige dēmde tō deáđe, Elen. Kmbl. 997; El. 500: Exon. Th. 247, 31; Jul. 87. Mec gesette Crist tō compe, 389, 3; Rä. 7, 2. His rīce đǣr wē tō gesceapene wǣron, Homl. Th. ii. 6, 27: Bt. 25; Fox 88, 7. (e) with words denoting address:—Đā cwæđ se Hǣlend tō him, Mt. Kmbl. 8, 4. Đæt hié tō đam beácne gebedu rǣrde, Cd. Th. 227, 23; Dan. 191. Ic clypige tō đē, Ps. Th. 21, 2. Wīte-brōgan đe đū tō mē beótast, Exon. Th. 250, 35; Jul. 137: Bd. 1, 27; S. 493, 30: 5, 12; S. 628, 43. Habbaþ wē tō đæm mǣran ǣrende, Beo. Th. 545; B. 270. (f) with words denoting hostility:—Đæt folc mǣnde tō him Arone (*contra se et Aaron*), Past. 28, 6; Swt. 201, 4: Ors. 3, 7; Swt. 120, 5: Beo. Th. 5994; B. 3001: Ps. Th. 70, 22. Monige đe tō mē feohtaþ *multi qui bellant me*, Ps. Th. 55, 3. Mē feóndas tō feohtaþ, 68, 17: 58, 1. (g) with words denoting preparation, aptness, readiness, or the reverse:—Fȳsan tō rāde, Elen. Kmbl. 1960; El. 982: Cd. Th. 173, 12; Gen. 2860. Hē đa leóde wenede tō wuldre, Andr. Kmbl. 3360; An. 1684. Hēt hié tō đam sīđe gyrwan, 1590; An. 796. Late tō đam orlege, 94; An. 47. Tō gefeohte gearu, Num. 21, 33: Elen. Kmbl. 45; El. 23. Ealdordōm tō hwōnlīc tō swā micelre bodunge, Homl. Th. i. 38, 6. Gleáwast tō wīge and tō gewinne, Ors. 4, 1; Swt. 154, 33. (h) marking the object of a feeling or operation of the mind:—Se đe næfþ lufe tō Godes sceápum, Homl. Th. i. 240, 18: 334, 7. Ic hæbbe geleáfan tō Gode, Cd. Th. 34, 27; Gen. 544. Næs him tō ēđle wynn, Andr. Kmbl. 2326; An. 1164. Ne biþ him tō hearpan hyge, ne tō wīfe wyn, ne tō worulde hyht, Exon. Th. 308, 23–26; Seef. 44, 45. Abraham tō Gode cȳđđe hæfde, Homl. Th. ii. 190, 12: 558, 1: i. 10, 3. Cynengas đe tō Gode lytelne ege hǣfdon, Lchdm. iii. 442, 24. Đa de tō đē egsan āhtan *qui timent te*, Ps. Th. 118, 79. Nān neát nyste nǣnne andan, ne nǣnne ege tō ōþrum, Bt. 35, 6; Fox 168, 10. Đæt hē hæbbe clǣne heortan tō mannum, Wulfst. 239, 18. Hié hæfdon ungeþwǣrnesse tō eallum folcum, Ors. 6, 3; Swt. 258, 1: Homl. Th. i. 38, 14. Swā hwæt swā gē habbaþ on eówrum mōde tō ǣnigum men, 266, 30. Sió heánes đe hié tō hopiaþ, Past. 41; Swt. 299, 5: Met. 7, 44. Đonne gelȳfe ic tō Gode, đæt hit đam men gehelpe, Lchdm. ii. 290, 9: Chr. 1036; Erl. 165, 16. Hī hogedon tō nīđe, Ps. Th. 77, 20. Tō đam beteran hycgan and hyhtan, Fragm. Kmbl. 82; Leas. 43. Tō swice þencan, Exon. Th. 317, 16; Mōd. 61: Beo. Th. 2281; B. 1138. Tō reáflāce rǣd āþencean *to devise counsel that has robbery for its object*, Ps. Th. 61, 10. Se cyning beþōhte swīđost tō Arpelles his ealdormenn, Ors. 1, 12; Swt. 52, 20. (i) marking a purpose to be effected, an end to be served, *to* some end, *for* some purpose:—Hē āsende đone sunu tō ūre ālȳsednesse, Homl. Th. ii. 6, 9. Đæt folc gedafode đæt sume leofodon tō wudunge and tō wæterunge, 222, 29. Âlesen tō lāre, Elen. Kmbl. 571; El. 286. Ofn onhǣtan tō cwale cnihta feorum, Cd. Th. 229, 32; Dan. 226. Hē up āhōf bord tō gebeorge, Byrht. Th. 135, 40; By. 131. Hié tō gebede feóllon *they fell down to pray*, Cd. Th. 48, 18; Gen. 777: Andr. Kmbl. 2054; An. 1029. Hē genam on eallum dǣl ǣhtum sīnum tō đam gielde, Cd. Th. 90; Gen. 1501: 175, 6; Gen. 2891. Hié werod læsse hæfdon tō hilde *a smaller band had they for battle*, Elen. Kmbl. 97; El. 49. Tō đam ic eom āsend *therefore am I sent*, Lk. Skt. 4, 43. Tō hwan ys điss forspilled *to what purpose is this waste?* Mt. Kmbl. 26, 8. Tō hwan becōm đū *wherefore art thou come?* 50: Soul Kmbl. 34; Seel. 17. Tō đam (đon) đæt *in order that, to the end that*, Ors. 1, 10; Swt. 48, 23: Lchdm. iii. 438, 19: Chart. Th. 436, 26. (j) marking an object for the benefit or service of which anything is intended, *for*:—Hē onfēng līchoman gegyrelan tō his godcundnesse, Blickl. Homl. 9, 27. Hē hæfde xx elpenda tō đæm gefeohte, Ors. 4, 1; Swt. 154, 30. Wēnen hī him māran mēde tō . . . Gif hī him māran mēde tō ne wēnaþ, Past. 59; Swt. 449, 12–13. Hē đē worhte tō mē, Cd. Th. 50, 32; Gen. 817. Hē gewyrceþ tō wera hilde helm oþþe hupseax, Exon. Th. 297, 5; Crä. 63. Hié wǣpna nāman tō đon đæt hié heora weras wrecan þōhton *they took arms for this reason, that they intended to avenge their husbands* (cf. Goth. du þē ei *pro eo quod*), Ors. 1, 10; Swt. 44, 32. (5) where position (lit. or fig.) is marked, (a) marking juxtaposition, *next to, at, by, alongside*:—Hī man bebyrigde tō hyre were *she was buried by her husband*, Homl. Th. i. 318, 1: ii. 188, 5. Hē gesette đa hālgan rōde tō his heáhsetle swilce him tō gefēran, H. R. 101, 10. Hié setton him tō heáfdum hilderandas, Beo. Th. 2488; B. 1242. Mid olfendes hǣrum tō līce (*next the body*) gescrȳdde, Homl. Th. ii. 506, 23: Homl. Skt. i. 12, 36. Wyrm tō fȳre *warm at the fire*, Lchdm. i. 374, 10: Exon. Th. 393, 36; Rä. 13, 11. Tō hire freán sittan *to sit by her lord*, Beo. Th. 1287; B. 641. Symle hī sǣton ætsomne tō gereorde, Homl. Th. ii. 506, 22. Gesittan tō symble, Cd. Th. 259, 33; Dan. 701: Judth. Thw. 21, 12; Jud. 15. Hiera sūþgemǣro licgeaþ tō đæm Reádan Sǣ, Ors. 1, 1; Swt. 10, 34: 16, 13. Seó forme India līþ tō đæra Sīlheorwena rīce, seó ōđer līþ tō Mēdas, seó đridde tō đam micclum gārsecge, Homl. Th. i. 454, 12–13. Þeáh đe se Hālga Gāst ne beó swutollīce genemned tō đam Fæder and tō đam Suna *along with the Father and the Son*, ii. 56, 29. (b) marking the place where an object is, *in, on*:—Ic cȳđe đām gerēfan tō gehwylcere byrig (þurh ealle mīne rīce, *other MS.*), L. Ath. i. prm.; Th. i. 194, 3. Hē gesette Iudas tō bisceope tō Godes temple, Elen. Kmbl. 2114; El. 1058. Tō horse *on horseback*, Exon. Th. 298, 7; Crä. 81. (c) fig., marking position or condition in which an object is placed:—Tō gewealde *in the power* of, *at the disposal* of, Cd. Th. 112, 7; Gen. 1867: 132, 32; Gen. 2202: 290, 15; Sat. 415. (d) with verbs of joining, adding to, cleaving, etc.:—Gesamnian sāwle tō līce, Met. 17, 12. Hē sǣlde tō sande scip, Beo. Th. 3838; B. 1917. Geđeódde sum wer him tō, Homl. Th. ii. 504, 22. v. clifian, geþeódan, īcan. (e) marking order, *next to, after*:—Tō mīnre mēder and geswystrum đū mē eart se leófesta freónd *secundum matrem meam sororesque meas, acceptissime*, Nar. 1, 12: Shrn. 108, 20. Scs Iohannes wæs ealra manna se mǽsta and se hālgosta tō Criste selnum, 123, 6: Homl. Skt. i. 6, 51: Cd. Th. 17, 3; Gen. 254: Ors. 2, 2; Swt. 66, 32. Hē wæs bufan eallum đǽm đe on đam rīce wǽron tō đæm cyninge, 3, 11; Swt. 148, 5. Sió is mǽst tō Babilonia byrig, Nar. 33, 17. Đū bist se đridda man tō mē on mīnum rīce, Homl. Th. ii. 436, 5, 17. Hē is geendebyrd tō Petre, 522, 2. (f) marking the position occupied, the purpose fulfilled by an object, *to, as, for*:—Wē habbaþ ūs tō fæder Abraham *we have Abraham to our father*, Lk. Skt. 3, 8: Mt. Kmbl. 14, 4: Exon. Th. 245, 34; Jul. 54. Hig hæfdon heom tō gewunan, đæt . . ., Mt. Kmbl. 27, 15. Ic hæbbe tō gewitnisse heofen and eorđan *testes invoco coelum et terram*, Deut. 4, 26. Hē hæfde Thesalium him tō fultume, Ors. 4, 1; Swt. 154, 30. Hié him đæt gold tō gode noldon, Cd. Th. 228, 5; Dan. 197. Hē is tō freónde gōd *he is good as a friend*, Exon. Th. 248, 28; Jul. 102. Ic genam hig tō wīfe, Gen. 20, 12: Bt. 8; Fox 24, 24. Hī him tō gewunon nāman, đæt . . ., Bd. 3, 5; S. 527, 7. Hē Agustinum him tō gespelian funde, Lchdm. iii. 434, 7. Ic clipie mē tō gewitnysse heofonan and eorđan, Deut. 30, 19. Him brego engla līg tō wræce sende, Cd. Th. 156, 6; Gen. 2584: 21, 2: Gen. 318. Hē sealde him tō bōte, đæs đe hē his brȳd genam, gangende feoh, 164, 21; Gen. 2718: 90, 24; Gen. 1500: 124, 29; Gen. 2070. Eal folc fæste tō gemǽnelīcre dǽdbōte, Wulfst. 180, 23. Hē is tō Cristes anlīcnesse āset *divina positus vice dispensat*, Past. 13; Swt. 79, 10. Hē gearwaþ đīnne innođ his suna tō brȳdbūre, Blickl. Homl. 9, 10. Tō lǽne *as a loan, on loan*, Deut. 15, 8: Past. pref.; Swt. 9, 7. Tō lāfe *as a remnant, remaining*. v. lāf, I. See also (j) below. (f 1) with verbs of making, appointing, being, accounting, naming, and the like, where often the preposition now has no representative, though *to, as, for* are sometimes used:—Mē feóndas geworhton him tō wæfersȳne *they made me a spectacle for themselves*, Rood Kmbl. 61; Kr. 31. God ne gesceóp hine nā tō deófle . . . ac hē weard tō deófle *God did not create him a devil . . . but he became a devil*, Homl. Th. i. 12, 20. Hē him dyde bearn tō weorcþeówum *he made them slaves*, Cd. Th. 220, 21; Dan. 74: 45, 6; Gen. 722: Andr. Kmbl. 53; An. 27. Hig ne fundon hwæt hī him tō gylte dydon *they could not find what they could make a charge against him*, Lk. Skt. 19, 48. Đam golde đe hē him tō gode teóde, Cd. Th. 229, 13; Dan. 216: Exon. 255, 18; Jul. 215. Hē sette hine on his hūse tō hlāfwearde *constituit eum dominum domus suae*, Ps. Th. 104, 17, 16: 108, 5: Elen. Kmbl. 2111; El. 1057: Blickl. Homl. 9, 5. God hine gesette manegum đeódum tō fæder (*a father of many nations have I made thee*, Gen. 17, 5), Homl. Th. i. 92, 16. Hine gecēs tō fæder and tō hlāforde Scotta cyning, Chr. 924; Erl. 110, 14: Cd. Th. 19, 3; Gen. 285: Exon. Th. 3, 15; Cri. 36: Andr. Kmbl. 647; An. 324. (v. *also* ge-hālgian, hālgian.) Beón tō tācnum, tō mete, Gen. 1, 14, 29. Næs him se swēg tō sorge, Cd. Th. 232, 22; Dan. 264. Đa þeódlogan đe taliaþ đæt tō wærscype, đæt . . ., Wulfst. 55, 15. Ne sete đū him đās dǽda tō synne, Homl. Th. ii. 34, 21. Heó hié sylfe tō đeówene genemde, Blickl. Homl. 9, 23. Hine tō sylfcwale secgas nemnaþ, Exon. Th. 330, 24; Vy. 56. Đeáh mon anweald and genyht tō twǽm þingum nemne, đeáh hit is ān, Bt. 33, 1; Fox 120, 20. (g) marking the place at which anything is sought, obtained, etc., *at, in*:—Sēcean hilde tō Heorote, Beo. Th. 3984; B. 1990. Tō dūnscræfum drohtođ sēcan, Andr. Kmbl. 3077; An. 1541. (h) marking the source from which anything is sought, desired, expected, deserved, obtained, etc., *of, from*:—Ǽlcum đe mycel geseald is him man mycel tō sēcþ *cui multum datum est, multum quaeretur ab eo*, Lk. Skt. 12, 48: Elen. Kmbl. 638; El. 319. Wē sēcaþ fultum tō đē (*a Domino*), Ps. Th. 7, 11. Hī tō Rōme him fultumes bǽdon, Bd. 1, 12; S. 480, 22. Hē iówan scolde đæt him mon tō āscaþ, Past. 22; Swt. 173, 2. Đū wilnodest tō ūs đæs gōdes đe đū tō him sceoldest, Bt. 7, 5; Fox 24, 3: Past. 58; Swt. 447, 15: Ors. 4, 6; Swt. 174, 24: L. Ath. v. 8, 3; Th. i. 236, 15: Wulfst. 277, 18. Girne hē tō Godes þeówum, đæt . . ., 180, 11. Swā ic đē wēne tō *as I expect of you*, Beo. Th. 2797; B. 1396: 5836; B. 2922. Ne þurfon wē nā tō ūrum mǽgum ne nān man tō his wīfe đencean tō đam swȳđe, đæt him man æfter his forđsȳþe tō đam micel fore gedǽle, đæt hī hine fram wītan ālȳsan *it is too much to expect of kinsmen or wife, that so much will be distributed for a man after his death as to release him from purgatory*, Wulfst. 306, 3. Đonne mōte wē đæs tō Gode earnian bet *we must better deserve it of God*, 157, 2: Ps. Th. 7, 3: Ors. 5, 4; Swt. 224, 33. Hē geceápade tō đǽm senatum, đæt hié ealle wǽron ymb hiene twywyrdige, 5, 7; Swt. 228, 17. Tō eorđan ǽtes tilian, Cd. Th. 94, 5; Gen. 1557: 59, 31; Gen. 972. (i) marking the object on which an action takes effect, *to* (in to do something *to* anything):—Hire man wōh tō ne dō, L. Edm. B. 7; Th. i. 256, 3: Cd. Th. 136, 28; Gen. 2265. Gūđrǽsa fela đara đe hē geworhte tō West-Denum, Beo. Th. 3161; B. 1578. (j) marking agreement, likeness, *according to, at, after*:—Hié ūs lǽrdon tō đæm đe hira willa wæs *secundum voluntatem suam erudiebant nos*, Past. 36; Swt. 255, 10: Bt. 8; Fox 24, 24: Homl. Th. i. 264, 23. Se đe tō Godes bisene gesceapen is (cf. gesceapene æfter đære biesene ūres Scippendes, 17), Past. 36; Swt. 249, 22: Cd. Th. 92, 14; Gen. 1528: Gen. 1, 27. Uton wircean him sumne fultum tō his gelīcnisse *faciamus adjutorium simile sibi*, 2, 18. Đū wāst đæt ic symle tilode tō lifigenne tō đīnes mūþes bebode *nosti quia ad tui oris imperium semper vivere studui*, Bd. 4, 29; S. 607, 28. Hī folgodon Cristes lāre tō đære nīwan ǽ (*according to the new law*), Ælfc. Gen. Thw. 2, 23. Đū đa unstillan gesceafta tō đīnum willan āstyrast, Bt. 33, 4; Fox 128, 9. Tō hwylcum gemete *after what manner*, Blickl. Homl. 5, 7. ¶ in adverbial phrases, equivalent to adverbs in *-lice*; but see also (f):—Ic secge eów tō sōđum *ego autem dico vobis* (in v. 34 the same words are translated: Ic secge eów sōđlīce), Mt. Kmbl. 5, 32. Tō sōđum ic secge eów *amen dico vobis* (cf. sōđlīce *amen*, 10, 15), 8, 11. Tō sōđan, Ælfc. T. Grn. 1, 6. Hwæt eart đū tō sōđe? St. And. 28, 8. Tō wissan *praesertim*, tō sōđan ł tō cūđan *pro certo, veraciter*, Hpt. Gl. 416, 40-43. Ic nāt tō gewissan hwǽr hē wunaþ nū *I don't know for certain where he lives now*, Homl. Skt. i. 21, 31. (k) marking comparison, *compared to, in comparison with, beside*:—Đes is ūre God, and nis nān ōđer geteald tō him, Homl. Th. ii. 12, 30. (l) *in addition to, besides*:—Đā sende hē æfter māran fultum, tō đæm đe đa burg ymbseten hæfdon (*in addition to the troops that had besieged the town*), Ors. 3, 7; Swt. 116, 23. Đæt is his andweorc đæt hē habban sceal tō đām tōlum, đām þrīm gefērscipum biwiste *that is his material, that he must have in addition to the tools, provision for the three classes*, Bt. 17; Fox 60, 3. Candidus and Uitalis and fela ōþre tō him (*many others besides them*), Homl. Skt. ii. 28, 19. Tō đam đe ic on līfe geūđe *besides what I granted in my lifetime*, Chart. Th. 563, 22. (m) marking price or equivalence, *for, at*:—Hū ne becȳpaþ hig twēgen spearwan tō peninge *nonne duo passeres asse veniunt*, Mt. Kmbl. 10, 29. Đis mihte beón geseald tō myclum wurđe (*multo pretio*), 26, 9. Geseald tō þrīm hund penegum, Mk. Skt. 14, 5. Ic sille eów hit, tō đam wurđe đe ic hit gebohte, Ap. Th. 10, 2. Heofonan rīce wæs ālǽten Zachēo tō healfum dǽle his ǽhta, and sumere wudewan tō ānum feórđlinge, and sumum menn tō ānum wæteres drence, Homl. Th. i. 580, 22-26. Hié hié selfe tō nōhte bemǽtan *they valued themselves at nothing*, Ors. 3, 7; Swt. 114, 37: 3, 9; Swt. 128, 4. Đises cwides hē geunn đam hīrēde tō đam forwyrdan (*as the price of, in return for, the agreement*), đæt hī hine wel healdan, Chart. Th. 329, 29. Wit đus baru ne magon wesan tō wuhte (*at any price, on any account*), Cd. Th. 52, 5; Gen. 839. (6) with the inflected infinitive, forming with the verb a phrase that is used (a) with a noun or its equivalent, (1) as a predicate expressing what shall or must be done to the object marked by the noun:—Mannes Sunu ys tō syllenne on manna handa *Filius hominis tradendus est in manus hominum*, Mt. Kmbl. 17, 22. Se anweald ne se weorþscipe ne beóþ tō wēnanne, đæt hit seó sōþe gesǽlþ sié. Swā hit is nū hrædost tō secganne be eallum đǽm woruldgesǽlþum, đæt đǽr nānwuht on nis đæs tō wilnianne seó, Bt. 16, 3; Fox 56, 27-31. (2) as attribute, (α) the verb having an active force:—Hē hæfþ anweald synna tō forgyfanne (*potestatem dimittendi peccata*), Mk. Skt. 2, 10. Ic hæbbe mihte đē tō forlǽtenne (-nde, MS. C.) *habeo potestatem demittere te*, Jn. Skt. 19, 10: Cd. Th. 18, 30; Gen. 280. Swā ūs neód is tō dōnne, L. Eth. vi. 42; Th. i. 326, 7. Tīd tō mildsiende his *tempus miserendi ejus*, Ps. Surt. 101, 14. (β) the verb having a passive force, the noun being the object of the action expressed by the verb:—Ic hæbbe đone mete tō etanne đe gē nyton *ego cibum habeo manducare, quem uos non scitis*, Jn. Skt. 4, 32. Ic hæbbe đē tō secgenne (-anne, MS. A.) sum đing *habeo tibi aliquid dicere*, Lk. Skt. 7, 40. Gif Drihten sylþ mē hlāf tō etenne and reáf tō werigenne *si dederit Deus mihi panem ad vescendum et vestimentum ad induendum*, Gen. 28, 20. Đæt hē genōh hæbbe tō etanne *quantum sufficit ad vescendum*, Ex. 16, 12. Nim đæt ic đē tō sillenne habbe, Ap. Th. 12, 2. Hē đæt feoh tō sellanne næfde *he had not the money to give*, Ors. 3, 7; Swt. 116, 15. Tō for nāht taliende *parvi pendenda, ad nihilum iudicanda*, Hpt. Gl. 418, 35. Suā suā sió leásung simle deret đǽm secggendum, suā dereþ eác hwīlum sumum monnum đæt sōđ tō gehiérenne *it harms some men that the truth should be heard; audita vera nocuerunt*, Past. 35; Swt. 237, 11. Đæm lāreówe is tō wietanne, đæt . . ., 63; Swt. 459, 6. (b) as object of a verb:—Hē ondrēd đyder tō farende (faranne, MS. A.: færenne, Lind.: færan, Rush.) *timuit illuc ire*, Mt. Kmbl. 2, 22. Ālȳfe mē tō farenne and bebyrigean mīnne fæder, 8, 21. Ys ālȳfed on restedagum wel tō dōnne (dōanne, Rush.) *licet sabbatis bene facere*, 12, 12. God geđafaþ Antecriste tō wyrcenne tācna, Homl. Th. i. 4, 30. Ne bud đū mē nā ælmessan tō syllanne, Ps. Th. 39, 7. Ūs gelustfullaþ tō sprecenne be đan hālgan were, Homl. Th. i. 360, 29. Hig begunnon đis tō wircanne, Gen. 11, 6. (c) adverbially, (1) with adjectives, (α) where the verb has an active force:—Đæs gescȳ neom ic wyrđe tō berenne *cujus non sum dignus calceamenta portare*, Mt. 3, 11. Heora fēt beóđ swīđe hrađe blōd tō āgeótanne *veloces pedes eorum ad effundendum sanguinem*, Ps. Th. 13, 6. Fūse tō farenne, Beo. Th. 3614; B. 1805. (β) where the verb has a passive force, governing the noun qualified by the adjective:—Hwæđer is ēđre tō secgenne? Mk. Skt. 2, 9. Đæt is nū hrađost tō secgenne, Bt. 17; Fox 60, 14: 16, 3; Fox 56, 29. Đeáh heó gladu wǽre on tō lōcienne, 6; Fox 14, 27: Exon. Th. 57, 15; Cri. 920. Langsumlīc biþ ūs tō gereccenne and eów tō gehȳrenne ealle đa deópnyssa [*there seems here a mixture of two constructions*, '*these things are tedious to hear* (tō gehȳrenne),' *and* '*to hear* (gehȳran) *these things is tedious*'], Homl. Th. i. 362, 32. Þeáh hē wyrđe ne sié tō ālǽtanne *though he deserve not to be pardoned*, Cd. Th.

39, 9; Gen. 622. (2) with verbs, where the verb in the phrase expresses an action that the subject of the main verb intends (*a*) to be done:—Ūt eode se sǣdere his sǣd tō sāwenne (*ad seminandum*), Mk. Skt. 4, 3. Gesceafta ðe hē gesceóp mannum tō ðeówianne, Ps. Th. 18, arg. Ne com ic rihtwīse tō gecīgeanne, Mt. Kmbl. 9, 13. Mellitum hē sende tō bodianne (bodiende, 20, 19) fulluht, Chr. 604; Erl. 21, 19. Tō dōnne rehtwīsnisse *ad faciendas justificationes*, Ps. Surt. 118, 112. Tō ondetende *ad confitendum*, 141, 8. Gesend englas tō ontȳnenne mīne sefan and tō andswariende ðyssum ārleásum, Nar. 40, 30. (*β*) to be suffered:—Cyning tō gefulliane com tō Rōme *the king came to Rome to be baptized*, Bd. 5, 7; S. 620, 26. (7) marking time, (a) marking a point of time at which anything takes place, *at*:—Tō midre nihte *at midnight*, Lk. Skt. 11, 5: Mt. Kmbl. 25, 6. Tō ðam ǣrdæge *at dawn*, Cd. Th. 190, 12; Exod. 198. Ðā āxode hē tō hwylcon tīman him bet wǣre. And hī sǣdon him, Gyrstandæg tō ðære seofoþan tīde se fefor hine forlēt, Jn. Skt. 4, 52. Ðæt hē him tō tīde gemetlīce gedǣle ðone hwǣte, Past. 63; Swt. 459, 12. Scyld gewāt tō gesceaphwīle, Beo. Th. 52; B. 26. (1 a) where the time is determined by that which takes place:—Āswearc ūre mōd tō eówrum infærelde, Jos. 2, 11. Tō ðȳssere dǣde wearð ðæs cynges heorte āblicged, Homl. Th. ii. 474, 19. (b) marking a space of time in the course of which something takes place, *in the course of, in, on*:—Gē etaþ næs tō ānum dæge, ne tō twām, ne tō fīfon, ne tō tȳnum, ne tō twēntigum, ac fullne mōnoð, Num. 11, 20. Swā micel swā hē tō ðam dæge geðicgan mihte *as much as he could eat in the day*, Homl. Th. ii. 194, 34: Lchdm. ii. 288, 26: Homl. Th. ii. 288, 7. Wē wǣron tō dæge ealle on ānnesse gemedemode, Blickl. Homl. 139, 26. Tō sunnedæge *in sabbato*, Jn. Skt. Lind. 7, 23. Tō heora symbeldæge (*at that feast*, A. V.), Mt. Kmbl. 27, 15. Tō ðisse næhte *in ista nocte*, Rush. 26. 31. Tō niht (cf. on ðisse nihte, Lk. 12, 20) ðū scealt ðīn līf ālǣtan, Wulfst. 286, 23. Hē biþ tō geáre deád *he will die in the course of the year*, Shrn. 83, 21. Nū tō geáre synd feówertȳne epactas *in the present year there are fourteen epacts*, Anglia viii. 327, 10: 329, 36. Tō dæge *to-day, at the present time*, Bd. 3, 16; S. 542, 35. (c) marking a space of time during which something continues, *for, during*:—Ðæt wæs tō suīðe scortre hwīle *that was for a very short time*, Past. 36; Swt. 255, 10: Cd. Th. 31, 22; Gen. 489. Tō langum fyrste *for a long while*, Homl. Th. i. 388, 18. Tō wyrcenne tācna tō feórþan healfan geáre *to work miracles for three years and a half*, 4, 31. Hē worhte his weorc tō seofon nihtum, ii. 356, 5. Syððan tō twelf mōnðum ne cymþ ðǣr nān ōðer scūr, Lchdm. iii. 254, 1. *See also* ealdor, feorh. (d) marking end of extent, *to*:—Hē frægn hū neáh ðære tīde wǣre ... Ðā andswaredon hī: 'Nis hit lang tō ðon,' Bd. 4, 24; S. 599, 5: Beo. Th. 5176; B. 2591: 5683; B. 2845. Is tō ðære tīde tælmet hwīle seofon and twēntig nihtgerīmes, Andr. Kmbl. 225; An. 113. Ðæt hit wǣre þrittig þūsend wintra tō ðīnum deáðdæge, Soul Kmbl. 73; Seel. 37. **II.** with gen. (1) marking the object to or towards which motion takes place, *to, for*:—Gewāt him se æðeling tō ðæs gemearces ðe him Metod tǣhte *the prince departed for the appointed place, which the Lord had shewed him*, Cd. Th. 174, 28; Gen. 2885. Gewāt him Andreas gangan tō ðæs ðe hē gramra gemōt gefrægen hæfde ōððæt hē gemētte be mearcpaðe standan stapul ǣrenne *Andrew went on his way towards the spot, where he had learned was the cruel ones' meeting, until he found standing by the path a brazen pillar*, Andr. Kmbl. 2120; An. 1061. Wōd hē tō ðæs ðe hē wīnreced wisse *thither he made his way, where he knew the hall was*, Beo. Th. 1433; B. 714: 3939; B. 1967: 4811; B. 2410. Tō ðæs gingran þider ealle urnon ðǣr se ēca wæs *thither ran all the disciples, to the place where the Eternal was*, Cd. Th. 298, 11; Sat. 531. Tō ðæs fōron Caldēa cyn tō ceastre forð ðǣr Israēla ǣhta wǣron *thither marched the Chaldeans, on to the city, where were the possessions of the Israelites*, 218, 19; Dan. 41. Cōmon hildfrecan tō ðæs ða hæftas ǣr hearm þrowedon *they came where the captives had suffered*, Andr. Kmbl. 2142; An. 1072. Tō hwæs hī gearwe bǣron *whither they should bear their arms*, Cd. Th. 190, 1; Exod. 192. (2) marking position, *in, at*:—Hē wæs tō middes wætres *he was in mid stream*, Homl. Skt. ii. 30, 176. Hē him ðæs leán forgeald tō ðæs ðe hē on reste geseah Grendel licgan *he paid him the reward for it, where he saw Grendel lying on the couch*, Beo. Th. 3175; B. 1585. *See* tō-middes, II. (3) marking purpose; see also (5):—Hié tō ðæs here samnodon, Andr. Kmbl. 2248; An. 1125. (4) marking extent or degree, *to* the extent, *to* such a degree:—Ðæt hē ðās hālgan tīde gehealde mid clǣnum fæstene tō ānes mǣles *that he keep this holy time with a pure fast to the extent of eating only once*, Wulfst. 285, 1. Nā tō ðæs hwōn *nequaquam*, Deut. 13, 11. *See* se, V (b 1). (5) forming with nouns adverbial or prepositional phrases:—Tō gyfes *gratis*, Hymn. Surt. 37, 20. Ic ðē tō leánes ðīnne noman mǣrsige *in recompense I will magnify thy name for thee*, Lchdm. iii. 436, 27. Womma tō leánes *in requital of sins*, Wulfst. 138, 23: 139, 2. God him sylþ tō mēdes ðæt ēce līf, Homl. Skt. i. 12, 139: St. And. 28, 20. Tō geflites *certatim, strenue*, Hpt. Gl. 408, 54: Ap. Th. 10, 5. Ðū dwollīce leofast swylce ðē tō gamenes *thou livest foolishly as if it were sport for you*, Homl. Ass. 6, 141. (6) marking time, (a) marking a point of time at which something takes place:—Etan tō middes dæges (*meridie*), Gen. 43, 16: Ps. Th. 36, 6: Btwk. 216, 14. Tō middes mergenes, Lchdm. ii. 116, 7. Tō undernes, 194, 5. Tō nōnes, 290, 7. Tō hwilces tīman, Homl. Th. i. 78, 18. Gif preóst tō rihtes tīman crisman ne fecce, L. N. P. L. 9; Th. ii. 290, 3. Tō ðises *now*, Jn. Skt. Lind. 2, 10. (b) marking a limit, *to, up to, until, till*:—Wæs hit ðā ān tīd tō ǣfenes *it then was an hour to evening*, Nar. 13, 6. Tō ǣfenes *usque ad vesperam*, L. Ecg. C. 4; Th. ii. 138, 1: Bd. 3, 23; S. 554, 32. Ðæt hī fæston tō nōnes (*ad nonam usque horam*), 3, 5; S. 527, 9. (c) marking a space of time in the course of which something takes place, *at, in, on*:—Hī ǣton ǣne on dæg, and ðæt wæs tō ǣfennes, Bt. 15; Fox 48, 8. Ðæt mon hiora tīd boega geuueorðiæ tō ānes dæges tō Osuulfes tīde *that the anniversary of them both be celebrated on the same day, on Oswulf's anniversary*, Chart. Th. 460, 6. **III.** with acc. (1) marking direction or motion (lit. and fig.):—Hē leát tō ðæs cāseres eáre, Homl. Th. i. 376, 28. Tō ða rīde, ðon andlang rīðe, eft on sǣ, Cod. Dip. Kmbl. iii. 12, 21. Ða ðe hweorfan sceoldan tō ðis enge lond, Exon. Th. 3, 6; Cri. 32. Nō hȳ hine tō deáð dēman mōston, 135, 8; Gū. 521. (2) with the infinitive (cf. Gothic infinitive with *du*) with the same force as with the inflected infinitive:—Micel is tō secgan eall æfter orde, ðæt hē ādreág, Exon. Th. 134, 4; Gū. 502. Mǣl is mē tō fēran, Beo. Th. 637; B. 316. Āfȳsed biþ āgenne eard tō sēcan, Exon. Th. 217, 5; Ph. 275. Hād tō hebban (hāt tō hebbanne, Cd. Th. 236, 14; Dan. 321), 187, 27; Az. 37. Him sēlle þynceþ leahtras tō fremman, 266, 34; Jul. 408. Ne bisorgaþ hē synne tō fremman, 95, 13; Cri. 1556. Ðā ongan hē tō cweðan *coepit dicere*, Mk. Skt. 13, 5. Hē onsende worn ðæs werudes west tō fēran, Cd. Th. 220, 25; Dan. 76. Hē tiolaþ ungelīc tō bión (biónne, Cott. MS.) ðam ōþrum, Bt. 39, 12; Fox 232, 7. Gié soecas mec tō cwella (cwellanne, Rush.) *quaeritis me interficere*, Jn. Skt. Lind. 8, 40. Hē sende ðegnas his tō geceiga (cēgan, Rush.) hiá sié gehlaðad *misit servos suos vocare invitatos*, Mt. Kmbl. Lind. 22. 3. (3) marking time:—Tō dæg *hodie*, Ps. Th. 2, 7: Hy. 7, 76. Tō ǣfen *vespere*, tō morgen *mane*, Ex. 16, 12: Cd. Th. 147, 12; Gen. 2438. **IV.** with instrumental, (1) marking end or purpose:—Hē com tō ðī ðæt hē wolde synna forgifan, Homl. ii. 226, 9. *See* se, **V**. Tō hwī *why*, Mt. Kmbl. 8, 26: 9, 4: 26, 65: Homl. ii. 134, 9. (2) marking end of extent (time):—Næs lang tō ðȳ ðæt his brōþor ðyses lǣnan līfes tīman geendode, Lchdm. iii. 434, 25. **V.** used adverbially, where a noun governed by the preposition might be supplied from the context, (1) where motion is expressed or implied:—Of ðære sōþan gesǣlþe cumaþ eall ða ōþre gōd, and eft tō, Bt. 34, 6; Fox 140, 17: 25; Fox 88, 29: 37, 2; Fox 188, 12. Gif twēgen men fundiaþ tō ānre stōwe and habbaþ emnmicelne willan tō tō cumenne, 36, 4; Fox 178, 10. Lā leóf, hē is deád; gang tō and ārǣr hine, Homl. Th. ii. 182, 10: Beo. Th. 5290; B. 2648. Ðā fērdon hī tō, Homl. Skt. ii. 30, 149. Seó eá on emtwā tōeode ..., and seó eá eft tō arn, Homl. Th. ii. 212, 24. Hē tō forð gestōp dracan heáfde neáh, Beo. Th. 4568; B. 2289: Byrht. Th. 136, 13; By. 150. Hē sende hys here tō *missis exercitibus suis*, Mt. Kmbl. 22, 7. Hē tō somnaþ ða ðe ūt gewitan, Ps. Th. 146, 2. Tō nā geneálǣc *ne accesseris*, Scint. 65, 15. Tō lǣtan *to admit*, Past. 45; Swt. 337, 16. Wē tilien, ðæt wē tō mōten, Exon. Th. 313, 5; Seef. 119. Tō sculon clǣne *to that place shall the pure go*, 450, 26; Dōm. 93. Hine se cyning tō gelaþode, Bd. 5, 19; S. 640, 8. (2) with verbs of placing (lit. or fig.), adding, etc.:—Ða ilcan studu tō gesette tō trymnesse, Bd. 3, 17; S. 544, 22. Sume ic tō ȳcte, pref.; S. 472, 30. Tō ætȳcean *superaddere*, 4, 30; S. 609, 33: 1, 27; S. 490, 22. Be ðām wītan ðē witan tō lēdan, L. E. G. 5; Th. i. 168, 27: Chart. Th. 370, 15. Swā hwæt swā ðū māre tō gedēst, Lk. Skt. 10, 35. (3) where position is marked:—Hū hié mid hiera wætrum tō licgeaþ *how they with their waters lie to one another*, Ors. 1, 1; Swt. 10, 5. (4) where direction is marked:—Ðǣr hȳ tō sēgun, Exon. Th. 31, 14; Cri. 495: Cd. Th. 232, 5; Dan. 255. Ðū ūre unriht āsettest ðǣr ðū sylfa tō eágum lōcadest *posuisti iniquitates nostras in conspectu tuo*, Ps. Th. 89, 8. Wē beótiaþ tō, Blickl. Homl. 33, 27. (5) *in addition, besides, too*:—Ða styriendan nētenu habbaþ eall ðæt ða unstyriendan habbaþ, and eác māre tō, Bt. 41, 5; Fox 252, 26. Manegu ōþru gōd tō eác ðām *many other goods too in addition to those*, 34, 6; Fox 140, 32. Hæfde hē nigon hund wintra and hundseofontig tō, Cd. Th. 74, 18; Gen. 1224. Ne bæd hē nō ðæt hē hiene mid ealle fortȳnde mid gehāle wāge, ac hē bæd dura tō (*he asked for a door to the wall*), Past. 38; Swt. 274, 23. **VI.** adverb, with adjectives or adverbs, *too*:—Hī sellaþ wið tō lytlum weorðe *they sell for too small a price*, Past. 59; Swt. 449, 14. Of tō micelre fylle, Lchdm. ii. 60, 19. Tō manega of ðam folce, Num. 25, 1. Wæs ðæt wīte tō strang, Cd. Th. 109, 8; Gen. 1819. Ðone ðe tō micelne andan hæfþ, ðū scealt hātan leó ...; and ðone sǣnan ðe biþ tō slāw, ðū scealt hātan assa, Bt. 37, 4; Fox 192, 18–20. Ðȳ læs hī hī tō up āhæbben, Bt. 39, 11; Fox 228, 23: Past. 13; Swt. 79, 17: 65; Swt. 461, 28. Ða untruman mōd mon ne scyle tō heálīce lǣran, 63; Swt. 459, 4. Ðū hæfst ðara wǣpna tō hraþe forgiten, Bt. 3, 1; Fox 4, 21. Ne fare gē tō feorr, Ex. 8, 28: 19, 12. Ðæt man mōte tō forð æfter luste libban and gȳman ne ðurfe nā oferlīce swȳðe ðæs ðe bēc beódaþ *that living as a man pleases may be carried too far, and over much heed need not be taken of what books* *bid*, Wulfst. 55, 17. [*O. Frs. O. Sax.* tō: *Du.* toe: *O. H. Ger.* zuo: *Ger.* zu.] v. hēr-, in-, þǽr-tō.

tō-, *a prefix denoting separation, division, like Latin* dis-, di-. [It occurs as late as the Authorized Version, in Jud. 9, 53, *to* brake. Cf. *Goth.* twis-: *O. Frs.* tō-, te-, ti-: *O. Sax.* te-, ti-: *O. H. Ger.* za-, zi-; zar-, zir-: *Ger.* zer-.]

tō-ætīcan *to increase*:—Swelce eác tōætēcte ðisse gedrēfnisse storm Sǽberhtes deáþ *auxit autem procellam hujusce perturbationis etiam mors Sabercti*, Bd. 2, 5; S. 507, 6. v. next word.

tō-ætīcness, e; *f. An increase, augmentation*:—Tōætȳcnys *augmentum*, Bd. 3, 22: S. 553, 14. v. tō-īcness.

tōan (?), tōian (?), tōgian (?) *to grow tough*:—Tōadan *lentescunt*, Wrt. Voc. ii. 52, 57: 92, 77. v. tōh, tēan.

tō-bǽd (? -blǽd. v. tō-blǽdan) *elevated, exalted*:—Tōbǽdne ł geufserodne *elevatum*, Ps. Lamb. 36, 35. Heó wyrd glædlīce on hyre heortan tōbǽd, Anglia viii. 324, 16.

tō-beátan; *p.* -beót *To beat to pieces, destroy by beating*:—Hig gebundon ðone bysceop be ðām fōtum on sumne fearr and ðone gegremedon, ðæt hē hleóp on unsmēðe eorðan and ðam bysceope ðæt heáfod tōbeót, Shrn. 152, 2. Com him swilc wind ongeán, swilce nān mann ǽr ne gemunde, and ða scipo ealle tōbeót, Chr. 1009; Erl. 142, 5. Scipia hēt ǽlcne hiéwestān tōbeátan *omni murali lapide in pulverem comminuto*, Ors. 4, 13; Swt. 212, 10. [Ure men hī tobetet *they knock our men about*, Laym. 3308. Me tobeot his cheoken, A. R. 106, 24. Euer euch man me tobeteþ, and hwanne heo habbeþ me ofslaȝe, O. and N. 1610.]

tō-beótiende. v. beótian.

tō-beran; *p.* -bær, *pl.* -bǽron; *pp.* -boren. I. *trans. To carry off in different directions, carry off*:—Hī tredaþ ðec and tergaþ, tōberaþ ðec blōdgum lāstum (*thy body will be torn to pieces*), Exon. Th. 119. 25; Gū. 260. Ðæt sǽd ðe feóll be ðam wege . . . wegfērende hit fortrǽdon, and fugelas tōbǽron (*birds carried it off in all directions*), Homl. Th. ii. 90, 15. Lētan hī his līchaman-licgan būtan ðære ceastre and woldon ðæt hine fuglas tōbǽron, Shrn. 32, 6. Ealle ða līchoman ðe wildeór ābiton, oþþe fuglas tōbǽron, oþþe fixas tōslitan, Blickl. Homl. 95, 16. Sȳn his bearn tōboren wīde *may his children be scattered far and wide; commoti amoveantur filii ejus*, Ps. Th. 108, 10. [As he me in his fete tobere, Chauc. H. of F. ii. 60.] II. *intrans. To move in different directions, separate*:—Sió wund wile tōberan gif hió ne biþ gewriðen *the edges of the wound will get further apart, if the wound is not bound up*, Past. 17; Swt. 123, 15. v. next word.

tō-berenness, e; *f. Difference*; differentia, Wrt. Voc. ii. 28, 42.

tō-berstan; *p.* -bærst, *pl.* -burston; *pp.* -borsten. I. *to burst asunder, to break* (intrans.) *in two*, or *in pieces, be rent asunder*:—Ic tōberste *crepo*, Ælfc. Gr. 24; Zup. 138, 5. Se heofon tōbyrst from ðæm eastdǽle ōþ ðone westdǽl, Blickl. Homl. 93, 22. Tōbirsteþ, Exon. Th. 420, 7; Rä. 39, 7. Se sceaft tōbærst *the shaft was shivered*, Byrht. Th. 135, 51; By. 136. Seó byrne tōbærst *the corslet was rent*, 135, 66; By. 144. Sum man feóll on īse ðæt his earm tōbærst *his arm was broken*, Homl. Skt. ii. 26, 34. Seó eorþe tōbærst and ðonan up wæs biernende fȳr wið ðæs hefones *hiatu terrae flamma prorupit*, Ors. 5, 10; Swt. 234, 7. Hē eode tō ðære burge wealle, and fleáh ūt ofer, ðæt hē eall tōbærst, 5, 12; Swt. 244, 3. Hē gefeól on ðone stocc and tōbærst on feówer dǽlas, Blickl. Homl. 189, 13. Ān hridder tōbærst on emtwā, Homl. Th. ii. 154, 16. Stānas tōburston *petrae scissae sunt*, Mt. Kmbl. 27, 51. Ða scittelsas tōburston, Homl. Skt. i. 3, 348. Tōborstenum bendum *ruptis vinculis*, Lk. Skt. 8, 29. I a. *to break out in sores*. v. tō-borstenness:—Wið springas and wið tōborsten līc *for carbuncles and for a body with breakings out*, Lchdm. i. 272, 18. His līchama barn wiðūtan mid langsumere hǽtan, and hē eal innan samod forswǽled wæs and tōborsten, Homl. Th. i. 86, 5. II. *to break out*:—Tōberstaþ *erumpunt*, Wrt. Voc. ii. 144, 8. [His brest tobrosten, Chauc. Kn. T. 1833. *O. Sax.* tebrestan: *O. H. Ger.* zar-brestan *crepare, discrepare*: *Ger.* zer-bersten.]

tō-berstung, e; *f. Bursting*:—Ðæs geswelles tōberstung, Lchdm. ii. 198, 10.

tō-bīgende *decrepit*:—Tōbīgende *decrepito*, Wrt. Voc. ii. 26, 26: 70, 4.

tō-blǽdan; *p.* de *To inflate, puff up*:—Sōð lufu nā byþ tōblǽdd *caritas non inflatur*, Scint. 82, 10. v. next word.

tō-blāwan; *p.* -bleów; *pp.* -blāwen. I. *to blow in different directions, scatter by blowing, blow away*:—Hī beóþ duste gelīcran ðonne hit wind tōblǽwþ *tamquam pulvis, quem projecit ventus a facie terrae*, Ps. Th. 1, 5. Tōdrifen mid winde, swā weorþaþ axe giond eorþan eall tōblāwen, Met. 20, 106. On ðam (helle) fȳre gē beóþ tōblāwene, Homl. Skt. i. 7, 139. II. *to inflate, puff up, distend with wind, swell*, (a) lit. v. next word:—Gif se maga biþ tōblāwen, Lchdm. iii. 58, 13. [Himm wærenn fet and þeos tobollenn and toblawenn, Orm. 8080.] (b) fig. *to cause the breast to swell* with emotion:—Tōblāwen (*superbie tumore*) *inflatus*, Anglia xiii. 441, 1084: Hpt. Gl. 423, 23. Murcnungum tōblāwene *questibus inflati*, 421, 11. Tōblāwene mid mōdignysse, Scint. 84, 19: R. Ben. 124, 6. [Mid a lutel wind of a word toblowen and tobollen, A. R. 122, 16.]

tō-blāwenness, e; *f. Inflation, distension*:—Ungelȳfendlīc tōblāwennys his innoð geswencte, Homl. Th. i. 86, 13.

tō-borstenness, e; *f. A breaking out, abscess*:—Hȳ ðæra innoða tōðundennysse and tōborstennysse (ῥήγματα) gehǽleþ, Lchdm. i. 322, 22. v. tō-berstan, I a.

tō-brǽdan; *p.* de. I. *to make broad, enlarge, extend, make great* in size or number, (a) of material objects:—Hig tōbrǽdaþ hyra healsbēc *dilatant philacteria sua*, Mt. Kmbl. 23, 5. (b) of non-material objects, *to make great, magnify, multiply, increase, improve the condition of* a person:—Ðeáh heora sȳ mycle mā ðonne ūre, þeáh ðū ūs tōbrǽdest ongeán hȳ, and wið hī gefriðast, Ps. Th. 11, 9. Ðū tōbrǽdest heorte mīne *dilatasti cor meum*, Ps. Spl. 118, 32. Tōbrēt *dilatat*, Kent. Gl. 648. Ðū nā tōbrǽddest fȳnd mīne ofer mē, Ps. Spl. 29, 1: 4, 1. Ðū ðīn sōðfæst weorc tōbrǽddest *multiplicasti justitiam tuam*, Ps. Th. 70, 20. Ða earfoðu mīnre heortan synd swȳðe tōbrǽd (*dilatatae*), 24, 15. II. *to expand, extend, spread out, open wide, distend*:—Gif ðū ðīnes scipes segl ongeán ðone wind tōbrǽdst, Bt. 7, 2; Fox 18, 32. Mid hū miclum gōdum willan Dryhten tōbrǽt (*expandit*) ðone greádan his mildheortnesse ongēn ða ðe tō him gecierraþ, Past. 52; Swt. 405, 9. Hē tōbrǽdde (*expandit*) his feðeru, Deut. 32, 11. Tōbrǽd ðīne handa swilce (ðū) sceát āstrecce, Techm. ii. 122, 24. Tōbrǽd mūð ðīn *open thy mouth wide* (A. V.), Ps. Spl. 80, 9. Āþened, tōbrǽd *distenta*, i. *extenta*, tōbrǽde *destentat*, Wrt. Voc. ii. 141, 22, 23. Tōbrǽddum *apertis*, 5, 15. Wē sǽton bōcum tōbrǽddon, Salm. Kmbl. 863; Sal. 431. III. *to extend, spread abroad, diffuse*:—Ðeós wyrt wið ða eorðan hyre telgran tōbrǽdeþ, Lchdm. i. 324, 3. Tō hwon wilnige gē, ðæt gē eówerne naman tōbrǽdan ofer ðone teóþan dǽl? Bt. 18, 1; Fox 62, 25. Ðonne mæg hine scamian ðære brǽdinge his hlīsan for ðam hē hine ne mæg furþum tōbrǽdan (tōbrēdan, Met. 10, 15) ofer ða nearwan eorþan āne *brevem replere non valentis ambitum pudebit aucti nominis*, 19; Fox 68, 25. His naman tōbrǽdan geond ealle eorþan, 30, 1; Fox 108, 12. God hafaþ his gemynd on heofonum and on eorðan tōbrǽd, Chr. 979; Erl. 129, 18. Binnan ðǽm feówer hyrnum ðises middangeardes is tōbrǽdd Godes folc *sancta ecclesia per quatuor mundi partes dilatata tenditur*, Past. 22; Swt. 171, 4. Tōbrǽdde *diffusa*, i. *sparsa, dispersa*, Wrt. Voc. ii. 140, 16. III a. intrans.:—Of ðyson eahta deófles cræftan ealle unþeáwas up āspringaþ and syððan tōbrǽdaþ ealles tō wīde, Wulfst. 68, 17. [*O. H. Ger.* ze-breiten.]

tō-brǽdedness, e; *f. Extent, an extensive place*:—On tōbrǽdednesse ł on brādnesse *in latitudine*, Ps. Lamb. 117, 5. On tōbrǽdednesse *in latitudinem*, 17, 20: Ps. Spl. 17, 22.

tō-brǽdness, e; *f. Extent, breadth*:—On tōbrǽdnysse *in latitudine*, Ps. Spl. 117, 5.

tō-brecan; *p.* -bræc, *pl.* -brǽcon; *pp.* -brocen *To break, break in pieces*:—Ic tōbrece *frango*, Ælfc. Gr. 28, 6; Zup. 176, 8: *rumpo*, 177, 4. Tōbrocen *contrita*, Hpt. Gl. 482, 67. I. in reference to material objects, *to break in two, to break to pieces, break up, to separate into parts* by striking or pulling:—Hē (*the patch of new cloth*) tōbrycþ hys stede on ðam reáfe, and se slite byþ ðe wyrsa, Mt. Kmbl. 9, 16. Ðū mē tōbrǽce (*disrupisti*) bendas grimme, Ps. Th. 115, 7. Hē ðone hlāf tōbræc on twā, Blickl. Homl. 181, 16. Ða ǽrenan scyttelas hē ealle tōbræc, 85, 7. Hē tōbræc hire (*the lion's*) ceaflas mid his barum handum, Ælfc. T. Grn. 7, 16. Hī ða gymstānas tōbrǽcon, Homl. Th. i. 60, 28. Hié ða scipu eall oðþe tōbrǽcon oþþe forbærndon, Chr. 894; Erl. 91, 25. Tōbrec hira anlīcnyssa *confringes statuas eorum*, Ex. 23, 24: Lchdm. i. 370, 22. Tōbrec ðīnne hlāf and syle ðone ōðerne dǽl hungrium men *break thy loaf in two and give one part to a hungry man*, Homl. Th. i. 180, 4. Man sceolde tōbrecan his stef, Chr. 1047; Erl. 177, 7. Ða wildan hors scealden iornan and him ða limo all tōbrecan, Shrn. 72, 2. Tō gehwylcum bryce, hundes brægen ālēd on wulle and ðæt tōbrocene tō gewriþen, Lchdm. i. 370, 19. Wiþ ealdre wunde tōbrocenre, ii. 92, 1. Tōbrocen wērun sconco hiora *frangeruntur eorum crura*, Jn. Skt. Rush. 19, 31. Ða bytta beóþ tōbrocene *rumpuntur utres*, Mt. Kmbl. 9, 17. Heora scipu sume þurh oferweder wurdon tōbrocene, Chr. 794; Erl. 59, 22. II. *to overthrow, break down, ruin, destroy, put into confusion, rout*, (a) of material objects:—Ceaster heora ðū tōbrǽce (*destruxisti*), Ps. Spl. 9, 6. Se ðe tōbræc (*destruebat*) ðone tempel Godes, Mt. Kmbl. Lind. 27, 40. Hyra setlu hē tōbræc (*evertit*), Mt. Kmbl. 21, 12: Mk. 11, 15. Wutun tiligean ðæt wē heora burh tōbrecan mōton *accipient in vanitate civitates tuas*, Ps. Th. 138, 17. Ðæs ne wēndon witan Scyldinga, ðæt hit (*the hall*) manna ǽnig tōbrecan meahte, Beo. Th. 1565; B. 780. Wæs ðæt beorhte bold tōbrocen swīðe, 1999; B. 997. Weard folc tōtwǽmed, scyldburh tōbrocen, Byrht. Th. 138, 58; By. 242. Āne tōbrocene byrgenne *sepulchrum dirutum*, Ors. 4, 10; Swt. 202, 4. Eal ðīn carcern hē hafaþ tōbrocen, Blickl. Homl. 85, 22. Hreósaþ tōbrocene burgweallas, Exon. Th. 61, 1; Cri. 978. (b) of persons, *to destroy, crush*:—Ic tōbrǽce hī *confringam eos*, Ps. Spl. 17, 40. Ðū hié tōbrǽce *attrivisti eos*, Past. 37; Swt. 267, 3. (c) of non-material objects:—Hit eallum ðǽm senatum ofþyncendum ðæt hē heora ealdan gesetnessa tōbrecan wolde (*would overthrow their old laws*), Ors. 5, 12; Swt. 244, 17. Ðonne biþ se glencg āgoten and se þrym tōbrocen, Wulfst. 263, 8. Hit ongeat ðæs wīsdōmes lâre swîþe tôtorenne and swîþe tôbrocenne, Bt. 3, 1; Fox 4, 31. III. *to take by assault*:—Tirus hē besæt and siþþan tôbræc and mid ealle tôwearp *Tyrum oppressit et cepit*, Ors. 3, 9; Swt. 126, 17. Ða gigantas woldon tôbrecan ðone heofon *lacessentes coelum gigantes*, Bt. 35, 4; Fox 162, 12. Hēr wæs tôbrocen Rōmāna burh fram Gotum, Chr. 409; Erl. 11, 10. On ðissum geáre wæs Bæbbanburh tôbrocon, 993; Erl. 133, 1. IV. *to break* a promise, pledge, etc., *to infringe, violate*:—Swā hwā swā halt ðis write . . . hwā swā hit tôbreceþ, Chr. 675; Erl. 38, 27. Man his riht tôbræc, 975; Erl. 126, 17. Twêgen gebróðra tôbrǣcon ðone regol, Homl. Th. ii. 166, 34. Gif hē his bebod tôbrǣce, Homl. Ass. 60, 217. Wed synd tôbrocene oft and gelōme, Wulfst. 161, 12. V. *to break, interrupt*:—Wē tôbrecaþ ūrne slǣp and gebiddaþ for eów, Homl. Ass. 51, 39. [The verb remains in the Authorized Version 'all to-brake his scull,' Jud. 9, 53. *O. Frs.* tō-breka (te-): *O. L. Ger.* te-brekan: *O. H. Ger.* ze-brechen *disrumpere, confringere*: *Ger.* zer-brechen.] v. tô-brocen, un-tôbrocen.

tô-brêdan, Met. 10, 15. v. tô-brǣdan, III.

tô-bregdan, -brēdan; *p.* -brægd, -brǣd, *pl.* -brugdon, -brūdon (-brudon?); *pp.* -brogden, -brōden (-broden? *in O. and N.* tobrode *rimes with* unsode). I. *to separate* (trans.) *by a quick movement*. (a) *to pull to pieces* (lit. and fig.):—Hū ǣnig mæg gangan in hūse stronges and fatu his tôbregdan (*diripere*), nymþe ǣr gebindaþ se stronge and ðonne hūs his tôbrægdeþ (*diripiat*), Mt. Kmbl. Rush. 12, 29. Hē tôbrǣd (*dilaceravit*) āne león tô sticcum, Jud. 14, 6. Metod tôbrǣd monna sprǣce *the Lord destroyed the unity of human speech*, Cd. Th. 102, 5; Gen. 1695. Hié tôbrugdon blōdigum ceaflum fira flǣschoman, Andr. Kmbl. 317; An. 159. Þrié wulfas ānes deádes monnes lîchoman styccemǣlum tôbrūdon (*cadaver sparsum membratim reliquerunt*), Ors. 4, 2; Swt. 160, 21. Ða nicoras tôbrūdon hié, Nar. 11, 11. Hit ongeat his lâre swîþe tôtorene and swîþe tôbrogdene, Bt. 3, 1; Fox 4, 31 note. Biþ se glencg āgoten and se þrym tôbrōden, Wulfst. 263, 8 note. Ðæt hē wǣre from ðām hundum tôbrōden, Shrn. 145, 4. (b) *to pull apart*:—Heora lima man ealle tôbrǣd ǣlc fram ōðrum *their limbs were torn from one another*, Homl. Skt. i. 23, 72. Ðā tôbrǣd Samson bēgen his earmas *Samson wrenched his arms apart*, Jud. 15, 14. II. *to separate* (intrans.) *by a quick movement, to break off, start* from sleep, cf. *Icel.* bregða svefni *to awake*:—Slǣpe tôbrægd folces weard, Cd. Th. 161, 15; Gen. 2665. Mid ðȳ heó ðā ðȳ slǣpe tôbrǣd *somno excussa*, Bd. 4, 23; S. 596, 5. Slǣpe tôbrugdon searuhæbbende, Andr. Kmbl. 3053; An. 1529. Ic gefrægn hæleð slǣpe tôbrēdan (-on, MS.), Judth. Thw. 25, 7; Jud. 247. III. *to separate by making a quick movement* with something (?):—Oft hȳ wordum tôweorpaþ ǣr hȳ bacum tôbrēden (*before they part and turn their backs on one another*, (?) cf. *Icel.* bregða hendi, fôtum, etc.), Exon. Th. 345, 20; Gn. Ex. 192. [Hi eteþ flesch unsode swich wulves hadde hit tobrode, O. and N. 1008. The fend him tobrayd *illum daemonium dissipavit*, Wick. Lk. 9, 42. He tobraide his clothes, Gow. ii. 53, 11.]

tô-brîtan; *p.* te. I. *to break in pieces, crush, bruise* (lit. and fig.):—Ic tôbrȳte *tero*, Ælfc. Gr. 28, 1; Zup. 165, 14: *confringo*, 28, 6; Zup. 176, 9. Ic tôbrȳte hî *confringam eos*, Ps. Lamb. 17, 39. Ðū tôbrȳtst hig *confringes eos*, 2, 9. Tôbrȳt (*confringet*) Drihten cederbeám, Ps. Lamb. 28, 5: 57, 7. Heó tôbrȳt (*conteret*) ðîn heáfod, Gen. 3, 15. Boga[n] tôbrȳteþ, Ps. Spl. 45, 9. Tēþ sinfulra ðū tôbrîttest (*contrivisti*), 3, 7. Folc ðū tôbrîttest (*confringes*), 55, 7. Gewît of ðære leásan anlîcnysse, and tôbrȳt hî eall and hire cræt samod, Homl. Th. ii. 496, 14. Tôbrȳt (*contere*) earm ðæs synfullan, Ps. Lamb. 9 second, 15. Flǣsces tôbrȳte (*terat*) mōdignesse, Hymn. Surt. 9, 22. Ne ūs gedweld tôbrȳte (*atterat*), 17, 24. Ðæt God ūre helpe and tôbrȳte ðisne here, Homl. Skt. ii. 25, 350. Ic bebeóde mînum þeówum þæt hî hî (*the idols*) ealle tôbrȳton, i. 5, 236. Tôbrȳtendes *confringentis*, Ps. Lamb. 28, 5. Tôbrȳtendne (*conterentem*) deóful, Hymn. Surt. 115, 15. Boga heora biþ tôbrȳt *arcus eorum confringatur*, Ps. Spl. 36, 16. Tôbrȳt ł tôbrocen *contrita, constricta*, Hpt. Gl. 482, 67. Tôbrȳt *contritus*, 515, 5. Tôbrȳttes *attritae, violatae*, 474, 75. Tôbrȳtte ł ofrorene *obruti, contriti*, 506, 6. Tôbrēttum *quassatis, confractis*, 421, 39. II. *to crush with feelings of sorrow, to make contrite*:—Heortan ða tôbrȳttan *cor contritum*, Ps. Lamb. 50, 19. Ða tôbrȳttan on heortan *contritos corde*, 146, 3. [Corineus heom tobrutte ban and heora ribbes, Laym. 1602.]

tô-brîtedness, e; *f.* I. *a bruise, breach*:—Hē gewrîð tôbrȳtednyssa heora *alligat contritiones eorum*, Ps. Lamb. 146, 3: 59, 4. II. *trouble, sorrow*:—Tôbrȳtednys and ungesǣlignys *contritio et infelicitas*, 13, 3.

tôbrîtend-lîc; *adj. Breakable*:—Ða tôbrȳtendlîcan *fragenda*, Wrt. Voc. ii. 150, 37.

'**tô-brîting**, e; *f. Crushing*, fig. *destruction*:—Tôbrȳtincge forestæpþ ofermōdignyss *contritionem precedit superbia*, Scint. 82, 12.

tô-brocen; *adj.* (*ptcpl.*) *Suffering from eruptions*:—Wiþ innan tôbrocenum mūðe, Lchdm. ii. 310, 19.

tôbrocen-lîc; *adj. Frail, perishable*:—Ðysse worulde wela is hwȳlwendlîc and feallendlîc and tôbrocenlîc *the wealth of this world is transitory and decaying and frail*, Wulfst. 263, 13.

tô-brȳsan *and* **-brȳsian**; *p.* de *To crush, break in pieces*:—Ic tôbrȳse *tero*, Ælfc. Gr. 28, 1; Zup. 165, 14 MS. T. Ealle ðîn bān ic tôbrȳsige, Nar. 41, 20. Se ðe fylþ uppan ðysne stān hē byþ tôbrȳsed (*confringetur*); and hē tôbrȳsþ (*conteret*) ðone ðe hē onuppan fylþ, Mt. Kmbl. 21, 44. Ðū ealle mîne bān tôbrîsdest, Nar. 45, 5. Ealle his bān heó tôbrȳsde, 44, 15. Tôbrȳsiende *confringens*, Ps. Lamb. 28, 5. Gif hwā tôbrȳsed sȳ *if any one be crushed* (convulsus), Lchdm. i. 122, 1. Tôbrȳsede tigelan, Homl. Skt. i. 8, 169. [ʒiff he wollde læpenn dun he munnde tobrisenn all himm sellfenn, Orm. 12032. Al tobrised bac and þe, Havel. 1950. Tobrusede *brake in pieces*, Wick. (2 Kings 18, 4).]

tô-brȳtan. v. tô-brîtan.

tô-ceorfan; *p.* -cearf, *pl.* -curfon; *pp.* -corfen. I. *to cut to pieces, cut in two, cut up*:—Hē tôcearf his basing on emtwā mid sexe, Homl. Th. ii. 500, 26. Hî tôcurfon ðone lîchaman on manugu sticceo, Shrn. 125, 10. Ða langnysse tôceorfan on pysena gelîcnysse, Lchdm. i. 260, 15. Rammes lungen smæl tôcorfen, 356, 21. Tôcorfen *lacerata*, Wrt. Voc. ii. 53, 32. Þeáh ðe se beám beó tôcoruen, H. R. 105, 15. II. *to cut off*:—Tôcearf him ða eárelipprica *amputavit illi auricula*, Mk. Skt. Lind. 14, 47. [Til he wyste who couþe uche kyndam tokerve, Allit. Pms. 88, 1700. *O. Frs.* tō-kerva.]

tô-ceówan; *p.* -ceáw, *pl.* -cuwon; *pp.* -cowen *To chew to pieces, break up by chewing, masticate*:—Ðæt hūsel biþ betwux tôðum tôcowen, Homl. Th. ii. 270, 33. [Deoflen torendeð ham ant tocheoweð ham euch greot, O. E. Homl. i. 251, 12. Hit tocheoweð ant touret Godes milce, A. R. 202, 16.]

tô-cînan; *p.* -cān, *pl.* -cinon; *pp.* -cinen *To break* (intrans.) *into chinks, split, crack*:—Tôcînit, tecînid *dehiscat*, Txts. 57, 653. Tôcîneþ, Wrt. Voc. ii. 25, 27: *dehiscit*, 27, 15. Gif hit (*an egg*) ne tôcîne, tôsleah hwōn *if it will not crack of itself, crack it slightly with a tap*, Lchdm. iii. 18, 2. Tôcinan (-en?) *rimosa*, Hpt. Gl. 529, 10. Gemētte hē be wege sumne lîcðrowere licgende eal tôcinen (*the skin all cracked with the disease*), Homl. Th. i. 336, 9. [Hie drinkeð þat hie tochineð, O. E. Homl. ii. 199, 32. Þe stan tochan, i. 141, 17. Þæ heorte tochan (-chon, 2nd MS.), Laym. 21235. Þe roche tochon, Misc. 92, 77.]

tôcir-hūs, es; *n. An inn*; diversorium (*di-vertere* = tô-cirran *q. v.*):—Tôcirhūs *diversorium*, Wrt. Voc. i. 38, 10.

tô-cirran; *p.* de *To turn in different directions, to part*:—Æfter ðon ðe wit nū tôcyrraþ and tôgāne beóþ *postquam ab invicem digressi fuerimus*, Bd. 4, 29; S. 607, 20 MS. B. Hî mid mycelon unsehte tôcyrdon *they parted on very bad terms*, Chr. 1094; Erl. 230, 6. Cf. tô-gān, -hweorfan.

tô-cleófan; *p.* -cleáf, *pl.* -clufon; *pp.* -clofen *To cleave asunder*:—Ic tôcleófe (-clefe, MS. J.) *findo*, Ælfc. Gr. 28, 6; Zup. 178, 5. Ic tôclǣfe, Engl. Stud. xi. 65, 38. Gif ðū ǣnne stān tôclîfst, ne wyrþ hē nǣfre gegaderod swā hē ǣr wæs, Bt. 34, 11; Fox 150, 26. Tôclȳfþ *findit*, i. *rupit*, Wrt. Voc. ii. 148, 63. Ðonne God ðysne middangeard tôcleófeþ, Blickl. Homl. 109, 35. Ða nȳtenu synd clǣne ðe tôcleófaþ heora clāwa, Homl. Skt. ii. 25, 55. Tôcleáf *findit*, Wrt. Voc. ii. 37, 32. Se rēða kyning hine tôcleáf on twā, Ælfc. T. Grn. 9, 21. Tôcleófende *sulcans*, Wülck. Gl. 254, 21. Monnes cinbān gif hit biþ tôclofen, gesette mon .xii. scill. tô bōte, L. Alf. pol. 50; Th. i. 94, 16. Ða sticcu ðæs tôclofenan hriddores, Homl. Th. ii. 154, 19. Oð ðone tôbrocenan beorg ðe ðǣr is tôclofen, Cod. Dip. Kmbl. ii. 251, 6. Æt ðam litlan tôclofenan beorge, iii. 421, 9. Tôcleofenan, ii. 249, 26. [*In later English the word is used transitively and intransitively.* His ban tocluuen, Laym. 1920. Drihhtin toclæf þe sæ, Orm. 14798. He smot and toclef þat heued, R. Glouc. 186, 3. Mine herte shal tocleve, Chauc. T. and C. v. 613. Þe holi goste heuene shal tocleue, Piers P. 12, 141. Þe shell tooclef, Alis. (Skt.) 1009.] v. un-tôclofen.

tô-clifrian; *p.* ode *To scratch* or *tear to pieces*:—Wæs tôclifrod *laniatur*, Germ. 398, 174. Hē unscrȳdde hine ealne, and wylode hine sylfne on ðam þiccum brēmlum and þornum swā lange, ðæt hē eall tôclifrod ārās, Homl. Th. ii. 156, 30.

tô-clipigend-lîc; *adj. Of address* or *appeal*:—O is tôclypigendlîc *abverbium*.

tô-clipung, e; *f. Invocation, appeal*:—Ǣlc man biþ gefullod on naman ðære Hālgan Ðrynnysse and hē ne mōt nā beón eft gefullod, ðæt ne sȳ forsewen ðære Hālgan Ðrynnysse tôclypung, Homl. Th. ii. 602, 3: Homl. Skt. i. 12, 143: Homl. Th. ii. 48, 15.

tô-cnāwan; *p.* -cneów; *pp.* -cnāwen *To discern, distinguish, know the difference between, understand*:—Tôcnāweþ *discernit*, Blickl. Gl. Tôcnāwen [beón] *dinosci, intellegi*, Wrt. Voc. ii. 140, 30. (1) with acc.:—Wē geseóþ þurh ūre eágan and ealle ðing tôcnāwaþ *by means of our eyes we see and distinguish all things*, Homl. Th. ii. 372, 27. Ðurh ða gesceádwîsnesse wē tôcnāwaþ good and yfel and geceósaþ ðæt gōd and āweorpaþ ðæt yfel *per discretionem virtutes eligimus, delicta reprobamus*, Past. 11; Swt. 65, 22. Ða searpþanclan witan ðe ðone twydǣledan wîsdōm hlūtorlîce tôcnāwaþ, Lchdm. iii. 440, 29. Him is neód ðæt hē his āgene wōdnesse tôcnāwe *it is necessary for him to discern his own madness*, Homl. Th. ii. 110, 29. Cunne gē tôcnāwan heofones hiw *faciem coeli dijudicare nostis*, Mt. Kmbl. 16, 3. Man mihte his lîf tôcnāwan *potuit ejus vita dinosci*, R. Ben. 108, 15: Homl. Th. ii. 154, 25. Irre oft āmirreþ monnes mōd, ðæt hē ne mæg ðæt riht tōcnāwan, Prov. Kmbl. 28: Homl. Th. i. 108, 23. Geseón and tōcnāwan ǣgðer ge gōd ge yfel *to see good and evil and know the difference between them*, 18, 4. Heora nān ne cūðe ōðres sprǣce tōcnāwan *not one of them could understand another's speech*, 318, 20. Heó ða mōd ðē geopenaþ ðīnra freónda and eác ðīnra feónda, ðæt ðū hié miht swutele tōcnāwan . . . Mid hū micelan feó woldest ðū habban geboht, ðæt ðū swutole mihtest tōcnāwan ðīne frīnd and ðīne fȳnd, Bt. 20; Fox 72, 13–21. Hī cræftas and unþeáwas ne cunnon tōcnāwan *they cannot distinguish virtues and vices*, 36, 6; Fox 180, 30. Lǣcas cunnon ǣlces medtrumnesse ongitan and tōcnāwan *medicus aegritudinis modum dignoscit*, 39, 9; Fox 226, 17. Priscianus segþ ðæt man sceal tōcnāwan ǣlces dǣles mihte and getācnunge and swā undergytan hwæt hē sȳ nā be ðære declinunge *Priscian says, that we must distinguish the force and signification of each part of speech, and in this way, not by the declension, understand what it is*, Ælfc. Gr. 18; Zup. 111, 14. Nis nān ðing tōcnāwen on sōðre eáwfæstnesse, ðæt his láreówdōm ne gestaðelode, Homl. Th. i. 392, 18. (2) with acc. and appositive adjective:—Wē tōcnāwaþ his rīce and ūre rīce ðǣr āwritene, ðǣr wē ǣr swilce be ōðrum mannum gereccednesse rǣddon *we discern his kingdom and our kingdom there described, where before we read the account as if about other men*, Homl. Th. ii. 64, 29. Ða tungelwītegan tōcneówon Crist sōðne mann *the astrologers discerned that Christ was really man*, i. 106, 33. (3) with a clause:—Gif wē gleáwlīce tōcnāwaþ, ðæt se swymmenda arc getācnode Godes gelaðunge, Homl. Th. ii. 60, 2. On ðam mūðe wē habbaþ swæcc, and tōcnāwaþ hwæðer hit biþ ðe wered ðe biter ðæt wē ðicgaþ, 372, 29. Ðæt ðeós menigu tōcnāwe, ðæt ðis hǣðengyld deófles biggeng is, i. 72, 3. Hū mihte Adam tōcnāwan hwæt hē wǣre, 14, 4. Tōcnāwan ðæt ūs is twyfeald neód, ii. 284, 23: Lchdm. iii. 236, 10: Homl. Ass. 107, 150. Ðus ðū miht tōcnāwan, hwænne nama cymþ of worde, hwænne word of naman, Ælfc. Gr. 36; Zup. 216, 5.

tō-cnāwenness, e; *f. Knowledge, discernment, understanding, knowledge which appreciates the difference between things*:—Ne sind hī ðrȳ Godas . . . ac seó Ðrynnys is ān sōð God . . . Ðeós tōcnāwennys is ēce līf, Homl. Th. ii. 362, 32.

tō-cnyssan; *p.* te; *pp.* ed *To crush to pieces, smash, shatter*:—Ne forbrȳte hē nā ðæt tōcnysede hreód (*arundinem quassatam*), R. Ben. 121, 6. [*O. H. Ger.* ze-cnussen *elidere*.]

tō-cumende; *adj.* (*ptcpl.*) *Coming to a strange place, strange, foreign*:—Hē for Godes lufon eode tō reordum mid ðām tōcumendum mannum *for the love of God he took his meals with the strangers who came*, Shrn. 129, 27.

tō-cwæstedness, e; *f. Destruction*:—Geswāc tōcwæstednys (-cwestedness, Ps. Lamb.) *cessavit quassatio*, Ps. Spl. 105, 29. [Cf. *Goth.* kwistjan *to destroy*; kwisteins *destruction*: *Dan.* kvæste *to hurt*.]

tō-cweþan; *p.* -cwæþ, *pl.* -cwǣdon; *pp.* -cweden *To forbid, prohibit*:—Wē nellaþ secgan . . . for ðan ðe hyt tōcwǣdon ða wīsan láreówas, and . . . ða hālgan bōceras forbudon tō secgenne, Homl. Ass. 24, 7. Tōcwedene *interdicta, prohibita*, Hpt. Gl. 421, 77. Wē forbeódaþ ordāl and āðas (ordāl and āðas ǣfre syndan tōcwedene, MS. B.) freólsdagum, Wulfst. 117, 14. Ordāl and āðas and wīfunga ǣfre sindan tōcwedene heáhfreólsdagum, L. Eth. vi. 25; Th. i. 320, 24: v. 18; Th. i. 308, 24: L. E. G. 9; Th. i. 172, 10. Cf. L. C. E. 17; Th. i. 370, 2.

tō-cwilman; *p.* de *To afflict grievously, torment*:—Ða druncengeornan nā ðæt ān ðæt hī on ðam tōweardan līfe mid ēcum tintregum tōcwylmede synt, ac eác hȳ synt on ðisum andweardan līfe mid mænigfealdum untrumnyssum gewǣhte, Homl. Ass. 146, 56.

tō-cwīsan; *p.* de *To shatter, break to pieces, crush, bruise*:—Ic tōcwȳse *quasso*, Ælfc. Gr. 24; Zup. 137, 10. Ic tōcwȳse *quatio*, tōcwȳsde *quassi*, tōcwȳsed *quassum*, 28, 4; Zup. 169, 6. Ofer ðæne ðe hē fylþ hē tōcwȳst (*comminuet*), Lk. Skt. 20, 18. Tōcwiésð, Ps. Lamb. 28, 6. Hē tōcwȳseþ heáfdu *conquassabit capita*, 109, 6. Gimstānas tōcwȳsan, Homl. Th. i. 60, 24. Ðā wolde hē ān eald hūs tōcwȳsan *he wanted to demolish an old house*, ii. 510, 12. Ætslād se hālga wer . . . swā ðæt hē forneán eal wearð tōcwȳsed, 512, 12. Sum cild bearn under ānum yrnendum hweóle and wearð tō deáðe tōcwȳsed, 26, 25: 166, 20. Tōcwȳsed hreód *arundinem quassatam*, Mt. Kmbl. 12, 20. Ðās gymstānas synd tōcwȳsede for ȳdelum gylpe, Homl. Th. i. 62, 6. ¶ The word seems used with a passive force in the following passage:—Feól se wāh uppan ðæs stuntan rǣdboran, þæt hē æll tōcwȳsde and sum ōþer cniht samod, Homl. Skt. i. 8, 173.

tō-cwīsedness, e; *f. Crushed condition*:—Iohannes gegaderode ðæra gymstāna bricas . . . Ðā fǣrlīce wurdon ða gymstānas swā ansunde, ðæt furðon nān tācen ðære ǣrran tōcwȳsednesse næs gesewen *that not even a trace of their having been crushed was visible*, Homl. Th. i. 62, 16.

tō-cyme, es; *m. A coming to* a place, *coming, approach, arrival, advent*:—Uncer efenþeówa uncet sceolde ūt ālǣdan, and uncer hlāford ābād uncres tōcymes, Homl. Ass. 206, 385. Ǣr ðære tīde his (*an attack of convulsions*) tōcymes, Lchdm. i. 364, 16. Ǣr Antecristes tōcyme, Wulfst. 156, 7. Foran tō ðon tōcyme dōmes dæges, Blickl. Homl. 35, 8. For Drihtnes cynedōmes tōcyme, 87, 5. Deáþ mid his dīgelan tōcyme, Homl. Ass. 54, 98. Gif se hīrēdes ealdor wiste ðæs ðeófes tōcyme, 54, 100. Ðone tōcyme ðæs Hālgan Gāstes, Blickl. Homl. 131, 12. Folc sceal gefeón on ðone his (*John the Baptist*) tōcyme, 167, 14. Se mæssepreóst, ðe se bisceop tō fundode . . . wyste his tōcyme, Homl. Skt. i. 3, 471. Hū hwōsta missenlīce on mon becume . . . Se hwōsta hæfþ manigfealdne tōcyme, Lchdm. ii. 56, 15. ¶ (1) *the coming of Christ to the world, the first* or *second Advent*:—Drihtnes tōcyme is his menniscnys. Hē com tō ūs ðā ðā hē genam ūre gecynd tō his Ælmihtigan Godcundnysse, Homl. Th. i. 600, 4. Swā byþ mannes Suna tōcyme, Mt. Kmbl. 24, 27, 37, 39. Hwilc tācn sī ðīnes tōcymes, 24, 3. Ðes middangeard ðe hē mid his tōcyme fram synnum gehǣlde, Homl. Ass. 47, 561. Ǣr Cristes tōcyme, Blickl. Homl. 81, 27. Ða ðe Cristes tōcyme wiston, 81, 10. Ða hālgan wītegan wītegodon ǣgðer ge ðone ǣrran tōcyme on ðære ācennednysse, and eác ðone æftran æt ðam micclum dōme, Homl. Th. i. 600, 23. (2) *the anniversary of Christ's coming, Advent*:—Ðeós tīd ōð midne winter is gecweden *Adventus Domini*, ðæt is Drihtnes tōcyme, Homl. Th. i. 600, 4. Ðū scealt healdan ðone tōkyme mid ealre ārwurðnesse, Lchdm. iii. 226, 7. [Efter Cristes tocyme, O. E. Homl. i. 89, 11.] v. hider-tōcyme.

tō-dǣl. v. tō-dāl.

tō-dǣlan; *p.* de *To divide, separate, distribute.* I. in the following glosses:—Ic tōdǣle *infindo*, Engl. Stud. xi. 66, 49: *discludo*, Wrt. Voc. i. 39, 31. Ic tōdǣle *dispono*, ii. 141, 45. Tōdǣlan *findere*, 37, 33. Tōdǣlende *discrepantes*, 25, 60: *dirimentes*, 28, 52: *diremtas*, 28, 32: 27, 48. Tōdǣled is *dispertitus est*, 26, 35: 73, 26. Sient tōdǣlede *dirimuntur*, 28, 53. Tōdǣlede *discretas*, 28, 33. Tōdǣldum *dilotis*, 25, 49. Tōdaeldum, 106, 36. Tōscirid ł tōdǣled *summotum*, Hpt. Gl. 528, 12. II. *to divide* a whole into parts, (1) *trans.*:—Hē tōdǣleþ hyne *he shall cut him asunder* (A. V.); dividet eum, Mt. Kmbl. 24, 51. Ðonne tōdǣlaþ hī his feoh on fīf oððe syx, Ors. 1, 1; Swt. 20, 27. Ðone ānne noman (woruld) ðū tōdǣldest on feówer gesceafta, Bt. 33, 4; Fox 128, 28. Hē Reádne Sǣ tōdǣlde *qui divisit Mare Rubrum in divisiones*, Ps. Th. 135, 13. Hié heora here on tū tōdǣldon *agmine diviso in duas partes*, Ors. 1, 10; Swt. 46, 16. Stānas bióþ earfoþe tō tōdǣlenne, Bt. 34, 11; Fox 150, 24. On twā tedǣled ys intinga tō syngienne *bipertita est causa peccandi*, Scint. 140, 13. Tōdǣldu wæteru *divisas aquas*, Past. 53; Swt. 413, 27. (2) *intrans.*:—Hēr tōdǣlde se foresprecena here on tū, Chr. 885; Erl. 82, 19. ¶ figuratively, *to destroy unity, make dissension in.* v. tō-dǣl, VIII:—Ǣlc rīce on hyt sylf tōdǣled byþ tōworpen. Gyf Satanas is tōdǣled on hine sylfne, hū stent his rīce? Lk. Skt. 11, 17, 18. II a. *to divide* a whole by assigning the limits of the different parts:—Iosue ðone eard gewann and ealne tōdǣlde, Ælfc. T. Grn. 6, 8. Philippus and Herodes tōdǣldun Lysiam, and Iudēam feówrīcum tōdǣldun, Chr. 12; Erl. 6, 4. Ðā wearþ ðæt rīce tōdǣled on .v., 887; Erl. 86, 1: 709; Erl. 42, 29. II b. *to divide* one number by another:—Tōdǣl ða twelf þurh fīf, Anglia viii. 328, 21: 304, 40. III. *to divide* one thing from another, *part, separate*, (a) *trans.*:—Ðonne se līchama and seó sāwul hī tōdǣleþ, Guthl. 20; Gdwin. 84, 13. Ðonne se earma līchama and seó wērige sāwul hī tōtwǣmaþ and tōdǣlaþ, Wulfst. 151, 11. Ongunnon ðæt monnes māgas hycgan, ðæt hȳ tōdǣlden unc, Exon. Th. 442, 14; Kl. 12. Hī ne māgon beón tōgædere genemnede, ac hī ne beóþ nǣfre tōdǣlede, Homl. Th. ii. 204, 28. (b) *intrans.*:—Swā tōdǣleþ se līchoma and seó sāwul, Wulfst. 149, 8. Nǣfre leófe ne tōdǣlaþ ne lāðe ne gemētaþ, 190, 2. IV. *to scatter, disperse*:—Drihten hig tōdǣlde of ðære stōwe geond ealle eorðan *the Lord scattered them abroad from thence upon the face of all the earth* (A. V.), Gen. 11, 8. Hē tōdǣlde ofermōdan *dispersit superbos*, Lk. Skt. 1, 51. Tōdael hié *dispertire eos*, Ps. Surt. 16, 14. Tōdǣlan heora geðeóde geond ðās woruld wīde, Ps. Th. 54, 8. Ealle his gefēran ðurh ōþre stōwe tōdǣlede wǣron *omnes socii per alia essent loca dispersi*, Bd. 3, 27; S. 558, 37: Gen. 10, 32. Wǣron tōdǣlede *dispargerentur*, Hpt. Gl. 518, 2. V. *to destroy*:—Ealle ðū his weallas wīde tōdǣldest *destruxisti omnes macerias ejus*, Ps. Th. 88, 33. Ne tōdēldun (hī) ðeóde *non disperdiderunt gentes*, Ps. Surt. 105, 34. VI. *to distribute, give away* parts of a whole. v. tō-dāl, VI:—Ic tōdǣle (*do*, Lk. 19, 8) healfne dǣl mīnra gōda ðearfum, Homl. Th. i. 582, 2. Hē tōdǣlþ his gife mannum, ii. 204, 10. Hē tōdǣlþ his hereреáf *spolia ejus distribuit*, Lk. Skt. 11, 22. Sume ealle hyra þearfum Godes tōdǣlaþ *quidam omnia sua pauperibus Dei distribuunt*, Scint. 58, 12. Tōdǣlan werum tō wiste fǣges flǣschoman, Andr. Kmbl. 303; An. 152. Tōdēlendes *distribuentis* (*dona*), Kent. Gl. 673. Hī wǣron tōdǣlende heora weoruldgōd syndrigum mannum, Bd. 1, 27; S. 489, 19. VII. *to divide* into shares, *to share*:—Sió sunne and se mōna habbaþ tōdǣled butwuht him ðone dæg and ða niht swīþe emne, Bt. 39, 13; Fox 234, 5. VIII. *to divide, distinguish, separate, make a difference between*:—Hū wundorlīce Drihten tōdǣlde ðæt Egiptisce folc and ðæt Israhēlisce folc, Ex. 11, 7. Beó nū leóht on ðære heofenan fæstnysse and tōdǣlon dæg and nihte, Gen. 1, 14. Hit hafaþ hāt baþo ǣlcere yldo and hāde ðurh tōdǣlede stōwe gescrǣpe (*per distincta loca accommodos*), Bd. 1, 1; S. 473, 22. IX. *to be different, be distinguished* from. v. tō-dāl, V:—Sacerd nāht tōdǣlþ fram folce *sacerdos nihil distat a populo*, Scint. 123, 19. Swā micelum swā tōdǣlan gewunaþ līf hyrdes fram hyrde *quantum distare solet uita pastoris a grege*, 120, 17. X. *to separate with the mind, discern, discriminate, distinguish.* v. tō-dāl, IX:—Gif geþanc yfel fram gōdum angytes mid gesceáde tōdǣlþ *si mens mala a* *bonis intellectus ratione discernit*, Scint. 141, 7. In gōman ðǽr mon ðone smæc tōdǽleþ *in palato*, Wrt. Voc. ii. 48, 4. Nū tōdǽlde Petrus swutelīce ðone sōðan geleáfan ðā ðā hē cwæð: 'Ðū eart ðæs lifigendan Godes sunu,' Homl. Th. i. 366, 31. Ðæt hig cunnon fægere tōdǽlan hwæt byþ betwux *ab animali ad animale* and *ab inanimale ad inanimale*, Anglia viii. 313, 35. Tōdǽled *discretus*, Scint. 123, 1. XI. *to give forth, utter* (?):—Ealle ða gehāt ðe ic ǽfre hēr mid mīnum welerum tōdǽlde (cf. mīn gehāt ðæt mīne weleras ǽr gedǽldan, v. 12, where Ps. Spl. and Ps. Surt. have tōdǽldon and the Latin is *vota quae distinxerunt labia mea*), Ps. Th. 65, 13. [*O. Sax.* te-dēlian: *O. Frs.* tō-dēla: *O. H. Ger.* ze-teilen *dividere, distribuere, dispertire, separare, spargere, scindere, distare*: *Ger.* zer-theilen: cf. *Goth.* dis-dailjan.]

tō-dǽledlīce; *adv. Separately, not in connection*:—Tōdǽledlīce *sigillatim*, Ps. Spl. 32, 15: *divise*, Ælfc. Gr. 38; Zup. 229, 9. Seó fīfte declinatio gebīgþ hire genitivum on *e* and *i* tōdǽledlīce (*the* e *and* i *are pronounced separately*), 7; Zup. 21, 14. Tōdǽledlīcor *differentius*, i. *eminentius*, Wrt. Voc. ii. 140, 14. v. tō-dǽlendlīce.

tō-dǽledness, e; *f. Division, distinction, separation*:—Tōdǽlednesse *discrimine*, Wrt. Voc. ii. 27, 63. I. *a division*, (a) *one of the different kinds of parts into which a whole may be divided*:—Feówertȳne tōdǽlednyssa synd on ðam dæge ... Ōðer tōdǽlednysse hātte *momentum*, þridde *minutum* ... feówerteóða *mundus*, Anglia viii. 318, 35-42. (b) *one of the parts into which a whole is divided*:—Wē wyllaþ tōdǽlan ða abecedaria on twā tōdǽlednyssa, 333, 5. II. *division, separation, break of connection* or *of continuity*, (a) local:—Fæder and Suna and se Hāliga Gāst būton ǽlcere tōdǽlednesse (-ennesse, MS.), Shrn. 167, 34. (b) temporal, *intermission, interruption*:—Fram Eástron ōð Pentecosten sȳ alleluia būtan tōdǽlednesse (*sine intermissione*) gecweden, R. Ben. 39, 14. III. *a division, dividing-point, break, pause*:—*Idus* tōdǽlednyssa ðæs mōnðes, Ælfc. Gr. 13; Zup. 85, 6. *Cesuras*, ðæt synd ða tōdǽlednyssa on ðām versum ... Ða tōdǽlednyssa on ðām versum synd feówer, Anglia viii. 313, 38.

tō-dǽlendlīc; *adj. Divisible, separable*:—Swā tōdǽlendlīc is līchama and sāwle, Wulfst. 264, 26.

tō-dǽlendlīce; *adv. Separably, distinctly*:—Ealle tōdǽlendlīce singende *omnia distincte psallendo*, Anglia xiii. 371, 78. Seó fīfte declinatio gebīgþ hire genitivum on *e* and *i* tōdǽlendlīce, Ælfc. Gr. 7; Zup. 21, 14 note. v. tō-dǽledlīce.

tō-dǽlness, e; *f. A division, distinct part*:—Tōdǽlnessa ðara wætera *divisiones aquarum*, Past. 53; Swt. 413, 26. In tōdǽlnesse *in divisiones*, Ps. Surt. 135, 13.

tō-dāl, -dǽl, es; *n. Division.* I. *a dividing* into parts, *partition*:—Mid þrȳnum tōdāle *trina partitione*, Anglia xiii. 380, 217. II. *separation*:—Tōdāl *distractio*, Hpt. Gl. 500, 35. Sume naman synd *dividua*, ða getācniaþ tōdāl, Ælfc. Gr. 5; Zup. 13, 12. III. *a part* of a whole, *separate portion, section*:—Stæfcræft hæfþ þrītig tōdāl (cf. sum ðæra dǽla is gehāten *nota*, 291, 9). Ðæt forme tōdāl is *vox* stemn ... Sume tōdāl sindon *pedes*, Ælfc. Gr. 50; Zup. 289, 15-290, 13. Tōdāl *divisiones*, Kent. Gl. 766. Capitulas, ðæt is tōdāla angin, R. Ben. 42, 1. Ðæra ǽgðer on þrīm tōdālum wunaþ, Lchdm. iii. 440, 31. IV. *a mark which divides, dividing-point*:—Tōdāl *comma*, Engl. Stud. xi. 65, 9. *Distinctiones*, ðæt sind tōdāl, hū man tōdǽlþ ða fers on rǽdinge. Se forma prica on ðam ferse is gehāten *media distinctio*, ðæt is on middan tōdāl . . . *Distinctio* is tōdāl, Ælfc. Gr. 50; Zup. 291, 2-7. Tōdālæ *commate, incisione*, Hpt. Gl. 473, 22. Þurh fīftan fōtes tōdāl *per penthemimerim*, 411, 12. Tōdāl *commata, incisiones, divisiones*, 411, 10. Tōdāla *incisiones*, Engl. Stud. xi. 66, 48. V. *distinction, difference*. v. tō-dǽlan, VIII, IX:—Tōdāl *differentia, divisio, distantia*, Hpt. Gl. 434, 48. Nā byþ tōdāl mǽþa *nulla erit distantia personarum*, Scint. 184, 1. *Differentia*, ðæt is tōdāl betwux twām þingum, Ælfc. Gr. 50, 20; Zup. 293, 18. Micel tōdāl is betwux ðām gecyrredum mannum, Homl. Th. i. 398, 20: 48, 35. Tōdāles *differentiae, distantiae*, Hpt. Gl. 439, 1. Tōdāl *distantiam*, 438, 28. VI. *distribution*. v. tō-dǽlan, VI:—On rāpincle tōdāles (-dǽles, Ps. Spl.) *in funiculo distributionis*, Blickl. Gl. Dihtung upplīces tōdāles, Scint. 227, 8. On tōdāle gyfa onfōþ mislīce gyfa *in divisione donorum diversi percipiunt diversa munera*, 133, 8. VII. *scattering, dispersing*. v. tō-dǽlan, IV:—On tōdāle *effusione*, Wrt. Voc. ii. 142, 67. VIII. *dissension, want of union* or *peace*. v. tō-dǽlan, II. ¶:—For ðam ðe ic com sybbe on eorþan sendan; ne secge ic eów, ac tōdāl (*separationem*), Lk. Skt. 12, 51. IX. *discretion*. v. tō-dǽlan, X:—Nēdbehēfes gerādes tōdāl *necessarie rationis discretio*, Anglia xiii. 375, 132. Fremfullum gesceádes tōdāle, 369, 52. Mid tōdǽle *cum discretione*, Scint. 81, 2. v. under-tōdāl.

tō-dāllīc. v. un-tōdāllīc.

tō-dēman; *p.* de *To judge between, distinguish*; dijudicare:—Tōscǽt ł tōdēmeþ *dijudicat*, Ps. Lamb. 81, 1. Mihtig Freá eall manna cynn tōdǽleþ and tōdēmeþ *the mighty Lord will divide and will distinguish in his judgement between all mankind*, Dōm. L. 20.

tō-dihtnian; *p.* ode *To dispose*:—Tōdihtnodon *disposuerunt*, Blickl. Gl.

tō-dōn; *p.* -dyde. I. *to put asunder, divide, separate*:—Ðæt wæter and seó eorðe wǽron gemengede ōð ðone ðriddan dæg; ðā tōdyde hī God, Hexam. 4; Norm. 8, 15. Gif hwylc wīf twēgen gebrōðra nimþ hire tō gemæccan, ōþerne æfter ōþrum, tōdō man hig (*separentur*), L. Ecg. P. ii. 11; Th. ii. 186, 10. Tōdō man hig on twā *separentur illi*, 19; Th. ii. 188, 27. II. *to undo, open*:—Tōdyde *solvit, disligat*, Germ. 402, 39. Hī tōdydon heora mūð ongeán mē *aperuerunt in me os suum*, Ps. Th. 21, 11. [Þat deor todede (undude, 2nd MS.) his chæfles, Laym. 6507. Ic uulle mine riche todon allen minen dohtren, 2945.]

tō-drǽfan; *p.* de *To drive asunder, drive in different directions, drive away, expel, dispel, scatter, disperse*:—God ða hǽðenan tōdrǽfþ (*disperdet*), Jos. 3, 10. Seó sunne tōdrǽfþ ða nihtlīcan þeóstru, Lchdm. iii. 234, 30. Hāligra manna ðe tōdrǽfaþ ða leahtras and deófla heom fram, Homl. Skt. ii. 25, 703. Hē is sōð leóht ðe tōdrǽfde ða þeóstra ðises līfes, Homl. Th. i. 144, 7. Hī mynstra tōstæncton, and munecas tōdrǽfdon, Chr. 975; Erl. 127, 22. Ðæt hē tōdrǽfe costnunga fram ūre heortan, Homl. Th. i. 156, 23. Fela wearð tōdrǽfed Godes ðeówa, Chr. 975; Erl. 126, 12. Heora heriges wæs mycel ofslægen and eall tōdrǽfed *cunctus eorum caesus sive dispersus exercitus*, Bd. 3, 18; S. 546, 36. Byþ seó heord tōdrǽfed *dispargentur oves gregis*, Mt. Kmbl. 26, 31. Beón ða scēp tōdrǽfede, Mk. Skt. 14, 27. [A lutel windes puf mei al todreven hit, A. R. 254, 1. Of þan folck þe wes todrefed, Laym. 330.] v. tō-drīfan.

tō-drǽfedness, e; *f. Dispersion, expulsion*:—Hē worhte āne swipe of rāpum and hī ealle ūt āscynde. Ðeós tōdrǽfednys getācnode ða tōweardan tōworpennysse, Homl. Th. i. 406, 8. On ðeóda tōdrǽfednysse *in dispersionem gentium*, Jn. Skt. 7, 35. Tōdrǽfednesse *dispersiones*, Ps. Lamb. 146, 2.

tō-drǽfness, e; *f. Division, difference*:—Tōdroefnise wæs him bituién ymb ðæt *schisma erat in eis*, Jn. Skt. Lind. 9, 16.

tō-dreósan; *p.* -dreás; *pl.* -druron; *pp.* -droren *To fall to pieces, fall away, decay*:—Ðæt goldgeweorc eall tōdreás, swā swā weax gemylt æt fȳre, Shrn. 156, 15. [He schal todreosen so lef on bouh, Misc. 94, 48. Alle þe bones beoþ todrore, 152, 182. Cf. *Goth.* dis-driusan.] Cf. tō-feallan.

tō-drīfan; *p.* -drāf, *pl.* -drifon; *pp.* -drifen *To drive in different directions, drive away.* I. *to drive asunder, separate*:—Wit ætsomne on sǽ wǽron fīf nihta fyrst, ōþþæt unc flōd tōdrāf, Beo. Th. 1095; B. 545. II. *to scatter, disperse*:—Se wulf tōdrīfþ (tōdrīfeð, Lind. Rush.) ða sceáp *lupus dispergit oves*, Jn. Skt. 10, 12. Wulfas tōdrīfaþ ðīne heorde, Blickl. Homl. 225, 18. Ðū hī wīde tōdrīf *disperge illos*, Ps. Th. 58, 11. Hē hī wolde on ðam wēstenne wīde tōdrīfan *ut prosterneret eos in deserto*, 105, 21. Wurde seó eorþe tōdrifen mid ðam winde swā swā dust, Bt. 33, 4; Fox 130, 8: Met. 20, 104. Licgaþ æfter lande loccas tōdrifene, Andr. Kmbl. 2852; An. 1428. III. *to scatter, destroy*:—Hē hī on heora fācne fæste tōdrīfeþ *in malitiis eorum disperdet illos Dominus*, Ps. Th. 93, 22. Ðū mīne feóndas tōdrīfe *disperdes inimicos meos*, 142, 12. IV. *to drive away, send elsewhere*:—Ðū ūs tōdrife *repulisti nos*, Ps. Th. 59, 1. Fram āswengde *vel* tōdrāf *excussit, i. dejecit*, Wrt. Voc. ii. 146, 18. Dryhten āwearp hine ðā of ðam wuldre and wīde tōdrāf, Salm. Kmbl. 928; Sal. 463. Se ðe æfter rihte wille æfter spyrian swā deóplīce, ðæt hit tōdrīfan ne mæg monna ǽnig ne āmerran ǽnig eorðlīc þincg *quisquis vestigat verum, cupitque nullis ille deviis falli*, Met. 22, 3. Ða tōdrifenan *actos*, Wrt. Voc. ii. 9, 58. V. *to drive away, dispel, put an end to*:—Gāte tord ða swylas tōdrīfþ, Lchdm. i. 356, 1. Ða springas hyt tōdrīfeþ, 7. Se hālga deófulgild tōdrāf and gedwolan fylde, Andr. Kmbl. 3372; An. 1690. Tōdrīf ðone mist ðe nū hangaþ beforan ūres mōdes eágum *disjice nebulas*, Bt. 33, 4; Fox 132, 32: Met. 20, 264. Wearð se hāta līg tōdrifen and tōdwæsced, Cd. Th. 238, 11; Dan. 353. [Al he todrof þes kinges here, Laym. 549. Hiss stren all shollde ben todrifenn and toskeȝȝredd, Orm. 16397. *O. Frs.* tō-drīva: *O. H. Ger.* ze-trīban *dispellere, dispergere, diverberare.*] v. tō-drǽfan.

tō-dwæscan; *p.* te *To extinguish*:—Wearð se hāta līg tōdrifen and tōdwæsced, Cd. Th. 238, 11; Dan. 353: Exon. Th. 190, 2; Az. 67.

tō-dwīnan; *p.* -dwān *To vanish away, to burst and vanish*:—Seó eádiga fǽmne hāl fram him gewænte and eall sticmǽlum tōdwān (-dwān? *but both* þwīneþ *and* dwīneþ *occur*, Lchdm. i. 84, 25: 82, 2) se draca ūt of ðan carcerne *the dragon burst all in pieces and vanished from the prison* (the Latin has: Crux crevit in ore draconis et in duas partes eum divisit. Cf. the later English version: His (*the dragon's*) bodi tobarst omiddheppes, Marh. 10, 22), Homl. Ass. 175, 200. v. dwīnan, for-dwīnan.

tō-eácan; *adv., prep.* I. *adv. In addition, besides*:—Hē beád his þegnum, ðæt hig lēdon hira ǽlces feoh on his sacc and fōrmete tōeácan (*datis supra cibariis in viam*), Gen. 42, 25. Ðū hæfst tōeácan eall ðæt ic ðē ǽr tealde, Bt. 10; Fox 28, 37. Ōþre fīfe ic tōēke gestriónde *alia quinque superlucratus sum*, Mt. Kmbl. Rush. 25, 20. Micel git hēr tōeácan, Wulfst. 165, 21. II. *prep. with dat. In addition to, besides*:—Tōeácan ðæs landes sceáwunge, Ors. 1, 1; Swt. 17, 35. Tōeácan hiere hwætscipe and hiere monigfealdum duguþum, 1, 10; Swt. 46, 24. Ða breósð tōeácan ðæm boge *pectusculum cum armo*, Past. 14; Swt. 81, 25. Tōēcan ðām dōmum, L. Ath. v. proem.; Th. i. 228, 9. Tōeácan ðon ðe hine God sylf innan manode, Blickl. Homl. 217, 5. Tōēcan ðæm ðe hē hiénende wæs his folc, hē wæs sinþyrstende monnes blōdes, Ors. 3, 9; Swt. 130, 30. v. þǽr-tōeácan; eáca.

tō-écness. v. tō-ícness.

tō-efnes, -emnes; *prep. with dat. On a level with, abreast of, alongside, beside*:—Andlang weges ōð tōemnes ðære micelan dīc *the boundary runs along the road until it comes on a level with the great dike*, Cod. Dip. Kmbl. ii. 251, 3. Ondlang brōces ōð hyt cymþ tōemnes ðæm ealdan lǽghrycge, iii. 437, 17. *See other instances under* emn.

tō-endebyrdness, e; *f. Order, series, succession*:—Hē eallum mannum megena weorc mid wordum bodode. And tōendebyrdnesse his gesihþa ðām mannum ānum hit cȳþan wolde, ðam ðe hine ācsodon for ðam luste inbryrdnesse *omnibus opus virtutum praedicabat sermonibus. Ordinem autem visionum suarum, illis solummodo qui propter desiderium compunctionis interrogabant, exponere volebat*, Bd. 3, 19; S. 549, 20.

tō-fær, es; *n. A going away, departure, decease*:—Tōfær his *excessum ejus*, Lk. Skt. Lind. 9, 31. v. next word, III.

tō-faran; *p.* -fōr; *pp.* -faren. I. *to go in different directions, go off separately, part*:—On sumera tōfōr se here, sum on Eást-Engle, sum on Norðhymbre, Chr. 897; Erl. 94, 25. Ðā hié tōgædere woldon, ðā com swā ungemetlīc rēn, ðæt heora nān ne mehte nānes wǽpnes gewealdan, and for ðæm tōfōran, Ors. 4, 10; Swt. 194, 19. Tōfōran on feówer wegas æðelinga bearn *they went off in four different directions*, Cd. Th. 102, 8; Gen. 1697. Ǽr ðam ðe his Apostolas tōfarene wǽron geond ealle eorðan tō lǽranne, L. Alf. 49; Th. i. 56, 4. II. *to disperse* (intrans.), *scatter*:—Swelce se bitresta smīc upp āstīge and ðonne wīde tōfāre, Ors. 3, 11; Swt. 142, 21. Ǽr seó mengeo eft tōfaran sceolde, Cd. Th. 100, 15; Gen. 1664. Ōþ his fird tōfaren wæs *until his army was dispersed*, Ors. 3, 11; Swt. 152, 21. Ðonne hié gind ðæt lond tōfarene wǽron, hié ðonne hié floccmælum slōgan, 2, 5; Swt. 78, 12: 3, 7; Swt. 116, 29. III. *to go away, pass off, depart, become extinct.* v. tō-fær:—Syle drincan . . . ðæt yfel tōfærþ, Lchdm. i. 118, 6. Syle drincan on wīne, eal ðæt āttor tōfærþ, 122, 18. [The folk . . . shall tofare on every clyve, Anglia iii. 546, 146. *O. Sax.* te-faran *to disperse; to pass away*: *O. L. Ger.* te-faran *deficere*: *O. H. Ger.* ze-faran *dissolvi, praeterire, transire, perire, defluere.*] v. tō-fēran, -gān, -gangan.

tō-feallan; *p.* -feóll; *pp.* -feallen *To fall to pieces, fall away, collapse, fall down*:—Ðā hié æt hiora theatrum wǽron, ðā hit eall tōfeóll (*collapsa est*), Ors. 6, 2; Swt. 256, 11. Ðā byfode seó eorðe, and stānas burstan, and stānweallas tōfeóllan, Shrn. 67, 19: Homl. Th. ii. 216, 4. Him ða lima ealle tōfeóllan *all his limbs fell off*, Shrn. 62, 3. [Scullen stanwalles biuoren him tofallen, Laym. 18867. Alls þatt temmple oferr hemm all tofelle, Orm. 16185. Þer no guod red ne ys þet uolk toualþ (*populus corruet*, Prov. 11, 14), Ayenb. 184, 11. *O. Sax.* te-fallan *to fall down* (of a house): *O. H. Ger.* ze-, zer-fallan *cadere, concidere, diruere*: *Ger.* zer-fallen.] v. tō-dreósan; tō-fillan.

Tōfe-ceaster *Towcester*:—Mon worhte ða burg æt Tōfeceastre, Chr. 921; Erl. 107, 26. [Cf. Tōfi, Tōfa, *Scandinavian proper names.*]

tō-feng (?: *but* cf. *the expression* fōn tō), es; *m. Taking, seizure*:—Se ðe ne sealde ūs on gehæfte ł tōfængce (tō fængce?) tōðum heora *qui non dedit nos in captionem dentibus eorum*, Ps. Lamb. 123, 6.

tō-fēran; *p.* de. I. *to go in different directions, go off separately*: —Ǽr ūres Drihtnes leorningcnihtas tōfērdan, ealswā heom beboden wæs (cf. Mk. 16, 15), Wulfst. 21, 5: Homl. Th. i. 318, 3. II. *to disperse* (intrans.):—Ðā ðæt gafol gelǽst wæs, ðā tōfērde se here wīde swā hē ǽr gegaderod wæs, Chr. 1012; Erl. 147, 27. Hī geswicon ðære getimbrunge, and tōfērdon geond ealne middangeard, Homl. Th. i. 22, 25: 318, 21. Hī tōfērdon tō fyrlenum lande on swā manegum gereordum swā ðæra manna wæs, Ælfc. T. Grn. 4, 12. [Ða apostoli er þon þet heo toferden, O. E. Homl. i. 93, 8. *O. H. Ger.* ze-fuoren.] v. tō-faran, -gān.

tō-ferian; *p.* ede *To carry in different directions*; differre. I. *to remove, get rid of*:—Hit ðæt sār tōfereþ, Lchdm. i. 114, 3: 108, 8: 130, 19: 190, 8. II. *to put off*:—Swā oft gebiddende nā raþe beóþ gehȳrede ūre ūs dǽda on eágum wē tōforan settan ðæt ðæt sylfe ðæt wē synd tōferede nā godcundre byþ geteald rihtwīsnysse ac gyltes ūres *quotiens orantes non cito exaudimur, nostra nobis facta in oculis proponamus, ut hoc ipsum quod differimur non divinae reputetur justitiae sed culpe nostre*, Scint. 35, 10. III. *to digest*; digerere:—Ðæt seó dæges þigen tōfered sȳ . . . and se maga gelȳht, ðæt hē ðe eáð his wæccean healdan mǽge *ut digesti surgant*, R. Ben. 32, 14.

tō-fesian; *p.* ede *To drive in different directions, disperse, scatter, rout*:—Gē eów tō gamene feónda āfillaþ oððe tōfesiaþ swā fela swā gē reccaþ, Wulfst. 132, 21. Gē tōfesede swīðe āfirhte oft litel werod earhlīce forbūgaþ, 133, 2.

tō-fillan; *p.* de *To cause to fall in different directions, to demolish, destroy, break to pieces*:—God heáfdas feónda gescǽneþ and hē tōfylleþ feaxes scādan ðe hēr on scyldum swǽrum eodon *Deus conquassabit capita inimicorum suorum; verticem capilli perambulantium in delictis suis*, Ps. Th. 67, 21. [*Ger.* zer-fällen.] v. tō-feallan.

tō-fleógan; *p.* -fleág, *pl.* -flugon; *pp.* -flogen. I. *to fly asunder, fly to pieces*:—Hē slōh ða næddran, ðæt heó on viiii tōfleáh *he struck the adder so that it flew into nine pieces*, Lchdm. iii. 34, 26. II. *to fly apart, to crack, have breakings out* (of a diseased body):—Wið hreófe and wið tōflogen līc *for leprosy and for a body that has breakings out on it*, Lchdm. i. 352, 18. [*O. H. Ger.* ze-fliogan *dissipari.*]

tō-fleón; *p.* -fleáh, *pl.* -flugon; *pp.* -flogen *To flee in different directions, be dispersed in flight, flee away*:—Gif wæter on eáran swīðe gesigen sȳ, genim ðysse ylcan wyrte seáw, drȳpe on ðæt eáre; sōna hyt tōflȳð (-flīhð, MSS. H. B.) *the water will run away directly*, Lchdm. i. 188, 8. [Þa cnihtes alle weoren wide toflo3en ut of þan wiðeruehte, Laym. 28668.]

tō-fleótan; *p.* -fleát; *pp.* -floten *To float in different directions, be dispersed by water, be carried away by water*:—Ða brycge ðe forneáh eall tōflotan wæs *the bridge that was almost quite carried away*, Chr. 1097; Erl. 24, 299. [Mid te fleotinde word tofleoteð þe heorte, so þ longe þer efter ne mei heo beon ariht igedered togederes, A. R. 74, 29. Forstoppeð ouwer þouhtes, ase 3e wulleð þ heo nout ne touleoten 3eond te world, 72, 22. *O. H. Ger.* ze-fliozan *defluere, liqui, fatiscere*: *Ger.* zer-fliessen.]

tō-flōwan; *p.* -fleów; *pp.* -flōwen *To flow different ways, disperse in flowing, flow away*:—Ic tōflōwe *defluo*, Ælfc. Gr. 28, 5; Zup. 175, 14. Tōfleówan ł ūt urnan *defluxerant*, Hpt. Gl. 473, 37. I. referring to material objects, (a) *to flow in different directions, be dispersed*:—Iudas tōbærst on emtwā and his innoð tōfleów, nāteshwōn gelōgod on nānre byrgene, Homl. Th. ii. 250, 26. Him (*the stream*) on innan felþ muntes mægenstān . . . hē on tū siððan tōsceáden wyrð . . . brōc biþ onwended of his rihtryne rȳðum tōflōwen, Met. 5, 20. (b) *to melt away, be destroyed*:—Swā hwæt swā ðeós gesyhþ oþþe hrepeþ, hyt tōflēwþ swā ðæt ðǽr nānwiht belīfeþ būton ða bān, Lchdm. i. 242, 26. Muntas swē swē wex tōfleówun (*fluxerunt*), Ps. Surt. 96, 5. II. metaphorically, (a) of want of concentration in the mind, *to wander, be drawn hither and thither, be distracted*:—Nān wuht nis on ūs ungestæððigre ðonne ðæt mōd, for ðæm hit gewītt suā oft fram ūs suā ūs unnytte geðohtas tō cumaþ, and æfter ǽlcum ðara tōflēwþ *nil in nobis est corde fugacius, quod a nobis toties recedit, quoties per pravas cogitationes defluit*, Past. 38; Swt. 273, 13. Hié nellaþ hié gehæftan and gepyndan hiora mōd, ac hē lǽt his mōd tōflōwan on ðæt ofdele giémeliéste, 39; Swt. 283, 14. Gebyreþ oft ðæt hié beóþ suā micle ungestæððelīcor tōflōwene on hiera mōde suā hié wēnaþ ðæt hié orsorgtran beón mǽgen *quae tanto latius diffluunt, quanto se esse securius aestimant*, 38; Swt. 271, 18. (b) *to be separated, take different directions*:—Hū ungelīc sprǽc eode of ðissa tuēga monna mūðe. . . . ðeáh heó an tū tefleówe, ðeáh wæs sió ǽspryng sió sōðe lufu, Past. 7; Swt. 49, 11. (c) *to spread*:—Suā willaþ ða synna weaxænde tōflōwan gif hié ne beóþ gebundne mid lāreówdōme, Past. 17; Swt. 123, 16. (d) *to pass away, be dissipated, scattered, rendered useless, brought to nothing*:—Ðæt wē gemundan ðæt ūre dǽde and ūre geþohtas nalæs on ðisne wind on īdelnesse tōflōwan (tōflōwenne, Bd. M. 440, 24) ac tō dōme ðæs heán dēman ealle gehealdene beón *ut meminerimus facta et cogitationes nostras non in ventum diffluere, sed ad examen summi judicis cuncta servari*, Bd. 5, 13; S. 633, 27. Of ðære tīde ongan se hyht and mægen Angelcynnes rīces tōflōwan and gewanod beón *ex quo tempore spes coepit et virtus regni Anglorum fluere, ac retro sublapsa referri*, 4, 26; S. 602, 28. (e) *to separate in confusion, become disconnected*:—Ic ongite ðæt ealle gesceafta tōfleówon swā swā wæter, and nāne sibbe ne nāne endebyrdnesse ne heóldon, gif hī næfdon ǽnne God ðe him eallum stiórde, Bt. 34, 12; Fox 154, 2.

tō-flōwedness, e; *f. A flowing, flux*; fluxus, Ælfc. Gr. 11; Zup. 79, 1.

tō-flōwende; *adj.* (*ptcpl.*) *Affluent, confluent*:—Ðæs tōflōwendan welan *affluentibus prosperitatibus*, Past. 50; Swt. 391, 11. Tōflōwendum *confluentibus*, Wrt. Voc. ii. 23, 62.

tō-foran; *prep. with dat., gen. Before.* I. of place, *in front of, in presence of*, (a) preceding the case:—Ealle þeóda beóþ tōforan (*ante*) him gegaderude, Mt. Kmbl. 25, 32. Hē ða hlāfas bræc and sealde his leorningcnihtum, ðæt hī tōforan him āsetton, Mk. Skt. 6, 41: 8, 6. Hē ðæt ylce gefæstnode tōforan ðam pāpan, Chr. 1070; Erl. 208, 19. (b) following the case:—Etaþ ðæt eów tōforan āset ys, Lk. Skt. 10, 8. Ic næbbe hwæt ic him tōforan lecge *non habeo quod ponam ante illum*, 11, 6. II. *of time, previous to*, (a) with dat.:—Tōforan eallum ðissum hig nimaþ eów *ante haec omnia inicient uobis manus suas*, Lk. Skt. 21, 12. Tōforan ðām Eástron, Chr. 1012; Erl. 146, 8. Tōforan ðam mōnðe Auguste, 1013; Erl. 147, 15. (b) with gen.:—Hit wæs tōforan dæges, Nar. 16, 11. III. marking degree, *above, in a greater degree than*:—Synfulle tōforan eallum *prae omnibus peccatores*, Lk. Skt. 13, 2. Gē beóþ gebletsod tōforan eallum ōðrum mannum, Deut. 7, 14: Homl. Th. i. 444, 30. Assa is stunt nȳten and tōforan ōðrum nȳtenum ungesceádwīs, 208, 12. IV. marking position or status, *superior to*:—Ðæt hē sȳ tōforan ōðrum mannum þurh his glencge geteald, Homl. Th. i. 528, 29. V. marking preference:—Habbaþ eów tōforan eallum ðingum ða sōðan lufe, Homl. Th. i. 606, 16: R. Ben. 55, 6. Tōforan eallum þingum wē myngiaþ, ðæt . . ., 58, 7: Wulfst. 239, 17. Tōforon, Bt. 42; Fox 260, 12. VI. marking excess, *over and above*, *beside, beyond*:—Tôforan ðám *praeterea*, Ælfc. Gr. 38; Zup. 234, 9. Tôforon ðám oððe bûtan ðám *praeter illa*, 47; Zup. 270, 9. Eall hit byþ oferflôwendnyss and ídel tôforan ðisum (ðæt tôforan ðysum is) *quod supra fuerit, superfluum est*, R. Ben. 90, 5. Swâ hwæt swâ tôforan ðám neádbehêfum belifen byþ, 138, 16. Salomon forgeaf ðære cwêne swâ hwæs swâ heó gyrnde æt him, tôforan (*over and above*) ðære cynelícan láce ðe hê hire geaf, Homl. Th. ii. 584, 31. For fela gewissungum ðe seó ân bôc hæfþ tôforan ðám ôðrum *for many directions which that one book has, and the others have not*, Ælfc. T. Grn. 6, 40. [*Piers P.* to-fore: *Ayenb.* to-vore: *O. Sax.* te-foran: *O. Frs.* tô-fora.] v. foran.

tô-forlǽten; *ptcpl. Dismissed*:—Tôforlǽten [is] *dimittitur*, Hpt. Gl. 420, 52. v. *next word, and* tô-lǽtan.

tô-forlǽtenness, e; *f. Intermission*:—Bûtan tôforlǽtennesse *sine intermissione*, R. Ben. Interl. 45, 11: Homl. Th. i. 596, 15: ii. 382, 1.

toft. A word apparently of Scandinavian origin, *Icel.* topt, tuft *a piece of ground, messuage, homestead; a place marked out for a house* or *building*; in the special later Icelandic sense *a square piece of ground with walls but without roof*: *Dan.* toft *an enclosed home-field.* It does not occur often in the earliest English, but it is found as the second part of many place-names in districts which were affected by the Danes. v. Taylor's Names and Places. In the Prompt. Parv. *toft* renders *campus*; in Piers Plowman it means an elevated piece of ground: I seigh a toure on a *toft*, Prol. 14; while later, according to Kennett, it is 'a field where a house or building once stood.' In the following passages it may mean *the enclosed ground in which the house stood*:—Healf ðæt land æt Súðhám, innur and útur, on tofte and on crofte, Cod. Dip. Kmbl. iii. 317, 7. Nǽfre myntan ne plot ne plôh, ne turf ne toft, L. O. 13; Th. i. 184, 7; Lchdm. iii. 286, 23. [Ic an] intô ðe túnkirke on Mardingford .v. acres and âne toft and .ii. acres mêdwe . . . And míne landseðlen here toftes tô ôwen aihte, Cod. Dip. Kmbl. iv. 282, 26-29. Alle míne men frê, and ilk habbe his toft and his metecû and his metecorn. And ic an þe prêstes toft intô þe kirke frê . . . And ic an Lêfquêne fiftêne acres and ân toft . . . And Alfwold habbe, mid tôn þe hê hêr hauede, .xvi. acres mid tofte mid alle, Chart. Th. 580, 6-27. v. Grmm. R. A. 539.

tog, es; *n. Strife, contention*:—Ða friðgeorne, ða ðe heá bûta êghwoelcum flíta and toge behaldan, Mt. Kmbl. Lind. 5, 9 note. [Cf. (?) *O. Frs.* toga *to treat with violence, pull about.*]

-tog. v. lang-tog (-toh), sceaft-tog.

toga *a leader* (only in compounds). [*O. Sax.* togo: *O. Frs.* toga: *O. H. Ger.* zogo: *Icel.* togi.] v. breóst-, folc-, here-toga.

tô-gædere, -gædre, -gadore; *adv. Together.* I. marking union, association, joining, mingling, etc.:—Ealle ðû nemdest tôgædere and hête woruld, Bt. 33, 4; Fox 128, 27: Met. 20, 56, 62. Gif ðû wið fŷre foldan and lagustreám ne mengdest tôgædere, 20, 112. Ðá com Godwine eorl and Swegen eorl and Harold eorl tôgædere, Chr. 1048; Erl. 178, 19: Ps. Th. 94, 1: Homl. Skt. ii. 30, 430. Ða stânas feóllon tôgædere, and wearþ geworht tô ânum wealle swâ, 27, 88. Ða ŷslan eft onginnaþ lúcan tôgædere, geclungne tô cleowenne, Exon. Th. 213, 17; Ph. 225. Hlemmeþ tôgædre grimme gôman, 363, 30; Wal. 61. In Danai ðære ié Asia and Europe hiera landgemircu tôgædre licgaþ, Ors. 1, 1; Swt. 8, 11. Heofon and eorðe hreósaþ tôgadore, Andr. Kmbl. 2875; An. 1440. II. marking hostile meeting:—Ðá hí tôgædere gân sceoldon ðá onstealdan ða heretogan ǽrest ðone fleám *when the battle should have been joined, the leaders were the first to fly*, Chr. 993; Erl. 132, 15: 998; Erl. 134, 18: Beo. Th. 5253; B. 2630. Ðá hí tôgædere cômon, ðá wolde se ealdorman beswícon ðone æþeling, and hí tôhwurfon bûton gefeohte, Chr. 1015; Erl. 152, 14: Ors. 4, 10; Swt. 202, 14. Hí ðǽr fæste tôgædere fêngon *they attacked one another fiercely*, Chr. 999; Erl. 134, 25: 1001; Erl. 137, 12. Hí fêngon tôgædere fæstlíce mid wǽpnum, Homl. Skt. ii. 25, 631. Hwænne hí tôgædere gâras bêron *when they should cross weapons*, Byrht. Th. 133, 48; By. 67. Ðá hí ǽrost tôgedore gerǽsdon ðá man ofslôh ðes Câseres gerêfan *at the first encounter Caesar's lieutenant was slain*, Chr. pref.; Erl. 5, 7. III. marking continuity:—Feówertig daga and feówertig nihta tôgædere, Gen. 7, 4: Homl. Th. i. 22, 3. Fæste .ii. dagas tôgædere, gif him mægen gelǽste, Lchdm. ii. 218, 2: 232, 19. [*O. Frs.* tô-gadera (-e).]

tôgædere-weard; *adv. In directions that will bring* (*people*) *together, will lead to meeting*:—Ða hwíle ðe hié tôgædereweard fundedon *while they were proceeding to meet one another*; Ptolemaeus occurrere bello Perdiccae parat, Ors. 3, 11; Swt. 146, 5. Ðá hié tôgædereweard fôron ðá flugon Pêne swâ hié eft selfe sǽdon . . . ǽr hié tôgædere geneálǽcten *when the armies were marching to meet one another, the Carthaginians fled, as they afterwards themselves said, before they were near meeting*; Ap. Claudius tam celeriter Poenos superavit, ut ipse rex ante se victum quam congressum fuisse prodiderit, 4, 6; Swt. 170, 22: 6, 36; Swt. 294, 21. Hê (= hié) hiera sundorsprǽce ðe hié betux ðǽm folcum tôgædereweard gesprǽcan tô unsibbe brohton and hié tô gefeohte geredon *their conference, which they* (*Scipio and Hannibal*) *held after going to meet one another between the armies, they brought to a hostile conclusion and prepared themselves for battle*, 4, 10; Swt. 202, 12.

tô-gægnes. v. tô-geagnes.

tô-gǽlan; *p.* de *To profane, violate*:—Míne rihtwísnessa gif hig besmítaþ ł tôgǽlaþ *si justitias meas profanauerint*, Ps. Lamb. 88, 32.

tô-gǽnan; *p.* de *To utter, pronounce*:—Hig spelliaþ ł hig tôgǽnaþ and sprǽcaþ unrihtwísnesse *effabuntur et loquentur iniquitatem*, Ps. Lamb. 93, 4. Cf. gânian.

tô-gân; *p.* -eode; *pp.* -gân. I. of living things, *to go in two different directions, to part, separate*:—Gif wíf and wer ǽne tôgâþ, Homl. Th. ii. 324, 2. Apollonius and Hellanicus tôeodon mid ðisum wordum, Ap. Th. 8, 23. Mycel wæl feóll on ǽgðre healfe, and ða heras him sylfe tôeodan, Chr. 1016; Erl. 156, 20. Æfter ðon ðe wit nû tôcyrraþ and tôgâne beóþ *postquam ab invicem digressi fuerimus*, Bd. 4, 29; S. 607, 20 MS. B. II. of material things, *to be sundered, to part*:—Ic tôgâ *dehisco*, Engl. Stud. xi. 65, 23. Hê slôh mid ânre gyrde on ða sǽ, and heó tôeode on twâ, Wulfst. 293, 15: Homl. Th. ii. 194, 19. Seó eá on emtwâ tôeode, 212, 22. Ðá tôeodon ða stânas, and geopenode ðæt get, H. R. 103. 22. III. *to go in many different directions, to disperse, go away*:—Ða wæteru tôeodon and wanedon *aquae ibant et decrescebant*, Gen. 8, 5. [Þe wlcne togað, O. E. Homl. i. 239, 25. Þe rede see toeode, 141, 6. He smat Frolle uppen þæne hælm þat he atwa helden (toȝeode, 2nd MS.), Laym. 23980. *O. H. Ger.* ze-gân: *Ger.* zergehen.] v. tô-gangan, -gengan, -faran.

tô-gang, es; *m. Access, approach*:—His tôgang (-gan, MS.) biþ ðearle strang, Lchdm. i. 364, 10. Sŷ getŷþod gebróþrum tôgang fŷres *concedatur fratribus accessus ignis*, Anglia xiii. 307, 457. Nânne hæfþ tôgang heortan onbryrdnyss *nullum habebit accessum cordis compunctio*, Scint. 173, 5.

tô-gangan; *p.* -gêng; *pp.* -gangen. I. *to go in different directions, to part*:—Æfter ðon ðe wit nû betweoh unc tôgongenne (tôgangne, Bd. M. 372, 3) beóþ *postquam ab invicem digressi fuerimus*, Bd. 4, 29; S. 607, 20. Ðá hié betwih him tôgangen (-gangende, Bd. M. 372, 20) wǽron *digredientes ab invicem*, S. 607, 36. II. *to go away, pass away*:—Ne tôgongeþ gumena hwylcum eáþe ðæt ic ðǽr ymb sprice *what I speak of does not easily pass away from any man* (it is a bow that speaks, and the reference is to a wound from a poisoned arrow), Exon. Th. 405, 30; Rä. 24, 10. v. tô-gân, -gengan, -faran.

tô-geagn; *prep. adv. Towards, in the direction of* an object:—Tôgeaegn iornaþ iúh monn *occurrit uobis homo*, Mk. Skt. Lind. 14, 13. [Wes heom toȝæn (aȝein, 2nd MS.) þe kaissere, Laym. 9792. *Du.* tegen: *Ger.* zu-gegen.] v. next word.

tô-geagnes, -gegnes, -geánes, -gênes. I. *prep.* (1) with dat. before or after it. (a) where there is motion towards the object governed by the word; (α) without idea of hostility, *towards, so as to meet*:—Sittas (*the translater has read* sed ite *as* sedite, *and taken it as* sedete) cuoeðað ðegnum his ðætte tôgeaegnes (-gægnes, Rush.) fǽres iúh *remain and tell his disciples that he will come to meet you*, Mk. Skt. Lind. 16, 7. Foerdon tôgægnes him *processerunt obviam ei*, Jn. Skt. Lind. Rush. 12, 13. Mann cumende heom tôgênes (tôgeegnas him, Lind.) *hominem venientem obviam sibi*, Mt. Kmbl. 27, 32. Eode seó ceasterwaru tôgeánes (-gægnas, Lind.) ðam Hǽlende, 8, 34. 'Ne côme gê nô tôgênes (-geánes, Cott. MSS.) mînum folce ðæt gê meahton standan on mînum gefeohte for Israhêla folce.' . . . Ðæt is ðonne ðæt hê fare tôgeánes Israhêla folce him mid tô gefeohtanne, Past. 15; Swt. 89, 17, 21. Ðá eode se cining him tôgeánes *egressus est rex in occursum ejus*, Gen. 14, 17. Symeon eode tôgeánes ðam cilde . . . Symeon eode hire tôgeánes, Homl. Th. i. 136, 14, 34. Faraþ him tôgênys (-geánes, MS. A.) *exite obviam ei*, Mt. Kmbl. 25, 6. Ðǽr him tôgênes manige cômon, Andr. Kmbl. 1313; An. 657. Bær man him tôgeánes ânre wydewan líc, Homl. Th. i. 60, 12: Blickl. Homl. 67, 7, 10. (β) with idea of hostility, *against, to meet*:—Hí fêrdon tôgeánes ðám hǽðenum *they marched to meet the heathens*, Homl. Th. i. 504, 27. Ðá fyrdode hê him tôgeánes, and wið him feaht, Chr. 835; Erl. 65, 24. Him ðǽr com tôgeánes Byrhtnoð ealdorman mid his fyrde, and him wið gefeaht, 993; Erl. 132, 5. Ða scipu fôran tôgênes him, 911; Erl. 100, 21. (b) where there is motion of the object governed by the word; (α) without idea of opposition, *in the way of, to meet the approach of, in readiness for, against the coming of*:—Biþ hit eft him togeánes gehealden *it shall be preserved against his coming*, Blickl. Homl. 53, 14. Ðæt folc, ðæt ðǽr beforan fêrde, streówodan heora hrægl him tôgeánes, 71, 8. Geseóþ ðæt hê ǽrest tô ðære sinoþstôwe cymeþ and gesiteþ, and gif hê âriseþ tôgeánes eów ðonne gê cumen (*si vobis adpropinquantibus adsurrexerit*), Bd. 2, 2; S. 503, 10: Homl. Th. ii. 52, 13. Gâstum tôgeánes, Cd. Th. 146, 30; Gen. 2430. Gewít ðû âwyrgda in ðæt wítescræf, ðê is susl weotod gearo tôgegnes, 308, 15; Sat. 693. Gearwian ûs tôgênes grêne strǽte, 282, 15; Sat. 287. Tôgeánes, Exon. Th. 450, 21; Dôm. 91. Ðǽr biþ oft open eádgum tôgeánes heofonríces duru, 198, 17; Ph. 11. (β) with the idea of opposition, *against, for the purpose of resisting*:—Hêr com Ôlâf cyng intô Norwegum, and ðet folc gegaderode him tôgeánes and him wið gefuhton, Chr. 1030; Erl. 163, 17. Hê forlêt his gingran tôgeánes ðære ceáste *he left his lieutenant to oppose the tumult*, Homl. Skt. i. 7, 212. Hæfde hê Grendle tôgeánes seleweard âseted, Beo. Th. 1336; B. 666. (c) marking the object towards or against which an action is directed:—

Ðā clypode se eádiga Godes ðeów him tōgeánes *the blessed servant of God cried out addressing him*, Homl. Th. ii. 168, 17. Hī biton heora tēð him tōgeánes *they gnashed on him with their teeth* (Acts 7, 54), i. 46, 28. Hnigon mid heáfdum heofoncyninge tōgeánes, Cd. Th. 16, 3; Gen. 238. Ðæt hē gewyrce deórum dǣdum deófle tōgeánes, Exon. Th. 310, 18; Seef. 76. Ne underfēhþ hē nā gerȳnu for him sylfum ac gecȳðnysse tōgeánes him sylfum, Homl. Th. ii. 276, 35. Hī cwǣdon gefeoht tōgeánes ðære burhware *they declared war against the citizens*, i. 504, 13. (d) marking time, *on the approach of, towards*:—Tōgeánes Eástron com ðæs pāpan sande *the pope's legate came towards Easter*, Chr. 1095; Erl. 232, 27. (e) marking comparison or contrast:—Hū mæg manna eádmōdnys beón mycel geþūht tōgeánes his eádmōdnysse ðe ælmihtig God is, Homl. Skt. i. 12, 288. (2) with acc.; instances of this government are rare, and the two following are doubtful:—Tōgeánes his fȳnd (feónd, MSS. C. U. W.: feónde, MS. D.) hē gǣþ *adversum inimicum pergit*, Ælfc. Gr. 47; Zup. 269, 6. Ðā geopenode seó sǣ tōgeánes Moysen (*the declension of the word in the translation of Exodous is dat.* Moise; *acc.* Moise, Ex. 8, 8. Moises, 8, 25: 4, 27: 16, 2, etc.), Ælfc. T. Grn. 5, 26. II. *adv.* (1) *again, in return*:—Ic him ōðerne (gār) eft wille sændan, fleógende flāne forane tōgeánes, Lchdm. iii. 52, 25. Ðā hēt se wiðersaca onfōn ðæra hlāfa, and āgifan ðam biscope tōgeánes gærs . . . Basilius underfēng ðæt gærs ðus cweðende: 'Wē budon ðē ðæs ðe wē sylfe brūcaþ, and ðū ūs sealdest tō edleáne (cf. ðū sealdest ūs tōgeánes, Homl. Skt. i. 3, 220) ungesceádwīsra nȳtena andlyfene' *then bade the apostate to take the loaves, and to give the bishop grass in return . . . Basilius took the grass saying: 'We offered thee what we ourselves use, and thou hast given us as requital (thou hast given us in return) the sustenance of irrational beasts,'* Homl. Th. i. 450, 2–8: Homl. Skt. i. 3, 215. Cūðberhtus him tōgeánes cwæð *Cuthbert said to them in reply*, Homl. Th. ii. 138, 34. Hió him andsware ǣnige ne meahton āgifan tōgēnes, Elen. Kmbl. 333; El. 167. Him tōgēnes ðā gleáwestan mǣldon *in reply the wisest said to him*, 1069; El. 536. (2) marking position or direction:—Heó grāp tōgeánes *she made a clutch at him*, Beo. Th. 3006; B. 1501. Hē ārās tōgēnes, Andr. Kmbl. 2021; An. 1013. [*Laym.* tō-ȝeines, -ȝænes: *Orm.* to-ȝænes: *Ayenb.* to-yens: *O. Sax.* te-gegnes.] v. þǣr-tōgeánes.

tō-gecorenness, e; *f.* *Adoption*:—Tōgicorenisse gāst *adoptionis spiritum*, Rtl. 29, 28.

tō-gegnes. v. tō-geagnes.

tō-gehlytto *fellowship*:—Tōgihlytto *consortio*, Rtl. 109, 31.

tō-geīcendlīc; *adj.* *Adjective*:—Ða ōðre naman synd *adjectiva*, ðæt synd tōgeīcendlīce, Ælfc. Gr. 8; Zup. 29, 4: 9, 18; Zup. 44, 4.

tō-geīht; *adj.* (*ptcpl.*) *Added*:—*Interpolares* vel *additi*, ðæt synd ða tōgeīhte dagas, Anglia viii. 306, 44. v. next word.

tō-geīhtness, e; *f.* *An addition, increase*:—*Adjectiones*, ðæt synt tōgeīhtnyssa, Anglia viii. 302, 32.

tō-gēnes, togenness. v. tō-geagnes, for-togenness.

tō-gengan; *p.* de *To go different ways, to separate*:—Hié tōgengdon on ðone grēnan weald, sǣton on sundran, Cd. Th. 52, 9; Gen. 841. v. tō-gān, -gangan.

tō-geótan; *p.* -geát, *pl.* -guton; *pp.* -goten. I. *to diffuse, spread*:—Tōgiót *diffundet* (*venena*), Kent. Gl. 914. Ðonne wē swīðe wīde ūt tōgeótaþ ða lāre *quando exterius late praedicationem fundimus*, Past. 48; Swt. 375, 10. Ǣr ðon sió yfele wǣte, se ðe on wintra gesomnad biþ, hié tōgeóte geond ōþera lima, Lchdm. ii. 228, 9. Tōgoten is geofu in weolerum dīnum *diffusa est gratia in labiis tuis*, Ps. Surt. 44, 3. Mid ða Cristes cyricean, seó geond ealne middangeard tōgoten is, Bd. 2, 4; S. 505, 26. II. *to pour away, to exhaust*:—Ādrugod and tōgoten *dried up and exhausted* (said of an ointment), Lchdm. ii. 28, 7. v. tō-gotenness.

tō-gesceádan *to separate things from one another*; metaph. *to expound, interpret*:—Wæs ingunnen from Moyse and allum wītgum tōgisceóde him in allum gewriotum ða ðe of him wērun *incipiens a Mose et omnibus prophetis interpraetabatur illis in omnibus scripturis quae de ipso erant*, Lk. Skt. Rush. 24, 27. v. tō-sceádan.

tō-geþeód[d]; *adj.* (*ptcpl.*) *Adjacent, contiguous, connected, adjoined*:—Ðæt eálond tōsceádeþ Wantsumo streám fram ðam tōgeþeóddan lande *insula, quam a continenti terra secernit fluvius Vantsumu*, Bd. 1, 25; S. 486, 20.

tō-geþeódende *adhering*:—Tōgeþeóden(d)ne *adhaerentem*, Hpt. Gl. 485, 29.

togettan; *p.* te (*used impersonally*):—Togetteþ betweox sculdrum *there are spasms between the shoulders*, Lchdm. ii. 216, 22.

tō-gewegen; *adj.* (*ptcpl.*) *Applied*:—Ðæt se bisceop ðæt tōgewegh-ene fȳr ðære cynelīcan burghe onweg gewende *ut episcopus admotum ab hostibus urbi regiae ignem amoverit*, Bd. 3, 16; S. 542, 12.

togian; *p.* ode *To tug, drag, pull*:—Ða Godes wiðerwinnan ða fǣmnan genāmon, ūt of ðære byrig ungerǣdelīce hī togoden, Homl. Ass. 178, 308. [Cf. toggen *to toy*, A. R. 424, 27: Marh. 14, 6. Toggyñ *idem quod* strogelyn, toggyñ or drawyñ *tractulo*, toggynge, drawynge *attractulus*, Prompt. Parv. 495. *O. Frs.* toga *to pull about, treat roughly*: *O. H. Ger.* zocchōn *rapere*; zucchen *rapere*: *Icel.* toga *to draw, pull.*] v. for-togian; togung.

tōgian. v. tōan.

tō-gīnan; *p.* -gān; *pp.* -ginen *To yawn, gape, open* as the mouth does:—Eorðe tōgaan and eall forswealh Dathanes weorod *aperta est terra, et deglutivit Dathan*, Ps. Th. 105, 15. Se stān tōgān, streám ūt āweóll, Andr. Kmbl. 3044; An. 1525. Biþ ðæt heáfod tōhliden, handa tōlið-ode, geaglas tōginene, Soul Kmbl. 215; Seel. 110.

tō-glīdan; *p.* -glād; *pp.* -gliden *To glide in different directions, glide away.* I. of a fluid:—Synt geárdagas forð gewitene, līfwynne ge-liden, swā lagu tōglīdæþ, Elen. Kmbl. 2536; El. 1269. II. of smoke, cloud, or the like, *to be dissipated, dispersed, dispelled, to disappear, vanish, pass away*:—Ðā gedwinon his drȳcræftas, swā swā rēc ðonne hē tōglīdeþ, oððe weax ðonne hit for fȳre gemelteþ, Shrn. 135, 3. Hit biþ gelīc rēna scūrum, ðonne hī of heofonum swȳðost dreósaþ and eft raðe eall tōglīdaþ, Wulfst. 149, 7: 264, 2. Ðæt wolcn tōglād, Homl. Th. ii. 242, 11: Chr. 979; Erl. 128, 7. Nihthelm tōglād, lungre leórde, Andr. Kmbl. 246; An. 123: Elen. Kmbl. 156; El. 78. II a. metaph. of pain, care, or the like:—Sele drincan, sōna ðæt sār tōglīt, Lchdm. ii. 356, 21. Ðenden him hyra torn tōglīde, Exon. Th. 345, 3; Gn. Ex. 182. Hyge wearð mongum blissad, sāwlum sorge tōglidene, 71, 31; Cri. 1164. III. *to fall to pieces, collapse*:—Grundweal gearone, se tō-glīdan ne þearf, ðeáh hit wecge wind, Met. 7, 34. IV. *to slip away*:—Ðeáh ðe ðās cāseras him hāton gewyrcean heora byrgene of marmanstāne and ūtan emfrætewian mid reádum golde, ðeáhhwæðere se deáð hit eal tōdǣlþ; ðonne biþ ðæt gold tōsceacen, and ða gymmas tōglidene (*the gems have slipped from their settings*), Wulfst. 148, 18–24: 263, 8. Gūðhelm tōglād, gomela Scylfing hreás *the war-helm slipped off, the aged Scylfing fell*, Beo. Th. 4967; B. 2487. [Þeo luue þat ne may her abyde . . . hit schal toglide, Misc. 94, 43. *O. Sax.* te-glīdan *to pass away, come to nought.*]

tō-gotenness, e; *f.* *Diffusion, spreading, effusion*:—Wyþ ǣwyrdlan ðæs lichoman ðe cymeþ of tōgotennysse ðæs geallan, Lchdm. i. 262, 11: 270, 5. v. tō-geótan.

togung, e; *f.* *Spasm*:—Wið sina togunge, Lchdm. i. 136, 9, 19. v. togian.

tōh; *adj.* *Tough, tenacious, holding fast together*; lentus:—Tōh, tōch, thōch *lenta*, Txts. 73, 1198. Tōh, Wrt. Voc. ii. 49, 64. Ðæm tōn *lento*, 62. Ðǣm tōn *ab lentis*, 3, 48. I. *tough, pliant*:—Tōh (tōch, thōh) gerd *lentum vimen*, Txts. 75, 1207: Wrt. Voc. ii. 50, 74. II. *tough, sticky, glutinous, clammy*:—Nim hwetstān brādne and guīd ða buteran on ðæm hwetstāne mid copore ðæt heó beó wel tōh, Lchdm. iii. 16, 22. [Makeþ ȝoure speres toȝe and strang, Laym. 5865. Mid toȝen his mæine, 9319. Thei hadden towȝ cley for syment, Wick. Gen. 11, 3. Towhhe, not tender *tenax*, Prompt. Parv. 498. *Du.* taai *pliant, tough, clammy, sticky*: *O. H. Ger.* zāhi *tenax*: *Ger.* zähe.] v. tóan, tēan, tōhlīce.

tō-haccian; *p.* ode *To hack to pieces, cut to pieces*:—Sume hig wǣron on feówer dǣlas tōhaccode, eall swā hig ðæs Hǣlendes tunecan on feówer tōdǣldon, Homl. Ass. 186, 166. [To smale peces ich hym wolde to-hakke, R. Glouc. 141, 14. *O. Frs.* tō-hakkia: *M. H. Ger. Ger.* zer-hacken.]

tō-heald; *adj.* *Inclined*:—Tōhald *adclinis* vel *incumbens*, Txts. 37, 74. Tōheald *adclinis*, Wrt. Voc. i. 287, 74: ii. 4, 41. Þeáh wuhta gehwilc wrigaþ tōheald, swīðe onhelded, wið ðæs gecyndes ðe him cyning engla æt frymðe getióde, Met. 13, 10. [Cf. *O. H. Ger.* zuo-hald *futurus, venturus.*]

tō-heáwan; *p.* -heów; *pp.* -heáwen *To hew to pieces, cut to pieces*:—Se cāsere cwæð þæt Basilla sceolde gebūgan tō ðam cnihte, oþþe hī man tōheówe mid swurde on twā, Homl. Skt. i. 2, 360. Man sceolde ða scipu tōheáwan, Chr. 1004; Erl. 139, 26. Wē synd ealle belēwde tō ūre līfleáste, ðæt wē beón tōheáwene mid heardum swurdum, Homl. Ass. 99, 255. [Turnus feol mid mechen toheawen, Laym. 178. The helmes thei tohewen and toschrede, Chauc. Kn. T. 1751. To zenne ne ssel he wende ayen, þaȝ me ssolde hine al toheawe, Ayenb. 178, 7. *O. Frs.* tō-hawa: *M. H. Ger.* zer-houwen: *Ger.* zer-hauen.]

tō-higung, e; *f.* The word glosses *affectus*, Rtl. 18, 32: 31, 40: 7, 27: *effectus*, 35, 37: 63, 20. v. higian.

tohl. v. tōl.

tō-hladan; *p.* -hlōd; *pp.* -hladen *To disband, disperse*:—Ne meahte hié (*the builders of the tower of Babel*) gewurðan weall forð timbran, ac hié earmlīce heápum tōhlōdon hleóðrunt gedǣlde *they could not combine to carry on the building of the wall, but, divided in speech, they miserably dispersed in troops*, Cd. Th. 101, 36; Gen. 1693. Cf. 235, 6; Dan. 302.

tō-hlecan (?); *p.* -hlæc; *pl.* -hlǣcon; *pp.* -hlocen *To disjoin, pull to pieces*:—Tōhlocene (tōlocene? v. tō-lūcan; *but see also* hlec, hlecan. *In the glosses among which the word occurs initial* h *before a consonant does not seem to be inserted elsewhere, though it is twice omitted, in* lecum *rimosae*, 400, 69, wisligendre *sibilantis*, 394, 278) *diuulsa*, Germ. 398, 112.

tō-hleótan; *p.* -hleát, *pl.* -hluton; *pp.* -hloten *To divide into lots, to divide into parts for which lots are to be cast*:—Hȳ gedǣldan him mīn hrægl and ðæt tôhlutan *diviserunt sibi vestimenta mea et super vestem meam miserunt sortem*, Ps. Th. 21, 16. Hié (*the apostles*) ðysne middangeard on twelf tânum tôhluton, and ǽghwylc ânra heora in ðæm dǽle ðe hê mid tân geeode manige þeóde ûrum Drihtne gestreónde, Blickl. Homl. 121, 8.

tôh-lîc; *adj. Tough, tenacious.* v. next word.

tôhlîce; *adv. Toughly, tenaciously*:—Tôhlîce, thôlîcae, tôchtlîcae *uscide, viscide* (viscide *fortiter*, Migne), Txts. 107, 2170. Tôlîce *huscide*, 69, 1033.

tô-hlîdan; *p.* -hlâd, *pl.* -hlidon; *pp.* -hliden *To yawn, gape, open, crack* (intrans.), *split* (intrans.) *asunder*:—Tôhlâd seó eorþe *terra dissiluit*, Ors. 3, 3; Swt. 102, 26. Tôhlâd seó eorþe and wæs byrnende fŷr up of ðære eorþan *flamma scisso terrae hiatu eructata*, 4, 2; Swt. 160, 24: Lchdm. iii. 428, 3. Se beorg tôhlâd eorðscræf egeslîc *the hill yawned, an awful cave it grew*, Andr. Kmbl. 3173; An. 1589. Heofonas tôhlidon, Blickl. Homl. 105, 13. Tôhlîdan *dehiscere*, Germ. 400, 482. Biþ ðæt heáfod tôhliden *the head shall be cloven*, Soul Kmbl. 213; Seel. 109. Hié gesâwon swelce se hefon wǽre tôhliden *coelum scindi velut magno hiatu visum*, Ors. 4, 8; Swt. 188, 26. Wæs ðæt beorhte bold tôbrocen . . . heorras tôhlidene *the hinges shewed gaping cracks*, Beo. Th. 2002; B. 999. Gimmas tôhlidene, Wulfst. 263, 8 note.

toh-lîne, an; *f. A tow-line*:—Tohlîne *remulcum*, Wrt. Voc. i. 63, 64: *remulcus*, 57, 5. [Cf. *Icel.* tog *a rope, line: Scott.* tow *a rope of any kind.*]

tô-hlocen. v. tô-hlecan.

tô-hlystend, es; *m. A listener*:—On ðara tôhlystendra heortan . . . Hê gedêþ ða sprǽce unnytte ðǽm tôhlystendum, Past. 15; Swt. 96, 8, 18.

tô-hnescian; *p.* ode *To soften away*:—Ðonne findest ðû ðæt hearde tôhnesced, Lchdm. ii. 250, 21.

tô-hopa, an; *m. Hope, expectation*:—Eádig byþ se wer ðe his tôhopa byþ tô swylcum Drihtne *beatus vir cujus est nomen Domini spes ejus*, Ps. Th. 39, 4. Hwæt is mîn tôhopa *quae est expectatio mea?* 38, 9. On ðê ys eall ûre hǽl and ûre tôhopa *Domini est salus*, 3, 7. Wâ eów welegum ðe eówer lufu eall and eówer tôhopa is on eówrum worldwelum, Past. 26; Swt. 180, 24. Sió lufu and se geleáfa and se tôhopa *fides spes et caritas*, 21; Swt. 167, 19, 25: Shrn. 179, 1: Bt. 10; Fox 30, 8. Se tôhopa ðære wræce, Bt. 37, 1; Fox 186, 23: Met. 25, 50. Ðû mê gesettest on tôhopan (*in spe*), Ps. Th. 4, 9: 15, 9. Ymbe ðone tôhopan ðe gê habbaþ on eów *de ea, quae in vobis est, spe*, Past. 22; Swt. 173, 9. Ealne his tôhopan sette hê on God, L. E. I. 21; Th. ii. 416, 17. [Nimeþ tohope to helme *sumentes galeam spei*, O. E. Homl. i. 155, 8. *O. L. Ger.* tô-hopa.] v. tô-hyht.

tô-hopian. v. hopian (tô).

tô-hopung, e; *f. Hope, expectation*:—Wæs eall heora myne fæst on tôhopunge ðæs êcean Drihtnes, Homl. Skt. i. 23, 155. v. tô-hopa.

tô-hreósan; *p.* -hreás; *pl.* -hruron; *pp.* -hroren *To fall to pieces.* I. of buildings, *to go to ruin*:—Monige ôþre ceastre tôhrorene wǽron *multis civitatibus conlapsis*, Bd. 1, 13; S. 482, 8. Mynstru tôrorene *coenobia diruta*, Anglia xiii. 366, 12. II. of flesh, *to decay, rot away*:—Beóþ ða lîchaman tôhrorene (cf. gebrosnode, 148, 24) and tô duste gewordene, Wulfst. 263, 9. Beóþ fingras tôhrorene, Soul Kmbl. 219; Seel. 112. [Portchestre, al heo gunnen toreosen (todrese, 2nd MS.), mid fure and mid fehte foruaren, Laym. 9245. Þus Portchestre toræs (toreos, 2nd MS.), & nauere seodden heo ne aras, 9426.]

tô-hrêran; *p.* de *To shake to pieces, to destroy*:—Tôhrêrde *diruit*, Hpt. Gl. 487, 75. Se grundweall ðara munta wæs tôhrêred *fundamenta montium conturbata sunt*, Ps. Th. 17, 7. Tôhrêrede *diruta, destructa*, Hpt. Gl. 459, 50.

tô-hrician; *p.* ode *To divide, separate, cut up*:—Tôhricod *secta*, Germ. 398, 183: *dissipatum*, 399, 303. Tôhricedum *resectis*, 398, 100. Cf. Hrycigende *resulcans*, 398, 144.

tohte, an; *f. A military expedition, war, battle*:—Nǽron ða twêgen tohtan sǽne, lindgeláces, land Perséa sôhton sîðfrome Simon and Thaddeus, Apstls. Kmbl. 150; Ap. 75. Gê dôm âgon, tîr æt tohtan, Judth. Thw. 24, 19; Jud. 197. Ðæt wîf ðîn heáfod tredeþ mid fôtum sînum ðû scealt fiersna sǽtan tohtan *the woman shall tread thy head with her feet, thou shalt lie in wait to attack her heels*, Cd. Th. 56, 18; Gen. 914. Æt sæcce oferswîðan feónda gehwylcne, ðonne fyrdhwate on twâ healfe tohtan sêcaþ, Elen. Kmbl. 2358; El. 1180. [Cf. *O. Frs.* tocht-man *a leader: Ger.* zug *a march: Dan.* tog *expedition, march;* togt *a cruise, expedition.*] v. ge-toht, tyht, II, toga, teón, IV; *and* cf. fird.

tô-hweorfan; *p.* -hwearf, *pl.* -hwurfon; *pp.* -hworfen *To go in different directions, to part, separate.* I. of two persons or parties:—Ða cyningas cômon tôgædere and heora freóndscipe gefæstnodon . . . And hî tôhwurfon ðâ mid ðisum sehte, Chr. 1016; Erl. 159, 5: 1091; Erl. 228, 8: 1093; Erl. 228, 39. II. of many persons, *to disperse*:—Eal seó fyrding tôhwearf, Chr. 1094; Erl. 230, 24. Ecgbryht lǽdde fierd wiþ Norþanhymbre, and hié him eáþmêdo budon, and hié on ðam tôhwurfon, 827; Erl. 64, 9. Siendon wê tôwrecene geond wîdne grund, heápum tôhworfene (-hworfne, Exon. Th. 186, 19; Az. 22) *we are scattered in exile through the wide world, dispersed in bands*, Cd. Th. 235, 6; Dan. 302. Cf. tô-cirran.

tô-hyht, es; *m. Hope, confidence, trust, glad expectation*:—Witena frôfur and eorla gehwam eádnys and tôhyht, Runic pm. Kmbl. 340, 10; Rûn. 4. Dæg byþ myrgð and tôhiht eádgum and earmum, 344, 12; Rûn. 24. Cf. tô-hopa.

tôian. v. tôan.

tô-îcness, e; *f. Increase*:—Mid ðŷ ðâ seó gesetenes ðæs heofonlîcan lîfes dæghwamlîce tôêcnesse nom *cum vitae coelestis institutio quotidianum sumeret augmentum*, Bd. 3, 22; M. 226, 31. v. tô-ætîcness.

tô-irnan; *p.* -arn, *pl.* -urnon; *pp.* -urnen *To run in different directions, run about*:—Þŷstru ðû gesettest on þearle niht on ðære ealle wildeór wîde tôeornaþ *posuisti tenebras, et facta est nox; in ipsa pertransibunt omnes bestiae sylvarum*, Ps. Th. 103, 19. v. tô-rinnan.

tô-irnende; *adj.* (*ptcpl.*) *Running together*:—Ðâ se Hǽlend geseah ða tôyrnendan menegu *cum videret Jesus concurrentem turbam*, Mk. Skt. 9, 25.

tôl, es; *n.* I. *that by which one makes things* (cf. *Goth.* taujan *to make, do*), *a tool, implement, instrument*, (a) literal:—Tôl *ferramentum*, Wrt. Voc. i. 84, 60. Tool *instrumentum*, 21, 37. Tohl, ii. 49, 22. Mid tôle *instrumento, materia*, Hpt. Gl. 443, 47. Ðŷ læs hié mid ðŷ tôle (*a surgeon's knife*) ðæt hâle lîc gewierden, ðe hié sceoldon mid ðæt unhâle âweg âceorfan, Past. 48; Swt. 365, 11. Gif ðû ðîn tôl (*cultrum*) âheíst ofer hyt *if thou lift up thy tool upon it* (A. V.), Ex. 20, 25. Hwîlon befeóll ân sîðe of ðam snǽde intô ânum deópan seáðe. Benedictus wolde gefrêfrian ðone wyrhtan ðe ðæt tôl âmyrde, Homl. Th. ii. 162, 12. Wîglîce tôl *instrumenta bellica*, Hpt. Gl. 424, 28. Eówer sûteres tôl *uestri sutoris instrumenta*, Ælfc. Gr. 15; Zup. 105, 15. Mid lâcniendlîcum tôlum *instrumentis medicinalibus*, Hpt. Gl. 478, 2. Ðâ cômon ða cempan (*the soldiers at the crucifixion*) mid cwylmbǽrum tôlum, and ðæra sceaðena sceancan tôbrǽcon, Homl. Th. ii. 260, 7. Be mynstres tôlum *de ferramentis monasterii*, R. Ben. 56, 2, 3. Sylle man ðam gebûre tôl tô his weorce and andlâman tô his hûse, L. R. S. 4; Th. i. 434, 26. Ða nŷdþearfe . . . ðæt is mete and drync and clâþas and tôl tô swelcum cræfte swelce ðû cunne ðæt ðê is gecynde, Bt. 14, 1; Fox 42, 6. Gif ðû nelle ânum ôlæcan, forlǽt eal ðæt ðû âge bûton wiste and wǽda and tô swylcum weorcum tôl swylce ðû cunne, Prov. Kmbl. 80. (b) metaph.:—Hwæt is hit elles bûtan getimbrunga and tôl hâligra manna (*instrumenta virtutum*), R. Ben. 133, 9. Ðis synt ða lâra and ða tôl gâstlîces cræftes, L. E. I. 21; Th. ii. 418, 17. Ðû wâst ðæt nân mon ne mæg nǽnne cræft cŷðan ne nǽnne anweald reccan bûtan tôlum and andweorce . . . Ðæt biþ cyninges andweorc and his tôl mid tô rîcsianne, ðæt hê hæbbe his land fullmannod; hê sceal hæbban gebedmenn and fyrdmen and weorcmen. Hwæt ðû wâst ðætte bûtan ðisum tôlum nân cyning his cræft ne mæg cŷðan . . . Ne mæg hê bûtan ðisum (*provisions of various kinds*) ðâs tôl gehealdan, ne bûtan ðisum tôlum nân ðara þinga wyrcan ðe him beboden is tô wyrcenne, Bt. 17; Fox 58, 28–60, 7. II. in a collective sense, *tools, machinery, apparatus*:—Decius cwæð: 'Æteówiaþ his gesihðum eal ðæt wîta tôl' (cf. eal ðæt pînungtôl, 428, 18). Ðâ wurdon hrædlîce forð âborene îsene clûtas, and îsene clâwa, and îsen bedd, and leádene swipa, Homl. Th. i. 424, 18. [*Icel.* tôl; *n. pl. tools*, cf. *Goth.* taujan *to do.*] v. pînung-, tow-, wîte-tôl.

tô-lǽtan; *p.* -lêt; *pp.* -lǽten *To let go in different directions, to cause to go different ways, to disperse, release, relax*:—Tôlǽte[þ] *relaxat*, Hpt. Gl. 405, 67. Gif mon sŷþ gârleác on henne broþe and selþ drincan, ðonne tôlǽt hió ðæt sâr (*costiveness*), Lchdm. ii. 276, 16. Hê forgiet hine selfne ðonne hê tôlǽtt and fægnaþ ongeagn ðara ôðerra word *oblitus sui in voces se spargit alienas*, Past. 17; Swt. 111, 10. Tôlǽtenum ǽddrum *laxis fibris*, Hymn. Surt. 102, 22. [*O. Sax.* te-lâtan *to scatter, disperse* (intrans.): *O. H. Ger.* ze-lâzzan *desinere, deserere, liquefacere: Ger.* zer-lassen *to dissolve.*]

tô-lǽtenness, e; *f. Abandonment, a giving up*:—Ðeós wyrt ealle ealde and unlâcnigendlîce âdlu tôfereþ, swâ ðæt hê byþ gelâcnud þeáh hê ǽr his hǽle on tôlǽtennesse wǽre *the patient will be cured, though before he had been in despair of his health*, Lchdm. i. 262, 3.

tolcendlîce; *adv. Wantonly*:—Tolcendlîcor *petulantius*, Germ. 401, 41. v. following words.

tolcettan; *p.* te *To be wanton*:—Tolcetende ł fleardiende *infruticans, luxurians*, Hpt. Gl. 435, 36. v. next word.

tolcettung, tolgettung, e; *f. An incentive, incitement*:—Tolgetunge, ontyndnesse *titillationis*, Hpt. Gl. 520, 32. Tolgetunge *titillationum, accensionum*, 457, 73. v. preceding words.

tô-leoðian, -lêsan. v. tô-liðian, -lîsan.

tô-licgan; *p.* -læg, *pl.* -lǽgon; *pp.* -legen. I. *intrans.* of roads, rivers, etc., *to lie* or *run in different directions*:—Heó (*the Nile*) tôlîþ on twâ ymb an îgland ðe mon hǽt Meroen *the stream runs in two channels round the island of Meroen;* faciens insulam nomine Meroën in medio sui, Ors. 1, 1; Swt. 12, 32. Ic wille ðara þreora landrîca gemǽre gereccan hû hié mid hiera wætrum tôlicgeaþ *I will describe the boundaries, in what different directions they run*; ipsarum partium (*the three divisions of the world*) regiones significare curabo, Swt. 10, 5. Nû hæbbe wê gesǽd ymbe ealle Europe landgemǽro hû hî tôlicgaþ. Nû wille wê ymbe Affrica secgan hû ða landgemǽro tôlicgaþ *we have now told in respect to all the boundaries of the countries in Europe the several directions they take.*

Now we will tell of Africa how the different boundaries of the countries run, Swt. 24, 21–23. Ðǽr ða wegas tólicgaþ *where the roads run in different directions*, Cod. Dip. Kmbl. iii. 411, 21. II. *trans. To lie between, to lie and part, to divide, separate*:—Seó eá tôlîþ Witland and Weonodland, Ors. 1, 1; Swt. 20, 6. Ǽlc ðæra sprǽca is tôdǽled on manega ðeóda, and ða sint tôlegena and tôdǽlda mid sǽ and mid wudum and mid muntum, Bt. 18, 2; Fox 62, 34.

tô-lísan; *p.* de *To unloose, undo, dissolve; solvere, dissolvere, exsolvere, resolvere.* I. *to undo* that which is bound, *release from a bond*, (a) literal:—Ðæt wíf tôlýsde hire feax, Homl. Th. ii. 30, 16. (b) figurative, (1) *to release* from captivity, difficulty, etc.:—Drihten tôlýseþ gecypsede *Dominus solvit compeditos*, Ps. Spl. 145, 6. Hé wæs gehyhtende ðæt hé sôna ðæs ðe hire mon gefullade his líchoman tôlýsed wǽre *sperans quia mox baptizatus carne solutus esset*, Bd. 5, 7; S. 620, 36. Tôlésed wǽran *extricaba[n]tur*, Wrt. Voc. ii. 83, 25. (2) *to do away with tension, relax, relieve*:—Hyt tôlýseþ ða blǽdran and ða stánas forð gelǽdeþ, Lchdm. i. 270, 9. II. *to put an end to the connection between, to separate*:—Tôlýsan líc and sâwle, Andr. Kmbl. 301; An. 151. Ðá tôsceáden wearð líg tôlýsed *then was the flame scattered, separated*, Exon. Th. 277, 23; Jul. 585. III. *to dissolve, put an end to, dissipate*, (a) of concrete objects:—Ðysse wyrte leáf tôlýsaþ gehwylce yfele springas and heardnyssa, Lchdm. i. 262, 9. Scadu sweþredon tôlýsed under lyfte, Exon. Th. 179, 17; Gú. 1263. (b) of abstract objects:—Ðære miltan sâr hyt tôlýseþ, Lchdm. i. 270, 11. Tôlýseþ leóna mægen Drihten *molas leonum confringet Dominus*, Ps. Th. 57, 5. IV. *to dissolve, relax, destroy the force of, weaken*:—Ymhídignyssa ofðriccaþ ðæt môd, and unlustas tôlýsaþ, Homl. Th. ii. 92, 15. Mid ðý ðe hié ðone drenc druncon, hraþe heora heorta wæs tôlésed and heora môd onwended, Blickl. Homl. 229, 13, 18. Seó sâwul on flǽsclícum lustum biþ tôlýsed, Homl. Th. i. 408, 16. Wǽrun míne ǽdra ealle tôlýsde *renes mei resoluti sunt*, Ps. Th. 72, 17. V. *to desolate, destroy.* v. tô-lísedness, -lísend, -lísendlíc:—Nú syndon hí gewordene tôlýsde *quomodo facti sunt in desolatione*, Ps. Th. 72, 15. VI. *to undo* a bond, (a) literal:—Ðá hét se apostol tôlýsan ða râpas, Homl. Th. i. 464, 21. Ðonne tôslupan ða bendas and tôlýsede wǽron *sunt vincula soluta*, Bd. 4, 22; S. 591, 13. (b) figurative:—Deáþes bend tôléseþ lífFruma, Exon. Th. 64, 25; Cri. 1043. VII. *to discharge* an obligation, *to pay*:—Ic tôlýsde ł âgeald *exolvebam*, Ps. Spl. 68, 6. VIII. *to break* a connection:—Seó geþeódnes ðæs heáfdes tôbrocen and tôlýsed wæs *ut capitis junctura solveretur*, Bd. 5, 6; S. 619, 25. Ða tôlýsdan geþeódnesse *dissolutam juncturam*, S. 620, 13. [*O. H. Ger.* ze-lôsen *dissolvere, resolvere, dividere, dirumpere.*] v. un-tôlísende.

tô-lísedness, e; *f. Dissolution, desolation, dispersion*:—Tôlésednes *dissolutio, dispersio*, Wrt. Voc. ii. 141, 40. Monige ðara bigengena ðonan gewitan for ðǽre burhge tôlýsednesse (*ob desolationem*), Bd. 4, 25; S. 601, 35. On tôlýsydnysse *in desolationem*, Ps. Spl. C. 72, 19.

tô-lísend, es; *m. A destroyer, desolater*:—Wéstend, tôlýsend *desolator, vastator*, Wrt. Voc. ii. 139, 34.

tô-lísendlíc; *adj. Destructive, desolating*:—Mid glédum tôlýsendlícum *cum carbonibus desolatoriis*, Ps. Lamb. 119, 4.

tô-lísing, e; *f.* I. *dissolution, destruction*:—Geleáfan tôlýsinge, Lchdm. iii. 206, 20. II. *release, redemption.* v. tô-lísan, I b:—Ðætte hé salde sâwel his lésnise ł tôlésinc fore monigum *ut daret animam suam redemptionem pro multis*, Mk. Skt. Lind. 10, 45.

tô-lísness, e; *f.* I. *dissolution, destruction*:—Sibbe tôlésness, Blickl. Homl. 115, 16. II. *dissolution, death*:—Seó tíd mínre tôlýsnesse and mínre forþfôre is swýþe neáh, Bd. 4, 29; S. 607, 21: 4, 9; S. 577, 16.

tô-liðian; *p.* ode *To dismember, disjoint*:—Ðá tôliðode se engel ðæt cild on ðam disce, Homl. Th. ii. 272, 18. Biþ ðæt heáfod tôhliden, handa tôliðode (-leoþode, Exon. Th. 373, 16), Soul Kmbl. 214; Seel. 109.

toll, es; *n. m.* (?) *Toll, tax, custom, duty, due.* I. that which is paid to the state. See also IV:—Cynelíc toll *fiscale tributum*, Hpt. Gl. 440, 43. Nim ðone wecg, and syle tô tolle for mé and for ðé, Homl. Th. i. 512, 5. Ǽt hwám nimaþ cyningas gafol oððe toll *reges terrae a quibus accipiunt tributum vel censum?* Mt. Kmbl. 17, 25. Ðæs câseres tolleras âxodon Petrus, ðá ðá hí geond ealne middangeard ðam câsere toll gegaderodon, 'Wyle eówer lâreów ǽnig toll syllan?' Homl. Th. i. 510, 26–29. Se cyng ne rôhte ná hú swíðe synlíce ða geréfan hit begeátan of earme mannon . . . Hý ârérdon unrihte tollas, Chr. 1086; Erl. 220, 15. II. that which is paid to individuals:—Sume men syllaþ cyrcan tô hýre swá swá wâclíce mylna . . . ac hit ne gedafnaþ ðæt man dô Godes hûs ânre mylne gelíc for lyðrum tolle, Homl. Skt. i. 19, 248–253. (Cf. *molta* pensitatio quam a vasallis exigit dominus pro frumenti molitura in molendinis suis, Migne.) Ðá hí nán þincg næfdon tô syllanne, ðá gyrnde hé ðæs wífes for ðam tolle (*passage money, fare*), ii. 30, 168. III. *taking toll*:—Matheus ârás ðǽrrihte fram his tolle, Homl. Th. ii. 468, 10. Hé hine geseah sittan æt tolle, 18. Óðer is ðæt man him ðurh fixnoðe bigleofan tilige, and óðer ðæt man ðurh toll feoh gadrige *it is one thing for a man to get his living by fishing, and another to get money together by toll-taking*, 288, 20. IV. as a technical term in England. In this connection *toll* is used to denote not only an amount payable to the king, but also freedom from the payment of such amounts. The word occurs not unfrequently in charters along with *sac, sócn, teám*, and other terms (v. Cod. Dip. Kmbl. i. xlv), and in the Latin version of an English charter is explained as 'in uendendis et emendis mercibus a tolneto immunitas,' Cod. Dip. Kmbl. iv. 203, 4–5. In like manner in the Laws of Edward the Confessor it is said: 'Tol, quod nos vocamus theloneum, scilicet libertatem emendi et vendendi in terra sua,' Th. i. 451, 30. Toll could be claimed by the king (1) on sales:—Si in strata publica seu in ripa emptorali quislibet mercauerit, thelon ad manum regis subeat; quod si intus in curte praedicta (*the bishop of Worcester's*) quislibet emerit vel uendiderit, thelon debitum ad manum episcopi reddatur, Cod. Dip. Kmbl. ii. 119, 7–12. Cf. the grant by Edward in 904 of 'villae mercimonium, quod Anglice *ðæs túnes cýping* appellatur,' v. 158, 37; and that by ealdorman Ǽðelréd and Ǽðelflǽd of a half of 'ǽlc gerihta ðe tô heora hlâforddôme gebyraþ on ceápstôwe,' 142, 33. The following passages give instances of the payment of toll:—Hér kýð on ðissere béc ðæt Leówine and his wíf gebohton Ǽlfilde tô feówer and sixtuge penegon and Ǽlfríc Hals nam ðæt toll for ðæs kynges hand, Chart. Th. 635, 24: 631, 28: 639, 15: 636, 2. Alword portgeréfa and Alwine fângon tô ðam tolle for ðæs cynges hand, 636, 30. Ǽilsig bohte ânne wífmann and hire sunu mid healfe punde, and sealde Ǽilsige portgeréfa and Maccosse hundredesmann .iiii. penegas tô tolle, 627, 14. Teolling gebohte Ǽlword and Édwine tô .vii. mancson tô cépe and tô tolle, and Ǽlword portgeréfa nam ðæt toll, 633, 2–7: 639, 20–24. Ǽilgyuu âlýsde Hig and Dunna and heora ofspring tô .xiii. mancson, and Ǽigunlf portgeréfa and Godsuc nâmon ðæt toll, 638, 12–17. (2) from ships coming into port. For a list of such tolls see L. Eth. iv. 2; Th. i. 300; and for instances of tolls being remitted see Cod. Dip. Kmbl. i. 94, where the toll (*vectigal*) on one ship entering the port of London is remitted to bishop Aldwulf; i. 101, where the king remits 'nauis onustae transvectionis censum qui a thelonearis nostris tributaria exactione impetitur; ut ubique in regno nostro libera de omni regali fiscu et tributo maneat.' See also pp. 114, 116. In a charter of Cnut the tolls of Sandwich are the subject of grant: 'nullus homo habet aliquam consuetudinem in eodem portu exceptis monachis aecclesiae Christi. Eorum autem est nauicula et transfretatio portus et theloneum omnium nauium cujuscumque sit et undecumque veniat,' iv. 21. (3) on transport by land or water. See the last passage: 'Eorum est transfretatio portus.' In another charter a grant of land carries with it 'theloneum aquarum,' Cod. Dip. Kmbl. iii. 369, 25. In the charter inserted in the Chronicle under the year 963, *se toll* of certain streams is the subject of grant, Erl. 123, 2. See Kemble's Saxons in England, ii. 73–78. [*O. Sax.* tol[l]: *O. H. Ger.* zol[l]: *Ger.* zoll; *m.*: *Icel.* tollr; *m.*: *Dan.* told; *m.*] v. scip-toll; toln, *and following words.*

tollere, es; *m. A toll-taker, tax-gatherer*:—Tollere *telonearius*, Wrt. Voc. i. 50, 56: *theolenarius*, 74, 45. Matheus wæs tollere, Homl. Th. i. 324, 3: ii. 288, 17. God hine âwende of tollere tô apostole, 468, 15. Ðone se Hǽlend geceás of woruldlícum tollere tô gâstlícum godspellere, Homl. Skt. i. 15, 129. Ðæs câseres tolleras âxodon Petrus . . . 'Wyle eówer lâreów ǽnig toll syllan?' Homl. Th. i. 510, 27. [Ryche Pers þe tollere, H. S. 5816. I seiȝ tolleres in marketes, Piers P. prol. 220. Tollare or takare of tol *telonearius*, Prompt. Parv. 496.] v. tolnere.

toll-freó; *adj. Free from toll, exempt from payment of toll*:—Tolfreó ofer ealle Engleland, wiðinne burhe and wiðútan, æt gârescépinge and on ǽfrice styde be wætere and be lande *per totam Angliam infra ciuitatem et extra, in omni foro et annuis nundinis et in omnibus omnino locis per aquam et terram, ab omni telonii exactione liberi sint*, Cod. Dip. Kmbl. iv. 209, 19.

toll-sceamol, es; *m. A seat where a receiver of toll sits, a place for receiving contributions*:—Hé geseah ǽnne man sittende æt tollsceamule (*in teloneo*), Mt. Kmbl. 9, 9. Ðæt folc hyra feoh torfude on ðone tollsceamul (*in gazophilacium*), Mk. Skt. 12, 41, 43. v. toll-setl.

toll-scír, e; *f. The office of taking toll, business of gathering taxes*:—Matheus ârás and forlét his tollscíre *Matthew arose and gave up his occupation as tolltaker*, Homl. Th. ii. 468, 25.

toll-setl, es; *n. A toll-booth, custom-house*:—Tolsetl *teloneum*, Wrt. Voc. i. 60, 36. Ðá geseah hé sittan sumne mannan æt tollsetle (*in teloneo*; in a tolbothe, Wick. Mt. 9, 9), Homl. Th. ii. 468, 9. Matheus nǽfre æfter his gecyrrednysse æt tollsetle ne sæt, 288, 18. v. toll-sceamul.

toln, e; *f. Toll*:—Hé begeat mid his sméhwrencan and mid his golde and seolfre eall dyrnunga æt Steorran, ðe ðá wæs ðæs kinges rǽdesman, ðæt him geweard se þridda pænig of ðære tolne on Sandwíc, Chart. Th. 339, 13: 340, 35. [Heore is ðæt scip . . . and se tolne of ealle scipen *eorum est navicula . . . et theloneum omnium navium*, 318, 1.] [*O. Frs.* tolen, tolne; *f.*; tolna *to impose toll*: *O. Sax.* tolna *toll*: *M. H. Ger.* zoln.] v. *next word, and* toll.

tolnere, es; *m. A toll-taker, tax-gatherer*:—Tolnere *telonearius*, Wrt. Voc. i. 50, 56: *exactor*, Germ. 395, 48. [*O. Frs.* tolner: *O. H. Ger.* zolnare, zollanari *telonarius, publicanus*: *Ger.* zöllner.] v. *preceding word, and* tollere.

tó-lúcan; *p.* -leác, *pl.* -lucon; *pp.* -locen *To tear to pieces, wrench asunder, dislocate.* I. literal:—Ðæs ne wêndon witan Scyldinga, ðæt hit (*the hall*) manna ǽnig tóbrecan meahte, listum tólúcan, Beo. Th. 1566; B. 781. Forðon ðe míne innoþas on ðam fylle tólocene wǽron *eo quod interanea essent ruendo convulsa*, Bd. 5, 6; S. 619, 31. Sint mê leoð tóloceu, líc sâre gebrocen, Andr. Kmbl. 2807; An. 1406. v. tó-hlecan. II. figurative, *to root out, destroy*:—Ic hæbbe ðê gesetne ofer ríce and ofer ðióda ðæt ðú hí tólúce and tóweorpe and forspilde and tóstence *constitui te super gentes et super regna, ut evellas et destruas et disperdas et dissipes*, Past. 58; Swt. 441, 31. [Hwil þ Marherete spec þus, me toleac hire, swa þ te reue fir þe stronge rune of þ blodi stream ne mahte for muchele grure lokin þiderweardes, Marh. 7, 11. Wâ is us þ we iseoð þi softe lich toluken swa ladliche, 6, 7. ȝef mi lich is toloken, 6, 12. Heo toluken þene king, and his leomen todrowen, Laym. 2602. Wilde deor limmel toluken ham, & tolimeden eauer euch lið from þe lire, Jul. 79, 5. Ich schal leoten toluken þi flesch þe fuheles of þe lufte *carnes volatilibus dilacerandas reiciam*, Kath. 2092. *O. H. Ger.* zi-lochan, -lohhan *devulsus, revulsus*.]

tó-lýsan, tom. v. tó-lísan; tam.

tóm; *adj. Empty*; figuratively, *free from*. Cf. leás:—Ðæt hý móstun mânweorca tôme lifgan and tíres blǽd êcne âgan (cf. the man farid imu an giwald Godes tionono tômig, Hêl. 2490), Exon. Th. 74, 26; Cri. 1212. [Tome saule (*animam inanem*) he filled with fode, Ps. 106, 9. Yee sal find þair tumbs tome (tume), C. M. 17798. Toom or voyde *vacuus*, Prompt. Parv. 496; temyn or maken empty *vacuo, evacuo*, 488. *Scott.* toom, tume: *Icel.* tômr: Dan. tom.]

tó-mearcian; *p.* ode *To distinguish, describe*:—Tômearcode *distinxit*, Ps. Spl. 105, 32. Ðæt eall ymbehwyrft wǽre tômearcod *ut describeretur uniuersus orbis*, Lk. Skt. 2, 1. v. next word.

tó-mearcodness, e; *f. A description*:—Ðeós tômearcodnes (*de-scribtio*) wæs ǽryst geworden fram ðam dêman Cirino, Lk. Skt. 2, 2. v. *preceding word, and* tó-writenness.

tó-meldan *to destroy* peace *by talebearing, by spreading reports*:—Ðǽr is helle grund ðam ðe sibbe ful oft tômældeþ mid his múþe (cf. Dante's Inferno, Canto 28, which describes the punishment of the sowers of scandal and schism), Exon. Th. 446, 22; Dôm. 26.

tó-middes; *prep.* (*adv.*) I. with dat. (1) marking rest, *in the midst of, amidst*, (a) preceding the governed word:—Gewurðe fæstnis tômiddes ðâm wæterum *fiat firmamentum in medio aquarum*, Gen. 1, 6. Iosue hêt âhebban ôðre twelf stânas tômiddes ðam streáme (*in medio Jordanis alveo*), Jos. 4, 9. Tômiddes eów stôd ðe gê ne cunnon *medius uestrum stetit quem uos non scitis*, Jn. Skt. i. 26. Hê stôd ðǽr âna tô-middes eallum ðam folce, Homl. Skt. i. 23, 639. (b) following the governed word:—Hê stôd him tômiddes, Homl. Skt. i. 23, 617. Ðǽr ic sylf beó him tômiddes, Homl. Th. ii. 284, 19. Sticaþ him tômiddes, Salm. Kmbl. 1010; Sal. 506. Holte tômiddes, Met. 13, 37: Cd. Th. 21, 15; Gen. 324. (2) marking motion, *into the midst of*:—Hwænne ðú miht tô ðam folce becuman mid ealre ðínre fare tômiddes Hierusalem, Homl. Ass. 110, 259. Hine ðanon ealle âtugan tômiddes ðære cýpinge, Homl. Skt. i. 23, 609. II. with gen. (here, perhaps, *middes* should rather be taken as noun governing the following word in the genitive). (1) marking rest, *in the midst of, in the middle of*:—Ðâ fundon hié hiene tômiddes ðara wietena ... ðâ wæs hê gemêt sittende tômiddes ðara láreówa *invenerunt illum sedentem in medio doctorum ... in medio doctorum sedens invenitur*, Past. 49; Swt. 385, 21–25. Ic sette míne hâlgan stôwe tômiddes eówre (*in medio vestri*), Lev. 26, 11. Tômiddes hyra *in medio*, Jn. Skt. 8, 3. Ðǽr ic beó tômiddes heora, L. E. I. 7; Th. ii. 406, 27. (2) marking movement, *into the midst of*:—Ðâ hê hiene tômiddes ðæs wêstennes hæfde gelǽdd *in deserta perductus*, Ors. 6, 31; Swt. 286, 17. III. as adverb:—Hê âhte geweald ealles ðæs splottes ðâr ðæt scræf wæs tômiddes, Homl. Skt. i. 23, 416. Sete on feówer healfe ðæs ceápes, and ân tômiddes, Lchdm. iii. 56, 9. Âlegdon ðâ tômiddes mǽrne þeóden, Beo. Th. 6273; B. 3141.

tó-nama, an; *m. A surname, cognomen*:—His tônama wæs Cambises gecweden, Homl. Ass. 103, 25. 'Huætd ðê tônoma (*or* tô noma (*dat.*)? *Rush. has* noma) is?' And cuoeð tô him: 'Here tônoma mê is' *quod tibi nomen est? Et dicit ei: 'Legio nomen mihi est,'* Mk. Skt. Lind. 5, 9. [Ðes wimman hadde on toname Magdalene, O. E. Homl. ii. 143, 13. Nu þu iherest of wuche gomen aras þer þe tonome ... tonome arised ofte of lutle þing þe long ilasted, Laym. 9383. God gyueth the riche fowl towname (v. Lk. 12, 20–21), Piers P. C-text 13, 211. *Ger.* zu-name. Cf. *Dan.* til-navn.] v. next word.

tó-namian; *p.* ode *To surname* [:—Simon ðone getônomade (getor-nomade, MS.) stân *Simonem quem cognominauit Petrum*, Lk. Skt. Lind. 6, 14]. v. preceding word.

tó-nemnan; *p.* -nemde *To name separately, distinguish by name into parts*:—Hié ða þrié dǽlas on þreó tônemdon, Asiam, Europem, and Affricam *they distinguished the three parts by the three names, Asia, Europe, and Africa*, Ors. 1, 1; Swt. 8, 4. Norþ óþ ðone gârsecg is eall Sciþþia lond binnan, þêh mon tônemne on twâ and on þrítig þeóda *north up to the ocean is all Scythia, though it is divided into thirty-two nations, each having its own name*, Swt. 14, 22. Swâ þeáh is tô geþencenne ðæt ða fíf þing þeáh hí tônemde sién mid wordum ðæt hit is eall ân þing ðonne hí gegaderode beóþ *atqui necessarium est confiteri nomina quidem esse diversa, nullo vero modo discrepare substantiam*, Bt. 33, 1; Fox 122, 11.

tonian; *p.* ode *To thunder*:—Ic tonige *tono*, Ælfc. Gr. 24; Zup. 138, 3. [From Latin.]

tó-niman; *p.* -nam, *pl.* -nâmon; *pp.* -numen. I. *to take to pieces, divide*:—Hæfde se cyning his fierd on tú tônumen, Chr. 894; Erl. 90, 17. II. *to take away*, cf. æt-beran:—*Tollite portas, principes* ... Ðæt byþ on Englisc: Gê ealdras, tônymaþ ða gatu, Nicod. 27; Thw. 15, 8.

tonwinto? The word occurs as a gloss to *adlido*, Txts. 39, 79.

topp, es; *m.* I. *a top, summit*:—Helmes top *apex, summitas galeae*, Wrt. Voc. i. 36, 1. II. *a lock of hair, tuft*; and fig. *a collection of rays of light* (?), as in the tail of a comet:—Se bróðor geseah eall ðæt hûs mid heofonlícre bryhto geondgoten, and hê ðǽr geseah fýrenne topp (*a stream of light* (?); cf. *Cometa* ... men cweþaþ on Englisc, ðæt hit sié feaxede steorra, for ðæm ðǽr stent lang leóma of, Chr. 891; Erl. 88, 19. But, perhaps, torr should be read, as the Latin has *turrim*; and the metrical version of the passage uses that word:—Heofonlíc leóma from foldan up swylce fýren tor ryht ârǽred, Exon. Th. 180, 26; Gú. 1285) up of ðære eorþan tô heofones heánnysse, Guthl. 20; Gdwin. 88, 11. III. *a top* to play with (?):—Mid gelǽtedre handa hê swang ðone top mid micelre swiftnysse (the passage is obscure, and perhaps the Latin original has been mistranslated. Thorpe, p. 41, note, cites two Latin versions, one of which has 'accepto ceromate, cum docta manu circumlavit ei cum subtilitate'; the other 'accepto cyramoco, docta manu circulavit eum': in each case the rubbing after the bath seems to be meant. But *swingan* (q. v.) elsewhere seems always used with the sense of *striking*, and hardly fits in with the meaning of the Latin), Ap. Th. 13, 13. [In later English the word seems mostly used of the hair at the top of the head, or of that which has a similarity with it, e. g. the leafy top of a tree:—Bi þone toppe (coppe, 2nd MS.) he hine nom, Laym. 684. Hongin bi þe toppe (teon bi þe top up, Bodl. MS.), Jul. 28, 6: Piers P. 3, 139. Top ouer tail, Will. 2776. En vostre chef vus avet toup (*a top of heer*), Wrt. Voc. i. 144, 21 (13th cent.). Ne rohte he þeȝ flockes were Imeind bi toppes and bi here, O. and N. 428. His heer was by his eres ful round ishorn, His top was docked lyk a priest biforn, Chauc. Prol. 590. Top or fortop, top of the hed *aqualium*, Prompt. Parv. 496. Up to þe toppe from þe more, O. and N. 1422: 1328. A top of flax *du lyn le toup*, Wrt. Voc. i. 144, 27. The word is used also of other things:—Teon seiles to toppa, Laym. 1339. Top or cop of an hey thynge *cacumen*, top of a maste *carchesia*, Prompt. Parv. 496. It is found, too, as the name of a plaything:—En la rue vus juvetz a toup (*a top of tre*), Wrt. Voc. i. 144, 25. Top of chylderys pley *trochus*, Prompt. Parv. 496. Sweype for a top *flagellum*, 482. *O. Frs.* top *a lock, tuft of hair*: *Du.* top *top, summit*: *O. H. Ger.* zopfe; *pl. cicinni, anciae*: *Ger.* zopf: *Icel.* toppr *a tuft* or *lock of hair; a top* of a mast: *Dan.* top *a top, summit; a tuft, crest; a top* to play with: *Swed.* topp *a top, summit*. The word was taken from the Teutonic into the Romance languages.]

tor *a tower; a rock*. v. torr.

tór; *adj. Difficult, hard*. v. tór-begete, -cirre [& tat iss harrd & strang & tor and hefiȝ lif to ledenn, Orm. 6350. Erueð (tor, MS. T.) for te paien, A. R. 108, 9. An honful ȝerden beoð erueð for te breken (arn tor to breken, MS. T.), 254, 2. Tor for to telle, Will. 1428. Toor, 5066. *O. H. Ger.* zuor-, zuir-, zuur-, zúr-: *Icel.* tor-].

toran-eáge. v. toren-íge.

tór-begete; *adj. Hard to get*:—Gif hê beget and yt rinde, sió ðe cymþ of neorxnawonge, ne dereþ him nân âtter. Ðonne cwæþ se ðe ðâs bóc wrât ðæt hió wǽre tórbegete, Lchdm. ii. 114, 3–6. Cf. éð-begete, *and see* tór.

tór-cirre; *adj. Hard to turn, hard to convert*:—Ða ðe wǽron ǽr swýðe heardes môdes and swýðe tórcyrres tô Crystes geleáfan, Shrn. 99, 1. Cf. earfoþ-cirre.

torcul *glosses* torcular, Mt. Kmbl. Rush. 21, 33. [*O. H. Ger.* torcul; *n.*; torcula; *f. torcular*.]

tord, es; *n. A turd, dung*:—Swínes tord, Lchdm. ii. 62, 22. Gâte tord, 122, 5. Genim níwe horses tord, 330, 27: 148, 13. Genim culfran tord, 322, 9. v. weorf-tord; tyrdlu, *and next word*.

tord-wifel, es; *m. A dung-beetle*; scarabaeus stercorarius:—Ðǽr ðú geseó tordwifel on eorþan up weorpan, ymbfô hine mid twâm handum mid his geweorpe, Lchdm. ii. 318, 15. [*Icel.* tord-yfill.] Cf. scearn-wifel.

tó-rendan; *p.* -rende *To rend in two, tear in pieces*:—Se hêh ðâ sacerd tôslât ł tôrende woedo his *summus autem sacerdos scindens vestimenta sua*, Mk. Skt. Lind. Rush. 14, 63. Wâghrægl temples tôre[n]ded (tôrended, Rush.) wæs in tuu *velum templi scissum est in duo*, 15, 38. Grin biþ tôrænded *laqueus contritus est*, Ps. Th. 123, 7. [Wurmes wullen todelen þine þermes, lifre and lihte torenden, Fragm. Phlps. 6, 59. He is of þe tetore uolke, þet toteređ his olde kurtel, and torendeđ þe olde pilche, A. R. 362, 29. Haue ruþe of þi faire bodi, þ^t me ne lete hit noȝt þus torende, Marg. 28, 132. *O. Frs.* tô-renda.]

toren-íge; *adj. Blear-eyed*:—Gif hē wǣre toreníge (-igge, Cott. MSS.) oððe fleáh hæfde on eágan *si lippus fuerit, si albuginem habens in oculo*, Past. 11; Swt. 65, 5. Wiþ eágena sār, ðæt is ðonne ðæt hwā torníge (toraneáge, MS. B.) sȳ *ad lippitudinem oculorum*, Lchdm. i. 108, 23. Wið eágena sāre, ðæt ys ðæt wē cwēðaþ torníge (-ēge, MS. H.) *ad epiphoras oculorum*, 156, 18.

torfian; *p.* ode. In the first instance *to throw with turf at* a person (cf. stǣnan), and then with stones or the like; so *Icel.* has tyrfa með grjóti ok með torfi, and *Swed.* tyrva med stenom. Afterwards in a more general sense *to throw*. I. *to throw at* an object, *strike* with a missile, *to stone* a person:—Seó clǣnnes ða fūlnesse mid flinte torfaþ *pudicitia libidinem cum saxo percutit*, Gl. Prud. 12 a. Ða deóflu mē swīðe geegsiaþ and eác swylce torfiaþ, Homl. Skt. i. 3, 424. Hī nāmon stānas, ðæt hī hine torfodon, Homl. Th. ii. 236, 21. Hī mid stānum torfodon ðone sōðfæstan Iacob, 300, 18. Hig nāmon stānas tō ðam ðæt hig woldon hyne torfian *tulerunt lapides, ut iacerent in eum*, Jn. Skt. 8, 59: *ut lapidarent eum*, 10, 31. Ða leásan gewitan hine ongunnon ǣrest tō torfienne, Homl. Th. i. 50, 15. II. *to throw, cast*, (a) with acc. of thing thrown:—Hē geseah hū ðæt folc hyra feoh torfude on ðone tollsceamul, and manega welige torfudon fela *aspiciebat quomodo turba iactaret aes in gazophilacium, et multi diuites iactabant multa*, Mk. Skt. 12, 41. (b) without an object:—Ic torfige oððe sceóte *iacio*, Ælfc. Gr. 28, 6; Zup. 178, 16. Ða Francisce men torfedon tōwærd ðam weofode, Chr. 1083; Erl. 217, 17. [Samuel þe sticches toruede (tarueden, 1st MS.) oueral þan strede, Laym. 16703. *Icel.* tyrfa *to pelt* a person with something.] v. of-, tō-torfian; turf, *and next word*.

torfung, e; *f.* I. *a throwing of stones, stoning*:—Ðæt hine (*a slave who had absconded*) man lǣdde tō ðære torfunge, L. Ath. v. 6, 3; Th. i. 234, 8. Cf. Si fur servus homo sit, eant sexaginta et viginti servi et lapident eum, iii. 6; Th. i. 219, 13. v. Grmm. R. A. 693. II. *a throwing, casting, hurling*:—Hié his wǣran swīðe ehtende ge mid scotum ge mid stāna torfungum, Ors. 3, 9; Swt. 134, 16.

torht; *adj.* [The word with its derivatives is almost confined to poetry. It is, however, found not unfrequently as one of the components in proper names. v. Txts. 576: cf. *beorht* in the same class of words. See, also, *torhtness*.] *Bright, splendid*. I. of the brightness of light, literal or figurative, (a) referring to things in this world:—Æþelast tungla, torht tācen Godes *the sun*, Exon. Th. 204, 11; Ph. 96. Leóma leóhtade leóda mǣgþum torht, 15, 12; Cri. 235. Upheofon torhtne mid his tunglum *the firmament splendid with its stars*, 60, 13; Cri. 969. Heofon torhtne tungolgimmum, 71, 6; Cri. 1151. Heofanas torhte *the bright skies*, 58, 11; Cri. 934. Tungla torhtast *the sun*, Menol. Fox 219; Men. 111. (b) of heavenly brightness:—Wæs mē swegles leóht torht ontȳned, Exon. Th. 131, 19; Gū. 457. Wuldres leóht torht, 102, 17; Cri. 1674: Andr. Kmbl. 3222; An. 1614: Cd. Th. 299, 28; Sat. 557. II. *of splendid appearance, bright, beautiful, splendid*, (a) of living creatures:—Se torhta fugel (*the phenix*), Exon. Th. 236, 15; Ph. 574. Ða torhtan mægþ (*Judith*: cf. ides ælfscīnu, 21, 11; Jud. 14), Judth. Thw. 22, 1; Jud. 43. Englas ælbeorhte, trume and torhte, Exon. Th. 55, 15; Cri. 884. (b) of inanimate objects:—Ðē is neorxna wang, boldwela fægrost . . . torht ontȳned, Andr. Kmbl. 209; An. 105. Ðæt torhte lond, Exon. Th. 199, 19; Ph. 28. Se torhta æsc, 429, 24; Rä. 43, 9. In ðære torhtan byrig, 34, 14; Cri. 542. Of ðam torhtan temple Dryhtnes, 12, 15; Cri. 186. Beám tānum torhtne, 435, 17; Rä. 54, 2. Him hildedeór hof torht getǣhte, Beo. Th. 631; B. 313. Torhtæ *vitreos, claros* (*gurgites*), Hpt. Gl. 406, 48. Tācna torhtost (*the cross seen by Constantine*; cf. ðæt wlitige treów, 330; El. 165), Elen. Kmbl. 327; El. 164. III. *splendid, glorious, noble, illustrious, having splendid qualities* or *properties*, (a) of persons:—Se torhta (*the Deity*), Cd. Th. 282, 29; Sat. 294. Ārās se wuldormago, spræc tō his onbehtþegne, torht tō his gesīþe, Exon. Th. 179, 29; Gū. 1269. Bearn Godes, torhtes tīrfruma[n], 13, 21; Cri. 206. Torhtne Drihten Hǣlend, Cd. Th. 301, 2; Sat. 575. Torhte and tīreádige twelfe *the twelve apostles*, Apstls. Kmbl. 7; Ap. 4: Exon. Th. 366, 10; Reb. 10. (b) of things:—Wuldres blēd torht, Cd. Th. 302, 5; Sat. 594. Seolf onfēng torhtum tācne (*circumcision*), 143, 6; Gen. 2375. Hē benam his feónd torhte tīre, 4, 23; Gen. 58. Ða hālgan duru heofona rīces torhte ontȳnan, Salm. Kmbl. 75; Sal. 38. Abraham wordum God torhtum cīgde, Cd. Th. 108, 16; Gen. 1807. Noldan hī ða torhtan tācen (*Christ's miracles*) oncnāwan, Exon. Th. 40, 21; Cri. 642. Torhte frætwe, 211, 20; Ph. 200. In ðone torhtestan þrȳnesse þrym, 140, 29; Gū. 617. IV. of sight or voice, *bright, clear*:—Blind sceal his eágna þolian, oftigen biþ him torhtre gesihþe, Exon. Th. 335, 29; Gn. Ex. 40. Ðūhte him ðæt engel stīgan cwōme and stefne ābeád, torhtan reorde, Cd. Th. 248, 10; Dan. 511. [*O. Sax.* torht: *O. H. Ger.* zoraht *clear, evident*.] v. freá-, geár-, gold-, heaðo-, heofon-, hilde-, hleór-, mǣre-, mere-, morgen-, rodor-, sige-, sigel-, swegel-, wlite-, wuldor-torht.

torhte; *adv.* I. *clearly*:—Frætwe mīne (*the swan's feathers*) swōgaþ hlūde, torhte singaþ, Exon. Th. 390, 9; Rä. 8, 8. Him torhte in gemynd his Dryhtnes naman dumba brohte, 440, 24; Rä. 60, 7. II. *beautifully, splendidly*:—Hē anlīcnesse geseh torhte gefrætwed, wlitige geworhte, Andr. Kmbl. 1430; An. 715. [*O. H. Ger.* zorahto *evidenter*.]

torhtian; *p.* ode *To make clear, shew*:—Tācnendi, torctendi *index*, Txts. 71, 1105. [Cf. *O. H. Ger.* gi-ougozorhtōn *manifestare*.]

torht-līc; *adj. Splendid*:—Eów ys wuldorblǣd torhtlīc tōweard, Judth. Thw. 23, 35; Jud. 157. Dryhten eallum dǣleþ . . . sumum torhtlīcne tiir, Exon. Th. 331, 18; Vy. 70. [*O. Sax.* torht-līk.]

torhtlīce; *adv. Splendidly*:—Ðæt is sigedryhten ðe ðone sele frætweþ, timbreþ torhtlīce, Exon. Th. 450, 25; Dōm. 93. His mildheortnyss is ofer ūs torhtlīce getrymed, Ps. Th. 116, 2: Andr. Kmbl. 3358; An. 1683. [*O. Sax.* torhtlīko.]

torht-mōd; *adj. Glorious, illustrious*; an epithet of the Deity, Judth. Thw. 21, 4; Jud. 6: 21, 35; Jud. 93: of Noah, Cd. Th. 90, 28; Gen. 1502.

torhtness, e; *f. Glory*:—Torhtnis, torchtnis *luculentum*, Txts. 75, 1243. Torhtnes, Wrt. Voc. ii. 51, 16. Gyf him þince (*seem in a dream*) ðæt his hūs byrnþ, micel blǣd and torhtnes him byþ tōweard, Lchdm. iii. 170, 10.

tō-rinnan; *p.* -rann *To run in different directions, disperse* (intrans.):—Suelce hit eall lytlum rīðum tōrinne, Past. 38; Swt. 277, 13. [*O. H. Ger.* ze-rinnan: *Ger.* zer-rinnen.]

tō-rīpan; *p.* te *To pluck in two, tear to pieces*:—Ðā hē fleáh ðā tōrȳpte hine ān brēmber ofer ðæt nebb. Ðā hē ætsacan wolde ðā sǣde him mon ðæt tō tācne *when he fled, a bramble scratched him all over the face. When he wanted to deny* (*the charge brought against him*), *they told him this as a token*, Chart. Th. 172, 27. [v. *Goth.* raupjan *to pluck*: *O. H. Ger.* roufen *vellicare, runcare*: *Ger.* raufen.] v. rīpan.

torn, es; *n.* [The word with its derivatives is almost confined to poetry; see, however, *torn-wyrdan*.] *Violent emotion of anger* or *grief* (cf. teran, *and Goth.* ga-taura *a rent*; ga-taurnan *to be torn*). I. of anger, (a) where there is just cause, *anger, indignation, wrath*:—Gewāt torne gebolgen dryhten Geáta (*Beowulf when the dragon ravaged the country*), Beo. Th. 4794; B. 2401. Ne mōton wyt on wǣrlogum wrecan Godes torn, Cd. Th. 152, 34; Gen. 2530: 4, 24; Gen. 58: 151, 13; Gen. 2508. Mē ðæt cynn hafaþ sāre ābolgen; nū mē Sethes bearn torn nīwiaþ, 76, 16; Gen. 1258. Līfes leóhtfruma leng ne wolde torn þrowigean *would not restrain his wrath*, 146, 14; Gen. 2422. (b) *unrighteous anger, rage*:—Wǣron teónsmiðas (*the evil spirits*) t[illegible] es fulle, cwǣdon ðæt him Gūðlāc earfeþa mǣst āna gefremede, Exon. Th. 114, 22; Gū. 176. Beóþ ða gebolgne . . . and heora torn wrecaþ *will wreak their rage*, 119, 24; Gū. 259. Synfull yrsaþ tōþum torn þolaþ teónum grimetaþ *peccator irascetur, dentibus suis fremet*, Ps. Th. 111, 9. II. of grief, *grief, affliction, trouble, distress*:—Cyning eallwihta Caines ne wolde tiber sceáwian; ðæt wæs torn were hefig æt heortan, Cd. Th. 60, 10; Gen. 979. Hȳ twēgen sceolon tæfle ymbsittan, ðenden him hyra torn tōglīde, forgietan ðara geócran gesceafte, habban him gomen on borde, Exon. Th. 345, 3; Gn. Ex. 182. Ðǣr wæs wōpes hring torne bitolden, 34, 6; Cri. 538. Ðā wæs wōpes hring, hāt heáfodwylm, ofer hleór goten; nalles for torne teáras feóllon, Elen. Kmbl. 2265; El. 1134. Hē lēt, torn þoliende, teáras geótan, Exon. Th. 165, 15; Gū. 1029. Inwidsorge ðe hié ǣr drugon and þolian scoldon, torn unlytel, Beo. Th. 1670; B. 833. Torn geþolode wine Scyldinga, weána gehwylcne, sīdra sorga, 297; B. 147. Torn dreógan, Exon. Th. 131, 20; Gū. 458. Gristbitian mid tōðon torn þoligende *gnashing their teeth in despair*, Judth. 25, 21; Jud. 272. Abraham bæd him fu[illegible]umes . . . cwæð ðæt him wǣre weorce on mōde, sorga sārost. . . . Hié Abrahame treówa sealdon, ðæt hié his torn mid him gewrǣcon on wrāðum, Cd. Th. 122, 36; Gen. 2037. Ne sceal nǣfre his torn tō rycene beorn of his breóstum ācȳþan, nemþe hē ǣr ða bōte cunne mid elne gefremman, Exon. Th. 293, 7; Wand. 112. Torna gehwylces, Beo. Th. 4385; B. 2189. [*O. Sax.* torn *grief, affliction*: *Du.* toorn *anger*: *O. H. Ger.* zorn *commotio, zelus, fervor, ira, indignatio, dolor, molestia*: *Ger.* zorn.] v. gār-, lyge-torn, *and next word*.

torn; *adj. Causing violent emotions of grief* or *anger, grievous, distressing, bitter*:—Hī him ermþu gehēton tornum teóncwidum *they threatened him with misery in grievous words of insult*, Exon. Th. 129, 10; Gū. 419. Ic sceal godscyld wrecan, torne teóncwide (*grievous blasphemies*), ðe ðū tǣlnissum wiþ ða sēlestan sacan ongunne, 254, 30; Jul. 205. Hī mē dǣdun (-m, MS.) torne tēlnysse, teónan mǣnige *detrahebant mihi*, Ps. Th. 108, 3. Ðæt wæs Hrōðgāre hreówa tornost *it was to Hrothgar the bitterest grief*, Beo. Th. 4265; B. 2129. [*O. Sax.* torn *bitter* (*tear*).] v. torne, torn-līc.

torn-cwide, es; *m. A speech that causes grief, bitter, grievous, distressing words*:—Heora tungan torncwidum serwaþ swā oft nædran dōþ *acuerunt linguas suas sicut serpentes*, Ps. Th. 139, 3. Ongunnon gromheorte (*the evil spirits*) Godes orettan in sefan swencan, swīþe gehēton, ðæt hē in ðone grimman gryre gongan sceolde . . .; woldun hȳ geteón mid torncwidum in orwēnnysse Meotudes cempan, Exon. Th. 36, 25; Gū. 546.

torne; *adv. In a way that causes grief* or *distress, grievously, distressingly*:—Hē wīse dōmas dēþ (ðām) ðe hēr deorce ǣr teonan manige torne geþoledan *facit judicium injuriam patientibus*, Ps. Th. 145, 6. Mē ys torne on mōde (cf. ys mē nū hige geómor, 22, 31; Jud. 87) *I am distressed in mind*, Judth. Thw. 22, 36; Jud. 93. Him ðæs wōpes hring torne gemonade, Exon. Th. 182, 22; Gū. 1314. Heó mec torne tǣle gerahte (-rǣhte?), 247, 3; Jul. 73.

torn-gemōt, es; *n. A meeting intended to cause trouble* or *molestation, an attack upon an enemy*:—Gif hē torngemōt þurhteón mihte *if he could bring about a meeting with his foe*, Beo. Th. 2284; B. 1140.

torn-genīðla, an; *m. A malignant, grievous, fierce enemy*:—Hēton hine ofer landsceare teón torngenīðlan, swā hié hit frēcnost findan meahton, Andr. Kmbl. 2462; An. 1232. Heó wǣron stearce, stāne heardran, noldon hire andsware ǣnige secgan torngenīðlan (*the Jews whom Elene asked about the cross*), Elen. Kmbl. 1132; El. 568. Hié (*the wicked after doomsday*) worpene beóþ in helle grund torngenīðlan, 2609; El. 1306.

torn-īge. v. toren-īge.

torn-līc; *adj. Grievous, bitter*:—Ða hēr on tornlīcum teárum (cf. wrēðan werk wōpu kūmian, tornon trahnon, Hēl. 5525) sāwaþ, Ps. Th. 125, 5. [*O. H. Ger.* zorn-līh *turbidus, iratus*.]

torn-mōd; *adj. Having the mind excited to anger, having rage in the heart*:—Gē (*the evil spirits*) mec nǣfre mōtan tornmōde teón in tintergu, Exon. Th. 141, 2; Gū. 621. [Cf. *O. H. Ger.* zorn-muot *turbor*; zorn-muotig *iracundus*.]

torn-sorh; *gen.* -sorge; *f. Anxious care*:—Tornsorgna ful eald ongon eaforan lǣran, Exon. Th. 304, 27; Fä. 76.

torn-word, es; *n. A word that causes distress* or *grief, a contemptuous, scornful word*:—Hī mē hosp sprecaþ, tornworda fela, Exon. Th. 11, 17; Cri. 172. v. torn-wyrdan.

torn-wracu, e; *f. Grievous revenge*:—Gē hēr āteóþ in ða tornwræce (*the destruction with which the evil spirits threatened Guthlac if he remained in his hermitage*) sigeleásne sīð, Exon. Th. 120, 16; Gū. 272.

torn-wyrdan; *p.* de *To address abusive words to, to vituperate*:—Hiera wīf him ongeán iernende wǣron, and hié swīþe tornwyrdon, and ācsedon, gif hié feohtan ne dorsten, hwider hié fleón woldon; ðæt hié ōðer gener næfden būton hié on heora wīf hrif gewiton (*the Latin, however, is*: Uxores eorum obviam occurrunt, orant, in praelium revertantur: cunctantibus obscoena corporis ostendunt, quaerentes, num in uteros uxorum vellent refugere), Ors. 1, 12; Swt. 54, 2. v. torn-word.

toroc *a bung, stopper of a cask* (?):—Toroc *dolua*, Wrt. ii. 141, 67. [*From Latin* (?) turachium *epistomium, dolii obturamentum*, Migne. Cf. (?), too, *French* douve *stave of a cask*. Another attempt at a meaning, however, may be suggested. Du Cange, who does not give *dolua*, gives *toroc* as a gloss for *gurgulio*; if this were the same word as that in the A. S. gloss, perhaps the latter is *tō-roc*; cf. ed-roc.]

torr, es; *m.* I. from Latin *turris, a tower*; the native word is *stīpel*; q. v.:—Ðīn nosu is suelc se torr (*turris*) on Liuano ðæm munte, Past. 11; Swt. 65, 24: Exon. Th. 266, 23; Jul. 402. Tor, Ps. Th. 60, 2: Exon. Th. 180, 26; Gū. 1285. Ðā hēt hire fæder hī bewyrcean on ānum torre mid twelf ðeówennum, Shrn. 105, 33. Æt torre *at the tower* (*of Babel*), Cd. Th. 101, 26; Gen. 1688. Tō beácne torr, 100, 19; Gen. 1666: Bt. 25, 4; Fox 162, 25. Monn getimberde torr (*turrem*), Mk. Skt. Lind. Rush. 12, 1. Torr (tor, Rush.), Lk. Skt. Lind. 14, 28. Āstāg Simon on ðone torr, Blickl. Homl. 187, 27. Hāt ðū mē ānne heáhne tor of mycclum beámum getimbrian, 183, 3. Hrōfas sind gehrorene, hreórge torras, Exon. Th. 476, 6; Ruin. 3: Andr. Kmbl. 1684; An. 844. Ceastre and torras (*farus*; v. fȳr-torr) and strēta and brycge geworhte wǣron, Bd. 1, 11; S. 480, 16. Mid ceastrum ða ðe wǣron mid weallum and torrum (*turribus*) and geatum getimbrade, 1, 1; S. 473, 28: Ps. Th. 47, 11: 121, 7. On ðæs sǣs waroþe tō sūþdǣle ðanon ðe hī sciphere on becom [hī] torras (*turres*) timbredon tō gebeorhge ðæs sǣs, Bd. 1, 12; S. 481, 11. Ða torras and ða scylfas on him bǣron ða elpendas, Nar. 4, 16. *O. Frs.* thoer: *O. H. Ger.* turri, turra *turris*.] Cf. tūr. II. from Celtic, *a projecting rock, a tor*:—Torr *scopulus*, Wrt. Voc. i. 38, 20. Ōð him (*the brook*) oninnan fel*þ* muntes mægenstān ātrendlod of ðæm torre (cf. micel stān wealwiende of ðam heáhan munte, Bt. 6; Fox 14, 29) *resistit rupe soluti objice saxi*, Met. 5, 17. Ǣrest on mercecumb (*in Dorset*), ðonne on grēnan pytt, ðonne on ðone torr æt mercecumbes ǣwielme, Cod. Dip. Kmbl. ii. 28, 32. On gyran torr (*in Devon*), iii. 412, 9. An horsa tor . . . on lytlan tor (*in Devon*), Cod. Dip. B. iii. 133, 10, 11. Stānrocca, torra *scopulorum*, Hpt. Gl. 449, 15. Torra *scopulorum*, 499, 68. Cf. Heáhtorra *alpium, montium*, 454, 42. v. fȳr-, geat-, heáh-, mere-, seoh-, stān-torr.

torrebrande, Wrt. Voc. ii. 61, 44, read *torre* brande; cf. *torribus* brandum, 94, 56.

tō-rȳpan. v. tō-rīpan.

tō-sǣlan; *p.* de; *impers. vb. To happen amiss* to a person (*dat.*) in respect to something (*gen.*), *to be lack* of something for a person:—Ne tōsǣleþ him gūþgemōtes siþþan ic þurh hylles hrōf gerǣce *he* (*the dog*) *will not want for fighting, when I* (*the badger*) *reach through the hill's roof*, Exon. Th. 397, 26; Rä. 16, 25. Ic beom strong ðæs gewinnes gif ic stille weorþe gif mē ðæs tōsǣleþ hī beóþ swīþran ðonne ic *I* (*the anchor*) *am strong for the struggle if I keep still; if I fail in that they will be stronger than I*, 398, 9; Rä. 17, 5. Tōsǣle, Prov. Kmbl. 65.

tō-samne, -somne; *adv. Together.* I. with verbs of motion, where meeting takes place, (1) without hostility:—Ðā cōman ðǣr tōsamne unārīmedlīco mengeo, Blickl. Homl. 191, 9. Ǣr hī tōsomne becōmun *antequam convenirent*, Mt. Kmbl. 1, 18. Hēht tōsomne ða heó sēleste wiste tō ðære hālgan byrig cuman, Elen. Kmbl. 2401; El. 1202. (2) with hostility:—Raðe ðæs ðe hié tōsomne cōmon *commisso praelio*, Ors. 4, 11; Swt. 208, 11. Fōron tōsomne wrāðe wælherigas, Cd. Th. 119, 19; Gen. 1982. II. with verbs implying collecting, assembling:—Beóþ ealle sǣfixas gegaderod tōsomne *omnes pisces maris in unum congregabuntur*, Num. 11, 22. Hī tōsomne eall werod clypedon *conuocant totam cohortem*, Mk. Skt. 15, 16. Leóde tōsomne bannan, Andr. Kmbl. 2188; An. 1095. Hēt ðā tōsomne sīne leóde, Cd. Th. 245, 26; Dan. 469. III. with verbs denoting joining, touching, mixing:—Tōsomne gerǣt *congelaverat*, Wrt. Voc. ii. 133, 37. Tōsomne cnyllaþ *conliserint*, 134, 66. Se wyrm gebeáh snūde tōsomne, Beo. Th. 5129; B. 2568. Ða stānas bióþ earfoþe tō tōdǣlenne and eác uneáþe tōsomne cumaþ, Bt. 34, 11; Fox 150, 25. Hié him geblendon tōsomne drync unheórne, Andr. Kmbl. 66; An. 33: Exon. Th. 88, 11; Cri. 1438. IV. of action, *in concert, at the same time*:—Ðā burston ða seofon weallas ealle tōsomne, Homl. Th. ii. 212, 31. Eall þreó nimeþ fȳres wælm tōsomne, Exon. Th. 60, 8; Cri. 966. Englas hlȳdaþ tōsomne, 55, 14; Cri. 883: Hy. 3, 16. Ðǣr gelāde leng ne mihton geseón tōsomne *the foes could not longer see one another*, Cd. Th. 190, 30; Exod. 207. V. of uninterrupted time:—Moyses fæste feówertig daga and feówertig nihta tōsamne, Homl. Th. ii. 100, 3. Tōsomne, 198, 13. Hē fæste hwīlum twēgen dagas, hwīlum þrȳ tōsomne, Shrn. 52, 20. Hit āgan rīnan .xl. daga and .xl. nihta tōsomne, Wulfst. 216, 33. [Heo ferden tosomne, Laym. 1393. Tosumne (togadere, 2nd MS.), 61. *O. Frs.* tō-samene: *O. Sax.* te-samne: *O. H. Ger.* zi-samane: *Ger.* zu-sammen.]

tō-samnian; *p.* ode *To assemble, collect*:—Ðā bæd hē hine ðæt hē sumne dǣl landes æt him onfēnge, ðæt hē mihte mynster on getimbrian and Godes ðeówas tōsomnian *he prayed him to receive from him a parcel of land, that he might thereon build a monastery and collect together servants of God*, Bd. 3, 23; S. 554, 11.

tō-sāwan; *p.* -seów *To sow broadcast, scatter seed*; fig. *to spread abroad, scatter, disperse*, (a) of concrete objects:—Sume hī cwǣdon, ðæt se līchoma ðe ǣne biþ tō duste gewend and wīde tōsāwon, ðæt hē nǣfre eft tōgædere ne cōme, Homl. Skt. i. 23, 376. Of Noes sunum ys tōsāwen (*disseminatum*) eall mancynn ofer eorðan, Gen. 9, 19. Is micel dǣl ðæs mancynnes gehwǣr wīde tōsāwen, Homl. Ass. 69, 94. (b) of abstract objects, *to disseminate* opinions, *distribute* favours, *sow* dissension:—Se mann ðe tōsǣwþ ungeþwǣrnysse betwux cristenum mannum, Homl. Th. i. 492, 14. Swā weorðlīce wīde tōsāweþ Dryhten his duguþe, Exon. Th. 299, 31; Crä. 110. Tōsāwaþ (*labia sapientium*) *disseminabunt* (*scientiam*, Prov. 15, 7), Kent. Gl. 511. Ða fyrmestan bydelas ðe Godes lāre geond ðās land tōseówon, Homl. Ass. 56, 143. Seó leáse gesetnys ðe þurh gedwolmen wīde tōsāwen is, Homl. Th. i. 438, 1.

tosca (-e; *f.* (?); *in the Ritual feminines sometimes end in* a), an; *m. A frog*:—Sceomiende (*the glosser has taken* rubeta *as connected with* rubeo) ða dió is ācuoeden tosca *rubeta illa quae dicitur rana*, Rtl. 125, 27. Sette him heard wīte hundes fleógan and hī ǣtan eác yfle tostan (toscan?) hæfdan hī eallunga ūt āworpen *immisit in eos muscam caninam, et comedit eos; ranam, et exterminavit eos*, Ps. Th. 77, 45. Sende on heora eorþan toscean teónlīce *misit in terram eorum ranas*, 104, 26. [Cf. (?) *O. H. Ger.* zuscen *to burn* (*so tosca might refer to the venomous character of the animal*), cf. (?), *also*, *Swed.* tossa *a toad*: *Dan.* tudse.]

tō-scādan, -scǣgde. v. tō-sceádan, -scecgan.

tō-scǣnan; *p.* de *To break to pieces*:—Bān ne tōscaenas (-scǣnas, Rush.) ł ni gebraecgaþ gē of him *os non comminuetis ex eo*, Jn. Skt. Lind. 19, 36. Ða feoturo forbræc ł tōscǣnde (-sceǣnde, Lind.) *compedes comminuisset*, Mk. Skt. Rush. 5, 4. Ne furðon ān bān næfde hē mid ōþrum ac tōscǣnede ofer eall lāgon and tōworpene geond ða wīdan eorþan *he had not even one bone along with another, but broken to pieces they lay in all directions and flung here and there throughout the wide world*, Homl. Skt. i. 23, 496. [Hi þe totorveþ . . . and þine fule bon toscheneþ, O. and N. 1120. In Layamon the word is intransitive:—Þu scalt toscæne mid mire eaxe . . . Corineus smat in enne stane . . . þe stan al tosceande (þat þe ston al tobrac, 2nd MS.), 2309-15.]

tō-sceacan, -scacan; *p.* -sceóc, -scōc; *pp.* -sceacen, scacen. I. *to shake to pieces, shake violently, to disturb*:—Tōscæcþ *concutit*, i. *turbat, terreat*, Wrt. Voc. ii. 136, 47. Stefn Drihtnes tōsceacende wēsten, Ps. Spl. 28, 7. II. *to shake off, drive away, disperse*:—Ic tōsceace *discutio*, Ælfc. Gr. 47; Zup. 277, 3. Hit ðæt āttor tōsceaceþ, Lchdm. i. 352, 14 note. Hundes sceanca tōsceaceþ ðone fefor, 362, 27. Hē tōsceóc ðone līg of ðam ofne, swā ðæt ðæt fȳr ne mihte him derigan, Homl. Th. i. 570, 14. Hē tōscōc ða dwollīcan nytennysse, 602, 35. Mōdes slǣp tōsceac *mentis somnum discute*, Hymn. Surt. 7, 23: *dissice*, 19, 17. Biþ ðæt gold tōsceacen, Wulfst. 148, 23: 263, 9. [Gromes . . . þe totwiccheþ and toschakeþ, O. and N. 1647. A wilde bor . . . man and houndes

. . . wiþ his taskes he al toshok, Beves 742. With shaking shal be toshaken pees, Wick. Is. 24, 20. Wynde may the plantes bigge toshake, Pall. 52, 240. The word is used also intransitively:—All þe worlde shall toshake, Anglia iii. 546, 156.]

tō-sceácerian; *p.* ode *To waste, devastate, scatter*:—Nū is eall mīn heord tōsceácerod *nunc omnis grex meus vastatus est; they were scattered* (Ezek. 34, 5), L. Ecg. P. iii. 16; Th. ii. 202, 28. Đā wurdon hī ealle đearle āfyrhte, and heora gesomnunga ealle wurdon sōna tōsceácerode *then* (*at the coming of the emperor Decius*) *they* (*the Christians*) *were all very frightened, and their congregations were at once scattered*, Homl. Skt. i. 23, 23. v. sceácere.

tō-sceád, es; *n.* I. *a separating, distinguishing, distinction*:—Ne sié fram abbode hāda tōsceád on mynstre gehealden *non ab abbate persona in monasterio discernatur*, R. Ben. 12, 7. Mid đæs micelum dōmes tōsceáde *cum magna examinis discussione*, Anglia xiii. 375, 141. II. *the faculty of distinguishing* objects presented to the mind, *discrimination, discerning*:—Se Hālga Gāst sylþ his gife đām đe hē wile. Sumum men hē forgifþ wītegunge, sumum tōsceád gōdra gāsta and yfelra (*to one is given by the Spirit prophecy; to another discerning of spirits* (discretio spirituum), 1 Cor. 12, 10), Homl. Th. i. 322, 27. III. *difference, diversity*:—Hū micel scyle bión đæt tōsceád & hū mislīce mon scyle menn lǣran mid đæm cræfte đæs lāreówdōmes *quanta debet esse diversitas in arte praedicationis*, Past. 23; Swt. 173, 12. Biþ tōsceád, swā swā se apostol sǣde: '*Stella ab stella differt in claritate*,' Homl. Ass. 43, 486. Betwuh đām þrim is swīþe micel tósceád, Bt. 42; Fox 256, 21. Dō sum tōsceád betwuh mē and unrihtwīsum folce *discerne causam meam de gente non sancta*, Ps. Th. 42, 1.

tō-sceádan, -scādan; *p.* -scēd, -sceád (*in the Northern Gospels weak forms are found, and* -sceádde *occurs in Bede*); *pp.* -sceáden. I. *to divide in two, separate* one thing from another, (1) literally, of local relations:—Swā swā sweord đa wunde tōsceát on tū, Past. 60; Swt. 453, 17. Se stream tōsceádeþ sūþfolc Angelđeóde and norþfolc *flumine meridiani et septentrionales Anglorum populi dirimuntur*, Bd. 1, 25; S. 486, 17. Neáh đam sǣ đe Engla land and Pehta land tōsceádeþ *in vicinia freti quod Anglorum terras Pictorumque disterminat*, 4, 26; S. 602, 36. Hē tōsceádes hiá betuih suā hiorde tōsceádas scīpo from ticgenum *separabit eos ab invicem, sicut pastor segregat oves ab haedis*, Mt. Kmbl. Lind. 25, 32. Đætte God efne-gigedraþ monno ne tōsceádeþ (tōsceáda, Lind.) hē (*separet*), Mk. Skt. Rush. 10, 9. On đæm dæge God tōscēd on twā eorđan and sǣ, Shrn. 63, 24: 62, 35. Đæt Severus onfēng micelne dǣl Breotone and đone mid dīce tōsceádde fram ōþrum þeódum *ut Severus receptam Brittaniae partem vallo a caetera distinxerit*, Bd. 1, 5; S. 476, 3. Đæt God gegeadrade monn ne tōslīte ł tōsceáđa (*separet*), Mt. Kmbl. Lind. 19, 6. Tōscādende *segregans*, Ps. Surt. 67, 10. Hē (*the stream*) on tū tōsceáden wyrđ, Met. 5, 18. Tōscāden, Wulfst. 26, 2. Đa syndon Temese streáme tōsceádene fram Centlande, Bd. 2, 3; S. 504, 16. Tōsceádenne mid Trēntan streáme wiþ Norþ-Myrcum *discreti fluvio Treanta ab Aquilonalibus Mercis*, 3, 24; S. 557, 37. .iiii. fȳr nōwiht miclum fæce betwyh him tōsceáden *quatuor ignes non multo ab invicem spatio distantes*, 3, 19; S. 548, 10. (2) figuratively, (a) *to divide* into parties, *cause division* or *dissension among*:—Hē tiolode hié betwux him tō tōscādanne . . . swā hē tōscēd đara ēhtera ānmōdnesse and Paulus com gesund đonon *inter semetipsos dividere studuit, quos contra se unitos vidit* . . . *facta in persecutorum unanimitate dissensio est, et divisa turba illaesus Paulus exivit*, Past. 47; Swt. 363, 1–8. (b) *to separate* contending parties *or* claims, *judge, decide between*:—God stōd godum on gemange, and hē hī on midle tōsceádeþ (*discernit*; he judgeth among the gods, A.V.), Ps. Th. 81, 1. Ic ne sēce mīn wuldor, is swā đeáh se đe sēcþ and tōscǣt (*judicat*, Jn. 8, 50), Homl. Th. ii. 232, 8. Tōscēd (*sors inter potentes*) *dijudicat* (Prov. 18, 18), Kent. Gl. 656. Tōscād *decerne* (*quod justum est*, Prov. 31, 9), 1134. Tōsceád *discerne* i. *dijudica*, Wrt. Voc. ii. 140, 62. (c) *to make a distinction* between things, *to distinguish, treat* or *regard differently*:—Sōđ lufu ne tōscǣt nǣnne be mǣglīcere sibbe *true love makes no distinction with respect to anybody on account of relationship*, Homl. Th. i. 128, 2. Se heofenlīca Fæder wuldraþ his bearn and tōscǣt his wuldor fram ōđra manna wuldre đearle unwiđmetenlīce *he distinguishes his glory beyond comparison from the glory of other men*, ii. 232, 9. Hwæt mǣnde Sanctus Paulus, đā hē his lāre suā cræftelīce tōsceád (-scēd, Cott. MSS.) (*gave such different counsel in the two cases*), and đone ōđerne lǣrde, đæt hē him anwald on tuge, ōđerne hē lǣrde geđyld? Past. 40; Swt. 291, 20. Đā đā hē đās eorđlīcan sibbe tōsceád (-scēd, Cott. MSS.) and đa hefonlīcan *cum terrenam pacem a superna distingueret*, 46; Swt. 351, 10. Ongiet georne hwæt sȳ gōd oþþe yfel and tōsceád simle *understand thoroughly what is good or evil, and always distinguish between them*, Exon. Th. 302, 34; Fä. 46. Tōsceáđ intingan mīnne of đeóde unhālgre *discerne causam meam de gente non sancta*, Ps. Spl. 42, 1. (d) *to separate* one thing from another with the mind, *to discern, distinguish, discriminate*:—Seó sāwul is on bōcum manegum naman gecȳged . . . Heó is *ratio*, đæt is gesceád, đonne heó tōscǣt, Homl. Skt. i. 1, 187. God gesyhþ ǣlces monnes geþanc, and his word and his dǣda tōscǣt (*cernit*), Bt. 40, 7; Fox 244, 1. Mid đære nose wē tōsceádaþ (*discernimus*) stencas, Past. 11; Swt. 65, 20. Is micel niéđđearf đæt se reccere đa đeáwas and đa unđeáwas cunne wel tōscādan *necesse est, ut rector animarum virtutes ac vitia vigilanti cura discernat*, 20; Swt. 149, 17. Mid hū micelan feó woldest đū habban geboht, đæt đū swutole mihtest tōcnāwan đīne frīnd and đīne fȳnd? Ic wāt đæt đū hit woldest habban mid miclan feó geboht, đæt đū hī cūþest wel tōscādan, Bt. 20; Fox 72, 22. Se đe gesceádwīsnesse hæfþ, se mæg tōsceádan hwæt hē wilnian sceal and hwæt hē onscunian sceal, 40, 7; Fox 242, 18: Shrn. 167, 4. Tōsceádan *discriminare*, Wrt. Voc. ii. 141, 2. Mǣden ācenned (*born on the first day of the moon*) biþ rihtlīce tōscēdende (-ne, MS.), Lchdm. iii. 184, 6. (e) *to separate* things from one another, *to order, dispose, appoint*:—Ic tōsceádo (-sceódo, Rush.) iuh suǣ tōsceádde (-sceódo, Rush.) mē fæder mīn đæt rīc *ego dispono uobis sicut disposuit mihi pater meus regnum*, Lk. Skt. Lind. 22, 29. Tōsceáda *disponere*, Mk. Skt. p. 2, 3. (f) *to separate* the parts of a confused whole, *to expound, interpret, render intelligible*:—Đegnum his tōsceádade (*disserebat*) alle, Mk. Skt. Lind. 4, 34. Tōsceádade *interpraetabatur*, Lk. Skt. Lind. 24, 27. Tōsceád (*dissere*) ūs bisen, Mt. Kmbl. Lind. 13, 36: *edissere*, 15, 15. (g) *to discuss*:—Tōsceádeþ *disputat*, Mt. Kmbl. p. 9, 18. II. *to send in different directions, to scatter, disperse*. v. sceádan, I. 3:—Manna bān Drihten tōsceádeþ *Deus dissipat ossa hominum*, Ps. Th. 52, 6. Tōscādeþ, 67, 14. Meolc wiđ wīne gemencged đæt āttor tōsceádeþ, Lchdm. i. 352, 14. Stefn Drihtnes tōsceádendis (*intercidentis*) lēg fȳres, Ps. Spl. 28, 7. Đā tōsceáden wearđ līg, tōlȳsed, Exon. Th. 277, 22; Jul. 584. III. *intrans. To be separated, to differ*:—Tōsceádaþ *discrepent, distant*, Wrt. Voc. ii. 141, 15. His līf tōscēd (e *has been made out of* æ, *and* g *erased before* d: MS. B. *has* tosced: v. tō-scecgan) fram ūssa tīda āswundenesse *vita illius a nostri temporis segnitia distabat*, Bd. 3, 5; M. 160, 25. [His lockes he toscædde, Laym. 30262. He wollde hire & te king todælenn and toshædenn, Orm. 19862. Englysche men usede þat tyme þe here of here ouerlyppes tosched & noȝt yschore, Trev. 3, 241. *O. H. Ger.* zi-sceidan *dividere, separare, segregare, discernere, distinguere*. Cf. *Goth.* dis-skaidan *differe, discernere*.] v. next two words.

tō-sceáden; *adj.* (*ptcpl.*) *Separate, distinct*:—Ǣlc þing đe tōsceáden biþ from ōþrum biþ ōþer, ōþer đæt þing, đeáh hī ætgædere sién. Gif đonne hwelc þing tōsceáden biþ from đam hēhstan gōde, đonne ne biþ đæt nō đæt hēhste gōd *quod a qualibet re diversum est, id non est illud, a quo intelligitur esse diversum. Quare quod a summo bono diversum est sui natura, id summum bonum non est*, Bt. 34, 3; Fox 138, 2–5. v. tō-sceadenness.

tō-sceádend, es; *m. One who divides* or *separates*:—Tōsceádend *discretor, divisor*, Wrt. Voc. ii. 141, 14.

tō-sceádenness, e; *f. Separation, distinction*:—Gē syndon clǣne, cwæđ hē tō his þegnum, næs nā hwæđere ealle. Hēr on đysum cwide wæs đæra apostola tōscādennys *here we have in these words a distinction made among the apostles*, Homl. Ass. 158, 162.

tō-scecgan (?); *p.* -scægde *To stand out distinctly, be separated* from surrounding objects:—His līf tōscægde fram ūssa tīda āswundennysse *vita illius a nostri temporis segnitia distabat*, Bd. 3, 5; S. 526, 35. v. scecgan; tō-sceádan, III.

tō-sceótan; *p.* -sceát, *pl.* -scuton *To rush in different directions, to disperse* (intrans.) *hurriedly, scatter*:—Tōscutan *dissiliunt*, Wrt. Voc. ii. 141, 9. Đā tōscuton đa deóflu (cf. đā wǣron tōstencte đa wiđerweardan gāstas *dispersi sunt spiritus infesti*, Bd. 5, 12; S. 629, 7; it is this passage in Bede which Ælfric is quoting), Homl. Th. ii. 352, 4. Đā wǣron đa munecas swīđe āfērede, nyston hwet heom tō dōnne wǣre, ac tōscuton; sume urnon intō cyrcean, Chr. 1083; Erl. 217, 12. [Þe shell toshett (*burst asunder*) on þe schire ground. Whan it cofli tooclef þer crep oute an addre, Alis. (Skt.) 1008.]

tō-sceótan, Met. 27, 19, *is rather to be taken under* sceótan. *The passage is*:—Ungesǣlge men deáþ ǣr willaþ foran tō sciótan = tōforan sceótan *anticipate, rush in front of*; cf. đa ungesǣligan menn forsceótaþ deáþ foran, Bt. 39, 1; Fox 212, 3; *and see passages under* foran, foran-tō.

tō-sciftan; *p.* te *To divide for the purpose of distribution, to divide and distribute*:—Se cyng intō Wealan fērde and his fyrde tōscyfte (*divided the force that the parts of it might take different routes*), and đæt land eall þurhfōr, swā đæt seó fyrd eall tōgædere com tō Snāwdūne, Chr. 1095; Erl. 232, 8. Se cyng lēt tōscyfton đone here geond eall đis land tō his mannon *the king had the troops divided and quartered all over the country on his men*, 1085; Erl. 218, 8.

tō-scirian; *p.* ede *To separate, part*:—Tōscereþ *separat*, Kent. Gl. 575: 603: 727. Bióþ tōscerede *separantur*, 669. Tōscirid ł tōdǣled *summotum*, Hpt. Gl. 528, 12. Tōscyrede *abjunctas*, Germ. 397, 441.

tō-scrīđan; *p.* -scrād *To flow in different directions, be dispersed*:—Đæt wæter unstille ǣghwider wolde wīde tōscrīþan, wāc and hnesce, ne meahte hit on him selfum ǣfre gestandan, Met. 20, 93. [*O. Sax.* ti-skrīdan:—Thie neƀal tiskrēd, Hēl. 5633.]

tō-scūfan; *p.* -sceáf *To thrust in different directions, thrust aside, scatter, disperse*, (1) literal:—Se đone līg tōsceáf hātan fȳres, Cd. Th.

237, 20; Dan. 340: Exon. Th. 189, 6; Az. 55. Engel đæt fŷr tôsceáf, 276, 11; Jul. 564. (2) figurative, *to do away, remove*:—Hê mid ælmessan ealle tôscûfeþ synna wunde, Exon. Th. 467, 28; Alm. 8. Tôsceáf (-sceóf, Rush.) đa mæhtigo of sedle *deposuit potentes de sede*, Lk. Skt. Lind. 1, 52.

tô-sencende, Gen. 9, 11. v. tô-stencan.

tô-sendan; *p.* de. I. *to send in different directions, send away, disperse, scatter*:—Âttru hit tôsend *venena diffundet*, Scint. 105, 9. Hê tôsende his geférau swilce for huntođes intingan, Homl. Skt. ii. 30, 104. Hê tôsende hî geond ealne middangeard, Homl. Th. i. 232, 5: 462, 15. Đæra cnapena hundnigontig đûsenda hî tôsendon tô gehwylcum leódscipum tô đeówte *ninety thousand boys they sent away to all nations to slavery*, 404, 15. Ehtatŷne sŷþum hundteóntig þûsenda hî tôsendon and wiđ feó sealdon wîde intô leódscipas, Blickl. Homl. 79, 23. II. *to destroy* (?): —Nabochodonosor com tô Hierusalem and đæt manncyn ofslôh and đa burh tôsende and đæt tempel tôwearp *destroyed* (the narrative in 2 Kings 25 or 2 Chron. 36 does not speak of the dispersion of the inhabitants of Jerusalem, but of the destruction of the city and the captivity of the inhabitants, so that *burh* seems to mean the city, not the citizens, and *tôsende* = destroyed: v. 2 Kings 25, 9, 10; 2 Chron. 36, 17–20) *the city and demolished the temple*, Ælfc. T. Grn. 8, 17.

tô-seóđan; *p.* -seáđ; *pp.* -soden *To boil to pieces*:—Seóđ on cetele and wylle ôþ đæt hió sié eal tôsoden, Lchdm. ii. 230, 8.

tô-sêđan; *p.* de *To prove*:—Drihten, đû ûs sealdest gesceádwîsnesse đæt wê mâgon tôsêđan and tôsceádan good and yfel, Shrn. 167, 3.

tô-settan; *p.* te *To set things apart from one another, to dispose; disponere*:—Se đe tôsetteþ ł gestiht spǽca his on dôme *qui disponet sermones suos in judicio*, Ps. Lamb. 111, 5: Blickl. Gl.: Ps. Spl. 111, 5. Tôsette *disposuit*, 83, 6: 104, 8.

tô-sîgan; *pp.* -sigen *To fall to pieces, to decay, get worn out*:—Nǽren tôsygene ł forgnidene *non extricabantur*; ic tôsîge ł forgnîde *extricor*, Hpt. Gl. 494, 36–39. Næs his reáf horig ne tôsigen, Homl. Th. i. 456, 20. Binnon feówertig geára fæce næs nân man gelegerod on eallum đam folce, ne heora reáf næs tôsigen (cf. vestimentum tuum nequaquam vetustate defecit, et pes tuus non est subtritus, en quadrigesimus annus est. Deut. 8, 4), ii. 196, 14. [Þe bodi schal tosie (*printed* -fye), Spec. 101.]

tô-sittan; *pp.* -seten *To sit at a distance from one another, to be placed apart*:—Đæs landes is .XLIII. þeóda wîde tôsetene for unwæstmbǽrnesse đæs londes *gentes sunt quadraginta duae, propter terrarum infoecundam diffusionem late oberrantes*, Ors. 1, 1; Swt. 14, 18.

tô-slacian; *p.* ode *To relax, to make* or *to become remiss*:—Tôslacad (*qui mollis et*) *dissolutus* (*est in opere suo*, Prov. 18, 9), Kent. Gl. 638.

tô-sleán; *p.* -slôh, *pl.* -slôgon; *pp.* -slegen *To strike to pieces, knock to bits*:—Tôslôg, tislôg *concidit*, Txts. 51, 516. Tôslôh, forheów *concidit*, Wrt. Voc. ii. 136, 16. (1) of material objects, (a) *to demolish, knock down* a building:—Þunor tôslôg heora hiéhstan godes hûs *aedes salutis ictu fulminis dissoluta est*, Ors. 4, 2; Swt. 160, 18: 6, 14; Swt. 268, 29. Swîđlîc wind tôslôh đæt hûs æt đâm feówer hwemmum *a strong wind broke down the house at the four corners*, Homl. Th. ii. 450, 18. Đa hǽþenan weras tôslôgon his glæsenne calic; đâ gesomnode se bisceoþ đa brocu, Shrn. 114, 25. (b) *to divide in two by a blow* or *stroke*:—Hê tôslôh sǽ *interrupit mare*, Ps. Lamb. 77, 13. Gif hit (*an egg*) ne tôcîne, tôsleah hwôn *if it will not crack, break it slightly with a blow*, Lchdm. iii. 18, 2. (2) of abstract objects, *to drive away* thoughts:—Đa yflan geþohtas đe him on môd becumaþ hê sceal sôna on Criste tôsleán . . . Đonne hê hié tôslyhþ on Criste đonne hê geđenceþ Cristes þrowunge and his wundra and mid đǽm geþohtum âflŷmeþ đa yfelan geþohtas *cogitationes malas cordi suo aduenientes mox ad Christum allidere*, R. Ben. 18, 2–6. [*O. Frs.* tô-slâ: *O. Sax.* te-slahan: *O. H. Ger.* zi-slahan: *Ger.* zer-schlagen.] v. un-tôslegen.

tô-slîfan; *p.* -slâf *To split in two, cleave, cut to pieces*:—Tôslâf, tôcleáf *findit*, Wrt. Voc. ii. 37, 32: 93, 8. [Thai laiden on with swerdes clere, Helm and scheld that stronge were Thai gonne hem al toschlîve. Gy of Warwike (in Halliwell's Dict.). *See* slîfan, *where the later form of that verb is cited from* Prompt. Parv. 459, *but the reference is omitted.*]

tô-slîtan; *p.* -slât, *pl.* -sliton; *pp.* -sliten *To tear in two, tear to pieces, tear asunder*:—Ic tôbrece ođđe tôslîte *rumpo*, Ælfc. Gr. 28, 6; Zup. 177, 4. Ic tôslîte *scindo*, Zup. 178, 6: *lacero*, 36; Zup. 214, 10: *lanio*, Zup. 216, 15. I. *to tear in two, in pieces, rend* material, e. g. a garment, a bond:—Đæt nîua tôslîtaþ *the new maketh a rent*, Lk. Skt. Lind. 5, 36. Se hêhsacerd tôslât ł tôrende (*scindens*) woedo his, Mk. Skt. Lind. 14, 63: Past. 3; Swt. 35, 20. Hê tôslât (*disrupisset*) đa raceteága, Mk. Skt. 5, 4. Ne tôslîte uê đæt cyrtel *non scindamus tunicam*, Jn. Skt. Lind. Rush. 19, 24. Đâ hêt ic eald hrægl tôslîtan and habban wiđ đæm fŷre *jussi scissas uestes opponere ignibus*, Nar. 23, 30. Đæs temples wâhryft wearđ tôsliten on twêgen dǽlas fram ufeweardon ôđ nyþeweard *the veil of the temple was rent in twain from the top to the bottom*, Mt. Kmbl. 27, 51. Tôslitten wæs đæt nett *rumpebatur retia*, Lk. Skt. Lind. 5, 6. I a. *to give a torn appearance to* anything, *to serrate* (of leaves):—Deós wyrt is gehwǽdon leáfun and tôslitenon, Lchdm. i. 290, 9. I b. figuratively:—Hê đone cræft briceþ and đa orđancas ealle tôslîteþ, Salm. Kmbl. 147; Sal. 72. Gif đê hwæt yfeles biþ, hraþe hyt byþ tôsliten, swâ wæs Abdias gyrdels đæs wîtegan, Lchdm. i. 328, 2. II. *to rend, cleave, break asunder* that which is hard or bulky:—Đû tôslite wyllas and burnan *tu dirupisti fontes et torrentes*; thou didst cleave the fountain and the flood (A. V.), Ps. Spl. 73, 16. Hê tôslât stân *dirupit petram*; he opened the rock (A. V.), 104, 39. Hê tôslât sǽ *interrupit mare*, Ps. Lamb. 77, 13. Stânas tôsliten ł tôbrocen wêron *petrae scissae sunt*, Mt. Kmbl. Lind. 27, 51. II a. figuratively:—Đâ ic đære heortan heardnesse mid geornfullîcre fandunge tôslât *cum cordis duritia studiosis percunctationibus scinditur*, Past. 21; Swt. 155, 5. III. *to tear* the flesh, *rend, bite, wound, lacerate*, generally of wounds made by animals, literally and figuratively:—Wurmas tôslîtaþ heora lîchaman mid fŷrenum tôđum, Homl. Th. i. 132, 17. Đa lîchoman đe wildeór âbiton, oþþe fixas tôslitan, Blickl. Homl. 95, 16. Gif hund mon tôslîte ođđe âbîte, L. Alf. pol. 23; Th. i. 78, 2. Đæt se werewulf tô swîđe ne tôslîte, ne tô fela ne âbîte of godcundre heorde, L. I. P. 6; Th. ii. 310, 31. Đe læs hig (*porci*) eów tôslŷton (-slîtas, Lind.) *ne dirumpant vos*, Mt. Kmbl. 7, 6. Tôslîtan (-en, MS.) *discerpere, dilaniare*, Hpt. Gl. 423, 54. Đam đe tôsliten (*bitten by a dog*) sŷ, Lchdm. i. 362, 25: 370, 16. Se đe tôsliten beó *he that is bitten by a snake*, Num. 21, 8: Homl. Th. ii. 240, 18. Swâ swâ sceáp from wildeórum beóþ fornumene, swâ đa earman ceasterwaran tôslitene wǽron fram heora feóndum (*discerpuntur ab hostibus*), Bd. 1, 12; S. 481, 26. Scîpo diówlîca ne forlǽt đû onerninge đætte wê sié tôsliteno *oves diabolica non sinas incursione lacerari*, Rtl. 36, 1. Gôman beóþ tôslitene, Soul Kmbl. 216; Seel. 110. Đa tôslitenan wunda heó forþrycceþ, Lchdm. i. 356, 14. IV. *to tear asunder, part, separate* what has been joined, *sever*:—Mon eáþe tôslîteþ, đætte nǽfre gesomnad wæs, Exon. Th. 380, 33; Rä. 1, 18. Sibbe tôslîtaþ sinhîwan tû, 284, 16; Jul. 698. Đæt God gegeadrade monn ne tôslîte *quod Deus conjunxit, homo non separet*, Mt. Kmbl. Lind. 19, 6. V. *to pull to pieces, destroy the existence of* an object, abstract or concrete, *to destroy, dissipate*:—Ic undôe ł tôslîto tempel đis *ego dissoluam templum hoc*, Mk. Skt. Lind. Rush. 14, 58. Hŷ sǽlđa tôslîtaþ, Salm. Kmbl. 697; Sal. 348. Tôslât *destruit*, Mt. Kmbl. p. 16, 16. Tôslîtende (eft gié tôslîtas, Lind. Rush.) Godes bebod *rescindentes uerbum Dei*, Mk. Skt. 7, 13. Rîc tôsliten biþ *regnum desolabitur*, Mt. Kmbl. Lind. 12, 25. Wæs semninga heofones smyltnes tôsliten *subito interrupta est serenitas*, Bd. 5, 1; S. 613, 24. Đurh đæt wierđ tôslieten (-sliten, Cott. MSS.) sió stilnes hiera hiéremonna môdes and biþ gedrêfed sió smyltnes hiera lîfes *subditorum vitam dissipata quietis tranquillitate confundunt*, Past. 40; Swt. 289, 7. VI. *to distract* the mind:—Hû oft sió bisgung đæs rîces tôslît đæt môd đæs recceres *quod plerumque occupatio regiminis soliditatem dissipet mentis*, Past. 4; Swt. 37, 11. VII. *intrans. To be different*:—Tôslittaþ *discordat*, Mt. Kmbl. p. 2, 8. [*O. H. Ger.* ze-slîzan *scindere, secidere, discerpere, lacessere, perdere, dissipare.*]

tô-slite, es; *m. A rent, tear, laceration, wound made by scratching, cutting,* or *biting*. v. slîtan, slite:—Gif hwâ tôbrŷsed sŷ, genim đâs wyrte . . . Eác swylce tôslite heó gehǽleþ, Lchdm. i. 122, 3. [*O. H. Ger.* zur-, zi-sliz *discidium, repudium.*] v. tô-slîtness, tô-slîtan, III.

tô-slîtere (?), es; *m. One who tears in pieces*; metaph. *one who causes dissension, a heretic*:—Tôslîterum (tôslitenum? v. sliten) *hereticis*, Lk. Skt. p. 2, 11. v. next word.

tô-slîtness, e; *f.* I. *a tearing in pieces, rending in pieces*:—Ungehêredre leoma tôslîtnysse wundade *inaudita membrorum discerptione lacerati*, Bd. 1, 7; S. 479, 14. II. fig. *dissension*:—Tôslîtnisse (-slittnise, Lind.) ł unsibbe *dissensio*, Jn. Skt. Rush. 7, 43.

tô-slûpan; *p.* -sleáp, *pl.* -slupon; *pp.* -slopen *To slip apart* or *away, be relaxed, dissolved*:—Heó wæs tôlêsed ł tôslopen *dissolvebatur, collabebatur*, Hpt. Gl. 502, 7. Tôslopen *remissus*, Germ. 393, 137: *dissipatum*, Wrt. Voc. ii. 139, 31. Âbogene, tôslopene *dimissa*, i. *humilia*, 140, 31. I. of that which is bound, *to have the connection between several objects* or *that between the parts of the same object relaxed*:—Gif hê hî ne bunde mid his unâbindendlîcum racentum, đonne tôslupan hî ealle *conjuncta naturarum ipsa diversitas dissociaret atque divelleret, nisi unus esset, qui quod nexuit contineret*, Bt. 35, 2; Fox 158, 1: 34, 12; Fox 154, 3. Hæfþ God geheaþorade ealle his gesceafta, đæt heora ǽlc wræđeþ ôþer, đæt hié ne môton tôslûpan, 21; Fox 74, 11. Se godcunda foreþonc heaþeraþ ealle gesceafta đæt hî ne môton tôslûpan of heora endebyrdnesse *providentia suis quaeque nectit ordinibus*, 39, 5; Fox 218, 31. Mid wriþan gewriþen grundweall nâ byþ tôslopen *loramento conligatum fundamentum non dissoluitur*, Scint. 200, 9. Gif se ân gestæđđega cyning ne staþelode ealla gesceafta, đonne wurdon hî ealle tôslopene and tôstencte, and tô nâuhte wurdon ealle gesceafta *quae nunc stabilis continet ordo, dissepta suo fonte fatiscant*, Bt. 39, 13; Fox 234, 27. I a. *to be dissipated, destroyed*:—Smyre đa sâr, hŷ tôslûpaþ, Lchdm. i. 268, 3. Môtan sǽs tôslûpan, iii. 36, 27. II. of that which binds, *to be loosed, undone*:—Đonne tôslupan đa bendas and tôlŷsede wǽron *sunt vincula soluta*, Bd. 4, 22; S. 591, 13, 22; 592, 7. Đâ wênde heó đæt seó snôd tôslupe, ac heó âfunde đa snôde mid eallum cnottum fæste gewriđen, Homl. Th. ii. 28, 25. Gif hê đa (brîdlas) lǽt tôslûpan *hic si frena remiserit*, Bt. 21; Fox 74, 33: Met.

11, 80. Nú syndon Satanases bendas swýðe tóslopene, Wulfst. 83, 9. **II a.** of illness:—Seó fæstnys (*costiveness*) tóslýpeþ (-slípeþ, MS. B.), Lchdm. i. 164, 20. **III.** *to get relaxed*, (a) of material things:—Liþa tóslopene *limbs relaxed in sleep*, Hymn. Surt. 2, 10. (b) of non-material things, *to be relaxed, get remiss*:—Ðonne mon lǽt tóslúpan ðone ege *nimia resolutione lenitatis*, Past. 40; Swt. 289, 2. Ðæt ungeornfulle mód and ðæt tóslopene *anima dissoluta*, 39; Swt. 283, 12. Ðænne geþanc orsorh byð ágyfen on slǽwþe mód byð tóslopen *cum mens secura redditur, in torporem animus laxatur*, Scint. 92, 17. **IV.** *to get paralysed, get powerless*, (a) physically:—Ðǽr ða sina tóslúpaþ, Lchdm. ii. 280, 3. Ðá wearð se líchama eal tóslopen, Homl. Th. i. 86, 25. Sum mǽden langlíce læg on legerbedde seóc, tóslopen on limum, sámcucu geðúht, ii. 510, 25. Se læg seofon geár tóslopenum limum, Homl. Skt. i. 6, 255. (b) in reference to the mind:—Ðá wearð heora heorte tóslopen and heora gást ne beláf on him *dissolutum est cor eorum et non remansit in eis spiritus*, Jos. 5, 1.

tó-slúping, e; *f. Dissolution*:—Tóslúpincg lífes *dissolutio uitae*, Scint. 68, 8.

tó-smeágan, -smeán; *p.* -smeáde *To examine in detail, enquire into the several parts of* a subject:—Betwuh ðám þrím is swíþe micel tósceád. Gif wit ðæt ealle sculon ásmeágan (tósmeágan, Cott. MS.), ðonne cume wit late tó ende ðisse béc, oððe nǽfre, Bt. 42; Fox 256, 21.

tó-snídan; *p.* -snád, *pl.* -snidon; *pp.* -sniden. **I.** *to cut in two, cut in pieces, cut up*:—Hé geteáh his seax and genam his sciccels ðe hé him on hæfde, tósnád ðá hine on twá, and healfne sealde ðæm þearfan . . . Ðá wǽron ðǽr manige men ðe . . . hine bismrodan, ðæt hé his gegyrelan tósnídan sceolde, Blickl. Homl. 215, 5-10. Tósnidenre hreáþemúse blód, Lchdm. ii. 236, 17. Uppan ðám sticceon ðe ðǽr tósnidene beóþ *membra quae sunt caesa*, Lev. 1, 8. **II.** *to cut away, cut off*:—Sum mon tósnáð (*amputauit*) him ðone æárliprica, Mk. Skt. Rush. 14, 47. [*O. Frs.* te-snítha: *O. H. Ger.* za-snídan *descindere, dirimere*.]

tó-sócness *and* tó-sócnung *gloss* adquisitio:—In tósócnisse *in adquisitionem*, Rtl. 28, 35. Tósócnung *adquisitio*, 81, 14.

tó-somne, -somnian. v. tó-samne, -samnian.

tó-sprǽc, e; *f. Speech addressed to a person, conversation*:—Hine God hiéwcúðlícor on eallum ðingum innan lǽrde ðonne óðre menn mid his gelómlícre tósprǽce *quem* (Moses) *de cunctis interius per conversationem cum Deo sedulam locutio familiaris instruebat*, Past. 41; Swt. 304, 20. [*O. H. Ger.* za-sprácha *eloquium*.]

tó-sprǽdan; *p.* de *To spread out, extend, expand, spread in different directions*:—Seó henn tósprǽt hyre fyðera and ða briddas gewyrmþ, Anglia viii. 309, 26. Heó tósprǽt hire bósm ðǽr ðǽr ða réðan wuniaþ . . ., and heó is genyrwed on ðone ende ðe ða gesceádwísan wuniaþ *she expands her bosom where the fierce dwell . . ., and is straitened in the quarter where the discreet dwell*, Homl. Th. i. 536, 18. Tósprǽd ðíne fingras, Techm. ii. 122, 25. Ðæs mannes sáwl biþ on Gode tósprǽd, swá ðæt heó oferstíhþ middaneard, and eác hí sylfe, Homl. Th. ii. 186, 8. Stríc mid tósprǽddum handum niðer ofer ðíne breóst, Techm. ii. 119, 25. Wíf tósprǽddum loccum *a woman with dishevelled locks*, Lchdm. iii. 208, 10. [His holie lichame was tospred on þe holie rode, O. E. Homl. ii. 21, 29. Tosprad, 205, 33. He tospret touward ou his ermes, A. R. 402, 9. Þe Brutones þat were tosprad here and þere, R. Glouc. 134, 15. With open hede . . . her hair tosprad, Gow. ii. 260, 4. *O. L. Ger.* te-spreidan *dispergere*: *O. H. Ger.* zar-, za-spreitan *spargere, expandere, dispergere*.]

tó-springan; *p.* -sprang, *pl.* -sprungon; *pp.* -sprungen *To spring asunder, fly to pieces, to crack, burst open*:—Tó ðám handum ðæt flǽsc tóspringaþ *for chapped hands*, Lchdm. iii. 114, 4. Se deófol wearp ǽnne stán tó ðære bellan, ðæt heó eall tósprang *the bell flew all to pieces*, Homl. Th. ii. 156, 10. Hí becómon tó ðam ísenan geate and ðæt tósprang ðǽrrihte him tógeánes *they came to the iron gate, and it burst open straightway at their approach*, 382, 12. Tósprang *dissilit*, Germ. 399, 272. Tóspringe *crepet*, 398, 112. [Er him þe herte tospringe, C. L. 593. *O. H. Ger.* zi-springan *dissilire*: *Ger.* zer-springen.]

tó-sprytting, e; *f. Instigation.* v. spryttan, **II b.**

tostan, Ps. Th. 77, 45. v. tosca.

tó-standan; *p.* -stód; *pp.* -standen. **I.** *to stand apart, be distant*; fig. *to differ, be different*:—Swé micel tóstondeþ eástdael from westdaele *quantum distat oriens ab occasu*, Ps. Surt. 102, 12. Tóstent, Blickl. Gl. Hú micel tóstent seó godspellíce sóðfæstnyss fram sceade ðære ealdan ǽ, Homl. Th. ii. 70, 29. Tóstænt *differt*, Wrt. Voc. ii. 140, 13. Tóstent *discrepat*, 141, 25: *dispartire*. Tóstandaþ *distent*, i. *separent*, 24. Tóstandendum mægna *distantes vires*, i. *discordes*, 26. **II.** *to stand aloof, not to be forthcoming*:—Be ðon ðe mon wíf bycgge, and ðonne sió gift tóstande. Gif mon wíf gebycgge, and sió gyft forð ne cume, L. In. 31; Th. i. 122, 3-6.

tó-stencan; *p.* -stencte; *pp.* -stenced, -stenct. **I.** *to scatter* the parts of a whole, *disperse* a number of objects gathered together:—Ðú tóstencst hig *dissipabis eos*, Ps. Spl. 143, 8. Se wulf cymþ tó ðám sceápum, sume hé ábítt, sume hé tóstencþ, Homl. Th. i. 240, 24: 238, 16. Ðinne líchoman geond ðisse ceastre lanan hié tóstenceaþ, Blickl. Homl. 237, 5. Ðú tóstenctest feónd ðíne *dispersisti inimicos tuos*, Ps. Spl. 88, 11: 43, 13. Gif wind tó cóme, ðonne tóstencte hé ða lác *sacrificium superveniens aura dispergeret*, Past. 33; Swt. 217, 22. Se godcunda anweald hí (*the builders of Babel*) tóstencte, Bt. 35, 4; Fox 162, 24: Homl. Th. i. 318, 18. Tósteng (*dissipa*) þeóda ðe gefeoht willaþ, Ps. Spl. 67, 34. Ða lác tóstencean (*dispergere*), Past. 33; Swt. 219, 5. Tóstencud biþ ðæt éde, Mk. Skt. Rush. 14, 27. Tóstenced, Exon. Th. 16, 21; Cri. 256. Tóstencte *dispersae*, Wrt. Voc. ii. 140, 71. Ðá wǽron tóstencte (*dispersi sunt*) ealle ða wiðerweardan gástas, Bd. 5, 12; S. 629, 7: 1, 16; S. 484, 14: Bt. 39, 13; Fox 234, 27: Homl. Th. ii. 244, 34. **II.** *to destroy* the integrity of a whole, *dissipate, bring to nought, overthrow*:—Tóstencþ (*disperdat*) Drihten ealle weleras fácnfulle, Ps. Spl. 11, 3. Drihten tóstenceþ (*dissipat*) geþeaht ðeóda, 32, 10. Tóstencþ goldhord *dissipabit thesaurum* (Prov. 21, 20), Kent. Gl. 793. Se (*Edwy*) þurh his cildhádes nytenesse his ríce tóstencte and his ánnesse tódǽlde, Lchdm. iii. 434, 36. Tóstencton (*dissipaverunt*) unrihtwíse ǽ ðíne, Ps. Spl. 118, 126. Hí munucregol myrdon and mynstra tóstæncton, Chr. 975; Erl. 127, 21. Ofermódignyss seó ðe englas cúþe beswícan, micele má menn tóstencean (*dissipare*), Scint. 83, 13. Gif ys of mannum geþeaht ðis oððe weorc, sí tostenct (*dissoluetur, dissipabitur*); gif hit of Gode ys, gé ne mágon tóstencean (*dissoluere*) (Acts 5, 38, 39), 199, 2-4. Tóstencendes *dissipantis* (*sua opera*, Prov. 18, 9), Kent. Gl. 639. Ne biþ flód tóstencende, (-sencende, MS.) ða eorðan *neque erit diluvium dissipans terram*, Gen. 9, 11. Se yfela willa biþ tóstenced, swá récels beforan fýre, gif mon ðæt weorc þurhtión ne mæg (*potuisse miserius est*) *sine quo voluntatis miserae langueret effectus*, Bt. 38, 2; Fox 196, 31. Sint tóstente *dissipantur* (*cogitationes*, Prov. 15, 22), Kent. Gl. 530. **II a.** *intrans. To perish*:—Hí tóstencton on ende *disperierunt in Endor*, Ps. Spl. 82, 9. v. next three words.

tó-stencedness, e; *f.* **I.** *dispersion*:—Drihten tóstencednyssa (*dispersiones*) somnigende, Ps. Spl. 146, 2. **II.** *dissipation, destruction*:—Hit is micel mægena tóstencennes (-stencednes, MS. T.) *plurima destructio est*, R. Ben. 128, 6. Ungeþyld is ealra mægna tóstencednys, Homl. Th. ii. 544, 6. Cometa, ðonne hé ætýwþ, ðonne tácnaþ hé hungor oððe cwealm oððe tóstencednysse ðæs eardes, Anglia viii. 321, 22. v. tó-stencan.

tó-stencend, es; *m. One who dissipates* or *squanders, a prodigal*:—Tóstencend *prodigus*, Lchdm. i. lxi, 7.

tó-stencness, e; *f. Dispersion*:—Tóstencnisse *dispersiones*, Ps. Surt. 146, 2.

tó-stician; *p.* ode *To stab to pieces, wound severely by stabs, destroy by thrusts*:—Funde hé hiene ǽnne be wege licgan mid sperum tósticad healfcucne *invenit in itinere solum relictum, confossum vulneribus et extrema vitae efflantem*, Ors. 3, 9; Swt. 128, 14. [Cf. *Ger.* zer-stechen.] Cf. tó-stingan.

tó-stincan; *p.* -stanc, *pl.* -stuncon *To distinguish by smell*:—Ðurh ða nosu wé tóstincaþ, hwæt clǽne biþ, hwæt fúl, Homl. Th. ii. 372, 30.

tó-stingan; *p.* -stang, *pl.* -stungon *To prick to pieces, break by pricking*:—Genim wulfes swýþre eáge and hyt tósting, Lchdm. i. 362, 2. Ðonne ðú ðæt geswel tóstinge oþþe sníþe, ii. 208, 20. [Olde men neddren tostyngeþ (*sting them all to pieces, wound severely with their stings*), Misc. 152, 177.] Cf. tó-stician.

tó-stregdan, -strédan. [*For conjugation see* stregdan.] **I.** *trans. To disperse, scatter, destroy.* The verb occurs mostly in glosses and renders the Latin verbs *spargere, aspergere, dispergere, disperdere, dissipare, dispertire, destruere*:—Mildheortnisse míne ic ne tóstregdo (-stréde, Ps. Spl., -stregde, C.) *misericordiam meam non dispergam*, Ps. Surt. 88, 34. Ic tóstréde, Scint. 230, 7. Tóstraigdes ł tódrífeþ *dispergit*, Jn. Skt. Lind. 10, 12. Tóstrét (-straegdæþ, Lind.: -stregdes, Rush.), Lk. Skt. 11, 23. Tóstrigeded *disperdet*, Ps. Surt. 77, 38. Tóstrédeþ *spargit*, Ps. Spl. 147, 5: *aspergit*, Blickl. Gl.: *dispersit*, Ps. Th. 111, 8. Fægere weras tóstrédaþ ðone líg ðæt hé ne mæg ná sceðþan ðisse fǽmnan *fair men scatter the flame, so that it cannot harm this virgin*, Shrn. 130, 31. Ðú tóstrugde úsic *dispersisti nos*, Ps. Surt. 43, 12. Tóstregdyst, Ps. Spl. C. 43, 13. Hé tóstregde *dispersit*, 111, 8. Tóstrægd, Lk. Skt. Lind. Rush. 1, 51: Rtl. 177, 15. Tóstregd hié *disperde illos*, Ps. Surt. 53, 7: *disperge*, 58, 12. Tóstrigden (-stregdyn, Ps. Spl. C.) wé hié *disperdamus eos*, 82, 5. Hé ne tóstrugde hié *ne disperderet eos*, 105, 23. Tóstrogden biþ *dispertiatur*, Mk. Skt. Rush. Lind. 3, 25. Ne biþ forléten stán ofer stáne se ðe ne sié tóstrogden (*destruatur*), 13, 2: Lk. Skt. Lind. 21, 6. Tóstrogden biðon (*dispargentur*) ða scípo, Mk. Skt. Lind. 14, 27. Ða ðe uoeron tóstrogden *qui erant dispersi*, Jn. Skt. Lind. 11, 52. Hié bióð tóstrogdne *dispergentur*, Ps. Surt. 58, 16: *dissipentur*, 67, 2. Tóstródne, 91, 10. Tóstréde synd (*dispersa sunt*) ealle bán míne, Ps. Spl. 21, 12. Geþancu and geþeahtu ðíne tóstrédde and tó náht getealde beón getácnaþ *the dream betokens that your thoughts and counsels will be dissipated and counted for nought*, Lchdm. iii. 214, 24. Scípa tóstrogdenra *ovium dissipatorum*, Rtl. 9, 38. **II.** *intrans. To be dispersed, not to keep within proper bounds*:—Ðonne ðæt mód flíhþ ðæt ðæt hit sié gebunden mid ege and mid láre, ðonne tóstrét (-strétt, Hatt. MSS.) hit on yfelre and on unnytte wilnunga and hæfþ ðæs suíðe micelne hunger *ut, quo se per* *disciplinam ligare dissimulat, eo se esuriens per voluptatum desideria spargat*, Past. 39; Swt. 283, 19.

tō-sundrian; *p.* ode *To separate*:—Hwanne hē tōsundrode bearn Adames *quando separabat filios Adam*, Cant. M. ad fil. 8. v. tō-syndrian.

tō-swāpan; *p.* -sweóp *To disperse by a sweeping movement, to sweep apart* or *away*:—Se đone līg tōsceáf, tōsweóp hine and tōswende þurh đa swīđan miht *he thrust back the flame on every side, swept and dashed it away by his strong might*, Cd. Th. 237, 23; Dan. 342. Tōsweóp and tōswengde, Exon. Th. 189, 13; Az. 59.

tō-swellan; *pp.* -swollen *To swell out, grow big*:—Ic tōswelle *turgeo*, Ælfc. Gr. 26, 3; Zup. 155, 12. Tōswyllaþ *grossescunt, intumescunt*, Hpt. Gl. 447, 29. Se earm wæs swā swīþe greát and tōswollen *brachio in tantum grossescente*, Bd. 5, 3; S. 616, 23. Wiþ tōtece ... đæt tōswollene lim fram đære uferan healfe beþe, Lchdm. ii. 68, 13. Wæs ān cnapa swīđe tōswollen þurh wyrmes slege, Homl. Th. ii. 514, 7: Homl. Skt. i. 3, 481. Đa tōswolnan *turgida*, Wrt. Voc. ii. 93, 7. Of đām tōswollenum fōtum (*feet swollen with dropsy*), Homl. Th. i. 86, 11. [Al ic æm toswollen, Laym. 17815. Heorte tobollen & toswollen, A. R. 282, 8. Toswelle *intumescere*, Wick. Jerem. 5, 22. Toswal; *p.* Mand. F. *O. H. Ger.* zi-suollan *tumida*.]

tō-swengan; *p.* de *To dash asunder, dispel by a stroke, drive apart.* v. tō-swāpan. [Cf. Mid sweorde toswungen (tohewe, 2nd MS.), Laym. 8026.]

tō-sweorcan *to make dark*:—Beóþ tōsworcene ł āþēstrede *obscurantur*, Hpt. Gl. 447, 36.

tō-swīfan *to move off in different directions*:—Ǣghwilc ōþer ūtan ymbclyppeþ, đȳ læs hī tōswīfen *each from without embraces other, lest they take their separate courses*, Met. 11, 36. v. Bt. 21; Fox 74, 11 *in* tō-slūpan, I.

tō-syndrian; *p.* ode *To separate*; fig. *to distinguish*:—Mid him hē tōsyndraþ gif beteran ōđrum wē beóþ gemētte *apud ipsum discernitur si meliores aliis inveniamur*, R. Ben. Interl. 14, 8. Đū settest on foldan swīđe feala cynna and tōsyndrodest hig siđđan, Hy. 9, 21; Btwk. 198, 6: Hy. 7, 65; Dom. L. 44, 65. Gescādene ł tōsendrede *discretas, segregatas*, Hpt. Gl. 411, 21. v. tō-sundrian.

tot *a projection* (?):—Tot *artura*, Wrt. Voc. ii. 100, 73. [Cf. Þe eorþe aroos in þe manere of a tote (*in modum cumuli*), Trev. v. 163, 11 note. Tot, tote *a tuft*, Halliwell's Dict. Tute *a jutting out, projection*; tute *to jut out*, Jamieson. *Icel.* tota *a protuberance*; tūtna *to be swelled up*: *Dan.* tude *a spout*.] v. ge-tot; tot-rida.

tō-talu, e; *f.* *Reputation*:—Fore đassum tōtales intinge *pro hac reputationis causa*, Rtl. 102, 5.

tō-tellan; *p.* -teled *To distinguish in counting, count separately*:—Ān īglond ligþ ūt on gārsecg đǣr nǣngu biþ niht on sumera ne wuhte đon mā on wintra dæg tōteled *an island lies out in the ocean, where in summer no night can be distinguished in reckoning time, any more than in winter day*, Met. 16, 15.

tō-teón; *p.* -teáh, *pl.* -tugon; *pp.* -togen. I. *to pull to pieces, tear to pieces* (lit. and fig.):—Se wyrm đa tungan tōtȳhþ, Soul Kmbl. 234; Seel. 121. His æfterfolgeras feówertiéne geár đisne middangeard tōtugon and tōtǣron (*dilaniaverunt*), Ors. 3, 11; Swt. 142, 23. Đām đe ūs mid tōđum tōteón woldan, Ps. Th. 123, 5. Biþ seó tunge tōtogen (beóþ hira tungan tōtogenne, Soul Kmbl. 222) on tȳn healfe, Exon. Th. 373, 25; Seel. 115. II. *to pull away*:—Tōtoghene *detracta*, Hpt. Gl. 515, 14. [Me þe sculde nimen and al tōteón mid horse, O. E. Homl. i. 9, 21. *O. H. Ger.* zi-ziohan *distranere, detrahere*.]

tō-teran; *p.* -tær, *pl.* -tǣron; *pp.* -toren *To tear to pieces*:—Ic tōtere *lanio*, Ælfc. Gr. 24; Zup. 137, 2. Tōteran *discerpere*, Hpt. Gl. 520, 75. Beón tōtoren *lacerari*, 527, 55. I lit. *to tear to pieces* a material:—Đū tōtǣre (*conscidisti*) mīn hwīte ; rægl, Ps. Th. 29, 11. Hē đæs beran ceaflas tōtær, Ælfc. T. Grn. 7, 15. Hē đone pistol tōtær, Homl. Th. ii. 122, 30. Hē tōtær his tunecan, 450, 21. Hī tōtǣron heora reáf, 454, 11. Fȳrene næddran đæt folc tōtǣron, Num. 21, 6. Swilce hē tōtǣre sum eáđelīc ticcen *quasi hoedum in frusta discerpens*, Jud. 14, 6. II. metaph. of violent feeling or action, *to tear to pieces, to harass, distract, destroy*:—Gȳtsung ealle middaneardes rīcu tōtyrþ *auaritia universa mundi regna discerpserit*, Scint. 99, 8. Welan đa sāwla tōteraþ mid pricungum mislīcra geđohta, Homl. Th. ii. 88, 22. His æfterfolgeras feówertiéne geár đisne middangeard tōtugon and tōtǣron (*dilaniaverunt*), Ors. 3, 11; Swt. 142, 24. Be gōde ōþres nā sāriga đū, for nānes gesun[d]fulnysse đū sī tōtoren *de bono alterius non doleas, nullius prosperitate lacereris*, Scint. 77, 9. Hit ongeat his lāre swīþe tōtorene ... se wīsdōm sǣde đæt his gyngran hæfdon hīne swā tōtorenne, Bt. 3, 1; Fox 4, 31–6, 2. [Wolde he teteren roted fleshs ... auh teteređ and tolimeđ cwike fleschs, A. R. 84, 5–8. Anne curtel þe wes swiđe totoren, Laym. 4994. Our lordes body they totere, Chauc. C. T. Group C. 474. Cf. *Goth.* dis-tairan.]

tōþ; *gen.* tōþes; *dat.* tēþ; *inst.* tōþe; *pl.* toeđ, tēþ, *and* tōþas; *m.* *A tooth, tusk*:—Tōđ *dens*, Wrt. Voc. i. 64, 54. Tōþ, 282, 70. Forrotad tōđ *dens putridus*, Kent. Gl. 966. Ǣt đām feówer tōđum fyrestum, æt gehwylcum .vi. scillingas; se tōđ se đanne bī standeþ .iv. scill.; se đe đonne bī đam standeþ .iii. scill.; and đonne siþþan gehwilc scilling *for knocking out the four front teeth, for each a fine of six shillings: the tooth that stands next must be paid for with four shillings; that which stands next to this with three shillings; and then each tooth afterwards with a shilling*, L. Ethb. 51; Th. i. 16, 2–4. Tōđ wiđ tēđ *dentem pro dente*, Ex. 21, 24: Lev. 24, 20. Tōđ fore tēđ, L. Alf. 19; Th. i. 48, 21. Sete on đone sāran tōþ, and hwīlum ceówe mid đȳ sāran tōþe, Lchdm. ii. 310, 16: Exon. Th. 495, 9; Rä. 84, 5. Gif hē tōđ of āsleá, Ex. 21, 27. Tōđ for tōđ, Mt. Kmbl. 5, 18. Tēđ *dentes*, tōđa flǣsc *gingivae*, đa eahta forworden tēđ betwux tuxum *adversi dentes*, Wrt. Voc. i. 43, 29–34. Wiđ đæt cildum būtan sāre tēđ wexen *to make teething easy for children*, Lchdm. i. 346, 13. Gif đa tēþ synd hole, ii. 310, 17. Oft mann smeáþ hwæđer tēþ bǣnene beón, Lchdm. iii. 104, 4, *and see whole article.* Heora tōþas wǣron gelīce horses twuxan, Guthl. 5; Gdwin. 34, 24: Exon. Th. 226, 18; Ph. 407. Mannes tōđa beóþ on eallum his līfe .ii. and .xxx., Salm. Kmbl. 192, 13. Tōđa sār, Lchdm. i. 72, 24. Tōþa wagung, 334, 9. Tōþa grystlung (grisbittung tōđana, Lind.) *stridor dentium*, Lk. Skt. 13, 28. Tōđa gebitt, Homl. Th. i. 126, 20. Tōđa geheáw, Cd. Th. 285, 18; Sat. 339. Būtan tōđum *suaeder*, Txts. 101, 1967. Hié (*walruses; so Icel.* tönn *is used of walrus-tusk*) habbaþ swīþe æþele bān on hiora tōþum; đa tēđ hié brohton sume đæm cyninge, Ors. 1, 1; Swt. 18, 1. Hē tōđum gristbitaþ *stridet dentibus*, Mk. Skt. 9, 18. Synfull tōþum torn þolaþ *peccatos dentibus suis fremet*, Ps. Th. 111, 9: Jdth. Thw. 25, 21; Jud. 272. Toeđ (tēþ, Ps. Spl.) synfulra, Ps. Surt. 3, 8: ii. p. 194, 19. Tēđ, Deut. 32, 24. Tōđ (tēđ, Ps. Spl.: tōđas, Ps. Th.), Ps. Surt. 57, 7. Hī biton heora tēđ him tōgeánes, Homl. Th. i. 46, 27. Tōþas, Exon. Th. 374, 5; Seel. 121: Salm. Kmbl. 230; Sal. 114. [*Goth.* tunþus: *O. Frs.* tōth, tond: *O. Sax. O. L. Ger.* tand: *O. H. Ger.* zand: *Icel.* tönn.] v. cweorn-, flǣsc-, fore-, grinde(-ig)-, wang-tōþ.

-tōþ, -tōþe *-toothed.* [*Icel.* -tannr.] v. blōdig-tōþ, twisel-tōþe.

tōþ-ece, es; *m.* *Tooth-ache*:—Tōđæcce mē forwyrnde ǣlcre leornunga ... Ic wāt đæt manig broc byđ mycle strengre đonne tōđæce, đeáh ic nǣfre nān strengre ne geđolode, Shrn. 185, 9–16. Lǣcedōmas wiþ đam uferan tōđece ge wiþ đam niþeran, Lchdm. ii. 50, 7: 52, 6, 7. v. tōþ-wærc.

tō-þegnung, e; *f.* *Administration*:—Tōþēnung *amministratio*, Anglia xiii. 441, 1085.

tō-þenedness, e; *f.* *Distension*:—Tōþenednyssum *distentionibus*, Hpt. Gl. 529, 1.

tō-þerscan; *p.* -þærsc, *pl.* þurscon *To knock to pieces*:—Đā com him swilc wind ongeán, swilce nān mann ǣr ne gemunde, and đa scipo ealle tōbeót and tōþræsc, Chr. 1009; Erl. 142, 5.

tōþ-gār, es; *m.* *A tooth-pick*:—Dō medmicel on đa eágan mid tōþgāre, Lchdm. ii. 36, 9. v. tōþ-sticca.

tō-þindan; *p.* -þand, *pl.* -þundon; *pp.* -þunden *To swell, grow big*:—Ic tōđinde *tumeo*, đū tōđindst (-þintst, MSS. F. R.: -þindest, MS. U.: -þinst, MS. W.) *tumes*, hē tōđint *tumet*, Ælfc. Gr. 16; Zup. 107, 8–9. I. in a physical sense:—Rif tōþand mǣdenes *alvus tumescit Virginis*, Hymn. Surt. 44, 1. Tōþindende *turgescens, intumescens* (*in cumulum*), Hpt. Gl. 465, 11. Tōþunden *gravis*, Germ. 390, 142. II. in a metaphorical sense, *to swell with pride, be puffed up, be arrogant*:—Tōþint *intumuerit, superbierit*, Hpt. Gl. 423, 25. Gif heora hwylc tōđint and hine on mōdignesse onhefþ and hē on đam leahtre biþ onfunden *si quisque ex eis inflatus superbia repertus fuerit reprehensibilis*, R. Ben. 46, 16. Gif hwylc brōđor ongyten biþ tōþunden (*contumax*), 48, 3. Tōđunden ođđe mōdig *contumax*, Ælfc. Gr. 9, 60; Zup. 69, 4. Is tōþundon (*inflammatum*) mīn heorte, Ps. Lamb. 72, 21. Tōþundenys gylpes *tumentis jactantiae*, Hpt. Gl. 527, 36. Gif ǣnig mid tōđundene mōdignesse *si aliquis tumido supercilio inflatus*, Chart. Th. 319, 13. Ofermōdignysse tōþondenre tōblāwen, Anglia xiii. 441, 1084. Hē hine mid tōđundenum mōde forseah, Homl. Th. i. 330, 20: 450, 33. Tōþundenne and āstrehtne hneccan *tumentem et erectam cervicem*, Scint. 83, 17.

tōþ-leás; *adj.* *Toothless*:—Tōþleásera *edentularum*, Germ. 394, 305. [*O. H. Ger.* zan(e)-lōs *edentulus, edentatus*: *Icel.* tann-lauss.]

tōþ-mægen, es; *n.* *Strength of teeth* or *tusks*:—Eofor tōþmægenes trum, Menol. Fox 499; Gn. C. 20.

tōþ-rima, -reoma, an; *m.* *A gum*:—Tōþrima *gingifa*, Wrt. Voc. ii. 41, 22. Tōđreoma *ingua* (*gingiua*?), i. 64, 55. Tōþriman *gingifa*, 282, 72. Wiđ tōþa sāre and tōđreomena, Lchdm. i. 318, 1, 4. Wiđ tōþreomena geswelle, 370, 29. Gnīd gelōme đa tōđreoman, 346, 14. Mid slītendum tōđreomum *rabidis gingivis*, Hpt. Gl. 423, 45.

tō-þringan; *p.* -þrang, *pl.* -þrungon; *pp.* -þrungen *To press asunder, scatter by pressure*:—Hwīlum ic wīde tōþringe lagustreáma full hwīlum lǣte eft slūpan tōsomne *sometimes I* (the storm) *drive wide apart the cups of the floods* (i. e. *the clouds*), *sometimes let them again glide together*, Exon. Th. 384, 34; Rä. 4, 37.

tōþ-sealf, e; *f.* *A tooth-salve*:—Wyrc đus tōþsealfe: ofersǣwisc rind and hunig and pipor, meng tōsomne, lege on, Lchdm. ii. 52, 3. Tōþsealfa, 4, 5.

tōþ-sticca, an; *m. A tooth-pick:*—Tōþsticca *dentile*, Wrt. Voc. ii. 138, 68. v. tōþ-gâr.

tō-þunden. v. tō-þindan.

tō-þundenness, e; *f.* I. physical, *swollenness:*—Wiþ đæra innoþa tōđundennysse, Lchdm. i. 282, 8: 198, 23. II. metaphorical, *pride, arrogance, contumacy:*—Mid đam âwyrigdan gâste tōþundennesse tōblâwen *maligno spiritu superbie inflatus*, R. Ben. 124, 5. Gif hē on tōþundennesse þurhwunaþ *si contumax fuerit*, 131, 8. For geþances tōþundennysse *propter mentis tumorem*, Scint. 183, 13. Đa eádmōdan đe nâne tōđundennysse nabbaþ, Homl. Th. i. 550, 1.

tō-þundenlīce; *adv. Proudly, arrogantly:*—Tōþundenlīce *arroganter, superbe*, Hpt. Gl. 422, 8. Gif hwylc cræftigra manna for đæs cræftes þingon hine tōþundenlīce onhefþ, R. Ben. 95, 5.

tō-þuniende *astonishing, amazing:*—Đæm tōđuniendan *adtonito*, Wrt. Voc. ii. 4, 24. v. þunian.

tōþ-wærc, -wræc, es; *m. Tooth-ache:*—Lǽcedōmas wiþ tōđwærce, Lchdm. ii. 50, 6, 8, 10, 21, 24. Wiđ tōþwræce, i. 370, 26. v. tōþ-ece.

tō-þwīnan. v. tō-dwīnan.

tōþ-wyrm, es; *m. A worm in a tooth:*—Wiđ tōþwærce, gif wyrm ete đa tēđ . . . Wiđ tōđwyrmum . . . lǽt reócan on đone mūđ, dō blæc hrægl under, đonne feallaþ đa wyrmas on, Lchdm. ii. 50, 10–20.

tōtian; *p.* ode *To peep* out, *look;* Halliwell gives *toot* = to pry inquisitively, as a Northern word:—Se ceác oferhelede đa oxan ealle būton đa heáfudu tōtodon ūt *the basin covered the oxen entirely, except that the heads peeped out;* luterem boves portant, qui facie exterius eminent, sed ex posterioribus latent, Past. 16; Swt. 105, 5. [Ech man þe cumeđ pleie to toten (*look at*) ođer to listen, O. E. Homl. ii. 211, 20. Is hit so ouer vuel uor te toten (lokin, MS. T.) utward? . . . Toten vt wiđuten vuel ne mei nouđer of ou, & nim ȝeme hwat vuel beo icumen of totinge, A. R. 52, 2–11. Euer se recluses toteđ more utwardes, 92, 7. Aȝein kunde hit is, ꝥ te deade totie, 50, 25. He bad me toten on þe tree, Piers P. 16, 22. He maketh him tote and pry, Gow. ii. 143, 6. He stod and totede in, Havel. 2106. Þanne totede y into a tauerne, Pl. Cr. 339. His bon toteden out, 425. *See also note on* totehylle, Prompt. Parv. 497, *and* tootere *speculator*, Wick. Is. 21, 6.]

tō-torfian; *p.* ode. I. *to fling in different directions, to toss about:*—Wæs đæt scyp of đâm ȳþum tōtorfod (*jactabatur*), Mt. Kmbl. 14, 24. Cf. tō-weorpan. II. *to stone to pieces, destroy by throwing stones.* [Me þe sculde al toteon mid horse, ođer þe al totoruion mid stane, O. E. Homl. i. 9, 21. Stones hi doþ in heore slitte and þe totorveþ, O. and N. 1119.]

tō-trǽgelian; *p.* ode *To pull to pieces, pull away, strip:*—Tōtrǽglion *exuent*, Germ. 396, 267. v. trǽgelian.

tō-tredan; *p.* -træd, *pl.* -trǽdon; *pp.* -treden *To tread to pieces, trample upon:*—Tetridtid *defecit*, Txts. 56, 344. Tetridit *desicit* (*deficit?*), 57, 654. Tetreþ *desicit*, Wrt. Voc. ii. 139, 21. [Sum of þe sede werđ totreden, O. E. Homl. i. 133, 22. Heo hit totreden mid horsen, Laym. 26771. Sixti hundred weoren totredene mid horsen, 27473. Wordliche þinges totreden & forhowien, A. R. 166, 22. Totrad *conculcavit*, Wick. Ps. 55, 2. *O. L. Ger.* te-tredan *conculcare: O. H. Ger.* zi-tretan: *Ger.* zer-treten.]

tot-rida, an; *m. That which swings on a projection, a swing* (?) or *a swinging figure* (?):—Totrida *oscida*, Wrt. Voc. i. 288, 52. Totridan *oscille*, ii. 63, 56: *oscillae*, Txts. 83, 1466. [Cf. scocga *oscille*, Grff. vi. 416: rita-scopha *oscilla*, 458: ii. 540. See Schmeller's Dict. 3, 320 and Diefenbach's Appendix to Du Cange, p. 402.] v. tot, *and* rīdan, III.

tō-twǽman; *p.* de *To divide, separate, disjoin:*—Ic tōtwǽme *disjungo*, Ælfc. Gr. 47; Zup. 277, 4. I. *to divide, stand between* objects, *separate* one object from another:—Gewurđe fæstnis tōmiddes đâm wæterum and tōtwǽme (*dividat*) đa wæteru fram đâm wæterum. And God geworhte đa fæstnisse and tōtwǽmde (*divisit*) đa wæteru, đe wǽron under đære fæstnisse, fram đâm đe wǽron bufan đære fæstnisse, Gen. 1, 6, 7. II. *to divide, part, dissociate, break the connection between:*—Sume hē (*the devil*) þurh graman tōtwǽmþ, Homl. Th. i. 240, 26. Đonne se līchama and seó sâuul hī tōtwǽmaþ *when body and soul part*, Wulfst. 151, 11. Wē nellaþ ūs nǽfre tōtwêman *we do not wish to be separated*, Homl. Skt. i. 2, 71. Hī siredon hū hī hié tōtwǽman mehten *Romani dolo divisere hostes*, Ors. 3, 10; Swt. 138, 7. Hié eft tōtwǽmde wǽron, 3, 7; Swt. 118, 20. Loth fērde fram eástdǽle, and hig wurdon tōtwǽmede (*divisi sunt*) heora ǽgđer fram his brēđer, Gen. 13, 11. Hī ne beóþ mid ǽnigum fæce fram him sylfum tōtwǽmede; on eallum weorcum hi beóþ tōgædere, Homl. Th. i. 500, 5. III. *to disperse, scatter:*—Seó sunne tōtwǽmþ đære nihte þȳstru mid hyre beorhtnysse, Anglia viii. 317, 6. Weard hēr on felda folc tōtwǽmed, Byrht. Th. 138, 57; By. 241. III a. where the object is abstract:—Beó đâm hâlgan tīdan eallum mannum sibb and sôm gemǽne and ǽlc sacu tōtwǽmed *let every cause of strife be removed*, L. Eth. vi. 25; Th. i. 320, 29: L. C. E. 17; Th. i. 370, 11. IV. *to divide* with the mind, *distinguish, discern:*—Se apostol tōtwǽmed đæs gâstes naman and đæs mōdes, Homl. Skt. i. 1, 189. Tōtwǽm ꝉ tōsceád intingan mīnne *discerne causam meam*, Ps. Lamb. 42, 1. Tōtwǽmendum (-þwæm-, MS.) *distinguente, dividente, ordinante*, Hpt. Gl. 438, 54. Ne gemengende hâdas ne edwiste tōtwǽmende *neque confundentes personas, neque substantiam separantes*, Ath. Crd. 4. [Þe eorđe totwemde *the earth yawned*, Marh. 17, 28. Ure louerd totweamede his soule urom his bodie, A. R. 396, 20.] v. un-tōtwǽmed.

tō-twǽmedness, e; *f. Division, want of union:*—Âwyrgede gâstas beóþ his lâtteówas and his gefēran būtan ǽlcere tōtwǽmednesse *accursed spirits will be his guides and comrades in close fellowship*, Wulfst. 194, 22.

tō-tyhting, e; *f. Instigation, prompting, suggestion:*—Đisses geáres đa Scottas heora cyng Duncecan ofslōgan, and heom syđđan his fæderan Dufenal tō cynge genâmon, þurh đes lâre and tōtihtinge hē weard tō deáđe beswicen, Chr. 1094; Erl. 231, 2.

tō-ward. v. tō-weard.

tow-cræft, es; *m. Skill in weaving* or *spinning:*—Heó (*the Virgin Mary*) weóx and weard fulfremed on gōdra mægna heányssum, and heó đâ sōna gōdum towcræftum onfēng, swȳđor đonne ǽnig đara đe heora bearn wǽron . . . Heó wolde beón fram đære þriddan tīde ōđ đa nigoþan tīd ymbe hyre webbgeweorc, Homl. Ass. 126, 339. Cf. 132, 545 sqq. According to the Protevangelion, when a new veil for the temple had to be made, it fell to Mary's lot to spin the true purple, c. ix. 4. v. tow-hūs, -līc.

tō-weard; *adj.* I. used attributively, (a) in an indefinite sense, *future, that is to come:*—*Praesens tempus* ys andwerd tīd . . . *futurum tempus* is tōwerd tīd, Ælfc. Gr. 20; Zup. 123, 17. Big đam ege đæs tōweardan dōmes *de terrore futuri judicii*, Bd. 4, 24; S. 598, 15: Bt. 39, 11; Fox 230, 12. Tōwurdre *futurae*, Hpt. Gl. 426, 48. Tō fleónne fram đan tōweardan yrre *a futura ira*, Mt. Kmbl. 3, 7. On tōweardre worulde *in saeculo futuro*, Mk. Skt. 10, 30: Blickl. Homl. 15, 4. Hē nolde ongytan đone tōwerdon deáþ (*death that sometime will come*), 195, 17. Đa misweaxendan bōgas of âscreádian, đæt đa tōweardan đeónde beón, Homl. Th. ii. 74, 13. Âwrītan đâm tōwerdum mannum *to write for future generations*, Homl. Skt. i. 21, 11. (b) of the near future, *about to come, coming, at hand, approaching:*—Se tōwarda winter *imminens hiems*, Bd. 4, 1; S. 564, 39. On đære tōweardan tīde đe đâ neálǽhte niđđa bearnum, Cd. Th. 77, 30; Gen. 1283. Hwylc tōweard yfel đū đē on neáhnysse forhtast *quae ventura tibi in proximo mala formidas*, Bd. 2, 12; S. 514, 1. II. used predicatively, (1) referring to future circumstances, *toward* as in Shakespere, e.g. What might be *toward*, that this sweaty haste Doth make the night joint labourer with the day, Hamlet i. 1. (a) (*that is*) *to happen* or *be* some time or other, (*that is*) *to come:*—Se đe æfter mē tōwerd ys *qui post me venturus est*, Mt. Kmbl. 3, 11. Gif hē wiste on hwylcere tīde se þeóf tōwerd wǽre, 24, 43. Georne wiste se Scyppend, hwæt tōweard wæs, Homl. Th. i. 112, 25. Hē nât hwæt him tōweard biþ *he knows not what is to happen to him*, Bt. 11, 1; Fox 32, 13. Hē wiste đæt wīte đæt him tōweard wæs, Blickl. Homl. 77, 29. Hē ys tōweard on micelre mǽgđe *futurus sit in gentem magnam*, Gen. 18, 18. Se đe wæs tōweard tō đisum middangearde, Homl. Th. i. 182, 24. Hē is tōweard tō dēmenne đâs world, Blickl. Homl. 81, 35. Đa þing đe eów tōwearde synd and hū eówer ǽlcon gebyređ ǽr his ende *quae ventura sunt vobis in diebus novissimis*, Gen. 49, 1. Eallum mannum, đâm đe nū sint and đâm đe tōwearde sint, Deut. 29, 15. (b) *about to happen*, (*that is*) *to come soon, imminent, impending:*—Mid đȳ hē ongeat đæt him deáþes dæg tōweard wæs *cum diem sibi mortis imminere sensisset*, Bd. 4, 11; S. 579, 24. Tōweard ys đæt Herodes sēcþ đæt cild tō forspillenne, Mt. 2, 13. Đonne wambâdl tōweard sié *when the disease is coming on*, Lchdm. ii. 216, 19. Tâcn hū sió âdl tōweard sié, 256, 21. Hī gesâwon đæt đǽr tōweard wæs *they saw what was about to happen*, Lk. Skt. 22, 49. Eów ys wuldorblǽd tōweard *glory is about to come to you*, Judth. Thw. 23, 35; Jud. 157. Noe sægde, đæt wæs þreālīc þing þeódum tōweard, Cd. Th. 79, 29; Gen. 1318. (c) where the time is fixed, *to take place, come to pass:*—On đære nihte đe đæt gefeoht on merigen tōweard wæs, Homl. Th. i. 504, 21. (2) marking motion, *coming* towards a place, *approaching, about to come:*—Se Hǽlend geseah đæt đǽr wæs mycel mennisc tōweard (cf. se Hǽlend geseah đæt micel folc com tō him *venit ad eum*, Jn. Skt. 6, 5), Homl. Th. i. 182, 5. Đâ ongeáton hié đæt se eádiga Michael đǽr wæs tōweard *they then perceived that the blessed Michael had come there* (or *had been present* (?) cf. hī undergeáton đæt Micahel đæt tâcen his andwerdnysse geswutelian wolde, Homl. Th. i. 506, 14), Blickl. Homl. 205, 2. (2 a) without inflection (or not adjective? v. III. 1 a):—Lōcian hwæþer hē đæt land gecneówe đæt hié tōweard wǽron *speculari quam regionem teneret*, Ors. 4, 10; Swt. 202, 3. (3) marking position, *with the face towards* a person, *facing:*—Geseoh đæt hé sié tōweard đonne đū in gange, Lchdm. ii. 352, 19. III. used appositively, (1) referring to future events, (a) where the futurity is indefinite:—Đa hâlgan ǽr Cristes cyme hyne tōweardne sægdon *said he was to come*, Blickl. Homl. 81, 31: Homl. Th. i. 354, 26, 32. Hē him đæt rīce tōwerd sǽde *he told him that the kingdom was in store for him*, Guthl. 21; Gdwin. 96, 8. Hē forestihte đa gecorenan tō ðam ēcan līfe, for ðan ðe hē wiste hī sw·lce tōwearde *he knew they were to become such*, Homl. Th. i. 112, 32, 34. D..hten ealle gōd him symle fremfullīce tōwearde dyde *the Lord ever had in store for him all good things to his advantage*, Lchdm. iii. 436, 23. ¶ Sometimes the word occurs without the inflexion that seems required, v. also II. 2 a; but perhaps in these cases the word should not be considered adjective. v. next word:—Wītgan hine tōweard sǣdon, Blickl. Homl. 71, 29. Ealle ða tācno & ða forebeácno ða ðe ūre Drihten ǣr tōweard sægde, 117, 31. Hī geseóþ heora wuldor and heora wlite and blisse hym tōweard, Wulfst. 238, 21. (b) of an immediate future:—Hēr is ūre sylfra forwyrd tōweard getācnod *here is our own destruction shewn to be imminent*, Judth. Thw. 25, 30; Jud. 286. Se engel him sige tōweardne gehēht *the angel promised them that victory should be theirs* (*on the morrow*), Blickl. Homl. 201, 33: 117, 14. Aidan ðām scypfarendum ðone storm tōwardne sægde (cf. sōna ðæs ðe gē on scyp āstīgaþ ofer eów cymeð mycel storm, 32), Bd. 3, 15; S. 541, 16. Hē foreseah Godes mynstrum micle frēcnesse tōwearde *monasteriis periculum imminere praevidens*, Bd. 3, 19; S. 549, 46. Hē wiste heora forwyrd hrædlīce tōweard, Homl. Th. i. 402, 12. (2) marking motion:—Ða leóde flugon ðā hié ðone here tōweardne wiston on ða burh Gerusalem *the people fled when they knew that the Roman army was on the march to Jerusalem*, Blickl. Homl. 79, 13. Hī gewunodon on gehwilcere byrig, ōð ðæt hī geāxodon ða apostolas tōwearde *they stopped in every town until they learned that the apostles were on the way thither*, Homl. Th. ii. 494, 2. [*O. Sax.* tō-ward.]

tō-weard; *prep. Toward, in the direction of.* I. *with gen.*:—Ða ðe gāþ on ryhtne weg tōweard ðæs hefonrīces, Past. 9; Swt. 59, 19. Hē wæs hym syððan tōweard hys scypes farende, Homl. Ass. 190, 258. II. *with dat. or uncertain*, (1) preceding the governed word:—Ðonne ærnaþ hȳ ealle tōweard ðæm feó, Ors. 1, 1; Swt. 20, 36. Hī torfedon tōwærd ðam weofode . . . and scotedon tōweard ðam hālig-dōme, Chr. 1083; Erl. 217, 17, 19. Crist wæs tōweard ðære rōde gelǣd, Btwk. 214, 27. (2) following the governed word:—Hē eów onet tōweard *mors propinquat*, Met. 27, 8. (3) where *tō* precedes and *weard* follows (cf. *to* God *ward*, *to* us *ward* in A. V.):—Hē hine bær tō mynstre weard, Homl. Th. i. 336, 12: Wulfst. 302, 26. Hē went ǣfre ðone hricg tō ðære sunnan weard, Lchdm. iii. 266, 24. Tō scipan weard, Chr. 1009; Erl. 143, 11. Hī wendon him tō ðære burge weard, 1048; Erl. 178, 1. Hī wǣron heom tō Lundene weard, 1052; Erl. 185, 4. Hē hēt ðæt hē biheólde tō his Drihtne werd, Homl. Skt. ii. 31, 78.

tō-weardes; *prep. with dat. Towards.* I. preceding the case:—Hī fērdon tōwardes Ou, Chr. 1094; Erl. 230, 31. II. following the case:—Mīne frȳnd standaþ ongeán mē and synt mē tōweardes *amici mei adversum me appropinquaverunt et steterunt*, Ps. Th. 37, 11. Deáð eów tōweardes onet, Bt. 39, 1; Fox 210, 27. Eów neálǣcþ se deáð tōweardes, Wulfst. 231, 34. [*O. Sax.* tō-wardes.]

tōweard-līc; *adj. Future*:—Mē þincþ ic stande and his āgene stefne gehȳre swā swā hit tōweardlīc is tō gehȳranne, Homl. Skt. i. 23, 831. Ðæt tācnaþ tōweardlīce firhto and brōgan, Lchdm. iii. 156, 10. God forgefe alle synne ðīno ondweardlīca and tōweardlīca (*futura*), Rtl. 170, 11.

tōweardlīce; *adv. In the future, in time to come*:—Hē forecwæþ ðæt hē tōwardlīce biscop beón sceolde *antistitem eum futurum esse praedixerat*, Bd. 4, 28; S. 606, 21.

tōweardness, e; *f.* I. *the time to come, the future*:—Ðæt hē on tōweardnesse (*in futuro saeculo*) ēcelīce mid Criste rīcsian mōste, Bd. 3, 29; S. 561, 22. Swā ðū on ðisum andweardum līfe mā earfoða drīgast, swā myccle ðū eft on tōweardnysse gefēhst, Guthl. 5; Gdwin. 32, 13. II. *a future coming*:—Ūre Drihten ðæt gefylde, ðæt hē þurh his ða hālgan tōweardnesse gehēt, Blickl. Homl. 119, 28.

tō-weccan; *p.* -wehte *To wake* (trans.) *up, stir up, arouse*:—Hū ða folc mid him fǣhþe tōwehton *how they stirred up strife amongst themselves*, Beo. Th. 5889; B. 2948.

tō-wegan; *p.* -wæg, *pl.* -wǣgon; *pp.* -wegen *To disperse, dispel*:—Heofones gim scīneþ, beóþ wolcen tōwegen *neu concreta nubes summoveat radios solis*, Exon. Th. 210, 11; Ph. 184.

toweht *a basket for putting wool in* (?):—The word occurs among terms connected with spinning and glosses *calatum* (= *calathus?* Calatum *is explained in Du Cange by* lignum piscatorum seu piscania e lignis confecta, *a meaning which seems not to belong to the word here*), Wrt. Voc. i. 282, 17: ii. 16, 35.

tō-wendan; *p.* de *To overthrow, upset, subvert, overturn*:—Hē tōwende *evertit*, Hpt. Gl. 459, 52. Tōwendum *erutis, subversis*, 433, 44. I. with reference to material objects, (a) where the object is not of great extent, *to overthrow, demolish*:—Ðā tōwende se hālga wer ðæt deófolgild grundlunge, Homl. Th. ii. 164, 16. Ðā tōwende se biscop ðæt weofod, 508, 5. Hæfde se deófol tōwend ðone weall *the devil had thrown down the wall*, 166, 19. Heora deófolgild wearð tōwend, Homl. Skt. i. 22, 158. (b) where the object is of great extent, *to overthrow, destroy*:—God ealne ðone eard tōwende *Dominus subvertit omnem regionem*, Gen. 19, 25. Ðā tōwænde se cy..ing heora winsuman burh, Homl. Ass. 102, 8. Hī tōwendon ðæt tempel, 68, 83. Hig heora burga tōwendon *subversis urbibus*, Num. 21, 3. Ðæt ic ða burh ne tōwende *ut non subvertam urbem*, Gen. 19, 21. II. with reference to non-materia.. .jects, *to destroy by changing, to repeal* a law, *abrogate, abolish, overthrow, destroy*:—Crist tōwyrpþ ðās stōwe and tōwent ða gesetnysse ðe ūs Moyses tǣhte, Homl. Th. i. 46, 3. Hī woldon tōwendon ealle ða gesetnessa ðe Domicianus hæfde ǣr geset, Ors. 6, 10; Bos. 120, 32 note. III. in a figurative sense:—Hāwa ðæt se inra wind ðē ne tōwende, Homl. Th. ii. 392, 32. [A sutare þet haueð forloren his el, he towent euerich strea uort he beo ifunden, A. R. 324, 18. Mid þusendfeld wrenches he þe herte towendeð, O. E. Homl. ii. 191, 26.]

tō-weorpan, -werpan, -worpan, -wurpan, -wyrpan; *p.* -wearp, *pl.* -wurpon; *pp.* -worpen *To throw in different directions, throw away, throw down, to scatter, disperse, destroy, overthrow*:—Tōwearp *discutit*, Wrt. Voc. ii. 28, 70. Tōwuorpon *destituunt*, tōworpne *destitutae*, 105, 81, 82. Tōwurpon, 25, 13. Tōworpenum *eruta*, 33, 16. *Destitutae, desertae*, i. *derelictae, vel* tōworpne, 139, 11. I. *to scatter* (lit. or fig.), *disperse*:—Se ðe ne gaderaþ mid mē, hē tōwyrpþ (*spargit*), Mt. 12, 30. Hē sendeþ his strǣlo and hī tōweorpeþ (*dissipavit*), Bd. 4, 3; S. 569, 20. Ðū ūs tōdrife and ūs tōwurpe geond werþeóda, Ps. Th. 59, 1. Hē ðæt fȳr tōsceáf and ðone līg tōwearp, Exon. Th. 276, 15; Jul. 566. Tōweorp ðū ða ðeóda *dissipa gentes*, Ps. Th. 67, 28. Ðæt hē heora oferhȳd tōweorpe *ut superbiam eorum dissipet*, Bd. 4, 3; S. 569, 24. Mid ðȳ ðe hē sceolde his gestreón tōweorpan, mid ðȳ hē hié gadraþ, Past. 8; Swt. 55, 11. Ūre bān syndon tōworpene *dissipata sunt ossa nostra*, Ps. Th. 140, 9. Ðætte suno Godes, ða ðe uoeron tōuorpen (*dispersi*), gesomnade in ān, Jn. Skt. Lind. 11, 52. I a. *to break in pieces, scatter the parts of a connected whole*:—Hē heora bendas tōwearp *vincula eorum disrupit*, Ps. Th. 106, 13. II. in a literal sense, *to overthrow*, (a) *to overturn* what is standing:—Hē āgeát ðara mynetera feoh, and tōwearp hyra mȳsan (*mensas subvertit*), Jn. Skt. 2, 15. (b) *to throw down* what is set up, *destroy* a building, *demolish*:—Gif eówer godes miht ða cyrcan tōwurpan ne mæg, ic tōwurpe eówer tempel, Homl. Th. i. 70, 30. Ðes tōwyrpþ (-wærpað, Lind.) Godes templ, and hyt eft getimbraþ *qui destruebat templum Dei, et illud reaedificabat*, Mt. Kmbl. 27, 40. Ðū tōwurpe weallfæsten his *deposuisti maceriam ejus*, Ps. Th. 79, 12. Ceaster heora ðū tōwurpe (*destruxisti*), Ps. Spl. 9, 6. God tōwearp (*subvertit*) ða burga, Gen. 19, 25: Ors. 3, 7; Swt. 114, 2. Hē tōwearp ðæt templ *Titus templum diruit*, 6, 7; Swt. 262, 20. Se godcunda anweald tōwearp ðone torr (*the tower of Babel*), Bt. 35, 4; Fox 162, 25. Æþelburg tōwearp Tántūn ðe Ine ǣr timbrede, Chr. 722; Erl. 44, 27. Hī tōwurpon ða heargas *destructis fanis*, Bd. 3, 30; S. 562, 15. Englas ðæt hūs tōwurpon þurh gāstlīcne cræft, Homl. Th. ii. 510, 15. Ðȳ læs eówer hūs windas tōweorpan, Exon. Th. 281, 22; Jul. 650. Hī mid æxum duru curfan, and teoledan ðæt hī mid adesan ealle tōwurpan (*dejecerunt*), Ps. Th. 73, 6. Tōwurpan (-worpan, MS. A.: -weorpan, Rush.: -worpa, Lind.) Godes templ *destruere templum Dei*, Mt. Kmbl. 26, 61: Homl. Th. ii. 510, 13. Tōworpon, Bd. 2, 13; S. 517, 14. Tōwyrpan hira geweorc, Bt. 35, 4; Fox 162, 13. Ne bið hēr lǣfed stān uppan stāne ðe ne beó tōworpen, Mt. Kmbl. 24, 2: Mk. Skt. 13, 2. Wearð Tirus seó mǣre burg eall tōworpenu *Tyrus excisa est*, Ors. 3, 9; Swt. 128, 28. Æfter tōworpenum templan *post deruta sacella*, Hpt. Gl. 467, 56. III. in a figurative sense, *to overthrow*, (a) where the object is a person, *to destroy the power of* a person, *to destroy*:—Hī tōweorp *destrue eos*, Ps. Th. 58, 11. Ðæt ðū tōwurpe feónd *ut destruas inimicum*, Ps. Spl. 8, 3. Hī wolde tōweorpan wuldres Aldor . . . ðæt hē hī ne tōwurpe geond werþeóda *dixit ut disperderet eos . . . ne disperderet eos*, Ps. Th. 105, 19. Swā sint tō teweorpanne ða ðe nān gōd ne dydon ðurh ðreáunge *qui nulla agere bona coeperunt, correctionis manu evertendi sunt*, Past. 58; Swt. 443, 33. Ic wolde tōwerpan bearn Hēlendes, Cd. Th. 270, 4; Sat. 85. Noldan hī tōworpan þeóde *non disperdiderunt gentes*, Ps. Th. 105, 26. Wutan hī tōwyrpan *disperdamus eos*, 82, 4. (b) where the object is not a person, *to overthrow* an institution, a practice, regulation, law, etc., *to put down, put an end to, destroy, make void, break, dissolve*:—Se ðe tōwyrpþ ān of ðysum bebodum *qui solverit unum de mandatis istis*, Mt. Kmbl. 5, 19. Hē ūre ǣ tōwyrpþ. Pilatus hym cwæð: 'Hwæt ys ðæt hē dēþ ðæt hē mǣge eówre ǣ tōwerpan?' Hī cwǣdon: 'On restedagum hē hǣlþ,' Nicod. 2; Thw. 1, 23–27. Hē com tō ðȳ ðæt hē wolde ǣlc yfel tōwurpan, and ǣlc good ārǣran. Nū tōwyrpþ hē on ūs leahtras . . . Hē tōwyrpþ mōdignysse . . . and ealle unðeáwas hē tōwyrpþ, Homl. Th. i. 144, 28–32. Se wind tōweorpþ ðære rosan wlite, Bt. 9; Fox 26, 19. Tōweorpeþ (-worpeþ, MS. B.), Salm. Kmbl. 149; Sal. 74. Ða heargas āīdlian and tōweorpan *fana profanare*, Bd. 2, 13; S. 516, 40. Hē wile ūre wītu tōweorpan *he will put an end to the pains we inflict*, Cd. Th. 289, 5; Sat. 393. Mīne āre tōweorpan *honorem meum repellere*, Ps. Th. 61, 4. Wutun symbeldagas Drihtnes on eorðwege ealle tōwurpan *comprimamus omnes dies festos Domini a terra*, 73, 8. Nelle gē wēnan ðæt ic cōme tōwurpan (*solvere*) ða ǣ; ne com ic nā tōwurpan (-wearpan, MS. A.), ac gefyllan, Mt. Kmbl. 5, 17. Uton tōwurpan ðās geflitu *dissolvamus has contentiones*, Coll. Monast. Th. 31, 23. Ælfhere hēt tōwurpon swȳðe manig munuclīf, Chr. 975; Erl. 127, 5. Oft becymþ se anweald ðisse worulde tō swīþe gōdum monnum for ðæm se anweald ðara yflana weorþe tôworpen *fit saepe, uti bonis summa rerum gerenda deferatur, ut exuberans retundatur improbitas*, Bt. 39, 11; Fox 228, 20. Ðone tôworpenan stal ðæs rîces *destructum regni statum*, Bd. 4, 26; S. 603, 8. Ðý læs tôwórpen sién fyrngewritu, Elen. Kmbl. 860; El. 430. IV. *to throw out.* v. tô-worpness, II:—Ðonne hió hié selfe tôweorpeþ ût of hiere selfre *cum se extra semetipsam ejicit*, Past. 38; Swt. 277, 24. [Ne bid naut his (*the wise man's*) lare fremful, ȝif he mid wercan towerped his bodunge, O. E. Homl. i. 109, 7. Þatt temmple wass all þurrh hæþenn follc toworrpenn, Orm. 16277. *O. Frs.* tô-, ti-werpa: *O. Sax.* te-werpan *to scatter, to destroy*: *O. H. Ger.* zer-, ze-werfan *dissipare, disjicere, dispergere, destruere, demoliri*: *Ger.* zer-werfen.]

tô-weorpendlîc, -wyrpendlîc; *adj. Destructible*:—Tôwyrpendlîcne *destructilem*, Germ. 394, 348.

tô-wesness, -wesenness, -wisness, e; *f.* I. *separation, dissolution, divorce*:—Tôwesnes *vel* tôlêsednes *dissolutio, dispersio*, Wrt. Voc. ii. 141, 40. Tôwesnisse *defortii*, Txts. 181, 41. II. *difference, disagreement, discord, dissension*:—Hê sǽwþ ðone sticel ðæs andan ôððæt ðǽr of âweoxþ tôwesnes, and of ðære tôwesnesse biþ ðæt fýr onǽled ðære feóunga . . . Se se ðæt wæter ût forlête wǽre fruma ðære tôwesnesse *seminantur stimuli, oriuntur rixae, accenduntur faces odiorum . . . Qui dimittit aquam, caput est jurgiorum*, Past. 38; Swt. 279, 9–13. Hû unâberendlîc gylt sió tôwesnes (*discordia*) biþ, 46; Swt. 349, 15. Wæs tôwesnes geworden *orta dissensione*, Bd. 4, 12; S. 581, 15. Ðâ sôhte Colemannus ðysse tôwisnesse (-wesennesse, MS. B.) and ðysse unsibbe lǽcedóm *quaesivit Colmanus huic dissensioni remedium*, 4, 4; S. 571, 6. Ðonne hê him ondrǽt ða tôwesnesse ûtane *dum humana foras jurgia metuunt*, Past. 46; Swt. 351, 23. [Cf. ge-weorþan *to agree*: *Goth.* ga-wairthi *peace*.]

towettan; *p.* te *To associate with*:—Riht is ðæt mynecena ne towettan woruldmannum ne ǽnige sundorcýððe tô heom habban ealles tô swîðe (*the other reading is* nǽfre wið worldmen ǽnige gemânan worldlîcre cýððe habban tô swîðe), L. I. P. 15; Th. ii. 322, 33.

tow-hûs, es; *n. A spinning-house*:—Towhûs of wulle *genitium* (= gynaeceum *locus seu aedes ubi mulieres lanificio operam dabant*. The women who worked were called *geniciariae pensiles*, Migne), Wrt. Voc. i. 59, 7. v. tow-cræft, -lîc, -tôl.

tô-wiðere, -wiðre; *prep. Against.* I. with dat. *in reply to*:—Hû mæg ic andsware findan wrâþum tôwiþere, Exon. Th. 12, 13; Cri. 185. II. with acc. *in opposition to*:—Wîg tôwiþre, 341, 20; Gn. Ex. 129. [*Ger.* zu-wider.]

tow-lîc; *adj. Pertaining to weaving*:—Towlîc weorc *textrinum opus*, Wrt. Voc. i. 26, 13: 82, 11.

tow-mýdrece, an; *f. A work-box, box for keeping materials connected with spinning or weaving* (?):—Ân hræglcysð and ân lytulu towmýderce, Chart. Th. 538, 21.

tô-worpenness, -worpedness, e; *f. Desolation, destruction*:—Heora tôworpennys *the destruction of the Jews by the Romans*, Homl. Th. i. 108, 3. Ða onsceonunge ðære tôworpennysse *abominationem desolationis*, Mt. Kmbl. 24, 15. Tôworpednysse (-worpennysse, MS. A.), Mk. 43, 14. Ðeós tôdrǽfednys (*the driving the money-changers out from the temple*) getâcnode ða tôweardan tôworpennysse ðurh ðone Rômâniscan here, Homl. Th. i. 406, 9. Ðæt se Hǽlend beweópe ðære ceastre tôworpennysse, ðe gelamp æfter his ðrowunge, 402, 7: Homl. Ass. 46, 548.

tô-worpness, -wyrpness, e; *f.* I. *dispersion.* v. tô-weorpan, I:—On tôwyrpnisse hǽðna *in dispersionem gentium*, Jn. Skt. Rush. Lind. 7, 35. II. *a throwing out, ejection.* v. tô-weorpan, IV:—Salde him mæhte gêmnisse tô untrymnissum and tôworpnisse (-wyrpnise, Lind.) diówla *dedit illis potestatem curandi infirmitates et eiciendi daemonia*, Mk. Skt. Rush. 3, 15. [*O. H. Ger.* zi-worfnessi *desolatio*.]

tô-wrecan; *p.* -wræc, *pl.* -wrǽcon; *pp.* -wrecen *To drive in different directions, scatter, disperse*:—Weorðaþ tôwrecene wîde ealle ða ðe unrihtes ǽror worhtan *dispergentur omnes qui operantur iniquitatem*, Ps. Th. 91, 8: 58, 15. Siendon wê tôwrecene geond wîdne grund, heápum tôhworfene, Cd. Th. 235, 4; Dan. 301: Exon. Th. 186, 17; Az. 21: 16, 24; Cri. 258: Elen. Kmbl. 261; El. 131.

tô-writenness, e; *f. A detailed writing, a description*:—Se câsere sette gebann, ðæt wǽre on gewritum âsett eall ymbhwyrft. Ðeós tôwritennys (*descriptio*. v. tô-mearcodness) wearð ârǽred fram ðam ealdormenn Cyrino, Homl. Th. i. 30, 2.

tô-wrîðan; *p.* -wrâð *To twist different ways, to distort*:—Ic tôwrîðe *distorqueo*, Ælfc. Gr. 26, 3; Zup. 155, 15.

tow-tôl, es; *n. An implement for spinning*:—Hê sceal fela towtôla habban, flexlînan, spinle . . ., Anglia ix. 263, 10.

tô-wunderlîc *glosses* admirabilis, Ps. Spl. 41, 4.

tô-wurpan. v. tô-weorpan.

tô-wyrd, e; *f. Occasion*:—Ðâ wǽron Seaxan sêcende intingan and tôwyrde heora gedâles wiþ Brittas *quaerentes occasionem divortii*, Bd. 1, 15; S. 483, 37.

tô-wyrpan, -wyrpendlîc, -wyrpness. v. tô-weorpan, -weorpendlîc, -worpness.

Trâci, Trâcia, Trâciana. v. þrâceas.

tract; trachtere, tractere. v. traht; trahtere.

træf, es; *n.* I. *a tent, pavilion*:—Lǽdan ða torhtan mægð tô træfe ðam heán (cf. wæs seó hâlige meówle on his bûrgetelde, 22, 10; Jud. 57), Judth. Thw. 22, 2; Jud. 43: 25, 12; Jud. 255. Beornas stôdon ymbe hyra þeódnes træf, 25, 19; Jud. 268. II. *a building*:—Tigelfâgan trafu, torras, windige weallas, Andr. Kmbl. 1683; An. 844. [Cf. (?) *Icel.* traf *a fringe, hem*: in mod. usage, *a kerchief*.] v. hearg-, hell-, wearg-træf.

trǽgelian, trǽglian; *p.* ode *To pluck*:—Trǽglian *carpere*, Germ. 398, 84. Tô trǽgelgenne *carpendum*, 399, 388. [Cf. (?) *Lat.* tragula.] v. tô-trǽgelian.

træppan, træppe. v. treppan, treppe.

trâg; *adj. Evil, bad*:—Tô trâg, Exon. Th. 354, 37; Reim. 57. Se feónd and se freónd, tîreádig and trâg, synnig and gesǽlig, Elen. Kmbl. 1906; El. 955. Ðæt hió ðære cwêne oncweðan meahton swâ tiles swâ trâges swâ hió him tô sôhte, 649; El. 325. [*O. L. Ger. O. H. Ger.* trâgi *iners, piger, segnis*: *Ger.* träge: *Du.* traag. Cf. earh *for the double sense of* slow *and* bad.]

trâg, e; trâgu; *indecl.*; *f. Ill, affliction*:—Hê wênde him trâge hnâgre *he expected humiliating affliction for himself*, Elen. Kmbl. 1333; El. 668. [*O. L. Ger. O. H. Ger.* trâgî *ignavia, torpor*.] v. preceding word.

tragan = dragan, Jn. Skt. Rush. 21, 8, 11.

trâge; *adv. Evilly, cruelly*:—Ðis is weorc ðara ðe oft wrâðe mê trâge tǽldan *hoc opus eorum, qui detrahunt mihi*, Ps. Th. 108, 20. [*O. H. Ger.* trâgo *tarde, segniter*.] v. trâg.

traht, tract, es; *m.*: e; *f.* I. *a text, passage*; textus, tractus (*tractus* ecclesiastici cantus species, Migne):—Æfter fyliaþ traht *sequitur tractus*: '*Eripe me, Domine*,' Anglia xiii. 417, 743. Traht *tractus*: '*Laudate Dominum*,' 425, 855. Mid trahte godspelles *cum textu euuangelii*, 416, 723. Nû bidde ic eów ðæt gê beón geðyldige on eówerum geðance ôððæt wê ðone traht oferrǽdan mâgon *I pray you to be patient in your thoughts until we have read the passage* (the passage is then given), Homl. Th. i. 166, 7. Ðæt man rǽde twâ rǽdinga mid twâm tractum and mid twâm collectum, L. Ælfc. C. 36; Th. ii. 358, 19. II. *a treating* of a subject, *an exposition, a commentary*:—Traht *expositio*, i. *tractatio*, Wrt. Voc. ii. 145, 84. Ðes traht is langsum eów tô gehýrenne, ac wê willaþ nû ûre sprǽce hêr geendian, Homl. Th. ii. 536, 22: 70, 13: i. 248, 21. Trahte *commentis*, Wrt. Voc. ii. 19, 58: 94, 31. Wê oferrǽddon ðis godspel . . . ac wê ne hrepodon ðone traht nâ swîðor ðonne tô ðæs dæges wurðmynte belamp *we read the gospel, but we did not further touch the exposition* (or *text*, under I?) *than pertained to the honour of the day*, Homl. Th. i. 104, 6. Trahtas *commentariola*, Wrt. Voc. ii. 24, 51. Rǽde man ðære godcundan lâre bêc, and eác swâ ða hâligan trahtas (*expositiones*) ðe fram namcûþum fæderum geworhte synt, R. Ben. 33, 20. Trahta *commenta, documenta*, Hpt. Gl. 512, 32. [*O. H. Ger.* trahta *tractatio*. From Latin.] v. godspell-, sealm-traht, *and following words.*

trahtaþ, es; *m. A commentary*:—Trahtaðum *commentis*, Wrt. Voc. ii. 19, 58.

traht-bôc; *f. A book of exposition, a treatise, commentary*:—Gregorius gedihte manega hâlige trahtbêc, Homl. Th. ii. 132, 15: i. 436, 10. Twâ and hundseofontig bôca ðære ealdan ǽ and ðære nîwan hê âwende . . . bûton ôðrum menigfealdum trahtbôcum ðe hê deópðancollîce âsmeáde, 15.

trahtere, es; *m. One who treats a subject, an expositor, interpreter, commentator*:—Mê ða treahteras tala wîsedon, Salm. Kmbl. 9; Sal. 5. Treahteras *commentarii*, Wrt. Voc. ii. 15, 41. Fram trehterum *a commentariis*, 7, 28. Of flîtendum trachterum *a vitiosis interpretibus*, Mt. Kmbl. p. i. 14. [*O. H. Ger.* pi-trahtari.] v. stǽr-trahtere; trahtnere.

trahtian; *p.* ode. I. *to expound, explain*:—Ðegnum his hê trahtade alle *he expounded all things to his disciples*, Mk. Skt. Lind. 4, 34. Se âwergda gâst ongan Godes bêc trahtian, and ðâ sôna leáh, Blickl. Homl. 29, 29. II. *to discuss*:—Ðâ ongunnon hý treahtigean, hwæðer mâ mǽrlîcra dǽda gefremed hæfde, ðe Philippus, ðe Alexander, Ors. 3, 9; Bos. 67, 3. [*O. H. Ger.* trahtôn *tractare, reputare*.] v. ge-trahtian; trahtnian, traht.

trahtnere, es; *m. An expositor, commentator*:—Gregorius se trahtnere, Homl. Th. ii. 72, 21. Se trahtnere cwið, ðæt ðæt gyftlîce hûs wæs ðryflêre, for ðan ðe on Godes gelaðunge sind þrý stæpas gecorenra manna, 70, 16: i. 338, 16. Hieronimus se wîsa trahtnere, Homl. Ass. 36, 296. v. trahtere.

trahtnian; *p.* ode. I. *trans. To expound, explain*:—Hægmon trahtnaþ ðis gospell, Homl. Th. i. 510, 26. Gregorius trahtnode ðis godspel, ii. 550, 1. Ic wolde eów trahtnian ðis godspel, ðe mann nû beforan eów rǽdde, i. 166, 3. Ðes cwyde is swîðor tô ondrǽdenne ðonne tô trahtnigenne, 332, 4: ii. 90, 5. I a. *to give as explanation* of (*be*) something:—Wê sprǽcon be ðam sǽde ðe betwux ðâm ðornum sprang . . . Drihten sylf trahtnode be ðisum ðæt ða sind ðe Godes word gehýraþ ac hî sind gebysgode mid heora welum *we spoke of the seed that sprang up among the thorns . . . The Lord himself gave as explanation of this, that they are those that hear God's word, but are occupied with their* *wealth*, Homl. Th. ii. 92, 7. II. with prep. *to treat* of (*be, ymbe*):—Manega trahtnedon ymbe ðis angin *de hoc principio multi tractaverunt*, Anglia viii. 307, 7. Mid were ǽwfæstum trahtna (*tracta*) be hálignysse, Scint. 200, 14. Nú wille wé be ðyssere freólstíde trahtnian, Homl. Th. i. 104, 9. Wé woldon gefyrn trahtnian be ðam lambe, ii. 278, 11. [Nimeþþ gom off þiss þatt her iss trahhtnedd, Orrm. 11680.] v. á-, ge-, ofer-trahtnian; trahtian.

trahtnung, e; *f. Exposition, explanation, comment*:—Uton nú fón on ðæs godspelles trahtnunge ðǽr wé hit forléton *let us resume the exposition of the gospel, where we left it*, Homl. Th. i. 114, 35: ii. 72, 22. Ús gedafenaþ ðæt wé mid árfæstum geleáfan underfón Drihtnes trahtnunge, 90, 4. Mid smeáþancelre trahtnunge *tenaci memoriae textu*, Hpt. Gl. 410, 65. Trah(t)nunge *commenta*, 479, 77. Mid gástlícum trahtnungum *commentariis, explanationibus*, 410, 24: Homl. Th. ii. 2, 8.

trahtung, e; *f. Exposition, comment*:—Trahtunga *commenta*, Wrt. Voc. ii. 24, 50. Þracþungum (*l.* tractungum *or* trahtungum) *commentis, doctrinis*, Hpt. Gl. 482, 16. [*O. H. Ger.* trahtunga *retractatio*.]

traisc, tráisc (?); *adj.* In the following passage this word is used to translate *tragicus*, which, however, seems to have been taken as an adjective formed from a proper name. In another passage the same word is rendered by *tróiesc, tróisc* (q.v.) Trojan, perhaps the same meaning is intended here:—Æfter ðon hé eall geár onwealh Norþanhymbra mǽgþe áhte nalas swá swá sigefæst cyning ac swá swá leódhata ðæt hé grimsigende forleás and hí on gelícnysse ðæs traiscan wæles wundade *dein cum anno integro provincias Nordanhymbrorum non ut rex victor possideret sed quasi tyrannus saeviens disperderet, ac tragica caede dilaceraret*, Bd. 3, 1; S. 523, 30.

tramet, es; *m. A page*:—Bóc *liber*, stæf *littera*, leáf *folium*, tramet *pagina*, Wrt. Voc. i. 80, 75–78: Ælfc. Gr. 7; Zup. 25, 5. Lá hwylc tramet (*pagina*) is, oððe hwylc sprǽc ðæs godcundan lareóudómes, áðer oðþe ðære ealdan cýðnesse oþþe ðære níwan, ðæt ne sý seó rihteste bysen úran menniscan lífes, R. Ben. 133, 2. Tramod, R. Ben. Interl. 118, 2. Swá fela trameta *tot paginae*, swá fela leáfa *tot folia*, Ælfc. Gr. 18; Zup. 117, 12. Trametas *paginas*, Germ. 398, 181.

trandan (?) *to roll, move hastily*:—Trondendi *praeceps*, Txts. 89, 1668. [Cf. (?) *Icel.* trandill (*as a nickname*).] v. trendan, trendel.

treaflíce; *adv. Grievously, painfully*:—Eallum ðe deópe and ful treaflíce teónan þolian *omnibus injuriam patientibus*, Ps. Th. 102, 6. [Cf. (?) *Welsh* traf *stir, strain*; trafu *to stir, agitate*.]

treágian; *p.* ode *To repair, sew together*:—Treágiende *sarcientes, consuentes, componentes*, Hpt. Gl. 445, 73. Getreágede (-ode) *consuta*, 412, 38.

treahtere, treahtigean. v. trahtere, trahtian.

tredan; *p.* træd, *pl.* trǽdon; *pp.* treden. I. *to tread, tread down, trample upon* (lit. and fig.):—Ðú trides (*conculcabis*) león and dracan, Ps. Surt. 90, 13. Hé trit mid ðæm fét *terit pede*, Past. 47; Swt. 357, 20. Hwílum mec (*an animal's skin*) brýd triedeþ fótum, Exon. Th. 393, 27; Rä. 13, 6. Mé man tredeþ *conculcavit me homo*, Ps. Th. 55, 1: Cd. Th. 56, 15; Gen. 912. Mé tredaþ feóndas míne, Ps. Th. 55, 2: Exon. Th. 119, 23; Gú. 259. Ðá hét ic ðone here ðæt hié mid fótum ðone snáw trǽdon *calcare militem niuem jubeo*, Nar. 23, 18: Jos. 10, 24. Ða ðe mé trǽdan *conculcantes me*, Ps. Th. 56, 3. Ðæt hig hine trǽdun, Lk. Skt. 12, 1. Trédun *proterunt*, Wrt. Voc. ii. 118, 2. Fótum tredene, Bd. 3, 22; S. 552, 15. I a. with prep.:—Anweald tó tredenne ofer snacan *potestatem calcandi supra scorpiones*, Lk. Skt. 10, 19. II. *to tread upon, step upon, walk upon*:—Ðonne ic hrúsan trede, Exon. Th. 389, 22; Rä. 8, 1. Hió grundbedd trideþ, 493, 3; Rä. 81, 24. Se ðe mórland trydeþ, Elen. Kmbl. 1221; El. 612. Se fótum tredeþ fiðru winda *qui ambulat super pennas ventorum*, Ps. Th. 103, 4. Ða ðe land tredaþ *those that move upon the earth* (Gen. 1, 28), Cd. Th. 13, 16; Gen. 203. Trædaþ, Exon. Th. 439, 5; Rä. 58, 5. Ðú flettpaðas míne trǽde, Cd. Th. 165, 12; Gen. 2730. Hé wræclástas træd, Beo. Th. 2709; B. 1352. Meodowongas træd, 3291; B. 1643. Mearh moldan træd, Elen. Kmbl. 109; El. 55. Forð gán, foldweg tredan, Andr. Kmbl. 1550; An. 776. Gewát him se hearda sǽwong tredan, Beo. Th. 3933; B. 1964. Tredan elþeódigra foldan, Exon. Th. 329, 4; Vy. 29. Ic seah turf tredan .vi. gebróðor, 394, 10; Rä. 14, 1. Ðú (*the serpent*) scealt ðínum breóstum bearm tredan brádre eorðan, faran féðeleás, Cd. Th. 56, 4; Gen. 907. III. in figurative senses, glossing Latin words:—Sáwl gefylled trytt (*calcabit*; tret, Kent. Gl. 1015) beóbreád *the full soul loatheth an honeycomb* (Prov. 27, 7), Scint. 50, 8. Tredaþ *terimus* (*otia temporum*), Wrt. Voc. ii. 78, 12. [*O. Frs.* treda: *O. L. Ger.* tredan: *O. H. Ger.* tretan: *Icel.* troða. Cf. *Goth.* trudan.] v. á-, be-, for-, ge-, of-, ofer-, tó-tredan; sin-tredende, *and following words*.

tredd. v. wín-tredd.

treddan; *p.* de. I. *to tread under foot, trample upon*:—Tréddun *proterunt*, Txts. 84, 749. II. *to investigate, examine*. v. á-treddan:—Weorð mé heorte forht ðǽr ic ðín hálig word tredde *a verbis tuis formidavit cor meum*, Ps. Th. 118, 161. [*O. H. Ger.* fortratta *proterit*; trettenti *terens*: *Icel.* tratta; *p.*; traddr; *pp.*]

treddian; *p.* ode *To tread, step, walk*:—Raþe æfter ðon on fiór feónd treddode, Beo. Th. 1455; B. 725. Cyning of brýdbúre tryddode, 1848; B. 922. Hié of ðam grimman gryre treddedon, Cd. Th. 243, 21; Dan. 439. Streámas ðú miht on treddian eorðan gelíce *flumina pertransivit pede*, Ps. Th. 65, 5. [*O. H. Ger.* trettôn *calcare, conculcare*.]

trede; *adj. Firm to tread on, that may be walked on*:—Sǽ cýðde hwá hine gesette, tírmeahtig cyning, for ðon hé hine tredne him ongeán gyrede, ðonne God wolde ofer síne ýðe gán *ready for his coming the sea made itself firm for his tread, when God would walk over its waves*, Exon. Th. 72, 2; Cri. 1166.

tredel, es; *m. A step*:—Tredelas *vel* stæpas *bases*, Wrt. Voc. i. 21, 48. [Grece or tredyl or steyre *gradus*, Prompt. Parv. 209. Tredyl or grece *gradus, pedalis*, 501. A tredel *subpedium*, Wülck. Gl. 614, 14: *suspendium*, 615, 3: *liciatorium*, 592, 33.]

tredend, es; *m. One who treads*:—Tredend *calcatrix*, Wrt. Voc. ii. 127, 42.

trég (treg ?), tríg (cf. (?) hég, híg *hay*, for the form), es; *n. A tray, trough*:—Trég *alueolum*, Wrt. Voc. i. 290, 70. Nim ðæt reáde ryden, dó on tríg; hǽt stánes swíþe háte, lege on ðæt tríg innan, Lchdm. ii. 340, 5–6. [Bye us vessel . . . Dysschys, cuppys, and sawsers, Bolles, treyes, and platers, Rich. 1490.] Cf. troh.

trega, an; *m. Pain, grief, vexation, hurt, ill*:—Trega ł anda ðínes húses *zelus domus tuae*, Ps. Lamb. 68, 10. Tregan *injuriam* (cf. teónan, R. Ben. 17, 11), R. Ben. Interl. 20, 10. Ic fleáh hlǽfdigan hete, tregan and teónan, Cd. Th. 137, 15; Gen. 2274. Ða twégen tregan (cf. ðyssa yfla hwæðer, 41), Met. 5, 42. Weá wæs árǽred, tregena tuddor, Cd. Th. 60, 27; Gen. 988. [Mid ham is muruhðe moniuold wiðute teone and treie, O. E. Homl. i. 193, 61. Alkyn sorow and trey and tene, Pr. C. 7327. Al that whilom was murthe is turned to treie and tene, P. S. 340, 380. *Goth.* trigó; us trigóm ἐκ λύπης, 2 Cor. 9, 7: *O. L. Ger.* trego *dolor*: *Icel.* tregi *difficulty*; *grief, sorrow*.] v. hell-trega, tin-treg, -trega.

tregian; *p.* ode *To vex, trouble, afflict, grieve*:—Gif gé on unriht ne tregiaþ ne earme ne tyrewiaþ (*if ye oppress not the stranger, the fatherless, and the widow*, Jer. 7, 6), Wulfst. 50, 2. Ða ðe tregiaþ mé *qui tribulant me*, Ps. Spl. T. 3, 1. [Eall þis wæs God mid tó gremienne and ðás arme leóde mid tó tregienne, Chr. 1104; Erl. 239, 40. Quað Balaam: 'For ðu tregest me,' Gen. and Ex. 3975. Þai traied þe *exacerbaverunt te*, Ps. 5, 11. *O. Sax.* tregan *to trouble*: *Icel.* trega *to grieve*.] v. tin-tregian.

trehing (*but* þrihing *in Lambarde*. v. Schmid, A. S. Gesetz. 508). The form given in L. Ed. C. to the Scandinavian word, which in Icelandic appears as *þriðjungr* = the third part of a shire:—De treingis. Erant potestates super wapentagiis quas trehingas vocabant, scilicet, terciam partem provincie, et qui super ipsam dominabantur, trehing-gref . . . Et quod illi vocabant tria hundreda, vel iiii, vel plura, isti (*those of Danish England*) vocabant trehing. Et quod trehinge non poterat diffiniri, in scira servabatur, L. Ed. C. 31; Th. i. 455, 17–25. In Magna Carta, § 25, trethingii (*pl.*) occurs. The Anglicized form of the word probably began with þ, and Halliwell gives Thirdings as the term used of the Ridings. The present form, Riding, seems to have arisen from a confusion of the initial dental with the final sound of East, West, North.

trehtere. v. trahtere.

trem, trym *a step*:—Ic ðæt gehâte ðæt ic heonon nelle fleón fótes trym *I vow that I will not flee hence one footstep* (cf. ðæt hé nolde fleógan fótmǽl landes, 139, 57; By. 275), Byrht. Th. 138, 68; By. 247. Fótes trem, Beo. Th. 5044; B. 2525. *The form is probably to be recognized in a gloss given* Anglia viii. 33, 163 note, ægne trem *rendering* pedetemtim, *for which perhaps* fægre, tremmǽlum *might be read*. Cf. Hpt. Gl. 477, 78, *where the gloss for the same passage is* fægre; fægre oððe fótmǽlum *gradatim*, Wrt. Voc. ii. 40, 47; fótmélum *pedetemptim*, Txts. 90, 834; stæpmǽlum *gradatim*, Hpt. Gl. 497, 54. Cf. *also*: Ðonne wiðtremð hé and onhupaþ *gressum post terga revocet*, Past. 58; Swt. 441, 27.

tremes, tremesa, tremese, tremesse. v. trimes.

tremian, tremman *to confirm*, tremman *to step*. v. trymman, wiðtremman.

trendan (?) *to turn, roll*. v. sin-trendende *teres*, *but perhaps* sintredende *should be read, see* tredan = *terere*. [Let hym rollen and trenden with inne hym self the lyht of his inward syhte *in se revolvat intimi lucem visus*, Chauc. Boet. 100, 2835. *Chaucer also uses* bi-trenden, *and* un-trenden *occurs elsewhere*. Cf. *O. Frs.* trind, trund *round*: *Dan.* trind.] v. trandan, trinda, *and next word*.

trendel, es; *m.* I. *a circle, ring*:—Án wunderlíc trendel (*mirabilis corona*) wearð ateówed ábútan ðære sunnan, Chr. 806; Erl. 60, 25. Gelden trendel *circulus aureus* (*in naribus suis*, Prov. 11, 22), Kent. Gl. 373. Brevis virgula (*the mark for short quantity*, i.e. ◡) ys ánes trendles dǽl ðus licgende, Anglia viii. 333, 29. On trendle *in rota*, Hpt. Gl. 471, 2. Stríc ðú mid ðínum scytefingre, swilce ðú trændel wyrce, Techm. ii. 129, 9. Trendla *circulorum* (the rings on a peacock's tail), Hpt. Gl. 419, 8. I a. *a circle used in calculation*:—Ðás þing wé geopeniaþ bet on ðissum trendle (cf. gȳm ðisses hwióles; hyt ðē ætȳwþ eall ðæs mōnan ryne, 33: *and:* Ðās circulas synt behēfe preóstum, 44), Anglia viii. 328, 38. I b. figurative:—Trendel (*benedicens*) *coronam* (*anni*), Blickl. Gl.: Ps. Spl. T. 64, 12. II. where a surface, plane or spherical, is denoted, *a disk, orb:*—Ðæs mōnan trendel is symle gelīc, þeáh ðe eall endemes eallunga ne scīne, Lchdm. iii. 242, 4: Hpt. Gl. 418, 16. Ðære sunnan trendel, Homl. Th. ii. 606, 12. Trendles *sphaerae,* trendel *sphaera,* Hpt. Gl. 489, 22, 23. Scīnendne trendel heofones, Hymn. Surt. 22, 17. Trendlum *orbibus,* Hpt. Gl. 490, 76. II a. *a round place, a circus:*—Trendles, hrincgsetles *circi,* Hpt. Gl. 488, 69. ¶ The word and the connected forms *trend, trind, trin* seem to occur in local names. v. Cod. Dip. Kmbl. vi. 343, 344. [*Wick.* trendil *sphaera: Prompt. Parv.* trendyl *troclea.* Trendel *giraculum,* Wülck. Gl. 586, 29: trendell *catantrum,* 571, 19. Halliwell gives *trindle* = wheel as a Derbyshire word.] v. sin-trendel; *adj., and following words.*

trendeled; *adj. Made round:*—Tryndyled reáf *circumtectum,* Wrt. Voc. i. 40, 29. [Panter is blac mid wite spottes sapen al, wit and trendled als a wel, Misc. 23, 737.]

trendlian; *p.* ode *To trundle, roll.* [Lefdis letten teares treondlin (trendlen, MS. C.: trondlin, MS. B.), Kath. 2329. Þeȝ appel trendli from þon treowe, O. and N. 135. Hit trendeled doun, Allit. Pms. 2, 41. Be trendlid *volvi,* Wick. Jud. 7, 13. Trendelyn a round thynge *trocleo, volvo,* Prompt. Parv. 502.] v. ā-trendlian; trendel.

treó. v. treów.

Treónta, Trēnta, an; *The Trent:*—Andlang Trēntan, Chr. 1013; Erl. 147, 18. Man ofslōh Ælfwine be Trēntan, 679; Erl. 41, 10. On Trēnton (Treóntan, Bd. M. 144, 14) streáme *in fluvio Treenta,* Bd. 2, 16; S. 519, 31. Mid Trēntan (Treóntan, Bd. M. 240, 1) streáme *fluvio Treanta,* 3, 24; S. 557, 37. Be Trēntan (Treóntan, Bd. M. 324, 15) ðære eá *juxta fluvium Treanta,* 4, 21; S. 590, 14. On Trēntan; of Trēntan, Cod. Dip. Kmbl. iii. 396, 20. Ða brycge ofer Treóntan, Chr. 924; Erl. 110, 10.

treów, es; *n.* I. *a tree:*—Treów *arbor,* Wrt. Voc. i. 32, 26. Iung treów *arbustum,* 41. Wudu *silva,* āhæáwan treów *lignum,* 33, 56: Ælfc. Gr. 8; Zup. 31, 13. Ðæt treów wæs gōd tō etanne, Gen. 3, 6. Treów (trēu, Lind.) *arbor,* Mt. Kmbl. 3, 10. Treów (trȳw, MS. B.: treó, Lind.), 7, 17. Hit wearð mycel treów (on treó miclum, Lind.: on tree miclum, Rush.) *factum est in arborem magnam,* Lk. Skt. 13, 19. Sunnan trió āgefeþ ondsware æt ðæm upgonge . . . and ðæt mōnan triów gelīce on niht dyde, Nar. 27, 16–19. Heó genam of ðæs treówes wæstme, Gen. 3, 6. Æppelbǣre treów westm wircende, 1, 11. Tree *arborem,* Lk. Skt. Lind. 13, 6: 19, 4. Gif man ōðres wudu heáweþ unāliéfedne, forgielde ǣlc greát treów mid .v. scill., L. Alf. pol. 12; Th. i. 70, 5. Oftost beóþ ða treówa getealde *feminini generis,* Ælfc. Gr. 6; Zup. 20, 14: Ps. Spl. 95, 12. Treówu, Scint. 56, 17: Ps. Th. 57, 8. Ða hālgan trió sunnan and mōnan . . . and ōþre treów, Nar. 27, 26–29. Treów, 32, 13. Triów, 28, 11. Treó sceolon brǣdan, Exon. Th. 343, 20; Gn. Ex. 160. Treó westmbēru *ligna fructifera,* Ps. Surt. 148, 9. Of ðæra treówa wæstme, Gen. 3, 2. Triówa heánnisse, Nar. 28, 1. Betwih ðǣm rindum ðæra trió, 27, 25. Trēa *lignorum,* Ps. Surt. 73, 5. Trēwna *arborum,* Mt. Kmbl. p. 15, 9. Ðæra treówa (trȳwa, MS. B.: trēuna, Lind.), Mt. Kmbl. 3, 10. Treóna, Rtl. 95, 23. Of ðam treówum, Lind.: trēum, Rush.), Mk. Skt. 11, 8. Sumu treówu hē watrode, Past. 40; Swt. 293, 4: Nar. 27, 21. Treówa, Gen. 1, 29. Behealdaþ ealle trȳwu (treówa, MS. A.: treó, Lind. Rush.), Lk. Skt. 21, 29. *The word occurs as the second part of many compounds,* e. g. æppel-, ceder-, corn-, cwic-, cyrs-, ele-, fīc-, gyr-, hwīting-, magdala-, palm-, persoc-, pīn-, plūm-, ulm-, wīn-, windel-treów; see also lād-, wudu-treów. II. a material, *wood:*—Hī worhton him anlīcnyssa, sume of golde, sume of seolfre, sume of stānum, sume of treówe, Homl. Th. i. 22, 30. Hē hēt getimbrian cyrican of treówe, Chr. 626; Erl. 23, 40. Hē of treówe (treó, Bd. M. 138, 21) cyricean getimbrede, Bd. 2, 14; S. 517, 26. Monige of ðam treówe (treó, Bd. M. 156, 5) ðæs hālgan Cristes mǣles spōnas nimaþ, 3, 2; S. 524, 30. III. in a collective sense, *trees, a wood:*—Ðā behīdde Adam hyne on middan ðam treówe neorxena wanges *Adam hid himself among the trees of the garden;* in medio ligni paradisi, Gen. 3, 8. Hē (*the Phenix*) sylf biereþ in ðæt treów innan torhte frætwe; ðǣr se wilda fugel ofer heánne beám hūs getimbreþ (cf. hē heánne beám on holtwuda wunaþ, 209, 15; Ph. 171), Exon. Th. 211, 19; Ph. 200. IV. *tree* as in roof-*tree,* saddle-*tree, a piece of wood, a beam, log, stake, staff, cudgel:*—Scort sinewealt stān *vel* treów *cilindrus,* Wrt. Voc. i. 41, 35. Ðonne seó sāwl hié gedǣleþ wiþ ðone līchoman, hwylc biþ hē ðonne būton swylce stān oððe treów (*a stone or a log*), Blickl. Homl. 21, 27. Of treówe *de stipite,* Wrt. Voc. ii. 27, 65. Gif mon mid treówe geslegen sié, Lchdm. ii. 8, 32: 94, 23. Gē fērdon mid swurdum and treówum mē gefōn, Mk. Skt. 14, 48. Gewyrcean tor of treówum and of mycclum beámum, Blickl. Homl. 187, 12. Swā hwā swā getimbraþ ofer ðisum grundwealle gold, oððe seolfor, oððe treówa, Homl. Th. ii. 588, 25. Treówu, 590, 13. Hié nāmon treówu and slōgon on ōþerne ende īsene næglas, Ors. 4, 1; Swt. 158, 4. v. fugol-, teld-, wægn-treów. IV a. *tree* as in gallows-*tree,* 'tree used of the cross:—Hǣlendes treów, Rood Kmbl. 50; Kr. 25. Wuldres treów, 28; Kr. 14. Ðū ðē on rōde treów āhōfe, Anglia xii. 506, 4: Elen. Kmbl. 411; El. 206. Ðurh treów ūs com līf, ðā ðā Crist hangode on rōde, Homl. Th. ii. 240, 22. v. gealg-, wulfheáfod-treów, *and* rōd. [*Goth.* triu *a tree; staff: O. Sax.* trio *a beam; the cross: O. Frs.* trē; *Icel.* trē *a tree; a beam; wood.*]

treów, trȳw, e; *f.* The word is sometimes used in the plural with the force of the singular. I. *truth* to a promise or engagement, *faith* (as in good or bad *faith,* to keep *faith* with a person), *troth:*—Treów, sió geond bilwitra breóst āríseþ, Exon. Th. 343, 21; Gn. Ex. 160. Hālegu treów seó ðū wið rodora weard healdest, Cd. Th. 127, 30; Gen. 2118. Wǣre gehealdan, treówe tācen, Andr. Kmbl. 427; An. 214. In swā hwylce tiid swā gē mid treówe (*truly*) tō mē on hyge hweorfaþ, and gē hellfirena geswīcaþ, Exon. Th. 366, 1; Reb. 5. On treówe gelǣton (-en ?) *fidei commissum,* Wrt. Voc. ii. 148, 76. His treówe (treówa, Bd. M. 130, 27) and his gehāt wið ðē gehealdon . . . his treówe for feógȳtsunge forleósan, seó ðe dȳrwurþre wǣre eallum māþmum *tibi fidem pollicitam servare . . . fidem suam, quae omnibus ornamentis pretiosior est, amore pecuniae perdere,* Bd. 2, 12; S. 514, 34–41. Ðȳ læs ic mīn gehāt and mīne treówe forleóse *ne fidem mei promissi praevaricer,* 4, 22; S. 592, 2. Āc fēreþ gelōme ofer ganotes bæð gārsecg fandaþ hwæðer āc hæbbe æðele treówe *oft fares the oaken vessel over the gannet's bath; ocean proves whether the oak keeps excellent faith,* i. e. whether the promise of safety, which its strength seems to give, is kept, Runic pm. Kmbl. 344, 22; Rūn. 25. Ne Hildeburh herian þorfte Eótena treówe, Beo. Th. 2148; B. 1072. Til biþ se ðe his treówe gehealdeþ, Exon. Th. 293, 6; Wand. 112. Ðū ðǣr tīrfæste treówe findest, 473, 8; Bo. 11: Ps. Th. 100, 6. Ðæt ǣfre on his dagum sceolde gewurðan swā lytle treówa, 13, arg. Mānum treówum woldon hié ðæt feorhleán, fācne gyldan, Cd. Th. 187, 11; Exod. 149. Ðū hæfst ongyten ða wonclan trūwa (treówa, Cott. MS.) ðæs blindan lustes, Bt. 7, 2; Fox 18, 3. Ða ðe mid tungan treówa gehātaþ, fācenlīce þencaþ, Fragm. Kmbl. 47; Leás. 25. Tīr healdeþ trȳwa wel wið æðelingas, Runic pm. Kmbl. 342, 22; Rūn. 17. II. *truth* to a person, *fidelity, fealty, loyalty.* Cf. hold:—Ðæs getreówan freóndes, ðone mon lufaþ for treówum, Bt. 24, 3; Fox 82, 35. Dauid forbær ðæt hē Saul ne dorste ofsleán for ðǣm ealdum treówum, Past. 28; Swt. 199, 3: 3; Swt. 37, 7. Cham ne wolde cȳðan hyldo and treówa, Cd. Th. 96, 9; Gen. 1592. III. *the truth* of the stronger to the weaker, *grace, favour, help.* Cf. hold:—Treów wæs gecȳþed, ðætte Gūðlāce God leánode ellen mid ārum, Exon. Th. 129, 11; Gū. 419. Treówe *latibulo* (protection, faithful care; the passage in which the word occurs refers to the entrusting of his mother by Christ to St. John's protection), Hpt. Gl. 415, 57. Git mē sibblufan and freóndscipe cȳðaþ, treówe and hyldo tīdiaþ mē, Cd. Th. 152, 6; Gen. 2516: 34, 21; Gen. 541. Heó treówe gehēt *she promised God's favour,* 44, 25; Gen. 714. Hē treówa gehēt, his holdne hyge, 41, 8; Gen. 653. IV. *an assurance of faith* or *truth, word* (in to give or pledge one's *word*), *a promise, an engagement, a covenant, league:*—Hū þearf mannes sunu māran treówe *what need has a son of man of a better assurance?* Cd. Th. 204, 26; Exod. 425. Ða eorlas ðe him treówe sealdon, 123, 17; Gen. 2046. Hē bæd hié ðæt hié gemunden ðara ealdena treówa *ad antiquorum jura foederum adhortatione persuadens,* Ors. 2, 5; Swt. 82, 9. Se ðe his nȳhstan swereþ, and hine mid treówum ne beswīcþ *he that swears to his neighbour, and does not deceive him with assurances of good faith,* Ps. Th. 14, 6. For ðām treówum ðe ðū genumen hæfdest tō Abrahame . . . Ðū him ðæt gehēte, ðæt . . ., Cd. Th. 235, 26; Dan. 312. Se wæs ofslagen ofer āþas and treówa (*or under* I) *contra fidem jurisjurandi peremptus est,* Bd. 2, 20; S. 521, 17. Norþhymbre and Eást-Engle hæfdon Ælfrēde cyninge āþas geseald, and Eást-Engle foregīsla vi; and þeh ofer ða treówa . . . fōron hié, Chr. 894; Erl. 90, 5. Ic eów treówa ðæs mīne selle, Cd. Th. 92, 28; Gen. 1535: 122, 35; Gen. 2037. Ðū treówa selle, wǣra ðīna, ðæt ðū wille mē wesan freónd, 170, 23; Gen. 2817. V. *faith* in something, *belief, trust, confidence:*—Treów in ðē (*the Virgin Mary*) weorðlīcu wunade, Exon. Th. 6, 11; Cri. 82. Nō him for egsan earmra gǣsta treów getweóde, 122, 25; Gū. 311: 134, 28; Gū. 515. Ðīna āgna treówa and seó godcunde lufu and se tōhopa ðē ne lǣtaþ geortrēwan be ðam ēcan līfe, Bt. 10; Fox 30, 8. Ða bebodu ðe giet māran sint . . . ðæt is, ryht dōm, and mildheortnes and treówa (cf. Mt. 23, 23 *where* geleáfa *renders* fides), Past. 57; Swt. 439, 31. Ða beraþ Godes fatu ða ðe ōðerra monna sāula underfōþ tō lǣdanne on ða treówa hira āgenra gearnunga *Domini vasa ferunt, qui proximorum animas perducendas in suae conversionis fide suscipiunt,* 13; Swt. 77, 4. Ðū gelȳfst ðīnum hlāforde bet ðonne ðē selfum, and ðīnum gefērum æmnwel and ðē selfum; ðū dēst swīðe rihte, mid ðȳ ðæt ðū swā gooda treówa wit hī hefst, Shrn. 196, 25. Hē (*Noah*) hæfde him on hreðre hālige treówa, Cd. Th. 201, 3; Exod. 366. Hē his treówa sceal, and his mōdgeþonc, mā up ðonne niþer habban tō heofonum, Met. 31, 18. [*Goth.* triggwa *a covenant: O. Sax.* trewa (*often pl.*): *O. L. Ger.* treuwa *foedus: O. Frs.* triuwe, treuwe: *O. H. Ger.* triuwa *fides, foedus.*] v. heáh-, hyge-, un-, wine-treów, *and next word.*

treówa, trýwa, an; *m. An assurance of good faith, a covenant.* v. treów, IV:—Se ēca treówa *the perpetual covenant* (cf. Ex. 31, 16), Wulfst. 210, 22. Nāđor ne wē on đone here faran, ne heora nān tō ūs, būton man trýwan and gýslas betwýnan sylle friđe tō wedde, L. A. G. 4; Th. i. 156, 8. Cf. trūwa.

treówan, triéwan, trīwan, trýwan; *p.* de. I. *to trust:*—Irnaþ ealle endemes, đa đe hiora ærninge trēwaþ *those who have confidence in their powers of running,* Bt. 37, 2; Fox 188, 10. Gehwylc hiora his ferhđe·treówde, đæt hē hæfde mōd micel, Beo.Th. 2337; B. 1166. II. *to prove* one's self *true, to clear* one's self *of a charge of untrue conduct.* Cf. *Icel.* tryggva *to make firm and trusty:*—Gif hē (*a person accused of plotting against his lord*) hine selfne trióvan wille, dō đæt be cyninges wergelde, L. Alf. pol. 4; Th. i. 64, 2. Treówan, 33; Th. i. 82, 8 note. Trýwan, 19; Th. i. 74, 7 note. v. ge-treówan, -triéwan, -trýwan, mis-trīwan, or-trýwan, *and* treówian.

treów-bytt (?), e; *f. A wooden vessel:*—*Flasce* trinnubyttæ (triuuu-? = treów-, cf. trýwen byt *flasco,* 149, 33), *eadem et flascones,* Wrt. Voc. ii. 39, 78.

treów-cynn, es; *n. A kind of tree* or *wood, a tree, a wood:*—*Abies* đæt treówcyn, Nar. 8, 21. Treócynn, Exon. Th. 472, 20; Bo. 2. Nim ǽlces treówcynnes dǽl đe on đæm lande sý gewexen, Lchdm. i. 398, 7. Hē āsmeáde be ǽlcum treówcynne fram đam heágan cederbeáme ōđ đæt hē com tō đære lytlan ysopan *he spake of trees, from the cedar tree that is in Lebanon even unto the hyssop that springeth out of the wall* (1 Kings 4, 33), Homl. Th. ii. 578, 4. Oftost on treówcynne beóþ đa treówa getealde *feminini generis* and se wæstm *neutri generis,* Ælfc. Gr. 6, 9; Zup. 20, 14. Man worhte Noes earce of đam treówcynne đe is genemned Sem, Salm. Kmbl. p. 184, 16: Nar. 10, 13. Đā ætýwde Drihten Moise ān treówcyn and hēt dōn đæt treów on đæt wæter, Ex. 15, 25.

treówe, triéwe, trýwe; *adj. True, faithful, trustworthy:*—Wæs hiera sib ætgædere, ǽghwylc ōđrum trýwe, Beo. Th. 2334; B. 1165. Hē spræc tō his onbehtþegne, tō his treówum gesīþe, Exon. Th. 179, 29; Gū. 1269. Hié ne beóþ nānum men getreówe (ne treówe, Bod. MS.), Bt. 7, 1; Fox 16, 17. Būton hē habbe twēgra trýwra manna gewitnesse, L. Eth. iii. 9; Th. i. 296, 18. Man namige .ii. trýwe þegnas, L. N. P. L. 57; Th. ii. 298, 31. His freónd se treówesta (getreówesta, Bd. M. 126, 30) *fidissimus amicus illius,* Bd. 2, 12; S. 513, 17. [*Goth.* triggws *true, faithful: O. Sax.* triuwi: *O. Frs.* triuwe: *O. H. Ger.* gi-triuwi: *Icel.* tryggr.] v. ge-, or-treówe (-triéwe, -trýwe).

treówen, trīwen, trýwen; *adj.* I. *of a tree:*—Hire hyrdeman sume āc āstāh, and his orf lǽswode mid treówenum helme, Homl. Th. ii. 150, 31. II. *of wood, wooden:*—Treówen *ligneus,* Ælfc. Gr. 5; Zup. 15, 14. Trīwen sceó *coturnus,* Wrt. Voc. i. 26, 21. Trýwen byt *flasco,* ii. 149, 33. On treówenum mortere, Lchdm. ii. 180, 4. Trýwenan, i. 220, 11: 230, 10. On treówenre cyste, Homl. Skt. i. 20, 69. On treówenre rōde, Nicod. 34; Thw. 20, 6. Hyre goldfāgan treówenan cuppan, Chart. Th. 536, 18. Wirce treówene earce *facies arcam ligneam,* Deut. 10, 1. Godu treówene and stǽnene, 4, 28. On treówenum fatum, Ex. 7, 19. Treówenu fatu mon weorþige, Bt. 36, 1; Fox 172, 19. [*Wick., C. M.* treen. *Goth.* triweins *wooden.*] v. pīn-treówen.

treów-fæst; *adj. Faithful:*—Tunge mīn triówfest, Ps. C. 114. Treówfæst (treóufæst, Lind.) *fidelis,* Lk. Skt. Rush. 19, 17. Trewufæst (treuw-?), Mt. Kmbl. Lind. 25, 21. Wē on bōcum rǽdaþ be sumum treówfæstum wīfe, Homl. Skt. i. 12, 179. Treófæsto, treófest *fideles,* Lk. Skt. Lind. 16, 11, 12. Wǽron his bebodu ealle treówfæste *fidelia omnia mandata ejus,* Ps. Th. 110, 5. [Trowfeste men, O. E. Homl. i. 89, 29. Cf. *Icel.* trū-fastr: *Dan.* troe-fast.] v. un-treówfæst.

treów-féging, e; *f. A joining together of planks;* commissoria, tabularum conjunctio, Wrt. Voc. ii. 132, 31.

treów-fugol, es; *m. A tree-haunting bird:*—Treófugla tuddor, Exon. Th. 146, 9; Gū. 707.

treów-geþofta, an; *m. A faithful comrade, trusty companion:*—Monig biþ uncūþ treówgeþofta, Exon. Th. 469, 20; Hy. 11, 5. Treówgeþoftan (*St. Matthew and St. Andrew*), Andr. Kmbl. 2101; An. 1052. Ic mid mec gelǽdde mīne þrié đa getreówestan frýnd, đa wǽron mīne syndrige treówgeþoftan *assumpsi mecum tres fidelissimos amicos,* Nar. 29, 28. [Cf. *Icel.* trygg-vinr *a trusty friend.*]

treów-geweorc, es; *n. A wooden structure:*—Treówgeweorc on gelīcnysse medmiceles hūses geworht *tumba lignea in modum domunculi facta,* Bd. 4, 3; S. 570, 16.

treów-gewrid, es; *n. A thicket of trees:*—Ys on Bretone land sum fenn unmǽtre mycelnesse . . . Đǽr synd . . . manige eáland and hreód and beorhgas and treówgewrido, Guthl. 3; Gdwin. 20, 7.

treówian, triéwian, trýwian; *p.* ode. I. *to trust, confide:*—Ǽghwylcum đe him on treówaþ *omnes qui confidunt in eis,* Ps. Th. 113, 17. Đa đe treówiaþ (*confidunt*) on Drihtne, Ps. Spl. 124, 1. On mannan tō treówianne *confidere in homine,* Ps. Th. 117, 8. On ealdormen tō treówianne *sperare in principibus,* 9. II. *to be true* to a person:—Dōþ swā ic hāte ic hāte ic eów treówige gif gē đæt tācen gegāþ sōđ geleátan *do as I bid; I will be true* (or *gracious,* v. treów, III) *to you, if you use that sign* (*circumcision*), *true sign of belief* (cf. sete tācn sōđ gif đū wille on mē habban holdne freónd, 139, 17–22; Gen. 2311–2313), Cd. Th. 140, 7; Gen. 2324. III. *to prove* one's self *true, clear* one's self *from a charge of untrue conduct:*—Gif hwā ōđerne tión wille . . . gif hē hine treówian wille, in .xii. ciricum dō hē đæt, L. Alf. pol. 33; Th. i. 82, 8. Gif hē hine triéwian wille, đæt hē tō đære lǽne fācn ne wiste, đæt hē mōt, 19; Th. i. 74, 7. [Þenne he þe treoweđe alre best, þenne beswikes tu heom, Laym. 3413. Him þ ha treoweđ on, Kath. 1327, note. Þeo luue . . . þu treowest hire, Misc. 94, 42. Putifar trewiđ his wiwes tale, Gen. and Ex. 2037.] v. ge-treówian (-trýwian); treówan, treówsian, trūwian.

treów-leás; *adj.* I. *faithless;* perfidus:—Wēnstū đæt ic sceole sprecan tō đissum treówleásan men (*the sorcerer, Simon*), Blickl. Homl. 183, 32. Simon cwæþ: 'Đis is đæt mennisc đe ealle mīne dǽda mid heora wordum onwendan.' Đā cwæþ Neron tō Petre: 'For hwon wǽron gyt swā treówleáse?' 175, 26. Treówleásra *perfidorum,* Wrt. Voc. ii. 66, 54: Wulfst. 186, 3. Đara treówleásra (*perfidorum*) cyninga beboda, Bd. 1, 7; S. 476, 35. Trióleásra, Rtl. 59, 23. Trīwleásra, 24, 21. II. *without belief, infidel;* infidelis:—Se đe ne gīmþ đara đe his beóþ hē wiđsæcþ Godes geleáfan and hē biþ treówleás *qui suorum curam non habet, fidem negavit, et est infideli deterior,* Past. 18; Swt. 139, 3. [*O. Sax.* treu-lōs *perfidus: Icel.* trygg-lauss.] v. ge-treówleás.

treówleásness, e; *f. Faithlessness:*—Trēuleásnis (-lēsnis) *perfidia,* Txts. 85, 1533. Đonne lǽrþ ūs Godes engel smeáunge ymbe Godes beboda. . . đonne lǽrþ ūs se deófol treówleásnesse Godes beboda (*unfaithfulness to God's commands*), Wulfst. 233, 19. v. ge-treówleásness.

treów-līc; *adj. True, faithful.* [*Icel.* trygg-ligr *trustworthy.*] v. ge-treówlīc, *and next word.*

treówlīce; *adv. Faithfully, truly:*—Ic dō swýđe treówlīce ymb hý *fiducialiter agam in eo,* Ps. Th. 11, 6. [Ich leote ham treowliche luuien ham, Marh. 13, 32. Þe luue is treouliche iuestned touward him, A. R. 218, 13. Þouȝ ȝe be trewe of ȝowre tonge and trewliche wynne, Piers P. i. 177. *O. H. Ger.* triulīhho *fideliter: Icel.* tryggliga.] v. ge-, un-treówlīce.

treów-loga, an; *m. One who fails to keep faith, one who fails in loyalty to his leader:*—Đa hildlatan holt ofgeáfon týdre treówlogan đa ne dorston ǽr daređum lācan on hyra mandryhtnes miclan þearfe *those laggards in fight relinquished the wood, pitiful false ones to plighted faith, who dared not with darts sport in their liege lord's great need,* Beo. Th. 5686; B. 2847. [The treulogo (*Judas*), Hēl. 4622.]

treów-lufu, e, an; *f. Faithful love:*—Wæs seó treówlufu (*the love of the disciples to Christ after the ascension*) hāt æt heortan, Exon. Th. 34, 7; Cri. 538.

treówness, e; *f. Trust, confidence:*—God đū eart mīn frōfer, mīn trēwnes, and mīn tōhopa, Bt. 42; Fox 260, 15. v. or-treówness (-trýwness).

treów-rǽden[n], e; *f. The state* or *condition of being faithful* or *true:*—Swā ic đē lǽre lǽst uncre wel treówrǽdenne *as I teach you, maintain our state of mutual faithfulness,* Cd. Th. 139, 5; Gen. 2305. Cf. hold-rǽden.

treówsian, trýwsian; *p.* ode. I. *to engage, pledge one's self:*—Him cōmon ongeán .vi. cyningas and ealle wiđ trýwsodon (wiđ hine getreówsodon, col. 1), đæt hī woldon efenwy[r]hton beón on sǽ and on lande *six kings came to meet him, and all solemnly engaged to co-operate on sea and on land,* Chr. 972; Th. i. 225, col. 2. Se munuc đe mynster næbbe cume tō scīre biscope and trýwsie (-ige) hine sylfne wiđ God and wiđ men đæt hē þreó þing healdan wille, L. Eth. v. 6; Th. i. 306, 7: vi. 3; Th. i. 314, 25. II. *to prove* one's self *to be true, to clear* one's self *from a charge of untrue conduct:*—Gif hē hine trýwsian wylle, đæt hē tō đære lǽne fācn ne wiste, đæt hē mōt, L. Alf. pol. 19; Th. i. 74, 7 note. [Þas weord ich wulle þe treosien þurh mine god *I will prove to thee the good faith of these words by an oath,* Laym. 8489. Trousien, 8315. The word also means *to trust:*—Þe king him treousede on, 9308.] v. ge-treówsian; treówan, treówian.

treów-steall, es; *n. A place where trees are planted, a plantation:*—Hit cymþ tō Wulfūnes treówstealle, Cod. Dip. Kmbl. iii. 404, 11. Ōđ đæt treówsteall; đonnon of đan treówstealle, v. 297, 24. Ōđ Æđelstānes treówsteal, 298, 12. Cf. wæter-steall, *and next word.*

treów-stede, es; *m. A place where trees are planted:*—Iung treów *vel* treówstede *arbusta,* Wrt. Voc. i. 39, 8.

treów-teoru *resin:*—Trēuteru *bapis,* Wrt. Voc. ii. 101, 58: *bapys,* 10, 76. v. teoru.

treówþ, triéwþ, trýwþ, e; *f.* The word is used sometimes in plural with force of singular. I. *truth, good faith, honour:*—Đǽr dydon þeáh Rōmāne lytla triéwþa đæt him đa wǽron lāđe đe hiera hlāford beswican *there, however, the Romans acted a little honourably* (in hoc solo Romanis circa eum fortiter agentibus), *in that those who had betrayed their lord were detestable to them,* Ors. 5, 2; Swt. 218, 17. II. *fidelity:*—Heora gemynd þurhwunaþ for heora trýwđe wiđ God, Ælfc. T. Grn. 1, 12. III. *a covenant, an assurance of good faith:*—Đis ys đære treówđe blōd đe Drihten eów behēt *hic est sanguis foederis, quod pepigit Dominus vobiscum,* Ex. 24, 8. In treówþe geþeóded gāstlīces freóndscipes *spiritalis amicitiae foedere copulatus*, Bd. 4, 29; S. 607, 9. Mid ǽnigere treówđe *quolibet pacto*, Hpt. Gl. 469, 34. Treówđa *foedera, pacta*, 404, 9. Treóŵđa *foedera*, 416, 47. Hié nânra treówþa him ne wēndon būton đæt hié mid ealle forweorþan sceolde *they expected no terms for themselves, but that they must entirely perish;* the Latin which this seems intended to translate is:—Non secus ac si capta esset, turbata civitas fuit, Ors. 4, 5; Swt. 166, 13. Ic gemunde mînra treówđa đe ic Abrahame behēt *recordatus sum pacti mei*, Ex. 6, 5. Gif gē mîne treówđa gehealdaþ *si custodieritis pactum meum*, 19, 5. [*O. H. Ger.* ga-triuwida *confidentia;* missa-triuwida *diffidentia, suspicio: Icel.* tryggð *faith, truce.*] v. ge-, un-treówþ.

treów-þrâg, e; *f. A season of good faith* or *trust:*—Men leahtras oft geceósaþ treówþrâg is tō trâg *men often prefer vice to virtue, the time when good faith is kept is all too short* (?), Exon. Th. 354, 37; Reim. 57.

treów-wæstm *fruit of a tree:*—Treówwæstmas wurdon đære nihte þurh forste swîđe fornumene, Chr. 1110; Erl. 243, 2. Þurh wæstma forweorþenesse, ǽgđer ge on corne and eác on eallon treówwæstman, 1103; Erl. 239, 3.

treów-weorþung, e; *f. Tree-worship:*—Wē lǽraþ đæt preósta gehwilc forbeóde treówwurþunga and stânwurþunga, L. Edg. C. 16; Th. ii. 248, 30. Cf. Wē forbeódaþ ǽlcne hǽđenscipe . . . đæt is, đæt man weorđige . . . stânas ođđe ǽniges cynnes wudutreówa, L. C. S. 5; Th. i. 378, 17-21. v. Grmm. D. M. c. 21.

treów-wyrhta, an; *m. A wood-wright, worker in wood, carpenter, joiner:*—Treówwyrhta *lignarius*, Wrt. Voc. i. 19, 10: 73, 29. Se Treówyrhta segþ:—Hwilc eówer ne notaþ cræfte mînon, đonne hūs and mistlîce fata and scypa eów eallum ic wyrce? Se Smiþ andwyrt:—Eálâ Trŷwwyrhta, for hwî swâ sprycst đū?, Coll. Monast. Th. 31, 9-17. Ic hæbbe treówwyrhtan *habeo lignarium*, 30, 1.

treów-wyrm, es; *m. A caterpillar:*—Hē salde treówyrme westmas heara *dedit erugini fructus eorum*, Ps. Surt. 77, 46. [A treworme *terudo, trunos*, Wrt. Voc. i. 223, col. 1.] v. leáf-wyrm.

trēpe (?), trype (?), trŷpe (?), es; *m. A troop, band:*—Blōdige trēpas ɫ werodu *sanguineas acies*, Hymn. Surt. 47, 18. [*From Low Latin* tropus *or* trupa (?); cf. *Fr.* troupe: *Span.* tropa: *Ital.* truppa.]

treppan; *p.* te. I. *to tread:*—Hē trepeþ *terit*, Kent. Gl. 144. [Cf. Halliwell's Dict. trap *to tramp: Du.* trappen *to tread, trample: O. Frs. Ger.* treppe *a step.*] II. *to trap:*—Hió [tr]e[p]te *inretivit*, Kent. Gl. 211. v. be-træppan, *and next word.*

treppe, træppe (v. (?) colte-træppe (=*colt-trap?*) *ramnus*, Wrt. Voc. i. 285, 47), an; *f. A trap:*—Ic beswîce fugelas mid treppan *decipio aves decipula*, Coll. Monast. Th. 25, 15. [*O. H. Ger.* trapo *tenda.* From this Low Latin *trappa*, hence French *trappe*, which perhaps helps to determine the form of the later English word:—To lacchenn þe þurrh trapp, Orm. 12301. A mous caught in a trappe, Chauc. Prol. 145. A trappe *brida*, Wrt. Voc. i. 264, 8. Trappe for myce *muscipula, decipula*, trappe to take wythe beestys *tenabulum*, trappyd or betrappyd *decipulatus, illaqueatus*, Prompt. Parv. 499.]

trēu, trēw *a tree*, trēwan, trēwness, tribulaþ. v. treów, treówan, treówness, trifulian.

-tricce *in* ge-tricce (q.v.) *tractable* (?). [Cf. (?) *Du.* trekken *to pull: Dan.* trække.]

tridwet ? *in* getridwet spere *hasta*, Wrt. Voc. i. 35, 40.

triēwan. v. treówan.

trifet, es; *n. Tribute:*—Trifetum *tributis*, Kent. Gl. 426. [*O. H. Ger.* tribuz. From Latin.]

trifulian; *p.* ode *To pound, grind, triturate:*—Se đe pîlaþ *vel* tribulaþ *pilurus* vel *pistor*, Wrt. Voc. i. 20, 26. Gebærn tō ahsan, dō eced tō, trifula swîđe, Lchdm. ii. 150, 3. Menge eall tōgædere, and trifolige, 186, 10. [*From Latin* tribulare.] v. ge-trifulian, *and next word.*

trifulung, e; *f. Grinding, pounding, threshing:*—In trifelunge *in tritura*, Wrt. Voc. ii. 46, 21.

trîg (trig?). v. trēg.

trimes(-is), es; trimessa, an; *m.:* trimes[s], e; trimes[s]e, an; *f.:* þrimes; *gender uncertain.* I. as a weight, *a drachm:*—Genime ânes trymeses gewǽge, Lchdm. i. 74, 21. Ânre tremese (trymese, MS. H.) gewihte, 110, 9. Ânre tremesse wǽge, 72, 11. Genim âne (ânne, MS. O.) trymesan gewǽge, 78, 13. Nime âne trymessan fulle, 76, 6. Twēgra trymesa, 78, 24. Twēga trymessa, 70, 15: 72, 26. .iiii. trymesan, 76, 22: 78, 8. Feówer trymessan, 76, 1, 10, 16. *De ponderibus incipit. Solidos tres* trymisas, Txts. 113, 80. II. as a coin, (a) not in England:—Trymes *staterem*, Mt. Kmbl. Lind. 17, 27. Lidrine trimsas (trymsas) *asses scorteas* (*corteas*), Txts. 38, 31. Liþerene trymsas *asses corteas*, Wrt. Voc. ii. 7, 18. (b) in England, *a coin of the value of three pence.* The gen. pl., *þrimsa, þrymsa*, occurs several times in the section headed Norđleóda laga, Th. i. pp. 186, 188. [*O. H. Ger.* drimisa (-issa), trimisa *dragma. From Latin* tremissis, tremisia.]

trinda, an; *m. A round lump, a ball:*—Geóte tō trindan . . . wyrce tō trindan, Lchdm. iii. 14, 10, 13. [Cf. Onn heffness whel all ummbetrin (*round about*), Orm. 17563. *O. Frs.* trind, trund *round: Dan. Swed.* trind; omtrent *about: Dan.* trindes *to grow round.*] v. trendan, trendel.

trinnu-byttae. v. treów-byt.

triumpha, an; *m. A triumph, the entry into Rome of a victorious general.* The following explanation of the term was inserted by Alfred in his translation of Orosius:—Đæt hié triumphan hēton, đæt wæs đonne hié hwelc folc mid gefeohte ofercumen hæfdon, đonne wæs heora þeáw đæt sceoldon ealle hiera senâtus cuman ongeán heora consulas æfter đæm gefeohte, siex mîla from đære byrig, mid crætwǽne, mid golde and mid gimstânum gefrætwedum, and hié sceoldon bringan feówerfēte twâ hwît. Đonne hié hâmweard fōran, đonne sceoldon hiera senâtus rîdan on cræt-wǽnum wiđæftan đǽm consulum, and đa menn beforan him drîfan gebundene đe đǽr gefongene wǽron, đæt heora mǽrþa sceoldon đŷ þrymlîcran beón. Ac đonne hié hwelc folc būton gefeohte on heora geweald geniéddon, đonne hié hâmweard wǽron, đonne sceolde him man bringan ongeán of đære byrig crætwǽn, se wæs mid seolfre gegiered, and ǽlces cynnes feówerfētes feós ân, hiora consulum tō mǽrþe, Ors. 2, 4; Swt. 70, 22-35. The explanation is called forth by the passage: Heora ân consul forsōc đone triumphan, đe him mon ongeán brohte . . . and sǽde, đæt hié hæfden bet gewyrht, đæt him mon mid heáfe ongeán cōme đonne mid triumphan, 17-21. Hió nolde đæt hié mon drife beforan đæm triumphan, 5, 13; Swt. 246, 29. Noldan hié dōn đone triumphan beforan hiora consulum, 4, 7; Swt. 182, 1: 4, 10; Swt. 202, 24.

trîwen. v. treówen.

trod, es; *n.:* trodu, e; *f. A track:*—Be trode gestolenes yrfes. Gif mon trode bedrîfþ forstolenes ŷrfes of stæđe on ōđer, đonne befæste mon đæt spor landes mannum . . . Gif mon secge đæt man đæt trod âwōh drîfe, đonne mōt se đe đæt yrfe âh trodađ (trod ōđ ?) tō stæđe lǽdan, L. O. D. 1; Th. i. 352, 3-11. Gyf him hundred bedrîfe trod on ōđer hundred, L. Edg. 4, 5; Th. i. 260, 3. Secga ǽnigum đara đe tîrleáses trode sceáwode, hū hē on weg đanon feorhlâstas bær, Beo. Th. 1691; B. 843. [Þe dunes underuođ þe treden (trodes, MS. T.) of him suluen, A. R. 380, 26. Cf. treoden, l. 18. Yf thou trowyde . . . That thi witt . . . Commys of thiselfe and noȝt of Gode, That es grett pryde and fals trode, R. Brunne. Of his trodus no sygne ther nasse, Chron. Vilodun. Halliwell, from whose Dictionary the last two passages are taken, gives *trod*=footpath: see also E. D. S. Pub. Lincoln. *Icel.* trođ; *n. a treading.* Cf. Þe þet troddeđ wel and ofsecheđ wel ut his owune feblesce, A. R. 232, 17.] v. wîg-, wiđer-trod.

trog, es; *m.* I. *a trough, tub, basin, vessel* for containing liquids or other materials:—Trog *albeus, genus vasis*, Txts. 109, 1140: *canthera*, 49, 425: Wrt. Voc. ii. 14, 7. Lege on hâtne stân on troge, geót hwōn wæteres on, Lchdm. ii. 326, 5: iii. 30, 9. Dō on troh hâte stânas, ii. 68, 5. Hē sende đæt wæter in trog (*peluem*), Jn. Skt. Lind. Rush. 13, 5. Man sceal habban trogas, Anglia xiii. 264, 14. v. wîn-trog. II. *a trough-shaped thing, a cradle, a boat:*—Cilda trog *conabulum*, Txts. 51, 492. Cf. ciltrog *cune*, 115, 154. Hē wæs biddende ânes lytles troges, đæt hē mehte his feorh generian *exiguo contentus latere navigio*, Ors. 2, 5; Swt. 84, 15. III. *a water-pipe, conduit.* v. mylen-trog. IV. *a basin of water* (?):—Of đæm forda on đone sǽtroh, of đæm troge on đone hǽþenan byrgels, Cod. Dip. Kmbl. iii. 456, 32. Tō trogan, 434, 15: 435, 11. [*O. H. Ger.* trog *alveus, alveolus, collectaculum, canalis: Icel.* trog.]

trog-hrycg *a ridge where there is a trough of water* (?):—On troh-hrycg, Cod. Dip. Kmbl. iii. 79, 17.

Trōgia. v. Trōia.

trog-scip, es; *n. Some kind of boat.* The Latin words which it translates are *littoraria* and *tonsilla;* the ordinary meaning of the latter is, *a sharp-pointed pole stuck in the ground to fasten vessels to the shore*, so perhaps trogscip means *a boat fastened to the shore, to which another was moored:*—Trohscip *littoraria* vel *tonsilla*, Wrt. Voc. i. 56, 29: *littoraria*, 48, 2: 64, 4.

troh, trōh. v. trog, þrōh.

Trōia, Trōgia *Troy:*—Trōia, Grēca burg, âwēsted wæs, Ors. 2, 2; Swt. 64, 20. Trōgia burg barn, Bt. 16, 4; Fox 58, 4. Trōia burg ofertogen hæfde lēga leóhtost, Met. 9, 16: 26, 20. [*O. H. Ger.* Trōia: *Icel.* Trōja.]

Trōiâna (-e?); *pl. The Trojans:*—Alra tâcna gehwylc swâ Trōiâna þurh gefeoht fremedon, Elen. Kmbl. 1287; El. 645. Ymb ealra đara Trōiâna gewin, Ors. 1, 8; Swt. 42, 13. Đæt mǽre gewinn Grēca and Trōiâna, 1, 11; Swt. 50, 9, 7: Bt. 38, 1; Fox 194, 3. (In the corresponding passage of the metres, Met. 26, 12, Fox has *Triōia gewin*, while Grein gives *Trōiâna.*)

Trōiânisc; *adj. Trojan:*—On đæm Trōiâniscan gefeohte, Ors. 1, 10; Swt. 48, 2: 1, 11; 50, 24. [*O. H. Ger.* Trōiânisc.]

Trōiesc, trōisc; *adj. Trojan:*—Hē gelîce đŷ Trōiescan (Trōiscan, Bd. M. 306, 20) wæle ealle đa landbigengan wolde ūt âmǽran *tragica caede omnes indigenas exterminare contendit*, Bd. 4, 16; S. 584, 6. [Of þan Troyscen monnen, Laym. 410.] v. traisc.

trondendi. v. trandan.

tropere, es; *m. One of the service books of the Church, that which contained the tropes* (*tropus* cantus ecclesiastici genus); troparium. v. Maskell's Monumenta Ritualia Ecclesiae Anglicanae, I. p. xxxvij:—.i.

tropere, Chart. Th. 430, 10. Ðonne ðū tropere haban wille, ðonne wege ðū ðīne swī[þ]ran hand, and tyrn mid ðīnum swīþran scytefingre ofer ðīne breóst foreweard, swilce ðū notian wille, Techm. ii. 119, 10-12. [A tropere *troparium*, Wülck. Gl. 617, 38: 755, 3. A tropery, 719, 34. A tropure, 648, 33 (all 15th cent. glosses).]

trūa. v. trūwa.

trucian; *p.* ode. I. *to fail* in doing something:—Ne trucaþ heora nān āna ðurh unmihte ac ðurh gecynde ānre Godcundnysse hī wyrcaþ ealle ǣfre ān weorc *no one of them alone fails through want of power, but through the nature of one divinity they all work always the same work*, Homl. Th. ii. 42, 27. Cneów truciaþ *the knees fail*, Lchdm. ii. 242, 14. II. *to fail* a person (*dat.*), *be wanting* in duty to a person:—Hē undergeat ðæt his geswowrene men him trucedan, and āgēfon hera castelas him tō hearme, Chr. 1090; Erl. 226, 32. III. *to fail, come to an end*:—Trucaþ *periclitatur*, ic trucige *periclitor* (the passage is: Propria manu perire non licet, absque eo ubi castitas *periclitatur*; but the glosser seems to have taken the word to mean more than *is endangered*, and to have taken it as meaning *is lost*), Hpt. Gl. 468, 78-469, 1. [Him trucode ealle his mycele cræftes, Chr. 1131; Erl. 260, 2. Him trukeþ his iwit, Fragm. Phlps. 5, 38. Heo is afered leste þeo eorðe hire trukie, O. E. Homl. i. 53, 15. Heo trukieð treoðen to halden, Laym. 16861. Þa iseh Hængest þ his help trukede, 16416. Wærc þe nauere nulle trukien, 17171. Ʒif bileaue him trukede, A. R. 230, 19. Ne schal him neauer tintreohe trukien *incredulos supplicio dampnat eterno*, Kath. 1796: 403. Þis bold ... neuer truke ne schal, Misc. 97, 122. Til domes dai ne sal it troken, Al middelerd ðerinne is loken, Gen. and Ex. 105.] v. ge-trucian.

trūgian. v. trūwian.

truht (trūht?) *a trout*:—Truht *tructa*, Wrt. Voc. i. 55, 74: 77, 64. [From Latin.]

trull. v. turl.

trum; *adj. Firm, strong*; firmus, Ælfc. Gr. 38; Zup. 236, 8. I. of material things, lit. or fig.:—Hē is mē trum weall, Homl. Skt. i. 7, 127. Seó burh Asor wæs swīðe trum gefyrn and manegra burga heáfod *Asor antiquitus inter omnia regna haec principatum tenebat*, Jos. 11, 10. Trumre underwreþincge *firmo fulcimento*, Wrt. Voc. ii. 148, 69. On trume stōwe *in locum munitum*, Ps. Th. 70, 2. Eálā wǣran ða ancras swā trume and swā þurhwuniende, Bt. 10; Fox 30, 10. Trume and torhte tungol, Exon. Th. 58, 11; Cri. 934. Ofer ealla truma ceastra ... Hwæt getācniaþ ða truman ceastra *super omnes civitates munitas ... Quid per civitates munitas exprimitur?* Past. 35; Swt. 245, 6. Weal ðȳ trumra, Exon. Th. 281, 23; Jul. 650. Biþ Drihten ūre se trumesta staþol, Blickl. Homl. 13, 10. Mid weallum and geatum and ðām trumestum locum getimbrade *muris, portis, ac seris instructa firmissimis*, Bd. 1, 1; S. 473, 27. II. of living things, (a) *strong, sound, having physical health* or *strength*:—Trum *validus* vel *vegetus*, Wrt. Voc. i. 51, 21. Gedafenaþ sacerde, ðonne hē mannum fæsten scrīfeþ, ðæt hē wite hwylc se man sig, trum þe untrum (*validus an invalidus*), L. Ecg. C. 1; Th. ii. 132, 25. Ðonne se mon his līchoman hǣlo forsihþ, ðonne ðonne hē wel trum biþ tō wyrceanne ðæt hē wile, Past. 36; Swt. 249, 5. Wæs eft swā ǣr on his līce trum, Andr. Kmbl. 2953; An. 1479. Heorot hornum trum, Beo. Th. 2742; B. 1369. Eofor tōþmægenes trum, Menol. Fox 499; Gn. C. 20. Ða truman (cf. hālan, l. 3) ... ða untruman *incolumes ... aegri*, Past. 36; Swt. 247, 5. (b) *strong, able to resist, fortified* against:—Wið eallum nǣdrum hē biþ trum, Lchdm. i. 92, 4. Wið eall næddercyn hē biþ trum, 244, 3. Trume wið deófla nīþum, Blickl. Homl. 171, 30. Sēcaþ gē Drihten and gē beóþ teónan gehwylce ful trume, Ps. Th. 104, 4. (c) in reference to moral qualities, *strong, steadfast, firm*:—Ne biþ nān man trum ðurh God, būton se ðe hine undergyt untrumne þurh hine sylfne, Homl. Th. ii. 392, 5. Iacobus trum in breóstum, Menol. Fox 266; Men. 134. Lǣt mē on ðīnum wordum weorðan trumne *confirma me in verbis tuis*, Ps. Th. 118, 28. God ēcne and trumne, Cd. Th. 297, 30; Sat. 525. Englas trume and torhte, Exon. Th. 55, 15; Cri. 884. III. of non-material things, *firm, stable, strong*:—Ðæt mōd ǣgðer ge trum ge untrum *animus et infirmus et fidelis*, Past. 51; Swt. 395, 3. Ān strica ðære ealdan ǣ ne biþ forgǣged, ōð ðæt hī ealle gefyllede beón. Þus trum is seó ealde ǣ, Homl. Th. ii. 200, 2. Trum *ratum*, Hpt. Gl. 528, 25. Gif ðū mid trumre heortan (*firmo corde*) gelȳfest, Bd. 3, 13; S. 538, 43. Heó āhte trumne geleáfan, Judth. Thw. 9; Jud. 6. Eówer geleáfa biþ þe trumra, gif gē gehȳraþ be Godes hālgum, Homl. Th. i. 556, 27. v. med-, mis-, un-trum.

-trum. v. ge-trum.

truma, an; *m.* I. *a troop* of soldiers. v. trymman, I. 6, II. 2:—Truma *acies, exercitus*, Hpt. Gl. 477, 13. Hē fērde mid fyrdlīcum truman and ða burh geeode, Jos. 11, 10: Homl. Ass. 113, 356. Truman *aciem*, Hpt. Gl. 426, 69. Hē gesette ða menn on ǣnne truman, ðe mon hiora mǣgas ǣr on ðæm londe slōg, Ors. 2, 5; Swt. 80, 19. Hē hæfde eahta and eahtatig coortana, ðæt wē nū truman hātaþ, 5, 12; Swt. 240, 33. Ða īsnodan truman *ferratas acies*, Wrt. Voc. ii. 147, 52. II. *order* of troops, *array*:—Hē ðæt folc būton truman lǣdde *he led the army without keeping any order*, Ors. 4, 8; Swt. 188, 14. III. *a support*. v. wyrt-truma. [Breken Modredes trume, Laym. 28352. Þat eadi trume of meidenes, H. M. 21, 33. Ðu (*Jacob*) and ðin trume ben ... to me welcume, Gen. and Ex. 1829. Hauelok was a ful god gome, He was ful god in eueri trome, Havel. 8.] v. fyrd-, ge-, scild-truma.

trumian; *p.* ode *To become strong, recover from illness*:—Ðā cwæþ hē ðæt gewunalīce word ðara frēfrendra: Truma ðē hraþe and wel *dixit solito consolantium sermone: Bene convalescas et cito*, Bd. 5, 5; S. 618, 9. Hine gestōd sumu untrymnis ... sōna swā hē trumian (*convalescere*) ongan, 4, 1; S. 564, 46. v. ge-trumian.

truming, e; *f. Gaining strength, recovery*:—Cwydas dōn truminge getācnaþ, Lchdm. iii. 210, 30.

trum-līc; *adj.* I. *firm, strong, stable*, (a) of material things, lit. or fig.:—Tǣceþ ūs se torhta trumlīcne hām, burhweallas beorhte scīnaþ, Cd. Th. 282, 30; Sat. 294. Ðā geseah ic gyldenne wīngeard trumlīcne and fæstlīcne *vineam solidam auro miratus sum*, Nar. 4, 28. Columnan swīðe trumlīce and fæste *columnae solidae*, 4, 21. (b) of non-material things:—Seó ealde gesetness ys eall swā trumlīc, swā swā se Hǣlend sǣde on his hālgan godspelle, Jud. 15; Thw. 159, 29. Kynewyrðe rǣd and trumlīc, Anglia viii. 308, 33. Ðæt ōðer līf ðætte fæstre beón scolde and trumlīcre (*stabilior*), Past. 52; Swt. 411, 1. II. *hortatory, of exhortation*:—Hē ðam cyninge sende trumlīc ǣrendgewrit, Bd. 2, 17; S. 520, 19 note. v. next word.

trumlīce; *adv.* I. *firmly, strongly, steadfastly*:—Trumlīce *firmiter*, Ælfc. Gr. 38; Zup. 236, 8. Ða gōdan weorc, ðeáh ðe hió beforan monna eágum ðyncen trumlīce gedōn *etiam quae humanis oculis fortia videntur*, Past. 34; Swt. 237, 2. Ðæt leód and lagu trumlīce stande, Wulfst. 74, 8. Eahta sweras syndon ðe rihtlīcne cynedōm trumlīce up wegaþ, L. I. P. 3; Th. ii. 306, 19. Trumlīcor *firmius*, Rtl. 34, 26. Freóndscype trumlīcust (*firmissime*) wunaþ, Scint. 197, 18. II. *in a way that encourages* (?):—Ungeleáffullnise trumlīce (*strongly* (?): but the Latin is *clementer*) geðreáð bið, Mk. Skt. p. 5, 13.

trumme. v. trymman.

trumnaþ, es; *m. Strengthening, confirmation*:—Swilc God wyrceþ gǣsta līfes tō trumnaþe, Exon. Th. 147, 18; Gū. 729.

trumness, e; *f.* I. *firmness, strength, certainty*:—Trumnesse *firmitatem*, Kent. Gl. 840. Ðīnes geleáfan trumnesse wē witon, Guthl. 5; Gdwin. 30, 18. Wē witon ðæt manega clericas nyton hwæt byþ *quadrans*, ac wē willaþ his mihta and his trumnysse hēr geswutelian, Anglia viii. 306, 28. II. *health*:—Ða truman sint tō manianne ðæt hié gewilnigen mid ðæs līcuman trumnesse ðæt him ne losige sió hǣlo ðæs mōdes ðȳ læs him ðȳ wirs sié gif hié ða trumnesse ðære Godes giefe him tō unnyte gehweorfaþ *admonendi sunt incolumes, ut salutem corporis exerceant ad salutem mentis; ne, si acceptae incolumitatis gratiam ad usum nequitiae inclinent, dono deteriores fiant*, Past. 36; Swt. 247, 6-8. III. *confirmation, support*:—Drihten trumnes mīn *Dominus firmamentum meum*, Ps. Spl. 17, 1: 24, 15: 72, 4. Ðæra apostola tweónung næs nā swā swīðe heora ungeleáffulnys, ac wæs ūre trumnys, Homl. Th. i. 300, 34. Hē tȳmde tō Basilies tǣcinge for his trumnysse, Basil prm.; Norm. 32, 10. Ealle trumnysse hlāfes hē forcnād *omne firmamentum panis contrivit*, Ps. Spl. 104, 15. IV. *a firm place, the firmament*:—Bið trumnys on lande on heáhnyssum dūna *erit firmamentum in terra in summis montium*, Ps. Spl. 71, 16. Weorc handa his bodaþ trumnyss[e] ł staþol (*firmamentum*), Ps. Spl. 18, 1. v. trymness.

trus, es; *n. Fallen leaves and branches or twigs as material for fuel*:—.vi. fōdra truses ǣlce geáre, Cod. Dip. Kmbl. iii. 169, 10. [*Icel.* tros; *n. leaves and twigs from a tree picked up and used for fuel.*]

trūð, es; *m. A player on a trumpet, an actor, buffoon*:—Trūð *liticen*, Ælfc. Gr. 9, 12; Zup. 40, 7: Wrt. Voc. i. 73, 66 (the word occurs in a list of terms connected with amusements). Com sum trūð tō ðæs bisceopes hīrēde, se ne gȳmde nānes lenctenes fæstenes, ac eode him tō kicenan, Homl. Skt. i. 12, 59. Trūþas *histriones*, gligmon *mimus, jocista, scurra, pantomimus*, tumbere *saltator*, Wrt. Voc. i. 39, 41-44. As an illustration of the character of the trūð see Strutt's Sports and Pastimes, Bk. iii. c. 3, §§ 4, 7, where one picture is given of dancers accompanied by trumpeters, and another of a dancing bear attended by a trumpeter. [*Icel.* trūðr *a juggler*.] v. next word.

trūð-horn, es; *m. The trumpet of a* trūð, q. v.:—Trūðhorn *lituus*, Wrt. Voc. i. 73, 67. Trūðhornes *salpistae* (the passage is: Horrorem belli et classicae salpistae metuentes), Hpt. Gl. 422, 77.

trūw, e; *f. Faith*:—Ðū hæfst ongyten ða wonclan trūwa ðæs blindan lustes, Bt. 7, 2; Fox 18, 3. [*O. H. Ger.* trūa, trūwa *fides*: *Icel.* trū.] Cf. treów.

trūwa, trūa, an; *m.* I. (*good*) *faith*:—Heriaþ ūrne Drihten, se ðe ne forlǣt on hine gelȳfende and ða ðe hihtaþ on his miclum trūwan, Homl. Ass. 112, 321. Ðam ānum ic healde mīnne trūwan ǣfre, Homl. Skt. i. 7, 56. II. *faith, belief, confidence, trust*:—Se trūwa (trūa, Cott. MSS.) micelre orsorgnesse *fiducia magnae securitatis*, Past. 35; Swt. 243, 12. Be geleáfan oþþe trūwan *de fide*, Scint. 126, 16. For ðam micclan geleáfan and for ðam sōðan trūwan ðe heó symle hæfþ tō

Gode, Homl. Ass. 29, 125. Hē hine gefullode mid fullum trūwan ðæt hē geleáfful wǽre, Ælfc. T. Grn. 17, 9. Se ðe mid dyslīcum trūwan and mid gylpe sum wundorlīc ðing on Godes naman dōn wile, Homl. Th. i. 170, 28. For ðæs cræftes trūwan (trūan) *from confidence on account of that art*, R. Ben. 95, 6: 46, 16. Habbaþ Godes trūwan *have faith in God*, Mk. Skt. 11, 22: Scint. 127, 1. Gif hopan trūwan wē nabbaþ *si spei fiduciam non habemus*, 33, 9. Habbaþ eów trūwan *habete fiduciam* (Mt. 14, 27), Homl. Th. ii. 388, 25. Hira godas on ðām hig trūwan hæfdon *dii eorum, in quibus habebant fiduciam*, Deut. 32, 37. Hig nefdon nānne trūwan tō nānum folce *they could not trust any people*, Nicod. 6; Thw. 3, 24. Gif heó it swā gehylt, swā ic hiræ trūwan tō hæbbe *as I have confidence in her* (*that she will do*), Chart. Th. 527, 34. III. *a solemn assurance of good faith, a covenant, word*:—Se Frysa lēt hine faran on his trūwan, Homl. Th. ii. 358, 22. Ic sette mīn wedd on ēcne trūwan (*in foedus sempiternum*), Gen. 17, 19. Ic behēt mīnne trūwan *pepigi foedus*, Ex. 6, 4. IV. *faithful care, protection*:—Ic hine nam on mīnne trūwan *ego in meam hunc recepi fidem*, Gen. 44, 32. [*O. Frs.* trouwa: *Icel.* trūa.] v. ge-, ofer-trūwa.

trūwian; p. ode *To trust, confide*:—Ic trūwige *fido* . . ., ic trūwige *confido*, ic trūwode *confisus sum*, Ælfc. Gr. 33; Zup. 204, 14–16. I. with dat., *to trust* to:—Ðonne ða fortrūwodan him selfum tō suīðe trūwiaþ *dum protervi valde de se praesumunt*, Past. 32; Swt. 209, 6. Ða ðe hyra weorcum trūwiaþ, Exon. Th. 52, 24; Cri. 838. Ðā ðā ic him betst trūwode, Bt. 2; Fox 4, 12: Beo. Th. 3991; B. 1993. Secgaþ ðǽm welegum, ðæt hī tō wel ne trūwigen ðissum ungewissum welum (*sperare in incerto divitiarum suarum*), Past. 26; Swt. 181, 15. Heó ongan his wordum trūwian, Cd. Th. 40, 35; Gen. 649. I a. *to trust* something to a person:—Se Hǽlend ne trūgude hine sealfne him, Jn. Skt. Lind. 2, 24. I b. *to trust* to a person for something (clause with *ðæt*):—Hygd bearne ne trūwode, ðæt hē wið ælfylcum ēþelstōlas healdan cūðe, Beo. Th. 4370; B. 2370. II. with gen. *to trust* in:—Geáta leód trūwode mōdgan mægnes, Beo. Th. 1343; B. 669. Hē his wīsna trūwade, drohtes on ðære ādle, Exon. Th. 171, 30; Gū. 1134. Hwȳ hié ðara gearnunga hiora dīgelnesse (and diégelnesse, Hatt. MS.) and ānette bet trūwien ðonne ðære hū hié ōðerra monna mǽst gehelpen *qua mente utilitati ceterorum secretum praeponit suum*, Past. 5; Swt. 46, 2. II a. with gen. and clause:—Hē wiðres ne trūwode ðæt hē sǽmannum onsacan mihte *he did not trust in resistance, that he should be able to repel the seamen*, Beo. Th. 5899; B. 2953. III. with prepositions (be, on, tō), *to be confident* about, *trust* in, on, *or* to:—Ða ðe trūwiaþ on him *qui confidunt in eis*, Ps. Spl. 134, 18. Ealle his wǽpnu ðe hē on trūwude *universa arma in quibus confidebat*, Lk. Skt. 11, 22. Ða burhware trūwodon tō ðam wealle, Homl. Skt. ii. 25, 446. Trūa on Crist, Homl. Th. ii. 392, 34. Ðæt ūre nān be him sylfum tō dyrstelīce ne trūwige *that none of us be over-confident about himself*, 82, 26. Ne trūwige nān man be ælmesdǽdum oððe on gebedum, būtan ðære foresǽdan lufe, i. 54, 11. IV. with a clause, *to trust* that:—Ic trūwige, ðeáh, ðæt sum wurðe ābrird þurh God, L. Ælfc. P. 3; Th. ii. 364, 17. [Muȝe we wel trowen al . . . he misfoð, O. E. Homl. i. 67, 209. Þu ne wolldesst nohht trowwenn mine wordess, Orm. 214. Wan hii þe troueþ alre best, Laym. 3413 (2nd MS.). Mon þe he wel trowede on, 2351. Wile he trowe me, Havel. 1656. *Chauc. Piers P. Wick.* trowe. *Goth.* trauan: *O. Sax.* trūōn (*with gen.* or *prep.*): *O. H. Ger.* trūēn, trūwēn (*same govt. as English*) *confidere*: *Icel.* trūa *to trust, believe* (*dat.* or *prep.*).] v. for-, ge-, or-trūwian; ofer-trūwod; treówian.

trūwung, tryccan, tryddian, trym, trymend-līc, trymeness, trymes, trymian, trymig. v. ge-trūwung, -trūgung, ge-tryccan, treddian, trem, trymmend-līc, trymness, trimes, trymman, un-trymig.

trymman, trymian; p. trymede. I. *to make firm* or *strong*, (1) of material objects, *to construct strongly*. v. trum, I:—Ðæt hē trymede getimbro, Cd. Th. 18, 20; Gen. 276. Gē ðone weall ne trymedon ymbe hira hūs *non opposuistis murum pro domo Israel*, Past. 15; Swt. 89, 19. (1 a) of non-material objects:—Se ðe him hālig gǽst wīsaþ and his weorc trymaþ, Exon. Th. 124, 2; Gū. 333. Dagas syndon trymede *dies firmabuntur*, Ps. Th. 138, 15. (2) of physical health or strength, *to give strength to, strengthen*. v. trum, II a:—Hlāf trymeþ heortan mannes *panis cor hominis confirmat*, Ps. Th. 103, 15. Onlegen tō trymmanne ðone magan and tō bindanne æfter ūtsihtan, Lchdm. ii. 180, 24. (3) of mental or moral strength, *to confirm, establish, give strength to* mind *or* heart. v. trum, II c:—Sōð Metod ðīn mōd trymeþ, Cd. Th. 170, 9; Gen. 2809. Hē trymede heora heortan mid Godes geleáfan, Blickl. Homl. 145, 21. Gǽst, se his hyge trymede, Cd. Th. 249, 23; Dan. 534. Engel hine elne trymede, Exon. Th. 113, 21; Gū. 161. Ðæt man Godes cyricean fæste tremede, ge lǽwede men ge hādode, Blickl. Homl. 43, 6. Ðæt hē hiera geleáfan trymede, Chr. 430; Erl. 10, 19. Ǽgðer ōðrum trymede heofonrīces hyht, Andr. Kmbl. 2104; An. 1053. Strangie man and trymme (trumme, L. I. P. 4; Th. ii. 308, 4) hī mid wīslīcre Godes lage, Wulfst. 267, 21. Hē ongon his sefan trymman, Exon. Th. 169, 4; Gū. 1089. On ðǽm medwīsan is tō trymmanne (trymmianne, Cott. MSS.) swā hwæt suā hié ongietan mǽgen ðæs godcundan wīsdōmes *in istis aedificandum est, quidquid de superna sapientia cognoscitur*, Past. 30; Swt. 203, 10. (3 a) as an ecclesiastical term, *to confirm*. v. un-trymed. (4) of abstract objects, *to corroborate, confirm* an agreement, a grant, testimony, statement, etc. v. trymmend, II:—Ic, Berhtwulf, ðās mīne gesaldnisse trymme and fæstna in Cristes rōde tācne, Cod. Dip. Kmbl. ii. 5, 33: 47, 20. Gif ic cȳðnisse trymmo *si ego testimonium perhibeo*, Jn. Skt. Lind. 5, 31. Ðæt trymeþ sió hālige ǽ, ðǽr hió cuæð, Past. 43; Swt. 309, 12. Wē trymmaþ *adstipulabimur*, Wrt. Voc. ii. 3, 28. Ic ðīne gewitnesse wordum trymede *servavi testimonia tua*, Ps. Th. 118, 168. Ðæt trymede sanctus Paulus, ðā hē cuæð ðæt . . ., Past. 11; Swt. 73, 2. Trymme hē eal mid wedde ðæt ðæt hē behāte, L. Edm. B. 5; Th. i. 254, 17. Trymmendre (*confirmante*) sprǽce, Mk. Skt. 16, 20. (5) *to give as surety*:—Trymide *commendabat*, Wrt. Voc. ii. 105, 22. Trymede, 15, 25. Hī gerǽddon ðæt man tremede gīslas on ǽgðer healfe, Chr. 1052; Erl. 187, 6. (6) *to trim, to set in firm order, array* troops. v. truma:—Hié hié būtan ðæm geate angeán Hannibal trymedon, Ors. 4, 10; Swt. 194, 17. Ðæt hié on morgenne hié forð trymedan ongeán heora feóndum, Blickl. Homl. 201, 35. Hī trymedon hī fæstlīce ongeán, Chr. 1048; Erl. 178, 31. Swylce ðǽr man fyrde trymme and samnige, Blickl. Homl. 91, 31. (6 a) of abstract objects, *to settle, arrange*:—Hē ðǽr ðone winter wunode and swā his sīþfæt trymede and tō Rōme com *ibi hiemem exigens sic Romam veniendi iter repetiit*, Bd. 5, 19; S. 639, 27. (7) *to strengthen* with words, *exhort, encourage, comfort*:—Hī hī mid wrāðum wordum trymmaþ, Ps. Th. 63, 4. Drihten is swīðe mildheort, se ūs trymede and lǽrde; hē cwæþ: 'Nelle ic ðæs synfullon mannes deáð,' Blickl. Homl. 97, 32: Bd. 1, 23; S. 485, 39: Andr. Kmbl. 927; An. 463. Heáhcyning sprǽce trymede tilmōdigne, Cd. Th. 130, 27; Gen. 2166. Gē hyra sefan trymedon on frōfre, Exon. Th. 83, 23; Cri. 1360. Swā hȳ hine trymedon, 110, 7; Gū. 104. Bēgen gebrōþru beornas trymedon, wordon bǽdon, Byrht. Th. 140, 49; By. 305. Ðīne lāreówas, ða ðec tō gōde trymmen, Exon. Th. 301, 4; Fa. 14. Lǽran sceal mon geongne monnan, trymman and tyhtan, 336, 10; Gn. Ex. 46: 280, 33; Jul. 638. Wordum trymman, Andr. Kmbl. 856; An. 428. Ðā ongunnon hī hine geornlīce trymman and lǽran *coeperunt diligenter exhortari*, Bd. 5, 14; S. 634, 30. Trymian, Byrht. Th. 132, 17; By. 17. Ðū trymmende earð mec *exhortatus es me*, Ps. Surt. 70, 21. Tremegende *monens*, R. Ben. 4, 15. II. *intrans.* (?) (1) *to become strong*:—Monig sceal siþþan wyrt onwæcnan; eác ðon wudubearwas tānum tȳdraþ trymmaþ eorðwelan *the woods teem with branches, grow strong* (?) *with the wealth of earth*, Exon. Th. 191, 7; Az. 84. (2) *to be arrayed*. v. truma:—Gāras trymedon, blicon bordhreóðan, bȳman sungon, Cd. Th. 187, 28; Exod. 159. Fōr fyrda mǽst, fēðan trymedan, Elen. Kmbl. 70; El. 35. v. getrymman.

trymmend, es; *m.* I. *one who strengthens* or *supports*:—Ðū mē wǽre trymmend *firmamentum meum*, Ps. Th. 70, 3. II. *one who makes a formal agreement*. v. trymman, I. 4:—Trymmend *stipulatorem*, Wrt. Voc. ii. 88, 2.

trymmend-līc; *adj. Hortatory*:—Trymendlīc *exortatorium*, Wrt. Voc. ii. 33, 17. Hē mid trymme[n]dlīce ǽrendgewrite hī gestrangode *epistola illos exhortatoria confortaverit*, Bd. 1, 23; S. 485, 15. Eác swylce ðæm cyninge hē sende trymmendlīce (-līc, Bd. M. 146, 9) gewrit *misit regi literas exhortatorias*, 2, 17; S. 520, 19.

trymmian. v. trymman.

trymming, e; *f.* I. *a strengthening, confirming, establishing, edification*:—Se cyning ðæt mǽre hūs (*the temple*) Gode betǽhte him and his folce tō trymminge and tō gescyldnysse wið ǽlces yfeles onscyte, Homl. Th. ii. 578, 22. Nū wylle wē eów secgan sum ðing ðe eów māge tō trymminge *that may serve for your edification*, Homl. Ass. 26, 50. Tō geleáfan trymminge *for the confirmation of belief*, 5, 111. Trimminge, Ælfc. T. Grn. 14, 8. II. *that which strengthens* or *supports*, (a) material, *a foundation*:—Curs mōder āwyrtwalaþ trymmincge *the curse of the mother rooteth out foundations* (firmamentum, Ecclus. 3, 9), Scint. 174, 7. (b) non-material, *that which edifies*:—Wē wyllaþ sume ōðre trimminge (*edifying matter*) be ðære mǽran Godes mēder gereccan tō eówre gebetrunge, Homl. Th. i. 448, 9. v. ge-, ymb-trymming.

trymness, trymeness, e; *f.* I. *firmness*. v. trumness, I:—Heora wītes ne biþ trymnes (trymenis, Ps. Surt.) *non est firmamentum in plaga eorum*, Ps. Th. 72, 3. Hiora trymnisse liomana *suorum firmitate membrorum*, Rtl. 32, 15. II. *that which makes firm, a support, prop*, (a) literal:—Man ða ilcan studu ūtan tō gesette tō trymnesse (wræðe, col. 1) ðæs wāges (*in munimentum parietis*) . . . tō trymnesse (fultume, col. 1) ðæs hūses *in fulcimentum domus*, Bd. 3, 17; S. 544, 21–36. (b) figurative:—Drihten, ðū eart mīn trymenes (-nis, Ps. Surt.) *Dominus firmamentum meum*, Ps. Th. 17, 1. Ðū eart mīn trymnes (trymenis, Ps. Surt.), 30, 4. (c) *a firm place, fastness*. v. trumness, IV:—Biþ trymenis (*firmamentum*; rodor, Ps. Lamb.) in eorðan in heánissum munta, Ps. Surt. 71, 16. III. *a strengthening, a confirmation*, (a) of a statement, agreement, etc.:—Trymnes *confirmatio, assertio*, Wrt. Voc. ii. 133, 27. Tō trymnisse *testamento*, Rtl. 191, 33. Trymnessum *adstipulationibus*, Wrt. Voc. ii. 1, 7: 3, 63. (b) of *or* in a purpose, belief, etc.:—Ðā wæs gestrangod Agustinus mid trymnysse ðæs eádigan fæder *roboratus confirmatione beati patris Agustinus*, Bd. 1, 25; S. 486, 13. (c) *a strengthening by words, an exhortation*:—Trymnes *exortatio*, i. *monitio, doctrina*, Wrt. Voc. ii. 145, 77. Trymnises *exortationis*, Mk. Skt. p. 2, 5. Mid stefne his hālígre trymenesse (trymnisse, Bd. M. 106, 26) and lāre *voce sanctae exhortationis*, Bd. 2, 4; S. 505, 18. Trymnyssum *exhortationibus*, 1, 7; S. 477, 3. Trymenessum, 5, 22; S. 644, 6. v. ge-, un-trymness.

trymsas. v. trimes.

trymþ, e; *f. Strength, support*:—Ealle getrymednesse ł trymðe hlāfes hē forgnād *omne firmamentum panis contrivit*, Ps. Lamb. 104, 16. v. un-trymþ.

tryndyled, trȳw, trȳwa, trȳwan, trȳwe, trȳwen, trȳwian, trȳwsian, trȳwþ. v. trendeled, treów, treówa, treówan, treówe, treówen, treówian, treówsian, treówþ.

tū (*two*), tū (*thou*), tuā, tuāes. v. twēgen, þū, tweó, tweógan.

tucian (*or* tūcian?; in Piers P. (v. infra) *touked* occurs, but the form of the noun is *tokkere* as well as *touker*, Prol. 100 A-text, and Halliwell gives *tucker* = fuller as a western word); *p.* ode *To treat ill, to afflict, harass, vex*:—Unrihtwīse cyningas ðe ðis wērige folc wyrst tuciaþ (*quos miseri torvos populi timent tyrannos*; ða unrihtwīsan cyningas . . . ðe ðis earme folc heardost ondrǣt, Bt. 36, 2; Fox 174, 26–29), Met. 24, 60. Hē heora fela ofslōh and tō sceame tucode *percussit Philisthiim ingenti plaga*, Jud. 15, 8: Homl. Skt. ii. 26, 11. Hī man swang and tō ealre yrmðe tucode *they were scourged and treated to* (*afflicted with*) *every misery*, i. 23, 106. Hī man tō wæfersȳne tucode mid gehwilcum wītum, ii. 28, 129. Swingan and tō ealre sorge tucigan, i. 23, 715. Noldon hī nā cweþan ðæt hit wǣre wīte . . . and noldan nǣnne þingere sēcan, ac lustlīce hī woldan lǣtan ða rīcan hié tucian æfter hiora āgnum willan *nec hos cruciatus esse dicerent, defensorumque operam repudiarent, ac se totos accusatoribus judicibusque permitterent*, Bt. 38, 7; Fox 210, 14. [Ure Louerd was on fele wise rewliche tuked, O. E. Homl. ii. 21, 32. He was so scheomeliche ituked and so seoruhfuliche ipined, A. R. 366, 3. Leccherie tukeð hire al to wundre & þreat to don hire schome, H. M. 17, 10. Ha tukeð ure godes to balewe & to bismere, Kath. 551. Þu tukest wroþe and uvele Hwar þu miht over smale fuȝele, O. and N. 63. Cloth with taseles cracched, Ytouked and ytented, Piers P. 15, 447. Tuck *to pinch severely*, Devonshire: *to smart with pain*, Wilts., Halliwell's Dict. *O. H. Ger.* zocchōn *rapere, diripere*.] v. ge-, mis-tucian.

tuddor. v. tūdor.

tude, an (?); *f. A shield*:—Tude *parma*, Hpt. Gl. 521, 9. Tudenarda (tudena, randa (?), tuderanda (?)) *scutorum*, 424, 5.

tūdor, tuddor, es; *n. That which grows from another* (used of animals or of plants), *offspring, progeny, product, fruit*:—Tūdor oððe cyn *propago*, Wrt. Voc. ii. 67, 33. On ða tīd wæs ofor eorþan tuddres æþelnes, Blickl. Homl. 115, 10. Hē tȳdreþ ǣlc tūdor, Bt. 39, 8; Fox 224, 10. I. of human beings, (a) *a child*:—Tudder *pignus*, Ælfc. Gr. 9, 32; Zup. 59, 9. Bearn *vel* tudder *soboles vel proles*, Wrt. Voc. i. 51, 64: *foetus*, i. *fructus, partus, filius, soboles*, ii. 148, 35. 'Ðū cennest sunu.' Mid ðȳ ðe heó gehȳrde ðone fruman ðæs godcundan tuddres, Blickl. Homl. 7, 20. Tūdre *foetu*, Wrt. Voc. ii. 36, 34. Gyf hwylc wīf hæbbe on hyre innoðe deádboren tuddur, Lchdm. i. 166, 4. Hyt ðæt tudder of ðam cwiðan gelǣdeþ, 296, 2. Tuddra *pignora*, Hymn. Surt. 52, 7. (b) in a general sense, *offspring, race, breed, family, children*:—Tuddor *prosapia*, Wrt. Voc. ii. 65, 71. Tudder (*maternae generationis*) *propago*, Hpt. 522, 30. Wē oncneówan ðæt ðæt tuddur ne grōwan mihte of swylcum gesinscype *didicimus ex tali conjugio sobolem non posse succrescere*, Bd. 1, 27; S. 491, 5. Moncynnes tuddor, Exon. Th. 86, 32; Cri. 1417. Fruma ælda tūdres, 151, 16; Gū. 796. Gōdes tūdres gesǣlig *bona sobole felix*, Bd. 3, 7; S. 529, 34: 3, 18; S. 546, 39. Wæstmbǣrnysse tuddres *faecunditatem sobolis*, 1, 27; S. 493, 8. Sunu gōdes tuddres *filium bone indolis*, Scint. 177, 6. Āra ðīnum earmum eorþan tūdre (cf. help ðīnum earmum moncynne, Bt. 4; Fox 8, 11), Met. 4, 31. Tūdre fyllaþ eorðan, incre cynne, sunum and dohtrum, Cd. Th. 13, 2; Gen. 196: 92, 27; Gen. 1535: 107, 12; Gen. 1788: 169, 18; Gen. 2801. Tō teónan manna tūdre *to the hurt of mankind*, Exon. Th. 270, 3; Jul. 459. Ðæs teámes wæs tuddor gefylled unlytel dǣl eorðan gesceafta, Cd. Th. 97, 16; Gen. 1613. Ðonne ðæt flǣsc nāuht elles ne sēcþ būton tūdor *nisi fructum propaginis non quaerere*, Past. 51; Swt. 399, 5. God weorðaþ eorþan tuddor, Exon. Th. 43, 13; Cri. 608. II. of animals:—Wōcor eorðan tūdres *every kind of animal*, Cd. Th. 79, 18; Gen. 1313: 86, 34; Gen. 1440. Setl ǣlcum eorðan tūdre, 79, 3; Gen. 1305. Deáþ spyreþ æfter ǣghwelcum eorþan tūdre, diórum and fuglum, Met. 27, 10. Treófugla tuddor cȳððon eádges eftcyme, Exon. Th. 146, 9; Gū. 707. Ðū seofone genim tūdra gehwylces, Cd. Th. 80, 29; Gen. 1336. II a. of human beings and animals:—Tuddor bið gemǣne incrum (*the woman and the serpent*) orlegnīð, Cd. Th. 56, 19; Gen. 914. Se egorhere eorðan tuddor eall ācwealde, būton ðæt earce bord heóld heofona freá, 84, 24; Gen. 1402. III. of plants:—Beorc byþ blǣda leás, bereþ tānas būtan tūdre, Runic pm. Kmbl. 342, 29; Rūn. 18. Brengþ eorþe ǣlcne westm and ǣlc tūdor ǣlce geáre, Bt. 39, 13; Fox 234, 14: Met. 29, 58. IV. metaphorical:—Weá wæs ārǣred, tregena tuddor, Cd. Th. 60, 27; Gen. 988. Ðonne mæg hē cennan ðæt tūder ryhtes geðohtes (*prolem rectae cogitationis*), Past. 15; Swt. 97, 8. Ōþre tuddru synna *cetere soboles peccatorum*, Scint. 112, 4. [Deor and fishshes and fugeles and here tuder, O. E. Homl. ii. 177, 17.] v. eorþ-, magu-, sige-tūdor, *and next word*.

tūdor (?); *adj. Prolific*:—Tuddre *fetose*, Wrt. Voc. ii. 148, 35. v. tūdor-full.

tūdor-fæst; *adj. Prolific, fruitful*:—Tūdorfæstum *foetosis*, Wrt. Voc. ii. 34, 15.

tūdor-fōster, es; *m. Nourishment of offspring*:—Æfter ðon tuddorfōstre *vel* of ðām sīþborenum *de post fetantes*, Wrt. Voc. ii. 138, 81.

tūdor-full; *adj. Prolific, fertile, fruitful*:—Tudderfulle, teámfulle *vel* tuddre *fetose*, Wrt. Voc. ii. 148, 34. On tudderfullum *fetosis, copiosis, fecundis*, Hpt. Gl. 484, 5, 7.

tūdor-spēd, e; *f. Abundance of offspring*:—Him engla helm tuddorspēd onleác . . . lēt weaxan eft heora rīmgetel, Cd. Th. 166, 24; Gen. 2752.

tūdor-teónde *producing offspring* or *fruit*:—Hēt sǣs and eorðan tuddorteóndra teohha gehwilcre wæstmas fēdan, Cd. Th. 59, 5; Gen. 959: 201, 14; Exod. 372.

tulge; *cpve.* tylg; *spve.* tylgest; *adv. Strongly, firmly*; but the word undergoes a similar change to that which is seen in the case of *swīðe* q. v., and is used with much the same force as that word:—Him beóþ under tungan tulge swearte ǣdra *he has under his tongue very black veins*, Lchdm. ii. 106, 23. Tylg *propensior* (-or from -us in Erfurt Gloss.), Txts. 84, 743. Ic bī mē tylgust secge ðis sārspell *I make this lament mostly about myself*, Exon. Th. 458, 5; Hy. 4, 95. [Nes ꝥ naht wunderlic ꝥ he þone deaþes deg swa unforht abad, for þon þe hit nes deaþes deg ac hit (his MS.) wes tylig Drihtnes blisse deg *it was not wonderful that he awaited the day of death so fearless, for it was not the day of death, but it was rather the day of the joy of the Lord*, Anglia x. 145, 160. Se ealles tylgest romanisce þeawe song in Godes circan *he sang chiefly after the Roman manner in God's Church*, 142, 36. (These two passages are from a MS. of the first half of the 12th century.) *O. Sax.* tulgo *very*. Cf. *Goth.* tulgus *steadfast*; tulgitha *safety, a stronghold*; tulgjan *to confirm*.]

tumbere, es; *m. A tumbler, dancer, player*:—Gligmon *mimus, jocista, scurra*, gligman *pantomimus*, tumbere *saltator*, Wrt. Voc. i. 39, 42–44. Tumbere oððe gligman *histrio*, Ælfc. Gr. 9, 3; Zup. 35, 6. [The feminine form *tumbestre* occurs in later English: Herodias douȝter, that was a tumbestere, and tumblede byfore him, Halliw. Dict. Than comen tombesteres Fetys and smale, Chauc. Pard. T. 477. See Strutt's Sports and Pastimes, Bk. iii. c. v. § 3. Cf. A tumbler *saltator* (in a list headed *nomina jugulatorum*), Wrt. Voc. i. 218, col. 1: *saltatrix*, 216, col. 2; *and see* tumbullere *saltatrix*, in the note. Tumlare, tumblar *volutator, volutatrix*, Prompt. Parv. 506. Tumbelyster *tornatrix*, Wülck. Gl. 616, 47.] v. next word.

tumbian; *p.* ode *To tumble, dance*:—Ðā tumbude (*saltavit*) ðære Herodidiscean dohtur beforan him, Mt. Kmbl. 14, 6. Tumbode, Mk. Skt. 6, 22. [Þe wenche ꝥat tombede (*v. r.* tomblede), Trev. iv. 365. Cf. Tumblide, Wick. Mt. 14, 6. Tumlyn̄ *voluto, volvo*, Prompt. Parv. 506. Eroud swore to here that tumbled yn the flore, Halliw. Dict.] v. preceding word.

tūn, es; *m.* I. *an enclosed piece of ground, a yard, court*:—Tuun *cors* (= *cohors*), Txts. 52, 281. Tūn *choors*, Wrt. Voc. ii. 17, 32: i. 291, 12. Yna (hȳna?) tūnes tācen is ðæt ðū sette ðīne swȳþran hand brādlinga ofer ðīnne innoð, Techm. ii. 126, 15 (cf. gang-tūn). Harewyrt lytelu oftost weaxeþ on tūne (*in a garden*), Lchdm. ii. 132, 8. v. æppel-, apulder-, ber-, cafer-, cyric-, deór-, gærs-, gang-, leáh-, līc-, wyrt-tūn. II. as a technical English term, (1) in its simplest form, *the enclosed land surrounding a single dwelling*:—Gif man in mannes tūn ǣrest geirneþ .vi. scillingum gebēte; se ðe æfter irneþ .iii. scillingas; siþþan gehwylc scilling, L. Ethb. 17; Th. i. 6, 16. (2) where there were many dwellings, *a manor, vill, 'an estate with a village community in villenage upon it under a lord's jurisdiction,'* v. Seebohm's English Village Community, c. v. See also Kemble's Saxons in England, ii. c. vii: Stubbs' Const. Hist. s. v. town: Green's Making of England, c. iv: Cod. Dip. Kmbl. iii. p. xxxix; in the last its frequent occurrence in English local names is noted:—Ego, Plegrēd, aliquam terre unculam emi et Eðelmōde, hoc est ān healf tūn, que ante pertinebat tō wilburgewellan, ðet land healf and healfne tūn hiis terminibus circumcincta . . . hanc casam supranominatam ic, Eðelmōd, Plegrēde donabo, Cod. Dip. Kmbl. ii. 66, 27–67, 3. Ic wille ðæt man frīgæ hæalue mīne men on ǣlcum tūne for mīne sāwlæ, and ðæt man dēle æal healf ðæt yrue ðæt ic hæbbæ on ǣlcum tūne, iii. 273, 4–6. Gif in cyninges tūne man mannan ofsleá, .L. scill. gebēte, L. Ethb. 5; Th. i. 4, 4. On eorles tūne, 13; Th. i. 6, 9. Ǣghwilc man æt ðam tūne, ðe hē tō hȳre, L. H. E. 5; Th. i. 30, 1. Beó hē on carcerne on cyninges tūne, L. Alf. pol. 1; Th. 60, 9: Chr. 787; Erl. 56, 14. Gif se gereáfa ðis oferheald, gebēte .xxx. sciłł., and sió ðæt feoh gedǣled ðǣm þearfum ðe on ða[m] tūn[e] synd, ðe ðis ungefremed wunie, L. Ath. i. prm.; Th. i. 198, 12. Hē wæs on ānum đæs cyninges tūne nōht feor fram đære foresprecenan byrig forđon đe hē đǣr hæfde āne cyricean and ān resthūs . . . Đæt eác swylce his đeáw wæs on ōþrum cyninges tūne tō dōnne *erat in villa* (in 544, 14 *tūn* translates *vicus*) *regia non longe ab urbe de qua praefati sumus. In hac enim habens ecclesiam et cubiculum . . .; quod ipsum et in aliis villis regis facere solebat*, Bd. 3, 17; S. 543, 20–29. Ciólulf sealde Eánmunde his mēge đisne tuun (cf. Ego Cialulf dabo Eanmunde cognito meo aliquam partem terre iuris mei, hoc est in Dorobernia ciuitate, id est in longitudo .vi. uirgis et in latitudo .iii., 87, 27–31), Cod. Dip. Kmbl. ii. 89, 10. Đis sind đara feówer tūna londgemǣra, iii. 77, 32. Đǣr hē rād betwuh his hāmum oþþe tūnum (*villas*), Bd. 2, 16; S. 520, 11. v. tūn-cyrice, -gebūr, -gerēfa, -incel, -land, -mann, -scīr, -steall, -stede; tūnes-mann, -tūningas. II a. where the residential character of the *tūn* is the prominent one, the buildings or inhabitants being referred to:—Đā ongan se tūn bernan, đā forburnon ealla đara monna hūs đe on đæm tūne wǣron, Shrn. 90, 3–5. Đes tūn (*villa*) wæs forlǣten, and ōþer wæs getimbred, Bd. 2, 14; S. 518, 11. Hē eode tō đære cyricean đæs tūnes (*villulae*), 5, 12; S. 627, 20. Hē hæfde đæt biscrīce .L. wint' æt Scīreburnan, and his līc līþ đǣr on tūne (*or* tūne = cyrictūne?), Chr. 867; Erl. 72, 20. Đone tūn đe hē oftust on eardode gyt mon his naman cneódeþ *cujus nomine vicus in quo maxime habitare solebat usque hodie cognominatur*, 2, 20; S. 522, 23. Wæs in đa tīd đeáu Ongelcynnes folcum, đæt đonne mæssepreóst in tūn (*villam*) com, hī ealle gesomnodon Godes word tō gehȳranne, 4, 27; S. 604, 16. Đæt cumende folc of eallum tūnum (*viculis*), 2, 14; S. 518, 9: 4, 27; S. 604, 26. Hē com tō đām ymbgesettum tūnum (*circumpositas ad villas*), and đām dwoliendum bodade, 604, 13. Se đe reáfaþ man leóhtan dæge, and hē hit kȳþe tō þrīm tūnan, L. Eth. iii. 15; Th. i. 298, 12. Hē āslāt đa tūnas ealle ymb đa burh *discissis viculis in vicinia urbis*, Bd. 3, 16; S. 542, 21. III. referring to the towns of Roman Britain:—On Swalewan streáme se ligþ be Ceterehtt tūne (*vicum Cataractam*; the Roman station, Cataractonium), Bd. 2, 14; S. 518, 15. Hēr Cynewulf and Offa gefuhton ymb Benesingtūn, and Offa nam þone tuun, Chr. 777; Erl. 54, 2. Cūþwulf feaht wiþ Bretwalas and iiii tūnas genom, 571; Erl. 18, 13. (See Green's The Making of England, c. iii.) Ceáwlin monige tūnas genom, 584; Erl. 18, 24. IV. in a general sense, *a habitation of men*:—Lengtentīma gǣđ tō tūne on .vii. id. Feb. (cf. sumor gǣđ tō mannum on .vii. id. Mai, 25) *spring comes to our dwellings on the 23rd of February*, Anglia viii. 312, 19. Se mōnþ gǣđ on Sunnandæge on tūne (cf. cymđ se mōnđ tō mannum, 14: 8), 304, 12. Cymeþ on đam ylcan dæge ūs tō tūne forma mōnađ, Menol. Fox 16; Men. 8: 69; Men. 34. Folcum bringđ morgen tō mannum mōnađ tō tūne Decembris drihta bearnum, 436; Men. 219. Yldum bringđ sigelbeorhte dagas sumor tō tūne, 176; Men. 89. Bringđ tiida lange ǣrra Līđa ūs tō tūne, Iunius on geard, 214; Men. 108. Oft mon fēreþ feor bī tūne (cf. *Icel.* fara um tūn *to pass by a house*) đǣr him wāt freónd unwiotodne *often a man travels far, passing the dwellings of men, and knows that he has no friend for himself in them*, Exon. Th. 342, 21; Gn. Ex. 146. Ǣr sumor on tūn gā, Lchdm. iii. 6, 1, 3. Hwylce dæge đa mōnđas gān on tūn, Anglia viii. 304, 5, 25. Cymeþ scrīđan on tūn Maius, Menol. Fox 153; Men. 78. Lencten on tūn geliden hæfde, 56; Men. 28. On folc fēreþ October on tūn, 363; Men. 183. [The phrase is found in later English, e. g. Elde cumid to tune, Misc. 133, 534.] V. where the word is used to translate Latin forms, or refers to places not in England, (1) *the residence or estate of a single person, an estate, farm*:—Đīn tūn *tua villa*, Ælfc. Gr. 15; Zup. 103, 7: Wrt. Voc. i. 84, 48. Hātan his tūn đæs anscōdan tūn *ejus habitaculum domum discalceati vocare*, Past. 5; Swt. 43, 17. Đā sende hē hine tō his tūne (*in uillam suam*; toun, Wick.), đæt hē heólde his swȳn, Lk. Skt. 15, 15: Mt. Kmbl. 22, 5. Tūne *ad prediolum suum*, Anglia xiii. 36, 258. Neáh đam tūne (*juxta praedium*; manere, Wick.) đe Iacob sealde his suna, Jn. Skt. 4, 5. Sceall beón se læsta dǣl nȳhst đæm tūne đe se deáda man on līđ, Ors. 1, 1; Swt. 20, 33, 31. Wespasianus gefōr on ānum tūne būton Rōme *Vespasianus in villa propria circa Sabinos mortuus est*, 6, 7; Swt. 262, 29. Hē gefōr on đæm ilcan tūne (*in eadem villa*) đe his fæder dyde, 6, 8; Swt. 264, 4: Blickl. Homl. 219, 8–9. On đone tūn (*villam*; toun, Wick.) đe is genemned Gezemani, Mt. Kmbl. 26, 36. Ic bohte ǣnne tūn (*villam*; lond, Lind. Rush.: toun, Wick.: ferme, Tindal), Lk. Skt. 14, 18: Homl. Th. ii. 372, 19–21. Iosep sealde his gebrōđrum tūn (*possessionem*), Gen. 47, 11. Fegerne tūn timbrian, Shrn. 163, 16. Tūnas *territorii*, Wrt. Voc. ii. 76, 68. Hē gemenigfylde his spēda ǣgđer ge on tūnum ge on landum (*tam in aedibus quam in agris*), Gen. 39, 5. Hī nemnaþ hiora land and hiora tūnas be heora naman *invocabunt nomina eorum in terris eorum*, Ps. Th. 48, 10. (2) *a collection of dwellings, a village, town*:—Tuun *vel* đrop *conpetum*, Txts. 54, 307. Tūn, þrop, Wrt. Voc. ii. 15, 7 (cf. *compitum*, i. *villa* þrop, 132, 55). Tūn *pagus*, i. 54, 2. Betfage se tūn, Blickl. Homl. 77, 15. In Bethania đæm tūne, Mt. Kmbl. Rush. 26, 6. Of. đæm tuune (tūne, Rush.) on Galilēes mēgđ *a Cana Galilaeae*, Jn. Skt. Lind. 21, 2. Of Abian tūne (lond, Lind. Rush.) *de uice* (vico *has been read*?) Abia, Lk. Skt. 1, 5. Of đæm tūne đe Scariot hātte, Blickl. Homl. 69, 6: 211, 17: 221, 19: Homl. Th. ii. 54, 3. Hē eode on đone tūn đe hātte Dadissus, and đǣr wunode . . . Đā bæd hē đæs tūnes hlāford, đæt hē mōste healdan heora æceras . . . His suna wǣron āfēdde on ōþran tūne, Homl. Skt. ii. 30, 213–217. Se resteþ on *uico longe*, đæt is on đæm langan tūne, Shrn. 76, 2. Đeáh đū on tūn (*uicum*; lond, Lind. Rush.) gā, Mk. Skt. 8, 26. Hē hēt đone tūn (*uicum*) forbærnan, Bd. 5, 10; S. 625, 2. Bedrifen on āune tūn *in cujusdan villulae casam deportatus*, Ors. 6, 34; Swt. 292, 1. Tūnas *oppida*, Wrt. Voc. ii. 64, 70. Com micel fȳrbryne on Rōmeburg, đæt đǣrbinnan forburnon xiv tūnas *quatuordecim vicos flamma consumsit*, Ors. 6, 1; Swt. 252, 21. Fare wē on gehende tūnas (*uicos*; lond, Lind. Rush.: townes, Wick.), Mk. Skt. 1, 38: *villas*, Lk. Skt. 9, 12. [Halliwell gives *town* = court, farmyard, as a Devonshire word; and in Jamieson's Dictionary *toun, town* = a farmer's steading, or a small collection of houses; a single dwelling-house. 'Waverley learned from this colloquy, that in Scotland a single house was called a *town*,' Waverley, c. ix. *O. Frs.* tūn *a fence*: *O. L. Ger.* tūn *maceria*: *Du.* tuin *a fence*; *a garden*: *O. H. Ger.* zūn *sepis, maceria*: *Ger.* zaun *a hedge*: *Icel.* tūn *an enclosure* within which a house is built; *a farm-house with its buildings, homestead*: *Norweg.* tun *court, farmyard*.] v. burg-, neáh-, wīc-tūn; tȳnan.

tūn-cressa, an; *m.*: -cærse, -cerse, an; *f. Town-cress* (v. E. D. S. Pub. Plant Names), *garden-cress, nasturtium*; lepidium sativum:—Tuuncressa *nasturcium*, Txts. 79, 1359. Tūncærse, Wrt. Voc. ii. 60, 4, 64: i. 67, 70. Tūnkerse, 31, 50. Nim tūncersan sǣd, Lchdm. ii. 90, 18.

tūn-cyrice, an; *f. A church in a* tūn (*q.v.*):—Habbe hē þat lond frē his day and his wīues, and after here bothere day intō þe tūnkirke, and þō men frē . . . þat lond schal intō tūnkirke . . . and þō men frē, Chart. Th. 572, 20–33. Intō đe tūnkirke on Mardingford, 593, 2.

tunece, an; *f. A tunic, coat*:—Tunece *tonica*, Wrt. Voc. i. 284, 62. Tunice, Scint. 144, 7. Tunicæ *tunica*, Wrt. Voc. i. 39, 71. Hit ys mīnes suna tunece, Gen. 37, 33: Exon. Th. 357, 1; Pa. 22. Hī nāmon his tunecan (*tunicam*; cyrtel, Lind. Rush.); seó tunece wæs unāsiwod, Jn. Skt. 19, 23. Đā dyde hē on his tunecan (cyrtil (-el), Lind. Rush.), 21, 7: Lk. Skt. 6, 29. Đam đe wylle niman đīne tunecan (cyrtel ł hrægl, Lind.: đīnne tonica, Rush.), lǣt him tō đīnne wǣfels, Mt. Kmbl. 5, 40. Đā sende him mon āne blace hacelan angeán him on bismer, and eft hié him sendon āne tunecan ongeán, đa đe hié tō gehēton, đæt hē ealles būton ārunge tō Rōme ne com (*the Latin seems to have been misunderstood, it is*: Senatus sagum, hoc est, vestem moeroris deposuit, atque antiquum togae decorem recuperavit), Ors. 5, 10; Swt. 234, 21–24, 31. Đæt hē ūs forgeáfe đa undeádlīcan tunecan đe wē forluron on đæs frumsceapenan mannes forgǣgednysse, Homl. Th. i. 34, 29. Hió becwiđ hyre betstan dunnan tunecan, Chart. Th. 537, 31. Hió an Ceóldrȳþe hyre blacena tunecena, swā đǣr hyre leófre beó, 538, 6. Se đe hæfþ twā tunecan (cyrtlas, Lind. Rush.), Lk. Skt. 3, 11: Blickl. Homl. 169, 13. [*O. H. Ger.* tunihha *tunica*. From Latin.] v. ge-tunecod.

tūnes-mann, es; *m. A man living on a manor* (tūn, *q.v.*):—Gif hwilc tūnesman ǣnigne pænig forhæbbe, gilde se landrīca đone pænig and nime ǣnne oxan æt đam men (cf. L. Edg. i. 4; Th. i. 264, 9: L. Eth. ix. 10; Th. i. 342, 25 in which 30 pence is fixed as a fine for not paying the *heorđ-penig* and *Rōmfeoh*, 30 pence being the value of an ox according to L. Ath. v. 3; Th. i. 232, 7: v. 6, 2; Th. i. 234, 1: v. 8, 5; Th. i. 236, 31), L. N. P. L. 59; Th. ii. 300, 5. Tūnes-men, L. Edg. S. 13; Th. i. 276, 23. Cf. 8; Th. i. 274, 27. v. tūn-mann.

tunge, an; tung [? *in the passage*: Ālēs sāwle mīne fram tunge fācenfulre *a lingua dolosa* (but in the next verse *linguam* is glossed by *tungan*, so that perhaps *tunge* is meant for nominative: O. L. Ger. and O. H. Ger., however, have strong as well as weak forms), Ps. Lamb. 119, 2], e; *f.* I. *a tongue*:—Tunge *lingua*, Wrt. Voc. i. 64, 56. Gif monnes tunge biþ of heáfde ōđres monnes dǣdum dōn, đæt biþ gelīc and eágan bōt, L. Alf. pol. 52; Th. i. 94, 20: Exon. Th. 373, 25; Seel. Ex. 115. His tungan (tungæs, Lind.: tunga, Rush.) bend *uinculum linguae eius*, Mk. Skt. 7, 35. Hē his tungan (tunga, Lind. Rush.) onhrān, 7, 33. Rōmāne đæm pāpan his tungon forcurfon, Chr. 797; Erl. 58, 13. II. *tongue*, (1) as representing the person who speaks with the tongue:—Sió tunge biđ gescinded on đam lāriówdōme, đonne hió ōđer lǣrđ ōđer hió liornode, Past. 1; Swt. 27, 11. Seó tunge đe swā monig hālwende word on đæs Scyppendes lof gesette, Bd. 4, 24; S. 599, 11. Mīn tunge mǣrde đīn weorc, Ps. Th. 70, 22. Ālȳs mīne sāwle from đære tungan đe teosu wylle. Hwæt biđ đē seald from đære inwitfullan tungan? 119, 2, 3. Heora tungan sprecaþ fācn, 5, 10. Wǣron hyra tungan tō yfele gehwam scearpe, 56, 5. (2) representing the words expressed by the tongue, *words, speech, language*:—Hī mid tungan heora fācenfullīce dydon, Ps. Spl. 5, 10. Mē inwit næs on tungan, Ps. Th. 138, 2. Fram swēsere tungan ūtoncumenre, Kent. Gl. 159. Đā betǣhte Ecgferđ on hālre tungan (*in plain language*) land and bōc Dūnstāne, Chart. Th. 208, 11: 272, 5. (v. hāl.) Wiđ andan and wiđ đa micelan mannes tungan, Lchdm. i. 384, 22. Mid đæm sueorde hiera tungna tǣlinge, Past. 28; Swt. 199, 6. (2 a) *a language, speech*:—Hī sprecaþ nīwum tungum, Mk. Skt. 16, 17. (3) representing power of speaking:—Ic hæfde đe lætran tungan, Ex. 4, 10. III. *a tongue-shaped thing*:—Heard is mīn tunge, Exon. Th. 489, 16; Rä. 78, 8. Hit hafaþ tungan lange, 439,

23; Rä. 59, 8. [*Goth.* tuggô: *O. Sax. O. L. Ger.* tunga: *O. Frs.* tunge: *O. H. Ger.* zunga: *Icel.* tunga.] v. under-tunge; ge-tynge.

tún-gebúr, es; *m. A tenant in villenage, villein*:—Túngebúr *inquilinus* (cf. genaeot *inquilinis*, Txts. 71, 1117; geneát, Wrt. Voc. ii. 45, 57; bigenga *tilia*, inbúend *colonus*, i. *incola, cultor, inquilinus*, 134, 24), Wrt. Voc. ii. 49, 56: i. 18, 50.

tungel. v. tungol.

tún-geréfa, an; *m.* I. *a reeve, steward, bailiff.* v. tún, II:—Túngeréfa *villicus*, Wrt. Voc. i. 84, 50: *villicus* vel *actor* vel *procurator* vel *rector*, 18, 48. Ðá eodon hí on sumes túngeréfan gestærn and hine bǽdon ðæt hé hí onsende tó ðam ealdormen ðe ofer hine wæs ... Ðá onféng hí se túngeréfa *intraverunt hospitium cujusdan villici, petieruntque ab eo, ut transmitterentur ad satrapam qui super eum erat ... Suscepit eos villicus*, Bd. 5, 10; S. 624, 19-28. Ðá com hé tó ðam túngeréfan se ðe his ealdormon wæs *veniens ad villicum qui sibi praeerat*, 4, 24; S. 597, 27. Ðá herede se hláford ðære unrihtwísnesse túngeréfan (*uilicum*), Lk. Skt. 16, 8. II. *a praetor.* v. tún, V. 2:—Ypolitus wæs túngeréfa on Róme, Shrn. 117, 9: 116, 9: Homl. Th. i. 422, 11. Hé hét betǽcan ðone diácon ðam túngeréfan Ypolite, 426, 35.

tunge-þrum *a ligament of the tongue*:—Tungeðrum (undertunge-þrum, lxxiv, 9) *sublinguae*, Lchdm. i. lxx, 9.

tung-full; *adj. Loquacious, talkative*:—Tungfull mann *linguosus homo*, Scint. 81, 9. [Cf. *O. H. Ger.* zungal *linguosus*.]

tungilsinwyrt *white hellebore* (Cockayne), Lchdm. ii. 120, 2. Cf. tunsing-wyrt.

tungl, tungla. v. tungol.

tunglen; *adj. Of the stars, sidereal*:—Seó tunglene heofon, Anglia vii. 12, 109, 115. Tunglenes éþeles wlite *sidereae patriae decus*, Hymn. Surt. 58, 2.

tunglere, es; *m. An astrologer, astronomer*:—Tunglera ł wiglera *Chaldaeorum*, Hpt. Gl. 483, 5. Tunglera *mathematicorum* (the passage is: Gentilitas, quae vitam veritatis expertem fato fortunae et genesi gubernari juxta mathematicorum constellationem arbitratur), Wrt. Voc. ii. 79, 64: 56, 68.

tungol (-ul, -el), tungl, es; *generally neuter, but pl.* tunglas *occurs*: tungla, an; *m.* I. *a heavenly body*:—Tungel *sidus*, Wrt. Voc. i. 41, 54. Mænig tungul máran ymbhwyrft hafaþ on heofonum, Met. 28, 20. Saturnes steorra wandraþ ofer óþrum steorrum ufor ðonne ǽnig óþer tungol, Bt. 36, 2; Fox 174, 14. Swá heofenes tunglu *sicut astra coeli*, Deut. 10, 22. Sume tunglu habbaþ scyrtran hwyrft ðonne sume habban, swá swá tunglu habbaþ ðe wé hátaþ wǽnes ðisla, Bt. 39, 3; Fox 214, 17-19, 22. Tungl, Met. 28, 6, 12. Men sǽdon ðæt heofones tungul (*astra*) hiora yfel flugon, Ors. 1, 8; Swt. 42, 24. Tungol, Exon. Th. 58, 12; Cri. 934: 204, 12: Ph. 96. Tunglan *lumina*, Hpt. Gl. 446, 23: Boutr. Scrd. 18, 31. Þás tunglan *haec sidera*, Ælfc. Gr. 14; Zup. 90, 5. Tunglan nǽron gesceapene ǽr on ðam feórðan dæge. On ðam feórðan dæge gesette se Ælmihtiga ealle tungla, Homl. Th. i. 100, 7-9. Saturnus yfmest is eallra tungla, Met. 24, 20. Se móna is ealra tungla nyþemest, Boutr. Scrd. 18, 38. *Astronomia*, ðæt ys tungla gang, Shrn. 152, 14. Æþelast tungla (*the sun*), Exon. Th. 204, 6; Ph. 93. Under tunglum *on earth*, Andr. Kmbl. 3; An. 2. Beheald ða tunglu ðæs heán heofnes, Bt. 39, 13; Fox 232, 25: Met. 29, 4. Tungl, 28, 5. Tungel, Cd. Th. 132, 8; Gen. 2190. II. *a heavenly body other than sun or moon, a star*:—Seó sunne and se móna and ealle tunglan (tungla, MS. R.), Lchdm. iii. 246, 23. Gewíteþ sunne and móna and eal tungla leóht áspringeþ, Blickl. Homl. 91, 23. Sunnan ... mónan ... tunglena (*siderum*), Hymn. Surt. 22, 29. Féran mid ðære sunnan betwyx ðám tunglum, Bt. 36, 2; Fox 174, 11. Sunnan leóma torht ofer tunglas, Exon. Th. 7, 26; Cri. 107. III. *a planet* (including the sun and moon):—Ða seofon dweligendan tunglan (cf. steorran, 26) ... Þone yfemestan héton ða hǽþenan Saturnus ... Se feórða is seó sunne ... Se seofoþa is se móna, Boutr. Scrd. 18, 29-38, 41. Tungel (*Saturn*), Met. 24, 23. Tungol (*the sun*), Exon. Th. 350, 25; Sch. 69: Chr. 937; Erl. 112, 14. Æðele tungol (*Venus*), Met. 29, 32. Móna, gǽstlíc tungol, Exon. Th. 44, 7; Cri. 699. Habbaþ æðele tungol emne gedǽled dæg and nihte, ... sunne and móna ... þa wlitegan tungl, Met. 29, 35-39. Ða mǽran tungl, 9. IV. *a fixed star*:—Seó tunglena heofon, Boutr. Scrd. 18, 24, 28. V. *a group of stars, a constellation, division of the zodiac*:—Arthon hátte án tungol on norðdǽle, se hæfþ seofon steorran ... ðone hátaþ lǽwede menn carles wǽn. Se ne gǽð nǽfre ádúne under ðyssere eorðan, swá swá óðre tunglan (tungla, MS. R.) dóð ... óðer tungel is on súðdǽle ðysum gelíc, Lchdm. iii. 270, 9-15. Ðé is nú cúð ðes mónan færeld, on hwilcum tungle hé nú is oððe on hwilce hé ðanon géð, Shrn. 173, 1. Under ðam circule (*the zodiac*) yrnð seó sunne and se móna and ða twelf tunglena tácna, Lchdm. iii. 242, 3. Hys geár is ðæt hé underyrne ealle ða twelf tunglan, 248, 21, 5. [*Goth.* tuggl (uf tugglam, Gal. 4, 3; cf. under tunglum, Andr. Kmbl. 3; An. 2): *O. Sax.* tungal: *O. H. Ger.* zungal: *Icel.* tungl *and* tungli (*wk.*) *the moon*: *Swed.* tungel *the moon*.] v. æðel-, heofon-, rodor-tungol.

tungol-ǽ; *f. Astronomy*:—Tungelǽ *astronomiam, legem astrorum*, Hpt. Gl. 528, 60: Anglia xiii. 38, 307.

tungol-bǽre; *adj. Starry*:—Tungelbǽrum *astriferis*, Hpt. Gl. 490, 75: 493, 12.

tungol-cræft, es; *m. Star-craft, astronomy, astrology*:—*Astralo(g)ia*, ðæt ys tungolcræft, Shrn. 152, 14. Tungelcræft *astronomia*, Hpt. Gl. 479, 47. Hí hí on tungolcræfte (*astronomiae*) lǽrdan, Bd. 4, 2; S. 565, 26. Wé rǽdaþ on tungelcræfte, ðæt seó sunne biþ hwíltídum þurh ðæs mónelícan trendles underscyte áðýstrod, Homl. Th. i. 608, 31.

tungol-cræfta, an; *m. An astrologer, astronomer*:—Tungelcræftum *Chaldeorum*, Wrt. Voc. ii. 18, 33: 82, 6. v. next word.

tungol-cræftiga, an; *m. An astrologer, astronomer*:—Tungelcræftig[um? v. *preceding word*] *caldeorum*, Wrt. Voc. ii. 20, 28. Þreó tungolcræftegan cóman fram eástdǽles mǽgðum tó Criste, Shrn. 48, 17. Ðreá tungelcræftigo, Rtl. 2, 15. Ða tungulcræftega (-kræftgu, Rush.) *Magi*, Mt. Kmbl. Lind. 2, 1. Tungulkræftgum *Magis*, Rush. 2, 7, 16. From drýum ł tungulcræftgum, Lind. 2, 16.

tungolcræft-wíse, an; *f. Astronomy*:—Tungelcræftwísan *astronomia*, Wrt. Voc. ii. 5, 4.

tungol-gesceád, es; *n. Astrology, astronomy*:—Tungelgesceád *astrologia*, Hpt. Gl. 479, 60: Anglia xiii. 38, 308.

tungol-gimm, es; *m. A starry gem, a star*:—Heofon ongeat, hwá hine torhtne getremede tungolgimmum, Exon. Th. 71, 6; Cri. 1151.

tungol-wítega, an; *m. One who prophesies by means of the stars, an astrologer*:—Tungelwítega *astrologus* vel *magus* vel *mathematicus*, Wrt. Voc. i. 17, 14: *mathematicus*, 60, 12. Ðá cómon ða tungolwítegan (*Magi*) fram eástdǽle, Mt. Kmbl. 2, 1. Tungelwítegan, 2, 10: Homl. Th. i. 78, 5: Chr. 2; Erl. 4, 28. Tuncgelwítegana, steorgleáwra *mathematicorum*, Hpt. Gl. 467, 74. Æfter ðære tíde ðe hé geáxode fram ðám tungolwítegum (*Magis*; drýum, Lind.), Mt. Kmbl. 2, 16. Hé clypode on sunderspræce ða tungelwítegan, 2, 7: Homl. Th. i. 78, 17.

tung-wód; *adj. Tongue-mad, violent in speech*:—Uppstige sandfull on fótum forealdudes swá wíf tungwód menn stillum *ascensus arenosus in pedibus ueterani, sic mulier linguata homini quieto*, Scint. 223, 13.

tunice. v. tunece.

túnincel, es; *n. A small* tún, *small farmstead* or *estate*:—Túnyncel *butiuncula*, Wrt. Voc. ii. 126, 82. Tó his túningclum *ad praediolum suum*, túnincle *ad villam*, Hpt. Gl. 515, 63, 64.

-túningas; *pl. m. People of a* tún (?):—Óþ ealdingctúninga mearce óþ níwantúninga mearce, and of níwantúninga mearce *to the mark of the people of Aldington, then to the mark of the people of Newington, and from the mark of the people of Newington*, Cod. Dip. B. ii. 526, 7-8. Wudetunnincga gemǽro, Cod. Dip. Kmbl. iii. 193, 10.

tuning-wyrt. v. tunsing-wyrt.

tún-land, es; *n. Land of an estate* or *a farm*:—Ðis sindon ða londgemǽra ðæra túnlonda ðe intó Perscóran belimpaþ *these are the boundaries of the lands forming the estate of Pershore*, Cod. Dip. Kmbl. iii. 76, 28.

tún-líc; *adj. Of a village, rustic*:—Túnlíc spǽc *comedia* (as if from κώμη = *vicus*), Wrt. Voc. i. 27, 13.

tún-mann, es; *m. A man belonging to a* tún:—Túnman *villanus*, Wrt. Voc. i. 84, 49. Furseus oncneów ða sáwle; se wæs his túnman ǽr on lífe (*he had lived on the estate* (tún) *belonging to Fursey's monastery*), Homl. Th. ii. 344, 18. v. túnes-mann.

tún-melde, an; *f. Orach*; atriplex hortensis:—Túnmelde *crysolachan*, i. *aureum olus* vel *atriplex*, Wrt. Voc. ii. 137, 6.

tunne, an; *f. A barrel, cask*:—Tunne *cuba*, Wrt. Voc. ii. 105, 56: 17, 29: *cupa*, i. 24, 54: 83, 26: *cantarus, ubi aqua mittitur*, vel *ydria*, ii. 128, 11. Twá tunnan fulle hlútres aloð, Cod. Dip. Kmbl. i. 203, 8; Chr. 852; Erl. 67, 38. Tunnena *cuparum, modiorum*, Hpt. Gl. 488, 73: *cuparum*, Wrt. Voc. ii. 18, 35. *Caupo* wínbyrels oððe on tunnum, 21, 13. Nim fela tunnan, and dó hí ðǽr on innan ... Hí wurdon ðá gebrohte ealle tó ðám tunnum, Homl. Skt. i. 4, 259-307. [*O. Frs.* tunne: *Du.* ton: *O. H. Ger.* tunna *ydria, crater*: *Ger.* tonne: *Icel.* tunna: *Swed.* tunna: *Dan.* tønde. There are both Celtic and Low Latin forms, *tunna*; from which the English is taken is uncertain.] v. wín-tunne.

tunne-botm, es; *m. The bottom of a cask*:—Tunnebotm (cf. bydenbotm *fundum*, in the same list 'nomina vasorum') *tympanum*, the bottom of a cask used as a drum?, Wrt. Voc. i. 24, 55. [*Dan.* tønde-bund *the bottom or the head of a barrel*.]

tún-rǽd, es; *m. A town-council*:—Man beád ðam túnrǽde ðe his suna on áfédde wǽron ðæt man sceolde twégen cempan gescyrpan *an order was given to the council of the town in which his sons had been brought up, that two soldiers should be equipped*, Homl. Skt. ii. 30, 297.

tún-scipe, es; *m. The inhabitants of a* tún:—Cýþe hé hit ðonne hé hám cyme; and gif hit cuce orf biþ mid his túnscipes gewitnysse on gemǽnre lǽse gebringe. Gif hé swá ne déð ǽr fíf nihtum, cýþan hit ðæs túnes men ðam hundredes ealdre, L. Edg. S. 8; Th. i. 274, 26. Hé hét ðone túnscipe ealne ofsleán and ðone tún forbærnan *mittens occidit vicanos illos omnes, vicumque incendio consumpsit*, Bd. 5, 10; S. 625, 1. [Gif twa men oþer iii coman ridend to an tun, al þe tunscipe flugæn for heom, Chr. 1137; Erl. 262, 35.]

tún-scír, e; *f. Stewardship*:—Ágyf ðíne scíre ne miht ðú lencg túnscīre bewitan . . . Đonne ic bescired beó fram tūnscīre *redde rationem vilicationis tuae, jam enim non poteris vilicare . . . Cum amotus fuero a vilicatione*, Lk. Skt. 16, 2-4.

tunsing-wyrt, e; *f. White hellebore :*—Tunsingwyrt. Đeós wyrt đe man *elleborum album*, and ōđrum naman tunsincgwyrt nemneþ, Lchdm. i. 258, 21-23: iii. 302, col. 1. Tun[s]ingwyrt, ii. 68, 25. Cf. tungilsinwyrt. [*Tunsing* occurs, Cod. Dip. Kmbl. vi. 236, 15.]

tūn-steall, es; *m. A farm-stead, farm-yard* (?):—Ober đane ealdan tūnsteall, Cod. Dip. B. ii. 202, 7. On đone tūnsteal eástweardne, Cod. Dip. Kmbl. iii. 193, 14. Cf. hām-, mylen-steall, and *town-place* = farm-yard, which Halliwell gives as used in Cornwall.

tūn-stede, es; *m. A village :*—Tūnstede *pagi*, Wrt. Voc. i. 36, 30.

tūn-weg, es; *m. A road on a tūn, a private road :*—Ealles hereweg *publica via*, tuunweg *privata via*, Wrt. Voc. i. 37, 39-40. Tō tūnweges ende, Cod. Dip. Kmbl. v. 281, 21. Đǣr tūnwegas ūt sceótaþ . . . þurh đone tūn, vi. 235, 6.

tūr, es; *m. A tower :*—Intō đam tūre on Lundene, Chr. 1100; Erl. 236, 31. Đone weall đe hī worhton onbūtan đone tūr, 1097; Erl. 234, 27. Sié ginyhtsumnisse in tūrum đīnum *fiat habundantia in turribus tuis*, Rtl. 176, 13. [Manega mynstras and tūras gefeóllon, Chr. 1117; Erl. 246, 21. The use of the word in the Chronicle would be due to the Norman French, but in the Ritual to Latin ?] v. torr.

turf; *gen. dat.* tyrf; *pl.* tyrf *and* turf; *f.* I. *a turf, sod, piece of earth with grass on it :*—Turf *gleba*, Wrt. Voc. i. 37, 20. Đeós wyrt of ānre tyrf manega bōgas āsendeþ, Lchdm. i. 290, 7. Hī đa flaxan gehȳddon under ānre tyrf, Guthl. 15; Gdwin. 64, 16. Under āne (ānre ?) tyrf, 23. Ne turf ne toft *not a sod nor a field* (i. e. neither little nor much ?), Lchdm. iii. 286, 23. Tyrb *cespites*, Wrt. Voc. ii. 103, 69. Tyrf, 23, 18: *glebe*, 40, 37. Genim feówer tyrf on feówer healfa đæs landes . . . drȳpe on đone stađol đara turfa . . . bere đa turf tō circean and mæssepreóst āsinge feówer mæssan ofer đan turfon, and wende man đæt grēne tō đan weofode, and siþþan gebringe man đa turf đǣr hī ǣr wǣron . . . Nim đonne đa turf and sete đǣr ufon on, Lchdm. i. 398, 4-24. Turfum *glebulis*, Wrt. Voc. ii. 40, 36: 80, 32. Turvum *glebulis, cespitibus*, Hpt. Gl. 470, 35. Đā gewrohte hē weall mid turfum (cf. vallum . . . de cespitibus, Bd. 1, 5), Chr. 189; Erl. 9, 25. On tyrf *in cespites*, Wrt. Voc. ii. 48, 16. Đa wæstmbǣre tyrf *feraces glebas*, 147, 51. II. *turf, greensward, the grassy surface of the earth :*—Blōwendre tyrf *florei cespitis*, Wrt. Voc. ii. 149, 50. Sum stān mid đynre tyrf bewrigen *lapis obtectus cespite tenui*, Bd. 5, 6; S. 619, 20. Wæter wynsumu of đære moldan tyrf brecaþ, Exon. Th. 202, 8; Ph. 66. Of đisse eorþan tyrf, 222, 15; Ph. 349: 423, 21; Rä. 41, 25. Ic seah turf tredan .vi. gebrōđor, 394, 10; Rä. 14, 1. [*O. Frs. O. L. Ger.* turf: *O. H. Ger.* zurba *cespes, terra avulsa : Icel.* torf; *n.*; torfa; *f. a turf, turf.*] v. ēđel-, wangturf; torfian.

turf-haga, an; *m. An enclosed space covered with turf, a grassy enclosure :*—Ongan hē eorđan delfan under turfhagan (cf. wangstede, 1584; El 794), Elen. Kmbl. 1656; El. 830.

turf-hleów, es; *n. A shelter built of turf* (?):—Æfter furan on rischrīđig; of rischrīđie on turfhleó; of turfhleó æfter heáfdan on Pydewyllan, Cod. Dip. Kmbl. iii. 15, 26.

turl, trull *a ladle, scoop, trowel :*—Turl, scofl *trulla*, Wrt. Voc. ii. 122, 67. [A trulle *trulla*, Wülck. Gl. 617, 46. From Latin.]

turnian; *p.* ode. I. *to turn* (intrans.), *revolve* round an axis or centre:—Đa ārleásan turniaþ on ymbhwyrfte, Homl. Th. i. 514, 23. Seó firmamentum tyrnþ symle onbūtan ūs . . . and ealle đa steorran, đe hyre on fæste synd, turniaþ onbūtan mid hyre, Lchdm. iii. 254, 16. Hwylces gecyndes is seó heofon ? Symle turniende (*volubilis*). Gif heó turniende (*volubile*) is, hūmeta ne feald heó ?, Anglia vii. 12, 108-110. Tyrnincg turniendre liđeran *vertigo rotantis* (*volventis*) *fundibuli*, Hpt. Gl. 422, 66. II. of giddiness, *to turn :*—Ad tornionem capitis. Þis ys se lācecræft be þan manne þat hym þing[þ] ꝥ hyt turnge ābōtan hys heáfod, Lchdm. iii. 90, 8.] v. tyrnan.

turnigend-līc; *adj. Revolving :*—Gif seó heofon turnigendlīc (*volubile*) is, Anglia vii. 12, 109 note. v. preceding word.

turnung, e; *f. Turning, rotation :*—Turnunge *rotatu*, Wülck. Gl. 253, 14.

turtle, an; *f.: but* turtla, an; *m. also is found. A turtle-dove :*—Turtle *turtur*, Wrt. Voc. i. 29, 33: 77, 43: Ælfc. Gr. 5; Zup. 14, 2. Đeós turtle *hic turtur*, 9, 22; Zup. 48, 16. Gemētt turtla nest him *invenit turtur nidum sibi*, Ps. Lamb. 83, 4. Geoffra mē tō lāce sume turtlan and sume culfran *sume mihi turturem et columbam*, Gen. 15, 9. Bringan tō lāce āne culfran and āne turtlan, Homl. Th. i. 140, 2. Bringe hē twā turtlan, Lev. 5, 7, 11: 1, 14: Lk. Skt. 2, 24: Homl. Th. ii. 210, 34. [Cf. *O. H. Ger.* turtul-tūba *turtur*. From Latin.] v. next word.

turtur, es; *m.:* turture, an; *f. A turtle-dove :*—Speara gemoeted him hūs and turtur nest *passer invenit sibi domum et turtur nidum*, Ps. Surt. 83, 4. Twēgen culfran briddas and twēgen turturan gemæccan, Blickl. Homl. 23, 27. Tuoe (twoege, Rush.) turturas *par turturum*, Lk. Skt. Lind. Rush. 2, 24. [*O. H. Ger.* turtur (Notker, Ps. 83, 4).]

Tuu, tuu, tuwa. v. Tīw, twēgen, twiwa.

tusc, tux, es: *a wk. pl.* tuxan *occurs; m. A canine tooth* or *a molar tooth, a tusk :*—Tusc *genuino* (-*um*), Txts. 67, 961. Tux *caninus*, Wrt. Voc. ii. 127, 81. Monnes tux biđ .xv. scill. weorđ *the compensation to be paid for knocking out a man's canine tooth is xv shillings*, L. Alf. pol. 49; Th. i. 94, 12. Cf. L. Ethb. 51; Th. i. 16. Hundes tux, Lchdm. i. 370, 29. Se flǣsctōþ wiþæftan đone tux *gigra*, Wrt. Voc. ii. 42, 9. Mannes tuxas *canini* vel *colomelli*, i. 43, 31. Tuxas *canini*, ii. 16, 50: 128, 21: Lchdm. iii. 202, 19. Wiđ tōþwræce, hundes tuxas, i. 370, 26. Tuscum *genuinis*, cweorntōđum *molaribus*, Wrt. Voc. ii. 76, 39. Tuxum, 40, 44. Mid tuxum *ingenuis* (= *in genuinis* ?), 48, 50. Grindetōþum, tuxum *molaribus* (but see 76, 39 *ante*), 54, 46. Tuxum *ginguinis* ꝉ *ginguinibus* (the passage is: Ursorum gingivis carperentur), Hpt. Gl. 492, 1. Tuxum *dentibus* (*porcorum*), 507, 52. Heora (*the evil spirits'*) tōþas wǣron gelīce horses twuxan, Guthl. 5; Gdwin. 34, 24. Hȳ habbaþ eoferes tucxas *habentes aprorum dentes*, Nar. 34, 32. Tuxan đara leóna *molas leonum*, Ps. Lamb. 57, 7. [*O. Frs.* tusk.] v. hilde-tusc, *and next word.*

tuscel, tuxl, es; *m. A canine tooth* or *a molar tooth, a tusk :*—Gefōh fox, āsleah of cucum đone tuxl, lǣt hleápan āweg *catch a fox, knock out while alive the canine tooth, let the fox run away*, Lchdm. ii. 104, 12. Hȳ heora bān gnagaþ brynigum tuxlum (cf. byrnendum tōđum, Wulfst. 139, 11) *lacerant ignitis dentibus ossa*, Dōm. L. 14, 211. Tuxlas (*molas*) leóna tōbrycþ Drihten, Ps. Spl. 57, 6. [Twey tuxlys out of hys mouth set as of a bore, Octov. 929.] v. preceding word.

twā. v. twēgen.

twā-dæg-līc; *adj. Lasting two days :*—Twādæglīc (twydæglīc, Bd. M. 350, 32) fæsten is genōh tō healdenne *biduanum sat est observare jejunium*, Bd. 4, 25; S. 600, 8. [Cf. *Ger.* zwei-tägig: *Icel.* tvī-dægra *the name of a mountain desert taking two 'dægr' to cross.*]

-twæccea. v. angel-twecca.

twǣde; *adj. Doubled* (?), *containing two of three parts* of a whole; the word occurs mostly as substantive, *two thirds, two parts of three :*—Wylle ōþ sié twǣde bewylled đæs wōses (cf. bewyl ōþ þriddan dǣl, 120, 15) *boil till two thirds of the juice are boiled away*, Lchdm. ii. 38, 11. Wylle ōþ đæt se wǣta sié twǣde on bewylled (cf. 266, 31) *boil till the liquor be boiled down to two thirds*, 332, 17. Dō twǣde đæs wīnes and þriddan dǣl đæs huniges *put two parts of wine to one of honey*, 306, 26. Dō đæs meluwes twǣde and đæs sealtes þriddan dǣl, 314, 5. Dō đæs huniges twǣde and đære buteran þriddan dǣl, 316, 7. Dō đæs swefles swilcan đara wyrta twǣde *to the quantity of sulphur put twice as much of the plants*, 78, 8. Se biscop and đa hīgen āhten twǣde đæs wuda and đæs mæstes, Chart. Th. 70, 29. Se cyning āh twǣdne dǣl (twegen dǣlas, MSS. B. H.) wetes, þriddan dǣl sunu oþþe mǣgas, L. In. 23; Th. i. 116, 15. [*O. L. Ger.* tuēdi *half: O. Frs.* twēde *two thirds*, also *half;* twēdnath *two thirds.*] Cf. twi-dǣl.

-twǣfan. v. ge-twǣfan.

twǣman; *p.* de *To divide, separate, part,* (1) *to prevent the joining of objects :*—*Dyple* (diple *signum in libris praesertim ecclesiasticis ad distinctionem oppositum*, Migne) . . . Þys tāken gesetton đa ealdan wrīteras on ciriclīcum bōcum, đæt hig twǣmdon ođđe ætȳwdon đa gewitnyssa hāligra gewrita, Anglia viii. 334, 11. (2) *to part* what has been joined: —Man wite, đæt hȳ þurh mǣgsibbe tō gelænge ne beón, đe læs đe man eft twǣme đæt man ǣr āwōh tōsomne gedydon (cf. hī (*William and his wife*) wǣron ziđđen tōtweamde for sibrēden, Chr. 1127; Erl. 255, 20), L. Edm. B. 9; Th. i. 256, 10. (3) *to divide, cause dissension among :*— Đæt wē ne lǣtan ūs deófol twǣman, Wulfst. 272, 24. (4) *intrans.* :— Wē nellaþ, Drihten, nǣfre fram đē twǣman, Homl. Skt. i. 11, 169. [Ic uulle mine kineþeode twemen mine bearnen, Laym. 2948. His attente is uorte unuestnen (tweamen, MS. C.) heorten, A. R. 252, 2. Ne mei unc nowđer lif ne deađ tweamin atwa, Marh. 5, 17.] v. ge-, tō-twǣman; tō-twǣmedness, *and next two words.*

twǣmendlīce; *adv. Separately :*—Twǣmendlīce *singulatim, separatim*, Hpt. Gl. 438, 51.

twǣming, e; *f.* I. *division, separation, severing the connection between* objects:—Nis seó godcundnys gemenged tō đære menniscnysse, ne đǣr nān twǣming nys . . . Hē (*Christ*) þurhwunaþ on ānum hāde untōtwǣmed, Homl. Th. i. 40, 24-30. Đǣr (*at the last day*) biþ seó twǣming rihtwīsra manna and ārleá ra, 616, 28. Twǣming (*separation of man and wife*) is ālȳfed đām đe lufiaþ swīđor đa heálīcan clǣnnysse đonne đa hohfullan gālnysse, ii. 324, 3. Biđ ūs sēlre đæt wē his flǣsclīcan lufe fram ūs āceorfon, and mid twǣminge (*by separation from him*) āwurpon, i. 516, 11. Ūre Drihten forbeád đa yfelan twǣmincge betwux twām ǣwum, ii. 322, 32. II. *separation, distinction :*—Hē cwæđ 'đæs lifigendan Godes' for twǣminge đæra leásra goda *he said 'the living God' to distinguish him from the false gods*, Homl. Th. i. 366, 19.

twaltiga *palma*, Wrt. Voc. i. 80, 14, *apparently an error for* palmtwig, *q. v.*

-twanc (?). v. ge-twanc.

twā-nihte; *adj. Two days old :*—On twānihtne mōnan far tō and bige land đæt đīne yldran āhton *when the moon is two days old, go and buy land that thy forefathers owned*, Lchdm. iii. 176, note 2.

twēgen (twegen ? *In the later MSS. of the Gospels* tweigen *and* twegen *are found, but* ei *may represent earlier* e, *e.g.* weig, Lk. 1, 79, eige, 2, 9; *or* ē, *e.g.* wreigende, 23, 10, wreigeð, 23, 14: *Layamon has* tweiȝe, tweien: *in the Ormulum the form is* tweȝȝen); *m.*: twā, twuā; *f.*: tū, tuu, twā; *n.*: *gen.* twēga, twēgea, tweágea, twīga, twēgera, twēgra (*later Gospels have* tweigre, tweire); *dat.* twām, twǣm. Besides these West Saxon are the following forms, *nom. acc.* twǣgen, twœgen, tuoegi, tuoege, tuōge, tuoe, tuē; *m.*: *f.* tuoege: *gen.* tuoega, tuoe, twēgen, tuoegara, twoegra, tuoera. *Two.* I. used adjectivally:—Tuēgen stridi *passus*, Txts. 85, 1510. Twēgen (twǣgen, MS. E.) aldormen, Chr. 822; Erl. 62, 12. Twēgen englas, Gen. 19, 1. Óþre twēgen sealmas, R. Ben. 37, 11. Twǣgen mīne mēgas, Cod. Dip. Kmbl. i. 310, 23. Twoegen gibrōþæra, Txts. 127, 1. Miððȳ wēron onfence fīf hlāfo and twē fiscas, Mk. Skt. Lind. 6, 41. Brȳda twā, Cd. Th. 65, 33; Gen. 1075. Twā þeóda . . . twā folc, Gen. 25, 23. Sinhīwan twā, Cd. Th. 49, 9; Gen. 789. Ðæt tweágea (twēgea, Hatt. MS.) bleó godweb, Past. 14; Swt. 86, 14. Of ðissa twēgea (tuēga, Hatt. MS.) monna mūðe, 7; Swt. 48, 10. Twēgra gebrōðra bearn oððe twēgea gesweostra sunu and dohtor, Bd. 1, 27; M. 70, 4–5. Ðissa twēga yfela āuþer, Bt. 6; Fox 16, 2. Ys ðeós wyrt twēgea (twēgra, MSS. B. O.) cynna, Lchdm. i. 204, 9. Twēgra (tuoegara, Lind.: twoegra, Rush.: tweire, later MS.) manna gewitnes, Jn. Skt. 8, 17. Twoega nētna *duorum animalium*, Ps. Surt. ii. p. 189, 6. Tuoera scyldigra, Lk. Skt. p. 5, 14. Hié wǣrun on twǣm (tuǣm, l. 30) gefylcum, Chr. 871; Erl. 74, 16. His wīfum twǣm, Cd. Th. 66, 26; Gen. 1090: Beo. Th. 2387; B. 1191. His twām gebrōðrum, Gen. 9, 22: 19, 30. Twām (tuǣm, Lind.: twǣm, Rush.) hlāfordum þeówian, Mt. Kmbl. 6, 24. On ðysum twām bebodum, 22, 40. On twām styccum, Exon. Th. 70, 15; Cri. 1139. Ic hæbbe twēgen suna, Gen. 42, 37. Heó geseah twēgen (tuoege, Lind.: twoege, Rush.) englas sittan, Jn. Skt. 20, 12: Lk. Skt. 10, 35. Twēgen (tuōge, Lind.: twoege, Rush.) briddas, 2, 24. Ymb twǣgen mōnðas, Chr. 871; Erl. 75, 28. Ðæt wæter stōd an twā healfa ðære strǣte, Ex. 14, 22. Twā turtlan (tuoe (twoege, Rush.) turturas, Lind.) *par turturum*, Lk. Skt. 2, 24. Hē gelǣrde twuā mǣgþa, Shrn. 131, 26. Wē habbaþ twā (tuā, Hatt. MS.) bebodu, Past. 7; Swt. 48, 13. Twā eágan (tuoe ēgo, Lind.) hæbbende, Mt. Kmbl. Rush. 18, 9. Bring mē twā ða betstan tyccenu, Gen. 27, 9. Ofer tū folc, Bd. 3, 21; S. 551, 33. II. used substantively, (1) absolutely:—Twēgen of his leorningcnihtum, Jn. Skt. 1, 35. Twēgen of eów, Mt. Kmbl. 18, 19. Ðǣr twēgen (tuoe, Lind.: twēge, Rush.: tweigen, later MS.) oððe þrȳ synt gegaderode, 18, 20. Twā (tuoege ł tuu wīf *duae*, Lind.: twā, Rush.) beóð æt cwyrne grindende, 24, 41: Lk. Skt. 17, 35. Tuu in līchome ānum, Rtl. 106, 32. Twēga sang *bicinium*, Wrt. Voc. ii. 13, 4. On twēgra gewittnesse (in mūð tuoe witnesa, Lind.: in mūþe twēgen gewitnesse, Rush.: tweigre, later MS.) *in ore duorum testium*, Mt. Kmbl. 18, 16. Ðā sende hē twēgen (tuoege, Lind.: twǣgen, Rush.) hys leorningcnihta, 11, 2. Ðara scipa tū (twā, MS. E.) hē genam, Chr. 882; Erl. 82, 11. Ðæt wē twā (tuu, MS. T.) oþþe ðreó gehȳron, Bd. 3, 9; S. 533, 28. (1 a) distributively:—Hē sende hig twām *misit illos binos*, Lk. Skt. 10, 1. Hē sende hī twām and twām, Homl. Th. ii. 528, 27: 530, 1. Ða wuniaþ twām and þrīm ætgædere (*bini aut terni*), R. Ben. 9, 15. Steorran of heofenan feóllan, nāht be ānan oððe twām, ac swā þiclīce ðæt hit nān mann āteallan ne mihte, Chr. 1095; Erl. 231, 21. (2) with qualifying or defining words:—Wit Adam twā *we two, Adam and I*, Cd. Th. 290, 6; Sat. 411. Wer and wīf, hī tū beóþ in ānum līchoman, Bd. 1, 27; S. 491, 13. Hwelce twā synd wiþerweardran ðonne gōd and yfel? Bt. 16, 3; Fox 56, 6. Wurdon ðam æðelinge bearn āfēded, freólīcu tū, Cd. Th. 102, 30; Gen. 1708. Uncer twēga, 110, 9; Gen. 1835: Beo. Th. 5057; B. 2532. Ðonne him mon ðissa twēgea (tuēga, Hatt. MS.) hwæðer ondrǣt, Past. 27; Swt. 188, 9. Hwæðer ðara twēgra (twēga, Cott. MS.) þincþ ðē mihtigra? Bt. 36, 4; Fox 178, 15. Ðyssa twīga mǣst, Lchdm. iii. 28, 15. Mon dyde him twǣm ðone triumphan, Ors. 6, 7; Swt. 262, 25. Wið him twǣm, 6, 36; Swt. 294, 16. Betwih him twām, Bd. 1, 13; S. 482, 1. Andreas wæs ōþer of ðām twām (tuǣm, Lind.: twǣm, Rush.) *erat Andreas unus ex duobus*, Jn. Skt. 1, 40. Be ðām neáhstan twām is æfter tō cweþanne, Bd. 4, 23; S. 594, 12. Him twām *duobus ex eis*, Mk. Skt. 16, 12. Ðā gebletsode Metod monna cynnes ða forman twā, fæder and mōder, Cd. Th. 12, 31; Gen. 194. Hē drāf of wīcum dreórigmōd tū, idese and his āgen bearn (*Hagar and Ishmael*), 169, 24; Gen. 2804. (3) in particular phrases:—Ōþer twēga, oððe . . . oððe *either . . . or*, Bt. 11, 1; Fox 30, 26: 11, 2; Fox 34, 23. Ðeáh heó an tū tefleówe, Past. 7; Swt. 49, 11: Exon. Th. 70, 19; Cri. 1141: Chr. 885; Erl. 82, 19. Tōsliten on twā (tuu, Lind. Rush.), Mk. Skt. 15, 38. On twā (tū, Cott. MS.), Bt. 34, 11; Fox 150, 32. On twā (twuā, Cott. MS.), 38, 4; Fox 202, 27. Hī on twā fērdon *they parted*, Homl. Th. i. 388, 20. Ðæt wæter wearð tō twā tōdǣled *divisa est aqua*, Ex. 14, 21. III. used in combination with other numerals, (1) with cardinals, (a) multiplicative:—Tū hund and þreó swylce þrittig eác wintra, Elen. Kmbl. 3; El. 2. Twā hund, 1264; El. 634. Twā (tuu, Lind.: tū, Rush.), hund elna, Jn. Skt. 21, 8. On twēgera hundred penega wurþe, 6, 7. Mid twām hundred penegon, Mk. Skt. 6, 37. Twā þūsendo, Cd. Th. 189, 14; Exod. 184. (b) added to the decades:—Twā (tuoege, Lind.: tū, Rush.) and hundseofantig *septuaginta duos*, Lk. Skt. 10, 1. Hundseofontig tuoegi, Rtl. 113, 22. Nānne ðara twā and twēntigra monna, Ors. 6, 2; Swt. 256, 1. (2) with ordinals:—Se twā and feówertigeða sealm, R. Ben. 37, 14. Ðane twā and syxtigeþan, 36, 16. On ðære twā and twēntugoðan wucan, Mt. Kmbl. 8, 14, rubric. Mōna se twā and twēntigoðe, Lchdm. iii. 194, 17. IV. with the force of an adverb:—Hē tōdǣlde hig twā *divisit ea per medium*, Gen. 15, 10. Ðǣr wearþ micel gefeoht tuā (tuwa *in three MSS.*) on geáre, Chr. 885; Erl. 84, 7. Tū swā lange swā ða ōðru *twice as long as the others*, 897; Erl. 95, 12. Nymaþ twā swā micel feós *pecuniam duplicem ferte*, Gen. 43, 12. Selle man him twā swylc swylce man æt him nime, Lchdm. i. 400, 17. Seó hell ys twā swā deóp, and heó ys ealswā wīd, Wulfst. 146, 10. Seóð ðū hit twā swā swīðe swā hit ǣr wæs, Lchdm. iii. 12, 21. [*Goth.* twai; *m.* twōs; *f.* twa; *n.*; *gen.* twaddjē; *dat.* twaim; *acc.* twans; *m.* twōs; *f.* twa; *n.*: *O. Sax.* twēne; *m.* twā, twō; *f.* twē; *n.*; *gen.* twēiō; *dat.* twēm: *O. Frs.* twēne; *m.* twā; *f.* twā; *n.*; *gen.* twēra, twīra; *dat.* twām: *O. H. Ger.* zwēne; *m.* zwā, zwō; *f.* zwei; *n.*; *gen.* zweio, zweiio, zweiero; *dat.* zweim: *Icel.* tveir; *m.* tvær; *f.* tvau; *n.*; *gen.* tveggja; *dat.* tveim; *acc.* tvā; *m.* tvær; *f.* tvau; *n.*]

twelf, *generally indeclinable if used adjectivally and preceding the noun, but generally in other cases declined; nom. acc.* twelfe; *gen.* twelfa; *dat.* twelfum. *Twelve.* I. adjectival:—Ða twelf ðīne þeówas sind gebrōðru, Gen. 42, 13. Wē twelf gebrōðru wǣron ānes esnes suna, 32. Twelf (tuoelf *altered from* tuoelfo, Lind.: twelf, Rush.) tīda ðæs dæges, Jn. Skt. 11, 9. Twelf wintra tīd, Beo. Th. 296; B. 147. Be twelf sealmum, R. Ben. 35, 6. Se tīreádga twelf sīþum hine bibaþaþ, Exon. Th. 205, 2; Ph. 106: 202, 13; Ph. 69: Cd. Th. 285, 17; Sat. 339. Mid hys twelf leorningcnihtum (ðǣm twelfum ðegnum, Lind.: ðǣm twælf leorneras, Rush.), Mt. Kmbl. 26, 20. Ymbe twelf mōnaþ *post annum*, L. Ecg. P. iv. 65; Th. ii. 224, 32. Tuoel ðegnas hē sendeþ, Mk. Skt. p. 2, 19. *In the following instance the word is inflected*:—Ān ðæra twelfa Drihtnes ðegena, Homl. Th. ii. 242, 15. I a. where the numeral follows the noun:—Ðā ongan hē sendan hālige weoras and geornfulle twelfe *holy men and diligent, twelve in number*; viros sanctos et industrios . . . erant numero duodecim, Bd. 5, 10; S. 623, 42. Hié getealdon fēðan twelfe, Cd. Th. 192, 2; Exod. 225. Mīne suna twelfe, Salm. Kmbl. 30; Sal. 15. II. substantival, (1) absolutely:—Twelfe wǣron dǣdum dōmfæste, Apstls. Kmbl. 8; Ap. 4. Hē twelfa sum āð sealde *cum undecim comparibus suis sacramentum fecit*, Chart. Th. 203, 1. Hē com twelfa sum (*cum duodecim militibus*), Bd. 3, 1; S. 523, 31. Gewāt xii.-a sum, Beo. Th. 4793; B. 2401. Lond twelfum hērra fæðmrīmes *per bis sex ulnas eminet ille locus*, Exon. Th. 199, 20; Ph. 28. Wē gefrunon twelfe under tunglum *we have heard of twelve men beneath the stars*, Andr. Kmbl. 3; An. 2. (2) with qualifying or defining words:—Hī twelfe (tuoelfo, Lind.), Lk. Skt. 8, 1. Hig twelfe (ða tuoelfo, Lind.) sǣdon him, 9, 12. Hē dyde ðæt hī twelfe mid him wǣron (ðætte hiá wēre twelfo mið him, Lind.), Mk. Skt. 3, 14. Hine āxodon ða twelfe, 4, 10. Ealra twelfa, Beo. Th. 6322; B. 3171. Eom ic ðara twelfa sum ðe hē gelufade, Exon. Th. 144, 20; Gū. 681. Hē wæs ān ðara twelfa (ān of ðǣm twelfum, Lind.), Jn. Skt. 6, 71. Ān of eów twelfum (ðǣm twelfum, Lind.), Mk. Skt. 14, 20. Hē ætȳwde him twelfum (ðǣm tuoelfum, Lind.), 16, 14. Ðū ūs twelfe trymman ongunne, Andr. Kmbl. 2837; An. 1421. Wē gesēgon eówre standan twelfe getealde, 1765; An. 885. *In the following instance the word is not inflected*:—Ðās twelf (tuelfe, Lind.: twælfe, Rush.) se Hǣlynd sende, Mt. Kmbl. 10, 5. [*Goth.* twalif: *O. Sax.* twelif: *O. Frs.* twelef, twilif, tolef: *O. H. Ger.* zwelif: *Icel.* tōlf. These forms are declinable as in English.]

twelf-feald; *adj. Twelve-fold*, (1) with a noun:—Hī gegaderodon twelf wilian fulle. Ðæt twelffealde getel getācnode ða twelf apostolas, Homl. Th. i. 190, 11: 542, 4. Twelffeald geþungennes *duodenus apex*, twelffealdum setle *duodeno solio*, Wrt. Voc. ii. 142, 14, 13. (2) used substantively:—Be .xii.-fealdum āgife hē ðone ciricsceat, L. In. 4; Th. i. 104, 11. Forgilde hē mid twelffealdan, L. Eth. ix. 11; Th. i. 342, 28: Wulfst. 311, 6.

twelf-gilde; *adj. To be restored twelve-fold*:—Godes feoh and ciricean .xii.-gilde *the property of the church, if stolen, is to be restored twelve-fold* (the word, however, might be a noun = a restoration of twelve times the amount stolen, cf. ān-gilde; or adverb (dat.?), cf. ix-gylde forgylde, 4; Th. i. 4, 3), L. Ethb. 1; Th. i. 2, 4.

twelf-hynde; *adj.* As applied to a person, *of the rank for which the wergild was twelve hundred shillings*; applied to the wergild, *that must be paid for a person of such rank.* As will be seen from the passages given below, the *twelfhynde man* was a *þegn*, and his importance, as marked by the wergild and otherwise, was six times that of the *ceorl*:—Ǣnig mǣgð, xii-hynde oþþe twyhynde, L. Ath. v. 8, 2; Th. i. 236, 10. Be xii-hyndum men. Gif hē sié twelfhynde, L. Alf. pol. 31; Th. i. 80, 14. Gif hió sié cirlisc mid .lx. scill. gebēte . . . Gif hió sié xii-hyndu .cxx. scill. gebēte, 18; Th. i. 72, 15. Be twelfhyndes monnes wīfe forlegenum. Gif mon hǣme mid twelfhyndes monnes wīfe, hundtwelftig scill. gebēte ðam were . . . Cierliscum men feówertig scill. gebēte,

10; Th. i. 68, 8-12. Twelfhyndes monnes burgbryce .xxx. scill . . . Ceorles edorbryce .v. scill., 40; Th. i. 88, 9-11. Twelfhyndes mannes wer is twelfhund scyllinga (cf. Ceorles wergild is on Myrcna lage .cc. scill. Đegnes wergild is syx swā micel, L. M. L.; Th. i. 190, 1. Twelfhindus est homo plene nobilis, i. thainus cujus wera est duodecies .c. sol., L. H. 76, 4; Th. i. 581, 17. Twelfhinde, i. thaini, 70, 1; Th. i. 572, 22. See also L. W. I. 8; Th. i. 470, 14), L. E. G. 12; Th. i. 174, 13. Twelfhyndes mannes āđ-forstent .vi. ceorla āđ; for đam gif man đone twelfhyndan man wrecan sceolde, hē biþ fullurecan on syx ceorlan, and his wergyld biþ six ceorla wergyld, L. O. 13; Th. i. 182, 19-22. xii-hyndum men twyfealdlīce be đæs syxhyndan bōte, L. Alf. pol. 39; Th. i. 88, 4. Æt twyhyndum were mon sceal sellan tō monbōte .xxx. scill. . . . æt twelfhyndum .cxx. (cf. ad manbotam de twelfhindo, i. thaino .cxx. sol., L. H. 69; Th. i. 572, 19), L. In. 70; Th. 146, 14. Æt twelfhyndum were·gebyriaþ twelf men tō werborge, L. E. G. 12; Th. i. 174, 18, 24. Cnut cing grēt . . . ealle mīne þegnas twelfhynde and twihynde, Chart. Th. 308, 16: Chart. Erl. 229, 20. ¶ In the following passage where the word is used without a noun perhaps *wer* may be supplied:—Hū man sceal gyldan twelfhyndes man (= twelfhyndes weres man *a man with a wergild of twelve hundred shillings*), L. E. G. 12; Th. i. 174, 12. v. six-, twi-hynde.

twelf-nihte; *adj. Twelve days old*:—On xii-niht[n]e mōnan byþ gōd tō fēranne ofer sǣ, Lchdm. iii. 178, 26.

twelfta; *ord. num. Twelfth*:—Se twelfta *duodecimus*, Ælfc. Gr. 49; Zup. 282, 19. Mōna se twelfta, Lchdm. iii. 190, 4. Hē wæs twelfta sylf, Andr. Kmbl. 1330; An. 665. ¶ Passages having reference to Twelfth-night, the twelfth day after Christmas, Epiphany:—Đæs (*the first of January*) embe fīf niht fulwihtiid ēces Drihtnes tō ūs cymeþ, đæne twelfta dæg tīreādige hæleþ hātaþ on Brytene, Menol. Fox 25; Men. 13. Đȳ twelftan dæge ofer Geohol *Epiphaniae*, Bd. 4, 19; S. 588, 8. Đys sceal on twelftan dæg, Rubc. Mt. Kmbl. 2, 1. On twelftan ǣfen, 2, 19. On Wōdnes dæg ofer twelftan dæg, 3, 13. Eádweard kingc com tō Westmynstre tō đam middan wintre . . . And hē forđfērde on twelftan ǣfen, and hyne man bebyrigde on twelftan dæig on đam ylcan mynstre, Chr. 1065; Erl. 196, 14-19.

twelftig. v. hund-twelftig.

twelf-wintre; *adj. Twelve years old*:—Ūre Hǣlend đā hē wæs twelfwintre, Past. 49; Swt. 385, 20: Lk. Skt. 2, 42. Tuoelfwintro *duodennis*, p. 4, 4. Heó wæs twelfwintre *erat annorum duodecim*, Mk. Skt. 5, 42. Se wæs xii-wintre cniht, Shrn. 118, 13. Hē hæfde āne dohtor neán twelfwintre *filia unica erat illi fere annorum duodecim*, Lk. Skt. 8, 42. Man ne sparige nānan þeófe ofer .xii. pæningas and ofer .xii.-wintre mann *no thief shall be spared above .xii. pence and above a twelve-year old person*, L. Ath. v. 1, 1; Th. 228, 13. Mon ne sparige nǣnne þeóf ofer .xii. winter (twelfwinterne, MS. B. L.) and ofer eahta peningas, 1, 1; Th. i. 198, 17. Gyf hine hwā āfylle ofer twelfwintre (ofer đæt hē biþ twelfwintre, MS. G.), L. C. S. 20; Th. i. 386, 22. Ǣlc man ofer twelfwintre sylle đone āđ, đæt hē nelle þeóf beón, 21; Th. i. 388, 6. Ǣlc man đe beó ofer twelfwintre, Wulfst. 136, 17. *Perhaps in the last five passages* ofer twelfwintre *should be taken as a compound.* [*Goth.* twalib-wintrus.]

twengan; *p.* de *To pinch, squeeze, twinge*:—Gyf đē gedrȳptes wīnes lyste, đonne dō đū mid đīnum swȳþran scytefingre on đīne wynstran hand, swylce đū tæppian wille, and wænd đīnne scytefinger ādūne and twængc hine mid đīnum twām fingrum, swylce đū of sumne dropan strīcan wylle, Techm. ii. 125, 19. Cyrsena tāc[n] is đæt đū sette đīnne winstran þūman on đīnes lytlan fingres liđ and twenge hine siđđan mid đara swīþran hande, 124, 23. Twenge đū mid đīnre swīđran neoþewearde þīne wynstran, 125, 1. [Þu havest clivres swiþe stronge, þu twengest þar mid so doþ a tonge, O. and N. 156. An holȝ stoc hwar þu þe miht hude þat me ne twenge þine hude, 1114. He twengde and schok hire bi þe nose, P. L. S. ix. 81. *O. H. Ger.* zwengen *remordere, praestringere.*]

twēntig, twēgentig; *num. Twenty.* I. used adjectivally, with the inflexions of the plural adjective in gen. and dat., but also with singular gen. (1) alone:—Đis synd đara twēntiges hīda landgemǣra, Cod. Dip. Kmbl. iii. 429, 25. Mid twēntigum (twoegentigum, Rush.: tuoentigum, Lind.) þūsendum, Lk. Skt. 14, 31. On twēntigum fōtmǣlum, Elen. Kmbl. 1657; El. 830. Næs tō ānum dæge, ne tō twām . . . ne tō twēntigum, Num. 11, 19. Intō đȳs twēntigum hīdum, Cod. Dip. Kmbl. v. 331, 1. (2) with other numbers, the inflection may be omitted if the noun does not immediately follow *twēntig*:—Nānne đara twā and twēntigra monna, Ors. 6, 2; Swt. 256, 2. Đæt mæsten is gemǣne tō đām ān and twēntigum hīdum, Cod. Dip. Kmbl. v. 319, 29. Ymb twēntig . . . and fīf nihtum, Menol. Fox 371; Men. 187. II. used substantively, (1) alone:—Gif đǣr beóþ twēntig rihtwīsra, Gen. 18, 31. Ān twēntig is đara bōca đe Adeluuold gesealde *of the books that Athelwold gave there is a score*, Chart. Th. 244, 21. Wæs ic mid đē twēntig wintra, Gen. 31, 38. Næfde hē mā đonne twēntig sceápa and twēntig swȳnas, Ors. 1, 1; Swt. 19, 14. Hē hæfde twǣm læs đe twēntig wintra, Blickl. Homl. 215, 34. Twēntig (fīfe and twoegentig, Rush.: tuēntig, Lind.) furlanga, Jn. Skt. 6, 19. (2) with other numbers:—Hundteóntig geára and seofon and twēntig geára, Gen. 23, 1. Seó menigu wæs ān hund manna and twēntig, Homl. Th. i. 296, 18. Onbīd hēr seofon and twēntig nihta, Blickl. Homl. 231, 5. (3) distributively:—Tȳnum and twēntigum on ānum inne ætgædere restan, R. Ben. 47, 7. [*Goth.* twai-tigjus: *O. Sax.* twēntig: *O. Frs.* twintege: *O. H. Ger.* zweinzug: *Icel.* tuttugu.]

twēntig-feald; *adj. Twenty-fold*:—Twēntigfeald getel *vicenarius*, Ælfc. Gr. 49; Zup. 285, 3. Twēntigfealde *uiceni*, 5; Zup. 13, 15.

twēntigođa; *ord. num. Twentieth*:—Se twēnteogođa (-tigođa) *uicesimus*, se ān and twēnteogođa *uicesimus primus*, Ælfc. Gr. 49; Zup. 283, 6. Mōna se twēntigoþa . . . mōna se ān and twēntigođa, Lchdm. iii. 194, 5-9. Se fīf and twēntugoþa dæg þæs mōnþes, Nic. 1; Thw. 1, 11. On đære twā and twēntugođan wucan, Rubc. Mt. Kmbl. 8, 14. Đȳ twēntigþan dæge, Bd. 4, 5; S. 572, 7. On đone tū and twēntegđan dæge, Shrn. 93, 1 (*and often*). On đone fīf and twēntigođan dæg, 96, 11.

twēntig-wintre; *adj. Twenty years old*:—Ōđ hē sȳ twēntigwintre ođđe gyt yldra, Wulfst. 3, 1.

tweó, twȳ; *gen.* tweón, twȳn; *m.* I. *doubt, uncertainty*:—Đonne đǣr ān tweó of ādōn biþ, đonne biþ đǣr unrīm āstyred *una dubitatione succisa innumerabiles aliae succrescant*, Bt. 39, 4; Fox 216, 18. 'Sum tweó mē hæfþ swīþe gedrēfed.' Đā cwæþ hē: 'Hwæt is se?' '*difficiliori ambiguitate confundor.*' '*Quaenam,*' *inquit* '*ista est?*' 41, 2; Fox 244, 14. Đū mē hæfst ārētne on đam tweón đe ic ǣr on wæs be đam freódōme, Fox 246, 12. Wē habbaþ litellne gearowitan būton tweón, 41, 6; Fox 254, 10. Đonne secge ic eów būton ǣlcum tweón, 16, 1; Fox 50, 27. Đæt hē đæt on gehđu gesprǣce and tweón, Elen. Kmbl. 1332; El. 668. Tō tweón weorđan *to become doubtful*, Exon. Th. 310, 4; Seef. 69. Būtan tweón *without doubt, undoubtedly, doubtless, certainly*; sine dubio, Bd. 1, 7; S. 478, 7: 1, 25; S. 486, 26. Hwæđer wǣre twēgra būtan tweón strengra, Salm. Kmbl. 854; Sal. 426. Būton ǣlcum tweón *beyond all question*, Bt. 22, 2; Fox 78, 11: 21; Fox 72, 28: Met. 11, 1. Būton twȳn, R. Ben. Interl. 17, 4: Homl. i. 190, 18. Būta tuā *utique*, Mt. Kmbl. Lind. 9, 18. Ic wāt đæt hine wile tweógan . . . Ne mæg se cyning đæne tweón eáđe gebētan? Wulfst. 3, 12. Đǣr seó wīse on tweón cyme *ubi res perveniret in dubium*, Bd. 1, 1; S. 474, 21. I a. where the subject of doubt is in the genitive:—Nis đæs nān tweó, đæt . . . *of this there is no doubt, that* . . ., Past. 6; Swt. 47, 10: Bt. 16, 3; Fox 54, 20. Nis đæs nān twȳ (tweó, Cott. MS.), đæt . . ., 40, 1; Fox 234, 36. Đām englum nis nān tweó nānes đæra đinga đe hī witon, 41, 5; Fox 254, 10. Đæt hit heofoncyninges tācen wǣre, and đæs tweó nǣre, Elen. Kmbl. 342; El. 171. Đæt nǣre nǣnig manna đæt mihte đæra twēgra tweón (*the doubt about the two*, cf. 854; Sal. 426, given above) āspyrian, Salm. Kmbl. 870; Sal. 434. I b. where the subject of doubt is expressed by a clause:—Nis nān tweó, đæt đæs andwearda wela āmerþ đa men, Bt. 32, 1; Fox 114, 2. Hit is nān tweó, đæt . . ., 36, 3; Fox 178, 4. Nis nān tweó đæt hē forgifnesse syllan nelle đam đe hié geearnian willaþ *there is no doubt about his not being ready to grant forgiveness to those that are ready to deserve it*, Blickl. Homl. 65, 8. Him tweó þūhte, đæt hē Gode wolde geongra weorđan, Cd. Th. 18, 21; Gen. 276. Đæt hālige gewrit, đæt mē nis tweó đæt đū geara canst *sacra scriptura, quam te bene nosse dubium non est*, Bd. 1, 27; S. 489, 2: 4, 7; S. 575, 13. Him wæs on mōde mycel tweó, hwæt hié be đære dorstan dōn, Blickl. Homl. 205, 10. Nā twȳ ys, đæt . . . *non dubium est, quod* . . ., Scint. 48, 10. Mid đȳ sumum monnum com on tweón hwæđer hit swā wǣre *cum hoc an ita esset quibusdam venisset in dubium*, Bd. 4, 19; S. 587, 26. II. *hesitation, delay*:—Būta tuiá đū onfindes *sine mora reperies*, Mt. Kmbl. p. 4, 4. III. *a doubtful state of things, state of indecision*:—On đæm tweón đe hié swā ungeorne his willan fulleodon đā becom him Antigonus mid firde on *in this state of indecision, in which they carried out his will so reluctantly, Antigonus fell upon them with an army*; qui fastidiose ducem in disponendo bello audientes ab Antigono victi sunt, Ors. 3, 11; Swt. 146, 24. [*O. Sax.* tweho: *O. H. Ger.* zweho *dubium, ambiguitas.*] v. un-tweó; tweógan (tweón), tweón *doubt.*

tweo-. v. twi-.

tweógan, tweón; *p.* tweóde. I. with impersonal construction, *to inspire doubt into* a person (*acc.*), (a) with gen. of object of doubt:—Wē witon đæt nānne mon đæs ne tweóþ, đæt se seó strong on his mægene đe mon gesihþ đæt stronglīc weorc wyrcþ, Bt. 16, 3; Fox 54, 28. Ne tweóþ mē đæs nāuht, 36, 3; Fox 176, 16: Exon. Th. 117, 13; Gū. 223. Nānne mon đæs tweógan ne þearf, đæt ealle men geendiaþ on đam deáþe, Bt. 11, 2; Fox 34, 34: 33, 1; Fox 120, 24. Tweógean, Blickl. Homl. 43, 1. (b) with a preposition:—Ymb đæt đe hiene tweóde, orn hē intō đæm temple, and frægn đæs Dryhten . . . Hié sculon, đonne hié ymb hwæt tweóþ, cyrran tō hiera āgnum inngeđonce, Past. 16; Swt. 102, 4-8. (c) with a clause:—Nǣnne mon ne tweóþ, đæt God sȳ swā mihtig, Bt. 35, 5; Fox 164, 4: 36, 3; Fox 176, 15. Ne đē nāuht ǣr ne tweóde, đætte God weólde ealles middaneardes, 35, 2; Fox 156, 30. Đēh đe hié ǣr tweóde, hwæđer hiene mon geflieman mehte, Ors. 4, 9; Swt. 192, 15. And đæt đȳ læs tweóge, hwæđer đis sōþ sȳ, ic cȳþe hwanan mē đās spell cōman *ut occasionem dubitandi subtraham, quibus auctoribus didicerim* *intimare curabo*, Bd. pref.; S. 471, 20. Hine wile tweógan, hwæðer heó him sóð secge, Wulfst. 3, 7. Nǽnigne tweógean ne þearf, ðæt seó wyrd geweorþan sceal, Blickl. Homl. 83, 9. Tweógan, Bt. 37, 3; Fox 190, 8. (d) absolute:—Ic wát ðætte wile woruldmen tweógan, Met. 4, 51. II. *to feel doubt, to doubt, hesitate*, (a) with gen. of object of doubt:—Ne tweóþ ðæs nán (nǽnne, Cott. MS.) mon, Bt. 35, 5; Fox 164, 5. Ne mæg ic ðæs nó tweógan (twiógean, Cott. MS.), 34, 9; Fox 146, 26: 35, 4; Fox 160, 18. Ðæs tweógan ne þearf ǽnig, Exon. Th. 147, 13; Gú. 726. (b) with preposition:—Ic nát ymbe hwæt ðú tweóst, Bt. 5, 3; Fox 12, 13. Gif gé tweógaþ be ðǽm ælmessum, Blickl. Homl. 41, 20. Ne tweóge ðis folc (*or acc.?*) be hire untrumnesse, 143, 12. Be ðam nis tó tweógenne, ac is tó gelýfanne, Bd. 3, 23; S. 555, 33. (c) with an infinitive:—Hí ne tweódon férende beón tó ðam écan lífe, Bd. 4, 16; S. 584, 38. (d) with a clause:—Ic náuht ne tweóge ðæt ðú hit mǽge gelǽstan, Bt. 36, 3; Fox 174, 31. Ðú cwist ðæt ðú náht ne tweóge ðætte God ðisse worulde rihtere sié, 5, 3; Fox 12, 13. (e) absolute:—Hé swýðor tweóþ ðonne se ǽrra, Wulfst. 3, 10. Se ðe cuoeðas and ne tuães ꝉ ne getuíga (ne twiás ꝉ ne twióge, Rush.) *qui dixerit et non haesitaverit*, Mk. Skt. Lind. 11, 23. Gif gé ne twígaþ *si non haesitaveritis*, Mt. Kmbl. Rush. 21, 21. Tuiáde *haesitabat*, Lk. Skt. Lind. Rush. 9, 7. Sume tweódun *quidam dubitaverunt*, Mt. Kmbl. Rush. 28, 17. Twiódun (tuiáton, Lind.) *haesitabant*, Jn. Skt. Rush. 13, 22. Ne tweóge *non cunctante*, Wrt. Voc. ii. 92, 49. Hé hine hét ðæt hé ne tweóde, ac ðæt hé wǽre ánrǽd, Guthl. 4; Gdwin. 30, 7. Ðá ðæt folc ongan tweógan on heora heortan, Blickl. Homl. 143, 8. Tó tweónne *nutabundum*, Hpt. Gl. 459, 5. Tuígendi *anceps*, Wrt. Voc. ii. 100, 40. Tweógende, 7, 2. Tweógende mód, Andr. Kmbl. 1542; An. 772. Nǽnig tweógende secgend *non quilibet dubius relator*, Bd. 3, 15; S. 542, 7. Tweógende cyningas *reges dubii*, 4, 26; S. 603, 17. Tweógende *hesitantes*, Wrt. Voc. ii. 43, 22: 74, 19. [*O. Sax.* twehón: *O. H. Ger.* zwehôn *dubitare, hesitare, cunctari.*] v. ge-tweógan, un-tweógende, -tweónde.

tweógend-líc; *adj.* *Doubtful, uncertain*, (1) where doubt is felt:—Tweógendlícre (*sine*) *ancipiti* (*ambiguitatis scrupulo veraciter credendum est*), Hpt. Gl. 422, 32. Hé on tweógendlícan onbide wæs (*quem cunctantem*), hwæðer hé winnan dorste, Ors. 4, 11; Swt. 204, 28. (2) where doubt is caused:—Is tweógendlíc ðysse worulde wela, Wulfst. 263, 11. Tweógendlícra gewrita *Apocryphorum*, Hpt. Gl. 522, 48. v. un-tweógendlíc.

tweógendlíce; *adv.* *Doubtingly, doubtfully*:—Sume hí twíendlíce be his lífe sprǽcon, and ðæt cwǽdon, ðæt hí nyston hwæðer hé on Godes mihte ða þing worhte ðe þurh deófles cræft, Guthl. 17; Gdwin. 70, 16. v. un-tweógendlíce.

tweógung, tweóung, e; *f.* *Doubt*:—Ðú mé hæfst gefrýlsod ðære tweóunge mínes módes be ðære ácsunga ðe ic ðé ácsode, Bt. 41, 3; Fox 248, 25.

tweohsn, tweoxn *occurs in the place name* Tweoxneám = *between streams*:—Ðone hám æt Winburnan and æt Tweoxneám (*Christchurch, in Hampshire*), Chr. 901; Erl. 96, 27. v. be-tweohsn; tweóne.

tweó-líc; *adj.* I. *doubtful, uncertain*:—Hit biþ twýlíc, hwæðer hit on lífe áðolige, Homl. Th. ii. 50, 24. *Dubii generis*, ðæt is twýlíces cynnes, Ælfc. Gr. 6, 6; Zup. 19, 17. Ðǽr beóþ kende *homodubii*, ðæt beóþ twílíce, Nar. 36, 18: 35, 3 note. II. *ambiguous*:—Ðá andwyrde hire se hálga mid twýlícere sprǽce, Homl. Th. ii. 146, 14. [*O. Frs.* twí-lík (twi-?) *doubtful.*] v. un-tweólíc, *and next word.*

tweólíce; *adv.* I. *doubtfully, uncertainly*:—Tweólíce and unfæsðlíce hé átiéfreþ ðæs ðinges onlícnesse on his móde, Past. 21; Swt. 157, 13. II. *ambiguously*:—Ondwyrdon hié him tweólíce *responso ambiguo*, Ors. 4, 1; Swt. 156, 3. v. un-tweólíce.

tweó-mann, es; *m.* *A creature about which it is doubtful whether it be human*:—*Homodubii* hý syndon hátene, ðæt beóþ twímen, Nar. 35, 3. v. tweó-líc.

tweón *doubt*:—Nis nán twýn, ðæt eów ne beó forgolden *there is no doubt, but that you will be requited*, Homl. Th. ii. 444, 10. Búton tweónne *without doubt*, Bt. 36, 6; Fox 182, 9. v. tweó.

tweón *to doubt*. v. tweógan.

tweóne. I. *two;* only in combination with the preposition *be*, either immediately following it (v. be-tweónum) or being separated from it by the governed noun, the two words together in either case having the force of *between*:—Be sǽm tweónum, ofer eormengrund, Beo. Th. 1721; B. 858: Exon. Th. 118, 10; Gú. 237. Be werum tweónum *among men*, Andr. Kmbl. 1116; An. 558. Hé wealdeþ be sǽ tweónum *dominabitur a mari usque ad mare*, Ps. Th. 71, 8. Cf. *O. H. Ger.* in zwiskên, untar zwiskên, *in later times* inzwischen, zwischen, *for a similar growth of adverb and preposition.* II. *double, not simple*:—Tweóne leóht *vel* deorcung *twilight, a mixture of light and darkness*, crepusculum, Wrt. Voc. i. 53, 3. v. tweónol, *and* cf. *O. H. Ger.* zwiski *biceps, non simplex, binus;* so iz under zuiskên liehten ist: *M. H. Ger.* zwischenlieht. [*Goth.* tweihnai: *Icel.* tvennr.]

tweónian, twínian, twýnian; *p.* ode. I. impersonal with dat. or acc. of person, *to cause doubt*, (a) absolute:—Mé twýnaþ (tweónaþ, MS. H.) *ambigo*, Ælfc. Gr. 28, 6; Zup. 176, 13. Gyt mé tweónaþ, Homl. Th. i. 72, 30. Gif hié giet ðǽr tweónaþ, Past. 16; Swt. 103, 9. Ðá twýnude (tweónode, MS. A.) him *haesitabat*, Lk. Skt. 9, 7: Homl. Th. ii. 392, 5. Hwí twýnode ðé?, 17. (b) with gen. of object of doubt:—Ðý læs ðe hwam twýnige ðyssere gereccednysse, Homl. Th. i. 598, 31. Hú mæg ðé nú twýnian ðæs écan leóhtes?, 160, 19. (c) with a preposition:—Gif hwam twýnige be ðam gemǽnelícum ǽriste, Homl. i. 132, 27. (d) with a gerundial infinitive:—Hwæt twýnaþ ðé, oþþe hwæt ondrǽst ðú ðé, ðone Hǽlend tó onfónne?, Nicod. 26; Thw. 14, 13. (e) with a clause:—Ðé ne twýnaþ nán ðing, ðæt ðú sáwle hæbbe, Homl. Th. i. 160, 21. Him twýnode be hwam hé hit sǽde *haesitantes de quo diceret*, Jn. Skt. 13, 22. Ús ne þearf ná twýnian, ðæt wé gebyrian ne sceolon odðe heofonwarena cyninge odðe hellewítes deóflum, Wulfst. 151, 19. II. with nom. of person, *to feel doubt, to doubt*, (a) absolute:—Se ðe ná twýnaþ on heortan his ac gelýfþ *qui non hesitauerit in corde suo sed crediderit*, Scint. 127, 1. Swá hwylc swá cwyþ . . . and on his heortan ne twýnaþ (tweónaþ, MS. A.), ac gelýfþ, Mk. Skt. 11, 23. Se is lytles geleáfan, se ðe hwæthwega gelýfþ and hwæthwega twýnaþ; se ðe mid ealle twýnaþ, hé is geleáfleás, Homl. Th. ii. 392, 17-19. Gif gé habbaþ geleáfan and ne twýniaþ (tweóniaþ, MS. A.), Mt. Kmbl. 21, 21. Hwí twýnedest (tweónedest, MS. A.) ðú *quare dubitasti?*, 14, 31. Sume hig tweónedon *quidam dubitaverunt*, 28, 17. (b) with gen. of object of doubt:—Ða beóþ áwyrigde ðe ðises twýniaþ, Homl. Skt. i. 5, 107. Hé beháte twíniende heofonlíces *ille promissi dubius superni*, Hymn. Surt. 103, 7. (c) with a preposition:—Ná twýna ðú ábútan ende *non dubites circa finem*, Scint. 27, 11. Ús is álýfed be ðisum tó twýnienne, Homl. Th. ii. 520, 16. (d) with a clause:—Hé árás, on his móde tweónigende hú heó mihte Iordanes wæteru oferfaran, Homl. Skt. ii. 23 b, 680. [Ȝunge monnan mei tweonian hweðer hí moten a libban, O. E. Homl. i. 109, 14. Þa wile þe heo tweoneden þus, Laym. 907.] v. ge-tweónian; tweógan.

tweónigend, es; *m.* *One who doubts* or *hesitates*:—Twýnigend *hic et haec anceps*, Ælfc. Gr. 9, 55; Zup. 67, 9.

tweónigend-líc; *adj.* *Expressing doubt*:—Sume syndon *dubitativa*, ðæt synd twýnigendlíce (tweóniend-, MS. H.), Ælfc. Gr. 38; Zup. 228, 16. Twýniendlíce, 44; Zup. 261, 2.

tweónol, twýnol; *adj.* *Doubtful*:—Tweónul leóht *maligna lux* vel *dubia*, Wrt. Voc. i. 53, 6. Swá swá his genyþerung ungewiss ys swá eác forgyfenyss twýnol *sicut ejus damnatio incerta est, sic et remissio dubia*, Scint. 46, 1. Ðæt deorc ys oþþe twýnol *quod obscurum est aut dubium*, 222, 3.

tweónum. v. tweóne.

tweónung, twínung, twýnung, e; *f.* *Doubt, uncertainty, hesitation*:—Ðam men biþ módes tweónung, Lchdm. ii. 194, 3. Ðæra apostola tweónung be Cristes ǽriste, Homl. Th. i. 300, 33. Ðam deófle wæs micel twýnung, hwæt Crist wǽre, 168, 10. Ðý læs ðe ǽnig twýning eów derian mǽge be ðam líflícan gereorde, ii. 262, 24. Tw(e)ónunge *ambiguitatis, dubietatis*, Hpt. Gl. 422, 32. Went nú moncyn on tweónunga *men will be in doubt*, Bt. 4; Fox 8, 18. Hí búton ǽlcere tweónunge sceolon on écnesse forwurðan, Homl. Ass. 145, 37. Bútan twýnunge *absque ambiguitate*, Ælfc. Gr. 272, 13: *sine dubitatione*, R. Ben. Interl. 52, 12: *sine scrupulo*, Anglia xiii. 367, 24. Gyt mé tweónaþ; ac gif ðú ðás deádan sceaðan árǽrst, ðonne biþ mín heorte geclǽnsod fram ǽlcere twýnunge, Homl. Th. i. 72, 32. Twúnunge, twínunge *scrupulum, dubitationem*, Hpt. Gl. 504, 77. Sume syndon *dubitativa*, . . . ðás getácniaþ twýnunge, Ælfc. Gr. 38; Zup. 229, 2. Ic mid tweóningum óðrum monnum bigleofan gesette *cum aliqua scrupulositate a nobis mensura victus aliorum constituitur*, R. Ben. 64, 11. Hí ádrǽfdon ealle twýnunga fram úre heortan, Homl. Th. i. 302, 3.

tweóung, tweowa. v. tweógung, twiwa.

twí *a twig*. v. twig.

twi-, *in composition with force of* two. v. following words. [*O. Frs. O. L. Ger.* twi-: *O. H. Ger.* zwi-: *Icel.* tví-.]

twía. v. twiwa.

twi-béte; *adj.* *Needing double compensation;* a term applied to an offence when from special circumstances the *bót* was twice that to be paid in an ordinary case:—Gif hwá nunnan mid hǽmedþinge oþþe on hire hrægl oþþe on hire breóst bútan hire leáfe gefó, sié hit twybéte, (twibóte, MS. B.: twybóte, MS. H.) swá wé ǽr be lǽwdum men fundon (*in the case of a nun the* bót *for the offences referred to was twice that in the case of a lay woman;* the case of the latter is the subject of sect. 11; Th. i. 68, 13-70, 2), L. Alf. pol. 18; Th. i. 72, 10. Gif hwá lengctenbryce gewyrce . . . þurh ǽnige heálíce misdǽda, sý ðæt twybéte (twibóte, MS. B.), L. C. S. 48; Th. i. 404, 1. [*O. Frs.* twi-béte (*with the same use as the English word*).] v. twi-bóte.

twi-bill, es; *n.*: twi-bile, es; *m.* *A two-edged axe*:—Twibill *bipinnis*, Wrt. Voc. ii. 12, 52. Twybill *bipennis*, i. 36, 5. Twilafte æx *vel* twibile *bipennis securis*, ii. 126, 28. Twybile (-bil, MS. W.) *bipennis*, Ælfc. Gr. 9, 28; Zup. 56, 9. Twibille *bipinnae* (= *bipenne*), Ps. Surt. 73, 6. Hé nam sum twibil and mid ðan þrý men tó deáðe ofslóh, Guthl. 12; Gdwin. 56, 23. Æcsa, twibilles (-as?) *bipennes* ꝉ *secures*, Hpt. Gl. 459, 2. [Twybyle (*printed* twybyl, Wrt. Voc. i. 196, 10) *bipennis* (in a list 'nomina armorum'), Wülck. Gl. 654, 2. Twybyl *bisacuta*, 568, 21 (both 15th cent. glossaries). Twybyl, wryhtys instrument *bisacuta*, *biceps*; twybyl or mattoke *marra*, *ligo*, Prompt. Parv. 505. A twybylle *biceps*, *bipennis*, *bisacuta*, Cath. Angl. 398, and see note. The word remains in some dialects, v. E. D. S. Pub. West Somerset Dialect, under *two-bill*, and Halliwell's Dict. *twibil*.] v. next word.

twi-bille; *adj. Double-edged*:—*Bipennis* twibille *vel* stānæx (the double gloss seems to render the double character of the Latin word as adjective and noun; a little later (see preceding word) in the same glossary *bipennis* as noun is rendered by *twybill*), Wrt. Voc. i. 34, 60.

twi-bleó; *adj. Double-dyed*:—Of twibleóum derodine *bis tincto cocco*, Wrt. Voc. ii. 126, 30. Tweobleóm (twiblīum, Cott. MSS.), Past. 14; Swt. 83, 23. Tōeácan ðæm twiblión (-bleón, Cott. MSS.) godwebbe, Swt. 87, 18.

twi-bōt (?) *double 'bōt.'* Perhaps in the passages given under twibōte; *adv.* the word might be taken as a case of this noun. Cf. twi-gilde. [Cf. the Scandinavian law phrases, liggi i tveböte, tväbötis drap, v. Grmm. R. A. 653. *Swed.* twe-böte a *double fine*.]

twi-bōte; *adj. Needing double compensation.* v. twi-bēte:—Se ðe stalaþ on Gehhol oþþe on Eástron oþþe on ðone Hālgan Ðunresdæg . . ., ðara gehwelc (*the offence in each of these cases*) wē willaþ sié twybōte, swā on Lenctenfæsten, L. Alf. pol. 5; Th. i. 64, 25. Gif ðisses hwæt gelimpe þenden fyrd ūte sié, oþþe in Lenctenfæsten, hit sié twybōte, 40; Th. i. 88, 12. v. next word.

twibōte; *adv. With double 'bōt'*:—Gif hē ōdswerian nylle, gebēte ðone mǣnan āð twibōte, L. In. 35; Th. i. 124, 13. ii-bōte gebēte, L. Ethb. 3; Th. i. 4, 2: 2; Th. i. 2, 9. v. twi-bōt.

twi-browen; *adj.* (*ptcpl.*) *Twice-brewed*:—On twybrownum ealað, Lchdm. ii. 120, 10.

twi-bytme (?); *adj. Double-bottomed*:—On ðæt twigbutme del; of ðam delle on beran del, Cod. Dip. Kmbl. v. 28, 19. v. bytm.

twiccere, es; *m. One who pulls to pieces*:—Twickere *offarius* vel *particularius* (particularius *minister in monasteriis, qui cibos per partes dissecat singulis monachis*, Migne), Wrt. Voc. i. 27, 20. v. next word.

twiccian; *p.* ode *To twitch, pluck*:—Twiccaþ *villicat*, Wrt. Voc. ii. 97, 14. Sume (*ants*) hió twiccedan ða grasu mid heora mūðe, Shrn. 41, 2. Teóh him ða loccas, wringe ða eáran and ðone wangbeard twiccige, Lchdm. ii. 196, 13. Twiccian *carpere*, *arripere*, Wrt. Voc. ii. 128, 69. [Twykkyn̄, twychyn *tractulo*, Prompt. Parv. 505. *In Mid. E. the past is* twighte. Cf. *O. H. Ger.* zwecchōn *carpere*: *M. H. Ger. Ger.* zwicken.]

twicen, e: twicene, an; *f. A place where two roads meet*:—Twicen *ambitus*, Wrt. Voc. i. 37, 46. On twycenan (-cinan, MS. B.) *in biuio*, Mk. Skt. 11, 4. Of ðære mere on ða twycene; of ðære twycenan, Cod. Dip. Kmbl. iii. 77, 4. On ða smalan twichenan; and swā andlang twichenan, 240, 20. Tō ðere twichenen; of ðere twichene, 201, 27.

twidæg-līc. v. twādæg-līc.

twi-dǣl *a double portion, two parts out of three*:—Dō gegrundenne pipor on, and cropleác, hwǣtenes melwes twidǣl swilce ðæs pipores *twice as much wheaten meal as pepper, two parts of meal to one of pepper*, Lchdm. ii. 52, 22. Genim heorotcrop and saluian, bewyl twydǣl on wætre *boil away two parts out of three*, 50, 12. Cf. twǣde.

twi-dǣlan; *p.* de. I. *to divide in two*:—Twidǣledre *bifori*, twidǣledu (v. Wülck. Gl. 194, 24) *bifida*, *bis divisa*, Wrt. Voc. ii. 126, 13, 16. Ðone twydǣledan wīsdōm, ðæt is andweardra þinga and gāstlicra wīsdōm, Lchdm. iii. 440, 29. Ðās twidǣledan *hanc bipartitam*, *divisam in duas partes*, Hpt. Gl. 434, 32. II. *to differ*:—Twydǣlþ *discrepat*, Scint. 125, 6. Hī cristenre lāre twydǣlaþ *christianae doctrinae dissentiunt*, 129, 10.

Twide, Tweode, an; *or indecl.* (cf. Humbre *for declension*); *f. The Tweed*:—In ōfre Tweode (Tuidon, Bd. M. 360, 29) streámes *in ripa Tuidi fluminis*, Bd. 4, 27; S. 603, 34.

twidig. v. lang-twidig.

twi-ecge; *adj. Two-edged*:—Twiicce *biceps* (*gladius*, Prov. 5, 4), Kent. Gl. 87. Mid twyecgum *bipenne*, Ps. Th. 73, 6. Hæfde hē twiecge handseax *habebat sicam bicipitem*, Bd. 2, 9; M. 122, 12. Genim ðæt micle greáte windelstreáw twyecge, Lchdm. ii. 44, 5. Sweord twiecge *gladii ancipites*, Ps. Surt. 149, 6. [*O. H. Ger.* zwi-ekki.]

twi-ecgede; *adj. Two-edged*:—Twyecgede *anceps*, *biceps*, Ælfc. Gr. 9, 55; Zup. 67, 9, 10. Sworde twyecgedes *gladii ancipites*, Ps. Spl. 149, 6. Hæfde hē twigecgede (twyecge, MS.B.) handseax *habebat sicam bicipitem*, Bd. 2, 9; S. 511, 15. [*Icel.* tvī-eggjaðr.]

twīendlīce. v. tweógendlīce.

twi-feald; *adj. Twofold*, *double*:—Twyfeald *duplex*, Ælfc. Gr. 9, 61; Zup. 70, 2: *geminus*, Wrt. Voc. ii. 42, 1: 44, 21: 41, 58. I. as a multiplicative, *twice as much*, *of twice the amount*:—Gyt synd manega getel on mislīcum getācnungum . . . *duplex* twyfeald, Ælfc. Gr. 49; Zup. 287, 2. Ic ādreáh mycel broc mid Petre; nū is mīn yfel twyfeald, nū Paulus ðæt ilce lǣreþ, Blickl. Homl. 175, 13. Twifealdum gāste (*Helisaeus Heliae*) *duplo* (*ditatus*) *spiritu*, Hpt. Gl 440, 47. Twifealdre gife *bino munere*, Wrt. Voc. ii. 126, 26: Blickl. Homl. 101, 23. Be twyfealdum ic forgylde *duplum*, Ælfc. Gr. 49; Zup. 286, 17: L. Alf. 25; Th. i. 50, 23: Homl. Th. ii. 562, 1. Hē him sylþ twifealdne mete (*cibos duplices*), Ex. 16, 29. 'Nymaþ twā swā micel fecs swā gē ǣr hæfdon' . . . Ðā nāmon hig twigfeald feoh '*pecuniam duplicem ferte*' . . . *Tulerunt ergo pecuniam duplicem*, Gen. 43, 12–15. II. *consisting of two items*:—Twyfealdre heolra *bilance*, Wrt. Voc. ii. 12, 1. Næbbe gē mid eów twyfeald hrægl (næbbe gē twā tunecan, Mt. Kmbl. 10, 10), Blickl. Homl. 233, 18. II a. *consisting of two parts*, *containing two elements*:—Ðæt twiefalde (twyfealde, Cott. MSS.) gesuinc . . . ðæt is ðæt hié ondrǣdaþ ðæt hī mon tǣlan wille . . . ; ōðer is ðara gesuinca ðæt hī sēceaþ endeleáse lādunga, Past. 35; Swt. 239, 4-8. Twufald intinge *duplex causa*, Mt. Kmbl. p. 1, 10. II b. *that belongs to one or other of two kinds*:—Ege is twyfeald, and ðeówdōm is twyfeald. Ān ege is būtan lufe, ōðer is mid lufe . . . Swā is eác ōðer ðeówt neádunge būton lufe, ōðer is sylfwilles mid lufe, Homl. Th. ii. 524, 3–6. Wē tweofealdne deáþ ðrowiaþ, oþþe sticode beóþ, oþþe on sǣ ādruncene *oriuntur duo genera funerum, aut jugulamur, aut mergimur*, Bd. 1, 13; S. 482, 1. III. *doubtful*, *irresolute*: v. twifealdness, II:—Hē ða yfelan and ða twyfealdan geþōhtas forlēt (cf. hē hine hider and þyder gelōmlīce on his mōde cyrde, 28, 8; hē ðām tweógendum geþōhtum widstōd, 18), and hine Scs Bartholomeus frēfrode, and hine hēt ðæt hē ne tweóde, ac ðæt hē wǣre ānrǣd, Guthl. 4; Gdwin. 30, 3–7. IV. *double* (as in *double* dealing), *not straightforward*, *deceitful*. v. twifealdness, III:—Dōmes dæg ārāfaþ ðæt cliwen ðære twifaldan (twyfealdan, Cott. MSS.) heortan *corda duplicitatibus involuta dissolvit*, Past. 35; Swt. 245, 22. Se ðe mid twyfealdum geðance tō mynsterlīcre drohtnunge gecyrþ, and sumne dǣl his ǣhta dǣlþ, sumne him sylfum gehylt, . . . hē underfēhþ ðone āwyrgedan cwyde mid Annanian and Saphiran, ðe swicedon on heora āgenum ǣhtum, Homl. Th. i. 398, 28–33: ii. 410, 32. Ðæt is syndrig yfel twiefealdra (twy-, Cott. MSS.) monna *est speciale duplicium malum*, Past. 35; Swt. 243, 24. Unclǣnu and twiefeald mōd *impura corda*, Swt. 245, 12. V. *double* (as in bent *double*), *placed together*:—Ǣlc wāg biþ gebiéged twiefeald on ðæm heale *duplex semper est in angulis paries*, Past. 35; Swt. 245, 13. Ðæt yfelwillende mōd gefielt hit self twyfeald oninnan him selfum, and sió twyfealdnes ðæs yflan willan hiene selfne twyfealdne gefielt oninnan him selfum *malitiosae mentis duplicitas sese infra se colligit*, 242, 6–9. [*O. Frs.* twi-fald: *O. L. Ger.* twi-veld, -fold: *O. H. Ger.* zwi-falt: *Icel.* tvī-faldr.] v. un-twifeald.

twifealdan. v. twifildan.

twifeald-līc; *adj. Double*:—Twyfealdlīc onbryrdnes eges and lufe, Homl. Th. i. 140, 16. Tuifallīco glædniso *geminata laetitia*, Rtl. 57, 2. Tuufallīce gāst *utriusque spiritus*, Mt. Kmbl. p. 14, 5. [Ðysra deáð wæs heora freóndan twyfealdlīc sār; ān, ðet hī swā feárlīce ðises līfes losedan; ōðer, ꝥ feáwa heora līchaman syððan fundena wǣron, Chr. 1120; Erl. 248, 12.] [*O. H. Ger.* zwifalt-līh: *Icel.* tvīfald-ligr.]

twifealdlīce; *adv. Doubly*, (1) *to twice the amount*:—On ðam sixtan dæge hig gaderodon twyfealdlīce *in die sexta collegerunt cibos duplices*, Ex. 16, 22: L. Alf. pol. 39; Th. i. 88, 4. Gē gedōþ hyne helle bearn twyfealdlīcor ðonne eów (*duplo quam vos*), Mt. Kmbl. 23, 15. (2) *in two ways*:—Ðis godspel mæg beón twyfealdlīce getrahtnod, ǣrest be Iudēiscum folce . . . , eft siððan be ǣlcum menn, Homl. Th. ii. 428, 5. Se biþ twyfealdlīce deád, se ðe on gōdnysse unwæstmbǣre biþ, and on yfelnysse wæstmbǣre, 406, 18.

twifealdness, e; *f.* I. *doubleness*, *doubling*. v. twi-feald, I:—Geedlǣcend twyfealdnys *iterata dupplicatio*, Anglia viii. 331, 23. II. *irresolution*. v. twi-feald, III:—Of ðære leóhtmōdnesse cymþ sió twiefealdnes and sió unbieldo *inconstantia ex levitate generatur*, Past. 42; Swt. 307, 3. III. *duplicity*, *deceitfulness*. v. twi-feald, IV:—Sió twyfealdness ðæs yflan willan *malitiosae mentis duplicitas*, Past. 35; Swt. 242, 8. Ða ðe nān sceadu ne geðiéstraþ ðære twiefaldnesse *quos nulla umbra duplicitatis obscurat*, Swt. 243, 23. Se iil getācnaþ ða twiefealdnesse ðæs unclǣnan mōdes ðe hit symle lytiglīce lādaþ *ericii nomine impurae mentis seseque callide defendentis duplicitas designatur*, Swt. 241, 8.

twi-ferclede. v. twi-fyrclede.

twi-fēre; *adj. Having two ways*, *accessible by two ways*:—Twifērum *bilustris* (cf. færeltu *lustra*, 53, 21, geondfērende *lustraturus*, 53, 54; *and see* un-fēre *invius*), Wrt. Voc. ii. 126, 22.

twi-fērlǣcan; *p.* -lǣhte *To dissociate*:—Ða ðe hī sylfe fram sōðre lufe twyfērlǣcaþ (-eþ, MS.) *qui semetipsos a caritate dissociant*, Scint. 6, 8.

twi-fēte; *adj. Two-footed*:—Twyfēte *bipes*, Ælfc. Gr. 9, 26; Zup. 51, 11: 49; Zup. 287, 20. Sume bīþ twiofēte, Bt. 41, 6; Fox 254, 27. [*Icel.* tvī-fættr.]

twifildan; *p.* de *To double*:—Ic twyfylde (-fealde, MSS. J. O. T.: -felde, MS. D.) *duplico*, Ælfc. Gr. 24; Zup. 138, 12: 49; Zup. 287, 4. Twyfeldende mæssehacelan *duplicans casulam*, Anglia xiii. 406, 587. [Cf. *O. H. Ger.* zwifaltōn *geminare*: *Icel.* tvīfalda.]

twi-fingre; *adj. Two fingers thick*, term applied to the fat on swine:—Æt twyfingrum (spic), L. In. 49; Th. i. 132, 19.

twi-fiðerede; *adj. Double-winged*, *shaped as if with two wings* (?), *forked*:—Twyfyrede (twyfyþerede, MS. C.: twifeðerede, MS. V.) *bisulcus* Ælfc. Gr. 49; Zup. 288, 11.

twi-fyrclede; *adj. Having two prongs, forked*:—Twyferclede *bifidus*, Ælfc. Gr. 49; Zup. 288, 10 note. [Cf. Wæs gesæwen swilce se beám (*the tail of a comet*) ongeánweardes wið ðes steorran ward fyrcliende wǽre *as if the tail were dividing in two, getting forked* (?), Chr. 1106; Erl. 240, 34. *Lat.* furculus *a fork with two or three prongs.*]

Twi-fyrd, -ford *Twyford*, a place-name occurring more than once in England and meaning *double ford*:—On ðære stówe ðe is cweden Æt Twyfyrde *in loco qui dicitur Ad Twifyrde, quod significat, ad duplex vadum*, Bd. 4, 28; S. 606, 5. Æt Twyfyrde, Cod. Dip. Kmbl. i. 114, 33. Tó Twyfyrde, iii. 203, 22. Of Twufyrde . . . æft on Twyfyrde, v. 147, 28–148, 22. On Twyfyrd; of Twyfyrde, iii. 444, 7. ¶ In Latin charters:—His nuncupantur uocabulis, Twyfyrde . . ., 153, 24. Apud Twyfird, v. 130, 31. *The form* Twyford *also occurs*:—Of Twyforde andlang Auene ðære eá swá ðæt mynstre stondeþ ofer Alne streám, vi. 220, 5. Cf. Circum fluuium Alne in loco qui dicitur Aet Tuiford, i. 29, 6. In loco qui Tuiforda appellatur, 74, 31.

twi-fyrede; *adj. Two-furrowed*; the word renders the Latin *bisulcus*, Ælfc. Gr. 49; Zup. 288, 11. [Cf. *O. H. Ger.* zwi-furhi, -furhig *bisulcus.*] v. furh.

twig, twí, es; *n. A branch, twig*:—Twig *ramus*, Wrt. Voc. i. 285, 80: *palmes*, Jn. Skt. 15, 6. Hys twig (twi *later MS.*) byþ hnesce, Mt. Kmbl. 24, 32. His twí (twig, MS. A.: twi *later MS.*) biþ mearu, Mk. Skt. 13, 28. Ic eom swá ðæt twig, ðæt biþ ácorfen of ðam treówe, Homl. Skt. ii. 30, 191. Hé déþ ǽlc twig áweg, Jn. Skt. 15, 2. Of ðam twige (*Abel's murder*) ludon réðe wæstme, Cd. Th. 60, 28; Gen. 988. Heó brohte án twig (*ramum*) of ánum elebeáme, Gen. 8, 11: Cd. Th. 88, 30; Gen. 1473. Gé synt twigu (*palmites*), Jn. Skt. 15, 5. Him ða twigu þincaþ merge, Met. 13, 44. Twigu *arbusta* (twigges, Ps.), Ps. Spl. 79, 11: Blickl. Gl. Ðonne ða twigo forburston, ðonne gewitan ða sáula niðer, ða ðe on ðǽm twigum hangodan, Blickl. Homl. 211, 3. Tán ł twiga *vimina, virgulas*, Hpt. Gl. 428, 34. Twiga *asserum*, Wrt. Voc. ii. 10, 10. Eft spryttendum ðám twigum (*virgultis*) ðæs Pelagianiscan wóles, Bd. 1, 21; S. 485, 5. Swilce se wudubeám oferfæðmde ealne middangeard twigum and telgum, Cd. Th. 247, 28; Dan. 504: 248, 18; Dan. 515. Sume twigu hé lehte mid wætere, Past. 40; Swt. 293, 7. Hí námon palmtrýwa twigu (*ramos palmarum*), Jn. Skt. 12, 13. Genim wiþowindan twigu, Lchdm. ii. 34, 17. Sume seóþaþ ðære reádan netlan twigu, 218, 6. Twigo settende *propagines pastinans*, Wrt. Voc. ii. 78, 63. [Heo nomen þa twigga, O. E. Homl. i. 5, 2. He suinged him mið smele twige, 149, 1. Þe uerþe tuyg, Ayenb. 22, 5. Twygge *virgula, ramusculus*, Prompt. Parv. 505: *vimen*, Wülck. Gl. 619, 27. *O. H. Ger.* zwíg, zwí: *Ger.* zweig.] v. ele-, ifig-, palm-, wín-twig; twigu, -twige.

twig-, twiga. v. twi-, twiwa.

twi-gǽrede; *adj. Cloven*:—Twygǽrede *bifidus*, Ælfc. Gr. 49; Zup. 288, 10. Cf. Bufan ðam hlince æt ðæs gǽredan (*pointed, angular*) landes ende, Cod. Dip. B. iii. 251, 42. v. gár, gára.

twige, twigea. v. twiwa.

-twige. v. líne-, þistel-twige.

twi-gedeágod; *adj. Double-dyed*:—Twigedeágodre deáge *bis tincto cocco*, Hpt. Gl. 431, 29.

twi-gilde (?), es; *n. A double payment*:—Hé ágife twygilde (*or adverb* (?) v. *passages under* twigilde; *adv., where, however, the word might be taken as a case of the noun*; cf. án-gilde *which is a noun*), L. Eth. iii. 4; Th. i. 294, 20. [*O. Frs.* twi-ielde, v. Richthofen s. v. ield, and Grmm. R. A. 653.] v. next word.

twi-gilde; *adj. To be paid double*:—Cyricfrið ii-gylde, m[ynster]frið ii-gylde, L. Ethb. 1; Th. i. 2, 6. ii-gelde seó mund sý, 76; Th. i. 20, 13. [*Icel.* tví-gildr *of double value.*] v. next word.

twigilde; *adv. With a double payment*:—Gif ðeós lád teorie, gylde twygylde (cf. gylde ángyldes, l. 15), L. O. D. 6; Th. i. 354, 31. Gif þeów steleþ, ii-gelde gebéte, L. Ethb. 90; Th. i. 24, 17. Béte hé ðam teónde twygylde, and ðam hláforde his were, L. Eth. i. 1; Th. i. 280, 20. Béte hé ðam teónde twygylde, and ðam hláforde his wer, L. C. S. 30; Th. i. 394, 6. Sió bót biþ twysceatte (twyggylde, MS. B.) máre *the bót shall be twice as much*, L. Alf. pol. 66; Th. i. 96, 31. v. two preceding words.

twigu (?), an; *f.*; *the forms in the Northern specimens may also be taken as weak*, tuigge, *pl.* tuiggo *A branch, twig*:—Steola *cauliculus*, twigu *ramunculus*, Wrt. Voc. ii. 129, 84. Twigge ł telge (telgra, Rush.) *ramus*, Mt. Kmbl. Lind. 24, 32: Mk. Skt. Lind. 13, 28. Ðe tuigga *palmes*, Jn. Skt. Lind. 15, 6. Ða tuiggo (twigan *late southern MS.*) *palmites*, 15, 5. Telgo míno and twiggo *ramos meos, et rami*, Rtl. 68, 32. Twigena ordum, Salm. Kmbl. 286; Sal. 142. In tyggum his *in ramis ejus*, Mt. Kmbl. Lind. 13, 32. Tuiggo *ramos*, 21, 8. Telgo ł twiggo, Mk. Skt. Lind. 4, 32: 11, 8. v. twig.

-twih (-twíh?). v. be-twih. [Cf. *Goth.* tweihnai.]

twi-heáfdode; *adj. Double-headed*:—Twyheáfdede *anceps, biceps*, Ælfc. Gr. 9, 55; Zup. 67, 9, 10. Twyheáfdede oððe se ðe hæfþ twégen líchaman *bicorpor*, 9, 21; Zup. 47, 17. [*O. H. Ger.* zwi-haupito *biceps*: *Icel.* tví-höfðaðr.]

twi-heolor, e; *f. A balance*:—Tuiheolore *bilance*, Wrt. Voc. ii. 102, 3. Twiwǽge *vel* (twi)heolore, 126, 20.

twi-híwe; *adj.* I. *of two forms* or *shapes*:—Twihiówe, swá swá biþ healf mon and healf fear *biformis*, Wrt. Voc. ii. 12, 31. Twihíwe *biformia*, 126, 12. II. *of two colours*:—Twihíwe *bicolor*, Wrt. Voc. i. 46, 34. Twihíwe godweb *coccum bis tinctum*, ii. 135, 44. Twiférum *vel* (twi)híwum *bilustris*, 126, 22. v. next word.

twi-híwede; *adj.* I. *double-shaped, having two forms*:—Twyhíwede *biformis*, Ælfc. Gr. 49; Zup. 287, 9. II. *double-coloured*:—Twyhíwedum wurman *bis tincto cocco*, Hpt. Gl. 431, 30.

twi-híwian; *p.* ode *To assume two shapes, to dissimulate*:—Oððe hé nát oððe hé twyhíwaþ *aut ignorat, aut dissimulat*, Scint. 44, 8.

twi-hlidede; *adj. Double-lidded, having two openings*:—Twyhlydede *bipatens*, Ælfc. Gr. 49; Zup. 288, 6.

-twihn (-twíhn?) *in* bi-twichn, Txts. 70, 546, bi-tuihn, 77, 1310.

twi-hweóle; *adj. Two-wheeled*:—Twihweólne *birotum*, Lchdm. i. lxii, 2.

twi-hwirft, es; *m. A double course, double period*:—Twyhwyrftum (*printed* -hwyrhtum) *bilustris*, Hpt. Gl. 465, 40.

twi-hycgan (?) *to think differently, dissent, disagree*:—Twy iccende (=twyhycgende?) *dissentiendo*, Anglia xiii. 367, 34.

twi-hynde; *adj.* As applied to a person, *of a rank for which the wergild was two hundred shillings*; applied to the wergild, *that must be paid for a person of such rank.* As will be seen from the passages given below, the *twihynde man* was a *ceorl*:—Twelfhyndes mannes wer is twelf hund scyllinga. Twyhyndes mannes wer is twá hund scill. (*the article then deals with the case of the former, and concludes*: Eal man sceal æt cyrliscum were be ðære mǽðe dón, ðe him tó gebyreþ, swá wé be twelfhyndum tealdan. Cf. too: Ceorles wergild is . . . ii hund scill. be Myrcna lage, L. Wg. 6; Th. i. 186, 11), L. E. G. 12; Th. i. 174, 14. Ǽnig mǽgð . . . xii-hynde oððe twyhynde, L. Ath. v. 8, 2; Th. i. 236, 11. Be twyhyndum were. Æt twyhyndum were mon sceal sellan tó monbóte .xxx. scill., L. In. 70; Th. i. 146, 12. Be twyhyndum men . . . Gif mon twyhyndne mon . . . ofsleá, L. Alf. pol. 29; Th. i. 80, 5–7. Cnut cing grét . . . ealle míne þegnas, twelfhynde and twihynde, Chart. Th. 308, 16. v. six-, twelf-hynde.

twi-icce. v. twi-ecge.

twi-læpped; *adj. Having two skirts* or *lappets*:—Twilæpped scrúd *cinctus gabinus*, Wrt. Voc. i. 41, 5.

twi-lafte; *adj. Two-edged*:—Twilafte æx *bipennis securis*, Wrt. Voc. ii. 126, 27. Cf. (?) læppa *or* læfer.

twi-líc, twi-lí (-li?); *adj. Double, woven of double thread.* Cf. *twill* coarse linen cloth:—Tuilí *biplex, duplex*, Txts. 109, 1151. Aenlí *simplex*, tilí *bilex*, 115, 156, 157. [*O. H. Ger.* zui-líh *bilex* (*tunica*), *bissina* (*tunica*), *biplex* (*pannus*): *Ger.* zwillich *ticking.*] Cf. þri-líc, *and see* twilíc-brocen.

twí-líc, -líce, -mann. v. tweó-líc, -líce, -mann.

twilíc-brocen; *adj. Woven of double thread and parti-coloured* (?) or *embroidered* (?):—Hió becwið hyre twilíbrocenan cyrtel, Chart. Th. 537, 23. [Cf. (?) *Swed.* brokig: *Dan.* broget *parti-coloured. Jamieson gives* brocked, broukit, broked *variegated, having a mixture of black and white.* Cf. (?) Celtic forms *Welsh* brech *brindled*: *Irish* breacan *a plaid, tartan*; breacaim *I chequer, embroider.*]

twin; *adj. Twin, double*:—Twinnum sangum *geminis concentibus*, Hpt. Gl. 467, 31. [An had off twinne (*double*) kinde, Orm. 1361. He spacc off hise twinne kindess (*two, twin, natures*), 17478. On ilc he brend twin der (*Balaam offered on every altar a bullock and a ram*, Num. 23, 2), Gen. and Ex. 4020. Iosep gaf ilc here twinne srud (*to all of them he gave each man change of raiment*, Gen. 45, 22), 2367. On twinne half, 3248. *O. Frs.* twiska tuine kindem: *Icel.* tvinnr.] v. ge-twin.

twín, es; *n. Linen*:—Tuum (tuuín?), tuigin, tuín *byssum*, Txts. 44, 138. Twín, Wrt. Voc. ii. 11, 14. Twiðrǽwen twín (*torta byssus*) . . . ðæt geðrǽwene twín, Past. 14; Swt. 87, 18, 42: Swt. 89, 2. Of twispunnenum twíne línenum *torta bysso*, Swt. 83, 23. Mid geedþrǽwenum twíne *cum bysso retorto*, Hpt. Gl. 431, 38: Wrt. Voc. ii. 11, 70: Kent. Gl. 1145. Gescrýdd mid twíne (mið linnenom, Lind. *bysso*), Lk. Skt. 16, 19. [*Later the word is used as in mod. English.* A twines (twined, 2nd MS.) þræd, Laym. 14220. Twyne, threede *filum torsum* vel *tortum*, Prompt. Parv. 505. *Du.* twijn *twine, twist.*] v. twínen.

twinclian; *p.* ode *To twinkle*:—Se spearca ðara gódra weorca ðe tuinclaþ beforan mannum *cuncta, quae coram hominibus rutilant*, Past. 14; Swt. 87, 6. Ic ðæt lytle leóht geseah twinclian, Bt. 35, 3; Fox 158, 32.

twi-nebbe; *adj. Having two faces*:—Twynebbe *bifrontem*, Germ. 397, 448.

twínen; *adj. Of linen, linen*:—Bam (*read* ham, v. *the corresponding gloss* ham *subucula*, Hpt. Gl. 526, 30: *at the same place*, byssina *is rendered by* línen) twínen *subucula bissina*, Anglia xiii. 37, 285. v. twín.

twing (twyng?) *what is pressed together* (?), *a mass, lump*:—Twinga *massas*, Hpt. Gl. 496, 70. v. next word.

twingan (?); *p.* twang; *pp.* twungen *To press, force*:—Se hrȳnđ (tringaþ (twingeþ?), MS. M.) muntas *qui tangit montes*, Ps. Spl. 103, 33. [I am twinged (twungen, MS. H.) and meked *incurbatus sum et humiliatus sum*, Ps. 37, 9. Whil þat twinges (*affligit*) me þe fo, 41, 10. *Ger.* zwingen.] v. twengan.

twînian. v. tweónian.

twi-nihte; *adj. Two days old*:—Twynihte grūt, Lchdm. ii. 74, 9. v. twā-nihte.

twinn, twînung. v. twin, tweónung.

twîn-wyrm (twin-?), es; *m.* The word glosses *buprestis* (= βούπρηστις *a poisonous beetle, which when eaten by cattle in the grass caused them to swell up*), Wrt. Voc. i. 24, 35.

twio-fête, twiógan, twio-rǣde. v. twi-fēte, tweógan, twi-rǣde.

twi-rǣde; *adj.* I. *of two minds, uncertain, undecided, irresolute*:—Geþenc be đē selfum hwæđer đū ǣnig đing swā fæste getiohhod hæbbe đæt đē þynce đæt hit nǣfre đīnum willum onwended weorþe . . . Ođđe hwæđer đū eft on ǣngum geþeahte swā twiorǣde sié đæt đē helpe hwæđer hit gewyrþe þe hit nō ne gewyrþe *consider in your own case whether you have so firmly determined anything, that it appears to you, that it will never with your consent be changed . . . Or again, whether in any plan you are so uncertain, that it may help you, if it is carried out, or if it is not*, Bt. 41, 3; Fox 250, 5-9. II. *of divided counsel, without unanimity*:—Ǣlc rīce đe byþ twyrǣde on him sylfum *omne regnum divisum contra se*, Mt. Kmbl. 12, 25. [Bruttes weoren alle twiræde, heore teone wes þa mare, Laym. 19416.] v. ān-ræde, *and next word.*

twirǣdness, e; *f. Discord, dissension, disagreement*:—Sacu and twirǣdnyss (*strife, seditions*, Gal. 5, 20), Homl. Skt. i. 17, 26. Đæt swā hweþer swā hit wǣre swā sibb swā twyrēdnys betweónan Saxan and Myrcenum, đæt đæt mynster beó ǣfre on sibbe, Cod. Dip. B. i. 156, 16. Se đe sibbe Drihtnes twyrǣdnysse mid hātheortnysse tōbrycþ *qui pacem Domini discordiae furore rumpit*, Scint. 10, 2. God nā ys twyrǣdnysse (*dissensionis*) God, 134, 6. Be twirǣdnysse *de discordia*, 133, 17. Se wæs for sumere twyrǣdnesse (*seditione*) on cwertern āsend, Lk. Skt. 23, 19. Đa đe ceáste and twyrǣdnysse styredon, Homl. Th. ii. 338, 11. Đonne gē geseóþ gefeoht and twyrǣdnessa (*seditiones*), Lk. Skt. 21, 9. Twyrēdnysse *dissensiones*, R. Ben. Interl. 109, 17. Twirēdnesse *discordias*, Kent. Gl. 1124.

-twis, -twisa. v. ge-twis, -twisa.

twi-sceatte; *adv. To the extent of a double payment*:—Sió bōt biþ twysceatte māre *the 'bōt' shall be twice as much*, L. Alf. pol. 66; Th. i. 96, 31. [*O. Frs.* twi-skette.] Cf. twi-gilde.

twi-scyldig; *adj. Liable to a double penalty*:—Gif se frigea sunnandæge wyrce . . . þolie his freótes oþþe sixtig scill., and preóst sī twyscildig, L. In. 3; Th. i. 104, 7. Cf. twi-gilde.

twi-seht; *adj. Discordant, at variance*:—Twysehte *discordes*, Scint. 192, 13.

twi-sehtan (?) *to disagree, be at variance*:—Ūđwitan gesihþ twysehtan (? *Cockayne prints* twyselican) hēnđe getācnaþ *if in a dream a man sees philosophers disagree, it betokens humiliation*, Lchdm. iii. 204, 24.

twisehtness, e; *f. Discord, dissension, variance*:—Fram twysehtnysse yfele *a dissensionis malo*, Scint. 6, 12.

twisel; *adj. Forked, double.* [Twisil tunge *double tongue* (Ecclus. 5, 14), Wick. *O. H. Ger.* der onocentaurus bizeichinōt die zuislen zungin der mennisken.] v. following words.

twisel-tōđe; *adj. Having the teeth forked* or *double*:—Twiseltōđe *scinodens*, Wrt. Voc. i. 17, 15.

twisla, an; *m. The fork* of a river, road, etc.:—Of đam mere on đan lace đǣr đa brōcas twisliaþ; đanne of đæm twislan, Cod. Dip. Kmbl. v. 198, 34. [Twissel, twistle *that part of a tree where the branches separate*, Halliwell's Dict. *O. H. Ger.* zwisila *furca.* Cf. *Icel.* kvísl *a fork; fork of a river.*]

twisled; *adj.* (*ptcpl.*) *Forked*:—On đone twisledan beám; of đam twisledan beáme on ceorla geat; andlang mearce on đa twysledan āc, Cod. Dip. Kmbl. iii. 14, 1-4. Twisld corn *scandula* (scandella *genus annonae apud Italos, q. alii dicunt hordeum distichum esse, alii vero hordeum cantherinum*, Migne), Wrt. Voc. i. 38, 45. [Cf. *Icel.* kvíslatrē *a forked tree*; tví-kvíslaðr *two-pronged.*] v. next word.

twislian; *p.* ode *To fork, branch*:—Đǣr đa wegas twisligaþ, Cod. Dip. Kmbl. iii. 409, 4: iv. 66, 15. Đǣr đa brōcas twisliaþ, v. 198, 34. [Tunge fele-twiselende *dispertite lingue*; cloven tongues (Acts 2, 3), O. E. Homl. ii. 117, 29. Cf. *Icel.* kvísla *to branch*, of a tree, stream, etc.]

twisliht; *adj. Forked, branched*:—In đa twislihtran biricean, Cod. Dip. Kmbl. iii. 391, 21. [*O. H. Ger.* zwisillochti *bifurcus.*]

twislung, e; *f. Forking, branching, partition*:—Se þurh his cildhādes nytenesse đis rīce tōstencte and his ānnesse tōdǣlde . . . Ǣfter his forđsīþe Eádgār ealne Angelcynnes anweald begeat, and đæs rīces twislunge eft tō ānnesse brōhte, Lchdm. iii. 436, 3.

twi-snæcce, -snæce, -snece; *adj. Double-pointed, cloven*:—Twysnæcce *bisulcus*, Ælfc. Gl. 49; Zup. 288, 11. (Cf. Snek *pessulum*, Wrt. Voc. i. 237, col. 2. Snekke or latche *clitorium, pessulum*, Prompt. Parv. 461. Snekk *obex, obecula*, Cath. Ang. 346 and see note. Sneck *a latch; a piece of land jutting into an adjoining field*, Halliwell's Dict. See also Jamieson's Dictionary *sneck.*) v. next word.

twi-snǣse; *adj. Double-pointed, cloven*:—Twysnēsum *bisulcis*, Germ. 393, 73. v. snās, *and preceding word.*

twi-sprǣc, e; *f. Double speech, unfair speech, detraction*:—Fācon and ēswico and æfisto and allo tuisprēco *dolum et simulationes et invidias et omnes detractiones*, Rtl. 25, 25. [Sowen we defles sed . . . ivele word, hoker and scorn, . . . and cheast, and twispeche, and curs, and leasinges, . . . and alle swikele speches, Rel. Ant. i. 129, 24.]

twi-sprǣce; *adj. Double-tongued*; bilinguis, Ælfc. Gr. 49; Zup. 288, 7. With a metaphorical meaning, *deceitful in speech, false in speech*, (with pleasant words) *flattering*, (with envy) *detracting*:—Se đe wǣre leássagol (twispǣce, MS. E.), weorđe se sōđsagol (sōđspǣce), Wulfst. 72, 16. Ne sȳn wē tō tǣlende ne tō twigsprǣce *let us not be too free with calumnies and detractions*, 253, 6. Ne beó đū nō tō tǣlende ne tō tweosprǣce . . . ac beó leófwende, Exon. Th. 305, 19; Fä. 90. Twisprēce *a flattering* (*mouth*, Prov. 26, 28); (os) lubricum, Kent. Gl. 1007. Word twispēces *the words of a talebearer* (Prov. 18, 8); verba bilinguis, 636. Twispēcne mūđ *the froward mouth* (Prov. 8, 13); os bilingue, 243. Gehega đīne eáran mid þornigum hege, đæt đū ne gehȳre lustum mōde đæra twysprǣcena word, Wulfst. 246, 10.

twisprǣcness, e; *f. Falseness in speech, detraction*:—Bebeorh đē wiđ twisprǣcnysse *cave tibi a biloquio*, L. Ecg. C. proem.; Th. ii. 132, 10. Uton beorgan ūs wiđ tǣlnysse and wiđ twysprǣcnysse and wiđ leáse gewitnysse *caveamus nobis a vituperatione et a biloquio et a falso testimonio*, L. Ecg. P. iv. 66; Th. ii. 226, 32. Twyspēcnessæ, Wulfst. 290, 30. Ic ondette æfste, twysprǣcnesse and leásunge, Anglia xi. 98, 26. Ic andette tǣlnessa and twisprǣcnessa, leásunga and unriht gilp, L. de Cf. 7; Th. ii. 262, 27.

twi-sprecan *to murmur*:—Hwisprendo ł tuispreccendo *murmurantes*, Jn. Skt. p. 4, 20. [Cf. *O. H. Ger.* zwi-sprehho *bifarius.*]

twi-spunnen; *adj.* (*ptcpl.*) *Double-spun, twice spun*:—Of twispunnenum twīne līnenum *torta bysso*, Past. 14; Swt. 83, 23. v. twi-þrāwen.

twist *a branch, fork* (?) [The faucon moste fallen fro the twiste, Chauc. Squieres Tale, 442. A twyste *frons, ramus*, Cath. Ang. 399, and see note. Twist *the fourchure; a twig*, Halliwell's Dict. Cf. *Icel.* kvistr *a branch.*] v. candel-, mæst-twist; twisel.

twi-strenge; *adj. Two-stringed*:—Twistrenge *bifidus* (as if from *fides*), Ælfc. Gr. 49; Zup. 288, 10.

twi-telged; *adj.* (*ptcpl.*) *Double-dyed*:—Of twitælgedum *bis tincto*, Wrt. Voc. ii. 126, 31. Twitælgade *depploide*, Ps. Surt. 108, 29.

twi-þrāwen; *adj.* (*ptcpl.*) *Double-twisted*:—Is beboden đæt scyle beón twiđrǣwen (-đrāwen, Cott. MSS.) twīn (*torta byssus*) on đæm mæssegierelan, Past. 14; Swt. 87, 18. Đæt tweođrǣwene (twyđrāwene, Cott. MSS.) twīn, Swt. 89, 2. v. twi-spunnen.

twiwa, tweowa, twuwa, tuwa, tuwwa, tua, twiga, twigea, twige, twīa; *adv. Twice*:—Hē hine twiwa (tuwa, MS. L.) mid fyrde gesōhte, Ors. 5, 2; Bos. 102, 37. Đæt heó on geáre twigea (twiwa, MS. H.: tuwa, MS. B.) blōwe, Lchdm. i. 320, 13. Hē gefeaht II (tweowa, MS. C.) wiđ đone cyning, Ors. 6, 30; Swt. 280, 9. Tweowa on dæg *bis in die*, Coll. Monast. Th. 20, 17. Twuwa, Scint. 80, 11. Hū ne mynegodest đū mē nū tuwa? Bt. 35, 2; Fox 156, 14. Tuwa (twiga, Bd. M.), Bd. 4, 1; S. 564, 16. Tuwa (twigea, Bd. M.) on geáre, 4, 5; S. 573, 6. Tuwa (tuiga, Lind.), Mk. Skt. 14, 30. Tua (tuwa, MSS. A. B. C.: twiga, Lind., Rush.), 14, 72. Ic fæste tuwa (tuigo, Lind.: twige, Rush.) on ucan, Lk. Skt. 18, 12. Ǣne ođþe tua (tuwa, MSS. T. F.), R. Ben. 74, 20: Homl. Skt. i. 16, 80. Oftor đonne tuwwa (tuwa, *other MSS.*), Chr. 894; Erl. 90, 20. Twiga þriga *bis terque*, Wrt. Voc. ii. 126, 35. ¶ With numerals:—Sió gestōd tuwa seofon hund wintra . . .; đæt is III C wintra and I M, Ors. 6, 1; Swt. 252, 6. Tuwa fīfe *binas quinquies*, Wrt. Voc. ii. 126, 25. Tuwa fīftig *bis quingentenum*, 11, 76. Twige, Hpt. Gl. 486, 77. Twīa seofon beóþ feówertȳne, Anglia viii. 302, 45. Twīa fīf beóþ tȳn, 328, 22. [*A. R.* twie, twien, twies: *Laym.* twien (twie, 2nd MS.): *Gen. and Ex.* twie: *O. E. Homl.* twiȝen, twies: *Orm.* twiȝȝess: *O. Frs.* twīa, tuiia.]

twi-wǣg, e; *f. A balance*:—Twiwǣge *bilance*, Wrt. Voc. ii. 126, 20. [*O. H. Ger.* zwi-wāga *bilibris.*]

twi-weg, es; *m. A place where two roads meet*:—Twiweg *bivia* vel *bivium*, Wrt. Voc. i. 53, 57.

twi-wintre, -winter; *adj. Of two years*:—Twiwintre *biennis*, Wrt. Voc. ii. 126, 11: *binus*, i. *biennius*, 126, 23. Twywintre *biennis, bimus*, Ælfc. Gr. 49; Zup. 287, 13, 18. Twiwinter *bimus* vel *biennis* vel *bimulus*, Wrt. Voc. i. 21, 58. Fram twywintrum cilde *a bimatu*, Mt. Kmbl. 2, 16: Homl. Th. i. 80, 16: 82, 11. Fram twiwintre fæce *a bimatu*, Ælfc. Gr. 49; Zup. 287, 19 note.

twi-wyrdig; *adj. Making contradictory* or *discordant statements, at* *variance in what is said*:—Hié swā twywyrdige sindon *they disagree in what they say* (ille promisit futura meliora, isti asserunt meliora praeterita), Ors. 2, 5; Swt. 86, 8. Hē com tō Rōme and diégellīce geceápede ðæt hié ealle wǣron ymb hiene twywyrdige *cum Romam ipse venisset, omnibus pecunia corruptis seditiones dissensionesque permiscuit*, 5, 7; Swt. 228, 18. [Cf. *Icel.* tvī-mæli *a dispute, a discordant report*, one saying this, another that.]

twuwa, -twux, twȳ, twy-, twycene, twy-iccende, twȳn, twȳnian, twȳnigend-līc, twȳnol, twȳnung. v. twiwa, be-twux, tweó, twi-, twicene, twi-hycgan, tweón, tweónian, tweónigend-līc, tweónol, tweónung.

tȳ; *indic., imper. subj. of* tȳn *to instruct.*

tyccen. v. ticcen.

tycgan; *p.* togde (?) *To move quickly, quiver, palpitate*:—Tolcetende, brottetende (v. brogdettan *palpitare, vibrare*), ticgende *infruticans*, Hpt. Gl. 435, 37. [Cf. *O. H. Ger.* zucchen; *p.* zuhta *rapere, eruere*: *Ger.* zucken *to shrug, writhe, palpitate*: *Icel.* tyggja *to chew*: *Dan.* tugge.] Cf. togian, togung, togettan.

tȳd *time*, tydder-, tyddre, tyddrian, tyddrung. v. tīd, tīder-, tīdre, tȳdran, tȳdrung.

tȳdran, tȳdrian; *p.* ede *To propagate*:—Ic tyddrige (teddrige, MS. D.) *propago*, Ælfc. Gr. 36; Zup. 216, 14. I. *trans.* (a) *To bring forth, produce*:—Se godcunda foreþonc geednīwaþ and tȳdreþ (tīdreþ, Cott. MS.) ǣlc tūdor and hit eft gehȳt *nascentia occidentiaque omnia per simileis foetuum seminumque renovat progressus*, Bt. 39, 8; Fox 224, 10. (b) *to propagate, nourish, foster*:—Ðīn hand plantode and tȳdrede ūre foregengan *plantasti eos*, Ps. Th. 43, 3. Hēr seó gālnese tȳdrode (tȳtrode, MS.) hir[e] cyn on hire sylfre *multitudinem vitiorum avaritia nigro lacte nutrit*, Gl. Prud. 57 b. Ælces landes gecynd is, ðæt hit him gelīce wyrta tȳdrige (tȳdre, Cott. MS.); and hit swā ðēþ; friþaþ and fyrþraþ swīþe georne, Bt. 34, 10; Fox 148, 29. Wyrd seó swīðe... heó wile late ādreótan, ðæt heó fǣhðo ne tȳdre *it will be long before she is weary of fostering hate*, Salm. Kmbl. 898; Sal. 448. Telgran tīdrian *surculos pastinare (plantare, nutrire)*, Hpt. Gl. 433, 48. Tȳdriende *pastinantem, rigantem*, 454, 13. Tytdriendum *propaganda*, Anglia xiii. 30, 75. Fācn wiþinnan tyddriende *dolum intus alentes*, Coll. Monast. Th. 32, 33. II. *intrans. To be prolific*, (a) absolute:—Tȳmaþ and tiédraþ, Cd. Th. 91, 14; Gen. 1512. Feoh sceal on eorðan tȳdran and tȳman, Menol. Fox 557; Gn. C. 48. Melce and tȳdrende *foetas*, Wrt. Voc. ii. 36, 32. (b) with dat. (inst.) of that in which anything is prolific:—Wæstmum tȳdreþ, Exon. Th. 493, 18; Rä. 81, 32. Wudubearwas tānum tȳdraþ, 191, 6; Az. 84. Wæstme tȳdraþ cederbeámas, Ps. Th. 103, 16. Tyddraþ, 64, 11. [Þenne men michel tuderið... and here tuder swiðe wexeð, O. E. Homl. ii. 177, 16. Þe33re time wass all gan to tiddrenn and to tæmenn, Orm. 18307. Of hem ben tudered manig on, Gen. and Ex. 630.] v. ā-, on-tȳdran, ge-tyddrian; tȳdred, un-tȳdrende, tȳdriend, tūdor.

tȳdre *weak*, -tȳdre. v. tīdre, on-, un-tȳdre.

tȳdred; *adj.* (*ptcpl.*) *Provided with offspring*:—Heora sceáp wǣron swylce tȳdred *oves eorum foetosae*, Ps. Th. 143, 17. v. tȳdran.

tȳdrian *to bring forth*, tȳdrian *to get weak.* v. tȳdran, tīdrian.

tȳdriend, es; *m. One that brings forth*:—Tȳdriend (tȳdriende?) *fecundus*, i. *copiosus, fructuosus*, vel *habundans*, Wrt. Voc. ii. 148, 47. [Cf. (?) Þe fule tuderende of flesliche lustes, O. E. Homl. ii. 55, 9.]

tȳdrung, e; *f.* I. *propagation*:—Uneácniendlīcre tēdrunge *infecunda sterilitate*, Hpt. Gl. 430, 61. Ic ongite ðæt ǣlc gesceaft willnaþ simle tō biónne; ðæt is swīþe switol on ðære tȳdrunge, Bt. 34, 12; Fox 152, 25. [Cf. (?) Þis woreld ebbeð þenne hit þat tuderinde wiðteoð *withholds its productivity*, O. E. Homl. ii. 177, 23.] II. *a branch*:—Tyddrung (tȳdrung, MS. T.: tiddrung, MS. V.) oððe bōh *propago*, Ælfc. Gr. 36; Zup. 216, 15.

tyge, tige (v. *double forms* togen, tigen, *pp. of* teón), es; *m.* I. *a pull, tug*:—Gange him tō mīnre byrgene and āteó āne hringan up, and gif seó hringe him folgaþ æt ðam forman tige, ðonne wāt hē ðæt ic ðē sende tō him. Gif seó hringe nele up þurh his ānes tige, ðonne ne sceall hē ðīnre sage gelȳfan, Homl. Skt. i. 21, 43–48. Ārena tīum *remorum tractibus*, Hpt. Gl. 406, 70. II. *a dragging*:—Valerianus hine hēt teón geond ðornas, and hē mid ðam tige his gāst āgeaf, Homl. Th. i. 432, 35. III. *leading, conducting*:—Ðone weterscype ðe hē intō Nīwan mynstre geteáh, and him se tige sume mylne ādilgade (*the diverting of the water had ruined his mill*), Chart. Th. 232, 7. Tiga *aquae ductuum*, Hpt. Gl. 418, 49. IV. *a draught* of drink:—Hālwende tige drincan, Anglia viii. 321, 32. V. *a drawing* of an inference, etc., *a deduction*:—Wē wyllaþ embe ðone geleáfan swīðor sprecan, forðan ðe ðises godspelles traht hæfþ gōdne tige *much good may be drawn from an examination of this gospel*, Homl. Th. i. 248, 21. Ðis godspel hæfþ langne tige on his trahtnunge *the exposition of this gospel might be drawn out to a great length*, ii. 72, 22. Petrus āwrāt twēgen pistolas, hig hebbaþ langne tige tō geleáfan trimminge *much matter for the confirmation of belief may be drawn from them*, Ælfc. T. Grn. 14, 8. [Ete nu enes o dai and drinke o tige atte mete, O. E. Homl. ii. 67, 11. *O. H. Ger.* zug, zugi (*in cpds.*) *ductus, motus.*] v. of-, on-, wæter-tyge.

tyge-hōc, es; *m. A hook to pull with*, the word occurs in a list of implements:—Scafan, sage, cimbīren, tigehōc, Anglia ix. 263, 2.

tyge-horn, es; *m. A cupping-glass*:—Mid tigehorne, Lchdm. ii. 120, 17.

tygel, es; *m. A strap to draw with, a trace*:—Tigel *tractorium* (cf. *tractorium* a trays, Wülck. Gl. 617, 7), Ælfc. Gl. Zup. 314, 16. [Ti3el *tractorium*, Wrt. Voc. i. 92, 74. Þe reines oþer þe tiels, Trev. 4, 77. *O. H. Ger.* zugil *habena, lorum*: *Icel.* tygill *a strap, thong.*]

tygele (?), an; *f. A lamprey*:—Tigle *murenula* (the word occurs in a list of the names of fishes; *murenula* is elsewhere glossed by *ǣl*, 66, 5: 281, 66; *sǣ-ǣl*, q. v.), Wrt. Voc. i. 55, 66. Cf. (?) preceding word.

tygele *a tile*, tyhhian. v. tigele, teohhian.

tyht, es; *m.* I. *way, manner of conducting one's self, usage, practice*:—Ic ðē giungne underfēng untȳdne and ungelǣredne and mē tō bearne genom and tō mīnum tyhtum getȳde... Ðū mē wǣre leóf ǣr ðon ðe ðū cūþest mīnne tyht and mīne þeáwas *I received thee young, uninstructed and untaught, and took as my child and brought thee up to my ways... Thou wast dear to me before thou knewest my way and my customs*, Bt. 8; Fox 24, 23–27. [Þat (*moderation*) is þeaw ant tuht forte halden, O. E. Homl. i. 247, 32. Cf. For þere ilke tuhtle (þinge, 2nd MS.) cnihtes weoren ohte, Laym. 24675. Elche untuhtle heo talden unwurðe, 24655.] II. *motion, move, march.* v. teón, IV, tohte, *and see passages from Layamon under* tyhtan, I:—Werod wæs on tyhte *the army was on the march*, Elen. Kmbl. 106; El. 53. Līg scrīþeþ... brond biþ on tyhte, Exon. Th. 51, 7; Cri. 812. Fȳr biþ on tihte, 233, 16; Ph. 525. III. *in* ofertyht (?) *a covering, what is drawn over.* v. ofer-teón; *and* cf. *Ger.* über-zug:—Þrong niht oferiiht londes frætwa *night, the covering drawn over the land's decorations, pressed on*, Exon. Th. 179, 3; Gū. 1256. [*Goth.* us-tauhts *a carrying out, completion*: *O. H. Ger.* zuht *disciplina, eruditio, nutrimentum.*]

tyhtan; *p.* te. I. *to draw, stretch* [:—Oferbrǣdels onbūtan getint *velamen in gyro tensum*, Anglia xiii. 421, 806]. [Tuhten is used in Layamon with the meaning of teón, IV:—Ure drihten heo bilæued, and to Mahune heo tuhted, Laym. 27321. Troynisce tuhten (to3e, 2nd MS.) to þon Gricken, 810.] II. but mostly in a metaphorical sense, *to draw* the mind to something, *to incite, exhort, provoke, solicit, prompt, urge, persuade*, (1) where the construction is uncertain:—Ic tyhte *ortor*, Ælfc. Gr. 25; Zup. 144, 18: *suadeo*, 26; Zup. 155, 6. Tyhto *sollicito*, tyhteþ, tyhtit *sollicitat*, tyhtan *sollicitare*, Txts. 97, 1887–3–9. Hē tihte *persuadet, docet*, Hpt. Gl. 491, 43: *incitavit*, 511, 28. Tyhton *irridabant*, Txts. 73, 1152: Wrt. Voc. ii. 45, 73. Tyctende (-i) *adridente*, Txts. 37, 70. Tyctendi *inlex*, 69, 1063. Tyhtende *adridens*, Wrt. Voc. i. 287, 70: ii. 4, 39. (2) where the object to which a person (*acc*) is exhorted, etc., is (a) marked by prep. *on* or *tō*:—Ne tyht nān mon his hiéremonna mōd ne ne bielt tō gǣstlīcum weorcum *nulla subditorum mentes exhortatio sublevat*, Past. 18; Swt. 129, 10. Deófol tiht ūs tō yfele, Homl. Th. i. 174, 31. Ōðer hine tyhteþ and on tæso lǣreþ, Salm. Kmbl. 983; Sal. 493. Hī (*devils*) on teosu tyhtaþ, Exon. Th. 362, 9; Wal. 34. God selfa tyhte (*suadente Deo*) Moyses on ðone folgoð, Past. 7; Swt. 51, 21. Heó hyre leófe bearn georne lǣrde and tō gōde tihte, Lchdm. iii. 428, 29. Hine his yldran tō woruldfolgaðe tyhton and lǣrdan *his parents urged him to temporal service*, Blickl. Homl. 211, 28. Hine tihtan tō his sāwle þearfe *eum hortari ad animae suae necessitatem*, L. Ecg. C. prm.; Th. ii. 130, 40. Ðreátian and tihtan (tyhtan, Cott. MS.) tō gōdum ðeáwum, Bt. 38, 3; Fox 200, 8. Tyhtan and gremian tō spīwanne *to provoke to vomit*, Lchdm. ii. 184, 1. (b) expressed by a clause:—Iohannes ðæt folc tihte, ðæt hī ufor eodon fram ðam deófles temple *John urged the people to go further away from the heathen temple*, Homl. Th. i. 70, 35. Ðā tihte (*or* III) heora sum, ðæt man ðæs cnapan līc smyrian sceolde, ii. 28, 3. (c) not expressed:—Ðū on ūs sāwle gesettest and hī styrest and tihtest, Met. 20, 178. Lǣran sceal mon geongne monnan, trymman and tyhtan, Exon. Th. 336, 10; Gn. Ex. 46. Ðæt se lāreów sceolde beón miehtig tō tyhtanne on hālwende lāre *ut potens sit exhortari in doctrina sana*, Past. 15; Swt. 91, 15. III. *to suggest, bring to the mind*:—Swā hwæt swā þurh unclǣnnysse on þeáwum hit tiht (*se suggerit*), Hymn. Surt. 28, 31. Gif mid rīcan mannan wē wyllaþ sum þinc tihtan (*suggerere*), R. Ben. Interl. 53, 6. IV. *to instruct, teach.* v. ge-tyhtan. [Þe deofel heom tuhte to þan werke, O. E. Homl. i. 121, 33. A þet wit cume forð ant tuhte ham þe betere, 247, 6. Tuhten and teachen, 267, 15. Þet tu ne schuldest nout tuhten ne chasten þi meiden uor hire gult, A. R. 268, 21. Tihhtenn and turrnenn folc to lefenn uppo Criste, Orm. 7048. *O. H. Ger.* zuhten, zuhtōn *nutrire, erudire*: *Ger.* züchten, züchtigen *to chastise*: *Dan.* tugte *to chastise, discipline.*] v. ā-, for- (fær-), ge-, leás-, mis-, on-tyhtan, *and following words.*

tyhten[n], e; *f. An incitement, inducement, allurement, incentive, enticement*:—Tyhten, tyctin, thyctin *lenocinium*, Txts. 73, 1199. Tyhtend (tyhtenn?) *allectio*, Wrt. Voc. ii. 9, 38. Tyhtinne, tyctinnae *incitamenta*, Txts. 69, 1074. Tyhtenne *lenocinia*, Wrt. Voc. ii. 50, 14: *incitamenta*, 48, 70. Tihtennum *inlecebris*, 48, 67. Tyctinnum, Txts. 68, 513.

tyhtend, tyhtiend, es; *m. One who exhorts, incites, instigates*:—Tyctaend, tychtend *inlex*, Txts. 68, 509. Tyhtend *incentor*, Wrt. Voc. ii. 111, 58: 44, 62: 83, 39: 94, 19. Tihtend *incentor, accensor, instigator*; tihtiend *adjutor, fautor*, Hpt. Gl. 495, 67, 70. v. yfel-tyhtend, fortihtigend.

tyhtend-līc; *adj. That serves for exhortation, encouragement*, etc. (v. tyhtan), *hortative*:—Wē wyllaþ sume tihtendlīce sprǣce wiđ eów habban, Homl. Th. ii. 574, 20. Sume *adverbia* syndon *ortativa*, đæt synd tihtendlīce, Ælfc. Gr. 38; Zup. 227, 16. Hē mid tihtendlīcum wordum heora gewǣhtan mōd getrymde and gefrēfrode, Homl. i. 562, 1.

tyhtere, es; *m. An inciter, instigator*:—Tyhtere *incentor*, Wrt. Voc. ii. 48, 48. Tihtere *leno*, i. 50, 55.

tyhting, e; *f. Persuasion, exhortation, encouragement, incitement, instigation, allurement, suggestion*:—Tihting *suasio*, Ælfc. Gr. 9, 3; Zup. 35, 10. Deófles costnung biþ on tihtinge . . . Deófol tiht ūs tō yfele, ac wē sceolon geniman nāne lustfullunge tō đære tihtinge . . . Seó yfele tihting is of deófle, Homl. Th. i. 174, 30–35: ii. 226, 29. Crist mid đyssere tihtinge Petrum gehyrte, 374, 17. God hira mōd onlīcht mid his fandunga and eác his tiehtinge (tihtinge, Cott. MSS.), Past. 35; Swt. 243, 22. For lāre and for tiehtinge his āgenes firenlustes *persuasione luxuriae*, 50; Swt. 393, 7. Mid godcundre tihtincge *divino instinctu*, Anglia xiii. 384, 266. Mid welwyllendre tihtincga myngiende *benevola intentione hortando*, 448, 1179: Scint. 34, 1. Se đe his brōđor hataþ đurh đæs deófles tihtinge, Basil admn. 4; Norm. 44, 17. Tihtinga *incitamenta*, Hpt. Gl. 520, 35. Tychtingum, Wrt. Voc. ii. 111, 3. Hē micclum mid his bēnum and tihtingum fylste *he helped much with his prayers and exhortations*, Homl. Th. ii. 126, 29. Se đe ōđerne tō leahtrum forspenþ, hē is manslaga, đonne hē đæs ōđres sāwle forpǣrþ þurh his yfelum tihtingum, 226, 32. Geþafian đæs deófles tihtinga, 546, 11. [Defles tuihting, O. E. Homl. ii. 29, 2. Tihting, i. 229, 19.] v. tō-tyhting.

tyhtle *a charge*. v. tihtle.

tyhtness, e; *f. Instigation*:—Tyhtnesse *instinctu*, Wrt. Voc. ii. 86, 20. Tihtnesse, 46, 63: 80, 28.

tyld-syle. v. teld-sele.

Tȳle *Thule*:—Ân īglond . . . đæt is Tīle hāten (þe isle þat hyȝt tile, Chauc. Boet. 3, 5. *This form is used also in Trevisa*, i. 325) *ultima Thule*, Met. 16, 15. [*Icel.* Tīle.] v. þȳle (*the usual form*).

tylg, tylian. v. tulge, tilian.

tyllan; *p.* tylde *To draw, attract*. Found only in the compound *fortyllan*, but see the following passages from later English. [Mi liht onswere tulde him upon me, A. R. 320, 13. Ne tulle ȝe to þe ȝete none unkuđe harloz, 414, 5. As muche place as myd a þong ich may aboute tille, R. Glouc. 115, 18. Of þe purse þat seluer heo tulleþ, Misc. 188, 40. Ille felawes hafd maistri To tille this yong man to foli, Met. Homl. 113, 8. Þe world tyl hym drawes And tilles . . . þam þat him knawes, Pr. C. 1183. To þe scole him for to till (tille), C. M. 12175. He hauede . . . Al þe folk tilled intil his hond, Havel. 438. *Also, like* teón, *with sense of* proceed, go:—Twei leomes stode þere; The gryttere tylde Est . . . þe oþer hadde branches . . . And westward thei drowe, R. Glouc. 151, 20: 152, 19. To gile ne to fraude wild he neuer tille, R. Brunne 128, 20. *Cf. also* tollen *to draw, attract*:—Þis tolled him towurd þe, A. R. 290, 5. Ha tolliþ togederes *they draw, come together*, Marh. 14, 6. (See instances quoted, p. 110.) Swa mai mon tolli him to Lutle briddes, O. and N. 1627. To drawen or tollen *allicere*, Chauc. Boet. 2, 7. Tollyn or mevyn *incito, provoco, excito*, Prompt. Parv. 496.]

tylþ, tylung, tȳma, tȳman. v. tilþ, tilung, tīma, tīman.

tym-bor (?) *a revolving borer, an auger*:—Timbor *rotum* vel *taratrum*, bor *desile*, scafa *olatrum*, Wrt. Voc. i. 287, 9–11. [Cf. (?) tumbian: *or* (?) *O. H. Ger.* tūmōn *rotari*.]

tymbran, tȳme, tymian, tȳn *ten*. v. timbran, tīme, temian, tīn.

tȳn; *p.* tȳde, tydde (tȳdde?); *pp.* tȳd *To instruct, educate, teach*:—Ic tȳ ođđe lǣre *imbuo*, Ælfc. Gr. 28, 3; Zup. 166, 14. Hē lǣrþ and hē tȳđ heorde his *docet et erudit gregem suam*, Scint. 146, 7. Se wīsdōm đe hit lange ǣr tȳde and lǣrde, Bt. 3, 1; Fox 4, 30. Hē hine geornlīce tȳde and lǣrde hū hē drohtian sceolde *eum erudire studuit qualiter conversari debuisset*, Bd. 1, 27; S. 489, 5. Hī mycelne đreát discipula on metercræfte and on tungolcræfte tȳdan and lǣrdan, 4, 2; S. 565, 26. Lāreówas đe hī (wudufuglas) tȳdon and temedon, Met. 13, 39. Swā hwilce men swā willnadon đæt hī on hālgum leornungum tȳde wǣron hī hæfdon gearuwe magistras đa đe hig lǣrdon and tyddon *quicumque lectionibus sacris cuperent erudiri, haberent in promptu magistros qui docerent*, Bd. 4, 2; S. 565, 34: 4, 3; S. 569, 6. Lāreów đū æþele þeáwas tȳ *doctor egregie mores instrue*, Hymn. Surt. 106, 5. Se đe đone mǣran noman abbodes underfēhþ hē sceal mid twyfealdre lāre đa wyldan and tȳn đe him underþeódde synt *cum aliquis suscipit nomen abbatis dupplici debet doctrina suis preesse discipulis*, R. Ben. 11, 12. Hē scole gesette in đære cneohtas tydde and lǣrde wǣron *instituit scholam in qua pueri literis erudirentur*, Bd. 3, 18; S. 545, 45. v. ge-tȳan, -tȳdan (*in each case read* -tȳn), and teón, III. 1.

tȳnan; *p.* de *To teen, tine* (v. Halliw. Dict.), *close*. I. *to fence, enclose*:—Me mæig on sumera tȳnan, Anglia ix. 261, 11. Gif ceorlas gærstūn hæbben gemǣnne oþþe ōđer gedālland tō tȳnanne, and hæbben sume getȳned hiora dǣl, sume næbben, L. In. 42; Th. i. 128, 6. II. *to close, shut* a door, book:—Midđȳ hīgna fæder tȳneþ đæt duro *cum paterfamilias cluserit ostium*, Lk. Skt. Lind. 13, 25. Đonne tȳnde hē his bēc *clauso codice*, Bd. 4, 3; S. 569, 10. Midđȳ đa duro uērun tȳndo *cum fores essent clausae*, Jn. Skt. Lind. 20, 19. III. *to close* a place, *prevent entrance into* a place, *shut up*:—Gié tȳndon rīc heofna *clauditis regnum coelorum*, Mt. Kmbl. Lind. 23, 13. III a. *to prevent* a person *granting access* to others (?), *render* a person *inaccessible*:—Tȳne hine Dryhten đam đe sār sprece sāwle mīnre *may the Lord shut His heart to him that speaks evil against my soul*, Ps. Th. 108, 20. IV. *to close, conclude, bring to an end*:—Se hālga Willfriþ æfter .xlv. wintra đæs onfongenan biscophādes đone ȳtemestan dæg tȳnde (*diem clausit extremam*), Bd. 5, 19; S. 636, 43. [An ancre nule nout tunen hire eiđurles aȝein dead of helle, A. R. 62, 17. Þa ȝæten heo tunden uaste, Laym. 15320. Tynyn̄ *sepio*; tynyd or hedgydde *septus*, Prompt. Parv. 494. *O. Frs.* be-tēna: *O. Du.* tuinen: *O. H. Ger.* zūnen *sepire*: *Ger.* zäunen.] v. ā-, ǣ-, an-, be-, bi-, for-, ge-, on-, un-tȳnan; fore-tȳn(e)d; tūn.

tȳnan *to vex*. v. tīnan.

tyncen *a barrel* (?), *a bladder* (?):—Đā gebeótode ân his đegna đæt hē mid sunde đa eá oferfaran wolde mid twām tyncenum, Ors. 2, 4; Swt. 72, 30.

tyndeht. v. tindiht.

tynder, e; tyndren (-in), e (?); tyndre, an; *f.* I. *tinder, fuel* (lit. and fig.):—Tyndir (-er) *napta, genus fomenti*, Txts. 80, 685. Geswǣlud spoon *vel* tynder *fomes*, Wrt. Voc. i. 39, 21. Tynder *fomes*, i. *incendium, astula minuta*, ii. 150, 4. Tyndrin, tyndirm (-in?) *isca* (= esca *fomes*, Migne; cf. *Span.* yesca *tinder*), Txts. 72, 562. Tyndre *isica*, Wrt. Voc. i. 284, 21: *isca*, ii. 45, 74: *fomentam* (*-um*?), 40, 7. Tyndre gōdes cynnes *fomentum bone indolis*, Scint. 206, 17. Tindre *sica* (l. *isica* or *isca*), Wrt. Voc. i. 66, 38. Wē habbaþ đone mǣstan dǣl đære tyndran đīnre hǣle . . . nū đū ne þearft đē nāuht ondrǣdan fordam đe of đam lytlan spearcan đe đū mid đære tyndran gefēnge līfes leóht đē onliéhte *habemus maximum tuae fomitem salutis . . . nihil igitur pertimescas; jam tibi ex hac minima scintillula vitalis calor illuxerit*, Bt. 5, 3; Fox 14, 9–14. Tyndri *isica*, Txts. 116, 179. Of gecyndelīcre tyndran *de ingenito fomite*, Wrt. Voc. ii. 139, 65. Tyndre *neptam*, 114, 59. Tynder, 60, 9. Tyndrum *fomitibus*, 33, 61. Deóful nā gewilnunge tyndran onǣlþ *diabolus non concupiscentiae fomenta succendit*, Scint. 210, 3. II. *a burner, an implement which burns*:—Mearcīsern *vel* tynder *cauterium*, Wrt. Voc. ii. 129, 76. Tynder *furnus*, 149, 84. Tyndre *cautere*, Txts. 114, 100. Tund[e]ri, 111, 19. [He tinder nom and lette i þan nutescalen don and fur þer on brohte, Laym. 29267. Of ston mid stel in đe tunder, Misc. 17, 535. Tondre, tunder, Piers P. 17, 245. Tundyr *fungus, napta*, Prompt. Parv. 506. *Du.* tonder: *O. H. Ger.* zuntra; *wk. f. fomes, isca*: *M. H. Ger.* zunder; *m. n.*: *Ger.* zunder: *Icel.* tundr; *n.*: *Dan.* tønder: *Swed.* tunder. Cf. *Goth.* tundnan *to be set on fire*.] v. tender, tendan.

tynder-cyn[n], es; *n. Combustibles*:—Tyndercyn *matteoli* (v. spæc), Wrt. Voc. ii. 56, 66: 78, 9.

tyndre, tyndrin, -tȳne. v. tynder, ge-tȳne.

tynge; *adj. Skilful with the tongue, rhetorical*:—Tingcum *rhetoricis, facundis*, Hpt. Gl. 460, 41. [Cf. *O. H. Ger.* zungal *linguosus*.] v. getynge.

tȳning, e; *f. A closing, fencing*. [Tynyn̄ or make a tynynge *sepio*, Prompt. Parv. 494.] v. be-, gafol-tȳning (-tīning); tȳnan.

tȳnness, e; *f. An enclosed place, a prison*:—Tēnys (= tȳnnysse?) þrexwealdum (heó) tō geþeódde *Anastasia lautomiae liminibus haerescit*, Hpt. Gl. 513, 65 (cf. l. 57 *lautomiae* cwearternes). v. on-tȳnness.

tȳr, tȳran. v. tīr, tīran.

tyrdlu, tyrdelu; *pl. n. Treddles* ('the droppings of sheep are called sheep's *tredles* in Somerset, *trattles* in Suffolk,' Lchdm. iii, Gl. *Treddle* excrement of rabbits, E. D. S. Pub. Old Farming Words. Halliwell quotes 'tak the *triddils* of an hare.' *Tyrdyl* schepys donge, Prompt. Parv. 494. Take scheps tridels or swynes muk, Rel. Ant. i. 53, 16):—Haran tyrdlu, Lchdm. ii. 214, 4. Genim gāte tyrdlu, 72, 16, 27. Tyrdelu, 282, 7. v. tord.

tyrf, tyrgan, tyrging, tyrian, tyriaca, tyring. v. turf, tirgan, tirging, tirgan, tiriaca, tirging.

tyrnan; *p.* de. I. *to turn* (intrans.), *revolve* on an axis, round a centre:—Seó heofon tyrnþ onbūtan ūs swiftre đonne ǣnig mylenhweól, Lchdm. iii. 232, 18: 254, 11: Boutr. Scrd. 18, 28: Homl. Th. ii. 214, 29. Se firmamentum went on đām twām steorran swā swā hwegol tyrnþ on eaxe, Lchdm. iii. 270, 22. Se cwyrnstān đe tyrnþ singallīce and nǣnne færeld ne đurhtihþ, Homl. Th. i. 514, 20. Đa steorran đe on đam rodere standaþ tyrnaþ ǣfre ābūtan mid đam brādan rodere, Hexam. 7; Norm. 12, 32. Hī tyrndon mid bodige and heora fōtwylmas āwendan ne mihton, Homl. Th. ii. 508, 19. Tyrn mid đīnum swīþran scytefingre *make circles with your right forefinger*, Techm. ii. 119, 11: 126, 1. Tyrnende *rotante*, Hpt. Gl. 517, 9. I a. figurative:—

Tyrnende swēgas *rotatiles trocheos*, Germ. 403, 8. II. *to turn* (trans.), *to cause to revolve*:—Ðā tyrndon ða hǣðenan hetelīce ðæt hweowl, Homl. Skt. i. 14, 93. [*O. H. Ger.* turnen. From Latin.] v. be-, ymb-tyrnan; turnian.

tyrn-geat, es; *n. A turn-stile*:—Tō tyrngeate, Cod. Dip. Kmbl. iii. 405, 4.

tyrning, e; *f.* I. *a turning round*:—Tyrnincg turniendre liðeran *vertigo rotantis fundibuli*, Hpt. Gl. 422, 65. II. *roundness*:—Sinewealtre trendla tyrnincge *tereti circulorum rotunditate*, 419, 9. v. turnung.

tyrwa (-e), tyrwan, tyrwen, tyrwian. v. tirwa (-e), tirwan, tirwen, tirgan.

tysca, an; *m. A buzzard*:—Glida *milvus*, tysca *butzus*, Wrt. Voc. i. 280, 22, 23. Tysca *bizus*, ii. 126, 39. Cf. (?) tusc.

tyslian; *p.* ode *To dress*:—Ic secge ðē, brōðor Eádweard, ðæt gē dōþ unrihtlīce ðæt gē ða Engliscan þeáwas forlǣtaþ ðe eówre fæderas heóldon and hǣðenra manna þeáwas lufiaþ ðe eów ðæs lifes ne unnon and mid ðam geswuteliaþ ðæt gē forseóþ eówer cynn and eówre yldran mid ðām unþeáwum ðonne gē him on teónan tysliaþ eów on Denisc āblerēdum hneccan and āblendum eágum. Ne secge ic nā māre embe ða sceandlīcan tyslunge būton ðæt ūs secgaþ bēc ðæt se beó āmānsumod ðe hǣðenra manna þeáwas hylt on his līfe and his āgen cynn unwurþaþ mid ðam *I tell you, brother Edward, that you do wrong to forsake the English customs that your fathers held and to love the customs of heathen men, that did not give you life, and that thereby you show that you despise your race and your forefathers, when to their shame you dress in Danish wise with bared* (? cf. blere *blurus, calvus*, Wrt. Voc. ii. 127, 13) *neck and darkened* (by hair falling over the eyes?) *eyes. I will say no more about that shameful fashion of dress, but that books tell us, that he is accursed, who holds the customs of heathen men in his life and thereby dishonours his own race*, Wanley Cat. pp. 121–122; see also Engl. Stud. viii. 62. Gedōnum tācne gān and hī mid dægþernum tyslian gescȳum *facto signo eant et se diurnalibus induant calciamentis*, Anglia xiii. 383, 260.

tyslung, e; *f. Dressing.* v. preceding word.

tȳtan; *p.* te *To stand out, be conspicuous* (?):—Ne tȳtaþ hēr tungul ac biþ tȳr scæcen *stars shall not shine forth, but glory shall have departed*, Exon. Th. 447, 26; Dōm. 45. [Cf. (?) *Icel.* tūta *a teat-like prominence*; tūtna *to be blown up*: *Dan.* tude *a spout*: *Swed.* tut: *Du.* tuit *a pipe, pike*.] Cf. tot.

tȳþa (-e). v. tīþe.

Þ

For the Runic þ, see þorn.

þā; *adv. conj. Then, when.* When the word stands at the beginning of a clause and may be translated by *then*, the verb generally precedes its subject; if it is to be translated by *when* the subject generally precedes the verb. I. *then, at that time*:—Ic ofstikode hyne. Swīþe þrȳste ðū wǣre þā (*tunc*), Coll. Monast. Th. 22, 19. Ðā wæs ðæt Agustinus gelaþode tō his sprǣce Brytta bisceopas *interea Augustinus convocavit ad suum colloquium episcopos Brittonum provinciae*, Bd. 2, 2; S. 502, 5. Godes ðeówas ðā nāne landāre hleótan ne mōston, Homl. Th. ii. 224, 4. On anginne ðissere worulde menn mōston lybban be heora lustum ðā . . . wē ne mōton lybban be ūrum lustum nū, Homl. Skt. i. 16, 233. Hit mæg eów nū fremian swā micclum swā hit ðā mihte, Homl. Th. ii. 378, 12. Se stān ðe ðæt wæter ðā of fleów, ii. 274, 1. Hē on fulluhte underfangen næs, forðan ðe Martinus ðā on neáwiste næs, 504, 24: Homl. Skt. i. 6, 112. On ðære tīde ðe Ehfrid and Æðelrēd wunnon, ðā æt sumon gefeohte wearð ān ðegen āfylled, Homl. Th. ii. 356, 24. II. marking sequence, *then, after that, thereupon*:—Ðā cwæð hē: 'Gā gē on mīnne wīngeard.' And hig þā fērdon, Mt. Kmbl. 20, 4. Sum iungling com mid gyrde tō mē, and wearp hī ðā tō mē, Homl. Th. ii. 312, 17. Se engel mē lǣdde ðā furðor . . . Efne ðā æteówdon līgas . . . Ic ðā beheóld ðone ormǣtan līg, 350, 15–21: 456, 24–26. Eft ðā on ðære þriddan nihte middan hē gewāt of ðisum līfe. Þā cōmon eft englas and hine gelǣddon, 336, 2–5. Hwæt ðā com sum man, 286, 19. Hwæt ða hǣþenan þā hine bestōdon, Homl. Skt. ii. 28, 104. Þā se bisceop dyde up ðone sanct, i. 21, 139. III. as adverbial connective, (1) of time, *when*:—Þā hē ūt eode embe underntīde, hē geseah ōðre īdele standan, Mt. Kmbl. 20, 3: 3, 7. Hwæt hē dyde, þā hine seó menego þreáde, Blickl. Homl. 19, 11, 31: 5, 25. (2) of cause or reason, *when, since, as*:—Hī hēton hine secgan hweþer hē cristen wǣre, þā hē wilnode þyllīces, Homl. Skt. ii. 28, 106. Hwā mæg āuht ōþres cweþan būtan ðū wǣre se gesǣligesta, ðā ðū mē wǣre ǣr leóf þonne cūþ, Bt. 8; Fox 24, 26. III a. where the form is doubled, or combined with *ðe*; v. also IV. (1) marking time, *when*:—Crist sylf gefæstnode his sprǣce, þā ðā hē spræc tō ānum Samaritaniscan wīfe, Homl. Th. i. 482, 24. Ðæt Drihten cwǣde tō Nichodēme, ān ðæra ealdra, ðā ðā hē his lāre sōhte, ii. 238, 4, 9. Ðā ðe (*cum*) hē in āre wes, Ps. Surt. 48, 21: 106, 6. (1 a) where the two forms are separated:—Þā heó þā in tō ðære hire moddrian eode, sōna ðæt cild onsprang, Blickl. Homl. 165, 28. (2) marking cause or reason, *when, since, as*:—Ðā cwæð his gefēra, ðæt hē gefyrn smeáde hwǣr hī bigleofan biddan sceoldon, ðā ðā hī ða fare fērdon būton wiste, Homl. Th. ii. 138, 33. (3) marking condition, *when, if*:—Ðæt hit wǣre geðūht ðæs ðe māre gemynd ðæs fæder, ðā ðā se sunu, his yrfenuma, wæs gecīged ðæs fæder naman, Homl. Th. i. 478, 11. IV. in correlative combinations, *then . . . when, when . . . then*:—Ðā se cyng ðæt hiérde, þā wende hē hine west, Chr. 894; Erl. 91, 9: 90, 22–24. Þā (*then*) þū cȳþdest ðæt þū nestest hwelces endes ǣlc angin wilnode, þā ðū wēndest ðæt steórleáse men wǣron gesǣlige, Bt. 5, 3; Fox 12, 34. Þā þā (*cum*) hē fæste feówurtig daga, þā ongan hyne syððan hingrian, Mt. Kmbl. 4, 2. Ðā ðā hē ealdode, þā clypode hē his yldestan cniht him tō, Homl. Th. ii. 234, 22: 286, 6: 390, 19–22. Þā hē ðā ūt faran wolde, þā hēt hē beódan, Chr. 905; Erl. 98, 21: 894; Erl. 90, 33. Ðā se wīsdōm ðā þis spell āreht hæfde, ðā ongan hē giddian, Bt. 19; Fox 68, 19. Þā þe . . . þā sōna, Blickl. Homl. 163, 15. Þā geseah Abraham Drihtnes dæg, þā þā hē ðās gerȳnu tōcneów, Homl. Th. ii. 234, 22. Se Frysa ðā, þā ðā hē hine gehæftan ne mihte, lēt hine faran, 358, 22. IV a. in combination with other demonstrative forms:—Mid ðȳ ðe heó gehȳrde ðone fruman, þā cwæþ heó þus, Blickl. Homl. 7, 20. Þǣr ðū cȳþdest ðæt ðū nystest mid hwilcan gerece God wylt ðisse worulde, þā ðū sǣdest ðæt . . ., Bt. 5, 3; Fox 14, 4. ¶ *See* git, gita, gēn, gēna, nū *for other instances of the word.* [*Chauc. Piers P.* tho, thoo: *O. Frs.* thā: *O. Sax.* thō, thuo: *O. H. Ger.* dō: *Icel.* þā.]

þaca, þeaca, an; *m. A covering, roof*:—Ðone song hē gehȳrde tō him neálǣcan, ōð ðæt hē becom tō ðeacan ðære cyricean (*ad tectum oratorii*), Bd. 4, 3; S. 567, 43. Cf. Bordðeaca, brodthaca *testudo*, Txts. 101, 1999. Bordþacan *latrariis*, Wrt. Voc. ii. 50, 52. v. ge-þaca *and* þæc.

þaccian; *p.* ode. I. *to pat, clap, strike gently*, with the open hand or the like:—Wildu hors, ðonne wē hié ǣresð gefangnu habbaþ, wē hié ðacciaþ and strāciaþ mid brādre handa *equos indomitos blanda prius manu tangimus*, Past. 41; Swt. 303, 10. Ðaccige hē hine selfne mid ðǣm fiðrum his geðōhta *cogitationum alis semetipsos feriant*, 64; Swt. 461, 17. Ælc ðara manna ðe ōðerne swīðe lufaþ, hine lyst bet þaccian and cyssan ðone ōðerne on bær līc, ðonne ðēr ðǣr clāðas beotweóna beóþ, Shrn. 185, 31. [This carter thakketh his hors uppon the croupe, Chauc. C. T. 7141. Nicholas had . . . thacked hire about the lendes wel, 3304.] II. *to clap, put* one thing to another:—Nim ða wyrta and wyrce tōgadere . . . þacc yt þanne gelōmelīce betwex ðan scaldrun *take the herbs and work together . . . clap the mixture often between the shoulders*, Lchdm. iii. 118, 14.

þacian; *p.* ode *To thatch*:—Me mæcg in Agusto and Septembri and Octobri ðacian, Anglia ix. 261, 17. [Thakkyn howsys *sartatego*, Prompt. Parv. 490. *M. H. Ger. Ger.* dachen *to roof*.] v. þeccan.

þadder; *adv. Thither, whither*:—Ðadder (ðider, Rush.) ðes færende is *quo hic iturus est*, Jn. Skt. Lind. 7, 35. [Perhaps a form due to Scandinavian influence. Cf. *Icel.* þaðra *there.* But see *þæder*.]

þæc, es; *n.* I. *a roof*:—Ðā gesēgon hī ðone hræfn ða glofe teran uppe on ānes hūses þæce . . . Wilfrið mid gyrde of ðæs hūses hrōfe ða glofe gerǣhte, Guthl. 11; Gdwin. 54, 16–22: Ps. Th. 128, 4. Gē þearfum forwyrndon, ðæt hī under eówrum þæce mōsten in gebūgan, Exon. Th. 92, 6; Cri. 1504. Se ðe on þæce siǽ *qui in tecto*, Mt. Kmbl. Rush. 24, 17. Hē mycelne aad gesomnode on beámum and on ræftrum and on wāgum and on watelum and on ðacum *advexit plurimam congeriem trabium, tignorum, parietum, virgeorum, et tecti fenei*, Bd. 3, 16; S. 542, 23. Bodigaþ on þacum *praedicate super tecta*, Mt. Kmbl. Rush. 10, 27. Nam ic wyrðe ðæt ðū gā under þacu mīnne (*sub tectum meum*), 8, 8. II. *the material of which a roof is composed, thatch*:—Ðæs hūses hrōf wæs mid ðæce beþæht *culmen domus erat foeno tectum*, Bd. 3, 10; S. 534, 32. Ða tær ðæt hors ðæt ðæc of ðære cytan hrōfe, Homl. Th. ii. 136, 16. [*Chauc.* thacke (in houses of thacke) *thatch*: *Prompt. Parv.* thak for howsys *sartatectum*: *tectura, tegimen*, Wrt. Voc. i. 237, col. 1. *O. H. Ger.* dah *tectum, opertorium*: *Ger.* dach: *Icel.* þak *roof*.] v. fen-þæc; þaca.

þæcele, an; *f. A torch, light*:—Þæcile *fax*, Wrt. Voc. i. 284, 20. Ðecele *facula*, ii. 77, 5. Ða fȳr feóllon on ða eorþan swelce byrnende þecelle *vise nubes ardentes de celo tanquam faces decidere*, Nar. 23, 26: 14, 15. Stōd se leóma him of swylce fȳren ðecelle (þecele, Bd. M. 476, 15) ongeán norðdǣle *portabant facem ignis contra aquilonem*, Bd. 5, 23; S. 645, 29. Ðæccilla (ðæcela, Rush.) *lucerna*, Lk. Skt. Lind. 11, 34: Mk. Skt. Lind. Rush. 4, 21. Þæccille (ðæcella, Rush.), Jn. Skt. Lind. 5, 35. Ðæccillæ (ðæcela, Rush.) *lucernae*, Lk. Skt. Lind. 12, 35. Dryhtnes ðecelan, Salm. Kmbl. 838; Sal. 418. Ðæccillas *lampades*, Mt. Kmbl. p. 9, 20. Mid brondum ł ðæccillum *cum facibus*, Jn. Skt. Lind. 18, 3. [Cf. Ælc beorn hæfde on heonde ane þechene bærninde, Laym. 8084.] v. fæcele.

þæcen. v. þecen.

þæc-tigele, an; *f. A tile for a roof*:—Þaectigilum *imbricibus*, Wrt. Voc. ii. 110, 56. [v. Halliwell's Dict. *thack-tiles*, and cf. Jamieson's Dict. *thack-stone*.]

þæder; *adv. Thither, whither*:—Gā ðū and lǣde ðis folc þæder þe ic þē ǣr sǣde *tu vade et duc populum istum, quo locutus sum tibi*, Ex. 32, 34. On mergen com se biscop þæder, Shrn. 139, 35. Hē þæder in eode, 156, 13. [Cf. *Icel.* þaðra *there*: *Goth.* þaþrō *thence.*] v. þadder, þider, *and next word*; *and* cf. hwæder.

þædres; *adv. Thither*:—Hidres ðædres (ðidres, Cott. MSS.) *hither and thither*, Past. 22; Swt. 169, 13. v. preceding word.

þæge, þage; *pron. pl. They, these*:—Þæge twēgen dagas, Lk. Skt. 11, 5 margin. Sume ðæge wǣron hǣðene *erant gentiles quidam ex his*, Jn. Skt. 12, 20. Hē wyrcþ māran ðonne þæge (þa, MS. A.) synt *majora horum faciet*, 14, 12. Saga mē hwanon wæs Adames nama gesceapen? Ic ðē secge, fram iiii steorrum. Saga mē, hwæt hātton ðage? Salm. Kmbl. p. 180, 1. [*Laym.* þaie, þaye *they, the* (pl.), *those.*]

þǣh *though*. v. þeáh.

þǣnan; *p.* de *To moisten*:—Gif tō stīð sié, þǣn (*printed* þæm; *but see* geþǣn mid hunige, 144, 1) mid ðȳ hunige, Lchdm. ii. 108, 17. Þēnda smerwunga wyrce of ele *make moist smearings of oil*, 182, 16. [Halliwell gives *thean* moist, damp, as a Westmoreland word; and Jamieson has *thain, thane* with the same meaning.] v. of-þænnan (*read* -þǣnan; *the form* ofþǣne *is subjunctive, not imperative*), þīnan, þwǣnan, þān, þānian.

þǣnian, þænnan, þænne. v. þānian, þennan, þanne.

þǣr, þār, þāra; *adv. There, where.* I. local, (a) with demonstrative force, (1) *there, in that place*:—Hig cōmon tō ðære stōwe, and hē gebæd hine þǣr (*ibi*) tō Gode, Gen. 13, 4: 18, 24. Gif ðū þǣr (ðēr, Lind.: ðǣr, Rush. *ibi*) geþencgst ðæt ðīn brōðor hæfþ ǣnig þing āgēn ðē, lǣt þǣr (*ibi*) ðīne lāc beforan ðam altare, Mt. Kmbl. 5, 23-24. Hē wæs āna þǣr (ðēr, Lind.: ðǣr Rush.) *solus erat ibi*, 14, 23. Hē his bigleofan þǣr feccan sceolde, Homl. Th. ii. 156, 6. Gif þār man ān bān findeð unforbærned, Ors. 1, 1; Swt. 21, 12. Hē fērde tō Bethania and lǣrde hī þār (þǣr, MS. A.), Mt. Kmbl 21, 17. Gē gegearwiaþ ūs þāra (ðēr, Lind. Rush.) *illic parate nobis*, Mk. Skt. 14, 15. Ic næs þāra (*ibi*), Jn. Skt. 11, 15, 31. Swīþe earfoþhāwe ac hit is ðeáh þāra *very difficult to see, but still it is there*, Bt. 33, 4; Fox 130, 31. (2) *thither, to that place*:—Wæs Hæsten þǣr cumen mid his herge, Chr. 894; Erl. 91, 16. Ne mæg þǣr inwitfull ǣnig gefēran, Cd. Th. 58, 18; Gen. 948: Elen. Kmbl. 1467; El. 735. Ic ðǣr cwom tō ðam hringsele Hrōðgār grētan, Beo. Th. 4023; B. 2009. (b) with relative force, (1) *where, in which place*:—Nellen gē goldhordian eów goldhordas on eorþan, þǣr (þār MS. A.: ðēr ł huēr, Lind.: þǣr, Rush. *ubi*) ōm and moððe hit fornimþ, and þǣr (þār, MS. A.: ðēr, Lind.: þǣr, Rush.) þeófas hit delfaþ and forstelaþ: goldhordiaþ eów goldhordas on heofenan, þǣr (þār, MS. A.) nāðor ōm ne moððe hit ne fornimþ, and þār þeófas hit ne delfaþ ne ne forstelaþ, Mt. Kmbl. 6, 19-20. On wēsten þǣr ǣr Adam forwearþ, Blickl. Homl. 29, 18: 39, 5. On ðære byrig þǣr se cyning ofslægen læg, Chr. 755; Erl. 50, 13. Sum feóll ofer stānscyligean þār hit næfde mycele eorðan, Mk. Skt. 4, 5. (2) *whither, to which place*:—Ic lǣrde on temple þār (þǣr, MS. A.: ðiddir, Lind.: ðider, Rush. *quo*) ealle Iudēas tōgædere cōmon, Jn. Skt. 18, 20. In ðam ēðle ðǣr hē ǣr ne cwom, Exon. Th. 27, 26; Cri. 436. Tō ðam lande þǣr ðē lust myneþ tō gesēcanne, Andr. Kmbl. 588; An. 294. (c) in correlative combinations, (1) þǣr . . . þǣr *there (where, thither, whither)* . . . *where (there, thither, whither)*:—Þǣr (þār, MS. A.) ðīn goldhord is ðǣr (þār, MS. A.) is ðīn heorte *ubi est thesaurus tuus, ibi est cor tuum*, Mt. Kmbl. 6, 21: 18, 20. Sceáwa þǣr dust and drȳge bān, þǣr þǣr ðū ǣr gesāwe fægre leomu, Blickl. Homl. 113, 21. (2) where the two forms are not separated, and may be translated by *where*:—God gefilde mid flǣsce þǣr þǣr ðæt ribb wǣs, Gen. 2, 21. Mīn þēn biþ þǣr þǣr (þār þār, MS. A.) ic eom *ubi sum ego illic minister meus erit*, Jn. Skt. 12, 26. Man mōt hine gebiddan, beó þǣr þǣr he beó, Homl. Skt. i. 13, 67. (d) with a demonstrative and relative force, as in modern *where, whither*:—Ðæt hī geworhten stǣnene weal ðǣr se cāsere hēt eorþwall gewyrcan, Bd. 1, 12; S. 481, 8. Ðæt hī woldan andlyfne niman ðǣr hī hit findan mihton, 1, 15; S. 483, 39. Se monlīca wunode þǣr hié strang begeat wīte, Cd. Th. 155, 4; Gen. 2567. Hē nǣnne ne mæg gebringan þǣr hē him gehēt, Bt. 32, 1; Fox 114, 4. Ðā becom hit þǣr se cynincg feóll, Homl. Skt. ii. 26, 208: Beo. Th. 718; B. 356. Far þǣr ðū freónda wēne, Exon. Th. 119, 29; Gū. 262. II. metaph. usages, (1) *there, in that case, then*:—Þǣr ðū cȳþdest ðæt ðū nystest . . . þā ðū sǣdest ðæt . . . , Bt. 5, 3; Fox 14, 2. Hū ne is se anweald þonne þǣr nāuht *is not, then, power in that case nought?* 16, 2; Fox 54, 7. Geðence hē ðæt hē biþ self suīðe gelīc ðām ilcan monnum ðe hē ðǣr ðreátaþ, Past. 17; Swt. 117, 16: 54; Swt. 425, 22: 12; Swt. 75, 13 (but see note on the last passage). (2) þǣr þǣr *then when, when*, þǣr *when*:—Ðȳ læs hié selfe ācwelen ðǣr ðǣr hié ða ōðre lācniaþ *ne alios medendo ipsi moriantur*, Past. 48; Swt. 371, 11. Ðǣr ðǣr ūs God forbeád *cum nos Deus prohiberet*, 59; Swt. 451, 5. Sīn ðīne suna and ðīne dohtra geseald ōðrum folce þǣr ðū on lōcie (*videntibus oculis tuis*), Deut. 28, 32. Hī clumiaþ mid ceaflum þǣr hī sceoldan clypian, L. I. P. 5; Th. ii. 308, 21. (3) *in case that, if*:—Ðǣr wē ūs selfum dēmden ðonne ne dēmde ūs nō God *si nosmet ipsos dijudicaremus, non judicaremur*, Past. 53; Swt. 415, 5. Ðǣr mīn āgen folc mē hȳran cūðan *si plebs mea audisset me*, Ps. Th. 80, 13: Bt. 32, 2; Fox 78, 1: 37, 3; Fox 100, 4: 36, 2; Fox 174, 5. Geornor wē woldon beón forsugiende, þǣr wē for eówerre āgenre gnornunge mōste, Ors. 3, 8; Swt. 122, 10: Exon. Th. 375, 20; Seel. 141: Cd. Th. 279, 7; Sat. 234. Ðǣr Moyses ne hulpe *si non Moyses stetisset*, Ps. Th. 105, 19: Past. 46; Swt. 355, 4: Cd. Th. 49, 24; Gen. 797: Ors. 2, 4; Swt. 70, 5. Ðār ðū nū gemyndest ða word ðe ic ðē sǣde on ðære forman bēc, ðonne miht ðū be ðām wordum genōg sweotole ongitan ðæt ðæt ðū ǣr sǣdest ðæt ðū nystest *si superiora concessa respicias, ne illud quidem longius aberit, quin recorderis, quod te dudum nescire confessus es*, Bt. 35, 2; Fox 156, 21. III. preparing the way for the subject, *there*:—Ðā com þǣr rēn and þǣr (þār, MS. A.) bleówun windas *et descendit pluvia et flaverunt venti*, Mt. Kmbl. 7, 25, 27. Þā æt sumum cirre cōmon þǣr sex scipu tō Wiht, Chr. 897; Erl. 95, 18. Eálā hwæt þǣr wæs fæger eáðmōdnes gemēted on ðære ā clǣnan fǣmnan, Blickl. Homl. 9, 21. Þǣr is mid Estum ān mǣgð, Ors. 1, 1; Swt. 21, 13. IV. in combination with suffixed prepositions the word has the force of a pronoun; see the forms given as compounds (though the attachment is rather slight, see e. g. *þær-on*) which follow. [*Laym.* þar, þare, þear: *Orm.* þær: *A. R.* þer: *Gen. and Ex.* ðor: *Hav.* þor, þore: *O. Sax. O. L. Ger.* thār: *O. Frs.* thēr: *O. H. Ger.* dār, dāra. Cf. *Goth. Icel.* þar.]

þǣr-ābūtan; *adv. Thereabout, about that place*:—On Antiochian byrig and ðǣrābūtan gehwǣr, Homl. Skt. ii. 25, 595. Tō ðām ðe ðārābūtan (-onbūtan, MS. A.) stōdon *circumstantibus*, Mk. Skt. 14, 69.

þǣr-æfter; *adv. Thereafter, after that*:—Gif se terminus gescȳt on sumon dæge ðære wucan, ðonne byþ se sunnandæg þǣræfter Eásterdæg, Lchdm. iii. 244, 18. Hié āhebbaþ hié ofer hiera hiéremenn, and ne ondrǣdaþ ðone dōm ðe ðǣræfter fylgþ, Past. 19; Swt. 145, 9.

þǣr-æt; *adv. Thereat*:—His horsbǣr wæs fram his discipulum gehealden, and monige unfrume ðǣræt hǣlo onfēngon, Bd. 4, 6; S. 574, 7.

þæran (? þærran) *to dry, wipe*:—Hē ðā hēt geótan wæter on mundleów and ongan his þegna fēt þweán and þæran (*other MSS. have* þar an, þær ana; *the Latin in* Jn. 13, 5 *is* extergere. The word intended seems to be one corresponding to Icelandic *þerra*, which, as well as the form *mundlaug*, the equivalent of the rather uncommon *mundleów*, the modern version in that language uses in this passage) mid ðȳ līne, ðe hē wæs begyrded, Homl. Ass. 155, 103.

þǣr-big; *adv. Thereby, by that* (person or thing):—Gif hwā gefare and nān bearn ne gestriéne, gif hē brōðor lǣfe, fō se tō his wīfe. Gif hē ðonne bearn ðǣrbig(-bié, Cott. MSS., *by the wife*) gestriéne, ðonne cenne hē ðæt ðam gefarenan brēðer ðe hié ǣr ǣhte, Past. 5; Swt. 43, 14.

þǣr-binnan; *adv. Therein*:—Philippus þǣrbinnan ne mehte, Ors. 3, 7; Swt. 112, 36. Se bisceop bebeád, ðæt hī heora lāc geoffrodon binnon ðam temple, and hēt hī ðǣrbinnon andbidigan, Homl. Th. i. 450, 25.

þǣr-bufan; *adv. Besides, over and above that*:—Hē cwæð: 'Biscepe gedafnaþ ðæt hē sié tǣlleás.' Ðǣrbufan (v. 1 Tim. 3, 2 sqq. *for the additional remarks referred to*) is geteald hwelc hē beón sceal, gif hē untǣlwierðe biþ, Past. 8; Swt. 53, 10.

þearf *need*, þærf *leavened*, þærh. v. þearf, þeorf, þerh.

þǣr-in; *adv. Therein, wherein*:—Hē wæs on Simones hūse, þǣrin geát ðæt wīf ða deórwyrþan smerenesse on his heáfod, Blickl. Homl. 73, 3.

þǣr-inne. v. þǣr-ūt, -ūte.

þǣr-mid; *adv.* I. *therewith, with that*:—Ðā geseah hē treów licgende, and ðæt lytel; ongan ðā þǣrmid delfan, Homl. Skt. ii. 23 b, 767. II. temporal, *straightway, at the same time*:—Ðā forceáw hē his āgenan tungan and wearp hine ðǣrmid on ðæt neb foran, Bt. 16, 2; Fox 52, 25.

þǣr-nēhst; *adv. Next to that*:—Godes grið is ealra griða geornost tō healdanne, and þǣrnēhst þæs cynges, L. Eth. vii. 1; Th. i. 330, 3.

þǣr-of; *adv. Thereof, of* or *from that*:—Genim ðās ylcan wyrte, wyrc clyþan þǣrof, Lchdm. i. 196, 23. Ðæt ic macige mete ðīnum fæder þǣrof *ut faciam ex eis escas patri tuo*, Gen. 27, 9.

þǣr-ofer; *adv. Thereover, over that*:—Se ficbeám oferseeadaþ ðæt lond, ðæt hit under him ne mæg gegrōwan, ne hē self nānne wæsðm ðǣrofer ne bireþ, Past. 45; Swt. 337, 12. Hig tōdǣldon hys reáf, and wurpon hlot þǣrofer, Mt. Kmbl. 27, 35.

þǣr-on; *adv.* I. *thereon*:—Hē com tō ðam treówe, sōhte wæstm ðǣron, and nǣnne ne gemētte, Homl. Th. ii. 408, 1. Se dēma hēt wyrcan āne hencgene and hēt hōn ðone bisceop þǣron, Homl. Skt. ii. 29, 253: Blickl. Homl. 71, 7. II. *therein*:—Hēr is ān lytele burg, ðǣr ic mæg mīn feorh on generian. Hió is ān lytel, and ðeáh ic mæg ðǣron libban, Past. 51; Swt. 399, 24. Āwyrtwala grǣdignysse of ðīnre heortan, and āplanta þǣron ða sōþan lufe, Homl. Th. ii. 410, 2. Segeþ þǣron (*in the book*), ðæt sum rīce man wǣre, Blickl. Homl. 197, 27. III. *thereinto*:—Ðū ne cymst þǣron *non ingredieris eam*, Deut. 32, 52. Ðā hēt hē gefeccan ǣnne ǣrenne oxan, and ða hālgan ðǣron dōn, Homl. Skt. ii. 30, 422. IV. *thereof*:—And hē ne cūðe nān þing þāron (cf. næs heora nān ðe þār ǣnig þing on cūðe, 41, 24), Gen. 39, 23.

þǣr-onbūtan. v. þǣr-ābūtan.

þǣr-ongeán; *adv. There against, on the contrary*; per contra:—Englas cȳðaþ ðīne dǣda beforan Godes gesihðe, and deófol āwrīt þǣrongēn ealle ðīne misdǣda, Wulfst. 248, 21.

þǽr-oninnan; *adv. Therein, thereinto*:—Healreced gewyrcean, and þǽroninnan eall gedǽlan, Beo. Th. 142; B. 71.

þǽr-onufenan. v. ufenan.

þǽr-onuppan; *adv. Thereupon, thereon*:—Ða hǽþenan byrnende glēda streáwodon, and ðǽronuppan deófle offrodon, Homl. Skt. i. 23, 35: 13, 25.

þǽr-riht; *adj. Straight*:—Þārrihtum *strictis* (*but the passage glossed is* strictis mucronibus; *the glosser seems to have given two senses of the word, as he gives* evaginatis *besides the English word*), Hpt. Gl. 495, 50. v. next two words.

þǽr-rihte; *adv. Straightway, forthwith, at once, immediately*:—Ðārrihte *confestim, continuo, statim, protinus*, Ælfc. Gr. 38; Zup. 229, 16–230, 1: *mox*, Zup. 241, 6: *confestim*, Scint. 236, 1. Gē gemētaþ þǽrrihte (sōna *statim*, Mt. Kmbl. 21, 2) getīgedne assan, Homl. Th. i. 206, 10: 494, 13: Mt. Kmbl. 3, 16: 27, 51. Ðā cwæð hē: 'Geweorðe leóht.' And leóht wæs þǽrrihte geworden, Lchdm. iii. 232, 9. Ðǽrryhte æfter rehte sanctus Paulus *paulo post subdit*, Past. 51; Swt. 395, 26. Hē wæs hālig þǽrrihte, swā hraðe swā hē mann wæs, Homl. Th. i. 200, 8. Sōna ł ðāriht *statim*, Mk. Skt. Rush. 1, 20. v. next word.

þǽr-rihtes; *adv. Straightway*:—Þǽrrihtes *protinus*, Hymn. Surt. 92, 37: 113, 35.

þærscan, þærsc-wald, -wold, þærst. v. þerscan, þerscold, ðærst.

þǽr-tō; *adv. Thereto.* (1) marking position or order, *next, then*:—Ðara is se forma Maximianus, ðǽrtō se ōþer Malchus, and se ðridda þǽrtō Martinianus, Homl. Skt. i. 23, 3–5. (2) marking addition, *besides*:—Ic gesett hæbbe wel feówertig lārspella and sumne eácan ðǽrtō, Ælfc. T. Grn. 14, 1. Hē nōwiht āgnes hæfde būtan his cyricean and ðǽrtō feówer æceras, Bd. 3, 17; S. 543, 32. (3) marking association:—Ðā stōd ðære sunnan cræt mid feówer horsum on āne healfe; on ōðre healfe stōd ðæs mōnan cræt and ða oxan ðǽrtō, Homl. Th. ii. 494, 24. Hē becwæð his lāford his beste scip, and ða segelgerǽda ðārtō, Cod. Dip. Kmbl. iii. 351, 25. (4) where movement, lit. or fig., is implied:—Ðæt hē ūs gebringe tō his ēcan gebeórscipe, se ðe ūs ðǽrtō gelaðode, Homl. Th. ii. 378, 6. Ðā dǽlde se cāsere ðæt rīce on feówer, and sette ðǽrtō feówer gebrōðra, i. 478, 20. Ðone ōþerne ðe hine ðǽrtō neádode, Homl. Skt. ii. 25, 227. (5) *thereto, for that end*:—Ūres Hǽlendes gerīp mænigfeald is and feáwa wyrhtan þǽrtō, Homl. Skt. ii. 29, 129.

þǽr-tōeácan; *adv. Besides, moreover*:—Hē ūrum gyltum miltsaþ, and ðǽrtōeácan ðæt heofenlīce rīce behǽt, Homl. Th. ii. 84, 8. On ðæt gerād ðæt se eorl him tō handan lēt Uescam, and þǽrtōeácan ðes cynges men sacleás beón mōston, Chr. 1091; Erl. 227, 9.

þǽr-tōgeánes; *adv.* I. local, *opposite*:—Ic ðǽrtōgeánes standende *ego e contra stans*, Coll. Monast. Th. 22, 15. Seó heofen . . . and seó eorðe þǽrtōgeánes, Homl. Skt. i. 13, 166. II. *on the contrary*:—Se gōda man biþ ðæs Hālgan Gāstes templ. Swā eác ðǽrtōgeánes se fordōna man biþ deófles templ, Homl. Th. i. 262, 17: Wulfst. 59, 3. III. *as an equivalent, as a set off, in return*:—Wē habbaþ heom geunnen . . . and hī ūs þārtōgēnes gifeþ . . ., Chart. Th. 436, 11–20. Se cyng ðone castel æt Bures gewann . . . Ðǽrtōgeánes se eorl gewann ðone castel æt Argentses, Chr. 1094; Erl. 230, 9. IV. *in reply, in refutation*:—Ðonne cweðaþ hī: 'Hū magon ðās bān beón geedcucode?' Ac wē cweðaþ þǽrtōgeánes, ðæt God mæg eal ðæt hē wile, Homl. Th. i. 236, 8: Homl. Skt. ii. 27, 162.

þǽr-under; *adv. Beneath*:—Ealle ða ðe ofer ōðre bióþ heáfda ðara ðe ðǽrunder bióþ, Past. 18; Swt. 131, 24.

þǽr-uppan; *adv. Thereupon*:—Him wæs his myxen forlǽten, ðæt hē þǽruppan sittan mihte, Homl. Skt. ii. 30, 200.

þǽr-ūt; *adv. Thereout, outside*:—Moyses oft eode inn and ūt on ðæt templ, for ðæm hē wæs ðǽrinne getogen tō ðære godcundan sceáwunga, and ðǽrūt (ðǽrūte, Cott. MSS.) hē wæs ābisgod ymb ðæs folces ðearfe, Past. 16; Swt. 101, 25.

þǽr-ūte; *adv. Without, outside*:—Nāhton hié nāþer ne þǽrinne mete ne þǽrūte freónd, Ors. 2, 8; Swt. 92, 34. v. preceding word.

þǽr-wiþ; *adv.* I. *therewith*:—Hī sint þǽrwiþ gemengde, Bt. 33, 4; Fox 130, 29. II. *in return, in exchange*:—Drīfaþ hider eówre orf and ic sylle eów þǽrwið mete *adducite pecora vestra, et dabo vobis pro eis cibos*, Gen. 47, 16.

þǽr-ymbe; *adv. About that*:—Hig tō lyt þǽrymbe þenceaþ, Wulfst. 273, 1.

þǽr-ymbūtan; *adv. Thereabouts*:—Hē (*the Roman name*) com tō Parþum . . . hē wæs ðǽrymbūtan manegum folce swīþe egefull, Bt. 18, 2; Fox 64, 13. On gehwylce healfe ðǽrymbūtan *circumquaque*, Bd. 3, 17; S. 543, 26.

þæslǽcan; *p.* -lǽhte *To agree, accord, fit*:—Þæslǽcan *congruant*, Wrt. Voc. ii. 133, 40. Þæslǽcende *congruentes, convenientes*, Hpt. Gl. 508, 5. v. ge-þæslǽcan.

þæs-līc; *adj.* I. *suitable, seemly, becoming, fit, meet, congruous*:—Gehӯþlīc, þæslīc *vel* gescrǽpe *commodus*, i. *honestus, congruus, utilis, aptus*, Wrt. Voc. ii. 131, 81. Ðæslīc (*operae*) *pretium* (v. *operae pretium, congruum* neádþearflīc, Hpt. Gl. 477, 38), Anglia xiii. 33, 163. Gif līf his on wyrþscype sī wel þæslīc *si vita honore sit condigna*, Scint. 125, 5. Swīðe þæslīc anginn menniscre ālӯsednysse wæs ðæt se engel wearð āsend fram Gode tō ðam mǽdene, Homl. Th. i. 194, 27. Hit nis nā gedafenlīc ne þæslīc, ðæt ic ðe swā grimlīce forworht eom, ðæt ic ðīne anlīcnysse sceáwige, Homl. Skt. ii. 23 b, 434. Nāht þæslīces deáðe *nihil dignum morte*, Lk. Skt. 23, 15. Forbærn mid fӯre þæslīcum (*congruo*), Hymn. Surt. 29, 25: Hpt. Gl. 443, 15. Ðæt hī Godes þēnunge mid þæslīcere endebyrdnysse gefyldon, Homl. Th. i. 508, 29. Þurh þǽslīce deádbōte *per dignam poenitentiam*, Scint. 40, 2. Swā þæslīc folc and him swā gecwēme, Lchdm. iii. 434, 8. Ða gelimplīcan, þæslīc *congrua*, i. *convenientia*, Wrt. Voc. ii. 133, 39. On þæslīcum tīman *competentibus horis*, 132, 66. Þæslīcum *congruis, aptis, opportunis*, Hpt. Gl. 437, 63. Hwæt mæg beón þæslīcre *what can be more fitting?* L. E. I. 27; Th. ii. 424, 5. II. *comely, fair, elegant*:—Mid þæslīce getingnysse *elegante* (*pulchra*) *sententia* ł *peritia*, Hpt. Gl. 528, 3. Ðā geseah ic tӯn geonge men genōh þæslīce on līchaman, Homl. Skt. ii. 23 b, 370. III. *accordant, in agreement, in harmony*:—Ða cӯðnessa nǽron þæslīce . . . And hyra cӯðnys næs þæslīc *convenientia testimonia non erant* . . . *Et non erat conveniens testimonium illorum*, Mk. Skt. 14, 56–59. v. ge-, un-þæslīc, *and next word*.

þæslīce; *adv.* I. *in that way, so*:—Þæslīce *ita*, Hpt. Gl. 417, 8. Hē ne dyde þæslīce ǽlcere þeóde *non fecit taliter omni nationi*, Ps. Lamb. 47, 20: Blickl. Gl. Hié ðæt gewinn ðā þæslīcost angunnan ðe hī hit ǽr ne angunnen *they began the contest then just as if they had never begun it before*; sic quasi ex integro nova bella nascuntur, Ors. 3, 11; Swt. 150, 31. II. *suitably, fitly, meetly*:—Se dǽdbōte þæslīce dēþ se ðe gylt his bōte lahlīcre beheófaþ *ille poenitentiam digne agit, qui reatum suum satisfactione legitima plangit*, Scint. 46, 1: R. Ben. 70, 21. Hē hlōd ða flōwendan lāre ðe hē eft þæslīce bealcette, Homl. Th. ii. 118, 22. Þæslīcor *dignius*, Germ. 390, 33. v. un-þæslīce.

þæslīcness, e; *f. Fitness, meetness, agreement with what is right*:—Ða hlāfordas hē manode ðæt hī milde wǽron heora ðeówum mannum mid þæslīcnysse (v. Col. 4, 1: Domini, quod justum est et aequum, servis praestate), Homl. Th. ii. 326, 27. v. un-þæslīcness.

þǽsma, an; *m. Leaven*:—Þǽsma godcundre rihtwīsnesse *fermentum divinae justitiae*, R. Ben. 10, 18. [*O. H. Ger.* deismo *fermentum*: *Du.* deesem *leaven*.]

þæt; *pron.* v. se.

þæt; *adv. After that, then*:—Ǽrest ymbe heora landgemǽra: andlang Temese, ðæt (ðonne *in other MS.*, v. l. 8) up on Legean, L. A. G. 1; Th. i. 152, 18. Ǽrest on Ucingford . . . þæt tō brocenan beorge; swā tō Wuduforda; þæt tō Luttes beorge; . . . þæt ðurh ðone mōr, Chart. Th. 186, 3–12. This use is very common in charters.

þæt; *conj. That.* I. introducing substantive clauses, (1) where the clause is equivalent to a noun in the nominative, and (a) stands as the subject of the verb in the main clause:—Genōh byþ ðam leorningcnihte þæt (þætte, Lind. Rush.) hē sӯ swylce his lāreów, Mt. Kmbl. 10. 25. On ðæs engles wordum wæs gehӯred þæt þurh hire beorþor sceolde beón gehǽled eall wīfa cynn, Blickl. Homl. 5, 23: Andr. Kmbl. 181; An. 91. Hū mænige geár synt þæt ðū on ðysum wēstene eardodest, Homl. Skt. ii. 23 b, 513. (b) where *þæt* or *hit* stands as subject in the main clause:—Hū hit beón mæg, þæt se Hālga Gāst cumeþ ufan on ðē, Blickl. Homl. 7, 35. Þæt geweorþeþ on dōmes dæge, þæt hē cymeþ tō dēmenne cwicum and deádum, 11, 3: Andr. Kmbl. 1147; An. 574. Ðæt is gedafenlīc, ðæt ðū Dryhtnes word healde, Elen. Kmbl. 2334; El. 1168. Mid ðæm cræfte ðe ðā scondlīcost wæs; þæt wæs, þæt hié from heora wīcstōwum under ðære eorþan dulfon, Ors. 2, 8; Swt. 90, 29. Nis þæt feor heonon, þæt se mere standeþ, Beo. Th. 2729; B. 1362. Hit is for seofon and feówertigum wintrum, þæt ic of ðære hālgan byrig ūt fōr, Homl. Skt. ii. 23 b, 516. (c) where it further explains a noun in the main clause:—Ðæs gāstes wæstmas synd ða gōdan ðeáwas, þæt se man lufige God . . . and beó gesibsum, Homl. Skt. i. 17, 53. Wæs ðæt weátācen wīde gefrēge, þæt hié ðæs cnihtes cwealm gesōhton, Andr. Kmbl. 2243; An. 1123. (2) where the clause is equivalent to a noun in the accusative, and (a) stands as object to the verb in the main clause:—God geseah þæt hit gōd wæs, Gen. 1, 4. Ic wāt ðæt ðū eart gecӯðed, Elen. Kmbl. 1627; El. 815. (b) where it is in apposition to *þæt* or *hit* standing as object in the main clause:—Gif his sunu and ðæs sunsunu þæt begyten, þæt hē swā micle landes habbaþ, L. Wg. 11; Th. i. 188, 23. Wē leornedon æt him ðæt wē flugen . . . and eác ðæt, ðæt wē his ege ūs ne ondrēden, Past. 3; Swt. 33, 23. Ic þæt wāt, þæt ūs gescildeþ weoruda Dryhten, Andr. Kmbl. 867; An. 434. (c) where it further explains the object of the verb in the main clause:—Helmstān ða undǽde gedyde, ðæt hē Æðerēdes belt forstæl, Chart. Th. 169, 19: Elen. Kmbl. 989; El. 496. Ǽlc man sylle ðone āð, ðæt hē nelle þeóf beón, L. C. S. 21; Th. i. 388, 7. Ic bebeóde wundor geweorðan, ðæt ðeós onlīcnes eorðan sēce, Andr. Kmbl. 1461; An. 731. (2 a) where the subject of the clause is omitted, and the clause taken with the accusative of the main clause is equivalent to the accusative and infinitive construction:—Þeóf ðone ðe wē geāxian, þæt ful sӯ, L. Ath. v. 1; Th. i. 228, 13. Woruldgerihta ic wille þæt standan on ǽlcum leódscipe, L. Edg. S. 2; Th. i. 272, 23. Se ðe mon gesihþ ðæt stronglīc weorc wyrcþ, Bt. 16, 3; Fox 54,

29: Homl. Th. i. 234, 3. Gif gē gesāwen hwelce mūs þæt wǣre hlāford ofer ōþre mȳs, Bt. 16, 2; Fox 52, 2. Ealle ða weód ðe hē geseó ðæt ðām æcerum derigen, 23; Fox 78, 23. Swā fela manna swā mán wite þæt ungelygne sȳn, L. Ath. iv. 1; Th. i. 222, 10. (3) where the clause is equivalent to a noun in the genitive or dative. (*a*) where in the main clause is a verb, verbal noun, or adjective taking after it such a case, and (a) where the substantive clause stands as object:—Ǣnig ne wēnde, ðæt hē lifgende land begēte, Andr. Kmbl. 755; An. 378. Saga þonc ðæt ic his mōdor geweard, Exon. Th. 13, 30; Cri. 210. Is nū þearf micel þæt wē wīsfæstra wordum hȳran, Andr. Kmbl. 2335; An. 1169. Ic āhebbe mīne hand ... þæt ic ne underfō ānne þwang *I lift my hand* (*in testimony of this*) *that I will not take a thing*, Gen. 14, 23. Ðonne hió geornast biþ þæt heó āfǣre fleógan, Ps. Th. 89, 10: Elen. Kmbl. 536; El. 268. (a 1) where the subject is omitted:—Ǣlc mynetere ðe man tīhþ þæt fals feoh slōge, L. Eth. iii. 8; Th. i. 296, 12. (b) where the main clause contains a case of a pronoun in apposition to the substantive clause:—Ne ðurfon wē ðæs wēnan, þæt ūs wuldorcyning wille eard ālēfan, Cd. Th. 272, 5; Sat. 115. Nānne mon ðæs ne tweóþ, ðæt se seó strong, Bt. 16, 3; Fox 54, 28. Hié þæs ðone willan næfdon, þæt hié heora noman hié benǣmon, Ors. 2, 8; Swt. 94, 7. Gif þæs geweorðe gesīðcundne mannan, þæt hē unrihthǣmed genime, L. Wih. 5; Th. i. 38, 4: Andr. Kmbl. 615; An. 308. Ne magon wē þæs wrace gefremman, þæt hē ūs hafaþ ðæs leóhtes bescyrede, Cd. Th. 25, 16; Gen. 394. (c) where the clause explains the noun in the main clause:—Wolde ic ānes tō ðē cræftes neósan, þæt ðū mē getǣhte hū ..., Andr. Kmbl. 969; An. 485. Gē widsōcon sōðe and rihte, ðæt in Bethleme bearn cenned wǣre, Elen. Kmbl. 781; El. 391. (*β*) where the clause is equivalent to a phrase, preposition and noun, with adjectival force, (a) defining the noun in the main clause:—Hit wæs ðā se tīma, þæt wīnberian rīpodon *now the time was the time of the first-ripe grapes* (A. V.), Num. 13, 21. Nis seó þrāh micel, þæt ðē wǣrlogan swencan mōton *the time of your affliction is not long*, Andr. Kmbl. 215; An. 108. Nis seó stund latu, þæt ðē wælreówe wītum belecgaþ, 2423; An. 1213. Nū is se dæg cumen, þæt ūre mandryhten mægenes behōfaþ, Beo. Th. 5297; B. 2646: Val. 1, 9. (b) in apposition to a pronoun in the main clause:—Wæs seó hwīl þæs lang, þæt ic Gode þegnode *the time of my serving God was long* (*or* þæs = so?), Cd. Th. 37, 5; Gen. 585. II. introducing clauses expressing end or purpose, *that, in order that*:—Sete ðīne hand ofer hī þæt (þætte, Lind. Rush.) heó hāl sȳ *ut salva sit*, Mk. Skt. 5, 23. Ðǣr se bisceop oft wæs, þæt hē fullade ðæt folc, Bd. 2, 14; S. 518, 15. Se deófol genam ðæt wīf him tō gefylstan, þæt hē ðone hālgan wer ðurh hī geswice, Homl. Th. ii. 454, 1. Hī cōmon him tō, þæt hī hine geneósodon, 7. II a. with a negative, *that ... not, lest*:—Ic ne underfō ānne þwang, þæt ðū ne secge eft (*ne dicas*): 'Ic gewelegode Abram,' Gen. 14, 23: Lk. Skt. 8, 12. Waciaþ and gebiddaþ þæt (þætte, Lind. Rush.) gē on costnunge ne gān (*ut non intretis*), Mk. Skt. 14, 38. Hig ne eodon intō ðam dōmerne, þæt (þætte, Lind. Rush.) hyg nǣron besmitene *ut non contaminarentur*, Jn. Skt. 18, 28. III. introducing clauses denoting result, manner, kind, degree, (1) where no demonstrative word in the main clause is antecedent to the subordinate clause, *that, so that, so as* (with infin.):—Hū mihtest ðū sittan on middum gemǣnum rīce, þæt ðū ne sceoldest ðæt ilce geþolian ðæt ōðre men? Bt. 7, 3; Fox 22, 17: Homl. Skt. ii. 23 b, 522. Asyrie hæfdon LX wintra and ān hund and ān þūsend, þæt hit nā būton gewinne næs, Ors. 1, 8; Swt. 42, 4. Nis nǣnigu gecynd, ... ðæt hē ne sȳ fȳres cynnes, Salm. Kmbl. 847; Sal. 423. Hē rād þæt hē wæs et Ceastre *he rode so that he was at Worcester*, Chart. Th. 71, 11: Andr. Kmbl. 1576; An. 789: 1474; An. 738. Man gecwǣman ne mæg twām hlāfordum ætsomne, þæt hē ne forseó þone ōðerne, Homl. Skt. i. 17, 220, 224. Þǣr is ān mǣgð þæt hī magon cyle gewyrcan, Ors. 1, 1; Swt. 21, 13. Tō ðām handum ðæt ðæt fel of gǣþ, Lchdm. iii. 114, 3. Hwylc man is þonne ǣfre, þæt hē wēne ... *whatever man is there* (*of such a kind*), *that he can suppose* ..., Wulfst. 214, 14: Cd. Th. 227, 20; Dan. 189. Hyge wæs oncyrred, þæt hié ne murndon, Andr. Kmbl. 73; An. 37. Gif mon sié dumb oþþe deáf geboren, þæt hē ne mæge his synna andettan, L. Alf. pol. 14; Th. i. 70, 14. Ǣfter ðære gebysnunge wurdon ārǣrede muneclīf mid ðære gehealdsumnysse, þæt hī drohtnian on clǣnnesse, Homl. Th. i. 318, 8. Gewunige hē fæstende, þæt hē wite þæt seó mæsse sȳ gesungen *let him continue his fast so, that he may know the mass has been sung*, L. E. I. 39; Th. ii. 438, 3. Gif ceorlisc man geþeó, þæt hē hæbbe .v. hīda landes, L. Wg. 9; Th. i. 188, 5: 10; Th. i. 188, 7. Ða Gotan læssan hwīle hergedan, þæt hié þurh Godes ege þæt hié nāþer ne þa burg ne bærndon ne þæs þone willan næfdon ..., Ors. 2, 8; Swt. 94, 5. (1 a) where the subject of the clause is omitted:—Nemne him mon .v. men, and begite þara .v. .1., þæt him mid swerige, L. Ath. i. 9; Th. i. 204, 11. Hwylc is manna þæt feores neóte ... oððe hwylc manna is þæt his āgene sāwle generige, Ps. Th. 88, 41: Elen. Kmbl. 750; El. 375: Exon. Th. 273, 20; Jul. 519. (2) where the clause stands as relative to a preceding demonstrative word:—Hē lǣrde hig swā þæt (*ita ut*) hig wundredon, Mt. Kmbl. 13, 54. Þæt wīte wæs tō þæs strang, ðæt ǣghwelc man sceolde mid sāre on þās world cuman, Blickl. Homl. 5, 28. Swelc wæs þeáw hira þæt hié ǣghwylcne ellþeódigra dydon him tō mōse, Andr. Kmbl. 51; An. 26. Swā is þære menigo þeáw, þæt ..., 355; An. 178. Ðȳn mægen is swā mǣre, mihtig Drihten, swā þæt ǣnig ne wāt eorðbūende þa deópnesse Drihtnes mihta, ne þæt ǣnig ne wāt engla hādes þa heáhnisse heofena kyninges, Hy. 3, 31–35. Gif his sunu and his sunu sunu þæt geþeóþ, þæt hī swā micel landes habban, L. Wg. 11; Th. i. 188, 10. (2 a) where the subject of the clause is omitted:—Nis nǣnig swā snotor, ne þæs swā gleáw, þæt āsecgan mæge, Cd. Th. 286, 12; Sat. 351. (*See also* se, V, swā.) IV. introducing clauses expressing cause, reason:—Hwæt þence gē betwux eów, þæt (forðon, Lind.: forþon þæt, Rush.) gē hlāfas nabbaþ *why reason ye among yourselves, because ye have brought no bread?* Mt. Kmbl. 16, 8. Byþ ðē meorð, þæt ðū ūs on lāde līðe weorðe, Andr. Kmbl. 551; An. 276. V. where the main clause is not expressed, (1) in narrative:—Ǣrþon ðe seó heánnes ðæs walles gefylled wǣre, þæt se cyning ofslegen wæs and þæt ylce geweorc Ōswalde forlēt (some form equivalent to *it happened* appears necessary before *þæt*, which word there is nothing in the Latin to suggest: Priusquam altitudo parietis esset consummata, rex ipse occisus opus idem Osualdo reliquit), Bd. 2, 14; S. 517, 31. Ðā æt nȳhstan mid fultume his freónda þæt hē gelȳfde, 3, 22; S. 552, 26: 3, 24; S. 556, 21: 4, 27; S. 604, 32 (cf. 3, 9; S. 533, 16–19: 4, 3; S. 569, 1–3). And þæs embe āne niht ðæt wē Marian mæssan healdaþ, Menol. Fox 39; Men. 20 and often. Nō þæt ðīn aldor wolde Godes goldfatu in gylp beran, Cd. Th. 262, 34; Dan. 754: 288, 9; Sat. 378: 304, 24; Sat. 634. (2) in the titles of chapters:—Caput II. Ðæt se ǣrra Rōmwara Cāsere Breotene gesōhte, Bd. 1, 2; S. 475, 2 and often. (3) in exclamations:—Wā þæt ðes tōwyrpþ Godes templ, Mt. Kmbl. 27, 40. Eálā þæt nān wuht nis fæste stondendes weorces, Bt. 9; Fox 26, 21: Met. 9, 55: 18, 1. Eálā, mīn Drihten, þæt ðū eart ælmihtig, 20, 1. Eálā, þæt ic eam ealles leás ēcan dreámes, Cd. Th. 275, 7; Sat. 168. VI. where the construction is elliptical:—Þrȳ dagas tō lāfe syndon þæt hié þē willaþ acwellan *three days remain before the day comes on which they mean to kill you*, Blickl. Homl. 237, 26. [*O. Sax.* that: *O. Frs.* thet: *O. H. Ger.* daz: *Icel.* at.] v. þætte; *conj.*

þætte (= þæt þe; v. se, IV. 3); *pron.* I. as a relative, *that, which*:—Ðæt ðū hyra frumcyn īcan wolde, ꝥte æfter him cenned wurde, Cd. Th. 236, 9; Dan. 318: 245, 32; Dan. 472. Ðæt hē ne forleóse his dreámes blǣd and his dagena rīm and his weorces wlite and wuldres leán, þætte heofones cyning syleþ tō sigorleánum, Exon. Th. 97, 11; Cri. 1589. Metod fēt eall ꝥte grōweþ, Met. 29, 70. Ðætte tǣlwyrðes sié, ðæt hié ðæt tǣlen, Past. 28; Swt. 195, 24. Wīslīce gē dyde, ꝥte mannum bedīgled wæs on eorðan þæt gē þæt on heofenas sōhtan, Blickl. Homl. 201, 1. II. combining antecedent and relative, *that which, what*:—On hire wæs gefylled ꝥte on Cantica Canticorum wæs gesungen, Blickl. Homl. 11, 15. Dō ā þætte duge, Exon. Th. 300, 10; Fä. 4. Wā ðæm ðe gemonigfealdaþ ðæte (ðætte, Cott. MSS.) his ne biþ, Past. 44; Swt. 329, 18.

þætte (= þæt þe; cf. eác wæs *ðæt ðe* beforan ðæm temple stōd ceác, Past. 16; Swt. 105, 1, *and*: Ðā wæs *ꝥte* scyttelas wurdan tōbrocene, Blickl. Homl. 87, 5. Þætte *is used in the same way as* þæt, q. v.); *conj. That.* I. introducing substantive clauses. (1) where the clause is equivalent to a noun in the nominative, and (a) stands as the subject of the verb in the main clause:—Cūþ is ꝥte Drihten fæstte, Blickl. Homl. 27, 23: 87, 5. Weard undyrne cūð, gyddum geómore, þætte Grendel wan wið Hrōðgār, Beo. Th. 305; B. 151. (a 1) where the subject of the substantive clause is omitted:—Nis eów forboden, ꝥte ǣhta habban, gif gē ða on riht strēnaþ, Blickl. Homl. 53, 27. (b) where *þæt* or *hit* stands as subject in the main clause:—Hit is āwriten ðætte Dauid, ðā hē ðone læppan forcorfedne hæfde, ðæt hē slōge on his heortan, Past. 28; Swt. 198, 16. Is þæt þeódnes gebod, ꝥte ..., Exon. Th. 202, 13; Ph. 69. Ðæt gelimpan sceal, þætte lagu flōweþ, 445, 2; Dom. 1. Þæt gesȳne weard, þætte wrecend lifde, Beo. Th. 2517; B. 1256. (c) where it further explains a noun in the main clause:—Ne biþ swylc cwēnlīc þeáw ..., þætte freoðuwebbe feores onsæce leófne mannan, Beo. Th. 3888; B. 1942. Treów wæs gecȳþed, þætte Gūðlāce God leánode, Exon. Th. 129, 12; Gū. 420: Cd. Th. 223, 3; Dan. 114. (2) where the clause is equivalent to a noun in the accusative, and (a) stands as object to the verb in the main clause:—Hēr sagaþ se godspellere, ꝥte Hǣlend wǣre lǣded on wēsten, Blickl. Homl. 27, 3: 41, 34. Hæbbe ic gefrugnen, ꝥte is feor heonan æþelast londa, Exon. Th. 197, 19; Ph. 1. (b) where it is in apposition to *þæt* or *hit* standing as object in the main clause:—Hī þæt ne gelȳfdon, ꝥte līffruma āhafen wurde, Exon. Th. 41, 16; Cri. 656. (c) where it further explains the object of the verb in the main clause:—Bodan sægdon sōðne gefeán, þætte sunu wǣre Meotudes ācenned, Exon. Th. 28, 24; Cri. 451. Men gesēgon þeódwundor micel, ꝥte eorðe āgeaf ða hyre on lǣgun, 71, 15; Cri. 1156. (3) where the clause is equivalent to a noun in genitive or dative:—Gode ælmiehtigum sī ðonc, ðætte wē nū ǣnigne onstāl habbaþ lāreówa, Past. pref.; Swt. 4, 1. Se ðæs onsōce, ꝥte sōð wǣre mǣre mihta waldend, Cd. Th. 244, 21; Dan. 451. II. introducing clauses expressing end or purpose, *that, in order that*:—Beforan ðæm temple stōd ǣren ceác, ðætte menn meahten hira honda đweán, Past. 16; Past. 105, 1. Sprec tō đīnum discipulum, ꝥte sȳ geblissad heora heorte, and hié sȳn ofergytende đisse sǣwe ege, Blickl. Homl. 233, 36. **III.** introducing clauses expressing result, manner, kind, degree. (1) where no demonstrative word is antecedent to the subordinate clause, *that, so that*:—Hī wēnaþ ꝥ hī mægen eall đās gōd gegaderian tōgædere, þætte nān būton đære gesomnunga ne sié, Bt. 24, 4; Fox 86, 3. Daniel sægde him wīslīce wereda gesceafte, ꝥte sōna ongeat cyning ord and ende đæs đe him ȳwed wæs, Cd. Th. 225, 28; Dan. 161. Woldon hié feorhleán fācne gyldan ꝥte hē ꝥ dægweorc dreóre gebohte *so that he should pay for that deed with blood*, 187, 14; Exod. 151. (1 a) where the subject of the clause is omitted:—Nis ǣnig man þætte swā bereáfod sié, Met. 22, 49. Nǣnig manna is þætte āreccan mæg, Andr. Kmbl. 1091; An. 546: Cd. Th. 210, 2; Exod. 509. (2) where there is a demonstrative form as antecedent:—Hē beóþ swā geþwǣra, þætte nō ꝥ ān ꝥ hī magon geféran beón, ac đȳ furþor ꝥ heora nān būton ōþrum beón ne mæg, Bt. 21; Fox 74, 17. Đǣr wæs swīþe swēte stenc swā ꝥte ealle đa slēpan đe đǣr wǣron, Blickl. Homl. 145, 29. Đīnne līchoman hié tōstenceaþ swā ꝥte đīn blōd flēwþ ofer eorđan swā swā wæter, 237, 6. (2 a) where the subject of the clause is omitted:—ꝥ nis nān man, ꝥte sumes eácan ne þurfe, Bt. 24, 4; Fox 86, 6. **IV.** where the main clause is not expressed:—Đonne hī niđer āstīgaþ tō āđweánne hiera niéhstena scylda, hié beóþ onlīcost suelce hī beren đone ceák . . ., đætte (*the case is such, that*) suā hwelc suā inweard higige tō gangenne on đa dura đæs ēcean līfes, hē ondette ǣlce costunge, Past. 16; Swt. 105, 14. Æfter đæm đe Rōmeburg getimbred wæs twā hunde wintra and IIIIX, þætte (*it came to pass, that*) Cambisis fēng tō Persa rīce, Ors. 2, 5; Swt. 78, 2: 4, 1; Swt. 154, 2. And đæs embe fīf niht đætte fulwiht tiid ēces Drihtnes tō ūs cymeþ, Menol. Fox 22; Men. 11, and often. Eálā ꝥte đis moncyn wǣre gesǣlig, gif heora mōd wǣre riht, Bt. 21; Fox 74, 40. Đætte oft đæs lāreówdōmes đēnung biþ swīđe untǣlwyrđlīce gewilnad, Past. 7, arg.; Swt. 47, 20, and often.

-þafa. v. ge-þafa.

þafet[t]ere, es; *m. One who agrees* or *consents, one who is remiss in allowing*:—Đȳ læs se đafetere, se đe wile forgiefan đæt hē wrecan sceolde, tō ēcum wītum geteó his hiéremenn *ne rector remittendo quod ferire debuit ad aeterna supplicia subditos pertrahat*, Past. 20; Swt. 149, 21. Đæt hē swā stiére đǣm ungeđyldegum irsunga, swā hē đone hnescan đafettere on recceléste ne gebrenge *sic ab impatientibus extinguatur ira, ut tamen remissis ac lenibus non crescat negligentia*, 60; Swt. 453, 25.

þafian; *p.* ode. **I.** *to consent to, agree with, approve of, assent to, allow, permit.* (a) with accusative:—Ic Beágmund đis đeafie and wrīte, Chart. Th. 472, 22, 24, 28, 19, and often. Swā hwylc swā morþorslege þafaþ and hine man đonne fremmeþ *quicunque ad homicidium consenserit, et id postea factum fuerit*, L. Ecg. C. 22; Th. ii. 148, 14. Heó hine monede đæt hē weoruldhād forlǣte and munuchāde onfēnge. Ond hē đæt well đafode *he readily consented to it*, Bd. 4, 24; S. 598, 3. Đē sint tū gearu swā līf swā deáđ, swā đē leófre biþ tō geceósanne; cȳđ hwæt đū đæs tō þinge þafian wille *say which alternative you mean to accept*, Elen. Kmbl. 1213; El. 608. Nǣfre ic đæs þeódnes þafian wille mǣgrǣdenne *I will never consent to marriage with the prince*, Exod. Th. 249, 8; Jul. 108. (b) with dative:—Gē þafiaþ eówer fædera weorcum *consentitis operibus patrum uestrorum*, Lk. Skt. 11, 48. Đafande woeron feh him tō seallanne *pacti sunt pecuniam illi dare*, Lind. 22, 5. (c) with a clause:—Gif hē þafaþ đæt hē ūt gā of minstre *si consenserit, ut egrediatur de monasterio*, R. Ben. Interl. 98, 17. Þafodest đū đæt mē þeówmennen drehte, Cd. Th. 135, 21; Gen. 2246. Þafa đæt ic ūt ādō đæt mot of đīnum eágan *sine eiciam festucam de oculo tuo*, Mt. Kmbl. 7, 4. Đa eorlas þafigan ne woldon đæt hié forlēton leófne lāreów, Andr. Kmbl. 804; An. 402. **II.** *to submit to, bear, suffer, endure*:—Đē þincþ se earmra se đæt yfel dēþ đonne se đe hit þafaþ *miserior tibi injuriae illator, quam acceptor esse videretur*, Bt. 38, 6; Fox 208, 19. Sum gewealdenmōd þafaþ in geþylde đæt hē sceal, Exon. Th. 297, 20; Crā. 77. Eal đæt hē for ūs þafode and đolode, Wulfst. 23, 22. Đa eádigan martyras mænigfealde earfođnyssa đafedon, Homl. Skt. i. 23, 12, 89. Se þeódcyning đafian sceolde Eofores ānne dōm, Beo. Th. 5919; B. 2963. Þafigan, Cd. Th. 227, 22; Dan. 190. Ic sceal þinga gehwylc þolian and þafian on đīnne dōm *I must suffer and submit to everything, as you decide*, Exon. Th. 270, 16; Jul. 466. Hié derede ǣgđer ge þurst ge hǣte, and ealne đone dæg wǣron đæt þafiende, Ors. 5, 7; Swt. 230, 17. **III.** *to bear with, tolerate*:—Hē ilde and đafode đa scylda and đeáh hē him gecȳđde *et dissimulavit culpas, et innotuit*, Past. 21; Swt. 151, 22. [*Non me demergat tempestas* louerd ne þaue þu þat storm me duue, O. E. Homl. ii. 43, 15. Ȝef ha ne letteđ me nawt, ah þauieđ ant þolieđ, Marh. 15, 19. Ne mahe ȝe nawt do me, bute þet he wule þeauien and þolien ow to donne, Jul. 19, 9. Þatt Godd ne þole nohht ne þafe laþe gastess to winnenn oferrhannd off uss, Orm. 5457. Euerilc husfolc đe mai it đauen on ger sep ođer on kide hauen, Gen. and Ex. 3139. Was neuere non þat mouhte þaue Hise dintes, noyþer knith ne knaue, Havel. 2696.] v. geþafian.

þafung, e; *f. Consent, permission*:—Be bisceopes þafunge *cum consensu episcopi*, L. Ecg. C. 26; Th. ii. 152, 3. Be his þafunge *permissionem suam*, R. Ben. Interl. 77, 6. Đū wēndest đæt seó weord đās woruld wende būton Godes geþeahte and his þafunge, Bt. 5, 1; Fox 8, 32. Ne mæg se deófol mannum derian būtan Godes đafunge, Homl. Skt. i. 17, 196. Þet weas mid Earnulfes þafunge (geþafunge, MS. A.), Chr. 887; Erl. 87. 3. [Vlesches fondunge gođ to uorđ upe me þurch min þafunge, A. R. 344, note.] v. ge-þafung.

þage, þāh *though*. v. þæge, þeáh.

þametaþ?:—Flōdas hafettaþ (þametaþ, MS. M.) handum *flumina plaudent manu*, Ps. Spl. 97, 8.

þan, þon; *adv.* **I.** *then, from that time, after that*:—Wæs wyrd ungemete neáh . . . nō þon lange wæs feorh æþelinges flǣsce bewunden, Beo. Th. 4838; B. 2423. [*Goth.* þan: *O. Sax. O. Frs. O. L. Ger.* þan.] **II.** *so, as*:—Wiþ đæs ic wāt đū wilt higian þon ǣr þe đū hine ongitest *towards it I know thou wilt hasten as soon as thou perceivest it*, Bt. 11, 2; Fox 34, 8. [Cf. *O. Sax.* than lango the hē mōsta is juguđi neotan, Hēl. 3498.] **III.** with comparatives, in negative sentences. (a) with adjectives, (α) followed by *đonne* or *đe, any*:—Gif hió bearn gestriéne, næbbe đæt đæs ierfes þon (þe, MS. H.) māre þe sió mōdor *if she have a child, it shall not have any more of the property than the mother*, L. Alf. pol. 8; Th. i. 66, 20. On ōđrum ærne đæt næbbe þon mā dura đonne sió cirice, 5; Th. i. 64, 15. Ne eart đū þon leófre, đonne se swearta hrefn *thou art not any more dear, than the black raven*, Exon. Th. 370, 4; Seel. 52. Nǣfre hlīsan āh meotud þan māran þonne hē wiđ monna bearn wyrceþ weldǣdum, 191, 10; Az. 86. Hē ne ūþe đæt ǣnig ōþer man ǣfre mǣrđa þon mā gehēdde, đonne hē sylfa, Beo. Th. 1012; B. 504. (α 1) where *þon* is preceded by *wihte, any at all*:—Ne mōt hē đara hyrsta lǣdan of đisse worulde wuhte þon māre đonne hē hider brōhte (cf. ne lǣt hē his nānwuht of đīs middanearde mid him māre đonne hē brōhte hider, Bt. 26, 3; Fox 94, 15–17), Met. 14, 10. (β) where the comparative takes the dative after it:—Hē đām đe on sceare māran wǣron on đām mægnum eáþmōdnesse and hȳrsumnesse nōhte đon læssa wæs *in respect to the virtues of humility and obedience he was not any less than those who were greater in the matter of the tonsure*, Bd. 5, 19; S. 637, 18. (γ) where neither particle nor case follows the comparative:—Næs đā wordlatu wihte þon māre þæt se stān tōgān *then was there not any more delay at all in obeying the command, so that the stone split open*, Andr. Kmbl. 3043; An. 1524. Nāhte ic đīnre nǣfre miltse þon māran þearfe *never had I any greater need of thy mercy* (*than I now have*), Judth. Thw. 22, 35; Jud. 92. (b) with adverbs, (α) followed by *đe*:—Hē nāt hwæt him tóweard biþ, þon mā þe đū wistest *he knows not what will happen to him any more than thou knowest*, Bt. 11, 1; Fox 32, 14. Wē his ne gefrēdaþ, þon mā đe mon his feax mæg gefrēdan būtan his felle, Past. 18; Swt. 139, 20. Him đæt nō ne derede, đon mā đe ceald wæter, Shrn. 83, 17: Exon. Th. 364, 33; Wal. 80. (β) without *đe*:—Ic đa word gehȳrde and nōht đon ǣr đære ærninge blon *ego audiens, nihilominus coeptis instití vetitis*, Bd. 5, 6; S. 619, 15. Hē georne wiđsōc Iōsepes hūse ne þon ǣr geceás Effremes cynn *he utterly refused the house of Joseph, nor any more readily did he choose the race of Ephraim*, Ps. Th. 77, 67. Æfre ic ne hȳrde þon cymlīcor ceól gehladenne *I have not ever heard of a vessel any more fairly laden*, Andr. Kmbl. 721; An. 361. Đā ne wolde se pāpa đæt geþafigean ne đa burhware đon mā *etsi pontifex concedere voluit, non tamen cives Romani potuere permittere*, Bd. 2, 1; S. 501, 33. Ne bewerede Penda đon mā gif hwylce men woldan Godes word lǣron đæt hī ne mōstan *nec prohibuit Penda, quin etiam verbum, si qui vellent audire, praedicaretur*, 3, 21; S. 551, 23. Ne đon mā se đe gehāt gehǣt, ne wēne hē đæt hē sié ā đȳ neár hefonrīce, gif hē hine from went đǣm gehātum *nor any more let him that vows a vow suppose that he be ever the nearer heaven, if he turns from those vows*, Past. 51; Swt. 403, 2. Ne biþ sond þon mā wiđ micelne rēn hūses hirde *nor any more is the sand a guard for a house against much rain*, Met. 7, 20: 8, 23: 11, 69. Būtan đū ūsic þon ōfostlīcor hreddan wille *if you do not save us any quicker*, Exon. Th. 17, 18; Cri. 272. (β 1) where *āwiht* or *wuhte* precedes *þon, any at all*:—Đǣr nǣnegu biþ niht on sumera, ne wuhte þon mā on wintra dæg tōteled tīdum, Met. 16, 14: 20, 108. Āwiht þon mā, Ps. Th. 63, 7. [*O. Sax.* ni . . . than mēr the *not . . . any more than*. Cf. *Goth.* ni . . . þana mais: *O. H. Ger.* dana mēr.]

þān; *adj. Moist*:—Þa þānan *madentia*, Wrt. Voc. ii. 93, 71: 57, 12. [*Thone, thoney* = damp, is found as a word of E. Norfolk and of some Midland counties in Marshall's Rural Economy (1795–6), and in Ray's North-country words (1691); v. E. D. S. Pub. Reprinted Glossaries, B. 3, 5, 15.] v. þānian, þǣnan.

þanan, þonan (-on, -un, -en); *adv.* **I.** with demonstrative force, *thence*:—Þanan *illic*(*-inc?*), Wrt. Voc. ii. 110, 55. Đonan *illinc*, 44, 54. (1) marking the point from which motion takes place:—Hē þanon (þonan, Rush.: þona, Lind. *inde*) eode, Mt. Kmbl. 4, 21. Þanon hē com on Iudéisce endas *inde exsurgens uenit in fines Iudaeae*, Mk. Skt. 10, 1. Hē wand up þanon, Cd. Th. 29, 7; Gen. 446. Hē fōr þanun (þanon, MS. A.: đonan, Rush.), Mt. Kmbl. 11, 1. Þanun (-en, MS. A.), 12, 9. Monige þonan gewitan, Bd. 4, 25; S. 601, 34. Þonan, Exon. Th. 235, 9; Ph. 554. Hē đa hālgan sāuwla þonon ālǣdde, Blickl. Homl. 67, 19. Hāt mīn blōd þonon ādrȳgan, 183, 27. (1 a) followed by a relative particle, the two words together having force of relative:—Þider cuman, þonan þe hit ǽr com, Bt. 25; Fox 88, 31. On ða rícu, þonon þe hē ǽr sended wæs, Blickl. Homl. 9, 25. Ðȳ læs hē āfealle ðonon ðe hē fæsðlīcost tō hopian scolde, Past. 51; Swt. 395, 11. (2) marking the point from or in regard to which direction or position is estimated:—Ðanon ðe hē blǽwþ him byþ nama gesett *from the quarter that the wind blows is a name made for it*, Lchdm. iii. 274, 11. Ðæt flōd ys þanon tōdǽled on feówer eán *from that point the stream runs in four separate channels*, Gen. 2, 10. Ðā hē on botme stōd, ðā him þūhte ðæt þanon wǽre tō helle duru hund þūsenda mīla gemearcodes, Cd. Th. 310, 7; Sat. 722. Hē ðǽr rom geseah unfeor þanon standan, 177, 9; Gen. 2927: Beo. Th. 3615; B. 1805. God wæs mīn on ða swīðran, ðanon ic ne wende ǽfre tō aldre onsión mīne, Elen. Kmbl. 696; El. 348. Hē sǽde ðæt ðæt land sié swīþe lang norþ þonan *he said that from that point the country stretches very far to the north*, Ors. 1, 1; Swt. 17, 4. Seó burh is west þonon from ðære stōwe on ānre mīle, Blickl. Homl. 129, 3. (3) marking the place from which an action or operation proceeds:—Nalles þanon (*from hell*) gehēran in heofonum hāligne dreám, Cd. Th. 284, 26; Sat. 327. Gesæt him be healfe . . . , þanon bāsnode hwæt him gūðweorca gifeðe wearð, Andr. Kmbl. 2131; An. 1067. Hié ealle on yppan wunedon, þonen bīdende ðæs Hālgan Gāstes, Blickl. Homl. 133, 26. God wunaþ on ðære ceastre his ānfealdnesse; ðonan hē dǽlþ manega gemetgunga eallum his gesceaftum, and þonon (-an, Cott. MS.) hē welt ealra, Bt. 39, 5; Fox 218, 18–21. Þonan ān cyning rīcsaþ . . . , ealra gesceafta waldeþ (cf. þǽr rīcsaþ ān cyning, se hæfþ anweald eallra ōþra cyninga *heic regum sceptrum dominus tenet*, Bt. 36, 2; Fox 174, 17), Met. 24, 31. (4) marking source, origin:—Mænige gefōþ hwælas and micelne sceat þanon (*inde*) begytaþ, Coll. Monast. Th. 25, 3. Þanon wōc fela geósceaftgāsta, Beo. Th. 2535; B. 1265. Þonon Eómer wōc, 3925; B. 1960. Ðære wrǽnnesse wōdþrāg . . . gedrǽfþ sefan ingehygd: þonan mǽst cymeþ unnetta saca, Met. 25, 43. (5) marking cause, reason:—Ne gehȳrdest ðū Drihten cweþende, for þon þe ic eów sende swā swā sceáp on middum wulfum? Þanon wæs geworden . . . ic bæd ūrne Drihten ðæt hē hine æteówde, and hraþe hē mē hine æteówde, and hē mē tō cwæð . . . 'Ic sende tō ðē Andreas,' Blickl. Homl. 237, 30. Þonne God gangeþ for his folc . . . þanon eorðe byþ onhrēred, Ps. Th. 67, 8. (6) temporal, *from that time, after that*:—Ðæt hē unæþele ā forð þanan wyrð, Met. 17, 28. Hē forlǽt his æþelo, and ðonan wyrþ anæþelad ōþ ðæt hē wyrþ unæþele, Bt. 30, 2; Fox 110, 22. Þanon forþ *exhinc*, Anglia xiii. 393, 404: *de cetero*, 439, 1059. Ðanon forþ *exinde*, 444, 1130. Hē ða gefeán ðæs heofonlīces ēðles þanon forð geseón ne mihte, Wulfst. 1, 6. Siððan ongon Cain ceastre timbran . . . Þanon his eaforan ǽrest wōcan bearn from brȳde on ðam burhstede. Se yldesta wæs Iared hāten *afterwards did Cain build a city . . . Not till after that were children born to his son* (*Enoch*) *in that town. The eldest was Irad* (v. Gen. 4, 17, 18), Cd. Th. 65, 4; Gen. 1061: 210, 14; Exod. 515. II. with relative force, *whence*, (1) referring to the point from which motion takes place:—Ic gecyrre on mīn hūs þanon (*unde*) ic ūt eode, Mt. Kmbl. 12, 44. Cunnaþ fȳr eft tō his ēðle, ðanon hit ǽror cwom, Salm. Kmbl. 834; Sal. 416. Hē gewāt on Hibernia, ðonan hē ǽr com, Bd. 4, 25; S. 600, 13. Þonan, Exon. Th. 17, 12; Cri. 269. Hē tō ðæm fæderlīcan setle eode, þonon hē nǽfre onweg ne gewāt, Blickl. Homl. 117, 1. (2) referring to the point from or in regard to which direction or position is estimated:—On heofonas, þonon hē nǽfre won wæs, Blickl. Homl. 131, 17: 91, 5. (3) referring to the place from which an action or operation proceeds:—Hē hine sylfne hefeþ on heánne beám, þonan ȳþast mæg sīð bihealdan, Exon. Th. 205, 15: Ph. 113. (4) referring to source or origin:—Ðæt sum gestreón mē ic begyte þanon ic mē āfēde *ut aliquod lucrum mihi adquiram, unde me pascam*, Coll. Monast. Th. 27, 21. (5) referring to cause or reason:—Hē mā gewunode on his smiþþan sittan, ðonne hē wolde on cyricean singan. Ðonon him gelamp ðæt sume men gewuniaþ cweþan *magis in officina sua residere, quam ad psallendum in ecclesia concurrere consuerat. Unde accidit illi, quod solent dicere quidam*, Bd. 5, 14; S. 634, 18. III. in correlative combinations:—Ðæt mē þincþ wiþerweard þing . . . ðætte þonan ðe hī teohhiaþ ðæt hī scylan eádigran weorþan, ðæt hī weorþaþ ðonan earmran, Bt. 26, 2; Fox 92, 24–27. Ðonon ðe hī ūtan bióþ āhæfene, ðanon hié bióþ innan āfeallene, Past. 50; Swt. 391, 12. [*O. Sax.* thanan: *O. Frs.* thana: *O. H. Ger.* danān *inde, illinc*.] v. *next word*, *and* þe, II. 1.

þanane; *adv.* I. *thence.* (1) local:—Ne gǽst ðū þanone (-ene, MS. A.: þonan, Rush.) *non exies inde*, Mt. Kmbl. 5, 26: Lk. Skt. 12, 59. Ðā gewāt ic þanone, Homl. Skt. ii. 23 b, 422. Ðanonne, Judth. Thw. 23, 21; Jud. 132. (2) temporal, *after that*:—*Rursum, dein vel* þonane, Wrt. Voc. ii. 139, 63. (3) causal:—Ðonne mon lǽt tōslūpan ðone ege . . . , ðonne wierþ gehnescad ðonone sió ðreáung ðæs anwaldes, Past. 40; Swt. 289, 3. II. *whence*:—Wīgheard tō Rōme wæs onsended, ðonone hī hider onsendon gewritu, Bd. 3, 29; S. 561, 3. [*O. L. Ger.* thanana: *O. H. Ger.* danana.] v. preceding word.

þanan-forþ. v. þanan, I. 6.

þanan-weard; *adj. Moving thence*:—Bebeád hē him, ðæt hē geara wiste, ðæt hē hine nǽfre underbæc ne besāwe, siþþan hē þononweard wǽre *lex dona coërceat, ne dum Tartara liquerit, fas sit lumina flectere*, Bt. 35, 6; Fox 170, 9. [Cf. þeone Godd warp hire (*pride*) sone se ha iboren wes; & as ha nuste hwuch wei ha come þeneward, ne con ha neauer mare ifinden na wei aȝainward, H. M. 43, 8.]

þanc, es; *m.* I. *thought*:—On ðeóstrum ne mæg þances gehygdum ǽnig wīslīcu wundur oncnāwan, Ps. Th. 87, 11. Þances gleáw þegn, Andr. Kmbl. 1113; An. 557. Þonces gleáw, Exon. 207, 19; Ph. 144. Þurh gemynda spēd, mōde and dǽdum, worde and gewitte, wīse þance, Cd. Th. 118, 1; Gen. 1958. Ge þanc ge þeáwas, word and weorc georne gerihtan, L. P. M. 3; Th. ii. 288, 16. Drihten, ūre mōd gebīg, þanc and þeáwas on ðīn gewil, Hy. 7, 78. [Þu þi þanc (þoht, 2nd MS.) al forhele, Laym. 4360. He put a swuc þonc in hire heorte, A. R. 222, 25.] II. *kindly thought, favour, grace*:—Oft hē þearfendra bēne þance (*graciously*) gehȳrde, Ps. Th. 101, 15. Ðis is landa betst, ðæt wit þurh uncres hearran þanc habban mōston (cf. hie thuru thes kēsures thank rīki habda, Hēl. 66), Cd. Th. 49, 22; Gen. 796. III. *agreeableness, pleasure, satisfaction*; in phrases, (a) æfter þance *according to what is agreeable, agreeably, pleasantly*:—Hē his līchoman forwyrnde woruldblissa . . . Him wæs Godes egsa māra in gemyndum ðonne hē menniscum þrymme æfter þonce þegan wolde *he refused his body worldly delights . . . There was too much fear of God in his mind for him to partake of human glory, following the dictates of pleasure*, Exon. Th. 112, 7; Gū. 140. (b) on þanc, tō þances, tō þance *to the satisfaction* of a person, *so as to please*, cf. *O. Frs.* tō thanke: *Icel.* til þakka eins, i þökk við einn *to one's liking*: *Ger.* zu Danke:—Hié nānwuht gōdes ne magon Gode bringan tō ðances *nullum boni operis Deo sacrificium immolant*, Past. 46; Swt. 349, 8. Ðū hæfst tō þance geþēnod ðīnum hearan, hæfst ðē wið Drihten dȳrne geworhtne (cf. habda ira Drohtine gethionōd te thanka, Hēl. 506), Cd. Th. 32, 20; Gen. 506: Beo. Th. 763; B. 379. Se bisceop ðæs getīðode on ealra ðæra witena þanc *the bishop granted it to the satisfaction of all the witan*, Chart. Th. 303, 2. Cūð dyde Nergend ðæt Noe ðæt gyld on þanc āgifen hæfde (*the sacrifice had been well pleasing*), Cd. Th. 91, 2; Gen. 1506. Him wīf sunu on þanc gebær *to his delight his wife bore him a son*, 167, 31; Gen. 2774. Ic ðē on hleóðre hearpan gecwēme . . . Ic ðē on þanc mōte sealmas singan, Ps. Th. 107, 3: Andr. Kmbl. 3242; An. 1624. On þonc, Exon. Th. 402, 7; Rä. 21, 26. Hē of stānclife burnan leódum lǽdde on leófne þanc, Ps. Th. 135, 17. (c) on þance *pleasing, agreeable, grateful*, cf. thīn thionost is im an thanke, Hēl. 118: *O. H. Ger.* in thanke, danche *gratus*:—On ðonce mē syndon ðīne word and ðīn lufu *gratias ago benevolentiae tuae*, Bd. 2, 12; S. 513, 23. Mē is ðīn cyme on myclum ðonce *gratus mihi est multum adventus tuus*, 4, 9; S. 577, 21: Exon. Th. 387, 22; Rä. 5, 9. Ðonne wǽron ǽgþer gōde, ge ða ǽrran ge ðās æfterran, and nǽron nāðere an þance *quid aliud colligi datur, nisi semper bona esse, sed ingrata?* Ors. 2, 5; Swt. 86, 10. Nǽnegum þūhte dæg on þonce gif sió dimme niht ǽr egesan ne brōhte (cf. þancwyrþre biþ ðæs dæges leóht for ðære egeslīcan þióstro ðære nihte, Bt. 23; Fox 78, 28), Met. 12, 16. IV. *thanks*:—Gode ælmiehtegum sī ðonc, ðætte . . . , Past. pref.; Swt. 2, 18. Him ðæs þanc sié, Cd. Th. 68, 13; Gen. 1116: Hy. 7, 58: Andr. Kmbl. 2900; An. 1453. Ðisse ansȳne Alwealdan þanc gelimpe, Beo. Th. 1861; B. 928. Swǽ gelǽrede biscepas, swǽ suǽ nū Gode ðonc wel hwǽr siendon, Past. prep.; Swt. 9, 4: 1; Swt. 27, 3: Andr. Kmbl. 2302; An. 1152. Ða gesceafta nǽron nānes ðonces ne nānes weorþscipes weorþe, gif hī heora unwillum hlāforde hērden, Bt. 35, 4; Fox 160, 20. Hié ða lāc þēgon tō þance (*thankfully, gratefully*), Andr. Kmbl. 2225; An. 1114. Hē him dǽda leán gieldeþ, ðām ðe his giefe willaþ þicgan tō þonce, Exon. Th. 109, 26; Gū. 96. Hié on þanc curon æðelinges ēst *they accepted Lot's kindness with thanks*, Cd. Th. 147, 20; Gen. 2442. Þanc āgan, habban *to have thanks, be thanked* for something (*gen., prep., or clause*):—Ðæs āge þrynesse þrym þonc, Exon. Th. 37, 27; Cri. 599. Hafa ārna þanc, Cd. Th. 147, 6; Gen. 2435. Hæfþ se þeówa ǽnigne þanc, forþam ðe hē dyde ðæt him beboden wæs, Lk. Skt. 17, 9. Þonc hafa, Iofes, ðæt ic ða mōste oferwinnan, Ors. 4, 1; Swt. 156, 27. Þanc cunnan, witan [cf. He cuðe him ðerof wel gret ðhanc, Gen. and Ex. 1659. Sche . . . can hem therfore as moche thank as me, Chauc. Kn. T. 950] *to feel grateful, be thankful* for something (*gen.*):—Ðām ðe þonc Gode wīta ne cūþun, ðæs ðe hē on ðone hālgan beám āhongen wæs *to those who felt no gratitude to God for his sufferings, for his being hung on the cross*, Exon. Th. 67, 22; Cri. 1092: 74, 29; Cri. 1213. Ðū Waldende ðīnre ālȳsnesse þonc ne wisses, 90, 5; Cri. 1474: 85, 5; Cri. 1386. Ðū ðæs ealles ǽnigne þonc ðīnum nergende nysses on mōde, 91, 29; Cri. 1498. God nele, ðæt him man his gifena þanc nyte, Wulfst. 261, 17. Þancas, þanc dōn *to give thanks*; gratias agere: þanca dǽd *gratiarum actio*, Scint. 50, 5:—Hē Gode þancas dyde *gratias agens*, Mk. Skt. 14, 23: Lk. Skt. 22, 17. Ðē ic þancas dō, forðam ðe ic ne eom swylce ōðre men, 18, 11: Jn. Skt. 11, 41: Scint. 50, 2, 3. Þanc ic dō, ðū gōda hyrde, forðon ðās sceáp mē efenþrowiaþ, Blickl. Homl. 191, 24. Þanc gegildan [cf. Me him ne yeldeþ þonkes of his guodes, Ayenb. 18, 6] *to pay thanks, give from a feeling of gratitude, to reward* a service:—Him God wolde æfter þrowinga þonc gegyldan, ðæt hē martyrhād gelufade, sealde him snyttra, Exon. Th. 130, 23; Gū. 442. Þanc, þancas secgan [cf. To zigge grat þank, Ayenb. 18, 17] *to* *express thanks* for something (*gen., prep. clause*), *give thanks*:—Hē Gode his gōda ðanc sægde (*gratias agebat*), Bd. 3, 12; S. 537, 26: Cd. Th. 16, 4; Gen. 238: Andr. Kmbl. 2937; An. 1471: Blickl. Homl. 103, 25: 217, 34. Ne sæcgaþ ūs nēnne þanc, Homl. Skt. i. 3, 332. Saga ēcne þonc, ðæt ic his mōdor gewearþ, Exon. Th. 13, 28; Cri. 209. Wē sculon simle secgan Gode ðoncas for eów, Past. 32; Swt. 213, 10. ¶ Þances, *genitive, used alone or in combination with noun or pronoun, and having adverbial force* (cf. *O. L. Ger.* thankis *gratis*: *O. H. Ger.* danches *sponte, ultro, gratis*). (1) *thanks* to a person on whom a result depends, *by* (*one's*) *grace, favour*:—Ðæt næs nā eówres þances ac þurh God *it was not thanks to you but by God's will*; non vestro consilio sed Dei voluntate, Gen. 45, 8. Sege mē hwæþer se ðīn wela ðīnes þances swā deóre seó ðe for his āgenre gecynde *tell me whether that wealth of thine is so precious thanks to thee or from its own nature*, Bt. 13; Fox 38, 6. Hié rīcsedon næs ðeáh mīnes ðonces *ipsi regnaverunt, et non ex me*, Past. 1; Swt. 27, 14. Godes þonces *by God's grace*, Chr. 897; Erl. 94, 29: 883; Erl. 83, 18. (2) where there is voluntary or unforced action, *of* (*one's own*) *accord, with* (*a person's*) *consent, willingly, voluntarily*:—Hē him hiera ðonces gestiéran ne meahte *he could not restrain himself from them* (his vices) *of his own accord*, Past. 3; Swt. 35, 18. Gewilde man hī tō rihte þances oþþe unþances *let them be compelled to right whether they will or no*, L. Eth. ix. 40; Th. i. 348, 28. Hē nam sume mid him, sume þances, sume unþances *he took some of them with him, some willingly, others against their will*, Chr. 1066; Erl. 198, 36. Ðā þancodon hȳ ðyses Gode and mē swȳþe georne, and heom eall ðis swȳþe wel līcode, and cwǣdon ðæt heora þances ðis on ēcnesse stande *they said that they approve of the arrangement remaining in perpetuity*, Chart. Th. 117, 7. Āgenes þances *sponte*, Germ. 395, 64: L. C. S. 75; Th. i. 416, 22. Gif hwā þeóf gemēte and hine his þances āweg lǣte būton hreáme *if any one come upon a thief and of his own accord let him get away without hue and cry*, 29; Th. i. 392, 14. Hwæþer ðe ðū hȳ forseó and ðīnes āgenes þonces hī forlēte būton sāre ðe ðū gebīde hwonne hī ðē sorgiendne forlētan *whether thou despise them and of thine own accord abandon them without a pang, or wait till the time comes when they abandon thee sorrowing*, Bt. 8; Fox 26, 12: 7, 2; Fox 18, 13. Ðonne sió sāul hire unðonces gebǣdd wierð ðæt yfel tō forlǣtanne ðæt hió ǣr hire āgnes ðonces gedyde, Past. 36; Swt. 251, 14. [Hi wenden alle fra þe king, sume here þankes and sume here unþankes, Chr. 1140; Erl. 265, 12. Bluðeliche he wule herkien þet þe preost him leið on; ah þenne þe preost hine hat aȝefen þa ehte þon monne þet hit er ahte, þet he nulle iheren his þonkes *he will not listen to that if he can help it*, O. E. Homl. i. 31, 8. Þe sulve mose hire þonkes wolde þe totose, O. and N. 70. Lordschipe wol not his thonkes han no felaweschipe, Chauc. Kn. T. 768.] (3) where there is uncontrolled or independent action, *at* (*one's*) *pleasure* or *will*:—Ðū wēndest ðæt seó wyrd ðās woruld wende heore āgenes þonces būton Godes geþeahte and his þafunge *thou didst suppose that fate turned this world at her own pleasure without the counsel and consent of God*, Bt. 5, 1; Fox 8, 31. (4) where there is independent condition, *in* or *of itself*:—Gif se weorþscipe and se anweald āgnes ðonces gōd wǣre, Bt. 16, 3; Fox 54, 9. Se anweald his āgenes ðonces gōd næs, ðā se gōd næs ðe hē tō com, 16, 4; Fox 58, 19. (5) *for* (*one's*) *sake*:—Wē biddaþ ðē. ðæt ðū hit ūs ðīnes fæder þances forgife *we pray thee to forgive us it for thy father's sake*, Gen. 50, 17. Gedǣle hē ðæt wurð Godes þances *pretium Dei gratia distribuat*, L. M. I. P. 43; Th. ii. 276, 23: L. Pen. 14; Th. ii. 282, 11: L. E. I. 25; Th. ii. 422, 8, 9: L. Ath. v. 8, 1; Th. i. 236, 8: Wulfst. 238, 28: Homl. Skt. i. 23, 200: Lchdm. i. 400, 9. Ic ann ðæs landes intō mynstre Scā Marian þances, Chart. Th. 558, 33. Ungeniédde mid eówrum āgenum willan gē sculon ðencean for eówre heorde Godes ðonces nals na for fraceðlecum gestreónum *providentes non coacte, sed spontanee secundum Deum, neque turpis lucri gratia, sed voluntarie*, Past. 18; Swt. 137, 20. Hié ða miclan feorme þigedon Cristes þonces ðe hié ǣr þigedon deófla þonces, Ors. 6, 21; Swt. 272, 22–24. [*Goth* thank fairhaitan χάριν ἔχειν, Lk. 17, 9: *O. Sax.* thank *grace, pleasure, thanks*: *O. Frs.* thank, thonk: *O. H. Ger.* danc, thanc *gratia*: *Icel.* þökk *pleasure, thanks*.] v. bealu-, fore-, ge-, hete-, hyge-, inge-, inwit-, nearu-, or-, searu-, un-þanc; un-þances.

þanc-ful[l]; *adj.* I. *thoughtful*:—Mǣden carful þancful nytwyrþe clǣne *a maiden born on the ninth day of the moon will be careful, thoughtful, useful, chaste*, Lchdm. iii. 188, 14. II. *spirited*; animosus:—Cild ācenned (*born on the thirteenth day of the moon*), þancfull (*animosus*), þrīste, reáful, ofermōd, him sylfum gelīcigende, Lchdm. iii. 190, 13. III. *pleasing, agreeable*, cf. *Icel.* þekki-ligr *handsome, pleasant*:—Ðonful *gratiosus*, Wrt. Voc. i. 61, 31. Þancfulle *idoneam*, ii. 44, 26. Wē hālsiaþ, God, ðæt þeów ðīn cync ūre . . . tō ðē . . . þancfull mæge becuman *quaesumus, Deus, ut famulus tuus rex noster . . . ad te . . . gratiosus ualeat pervenire*, Anglia xiii. 381, 228. Þancfullust hȳrsumnysse wæstm *gratissimus obedientie fructus*, 371, 84. IV. *thankful, grateful*:—Ðæt folc wearð swā fægen his cystignessa and swā þancful, ðæt hig worhton him āne anlīcnesse of āre, Ap. Th. 10, 10. Beóþ þancfulle *grati estote* (Col. 3, 15), Homl. Th. i. 606, 18. Wesaþ þancfulle þon Hǣlende eóweres andleofan, Blickl. Homl. 169, 16. V. *content, satisfied*:—Ðancful *contentus*, Wrt. Voc. ii. 16, 6. Þancfull, 24, 66. Ðæt hē ðoncfull sī stȳre him ðæs bebodenan folces *contentus sit gubernatione creditae sibi plebis*, Bd. 4, 5; S. 572, 33. Ælþeódige bisceopas sȳn ðoncfulle (*contenti*) heora gæstlīþnesse and feorme, S. 573, 3. Scottas wǣron ðancfulle (*contenti*) heora gemǣrum, 5, 23; S. 646, 36. [*O. H. Ger.* un-dancfol *ingratus*.] v. un-þancful[l].

þancfullīce; *adv. Thankfully, gratefully*:—Ðā ongeat Eustachius ðæt seó foresǣde costnung him ðā æt wæs, and þancfullīce hī underfēng, Homl. Skt. ii. 30, 144. v. scearp-þancfullīce.

þanc-hycgende *thoughtful*:—Hē, gumena nāt hwylc, þanchycgende ðǣr gehȳdde deóre māðmas, Beo. Th. 4462; B. 2235.

þancian; *p.* ode. I. *to thank, give thanks, express in words* or *have in mind feelings of gratitude*, (1) absolute:—Drihten ðancode, ǣrðan ðe hē ða hlāfas tōbrǣce, Homl. Th. ii. 400, 16. Hē genam ðone calic þanciende *accipiens calicem gratias egit*, Mt. Kmbl. 26, 27. (2) with dat. of person to whom thanks are given:—Ðē panciaþ Cristes þegnas, Hy. 7, 52, 49. Hī tō ðē cleopiaþ and ðē lofe þanciaþ *clamabunt et hymnum dicent*, Ps. Th. 64, 14. Hē Gode þancode, Mk. Skt. 8, 6: Homl. Skt. i. 3, 454. Hē feóll tō his fōtum and him þancode *cecidit ante pedes ejus gratias agens*, Lk. Skt. 17, 16. Þearfan ic lǣrde ðæt hié Gode þancodon, Blickl. Homl. 185, 18. Wē sceolon him ðancian, Homl. Th. ii. 400, 18. Hig ðone hlāf ǣton Drihtne þanciende, Jn. Skt. 6, 23. (3) with gen. of that for which thanks are given:—Wē þanciaþ ðīnes weorðlīcan wuldordreámes, Hy. 8, 9. Hié þanciaþ þrymmes þrīstum wordum, Cd. Th. 242, 26; Dan. 425. Ne sceal hē beón tō georn deádra manna feós, ne tō lyt þancian heora ælmessan, Blickl. Homl. 43, 13. (4) with dat. of person to whom thanks are given, and (a) gen. of thing for which:—Hī Gode þonciaþ blǣdes and blissa, Exon. Th. 77, 14; Cri. 1256. Hē ðæs þancode Gode, Homl. Skt. i. 4, 237. Hié Gode þancudan ðæs siges, Blickl. Homl. 203, 33. Ðanca Gode ðīnre gesundfulnysse, Homl. Th. i. 400, 13. Þeáh hī his ðē ne ðancien, Ps. Th. 4, 8. Sceolde hē his Drihtne þancian ðæs leánes, Cd. Th. 17, 10; Gen. 257. (b) with gen. of a pronoun and clause stating cause of thanks:—Se gomela Gode þancode ðæs se man gespræc, Beo. Th. 2799; B. 1397: Elen. Kmbl. 1921; El. 962. Heó Gode þancode ðæs ðe hió sōð gecneów, 2276; El. 1139: Beo. Th. 1255; B. 625: Andr. Kmbl. 2022; An. 1013. Þoncade, Exon. Th. 148, 25; Gū. 750. Hī Gode þancodon ðæs ðe hī hyne gesundne geseón mōston, Beo. Th. 3257; B. 1626. Þancedon, 460; B. 227. (c) the cause of thanks given in a clause introduced by *ðæt*:—Ic ðancige ðē, ðæt ic ne eom nā swilce ōðre mannum, Homl. Th. ii. 428, 19. Hī þanceden þeódne, ðæt hit þus gelomp, Cd. Th. 298, 16; Sat. 534. Ðanca Gode, ðæt hē ðē gefultumode, Bt. 5, 3; Fox 14, 8. (5) combining the construction of (2) and (3):—Ic þancige Gode and eów eallum ðe mē wel fylston, and ðæs friðes ðe wē nū habbaþ, L. Edm. S. 5; Th. i. 250, 4. II. *to express thanks by action, shew gratitude*:—Wē ðē freóndlīce wīc getǣhton ðū ūs leánest nū unfreóndlīce fremena þancast *as friends we assigned thee a dwelling, thou dost now unkindly requite us and shew thy gratitude for benefits*, Cd. Th. 162, 31; Gen. 2689. Sceolde hē mid lāce his clǣnsunge Gode ðancian *he should shew his gratitude to God for his cleansing by a gift*, Homl. Th. i. 124, 10. III. *to feel gratified, to rejoice*:—Þancaþ ł blissaþ *gratatur*, Hpt. Gl. 522, 60. Ðām ðe þanciaþ yfelum mīnum *qui gratulantur malis meis*, Ps. Spl. 34, 29. [*O. Sax.* thankian: *O. Frs.* thonkia: *O. H. Ger.* danchōn *satisfacere, benedicere, remunerare*: *Icel.* þakka.] v. ge-þancian.

þanc-metegung, *deliberation*. v. next word.

þanc-metung, e; *f. Deliberation, consideration*:—Gif hē mid ðancmetuncge (-metegunge, MS. B.: þoncmeotunge, Bd. M. 88, 4) and ðreodunge geþafaþ *si ex deliberatione consentit*, Bd. 1, 27; S. 497, 23.

-þancness. v. nearu-þancness.

þancol; *adj. Addicted to thought, acute*:—Cild ācenned (*born on the sixteenth day of the moon*) þancul (*efficax*; cf. scearpþancfullīce *efficaciter*, Scint. 206, 14; *and see* scearpþanclīce), staþolfæst, Lchdm. iii. 192, 8. Saga, þoncol mon, hwā mec bregde of brimes fæþmum, Exon. Th. 382, 17; Rä. 3, 12. v. deóp-, fore-, ge-, gearo-, hete-, hyge-, scearp-, searu-þancol; þancol-mōd.

-þancollīce. v. deóp-þancollīce.

þancol-mōd; *adj. Having the mind addicted to thought, of acute mind, wise, intelligent*:—Þancolmōd wer, þeáwum hȳdig, Cd. Th. 102, 24; Gen. 1705. Seó gleáwe hēt hyre þīnenne þancolmōde heáfod onwrīðan, Jud. Thw. 24, 5; Jud. 172. Ealle witen eorðbūende þoncolmōde ðæt hī ðǣr ne sint, Met. 19, 14.

þanc-snot[t]or; *adj. Wise in thought, wise*:—Þoncsnottor guma breóstgehygdum his bearn lǣrde, Exon. Th. 301, 19; Fä. 21. Fore there neidfaerae naenig uuiurthit thoncsnottura than him tharf sié, Txts. 149, 17.

þancung, e; *f. Thanking, thanks, thanksgiving*:—Gode sié lof and wuldor and dǣda þoncung ealra ðæra gōda ðe hē ūs forgifen hafaþ, Chart. Th. 136, 32. Sāwla þancung *thanksgiving by souls*, Hy. 9, 45. Ic ete mid micelre þancunge *manduco cum gratiarum actione*, Coll. Monast.

Th. 34, 29. Mid ealre þoncunga, Blickl. Homl. 31, 21. Hē underfēng ða lāc mid ðancunge, Homl. Th. ii. 170, 16. [Be] ðæncunge ðǣm ðe wið ðȳfðe fylstaþ, L. Edm. S. 5; Th. i. 250, 3. Ongan se bisceop ðancunge dōn Drihtne *episcopus gratias coepit agere Domino*, Bd. 2, 9; S. 511, 31: 4, 23; S. 595, 19. Ðoncunge, 5, 19; S. 641, 2. Ic ðæs þoncunge dō Grēca herige, Nar. 2, 30. Þæs þancunga þīne scealcas ealle hæfdan *all thy servants gave thanks for this*, Ps. Th. 101, 12. Wyrþe ðū eart, ðæt ðū onfō wuldor and dǣda þancunga, Blickl. Homl. 75, 2. Ðē ic sylle þancunga *tibi reddo gratias*, Ælfc. Gr. 15; Zup. 95, 15. Ðæt is tō wundrianne, ðæt hī swā lytle þoncunge wiston Iōsepe ðæs ðe hē hī æt hungre āhredde *it is wonderful that they felt so little gratitude to Joseph for saving them from famine;* hunc Ioseph, quem constituit Deus Aegyptiis conservatae salutis auctorem, quis credat ita in brevi eorum excidisse memoriae, Ors. 1, 5; Swt. 34, 32. v. þanc, IV.

þanc-weorþ, -wurþ, -wirþe; *adj. Thankworthy, deserving thanks, acceptable:*—Þurh ðære þancweorþan Cristes gyfe *through the help of Christ's grace, which is deserving of all thanks*, Lchdm. iii. 432, 23. Þancwurðre *gratuita* (*Christi gratia fretus*), Hpt. Gl. 420, 76. Ūrum godum geoffrian ðancwurðe onsægednysse *to offer to our gods an acceptable sacrifice*, Homl. Th. i. 592, 34. Būtan ðū him þoncwyrþe lāc onsecge, Exon. Th. 254, 17; Jul. 198. Ic eów secgan mæg þoncwyrþe þing, ðæt gē ne ðyrfen leng murnan on mōde, Judth. Thw. 23, 33; Jud. 153. Þancwurðe gifa *grata* (*accepta*) *libamina*, Hpt. Gl. 415, 7. Gecwēme (?) þancwurde gife *grata munuscula*, 510, 71. Þancwurde *gratos, acceptos, caros*, 416, 51. Ða ðe ic ðām bigengum ðancwyrþe gelȳfde *quae incolis grata credideram*, Bd. pref.; S. 472, 38. Smylte weder biþ ðȳ þancwyrþre (*gratius*) gif hit hwēne ǣr biþ stearce stormas . . . And þancwyrþre biþ ðæs dæges leóht for ðære egeslīcan þióstro ðære nihte, Bt. 23; Fox 78, 26–29. Þancwurðra *gratuita*, Hpt. Gl. 442, 26. Hē gearcode him gebeórscipe on his hūse, ac hē gearcode him micele þancwurðran gereord on his heortan, Homl. Th. ii. 468, 30. Þancwur[ðe]ste *gratissimum, acceptissimum, amantissimum*, Hpt. Gl. 441, 66. v. un-þancweorþ.

þancweorþlīce; *adv. Gladly, willingly, in a way that shews acceptance:*—Hī ðancweorþlīce (*gratanter*) wǣron fram him onfangene, Bd. 5, 10; S. 624, 2. Hē ðære gife ðancwurþlīce (*gratanter*) onfēng, 4, 30; S. 609, 9. Gif hē ǣr ne geæfstgode ðætte his brōður lāc wǣron ðancweorðlīcor onfongne ðonne his *nisi Cain invidisset acceptam fratris hostiam*, Past. 34; Swt. 235, 3. *In* Jn. Skt. 6, 11 þancwurðlīce dōn *translates* gratias agere.

þanc-word, es; *n. A word of thanks:*—Swā scrīþende hweorfaþ gleómen, þearfe secgaþ, þoncword sprecaþ, simle sumne gemētaþ geofum unhneáwne, Exon. Th. 326, 32; Vīd. 137.

þanēcan þe *whenever, as soon as ever:*—Ðonēcan þe heó ūtan behwerfed sié (cf. þonne hió ǣrest sié ūtan behwerfed, Met. 13, 77), Bt. 25; Fox 88, 34. Þeáh hī nū eall hiora līf āwriten hæfdon, hū ne forealldodon ða gewritu þeáh and losodon ðonēcan þe hit wǣre swā some swā ða wrīteras dydon and eác ða þe hī ymbe writon *though they indeed had written all their life, yet would not the writings have become antiquated and have perished, as soon as ever it was done, in the same way as the writers did, and those too about whom they wrote;* quamquam quid ipsa scripta proficiant, quae cum suis auctoribus premit longior atque obscura vetustas? 18, 3; Fox 64, 28. Ac þonēcan (þan-, Bod. MS.) þe hē ðone anweald forlǣt, oððe se anweald hine, ðonne ne biþ hē ðam dysegan weorþ, 27, 1; Fox 94, 20. v. (?) ēce.

þānian; *p.* ode *To be or to become moist:*—Þǣnie *madeo*, Wrt. Voc. ii. 58, 44. Ðāniaþ *madescunt*, 57, 39. v. þān.

þanne, þænne, þonne; *adv. conj. Then, when.* Generally if the subject follows the verb the word is to be rendered by *then*, if the subject precedes the verb, by *when*. [*Þanne* and *þā* differ in force; the former is used where the time of an action is indefinite, and is found with the future, the indefinite present and the indefinite past; the latter is used where a definite action has taken place. Cf. Þonne faraþ hig on ēce susle, Mt. Kmbl. 25, 46, with: Ðā fērde se ðe ða fīf pund underfēng, 25, 16. Þonne ðū fæste, smyra ðīn heáfod, 6, 17, with: Þā þā hē fæste feówertig daga, 4, 2. Symle ic gehȳrde, þonne heofones gim west onhylde, Exon. Th. 174, 30; Gū. 1185, with: Þā hī ðis gehȳrdon, hī fahnodon, Mk. Skt. 14, 11.] A.—demonstrative, *then*. I. of time, *then, at that time:*—Fōron hié bī swā hwaþerre efes swā hit þonne (*at the time of their going, whenever it was*) fierdleás wæs, Chr. 894; Erl. 90, 13. Ðæt geweorþeþ on dōmes dæge . . . þonne forhtiaþ ealle gesceafta, Blickl. Homl. 11, 3: 95, 29: Exon. Th. 372, 21; Seel. 96. Þonne hī clypiaþ tō mē, and ic hī ne gehȳre, Homl. Th. ii. 378, 2. Se deófol ðe beswāc ðone þeóf nele nāht on his ende geðafian, ðæt hē þonne gecyrre tō ðam Hǣlende, Homl. Skt. i. 19, 191. II. marking order or sequence, *then, after that*, (1) of time:—Swā hwylc swā morþorslege þafaþ, and hine man þonne fremmeþ *quicunque ad homicidium consenserit, et id postea factum fuerit*, L. Ecg. C. 22; Th. ii. 148, 14. Gang ǣr and gesybsuma wið ðīnne brōðer, and þonne cum ðū syððan and bring ðīne lāc, Mt. Kmbl. 5, 24. Būton hē gebinde ǣrest ðone strangan, and þonne hys hūs bereáfige, 12, 29. Nū wē faraþ tō Gerusalem, and þonne beóþ gefylde ealle ða hālgan gewreotu, Blickl. Homl. 15, 8. Se ðe gōd onginneþ, and þonne āblinneþ, 21, 34. Ðam ðe for his synnum onsǣgd weorþeþ, and þonne ā tō ealdre orleg dreógeþ, Exon. Th. 446, 28; Dōm. 29. Ealle ða hwīle sceal beón gedrync, ōð ðone dæg ðe hī hine forbærnaþ. Þonne ðȳ ylcan dæge ðe hī hine tō ðæm āde beran wyllaþ, þonne tōdǣlaþ hī his feoh . . . Ðonne sceolon beón gesamnode . . . menn . . . Þonne ærnaþ hȳ ealle . . .; ðonne cymeþ . . . se ðæt swiftoste hors hafaþ tō ðæm ǣrestan dǣle, Ors. 1, 1; Swt. 20, 25–36. Ālecgaþ hī ðone mǣstan dǣl, þonne ōðerne, ðonne ðæne þriddan, Swt. 20, 31. Gē cweðaþ: 'Drihten, ātȳn ūs.' Þonne cwyð hē: 'Ne can ic eów.' Ðonne ongynne gē cweþan. . . . Þonne segþ hē . . ., Lk. Skt. 13, 25–27. Gif gē þonne git (*after that still*) nellaþ eów wendan tō mē, Homl. Skt. i. 13, 169: Lk. Skt. 14, 32. Monige men syndon ðe cweþaþ ðæt hié on God gelȳfon, and þonne hweþere (*and yet after saying so*) nellaþ āblinnan from heora unrihtum gestreónum, Blickl. Homl. 25, 5: 55, 21. (2) of place or position:—Æt ðām feówer tōðum fyrestum . . . se tōð se þanne bī standeþ . . . se ðe þonne bī ðam standeþ . . . and þonne siþþan gehwilc, L. Ethb. 51; Th. i. 16, 3–4. Is se ðridda Martinianus, þonne se feórða Dionisius . . . þonne ðæs sixtan Seraphun nama is, Homl. Skt. i. 23, 5–6. II a. marking addition, *yet, besides:*—Hwæt māre dēst ðū? Gewyslīce þænne māre ic dō *certe adhuc plus facio*, Coll. Monast. Th. 19, 35. III. marking the succession of subjects treated of in narrative, *then, again:*—Næs ðæt þonne mǣtost mægenfultuma, ðæt him lāh þyle Hrōðgāres *and then* (the helmet and byrnie having been already spoken of) *that was not meanest of aids that Hunferth lent him*, Beo. Th. 2914; B. 1455. Ðænne (cf. And, 21; Men. 11; 38; Men. 19), Menol. Fox 46; Men. 23. IV. in a clause that is a qualification or contrast to a preceding clause, *then, yet, but:*—Feówertig daga, gif hit hysecild wǣre; gif hit þonne mǣdencild wǣre, . . . hundeahtatig daga, Homl. Th. i. 134, 18. Ða ðe mihton ðurhteón sceoldon bringan lamb and culfran. Gif þonne hwylc wīf tō ðam unspēdig wǣre, ðæt heó ðās ðing begytan ne mihte . . ., 140, 2, 13: Homl. Skt. i. 13, 163. Līfes ic ðē geann, gif ðū gelȳfst . . . Gif ðū þonne elles dēst, ðū scealt deáþe sweltan, ii. 27, 73. Syndon ealle hǣþene godu hildedeóful; heofenas þænne (*autem*) worhte Drihten, Ps. Th. 95, 5. Ðæt hālige gewrit ðæt cȳþeþ . . . Ðonne is ðeáw ðæs apostolīcan setles *sacra scriptura testatur . . . Mos autem sedis apostolicae est*, Bd. 1, 27; S. 489, 5. Eác is swīðe micel þearf ðæt gē cȳðon hū ungeföhlīcu scyld ðæt (*perjury*) is . . . Þonne habbaþ wē geāhsod ðæt hit sume men dōþ tō lytelre scylde; þonne nis hit nā swā, ac is ān ðæra mǣstena scylda, L. E. I. 26; Th. ii. 422, 19–24: Blickl. Homl. 175, 34. Twēgen beámas stōdon . . . ōðer wæs swā wynlīc . . . Þonne wæs se ōðer sweart, Cod. Th. 30, 34; Gen. 477. Þeáh wē þillīco wīto witan, þonne hwæðere ne sceolon wē nǣfre geortrȳwan be Godes mildheortnesse, L. E. I. proem.; Th. ii. 398, 42. Wē leorniaþ ðæt seó tīd sié dēgol . . . wē witon þonne hweþre ðæt hit nis nō feor tō ðon, Blickl. Homl. 117, 29. IV a. in an interrogative clause:—Wæs Cristes tōcyme ǣgðer ge hryre ge ǣrist. Hū ðonne? Homl. Th. i. 144, 27: Exon. Th. 446, 30; Dōm. 30. V. marking a conclusion, inference or result based on a previous statement, *then, therefore, consequently:*—Ðæt ðonne (*from the statements already made*) biþ ðæs recceres ryht, ðæt hē ðurh ða stemne his lāriówdōmes ætiéwe ðæt wuldor ðæs uplīcan ēðles, Past. 21; Swt. 159, 22: Blickl. Homl. 39, 23. Drihten cwæþ: 'Bringaþ gē eówerne teóðan sceat.' . . . Þonne sægþ on ðissum bōcum, ðæt Drihten sylf cwǣde, ðæt ðis mennissce cyn ne sceolde āgīmeleásian, ðæt hié sealdon heora wæstma fruman for Gode, 41, 3. On ðone dæg hē sende ðone Hālgan Gāst. Þonne forþon (*it may be inferred that on that account*) is hit swȳðe micel cyn, ðæt gehwylc cristen man ðone dæg weorðige, L. E. I. 24; Th. ii. 420, 30: Blickl. Homl. 63, 7. Hē mā cēgde . . . ðæt is þonne (*we may infer*) ðæt wē sceolan beón gelǣrede mid ðysse bysene . . ., 19, 13: 23, 9. Gifeón wē þonne (*for reasons contained in the preceding statement*) on þone gemǣnan Godes and manna, 11, 4: 13, 24. Hæbbe ic geāhsod, ðæt hē wǣpna ne recceþ; ic ðæt þonne (*consequently*) forhicge, ðæt ic sweord bere tō gūþe, Beo. Th. 874; B. 435: 3346; B. 1671. Ðū ūs wel dohtest. Gif ic þonne mæg ðīnre mōdlufan māran tilian, ic beó gearo sōna, 3648; B. 1822. Hwylc beren mǣnde hē þonne elles būton heofona rīce *what other barn can it be inferred that he meant, but heaven?* Blickl. Homl. 39, 27, 29. VI. marking a consequence dependent upon a hypothesis, *then, in that case*, (a) where the hypothesis is expressed in a clause introduced by *gif:*—Gif man frigne man gefō, þanne wealde se cyning . . ., L. Wih. 26; Th. i. 42, 15. Gif wē willaþ on Drihten gelȳfan, þonne beó wē sittende be ðæm wege, Blickl. Homl. 23, 8: 13, 10: Mt. Kmbl. 24, 50: Coll. Monast. Th. 29, 25. Gif wē deóplīcor ymbe ðis sprecaþ, þonne wēne wē ðæt hit wile ðincan ðām ungelǣredum tō menigfeald, Homl. Th. ii. 582, 24. Gif hwā cwyð ðæt hē lufige God, and his beboda ne hylt, hē biþ leás ðonne, 314, 31. Gif ðū wilt ðæt ðis feoh becume tō ðīnre sāwle ðearfe, tōdǣl hit ðonne ðearfum, 484, 32. Gyf þonne Frysna hwylc ðæs morþorhetes myndgiend wǣre, þonne hit sweordes ecg swedrian scolde, Beo. Th. 2216; B. 1106. Ðonne wēne ic tō ðē wyrsan geþingea, gif ðū Grendles dearst bīdan, 1054; B. 525. (b) where the hypothesis is otherwise expressed:—Se ðe wille anwald âgon (=*if any one desires to have power*), þonne sceal hē ǣrest tilian ðæt hē his selfes âge anwald, Met. 16, 1. Se ðe feohtan ne dear mid Godes gewǣpnunge ongeán ðone feónd, hē biþ þonne mid ðām deófellīcum bendum gewyld, Homl. Th. ii. 402, 18. (c) where the hypothesis is implied:—Wē sceolon ðone geleáfan mid gōdum dǣdum gefyllan, þonne (*if we do so, then*) beó wē ūrum Hǣlende fylgende, Blickl. Homl. 23, 10. Ic ðē lǣre, ðæt ðū hospcwide ne fremme; ðonne ðū geearnast ðæt ðē biþ ēce līf seald, Elen. Kmbl. 1049; El. 526. Weorþiaþ gē eówerne God . . .; þonne gefylleþ Drihten eówer beren, Blickl. Homl. 41, 10. Lufian wē hine . . .; þonne ne lǣteþ hē ūs nō costian, 13, 8, 26. Hwæt mǣnde hē elles, būton ðæt wē gefyllon ðæs þearfan wambe? þonne (*if we do fill*, etc., *then*) ne hingreþ ūs nǣfre, 39, 30. 'Hwæt dēstū gif ic tō mergen middeges gebīde?' Hē cwæð: 'Sylf ic swelte þonne,' Homl. Skt. i. 3, 591. Ðes man is sōþfæst, ac þonne hwæþere git sindon bigswicon *this man is true, but yet* (*if that be so*) *then ye are deceivers*, Blickl. Homl. 187, 30. **VI a.** in questions, and referring to a condition contained in another sentence, *then, in that case*:—Wilt ðū syllan þingc ðīn hēr ealswā ðū hī gebohtest þǣr? Ic nelle. Hwæt þænne mē fremode gedeorf mīn? Coll. Monast. Th. 27, 17. Hig beóþ tōdǣlede. Hū mæg þonne hys rīce standan? Mt. Kmbl. 12, 26: Salm. Kmbl. 715; Sal. 357. **B.**—relative, *when*. **I.** of time. (1) of the time of a single action in the future:—Hwylc tācen biþ, þænne ealle ðās ðing onginnaþ beón geendud, Mk. Skt. 13, 4. Ðænne mannes sunu cymþ, gemēt hē geleáfan? Lk. Skt. 18, 8: 13, 28. Ðonne ic cume tō ðē tǣc mē *quando veniam ad te, doce me*, Ælfc. Gr. 38; Zup. 224, 7. Ðonne se hīrēdes ealdor ingǣð, gē standaþ þǣr ūte, Lk. Skt. 13, 25. Ðonne ðū for unc ondwyrdan scealt, Exon. Th. 372, 5; Seel. 88. Hwænne wylle gē singan ǣfen oþþe nihtsangc? þonne hyt tīma byþ, Coll. Monast. Th. 34, 5. Geþence mē, þonne ðē ðīn wīse līcie, Gen. 40, 14. Ic nāme þænne ic cōme *veniens ego recepissem*, Mt. Kmbl. 25, 27. (2) referring to the times of an action which may occur an indefinite number of times, *when, at such times as*:—þænne se yrþlingc unscenþ ða oxan, ic lǣde hig tō lǣse, Coll. Monast. Th. 20, 25. Būtan ðænne bises geboden weorþe, Menol. Fox 64; Men. 32. Eádige synt gē, þonne hī wyriaþ eów, Mt. Kmbl. 5, 11. þonne ðū ðīne ælmessan sylle, ne blāwe man bȳman beforan ðē, 6, 2, 3, 5, 6. Symle hē sceal singan, ðonne hē his sweord geteó, Salm. Kmbl. 334; Sal. 166: Beo. Th. 46; B. 23: Andr. Kmbl. 503; An. 252: Exon. Th. 42, 18; Cri. 674. Saga ðū ðæt ðū sié sweostor mīn, þonne ðē leódweras fricgen (*whenever you are asked*), Cd. Th. 110, 5; Gen. 1833. Ðæt wǣron men fyrdhwate, þonne rond and hand helm ealgodon, Andr. Kmbl. 18; An. 9. Symle ic gehȳrde, þonne heofones gim west onhylde, Exon. Th. 174, 30; Gū. 1185: 122, 11; Gū. 304: Cd. Th. 33, 21; Gen. 523. Ic ðonne (*dum*) mē hefie wērun, ic gegerede mec mid hēran, Ps. Surt. 34, 13. (3) where the order in time of two circumstances is to be marked, *when, after*:—Eallum geleáffullum mannum englas þegniaþ, þonne hī habbaþ deófol oferswīþed, Blickl. Homl. 35, 3. Ðīn âgen bearn frætwa healdeþ, þonne ðīn flǣsc ligeþ, Cd. Th. 132, 5; Gen. 2188. Hwæt dō wē, þonne hē unc hafaþ geedbyrded ōþre sīþe, Exon. Th. 372, 29; Seel. 100. **II.** denoting a cause, *when, since, seeing that*:—Sindon monige tō ðreágenne, ðonne hié selfe nellaþ ongietan hiera scylda, Past. 21; Swt. 159, 17. Ealle clǣne þingc ic ete. Swīþe waxgeorn eart ðū, þonne (*cum*) ðū ealle þingc etst, Coll. Monast. Th. 34, 31. Hī beóþ slītende wulfas, þonne hié for feós lufan earmne fordēmaþ būton scylde, Blickl. Homl. 63, 10: Homl. Th. ii. 226, 31. Wēn is ðæt hē wille bewitan his menn ge on līfe ge on deáðe, þonne se lytla fugel ne befylþ on grin būtan Godes willan, Homl. Skt. i. 17, 188, 197. **II a.** in questions denoting the cause or reason for that not being done about which the question asks:—Hū lange wilt ðū bewēpan Saules sīð, þonne ic hine âwearp, ðæt hē leng ne rīxige *how long wilt thou mourn for Saul, seeing I have rejected him from reigning?* (A. V. 1 Sam. 16, 1) Homl. Th. ii. 64, 5. Hwā sceal tō his rīce fōn, þonne hē brōðer næfþ, ne hē bearn ne belǣfþ? 146, 19: i. 48, 12, 25. Hū mæg ic yrnan mid eów, þonne ic ne ârās of ðysum bedde nū for nigon geárum? Homl. Skt. i. 21, 344. Hwæt wille wē furðor secgan hū se cāsere his fyrdinge geendode, þonne hē forfērde on ende, ii. 28, 118. **III.** *although*:—Ðū gelȳfdest on mē, þonne ðū mē ne gesāwe *credidisti in me, cum ipse me non uideris*, Homl. Skt. ii. 24, 114. **IV.** denoting condition, case, *when, the case in which*:—*Iactantia*, ðæt is ȳdel gylp; ðæt is ðonne se man biþ lofgeorn and mid līcetunge fǣrþ, Homl. Skt. i. 16, 302. Óðer deófolgild is, . . . ðonne se man forsihþ his Scyppendes beboda, 17, 50. Mīne eágan synt ealra gelīcast þonne esne biþ þonne his hlāforde hēreþ *my eyes are most like the case of the servant obeying his lord*, Ps. Th. 122, 2. Ealle wē syndon ungelīce, þonne þe wē in heofonum hæfdon ǣrror wlite *we are all unlike what we were when in heaven we formerly had beauty*, Cd. Th. 274, 8; Sat. 151. Ðonne se mōna wexeþ (*in its crescent condition*), hē biþ gelīc ðæm gōdum men, Blickl. Homl. 17, 22. **C.** correlative, þanne . . . þanne *then . . . when, when . . . then*:—Ðonne ðū ealle gedǣlde hæfst, þonne bist ðū ðē self wædla, Bt. 13; Fox 38, 34. Ðonne eów mislīciaþ ða mettrumnessa ðe gē on ōðrum monnum geseóþ, ðonne geðence gē hwæt gē sién, Past. 21; Swt. 159, 13–14, 19–21: Blickl. Homl. 17, 2–3. þonne se mōna wanaþ, þonne tācnaþ hē ūre deáþlīcnesse, 17, 24: 19, 14–15, 28–29. þonne Godes gecorenan becumaþ tō deáðe, ðonne gemētaþ hī yrfwyrdnysse, Homl. Th. ii. 526, 29–30: Exon. Th. 83, 7–10; Cri. 1352. Ðætte ðonne, ðonne hié ða untruman lācnian willaþ, ðætte hié ǣr gesceáwien, Past. 48; Swt. 370, 9. **D.** after comparatives, *than*. **I.** where the comparison is between different objects, (1) where the objects are expressed by single words or phrases:—Hē wæs ǣr þonne ic, Jn. Skt. 1, 15. Gē synt sēlran þonne manega spearuan, Mt. Kmbl. 10, 31. Ðē wæs leófra his sibb and hyldo þonne ðīn sylfes bearn, Cd. Th. 176, 34; Gen. 2921: Andr. Kmbl. 2856; An. 1430. Leófre ys ūs beón beswungen for lāre þænne hit ne cunnan, Coll. Monast. Th. 18, 20: 24, 23. (1 a) where there is a negative with the comparative:—Næfþ nān mann māran lufe þonne ðeós ys, Jn. Skt. 15, 13. (2) where one or each object is expressed by a clause:—Sēlre biþ ǣghwæm, ðæt hē his freónd wrece, þonne hē fela murne, Beo. Th. 2775; B. 1385. Ðē wǣre sēlle, ðǣr ðū wurde fugel, þonne ðū ǣfre mon gewurde, Exon. Th. 372, 1; Seel. 85. (2 a) where there is a negative with the comparative:—Nis nǣnig māre mægen, þonne hē ðone âwyrgdan gāst oferswīþe, Blickl. Homl. 31, 31. Nyston beteran rǣd þonne hié ða behlidenan him tō līfnere gefeormedon, Andr. Kmbl. 2179; An. 1091. (2 b) in questions:—On hwam mæg se iunga rǣdran rǣd gemittan, þonne hē ðīne wīsan word gehealde? Ps. Th. 118, 9. Hwæs wǣre mē māre þearf, þonne ic mid cilde wǣre? Gen. 25, 22. **II.** where the comparison is between the same object under different conditions:—Âcumendlīcre byþ Sodoma lande on dōmes dæg þonne þære ceastre, Mt. Kmbl. 10, 15. Ic wylle cȳpan hēr luflīcor þonne ic gebicge ðǣr (*the price is higher in one case than in the other*), Coll. Monast. Th. 27, 19. Sceolan wē beón geornran ðæt wē Godes bebodu healdan, þonne wē ūrne teónan gewrecan *our zeal to keep God's commands must be greater than our zeal to avenge our wrong*, Blickl. Homl. 33, 24. Nǣfre hlīsan âh Meotud þan māran, þonne hē wið monna bearn wyrceþ weldǣdum *the glory is never greater than when working benevolently*, Exon. Th. 191, 11; Az. 86. Hē biþ on ðæt wynstre weorud wyrs gesceáden, þonne hē on ða swīþran hond swīcan mōte, 449, 24; Dōm. 76. **III.** where the comparative with *þanne* may be rendered by the positive preceded by *too* and followed by *for* with an infinitive or by an infinitive:—Seó is brādre þonne ǣnig man ofer seón mæge *it is too broad for anybody to be able to see across*, Ors. 1, 1; Swt. 19, 19. Ðæt his mōd wite, ðæt migtigra wīte wealdeþ, þonne hē him wið mæge (*one too mighty for him to prevail against*), Cd. Th. 249, 1; Dan. 523. Him wæs Godes egsa māra in gemyndum, þonne hē menniscum þrymme þegan wolde (*too much fear of God for him to wish for human glory*), Exon. Th. 112, 6; Gū. 139. Deóplīcor mid ūs ðū smeágst, þonne yld ūre anfōn mæge (*too deeply for our age to be able to take it in*), Coll. Monast. 33, 11. Se wæs mid his dǣdum snelra þonne hē mægenes hæfde *he was too quick in his actions to have enough strength for them*; celeritate magis quam virtute fretus, Ors. 2, 5; Swt. 78, 27. **IV.** where the adjective is in the positive, and the comparative required by *þanne* must be inferred:—Gōd ys on Dryhten tō þenceanne, þonne on mannan wese mōd tō treówianne *bonum est confidere in Domino, quam confidere in homine*, Ps. Th. 117, 8, 9. [*O. H. Ger.* danne.] v. þan; þā.

þanon, þanone, þār, þāra, þarf, þāriht, þār-riht, -rihte, þās, þasser, þassum. v. þanan, þanane, þǣr, þearf, þǣr-rihte, -riht, -rihte, þes.

þawenian. v. ge-þawenian.

þāwian (þawian?); *p.* ode *To thaw* (trans.):—Se þridda heáfodwind hātte zephirus . . . se wind tōwyrpþ and ðāwaþ ǣlcne winter, Lchdm. iii. 274, 22. [Thowes *degelat* (*Deus*), Wrt. Voc. i. 201, col. 2 (15th cent.). Thowyn or meltyn, as snowe *resolvo*, thowyn, as yce *degelat*, *resolvit*, thowe, of snowe or yce *resolucio*, *liquefaccio*, Prompt. Parv. 492. Her names . . . were almost ofthowed so, that of the lettres oon or two were molte away, Chauc. H. of Fame, iii. 53. Cf. *O. H. Ger.* douwen, dewen, *digerere, consumere*: *Icel.* þeyja *to thaw* (intrans.).]

þe; *indecl. particle*. **I.** as relative pronoun of any number, gender, or case, (1) where the antecedent clause does not contain a demonstrative:—Ic hit eom, þe wið ðē sprece, Jn. Skt. 4, 26. Ðæt ðū ne sȳ gesewen fram mannum fæstende, ac ðīnum Fæder þe ys on dīglum: and ðīn Fæder þe gesyhþ on dȳglum hit âgylt ðē, Mt. Kmbl. 6, 18: Beo. Th. 5264; B. 2635. Idesa scēnost þe on woruld cōme, Cd. Th. 39, 18; Gen. 627. Swȳðe manega synt þe þurh ðone weg faraþ, . . . Swȳðe feáwa synt þe ðone weg findon, Mt. Kmbl. 7, 13, 14. Gē þe yfle synt cunnun gōde sylena syllan, 7, 11. Wið gehwylce yfelu þe on ðam innoðe dereþ, Lchdm. i. 280, 18. (2) where the antecedent clause contains a demonstrative:—Hē fōr tō ðæm iglande þe monn ðæt folc Mandras hǣtt (*the people of which are called Mandras*), Ors. 3, 9; Swt. 134, 5. Habbe hē ðone ilcan dōm þe (*the same sentence as*) se þe ðæt fals worhte L. C. S. 8; Th. i. 380, 22. *For other instances* v. se. (3) used in combination with the personal pronouns:—Saga hwæt ic hātte, þe ic lond reáfige, Exon. Th. 394, 6; Rā. 13, 14. Wē ðās word sprecaþ . . . þe wē in carcerne sittaþ, 2, 27; Cri. 25. Wē, þe ūs befæst is seó gȳming

Godes folces . . . *we, to whom is committed the care of God's people* . . ., L. E. I. 1; Th. ii. 402, 9. Fæder úre ðú þe eart on heofenum *Pater noster, qui es in coelis*, Mt. Kmbl. 6, 9. Ðú þe reccest, ðú nú beheald *qui regis, intende*, Ps. Th. 79, 1. Ðonne se scrift ongit ðæs costunga ðe hē him ondetteþ *when the confessor hears the temptations of the man who confesses to him*, Past. 16; Swt. 105, 20. Ðære fǽmnan tíd þe hire (*whose*) noma wæs Scā Anatolia, Shrn. 102, 34. Sceáweras þe hira naman hēr sint āwritene *viros, quorum ista sunt nomina*, Num. 13, 5: Lev. 11, 3. Ða men þe mon hiora mǽgas ǽr slōg, Ors. 2, 5; Swt. 80, 19. *For other instances see* hē. (4) where relative and antecedent are included in one form:—Eart ðú ðe tō cumenne eart? Lk. Skt. 7, 20. Wēn ne brūceþ ðe can weána lyt, Runic pm. Kmbl. 340, 30; Rūn. 8. Tō middes eów stōd þe gē ne cunnon, Jn. Skt. 1, 26. Hēr syndon þe ðīne deórlingas beón sceoldon, Homl. Skt. i. 23, 147. **II.** as adverb. (1) a relative adverb:—Ðonon ðe hī ūtan bióþ āhæfene, ðanon hié bióþ innan āfeallene, Past. 50; Swt. 391, 12. Ðæt ūre ende geendige on God, þanon þe ūs þæt angin com, Homl. Skt. i. 16, 8. On ðæs sǽs waroþe, ðanon ðe hī sciphere on becom, Bd. 1, 12; S. 481, 11. Þider ðe Stephanus forestōp, ðider folgode Paulus, Homl. Th. i. 52, 5. (2) before comparatives, (*a*) *any*. v. þan:—Ne ðearft ðú nō be ðǽm gesceaftum tweógan þe (þon, Cott. MS.) mā þe be ðǽm ōþrum *you need not doubt about those creatures any more than about the others*, Bt. 34, 10; Fox 148, 18: 34, 1; Fox 134, 15: L. Pen. 7; Th. ii. 280, 5: Homl. Skt. i. 7, 20. Nys mē ðȳnes weales hǽmed nǽfre þe leófre þe mē nǽdre tōslȳte, Shrn. 154, 22. Nis þeós woruld ðe geliccre ðære ēcan woruldе þe is sum cweartern leóhtum dæge *this world is no more like the eternal world than a prison is like bright day*, Homl. Th. i. 154, 18. Nǽre hit þe geliccre ðære ēcean myrhðe, þonne biþ ðam menn þe sitt on cwearterne wið ðam menn þe færþ frig geond land, Homl. Skt. i. 12, 107. Gif hwylc gōd man from gōde gewīte, ðonne ne biþ hē þe (þon, Cott. MS.) mā fullīce gōd (cf. *Goth.* ni magt thana mais fauragaggja wisan, Lk. 16, 2), Bt. 37, 3; Fox 190, 29. (*β*) = þȳ, *the*:—Swā biþ micle þe winsumre sió sōþe gesǽlð tō habbenne æfter ðām eormþum ðisses līfes, Bt. 23; Fox 78, 30. Hē hæfde giet ðe mā unþeáwa þonne his eám hæfde *avunculi sui erga omnia vitia ac scelera sectator, immo transgressor*, Ors. 6, 5; Swt. 260, 28. Swā þincþ ānra gehwæm sió sōðe gesǽlð þe betere and þȳ wynsumre, þe hē wīta mā hēr ādreógeþ, Met. 12, 20. Symle bið þȳ heardra, þe hit sǽstreámas swȳðor beátaþ, Cd. Th. 80, 8; Gen. 1325. Þe læs *lest*, Ex. 19, 21, 24: Mk. Skt. 4, 12: 13, 36. **III.** as conjunction. (1) introducing noun or adverb clauses, *that*, cf. þæt. (*a*) noun clauses:—Eác wæs ðæt ðe beforan ðæm temple stōd ǽren ceác, Past. 16; Swt. 105, 1. Heó ðā fǽhðe wræc, þe ðú Grendel cwealdest, Beo. Th. 2672; B. 1334. Āras sceoldon wilspella mǽst gesecgan, ðe ðæt sigorbeácen mēted wǽre, Elen. Kmbl. 1967; El. 985. Ðæt dysig is anlīccost þe sum cild sié full hāl geboren . . . *such folly is most like, that* (*just as if*) *a child were born quite healthy* . . ., Bt. 38, 5; Fox 206, 21. Hit is ðæm gelīcost þe ic sitte on ānre heáre dūne, Ors. 3, 11; Swt. 142, 13. (*β*) adverb clauses:—Hwæt is se manna þe ðú him cȳþan woldest *quid est homo, quod innotuisti ei?* Ps. Th. 143, 4. Hē wolde ðæt ða folc him ðȳ swīþor tō buge, þe hē hæfde hiera ealdhlāfordes sunu on his gewealde, Ors. 3, 11; Swt. 148, 32. Hē wæs sundes þe sǽnra, þe hyne swylt fornam, Beo. Th. 2877; B. 1436: Exon. Th. 432, 15; Rä. 48, 6. Hié ðæt gewinn ðæslīcost angunnan, þe hī hit ǽr ne angunnen, Ors. 3, 11; Swt. 150, 31. (*γ*) in combination with other particles, where the combination may be rendered by a conjunction:—Ðeáh þe . . . swā ðeáh, Homl. Skt. i. 12, 106. Ōþ þe (*until*) hyt eall ālēd biþ, Ors. 1, 1; Swt. 20, 31: Bt. 38, 5; Fox 206, 24. *See* þeáh, ōþ, *and* se, **V.** (2) *than*:—Hē hæfde twǽm læs þe twēntig wintra, Blickl. Homl. 215, 34: Chr. 901; Erl. 96, 24. Ne hī hié selfe ðȳ beteran ne taligen, ðe ða ōðre, Past. 44; Swt. 319, 18. *See* **II.** 2 *a above, and* þan. (3) *or*, (*a*) alone:—Ys hyt ālȳfed, þe nā? Mt. Kmbl. 22, 17: Lk. Skt. 7, 20. God āna wāt hū his gecynde biþ, wífhādes þe weres, Exon. Th. 223, 9; Ph. 357. Hwæðer wǽre twēgra strengra, wyrd ðe warnung, Salm. Kmbl. 855; Sal. 427. (*β*) þe . . . þe *whether* . . . *or*:—Hwyder hē gelǽded sȳ, þe tō wīte, þe tō wuldre, Blickl. Homl. 97, 22. Gē nyton hwænne ðæs hūses hlāford cymþ; þe on ǽfen, þe on midre nihte, þe on hancrēde, þe on mergen, Mk. Skt. 13, 35. (*β* 1) hwæðer (*pronoun*) . . . þe . . . þe:—Ðæt ic wite hwæðer hit sig, þe sōð þe leás, ðæt gē secgaþ, Gen. 42, 16. Hwæþer ðincþ ðē ðonne, ðæt ða ðing sién, þe ðara sōþena gesǽlþa limu, ðe sió gesǽlþ self? Bt. 34, 6; Fox 142, 10. Hwæðer is ðē leófre, þe ðú nū onfō ða costnunga, þe neár ðīnum ende? Homl. Skt. ii. 30, 131. (*γ*) hwæðer, þeáh . . . þe *whether* . . . *or*:—Hwæþer hē wacode ðe slēpte, Bd. 2, 12; S. 513, 39. Hwæðer ðæs landes folc cristen wǽre ðe hǽðen, Homl. Th. ii. 120, 23. Ongitan hwæþer hit hysecild þe mǽdencild beón wille, Lchdm. ii. 172, 17: Exon. Th. 80, 16; Cri. 1307: Blickl. Homl. 117, 19. Ic nāt þeáh ðú mid ligenum fare, þe ðú Drihtnes eart boda, Cd. Th. 34, 4; Gen. 532. [*O. Sax.* the.]

þe = se, *in Northern Gospels*:—Ðe ł hē *ipse*, Mt. Kmbl. Lind. 15, 24. Ðe ilca *ipse*, 3, 4. Ðe ðe *qui*, 3, 2. Ðe Hǽlend, Jn. Skt. Rush. 4, 2, 6.

þeá, þeaca, þeaclīce, þeád, þeáf. v. þeów, þaca, þearllīce, II, þeód, þeóf.

þeáh, þāh, þǽh, þēh; *adv. conj.* **I.** *yet, still, however, nevertheless*:—Ðeáh (ðēh, MS. A.) ic secge inc *verumtamen dico vobis*, Mt. Kmbl. 11, 22. Hē ðafode ða scylda, and ðeáh hē him gecȳðde, Past. 21; Swt. 151, 23: Blickl. Homl. 55, 26. Hié hæfdon āþas geseald, and þēh ofer ða treówa fōron hié, Chr. 194; Erl. 90, 4. Dydon swā hwæþer swā hȳ dydon, ne dohte him nāwþer; ðeáh hī sceoldon ðæt feorh ālǽtan *let them do which they would, neither did them any good; they had nevertheless to lose their lives*, Bt. 29, 2; Fox 106, 2. Wǽron manige eác him þēh ic ða geðungnestan nemde *there were many besides them; however, I have named the chief*, Chr. 897; Erl. 95, 6. Āgife hē ðone teóþan sceat Gode, and dǽle þeáh his ælmessan forþ of ðon nigeoþan dǽlon *let him pay the tithe to God, and still go on distributing alms from the other nine parts*, Blickl. Homl. 53, 11. Ne magon ðis þeáh ealle men dōn *all men, however, cannot do this*, 37, 34: Cd. Th. 44, 12; Gen. 708. Hwæt is ðe deórast þince hwæþer þe gold, þe hwæt? Ic wāt þeáh gold, Bt. 13; Fox 38, 11. Gif ðú þeáh mīnum wilt wordum hȳran, Cd. Th. 35, 24; Gen. 559. Hē ne wisse word ne angin swefnes sīnes, hēt him secgan þeáh, 223, 28; Dan. 126. **I a.** combined with other particles, *hwæðere, swā, se . . . þeáh*:—Ðú ealle gesceafta ǽrest gesceópe swīðe gelīce, sumes hwǽþre þeáh ungelīce, nemdest swā þeáh mid āne noman ealle tōgædere, Met. 20, 52–56. Hwæþer (hwæþre?) ic ðē secge þeáh, ðæt . . ., Bt. 13; Fox 38, 7. Ac swā ðeáh wīse lāreówas tōdǽldon ðone praeteritum tempus, Ælfc. Gr. 20; Zup. 124, 1: 38; Zup. 226, 1. And ābād swā þeáh (*nihilominus*) seofon dagas, Gen. 8, 12. Ic dēme swā þeáh ða þeóde *verumtamen gentem ego judicabo*, 15, 14. Ðæt ðæs Hālgan Gāstes þēnung wǽre on ðære gyfe ðæs fullwihtes swā þeáh (*nihilominus*), nalles ðæs mannes, L. Ecg. C. 7; Th. ii. 140, 3: H. R. 101, 8. Sceolde hwæðre swā þeáh æþeling unwrecen ealdres linnan, Beo. Th. 4876; B. 2442. [*Goth.* swē þauh.] *See* þeáh-hwæðere, *and* se, weald. **II.** *though, although*, (1) in clauses which express no uncertainty:—Þeáh (ðæch, Lind.: ðēh ðe, Rush.) se Hǽlend ne fullode *quamquam Jesus non baptizaret*, Jn. Skt. 4, 2. Wǽron Rōmware sōna gegearwod, ðeáh hié werod læsse hæfdon tō hilde, Elen. Kmbl. 96; El. 48. Þeáh hié ǽr ðæs ēcan līfes orwēne wǽron, hié synt nū swīþe blīþe, Blickl. Homl. 85, 27. (1 a) combined with *þe*:—Hī wǽron ðæs Hǽlendes gewitan, ðeáh ðe hī hine ðāgyt ne cūðon, Homl. Th. i. 84, 4: 82, 33. Þeáh ðe hē geong sȳ, Beo. Th. 3667; B. 1831. Ne beóþ gē tō forhte, þēh þe synnigra cynn swylt þrowode, Andr. Kmbl. 3217; An. 1611. (2) in hypothetical clauses, *though, if, even if*:—Ic ðē sylle swā hwæt swā ðú mē bitst, þeáh (*licet*) ðú wylle healf mīn rīce, Mk. Skt. 6, 23: Bt. 18, 3; Fox 66, 10. Hwæt fremaþ ǽnegum menn, þeáh (ðāh, Lind.: ðeáh þe, Rush.) hē ealne middaneard gestrȳne *si mundum universum lucretur*, Mt. Kmbl. 16, 26. On hwan mæg se mann mōdigan, þeáh hē wille *on what can man pride himself, even if he wishes?* Hom. Skt. i. 16, 371. Hwæt hæfst ðú æt ðām gifum, ðeáh hī nū ēce wǽron? Bt. 13; Fox 38, 5. Nāt þeáh ðú mid ligenum fare, Cd. Th. 34, 2; Gen. 531. Þǽh, 281, 2; Sat. 265. Ðēh ðú þersce *si contuderis*, Kent. Gl. 1034. Þeáh man āsette twēgen fætels full ealað oððe wæteres, hȳ gedōþ ðæt ǽgþer biþ oferfroren, Ors. 1, 1; Swt. 21, 15. (2 a) in combination with *þe*:—Þeáh (ðēh, Lind.: þǽh, Rush.) þe ic scyle sweltan mid ðē, ne wiðsace ic ðē *etiamsi opportuerit me mori tecum, non te negabo*, Mt. Kmbl. 26, 35. Ðeáh þe *etsi*, 26, 33. Þeáh ðe (ðǽh, Lind.: ðēh, Rush.), Mk. Skt. 14, 29. Þeáh ðe ðē man bere mete tōforan, hwōnlīce ðē fremaþ ðæt ðú hine geseó, būton ðú his onbyrige, swā eác ðē ne fremaþ, þeáh ðe ðú ða hālgan lāre gehȳre, būtan ðú hī tō gōdum weorcum āwende, Homl. Th. ii. 402, 2–5. **III.** in correlative clauses:—Þeáh (ðāh, Lind. *etsi*) ic God ne ondrǽde, þeáh (*tamen*) ic wrece hig, Lk. Skt. 18, 4–5: Bt. 13; Fox 38, 11. Ac þeáh ðú nū fier sié ðonne ðú wǽre, ne eart ðú þeáh ealles of ðam earde ādrifen, 5, 1; Fox 8, 35: 7, 4; Fox 22, 26. Ðeáh ðe hē wið ða scyldgiendan swugode, hē hit him ðeáh suīgende gesǽde, Past. 21; Swt. 151, 23. Þeáh þe man wafige wundorlīce mid handa, ne biþ hit þeáh bletsung . . ., Homl. Skt. ii. 27, 151. Þeáh lǽwedum mannum wīf sī ālȳfed, swā ðeáh hī āgan micele þearf, ðæt . . ., Wulfst. 305, 17. Ðeáh hē nǽre fullīce gefulwad, hweðre hē ðæt gerȳne ðære hālgan fulwihte mid gōdum dǽdum heóld, Blickl. Homl. 213, 13. Hwæþre hē getrymede heora geleáfan, þeáh hié ðæt word ne ongeáton, 17, 8. Ðaeh ðe . . . hweðre *quanquam . . . tamen*, Ps. Surt. 38, 7. Ðeáh hwæðere, þeáh heó synderlīce Iōhannes gȳmenne betǽht wǽre, hwæðere heó drohtnode gemǽnelīce mid ðam apostolīcum werode, Homl. Th. i. 438, 31. [*Goth.* þauh: *O. Sax.* thōh: *O. Frs.* thāch: *O. H. Ger.* doh: *Icel.* þō.]

þeáh-hwæðere; *adv. conj. Yet, but, nevertheless, however*:—Ðeáhhwæðere (*verumtamen*) ic secge eów, Mt. Kmbl. 11, 24: Lk. Skt. 10, 20. Ðeáhhwæðere (*autem*) gang tō ðære sǽ, Mt. Kmbl. 17, 27. Þeáhhwæþere, Blickl. Homl. 97, 25. Monige sint ðe mon sceal wærlīce līcettan, and ðeáhhwæðre eft cȳðan, Past. 21; Swt. 151, 13. And hwæðre him mæg wīssefa wyrda gehwylce gemetigian, . . . ðeáhhwæðre godcundes gāstes brūcan *and yet can the wise-minded man moderate every fate for himself, . . . yet can he enjoy the divine spirit*, Salm. Kmbl. 883; Sal. 441. And þeáhhwæþere *et tamen*, Coll. Monast. Th. 29, 27. Þeáhhweðere, Blickl. Homl. 31, 18. Þeáhhweþre, 93, 17.

Ac þeáhhwæþere *sed tamen*, Coll. Monast. Th. 18, 32: Chr. 1009; Erl. 142, 26. Gyt þeáhhwæþere *adhuc tamen*, Coll. Monast. Th. 33, 9. Nyste þeáhhweđre hwæt hē him dōn sceolde, Blickl. Homl. 215, 2. Gif hē ne ārīst forđam đe hē his freónd ys, þeáhhwæþere for hys onhrōpe hē ārīst, Lk. Skt. 11, 8. ¶ combined with swā:—And swā þeáhhwæþere ōþ đone deáþ hē hine tintregaþ, Blickl. Homl. 59, 30. Ac swā đeáhhwæđere seó menniscnys wæs ǣfre forestiht, Homl. Th. ii. 364, 25. Nolde ic cwic ǣfre swā þeáhhwæđere đīne gewitnesse forlǣtan, Ps. Th. 118, 157.

þeaht, e; *f. Counsel:*—Sum bisceop tō him fērde, efne swā swā hē wǣre mid heofonlīcre þeahte gelǣred, đæt hē tō đære sprǣce fērde đæs Godes mannes, Guthl. 17; Gdwin. 70, 8. Hī rǣddon đæt man hine gebunde, and ōđ deáđ swunge. Nero, đā đā hē đæs folces đeaht geácsode, wearđ tō feore āfyrht, Homl. Th. i. 384, 7. On mōdes þeaht, Elen. Kmbl. 2482; El. 1242. v. ge-þeaht.

-þeahta, -þeahtend, -þeahtendlīc, -þeahtendlīce. v. ge-þeahta, -þeahtend, -þeahtendlīc, un-geþeahtendlīce.

þeahtere, es; *m. A counsellor:*—On .v. nihte mōnan gang tō đīnum þeahtere, Lchdm. iii. 170, 3. Đæs cyninges þeahteras *regis consiliarii*, Bd. 2, 13; S. 516, 25. Gē yfelan þehteras! ic nǣfre mē ne gebidde on eówer god, Nar. 42, 6. v. ge-, rǣd-þeahtere.

þeahtian; *p.* ode *To take counsel, to consult:*—Hié smeágeaþ and đeahtigaþ on hiera mōdes rinde monig gōd weorc tō wyrcanne, Past. 9; Swt. 55, 22. Hē mid his ealdormannum đeahtode and sōhte hwæt be đyssum đingum tō dōnne wǣre *cum suis primatibus curavit conferre, quid de his agendum arbitrarentur*, Bd. 2, 9; S. 512, 11. Đā þeahtode þeóden ūre mōdgeþonce, hū hē đa mǣran gesceaft eft gesette, Cd. Th. 6, 21; Gen. 92. Hȳ þeahtodon hū hī mihton geniman mīne sāwle *ut acciperent animam meam consiliati sunt*, Ps. Th. 30, 16. Weras þeahtedon, Elen. Kmbl. 1091; El. 547. Hī þeahtedon ongēn hine, hū hī hine fordōn mihton *consilium faciebant aduersus eum, quomodo eum perderent*, Mk. Skt. 3, 6. Hī đeahtodon embe đæra apostola forwyrd, Homl. Th. i. 572, 30. Hē đa monnđwǣrnesse đe hē ǣr đurhtogen hæfde eft đeahtigende on yfel gewend *mansuetudinem, quam tolerantes habuerunt, retractantes in malitiam vertunt*, Past. 33; Swt. 225, 22. Đā wǣron đa hǣþenan betwih him đeahtiende and sprecende, Bd. 5, 10; S. 624, 35. v. ge-, ymbe-þeahtian; rǣd-þeahtende.

þeahtung, e; *f. Counsel, consultation:*—Tō đæhtunge *consilio*, Mt. Kmbl. Lind. 27, 7. Đætung *consilium*, 28, 12. Đæhtung, p. 16, 14: Mk. Skt. Lind. 3, 6: 15, 1: Lk. Skt. Lind. 7, 30. Đæhtunge, Mk. Skt. Rush. 3, 6. v. for-, ge-, rǣd-þeahtung.

þeána (*combined with* swā, se); *adv. conj. Yet:*—Pāpa on Rōme swā þeána gesette *papa Romanus tamen statuit*, L. Ecg. C. 7; Th. ii. 138, 36. Līfe ne gielpeþ hlāfordes gifum, hȳreþ swā þeána þeódne sīnum, Exon. Th. 440, 6; Rä. 59, 13: 108, 32; Gū. 81. Nō God wolde đæt seó sāwl sār þrowade, lȳfde se þeána đæt hȳ him mid hondum hrīnan mōsten, 127, 3; Gū. 380.

þearf, e; *f.* I. *need:*—Wē sceolan beón gemyndige Godes beboda, and ūre sāwle þearfe, Blickl. Homl. 25, 27. Gemyndige ūre sāula þearfe, 101, 16. God, đe ǣlces monnes đearfe wāt, Bt. 39, 10; Fox 226, 25. Hē ealle can ūre þearfe, Ps. Th. 102, 13. Seleþegn ealle beweotede þegnes þearfe, Beo. Th. 3598; B. 1797. Gleómen þearfe secgaþ, Exon. Th. 326, 31; Vīd. 137. Đæt hē ne āgǣle gǣstes þearfe, 51, 17; Cri. 817: 298, 17; Crā. 86. Miltsa đū ūs, and gemyne đū ūre þearfa, Blickl. Homl. 225, 21. II. *need* for or of something, which is expressed (1) by a genitive (α) of a noun, or of a pronoun referring to a noun:—Hwylc đearf is đē hūsles *quid opus est eucharistia?* Bd. 4, 24; S. 598, 37: Cd. Th. 54, 19; Gen. 879. Him wæs manna þearf, Beo. Th. 405; B. 201. Nǣnges þinges māre þearf nǣre, Blickl. Homl. 175, 9. Nalas þȳ þe ūre Drihten đæs wolcnes fultomes þearfe hæfde, 121, 13. Nāhte ic đīnre miltse þon māran þearfe, Judth. Thw. 22, 35; Jud. 92. Drihten đæs (*the ass*) āh þearfe, Blickl. Homl. 71, 1. (β) of a pronoun that represents a clause:—'Ic bidde đē, đæt đū nyme đē lādmenn.' Đā cwæđ hē: 'Nys mē đæs nān þearf' (*non est necesse*), Gen. 33, 15. Hī bǣdon đæt hī mōston on ōđerne weg faran, and sǣdon đæt him đæs neód wǣre and eác þearf, Guthl. 14; Gdwin. 62, 6. Hwæs wǣre mē māre þearf, þonne ic mid cilde wǣre *quid necesse fuit concipere?* Gen. 25, 22. Đæs ānes ic āh þearfe, đæt đū mīn freónd sig and ic đīne miltse hæbbe *hoc uno tantum indigeo, ut inveniam gratiam in conspectu tuo*, Gen. 33, 15. Wē đæs nāne þearfe nāgon, đæt wē him ǣfre fram ābūgan, Homl. Skt. i. 23, 454. (γ) of a pronoun that refers to a gerundial infinitive; cf. (3):—Forþon nis mē đæs þearf, cwæđ Orosius, tō secgenne, Ors. 1, 11; Swt. 50, 15. (2) by a clause:—Him næs nān þearf (đarf, Lind. *opus*), đæt ǣnig man sǣde gewitnesse be men, Jn. Skt. 2, 25: 16, 30. Ūs is eallum þearf, đæt ūre ǣghwylc ōþerne bylde, Byrht. Th. 138, 41; By. 233. Is đam weorce þearf, đæt . . ., Exon. Th. 1, 21; Cri. 11. Ūs is mycel đearf, đæt wē teolian, Blickl. Homl. 125, 11. Him wæs þearf micel, đæt . . ., Cd. Th. 123, 32; Gen. 2054. Ic wēne đæt hit sié nū ǣrest þearf, đæt ic đē gerecce hwǣr đæt hēhste gōd is *nunc demonstrandum reor, quonam haec felicitatis perfectio constituta sit*, Bt. 34, 1; Fox 134, 3. Gē habbaþ micle đearfe, đæt gē simle wel dōn, 42; Fox 258, 26. Ic āh mǣste þearfe, đæt đū mīnum gāste gōdes geunne, Byrht. Th. 136, 61; By. 175. (3) by the gerundial infinitive:—Monige menn angiennaþ smeágean suīđor đonne him đearf sié tō begonganne *nonnulli se in quibusdam inquisitionibus plus quam necesse est exercentes*, Past. 11; Swt. 67, 4. Ūs is mycel þearf tō witenne, Blickl. Homl. 63, 5. Hwæt is đæt đæm men sȳ māre þearf tō þencenne? 97, 19. Nis mē wihtæ þearf hearran tō habbanne, Cd. Th. 18, 25; Gen. 278. (4) where that for which there is need is not expressed:—Gē đone hlīsan habban tiliaþ ofer þióda mā, þonne eów þearf sié, Met. 10, 22. Hit is eów uncūđre, đonne gē þearfe āhton *you have less knowledge on the point than you have need of*, Wulfst. 292, 8. Ic ādrǣde, đæt gē willan heora læs gȳman, đonne gē þearfa āhton, 297, 20. III. *needful things, what is needful:*—Đā hēt hē him heora đearfe forgyfan *eis necessaria ministrari jussit*, Bd. 1, 25; S. 486, 29. Wē willaþ eów andlyfne syllan and eówre þearfe forgifan *quae victui sunt vestro necessaria ministrare curamus*, S. 487, 15. Ǣghwylc mon wile đæt him Drihten selle ealle his þearfe, Blickl. Homl. 51, 15. Mē Dryhten sendeþ þurh monnes hond mīne þearfe, Exon. Th. 121, 24; Gū. 293. IV. *what is required of a person, duty:*—Gif munuc wiđersaca wurđe mid ealle, hē sī āmānsumod ǣfre, būton hē gebūge tō his þearfe, L. Eth. ix. 41; Th. i. 348, 33. Āfæstnie man symle georne on heortan godcunde þearfe (*duty towards God*), Wulfst. 75, 5. God sceáwaþ sylf, mid hwylcum geþance man tō cyrican fare, and hwæt đǣr man dreóge wordes ođđe weorces. And se đe đǣr đæt dēþ, đæt his þearfa beóþ, se gegladaþ God, 279, 1. Men forgȳmdon Godes laga swȳđor, đonne heora þearfa wǣron, 292, 13. V. *use, service, behoof, good, advantage, profit* [v. þearf-līc, II, *and* cf. *Icel.* þarfr *useful: Dan.* tarv. *behoof, good, benefit: O. H. Ger.* bi-darbi *utilis*]:—Nyttung *vel* þearf *vel* gewuna *usus*, Wrt. Voc. i. 54, 68. His wylla is, đæt wē aa æfter ūre āgenre þearfe geornlīce winnan *his will is that we ever strive diligently after our own profit*, Wulfst. 109, 8. For eówre þearfe mē sende God *pro salute vestra misit me Deus*, Gen. 45, 5. On đa gerād đæt đū đa eorþan sēcan wille for gōdra manna þearfe, Bt. 7, 3; Fox 22, 8. Bisceopas āscādaþ ūt of cyrican for heora āgenan þearfe đa, đe healīce hȳ sylfe forgyltan, Wulfst. 104, 11. Hē earfeþu geþolade fore þearfe þeódbūendra, lāđlīcne deáđ leódum tō helpe, Exon. Th. 72, 15; Cri. 1173. Đæs mūđes tunge sceal faran on đara eárena đearfe *ad usum suum auribus oris lingua concurrat*, Past. 34; Swt. 233, 8: Andr. Kmbl. 3302; An. 1654: Beo. Th. 2916; B. 1456. Þonne wē biddaþ ongeán ūre āgenre þearfe þonne forwyrnþ God ūs đæs đe wē ungesceádwīslīce biddaþ *when we ask for what is opposed to our own good, God refuses us that which we ask indiscreetly*, Homl. Th. ii. 528, 8. Đæt hī sȳn gewordene bysen tō forwyrde swȳđor þonne tō þearfe *that they have become an example to perdition rather than to profit*, L. I. P. 23; Th. ii. 334, 14. Ūre ǣlc scute .iiii. pæng. tō ūre gemǣn[r]e þearfe *each of us should contribute four pence to our common use*, L. Ath. v. 2; Th. i. 230, 16. Tō đæs heres þearfe *to the service of the Danes*, Chr. 874; Erl. 76, 32. Eallum þeódscipe tō þearfe *for the good of the whole nation*, 1006; Erl. 141, 7. Mann wīsdōm spreċþ manegum tō þearfe and tō rihtinge, Ælfc. T. Grn. 21, 27: Wulfst. 32, 9. Ūre Drihten đe eallum manncynne com tō đearfe (helpe, MS. E.), 14, 17. Godes hūs sēce hē gelōme him sylfum tō þearfe, 73, 16. Hit wearđ mancynne tō mycelre þearfe, 23, 5: 119, 16. Tō þearfe *usefully, profitably*, 49, 2: Byrht. Th. 138, 38; By. 232: Menol. Fox 426; Men. 214. Se đe đæt dēþ, hē dēþ him sylfum mycle đearfe, Wulfst. 113, 13: 119, 11: 303, 7. Fremmaþ gē leóda þearfe, Beo. Th. 5594; B. 2801. Ic wāt đæt đū sēcst mīne đearfe *I know that you seek my good*, Shrn. 182, 32. Gif eall geférrǣden đone rǣd missrǣdaþ, and þeáh feáwa witena on đam geférscipe beón, đæt đa þearfe wīslīcor tōcnāwan cunnon þonne sume, stande đæra rǣd đe đa đearfe geceósaþ, R. Ben. 116, 20. V a. *a useful thing, profitable employment:*—Đæs hādes men đe hwȳlum wǣron nyttoste and geswincfulleste on godcundan þeówdōme and on bōccræfte, đa syndon nū unnyttaste, and ne swincaþ ā swīđe ymbe ǣnige þearfe for Gode ne for woruldе, L. I. P. 14; Th. ii. 322, 22. VI. *need, distress, straits, difficulty:*—Gif him þyslīcu þearf gelumpe, Beo. Th. 5268; B. 2637: 2504; B. 1250. Mec þearf monaþ, micel mōdes sorg, Exon. Th. 285, 21; Jul. 717. Gefultumend æt ǣlcere đearfe *adjutor in opportunitatibus, in tribulatione*, Ps. Th. 9, 10. Swā đæt se man ābrȳđ æt ǣlcere þearfe (cf. ābreóđe on ǣlcere neóde, 59, 12), Wulfst. 53, 13. Gif ic æt þearfe đīnre scolde aldre linnan, Beo. Th. 2958; B. 1477. On hyra mandryhtnes miclan þearfe, 5691; B. 2849. Seó ecg geswāc þeódne æt þearfe, 3054; B. 1525. Swylc sceolde secg wesan æt þearfe, 5411; B. 2709: Byrht. Th. 140, 52; By. 307. Þonne weorđe ic mid eów ǣfre æt đearfe, and eów ne forlǣte ǣfre æt neóde, Wulfst. 50, 5: Ps. Th. 62, 7: 70, 6. Đa đe hine seóslige sōhtun on đearfe, Exon. Th. 157, 30; Gū. 899. Wāst đū hū ic gewand ymbe Creosos þearfe, đā đā hine Cirus gefangen hæfde? Bt. 7, 3; Fox 22, 10. Hwæt miht đū on đa tīd þearfe gewēpan? Dōm. L. 176. Đec nū for þearfum đīn āgen geweorc bīdeþ, Exon. Th. 8, 3; Cri. 112. Wē đec for þearfum and for þreánȳdum ārena biddaþ, 186, 3; Az. 14. Đonne hwā tō his scrifte cymeþ, on đa gerād đæt hē wille his þearfa tō him sprecan and his synna andettan, L. E. I. 31; Th. ii. 428, 9. [Gif hwa is swa sunful þet nulle his scrift ihalden, þenne segge ic eou, þet nis hit nan þerf (*it is no use*), þet me her on þisse liue for his saule bidde pater noster, O. E. Homl. i. 9, 31. Alle þatt haffdenn ned and þarrfe to þin hellpe, Orm. 12247. *Goth.* þarba *need, want: O. Frs.* therve: *O. L. Ger.* therva *opus: O. H. Ger.* darba *privatio: Icel.* þörf.] v. feorh-, firen-, heáh-, nearu-, nīd-, ofer-, sāwel-, un-, weá-, weoruld-þearf; þurfan.

þearf. v. þurfan.

þearfa; *adj.* I. *destitute of, needing* (with gen.):—Hrægles þearfa ic wreó mē wǣda leásne, Cd. Th. 53, 25; Gen. 866. [*Goth.* þarba (*with gen.*).] II. the word is generally used substantively, *a needy, poor person*:—Ðearfa *pauper*, wædla *egenus*, Wrt. Voc. i. 74, 21. Ðā sæt ðǣr sum þearfa æt ðæm burggeate, Blickl. Homl. 213, 32. Ðā sæt ðǣr sum blind þearfa, 15, 16. Nā ðæt ān ðæt hē wolde mann beón, ac eác swylce hē wolde beón þearfa for ūs, Homl. Th. i. 140, 10. Fela sind ðearfan þurh hafenleáste . . . Sind ōðre ðearfan on gāste . . . on ðās wīsan wæs Abraham ðearfa, and Dauid, se ðe hine sylfne geswutelode þearfan on gāste, þus cweðende: 'Ic eom wædla and þearfa.' Ða mōdigan rīcan ne beóþ þearfan ne þurh hafenleáste ne on gāste, 550, 2–11. Nafa ðū nānes þearfan wedd mid ðē nihtlangne fyrst, Deut. 24, 12. Gefyllan ðæs þearfan wambe, Blickl. Homl. 39, 29. Mec mon biþeahte mid þearfan wǣdum (*with the garments of a pauper*), Exon. Th. 87, 10; Cri. 1423. Se biscop nǣre miltsiende nānum Godes þearfan, Blickl. Homl. 45, 2. Ða gāstlīcan þearfan (ðaerfe, Lind.) *pauperes spiritu*, Mt. Kmbl. 5, 3. Eádige sind gē þearfan on gāste, Lk. Skt. 6, 20. Gener ðearfena *refugium pauperi*, Ps. Spl. 9, 9. Ðearfena and earmra manna *inopum*, Bd. 3, 6; S. 528, 17. Ic sylle ðearfum (*pauperibus*) healfe mīne ǣhta, Lk. Skt. 19, 8. Syllan þearfon (*egenis*), Jn. Skt. 12, 5. Him gebyrode tō ðām þearfon (ðorfum, Lind.: ðarfum, Rush.), 12, 6. Ðæt hē dǣlde þearfum and wædlum, Homl. Skt. ii. 26, 59. Þearfum *matriculariis* (matricularius *a poor person supported by a church*), Wrt. Voc. ii. 86, 50: 57, 1. Þearfum *pauperculis, miseris*, Hpt. Gl. 458, 13. Hē dēmeþ fyrhte þearfan swylce hē þearfena bearn hǣleþ *judicabit pauperes, et salvos faciet filios pauperum*, Ps. Th. 71, 4. Þearfan ic lǣrde, ðæt hié heora wædle gefeán hæfdon, Blickl. Homl. 185, 17. Ic lǣre ge ða welegan ge þa þearfan, 107, 12. ¶ Besides enjoining almsgiving the church directly assisted the poor by assigning a certain proportion of the tithes to those whom it called *Godes þearfan*. Thus in general terms it is said:—Wē willaþ myngian freónda gehwylcne, ðæt hī Godes þearfan frēfrian and fēdan, L. Eth. vi. 46; Th. i. 326, 24; and in reference to tithe:—Þridda dǣl ðare teóðunge, ðe tō circan gebyrige, gā Godes þearfum and earmum þeówetlingum, ix. 6; Th. i. 342, 9: in return the poor were exhorted to intercede for the people whose alms they received:—Wē lǣraþ, ðæt preóstas, þonne hī ða ælmessan dǣlan, ða þearfan georne biddan, ðæt hig for ðæt folc þingian, L. Edg. C. 56; Th. ii. 256, 11. From other sources the poor derived benefit; certain fines were devoted to their use:—Gebēte hē .xxx. scill., and sié ðæt feoh gedǣled ðǣm þearfum, ðe on ða[m] tūn[e] synd, L. Ath. prm.; Th. i. 198, 12. Gif feohbōt ārīseþ, ðæt gebyreþ rihtlīce . . . tō þearfena hyðde, L. Eth. vi. 51; Th. i. 328, 6. [*Ego egenus et pauper sum*, þet is: Ic em þarua and wrecche, O. E. Homl. i. 115, 8. *Goth.* þarba *a poor person.*] v. ofer-, weoruld-þearfa; þorfa.

þearfan; *p.* de; *pp.* ed *To need, suffer need*:—Nū ðū ðæt swā openlīce ongiten hæfst, ne þearfe ic nū nāuht swīþe ymbe ðæt swincan, Bt. 35, 3; Fox 158, 8. Ūre ceaster is þearfende . . . wē þoliaþ ðone heardestan hungor, Ap. Th. 9, 7. Ðū, þīne þearfende *thou, needing food* (? v. þigen, II), Cd. Th. 149, 25; Gen. 2480. Ðæt ðū miltsige mē þearfendum, Exon. Th. 269, 13; Jul. 449. Ic ðē biddan wille miltse ðīnre mē þearfendre, Judth. Thw. 22, 29; Jud. 85. Wē ðearfende þearle syndon *pauperes facti sumus nimis*, Ps. Th. 78, 8. Ða ðe hira hlāf sellaþ ðǣm synfullum ðe ðearfende beóþ, nalles for ðæm ðe hié synfulle beóþ ac for ðæm ðe hié menn beóþ and ðearfende beóþ *qui indigenti etiam peccatori panem suum, non quia peccator, sed quia homo est, tribuit*, Past. 44; Swt. 327, 8. ¶ *The present participle, as adjective or as substantive, often occurs*, (1) as adjective, *indigent, needy, poor*:—Hē sǣde ðæt hē folclīc man wǣre and ðearfende *rusticum se et pauperem fuisse respondit*, Bd. 4, 22; S. 591, 6. Widua ðiós ðærfen[de] (ðorfende, Rush.) *uidua haec pauper*, Mk. Skt. Lind. 12, 43. On ðearfendum līfe and on earmlīcum *in humili et paupere vita*, Bd. 4, 13; S. 582, 23: 1, 15; S. 484, 7. Of ðearfendum folce *de paupere vulgo*, 4, 22; S. 591, 34. Ða ðearfendan lāfe Brytta *pauperculae Brittonum reliquiae*, 1, 13; S. 481, 41. Ǣnig gemynd þearfendra manna, Blickl. Homl. 69, 10. Brec ðinne hlāf þearfendum mannum, 37, 20: 75, 23: 109, 14. Ðæt hē sealde sum þing þearfendum mannum (*egenis*), Jn. Skt. 13, 29. (2) as substantive, (a) *a poor person*; mostly in plural, *the poor*:—Ðone þearfendan ārecean *erigens pauperem*, Ps. Th. 112, 6. Eádge biðon ða ðærfendo (ðorfendo, Lk. Skt. Lind. 6, 20) *beati pauperes*, Mt. Kmbl. Lind. 5, 3. Þearfendra bēne *orationes pauperum*, Ps. Th. 101, 15: 108, 30. Hleó ðarfendra *refugium pauperum*, Rtl. 40, 25. Hē þearfendra ēhte *persecutus est hominem pauperem*, Ps. Th. 108, 16. Se ðe his ǣhta þearfendum (*pauperibus*) gedǣleþ, 111, 8. Ðearfendum, Past. 44; Swt. 327, 20. Ðarfendum *egenis*, Lk. Skt. Rush. 12, 5. Þearfendum and ælþeódigum *peregrinis et egentibus*, Cod. Dip. B. i. 155, 5. Hē fēdde þearfende, Homl. Skt. ii. 31, 53. Ða þearfendan Drihten gehȳreþ, Ps. Th. 68, 34. (b) *a miserable person*:—Biþ ðæt þridde þearfendum (*the wicked*) sorg, Exon. Th. 79, 4; Cri. 1285. [*Goth.* ga-þarban matē ἀπέχεσθαι βρωμάτων, 1 Tim. 4, 3: *O. H. Ger.* darbēn *carere.*] v. be-, mete-, weoruld-, wine-þearfende; þearfedness, þearfend-līc; þearfian.

þearfedness, e; *f. Poverty*:—On wilsumlīcre ðearfednesse *voluntaria paupertate*, Bd. 4, 3; S. 569, 3: Anglia x. 145, 163. Mid ðearfednesse ge mid heora ungelǣrednesse *paupertate ac rusticitate sua*, Bd. 4, 27; S. 604, 28. In ðearfednisse *in paupertate*, Ps. Surt. 30, 11.

þearfende. v. þearfan.

þearfend-līc; *adj. Poor*, (a) of persons, *indigent, destitute*:—Monnes bearn (*Guthlac in his hermitage*) swā þearfendlīc, Exon. Th. 128, 11; Gū. 402. (b) of things, *scanty, insufficient*:—Ðæt ðū ne forgite mīne þearfendlīcan gegirlan (cf. se fiscere tōslāt his wǣfels on twā and sealde Apollonige ðone healfan dǣl, 11, 27), Ap. Th. 12, 8.

þearfian; *p.* ode *To be in need*:—Hē þearfigendra sāwla gehǣleþ *animas pauperum salvas faciet*, Ps. Th. 71, 13. [*Icel.* þarfa; *p.* þarfaði.] v. be-þearfaþ, ge-þearfian; þearfan.

þearf-leás; *adj. Without having need* or *reason* to do something. v. þearf, II, þurfan, II. 4:—Þearflǣs hē syrwde ymbe Crist *he plotted against Christ, but he had no need to do it*, Homl. Th. i. 82, 20. Ic ðearfleás (þearfleáse, Job. Thw. 166, 22) hine geswencte *without having cause I afflicted him*, ii. 452, 16. [*Icel.* þarf-lauss *needless.*]

þearfleáse; *adv. Needlessly, without cause.* v. preceding word.

þearf-līc; *adj.* I. *necessary*:—Lā hū þearflīc hit is *quanto magis*, Hpt. Gl. 454, 6. Nēd ɫ ðarflīc is *necesse esse*, Mt. Kmbl. Lind. 18, 7. Ðarflīc ɫ nēd is *necessarium est*, p. 13, 1. II. *useful, profitable*, v. þearf, V:—Behōflīc ɫ ðarflīc *utile*, Mt. Kmbl. p. 13, 6. Hēr is hālwendlīc lār and ðearflīc lǣwedum mannum, Wulfst. 134, 9. Ðæt is þearflīc gewuna, 104, 17: 108, 19: L. Ath. v. 8, 9; Th. i. 238, 18. On gōdum lǣce biþ gelang þearflīc broces bōt, L. Pen. 9; Th. ii. 280, 13. Ðæt him ðearflīc nǣre, ðæt hē ðǣs hālgan hǣse forhule his hlāforde *that it would not be well for him to conceal the saint's bidding from his lord*, Homl. Skt. i. 21, 80. On gōdan þeáwan and on þearflīcan dǣdan, Wulfst. 121, 2. Sēlre ūs is and ðearflīcre, ðæt wē ūre gyltas andetton, 136, 1. Ðarflīcro (ðaroflīcra, Rush.) is *utilius est*, Lk. Skt. Lind. 17, 2. Swā swā him þincæ ðæt mǣ þearfliicustþ sī, Chart. Th. 554, 36. [*Icel.* þarf-ligr *useful.*] v. beþearf-līc, nīdþearf-līc.

þearflīce; *adv. Usefully, profitably, with profit, to good purpose*:—Wē mihton ðās hālgan rǣdinge menigfealdlīcor trahtnian, ac ūs twȳnaþ hwæðer gē magon māran deópnysse ðǣron þearflīce tōcnāwan *whether you can with profit know the profounder parts of the subject*, Homl. Th. i. 556, 15. Angan listum ymbe þencean þearflīce hū hē þider meahte Crēcas oncerran, Met. 1, 60. [*Icel.* þarfliga *usefully.*]

þearflīcness, e; *f. Poverty, neediness*:—Þærflīcnys *paupertas*, Hpt. Gl. 438, 60. Þerflīcnes *mendicitas*, Kent. Gl. 950. On þearflīcnysse *in paupertate*, Ps. Spl. 30, 13: Scint. 127, 18: 148, 2. Þearflīcnysse hē ondrēt *paupertatem ueretur*, 179, 8. Þearflīcnysse lufian *paupertatem diligere*, Cod. Dip. B. i. 155, 7.

þearl; *adj.* (1) of persons, *severe, strict*:—Se ðearla and se ryhtwīsa Dēma *districtus judex*, Past. 21; Swt. 167, 22. (2) of things, (a) pain, punishment, effort, and the like, *severe*:—Hē dȳ wyrs meahte þolian ða þrāge, ðā hió swā þearl becom, Met. 1, 77. Þreánȳd þearl, Elen. Kmbl. 1404; El. 704. Wæs seó ādl þearl, Exon. Th. 160, 30; Gū. 951. And suā ðȳ ðearlan dōme hē forleás his mennisce *ut districto justoque judicio homo esse perderet*, Past. 4; Swt. 39, 23. Heó þrowedon þearl æfterleán, Cd. Th. 5, 24; Gen. 76. Þreá wǣron þearle, Exon. Th. 135, 4; Gū. 519: Ps. Th. 104, 12: 149, 7. Wēndon hié wera cwealmes, þearlra geþinga, Andr. Kmbl. 3194; An. 1600. Ðirst and hungor and ðearle gewin, Salm. Kmbl. 946; Sal. 472. (b) *utter, excessive*:—Þȳstru ðū gesettest on þearle niht (*night utterly dark*) *posuisti tenebras, et facta est nox*, Ps. Th. 103, 19.

þearle; *adv. Severely, sorely, strictly, hard.* This word, as does *swīþe* (q. v.), tends to become an adverb of degree rather than one of manner or quality; where it qualifies words denoting pain, effort, or the like, it may be considered as keeping much of its old force, but even there it is used to translate Latin words marking degree; while in the case of words which do not convey such an idea, it becomes equivalent to *very, very much, exceedingly*, and the like. I. where there is the idea of pain, trouble, etc. (*a*) where the idea of manner is more prominent:—Þearle ys mē nū ðā, heorte ys onhǣted *matters go hardly with me now, my heart burns within me*, Judth. Thw. 22, 30; Jud. 86. Se ðe his þeóden ǣr þearle gerǣhte (*severely wounded*), Byrht. Th. 136, 29; By. 158. Hī fuhton ðearle *they fought hard*, Judth. Thw. 25, 16; Jud. 262: Chr. 937; Erl. 112, 23. Hī hungre wǣron þearle geþreátod, Andr. Kmbl. 2231; An. 1117: Beo. Th. 1124; B. 560: Rood Kmbl. 103; Kr. 52. Ðis is ðeóstræ ham ðearle gebunden fæstum fȳrclommum, Cd. Th. 267, 15; Sat. 38. Þearle hē dēmde *tantopere taxaverat*, Hpt. Gl. 454, 2. Ūs stalu and cwalu . . . derede swȳðe þearle *injured us very severely*, Wulfst. 159, 11. Ðæt hē him ðonne ðearlur (*districtius*) dēman scyle,

Past. 53; Swt. 419, 5. (β) where the idea of degree is more prominent, *very, very much, exceedingly, excessively*:—Sáwl mín gedréfed is ðearle *anima mea turbata est valde*, Ps. Spl. 6, 3. Geeádmét ic eom ðearle (*nimis*), 37, 8: Ps. Th. 78, 8. Þearle ic deorfe *nimium laboro*, Coll. Monast. Th. 19, 13. Forþóht þearle (cf. swíþe unrót, Bt. 1; Fox 4, 4), Met. 1, 82. Ðæt folc wearð þearle geswenct mid ðam síðfate *taedere coepit populum itineris ac laboris*, Num. 21, 4: Ps. Th. 103, 8: Homl. i. 80, 14. II. where there is no idea of pain, trouble, etc., *very, to a great degree, very much, to a great extent, exceedingly*:—Geðancas þearle deópe *nimis profundae cogitationes*, Ps. Th. 91, 4. Þearle mildheort *multum misericors*, 144, 8: Judth. Thw. 22, 23; Jud. 74. Swíðe gelýfed mann and ðearle eáwfæst, Homl. Th. ii. 306, 4. Ðú eall geworhtest þing þearle gód (cf. swíþe góde, Bt. 33, 4; Fox 128, 22), Met. 20, 45. Behéfe þearle *utilis valde*, Coll. Monast. Th. 27, 27: 29, 31. Þearle deóplíce *valde profunde*, 32, 9. Þearle swíþe tó herienne, Lchdm. iii. 436, 18: 438, 27. Hé geíhte folc his ðearle (*vehementer*), Ps. Spl. 104, 22. Þearle fremaþ cræft mín eów *multum prodest ars mea vobis*, Coll. Monast. Th. 28, 7: Judth. Thw. 26, 3; Jud. 307. Ic ðé gemenigfilde swíðe þearle (*vehementer nimis*), Gen. 17, 2. Drig swýþe þearle *dry very thoroughly*, Lchdm. i. 70, 10. Ðis godspel belimpþ swíðe þearle tó ðære mǽran freólstíde *this gospel belongs very specially to the great festival*, Homl. Th. ii. 360, 10. Hig þearle etaþ *nimium comedunt*, Coll. Monast. Th. 26, 11. Gehwylc mé drincan sealde þearle *each gave me abundance to drink*, Exon. Th. 485, 1; Rä. 71, 7. Drinc swýþe þearle *drink very largely*, Lchdm. i. 78, 10. Hit on wolcnum oft þearle þunraþ, Met. 28, 25. v. for-þearle.

þearl-líc; *adj. Severe, hard to bear*:—Ðá ðæt Andrea earmlíc þúhte, þeódbealo þearlíc tó geþolianne, ðæt hé swá unscyldig ealdre sceolde lungre linnan, Andr. Kmbl. 2273; An. 1138. Sceal se dæg weorþan, ðæt wé forð beraþ firena gehwylce; ðæt biþ þearlíc gemót (*a meeting that will be a severe ordeal for all*), Exon. Th. 447, 9; Dóm. 36. Deáþes cwealm, þearlíc wíte, 240, 25; Ph. 644. Þurh þearlíc þreá, 283, 10; Jul. 678.

þearllíce; *adv.* I. *severely*:—Ðonne sint eác ðǽm ilcan monnum suíðe ðearllíce (ðearlíce, Cott. MSS.) tó recceanne ða godcundan cwidas *districte itaque contra illos divinae sententiae proferendae sunt*, Past. 37; Swt. 265, 22. Forðon is néd, ðætte sume mid woningum, sume þearlícor (ðearflícor, Bd. S. 490, 11), sume líðelecor, synd gerehte *unde necesse est ut quidam damnis, quidam districtius, quidam levius, corrigantur*, Bd. 1, 27; M. 68, 5. II. *strictly, exactly, thoroughly*:—Drig swýþe þearle (þeaclíce (þearlíce?), MS. O.), Lchdm. i. 70, 10. III. *violently*:—Swá biþ be ðám heáclifum and torrum, ðonne hí hlifiaþ feor up ofer ða óðre eorðan, hý ðonne feallan onginnaþ and full þearlíce hreósan tó eorðan (*come with a great crash to the ground*), Wulfst. 262, 12. v. for-þearlíce.

þearl-mód; *adj. Of severe mind*, (1) in a bad sense, *stern, cruel*:—Hæfde his ende gebidenne unswǽslícne, swylcne hé ǽr æfter worhte, þearlmód þeóden gumena (*Holofernes*), Judth. Thw. 22, 18; Jud. 66. (2) in a good sense, *severe* in dealing with evil. v. þearl, I:—Þearlmód þeóden gumena (*the Deity*), 22, 34; Jud. 99.

þearl-wís; *adj. Severe, strict*:—Ierre ðæs ðearlwísan déman *districti iram judicis*, Past. 10; Swt. 63, 15. Beforan ðæm ðearlwísan déman *apud districtum judicem*, 16; Swt. 105, 10: Bd. 4, 25; S. 599, 36. Þearlwísere gýmene *districto regimine*, Hpt. Gl. 486, 61. God sylfa ðonne ne gýmeþ nǽnges mannes hreówe, ac biþ ðonne réþra and þearlwísra ðonne ǽnig wilde deór, Blickl. Homl. 95, 30.

þearlwís-líc; *adj. Severe, hard*:—Drihten hyne þreáde myd þearlwýslícere swingle *the Lord punished him with a severe flogging*, Shrn. 98, 15.

þearlwíslíce; *adv. Severely, strictly*:—Ðreáge hé hine selfne ðearlwíslíce on his geðóhte *se districta animadversione corrigant*, Past. 64; Swt. 461, 20. Hié ða scyldigan þearlwíslíce démaþ, Blickl. Homl. 63, 20. Ðý læs hié wyrðen ðearlwíslecor gedémede *ne districtius puniantur*, Past. 28; Swt. 191, 15.

þearlwísness, e; *f. Severity, strictness*:—Seó ðearlwísnes ðæs heardan lífes *districtio vitae arctioris*, Bd. 4, 25; S. 599, 31. Hé hine wæs frignende mid ða apostolícam ðearlwísnesse *sciscitabatur apostolica districtione*, 2, 6; S. 508, 14.

þearm, es; *m. A gut, an intestine* [*Tharm* = guts washed for making hogs' puddings, is given as a Lincolnshire word in Bailey's Dictionary; with the meaning, 'material of which fiddle-strings are made,' it is given in E. D. S. Pub. Cumberland Glossary; and in Jamieson's Dictionary *therm, tharme* = the intestines; a gut prepared, especially as a string for a musical instrument]:—Þearm, thearm *intestinum*, Txts. 69, 1058. Þearm *fibra*, 63, 870: Wrt. Voc. ii. 148, 55: *intestinum*, 44, 2. Þearm *fibra*, þearma *fibrarum*, þearmas *fibre*, 35, 39–41. Blind þearm *cecum*, 16, 59. Lǽcedómas wiþ þearmes útgange, and gif men bilyhte sié ymb ðone þearm, Lchdm. ii. 170, 27. Þearmas *fibrae*, Wrt. Voc. i. 45, 16: *intestina*, ii. 49, 50: *exta*, Ælfc. Gr. 13; Zup. 85, 10. Ðearmas, Wrt. Voc. i. 71, 14. Smæle þearmas *ilia*, 44, 46. Þearma *fibrarum*, Hpt. Gl. 520, 62. Darmana, Txts. 111, 27. Þearmas *fibras*, Wrt. Voc. ii. 38, 5: Hpt. Gl. 453, 14. [Þærmes (þarmes, 2nd MS.), Laym. 818. Þermes, 18451. Þine þarmes þralinge, H. M. 35, 26. Thaarme or gutte *sumen, viscus*, Prompt. Parv. 490. A tharme *trutum*, Wrt. Voc. i. 247, 5 (15th cent.). *O. Frs.* thermar; *pl.*: *O. L. Ger.* thermi; *pl. exta*: *O. H. Ger.* darm *fibra*; *pl.* darma *intestina, ilia*: *Ger.* darm: *Icel.* þarmr; *pl.* þarmar: *Dan. Swed.* tarm *gut.*] v. bæc-, smeoru-, snǽdel-þearm, smæl-þearmas, *and next word*.

þearme(, es; *n.?* v. smæl-þearme) *the entrails*:—Tharme *viscera*, Txts. 107, 2140.

þearm-gewind, -wind, es; *m.* The words seem to mean '*that which enwraps the intestines*,' cf. *plecta* wǽfelsa, gewynde, Hpt. Gl. 462, 64, but they are used to gloss *jugulam* (-*um?*), so should mean *the collar-bone*, or *the hollow part of the neck above the collar-bone*, or *the throat*:—Gescyld ðearmgewind (ðearmwind, lxxiv, 24), breóstbán, breóst *tege jugulam, pectusculum, mamillas*, Lchdm. i. lxxii, 1.

þearm-gyrd *a belly-band, girth*:—Þearmgyrd *subligar* (the word occurs in a list of terms connected with horses), Wrt. Voc. i. 23, 16. [Cf. *O. H. Ger.* darm-gurtil *cingula*.] Cf. forþ-gyrd.

þeáter (*with declension like* winter?) *a theatre*:—Æt heora þeátra, Ors. 4, 1; Swt. 154, 2.

þeáw, es; *m.* I. *a custom, usage, general practice* of a community:—Swá Iudéa þ[e]áw (ðeáu, Lind.: ðeów, Rush.) ys tó bebyrgenne *sicut mos Iudaeis est sepelire*, Jn. Skt. 19, 40. Hit wæs Iudisc þeáw, Blickl. Homl. 67, 8. Feówertig daga hit wæs þeáw (*mos*) ðæt man sceolde wépan ǽlcne deádne mann, Gen. 50, 3. Siþþan wæs hiera (*the Amazons*) þeáw, ðæt hié ǽlce geáre tósomne férdon, Ors. 1, 10; Swt. 46, 8: Beo. Th. 2497; B. 1246: Andr. Kmbl. 50; An. 25. Wæs in ða tíd ðeáu Ongelcynnes folcum, ðæt . . ., Bd. 4, 27; S. 604, 15. Gyf hit on lande ðeáw sý, L. R. S. 3; Th. i. 432, 24. Hwæt ðeóde ðeáw sý, 4; Th. i. 434, 34: 21; Th. i. 440, 21. Be ðære ðeóde ðeáwe ðe wé ðænne on wuniaþ, 440, 23. Ðara ðeóda þeáwas sint swíþe ungelíca, Bt. 18, 2; Fox 64, 22. Efenfela þeóda and þeáwa, Exon. Th. 334, 18; Gn. Ex. 18. Ðeóda ungelíca ǽgþer ge on sprǽce ge on ðeáwum, Bt. 18, 2; Fox 62, 29. II. *mode of conduct, custom, manner, practice, way, usage* of a class or kind, (a) referring to human beings:—Ne bið swylc cwénlíc þeáw, Beo. Th. 3885; B. 1940. Swá bið geóguðe þeáw, Exon. Th. 127, 23; Gú. 390. Hýrena ðeáwe gé fleóþ *ye flee after the manner of hirelings*, Past. 15; Swt. 89, 14. Hé for eaxlum gestód Deniga freán, cúþe hé duguðe þeáw, Beo. Th. 724; B. 360. (b) *referring to animals*:—Hiora ðeáwe *suatim* (cf. *suatim, suarum more*, 77, 43), Wrt. Voc. ii. 88, 14. Ðú (*Nebuchadnezzar*) ne gewittes wást bútan wildeóra þeáw, Cd. Th. 252, 2; Dan. 572. (c) referring to inanimate things:—Ðæt mennisce mód hæfþ wætres ðeáw (*aquae more*), Past. 38; Swt. 277, 6. Ǽlces mannes mód hæfþ scipes ðeáw (*more navis*), 58; Swt. 445, 10. Nú ðú wást hwelce þeáwas ða woruldsǽlþa habbaþ . . . Gif ðé heora þeáwas líciaþ, Bt. 7, 2; Fox 18, 5–7. (d) referring to all created things:—God gesette unáwendendlícne sido and þeáwas eallum his gesceaftum, Bt. 21; Fox 74, 1: Met. 11, 12. III. *a practice* of religion, *method* of belief, *way* of thinking, legal *usage*:—Gecynde riht *jus naturale*, þeáw *vel* wíse *solempnitas*, Wrt. Voc. i. 20, 32. Swylc wæs þeáw hyra *such was their religion*, Beo. Th. 359; B. 178. Ánmóde þeáwes *those who think alike*; unius moris (cf. un[i]animes, Ps. Th. Surt.), Ps. Spl. 67, 6. Se forlét his fulluht, and leouode on hǽðenum þeáwe, Chr. 616; Erl. 20, 40. Hé nǽnigne nýdde tó Cristenum ðeáwe (*ad Christianismum*), Bd. 1, 26; S. 488, 15. Tó reogollícum ðeáwe rihtra Eástrena *ad ritum Paschae canonicum*, 5, 22; S. 643, 38. Þis folc æfter ðeáwe tó húsle gange, Blickl. Homl. 207, 5. Heó ðone ðeáw ðæs Cristenan geleáfan (*ritum fidei*) healdan móste, Bd. 1, 25; S. 486, 34. Hǽþennysse ðeáw forlǽtan *gentilitatis ritum relinquere*, 1, 26; S. 488, 12. Ðone ealdan ðeáw . . . ðý apostolican ðeáwe *inveteratam illam traditionem . . . apostolico more*, 5, 22; S. 644, 6–8. Hé hæfde beteran ðeáw, leóhtran geleáfan, Cd. Th. 256, 18; Dan. 642. Ða ðe on hǽðnum þeáwum dwelgende wǽron, Blickl. Homl. 201, 20. Geset is on cyrclícum þeáwum, Homl. Th. i. 150, 26. Hé áwrát áne bóc be cyrclícum ðeáwum, ii. 84, 23. Onféngon hí rihtgelýfede ðeáwas on tó lifianne *susceperunt ritus vivendi catholicos*, Bd. 5, 22; S. 644, 23: Hy. 9, 28. Ðone naman ánne wé hæfdon ðætte wé Cristene wǽron and swíðe feáwe ða ðeáwas *we should have the name only of being Christians, and very few of the practices of Christianity*, Past. pref.; Swt. 4, 8. Þeáwas (*Epicuri*) sectas, Wrt. Voc. ii. 84, 67: Hpt. Gl. 503, 59. IV. *a custom, habit, manner, mode of conduct* of an individual; the pl. often may be rendered by *conduct, behaviour*:—Ðeáw wæs ðam ylcan biscope, ðæt hé ðæt weorc má ðurh his fóta gange fremede, ðonne on his horsa ráde *moris erat eidem antistiti, opus magis ambulando quam equitando perficere*, Bd. 4, 3; S. 566, 31. Ǽlces gódes þeáwas wísdóm gefyllþ ðone, ðe hine lufaþ, Bt. 27, 2; Fox 98, 2. Wá him ðæs þeáwes, gif hí unrǽdes ne geswícaþ, Exon. Th. 393, 11; Rä. 12, 8. Hé wæs swíþe yfel monn ealra þeáwa, búton ðæt hé wæs céne *his conduct was very bad in every respect, except that he was brave*, Ors. 6, 14; Swt. 268, 27. Weorðe hé worda and dǽda, þeáwa and geþonca, ðæt hé ne forleóse his dreámes blǽd, Exon. Th. 97, 1; Cri.

1584. Ic geseó on eówres fæder þeáwum ðæt hē nys swā wel wið mē geworht, swā hē wæs gyrstandæg *I see by your father's behaviour that he is not so well disposed to me as he was yesterday*, Gen. 31, 5. Hē ongiet be sumum ðingum oððe ðeáwum ūtanne ætiéwdum eall ðæt hié innan ðenceaþ, Past. 21; Swt. 155, 10. Wer gecorene on his ðeáwum *virum probum moribus*, Bd. 3, 23; S. 554, 9. Wæs hē swīðe geþungen on his ðeáwum *he was most excellent in his conduct*, Blickl. Homl. 217, 7: Judth. Thw. 23, 19; Jud. 129: Exon. Th. 126, 10; Gū. 369: 297, 14; Crä. 68. Þeáwum geþancul *habitually thoughtful*, Andr. Kmbl. 923; An. 462: Cd. Th. 102, 25; Gen. 1705. Lifian rihtum þeáwum *to live righteously*, 160, 4; Gen. 2646. Þeáwum lifian *to live virtuously*, Exon. Th. 319, 13; Vīd. 11: Beo. Th. 4295; B. 2144. Ǽlc ðara ðe healdan wile hālige þeáwas *every one who will maintain habits of holiness*, Cd. Th. 92, 20; Gen. 1531. [*O. E. Homl.* þeau, þeu: *A. R.* þeau: *Laym.* þeauwes, þewes, þæwes; *pl.*: *Orm.* þæw: *O. and N. Chauc.* þewes; *pl.*: *Prompt. Parv.* thewe, maner or condycyon *mos*: *O. Sax.* thau: *O. H. Ger.* dau.] v. freoðo-, fulwiht-, leód-, mann-, mynster-, regol-, un-þeáw; ge-þȳwe, un-geþeáwe.

þeáw *a slave*. v. þeów.

þeáw-fæst; *adj.* I. *of good manners, of well-ordered life, moral, virtuous*:—Loth hine fægre heóld, þeáwfæst and geþyldig, on ðam þeódscipe, Cd. Th. 116, 26; Gen. 1942: (*Abraham*), 161, 8; Gen. 2662. Wunige hē mid þeáwfæstum mannum *maneat cum bene moratis hominibus*, L. Ecg. P. i. 10; Th. ii. 176, 23. II. *gentle*:—Sumum hē syleþ monna milde heortan, þeáwfæstne geþōht, Exon. Th. 299, 28; Crä. 109. v. un-þeáwfæst.

þeáwfæstness, e; *f.* *Adherence to the rules of right conduct* or *method, discipline, obedience to rule*:—Þeáwfæstnesse *disciplinae*, Hpt. Gl. 432, 34. Be sealmsanges ðeáwfæstnesse *de disciplina psallendi*, R. Ben. 45, 2. Ða cild mid steóre and þeáwfæstnysse (*cum disciplina*) heora endebyrdnysse healdon, 116, 9: R. Ben. Interl. 106, 12. On hāligre þeáwfæstnesse, Homl. Ass. 40, 406, 404: Homl. Skt. ii. 28, 138. Þēningmen ðe þeáwfæstnysse him gebeódon (cf. þēnas ðe his willan gefyllaþ, 65), Homl. Skt. i. pref., 62. Regoles gehȳrsumnesse and þeáwfæstnesse *regule oboedientiam et disciplinam*, R. Ben. Interl. 103, 16. Ðū hatast ðeáwfæstnysse (*disciplinam*, Ps. 50, 17), Homl. Th. ii. 532, 2.

þeáw-full; *adj.* *Moral, virtuous*:—Oft hig (*devils*) beswīcaþ þeáwfulle weras (ða ðeáwfullan, MS. A.), Wulfst. 250, 4. [Heo Godd thonkeden mid þeufulle (witfolle, 2nd MS.), worden, Laym. 1797. Mid þeaufule talen schurteð ou, A. R. 422, 19. Ne beo þu nawt tu trusti ane to þi meidenhad wiðuten oðer god and þawfulle mihtes, H. M. 45, 4.] v. un-þeáwfull.

þeáwian *to serve*. v. þeówian.

þeáwian *to make* (*well*) *mannered*. [Wel ðewed, Gen. and Ex. 1914. So boner and þewed, Allit. Pms. 59, 733.] v. ge-þeáwian.

þeáw-leás; *adj.* *Ill-mannered, ill-conditioned*:—Swȳn ðe cyrþ tō meoxe æfter his ðweále, þeáwleás nȳten, Homl. Th. ii. 380, 11. [For lust hath leve, the lond is theweles, P. S. 255, 19.]

þeáw-līc; *adj.* I. *usual, customary*:—Sum wīt mid sealfe his fēt smyrode, swā swā hit þeáwlīc wæs on ðære þeóde, Homl. Ass. 41, 439. II. *moral, figurative*:—Þeáwlīc[r]e spǣce *tropologiae, figurati sermonis*, Hpt. Gl. 432, 13. Þeáwlīcre spǣce *tropologiam misticum, moralem*, 410, 43. Wē willaþ secgan hū ðās lāc tō ūs belimpaþ æfter ðeáwlīcum andgite, Homl. Th. i. 116, 33: ii. 110, 26: 210, 27: Wulfst. 234, 10. [*O. H. Ger.* dau-līh *moralis*.]

þeáwlīce; *adv.* *In accordance with good manners, properly*:—Gāþ þeáwlīce . . . and standaþ þeáwlīce *incedite morigerate* . . . *et state disciplinabiliter*, Coll. Monast. Th. 36, 1-5. Ðā hē ðæt hæfde ðeáwlīce (*rite*) gesett, Bd. 3, 19; S. 549, 37.

þec. v. þū.

þeccan; *p.* þeahte, þehte; *pp.* þeaht *To cover*, (1) *to cover* an object with something:—Ic wreó mē, leáfum þecce, Cd. Th. 53, 29; Gen. 868. Ðū ðīn sylf þecest līc mid leáfum, 54, 15; Gen. 877. Se ðe heofen þeceþ wolcnum *qui operit coelum nubibus*, Ps. Th. 146, 8. Mec (*a horn*) þeceþ mon golde and sylfore, Exon. Th. 395, 2; Rä. 15, 1. Hē þeahte bearn middangeardes wonnan wǣge, Cd. Th. 83, 10; Gen. 1377. Git eágorstreám earmum þehton, Beo. Th. 1031; B. 513. Saga hwā mec þecce, Exon. Th. 381, 21; Rä. 2, 14. Mec ongon hold gewēdum þeccan, 391, 13; Rä. 10, 4. Hine mid hrægle wryón and sceome þeccan, Cd. Th. 95, 3; Gen. 1573: 58, 7; Gen. 942. Wæstmum þeaht, 115, 20; Gen. 1922. Hleówfeðrum þeaht, 165, 31; Gen. 2740. Ȳþum þeaht, Exon. Th. 392, 7; Rä. 11, 4. Helmum þeahte, Cd. Th. 120, 3; Gen. 1989. (2) *to serve as covering to* an object. Earn ðeceþ (*tegit*) nest his, Ps. Surt. ii. p. 192, 31. Mec hrīm þeceþ, Exon. Th. 490, 11; Rä. 79, 9. Forst and snāw eorþan þeccaþ, 215, 7; Ph. 249. Ic gealgan þehte *I was stretched upon the cross*, Andr. Kmbl. 1932; An. 968: Apstls. Kmbl. 44; Ap. 22. Ealne middangeard mereflōd þeahte, Exon. Th. 200, 18; Ph. 42: Cd. Th. 8, 1; Gen. 117. Līca gehwilc ðara ðe līfes gāst þeahte *every body that had within it a living spirit*, 77, 28; Gen. 1282. On hwelcum hī (*Weland's bones*) hlǣwa hrūsan þeccen, Met. 10, 43. Sió filmen biþ þeccende and wreónde ða wambe, Lchdm. ii. 242, 17. ¶ In the following passages Grein suggests that the form is quite a different word = *comburere*, and Cosijn (P. B. 8, 574) takes it to be connected with *þicgan* (but see *þecgan*); but, perhaps, the verb may be the same here as in the previous instances, and used with much the same force as *wrap* in such a phrase as *wrapt* in flames:—Byrneþ þurh fȳres feng fugel (*the phenix*) mid neste . . . þonne brond þeceþ heoredreórges hūs, Exon. Th. 212, 27; Ph. 216. Hine ād þeceþ, 223, 26; Ph. 365. Seó hyre bearn gesihþ brondas þeccan, 330, 7; Vy. 47. Beágas sceal brond fretan, ǣled þeccean, Beo. Th. 6022; B. 3015. [To dyche and to thecche, Piers P. 19, 232. *O. L. Ger.* thekkan: *O. Frs.* thekka: *O. H. Ger.* decchen *tegere, operire, velare*: *Icel.* þekja *to cover*.] v. be-, (bi-), ge-, ofer-, un-þeccan; þeccend; þacian.

þecc-bryce, es; *m.* *A tile*:—Þeccbrycum *imbricibus*, Hpt. Gl. 459, 42. Cf. þæc-tigele.

þeccend, es; *m.* *One who covers* or *protects, a protector*:—Ðū eart þeccend (*protector*) mīn, Ps. Th. 70, 5, 2.

þecel[l]e. v. þæcele.

þecen, e; *f.* *A roof*:—Þecen *vel* rōf *tectum*, Wrt. Voc. i. 26, 34. Þæcen, 81, 9. Of daliscre þecene *dedalei tecti*, ii. 139, 68: Exon. Th. 493, 21; Rä. 81, 34. Swā swā spearwa on ðecene (on efese ł on þecene, Ps. Lamb.) *sicut passer in tecto*, Ps. Spl. 101, 8. Under mīne þecene, Mt. Kmbl. 8, 8: Lk. Skt. 7, 6: Homl. Th. i. 126, 30: Mk. Skt. 13, 15: Exon. Th. 431, 18; Rä. 46, 2. Hīg þecena (getimbrena ł þæcena, Ps. Lamb.) *foenum tectorum*, Ps. Spl. 128, 5. [*O. L. Ger.* thecina.]

þecgan; *p.* þegde; *pp.* þeged *To take, consume*:—Hine þegeþ þurst *he is consumed by thirst*, Lchdm. ii. 60, 7: 74, 22. v. ā-, ge-, of-þecgan; þicgan.

þecge (?), an; *f.* *A receptacle* (?):—On hærfeste man sceal ðacian, ðecgan and fald weoxian, scipena behweorfan, Anglia ix. 261, 17. Cf. þicgan.

þēde, þēdum, þēfel, þēfan-, þēfe-þorn. v. þeówan, þȳfel, þīfe-þorn.

þefian *to pant, to be agitated*:—Þefiendra *anhelantium*, Hpt. Gl. 406, 8. Þefian *aestuare in animo*, Dial. 1, 9 (Lye). [Cf. (?) *Icel.* þefja *to smell*.]

þeften. v. þyften.

þegan (*this seems the regular strong form for the verb which usually has weak forms in the present*, þicgan, q. v.) *to take, accept*:—Him wæs Godes egsa māra in gemyndum ðonne hē menniscum þrymme þegan wolde *there was too great fear of God in his thoughts for him to wish to get human glory*, Exon. Th. 112, 8; Gū. 140.

þegen, þegn, þeng, þēn, es; *m.* I. *a servant, one who does service for another*:—Þēn *minister*, Wrt. Voc. i. 82, 24. Swā hwylc swā wyle betweox eów beón yldra, sȳ hē eówer þēn (*minister*), Mt. Kmbl. 20, 26: 23, 11. Ðā bæd hē his ðeng (*ministrum*), ðæt hē him stōwe gegearwode. Ðā wundrade se ðeng, Bd. 4, 24; S. 598, 29. Geleáffull ðegn (esne, Rush.: þeów, W. S.) *fidelis servus*, Mt. Kmbl. Lind. 24, 45, 46. Ðā þēnas ðe ðæt wæter hlōdon, Jn. Skt. 2, 9. II. where the service is of a public or official character, *an officer, minister*:—Þegn *lictor*, Wrt. Voc. ii. 93, 10: 52, 59. Ðe læs se dēma ðē sylle ðam þēne (ðegne, Lind.: dægne, Rush.), Mt. Kmbl. 5, 25. Ða weorcgerēfan and ða þēnas (*praefecti operum et exactores*) cwǣdon tō ðam folce: 'Pharao bȳt, ðæt eów mann ne sylle leng nān cef,' Ex. 5, 10. Ða þeówas and ða þegnas *serui et ministri*, Jn. Skt. 18, 18. Þegna *lictorum*, Wrt. Voc. ii. 84, 24: 52, 41. Ābeád þeódcyning þegnum sīnum, ombihtscealcum, Cd. Th. 112, 12; Gen. 1869. Ða ealdras sendon hyra þēnas, ðæt hig woldon hine gefōn, Jn. Skt. 7, 32. Sangeras and mæssepreóstas and manigfealdlīce cirícean þegnas, Blickl. Homl. 207, 32. II a. figurative:—Deófolgieldum, ðām wyrrestum wītes þegnum, Exon. Th. 251, 29; Jul. 152. III. where the service is military, *a soldier*:—Ān Ueriatuses þegn *unus ex iis* (one of the victorious Lusitanians), Ors. 5, 2; Swt. 216, 21. Þa þēnas (ðegnas, Lind. Rush.) *milites*, Jn. Skt. 19, 2. Ðā hēt hē his ðegnas (*milites*) hine sēcan . . . 'Ðone forhycgend ūra goda ðū mē helan woldest swȳþor ðonne mīnum ðegnum (*militibus*) secgean,' Bd. 1, 7; S. 477, 7-20. Hī sealdon ðām þegenum (*militibus*) micyl feoh, Mt. Kmbl. 28, 12. Ic hæbbe þegnas (ðeignas, Lind.) under mē *habens sub me milites*, 8, 9. IV. *a follower of a great man, a retainer*:—Þegn, gesīþa *cliens*, i. *socius*, Wrt. Voc. ii. 131, 70. Thegn, degn, þegn *adsaeculam*, Txts. 42, 101. Þegn, Wrt. Voc. ii. 4, 43. Ðæs degenes lof is ðæs hlāfordes wurðmynt, Homl. Th. ii. 562, 6. Ðā wæs ðǣrinne Dauid mid his monnum. Ðā cleopedon his ðegnas him tō and hine lǣrdon ðæt hē hine ofslōge *illic cum viris suis Dauid inerat, cum eum viri sui ad feriendum Saul accenderent*, Past. 28; Swt. 197, 17. Ārās se rīca (*Beowulf*), ymb hine rinc manig, þegna heáp, Beo. Th. 805; B. 400. Þēna, cnihta, forspillendra þēna *parasitorum*, incniht *parasitus*, Hpt. Gl. 504, 18-21. Þēnum *parasitis*, incnihttum *clientibus*, 514, 52-54. Ðegnum *pedisequis*, Wrt. Voc. ii. 84, 75. IV a. figurative:—Ðū wāst hwelce þeáwas ða woruldsǣlþa habbaþ . . . Gif ðū heora þegen beón wilt, Bt. 7, 2; Fox 18, 6. V. *a follower of a teacher, a disciple*:—Iōhannes, se deóra þegn, Blickl. Homl. 67, 22. His þegnas lǽddon him tó ðone eosol, 71, 5: 15, 13. On Sancte Petres naman, Cristes ðegnes, 205, 14. Ðeignas his (his discipuli ł his þegnas, Rush.) *discipuli ejus*, Mt. Kmbl. Lind, 5, 1. Cuǽdon tó ðeignum his, 9, 11. Ðegnum, 10: Jn. Skt. Lind. Rush. 18, 19. **V a.** in poetry, borrowing the terms of war:—Sint geþreáde þegnas míne (*St. Andrew's disciples*), geonge gúðrincas, Andr. Kmbl. 782; An. 391. **VI.** *one engaged in a king's* or *queen's service*, whether in the household or in the country, *a thane*. The word in this case seems gradually to acquire a technical meaning, and to become a term denoting a class (v. þegen-riht, -wér), containing, however, several degrees. To illustrate the wider sense in which the word could be used, when the þegen is spoken of in relation to the king, the following passages may be cited. In the Chronicle an. 897 'manige ðara sélestena cynges þéna' includes two bishops and three aldermen, as well as a cynges þegn and a cynges horsþegn. In a charter Cnut greets 'ealle míne þegnas, twelfhynde and twihynde' (*the twihynde man is a ceorl:* cf. too, 'ealne his leódscype, twelfhynde and twyhynde,' Chart. Erl. 229, 19), Cod. Dip. Kmbl. iv. 9, 30. The word seems general, too, in the passage, 'Weorðscipes wyrþe ǽlc be his mǽðe, eorl and ceorl, þegen and þeóden,' L. R. 1; Th. i. 190, 13. The more limited sense seems to belong to the word in the following:—Gif þegen geþeáh ðæt hé wearð tó eorle, L. R. 5; Th. i. 192, 7. Cf. §§ 2, 6; and see L. In. 45, L. C. S. 72, L. M. L. given below. In some cases, too, it will be seen that the term implies military service, as when *de militia regis juvenis* is translated *sum geong ðæs cyninges ðegin* (see also other passages below from Bd. 4, 3, and 5, 13); in others, the service is that of the household, v. Bd. 4, 3; S. 567, 21, and búr-, disc-, hrægl-þegen; in others it is official work in the country. For the development of the class of thanes in England, see Stubbs' Const. Hist. s. v. thegn; Kemble's Saxons in England, I. c. 7, II. c. 3; Schmid, A. S. Gesetz. s. v. þegen. (1) where the word is used of other than Teutonic peoples:—Wæs his (*St. Martin's*) fæder ǽrest cyninges þegn, and geðeáh ðæt hé wæs cininges þegna aldorman, Blickl. Homl. 211, 21. (Cf. His (*St. Martin's*) fæder wæs æðelboren, ǽrest cempa, and siððan cempena ealdor, Homl. Th. ii. 498, 25. St. Martin's father was a military tribune.) Þegn *satrapa*, Wrt. Voc. i. 42, 17. Xersis þegn wæs háten Marðonius, Ors. 2, 5; Swt. 82, 28. Wé sǽdon, ðæt hé wǽre ryhtwísra ðá ðá hé ðeng wæs ðonne hé wǽre siððan hé kyning wæs. Ðá ðá hé ðegn wæs hé his feónd ne dorste ofsleán *David rectior fuit in servitio, quam cum pervenit ad regnum. Servus adversarium ferire timuit*, Past. 50; Swt. 393, 2–6. Tarcuinius óðerne ðegn ongeán sende, Ors. 2, 3; Swt. 68, 17. Pharaones þegnas *servi Pharaonis*, Ex. 10, 7. His (*Ulysses'*) þegnas him ne mihton leng mid gewunian, Bt. 38, 1; Fox 194, 27. Mænegum cyninges (*king of Egypt*) þegnum, Cd. Th. 111, 5; Gen. 1851. (1 a) where the Deity is the king served:—Metodes ðegn, Abraham, Cd. Th. 176, 6; Gen. 2907. Dryhtnes þegn (*Guthlac*), Exon. Th. 143, 22; Gú. 665. Ðú cyninges eart þegen geþungen, Andr. Kmbl. 1055; An. 528. Wuldres þegn, engel Drihtnes, Cd. Th. 136, 31; Gen. 2266. Ðæt is micel wundor, ðæt wolde þeóden þolian, ðæt wurde þegn swá monig forlǽdd, 37, 30; Gen. 597. (1 b) figurative:—Fuglas þringaþ ymbe æþelne (*the phenix*), ǽghwylc wille wesan þegn and þeów þeódne mǽrum, Exon. Th. 209, 3; Ph. 165. (2) where the word applies to Englishmen or to other Teutonic peoples:—Hér Hengest and Æsc gefuhton uuiþ Walas and hiera þegn án wearþ ofslægen, Chr. 465; Erl. 12, 23. Gest hine clǽnsie sylfes áðe, swylce cyninges þeng, L. Wih. 20; Th. i. 40, 20. Lilla se cyninges ðegn him se holdesta *minister regi amicissimus*, Bd. 2, 9; S. 511, 22. Sum geong ðæs cyninges ðegin *de militia ejus juvenis*, 4, 22; S. 590, 33. Ðá ondrǽdde hé andettan ðæt hé cyninges ðegen wǽre, ac sǽde, ðæt hé folclíc man wǽre, and ðæt hé forðon in ða fyrd cóme, ðæt hé sceolde cyninges ðegnum heora mete lǽdan *timuit se militem fuisse confiteri; rusticum se fuisse respondit, et propter victum militibus adferendum in expeditionem se venisse testatus est*, S. 591, 5–9. Hé sægde ðæt hé wǽre cyninges ðeng *ministrum se regis fuisse manifestans*, 591, 38. Hé ðære ylcan cwéne ðeng (*minister*) wæs, 592, 13. Sum wer wæs on lǽwedum háde ðæs cyninges ðegn *vir in laico habitu atque officio militari positus*, 5, 13; S. 632, 8. Þegn, se ðe on handa bær ealowǽge, Beo. Th. 993; B. 494. Þegn Hróðgáres, égweard, 475; B. 235. Eádwold cynges ðegen, Chr. 905; Erl. 98, 28. Gif mon cyninges þegn beteó, gif hé hine ládian dyrre, dó hé ðæt mid .xii. cininges þegnum. Gif man ðone man betýhþ ðe biþ læssa maga (mága?) ðonne se cyninges þegn, ládige hé hine mid .xi. his gelícena and mid ánum cyninges þægne, L. A. G. 3; Th. i. 154, 5–9. Gif cyninges þegn ætsace ... gilde .x. healfmearc (cf. the next two sections), L. N. P. L. 51; Th. ii. 298, 7: 58; Th. ii. 300, 3: 60; Th. ii. 300, 9. Burgbryce mon sceal bétan eoldormonnes .lxxx. scill., cyninges þegnes .lx. scill., gesíðcundes monnes landhæbbendes .xxxv. scill., L. In. 45; Th. i. 130, 9. Eorles heregeata syndon ... And syþþan cyninges þegenes (þegnas, MS. G.) ðe him nýhste syndon ... And medemra þegna ... And cyninges þegnes heregeata inne mid Denum ðe his sócne hæbbe feówer pund. And gif hé tó ðam cyninge furðor cýððe hæbbe ..., L. C. S. 72; Th. i. 414, 4–20. Ðegenes lagu is, ðæt hé sý his bócrihtes wyrðe, and ðæt hé ðreó ðinc of his lande dó, fyrdfæreld and burhbóte and brycgeweorc. Eác of manegum landum máre landriht árist tó cyniges gebanne, L. R. S. 1; Th. i. 432, 4–7. Ðegnes wergild is syx swá micel (swá ceorles). Ðonne biþ cynges ánfeald wergild .vi. þegna wer be Myrcna lage, L. M. L.; Th. i. 190, 2–5. Hié (*the Danes*) sealdon (Ceólwulfe) ánum unwísum cyninges þegne Miercna ríce tó haldanne, Chr. 874; Erl. 76, 27. Nán man náge náne sócne ofer cynges þegen búton cyng sylf, L. Eth. iii. 11; Th. i. 296, 23. Ðæs cyninges þegnas (cf. ða men ðe mid ðam cyninge wǽrun, Erl. 48, 31), Chr. 755; Erl. 50, 3, 9. Hé wæs hyre (*the queen's*) ðéna hire húses and hire geférscipes oferealdormonn *erat primus ministrorum et princeps domus ejus*, Bd. 4, 3; S. 567, 21. Se cyning gestód æt ðam fýre mid his ðegnum (*ministris*), 3, 14; S. 540, 34. Wé willaþ ðæt man namige on ǽlcon wǽpengetæce .ii. trýwe þegnas and ǽnne mæssepreóst, L. N. P. L. 57; Th. ii. 298, 31. *In the two following passages, though translations, the ideas are probably English:*—Cyningas ne magan nǽnne weorþscipe forþ bringan búton heora þegna (*servientium*) fultume. Hwæt wille wé secgan be ðám ðegnum (*familiaribus*; cf. folgerum, l. 10), Bt. 29, 1–2; Fox 104, 12–15. Mid miclon geférscipe hiora þegna, and ða bióþ mid fetlum and mid gyldenum hyltsweordum and mid manigfealdum heregeatwum gehyrste, 37, 1; Fox 184, 4. **VI a.** *a thane who served a bishop:*—Wulfhere bisceopes ðegn, Chr. 1001; Erl. 136, 8. Ic Leófinc bisceop gebócige sumne dǽl landes mínan holdan and getreówan þegene, ðam is Ægelríc nama, for his eádmódre gehérsumnysse, Chart. Erl. 242, 11. Ic (*Cnut*) cýðe, ðæt ic hæbbe geunnen him (*archbishop Æthelnoth*), ðæt hé beó his saca and sócne wyrðe ofer his ágene menn and ofer swá feala þegna swá ic him tólǽtan hæbbe, 233, 6. **VI b.** *one engaged in the service of a republic:*—Scipia, se betsta Rómána þegn (se besta and se sélesta Rómána witena and þegena, MS. C.), Ors. 5, 4; Swt. 224, 24. **VII.** *a person of rank, one of a class higher than the ordinary freeman* (ceorl). v. þegen-boren:—Þegn *primas*, Wrt. Voc. i. 42, 14. Ðegn *optimas*, Ælfc. Gr. 9, 25; Zup. 50, 3. Ðeáh þrǽla hwylc hláforde æthleápe, and hit æfter ðam geweorðe, ðæt wǽpngewrixl weorðe gemǽne þegene and þrǽle, gyf þrǽl ðæne þegen áfylle, licge ǽgylde; and gyf se þegen ðæne þrǽl, ðe hé ǽr áhte, áfylle, gylde þegengylde, Wulfst. 162, 5–10. Ælc dohtig man on Kænt and on Súð-Sexan, on þegenan and on ceorlan, Cod. Dip. Kmbl. iv. 11, 7. **VIII.** *a brave man, noble man, good warrior;* vir fortis. v. þegen-líc, -líce, -scipe, III:—Gif gé swelce þegnas synt, swelce gé wénaþ ðæt gé sién, ðonne sceoldon gé lustlíce eówre ágnu brocu áræfnan, Ors. 3, 7; Swt. 120, 7. Ðæt wæs swíðe sweotol, ðæt hié ðá wǽron beteran þegnas ðonne hié nú sién, ðæt hié ðæs gewinnes geswícan noldon, 4, 9; Swt. 192, 32. **VIII a.** in poetry the word is used, like *eorl*, as a complimentary term for *man, warrior:*—Swylc sceolde secg wesan, þegn æt ðearfe, Beo. Th. 5411; B. 2709. Se þegn (*St. John*) wæs on wynne, Exon. Th. 462, 21; Hö. 55. Þances gleáw þegn (*St. Andrew*), Andr. Kmbl. 1114; An. 557. Ðam þegne (*Adam*) ongan his hige hweorfan, Cd. Th. 44, 7; Gen. 705. Scyle áscian deóphýdig mon ... ne sceal ðæs áþreótan þegn módigne, Exon. Th. 348, 1; Sch. 21. Ðæt micle morð menn ne þorfton, þegnas þolian, Cd. Th. 40, 18; Gen. 641. Wlance þegenas, unearge men, Byrht. Th. 137, 53; By. 205. Ne sceolon mé on ðære þeóde þegenas ætwítan (cf. stedefæste hæleð, 139, 5; By. 249), 138, 15; By. 220. ¶ The word is applied to Christ:—Þegen mid þreáte, þeóden engla, Cd. Th. 288, 27; Sat. 388. [*O. Sax.* þegan: *O. H. Ger.* degan *masculus, herus, miles, defensor: Icel.* þegn.] v. ærn-, ambeht-, bed-, búr-, burh-, cyric-, disc-, duru-, ealdor-, forþ-, gum-, hand-, heáh-, heal-, helle-, hrægl-, mægen-, mæsse-, magu-, mete-, scír-, scóh-, sele-, tintreg-, weofod-, weoruld-, wic-, wíf-þegen (-þegn).

þegen-boren; *adj. Of gentle birth.* v. þegen, VII:—Sý hé þegenboren, sý hé ceorlboren, L. O. D. 5; Th. i. 354, 20.

þegen-gilde, es; *n. The wergild for a thane:*—Gyf þrǽl þegen fullíce áfylle, licge ǽgylde; and gyf se þegen þæne þrǽl, ðe hé ǽr áhte, fullíce áfylle, gylde þegengylde, Wulfst. 162, 10. [*Icel.* þegn-gildi *the wergild for a þegn.*]

þegen-hyse; *pl.* -hyssas; *m. A follower, attendant:*—Ðegnhyssas *clientes* (the passage in Aldhelm is: Ejusdem nefandae militiae tam calones et clientes ... quam satrapae et proceres), Wrt. Voc. ii. 76, 73: 17, 74.

þegen-lagu, e; *f. Thane-law, the legal rights and privileges which attached to the rank of thane:*—Se (*the priest*) ðe ðæs (*concubinage*) geswícan wille and clǽnnesse healdan, hæbbe hé Godes miltse, and tó woruldwurðscipe sí hé þegenlage wyrðe *as regards worldly dignity let him rank as a thane*, L. C. E. 6; Th. i. 364, 16: Wulfst. 270, 32. v. þegen-riht.

þegen-líc; *adj. Manly, brave, manful.* v. þegen, VIII:—Andreas is gereht ðegenlíc, Homl. Th. i. 586, 11. Máran lufe nimþ se heretoga on gefeohte tó ðam cempan, ðe æfter fleáme his wiðerwinnan ðegenlíce oferwinþ, ðonne tó ðam ðe mid fleáme ne ætwand, ne ðeáh on nánum gecampe náht ðegenlíces ne gefremode, 342, 5.

þegenlíce; *adv. Bravely, manfully, like a brave man, gallantly:*—Beó ðú gehyrt and hicg þegenlíce *tu confortare et viriliter age*, Jos. 1, 18: Homl. Skt. ii. 25, 248. Heó tó ðám þegnon cwæð: 'Dóð þegnlíce and wel; ábeódaþ míne ǽrende tó ðam gemóte,' Chart. Th. 337, 36.

Gif hē đegenlīce earfođnysse forberþ, Homl. Th. i. 586, 19: Homl. Skt. i. 11, 3. Ealle þeóda sprǣcon hū đegenlīce hī fuhton, ii. 25, 324. Hē læg đegenlīce đeódne gehende *he lay like a warrior close to his lord*, Byrht. Th. 140, 26; By. 294. [*O. L. Ger.* thegenlīcho *viriliter*: *O. H. Ger.* thegan-, degan-līcho.] v. preceding word.

þegen-rǣden[n], e; *f. The condition of being a* þegen, *service*:—Þegnrǣdenne ođđe hīwrǣdenne *clientele*, Wrt. Voc. ii. 24, 44. Hīrēdlīcre þēnrǣdene *familiaris clientelae*, Hpt. Gl. 504, 46. Manige men of cyninges þegenrǣdene tō Cristes þeówdōme gecyrdon, Blickl. Homl. 173, 17. Cf. þegen-scipe.

þegen-riht, es; *n. Thane-right, the legal rights and privileges which attached to the rank of thane* (e.g. Mæssepreóstes āđ and woruldþegenes is on Engla lage efendȳre... Twelfhyndes mannes (*a thane's*) āđ forstent .vi. ceorla āđ, L. O. 12, 13; Th. i. 182, 14–19):—Se mæssepreóst biþ þegenrihtes wyrđe, L. O. 12; Th. i. 182, 17: L. Eth. v. 21; Th. i. 306, 21: vi. 5; Th. i. 316, 14. Gif ceorl geþeáh đæt hē hæfde fullīce fīf hīda āgenes landes... and sundernote on cynges healle, đonne wæs hē đonon forđ þegenrihtes weorđe, L. R. 2; Th. i. 190, 18. Gif massere geþeáh đæt hē fērde þrige ofer wīdsǣ, se wæs þegenrihtes weorđe, 6; Th. i. 192, 10. v. þegen-lagu, -wer.

þegen-scipe, es; *m.* I. *thaneship, the status of thane*:—Se dēma đe ōđrum wōh dēme... þolige hē his þegenscipes, L. Edg. ii. 3; Th. 266, 18: L. C. S. 15; Th. i. 384, 13. II. *a body of thanes*:—Scē Adrianes wæs đæs cāseres đegnscipes ealdorman, đe Maximianus wæs nemned, Shrn. 59, 24. III. *bravery, manfulness, gallantry.* v. þegen, VIII, þegenlīc:—Beóþ nū gehyrte, and healdaþ mid đegenscipe đa hālgan Godes ǣ, Homl. Skt. ii. 25, 258. Hē him eft his rīce tō forlēt for his þegnscipe (*ob testimonium virtutis*), Ors. 3, 9; Swt. 132, 24. Alexander his ǣrestan đegnscipe on đon gecȳþde, đā hē ealle Crēcas mid his snyttro on his geweald geniédde, ealle đa đe wiđ hiene gewin up āhōfon *Alexander primam experientiam animi et virtutis suae, compressis celeriter Graecorum motibus, dedit*, Swt. 122, 32. IV. in that part of the Genesis which is thought to show Old Saxon influence, the word occurs with the meaning of *service to a lord*, like the Old Saxon *thegan-skepi*:—Nis mē on worulde mōd ǣniges þegnscipes, Cd. Th. 51, 33; Gen. 836. On þegnscipe þeówian, 46, 15; Gen. 744. Hié þegnscipe Godes forgȳmdon, 21, 19; Gen. 326. [*Icel.* þegnskapr *honour* (as in *on one's honour*); *liberality; allegiance of a* þegn.]

þegen-scolu, e; *f. A band of thanes, a following*:—Þegenscole *clientele*, Wrt. Voc. ii. 18, 1.

þegen-sorh; -sorge; *f. Sorrow for the loss of thanes*:—Grendel on reste genam þrītig þegna... Mǣre þeóden þegnsorge dreáh, Beo. Th. 263; B. 131.

þegen-weorod, es; *n. A host of thanes*:—Đæt wē tō đam hȳhstan hrōf gestīgan, đǣr is geþungen þegnweorud, Exon. Th. 47, 6; Cri. 751.

þegen-wer, es; *m. The* wer-gild *of a thane*:—Hē sȳ þegenweres and þegenrihtes wyrđe, L. Eth. v. 9; Th. i. 306, 21: vi. 5; Th. i. 316, 14. Gif weofodþēn be bōca tǣcinge his āgen līf rihtlīce fadige, đonne sī hē fulles þegnweres and weorđscipes wurđe, ix. 28; Th. i. 346, 18. Cf. Mǣsseþegnes and woruldþegnes wergyld is .ii. þūsend þrymsa, L. Wg. 5; Th. i. 186, 10. v. þegen-riht.

þégh, þegin, þegn, þegnen. v. þeóh, þegen, þignen.

þegnest (? *related to* þegnian *as O. Sax.* thionost, *O. L. Ger.* thianust, thienest, *O. H. Ger.* dionōst, *Icel.* þjónusta *are to verbs* thionōn, dionōn, þjóna *respectively; or* (?) þēnest, þeónest *the English form corresponding to the nouns given above. The passage in which the word occurs separately refers to Germany, so perhaps the German form has been borrowed* (?): *where it occurs as the first part of a compound the form is* þeónest; *in the same passage, which is late,* eó *is written where* ē *is the more regular form, as* heót *for* hēt; *perhaps, however, the Scandinavian form has influenced the English*) *Service*:—Þæs ilcan gēres fōr Aldrēd biscop tō Colne ofer sǣ, and wearđ đǣr underfangen mid mycclan weorđscipe, and him geaf ǣgđer þēneste ge se biscop on Colone and se cāsere, Chr. 1054; Erl. 189, 25. (This passage occurs in only one MS.) v. *next word, and* þegnisc.

þegnest-mann (?), es; *m. A thane*:—Þās (*a number of bishops, aldermen and others, who are named*) and feola ōþre kyninges þeónestmen (*but cf. Icel.* þjónustu-maðr *a liegeman*), Chr. 656; Erl. 33, 9. v. preceding word.

þegnestre, þēnestre, an; *f. A female servant*:—Þēnestran *cultricem, ministram*, Hpt. Gl. 438, 33. v. next word.

þegnian; *p.* ode; *pp.* od. I. *to serve* a person (*dat.*), *do* a person (*dat.*) *service, minister to, attend* upon:—Hwæđer ys yldra đe se đe đēnaþ đe se đe sitt *quis major est, qui recumbit? an qui ministrat?* Lk. Skt. 22, 27. On heáhsetle siteþ self cyning (God), and điós sīde gesceaft þēnaþ and þiówaþ, Met. 29, 77. Gif him ǣrlīce esne þēnaþ, Exon. Th. 430, 9; Rä. 44, 5: 403, 28; Rä. 22, 14. Þēnaþ *prosequitur*, Hpt. Gl. 451, 57. Hē (*a king*) bioþ swīþe anlīc đara his þegna sumum đe him þēniaþ, Bt. 37, 1; Fox 186, 12. Gif hē nǣre sōþ God, nā him englas ne þegnodon. On đisse bysene is gecȳþed, đæt eallum geleáffullum mannum englas þegniaþ, đonne hī habbaþ deófol oferswīþed, Blickl. Homl. 35, 1–4. Ic geornlīce Gode þegnode þurh holdne hyge, Cd. Th. 37, 7; Gen. 585. Hē mē holdlīce đegnade *mihi ministrabat*, Ps. Th. 100, 6. Ne com ic tō đon on eorđan đæt mē mon đēnode, ac tō đon đæt ic wolde đegnian *filius hominis non venit ministrari, sed ministrare* (Mt. 20, 28), Past. 41; Swt. 301, 2. Iōsep hæfde mycele gife æt his hlāforde and þēnode (*ministrabat*) him, Gen. 39, 4: 40, 4. Englas him þegnedan, Blickl. Homl. 27, 22. Þegnedon, 33, 34. Þēna me *ministra mihi*, Lk. Skt. 17, 8. Ǣlc wēnþ đæt hē þenige Gode *omnis arbitretur obsequium se praestare Deo*, Jn. Skt. 16, 2. Se biscop and se mæssepreóst, gif hī mid rihte willaþ Gode þeówian, đonne sceolan hī þegnian dæghwamlīce Godes folce *the bishop and the priest, if they desire to serve God aright, must minister daily to God's people*, Blickl. Homl. 45, 30. Ne þūhte hit mē nāuht rihtlīc, gif him sceoldan þeówe men þēnigan (þēnian, Cott. MS.), Bt. 41, 2; Fox 244, 27. On đam hūse hyra đeáw wæs, đæt hī đa untruman in lǣdan sceoldan, and him ætsomne đēnigean, Bd. 4, 24; S. 538, 29. I a. where the instrument with which service is performed is given:—Mec lāđgeteónan þreátedon; ic him þēnode deóran sweorde swā hit gedēfe wæs *I served my foes with my good sword, as was fitting*, Beo. Th. 1125; B. 560. Đās bōc Leófrīc gef Scō Petro and eallum his æftergengum intō Exancestre Gode mid tō þēnienne, Chart. Erl. 253, 12. II. *to serve* food, *to supply* wants, *minister* to necessities, *provide.* v. þegnung, V:—Đæt ylce wæter eallum đyder cumendum his heofonlīcre gife genihtsumnesse đegnaþ *aqua sufficientem cunctis illo advenientibus gratiae suae coelestis copiam ministrat*, Bd. 4, 28; S. 605, 32. Seó mȳse is seó bōclīce lār, seó đe ūs đēnaþ līfes hlāf, Homl. Th. ii. 114, 26. Martha gearwode đam Hǣlende ǣfengereordu... Martha wæs geornful đæt heó đon Hǣlende tō gecwēmnesse þegnode (þēnode, Lk. Skt. 10, 40): heó him tō cwæþ: 'Hwȳ nelt đū gēman đæt mīn sweostor mē lǣt āne þegnian (þēnian, Lk. Skt.)?, Blickl. Homl. 67, 25–31. Malchus, đa þēnunga đe hē đider brōhte, heom geornlīce þēnode, đæt hī be dǣle hī gereordodon, Homl. Skt. i. 23, 240. Se him đa gerȳno đēnode (*ministrare solebat*) đæs hālgan geleáfan, Bd. 3, 23; S. 554, 17. Hwænne gesāwe wē đē hingrigendne ođđe þyrstendne... and wē ne þēnedon đē?, Mt. Kmbl. 25, 44. Eallum Godes đearfum man sceall weldǣda þēnian, Homl. Th. i. 514, 5. Hē him bigleofan đēnian wolde, ii. 128, 29. Hē hēt hire þēnian of his ēstmetum, Homl. Ass. 110, 268. III. *to serve* an office, *administer, perform the duties of* an office:—Đā hē đā monig geár biscophād đegnade *qui cum annis multis episcopatum administraret*, Bd. 3, 23; S. 555, 7. Đēnade, 4, 3; S. 566, 28, 40. Đegnode Willferþ đa bisceopđēnunge fīf geār *Vilfrid annos quinque officium episcopatus exercebat*, 4, 13; S. 583, 14. Medomlīce đēnian đa đēnunga *officium ministrare digne*, Past. 1; Swt. 27, 10. [Þe king him gon to þeinen, þæ quene bar to drinken, Laym. 30786. A þusen cnihtes þeineden þan kinge... þas beorn þa sunde from kuchene to þan kinge, 24595.] v. ge-, under-þegnian.

þegnisc (? cf. *-ska* nouns in Icelandic (?); or see *þegnest* (?)) *service*:—Þat sāwulgesceot sceulon đa canonicas habban, and swilce þēnisce dōn for hig swilce hig āgon tō dōne, Chart. Th. 609, 16.

-þegnsum. v. ge-þēnsum.

þegnung, e; *f. Service, ministration.* I. *service, good office* done by one to another:—Englas beóđ tō đegnunge gǣstum fram Gode hider on world sended, Blickl. Homl. 209, 23. Ne mihte se mānfulla ēhtere mid nānre đēnunge đām lytlingum swā micclum fremian, Homl. Th. i. 84, 10. Þēnunge *patrocinium* (ut puellulas ad patrocinium vitae impendant, Ald. 69), Hpt. Gl. 519, 2. Đa Ebrēiscan wīf cunnon þēnunga *obstetricandi habent scientiam*, Ex. 1, 19. v. þignen. Hē brǣd hine on feala bleóna þurh deófles þegnunga *he changed himself into many forms by the devil's good offices*, Blickl. Homl. 175, 5. I a. *service* rendered by things, *use*:—Hē wæs lama and eallra his lima đēnunge benumen *deficiente omni membrorum officio*, Bd. 5, 5; S. 617, 38. In đegnunge *in use*; in procinctu, Wrt. Voc. ii. 111, 16. Hē him beád his recedes hleów and þegnunge *he offered them the shelter and use of his house*, Cd. Th. 147, 19; Gen. 2442. I b. *use* made of things:—Nǣnig hī (*the cups*) hrīnan dorste, ne ne wolde, būtan tō his neódþearflīcre đēnunge (*ad usum necessarium*), Bd. 2, 16; S. 520, 8. II. *service* to a lord or master:—Ā tō his (*king Oswine*) folgoþe and tō his đēnunge đa æþelestan men cōman *ad ejus ministerium viri nobilissimi concurrerent*, Bd. 3, 14; S. 540, 12. Wuldres āras đū tō þegnunge đīnre gesettest, Elen. Kmbl. 1474; El. 739. Ōþþæt đū gefylle đīne þegnunge, tō đære đe đū sended eart, Blickl. Homl. 233, 28. Pharao geþencþ đīne þēnunga *recordabitur Pharao ministerii tui*, Gen. 40, 13. Đēnunga *obsequia*, Wrt. Voc. ii. 62, 44. Gif him mon oftīhþ đara þēnunga, Bt. 37, 1; Fox 186, 10, 14. Þegnunga, Met. 25, 24, 32. Đara gumena đē him mid þegnungum þringaþ ymbe ūtan, 25, 28. For đȳ đa ōþra gesceafta þeówe sint, hī healdaþ hiora þēnunga, Bt. 41, 3; Fox 248, 18. Þegnunga, Met. 11, 46. II a. *service, obedience, suit and service*:—Đæt selfe wæter þegnunge gearwode beforan his fōtum *the very water showed itself to be at his command by retreating before his feet* (cf. him gearu sōna þurh streámræce strǣt wæs gerȳmed, symble wæs drȳge folde fram flōde, swā his fōt gestōp, Andr. Kmbl. 3157–; An. 1581–), Blickl. Homl. 247, 10. III. *service* of an official, *office, official employment, ministry*:—Đæs lāreówdōmes đēnung *praedicationis officium*, Past.

7; Swt. 47, 20. Hē wilnode ðære ðegnunga ðæs lāriówdōmes, Swt. 49, 15. Ðære clǣnan ðegnenga ðæs sacerdhādes, Swt. 51, 2. Gefyldum dagum his (*St. Augustine*) ðēnunge *completis diebus officii sui*, Bd. 2, 3; S. 505, 3. Gif ðū wāst ðæt ic unrihtlīce bisceophāde onfēnge, ic lustlīce fram ðære ðēninge (*officio*) gewīte, 4, 2; S. 566, 6. Ic wæs gesett tō mīnre þēnunge (*officio; office of cupbearer*), Gen. 41, 13. Nǣnig sȳ belādod fram ðære kycenan þēnunge *nullus excusetur a coquine officio*, R. Ben. 58, 14. Hē ðæs godspelleres þegnunga gefylde *he filled the office of evangelist*, Blickl. Homl. 167, 9. Ða eorðlīcan hlāfordas sint tō ðæm gesette ðæt hié ða endebyrdnesse and ða ðegnunga hiora hiérēdum gebrytnige *terrenae domus dominus famulorum ordines ministeriaque dispertiens*, Past. 44; Swt. 319, 20. **IV.** *the act of serving* in an official capacity:—Ðæt Leuies mǣgð stōde beforan him on þēnunge, Deut. 10, 8. **IV a.** *a service, an official performance, a service* of religion, *an office* of the church, *a ceremonial* or *ritual service*:—Þēnung *officium*, onsægung *immolatio*, Wrt. Voc. i. 28, 48–49. Þēnunge *sacrificio*, Hpt. Gl. 521, 70. Ðis godspel belimpþ tō ðysses dæges ðēnunge, Homl. Th. i. 104, 4. Byrgincge þēnuncge *sepulturae officio*, Anglia xiii. 444, 1124. Nǣnigum heora ālȳfed sī ǣnige sacerdlīce ðēnunge dōn *nulli eorum liceat ullum officium sacerdotale agere*, Bd. 4, 5; S. 573, 4. Ðæt gē ða ðēnunge fulwihte (*ministerium baptizandi*) æfter ðeáwe ðære hālgan Rōmāniscan cyricean gefyllan, 2, 2; S. 503, 21. Ða clǣnan þēnunga *lauta* (*supernarum*) *munia* (*rerum*, Ald. 144), Wrt. Voc. ii. 90, 9: 52, 51. Ðegnunge *munia*, 91, 32. Þēnunge, 57, 8. Ðā his þēnunga dagas (*dies officii eius*) gefyllede wǣron, Lk. Skt. 1, 23. Þēnungum *culturis, ministeriis*, Hpt. Gl. 495, 27. Mænigfealdum þēnungum *exequiis pluribus*, Wrt. Voc. ii. 144, 79. **IV b.** *a service, the formulas used in a service*:—Swīðe feáwa wǣron behionan Humbre ðe hiora ðēninga cūðen understondan, Past. pref.; Swt. 3, 14. **V.** *service* of food, *a meal, food served, food, provision*. v. þegnian, II, *and* cf. gēmung *for similar specialization of a general term*:—Ðā Drihtnes þēnung wæs gemacod *cena facta*, Jn. Skt. 13, 2. Hē ārās fram his þēnunge *surgit a cena*, 4. Gearwa ūre þēnunga ðæt hig magon etan mid mē *instrue convivium, quoniam mecum sunt comesturi*, Gen. 43, 16: Mt. Kmbl. 26, 17. Ic wolde ðīne ðēnunge sylf nū gearcian, gif ic mē mid fēdunge ferian mihte, Homl. Th. ii. 134, 31. Malchus hæfde mid him eáþelīcan fōdan, and com tō his gefēran ... and ða eáðelīcan þēnunga ðe hē ðider brōhte heom þēnode, ðæt hī be dǣle hī gereordodon, Homl. Skt. i. 23, 233–240. Ðonne man fæste, ðonne dǣle man ða þēnunga ðe man brūcan sceolde ealle Godes þearfan *when a man fasts, then let all the food that would have been used be distributed to the poor*, L. P. M. 3; Th. ii. 286, 28. Hē hēt hire þēnian of his āgenum þēnungum and his ēstmetum, ac heó nolde his sanda brūcan, Homl. Ass. 110, 269. **VI.** in a personal sense, *a following, retinue, train*, cf. folgaþ:—Seó hell and se deáð and heora ārleásan þēnunga wǣron āforhtode, Nic. 28; Thw. 16, 10. [Fer (werpð) manifeald þeninge *fire does service of many kinds*, O. E. Homl. i. 233, 26.] v. ǣfen-, bisceop-, cyric-, fulluht-, geár-, heáh-, līc-, mynster-, tīd-, tō-, ūht-, weofod-, wic-þegnung (-þēnung), *and following words*.

þegnung-bōc, e; *f. A service-book, a book giving the religious services that were to be performed*:—Leviticus on Grēcisc and ministerialis on Lȳden, ðæt ys þēnungbōc on Englisc, for ðam ðara sacerda þēnunga sind ðār āwritene, Lev. pref. Sume ūre ðēningbēc onginnaþ on Aduentum Domini, Homl. Th. i. 98, 26.

þegnung-fæt, es; *n. A vessel used in the service of the kitchen*:—Ðære kycenan wicþēnas . . . heora þēningfata clǣne and hāle ðam hordere betǣcen; se hordere eft ðære tōweardan wucan wicþēnum ða ylcan þēningfata betǣce, R. Ben. 59, 6–12.

þegnung-gāst, es; *m. A ministering spirit*:—Englas beóþ tō ðēninggāstum fram Gode hider on worulde āsende, ðæt hī beón on fultume his gecorenum (*nonne angeli sunt administratorii spiritus, in ministerium missi propter eos, qui haereditatem capient salutis?* Heb. 1, 14), Homl. Th. i. 510, 15.

þegnung-hūs, es; *n. A house in which an employment is carried on, a workshop*:—Þēninghūsum *officinis*, Germ. 394, 267.

þegnung-mann (þēning-, þēnig-), es; *m.* **I.** in a general sense, *a serving-man, attendant*:—Wæs amang ðām Malchus heora ðēnigmann, and ða eáðelīcan þēnunga ðe hē ðider brōhte heom geornlīce þēnode, Homl. Skt. i. 23, 239. Ārās Malchus heora þeningmann, and dyde eall swā his gewuna wæs, nam mid him sumne dǣl feós ... ðæt feoh bær tō porte, 472–486: 447. Se Hǣlend hēt ða ðēnigmen āfyllan six stǣnene fatu, Homl. Th. i. 58, 12. **II.** *a servant of a lord* or *king, a thane, minister*, (a) in a general sense:—Sint tō manienne ða ðe mildheortlīce sellaþ ðæt hié habbaþ, ðæt hié angieten ðæt hié sint gesette ðæm hefencundan Gode tō ðēningmannum tō dǣlanne ðās lǣnan gōd (*ut a coelesti Domino dispensatores se positos subditorum temporalium agnoscant*), Past. 44; Swt. 321, 7. Ān woruldcyningc hæfþ fela þegna; hē ne mæg beón wurðful cyningc būton hē hæbbe swylce þēningmen ðe þeáwfæstnysse him gebeódon, Homl. Skt. i. pref., 62. (b) as a technical English term:—Mīne (*Alfred's*) ealdormenn and mīne þēnigmenn, Chart. Th. 490, 22. On cinges þēningmanna gemōte, Cod. Dip. Kmbl. vi. 80, 20. See Kemble's Saxons in England, ii. 47; Stubbs' Const. Hist. i. 186.

þegnung-weorod, es; *n. A body of attendants* or *serving-men*:—Manege of ðæs ealdormannes þēnungwerode, Shrn. 154, 26.

þegu, e; *f. A taking, accepting*. v. beáh-, beór-, fōd(d)or-, hring-, sinc-, wil-, wīn-þegu; þicgan.

þeh = þec, þēh. v. þū, þeáh.

þel (þell), es; *n. A thin piece of wood* or *metal, a plank, plate*:—Gylden þel āslægen *bratea*, Wrt. Voc. ii. 12, 42. Weel *planca* (þell? þele? *the line is*: Corpus virgineum natat ceu *plana carina*, Ald. 199), 95, 79. Þeáh man gesette ān brād īsen þell ofer ðæs fȳres hrōf . . . and þeáh man mid ðām hameron beóte on ðæt īsene þell, Wulfst. 147, 2–7. Ða wāgas wǣron gyldne mid gyldnum þelum ānæglede fingres þicce *auratos parietes laminarum digitalium grossitudine*, Nar. 4, 25. Wǣpenu mid gyldenum þelum bewyrcean *arma aureis includere laminis*, 7, 12. [Cf. *Icel*. þili; *n. a plank*.] v. benc-, ceól-, wǣg-þel; þel-brycg, -fæsten; þelu; þiling, þille.

þel-brycg, e; *f. A bridge of planks*:—On herepaþ ōþ ðelbrycge, Cod. Dip. B. iii. 682, 18. Of ðam brōcæ in þælbricge; of þælbricge in hēhstræte, Cod. Dip. Kmbl. vi. 60, 21. Cf. stān-brycg.

þele. v. þyle.

þel-fæsten(n), es; *n. A fortress of planks* (Noah's ark):—Nolde seó culufre under salwed bord syððan ætȳwan on þellfæstenne, Cd. Th. 89, 17; Gen. 1482.

þelma, an; *m. A trap*:—Þelman *tendiculum*, Hpt. Gl. 429, 17. Cf. (?) þel.

þelma (?), an; *m. Heat*:—Se þelma and sió hǣto, Lchdm. ii. 82, 10. [Cockayne compares the word with *for-þylman*; but perhaps *welma* or *welm* should be read. The form *welm*, referring to the inflammation which 'þelma' denotes, occurs three times in the section.]

þelu. v. buruh-þelu; þel.

þēn. v. þegen.

þencan; *p.* þōhte (þohte?) *To think*. **I.** absolute, *to meditate, cogitate, consider*:—Sceal scearp scyldwīga gescād witan worda and worca, se ðe wel þenceþ, Beo. Th. 584; B. 289. Ða leásan men treówa gehātaþ fægerum wordum, fācenlīce þencaþ, Fragm. Kmbl. 49; Leás. 26. Ðara sacerda ealdras þōhton ðæt hig woldon Lazarum ofsleán *cogitaverunt principes sacerdotum, ut Lazarum interficerent*, Jn. Skt. 12, 10: Blickl. Homl. 69, 26: 77, 8. Weras þeahtedon and þōhton, Elen. Kmbl. 1094; El. 549. Ðā āgunnon þencan ða bōcerns *coeperunt cogitare scribce*, Lk. Skt. 5, 21. Ne mæg se flǣschoma, ðone him ðæt feorg losaþ, mid hyge þencan, Exon. Th. 311, 23; Seef. 96. Hē eode ūt on ðæt land þencende *egressus fuerat ad meditandum in agro*, Gen. 24, 63. **II.** where the thought is the object of the verb, *to think, have in the mind*:—Secge hē hwæt ic þence *let him say what my thoughts are*, Blickl. Homl. 181, 7. Ðeáh hwā mæge ongitan hwæt ōþer dō, hē ne mæg witan hwæt hē ðencþ, Bt. 39, 9; Fox 226, 7. Gedō ðæt hȳ nægen dōn ðæt yfel ðæt hȳ þencaþ and sprecaþ *decidant a cogitationibus suis*, Ps. Th. 5, 11. Weras ðe ðæt on geþōhtum þenceaþ: Wutun . . ., 138, 17. Ealle ða geþōhtas ðe hī þōhtan *omnes cogitationes eorum*, 145, 3. **II a.** where the thought is expressed:—Ðæt mæg beón, ðæt sume men þencan, 'hū mæg ic sēcan ðæt gāstlīce leóht?' Blickl. Homl. 21, 18. **III.** *to think, suppose, hold as an opinion* or *belief*:—Hē þenceþ ðæt his wīse wel hwam þince eal unforcūþ, Exon. Th. 315, 12; Mōd. 30. Nǣnig heora þōhte, ðæt hē ðanon scolde gesēcean folc, Beo. Th. 1386; B. 691. **IV.** *to think of, consider, employ the mind on* a subject, (1) where the subject of thought is in the accusative:—Ic ðīne sōðfæstnysse þence *meditabor in justificationibus tuis*, Ps. Th. 118, 117. Ðā þōhton hig ðis word, Lk. Skt. 9, 45. Him ðās þing þencendum *haec eo cogitante*, Mt. Kmbl. 1, 20. (2) where the subject of thought is in genitive:—Hē ðencþ ðæs tīman hwonne hē hit wyrs geleánian mæge *deteriora, si occasio praebeatur, quaerat*, Past. 33; Swt. 227, 23. Ðenc ðara worda mīnra gebeda *intende voci orationis meae*, Ps. Th. 5, 1. Gif ðū ðone mon lācnian wille, þænc his gebǣra *consider his gestures*, Lchdm. ii. 348, 13. Hié nyllaþ ðæs ðencean, hū hié mægen nyttweorðuste beón hiera niéhstum, Past. 5; Swt. 45, 18. Wē mōton ðæs þencan ðe egeslīc on ðissum bōcum is gewriten, L. Ath. i. prm.; Th. i. 196, 23. (3) where the subject of thought is governed by a preposition, *to think* about, of, on a subject:—Ic ymb sīþ spræce and on lagu þence, Exon. Th. 458, 9; Hy. 4, 97. Myccle swīðor wē sceolan þencan be ðǣm gāstlīcum þingum ðonne bē ðǣm līchomlīcum, Blickl. Homl. 57, 13. Be ðan morgendæge þencean *de crastino cogitare*, 213, 23. Onginnaþ ymb ða fyrde þencean, Cd. Th. 26, 18; Gen. 408. Hwæt is ðæt ðæm men sȳ māre þearf tō þencenne ðonne embe his sāuwle þearfe, Blickl. Homl. 97, 19. Gōd ys on Dryhten tō þenceanne *bonum est confidere in Domino*, Ps. Th. 117, 8. (4) where the subject of thought is given in a clause introduced by an indirect interrogative:—Hē þencþ hū hē hine ēþelīcost beswīcan mæge, Blickl. Homl. 55, 21. Hē þōhte hū hē him stōl geworhte, Cd. Th. 18, 13; Gen. 272. Maria swīgende ðōhte hwæt seó hālettung wǣre, Blickl. Homl. 7, 16. Hié þōhton hū hié hine ācwellan meahton, 241, 18: Ps. Th. 72, 6. Is wēn ðæt feala manna þence hwylcum edleáne hē onfō æt Drihtne, Blickl. Homl. 41, 14. Smeágean wē and þencan hwæt ðæt tācnode, 19, 4. Smeágan and þencan hwylce ðæs gōdan mannes weorc and his dǣda wǽron, 55, 12. (5) where the construction is uncertain:—Ðenđ *excogitat* (*de domo impii*, Prov. 21, 12), Kent. Gl. 775. V. *to direct the thoughts* to an object, (a) *to look* to with attention, *turn the thoughts* to:—Þenc nū swīđe geornlīce tō đam đe ic ǽr sāde *turn your thoughts very carefully to what I said before*, Shrn. 177, 35. Ðǽm welwillendum is tō secganne, đonne hié gesióđ hiera geférena gōd weorc, đæt hié eác đencen tō him selfum *dicendum est benevolis, ut, cum proximorum facta conspiciunt, ad suum cor redeant*, Past. 34; Swt. 231, 11. Riht is đæt munecas dæges and nihtes inweardre heortan ā tō Gode þencan and geornlīce clypian *it is right that monks day and night ever earnestly direct their thoughts to God and diligently cry to him*, L. I. P. 14; Th. ii. 322, 3. (b) *to look* to with trust, expectation, *expect* of. Cf. *Ger.* zu-denken:—Næs heó swicol nānum đæra đe hyre tō đōhte, Lchdm. iii. 430, 1. Ðā seonde hē đæt man sceolde đa scipu tōheáwan; ac hī ābruđon đa đe hē tō þōhte, Chr. 1004; Erl. 139, 26. Ne þurfon wē nā tō ūrum mǽgum ne nān man tō his wīfe đencean tō đam swȳþe, đæt him man æfter his forđsȳþe tō đam micel fore gedǽle, đæt hī hine fram wītan ālȳsan, gif hē hēr hine sylfne forgȳmde *we need not expect so much of our kinsmen, and no man need expect so much of his wife, as that enough will be given for him after his death to redeem him from torment, if he neglected himself before*, Wulfst. 306, 4. (c) where purpose or intention is implied, *to turn the thoughts* to action, *to be bent* upon something, *have an intention* to do something:—Hī beóđ gewǽpnode on đa wīsan, đe man hors gewǽpnaþ, đonne man tō wīge þencþ (*intends to go to war*), Wulfst. 200, 11. Feówer þing synt ealra þinga behēfost đam ārwyrđan men, đam đē þencþ tō đam ēcan līfe, 247, 12. Hē tō gyrnwræce swīđor þōhte đonne tō sǽlāde *his thoughts were turned rather to vengeance than to voyage*, Beo. Th. 2282; B. 1139. Hī tō swice þōhton, and þrymcyning þeódenstōles berȳfan, Exon. Th. 317, 6; Mōd. 61. Gif hwylc mǽdenman mid gehādodum wunaþ, and heó tō đam ylcan hāde þence *si puella aliqua cum ordinatis habitet, et se eidem ordini destinet*, L. Ecg. P. ii. 17; Th. ii. 188, 10. VI. *to think* of something, where it is implied that effect will be given to the thought, *to determine, devise, mean, purpose, intend*, (a) with gen.:—Ne þence wē nānes yfeles *nec ullas molimur insidias*, Gen. 42, 31. Geheald mē, đæt mē ne beswīce synwyrcende, đa đe unrihtes ǽghwǽr þenceaþ *custodi me a scandalis operantium iniquitatem*, Ps. Th. 140, 11. Ða đe mē đenceaþ yfeles *qui cogitant mihi mala*, 34, 5. Ealle mīne fȳnd þōhton mē yfeles, 40, 8. Ðæt ic mān fleó and mid rihtheortum rǽdes þence, 93, 14. Ne mæg đīn rīce leng stondan, būton đū heora forwyrde đe geornor þence, Blickl. Homl. 175, 15. Ne þenđū *ne moliaris* (*amico tuo malum*, Prov. 3, 39), Kent. Gl. 55. (b) followed by an infin., *to think* of doing something, *intend* to do:—Ic his swīđran hand settan þence *ponam manum ejus*, Ps. Th. 88, 22: 107, 8: 118, 109. Ic mē be healfe mīnum hlāforde licgan þence *I mean to lie by the side of my lord*, Byrht. Th. 141, 9; By. 319. Nō ic eów sweord ongeán ōđberan þence . . . ac ic mīnum Criste cwēman þence, Exon. Th. 120, 18–26; Gū. 274–277. Gif đū ūre bīdan þencest, 119, 26; Gū. 260. Se đe wrecan þenceþ freán, Byrht. Th. 139, 23; By. 258: Beo. Th. 3075; B. 1535: Cd. Th. 287, 9; Sat. 364. Ðonne wē tō hēhselde hnīgan þencaþ, 277, 22; Sat. 208. Mid đȳ hī wrecan þenceaþ *ad faciendum vindictam*, Ps. Th. 149, 7, 8. Hī unscyldige scotian þenceaþ *ut sagittent immaculatum*, 63, 3. Ic hine wrīþan þōhte . . . ic hine ne mihte ganges getwǽman *I meant to bind him . . . but I could not stop him*, Beo. Th. 1933; B. 964: 1483; B. 739. Hē đæt gewrecan þōhte *he determined to punish that*, Cd. Th. 77, 13; Gen. 1274. Hié wyrnan þōhton Moyses māgum leófes sīđes, 180, 27; Exod. 51. Hié wǽron wiđ đæs fȳres weard tō đon đæt hié hit ācwencean þōhton *ad extinguendum ignem concurrerunt*, Ors. 4, 10; Swt. 200, 17: 1, 10; Swt. 44, 32. Se đe gōd beginnan þence hē đæt angin on him sylfum āstelle *he who intends to begin reformation, let him make a beginning with himself*, Lchdm. iii. 438, 32. (b 1) with the gerundial infin.:—Hī đǽr swā longe đōhton tō beónne, Ors. 1, 14; Swt. 56, 22. Se đe đa āre þænce tō þeófigenne ođđe on ōđđre wīs on tō āwendenne *qui quid illinc abstulerit sive in alium usum converterit*, Chart. Th. 177, 13. (b 2) with infin. omitted:—Ða Iudēas sōhton Iōsep and đa twelf cnyhtas and Nichodemus . . . Ealle hig hig selfe bedȳglodon . . . būton Nichodemus sylfa . . . Com hē tō hym . . . Eall swā gelīce Iōsep æfter đam hyne ætȳwde, and heom tō com . . . Hig cwǽdon tō hym: 'Oncnāw nū đæt hyt đē lyt sceal fremian đæt đū tō þōhtest' (*know that it shall benefit you little, that you have determined to come to us*), Nicod. 12–13; Thw. 6, 14–38. Ðara ǽlces đe đæs wordes wǽre đæt from Rōmebyrg þōhte *of each one that should give expression to an intention of leaving Rome*, Ors. 4, 9; Swt. 190, 25. (c) followed by a clause:—Ða đe swā þenceaþ, đæt heó gehȳden hǽlun mīne *ipsi calcaneum meum observabunt*, Ps. Th. 55, 6. Heó ǽr þōhte đæt heó Godes brȳd wurþan wolde *antea statuerat, quo Dei sponsa fieret*, L. Ecg. P. ii. 17; Th. ii. 188, 13. 'Uton ārīsan and ācwellan đa apostolas' . . . Ða Iudēas đā ārison, and hié ongunnon mid sweordum đyder gān; þōhton đæt hié woldan ofsleán đa apostolas, Blickl. Homl. 151, 1. (d) with an accus. to which a clause stands in apposition:—His đegna đreát đe đæt þence nū, đæt hī his willan wyrcean georne *ministri ejus, qui facitis voluntatem ejus*, Ps. Th. 102, 20. VII. *to think* of doing something with hope or expectation, *to desire, seek*:—Ðurh đa rōde sceal rīce gesēcan ǽghwylc sāwl, seó đe mid Wealdende wunian þenceþ, Rood Kmbl. 240; Kr. 121. Hwæþer đū đonne ongite đæt ǽlc đara wuhta đe him beón þencþ đæt hit þencþ ætgædere beón gehāl undǽled *quod autem subsistere ac permanere appetit id unum esse desiderat*, Bt. 34, 12; Fox 152, 26. Ðara gesǽlđa wilniaþ ealle deáþlīce men tō begitanne, đeáh hē đurh mistlīce wegas đencan tō cumanne, 24, 2; Fox 80, 31. VIII. *to think, call to mind, originate* in the mind:—Hié đonne forhtiaþ, and feá þencaþ hwæt hié tō Criste cweđan onginnen *then will they fear, and few will think what to say to Christ*, Rood Kmbl. 228; Kr. 115. [*Goth.* þag(g)kjan; *p.* þāhta *to think, consider, consult, debate*: *O. Sax.* thenkian; *p.* þāhta: *O. L. Ger.* thenkan; thāhta: *O. Frs.* thanka, thenkia; *p.* thōgte: *O. H. Ger.* denchen; *p.* dāhta: *Icel.* þekkja; *p.* þātti *to perceive, know.*] v. ā-, be-, bi-, for-, fore-, ge-, geond-, of-, under-, ymbe-þencan.

þencan in the following passage seems an error:—Sum on bǽle sceal brondas þencan (*Thorpe would read* þeccan; *Grein suggests* sumne on bǽle sceal brond āswencan. Cf. ge-swencan), Exon. Th. 329, 33; Vy. 43.

þēnda, Lchdm. ii. 182, 16. v. þǽnan.

þende; *conj. While*:—Ðendi hē đæt þōhte engel Drihtnes æteáwde him *haec eo cogitante angelus Domini apparuit ei*, Mt. Kmbl. Rush. 1, 20. Þende hē đā gespræc *adhuc eo loquente*, 17, 5. Ðende wæs hē sprecende ł đa hwīle hē spræc *adhuc ipso loquente*, Lind. 26, 47. Ðende đonne (mid þȳ þonne þende, Rush.) wæs đe Hǽlend in Bethania *cum autem esset Jesus in Bethania*, 26, 6. Þende *regente* (perhaps here the word is the beginning of a rendering of the absolute construction, as in the previous passages; or it might be (?) a mistake for *þeódne*), Germ. 403, 35. [*Goth.* þandē, þandei *while, as long as; since*: *O. H. Ger.* danta *quia, ideo.*] v. next word.

þenden. I. *conj. While.* (1) where the periods of the actions marked by the verbs in the conjoined clauses are co-extensive, *as long as*, (*all the*) *while* (*that*):—Ic Drihtne singe þenden ic wunige on woruldreámum *psallam Deo, quamdiu ero*, Ps. Th. 103, 31. Byþ his sōþfæstnys mǽre þenden þysse worulde wunaþ ǽnig dǽl *justitia ejus manet in seculum seculi*, 111, 3: 101, 10: Cd. Th. 93, 9; Gen. 1542: 56, 7; Gen. 908. Ne þearft đū đē wiht ondrǽdan, þenden đū mīne lāre lǽstest, 130, 33; Gen. 2169: Beo. Th. 574; B. 284. Mon mæg gelācnian, þenden of đære lifre sió blōdsceáwung geondgēt ealne đone līchoman, Lchdm. ii. 222, 9. Heó wǽron leóf Gode, đenden heó his word healdan woldon, Cd. Th. 16, 18; Gen. 245. Þenden, 73, 5; Gen. 1200: 194, 3; Exod. 255: 216, 17; Dan. 8: Beo. Th. 59; B. 30: 114; B. 57: Exon. Th. 157, 34; Gū. 901. Þendan, 37, 8; Cri. 590: 50, 14; Cri. 800. Þendon, Andr. Kmbl. 3422; An. 1715. Þynden, 2648; An. 1325. Þenden wē on eorđan eard weardigen, Exon. Th. 48, 15; Cri. 772: Ps. Th. 105, 5. (2) where the verbs of the conjoined clauses denote contemporaneous actions. v. II:—Hȳ sceolon tæfle ymbsittan þenden him hyra torn tōglīde *they shall sit at their play, while their grief slips away*, Exon. Th. 345, 3; Gn. Ex. 182. (3) where the period of the action of the verb in the first clause is included within that of the verb in the subjoined clause, *while, at some time during the period when*:—Gif ic ǽnegum þegne þeódenmādmas forgeáfe, þenden wē on đan gōdan rīce sǽton, Cd. Th. 26, 22; Gen. 410. Hē frægn đa mænigeo hwæt hine gemǽtte, þenden reordberend reste wunode, 223, 21; Dan. 123. II. *adv. Meanwhile*:—Heorot innan wæs freóndum āfylled, nalles fācnstafas þeód-Scyldingas þenden fremedon, Beo. Th. 2043; B. 1019. Dǽdum mildheort, þenden geđyldig, Ps. Th. 85, 14: 91, 13. v. preceding word.

þenedness, þeneness, þēnest, þēnestre, þeng. v. tō-þenedness, ā-þeneness (đenenis *is given in* Ps. Surt. ii. p. 194, 15, *but* āđenenes *in* Txts. 411, 48), þegnest, þegnestre, þegen.

þengel, es; *m. A prince*:—Segncyning, manna þengel, Cd. Th. 188, 24; Exod. 173. Hringa þengel (*Beowulf*), Beo. Th. 3018; B. 1507. [*Icel.* þengill *a prince* (only in poetry).] Cf. fengel, strengel.

þenian, þēnian, þēnisc, þēning. v. þennan, þegnian, þegnisc, þegnung.

þennan, þenian; *p.* þenede. I. *to stretch, spread out, extend, bend* (a bow):—Ic mīne handa tō đē hebbe and đenige *expandi manus meas ad te*, Ps. Th. 87, 9. Bogan his đeneþ *arcum suum tetendit*, Ps. Surt. 7, 13. Ic mīne handa tō đē þenede *expandi manus meas ad te*, Ps. Th. 142, 6. Ða synfullan đenedon (*intenderunt*) bogan, Ps. Surt. 10, 3. Ðene (*praetende*) mildheortnisse đīne weotendum đec, 35, 11. Ðænne đone swīđran earm swā hē swīþast mǽge *let him stretch out the right arm as hard as he can*, Lchdm. iii. 22, 11. Swā hwider swā se cining his rīce mihte þennan *whithersoever the king could extend his power*, Anglia x. 142, 47. Hē đa fǽmnan hēt nacode þennan and mid sweopum swingan *he bade stretch the maiden out naked and scourge her with whips*, Exon. Th. 253, 29; Jul. 187. Þenian *to stretch on the cross*, Rood Kmbl. 103; Kr. 52. Ðennende đū āđenes bogan đīne *tendens extendes arcum tuum*, Ps. Surt. ii. p. 190, 5. II. *to prostrate, overthrow*:—Ðæt hē þenede hig on wēstene *ut prosterneret eos in deserto*, Ps. Spl. 105, 25. III. *to strain, make an effort, exert one's self, press on* (v. Gothic):—Ðæt geswinc his sȳđfætes ne understandende mid hrædestan ryne þenigende arn (*he exerted himself in running*), for ðam ðe hē gewilnode hine geðeódan ðam ðe ðǣr fleáh, Homl. Skt. ii. 23 b, 186. [*Goth.* sik ufþanjan *se extendere* (Phil. 3, 14): *O. Sax.* sie netti thenidun, Hēl. 1155: *O. L. Ger.* thenan *intendere, extendere: O. H. Ger.* dennen *extendere, expandere, distendere: Icel.* þenja *to stretch, extend.*] v. ā-, be-, ge-þennan, -þenian.

þenning, e; *f. Stretching, extension:*—Be Cristes earm[a] þenninge and his honda on rōde, Anglia xi. 172, last line.

þēnsum, þēnung, þeó. v. ge-þēnsum, þegnung, se.

þeód, e; *f.* I. *a nation, people:*—Ðeód winþ ongēn þeóde *consurget gens in gentem*, Mt. Kmbl. 24, 7. Of ðām frumgārum folc āwæcniaþ, þeód unmǣte, Cd. Th. 138, 15; Gen. 2292. Eást-Engla cyning and seó þeód gesōhte Ecgbryht cyning, Chr. 823; Erl. 62, 24. Eal seó þeód ðe on Eást-Englum beóþ, L. A. G. prm.; Th. i. 152, 3. Myrcena ðeód onfēng fulluht, Lchdm. iii. 430, 21. Ðeós þeód (*the Jews*), Elen. Kmbl. 934; El. 468. Ðā wæs þeód (*the citizens of Mermedonia;* cf. burhwaru, 2189; An. 1096) gesamnod, Andr. Kmbl. 2198; An. 1100. Cham ys fæder ðære Cananēiscre þeóde, Gen. 9, 18. Ðǣr wæs micel unþuǣrnes ðære þeóde (*the Northumbrians*) betweox him selfum, Chr. 867; Erl. 72, 8. Mid ðǣm ieldstan witum mīnre þeóde, L. In. prm.; Th. i. 102, 6. Þióde aldor, Dauid, Ps. C. 146. In lond ðara ðeáde *in regionem Gerasenorum*, Mt. Kmbl. Lind. 8, 28. Hēr Ēdwine kyning wæs gefulwad mid his þeóde, Chr. 627; Erl. 24, 2. Ic dēme ða þeóde (*gentem*, the Egyptians), Gen. 15, 14. Clǣnsie man ða þeóde, L. E. G. 11; Th. i. 174, 2. Ealla ōðræ Cristnæ ðióda, Past. pref.; Swt. 7, 5. Of ðām frumgārum twā þeóda (*the Moabites and the Ammonites*) āwōcon, Cd. Th. 158, 11; Gen. 2615. Þeóda *gentes*, Ps. Th. 65, 7. Þeóde, 78, 1: 113, 10. Manegra þeóda fæder *pater multarum gentium*, Gen. 17, 4. Ofer þeóda gehwylce, Beo. Th. 3414; B. 1705. Drihten, ðeóda waldend, Cd. Th. 238, 27; Dan. 361. Eardas rūme Meotud ārǣrde for moncynne, efenfela þeóda and þeáwa (i. e. *each people has its own customs*), Exon. Th. 334, 18; Gn. Ex. 18. Ðiéda *gentium*, Ps. Surt. 17, 44: ii. p. 192, 17. On ðeódum *inter gentes*, Ps. Th. 107, 3. Ofer ealle þeóde *super gentes*, 65, 6. Hī þreátiaþ ymbsittenda ōþra þeóda, Met. 25, 14. Lǣraþ ealle þeóda *docete omnes gentes*, Mt. Kmbl. 28, 19. I a. where the general term is used, but only a part of the people is actually concerned:—Sió þeód geseah in Hierusalem, godwebba cyst ufan eall forbærst, Exon. Th. 70, 6; Cri. 1134. Inne on healle wæs ðeód on sǣlum, Beo. Th. 1291; B. 643. Heó ðæs āð lǣdde on ealre ðeóde gewitnesse tō Ǣglesforda, Chart. Th. 202, 3. Ǣþelrēd Norþanhymbra cyning wæs ofslægen from his āgenre þeóde, Chr. 794; Erl. 58, 5. I b. in pl. *the gentiles:*—Se þeóda lāreów Paulus, Homl. Th. i. 96, 35: Shrn. 58, 33. Þara þeóda (ðeáda, Lind.) Galilea, Mt. Kmbl. Rush. 4, 15. I c. *a race:*—Giganta cyn . . . ðæt wæs fremde þeód ēcean Dryhtne, Beo. Th. 3387; B. 1691. I d. in a general sense, particularly in pl., *people, men:*—Gif ðū eáðmōdne eorl gemēte, þegn on þeóde (*among men*), Exon. Th. 318, 7; Mōd. 79: 176, 4; Gū. 1204. Ðæt wē siþþan forð ða sēllan þing mōten geþeón on þeóde, 23, 31; Cri. 377: 8, 33; Cri. 127: 208, 23; Ph. 160. Cristes þegnas biddaþ God āre ealre þeóde; ðū him tīðast, swā ðū eádmōd eart ealre worlde, Hy. 7, 55. Grēcas . . . Egiptisce þeóda . . . Romani and Englisce þeóda, Anglia viii. 309, 19–21. Þeóda wlītaþ . . . hū seó wilgedryht wildne weorþiaþ, Exon. Th. 221, 28; Ph. 341. Hē þeóda gehwam (*to every one on earth*) hefonrīce forgeaf, Cd. Th. 40, 19; Gen. 641: Exon. Th. 429, 4; Rä. 42, 8. Geþola þeóda þreá *endure men's oppression*, Andr. Kmbl. 213; An. 107. Se ðisne ār hider onsende þeódum tō helpe (*to help people*), 3209; An. 1607. Is wīde cūð ðeódum, ceorlum and eorlum, Menol. Fox 61; Men. 30. David wæs swīðe geðancol tō ðingienne þiódum sīnum wið ðane Sceppend, Ps. C. 7. II. in a local sense, *the district occupied by a people, a country:*—Ān hearpere wæs on ðære þeóde ðe Thracia hātte, Bt. 35, 6; Fox 166, 28. Se wæs on ðære ðeóde ðe hātte Babilonige, Cd. Th. 226, 16; Dan. 172. Ða beorgas onginnaþ in Narbonense ðære ðeóde, Ors. 1, 1; Swt. 22, 20. In ðær ðeáde *in Galilaeam*, Jn. Skt. Lind. 4, 45. Aulixis hæfde twā ðióda under ðam Kāsere. Ða ðióda wǣron hātene Iþacige and Rētie, Bt. 38, 1; Fox 194, 4. III. *a language.* v. ge-þeóde:—Þeáh ðe seofan men sittan on middanearde, and heó mihton sprecan on ǣghwylcere þeóde ðe betwux heofonum and eorðan wǣre, ðara is twā and hundseofontig, Wulfst. 214, 29. [*Goth.* þiuda *a nation, people; pl. the gentiles: O. Sax.* thiod, thioda *a people;* in pl. *men: O. L. Ger.* thiad *gens, natio: O. Frs.* thiade *people, men: O. H. Ger.* diot, diota *gens, populus, plebs, natio: Icel.* þjóð *a nation, people;* in a local sense, *a land, country.*] v. el- (æl-), eást-, gum-, heáh-, neáh-, norþ-, sige-, Sweó-, wer-þeód, irmen-þeóde; in-geþeóde.

þeód-. As the first part of several compounds (see below) *þeód* has the force of *general, great;* a similar use is found in *O. Sax.* and *Icel.* The form is also found in proper names, e. g. Ðeód-bald, Bd. 1, 34; S. 499, 33. Ðeód-rīc, Bt. 1; Fox 2, 5. Þeód-Scyldingas, Beo. Th. 2042; B. 1019. Cf. regn-.

þeódan, þiédan, þīdan, þȳdan; *p.* de *To join* (trans. or intrans.), *attach:*—Be ðām ðe wið ða dǣdbētendan ðeódaþ *de is qui junguntur excommunicatis*, R. Ben. 50, 9. Ðonne hȳ sume mid geficum wið ðone ānne þeódaþ and leásettaþ, sume wið ðone ōþerne *dum adulantur partibus*, 125, 2. Ða woruldgesǣlþa hū hié simle tō ðām gōdum ne ðeódaþ ne ða yfelan gōde ne gedōð ðe hié hié oftost tō geðeódaþ *fortuna nec se bonis semper adjungit, et bonos, quibus fuerit adjuncta, non efficit*, Bt. 16, 3; Fox 56, 33. Ðā weóxon ða fȳr swȳþe and hī tōgædere þeóddon and samnedon ōþ ðæt ðe hī wǣron on ǣnne unmǣtne lēg geānede *crescentes ignes usque ad invicem sese extenderunt, atque in immensam adunati sunt flammam*, Bd. 3, 19; S. 548, 20. Nān brōðor wið ōþerne ne þeóde, ne mid his geþeódrǣdenne ne lette on unþæslīcum tīman *neque frater ad fratrem jungatur horis incompetentibus*, R. Ben. 74, 23. Ðæt hē hiene nānwuht ne āhebbe ofer his gelīcan ne from hiera geferrǣdenne ne ðiéde *quia per elationem se minime a proximorum societate disjungit*, Past. 46; Swt. 349, 5. Þæt wē ūs georne tō Gode þȳdon *that we diligently attach ourselves to God*, Blickl. Homl. 115, 21. Mid cnottum (wǣre) þeód *nexibus nodaretur*, Hpt. Gl. 481, 31. Þiód *subjugatae, subjunctae*, 519, 4. [Cf. *Icel.* þȳða *to associate, attach.*] v. ā-, be-, ge-, ōþ-, under-þeódan (-þiédan, -þīdan, -þȳdan).

þeód-bealu, wes; *n. Great ill, grievous ill:*—Þeódbealu on þreó healfa (*referring to three elements in the misery of the lost;* cf. *O. Sax.* thiod-arbēdi, *applied to the expulsion from Eden*), Exon. Th. 78, 2; Cri. 1268. Andrea þūhte þeódbealo þearlīc tō geþolianne, ðæt hē swā unscyldig ealdre sceolde linnan (cf. *O. Sax.* thiod-quālu, *applied to the crucifixion, and to the agony in the garden*), Andr. Kmbl. 2273; An. 1138. Cf. þeód-þreá.

þeód-būend[e]; *pl. Those living in nations, mankind, men:*—Hē (*Christ*) earfeþu geþolade fore þearfe þeódbūendra, lāðlīcne deáð leódum tō helpe, Exon. Th. 72, 16; Cri. 1173. Hē geðingade þeódbūendum wið fæder swǣsne fǣhþa mǣste, 39, 3; Cri. 616: 84, 11; Cri. 1372.

þeód-cwēn, e; *f. A great queen, an empress:*—Þeódcwēn *the empress* (*Elene*), Elen. Kmbl. 2310; El. 1156. v. next word.

þeód-cyning, es; *m.* I. *the king of a whole nation, a monarch, an independent sovereign.* [Ei mā þā kalla þjóðkonunga er skattkonungar eru, Edda. Ef hann (*Harold Fairhair*) vill leggja undir sik allan Noreg ok rāða þvī rīki jafnfrjālsliga, sem Eirīkr konungr Svīaveldi, eða Gormr konungr Danmörku, þā þykkir mēr hann mega heita þjóðkonungr, Haralds Saga, c. 3.]:—Þeódcyning (*the king of Egypt;* cf. folcfreá, 111, 7; Gen. 1852), Cd. Th. 112, 11; Gen. 1869. Ðeódcyning (*Ongentheow*), Beo. Th. 5932; B. 2970. Se ðeódcyning (*Hrothgar*), 4294; B. 2144. Ðiódcyning (*Beowulf*), 5151; B. 2579. Ǣt þearfe þeódcyninges, 5382; B. 2694. Ðæs þeódkyninges (-kyngces, MS. D.) (*Edward the Confessor*), Chr. 1066; Erl. 198, 15. Fore þrymme ðeódcyninges ǣniges on eorðan, Apstls. Kmbl. 36; Ap. 18. Gewiton hié feówer þeódcyningas (cf. Thadal rex gentium, Gen. 14, 1) þrymme micle, Cd. Th. 118, 14; Gen. 1965. Ðǣr beóþ þearfan and þeódcyningas (*paupers and monarchs;* pauperque potensque), Dōm. L. 161. Wē Gār-Dena in geārdagum þeódcyninga þrym gefrunon, Beo. Th. 3; B. 2. Ond swā micel wundor and wæfersién wæs mīnes weoredes on fægernisse ofer ealle ōþre þeódkyningas ðe in middangearde wǣron *fuitque inter uarietates spectaculorum in conspiciendo talem exercitum, qui ornatu pariter ac uiribus inter gentes eminebant*, Nar. 7, 19. II. *the king of all nations, the monarch of the world, the Deity:*—Būtan ǣr þeódcyning (cf. Exon. Th. 367, 25 *which has here* ēce Dryhten), ælmihtig God ende worulde wyrcan wille, weoruda Dryhten, Soul Kmbl. 24; Seel. 12. [*O. Sax.* thiod-kuning (*used of Christ and of Herod*): *Icel.* þjóðkonungr.] Cf. þeóden.

þeóddon *served.* v. þeówan.

þeód-egesa, an; *m. A terror that affects whole nations, a mighty, general terror:*—Ðonne mægna cyning on gemōt (*at the day of judgement*) cymeþ, þeódegsa biþ hlūd gehȳred, Exon. Th. 52, 16; Cri. 834.

þeóden, es; *m.* I. *the chief of a* þeód [cf. dryhten, dryht *for connexion of* þeóden, þeód], *a prince, king;* the word is used almost exclusively in poetry, but occurs once in the Laws in an alliterative phrase:—Ǣlc be his mǣðe, eorl and ceorl, þegen and þeóden, L. R. 1; Th. i. 190, 14. Eádmund cyning, Engla þeóden, Chr. 942; Erl. 116, 7. Cyning, þeóden Scyldinga, Beo. Th. 3746; B. 1871. Gūðcyning, Wedera þeóden, 4661; B. 2336. Ðeóden gumena (*Holofernes*), Judth. Thw. 22, 18; Jud. 66. Hēr Eádgār wæs, Engla waldend, tō cyninge gehālgod . . . on ðam xxx wæs ðeóden gehālgod, Chr. 973; Erl. 124, 28. Se mondryhten, se eów māðmas geaf . . . hē oft gesealde helm and byrnan, þeóden his þegnum, Beo. Th. 5730; B. 2869: Cd. Th. 158, 34; Gen. 2627. Rīce þeóden, 161, 31; Gen. 2673: 222, 24; Dan. 109. Mǣre þeóden, Beo. Th. 259; B. 129: 3434; B. 1715. Wealhþeów ðeódnes dohtor, 4354; B. 2174: 3678; B. 1837: 2174; B. 1085. Þrȳ wǣron on ðæs þeódnes byrig, ðæt hié noldon hyra þeódnes dōm þafigan onginnan, Cd. Th. 227, 18; Dan. 188. Þeódnes (*Constantine*) willan, Elen. Kmbl. 534; El. 267. Āsecgan suna Healfdenes, mǣrum þeódne, mīn ǣrende, aldre ðīnum, Beo. Th. 695; B. 385: Cd. Th. 221, 25; Dan. 93. Þegnas þeódne sægdon, 228, 20; Dan. 205. Þeóden mǣrne þegn, winedryhten his, wætere gelafede, Beo. Th. 5435; B. 2721: 5570; B. 2788. Leófne þeóden, rīces hyrde, 6151; B. 3079. Mǣrne þeóden, hlāford leófne,

6274; B. 3141. II. *a great man, a lord, chief*:—Úre þeóden (*Byrhtnoth*) líð, eorl on eorðan, Byrht. Th. 138, 39; By. 232: 135, 18; By. 120. Þrymfæst þeóden (*Noah*), Cd. Th. 200, 27; Exod. 363. Þeóden leófesta, Andr. Kmbl. 575; An. 285: (*Guthlac*), Exon. Th. 163, 1; Gú. 987. Þurh ðæs þeódnes word, 174, 2; Gú. 1171. Eorl Beówulfes wolde freádrihtnes feorh ealgian, mǽres þeódnes, Beo. Th. 1598; B. 797: 3259; B. 1627. Seó ecg geswác þeódne (*Beowulf, not yet a king*) æt þearfe, 3054; B. 1525. Hé læg ðegenlíce ðeódne (*Byrhtnoth*) gehende, Byrht. Th. 140, 27; By. 294. Mec ides freán sealde, holdum þeódne, swá hió háten wæs, Exon. Th. 479, 7; Rä. 62, 4. Hæleð, þeódnas þrymfulle, þegnas wlitige, Andr. Kmbl. 725; An. 363. II a. referring to other than men:—Fuglas þringaþ ymbe æþelne, ǽghwylc wylle wesan þegn and þeów þeodne mǽrum (*the Phenix*), Exon. Th. 209, 4; Ph. 165. III. referring to the Deity, (1) to God:—Wæs freá eallum leóf, þeóden his þegnum, Cd. Th. 5, 31; Gen. 80: 37, 29; Gen. 597: 218, 4; Dan. 34. Þeóden, rodera waldend, 73, 10; Gen. 1202. Freá ælmihtig, mǽre þeóden, 52, 34; Gen. 853. Swegles aldor, ríce þeóden, 53, 21; Gen. 864. Engla þeóden, 205, 6; Exod. 431. Swegles ealdor, þearlmód þeóden gumena, Judth. Thw. 22, 34; Jud. 91. Se þióden, Met. 11, 80. Þegnas þrymfæste þeóden heredon, Cd. Th. 2, 7; Gen. 15. (2) to Christ:—Lífes ceápode þeóden moncynne, Exon. Th. 68, 1; Cri. 1097. Se brego mǽra tó Bethania, þeóden þrymfæst, his þegna gedryht gelaðade, 29, 3; Cri. 457. Crist, cyninga wuldor, mǽre ðeóden, Menol. Fox 4; Men. 2. Se drihten, se ðe deáð for ús geþrowode, þeóden engla, Cd. Th. 306, 19; Sat. 666: Elen. Kmbl. 971; El. 487. [*Goth.* þiudans βασιλεύς: *O. Sax.* thiodan (*used of God and Christ, as also of earthly rulers*): *Icel.* þjóðann (*poet.*) *a king, ruler; a great man.*]

þeódend-líc. v. under-þeódendlíc.

þeóden-gedál, es; *n. The separation from a lord* by his death:—Ellen biþ sélast ðam ðe sceal dreógan dryhtenbealu, behycgan þeódengedál . . . se wát his sincgiefan holdne biheledne, Exon. Th. 183, 8; Gú. 1324.

þeóden-hold; *adj. Faithful to a lord, loyal*:—Þegn þeódenhold, Andr. Kmbl. 767; An. 384. Petrus and Paulus ðeódenholde ðrowedon on Róme, Menol. Fox 243; Men. 123. Wígend unforhte, þeódenholde, Cd. Th. 189, 10; Exod. 182. Hé wígena fand æscberendra .xviii. and .ccc. eác þeódenholdra (þeonden, MS.), 123, 10; Gen. 2042. Hé mid wuldre geweorðode þeódenholde, 183, 5; Exod. 87. Cf. dryhten-hold, Cd. Th. 137, 32; Gen. 2282.

þeóden-leás; *adj. Without a lord, deprived of one's prince*:—Hié hira beággyfan banan folgedon þeódenleáse, Beo. Th. 2210; B. 1103. Cf. hláford-leás.

þeóden-máðum, es; *m. A treasure given by a prince*:—Gif ic (*Satan*) ǽnegum þegne þeódenmádmas forgeáfe, Cd. Th. 26, 20; Gen. 409.

þeóden-stól, es; *m. The seat of a king, a throne*:—Þrymcyning þeódenstóles berýfan, Exon. Th. 317, 8; Mód. 62. Ymb þeódenstól hý þringaþ, 25, 7; Cri. 397: 319, 16; Víd. 13.

þeód-eorþe, an; *f. The whole inhabited earth, the world*:—Hwæt sceoldon ðé (*the guilty soul*), þeódeorðan fýlnes (cf. Exon. Th. 368, 7), úre ælmessan? Wulfst. 240, 15.

þeód-feónd, es; *m. The arch-enemy*:—Se þeódfeónd, Antecrist sylfa, Wulfst. 83, 16. Hé fordéþ ðæne þeódfeónd and on helle grund besenceþ, 86, 20: 85, 19: 54, 20.

þeód-fruma, an; *m. A prince of a people, a lord, ruler*:—Ðæt hí þiówien swilcum þiódfruman (hláforde, Bt. 39, 13; Fox 234, 29), Met. 29, 94. Cf. land-fruma.

þeód-gestreón, es; *n. A great treasure*:—Brúc ðisses beáges, and ðisses hrægles neót, þeódgestreóna, Beo. Th. 2440; B. 1218. Nalæs hí hine læssan lácum teódan, þeódgestreónum, 87; B. 44.

þeód-guma, an; *m. A chief man of a people, a great man*:—Ða þeódguman (cf. eorlas æscrófe, 26, 20; Jud. 337), Judth. Thw. 26, 17; Jud. 332: 24, 26; Jud. 208. [*O. Sax.* thiod-gumo:—Thiodgumo, mári mahtig Krist, Hél. 2576. The word is also used of John the Baptist, 2748.]

þeód-here; *gen.* -her(i)ges; *m. The army of a nation, the military force of a people*:—Þeódherga wæl *the slain of the nations who fought*, Cd. Th. 130, 15; Gen. 2160.

þeód-herpaþ (-æþ, -oþ), es; *m. The highway, public road*:—On ðæne þeódherpað, Cod. Dip. Kmbl. iii. 24, 2. Þeódherpoð, v. 157, 14, 16. On ðone þeódherpað west on herpað, Chart. Erl. 330, 5. [Cf. *O. H. Ger.* diet-uuec *via publica*, Grff. i. 669: *Icel.* þjóð-braut, -gata, -leið, -vegr *a high road.*] Cf. þeód-weg.

-þeódig. v. el- (æl-) þeódig. [*O. Sax.* eli-thiodig: *O. H. Ger.* eli-diotic.]

þeódisc; *adj. Belonging to a people, gentile*:—Þeódisce *gentiles*, Anglia xiii. 37, 268. [Þa þeodisce men (þe Romanisse, 2nd MS.), Laym. 5838. *O. L. Ger.* thiudisca liudi *germania*: *O. H. Ger.* diutisk *teutonicus*. Cf. *Goth.* þiudiskō ἐθνικῶς, *gentiliter.*] v. el- (æl-) þeódisc, *and next word.*

þeódisc, es; *n. A language*:—Ðeáh hit gebyrige ðæt ða útemestan ðióda eówerne naman up áhebban and on manig þeódisc eów herigen *licet remotos fama per populos means diffusa linguas explicet*, Bt. 19; Fox 68, 30. Þiódisc, Met. 10, 26.

þeód-land, es; *n.* I. *an inhabited district, a region, country*:—Fromcyme folde weorðeþ, þeódlond monig, ðíne gefylled, Cd. Th. 106, 4; Gen. 1766. Ðá becwom ic on Caspiam ðæt lond; ðá wæs ðǽr seó wæstmberendeste eorþe ðæs þeódlondes, and ic swíðe wundrade ða gesǽlignesse ðære eorðan *Caspias portas peruenimus, ubi cum fertilissimarum regionum admirarer felicitatem*, Nar. 5, 21. Tó wrítanne be ðæm þeódlonde Indie *scribendum de regionibus Indie*, 1, 15. Wé neálǽhtan ðæm þeódlonde (*regioni*), 26, 12. Hé forþférde on Middel-Englum on ðam ðeódlande (*regione*) ðe is nemned on Feppingum, Bd. 3, 21; S. 551, 35. On ðam ðeódlande (*regione*) ðe is gecýged Élíge, 4, 19; S. 588, 1. Gotan geþrungon þeódlond monig, Met. 1, 3. Sculon ágan eaforan ðíne þeódlanda gehwilc, Cd. Th. 133, 15; Gen. 2211. On Cantwara mǽgþe and eác on ðám ðeódlandum ðe ðǽrtó geþeódde wǽron (*in contiguis eidem regionibus*), Bd. pref.; S. 471, 26. Ðá férdon wé on óþer þeódlond India *in alias Indie profecti regiones*, Nar. 22, 2. Wé fram dæge tó óþrum geáxiaþ ungecyndelíco wítu geond þeódland (*throughout the world*) tó mannum cumene, Blickl. Homl. 107, 26. Hé wearð wíde geond þeódland geweorðad, Chr. 959; Erl. 119, 23: Exon. Th. 19, 26; Cri. 306. II. *the continent* (?):—Fýr cymþ and hit gefealþ ǽrest on Sceotta land . . . and hit ðonne færþ on Brytwealas . . . and ðonne hit færþ on Angelcyn . . . Ðonne hit færþ súð ofer sǽ geond ðæt þeódland (on ða þeódland, 215, 18), and hit ðǽr forbærnþ ðæt mancyn, swá hit hér ǽr dyde, Wulfst. 205, 13. [*Icel.* þjóð-land *a country.*]

þeód-líc; *adj. Of a people*:—Ðeódlíc nama *gentile nomen*, Ælfc. Gr. 9, 45; Zup. 65, 6. [*O. H. Ger.* diete-líh.]

þeód-lícettere, es; *m. An arch-hypocrite*:—Se þeódlícetere (*Antichrist*) hit gehíwaþ swá ðæt læst manna wát, hú hé him wið ðone ðeódfeónd gescyldan sceal, Wulfst. 54, 18.

þeód-loga, an; *m. An arch-impostor, a great liar*:—Ða gódan Godes þegnas sǽdan, ðæt hé (*Simon the sorcerer*) luge, and hý geswutelodon, ðæt hit eal leás wæs, ðæt se þeódloga sǽde, Wulfst. 99, 23. Antecrist lǽrþ unsóðfæstnysse and swicolnesse . . . and swá dóð ða þeódlogan, ðe taliaþ ðæt tó wærscype, ðæt man cunne lytelíce swician and mid unsóðe sóð oferswíðan, 55, 15.

þeód-mægen, es; *n. A tribal force*:—Þridde þeódmægen (*the tribe of Simeon, which came third*), Cd. Th. 199, 21; Exod. 342. Cf. folcmægen fór æfter óðrum, 199, 31; Exod. 347.

þeód-mearc, Cd. Th. 187, 33; Exod. 158, *read* þeód mearc.

þeódness, e; *f. A junction, joining*:—Gedafenlíc þeódnys *habilis conjunctio*, Wrt. Voc. i. 54, 60. Þeódnysse *copulam, conjunctionem*, Hpt. Gl. 481, 51. v. ge-, under-þeódness.

þeód-sceaþa, an; *m. A criminal against the community, a spoiler of the community, a great criminal* or *spoiler*:—Wác biþ se hyrde, ðe nele ða heorde bewerian, gyf ðǽr hwylc þeódsceaða sceaðian onginneþ. Nis nán swá yfel sceaða swá is deófol sylf. Ðonne móton ða hyrdas beón swíðe wacore, ðe wið ðone þeódsceaðan folce sceolon scyldan, L. C. E. 26; Th. i. 374, 22–28: Wulfst. 191, 6–13. Þeódsceaða, fýrdraca, Beo. Th. 5369; B. 2688: 4545; B. 2278. Se þeódsceaða (*famine*), Andr. Kmbl. 2232; An. 1117. Gyf God ne gescyrte ðæs þeódscaðan (*Antichrist*) lífdagas, Wulfst. 86, 17. God biddan, ðæt hé ús gescylde wið ðæne þeódscaðan (*Antichrist*), 80, 6. Ðider (*to hell*) sculon þeófas and ðeódscaðan, 26, 18: 165, 36: Exon. Th. 98, 20; Cri. 1610. Lácende lég láðwende men þreáð, þeódsceaþan, 97, 25; Cri. 1596. [*O. Sax.* thiod-skaðo (*the devil*).] Cf. folc-, leód-sceaþa.

þeód-scipe, es; *m. A people*:—Him cierde tó eall se þeódscype on Myrcna lande *all the people of Mercia*, Chr. 922; Erl. 108, 25. Eal þeódscype hine hæfde for fulne cyng, 1013; Erl. 148, 36. Þes þeódscype *the English*, Wulfst. 163, 19. Se ðeódscype *the Jews*, 14, 7. Cyning sceal geþeón and his þeódscipe eác swá, 266, 21. *Oratores* syndon gebedmen, ðe sceolon for ðæne cyngc and for ealne þeódscipe þingian georne. *Laboratores* syndon weorcmen, ðe tilian sceolon ðæs, ðe eall þeódscipe big sceal lybban, 267, 10–15; L. I. P. 2; Th. ii. 304, 15: 4; Th. ii. 306, 33–36. Hí léton ealles ðeódscipes geswincg forwurðan, Chr. 1009; Erl. 142, 12: 1048; Erl. 178, 23. An hé (*king Eadred*) his sáwla tó anliésnesse, and his ðeódscipe tó þearfe sixtýne hund punda, Cod. Dip. B. iii. 75, 1. On ðam þeódscipe (*the people of Sodom*), Cd. Th. 116, 27; Gen. 1942. Wið þeódscipe Assiriæ, 15, 11; Gen. 231. Hí nimaþ úre land and úrne þeódscipe (*gentem*), Jn. Skt. 11, 48: Guthl. 12; Gdwin. 58, 11. Hét se cyng ábannan út ealne þeódscipe, Chr. 1009; Erl. 142, 25. Hú heó rihtlícost heora þeódscipe gehealdan mehton, Chart. Th. 139, 22. Þeódscypas winnaþ heom betweónan, Wulfst. 86, 7. Fela mǽrra manna of manegan þeódscipan, Chr. 1049; Erl. 172, 24. Æfter sumum þeódscipum byþ ðes saltus on .xv. kl. Decembris, Anglia viii. 309, 18. Cf. folc-, leód-scipe.

þeód-scipe, es; *m. Connexion, association, fellowship.* v. þeód-ness, þeódan:—Uton witan hwá hine ðæs wurðscipes cúðe ðe hé sceolde gestandan on ðam rímcræfte. Ic wát gere, ðæt hé ys þeódscipes wyrðe *it is entitled to be connected with arithmetic*, Anglia viii. 308, 23. Ðæt wé gésine ne sýn Godes þeódscipes, metodes miltsa *that we lack not fellowship with God, the Maker's mercies*, Cd. Th. 211, 19; Exod. 528.

Nǽfre ðú geþreátast ðínum beótum, ðæt ic þeódscype ðínne lufie, Exon. Th. 253, 10; Jul. 178.

þeód-scipe, es; *m.* I. *teaching, instruction*:—Ðeódscipe ðín hē mē lǽrde *disciplina tua ipsa me docebit*, Ps. Surt. 17, 36. I a. *instruction, being taught*:—Ðū fiódes ðeódscipe and ðū āwurpe word mīn efter ðē *odisti disciplinam et projecisti sermones meos post te*, Ps. Surt. 40, 17. I b. *testimony*:—Forebodan bið ðis godspell in ðeódscip ł cȳðnise (*in testimonium*) allum cynnum, Mt. Kmbl. Lind. 24, 14. II. *what is taught* or *enjoined, a rule, regulation, law, injunction*:—Ðū him ǽrest ne sealdest, æfter ðam apostolīcan ðeódscipe, meolc drincan, Bd. 3, 5; S. 527, 33. II a. *a collection of regulations, law, religion*:—Swā swā bī ðan ealdan ðeódscipe ða ūttran weorc wǽron behealden, swā on ðam nīwan ðeódscype ... *sicut in Testamento* (v. I b) *veteri exteriora opera observantur, ita in Testamento novo* ..., 1, 27; S. 494, 30. Ealle ða þing ðe hālige men writon on ealdum oþþe on neówum þeódscipe, Blickl. Homl. 133, 2. .vii. gebrōðor geþrowedon deáþ for ðære ealdan ǽ bebode ... Ðā cwæþ se cniht (*the seventh brother*): 'Ic sylle mīnne līchoman for ūssa fædera ðeódscipe, swā mīne brōþor dydon,' Shrn. 111, 20. Ic geseah manige gōde and on Godes þeódscipe wel heora līf lǽddon *alios fuisse narrabat verae religionis cultores*, Guthl. 17; Gdwin. 70, 24. Ðū hine þeódscipe ðīnne lǽrest *de lege tua docueris eum*, Ps. Th. 93, 12. III. *discipline, a disciplinary regulation*:—On strengo þeódscipes and þreá tō wlæc *in disciplinae vigore tepidus*, Bd. 1, 27; S. 492, 18. Ǽfæstnia untrymnisse hire mægne ðeátscip[es] *muniat infirmitatem suam robore discipline*, Rtl. 110, 3. On reogollīcne ðeódscipe *observatione disciplinae regularis*, Bd. 3, 3; S. 526, 9. Hē micele gȳminge hæfde mynsterlīcra ðeódscipa *curam non modicam monasticis exhibebat disciplinis*, 3, 19; S. 547, 28. Reogollīcum ðeódscipum underþeóded *regularibus disciplinis subditus*, 4, 24; S. 598, 21: 3, 19; S. 547, 20. In cyriclīcum ðeódscipum and in mynsterlīcum heálīce intimbred *ecclesiasticis ac monasterialibus disciplinis summe instructus*, 5, 8; S. 621, 34. Þætte ūs fæstern giðii ðōhto ūsra heofonlīcum gilǽr ðeádscipum *ut nobis jejunium proficiat, mentes nostras coelestibus instrue disciplinis*, Rtl. 14, 28. On mynstrum hē leornade gāstlīce ðeódscipas, Shrn. 50, 26. IV. (*regular*) *custom*, (*proper*) *mode of conduct*:—Bēte ðara ǽghwelc mid ryhte þeódscipe ge mid were ge mid wīte *let him make amends for each in the regular way both with* wer *and with* wīte, L. Alf. pol. 2; Th. i. 62, 4. Wæs Godes lof hafen þrymme micle ōþ ðisne dæg mid þeódscipe (*with proper observance?* or *among the people?* v. þeódscipe *a people*), Exon. Th. 284, 10; Jul. 695. Hē wolde habban ða ðēnunga ðeáwas and ðeódscipe tō lǽranne, Past. 17; Swt. 121, 18. Ða men, ðe bearn habban, lǽran hié ðām rihtne þeódscipe, and him tǽcean līfes weg and rihtne gang tō heófonum, Blickl. Homl. 109, 17. Fæderas ic lǽrde, ðæt hié heora bearnum þone þeódscipe lǽrdon Drihtnes egsan (*fathers, bring up your children in the nurture and admonition of the Lord*, Eph. 6, 4), 185, 19. V. *learning, knowledge, understanding*:—Nis in him ðiódscipe *non est in eis disciplina*; neither is there any understanding in them (Deut. 32, 28), Ps. Surt. ii. p. 194, 41. Nis nū fela folca ðætte fyrngewritu healdan wille, ac him hyge brosnaþ, īdlaþ þeódscype (*or under* IV?), Exon. Th. 304, 13; Fä. 69. Hē wæs on godcundlīcan þeódscipe getȳd and gelǽred (*sacris litteris et monasticis disciplinis erudiebatur*)... Hē wæs twā geár on ðære leornunge, ðā hæfde hē his sealmas geleornode, Guthl. 2; Gdwin. 18, 11. Ðū mē þeódscipe lǽr ðīnne tilne and wīsdōmes word *bonitatem et disciplinam et scientiam doce me*, Ps. Th. 118, 66. Hē forget hine selfne and ða lāre and ðone ðiódscipe ðe hē geliornode, Past. 50; Swt. 393, 17. Heó hēht gefetigean forðsnotterne, and his lāre geceás ðurh þeódscipe (*on account of his learning?* or *with a view to learning?* the Latin has: convocans virum disciplinatum), Elen. Kmbl. 2331; El. 1167.

þeód-stefn, es; *m. A stock, people*:—Betere is tō gebīdanne ānne dæg mid ðē, ðonne ōdera on þeódstefnum þūsend mǽla, Ps. Th. 83, 10. Cf. leód-stefn.

þeód-þreá *a great calamity*:—Hié wordum bǽdon, ðæt him gāstbona geoce gefremede wið þeódþreáum (*the injuries inflicted by Grendel*), Beo. Th. 358; B. 178. Cf. þeód-bealu.

þeód-weg, es; *m. A highway*:—In þiódweg; æftær þiódwege, Cod. Dip. Kmbl. v. 187, 30. On ðeódweg norð ofer ðone weg, 42, 30. [*Icel.* þjóð-vegr *a high road.*] Cf. þeód-herpaþ.

þeód-wīga, an; *m. A mighty warrior*:—Se þeódwīga (*the panther*) ... ellenrōf, Exon. Th. 357, 33; Pa. 38.

þeód-wita, an; *m.* I. *one of the wise men of a nation, one whose knowledge fits him for a place in the councils of the nation, a senator*:—*Senatores*, ðæt synd þeódwitan, Jud. p. 161, 32. Ðā wǽron þeódwitan (leód-, MS. H.) weorðscipes wyrðe, L. R. 1; Th. i. 190, 12. Be ðeódwitan. Cyningan and bisceopan, eorlan and heretogan, gerēfan and dēman, lárwitan and lahwitan gedafenaþ mid rihte ðæt hī ānrǽde weorðan, L. I. P. 5; Th. ii. 308, 12. II. *a man of great wisdom* or *learning, a sage*:—Wā eów ðe taliaþ eów sylfe tō ðeódwitan *ve, qui sapientes estis coram oculis vestris*, Wulfst. 46, 26. II a. used of a poet:—Se þeódwita Virgilius, Anglia viii. 320, 30. Oft ða þeódwitan ðus heora meteruers gewurðiaþ, 332, 15. II b. used of a historian or philosopher or man of science:—Ān þeódwita wæs on Britta tīdum, Gildas hātte, Wulfst. 166, 17. Manega þing wē mihton of þeódwitena gesetnysse geīcean, Anglia viii. 321, 24. [Cf. *Icel.* þjóð-skáld, -smiðr *a great poet, craftsman.*] Cf. leód-wita.

þeód-wrecan *to avenge thoroughly, take great vengeance for*:—Grendles mōdor gegān wolde sorhfulne sīð, sunu þeódwrecan (*Ettmüller would read* suna deáð wrecan; *but perhaps the force of* þeód- *here and its composition with a verb may be illustrated by the case of* full-, *which is compounded with verbs, and has the force of* per-; *see the verbs in the Dictionary. The parallel between* full- *and* þeód- *might be further illustrated from compound adjectives in Icelandic*, e.g. full-glaðr *and* þjóð-glaðr, full-góðr *and* þjóð-góðr), Beo. Th. 2561; B. 1278.

þeód-wundor, es; *n. A great wonder, mighty miracle*:—Men gesēgon þeódwundor micel, ðætte eorðe āgeaf ða hyre on lǽgun, Exon. Th. 71, 14; Cri. 1155.

þeóf, es; *m. A thief* [the secrecy implied by the word is marked in the following passage from the Laws dealing with injury done to a wood: Fȳr biþ þeóf ... sió æsc biþ melda, nalles þeóf, L. In. 43; Th. i. 128, 19–23. Cf. *Goth.* þiubjō ἐν κρυπτῷ]:—Þeóf *fur*, scaþa *latro*, Wrt. Voc. i. 74, 23. Gyf se hīrēdes ealdor wiste on hwylcere tīde se þeóf (ðeáf, Lind. *fur*) tōwerd wǽre, Mt. Kmbl. 24, 43. Ealle ða ðe cōmun wǽron þeófas (ðeáfas, Lind.) and sceaþan (*fures et latrones*) ... Þeóf (ðeáf, Lind. *fur*) ne cymþ būton ðæt hē stele and sleá, Jn. Skt. 10, 8–10. Þeóf ðe on þȳstre færeþ, on sweartre niht, Exon. Th. 54, 21; Cri. 872: 432, 10; Rä. 48, 4. Ðeóf sceal gangan in ðȳstrum wederum, Menol. Fox 543; Gn. C. 42. Ðǽr þeófas (ðeáfas, Lind. *fures*) hit delfaþ and forstelaþ, Mt. Kmbl. 6, 19. On helle beóþ þeófas and gītseras ðe on mannum heora ǽhta on wōh nimaþ, Blickl. Homl. 61, 21. Hēr syndan rȳperas and reáferas and woruldstrūderas and ðeófas and þeódscaðan, Wulfst. 165, 36. Þeófum *grassatoribus*, Wrt. Voc. ii. 40, 35. Ealle niht ic (*the ox-herd*) stande ofer ða oxan waciende for þeófan (*propter fures*), Coll. Monast. Th. 20, 29. ¶ The passage last cited suggests a state of society in which property was not very secure, and the suggestion seems borne out by the many passages, dealing with thieves, that are to be found in the Laws. Thieving was so far common, that the law enacted: Gif feorrancumen man oþþe fræmde būton wege gange, and hē ðonne nāwðer ne hrȳme, ne hē horn ne blāwe, for þeóf hē biþ tō prōfianne, L. Wih. 28; Th. i. 42, 23: L. In. 20; Th. i. 114, 15; and on such a scale was it conducted that according to the numbers of the depredators acting together were different terms used of them: Ðeófas wē hātaþ ōð .vii. men; from .vii. hlōð ōð .xxxv.; siþþan biþ here, L. In. 13; Th. i. 110, 13. The frequency of this particular form of crime may also be inferred from the later enactment: Wē wyllaþ ðæt ǽlc man ofer twelfwintre sylle ðone āð, ðæt hē nelle þeóf beón ne þeófes gewita, L. C. S. 21; Th. i. 388, 6. But far stronger measures than the exacting of such an oath were in force. The law made provision for the pursuit of thieves, L. Edg. H. 2; Th. i. 258, 6, and imposed penalties on those who, being summoned, or hearing the hue and cry, neglected to take part in the pursuit, 3; Th. i. 258, 14: L. C. S. 29; Th. i. 392, 17: while a reward was given to him who seized a thief: Se ðe þeóf gefēhþ, hē āh .x. scill., L. In. 28; Th. i. 120, 5. To let a thief go, when caught, was a crime, L. In. 36; Th. i. 124, 14; so, also, to allow him, when discovered, to escape without raising hue and cry, L. C. S. 29; Th. i. 392, 14: to harbour a thief, except in those cases where the right of asylum might for three or nine days be extended to him, was to become liable to the fate of a thief, L. Ath. iii. 6; Th. i. 219, 6: iv. 4; Th. i. 224, 4: v. 1, 2; Th. i. 228, 21; to fight for him was equally penal, v. 1, 3; Th. i. 228, 23: v. 8, 3; Th. i. 236, 18. And the laws which affected the thief himself were very severe. Any one above the age of twelve, who was caught stealing property above the value of eight pence, was liable to capital punishment, L. Ath. i. 1; Th. i. 198, 15; according to other regulations, for a theft which, on conviction, rendered the thief liable to be slain, the limit of age was made fifteen years, L. Ath. v. 12, 1; Th. i. 240, 28, and the limit of value was twelve pence, L. Ath. v. 1, 1; Th. i. 228, 12: v. 12, 3; Th. i. 242, 8. The extreme penalty was not in all cases exacted; but in case of repeated conviction there was to be no remission, L. Ath. v. 1, 4; Th. i. 230, 3. Cf. too the passages: Gesēce ǽbera þeóf ðæt ðæt hē gesēce, oððe se ðe on hlāfordsearwe gemēt sȳ, ðæt hī nǽfre feorh ne gesēcen, būton se cyningc him feorhgeneres unne, L. Edg. ii. 7; Th. i. 268, 22: L. C. S. 26; Th. i. 390, 27. Sȳ hē þeóf, and þolige heáfdes and ealles ðæs ðe hē āge, L. Edg. S. 11; Th. i. 276, 13. The kinds of death mentioned in L. Ath. iii. 6; Th. i. 219, are throwing from a rock or drowning in the case of a free woman; in the case of a *servus homo*, stoning by slaves; in that of a *serva ancilla*, burning. Further a thief who was taken in the act, or taken in flight, or who resisted, instead of being handed over to justice (on cyninges bende, L. In. 15; Th. i. 112, 4: se cyning āh ðone þeóf, 28; Th. i. 120, 6), might be slain without the intervention of the law, and the death called for no 'wergild,' L. Wih. 25; Th. i. 42, 13: L. In. 12; Th. i. 110, 7: 16; Th. i. 112, 7: 35; Th. i. 124, 6: L. Ath. i. 1; Th. i. 198, 20; and in cases of flight or resistance the fact that the value of the stolen property was less than twelve pence was to be no bar to the slaying, L. Ath. v. 12, 3; Th. i. 242, 10. He who struck down a thief in public was rewarded: Se ðe þeóf fylle beforan ōðrum mannum, ðæt hē wǽre of ūre ealra feó .xii. pæng̃ đe betera for đære dǽda and đon anginne, L. Ath. v. 7; Th. i. 234, 22. Short of death were the punishments of selling into slavery, of imprisonment, fine, and mutilation: Gif man frigne man æt hæbbendre handa gefó, đanne wealde se cyning þreora ānes: oþþe hine man cwelle, oþþe hine ofer sǽ selle, oþþe hine his wergelde ālēse, L. Wih. 26; Th. i. 42, 15. Gif þeóf sié gefongen, swelte hē deáđe oþþe his līf be his were man āliése, L. In. 12; Th. i. 110, 8. Gif man þeóf on carcerne gebringe, đæt hē beó .xl. nihta on carcerne, and hine mon đonne ālȳse ūt mid .cxx. scill., L. Ath. i. 1; Th. i. 198, 21. Cutting off the hand or foot of a 'cirlisc þeóf' is mentioned, L. In. 18; Th. i. 114, 5: 37; Th. i. 124, 20. The same punishment is mentioned, L. C. S. 30; Th. i. 394, 10; and in aggravated cases the more severe sentence was passed, that the eyes were to be put out, and the nose, ears, and upper lip to be cut off, *ib.* An instance of punishment for theft, in which the eyes were put out and the ears cut off after (wrongful) conviction is given, Homl. Skt. i. 21, 265. If the thief managed to escape, he was declared an outlaw: Beó se þeóf ūtlah wiđ eall folc, L. C. S. 30; Th. i. 394, 24. v. Grmm. R. A. 635 sqq.; Schmid, A. S. Gesetz. s. v. Diebstahl. [*Goth.* þiubs: *O. Sax.* thiof: *O. Frs.* thiaf: *O. H. Ger.* diob: *Icel.* þjófr.] v. beó-, gold-, mann-, mūs-, regn-, sǽ-, stōd-, wergild-þeóf; infangene-þeóf; þīfþ.

þeóf, e; *f. Theft*:—Nā dōn þeófæ *non facere furtum*, R. Ben. Interl. 19, 12. [*O. H. Ger.* diuba *furtum.*]

þeóf-denn, es; *n. A thieves' cave*:—Andlang weges tō đam þeófdenne, Cod. Dip. Kmbl. iii. 15, 28.

þeófend, þeófent, e; *f.* (*the word seems to occur only in the plural*) *Theft*:—Of hearte ūtgaas . . . điófunta *de corde exeunt* . . . *furta*, Mt. Kmbl. Lind. 15, 19. Điófunto (-ento, Rush.) *furta*, Mk. Skt. Lind. 7, 22. Wiđ þeófentum, Lchdm. iii. 58, 1. Ic heó tō þeófendum and tō geflitum stihte, Wulfst. 255, 11. Ne leásunga tō sæcganne, ne þeófenda tō begangenne, 253, 8. Ne dōe đū điófonto ł stalo *non facies furtum*, Mt. Kmbl. Lind. 19, 18: Lk. Skt. Lind. 18, 20. Đióf[]nto, Rtl. 103, 3.

þeófe-þorn. v. þīfe-þorn.

þeóf-feng, es; *m. Seizing of thieves;* the Latin rendering of the term in Charters is *comprehensio* (or *captio*) *furis* (*-um*). I. The word seems to denote the obligation of one who holds land to arrest and bring to justice those who committed theft on that land, and occurs generally in connection with the burdens from which land, when granted, was relieved:—Ic forgyfe đisne freóls tō đære hālgan stōwe æt Scīreburnan, đæt hit sȳ gefreód alra cynelīcra and alra dōmlīcra þeówdōma, ge þeóffenges ge ǽghwelcre [un]iéđnesse ealles worldlīces broces, nymđe fyrde and bryceweorces, Chart. Th. 125, 11. Đæt hit (*the monastery at Horton*) sȳ gefreód ealra cynelīcra and ealdordōmlīcra þeówdōma, ge þeóffengces ge ǽghwylcere uneáđnesse ealles woroldlīces broces būton fyrdsōcne and burhgeweorce and bryggeweorce, 389, 28. *Corresponding cases in Latin charters are the following*:—Ego Ecgberhtus . . . hanc libertatem donabi aecclesiae . . ., ut omnes agros sint libera ab omni regali seruitio (*then follows a list of exemptions*), . . . et ab omnibus difficultatibus regalis uel saecularis seruitutis, cum furis comprehensione intus et foris, praeter pontis constructione et expeditione liberata permaneat, Cod. Dip. Kmbl. i. 288, 5. Terra predicta liber et securus omnium rerum permaneat, id est, regalium et principalium tributum, et ui exactorum operum siue poenalium causarum, furisque comprehensione, et omni saeculari grauidine, ii. 28, 22. Ui exactorum operum et penalium rerum, principali dominatione, furisque comprehensione, et cuncta seculari grauidine . . . secura et immunis, 65, 14. Omnium regalium debitorum et principalium rerum, caeterarumque causarum, furisque comprehensione, et ab omnium saecularium seruitutum molestia secura et inmunis, 95, 33. Furum comprehensione, iii. 277, 4. Captio furum, iv. 2, 26. II. In other passages, however, the word implies advantage, and seems to refer to the right to receive the fines which might be exacted in case of conviction for theft. For such emoluments cf. Gif frigman stelþ . . . cyning āge đæt wīte and ealle đa ǽhtan, L. Ethb. 9; Th. i. 6, 2. Ealle wītu (*in cases of theft*) sint gelīce, .cxx. scill., L. Alf. pol. 9; Th. i. 68, 7: L. Ath. i. 1; Th. i. 198, 23. Gif þeuw stele . . . hine man ālēse .lxx. scill., L. Wih. 27; Th. i. 42, 20. Hine man his wergelde ālēse, 26; Th. i. 42, 17: L. In. 12; Th. i. 110, 8. These emoluments of the crown are made the subject of grant:—Concedo consuetudines, ut ab omnibus apertius et plenius intelligantur Anglice scriptas, scilicet, mundbryce, feardwītæ, fihtwīte . . . þiéfphang, hangwīte, grydbryce . . . toll et teám, aliasque omnes consuetudines quae ad me pertinent, Chart. Th. 384, 24. Terram liueram ab omni seruitute, cum omnibus ad se rite pertinentibus, cum furis comprehensione, et cum omnibus rebus quae ad aecclesiam Sancti Andreae pertinent, cum campis, etc., Cod. Dip. Kmbl. ii. 109, 21.

þeóf-gild, es; *n. Payment made in the way of fine or compensation by one convicted of stealing*:—Swerian hī đæt him nǽfre āđ ne burste, ne hē þeófgyld ne gulde (i. e. *that he had never been convicted of stealing*), L. Eth. i. 1; Th. i. 280, 13: iii. 4; Th. i. 294, 13: L. C. S. 30; Th. i. 392, 28. [Cf. *Icel.* þȳfi-gjöld *fine for theft.*]

þeófian (*and* þeófan? *The Lindisfarne gloss has* đæt đū ne forstele ł ne forđiófe, Mk. 10, 19; *the Kentish Glossary,* điófende *furtivus; but this might imply the form* điófian, cf. tācnendi *and* tācnian: cf. *also, for both force and form of the participle* styrende *agitatam*, Mt. Kmbl. Lind. 11, 7) *to thieve, steal*:—Se đe đa āre þænce tō þeófigenne *qui quid illinc abstulerit*, Chart. Th. 177, 13. Điófende weteru *stolen waters;* aque furtive, Kent. Gl. 309. [*O. H. Ger.* thaz sie mit stalu nan nirzuken noh inan thar githiuben, Ot. iv. 36, 12.] v. ge-þeófian.

þeóf-mann, es; *m. A robber, bandit, brigand*:—Ān hirde wæs Ueriatus hāten, and wæs micel þeófmon *Viriathus homo pastoralis et latro*, Ors. 5, 2; Swt. 216, 7.

þeóf-scip, es; *n. A pirate-vessel*:—Đeófscip (thēb-) *mimopora* (= myoparo), Txts. 79, 1316: Wrt. Voc. ii. 55, 67.

þeóf-scolu, e; *f. A gang* or *band of thieves*:—Gif đū wǽre wegfērende and hæfdest micel gold on đē, and đū đonne becōme on þeófsceole (þiófscole, Cott. MS.), đonne ne wēndest đū đē đīnes feores, Bt. 14, 3; Fox 46, 26.

þeóf-scyldig; *adj. Guilty of theft*:—Stent đonne þeófscyldig se đe hit on handa hæfþ, L. Eth. ii. 9; Th. i. 290, 16.

þeóf-slege, es; *m. Thief-slaying*:—Be đeófslege. Se đe þeóf ofslihþ, L. In. 16; Th. i. 112, 6.

þeóf-sliht, es; *m. Thief-slaying*:—Be đeófslihte. Se đe þeóf slihþ, hē mōt āđe gecȳđan đæt hē hine fleóndne for þeóf slōge, L. In. 35; Th. i. 124, 4.

þeóf-stolen; *adj.* (*ptcpl.*) *Stolen, taken by thieves*:—Swā ic sprǽce drīfe . . . swā mē þeófstolen (forstolen, MS. H.) wæs đæt orf, L. O. 2; Th. i. 178, 14: L. O. D. 8; Th. i. 356, 12. Ǽt ǽlcon đeófstolenan orfe, L. Ff.; Th. i. 226, 2. [*Icel.* þjóf-stolinn. Cf. *M. H. Ger.* diep-, diup-stāle: *Ger.* dieb-stahl.]

þeófþ, þeóft. v. þīfþ.

þeóf-wracu, e; *f. Punishment for theft*:—Gif hē eft ofer đæt stalie . . . sleá man hine on đa þeófwrace, L. Ath. v. 1, 4; Th. i. 230, 4.

þeóging, e; *f. Profiting, thriving, progress, advancement*:—þeógincg đīn swutul sȳ eallum *profectus tuus manifestus sit omnibus;* that thy profiting may appear to all (A. V. 1 Tim. 4, 15), Scint. 203, 8. þeóginc (*profectus*) mannes gyfu Godes ys, 132, 17. Swylcre þeógincge *tanti profectus*, Anglia xiii. 372, 94. þeógincgum *profectibus*, Scint. 210, 1. [*O. H. Ger.* dīhunga *provectus.*] v. þeón.

þeóh; *gen.* þeós; *dat.* þeó; *pl.* þeóh; *gen.* þeóna; *dat.* þeón; *n. A thigh*:—þeóh, thēgh *coxa*, Txts. 54, 295. þeóh, Wrt. Voc. ii. 15, 6. þeóh *femur, femoris*, ys swā đeáh eft gecweden *femen, feminis*, Ælfc. Gr. 9, 22; Zup. 49, 10. Inneweard þeóh *femen*, þeóh *coxa*, ūtanweard þeóh *femur*, Wrt. Voc. i. 44, 60–62. þeóh *femur*, þeóh *coxa*, hype *clunis*, 71, 46–49. þeóh *femor*, innewerd þeóh *femina*, þeóhscanca *coxa*, 283, 63–65. þeóh *vel* hype *femur*, ii. 148, 18. Đæt đeóh getācnode his cynn, Homl. Th. ii. 234, 33. Gif þeóh gebrocen weorđeþ, .xii. scillingum gebēte, L. Eth. 65; Th. i. 18, 13. Gif man þeóh þurhstingđ, stice gehwilce .vi. scillingas, 67; Th. i. 18, 16. Gif monnes þeóh biþ þyrel, geselle him mon .xxx. scill. tō bōte; gif hit forad sié, sió bōt eác biþ .xxx. scill., L. Alf. pol. 62; Th. i. 96, 13. Đā æthrān hē his sine on his þeó *tetigit nervum femoris ejus*, Gen. 32, 25. 'Hæbbe eówer ǽlc his sweord be his đeó.' Đonne mon hæfþ his sweord be his đió, đonne . . ., Past. 56; Swt. 433, 11: Exon. Th. 431, 2; Rä. 45, 1. Under mīn þeóh *subter femur meum*, Gen. 24, 2: 47, 29: Ps. Th. 44, 4. Bind on đæt winstre þeóh up wiđ đæt cennende lim, Lchdm. ii. 328, 22. þeóh *bathma*, i. *femora*, Wrt. Voc. ii. 125, 28. Đeeoh (đyóh, lxxiv, 3) *bathma*, Lchdm. i. lxx, 2. Gif men his đeóh acen, 78, 23: ii. 66, 4. Hyre (*the bee's*) đa rūwan þeóh wurđaþ swȳđe gehefegode, Anglia viii. 324, 13. Bāna, þeóna *coxarum*, Wrt. Voc. ii. 75, 27: Lchdm. i. 208, 3. Đæra đeóna sār, 80, 2. On þeón *in femoribus*, Anglia xi. 117, 25. Smyre đa þeóh, sōna hȳ beóþ hāle, Lchdm. i. 354, 20: ii. 64, 26: Ors. 1, 7; Swt. 38, 3. [*O. Frs.* thiach: *O. L. Ger.* thio *femur*: *O. H. Ger.* dioh *femur, femen, coxa*: *Icel.* þjó.]

þeóh-ece, es; *m. Thigh-ache*:—Lǽcedōmas wiþ þeóhece, Lchdm. ii. 6, 6: 64, 26.

þeóh-gelǽte, es; *n. A thigh-joint, the meeting of the thigh with the part of the body above it*:—Ersendu mid đām đeóhgelǽtum (þeóhsconcum, lxxiv, 19) *nates cum femoribus*, Lchdm. i. lxx, 10. [Cf. *O. H. Ger.* lidi-gilāz *artus, compago.*] v. ge-lǽte.

þeóh-geweald; *pl. n. Genitalia*:—Đa þeóhgeweald mid đǽm þeóhhweorfan *genitalia cum genuclis*, Lchdm. i. lxxiv, 20. v. ge-weald.

þeóh-hweorfa, an; *m. A knee-joint;* genuculum (cf. cneów-wyrste *geniculi*, Wrt. Voc. i. 44, 70). v. preceding word.

þeóh-sceanca, an; *m. A thigh-shank, the upper part of the leg*:—Earsendu *nates*, þeóh *femur*, þeóhscanca *coxa*, Wrt. Voc. i. 65, 36–38: 283, 61–65. Đa hypbān đa earsenda mid đǽm þeóhsconcum *catacrinas, nates cum femoribus*, Lchdm. i. lxxiv, 19. [*O. Frs.* thiach-schonk. Cf. *Icel.* þjó-leggr *the thigh-bone.*]

þeóh-seax, es; *n. A short sword that could be worn on the thigh*:—þeóhsaex *semispatium* (= *-spathium*), Wrt. Voc. ii. 120, 26. Sweord *macheram*, þeóhseax *senspatium*, 96, 29. Cf. hup-seax.

þeóh-wærc, -wræc, es; *m. Pain in the thighs*:—Wiđ þeóhwræce . . . smyre đa þeóh, sōna hȳ beóđ hāle, Lchdm. i. 354, 19.

þeón [*from* þīhan; *and this from an earlier nasal stem, of which traces are preserved in the past forms, where* g *has replaced* h *by Verner's law*: —Đunge *pollesceret*, Wrt. Voc. ii. 66, 40. Frōd fæder freóbearn lǽrde wordum wísfæstum, ðæt hē wel þunge, Exon. Th. 300, 9; Fä. 3. *See also the passages given under* ge-þingan; ofer-þeón; ge-, heáh-, wel-þungen; on-þungan, Exon. Th. 497, 3; Rä. 85, 23 (*omitted in its place*)]; *p.* þāh *and* þeáh, *pl.* þigon *and* þugon; *p. pr.* þīende *and* þeónde; *pp.* þigen *and* þogen *To thrive, grow, flourish, prosper:*—Þīhþ *cluit, pollet, viget, nobilitat,* Wrt. Voc. ii. 131, 75. Þāh *pubesceret,* 66, 22. Þeó *vigeat,* Wülck. Gl. 257, 17. I. of persons in respect to either physical or moral growth. (1) absolute:—Se his yldrum ðāh tō frōfre *he grew up a comfort to his parents,* Cd. Th. 67, 28; Gen. 1107. Sunu weóx and ðāh, 138, 30; Gen. 2299. Þāg, 167, 25; Gen. 2771. Ðæt cynn þeáh, Wulfst. 13, 11. Heó ðurh mægðhād mǣrlīce þeáh, Homl. Skt. i. 2, 3. Cnæplingc weóx ɫ þēh *puer pollesceret,* Hpt. Gl. 466, 60. Hyhtful *vel* ðīendi *indolis,* Wrt. Voc. ii. 111, 54. Þiónde, 45, 58. (2) where that, in which the growth, etc., takes place, is stated:—Se gǣst þīhð in þeáwum, Exon. Th. 126, 10; Gū. 369. Sume on ǣgþrum þeóþ *quidam in utrisque pollent,* Scint. 221, 1. Hē weóx under wolcnum, weorþmyntum þāh, Beo. Th. 16; B. 8. Se Hǣlend þeáh on wīsdōme and on ylde *Jesus proficiebat sapientia et aetate,* Lk. Skt. 2, 52: Homl. Skt. i. 2, 23. Þeáh hwā þeó on eallum welum and on eallum wlencum, Bt. 19; Fox 68, 31. Þió, Met. 10, 28. Ðeónde on cræftum *virtutibus pollens,* Past. 9; Swt. 59, 11. Ðiónde, Bt. 38, 5; Fox 206, 22. Ðiiende on wæstum *proficiens incrementis,* Rtl. 38, 41. (3) where that, in relation to which the growth, etc., takes place, is stated:—Monge lifgaþ gyltum forgiefene, nales Gode þīgaþ, Exon. Th. 130, 3; Gū. 432. Wǣron hālige sacerdas Gode ðeónde, Homl. Th. i. 544, 11. II. of things abstract or concrete:—Andgyt þȳhð *sensus uiget,* Scint. 52, 8. Þȳhð (*virginitatis gratia*) *adolescit,* Hpt. Gl. 436, 67. Ic þǣh ōþþæt ic wæs yldra, Exon. Th. 485, 2; Rä. 71, 7. Se sīð ne þāh ðam ðe unrihte inne gehȳdde wræte *the journey did not turn to the profit of him who unrighteously had hidden treasure within,* Beo. Th. 6109; B. 3058: 5665; B. 2836. Hine (him?) se cwealm ne þeáh, Exon. Th. 278, 30; Jul. 605. Þeáh, bleów (*gratia*) *floruerit,* Hpt. Gl. 441, 48. His wæstmas genihtsumlīce þugon (*uberes fructus ager attulit,* Lk. 12, 20), Homl. Th. ii. 104, 15. Se līchama þeónde on strangum breóste, on fullum limum and hālum, i. 614, 11. Ðās wanunge getācnaþ se wanigenda dæg his (*John's*) gebyrdtīde, and se ðeónda (*increasing, lengthening*) dæg ðæs Hǣlendes ācennednysse gebīcnaþ his ðeóndan mihte, 358, 4. Betweox ōðrum mægenum bið ðeónde (ðiónde, Hatt. MS.) sió earnung ðæs geswenctan flǣsces *inter virtutes ceteras afflictae carnis meritum proficit,* Past. 14; Swt. 86, 25: Hpt. Gl. 420, 37. Þeónde *florentis* (*pudicitiae*), 511, 50. [Here tuder swiðe wexeð and wel þieð, O. E. Homl. ii. 177, 18. He was þogen on wintre and on wastme, 127, 15. His welðe ðeg, Gen. and Ex. 2012. Wexen he (*they*) and ðogen wel, 2542. So wex here erue, and so gan ðen, 803. So mot I the, Chauc. N. P. T. 156. Theen or thryvyn *vigeo,* Prompt. Parv. 490. *Goth.* þeihan: *O. L. Ger. O. Sax.* thīhan: *O. H. Ger.* dīhan *proficere, pollere, florere, crescere, excellere.*] v. for-, fore-, ge-, mis-, ofer-, on-þeón.

þeón; *p.* þeóde *To do, perform, effect:*—Wē ðæt ǣbylgð nyton, ðæt wē gefremedon, þeódon bealwa wið ðec ǣfre, Elen. Kmbl. 805; El. 403. v. ge-þeón.

þeón *to press.* v. þeówan.

þeónest-mann. v. þegnest-mann.

þeór, es (?), e (?), gender is uncertain: in the following passages, which might be decisive, the forms are doubtful:—Wiþ þeóre drenc, and eft wiþ þære (*if* þære *refers to* þeór *the word would be feminine, but perhaps* þeore *should be read; cf. the text:* Wyrc gōdne ðeórdrenc . . . Wiþ þeóre and sceótendum wenne, 324, 15–25) and sceótendum wenne and eft beþing wiþ þam (*the* beþing *is for* þeór, v. 326, 3, *so if* þam *refers to* þeór *the word is masc. or neuter*) gif þeór gewunige on ānre stōwe, Lchdm. ii. 300, 30. Drenc wiþ þeórādle . . . gif hē on þam innoþe biþ þonne ādrīfþ hine ðes drinc ūt (hē *and* hine *may, perhaps, be taken as referring to* þeór, *as* ādl *is fem.*), 118, 1–12. The meaning, too, is doubtful. It seems to denote an inflamed swelling or ulcer; it is mentioned in connection with wens (Lchdm. ii. Bk. ii. §§ 30, 31); in reference to the eye it is said to be the same as 'fig' (ii. 38, 5), and is mentioned in close connection with the same disease (iii. 30, 3–16); the same prescription is good 'wið ðam micclan līce and wið ōþrum giccendum blece and þeórgeride' (iii. 70, 28); *þeórwyrt* is used against *hreófl* (ii. 78, 13); purgative and emetic drinks are used for its cure (ii. 115, 23), and bleeding (118, 21: 120, 12), cupping (120, 16), and fomentation (326, 3) are prescribed:—Gif þeór gewunige on ānre stōwe, wyrc beþinge, Lchdm. ii. 326, 2: iii. 30, 6. Drenc gif þeór sié on men, ii. 354, 16: iii. 28, 13. Sealf wiþ þeóre . . . Wiþ þeóre on fēt, ii. 118, 12, 28. Wið ðeóre, iii. 20, 15: 28, 7, 19: 30, 3, 13. v. next word.

þeór-ādl, e; *f. Some disease.* v. preceding word:—Wiþ þeórādle on eágum ðe mon gefigo hǣt, Lchdm. ii. 38, 5. Lǣcedōmas wið þeórādlum . . . Drenc wiþ þeórādle, 116, 1, 13: 118, 1, 18: 172, 30. Drencas and sealfa wiþ þeórādlum, 12, 1, 3.

þeorcung, Anglia xiii. 398, 475: 400, 508. v. deorcung.

þeór-drenc, es; *m. A drink for* þeór-ādl, Lchdm. ii. 324, 18: iii. 28, 25. v. þeór-ādl.

þeorf; *adj.* I. *unleavened,* used substantively, *unleavened bread:*—Gehafen hlāf *fermentacius panis,* ðeorf *azimus,* Wrt. Voc. i. 41, 15–16. Þeorf *azimum,* ii. 6, 8. Sȳfernysse þearf *sinceritatis azima,* Hymn. Surt. 82, 31. Þeorfne hlāf ðū scealt etan *vesceris azymis,* Ex. 34, 18: Homl. Th. ii. 264, 16. Etaþ þeorf *azyma comedetis,* Ex. 12, 15, 18. Doege ðara ðorofra (ðefra, Rush.) mæta *die azymorum,* Mt. Kmbl. Lind. 26, 17. Lactuca hātte seó wyrt ðe hī etan sceoldon mid ðām þeorfum hlāfum, Homl. Th. ii. 278, 26, 18. On ðærfum biluitnises *in azymis sinceritatis,* Rtl. 25, 19. Healdaþ þeorfe mettas *observabitis azyma,* Ex. 12, 17. Hī worhton þeorfe heorðbacene hlāfas *fecerunt subcinericios panes azymos,* 12, 39: Lev. 8, 2: Homl. Th. ii. 210, 34: 264, 2. I a. in the Lindisfarne gloss *fermento* is glossed by *ðærfe,* Mt. 16, 6, 11. II. of milk, *fresh* (as opposed to sour? cf. *Icel.* þjarfr, of water, *fresh* as opposed to salt), *skim* (? so Cockayne):—Dō on beór swā on wīn swā on þeorfe meoluc, Lchdm. ii. 270, 29. [Bræd all þeorrf wiþþutenn berrme, Orm. 997. Þerue kakeȝ, Allit. Pms. 57, 635. Þerf bred, Mand. 19, 1. Of þerf brede *de azymo pane,* Trev. v. 9, 6: Wick. Gen. 19, 3. Therf, not sowyryd *azimus,* Prompt. Parv. 490. A[e] tharf bred *panis siliginus, sigalinus,* Wrt. Voc. i. 198, 8, 9. *O. H. Ger.* derb brōt *azymus: Icel.* þjarfr *unleavened; fresh* (water).]

þeorf-dæg, es; *m. A day on which unleavened bread was to be eaten:*—Ðæt gerīst preóstum tō witanne hwæt beó betwyx Eástron and ðeorf-dagum. Eásterdæg wæs se forma dæg on ðære ealdan ǣ, þonne se mōna wæs .xiiii., and ða seofon dagas, ðe ðǣr æfter wǣron, wǣron gecīged *dies azimorum,* Anglia viii. 330, 19.

þeorf-hlāf, es; *m. A loaf of unleavened bread:*— Hī ǣton þeorfhlāfas, Jos. 5, 11.

þeorfling, es; *m. An unleavened loaf:*—Ðeorflingas *azimos,* Wrt. Voc. ii. 6, 32. [Þerrflinng bræd iss clene bræd, forr þatt itt iss unnberrmedd, Orm. 1590.]

þeorfness, e; *f. Unleavenedness;* metaphorically, *freedom from impurity, purity:*—Ðonne wē būton yfelnysse beorman on ðeorfnysse sȳfernysse and sōðfæstnysse faraþ, Homl. Th. ii. 212, 1. On ðeorfnyssum sȳfernysse and sōðfæstnysse, 278, 25.

þeorf-symbel, es; *n. The feast of unleavened bread:*—Ðū ytst þeorf-symbel, Ex. 23, 14.

þeór-gerid, es; *n. The inflammation accompanying* þeór (?):—Gōdne morgendrænc . . . wið ðam micclan līce and wið ōþrum giccendum blece and þeórgeride and ǣghwylcum āttre, Lchdm. iii. 70, 28. v. þeór; *and* cf. (?) *O. H. Ger.* rito *febris.*

þeorscwold. v. þerscold.

þeór-wærc, es; *m. The pain caused by* þeór (q. v.):—Wiþ þeórwærce, Lchdm. ii. 120, 7.

þeór-wenn, es; *m. An inflamed wen, a carbuncle* (?):—Wiþ þeór-wenne, Lchdm. ii. 342, 16.

þeór-wyrm, es; *m. A worm in a boil:*—Wiþ þeórwyrme on fēt, Lchdm. ii. 12, 2: 118, 25.

þeór-wyrt, e; *f. Ploughman's spikenard;* inula conyza:—Wiþ hreófle . . . þeórwyrt, Lchdm. ii. 78, 13. Wyrc gōdne ðeórdrenc . . . þeórwyrt, 324, 20. Ðyórwyrt, iii. 28, 27.

þeóster-cofa, an; *m. A dark chamber,* used of the place where a person or thing is buried:—Under neólum niðer næsse gehȳdde in þeóstorcofan, Elen. Kmbl. 1662; El. 833. Ðæt heó ðis bānfæt beorge bifæste, lāme bilūce līc orsāwle in þeóstorcofan, Exon. Th. 173, 29; Gū. 1168. v. þeóster-loca.

þeóster-full (þīstre-, þrȳstre-); *adj. Full of darkness, dark, obscure:*—Þeóstorfull wæter *tenebrosa aqua,* Ps. Spl. 17, 13. Ðīn līchama byþ þȳsterfull (*tenebrosum*), Mt. Kmbl. 6, 23. Þēstreful *tenebrosa, obscura,* Hpt. Gl. 483, 53. Of þrȳstrefulre *de latebroso, tenebroso,* 458, 52. Se engel mē lǣdde tō ānre þeóstorfulre stōwe . . . ealle ða ðeóstorfullan stōwe, Homl. Th. ii. 350, 15–26. Hē geseah swilce ān ðeóstorful dene, 338, 5. Ðeósterfulle wununga, i. 68, 4. Þēsterfulle dimhoua *latebrosa latibula,* Hpt. Gl. 446, 5.

þeósterfullness, e; *f. Darkness, obscurity:*—Þēstrefulnysse *latebras, tenebras,* Hpt. Gl. 488, 33.

þeóster-líc; *adj. Dark:*—Ðæs muntes cnoll mid þeósterlīcum genipum oferhangen wæs, Homl. Th. i. 504, 30. [Cf. Þe clene of herte þet hier ssolle ysy him be byleaue, ac alneway þiesterliche, Ayenb. 244, 10.]

þeóster-loca, an; *m. A dark enclosure, a tomb:*—In byrgenne bīdende wæs under þeósterlocan, Elen. Kmbl. 967; El. 485.

þeósterness, e; *f. Darkness:*—Wearð micel þeósternes ofer eallne middangeard *tetra nox obducta terris est,* Ors. 6, 2; Swt. 256, 16. Ðā com ðære nihte þȳsternys, Homl. Ass. 203, 265. Þǣsternes (cf. þióstro, Met. 21, 40), Bt. 34, 8; Fox 146, 4. On ðȳsternesse *in obscuro,* Ps. Spl. 10, 2. [*A. R.* þeosternesse: *Orm.* þeossterrnesse: *Gen. and Ex.* ðisternesse: *Piers P.* þesternesse: *O. L. Ger.* thiusternussi.]

þeóstre *darkness.* v. þeóstru.

þeóstre, þeóster (-or, -ur), *and* þiéstre, þīstre, þȳstre; *adj. Dark.* I. in a physical sense, *without light:*—Ðis (*hell*) is ðeóstræ hām, Cd. Th. 267, 14; Sat. 38. Ðā hangode swīðe þȳstru wæter on ðām wolcnum *tenebrosa aqua in nubibus,* Ps. Th. 17, 11. Wæs se ōðer beám eallenga sweart, dim and þȳstre, Cd. Th. 30, 36; Gen. 478. Þȳstre genip, 9, 9; Gen. 139. Se þeóstra, Wulfst. 186, 4. Niht seó þȳstre, Judth. Thw. 21, 25; Jud. 34. Hit wearð þȳstre *tenebrae factae erant*, Jn. Skt. 6, 17. On óþre healfe ys þȳstre land, Shrn. 120, 20. Ða fūlnessa ðæs ðȳstran ofnes *foetorem tenebrosae fornacis*, Bd. 5, 12; S. 629, 21. Under ðam scūwan ðære ðȳstran nihte *sub nocte per umbras*, S. 628, 15. Wæs heora sum ðȳstran onsȳne (*tenebrosae faciei*), 5, 13; S. 633, 3. In ðære sweartan niht and in ðære þȳstran, Nar. 15, 1. In ðam þȳstran hām (*hell*), in ðam neólan scræfe, Exon. Th. 283, 21; Jul. 683. Þȳstre land (*hell*), Cd. Th. 46, 1; Gen. 737. Sume ðara ðȳstra gāsta *quidam spirituum obscurorum*, Bd. 5, 12; S. 628, 40. Þeóstrum nihtum, Bt. 7, 4; Fox 22, 28. Ðeóf sceal gangan in ðȳstrum wederum, Menol. Fox 544; Gn. C. 42. Niht biþ wedera þeóstrost, Salm. Kmbl. 621; Sal. 310. II. metaphorically, of absence of spiritual or mental light, or of cheerfulness:—Gif ðīn eáge byþ deorc, eall ðīn līchama byþ þȳstre (ðióstor, Rush.), Lk. Skt. 11, 34. Biþ seáð ðam fyrenfullan deóp ādolfen, deorc and ðȳstre, Ps. Th. 93, 12. Tōdrīf ðone þiccan mist, ðe wið ða eágan foran ūsses mōdes hangode, hefig and þȳstre, Met. 20, 266. On hū ðióstrum horaseáþe ðara unþeáwa, Bt. 37, 2; Fox 188, 1. On ðās þeóstran weorulde, Exon. Th. 86, 18; Cri. 1410. Ðióstur (*caecatum*) habbas gē heorta iówre, Mk. Skt. Rush. 8, 17. Breóst innan weóll þeóstrum geþoncum, Beo. Th. 4653; B. 2332: Elen. Kmbl. 623; El. 312. [*Laym.* þe þestere (þustere) niht: *Orm.* þessterr: *O. and N.* bi þeostre nihte: *Ayenb.* þiestre: *O. Sax.* thiustri: *O. Frs.* thiustere.]

þeóstrian, þēstrian, þiéstrian, þīstrian, þȳstrian; p. ode. I. *to make dark* or *dim, to make* the eye *less capable of seeing, dim* the sight:—Se dæg blent and ðióstraþ hiora eágan, Bt. 38, 5; Fox 206, 5. II. *to grow dark* or *dim*:—His eágan þȳstrodon *caligaverunt oculi ejus*, Gen. 27, 1: 48, 10. Ðȳstrodan, Bd. 4, 10; S. 578, 19. Geseah ic onginnan ðȳstrian ða stōwe *vidi obscurari incipere loca*, 5, 12; S. 628, 10. [Þa þestrede þe dai, Chr. 1135; Erl. 260, 32. Steorren sculen þeostren, O. E. Homl. i. 143, 20. Heó þeostreð (*make dark*) ham suluen, A. R. 94, 20. Aras a ladlich weder, þeostrede (þustrede, 2nd MS.) þa wolcne, Laym. 4575.] v. ā-, for-, fore-, ge-, of-þeóstrian (-þióstrian, -þēstrian, þiéstrian, -þīstrian, -þȳstrian).

þeóstrig; *adj. Dark*:—All līchoma ðīn ðióstrig (*tenebrosum*) biþ, Mt. Kmbl. Lind. 6, 23: Lk. Skt. Lind. 11, 34. Ðióstrig ł blind hearta *caecatum cor*, Mk. Skt. Lind. 8, 17. Ðurh ðrióstrie wegas *per vias tenebrosas*, Kent. Gl. 21.

þeóstru (*sometimes written* þr- *instead of* þ-) *and* þiéstru, þīstru, þȳstru; *f.*: *and* þeóstre, þȳstre; *n.* [cf. *O. Sax.* thiustri; *n.*] *Darkness* (lit. and metaph.); *dimness* of sight (lit. or metaph.); like the Latin *tenebrae*, which it translates, it is often used in the plural:—Ðǣr wæs deorc þeóstru, Ps. Th. 87, 6. Leóht and þeóstro, Cd. Th. 239, 27; Dan. 376. Þióstro, Met. 21, 41. Gif ðæt lēht, ðætte in ðē is, þeóstru sint, ðæt þeóstre hū micel biþ, Mt. Kmbl. Rush. 6, 23. On ðæt gemǣre leóhtes and þeóstro, Bt. 35, 6; Fox 170, 13. Mid þȳstro genipum, Blickl. Homl. 203, 8: 209, 33. On ðȳstres onlīcnisse . . . on leóhtes onlīcnisse, Salm. Kmbl. p. 144, 30. For ðære egeslīcan þióstro ðære nihte, Bt. 23; Fox 78, 29. Ne gǣþ hē on þeóstro, Blickl. Homl. 103, 31. In þȳstro, Exon. Th. 432, 10; Rä. 48, 4. Mid þȳstro, Cd. Th. 148, 1; Gen. 2450. Wið eágena þȳstru and genipe, Lchdm. i. 366, 13. On þeóstre, Exon. Th. 87, 11; Cri. 1423: 94, 27; Cri. 1546. Þeóf ðe on þȳstre færeþ, on sweartre niht, 54, 22; Cri. 872. Mid þȳstre, 462, 20; Hö. 55: 470, 12; Hy. 11, 14. Þeóstru *tenebre*, Wrt. Voc. i. 76, 48. Þeóstru wǣron, Gen. 1, 2. Becōmon ðicce ðeóstru, Homl. Th. ii. 194, 4. Swā dōþ ða þeóstro ðīnre gedrēfednesse, Bt. 6; Fox 14, 30. Beóþ þeóstra gewordene, Blickl. Homl. 93, 18. Ðære nihte þióstro hī onlīhtaþ, Bt. 38, 5; Fox 206, 5. Ðióstro, Jn. Skt. Lind. Rush. 6, 17. Gif ðæt leóht, ðe on ðē is, synt þȳstru (ðióstræ, Lind.: þeóstru, Rush.), hū mycle beóþ ða þȳstru (ðióstro, Lind.), Mt. Kmbl. 6, 23: Lk. Skt. 11, 35. Ðæt þȳstro eów ne befōn *ut non tenebrae vos compraehendant*, Jn. Skt. 12, 35: 1, 5. Æfter ðǣm clammum helle þeóstra, Blickl. Homl. 83, 22: Exon. Th. 143, 28; Gū. 668. Se beorhta dæg tōdrǣfþ ða dimlīcan þeóstru ðære sweartan nihte . . . Crist ūs fram deófles ðeóstrum ālȳsde . . . 'Uton āwurpan þeóstra weorc . . .,' Homl. Th. i. 604, 1–5. Ðara þióstra ðisse worulde, Bt. 36, 2; Fox 174, 26. Þȳstra (ðióstrana, Lind. Rush.) anweald, Lk. Skt. 22, 53: 11, 36. Ðiéstra dæg and mistes, Past. 35; Swt. 245, 5. On þȳstra bealo, Exon. Th. 76, 32; Cri. 1248. Þrȳstra wræce, 37, 15; Cri. 593. Hē gedǣlde ðæt leóht fram ðām þeóstrum, Gen. 1, 4: Cd. Th. 8, 21; Gen. 127: Blickl. Homl. 65, 17. Þióstrum, Bt. 39, 3; Fox 214, 30. Ðyóstrum, Mt. Kmbl. Lind. 8, 12. Mid ðǣm ðiéstrum (ðīstrum, Hatt. MS.) ðisses andweardan līfes . . . on ðǣm ðīstrum (ðiéstrum, Hatt. MS.), Past. 65; Swt. 64, 8, 12. Ðȳstrum, Ps. Th. 106, 9. ¶ *The acc. sing. and pl. are given together, as often the two cannot be distinguished*:—God hēt ða þeóstra niht, Gen. 1, 5: Blickl. Homl. 17, 36. Ðeós India hæfþ on ānre sīdan þeóstru, Homl. Th. i. 454, 14. On ða ūttran þȳstru (in þeóstra ðæt ȳtterre, Rush.), Mt. Kmbl. 25, 30. Ðara deófla þeóstro hē oforgeát mid his leóhte, Blickl. Homl. 85, 8, 21. Āweorpan ða ðióstro his mōdes, Bt. 35, 6; Fox 166, 26: Met. 24, 56: Rtl. 37, 9. On ða ūttran þȳstro (in ðióstre ðæt ȳtemæst ł ȳterræ, Rush.), Mt. Kmbl. 22, 13: 8, 12. Þȳstro (ðióstro, Lind.: ðióstru, Rush.) *tenebras*, Jn. Skt. 3, 19. Þīstro, Bt. 3, 2; Fox 6, 10. Ðīstro, Past. 56; Swt. 433, 13. Þȳstru, Ps. Th. 103, 19. Þrióstre senna, Hy. 8, 28. [Of þeóstran *de tenebris*, O. E. Homl. i. 131, 12. Hit luveþ þuster and hateþ liht, O. and N. 230. *O. Sax.* thiustria; *f.*: thiustri; *n.*] v. carcern-, hinder-þeóstru.

þeóstrung, þȳstrung, e; *f. Darkness, gloom, obscurity*:—Hī on ðære þȳstrunge hine swencton, Guthl. 5; Gdwin. 36, 14. Næhtes [ðió]strung *noctis caliginem*, Rtl. 182, 35.

þeótan *and* þūtan; *p.* þeát, *pl.* þuton. I. *to howl* like a wolf:—Wulf ðȳtt *lupus ululat*, Ælfc. Gr. 22; Zup. 129, 1. Hwīlum hī ðuton eall swā wulfas, Shrn. 52, 29: Bt. 38, 1; Fox 194, 36. Sume hī tō wulfum wurdon . . . hió þióton ongunnon, Met. 26, 80. Ðeótende swā swā wulf, Homl. Th. i. 374, 9. Hwīlum swā swā þeótende wulf, hwīlum swā beorcende fox, Shrn. 141, 12. II. of other sounds:—Þeótende *murmurans*, Germ. 399, 417. Hlōwende, þūtende *bombosa*, Wrt. Voc. ii. 126, 51. Ðære þūtendan *bombose*, 11, 71. Him on gafol forlēt ferðfriþende feówer wellan scīre sceótan on gesceap þeótan (*or* gesceap-þeótan. ? v. gesceap, III, *and* þeóte. *The passage describes a calf sucking from its mother; if* þeótan *is an infinitive, it must refer to the sound made by the milk coming from the teat, but perhaps* gesceap-þeóte *may be a compound noun meaning the teat*), Exon. Th. 420, 2; Rä. 39, 4. [Bigunnen to þeoten and to ȝellen alle þe untrume weren, Marh. 22, 29. Wummone wroð is wuluene . . . ne deð heo bute þeoteð, A. R. 120, 12. Ȝeinde ȝurinde & þeotinde wið reowfule reames *queruloso gemitu deplorantes*, Kath. 161. Giff mann wollde tælenn þatt, and hutenn hire & þutenn, Orm. 2034. *O. H. Ger.* diozan *stridere, fremere, strepere, mussare*: *Icel.* þjóta *to whistle* (of the wind, etc.), *to howl* (of a wolf), *to rush*: *Dan.* tude *to howl.* Cf. *Goth.* þut-haurn, -haurnjan.] v. ā-þeótan; ge-þeót, -þot, *and next word.*

þeóte, an; *f. A pipe* or *channel* through which water rushes:—Þeóte *canalis*, Wrt. Voc. i. 38, 17: *fistula*, 39, 56. Of þeótan (þeóte, Wrt. Voc. ii. 76, 4, *the passage glossed is the same*) *tubo*, Hpt. Gl. 418, 61. Þeótan *organa*, Wrt. Voc. ii. 64, 51: 97, 24. Þeótan, wæterþrūh *cataractae*, 13, 15. Ealle heofones þeótan wǣron mid wætere gefylde, Wulfst. 206, 17. In stefne ðeótena (*cataractarum*) ðīnra, Ps. Surt. 41, 8. Þeótum *fistulis*, Wrt. Voc. ii. 108, 67: 35, 59. Hē wundorlīce mid þeótum wæter ūt āteáh, Homl. Skt. ii. 27, 32. Hē ūs ontȳneþ heofenes þeótan, Blickl. Homl. 39, 31: 51, 11. [*O. H. Ger.* watar-dioza *cataractae.* Cf. *Icel.* þjótandi *the name of an artery.*] v. līc-, wæter-þeóte, *and previous word.*

þeów, es; þeówa, an; *m. A servant*; often with the stronger sense of *slave*; servus, famulus, mancipium:—Ic Bēda Cristes ðeów and mæsse-preóst *Baeda famulus Christi et presbyter*, Bd. pref.; S. 471, 7. Se ðe wyle betweox eów beón fyrmest, sȳ hē eówer þeów (ðeá ł ðegn *servus*, Lind.), Mt. Kmbl. 20, 27: 18, 26: 10, 24. Se Godes þeów *the priest*, Blickl. Homl. 49, 3. Metodes þeów (*Abraham*), Cd. Th. 146, 29; Gen. 2429. Dryhtnes þeów (*Guthlac*), Exon. Th. 121, 8; Gū. 285. Þegn and þeów þeódne mǣrum, 209, 3; Ph. 165. Þeów *mancipium*, Wrt. Voc. ii. 80, 31. Ðeówa *servus*, Ælfc. Gr. 5; Zup. 12, 18. Þeówa, Wrt. Voc. i. 50, 15. Cham biþ þeówena þeówa (*servus servorum*) his ge-brōðrum . . . beó Chanaan Semes þeówa (*servus*), Gen. 9, 25–26. Wē synd ealle ðīne þeówas . . . Sig se mīn þeówa, ðe ðone læfyl forstæl, and fare gē frige, 44, 17–18. Ðū gōda þeówa, Lk. Skt. 19, 17: Mt. Kmbl. 25, 23. Se yfela þeówa, 24, 48. Se hlāford and se þeówa gelīce clypiaþ tō ðam heofonlīcan Fæder, Homl. Th. ii. 326, 28. Gif ōðer wyle Godes þeówa beón *if one wishes to enter a monastery*, L. Ecg. C. 25; Th. ii. 150, 28. Biþ hē deófles ðeówa, Homl. Th. i. 172, 20. Hē biþ ðæra ǣhta ðeówa, 66, 7. Fram Gode hē is send, and hē is Godes þeówa, Blickl. Homl. 247, 19. Ðæs Godes þeówes synna, 49, 6. Moises gelīca mīnes þeówes, Num. 12, 7. Ðæs þeówan hlāford, Lk. Skt. 12, 46. Ic cweðe tō mīnum þeówe (ðeua, Lind.), Mt. Kmbl. 8, 9. Geseoh hū ðās men ðīnum ðeówe dōþ, Blickl. Homl. 229, 23: Ps. Th. 118, 49. Gecum tō mīnum ðeówan Saulum, Homl. Th. i. 386, 19: Exon. Th. 157, 19; Gū. 894. Ðissum ðeá (*famulo*) ðīnum, Rtl. 103, 13. Ðiosne ðeá *hunc famulum*, 97, 4. Sēc ðīnne þeów, Drihten, Blickl. Homl. 87, 31. Ðone unnyttan þeówan, Mt. Kmbl. 25, 30: Homl. Th. i. 64, 17: ii. 578, 26. Wit syndon Cristes þeówas, Blickl. Homl. 187, 32: Wulfst. 157, 19. Eálā gē mīne ðeówan beóþ getreówe *o mea mancipia, estote fideles*, Ælfc. Gr. 15; Zup. 102, 3. Ðeás *servi*, Mt. Kmbl. p. 18, 7. Ða þeówan drincaþ medo, Ors. 1, 1; Swt. 20, 17. Micel menigu Godes ðeówa (ðiówa, Hatt. MS.), Past. pref.; Swt. 4, 11. Wītniendra þiówa *lictorum*, Wrt. Voc. ii. 52, 77. Seó myccle menigo heora þeówa, Blickl. Homl. 99, 34. Ðæra þeówa (ðeána, Lind.) hlāfurd, Mt. Kmbl. 25, 19. Ān ðæs bisceopes þeówena, Jn. Skt. 18, 26: Wulfst. 199, 22. Ðǣm earmestan Godes þeówum, ðe ða cyrican mid godcundum dreámum weorþiaþ, Blickl. Homl. 41, 26. Ðā clypode hē his tȳn þeówas, Lk. Skt. 19, 13. Ðeá ðīno *famulos tuos*, Rtl. 100, 22: 170, 31. Ðiúwas (ða ðiówe, Rush.) *ancillas*, Lk. Skt. Lind. 12, 45. ¶ Slavery, which is mentioned by Tacitus (Germania, cc. 24, 25) as existing among the Germans, is recognized by the earliest English laws, and early traces of it are to be found in the English slaves whom Gregory saw at Rome. It was a condition that was due to many causes. The fortune of war might put life and liberty at the disposal of another, as in the case of the Northumbrian, Imma, who, falling into the hands of a hostile Mercian, was by him sold to a Frisian, Bd. 4, 22. Kidnapping, to judge by Theodore's Penitential, was not unknown: Si quis Christianus alterum Christianum vagantem reppererit, eumque furatus fuerit, ac vendiderit, Th. ii. 50, § 5; and cf. Earme men beswicene and hreówlíce besyrwde, and út of ðisan earde gesealde swýðe unforworhte fremdum tó gewealde, Wulfst. 158, 13. Freedom might be forfeited as the punishment of crime; e. g. Gif hwá stalie on gewitnesse ealles his hírédes, gongen hié ealle on þeówot .x.-wintre cniht mæg bión þiéfðe gewita, L. In. 7; Th. i. 107, 16; and cf. Wulfst. 158, 14. Gif se frigea on Sunnandæg wyrce, þolie his freótes, L. In. 3; Th. i. 104, 6. See also L. Eth. vii. 16; Th. i. 332, 18. v. wíte-þeów. Again, the power which one relative had over another was at times exercised to enslave the latter. A child of less than seven years might, in case of need, be sold by its father: Se fæder his sunu, gif him mycel neód byþ, hé hine mót on þeówet gesyllan óð ðæt hé biþ .vii. winter; ofer ðæt, bútan ðæs suna willan, hé hine ne mót syllan, L. Ecg. C. 27; Th. ii. 152, 17: L. Th. P. 19, 28; Th. ii. 19, § 28. Cf. L. Alf. 12; Th. i. 46, 12. The sale of kindred is elsewhere, and not without occasion, denounced: Gif hwylc cristen man his ágen bearn, oððe his néhstan mǽg wið ǽnigum wurðe sylle, næbbe hé nánne gemánan mid cristenum mannum, ǽr hé hine álýsed hæbbe of ðam þeówdóme, L. Ecg. P. 26; Th. ii. 212, 8; cf. Wé witan ful georne, hwǽr seó yrmþ geweard, ðæt fæder gesealde bearn wið weorðe, and bearn his módor, and bróðor óþerne fremdum tó gewealde, Wulfst. 161, 6. Further, slavery was at times entered into voluntarily; such cases seem contemplated in Theodore's Penitential: Homo .xiii. annorum sese potest servum facere, Th. ii. 19, § 29; and that such cases did occur may be seen from the following passage: Geatfleda geaf freóls . . . ealle ða men ðe heó nam heora heáfod for hyra mete (cf. On .xii. mónðum ðú scealt sillan ðínum þeówan men .vii. hund hláfa and .xx. hláfa, búton morge[n]metum and nónmetum, Salm. Kmbl. p. 192, 18) on ðám yflum dagum, Chart. Th. 621, 9. And besides the causes enumerated there was that which must have been the most efficient—birth; the child of slaves was itself a slave: cf. the phrase in the document last cited, in which freedom is given to certain persons and to 'eall heora ofsprinc, boren and unboren.' See also þeów-boren. The terms used in connection with the slave shew him to be the property of his master: Gif þeów stele and hine man ácwelle, ðam ágende hine man healfne ágelde, L. Wih. 27; Th. i. 42, 20. Gif hwylc man his ǽht (*servum*) ofslyhþ, L. Ecg. P. ii. 3; Th. ii. 182, 29: L. M. I. P. 11; Th. ii. 268, 9. Wéron ðǽr ðreó wíteþeówe men búrbærde and ðreó ðeówberde; ða mé salde bisceop tó ryhtre ǽhta, and hire teám, Chart. Th. 152, 22. Bought and sold like an animal, his treatment in other respects was that of an animal. Tacitus (Germania, c. 25) had remarked that the Germans often killed their slaves on the impulse of passion, and that it was done with impunity. The same might be said of the English: Gif hwylc man his ǽht (*servum suum*) ofslyhþ, and hé náne gewitnysse næbbe ðæt hé forworht sig, bútan hé hine for his hátheortnesse and for gýmeleáste ofslihþ, L. Ecg. P. ii. 3; Th. ii. 182, 29: L. M. I. P. 11; Th. ii. 268, 9: L. Th. P. 21, 12; Th. ii. 23, § 12. Gif hwylc wíf for hwylcum lyþrum andan hire wífman swingþ, and heó þurh ða swingle wyrð deád, and heó unscyldig biþ, L. Ecg. P. ii. 4; Th. ii. 182, 32: L. M. I. P. 12; Th. ii. 268, 11: L. Th. P. 21, 13; Th. ii. 24, 1. The inferiority of the slave is marked in many ways by the law. The price of redemption in the case of the þeów who stole was seventy shillings, L. Wih. 27; Th. i. 42, 20; in the case of the free man it was 120 shillings, L. Ath. i. 1; Th. i. 198, 23. Ðeówæs wegreáf sé .iii. scillingas, L. Ethb. 89; Th. i. 24, 16; in the case of the ceorl it is six shillings, 19; Th. i. 8, 1. Gif þeów steleþ, .ii. gelde gebéte, 90; Th. i. 24, 17. Gif frigman fréum steld, .iii. gebéte, 9; Th. i. 6, 2. So, too, in the matter of punishments; where the freeman can pay a fine, the slave pays with his hide, i. e. is scourged; see L. In. 3; Th. i. 104, 2: L. E. G. 7; Th. i. 172, 1: 8; Th. i. 172, 6: L. C. S. 45; Th. i. 402, 15: L. In. 13: 15; Th. i. 40, 7, 11. Gif þeów man fúl wurðe . . . swinge hine man þriwa, L. Ath. i. 19; Th. i. 208, 22. Or mutilation was inflicted, where a freeman was fined, L. Alf. pol. 25; Th. i. 78, 14. The manner in which the punishment of death was executed was an ignominious one—stoning by slaves, L. Ath. iii. 6; Th. i. 219, 13: v. 6, 3; Th. i. 234, 8. The slave could not be vouched to warranty, L. In. 47; Th. i. 132, 5; and he was not allowed the holidays given to freemen, L. Alf. pol. 43; Th. i. 92, 3. Three days, however, in the year were granted, the Monday, Tuesday, and Wednesday before Michaelmas: Sit omnis servus liber ab opere illis tribus diebus, quo melius jejunare possit, et operetur sibimet quod vult, L. Eth. viii. 2; cf. Wulfst. 181, 18; and one of Alfred's laws speaks of fragments of time in which it was possible for the slave to earn something: Ǽghwæt ðæs ðe ðeówum monnum ǽnig mon for Godes noman geselle, oþþe hié on ǽnegum hiora hwílsticcum gearnian mægen, L. Alf. pol. 43; Th. i. 92, 12. It was thus possible for a slave to acquire property, and the church endeavoured to render his possession secure: Ne biþ álýfed æt ðam þeówan his feoh tó nimanne, ðæt hé mid his swynce begiteþ, L. Ecg. P. Addit. 35; Th. ii. 238, 6: L. Th. P. 19, 30; Th. ii. 19, § 30. Throughout the influence of the church seems to have been exerted in favour of the slave. The sale of slaves into heathen lands was denounced: Gif hwá cristene man on hǽðendóm sylle, se ne biþ wurðe ǽnigre reste mid cristenum folce, bútan hé gebycge eft hám ongeán, ðæt hé út sealde, L. M. I. P. 43; Th. ii. 276, 20; see, too, L. Th. P. 42, 3, 4; Th. ii. 50, §§ 3, 4: L. Ecg. E. 150; Th. ii. 124, 2: and probably freedom was not unfrequently granted at the suggestion of the church. Cf. such expressions as: Geatfleda geaf freóls for Godes lufa and for heora sáwla þearfe, Chart. Th. 621, 3. Ðá freóde Folcerd Agelwine his man and his ofspring Criste tó lofe and Scá Maria, and his sáwle áliésednisse, 634, 20. Cf. too, L. Wih. 8; Th. i. 38, 15, and L. In. 3; Th. i. 104, 2. Gif þeów mon wyrce on Sunnandæg be his hláfordes hǽse, sié hé frioh. To the same effect is L. C. S. 45; Th. i. 402, 18: Gif hláford his þeówan freólsdæge nýde tó weorce, þolige ðæs þeówan, and beó hé syþþan folcfrig. See on the question of slavery Kemble's Saxons in England,' i. c. 8, Andrews' Old English Manor, c. 3, Grimm's R. A., pp. 300 sqq. [*Goth.* þius; *pl.* þiwós; *m.: O. H. Ger.* deo; *Icel.* þý; *n.*] v. efen-, níd-, under-, weorc-, wíte-þeów; lád-teów, *and following words.*

þeów, e; þeówe, an; *f. A female servant* or *slave:*—Seó foresprecene Cristes þeówe *praefata Christi famula,* Bd. 4, 9; S. 577, 13: 4, 10; S. 578, 5: 4, 23; S. 592, 36. Seó Cristes þeówe, Guthl. 20; Gdwin. 92, 2. Án menen ł þeówæ (ðíua, Lind.) *ancilla,* Mt. Kmbl. Rush. 26, 69. Ðínre þeówan sunu *filium ancillae tuae,* Ps. Th. 85, 15: 115, 6. On Marian ðínre þeówan, Blickl. Homl. 157, 3. Ðió *famulam,* Rtl. 103, 40. Ðióe, 104, 18. Ðá wǽron ða Cristes ðeówe út gangende of cyricean *egressae de oratorio famulae Christi,* Bd. 4, 7; S. 575, 3. Ða hús ðara untrumra Cristes ðeówna *casulas infirmarum Christi famularum,* 3, 8; S. 531, 33. Ne gǽð heó út swá þeówena gewuna ys *non egredietur, sicut ancillae exire consueverunt,* Ex. 21, 7. Án from ðǽm ðiówum *una ex ancillis,* Mk. Skt. Lind. Rush. 14, 66. [*Goth.* þiwi: *O. Sax.* thiu; thiwa: *O. H. Ger.* diu; diwa: *Icel.* þýr.] v. þeówen.

þeów; *adj. Servile, not free, bond:*—Ðes ðeówa mann *hic manceps,* Ælfc. Gr. 9, 55; Zup. 67, 2. Gif þeów monn wyrce on Sunnandæg be his hláfordes hǽse, sié hé frioh, L. In. 3; Th. i. 104, 2. Ðeów swán and ðeów beócere, L. R. S. 6; Th. i. 436, 19. Ðeáh hwá bebycgge his dohtor on þeówenne, ne sié hió ealles swá þeówu swá óðru mennenu, L. Alf. 12; Th. i. 46, 13. Þeów mennen, Agar, Cd. Th. 135, 22; Gen. 2246. On þeówum dóme ł tó ðeówan wæs geseald *in seruum venundatus est,* Ps. Lamb. 104, 17. Se ðe sleá his ágenne þeówne esne, L. Alf. 17; Th. i. 48, 12. Feówertýnewintre man hine sylfne mæg þeówne gedón (*se servum facere*), L. Ecg. C. 27; Th. ii. 152, 27. Hit þurh ǽnne þeówne mon geypped wearð *quadam ancilla indice,* Ors. 3, 6; Swt. 108, 31. Gif hé þeów oþþe þeów mennen ofstinge, L. Alf. 21; Th. i. 50, 3: Cd. Th. 134, 32; Gen. 2233. Gif hwylc swíþe ríce cyning næfde nǽnne frýne mon on eallon his ríce, ac wǽron ealle þeówe . . . Gif him sceoldan þeówe men þénigan, Bt. 41, 2; Fox 244, 24-27. Ealla gesceafta hé hæfde getiohhod ðeówe (þeówu, Cott. MS.) búton englum and monnum, ða óðra gesceafta þeówe sint, 41, 3; Fox 248, 16-18. Gé giet tó dæge wǽron Somnitum þeówe *hodie Romani Samnio servirent,* Ors. 3, 8; Swt. 122, 12. Þeówe men ða ðrig dagas beón weorces gefreóde, Wulfst. 181, 18. Seofæn þeówæ mæn, Chart. Th. 163, 10. Ne freó ne þeówe, Cd. Th. 166, 12; Gen. 2746. Freóra and þeówra, 166, 26; Gen. 2753. Míne wealas eriaþ *mea mancipia arant,* mínra þeówra manna æceras *meorum mancipiorum segetes,* mínum ðeówum mannum (*mancipiis*) ic dǽle penegas, míne þeówan men (*mancipia*) ic ðreáge, fram mínum þeówum mannum ic eom gefultumod, Ælfc. Gr. 15; Zup. 101, 19-102, 5. Þeówe men manode se apostol . . . Ða hláfordas hé manode ðæt hí milde wǽron heora ðeówum mannum, Homl. Th. ii. 326, 21-27. Nelt ðú nán ðing yfeles habban . . . ne yfele cild, ne yfele ðeówe men, 410, 16. [Cuð me ȝef þu art foster of freo monne oðer þeow wummon, Marh. 4, 2. Heo weren þeowe, Laym. 334. Ȝonge and olde, thewe and freo, Al. 3. *O. H. Ger.* frie getuon nals teuue.] v. wíte-þeów, *and preceding words.*

þeówa. v. þeów; *m.*

þeówan, þéwan, þíwan, þýwan, þýgan, þeón, þían, þýn, *and* þeówian, þíwian, þýwian; *pres.* ic þý, hé þýþ; *p.* þeówde, þéwde, þíwde, þýwde, þýgde, þeóde, þýde; *ppr.* þýwende, þíende; *pp.* þéd, þýd. I. *to press:*—Hwílum mec (*an animal's skin*) wonfeax wale wegeþ and þýð, Exon. Th. 393, 31; Rä. 13, 8. [Hé mec (*a cup*) fin]grum þýð, 480, 24; Rä. 64, 6. Þýde *conpressit* (the line in Aldhelm is: Dulcia sed Christi compressit labra labellis), Wrt. Voc. ii. 95, 33. Ðýde, 19, 67. Hé ðá hit eft sette on ðæt ylce þyrh and þýde mid his fét, Homl. Skt. i. 21, 72. Hé sum fæc ðone swyle mid ðýgde (*or* midðýgde? mid þýde, Bd. M. 382, 29) *aliquandiu tumorem horum adpositione comprimere curabat,* Bd. 4, 32; S. 611, 41. Sceal mon ðam men mid dríum handum ða handa and ða fét gnídan swíðe and þýn *with dry hands must the hands and feet be rubbed hard and squeezed for the man,* Lchdm. ii. 182, 9. Ðæs mannes fét and handa man sceal swíþe þýn, 182, 25. II. *to* *press on, urge on, drive*:—Weard æt steorte wegeþ mec (*a plough*) and þýd, Exon. Th. 403, 10; Rä. 22, 5. Se mec on þýd æftanweardne, 480, 2; Rä. 63, 5. Hwílum ic (*a storm*) sceal tó staþe þýwan (þyran, MS.) flintgrǽgne flód, 383, 30; Rä. 4, 18. Þēwende (? þerende, MS.) *inruens*, Wrt. Voc. ii. 111, 12. III. *to press* with a weapon, *to stab, pierce*:—Ðá hēt hē him his seax árǽcan, and hine sylfne hetelíce ðýde, Homl. Th. i. 88, 10. Ðá ðýde se cwellere hine bæftan mid átogenum swurde, ii. 478, 19. Se fear arn him tógeánes and hine ðýde, ðæt hē his feorh forlēt, Homl. Skt. i. 12, 73. Hí hine ufan mid ísenum geaflum ðýdon . . . Hí mid heora forcum hine ðýdon, Homl. Th. i. 430, 5–11. IV. *to press, threaten, rebuke*:—Seó módinys on horse ðýwð ðæt folc *superbia in equo minatur turbis*, Gl. Prud. 31 b. Hē þýwþ (*arguet*) ðysne middaneard be synne, Jn. Skt. 16, 8. Hē ondrǽde ða þeówwrace ðe Drihten þurh his wítigan ðýwð ðus cweþende *metuat prophete comminationem per quem dicit Deus*, R. Ben. 51, 14. Se ðe brimu bindeþ, brúne ýða þýð and þreátaþ, Andr. Kmbl. 1039; An. 520. Hē ne þíwaþ *non comminabitur*, Ps. Lamb. 102, 9. Hē ðýwaþ mē *increpabit me*, 140, 5. Gif ic ðæt gefricge, ðæt ðec ymbsittend egesan þýwaþ, Beo. Th. 3659; B. 1827. Hē hine þeówde tó ofsleánne, Homl. Ass. 112, 342. Ðíwde, Homl. Th. ii. 174, 32. Ðýwde, 308, 16. Seó ofermódnes þýwde (*minatur*) ðæt folc, Gl. Prud. 31 a. Ðú hine þíwe *commineris*, Scint. 114, 10. Næs se folccyning ymbsittendra ðe mec dorste egesan ðeón, Beo. Th. 5465; B. 2736. Þeówigende, þēwende *minax*, Ælfc. Gr. 9, 60; Zup. 69, 7. Ic gā út þýwende (*minando*) oxan . . . Ic hæbbe sumne cnapan þýwende (*minantem*) oxan mid gādísene, Coll. Monast. Th. 19, 15, 27. V. *to oppress, subjugate*: —Þēde *mancipium*, Wrt. Voc. ii. 56, 70. Cf. geðēdum *subjugatis*, 121, 69. Þēdum *teste* (? the passage is:—Teste tyranni (*Holofernes*) capite), Hpt. Gl. 525, 53. [Þat he miȝte þat liþere folc so þewe, P. L. S. 24, 57. *Goth.* ga-þiwan *to pierce; to subject*; ana-þiwan *to subject*: *O. H. Ger.* theuwe *humiliat*; gi-diota, -dieti *confracti*: *M. H. Ger.* diuwen *to oppress*: *Icel.* þjá *to constrain; chastise, afflict*.] v. ā-, for-, ge-, þurh-þeówan (-þēwan, -þíwan, -þeón, -þían, -þýan, -þýn); *and see* þyddan.

þeówan; *p.* þeówde, þeódde *To serve* (with dat.):—Ðæt sind ða gecostan cempan, ða ðam cyninge þeówaþ, Exon. Th. 107, 22; Gú. 62. Hē Dryhtne þeówde, 146, 20; Gú. 712. Israhēla folc on hæftnēde Babiloniscum cyninge þeówde, Homl. Th. ii. 84, 27: 66, 9. Hē Drihtne ðeówde *Domino servierat*, Bd. 4, 24; S. 599, 9. Ic him geornlícor ðeódde *illis impensius servire curavi*, 2, 13; S. 516, 9. Ic bebeád ðeówum mannum, ðæt hí getreówlíce heora hláfordum þeówdon, Homl. Th. i. 378, 33: Homl. Skt. i. 2, 85. Ða óðre beóþ frige, ðeáh ðe hí on lífe lange ǽr ðeówdon, Homl. Th. ii. 326, 33. Ðæt hié þeówdon Godes ciricum, Blickl. Homl. 185, 29: Bd. 4, 11; S. 579, 15. Ðeówdun *servierunt*, Ps. Surt. 80, 7. Hí hǽþenum bigangum ðeówdon *paganis cultibus provincia serviebat*, Bd. 4, 13; S. 582, 5. Hí swā frige Drihtne gefeónde ðeóddon (þeówodon, Bd. M. 240, 13) *sic liberi Christo servire gaudebant*, 3, 24; S. 558, 1. v. þeówian.

þeów-beócere. v. þeów; *adj.*

þeów-boren; *adj. Slave-born, born of parents in slavery*:—Ne sceal hē (*the abbot*) ðone æþelborenan settan beforan ðane þeówborenan, gif se þeówborena ǽr on ðæm mynstre wæs, bútan hē for hwylcum gesceáde hit dó *non preponatur ingenuus ex servitio convertenti nisi forte aliqua rationabilis causa existat*, R. Ben. 12, 13.

þeów-byrde, -berde; *adj. Of servile birth*:—Wēron ðǽr ðreó wíte-þeówe men búrbærde, and ðreó ðeówberde, Chart. Th. 152, 20.

þeów-cnapa, an; *m. A servant-lad*:—His ðeówcnapena ān wearð þearle āwēd; ðā sette Martinus his handa him onuppon, and se feónd fleáh forht for ðam hālgan, and se ðeówa siððan gesundful leofode, Homl. Th. ii. 510, 27.

þeów-dōm, es; *m. Service*; in an unfavourable sense *servitude, slavery, bondage, thraldom*:—Ðes þeówdōm *haec seruitus*, Ælfc. Gr. 9, 33; Zup. 60, 7. Þeówdōm *mancipatio*, Wrt. Voc. i. 59, 57: *famulatus*, ii. 147, 35. Þeówdōmum *famulatibus*, 34, 3. Ðeówdōm is twyfeald . . . Is óðer ðeówt neádunge būton lufe, óðer is sylfwilles mid lufe, se gedafenaþ Godes ðeówum, Homl. Th. ii. 524, 3. I. in the more favourable sense:—For lufan ðæs godcundan ðeówdōmes, Bd. 4, 23; S. 593, 31. Godes þeówdōmes, Blickl. Homl. 23, 18. Ne þearft ðú nó wēnan, ðæt ða wlitegan tungl ðæs þeówdōmes āþroten weorðe, Met. 29, 40. Embichta ðeádōmes *obsequium servitutis*, Mt. Kmbl. p. 8, 3: Rtl. 9, 13. Wyrta ðeówdōme manna, Ps. Spl. 103, 15. Swā hwā swā ðæs wyrþe biþ, ðæt hē on heora ðeówdōme beón mōt, ðonne biþ hē on ðam hēlstan freódōme, Bt. 5, 1; Fox 10, 13. On Godes ðone sōþan þeówdōm, Blickl. Homl. 45, 24: Elen. Kmbl. 402; El. 201. Hē hine sylfne on ðeówdum (-dōm, Bd. M. 450, 29) gesealde ðara muneca *monachorum famulatui se contradens*, Bd. 5, 19; S. 637, 12. I a. *service* of the church, *divine service*:—On mynstre ðǽr lytel þeówdōm sý, L. C. E. 3; Th. i. 360, 22. Nū habbaþ hig ðæt mynster gesett mid preóstan, and willaþ ðǽr habban þeówdōm eall swā man hæfþ on Paules byrig on Lundene, Chart. Th. 370, 22. II. in the less favourable sense:—Gif se Godes þeów nelle ðære cyrican on riht þeówian, ðæt hē ðonne mid lǽwedum mannum onfō ðæs heardestan þeówdōmes, Blickl. Homl. 49, 5. Se freódōm ðæs unāræfnedlícan þeówdōmes *freedom from the intolerable bondage*, 137, 13. From deófles þeówdōme, 65, 33: 73, 8. Hí synd of miclum dǽle heora sylfes anwealdes, hwæþere of miclum dǽle hí syndon Angelcynnes ðeówdōme betǽhte (*Anglorum sunt servitio mancipati*), Bd. 5, 23; S. 647, 4. Nales ðæt ān ðæt men hié mehten āliésan mid feó of þeówdōme, ac eác þeóda him betweónum būton þeówdōme gesibbsume wǽron, Ors. 1, 10; Swt. 48, 34. Ealle ða men ðe hié on ðeówdōme hæfdon, hié gefreódon, 4, 9; Swt. 190, 31: L. Alf. prm.; Th. i. 44, 5. In nēdhērnisse ł in ðeádōme ic bēgo *in servitutem redigo*, Rtl. 6, 9. Þeówdōm þolian, Cd. Th. 135, 9; Gen. 2240: 136, 24; Gen. 2263. Ðeádōm *captivitatem*, Lk. Skt. p. 10, 16. [Heo woneð inne þeowedome (þeu-, 2nd MS.), þrelwerkes doð, Laym. 454. I þeowwdom unnderr laferdd, Orm. 3611. Leden ut of þeoudome (þeowedom, MS. C.), A. R. 218, 28. Leaden in to þeowdom, H. M. 5, 5.] v. ǽfen-þeówdōm.

þeówdōm-hād, es; *m. Service*:—Monige hí sylfe and heora bearn mā gyrnaþ on mynster and on Godes ðeówdōmhād tó syllanne ðonne hí synd bigongende woruldlícne camphād *plures se suosque liberos, depositis armis, satagunt magis accepta tonsura monasterialibus adscribere votis, quam bellicis exercere studiis*, Bd. 4, 23; S. 647, 8.

þeówe. v. þeów; *f.*

þeówen, þíwen, [n]e; þeówene, an; *f. A female servant* or *slave, a handmaid*:—Ic eom Drihtnes þeówen (*ancilla*, Lk. 1, 38), Blickl. Homl. 9, 20. Ðā com tó hym ān þeówyn (-en, MS. A.) *accessit ad eum una ancilla*, Mt. Kmbl. 26, 69. Seó Godes ðeówen, Bd. 4, 9; S. 576, 14: Homl. Skt. ii. 23 b, 192. Nergendes þeówen (*Judith*), Judth. Thw. 22, 23; Jud. 74. Ic Luba eáðmōd Godes ðíwen, Chart. Th. 475, 21. Hē sceáwode ða eáþmōdnesse his þeówene, Blickl. Homl. 7, 4. Swā eágan gāð earmre þeówenan (*ancillae*), ðonne heó on hire hlǽfdigean handa lōcaþ, Ps. Th. 122, 3. Heó hié sylfe tó ðeówene genemde, Blickl. Homl. 9, 24. Þeówene, 89, 12. Gif hwā āsleá his þeówne oþþe his þeówenne (-ene, MS. H.) ðæt eáge ūt, L. Alf. 20; Th. i. 48, 24. Þeówne (*or adj.?*) *bernam*, Wrt. Voc. ii. 12, 24. Ðeáh hwā bebycgge his dohtor on þeów-enne, L. Alf. 12; Th. i. 46, 12. Se fæder hire sealde āne þeówene (*servam*), Gen. 29, 29. Ðióenne *famulam*, Rtl. 104, 2: 34, 10 (see Skeat's collation). Ðióen, 25. Scā Affra and hire þreó ðeówena . . . Sió Affra wæs ǽrest forlegor wíf mid hire þeówenum, Shrn. 115, 3–5. Ðā hēt hire fæder hí bewyrcean on ānum torre mid twelf ðeówennum, 106, 1. Þeówenna *bernas*, Wrt. Voc. ii. 95, 59: 12, 17. Ic hæbbe þeówas and þeówena (*servos et ancillas*), Gen. 32, 5. v. efen-þeówen.

þeówene. v. preceding word.

þeówet(-ot, -ut), þeówt, [t]es; *m. Service*; in an unfavourable sense, *servitude, bondage, slavery*:—Is óðer ðeówt neádunge būton lufe, óðer is sylfwilles mid lufe, se gedafenaþ Godes ðeówum, Homl. Th. ii. 524, 5. I. of voluntary service:—Githro sǽde ðæt Moyses on dyslícum gesuincum wǽre mid ðæs folces eorðlícan ðeówote *quod terrenis populorum negotiis stulto labore deserviat*, Past. 18; Swt. 131, 14. II. of forced service:—Ælc ðeówt biþ geendod on ðisum andweardan life, būton ðæra ānra ðe synnum ðeówiaþ; hí habbaþ ēcne ðeówt, Homl. Th. ii. 326, 30. Sí þreora ān for his feore, wergild, ēce þeówet, hengenwítnung, L. Eth. vii. 16; Th. i. 332, 18. Of þeówetes hūse *de domo servitutis*, Deut. 6, 12. Þeówettes, 13, 10. Se synfulla ðeówaþ ðam wyrstan ðeówte *the sinner is a slave to the worst slavery*, Homl. Th. ii. 228, 10. Of þeówete ūt ālǽdan *de servitute eruere*, Ex. 6, 6. Þeówette, Deut. 5, 6. Of þeówte gelǽdan, Ælfc. T. Grn. 5, 19. Of þeówte ālísan, 2, 11. On þeówote gebringan *to enslave*, Ors. 3, 9; Swt. 128, 29. Ðeówte, Homl. Th. ii. 190, 90. Tó ðeówte gelǽdan, 66, 34. Hē wolde ðæt folc habban ongeán tó his lande tó his lādum þeówte, Ælfc. T. Grn. 5, 26. Bige ūs tó ðæs cynges þeówette *eme nos in servitutem regiam*, Gen. 47, 19. Tó þeówte bebycggan *to sell into slavery*, L. Alf. 12; Th. i. 46, 12 MS. H. On þeówete standan *to remain in bondage*, L. Ath. v. 12, 2; Th. i. 242, 5. Ðære wylne sunu wunaþ eal his líf on ðeówte, Homl. Th. i. 110, 29. Drihtenes āre oððe deófles þeówet, Hy. 7, 98. Tōdǽlan freót and þeówet *to distinguish between freedom and slavery*, i. e. between the free and the bond, L. C. S. 69; Th. i. 412, 10. On þeówot gangan, L. In. 7; Th. i. 106, 17. On þeówot sellan, Ors. 3, 7; Swt. 112, 30. Þeówet, L. Ecg. C. 27; Th. ii. 152, 17. [Cf. Swa summ þu þeowwtesst tin eorþlike laferrd swa shall þin sune himm þeowwtenn, butt iff he wurrþe lesedd ut off hiss þeowwdomess bandess, Orm. 43–46.]

þeówet-dōm, es; *m. A service*:—Georne ymb ealle ða ðeówutdōmas (ðíowot-, Hatt. MS.) ðe hié Gode dōn sceoldon, Past. pref.; Swt. 2, 10.

þeówet-líc; *adj. Servile*:—Þeówtlíc (þeówet-, þeówot-) *servilis*, Ælfc. Gr. 9, 28; Zup. 55, 1. Þeówtlícum inhírēde *vernacula clientela*, Hpt. Gl. 483, 71. Mid þeówetlícum mōde *seruili mente*, Scint. 63, 13. Þeówtlícne líchoman *servile corpus*, Hymn. Surt. 50, 12. Gif wē ðeówtlícera weorca, ðæt sind synna, geswícaþ, Homl. Th. ii. 208, 6. Ðæt Sunnandæg freóls beó fram þeówetlícum weorcum, Wulfst. 292, 7.

þeówetling, es; *m. A* (*poor*) *slave*; the diminutive form seems to be depreciatory in this case:—Quintianus wæs grǽdig gítsere, deófles þeówetlincg *a miserable slave of the devil*, Homl. Skt. i. 8, 6. Þeáh ðe hē brūce brādes ríces hē is earm ðeówtling nā ānes hlāfordes *though he exer-*

cise extensive power, he is a poor miserable slave, and not of a single master, Homl. Th. ii. 228, 11. Ǽlc hysecild ǽgðer ge æþelboren ge þeówetling, i. 92, 1. Ǽlces mannes þeówetlingas ða ðrý dagas weorces beón gefreóde, Wulfst. 171, 19. Be teóðunge . . . þridda dǽl gā þearfum and earman þeówetlingan, L. Eth. ix. 6; Th. i. 342, 9. Þearfena helpan and þeówetlingan beorgan, L. I. P. 11; Th. ii. 318, 26. Þeówetlingum *servulis,* Hymn. Surt. 25, 18. Þeówtlingas *servulos,* 124, 13: 125, 5. v. nīd-þeówetling.

þeówetscipe, es; *m. Service:*—Hē ealle ðæs regoles bebodu and fulfremednysse ðæs munuclīcan þeówtscypes geheóld, Homl. Skt. ii. 23 b, 26.

þeów-hād, es;.*m. The condition of a servant, service:*—Heó hāligryfte onfēng and Godes ðeówhāde *she took the veil and accepted the condition of a servant of God;* accepto velamine sanctimonialis habitus, Bd. 4, 19; S. 587, 42. Hē Godes ðeówhāde and sceare onfēng *accepta tonsura,* 5, 12; S. 627, 26.

þeówian; *p.* ode. I. *to serve* (of animate or inanimate objects), *be a servant* or *slave.* (1) in the more favourable sense, (a) absolute:—Ðiós sīde gesceaft þēnaþ and þiówaþ, Met. 29, 77. Gehērsumendre stilnesse ł þieówiende *quiete,* Hpt. Gl. 413, 20. (b) followed by dat. of the person or institution served:—Ic (*an animal's skin*) dryhtum þeówige, Exon. Th. 394, 9; Rä. 13, 15. Him ānum ðū þeówast (þēwige, Rush.) *illi soli servies,* Mt. Kmbl. 4, 10. Ðam (*God*) þeówiaþ ealle, ða ðe þeówiaþ . . . ge ða ðe hit witon, ðæt hié him þeówiaþ, ge ða ðe hit nyton, Bt. 21; Fox 72, 30-32: Exon. Th. 106, 34; Gū. 40. Hū ne þeówode ic ðē for Rachele *nonne pro Rachel servivi tibi?* Gen. 29, 25: Lk. Skt. 15, 29. Hī ne mihton elles beón, gif hē ne þiówedon hiora fruman, Bt. 39, 13; Fox 234, 30. Þiówoden, Met. 29, 99. Ða ðe fram cildhāde Gode þeówodon, Homl. Th. ii. 78, 17. Him ānum ðū þeówa, Blickl. Homl. 27, 21. Eall ðeós eorðe Gode þeówie, Ps. Th. 99, 1. Sume secgaþ ðæt se milte ðām sinum þeówige, Lchdm. ii. 242, 22. Ðæt wē ðīwgen him *ut serviamus illi,* Ps. Surt. ii. p. 199, 26. Ne mæg nān man twām hlāfordum þeówian (ðeówigan, Rush.), Mt. Kmbl. 6, 24: Lk. Skt. 16, 13. Drihtne on dǽdum þeówian, Blickl. Homl. 31, 12. Gif hī mid rihte willaþ Gode þeówian, ðonne sceolan hī þegnian Godes folce, 45, 30. Ðære cyrican þeówian, 49, 4. Hē nolde Gode þeówian, Cd. Th. 17, 24; Gen. 264. ¶ In special reference to the services of religion:—Þeówian his Drihtne swā wel swā hē (*the monk*) betst mæge, L. Eth. v. 6; Th. i. 306, 9. Ic ðǽr Englisce scole gesette, ðe ǽfre for ūre þeóde Gode þýwian scolde, Chart. Th. 116, 35. Þeówigende (ðió hērde Gode, Rush.) on fæstenum and on hālsungum, Lk. Skt. 2, 37. Wæs heó Drihtne ðeówiende on ðam mynstre, Bd. 3, 8; S. 531, 15. On ðam mynstre wǽron fīf bróþra oþþe syxe Drihtne ðeówiende, 4, 13; S. 582, 23. (c) with dat. of practice in which a person labours, *to be devoted* to, *attend* to, *bestow pains* on, *work* at:—Hē wæs manod ðæt hē his ðam gewunelīcan wæccum and gebedum geornlīce ðeówode *admonitus est vigiliis consuetis et orationibus indefessus incumbere,* Bd. 3, 19; S. 547, 15. Sealmsangum hig þeáwian *psalmodiis inseruiant,* Anglia xiii. 373, 117. (d) with acc. (?) of service done, *to perform* a service:—Ealle ða ðēnunga ðe (*acc. or dat.?*) wē nū ðiówiaþ and wyrceaþ *quod in actione servemus,* Past. 34; Swt. 233, 10. (2) in the less favourable sense, (a) absolute:—Eálā gē ðeówan . . . ne ðeówige gē tō ansýne, Homl. Th. ii. 326, 24. Gif ðū þeów bigst, þeówie hē six gēr and beó him freoh on ðam seofoðan, Ex. 21, 2. Gilde hē, þeówige hē *whether he pay or serve* (*as a slave*), L. Eth. vii. 17; Th. i. 332, 19. (b) with dat. of that which is served:—Hē biþ ðæra ǽhta ðeówa ðonne hē him eallunga þeówaþ (*he is entirely in bondage to them*), Homl. Th. i. 66, 7. Se synfulla ðeówaþ ðam wyrstan ðeówte *the sinner is a slave to the worse slavery,* ii. 228, 10. Pharao āh ǽgðer ge eów and eówer land . . . Hig cwǽdon: 'We þeówiaþ blīðelīce ðam cynge,' Gen. 47, 25. II. *to enslave, reduce to a state of slavery, deprive of freedom:*—Ðæt hē ūs þeówige *ut violenter subjiciat servituti nos,* Gen. 43, 18. Sý ǽlc cirice on Godes griðe and on ðæs cynges and on ealles cristenes folces, and ǽnig man heonanforð cirican ne þeówige, L. Eth. v. 10; Th. i. 306, 27; vi. 15; Th. i. 318, 26. [Þa hwile þu þeowest þire sunne, O. E. Homl. i. 25, 1. Heo hine beden þat he nomen heom to þrallen & heo him wolden þiwien (hii him wolde be þeouwe, 2nd MS.), Laym. 10015.] v. ge-þeówian, þeówan.

þeówincel, es; *n. A young slave, a slave:*—Ðiówincelu *familici* (the word has been taken as if connected with *famulus*), Ps. Surt. ii. p. 186, 15.

þeów-līc; *adj. Servile:*—Þeóulīc *servilis,* Ælfc. Gr. 9, 28; Zup. 55, 1 MS. W. [Ressteda33 off alle þewwlike dede, Orm. 4177. *O. H. Ger.* deo-līh.]

þeówling, es; *m. A slave:*—Þeówlincgas ða þrý dagas ǽlces weorces beón frige, Wulfst. 173, 23. Cf. þeówetling.

þeów-men[n]en. v. þeów; *adj.*

þeów-nīd, e; *f. Violence* or *force that enslaves* or *subdues, oppression, enslavement:*—His suhtriga (*Lot*) þeównýd þolode; bæd hē (*Abraham*) ða rincas ðæs rǽd āhicgan, ðæt his hyldemǽg āhred wurde, Cd. Th. 122, 21; 2030. Wē nū hǽðenra þeównēd (þreánýd, Exon. Th. 187, 1; Az. 28), 235, 18; Dan. 308: Elen. Kmbl. 1536; El. 770. For þreáum and for þeónýdum (for þearfum and for þreánýdum, Exon. Th. 186, 4; Az. 14) *on account of afflictions and oppression,* Cd. Th. 234, 19; Dan. 294.

þeówot, þeówracian, þeówracu, þeówt, þeówut. v. þeówet, þeów-[w]racian, þeów-[w]racu, þeówet.

þeów-weorc, es; *n. Servile work, work to be done by a slave:*—Gif hwā freót forwyrce . . . sý hē ðæs þeówweorces wyrðe ðe ðǽr tō gebyrige *if any one forfeit his freedom . . . let him have such servile work assigned him as pertains thereto,* L. Ed. 9; Th. i. 164, 12. Gif esne ofer dryhtnes hǽse þeówweorc wyrce an Sunnanǽfen (v. þeówet-līc, *last passage*), L. Wih. 9; Th. i. 38, 18.

þeów-[w]racian; *p.* ode *To threaten:*—Ne on ēcnysse hē þeówracaþ *neque in aeternum comminabitur,* Ps. Spl. 102, 9. v. next word.

þeów-, þīw-, þýw- [w]racu, e, an; *f. A threat, threatening:*—Martianus hēt hī gebūgan tō his deófolgyldum, ðe læs ðe hī fordēmede wurdon; ac Iulianus ne rōhte ðæs rēðan þýwrace (*cared not for the cruel one's threat*), Homl. Skt. i. 4, 114. Þreále oððe þeówraca[n?] *invectionis, inlationis,* Hpt. Gl. 448, 52. Heó næs āfyrht for his þeówracan, Homl. Skt. i. 7, 87. For ðeówracan sweartra deófla, Homl. Th. ii. 142, 32. Hē ondrǽde ða þeówwrace ðe Drihten þurh his wītigan ðýwþ *metuat prophete comminationem,* R. Ben. 51, 13. Basilius cýdde ðæs rēðan cāseres ðeówrace, Homl. Th. i. 450, 17. *Uae* getācnaþ hwīlon wānunge, hwīlon ðeówracan (þeówrace, MS. D.: þīwrace, MS. C.: ðīwwrace, MS. U.), hwīlon wyrigunge, Ælfc, Gr. 48; Zup. 278, 17. Ðīne ðeówracan synd hwīlwendlīce, Homl. Skt. i. 14, 100. Mid menigfealdum ðeówracena teartnyssum gebrēgede, Homl. Th. i. 578, 27. Hē ne mihte mid nānum þeówracan ða cristenan geegsian, 564, 2. Mid þīwracum *minis,* Scint. 63, 8. Þeówwracan *minas,* Wülck. Gl. 252, 19. Hī him ne ondrēdon hǽðenra cyninga þeówracan, Homl. Th. ii. 44, 12. Ic forseó ðīne þeówracan, Homl. Skt. i. 7, 124. Ic gehýre hyra egeslīcan þīwracan, 3, 432. v. þeówan, IV.

þeox *a spear:*—Īsenum bārsperum ł þioxum *ferratis venabulis,* Hpt. Gl. 423, 68. [Cf. (?) Thyxyl *ascia,* Prompt. Parv. 491, and see note there. Thyxylle, Wrt. Voc. i. 234, 18. *O. H. Ger.* dehsa *ascia;* dehsīsen *confertorium;* dehsala *ascia, ferrum confertorium: Icel.* þexla *an adze.*]

þerende *inruens,* Wrt. Voc. ii. 111, 12, (se) þe rende (? *from* rennan), *or* (?) þēwende. v. þeówan, II.

þerh. v. þurh.

þero?:—.vii. hrīðru and six weðeras and .xl. cýsa and .vi. lang þero and þrītig ombra rūes cornes, Chart. Th. 40, 8.

þerscan; *p.* þærsc, *pl.* þurscon; *pp.* þorscen *To thrash.* I. *to strike, beat, flog, scourge:*—Ðū ðe rehtlīce ðersces synfullo *qui juste verberas peccatores,* Rtl. 43, 9. Ða wēregan neát ðe man drīfeþ and þirsceþ, Elen. Kmbl. 716; El. 358. Se ðunor ðæt deófol ðrysceþ mid ðære īýrenan æcxe, and hit drīfeþ tō ðære īrenan racenteáge ðe his fæder on eardaþ, Salm. Kmbl. p. 148, 6. Sume hiá ðurscun *quosdam caedentes,* Mk. Skt. Lind. 12, 5. Hī þurhsun (þurcsun, MS. A.) his nebb *percutiebant faciem ejus,* Lk. Skt. 22, 64. Ðā hēt hē hine mid stengum ðyrscan, Shrn. 55, 10. Ongunnun sume mið fýstum hine slā ł ðarsca (*caedere*), Mk. Skt. Rush. 14, 65. Ðærscende hine stānum *concidens se lapidibus,* Lind. 5, 5. Swoelce lyft ðerscende (*verberans*), Rtl. 6, 7. II. *to thrash* corn:—Hē corn ðærsc and ðæt windwode, Shrn. 61, 19. Mænige inweorc wyrcean, ðerhsan, wudu cleófan, Anglia ix. 261, 25. Flōr on tō þerscenne *area,* Wrt. Voc. i. 37, 59. III. *to pound, batter:*—Ðēh ðū þercce . . . swā berecorn ðercce[n]dum *si contuderis* (*stultum in pila*) *quasi ptisanas feriente,* Kent. Gl. 1034-6. Ðerscaþ ðone weall mid rammum, Past. 21; Swt. 161, 6. [Þin þrosshenn corn, Orm. 1530. *Goth.* þriskan *triturare: O. H. Ger.* drescan *triturare: Icel.* þryskva (*wk.*) *to thrash* corn.] v. be-, ge-, tō-þerscan.

þerscel, es; *m. An implement for thrashing corn, a thrashle, threshel* (v. Halliwell's Dictionary), *a flail:*—Þerscel *tritorium,* Wrt. Voc. i. 16, 36: 34, 49: *bainus,* ii. 115, 2. Ðerscel, 12, 73. [*O. H. Ger.* driscil *tribula.*]

þerscel-flōr, e; *f. A threshing-floor:*—Hē āfeormaþ his þyrscelflōre (*aream suam*), Mt. Kmbl. 3, 12. v. þirsce-flōr.

þerscold, þerxold, þrexold, þersc-wold, -wald, es; *m. A threshold:*—Oferslege oððe þerexwold (þræx-, þreox-, þerx-wold, ðrexold) *limen,* Ælfc. Gr. 9, 12; Zup. 40, 15. Þrexwold, Wrt. Voc. i. 85, 65. Þerxwald, 290, 16. Þerscwold oððe duru, ii. 52, 5. Wrīte on ðīnum þerscolde (*limine*), Deut. 6, 9. On ðam þerxolde, Ex. 12, 22. Fram deáþes ðrecswalde (þirsc-, Bd. M. 398, 23) *ab ipso mortis limite,* Bd. 5, 6; S. 618, 34. Of ðæs portices dura ðærscwolde, Blickl. Homl. 207, 11. Ofer ðone ðerscold, Past. 13; Swt. 77, 22. Ðerscwold, Homl. Skt. ii. 23 b, 413. Þerscwold, Shrn. 141, 17. Þeorscwold, Bt. 21; Fox 74, 26. Þyrscwold, Met. 11, 68. Þerxwold, Lchdm. ii. 142, 12. Þrexwealdum *liminibus,* Hpt. Gl. 513, 66. Ðærscwaldas *limina,* Bd. 5, 7; S. 620, 27. [*Icel.* þresköldr.]

þes, þæs; *m.:* þeós, þiós, þiús; *f.:* þis, þiss, þys; *n. demons. pron. This:*—*Iste,* þes (þæs, MS. F.), ys æteówiendlīc, and ðǽr biþ, ðǽr man swā bīcnaþ be him; *ille,* hē, ne biþ ðǽr ætforan andwerd, ðǽr men swā be him clypaþ . . . *ille* hē, *ipse* hē sylf, *iste* ðes, *hic* ðes, Ælfc. Gr. 15; Zup. 93, 8-13. I. used adjectivally. (1) alone with a noun:—Eal þes middangeard, and þās windas, and þās regnas, Blickl. Homl. 51, 19.

Ðes eorl, Beo. Th. 3409; B. 1702. Þes Paulinus, Chr. 627; Erl. 25, 5. Ymbhwyrft þes, Exon. Th. 424, 21; Rä. 41, 42. Þeós (ðiós, Lind., Rush.) sealf *unguentum istud*, Mk. Skt. 14, 5. Þeós (ðiús, Lind.: ðiós, Rush.) stefn *uox haec*, Jn. Skt. 12, 5. Þeós wundrung, Exon. Th. 6, 24; Cri. 89. Þiós eorðe, Met. 20, 118. Snytry ðiós *sapientia haec*, Mt. Kmbl. Lind. 13, 54. Þis word *verbum istud*, Mt. Kmbl. 28, 15. Þis (ðis, Lind.) godspel *hoc evangelium*, 24, 14. Þisses middangeardes, Blickl. Homl. 27, 17. Þisses lîfes, Cd. Th. 68, 21; Gen. 1120. Þysses, Beo. Th. 397; B. 197: Blickl. Homl. 31, 3. Þyses, 115, 5. Heofones þisses, Met. 24, 3. Þisse worulde *saeculi istius*, Mt. Kmbl. 13, 22: Blickl. Homl. 17, 17. Ðisse, 119, 9: Beo. Th. 1860; B. 928. Þysse eorðan *terrae*, Ps. Th. 70, 19. Ðeosse wîsan geweotan, Cod. Dip. Kmbl. ii. 121, 36. Weorulde þisse, Met. 29, 82. Þissum hysse, Andr. Kmbl. 1099; An. 550: Blickl. Homl. 11, 28. Þyssum, 7, 13. Ðyssum, 209, 4. Þisum, Mt. Kmbl. 21, 21. Þysum, Blickl. Homl. 151, 35. Of ðæssum (þissum, Rush.) cynne *de hoc genimine*, Mt. Kmbl. Lind. 26, 29. Tô dæge þissum, Cd. Th. 63, 13; Gen. 1031. On þisse meoduhealle, Beo. Th. 1280; B. 638: Blickl. Homl. 23, 3. Ðisse, 139, 32. Þysse, 35, 33. On þysse (ðasser, Lind.: þisse, Rush.) nihte *in ista nocte*, Mt. Kmbl. 26, 31. On þissere (ðisser, Lind.: ðisse, Rush.) nihte *in hac nocte*, 26, 34. Tô dûne þissere, Rush. 21, 21. Þissere þeóde, Chr. 1057; Erl. 192, 22, 27. Þisne ælþeódigan, Blickl. Homl. 247, 13. Þysne, 11, 8. Ðysne, Elen. Kmbl. 624; El. 312. Wîngeard ðeosne *vineam istam*, Ps. Surt. 79, 15. Þâs woruld ofgifan, Cd. Th. 68, 32; Gen. 1126: Blickl. Homl. 5, 28. Ðâs, 117, 35. Ðiós (þâs, Rush.) *istam*, Mt. Kmbl. Lind. 15, 15. Ðæt folc þis wundor geseah, Blickl. Homl. 15, 29. On þŷs geáre, 119, 2. Mid þisse sealfe and mid þŷs drence, Lchdm. ii. 118, 17. Mid ðŷs beácne, Elen. Kmbl. 184; El. 92. Of þîs middanearde, Bt. 26, 3; Fox 94, 16. Fram þis wîgplegan, Byrht. Th. 141, 2; By. 316. Ealle þâs gôd cumaþ, Blickl. Homl. 29, 10. Ðâs men, 189, 28. Þissa leóda land, Andr. Kmbl. 535; An. 268. Þyssa, Met. 7, 54. Þeossa, Blickl. Homl. 15, 13. Ealra ðeassa portweorona gewitnisse, Cod. Dip. Kmbl. ii. 3, 11. Worda þissa, Exon. Th. 246, 6; Jul. 57. Of þissum lioðobendum, Cd. Th. 24, 23; Gen. 382. Þyssum, Andr. Kmbl. 175; An. 88: Blickl. Homl. 25, 9. Þisum, Met. 20, 255. Þysum, 26, 98: Blickl. Homl. 145, 5. Þeossum, 95, 11: 135, 31. Þiossum, Met. Einl. 4. Þâs folc sleán, Cd. Th. 151, 10; Gen. 2506. Þâs dǽda, Blickl. Homl. 31, 20. Ðâs word, 177, 33. Þǽs, 5, 30. (1 a) where objects are contrasted, *this* as opposed to *that*, *one* as contrasted with others:—Ðonne hî eów êhtaþ on þysse (ðissær, Lind.) byrig, fleóþ on ôðre, Mt. Kmbl. 10, 23. Þis leóht wê habbaþ wið nŷtenu gemǽne, ac ðæt leóht wê sceolan sêcan, ðæt wê môtan habban mid englum gemǽne, Blickl. Homl. 21, 13. Ânra gehwylc hæfþ syndrige gife of Gode, sume þâs gife, sume ôðre gife, Homl. Ass. 34, 242. (2) with numerals or adjective forms used substantively:—Ðæt fæsten þyses feówertiges daga, Blickl. Homl. 35, 5. On þyssum feówertigum nihta, 35, 17. For ðissum (ðeosun, Hatt. MS.) ilcan is gesǽd, Past. 17; Swt. 120, 9. Ðioson, Swt. 125, 6. Be ðŷs ilcan, 22; Swt. 168, 19. Þâs þyllîce mê tugon tô helle, Homl. Skt. i. 4, 290. Mon ðissa twêga hwæðer ondrǽtt suîður ðonne ôðer, Past. 27; Swt. 189, 9. Menn þisra seofona hêddon, Homl. Skt. i. 23, 137. (3) where the noun is qualified by an adjective:—Þes ealda man, Blickl. Homl. 43, 33: Cd. Th. 7, 11; Gen. 104. Ðæs andweardа wela, Bt. 32, 1; Fox 114, 2. Þeós swîðre hand, Cd. Th. 195, 22; Exod. 280: Blickl. Homl. 5, 29. Þiós, Bt. 5, 3; Fox 14, 4. Ðiós unstille gesceaft and þeós (þiós, Cott. MS.) hwearfiende, 39, 6; Fox 220, 23. Þis mennisce cynn, Blickl. Homl. 17, 14. Ne þyses lǽnan welan, ne þyssa eorþlîcra geofa, 21, 11. On ðissum andweardan dæge, 171, 3: Cd. Th. 271, 27; Sat. 111. Ðeossum, 271, 20; Sat. 108. Þysum, Hy. 3, 53. Be þisse ondweardan tîde, Blickl. Homl. 15, 4. Þeosne andweardan dæg, Homl. Skt. ii. 23 b, 579. Þŷs uferan Sunnandæge, Blickl. Homl. 119, 15. Hwelc þǽs flǽsclîcan gôd sién, Bt. 32, 2; Fox 116, 28. (3 a) with a numeral used adjectivally:—Intô ðŷs twêntigum hîdum, Cod. Dip. Kmbl. v. 331, 1. On þŷs ylcum þrîm dagum, Lchdm. iii. 76, 26. II. used substantivally, (1) pointing out a person or object:—Þes ys smiðes sunu, Mt. Kmbl. 13, 55: Jn. Skt. i. 34. Nys þes Iôsepes sunu? Lk. Skt. 4, 22. Hê wæs gehâten Zosimus. Ðes on ânum mynstre drohtnode, Homl. Skt. ii. 23 b, 22. Æfter ðyses forðsîðe, 25, 142. Hwanon ys þysum (ðissum, Lind.) þes wîsdôm? Mt. Kmbl. 13, 54, 56. Tô hwon lǽddest ðû hider þeosne? Blickl. Homl. 85, 25: 87, 1. Wê þissa wundra gewitan sindon; eall þâs geeodon in ûssera tîda tîman, Exon. Th. 147, 11; Gû. 725. Þysum (*for these men*) is tô gearcigenne ða rêþestan wîta, Homl. Skt. ii. 24, 21. Ðeossum ða *his qui*, Ps. Surt. 30, 24. Þassum, Mt. Kmbl. Rush. 8, 32. (1 a) *this, the present*:—Ǽr ðissum (ðŷsum, Cott. MSS.), Past. pref.; Swt. 7, 16. Of þisson forð âwa tô worulde *ex hoc nunc et usque in seculum*, Ps. Th. 120, 7. Ðyssum, 130, 5. Ðyssan, 113, 25. Ôð ðiss (ðis, Cott. MSS.) *hitherto*, Past. 23; Swt. 173, 14. Þis, Homl. Skt. i. 22, 44. (1 b) where there is a contrast between two objects, *this* as opposed to *that* or *the other*:—Ðeós wyrt ys twêgea cynna; þonne ys þeós reád . . .; þonne ys ôðer byterre on byrgincge, Lchdm. i. 320, 15. Þeós . . . seó ôþer, Exon. Th. 91, 9; Cri. 1489. Of þysum on þæt, Ps. Th. 74, 8. ¶ *Þis*, like *þæt*, is used with the substantive verb in reference to a subject of any gender or number:—Þis is mîn se leófa sunu, Blickl. Homl. 29, 28. Þis ys se dæg, Ps. Th. 117, 22: Cd. Th. 195, 7; Exod. 273. Eart ðû þis, Drihten? 298, 22; Sat. 537. Þis is seó eorðe, 107, 10; Gen. 1787. Þis (ðiós, Lind. Rush.) is eówer tîd *haec est hora uestra*, Lk. Skt. 22, 53. Þis is landa betst, Cd. Th. 49, 21; Gen. 795. Þiss wǽron ealle Crêca leóde, Ors. 3, 1; Swt. 100, 13. Þis sint ða ðe sceolon standan *hi stabunt*, Deut. 27, 12: Jos. 12, 1. Þis synd ða bebodu and dômas and laga *haec sunt judicia atque praecepta et leges*, Lev. 26, 46: Num. 3, 2. Þe þis sint hira naman *quorum ista sunt nomina*, 1, 5. Ne synt nâ þis wôdes mannes word *haec uerba non sunt daemonium habentis*, Jn. Skt. 10, 21. Sint þis ða gôd and ðæt edleán ðe ðû gehête? Bt. 3, 4; Fox 6, 19. (2) where the pronoun refers to that which has just been stated:—'Ðû cennest sunu.' Ðâ cwæþ heó: 'Hû mæg þis geweorþan?' Blickl. Homl. 7, 21. Hwâ ne wafaþ ðæs ðonne se fulla môna wyrþ ofertogen mid þióstrum? oððe eft ðæt ða steorran scînaþ beforan ðam mônan and ne scînaþ beforan ðære sunnan? Ðisses hî wundriaþ, Bt. 39, 3; Fox 214, 31. Þisses, Exon. Th. 15, 18; Cri. 238. Hwanun wât ic þis? Lk. Skt. 1, 18. Swâ lange swâ ge ðis dydon, Blickl. Homl. 169, 21: Exon. Th. 39, 24; Cri. 627. For þîs (þŷ, Cott. MS.) is se cwide sôþ *for this reason is the saying true*, Bt. 36, 7; Fox 184, 18. Þiss, Mt. Kmbl. 28, 14. Wê ðiss (ðis, Cott. MSS.) feáwum wordum sǽdon, Past. 3; Swt. 33, 6: 22; Swt. 169, 3. Wê sculon ðissa ǽgðer underðencean, 7; Swt. 49, 23. ¶ Referring to a circumstance which serves to mark time:—Æfter ðrîm mônðum ðises (*the circumstance just mentioned*), Homl. Th. ii. 496, 29. Æfter þisson, Jn. Skt. 11, 7. Betwux ðisum, Homl. Th. i. 480, 27. Æfter þiossum, Blickl. Homl. 239, 32. (2 a) where the pronoun refers to a statement immediately following:—Þis næs gecweden be Criste, ðæt his fôt æt stâne ôþspurne, Blickl. Homl. 29, 30. Þis þinceþ riht, ðæt ðû ðê âferige of þisse folcsceare, Cd. Th. 149, 17; Gen. 2476: 294, 2; Sat. 465. For ðeosum wæs geworden . . . for ðæm, Past. 15; Swt. 91, 26. [*O. Sax.* thius; *f.*; thit; *n.*: *O. Frs.* this, thisse; *m.*; thius, thisse; *f.*; thit, this; *n.*: *O. H. Ger.* dese; *m.*; desiu; *f.*; diz; *n.*: *Icel.* þessi; *m. f.*; þetta; *n.*]

þêwan, þî, þîan. v. þeówan, þŷ, þeówan.

þicce; *adj. Thick*:—Þicce *condensa*, i. *spissa*, Wrt. Voc. ii. 135, 64. Þicce and þynne, Exon. Th. 424, 8; Rä. 41, 36. I. of substances, (1) of liquids or moist materials, *thick, viscous*:—Gegnîd on gewleced wæter, ôþ ðæt hit sié swâ þicce swâ huniges teár, Lchdm. ii. 74, 4. Nâne ôþre wǽtan ðæt þicce and stille sié, 138, 13. Ôþ hit sié þicce swâ þynne brîw, 314, 3: 316, 24. Swâ þicce swâ molcen, 332, 18. Wyl on swîþum beóre ðæt hit sié þicce, 358, 19. Þat hê ût hrǽcþ byþ swîþe þicce, iii. 126, 11. Ðicce, ii. 262, 21. Tôsoden and þicge geurnen, 230, 8. Mid þiccere wǽtan, 280, 4. Ne drince hê þicce wîn (cf. þynne wîn, l. 18), 254, 26. Of þiccum *lento* (*defruto*), Hpt. Gl. 408, 38. 'Wâ ðæm ðe gaderaþ an hine selfne ðæt hefige fenn (*densum lutum*)' . . . Ðæt is ðonne ðæt mon gadrige ðæt ðicke (ðicce, Cott. MSS.) fenn (*densum lutum*) on hine, Past. 44; Swt. 329, 19. (2) of solid material, *dense*:—Sió eorþe is hefigre and þiccre þonne ôþra gesceafta, Bt. 33, 4; Fox 130, 19. Þicre, Met. 20, 134. II. of air, cloud, darkness, etc., *thick, dense*:—Þicce genip (*nubes densissima*) oferwrêh ðone munt, Ex. 19, 16. Ǽr se þicca mist þinra weorðe, Met. 5, 6. Sió þicce ǽrlyft *gravis*, Wrt. Voc. ii. 41, 74. Þiccre *crassae, densae* (*noctis*), Hpt. Gl. 446, 25. Tôdrîf ðone þiccan mist, Met. 20, 264. Anlîce swâ ðû bærne þornas þyre þicce fŷre, Ps. Th. 117, 12. Ða ðŷstru swâ ðicce wǽron *tenebrae in tantum condensatae sunt*, Bd. 5, 12; S. 628, 12. Becômon ðicce ðeóstru, Homl. Th. ii. 194, 3. III. where objects are placed close together, *thick, dense*:—Gif hǽr tô þicce sié, Lchdm. ii. 156, 8. Of þiccum (*thickly planted?*) felde *de denso campo*, Wrt. Voc. ii. 138, 59. Ðû lǽtst mê on þicne wudu, Bt. 35, 5; Fox 164, 13. On þiccon bearwum, Lchdm. i. 322, 25. Intô ðam wudu ðǽr hê þiccost wæs, Homl. Skt. ii. 30, 31. In ðone þiccestan wudu, Shrn. 118, 16. III a. *growing thickly, abundant*:—Gebeorh Godes bringeþ tô genihte wæstme weorðlîce and wel þicce (*or adv.?*) *montem Dei, montem uberem; mons coagulatus, mons pinguis*, Ps. Th. 67, 15. Seó eá (*Nile*) gedêþ mid ðæm flôde swîþe þicce eorþwæstmas, Ors. 1, 1; Swt. 12, 36. IV. marking dimension, (1) in a general sense, *thick, stout*:—Dô on ânne þicne (þynne, MS. H.) lînenne clâð, Lchdm. i. 240, 21. Lege on þone þiccestan clâð opðe on fel, ii. 200, 11. (2) of more exact measurement, *thick*:—Hî woldon witon hû heáh hit wǽre tô ðæm hefone, and hû ðicke (þicce, Cott. MS.) se hefon wǽre, oððe hwæt ðǽr ofer wǽre, Bt. 35, 4; Fox 162, 22. Se weall wæs .xx[x]. fôta ðicce *is locus murum triginta pedes latum habuit*, Ors. 4, 13; Swt. 210, 30. Seó eá oferfleów mid fôtes þicce flôde, 1, 3; Swt. 32, 6. Ða wâgas wǽron gyldne mid gyldnum þelum ânæglede fingres þicce *auratos parietes laminarum digitalium grossitudine*, Nar. 4, 26. [*O. Sax.* thikki: *O. Frs.* thikke: *O. H. Ger.* dicchi *crassus, spissus, densus, torosus, grossus, frequens*: *Icel.* þykkr.] v. þicness.

þicce; *adv.* I. marking closeness in the texture or composition of a whole, *closely*:—Þicce gewefen hrægel *pavidensis*, Wrt. Voc. i. 40, 11. II. marking closeness of separate objects, *thickly, densely, closely*:—Ðâ flugon ða lêgetu swylce fŷrene strǽlas tô ðæm þicce ðæt . . .,

Blickl. Homl. 203, 10. Swā þicce is þeó heofon mid steorrum āfylled on dæg swā on niht, Lchdm. iii. 234, 31. Wæl þicce gefylled *the corpses lying thick on the ground*, Cd. Th. 130, 16; Gen. 2160. Swā þicce hié āweóllon swā æmettan *they swarmed as thick as ants*, Nar. 11, 12. III. marking action that occurs with frequency or with little intermission:—Feónda feorh feóllon đicce, Cd. Th. 124, 20; Gen. 2065. Hió spræc him þicce tō *she spoke to him again and again*, 43, 1; Gen. 684. IV. marking abundance, *thickly*:—Lege đæt dust swīþe þicce on clāđ, Lchdm. ii. 148, 15: 340, 21. Weard beám monig blōdigum teárum birunnen reáde and þicce, Exon. Th. 72, 22; Cri. 1176. [*O. Sax.* thikko (mid thiodu gisetan): *O. H. Ger.* diccho *dense, frequenter, saepe.*] v. þiclīce.

þiccet[t], es; *n. A place where there is dense growth* (v. þicce, III), *a thicket*:—On þyccetum *in condensis*, Ps. Lamb. 117, 27. Stefn Drihtnes āwrīhþ þiccettu (þiccetu, Ps. Lamb.) *vox Dominis revelabit condensa*, Ps. Spl. 28, 8.

þiccian; *p.* ode *To thicken* (trans. and intrans.), *to make* or *to become thick*, of persons, *to throng*:—Ic điccige *denso* and *denseo*, Ælfc. Gr. 37; Zup. 220, 8. þiccaþ *densescit, spissat*, Wrt. Voc. ii. 138, 74. Đā þiccodan þider semninga þa Ismahēli, Shrn. 38, 4. [Hit bicometh to a thikke blod . . . neoȝe dayes hit thicketh so, Wrt. popl. science 139, 3. Thykkyñ or make thykke, as wodys *condenso*, thykkyñ or make thykke, as lycurys *spisso, inspisso*, Prompt. Parv. 491. *O. H. Ger.* dicchēn *glomerare, grossescere, crebriscere.*]

þiccness. v. þicnes.

þiccol(-ul); *adj. Stout, corpulent*:—þiccol *corpulentus*, Wrt. Voc. i. 83, 47. Điccul, 51, 13.

þic-feald; *adj. Dense, close*:—þicfealdum þreátum *spissis cohortibus*, Hpt. Gl. 413, 1. v. next word.

þicfildan. v. ge-þicfyldan (*l.* geþycfyldan *densere*, Germ. 401, 21). v. preceding word.

þicgan; *p.* þah, þeah, *and* þigde, þigede, *pl.* þǣgon, þēgon, *and* þigdon, þigedon; *pp.* þegen, *and* þiged. I. *to take, receive, accept*:—Hē him brād syleþ lond tō leáne, hē hit on lust þigeþ, Exon. Th. 331, 31; Vy. 76. Hié đa lāc þēgon tō þance, Andr. Kmbl. 2225; An. 1114. Đeáh hē māđmas þēge, Elen. Kmbl. 2516; El. 1259. Đæt hȳ beágas þēgon, Exon. Th. 283, 29; Jul. 687. Heó hafaþ gefreód đa men đe heó þigede æt Cwæspatrike, Chart. Th. 621, 18. Welan þicgan, Exon. Th. 331, 1; Vy. 61. Feoh þicgan, 332, 7; Vy. 81. His giefe þicgan tō þonce, 109, 26; Gū. 96. Lāfe þicgan, 498, 9; Rä. 87, 10. Ne gē đæt geþyldum þicgan woldan, 131, 12; Gū. 454. Se æđeling gehwilcan feoh and feorh beád, and heó nǣnig þicgan noldan, Chr. 755; Erl. 51, 5. II. *to take* food, poison, medicine, etc., *to eat* or *drink, consume*:—Hū đæt ne gemylt, đæt se maga þigeþ, Lchdm. ii. 158, 16. þigđ, 186, 21. Fȳr þigeþ lǣnne līchoman, Exon. Th. 213, 4; Ph. 219. Nō hē þigeþ mete, 215, 27; Ph. 259: 357, 28; Pa. 35. Of đam mete đe wē þicgaþ, Bt. 34, 11; Fox 150, 35. Đonne hig mete þicgeaþ *cum panem manducant*, Mt. Kmbl. 15, 2. Hī hyra hlāf þicgaþ, Mk. Skt. 7, 5. Hē on his hūs eode and his swǣsendo đeah *intravit epulaturus domum ejus*, Bd. 3, 22; S. 553, 30. Đæt hē nǣfre oftor swǣsendo đeah (*reficeret*), 4, 25; S. 600, 16. Swā đæt hē nǣfre mete onfēng ne swǣsendo đeah *ita ut nihil unquam cibi vel potus perciperet*, S. 599, 30. Wē medu þēgon, Beo. Th. 5260; B. 2633: Judth. Thw. 21, 15; Jud. 19. Hī wiste þēgon, Andr. Kmbl. 1186; An. 593. Hié fira flǣschoman þēgon, 49; An. 25. Hī þēgun æppel, Exon. Th. 226, 8; Ph. 402. Đæt hē mæte đygde *ad prandendum*, Bd. 5, 4; S. 617, 11. Israhēl đigde đæs lambes flǣsc, Homl. Th. ii. 278, 18. þigde *consumeret, biberet*, Hpt. Gl. 450, 32. þigede, Guthl. 4; Gdwin. 26, 18: 5; Gdwin. 34, 7. Đygede, Bd. 5, 4; S. 617, 17. Wit eaples þigdon, Cd. 290, 7; Sat. 411. Hē sumum liéfde tō đicganne đætte hē nolde đæt hī ealle đigden, Past. 59; Swt. 451, 29. þigedan, Ors. 3, 6; Swt. 110, 1: 6, 21; Swt. 272, 23. Đæt hī of his swǣsendum mete ne đygedon *ne de cibis illius acciperent*, Bd. 3, 22; S. 553, 28. Ceorf nygan penegas, and đige đa, Lchdm. iii. 8, 2. Nǣfre gē beódgereordu unārlīce eówre þicgeaþ, Cd. Th. 91, 29; Gen. 1519. Ne hē nāht fūles ne þicge (*comedat*), Jud. 13, 4. Wiþ þon þe mon þicge ātor, Lchdm. ii. 110, 24. Đæt hī mōston onfōn and đicgean đa foresetenysse hlāfas *ut panes propositionis acciperent*, Bd. 1, 27; S. 496, 14: 5, 4; S. 617, 14. Nolde ic mid þæm men mīnne mete đicgean *cum hoc simul non edebam*, Ps. Th. 100, 5. Đicgan, Bd. 4, 19; S. 588, 12: Homl. Th. ii. 244, 11: 40, 13. Syle đone wyrttruman đam seócan þicgean . . . Gyf đū đās wyrte sylst þicgean on strangon wīne, Lchdm. i. 172, 10–13. On drince þicgean, 198, 25. Genim đās ylcan wyrte, seóđ on hunige, syle þiggean (þiggcan, MS. H.: þicgan, MS. B.), 150, 9. Symbel þicgan, Beo. Th. 2025; B. 1010. Đonne āliéfþ hē đæm siócan eal đæt đæt hine lysđ tō dōnne and tō đycganne, Past. 50; Swt. 391, 25. Biđ seó ān snǣd sēlre tō þicganne, Salm. Kmbl. 813; Sal. 406. Se forbeád blōd tō þicgenne, Ælfc. T. Grn. 4, 43. Đicgendum (điccendum, Rush.) miđ him and etendum *discumbentibus cum eis et manducantibus*, Mk. Skt. Lind. 14, 18. [þet mon to muchel ne þigge on ete and on wete, O. E. Homl. i. 105, 3. *But later the word means* to beg:—He haueth me do mi mete to thigge, Havel. 1373. Beggyn or thyggyn *mendico*, Prompt. Parv. 28. Cf. thyggynge or beggynge *mendicacio*, 490. Thiggand *egenus*, Ps. 39, 18. See also Halliwell's Dict. and Jamieson's Dict. *O. Sax.* thiggean (*wk.*) *to receive, to ask*: *O. H. Ger.* diggen (*wk.*) *impetrare, petere, expetere*: *Icel.* þiggja; *p.* þā, *pl.* þāgu; *pp.* þeginn *to receive, accept.*] v. ge-þicgan, þegan; þegu.

þiclīce; *adv. Thickly, in great numbers, in quick succession*:—Đā hié gesāwan đa deádan men swā þiclīce tō eorþan beran, Ors. 3, 10; Swt. 138, 25. Steorran of heofenan feóllan, nāht be ānan ođđe twām, ac swā þiclīce đæt hit nān mann āteallan ne mihte, Chr. 1095; Erl. 231, 21. v. ful-þiclīce; þicce.

þicness, e; *f.* I. referring to the consistency of matter, *thickness, viscosity*. v. þicce, I:—Cnuca mid wīne on huniges þicnysse, Lchdm. i. 126, 12. Gyf hwā mycelne hracan þolige, and hē đone him eáþelīce fram bringan ne mæge for đycnysse, 284, 24. Seóþ ōþ đæt đæt hæbbe huniges þicnesse, ii. 190, 5. II. referring to the lack of transparency, *thickness, obscurity, cloud, darkness*. v. þicce, II:—Genipu and þicnæs *nubes et caligo*, Ps. Spl. 96, 2. Tegānre þicnysse *rupto tenebrarum situ*, Germ. 388, 43. Of nyþerhreósendre þicnysse *deciduo imbre*, 390, 79. Wē ne magon for đære fyrlynan heáhnysse and đæra wolcna đicnysse and for ure eágena tyddernysse hī (heofenan) nǣfre geseón, Lchdm. iii. 232, 16. Đa þicnyssa smīces stigon upp *the clouds of smoke rose up*, Homl. Skt. i. 23, 36. III. *a thicket*. v. þicce, III:—On đicnessum *in condensis*, Ps. Lamb. 117, 27. Đicnyssa *condensa*, 28, 9. IV. referring to dimension, *thickness, depth, a thick body*. v. þicce, IV:—Hreóflīcre þicnesse *elephantina callositate*, Hpt. Gl. 519, 31. Hit næfde eorþan þiccnesse *non habebat altitudinem terrae*, Mk. Skt. 4, 5. Sweflenum þicnyssum *sulphureis flammarum globis*, Hpt. Gl. 499, 41. [*O. H. Ger.* diknissa *densitas.*]

þīdan, þiddan. v. þeódan, þyddan.

þider, þieder; *adv. Thither, whither*, where motion is expressed or implied. I. as absolute demonstrative, *thither, to that place*:—Ne færst đū þider (*illuc*), Deut. 1, 37. Đa đe hine þider lǣddon, Gen. 39, 1. þyder (đider, Lind.) faran *illuc ire*, Mt. Kmbl. 2, 22. Hē com þyder (đidir, Lind.: þidera, Rush.), Jn. Skt. 18, 3. Đyder (đidder, Lind.: đider, Rush.), 11, 8. Hī tō đon đider (*illo*) sende wǣron, đæt hī sceoldon đæt gyldene mynet mid him geniman đætte đider (*eo*) of Kent com, Bd. 3, 8; S. 530, 40. Đā fērde hē đyder, Blickl. Homl. 225, 7. Nū þyder ingongaþ and mē ætstondaþ, 207, 2. Uton mid him þyder geond gān, Homl. Skt. i. 23, 748, 321. Đæt gifeđe đe đone þyder ontyhte, Beo. Th. 6164; B. 3086. Hit witena nān þider (cf. þǣr, Bt. 32, 3; Fox 118, 9) ne sēceþ *no wise man goes thither to look for it*, Met. 19, 8. þider wǣron fūse, Cd. Th. 190, 9; Exod. 196. Hē þyder folc samnode, 230, 5; Dan. 228: Blickl. Homl. 67, 20. Se siþfæt is þyder tō lang, 231, 26. Ǣrende wē þyder habbaþ, 233, 11. I a. in an indefinite sense:—Đæt hió on ǣnige healfe ne heldeþ; ne mæg hió hider ne þider sīgan, Met. 20, 164. On healfa gehwǣr, sume hyder, sume þyder, Elen. Kmbl. 1093; El. 548. II. as antecedent:—Đā ferede hine Godes hand þider, þǣr hine men siđđan āredon, Shrn. 57, 5. Uton ācerran þider, þǣr hē sylfa sit, Cd. Th. 278, 6; Sat. 217. Gingran þider ealle urnon, þǣr se ēca wæs, 298, 11; Sat. 531. þider cuman, þonan þe hit ǣr com, Bt. 25; Fox 88, 30. III. in correlative clauses, *thither . . . whither*:—Đider becuman . . . đieder đe hē wilnaþ, Past. 11; Swt. 65, 16. Đyder đe hē sylfa tōweard wæs æfter deáþe, đider hē his mōdes eágan sende ǣr his deáþe *ubi erat futurus post mortem, ibi oculos mentis ante mortem misit*, Bd. 5, 14; S. 634, 41. þider đe Stephanus forestōp, đider folgode Paulus, Homl. Th. i. 52, 6. IV. where antecedent and relative are contained in the one form, *to the place to which, whither*:—Cuman þyder (đidder, Lind.) ic fare *quo ego vado venire*, Jn. Skt. 8, 21. Đū mōst fēran þider đū fundadest, Exon. Th. 102, 12; Cri. 1671: Met. 26, 119: 13, 3. Đæt heó mē gerihte þyder hire willa wǣre, Homl. Skt. ii. 23 b, 509. V. as a relative, *whither*:—Tō heofenum, þider hié witon đæt hē āstāg, Blickl. Homl. 125, 29. Hē tō heofenum lōcade, þyder his mōdgeþanc ā geseted wæs . . . tō Drihtne þyder hē fēran sceal, 227, 17–22. v. þæder.

þideres, þidres; *adv. Thither*:—Đæt sió ūterre ābisgung đissa woridđinga đæs monnes mōd gedrēfđ and hiene scofeđ hidres đidres, ōđđæt hē āfilþ of his āgnum willan *quod cor externis occupationum tumultibus impulsum a semetipso corruat*, Past. 22; Swt. 168, 13. Hidres þidres, Bt. 40, 5; Fox 240, 21. Hē lange hyderes and þyderes sēcende fōr, Homl. Skt. ii. 23 b, 730. v. þædres.

þider-inn, -in; *adv. Into that place*, (1) where motion is expressed or implied:—þeáh hwā his āgen spere sette tō ōđres mannes hūses dura, and hē þiderinn (-in, MS. B.) ǣrende hæbbe, L. C. S. 76; Th. i. 418, 5. Ic mē þyderinn eode, Homl. Skt. ii. 23 b, 500. Hié þyderin wǣron gesamnode *they were got together into the place*, Blickl. Homl. 207, 36. (2) of other relations:—Eal seó sōcna đe đærto hēreþ and đæt land þiderinn *the land belonging to it*, Chart. Th. 547, 2. Ic wille đæt se cyng beó hlāford đæs mynstres and đære landāra đe ic þyderinn becweden hæbbe (*that I have bequeathed to the monastery*), 547, 32. His bēc ealle hē cwæđ þyderin, 550, 23. Ōsanīg gange þyderin, 550, 19.

þider-leódisc; *adj. Of that people:*—Hē geleórde on Burgenda mǣgðe, and hē wæs bebyrged mid micle wōpe ge Angelcynnes monna ge þiderleódiscra, Shrn. 134, 24.

þider-weard; *adv. Thitherward, in that direction, towards that place* or *point:*—Iosue fērde mid his fyrde þiderweard *ascendit Iosue et omnis exercitus cum eo*, Jos. 10, 7. Ðā hē þiderweard seglode *as he sailed towards that port*, Ors. 1, 1; Swt. 19, 24. Ealle þiderweard ēfeston *all hastened towards the spot*, Guthl. 1; Gdwin. 8, 20. Hié wǣron flocmǣlum þiderweard *they were flocking to the place*, Ors. 4, 10; Swt. 200, 19: 5, 13; Swt. 246, 21. Ðā hē ðyderweard wæs *when he was on the way to it*, Homl. Skt. ii. 30, 179: Chr. 1009; Erl. 142, 3. Beheóld Abraham þyderweard *Abraham looked in that direction*, Gen. 19, 27. Beseah hē þiderweard, Homl. Skt. i. 23, 499. Þinga gehwilc þiderweard fundaþ, Met. 13, 14. Wuhta gehwilc wilnaþ þiderweard, 20, 159.

þiderweardes; *adv. Thitherwards:*—Wæs se cyng þiderweardes on fære . . . Þā hē þā wæs þiderweardes and sió ōþeru fierd wæs hāmweardes *the king was on the march thither . . . When he was on the way thither and the other troops were on the road home*, Chr. 894; Erl. 90, 32. Swā heó ǣr dyde þyderweardes *as she did before when on the way to that place*, Homl. Skt. ii. 23 b, 724. Ðā ongon hē sprecan swīþe feorran ymbūton, swilce hē nā þa sprǣce ne mǣnde, and tiohhode hit þeáh þiderweardes (*towards that point*), Bt. 39, 5; Fox 218, 12.

þidres, þiédan, þiéfan, þiéfe-feoh, þiéfþ, þiéstru. v. þideres, þeódan, ge-þiéfian (*read* -biéfan), þīfe-feoh, þīfþ, þeóstru.

þīfe-feoh *stolen goods:*—Gif þiéfefeoh (forstolen feoh, MS. H.) mon æt ciépan befō, L. In. 25; Th. i. 118, 13. [Cf. *Icel.* þýfi; *n. stolen goods.*]

þīfe-, þeófe-, þēfe-, þȳfe-, þēfan-þorn, es; *m. Buckthorn:*—Ðeófeðorn, thēbanthorn *ramnus*, Txts. 93, 1710. Þīfeþorn, Wrt. Voc. i. 33, 43. Þēfeþorn, 68, 34. Þȳfeþorn *ramnus* vel *sentix ursina*, 39, 23. Þēfanðorn, coltetræppe *ramnus*, 285, 47. Þēfanþorn, Lchdm. ii. 312, 15: 352, 12: 354, 24. Nim ðēfeþorn, iii. 56, 27. Þēfeðorn *ramnum*, Ps. Spl. T. 57, 9. [Wicklif uses *thevethorn* in the passage last cited, as also in Jud. ix. 14; see, too, Ps. 57, 10, and Prompt. Parv. *thevethorn tre* ramnus. *Thief* is given as a word for *bramble* in E. D. S. Leicestershire Glossary. *O. H. Ger.* dēpan-dorn *ramnus.*] v. þūfe.

þiffe?:—*Defruto* ł felde ł þiffe (þīfe? Cf. (?) theve, brusch, Prompt. Parv. 490; *or* þīfele (?). The passage glossed is *lento careni defruto*, in which the first word is glossed by *of þiccum*, but in the margin by *of þiccum þēfele*. Cf. too Wrt. Voc. ii. 138, 59 *de lento fruto* of þiccum felde), Hpt. Gl. 408, 50.

þīfþ, þiéfþ, þȳfþ, þeófþ, þeóft, e; *f.* I. *theft, act of thieving:*—Be ānre nihtes (nihte, MS. B.) ðiéfðe (þȳfte, MS. B.: þȳfðe, MSS. G. H.). Gif hit bið nihteald þiéfð (þȳfð, MS. H.) *if a day has elapsed since the theft was committed*, L. In. 73; Th. i. 148, 10. Mōna se syofoða . . . þȳfð gestrangaþ, Lchdm. iii. 186, 22. Gif hwā stalie on gewitnesse ealles his hīrēdes, gongen hié ealle on þeówot .x.-wintre cniht mæg bión þiéfðe (þȳfðe, MSS. B. H.) gewita (cf. wǣron cradolcild geþeówode þurh wælhreówe unlaga for lytelre þȳfðe, Wulfst. 158, 15), L. In. 7; Th. i. 106, 18. Betygen þiéfðe (þīfðe, MS. H.), 37; Th. i. 124, 22. Be ðȳfðe betogenum. Gif hwā þīfðe betogen sȳ, L. Ed. 6; Th. i. 162, 16. Onsacan ðære þiéfðe (þeófðe, MS. B.), L. In. 46; Th. i. 130, 14. Se ðe þȳfðe forworht wǣre openlīce, L. Ath. v. 1, 4; Th. i. 228, 25. Gif man leúd ofsleá an þeófðe, licge būtan wyrgelde, L. Wih. 25; Th. i. 42, 13. Be ðeófes onfenge æt ðiéfðe, L. In. 28; Th. i. 120, 4: 37; Th. i. 124, 20. Þȳfðe, L. Ath. i. 3; Th. i. 200, 20. Æt openre þȳfðe, L. C. S. 26; Th. i. 392, 3. Ðā geácsode se biscop ðæt ða bēcc forstolene wǣron, bæd ðara bōca geornlīce . . . man gerehte ðam biscope ða forstolenan bēcc, and bōte æt ðære þȳfðe, Chart. Th. 265, 10. For þeófte oþþe for manslihte, L. Wil. ii. 1; Th. i. 489, 6. Gif hē ða þiéfðe gedierne, L. In. 36; Th. i. 124, 17. Ðæt hȳ on heora mǣge nāne þȳfðe (þeófðe) nyston, L. Ath. i. 13; Th. i. 206, 2: iv. 4; Th. i. 224, 6. Man forgā þȳfðe (-a), i. 20; Th. i. 210, 3. Ealles folces þing byþ ðe betere æt ðām þȳfðum, v. 8, 9; Th. i. 238, 20. Ðæncunge ðǣm ðe wið ðȳfðe fylstaþ. Ic þancige Gode and eów eallum ðæs friðes ðe wē nū habbaþ æt ðǣm þȳfðum, L. Edm. S. 5; Th. i. 250, 5. II. *what is stolen, theft:*—Tō ðȳ ðæt earm and eádig mōte āgan ðæt hȳ mid rihte gestrȳnaþ, and þeóf nyte hwǣr hē þȳfðe (þeófte, MS. C.) befæste, þeáh hē hwæt stele, L. Edg. S. 2; Th. i. 274, 3. [*O. E. Homl. Laym. A. R.* þeofðe: *R. Glouc.* þufþe: *Gen. and Ex.* ðefte: *Ayenb.* þiefþe: *Chauc.* thefte. *O. Frs.* thiufthe, thiufte: *Icel.* þȳfð, þȳft.]

þigaþ, Exon. Th. 130, 3; Gū. 432. v. þeón.

þigen, e; *f.* I. *the taking* of food, *partaking, eating* or *drinking:*—Ne sȳ him gemǣne þigen mid gebrōðrum geþafod *non permittatur ad mense communis participationem*, R. Ben. 69, 13. Ðæs hālgan hūsles ðygen *partaking of the eucharist*, Homl. Th. i. 266, 17. Se frumsceapena man wearð ādrǣfed of neorxenawanges myrhðe for ðigene ðæs forbodenan bigleofan, 118, 25. Lactuca is biter on ðigene *lettuce is bitter in the eating*, ii. 278, 27. Mid unālȳfedre ðigene, 332, 1. Æt ðære ðigene (*at the Passover*), 280, 34. Sȳ hē āscyred fram gemǣnre mȳsan þigene *from eating at the common table*; a mensa, R. Ben. 49, 15; 70, 4. Sȳ ā on ðære þigene forhefednes *let there ever be moderation in taking wine*, 65, 3. Wið āttres ðigne, Lchdm. i. 150, 3. His gereordes þigene hē āna underfō *refectionem cibi solus accipiat*, R. Ben. 49, 6: Wulfst. 284, 25: Homl. Th. ii. 98, 30. Ðurh ðæs hālgan hūsles þygene ūs beóþ ūre synna forgyfene, i. 266, 8. Ðurh ānes æpples ðigene *through eating an apple*, ii. 330, 33. Ða oferflōwendlīcan ðygene *excessive eating and drinking*, i. 360, 13. II. *what is taken, food, meat* or *drink:*—Þigen *edulium*, Hpt. Gl. 513, 63. Ðæt seó dæges þigen tōfered sȳ and seó hǣte ðære þigene oferslegen *ut digesti surgant*, R. Ben. 32, 14. Ne sȳ him nānre ōðere þigene getīðod *let him have no other food given him*, 69, 21. Werede ðigene *nectareum edulium*, Hpt. Gl. 413, 38. Ða hālgan ðigene (*the eucharist*) onfōn, Homl. Th. ii. 280, 29. Heora þigne gehealdan *to retain their food*, Lchdm. i. 90, 12. Þygne, 8, 6. Ðū ðās werðeóde wræccan lāste freónda feásceaft gesōhtest þīne þearfende (þīne *for* þigne? *needing food; or* þīne *pron.* (v. þīn, III) *thy men being in need*), Cd. Th. 149, 25; Gen. 2480. Fram eallum ðām þigenum ðe hracan oþþe innoþ tō miclum luste getȳhþ, R. Ben. 138, 14. Āwendan ūrne swæcc fram unālȳfedum, ðigenum, Homl. Th. ii. 374, 5. v. blōd-þigen; þicgan.

þiging, e; *f. The taking* of anything to eat or drink, *eating* or *drinking:*—Of metta and of drincena þiginge, Lchdm. ii. 244, 12.

þignan *to eat:*—Hȳ ðȳnde *depastus est eam*, Ps. Spl. C. 79, 14.

þignen[n], þīnen[n], þinnen[n], e; *f.* I. *a female servant, female attendant, handmaid:*—Ðignen *pedisequa*, Wrt. Voc. ii. 116, 63. Þīnen, i. 282, 15: *ancilla*, ii. 4, 12. Þīnen, wyln *abra*, i. *ancilla*, i. 17, 26. Þȳnen *vernacula, servula, ancilla*, Hpt. Gl. 498, 20. Sum þīnen (ðignen, Lind.) *a certain maid*, Lk. Skt. 22, 56. Sió ðignen (ðegnen, Rush.) durehaldend *ancilla ostiaria*, Jn. Skt. Lind. 18, 17. Ic eom Godes ðīnen *behold the handmaid of the Lord* (Lk. 1, 38), Homl. Th. i. 200, 10: Homl. Skt. ii. 23 b, 237. Heó cwæð tō him: 'Ic eom deófles ðīnen, Shrn. 140, 18. Þīnene *ancillae*, Gen. 35, 25, 26: Scint. 229, 6. Þīnenne, Ps. Lamb. 115, 6: 85, 16. Þinnenre (-ne?), Ps. Spl. 85, 15. Þinnenne *abrâ*, Wrt. Voc. ii. 87, 49. Seó abbudisse eode mid ānre hire ðignenne (*cum una sanctimonialium feminarum*) . . . Ðā hēt heó hire ðīnenne (*ministram*) gān, Bd. 3, 11; S. 536, 18–27. Þīnenne, Judth. Thw. 24, 4; Jud. 172. Heó hæfde āne þīnene (*ancillam*), Gen. 16, 1. Āne hire þīnena *unam e famulabus suis*, Ex. 2, 5. Þīnennum *pedisequis*, þīnenna *pedisequas*, Wrt. Voc. ii. 67, 9, 10. Þīnum *vernaculis*, Hpt. Gl. 523, 26. Þīnenne *vernaculas*, 404, 56. Þīnena *ancillas*, Lk. Skt. 12, 45: Gen. 33, 2: Homl. Th. ii. 478, 10. II. *used with the meaning of* byrþ-þignen, *a mid-wife:*—Se cyning cwæþ tō ðām þīnenum ðe ðām Ebrēiscean wīfun þēnodon (*obstetricibus Hebraeorum*) . . . Ða þīnena (*obstetrices*) him ondrēdon God, Ex. 1, 15, 17, 20, 21. v. beorþor- (*written* broþor-), byrþ-, duru-, in-þignen (-þīnen).

þiht; *adj. Tight, firm, strong.* This word seems to be the second part in each of the two compounds found in the following charm:—Gehwēr fērde ic mē ðone mǣran magaþīhtan mid ðysse mǣran meteþīhtan ðonne ic mē wille habban and hām gān, Lchdm. iii. 68, 17. [Thyht, hool fro brekynge *integer, solidus*; thyhtyn or make thyht *integro, consolido, solido*, Prompt. Parv. 491. Halliwell gives *thiht* close, compact, as an Eastern counties word. *M. H. Ger.* dihte: *Ger.* dicht: *Icel.* þēttr.]

Thīla(-e). v. Thyle.

þilian, þillian, þillan *to plank, lay planks* as in making a bridge:—Ðā hēt Maxentius oferbricgian ða eá eal mid scipum, and syððan ðylian swā swā ōðre bricge, Homl. Th. ii. 304, 22. Tō þilianne *plancas ponere*, Cod. Dip. B. iii. 659, 33. Tō þillianne, 5, 8, 10, 14. Tō þelliene, 26. Tō þillanne, 28. Tō þyllanne, 24. (The section is headed: Ðis is ðære bricge geweorc on Hrōuecæstre.) [*O. H. Ger.* gi-dillōn *insternere* (*pontes*): *Ger.* dielen *to board, plank: Icel.* þilja *to cover with deals, to board, plank.*] v. next two words.

þiling, e; *f. A boarding, flooring, something composed of planks:*—Breda þiling *vel* flōr on tō þerscenne *area*, Wrt. Voc. i. 37, 59. Hig fæstniaþ ðone stepe þurh ða þilinge (*deck*; cf. *Icel.* þiljur; *pl. the deck*), Shrn. 35, 15. v. wāh-þiling.

þille, an; *f. A boarding, flooring, floor:*—Ðille *tabulata, tabulamen*, Wrt. Voc. ii. 122, 8, 10. Þille *tabulamen*, i. 290, 73. [*O. H. Ger.* dilla; *f.*; dil, dillo; *m. planca, ima pars navis, pluteus, tabula parietis: Ger.* diele: *Icel.* þilja; *f. a deal, plank, planking.*] v. þel.

þillic. v. þyllic.

þīn; *pron. poss.* I. attributive, *thy, thine*, (1) with noun alone:—Tō become þīn (ðīn, Lind.) rīce. Gewurðe þīn willa, Mt. Kmbl. 6, 10. Þīnes fæder God, Gen. 31, 29. Far of þīnum lande and of þīnre mǣgðe and of þīnes fæder hūse, 12, 1. Þīnre dura belocenre, Mt. Kmbl. 6, 6. (1 a) where the noun is to be inferred:—Ða ilcan ðē habbaþ nū heora āgnes þances forlētan, nales þīnes, Bt. 7, 2; Fox 18, 13. (1 b) strengthened by *āgen*:—Þīn āgen geleáfa þē hæfþ gehǣledne, Blickl. Homl. 15, 26. Þurh þīne āgene gemeléste, Bt. 5, 1; Fox 10, 1. Gif ðæt þīne āgne (āgnan, Bod. MS.) welan wǣron, 7, 3; Fox 29, 17. (2) where the noun is qualified by an adjective:—For þīnum īdlan gilpe, Blickl. Homl. 31, 14. For þīnum gōdan willan . . . ða leán eallra þīnra gōdena weorca, Bt. 7, 3; Fox 22, 14–16. Þurh þīne æðelan hand, Hy. 7, 5. Ða mōd ðínra getreówra freónda . . . nimaþ hí heora men mid him and lǽtaþ þíne feáwan getreówan mid þé, 20; Fox 72, 14-17. (3) where a demonstrative pronoun is used with the noun:—Þes þín sunu, Lk. Skt. 15, 30. Þín se fægresta fæþm *that fairest bosom of thine*, Blickl. Homl. 7, 24. Sege mē hwæþer se þín wela swā deóre seó, Bt. 13; Fox 38, 6: Met. 20, 29. Āles þíne þa liófan gesceft, Hy. 8, 33: Ps. Th. 90, 7. Hí ðæt þín fægere hūs forbærndan, 73, 7. Ðæt wē ðæt yrfe þín herige, 105, 5. (4) used in the genitive where the personal pronoun might be expected:—On þínes silfes hand, Hy. 7, 83. Þurh þínes sylfes geweald, Exon. Th. 466, 26; Hö. 127. Þínre sylfre sunu, 21, 23; Cri. 339. Mid þínes ānes geþeahte *with the counsel of thee alone*, Bt. 33, 4; Fox 128, 19: Met. 20, 40. ¶ In poetry the pronoun may be separated from the words to which it belongs:—Blǽd is ārǽred geond wídwegas, wine mín Beówulf, þín ofer þeóda gehwylce, Beo. Th. 3414; B. 1705. Ðæt ic mǽgburge móste þínre rím miclian, Cd. Th. 134, 6; Gen. 2220. Gewít þū þínne eft waldend sēcan, 138, 16; Gen. 2292. II. used predicatively, *thine*:—Gilpan ðæt heora fægernes þín sié, Bt. 14, 1; Fox 40, 22. Nān ðara gōda þín nis, 14, 2; Fox 42, 29. Ealle míne þing synt þíne (ðíno, Lind.), Lk. Skt. 15, 31. Hig wǽron þíne (ðíno, Lind.), Jn. Skt. 17, 6. III. used substantively, *thine*:—Nis sceat ðæs ic þínes āhredde *not a penny of what I saved of thine*, Cd. Th. 129, 16; Gen. 2144. Ðonne þū and þíne beóþ ālýsde *when thou and thine are released*, Lchdm. i. 328, 25. Þū ðās werðeóde gesōhtest þíne þearfende (*thy men being in need* (?); v. þigen, II), Cd. Th. 149, 25; Gen. 2480. Ealle míne synt þíne, and þíne (ðíno, Lind.) synt míne, Jn. Skt. 17, 10. [*Goth.* þeins: *O. L. Ger. O. Frs.* thín: *O. H. Ger.* dín: *Icel.* þinn.]

þínan; *p.* þān; *pp.* þinen *To get moist* or *damp*:—Dō on næsc, hæbbe him on, ðý læs hit þíne, Lchdm. ii. 36, 8. v. of-þinen; þǽnan.

þincan, þind. v. þyncan, ge-þind.

þindan; *p.* þand; *pp.* þunden. I. *to swell up*:—Þindeþ him se milt *his milt swells up*, Lchdm. ii. 232, 11. Þint sió lifer, 198, 23. Gif innoþ þinde, i. 354, 1. Þindan, Exon. Th. 431, 17; Rä. 46, 2. Se streám ongan tō þindenne ongeán swilce hit wǽre ān heáh dūn (*ad instar montis intumescentes*), Jos. 3, 16. Hit biþ þindende, Lchdm. ii. 210, 22. Gif ómihte blōd and yfel wǽte on ðam milte sié þindende, þonne sceal him mon blōd lǽtan, 252, 25: 168, 11. II. figurative, *to swell with indignation, pride*, etc.:—Synful yrsaþ, tōþum torn þolaþ, þearle þindeþ (in this and the next passage the Latin verb is *tabescere*, but *tumescere* seems in each case to have been read), Ps. Th. 111, 9. Ic þand (*I was angry*) wið ðan ðe hí teala noldan þínre sprǽce spēd gehealdan, Ps. Th. 118, 158. Ðindende weleras *labia tumentia*, Kent. Gl. 1002. v. ā-, tō-þindan; for-þunden; ge-þind.

þinen. v. þignen.

þing, es; *n.* I. *a thing*, (1) *a single object*, material or immaterial:—Hweðer ðū wēne ðæt ǽnig ðing on ðisse worulde swā gōd sié, Bt. 34, 1; Fox 134, 6. Ðonne ða fíf þing ealle gegadorade beóþ, ðonne beóþ hit eall ān ðing, and ðæt ān þing biþ God, 33, 2; Fox 122, 18. Ðæt ilce ðū miht geþencan be ǽlcum ðinge, ðæt nān þing ne biþ swelce hit wæs, siþþan hit wanian onginþ, 34, 9; Fox 148, 9: Met. 20, 37. Ǽghwilc þing ðe on ðís andweardan lífe lícaþ, 21, 28. Ǽlc þing ðe líf hæfde, Gen. 7, 22. Ic seah sellíc þing singan, Exon. Th. 413, 10; Rä. 32, 3. Hefon and eorþe and sǽ and ealle ða þing ðe on ðǽm syndon, Blickl. Homl. 91, 21. Ðinga scæpend *rerum creator*, Rtl. 180, 9. Wē āgyltaþ þurh feówer þing, þurh geþōht and þurh word and þurh weorc and þurh willan, Blickl. Homl. 35, 14. (1 a) of particular classes of objects, (*a*) *a thing* of value, *property*, *a thing* for sale; generally in pl., *things, goods*:—Him eallum wæs gemǽne heora ðing, Homl. Th. i. 316, 9. Nān man nān þing ne bycge ofer feówer peninga weorð ne libbende ne licgende, L. C. S. 24; Th. i. 390, 2. Breng ðing *offer munus*, Mt. Kmbl. Lind. 8, 4. Him eallum wǽron heora ðing gemǽne, Homl. Th. ii. 506, 18. 'Būton ðū mē sylle sum ðínra þinga' . . . se apostol cwæð: 'Hafa mínne stæf,' 416, 34. Hū Wulfgyð gean hire þinga æfter hire fordsíðe, Chart. Th. 563, 3. Ðingum *muneribus*, Mt. Kmbl. p. 14, 2: Lk. Skt. Lind. 21, 4. Ða teóþan sceattas ge on lande ge on ōþrum þingum ge on ōþrum gestreónum, Blickl. Homl. 51, 8. Hié mid miclum þingum hāmweard fōran *ingentem praedam ad classem devexerunt*, Ors. 4, 6; Swt. 176, 27. Ðe ealle his þing bewiste *qui praeerat omnibus quae habebat*, Gen. 24, 2. Ðinga ł geafa *munera*, Mt. Kmbl. Lind. 2, 11. Ða felarícan brōhton micele ðing, Homl. Th. i. 582, 14. Hē hæfde ǽr his ðing þearfum gedǽlede, ii. 500, 24. Hē becwæð his ðincg, Homl. Skt. i. 19, 211: 18, 414: 9, 41. Hē on swilce weorc āspende his ðing, ii. 31, 68. Wilt ðū syllan þingc ðíne? Coll. Monast. Th. 27, 15. (*β*) *a thing* to eat:—Eal ða wǽtan þing, and ða smerewigan, and eal swēte þing, Lchdm. ii. 210, 27. Mid wyrmendum þingum swilc swā pipor, 62, 2: 82, 4, 15. (2) *a thing* that is done, *an action, a proceeding, way* of conduct:—Ān þing ðē is wana (*one thing remains for you to do*); gesyle eall ðæt ðū āge, Mk. Skt. 10, 21. Plyhtlíc þingc hit ys gefōn hwæl, Coll. Monast. Th. 24, 21. Hē on axan and on duste licge: gif ic eów ōþres ðinges bysene onstelle ðonne āgylte ic, Blickl. Homl. 227, 15. Wes ðū gemyndig Marian þinga *be mindful of Mary's conduct*, 67, 33. Ǽfter þissum þingum hyra fæderas dydon ðām wītegum *in these ways their fathers treated the prophets*, Lk. Skt. 6, 23. Tō morgen dēð Drihten ðās þing, Ex. 9, 5: Mk. Skt. 11, 33: 7, 8: Ps. Th. 28, 4. Ealle ða þing ðe wē ofor his bebod gedydon, Blickl. Homl. 91, 16: 131, 33. (3) *a thing* that happens, *an event, what takes place*:—Nǽnges þinges nāre þearf nǽre ðonne his unriht yppe wurde *nothing better could happen than that his wickedness should become manifest*, Blickl. Homl. 175, 9. Þās þing ealle geweorþan sceoldan, 109, 8: Homl. Th. ii. 538, 3. Ðara þinga (ðingana, Lind., Rush.) race ðe on ūs gefyllede synt, Lk. Skt. 1, 1. Ǽfter þeossum þingum, Blickl. Homl. 95, 11. (4) where the word has much the same force as a cognate accusative, or where the meaning of the indefinite *þing* is determined by a verb:—Hē hine ǽlces þinges geclǽnsode ðe him mann on sǽde *he cleared himself of every charge that was brought against him*, Chr. 1022; Erl. 161, 37. Hū manigfeald þing Drihten geþrowode *what manifold suffering the Lord endured*, Blickl. Homl. 91, 11. Ic sceal þinga gehwylc þolian, Exon. Th. 270, 15; Jul. 465. Hine betellan æt ǽlc ðæra þinga þe him man on lēde, Chr. 1048; Erl. 180, 12. Ealle ða þing ðe hālige men writon, Blickl. Homl. 133, 1. (5) *a thing, circumstance*; in combination with an adjective nearly the same as the neuter of the adjective used as substantive, or as an abstract noun formed from the adjective:—Is ðæt earmlíc þing, ðæt his gebīdan ne magon burgsittende, Met. 27, 16: 28, 53. Þreálíc þing, rēðe wíte, Cd. Th. 79, 28; Gen. 1318. Ǽfter sōðum ðincge *according to the truth*, Homl. Th. ii. 230, 14. Swā hit āgǽð mid sōðum ðincge *as it actually happens*, Homl. Skt. i. 17, 109. Wundorlíc ðingc, Lchdm. i. 112, 13. Manegu dígln ðing sindon tō smeágeanne, Past. 21; Swt. 153, 13. On ðǽm sēlran þingum and on ðǽm gesundrum *in secundis rebus*, Nar. 7, 26. Næs nō on gesundum þingum ānum ac eác swylce on wiðearweardum þingum *not only in prosperity but also in adversity*, Blickl. Homl. 13, 7: 35, 33: Exon. Th. 337, 1; Gn. Ex. 58. Tō ēcum ðingum *to eternity*, Homl. Th. i. 16, 18: 616, 21: 568, 25. Tō sōþan þingon *truly*, Homl. Skt. i. 23, 736. Mid unrihtum þingum *per fraudem*, L. Ecg. P. ii. c. 13; Th. ii. 180, 23. Be fullum ðingum *fully*, Wulfst. 51, 11: 57, 8. (6) *state, condition*:—Ealles folces þing byþ ðe betere æt ðām þýfðum *the condition of the whole people will be the better in the matter of the thefts*, L. Ath. v. 8, 9; Th. i. 238, 20. Sēna hine gelōme; his þing biþ sōna sēlre, Lchdm. ii. 344, 19: Exon. Th. 378, 1; Deór. 9. Tō hwan ðínre sāwle þing (sið, Exon. Th. 368, 11) siððan wurde, Soul Kmbl. 39; Seel. 20. Cýð hwæt ðū ðæs tō þinge þafian wille *declare to which (life or death) thou wilt assent as thy condition*, Elen. Kmbl. 1212; El. 608. (7) *a thing, matter, subject* of consideration or enquiry:—Ānes þinges ic ðē wolde ācsian, Bt. 34, 1; Fox 134, 5: Blickl. Homl. 117, 20. Uton ðās þing geþencean, 97, 1. (8) *concern, affair*:—Hē þearfendra þinga teolode *he attended to the concerns of the needy*, Ps. Th. 108, 30. Sió geornfulnes eorðlícra ðinga *terrena studia*, Past. 18; Swt. 128, 15. Hē mínre geðylde þingum wealdeþ *ab ipso est patientia mea*, 61, 5. On menniscum ðingum *in human affairs*, Blickl. Homl. 213, 6. Hē wolde beón embe his þincg, Homl. Skt. i. 6, 120. (9) *a cause, sake, account, reason*; in the phrase *for . . . þingum*:—Þinge *causam*, Wrt. Voc. ii. 20, 12. For hwylcum þinge *ob quam causam*, Lk. Skt. 8, 47. For ǽnegum þinge *quacumque ex causa*, Mt. Kmbl. 19, 3. Āris tō mínum þinge (*in causam meam*), Ps. Th. 34, 22. For hira þinge *because of them*, Deut. 28, 34. For ðan miceles blōdes þinge, Lchdm. iii. 140, 30. For feós þinge *pecuniae causa*, L. Ecg. P. addit. 20; Th. ii. 234. 30. Būton forlegennysse þingum *excepta fornicationis causa*, Mt. Kmbl. 5, 32. For þisum þingum *igitur*, Bt. 26, 2; Fox 92, 19. For ðām þingum *for those reasons*, Homl. Skt. ii. 23 b, 12. For þrím þingum Hǽlend eode on wēsten, Blickl. Homl. 29, 19. For monigra monna ðingum, Past. 5; Swt. 41, 22: Ps. Th. 50, arg. For mínes wífes þingon *propter uxorem meam*, Gen. 20, 11: 43, 30. For Iōsefes þingon, 39, 5: Homl. Skt. i. 23, 304. For his sceatta ðingon *for the sake of his money*, Basil admn. 9; Norm. 52, 29. For ðæs āðes þingum *propter juramentum*, L. Ecg. P. ii. 29; Th. ii. 194, 12. For mínon þingon, for eówrum þingon *propter me, propter vos*, Jn. Skt. 12, 30: 11, 15. For mínum ðingum, Bt. 7, 3; Fox 20, 3. For ðínum þingum, 7, 2; Fox 18, 28. Þurh þon þingum ðū eart eádig on ēcnesse, Nar. 46, 23. Incan *vel* þing *causas, res*, Wrt. Voc. ii. 130, 12. (10) *an object, a purpose*:—Gode wē cyrican betǽcaþ tō ðām þingum, ðæt cristene men ðǽrtō faran magan and ðǽr heora neóda tō Gode mǽnan and synna forgifenesse biddan, Wulfst. 278, 19. Hē wearð man geboren tō ðām þingum, ðæt hē mid his āgenum feore mancynn ālýsde of deófles gewealde and of helle wíte, 16, 11. Þingum *purposely*, Exon. Th. 472, 10; Rä. 61, 14. (11) *a relation, respect*:—Hē ðone welegan wædlum efnmǽrne gedēð ǽlces þinges *in every respect*, Met. 10, 32, 50. Unmǽle ǽlces þinges, Exon. 21, 12; Cri. 333. Ne wēne hē nānes ðinges hine selfne beteran, Past. 17; Swt. 107, 16. Sōð hí sǽdon sumera ðinga (*in some respects*), Homl. Th. i. 190, 16: 236, 11. Ðæt ic ðē geþeó þinga gehwylce, Hy. 4, 12. God hine gebletsode on eallum þingum, Gen. 24, 1. Wæs heó on eallum þingum þe eáþmōddre, Blickl. Homl. 13, 3. On ǽnigum þingum cræftig, 49, 28. On eallum ðingum gehýrsum, Bd. 2, 12; S. 514, 17. (12) *a condition*:—Hié bǽdon friðes, ac hit Scipia nolde him āliéfan wið nānum ōþrum þinge būtan hié him ealle hiera wǽpeno āgeáfen, Ors. 4, 13; Swt. 210, 20. (13) *a way, means, wise*; mostly in phrases, every *way*, by no *means*, in any *wise*, etc.:—Ðæt đæt nǽnig đing ne gedafenade *quia nulla ratione conveniat*, Bd. 2, 12; S. 514, 38. Ne mihte hine nān man þurh ǽnig þing (*by any means*) āteón, Homl. Skt. i. 4, 194. Gif gē mīne lima þurh ǽnig þing gehǽlan magon, 5, 198: Wulfst. 49, 7. Þurh ǽlc þing *by all means*, L. I. P. 2; Th. ii. 304, 13. Oeghwelce đinga *omni modo*, Wrt. Voc. ii. 115, 50. Đā wolde hē ǽlce þinga đæt gyld ābrecan, Blickl. Homl. 221, 21. Hwæđer wēn wǽre đæt wē ǽnige đinga furþon đæt eálond gesēcean mihte *si forte insulam aliquo conamine repetere possemus*, Bd. 5, 1; S. 613, 29. Ne hī his bēnum ǽnige đinga geþafigean woldan *nor would they in any wise assent to his prayers*, 2, 1; S. 502, 14. Ne magon gē ǽnige đinga līfes hlāfe onfōn *nullatenus valetis panem vitae percipere*, 2, 5; S. 507, 20: Beo. Th. 4738; B. 2374: Homl. Skt. ii. 23 b, 721. Ðæt hē nāne đinga đæt ryht tō suīđe ne bodige *ut ne recta quidem nimie proferantur*, Past. 15; Swt. 95, 17. Hē nāne þinga beór ne drince, Lchdm. ii. 88, 11. Nǽnig þinga, L. E. I. 21; Th. ii. 406, 21. Nǽnige đinga *nequaquam*, Bd. 2, 5; S. 507, 23: 5, 6; S. 619, 8: *nullatenus*, 1, 27; S. 495, 20. Hié nǽnige þinga ongeán lōcian ne mihton, Blickl. Homl. 203, 10: Homl. Skt. ii. 23 b, 12: Met. 10, 16. Mid nānum đingum *by no means*, Past. 21; Swt. 167, 24. Mid đām þingum *by those means*, Lchdm. ii. 208, 26. Ōđero đingo *alioquin*, Lk. Skt. Lind. 14, 32. (14) *thing*, as in some*thing*, any*thing*, etc.:—Nān þing grēnes *nihil virens*, Ex. 10, 15. Gē ne biddaþ mē nānes þinges *me non rogabitis quicquam*, Jn. Skt. 16, 23. Mid ǽnige þinge *in aliquo*, Chart. Th. 422, 28. Ge on mete, ge on hrægle, ge on ǽghwylcum þinge, Blickl. Homl. 219, 30. Nyste ic nān þing þises *I knew nothing of this*, Gen. 21, 26: Lk. Skt. 9, 36: Mt. Kmbl. 26, 72. Styrigendlīces nān þincg findan, Homl. Skt. ii. 23 b, 735. Sum đing miccles gebīcnodon đa tungelwītegan Homl. Th. i. 118, 20: ii. 24, 19. Hæfđ se mann ealra gesceafta sum đing, i. 302, 19. Canst đū ǽnig þing *scis tu aliquid?* Coll. Monast. Th. 20, 37. Beó đæt þinga đæt hit beó *be it what it may*, Btwk. 222, 8. Hūru þinga *praesertim*, Ælfc. Gr. 38; Zup. 238, 6. Ǽrost þinga *first of all*, Wulfst. 32, 9: L. I. P. 10; Th. ii. 316, 11. Raþost þinga *at the earliest*, L. C. S. 24; Th. i. 390, 14. II. *a meeting, court*:—An medle oþþe an þinge, L. H. E. 8; Th. i. 30, 12. Hē Freán gesihđ faran tō þinge (*the meeting held at the day of judgement*), Exon. Th. 57, 32; Cri. 927. Þing gehēgan *to hold a meeting*, Andr. Kmbl. 314; An. 157: 1859; An. 932. Þing sceal gehēgan frōd wiþ frōdne, biþ hyra ferđ gelīc, Exon. Th. 334, 19; Gn. Ex. 18. Ic wiđ Grendel sceal āna gehēgan đing, Beo. Th. 856; B. 426. [*O. Sax.* thing *res*; thing-hūs *court-house*: *O. Frs.* thing *res*; *meeting, court*: *O. H. Ger.* ding *res, substantia, negotium*; *concio, conventus, concilium*: *Icel.* þing; *pl. things, articles*; þing *an assembly, meeting*; *Norweg.* stor-thing *parliament*.] v. breóst-, brȳd-, cīpe-(cȳpe-), cyric-, ge-, woruld-þing.

þingan; *p.* de *To invite, address*:—Hē him thinget *invitat se*, Wrt. Voc. ii. 49, 39. Þinge *interpella*, Hymn. Surt. 127, 14. [Cf. *O. H. Ger.* dingen; *p.* dingta *conducere, convenire*; gi-dingen *appellare*.] v. ge-þingan; un-þinged.

þingere, es; *m.* I. *an advocate, intercessor*:—Þingere *advocatus*, Wrt. Voc. ii. 99, 39. Ðingere, 4, 48: *interventor*, Rtl. 79, 36. Beón đingere for ōđerra scylde *intercessor fieri pro culpis aliorum*, Past. 10; Swt. 63, 20. Ðæs wordes (*Paraclete*) andgit is swā mon cweþe þingere, Blickl. Homl. 135, 33. Ðæt heó ūs sȳ milde þingere wiđ ūrne Drihten, 159, 33. Ic beó eówer þyngere tō Gode, Shrn. 155, 2: Homl. Ass. 137, 701. Mid đa gife his đingeres *gratia suo intercessori*, Bd. 4, 29; S. 608, 3. Mid þingere *cum advocato*, Wrt. Voc. ii. 79, 56: *advocato, interpellatore*, Hpt. Gl. 466, 72. Hī noldon nǽnne þingere sēcan *defensorum operam repudiarent*, Bt. 38, 7; Fox 210, 13. Ða þingeras (*oratores*) þingiaþ nū đǽm đe læssan þearfe āhton, Fox 208, 25. Þingeras wiđ Drihten, Cod. Dip. Kmbl. i. 114, 18: Wulfst. 240, 10. II. *a priest*, who in his office intercedes for the people. v. þingian, I a:—Preóst *vel* þingere *clericus*, Wrt. Voc. i. 42, 24. [*O. Frs.* thingere: *O. H. Ger.* dingari *advocatus*.] v. cyrc-, fore-, ge-þingere.

þingestre, an; *f. A female advocate*:—Ðæt heó ūs beó þingestre tō đam heofenlīce mægenđrymme, Homl. Ass. 137, 698.

þing-gemearc, es; *n. Measuring* (*time*) *by events* (? cf. other compounds of *gemearc*, e. g. *fōt-, geár-gemearc*, where the first part determines the character of the measurement, measurement by feet, by years; in the case of almost all such compounds it is an (adverbial) genitive that is found):—Đā wæs āgangen tū hund and þreó geteled rīmes swylce þrittig eác þinggemearces wintra *measuring by the events that had happened two hundred and thirty-three years would be counted as past, things had been going on for two hundred and thirty-three years*, Elen. Kmbl. 6; El. 3. Đā wæs first āgān þinggemearces būtan þrīm nihtum *things had gone on till there remained only three days of the allotted time*, Andr. Kmbl. 295; An. 148.

þingian; *p.* ode. I. *to intercede, ask favour, supplicate, plead, intervene*, (1) absolute:—Đǽr Satanus þingaþ, Cd. Th. 292, 28; Sat. 447. (2) *to intercede* for a person (*dat. or* for *with dat. or acc.*):—Ic for mīnes Godes hūse þingie, Ps. Th. 121, 9. Đa þingeras þingiaþ đæm đe læssan þearfe āhton; þingiaþ đǽm đe man yflaþ, and ne þingiaþ đām đe đæt yfel dōþ *oratores pro his, qui grave quid perpessi sunt, miserationem judicum excitare conantur*, Bt. 38, 7; Fox 208, 26. Ic (*Christ*) eów þingade, đā mē on beáme beornas sticedon, Cd. Th. 296, 29; Sat. 509. Him (*himself*) đingode David, and tō Drihtne gebæd, Ps. C. 26: Elen. Kmbl. 985; El. 494. Gif hē wyle him sylfum þingian *si pro seipso supplicare velit*, L. Ecg. P. iv. 62; Th. ii. 222, 25. Hwæđer hīs māgas him fore þingian willon *num amici ejus pro eo intervenire vellent*, L. Ecg. P. addit. 29; Th. ii. 236, 32. (3) *to ask* for (*for* with acc.) a person that some favour may be granted (*clause*):—Ðæt hē sceolde for hī đingian (*supplicatu obtineret*) đæt hī ne đorftan fēran, Bd. 1, 23; S. 485, 36. (4) *to intercede, plead* before a person:—Þinga for đeódne ǽr đam seó þrāh cyme, đæt hē đec āworpe of woruldrīce, Cd. Th. 252, 33; Dan. 588. (5) *to intercede* for a person (*dat. or* for *with dat. or acc.*) to or with another (*tō, mid, wiđ*):—Đā spæc ic him fore and þingade him tō Ælfrēde cinge. Đā lȳfde hē đæt hē mōste beón ryhtes wyrđe for mīnre forspǽce, Chart. Th. 169, 30. Wǽre þearf đæt him mon þyngode tō đam rīcum, Bt. 38, 7; Fox 208, 29. Se đe bitt đone monn đæt him đingie wiđ ōđerne đe hē biþ eác ierre *cum is, qui displicet, ad intercedendum mittitur*, Past. 10; Swt. 63, 12. Hū mæg ǽnig man tō his hlāforde ōđrum þingian, gif hē his hlāforde sylf hæfđ ābolgen, L. I. P. 21; Th. ii. 332, 5. Earmum đingian tō đam rīcan, Homl. Th. ii. 558, 2. Tō đingienne þiódum sīnum wiđ đane Sceppend, Ps. C. 7. (6) *to make intercession* to (*tō*) a person that something may be granted (*clause*):—Þingode Dauid tō Dryhtne, đæt . . ., Ps. C. 146. I a. referring to intercession to the Deity. v. þingere, II:—Ða đe on heofenum syndon, hī þingiaþ for đa đe đyssum sange fylgeaþ, Blickl. Homl. 45, 36. Swā oft swā hig clypiaþ tō Criste, and for folces neóde þingiaþ, L. C. E. 4; Th. i. 362, 4. Ic for đē þingode, Homl. Skt. i. 5, 416. Būton sum hālga mē þingie tō đam Hǽlende, ii. 26, 255. Ðingige, Homl. Th. ii. 518, 34. Hē cleopie tō Godes hālgum, and bidde đæt hig him tō Gode þingien, L. E. I. 23; Th. ii. 420, 10. Hū dearr hē đingian ōđrum monnum, and nāt hwǽđer him selfum geđingod biđ *quomodo aliis veniam postulat qui, utrum sibi sit placatus, ignorat?* Past. 10; Swt. 63, 9: Homl. Th. ii. 388, 4: 528, 15: i. 174, 10: L. I. P. 21; Th. ii. 332, 6. For heora campwered gebiddan and tō Gode đingian *ad exorandum Deum pro milite*, Bd. 2, 2; S. 503, 40. For hine đingian and for sibbe his đeóde *ad supplicandum pro pace gentis ejus*, 3, 24; S. 556, 43. Ðæt hī for mīnum untrumnessum đingian mid đa upplīcan ārfæstnesse *ut pro meis infirmitatibus apud supernam clementiam intervenire meminerint*, pref.; S. 472, 35. II. *to make terms, settle*, (1) absolute:—Āge hē þreora nihta fierst him tō gebeorganne, būton hē þingian wille, L. Alf. pol. 2; Th. i. 62, 2. (2) *to settle* a dispute:—Siđđan ic đa fǽhđe feó þingode, Beo. Th. 945; B. 470. Feorhbealo feó þingian, 315; B. 156. (3) *to settle* the terms of an agreement, *to agree* that . . .:—Būton hiora hwæđer ǽr þingode đæt hē hit āngylde healdan ne þorfte, L. Alf. pol. 19; Th. i. 74, 11. (4) *to settle* with (*wiđ*) a person, *to come to terms, be reconciled*. v. (6):—Heom man raþe đæs wiđ þingode *soon after people came to terms with them*, Chr. 1001; Erl. 136, 32. Hē sceal þingian wiđ đone đe hē ābylgþ *debet reconciliari ei quem offendebat*, L. Ecg. P. addit. 19; Th. ii. 234, 27. (5) *to make terms* for:—Be đǽm đe for ordāle đingiaþ. Gif hwā þingie for ordāl, þingie on đam ceápgilde, and nāht on đam wīte, L. Ath. i. 21; Th. i. 210, 15. Weorpe đæt neát tō honda oþþe fore þingie *let the beast be handed over, or terms settled for it*, L. Alf. pol. 24; Th. i. 78, 10. (6) *to make terms* for a person (*dat. or* for) with (*wiđ*) another, *to reconcile*. v. (4):—Gif gesīđcund mon þingaþ wiđ cyning for his inhīwan, ođđe wiđ his hlāford for þeówe, L. In. 50; Th. i. 134, 2. Þinga þē wiđ God *concilia tibi Deum*, L. Ecg. P. iv. 66; Th. ii. 226, 17. Ðæt wē ūs beþencan and wiđ God sylfne þingian, Wulfst. 166, 35. (6 a) where the person with whom is not stated:—Ne sié him nō đȳ þingodre *none the more shall the case be settled for him*, L. In. 22; Th. i. 116, 12. III. *to settle* to do something, *to determine*. v. ge-þingan, geþingian, II:—Hū hē him on đās world þingian ongan *how he settled for himself to come into this world*, Blickl. Homl. 105, 8. IV. *to speak, discourse*:—Đē đa wordcwydas wittig Drihten on sefan sende; ne hȳrde ic snotorlīcor, on swā geongum feore, guman þingian, Beo. Th. 3691; B. 1843. IV a. *with* geán, ongeán, wiđ, *to address, accost*. v. þingan:—Him brego engla geán þingade, Cd. Th. 62, 5; Gen. 1009. Iudas hire ongēn þingode, Elen. Kmbl. 1214; El. 609: 1330; El. 667: Exon. Th. 116, 20; Gū. 210. Hyre se wræcmæcga wiđ þingade, 258, 5; Jul. 260: 268, 9; Jul. 429: Andr. Kmbl. 612; An. 306: 1264; An. 632: Elen. Kmbl. 154; El. 77. [Do we mid ure weldede þingen us wiđ ure helende, O. E. Homl. ii. 43, 30. To þingenn uss wiþþ ure Godd, Orm. 8997. *O. Sax.* thingōn: Hie gēng im wiđ thena heritogon mahlian, thingōn wiđ thena thegan kēsures, Hēl. 5725. *O. Frs.* thingia *placitare*: *O. H. Ger.* dingōn *concionare, judicare, disceptare, pacisci*: *Ger.* dingen *to bargain for, agree on*: *Icel.* þinga *to hold a meeting; to consult about, discuss*.] v. for-, fore-, ge-, ōþ-þingian.

þingiend. v. fore-þingiend.

þing-leás; *adj. Exempt*:—Unscyldigo and đingleáso from đissum synne *innocentes et immunis ab hoc crimine*, Rtl. 114, 7. [*O. Frs.* thing-lōs.]

þing-rǽden[n], e; *f. Intercession, advocacy, pleading, intervention, mediation,* (1) in a general sense:—Ða apostoli hí ástrehton æt ðæs ealdormannes fótum, biddende ðæt ða hǽðengildan nǽron for heora intingan ácwealde ... Ðá cwæð se ealdorman: 'Wundor mē ðincþ eówer ðingrǽden,' Homl. Th. ii. 484, 14. God heora synne ðurh his (*Job's*) ðingrǽdene forgeaf, 458, 4: 292, 1. Gif ðú geþafian nelt þingrǽdenne (*pleading on behalf of a lover*), Exon. Th. 250, 13; Jul. 126. (2) of intercession to the Deity. v. þingian, I a:—Mid ðínre (*Stephen's*) þingrǽdene *tuo interventu*, Hymn. Surt. 46, 24. Þissere for þingrǽdene *hujus obtentu*, 139, 27. Þurh his hálgena þingrǽdene, Chart. Erl. 231, 28. Þurh his móder ðingrǽdene, Homl. Th. i. 450, 26. Þa þingrǽdene for ðam folce, ii. 536, 11. Mid ðínum (*St. Andrew's*) þingrǽdenum *tuis intercessionibus*, Hymn. Surt. 126, 8. Þurh heora menigfealdan þingrǽdena, Homl. Th. i. 556, 19. v. fore-þingrǽden.

þing-stede, es; *m. A place where a meeting* (v. þing, II) *is held*:—On ðam þingstede (*in the place to which Christ had summoned his disciples to speak with them for the last time.* Cf. tó Bethania þeóden his þegna gedryht gelaðade; hý ðæs láreówes word ne gehyrwdon, hyra sincgiefan, 29, 2-9; Cri. 456), Exon. Th. 31, 17; Cri. 497. Ic gefrægn leóde tósomne bannan ... Ðá wæs tó ðam þingstede þeód gesamnod, Andr. Kmbl. 2197; An. 1100. [An that hús innan, thár Pilatus was an thero thingstedi, Hél. 5307. *O. H. Ger.* ding-stat *forum, conciliabulum*: *Icel.* þing-staðr *place where a* þing *is held.*] v. next word.

þing-stów, e; *f. A place of meeting, a public place*:—*Compitum*, i. *villa vel* þingstów *vel* þrop, Wrt. Voc. ii. 132, 55. In sprec[stów] ꝉ in ðingstów *in foro*, Mt. Kmbl. Lind. 20, 3. From ðingstówe (-stów, Lind.) *a foro*, Mk. Skt. Rush. 7, 4. v. geþing-stów, *and preceding word.*

þingung, e; *f. Intercession, intervention, mediation*:—Þingunge *interventu*, Wrt. Voc. ii. 111, 28: 48, 76. Hí on friþe wunedon þurh ðære cwēne þingunge, Homl. Ass. 101, 313. ¶ Especially intercession to the Deity:—Ðæt ic mid eallum ðone wæstm árfæstre ðingunge gemēte *ut apud omnes fructum piae intercessionis inveniam*, Bd. pref.; S. 472, 39. Hē ðære eádigan Marian fultumes and ðingunge bæd, Homl. Th. i. 448, 19. Gif wē for synfullum mannum gebiddaþ and hí ðære ðingunge unwurðe synd, ii. 528, 12. Biddaþ eów þingunge æt ðysum martyrum, i. 88, 33: ii. 110, 30. Eádges Iōhannes ðincgunge (*intercessione*), Rtl. 46, 30: 51, 16. Ús tó þingunge, Chart. Th. 240, 24. Ðurh ða bróþorlícan ðingunge *per intercessionem fraternam*, Bd. 4, 22; S. 592, 22: 5, 19; S. 640, 42: Homl. Th. i. 76, 22. Ðǽr nǽnige þingunga ne beóþ, Blickl. Homl. 95, 30. Wē biddaþ þingunga æt hálgum mannum, Homl. Th. i. 174, 9. Mid hira ðingengum, Past. 10; Swt. 63, 15. Þurh bisceopes þingunga *ex episcopi interventu*, L. Ecg. P. i. c. ix; Th. ii. 170, 17. v. fore-, ge-þingung.

þinne, þió *a slave*, þió, *pron.* (Jn. Skt. Lind. Rush. 4, 5), þio-, þió-, þióen. v. þynne, þeów, se, þeo-, þeó-, þeówen.

þír *a female servant*:—Ðír ꝉ sió ðignen (ðír ꝉ ðegnen, Rush.) *ancilla*, Jn. Skt. Lind. 18, 17. [*The Scandinavian form* þýr?]

þirda, þirding, þirel, þirlian. v. þridda, þridding, þyrel, þyrlian.

þirran, þierran *to dry, wipe.* [*O. H. Ger.* derren *torrere, exsiccare*; ar-derren *arefacere*: *Icel.* þerra *to dry, wipe dry.* Cf. *Goth.* ga-þairsan *to wither.*] v. á-þierran.

þirsce-flōr *a threshing-floor*:—Hig cómon tó ðære þirscefló̄re *venerunt ad aream*, Gen. 50, 10. v. þerscel-flōr.

þirscwald, þis, þísl, þislíc. v. þerscold, þes, þíxl, þyslíc.

þistel, es; *m. A thistle*:—Þistel, thistil *cardu[u]s*, Txts. 47, 384. Ðystel, Wrt. Voc. i. 79, 56. Þistel *carduus*, 31, 53. Se onscunienda þystel *carduus orrens*, ii. 22, 43. Se unbráda þistel *scolimbos*, i. 69, 12. (Se unbráde thistel, Lchdm. iii. 305, col. 1. Brád thistle *erithius*, 302, col. 1.) Þúfe þistel *sow thistle*, Lchdm. ii. 312, 20. Genim ðæs scearpan þistles moran, 314, 11. Þistles blóstm *thistle-down*; pappus, Wrt. Voc. i. 32, 23. Þistlum *card[u]is*, ii. 128, 63. ¶ The word is found in compounds which are names of places. Þistel-beorh, Cod. Dip. B. iii. 396, 33: þistel-mere, Cod. Dip. Kmbl. iii. 82, 15: þistel-leáh, iv. 49, 2. [*O. H. Ger.* distil: *Icel.* þistill.] v. þú-, wudu-þistel.

þistel-geblǽd *a blister caused by the prick of a thistle*:—Wið þorngeblǽd, wið þys[tel]geblǽd, Lchdm. iii. 36, 22.

þistel-twige, an; *f. A goldfinch* or some other bird that eats thistledown. [In E. D. S. Pub. Bird Names, p. 58, *thistle-finch* is given as a name of the goldfinch: Halliwell quotes: '*Carduelis* a linnet, a thistlefinch' (1585). Cf. *O. H. Ger.* distil-finco *carduelis*: *Ger.* distel-fink *a linnet*: *O. H. Ger.* distil-ziu *carduelus*]:—Þisteltuige, distiltige *cardella*, Txts. 47, 381. Þisteltwige, Wrt. Voc. i. 281, 19.

þistra, þrístra *a trace* (?), *part of an animal's harness*:—Þístra *conjuncta*, Wrt. Voc. ii. 136, 34. Þrístra, i. 16, 9. [*For similar double form* cf. þeóstru, *for meaning* cf. (?) *Goth.* þinsan: *O. H. Ger.* dinsan *trahere*: '*Bavarian* dünsel *a twisted withy or other thin branch, used to bind rafts of wood to the shore,*' Cod. Dip. Kmbl. iii. xlii; *and see Du Cange* coniuncta.]

þístru, þiú (Mt. 24, 15). v. þeóstru, se.

þiustra, Wrt. Voc. ii. 100, 18; *according to form the word might belong to* þeóstru, *but it glosses* ambulas, *the meaning of which, according to the dictionary, is* endive *or* chicory.

þíwan, þíwen, þíwracan. v. þeówan, þeówen, þeó[w]-wracu.

þíxl, þísl, e; þísle, an; *f.* I. *a beam* or *pole of a waggon*; temo: used, also, like *temo*, to denote a constellation, *the Bear*:—Wǽnes ðísl (wægne þíxl (wægnes?), 100, 72) *archtoes*, Wrt. Voc. ii. 7, 23. Þísl *temo* vel *arctoes*, i. 16, 24: *themon* (in a list 'de plaustris'), 284, 46. Þístle *temo* (*Wülcker prints* þísle *themon*, Gl. 295, 14), 66, 53. Díxl *arquamentum*, Txts. 109, 1147. Tunglu ðe wē hátaþ wǽnes ðísla, Bt. 39, 3; Fox 214, 19. Án ðara tungla woruldmen hátaþ wǽnes þísla, Met. 28, 10. Þíx[l]um, díxlum, díslum *temonibus*, Txts. 101, 2007. II. *a pole* (?):—Of ðære ác in ða heortsole; of ðære sole in ða þísle; of ðære þísle eft in ða mýðan, Cod. Dip. Kmbl. iii. 380, 6. [*O. L. Ger.* thísla; *f. wk. temo*: *Du.* dissel *axle-tree*; dissel-boom *beam* or *pole of a carriage*: *O. H. Ger.* díhsel, díhsila, dísala; *f. temo*: *Ger.* deichsel: *Icel.* þísl; *Swed.* tistel-stång *coach-pole.*]

þó, þóae. v. þóhe.

þocerian; *p.* ode *To run to and fro, run about*:—Þoceraþ *cursat, currit, cursitat*, Wrt. Voc. ii. 137, 53. Þocerodan (*vitae late praeconia*) *cursant*, 95, 19: 19, 65. Sitte him ðín mód on mínum hrædwǽne, þocrige him on mínne weg *mea semita, meis vehiculis revertaris*, Bt. 36, 1; Fox 174, 1. [Cf. *Icel.* þoka *to move.*]

þoddettan; *p.* te *To push, strike, batter*:—Ða deóflu þoddetton ða earme sáwle and hēton hý út faran of ðam líchaman, Wulfst. 235, 15. Þoddetton *pulsent*, Germ. 399, 264. v. þyddan.

þoden, es; *m. A violent wind, a whirlwind*; also, *a whirlpool*; turbo:—Þoden *alcanus* (l. *altanus*), Wrt. Voc. ii. 100, 3: *altanus*, i. 17, 34. Ðoden *turbo*, Ælfc. Gr. 9, 3; Zup. 37, 10. Þoden ða nán ne tócwíse oþþe worigende tówurpon windas *turbo quam nullus quatit aut vagantes diruunt venti*, Hymn. Surt. 142, 26. Cumendum swá þoden tó tóstæncanne mē *venientibus ut turbo ad dispergendum me*, Cant. Ab. 14. Ðonne sió geornfulnes eorðlícra ðinga ábisgaþ ðæt ondgit and áblent ðæs módes eágan mid ðære costunge ðæm folce, suǽ suǽ dust dēð ðæs líchoman eágan on sumera mid ðodene (ðodne, Hatt. MS.) *dum pastoris sensus terrena studia occupant, vento tentationis impulsus ecclesiae oculos pulvis caecat*, Past. 18; Swt. 128, 17. Hēr wǽron rēðe forebēcna cumen ofer Norðhymbra land ... ðæt wǽron ormēte þodenas and lígrescas, Chr. 793; Th. 101, 5, col. 1. Þurh ðæs windes blǽs, ðe swýðlíce ða heánnyssa ðæs roderes sceeð mid his þodenum, Anglia viii. 320, 34. Lageflódum þodenum *ceruleis turbinibus*, Wrt. Voc. ii. 130, 38. [Swa þode [þodde, 2nd MS.) on felde þenne he þat dust heȝe aȝiueð from þere eorðe, Laym. 27645.]

þóe. v. þóhe.

þoft (?), e; þofte, an; *f. A rower's bench*:—Scipsetl *transtra*, þofta (þoftan?) *trastra* vel *juga*, Wrt. Voc. i. 48, 15. Þoftan *transtra*, 56, 41: 63, 43. (All three occur in lists 'de navibus.') [*Du.* doft; *f. a rower's bench*: *Icel.* þopta; *wk. f. a rowing bench.* Halliwell gives *thoft-fellow* a fellow-oarsman.]

-þofta, -þoftian. v. ge-þofta [*Icel.* þopti *a bench-fellow*], ge-þoftian.

þoft-rǽden[n], e; *f. Fellowship*:—Ðú hopast ðæt ðú hæbbe ðoftrǽdene tó ðam áwyrigedan deófle, ðonne ðú bǽde ðæt hē ðē ásende his englas tó mínre dare, Homl. Th. ii. 416, 14. v. ge-þoftrǽden.

þoftscipe, es; *m. Fellowship*:—Sum bróðor ... se him wæs on gástlícum (-re, MS.) þoftscipe geþeóded, Guthl. 10; Gdwin. 52, 5: 14; Gdwin. 62, 2. v. ge-þoftscipe.

þóhe, þóe, þó; *gen.* þón; *f. Clay*:—Thóhae, thóae *argilla*, Txts. 36, 3. Ðó, Wrt. Voc. ii. 6, 16. Þóe *creta*, 136, 78. [*Goth.* þáhó πηλός: *O. H. Ger.* dáha *argilla, testa*: *Ger.* thon: *Icel.* þá *muddy ground.*] v. next word.

þóhiht, þóiht; *adj. Clayey*:—Ðóihte *argillosa*, Wrt. Voc. ii. 6, 15.

þóht, es; *m. Thought, mind*:—Pund gefe of ðon is ðóht monnes *pondus gratiae, inde est sensus hominis*, Rtl. 192, 23. Suǽ líchomes suǽ ðóhtes (*animae*) hǽlo, 99, 13. Háles ðóhtes *sane mentis*, Mk. Skt. Lind. 5, 15. Mid þóhtes wilnunga besmiten *desiderio cogitationis coinquinatus*, L. Ecg. C. 5; Th. ii. 138, 15. In alle ðóht ðínne *in tota mente tua*, Mt. Kmbl. Lind. 22, 37. In ðon ilco ðócht *in eundem sensum*, p. 9, 18. Unstaðolfæstnis ðóhta *instabilitas mentium*, Rtl. 192, 21. [*Icel.* þóttr, þótti.] v. ge-þóht.

þol. v. þoll.

þole-byrde; *adj. Bearing patiently, patient, long-suffering*:—Þolobyrde mann *patiens homo* ... Wer þolebyrde *vir patiens*, Scint. 13, 11, 13. [He beð þoleburde, O. E. Homl. ii. 79, 25.]

þolebyrdness, e; *f. Patience, long-suffering, endurance*:—Tó þolibyrdnysse þrowunga strange *ad tolerantiam passionum fortes*, Scint. 3, 8. [On giwer þoleburdnesse *in patientia vestra*, O. E. Homl. ii. 79, 9.]

þole-mód; *adj. Of a patient disposition, patient, long-suffering*:—Þolemód *longanimis*, Hpt. Gl. 437, 43. Heó wæs þolemód and gestæððig on hire gebǽran, and ne geseah hí nán man yrre, Homl. Ass. 127, 367. Þolemód on wiþerweardum þingum *patient in adversity*, R. Ben. 26, 18. His mon fandige hwæðer hē þolemód (þolo-, Wells Frag.) sý and geþyldig *probetur in omni patientia*, 99, 4. Þolomód *patiens*, Scint.

8, 12, 14. Ðæt se mann beó geðyldig and ðolomód (þol-, MSS. U. D.), Homl. Skt. i. 16, 335. Geðyldig and ðolmód, 17, 55. On ðære écan worulde, ðe gewelgaþ ða þolmódan, Homl. Th. ii. 456, 2. [Gordoille wes þolemod, Laym. 3141. Katerine wes þuldi & þolemod, Kath. 173. Þolemod is þe þet þuldeliche abereð wouh þet me deð him, A. R. 158, 4. Cf. *Icel.* þolin-móðr *patient: Dan.* taal-modig.]

þole-mód (?) *patience:—Patientia* ðæt is ðolmód, Homl. Skt. i. 16, 334, MS. D. [Habbe we edmodnesse and þolemod, O. E. Homl. i. 69, 266.] v. next word.

þolemódness, e; *f. Patience, long-suffering, endurance:—Patientia*, ðæt is geðyld and þolmódnys gecwæden, Homl. Skt. i. 16, 334. Se geþyldiga man mid his þolmódnysse his sáwle gehylt, ii. 28, 146. Ða getreówfullan ealle lífes wiðerweardnesse forþyldigian scylun, be hiora þolemódnesse (þolo-, MS. T.) is þus áwriten, R. Ben. 27, 8, 13. Wurðigan ða gódan þeáwas . . . geþyld and þolemódnysse, Guthl. 2; Gdwin. 18, 16. [Þolemodnesse and edmodnesse, of mild and meek heart, A. R. 158, 2. Þolemodnesse, H. M. 41, 10: Ayenb. 68, 4.]

þolian; *p.* ode *To thole* (still used in some dialects), *suffer, endure.* I. *to suffer* what is evil, punishment, reproach, illness, grief, etc.:—Hwílon forlidenesse ic þolie *aliquando naufragium patior*, Coll. Monast. Th. 27, 1. Þolige, Exon. Th. 499, 18; Rä. 88, 17. Hé þreánýd þolaþ, Beo. Th. 573; B. 284. Synfull tóþum torn þolaþ *peccator dentibus suis fremet*, Ps. Th. 111, 9. Þoliaþ wé þreá on helle, Cd. Th. 25, 5; Gen. 389. Hí hosp þoliaþ *contumeliam toleravit*, Hpt. Gl. 506, 25. Þú þoladest *ferres*, i. *sustinebas, contuleras*, Wrt. Voc. ii. 147, 55. Ðú þolades mægenearfeþu, Exon. Th. 86, 19; Cri. 1411. David his éhtnesse ðolade, Past. 28; Swt. 197, 17. Hé þeównýd þolode, Cd. Th. 122, 21; Gen. 2030. Hí bryne þolodon, Rood Kmbl. 296; Kr. 149. Ða ðe elþeódigra edwít þoledon, hæþenra hosp, Judth. Thw. 24, 30; Jud. 215. Þoledan and þrowedan *luebant*, Wrt. Voc. ii. 53, 19. Þéh ðú drype þolie, Andr. Kmbl. 1910; An. 957. Gif wíf ðone fléwsan ðæs wǽtan þoligen, Lchdm. i. 308, 2. Fela þinga þolian fram yldrum *multa pati a senioribus*, Mt. Kmbl. 16, 21. Þoligean, Lk. Skt. 24, 26. Ðæt micle morð þolian, Cd. Th. 40, 18; Gen. 641. Þeówdóm þolian, 135, 9; Gen. 2240. Hýnðo þolian, 198, 18; Exod. 324. Torn þolian, Beo. Th. 1669; B. 832. Wítu þolian, Andr. Kmbl. 2828; An. 1416. Ðæt ðam weligan wæs weorc tó þolianne, Exon. Th. 276, 21; Jul. 569. Hé lét, torn þoliende, teáras geótan, 165, 15; Gú. 1029. Syle ðam þoligendan ðicgean . . . ðú hine gelácnast wundorlíce, Lchdm. i. 220, 17: 17: 188, 1. Mid tóðon torn þoligende, Judth. Thw. 25, 21; Jud. 272. I a. *to suffer, undergo, submit to* discipline, treatment:—Se ðe ðysne lǽcedóm þolaþ, Lchdm. i. 300, 20. Ðæt wíf ðe on blódryne wæs fram manegum lǽcum fela þinga þolode, Mk. 5, 26. Tó ðolienne ðínne willan, Ps. C. 90. I b. of things which are used to do hard work:—Seó ecg geswác þeódne æt þearfe; þolode ǽr fela hondgemóta, Beo. Th. 3055; B. 1525. II. *to suffer* a person, *bear with, tolerate* a condition of things, *let come to pass:*—Swá lange swá ic mid eów beó, swá lange ic eów þolige (ðola, Lind.: ðolo, Rush.), Mk. Skt. 9, 19. Þolie (ðola, Lind.: ðolo, Rush.), Lk. Skt. 9, 41. Ðæt is micel wundor, ðæt hit God wolde þolian, ðæt wurde þegn swá monig forlǽdd, Cd. Th. 37, 29; Gen. 597. III. *to suffer lack* or *loss* of something (*gen.*), *to lose* what one has, *to fail to get* what one desires; in many cases the loss or failure is the result of wrong either done or suffered by the subject of the verb, *to forfeit, be* (*wrongfully*) *deprived of:*—Ic ðolige sumes ðinges *careo*, Ælfc. Gr. 26, 2; Zup. 154, 16. Ic ðolige mínes feós *careo mea pecunia*, ðoligende his þinges *carens sua re*, 41; Zup. 250, 11. Ðonne þolie ic ðus miceles ðæs ðe míne foregengan hæfdon *in that case I shall be* (*unfairly*) *deprived of thus much of what my predecessors had*, Cod. Dip. Kmbl. iii. 327, 16. Gif ðú Drihten forgitst, ðú ðolast ðære écan méde, Homl. Th. i. 140, 32. Ðolaþ *carebit* (*benedictione*), Prov. 20, 21. Gé þoliaþ ðæs ðe eów God behét for eówre ungehírsumnisse, Deut. i. 40. Hý (*evil spirits*) háma þoliaþ, Exon. Th. 115, 22; Gú. 193. Ic þolade gódes ealles, 457, 16; Hy. 4, 84. Hé férde swá swá his forcúða fæder, and his lífes ðolode and his lǽnan ríces, Homl. Skt. i. 18, 231. Hé (*Job*) hæfde his wíf, þeáh hé his bearna þolode, ii. 30, 204. Þolade *caruerit*, Wrt. Voc. ii. 23, 83. Ne forgit ðú deáð, ðý læs ðú þolie ðæs écan lífes, Prov. Kmbl. 17. Þeáh God wille hwam hys willan tó forlǽtan, and hé ðæs eft þolige, Ors. 1, 5; Swt. 34, 36. Þolige hé his wǽpna and his ierfes, L. Alf. pol. 1; Th. i. 60, 14: L. Edg. i. 4; Th. i. 264, 15. Þolie se þeówa his hýde oþþe hýdgyldes . . . þolie se frigea his freótes, L. In. 3; Th. i. 104, 4, 6. Þolige se déma, ðe ódrum wóh déme, á his þegenscipes, L. Edg. ii. 3; Th. i. 266, 17: Chart. Th. 606, 30: Homl. Th. ii. 94, 33. Hefonríces þolian, Cd. Th. 40, 3; Gen. 633: Exon. Th. 402, 8; Rä. 21, 26. Blind sceal his eágna þolian, 335, 28; Gn. Ex. 39. III a. with a preposition:—Þolige hé be healfre ðære bóte, L. Alf. pol. 11; Th. i. 68, 19. IV. *intrans. To hold out, exercise endurance, endure, not to give in:* of things, *to last, continue to be serviceable:*—Ic tó aldre sceal sæcce fremman, þenden ðis sweord þolaþ, Beo. Th. 4992; B. 2499. Gif mín (*an anchor's*) steort þolaþ *if my tail can stand the strain on it*, Exon. Th. 398, 16; Rä. 17, 8. G[esǽlig?] biþ ðæt, ðonne mon him sylf ne mæg wyrd onwendan, ðæt hé ðonne wel þolige, 459, 16; Hy. 4, 117. Æt ðearfe þolian, unwáclíce wǽpna neótan, Byrht. Th. 140, 53; By. 307: 137, 45; By. 201. [*Goth.* þulan *to tolerate, endure: O. Sax.* tholian, tholón (*trans. acc. and gen., and intrans.*) *to suffer, endure, lose, hold out: O. L. Ger.* tholón *pati, sustinere: O. Frs.* tholia: *O. H. Ger.* dolén, dolón *pati, sustinere, tolerare, luere: Icel.* þola; *p.* þolði.] v. á-, for-, ge-, mid-þolian.

þoligend, þoligendlíc, þolibyrdness. v. mid-þoligend, un-þoligendlíc, þolebyrdness.

þoll, es; *m. A thole* or *thowl, a peg in the side of a boat to keep the oar in place:*—Þoll *scalmus*, Wrt. Voc. i. 63, 79. Thol, ii. 120, 15. [Tholle, cartepynne *cavilla*, Prompt. Parv. 492. *Du.* dol *a thole: Icel.* þollr *a wooden peg*; esp. *the thole* of a row-boat: *Dan.* tol *a thole*; tolle-gang *a row-lock*.]

þolle, an; *f. A frying-pan:*—Hwer ł þollan *sartaginem*, Hpt. Gl. 503, 16. v. fýr-þolle.

þol-mód, þolo-byrde, þolo-mód, þon, þonan, þonc, þon-écan, þonne, þonon. v. þole-mód, þole-byrde, þole-mód, þan, þanan, þanc, þan-écan, þanne, þanan.

Thómas *Thomas:*—Thómas án of ðám twelfon, Jn. Skt. 20, 24. Þómas, 26. Ðómas, 28. Thómas geneðde, Apstls. Kmbl. 99; Ap. 50. Scē Thómas týd ðæs apostoles, Shrn. 155, 28. Nergend Thómase forgeaf éce ríce, Menol. Fox 444; Men. 223. Cf. Hé sǽde þómé (thómase, *later MS.*), Jn. Skt. 20, 27. Hé nýdde ðysne Thómam, ðæt hé weorðode sunnan deófolgild, Shrn. 156, 9: Mk. Skt. 3, 18.

þoot, Txts. 64, 444. v. wóþ.

Þór *the Scandinavian form of a name which in English is* Þunor (-er), *one of the gods, Thor:*—Nú secgaþ sume ða Denisce men on heora gedwylde, ðæt se Iouis wǽre, ðe hý Þór hátaþ, Mercuries sunu, ðe hí Óðon namiaþ; ac hí nabbaþ ná riht: for ðan ðe wé rǽdaþ on bócum, ge on hǽþenum ge on cristenum, ðæt se hetula Iouis tó sóðan is Saturnes sunu, Wulfst. 107, 8–13. Þór and Ówðen, ðe hǽðene men heriaþ swíðe, 197, 19. Fled (fleó?) þór (? þr̄, MS.) on fyrgen hæfde (fyrgenheáfde?), Lchdm. iii. 54, 17. v. Þunor.

þorch. v. þurh.

þorfa; *adj. Destitute, poor*; used as a substantive, *a needy person:*—Of ðorfum *de egenis*, Jn. Skt. Lind. 12, 6. [*Icel.* þurfi *or* þurfa *wanting, in need* of. Cf. *Goth.* ga-þaurbs *continens*.] Cf. þearfa.

þorfan; *p.* te *To need:*—Ne ðorfeþ (-æþ, Lind.) *non indiget*, Jn. Skt. Rush. 13, 10. Ne ðo[r]feþ ða ðe hálo sint tó léce *non egent qui sani sunt medico*, Lk. Skt. Lind. 5, 31. Cf. þearfan, *and see next word.*

þorfend, es; *m.*: þorfende; *adj.* (*ptcpl.*) *used substantively. A needy person, a poor person:*—Wæs sum ðærfe ł ðo[r]fond (*mendicus*) . . . wæs deád se ðorfendo (*mendicus*), Lk. Skt. Lind. 16, 20, 22. Ofer armne and ðorfend *super egenum et pauperem*, Rtl. 175, 33. Ðorfendo *pauperes*, Mk. Skt. Lind. 14, 7. Eádgo ða ðorfendo *beati pauperes*, Lk. Skt. Lind. 6, 20. Ic sello ðorfendum *do pauperibus*, 19, 8: Mk. Skt. Lind. Rush. 14, 5. Ðorfendum ł næfigum (ðarfendum, Rush.) *egenis*, Jn. Skt. Lind. 12, 5. Cf. þearfende, *and see preceding and following words.*

þorfendness, e; *f. Poverty, destitution:*—In ðorfendnisse *in paupertate*, Rtl. 105, 11.

þorf-fæst; *adj. Useful:*—Ne on eorðo ne in feltúne ł on mixenne ðor[f]fæst is *neque in terram neque in sterculinium utile est*, Lk. Skt. Rush. Lind. 14, 35. Ðor[f]fæst *utilis*, Rtl. 192, 7. Sié ðor[f]fæsta ús *prosint nobis*, 91, 27. [Cf. All þatt hemm wass þurrfe, Orm. 9628. *Icel.* þurf-samr *helping*.] Cf. þearf, V, þearf-líc, II, *and next word.*

þorf-leás; *adj. Useless:*—Ðe ðor[f]leása ðegn *inutilis servus*, Mt. Kmbl. Lind. 25, 30. Ðor[f]leáse ł sum óðer gefeóllon néh strǽt *quaedam ceciderunt secus viam*, 13, 4. Esnas ðor[f]leáse (-leóse, Rush.) wé sindon *servi inutiles sumus*, Lk. Skt. Lind. 17, 10. Cf. þearf-leás, *and preceding word.*

þorh. v. þurh.

þorian (?) *to dare:*—Thorie *dosmui* (*domui?*), Wrt. Voc. ii. 141, 82. [*Icel.* þora *to dare.*]

þorn, es; *m. A thorn, the prickle of a plant* or *a plant on which such prickles grow:*—Þorn *spina*, Wrt. Voc. i. 33, 44: 80, 22: *tribulus*, 33, 45: *dumus*, ii. 25, 70. On ða þyrnan westeweardes, ðǽr se mycla þorn stód, Cod. Dip. Kmbl. iii. 404, 13. Tó hafucðornæ; of ðam þornæ on ðone brádan stán . . . on hælnes þorn; of ðam þorne on ðone bróc, v. 348, 21. On weocan þorn; of ðam þorne, vi. 92, 3. Ðornas *sentes*, Wrt. Voc. ii. 120, 28. Þornas, i. 33, 41: 80, 19. Hí wundon cynehelm of þornum *plectentes coronam de spinis*, Mt. Kmbl. 27, 29: Exon. Th. 88, 27; Cri. 1446. Of ðæm hylle ðæt swá be ðǽm .IIII. þornan; of ðǽm þornan be ðǽm heáfdon, Cod. Dip. Kmbl. iii. 263, 31. Þornas and brémelas *spinas et tribulos*, Gen. 3, 18. Sume feóllon on þornas; and ða þornas weóxon and fordrysmudon ða, Mt. Kmbl. 13, 7: Mk. 4, 7. Swá ðú bærne þornas fýre *sicut ignis in spinis*, Ps. Th. 117, 12. Átió hé of lande ða þornas and ða fyrsas and ðæt fearn and ealle ða weód ðe hé gesió ðæt ðám æcerum derigen *liberat arva fruticibus, falce rubos filicemque resecat*, Bt. 23; Fox 78, 22: Met. 12, 3. [The word is found in many local names. v. Cod. Dip. Kmbl. vi. 341.] ¶ *The name of the letter* þ *was* þorn:—Þ byþ þearle scearp, Runic pm. Kmbl. 339, 13; Rūn. 3. [*Goth.* þaurnus: *O. Sax. O. Frs. O. L. Ger.* thorn *spina, dumus*: *O. H. Ger.* dorn: *Icel.* þorn *a thorn; the name of the letter* þ.] v. appel-, brēmel-, gemǣr-, hæg-, haga-, lūs-, mǣr-, pōl-, pric-, set-, slāh-, þīfe-þorn, *and following words.*

þorn-geblǣd *a blister caused by the prick of a thorn,* Lchdm. iii. 36, 21.

þorn-grǣfe, an; *f. A thorn-copse*:—Andlang ðære þorngrǣfan, Cod. Dip. Kmbl. v. 148, 4.

þornig; *adj. Thorny, full of thorns.* v. þorn:—Se yrðling lufaþ ðone æcer ðe æfter ðornum and brēmelum genihtsume wæstmas āgifþ swīðor ðonne hē lufige ðone ðe ðornig næs, Homl. Th. i. 342, 8. Gehega þīne eáran mid þornigum hege, Wulfst. 246, 9. [*O. H. Ger.* dornig: *Ger.* dornig.]

þorniht; *adj. Thorny, full of thorns* (v. þorn) *or briars*:—Þorniht *senticosus*, Wrt. Voc. i. 33, 41. Tō ðæm þornihtan heáfodlonde, Cod. Dip. Kmbl. iii. 263, 32. On ðam þornehtan dūne, 421, 24. On ða þornihtan leáge, v. 389, 14. Ðǣm ðornihtum *senticosis* (velut rosa *senticosis* exorta surculis, Ald. 18, 14), Wrt. Voc. ii. 77, 47. [*O. H. Ger.* dornohti *spinosus*: *Ger.* dornicht.]

þorn-rǣw, e; *f. A row of thorn-bushes*:—On ða þornrǣwe, Cod. Dip. Kmbl. iii. 77, 28. On ða ealdan þornrǣwe, 199, 33, 34.

þorn-rind, e; *f. The bark of a thorn-tree*:—Hnutbeámes rinde and þornrinde gecnūa tō dūste, Lchdm. ii. 52, 1.

þorn-stybb, -stubb, es; *m. The stump of a thorn-tree*:—Tō ðæm þornstybbe; of ðam þornstybbe, Cod. Dip. Kmbl. v. 252, 28. Tō ðan þornstybbe, vi. 8, 33, 37. On ðonæ þornstub, v. 291, 11. On ðone þornstyb; of ðam stybbe, Cod. Dip. B. iii. 169, 33.

þorof. v. þeorf.

þorp, þrop, es; *m.* Perhaps the idea at first connected with the word is that of an assemblage, cf. the use in Icelandic: Maðr heitir einnhverr . . . þorp ef þrīr ero, Skāldskaparmāl; þyrpast *to crowd, throng;* þyrping *a crowd:* later the word may have been used of the assemblage of workers on an estate, and also of the estate on which they worked; all three ideas seem to be implied in one or other of the following glosses:—Tuun, þrop, ðrop *conpetum*, Txts. 53, 557: Wrt. Voc. ii. 15, 7. *Compitum* i. *villa vel* þingstōw *vel* þrop, 132, 56. Þrop *fundus*, i. 37, 51. The idea of an estate belongs to the word in Gothic: þaurp ni gastaistald ἀγρὸν οὐκ ἐκτησάμην, Neh. 5, 16. In the end the meaning came to be *hamlet, village,* in which sense it remained for some time in English, e. g.: Ic Ǽdgar gife freodom Sc̄e Petres mynstre Medeshamstede of kyng and of biscop, and ealle þa þorpes þe ðærto lin: ðæt is, Ǽstfeld and Dodesthorp and Ege and Pastun, Chr. 963; Erl. 121, 40. He com to Bethfage, swo hatte þe þrop, O. E. Homl. ii. 89, 13. Ther stod a throp . . . in which that poure folk hadden her bestes and her herbergage, Chauc. Cl. T. 199. Thorp, litell towne or thoroughfare *oppidum*, Prompt. Parv. 492. The word is now obsolete, but it remains in a great many local names, either alone or in composition; though, as such names are found mostly in those parts of England which were affected by the Danes, its occurrence in them may be due rather to Scandinavian than to English influence. v. Leo, Anglo-Saxon Names of Places, p. 43 sqq.; Taylor's words and Places, s.v. [*Goth.* þaurp: *O. Frs.* thorp, therp: *O. L. Ger.* thorp, tharp: *Du.* dorp: *O. H. Ger.* dorf *villa, vicus, praedium, oppidum, municipium*: *Icel.* þorp *a hamlet, village.*]

þost, es; *m. Dung, ordure;* with this meaning *thoste* (according to a MS. glossary cited by Halliwell) is used in Gloucestershire:—Wyrc drenc of hwītes hundes þoste, Lchdm. i. 364, 5. Bærn hundes ðost and gnīd smale, 7. Nim drīgne hundes þost, 11: ii. 48, 8. [Þost, thoste *stercus*, Ps. 82, 11. An horse thoste, P. S. 237, 14. As a thost in the weie totreden, Wick. Ecclus. 9, 10. Ass uryne and swynes thost, Pall. 116, 348. Thoste or toord *stercus*, Prompt. Parv. 492. *O. H. Ger.* dost *stercus, coenum.*]

-þot. v. ge-þot. [Cf. *Icel.* upp-þot *a great stir.*]

þoterian; *p.* ode *To howl, wail, cry out*:—Þotraþ *clamat*, Wrt. Voc. ii. 21, 12. Geómriende hell þoteraþ *gemens infernus ululat*, Hymn. Surt. 84, 34. Gē wēpaþ and þoteriaþ *plorabitis et flebitis*, Scint. 167, 3. Hī ðotorodon swilce ōðre wulfas, Homl. Th. ii. 488, 27. v. þeótan.

þoterung, e; *f. Howling, wailing, crying*:—Stefn wæs gehȳred wōp and mycel þotorung (þoterung, MS. A.) *vox audita est, ploratus et ululatus multus*, Mt. Kmbl. 2, 18: Homl. Th. i. 80, 19. Ne āblinþ grānung and þoterung (on helle), 68, 7. Geómerung and singal þoteruncg, Wulfst. 114, 27. Hē weóp swīðe biterlīce and hē feóll tō Iōhannes fōtum mid geómerunge and þoterunge, Ǽlfc. T. Grn. 18, 32. Hē symle clypode mid swīðlīcere þoterunge: 'And wā ðissere burhware,' Homl. Th. ii. 302, 12.

þōþer (-or, -r), es; *m. A ball, sphere*:—Thōthr, thōthor *pila*, Txts. 87, 1584. Ðōþor, Wrt. Voc. ii. 68, 17. Þōðer, i. 86, 6. Þōþor, 287, 15. Ðōþer *pila* vel' *sfera*, 39, 51. Þōþer *ballum*, ii. 125, 14. Ðū leornodest ðone cræft ðe wē hātaþ geometrica; on ðam cræfte ðū leornodest onn ānum þōðere odþe on æpple ātēfred, ðæt ðū meahtest be ðære tēfrunge ongytan ðises rodores ymbehwirft . . . Ðū leornodest be ānre līnan wæs āwriten anlang middes ðæs þōþeres . . . Ðū secgst ðæt ðū ymbe ða līnan wite ðe on ðam þōðere ātēfred wæs . . . Ic wolde witan hweðer ðū eác wite ymbe ðone þōðer ðe seó lȳne on āwriten is, Shrn. 174, 16–175, 1. Ðā āgan se cyngc plegan wið his geféran mid þōðere, and Apollonius yrnende ðone ðōðor gelǣhte, Ap. Th. 13, 1–3.

Thrāceas, þrācie (?); *pl. The Thracians*:—Ðrācia cyning, Met. 26, 22, 59, 7. Dorus Thrācea cyning, Ors. 3, 11; Swt. 152, 3. *In other passages Latin forms occur,* Traci, Thraci:—Be westan ðære byrig sindon Traci, 1, 1; Swt. 22, 8. Hē wæs farende on Thraci and hié tō him gebīgde *Thracas domuit*, 3, 9; Swt. 124, 9: 4, 11; Swt. 204, 16. *Another form is* Trāciane; *pl.*:—Trāciana *Tracium* (*provincias*, Ald. 64, 10), Wrt. Voc. ii. 85, 74. *The name of the country is given as* Trācia, Thrācia:—On Trācia (Thrācia, MS. C.) ðæm londe, Ors. 3, 7; Swt. 114, 15. Lysimachus befēng Thrāciam *Thracia Lysimacho data*, 3, 11; Swt. 142, 33.

þracian. v. ā-, an-, on-þracian.

þracu; *gen.* þræce; *f.* I. not in a bad sense, *power, force*:—Þracu (-a, MS.) wæs on ōre, heard handplega, hægsteald mōdige, wīgend unforhte, Cd. Th. 198, 22; Exod. 326. Sigores tācn wið þeóda þræce *a token of victory against the power of nations*, Elen. Kmbl. 369; El. 185. Se cāsere hēht bannan tō beadwe, beran ūt þræce . . . wǣron Rōmware sōna gegearwod *the emperor bade give the summons to war, bade put forth their power* (?) . . . *At once were the Romans prepared*, 90; El. 45. Geceósan swā þrymmes þræce swā þrȳstra wræce *to choose either the power of glory or the misery of darkness*, Exon. Th. 37, 14; Cri. 593. Oft wē ofersēgon þeóda þeáwas, þræce mōdigra *the power of the proud*, 118, 12; Gū. 238. II. in a bad sense, *violence*:—Oft hī þræce rǣrdon . . . feóndscipe rǣrdon . . . hālge cwelmdon . . . bærndon gecorene, Exon. Th. 243, 18; Jul. 12: 262, 16; Jul. 333. [*O. Sax.* mōd-thraka.] v. ādl-, æsc-, bǣl-, ecg-, flān-, gār-, gūð-, hild-, holm-, līg-, mōd-, wǣpen-, wīg-þracu; þrece.

þræc. v. ge-þræc, *and preceding word.*

-þræc. v. on-þræc.

þræc-heard; *adj. Brave in battle*:—Þrungon þræchearde, Elen. Kmbl. 245; El. 123.

þræc-hwīl, e; *f. A time of suffering, a hard time*:—Ongan ðā hreówcearig sār cwānian . . . 'Ðū mec þreádes þurh sārslege . . .' Hine seó fǣmne forlēt æfter þræchwīle, Exon. Th. 275, 22; Jul. 554. [Cf. *Icel.* þrekaðr *wearied, exhausted.*]

þræc-rōf; *adj. Valiant*, Cd. Th. 122, 22; Gen. 2030.

þrǣc-wīg, es; *m. Hard fighting*:—Þurstige þræcwīges, Cd. Th. 189, 9; Exod. 182.

þræc-wudu, a; *m. A spear*:—Helm, byrne, þræcwudu, Beo. Th. 2496; B. 1246.

þrǣd, es; *m. A thread*:—Ðrēd *filum*, Wrt. Voc. ii. 108, 59: i. 66, 28. Þrǣd, ii. 35, 44: i. 81, 65: *fila*, 282, 11. Se gyldna ðrǣd *bratea fila*, ii. 89, 37: 12, 3. Þrǣd mē (*a coat of mail*) ne hlimmeþ, ne æt mē hrisil scrīþeþ, Exon. Th. 417, 18; Rä. 36, 6. Cnyte mid ānum ðrǣde, Lchdm. i. 218, 20. Mid ānum reádum þrǣde, 100, 19. Mid wyllenan þrǣde, ii. 310, 22. Him ne hangaþ nacod sweord ofer ðam heáfde be smalan þrǣde, Bt. 29, 1; Fox 102, 28. Þrǣda *filorum*, Hpt. Gl. 494, 18. Āþrāwenum ðrǣdum *contortis*, Wrt. Voc. ii. 21, 18. Webb byþ gefylled mid þrǣdum *tela consummatur filis*, Scint. 216, 2. [*O. L. Ger.* thrād *filum*: *O. Frs.* thrēd: *Du.* draad: *O. H. Ger.* drāt: *Ger.* draht *Icel.* þrāðr: *Dan.* traad.] v. col-, gold-, hefeld-, rihtung-, weall-þrǣd þrāwan.

þræft *a quarrel, dispute, contention, chiding*:—Siteþ symbelwlonc searwum lǣteþ wīne gewǣged word ūt faran þræfte þringan þrymme gebyrmed æfæstum onǣled oferhygda ful *flushed with the feast he sits, affected with wine, words he guilefully lets fare forth, crowd out with quarrel in their train, leavened as he is with pride, inflamed with ill-will, full of overweening*, Exon. Th. 316, 1; Mōd. 42. [*Icel.* þrapt *quarrel;* þrefa *to wrangle.* Jamieson gives *thraftly* in a chiding or surly manner.] v. (?) þrafian.

þrægan (cf. *Goth.* þragjan, *and for conjugation* cf. plegan); *p.* de *To run, proceed in a course*:—Sume tungul læsse gelīðaþ, ða ðe lācaþ ymb eaxe ende, odðe micle māre gefēraþ, ða hire midore ymbe þearle prægeþ (-aþ?) (cf. sume tunglu habbaþ lengran ymbhwyrft ðonne sume habban, and ða lengestne ðe ymb ða eaxe middewearde hwearfaþ, Bt. 39, 3; Fox 214, 24), Met. 28, 24. Ðǣr him eoh fore mīlpaðas mæt, mōdig þrægde, Elen. Kmbl. 2524; El. 1263. Ic seah hors swīþe þrægan, Exon. Th. 400, 4; Rä. 20, 3.

-þrǣge. v. wǣpen-þrǣge.

þrǣl, es; *m. A thrall, slave, servant*:—Ðe yfle ðrael *malus servus*, Mt. Kmbl. Lind. 24, 48. Allra ðrǣl ł esne *omnium servus*, Mt. Skt. Lind. Rush. 10, 44. Se ðe dōeð synne ðrǣl is synnes, Jn. Skt. Rush. 8, 34. Ne cweðo ic iów ðrǣlas (ðrǣllas, Lind.), for ðon ðrǣl (ðrǣll, Lind.) nāt hwæt wyrceð hlāford his, 15, 15. Wē witan ðæt þurh Godes gyfe þrǣl weard tō þegene, and ceorl tō eorle, L. Eth. vii. 21; Th. i. 334, 8. Ðeáh þrǣla hwylc hlāforde æthleápe and of cristendōme tō wīcinge weorðe, and hit æfter ðam eft geweorðe, ðæt wǽpngewrixl weorðe gemǽne þegene and þrǽle, gyf þrǽl ðæne þegen fullíce áfylle, licge ǽgylde ealre his mǽgðe; and gyf se þegen ðæne þrǽl, ðe hē ǽr āhte, fullíce āfylle, gylde þegengylde, Wulfst. 162, 5-10. Oft þrǽl ðæne þegen, ðe ær wæs his hláford, cnyt swȳðe fæste and wyrcþ him tō þrǽle, 163, 1. Gebēte þrǽl mid his hīde, þegn mid .xxx. scillingan, 181, 9. Ðe hlāferd ðrǽles ðæs *dominus servi illius*, Mt. Kmbl. Lind. 24, 50. Ðrǽles (ðrǽlles, Lind.), Lk. Skt. Rush. 12, 46. Ic cuoeðo ðrǽle mīnum, Lind. 7, 8. Hē sende ōðerne ðrael, Mk. Skt. Lind. 12, 4. Gif Englisc man Deniscne þrǽl ofsleá, gylde hine mid punde, and se Denisca Engliscne eal swā, gif hē hine ofsleá, L. Eth. ii. 5; Th. i. 286, 24. Þrǽlas ne mōton habban ðæt hī āgon on āgenan hwīlan mid earfeðan gewunnen, Wulfst. 158, 38. Antecristes þrǽlas, 55, 9. Ðonne beó gē ealle þrǽlas *tunc eritis omnes servi*, Coll. Monast. Th. 29, 25. [*From Icel.* þræll.]

þrǽl-riht, es; *n. Thrall-right;* in pl. *the legal rights and privileges which belonged to the thrall*:—Freóriht wǽron fornumene and ðrǽlriht generwde . . . Frige men ne mōtan wealdan heora sȳlfra, ne faran ðār hī willaþ, ne āteón heora āgen, swā swā hī willaþ; ne þrǽlas ne mōton habban ðæt hī āgon on āgenan hwīlan mid earfeðan gewunnen, ne ðæt ðæt heom on Godes ēst gōde men geúðon and tō ælmesgife for Godes lufan sealdon, Wulfst. 158, 15.

þrǽs *a fringe, border*:—Ðrēs, liste *limbus*, Txts. 75, 1228. Ðrēs, thrēs *oresta*, 85, 1455. Ðrǽs, Wrt. Voc. ii. 63, 51. Þrǽs *instita*, i. 26, 10. Ðrēsi *lymbo*, Txts. 75, 1264. Liste oððe þrǽs *lembum*, listum oððe þrǽsum *limbus(-is?)*, Wrt. Voc. ii. 50, 68, 69.

þræsce, an; *f. A thrush*:—Ðrostle *trita*, ðraesce *truitius*, Wrt. Voc. ii. 122, 79. [Cf. *Icel.* þröstr; *gen.* þrastar *a thrush.*] v. þrysce.

þræscende. v. þrǽstan.

þræst. v. dærst.

þrǽstan; *p.* te. I. *to twist, writhe, roll about*:—Ðæt hors on misenlīce dǽlas hit wond and ðrǽste *cum diversas in partes se torqueret*, Bd. 3, 9; S. 533, 36. Hē misenlīcum styrenessum ongan his limu ðrǽstan *diversis motibus coepit membra torquere*, 3, 11; S. 536, 15. II. *to torture, torment, harass, plague, afflict*:—Ǽnne of ðām mannum ðe hī on ðam fȳre bærndon and ðrǽston *unum de eis quos in ignibus torrebant*, 3, 19; S. 548, 48. Ðætte Bryttas hié sylfe ðrǽston (*contriverint*) on ingefeohtum, 1, 22; S. 485, 11. Mē þræscende (þrǽstende?), Homl. Skt. ii. 23 b, 554. Hē grimme sāre ongan ðrǽsted beón (*torqueri*), Bd. 5, 13; S. 632, 19. Ða unrīman mænigeo ðrǽste wǽron *innumerabilis multitudo torqueretur*, 5, 12; S. 628, 4. Missenlīcum cwealmnyssum ðrēste *diversibus cruciatibus torti*, 1, 7; S. 479, 13. III. *to press, constrain*:—Tō nirwienne ł tō þrǽstenne *artandum, constringendum*, Hpt. Gl. 480, 32. [Is] þrǽst *compellitur, coartatur*, 469, 20. [In later English the word seems mostly used intransitively, *to press* in, on, out:—Monie þurles, þer þet water þrest in, A. R. 314, 14. Þreaste smoke ut, Marh. 9, 6. He þraste to þan fihte, Laym. 27644. Moni þusenden þrasten ut of telden, 26318. Heo þresten in uppon me *irruerunt super me*, A. R. 220, 31. Mine cnihtes scullen þræsten (þreaste, 2nd MS.) biforen me, Laym. 23373. He thurgh the thikkeste of the throng gan threste, Chauc. Kn. T. 1754.] v. ā-, for-, ge-þrǽstan.

þrǽstedness, þrǽstness. v. for-þrǽstedness, for-, ge-þrǽstness.

þrǽsting, e; *f. Torment, affliction*:—Swā hē sceal etan ðætte hiene sió gewilnung ðære gīfernesse of his mōdes fæstrǽdnesse ne gebrenge, ne eft sió ðrǽsting (ðrǽsðing, Hatt. MS.) ðæs līchoman ðæt mōd ne āscrence mid upāhæfennesse *ne aut illos appetitus gulae a mentis statu dejiciat, aut istos afflicta caro ex elatione supplantet*, Past. 43; Swt. 316, 7.

þræxwold. v. þerscold.

þrafian; *p.* ode. I. *to urge, press*:—Ic ðrafige *urgeo*, Ælfc. Gr. 26, 3; Zup. 155, 12. Gif ic mīne heorde tō swīðe þrafige on gancge and swence hig ealle hig sweltaþ ānes dæges *si greges meos plus in ambulando fecero laborare, morientur cuncti una die*, R. Ben. 120, 20. Mec mīn freá þrafaþ on þȳstrum, hætst on enge, Exon. Th. 383, 1; Rä. 4, 4. Se biscop sceal þrafian ða mæssepreóstas mid lufe ge mid lāþe, ðæt hié healdan Godes ǽwe on riht, Blickl. Homl. 45, 8. II. *to reprove, rebuke, correct.* v. þrafung:—Se Hǽlend on manegum wīsum ðrafode and āfandode his gingran, and geedlǽhte ðæt ðæt hē ǽr tǽhte tō fulre lāre, Homl. Th. ii. 296, 22. Drihten, ne þreá ðū me ne ne þrafa on ðīnum yrre *Domine, ne in ira tua arguas me*, Ps. Th. 37, 1. Hwīlum līðelīce tō ðreátianne, hwīlum suīðlīce and strælīce tō ðrafianne *aliquando leniter arguenda, aliquando vehementer increpanda*, Past. 21; Swt. 151, 12. [Cf. (?) *Goth.* þrafstjan *to exhort, encourage, comfort.*] v. (?) þræft.

þrafung, e; *f. Reproof, rebuke, censure*:—Þrafunge *argumenti* (v. þrafian, II), Hpt. Gl. 487, 20. Ðæt is ðonne swelc mon mid forewearde orde stinge, ðæt mon openlīce and unforwandodlīce on ōðerne rǽse mid tǽlinge and mid ðrafunga *ex mucrone quippe percutere, est impetu apertae increpationis obviare*, Past. 40; Swt. 297, 13. Se Hǽlend æteówde hine sylfne cucenne his gingrum æfter his ǽriste on manegum ðrafungum, Homl. Th. i. 294, 16. Hī (*Job's friends*) mid manegum ðrafungum hine (*Job*) geswencton, ii. 454, 21. v. nīd-þrafung.

þrāg, þrāh, e; *f.* I. *a time, season*:—Ðonne seó þrāg cymeþ wefen wyrdstafum, Exon. Th. 183, 9; Gū. 1324. Wergendra tō lyt þrong ymbe þeóden, ðā hyne sió þrāg becwom, Beo. Th. 5759; B. 2883. Ǽr ðam seó þrāh cyme, ðæt hē ðec āworpe of woruldrīce, Cd. Th. 252, 34; Dan. 588. Nis seó þrāh micel, ðæt hī ðē swencan mōton, Andr. Kmbl. 214; An. 107. Ða æfterwritenan lǽcedōmas ne sculon on āne þrāge tō lange beón tō gedōne, Lchdm. ii. 186, 12. Nis ðæt eówer ðæt gē witan ða þrāge and ða tīde *non est vestrum nosse tempora vel momenta*, Blickl. Homl. 117, 24. II. having reference to the condition of things at any time, *time* as in good, bad, hard, etc. *times*:—Hū seó þrāg (*the happy time just described*) gewāt, swā heó nō wǽre, Exon. Th. 292, 7; Wand. 95. Is ðeós þrāg ful strong, ic sceal þinga gehwylc þolian, 270, 13; Jul. 464. Onwæcnaþ sió wōde þrāg ðære wrǽnnesse and gedrēfþ hiora mōd *libido versat avidis corda venenis*, Bt. 37, 1; Fox 186, 18: Met. 25, 41. Ic mē þyslīcre ǽr þrāge ne gewēnde *I did not expect such a time as I have had*, Exon. Th. 269, 21; Jul. 453. Wēndon hié þearlra geþinga, þrāge hnāgran, Andr. Kmbl. 3195; An. 1600. Ōð ðæt rīmgetæl rēðre þrāge daga forð gewāt, Cd. Th. 85, 26; Gen. 1420. Hē ðȳ wyrs meahte þolian ða þrāge, ðā hió swā þearl becom (cf. Ðā hit gelomp ðæt hē on swā micelre nearunesse becom, Bt. 1; Fox 2, 26), Met. 1, 77. III. adverbial uses. Cf. hwīl:—Þrāge *interim*, Wrt. Voc. ii. 110, 76. Hē þrāge mid ūs wunode *he dwelt with us for a time*, Blickl. Homl. 131, 19: Exon. Th. 208, 24; Ph. 160: Ps. Th. 81, 5: 111, 4: Met. 20, 134. Tōdrīf ðone mist ðe þrāge nū hangode hwȳle, 20, 264. Hē þrāge siððan wīcum wunode, Cd. Th. 108, 25; Gen. 1811: 74, 5; Gen. 1217. Hit þrāge sceal in sondhofe siþþan wunian, Exon. Th. 173, 30; Gū. 1168. Swelge hē ða ðrāge ðe (*while, as long as*) hē mæge, Lchdm. ii. 284, 14. Geærndon hī sume ðrāge *they raced for some time*, Bd. 5, 6; S. 619, 9. Ealle þrāge *all the time*, Ps. Th. 101, 25: Exon. Th. 324, 2; Vīd. 88: Judth. Thw. 25, 2; Jud. 237: Apstls. Kmbl. 60; Ap. 30. Ðū sægdest ðæt ic sceolde lifigan lange ðrāge, Ps. Th. 118, 116. Bād sunu Lameches sōðra gehāta lange þrāge, Cd. Th. 86, 5; Gen. 1426: 153, 25; Gen. 2544: 252, 4; Dan. 573: Beo. Th. 108; B. 54: Andr. Kmbl. 1580; An. 791. Wǽran hī ǽr on hǽþenra hæfteclommum lange þrāga, Chr. 942; Erl. 116, 17. Þēh mīn līchama lytle ðrāge on niðerdǽlum eorðan wunige, Ps. Th. 138, 13. Swā ic þrāgum (*at times, sometimes*) winne, hwīlum . . ., hwīlum, Exon. Th. 386, 26; Rä. 4, 67: 381, 1; Rä. 2, 4: 494, 6; Rä. 82, 4: Cd. Th. 271, 29; Sat. 112: Elen. Kmbl. 2475; El. 1239. Wæter wynsumu mōnþa gehwam bearo geondfaraþ þrāgum (*at appointed times*), is ðæt þeódnes gebod, ðætte twelf sīþum ðæt tīrfæste lond geondlāce laguflode wynn, Exon. Th. 202, 11; Ph. 68: Ps. Th. 138, 11. [Habben an alpi þraȝe summe lisse, O. E. Homl. i. 35, 10. He tah hine aȝein ane þrowe, Laym. 640. God þraȝhe *a good while*, Orm. 3475. Lat me nu habbe mine þroȝe (*rimes with* oȝe), O. and N. 260. Sume þroȝe *for a while*, 478. Or he reste hym ony thrawe, Rich. 5062. Liþe me a litel þroȝe, Horn. 336. Þrawe, Havel. 276: R. Brun. 180, 11: Alis. 3836. Thi pynes lastes bot a thrawe, Met. Homl. 142, 2. Throwe, Ch. M. of L. T. 953. Many a throwe, Ch. Yem. T. 941. Any throwe, Monk's T. 3326. Throwe, a lytyl wyle *momentum*, Prompt. Parv. 493.] v. earfoþ-, ryne-, treów-þrāg.

þrāg-bisig; *adj. Occupied for a time* (?), *periodically employed* (?):—Ic sceal þrāgbysig þegne mīnum hȳran georne, Exon. Th. 387, 6; Rä. 5, 1. The subject of the riddle is a millstone, and the Latin riddles on which the English one is based seem to suggest that the epithet might refer to running; Aldhelm has: Par labor ambarum . . . altera currit; Symphosius: Non desinit ille moveri. v. Prehn's Rätsel des Exeterbuches. But the verse requires *þrāg*, while the verb, *þrægan*, has a short vowel; and *þrāg* seems always (?) used in the sense of *time.*

þrāg-mǽlum; *adv. From time to time, at times, at intervals*:—Ic wæs nȳde gebǽded, þrāgmǽlum geþreád, ðæt ic ðē sōhte, Exon. Th. 263, 3; Jul. 344. Ne meahton hió word forðbringan, ac hió þrāgmǽlum þióton ongunnon, Met. 26, 80. Hit on wolcnum oft þearle þunraþ, þrāgmǽlum eft ānforlǽteþ (cf. hit hwīlum þunraþ, hwīlum nā ne onginþ, Bt. 39, 3; Fox 214, 34), 28, 55. Ðrāgmǽlum, Andr. Kmbl. 2461; An. 1232.

þrang (?) *a throng, crowd*:—Wæterberendra þran[gum] *lixarum coetibus*, Hpt. Gl. 427, 15. [Grete thrang of men, Pr. C. 4704. A þral in þe þrong, Allit. pms. 42, 135. *Du.* drang *a crowd*: *M. H. Ger.* dranc: *Ger.* drang: *Icel.* þröng.] v. ge-þrang; þringan.

þrāwan; *p.* þreów; *pp.* þrāwen *To throw* (v. throw, thraw *to turn wood, to twist*; throwster *one that throws or winds silk* or *thread*; throwing-clay *clay that will work on the wheel*, Halliw. Dict. See, also, E. D. S. Pub. Holderness, Lincolnshire and Huddersfield dialects, *thraw, thrown*: Jamieson's Dict. *thraw.*), *twist*:—Ic samod þrāwe *contorqueo*, Ælfc. Gr. 26, 3; Zup. 155, 16. I. *trans. To twist, rack, torture*:—Hē hēt hī on hencgene āstreccan and ðrāwan swā swā wiððan, Homl. Skt. i. 8, 113. Hē hēt hine hōn on hengene, and mid hengene ðrāwan tō langere hwīle, Homl. Th. ii. 308, 31. II. *intrans. To twist, turn round,* (1) *to take a different direction*:—Se līg sōna ðreów ðwyres wið ðæs windes *the flame at once turned round in a contrary direction towards the wind*, Homl. Th. ii. 510, 8. (2) *to turn round, revolve*:—Þrāwende *rotante* (*fusa*, Ald. 175, 34), Wrt. Voc. ii. 93, 78. (3) *to curl*:—Þrāwendum ł cyrpsiendum loccum *crinibus crispantibus*, Hpt. Gl. 435, 9. [Haremarken þrauwen mid winde, Laym. 27359. *But Layamon uses the word intransitively also of movement:*—Of his horse he þreou (cf. anan swa ich lihte of blonken, 793), 807. Þa cheorles up þreowen (þreuwen, 2nd MS.) *the churls started up,* 12321. Þrawen wyth a þwong, Gaw. 194. *The word, however, early gets the meaning of* throwing:—Horn þreu þe ring to grunde . . . 'Palmere trewe, þe ring þat þu þrewe,' Horn 1160–72. Ded he threow him to grounde, Alis. 2425. In fire saltou thrawe þam *in igne dejicies eos,* Ps. 139, 11. *O. L. Ger.* thrāan *rotare: Du.* draaijen *to turn, twist: O. H. Ger.* drājan; *wk. tornare, torquere: Ger.* drehen.] v. ā-, be-, ge-, ge-ed-, þurh-þrāwan; twi-þrāwen.

þrāwing-spinel, e; *f. A curling-iron, crisping-pin:*—Þrāwincspinle ł hǽrnǽdla *calamistro,* Hpt. Gl. 435, 7: 513, 75: 526, 46.

þreá, þrawu; *gen.* þreá; *pl.* þreá; *f.:* þreá; *gen.* þreán, *also* þreás (?); *m.; also neuter.* I. *rebuke, reproof, threat:*—Thrauuo, thrauu, trafu *argutiae,* Txts. 41, 200. Se ðe ege healdeþ eallum þeódum and his þreá ne sí ðǽr for āwiht *qui corripit gentes, non arguet?* Ps. Th. 93, 10. For ðínre þreá *ab increpatione tua,* 75, 5. Hē mid heardre ðreá hí on spræc *aspera illos invectione corrigebat,* Bd. 3, 5; S. 527, 11. Ðreán *adversione,* Wrt. Voc. ii. 2, 29. Ðǽm scamleásan ne wyrð nō gestiéred būtan micelre tǽlinge and miclum ðreán *impudentes ab impudentiae vitio non nisi increpatio dura compescit,* Past. 31; Swt. 205, 23. For ðínum þreán and for ðínum yrre *ab increpatione tua, ab inspiratione spiritus irae tuae,* Ps. Th. 17, 16. Ða him þreá ðíne þearle ondrǽdaþ *ab increpatione tua fugient,* 103, 8. Hē for him þreá geaf kyningum *corripuit pro eis reges,* 104, 12. Gē hlāfordas, dōð gē eówrum monnum ðæt ilce, and gemetgiaþ ðone ðreán *vos domini eadem facite illis, remittentes minas,* Past. 29; Swt. 203, 1. Ne hí Agustinus lārum ne his bēnum ne his ðreám (*increpationibus*) geþafigean woldan, Bd. 2, 2; S. 502, 14. Ðreá þeódum eáwan *ad faciendas increpationes in populis,* Ps. Th. 149, 7. II. *chastisement, correction, punishment, an infliction* that has been deserved, justifiable *severity:*—Se egsan þreá *the pain caused by the terror of the day of judgement,* Exon. Th. 65, 34; Cri. 1064. Seó lufu ðæt gemet ðære ðreá (*the punishment to be imposed for stealing*) dihtaþ, Bd. 1, 27; S. 490, 21. On strengo þeódscipes and þreá tō wlæc *in disciplinae vigore tepidus,* S. 492, 18. Ðære uplecan ðreá sweopon *supernae flagella districtionis,* 2, 5; S. 507, 2. Æfter ðære ðreá (*flagello*), 4, 31; S. 611, 1. Ðæt weorþeþ þeódum tō þreá, ðām ðe þone Gode ne cūþun, Exon. Th. 67, 21; Cri. 1092. Ðoliaþ wē þreá on helle, Cd. Th. 25, 5; Gen. 389. Þurh egsan þreá, Exon. Th. 83, 32; Cri. 1365. Næs ǽnig ðæt mec þus bealdlíce bendum bilegde, þreám forþrycte, 273, 22; Jul. 520. III. *an infliction* (where no idea of correction is implied), *evil, ill, pang, plague, calamity, affliction:*—Tō ne geniólaecað tō ðē yfel and ðreá (*flagellum*) ne geneólaeceþ getelde ðínum, Ps. Surt. 90, 10. Hí gesomnadon in mec ðreá (*flagella*), 34, 15. Heó fleón gewāt þreá (*ill treatment,* cf. Gen. 16, 6) and þeówdōm, Cd. Th. 136, 24; Gen. 2263. Geþola þeóda þreá *bear the ills inflicted on thee by the gentiles,* Andr. Kmbl. 213; An. 107. Swylt ealle fornom . . . þurh þearlíc þreá *death carried off all . . . by a terrible calamity* (*shipwreck*), Exon. Th. 283, 10; Jul. 678. Þreá wǽron þearle, þegnas grimme, 135, 4; Gū. 519. Monge ðreá (*flagella*) synfulra, Ps. Surt. 31, 10. Wē ðec for þreáum and for ðeónȳdum (for þearfum and for þreánȳdum, Exon. Th. 186, 3) ārna biddaþ, Cd. Th. 234, 18; Dan. 294. Bonan mǽndon ðæt hȳ monnes bearn þreám oferþunge and him tō earfeðum āna cwōme gif hȳ him ne meahte māran sārum gyldan gyrnwræce *the murderous spirits made moan, that a child of man would have surpassed them in afflictions* (i.e. *would have caused them greater miseries than they had done to him*), *and alone would have come to their distress, if they could not requite their misery on him with greater pains,* Exon. Th. 128, 10; Gū. 402. Þreám forþrycced þurh ðæs þeódnes word *grievously oppressed by the prince's words* (*which announced his death*), 174, 1; Gū. 1171. Hí beág ymb mín heáfod þreám (*painfully* or *with reproaches?*) biþrycton, 88, 26; Cri. 1446. Hē Godes ðeówdōm miccle swíðor lufode þonne ða ídlan þreás ðisse worlde *he loved God's service much more than the vanities and vexations of this world,* Blickl. Homl. 211, 27. III a. in reference to inanimate things:—Sunne wearð þreám āþrysmed *the sun was miserably darkened* (*at the crucifixion*), Exon. Th. 70, 5; Cri. 1134. Wind nearwe geheaðrod, þreám forþrycced *the wind, straitly confined, strictly repressed,* Elen. Kmbl. 2551; El. 1277. [Hie nimeð swo bittere þrowes, þat hie ne mai hire mud holden, O. E. Homl. ii. 181, 2. A thrawe hire cam, Alis. 616. Wa geres us thol hard traues (thrawes, MS. C.), Met. Homl. 36, 16. In his harde þrowe, L. H. R. 150, 18. On his last þrowe, Ass. B. 533. Throwe, womannys pronge *erumpna,* Prompt. Parv. 493. *O. Sax.* thrā (*in* thrā-werk): *O. H. Ger.* drauua, drouua, drōa *animadversio, comminatio, mina; drōa passio: Icel.* þrā *a throe, pang.*] v. brōh-, cwealm-, heáh-, mōd-, þeód-þreá, *and next word.*

þreágan, þreán, *and* þreáwian (v. þreápian); *p.* þreáde [*in* Bt. 38, 1; Fox 196, 7 *a form occurs that might be a strong past of* þreán, *on the analogy of* þweán, sleán:—Ðæt gewit wæs swíþe sorgiende for ðām ermþum ðe hí ðrōgan; cf. *the rendering of the same passage in the metres:* Ðæt mōd wæs swíðe sorgum gebunden for ðǽm earfoþum ðe him on sǽton, Met. 26, 97. *But, perhaps,* drugon *should be read, as Latin is:* Mens super monstra, quae *patitur,* gemit]; *pp.* þreád. I. *to reprove, rebuke, reproach:*—Ic hine þreáge (ðreá, Lind.: ðriá, Rush.) and forlǽte *corripiam illum et dimittam,* Lk. Skt. 23, 22. Ne þreáge (drēgu, Surt.: þreá, Spl. C.: þrǽwie, Spl. T.) ic eów *non arguam te,* Ps. Th. 49, 9. Þreáge (ðrēu, Surt.: ðreáge, Spl.), 49, 23. Ðū ðreást (ðreádes, Surt.: þreádest, Spl.) ðeóda *increpasti gentes,* 9, 5. Gif ðū ðreást (dreast, MS.) *si corripueris,* Kent. Gl. 714. Ðreáð *corripit,* 514: *arguit,* 290. Ðū oferhȳdige þreádest (ðreádes, Surt.) *increpasti superbos,* Ps. Th. 118, 21. Abraham þreáde Abimelech mid wordum *Abraham increpavit Abimelech,* Gen. 21, 25: Andr. Kmbl. 3371; An. 1689. Hē ðreáde ðæne wind, Lk. Skt. 8, 24: 23, 40. Ðreáde *corripit,* Past. 21; Swt. 151, 20. Þreádon *increpabant,* Mt. Kmbl. 19, 13. Ne þreá ðū mē *ne arguas me,* Ps. Th. 6, 1: 37, 1. Þreá hine openlíce *publice argue eum,* Lev. 19, 17: R. Ben. 13, 9. Mē sōðfæst gerecce (ðreáð, Surt.) and þreáge (ðreáð, Surt.) *corripiet me justus et increpabit me,* Ps. Th. 140, 7. Ðreágan *redarguere,* Past. 2; Swt. 31, 12. Hē ongan hine þreágean (þreágan, MS. B.) *coepit increpare eum,* Mk. Skt. 8, 32. Ðreiga, Mt. Kmbl. Rush. 16, 22. Hē sceall stíðlícor þreán (*arguere*), R. Ben. Interl. 15, 1. Monige sindon suíðe líðelíce tō ðreágeanne *nonnulla sunt leniter arguenda,* Past. 21; Swt. 157, 24. Sindon monige suíðe suíðe tō ðreágeanne ðæt hí gehiéran ðreágende of ðæs lāriówes mūðe hū micle byrðenne hié habbaþ on hiera scyldum *nonnulla sunt vehementer increpanda, ut quanti sit ponderis culpa ab increpantis ore sentiatur,* Swt. 159, 16–18. Ðā andwyrde se ōðer ðreágende '*the other answering rebuked him* (Lk 23, 40), Homl. Th. ii. 256, 12. Ðreágende wer *uir objurgans,* 530, 28. Wæs hē fram ðām brōþrum ðreád *corripiebatur a fratribus,* Bd. 5, 14; S. 634, 10. Wē beóþ þreád *corripiemur,* Ps. Spl. 89, 12. II. *to punish* one who deserves punishment, *to chastise* by way of discipline, with a view to amend, *to chasten, correct:*—Ða ðe ic lufige, ða ic ðreáge and beswinge, Homl. Th. i. 470, 26. God beswingð and þreáð ða ðe hē lufaþ, ii. 548, 18: Exon. Th. 63, 23; Cri. 1024. Lēg þreáð þeódsceaþan, 97, 25; Cri. 1596. Wē sculon men ðreágean swā swā ða gōdan fæderas gewuniaþ heora bearn ða hí for heora synnum ðreágeaþ and swingaþ and hwæðere ða sylfan ðe hí mid ðām wītum ðreágeaþ and swenceaþ lufiaþ eác *sic nos fidelibus tenere disciplinam debemus, sicut boni patres filiis solent, quos et pro culpis verberibus feriunt, et tamen ipsos quos doloribus adfligunt amant,* Bd. 1, 27; S. 490, 15–18. Ðū mē þreádes þurh sārslege, Exon. Th. 275, 7; Jul. 546. Drihten hyne þreáde myd þearlwȳslícere swingle for his ungehȳrsumnysse, Shrn. 98, 14. Hē hine sylfne þreáge swíðe þearle mid forhæfednesse ǽtes and drinces, L. Pen. 14; Th. ii. 282, 18. Synrust þweán, hine sylfne þreán, Exon. Th. 81, 10; Cri. 1321. Mid þȳstrum þreán, Ps. Th. 104, 24. Ðrēgende ðreáde mec Dryhten *castigans castigavit me Dominus,* Ps. Surt. 117, 18. Hē him eáwde mid hū miclum swingum hē ðreád and wītnod wæs, Bd. 2, 6; S. 508, 24. Hē (*the man who will not give tithes*) bið mid wītum þreád æfter his deáþe, Blickl. Homl. 49, 25. Synfulle (*those in purgatory*) beóþ þreád, Elen. Kmbl. 2590; El. 1296. III. of undeserved punishment, *to torture, torment, afflict, distress, vex, oppress:*—Seó wyrd þreáþ ða unscildigan and nāuht ne þreáþ ðām scildigum *fortuna premit insonteis debita sceleri noxia poena,* Bt. 4; Fox 8, 13. Se hine mid miclum wītum þreáde, ðæt hē Criste wiðsōce, Shrn. 93, 33. Ðreáde, 118, 19, 21. 'Þreá hig lōca hū ðū wylle.' Sarai hig ðā geswencte, Gen. 16, 6. Ic hālsige ðē ðæt ðū mē ne þreáge (*torqueas*), Mk. Skt. 5, 7: Lk. Skt. 8, 28. Ðrēge *urgeat,* Ps. Surt. 68, 16. Ðā hēt hē hí āhōn be hire loccum and hí þreágean mid missenlícum wītum, Shrn. 75, 21: 104, 16. Swingan and þreágan, Exon. Th. 251, 9; Jul. 142. Cōme ðū ūs tō þreágenne (*torquere*), Mt. Kmbl. 8, 29. Ðreágende *torquens,* Kent. Gl. 662. Mid sumre untrumnesse his líchaman ðreád *quadam infirmitate corporis arreptus,* Bd. 3, 19; S. 547, 12. (Wē) biád þreáde *aporiamur* (aporiare *ad angustiam reducere,* Migne), Wrt. Voc. ii. 100, 44: 7, 6. (Wǽron) þreád (*cruciatibus*) *artabantur, stringebantur,* Hpt. Gl. 484, 10. III a. where the subject of the verb is not a person:—Seó langung hine þreáde, Blickl. Homl. 113, 14. Gif strongra storm and genip swȳþor ðreáde *si procella fortior aut nimbus perurgeret,* Bd. 4, 3; S. 569, 12. [Þraghand *castigans,* Ps. 117, 18. What if þretty þryuande be þrad (*punished*), Allit. Pms. 60, 751. *O. Sax.* gi-þrōōn *corripere* (Lk. 23, 22, v. *first passage in* I *above*): *O. H. Ger.* drauwen, drouwen *arguere, redarguere, increpare, minari, minitari.*] v. ge-þreán.

preágend, es; *m. One who reproves* or *corrects:*—Þreágendes (*vox*) *correctoris* (*amici*), Hpt. Gl. 527, 48.

þreágung, þreáwung (v. þreápung), þreáung, þreáng, e; *f.* I. *reproof, rebuke:*—Þreáiunge *castigationis* (*censura*), Hpt. Gl. 476, 48. For ðære strenge ðínre þreáunga, Ps. Th. 38, 11. Of þreáunga (þrǽgunge, MS. T.: ðreánge, Surt.) ðínre *ab increpatione tua,* Ps. Spl. 17, 18: 79, 17: 103, 8. Fram ðreáwunge (ðreánge, Surt.), 75, 6. Hū gesceádwís se reccere sceal bión on his ðreáunga *quae esse debet rectoris discretio correptionis,* Past. 21; Swt. 151, 5. Ðreáunge *correptionibus,* Swt. 155, 5. Ðreánge *increpationem,* Ps. Surt. 37, 15. Ðreángum *increpationibus,* 38, 12. Ðreánge *increpationes,* 149, 7. II. *a threat:*—Ælc gleáw mōd hit gewarenaþ ǽgðer ge wiþ heora þreáunga ge wið ōlecunga *prudentia nec formidandas fortunae minas, nec exoptandas facit esse* *blanditias*, Bt. 7, 2; Fox 18, 24. III. *chastisement, punishment*:—Ic wæs beswungen ǽlce dæg and þreáung (*castigatio*) mín on dægrǽde, Ps. Spl. 72, 14. Ðæt ic ídel heonone ne hwyrfe míne synna on þreágunge berende *that I may not go hence with nothing accomplished, bearing my sins to punish me*, Homl. Skt. ii. 23 b, 672. III a. *correction*:—Ǽfter deáþe nán þreágincge ys leáf *post mortem nulla correctionis est licentia*, Scint. 48, 16. [*O. H. Ger.* drowunga, drôunga *animadversio, comminatio.*]

þreahs. v. þreax.

þreál, e; *f. Correction*:—Þreál *correctio*, Wrt. Voc. ii. 135, 81. I. *correction by words, reproof, rebuke*:—Ðreál *correptio*, Kent. Gl. 1061. Þreále *invectionis*, Hpt. Gl. 448, 52. Hé (*John the Baptist*) ða heard-heortan ðeóde mid stearcre ðreále and stíðre myngunge tó lífes wege gebígde, Homl. Th. i. 362, 34. II. *correction by acts, chastisement, punishment, discipline*:—Gif hé bétan nele underlicgge hé rihtlícre þreále *si non emendaverit, discipline regulari subjaceat*, R. Ben. 56, 13. Ðú (*Belshazzar*) noldest ðé warnian þurh ðínes fæder ðreále, Homl. Th. ii. 436, 8. Mistlíce þreála gebyriaþ for synnum, bendas oððe dyntas . . ., L. Pen. 3; Th. ii. 278, 25. Hine man mid líchamlícum þreálum gewylde, R. Ben. 57, 12: 58, 10. Ðonne wurð seó heardnis stíðmódre heortan swíðe gehnescad þurh grimlíce steóra and heardlíce ðreála, ðe ic on mancyn sænde, Wulfst. 133, 19.

þreá-líc; *adj. Miserable, woeful, calamitous*:—Godes ágen bearn héngon fæderas ússe; ðæt wæs þreálíc geþóht, Elen. Kmbl. 851; El. 426. Wæs þreálíc þing (*the deluge*) þeódum tóweard, réðe wíte, Cd. Th. 79, 28; Gen. 1318. Ða apostolas þrowedon folcbealo ðreálíc, mǽrne martyrdóm, Menol. Fox 248; Men. 125.

þreán. v. þreágan.

þreá-níd, es; *n.*: e; *f. Force* or *compulsion that punishes* or *causes misery, affliction that comes from punishment*:—Ic hit leng ne mæg helan for hungre; is ðes hæft tó ðan strang, þreáným ðæs þearl *this imprisonment is so hard, so severe the pain of my punishment*, Elen. Kmbl. 1404; El. 704. Þrowigean þreániéd micel fýres wylm *to suffer much torturing violence, the fervor of fire*, Cd. Th. 229, 7; Dan. 213. Þreáným þolian, Beo. Th. 573; B. 284: Exon. Th. 187, 1; Az. 28. Þreánéd, 270, 12; Jul. 464. Blíðheort wunode eorl in þreánédum *cheerful the man remained in his misery*, Andr. Kmbl. 2530; An. 1266. Wé ðec for þearfum and for þreánýdum árena biddaþ *we pray thee for mercy on account of our needs and afflictions*, 186, 4; Az. 14: Beo. Th. 1668; B. 832. Ðone feónd hé gefetrode fýrnum teágum, biþeahte þreánýdum (*with penal restraints*), 359, 11; Pa. 61. Þreánédum beþeaht, Elen. Kmbl. 1764; El. 884.

þreá-nídla, an; *m. Painful constraint, restraint of punishment, oppression*:—Béc ámyrgaþ módsefan of ðreánýdlan ðisses lífes *books bring the mind to mirth from the painful pressure of this life*, Salm. Kmbl. 481; Sal. 241. Ðonne wyrd and warnung winnaþ mid hira ðreánýdlan hwæðerne ǽðreóteþ ǽr *when fate and prudence strive, each with its own hard constraint, which of the two tires first?* 857; Sal. 428. Nealles sylfes willum ac for þreánédlan, Beo. Th. 4450; B. 2224. Hé þeóstra þegnas þreániédlum bond *he bound the ministers of darkness with penal restraints*, Exon. Th. 143, 29; Gú. 668.

þreáníd-líc; *adj. That entails painful violence, calamitous, afflictive*:—Micel is ðæt ongin and þreániédlíc ðínre gelícan ðæt ðú forhycge hláford úrne *great is the undertaking and calamitous for the like of thee to despise our lord*, Exon. Th. 250, 16; Jul. 128.

þreáp (?) *a troop, band*:—Þreápum *commanipularibus, sociis* (*perhaps* heápum *should be read*, cf. efenheápum *conmanipularibus*, Wrt. Voc. ii. 20, 27; *or* þreátum; v. þreát: *but* þreáp *may have a double sense as* þreát *has* (*see, too*, þreápian, þreátian); *in later English it remains with the meaning* strife, contest, e. g.: Wituten threp (ani enuy, alle chidyng) or strijf, C. M. 13310. This þrepe (*the siege of Troy*) for to leue, Destr. Tr. 9845: *perhaps, also, in sense of troop*:—An feondes trume . . . þe saules . . . awarieþ al a-þrep (*in a troop?* or = *Ital.* a gara) al so wulues doþ þe scep, Misc. 149, 85. Halliwell gives *thrap* to crowd, as an Essex word), Hpt. 477, 52: 487, 33.

þreápian; *p.* ode *To rebuke, reprehend*:—Oft gelimpeþ, ðonne hé tó suíðe and tó ðearllíce ðreápian (ðreáwian, ðreátian, Cott. MSS.) wile his hiéremenn, ðæt his word beóþ gehwyrfedo tó unnyttre ofersprǽce *plerumque contingit, ut, dum culpa subditorum cum magna invectione corripitur, magistri lingua usque ad excessus verba pertrahatur*, Past. 21; Swt. 165, 17. [Þrepe *arguere*, Ps. 93, 10. Himm birrþ þræpenn wiþþ skill onnȝæness alle sinness *he must with discretion contend against all sins*, Orm. 5744. Whan ȝe aȝens the prechur threpe *when ye blame the preacher* (quotation in Halliwell's Dict.). Ha þreapeð aȝein þe, Kath. 1916. Bihat al ꝥ tu wult, þreap (*threaten*) þrefter inoh, 1499. In þraldom to þrepe (*contend*) with þe werld, Destr. Tr. 12134. Þai þrappit with stormys, 2003. They threpide wyth the throstille, D. Arth. 930. See also Halliwell's Dict. *threap, thripe*; Jamieson's Dict. *threpe*. Cf. Al þet fortune may þreapny (*threaten*) an do, Ayenb. 84, 20.] v. þrípel, *and next word*.

þreápung, e; *f. Rebuke, reproof*:—Ðæt geðreátade mód bið suíðe raðe gehwierfed tó fióunga gif him mon tó ungemetlíce mid ðære ðreápunga (ðreáwunga, Cott. MSS.) oferfylgð suíður ðonne mon ðyrfe *correpti mens repente ad odium proruit, si hanc immoderata increpatio, plus quam debuit, affligit*, Past. 21; Swt. 167, 14. [Þrepyng *strife*, Allit. Pms. 43, 183. Cf. Cheaste. Þes boȝ him todelþ ine .vij. oþre boȝes . . . þe zixte þreapninge (*threatening*) . . . Efterward comeþ þe þreapnynges and beginneþ þe medles and þe werres, Ayenb. 65–66.] v. two preceding words.

þreát, es; *m.* I. *a troop, band, crowd, body of people, swarm, press, throng*, (1) indefinite:—Þreát *turba*, Wrt. Voc. ii. 137, 29. Ðreát (ðreátt, Rush.), Mk. Skt. Lind. 3, 32. Ðreót (ðæt folc ł ðreátas, Lind.) *turbae*, Lk. Skt. Rush. 3, 10. Menigo ðreád (monige ðreátas, Rush.) *multa turba*, Mk. Skt. Lind. 3, 7: 5, 21: Lk. Skt. Lind. 8, 40. Þreát *chorus*, Wrt. Voc. ii. 17, 33: i. 291, 13. Se ðreát (*caterva*) ðara Godes ðeówa, Bd. 4, 7; S. 574, 34. His ðegna ðreát *ministri ejus*, Ps. Th. 102, 20. Heofonengla þreát, Exon. Th. 57, 34; Cri. 928. Wítgena weorod, wífmonna þreát, 462, 7; Hö. 48. Þreátes *classis*, Wrt. Voc. ii. 24, 78. Þreáte *examine*, 33, 26. Gesomnadum ðreáte (*coetu*) bisceopa, Bd. 4, 17; S. 585, 12: Blickl. Homl. 95, 6. Se wæs on ðam ðreáte þreotteóða secg, Beo. Th. 4803; B. 2406. Cyning þreáte fór, herge tó hilde, Elen. Kmbl. 102; El. 51: Cd. Th. 288, 27; Sat. 388. Hió þrungon on þreáte *they pressed in a crowd*, Elen. Kmbl. 657; El. 329. In ðreáte *in choro*, Ps. Surt. 149, 3: 150, 4. Hí gesomnodan mycelne ðreát discipula *congregata discipulorum caterva*, Bd. 4, 2; S. 565, 25. Wyrma þreát, Cd. Th. 285, 12; Sat. 336. Gif hé on þreát cymeþ, Exon. Th. 380, 4; Rä. 1, 2. Ofer ðreótt, Mk. Skt. Rush. 8, 2. Menigo ł ðreátas *turbae*, Mt. Kmbl. Lind. 13, 2. Engla þreátas, Blickl. Homl. 11, 12. Ealle ða mycclan þreátas ðe him mid férdon, 99, 35. Þurh þreáta geþræcu, Exon. Th. 417, 17; Rä. 36, 6. Mid engla ðreátum *ducibus angelis*, Bd. 4, 23; S. 596, 12. Þreátum *festis choreis*, Wrt. Voc. ii. 148, 14. Weras ðreátum and þrymmum þrungon and urnon, Judth. Thw. 23, 39; Jud. 164. Meara þreátum, Exon. Th. 119, 19; Gú. 257. Ðreáttum *turbis*, Rtl. 95, 6. (2) in a more definite sense:—Ðreát *turma .i. xxxii equites*, Jn. Skt. Lind. 18, 12 margin. Ðes ðreát *haec cohors*, Ælfc. Gr. 9, 44; Zup. 64, 12. *Cohors, d. milites vel* þreát, Wrt. Voc. ii. 136, 1. Þreát *falanx, multitudo militum, cohors*, 147, 6. Of þreáte *ex falange*, 29, 66. Ðreóte, 107, 59. Ðæs déman cempan gegaderodon ealne ðone þreát (ðreád, Lind. *cohortem*), Mt. Kmbl. 27, 27. Þicfealdum þreátum eóroda *spissis legionum cohortibus*, Hpt. Gl. 413, 1. II. *violence, compulsion, force, oppression, punishment, ill-treatment.* v. þreátend:—Is ðeós þrág ful strong, þreát ormǽte; ic sceal þinga gehwylc þolian, Exon. Th. 270, 14; Jul. 465. Hé wæs gebunden fýre and líge; ðæt wæs fæstlíc þreát (*a punishment that pressed on him without remission*), Cd. Th. 284, 22; Sat. 325. Gotan eástan sceldas lǽddon þreáte (*by force* or (?) *with their army*) geþrungon þeódlond monig, Met. 1, 3. Stódan him ábútan swearte gástas and mid micclum ðreáte (*with great violence*) him onsigon, Homl. Th. i. 414, 9. Ða ðe hæfdon sum þing lytles tó bigleofan, ðæt gelæhton reáferas and of ðam múðe him ábrudon unmǽdlíce mid þreáte, Homl. Ass. 68, 73. Mid swíðlícum þreáte, Ælfc. T. Grn. 21, 12: Homl. Skt. ii. 28, 105: 29, 217. Godes ǽ forgǽgan for his gramlícan ðreáte, 25, 220. Ne forhtige gé for ðæs fyrnfullan þreátum (*cruelties*, or (?) *troops*), 25, 260. Hié ealle worlde weán and ealle þreátas (*all the woes of the world and all miseries*) oferhogodan . . . hié ealle worldlíce tintrega and ealle lichomlícu sár oforhogodan, Blickl. Homl. 119, 16. [Riden ut þritti þusend, þe þræt (*throng*) wes þa mare, Laym. 9791. Listeð wich þreat (*punishment, trouble*, cf. God wile his swerd dragen, 22), Dauid setted uppen us, O. E. Homl. ii. 61, 20. Þrat moste I þole and unþonk, Allit. Pms. 93, 55. 'Herekempen scullen þi lond wasten . . .' þis iherde þe king, þræt (*threat*) þas kaiseres, Laym. 22582. For scrið ne ðret *neither for entreaty nor threat*, Gen. and Ex. 2021. Ne recche ich noht of þine þrete, O. and N. 58. Grete wordis and moche grym þrete, Destr. Tr. 2595. Hire sire and hire dame þreteþ hire to bete, nule heo forgo Robin for al heore þrete, Misc. 190, 84. *M. H. Ger.* drôz *annoyance, molestation*. Cf. *Icel.* þraut; *f. a struggle, labour, hard task.*] v. á-, beadu-, beorn-, eóred-, ge-, gúð-, here-, heofon-, íren-, mægen-, mearc-, sige-, wǽg-þreát.

þreátend, es; *m. A violent person, one using violence* or *compulsion*:—Ðæm ðreátende *violenti*, Mt. Kmbl. Lind. 11, 12. Ðæm nédende ł ðæm ðreátende *volenti* (l. *violenti*), 5, 42. Ðæm ðreáddende *angarianti*, p. 14, 17. v. þreát, II.

þreátian; *p.* ode. I. *to urge, press*:—Threátade *urguet*, Wrt. Voc. ii. 124, 21. (1) *to oppress, afflict, vex, trouble, exercise, harass*:—Ðú ðreást ða ðeóda ðe ús ðreátigeaþ, Ps. Th. 9, 5. Mec láðgeteónan þreátedon þearle *my foes harassed me sorely*, Beo. Th. 1124; B. 560. Wyrd . . . for ðý cymþ tó ðæm gódan, ðæt hió óþer twéga dó, oððe hine þreátige tó ðon ðæt hé bet dó ðonne hé ǽr dyde, oððe him leánige ðæt hé ǽr tela dyde *fortuna . . . remunerandi exercendive bonos causa deferatur*, Bt. 40, 1; Fox 236, 3. Þreátende *maceratus*, Wrt. Voc. ii. 113, 49: 55, 43. (2) *to urge* a person to something, *press* for something, *force* to do something:—For ðí ic ðreátige ðé tó úra goda offrunge, ðæt ðis folc, ðe ðú beþǽhtest, forléton ða ídelnysse ðínre láre, Homl. Th. i. 592, 31.

Seó wyrd ðe þreátaþ ða yflan tō wītnianne *fortuna quae justo supplicio malos coercet*, Bt. 40, 2; Fox 236, 25 note. Hē þreátode hine tō hǣþenscipe, Shrn. 33, 10. Ǣghwylc hine þreátode æfter ðām bōcum *every one tormented him for the books*, 123, 29. Ða cempan hine ðreátodon ðæt hē his lāc offrian sceolde *the soldiers urged him to offer his sacrifice*, Homl. Th. i. 416, 27. Men ðreátian and tihtan tō gōdum ðeáwum for ðam ege ðæs wītes *ad rectum supplicii terrore deducere*, Bt. 38, 3; Fox 200, 7. Sceolan ða bisceopas men georne þreátigean, and him bebeódan, ðæt hī Godes dōmas on riht healdan, Blickl. Homl. 47, 35. Ongan se cāsere hine ðreátian tō hǣðengylde, Shrn. 121, 12. Ða fǣmnan Simfronius ongan þreátian his suna tō wīfe *that virgin* (*St. Agnes*) *Simfronius attempted to force to be wife to his son*, 56, 7. Geneáded ł þreátod *coacta*, Hpt. Gl. 508, 22. II. *to reprove, rebuke*:—On wuda ðū wildeór wordum þreátast *increpa feras silvarum*, Ps. Th. 67, 27. Geðence hē ðæt hē biþ self suīðe gelīc ðām ilcan monnum ðe hē ðǣr ðreátaþ and hēnð *aequales se ipsis fratribus, qui corriguntur, agnoscant*, Past. 17; Swt. 117, 16. Se ðe brūne ȳða þreátaþ *he that rebukes the waves* (cf. geðreádade tō sae *increpavit mari*, Mt. Kmbl. Lind. 8, 26), Andr. Kmbl. 1039; An. 520. God þreátode (*arguit*) ðē, Gen. 31, 42. Ðā þreátode (*increpavit*) se fæder hine, 37, 10. Ðonne se lāreów sēcð ðone tīman ðe hē his hiéremen on ðreátigean (ðreágean, Cott. MSS.) mæge *cum tempus subditis ad correptionem quaeritur*, Past. 21; Swt. 153, 6. Līðelīce tō ðreátianne (ðreátigeanne, Cott. MSS.) *leniter arguenda*, Swt. 151, 11. III. *to threaten*:—Hē þreátaþ ðone earman mid his eágum *oculi ejus in pauperem respiciunt*, Ps. Th. 9, 29. Hī þreátiaþ eall moncynn mid hiora þrymme *ore torvo comminantes*, Bt. 37, 1; Fox 186, 6: Met. 25, 13. [*In later English the forms from* þrētan, þriétan (e. g. *p.* þrette) *occur, though in the earlier time this form seems very rare.* v. þrītan. He gon þretien swiðe, þat al he wolde heom todrive, Laym. 17300. Mine þralles me þretiað (*threaten*), 493. Þe king þræted Brutun, þat . . ., 504. Summe þrætteden heore ueond, 27131. Oluhnen oðer þreaten, A. R. 248, 8. He þrette us for to smiten, 366, 16. He bigon to þreatin hire *vehementius adversus eam in vocem erupit*, Kath. 2078. Þreatin *minari*, 626. To þrete *to complain* (cf. pleny, 548), Allit. Pms. 17, 560. Þat þretes (*reproves*) þe of þyn unþryfte, 89, 1728. Euereuch man me mid stone þreteþ (*ill-treats*), O. and N. 1609. Sho was adrad, for he so þrette (*threatened*), Havel. 1163: Gen. and Ex. 2023. An canticle ðæt ðreated (*rebuked*) ðo men, 4125. Ne threte (*arguis*) me, Ps. 6, 2. He watȝ þreted (*abused*) and þef called, Gaw. 1725. Of thralles y am thrat (*ill-used?*), P. S. 158, 17.] v. ā-, ge-þreátian; þrītan; þreátnian; þreátung; þreótan.

þreát-mǣlum; *adv. In troops, in crowds*:—Þreátmǣlum *manipulatim*, Wrt. Voc. ii. 113, 38.

þreátnian; *p.* ode *To urge, force, compel*:—For hwilcum ðingum neádaþ se deófol eów ðæt gē cristene men tō his biggengum ðreátniaþ *for what reasons does the devil compel you to force Christian men to his worship?* Homl. Th. i. 424, 3. [Myd word he þretneþ muche, and lute deþ in dede, R. Glouc. 457, 14. Disciplis thretenyden (*comminabantur*) to men offringe, Wick. Mk. 10, 13.] v. þreátian.

þreátung, e; *f.* I. *compulsion, force, violence, oppression, ill-treatment.* v. þreátian, I:—Hī bestungon him on mūþ mid mycelre ðreátunge ðone fūlan mete, Homl. Skt. ii. 25, 34. Pilatus hē hæfde on þreátunge ōþ hē hiene selfne ofstong *Pilatus tantis angoribus coarctatus est, ut sua se manu transverberaverit*, Ors. 6, 3; Swt. 258, 10. Hié heora land tō bismere oferhergodan, and him ðæs nǣnige bōte dydon būton ofermōdlīce wīg and þreátunge *they harried their land, and for that they made them no amends, but in their arrogance made war on them and harassed them*, Blickl. Homl. 201, 24. II. *rebuke, reproof.* v. þreátian, II:—Mid ðreátunge *correptionibus*, Past. 21; Swt. 154, 5. Ðonne of ðære ðreátunga gāþ tō stīðlīco word *cum de correptione sermo durior excidit*, Swt. 167, 10. Ðurh ðæt īsern is getācnod ðæt mægen ðara ðreátunga *per ferrum increpationis fortitudo signatur*, Swt. 163, 24. II a. *correction*:—Tō ðam yflum cymþ rēþu wyrd tō edleáne his yfla oððe tō þreátunge and tō lāre ðæt hē eft swā ne dō *fortuna aspera puniendi corrigendive improbos causa deferatur*, Bt. 40, 1; Fox 236, 8. III. *threatening*:—On ðam geáre gegaderade Eádward cyng mycele scypferde on Sandwīc þurh Magnus þreátunge on Norwegon (v. Saga Magnūs gōða, cc. 37, 38: Magnūs konungr gerði sendimenn til Englands . . . en þat stōð ā brēfum . . . 'Vil ek, at þū gefir upp rīkit fyrir mēr; en at öðrum kosti mun ek sœkja til með styrk hers'), Chr. 1046; Erl. 171, 25. [Ihorde þe king of þisse herde þreting, Laym. 22582. Vre Louerd hefde ifuld him of his þreatunge *comminatione tua replesti me*, A. R. 156, 3. Þreting ne bene, Misc. 156, 17.]

þreáung. v. þreágung.

þreá-weorc, es; *n. Pain inflicted as a punishment*, used of the misery of hell, as in *O. Sax.* the phrase *thrā-werk tholōn*:—Wit hearmas, þreáweorc þoliaþ, and þȳstre land, Cd. Th. 45, 35; Gen. 737.

þreáwian, þreáwung. v. þreágan, þreágung.

þreax, þreahs *rottenness*:—Þreahs *caries*, Wrt. Voc. ii. 20, 56. Swā swā forrotod þreax, Basil admn. 7; Norm. 48, 20.

þrece, es; *m. Force, oppression*; the result of oppression, *weariness, exhaustion*:—Ðǣr synt tō sorge ætsomne gemenged se þrosma (þrosmiga, Wulfst. 138, 26) līg and se þrece gicela *there to their sorrow are mingled together the stifling flame and the violence of cold*; frigora mista simul ferventibus algida flammis, Dom. L. 191. Hneppade sāwle mīn for ðrece *dormitavit anima mea prae taedio*, Ps. Lamb. 118, 28. [*O. Sax.* wāpanthreki *force of arms*: *Icel.* þrekr; *m.*; þrek; *n. strength, fortitude*; þrekinn *enduring*; þrekaðr *wearied, exhausted.*] v. þracu.

þrecswald, þreiga, þremma, þreó, þreo-. v. þerscold, þreágan, þrymma, þrī, þri-.

þreodian, þridian; *p.* ode. I. *to deliberate, take thought*:—Hē on his mōde ðōhte and ðreodode ðæt hē wolde eall Angolcyn of Breotone gemǣrum āflȳman *totum genus Anglorum Brittaniae finibus erasurum se esse deliberans*, Bd. 2, 20; S. 521, 28. Hē þreodode and smeáde on his mōde, hwæt hē embe ðæt dyde, Homl. Ass. 124, 242. Ic frōd þrāgum þreodude, Elen. Kmbl. 2475; El. 1239. Weras þeahtedon, þrydedon and þōhton, 1094; El. 549. II. *to deliberate, hesitate*:—Þrydaþ *hesitat*, Wrt. Voc. ii. 137, 35. Ne þreodode hē fore þrymme ðeódcyninges ǣniges on eorðan, ac him ēce geceás līf *he did not hesitate before the glory of any king on earth, but* (*at once*) *chose life eternal*, Apstls. Kmbl. 35; Ap. 18. v. ymb-þreodiende, *and next word.*

þreodung, þridung, e; *f.* I. *deliberation*:—Þridung *discrepatio*, Wrt. Voc. ii. 25, 63. Gif hē mid þancmetunge and ðreodunge (ðrydunge, MS. B.) geþafaþ *si ex deliberatione consentit*, Bd. 1, 27; S. 497, 23. II. *hesitation*:—Geseah hē sume earme sāwle ūt fundigende of hyre līchaman, ac heó ne dorste ūt gān, for ðam ðe heó geseah ða āwyrgedan gāstas beforan hyre standan. Ðā cwæð ān ðæra deófla tō hyre: 'Hwæt is ðīn þriding? hwī nelt ðū ūt gān?' Wulfst. 140, 13. Tweógendlīcere tweónunge þrydunge *ancipiti ambiguitatis scrupulo*, Hpt. Gl. 422, 34. v. ymb-þreodung.

þreohtig. v. þrohtig.

þreóhund-wintre; *adj. Three hundred years old*:—Hē wæs on ðisum līfe þreóhundwintre and fīf-and-sixtigwintre, Gen. 5, 23.

þreó-niht; *pl. Three days*:—Hē þreónihta (*or ?* þreó nihta, þreó *being undeclined after the manner of* feówer, *etc.*) fæc swefeþ, Exon. Th. 357, 34; Pa. 38.

þreosel-līc. v. þrisel-līc.

þreótan; *p.* þreát; *pp.* þroten *To weary*:—Ic ðē bydde ðæt ðē ne ðreóte, ne ðū ða sprēce ðǣr ne forlēte *I pray thee that it may not weary thee, and that thou do not leave the conversation there*, Shrn. 188, 20. [*Goth.* us-þriutan *to trouble, be troublesome to*: *O. H. Ger.* bi-, gi-, ir-driozan *to weary, trouble*: *Ger.* ver-driessen: *Icel.* þrjóta *to lack, want.*] v. ā-þreótan, un-āþreótende, ā-þrotennes, -þrotsum; þreát, þreátian.

þreó-teóða, þreotteóða *thirteenth*:—Se þreotteóða (þriot-, þret-, þreó-) *tertius decimus*, Ælfc. Gr. 49; Zup. 282, 20. Se wæs on ðam ðreate þreotteóða secg, Beo. Th. 4804; B. 2406. Paulus is se ðreotteóða ðyses heápes, Homl. Th. ii. 520, 30. Seó ðreotteóðe mǣigð, i. 396, 4. On ðære þrytteóðan wucan, Mt. Kmbl. 11, 20 rubc. On ðæm þreóteóðon geáre, Ors. 4, 10; Swt. 200, 33. Þrytteóðan, Homl. Skt. i. 6, 272.

þreó-tīne *thirteen*:—Ðreótēno, Salm. Kmbl. 581; Sal. 290. Ðreótȳne, Menol. Fox 229; Men. 116. Þreottȳne *tredecim*, Ælfc. Gr. 49; Zup. 281, 11: Bd. 1, 23; S. 485, 23. Ðǣr syndon betweónan ðām twām mynstrum ðreottȳne mīla āmetene, 4, 23; S. 596, 26. Þreótiénum *terdenis*, Wrt. Voc. ii. 82, 38.

þreótīne-geáre; *adj. Thirteen years old*:—Seó fǣmne wæs .xiii. geáre, Shrn. 153, 32.

þreoxwold, þrēpel, þrescwald, þrexweald. v. þerscold, þrīpel, þerscold.

þrī, þrȳ, þrié, þreó; *m.*: þreó, þrió, þrē; *f. n.* (ðreá, ðriá, ðreó, ðrió *in North.*); *gen.* þreóra, þrióra (*and* ðreána *in North.*); *dat.* þrim (þrīm? ðriim *in North., but cf. Goth.* þrim), *later* þreom. *Three*:—*Tres* þrȳ gebyriaþ tō masculinum and femininum, *tria* þreó tō neutrum, Ælfc. Gr. 49; Zup. 281, 3. I. used adjectivally:—Þrié Scottas cuōmon, Chr. 891; Erl. 88, 5. Ða þreó clystru ðæt sind þrī dagas, Gen. 40, 12. Ða þrī windlas ðæt sind þrī dagas, 18. Ða brōðor þrȳ, Cd. Th. 122, 28; Gen. 2033. Þreó godas, Hy. 10, 44. Ða þrē fǣmnan, Blickl. Homl. 145, 31. Nū synt þreó (ðrió, Lind., Rush.) gēr, Lk. Skt. 13, 7. Tō ðara ðreóra burga ānre, Past. 21; Swt. 167, 17: Ors. 1, 1; Swt. 10, 4. Þrióra, Swt. 4, 10. On þrim (ðriim, Lind.: ðrim, Rush.) dagon, Mk. Skt. 15, 29: Jn. Skt. 2, 19, 20. Ðrīm, Lk. Skt. Lind. 4, 25: Mt. Kmbl. Lind. 27, 63. On ðǣm þrim geárum on þrim folcgefeohtum, Ors. 3, 9; Swt. 128, 21. Of ðām þrim sunum, Anglia xi. 2, 37. On þȳs ylcum þrim dagum, Lchdm. iii. 76, 26. Þreom nihton ǣr Candelmæssan, Chr. 1078; Erl. 215, 28. Hié ða þrié dǣlas on þreó tōnemdon, Ors. 1, 1; Swt. 8, 3: Swt. 10, 3. Mīne þrié ða getreówestan frȳnd, Nar. 29, 27. Hē gestrīnde þrī suna, Gen. 6, 10: Ex. 2, 2. Lǣn me þrȳ (ðreó, Lind.: ðriá, Rush.) hlāfas, Lk. Skt. 11, 5. Þrȳ (þreó, Rush.) dagas and þreó (þreó, Rush.) niht, Mt. Kmbl. 12, 40. Ymbe þreó mōnað, Ors. 5, 11; Swt. 238, 11. On ðrió wīsan, Past. 53; Swt. 417, 20. Þrió mīla, Ors. 4, 10; Swt. 194, 7. Ymb þreó niht, 3, 11; Swt. 152, 19: Elen. Kmbl. 1663; El. 833: Gen. 29, 2. Þreó eardungstōwa (ðreá hūso, Lind.: ðreó selescotu, Rush.), Mt. Kmbl. 17, 4. Ðreá hūsa (ðriá hūs, Rush.), Mk. Skt. Lind. 9, 5. Þrió mydd hringa, Ors. 4, 9; Swt. 190, 12. Ðrió gecynd, Bt. 33, 4; Fox 132, 3: 35, 6; Fox 168, 19. Gif hē ðās þreó þing ne dēð, Ex. 21, 11. Þreó gēr, Lk. Skt. 4, 25. II. used substantivally, (1) absolutely:—Ðǽr twēgen oððe þrȳ (þreó, MS. A.: ðreó, Lind.: þreó, Rush.) synt gegaderode, Mt. Kmbl. 18, 20. Beóð fīfe on ānum hūse tōdǽlede, þrȳ (ðrió, Lind.: ðriá, Rush.) on twēgen and twēgen on þrȳ (þreó, MS. A.: ðrió, Lind., Rush.), Lk. Skt. 12, 52. Ðæt ǽlc word stande on twēgra oððe þreóra (ðreá, Lind.: þreó, Rush.) gewittnesse, Mt. Kmbl. 18, 16. Ðæt wē twā oððe ðreó gehȳron, Bd. 3, 9; S. 533, 29. (1 a) distributively:—Ða wuniaþ twām and þrim ætgædere, R. Ben. 9, 15. (2) with qualifying or defining words:—Þa þrȳ cōmon, Cd. Th. 221, 24; Dan. 93. Wē þrȳ, 242, 3; Dan. 413. Ða mōdhwatan þrȳ, 238, 21; Dan. 413. Cōmon þrȳ gelǽrede weras ... hī ða ealle þrȳ tōgædere grētton ðone cyngc, Ap. Th. 19, 22: Homl. Th. ii. 384, 4. Ða þreó ðē ne lǽtaþ geortrēwan, Bt. 10; Fox 30, 8. Hwylc ðara þreóra (ðīsra ðreána, Lind.), Lk. Skt. 10, 36: Homl. Th. i. 288, 27. Of ðisum þrim Noes sunum, Gen. 9, 19. Of him þrim, Anglia xi. 2, 45. Betwuh ðam þrim, Bt. 42; Fox 256, 20. Se ðe ðās ðreó hæfþ, 14, 2; Fox 44, 26. (3) in the phrase *on þreó*:—On þreó tōnemnan, Ors. 1, 1; Swt. 8, 3. On ðreó tōdǽlan, Bd. 5, 12; S. 627, 21. III. in combination with other numerals, (1) with cardinals, (a) multiplicative:—Þreó hund fæðma, Gen. 6, 15. Þreó hund wera, Jud. 7, 6. On þisum þrim hundrydum, 7. Wiþ þrim hundred (ðriim hundum, Lind.) penegon, Jn. Skt. 12, 5. (b) added to the decades:—Þreó and twēntig, Ex. 32, 28. Þreo-and-hundeahtatig-wintre, 7, 7. (2) with ordinals:—Se þreó-and-syxtigeða, R. Ben. 37, 16. Mōna se þrī-and-twēntigoða, Lchdm. iii. 194, 21. [*Goth.* þrija; *n.*; *gen.* þrijē; *dat.* þrim; *acc.* þrins; *m. f.*; þrija; *n.*: *O. Sax.* thrie, threa; *dat.* thrim: *O. L. Ger.* thrie; *m.*; thriu; *n.*; *dat.* thrim: *O. Frs.* thrē; *m.*; thria; *f.*; thriu; *n.*; *gen.* thrīra; *dat.* thrium, thrim, threm: *O. H. Ger.* drī; *m.*; drīo; *f.*; driu; *n.*; *gen.* drīo; *dat.* drim, drin: *Icel.* þrír; *m.*; þrjár; *f.*; þrjú; *n.*; *gen.* þriggja; *dat.* þrim(r), þrem(r); *acc.* þrjá; *m.*; þrjár; *f.*; þrjú; *n.*]

þría. v. þriwa.

þri-beddod; *adj. Having three beds* or *couches*:—Būr þrybeddod *triclinium*, Wrt. Voc. i. 58, 5.

þridæg-lic; *adj. Lasting three days*:—Þreodæglīc fæsten *jejunium triduanum*, Bd. 4, 25; S. 600, 8.

þri-dǽled; *adj. Divided into three parts, tripartite*:—Þreodǽledes *tripertiti*, Hpt. Gl. 511, 10. Þreodǽled *tripartitam*, 438, 27. Þreodǽlede *tripertitas, in tribus partibus divisas*, 451, 15. [*Icel.* þrī-deildr.]

þridda, þirda (*in North.*) *third*:—Se ðridda *tertius*, Ælfc. Gr. 49; Zup. 282, 16. I. as an ordinal:—Se forma ... se ōðer ... se þrydda (ðirda, Lind.: þridde, Rush.), Mt. Kmbl. 22, 26. Se þridda (ðirdda, Lind.: ðirda, Rush.), Mk. Skt. 12, 21. Twēgen men ... mǽg wæs his āgen þridda, hē feórða sylf, Cd. Th. 173, 29; Gen. 2868: Elen. Kmbl. 1707; El. 855. Heofonwaru and eorðwaru, helwaru þridde, Hy. 7, 95. Ðære þriddan eá nama, Gen. 2, 14. On nānum heolstrum heofenan, oþþe eorþan, oþþe sǽ þriddan, Homl. Th. ii. 146, 32. Ðȳ þryddan dæge (ðe ðirda dæg, Lind.), Mt. Kmbl. 16, 21. On ðære þriddan (ða ðirdda, Lind.: ðirda, Rush.) wæccan, Lk. Skt. 12, 38. Æfter ðon ðridan dæge, Blickl. Homl. 181, 2. Nān þridde be him sylfum ne lēt hē *he admitted no third hypothesis about himself*, Homl. Skt. i. 23, 633. I a. marking degrees of relationship:—Þridde fæder *proavus*, þridde mōder *proavia*, Wrt. Voc. i. 51, 55, 56. Þridde fæder *abavus*, 72, 21. Mīnes fæderan þridda fæder *abpatruus meus*, ii. 8, 24. Þridda sunu *pronepus*, 62, 36. II. fractional. v. twǽde:—Bewyl ōþ þriddan dǽl, Lchdm. ii. 120, 15. Seóþe tō þriddan dǽle, i. 98, 7. [*Goth.* þridja: *O. Sax.* thriddio: *O. Frs.* thredda: *O. H. Ger.* dritto: *Icel.* þriþi (*gen.* þriþja).]

þridding (?), e; *f. The doing of a thing for the third time* (? Halliwell gives *thirding* with this meaning as a Suffolk word):—Ðirding (*but the word has been altered to* ðirde. v. Skeat's collation) scipdrincende *tertio naufragantem*, Rtl. 61, 31.

þridung, þrie-, þrielig, þriétan. v. þreodung, þri-, þrilig, þrītan.

þri-ex; *n.* ?:—On ðæt þri ex; of ðam þri exe, Cod. Dip. Kmbl. iii. 436, 28.

þri-feald; *adj. Threefold, triple*:—Ic cwæþ ðæt sió sāwul wǽre þriofeald, Bt. 33, 4; Fox 132, 2. Þriefald, Met. 20, 183. Ðrifald *trinus*, Rtl. 111, 8: Mt. Kmbl. p. 14, 6. Ðryfeald, Homl. Th. ii. 606, 24. Ðryfeald *triplex*, Ælfc. Gr. 9, 61; Zup. 70, 2: 49; Zup. 284, 17. From ðæm þriefealdan (*triplici*) brægene, Wrt. Voc. ii. 80, 57. On þreofealdum hūse *in triclinio*, 45, 80. Þreofealdum fæce *terna intercapedine*, Hpt. Gl. 462, 76. Mid þreofealdre lencge *terna proceritate*, 445, 7. Ðū þriefalde on ūs sāwle gesettest, Met. 20, 176. Þryfealdne (þreo-, MS. B.) āð ... þryfealde (þri-, MS. B.) lāde mid þryfealdan forāðe, L. C. S. 22; Th. i. 388, 12–15. Ða þriefealdan sāwla, Bt. 33, 4; Fox 130, 39. Ðrifaldo *ternos*, Rtl. 193, 33. [*O. Frs.* thri-fald: *O. H. Ger.* dri-falt: *Icel.* þrī-faldr.]

þrifealdlīce; *adv. Triply*:—Ðriof[e]aldlīce *tripliciter*, Kent. Gl. 839. Þriefealdlīce (þry-, MS. B.: þri-, MS. H.), L. Alf. pol. 39; Th. i. 88, 3.

þri-feoðor; *adj. Triangular*:—Ðrifeoðor, ðrifedor, trifoedur *triquadrum*, Txts. 103, 2052.

þri-fēte; *adj. Having three feet*:—Þryfēte *tripes*, Ælfc. Gr. 9, 26; Zup. 51, 12: 49; Zup. 287, 20. Þriefēte rīcelsfæt *cythropodes*, Wrt. Voc. ii. 15, 60. [*Icel.* þrī-fættr.]

þrifildan; *p.* de *To triple*:—Ic þryfylde *triplico*, Ælfc. Gr. 49; Zup. 287, 4. [*Icel.* þrīfalda.]

þri-fingre; *adj. Three fingers thick*:—Æt þryfingrum (spic *is added in MS. B.*), L. In. 49; Th. i. 132, 18.

þri-fingre; *adv. By a distance equal to the breadth of three fingers*:—Gif se ord sió þreofingre ufor ðonne hindeweard sceaft, L. Alf. pol. 36; Th. i. 84, 17. Cf. Grmm. R. A. 101.

þri-flēre; *adj. Having three floors, three-storied*:—Ðæt gyftlīce hūs wæs ðryflēre, for ðan ðe on Godes gelaðunge sind þrȳ stæpas gecorenra manna, Homl. Th. ii. 70, 17.

þri-fōtede, -fōtad; *adj. Three-footed*:—Þrifōtede *tripes*, Ælfc. Gr. 49; Zup. 287, 20 note. Þryfōtad fæt *trisilis*, Wrt. Voc. i. 25, 30.

þri-fyrede; *adj. Three-furrowed*; the word renders Latin *trisulcus*, Ælfc. Gr. 49; Zup. 288, 12 note.

þriga. v. þriwa.

þri-gǽrede; *adj. Cloven into three parts, three-pronged*:—Þrygǽrede (þreo-, þrio-) *trifidus*, Ælfc. Gr. 49; Zup. 288, 10. v. gār, gāra.

þri-geáre; *adj. Three years old*:—Se onfēng fulwihte ðā hē wæs þrigeáre cniht, Shrn. 119, 19. [*Icel.* þrī-ærr.]

þri-geáre, es; *n. A space of three years*:—Þrigeáre (þreóra geára ferst) *triennio*, Hpt. Gl. 519, 15. [*Icel.* þrī-æri; *n.*]

þri-gilde; *adj. To be paid threefold*:—Cleroces feoh .iii. -gylde, L. Ethb. 1; Th. i. 2, 6. [*Icel.* þrī-gildr *of threefold value*; þrī-gilda *to pay threefold*.] v. twi-gilde; *adj.* and *subst.*

þri-gilde; *adv.* (*or case of a noun* þri-gilde. v. twi-gilde; *subst.* and *adv.*) *With a treble payment*:—Gif man inne feoh genimeþ, se man .iii.-gelde gebēte, L. Ethb. 28; Th. i. 10, 1. Gylde hē hit þrygylde, L. A. G. 3; Th. i. 154, 11. Gange hē tō ānfealdum ordāle oþþe gilde .iii.-gylde, L. Eth. iii. 4; Th. i. 294, 15.

þri-heáfdede; *adj. Three-headed*:—Þryheáfdede *triceps*, Ælfc. Gr. 9, 55; Zup. 67, 11. [*Icel.* þrī-hōfðaðr.]

þrihing *for* (?) þriþing. v. trehing.

þri-hīwede; *adj. Having three forms*:—Ðryhīwede *triformis*, Ælfc. Gr. 49; Zup. 287, 10.

þri-hlidede; *adj. Three-lidded, having three openings*:—Ðryhlidede *tripatens*, Ælfc. Gr. 49; Zup. 288, 6.

þri-hyrne; *adj. Three-cornered, triangular*:—Ðæt sǽd byþ þreohyrne, Lchdm. i. 316, 10.

þri-hyrnede; *adj. Triangular*:—Þryhyrnede *triangulus*, Ælfc. Gr. 49; Zup. 289, 4. [*Icel.* þrī-hyrndr.]

þri-leáfe, -lēfe, an; *f. Trefoil* (cf. later, *three-leaved grass, triple grass.* v. E. D. S. Pub. Plant Names):—Geáces sūre *vel* þrilēfe *trifolium*, Wrt. Voc. i. 30, 24.

þrilen; *adj. Woven with three threads*:—Þrylen hrægel *trilicis vestis*, Wrt. Voc. i. 40, 19.

þrili. *This word has the form of an i-stem adjective in the glosses* ðrili *trilex*, Txts. 35, 29; drili *triplex*, 115, 158; *and that* þril- *is the main part of the word seems suggested by* þrilen (q.v.), *by* þrielig *in* þrielig hrægil *triligium*, Wrt. Voc. i. 289, 53, *and by later English* þrile, e.g. An God, þrile in þreo hades, A. R. 26, note a; þrumnesse þreofald ant anfaldte, þrile i þreo hades, Marh. 11, 27. Þrille-hod *trinity*, C. L. 1239. Cf. *too, O. H. Ger.* drilero *triplici* (*catena*). *On the other hand it might seem that the form is* þri-li *from comparison with* aen-li *simplex*, Txts. 115, 156; cf. *too, O. H. Ger.* dri-līch *drilex* (*tunica*), dri-līha *trilicem* (*tunicam*): *Ger.* drillich *ticking*. *Perhaps the word has been influenced by the Latin which it translates.* v. twi-līc, *and next word.*

þri-līc; *adj. Threefold*:—Ān myhtylīce and þrylīc hādelīce *unus potentialiter trinusque personaliter*, Hymn. Surt. 29, 13: 55, 13: 105, 15. Eálā ðū ðrilīc godcundnyss, 133, 5. Ðē þrylīcne and ǽnne, 146, 32. v. preceding word.

þrilig; *adj. Woven with three threads*:—Þrielig hrægil *triligium*, Wrt. Voc. i. 289, 53. v. þrili.

þri-līðe (?); *adj. Having three months named* Līða, a term applied to the year in which a fourth summer month was intercalated; the passage in which the Latinized form of the word occurs is as follows: Quotiescunque communis esset annus, ternos menses solares singulis anni temporibus dabant, cum vero embolismus, hoc est xiii mensium lunarium annus occurreret, superfluum mensem aestati apponebant, ita ut tunc tres menses simul Lida nomine vocarentur, et ob id annus thrilidus cognominabatur habens quatuor menses aestatis, ternos, ut semper, temporum caeterorum. Beda de temporum ratione, c. 13. v. Grmm. Gesch. D. S. c. vi.

þrimen *a third*:—Nim sealtes þrymen, Lchdm. ii. 124, 4. [*O. Frs.* thrimen (-in) *amounting to a third*; thrimenath *a third part*.]

þri-milce, es; *m.* (?) *The early name for the month of May*:—Se fīfta mōnað is nemned on ūre geðeóde Ðrymylce, for ðon swylc genihtsumnes wæs geó on Brytone and eác on Germania lande, of ðæm Ongla ðeód com on ðás Breotone, ðæt hí on ðæm mônðe þriwa on dæge mylcedon heora neát (Bede's Latin is: Thrimilci dicebatur, quod tribus vicibus in eo per diem pecora mulgebantur; talis enim erat quondam ubertas Britanniae vel Germaniae, e qua in Britanniam natio intravit Anglorum, De temp. rat. c. 13), Shrn. 77, 37. Ðonne Ðrymelces mônað bið geendod ðonne bið seó niht eahta tída lang, 87, 28. Ðrymylce mônað, Chr. Erl. Introd. xxxi, margin.

þrim-feald; *adj. Threefold:*—On ðam þrimfealdan (þry-, MSS. B. L.) ordâle, L. Ath. i. 4; Th. i. 202, 4. On ðam þrimfealdum (þry-) ordâle, 6; Th. i. 202, 13. Æt þrimfealdre (þryfealdre, 17) spræ̂ce, L. Eth. ix. 19; Th. i. 344, 13. Be ânfealdum *simplum*, be twyfealdum *duplum*, be þrimfealdum *triplum*, Ælfc. Gr. 49; Zup. 286, 18. [Cf. Ileafan on þa halȝa þreomnesse, O. E. Homl. i. 99, 34. Þe heuenliche þremnesse was mid him, ii. 137, 7. Þrumnesse, A. R. 160, 10. Þrimmnesse, Orm. 11177. Cf. *also O. Frs.* thrim-dêl (threm-) *a third.*]

þrimsa, þrindende, Exon. Th. 431, 23; Rä. 46, 5. v. trimes, þindan (?), þrintan (?).

þrinen; *adj. Threefold;* trinus:—God ânfeald and samod þrynen (*trinus*), Hymn. Surt. 105, 3. God þrynen and ân, 115, 37: 137, 31. Þrynenum gebede *trina oratione* . . . Mid þrynum tôdâle *trina partitione*, Anglia xiii. 380, 214, 217. God ðæne ðrynenne on ânnesse and ǣnne on ðrynnesse wê andettaþ *Deus quem trinum in unitate et unum in trinitate confitemur*, Wanl. Cat. 292, col. 1. [Cf. *Icel.* þrinnr.]

þring. I. *a press, crowd.* [Utforen al þan dringe (þringe, 2nd MS.), Laym. 14966. Amidden þan þrunge (þringe, 2nd MS.), 27524. Cf. Among þe þrenge of sipmen, 2229 (2nd MS.). Myd wel muchel þrynge, Misc. 86, 72. Cf. No þrung of folc, A. R. 162, 8.] v. eofor-, ge-þring. II. (*or* þryng?) *what presses or confines:*—Þryng *cannalis*, Wrt. Voc. ii. 128, 5. [Cf. *Icel.* þröng *a strait, a narrow place.*]

þringan; *p.* þrang, *pl.* þrungon; *pp.* þrungen. I. *trans. To press, crowd, throng:*—Ðás menegeo ðe ðringaþ *turbae te comprimunt*, Lk. Skt. 8, 45. Ðæt folc hine þrang, Homl. Th. ii. 394, 17. Þrungun *torquent*, Wrt. Voc. ii. 122, 56. Hí þrungon (geðringdon, Lind.: on ðrungun, Rush.) *comprimebant illum*, Mk. Skt. 5, 24. Ðû gesyxst ðás menigu ðê ðringende (ðringende on ðec, Rush.) *uides turbam comprimentem te*, 31. II. *to throng, press* round, upon, *crowd* together:—Hŷ ymb þeódenstôl þringaþ georne, Exon. Th. 25, 8; Cri. 397: 208, 30; Ph. 163. Fugla cynn on healfa gehwone heápum þringaþ *contrahit in coetum sese genus omne volantum*, 221, 18; Ph. 336. Gelíc sumum ðara gumena ðe him geornost mid þegnungum þringaþ ymbe ûtan, Met. 25, 28. Wergendra tô lyt þrong ymbe þeóden, Beo. Th. 5758; B. 2883. Ðâ him ðæt folc swíðost an þrang *ubi se obrui a circumfusa multitudine persensit*, Ors. 3, 9; Swt. 134, 18. Duguð samnode, hildfrecan heápum þrungon, Andr. Kmbl. 252; An. 126. III. *to press, move with violence, eagerness* or *hurry, press* on, *press* forward, *force a way:*—On hû grundleásum seáðe ðæt môd þringþ . . . hit þringþ on ða fremdan þîstro *tendit in externas ire tenebras*, Bt. 3, 2; Fox 6, 7-10: Met. 3, 7. Sum on oferhygdo þryme þringe (þrymme þringeþ? cf. below Homl. Skt. ii. 25, 781: Rä. 4, 61), Exon. Th. 314, 34; Môd. 24. Hê on ðæt weorod þrong for ðon ðe him wæs leófre ðæt hiene mon ofslôge ðonne hiene mon gebunde *he pressed into the host* (*of the enemy*), *because he would rather be slain than made prisoner*, Ors. 5, 12; Swt. 244, 12. Se ðe mid gebeóte and mid micclum þrymme þrang intô ðam temple, Homl. Skt. ii. 25, 781. Him arn on lâst, þrang þŷstre genip *dark cloud made its resistless way*, Cd. Th. 9, 9; Gen. 139: Exon. Th. 179; Gû. 1255. Wræccan þrungon (*pressed forward*), 461, 28; Hö. 42: Elen. Kmbl. 245; El. 123. Hí þrungon and urnon ongeán ða ðeódnes mægþ, Judth. Thw. 23, 40; Jud. 164. Tô weallgeatum wîgend þrungon, Andr. Kmbl. 2408; An. 1205: Beo. Th. 5913; B. 2960. Tô ðam swicce men on healfa gehwone heápum þrungon, Exon. Th. 359, 24; Pä. 67. Hê lǣteþ word ût faran, þræfte þringan, 316, 1; Môd. 42. Ic gewíte þringan þrymme micle, 386, 13; Rä. 4, 61. Ne þurfon gê nô hogian on ðæm anwealde, ne him æfter þringan, Bt. 16, 1; Fox 50, 30. Hê lêt willeburnan on woruld þringan, Cd. Th. 83, 2; Gen. 1373. Tô ðâm wícum hí cwômun hlôþum þringan, Exon. Th. 156, 1; Gû. 868. Ðâ ongan ic nŷdwræclíce gemang ðam folce wið ðæs folces (temples?) þringan, Homl. Skt. ii. 23 b, 405: Judth. Thw. 25, 8; Jud. 249. [(1) His sporis he gynneth in hors thryng, Alis. 2388. Cumpanyes thringen thee, Wick. Lk. 8, 45. Gif eiþer oþer faste þringe, O. and N. 756. To noght he thrange (*redegit*) Israele, Ps. 77, 59. Liknes of þa to noght thryng saltou (*rediges*), 72, 20. I am to noghte thrungen, 22. (2) Þe folc cumþ fastlice and elce deȝie þicce þringeð, O. E. Homl. i. 237, 29. A thousand of men thrungen togyderes, Piers P. 5, 517. (3) Iudas him com þrynge, Misc. 42, 177. Into þe deueleȝ þrote man þryngeȝ bylyue, Allit. Pms. 43, 180. Carrais him on þrong (Carais to þrong, 2nd MS.), Laym. 10652. Through her hert the swerd throng, Gow. iii. 262, 7. Þrungen euchan biuoren oðer forte beo bihefdet, Jul. 67, 11. Binnen heo þrungen (alle in þronge, 2nd MS.), Laym. 9421. *O. Sax.* thringan (*trans.* and *intrans.*): *O. H. Ger.* dringan *urgere, stipare: Icel.* þryngva. Cf. *Goth.* þreihan.] v. â-, æt-, be-, for-, ge-, of-, on-, ôþ-, tô-, ymb-þringan; ût-âþrungen.

þri-nihte; *adj. Three days old:*—Gif hê biþ âcenned on .iii.-nihtne mônan, Lchdm. iii. 160, 20: 176, 22, and note 2. [*Icel.* þrí-nættr.] v. twi-nihte.

þrinna. This seems a Scandinavian form [cf. *Icel.* þrennar tylftir *three twelves;* e. g. þrennar tylftir eigu at dæma mâlit, Njála c. 144]:—Lâdige hê hine mid þrinna .xii., L. Eth. iii. 13; Th. i. 296, 29.

þrinness, þriness, e; *f. Trinity,* mostly in the special sense *the Trinity:*—Ðæs mannes sâwl hæfð ðære hâlgan þrynnysse anlícnysse; for ðan ðe heó hæfð on hire ðreó ðing . . . Is hwæðere se man ân man, and nâ ðrynnys, God . . . þurhwunaþ on ðrynnysse hâda and on ânnysse ânre godcundnysse; nis nâ se man on ðrynnysse wunigende, swâ swâ God, Homl. Th. i. 288, 17-35. Ðeós þrynnys is ân God, 10, 7. Is seó hâlige þrinnis on ðisum þrim mannum, Ælfc. T. Grn. 2, 8. For ðí is gecweden 'uton wyrcan,' ðæt wǣre geswutelod ðære hâlgan þrynnysse weorc on ânnysse. Seó hâlige þrynnys is undergiten on ðam worde 'uton wyrcan,' Boutr. Scrd. 19, 12. Ðrines *trinitas*, Ps. Surt. ii. p. 202, 23. Þrynes, Exon. Th. 24, 4; Cri. 379. Þrynis, 286, 3; Jul. 726. Þrynysse þrym, 37, 26; Cri. 599. Of ðæm mægene ðære hâlgan þrynesse, Blickl. Homl. 29, 12. On ðære hâlgan þrynnysse, 249, 23. Mid þrym fingrum man sceall sênian for ðære hâlgan þrynnysse (ðrymnysse, MS. U.; v. *Middle English quoted under* þrim-feald), Homl. Skt. ii. 27, 156. Clypung tô ðære hâlgan Ðrynnisse *invocatio ad sanctam trinitatem*, Hymn. Surt. 1, 1. Wê andettaþ . . . ðrynnesse in ânnesse and ânnesse on ðære ðrynnesse, Bd. 4, 17; S. 585, 36. For ða hâligan ðrinesse, Rtl. 114, 17. Þrynesse, Blickl. Homl. 205, 30. [*O. H. Ger.* drinissa.]

þrintan; *p.* þrant, *pl.* þrunton; *pp.* þrunten *To swell:*—Þrinteþ, Exon. Th. 315, 1; Môd. 24. v. â-þrintan.

þrió, þriostrig. v. þrî, þeóstrig.

þrípel, es; *m. An instrument of punishment, a kind of cross:*—*Eculeus vel* þrŷpel *genus tormenti*, Wrt. Voc. ii. 142, 25. Unhêh þrêpel *eculeus* (equuleus *patibulum, furca cui decollatorum martyrum cadavera affigebant*, Migne), i. 21, 18. v. þreápian, *and next word.*

þrípel-úf (?) *an instrument of punishment:*—Wæarhrôd *vel* þrŷpelûf *eculeus* vel *catasta*, Wrt. Voc. i. 55, 52. v. þrípel.

þri-rêðre; *adj. Having three banks of oars;* used substantively *trireme:*—Ðâ næfde hê mâ scipa ðonne ân; ðæt wæs ðeáh þrerêþre, Bt. 38, 1; Fox 194, 10. Þrierêþre ceól, Met. 26, 27. Ân .C. ðara miclena þrierêðrena *centum triremes*, Ors. 3, 1; Swt. 96, 27: 5, 13; Swt. 246, 6. [*O. H. Ger.* dri-ruodri.]

þrisce. v. þrysce.

þri-scíte; *adj. Triangular, three-cornered:*—Ispania land is þryscyte *Hispania trigona est*, Ors. 1, 1; Swt. 24, 1. Sicilia is ðryscŷte *Sicilia tria habet promontoria*, Swt. 28, 2. On ðone þryscŷtan crundel, Cod. Dip. Kmbl. v. 374, 26. [Cf. *Icel.* þrí-skeyta *a triangle.*]

þrisel; *adj. Divided into three.* v. twisel, *and next word.*

þrisel-líc; *adj. Tripartite:*—Ðǣr beóþ men âcende þreosellîces hîwes *nascuntur homines tripartito colore*, Nar. 35, 29. v. twisel.

þri-slite, -slitte (?); *adj. Three-forked, three-pointed:*—Hæfdon ða wyrmas þriesli[ ]te (*a letter has been erased before the* t, *see note, and* Anglia i. 510, iv. 151) tungan *cum trisulcis linguis*, Nar. 14, 12. Cf. next word.

þri-snæcce, -snæce, -snece; *adj. Three-pointed, cloven in three:*—Þrysnece (-snæcce, -snæce) tungan hæfþ seó næddre *trisulcam linguam habet serpens*, Ælfc. Gr. 49; Zup. 288, 12. v. twi-snæcce.

þriste *and* þríst; *adj. Bold,* (1) in a good sense:—Môna se sixta . . . se ðe bið âcenned, þríste, mǣre, Lchdm. iii. 186, 15. Ic ofstikode bâr. Swîþe þrŷste (*audax*) ðû wǣre ðâ, Coll. Monast. Th. 22, 19. Þríste sceal mid cênum, Exon. Th. 337, 8; Gn. Ex. 61. Gewât hê (*Andrew*) þríste on geþance, Andr. Kmbl. 473; An. 237. Elene, þríste on geþance, Elen. Kmbl. 533; El. 267. Eorl unforcûð, elnes gemyndig, þríst and þrohtheard, Andr. Kmbl. 2529; An. 1266. Þríst, þonces gleáw, Exon. Th. 207, 19; Ph. 144. Geþinga ûs þrístum wordum, 21, 30; Cri. 342: Cd. Th. 242, 27; Dan. 425. Ic ǣnig ne mêtte þrístran geþôhtes, mægþa cynnes, Exon. Th. 275, 14; Jul. 550. (2) in a bad sense, *bold, presumptuous, audacious, shameless:*—Ðŷ læs hê tô ðríste sié for ðŷ underfenge his lâreówdômes *ne doctrinam praesumtio extollat*, Past. proem.; Swt. 23, 23. Ðonne hê wilnaþ on his môde ðæt hê sciele rícsian hê bið swíðe forht and swíðe behealden; ðonne hê hæfð ðæt hê habban wolde, hê bið swíðe ðríste *mens principari appetens fit ad hoc pavida, cum quaerit, audax cum pervenerit*, 9; Swt. 57, 4. Mǣden ofermôdig, þríste on lîchaman mid manegum werum, Lchdm. iii. 190, 16. (Cf. mǣden môdig, dyrstig, manega weras wilnigende, 25.) Ic (*the devil*) wênde þríste geþoncge, ðæt ic ðê meahte bûtan earfeþum âhwyrfan from hâlor, Exon. Th. 264, 2; Jul. 358. Forhwon beóð suǣ ðríste ða ungelǣredan ðæt hí underfôn ða heorde ðæs lâriówdômes *ab imperitis pastorale magisterium qua temeritate suscipitur?* Past. 1; Swt. 25, 16. Ða ðe tô ðam þríste sŷn, ðæt hig God oferseóð, Wulfst. 270, 23. Hié wǣron womma ðríste, inwitfulle, Cd. Th. 77, 9; Gen. 1272. Tô frece, synna þríste, 155, 31; Gen. 2581. Wǣron Sodomisc cynn synnum þríste, 116, 13;

Gen. 1935. Wed gesyllan eallra unsnyttro, þrîstra geþonca, Elen. Kmbl. 2569; El. 1286. Ic þrîsta sum þeófes cræfte, Exon. Th. 486, 24; Rä. 72, 20. [Ȝif he were swa þriste, and he hit don durste, þ he heom wolde leaden, Laym. 356. Þer þe dusie mon bid þriste, O. E. Homl. i. 117, 23. Ne helpþ noht þat þu beo so þriste, ich wolde fihte bet mid liste þan þu mid alle þine strengþe, O. and N. 171. To uvele we beoþ al to þriste, P. L. S. 8, 10. *O. Sax.* thrîsti: *Ger.* dreist.] v. ellen-, gâr-, un-, wîg-þrîste(-þrîst).

þrîste; *adv. Boldly*, (1) in a good sense, *confidently, without apprehension, fear, hesitation, reserve*:—Hê þrîste genêdde on ôðre dǽlas, Apstls. Kmbl. 100; Ap. 50. Hê þrîste bebeád, ðæt hié his lâre lǽston, Andr. Kmbl. 3303; An. 1654: Elen. Kmbl. 818; El. 409. Ne wæs ǽnig ðæt nê þus þrîste hrînan dorste, Exon. Th. 273, 4; Jul. 511. Heó ne meahte þrîste geþencan, hû ymb ðæt sceolde *she could not think with confidence of the event*, 378, 6; Deór. 12. Ic mundbyrd on ðê þrîste hæfde *in te confirmatus sum*, Ps. Th. 70, 5. Ic ðîn bebod þrîste gelýfde, 118, 66. (2) in a bad sense, *without sense of shame, presumptuously, audaciously*:—Heó þrîste ongan wið Sarran swîðe winnan, Cd. Th. 135, 10; Gen. 2240. Gê him þrîste oftugon *ye had no misgivings when ye refused them help*, Exon. Th. 92, 18; Cri. 1510. (3) in the Psalms *þrîste* seems used several times with an intensive force, much as *swîðe* is used:—Þa þearfendan þrîste Drihten gehýreþ holdlîce *hears attentively and graciously*; exaudivit pauperes Dominus, Ps. Th. 68, 34. Hê þearfena bearn þrîste hǽleþ *completely saves*; salvos faciet filios pauperum, 71, 4: 81, 4: 112, 6. Ealle hine þeóda þrîste heriaþ *greatly praise*; magnificabunt, 18. Þrîste ongunnon georne slêpan ða ðe on horsum wǽron, 75, 5. Ðû mîne geðóhtas þrîste oncneówe *thou didst thoroughly know my thoughts*; intellexisti cogitationes meas, 138, 2. Hê þearfendra ðrîste êhte *he persecuted the poor exceedingly*; persecutus est hominem pauperem, 108, 16.

þrîst-full; *adj. Presumptuous*:—Þrîstfulle *presumptuosi*, Anglia xiii. 369, 55.

þrîst-hycgende; *adj.* (*ptcpl.*) *Thinking* or *intending boldly, firm of purpose, having bold resolve*:—Ðû geþôhtest þrîsthycgende, ðæt ðû ðînne mægðhâd Meotude sealdes bûtan synnum, Exon. Th. 18, 24; Cri. 288. On þeóde geþeón, ðæt hê wese þrîsthycgende, 336, 17; Gn. Ex. 50.

þrîst-hygdig, -hýdig; *adj. Bold-minded, courageous*:—Þióden þrîsthýdig, Beo. Th. 5612; B. 2810. Nergend ðrîsthýdigum Thômase forgeaf êce rîce, bealdum beornwigan bletsunga his, Menol. Fox 443; Men. 223. Sum biþ æt þearfe þrîsthýdigra þegn mid his þeódne, Exon. Th. 298, 1; Crä. 78. [Cf. *O. Sax.* thrîst-môd thegan (*Peter*).]

-þrîstian. v. ge-þrîstian.

þrîst-lǽcan; *p.* -lǽhte; *pp.* -lǽht *To become bold, to dare, presume*:—Wê þrîstlǽcaþ biddan *audemus rogare*, Hymn. Surt. 111, 34. Hié sint tô manianne ðæt hié nô ðý swîður wið hié ne ðrîstlǽcen (ðrîsð-, Hatt. MS.) *admonendi sunt, ne contra eos audaciores fiant*, Past. 28; Swt. 196, 5. Be ðære ârfæstan Godes cennestran mildheortnysse þrýstlǽcende, ic mê of ðære stôwe âstyrede, ðe ic ðis gebæd, Homl. Skt. ii. 23 b, 457. [Awah þet he efre wulle þristelechen oðer biþenchen mid his fule heorte þe heo wulle underfon swa heȝ þing swa is Cristes licome in his sunfulle buke, O. E. Homl. i. 25, 30.] v. ge-þrîstlǽcan.

þrîstlǽcness, e; *f. Boldness, audacity, temerity, presumption*:—Ic eom ondetta . . . ðrîstlǽcnesse mînra synna, Anglia xi. 98, 22. Gyf man þurh þrýstlǽcnysse man fullaþ *si quis ex temeritate aliquem baptizaverit*, L. Ecg. P. addit. 30; Th. ii. 236, 34.

þrîstleásness (?), e; *f. Want of boldness*:—Ic eom andetta . . . þrîstleásnyssa mînra synna, Anglia xi. 101, 34. v. preceding word.

þrîstlîce, þrîstelîce; *adv. Boldly, confidently*, (1) in a good sense:—Hê spræc þrîstlîcor mid hine *confidenter ait*, Gen. 44, 18. (2) in a bad sense:—Ða underðióddan sint tô manianne ðæt hié ðara undeáwas ðe him ofergesette bióð tô swîðe and tô ðrîstelîce (ðrîsðlîce, Hatt. MS.) ne eahtigen *admonendi sunt subditi, ne praepositorum suorum vitam temere judicent*, Past. 28; Swt. 196, 1. Oft þeóf þrîstlîce sorgleáse hæleð forfêhð, Exon. Th. 54, 21; Cri. 872. Ðû (*the devil*) þrîstlîce þeóde lǽrest, Andr. Kmbl. 2371; An. 1187.

þrîstling (?), es; *m. A bold person*; found in the local name which occurs in the following passage:—On þrîstlinga dene; of þrîstlinga dene ufeweardre, Cod. Dip. Kmbl. iii. 82, 28. v. þrîste.

þrîstness, e; *f. Boldness, presumption, temerity*:—Ðrîsnes *praesumptio*, Kent. Gl. 1169. Mid þrýstnesse dyrstigere *praesumptione temeraria*, Anglia xiii. 383, 262. On þrîstnysse *in temeritate*, Scint. 139, 3. Hê yfel þurh þrîstnysse gefremede *malum per audaciam perpetravit*, 40, 5.

þri-strenge; *adj. Three-stringed*:—Þrystrenge (þreo-, þrio-) *trifidus*, Ælfc. Gr. 49; Zup. 288, 10. v. twi-strenge.

þrîtan; *p.* te. I. *to weary*:—Ðæt folc wearð þrît and þearle geswenct mid ðam sîðfæte *taedere coepit populum itineris ac laboris*, Num. 21, 4. II. *to urge, press, force*:—Seó wyrd ðe þriétaþ (-eþ?) ða yflan tô wîtnianne *fortuna quae justo supplicio malos coercet*, Bt. 40, 2; Fox 236, 25. [*Icel.* þreytask *to be exhausted*; þreyttr *tried, exhausted*: *Dan.* træt *wearied*.] v. â-, ǽ-þriétan (-þrîtan); þreátian.

þrîtig, þrittig; *num. Thirty*:—Þrittig, þrîtig *triginta*, Ælfc. Gr. 49; Zup. 281, 17. I. used substantivally as a neuter. (1) governing a noun in the genitive, when the inflections are *gen.* -es, *dat.* -um. (*a*) alone:—Ðam sceal .xxx. sciħ. tô bôte (cf. *in next line*: Ðam sculon .v. sciħ. tô bôte), L. Alf. pol. 56; Th. i. 94, 28. Hwæt gif ðǽr beóð þrîtig? God cwæð: Ne dô ic him nâ lâð, gif ðǽr beóþ þrîtig rihtwîsra, Gen. 18, 30. Þrittig fæðmâ biþ se arc on heáhnisse, 6, 15: Jn. Skt. 6, 19. Ymb þrittig wintra, Bt. 39, 3; Fox 214, 25. Ymb þrîtig wintergerîmes, Met. 28, 25. Ymb þrîtig geárgerîmes, 29. Hê genam þrîtig þegna, Beo. Th. 246; B. 123. Dô hî ealle tôgæderc, ðæt þrîtig seolforsticca, Anglia xi. 8, 19. Wintra ðrittih (ðrîtig, Rush.), Lk. Skt. Lind. 3, 23. Hê wæs ðrîtiges geára eald, Past. 49; Swt. 385, 15. Þrîtiges mîla brâd, Chr. 893; Erl. 88, 29. Ðrittiges heáh elngemeta, Cd. Th. 79, 8; Gen. 1308. xxx.-tiges manna mægencræft, Beo. Th. 764; B. 379. Ða hǽþenan ðrittigum sîþa mâre weorud hæfdon, Bd. 3, 24; S. 556, 22. (*β*) in combination with other numerals:—Þreó and þrîtig geára, Cd. Th. 296, 16; Sat. 503. Eahta and þrittig (ðrittih, Lind.: ðrîtig, Rush.) wintra, Jn. Skt. 5, 5. Hê rîxode twâ læs xxx geára, Chr. 641; Erl. 27, 16. Mid feówer hunde scipa and þrîtigum, Ors. 4, 6; Swt. 172, 31. (2) as a plural with *gen.* -a:—Com se cyning þrîtiga sum (þrittigum sum, MS. E.) ðara monna ðe in ðam here weorþuste wǽron, Chr. 878; Erl. 80, 20. II. used adjectivally, (1) alone:—Þrîtig þûsend wera, Jos. 8, 3. Þrîtigon sîðon *tricies*, Ælfc. Gr. 49; Zup. 286, 2. Cf. Þrittig sîðon seofon beóð twâ hundred and týn, Anglia viii. 303, 7. Þrittig sîðon twelf, 29. Þrittigun sýþum hundteóntig þûsenda, Blickl. Homl. 79, 25. Ða þryttig scyllingas, Mt. Kmbl. 27, 3. (2) in combination with other numerals:—Ðæt is ealles .xxx. and vi. peningas, Anglia xi. 8, 18. Mid þrym and ðrittigum mannum, Homl. Skt. i. 5, 128. Mid ðâm âþelestum ceastrum ânes wana ðrittigum *civitatibus viginti et octo nobilissimis*, Bd. 1, 1; S. 473, 26. ¶ In the following passage the construction is unusual:—On þrýtiges wintres ylde, Anglia xi. 2, 26. II a. of age, *thirty* (*years old*):—Se Hǽlend wæs þrittig ðâ hine mann fullude, Anglia xi. 3, 77. III. used in forming ordinals:—Se wæs fram Agusto ðridde eác ðrittigum *tricesimus tertius ab Augusto*, Bd. 1, 6; S. 476, 17. [*Goth.* þrins tiguns (*acc.*): *O. Sax.* thrîtig: *O. Frs.* thrîtich: *O. H. Ger.* drîzug: *Icel.* þrír tigir.]

þrîtig-feald; *adj. Thirty-fold*:—Mid þrittifealdne hêhnysse *tricena altitudine*, Hpt. Gl. 445, 8. Sum berð þrittigfealdne wæstm, Homl. Ass. 21, 175: Mt. Kmbl. 13, 8. Þrîtigfealdne, Mk. Skt. 4, 20. Ða habbaþ þrittigfealde mêde, Homl. Ass. 21, 179.

þrîtigoða; *num. adj. Thirtieth*:—Se þrittigoða (ðrîtogoða, þritteogoða, þreotteogaþa) *tricesimus*, Ælfc. Gr. 49; Zup. 283, 10. Ðý ðrittigoþan geáre, Bd. 5, 23; S. 647, 29.

þrîtig-wintre, -wintra; *adj. Thirty years old*:—Iôsep wæs þrîtigwintre *triginta annorum erat Joseph*, Gen. 41, 46: Lk. Skt. 3, 23: Homl. Th. i. 26, 3. Ðâ ðâ Crist wæs þrîtigwintra (*or* þrîtig wintra), Homl. Th. ii. 38, 25.

þriwa, þrywa, þreowa, þriowa, þriuwa, þriga, þrige, þrîa; *adv. Thrice, three times*:—Þriwa (þreowa) *ter*, Ælfc. Gr. 49; Zup. 285, 14: 38; Zup. 232, 7: Exon. Th. 207, 20; Ph. 144. Þriwa on gêre *tribus vicibus per singulos annos*, Ex. 23, 14: *ter in anno*, 17. Ne sint ðæt þreó godas þriwa genemned, ac is ân God, Hy. 10, 44. Þriwa (ðriga, Lind.: þriowa, Rush.) *ter*, Mt. Kmbl. 26, 34. Þriuwa, Rush. 75. Þriwa (ðrîa, Lind.: ðrige, Rush.), Mk. Skt. 14, 30, 72. Þriwa (ðriga, Lind.: ðrige, Rush.), Lk. Skt. 22, 61. Þriwa (þrywa, MS. A.), Jn. Skt. 13, 38: 21, 14. Þriga, Wrt. Voc. ii. 126, 35. Ðriga, Bd. 1, 13; S. 481, 42. ¶ With numerals:—Cweð þriwa nigon sîþan, Lchdm. i. 202, 11. Þriwa seofon beóð ân and twêntig, Anglia viii. 302, 43. Þriwa feówer beóð twelf, 328, 21. [Þrie twenti *sixty*, H. M. 23, 29. Þrie he eode abuten, Laym. 17432. Þreie (þries, 2nd MS.), 26066. Þrien, 14352: þreoien, 14338. Þries, A. R. 106, 18. Þriȝess, Orm. 1149. Þriȝȝess, 5945. Thrie, Alis. 1263. Þrye, R. Glouc. 191, 14. Þries, Ayenb. 35, 11. *O. Sax.* thriwo, thriio: *O. L. Ger.* thrio: *O. Frs.* thrîa, thriia.]

þri-wintre, -wintra, -winter; *adj. Of three years, three years old*:—Thriuuintri (ðriuuintri, Corpus Gl.) steór *prifeta*, Txts. 86, 780. Þrywintre (-wintra) *triennis, trimus*, Ælfc. Gr. 49; Zup. 287, 13, 18. Þriwinter *trimus*, vel *triennis*, vel *trimulus*, Wrt. Voc. i. 21, 59. Þrywinter *triennis*, 23, 53. Wæs cnihtcild sum ne wæs yldre ðonne ðrywintre *erat puer trium circiter, non amplius, annorum*, Bd. 4, 8; S. 575, 27. Geoffra mê ân þriwintre hrýðer and ǽnne þriwintre ramm and âne þriwintre gât *sume mihi vaccam triennem et capram trimam et arietem annorum trium*, Gen. 15, 9. Hê âsende him tô ân ðrywintre cild, Homl. Th. ii. 134, 7. [*Icel.* þrí-vetr *three years old*.]

þroc, es; *n.* I. *a throck* (v. E. D. S. Pub., Cheshire Gloss., where is quoted: 'The *Throck* is the piece of Timber on which the suck (*share*) is fixed.' *Academy of Armory* by Randle Holmes. Also spelt *thruck*):—*Dentale*, s. *est aratri pars prima in qua uomer inducitur quasi dens* sule reóst *vel* þroc, Wrt. Voc. ii. 138, 72. (v. Wülck. Gl. 219, 4.) II. *a table*:—Mynetera þrocu hê tôbræc *mensas nummulariorum euertit*, Mk. Skt. 11, 15. [Cf. *O. H. Ger.* druh; *f. cippus, compes*.]

ðrogan, Bt. 38, 1; Fox 196, 7. v. þreágan.

þrôh *glosses* rancor:—*Rancor* thrôh (thrôch, Erfurt Gl.) *vel invidia, vel odium* (trôh *rancor*, Corpus Gl.), Txts. 92, 874. v. next word.

þróh; *adj. glosses* rancidus:—Of ðrôn æfðancan *rancida invidia*, Anglia xiii. 33, 156. Swá ðrógum *tam rancidis* (v. Hpt. Gl. 472, 61: *tam rancidis* (*fetidis, amaris, s. invisis, abominatis*) þrôn, biterum, mid swá biterum), 148. v. preceding word.

þroht, es; *m. Oppression, affliction, hardship*:—Ic hit leng ne mæg helan for hungre, is ðes hæft tó ðan strang, þreanýd ðæs þearl, and ðes þroht tó ðæs heard, Elen. Kmbl. 1405; El. 704. [Cf. *Icel.* þróttr *fortitude*.]

þroht; *adj. Oppressive, grievous*:—Him sorgendum sár ǒðclífeþ, þroht þeódbealu, Exon. Th. 78, 2; Cri. 1268. Ellen biþ sélast ðam ðe oftost sceal dreógan dryhtenbealu, deópe behycgan þroht þeódengedál, 183, 8; Gú. 1324.

þroht-heard; *adj.* I. *strong under afflictions, having fortitude or endurance in trouble*:—Ne geald hé (*Stephen*) yfel yfele, ac his ealdfeóndum þingode þrohtheard *he requited not evil with evil, but strong to bear his sufferings he interceded for his foes*, Elen. Kmbl. 985; El. 494. Blíðheort wunode eorl unforcúð elnes gemyndig, þríst and þrohtheard in þreánédum, Andr. Kmbl. 2529; An. 1266. Héton lǽdan út þrohtheardne þegn, woldon ellenróffes mód gemiltan; hit ne mihte swá, 2781; An. 1393. Þegnas þrohthearde þafigan ne woldon, ðæt hié forléton leófne láreów, 803; An. 402. II. *grievously hard*:—Wæs se leódhete þrohtheard, Andr. Kmbl. 2279; An. 1141.

þrohtig (?); *adj. Enduring, firm, persevering, laborious*:—Ðrohtig (*in the MS.* e *is written over* o) *pervicax*, Txts. 87, 1556. Ic eom swiftre ðonne hé, þrágum strengra, hé þreohtigra, Exon. Th. 494, 7; Rä. 82, 4. [Cf. *Icel.* þróttigr *powerful*.]

þrop, þrosle. v. þorp, þrostle.

þrosm, es; *m.* I. *smoke, vapour*:—Se þeóstra þrosm, Wulfst. 186, 4. On forsworcennesse sweartes þrosmes and ðæs weallendan pices, 139, 1: Dóm. L. 199. Eft átogenum ðara fýra ðrosmum . . . eác fúlnes wæs mid ðæs fýres ðrosme *retractis ignium vaporibus . . . et foetor cum eisdem vaporibus*, Bd. 5, 12; S. 628, 24–26. Ða ðe þrosme beþeahte in þeóstrum sǽton, Exon. Th. 8, 11; Cri. 116: Elen. Kmbl. 2593; El. 1298. Ða biteran récas, þrosm and þýstro, Cd. Th. 21, 18; Gen. 326. Se þrosma (*but see* þrosmig) líg, Dóm. L. 191. II. *darkness, a dark space*:—Sweart þrosm onáslít *tetrum chaos inlabitur*, Hymn. Surt. 13, 36. Betwux ús and eów is gefæstnod micel ðrosm (*inter uos et nos chaos magnum firmatum est*, Lk. 16, 26), Homl. Th. i. 332, 17. III. *in* Germ. 398, 230 þrosm *glosses* chautêrem. v. swefel-þrosm; þrysman.

þrosmig; *adj. Smoky, vaporous*:—Ðǽr synd sorhlíce tósomne gemencged se þrosmiga líg and se þrece gycela (*frigora mista simul ferventibus algida flammis*, Dóm. L. 25, 95), Wulfst. 138, 26.

þrostle, þrosle, an; *f. A throstle, singing-thrush*:—Ðrostle *trita*, Txts. 103, 2062: *turdella*, 2068. Þrostle, Wrt. Voc. i. 281, 16: *merula*, 62, 45: 77, 19. Ðrostle, ii. 55, 61. Þrosle *merula vel plara*, i. 29, 57. Án blác þrostle flicorode ymbe his neb, Homl. Th. ii. 156, 22. Of ðam leá on þrostlan wyl, Cod. Dip. Kmbl. v. 345, 3. [*M. H. Ger.* drostel.] Cf. þrysce.

-þrot. v. ǽ-þrot, á-þrotsum.

þrot-bolla, an; *m. The gullet, windpipe*:—Ðrotbolla *gurgulio*, Ælfc. Gr. 9, 3; Zup. 35, 7: Wrt. Voc. ii. 110, 15. Þrotbolla, i. 43, 41: 64, 62: 282, 82: *ceutrum*, ii. 131, 1. Eal þrotbolla *chautrum*, i. 43, 42: ii. 22, 59. Gif monnes þrotbolla biþ þyrel, gebéte mid .xii. scill., L. Alf. pol. 51; Th. i. 94, 18. Ðrotbollan *gurgilioni*, Lchdm. i. lxx, 9. Þrotbollan *gurguliones*, Wrt. Voc. ii. 40, 45: Hpt. Gl. 490, 20. [Nu schal forrotien . . . þi protebolle þat þu mide sunge, Misc. 178, 173. And by the throtebolle he caught Aleyn, Chauc. Reeve's T. 353. The throtebolle *epyglotum*, Wülck. Gl. 580, 21 (15th cent.). Throte bolle *frumen hominis est, rumen animalis est, ipoglotum*, Cath. Angl. 386.]

þrotu, an; *f. The throat*:—Þrotu *guttur*, Wrt. Voc. i. 43, 39: Ps. Lamb. 5, 11: Scint. 97, 16: Lchdm. ii. 46, 22. Þeós ðrotu *hoc guttur*, Ælfc. Gr. 9, 22; Zup. 49, 3. On ðære ðrotan, Lchdm. ii. 2, 18. On ða þrotan, Bt. 22, 1; Fox 76, 30. Hé (*Judas*) gewrâð ða forwyrhtan ðrotan, seó ðe lytle ǽr belǽwde Drihten, Homl. Th. ii. 250, 16. Woruldcara forsmoriaþ ðæs mõdes ðrotan, 92, 11. Þrotan *gurguliones*, Wrt. Voc. ii. 82, 52. [*O. H. Ger.* droza, drozza *gurgulio*.] v. æsc-, eofor-þrotu(-e).

-þrowen *in* á-þrowen, *read* á-dropen.

þrowend, es; *m. A scorpion*:—Hí habbaþ tæglas ðám wyrmum gelíce ðe men hátaþ þrowend, Wulfst. 200, 15. *Scorpius*, ðæt is þrowend, Lchdm. iii. 246, 1. Se wyrm ðrowend slihþ mid ðam tægle tó deáðe . . . Ondrǽd ðé ðone ðrowend . . . Bið hiht geǽttrod mid ðæs ðrowendes tægle, Homl. Th. i. 252, 4–11. Se ðe gegrípð þrowend (*scorpionem*), Scint. 86, 11: 225, 4. Þrowendra *regulorum, serpentium*, Hpt. Gl. 450, 17.

þrowende(-as?); *pl. The Thronds* (?), people in North Norway (*Icel.* Þrændir: *Norw.* Thrönder):—Mid þyringum ic wæs and mid þrowendum and mid Burgendum, Exon. Th. 322, 17; Víd. 64.

þrowere, es; *m.* I. *a sufferer*:—Gif mann bið ǽkenned on .x. nihta ealdne mónan se bið þrowere, Lchdm. iii. 156, 27. v. líc-þrowere. II. *a sufferer for religion, a martyr*:—Ðe fruma ðrowere *protomartyr*, Rtl. 197, 9. Ðroweres ðínes *martyris tui*, 75, 41. Ðæs þroweres gemynd Sc̄i Ypolyti, Shrn. 117, 8. Sc̄e Ciricius tíd ðæs þroweres, Chr. 916; Th. i. 190, col. 2. Ðrowres, Rtl. 50, 15. Ðrowre *martyrem*, 2. Monge Godes þrowera, Exon. Th. 113, 5; Gú. 153: 111, 25; Gú. 132. Ðrowara ðínra *martyrum tuorum*, Rtl. 63, 16, 34. Ðrowerana, 44, 32. Wuldrigo ðrowras *gloriosos martyres*, 75, 34.

þrowian (þrówian?), þreowian (þreówian?); *p.* ode *To suffer*:—Ic ðrowige *patior*, Ælfc. Gr. 29; Zup. 186, 9. I. *to suffer* as opposed to to act:—*Verbum* ys word . . . getácniende oððe sum ðing tó dônne oððe sum ðing tó þrowigenne oððe náðor, Ælfc. Gr. 19; Zup. 119, 10. II. *to suffer* what is painful. (1) with acc.:—Mid gewyrhtum ic ðás þrowige, Blickl. Homl. 89, 7. Ðú ne þrowast nǽnige þrowunge, 157, 14. Wíf ácenþ bearn and þrowaþ micel earfoþu, Bt. 31, 1; Fox 112, 2. Hungor hí þrowiaþ *famem patientur*, Ps. Spl. 58, 7: Andr. Kmbl. 562; An. 281: Exon. 98, 30; Cri. 1615. Hé ðæs gewinnes weorc þrowade, Beo. Th. 3447; B. 1721. Hé drepe þrowade, 3183; B. 1589: Exon. Th. 256, 10; Jul. 229. Hé for ælda lufan fela þrowade, 69, 10; Cri. 1118: Blickl. Homl. 23, 35. Hí ermða þrowodan, 17, 17. Ðrowedon, Menol. Fox 244; Men. 123. Hí heora scylde wíte ðrowedon *poenas sui reatus luerent*, Bd. 4, 26; S 602, 14. Swá oft swá wé óht uneáþes þrowian æt ysflum monnum, Blickl. Homl. 33, 22. Þǽh þe ealle ǽswice þrowige on þé ic nǽfræ þrowe *si omnes scandalizati fuerint in te, ego numquam scandalizabor*, Mt. Kmbl. Rush. 26, 33. Hira untrymnesse hé sceal ðrowian on his heortan *ex affectu cordis alienae infirmitati compatitur*, Past. 10; Swt. 61, 16. Éce wíte ðrowian, Homl. Th. i. 66, 14. Sceame þrowian, Soul Kmbl. 98; Seel. 49. Sár þrowian synna tó wíte, Exon. Th. 77, 1; Cri. 1250. Wrace þrowian, biterne bryne, Andr. Kmbl. 1230; An. 615. Wóp ðrowian, heáf under heofonum, Salm. Kmbl. 934; Sal. 466. Torn þrowigean, Cd. Th. 146, 14; Gen. 2422. Þrowigean þreániéd micel, fýres wylm, 229, 6; Dan. 213. Manega earfoðnesse fram Iudéum ic wæs ðrowiende, Blickl. Homl. 237, 10. (2) without acc., generally *to suffer martyrdom*:—Ic þrowode, Cd. Th. 296, 17; Sat. 503. Mín Drihten, áne tíd on róde ðú þrowodest, Blickl. Homl. 243, 28. Godes sunu on róde galgan þrowode, 27, 28: Elen. Kmbl. 841; El. 421: Rood Kmbl. 165; Kr. 84. Ðrowode, Menol. Fox 167; Men. 85. Þrowode *martyrizavit*, Wrt. Voc. ii. 55, 14. His mæssepreóst þreowude mid him, Shrn. 124, 1. Þrowedon *agonizarunt*, Wrt. Voc. ii. 3, 6. Þreowedan, 81, 50. Hú Drihten wolde cuman tó ðære stówe ðe hé on þrowian wolde, Blickl. Homl. 15, 5. Hé wolde þrowian for ealra manna hǽle, 65, 32: 77, 13. Hiǽ lǽddun hine ðæt hé þrowigan salde *duxerunt eum ut crucifigerent*, Mt. Kmbl. Rush. 27, 31. Ys mannes sunu fram him tó þrowigenne (þrowende bið, Rush.) *Filius hominis passurus est ab eis*, Mt. Kmbl. 17, 12. Tó ðrowienne, Homl. Th. i. 82, 27. Ðrouande *passurum*, Lk. Skt. p. 6, 9. Þrowigende *laturi*, Wrt. Voc. ii. 86, 39: 52, 46. ¶ The past participle is used as if the verb were a causative = *to make to suffer, to crucify*:—Æfter ðonne ðe hé þrowad wæs *after he was crucified*, Mt. Kmbl. Rush. 27, 44. Cf. Geðrowod under Pilate, Homl. Th. ii. 596, 15. Ðone geðrowodan Crist, 292, 13. (2 a) with gen. of instrument inflicting death:—Hé sceolde deófolgeldum geldan, oððe sweordes þrowian *suffer death by the sword*, Shrn. 129, 3. III. *to suffer for* something, *pay for, atone for*:—Ic ðrouuio *persolvio*, Wrt. Voc. ii. 117, 16. Ðrowode *expe[n]disset*, throuadae *expendisse[t]*, Txts. 61, 783. Þrowode *expendisset*, Wrt. Voc. ii. 29, 63. Hé þrowade ðæs þeówes sleacnysse *he suffered for the slowness of the servant*, Shrn, 43, 15. Þoledan and þrowedan *luebant*, Wrt. Voc. ii. 53, 19. Ðú scealt þrowian ðínra dǽda gedwild *thou shalt expiate the error of thy deeds*, Cd. Th. 57, 2; Gen. 921. Þrowgende *luendi*, Wrt. Voc. ii. 94, 51: 52, 65. [Crist þrouwede deð, O. E. Homl. i. 17, 29. Þrowede, ii. 101, 9. Hwi walde he þrowin as he dude, Kath. 1135. He ðrowede and ðolede, Gen. and Ex. 1180. *O. H. Ger.* drôen, druoen *pati*.] v. á-, efen-, ge-þrowian.

þrowiend-líc, þrowigend-líc; *adj.* I. *capable of suffering*:—Ðá wearð hé (*Christ*) gesewenlíc on úrum gecynde and þrowigendlíc, Homl. Th. i. 120, 26: ii. 6, 32. Ðis is ðín gecynd ðus ðrowigendlíc, ðe ic of ðé genam, 256, 28. Hélias wæs ús mannum gelíc, ðrowiendlíc, swá swá wé, 330, 16. II. as a grammatical term, *passive*:—*Passiva verba*, ðæt synd þrowiendlíce word, Ælfc. Gr. 19; Zup. 121, 1. Eal swá gǽð ða óðre ðrowigendlícan word, 27; Zup. 161, 15. v. un-þrowi(g)endlíc.

þrowing, þreowing, e; *f.* I. *suffering* as opposed to doing:—*Verbum* is word, and word getácnaþ weorc oððe ðrowunge oððe geþafunge, Ælfc. Gr. 5; Zup. 9, 3. Him (*the verb*) gelimpþ *significatio*, ðæt ys getácnung, hwæt ðæt word getácnige, dǽde oððe þrowunge oððe náðor, 19; Zup. 119, 14. II. *suffering* which is painful:—Ic geteorode on ðære þrowunga, Ps. Th. 38, 11. Ðú ne þrowast nǽnige þrowunge on ðínum líchoman, Blickl. Homl. 157, 15. Wæs monigu ðrowunga from swíðe monigum lécum *fuerat multa perpesa a compluribus medicis*, Mk. Skt. Rush. 5, 26. Hé gehýrde heora þrowunga *he heard of their sufferings* (they had been struck blind), Blickl. Homl. 153, 35. II a. as a medical term, *a painful symptom*:—Tácn ðæs ofercealdan magan, ðæt ða men ne þyrst, ne hí swól gefélaþ on magan, and ne biþ him ǽnig wearm þrowung getenge, Lchdm. ii. 194, 13. III. *suffering* that is undergone for the sake of religion, *suffering* of persecution, *cross* (in the phrase to take up one's *cross*):—Him

God wolde æfter þrowinga þonc gegyldan, ðæt hē martyrhād mōde gelufade, Exon. Th. 130, 22; Gū. 442. Lǽdæ ðrōunc his and fylge meh *tollat crucem suam et sequatur me*, Mk. Skt. Lind. 8, 34. Ðrowung (ðrowunge, Rush.), Lk. Skt. Lind. 9, 23. Ðrōung (ðrowunge, Rush.), 14, 27. Se ðe in þrowingum þeódnes willan dreógeþ, Exon. Th. 125, 18; Gū. 356: 148, 26; Gū. 750. Gehȳran heora þrowunga *to hear of the sufferings of St. Peter and St. Paul*, Blickl. Homl. 173, 2. III a. *suffering which ends in death, passion, martyrdom*:—Ðrouinges *martyrii*, Rtl. 64, 18. Ðrōunges *passionis*, 50, 23. Ic, eówer emnðeówa and Cristes ðrowunge gewita, Past. 18; Swt. 137, 16. Se ðe biþ gemyndig Drihtnes þrowunge and his ǽriste, Blickl. Homl. 83, 14. Ða mōddru on heora cildra martyrdōme þrowodon . . . neód is ðæt hī beón efenhlyttan ðæs ēcan edleánes, ðonne hī wǽron geféran ðære ðrowunge, Homl. Th. i. 84, 20. On hwæs tīman hē ðrowunge underhnige *in whose time he had submitted to martyrdom*, ii. 506, 31. Ðæt hē tō ðrowunge becōme *ad martyrium pervenire*, Bd. 1, 7; S. 478, 12. Be Cristes ðrowunge *de passione dominica*, 4, 24; S. 598, 13. Drihten ūs mid his þrowunga ālēsde, ðā hē on rōde galgan āstāg, Blickl. Homl. 97, 10: 35, 7: 81, 31. Ðrowenge *passione*, Rtl. 50, 4. Hē ongan ārweorþian ða ðrowunge hāligra martyra *honorem referre incipiens caedi sanctorum*, Bd. 1, 7; S. 479, 1. Þurh his þrowinga, Exon. Th. 29, 29; Cri. 470: 69, 33; Cri. 1130. III b. *the anniversary of a martyr's suffering*:—On ðone feówer and twēntygoðan dæg ðæs mōnðes byð Sci. Crissoȝones tȳd and þrowung, Shrn. 151, 17, 31. Þreowung, 114, 21. [Vre drihtnes halie passiun, þet is his halie þrowunge, O. E. Homl. i. 119, 26. Inntill þrowwinnge and pine, Orm. 15205. Cheosen er licomes hurt þen soule þrowunge, A. R. 372, 6. Wiðuten ðhrowing and figt, Gen. and Ex. 1317. *O. H. Ger.* druuunga *passio*.] v. following words.

þrowing-rǽding, e; *f. A martyrology*:—Sī rǽdd þrowungrǽding *legatur martyrlogium*, Anglia xiii. 385, 286.

þrowing-tīd, e; *f.* I. *the time at which a person suffered martyrdom*:—Fram ðissere worulde fruman ōð Xp̄es þrowungtīd, ðæt is six þūsend geára and .c. geára and lviii geára, Anglia xi. 7, 18. Weorðian wē on ðissum andweardan dæge Sancte Petres þrowungtīde, Blickl. Homl. 171, 4. II. *the anniversary of the time when some one suffered*:—Ðeós tīd fram ðisum andwerdan dæge (*fifth Sunday in Lent*) ōð ða hālgan Eástertīde is gecweden Cristes ðrowungtīd, Homl. Th. ii. 224, 19. On ǽlces geáres ymbryne ymbe his ðrowungtīde, i. 564, 24.

þrowing-tīma, an; *n. A time of suffering*:—Ðonne mīn ðrowungtīma cymþ, ðonne geswutelaþ seó menniscnys hire untrumnysse, Homl. Th. ii. 56, 2.

þrūh (*also* þrȳh, Bd. S. 580, 14); *gen. dat.* þrȳh, *and dat.* þrūh; *f.*: *dat.* þrūge; *m. n. Wood* or *stone hollowed out.* I. *a trough, pipe, conduit*:—Ðrūh, thruuch, thruch *tubo*, Txts. 103, 2067. Þrūh *vel* mylentroh *canalis*, Wrt. Voc. ii. 128, 16. Of þrȳh ł þeótan *tubo*, Hpt. Gl. 418, 61. Of ðam brōce in ðæt þrūh; of ðam þrūge, Cod. Dip. Kmbl. iii. 380, 3. Ðā gesomnodon ða sticceo hī in ða þrūh, þurh ða ðe ðæt wæter fleów; ðā ne meahte ðæt wæter flōwan, Shrn. 125, 12. II. *a box, chest*:—*Fiscella* spyrte ł þrūh, Germ. 400, 492. III. *a coffin, sarcophagus, tomb*:—Þrūh *sarcofagum*, Wrt. Voc. i. 49, 28. Ðūrh, 85, 78. Ðrūh oððe ofergeweorc *mausoleum*, 85, 76. Ðā gearwodan hī his līchoman tō bebyrigeanne on stǽnenre ðrūh (byrgenne stǽnenne ðrūh, MS. T.) . . . ðā wæs se līchoma sponne lengra ðære ðrȳh (ðonne seó ðrȳh, MS. B.) . . . Hī tōætȳcton lengeo ðære ðrȳh . . . Ðā ðōhton hī ðæt hī ōþre ðrȳh (ðūrh, MS. B.) sōhton . . . Ðā wæs seó ðrȳh (þrūh, Bd. M. 296, 28) gemēted gerisenlīcre lengo . . . seó ðrūh wæs ðam līchoman lengre *cujus corpori tumulando praeparaverant sarcofagum lapideum . . . invenerunt hoc mensura palmi longius esse sarcofago . . . addiderunt longitudini sarcofagi cogitabant aliud quaerere loculum . . . Inventum est sarcofagum illud congruae longitudinis*, Bd. 4, 11; S. 580, 3–14. Wæs him ðrūh (*loculus*) gegearwod, 5, 5; S. 617, 39. Ðā stōd on ðære stōwe sum stǽnen ðrūh . . . Ðā lēdon ða þegenas ðone Hǽlend ðǽron . . . Hī ða ðrūh geinnsegelodon, Homl. Th. ii. 262, 1–11. Þrēh *sarcophagi*, Hpt. Gl. 499, 58. Of þrīh *de tumba*, 450, 73. Se engel āwylte ðæt hlid of ðære ðrȳh . . . Crist mihte, belocenre ðrīh, faran of middangearde, Homl. Th. i. 222, 8–13. Hī gemētton nīwe ðrūh of marmanstāne on cyrcan wīson gesceapene . . . Ǽt ðære hālgan þrȳh sind getīdode heofonlīce lācnunga, 564, 19–31. On eallhwītre ðrȳh of marmstāne geworht, Cod. Dip. Kmbl. iii. 60, 21. Of ðære stǽnenan þrȳh ðe stent wiðinnan, Homl. Skt. i. 21, 22. On treówene ðrūh *ligneo in locello*, Bd. 4, 19; S. 588, 21, 25, 31, 34. On ða stǽnenan ðrūh *in sarcophago*, S. 589, 40. Ða ðūrh (*loculum*) be him gesett, 5, 5; S. 618, 6. Hī his līc gedydon on þrūh, Blickl. Homl. 191, 33: Guthl. 20; Gdwin. 84, 7, 14. Hē worhte āne ðrūh on hwītum seolfre tō ðæra apostola līce, Homl. Th. ii. 498, 3. ¶ The word seems left in local names, *Thrubrook, Througham*, v. Cod. Dip. Kmbl. vi. 342. [Me leið þene licome in þere þruh, O. E. Homl. i. 51, 5. Strikeð a stream ut of þ stanene þruh (*de sepulchro*), Kath. 2480. Ine stonene þruh biclused . . . þeos þruh, A. R. 378, 12: Misc. 51, 511. In throghes *in sepulcris*, Ps. 67, 7. Thurhwe stone, throwe or throwstone *sarcofagus*, Prompt. Parv. 493. A thrughe *mauseolum*, Cath. Angl. 386, *and see note there. Icel.* þrō; *f. a trough*; stein-þrō *a stone coffin*.] v. wæter-þrūh.

þrum. v. tunge-þrum. [Thrumm of a clothe *filamen*, Prompt. Parv. 493. Throm *licium*, Wrt. Voc. 235, 5. *O. H. Ger.* drum, thrum *meta, finis*.]

þrust-fell, es; *n. A cutaneous disease, leprosy*:—Blaec thrustfel *bitiligo*, Txts. 45, 296. [*Goth.* þruts-fill *leprosy*; þruts-fills *leprous*. Cf. *Icel.* þroti *a tumour*.]

þrūtian; *p.* ode *To swell* with pride *or* anger:—Hē āsende his swurdboran, Riggo gehāten, gescrȳdne mid his cynelīcum gyrelum, swilce hē hit sylf wǽre. Ðā gesæt Benedictus forn ongeán ðam Riggon, ðe mid ðam leáslīcum getote inn eode ðearle ðrūtigende (*he entered in a very pompous manner*), Homl. Th. ii. 168, 16. Hē cwæþ hire þus tō mid þrūtigendum mōde (*angrily, passionately*), Homl. Skt. i. 10, 273. [Cf. *Icel.* þrūtinn *swoln*; reiði-þrūtinn *swoln by anger*; þrūtna *to swell*.]

þrūtung, e; *f. A swelling* of the mind from anger, etc., *angry emotion*:—Hē befrān mid mycelre ðrūtunge, hwæt se brȳdguma wǽre, Homl. Skt. i. 7, 76.

þrȳ, þry-, þrȳan. v. þrī, þri-, ā-þrȳan, ge-þrȳde.

þryccan; *p.* þrycte, þryhte; *pp.* þrycced, þryht. I. *trans. To press, crush, oppress, repress, trample*:—Sittaþ mānfulle on heáhsetlum and hālige under heora fōtum þryccaþ *perversi resident celso mores solio, sanctaque calcant colla*, Bt. 4; Fox 8, 14: Met. 4, 38. Ðæt sió manung hié ne ðrycte *ne admonitio eos concuteret*, Past. 32; Swt. 213, 22. Ða gāstas ðe mē swenctan and ðrycton *qui me premebant spiritus*, Bd. 3, 11; S. 536, 37. Ðrycce se magister ða belde *reprimatur praecipitatio*, Past. 61; Swt. 455, 21. Swā hié se stān and seó eorþe þrycce, Blickl. Homl. 75, 9. Hē mid wēdenheortnesse mōdes ðrycced wæs *mentis vesania premebatur*, Bd. 2, 5; S. 507, 4. Untrumnesse ðrycced and hefigod *infirmitate pressus*, 4, 24; S. 598, 25. II. *intrans. To press, force a way*:—Wē ðās wīc magun fōtum āfyllan; folc in ðriceþ meara þreátum and monfarum, Exon. Th. 119, 18; Gū. 256. [He wænde mid his crucche us adun þrucche, Laym. 19483. Þre at þe fyrst þrast he þryȝt to þe erþe, Gaw. 1443. A þral þryȝt in þe þrong, Allit. Pms. 42, 135. *To thrutch* is still used in some dialects; see E. D. S. Pub. Lancashire and Cheshire Glossaries, where see also *thrutchings* = whey squeezed out whilst the cheese is under pressure. *O. H. Ger.* drucchen *premere, comprimere*.] v. bi-, ge-, of-, on-þryccan.

þrycness, e; *f. Oppression, affliction, tribulation*:—Biþ ðrycnisse micelu *erit tribulatio magna*, Mt. Kmbl. Rush. 24, 21. In ðrycnisse *in tribulationem*, 9. [*O. H. Ger.* thrucnessi *pressura* (Jn. 16, 33).] v. ge-, of-þrycness.

þrydian, þrȳdge, þrydlīce, þrydung, þrȳh. v. þreodian, þrȳþig, þrȳþlīce, þreodung, þrūh.

ðryhte, *in* Mt. Kmbl. Rush. 27, 31, *seems an error for* ðȳ ryfte *which glosses* clamyde *in the same passage of the Lindisfarne Gloss.*

þrylen, þryl-hūs, þrym. v. þrilen, þyrl-hūs, þrymm.

þrym-cyme, es; *m. A glorious coming*:—Ic (*Guthlac*) on mōde māð monna gehwylcne þeódnes þrymcyme (*the coming of the angel* (wuldres wilboda) *each evening to Guthlac*), Exon. Th. 177, 20; Gū. 1230.

þrym-cyning, es; *m. The king of glory, the Deity*:—Ðū, sigora waldend, þeóda þrymcyning, Met. 20, 205. Þrymcyning rīcne, Exon. Th. 317, 7; Mōd. 62: Elen. Kmbl. 986; El. 494. Cf. wuldor-cyning.

þrym-dōm, es; *m. Glory*:—Ðæt eorðlīce mægn ðe tō dōme (þrymdōme, MS. D.) cumen is, Wulfst. 254, 14. v. þrymness.

þrymen. v. þrimen.

þrym-fæst; *adj. Glorious, majestic, illustrious, mighty*, (1) as epithet of the Deity:—Mægencyninga Meotod, þrymfæst þeóden, Exon. Th. 58, 31; Cri. 944. Se brego mǽra, þeóden þrymfæst (*Christ*), 29, 3; Cri. 457: Andr. Kmbl. 645; An. 323. (2) in other connections:—Eorl unforcūð . . . þeóden þrymfæst, Andr. Kmbl. 957; An. 479. Þrymfæst þeóden (*Noah*), Cd. Th. 200, 27; Exod. 263. Ic (*the cross*) þrymfæst hlīfige under heofonum, Rood Kmbl. 166; Kr. 84. Se wyrm (*a bookworm*) forswealg þrymfæstne cwide, Exon. Th. 432, 11; Rä. 48, 4. Þegnas þrymfæste (*angels*), Cd. Th. 2, 6; Gen. 15. Þeóda þrymfæste, 114, 22; Gen. 1908: 158, 10; Gen. 2615.

þrym-full; *adj. Glorious, magnificent, illustrious, mighty*:—Nergendes þeówen ðrymfull (*Judith*), Judth. Thw. 22, 23; Jud. 74. Wǽre ðū (*the body*) ðē wiste wlonc . . . , þrymful, Exon. Th. 369, 12; Seel. 40. Ic (*a storm*) āstīge strong, stundum rēþe, þrymful þunie, 380, 42; Rä. 2, 4: 386, 25; Rä. 4, 67. Ic bidde ðīnne þrymfullan cynescype, Homl. Skt. i. 23, 793. Þeódnas þrymfulle, þegnas wlitige, Andr. Kmbl. 725; An. 363. Þegnas þrymfulle (*the disciples*), Exon. Th. 34, 12; Cri. 541.

þrym-līc; *adj. Magnificent, splendid, glorious*:—Ða apostolas cwǽdon ðæt hit (*the temple*) wǽre þrymlīc geweorc and fæger, Blickl. Homl. 77, 32. Swīðe mycel cyrice and þrymlīc, 125, 20. Þrecwudu þrymlīc, Beo. Th. 2496; B. 1246. Lidweardas þrymlīce, Andr. Kmbl. 489; An. 245. Ðrymlīc swǽsendo, Judth. Thw. 21, 7; Jud. 8. Swā hē ūs mǽrlīcor gifeþ, swā wē him mǽrlīcor þancian scylon; swā þrymlīcre ār, swā māre eádmōdnes, Wulfst. 261, 21. Sceoldon hié ða menn beforan him drīfan gebundene ðe gefongene wǽron, ðæt heora mǽrþa sceoldon ðȳ þrymlīcran beón, Ors. 2, 4; Swt. 70, 30.

þrymlíce; *adv. Magnificently, splendidly, gloriously*:—Hú þrymlíce ðú (*God*) ðíne gife dǽlest, Andr. Kmbl. 1093; An. 547: Elen. Kmbl. 1558; El. 781: Exon. Th. 18, 23; Cri. 288. Cyning þrymlíce of his heáhsetle scíneþ, 232, 30; Ph. 514. Wæter wynsumu bearo geondfaraþ þrymlíce, 202, 11; Ph. 68: Menol. Fox 153; Men. 78. Án and þryttig geára hē ríxode þrymlíce on Hierusalem, Homl. Skt. i. 18, 470.

þrymm, es; *m.* I. *a host, great body of people, a force, multitude*:—Eall heofonlíc þrym (cf. ðæt heofonlíce werod, l. 9) hire tócymes fægnian wolde. Eác wē gelýfaþ ðæt Drihten sylf hire tōgeánes cōme *all the heavenly host would rejoice at her advent. We believe, too, that the Lord himself would come to meet her*, Homl. Th. i. 442, 13. Ðē þanciaþ þúsenda fela, eal engla þrym ánre stefne, Hy. 7, 50: Cd. Th. 267, 11; Sat. 36. Ealle ábúgaþ tō ðē, ðínra engla þrym, Hy. 7, 11. Seó heá dugud and se engla þrym, Exon. Th. 65, 33; Cri. 1064. Glæd gumena weorud, . . . heofonduguða þrym, 101, 7; Cri. 1655. Hē wile cuman in wolcne and mid engla þrymme, Blickl. Homl. 121, 19. Hē ásende Rapsacen mid micclum ðrymme (*with a great army*, A.V. Is. 36, 2), Homl. Th. i. 568, 6: ii. 304, 6: Homl. Skt. ii. 25, 531. Se ðe mid micclum þrymme (cf. hē com mid werode, 763) þrang intō ðam temple, 781. Se hundredes ealdor com mid mycclum þrymme, 841. Heora godas ne mihton hí gescyldan wið mínne ðrymm (*host* or *power*?), Homl. Th. i. 568, 10. Hý forheówan Heaðobeardna þrym, Exon. Th. 321, 21; Vid. 49: 461, 14; Hö. 35. Cyning (*God*) on gemōt cymeþ þrymma mǽste, 52, 15; Cri. 834. Ðú (*Christ*) ǽr wǽre eallum geworden worulde þrymmum, 14, 10; Cri. 217. Of ðǽm engelícum þrymmum *from the angelic hosts* (or *glories*?), Blickl. Homl. 5, 13: 21, 15. Weras and wíf, wornum and heápum, ðreátum and þrymmum þrungon and urnon, Judth. Thw. 23, 40; Jud. 164. Se ðe herga þrymmas on geweald gebræc, Cd. Th. 127, 14; Gen. 2110. I a. *a great body* of water:—Flōda þrym (*the host of waters*) sealte sǽstreámas sǽlðe habbaþ *commoveatur mare et plenitudo ejus*, Ps. Th. 95, 11. Ýþa ðrym *the host of waves*, Beo. Th. 3841; B. 1918. Swá wætres þrym ealne middangeard mereflōd þeahte *cum diluvium mersisset fluctibus orbem*, Exon. Th. 200, 16; Ph. 41: Andr. Kmbl. 3070; An. 1538. Wē þuruh flōda þrym faraþ *transivimus per aquam*, Ps. Th. 65, 11. Com æfter niht lagustreámas (=es?) wreáh þrym mid þýstro *night covered the great mass of water with darkness*, Cd. Th. 148, 1; Gen. 2450. II. *force, power, might*:—Ðǽr wæs mōdigra mægen forbēged, wígendra þrym, Andr. Kmbl. 3142; An. 1574: 6; An. 3. Clang wæteres þrym *the water's might withered*, i. e. *the water was frozen*, 2522; An. 1262. On ðære fyrde wǽron feówertig þúsenda and seofon þúsenda swýðe gewǽpnode, and cōmon ðá mid þrymme tō Iudéiscum cynne, Homl. Skt. ii. 25, 334. Hié wið Drihtne dǽlan meahton wíc werodes þrymme *by the might of their band*, Cd. Th. 2, 31; Gen. 27. Eall ðæt ða þeódguman þrymme (*by force* or *gloriously*?) geeodon, Judth. Thw. 26, 17; Jud. 332. Se mec mæg ēcan meahtum, geþeón þrymme, Exon. Th. 427, 14; Rä. 41, 91. Bewyl þrimme (*strongly, thoroughly*) ðæt ealo on ðære wyrte, Lchdm. ii. 276, 14. Hē þrymmum (*mightily, with power*) cwehte mægenwudu mundum, Beo. Th. 476; B. 235. Seraphinnes cynn unáþreótendum þrymmum singaþ *the seraphim with unwearying powers sing*, Exon. Th. 24, 22; Cri. 388. III. *glory, majesty, magnificence, greatness, grandeur*:—Mín þrym is from eastewearde middangearde ōþ ðæt westanweardne *majestas mea peruenit ab occidente usque in orientem*, Nar. 25, 24. Drihtenes þrym *the majesty of the Lord*, 274, 34; Sat. 164: Exon. Th. 37, 26; Cri. 599: Judth. Thw. 22, 30; Jud. 86. Wæs him (*the fallen angels*) forbíged þrym, wlite gewemmed, Cd. Th. 5, 12; Gen. 70: 306, 11; Sat. 662. Lof wíde sprang, miht and mǽrðo, þrym unlytel, Apstls. Kmbl. 16; Ap. 8. Þín heáhsetl is þrymmes áfylled, Wulfst. 254, 18. Wuldres dēma, ðrymmes hyrde, Judth. Thw. 22, 15; Jud. 60: Blickl. Homl. 65, 32. On ðone gefeán ðæs heofonlícan þrymmes, 63, 27. Þremmes, 73, 34. Gif him (*a king*) geberede, ðæt him wurde oftogen þrymmes and wǽda and þegnunga, Met. 25, 32. Mið ðý cymeþ in ðrymme his *cum uenerit in majestate sua*, Lk. Skt. Rush. 9, 26, 31: 21, 27: Bd. 3, 22; S. 552, 16: Exon. Th. 106, 22; Gú. 45: Hy. 8, 40. Babilon ðe ic self átimbrede tō kynestōle and tō ðrymme *Babylon quam ego aedificavi in domum regni*, Past. 4; Swt. 39, 17: Homl. Th. ii. 432, 32. Mín werod fōran ymb mē úton mid þrymme (*with magnificent array*), and herebeácen and segnas beforan mē lǽddon, Nar. 7, 16. Hē fōr mid ðrymme and mid prasse, Homl. Skt. i. 23, 26: Elen. Kmbl. 658; El. 329: Bt. 37, 1; Fox 186, 7: Met. 25, 13. Ne þreodode hē fore þrymme ðeódcyninges ǽniges, Apstls. Kmbl. 35; Ap. 18: Exon. Th. 112, 7; Gú. 140. Hiá gesēgon ðrymm (ðrym, Rush.) his *uiderunt majestatem ejus*, Lk. Skt. Lind. 9, 32: Exon. Th. 63, 23; Cri. 1024: 234, 17; Ph. 541. Ðínes mihtes þrym *potentiam tuam*, Ps. Th. 70, 18: Exon. Th. 349, 19; Sch. 48. Þone þrym and þa fægernesse ðæs temples *the magnificence and beauty of the temple*, Blickl. Homl. 77, 30. Wē Gár-Dena in geárdagum þeódcyninga þrym gefrunon, hú ða æþelingas ellen fremedon, Beo. Th. 4; B. 2. Þrymmas weóxon duguða dreámhæbbendra, Cd. Th. 5, 32; Gen. 80: Menol. Fox 468; Gn. C. 4. Eallra þrymma God, Elen. Kmbl. 1036; El. 519. Cyninga setl þrymmum (*magnificently*) gefrætewad, Wulfst. 253, 22. Heágum þrymmum *most gloriously*, Cd. Th. 1, 16; Gen. 8. Hē hié álǽdde of helle grunde on ða heán þrymmas (*the high glories*) heofona ríces, Blickl. Homl. 67, 22. IV. denoting a glorious, magnificent person *or* object:—Ealra cyninga þrym (*the Deity*), Hy. 7, 45: Elen. Kmbl. 1629; El. 816. Ealra þrymma þrym, Exon. Th. 45, 28; Cri. 726. Rodera þrim, heofona heáhfreá, 26, 28; Cri. 423. Wuldres þrym, 6, 13; Cri. 83. Ðú ðe sitst ofer engla ðrymm (*qui sedes super cherubim*, Is. 37, 16) (*or* (?) ðrymm = *host*), Homl. Th. i. 568, 15. Mec (*a hurricane*) þrymma sumne *one of glorious things*, Exon. Th. 383, 2; Rä. 4, 4. [Her throme fourti thousand men thai founde (quoted in Halliwell). A god man on þat throm, C. M. 7423. Cf. Heo folc funden feouwer þrumferden (fouruald ferde, 2nd MS.), Laym. 1356. *O. Sax.* heru-thrummi in mid heruthrummeon *violently*: *Icel.* þrymr *an alarm, noise* (*poet.* of battle); used, too, in cpds. denoting a warrior.] v. cyne-, ēðel-, god-, heáh-, heofon-, here-, hilde-, hyge-, mægen-, ofer-, wuldor-þrymm.

þrymma, an; *m. A strong* or *great man, a warrior*:—Þrymman sceócan, mōdige maguþegnas, morðres on luste, Andr. Kmbl. 2280; An. 1141. [Cf. *Icel.* þrymr *glorious*; and the poet. cpds. in *þrym-*, denoting a warrior.] v. hilde-þremma.

þrymness. v. heáh-, mægen-þrymness; *and* cf. þrym-dōm.

þrym-ríce, es; *n. A glorious kingdom, heaven*:—Drihten wolde cuman of ðam cynestōle and of ðæm þrymríce hider on ðás world, Blickl. Homl. 105, 11.

þrymsa. v. trimes.

þrym-seld, es; *n. A throne*:—Ofer ðrymseld *super thronum*, Ps. Surt. 9, 5: 88, 30. Þrymseld *thronos*, Lchdm. i. lxxiii, 22.

þrym-setl, es; *n. A throne*:—Heofon ys Godes þrymsetl (*thronus*), Mt. Kmbl. 5, 34. On Godes þrymsetle, 23, 22. Se cásere feóll of his ðrymsetle, Shrn. 76, 31. Beforan þrymsetle Cristes *ante tribunal Christi*, Anglia xiii. 387, 311: Blickl. Homl. 101, 29. *Throni* sind þrymsetl, Homl. Th. i. 342, 34. Gē sitton ofer þrymsetl (*thronos*) dēmende twelf mǽgða Israhēl, Lk. Skt. 22, 30: Blickl. Homl. 31, 8. [Þrimsetles *troni*, O. E. Homl. i. 219, 10.]

þrym-sittende; *adj.* (*ptcpl.*) *Dwelling in glory, inhabiting heaven*:—Seó þrynis þrymsittende, Exon. Th. 286, 3; Jul. 726. Þegn þrymsittendes wuldorcyninges, Andr. Kmbl. 834; An. 417: 1056; An. 528. Sié ðē þrymsittendum þanc, Elen. Kmbl. 1618; El. 811: Exon. Th. 239, 19; Ph. 623. Ēcne God þrymsittendne, 268, 20; Jul. 435.

þrym-wealdend; *adj. Glory-ruling, ruling heaven*:—Seó Hálige Ðrynnys ðe is þrymwealdend God, Homl. Th. ii. 316, 4. Þrimwealdend, Homl. Skt. ii. 27, 156. Se ðrimwealdenda Scyppend, Homl. Th. i. 112, 10. Wē sceolon biddan ða hálgan ðæt hí ús þingion tō ðam þrymwealdendum Gode, Homl. Skt. i. 21, 288.

þrynen, þryness, þryng, þrýpel. v. þrinen, þrinness, þring, þrípel.

þryscan *to press*. v. ge-, of-þryscan.

þrysce, an; *f. A thrush*:—Þryssce *strutio*, Wrt. Voc. i. 63, 2. Þrisce *trutius*, 281, 23. [Þrusche and þrostle, O. and N. 1659. Thryshe *mauiscus*, Wülck. Gl. 595, 20. *O. H. Ger.* drosca.] v. þræsce, þrostle.

ðrysceð, Salm. Kmbl. p. 148, 6. v. þerscan.

þrysman(-ian); *p.* de, ode *To choke, stifle, suffocate*; fig. *to keep in subjection*:—Alexander .xii. geár ðisne middangeard under him þrysmde and egsade *Alexander per duodecim annos trementem sub se orbem ferro pressit*, Ors. 3, 11; Swt. 142, 22. [*O. Frs.* thresma, tresma *to choke, stifle, strangle*.] v. á-, for-, of-þrysman(-ian).

þrýste, þrystig, þrýstru, -þryt, -þrytness. v. þríste, þyrstig, þeóstru, ǽ-þryt, á-þrytness.

þrýþ, e; þrýþu (? *indecl.* v. mōd-þrýþu); *f. Force, power, strength*; the word seems to occur only in the plural, *forces, troops, hosts*:—Of ðam stáne wæter cwōman swýþe wynlíce wætera þrýðe (*the waters' forces*); eduxit aquam de petra, et eduxit tamquam flumina aquas, Ps. Th. 77, 18. Heofon weardiaþ ufan wætra ðrýðe *the waters' forces guard heaven above*, 103, 3. Sōna wǽrun geworht wætera ðrýþe, 148, 5. Wætra þrýþe stille stondaþ, Exon. Th. 210, 12; Ph. 184. Eorlas fornōman asca þrýþe, wǽpen wælgífru *hosts of spears, weapons ravenous for slaughter, have swept off the men*, 292, 15; Wand. 99. Þrýþa dǽl *some forces* (?), 481, 15; Rä. 65, 4. Eóredciestum hí faraþ, folca þrýþum, 220, 27; Ph. 326. Beornþreát monig faraþ folca þrýþum, eóredcystum, 358, 26; Pa. 51. Æfter him folca þrýðum sunu Simeones sweótum cōmon, Cd. Th. 199, 18; Exod. 340. Wæteregsa stōd þreáta þrýðum *the terrible waves stood in battalions*, Andr. Kmbl. 751; An. 376. Ecga þrýðum *with hosts* (or *force*?) *of swords*, 2298; An. 1150. ¶ Þrýþum *vehemently, mightily, fiercely, greatly*:—Teónlēg þrýþum bærneþ þreó eal on án, grimme tōgædre, Exon. Th. 60, 15; Cri. 970. Ic seah wiht (*a cask*), wombe hæfde micle þrýþum geþrungne, 495, 3; Rä. 84, 2. Ic wiht (*bellows*) geseah, womb wæs þríþum áþrunten, 419, 7; Rä. 38, 2. Þrýðum dealle, Beo. Th. 992; B. 494. ¶ Þrýþ *is used in the formation of many proper names*. v. Txts. 638. [*Icel.* Þrúðr *the name of a daughter of Thor and Sif*; it is used in the formation of proper names.] v. hilde-, hyge-, wæter-þrýþ; mōd-þrýþu.

þrýþ-ærn, es; *n. A splendid house, a palace:*—Nǽfre ic ǽnegum men ǽr álýfde ðrýþærn (cf. heáhsele, 1298; B. 647) Dena. Hafa nú húsa sēlest, Beo. Th. 1318; B. 657.

þrýþ-bearn, es; *n. A mighty youth:*—Ic ǽfre ne geseah ǽnigne mann, þrýðbearn hæleð, ðē gelícne, steóran ofer stæfnan, Andr. Kmbl. 987; An. 494.

þrýþ-bord, es; *n. A strong shield*, E'en. Kmbl. 302; El. 151. [Cf. *Icel.* þrúð-hamarr *the mighty hammer of Thor.*]

þrýþ-cyning, es; *m. A mighty king* (*the Deity*), Andr. Kmbl. 872; An. 436. Cf. þrym-cyning.

þrýþ-full; *adj. Mighty, strong, powerful:*—Fóron æfter burgum þegnas þrýðfulle, oft hí þræce rǽrdon, Exon. Th. 243, 17; Jul. 12. Ic (*the devil*) bebeóde bearnum mínum, þegnum þrýðfullum, ðæt hié ðē hnǽgon, Andr. Kmbl. 2659; An. 1331.

þrýþ-gesteald, es; *n. A splendid abode:*—Þeódnes þrýðgesteald (*heaven*), Exon. Th. 22, 19; Cri. 354. Cf. wuldor-gesteald.

þrýþian. v. ge-þrýþian.

þrýþig (?); *adj. Mighty, powerful, strong:*—Hæleð onetton mōdum þrydge (þrýðge?), Cd. Th. 119, 28; Gen. 1986. [*Icel.* þrúðigr *doughty; and* cf. þrúð-móðigr *heroic of mood.*] v. þrýþlíce *for* d *instead of* ð, *and next word.*

þrýþ-líc; *adj. Mighty, powerful:*—Rinc manig, þrýðlíc þegna heáp, Beo. Th. 805; B. 400. Ðrýðlíc, 3258; B. 1627.

þrýþlíce (?); *adv. Mightily:*—Bissextus ðe on gewunan hæfþ ðæt hē binnan ðam feórðan geáre ealle ðære wucan dagas þrydlíce (þrýþlíce?) æthríne, Anglia viii. 302, 14. Hē oft gesealde healsittendum helm and byrnan swylce hē þrydlícost (þrýþlícost?) ōhwǽr feor oððe neáh findan meahte *he often gave to his followers helm and corslet such as for greatest strength anywhere far or near he could find* (cf. for similar use of the adverb: Hē sōhte, hū hē sārlícast meahte feorhcwale findan, Exon. Th. 276, 25; Jul. 571), Beo. Th. 5731; B. 2869. [*Or, perhaps,* þrydlíce = *deliberately, might be read.* v. þreodian.]

þrýþ-swíþ; *adj. Exceedingly powerful:*—Mǽre þeóden unblíðe sæt, þolode ðrýðswýð, þegnsorge dreáh *the great prince sat cheerless, he, mighty, suffered, grief for his thanes' loss he endured*, Beo. Th. 262; B. 131. Þrýðswýð beheóld, mǽg Higeláces, hū se mānscaða gefaran wolde, 1477; B. 736. [Cf. *the proper names Æþel-swíþ, Beorht-swíþ.*]

þrýþ-weorc, es; *n. A splendid, mighty work:*—Þrýðweorc (*a statue;* v. the description: Wrætlíce wundorāgræfen anlícnes engla . . . torhte gefrætwed, wlitige geworht . . . anlícnes engelcynna ðæs brēmestan, 1423–35; An. 712–8), Andr. Kmbl. 1546; An. 774.

þrýþ-word, es; *n. A brave word, noble speech:*—Ðā wæs eft swā ǽr (cf. word wǽron wynsume, 1228; B. 612) inne on healle þrýðword sprecen, ðeód on sǽlum, sigefolca swēg, Beo. Th. 1290; 643.

þū; *pers. pron. Thou.* I. alone:—Ðis land ðe þū gesihst, Gen. 13, 15. Hwæt eart þū þe þýn ansýn is swylce ānes sceapan, and hwæt ys ðæt tācen þe þū on uppan þínum exlum byrst? Nicod. 32; Thw. 18, 19. Gewít þū, Abraham, fēran . . . þū scealt Isaac mē onsecgan, Cd. Th. 172, 24; Gen. 2849: Andr. Kmbl. 1899; An. 952. Ic āscige ðē, ðū Boetius, hwí þū swā manigfeald yfel hæfdest? Bt. 27, 2; Fox 96, 12. Eá lā þū mín Drihten God, hwæt gifst þū mē? Ger. 15, 2. Westū gearo, Bd. 5, 19; S. 640, 44. Scealtū ceól gestīgan, Andr. Kmbl. 439; An. 220. Hié woldon þín onbídan, Blickl. Homl. 233, 27. Se ðe mid þē (ðec mið, Lind. Rush.) wæs *qui erat tecum*, Jn. Skt. 3, 26. Ne biþ þec mǽlmete, nymþe mōres græs, ne rest witod, Cd. Th. 252, 7; Dan. 575. Þū gesyxst þās menigu þē (ðec, Lind.: on ðec, Rush.) ðringende, Mk. Skt. 5, 31. Se hālga gāst on þē (ðeh, Lind.: ðec, Rush.) becymþ, Lk. Skt. 1, 35. Þec Sarre āh, Cd. Th. 137, 8; Gen. 2270. Ne forlǽte ic þē, 136, 10; Gen. 2256. I a. used reflexively:—Ne ondrǽd þū þē, Gen. 15, 1: Lk. Skt. 1, 30. Ðū hafast þē on fyrhðe eorles ondsware, Andr. Kmbl. 1013; An. 507. Nim þē þis ofæt on hand, Cd. Th. 33, 11; Gen. 518. Āsend þē (ðeh, Lind.: þec, Rush.) nyþer, Mt. Kmbl. 4, 6. Þonne þū þē gebidde, 6, 6. II. strengthened with *self* or *āna:*—Þū sylf ne gesyhst þæne beám on þínum āgenum cágan, Lk. Skt. 6, 42. Þū (*Juliana*) sylfa meaht gecnāwan, Exon. Th. 262, 32; Jul. 341: Cd. Th. 36, 12; Gen. 570. Ðū eart seolfa geong, Andr. Kmbl. 1010; An. 505. Þū meaht þē self geseón, Cd. Th. 38, 23; Gen. 611. Þæt þū þa beorhtan ūs sunnan onsende, and þē sylf cyme, Exon. Th. 8, 8; Cri. 114. Hwí swingst þū āna? . . . Ne miht þū āna hit ācuman, Ex. 18, 14, 18. Þū āna canst ealra gehygdo, Andr. Kmbl. 135; An. 68. Þē wæs leófra his hyldo, þonne þín sylfes bearn, Cd. Th. 176, 34; Gen. 2921. Lufa þínne nēhstan swā þē sylfne (ðec seolfne, Lind.), Mt. Kmbl. 19, 19. III. combined with *þe* to express the relative:—Fæder ūre þū þe eart on heofenum *Pater noster, qui es in coelis*, Mt. Kmbl. 6, 9. Drihten þū þe míne fæderas on þínre gesihþe eodon, God þū þe mē fēddest *Deus, in cujus conspectu ambulaverunt patres mei, Deus, qui pascit me*, Gen. 48, 15: Elen. Kmbl. 1448; El. 726. Wē þē þanciaþ, þe þū hafest on gewealdum hiofen and eorþan, Hy. 8, 12. Eálā þū Hǽlend þurh þíne þrowunga þe þū getuge tō þē ealle ða sāwla, H. R. 15, 3. [*Goth.* þu; *gen.* þeina; *dat.* þus; *acc.* þuk: *O. Sax.* thu; *gen.* thín; *dat.* thi; *acc.* thik: *O. Frs.* thu; *gen.* thín; *dat. acc.* thi: *O. H. Ger.* dū; *gen.* dín; *dat.* dir; *acc.* dih: *Icel.* þú; *gen.* þín; *dat.* þér; *acc.* þik.] v. gē, git.

þúf, es; *m. A tuft.* I. applied to foliage:—Þūfum *crinibus* (the passage is: Dum virgas steriles atque superfluas flammis de fidei palmite concremant, ut concreta vagis vinea crinibus silvosi inluviem poneret idoli), Germ. 402, 71. v. þūf-bǽre, *and following words.* II. *the crest of a helmet* (?). v. Lydus de magistrat.:—καλοῦσι δὲ αὐτὰς οἱ μὲν Ῥωμαῖοι ἰούβας, οἱ δὲ βάρβαροι τουφάς. v. next section. III. *a kind of standard*, made with tufts of feathers:—Illud genus vexilli, quod Romani *Tufam* (tufa *genus vexilli ex confertis plumarum globis*, v. Du Cange s. v.), Angli vero Tuuf (v. ll. thuuf, thuf, Txts. 137, 1), ante eum ferri solebat (the A.-S. version has only:—Him mon symle ðæt tācen beforan bær), Bd. 2, 16. Ðā wæs þūf hafen, segen for sweótum, Elen. Kmbl. 246; El. 123. Sunu Simeones sweótum cōmon, þūfas wundon ofer gārfare, Cd. Th. 199, 22; Exod. 342. Hié gesāwon þūfas þunian, 187, 32; Exod. 158. v. sige-þūf.

þúf-bǽre; *adj. Bearing foliage, leafy:*—Bōh þūfbǽres pīntreówes *frondentis pini stipitem*, Hpt. Gl. 458, 67.

þúfe; *adj. Tufted, having leaves in tufts* (?), *bushy:*—Þūfe þistel *sow thistle*, Lchdm. ii. 312, 20. v. ge-þūf, þīfe-þorn, *and preceding and following words.*

þúfian; *p.* ode *To become leafy* or *bushy:*—Þūfaþ and wridaþ *frutescit*, Wrt. Voc. ii. 38, 13.

þúfig; *adj. Full of leaves, with thick foliage:*—Þūfigum *frondosis*, Wrt. Voc. ii. 38, 14.

þúft, es; *m. A place full of bushes:*—Gewrid oþþe þūftas *frutecta*, Wrt. Voc. ii. 38, 25. v. þýfel.

þuhsian, þux[s]ian; *p.* ode *To make misty, dark:*—Eall upheofon biþ sweart and gesworcen and swýðe geþuhsod (cf. Dōm. L. 8, 105, *which has* geþuxsað), deorc and dimhíw and dwolma sweart, Wulfst. 137, 9. [Cf. *Icel.* þoka *fog, mist.*]

þullic. v. þus-líc.

þúma, an; *m. The thumb:*—Ðūma, thūma, thūmo *pollux*, Txts. 89, 1617. Swā greáte swā ðín þūma, Lchdm. iii. 18, 25. Ic com mid handa on ðone stān drífan, and se ðūma gebroceu wæs, Bd. 5, 6; S. 619, 24. Gif se þūma biþ of āslægen, ðam sceal .xxx. scill. tō bōte. Gif se nægl biþ of āslegen, ðam sculon .v. scill. tō bōte, L. Alf. pol. 56; Th. i. 94, 28. Gif man þūman of āslæhþ, .xx. scill. Gif þūman nægl of weorðeþ, .iii. scill. gebēte, L. Ethb. 54; Th. i. 16, 9. Hē æthrān his swíðran þūman (*pollicem manus ejus dextrae*), Lev. 8, 23. Þūman *pollices*, Wrt. Voc. ii. 82, 48: Ex. 29, 20. [Mid te þume, A. R. 18, 14. Þe nayle of þe þoume, Ayenb. 43, 14. To the thowme, Rel. Ant. i. 190, 22 (end of 14th cent.). Thombe, Chauc., Piers P. Thowmbe, Prompt. Parv. 492. *In other glossaries of 15th cent. it is spelt* thome, Wrt. Voc. i. 184 (*where also* thombe): 207, col. 2: thowme, 186, col. 1: thombe, 179: 247, col. 2: (*in same glossary also*) thumb, 246, col. 1. *O. Frs.* thūma: *O. L. Ger.* thūmo: *O. H. Ger.* dūmo: *Dan.* tomme: *Swed.* tumme.] v. þýmel.

þumle *entrails:*—Tharme, thumle *viscera*, Wrt. Voc. ii. 123, 72.

-þunca, -þuncan, þundende, þune-líc, þuner. v. æf-þunca, be-þuncan, þunian, þunor-líc, þunor.

þung, es; *m. A poisonous plant,* (*vegetable*) *poison;* the word is used to translate *aconitum, eleborus, mandragina*, as well as the more general term *toxa* (cf. letali toxa = mortali veneno, Hpt. Gl. 427, 54):—Þung, woedeberge *eleborus*, Wrt. Voc. ii. 107, 12: 29, 21. Þung *mandragina*, 59, 42: *aconita*, i. 31, 58: *aconitum*, 67, 16: *toxa*, 68, 26: *coxa* (r. *toxa*), 67, 15. Þung *toxa* or *toxicum* (printed *toxi* pang), 289, 52. Gif mon þung ete, āþege buteran and drince; se þung gewít on ða buteran. Eft wiþ ðon, āsleá him mon fela scearpena on ðam scancan, ðonne gewít ūt ðæt āttor þurh ða scearpan, Lchdm. ii. 154, 1–4. Sealf wiþ ðam miclan líce . . . þung . . ., 78, 25. Āmber fulne holenrinda and æscrinda and þunges, 332, 16. Nim ðone miclan þung, 154, 14. Thungas, þungas *aconita*, Txts. 36, 23. Þungas, Wrt. Voc. ii. 4, 20. v. cluf-þung; *f.*

þunge, -þungen. v. þeón, ful-, ge-, heáh-þungen.

þungenness, e; *f. Excellence, virtue:*—Mid hū monigum mēdum mín fæder and mín mōder mē [wǽron] biddende, ðæt ic forlēte míne (ge-?)þungenesse (*the speaker wished to become a monk*), Shrn. 36, 26. v. ge-þungenness.

þunian; *p.* ode. I. *to stand out, be prominent, be lifted up, stick up:*—On ðam forman dæge on ðam middangeard þunaþ gesceapen *primo dierum quo mundus extat conditus*, Hymn. Surt. 4, 4. Þunie (þu me, Th.) him gewinnes wearn ofer wealles hrōf *may much strife be lifted up for it above the top of its wall;* circumdabit eam super muros ejus iniquitas, Ps. Th. 54, 9. Hié gesāwon fyrd wegan . . . þūfas þunian *they saw the host march . . . saw the standards lift their tops above the ranks*, Cd. Th. 187, 32; Exod. 158. Þindan and þunian, þecene hebban, Exon. Th. 431, 17; Rä. 46, 2. I a. fig *to be lifted up, be proud*, cf. colloquial *to be stuck up:*—Wǽre ðū (*the body*) ðē wiste wlanc, þrymful ðunedest, Soul Kmbl. 79; Seel. 40. v. on-þunian, *and* cf. þennan. II. *to make a noise, to sound, resound, creak:*—Ic (*a storm*) āstīge strong, þrymful þunie, Exon. Th. 380, 42; Rä. 2, 4. Sundwudu þunede *the ship's timbers creaked*, Beo. Th. 3817; B. 1906. Þunode oððe hleóþrede *increpuerit*, Wrt. Voc. ii. 44, 14. Dynedan and þunedan *crepitabant*, 21, 17. Ðære thundendan (thuniendan? *but* cf. (?) *Icel.* Þundr *a name of Odin;* Þund *the name of a mythical river*) *bombosae* (*vocis mugitum*), Wrt. Voc. ii. 77, 59. v. tō-þuniende, þunung, ge-þun, þunor, *and* cf. *Lat.* tonare, tonitrus.

þunor (-ar, -er, -ur), es; *m.* I. *thunder* (implying not only sound but also striking); tonitrus, fulmen:—Þunor *tonitruum* vel *tonitrus*, Wrt. Voc. i. 52. 45: 76, 34: Blickl. Homl. 91, 34. Ðuner (ðunor, Rush.), Jn. Skt. Lind. 12, 29. Ðunar byð hlūdast, Menol. Fox 467; Gn. C. 4. Ðunor cymð of hǣtan and of wǣtan . . . seó hǣte and se wǣta winnaþ him betweónan mid egeslīcum swēge, and ðæt fȳr ābyrst ūs ðurh līgett . . . Swā hāttra sumor, swā māra ðunor and līget on geáre. Ða þuneras (þunras, MS. R.) . . . on Apocalipsin . . . ne belimpaþ tō ðam ðunere (þunre, MS. R.) ðe on ðyssere lyfte oft egeslīce brastlaþ. Se byþ hlūd for ðære lyfte brādnysse, and frecenfull for ðæs fȳres sceótungum, Lchdm. iii. 290, 2–15. Þunor tōslōg heora godes hūs *aedes Salutis ictu fulminis dissoluta est*, Ors. 4, 2; Swt. 160, 18. Ān þunor tōslōg hiora Capitoliam *fulmine Capitolium ictum*, 6, 14; Swt. 268, 29. Hiene ofslōg ān þunor *fulmine ictus interiit*, 6, 29; Swt. 278, 17. Ðunres bearn *filii tonitrui*, Mk. Skt. 3, 17. Þunres slege *a clap of thunder*, Nicod. 23; Thw. 13, 3. Þunres slege *fulgura*, Ps. Spl. T. 96, 4. Stefne ðunures micles, Rtl. 47, 22. God āsende rēn mid ðunore, and manega menn mid ðam ðunore swulton, Homl. Skt. i. 15, 93. Beóþ myccle þuneras on heofnum, Blickl. Homl. 93, 15. Ðā sceolde hē sendan ðunras and lȳgetu, Bt. 35, 4; Fox 162, 13. II. *one of the Teutonic gods, to whom, among the Roman, Jupiter seems to have been considered most nearly to correspond;* hence Jupiter is translated by Þunor:—Þunor oððe Ðūr *Joppiter*, Wrt. Voc. ii. 47, 33. Þunor, 93, 59. Þuner *Jovem*, 112, 5. II a. it is mostly in connection with the fifth day of the week that the word occurs:—On ðam fīftan dæge ðe gē Ðunres hātaþ, Homl. Th. ii. 242, 23. Ðunres-dæges nama is of Iove, Anglia viii. 321, 16. On ðone Hālgan Ðunres-dæg, L. Alf. 5; Th. i. 64, 24. Tō ðam hālgan Þurres-dæge, Homl. Skt. ii. 23 b, 621. Gang on Þunres-ǣfen (*Wednesday evening*), Lchdm. ii. 346, 10. *It is found also in local names*, e.g. Ðunres-feld, Ðunres-leáh, Cod. Dip. Kmbl. vi. 342. [Þa Þunre heo ȝiuen þunres dæi (þoris dai, 2nd MS.), Laym. 13929.] III. *a thane of king Egbert of Kent:*—Ermenrēd gestrȳnde twēgen sunu ða syððan wurðan gemartirode of Ðunore, Chr. 640; Erl. 26, 4. See for more details of the event thus recorded, Lchdm. iii. 422 sqq., and the Latin charter, Cod. Dip. Kmbl. iv. 236. [*O. L. Ger.* Thuner:—Ec forsacho Thuner ende Uuōden: *O. Frs.* thuner, tonger; Thunres-dei: *O. H. Ger.* donar; Toniris tac: *Icel.* Þōrr. See Grmm. D. M. c. 8.] v. Þōr, Þūr.

þunor-bodu *a gilthead* (a kind of fish):—Ðunorbodu *sparus*, Wrt. Voc. i. 55, 71 (in a list 'nomina piscium').

þunor-clāfre, -clǣfre, an; *f. Bugle;* ajuga reptans (cf. Þundre clovere *consolida media*, Wrt. Voc. i. 140, 68, and *consound* in E. D. S. Pub. Plant Names):—Þis is seó æðeleste eáhsealf . . . Genim . . . ðunorclǣfran blōsman, Lchdm. iii. 4, 7. Ðunorclāfran, i. 374, 4.

þunor-līc; *adj. Thunderous, of thunder:*—Þune[r]līcum cirme *tonitruali fragore*, Hpt. Gl. 451, 47.

þunor-rād, e; *f. Thunder, a peal of thunder:*—Ne biþ þǣr līget . . . ne þunerrād (þunor, Wulfst. 139, 31) *non fulmina*, . . . *tonitru*, Dōm. L. 16, 263. Ðā com þunerrād and lēgetsleht and ofslōh ðone mǣstan dǣl, Shrn. 57, 35. Ðā wæs geworden mycel þunorrād, Blickl. Homl. 145, 29. Ðonne þunorrād biþ, ne sceþeð ðam men ðe ðone stān (*agate*) mid him hæfð, Lchdm. ii. 296, 30: iii. 374, col. 2. From stefne ðunurrāde (þunurāde, Spl.) *a voce tonitrui*, Ps. Surt. 103, 7: 76, 19. Þunurrāda ðīnre *tonitrus tui*, Ps. Spl. 76, 17. Hió āhōf ðæt heáfod of ðære mȳsan somod mid ðære þunorāde, Lchdm. iii. 374, col. 2. Biddaþ Drihten, ðæt his þunorrāda (*tonitrua*) geswīcon, Ex. 9, 28, 33, 34. Gif līgette and ðunorrāde (*tonitrua*) eorþan and lyfte brēgdon, Bd. 4, 3; S. 569, 12. Þunerāda, Hpt. Gl. 509, 22. Ðunorrāda hlynn, Wulfst. 186, 3. Mycel mægen liégetslyhta and þunerāda, Lchdm. iii. 374, col. 2. Gōd wið līgetta and wið þunorrāda, ii. 290, 16. Hē worhte þunorrāda on heofonum *intonuit de caelum Dominus*, Ps. Th. 17, 13: Ex. 9, 23. [Cf. *Icel.* reið *a clap of thunder*, from the notion of Thor *driving* through the air. See Grmm. D. M. c. 8.]

þunorrād-līc; *adj. Thunderous, of thunder:*—Of þunerādlīcan cerme *tonitruali fragore*, Hpt. Gl. 451, 46.

þunorrād-stefn, e; *f. A voice of thunder:*—Wæs þunurrādstefn strang on hweóle *vox tonitrui tui in rota*, Ps. Th. 76, 14.

þunor-wyrt, e; *f. Thunder-plant* (v. E. D. S. Pub. Plant Names), *house-leek;* sempervivum tectorum:—Nime þunorwyrt, Lchdm. ii. 118, 2. [On plants that were a protection against thunder, see Grmm. D. M. pp. 167, 1147.]

þunres dæg. v. þunor, II a.

þunrian; *p.* ode *To thunder:*—Hē is mægenþrymmes God. and hē þunraþ ofer manegum wæterum *Deus majestatis intonuit, Dominus super multas aquas*, Ps. Th. 28, 3. Hit ðunraþ *tonat*, Ælfc. Gr. 22; Zup. 128, 17. Hit hwīlum þunraþ, Bt. 39, 3; Fox 44, 34: Met. 28, 55. Seó menio sǣdon ðæt hyt þunrode (*tonitruum factum esse*), Jn. Skt. 12, 29. Þunerode of heofonum Drihten *intonuit de coelo Dominus*, Ps. Spl. T. 17, 15. [*O. H. Ger.* donarōn.]

þunring, e; *f. Thundering, thunder:*—Swā stōr þunring and lǣgt wes, swā ðæt hit ācwealde manige men, Chr. 1085; Erl. 219, 22.

þunung, e; *f. A creaking, a rattle:*—Þunange *crepitum*, Wrt. Voc. ii. 21, 25. Þununga *crepundiorum*, 23, 64.

þun-wang, e: -wange, -wenge, an; *f.* (and *n.*? Wange, wenge *are both found neuter, though also the plurals* wangas, wangan *occur*) *A temple:*—Þunwang *timpus*, Wrt. Voc. i. 42, 50. Þunwange *tempus*, 64, 32. Þunwencge (-wenge, -wange) *timpus*, Ælfc. Gr. 9, 32; Zup. 59, 5: 298, 2. Gif ic on þunwange gereste *si dedero requiem temporibus meis*, Ps. Th. 131, 4. Bufan his þunwengan *supra tempus capitis ejus*, Jud. 4, 21. Þunwonge *tympora*, Wrt. Voc. i. 282, 44. Þunwonga sār *dolor timporum*, ii. 143, 34: Lchdm. i. 156, 22. Þunwongena *timporum*, Wrt. Voc. ii. 87, 61. Þunwangena, Anglia xiii. 37, 291. Þunwængum (-wengum, Spl. C.) *timporibus*, Ps. Lamb. 131, 5. Ðunwoengum, Rtl. 181, 13. Þunwange *malas*, Wrt. Voc. ii. 57, 30. Smire ðone man mid on þa þunwonge, Lchdm. ii. 334, 15. Smyre ða ðunwonga, i. 216, 8. Gnīd on ða þunwunge, 380, 15. Smire ða þunwangan mid, ii. 20, 8. Þunwongan, 306, 2. [Þungana, Lchdm. iii. 292, 22. Lay on the forheyd and on the thunwanges, Rel. Ant. i. 54, 26, 43 (quoted in Halliwell's Dict.). Thunwonge of mannys heede *tempus*, Prompt. Parv. 493. Thunwange *tempus*, Cath. Angl. 387, and see note. Thonwangnes, Wrt. Voc. i. 185, col. 2 (15th cent.). *O. H. Ger.* dun-wengi: *Icel.* þunn-wangi; *m.;* þunnwengi; *n.*] v. (?) þynne *and* wange.

þūr, es; *m. Thor*, the god who most nearly corresponded to Jupiter; hence Jupiter is translated by Þūr:—Þunor oððe Ðūr *Joppiter*, Wrt. Voc. ii. 47, 33. Þūres mōdur *Latona*, 53, 4. On Galienus dagum ðæs kāseres hēt Necetius Rōme burge gerēfa hī lǣdan tō Þūres deófulgeldum, Shrn. 128, 9. Ðys godspel sceal on Þūres-dæg, Rubc. Jn. 7, 40. On Þūrs-dæg, Rubc. Jn. 5, 30. The word is found also in local names, e.g. Ðūres-leáh, Ðūrgārtūn, Cod. Dip. Kmbl. vi. 342. [A. R. Þurs-dei.] v. Þunor, Þōr.

þuren. v. ge-þuren.

[**þurfan**;] *prs.* ic, hē þearf, ðū þearft, *pl.* wē þurfon; *p.* þorfte; *subj. prs.* ic þurfe, þyrfe, *pl.* þurfen, þyrfen; *prs. ptcpl.* þurfende, þyrfende *To need.* I. *to be in need, have need* of something, (1) absolute:—Gif ðū clāþa þe mā on hæfst, þonne ðū þurfe, Bt. 14, 1; Fox 42, 15. Ðū gæderast māre, þonne ðū þurfe (þyrfe, Cott. MS.), 14, 2; Fox 44, 8. Nis hit gōd, ðæt hié sién on ðam lāðe leng, þonne ðū þurfe, Cd. Th. 243, 3; Dan. 430. Sam hī þyrfon, sam hī ne þurfon, hī willaþ þeáh, Bt. 26, 2; Fox 92, 30. Ða þurfende *pauperes*, Mt. Kmbl. Rush. 5, 3. Þyrfendra *egentum*, Wrt. Voc. ii. 142, 69. (2) with gen. of thing needed:—Beó ðē be ðīnum, and lǣt mē be mīnum; ne gyrne ic ðīnes, ne ðū mīnes ne þearft (ðærft, Lchdm. iii. 288, 9), L. O. 13; Th. i. 184, 16. Ne ðearf hē nānes þinges būton ðæs, ðe hē on him selfum hæfþ, Bt. 24, 4; Fox 86, 8: Cd. Th. 204, 27; Exod. 425. Hwæt ðurfe (ðurfu, Lind.) wē leng gewitnisse *quid adhuc egemus testibus*, Mt. Kmbl. Rush. 26, 65. Ða þurfon swīþe lytles, ðe māran ne willniaþ þonne genōges, Bt. 14, 2; Fox 44, 13. Ne ðorfte hē nā māran fultumes, 26, 2; Fox 92, 22. Hī his sume ðorfton, Past. pref.; Swt. 9, 16. Ðǣm ðe micles ðorfton . . . ðæm ðe lytles ðyrfe, 44; Swt. 325, 5–7. Swā welig ðæt hē nānes þinges māran ne þurfe, Bt. 24, 2; Fox 82, 4. (3) with acc.:—Mūþa gehwylc mete þearf, Exon. Th. 341, 12; Gn. Ex. 125. Mete bygeþ, gif hē māran (*or gen.?*) þearf, 340, 14; Gn. Ex. 111. II. *to need* to do something. (1) where a want has to be satisfied, a purpose to be accomplished, or the like:—Ðū meaht ðē self geseón, swā ic hit ðē secgan ne þearf, Cd. Th. 38, 24; Gen. 611. Gif hit sié sumor, dō wermōdes sǣdes dust tō; gif hit sié winter, ne þearft ðū ðone wermōd tō dōn, Lchdm. ii. 180, 29. Hē ne ðearf nā faran fram stōwe tō stōwe, Homl. Th. i. 158, 4. Hwæt ðurfon (þurfe, Bod. MS.) wē nū mā sprecan? Bt. 24, 4; Fox 86, 22. Hī witan, hwǣr hī eáfiscas sēcan þurfan (*where they must seek them, if they are to find them*), Met. 19, 25. Syle mē ðæt wæter, ðæt mē ne þyrste, ne ic ne ðurfe hēr feccan, Jn. Skt. 4, 15. Ðȳ læs wē leng sprecen ymbe ðonne wē þyrfon (wē ne þyrfen, Cott. MS.), Bt. 34, 2; Fox 136, 14. (2) where the need is based on grounds of right, fitness, law, morality, etc., *to be bound* to do something because it is right, etc.:—Nō ðū mīnne þearft hafelan hȳdan *the duty of burying me will not fall upon you*, Beo. Th. 895; B. 445. Gif hē gewitnesse hæbbe, ne þearf hē ðæt geldan (*he is not bound by law to pay*), L. Alf. 28; Th. i. 52, 3. Ne þearf hē him onfōn, L. In. 67; Th. i. 146, 4. Mē ðæt riht ne þinceþ, ðæt ic ōleccan þurfe Gode, Cd. Th. 19, 13; Gen. 290. Ðæt ðū ne wēne, ðæt ðū Iudēa leásungum gelȳfan þurfe *that you may not think, that you are bound to believe the Jews' false tales*, Blickl. Homl. 177, 35. Hē suīðor his mōd gebint tō ðǣm unnyttran weorcum, ðonne hē ðyrfe (*more than is fitting for him*), Past. 4; Swt. 37, 21. Ðonne mon mā fæst, ðonne hē ðyrfe (*more than religion requires*), 43; Swt. 313, 2. Gif ða gyltas tō ðam hefelīce beón, ðæt hē tō bisceopes dōme tǣcan þurfe (*he must do it because the church has prescribed such a course*), L. Ecg. P. i. 11; Th. ii. 176,

30. Gedōn hī ðæt hira synna ne ðyrfen (*need not, because of the divine ordinance*) bión gesewene æt ðæm nearwan dōme, Past. 53; Swt. 413, 16. (3) with the idea of compulsion, or where the inevitability of a consequence is expressed; in some cases the word might be taken almost as an auxiliary, of much the same force as *shall; to be obliged, be compelled by destiny*:—Gē ne þurfon hēr leng wunian *you shall not be obliged to stop here longer*, Ex. 9, 28. Nis ðæt þonne nǣnig man, ðæt þurfe ðone deópan grund ðæs hātan lēges gesēcean, Blickl. Homl. 103, 14. Næs him ǣnig þearf, ðæt hē sēcean þurfe *there was no need to force him to seek*, Beo. Th. 4984; B. 2495. Feallaþ ofor ūs, ðæt wē ne þurfon ðysne ege leng þrowian, Blickl. Homl. 93, 34. Þȳ læs gyt lāð Gode weorðan þyrfen *lest the inevitable consequence, your becoming hateful to God, follow*, Cd. Th. 36, 26; Gen. 577. Þȳ læs ða tȳdran mōd ða gewitnesse wendan þurfe, Exon. Th. 147, 21; Gū. 730. Nāuht ðæs ðe hē ondrēde, ðæt hē forleósan þorfte (*should be obliged to lose*), Bt. 26, 2; Fox 92, 22. Hwȳ him on hige þorfte (*should necessarily follow*) ā þȳ sǣl wesan, Met. 15, 9. Hū hē ðisse worulde wynna þorfte læsast brūcan *how he should be least under the necessity of enjoying the delights of this world*, Exon. Th. 122, 20; Gū. 308. Ðæt ðæt micle morð menn ne þorfton þolian *that men would not necessarily have to suffer that great perdition*, Cd. Th. 40, 17; Gen. 640. (4) *to have good cause* or *reason* for doing something:—Ðū sorge ne þearft beran on ðīnum breóstum, Cd. Th. 45, 28; Gen. 733. Ic ðē scylde, ne þearft ðū forht wesan, 131, 5; Gen. 2171: Blickl. Homl. 191, 18: Beo. Th. 3353; B. 1674. Ðū ðec sylfne ne þearft swīþor swencan, gif ðū God lufast, Exon. Th. 245, 18; Jul. 46. Ðæt is genōg sweotol, ðætte nānne mon ðæs tweógean ne þearf, Bt. 11, 2; Fox 34, 34: Blickl. Homl. 41, 36: 83, 9. Ne þearf ðæs nān mon wēnan, 101, 13: 109, 30. Ne ðarf mon nā ðone medwīsan lǣran, ðæt hē ða lotwrencas forlǣte, forðonðe hē hié næfþ, Past. 30; Swt. 203, 15. Ne þearf hē gefeón *he will have no cause to rejoice*, Cd. Th. 92, 4; Gen. 1523: Exon. Th. 449, 9; Dōm. 68: Beo. Th. 4016; B. 2006. Mē wītan ne ðearf Waldend, 5475; B. 2741: Cd. Th. 165, 7; Gen. 2728. Ne ðurfe wē ceorian, Homl. Th. ii. 438, 27. Ne þurfan gē nōht besorgian, hwæt gē sprecan, Blickl. Homl. 171, 18. Ne þurfe gē beón unrōte, 135, 24. Ne þurfun gē wēnan, Exon. Th. 142, 16; Gū. 645. Ne þurfon mē hæleð ætwītan, Byrht. Th. 139, 4; By. 249. Ic eów secgan mæg, ðæt gē ne ðyrfen leng murnan, Judth. Thw. 23, 33; Jud. 153. Sume him ondrǣdaþ earfoþu swīþor þonne hȳ þyrfen, Bt. 39, 11; Fox 228, 24. Gif hē nāne ǣhta næfde, ne þorfte hē nānne feónd ondrǣdan . . . Gif ðū swelces nānuuht næfdest ne þorftest ðū ðē nānwuht ondrǣdan, 14, 3; Fox 46, 23–28. Nō hē ðære feohgyfte scamigan þorfte, Beo. Th. 2057; B. 1026: 2147; B. 1071. Hwǣr hē ðara nægla swīðast wēnan þorfte *where he had most reason to expect that he should find the nails*, Elen. Kmbl. 2206; El. 1104. Nō wē þus swīðe swencan þorftan, þǣr ðū freónda lārum hȳran wolde, Exon. Th. 129, 19; Gū. 423. Ne þorfton hī hlūde hlihhan, Cd. Th. 5, 17; Gen. 73. Hī gearowe wǣron deáðe sweltan, gif hī ðorfton (*if the occasion demanded it*), Homl. Th. ii. 130, 5. (5) where the need arises from an advantage to be gained, or purpose to be served, *to be use, to be good* for a person to do something:—Ne þearf ic yrfestōl bytlian *it is no good* or *use for me to build an hereditary seat*, Cd. Th. 131, 14; Gen. 2176. Ne þearft ðū sæce rǣran, Elen. Kmbl. 1876; El. 940. III. *to owe*, cf. sculan, I:—Ne þearf ic N. sceatt ne scilling, ne pænig ne pæniges weorð; ac eal ic him gelǣste ðæt ðæt ic him scolde, L. O. 11; Th. i. 182, 9. [*Goth.* þarf, *pl.* þaurbum; *prs.*; þaurfta; *p.*; þaurbands; *prs. ptcpl.*: *O. Sax.* tharf, *pl.* thurðun; *prs.*; thorfta; *p.*: *O. Frs.* thurf, thorf, *pl.* thurvon; *prs.*: *O. H. Ger.* darf, tharf, *pl.* durfun, thurfun; *prs.*; dorfta; *p.*: *Icel.* þurfa; þarf, *pl.* þurfum; *prs.* þurfti; *p.*; þurfandi; *prs. ptcpl.*] v. be-þurfan; þearfan, þearfian, þorfan.

þurh, þurg, þuruh, þorh, þorch, þerh, þerih, þærh; *prep. Through*. A. with acc. v. also C. I. local, (1) marking motion into and out at the opposite side:—Þorh (dorh, ðorh) ludgaet *per seudoterum*, Txts. 84, 741. Ðurh ða duru wē gāð in *per hostium intramus*, Ælfc. Gr. 47; Zup. 269, 18: Cd. Th. 29, 8; Gen. 447. Gangaþ inn þurh (ðerh, Lind.) ðæt nearwe geat, Mt. Kmbl. 7, 13: Lk. Skt. 18, 25. Syllan drincan þurh þyrel, Exon. Th. 485, 1; Rä. 71, 7. Ðā fērde hē þurh (ðerh, Lind.) hyra mydlen, Lk. Skt. 4, 30. Wē þuruh fȳr faraþ and þuruh flōda þrym *transivimus per ignem et aquam*, Ps. Th. 65, 11. Hē wæs on breóstum wund þurh ða hringlocan, Byrht. Th. 136, 2; By. 145. (1 a) where the preposition follows the governed word:—Duru, ðe ic wæs þurh hider onsended, Blickl. Homl. 9, 1. (2) marking motion over *or* in, cf. geond:—Hē fērde þurh ða ceastre and ðæt castel bodiende, Lk. Skt. 8, 1. Hē āstyraþ ðis folc, lǣrende þurh ealle Iudēam, 23, 5. Hē hleóþrede þurh hātne līg, Exon. Th. 185, 4; Az. 2. Ic þurh ðīn hūs middan eode *perambulabam in medio domus meae*, Ps. Th. 100, 2. Ðæt fȳr nimeþ þurh foldan gehwæt, Exon. Th. 62, 18; Cri. 1003. II. temporal, marking continuity, *through, for, during*:—Ðurh twēgen dagas *per biduum*, Bd. 4, 19; S. 589, 2. Þurh ealne dæg *tota die*, Ps. Th. 73, 21. Þuruh, 87, 9. Ðorh syndrie neht *per singulas noctes*, Ps. Surt. 6, 7. Þurh scīrne dæg, Exon. Th. 439, 15; Rä. 59, 4. Þurh lytel fæc, 115, 6; Gū. 185. Þurh ælda tīd, 152, 11; Gū. 807. Þurh ealra worulda woruld, Ps. Th. 71, 5. III. other relations, (1) marking the agent, *through, by*:—Þorch (dorh, ðorh) byrgeras *per vispelliones*, Txts. 86, 760. Ðerih, 151, 6. Wā ðam menn þurh ðone ðe (ðe ðorh hine, Lind.) byð mannes Sunu belǣwed, Mt. Kmbl. 26, 24: Chr. 1014; Erl. 151, 8. Hié hié wendon ealla ðurh wīse wealhstōdas on hiora āgen geðiόde, Past. pref.; Swt. 7, 4. Seó hergung wæs ðurh Alaricum geworden, Bd. 1, 11; S. 480, 11. Hē ða bisceopðēninge ðurh hine sylfne (*per se*) ðēnian ne mihte, 4, 23; S. 594, 27. Wiste Cūðberhtus eal be ðam wīfe, and wolde þurh hine sylfne hī geneósian (*would visit her in person, the visit should be made by himself*), Homl. Th. ii. 142, 11. Gif hwā ymb cyninges feorh sierwie þurh hine oþþe þurh wreccena feormunge (*by his own direct acts or by the harbouring of criminals*), L. Alf. pol. 4; Th. i. 62, 15. (1 a) preposition following case:—Wā ðam ðe hig þurh (ðerh, Lind. Rush.) cumaþ *uae illi per quem ueniunt*, Lk. Skt. 17, 1. (2) marking the means or instrument, *through, by, by means of, by use of*:—Swā hē spræc þurh hys hālegra wītegena mūð (*per os sanctorum*), Lk. Skt. 1, 70. Hē ðurh ðæra wealhstōda mūð ðam cyninge bodade, Homl. Th. ii. 128, 21: 148, 12. Ic þurh mūþ sprece mongum reordum, Exon. Th. 390, 13; Rä. 9, 1. Þurh his sylfes mūð, 464, 6; Hö. 83: Andr. Kmbl. 1301; An. 651. Tōdǣl þurh seofon *divide by seven*, Anglia viii. 304, 41. Cnuca hȳ þurh hȳ selfe *pound it by itself* (per se), Lchdm. i. 130, 4: 192, 17. Wē ðæt gehȳrdon þurg hālige bēc, Apstls. Kmbl. 126; Ap. 63. Þurg wītgena wordgeryno, Elen. Kmbl. 577; El. 289. Hié lufodon wīsdōm and ðurh ðone hié begeáton welan, Past. pref.; Swt. 5, 14. Hē gefērde þurh feóndes cræft, Cd. Th. 29, 21; Gen. 453: 1, 21; Gen. 11: Blickl. Homl. 17, 11. Þuruh, Ps. Th. 70, 1. Hē hié tō heofona rīce laþode þurh his wundorgeweorc and þurh ða godspellīcan lāre, Blickl. Homl. 7, 9: Andr. Kmbl. 1949; An. 977. Ðæt hī heora synna wītnade and bētte ðurh fæsten and ðurh wōpas and ðurh gebedo, Bd. 4, 25; S. 599, 25. Wē witon unrīm ðara monna ðe ða ēcan gesǣlða gesōhtan nallas ðurh ðæt ān ðæt hī wilnodon ðæs līchomlīcan deáðes ac eác manegra sārlīcra wīta hié gewilnodon wið ðan ēcan līfe *multos scimus beatitudinis fructum non morte solum, verum etiam doloribus suppliciisque quaesisse*, Bt. 11, 2; Fox 36, 3. Gif hine mon geyflige mid slege oþþe mid bende oþþe þurh wunde, L. Alf. pol. 2; Th. i. 62, 4. (3) marking the efficient cause or reason, *through, in consequence of, as the result of, by reason of, on account of*:—Heofonrīces duru belocen standeþ þurh ða ǣrestan men, Blickl. Homl. 9, 2. Wæs micel unfrið þurh sciphere, Chr. 1001; Erl. 136, 2. Gif seó hringe nele up þurh his ānes tige, Homl. Skt. i. 21, 47: Ps. Th. 64, 11. Ðurh Æþelrēdes hǣse (*jubente Ædilredo*) Wilfriþ hine tō biscope gehālgode, Bd. 4, 23; S. 594, 29: Andr. Kmbl. 3038; An. 1522. Ic þurh his willan āsend wæs *Dei voluntate missus sum*, Gen. 45, 8: Exon. Th. 194, 3; Az. 133. Þurh clǣne gecynd *in consequence of a pure nature*, Hy. 9, 11: 7, 24. Ðā mihte heó wīde geseón þurh (*in consequence of*) ðæs lāðan lǣn, Cd. Th. 38, 3; Gen. 601: 39, 25–27; Gen. 631–2. Þurg, Apstls. Kmbl. 25; Ap. 13. Hē ðurh his gylt on ðām inrum þeóstrum befeóll, Homl. Th. ii. 556, 20: Cd. Th. 21, 29, 30; Gen. 331–2. Þurh ða eáðmōdnesse mid geleáfullum hē gefylde ðysne middangeard, Blickl. Homl. 11, 7. Hine mǣtte, and hē rehte ðæt his brōðrum; þurh ðæt hig hine hatedon ðe swīðor (*quae causa majoris odii seminarium fuit*), Gen. 37, 5. Hit wearð gelet þurh ðæt ðe Magnus hæfde micelne scypcræft, Chr. 1048; Erl. 173, 7: Wulfst. 161, 1. Wearð ðǣr ǣfre ðuruh sum þing fleám āstiht, Chr. 998; Erl. 134, 19. Þurh hwæt ðū ðus hearde ūs eorre wurde, Elen. Kmbl. 799; El. 400. Man þurh ǣlc þingc rihtwīsnesse lufige, Wulfst. 266, 18. (4) marking motive or feeling that prompts action, *through, from*:—Ðurh (ðerh, Lind.: ðærh, Rush.) andan hine sealdon ða heáhsacerdas, Mk. Skt. 15, 10. Se forhātena spræc þurh feóndscipe, Cd. Th. 38, 21; Gen. 610. Ic Gode þegnode þurh holdne hyge, 37, 7; Gen. 586: Ps. Th. 77, 38. Hyre þurh yrre āgeaf andsware fæder feóndlīce, Exon. Th. 249, 25; Jul. 117. Gif wē þurh eáþmōdnesse eall ārǣfnaþ, Blickl. Homl. 13, 91. Hī fricgaþ þurh fyrwet, Exon. Th. 6, 30; Cri. 92. (5) marking the circumstance which renders state or action possible or right, *through, in virtue of, by right of*:—Ðæt Martinus wǣre wyrðe ðæs hādes, and ðæt folc gesǣlig ðurh swelcne biscop *that Martin was worthy of the office, and the people happy in such a bishop*, Homl. Th. ii. 506, 9. His blōd āgeát God on galgan þurh his gāstes mægen *in virtue of his spirit's strength*, Cd. Th. 299, 16; Sat. 550. Hē fæste feówertig daga þurh his mildsa spēd, 306, 23; Sat. 668. Heó hit þurh monnes geþeaht ne sceáwode, 38, 12; Gen. 605. Him bearn Godes dēman wille þurh his dǣda spēd, 304, 2; Sat. 623: 301, 30; Sat. 589. (6) marking manner, state, *in, by, in the character of, by way of*:—Þorch (dorh, ðorh) ōbst *per anticipationem*, Txts. 84, 757. Ðurh endebyrdnesse singan *per ordinem cantare*, Bd. 4, 24; S. 597, 6. Ðæt fȳr ābyrst ūt ðurh līgett *in the shape of lightning*, Lchdm. iii. 280, 6: Elen. Kmbl. 2210; El. 1106. Ācenned in middangeard þurh mennisc heó *born into the world in human shape*, 12; El. 6. Onsȳne þurh cnihtes hād *visible in the form of a youth*, Andr. Kmbl. 1824; An. 914. Hnīgan mid heáfdum þurh geongordōm *to bow the head as vassals*, Cd. Th. 46, 12; Gen. 743. Ne can ðara idesa ōwðer þurh gebedscipe beorna neáwest, 148, 35; Gen. 2467. Hē ðolode ðurh wīte (*as punishment*) ða ȳttran blindnysse . . . Hé ðolaþ þeóstra ðurh wrace, Homl. Th. ii. 556, 19–21. Wundorgiefe þurh goldsmiþe *wondrous gifts in the goldsmith's art*, Exon. Th. 331, 24; Vy. 73. Stôd him sum man æt ðurh swefen (*per somnium*), Bd. 4, 24; S. 597, 11: Cd. Th. 159, 16; Gen. 2635: 160, 21; Gen. 2653. Him synna brytta þurh slǽp (*in sleep*) oncwæð, 159, 28; Gen. 2641. (7) marking accompanying circumstances of an action, *in, with*:—Ðû scealt þurh wôp and heáf on woruld cennan, þurh sâr micel, sunu and dohtor, Cd. Th. 57, 4–7; Gen. 923–4. Líg þurh lust geslôh micle mâre ðonne gemet wǽre, 231, 19; Dan. 249. Ðara ðe hyra lîfes þurh lust brûcan, Exon. Th. 127, 19; Gû. 388. Ða wácran ðás woruld healdaþ, brûcaþ þurh bisgo, 311, 6; Seef. 88. (8) marking aim, *with a view to*:—Hê Drihten mid hondum genom þurh edwît (*with a view to disgrace him*), Cd. Th. 307, 17; Sat. 681. Heó his lâre geceás ðurh þeódscipe (*with a view to instruction* (?), *in order to be instructed*; or *on account of his learning* (?)), Elen. Kmbl. 2331; El. 1167. (9) with verbs of swearing, adjuring, etc., *through, by, in*:—Sume synd *jurativa*, ðæt synd swerigendlîce, *per* ðurh: *juro per Deum* ic swerige ðurh God, Ælfc. Gr. 38; Zup. 227, 3. Ic swerige þurh mê sylfne *per memetipsum juravi*, Gen. 22, 16. Ðæt gê ne swerion ne þurh heofon . . . ne þurh eorðan . . . ne ðû ne swere þurh ðîn heáfod, Mt. Kmbl. 5, 34–36: Cd. Th. 205, 10; Exod. 433: Elen. Kmbl. 1369; El. 686. Ðû deópe âðe þurh ðînes sylfes sôð benemdest, Ps. Th. 88, 42. Ic ðec hâlsige þurh gǽsta weard, Exon. Th. 174, 14; Gû. 1177. Hý þurh mînne noman bǽdan, 92, 12; Cri. 1507. Eallum ðǽm ðê mê gecêgaþ þorh ðînne noman, Shrn. 105, 6. Ic ðê hâte þurh ða hêhstan miht, Cd. Th. 308, 18; Sat. 694. (10) marking extent:—Hwî is ðis fæsten þus geteald þurh feówertig daga *why is this fast reckoned at forty days?* Homl. Th. i. 178, 19. **B.** with dat. v. also **C.** **I.** local, (1) marking motion into and out at the opposite side:—Englas flugon swilce ðurh ânre dûna intô ðære heofenan, Homl. Th. ii. 342, 6. Gif ðǽr biþ ân hwem open forlǽten, ðæt se here þurh ðam infær hæbbe, 432, 5. Ðerh middum, Lk. Skt. Lind. 4, 30. (2) marking motion over or in:—Ic wæs getogen þurh ðisse ceastre lanum, Blickl. Homl. 243, 29. **II.** in other relations, (1) marking means or instrument:—Geufered þurh lârewlîcum basincge *exaltatus melote*, Hpt. Gl. 440, 71. Heó wolde þurh his mynegungum hire môd getrymman, Homl. Th. ii. 146, 10: 448, 27. Ðurh ðînum drýcræftum, 414, 4. Þurh ðam eárplættum, 248, 25. Þurh twâm gewritum, Wulfst. 230, 3. Ðerh mûðe hâligwara, Lk. Skt. Lind. 1, 70. (2) marking cause:—Hê næs âcweald ðurh ðam heálîcan fylle, Homl. Th. ii. 300, 19. Seó geladung ys weaxende þurh âcennedum cildum and waniende þurh forðfarenum, Lchdm. iii. 238, 2. (3) marking manner, state:—Hê ðæt weorc ðæs godspelles mâ ðurh his fôta gange fremede ðonne on his horsa râde (*more on foot than on horseback*), Bd. 4, 3; S. 566, 32. Ðâ com ûre Drihten þurh wolcnum (*in clouds*), Blickl. Homl. 145, 35. **C.** in the following passages both acc. and dat. are used:—Ðâ âxode se ealdorman ðone hæftling, hwæðer hê ðurh drýcræft oððe ðurh rûnstafum his bendas tôbrǽce, Homl. Th. ii. 358, 10–11. Hî sume þurh freónda fultum and ælmesdǽdum, and swîðost þurh hâlige mæssan beóð âlýsede, 352, 25–27. Ðurh ða treówu and ðam streáwe and ðam ceafe sind getâcnode leóhtlîce synna, 590, 12–14. **D.** with gen.:—Wê beóð geclǽnsode þurh ðæs hâlgan hûselganges, Homl. Th. ii. 266, 23. **E.** as adverb; see also the following compounds:—Hê sǽ tôslât and hî fôran þurh, Ps. Th. 77, 15. Ðǽr wæs fleóhnet ymbe ðæs folctogan bed âhongen, ðæt se bealofulla mihte wlîtan ðurh, and on hyne nǽnig monna cynnes, Judth. Thw. 22, 5; Jud. 49. [*O. E. Homl.* þurh, þurch, þuregh: *Laym.* þurh, þorh: *Orm.* þurrh: *A. R.* þurh, þuruh: *Gen. and Ex.* ðurg: *Havel.* þoru: *R. Glouc.* þoru, þorw: *Chauc.* thurgh: *Piers P.* þorowȝ, thorw: *Goth.* þairh: *O. Sax.* thurh, thuru: *O. L. Ger.* thurh, thuru(-o): *O. Frs.* thruch: *O. H. Ger.* durh, duruh (-ah, -eh).]

þurh-. With words expressing motion the prefix signifies *through, over*; in other cases it implies *thoroughness, completeness, continuity*; with adjectives of quality it has an intensive force. It is often a rendering of the Latin prefix *per-*; sometimes of *trans-*.

þurh-beorht; *adj. Very bright, splendid*, (1) lit.:—Heora nebwlite ongann tô scînenne swilce seó þurhbeorhte sunne, Homl. Skt. i. 23, 820. (2) fig.:—Swâ micele mâran eádmôdnysse ðû sý þurhbeorht (*perspicuus*), swâ mîcele swâ mâran wurþnysse foresett ðû eart, Scint. 22, 17. Yrfweardnes mîn þurhscînendlîc ł þurhbeorht (*praeclara*) is, Ps. Lamb. 15, 6.

þurh-bitter; *adj. Very bitter, exasperating*:—Þweor mǽgþ and tyrwiende ł þurhbitter *generatio prava et exasperans*, Ps. Lamb. 77, 8.

þurh-blâwen; *adj.* (*ptcpl.*) *Inspired*:—Mid forewitigum þurhblâwen gâste *presago afflatus spiritu*, Anglia xiii. 370, 65.

þurh-borian *to bore through, perforate*:—Ðâ wolde ic witan hwæðer ða gelîcnissa wǽron gegotene ealle swâ hê sǽde; hêt hié ðâ þurhborian *simulacra quae an solida essent scire ego cupiens omnia perforavi*, Nar. 20, 1. [*O. H. Ger.* durh-porôn *perforare, terebrare*.]

þurh-brecan *to break through*:—Wordes ord breósthord þurhbræc, Beo. Th. 5577; B. 2792. [*O. H. Ger.* durh-brehhan *dissecare*.]

þurh-brengan *to bring through*:—Hê tôslât sǽ and hê þurhbrôhte (*perduxit*) hig, Ps. Lamb. 77, 13. [*O. H. Ger.* durh-bringan *perferre*.]

þurh-brogden; *adj.* (*ptcpl.*) *Transported*:—Ðorhbrogden *trajectus*, Wrt. Voc. ii. 122, 63.

þurh-brûcan *to enjoy thoroughly*:—Hwylc manna þurhbrýcþ (*perfruitur*) mettum bûton swæcce sealtes, Coll. Monast. Th. 28, 15.

þurh-burnen; *adj.* (*ptcpl.*) *Thoroughly burnt, burnt through*:—Bærn swâ ðæt hit sî þurhburnen, Lchdm. iii. 40, 11.

þurh-clǽnsian *to cleanse thoroughly*:—Þurhclǽnsaþ (ðerhclǽnsade, Lind. *permundavit*) *he will throughly purge*, Mt. Kmbl. Rush. 3, 12.

þurh-creópan *to creep through*:—Swâ swâ mon melo sift, ðæt melo ðurhcrýpþ (þurg-, Cott. MS.) ǽlc þyrel, Bt. 34, 11; Fox 152, 2.

þurh-delfan *to dig through, bore through, pierce*:—Ic ðurhdelfe *perfodio*, Ælfc. Gr. 28, 6; Zup. 179, 10. Þurhdelfeþ, Ps. Th. 79, 15. Hý þurhdulfon (*foderunt*) mîne handa and mîne fêt, 21, 15. Þurhdol[fen] *confossa, transfixa*, Hpt. Gl. 501, 29.

þurh-dreógan *to carry through, perform, pass* time:—Ârîsende ôþre þurhdreógan *surgentes cetera peragant*, Anglia xiii. 423, 825. Nihte þurhdreógan *noctem peragere*, 394, 420.

þurh-drîfan. **I.** *to drive through, pierce, transfix*:—Him man ǽgðer þurhdrâf mid îsenum næglum ge fêt ge handa, Wulfst. 22, 21. Þurhdrifon hî mê mid næglum, Rood Kmbl. 91; Kr. 46. Hê lêt hine sylfne bindan and him ǽgðer þurhdrîfan mid næglum ge fêt ge handa, Wulfst. 110, 15: Exon. Th. 68, 27; Cri. 1110. Dolgbennum þurhdrifen, Andr. Kmbl. 2793; An. 1399. Mîne handa mid næglum þurhdrifene, Homl. Th. i. 220, 17. Þurhdryfene, L. E. I. 21; Th. ii. 416, 30. **I a.** fig. *to penetrate, permeate, imbue*:—Ðeáh ic ǽr mid dysige þurhdrifen wǽre, Elen. Kmbl. 1410; El. 707. **II.** *to drive violently*; perpellere:—Word spearcum fleáh, ðonne hê ût þurhdrâf (*when he sent out his words vehemently, exclaimed vehemently*), Cd. Th. 274, 33; Sat. 163. [He let þurhdriuen þe spaken mid gadien, Kath. 1920. Wes mon þurhdriuen upon þe rode *homo cruci affixus est*, 1198.]

þurh-dûfan *to dive through*:—Hê wæter up þurhdeáf, Beo. Th. 3243; B. 1619.

þurh-etan *to eat through, eat out*:—Se wyrm ða eágan þurheteþ, Soul Kmbl. 236; Seel. 122. Âholad, þurhetan (-en?) *exesum* vel *comessum*, Wrt. Voc. ii. 144, 76. Swyrd ômige, þurhetene, Beo. Th. 6090; B. 3049.

þurh-fær, es; *n. An inner, secret place*:—Ǽlc synful on his þurhfærum (*penetrabilibus*) byð bedîglod, Scint. 39, 2. v. þurh-fêre, -farenness, -faran, IV.

þurh-fæstnian *to transfix*:—Ðorhfæstnadon *transfixerunt*, Jn. Skt. Lind. Rush. 19, 37.

þurh-faran. **I.** *to go through* or *over, to traverse*; pertransire, (1) *trans.*:—Burnan þurhfôr (ł -færþ) sâwla ûre wênunga þurhfôr sâwla ûre wæter *torrentem pertransivit anima nostra, forsitan pertransisset anima nostra aquam*, Ps. Spl. 123, 4. Hê ðæt land eall þurhfôr, Chr. 1095; Erl. 232, 8: 1097; Erl. 233, 38. (2) *intrans. To pass*:—Mid ðî ðe ðû þurhfærst (*pertransires*) on wêstene, Ps. Spl. 67, 8. On anlîcnysse þurhfærþ man *in imagine pertransit homo*, 38, 9: 102, 15. Ðǽr scipu þurhfaraþ (ðorhfearaþ, Surt.) *illic naves pertransibunt*, 103, 26. **II.** of a weapon, *to pierce, pass through*:—His swurd ðîne sâwle þurhfærþ, Lk. Skt. 2, 35. Îsen þurhfôr sâwla his, Ps. Spl. 104, 17. **III.** *to pass beyond, transcend*:—Hefonas hê ðurhfôr (*transcendit*), Past. 16; Swt. 99, 23. **IV.** *to penetrate*:—Sió stefn ðæs lâriówes ðurhfærþ ða heortan ðæs gehîrendes *illa vox auditorum cor penetrat*, Past. 14; Swt. 81, 9: 21; Swt. 155, 11: Bt. 13; Fox 38, 27. Ðeáh ðû ðæt hêhste ðurhfare *cum summa penetras*, Past. 65; Swt. 467, 1. Þurhfare *penetret*, Anglia xiii. 378, 192. Ðæt word ðære lâre ne mæg ðurhfaran ðæs wædlan heortan *egentis mentem doctrinae sermo non penetrat*, Past. 18; Swt. 137, 6. Þurhfarende *penetrans*, Hymn. Surt. 84, 9. [*O. H. Ger.* durh-faran *transire, permeare, penetrare*.] v. þurh-fêran.

þurh-farenness, e; *f. An inner, secret place*; penetrale:—On þurhfarennyssum cyninga heora *in penetralibus regum ipsorum*, Ps. Spl. 104, 28. v. þurh-fær, -fêre, -faran, IV.

þurh-fêran. **I.** *to pass through* or *over*:—Ðæt geðyld ðurhfêrde ðara leahtra truman *patientia medias acies transit*, Gl. Prud. 26 b. Hê þurhfêrde hǽðenre þeóde eard, Shrn. 155, 34. Hî þurhfêrdon ealle ða land . . . óððæt hî cômon ðǽr hê wunode, Homl. Skt. ii. 30, 231. Þurhfêrende (*humida cum siccis*) pervadens (*caerula plantis*), Wrt. Voc. ii. 96, 38. **II.** *to penetrate, get into*:—Hêr Rodla ðurhfêrde (*penetravit*) Normandi mid his here, Chr. 876; Th. i. 145, col. 3. [He þe þurhferde deað, Kath. 1142.] v. þurh-faran.

þurh-fêre; *adj. That may be passed through* or *over, passable, pervious*:—Geat þurhfêre *porta pervia*, Hymn. Surt. 112, 9. *The neuter used substantivally translates* penetrale:—On þurhfêrun *in penetralibus*, Mt. Kmbl. 24, 26. v. þurh-fær.

þurh-fleón *to fly through*:—Cume ân spearwa and hrædlîce ðæt hûs þurhfleó *adveniens unus passerum domum citissime pervolaverit*, Bd. 2, 13; S. 516, 18.

þurh-fôn *to get through, penetrate*:—Heó ðone fyrdhom þurhfôn ne mihte lâþan fingrum, Beo. Th. 3013; B. 1504.

þurh-gân. I. *to go over* or *through*:—Fixas þurhgâð (*perambulant*) paðas sǽs, Ps. Spl. 8, 8. Ic wille ðurhgân orsorh ðone here, Homl. Th. ii. 502, 11. II. of a weapon, *to pass through, pierce*:—Hē sette his swurdes ord tōgeánes his innoðe, and feól him on uppon, ðæt him ðurheode (*or* him ðurh eode, *under* þurh, B. I (1)), Homl. Th. ii. 480, 15. His swurd sceal ðurhgân ðīne sāwle, i. 146, 8. III. *to penetrate, permeate, pervade*:—Seó eorðe byð mid ðam winterlīcan cyle þurhgân, Lchdm. iii. 252, 7. [Heo þurheoden Francene þeode, Laym. 5217. Læten heom þurhgon al þa duȝeðe, 19645. Þeȝȝ shollden all þurrhgan þiss middellærd, Orm. 12860. *Goth.* þairh-iddja; *p.*: *O. H. Ger.* durh-gân *pertransire, penetrare.*] v. next word.

þurh-gangan. I. *to go over* or *through, perambulate*:—Þurhgangende *perambulante*, Ps. Spl. 90, 6. II. *to pierce*:—Ne forhtast ðū ðē on dæge flān on lyfte, ðæt ðē þuruhgangan gāras on ðeóstrum, Ps. Th. 90, 6. [*Goth.* þairh-gaggan: *O. H. Ger.* durh-gangan.]

þurh-gefeoht, es; *n. War*:—Þorhgefeht, þorgifect *perduellium*, Txts. 85, 738.

þurh-geótan. I. *to pour over, cover by pouring* (lit. and fig.):—Ðū þurhgute hine gedrēfednysse *perfudisti eum confusione*, Ps. Spl. 88, 44. Ic mid ða līffæstan ȳþe ðurhgoten wæs *vitali unda perfusus sum*, Bd. 5, 6; S. 620, 18. II. *to fill, saturate*:—Ðonne se sacerd gehālgodne tapor in ðæt wæter dēð, ðonne wyrð ðæt wæter mid ðam hālgan gāste ðurhgoten, Wulfst. 36, 6. II a. *to fill, imbue, inspire*:—Gleáwnysse þurhgoten, Elen. Kmbl. 1920; El. 962. [*O. H. Ger.* durh-giozan *perfundere.*]

þurh-glēded; *adj.* (*ptcpl.*) *Thoroughly furnished with burning coals*:—Wæs se ofen onhǽted, īsen eall ðurhglēded, Cd. Th. 231, 8; Dan. 244.

þurh-hǽlan *to heal thoroughly*; persanare:—Ealle ða þincg, ðe on ðæs mannes līchoman tō lāðe ācennede beóþ, heó ðurhhǽleþ (þur-, MS. O.), Lchdm. i. 124, 22.

þurh-hǽlig; *adj. Very holy*:—Þurhhāligere gerde *sacrosancti viminis* (Moses' rod), Hpt. Gl. 409, 70. Þurhhāliges blōdes *sacrosancti cruoris*, 503, 46. Tō ðam þurhhāligum hāligdōme Drihtnes līchaman and blōdes *ad sacrosanctum sacramentum corporis et sanguinis Domini*, Wanl. Cat. 79, 4.

þurh-hefig; *adj. Very heavy*; praegravis, Dial. 2, 3 (Lye).

þurh-hwīt; *adj. Very white*:—Þurhhwīt *candidus*, Wülck. Gl. 163, 6 (omitted in Wrt. Voc. i. 46, 30).

þurh-irnan *to run through*:—Þurharn *cucurrit*, Wrt. Voc. ii. 137, 60. Ðæt swurd ðe ðæra cildra lima þurharn, Homl. Th. i. 84, 18.

þurh-lǽran *to persuade*:—Nele God wrecan yfelnysse se andettan gyltas þurhlǽrþ *non uult Deus ulcisci malitiam, qui confiteri delicta persuadet*, Scint. 38, 12.

þurh-lǽred; *adj. Very learned*:—Þurhlǽred *vel* gleáw *expertus*, i. *multum peritus*, Wrt. Voc. i. 22, 35.

þurh-lāð; *adj. Very hateful, odious*:—Þurhlāð *odiosus*, Wrt. Voc. i. 28, 66.

þurh-leóran *to pass through*:—Ðorhleórdun *pertransierunt*, Ps. Surt. 76, 18.

þurh-lōcung, e; *f. A looking through* or *over, a preliminary examination* (?) of a book; but the word glosses *prohemium*:—Ðurhlōcung *prohemium*, forespǽc *praefatio*, Wrt. Voc. i. 51, 38. [Cf. Illc an ferrs to þurrhlokenn offte, Orm. dedic. 68.]

þurh-rǽsan *to rush through*:—Hwīlum ic þurhrǽse, Exon. Th. 384, 31; Rä. 4, 36.

þurh-sceótan *to shoot through, transfix, pierce*:—Þurhscēt *transfigat*, Hpt. Gl. 526, 3. Hē his byrnsweord getȳhþ, and ða līchoman þurhsceóteþ, Blickl. Homl. 109, 35. Ðǽr wearð Alexander þurhscoten mid ānre flān . . . hē þurh ðæt folc geþrang ðæt hē ðone ilcan ofslōg ðe hiene ǽr þurhsceát *in eo praelio sagitta trajectus eatenus pugnavit, donec eum, a quo vulneratus esset, occideret*, Ors. 3, 9; Swt. 134, 22-27. Besyrian ðone earman and þurhsceótan ða unscæðfullan heortan, Ps. Th. 36, 13. Ðā wurdon hī mid deófles flān þurhscotene, Homl. Th. i. 62, 28. [*O. Frs.* thruch-skiata: *O. H. Ger.* durh-sciozan.]

þurh-scīne; *adj. Transparent*:—Þurhscȳne stān *specularis*, Wrt. Voc. i. 38, 30. [Cf. *O. Frs.* thruch-skīnich.]

þurh-scīnendlīc; *adj. Splendid*; praeclarus, Ps. Lamb. 15, 6. v. þurh-beorht.

þurh-scrīþan. I. of physical movement, *to pass through, glide through*:—Synd twelf tācna on ðam foresprecenan circule ðe seó sunne þurhscrīð, Anglia viii. 298, 18. II. *to go through* a subject, *examine, consider*; perlustrare:—Ǽlc ðæra ðe wyle ða eásterlīcan blisse mǽrsian, ne sceal hē nāðer ne ðæs lambes flǽsc hreáw etan, ne gesoden, ac gebrǽd; ðæt ys, ðæt hē ne sceal þurh menniscnysse wīsdōm þurhscrīðan ða hālgan flǽscennysse ūres Drihtnes (*he shall not by the aid of human wisdom examine* (?) *our Lord's nature according to the flesh*), ne on him gelȳfan swylce hē sȳ ānfeald man būton his godcundnysse, ac wē sceolon gelȳfan ðæt hē ys sōð man and sōðlīce God, Anglia viii. 324, 1. [Al þa londes ic scal þurhscriðen (þorhride, 2nd MS.), Laym. 10887.]

þurh-scyldig; *adj. Very guilty*:—Hī (*the Jews who plotted against Christ*) synd þurhscyldige for heora syrwunge, Homl. Skt. i. 11, 321.

þurh-sēcan. I. *to make search for, seek out*:—Þurhsēcende *conquirens*, Scint. 209, 3. [II. *to search through, examine* (?), as in later English:—He þurhsecheð al þe soule, O. E. Homl. ii. 191, 28. Twa Goddspelless uss birrþ þurrhsekenn, Orm. 242. He hefde al þ lond ouergan and þurhsoht *peragratis provincie finibus*, Kath. 519. Þe poyson þe veynes so þorwsouȝte, R. Glouc. 151, 11. *O. H. Ger.* durh-suohhan *to search through.*]

þurh-seón *to see through, see into, penetrate with the sight* (lit. or fig.):—God geseóþ and þurhseóþ ealle his gesceafta, Bt. 41, 1; Fox 244, 11. Þurhsyhþ, Met. 30, 16. Gif hwā biþ swā scearpsēne, ðæt hē mæge hine (*Alcibiades*) ðurhseón, swā swā Aristoteles sǽde ðæt deór wǽre, ðæt mihte ǽlc wuht þurhseón . . . gif ðonne hwā wǽre swā scearpsēne, ðæt hē mihte ðone cniht ðurhseón, ðonne ne þūhte hē him nō innon swā fæger, swā hē ūtan þūhte *si, ut Aristoteles ait, lynceis oculis homines uterentur, ut eorum visus obstantia penetraret, nonne introspectis visceribus, illud Alcibiadis superficie pulcerrimum corpus, turpissimum videretur*, Bt. 32, 2; Fox 116, 19-25. Wē sceolon gleáwlīce þurhseón ūsse hreþercofan heortan eágum, Exon. Th. 81, 24; Cri. 1328. [He þurhsihð elches mannes þanc, O. E. Homl. ii. 222, 90: i. 165, 90. Þe blake cloð is wurse to þurhseon, A. R. 50, 16. *O. H. Ger.* durh-sehan *visu penetrare.*]

þurh-seón *to strain through, penetrate*:—Ealle ða fūllnessa ðæs fūllan ofnes and ðæs þeóstran ðe mec ǽr ðurhseáh *omnem foetorem tenebrosae fornacis, qui me pervaserat*, Bd. 5, 12; M. 430, 6.

þurh-sleán. I. *to smite through, strike through* (lit. and fig.):—Hē his byrnsweord getȳhþ and ðās world ealle þurhslyhþ, Blickl. Homl. 109, 34. Hire swiora næs þurhslagen, Homl. Skt. i. 12, 235. Ðā wearð heó mid micelre sārnysse ðurhslegen, Homl. Th. ii. 30, 21. II. *to smite*:—Ic ðerhslǽ ł hrīno ðone hiorde *percutiam pastorem*, Mk. Skt. Lind. Rush. 14, 27. [*O. Frs.* thruch-slā: *O. H. Ger.* durh-slahan *percutere, pulsare.*]

þurh-smeágan, -smeán *to search through, inquire into, examine into, investigate*:—Ða ðe mid carfulre gȳmene gāstlīce bebodu þurhsmeágeaþ *qui solerti cura spiritalia precepta perscrutantur*. Ðā hē ða seofon cræftas ealle hæfde þurhsmeáde, Shrn. 152, 18. Hē rīxade ofer Englæland, and hit mid his geápscipe swā þurhsmeáde (*made such a thorough inquisition*), ðæt næs ān hīd landes innan Englælande, ðæt hē nyste hwā heó hæfde, oððe hwæs heó wurð wæs, Chr. 1086; Erl. 222, 10. Þurhsmeágean *perscrutari*, Scint. 32, 11.

þurh-smūgan. I. of movement (lit. or fig.), *to creep through, move slowly through*:—Se wyrm ða tungan tōtȳhþ, and ða tēð þurhsmȳhþ, Soul Kmbl. 235; Seel. 121. Ðæt gēr, ðe man hǽt *solaris*, þurhsmīhþ *Zodiacum* ðone circul on þrim hund dagum and fīf and syxtigum, Anglia viii. 303, 22. II. *to go carefully through* a subject, *go over the details*:—Hē sceal snotorlīce smeágean and georne þurhsmūgan ealle ða ðing ðe hlāforde magan tō rǽde *he must prudently consider and diligently go over in his mind all those matters which may be to his lord's advantage*, Anglia ix. 259, 18. Nū wille wē ūre sprǽce āwendan tō ðam iungum munecum ðe heora cildhād habbaþ ābīsgod on cræftigum bōcum . . . Hig habbaþ āscrutnod Serium and Priscianum, and þurhsmogun Catus cwydas *they have gone carefully through Cato's Disticha*, Anglia viii. 321, 28.

þurh-spēdig; *adj. Very wealthy*:—Ðǽr eardode sum þurhspēdig mann (cf. *of the same person* sum rīce man and for worlde ǽhtspēdig, Blickl. Homl. 197, 27), Homl. Th. i. 502, 8.

þurh-stician *to stick through, pierce, transfix*:—Ðorhsticadun *transfixerunt*, Jn. Skt. Lind. 19, 37. [Cf. Heo þuruhstihten Isboset adun into þe schere (*percusserunt eum in inguine*, 2 Sam. 4, 6), A. R. 272, 12. *O. Frs.* thruch-steka: *O. H. Ger.* durh-stehhan *confodere, transfigere.*]

þurh-stingan *to stab through, pierce, thrust through*:—Gif man þeóh þurhstingð *if the thigh is thrust through*, L. Ethb. 67; Th. i. 18, 16. Þurhstinð, 32; Th. i. 12, 1. Hē ðurhstong ðone cyninges ðeng and ðone cyning gewundade *tanta vi hostis ferrum infixit, ut per corpus militis occisi etiam regem vulneraret*, Bd. 2, 9; S. 511, 24. Þurhsting his eáre *perforabis aurem ejus*, Deut. 15, 17. Ðæt hē hine selfne ne ðurhstinge mid ðȳ sweorde unryhthǽmedes *ne luxuriae se mucrone transfigant*, Past. 43; Swt. 313, 8. Hē hēt hine mid sweorde þurstingan, Shrn. 131, 33. Þurhstungen *confosa*, Wrt. Voc. ii. 24, 42. [Weren his fet mid irnene neiles þurhstungen, O. E. Homl. i. 147, 32.]

þurh-swimman *to swim through* or *over, pass by swimming*:—Ðorhsuimmaþ *tranant*, Wrt. Voc. ii. 122, 74.

þurh-swīðan *to prove very strong*:—Hē þurhswīðde on īdelnesse *praeualuit in vanitate*, Ps. Lamb. 51, 9.

þurh-swōgan *to press through, penetrate, pervade*:—Ealle ða fūllnessa ðæs ðȳstran ofnes ðe mē ǽr ðurhsweógh(-swēg, Bd. M. 430, 6 note) *omnem foetorem tenebrosae fornacis, qui me pervaserat*, Bd. 5, 12; S. 629, 21.

þurh-teón. I. *to carry through, get a proposal accepted*, a request *granted*:—Ðā hē ðæt (*his proposal*) uneáþe ðurhteáh *quod dum* *aegre impetraret ab ea*, Bd. 4, 11; S. 579, 17. Lucius bæd ðæt hē cristen geðón wǣre, and hē þurhteáh ðæt hē bæd (*by a later hand this is turned into* him wærð tīþod ðæt hē bæd), Chr. 167; Erl. 8, 15. **II.** *to carry out* a plan, orders, etc., *give effect to* an intention:—Bið oft synleás yfel geðōht ðǣm gōdum, ðonne hī hit mid weorcum ne ðorhtióð, Past. 54; Swt. 423, 4. Hē nōhwæþer ðyssa (*neither of these plans*) gefremede ne ðurhteáh *ne aliquid horum perficeret*, Bd. 5, 9; S. 622, 23. Mennisclīc is ðæt mon on his mōde costunga ðrowige on ðæm luste yfles weorces, ac ðæt is deófullīc ðæt hē ðone willan ður[h]teó, Past. 11; Swt. 71, 15. Gif hē ðæt þurhtió, ðæt hē getihhod hæfþ, Bt. 34, 7; Fox 144, 4. Cweþan ðæt sió godcunde foretiohhung getiohhod hæfde ðæs ðe hió ne þurhtuge, 41, 3; Fox 248, 21. Hī nōhwæþere heora willnunge habban ne ðurhteón magan *in neutro cupitum passunt obtinere propositum*, Bd. 5, 23; S. 647, 3; Ors. 1, 2; Swt. 30, 22. Ðæt hē ðæt mihte mid ðȳ māran ealdorlīcnesse ðurhteón and gefremman, Bd. 5, 21; S. 642, 30. **III.** where continuous action is implied, *to carry through, carry on to a* (*successful*) *end, to accomplish, perform*; of evil actions, *to perpetrate*:—Se cwyrnstān ðe tyrnð singallīce and nǣnne færeld ne ðurhtīhþ, Homl. Th. i. 514, 20. Micel tōsceád is betwuh ðære synne, ðe mon longe ymbsireð, and ðære ðe mon fǣrlīce ðurhtiéhð, Past. 56; Swt. 435, 6. Hī ðæt yfel þurhtióþ (þurgtióð, Cott. MS.) *scelus perficiunt*, Bt. 38, 2; Fox 196, 34. Ðurhteáh *patraverat*, Wrt. Voc. ii. 67, 51. Ða scylde ðe se him self ǣr nyste se hié þurhteáh *culpam, quam nescit ipse etiam, qui perpetravit*, Past. 15; Swt. 91, 14. Silla wið Marius heardlīce gefeaht þurhteáh (*fought and won*) and hiene gefliémde *Sulla Marium gravissimo praelio tandem vicit*, Ors. 5, 11; Swt. 236, 21. Ðonne gē ymb ðæt ān gefeoht alneg ceoriað ðe eów Gotan gedydon, hwȳ nyllaþ gē geþencan ða monegan ǣrran ðe eów Gallie oftrædlīce bismerlīce þurhtugon *the many former fights that the Gauls often fought and won against you to your disgrace*, Ors. 3, 11; Swt. 142, 9. Hī lǣrdan hine ðæt hē ða fōre ðurhtuge *they persuaded him to perform* (perficere) *the journey*, Bd. 5, 19; S. 637, 27. Ðæt ðæt mōd ðurhtuge swelce synne, Past. 56; Swt. 435, 4. Ne mæg se ælmihtiga Wealdend þurhteón ðæt hē dō his ðeówan rīce *cannot the almighty Ruler accomplish the enriching of his servants?* Homl. Th. i. 64, 17. Wē ne magan for ūre tyddernysse þyllīc fæsten þurhteón *we cannot on account of our weakness accomplish such a fast*, Wulfst. 285, 27. Þurhtión (þurg-, Cott. MS.) ðæt yfel ðæt hī lyst *cupita perficere*, Bt. 38, 2; Fox 196, 28, 32. Þurhtión nāwuht goodes (cf. nān gōd dōn, Bt. 37, 1; Fox 186, 27), Met. 25, 59. Ðæt hié nāne mildheortnesse þurhteón ne mehtan, Ors. 2, 1; Swt. 64, 17. Ðā wearð eft Ianes duru andōn, þēh ðǣr nān gefeoht þurhtogen ne wurde *though no battle had actually been fought*; nulla bella sonuerunt, 6, 1; Swt. 254, 19. Ne biþ ðǣr sin ðurhtogen *peccatum perpetratum non est*, Bd. 1, 27; S. 497, 21: Exon. Th. 128, 1; Gū. 397: 270, 1; Jul. 458. Þurhtogen *conlatum* (v. þurhtogenness), Wrt. Voc. ii. 134, 41. Mid ðȳ ðurhtogenan weorce, Past. 48; Swt. 367, 12. Ða ðe ða ðurhtogenan (cf. geworhtan, 53; Swt. 413, 3) synna wēpaþ *qui peccata deplorant operum*, 23; Swt. 176, 22. **III a.** of continuous but uncompleted action, *to carry on, continue*:—Hē swā six and twēntig daga ðæt færeld þurhteáh swilce hē tō sumum menn mid gewisse fōre *so for six and twenty days he continued the journey, as if he were with certainty travelling to some one*, Homl. Skt. ii. 23 b, 159. **IV.** where a result is marked, *to bring to a successful issue, to achieve, bring about, bring to pass*:—Gif hē torngemōt þurhteón mihte *if he could bring about a meeting*, Beo. Th. 2284; B. 1140. His sige tō tācne ðe hē ðurhteón þōhte *as a monument of the victory that he thought to achieve*, Ors. 2, 5; Swt. 84, 5. On Criste ānum is ealles siges fylnes þurhtogen *in Christ alone does the fullness of all victory come to pass*, Blickl. Homl. 179, 7. **V.** *to afford*:—Hit wæs geset on ðære ealdan ǣ, ðæt ða ðe mihton ðurhteón sceoldon bringan ānes geáres lamb, and āne culfran . . . Gif hwylc wīf tō ðam unspēdig wǣre, ðæt heó ðās ðing begytan ne mihte . . ., Homl. Th. i. 138, 35. Āne feorme swā gōde swā hī bezte þurhteón magon *a refection as good as ever they can afford*, Chart. Th. 531, 15. Gif hwā ne mage ðurhteón ða spēda ðæt hē gesewenlīc lāc Gode offrige *if any man cannot afford such means, that he may offer a visible gift to God*, Homl. Th. i. 584, 2. Sȳ him gefultumad and frōfor þurhtogen *solacia accomodentur eis*, R. Ben. 85, 18. **VI.** *to go through, undergo*:—Swā swā wīf ācenþ bearn and þrowaþ micel earfoþu æfter ðam ðe heó ǣr micelne lust þurhteáh, Bt. 31, 1; Fox 112, 3. Hefige geswincu wē þurhteón, ðæt wē tō heofenan āstīgan magan, Scint. 101, 11. Gif hē ða beþinge þurhteón ne mæge, Lchdm. ii. 340, 10. **VII.** *to draw, drag*:—On wītu helle mann gālnys þurhtȳhð *in poenas tartari hominem libido pertrahat*, Scint. 89, 5. Ða ðe ōþre tō unrihtwīsnysse lǣrende þurhteóð (*pertrahunt*), 192, 4.

þurh-þeówan, -þīan, -þȳgan, -þȳn *to thrust through, pierce through, transfix*:—Ic ðurhðȳ (-þȳge, MS. J.) *perfodio*, Ælfc. Gr. 28, 6; Zup. 179, 10. Seó clǣnnys ðurhðȳð (*transfigit*) ða gālnysse mid swurde, Gl. Prud. 13 b. Hē siwode scōs and ðurhþīde his hand, Homl. Skt. i. 15. 24. Ðurhðȳde, Homl. Th. i. 452, 14. Hī þurhðȳdon (ðurhðȳgdon, Ps. Lamb. 21, 17) mīne handa *foderunt manus meas*, ii. 16, 23. Dauides þegnas hine (*Absalom*) þurhðȳdon, Homl. Skt. i. 19, 223. Ðā wolde hē þurhþȳn hī mid swurde, 12, 225. Þurhþīende *transverberans, transfigens*, Hpt. Gl. 411, 66. Þurhþēd *confossa, transfixa*, 501, 29. Mīn bān bið mid sārnysse þurhðȳd os *meum perforatur doloribus* (Job 30, 17), Homl. Th. ii. 456, 12. Ōþre wǣron mid stengum þurhðȳde, i. 542, 28. v. þeówan, *and* þurh-þyddan.

þurh-þrāwan *to twist through* [:—Se wǣte of hūse dropaþ on stān . . . and ðane stān þurhþurleþ and þurhþreáwþ, Lchdm. iii. 104, 11].

þurh-þyddan *to thrust through, pierce through*:—Ðā com sum cempa swīþe gewǣpnod, and hyne sōna þurhþydde, Homl. Skt. i. 3, 273. v. þyddan, *and* þurh-þeówan.

þurh-þȳn. v. þurh-þeówan.

þurh-þyrel; *adj. Pierced through, perforated*:—Gif hrif wund weorðeþ, .xii. scill. gebēte. Gif hē þurhþirel weorðeþ, .xx. scill. gebēte, L. Ethb. 61; Th. i. 18, 7. Gif sió lendenbrǣde biþ on bestungen, geselle .xv. scill. tō bōte; gif hió biþ þurhþyrel (-þyrl, MS. B.), ðonne sceal ðǣr .xxx. scill. tō bōte, L. Alf. pol. 67; Th. i. 98, 3. Cf. þurh-wund.

þurh-þyrelian, -þyrlian *to pierce through, make a hole through, perforate*:—[Se wǣte of hūse dropaþ on stāne . . . and ðane stān þurhþurleþ, Lchdm. iii. 104, 11.] 'Ðurhðyrela ðone wāg.' Ðā ic ðone wāh ðurhðyreludne hæfde '*fode parietem.*' *Cum fodissem parietem*, Past. 21; Swt. 153, 17. Ðæt mon ðurhðyrelige ðone weall . . . Hē cuæð: 'Ðā ic hæfde ðone weall ðurhðyrelod, Swt. 155, 1–3. Þurhþyrlige his hlāford his eáre *dominus perforabit aurem ejus* (Ex. 21, 6), L. Alf. 11; Th. i. 46, 10. Wǣron ða eáran him þurhþyrelode *perforatis auribus*, Nar. 26, 30.

þurhtogenness, e; *f. A religious reading in monasteries, especially after meals*; collatio:—Þurhtogenessa and gesetnessa heora līfes *conlationes patrum et instituta vite eorum*, R. Ben. Interl. 118, 7. Cf. þurh-togen *conlatum*, Wrt. Voc. ii. 134, 41.

þurh-trymman *to confirm thoroughly, corroborate*:—Werc cȳðnisse ðerhtrymmaþ of mē *opera testimonium perhibent de me*, Jn. Skt. Rush. Lind. 10, 25.

þurh-ūt; *prep. adv. Throughout, quite through*:—Ðæt spere him eode þurhūt, Homl. Skt. i. 12, 55. Hē fōr þurhūt Eoferwīc, Chr. 1066; Erl. 200, 33. [Mid helle sweordes al snesien ham þuruhut, A. R. 212, 23. He sahede hire þurhut, Marh. 22, 11. Ðis lond ðurgut he charen, Gen. and Ex. 3704. Ane stræte þurhut al þis kinelond, Laym. 4826. Sunne þurhut forleten, O. E. Homl. i. 23, 10. Þurhut gode and þurhut clene on mode, O. and N. 879. *Ger.* durch-aus.]

þurh-wacol; *adj. Very watchful, vigilant*:—Wacul *vigil* vel *vigilans*, ðurhwacul *pervigil*, Wrt. Voc. i. 46, 3. Þurhwacol, 75, 66. Þurhwacol *pernox*, Ælfc. Gr. 9, 65; Zup. 71, 15. (1) in reference to persons:—Þurhwacol emhīdignys *pervigil sollicitudo*, Hpt. Gl. 426, 51. Hē ābād on ðam legere . . . Þurhwacol on gebedum, Homl. Th. ii. 516, 30. Wē hālsiaþ eów ðæt gē beón on gebedum þurhwacule *hortamur vos orationibus pervigiles existere*, Cod. Dip. B. i. 154, 36. Hī on heora gebedum wunodon þurhwacole ōð midde niht, Homl. Skt. i. 11, 44. Hī ealle ða niht mid hālgum sprǣcum ðæs gāstlīcan līfes ðurhwacole āspendon, Homl. Th. ii. 184, 14. Hī heom weardas setton, þurhwacole menn, Homl. Skt. i. 11, 147. (2) in reference to time, *very wakeful, quite sleepless*:—Hine gedrehte singal slǣpleást, swā ðæt hē þurhwacole niht būton slǣpe ādreáh, Homl. Th. i. 86, 17. [Cf. *Goth.* þairh-wakan *pernoctare, vigilare*: *O. H. Ger.* durh-wahhēn; durh-wacha *pervigilium.*]

þurh-wadan. **I.** *to pass through*:—Ða hyssas þrȳ wylm þurhwōdon, Cd. Th. 245, 16; Dan. 464. **II.** of a weapon (lit. or fig.), *to pierce* through, *penetrate*:—Ðæt swurd þurhwōd wyrm, ðæt hit on wealle ætstōd, Beo. Th. 1785; B. 890: 3139; B. 1567: Byrht. Th. 140, 31; By. 296. For ðām næglum ðe ðæs Nergendes fēt þurhwōdon, Elen. Kmbl. 2139; El. 1066. Swylce hit seaxes ecg þurhwōde, Exon. Th. 70, 21; Cri. 1142. Ða syngan flǣsc, scaudum þurhwaden, 78, 32; Cri. 1283. [*O. H. Ger.* durh-watan *pertransire.*]

þurh-wæccendlīc; *adj. Very vigilant*:—Mid þurhwæccendlīcan mōde, Homl. Skt. ii. 23 b, 43.

þurh-werod (?); *adj. Very sweet*:—Hwylc manna þurhwerodum (*dulcibus*; perhaps *þurh* is an error of the scribe brought about by the *þurh* of the following word) þurhbrȳcþ mettum būton swæcce sealtes, Wrt. Voc. i. 9, 21.

þurh-wlītan *to look through, penetrate with the sight*:—Glæs ðæt mon mæg eall þurhwlītan, Exon. Th. 79, 2; Cri. 1284. Wē ne magun hygeþonces ferð eágum þurhwlītan, 82, 1; Cri. 1332.

þurh-wrecan *to thrust through*:—Sumne heó mid sweorde ofslōgen, sumne mid spiten betweón felle and flǣsce þurhwrǣcon, Homl. Ass. 171, 39. Ōð hielt þurhwrecen (*ense*) *capulo tenus* (*per utraque latera*) *adacto*, Wrt. Voc. ii. 86, 69.

þurh-wund; *adj. Wounded by a weapon which has passed quite through*:—Gif mon biþ on hrif wund, geselle him mon .xxx. scill. tō bōte; gif hē þurhwund biþ, æt gehweðerum mūðe .xx. scill., L. Alf. pol. 61; Th. i. 96, 11. [Cf. Sinness þatt stinngenn and þurrhwundenn all þatt bodig and tatt sawle, Orm. 17443.] Cf. þurh-þyrel.

þurh-wunian. **I.** *to continue, last, not to come to an end, not to* *pass away*:—Godes ege þurhwunaþ â worlda world *timor Domini permanens in seculum seculi*, Ps. Th. 18, 8. His rîce þurhwunaþ on êcnesse, Blickl. Homl. 65, 16. Hûs rihtwîsra þurhwunaþ (*permanebit*), Scint. 73, 2, 16. Heora gemynd þurhwunaþ â tô worulde, Ælfc. T. Grn. 1, 11. God, se đe ǽfre þurhwunode bûton ǽlcum anginne, 2, 3. Þurhwunedan *duraverunt*, Wrt. Voc. ii. 28, 58: Wülck. Gl. 256, 2. Úre nâ þurhwunedun fæderas *nostri non mansere parentes*, 6. Þa leornian on eorþan đæra ûs cýþ þurhwunige on heofenum *illa discere in terris quorum nobis notitia perseueret in coelis*, Scint. 218, 13. Lang mid þingum ûrum þurhwunian (*durare*) wê nâ magan, 183, 4. Âdl þurhwunigende *languor perseuerans*, 153, 17. II. *to continue* in a place, with a person, *to remain, not to leave*:—Ic þurhwunode (*perseveravi*) on đam munte feówertig daga and feówertig nihta, Deut. 9, 9. Gê synt đe mid mê þurhwunedon (đerhwunadon(-un) *permansistis*, Lind., Rush.) on mînum geswincum, Lk. Skt. 22, 28. Þurhwunedan munecas on Xp̄es cyrican *monks have continued to live* (permanserunt) *in Christchurch*, Chr. 995; Th. i. 244, 29. Đæt hê symle on ûs eardige, and wê on him þurhwunian (*permaneamus*), Scint. 16, 11. Đæt gê þurhwunion lange on đam lande, Deut. 4, 40. Eálâ wǽran đa ancras swâ trume and swâ þurhwuniende, đonne mihte wê dý ěþ geþolian swâ hwæt earfoþnessa swâ ûs on becôme *haereant ancorae, precor; illis namque manentibus, utcumque se res habeant, enatabimus*, Bt. 10; Fox 30, 10. III. *to continue* in a condition, *not to change*; where purpose or effort is implied, *to persevere, persist, hold out*, (1) absolute:—Se þurhwunaþ (đerhwunes ł đerhwunia wælla, Lind.) ôđ ende, se byþ hâl *qui perseveraverit usque in finem, hic salvus erit*, Mt. Kmbl. 10, 22: Scint. 90, 2: Blickl. Homl. 21, 36. Se đe ôđ ende þurhwunaþ (*sustenuerit*), Mk. Skt. 13, 13. Nâ ongynnendum mêd ys behâten ac þurhwunigendum (*perseverantibus*) ys geseald, Scint. 91, 3, 1. (2) where the condition is given by a complementary noun or adjective:—Ǽfre hê biþ ânes môdes, and glæd þurhwunaþ, Homl. Th. i. 456, 25. Heó þurhwunode mǽden, 24, 27. Heó onwealg on hiere onwalde æfter þurhwunade *manet adhuc et regnat incolumis*, Ors. 2, 1; Swt. 62, 24. Heó â clǽne þurhwunode, Blickl. Homl. 3, 18. Hê þurhwunode unspecende and mihteleás forđ ôđ đone Đunresdæg, Chr. 1053; Erl. 186, 23. Is rihtost đæt hê đananforđ wydewa þurhwunige, L. I. P. 22; Th. ii. 332, 32. (3) where the condition is given in a phrase:—On gôde on đam hê ongan ôþ ende hê þurhwunaþ *in bono quo coepit usque in finem perdurat*, Scint. 227, 15. Gyt git þurhwuniaþ on incre ânwilnesse *ye still persist in your obstinacy*, Blickl. Homl. 187, 33. His (*Adam's*) bendas wǽron onlýsde . . . Eua dǽgyt on bendum þurhwunode, 89, 6. Hié þurhwunian on rihtum geleáfan, 77, 19. Hê nolde þurhwunian on đære sôđfæstnisse đæs sôđfæstan Godes sunu, Ælfc. T. Grn. 2, 41. Se đe on đâm gesǽlþum đurhwunian ne môt, Bt. 2; Fox 4, 15. IV. *to continue* an action, *persevere* with or in, *not to desist from, not to leave off*:—Eua đǽgyt on wôpe þurhwunode, Blickl. Homl. 89, 6. Hié forþ on heora yfelum þurhwunedon, 79, 8. Đâ hig þurhwunedon (*perseuerarent*) hine âxsiende, Jn. Skt. 8, 7. On đam gewinne þurhwunian, Bt. 37, 1; Fox 186, 31: Met. 25, 70. Þurhwunian on fulfremedlîcum weorcum, Blickl. Homl. 77, 19. Þurhwunian his bêne *persistere petitioni sue*, R. Ben. Interl. 95, 16. Hê þurhwunigende mid gebedum wæs Drihtnes lôf singende, Blickl. Homl. 231, 9. Drihten eallum mannum þurhwuniggendum on sôþre andetnesse cwæþ, 171, 15. [An lond þer he mihte þurhwunian (wonie, 2nd MS.), Laym. 1384. Þu wiđ Godd þurhwunest in alre worlde world, Kath. 663. Cf. *Goth.* þairh-wisan *manere, permanere*.]

þurhwunigendlîce; *adv. Perseveringly, persistently, continuously*:—Þurhwunigendlîce begýman hit gedafenaþ môd ûre *perseveranter intendere oportet animum nostrum*, Scint. 33, 18.

þurh-wunung, e; *f.* I. *continued dwelling, residence*:—Óþer cyn is muneca, đæt is wêstensetlan, đe feor fram mannum gewîtaþ . . . geefenlǽcende Élian and Iôhannem, đa þurhwununge on wêstenes innoþe heóldon, R. Ben. 134, 14. II. *perseverance, persistence, constancy*:—Be þurhwununge . . . Mægen gôdes weorces þurhwunung ys *de perseverantia . . . Virtus boni operis perseuerantia est*, Scint. 90, 1-14. Gif hê behǽt stađolfæste þurhwununge *si promiserit de stabilitate sua perseuerantiam*, R. Ben. 97, 20.

þurruc. I. *a small ship*:—Þurruc *cumba* vel *caupolus* (the word occurs in a list of names for different kinds of ships), Wrt. Voc. i. 56, 30. II. *the bottom part of a ship* (?):—Se æften-stemn *puppis*, þurruc *cumba* (cf. scipes botm *cimba* vel *carina*, 56, 32), bytme *carina*, scipes flôr *tabulata navium*, Wrt. Voc. i. 63, 37-40. In this instance the word seems to mean rather part of a ship than the whole, and in this sense it is used later. It occurs in the Persones Tale: 'Smal dropes of water, that enteren thurgh a litel crevis in the *thurrok*, and in the botom of a ship.' Tyrwhitt in explanation quotes the following: 'Ye shall understande that there ys a place in the bottome of a shyppe, wherin ys gathered all the fylthe that cometh into the shyppe, and it is called in some contre of thys londe a *thorrocke* . . . Some calle yt the *bulcke* of the shyppe.' See also *thurrok* of a shyppe *sentina*, Prompt. Parv. 493.

þûrs-dæg. v. þûr.

þurst, es; *m. Thirst* (lit. and fig.):—Ne biþ đǽr hungor ne þurst, Blickl. Homl. 65, 19: Exon. 101, 20; Cri. 1661. Beóđ đê hunger and þurst hearde gewinnan, 118, 27; Gû. 246. Hungor se hâta ne se hearde þurst, 238, 33; Ph. 613. Se hâta þurst, 430, 6; Râ. 44, 3. Ne biþ se đurst gefylled heora gîtsunga, Bt. 7, 4; Fox 22, 31. Đû woldest ûs ofsleán mid þurste (*siti*), Ex. 17, 3. On đurste mînum hî drencton mê mid ecede, Ps. Spl. 68, 26: 103, 12. On hungre and on þurste hê biþ âfêded, Blickl. Homl. 59, 35: Homl. Th. i. 392, 7. Drihten âsent hungor on eów and þurst and næcede, Deut. 28, 48. Đeós wyrt þyrstendon đone þurst gelîþigaþ, Lchdm. i. 268, 12. [*Goth.* þaurstei; *f.*: *O. Sax. O. L. Ger.* thurst: *O. H. Ger.* durst: *Icel.* þorsti.] v. ungemet-þurst, þyrst.

þurstig; *adj. Thirsty* (lit. and fig.):—Hê sylfa þursti wæs *ipse sitiens*, Nar. 8, 4. Þurstig wyll *bibulus fons*, Scint. 13, 12. Swâ swylgþ seó gîtsung đa dreósendan welan, for đam hió hiora simle biþ đurstegu, Bt. 12; Fox 36, 14. Swâ hwâ swâ sylþ ceald wæter drincan ânum þurstigan menn, Homl. Th. i. 582, 24: ii. 106, 15: Wulfst. 287, 20. Hwænne gesâwe wê đê þurstine? 288, 21. Þurstige mûđe, Ps. Th. 61, 4. Þurstige þræcwîges, Cd. Th. 189, 9; Exod. 182. Heolfres þurstge, Exon. Th. 373, 24; Seel. 114. [*O. H. Ger.* durstig.] v. þyrstig.

þuruh. v. þurh.

þus; *adv. Thus, in this manner, degree, etc.* I. where the manner, etc., is determined by what precedes, (1) with verbs:—'Mîn Drihten, gestranga mîne heortan. Đus gebiddende đam hâlgan Andrea Drihtnes stefn wæs geworden, Blickl. Homl. 245, 3: Exon. Th. 236, 6; Ph. 570: 43, 9; Cri. 686. Đus (*sic*) unc gedafnaþ ealle rihtwîsness gefyllan, Mt. Kmbl. 3, 15: Lk. Skt. 24, 46. Hû mæg đis đus geweorþan? Blickl. Homl. 7, 21. Đâs dǽda þus gedône from Drihtne, 31, 20. Cucler fulne þus geworhtes drincan, Lchdm. ii. 182, 23. Lǽtaþ þus *sinite usque huc*, Lk. Skt. 22, 51. (2) with adjectives:—Đis wîf wæs âfundyn on unrihton hǽmede. Moyses ûs bebeád đæt wê sceoldon þus gerâde mid stânum oftorfian, Jn. Skt. 8, 5: Deut. 4, 32. Þuss gerâdum âdle, Anglia xiii. 434, 995. Þus manige men, Beo. Th. 679; B. 337. Ic nǽfre đê gemêtte þus mêdne, Exon. Th. 163, 3; Gû. 988: 376, 19; Seel. 376: 447, 4; Dôm. 34. (3) with adverbs:—Nô wê đê þus swîđe swencan þorftan, Exon. Th. 129, 18; Gû. 423: 268, 16; Jul. 433: Judth. Thw. 22, 36; Jud. 93. II. where the manner, etc., is determined by what follows, (1) with verbs:—God spræc þus: 'Ic eom Drihten þîn God,' Ex. 20, 1. Se engel þus cwæþ: 'Wes đû hâl,' Blickl. Homl. 5, 3: Andr. Kmbl. 124; An. 62: Mt. Kmbl. 2, 5. Þus sindon hâten fæder and môdur, đæs wê gefrægen habbaþ . . . Maria and Iôseph, 1371; An. 686. Sôđlîce þus wæs Cristes cneóres *now the birth of Jesus Christ was on this wise*, Mt. Kmbl. 1, 18. Ic wêne þus, đæt . . ., Exon. Th. 468, 8; Phar. 4. Đû đa sâwle þus gesceópe, đæt hió hwearfode on hire selfre (cf. swâ đû gesceópe đa saûle, đæt hió sceolde hwearfian on hire selfre, Bt. 33, 4; Fox 132, 11), Met. 20, 205. Þuss, Gen. 2, 16. (2) with adjectives:—Ic wêne đæt đû nǽfre tô đus mycles mægnes lǽcedômum becôme swylcum swâ ic gefregn đa đe fram Æscolapio ferdon, Lchdm. i. 326, 5. III. used in place of a definite expression:—Đâ cwæđ Petrus: 'Beceápode gê đus micel landes?' Heó andwyrde: 'Geá, leóf, swâ micel' *Peter answered unto her, Tell me whether ye sold the land for so much? And she said, Yea, for so much* (Acts 5, 8), Homl. Th. i. 316, 32. [*O. Sax. O. Frs.* thus.]

þûsend. I. as a numeral noun, neuter and fem. (v. Ps. Th. 118, 72, and cf. cognates), *a thousand*; *gen.* þûsendes, *pl.* þûsendu (-o, -a, -e); *also* þûsend *sometimes in the multiples, though, perhaps, in these cases the whole number is to be considered as singular*, e. g. Tele đa lenge đære hwîle wiđ tên þûsend wintra . . . Tele nû đæt tên þûsend geára wiđ đæt êce lîf, Bt. 18, 3: Fox 66, 6-10. Wæs þreó þûsend đæra leóda âlesen, Elen. Kmbl. 569; El. 285: Blickl. Homl. 119, 3. v. under (2) other examples. (1) without other numerals, (a) governing a genitive:—Þûsend wintra biþ swâ geostran dæg *mille anni sicut dies hesterna*, Ps. Th. 89, 4: Exon. Th. 223, 23; Ph. 364. Fealleþ đê on đa wynstran wergra þûsend, Ps. Th. 90, 7. Mænigfeald þûsend môdblissiendra *millia laetantitium*, 67, 17. Ân þûsend manna, Ors. 1, 10; Swt. 46, 34. Đeáh hê erige his land mid đûsend sula, Bt. 26, 3; Fox 94, 14. Erigan æcera þûsend, Met. 14, 5. Ôđ đæt hê þûsende đisses lîfes wintra gebîdeþ *postquam vitae jam mille peregerit annos*, Exon. Th. 208, 5; Ph. 151. Hê ofslôg fela þûsend monna, 6, 13; Swt. 268, 17. Hê heora monig đûsend ofslôg, Ors. 3, 7; Swt. 110, 33. Đurh đâs bodunge gelýfdon fela đûsend manna, Homl. Th. ii. 296, 22. Manega đûsenda engla, 334, 16. Heora fela đûsenda gefongen wæs, Ors. 3, 4; Swt. 104, 11. Ic đê þûsenda þegna bringe, Beo. Th. 3662; B. 1829. (b) where the genitive of the objects numbered is not given:—Hwæþer đis þûsend sceole beón scyrtre đe lengre, Blickl. Homl. 119, 6. Đæt forme þûsend, đæt ys seó forme yld, Anglia viii. 335, 45. Þûsendes ealdor *ciliarcus*, Wrt. Voc. i. 18, 10. Æfter đam þûsende biþ se deófol unbunden, Wulfst. 243, 23. On þûsende đære cneórisse *in mille generationes*, Ps. Th. 104, 8. Hié đone here gefliémdon and his fela þûsenda ofslôgon, Chr. 911; Erl. 100, 28: Ors. 3, 7; Swt. 118, 8: Cd. Th. 289, 23; Sat. 402: 290, 26; Sat. 421. Hê fôr mid monegum þûsendum, Ors. 5, 4; Swt. 224, 19. Ic mê nâ ondrǽde þûsendu folces *non timebo millia populi*, Ps. Th. 3, 5. Betere đonne mon mê geofe đûsende goldes and seolfres *super millia auri et* *argenti*, 118, 72. (2) with other numerals as multipliers, (a) alone:—Twá þúsend, Ælfc. Gr. 49; Zup. 282, 12: Ors. 2, 4; Swt. 76, 30. iiii þúsend monna, 2, 5; Swt. 80, 13. v þúsend wera, Chr. 508; Erl. 15, 18. Syx þúsend olfenda, Homl. Th. ii. 458, 18. Wæs Rómána eahta þúsend ofslagen, Ors. 4, 1; Swt. 158, 11: 4, 9; Swt. 192, 24. Týn þúsend punda, Mt. Kmbl. 18, 24. Tén ðúsend, Ps. Surt. 90, 7. Endlefan þúsend monna, Ors. 2, 5; Swt. 78, 24. Feówertýne þúsend sceápa, Homl. Th. ii. 458, 17. xvi þúsend punda, Chr. 994; Erl. 133, 27. Ðæt wǽre þrítig þúsend wintra, Exon. Th. 369, 5; Seel. 36: Salm. Kmbl. 544; Sel. 271. cxi þúsend, Chr. 71; Erl. 9, 2. Án hund þúsend manna and hundeahtatig ðúsend, Homl. Skt. i. 18, 403. Ðæt wǽron fíftiéne hund þúsend monna, Ors. 3, 9; Swt. 128, 22. Twá þúsendo, Mk. Skt. 5, 13: Cd. Th. 189, 14; Exod. 184. Twá ðúsendu swína, Chart. Th. 481, 5. Twá þúsenda, 471, 22: Jos. 7, 3. Ðá férdon þreó þúsenda feohtendra wera, 7, 4. iii þúsendo (-a, MS. E.) londes, Chr. 648; Erl. 26, 16. Ágefe hé feówer ðúsendo, Chart. Th. 471, 24. v þúsendu wera, Chr. 508; Erl. 14, 17. Fíf þúsendo. Andr. Kmbl. 1181; An. 591. Hé him gesealde seofon þúsendo, Beo. Th. 4397; B. 2195. Týn þúsendo, Ps. Th. 90, 7: 67, 17. Téno ðúsendo (þúsende, Rush.), Mt. Kmbl. Lind. 18, 24. Geselle et ðem londe .x. ðúsenda, Chart. Th. 465, 30. Cantwara him gesealdon xxx þúsenda, Chr. 694; Erl. 43, 21. Ðǽr wæs ofslagen eahtatig þúsenda, Ors. 5, 8; Swt. 232, 2. Hundeahtatig þúsenda, 2, 5; Swt. 78, 17. Án hund þúsenda gehorsedra, 3, 9; Swt. 124, 34: Cd. Th. 310, 9; Sat. 723. Hund þúsenda landes and locenra beága, Beo. Th. 5981; B. 2994. cxi þúsenda, Chr. 71; Erl. 8, 2. Ðone sang ðe nán mon elles singan ne mæg, búton ðæt hundteóntig and feówertig and feówer ðúsendo, Past. 52; Swt. 409, 10. Wearð tú hund þúsenda ofslægen, Ors. 2, 5; Swt. 78, 28. Ðá com him ongeán twá hund þúsenda monna, 3, 9; Swt. 132, 30. His heres wæs seofon hund þúsenda, 2, 5; Swt. 78, 10. viii c þúsenda, Swt. 80, 4. Ðæt wæs nigon x hund þúsenda, Swt. 84, 29. Þúsend ðúsenda ðénodon him, Homl. Th. i. 348, 2. Tó twǽm ðúsendum, Mk. Skt. Lind. Rush. 5, 13. Tén ðúsendum, Ps. Surt. 67, 18. Mid týn þúsendum cuman ágén ðone ðe him ágén cymþ mid twéntigum þúsendum, Lk. Skt. 14, 31. Fíf hund þúsendum *quinquagenis milibus*, Hpt. Gl. 426, 11. (b) in combination with hundreds, tens, units:—Twá þúsend wintra and twá hund and twá and feówertig geára gerímes, Anglia viii. 336, 1. Feówer þúsend wintra and feówer hund and twá and hundeahtatig, Ors. 1, 14; Swt. 58, 9. Wǽron ágán .v. þúsend wintra and .cc. wintra, Chr. 11; Erl. 7, 2. v. þúsend wintra and cc. and xxvi, 33; Erl. 7, 10. Gersones hírédes wǽron seofon þúsenda and fíf hundredu . . . Gaathes hírédes wæron eahta þúsendo and six hundredu . . . Meraries hírédes wǽron six þúsendo and twá hundrydo . . . ðá wǽron hira twá and twéntig þúsenda, Num. 3, 21–39. Rómána wæs án C and án M ofslagen *Romanorum mille centum periere milites*, Ors. 4, 6; Swt. 176, 14. Ðæt wæs v hund monna and án M, 5, 12; Swt. 240, 34. II. as an adjective indecl.:—Þúsend getýme oxena and þúsend assan, Homl. Th. ii. 458, 18. Mid þúsend gemetum *mille modis*, Wülck. Gl. 254, 44. On hund þúsend wintrum . . . on syx þúsend wintrum, Anglia viii. 335, 46–336, 20. On six þúsend wintrum, Wulfst. 244, 2. Tén ðúsend síðan hundfealde ðúsenda, Homl. Th. i. 348, 3. III. the word is sometimes used of value without expressing the unit (cf. the Icelandic use of *hundrað*); see the passages (quoted above), Chr. 648; Erl. 26, 16: 694; Erl. 43, 21: Beo. Th. 4397; B. 2195: 5981; B. 2994: Chart. Th. 465, 30: 471, 22, 24: Ps. Th. 118, 72. [*Goth.* þúsundi; *f. n.*: *O. Frs.* thúsend: *O. L. Ger.* thúsint: *O. Sax.* thúsundig: *O. H. Ger.* dúsunt, túsunt; *f. n.*: *Icel.* þúsund; *f.* (later *f.* and *n.*)]

þúsend-ealdormann, es; *m. A captain of a thousand men*:—Þúsendealdermen *chiliarcho*, Hpt. Gl. 515, 76.

þúsend-feald; *adj. Thousand-fold, a thousand*:—Ðæt þúsendfeald getæl is fulfremed, Wulfst. 243, 26, 23. Þúsendfealdre gegaderunge *millena congerie*, Hpt. Gl. 416, 63. Ðæt wǽron þúsendfealde onsægednyssa, Homl. Th. ii. 576, 8. Ongǽn þúsendfealde deriende cræftas *contra mille nocendi artes*, Wrt. Voc. ii. 135, 30: Hpt. Gl. 424, 45. [Mid þusendfeld wrenches he þe herte towendeð *per mille meandros agitat quieta corda*, O. E. Homl. ii. 191, 26.]

þúsend-gerím, es; *n. Numeration by thousands, counting with the unit a thousand*:—Ðría ðreóténo ðúsendgerímes *thirty-nine thousand*, Salm. Kmbl. 582; Sal. 290.

þúsend-getæl, es; *n. The number a thousand*:—Þúsendgetel biþ fulfremed, and ne ástíhþ nán getel ofer ðæt, Homl. Th. i. 188, 34.

þúsend-híwe; *adj. Of a thousand shapes*:—Þúsendhíwe *milleformes*, Coll. Monast. Th. 32, 29.

þúsend-líc; *adj. Numbered by thousands*:—Ðúsendlícre *milleno*, Wrt. Voc. ii. 57, 40. Ðæt hé ús gescylde wiþ ða þúsendlícan cræftas deófles costunga, Blickl. Homl. 19, 16.

þúsend-mǽle (?); *adj. A thousand each, a thousand*:—Ðúsendmǽle *mellena*, Wrt. Voc. ii. 58, 19. Betere is tó gebídanne ánne dæg mid ðé ðonne óðera on þeódstefnum þúsendmǽla, Ps. Th. 83, 10.

þúsend-mǽlum; *adv. In thousands*:—Weras and wíf somod wornum and heápum þrungen and urnon þúsendmǽlum, Judth. Thw. 23, 40; Jud. 165: Cd. Th. 190, 8; Exod. 196: 304, 18, Sat. 632. Him ymb flugon engla þreátas þúsendmǽlum, 300, 23; Sat. 569: 279, 11; Sat. 236: 296, 28; Sat. 509: Andr. Kmbl. 1744; An. 874.

þúsend-mann, es; *m. A captain of a thousand men*:—Gesete of him þúsendmen and hundrydmen *rulers of thousands and rulers of hundreds* (A. V.), Ex. 18, 21, 25.

þúsend-ríca, an; *m. A ruler of a thousand men*:—Þúsendríca *millenarius*, Wrt. Voc. i. 18, 9.

þus-líc, þul-líc; *adj. Such*:—Nǽfre adeáwde ðuslíc (swylc, W. S.), Mt. Kmbl. Lind. 9, 33. Ðuslíc *talem*, 18, 5. Mæhto ðullíco *uirtutes tales*, Mk. Skt. Lind. 6, 2. Ðuslíca is ríce Godes *talium est regnum Dei*, 10, 14. Of ðuslícum cnæhtum *ex hujusmodi pueris*, 9, 37. Mid ðullucum (ðuslícum, Rush.) monigum bíspellum *talibus multis parabolis*, 4, 33. Ðuslícum fultumum, Rtl. 64, 33. Ðuslíco (-u, Rush.) monigo gié dóas *hujusmodi multa facitis*, Mt. Skt. Lind. 7, 13. Ðe fæder ðullíco (ðuslíco, Rush.) soecað *pater tales quaerit*, Jn. Skt. Lind. 4, 23. [Of þulliche wepnen, O. E. Homl. i. 255, 15. Þeos and swuche (þullich, MS. C.) oþre, A. R. 8, 7. Gon and iseon swuch (þullich, MS. C.), 10, 13. Of swuche (þullic, MS. C.), 82, 3. Swuche (þulliche, MS. C.), men, 84, 20. Þulli, Marh. 7, 27: H. M. 9, 25. Þullich, Kath. 847. Þellich, Ayenb. 6, 12.]

þútende. v. þeótan.

þú-þistel, es; *m. Sow-thistle*:—Þúðistel (-þistil) *lactuca*, Txts. 73, 1179: Wrt. Voc. ii. 50, 57. Cf. þúfe.

þuuf, þuxsian. v. þúf, þuhsian.

þwǽle (*or* -a? ; *m.*), an; *f. A band, fillet*:—Ðuaelum *taenis*, Txts. 101, 1991. Thuélan *vittas*, 107, 2120. From its form the word, apparently, should mean *towel*, cf. *O. H. Ger.* dwahila, dwehila; *f. mantile, mappula, manutergium*: *M. H. Ger.* dwehele, dwéle: *Du.* dwaal *a towel; a shroud.*

þwǽnan; *p.* de *To soften* by moisture, ointment, etc., *to soften*:—Rysele oþþe gelyndo wiþ gárleác gemenged and on áléd ðone swile þwǽnþ, Lchdm. ii. 72, 5. Ðæt (*the ointment*) ða áheardodan swilas bét and þwǽnþ, 246, 17. Ðá hé ðam feaxe onféng ðæs hálgan heáfdes ðá wæs hé monad ðæt hé tó gesette and sum fæc ðone swyle mid ðýgde and ðwénde (ðwǽnde, MSS. B. T.) *admonitus, cum accepisset capillos sancti capitis, adposuit, et aliquandiu tumorem horum adpositione comprimere ac mollire curabat*, Bd. 4, 32; S. 611, 41. Sceal mon mid útyrnendum drencum áteón út ða horhehtan wǽtan. Þwǽne mid ðý ǽrest, Lchdm. ii. 222, 26. Gif ðú wylle mannes wambe þwǽnan, i. 82, 11. v. á-, ge-þwǽnan, *and* cf. (?) þǽnan.

þwǽre, an; *f. An instrument for beating* or *stirring*:—Thuaere, thuérae, thuére *tudicla, tudica*, Txts. 103, 2072. v. þweran.

þwǽre; *adj. Gentle, agreeable*:—Scs Arculfus sǽde ðæt ðǽr hangade úþmǽte leóhtfæt and ðwǽre (*a lamp giving an agreeable light* ?), Shrn. 81, 17. [Gif hé on Tíwesdæg biþ ácenned, se biþ ǽwerd on his lífe and biþ mán and ðwǽre (*effeminate* ?, *but perhaps* manþwǽre *should be read, the text is late*), Lchdm. iii. 162, 11.] v. efen-, ge-, mann-, un-þwǽre.

þwǽrian. v. ge-, mid-þwǽrian; þwárian.

þwǽrlǽcan; *p.* -lǽhte *To consent*:—Þwǽrlǽhte *consentiret*, Hpt. Gl. 465, 63. v. ge-þwǽrlǽcan.

þwǽrness, e; *f. Agreement*:—Hí him ðǽr eádmédo budon and þwǽrnessa (geþuǽrnesse, MS. A.), Chr. 827; Erl. 65, 7. v. ge-þwǽrness.

þwang, es; *m.*: e; *f. A thong, strip of leather*:—Ðwangc *corrigia*, Wrt. Voc. i. 84, 2. Gréne hýde, þwanges *recentis corii*, Hpt. Gl. 483, 31. Ic ne underfó ánne þwang (*corrigiam caligae*), Gen. 14, 23. Mid ðuongum (ðwongum, Rush.) *sandalis*, Mk. Skt. Lind. 6, 9. Ðæs ne eom ic wyrðe ðæt ic his sceóna þwanga (ðuongas, Lind.: þwongas, Rush.) búgende uncnytte *cujus non sum dignus procumbens soluere corrigiam calciamentorum ejus*, Mk. Skt. 1, 7. [*Orm. Laym.* þwang, þwong: *R. Glouc.* þong: *O. H. Ger.* dwang *frenum.*] v. brídel-, ól-, scóh-þwang; þweng.

þwárian; *p.* ode *To bring into agreement, make harmonious*:—Hé gemetgaþ ða feówer gesceafta, ða hé þwáraþ and gewlitegaþ (geþwǽraþ and wlitegaþ, Cott. MS.), hwílum eft unwlitegaþ and on óþrum híwe gebrengþ and eft geedníwaþ *elementa in se invicem temperat, et alterna commutatione transformat*, Bt. 39, 8; Fox 224, 9. [Cf. *O. H. Ger.* twárón *misceri.*] v. þwǽrian.

þwarm. v. þwearm.

þwástrian (=? hwástrian, q. v.) *to murmur, speak low*:—Þis ic spece nú gyt mid swá miccle ege ðæt mé þinceþ ðæt mé sió tunge stomrige nis hit gyt forðun ðæt ic þwástrian durre *I dare not yet even speak low*, Shrn. 42, 35.

þweál, es; *n. m.* I. *washing*:—Ðhuehl, thuachl *delumentum*, Txts. 55, 641. Þweál, Wrt. Voc. i. 61, 20: ii. 25, 18: *delumentum*, i. *lavatio*, 138, 52: *lustramentum*, Hpt. Gl. 483, 20. Ðeáh swín ádwægen sié, gif hit eft filþ on ðæt sol, ðonne biþ hit fúlre ðonne hit ǽr wæs, and ne forstent ðæt ðweál náuht, Past. 54; Swt. 421, 3. Hwæt forstent him ðæt ǽrre ðweál (*lavatio*), 21. Ðæt wæter his bána ðweáles *aqua lavacri*, Bd. 3, 11; S. 536, 6. Clǽnsunge ðweáles and bæþes *lavacri purificationem*, 1, 27; S. 495, 16. Be weres þweále *de viri lotione*, L.

Ecg. C. xxvi. tit.; Th. ii. 130, 10. Æfter fóta ðweále *post pedum lavationem*, Anglia xiii. 392, 392: R. Ben. 83, 23. For ðæs reáfes þweále, 91, 4. Swýn ðe cyrþ tō meoxe æfter his ðweále, Homl. Th. ii. 380, 11. Se Hǣlend hī āþwōh mid þweále, 242, 29: Blickl. Homl. 147, 22. Mid þweále ðæs hālgan fulluhtes, Lchdm. iii. 434, 2. Eádig ðū eart ðe onfēnge ðone þweál mīnre gife, Homl. Skt. ii. 30, 111. Þweálu clǣnes wǣles *lavacra puri gurgitis*, Hymn. Surt. 52, 13. Þweála (þweálu, MS. A.) calica *baptismata calicum*, Mk. Skt. 7, 8. [Forhabbe hē hyne wyð ǣlc þweald, Lchdm. iii. 134, 25.] II. *what is used in washing, ointment.* (Cf. *Icel.* þvāl *a kind of soap*, þvæla *to wash with soap: Swed.* twål *hard soap.*) v. þweán, II:—Pund ðuahles *librum ungenti*, Jn. Skt. Lind. 12, 3. [*Goth.* þwahl; *n. lavacrum: O. H. Ger.* dwahal.] v. fōt-, hand-, heáfod-þweál.

þweán; *p.* þwōh, *pl.* þwōgon; *pp.* þwagen, þwægen, þwegen, þwogen. I. *to wash.* (1) with object of that which is to be cleansed:—Petrus cwæð tō him: 'Ne þwyhst (ðuōas, Lind.: ðwǣs, Rush.) ðū nǣfre mīne fēt.' Se Hǣlend cwæþ: 'Gif ic ðē ne þweá (āðōa, Lind.: ðwǣ, Rush.), næfst ðū nānne dǣl myd mē, Jn. Skt. 13, 8. Ðū ðwehst (ðwēs, Surt.) mē *lavabis me*, Ps. Lamb. 50, 9. Hē his handa ðwehþ (ðwēð, Surt.), Ps. Th. 57, 9. Ne þweáð (ðwās, Lind.: thuāð, Rush.) hī hyra handa, Mt. Kmbl. 15, 2. Gif ic þwōh (geðuōg, Lind.: ðwōg, Rush.) eówre fēt, Jn. Skt. 13, 14. Ic þwōh (ðwōg, Surt.), Ps. Th. 72, 11. Ic in ða eá āstāh and of ðam wætere mīne handa þwōh, Homl. Skt. ii. 23 b, 502. Hē hire fēt mid his teárum þwōh, 744. Hē þwōh Aaron and his suna, Lev. 8, 6. Heó hī ðwōhg, Bd. 3, 9; S. 534, 13. Ðæt sylfe wæter ðæt hī ða bān mid ðwōgan, 3, 11; S. 535, 33. Ðæt wæter wæs gedrēfed, ðonne ðǣr micel folc hiera fēt and honda on ðwōgon, Past. 16; Swt. 105, 22. Þwōgan, Blickl. Homl. 149, 6. Þwōgon, Gen. 43, 24. Þweah (ðuah, Lind.: þwah, Rush.) ðīne ansȳne, Mt. Kmbl. 6, 17. Ne þweh ðū nā mīne fēt āne, Jn. Skt. 13, 9. Þweáð eówre fēt, Gen. 19, 2. Ne beðearf būton ðæt man his fēt þweá (āðōa, Lind.: ðwǣ, Rush.), Jn. Skt. 13, 10. Būton hī hyra handa þweán, Mk. Skt. 7, 3. Scealt ðū ðweán (geðōas, Lind.: ðū mē ðwoege, Rush.) mīne fēt, Jn. Skt. 13, 6. Heó wolde hig þweán æt ðam wætere, Ex. 2, 5. Hē underfēhð ðæt fenn ðara ðweándra, Past. 16; Swt. 105, 24. (2) with object of that which is to be cleansed away:—Mid hū micle elne ǣghwylc wille synrust þweán, Exon. Th. 81, 9; Cri. 1321. II. *to anoint.* v. þweál, II:—Ðuah heáfud ðīn *unge caput tuum*, Mt. Kmbl. Lind. 6, 17. [*Goth.* þwahan: *O. Sax.* thwahan: *O. H. Ger.* dwahan: *Icel.* þvā.] v. ā-, be-, ge-þweán.

þwearm, es; *m.* (?) *A cutting instrument*:—Thuearm, duæram, þuarm *scalprum*, Txts. 94, 891.

þwēnan. v. þwǣnan.

þweng, e; *f.* (?) *A band*:—Ðuencgu (þwænge, Rush.) *philacteria*, Mt. Kmbl. Lind. 23, 5. [*Icel.* þvengr *a thong.*] v. þwang.

þweora, an; *m. Crossness, peevishness*:—Ǣlc ðweora and ǣlc ierre and unweorðscipe . . . sié ānumen fram eów *omnis amaritudo, et ira, et indignatio . . . tollatur a vobis* (Eph. 4, 31), Past. 33; Swt. 222, 8. His mūð hē sceal from ǣlcum þweoran (*or adj.?* v. L. E. I. 21; Th. ii. 416, 33) and yflum wordum gehealdan *debet os suum a malo vel pravo eloquio custodire*, R. Ben. 18, 7. [Cf. *Goth.* þwairhei *indignatio* (in the verse just given): *Icel.* þver-leikr *crossness.*] v. þweorh, III.

þweores, þwires, þwyres. I. *across* as opposed to along, *athwart, transversely, crosswise* as opposed to lengthways:—Lege bred þweores ofer ða fēt *lay a board across over the feet*, Lchdm. ii. 342, 6. Ðonon þweores ofer ðone beorh, Cod. Dip. Kmbl. v. 353, 16. Adam wæs on længe sīf and hundnigontiges fingra lenge ofer þweoras ða fingras (i. e. *taking the breadth, not the length, of the fingers*), Anglia xi. 2, 28. Andlang ðære þorngrǣfan þwyres ofer Hysseburnan on gōsdæne; ðonne andlang ðæs weges ðe līð andlang gōsdæne þwyres ofer in waldes weg, Cod. Dip. Kmbl. v. 148, 4-7. Þwyres ofer þrȳ crundelas; ofer ða strēt; þwyres ofer ða dūne, 13, 32: vi. 226, 15. Hē hēt ǣnne weall þwyres ofer eall ðæt lond āsettan from sǣ ōþ sǣ, Ors. 6, 15; Swt. 270, 13. Binnan ðam dīce ðe wē gemynegodon ðæt Severus hēt ðwyrs ofer ðæt eálond gedīcian *intra vallum quod Severum trans insulam fecisse commemoravimus*, Bd. 1, 11; S. 480, 19. Ðā wolde hē þurhþȳn hī þwyres mid ðam swurde *then he wanted to thrust her through, from one side to the other, with the sword*, Homl. Skt. i. 12, 225. Hī wurdon āworpene intō ðam byrnendum ofne gebundene ðwyres (*bound across, with their arms bound to their sides*), Homl. Th. ii. 312, 1. II. *on the flank*:—Ðā hēt hē ðæt hiere (*the serpent*) mon mid ðǣm palistas þwyres on wurpe. Ðā wearð hiere mid ānum wierpe ān ribb forod, Ors. 4, 6; Swt. 174, 10. Hē gesette twā folc diégellīce on twā healfa . . . and bebeád ðǣm twām folcum, . . . ðæt hié on Reguluses fird on twā healfa þwyres on fōre (*that they should attack Regulus's army on both flanks*), 176, 3. Hannibal him com þwyres on, 4, 8; Swt. 188, 15. III. *perversely, wrongly*:—Godes wiþerwinnan ðe willaþ ǣfre þwires, Jud. Thw. 157, 30. Se ðe his neáxtan hataþ, se bið gehāten ðæs āwyrgedan deófles bearn, ðe wyle ǣfre ðwyres, Basil admn. 4; Norm. 44, 14. [*O. H. Ger.* tweres *oblique*; cf. *Ger.* quer, quer über: *Icel.* þvers, þvers um *across: Dan.* tværs, tværs over *across.*] v. next word.

þweorh, þwerh, þwyrh; *adj.* I. *crooked, cross,* (1) for the literal sense see *þweores.* (2) fig.:—Ðuer wig *perversa via*, Kent. Gl. 772. On ðweorum wige *in via perversi*, 812. Þwuru (þweoru, MS. A.) beóþ on gerihte *erunt prava in directa*, Lk. Skt. 3, 5. II. *adverse, opposed* (cf. *Icel.* þver-ūð *discord*). v. þweorian, þweor-līc, II:—Þwyr oððe wiðerrǣde *adversus*, Ælfc. Gr. 38; Zup. 240, 1. Gif gē beóð þwyre tō ðisum, Homl. Skt. i. 11, 94. Ungeþwǣre and þwyre him betwȳnan *at variance among themselves*, 13, 236. III. *cross, angry, bitter.* v. þweora:—Ðǣm þweorum (þreorum, Wrt.) *rancidis*, Wrt. Voc. ii. 80, 59. v. þrōh. IV. *perverse, wrong, evil, depraved, froward*:—Heorte ðuerh (þweor, Spl.: þweorr, Lamb.) *cor pravum*, Ps. Surt. 100, 4. Cyn ðuerh (þweor, Spl. Lamb.) *genus pravum*, 77, 8. Þwyr geþanc *praua mens*, Scint. 68, 3. Mann þwyr *homo peruersus*, 134, 11. Þwyr mōd *proteruus animus*, 19. Hē wæs þwyr on dǣdum, Homl. Th. i. 534, 2. Seó hīwrǣden is swīðe ðwyr *domus exasperans est*, ii. 530, 29. Decius se þweora heóld rīce, Homl. Skt. i. 23, 12. Eálā þwyre (þweóre, MS. A.) cneóres *O generatio perversa*, Mt. Kmbl. 17, 171. Þwure (þweore, MS. A.), Lk. Skt. 9, 41. Seó ðwyre sāwul, Homl. Th. i. 408, 13. Ðæt ðwyre mōd, 410, 21. Ðwerre heortan *peruersi cordis*, Kent. Gl. 612. Mid þweorum (ðȳ ðweoran, Surt.) *cum perverso*, Ps. Spl. 17, 28. Hē eall ðurh his unrihtdǣde mid ðweorum līfe āþȳstrade *universa prave agendo obnubilavit*, Bd. 5, 13; S. 633, 33. On þwerre sprǣce *in locutione perversa*, Confess. Peccat. Ðweran *perverso*, Kent. Gl. 142. On bogon þweorne (ðone ðweoran, Surt.) *in arcum pravum*, Ps. Spl. 77, 63. On ōðre wīsan sint tō manienne ða bilwitan on ōðre ða ðweoran and ða lytegan *quomodo admonendi simplices et versipelles*, Past. 35; Swt. 237, 5. Ða ðweoran hī ofslōgon, Homl. Th. i. 232, 7. Ða ðwyran beón geðreáde, ðæt hī tō Godes rihte gebūgan, ii. 96, 5. On þweorra (ðwyrra, Wells Frag.) manna (*pravorum*) gewit, R. Ben. 119, 13. Ðwyrra, Homl. Th. i. 552, 35. Ðweorum *pravis*, Wülck. Gl. 251, 13. Mid þweorum ðeáwum, Homl. Th. i. 302, 30. From þweorum and yfelum wordum, L. E. I. 21; Th. ii. 416, 33. Geðyldig wið ðwyrum mannum, Homl. Th. ii. 514, 11. Ða ðwyran *improbos*, R. Ben. Interl. 15, 10. ¶ On þweorh *wrongly, evilly*:—Ðæt hī ðȳ māre wīte hæbben ðe hī gere witon ðæt hī on ðweorh dōð, Past. 55; Swt. 429, 9. Hē ongeat ðæt hē hæfde on ðweorh gedōn, ðæt seó mǣgþ wæs būtan biscope, Bd. 3, 7; S. 530, 22. Ðonne hig eów tela tǣcean, and him sylf on ðweorh dōð, L. E. I. 21; Th. ii. 418, 7. Hié on þweorh sprecaþ, Cd. Th. 145, 30; Gen. 2413. [*Goth.* þwairhs *angry: O. H. Ger.* dwerah *transversus*; in duerh *in transversum: Icel.* þverr *cross, transverse.*] v. ire-þweorh.

þweorh-furh (?) *a cross furrow, a rough place*:—Þuerhfyri *salebrae* (cf. *O. H. Ger.* furihi *salebras; sulcos*), Txts. 95, 1761. Ða unsmēþan ðwerfuru *salebrosos* (*complanans*) *anfractus* (Ald.), Wrt. Voc. ii. 78, 26. Þwyrhfero *anfractus* (the passage in Aldhelm is: Errabundis anfractibus exorbitans), 83, 6. Ðweorhfyro, 2, 20. *See also* þwyres fura *salebroso* (the passage is: Genus explanat salebroso pagina versu), 90, 60.

þweorian, þwyrian; *p.* ode *To be opposed, adverse* to (*wið*), *to be at variance.* v. þweorh, II:—Ic ðwyrige oððe ic wiðerige *adversor*, Ælfc. Gr. 25; Zup. 145, 18. On sibbe is fulfremednyss ðǣr ðǣr nān ðing ne þwyraþ (*there are no conflicting elements*), Homl. Th. i. 552, 21. Ic eom sōðfæstnys, ac ðās ðweorigaþ wið mē *these men are opposed to me*, 380, 8. Ne mæg ðeós offrung beón on ðære heortan ðe mid gȳtsunge oððe andan gebysgod bið, for ðan ðe hī ðwyriaþ wið ðone gōdan willan *they are adverse to the good will*, 584, 20. Oððe hī his fēt gesōhton, him and Gode gehȳrsumigende, oððe gif heora hwylc ðwyrode (*if any one of them was adverse*), hē his andweardnysse forfleáh, 560, 10. Ða heáfodmen wiðcwǣdon and symle ðwyrodon *ever proved adverse*, ii. 260, 2. Widersaca[n]dan ł þw[r]eredon *apostataverant*, Hpt. Gl. 510, 50. Ðā ongunnon Pharisēi him betwȳnan ðwyrian *the Pharisees began to be at variance among themselves*, Homl. Th. ii. 298, 28.

þweor-līc, þwyr-līc; *adj.* I. *reversed, contrary, opposite*:—Ða word, ðe synd *passiva*, beóð *activa* gif se *r* byþ āweg gedōn; . . . twā dǣdlīce word synd ðe habbaþ þwyrlīce getācnunge; ðæt ðe geendaþ on o getācnaþ þrowunge, and ðæt ðe geendaþ on *or* getācnaþ dǣde, Ælfc. Gr. 19; Zup. 122, 17. Bið swīðe þwyrlīc, ðæt ðearfa beó mōdig *it is quite reversing the proper order of things for a needy person to be proud*, Homl. Skt. i. 13, 123. II. *adverse.* v. þweorh, II:—Antecrist is gereht ðwyrlīc Crist, Homl. Th. i. 4, 22. III. *perverse, evil, depraved*:—Hē wæs ācenned būton synne, and næs nān ðing ðwyrlīces on him, Homl. Th. i. 176, 5. Fram þwyrlīce sprǣce *a pravo eloquio*, R. Ben. Interl. 21, 9. Gesamnodon gehwylce ðwyrlīce wiðercoran, Homl. Th. i. 468, 5. Ðonne ðwyrlīcra manna heortan beóð geemnode, 362, 26. Þwyrlīcra *pravorum*, R. Ben. Interl. 107, 11.

þweorlīce; *adv.* I. *awry, askew, in reversed order*:—Þwyrlīce færð æt ðam hūse ðǣr seó wyln bið ðære hlǣfdian wissigend and seó hlǣfdige bið ðære wylne underðeódd, Homl. Skt. i. 17, 10. II. *in a way that offers opposition, obstinately, flatly* (of refusal):—Hē wiðcwæð þwyrlīce (*flatly*; cf. *Icel.* synja, neita þverliga; or *angrily*, v. þweorh, III) and hī mid gedrēfedre ǣbilignysse him fram ādrāf, Homl. Th. ii. 24, 29. III. *perversely, evilly*:—And suā ðeáh hē mid wōn weorcum hit tō ðweorlīce ne fremeþ ðeáh hē hit on his mōde forlǣtan ne mæge *et quamvis prava non exerceat opere, ab his tamen non evellitur mente*, Past. 11; Swt. 73, 13. *Enervatius*, i. *debilius* sleaclīce, þweorlīce; *eneriter*, wāclīce, *turpiter*, Wrt. Voc. ii. 143, 55. Þwyrlīce lybbende *praue uiuendo*, Scint. 45, 18.

þweorness, e; *f.* I. *crookedness* (fig.) v. þweorh, I. 2:—Ðwyrnyssa beóð gerihte, Homl. Th. i. 362, 22. II. *opposition*. v. þweorh, II, þweorlīce, II:—*Aduersus* ongeán mid þwyrnysse (.i. *discordia*, MS. W.), Ælfc. Gr. 38; Zup. 239, 14. Ðā sceorede ðāgyt se yldesta hǣðengylda mid mycelre þwyrnysse *the chief idolater still refused most flatly*, Homl. Th. i. 72, 10. III. *perversity, iniquity, evil, depravity*:—Mycel is seó þwyrnes (cf. *abundabit iniquitas*, 8), Wulfst. 82, 17. Fram þwyrnysse *a prauitate*, Scint. 32, 3. For heora līfes ðwyrnysse, Homl. Th. ii. 530, 24. Forbeóde hē ða þwyrnesse hyra ungeþeahtes *prohibeant pravorum prevalere consensum*, R. Ben. 119, 9. Hrædlīce bið se Dēma tō ūrum bēnum gebīged, gif wē fram ūrum ðwyrnyssum beóð gerihtlǣhte, Homl. Th. ii. 124, 35: Lchdm. iii. 276, 18. Manna þwyrnyssa *hominum prauitates*, Scint. 44, 9.

þweorscipe, es; *m.* *Perversity, iniquity, depravity*:—Se bið ðæm īsene gelīc inne on ðæm ofne, se ðe for ðære suingellan nyle his ðweorscipe forlǣtan, ac ofan his nīhstan his līfes, Past. 37; Swt. 269, 6.

þweor-timbre (?); *adj.* *Cross-grained* (?), *stubborn*:—Ic wāt ðæt ic ǣr ne sīð ǣnig ne mētte þrīstran geþōhtes ne þweorhtimbran (*Grein suggests* -tīmran, v. *next word*) mægþa cynnes, Exon. Th. 275, 15; Jul. 550.

þweor-tīme; *adj.* I. *given to opposition, contentious*. v. þweorh, II:—Ðone rēþan, ðe biþ þweortēme, ðū scealt hātan hund, nallas mann *ferox, atque inquies linguam litigiis exercet ? cani comparabis*, Bt. 37, 4; Fox 192, 16. II. *given to evil, wicked, depraved*:—And ðeáh ðonne hē ongiete ða scylda ðāra ðweortiémena, ðonne geðence hē ðone ealdordōm his onwealdes *cum pravorum culpa exigit, potestatem sui prioratus agnoscat*, Past. 17; Swt. 107, 12. Ðǣm gōdum hē sceal mid wordum stȳran and ðǣm þweortȳmum mid swingellum *honestiores animos verbis corripiat, improbos autem verberum castigatione*, R. Ben. 13, 20.

þwer. v. þweorh.

þweran; *p.* þwær, *pl.* þwǣron; *pp.* þworen, þuren:—*To twirl, stir*. [*O. H. Ger.* dweran; *p.* dwar; *pp.* dworan *miscere*.] v. ā-, ge-þweran; þwirel.

þwinan; *p.* þwān, *pl.* þwinon; *pp.* þwinen *To get less, dwindle, be reduced* (of a swelling):—Beþe ða fēt and smyre, ðonne þwīnaþ (-eþ, MS.) hȳ sōna (*the swelling goes down*), Lchdm. i. 84, 25. Ðonne þwīnaþ ða āswollena sina, ii. 282, 8. Tācn ðæt se swile þwīnan ne mæg, ne ūt yrnan on ðære lifre, 162, 3: 212, 9. Cf. dwīnan.

þwirel; es; *m.* *A stick for whipping milk*:—Meolc *lac*, fliéte *verberatum*, molcen *lac coagolatum*, þwiril *verberaturium*, Wrt. Voc. i. 290, 26–30. [*O. H. Ger.* dwiril: *M. H. Ger.* twirel, twirl: *Ger.* querl, quirl *a twirling-stick*; querlen *to beat up*: *Icel.* þyrell *a whisk* to whip milk; flauta-þyrell *a stick for whipping milk*; þyrla *to whirl*; cf. þwara *a stick used to stir up a cauldron*.] v. þweran.

þwires. v. þweores.

þwītan; *p.* þwāt, *pl.* þwiton, þweoton; *pp.* þwiten *To thwite* (still in some dialects, e. g. Lancashire), *to cut, cut off*:—Þwīteþ, Exon. Th. 354, 50; Reim. 63. Monige of ðam treówe ðæs hālgan Cristes mǣles spōnas and sceafþan nimaþ (spōnas ðwītaþ, MS. B.) *multi de ipso ligno sacrosanctae crucis astulas excidere solent*, Bd. 3, 2; S. 524, 31. Monige of ðære ilcan styþe spōnas ðweoton and sceafþan nōmon (ðæt geþwit nāman, MS. B.) *astulis ex ipsa destina excisis*, 3, 17; S. 544, 44, col. 2 (sprytlan ācurfon, col. 1). Genim ðone wyrttruman, delf up, þwīt nigon spōnas on ða winstran hand, Lchdm. ii. 292, 2. [Telwyñ or thwytyñ *abseco, reseco*, Prompt. Parv. 488. To thwyte *dolare*, Cath. Angl. 388, and see note. Cf. *Icel.* þveita *a small axe*, þvita *a kind of axe*, þveit, þveiti *a cut-off piece, a parcel of land*.] v. ā-, for-þwītan; ge-þwit.

þwur, þwyr, þwyr-, þwyre, þȳ, þȳan. v. þweor, þweor-, þweores, þe, þeówan.

þȳ-dǣges; *adv.* *On that day, then*:—Gif ðǣr byð ān ofer ða seofon, ðonne tācnaþ ðæt ðæt se mōnð gǣð on Sunnandæg on tūne; gif ðǣr beóð ofer ða seofon twā oððe þreó, feówer oððe fīfe oððe syxe, wite ðū tō sōðe ðæt ðȳdæges cymð sē mōnð tō mannum, Anglia viii. 304, 13: 310, 39.

þyddan; *p.* de *To strike, thrust, push*:—*Impingere* on besettan (*in margin* on þidden, ic on þydde), Hpt. Gl. 505, 46. Ðā ðydde Æfner hine mid hindewerde sceafte on ðæt smælðearme ðæt hē wæs deád *percussit eum Abner aversa hasta in inguine, et transfodit eum, et mortuus est*, Past. 40; Swt. 295, 17. Se assa þidde his hlāfordes fōt þearle tō ðam hege *junxit asina se parieti et attrivit sedentis pedem*, Num. 22, 25. Ðā ābrǣd Aoth his swurd and hine hetelīce þidde swā ðæt ða hiltan eodon in tō ðam innoðe *Aoth tulit sicam, infixitque eam in ventre ejus, tam valide, ut capulus sequeretur ferrum in vulnere*, Jud. 3, 21. Ðæt is ðæt mon mid hindewearde sceafte ðone ðydde ðe him oferfylge *aversa hasta persequentem ferire est*, Past. 40; Swt. 297, 14. [Þenne þudde ich in ham lueliche þohtes, Marh. 14, 7. Þa þudde ha uppon þe þurs feste wið hire fot, 12, 17. He þudde (þraste, 2nd MS.) frommard his breoste, Laym. 1898.] v. þurh-, wiþ-þyddan; þoddettan; *see also* þeówan.

þyder, þȳfe. v. þider, þīfe.

þȳfel, es; *m.* *A bush; a thicket; a leafy plant*:—*Frutectum*, i. *arborum densitas* vel *ramus* (*ramnus ?*) þȳfel, *frutices, ramos* (*ramnos ?*) þyrne, *frutex, frutecta* þȳfel, Wrt. Voc. ii. 151, 42–45. Þȳfel *frutex*, i. 33, 42. Ðȳfel, 80, 20. Þȳfel *spartus*, 32, 40: *spina, sentrix*, 33, 47. Of þiccum þēfele, Hpt. Gl. 408, 38. On ðone hundes þȳfel; of hundes þȳfele forþ on ðone þorn, Cod. Dip. Kmbl. iii. 425, 29. Andlang paðes on ðone hyndes þȳfel; of ðæm þȳfele andlang weges, vi. 36, 4. Þȳfelas *frutecta*, Wrt. Voc. i. 39, 9. His þȳfelas ł twygu *arbusta ejus*, Ps. Lamb. 79, 11. Þȳfela *vel* boxa *belsarum*, Wrt. Voc. ii. 125, 44. Genim ðysse wyrte, ðe wē león fōt nemdon, fīf ðȳfelas būtan wyrttruman, Lchdm. i. 98, 16. [Smale fuȝele þat fleoþ bi grunde and bi þuvele, O. and N. 278.] v. brēmel-, rysc-, sceald-, wiðig-þȳfel; þūf.

þȳflen (?); *adj.* *Bushy*:—Þȳflen (*printed* ryplen) *sparteus* (cf. þȳfel *spartus*), Germ. 399, 457.

þyften, e; *f.* *A female servant*:—Þyften *verna, famula, servus*, Hpt. Gl. 470, 9. Þeftan *vernacula, servula, ancilla*, 461, 56. [Þe oðer is ase lefdi; þeos is ase þuften, A. R. 4, 11. Mi lauerd biseh his þufftenes mekelec *respexit humilitatem ancillae suae*, H. M. 45, 12.] v. ge-þofta.

þȳgan. v. þeówan.

þyhtig; *adj.* *Strong, firm*:—Sweord ecgum þyhtig, Beo. Th. 3121; B. 1558. v. hyge-, un-þyhtig.

þylc; *pron.* *Such*:—Þes þylc fela spycð *iste talis multum loquitur*, Scint. 80, 19. Gif hē āwiht þylces dō *si tale quid fecerit*, L. Ecg. C. 15; Th. ii. 142, 27. Þylces fela *his similia*, Coll. Monast. Th. 27, 11. Āne þilīcne lytling *unum parvulum talem*, Mt. Kmbl. 18, 5. Hwæt is þes be þam ic þilc gehȳre *de quo audio ego talia*, Lk. Skt. 9, 9. Manega ōþre þylce (þyilīce, MS. A.) gē dōð *alia similia his facitis multa*, Mk. Skt. 7, 8. Feáwa synd ða þylce gebedu habban *pauci sunt qui tales orationes habeant*, Scint. 33, 3. [*Laym. Chauc.* þilk: *R. Glouc.* þulk: *Icel.* þvī-līkr.]

þyl-cræft, es; *m.* *Rhetoric*:—Þelcræft *rethorica*, Hpt. Gl. 479, 55. v. þyle.

þyld *patience*:—On ðylde iówre settas gē sāwle iówre *in patientia uestra possidebitis animas uestras*, Lk. Skt. Rush. 21, 19. [Þild to þolenn unnseollþe, Orm. 2603. Þild *patientia*, Ps. 9, 19. *O. H. Ger.* dult.] v. ge-þyld.

þyldig; *adj.* *Patient*:—Strong and ðyldig *fortis et patiens*, Rtl. 101, 8. [Þuldi and þolemod, Kath. 174. *O. H. Ger.* dultīg *patiens*.] v. ge-, un-þyldig.

þyldigian; *p.* ode *To endure*:—Wel þyldigende hī beóð *bene patientes erunt*, Ps. Spl. 91, 14. v. ā-, for-, ge-ðyldigian (-þylgian).

þyle, es; *m.* *An orator, spokesman*:—Gelǣred þyle fela spǣca mid feáwum wordum geopenaþ *doctus orator plures sermones paucis verbis aperit*, Scint. 119, 3. Þylas *oratores*, Wrt. Voc. ii. 63, 1. *As a proper name* Þyle *is found in* Exon. Th. 320, 5; Vīd. 24:—Þyle weóld Rondingum. ¶ In Beowulf the *þyle* of the Danish king is mentioned:—Hūnferþ þyle, Beo. Th. 2335; B. 1165. Þyle Hrōðgāres, 2917; B. 1456. In two passages it is noted that he sat at his lord's feet:—Hūnferð maþelode ðe æt fōtum sæt freán Scyldinga, 1002; B. 499: 2335; B. 1165. He is the only one of the courtiers who is actually stated to have addressed Beowulf, so that the duty of leading the conversation seems to have fallen to him. If a gloss in Wrt. Voc. ii. 25, 31—*descurris* hofðelum—may be read *de scurris* of ðelum (=ðylum) *or* hofðylum, perhaps his function was something like that of the later court jester, and the style of his attack on Beowulf hardly contradicts the supposition. [*Icel.* þulr; cf. þylja *to say, chant*.] v. þyl-cræft.

Þȳle, Thīla *Thule*, some island in the north-west of Europe:—Be westannorðan Ibernia is ðæt ȳtemeste land ðæt man hǣt Thīla (*insula Thule*), and hit is feáwum mannum cūð for ðære oferfyrre, Ors. 1, 1; Swt. 24, 20. Ðæt īland ðe wē hātaþ Thȳle, ðæt is on ðam norþwestende ðisses middangeardes *ultima Thule*, Bt. 29, 3; Fox 106, 23. Thīle hātte ān īgland be norðan þysum īglande, syx daga fær ofor sǣ, Lchdm. iii. 260, 2. v. Tȳle.

þylian, þylīc, þyl-līc, þylman. v. þilian, þylc, þys-līc, for-þylman.

þȳmel, es; *m.* *A thumbstall, fingerstall, thimble*:—Wiþ scurfedum nægle . . . wyrc þȳmel tō, and lege eald spic onufan ðone nægl, Lchdm. ii. 150, 6. [Themyl *digitale*, Wülck. Gl. 578, 29 (15th cent.). Themelle, thymbylle, thymle *digitale, parcipollex, pollicium*, Cath. Ang. 383, where see note. Thymbyl *theca*, Prompt. Parv. 491. *Icel.* þumall *the thumb of a glove*.]

þȳmel; *adj.* *A thumb thick*, applied to the fat of swine:—Æt þȳmelum, L. In. 49; Th. i. 132, 19.

þȳn *to press*. v. þeówan.

þyncan; *p.* þūhte. I. *to seem, appear*. (1) where the subject of the verb is expressed:—Ðynceþ him swīðe leoht sió byrðen ðæs lāreówdōmes *pondus magisterii levius aestimant*, Past. proem.; Swt. 24, 9. Mē ðeós (rōd) heardra þynceþ, Exon. Th. 91, 9; Cri. 1489: 383, 14; Rä. 4, 10: Met. 12, 8. Þincð, Bt. 23; Fox 78, 25: Met. 12, 18. Þis þinceþ riht micel, ðæt . . ., Cd. Th. 149, 17; Gen. 2476. Mē ðæt riht ne þinceþ, ðæt . . ., 19, 11; Gen. 289. Þynceþ, Andr. Kmbl. 1218; An. 609. Hī ne wundriaþ mæniges þinges ðe monnum wunder þynceþ, Met. 28, 82. Ðæs ðe mē þynceþ, Andr. Kmbl. 944; An. 472: Ps. Th. 101, 3. Him ða twigu þincaþ merge, Met. 13, 44. Hȳ wyrðe þinceaþ, Beo. Th. 742; B. 368. Lytel þūhte ic leóda bearnum, Exon. Th. 87, 14; Cri. 1425. Ne þūhte hē him nō innon swā fæger swā hē ūtan þūhte. Þeáh ðū nū hwam fæger þince, ne biþ hit nō ðȳ raþor swā, Bt. 32, 2; Fox 116, 24. Hē ðūhte him selfum suīðe unlytel *se parvulum non videbat*, Past. 17; Swt. 113, 12. Hire þūhte hwītre heofon and eorðe, Cd. Th. 38, 7; Gen. 603: 111, 4; Gen. 1850: Beo. Th. 1688; B. 842: Met. 12, 15. Tō lang hit him þūhte, hwænne hī tōgædere gāras bēron, Byrht. Th. 133, 47; By. 66. Him ðæt wræclīc þūhte, Cd. Th. 233, 4; Dan. 270. Ðæt wundra sum monnum þūhte, ðæt . . ., Exon. Th. 133, 13; Gū. 489: 169, 27; Gū. 1101. Hié ðam were geonge þūhton men, Cd. Th. 146, 27; Gen. 2428. Ealle brimu blōdige þūhton, 214, 20; Exod. 572: Andr. Kmbl. 880; An. 440: Beo. Th. 1737; B. 866. Ðȳ ðe hȳ him sylfum sēllan þūhten, Exon. Th. 455, 24; Hy. 4, 54. Hē þenceþ ðæt his wīse welhwam þince unforcūþ, 315, 13; Mōd. 30. Þeáh hit lang þince, Met. 10, 66. Hwæt eów sēlest þynce, Elen. Kmbl. 1062. Hié wilniaþ ðæt hié ðyncen ða betstan, Past. 18; Swt. 134, 18. Hwelc wīte sceal ūs tō hefig ðyncan? 36; Swt. 255, 3. Hī woldon mē swīþe bitere þincan, Bt. 22, 1; Fox 76, 19. Swā hit þincan mæg, L. I. P. 19; Th. ii. 326, 36. (2) where the subject is not expressed, as in *methinks*:—Swā mē ðincþ, Bt. 33, 1; Fox 120, 21: 36, 3; Fox 176, 30. Swā ðē ðyncþ, 38, 2; Fox 196, 22. Hū þincþ eów *quid vobis videtur*, Mt. Kmbl. 21, 28. Þincþ him genōg on ðam ðe hī binnan heora ǣgenre hȳde habbaþ, Bt. 14, 2; Fox 44, 22. Dēm ðū hī tō deáþe, gif ðē gedafen þince, Exon. Th. 247, 32; Jul. 87. Ðeáh monnum swā ne þince, Bt. 39, 8; Fox 224, 17. (2 a) where the verb is followed by a clause:—Mē þincþ ðæt hit hæbbe geboht sume leáslīce mǣrþe, Bt. 24, 3; Fox 82, 24. Ne þynceþ mē gerysne, ðæt wē rondas beren, Beo. Th. 5299; B. 2653. Hwæt þincþ ðē ðæt ðū sȳ?, Jn. Skt. 8, 53. Þyncþ him ðæt hē næbbe genōg, Bt. 33, 2; Fox 124, 4. Him selfum þincþ ðæt hē nǣnne næbbe, swā swā manegum men þincþ ðæt hē nǣnne næbbe, 29, 1; Fox 104, 8. Wrætlīc mē þinceþ, hū seó wiht mæge wordum lācan, Exon. Th. 414, 11; Rä. 32, 18. Þinceþ ðē miht ðū libban *potes vivere?* Bd. 5, 6; S. 619, 40. Ðūhte heom ðæt hit mihte swā, Cd. Th. 266, 14; Sat. 22. Ne þūhte gerysne rodora wearde, ðæt Adam leng āna wǣre, 11, 9; Gen. 169. Ðeáh ūs þince ðæt it on wōh fare, Bt. 39, 8; Fox 224, 20. Higesnotrum mæg þincan, ðæt . . ., Met. 10, 8. II. *to seem fit*:—Swā mycel swā ðē þince *as much as to you seems good*, Lchdm. ii. 74, 2. Dō swā ðē þynce, gif ðū frygnen sié, Elen. Kmbl. 1078; El. 541. [*Goth.* þug[g]kjan: *O. Sax.* thunkian: *O. H. Ger.* dunchan: *Icel.* þykkja.] v. ge-, mis-, of-, on-þyncan.

þyncþ[u]; *f. Honour, dignity, rank*:—Suā suǣ hē on ðyncðum (geðyncðum, Cott. MSS.) bið furður ðonne ōðre *sicut honore ordinis superat*, Past. 14; Swt. 81, 23. v. ge-þingþu.

þȳnde. v. þignan.

þyng, es; *m.* (?) *Growth, progress, profit*:—Mið ðynge *proficiendo*, Rtl. 83, 40. v. ge-þynge.

þyn-hlǣne; *adj. Wasted, shrunk*:—Ða gescruncenan and ða þynhlǣnan *marcida*, Wrt. Voc. ii. 57, 23.

þynne; *adj. Thin*:—Ðæt ic reccan mōste þicce and þynne, Exon. Th. 424, 8; Rä. 41, 36. Ic dō sum ðing ðinre *tenuo*, Ælfc. Gr. 24; Zup. 137, 9. I. of dimension, (1) *thin, lean, the opposite of fat* or *stout*:—Þynne monn *galbus*, Wrt. Voc. ii. 42, 11. Ne mæg him se līchoma batian, ac bið blāc and þynne, Lchdm. ii. 206, 11. (2) *thin, the opposite of thick*:—Mid ðynre tyrf bewrigen *obtectus cespite tenui*, Bd. 5, 6; S. 619, 20. Hē hæfde midmycle neosu ðynne *vir naso pertenui*, 2, 16; S. 519, 34. Seóh þurh þynne hrægl, Lchdm. ii. 290, 4. Seó wyrt hafaþ þynne leáf, Lchdm. i. 288, 16. (3) *thin, the opposite of broad*:—Ðæt seó ðynneste dolhswaþo ætȳwde *ut tenuissima cicatricis vestigia parerent*, Bd. 4, 19; S. 589, 19. II. of density, (1) where the parts of a whole are not close together, *thin*:—Oft of ðinnum rēnscūrum flēwð seó eorðe, Homl. Th. ii. 466, 7. In sceagan ðǣr hē þynnest is, Cod. Dip. Kmbl. iii. 391, 15. (2) applied to liquids, air, etc., *thin*:—Sum ūtgang biþ þynne, sum mid þiccum wǣtum geondgoten, Lchdm. ii. 276, 24. Hit sié þicce swā þynne brīw, 314, 4. Lyft is līchamlīc gesceaft, swȳðe þynne, iii. 272, 17. Þynne wīn, ii. 254, 18. Snāw cymð of ðam þynnum wǣtan, iii. 278, 23. Hē elles ne ðeah nemne medmicel hlāfes mid ðynre meolce *lac novum in phiala ponere solebat, et post noctem ablata superficie crassiore, ipse residuum cum modico pane bibebat*, Bd. 3, 27; S. 559, 35. Ǣr se þicca mist þynra weorðe, Met. 5, 6. III. fig. (1) *thin, weak, feeble*:—Hwilc sié sió gecynd ðæs līchoman, hwæðer hió sié strang ðe heard . . . ðe hió sié hnesce and mearwe and þynne, Lchdm. ii. 84, 14. Ðynre ēþunge ānre ætȳwde ðæt hē līfes wæs *halitu tantum pertenui quia viveret demonstrans*, Bd. 5, 19; S. 640, 24. (2) *delicate, fine*:—Andgyt þēnunge gearwigende Gode þȳhð symle and þynne hit byð *sensus officium exhibens Deo uiget semper et tenuis fit*, Scint. 52, 9. [*O. H. Ger.* dunni *tenuis*: *Icel.* þunnr.]

þynness, e; *f.* I. *thinness, slightness of density*. v. þynne, II. 2:—Metta meltung and þynnes, Lchdm. ii. 198, 3. II. *weakness*. v. þynne, III. 1:—Hit gehǣlð ða þynnysse ðære gesihðe, Lchdm. i. 134, 27 (see note).

þynnian; *p.* ode *To make* or *to become thin*:—Ðynnade *obtenuerat*, Txts. 182, 80. Ðæt þicce horh ðū scealt mid ðām lǣcedōmum wyrman and þynnian, Lchdm. ii. 194, 22. [*O. H. Ger.* gi-dunnōt *attenuatus*; dunnēn *rarescere*: *Icel.* þynna *to make thin*.] v. ā-, ge-þynnian.

þynnol(-ul); *adj. Lean, meagre*:—Ðynnul *macilentus*, Wrt. Voc. i. 51, 16.

þynnung, e; *f. Thinning, making thin*:—Lǣcedōmas ðe þynnunge mægen hæbben and smalunge, Lchdm. ii. 260, 23.

þyn-wefen; *adj. Thin-woven*:—Thynwefen hrægl *levidensis*, Wrt. Voc. ii. 54, 17.

þyrel (*from* þyrhel, v. þurh), þyrl, es; *n. A hole made through anything, an aperture, orifice*:—Ǣlces kynnes mūð *vel* ðyrl *orificium*, Wrt. Voc. i. 19, 57. Ic borige *terebro*. ðyrl *foramen*, 84, 65: Ælfc. Gr. 9, 12; Zup. 40, 16. Is on ðam wāge ðyrl geworht *est foramen in pariete*, Bd. 4, 3; S. 570, 17. Gif ān þyrl (*foramen*) open byð forlǣten, ðanon fram feóndum beó inn āgan, Scint. 140, 6. Ðæt wǣre ðyrel on middum ðæm hweóle, Shrn. 81, 13. Gerȳme ðæt ðæt þyrel (*the aperture made by a lancet*) tō nearo ne sié, Lchdm. ii. 208, 25. Stōl niþan ðyrele, 76, 22. Ðæt īsen (*a scythe*) becom swymmende tō ðam snǣde and tō ðam ðyrle ðe hit ǣr of āsceát, Homl. Th. ii. 162, 14. Swā swā mon melo sift; ðæt melo ðurhcrȳpþ ǣlc þyrel, Bt. 34, 11; Fox 152, 2. Þurh nǣdle þyrel (ðyril, Lind.) *per foramen acus*, Mk. Skt. 10, 25: Wrt. Voc. ii. 73, 1. Ðyrl, Lk. Skt. Lind. 18, 25. Gif wyrm þyrel gewyrce . . . drype on ðæt þyrel, Lchdm. ii. 114, 14. Drincan syllan þurh þyrel, Exon. Th. 485, 1; Rä. 71, 7: 397, 18; Rä. 16, 21. Ne furþon ān þyrl (*foramen*) būton cræfte mīnon (*the smith's*) ðū ne miht dōn, Coll. Monast. Th. 31, 17. Hē ðæt īsen sette on ðæt ylce þyrl, and hit fæste stōd, Homl. Skt. i. 21, 71. Þyrel *foramina*, Wrt. Voc. ii. 149, 73. Þyrlum *finistris*, 148, 60. Ðyrelum *foraminibus*, Bd. 3, 17; S. 544, 30, col. 2. Ðurh ða ðyrlo, 544, 32, col. 1. Ic hēt hié þurhborian . . . hēt ic eft ða ðyrelo mid golde forwyrcean, Nar. 20, 3. [*A. R.* þurl *a window*: *Ayenb.* þerle.] v. eág-, ears-, hūn-, næs-, nos-, teol-þyrel (-þyrl, -þerl), *and next word*.

þyrel; *adj. Perforated, having a hole* or *holes, pierced through*:—Gif eáre þirel weorðeþ, .iii. scill. gebēte, L. Ethb. 41; Th. i. 14, 6: 49; Th. i. 14, 15. Þyrel, 45; Th. i. 14, 10. Gif monnes þeóh biþ þyrel (þyrl, MS. B.), L. Alf. pol. 62; Th. i. 96, 13: 63; Th. i. 96, 16. Gif se wāh bið ðyrel *if the wall have a hole through it*, Past. 21; Swt. 157, 17. From ðyrelan stāne, Cod. Dip. Kmbl. ii. 29, 2. On ðone þyrlan stān, iii. 406, 11. Þyrllan, 436, 34. Se ðe mēdsceattas gaderaþ, hē legeþ hié on ðyrelne pohchan (*in sacculum pertusum*), Past. 45; Swt. 343, 20. Gif ðegna hwelc ðyrelne kylle brōhte tō ðȳs burnan, bēte hine georne, 65; Swt. 469, 10. Heáfodwunde tō bōte. Gif ða bān beóð būtū þyrel (þyrle, MSS. B. H.) . . . Gif ðæt ūterre bān bið þyrel . . ., L. Alf. pol. 44; Th. i. 92, 14. Gif būtū þyrele sién, L. Ethb. 47; Th. i. 14, 12. Hē eówaþ ūs his þyrlan handa, Wulfst. 90, 6. [*O. H. Ger.* durchil *pertusus*.] v. þurh-þyrel.

þyrelian, þyrlian; *p.* ode. I. *to make a hole through, pierce through, perforate*:—Þirlie his hlāford his eáre mid ānum ǣle *dominus perforabit aurem ejus subula*, Ex. 21, 6. Þirlige, Lev. 25, 10. II. *to make hollow*; fig. *to make vain*:—Āīdlie ł þyrlie *obunco* (? obunco *is glossed by* ymbclipe, Wrt. Voc. i. 22, 31), Engl. Stud. xi. 66, 66. Þyrliaþ *cavantur, evacuantur*, hol *cava*, Wrt. Voc. ii. 129, 62. [He lette þurlen his scheld, A. R. 392, 24. To þurlin godes side wið speres ord, Jul. 41, 14. With a spere was thirled his brestboon, Ch. Kn. T. 1852. To hem þat his herte þirled, Piers P. i. 172. Thyrlyn (thryllyn) or peercyn *penetro, terebro, perforo*, Prompt. Parv. 491.] v. þurh-þyrelian.

þyrelung, e; *f. Perforation, piercing through*:—'Ðurhðyrela ðone wāg' . . . Hwæt is sió ðyrelung ðæs wāges '*fode parietem*.' . . . *Quid est parietem fodere?* Past. 21; Swt. 153, 25. [In his side þurlunge, O. E. Homl. i. 207, 13.]

þyrel-wamb; *adj. Having the stomach pierced*:—Þyrelwombne, Exon. Th. 490, 13; Rä. 79, 11.

þyrfende. v. þurfan.

þyringas; *pl. The Thuringians*:—Wōd weóld Þyringum, Exon. Th. 320, 17; Vīd. 30: 322, 16. Mid Eást-Þyringum, 323, 30; Vīd. 86. Maroara habbaþ bewestan him Þyringas, Ors. 1, 1; Swt. 16, 11. v. Grm. Gesch. D. S. c. xxii.

þyrl, þyrlian. v. þyrel, þyrelian.

þyrl-hūs, es; *n. A turner's shop*:—Þrylhūs *tornatorium*, Wrt. Voc. i. 58, 45.

þyrn-cin, es; *n.* (?) *A small prickly plant* (-cin *diminutive suffix?*), *a thistle*:—Cwyst ðū gaderaþ man wīnberian of þornum oððe fīcæppla of þyrncinum (*tribolis*), Mt. Kmbl. 7, 16.

þyrne, an; *f. A thorn-bush*:—Þyrne, thyrnae *dumus*, Txts. 57, 710. Þorn oþþe þyrne *dumus*, Wrt. Voc. ii. 25, 70. Þyrne *frutices, ramos*, 151, 44: *dumus*, i. *spina, spineta*, Wülck. Gl. 225, 23. Hē geseah ðæt seó þyrne (*rubus*) . . . næs forburnen, Ex. 3, 2, 3. On ða þyrnan westewarde ðǽr se mycla þorn stód, Cod. Dip. Kmbl. iii. 404, 12. On ða rūgan þyrnan; of ðære þyrnan on ða brēmbelþyrnan, 419, 12. On gāte þyrnan; of ðære þyrnan on blace þyrnan, vi. 2, 5. On ða blacan þyrnan; of ðære þyrnan, 220, 20. On ða ealdan þyrnan, Cod. Dip. B. iii. 336, 25. Þyrnan *dumos*, þyrnum *dumis*, Wrt. Voc. ii. 27, 43, 44. [Cf. *Icel.* þyrnir *a thorn.*] v. brēmel-, brēr-, mǽr-þyrne.

þyrnen; *adj. Of thorns*:—Hē hæfde fiþru swylce þyrnen besma, Shrn. 120, 28. Hī mid þyrnenum helme his heáfod befēngon, Homl. Th. ii. 252, 26. Þyrnenne helm (ðyrnenne bēg, Lind., Rush.) *spineam coronam*, Mk. Skt. 5, 17: Jn. Skt. 19, 5. Þyrnenne cynehelm (sigbēg of ðornum, Lind., Rush.) *coronam de spinis*, 2. Ðyrnenne beág, Past. 36; Swt. 261, 14. Þyrnenne, Exon. Th. 69, 27; Cri. 1127. Ðone ðyrnenan helm, Homl. Th. ii. 254, 10. Þyrnenan, Wulfst. 124, 5. [*O. Frs.* thornen: *O. H. Ger.* durnīn *spineus.*]

þyrnet[t], es; *n. A place full of thorns, a thicket of thorn-bushes*:—Þirnetum *spinetis*, of ācynnendlīcum ł fexedum þyrnetum *de spinetis nascentibus* (*gignentibus*), Hpt. Gl. 463, 32–36. Of þiccum þyrnetum *senticosis, spinosis*, 436, 47.

þyrniht; *adj. Thorny, prickly*:—Ðeós wyrt hafaþ leáf . . . þyrnyhte, and heó hafaþ sumne sinewealtne crop and þyrnyhtne, Lchdm. i. 282, 14–17. Þynne leáf and ða hwōnlīce þyrnihte, 288, 17. [*O. H. Ger.* dornoht *spinosus*: *Ger.* dornicht.]

þyrran. v. þyrrian.

þyrre; *adj.* I. *dry, lacking water*:—On þyrran mæræ, Cod. Dip. Kmbl. v. 117, 5. II. *lacking sap* or *moisture*:—Þornas þyre (þyrre? *but* cf. *O. L. Ger.* thiori holt), Ps. Th. 117, 12. III. as a medical term, *dry*:—Hine dreceþ þyrre hwōsta, Lchdm. ii. 264, 13. Eallum þyrrum līchomum hǽmedþing ne dugon ac swīþost þyrrum and cealdum; ne dereþ hit hātum and wǽtum, 222, 28–30. [*Goth.* þaursus *dry, withered*: *O. H. Ger.* durri *aridus, siccus, torridus*: *Icel.* þurr: *O. L. Ger.* thurritha *dryness.*]

þyrrian(-an?) *to make* or *to become dry*:—Corfen, sworfen, cyrred, þyrred, Exon. Th. 410, 25; Rä. 29, 4. [Cf. *Goth.* thaurseith mik *I thirst*: *O. Sax.* thorrōn *to be withered up, consumed*: *O. H. Ger.* dorrēn *arescere*: dorren *arefacere.*] v. for-þyrrian.

þyrs, es; *m. A giant, an enchanter, a demon*:—Ðyrs, heldióbul *Orcus*, Wrt. Voc. ii. 115, 64. Ðyrs sceal on fenne gewunian āna innan lande, Menol. Fox 545; Gn. C. 42. Þyrses *Caci*, Wrt. Voc. ii. 20, 62. Þyr[ses] *colossi*, Hpt. Gl. 445, 2. Gehēgan ðing wiþ þyrse (*Grendel*), Beo. Th. 856; B. 426. Ealdum þyrse (þyrre, MS.), Exon. Th. 425, 29; Rä. 41, 63. Þyrsa oððe wyrmgalera *Marsorum*, þyrsas ł wyrmgaleras *Marsi*, Hpt. Gl. 483, 13–15. Cf. Wrt. Voc. ii. 82, 9. Ānīge þyrsas *Cyclopes*, Wrt. Voc. ii. 22, 37. Ðyrsa *Cyclopum*, 21, 72. [Com þe þurs Maxence, Kath. 1858. Ichabbe isehen þene þurs of helle, Marh. 11, 7. Thykke theefe as a thursse, Halliwell's Dict. Ther shal lyn lamya (satyr, A. V.), that is a thirs (thrisse), or a beste hauende the bodi lic a womman and horse feet, Wick. Isaiah 34, 15. *O. H. Ger.* durs *Dis, daemonium*: *Icel.* þurs *a giant.*] v. orc-þyrs.

þyrscel, þyrscwold. v. þerscel, þerscold.

þyrstan; *p.* te *To thirst.* I. used impersonally, (1) with acc. of person:—Mē þyrst (ic ðyrsto, Lind., Rush.) *sitio*, Jn. Skt. 19, 28. Ne þyrst ðone nǽfre ðe on mē gelȳfð (se ðe gilēfeð(-es, Lind.) on mec ne ðyrsteð(-es, Lind.) ǽfre, Rush.) *qui credit in me non sitiet umquam*, 6, 35. Mīne sāwle þyrst *sitivit anima mea*, Ps. Th. 41, 2. Ða men ne þyrst, Lchdm. ii. 194, 12. Mē þyrste (mec þyrste, Rush.) *sitivi*, Mt. Kmbl. 25, 35 Mīnne þegn þyrste and mīnne here, Nar. 8, 11. Hine ðyrstte, Past. 36; Swt. 261, 16. Ðæt mē ne þyrste (þ ic ne ðyrste(-o, Lind.), Rush.) *ut non sitiam*, Jn. Skt. 4, 15. Cume tō mē se ðe hine þyrste (se ðe ðyrsteð, Lind.: gif hwelc ðyrste, Rush.) *qui sitit veniat ad me*, 7, 37. Ongan ðone oferhȳdygan þyrstan on deáþ, Shrn. 130, 1. Drihten ealle ða gefylde, ða ðe hié on eorþan lēton hingrian and þyrstan for his noman, Blickl. Homl. 159, 17. (1 a) with acc. of person and gen. of object of thirst:—Ðeáh ðæt folc ðyrste ðære lāre, Past. 2; Swt. 31, 7. (2) with dat. of person:—Ðyrste sāwle mīnre *sitivit anima mea*, Ps. Spl. 41, 2: 62, 2. Swā hwam swā ðyrste, cume tō mē, Homl. Th. ii. 274, 3. II. with nom. of person suffering thirst; see also extracts from Northern Gospels in I. (1) absolute:—Mīn sāwl on ðē þyrsteþ *sitivit in te anima mea*, Ps. Th. 62, 1. Ðyrsteþ sāwul mīn, Ps. Surt. 42, 3: 62, 2. Hwænne gesāwe wē ðē þyrstendne, Mt. Kmbl. 25, 37, 44. Heó þyrstendon ðone þurst gelīþigaþ, Lchdm. i. 268, 11. (2) with gen. (or acc.?) of object of thirst:—Flǽsc ðonne hit God þyrst *caro tunc Deum sitit*, Scint. 54, 6. Eádige ða ðe þyrstaþ rihtwīsnysse (*iustitiam*), 49, 17. Ða ðe rihtwīsnesse þyrstaþ (lǽt hig þyrstan, MS. A.), Mt. Kmbl. 5, 6. Ðū ðe þyrstende wǽre monnes blōdes, Ors. 2, 4; Swt. 76, 33. Hió ðyrstende wæs on symbel mannes blōdes, 1, 2; Swt. 30, 27. [*O. Sax.* thurstian (*impers.*): *O. H. Ger.* dursten (*pers. and impers.*): *Icel.* þyrsta (*impers.*), cf. *Goth.* þaursjan (*impers.*) *to thirst.*] v. ge-þyrst, of-þyrsted, sin-þyrstende; þyrre.

þyrstig; *adj. Thirsty*:—Ic wæs ðyrstig *sitivi*, Mt. Kmbl. Lind. 25, 35. Ðyrstende ł ðrystig (þyrstigne, Rush.) *sitientem*, 37. v. þurstig.

þys, es; *m. A storm*:—Seó orsorhnes gǽþ scȳrmǽlum swā þæs windes þys *prosperam fortunam videas ventosam*, Bt. 20; Fox 72, 5 note. [*Icel.* þyss *uproar, tumult*; þysja *to rush.*]

þys-lic, þyl-līc; *pron. Such.* I. used adjectivally, (1) qualifying a noun:—Gif him þyslīcu þearf gelumpe, Beo. Th. 5267; B. 2637. Wēnst ðū ðæt ðē ānum þyllīc (þellecu, Cott. MS.) hwearfung and þillīc (þillīcu, Cott. MS.) unrōtnes on becumen, and nānum ōþrum mōde swelc ne on becōme, Bt. 8; Fox 24, 35. Ic mē þyslīcre þrāge ne gewēnde, Exon. Th. 269, 20; Jul. 453. Þyslīcne þegn, 316, 7; Mōd. 45: Elen. Kmbl. 1087; El. 546. Ða ðe ðyllīcne gylt þurhteóð, Homl. Ass. 148, 122. Ðā ongan hē forð sendan þyllīce stemne and þus cwæð . . ., Homl. Skt. ii. 23 b, 190. Ðyllīce, 204. Þislīc ǽrende se pāpa eft onsende and ðās word cwæð . . ., Blickl. Homl. 205, 22. Ne geceás ic nō ðis fæsten, ac ðyllīc fæsten ic geceás: brec ðæm hyngriendum ðīnne hlāf, Past. 43; Swt. 315, 13. Ðæt mōd þillīc sār cweþende wæs, Bt. 5, 1; Fox 8, 24. Mid þyslīce þreáte hlāford fergan, Exon. Th. 32, 23; Cri. 517. Þyllīcu þing syndon gereht, Homl. Ass. 199, 142. Ðyllecum unrihtum, Bt. 16, 4; Fox 58, 10. Ðyslīce gife and swā mycle *tanta taliaque dona*, Bd. 2, 12; S. 514, 13. Ðyllīca giefa, Past. 5; Swt. 41, 13. Ðyllīce gyltas, Homl. Ass. 149, 132. Ðyllīce weorc, Homl. Skt. i. 17, 28. Manega ōþre þyllīce ðing *alia similia his multa*, Mk. Skt. A. 7, 8. (2) predicative:—Ðæt seó onwrihgnes ðyslīc wǽre *revelationem hujusmodi esse*, Bd. 3, 8; S. 531, 37. Ðyslīc mē is gesewen ðis līf *talis mihi videtur vita*, 2, 13; S. 516, 13. Ðonne ðis tācen ðyslīc ðē tō cume, 2, 12; S. 514, 22. Sió onsȳn biþ þyslīcu, Lchdm. ii. 348, 21. Þyllīc bið se ende ðæs līchoman fægernesse, Blickl. Homl. 59, 21: Homl. Th. i. 88, 10. Þyllīc byð ðæt cyn *haec est generatio*, Ps. Th. 23, 6. Ic nǽfre ðē þyslīcne gemētte, þus mēðne, Exon. Th. 163, 2; Gū. 987. Þās tācno þyslīco syndon, Blickl. Homl. 109, 6. Ða ðe ðyllīce beóð, Past. 5; Swt. 41, 20: Homl. Ass. 146, 63. II. used substantively:—Þes þyllīca sȳ gemyngod *hic ammoneatur*, R. Ben. 48, 6. Gif ōwiht þislīces gelimpe *si hujus simile quid acciderit*, L. Ecg. C. 15; Th. ii. 144, 2. Ðises hī wundriaþ and manies þyllīces, Bt. 39, 3; Fox 214, 32: Ps. Th. 9, 31: Homl. Th. ii. 158, 2: Homl. Skt. i. 12, 275: ii. 28, 106. Ymb ðyllīc is tō geðencenne, Past. 9; Swt. 59, 21. Þyllīc, Homl. Skt. ii. 28, 119. Sege hwænne ic ǽfre ǽr þillīc ðē gedyde *dic, quid simile unquam fecerim tibi*, Num. 22, 30. Nǽfre wē ǽr þyllīc ne gesāwon *numquam sic vidimus*, Mk. Skt. 2, 12: Ors. 4, 4; Swt. 164, 3. Hwam beóð ðās ðyllecan gelīcran *quibus isti sunt similes?* Past. 33; Swt. 226, 23. Ðās ðyllīce bringaþ gestreón, Homl. Th. ii. 550, 35: Homl. Skt. i. 4, 290. For ðyllecum næs hē geunrōtsod, Bt. 16, 4; Fox 58, 8. Mid þyllīcum and mid manegum þyllīcum, Ps. Th. 10, 7. Ða ðe heora lustum folgiaþ and ðyllīce ādreógaþ, Homl. Ass. 196, 45. Wē gehȳrdon þyllīce gereccan, Homl. Skt. i. 6, 184, 189. [*O. E. Homl. Kath. A. R. H. M.* þullich: *Ayenb.* þellich.] Cf. þus-līc.

þȳster-, þȳstre, þȳstrian, þȳstru, þȳstrung. v. þeóster-, þeóstre, þeóstrian, þeóstru, þeóstrung.

þȳþel, Ps. L. 79, 11, -þȳtiþ, þȳwan, þȳwen. v. þȳfel, ā-þȳtiþ, þeówan, þeówen.

U

For the Runic U, see ūr.

u *the letter u*:—*Mortuus* on twām uum, Ælfc. Gr. 31; Zup. 197, 16.

ūder *an udder, a breast*:—Of ūdrum *uberibus*, Kent. Gl. 203. [Iddyr or uddyr of a beeste, pappe *uber*, Prompt. Parv. 258. *O. Du.* uder, uyder: *Du.* uijer: *O. H. Ger.* ūtar, ūtiro *uber*: *M. H. Ger.* iuter, ūter: *Ger.* euter: *Icel.* júgr: *Dan.* yver: *Grk.* οὖθαρ.]

ūf, es; *m. An owl*; the word also glosses *vultur*:—Uuf *bubo*, Wrt. Voc. ii. 102, 28. Ūf, i. 29, 45. Ðes ūf *hic uultur*, Ælfc. Gr. 9, 22; Zup. 48, 17 note. [*O. H. Ger.* ūvo *bubo*: *Icel.* ūfr *some kind of bird.*] v. hūf; þrīpel-ūf?

ūf, es; *m. The uvula*:—Mūðes hrōf *palatum*, ūf *sublingua*, Wrt. Voc. i. 64, 59. Cf. Undertungan *sublinguae*, 282, 79. [*From Latin* uva?] v. hūf.

ufan; *adv.* I. *from above, down*, (1) where motion is expressed or implied:—God him sende ufan greáte hagolstānas *Dominus misit super eos lapides magnos de coelo*, Jos. 10, 11: Blickl. Homl. 51, 12. Him feóll ufan flǽsc *pluit super eos carnes*, Ps. Th. 77, 27. Seó lyft tȳhð ðone wǽtan tō hyre neoðan and ða hǽtan ufon, Lchdm. iii. 280, 3. Ic eom engel Godes ufan sīþende, Exon. Th. 258, 7; Jul. 261. Hine ufan neósade Meotud, 159, 24; Gū. 931: Beo. Th. 3005; B. 1500. Se ðe ufa cuom *qui desursum uenit*, Jn. Skt. 3, 31. Se Hālga Gāst cumeþ ufan on ðē, Blickl. Homl. 7, 35. Ic on andwlitan sīgan lǽte wællregn ufan wīdre eorðan, Cd. Th. 81, 24; Gen. 1350. Hē ða eágan þurheteþ ufon on ðæt heáfod *it eats its way through the eyes down into the head*, Exon. Th. 374, 7; Seel. 122. Ic fērde tō foldan ufan from ēðle, Cd. Th. 296, 2; Sat. 496. Hī feóllon ufon of heofonum, 20, 11; Gen. 308. Ufan cumende of heánisse *oriens ex alto*, Ps. Surt. ii. p. 199, 40: Cd. Th. 248, 7; Dan. 509. Of roderum ufan onsended, 237, 14; Dan. 337: Exon. Th. 368, 20; Seel. 27. (2) where an action is directed from a higher to a lower point :—Seó sunne lôcaþ ufan on helle, Salm. Kmbl. p. 200, 2. Ufan engla sum cȳgde . . . ufan of roderum wuldergâst mǣlde, Cd. Th. 176, 7-16; Gen. 2908-2911. Ðæt eów ne bið ufan âlȳfed, Exon. Th. 138, 31; Gû. 584. Âmet ufan tô grunde *measure from top to bottom*, Cd. Th. 309, 2; Sat. 703. Godwebba cyst ufan eall forbærst, Exon. Th. 70, 13; Cri. 1138. II. marking position, *above, at the top* :—Synd ðǣr þrȳ porticas . . . fægere ufan oferworhte and oferhrȳfde. Seó cyrice is ufan open . . . and þeáh ðe ðæt hûs ufan open sȳ, hweþre hit biþ â þurh Godes gife ufan wiþ ǣghwilc ungewidro gescylded, . . . and nǣfre nǣnig man ða lǣstas ufan oferwyrcean ne mihte, Blickl. Homl. 125, 24-35: 19, 27: Exon. Th. 219, 17; Ph. 308: 446, 14; Dóm. 22. Æscholt ufan grǣg, Beo. Th. 665; B. 330. Hæfdon hî Dryhtnes leóht ufan (*above, in heaven*) forlēten, Cd. Th. 269, 7; Sat. 69. Hēr is fȳr micel ufan and neoðone, 24, 9; Gen. 375. On ǣlcere stôwe hē is hire emnneáh ge ufan ge neoþon, Bt. 33, 4; Fox 130, 23. ¶ Associated with prepositions :—Saturnus yfemest wandraþ ofer eallum ufan ôþrum steorrum, Met. 24, 24. On ðâm ufan stôdon scyttan, Nar. 4, 15. On ðam seáðe ufan hē hûs getimbrode, Guthl. 4; Gdwin. 26, 9. Ðâ gefeóll hē on his earm ufan, Bd. 3, 2; S. 525, 2. [*Icel.* ofan *from above*; ofan â *upon*: *O. Sax.* bi-oƀan.] v. be-, on-ufan; ufane, ufenan.

ufan-cund; *adj. Heavenly, celestial*; supernus :—Segnbora ðæs ufancundan kyninges, Blickl. Homl. 163, 22. Ufancundes engles word, Exon. Th. 169, 19; Gû. 1097. Engel ufancundne, 176, 26; Gû. 1216. Ufancundne ege *fear from heaven*, 143, 8; Gû. 658. Ðonne hē ongiete ðone ufancundan willan *cum superna voluntas agnoscitur*, Past. 7; Swt. 51, 8. Âras ufancunde *celestial messengers*, Exon. Th. 31, 29; Cri. 503.

ufane(-en(n)e); *adv.* I. *from above, down*, (1) where motion is expressed or implied :—Hié sǣdon ðæt hit ufane of ðære lyfte côme, Ors. 3, 6; Swt. 108, 30. Hē dēð ðæt fȳr cymð ufene, Wulfst. 97, 21. Steorran hreósaþ ufene of heofonum, 93, 8. (2) where an action is directed from a higher to a lower point :—Ufone sceal ðæt heáfod gîman ðæt ða fêt ne âslîden *caput debet ex alto providere, ne pedes torpeant*, Past. 18; Swt. 131, 25. Clypigende ufenne, Homl. Skt. i. 9, 25. I a. *from above, from heaven* :—Ic eom ufane *ego de supernis sum*, Jn. Skt. 8, 23. Ôð gē sȳn ufene (*ex alto*) gescrȳdde, Lk. Skt. 24, 49. II. marking position, *above* :—Ne hire on nânre ne môt neár ðonne on ôðre stôwe gestæppan, strîceþ ymbûtan ufane and neoðane efenneáh gehwæðer, Met. 20, 141. [*O. Sax.* oƀana *from above*: *O. H. Ger.* obana *desuper, superne, super, supra.*] v. ufan.

ufan-weard; *adj.* The word may be translated by *top of* (the noun with which it agrees) :—Sôna wǣron wit on his heánesse on ðam wealle ufanweardum *statim fuimus in summitate ejus* (i. e. muri), Bd. 5, 12; S. 629, 18. On ðysse dûne ufanweardre *in hujus* (*montis*) *vertice*, 1, 7; S. 478, 25. Ðâ gesâwon wē westan ðone leóman sunnan and se leóma gehrân ðǣm treówum ufonweardum *videmus ab occidente jubare fulgentibus Phebi radiisque percussa arborum cacumina*, Nar. 28, 25. [*Icel.* ofan-verðr. Cf. *O. Sax.* oƀan-wardan; *adv.*] v. ufe-weard.

ufemest. v. ufera *and* ufor.

ufenan. I. *adv. From above* :—Se ðe ufenan com *qui desursum uenit*, Jn. Skt. 3, 31. Hē dēð ðæt fȳr cymð ufenon, Wulfst. 97, 21 note. Seó landfyrd com ufenon and trymedon hig be ðam strande, Chr. 1052; Erl. 184, 24. II. *prep. with acc. Above, besides* :—Ufenan eall ðis *insuper*, Dom. L. 10, 144: 18, 271. Ufenon eal ðis, 14, 212. Hē ða bôc hire tô lêt . . . , and ufenan ðæt hire âð sealde, Chart. Th. 203, 1. ¶ Þǣr on ufenan *thereupon* :—Hē cwæð, ðæt ân culfre him fluge wið ðæt heáfod, swilce heó ðǣr on ufenan settan wolde, Homl. Ass. 198, 112. [Þe munt þe Vther wes ufenan (þar Vther lay ouenan, 2nd MS.), Laym. 18337. Swa deð ælc witer mon þa neode cumeð uuenan, 28501. He smat hine uuenen (ouenon, 2nd MS.), þat hæued, 18090. Þe eotend smat þer an ouenan (ouenan, 2nd MS.), 26051. He smat in enne stane þer Locrin stod vuenan, 2314. *O. H. Ger.* obenan.]

ufene. v. ufane.

ufer(r)a; *cpve.*: ufemest; *spve.* I. local, *upper, higher; upmost, highest* :—Ufre scrûd *an upper garment*; ependeton, Wrt. Voc. i. 59, 52. Ðæt uferre hrif, Lchdm. ii. 224, 8. On ðam uferan dǣle ðæs heáfdes *in superiore parte capitis*, Bd. 5, 2; S. 614, 45. Ðone wîsdôm ðara uferrena gâsta *supernorum spirituum scientiam*, Past. 3; Swt. 32, 13. Ðâm uferum (uferrum, Ps. Surt.) *superioribus*, Ps. Spl. 103, 14. Ða uferan (uferran, Ps. Surt. 103, 3) *superiora*, Blickl. Gl. On ðam ufemystan windle *in uno canistro quod erat excelsius*, Gen. 40, 17. On midne dæg bið seó sunne on ðam ufemestum ryne stîgende, Homl. Th. ii. 76, 18. II. temporal, *later, after*. v. uferian, II, ufeweard, II :—Oððe eft uferran dôgore oððe ðonne *either at a later day or at the time*, Past. 38; Swt. 281, 12. Hē ðē teóþan dæge him ðone Hâlgan Gâst onsende . . . on ðâs hâlgan tîde ðe nû ðȳs uferan Sunnandæge bið *he sent them the Holy Ghost on the tenth day . . . at the holy time which will be on the Sunday after next*, Blickl. Homl. 119, 15. Ðȳ læs hit monn uferan dôgore wrǣce *ne quis eum umquam ulcisci meditaretur*, Ors. 4, 5; Swt. 168, 6. Gif eówre bearn eów befrînaþ eft on uferum dagum *quando interrogaverint vos filii vestri cras*, Jos. 4, 6. On uferan dagum, Wulfst. 88, 20: Chart. Th. 356, 7. Uferan dôgrum, Beo. Th. 4407; B. 2200: 4773; B. 2392. On uferum tîdum, Lchdm. iii. 438, 15. On uferan tîdan, Wulfst. 89, 1. [Þe ufere (ouere, 2nd MS.) hond habben of þan kinge, Laym. 1520. An uuere daȝe (þar after, 2nd MS.), 27794. Þe huuemeste bou, O. E. Homl. ii. 219, 15. *O. H. Ger.* obero, oberoro: *Icel.* efri *upper*; of time, *later*.] v. yfemest.

uferian; *p.* ode. I. *to elevate, make higher* :—Ufered (uffred, MS.) *sublimatus*, Hpt. Gl. 473, 42. II. *to make later, to delay*. v. ufera, II :—Mîn hlâfurd uferaþ hys cyme *moram facit dominus meus venire*, Mt. Kmbl. 24, 48; Lk. Skt. 12, 45. [*O. H. Ger.* obarôn *differre*.] v. ge-uferian.

ufe-weard, uf-weard; *adj.* I. local, *upper*; generally may be translated by *upper part of* (the noun which it qualifies); used substantively, *upper part* :—Is se hals grēne nioþoweard and ufeweard *the lower and upper parts of the neck are green*, Exon. Th. 218, 23; Ph. 299. Ufeweard swer *epistilia*, Wrt. Voc. ii. 30, 29. Ufeweard eáre *pinnula*, i. 282, 62. Ufweard eáre, 43, 15. Ufeweard lippa *labium*, niðera lippe *labrum*, 43, 24-5. Ufeweard exle ðæs æftran dǣles *ola*, 43, 46. Eal ufweard nosu *columna*, 43, 18. Up tô ânre dûne tô ufeweardum ðam cnolle *ad verticem montis*, Jud. 16, 3. Ða eágan bióð on ðam lîchoman foreweardum and ufeweardum *oculi sunt in ipsa honoris summi facie positi*, Past. 1; Swt. 29, 13. Þreó stôdon æt ufeweardum ðæm mûðan, Chr. 897; Erl. 95, 23. Fram his hnolle ufewerdan, Homl. Th. ii. 452, 26. Hē geseah Drihten on ufeweardre ðære hlǣdre *vidit Dominum innixum scalae*, Gen. 28, 13. Seó stôw is on Oliuetes dûne ufeweardre, Blickl. Homl. 125, 19. Fram ufeweardon ôð nyþeweard *a summo usque deorsum*, Mt. Kmbl. 27, 51: Mk. Skt. 15, 38. On ufeweardum *at the top*, Gen. 6, 16. On ufeweardan, Homl. Th. i. 536, 9. Fram ufeweardan ôð neoþeweardan, ii. 496, 26. Bûtan ðam heáfde ufweardum *except the upper part of the head*, Homl. Skt. i. 18, 353. Of ufeweardum bergum *de vertice*, Wrt. Voc. ii. 27, 74. Se môna gehrân mid his scîman ðǣm triówum ufeweardum, Nar. 30, 8. II. temporal, *later, latter part of* a time. v. ufera, II :—On foreweardne sumor and eft on ufeweardne hærfest *in the early part of the summer and again in the latter part of autumn*, Chr. 913; Th. i. 186, col. 2.

ufon. v. ufan.

ufor; *cpve.*: ufemest; *spve. adv. Higher; highest* :—Ufor *superius*, ufemest *supreme*, Ælfc. Gr. 38; Zup. 240, 10. I. local, (a) *at* or *to a greater height* :—Seó sunne stîgþ ufor and ufor, Bt. 25; Fox 88, 27. Saturnus wandraþ ofer ôþrum steorrum ufor ðonne ǣnig ôþer tungol, 36, 2; Fox 174, 14. Seó sunne is micle ufor (furþor, MS. R.) ðonne se môna, Lchdm. iii. 242, 11. Nâþor ne ufor (ufror, MS. R.) ne nyðor, 254, 17: 266, 18. Swâ hî ufor fērdon, Homl. Th. ii. 548, 15. Gif se ord sié ufor ðonne hindeweard sceaft, L. Alf. pol. 36; Th. i. 84, 17. Se earn flȳhð ealra fugela ufemest, Homl. Skt. i. 15, 198. (b) where distance rather than height is marked (cf. to go *up* country), *farther* from a coast, from a spot :—Hēr fôr se here ufor on Fronclond *in this year the Danes made their way further inland in France*, Chr. 881; Erl. 82, 4: Beo. Th. 5895; B. 2951. Ðâ hêt ic hî hwæthwega ufor gân *I bade them retire somewhat from the spot*, Homl. Th. ii. 32, 22: i. 70, 35. (c) of position, *higher, at* or *to a more honourable place* :—Lâ freónd site ufur *amice ascende superius*, Lk. Skt. 14, 10. II. metaphorical, *higher* :—Hē bið suâ micle sēl gehiéred suâ hē ufor gestent on his lifes gearnungum, Past. 14; Swt. 81, 17. Nabbaþ hî nân gôd ofer ðæt tô sêcanne, ne hî nânwuht ne magon ne ufor ne ûtor findan, Bt. 34, 12; Fox 154, 16: Exon. Th. 427, 8; Rä. 41, 88. III. temporal, *later*. v. ufera, II :—Fîf nihtum ufor *five days later*, Menol. Fox 355; Men. 179: 68; Men. 34. Ðonne ymb .iii. niht gesēcæn hiom sǣmend, bûton ðam ufor leófre sió ðe ða tihtlan âge *then after three days let them seek themselves an arbitrator, unless the prosecutor would liever do it later*, L. H. E. 10; Th. i. 30, 19. [All þiss icc seȝȝde her uferr mar, Orm. 1715. *Icel.* ofarr *higher up*; of time, *later*.]

uf-weard, uht. v. ufe-weard, wiht.

ûht, es; *m. The time just before daybreak* :—Ðâ hit wæs foran tô ûhtes *antelucanum demum tempus*, Nar. 15, 31. Gang eft tô ðonne dæg and niht furþum scâde on ðam ilcan ûhte, Lchdm. ii. 346, 14. [*O. Sax.* adro an ûhta *primo mane* (Mt. 20, 1).] v. next word.

ûhta, an; *m.* I. *the last part of the night, the time just before daybreak* :—Þis wæs on ûhtan eall geworden ǣr dægrēde, Cd. Th. 294, 2; Sat. 465. On ûhtan mid ǣrdæge, Beo. Th. 252; B. 126: Andr. Kmbl. 469; An. 235: 2775; An. 1390: Elen. Kmbl. 209; El. 105. Syle drincan ǣr ûhton, Lchdm. iii. 20, 2. Cymð on ûhtan eásterne wind, Cd. Th. 20, 26; Gen. 315: 289, 31; Sat. 406: Exon. Th. 443, 24; Kl. 35. On ûhtan *very early in the morning*; ualde mane (Mk. 16, 2), ualde diluculo (Lk. 24, 1), Exon. Th. 459, 17; Hö. 1: 460, 14; Hö. 17. Ûhtna gehwylce, 287, 3; Wand. 8: 471, 24; Rä. 61, 6. II. as an ecclesiastical term, *the time at which the earliest of the seven canonical services was held, the time of nocturns* :—*De nocturna celebratione.* On ûhtan wē sculon God herian, ealswâ Dauid cwæð: 'Media nocte surgebam ad confitendum tibi,' Btwk. 220, 17. Hit gedafenaþ ðæt gehwylce cristene men on Sæternesdæg cume tô cyrcean, and ðǣr ǽfensang gehýran, and on úhtan ðone úhtsang, L. E. G. 24; Th. ii. 420, 35. Eallum cristenum mannum is beboden ðæt hí ealne heora líchoman seofon síþum gebletsian mid Cristes róde tácne, ǽrest on ǽrnemorgen . . . seofoþan síþe on úhtan, Blickl. Homl. 47, 19. [Godess enngell comm himm to onn uhhtenn þær he sleppte, Orm. 2484. Hi sloȝen and fuȝten þe niȝt and þe uȝten, Horn 1376. Ruddon of þe dayrawe ros upon uȝten, when merk of þe mydnyȝt moȝt no more last, Allit. Pms. 64, 893. *Goth.* air úhtwōn πρωῒ ἔννυχα λίαν, Mk. 1, 35. *O. Sax.* adro an úhton *primo mane*, Mt. 20, 1. *O. H. Ger.* uohta *diluculum*: *Icel.* ótta *the last part of the night.*] v. mæsse-, sunnan-úhta; úht, *and following words.*

úhtan-tíd, e; *f. The time of early morning*:—Úhtan(-en, MS.)-tíd *matutinum*, Wrt. Voc. i. 53, 7. On úhtan-tíde *matutinis horis*, Bd. 4, 12; S. 581, 14. On úhtu-tíd (úhte-, Lind.) *galli cantu*, Mk. Skt. Rush. 13, 35. [Crist ras onn uhhtenntid, Orm. 5832. *Icel.* óttu-tíðir *matins.*] v. úht-tíd.

úhtan-tíma, an; *m. The time of nocturns*:—On úhtan-tíman, Btwk. 194, 14.

úht-cearu, e; *f. Care that comes in the early morning*, Exon. Th. 442, 4; Kl. 7.

úht-floga, an; *m. A creature that flies in the early morning*:—Ðæs wyrmes denn, ealdes úhtflogan, Beo. Th. 5513; B. 2760.

úht-gebed, es; *n. A prayer repeated in the early morning, matins*:—Úhtgebed *vel* þénung *matutinum officium*, Wrt. Voc. i. 28, 29. Se eádiga wer his úhtgebedum befeal, Guthl. 6; Gdwin. 42, 12.

úht-hlem[m], es; *m. A din made in the early morning* (the noisy conflict of Beowulf and Grendel; cf. dryhtsele dynede . . . reced hlynsode . . . swég up ástág, 1540–1569; B. 767–782), Beo. Th. 4019; B. 2007.

úht-líc; *adj.* I. *of early morning*; matutinus:—Tó ðǽm úhtlícum *ad matutinum*, Ps. Spl. T. 29, 6. On úhtlícum *in matutino*, 100, 9. II. *of matins*:—Fram ðære tíde ðæs úhtlícan lofsanges *a tempore matutinae laudis*, Bd. 3, 12; S. 537, 23: 4, 7; S. 575, 2. Tó úhtlícum lofsangum *ad matutinales laudes*, Anglia xiii. 382, 243.

úht-sang, es; *m. One of the services of the church, nocturns* or *matins*:—Hú fela sealma on nihtlícum tídum tó singenne synt. On wintres tíman is se úhtsang þus tó beginnenne . . . *quanti psalmi dicendi sunt nocturnis horis. Hiemis tempore premisso in primis versu* . . ., R. Ben. 33, 7. Seofon tídsangas hí gesetton . . . Se forma tídsang is úhtsang mid ðam æftersange ðe ðǽrtó gebiraþ, L. Ælfc. P. 31; Th. ii. 376, 5: L. Ælfc. C. 19; Th. ii. 350, 6. Of ðære tíde úhtsanges *ex tempore matutinae synaxeos*, Bd. 4, 19; S. 588, 13: Shrn. 94, 32. Hwá áwecþ ðé tó úhtsancge (*ad nocturnos*)? Coll. Monast. Th. 35, 27. Tó úhtsange, tó æftersange *ad nocturnam, ad matutinam*, Anglia xiii. 396, 449: 401, 523. Ðæt ðære nihte tó láfe sié æfter ðam úhtsange *quod restat post vigilias*, R. Ben. 32, 17. From Eástron oð ða kalendas Nouembris sý se ǽrest ðæs úhtsanges swá gemetegad, ðæt lytel fæc gehealden sý betwyh ðæm úhtsange and ðæm dægrédsange, and upásprungenum dægriman dægrédsang sý begunnen *a Pasca usque ad kalendas Novembris sic temperetur hora vigiliarum agenda, ut parvissimo intervallo custodito mox matutini, qui incipiente luce agendi sunt, subsequantur*, 32, 19–33, 1: 34, 7. Ða þénunga ðe wé habbaþ on Godes þeówdóme tó mæssan, and tó úhtsange, and tó eallum tídsangum, L. Ælfc. P. 30; Th. ii. 374, 34. Ic sang úhtsang *cantavi nocturnam*, Coll. Monast. Th. 33, 25: Anglia xiii. 380, 220. Úhtsang singan *nocturnas laudes dicere*, Bd. 4, 24; S. 599, 4. On úhtan ðone úhtsang gehýran, L. E. I. 24; Th. ii. 420, 35. Tíd úhtsanga *hora vigiliarum*, R. Ben. Interl. 37, 12. Be nihtlícum úhtsangum *de nocturnis vigiliis*, 46, 9. [Ure Leafdi uhtsong sigged oþisse wise, A. R. 18, 19. Uhtsong bi nihte ine winter, ine sumer iþe dawunge, 20, 19. Daȝȝsang and uhhtennsang, Orm. 6360. *O. H. Ger.* úhti-sang *orgia*: *Icel.* óttu-söngr *matins.*] v. next word.

úhtsang-líc; *adj. Of nocturns*:—Úhtsanglíc lof *nocturna laus*, Anglia xiii. 436, 1014.

úht-sceaþa, an; *m. One who robs in the night* or *early morning*:—Eald úhtsceaða . . . nacod níðdraca nihtes fleógeþ, Beo. Th. 4534; B. 2271.

úht-þegnung, e; *f.* v. úht-gebed.

úht-tíd, e; *f. Early morning time, the time before daybreak*:—Úhttíd *vel* beforan dæge *matutinum*, Wrt. Voc. ii. 58, 64. On úhttíde *in matutino*, Ps. Spl. 48, 15. Moyses bebeád eorlas on úhttíd folc somnigean, frecan árísan, Cd. Th. 191, 17; Exod. 216. v. úhtan-tíd.

úht-wæcce, an; *f. A nightly vigil*:—Be ðám úhtwæccum *de nocturnis vigiliis*, R. Ben. 40, 10.

úle, an; *f. An owl*:—Úlae *cavanni*, Txts. 47, 378: *ulula*, 107, 2150. Úle *noctua, ulula*, 81, 1382: *ulula*, Wrt. Voc. i. 281, 7: ii. 62, 35: *noctua*, i. 281, 6: ii. 60, 35: *noctua* vel *strinx*, i. 77, 41: *strix* vel *cavanna* vel *noctua* vel *ulula*, 29, 11. Ne ete gé úlan (*noctuam*), Lev. 11, 16. Úlena *cavannarum*, Wrt. Voc. ii. 87, 69: 19, 20: Hpt. Gl. 526, 62. [*O. H. Ger.* úwila, úla *noctua, ulula, bubo*; *Icel.* ugla.]

ulm-treów, es; *n. An elm-tree*:—Ulmtreów *ulmus*, Wrt. Voc. i. 32, 63. [*Wicklif uses* ulmtree, Is. 41, 19.]

uma, huma, an; *m.* I. *a weaver's beam*:—Uma *scapus*, Wrt. Voc. i. 66, 25: *scafus*, 282, 8 (in each case the word occurs in a list of terms connected with weaving). Huma *scafus*, Corpus Gl. ed. Hessels 106, 206 (the word is omitted by Wright in Voc. ii. 120, 26, and in Txts. 97, 1832). II. *the name of some plant*:—Genim uman, and medmicelne bollan fulne ealað; bewyl ðæt ealo on ðære wyrte, Lchdm. ii. 276, 12.

umbor, es; *n. A child*:—Hwæt wit tó willan umbor wesendum ǽr árna gefremedon, Beo. Th. 2378; B. 1187. Ða ðe hine forð onsendon ǽnne ofer ýðe umbor wesende, 92; B. 46. Meotud ána wát hwǽr se cwealm cymeþ ðe heonan of cýþþe gewíteþ umbor ýceþ ðá ǽr ádl nimeþ dý weorþeþ on foldan swá fela fira cynnes *the Lord only knows what becomes of the pestilence that departs away from the land. He increases the children then, before disease carries them off* (a great many children are born before pestilence returns to a country), *so it happens that there are so many of mankind on earth*, Exon. Th. 335, 9; Gn. Ex. 31. Cf. cniht-wesende.

un-. *The prefix* (1) *expresses negation*; (2) *gives a bad sense, as in* un-dǽd, un-dóm, un-lagu, un-lǽce; (3) *reverses an action, as in* un-bindan, un-dón; (4) *is intensive* (?) v. un-hár.

un-ábeden; *adj. Unbidden, unasked*:—God beád mancynne ðæt hí hine biddan sceoldon, and hé wile syllan unábeden ðæt ðæt wé ús ne wéndon þurh úre béne, Homl. Th. ii. 372, 16: L. O. 8; Th. i. 180, 28.

un-áberendlíc; *adj. Unbearable, intolerable*:—Unáberendlíc gyhða, Homl. Th. i. 86, 11. On ðam ne eardaþ nán eorðlíc mann for ðam unáberendlícum (unáberiendan, MS. R.) bryne, Lchdm. iii. 260, 23 note. Unáberendlíce *intolerabilem*, Ps. Lamb. 123, 5. Unáberendlíce broc, Bt. 39, 10; Fox 228, 4. Dyslícu gehát and unáberendlícu *vota stulta et intoleranda*, L. Ecg. C. 19; Th. ii. 146, 33.

un-áberendlíce; *adv. Unbearably, intolerably*:—Ðæt hé ðæt ryht tó suíðe and tó ungemetlíce and tó unáberendlíce ne bodige *ne recta nimie et inordinate proferantur*, Past. 15; Swt. 95, 18. Ðæt hí tó unáberendlíce ne beóden *ne plus justo jubeant*, 28; Swt. 189, 19. Wé wǽron unáberendlíce fornumene, Homl. Th. ii. 416, 12.

un-áberiende. v. un-áberendlíc.

un-ábígendlíc; *adj. Inflexible*:—Unabégendlícre *inflexibili*, Wrt. Voc. ii. 45, 23.

un-ábindendlíc; *adj. That cannot be unbound, indissoluble*:—Hine gebindaþ ða wón wilnunga mid heora unábindendlícum racentum *quem vitiosae libidines insolubilibus adstrictum retinent catenis*, Bt. 16, 3; Fox 56, 18: 33, 4; Fox 130, 31. v. un-onbindendlíc.

un-áblinn, es; *n. A not ceasing*:—Ic geseó ða mánfullan smeáunge ðínre heortan; manna kynnes costere hafaþ ácenned on ðé ða unablinnu (-blinnunge?) ðæs yfelan geþóhtes *I see the wicked device of thy heart; the tempter of the race of men hath begotten in thee those incessant recurrences of* (that never ceasing from) *that evil thought*, Guthl. 7; Gdwin. 46, 10.

un-áblinnende; *adj.* (*ptcpl.*) *Unceasing*:—Mid unáblinnendre stemne *incessabili voce*, Hymn. ad Mat. 4.

un-áblinnendlíc; *adj. Unceasing, incessant*:—Ðǽr wæs unáblinnendlíc staþolfæstnys Godes herunge ǽghwylcne dæg and eác nihtes, Homl. Skt. ii. 236, 86.

un-áblinnendlíce; *adv. Unceasingly, incessantly, without ceasing, without intermission*:—Unáblinnendlíce *incessanter*, Rtl. 3, 17: 23, 32: *indesinenter*, Past. 13; Swt. 77, 20. Heó ðurh syx singal geár ðære ylcan hefignesse ádle unáblinnendlíce won *per sex continuos annos eadem molestia laborare non cessabat*, Bd. 4, 23; S. 595, 18: Homl. Skt. i. 19, 9: ii. 23 b, 328, 155. Hí gebiddaþ unáblinnendlíce, i. 5, 446: Blickl. Homl. 123, 16. Gnættas ǽgþær ge ða men ge ða nýtenu unáblinnendlíce píniende wǽron *ciniphes nusquam evitabiles*, Ors. 1, 7; Swt. 36, 31.

un-ábrecendlíc; *adj. Inextricable*:—Ða unábrecendlícan *inextricabilem*, Wrt. Voc. ii. 43, 69.

un-ácenned; *adj. Unbegotten*:—Ðú eart unácenned Fæder, hé is Sunu of ðé ǽfre ácenned, Homl. Th. i. 464, 34.

un-ácnycendlíc; *adj. Not to be knocked off* (of bonds), *indissoluble*:—Unácnycendlícre sibbes bende *insolubili pacis vinculo*, Rtl. 108, 21.

un-ácumendlíc; *adj. Unbearable, intolerable, impossible to be borne, excessive*:—Be unácumenlícra (-endlíca, 8, 24) ðinga gebode. Gif hwylcum bréþer hwæt hefelíces and unacumenlíces beboden sý *si fratri impossibilia jubentur. Si cui fratri aliqua gravia aut impossibilia* (unácumendalíce, R. Ben. Interl. 114, 5) *injunguntur*, R. Ben. 128, 9–11. Ða wiðercoran unácumendlíce hǽtu þrowiaþ, Homl. Th. i. 532, 1. Unácumenlícum *inextricabili, infatigabili, inextinguibile*, Hpt. Gl. 497, 68. Unácumendlícum hagelum *inexhaustis* (*inconsummatis, investigabilibus*) *imbribus*, 414, 63.

un-ácumendlícness, e; *f. Unbearableness, impossibility to be borne*:—Unácumenlícnesse *impossibilitatis*, R. Ben. Interl. 114, 9.

un-ácwencedlíc; *adj. Unquenchable, inextinguishable*:—On helle unácwencedlíces fýres *in gehennam ignis inextinguibilis*, Mk. Skt. 9, 45. On unácwencedlícum fýre, Lk. Skt. 3, 17. On unácwencedlíc fýr, Mk. Skt. 9, 43.

un-âdrugod; *adj. Undried*:—On nîwne weall unâdrugodne and unâstîđodne, Past. 49; Swt. 383, 32.

un-âdrysendlîc; *adj. Unquenchable, inextinguishable*:—Unâdrysendlîc *inextinguibilis*, Mk. Skt. Lind. Rush. 9, 43: Rush. 9, 45. v. next word.

un-âdrysnende; *adj. Not to be quenched* or *extinguished*:—Mid đæccille his unâdrysnendre *cum lampade sua inextinguibili*, Rtl. 106, 10.

un-âdrysnendlîc; *adj. Unquenchable, inextinguishable*:—Unâdrysnendlîc *inextinguibilis*, Mk. Skt. Lind. 9, 45: Lk. Skt. Lind. 3, 17 (unâdryssenlîc, Rush.). v. preceding word.

un-âdwæsced; *adj. Unquenched, unextinguished, never extinguished*:—Þâr bid unâdwæsced fȳr *there shall be fire that is not quenched*, Homl. Ass. 168, 115, 129.

un-âdwæscedlîc; *adj. That is not quenched* or *extinguished*:—On đæt unâdwescedlîce fȳr *into the fire that is not quenched*, L. E. I. prm.; Th. ii. 394, 17. Of đǽm unâdwæscedlîcum lîgum, Th. ii. 396, 5.

un-âdwæscendlîc; *adj. Unquenchable, inextinguishable*:—On middel đæs unâdwæscendlîcan lîges *in medium flammarum inextinguibilium*, Bd. 5, 12; S. 628, 2. On unâdwæscendlîcum fȳre, Mt. Kmbl. 3, 12: Homl. Th. i. 526, 22: Homl. Skt. i. 17, 32.

un-ǽmetta, -ǽmta, an; *m. Want of leisure for doing something, occupation, business*:—Unēmetta *negotia* (unemotan *negotio*, Ep. Gl. 680), Txts. 81, 1371. Gif hit sié se đe đæt land hæbbe đæt hē đis forgȳmeleásie būton hit hæres unǽmetta sié, đonne ... *if it happen that he who has the land neglect this arrangement, unless occupation in connection with the Danes be the cause of the neglect, then* ..., Chart. Th. 159, 7. Gif man hwylc metrum cild tō mæssepreóste bringe, đonne fullie hē hit sōna, and for nǽnigum unǽmtan ne forlǽte [đæt] hē hit ne fullie *if any sick child be brought to a priest, let him baptize it at once, and do not let him be prevented by any occupation from baptizing it*, L. E. I. 17; Th. ii. 412, 22. Gif hwā mid hwylcum unǽmtan genȳd sȳ, đæt hē tō đære mæssan cuman ne mæge, 39; Th. ii. 438, 1. Misenlîce intingan and unǽmtan oft gelimpaþ *diversae causae impediunt*, Bd. 4, 5; S. 573, 7.

un-ǽmtig(i)an *to prevent* a person *being at leisure, to deprive of leisure*:—Ne lyste đē wîfes đe đē on nānum þingcum ne âbysige ne đē ne unǽmtige tō đînum wyllan *do not you desire a wife that may worry you in nothing, and may not prevent you being at leisure to follow your own will*, Shrn. 183, 12.

un-ǽt, es; *m. Excessive eating, revelling*:—Hē begǽđ unǽtas and oferdrincas and gâlscipe *comessationibus vacat et luxuriae atque conviviis*, Deut. 21, 20.

un-æþelboren; *adj. Not nobly born, not of noble birth*:—Gif se æþelborena đone unæþelborenan oferþȳhđ, sȳ hē gemedemad furđur be his geearnungum đonne se unæþelborena, R. Ben. 12, 15–17. Ealle cristene men, ǽgđer ge rîce ge heáne, ge æđelborene ge unæđelborene, and se hlâford and se đeówa, ealle hî sind gebrōđra, Homl. Th. i. 260, 20. [Æþelboren [*nobi*]*lis* (v. 85, 60), unæþelboren *ignobilis*, Wrt. Voc. i. 95, 16.]

un-æþele; *adj.* I. of persons, *not noble*, (1) as regards birth:—Gedence hē simle, sié suā æđele suā unæđele, Past. 14; Swt. 85, 15. Hwî ofermōdige gē ofer ōþre men for eówrum gebyrdum, nū gē nānne ne magon mētan unæþelne, ac ealle sint emnæđele, gif gē willaþ đone fruman sceaft geþencan, Bt. 30, 2; Fox 110, 16: Met. 17, 17. Sume beóþ swîđe æþele and wîdcūþe on heora gebyrdum, ac hî beóþ mid wædle ofþrycte, đæt him wǽre leófre đæt hî wǽran unæþele đonne swā earme, Bt. 11, 1; Fox 32, 1. Æþele and unæþele *nobiles, ignobiles*, Bd. 5, 7; S. 621, 14. Ge æþele ge unæþele *tam nobiles quam privati*, 5, 23; S. 647, 7. Frige and þeówe, æđele and unæđele, Ap. Th. 12, 20. Unaeđilra (-sa, MS., aedilra, Ep. Erf.) *gregariorum*, Txts. 67, 993. Unæþelra, Wrt. Voc. ii. 41, 7. Leófre mē is đæt hē (*the king*) mē tō deáþe gesylle đonne unæþelra (*ignobilior*) man, Bd. 2, 12; S. 513, 27. (2) as regards character:—Wæs se cyning æþelre gebyrde đeáh đe hē on dǽde unæþele wǽre *erat rex natu nobilis quamlibet actu ignobilis*, Bd. 2, 15; S. 518, 37. Ǽlc mon đe allunga underþeóded biþ unþeáwum . . . wyrþ anæþelad ōþ đæt hē wyrþ unæþele (*degener*), Bt. 30, 2; Fox 110, 22: Met. 17, 28. II. of things, *ignoble, mean, infamous*:—Unæþelre âdle *degeneri languore*, Wrt. Voc. ii. 138, 33. Mid đȳ unæþelan gidde *cum infami eulogio*, 87, 40: 19, 16: 137, 42.

un-æþellîce; *adv. Ignobly*:—Ic cūþe sumne brōþor ... wæs hē geseted on æþelum mynstre, ac hē unæþelîce his lîf lifede *novi fratrem ... positum in monasterio nobili, sed ipsum ignobiliter viventem*, Bd. 5, 14; S. 634, 9.

un-æþelness, e; *f. Ignobility*; ignobilitas, infamia, Dial. 2, 23.

un-ætspornen; *adj. That is not hindered*:—Unætspornenum fōtum *inoffensis pedibus*, Dial. 1, 9.

un-ǽwisc; *adj. Modest, bashful*:—Unēwisc *pudicus*, Wrt. Voc. i. 65, 1.

un-âfandod; *adj. Untried, unproved*:—Ic wolde witan hū đū đæt ongytan woldest, hweđer đe đū woldest unâfand(o)des geleáfan đe âfandud witan, Shrn. 181, 2.

un-âfeohtendlîc; *adj. Not to be overcome*:—Unâf(e)ohtendlîc *ineluctabilis*, Wrt. Voc. ii. 48, 52. Unâfæhtendlîc *inexpugnabile*, Rtl. 92, 18.

un-âfunden; *adj.* I. *not found out, undiscovered*:—Hē hæfde ǽnne lîcđrowere belocen on ânum clyfan, and hine đǽr âfēdde unâfunden ōđ đæt, Homl. Skt. i. 3, 482. II. *not tried*:—Unâfundenum *inexperto*, Wrt. Voc. ii. 44, 28.

un-âfȳled; *adj. Undefiled*:—Unâfîlede wegas *inpolluta via*, Ps. Lamb. 17, 31.

un-âfylledlîc; *adj. Insatiate*:—Hî (*hell and avarice*) habbaþ unâfylledlîce grǽdignysse đæt hî fulle ne beóđ nǽfre, Homl. Skt. i. 16, 285.

un-âfyllendlîc; *adj. Insatiable*:—Ic hæfde unâfyllendlîce gewilnunga, Homl. Skt. ii. 23 b, 341. [Unafillendliche gredinesse, O. E. Homl. i. 103, 17.]

un-âfyllendlîce; *adv. Insatiably*, Homl. Skt. ii. 23 b, 329.

un-âga, an; *m. One without possessions, a poor person*:—Hē of eorđan mæg đone unâgan wccan *suscitans a terra inopem*, Ps. Th. 112, 6.

un-âgǽledlîce; *adv. Unremittedly*:—Hié sceoldan mancynne bodian; swā đæt cūþ gewearþ đæt hié đæt scoþþan dydon unâgǽledlîce, Blickl. Homl. 121, 5.

un-âgân; *adj. Not lapsed, with the time of its lease not run out*:—Ego Ealdulf . . . quandam ruris particulam . . . cuidam militi nomine Leofenađ . . . largitus sum . . . et post uitae suae terminum duobus tantum haeredibus immunem derelinquat; quibus defunctis, aecclesiae ... restituatur. Đis is seó gerǽdnes đe Ealdulf hæfđ gerād tō setnesse. đa hwîle đis land unâgân sē *as long as the lease of the land runs*, Cod. Dip. Kmbl. iii. 295, 22–33. Nū gewrîte ic Cyneswîđe đæt đreóra hîda lond on đreóra monna daeg . . . and ēc ic hire lēte tō . . . đæt twēga hîda lond . . . đa hwîle hit unâgaen seó, ond Cyneswîđ hit tō nǽngum ōđrum men ne lēte đa hwîle hit unâgaen sē, būtun tō hire bearna sumum . . . Ond ic biddu đæt đis đreóra hîda lond and ēc đæt twēga, đonne hit âgǽn seó (*when its lease has run out*), đæt hit sē âgefen intō Clife; and ēc ic and all hîgen hâlsigaþ ūsse æfterfylgend, đæt heora nǽnig đæt gefe gewonige, ǽr hit swā âgǽn sî, swā hit on đissum gewrite stondeþ, ii. 100, 12–29.

un-âgen; *adj. Not one's own, not in a person's possession* or *under his control*:—Gehiéren đa eádmōdan hū ēce đæt is đæt hié wilniaþ, and hū gewîtende and hū unâgen đæt is đæt hié onscuniaþ *audiant humiles, quam sint aeterna, quae appetunt, quam transitoria, quae contemnunt*, Past. 41; Swt. 299, 9. Gif man widuwan unâgne (*a widow of whom he is not the guardian*) genimeþ, L. Ethb. 76; Th. i. 20, 13, and see note. Hié sculon suā micle ēstelîcor dǽlan suā hié ongietaþ đæt him lǽnre and unâgenre biđ đæt hié đǽr dǽlaþ *tanto humiliter praebeant, quanto aliena esse intelligunt, quae dispensant*, Past. 44; Swt. 321, 9.

un-âgifen; *adj. Not given up, not repaid*:—Nolde Sigelm tō wigge faran mid nānes mannes scette unâgifnum *Sigelm would not go to battle with the money owing to any man unpaid*, Chart. Th. 201, 24.

un-âgunnen; *adj. Not begun, without a beginning*:—On unâgunnenre Godcundnysse and on ongunnenre menniscnysse *of Divinity without beginning and of humanity with beginning*, Homl. Th. iii. 292, 16.

un-âlîfed; *adj. Unallowed, illicit, unlawful*:—Be unâliéfedes mæstennes onfenge. Gif mon on his mæstene unâliéfed swîn gemēte, L. In. 39; Th. i. 132, 11. Unâlȳfedre willunge *inlicitae concupiscentiae*, Bd. 1, 27; S. 495, 9. Ne sceal hē nāht unâliéfedes dōn, ac đæt đætte ōđre menn unâliéfedes dōt hē sceal wēpan *qui nulla illicita perpetrat, sed perpetrata ab aliis deplorat*, Past. 10; Swt. 61, 14. Eall đæt hié unâliéfedes đenceaþ, 21; Swt. 155, 12. Unâlȳfedne gesynscipe *inlicitum conjugium*, Bd. 3, 22; S. 553, 25. Đone unâlȳfedan bryne mînra leahtra, Homl. Skt. ii. 23 b, 331. Wiþsacaþ đām unâlȳfdum gestreónum, Blickl. Homl. 53, 23. Unâliéfde geþōhtas *cogitationes illicitas*, Past. 13; Swt. 77, 21.

un-âlîfedlîc; *adj. Not allowable, unlawful, illicit*:—Unâlȳfedlîc þing *hoc nefas*, Ælfc. Gr. 9, 25; Zup. 51, 2. Swȳnen flǽsc Iudēum unâlȳfedlîc ys tō etanne, Ps. Th. 16, 14: Homl. Th. ii. 456, 35. Hî ne mōstan for him nāht unâlȳfedlîces begangan, Shrn. 65, 11. On hūs gehwyrfed unâlȳfedlîcra scylda *in inlecebrarum cubilia conversae*, Bd. 4, 25; S. 601, 14.

un-âlîfedlîce; *adv. Unlawfully*:—Ne sceal mon unâlȳfedlîce gelustfullian *non concupiscere*, R. Ben. 16, 19. Unâlȳfedlîce *illicite*, Dial. 2, 2.

un-âlîfedness, e; *f. What is not allowed, licence, licentiousness*:—Lîchomlîcre unâlēfednesse *corporalis inlecebre*, Wrt. Voc. ii. 135, 83. Ūrum lîcumlîcum unâlȳfednessum đeówigende *carnis inlecebris servientes*, Bd. 4, 25; S. 601, 37: 5, 6; S. 618, 39: 5, 14; S. 634, 5. Hî đis lîf forseóđ and ealles đysses lîfes unâlȳfednessa, R. Ben. 136, 31.

un-âlîfendlîc; *adj. Unallowable, illicit*:—Unâlȳfendlîcum *illecebrosis, inlicitis*, Hpt. Gl. 505, 42. From unâlîfendlîcum *ab inlecebrarum*, Wrt. Voc. ii. 2, 12: 44, 13.

un-âlîfendlîce; *adv. Unallowably, unlawfully*:—Unâlȳfendlîce *inlicite*, Scint. 141, 4.

un-âlîsendlîc; *adj. Not to be remitted* or *forgiven, without remission*:—Biđ his scyld unâlȳsendlîc, Homl. Th. i. 500, 18.

un-âmânsumod; *adj. Unexcommunicated, relieved from sentence of excommunication*:—Đā wǽron đa âmânsumedan mynecena bebyrigede

... Benedictus hēt mæssian for đām mynecenum; cwæđ đæt hī siđđan unāmānsumode wǣron, Homl. Th. ii. 174, 28.

un-āmelt; *adj. Unmelted*:—Unāmaelte (-melti, Erf.) smeoruue *pice, saevo*, Txts. 87, 1581.

un-āmeten; *adj. Unmeasured.* (1) *not having determined limits*:—Unāmeten is se Fæder, unāmeten is se Sunu, (unāmeten is se Hālga Gāst) ... Ne synt þrȳ unāmetene ... ac is ān unāmeten *immensus Pater, immensus Filius, immensus Spiritus Sanctus ... Non tres immensi ... sed unus immensus*, Ath. Crd. §§ 9, 12. (2) *very great, immense, boundless*:—God unāmetenre ārfæstnysse *Deus immense pietatis*, Anglia xi. 112, 2. Nis ūs nān gemet on đam ǣrran bebode, forđan đe wē sceolon ūrne Scyppend lufian mid unāmetenre lufe, Homl. Th. ii. 314, 12: Homl. Skt. i. 16, 254.

un-anbundenlīc. v. un-onbundenlīc.

un-andcȳđigness, e; *f. Ignorance*:—Scyld unondcȳđignesse mīnre *delicta ignorantiae meae*, Ps. Surt. 24, 7. [Cf. *O. H. Ger.* ant-kundig *expertus*.]

un-andergilde; *adj. Not to be paid back* (?), *that may be retained* (?):—Geđenc nū hwæt đīnes āgnes seó ealra đissa woruldǣhta and welena, ođđe hwæt đū đǣron āge unandergildes, gif đū him sceádwīslīce æfter spyrast. Hwæt hæfst đū æt đām gifum đe đū cwist đæt seó wyrd eów gife, and æt đām welum, đeáh hī nū ēce wǣron? *age enim, si jam caduca et momentaria fortunae dona non essent, quod in eis est, quod aut vestrum umquam fieri queat, aut non perspectum consideratumque vilescat*, Bt. 13; Fox 38, 1–5. v. andergilde.

un-andet; *adj. Unconfessed*:—Ǣnig man mid unandettan heáfodleahtrum hūsles ne ābyrige, ac andette and bēte, Wulfst. 71, 7.

un-andgitfull; *adj. Not intelligent, without understanding*:—Unondgetfulle *insensati*, Ps. Surt. ii. p. 195, 11. Đæt đa andgytfullan mid worda lāre tō Godes willan gemyngode sȳn and đa unandgytfullan mid gōdum dǣdum getrymede *ut capacibus discipulis mandata Domini verbis proponat, et simplicioribus factis suis divina precepta demonstret*, R. Ben. 11, 16. Đǣm unandgytfullum (*infirmis intellectibus*) đæt gāstlīce angyt is earfoþe tō understandenne, 66, 19.

un-andhēfe; *adj. Insupportable*:—Byrþenne hæfige and unandhoife *onera gravia et inportabilia*, Mt. Kmbl. Rush. 23, 4. [Cf. *O. H. Ger.* ant-heffen *sustentare*.]

un-andweard; *adj. Not present*:—Drihten nolde līchamlīce sīđian tō đæs cyninges untruman bearne, ac unandweard mid his worde hine gehǣlde, Homl. Th. i. 128, 17.

un-andwendlīc; *adj. Immovable, unchangeable*; immobilis, Bt. 39, 6; Fox 220, 16 note. v. un-āwendendlīc.

un-andwīs; *adj. Inexperienced*:—Unandwīs *inexpertus*, Wrt. Voc. ii. 84, 13: 46, 76. Đȳ unandwīsan *inexperto* (the passage, however, is *in experto terrore*, Ald. 34), 79, 39.

un-ānrǣdness, e; *f. Inconstancy*:—Hē (*the devil*) nǣnige mehte wiđ ūs nafaþ, būton hwylc man þurh đa unānrǣdnesse his mōdes him wiđstandan nelle, Blickl. Homl. 31, 34.

un-anwendenlīc. v. un-onwendendlīc.

un-āpīnedlīce; *adv. With impunity*:—Unāpīnedlīc(e) *inpune*, Rtl. 113, 36.

un-ār, e; *f. Dishonour*:—Tō unāre *to the dishonour* (*of God*), Anglia xi. 98, 45. Hē wēpende mǣnde đa unāre đe him mon būton gewyrhton dyde *deplorans injurias suas*, Ors. 5, 12; Swt. 240, 9: Ps. Th. 68, 7. [*O. L. Ger. O. H. Ger.* un-ēra *dedecus, contumelia, damnum*.]

un-āræfned; *adj. Intolerable, insupportable*:—Đa unāræfnodan wurþaþ tōbrocenne *quae non toleranda sunt, dirimantur*, L. Ecg. C. 19; Th. ii. 146, 4. Þurh đa wædlan stōwe wætres and þurh đa unārefndon lond wildeóra and wyrma *per immania et egentia plerumque aquarum, per aliquot serpentium ferarumque loca*, Nar. 26, 8.

un-āræfnedlīc; *adj. Intolerable, impossible to bear*:—Būton hit unāræfnedlīc sȳ tō ofercumenne đa þing đe ūs synd fram đē forestihtode *unless it be beyond our powers of endurance to overcome the things that are fore-ordained for us by thee*, Homl. Skt. ii. 30, 133. Seó unāræfnedlīce byrþen synna, Blickl. Homl. 75, 9. Se freódōm đæs unāræfnedlīcan þeówdōmes, 137, 13. Mid unārefnedlīce þurste geswencte, Nar. 9, 17: 8, 21. Wæter unārefnedlīc *aquam intolerabilem*, Ps. Lamb. 123, 5. Þurh đa lond đe đa unārefnedlīcan cyn nædrena in wǣron *in execrabilia serpentum genera*, Nar. 6, 22.

un-āræfnendlīc; *adj. Intolerable*:—Unāræfnendlīc *intolerabile*, Bd. 5, 12; S. 627, 38. Unāræfnendlīce fūlnes *foetor incomparabilis*, S. 628, 25. Weter unārefnendlīc *aquam intolerabilem*, Ps. Surt. 123, 5. Be đām tintregum unāræfnendlīcum (*intolerabilibus*), Bd. 5, 12; S. 628, 5. Grimme hergunge and unāræfnendlīce *acerbas atque intolerabiles irruptiones*, 3, 24; S. 556, 5.

un-āreccendlīc; *adj. Not to be related, indescribable*:—Unāreccendlīc blis *inenarrabile gaudium*, Scint. 26, 15.

un-āreht *undiscussed, not expounded*:—Nū hæbbe wē gereht be welan and be anwealde, and đæt ilce wē magon reccan be đām þrīm đe wē unāreht (unreht, Cott. MS.) habbaþ *similiter ratiocinari de honoribus, gloria, voluptatibus licet*, Bt. 33, 2; Fox 124, 21.

un-ārian *to dishonour*:—Se unārade sc̄s Georgies anlīcnysse, Shrn. 73, 13. v. ge-unārian.

un-ārīmed; *adj. Unnumbered, numberless, countless*:—Unārīmed mengeo, Blickl. Homl. 199, 1. Seó unārīmede menigo, 87, 18. Mid đȳ unārīmedan weorode, 25, 35. Mid hū miclan feó woldest đū habban geboht...? Ic wolde mid unārīmedum feó gebycgan *quanti aestimabis*...? *Infiniti*, Bt. 34, 9; Fox 146, 11. Unārīmede untrumnessa, Blickl. Homl. 209, 13. Unārīmedum *numerosis*, Hpt. Gl. 408, 67: Bt. 1; Fox 2, 11. Be đǣm unārīmdum cynnum *de innumeris generibus*, Nar. 1, 17.

un-ārīmedlīc; *adj.* I. *innumerable, countless*:—Se cāsere gegaderode unārīmedlīce fyrde ... seó fyrd wæs unārīmedlīc đe hē gegaderad hæfde, Chr. 1050; Erl. 173, 21–24. Seó unārīmedlīce menigo hāligra sāula, Blickl. Homl. 87, 6. Be đære unārīmedlīcan mengeo his weoredes, đæs wæs būton unārīmedlīcan fēþum ... *de innumerabili exercitu, in quo fuerint permultae peditum copiae* ... Nar. 4, 10–12. Cōman tōsamne unārīmedlīco mengeo, Blickl. Homl. 199, 9. Hī genāmon unārīmedlīco herereáf, Chr. 473; Erl. 12, 26: 584; Erl. 18, 25. II. *boundless, infinite, shewn in countless instances*:—Đæt mid Drihtne sig unārīmedlīcu mildheortnys *quod apud Dominum sit innumerabilis misericordia*, L. Ecg. P. i. 9; Th. ii. 176, 14. Hē bæd hié đæt hié gemunden đæs unārīmedlīcan freóndscipes đe hié hæfdon on ealddagum, Ors. 2, 5; Swt. 82, 19.

un-ārīmedlīce; *adv. Innumerably*:—Đa geswinc đe hē fela wintra dreógende wæs unārīmedlīce oft (*times without number*), Ors. 5, 4; Swt. 224, 29.

un-ārlīc; *adj.* I. *dishonourable, disgraceful, shameful*:—Đīn mōdor gewīteþ of weorulde þurh scondlīcne deáđ and unārlīcne and heó ligeþ unbebyrged in wege fuglum tō mete and wildeórum *mater tua miserando turpissimoque exitu sepultura carebit, iacebitque in uia praeda auium ferarumque*, Nar. 31, 29. Sægde Lameh unārlīc spel (*a tale of shame*); 'Ic honda gewemde on Caines cwealme,' Cd. Th. 66, 31; Gen. 1092. II. *unkindly*:—Unārlīce yrfebēc *a will in which nothing is left to nearest relatives*; inofficiosum testamentum, Wrt. Voc. ii. 49, 17.

un-ārlīce; *adv.* I. *disgracefully, shamefully*:—Mē þeówmennen drehte dǣdum and wordum unārlīce, Cd. Th. 135, 29; Gen. 2250. II. *mercilessly, cruelly*:—Nǣfre gē mid blōde beódgereordu unārlīce eówre þicgeaþ, Cd. Th. 91, 28; Gen. 1519.

un-arodscipe, es; *m. Inactivity, spiritlessness*:—Oft mon biđ suīđe wandigende æt ǣlcum weorce and suīđe lætrǣde, and wēnaþ men đæt hit sié for suārmōdnesse and for unarodscipe, and biđ đeáh for wīsdōme and for wærscipe *sæpe agendi tarditas gravitatis consilium putatur*, Past. 20; Swt. 149, 15.

un-ārweorþian *to dishonour*:—Ic ārwurđige (-weorđige, Jn. Skt. 8, 49, MS. A.) mīnne Fæder and gē unārwurđiaþ (-weorđodon, Jn. Skt. MS. A.) mē *honorifico Patrem meum et uos inhonoratis me*, Homl. Th. i. 442, 21.

un-ārweorþness, -wirþness, e; *f. Disrespect, irreverence*:—Unārwyrđnyss *irreverentia*, Scint. 224, 1.

un-āsaedde. v. un-āsedd.

un-āscended; *adj. Unharmed, not to be harmed*:—Unāscended fruma *incorruptibile principium*, Jn. Skt. p. 1, 12. Unāscendedo *interos*, Rtl. 114, 7. Unāscendado, 101, 36: 172, 3: 179, 1.

un-āscirigendlīc; *adj. Inseparable*:—Đære Hālgan Þrynnysse is ān godcundnyss, and ān gecynd, and ān willa, and ān weorc unāscyrigendlīce (*inseparable*; or *inseparably?*), Homl. Th. i. 326, 27.

un-āscirod; *adj. Not separated*:—Unāscyrod *inremota, s. inseparata*, Wülck. Gl. 253, 3.

un-āscruncen; *adj. Unwithered, unfading*:—Unāscryuncan *immarcessibilem*, Rtl. 24, 32.

un-āsecgende; *adj. Not to be told, unspeakable, ineffable*:—Mid unāsecgendre swētnysse *cum ineffabili dulcedine*, Bd. 4, 3; S. 568, 3.

un-āsecgendlīc; *adj.* I. implying greatness, *beyond the powers of language to describe, unspeakable, indescribable, ineffable*:—Hwæt wundor is, gif se ælmihtiga God is unāsecgendlīc? Homl. Th. i. 286, 26: 322, 9: ii. 232, 5: Homl. Skt. i. 1, 33: Elen. Kmbl. 929; El. 466. Unāsæcgendlīc clǣne girȳno *ineffabile sacramentum*, Rtl. 33, 8. Unāsægcgendlīc, 35, 15. Đæt unāsecgenlīce wræc, Blickl. Homl. 25, 24. Unāsecggenlīce, 65, 21. Đæt wæs unāsecgendlīc ǣnigum menn hū mycel đæs folces wæs *it was impossible for any man to say how much people there was*, Chr. 1011; Erl. 145, 14. God unāsecgendlīcere mildheortnesse *Deus inestimabilis misericordie*, Anglia xi. 112, 1. Wundriende đære unāsecgendlīcan gesǣlignesse đæra manna, đe him God forgifþ ealle heora scylda, Ps. Th. 31, arg. Ǣfter his unāsecgendlīcum foreþonce, Bt. 39, 5; Fox 220, 2. Unāsæcendlīcum *inenarrabili*, Rtl. 38, 5. Unāsecggendlīcum, Blickl. Homl. 87, 21. Mid unāsecgendlīcre wurđmynte, Ap. Th. 10, 21. Hē hæfde fulneáh unāsecgendlīcne sige, Bt. 16, 2; Fox 54, 1: Homl. Th. i. 532, 1, 2. Hī nāmon unāsecgendlīce herehūđe, Chr. 1046; Erl. 171, 1. Đa unmǣtan tyntregu and đa unāsecgendlīcan wīta, L. E. I. prm.; Th. ii. 396, 35. Hē nam of hire eall đæt heó āhte on golde and on seolfre and on unāsecgendlīcum þingum (*things innumerable*), Chr. 1042; Erl. 169, 21. Unāsæccendlīcum costum *ineffabilibus modis*, Rtl. 108, 27. II. *not proper to tell, not to be told*:—Đa unāsecgendlīcan *nefandas*, Wrt. Voc. ii. 61, 40.

un-āsecgendlīce; *adv. Unspeakably, in a way that cannot be told, ineffably*:—Hāligne Gāst forþleórendne of Fæder and of Suna unāsecgendlīce (*inenarrabiliter*), Bd. 4, 17; S. 586, 14.

un-āsedd; *adj. Unsated*:—Unāsaedde (-seddae) *inopimum*, Txts. 71, 1102. Unāsedde, Wrt. Voc. ii. 48, 81.

un-āseolcendlīc; *adj. Eager, energetic, vehement*:—Of geornum *subnixis*, unāseolcendlīcum (-seoclendlīcum, MS.) menegungum *hortamentis* (the whole passage is: Puberem subnixis precibus et inauditis blandimentorum hortamentis flectere nitebantur, Ald. 46), Hpt. Gl. 485, 50. v. un-āsolcenlīce, ā-seolcan.

un-āseowod; *adj. Unsewed, without seam*:—Seó tunece wæs unāsiwod (-seowod, MS. A.) *erat tunica inconsutilis*, Jn. Skt. 19, 23.

un-āsēđendlīc (-sēdendlīc? v. sēdan); *adj. Insatiable*:—Unāsēđendlīc *insaturabilis*, Kent. Gl. 471. Unāsēđenlīc *insatiabilis*, 522: 1031: *insaturabilis*, 1087.

un-āsmeágendlīc; *adj. Unsearchable, past finding out, inscrutable*:—Seó godcundnys is unāsmeágendlīc, Homl. Th. ii. 232, 4: Homl. Skt. i. 1, 33. Đīn myldheortnys is swīđe mycel and unāsmǣgendlīc, 3, 548. Đære sāwle brōgan, unāsmeágendlīcu yrmđu (*misery beyond the power of man to explore*), Wulfst. 249, 19. Hē mē gefrætwode mid unāsmeágendlīcra wurđfulnesse, Homl. Skt. i. 7, 31. Đa ōđre heofenan, đe bufan hyre synd and beneođan, synd mannum unāsmeágendlīce (*are beyond the reach of men's investigation*), Lchdm. iii. 232, 23. His lāra and his drohtnunga sind ūs unāsmeágendlīce, Homl. Th. i. 392, 23.

un-āsolcenlīce; *adv. Not lukewarmly, heartily, energetically, with vigour*:—Gif đæt gebodene biđ gefremed unforhtlīce and unsleaclīce and unāsolcenlīce *si quod jubetur non trepide, non tarde, non tepide efficiatur*, R. Ben. 20, 19.

un-āspringende; *adj. Unfailing*:—Geunne mē đæt đis wæter sȳ mē tō fulwihtes bæþ unāspringende (*fiat mihi haec aqua fons baptismi indeficiens*, Homl. Ass. 217, 326), Nar. 46, 9.

un-āspyrigendlīc; *adj. That cannot be investigated, that cannot be learnt by inquiry*:—Unāsperiendlīc *in[inve]stigabilis*, Kent. Gl. 91. Unāsporiendlīc, Dial. 2, 16.

un-āstīđod; *adj. Not made firm*:—Gif mon on nīwne weall unādrugodne and unāstīđodne micelne hrōf and hefigne onsett, đonne ne timbreþ hē nō healle ac hryre *quod structuris recentibus necdum solidatis, si tignorum pondus superponitur, non habitaculum sed ruina fabricatur*, Past. 49; Swt. 383, 32.

un-āstyrigendlīc; *adj. Motionless*:—Ic fōr of dūne on đa eorđan, and forneáh eallunga unāstyrigendlīc būtan gāste læg, Homl. Skt. ii. 23 b, 576. Beón hig unāstyriendlīce (*immobiles*) swylce stān, Cant. M. 16 (Ex. 15, 16).

un-āstyrod; *adj. Unmoved*; inmotus, Hymn. Surt. 11, 4.

un-āsundrodlīc; *adj. Inseparable*; inseparabilis, Rtl. 122, 10: 109, 13.

un-āswundenlīce; *adv. Not languidly, not slowly, promptly*:—Đā đōhte hē đæt hē sceolde weorulde wiþsacan, and đæt unāswundenlīce swā gedyde (*non hoc segniter fecit*), Bd. 4, 3; S. 567, 23. Heó đæt weorc unāswundenlīce gefylde *opus non segniter implevit*, 4, 23; S. 593, 36.

un-ātalodlīc; *adj. Unnumbered, innumerable*:—Gyltingum unātaladlīcum *delictis innumerabilibus*, Rtl. 124, 42.

un-āteald; *adj. Uncounted*:—Gif se dæg biđ forlǣten unāteald, đǣrrihte āwent eal đæs geáres ymbrene đwyres, Boutr. Scrd. 28, 32. v. un-teald.

un-ātellendlīc; *adj. Innumerable*:—Seó fyrd wæs unātellendlīc đe hē gegaderod hæfde, Chr. 1049; Erl. 172, 23. Hī bereáfedan hī æt eallon đan gærsaman đe héo āhte; đa wǣron unātellendlīce, 1043; Erl. 168, 34. Đam se fæder becwæđ gersuman unāteallendlīce, 1086; Erl. 221, 8. Mīne unātellendlīce (*innumerabilia*) beón ic oncnāwe gyltas, Anglia xi. 118, 62.

un-ātemed; *adj. Untamed, unsubdued*:—Severus micelne dǣl Breotone mid dīce tōsceádde fram ōþrum unātemedum đeódum, Bd. 1, 5; S. 476, 3.

un-ātemedlīc; *adj. Untameable*:—Forđon đe đa men wǣron unātemedlīce and heardes mōdes and ellreordes *eo quod essent homines indomabiles et durae ac barbarae mentis*, Bd. 3, 5; S. 527, 25.

un-āteoriende; *adj. Unwearying, indefatigable*:—Unāteoriendum þēnungum *indefessis* (*infatigabilibus*) *famulatibus*, Hpt. Gl. 463, 8.

un-āteorigendlīc; *adj.* I. *indefatigable, unwearied*:—Mid unāteriendlīce strecnysse *indefessa instantia*, Hpt. Gl. 434, 22. II. *that shall not fail, unending, imperishable*:—Hī befæston Godes lāre heora underþeóddum tō unāteorigendlīcum gafele, Homl. Th. i. 544, 18. Wē habbaþ unāteorigendlīce sāule, 96, 18. Wē đe sind ēce on ūrum sāwlum, and eác beóđ on līchaman unāteorigendlīce æfter đam gemǣnelīcum ǣriste, ii. 462, 30.

un-āteorigendlīce; *adv.* I. *indefatigably*:—Unāteorien[d]līce *infatigabiliter*, Hpt. Gl. 424, 17. II. *unceasingly, without failing*:—Unāteoriendlīce *incessabiliter*, R. Ben. Interl. 22, 13. God đe wē unātirendlīce (*incessanter*) ondrǣden, Chart. Th. 316, 33.

un-āteorod; *adj. Unwearied, unexhausted, unfailing*:—Unāteorodne *inexhaustam* (*indefessam, indeficientem*), Hpt. Gl. 463, 18.

un-āþreótende; *adj. Unwearying, inexhaustible*:—Hī unāþreótendum þrymmum singaþ, Exon. Th. 24, 21; Cri. 388.

un-āþroten; *adj. Unwearied, persevering*:—Sindon tō sēceanne stronge and unāđrotene lāreówas and đurhwuniende *fortes perseverantesque doctores quaerendi sunt*, Past. 22; Swt. 171, 9.

un-āþrotenlīce; *adv. Unweariedly, unceasingly*:—Hī sint tō manienne đæt hī unāđrotenlīce đa gedōnan synna gelǣden beforan heora mōdes eágan *admonendi sunt, ut incessanter admissa ante oculos reducant*, Past. 53; Swt. 413, 14. Ealne đisne andweardan welan hī swīþe unāþrotenlīce sēcaþ, Bt. 32, 3; Fox 118, 21: 39, 13; Fox 234, 7.

un-ātweógendlīce. v. un-tweógendlīce.

un-āwæscen; *adj. Unwashed*:—Unāwæscen wull *lana succida* vel *sucilenta*, Wrt. Voc. i. 61, 8. Unāwaxen wul *lana sucida*, ii. 54, 6.

un-āwegendlīc; *adj. Immovable, unshaken*:—Seó gefæstnung stađelfæst and unāwægendlīc mid þurhwuniende rihte beó gefæstned *confirmatio stabilis et inconcussa perseverantissimo jure consolidetur*, Chart. Th. 319, 9.

un-āwemmed; *adj. Unstained, undefiled, immaculate*:—Unāwoemmed *immaculatus*, Rtl. 24, 42: 29, 11, 15. Unāwemdo *eunuchi*, Mt. Kmbl. Lind. 19, 12.

un-āwemmedlīc; *adj. Incorruptible, immaculate*:—Eádignisse unāwoemmedlīcum *beata immortalitate*, Rtl. 33, 12.

un-āwemmedness, e; *f. Incorruption*:—Crist gewāt of deáđe tō līfe, and of brosnunga tō unāwemmednysse, and of wīte tō wuldre, Anglia viii. 330, 10.

un-āwend, -āwended; *adj. Unchanged, unaltered*:—Hlāfordes rihtgifu stande ǣfre unāwend (-āwended, MS. B.), L. C. S. 82; Th. i. 422, 3: Cod. Dip. Kmbl. iv. 231, 17. Ic wille đæt se fréols stonde unāwent, 219, 20.

un-āwendedlīc, -āwendlīc; *adj. Unchangeable, fixed, invariable*:—Đū đe ealle đa unstillan gesceafta tō đīnum willan āstyrast and đū self simle stille and unāwendedlīc đurhwunast *qui stabilis manens das cuncta moveri*, Bt. 33, 4; Fox 128, 10. Unāwendedlīce, unāwendlīce *fixa*, Ælfc. Gr. 43; Zup. 254, 17 note. v. un-āwendendlīc.

un-āwendende; *adj. Unchanging*:—Se ūs gesette sido unāwendendne, Met. 11, 13. v. next word.

un-āwendendlīc; *adj. Unchangeable, unalterable, invariable*:—Heora nān nǣfre of đam hāde đe hē is ne āwent, forđan đe God is unāwendendlīc, Homl. Th. ii. 606, 27: Bt. 35, 2; Fox 158, 4. God is ealra đinga reccend and hē āna unāwendendlīc wunaþ and eallra đara āwendendlīcra welt *rerum orbem mobilem rotat, dum se immobilem ipsa conservat*, 35, 5; Fox 166, 9. Sió godcunde foreteohhung is ānfeald and unāwendendlīc (*simplex immobilisque*), 39, 6; Fox 220, 16. God gesette unāwendendlīcne sido, 21; Fox 74, 1. Eorþan đū sealdest unāwendendlīce *terram dedisti immobilem*, Hymn. Surt. 19, 33. Gif hī beóđ *participia*, đonne beóđ hī ... *mobilia*; gif hī beóđ naman, đonne beóđ hī ... *fixa*, đæt is unāwendendlīce, Ælfc. Gr. 43; Zup. 254, 17. Đa habbaþ đa ēcean reste and unāwendendlīce welan, Homl. Skt. i. 22, 219.

un-āwendendlīce; *adv. Unalterably, without possibility of change*:—Ic nāt hwæþer hit eall gewyrþan sceal unāwendendlīce, đæt hē wāt and getiohhod hæfþ. Đā cwæþ hē: 'Ne þearf hit nō eall gewiorþon unāwendendlīce; ac sum hit sceal geweorþan unāwendendlīce, Bt. 41, 3; Fox 248, 30–250, 2.

un-āwidlod; *adj. Uncontaminated, undefiled*:—Lombes unāwidlades *agni incontaminati*, Rtl. 24, 40. Erfeueardnisse unāwidlad *hereditatem incontaminatam*, 32.

un-āwirded; *adj. Uninjured, uncorrupted*:—Unāwerded *incorruptibilis*, Jn. Skt. p. 1, 12. Unāwoerdedo *inlaesos*, Rtl. 102, 31.

un-āwriten; *adj. Unwritten*:—Thomes đrowunge wē forlǣtaþ unāwritene, Homl. Th. ii. 520, 9. Unāwritten *cautionem*, Lk. Skt. Lind. 16, 6.

un-bældo. v. un-bildu.

un-banden; *adj. Released from bonds*:—Ǣfter đam þūsende byđ se deófol unbanden (-bunden?), Anglia viii. 336, 15.

un-beald; *adj. Not bold, not confident, irresolute*:—Oft gebyreþ đæm manđwǣran, đonne hē wierđ rīce ofer ōđre men, đæt hē for his manđwǣrnesse āslāwaþ and wierđ tō unbald (-beald, Hatt. MS.), forđæm sió unbieldo and sió manđwǣrnes bióđ swīđe anlīce *nonnunquam mansueti, cum praesunt, vicinum et quasi juxta positum torporem desidiae patiuntur*, Past. 40; Swt. 288, 1. On ōđre wīsan sint tō manianne đa ānfealdan strǣcan, on ōđre đa unbealdan ... Đǣm unbealdum is tō cȳđanne hū giémeleáse hié bióđ đonne hié hié selfe tō suīđe forsióđ *aliter admonendi sunt pertinaces, atque aliter inconstantes ... istis intimandum est, quod valde se despicientes negligunt*, 42; Swt. 305, 12–16. Wēnde ic đæt đū đȳ wærra weorþan sceolde, and đȳ unbealdra, Exon. Th. 268, 4; Jul. 427. [*Laym.* un-bald.]

un-bealu; *gen.* -beal(u)wes; *n. Innocence*:—Mid unbealuwe ealre heortan *in innocentia cordis mei*, Ps. Th. 100, 2.

un-bealufull; *adj. Innocent, harmless*:—Of unbealafullum feoh gerǣcan, L. I. P. 12; Th. ii. 320, 26: Wulfst. 83, 13.

un-beboht; *adj. Unsold*:—Hē hæfde tamra deóra unbebohtra syx hund, Ors. 1, 1; Swt. 18, 10.

un-bebyriged; *adj. Unburied*:—Ðīn mōdor ligeþ unbebyriged *mater tua sepultura carebit*, Nar. 31, 30: Shrn. 40, 4. Heora līchaman licgaþ unbebyrgede (-byrigde, MS. F.), Wulfst. 199, 10. [Unbiburiet *inhumatus*, Kath. 2243.]

un-beceás; *adj. Not giving occasion to litigation, indisputable, incontestable*:—Bidde hē ða hond ðe ðæt ierfe hafaþ, ðæt hē him gedō ðone ceáp unbeceásne (*that he shew the chattel to be his by incontestable right*), L. In. 53; Th. i. 136, 7.

un-becrafod; *adj. Not subjected to claims*:—Ðǣr se bōnda sæt unbecrafod *where the husband dwelt without having had any claims made upon him*, L. C. S. 73; Th. i. 414, 22. v. un-crafod.

un-becweden; *adj. Unbequeathed, not left by will*:—On ǣlcum þingum ðe ðǣr unbecweden bið, on bōcum and an swilcum lytlum, Chart. Th. 538, 24. Ðæt land æt Sendan and æt Sunnanbyrg unbecwedene and unforbodene wið ǣlcne man, 208, 38.

un-beden; *adj. Unbidden, unasked*:—Sume preóstas . . . unbedene gaderiaþ hī tō ðam līce, swā swā grǣdige ræmmas ðǣr ðǣr hī hold-geseóð, L. Ælfc. P. 49; Th. ii. 386, 2. [Toc Crist unnbedenn and unnbonedd to mælenn, Orm. 17081.]

un-befangenlīc; *adj. Incomprehensible*:—God is unāsecgendlīc and unbefangenlīc, Homl. Th. i. 286, 27.

un-befliten; *adj. Uncontested, undisputed*:—Ðā wæs hīgen and hlāforde lond unbefliten ēghwæs and seoððan ā ōð his daga ende, Chart. Th. 48, 1: 481, 14: 483, 3.

un-befohten; *adj. Unfought, unopposed*:—Ðā wēnde se here . . . ðæt hié mehten faran unbefohtene ðǣr ðǣr hié wolden, Chr. 911; Erl. 100, 23: Byrht. Th. 133, 28; By. 57.

un-befōndlīc (?). v. un-beseóndlīc.

un-begān; *adj.* I. *uncultivated*:—Unbegānum *incultis* (*arvis*, Ald. 200), Wrt. Voc. ii. 96, 2: 47, 38. Ðeós wyrt byþ cenned on dūnum and on unbegānum stōwum, Lchdm. i. 230, 4: 238, 17. II. *unadorned*:—Unbegān *inculta, non ornata*, Hpt. Gl. 435, 26.

un-begrīpendlīc; *adj. Incomprehensible*:—Se myccla mægenþrym and se unbegrīpendlīca, Blickl. Homl. 179, 9. Unbegrīpendlīc and ungesȳnelīc God, 185, 31.

un-begunnen; *adj. Without beginning*:—*Sum* ic eom is edwistlīc word and gebyraþ tō Gode ānum synderlīce, forðan ðe God is ǣfre unbegunnen and ungeendod on him sylfum and ðurh hine sylfne wunigende, Ælfc. Gr. 32; Zup. 201, 9: Wrt. Voc. i. 70, 1: Homl. Th. ii. 204, 12: Homl. Skt. i. 1, 16: Homl. Ass. 25, 25. Hē wæs ǣfre unbegunnen Scyppend, Hexam. 1; Norm. 4, 3.

un-beheáfdod; *adj. Unbeheaded*:—Ic eów lǣte unbeheáfdod, Homl. Skt. i. 23, 185.

un-behēfe; *adj.* (or *subst.*?) *Unsuitable, inconvenient, unprofitable*:—Unbehēfe *incommodum*, Wrt. Voc. ii. 85, 35. [Al þat ure sowle and ure lichame beð unbiheue, O. E. Homl. ii. 7, 30. *Also subst.* Hie turnden fro him hem seluen to unbihefe, 121, 26.] Cf. un-brȳce.

un-behelendlīce; *adv. Without the possibility of concealment*:—Ðæt bið eallum open unbehelendlīce, ðæt man ǣr hæl, Wulfst. 138, 3.

un-behelod; *adj. Uncovered, naked*:—Hē læg on his getelde unbehelod (*nudatus*), Gen. 9, 21, 22.

un-behreówsigende; *adj. Unrepenting, impenitent*:—Se ðe mid unbehreówsigendre heortan þurhwunaþ on māndǣdum, Homl. Th. i. 500, 15.

un-belimp, es; *n. Mischance, accident*:—Of unbelimpum (*fortunae*) *casibus* (*oppressos*, Ald. 42), Hpt. Gl. 478, 25.

un-beorhte; *adv. Not brightly*:—Ealle steorran weorþaþ gebirhte of ðære sunnan, sume þeáh beorhtor, sume unbeorhtor (*less brightly*), Bt. 34, 5; Fox 140, 6. Sume beorhtor, sume unbyrhtor, 33, 4; Fox 132, 21.

un-bereáfigendlīc; *adj. Not to be taken away*:—Syle mē ðæt unbereáfigendlīc gebæd ðīnre fulfremednysse, Homl. Skt. ii. 23 b, 242.

un-berende; *adj.* I. *not bearing, barren, sterile*:—Elizabeth wæs unberende (-berend, Lind. *sterilis*), Lk. Skt. 1, 7. Unbeorendu (*sterilis*) cende monige, Ps. Surt. ii. p. 186, 17. Ne biþ mid eów nān þing unberendes ne on mannum ne on nȳtenum, Deut. 7, 14. Ðæt unberende treó hē genimes *palmitem non ferentem fructum tollet*, Jn. Skt. Lind. 15, 2 margin. Unbeorende *sterilem*, Ps. Surt. 112, 9. Eádige syndon ða men ða ðe wǣron unberende, Blickl. Homl. 93, 30. Unberende telgan *spadones*, Wrt. Voc. i. 38, 58. II. *unbearable*:—Byrðenna unbærende *onera importabilia*, Mt. Kmbl. Lind. 23, 4. [*Goth.* un-bairands *barren*.]

un-berendlīc; *adj. Unbearable, intolerable*:—On ðam ne eardaþ nān eorðlīc mann for ðam unberendlīcum bryne, Lchdm. iii. 260, 23.

un-berendness, e; *f. Barrenness, sterility*:—Unberendnise *sterilitas*, Rtl. 118, 1. Unbeore[n]dnisse *sterilitatem*, Ps. Surt. 34, 12.

un-besacen; *adj.* I. of persons, *unmolested by litigation*:—Ðǣr se bōnda sæt uncwyd and unbecrafod, sitte ðæt wīf and ða cild on ðam ylcan unbesacen, L. C. S. 73; Th. i. 414, 23. II. of things, *not made the subject of litigation, uncontested*:—Ðæt ðæt land swā unbesæccen gange intō ðære cyrican swā hit ðā on dæg wes ðā hit man him tō lǣt *that the land pass into the possession of the church as uncontested as it was on the day when it was let to him*, Chart. Th. 159, 24. Ðā sealde hē Æþelrige unbesacen land on hand, ðæt hē þanonforð syþþan ðǣron ne sprǣce *he gave the land up to Æþelrige uncontested, so that thenceforth he would not lay claim to it*, 289, 31. Hió ðæt land hæbben unbesacen wið ǣlce hand (*not liable to suits from any side*) ða hwīle ðe hió lifgean, and gif Ælfw̄ leng sió, ðonne sȳ hit hyre unbesacen, Cod. Dip. Kmbl. ii. 150, 22–25: L. C. S. 80; Th. i. 420, 21. Hē him gedō ðone ceáp unbesacene *let him make the chattel secure from being the subject of litigation*, L. In. 53; Th. i. 136, 7 note. v. un-forboden.

un-besceáwod; *adj. Inconsiderate, heedless*:—Se ðe unbesceáwud ys tō specenne hē ongytt yfele *qui inconsideratus est ad loquendum sentiet mala*, Scint. 78, 7. Unbesceawad, Kent. Gl. 433. Unbesceáwode *improvida* vel *inconsiderata*, Wrt. Voc. i. 55, 13.

un-besceáwodlīce; *adv. Inconsiderately, heedlessly*:—God swȳþor tō yrsunge unbesceáwudlīce forþclypian ðænne foresceáwudlīce tō synna forgyfenyssa innlaþian *Deum potius ad iracundiam inconsiderate prouocare quam prouide ad peccaminum ueniam inuitare*, Anglia xiii. 370, 76.

un-bescoren; *adj. Unshorn, without the tonsure*:—Sume sīdfeaxe gāþ, ðæt seó bescorene hālignes ne sȳ weorþre ðenne seó unbescorene, R. Ben. 135, 29.

un-besenged; *adj. Unsinged, unscorched, unburnt*:—Se bið swȳðe clǣne ǣlcere synne, se ðe ðæne bryne ðurhfærð unbesencged (-sænged, MS. C.), Wulfst. 25, 19.

un-beseóndlīc; *adj. Incomprehensible*:—God on ðrymme unbeseóndlīcne (-fōndlīcne?) *Deum majestate incomprehensibilem*, Bd. 3, 22; S. 552, 16.

un-besmiten; *adj. Undefiled, unpolluted, unsullied, pure*:—Unbesmiten weg *impolluta via*, Ps. Spl. 17, 32. Gif heó unbesmiten (*impolluta*) tō him cyrre, L. Ecg. Addit. 12; Th. ii. 234, 6: Nar. 41, 11. Ðæs unbesmitenan līchaman ūres Drihtnes, Homl. Skt. ii. 23 b, 113: Blickl. Homl. 155, 32: 3, 15: Homl. Skt. i. 4, 69: 23 b, 503. Healdaþ eówre handa unbesmitene (*innoxias*), Gen. 37, 22.

un-besorh; *adj. Not the object of care, that one does not care about*:—Ðā hēt se cyning clypian him tō unbesorge men (*men that he didn't care about*), Homl. Th. ii. 486, 9. v. be-sorg.

un-bēted; *adj. For which amends has not been made*:—Nǣnig bihelan mæg on ðam heardan dæge wom unbēted, Exon. Th. 80, 25; Cri. 1312.

un-beþōht; *adj. Unreflecting, inconsiderate*:—Micle hrædlīcor hī wǣren ādwægene ðæra scylda mid ðære hreówsunga, gif hī fǣrlecor syngoden unbeðōhte *citius delicta poenitendo abluerent, si in his sola praecipitatione cecidissent*, Past. 56; Swt. 435, 2.

un-beþirfe. v. un-biþirfe.

un-beweddod; *adj.* I. *unbetrothed*:—Gif hwā līð mid unbeweddudre fǣmnan *si quis dormierit cum virgine necdum desponsata*, Ex. 22, 16. Gif hwā fǣmnan beswīce unbeweddode and hire mid slǣpe, L. Alf. 29; Th. i. 52, 5. Unbeweddod mǣden *puellam virginem, quae non habet sponsum*, Deut. 22, 28. II. *unmarried*:—Unbeweddod *innuba*, Wrt. Voc. i. 52, 35. Mǣden seó ðe unbeweddud ys *uirgo quae innupta est* (1 Cor. 7, 34), Scint. 69, 3. Gif Maria unbeweddod wǣre and cild hæfde, ðonne wolde ðæt folc mid stānum hī oftorfian, Homl. Th. i. 196, 11.

un-bewilled; *adj. Not boiled away*:—Seóþ on wætre ōþ ðæt ðæs wætres sié þridda[n] dǣl unbewelled, Lchdm. ii. 248, 18.

un-biddende; *adj. Not praying, without praying*:—Gif hē nele biddan ðæs ēcan leóhtes, hē sitt ðonne blind be ðam wege unbiddende, Homl. Th. i. 156, 4.

un-bildu(-o); *indecl. f. Want of boldness, weakness, irresolution, inconstancy*:—Sió unbieldo and sió manðwǣrnes bióð swīðe anlīce *weakness and gentleness are very much alike*, Past. 40; Swt. 288, 1. Of ðære leohtmōdnesse cymð sió twiefealdnes and sió unbieldo *inconstantia ex levitate generatur*, 42; Swt. 307, 3. Sió unfæsðrǣdnes and sió unbieldo ðara geðōhta *cogitationum inconstantia*, Swt. 308, 5. Ðonne hié of unwīsdōme oððe of wācmōdnesse and of unbieldo oððe of untrymnesse mōdes oððe līchoman gesyngaþ *cum sola ignorantia vel infirmitate delinquitur*, 21; Swt. 159, 1. Ða lytelmōdan and ða unðrīstan ðonne hié ongietaþ hiera unbældo and hiera unmiehte *pusillanimes dum nimis infirmitatis suae sunt conscii*, 32; Swt. 209, 7.

un-bindan; *p.* -band, *pl.* -bundon; *pp.* -bunden *To unbind, untie*:—Ne eom ic wyrðe ðæt ic unbinde (*soluam*) his sceóþwang, Jn. Skt. 1, 27. 'Æfter his behāte ic ðē unbinde' . . . . Se engel hine ðā unband, Homl. Th. i. 466, 31. Swā hwæt swā ðū unbindst (*solveres*) ofer eorðan, ðæt byð unbunden (*solutum*) on heofonum, Mt. Kmbl. 16, 19: 18, 18. Ðæs fæder tungan his nama unband, Homl. Th. i. 352, 31. Ālēsde ł unband *soluit*, Ps. Lamb. 104, 20. Unband *dissoluit*, Cant. Abac. 6. Hiá onfundun fola gibundenne, and unbundun hine, Mk. Skt. Rush. 11, 4. Sceal se lāreów hine unbindan fram ðam ēcum wīte, swā swā ða apostoli līchamlīce Lazarum ālȳsdon, Homl. Th. i. 234, 14, 9. Ǣr ðon God heó ðæs wræces unbindan wolde, Anglia xi. 2, 24. Æfter þūsend geárum bið Satanas unbunden *post mille annos soluetur Satanas*, Wulfst. 83, 6. Beón unbunden *dissolui* (*a peccato*), Scint. 38, 12. Hī wurdon unbundene, Homl. Th. ii. 20, 8. From synna bendum unbundeno *a peccatorum vinculis absolutos*, Rtl. 7, 13. [Cf. *Goth.* and-bindan: *O. Sax.* ant-bindan: *O. H. Ger.* int-, in-bindan.] v. on-bindan.

un-birnende; *adj. Without burning, without being on fire*, Beo. Th. 5089; B. 2548.

un-bisc[e]opod; *adj. Unconfirmed*:—Wē lǽraþ . . . ðæt ǽlc cild sȳ gefullod binnon .xxxvii. nihtum, and ðæt ǽnig man tō lange unbiscopod ne wurðe, L. Edg. C. 15; Th. ii. 246, 28. Unbiscpod (-biscopod, MSS. C. E.), Wulfst. 120, 15. Wē secgaþ eów, ðæt ǽlc cild sceall beón binnon þryttigum nihtum gefullod . . . Ne nǽnne man man ne lǽte unbisceopod tō lange . . . And witan ða ðe cildes onfōn æt fulluhte oððe æt bisceopes handum, ðæt hī hit on rihtum geleáfan gebringan, 300, 16–30. [Longe beon unbishoped, A. R. 204, 29.]

un-biþirfe; *adj. Useless, vain, unprofitable*:—Ðū hafast unbiþyrfe ofer witena dōm wīsan gefongen *you have taken an unprofitable course contrary to the judgement of wise men*, Exon. Th. 248, 18; Jul. 97. Ða (*false gods*) sind geásne gōda gehwylces, īdle, orfeorme, unbiþyrfe, ne ðǽr freme mēteþ fira ǽnig, 255, 21; Jul. 217. [*O. Sax.* un-bitherbi: *O. H. Ger.* un-biderbi *inutilis, vanus, inanis.*]

un-blanden; *adj. Unmixed*:—Unblonden *non mixtum*, Rtl. 68, 30.

un-bleoh; *adj. Not coloured, clear, bright, splendid*:—Is mīn land foremǽre and mē swȳðe unbleó *haereditas mea praeclara est mihi*, Ps. Th. 15, 6. Hwæt mæg beón heardes hēr on līfe wið ðam ðū mōte gemang ðam werode eardian unbleoh on ēcnesse (*but there is no corresponding word in the Latin, which is:* Quid durum saeclo consetur in isto, utque illas inter liceat habitare cohortes?), Dōm. L. 302. Cf. ungebleoh.

un-bletsung, e; *f. Cursing*:—Fela is ðæra ðe . . . . embe bletsunga oððe unbletsunga leohtlīce lǽtaþ, and nā understandaþ . . . 'Quodcumque benedixeritis et cetera,' L. I. P. 6; Th. ii. 310, 36.

un-blinnendlīce; *adv. Incessantly*:—Unblinnendlīce dōn wæs *incessabiliter acta est*, Bd. 1, 6; S. 476, 26.

un-bliss, e; *f. Unhappiness, grief, sorrow, misery*:—Mycel is mē unbliss mīnra dȳrlinga miss, Homl. Skt. i. 23, 271. Nū wē beóð blīðe, and eft on micelre unblisse, Homl. Th. i. 184, 3. Manege unblissa and micele sorga becōmon ðām Iudēiscum æfter Cristes slege, Homl. Ass. 79, 179.

un-blīðe; *adj.* I. *sad, sorrowful, grieved*:—Unblīðe *tristis*, Mt. Kmbl. Rush. 19, 22: Beo. Th. 261; B. 130. Giómormōd, unblīðe, 4529; B. 2268. Wæs hē swȳðe unblīðe . . . Ðā geseah Gūðlāc ðone brōþor sārig, Guthl. 9; Gdwin. 50, 6. Beón in unblīðum mōde *moestus esse*, Mt. Kmbl. Rush. 26, 37. Ðām unblīðum (*tristibus*) sint tō cȳðanne ða gefeán ðe him gehātene sindon . . . Gehiéren ða unblīðan (*tristes*) ða leán ðæs gefeán ðe hié tō hopiaþ . . . Monige beóð ðeáh blīðe and eác unblīðe (*laeti vel tristes*) for ðæs blōdes styringe, Past. 27; Swt. 187, 16–24: 61; Swt. 455, 10. Hū blinde hī (*the envious*) beóð, ðonne hī beóð unrōte for ōðerra monna gōdan weorcum and for hira ryhtum gefeán beóð unblīðe *quantae caecitatis sint qui alieno provectu deficiunt, aliena exultatione contabescunt*, 34; Swt. 231, 17. Hȳ āswindaþ *vel* heó beóþ unblīþe *contabescunt*, i. *exsiccant*, Wrt. Voc. ii. 134, 74. Weorod eall ārās, eodon unblīðe, weóllon teáras, Beo. Th. 6054; B. 3031: Cd. Th. 223, 29; Dan. 127. Gemynd hē ða ungelimp ðe hē hæfde on his wrecsīðe and ne byð þeáh nā ðe unblīðre (*not less glad*), Shrn. 204, 11. Ðonne hwylcum men gelimpeþ ðe his leóf fæder gefærþ, ne mæg ðæt nā beón ðæt ða bearn ðe unblīðran ne sȳn *it cannot be that the children are not the sadder*, Blickl. Homl. 131, 25. II. *unkind, shewing ill-will* or *displeasure, stern, angry*:—Gif ēgo ðīn unblīðe sē *si oculus tuus nequam fuerit*, Mt. Kmbl. 6, 23. Ðā wearð unblīðe Abrahames cwēn hire worcþeówe, wrāð on mōde, heard and hrēðe, Cd. Th. 136, 16; Gen 2259. Him unblīðe andswarode wulfheort cyning, 224, 10; Dan. 134. III. *unquiet, not peaceful*:—Giðreáð ðe unblīðo *corripite inquietos*, Rtl. 11, 37. [*O. H. Ger.* un-blīdi *tristis.*]

un-blīðemōde; *adj. Sadhearted, sorrowful*:—Unblīðemoede *moestus*, Mt. Kmbl. Lind. 26, 37.

un-blōdig; *adj. Bloodless*:—On unblōdium gefeohte *incruento prelio*, Germ. 395, 16.

un-boht *unbought, free*:—Unboht ł unceáped *gratis*, Mt. Kmbl. Lind. 10, 8. Sacleás ł unsynnig ł unbocht *gratis*, Jn. Skt. Lind. 15, 25.

un-boren; *adj. Unborn*:—Se ðe unborenum cildum līf sylð, Homl. Skt. i. 23, 429. Ða unborenan bearn, Past. 48; Swt. 367, 20. [*Goth.* un-baurans.]

un-brād; *adj. Not broad, narrow*:—Eall swā brād seó sunne is swā eall eorðan ymbhwyrft, ac heó þingð ūs swȳðe unbrād, Lchdm. iii. 236, 8. Se unbrāda þistel *scolimbos*, Wrt. Voc. i. 69, 12. On brǽde, ðār hit brādest is, fīf geurda, and ðǽr hit unbrādost is, ānne geurde, Chart. Th. 156, 29. Ðǽr ðæt land unbrādest is, ðēr hit sceol beón eahtatȳne fōta brād, 236, 8.

un-brǽce; *adj. Unbreakable, indestructible*:—Flint unbrǽcne, Exon. Th. 1, 11; Cri. 6. Tīr unbrǽcne, Apstls. Kmbl. 172; Ap. 86.

un-brice, un-briéce. v. un-bryce, un-brȳce.

un-brocheard; *adj. Tender, delicate*:—Unbrocheard *vel* sēfta *delicatus*, i. *tenerus*, Wrt. Voc. ii. 138, 39. Hwī ne miht ðū ongitan, ðætte ǽlc wuht cwices biþ innanweard hnescost and unbrocheardost *quid, quod mollissimum quodque, sicuti medulla est, interiore semper sede reconditur?* Bt. 34, 10; Fox 150, 6.

un-brosnigendlīc; *adj. Incorruptible, imperishable*:—His līchama wæs grāpigendlīc, and ðeáhhwæðere unbrosnigendlīc; hē æteówde hine grāpigendlīcne and unbrosnigendlīcne, Homl. Th. i. 230, 26: 300, 10: Homl. Skt. ii. 27, 146. Ðū unscrȳddest ðē ðone brosnigendlīcan mann and ðē gescrȳddest ðone unbrosnigendlīcan mann, 30, 114: Homl. Ass. 45, 521. On ðam gemǽnelīcum ǽriste beóð ūre līchaman geedcennede tō unbrosnigendlīcum līchaman, Homl. Th. i. 394, 33.

un-brosnung, e; *f. Incorruption*:—Beóð ūre līchaman geedcynnede tō unbrosnunge, ðæt is tō ēcum ðingum, Homl. Th. i. 394, 27. Āwende fram brosnunge tō unbrosnunge, ii. 206, 2.

un-bryce; *adj. Unbroken, inviolate, uninjured*:—Hwæþre his meahta spēd hālig wunade, dōm unbryce, þeáh hē deáþes cwealm ræfnan sceolde, Exon. Th. 240, 21; Ph. 642. Hyre wæs mægen unbrice, 256, 22; Jul. 235.

un-brȳce; *adj.* (or *subst.?*) *Useless, unprofitable*:—Unbrȳce, unbrȳce, unbrycci *incommodum*, Txts. 69, 1050. Unbriéce *incommodum, inutile*, Wrt. Voc. ii. 44, 76. Nyle hē ða dærstan him dōn unbrȳce *faex ejus non est exinanita*, Ps. Th. 74, 8. [But calleth hym yn the gospel ryche, As unkynde and unbryche, Halliwell's Dict. *Goth.* unbrūkjai skalkōs *servi inutiles*, Lk. 17, 10.] Cf. un-behēfe.

un-brȳde. v. next word.

un-brygd (?), es; *m. A not unfair turn, fair dealing* (?):—Swā ic hit hæbbe, swā hit se sealde, ðe tō syllanne āhte, unbrȳde and unforboden, and ic hit āgnian wille tō ǽgenre ǽhte *so I have it, as he gave it, who had the right to give, without fraud and unforbidden, and I mean to possess it as my own property*, L. O. 13; Th. i. 184, 4. Cf. brægd, brygd (bryd). *Or, perhaps,* unbrȳde = un-brigde *without liability to be reclaimed;* cf. *Icel.* brigð *a right to reclaim*, chiefly of landed property.

un-bunden; *adj. Not bound*:—Nelle ic (*a bow*) unbunden ǽnigum hȳran nymþe searosǽled, Exon. Th. 406, 10; Rä. 24, 15. Gif hē hine bescire unbundenne . . . Gif hē hine gebinde and ðonne bescire, L. Alf. pol. 35; Th. i. 84, 7.

un-burh (?). v. un-bȳing.

un-bȳed; *adj. Uninhabited, desert*:—Unbȳed is styd *disertus est locus*, Mk. Skt. Lind. Rush. 6, 35. Wēstig ł unbȳed *deserta*, Mt. Kmbl. Lind. 23, 38. In unbȳedum londæ *in deserto*, p. 9, 14.

un-bȳing (?) *a solitude*:—Unbyergo (-bȳengo? *or* -byrego, *from* -burh? Cf. un-lond) *solitudines*, Rtl. 1, 17.

un-byrged; *adj. Unburied*:—Se cāsere bebeád ðæt hine man forlēte unbyrgedne, Shrn. 57, 1.

unc; *dat.*: unc, uncet (-it), *acc.*: uncer; *gen. Us two, me and thee, me and him.* (1) *alone*:—'Hwæt wylle gyt ðæt ic inc dō?' Ðā cwǽdon hī: 'Syle unc ðæt wit sitton, ān on ðīne swȳðran healfe and ōþer on ðīne wynstran,' Mk. Skt. 10, 37. Hē sǽde unc eall, Gen. 41, 13. Ðū mē behēte hāl ðæt ðæt ðū mē sealdest, on ða gewitnesse ðe unc ðā mid wæs, L. O. 7; Th. i. 180, 24. Unc is his hyldo þearf, Cd. Th. 41, 30; Gen. 664. Æfter ðon ðe wit nū betweoh unc tōgongenne beóþ, ne geseó wit unc ofer ðæt in ðysse weorulde, Bd. 4, 19; S. 607, 20. Beforan ungc, 5, 12; S. 628, 15. Mid ðȳ ic unc wēnde ingangende beón, S. 629, 39. Wit unc werian þōhton, Beo. Th. 1085; B. 540. Gif hē forhigeþ uncet fyrenfulle, Shrn. 42, 27. Ðā sende hē uncerne efenþeówan mid unc, ðæt hē uncet sceolde ūt ālǽdan . . . ðā ne mihte hē unc gesión, 43, 1–5. Sege mīnum brēðer ðæt hē dǽle uncer ǽhta wið mē, Lk. Skt. 12, 13. Wit be uncer ǽrdǽdum onfōð, 23, 41. Ðū hæfst yfele gemearcod uncer sylfra sīð, Cd. Th. 49, 14; Gen. 792. Mid uncer āgene swurde, Shrn. 39, 35. Wit gerehton bi ealre uncer fōre, 43, 34. Uncer lāþette ǽgðer ōðer, 39, 22. Ne nǽfre uncer āwþer his ellen cȳðde, Exon. Th. 496, 29; Rä. 85, 22. (2) *with numeral forms*:—Ic wið ðē sceolde for unc ānum twām ǽrendsprǽce ābeódan, Exon. Th. 472, 12; Rä. 61, 15. Unc mǽran twām, 496, 6; Rä. 85, 10. Bismærædu ugket men bā ætgadre, Txts. 126, 8. Hwæðer uncer twēga, Beo. Th. 5057; B. 2532: Cd. Th. 110, 9; Gen. 1835. Ic rǽd sprece bēgra uncer, 115, 4; Gen. 1914. (3) with the name of the person who is associated with the speaker:—Sceolde unc Adame (*for me and Adam*) yfele gewurðan ymb ðæt heofonrīce, Cd. Th. 25, 1; Gen. 387. Is ðæt land healf ðæs einges, healf uncer Brentinges, Cod. Dip. Kmbl. iii. 422, 11. Uncer Grendles *of me and Grendel*, Beo. Th. 4009; B. 2002. [*Laym. Marh. Gen. and Ex.* unc: *Orm.* unnc baþe: *Kath.* bituhten unc tweien (us twa, *v. r.*): *Laym. O. and N.* hwaðer unker. *Goth.* ugkis; *dat.*; ugkis, ugk; *acc.*; ugkara; *gen.*: *O. Sax.* unk; *dat. acc.*; unkerō; *gen.*: *O. H. Ger.* unker (zweio); *gen.*: *Icel.* okkr; *dat. acc.*; okkar; *gen.*] v. wit, uncer.

un-cáfscipe, es; *m. Inactivity, sluggishness*; ignavia:—Ðā fēng Nero tō rīce; se æt nēxtan forlēt Brytene īgland for his uncáfscipe (cf. se nāht freomlīces ongan on ðære cynewīsan, ac . . . hē Breotona rīce forlēt *nihil omnino in re militari ausus est . . . Brittaniam pene amisit*, Bd. 1, 3; S. 475, 20), Chr. 47; Erl. 7, 26.

un-camprōf; *adj. Unwarlike, not bold in battle*:—Uncamprōfes *in-bellis*, Germ. 399, 420.

un-capitulod; *adj. Not provided with titles to the several sections*:—Hyt is tō witanne hwī ðeós feórþe bōc sig uncapitulod nū þa ǽrran bēc synt gecapitulode *sciendum est, quare liber hic quartus sit sine capitulis, cum priores libri capitulis instructi sint* (v. pp. 170, 180, 194, where the titles to the sections of bks. I, II, III are given), L. Ecg. P. iv; Th. ii. 204, 1.

un-ceáped. v. un-boht, *and* cf. un-cīpe.

un-ceápunga; *adv. Without payment* or *recompense*; gratis:—Nō ic wið feohsceattum ofer folc bere Drihtnes dōmas, ac ðē unceápunga orlæg secge, Cd. Th. 262, 18; Dan. 746.

un-ceás, -ceást, es (*but* ceás *and* ceást *are both fem.*) *Absence of quarrel, inhostility*:—Se ðe þeóf slihð hē mōt āðe gecȳðan ðæt hē hine fleóndne for þeóf slōge, and ðæs deádan mǽgas him swerian unceáses (-ceástes, MS. H.) āð *the kinsmen of the dead man shall swear to the slayer an oath that they will have no quarrel with him*, L. M. 35; Th. i. 124, 8. Cf. the similar phrase in reference to the seizing of a thief: Ða mǽgas him (*the captor*) swerian āðas unfǽhða, 28; Th. i. 120, 6.

un-cenned; *adj. Not begotten*:—Wuldor Fæder ðam uncænnedan *gloria Patri ingenito*, Hymn. Surt. 120, 13.

uncer; *pron. poss. Of us two, our* (of two persons):—Uncer hlāford hióld hiora olfendu and ābād uncres tōcymes . . . wit gesēgon ðæt uncer efenþeów wæs forworden . . . and se uncer hlāford ābād uncres tōcymes . . . sió lió forswealh uncerne hlāford . . . Wit geseágon uncre feónd forwordene, Shrn. 43, 2–21. Uncres gewinnes, Exon. Th. 254, 1; Jul. 190. Of uncrum wege, Bt. 40, 5; Fox 240, 18. Of uncrum feó, Bd. 3, 14; S. 540, 8. Uncerne hwelp, Exon. Th. 380, 31; Rä. 1, 16. Crist wāt uncre clǽnnysse, Shrn. 40, 20: 42, 3: Cd. Th. 139, 4; Gen. 2304. Uncre eágan, Mt. Kmbl. 20, 33: Homl. Skt. ii. 30, 374. Mid uncrum fōtum, Shrn. 42, 1: Gen. 31, 16. For uncera sāule, Cod. Dip. Kmbl. iii. 304, 33. [*O. Sax.* unka: *Icel.* okkarr.]

uncet. v. unc.

un-cīpe; *adj. Given without payment, gratuitous*:—Sió uncȳpe *gratuita* (*Dei gratia*, Ald. 78), Wrt. Voc. ii. 88, 9. [Cf. *Icel.* ū-keypis *gratuitously.*] v. un-ceáped.

un-clǽmod; *adj. Rough-cast, unsmoothed*:—Unclǽmodum *impolitis*, Germ. 398, 258.

un-clǽne; *adj.* I. in a physical sense, *unclean, foul, filthy.* v. un-clǽnness, clǽne. I a. as applied to animals or things, *unclean, not fit for food*:—Seó ǽ monig ðing bewereþ tō etanne swā swā unclǽne (*inmunda*), Bd. 1, 27; S. 494, 33. Hwæt gif hit unclǽne (*immundi*) beóþ fixas? Ic wyrpe ða unclǽnan ūt, and genime mē clǽne tō mete, Coll. Monast. Th. 23, 15. Ða ōðre synd unclǽne (*polluta*), Lev. 11, 12. Be swȳnum and be ōðrum unclǽnum nȳtenum *de porcis et de aliis impuris animalibus*, L. Ecg. C. 40, tit.; Th. ii. 130, 31. II. in a moral sense, *unclean, impure*:—Unclǽne *incestus* vel *impurus*, Wrt. Voc. i. 50, 13: *incestus*, 51, 35: 72, 13. Se unclǽna (*inmundus*) gāst, Mk. 1, 26. Woruldmonna seó unclǽne gecynd, Exon. Th. 63, 9; Cri. 1017. Besmitene mid ðem unclǽnan firenluste, Blickl. Homl. 25, 8. Wæs sum man unclǽne (*inmundum*) deófol hæbbende, Lk. Skt. 4, 33. Unclǽne ingeþoncas, Exon. Th. 80, 33; Cri. 1316. Unclǽnra *inpudicarum*, Wrt. Voc. ii. 45, 14.

un-clǽnlic; *adj. Uncleanly, impure*:—Cunnunga ða unclǽnlīco gifliǽ *contactus inlicitorum fugat*, Rtl. 110, 1.

un-clǽnlīce; *adv. Impurely*:—Swā hwilc man swā Godes weorc clǽnlīce wirceþ, hē bið ēcelīce gehealden. Se ðe hit unclǽnlīce wyrceþ, hē bið āwyrged intō helle, Homl. Ass. 168, 121. Wē wilniaþ mid ūrum hlāforde clǽnlīce sweltan, swīðor ðonne unclǽnlīce mid eów lybban, Homl. Th. i. 432, 26.

un-clǽnness, e; *f.* I. in a physical sense, *uncleanness, impurity, foulness, squalor*:—Suǽ huæd in hūsum ðās ȳð eft āstrægde beuærle unclǽnnisse *quicquid in domibus haec unda resperserit careat inmunditia*, Rtl. 121, 36. Fūle unclǽnnessa *olidos* (*ergastulorum*) *squalores*, Hpt. Gl. 509, 75. II. in a moral sense, *uncleanness, impurity, obscenity*:—Lāð unclǽnnys *detestanda obscenitas*, Hpt. Gl. 506, 74. Se reccere sceal beón simle clǽne on his geðōhte, ðætte nān unclǽnnes (*immunditia*) hine ne besmīte, Past. 13; S. 75, 20: Rtl. 97, 29. Wrǽnre unclǽnnysse *lascivae obscenitatis*, Hpt. Gl. 505, 38. Hwā unclǽnnisse līf ālifde, Exon. Th. 448, 31; Dōm. 62. Unclǽnnysse *spurcitia*, Hpt. Gl. 439, 8.

un-clǽnsian; *p.* ode *To defile, pollute*:—Unwyrtrumias ł unclǽnsias *eradicetis*, Mt. Kmbl. Lind. 13, 29. Unclaensia *inquinare*, p, 17, 12. v. ge-unclǽnsian, *and next word.*

un-clǽnsod; *adj. Not purified*:—Ðȳ læs ǽnig unclǽnsod dorste on swā micelne hāligdōm fōn ðære clǽnan ðegnenga ðæs sacerdhādes *ne non purgatus adire quisque sacra ministeria audeat*, Past. 7; Swt. 51, 1. v. un-geclǽnsod.

un-clǽnu(-o); *f. Uncleanness, impurity*:—Fulle sint unclǽno *pleni sunt inmunditia*, Mt. Kmbl. Lind. 23, 25. Fulla sint all ł ēghuelc unclǽnæ *plena sunt omni spurcitia*, 27.

un-cnyttan; *p.* te *To unknot, untie*:—Ðæs ne eom ic wyrðe ðæt ic his sceóna þwanga būgende uncnytte *cujus non sum dignus procumbens soluere corrigiam calciamentorum eius*, Mk. Skt. 1, 7: Lk. 3, 16. (Wǽron) uncnytte (*vinculorum ligamina*) *enodarentur, solverentur*, Hpt. Gl. 482, 59.

un-coðu, e; *f.*: -coða, an; *m. Disease*:—Ūs stalu and cwalu, stric and steorfa, orfcwealm and uncoða (*murrain and disease*) derede swȳðe þearle, Wulfst. 159, 10. Gē gehwilce uncoðe gehǽldon, Homl. Th. i. 64, 23. Hē mid īsene ðone uncoðan (ða uncoðe, *v. rr.*) āceorfe, R. Ben. 52, 19. Orfcwealm oþðon mancwealm þurh fǽrlīce uncoða, Wulfst. 170, 2.

un-cræft, es; *m. An evil art, ill practice*:—Gif hē þurh gedrinc oððe þurh ōðerne uncræft man ācwelle *si ex ebrietate vel alia prava arte hominem occiderit*, L. Ecg. P. iv. 68, 22; Th. ii. 230, 28. Gyf hit geweorðe ðæt man mid tyhtlan and mid uncræftum sacerd belecge, L. C. E. 5; Th. i. 362, 8. Utan sume getrȳwða habban ūs betweónan būtan uncræftan, Wulfst. 167, 5.

un-cræftig; *adj. Powerless*:—Se earma flȳhð uncræftiga slǽp sleác mid sluman slincan on hinder *somnus iners torporque gravis, desidia pigra cessabunt*, Dōm. L. 239.

un-crafod; *adj. With no claim made upon one*:—Se ðe sitte uncrafod on his āre on līfe, ðæt nān man on his yrfenuman ne sprece æfter his dæge *he that dwells on his property without any claims being made on him in his lifetime, that no man shall bring an action against his heir after his death*, L. Eth. iii. 14; Th. i. 298, 9. v. un-becrafod.

un-cristen; *adj. Not Christian*:—Ðeáh ðe hī ðāgyta uncristene wǽron *thought they were not yet Christians*, Bd. 4, 16; S. 584, 9 note.

un-cumlīðe; *adj. Inhospitable*:—Se Hǽlend spræc tō sumum weligum men, ðe . . . him wæs lāð þearfendum mannum mete tō syllenne, and hē wæs uncumlīðe, Wulfst. 257, 14.

un-cūþ; *adj. Unknown*; incognitus, Ælfc. Gr. 33; Zup. 205, 10. I. *unknown, strange*:—Wæs Breotone eálond Rōmānum uncūþ (*incognita*), Bd. 1, 2; S. 475, 3: Beo. Th. 4434; B. 2214. Gif men uncūð swyle on gesitte, Lchdm. i. 194, 27. Ðæt wǽre gelæht ān uncūð geong man, Homl. Skt. i. 23, 613: Ors. 6, 31; Swt. 286, 22. Heó on wēstenne gewunade eallum monnum uncūð, Shrn. 107, 24. Mon uncūþes andwlitan and uncūþes gegyrlan *hominem vultus habitusque incogniti*, Bd. 2, 12; S. 513, 35. Firum uncūþ, hwī . . ., Met. 4, 39. Word āres uncūþes, Exon. Th. 175, 5; Gū. 1190. Nis ðæs nān tweó. Ac ic wolde nū ðæt ðū mē sǽdest hwæthwegu uncūþes, Bt. 34, 6; Fox 142, 24: Beo. Th. 1757; B. 876. Ne fyligeaþ hig uncūþum (*alienum*), for ðam ðe hig ne gecneówun uncūðra (*alienorum*) stefne, Jn. Skt. 10, 5. Uncūðum gode *deo ignoto*, Homl. Skt. ii. 29, 23. Be uncūðum yrfe (cf. ignotum pecus, L. Edm. C. 5; Th. i. 253, 7), L. Edg. H. 4; Th. i. 258, 21. Ðā ālēde ic mīnne kynegyrylan and mē mid uncūþe hrægle gegerede (*I went incognito*), Nar. 18, 2. Hwā gifþ ðam uncūðan līfes fultum, Ap. Th. 11, 15. Gehȳrde hē ōðerne sang swilce uncūðne, Homl. Th. ii. 334, 16. Uncūðne weg, Met. 13, 58: Cd. Th. 181, 9; Exod. 58: Beo. Th. 2825; B. 1410. Drihten sent uncūðe þeóde ofer eów ða ðe gē ne cunnon *ducet te Dominus in gentem, quam ignoras*, Deut. 28, 36. Geopenigean uncūðe wyrd, hwǽr hē ðara nægla wēnan þorfte, Elen. Kmbl. 2202; El. 1102. Nime man uncūþ sǽd æt ælmesmannum, Lchdm. i. 400, 17. Uncūð ādle *pestilentiae*, Mt. Kmbl. Lind. 24, 7. Cf. Se hwīta stān mæg wið eallum uncūþum (*unknown, and so caused by witchcraft?*) brocum, Lchdm. ii. 290, 11. Ðǽr him folcweras fremde wǽron, wine uncūðe, Cd. Th. 110, 32; Gen. 1847. Ðæm folce seldsiéne and uncūðe wǽron wīnes dryncas, Ors. 2, 4; Swt. 76, 12. Mīnra firena ðe mē uncūðe wǽron *delicta ignorantiae meae*, Ps. Ben. 24, 6. Ðās ðē sint unncūðo *haec ignoras*, Jn. Skt. Lind. 3, 10. Hié uncūðra ǽngum ne willaþ feóres geunnan *they will grant no stranger life*, Andr. Kmbl. 355; An. 178: Cd. Th. 163, 14; Gen. 2698. Se ūtancumena munuc ðe of uncūðum eardum cymð *si quis monachus peregrinus de longinquis provinciis supervenerit*, R. Ben. 109, 4. Gif wē scomiaþ ðæt wē tō uncūðum monnum (*men we do not know*) suelc sprecen, Past. 10; Swt. 63, 6. Oft ic nū miscyrre cūðe sprǽce, and þeáh uncūðre ǽrhwīlum fond, Met. 2, 9. II. *unknown, not understood*:—God sealde heora ǽlcum synderlīce sprǽce, ðæt heora ǽlcum wæs uncūð, hwæt ōðer sǽde, Ælfc. T. Grn. 4, 11. III. *unknown, uncertain*:—Ðære tīde ðe ūs uncūþ is *ejus quod nobis incertum est temporis*, Bd. 2, 13; S. 516, 15. Heora sylfra forþfōre ðære tīd[e] is uncūþ *suum exitum, cujus hora incerta est*, 4, 3; S. 568, 21: Blickl. Homl. 125, 7. Ūs is swīþe uncūþ hwæt ūre yrfeweardas getreówlīces dōn willon, 51, 35: 119, 7. Clypiaþ gyt hlūdor uncūð þeáh ðe hē slǽpe (*cry aloud . . . peradventure he sleepeth*, 1 Kings 18, 27), Homl. Skt. i. 18, 119. Monig biþ uncūþ treówgeþofta teoraþ hwīlum wāciaþ wordbeót *many a thing is uncertain, trusty comrade sometimes fails, weak prove words of promise*, Exon. Th. 469, 19; Hy. 11, 4. Fægere word ðis synd ðe gē brōhton, ac hī nīwe syndon and uncūþe *pulchra sunt verba quae adfertis, sed nova sunt et incerta*, Bd. 1, 25; S. 487, 10. Ðonne cuman fǽrlīce on uncūðum tīdum tō mynstre cumaþ *incertis horis supervenientes hospites*, R. Ben. 85, 9. IV. *ungentle, unkind, hostile, harsh, unfriendly.* v. un-cūþlīce:—Brōga cwom egeslīc and uncūð, ealdfeónda nīð, Exon. Th. 110, 23; Gū. 112. Mōna se ehtoða . . . cild âcenned uncúð (*unfriendly?*), strang, Lchdm. iii. 188, 3. Wê genêðdon eafoð uncûþes (*Grendel*); ûþe ic swîþor, ðæt ðû hine selfne geseón môste, feónd fylwêrigne, Beo. Th. 1924; B. 960. Sceaþa eáweþ uncûðne nîð, 558; B. 276. Mec ongon hreówan ðæt mîn hondgeweorc on feónda geweald fêran sceolde, sceolde uncûðne eard cunnian, sâre sîþas, Exon. Th. 86, 34; Cri. 1418. [*Goth.* un-kunþs *ignotus*: *O. H. Ger.* un-kund *ignotus, incognitus, peregrinus, agrestis, incertus*: *Icel.* û-kunnr *unknown.*]

un-cûþlic; *adj. Unknown, strange, uncanny*:—Ða stânas sint ealle swîðe gôde of tô drincanne wiþ ealle uncûþlîcu þing, Lchdm. ii. 290, 14.

un-cûþlîce; *adv. Unkindly*:—Ðam elþeódigan and ûtancumenan ne lǽt ðû nô uncûðlîce wið hine ne mid nânum unrihtum ðû hine ne drecce (*peregrino molestus non eris*, Ex. 23, 9), L. Alf. 47; Th. i. 54, 21. [He spacc till hiss moder þuss unncuþliȝ (v. Jn. 2, 4), Orm. 14341. *Icel.* û-kunnliga *like a stranger.*] v. un-cûþ, IV.

un-cwaciende; *adj. Without shaking* or *tottering*:—Ða ðe ne magon uncwaciende gestondan on emnum felda *qui in planis stantes titubant*, Past. 4; Swt. 41, 7.

un-cweden; *adj. Unsaid, revoked*:—Uncwedene yrfebêc *ruptum testamentum*, Wrt. Voc. i. 20, 42.

un-cweþende; *adj.* I. *not having speech*:—Ðeáh ðe gesomnod sý eal ðætte heofon oððe hel oððe eorðe ǽfre âcende, and ânra gehwylc ge ðæra cweðendra ge ðæra uncweðendra hæbbe gyldene býman on mûðe, Salm. Kmbl. p. 152, 9. II. *not having a voice, inanimate*:—Hweþer ðû ongite ðæt ða uncweþendan gesceafta wilnodon tô biónne on êcnesse swâ ilce swâ men gif hî mihton *ea quae inanimata esse creduntur, nonne quod suum est quaeque simili ratione desiderant?* Bt. 34, 11; Fox 150, 17. [Cf. Waldandes dôð unqueðandes sô filo antkennian scolda . . . erða . . . bergôs . . . stênôs, Hêl. 5663.]

un-cwid[d]; *adj. Undisturbed by charges, in undisputed possession*:—Se ðe sitte uncwýdd and uncrafod on his âre on lîfe, L. Eth. iii. 15; Th. i. 298, 9. Ðǽr se bônda sæt uncwýd (-cwýdd, MS. G.) and unbecrafod (cf. ubi bunda manserit sine calumpnia, L. H. I. 14, 5; Th. i. 526, 3), L. C. S. 72; Th. i. 414, 22. [Cf. *Icel.* û-kvíðinn *unconcerned.*] v. cwiðan.

un-cwisse; *adj. Speechless*:—Ðære tungan onstyrenesse beswicade (*linguae motu caruit*). Ðâ wǽron ðrý dagas and ðreó niht fulle ðæt heó wæs uncwisse, Bd. 4, 9; S. 577, 18.

un-cyme; *adj. Mean, paltry, poor*:—On uncymre byrigenne geseted *ignobili traditus sepulturae*, Bd. 1, 33; S. 499, 7. Wæs his æþeleste ræst on nacodre eorðan. Ðâ bǽdon hine his discipulos ðæt hié môstan hûru sume uncyme streównesse him under gedôn for his untrumnesse, Blickl. Homl. 227, 12. Ne hæfde wit monig ôðer uncymran hors *nunquid non habuimus equos viliores plurimos?* Bd. 3, 14; S. 540, 26.

un-cynde; *adj. Unnatural*:—Nim swâ wuda swâ wyrt of ðære stôwe ðe his eard and æþelo biþ on tô weaxanne and sette on uncynde stôwe him, ðonne ne gegrêwþ hit ðǽr nâuht, Bt. 34, 10; Fox 148, 27. v. ungecynde.

un-cynlîc; *adj. Unsuitable, improper*:—Ðæt wǽre uncynlîcre, gif God næfde on eallum his rîce nâne frige gesceaft, Bt. 41, 2; Fox 244, 28 note.

un-cyn[n]; *adj. Unsuitable, unfitting, improper*:—Ðæm ne is uncynn mæht bið sald *cui non inmerito potestas datur*, Lk. Skt. p. 3, 3.

un-cýpe. v. un-cîpe.

un-cyst, e; -cyste, an; *f. A vice, defect, fault.* I. of the body, *a disorder*:—Wið wîfa earfoðnyssum; ðâs uncyste Grêcas hâtaþ hystem cepnizam, Lchdm. i. 334, 18. Tô eallum uncystum ðe on gômum beóð âcenned, 348, 12. II. of diction, *a fault, solecism*:—Ðære uncyste *sylocismi, laudacismi*, ða uncyste *barbarismi* (the passage is: Inter Scillam soloecismi et barbarismi baratrum . . . scopulosas lautacismi collisiones, Ald. 80), Wrt. Voc. ii. 88, 27–33: 52, 49. III. of morals, *a vice, fault*:—Ðæt on ûs ne sý gemêted nǽnigu stôw ǽmetig gâstlîcra mægena, ðæt ðǽr mæge yfelu uncyst on eardian, Blickl. Homl. 37, 10. Ðeós deáþberende uncyst (*envy*), 65, 13. Hê bær ða wǽtan ðære uncystan (-cyste, Bd. M. 82, 13) in ðam telgan *portat in ramo humorem vitii*, Bd. 1, 27; S. 495, 26. Ða uncyste ðære ânwielnesse *vitio obstinationis*, Past. 6; Swt. 47, 16. Gif ðû nân gôd dôn nelt Gode tô wurðmynte, ðonne geswutelast ðû mid ðære uncyste ðîne yfelnysse, Homl. Th. i. 142, 2. Fýr ǽleþ uncyste, Exon. Th. 233, 17; Ph. 526: 81, 27; Cri. 1330. Gif hwylce uncysta on biscopum gemêtte sýn *si qua sunt in episcopis vitia*, Bd. 1, 27; S. 492, 17. Ða unsýfernysse uncysta *rudera vitiorum*, 4, 3; S. 569, 32: 1, 27; S. 495, 32. Uncysta *passionum*, Wrt. Voc. ii. 77, 33. Ða men ðe ðyssum uncystum (*covetousness, envy, lust*) fylgaþ, Blickl. Homl. 25, 9. Hwâ ongyt his uncysta *delicta quis intelligit?* Ps. Th. 18, 11. Sume wealdaþ ealle uncysta and leahtras on him sylfum, Homl. Th. i. 344, 35. III a. *the vice of avarice, niggardliness, parsimony, want of liberality.* v. un-cystig:—Ðises mannes (*the rich man who gave nothing to Lazarus*) uncyst and upâhefednys hine besencte on cwicsûsle, Homl. Th. i. 328, 22. Spærnesse ł uncyste *frugalitatis*, Hpt. Gl. 425, 66. Ne hê uncysta nâ begange *nec avaritie studeat*, R. Ben. 55, 3. [*O. H. Ger.* un-kust *vitium, scelus, dolus.* Cf. *Icel.* û-kostr *a fault.*]

un-cystig; *adj. Niggardly, parsimonious, not liberal*:—Uncystig *frugus*, Wrt. Voc. ii. 109, 18: 36, 5: *frugi* vel *parcus*, i. 47, 37: *parcus*, Ælfc. Gr. 28, 7; Zup. 180, 13. Uncystig oððe spærhynde *frugi*, 9, 78; Zup. 74, 12. Fæsthafol oððe uncystig *tenax*, Wrt. Voc. i. 76, 5. Ne sǽde ðæt hâlige godspel (Lk. c. 16) ðæt se rîca reáfere wǽre, ac wæs uncystig and môdegode on his welum, Homl. Th. i. 328, 19. 'Gê noldon him on mînum naman tîðian' . . . Ðonne faraþ ða uncystigan intô êcere cwicsûsle, ii. 108, 30: Wulfst. 289, 8. Ða uncystgan hê cysta lǽre, swâ hê ða cystgan on merringe ne gebringe; ond swâ eft ða rûmmôdan fæsthafolnesse lǽren, swâ hî ða uncystegan on yfelre hneáwnesse ne gebrengen *sic tenacibus infundatur tribuendi largitas, ut tamen prodigis effusionis frena minime laxentur; sic prodigis praedicetur parcitas, ut tamen tenacibus periturarum rerum custodia non augeatur*, Past. 60; Swt. 453, 27–29. [*O. H. Ger.* un-kustig *rudis, impurus, dolosus, improbus.*]

un-cýðig; *adj. Ignorant, unacquainted*:—Wittende *sciens* . . . uncýðig ł unwittende *ignorans*, Lk. Skt. p. 7, 18. Ðâ wundrade heó ymb ðæs weres snyttro, hû hê swâ geleáfful on swâ lytlum fæce ond swâ uncýðig ǽfre wurde gleáwnysse þurhgoten *she wondered at the man's wisdom, how in so little space and* (*previously*) *so ignorant he should ever become so full of belief, saturated with prudence*, Elen. Kmbl. 1918; El. 961. Elnes uncýðig *ignorant* (i. e. *devoid*) *of strength*, Exon. Th. 175, 23; Gû. 1199. [*Icel.* û-kunnigr *unacquainted*: *Ger.* un-kundig.] v. on-cýðig; un-and-cýðigness.

un-cýððu(-o); *indecl.*: -cýðð, e; *f.* I. *ignorance*:—Ne spræc hê (*Moses*) hit nô forðýðe his môd âuht genierwed wǽre mid ðære uncýððe ðæs sîðfætes *neque enim Moysi mentem ignorantia itineris angustabat*, Past. 41; S. 304, 17. Mîn sceal of lîce sâwul on sîðfæt, nât ic sylfa hwider, eardes uncýðþu (*in ignorance of the land to which it is bound*), Exon. Th. 284, 22; Jul. 701. II. *a country not one's own, a strange land*:—Siþþan se êþel ûðgenge wearð Adame and Euan . . . ðâ hý on uncýððu scofene wurdon, on gewinworuld, Exon. Th. 153, 18; Gû. 827. [Þe soule is her in uncuððe . . . and nout eðcene hwuch heo schal iwurðen in hire owune riche. Þet fleshe is her et home, A. R. 140, 17–20.]

un-dǽd, e; *f. An ill deed, evil action, a crime, misdeed*:—On yfelan geðance and on undǽde, Wulfst. 165, 5. Ðâ Helmstân ða undǽde gedyde ðæt hê Æðerêdes belt forstæl *when Helmstan committed the crime of stealing Æthered's belt*, Chart. Th. 169, 19, 28. Yflo uerco ł undêdo *mala opera*, Jn. Skt. Lind. 3, 19. Scyldig and mânful mid undǽdum eall gesýmed *sceleratis impius actis*, Dôm. L. 58. Man deófol georne forbûge and his undǽda ealle oferhogie, Wulfst. 68, 12. [*O. H. Ger.* un-tât *delictum, macula, flagitiosum*: *Ger.* un-that.]

un-dæftelîce. v. un-gedæftlîce.

un-dǽled; *adj. Undivided, not separated*:—Hit þencþ ætgædere beón gehâl undǽled, forþam gif hit tôdǽled biþ, ðonne ne biþ hit nô hâl, Bt. 34, 12; Fox 152, 27. Ða hwîle ðe seó sâwl and se lîchoma undǽlde beóþ, 34, 9; Fox 148, 5.

Undalan; *pl. The name which remains as Oundle, a town in Northamptonshire*:—Fêrde hê forþ on his mynstre ðe hê hæfde on Undalana mǽgþe (*in provincia Undalum*), Bd. 5, 19; S. 641, 16. On ðære mǽgþe seó is gecýged In Undalum *in provincia quae vocatur In Undalum*, S. 636, 43. Wilferð biscop forðfêrde in (on *v. r.*) Undalum, Chr. 709; Erl. 45, 1. *In Latin charters the form is* Undale:—Uillam Undale . . . de ipsa uilla Undale, Cod. Dip. Kmbl. iii. 93, 1, 8. Uillam de Undale, v. 6, 22. *In later English it is* Undela:—Ic gife ðone tûn ðe man cleopeþ Undela, Chr. 963; Erl. 122, 4.

un-deáded; *adj. Not deadened*:—Wiþ springe ge âdeádedum ge undeádedum, Lchdm. ii. 8, 7.

un-deádlîc; *adj. Immortal, undying, imperishable, endless*:—God hâlig and undeádlîc (*immortalis*), Rtl. 169, 17. Hê wunaþ undeádlîc, se ðe wæs deádlîc, Homl. Th. i. 150, 22. Se mann wǽre ǽfre undeádlîc, gif hê his Drihtne gehýrsumode, Hexam. 15; Norm. 22, 27. Undeádlîc, wyrm *the worm that never dies*, Homl. Skt. i. 4, 385. Tô onfônne ðæs undeádlîcan gegyrlan on neorxna wange, Homl. Ass. 142, 105. Hî wǽron gehâtene ealle *immortalis*, þæt sindon undeádlîce, Jud. Thw. p. 162, 31. Þurh undeádlîce worulda *per immortalia secula*, Anglia xi. 119, 77. v. un-deáþlîc.

un-deádlîcness, e; *f. Immortality*:—Ûre ǽhta sind êce on heofenum, ðǽr ðǽr undeádlîcnys rîcsaþ, Homl. Th. ii. 484, 28. Hyht hiora undeádlîcnise (*immortalitate*) full is, Rtl. 86, 22: Homl. Th. i. 544, 3. Hæfde God ðæs mannes sâwle gegôdod mid undeádlîcnysse . . . we ne forluron nâ ða undeádlîcnyssæ, 20, 1–4: Bd. 1, 27; S. 493, 4: 3, 21; S. 551, 3. v. un-deáþlîcness.

un-dearninga(-unga), -deornunga; *adv. Without secrecy* or *concealment, openly*:—Elene for eorlum spræc undearninga, ides reordode hlûde for herigum, Elen. Kmbl. 809; El. 405: Fins. Th. 45; Fin. 22. Undearnunga, Elen. Kmbl. 1237; El. 620. Ðû ofer ealle undearnunga ðîne bearn sprecest and bealde cwyst *locutus es in aspectu filiis tuis et dixisti*, Ps. Th. 88, 16. Ic seah wyhte twâ undearnunga plegan, Exon. Th. 429, 9; Râ. 43, 2. Gecýþe hê ðæt hê ðæt feoh undeornunga his cûðan ceápe in wîc gebohte, L. H. E. 16; Th. i. 34, 10.

un-deáþlíc; *adj. Immortal*:—Se líchoma bið ðonne undeáþlíc, þeáh hē ǽr deáþlíc wǽre, Blickl. Homl. 21, 31. Se ðe com deáðlíc tō ðissum middangearde . . . hē ārās undeáðlíc, Homl. Th. i. 222, 12, 18. Wē sprecaþ ymbe God, deáðlíce be undeáðlícum, 286, 8. Monna sāwla sint undeáþlíce (undeádlíca, Cott. MS.) and ēce, Bt. 11, 2; Fox 34, 33. v. un-deádlíc.

un-deáþlíce; *adv. Immortally, to immortality*:—Ūre Drihten on ðam ðriddan dæge undeáþlíce of deáðe ārās, H. R. 5, 24.

un-deáþlícness, e; *f. Immortality*:—Bið ūre deádlíca líchama āwend tō undeáðlícnýsse, Homl. Th. ii. 70, 4. v. un-deádlícness.

un-deáw; *adj. Without dew*:—Gewyrc ða wyrt on morgenne ðonne hió gedeáw sié, sume beóð undeáwe, Lchdm. ii. 92, 15.

un-declínigendlíc; *adj. Indeclinable*:—*Nihil* nāht *indeclinabile*, ðæt is, undeclínigendlíc, Ælfc. Gr. 9, 8; Zup. 39, 6: 38; Zup. 223, 1: 44; Zup. 258, 1. *Indeclinabilia*, ðæt synd, undeclíniendlíce, 9, 78; Zup. 75, 3.

un-deógollíce. v. undígellíce.

un-deóp; *adj. Not deep, shallow* (lit. and fig.):—Nis ðæt rǽdlíc ðing, gif swā hlūtor wæter hlūd and undióp tōflōweþ æfter feldum ōð hit tō fenne werð, Past. 65; Swt. 469, 6. Ðý læs mon mā geóte on ðæt undiópe mōd ðonne hit behabban mæge ðæt hit ðonne oferflōwe *ne cum angusto cordi incapabile aliquid tribuitur, extra fundatur*, 63; Swt. 459, 14. [Sume hi diden in crucethus ð is in an cæste þat was scort and nareu and undep, Chr. 1137; Erl. 262, 9.]

un-deópþancol; *adj. Not given to think deeply, shallow*:—Nū smeáð sum undeópðancol man hū God mæge beón ǽghwǽr ætgædere, and nāhwār tōdǽled, Homl. Th. i. 286, 29.

un-deór(-deóre?); *adj. Not dear, cheap, common*:—Undeór hit is *vile valet*, Wrt. Voc. i. 28, 61. Ðæt hié mon nā undeórran weorðe mōste lēsan ðonne hié mon be ðam were geeahtige, L. Alf. pol. 32; Th. i. 82, 1. Hē nemde ða undiórestan wyrta ðe on wyrttūnum weaxe and ðeáh swíðe welstincenda *cum decimari minima diceret, extrema quidem de oleribus maluit sed tamen bene olentia memorare*, Past. 57; Swt. 439, 32. [Undeore he makeð God, þet for eni worldliche luue his luue trukie, A. R. 408, 14. *O. H. Ger.* un-tiuri *vilis*: *Icel.* ū-dýrr *cheap, of little value*.]

un-deóre; *adv. Cheaply, at a small cost*:—Undeóre hē bohte *vile vendidit*, Wrt. Voc. i. 28, 63. Gā seó wǽge wulle tō .cxx. ꝥ. and nān man hig nā undeóror ne sylle, L. Edg. ii. 8; Th. i. 270, 4. Ðæt sý undeóror geseald ðonne hit woroldmannum gewunelíc sý *vilius detur quam ab aliis secularibus*, R. Ben. 95, 17. Swylce mon undeórest bicgan mæge *quid vilius comparari potest*, 89, 17.

un-deornunga. v. un-dearnunga.

under; *prep. adv. Under*. I. with dat. (1) local, without motion to bring one object under another, (a) where one object has another vertically above it:—Ða wæteru ðe wǽron under ðære fæstnisse, Gen. 1, 7. Under heofenum, 6, 17. Heó ālēde ðone sunu under sumum treówe, 22, 15. Ic geseah ðē ðā ðū wǽre under ðam fíctreówe, Jn. Skt. 1, 48. (a 1) where one object is supported by another:—Mearh under mōdegum, Elen. Kmbl. 2383; El. 1193. Ðæt scip wæs yrnende under segle, Ors. 1, 1; Swt. 19, 34: Andr. Kmbl. 1009; An. 505. Wedera leód heard under helme, Beo. Th. 689; B. 342. Cwom Wealhþeów gān under gyldnum beáge, 2330; B. 1163. (b) where one object is at the lower part of another, *under, at the foot of*:—Wæs bāt under beorge, Beo. Th. 427; B. 211. Ðā com of mōre under misthleoþum Grendel gongan, 1425; B. 711. Under weallum, Cd. Th. 146, 6; Gen. 2418. v. neoþan. (c) where an object is surrounded, covered, shut in, etc. by another, *under, within*:—Heora andwlitan inbewrigenum under loðum, Cd. Th. 95, 29; Gen. 1586. Under lindum, 192, 7; Exod. 228. Under gyrdelse, Exon. Th. 436, 34; Rä. 55, 11: 431, 3; Rä. 45, 2. Under heolstorlocan bīdan *to wait in prison*, Andr. Kmbl. 288; An. 144: Beo. Th. 3860; B. 1928. Heó under breóstcofan bearn ǣcende, Hy. 10, 16. Hwæþer him yfel þe gōd under wunige *whether evil or good dwell within the mind*, Exon. Th. 82, 4; Cri. 1333. (d) where an object is surrounded by others, *among*:—Ne mehton ða senātus nǽnne consul under him findan, Ors. 4, 10; Swt. 196, 10. Sang se wanna fugel under deoredsceaftum, Cd. Th. 119, 23; Gen. 1984. (2) local, where motion is implied:—Mec mīn freá sendeþ under sǽlwonge, Exon. Th. 382, 27; Rä. 4, 2. (3) figurative, (a) marking subordination, subjection, rule, etc.:—Sete hig under Aarone, ðæt hig þénigeon him . . . Beón hig þēnas under Aarone and his sunum, Num. 3, 6, 9. Ða ðe under Alexandre fyrmest wǽron, Ors. 3, 11; Swt. 142, 17. Aulixes hæfde twā ðióda under ðam Kásere, Bt. 38, 1; Fox 194, 4: Met. 26, 5. Under Rōmwarum, Hy. 10, 26. Burgā fífe wǽran under Norðmannum gebēgde, Chr. 942; Erl. 116, 15. Ic eom man under anwealde gesett, and ic hæbbe þegnas under mē, Mt. Kmbl. 8, 9. Ealle ða rícu ðe him under beóð, Bt. 16, 1; Fox 50, 3. Būtan ðam dǽle ðe under Dena onwalde wæs, Chr. 901: Erl. 96, 23. Under hǽþenra hyrda gewealdum, Exon. Th. 44, 19; Cri. 705. Eáþmōdgiaþ eów sylfe under ðære mihte Godes handa, Blickl. Homl. 99, 3. Óðer tíd is seó ðe wæs under ǽ; seó ðridde . . . is gecweden under Godes gife, Homl. Th. i. 312, 31. Cild ic eom under gyrde (*sub virga*) drohtniende, Coll. Monast. Th. 34, 21. (b) marking protection, shelter:—Under mundbyr[d]e *sub pretextu*, Wrt. Voc. ii. 79, 84: 84, 15. Under wealla hleó, Cd. Th. 259, 13; Dan. 691. (c) marking pretence:—Under intingan *sub obtentu* (Mk. 12, 40), Wrt. Voc. ii. 73, 43. (d) marking exposure, suffering:—Hū se mānscaða under fǽrgripum gefaran wolde, Beo. Th. 1480; B. 738. Under stormum, Exon. Th. 476, 21; Ruin. 11. Fela ðæs ðe hē ādreág under nīðgysta nearwum clommum, 134, 21; Gū. 511. Under Godes egsan, 146, 2; Gū. 703. (e) marking rank, degree:—Under hire selfre hió biþ ðonne, ðonne heó lufaþ ðās eorþlícan þing, Bt. 33, 4; Fox 132, 17. (f) marking circumstances or conditions under, among, or during which something takes place:—Be ðam men ðe bið hūsl forboden and under þam (*interim*) forðfǽrð, L. Ecg. P. i. 13, tit.; Th. ii. 170, 25: *interea*, 13; Th. ii. 178, 15: Chr. 876; Erl. 78, 12: 1046; Erl. 173, 5. Hē him gehēt ðæt hē his ríce wið hiene dǽlan wolde and hiene under ðæm ofslōg *Titum, mox ut in societatem regni adsumpsit, occidit*, Ors. 2, 2; Swt. 66, 12. Under ðæm ðe hē him onwinnende wæs *while he was warring upon them*, 1, 2; Swt. 30, 5. Under ðæm gewinne hié genāmon friþ *in the course of the struggle they made peace*; pace armis quaesita, 1, 10; Swt. 46, 7. Swā wæs ðæt hié under ðære sibbe tō ðære mǽstan sace becōme, 4, 7; Swt. 182, 28: 4, 12; Swt. 210, 10: Chr. 865; Erl. 70, 33. Wē sceolan under ðæm feówerte[g]oþan gerīme syllan ðone teóþan dǽl ūre worldspēda *we must during that forty days give the tithe of our worldly wealth*, Blickl. Homl. 35, 18. (g) marking manner:—Under earhfære bannan tō beadwe *to summon to war by sending round an arrow* (v. Grmm. R. A. 162), Elen. Kmbl. 87; El. 44. II. with acc., (1) local, where motion is expressed or implied, (a) where one object comes to have another vertically above it:—Ne eom ic wyrðe ðæt ðū gā under míne þecene, Lk. Skt. 7, 6. Sume steorran gewītaþ under ða sǽ, Bt. 39, 3; Fox 214, 26. Stefn in becom under hārne stān, Beo. Th. 5100; B. 2553. Hió ðæt līc ætbær under firgenstreám, 4263; B. 2128. Ðā nāmon hig ānne stān and lēdon under hine, Ex. 17, 12. Lǽd under earce bord eaforan ðīne, Cd. Th. 80, 23; Gen. 1333. Under helm drepen biteran strǽle, Beo. Th. 3495; B. 1745. ¶ Combined with on:—Lecgan uppan ðone stān and on under, Lchdm. iii. 38, 18. (b) where one object comes to the lower part of another:—Weorod eodon unblīðe under Earna næs wundur sceáwian; fundon on sande sāwulleásne ðone ðe him hringas geaf, Beo. Th. 6055; B. 3031. (c) where one object comes to be surrounded, covered, shut in, etc. by another:—Hē gelǽdde brýd under burhlocan, Cd. Th. 153, 12; Gen. 2537: Andr. Kmbl. 1879; An. 942. Under heolstorhofu hreósan, Elen. Kmbl. 1524; El. 764. In under eoderas, Beo. Th. 2068; B. 1037: Cd. Th. 147, 25; Gen. 2445. Under sceát, 124, 17; Gen. 2064: Exon. Th. 436, 21; Rä. 55, 4. (d) where extension under a surface is implied:—God under roderas feng wolde ðæt eorðe geseted wurde woruldsceafte, Cd. Th. 6, 33; Gen. 98: 71, 5; Gen. 1166. Under heofenes hwealf, Beo. Th. 1156; B. 576: 4033; B. 2015. Under swegles begong, 1724; B. 860: 3550; B. 1773: An. 415; An. 208. Siððan ǽfenleóht under heofenes hādor beholen weorþeþ *after the evening light has died out everywhere beneath the sky*, Beo. Th. 832; B. 414. (2) figurative, (a) marking subordination, subjection, rule, etc:—Under hand hǽðenum dēman *in subjection to a heathen ruler*, Cd. Th. 220, 14; Dan. 71. Gewāt him Abraham under Abimelech ǽhte lǽdan, 158, 22; Gen. 2621. Under ānes meaht ealle forlǽtan, Exon. Th. 294, 30; Crä. 23. Hí wǽran geseald under sweordes hand *tradentur in manus gladii*, Ps. Th. 62, 8. (b) marking exposure, suffering:—Se eów in hæft bedrāf, under nearowe clom, Exon. Th. 138, 2; Gū. 570. (c) in various other senses:—Ne þurfon gē wēnan ðæt gē ðæt orceápe sellon, ðæt gē under Drihtnes borh syllaþ, Blickl. Homl. 41, 13. Hī him his forwierndon and hit under ðæt lādedon for ðon ðe hē æt ðæm ōþrum cirre sige næfde *they refused him the triumph, and sheltered themselves under the excuse, that he had not on the other occasion been victorious*, Ors. 5, 2; Swt. 216, 31. Under monnes hīw *in human form*, Exon. Th. 144, 22; Gū. 682. Ne swerigen gē nǽfre under (cf. þurh, Ex. 23, 13) hǽðene godas, L. Alf. 48; Th. i. 54, 23. Se king swōr under God ǽlmihtine and under ealle hālgan ðārtō, Chart. Th. 340, 2. Symle byð under dæg and niht feówer and xx[tig] tída, Lchdm. iii. 260, 12. Ðū āhst tō fyllene ðīne seofen tídsangas under dæg and niht, Wulfst. 290, 18. III. adverbial; see also the compound forms given below. (1) where one object has another vertically above it:—Ān treów ðæt mæge .xxx. swīna under gestandan *a tree so big that thirty swine can stand beneath*, L. In. 44; Th. i. 130, 3. His hors wearð under ofscoten *his horse was killed under him*, Chr. 1079; Erl. 216, 25. Sume crupon under *some crept beneath*, 1083; Erl. 217, 22. Hē hēt fýr under bētan, Homl. Th. i. 4, 393. Ðǽr ðæs Hǽlendes fōtlāstas syndon under, Shrn. 81, 29. (2) where relative height is marked, *below, beneath*:—Hē funde wynleásne wudu, wæter under stōd, Beo. Th. 2837; B. 1416. (3) *down* as opposed to up:—Wið ðone ðe him mete under ne gewunige *if his food do not remain down*, Lchdm. ii. 190, 1: 198, 23. [*Goth.* undar: *O. Sax.* undar: *O. Frs.* under: *O. H. Ger.* untar: *Icel.* undir.] v. þǽr-under.

under-ágenlíc; *adj. The word glosses* subnixus *in*: Underāgenlícum beadum *subnixis precibus*, Rtl. 182, 33.

under-andfōnd *glosses* susceptor *in:* Underondfōendo *susceptores,* Rtl. 193, 11.

under-bæc; *adv.* I. where there is motion of a person in the direction towards which the back is kept turned, *backwards,* (a) approaching an object:—Sem and Iafeth eodon underbec *Shem and Japhet went backward;* incedentes retrorsum, Gen. 9, 23. (b) motion from:—Ðā eodon hig underbæc *they went backward;* abierunt retrorsum, Jn. Skt. 18, 6. Hwīlum ic underbæc bregde nebbe, Exon. Th. 498, 5; Rä. 87, 8. Feallan underbæc *to fall backwards,* Homl. Th. ii. 392, 8: Homl. Skt. i. 12, 63. Sceófan underbæc, 14, 88: 18, 345: Homl. Th. ii. 300, 15. II. marking retreat, where there is motion of a person in the direction to which his back has been turned, *back:*—Diabolo non dicitur: 'Uade retro me,' sed: 'Uade retro' . . . Crist cwæð tō ðam deófle: 'Gā ðū underbæc.' Deófles nama is gereht, nyðerhreósende. Nyðer hē āhreás and underbæc hē eode ðā ðā hē wæs āscyred fram ðære heofonlīcan blisse, Homl. Th. i. 172, 30–35: Wrt. Voc. ii. 71, 70. Nū næfð Israēl nānne stede wið his fȳnd ac flīhð underbæc *nec poterit Israel stare ante hostes suos, eosque fugiet,* Jos. 7, 12. Underbæc cyrran *to turn back,* Exon. Th. 405, 2; Rä. 23, 17: Ps. Lamb. 34, 4. (Under bæce, Ps. Spl. 34, 5.) Ðū gehwyrfdest mīne fȳnd underbæc *in convertendo inimicum meum retrorsum,* Ps. Th. 9, 3. III. where an action is directed towards a point behind the agent's back, *behind, back:*—Ðū forwurpe mīn word underbæc fram ðē *projecisti sermones meos postea,* Ps. Th. 49, 18: Homl. Th. ii. 532, 3. Ne beseoh ðū underbæc *noli respicere post tergum,* Gen. 19, 17: Cd. Th. 154, 28; Gen. 2562: Jos. 8, 20. Ðā beseah hē hine underbæc wið ðæs wīfes, Bt. 35, 6; Fox 170, 14. Hāwian underbæc *respicere retro* (Lk. 9, 62), Past. 51; Swt. 403, 2. IV. where the point from which something proceeds is behind the recipient:—Ðīn eáran gehīraþ underbæc *thine ears shall hear a word behind thee* (Is. 30, 21); aures tuae audient verbum post tergum monentis, Past. 52; Swt. 405, 26: 407, 12. v. next word.

under-bæcling; *adv. Back:*—Ðonne gecerraþ mīne fȳnd underbæcling *tunc conuertentur inimici mei retrorsum,* Ps. Lamb. 55, 10. Underbæclinc, Blickl. Gl.

under-beginnan *to attempt:*—Nū þincþ mē ðæt ðæt weorc is swīþe pleólīc mē oþþe ǣnigum men tō underbeginnenne, Ælfc. Gen. Thw. 1, 14. v. under-ginnan.

under-beran *glosses* supportare, sustinere, subsistere:—Underbearaþ *subportantes,* Rtl. 13, 35. Underbær *sustinuit,* 27, 31. Underbeara *subsistere,* 7, 38. Underberende *supportantes,* Scint. 24, 1.

under-bīgan *to subject:*—Underbēged *subjectus,* Rtl. 125, 25: Mt. Kmbl. p. 3, 10. v. under-būgan.

under-brǣdan *glosses* substernere *in:* Underbrǣddon gegerelo *substernebant uestimenta,* Lk. Skt. Lind. 19, 36.

under-bregdan *to spread under:*—Óþer eáre hī him on niht underbrēdaþ and mid óðran hī wreóð *unam aurem sibi noctem substernunt, de alia se cooperiunt,* Nar. 37, 12.

under-būgan *to submit:*—Paulus underbeáh swurdes ecge, Homl. Th. i. 382, 6. Ūre Hǣlend rōdehengene underbeáh, ii. 600, 7.

under-burh *a suburb:*—Of Gomorra underburgum *de suburbanis Gomorrhae,* Deut. 32, 32.

underburh-ware; *pl. The inhabitants of a suburb:*—Of underburhwarum *de suburbanis,* Cant. M. ad fil. 32. v. preceding word.

under-cirran *glosses* subvertere *in:* Undercerrende *subvertentem,* Lk. Skt. Lind. Rush. 23, 2.

under-crammian *to stuff full below;* suffercire:—Hī mid byrnendum glēdum ðæt bed undercrammodon, Homl. Th. i. 430, 4.

under-creópan *to enter surreptitiously;* surrepere:—Ðā wæs ðæs wītegan cnapa mid gītsunge undercropen *avarice crept into the heart of the prophet's servant,* Homl. Th. i. 400, 16. Ðæt ne feónd ūs undercreópe (*but the Latin is* subripiat), Hymn. Surt. 12, 28.

under-cuman *glosses* subvenire, succedere *in:* Undercwom *succedente,* Mt. Kmbl. p. 8, 9. Undercyme *subveniat,* Rtl. 66, 35. Undercymende *succedente,* 37, 35.

under-cyning, es; *m. A dependent, tributary king, one who rules under another.* Cf. þeód-cyning:—Cyning *rex,* lytel cyning oððe undercyning *regulus,* Ælfc. Gr. 5; Zup. 16, 19. Kyning *basileus,* undercyning *regillus,* Wrt. Voc. i. 17, 47. Sum undercyning wæs *erat quidam regulus,* Jn. Skt. 4, 46, 49: Homl. Th. i. 128, 5. Ic Offa, Myrcena kining . . . Ic Aldrēd, Wigraceastres undercining (*subregulus*), Cod. Dip. Kmbl. i. 186, 13. Griffin swōr āðas ðæt hē wolde beón Eádwearde kinge hold underkingc, Chr. 1056; Erl. 190, 35. Tiberius hæfde anweald ofer eall Rōmāna rīce, and him wæs undercyning Herōdes, Nicod. 1; Thw. 1, 8. Ðe Hǣlend stōd befar ðone undercynige (*praesidem*), and gefrægn hine ðe undercynig (*praeses*), Mt. Kmbl. Lind. 27, 11, 21. Tō undercyningum *ad praesides,* 10, 18: Mk. Skt. Lind. 13, 9. Ic ðǣr gemētte Tȳtum and Vespasianum ðȳne (*Tiberius'*) getrȳwestan undercyningas, Homl. Ass. 191, 285. [*Icel.* undir-konungr.]

under-delf *glosses* suffossum, Ps. Spl. 79, 17. v. under-holung.

under-delfan *to dig under, undermine, dig out* (lit. or fig.):—Ic underdelfe *subfodio,* Ælfc. Gr. 28, 6; Zup. 179, 11. Æt dura hē underdelfeþ (*suffodiet*) fōtwylmas ðīne, Scint. 196, 8. Ðū beswice oððe underdulfe (*supplantasti*) onārīsende on mē under mē, Ps. Lamb. 17, 40. Seáþ hē geopnode and hē underdealf ðæne *lacum aperuit et effodit eum,* 7, 16. Hē nolde geþafigan ðæt man hys hūs underdulfe *non sineret perfodi domum suam,* Mt. Kmbl. 24, 43: Lk. 12, 39. Hē nolde geþafian ðam þeófe nāteshwōn ðæt hē underdulfe dīgellīce his hūs, Homl. Ass. 50, 13. Ne beóþ underdolfene ł ne beóþ forscræncte stæpas his *non supplantabuntur gressus ejus,* Ps. Lamb. 36, 31. ¶ underdelfan *glosses* suffocare, Mt. Kmbl. Lind. 13, 7, 22: Mk. Skt. Lind. Rush. 4, 7, 19.

under-diácon, es; *m. An under-deacon, a sub-deacon:*—Underdiácon *subdiaconus,* Wrt. Voc. i. 42, 26: Rtl. 194, 9. Subdiaconus is sōðlīce underdiácon, se ðe ða fatu byrð forð tō ðam diácone, and mid eádmōdnysse þēnaþ under ðam diácone æt ðam hālgan weofode mid ðām hūselfatum, L. Ælfc. C. 15; Th. ii. 348, 9.

under-dōn *to put under;* subjicere:—Ðone wudu ðe man ðæt fȳr sceal underdōn *ligna quibus subjiciendus est ignis,* Lev. 1, 12.

under-drencan *glosses* suffocare *in:* Underdrencdo *suffocati,* Mk. Skt. Lind. 5, 13.

under-drifenness *glosses* subjectio *in:* Of underdrifenise diówla *de subjectione daemonum,* Lk. Skt. p. 6, 16.

under-etan *to eat away below, to sap;* subedere:—Ðæt mennisce mōd bið undereten and āweged of his stede ðonne hit se wind strongra geswinca āstyroþ, Bt. 12; Fox 36, 17.

under-fang *glosses* susceptor, Ps. Spl. 3, 3: 17, 3: 45, 7: 143, 2.

under-fangelnes *glosses* susceptio *in:* Underfangelnes heáfdes mīnes *susceptio capitis mei,* Ps. Lamb. 107, 9.

under-fangenness, e; *f. Undertaking, assumption:*—Mid underfangennysse menniscnysse *assumptione humani,* Ath. Crd. 35.

under-feng, es; *m. Undertaking, acceptance:*—Ðȳlæs hē for ðȳ underfenge (*the undertaking the office of teacher*) his eáðmōdnesse forlǣte, oððe eft his līf sié ungelīc his ðēnunga, oððe hē tō ðriste and tō stīð sié for ðȳ underfenge his láreówdōmes *ne aut humilitas accessum* (*ad culmen regiminis*) *fugiat; aut perventioni vita contradicat; aut vitam doctrina destituat; aut doctrinam praesumtio extollat,* Past. proem.; Swt. 23, 22.

under-flōwan *to flow under:*—Wæs ic neoþan wætre, flōde underflōwen *beneath had I water, the flood flowing under me,* Exon. Th. 392, 3; Rä. 11, 2.

under-folgoþ, es; *m. An office under a superior:*—Hē (*Julian*) sǣde ðæt nān cristen man ne mōste habban nǣnne his underfolgoþa (sunderfolgeþa, Swt. 286, 5), Ors. 6, 31; Bos. 128, 24.

under-fōn; *p.* -fēng, *pl.* -fēngon; *pp.* -fangen. I. *to receive, to have given, to get:*—Ne underfō ic nāne beorhtnesse æt monnum *claritatem ab hominibus non accipio,* Jn. Skt. 5, 41. On ðam lande ðe ðū underfēhst *in the land which the Lord giveth thee* (A.V.); in terra quam acceperis, Deut. 28, 8. Eálā ðæt hit is gōd ðæt mon micelne welan āge, nū se nǣfre ne wyrþ orsorg ðe hine underfēhþ *O praeclara opum mortalium beatitudo, quam cum adeptus fueris, securus esse desisti,* Bt. 14, 3; Fox 46, 34. Hū micelne unweorþscipe se anwald brengþ ðam unmedeman, gif hē hine underfēgþ, 27, 2; Fox 96, 10. Mid ðam casu (*ablative*) byð geswutelod, swā hwæt swā wē underfōð æt ōðrum . . . *ab hoc homine pecuniam accepi* fram ðisum men ic underfēng feoh, Ælfc. Gr. 7; Zup. 23, 7–11. Ða Godes þeówas ðe ða sceattas underfōð ðe wē Gode syllaþ, L. Edg. S. 1; Th. i. 272, 15. Ðā underfēng Iudas ðæt folc æt ðām bisceopum, Jn. Skt. 18, 3. Ne cwæð hē nū, 'ðū hēte mē,' ac 'forgeáfe mē'; mid ðam worde is seó gifu geswutelod ðe hē on ðǣre menniscnysse underfēng. Seó menniscnys wæs underfangen fram ðam godcundum worde, Homl. Th. ii. 364, 11–14. Hī heora mēde underfēngon, 80, 2: i. 68, 30. Ðæt hē ne cnytte ðæt underfongne feoh on ðæm swātlīne, Past. 9; Swt. 59, 13. II. *to receive, submit to* a rite, etc.:—Godes ðeów, se ðe hād underfēhð *God's servant, who takes orders,* Homl. Th. ii. 48, 31. Ðā wē fulluht underfēngan, Wulfst. 167, 1. III. *to receive* a person, (1) *to receive* for the purpose of entertaining, sheltering, harbouring, etc.:—Florus fērde him tōgeánes and ða ædelan Godes menn underfēng tō him, and foresceáwode him wununge, Homl. Skt. i. 6, 138. Ðæt nān man nǣnne man ne underfō nā leng ðonne þreó niht, L. C. S. 28; Th. i. 392, 9. Ðæt nāðor ne hȳ ne wē ne underfōn ōðres wealh, ne ōðres þeóf, ne ōðres gefān, L. Eth. ii. 6; Th. i. 288, 4. (2) *to receive* for safe conduct, custody, etc.:—Ðā underfēngon ðæs dēman cempan ðone Hǣlend on ðam dōmerne, Mt. Kmbl. 27, 27. Nāh tō farenne Wylisc man on Ænglisc land būtan gesettan landmen, se hine sceal æt stæðe underfōn, and eft ðǣr būtan fācne gebringan, L. O. D. 6; Th. i. 354, 25. (3) *to receive* as a servant or dependent:—Be ðon ðe ōðres mannes man underfēhð būtan leáfe. Ne underfō nān man ōðres mannes man būtan ðæs leáfe ðe hē ǣr fyligde, L. Ed. 10; Th. i. 164, 14: L. Ath. i. 22; Th. i. 210, 20: iv. 1; Th. i. 220, 18. 'God underfēng his cnapan Israhēl.' Mid ðam naman syndon getācnode ealle ða ðe Gode gehȳrsumiaþ, ða hē underfēhð tō his werode, Homl. Th. i. 204, 13. (4) *to receive, admit* into a society:—Hē sī underfangen on gegæderunge *suscipiatur in congregatione,* R. Ben. Interl. 97, 4. (5) *to receive* as a master, *to submit to:*—Gif se anweald of his āgenre gecynde gōd wǣre, ne underfénge hé nǽfre ða yfelan ac ða gódan, Bt. 16, 3; Fox 54, 23. (6) *to receive, admit the claims of*:—Se ðe eów underféhð, hé underféhð mé, and se ðe mé underféhð, hé underféhð ðone ðe mé sende, Mt. Kmbl. 10, 40. Ic com on mínes Fæder naman and gé mé ne underféngon. Gyf óðer cymþ on his ágenum naman, hyne gé underfóð, Jn. Skt. 5, 43. (6 a) *to receive, admit the force of* a person's words, *accept* testimony:—Hé cýð ðæt hé geseah and gehýrde, and nán man ne underféhþ his cýðnesse, Jn. Skt. 3, 32. Se ðe míne word ne underféhð, hé hæfþ hwá him déme, 12, 48. Ne underfóð ealle menn ðis word, Mt. Kmbl. 19, 11. **IV.** *to receive* what is offered, *to accept*:—Drihten gebed mín hé underféng (-fang, MS.) *Dominus orationem meam suscepit*, Ps. Spl. 6, 9. Hé nolde náne fréfrunge underfón *noluit consolationem accipere*, Gen. 37, 35. **V.** of things, *to receive, serve as a receptacle for*:—Underfó *receptet* (*the passage is*: Cadaver nequaquam sepulchri sarcophagus receptet, Ald. 52), Hpt. Gl. 496, 11. **VI.** *to receive* or *accept* an office, a duty, etc., *to take upon one's self, to undertake* a labour, task, etc., (a) where the object of the verb is a word implying action or effort:—Regulus underféng Cartaina gewinn *Regulus, bellum Carthaginense sortitus*, Ors. 4, 6; Swt. 174, 1: 2, 2; Swt. 66, 13. Ðæt ilce (ða ðegnunga ðæs láreówdómes) ðæt hé untǽlwierðlíce ondréd tó underfoonne, Past. 7; Swt. 48, 19. Sió giémen ðæs underfangenan láreówdómes *suscepta cura regiminis*, 4; Swt. 37, 13. Ðá hié gewin hæfdon underfongen *bella suscepta*, Ors. 4, 9; Swt. 192, 29. Ǽr hé hæbbe godcunde bóte underfangen, L. Edm. S. 4; Th. i. 248, 25. Underfangenre andwealhnysse *adeptae integritatis*, Hpt. Gl. 465, 70. (b) where the object of the verb denotes that in respect to which action or effort is needed:—Gif wífman híwrǽdene underféhð *si mulier familiam susceperit*, L. Edg. C. 25; Th. ii. 272, 7. Ðonne hié monna heortan underfóð tó lǽronne, Past. 21; Swt. 161, 12. Hig underfóð ðis folc mid ðé *ut sustentent tecum onus populi*, Num. 11, 17. On ða rícu ðe hé underfangen hæfde, Bt. proem.; Fox viii, 8. **VII.** *to receive* what is burdensome, *undergo, bear*:—Gé underfóð eówere unrihtwísnissa (*ye shall bear your iniquities*, A.V.), ðæt gé witon míne wrace *recipietis iniquitates vestras, et scietis ultionem meam*, Num. 14, 34. **VIII.** *to take surreptitiously, to steal*:—Gyf feoh sý underfangen (*or* ? under fangen), Lchdm. iii. 286, 4. [*O. E. Homl. Laym. Kath. Gen. and Ex.* under-fon: *Orm.* unnderr-fon; *A. R.* under-von: *Piers P.* under-feng; *p.*: *Ayenb.* onderving: *O. H. Ger.* untar-fáhan.] v. under-niman.

under-fónd *glosses* susceptor, Ps. Lamb. 3, 4: 53, 6: 90, 2.

under-fóndlic; *adj. To be received*:—Se underfónlíca *suscipiendus*, R. Ben. Interl. 97, 8.

under-fylgan *glosses* subsequi *in*: Underfylgdon (-fyligdon, Rush.) *subsecutae*, Lk. Skt. Lind. 23, 55.

under-gán *to undermine, ruin*:—Gif hwylcne man deóful tó ðam swýþe undergán hæbbe *si diabolus hominem aliquem adeo perdiderit*, L. Ecg. P. iv. 14; Th. ii. 208, 12. Ne sý nán eorðcund cyning mid gítsunge tó ðæm swíþe undergán, Lchdm. iii. 444, 3. [Ðis maidenes redden . . . hu he migten undergon (*deceive*) here fader, Gen. and Ex. 1147.]

under-gangan *to undergo*:—Ic undergange *subeo*, Ælfc. Gr. 37; Zup. 217, 17. [Me birrþ beon fullhtnedd att tin hannd þin blettsinng tunnderrganngenn, Orm. 10661.]

under-geoc; *adj. Accustomed to the yoke, tame*:—Ofer ðone fola suna undergeocas (cf. on folan sunu ðære teoma, Rush.) *super pullum filium subjugalem*, Mt. Kmbl. Lind. 21, 5.

under-geréfa, an; *m. An under-officer*:—Geréfa *consul*, undergeréfa *proconsul*, Wrt. Voc. i. 18, 5. Se undergeréfa *the pro-prefect*, Homl. Skt. i. 4, 332: 7, 216.

under-geþeóded *subject*:—Nǽnig ealdormonna ne ús undergeþeóddra (-endra, MSS. B. H.), L. In. proem.; Th. i. 102, 11. v. under-þeódan.

under-ginnan; *p.* -gann; *pl.* -gunnon; *pp.* -gunnen *To begin, attempt*:—Ic gedyrstlǽhte ðæt ic ðás gesetnysse undergann *I ventured to attempt this work* (the translation of a Latin work), Homl. Th. i. 2, 27. Gregorius ús trahtnode ðyses godspelles dígelnysse ðus undergynnende: 'Dryhten ús gewilnaþ . . . etc.,' 608, 9.

under-gitan; *p.* -geat, *pl.* -geáton; *pp.* -giten *To understand, perceive, know*:—Ic gefréde oððe undergyte *sentio*, Ælfc. Gr. 30, 2; Zup. 190, 11. Ic undergyte *perpendo*, 28, 7; Zup. 181, 6. Gif folces man syngaþ þurh nytenyss[e] and his gylt undergit (*et cognoverit peccatum suum*), Lev. 4, 28. Fram hyra wæstmum gé hí undergytaþ (*cognoscetis*), Mt. Kmbl. 7, 16. Ðá Samson heora syrwunga undergeat and árás, Jud. 16, 3: Homl. Th. i. 62, 30. Ðá undergeat Noe, ðæt ða wæteru wǽron ádrúwode ofer eorðan, Gen. 8, 11. Ðá Ulfcytel ðæt undergeat, Chr. 1004; Erl. 139, 25. Ðá Eádwine eorl and Morkere eorl ðæt undergeáton, 1066; Erl. 198, 39: Ors. 3, 7; Swt. 112, 26. Hig ne undergéton (-geáton, MS. A.) ðæt hé tealde him God tó fæder *non cognouerunt quia patrem eis dicebat*, Jn. Skt. 8, 27. Ne undergéton (-geáton, MS. A.) (*cognouerunt*) hys leorningcnihtas ðás þing ǽrest, 12, 16. Gif hwam gelustfullaþ tó witanne hwæt sý *quadrans*, ðonne undergite hé ðæt *quadrans* byð se feórða dǽl, Anglia viii. 298, 10. Understandan *capere, intelligere*, undergite *capiat*, Hpt. Gl. 437, 28. Undergitende heortan *cor intelligens*, Deut. 29, 4. Beón undergiten *colligi, cognosci, intelligi*, Hpt. Gl. 460, 13. Þe beóð undergitene *noscuntur, intelleguntur*, 430, 11.

under-hebban *glosses* accipere, sustollere, sublevare *in*:—Onfoeng ł underhóf *accepit*, Mt. Kmbl. Lind. 8, 17. Genom ł underhóf *sustulit*, Jn. Skt. Lind. Rush. 5, 9. Underhóf *subleuasset*, 6, 5. Underhebendum égum *subleuatis oculis*, Lind. 17, 1. Ðæt ué sié underhefen *sublevari*, Rtl. 80, 1.

under-hlystan *renders* subaudire *in*: *Subaudio* ic underhlyste, *subaudis* ðú underhlyst, *subaudit* hé underhlyst, Ælfc. Gr. 26; Zup. 151, 2-4.

under-hlýstung *renders* subauditio *in*: *Subauditionem et personam*, ðæt ys, underhlystunge and hád, Ælfc. Gr. 26; Zup. 151, 1.

under-hnígan; *p.* -hnáh; *pl.* -hnigon; *pp.* -hnigen. **I.** *to descend beneath, go lower than* a place:—Grundum ic hríne, helle underhníge, heofonas oferstíge, Exon. Th. 482, 23; Rä. 67, 6. Hwílum ýða ic sceal underhnígan, 386, 29; Rä. 4, 69. **II.** *to submit to* what is laborious or painful, *be subjected to* evil, *undergo* punishment, etc., (a) with acc. of that which is undergone:—Ðonne hí ða scandlícan lustas ðisses middangeardes mid hira módes willan underhnígaþ *cum turpi hujus mundi desiderio humanae mentis voluntas substernitur*, Past. 52; Swt. 405, 3. For intingan hérsumnesse ic háten geþafode ðæt ic ðone hád underhnáh (-nágh, S. 566, 8) þeáh ðe ic unwyrðe wǽre *obedientiae causa jussus subire hoc quamvis indignus consensi*, Bd. 4, 2; M. 260, 8. Hí underhnigon ðone hwílendlícan deáþ *mortem subiere temporalem*, 4, 16; S. 584, 37. Hé underhníge menniscne þeówdóm *se humano servitio subjiciat*, L. Ecg. P. Addit. 18; Th. ii. 234, 24. Ic eom nýded ðæt ic sceal hraþe deáþ underhnígan *ad articulum subeundae mortis compellor*, Bd. 3, 13; S. 538, 26. Beheáfdunge underhnígan *capitalem sententiam subire*, Hpt. Gl. 477, 74. (b) with dat.:—Sixtus underhnáh swurdes ecge, and his twégen diáconas samod, Homl. Th. i. 420, 17. Hé ðam deáðe underhnáh and ðone deófol oferswýðde, Homl. Skt. i. 16, 115. Regolícore stýre hé underhníge *disciplinae regulari subjaceat*, R. Ben. Interl. 19, 1. Ðonne sceal hé underhnígan ðære steóre regollícre láre, R. Ben. 16, 4. Hí sceoldon underhnígan nacodum swurde, Homl. Skt. i. 5, 28. Hét se réða cwellere hine underhnígan swurdes ecge, Homl. Th. i. 428, 8. (c) case uncertain:—Hé sáres wite underhníhð *doloris poenae succumbit*, Scint. 12, 9. Ðú galgan underhnige, Anglia xii. 506, 1. Nyste heora nán on hwæs tíman hé ðrowunge underhnige, Homl. Th. ii. 506, 31.

under-holung *glosses* suffossum *in*: Underholunga *suffossa*, Ps. Lamb. 79, 17.

under-hwítel, es; *m. An under-whittle*; ragana, Wrt. Voc. i. 59, 28. [Migne gives *racana* vêtement déchiré, de peu de valeur.]

under-hwrǽdel. v. under-wrǽdel.

under-ícan *glosses* subjungere *in*: Underýcende *subjungentes*, Anglia xiii. 385, 292.

un-derigende; *adj. Harmless, innocent*:—*Nocens*, derigende, is nama and *participium*, and *innocens*, underigende, of ðam geféged ys ǽfre nama, Ælfc. Gr. 9, 38; Zup. 62, 16. Underigende handum *innocens manibus*, Ps. Spl. 23, 4. Hió mid wíflíce níðe wæs feohtende on ðæt underiende folc, Ors. 1, 2; Swt. 30, 19.

un-derigendlíc; *adj. Harmless, innoxious*:—Se Hálga Gást hí ealle onǽlde mid undergendlícum fýre, Homl. Th. i. 298, 6.

under-irnan *to under-run, run beneath*:—Hé underyrnþ ealle ða twelf tácna, Lchdm. iii. 248, 1. Ðonne seó sunne hí hæfð ealle underurnen, 246, 10. ¶ *As a gloss of* succurrere:—Underiorn *succurre*, Rtl. 43, 17.

under-ládteów, es; *m. A subordinate ruler*, applied to the consuls in comparison with the kings:—Him ðá Rómáne æfter ðæm ládteówas (underlátteówas, MS. C.) gesetton ðe hié consulas héton ðæt heora ríce heólde án geár án monn *igitur regibus urbe propulsis, Romani consules creaverunt*, Ors. 2, 2; Swt. 68, 2.

under-lǽded *glosses* subductus, Lk. Skt. Lind. 5, 11: sublatus, Mt. Kmbl. p. 3, 10.

under-lecgan. **I.** *to underlay, support*:—Ic underlecge *fulcio*, Ælfc. Gr. 30, 2; Zup. 190, 5. Ðá bæd hé hí ánre sylle, ðæt hé mihte ðæt hús mid ðære underlecgan, Homl. Th. ii. 144, 33. Ðeáh hit mid náne anwald ne sié underléd *cum nulla potestate fulcitur*, Past. 17; Swt. 113, 25. Ðonne bið se elnboga underléd mid pyle and se hnecca mid bolstre *pulvillo cubitus vel cervicalibus caput jacentis excipitur*, 19; Swt. 143, 17. **II.** *rendering* supponere, substernere, etc.:—Ic underlecge *subpono*, Ælfc. Gr. 28, 3; Zup. 167, 17: 47; Zup. 276, 9. Underlegdon *substernebant*, Lk. Skt. Lind. 19, 36. Of underlédum brandum *suppositis torribus*, Hpt. Gl. 489, 6. [*O. H. Ger.* unter-leccen *fulcire.*]

under-licgan *to be subject, submit, yield*:—Ne mæg se preóst mannum ðingian, gif hé synnum underlíð, Homl. Th. ii. 320, 21: Homl. Skt. i. 1, 155. Ne underlicga wé synnum *nec succumbamus vitiis*, Rtl. 82, 25. Underlicgge hé þreále *discipline subjaceat*, R. Ben. 56, 12. Ða underdiéddan mon sceal lǽran ðæt hí him eáðmódlíce underlicgen *subditi* *admonendi sunt ut humiliter subjaceant*, Past. 28; Swt. 189, 20. [*O.H. Ger.* unter-ligan *subjacere.*]

under-lihtan *glosses* sublevare *in:* Uē underlihtad sié *sublevemur*, Rtl. 51, 23. Ðætte uē sié underlihtado *sublevari*, 72, 3.

underling, es; *m.* (the word seems to occur only in late texts) *An underling, a subordinate, a subject:*—Heó (*the Jews*) syððen ǽfre unwurðe wǽron on heora lífdagen and get synden underlinges, Homl. Ass. 194, 50. Eádward kyng grēt Harald eurl and alle his undurlynges (*omnes meos ministros*) in Herefordeshīre, Cod. Dip. Kmbl. iv. 218, 14. [Leir king scal beon eouwer lauerd . . . & Aganippus ure king scal beon his underling, Laym. 3657. Inobedience, þet is . . . underling þet ne buhð nout his prelat, A. R. 198, 18.]

under-lūtan; *p.* -leát, -luton; *pp.* -loten *To stoop beneath* something in order to raise or support it, *to support, bear, submit to:*—Ða ðe beóð mid hira āgnum byrðennum ofðrycte, ðæt hié ne magon gestondan, hié willaþ lustlīce underfōn ōðerra monna, ond unniédige hié underlūtaþ mid hira sculdrum ōðerra byrðenna *qui ad casum valde urgetur ex propriis, humerum libenter opprimendus ponderibus submittit alienis*, Past. 7; Swt. 51, 25. Hē ārās underléat ðæt bēr eode *ille surrexit sublato grauato abiit*, Mk. Skt. Lind. Rush. 2, 12. Eálā ofermōdan! hwī gē wilnigen ðæt gē underlūtan mid eówrum swiran ðæt deáþlīcne geoc *quid o superbi colla mortali jugo frustra levare gestiunt?* Bt. 19; Fox 68, 26. Hwī eów ā lyste mid eówrum swiran selfra willum ðæt swǽre gioc underlūtan, Met. 10, 20.

undern, es; *m. The third hour of the day, nine in the morning;* in later English (v. infra) it is used of the *sixth hour*, a use it seems to have in *undern-rest*, q.v.:—Undern *tertia*, middæg *sexta*, Wrt. Voc. i. 53, 11. Undern is dæges þridde tīd, Btwk. 214, 33. Ðæs hīrēdes ealdor gehȳrde wyrhtan on ǽrnemerigen, eft on undern . . . Se ǽrmerigen wæs fram Adam ōð Noe, se undern fram Noe ōð Abraham, Homl. Th. ii. 74, 7–19. Tō undernes, Lchdm. ii. 194, 6. Byð seó sceadu tō underne and tō nōne seofon and twēntigoþan healfes fōtes *the shadow at nine and at three is twenty-six and a half feet long*, iii. 218, 3, and often. Æt underne . . . ǽr underne, Blickl. Homl. 93, 22, 36. Ǽr undern . . . ofer undern *mane . . . vespere*, Lev. 6, 20. On ða þriddan tīd dæges, ðæt is on undern, Shrn. 79, 35. Wē etaþ on ðam Sunnandagum on undern and on ǽfen, Homl. Skt. i. 12, 3. Sele drincan on þreó tīda, on undern, on middæg, on nōn, Lchdm. ii. 140, 1. Fram hancrēde ōð undern, Homl. Th. i. 74, 21: Chr. 538; Erl. 16, 2. Ofor undern, Blickl. Homl. 93, 15. Healfe tīd ofer undern, 540; Erl. 16, 4. Ōð heáne undern *usque ad tertiam plenam*, R. Ben. 74, 11. [Abuten undern deies . . . abute swucke time alse me singeð messe (from prime oðet midmareȝen, hwenne preostes singeð heore messen, MS. C.), A. R. 24, 11. So ha dede at undren and and at midday also (Mt. 20, 3), Misc. 33, 22. At þon heye undarne (Acts 2, 15), 56, 657. It was the thridde our (that men clepen undrun), Wick. Mk. 15, 25. The time of undern of the same day, Ch. Cl. T. 260. *But the word sometimes denotes a later hour:*—Bi þis was undren (under, undrin) on þe dai (*the sixth hour*, Lk. 23, 44), C. M. 16741. Undorne, 19830. The our was as the sixte or undurn, Wick. Jn. 4, 6. An orendron̄, ornedrone *meredies*, Cath. Angl. 261, where see note. *See also the later English forms given under* undern-mǽl, -mete, -tīd. *O. Sax.* undorn *the third hour: O. Frs.* ond, unden (*and see Richthofen Wtbch.*): *O. H. Ger.* untarn *midday: Icel.* undorn *nine o'clock* A.M. or *three o'clock* P.M.; *a meal.* Cf. *Goth.* undaurni-mats ἄριστον. As in the case of *mǽl* = meal, the word seems to have come to denote the eating that takes place at the time, which at first the word denoted. v. Halliwell's Dict. *aandorn*, and see the forms in other dialects in Cl. & Vig. Icel. Dict. s.v. undorn.] v. *compounds with* undern-.

un-derne. v. un-dirne.

under-neoþan, -nyþan; *prep. adv. Underneath:*—Þurhscoten mid ānre flān underneoðan ōðer breóst *sagitta sub mamma trajectus*, Ors. 3, 9; Swt. 134, 23. Ðū nymst cealfes blōd mid ðīnum fingre on ðæs weofodes hyrnan and gīst ðæt ōðer undernyðan (*reliquum sanguinem fundes juxta basim altaris*), Ex. 29, 12. [Þet fotspure þe wæs underneðen his fote, Chr. 1070; Erl. 209, 8.] v. neoþan.

under-neoþemest *lowest:*—Eorðe stōd ealra gesceafta underniþemæst (under niþemæst? Cf. sió eorðe is nioþor ðonne ǽnig ōðru gesceaft, Bt. 33, 4; Fox 130, 20), Met. 20, 135.

undern-gereord, es; *n. A morning meal, breakfast:*—Underngereord *prandium*, ǽfengereord *cena*, nōnmete *merenda*, Wrt. Voc. i. 38, 12. Æt his underngereorde ǽr hē tō ðæm gefeohte fōre, Ors. 2, 5; Swt. 84, 34. Gif wē fæstaþ and ðæt underngereord tō ðam ǽfengifle healdaþ, ðonne ne bið ðæt nān fæsten, L. E. I. 38; Th. ii. 436, 28. Heora underngereordu and ǽfengereordu hié mengdon tōgædere, Blickl. Homl. 99, 22.

undern-gifl, es; *n. Food eaten in the morning, breakfast:*—Ðonne ðū hæbbe gegearwod underngifl (-giefl, Hatt. MS.) oððe ǽfengifl *cum facis prandium aut coenam*, Past. 44; Swt. 322, 19.

under-niman; *p.* -nam, *pl.* -nāmon; *pp.* -numen. I. *to take surreptitiously, to steal.* v. under-fōn, VIII:—Gif feoh sȳ undernumen (under numen?), Lchdm. i. 392, 8. II. in figurative senses, (1) *to take into the mind, receive* what is said, taught, etc.:—Gehādede men hit sceolon him āsecgan, undernimð se ðe wile, Wulfst. 305, 20. Hē deóplīce undernam Drihtnes lāre æt him, Homl. Skt. ii. 29, 76. Abraham undernam hefiglīce ðās word *dure accepit hoc*, Gen. 21, 11. Ðis sind ðæra apostola word, undernimaþ, hī mid carfullum mōde, Homl. Th. i. 236, 4: H. R. 7, 29. Ne underfōð ealle menn ðis word . . . Undernyme se ðe undernyman mæge (cf. ne underneomeð (uoð, MS. B.) nawt þis ilke word alle . . . Hwase hit me underneomen, underneome, H. M. 19, 27) *non omnes capiunt verbum istud . . . Qui potest capere, capiat*, Mt. Kmbl. 19, 11–12. Man mæg swīðe eáðe witan, se ðe hit underniman wile, ðæt hit riht nis . . ., Wulfst. 305, 1: Homl. Ass. 26, 53. [Hire fader hefde iset hire to lare and heo undernom (-ueng, MS. R.) hit wel, Kath. 117.] (2) *to take upon one's self:*—Gif ðū leornian wille hū ðæt gewurðan mæge, ðonne undernim ðū leorningcnihtes hīw, Homl. Th. i. 590, 20. [We þis feht habbeoð undernumen buten Arðures rede, Laym. 26734. To poure iheorted eni heih þing to undernimen ine hope of Godes helpe, A. R. 202, 6. Hardy to greate þinge ondernime, Ayenb. 83, 19.] (3) *to blame, resent* (?):—Ðā undernam Godwine eorl swȳðe ðæt on his eorldōme sceolde swilc geweorðan, Chr. 1052; Erl. 179, 16. [He cometh not to the light, that his workis be not undirnomun *ut non arguantur opera ejus*, Wick. Jn. 3, 20. Impacient is he that wil not ben itaught ne undernome of his vices, Chauc. Pers. T. Whoso undernymeth me hereof, Piers P. 5, 115. Underneme *reprehendo, deprehendo, arguo;* undernemynge *deprehensio, reprehensio*, Prompt. Parv. 511.]

under-niþemæst. v. under-neoþemest.

undern-mǽl, es; *n. Morning-time:*—On undernmǽl, Beo. Th. 2860; B. 1428. An undermǽl, Homl. Skt. ii. 30, 319. [Ther walkith noon but the lymytour himself in undermēles and in morwenynges, Chauc. W. of B. T. 19. Undermele *postmeridies, postmessimbria, merarium*, Prompt. Parv. 511. Cf. In an undermele tyde *meridiano tempore*, Trev. v. 373, 9. See also Nares' Dict. *undermeal.*]

undern-mete, es; *m. Food eaten in the morning, breakfast:*—Undermete *prandium*, ǽfenmete *cena*, Wrt. Voc. i. 290, 65. Uton brūcan ðisses undernmetes swā ða sculon ðe hiora ǽfengifl on helle gefeccean sculon *prandete tamquam apud inferos coenaturi*, Ors. 2, 5; Swt. 86, 1. Undernmete *prandium*, Mt. Kmbl. Rush. 22, 4. [An orendron̄ mete, ordrone mete *merenda;* to ete orendron̄ mete *merendare*, Cath. Angl. 261, where see note. *Goth.* undaurni-mats ἄριστον, *prandium.*]

undern-rest, e; *f. Rest in the morning:*—Ðā hē ārās on dæge of undernræste (*postquam de meridiana quiete surrexerunt*, Bede's Vita Cudberci, c. 35), Shrn. 64, 7.

undern-sang, es; *m. The service at the third hour of the day, tierce:*—Undernsang *tertia*, R. Ben. 39, 19: 40, 6: L. Ælfc. C. 19; Th. ii. 350, 6. Undernsanges gebed *tertie oratio*, R. Ben. Interl. 47, 10. Æt ǽfensonge and æt undernsonge, Chart. Th. 137, 34.

undern-swǽsendu; *pl. Breakfast:*—Ðæt hē mid ðȳ biscope sǽte æt his undernswǽsendum (*ad prandium*), Bd. 3, 6; S. 528, 13.

undern-tīd, e; *f.* I. *the third hour of the day, nine o'clock* A.M.:—Ðā wæs underntīd *erat hora tertia*, Mk. Skt. 15, 25: Homl. Th. i. 314, 22 (see Acts 2, 15). Ūres andgites merigen is ūre cildhād, ūre cnihthād swylce underntīd, on ðam āstīhð ūre geógoð, swā swā seó sunne dēð ymbe ðære ðriddan tīde, ii. 76, 15. From underntīde (underne tīde, S. 592, 7), ðonne mon mæssan oftost singeþ *a tertia hora quando missae fieri solebant*, Bd. 4, 22; S. 328, 32. Embe underntīde *circa horam tertiam*, Mt. Kmbl. 20, 4. Ǽrest on ǽrnemorgen, ōþre sīþe on underntīd, Blickl. Homl. 47, 17: 133, 27. II. *the service at the third hour:*—Wē sungon underntīde and dydon mæssan *cantavimus tertiam et fecimus missam*, Coll. Monast. Th. 33, 31. [Hit is undertid (Acts 2, 15), O. E. Homl. i. 91, 2: Mk. Skt. 15, 25, col. 2. Þe soðe sunne iðe undertid was istien on heih, A. R. 400, 15. Þan was it underntide (undrin-, undir-) o þe dai *about the sixth hour* (Acts 10, 9), C. M. 19830.]

undern-tīma, an; *m. The third hour of the day*, nine o'clock A.M.:—On undern wē sculon God herian, forðam on underntīman Crist wæs tō deáþe fordēmed . . . And eft com se Hālga Gāst on underntīman ofer ða apostolas, Btwk. 214, 26–30. [Godess Gast com i firess onnlicnesse an daȝȝ att unnderrntime, Orm. 19458.]

under-plantian *glosses* supplantare *in:* Ðū underplantedest *supplantasti*, Ps. Spl. 17, 41. Dysig byð underplantud *stultus supplantatur*, Scint. 169, 2.

under-sceótan; *p.* -sceát, *pl.* -scuton; *pp.* -scoten. I. *to move to a place beneath, to intercept:*—His (*the moon's*) trendel underscȳt ðære (ða, MS. R.) sunnan tō ðam swīðe ðæt heó eall āþeóstraþ, Lchdm. iii. 242, 20. II. *to under-prop, support:*—Hī ne beóð mid nānre sylle underscotene ðæs godcundlīcan mægenes *nullis fulti virtutibus*, Past. 1; Swt. 27, 17. Cf. under-stingan.

under-scyte, es; *m. Intercepting, intervention:*—Se mōna mæg þurh his underscyte ða sunnan āþeóstrian, Lchdm. iii. 242, 25. Wē rǽdaþ on tungelcræfte ðæt seó sunne bið hwīltīdum þurh ðæs mōnelīcan trendles underscyte āðȳstrod, Homl. Th. i. 608, 32.

under-sēcan; *p.* -sōhte *To investigate;* discutere (cf. discutiens, i.

judicans, querens, Wrt. Voc. ii. 141, 42) :—Ðæt is ðæt hié ðara ðing ðe him underðióddе bióð for ðam ege ānum ðæs innecundan dēman undersēce *est subjectorum causas pro sola interni judicis intentione discutere*, Past. 13; Swt. 79, 8. Ðæm lāreówe is swíðe smeálíce tō undersēceanne be ðæm weorcum ðara ofertrūwedena *subtiliter ab arguente discutienda sunt opera protervorum*, 32; Swt. 209, 12. [Huo þet heþ þise yefþe, he onderzekþ þe redes þet me him yefþ, Ayenb. 184, 23. *Ger.* untersuchen.]

under-serc, es; *m. An under-garment* :—Undersyrc *colophium* (= *colobium*), Wrt. Voc. ii. 22, 45.

under-singan *renders* succinere *in:* Ic undersinge *succino*, Ælfc. Gr. 28, 7; Zup. 181, 2.

under-sittan *renders* subsidere *in:*—Ic undersitte *subsideo*, Ælfc. Gr. 26, 5; Zup. 157, 5.

under-smeágan *glosses* subrepere, subripere *in:* Undersmǣge *subripiat*, R. Ben. Interl. 71, 6. Undersmēge *subrepat*, 72, 9. v. next word.

under-smūgan; *p.* -smeáh, *pl.* -smugon; *pp.* -smogen *To creep under, come upon unawares, surprise* :—Īdelnysse underþeódde gālscype undersmȳhð *otio deditos luxuria subripit*, Scint. 89, 8. Ne undersmūge gītsunge yfel *non subripiat* (but other MS. *subrepat*) *avaritie malum*, R. Ben. Interl. 95, 7. Ðæt ǣnig þinc ne undersmuge on wege gesyhðe *ne quid forte subripuerit in via visus*, 113, 11. Swā hȳ nǣfre mid oferfylle undersmogene and beswicene ne weorðan *ne subrepat satietas aut ebrietas*, R. Ben. 64, 19.

under-standan; *p.* -stōd, *pl.* -stōdon; *pp.* -standen. I. *to understand, have insight into* :—Ðū genōh wel understentst ðæt ic ðē tō sprece, Bt. 13; Fox 38, 1. Se godcunda foreþonc hit understent eall swīþe ryhte . . . wē ne cunnon ðæt riht understandan, 39, 8; Fox 224, 19–21. Gecȳðnessa ðīne ic ongeat ł understōd *testimonia tua intellexi*, Ps. Lamb. 118, 95. Understand ðās gesihðe *intellige visionem* (Dan. 9, 23), Homl. Th. ii. 14, 9. Ðam men is gemǣne mid englum ðæt hē understande i. 302, 22. Eal ðæt syndon micle and egeslīce dǣda, understande se ðe wille, Wulfst. 161, 9. Understande se ðe cunne, 162, 12. Snotornys, þurh ða seó sāwel sceal hyre Scippend understandan, Homl. Skt. i. 1, 157. Ðæt wē magon understandan ða þing ðe ðū specst *ut possimus intelligere quae loqueris*, Coll. Monast. Th. 32, 15. Swǣ clǣne hió (*learning*) wæs ōðfeallenu on Angelcynne ðæt swíðe feáwa wǣron behionan Humbre ðe hiora ðēninga cūðen understondan, Past. pref.; Swt. 3, 14. Gehwā ðe his āgene þearfe wille understandan, L. Eth. vi. 27; Th. i. 322, 9. I a. *with prep.* ymbe :—Ne mæg nān gesceaft fulfremedlīce smeágan ne understandan ymbe God . . . Englas ne magon fulfremedlīce understandan ymbe God, Homl. Th. i. 10, 2–5. II. *to understand, perceive, know certainly* :—Understand be ðām hū se ælmihtiga God hī ealle gesceóp būtan antimbre *know certainly concerning them, how that the almighty God created them all without matter*, Homl. Skt. ii. 25, 178. Understandaþ eác georne, ðæt deófol ðās þeóde dwelode, Wulfst. 156, 7. Understanden (beón) *deprehendi*, Hpt. Gl. 526, 18: *conjici*, 469, 30. [I do gowe to understonden *ego notifico nobis*, Cod. Dip. Kmbl. iv. 218, 15.] III. *to understand in such and such a sense, to conceive of, consider* :—Ne understand ðū hit mē tō unrihtwīsnesse *do not consider it as unrighteousness in me*, Ps. Th. 21, 2. Gif ic eáðmōdlīce mē sylfne ne understōde, ac mīn mōd on mōdignesse anhōfe *si non humiliter sentiebam, sed exaltavi animam meam*, R. Ben. 22, 18. III a. *with prep.* be :—Ǣwfæstlīce understandende be ūre ealra ǣriste *piously conceiving of the resurrection of us all*, Homl. Skt. ii. 25, 472. III b. *to accept as correct* :—Ðis ylce understand be ðām ōðrum dagum *take the same rule as applicable in the case of the other days*, Anglia viii. 304, 29. IV. *to observe, notice, consider* :—Understand (*or* I) rǣdere, hwæt seó rǣding cwyð, Anglia viii. 309, 1. Understand mīne sprǣce *animadverte sermonem* (Dan. 9, 23), Homl. Th. ii. 14, 9. Ðæt tō understandenne ealle gedēmdon *hoc adtendendum cuncti decreuerunt*, Anglia xiii. 371, 90. Ðæt geswinc his sȳðfætes ne understandende hē mid hrædestan ryne arn, Homl. Skt. ii. 23b, 186. On dehter nā understandendre *in filia non aduertente se*, Scint. 225, 7.

under-standenness *glosses* substantia *in:* Understondennisse *substantia*, Rtl. 31, 40.

under-standing, e; *f. Intelligence* :—On andgyte inran understandincge *sensu interioris intelligentie*, Scint. 221, 13.

under-stapplian *glosses* supplantare *in:* Understappla ł forscrænc hine *supplanta eum*, Ps. Lamb. 16, 13.

under-staþolfæst. v. un-staþolfæst.

under-stingan *to under-prop, support* :—Understungen and āwreðed mid ðȳs hwīlendlīcan onwalde *fultus temporali potentia*, Past. 17; Swt. 113, 11. Cf. under-sceótan.

under-stregdan *to under-strew* :—Hē wæs nacod and on carcern onsǣnded, and ðǣr wæs understregd mid sǣscellum and mid scearpum stānum *he was stripped and sent to prison, and there had sea-shells and sharp stones strewed under him*, Shrn. 51, 13.

under-þegnian *glosses* subministrare *in:* Underþēnaþ *subministrat*, Scint. 5, 6.

under-þencan *to look into, consider* :—Wē sculon swíðe smeálīce ðissa ǣgðer underðencean *hoc in utrisque subtiliter intuendum*, Past. 7; Swt. 49, 23.

under-þeód; *adj.* (*ptcpl.*) *used substantively. Subject, subordinate* :—On ōðre wīsan sint tō manianne ða underðióddan, on ōðre ða ofergesettan. Ða underðieddan (-ðióddan, Cott. MSS.) mon sceal lǣran ðæt hié elles ne sién genǣt *aliter admonendi sunt subditi, atque aliter praelati. Illos ne subjectio conterat*, Past. 28; Swt. 189, 14. Ðonne ðæt mōd ðara underðiédra (-ðiéddra, Cott. MSS.) hwæthwugu ryhtlīces ongitan mæg *subditorum mens cum quaedam recte sentire potuerit*, 19; Swt. 147, 1. On his (*the abbot's*) underþeóddera mōdum *in discipulorum mentibus*, R. Ben. 10, 18. Se lāreów sceal ǣrest on him sylfum ǣlcne leahter ādwæscan, and siððan on his underðeóddum, Homl. Th. i. 320, 30. Landfranc wæs gehāded on his āgenum biscopsetle fram eahte biscopum his underðióddum, Chr. 1070; Erl. 206, 5. [Prost scal spenen among al his underþede, O. E. Homl. i. 85, 14.] v. next word.

under-þeódan, -þiédan, -þīdan; *p.* de. I. *to subject, subjugate, render subject*, (1) with dat. :—Se līchoma hine him (*the devil*) underðiéd mid ðære lustfulnesse . . . Swā swā sió nædre lǣrde Euan on wōh and Eue hī hire underðiód[d]e mid lustfulnesse, swā swā līchoma *caro se delectatione subjicit . . . Unde et ille serpens prava suggessit, Eva autem quasi caro se delectationi subdidit*, Past. 53; Swt. 417, 24–27. Hī hī underþiódaþ unþeáwum, Bt. 37, 1; Fox 186, 28. God ðū ðe mē sealdest ðæt ic meahte swylc wīte dōn mīnum feóndum, and mē swylc folc underþȳdes (-þeodes, Ps. Surt.) *Deus qui das vindictas mihi, et subdidisti populos sub me*, Ps. Th. 17, 45. Hē ūs underþeódde ūre folc *subjecit populos nobis*, Ps. Th. Spl. Surt. 46, 3. Claudius Orcadus Rōmāna cynedōme underþeódde, Chr. 47; Erl. 6, 26. Ðū mē folc mænig underþeóddest *subjiciens populum meum sub me*, Ps. Th. 143, 3. Tō ðara hlāforda dōme ðe hē hine ǣr underþeódde (-þiódde, Met. 25, 66), Bt. 37, 1; Fox 186, 29. Ic mīne sāwle wylle Gode underþeódan *nonne Deo subdita erit anima mea?* Ps. Th. 61, 1: Met. 25, 63. Hī druncennesse and oferhȳdo . . . wǣron heora swiran underðeóddende (*subdentes*), Bd. 1, 14; S. 482, 27. Reogollīcum ðeódscipum underþeóded *regularibus disciplinis subditus*, 4, 24; S. 598, 21. His anwealde underþeóded, Bt. 26, 3; Fox 94, 15. Ǣlc mon ðe underþeóded (-þiéded, Met. 17, 23) bið unþeáwum, 30, 2; Fox 110, 20. Underþeód (-þȳded, Met. 16, 4), 29, 3; Fox 106, 19. Næs him nō ðȳ læs underðeód eall ðes middangeard, 16, 4; Fox 58, 10. Hē wæs him underþeód (-ðióded, Lind., Rush.) *erat subditus illis*, Lk. Skt. 2, 51. Underþeód (-þȳd, Th.: -ðióded, Surt.) beó ðū Drihtne *subditus esto Domino*, Ps. Spl. 36, 6: *subjecta*, 61, 5. Him se mǣsta dǣl wearð underþiéded, Ors. 1, 10; Swt. 44, 5. Gif hē wiðcwǣde ðæt hē nære underðiódd (-ðidd, Hatt. MS.) his Scippende *si auctoris imperio obedire recusaret*, Past. 7; Swt. 50, 13. Him wesan underþȳded, Exon. Th. 138, 13; Gū. 575. Syndan mē fremde cynn underþeóded *mihi allophili subditi sunt*, Ps. Th. 107, 8. Deófolseócnessa ūs synt underþeódde *daemonia subjiciuntur nobis*, Lk. Skt. 10, 17. Ealle ðās mǣgþe Æþelbalde on hȳrsumnesse underþeódde syndon *hae omnes provinciae Ædilbaldo subjectae sunt*, Bd. 5, 23; S. 646, 27. Ðām ānum ðe Gode underþeódde syndon mid myclum hādum, Blickl. Homl. 109, 22. Swǣsum wordum underþeódde (*dediti*), Coll. Monast. Th. 32, 33. Ða ðe him underðiédde (-ðidde, Cott. MSS.) bióð *subjecti*, Past. 4; Swt. 39, 7. Wē ealle ðære hnescnesse ūres flǣsces beóð underðiédde (-ðidde, Cott. MSS.) *cuncti corruptionis nostrae infirmitatibus subjacemus*, 21; Swt. 159, 6. Eall ða ðing ðe hire underþiéd sint, sint underþiéd ðam godcundan foreþonce, Bt. 39, 6; Fox 220, 20. Ða ealdormen beóð Gode underðȳdde, Ps. Th. 46, 9. (2) with a preposition :—Ðū underþeódest folc mīn under mē *subdis populum meum subter me*, Ps. Spl. 143, 3. Gē underþiódaþ eówre hēhstan medemnesse under ða eallra nyþemestan gesceafta *vos dignitatem vestram infra infima quaeque detruditis*, Bt. 14, 2; Fox 44, 33. Ðū underþeóddest folc under mē *subdis populos sub me*, Ps. Spl. 17, 49. Ne wæs ǣfre ǣnig cyning ðæt mā heora landa him tō gewealde underþeódde, Bd. 1, 34; S. 499, 23. Underðeódende folc under mē *subjiciens populos sub me*, Ps. Surt. 143, 2. (3) where that to which there is subjection is not stated :—Ðonne hē underðiód *quando summiserit*, Kent. Gl. 1004. Ðæt hit ungedafenlīc sig, ðæt se dǣdbēta hine nā on ða wīsan ðissa woroldlīcra þinga ne underþeóde *quod indecorum sit, poenitentem in re mundanorum horum negotiorum se non cohibere*, L. Ecg. P. i. 7; Th. ii. 174, 25. Ūs is tō gelȳfenne ðæt se Hǣlend þyder cōme, næs nō genēded, ne underþeóded, ac mid his wyllan, Blickl. Homl. 29, 15. Underþeód *dedito*, Hpt. Gl. 509, 62. II. *to subject, cause to endure, render liable* :—Hefigran scylde and hefigran wītum hē hine underðiét *poenae gravioris culpae se subjicit*, Past. 54; Swt. 421, 6. Ðā hēt se cāsere ðone diácon miclum wītum underþeódan, Shrn. 56, 34. III. *to subjoin, add* :—Hē underþeódde and him sǣde ðæt se dæg swīþe neáh stōde his forþfōre *subjunxit diem sui obitus jam proxime instare*, Bd. 4, 3; S. 568, 15. IV. *to support* :—Underþiód *subnixa, suffulta*, Hpt. Gl. 467, 21. Underþeódne *subnixum*, 507, 57.

under-þeódendlīc *renders* subjunctivus *in:* *Subjunctivum*, ðæt ys underðeódendlīc, Ælfc. Gr. 15; Zup. 98, 23. *Subjunctivae*, ðæt sind underþeódendlīce, 46; Zup. 267, 7.

under-þeódness, e; *f. Subjection, submission*:—For yrmþo ðære underþeódnysse *ob aerumnam subjectionis*, Bd. 4, 16; S. 584, 41. Wite hē ðæt hē micle eádmōdra beón sceal on regoles underðeódnysse *sciens se multo magis discipline regulari subditum*, R. Ben. 112, 1. Micle swȳþor is tō hālsienne Drihten mid ealre eádmōdnesse and mid ealre underþeódnysse (*cum omni humilitate*), 45, 18. Him gehȳrsumiaþ ōðra engla werod mid micelre underðeódnysse, Homl. Th. i. 342, 34: 346, 34: Ælfc. T. Grn. 1, 31. Hī him gehētan eáþmōde hȳrnysse and singale underþeódnysse *subjectionem continuam promittebant*, Bd. 1, 12; S. 480, 27.

under-þeów, es; *m. One reduced to slavery, one who serves under* or *is subject to another, a slave, servant*:—Hē geniédde Arhalaus ðone lātteów ðæt hē wæs his underþeów, Ors. 5, 11; Swt. 238, 2. Ða burgware bǣdon ðæt hié mōsten beón hiera underþeówas ðā hī hié bewerian ne mehton *petentes, ut quos belli clades reliquos fecit, saltem servire liceat*, 4, 13; Swt. 212, 5: 2, 8; Swt. 92, 23. Ealle wurdon Iuliuse underþeówas *Caesar omnes ad deditionem compulit*, 5, 12; Swt. 242, 27.

under-þīdan, -þiédan, -þȳdan. v. under-þeódan.

under-tōdāl *renders* subdistinctio *in*: *Subdistinctio*, ðæt is undertōdāl, Ælfc. Gr. 50, 14; Zup. 291, 5.

under-tunge *glosses* sublingua *in*: Undertungan *sublinguae*, Wrt. Voc. i. 282, 79.

under-tungeþrum. v. tunge-þrum.

under-weaxan *glosses* succrescere *in*: Underwexaþ *succrescunt*, Scint. 104, 8.

under-wed[d], es; *n. A pledge, security*:—'Gif ðū mē sylst underwedd (*arrhabonem*), ōð ðæt ðū mē sende ðæt ðū mē behǣtst' . . . 'Hwæt wilt ðū tō underwedde (*pro arrhabone*) nyman?' . . . Iudas sende ān tyccen wið his hirde, ðæt hē fette ðæt underwedd, Gen. 38, 17-20. Gylde hē ðæt yrfe oþþe underwed lecge, L. O. D. 1; Th. i. 352, 8: 8; Th. i. 356, 10.

under-wendan *glosses* subvertere *in*: Hē underwende *subuertat*, Scint. 196, 6.

under-wrǣdel *glosses* subfibulum *vel* subligaculum, Wrt. Voc. i. 40, 61.

under-wreðian, -wreoðian, -wriðian *to support, sustain*:—Ic underwreðige (-wreoðige, MSS. F. O.) *fulcio*, Ælfc. Gr. 30, 2; Zup. 190, 5. Underwreðie, Engl. Stud. xi. 65, 34. Ðū underwreðdes *sustentas*, Rtl. 45, 9. Underwreoðaþ his untrumnesse *sustentat inbecillitatem suam*, Kent. Gl. 644. Ealle stōwa Drihten ymbfēhþ and neoþan underwreþeþ, Blickl. Homl. 23, 21. Man ða ræftras tō ðære fyrste gefæstnaþ and mid cantlum underwriðaþ, Anglia viii. 324, 10. Hē mid criccum his fēdunge underwreðode, Homl. Th. ii. 134, 25. Hī underwriðedon his handa *sustentabant manus ejus*, Ex. 17, 12. Ðæt hī underwreþigen *ut leuent*, Germ. 390, 173. Ða ðe bet cunnon, sceolon gȳman ōðra manna, and mid heora fultume underwryðian, Homl. Th. ii. 282, 2. Sceancan mīne mē tō underwreðigenne on yfel strange wǣron *crura mea ad me sustinendum in malum fortes fuere*, Anglia xi. 117, 23. Mid gōdum weorcum underwreðed *bonis actis fultus*, Past. 19; Swt. 141, 18: Homl. Skt. ii. 23 b, 228: Hpt. Gl. 430, 36: Rtl. 76, 3. Treów wyrtrumum underwreðyd, Runic pm. Kmbl. 341, 30; Rūn. 13. Underwreoþod ǣghwanone *circum fultus undique*, Hymn. Surt. 46, 12. Hyt ys underwryðed mid þrīm swerum, Anglia viii. 301, 37. Mid tȳn rihtingum underwriðode, 304, 32: Homl. Th. i. 444, 35. Underwreðdedo *suffulti*, Rtl. 71, 17. ¶ *The word glosses* supponere *in*: Drihten underwriðaþ ł [under]set handa his *Dominus supponet manum suam*, Ps. Lamb. 36, 24.

under-wreðung, e; *f. Support, sustentation*: — Underwreþung līchaman *sustentatio corporis*, Scint. 56, 10. Trumre underwreþincge *firmo fulcimento*, Wrt. Voc. ii. 148, 69.

under-wrītan *to subscribe, sign*:—Wē ealle mid Cristes rōdetācn fæstnedon and underwritan *nos omnes subscripsimus*, Bd. 4, 17; S. 586, 16.

under-wriðian. v. under-wreðian.

under-wyrtwalian *glosses* supplantare *in*: Ðū underwyrtwæledæst *supplantasti*, Ps. Spl. T. 17, 41.

un-dīgollīce; *adv. Not secretly, openly, clearly, plainly*:—Se dīgla Dēma him swīðe undīgellīce (-deógollīce, Hatt. MS.) (*aperte*) geondwyrde, Past. 4; Swt. 38, 19. Þus spræc God gefyrn, hit is swā ðeáh swā gedōn swȳðe neáh mid ūs . . . and undīgollīce, Homl. Skt. i. 13, 177.

un-dilegod; *adj. Not blotted out, not effaced*:—Swā se wrītere, gif hē ne dilegaþ ðæt hē ǣr wrāt, ðeáh hē nǣfre mā nāuht ne wrīte, ðæt bið ðeáh undilegod, ðæt hē ǣr wrāt *neque enim scriptor, si a scriptione cessaverit, quia alia non addidit, etiam illa, quae scripserat, delevit*, Past. 54; Swt. 423, 33.

un-dirne, -dierne, -dyrne; *adj. Not hidden, discovered, revealed, manifest*:—Gif mon āfelle on wuda wel monega treówa and wyrð eft undierne (-dyrne, MS. B.), L. In. 43; Th. i. 128, 20: 44; Th. i. 130, 3. Ðæt wearð underne eorðebūendum, ðæt Meotod hæfde miht, Cd. Th. 265, 1; Sat. 1. Wīde wearð wyrd undyrne, Apstls. Kmbl. 84; Ap. 42. Ðā wæs Grendles gūðcræft gumum undyrne, Beo. Th. 255; B. 127: 4004; B. 2000. Bið him synwracu andweard undyrne *the punishment of sin shall stand revealed before them*, Exon. Th. 94, 16; Cri. 1541. Nū is undyrne werum, hū ða wihte hātne sindon, 429, 19; Rä. 43, 15. Ic wordum wemde wyrd undyrne, Andr. Kmbl. 2959; An. 1482. Ic gearwe wāt ðæt ðē (*God*) sieudan ealle wīsan (*printed* wifan) undierne and cūðe ðīnre ðære hālgan þrynesse, Anglia xi. 97, 7. *Nuncupatio est* undyrne yrfebēc, Wrt. Voc. ii. 62, 24.

un-dirne; *adv. Openly, clearly, plainly*:—Wearð ylda bearnum undyrne cūð ðætte Grendel wan wið Hrōðgār, Beo. Th. 303; B. 150: 825; B. 410.

un-dōm, es; *m. Unjust judgement*:—Wā ðam ðe rǣreþ unriht tō rihte and undōm dēmeþ earmum tō hȳnðe *vae qui condunt leges iniquas; et scribentes, injustitiam scripserunt; ut opprimerent in judicio pauperes* (Is. 10, 1-2), Wulfst. 47, 26: 128, 10: 268, 1. Se ðe unlage rǣre oþþe undōm gedēme for lǣððe oþþe for feohfange, L. C. S. 15; Th. i. 384, 9. Hī geūtlageden ealle Frencisce men ðe ǣr unlage rǣrdon and undōm dēmdon and unrǣd rǣddon, Chr. 1052; Erl. 186, 2. Wē cȳðaþ dēman and gerēfan, ðæt hig āgan þearfe, ðæt hī unrihtes geswīcan and nāhwār þurh undōm for feó ne for freóndscipe forgȳman heora wīsdōm, Wulfst. 267, 28. Wearð ðes ðeódscipe swīðe forsingod þurh undōmas, 130, 4.

un-dōmlīce; *adv. With bad judgement, indiscreetly*:—Hyrde oþþe unbindan undōmlīce ondrǣde oþþe gewrīþan *pastor vel absoluere indiscrete timeat uel ligare*, Scint. 202, 14.

un-dōn; *p.* -dyde; *pp.* -dōn *To undo*. I. *to undo* that which is closed, *to open*:—Ðā heó ðone windel undyde *aperiens fiscellam*, Ex. 2, 6. Ðā undyde hira ān his sacc *aperto sacco*, Gen. 42, 27. Hē undyde his mūð, Homl. Th. i. 548, 14. Ðā undydon wē ūre saccas *aperuimus saccos nostros*, Gen. 43, 21. Ðæt hē undō his eágan, Anglia viii. 317, 5. II. *to undo* that which is bound, *to release*, (1) literal:—Beón þreó niht ǣr man ða hand undō, L. Ath. i. 23; Th. i. 212, 4. (2) figurative, *to release, absolve*:—From allum ūsig synnum undō *ab omnibus nos peccatis absolve*, Rtl. 42, 3. Ða ðe synna racentēg gifæstnigaþ milsa ðīnræ ārfæstnisse undōe *quos delictorum catena constringit miseratio tuae pietatis absolvat*, 40, 23. Ðæs on .ix. nihton ðæt wed undō hē mid rihtan gylde *nine days after let him release the pledge by lawful payment*, L. O. D. 1; Th. i. 352, 9. III. *to undo* that which closes, *to open* a door, etc.:—Undōð mē duru sōðfæstra *aperite mihi portas justitiae*, Ps. Th. 117, 19: 23, 7. Undōnde *reserando* (*valvam*), Hpt. Gl. 478, 11. Ðā wearþ eft Ianes duru undōn (andōn, Swt. 254, 17) *apertus est Janus*, Ors. 6, 1; Bos. 116, 25. Undōnum remmingum *apertis obstaculis*, Hpt. Gl. 489, 73. IV. *to undo* that which binds or fastens, *to undo* a bolt, a knot, etc.:—Godes engel undyde ða locu ðæs cwearternes, Homl. Th. i. 572, 26. Ic ne am wyrðe ðætte ic undōe (*soluam*) his ðuong scōes, Jn. Skt. Lind. 1, 27. Undōn (undōa, Lind.) ł loesan þwongas *soluere corrigiam*, Mk. Skt. Rush. 1, 7. V. *to undo* what has been done, *to abrogate, destroy*, (1) where the object is material:—Ic undōe tempel ðis *ego dissoluam templum hoc*, Mk. Skt. Lind. Rush. 14, 58. (2) where the object is not material:—Ðet hyra nān næ undō ðet ic tō ðām hāligum mynstrum gedōn hebbe, Chart. Th. 232, 28. Ne mæg undōa ða gewriota *non potest solui scribtura*, Jn. Skt. Rush. 10, 35. Nællas gié woenæ forðon ic cuom tō undōenne (*solvere*) ae, Mt. Kmbl. Lind. 5, 17. Ðætte ne sē undōen ae *ut non soluatur lex*, Jn. Skt. Lind. Rush. 7, 23. v. on-dōn.

un-drēfed; *adj. Untroubled, not made turbid*:—Gē gedrēfdon hiora wæter mid iówrum fōtum, ðeáh gē hit ǣr undrēfed druncen, Past. 2; Swt. 31, 3.

un-drifen; *adj. Not driven*:—Ǣlc ceápscip frið hæbbe, ðe binnan mūðan cuman[mæg?], þēh hit unfriðscyp sȳ, gyf hit undrifen bið (*si non sit abacta tempestatibus* (Lat. vers.). For the fate of what was driven, cf. such a grant as the following:—Ic cȳðe eów ðæt Urk habbe his strand . . . and eall ðæt tō his strande gedryuen hys, Cod. Dip. Kmbl. iv. 221, 5-8), L. Eth. ii. 2; Th. i. 284, 21.

un-druncen; *adj. Not drunk, sober*:—Hē suā micle bet his āgen dysig oncnēw suā hē undruncenra wæs *he recognized his own folly so much better as he was more sober*, Past. 40; Swt. 295, 8. [*Icel.* ū-drukkinn.]

un-drysnende *inextinguishable*; inextinguibilis, Mt. Kmbl. Lind. 3, 12.

un-dyrne. v. un-dirne.

un-eácniendlīc; *adj. Unproductive, sterile*; infecundus, Hpt. Gl. 430, 57.

un-earh; *adj. Undaunted, intrepid, fearless*:—Unærh *impavidus, intrepidus*, Hpt. Gl. 502, 61. Sum cāsere wæs on ðām dagum unearh on gefeohtum, Homl. Skt. ii. 27, 47. Gif mann bið ākenned on .xxii. nihta ealdne mōnan se bið unearh fihtling, Lchdm. iii. 158, 11. Ðǣr mihton geseón Winceastre leódan rancne here and unearhne, ðæt hī be hyra gate tō sǣ eodon, and mæte and mādmas ofer .L. mīla him fram sǣ fættan, Chr. 1006; Erl. 140, 26. Wendon forð wlance þegenas, unearge men, Byrht. Th. 137, 54; By. 206.

un-earhlīc; *adj. Intrepid, dauntless*:—Hē cwæð tō ðam cāsere unearhlīcere stemme, Homl. Skt. i. 23, 164.

un-eáðe *and* un-iéðe (-ēðe, -īðe, -ȳðe); *adj.* I. of that which is not easy to do, *difficult, hard*:—Nis ðæt uneáðe ealwealdan Gode tō gefremmanne, Andr. Kmbl. 409; An. 205. Hē sǣde ðæt se cræft uniéðe wǣre tō gehealdenne *praedicit quia difficile capitur*, Past. 52; Swt. 409, 20. Hit is uniéðe tō gesecgenne hū monege gewin wǣron, Ors. 1, 12; Swt. 52, 8. II. of that which is not easy to bear, *troublesome, unpleasant, grievous*:—Se līchoma on ðone fūlostan stenc bið gecyrred . . . and hē byð uneáðe ǣlcon men on neáweste tō hæbbenne, Blickl. Homl. 59, 15. Uneáðe mē is ðis *I am in a great strait* (2 Sam. 24, 14), Homl. Skt. i. 13, 247. Ðæt folc hine hæfde swā yfele swā hē sumes þinges scyldig wǣre . . . and him wæs swā uneáðe amang ðām, and him ða eágan floterodon, and bitere teáras āleton, 23, 654. For hwȳ sceal ǣnigum menn ðyncan tō rēðe oððe tō uniéðe ðæt hē Godes suingellan geðafige *cur asperum creditur, ut a Deo homo toleret flagella?* Past. 36; Swt. 261, 20. Seó wīse wæs mīne (in mē, *v.l.*) on twā healfa unēþe *quae res dupliciter me torsit*, Nar. 9, 23. Him bið unēþe þurst getenge *he will be oppressed by troublesome thirst*, Lchdm. ii. 174, 23. Wamb ungewealden and unȳþe, 242, 5. Unȳþe *molestus*, Wrt. Voc. ii. 56, 12. Swā oft swā wē ōht uneáþes þrowian æt yfflum monnum, Blickl. Homl. 33, 22. Hē Gode þancie ealles ðæs ðe hē him forgeaf, ǣgðer ge ȳðran ge unȳðran, L. E. I. 29; Th. ii. 426, 11. Hē was underfange[n] of ðām hādesmannum ðe him ealra uneáþest was, ðæt was clerican *he was received by those of the clergy that it was most distasteful to him to be received by, that is by the secular clergy* (cf. Aþelwold drāf ūt ða clerca of þe biscoprīce, 963; Th. i. 220, 19), Chr. 995; Th. i. 244, 6. III. of that which is not readily done, to which one is not easily moved, and so is little done:—Ðū gionga, bió ðē unīðe tō clipianne and tō lǣranne *do not let it be an easy matter to you to call and to teach; adolescens loquere vix*, Past. 49; Swt. 385, 10. [Þeih hem be uneáðe ne sal nafre eft Crist þolien deað for lesen hem of deaðe, O. E. Homl. ii. 225, 183. Corineus was uneðe and wa on his mode, Laym. 2259.]

un-eáðe; *adv.* I. where a thing is not easily done, *with difficulty*:—Se weliga uneáþe (-eáðe, Lind.) gǣþ in heofuna rīce *dives difficile intrabit in regnum coelorum*, Mt. Kmbl. Rush. 19, 23. Swīðe uneáðe (-eáða, Lind.) ł hefige, Mk. Skt. Rush. 10, 23: Lk. Skt. Lind. 18, 24. Hē uneáðe āwæig com, and him ðǣr micel forfērde, Chr. 1052; Erl. 181, 18. Swīðe strang gyld, ðæt man hit uneáðe ācom, 1040; Erl. 166, 21. Ða lufe mon mæg swīðe uneáþe oððe nā forbeódan, Bt. 35, 6; Fox 170, 11. Ongit hē swā micle māran sige on him selfum swā hē uniéð wiðstōd *he will feel so much greater victory in himself as he had greater difficulty in withstanding*, Past. 52; Swt. 407, 26. Ðisse ādle fruman mon mæg ȳþelīce gelācnian . . . and æfter unēð, gif hió bið unwīslīce tō lange forlǣten, Lchdm. ii. 232, 17. Cumaþ æalle tō ānum hlāforde, sume ēð sume unēð, Shrn. 187, 15. II. where a thing is not easily borne, *grievously, hardly*:—Sume uneáþe gedrycnede (gedrehte, MS. C.) āweg cōman *turpi macie exinanitos adflictosque pestilentia dimiserit*, Ors. 3, 3; Swt. 102, 10. Rīc heofna uneáðe geðolas *regnum caelorum vim patitur*, Mt. Kmbl. Lind. 11, 12. III. where a thing is not readily done, *unwillingly, hardly*:—Ðā geþafedon ðæt uneáþe ða his gesacan *quod cum adversarii inviti concederent*, Bd. 2, 2; S. 502, 24. Ðā underfēng hē hig uneáðe *vix fratre compellente suscipiens*, Gen. 33, 11. IV. with a force only slightly removed from a negative, *hardly, scarcely, only just*:—Uneáþe cwic ætberstende *vix vivus evadens*, Coll. Monast. Th. 27, 3. Uneáðe Isaac geendode ðās sprǣce ðā com Esau *vix Isaac sermonem impleverat, venit Esau*, Gen. 27, 30. Hē uneáþe ðurh hine sylfne oþþe ārīsan oþþe gangan mihte *vix ipse per se exsurgere aut incedere valeret*, Bd. 4, 31; S. 610, 19. Uneáþe ic mæg forstandan ðīne ācsunga and cwist þeáh ðæt ic ðē andwyrdan scyle *vix rogationis tuae sententiam nosco, ne dum ad inquisita respondere queam*, Bt. 5, 3; Fox 12, 15. Ic hit mæg uneáþe mid wordum gereccan *sententiam verbis explicare vix queo*, 20; Fox 70, 27. Uneáþe ǣnig com tō ende ðære sprǣce *ad rem . . . cui vix exhausti quidquam satis sit*, 39, 4; Fox 216, 16. Uneáðe (*pretium scorti*) *vix* (*est unius panis*, Prov. 6, 26), Kent. Gl. 163. Ungeáþe (uneáþe, Cott. MS.), Bt. 35, 3; Fox 158, 28. [Itt wass till ennde brohht unnæþe and all wiþþ ange, Orm. 16289. Þu me hauest sore igramed þat ic mai uneaþe speke, O. and N. 1605. Cf. He spac uneðes, so e gret, Gen. and Ex. 2341. *Chauc.* unnethe, unnethes, and v. Halliwell's Dict. *unnethe*.]

un-eáðelic; *adj.* I. *difficult* to do, *impossible*:—Uneáðelīc ðæt ys mid mannum *apud homines hoc impossibile est*, Mt. Kmbl. 19, 26. Uneáþelīc, Mk. Skt. 10, 27. Līg fȳres on ceafa yrnende æthabban ys uneáþelīc *flammam ignis in paleas currentem retinere est impossibile*, Scint. 57, 7. II. *difficult* to bear, *grievous, troublesome*:—Ne heó (*a sin*) nǣfre ne þince eów tō ðan hefig ne tō ðan uneáðelīc ne tō ðam fracodlīc, ðæt gē ǣfre lǣton ǣnig ðing ungeandett, Wulfst. 135, 12. Unēþelīcne wæterbollan *a grievous dropsy*, Lchdm. ii. 204, 13. Ðās onfōað unēðelīc (-ēðlīc, Lind.) dōm *hi accipient prolixius judicium*, Mk. Skt. Rush. 12, 40.

un-eáðelice; *adv.* I. *with difficulty*:—Mid ðȳ wit ðæt unēþelīce ðurhtugan ðæt hē ðæs geþafa beón wolde *cum hoc difficulter impetraremus*, Bd. 5, 4; S. 617, 17. Hē geseah ðæt hē unȳþelīce (*difficulter*) mihte ða heánnesse ðæs cynelīcan mōdes tō eádmōdnesse gecyrran, 2, 12; S. 512, 27. II. *with trouble* or *inconvenience, under difficulties*:—Hē uniéþelīce æfter wudum fōr and on mōrfæstenum, Chr. 878; Erl. 78, 33. Ða scipu wurdon swīðe unēðelīce āseten *the ships were stranded in a most inconvenient manner*, 897; Erl. 95, 29.

un-eáðelicness, e; *f.* *Difficulty*:—Ðā wæs mycel unēþelīcnes geworden be his byrignesse *facta difficultate tumulandi*, Bd. 4, 11; S. 580, 8.

un-eáðlǣcn[e ?], -lǣcne; *adj.* *Not easily cured*:—Biþ ðonne se milte uneáþlǣcne, ðonne ðæt blōd āheardaþ on ðǣm ǣdrum, Lchdm. ii. 250, 5. Cyrnelu uneáðlācnu, 240, 21. Ða dolh beóþ uneáðlācnu, 242, 10. Uneáðlācno, 242, 3. Seó wǣte wyrcþ uneáþlācna ādla, 226, 15.

un-eáðlǣce; *adj.* *Not easily cured*:—Gif hit biþ of yfelre inwǣtan hit biþ ðe uneáþlǣcra, Lchdm. ii. 258, 27.

un-eáðmilte; *adj.* *Not easily digested, indigestible*:—Sió melt mete wel, swīþost ða ðe hearde beóð and uneáðmylte, Lchdm. ii. 220, 23.

un-eáðness, e; *f.* I. *uneasiness of mind, anxiety, trouble, grief, difficulty*:—Hē ealle ða word gehȳrde, and ǣfre wæs his uneáðnys wexende, Homl. Skt. i. 23, 621. Ne biþ ðǣr sār ne gewinn, ne nǣnig unēþnes, ne sorg ne wōp, Blickl. Homl. 103, 35. Hē swȳþe weóp and mid mycelre unēðnysse his eágospind mid teárum leohte. Ðā frēfrode hine Gūthlāc and him cwæð tō: 'Ne beó ðū nā geunrōtsod, forþon ne bið mē nǣnig unēðnysse ðæt ic tō Drihtne fare, Guthl. 20; Gdwin. 82, 2–8. Hī on wōpe wǣron and hī on uneáðnysse sprǣcon, Homl. Skt. i. 23, 247. Ðū manigfeald yfel hæfdest and micle unēþnesse on ðam rīce, Bt. 27, 2; Fox 96, 13. Ealle angnysse and uneáðnysse, Lchdm. iii. 156, 13. Gif hit geberige ðæt hē ða unǣtnessa ābidan scel, Chart. Th. 509, 33. Hwæt wylt ðū tō mēde gesyllan ðam ðe ðe fram ðissum unēðnyssum ālȳseþ? Shrn. 16, 29. Ðū canst mīne yrmþa, ðū mē wǣre symble on fultume on mīnum unȳðnyssum, Guthl. 21; Gdwin. 94, 11. II. *severity, harshness*:—Ða ðe ðǣr gefongne wǣron hié tawedan mid ðære mǣstan uniéðnesse; sume ofslōgon, sume ofswungon, sume wið feó gesealdon, Ors. 4, 1; Swt. 154, 8.

Unecunga? The word occurs in a list of territorial names:—Unecung(a ?)ga (Ynetunga, p. 415; Unecung-ga, p. 416) twelf hund hȳda, Cod. Dip. B. i. 414, 26.

un-efn, -efen, -emn, -emne (?); *adj.* *Unequal, unlike, dissimilar, diverse, irregular*:—Hū ðǣr wæs unefen racu unc gemǣne, ic onfēng ðīn sār ðæt ðū mōste gesǣlig mīnes ēþelrīces neótan, Exon. Th. 89, 20; Cri. 1460. Dysigra monna mōd bið suīðe unemn and suīðe ungelīc . . . Ac ðara monna mōd bið suīðe unemn, for ðæm hit gedēð hit self him selfum suīðe ungelīc for ðære gelōmlīcan wendinge, for ðæm hit nǣfre eft ne bið ðæt hit ǣr wæs *cor stultorum dissimile erit . . . Cor vero stultorum dissimile est, quia, dum mutabilitate se varium exhibet, numquam id, quod fuerat, manet*, Past. 42; Swt. 306, 12–18. Sume word synd gehātene *anomala* oþþe *inequalia*. *Anomalus* is unemne, *inequalis* ungelīc, Ælfc. Gr. 32; Zup. 199, 3. Ða unefne ł ungelīco burna woegas *diversos rivulorum tramites*, Mt. Kmbl. p. 2, 9.

un-efne; *adv.* *Unequally, diversely*:—Swā unefne is eorþe þicce *sicut crassitudo terrae*, Ps. Th. 140, 9.

un-efnlic; *adj.* *Unequal, diverse*:—Unefenlīcra *diversarum*, Mt. Kmbl. p. 7, 5.

un-endebyrdlice; *adv.* *In a disorderly manner, without order, irregularly*:—Gif hē unendebyrdlīce onet mid ðære sprǣce *si inordinate ad loquendum rapitur*, Past. 15; Swt. 93, 18. Ðonne ðæt mōd bið forlǣten and onstyred and tōdǣled ungedafenlīce and unendebyrdlīce on unðeáwas *si inordinatis dimissa motibus mens vitiis dissipatur*, 43; Swt. 315, 7. Unendebyrdlīce *inordinate*, Scint. 101, 14: 191, 3.

un-ered; *adj.* *Unploughed*:—Unered land *rus*, Wrt. Voc. i. 37, 49.

un-ēðe, un-ǣwisc. v. un-eáðe, un-ǣwisc.

un-fǣcne, -fācne; *adj.* *Without deceit, without fraud*:—Unfaecni, -fēcni *non subscivum*, Txts. 81, 1386. Unfǣcne (*printed* -sæcne), Wrt. Voc. ii. 60, 16. Gif man mægð gebigeþ ceápi, geceápod sȳ, gif hit unfācne is, L. Ethb. 77; Th. i. 22, 2. Gif man mannan ofsleá, unfācne feó gehwilce gelde (*there should be no fraud as regards anything given in payment of the* wergild), 30; Th. i. 10, 4. Ic Heaþobeardna hyldo ne talige Denum unfǣcne, freóndscipe fæstne, Beo. Th. 4143; B. 2068. Hæbbe hē him twēgen oþþe þreó unfācne ceorlas tō gewitnesse, L. H. G. 16; Th. i. 34, 4.

un-fæderlice; *adv.* *In an unfatherly manner*:—Saturnus wæs swā wælhreów, ðæt hē fordyde his āgene bearn ealle būtan ānum and unfæderlīce macode heora līf tō lyre, Wulfst. 106, 6.

un-fǣge; *adj.* *Not fey, not appointed to die*:—Mæg unfǣge eáðe gedīgan weán and wræcsīð, se ðe Waldendes hyldo gehealdeþ *out of misery and exile may easily come one not appointed to die, who possesses God's favour*, Beo. Th. 4571; B. 2291. Wyrd oft nereþ unfǣgne eorl, ðonne his ellen deáh, 1150; B. 573. [*Icel.* ū-feigr *not fey*.] v. un-fǣglīc.

un-fæger; *adj.* *Not fair, not beautiful, foul, ugly, horrid*:—Sió gefrēdnes mæg gefrēdan ðæt hit līchoma biþ, ac hió ne mæg gefrēdan hwæþer hē biþ ðe blac ðe hwīt, ðe fæger þe unfæger, Bt. 41, 4; Fox 252, 12. Þincð his (*a dead man's*) neáwist lāþlīco and unfæger, Blickl. Homl. 111, 30. Him of eágum stōd līge gelīcost leóht unfæger *from*

Grendel's eyes there shot a horrid light like flame, Beo. Th. 1459; B. 727. Se unfægera *larbata* (cf. hreófe *larbatos*, 86, 64: egisgrîma *larbula*, 112, 21), Wrt. Voc. ii. 95, 68. [*Goth.* un-fagrs *ingratus*: *Icel.* û-fagr *ugly*.]

un-fægere; *adv. Unpleasantly, ungently, terribly, cruelly*:—Hê ðæt unfægere wera cneórissum gewrecan þôhte, Cd. Th. 77, 11; Gen. 1273. Gripon unfægre under sceát werum scearpe gâras, 124, 16; Gen. 2063. Sampson hewis doun of þa hirdis, hurtis þam unfaire, Alex. (Sk.) 1224, [and see Glossary.]

un-fægerness, e; *f. Foulness, ugliness, abomination*:—Unfegernis slitnese *abominatio desolationis*, Mt. Kmbl. Lind. 24, 15.

un-fǽglic; *adj. Not indicating impending death*:—Ðæt is tâcn ðînre hǽle; swâ swâ lǽca gewuna is, ðæt hê cweþaþ ðonne hió seócne mon gesióþ, gef hê hwelc unfǽglîc (ungefǽglîc, Cott. MS.) tâcn (*a symptom which does not indicate that a disease is mortal*) him on geseóþ: mê þincþ nû ðæt ðîn gecynd flîte swîþe swîþlîce wiþ ðæm dysige *id, uti medici sperare solent, indicium est erectae jam resistentisque naturae*, Bt. 36, 4; Fox 178, 27. v. un-fǽge.

un-fǽhð, e; *f. Absence of hostility*; the word refers to the abstention from the prosecuting of the feud, which under certain conditions it would be allowable for the kinsmen of a man to follow up:—Se ðe þeóf gefêhð, hê âh .x. sciłł.... and ða mǽgas him swerian âðas unfǽhða (cf. unceáses âð, 35; Th. i. 124, 8, the circumstances in the two cases being similar), L. In. 28; Th. i. 120, 6. v. un-fâh.

un-fǽle; *adj. Evil, ill, bad*:—Unfǽle (*printed* -sǽle), gemâh *improbus*, Wrt. Voc. ii. 45, 16. (1) applied to living objects:—Hî wêndon ðæt hit unfǽle gâst (*phantasma*) wǽre, Mk. Skt. 6, 49. *Satiri* vel *fauni* vel *selini* vel *fauni ficarii* unfǽle men, wudewâsan, unfǽle wihtu, Wrt. Voc. i. 17, 20. Unfǽle men *satyri* vel *fauni*, wudewâsan *ficarii* vel *invii*, 60, 23-4. [Gif þe unfele man his wille folgeð, and teð him to unwrenches, O. E. Homl. ii. 79, 27. Þe laþe gast cwelleþþ hemm þurrh his unnfæle þeowwess, Orm. 8034. Iðisse wildernesse beoð monie vuele bestes (unfeale bestes monie, MS. T.), A. R. 198, 2. Ȝef heo is atbroide þenne heo is unfele and forbrode, O. and N. 1381.] (2) applied to inanimate objects:—Ofet unfǽle (*the forbidden fruit*), Cd. Th. 45, 7; Gen. 723. Unfǽle *dira* (the passage is: *dira vinculorum ligamina*, Ald. 44), Anglia xiii. 34, 178. [Þat water is unfæle, Laym. 22018. Þat lond is grislich and unfele, þe men beoþ wilde and unisele, O. and N. 1003. Þe stude (*hell*) is swiþe unvele (*rimes with* hele = *heal*), Misc. 73, 45. Cf. A seolcuð mere . . . mid uniuele þingen, Laym. 21744.]

un-fæst; *adj. Not firm, unstable, unsteady, weak*:—Hû ne is ðê nû genôh sweotole gesǽd ðæt seó wyrd ðê ne mæg nâne gesǽlþa sellan, for ðam ðe ǽgþer is unfæst ge seó wyrd ge seó gesǽlþ *manifestum est, quod ad beatitudinem percipiendam fortunae instabilitas aspirare non possit*, Bt. 11, 2; Fox 34, 21. Hwæt getâcnaþ ðonne ðæt flǽsc bûton unfæsð weorc and hnesce . . .? Oft ðeáh gebyreþ ðætte sume on monegum weorcum unfæste beóð ongietene *quid per carnes nisi infirma quaedam ac tenera acta signantur? Et plerumque contigit, ut quidam in nonnullis suis actibus infirmi videantur*, Past. 34; Swt. 235, 14-17. Ðonne ðæt môd bið on monig tôdǽled, hit bið on ânes hwæm ðe unfæstre *impar quisque invenitur ad singula, dum confusa mente dividitur ad multa*, 4; Swt. 37, 15. [*O. H. Ger.* un-festi *infirmus*.]

un-fæstende; *adj. Not fasting*:—Ðæt ǽnig unfæstende man hûsles ne âbirige, L. Edg. C. 36; Th. ii. 252, 1.

un-fæstlîce; *adv. Not firmly, uncertainly, vaguely*:—Ðonne mon smeáð on his môde ymb hwelc eorðlîc ðing, ðonne dêð hê swelce hê hit âtîfre on his heortan, and swǽ tweólîce and unfæstlîce hê âtîfreþ ðæs ðinges onlîcnesse on his môde ðe hê ðonne ymb smeáð, Past. 21; Swt. 156, 13.

un-fæstrǽd[e], -râd; *adj. Infirm of purpose, inconstant, unstable, weak*:—Unfæstrǽd *inconstans*, Wrt. Voc. ii. 49, 4. Ðâ ongon hê ǽresð herigean on him ðæt ðæt hê fæsðrǽdes wiste and sôna æfter ðon suîðe lîðelîce hierd[d]e ða ðe hê unfæsðrâde (unfæstrǽdes, Cott. MSS.) wisse *prius in eis, quae fortia prospicit, laudat, et caute monendo postmodum, quae infirma sunt roborat*, Past. 32; Swt. 213, 9. Ða ungestæððegan and unfæsðrǽdan *inconstantes*, 23; Swt. 177, 4: 42; Swt. 305, 11.

un-fæstrǽdness, e; *f. Instability, inconstancy, levity*:—Hié wêndon ðæt hê nyste hiera leohtmôdnesse and hiera unfæstrǽdnesse *dum de ipsa levitate motionis praedicatori suo se incognitos crederent*, Past. 32; Swt. 214, 2. On heora wandlunga hié gecýþdon heora unfæstrǽdnesse, Bt. 7, 2; Fox 16, 32 note.

un-fâh; *adj. Not regarded as a foe*, used of the kinsmen of a criminal when not involved in the feud which their kinsman's guilt occasioned:—Gif hwâ heonanforð ǽnigne man ofsleá, ðæt hê wege sylf ða fǽhðe . . . Gif hine seó mǽgð forlǽte . . . ðonne wille ic ðæt eall seó mǽgð sý unfâh, bûtan ðam handdǽdan, L. Edm. S. 1; Th. i. 248, 2-7. [*O. Frs.* unfâch.] v. un-fǽhþ.

un-fealdan; *p.* -feóld *To unfold, unroll*:—Unfealdaþ *replicant*, i. *reuoluunt*, Scint. 140, 2. Hê ða bôc unfeóld *reuoluit librum*, Lk. Skt. 4, 17.

un-feferig; *adj. Not feverish*:—Syle drincan on wîne, gif hê unfeferig sý; gif hê on fefere sý, syle drincan him on wætere, Lchdm. i. 164, 19.

un-fêlende; *adj. Unfeeling, callous*:—Yfele swilas unfêlende, Lchdm. ii. 264, 13.

un-feor[r]; *adv. Not far off.* I. marking position, *at no great distance off*, (1) where the point from which the distance is measured is given by an adverb:—Ðǽr wæs unfeorr (-feor, MS. A.) ân swýna heord *erat non longe ab illis grex porcorum*, Mt. Kmbl. 8, 30. Ðâ geseah hê deófol ðǽr unfeor standan, Blickl. Homl. 227, 24. (2) with dative:—Ðâ hê wæs unfeor ðam hûse *cum non longe esset a domo*, Lk. Skt. 7, 6. Ðæt is unfeor ðære byrig Neapoli *quod est non longe a Neapoli*, Bd. 4, 1; S. 563, 30: Cd. Th. 125, 22; Gen. 2083. Unfeor herge *haud procul a delubro*, Hpt. Gl. 493, 36. (3) with dative and adverb:—Se rinc him ðǽr rom geseah unfeor þanon standan, Cd. Th. 177, 9; Gen. 2927. (4) with preposition:—Hî wǽron unfeor fram lande *non longe erant a terra*, Jn. Skt. 21, 8. Fram ðam mynstre unfeor wæs ðære abbudissan mynster *a quo (monasterio) non longe illa monasterium habebat*, Bd. 3, 11; S. 536, 1. (5) where the point from which distance is measured is implied:—Wutað ðætte unfeorr sié *scitote quod in proximo sit*, Mk. Skt. Lind. 13, 29. II. with verbs of motion, (*to*) *no great distance*:—Hig wendan unfeorr ût on Wealas *they marched a short distance into Wales*, Chr. 1055; Erl. 190, 12.

un-feormigende *inexpiable*:—Ðâ onhrân mîn môd hǽlo andgit mid mê sylfre þencende ðæt mê ðone ingang belucen ða onfeormeganda mînra misdǽda *the inexpiable circumstances of my misdeeds had closed the entrance for me*, Homl. Skt. ii. 23 b, 426. v. feormian, III.

un-fêre; *adj. Incapacitated, disabled, infirm, feeble*:—Se wæs Æþelstânes biscopes gespelia syððan hê unfêre wæs, Chr. 1055; Erl. 190, 21. [Þa iwærð þe king unfere. Swa þe king seoc læi . . . ne mihte he þer of beon hæl, Laym. 6780. Al unfer he it (*Moses's leprous hand*) fond, Gen. and Ex. 2810. Þat licour for to dele unto þe unfere, L. H. R. 115, 277. See also Halliwell's Dict. *Icel.* û-fœrr *disabled*.]

un-flitme; *adv. Without dispute*:—Fin Hengeste elne unflitme âðum benemde ðæt hê ða weálâfe ârum heólde (*Fin confirmed with oaths the terms he made with Hengest, and there was no dispute about the terms which were settled*), Beo. Th. 2198; B. 1097.

un-forbærned; *adj. Unburnt, not burnt up, not consumed by fire*:—Ðǽr is deáw, ðonne ðǽr bið man deád, ðæt hê lîð inne unforbærned mid his mâgum and freóndum mônað, . . . hwîlum healf geár ðæt hî beóð unforbærned, Ors. 1, 1; Swt. 20, 19-24. Gyf man ân bân findeþ unforbærned, hî hit sceolan miclum gebêtan, Swt. 21, 12. Tiburtius eode ofer ða byrnendan glêda unforbærnedum fôtum, Homl. Skt. i. 5, 380.

un-forboden; *adj. Unforbidden, not prohibited, free from any moral* or *legal hindrance*:—Ðæt hî môston him beran unforboden flǽsc, Homl. Skt. ii. 25, 91. Swâ ic hit hæbbe, swâ hit se sealde, ðe tô syllanne âhte, unforboden (*no one had a right to forbid the entering into possession of the property*), L. O. 13; Th. i. 184, 5. Unforboden and unbesacan, Cod. Dip. Kmbl. iv. 234, 20. Gebohte se arcebisceop æt Ælfhêge ðæt land æt Sendan mid .xc. pundum, and æt Sunnanbyrg mid .cc. mancussan goldes, unbecwedene and unforbodene wið ǽlcne man tô ðære dægtîde; and hê him swâ ða land geágnian derr, swâ him se sealde ðe tô syllenne âhte, Chart. Th. 208, 38.

un-forbûgendlîc; *adj. Unavoidable, inevitable*:—Unforbûgendlîc *inevitabile*, Hpt. Gl. 440, 40.

un-forbûgendlîce; *adv. Without turning aside, constantly, fixedly*:—Ic cwæð tô hire geornlîce and unforbûgendlîce behealdende and cweðende: Eálâ . . ., Homl. Skt. ii. 23 b, 431.

un-forburnen; *adj. Unburnt, not consumed by fire*:—Se wind âbær ðone lîg tô ðæs cyninges botle, swâ ðæt him ne belǽfde nân þing unforburnen, and hê sylf earfoðlîce ðam fýre ætbærst, Homl. Th. ii. 480, 7.

un-forcûþ; *adj. Not despicable, not ignoble, not wicked, honourable, noble, good*:—Ic eom heard and strong, forðsîdes from, freán unforcûð, Exon. Th. 479, 22; Rä. 63, 2. Hêr stynt unforcûð eorl ðe wile gealgian êþel ðysne, Byrht. Th. 133, 16; By. 51. Eorl unforcûð elnes gemyndig, Andr. Kmbl. 2527; An. 1265. Nǽfre ic sǽlidan sêlran mêtte . . . ic wille ðê, eorl unforcûð, biddan, 949; An. 475. Ðegn unforcûð, Menol. Fox 338; Men. 170. Hê þenceþ ðæt his wîse þince eal unforcûþ, Exon. Th. 315, 14; Môd. 31. Cweðan ealle ðæt unforcûðe ðe him on standeþ egsa Dryhtnes *dicant qui timent Dominum*, Ps. Th. 117, 4.

un-forcûþlîce; *adv. Nobly, excellently*:—Metode geþungon Abraham and Loth unforcûðlîce, swâ him from yldrum æðelu wǽron, Cd. Th. 103, 9; Gen. 1715.

un-fordyt[t]; *adj. Unobstructed, unstopped*:—Ða unfordyttan gemâgnesse *obstinatam importunitatem (garrulitatem)*, Hpt. Gl. 491, 24.

un-forebyrdig; *adj. Impatient*; inpatiens, Scint. 8, 13.

un-fored. v. un-forod.

un-foresceáwod; *adj. Unconsidered, hasty, without due consideration*:—Næs hit nâ fǽrlîc geðôht oððe unforesceáwod rǽd, ðæt se ælmihtiga God ðysne middangeard gesceóp, ac wæs ǽfre æt fruman on his êcum rǽde, Hexam. 14; Norm. 22, 5.

un-foresceáwodlîc; *adj. Hasty, inconsiderate, rash*:—On scyterǽs oþþe on fǽrfyll, unforesceáwodlîc *in precets*, Wrt. Voc. ii. 47, 44. v. un-forsceáwodlîc.

un-forfeored (un-forfored (?). v. un-forodlíc; *also* ungebrocenre *extricabili*, 33, 7: perhaps in each case *inextricabilis* should be read, cf. untōsliten *inextricabilis*, 110, 60); *adj. Unbroken;* extricabile, Wrt. Voc. ii. 145, 22. v. forod.

un-forgifen; *adj.* I. *unforgiven:*—Ealle scylda đe wiđ God beóđ ungebētta beóđ unforgifne on dōmes dæge, Past. 33; Swt. 220, 17. II. *not given in marriage* (cf. *Goth.* fra-gifts *espousal; Icel.* ū-gefinn *unmarried*):—Unforgifenum *innupti*, Wrt. Voc. ii. 45, 19.

un-forgitende; *adj. Not forgetful, mindful:*—Đīnra gewinna and earfođa ic eom unforgitende, Guthl. 19; Gdwin. 76, 22.

un-forgolden; *adj. Unremunerated, not paid for:*—Nafa đū āne niht unforgolden đæs weorc đe đē wirce *do not leave unpaid for a night the work of him that works for thee*, Lev. 19, 13.

un-forhæfedness, e; *f. Incontinence:*—Gӯfernyss mōder ys unforhæfednysse (*incontinentiae*), Scint. 89, 14. Unforhæfdnysse, Bd. 1, 27; S. 493, 36.

un-forhladen; *adj. Unexhausted:*—Unforhladenum *inexaustis*, Wülck. Gl. 255, 39.

un-forht; *adj. Not frightened, not afraid, fearless, intrepid:*—Đæt geđyld stent unforht betweónan đara leahtra truman *patientia inter acies vitiorum intrepida stat*, Gl. Prud. 17 b. Hwæt eart đū, đū đe swā unforht ūs tō eart cumen? Nicod. 28; Thw. 16, 33: Homl. Skt. i. 18, 262: Cd. Th. 199, 7; Exod. 335: Exon. Th. 278, 21; Jul. 601: Rood Kmbl. 218; Kr 110. Se Hǣlend unforht āxode, Homl. Th. ii. 246, 13: Exon. Th. 255, 5; Jul. 209. On wicge sæt ombeht unforht, Beo. Th. 579; B. 287. Him seó unforhte āgeaf andsware, Exon. Th. 251, 18; Jul. 147. Unforhte mōde hē geneálǣhte đære stōwe, Blickl. Homl. 67, 1. Se man hӯwaþ hine sylfne mihtine and unforhtne, Wulfst. 53, 15. Wīgend unforhte, Cd. Th. 189, 6; Exod. 180: Byrht. Th. 134, 5; By. 79. Hī unforhte and blīþe underhnigon deáþ *mortem laeti subiere*, Bd. 4, 16; S. 584, 37. Đæt hī đӯ baldran and đӯ unforhtran wǣron (đæt heora compweorodes mōd đӯ unforhtre beón sceolde, col. 2) *sperantes minus animos militum trepidare*, 3, 18; S. 546, 24.

un-forhte; *adv. Fearlessly:*—Hē wille leóde etan unforhte, Beo. Th. 892; B. 444.

un-forhtigende; *adj. Not fearing, fearless:*—Hē wolde leódum bodian on fyrlenum lande unforhtigende, Homl. Th. ii. 140, 29.

un-forhtlīce; *adv. Fearlessly, without fear:*—Unforhtlīce *non trepide*, R. Ben. 20, 18. Hē unforhtlīce đa strǣle đara āwerigdra gāsta him fram āsceáf, Guthl. 6; Gdwin. 42, 24. Twā swalewan hī setton unforhtlīce on đa sculdra Gūđlāces, 10; Gdwin. 52, 9: Homl. Th. i. 508, 1: ii. 558, 30. Hē đӯ unforhtlīcor đone deáþ ārǣfnode, Shrn. 129, 21.

un-forhtmōd; *adj. Fearless:*—Ic unforhtmōd đæs drences onfō, Homl. Th. i. 72, 17. Sixtus unforhtmōd tō his preóstum clypode: 'Mīne gebrōđra, ne beó gē āfyrhte, and eówer nān him ne ondrǣde đa scortan tintregunga,' 416, 6.

un-forlǣten; *adj. Not left:*—Unforlētne *non relicto*, Mk. Skt. Lind. Rush. 12, 20.

un-formolsniendlīc; *adj. Undecaying, incorruptible:*—Unforwurdenlīcne ɫ [unfor]molsniendlīcne (*or* [un]molsniendlīcne?) *incorruptam, immarcescibilem*, Hpt. Gl. 407, 37.

un-formolsnod; *adj. Undecayed:*—His līchama līđ unformolsnod, Th. An. 124, 4.

un-formolten; *adj. Unconsumed, undigested:*—Se wītega wæs gehealden unformolten on đæs hwæles innođe, Homl. Th. i. 488, 7.

un-forod(-ed); *adj. Unbroken, inviolate:*—Werige hine se Frǣncisca mid unforedan āþe, L. W. ii. 3; Th. i. 489, 25. Wē sceolon healdan đone brōđerlīcan bend unforedne, Homl. Th. i. 260, 29. v. next word.

un-forodlīc; *adj. Indissoluble:*—Unforedlīcre racent[e]āgæ *inextricabili collario*, Hpt. Gl. 455, 9. Unforedlīcum bende *inextricabili* (*indissolvibili*) *repagulo*, 462, 73. Unforadlīce *inextricabile* (*vinculum*), 521, 75.

un-forrotigendlīc; *adj. Not liable to decay, imperishable, incorruptible:*—Beó his calic of clǣnum antimbre geworht unforrotigendlīc, gylden ođđe seolfern ođđe tinen, L. Ælfc. C. 22; Th. ii. 350, 23. Unforrotiendlīc, 36; Th. ii. 360, 42.

un-forrotodlīc; *adj. Not liable to decay, incorruptible, imperishable:*—Unforrotedlīces *immarcescibilis, imputribilis*, Hpt. Gl. 467, 45.

un-forsceáwodlīce; *adv.* I. *unexpectedly:*—Ōþ đæt đe hig (wildeór) cuman tō đām nettan unforsceáwodlīce *usque quo perveniant ad retia improvise*, Coll. Monast. Th. 21, 17. II. *without forethought, without consideration:*—Ne getīmode Thōme unforsceáwodlīce đæt hē ungeleáfful wæs, ac hit getīmode þurh Godes forsceáwunge, Homl. Th. i. 234, 19. Gif hē hit ǣne and unforsceáwodlīce gedyde *si semel et inconsiderate fecerit*, L. Ecg. C. 39; Th. ii. 164, 24. v. un-foresceáwodlīc.

un-forswǣled; *adj. Unburnt, unscorched:*—Ic geseó feówer weras gangende onmiddan đam fӯre ungewemmede and unforswǣlede *ego video quatuor viros . . . ambulantes in medio ignis, et nihil corruptionis in eis est* (Dan. 3, 25), Homl. Th. ii. 20, 15.

un-forswigod; *adj. Not passed over in silence, not omitted:*—Ān weorc hē hæfde unforswigod . . . đæt wæs sealmsang *one work he never allowed to pass in silence . . . that was psalmsinging*, Homl. Skt. ii. 23 b, 35.

un-forswīþed; *adj. Unconquered:*—Ic đæs þoncunge dō đæm unforswӯþdum ūrum weorode *ago gratias inuicto exercitui nostro*, Nar. 2, 31.

un-fortredde *not destroyed by treading;* a name given to a plant that can grow in trodden paths, *knot-grass;* polygonum aviculare:—*Pilogonus et sanguinaria* đæt is unfortredde, Wrt. Voc. i. 68, 66. Unfortrædde. Đeós wyrt đe man *proserpinacam* and ōđrum naman unfortredde nemneþ, heó biđ cenned gehwǣr on begānum stōwum, Lchdm. i. 112, 4-7. [Cf. way-grass, E. D. S. Plant Names: *O. H. Ger.* wege-trat *centenodia; umbi-trat *serpinacia;* ana-tret *proserpinaca*.] v. next word.

un-fortreden; *adj. Not destroyed by treading:*—Unfortreden wyrt *appoligonius* (=*polygonum*), Lchdm. iii. 299, col. 2. v. preceding word.

un-forwandigendlīce; *adv. Unhesitatingly, freely, without regard to fear* or *shame:*—Gif đū wundrige đæt swā scamfæst fǣmne swā unforwandigendlīce đās word āwrāt, đonne wite đū đæt ic hæbbe þurh weax āboden, đe nāne scame ne can, đæt ic silf đē for scame secgan ne mihte, Ap. Th. 21, 9.

un-forwandodlīc; *adj. Undeterred by fear* or *shame, fearless, free:*—Đæt hē wiđstande mid his sprǣce đām unryhtwillendum đe đyses middangeardes waldaþ mid freóre and unforwandodlīcre stefne *voce libera hujus mundi potestatibus contraire*, Past. 15; Swt. 89, 23. Đonne wēnaþ hié đæt hié sprecen for unforwandodlīcre and orsorglīcre ryhtwīsnesse *se credunt loqui per libertatem rectitudinis*, 41; Swt. 302, 5.

un-forwandodlīce; *adv.* I. *without swerving, directly:*—Forđrihte, unforwandedlīce *indeclinabiliter, inevitabiliter* (ad destinatum indeclinabiliter dirigit locum, Ald. 2), Hpt. 406, 4. II. *unexpectedly, suddenly:*—Unforwandedlīce *ex improviso, extemplo, subito*, Hpt. Gl. 457, 35. III. *with a disregard of fear, unhesitatingly, freely, fearlessly:*—Ne durron ryht freolīce lǣran and unforwandodlīce sprecan *loqui libere recta pertimescunt*, Past. 15; Swt. 89, 12: 41; Swt. 302, 2. Đæt mon openlīce and unforwandodlīce on ōđerne rǣse mid tǣlinge *impetu apertae increpationis obviare*, 40; Swt. 297, 12. Ǣghwylc cristen man dō swā him þearf is . . . unforwandodlīce his synna gecӯþe, L. Eth. v. 22; Th. i. 310, 6: Wulfst. 180, 6: Homl. Ass. 141, 69. IV. *rashly, recklessly, inconsiderately, heedlessly:*—Unrǣdlīce, unforwandedlīce *inconsulte, inconsiderate*, Hpt. Gl. 474, 57: 509, 64. Đǣr biđ dæghwomlīce wōp . . . and endeleás cwylming, tō đām Egeas onet unforwandodlīce, Homl. Th. i. 592, 17.

un-forwealwod; *adj. Unwithered, undecayed:*—Bringan Drihtne unforwealwod wæstm gōdra weorca, Blickl. Homl. 73, 25.

un-forwordenlīc; *adj. Undecayed, uncorrupt:*—Unforwurdenlīcne *incorruptam*, Hpt. Gl. 407, 36.

un-forworht; *adj. Not criminal, innocent:*—Wǣron earme men beswicene and ūt of đisan earde gesealde swӯđe unforworhte fremdum tō gewealde, Wulfst. 158, 13. Ūre hlāfordes gerǣdnes is đæt man cristene menn and unforworhte of earde ne sylle, L. Eth. v. 2; Th. i. 304, 15. Se đe hit āwende æt unforworhtum þingum *he who sets aside the grant when there is no criminality on the part of the grantee* (cf. the phrase frequent in Oswald's charters: Gif hwā būton gewyrhtum hit ābrecan wille, iii. 21, 30, and often. See also, in another of Oswald's charters: Si quid praefatorum delicti praeuaricantis causa defuerit jurum, praevaricationis delictum secundum quod praesulis jus est emendet, aut illo quo antea potitus est dono et terra careat, vi. 125; and see Kemble's Saxons in England, i. 311), Cod. Dip. Kmbl. ii. 408, 5. [*O. Frs.* un-forwrocht *not forfeited*.] v. for-wyrcan.

un-forworht [*different from preceding word.* v. fōr-wyrcan (*l.* for-), *and* cf. *O. H. Ger.* furi-wurchen *obstruere*]; *adj. Unobstructed, without hindrance, free;* the term is used of land that after several lives was to revert to the grantor, and seems to render the word *immunis* in the Latin charters:—On đa gerād, weorce hē đæt hē weorce, đæt đæt land seó unforworht intō đære hālgan stōwe (the Latin previously in the same charter is: Ad usum primatis in Weogornaceastre redeat inmunis. See also the passage: Tellus episcopali restituatur cathedrae absque ullius controversiae obstaculo, iii. 232, 24), Cod. Dip. Kmbl. ii. 396, 33: 397, 29: 384, 22. (The formula is common in Oswald's charters. See Cod. Dip. Kmbl. i. xxxiii, and Kemble's Saxons in England, i. 312.)

un-fracodlīce; *adv. Not dishonourably, honourably, virtuously:*—Ic wilnode andweorces tō đām weorce đe mē beboden wæs tō wyrcanne, đæt wæs, đæt ic unfracodlīce and gerisenlīce mihte steóran and reccan đone anweald đe mē befæst wæs *materiam gerendis rebus optavimus, quo ne virtus tacita consenesceret*, Bt. 17; Fox 58, 27.

un-frætewod; *adj. Unadorned, unpolished:*—Unfratewode *inculta*, Germ. 396, 180.

un-fremful; *adj. Unprofitable, not advantageous:*—Unfremful biđ đæt folc beó būtan steóre ođđe būtan ǣ him eallum tō hearme, Homl. Skt. i. 13, 126. Unfremful *imperfectum* (incomplete, not of use), Hpt. Gl. 524, 66.

un-fremu, e; *f. Hurt, loss, damage, detriment:*—Hū nyt bið ðæt, ðeáh ðū ðē ealne middaneard and ealle eorðan wille gestrȳnan, gif ðū ðīnre sāwle unfreme and forlorenesse gewyrcst? Anglia xi. 8, 29. Ðū blǣda nāme on treówes telgum, and mē on teónan ǣte ða unfreme, Cd. Th. 55, 12; Gen. 893. [Ðe man noteð wel his ȝiepshipe, þe birgeð him seluen wið his aȝene soule unfreme, and erneð after his soule freme, O. E. Homl. ii. 195, 9.]

un-freóndlīce; *adv. In an unfriendly manner:*—Wē ðē freóndlīce wīc getǣhton, ðū ūs leánest nū unfreóndlīce, Cd. Th. 162, 30; Gen. 2689.

un-fricgende *not questioning:*—Mē sægde ðæt wīf hire wordum selfa unfricgendum *the woman of her own accord told me without my asking*, Cd. Th. 160, 12; Gen. 2649.

un-friþ, es; *n.* I. *absence of peace, hostilities:*—Hēr wæs micel unfrið on Angelcynnes londe þurh sciphere, and wel gehwǣr hergedon and bærndon *in this year there were constant hostilities in England through the Danes, and they harried and burned pretty well everywhere*, Chr. 1001; Erl. 136, 1. Hēr āspōn Æðelwald ðone here tō unfriðe, ðæt hié hergodon ofer Mercna land *in this year Ethelwold enticed the Danes to hostilities, so that they went across Mercia harrying*, 905; Erl. 98, 14. Hē behēt ðæt hē nǣfre eft tō Angelcynne mid unfriðe cumon nolde *he promised that he would never again come and disturb the peace of England*, 994; Erl. 133, 33. Se cyng bæd Godwine eorl faran intō Cent mid unfriða, ac se eorl nolde nā geðwǣrian ðære infare, forþan him wæs lāð tō āmyrrenne his āgenne folgað, 1048; Erl. 178, 8. For unfriðe *on account of hostilities*, L. N. P. L. 56; Th. ii. 298, 26. Hié ne dorston forþ bī ðǣre eá siglan for unfriþe; for ðæm ðæt land wæs eall gebūn on ōþre healfe ðære eás *they durst not sail on past the river for fear of being attacked; for the land was all cultivated on the other side of the river*, Ors. 1, 1; Swt. 17, 22. II. referring to the king's peace, *the state of being out of the king's peace:*—Fare se ealdorman tō; gif hē nelle, fare se cyning tō; gif hē nelle, licge se ealdordōm on unfriðe (*the old Latin version renders this:* adeat aldremannus; si nolit, rex; si nolit, sit pars illa praeter pacem), L. Eth. ii. 6; Th. i. 286, 34. [Membriz hefde inomen grið, ah sone he makede unfrið, Laym. 2557. *O. Frs.* on-frede, un-fretho: *O. H. Ger.* un-fridu: *Ger.* un-friede: *Icel.* ū-friðr.]

unfriþ-flota, an; *m. A hostile fleet:*—Se[o] unfriðflota wæs ðæs sumeres gewend tō Rīcardes rīce, Chr. 1000; Erl. 137, 5.

unfriþ-here, es; *m. A hostile army, an army that is carrying on hostilities:*—Com se ungemetlīca unfriðhere tō Sandwīc, Chr. 1009; Erl. 142, 16. On ðissum geáre wæs ðet gafol gelǣst ðam unfriðehere, 1007; Erl. 141, 13.

unfriþ-land, es; *n. A hostile country, a country with which hostilities are being carried on:*—Gyf Æðelrēdes cynges friðman cume on unfriðland (*terram hostilem*, Latin version), and se here ðǣrtō cume, hæbbe frið his scip and ealle his ǣhta, L. Eth. ii. 3; Th. i. 286, 7.

unfriþ-mann, es; *m. A man of a country not at peace with another, a man of a hostile country:*—Gif hē his ǣhta bere geman[g] ðara unfriðmanna ǣhta intō hūse, þolie his ǣhta *si pecuniam suam inter pecuniam unfriðmannorum*, i. e. *pacem non habentium, in domo mittat, perdat pecuniam suam* (Lat. vers.), L. Eth. ii. 3; Th. i. 286, 11. [*O. Frs.* unfreth-monn.] v. preceding word.

unfriþ-scip, es; *n.* I. *a ship which is carrying on hostilities:*—Ðam cynge com word ðæt unnfriðscipa lǣgen be westan and hergodon, Chr. 1046; Erl. 173, 5. II. *a ship belonging to a hostile country:*—Ǣlc ceápscip frið hæbbe ðe binnan mūðan cuman(-e?), þēh hit unfriðscyp sȳ, gyf hit undrifen bið *omnis ceapscip*, i. e. *navis institoris, pacem habeat, quae in portum veniet, licet navis sit inimicorum, si non sit abacta tempestatibus* (Lat. vers.), L. Eth. ii. 2; Th. i. 286, 21.

un-frōd; *adj.* I. *not old:*—Ðā wæs gegongen guman(-ū, MS.) unfrōdum (cf. geongum, 5712; B. 2860) earfoðlīce, ðæt hē on eorðan geseah ðone leófestan bleátne gebǣran, Beo. Th. 5635; B. 2821. II. *not wise, ignorant, rude.* [*Goth.* un-frōþs *foolish*: *Icel.* ū-frōðr *ignorant.*] v. next word.

un-frōdness, e; *f. Ignorance, rudeness:*—Unfrōdnyssa (cf. edwītu, R. Ben. 97, 7) geþyldelīce beran *difficultatem patienter portare*, R. Ben. Interl. 95, 14.

un-from; *adj. Not strong, feeble, weak:*—Ðæt hē sleac wǣre, æðeling unfrom, Beo. Th. 4382; B. 2188. Eágan ðīne gesāwon ðæt ic ealles wæs unfrom on ferhþe *imperfectum meum viderunt oculi tui*, Ps. Th. 138, 14.

un-fūl; *adj. Not foul, good;* but the word glosses *insulsum*, Mk. Skt. Lind. Rush. 9, 50.

un-fulfremed; *adj. Imperfect:*—*Praeteritum imperfectum*, ðæt is unfulfremed forðgewiten, Ælfc. Gr. 20; Zup. 124, 3. Ðæt hī didon unfulfremed (*inperfectum*) forlǣtende, R. Ben. Interl. 24, 1. Ða ðing ðe hē unfullfremed gemētte *ea quae minus perfecta reperit*, Bd. 4, 2; S. 566, 2.

un-fulfremedness, e; *f. Imperfection:*—Ðæt hī murkien for hira unfullfremednesse *ut imperfectionis suae taedio tabescant*, Past. 65; Swt. 467, 13. Unfulfremednisse mīne (*inperfectum meum*) gesēgun ēgan ðīn, Ps. Surt. 138, 16.

un-fulfremming, e; *f. Imperfection:*—Unfulfremmingce mīne *imperfectum meum*, Ps. Lamb. 138, 16.

un-fūliende; *adj. Incorruptible:*—Unfūliendre clǣnnysse *imputribilis pudicitiae*, Hpt. Gl. 467, 46.

un-fūliendlīc; *adj. Incorruptible:*—Unfūliendlīcere gecynde *imputribilis naturae*, Hpt. Gl. 419, 36.

un-fullod; *adj. Unbaptized:*—Swā hwylc mæssepreóst se ðe wite ðæt hē unfullod sȳ, fullige man hine *omnis presbyter, qui noverit quod non sit baptizatus, baptizetur*, L. Ecg. C. 7; Th. ii. 138, 23. Be unfullodon mæssepreóste, Th. ii. 128, 17.

un-fulworht; *adj. Unfinished, uncompleted, imperfect:*—Ða ðe . . . swā hwylce bysiga swā hȳ on handa hæfdan unfulworhte lǣtaþ *ex occupatis manibus quod agebant inperfectum relinquentes*, R. Ben. 20, 3.

un-fyrn; *adv.* I. of past time, *not long ago:*—Weorþodan wē nū unfyrn for tēn nihtum ðone symbeldæg foran tō ðyssum ondweardan dæge *not long ago now, ten days from to-day, we celebrated the festival*, Blickl. Homl. 131, 9. II. of future time, *before long:*—Secgas mīne gearwe sindon; ða ðē unfyrn faca feorh ætþringan, Andr. Kmbl. 2741; An. 1373. Nū ic fundige tō ðē of ðisse worulde; nū ic wāt ðæt ic sceal ful unfyr[n] faca, Exon. 454, 32; Hy. 4, 42. [Cf. *Icel.* ū-forn *not old.*] Cf. un-gefyrn, -geára.

un-gænge, ungc, un-geæhtendlīc. v. un-genge, unc, un-geeahtendlīc.

un-geǣwed; *adj. Unmarried:*—Uniǣwedan *innuptis*, Hpt. Gl. 525, 17.

un-geandet[t]; *adj. Unconfessed:*—Ðæt gē nǣfre ne lǣton ǣnige synne ungeandet . . . ðæt gē lǣton ǣnig ðing ungeandett . . . ðæt se deófol eów nāge nāht on tō bestelenne ungeandettes, Wulfst. 135, 9-32.

un-geára; *adv.* I. of past time, *not long ago, lately:*—Ic wæs ungeára on niht ābysgod on wæccum *nuper occupatus noctu vigiliis*, Bd. 4, 25; S. 600, 39. Ðæt wæs ungeára, ðæt ic ǣnigra mē weána ne wēnde bōte gebīdan, Beo. Th. 1868; B. 932. II. of the future, *before long, soon:*—Ðone egesfullan dōmes dæg, se cymeþ nū ungeára, Blickl. Homl. 101, 28. Ungeára nū, Cd. Th. 289, 9; Sat. 395: Beo. Th. 1209; B. 602. Ðū ungeára deáþe sweltest, Exon. Th. 250, 8; Jul. 124. Cf. un-fyrn.

un-gearu; *adj.* I. *not ready, not prompt, indisposed* to act:—Se sixta leahter is *accidia* gehāten, ðæt is slǣwð on Englisc, ðonne ðam menn ne lyst nān gōd dōn and hē bið ǣfre ungearu tō ǣlcere duguðe, Homl. Skt. i. 16, 299. [Ungearu to elchere duȝeðe, O. E. Homl. i. 103, 28.] II. *not ready, not in a fit state* for use:—Ðȳ læs sió earc sī ungearo tō beranne *ut ad portandum arcam nulla mora praepediat*, Past. 22; Swt. 173, 11. Ðȳ læs hine ǣnig wuht gǣlde ungearowes (-ewes, Cott. MSS.), ðonne mon ða earce beran scolde *ut, cum portari arcam opportunitas exigit, portandi tarditas nulla generetur*, Swt. 171, 23. IIa. of land, *uncultivated:*—Gūðlāc ðæs wīdgillan wēstenes ða ungearawan stōwe ðǣr gemētte, Guthl. 3; Gdwin. 20, 10. III. *not ready, not prepared* for attack:—Wē ðē beóð holde, gif ðū ūs hȳran wilt, oþþe ðec ungearo (-geára ?) eft gesēcaþ, Exon. Th. 119, 9; Gū. 252. Hē on ungearone ðone Ōsrīc mid his fyrde becom and hine mid ealle his weorude ādylgode *Osricum erumpens subito cum suis omnibus imparatum cum suo exercitu delevit*, Bd. 3, 1; S. 523, 26. Ǣlc here hæfð ðȳ læssan cræft ðonne hē cymð, gif hine mon ǣr wāt, ǣr hē cume; for ðæm hē gesihð ða gearwe ðe hē wēnde ðæt hē sceolde ungearwe findan. Him wǣre ðonne iéðre ðæt hē hira ǣr gearra wēnde, ðonne hē hira ungearra wēnde, and hī gearuwe mētte *dum contra ictum quisque paratior redditur, hostis, qui se inopinatum credidit, eo ipso, quo praevisus est, enervatur*, Past. 56; Swt. 433, 27-31. Þeóf forfēhð slǣpe gebundne eorlas ungearwe, Exon. Th. 54, 27; Cri. 875. Andra besierede ðæt folc ðe hié ymbseten hæfde on ānre niht ungearwe *exercitum incautum Andro oppresserat*, Ors. 4, 5; Swt. 170, 2. Hié fōron ūt nihtes and cōmon on ungearwe men, Chr. 921; Erl. 106, 13. Hē nihtes on ungearwe hī on bestæl *ex improviso adgredi et insperatas circumvenire maluerit*, Ors. 1, 10; Swt. 46, 34. Hié on Ahtēne ungearwe becōman and hié gefliémdon *Agesilaus improvisus bello supervenit*, 3, 1; Swt. 98, 15. Ðæt hē on ða burgware on ungearwe becōme *quibus repente incautam urbem opprimeret*, 4, 5; Swt. 166, 32: 4, 10; Swt. 196, 25. Hē on ungearwe on Ahtēne mid firde gefōr, 3, 7; Swt. 118, 20. [*O. H. Ger.* un-garo *imparatus.*]

un-geārwyrd; *adj. Not honoured, not respected:*—Ungeārwyrd *intemerata*, Wrt. Voc. ii. 45, 25.

un-geáþe = un-eáþe, Bt. 35, 3; Fox 158, 28.

un-geāxod; *adj. Unasked:*—Hē ungeāxod clypode: 'Ic eom cristen,' Homl. Th. i. 428, 6.

un-gebeard[e ?], -bierde, -bird (-byrd); *adj. Beardless, young:*—Ungebyrd *investis*, Wrt. Voc. ii. 47, 28: 92, 54. Ungebarde hysse *effebo hircitallo* (cf. beardleás hysse, Hpt. 487, 78), ii. 82, 32. Ða ungebyrdan heápas *investes catervas*, 44, 41. [*O. H. Ger.* un-giparta *sine barba, impubis.*]

un-gebeorhlīce; *adv. Not safely, rashly* (?), *intemperately* (?):—

Lufiaþ, gē weras, eówere wīf on ǣwe; ne beó gē bitere him ungebeorhlīce (*nolite amari esse ad illas*, Col. 3, 19), Homl. Th. ii. 322, 26.

un-gebēt[t]; *adj.* I. of things, *unamended, uncorrected;* in reference to sin, *not amended through the penance prescribed by the church:*—Scylde ðe an hiera ealra gewitnesse gedōn wæs and ðāgiett ungebētt (-bēt, Hatt. MS.) *culpam quae apud eos et perpetrata fuerat, et incorrecta remanebat*, Past. 32; Swt. 210, 7. Gyf hē ǣnigne gylt ungebēt hæfð, L. Ælfc. C. 32; Th. ii. 354, 29. Ealle scylda, ðe wið God beóð ungebētta, beóð unforgifne on dōmes dæge, Past. 33; Swt. 220, 17. II. of persons, *unatoned* because 'bōt' has not been made:—Ðā wæs hē ðisse spǣce, ǣgðer ge on līfe and æfter, ungelādod ge ungebētt *he was, both when alive and afterwards, uncleared from this charge and unatoned* (i. e. neither was his innocence proved nor was the case settled by the payment of 'bōt'), Chart. Th. 540, 4. [*Icel.* ū-bættr *unatoned*]

un-gebierde. v. un-gebearde.

un-gebīged; *adj. Unbent:*—Unibīgedre *inflexi*, Hpt. Gl. 476, 23.

un-gebīgendlīc; *adj. Inflexible;* in grammar, *indeclinable:*—Ungebīgendlīc *inflexibile*, Hpt. Gl. 425, 34. Ðās naman synd *indeclinabilia*, ðæt synd ungebīgendlīce . . . *nugas* is ungebīgendlīc on declīnunge, Ælfc. Gr. 9, 25; Zup. 51, 2-6.

un-gebleoh; *adj. Of different colours, unlike:*—Ungebleoh *discolor*, Ælfc. Gr. 9, 21; Zup. 47, 16: *discolor*, i. *dissimilis*, Wrt. Voc. ii. 140, 79.

un-gebletsod; *adj. Unblessed:*—Sume ic funde būtan Godes tācne, gȳmeleáse, ungebletsade, Exon. Th. 271, 34; Jul. 492.

un-geblȳged; *adj. Undismayed:*—Him fǣringa ādl in gewōd; hē on elne swā þeáh ungeblȳged bād beorhtra gehāta blīþe in burgum, Exon. Th. 158, 23; Gū. 913. [Cf. Þa iwarð þat folc swiðe abluied (*stupebant omnes*, Acts 2, 7), O. E. Homl. i. 89, 31. *O. H. Ger.* plūcheit *diffidentia: M. H. Ger.* er-bliugen *to frighten: Icel.* bljúgr *shy: Dan.* bly: *Swed.* blyg. See also Diefenbach's Gothic Dict. i. 307, § c.] Cf. ā-blīcgan.

un-geboden; *adj. Unsummoned, unbidden:*—Þreó mōtlǣþu ungeboden on .xii. mōnþum *the tenant attended three courts without summons in the year*, Chart. Th. 433, 22. *Perhaps the word is to be found in the phrase* de placito ungebendro (ungebendeo, MS. R. = ungebodene?), L. Eth. iv. 4; Th. i. 301, 21. Cf. Tribus principalibus mallis, qui vulgo *ungeboden ding* vocantur . . . tria plebiscita, quae dicuntur *ungeboten* . . . tria judicia per annum, quae dicuntur judicia *non indicta*, Grmm. R. A. 823.

un-geboht; *adj. Unbought:*—Ic hēr on sōðre gewitnesse stande, unābeden and ungeboht, L. O. 8; Th. i. 180, 28.

un-geboren; *adj. Unborn:*—Ge for geborene ge for ungeborene, L. A. G. proem.; Th. i. 152, 6.

un-gebrocen; *adj. Unbroken:*—Ungebrocenre *extricabili*, Wrt. Voc. ii. 33, 7. v. un-forfeorod.

un-gebrocod; *adj. Unafflicted, uninjured:*—Ðonne wē manna līchaman derigaþ, būton wē ðære sāwle derian magon, ða līchaman þurhwuniaþ on heora āwyrdnysse . . . Ðonne hī gelȳfaþ ðæt wē godas sind . . . wē forlǣtaþ ðone līchaman ungebrocodne, and cēpaþ ðære sāwle, Homl. Th. i. 464, 6.

un-gebrosnendlīc; *adj. Incorruptible:*—Ða ungebrosnendlīcan limo *incorrupta membra*, Bd. 4, 30; S. 609, 29.

un-gebrosnod; *adj. Uncorrupted, undecayed:*—Ungebrosnad *incorruptus*, Bd. 3, 6; S. 528, 29. Ðā wæs heó swā ungebrosnad gemēted swā heó ðȳ ilcan dæge wǣre forðfēred, Shrn. 94, 36. His handa siondan ungebrosnode in ðære cynelīcan ceastre, 114, 1: Chr. 641; Erl. 27, 11: Homl. Th. ii. 568, 24.

un-gebrosnung, e; *f. Incorruption:*—Ungebrosnunge onfēhð *incorruptionem recipit*, Scint. 71, 2.

un-gebunden; *adj. Unbound:*—Sume syndon *absolutiuae*, ðæt synd ungebundene, Ælfc. Gr. 5; Zup. 14, 13.

un-gebyde, un-gebyrd. v. un-gebyrde, un-gebearde.

un-gebyrde; *adj. Not natural, uncongenial:*—Ǣlc gesceaft flīhþ ðætte him wiþerweard biþ and ungebyrde (? -byde, Fox) and ungelīc, Bt. 34, 11; Fox 150, 23.

un-gebyredlīc; *adj. Unsuitable, incongruous:*—Ungebyredlīc *incongruum*, Rtl. 179, 34.

un-gecirred; *adj. Unconverted:*—Ðȳ læs ðe ǣnig ungecyrred woroldman mid ungewitte regules geboda ābrǣce, Lchdm. iii. 442, 1.

un-geclǣnsod; *adj. Uncleansed, unpurified:*—Swā hwā swā ungeclǣnsod byð, hē gefrēt ðæs fȳres ǣðm, Homl. Th. i. 616, 23: L. E. I. 44; Th. ii. 440, 21. v. un-clǣnsod.

un-gecnāwen; *adj. Unknown:*—Hē fela þinga forðteáh ðe ðam folce ungecnāwe[n] wæs and ungewunelīc, Ap. Th. 17, 13.

un-gecnirdness, e; *f. Negligence, want of diligence:*—Menige sind ðe ðurh ungecnyrdnysse ðisum ðeówan (*the slothful servant in the parable*) geefenlǣcaþ, Homl. Th. ii 552, 35.

un-gecoplīc; *adj. Unfit, inconvenient, troublesome;* importunus:—Saca mid ungecoplīcum *quarrels with rude fellows*, Lchdm. iii. 200, 18. v. un-gedafenlīc.

un-gecoplīce; *adv. Unsuitably, unseasonably:*—Ongecoplīce *inportune*, Scint. 80, 14.

un-gecoren; *adj.* I. *unchosen, unselected;* used in reference to those who swore along with another, when they were not selected by the party making oath from a number of persons named to him, as was the case in the *cyre-āð*, q. v.:—Ðæt hē ðone āð funde, gif hē mæhte, ungecorenne, ðe se onspeca on gehealden wǣre. Gif hē ðone ne mehte, ðonne namede him man six men and begēte ðara syxa ǣnne æt ānum hrȳðere, i. e. *if he could bring those to swear with him, that the claimant was satisfied with, there was no need to nominate persons from whom he was to choose; if he could not, then six men were to be nominated and from them he was to get one for every ox (or its equivalent) that was in dispute*, L. Ed. 1; Th. i. 158, 20. Ðonne mōt hē syxa sum ungecorenra, ðe getrȳwe sȳn, ðone āð syllan, L. O. D. 1; Th. i. 352, 12. II. *reprobate, evil:*—For ðissum lǣnan līfe ic sylle ðæt unlǣne, for ðyssum ungecorenum ðæt gecorene, Wulfst. 264, 19. Ða burhware (*of Jerusalem*) him (*Christ*) wǣron for heora ungeleáfan and māndǣdum swīþe forhogde and ungecorene, Blickl. Homl. 77, 28. [*Goth.* un-gakusans ἀδόκιμος, *reprobus.* Cf. *Icel.* ū-kjörligr *wretched.*] v. next word.

un-gecost; *adj. Bad, evil, vicious:*—On ungecostum ðeáwum *moribus improbis*, Bd. 5, 23; S. 647, 1. v. un-cyst, *and preceding word.*

un-gecwēme; *adj. Unpleasant, disagreeable;* ingratus, Scint. 38, 15.

un-gecȳd[d], -gecȳðed; *adj. Undeclared:*—Gif ceáp ofer .v. niht ungecȳd on gemǣnre lǣse wunaþ, L. Edg. S. 9; Th. i. 276, 1.

un-gecynde; *adj. Unnatural:*—Nim swā wuda swā wyrt of ðære stōwe ðe his eard and æþelo biþ on tō weaxanne, and sette on ungecynde stōwe him, ðonne ne gegrēwþ hit ðǣr nāuht, Bt. 34, 10; Fox 148, 27 note. Hié hæfdun hiera cyning āworpenne Ōsbryht and ungecyndne (*not of the royal race;* cf. 'non de regali prosapia progenitum,' Asser) cyning underfēngon, Chr. 867; Erl. 72, 10. [We scullen of londe driuen unicunde (*foreigners*), Laym. 18429.] v. next word.

un-gecyndelīc; *adj.* I. *unnatural, not in accordance with the nature of a thing:*—Ungecyndelīc is ǣlcre wuhte, ðæt hit wilnige deáþes, Bt. 34, 11; Fox 152, 7. II. *not natural, supernatural:*—Ungecyndelīc fȳr cymð fǣrunga on eówre burga, Wulfst. 297, 13. III. *unnatural, contrary to nature, monstrous:*—Hit is ungecyndelīcu ofermōdgung ðæt se monn wilnige ðæt hine his gelīca ondrǣde *contra naturam superbire est, ab aequali velle timeri*, Past. 17; Swt. 109, 11. Swīþe ungecyndelīc yfel, ðæt ða bearn sieredon ymbe ðone fæder, Bt. 31, 1; Fox 112, 12. Gecyndelīcra synna oþþe ungecyndelīcra, L. de Cf. 6; Th. ii. 262, 24: Anglia xi. 98, 19. On ungecyndelīcum þingum *in rebus naturae contrariis*, L. M. I. P. 40; Th. ii. 276, 7: Anglia xi. 3, 78. Wē fram dæge tō ōþrum geāxiaþ ungecyndelīco wītu and ungecyndelīce (-cynelīce, MS.) deáþas tō mannum cumene, Blickl. Homl. 107, 26. Hwæt wǣre ungecyndlīcre, gif God næfde on eallum his rīce nāne frige sceaft under his anwealde, Bt. 41, 2; Fox 244, 28.

un-gecyndelīce; *adv. Unnaturally:*—And sǣ hē dēð beón ungemetlīce and ungecyndelīce swīþe āstyrode, Wulfst. 196, 3.

un-gedæftlīce, -gedæftelīce; *adv. Unseasonably, unsuitably:*—'Ðæt ðū lǣre ǣgðer ge gedæftlīce ge ungedæftlīce (-dæfte-, Cott. MSS.).' Ðeáh hē cuǣde un[ge]dæftelīce, hē cuæð ðeáh ǣr gedæftelīce '*insta opportune, importune.*' *Dicturus importune praemisit opportune*, Past. 15; Swt. 97, 16.

un-gedæftness, e; *f. Importunity, unseasonableness:*—Ðonne sió ungedæftnes hit ne cann eft gedæftan *si habere importunitas opportunitatem nescit*, Past. 15; Swt. 97, 19.

un-gedafenlīc; *adj. Unbecoming, unseemly, unmannerly:*—Ungedafenlīc *indecens*, Ælfc. Gr. 14; Zup. 87, 12. Ðæt hit ungedafenlīc sig *quod indecorum sit*, L. Ecg. P. i. 7; Th. ii. 174, 22. Ðæt man intō circan ǣnig þingc ne lōgige, ðæs ðe ðārtō ungedafenlīc sī, L. Edg. C. 27; Th. ii. 250, 11. Mid ungedafenlīcre and unwærlīcre ofersprǣce *loquacitatis incauta importunitate*, Past. 15; Swt. 95, 19. Saca mid ungedafenlīcum *quarrels with unmannerly fellows* (v. un-gecoplīc), Lchdm. iii. 204, 20. Wē oft ymb ungedafenlīce wīsan smeágeaþ, Past. 18; Swt. 139, 22. Gif preóst on circan ungedafenlīce þingc gelōgige, gebēte ðæt, L. N. P. L. 26; Th. ii. 294, 12.

un-gedafenlīce; *adv. Unbecomingly, unseasonably, inordinately, in an unseemly manner, indecently:*—Ōðer ðara irsunga bið tō ungemetlīce and tō ungedafenlīce ātyht on ðæt ðe hió mid ryhte irsian sceall *illa ira in hoc, quod debet, inordinate extenditur*, Past. 40; Swt. 293, 13. Ðeáh hwelc man ungemetlīce and ungedafenlīce wilnige ðæt hē scile his hlīsan tōbrǣdan, Bt. 18, 2; Fox 64, 20. Boda Godes word ǣgðer ge gedafenlīce ge ungedafenlīce *preach God's word both in season and out of season*, Homl. Ass. 12, 306. Be ðam men ðe ungedafenlīce hǣmð *de homine qui turpiter fornicatur*, L. Ecg. P. ii. 6 tit.; Th. ii. 180, 9.

un-gedafenlīcness, e; *f. Inconvenience:*—Ungedafenlīcnyssum *inopportunitatibus*, Ps. Spl. C. second 9, 1. v. gedafenlīcness.

un-gedafniendlīc; *adj. Unseemly, indecent:*—Unidafniendlīc fūlnes *indecens obscenitas*, Hpt. Gl. 492, 60.

un-gedēfe; *adj. Troublesome, disagreeable:*—Cild ācenned ungedēfe, ofermōd, felasprecol, Lchdm. iii. 192, 22. Hēr ys seó bōt hū ðū meaht ðīne æceras bētan, gif hī nellaþ wel wexan oþþe ðǣr hwilc ungedēfe þing on gedōn bið, i. 398, 2. Mannum ungedēfum *hominibus importunis*,

Scint. 38, 15. Ungeþeáwfæstan and ða ungedēfan þreán *indisciplinatos et inquietos arguere*, R. Ben. Interl. 15, 1.

un-gedēfelīce; *adv. Unfitly, in a way that ill suits the conditions of a case*:—Wæs ðam yldestan ungedēfelīce mǽges dǽdum morþorbed strēd . . . Hǽðcyn his mǽg ofscēt, brōðor ōðerne *for the eldest unfitly, by a kinsman's deeds, was the death-couch spread . . . Hæthcyn with his arrow slew his kinsman, brother slew brother*, Beo. Th. 4862; B. 2435.

un-gedered(-od); *adj. Unhurt, uninjured*:—Ic bidde ðē, uca peruica, . . . ðæt ðū mē gegearwie, ðæt ic sȳ ungedered fram āttrum and fram yrsunge *te precor, uica peruica, ut ea mihi prestes, ut a uenenis et ab iracundia interus sim*, Lchdm. i. 314, 10. Hē æfter ðam drence ansund and ungederod ðurhwunode, Homl. Th. i. 574, 12. Ne sceal hē ungederod ðæs ēcan līfes brūcan, ii. 336, 20. Hē wunade betwux eallum deórcynne ungederod, i. 486, 35: Homl. Ass. 71, 169. Ān man mihte faran ofer his rīce mid his bōsum full goldes ungederad, Chr. 1086; Erl. 222, 5. Ðære ungederedan *inlibatae*, Wrt. Voc. ii. 44, 16. Seó leó heóld ðæt cild ungederod, Homl. Skt. ii. 30, 183.

un-gedrehtlīce; *adv. Unweariedly, indefatigably*; infatigabiliter, Wrt. Voc. ii. 48, 51.

un-gedyrstig; *adj. Faint-hearted, diffident*:—Ða unmōdigan and ða ungedyrstigan wēnaþ ðæt ðæt suīðe forsewenlīc sié ðætte hié dōð and forðon weorðaþ oft ormōde *pusillanimes vehementer despecta putant esse, quae faciunt, et idcirco in desperatione franguntur*, Past. 32; Swt. 209, 10.

un-geeahtendlīc; *adj. Inestimable*:—Mid ða sylfan mycelnysse ðes ungeæhtendlīcan (ungeendedlīcan and [un]geeahtendlīcan, MS. B.) gerȳnes *ipsa inaestimabilis mysterii magnitudine*, Bd. 1, 27; S. 496, 11.

un-geendigendlīc; *adj. Indefinite, infinitive*:—Gif ic cweðe: *Nescio, quis hoc fecit*, ðonne byð se *quis* infinitivum, ðæt is, ungeendigendlīc, Ælfc. Gr. 18; Zup. 113, 16: 116, 14. Ðæt fīfte gemet is *infinitivus*, ðæt is ungeendigendlīc, forðan ðe ðǽr ne byð nān sprǽc geendod, 21; Zup. 126, 7.

un-geendod; *adj.* I. *endless, without end, not coming to an end*:—God is ǽfre unbegunnen and ungeendod, Ælfc. Gr. 32; Zup. 201, 10: Homl. Th. i. 8, 27: Homl. Skt. i. 1, 16. Ðǽr is ðæt ēce blis and ðæt ungeendode rīce, Blickl. Homl. 25, 30, 24. Gif ðū getælest ða hwīle ðisses hwīlendlīcan wið ðæs ungeendodan līfes hwīla, Bt. 18, 3; Fox 66, 5. Swā ēcum līfe swā ungeendodon wīte *sive vitam aeternam, sive infinitum supplicium*, L. Ecg. P. iv. 65; Th. ii. 226, 14. Geond ungeendode worulde, Homl. Th. i. 76, 7. Ðæra gesǽlða ðe him ungeendode becuman sculon *felicitas, quae sine transitu attingitur*, Past. 52; Swt. 407, 30. II. *infinite, very great* in number, extent, etc.:—Se hine slōh on ðæt næsþyrl, ðæt ðǽr ūt fleów ungeendod blōd, Shrn. 112, 31. Ungeendodre lengo *infinitae longitudinis*, Bd. 5, 12; S. 627, 36. Ungeendedum forbeácnum *infinitis prodigiis*, Hpt. Gl. 490, 67.

un-geendodlīc; *adj. Infinite*:—Nis nō tō metanne ðæt geendodlīce wiþ ðæt ungeendodlīce *infiniti atque finiti nulla poterit esse collatio*, Bt. 18, 3; Fox 66, 13. v. un-geeahtendlīc.

un-gefǽglīc, un-gefǽrum. v. un-fǽglīc, un-gefēre.

un-gefandod; *ptcpl. Not tried, not experienced*:—Sint tō manigenne ða ðe ðonne giet ungefandod habbaþ flǽslīcra scylda *admonendi sunt peccata carnis ignorantes*, Past. 52; Swt. 407, 19: 409, 16, 22.

un-gefaren; *adj. Untravelled, without a road*:—On ungefarenum and on wæterigum *in invio et in aquoso*, Blickl. Gl. (Ps. 62, 3: 106, 40). v. un-gefēre, -gefēred, -gefērne.

un-gefeálīce; *adv. Joylessly, miserably*:—Beornrǽd fēng tō rīce and lytle hwīle heóld and ungefeálīce, Chr. 755; Erl. 52, 3.

un-gefēge; *adj. Unsuitable, absurd*; ineptus, Wrt. Voc. i. 61, 38. [Ferde he hauede inoh, muchel and unifeie (onimete, 2nd MS.), Laym. 5573. *O. H. Ger.* un-gifōgi *importunus, enormis*.] v. un-gefōg.

un-gefēle; *adj. Without feeling, without sensation, insensible*:—Ða lǽcedōmas ðe wē lǽrdon ðæt mon dyde tō ðære ungefēlan heardnesse ongunnenre on ðære lifre, Lchdm. ii. 212, 15.

un-gefēled; *adj. Not possessed of feeling, insensible*:—Ðonne seó ungefēlde āheardung ðære lifre tō langsum wyrð, Lchdm. ii. 210, 3. Gif ðæt līc tō ðon swīþe ādeádige, ðæt ðǽr nān gefēlnes on ne sié, ðonne scealt ðū eal ðæt deáde and ðæt ungefēlde of āsnīþan, 82, 27.

un-gefēre; *adj.* I. lit. *impassable*:—Ungefēre *vel* wegleás pæð *invium*, Wrt. Voc. i. 53, 61. On ungefērum *in invio*, Ps. Spl. C. 106, 40. Mid wēstenum and ungefǽrum londum, Bt. 18, 2; Fox 62, 36. II. fig. *impervious, impenetrable*:—Ða mōd ðe Dryhtne ungefēru sint *mentes Deo impenetratae*, Past. 35; Swt. 245, 23.

un-gefēre; *adv. Impassably*:—Ungefēre [*im*]*pervie*, Wrt. Voc. ii. 68, 61: 69, 17.

un-gefēred; *adj. Unapproached, inaccessible*:—Feldas and wudu and dūna, ða wǽron monnum ungefērde for wildeórum and wyrmum, Nar. 20, 11. In ān nearo fæsten micel ungefēredra mōra *in angustias inaccessorum montium*, Bd. 4, 26; S. 602, 20. v. un-gefaren.

un-gefērendlīc (?); *adj. Inaccessible, difficult of access*:—Fōran wē þurh ða ungefērenlīcan (-fērend-?) eorþan, Nar. 17, 7.

un-gefērlīc; *adj. That cannot be united* or *that separates*; applied to war in which those, who naturally should be comrades, are opposed, *civil, social*:—Wearþ ofer ealle Italia ungefērlīc unsibb *sociale bellum tota commovit Italia*, Ors. 5, 10; Swt. 232, 31: 5, 10 tit.; Swt. 5, 31. Ungefērlīces *dissociabile*, Wrt. Voc. ii. 141, 39. v. next word.

un-gefērlīce; *adv. In civil war*:—Hē .v. gefeoht ungefērlīce (wel cynelīce gefeaht and, MS. C.) þurhteáh *bella civilia quinque gessit*, Ors. 5, 13; Swt. 244, 25. v. preceding word.

un-gefērne; *adj. Impassable*:—In ungefoernum *in invio*, Ps. Surt. 106, 40. In ðæm ungefoernan, 62, 3.

un-gefeþered; *adj. Unfeathered*:—Ungefeþeredne *inplumem*, Wrt. Voc. ii. 48, 21.

un-gefōg(-fōh); *adj.* I. *immense*:—Hī nāmon sceattas genōge sylfrene and gyldene ungefōge, Homl. Skt. i. 23, 199. II. in a bad sense, *intemperate, immoderate excessive*:—Seó þwyre sāwul on hwīlwendlīcum bricum biþ ungefōh, Homl. Th. i. 408, 15. Hefigtȳme leahter is ungefōh fyrwitnys, ii. 374, 3. Hē wæs mid ungefōhre gȳtsunge ontend, i. 414, 5. [He sloh þer uniuoȝe, moni and inoȝe, Laym. 21793. Noldest þu nefre ben inouh, buten þu hefdest unifouh, Fragm. Phlps. 7, 23. *O. Frs.* un-efōg.]

un-gefōge; *adv. Immensely, exorbitantly*:—Ðǽr beóð ða swiftan hors ungefōge dȳre, Ors. 1, 1; Swt. 21, 6.

un-gefōglīc; *adj. Immense, enormous*, (1) in a physical sense:—Ungefōhlīc hreám *immensus clamor*, Greg. Dial. 1, 9. Ymbūtan ðone weall is se mǽsta dīc, on ðam is iernende se ungefōglecesta streám *fossa extrinsecus late patens vice amnis circumfluit*, Ors. 2, 4; Swt. 74, 18. (2) in a moral sense:—Is swīðe micel þearf ðæt gē georne mǽnra āða stȳran, and eówrum hȳremonnum cȳðon, hū ungefōhlīcu scyld ðæt is, L. E. I. 26; Th. ii. 422, 20.

un-gefōglīce; *adv. Excessively, intemperately, immoderately*:—Hī ongann ungefōhlīce swǽtan, Homl. Th. i. 414, 12. Hī mid eorþlīcum teolungum ungefōhlīce hī gebysgiaþ, 524, 14: Boutr. Scrd. 20, 11.

un-gefrǽge; *adj. Unheard of*:—Ungefrǽge *inauditum*, Wrt. Voc. ii. 46, 66: 80, 60. [Cf. *Icel.* ū-frægr *not famous*.]

un-gefrǽgelīc; *adj. Unheard of, unusual, extraordinary*:—Gyf hyra (*gallinarum*) hwylc man æthrīneþ, ðonne forbærnaþ hī sōna eall his līc; ðæt syndon ungefrǽgelīcu (unge frelicu, un ge fræ licu, MSS. v. Anglia i. 332) lyblāc, Nar. 34, 3. Ða deór habbaþ eahta fēt, and wælkyrian eágan, and twā heáfda . . .; ðæt syndon ungefrǽgelīcu (-fregelicu, MS. T.) deór, 34, 8.

un-gefrǽglīce; *adv. In an unheard of manner, to an unheard of extent, unusually, extraordinarily*:—Catulus swā ungefrǽglīce forcwæð Nonium *Catullus Nonium strumam appellat*, Bt. 27, 1; Fox 94, 32. Swīþe ungefrǽglīce upāhafen on his mōde, 37, 1; Fox 186, 8. Se hearpere wæs swīþe ungefrǽglīce gōd, 35, 6; Fox 166, 29.

un-gefrætwod; *adj. Unadorned*:—Ungefrætwodu *incompta*, Wrt. Voc. ii. 44, 3.

un-gefrēdelīce; *adv. With insensibility, callously*:—Hié beóð tō ðreágeanne and tō swinganne mid swā micle māran wīte suā hié ungefrēdelīcor beóð āheardode on hiera unðeáwum *tanto acriori invectione feriendi sunt, quanto majori insensibilitate duruerunt*, Past. 37; Swt. 265, 16.

un-gefremed; *adj. Not accomplished, not done*:—Ungeffremed *infectum*, Wrt. Voc. ii. 87, 36. Ungefremed, L. Ath. i. proem.; Th. i. 198, 13.

un-gefullod, -gefulwad; *adj. Unbaptized*:—Gif ungefullod cild fǽrlīce bið gebrōht tō ðam mæssepreóste, ðæt hē hit mōt fullian sōna, ðæt hit ne swelte hǽðen, L. Ælfc. C. 26; Th. ii. 352, 15: Homl. Th. ii. 50, 20. Ðeáh ðe hē ungefullod gyt farende sȳ, 500, 35. Hine swā fǽrlīce deáð fornam, ðæt hē ungefullad forðferde. Ðā Sanctus Martinus ðæt geseah . . . him wæs ðæt swīþe myccle weorce ðæt hē swā ungefulwad forðferan sceolde, Blickl. Homl. 217, 18-23.

un-gefullod; *adj. Unfulfilled*:—Ðære bēne ungafullodre, Exon. Th. 441, 7; Rä. 60, 14.

un-gefylled; *adj. Unfilled, unsatisfied*:—Ic eom getogen tō fremdum þeáwum ðurh ða ungefyldan (-gefylledan, Cott. MS.) gītsunge woruldmonna *nos ad constantiam, nostris moribus alienam, inexpleta hominum cupiditas alligabit?* Bt. 7, 3; Fox 20, 26.

un-gefylledlīc; *adj. Insatiable*:—Ðam ungefylledlīcan *insatiabili*, Ps. Lamb. 100, 5: Nar. 42, 12.

un-gefyllendlīc; *adj. Insatiable*; insatiabilis, Scint. 50, 8: 110, 16.

un-gefynde; *adj. Not to be found* or *provided as food* (?) (cf. (?) *the phrase* mete findan *to provide food*):—Se æcer ðe stent on clǽnum lande, and bið unwæsdmbǽre oððe ungefynde corn bringð oððe deáf *terra, quae exculta sterilem segetem gignit*, Past. 52; Swt. 411, 19.

un-gefyrn; *adv. At no distant date, before long, soon*:—Ðū āfindst his mihte ungefyrn on ðē sylfum, Homl. Skt. ii. 25, 153. Eallum folce ðæs swīðe ungefyrn (*very soon after that*) hē geswutelian wolde hwæs gehwā gelȳfan sceolde, i. 23, 405. v. un-fyrn.

un-gegearwod, -gegered; *adj. Not dressed*:—Ungigearuad woede *non vestitum veste*, Rtl. 108, 1. Ungeraradne, Mt. Kmbl. Rush. 22, 11.

un-gegrēt; *adj. Ungreeted*:—Hē wolde tō ðam mynstre faran and his gebrōðra grētan, forþan hē ǽr fram heom ungegrēt gewāt, Guthl. 3; Gdwin. 22, 20.

un-gehâdod; *adj. Not ordained, not in holy orders*:—Be ungehâdedan mǽdene. Gif hwylc mǽdenman mid gehâdodum wunaþ, and heó tó ðam ylcan hâde þence . . . ne biþ heó nâ wið God unscyldig, þeáh heó ungehâdod wǽre *de puella non ordinata. Si puella aliqua cum ordinatis habitet, et se eidem ordini destinet . . . non erit insons coram Deo, etiamsi non sit ordinata*, L. Ecg. P. ii. 17; Th. ii. 180, 19–188, 9–12. Gewylces ungehâdodes wîfes tâcen is . . ., Techm. ii. 129, 18. [Artu ihoded oþer þu cursest al unihoded, O. and N. 1178.] v. un-hâdod.

un-gehǽledlîc; *adj. Incurable*; insanabilis, Ps. Surt. ii. p. 195, 21.

un-gehǽlendlîc; *adj. Incurable*; insanibilis, Ps. Surt. ii. p. 194, 17.

un-gehǽmed; *adj. Unmarried*:—Ungehǽmed *innupta*, Hpt. Gl. 434, 37. v. un-hǽmed.

un-gehæplîc; *adj. Unsuitable, incongruous*:—Ungehæplîc (-geþæslîc, Wrt., *but see* Anglia viii. 452) *incongruus*, Wrt. Voc. i. 61, 39.

un-gehâlgod; *adj. Unhallowed, unconsecrated*:—On ungehâlgedum Cristes mǽle *in cruce non consecrata*, L. Ecg. C. 34; Th. ii. 158, 36. Mid wîne ungehâlgudum, Anglia xiii. 422, 818. Ungehâlgod fŷr *ignem alienum*, Lev. 10, 1. v. un-hâlgod.

un-gehâten; *adj. Not promised*:—Ðæt ungehâten is sceal beón geendod, Blickl. Homl. 189, 27.

un-geheáfdod; *adj. Not come to a head*:—Gif se slyte blind bið and mid ðam geswelle ungeheáfdud, ðonne lege ðû ða wyrte ðǽrtô, sôna hit sceal openian, Lchdm. i. 92, 26.

un-gehealdsum; *adj. Incontinent*:—Se ôðer heáfodleahter is gecweden forliger oððe gâlnyss, ðæt is ðæt se man ungehealdsum sŷ on hǽmede, and hnesce on môde tô flǽsclîcum lustum, Homl. Th. ii. 220, 4. Ðæt gê (*maidens*) wislîce lybbon and wel geþeáwode beón . . . nâ tô ungehealtsume (-heald-, *in one MS.*), Homl. Ass. 47, 575.

un-gehealdsumlîce; *adv. Incontinently*:—Ðæt eald wîf sceole ceorles brûcan ungehealtsumlîce, Homl. Ass. 20, 159.

un-gehealdsumness, e; *f. Incontinence*:—Hî (*a widow or widower marrying again*) sculon dǽdbôte dôn for heora ungehealdsumnesse, L. Ælfc. P. 43; Th. ii. 382, 34. Ðes þeódscype þurh ungehealdsumnesse âwyrd is, Cod. Dip. Kmbl. iii. 349, 7.

un-gehende; *adv. Not near, at a distance, far off*:—Se ðe tô ðam ungehænde sŷ, ðæt hê dæghwamlîce his circan gesêcan ne mæge, Homl. Ass. 144, 8.

un-gehendness, e; *f. Remoteness, distance*:—Sume naman syndon *localia*, ðæt synd stôwlîce, ða geswuteliaþ gehendnysse oððe ungehendnysse, Ælfc. Gr. 5; Zup. 14, 19.

un-geheort; *adj. Disheartened, without courage*:—Ðâ ðâ hî gesâwon swâ mænigfealde ôgan on mistlîcum wîtum, ðâ wurdon hî sôna ungeheorte (*they lost heart*), and deófle offredon, Homl. Skt. i. 23, 62. v. un-gehirt.

un-gehîred; *adj. Unheard of*:—Ungehêredre leoma tôslîtnysse wundade *inaudita membrorum discerptione lacerati*, Bd. 1, 7; S. 479, 13.

un-gehîrness, e; *f. Hardness of hearing, deafness*:—Wiþ eágwærce and wiþ ungehŷrnesse, Lchdm. ii. 316, 1. Wið eágena dimnessa, wið eárena swinsunge and ungehŷrnesse, iii. 70, 23.

un-gehîrsum; *adj. Inattentive to what is said, unsubmissive, disobedient*:—Hû lange wylt ðû beón ungehîrsum *usque quo non vis subjici mihi?* Ex. 10, 3. Oððe hê bið ânum gehŷrsum, and ôðrum ungehŷrsum *aut unum sustinebit, et alterum contemnet*, Mt. Kmbl. 6, 24. Ðis is uncer ungehîrsuma sunu, hê forhogaþ ðæt hê hîre uncre lâre *filius noster iste protervus et contumax est, monita nostra audire contemnit*, Deut. 21, 20. Ne forlǽte hê ða ungehiérsuman (-hîr-, Hatt. MS.), Past. 12; Swt. 74, 16. v. un-hîrsum.

un-gehîrsumness, e; *f. Want of submission, disobedience*:—Môdignys âcenð forsewennysse and ungehŷrsumnysse, Homl. Th. ii. 222, 7. [Þane stede þe se deofel of hafel þurh unihersamnesse, O. E. Homl. i. 221, 30. Cf. *O. H. Ger.* un-gihôrsamî *inobedientia*.] v. un-hîrness.

un-gehîrsumod; *adj. Not subject, disobedient*:—Ungehŷrsumude *inoboedienti*, R. Ben. Interl. 12, 8. v. ge-hŷrsumian, II, un-hîrsumness.

un-gehirt; *adj. Disheartened, cowardly*:—Ða ungehyrtan of heora wege âflŷman, Wulfst. 192, 24. v. un-geheort.

un-gehîwod; *adj.* I. *not formed, without form*:—On ðam ungehîwoðum antimbre ðe hê ða gesceafta of gesceóp *in materia informi creavit omnia*, Btwk. Scrd. 18, 15. Tô gescippenne ðæt ungehîwode antimber *ad formandam informem materiam*, 19, 3. II. *not feigned, unfeigned*:—Unihîwidre (*gloriosa*) *non fictae* (*puritatis palma*, Ald. 24), Hpt. Gl. 447, 46.

un-gehleóþor; *adj. Dissonant, discordant*:—Ungeswêga *vel* [un]-gehleóþre *vel* ungerâde *dissona, i. discordantia, incongrua*, Wrt. Voc. ii. 141, 37. v. ge-hleóþ (*read* -hleóþor).

un-gehrepod; *adj. Untouched, intact*:—Ne þorfte Adam deáðes onbyrian, gif ðæt treów môste standan ungehrepod, Homl. Th. i. 18, 25. God wolde ðæt hî ungehrepode on ðam scræfe slêpon, Homl. Skt. i. 23, 317.

un-gehrinen; *adj. Untouched, intact*:—Seó studu ungehrinen (*intacta*) fram ðam fŷre âwunede, Bd. 3, 10; S. 534, 36.

un-gehwǽde; *adj. Not slight, considerable, much*:—Gif mete sŷ âwyrd and ungehwǽde mylcen, Lchdm. ii. 142, 14.

un-gehwǽrness, -gehŷrness, -gehŷrsum, -gehyrt. v. un-geþwǽrness, -gehîrness, -gehîrsum, -gehirt.

ungel, es; *m.* (?) *Fat*:—Ungel *arvina*, Wrt. Voc. i. 71, 11. Mid ungle ɫ mid fǽtnysse lamba *cum adipe agnorum*, Cant. M. ad fil. 14. Beó mîn sâwul gefylled swâ swâ mid rysle and mid ungele *sicut adipe et pinguedine repleatur anima mea* (Ps. 63, 5), Homl. Th. i. 522, 35. [*Du.* ongel; *m. suet.*]

un-gelâcnod; *adj. Uncured*:—Næs nǽnig untrum ðæt hê ungelâcnod fram him fêrde, Guthl. 15; Gdwin. 66, 16. v. un-lâcnod.

un-gelâdod; *adj. Not acquitted, uncleared* of a charge:—Ðâ wæs hê ðisse spǽce, ægðer ge on lîfe ge æfter, ungelâdod ge ungebêtt, Chart. Th. 540, 4.

un-gelæccendlîc; *adj. Irreprehensible*; inreprehensibilis, Scint. 119, 11.

un-gelǽred; *adj. Untaught, unlearned, ignorant, unskilled*:—Ungelǽred *idiota*, Wrt. Voc. i. 55, 48. Swîðe eáðe mæg on smyltre sǽ ungelǽred scipstiéra genôh ryhte stiéran *quieto mari recte navem et imperitus dirigit*, Past. 9; Swt. 59, 1. Ceahhetung swâ swâ ungelǽredes folces *cachinnum quasi vulgi indocti*, Bd. 5, 12; S. 628, 30. Dysine and ungelǽredne ic ðê underfêng, Bt. 7, 3; Fox 20, 9. Tô hwon ðû sceole for ôwiht ðysne man habban ungelǽredne fiscere (*St. Peter*), Blickl. Homl. 179, 14. Ungelǽrede wê syndon *idiotae sumus*, Coll. Monast. Th. 18, 8. Forhwon beóð ǽfre suǽ ðrîste ða ungelǽredan ðæt hî underfôn ða heorde ðæs lâriówdômes *ab imperitis pastorale magisterium qua temeritate suscipitur?* Past. 1; Swt. 25, 16. v. un-lǽred.

un-gelǽredlîce; *adv. Without instruction, ignorantly, in an undisciplined manner*:—Swîþe unwîslîce and ungelǽredlîce (*indocte*) gê dydon, ðæt gê scoldan on feówernihte mônan blôd lǽtan, Bd. 5, 3; S. 616, 13. Ungelǽredlîce (*indisciplinate*) nâ geþwǽrlǽce mûþ ðîn, Scint. 136, 2.

un-gelǽredness, e; *f. Uninstructedness, ignorance, inexperience, rudeness*:—Monige sindon mê swîðe onlîce on ungelǽrednesse *sunt plerique mihi imperitia similes*, Past. proem.; Swt. 25, 8. Hê hié ðreáde for hira ungelǽrednesse *pastorum imperitia increpatur*, 1; Swt. 27, 24. Mid ðearfednesse ge mid heora ungelǽrednesse *paupertate ac rusticitate sua*, Bd. 4, 27; S. 604, 28.

un-gelaðod; *adj. Uninvited*:—Drihten nolde gelaðod sîðian tô ðæs cyninges bearne . . . and hê wæs gearo ungelaðod tô sîðigenne mid ðam hundredes ealdre, Homl. Th. i. 128, 18.

un-geleáf; *adj. Unbelieving*:—Ne magon ðǽr eard niman ungeleáfe menn *qui non credunt inhabitare in eo*, Ps. Th. 67, 19. [Cf. Þu art unlef mine worde *non credidisti uerbis meis*, O. E. Homl. ii. 125, 24.]

un-geleáfa, an; *m. Unbelief*:—Hê wundrode for heora ungeleáfan (*incredulitatem*), Mk. Skt. 6, 6: Blickl. Homl. 77, 27. Ungeleáuon, Chr. 616; Erl. 22, 21. For ungeleáfa heora, Mt. Kmbl. Rush. 13, 58: 17, 20. [*O. Sax.* un-gilôbo: *O. H. Ger.* un-giloubo. Cf. *Goth.* ungalaubeins.]

un-geleáfful[1]; *adj. Unbelieving, incredulous*:—Ne beó ðû ungeleáfful (-full, MS. C.) *noli esse incredulus*, Jn. Skt. 20, 27. Eálâ ungeleáffulle cneórys, Mk. Skt. 9, 19. Eálâ gê ungeleáffulle cneóres, Mt. Kmbl. 17, 17. Hê ungeleáfful wæs Cristes ǽristes, Homl. Th. i. 234, 20. Ne sŷ mê nân man tô ungeleáful be ðâm þingum wrîtende ðe ic gehŷrde, Homl. Skt. ii. 23 b, 16. Ða deófolgyldan ðe ðâgyt ungeleáffulle wǽron, Homl. Th. i. 70, 24. Tô beswîcenne ungeleáffulra manna heortan, Blickl. Homl. 189, 8. Hê æteówde ða wunda ðǽm ungeleáffullum mannum, 91, 2.

un-geleáffullîc; *adj.* I. *unbelieving, incredulous*:—Gif hwâ ðises ne gelŷfð hê ys ungeleáfulîc, Jud. 15, last line. II. *unbelievable, incredible*:—Ic wât ðæt hit wile ðincan swŷðe ungeleáffullîc ungelǽredum mannum, Lchdm. iii. 270, 7. v. un-geleáflîc.

un-geleáffullîce; *adv. Incredibly*; incredibiliter, Scint. 54, 9: Basil admn. 7; Norm. 48, 20.

un-geleáffulness, e; *f. Unbelief, incredulity*:—Gefylst mînre ungeleáffulnysse (*incredulitatem*), Mk. Skt. 9, 24. Ne dô ðû æfter heora ungeleáffulnesse, Blickl. Homl. 237, 9. Ungeleáfulnesse, 241, 34. For hyra ungeleáffulnysse, Mt. Kmbl. 13, 58: 17, 20. Hê tǽlde hyra ungeleáffulnesse, for ðam ðe hî ne gelŷfdon ðâm ðe hine gesâwon of deáþe ârîsan, Mk. Skt. 16, 14.

un-geleáflîc; *adj. Incredible*:—Ðæt ân þing wǽre ungeleáflîc on ðære race geset, Homl. Th. ii. 520, 12. Ðæt wile þincan ungeleáflîc eallum ðǽm ðe ða stôwe on uferum tîdum geseóð, Lchdm. iii. 438, 14: Chr. 1036; Erl. 165, 9.

un-geleáfsum; *adj. Unbelieving, infidel, not Christian*:—Se ðe ðam suna is ungeleáfsum ne gesyhþ hê lîf *qui incredulus est filio non uidebit vitam*, Jn. Skt. 3, 36. Ða ungeleáfsuman ðeóde gesêcan *incredulam gentem adire*, Bd. 1, 23; S. 485, 33. Gif hî ungeleáfsume (*infideles*) wǽron, hê hî laþede ðæt hî onfêngon ðam gerŷne Cristes geleáfan, 3, 5; S. 526, 30. Manige hǽþne men ungeleáfsume, Blickl. Homl. 129, 24. Ðâm ungeleáfsumum (*infidelibus*) nôht biþ clǽne, Bd. 1, 27; S.

494, 40. Hē ungeleáfsume (*incredulos*) tō Cristes geleáfan getrymede, 3, 19; S. 547, 10.

un-geleáfsumness, e; *f. Unbelief, infidelity, heathenism*:—Monige on Angelðeóde, mid ðȳ hī ðāgyta on ungeleáfsumnysse (*infidelitate*) wǣron, Bd. 1, 27; S. 491, 22.

un-gelīc; *adj. Unlike, different, dissimilar, diverse*:—Ungelīc *dispar*, Ælfc. Gr. 9, 17; Zup. 43, 2: *dissimile*, Kent. Gl. 512. Ðē is ungelīc wlite siððan ðū lǣstes mīne lāre *you have a different beauty, since you followed my teaching*, Cd. Th. 38, 26; Gen. 612: 222, 29; Dan. 112. Ðonne is ungelīc be ðon ēcan līfe *now with the life eternal it is different*, Blickl. Homl. 97, 28. Ungelīc is ūs *our lots are different*, Exon. Th. 380, 5; Rä. 1, 3. Hē tiolaþ ungelīc tō biónne ðam ōþrum, Bt. 39, 12; Fox 232, 7: Cd. Th. 23, 9; Gen. 356. Hit is ungelīc ūrum gecynde, Met. 20, 33. Unilīcum hāde *dispari sexu*, Hpt. Gl. 461, 5. Ungelīce, Wrt. Voc. ii. 28, 41. Hē reorde gesette eorðbūendum ungelīce, Cd. Th. 101, 21; Gen. 1685. Se ðe bīspell secgan wolde, ne sceolde fōn on tō ungelīc bīspell ðære sprǣce ðe hē ðonne sprecan wolde *cognatos, de quibus loquimur, rebus oportere esse sermones*, Bt. 35, 5; Fox 166, 20. Syndon dryhtguman ungelīce, Exon. Th. 314, 32; Mōd. 23. Wē syndon ungelīce ðonne ðe wē in heofonum hæfdon wlite *we are different from what we were when we had beauty in heaven*, Cd. Th. 274, 7; Sat. 150. Hē cwæþ ðæt hē gesāwe ungelīce bēc him berende beón ðurh ða gōdan gāstas oþþe ðurh ða gālan *quod codices diversos per bonos sive malos spiritus sibi vidit offerri*, Bd. 5, 13; S. 633, 24. Hī wilniaþ þurh ungelīce earnunga cuman tō ānre eádignesse, Bt. 24, 1; Fox 80, 9. Ealle gesceafta ðū gesceópe him gelīce, and eác on sumum þingum ungelīce, 33, 4; Fox 128, 26; Met. 20, 55.

un-gelīca, an; *m. One not like another*:—Ic hæbbe ōðerne lufiend, ðīnne ungelīcan (*a very different person from you*), Homl. Skt. i. 7, 28. [Ever ich am þin unilike, O. and N. 806.] v. ge-līca.

un-gelīce; *adv. Not in like manner, differently, diversely*:—Hwæðer ðū mæge gemunan ðætte ǣlces monnes ingeþanc wilnaþ tō ðære sōþan gesǣlþe tō cumenne, ðeáh hē ungelīce hiora earnige *meministine intentionem omnem voluntatis humanae, quae diversis studiis agitur, ad beatitudinem festinare?* Bt. 36, 3; Fox 176, 21. Ða strengas se hearpere suīðe ungelīce styreþ, and mid ðȳ gedēð ðæt hī nāwuht ungelīce ðæm sōne ne singaþ ðe hē wilnaþ. Ealle hē grēt mid ānre honda, ðeáh hē hié ungelīce styrige *chordas tangendi artifex, ut non sibimetipsi dissimile canticum faciat, dissimiliter pulsat. Chordae uno quidem plectro, sed non uno impulsu feriuntur*, Past. 23; Swt. 175, 7–10. Is hām sceapen ungelīce englum and deóflum, Exon. Th. 56, 11; Cri. 899: 56, 34; Cri. 910: 83, 29; Cri. 1363: 283, 31; Jul. 688. Bið ðām ōþrum ungelīce willa geworden, 77, 28; Cri. 1263. Biþ ðam ōþrum ungelīce, se ðe on eorþan eáðmōd leofaþ, 317, 18; Mōd. 67: Elen. Kmbl. 2611; El. 1307: Exon. Th. 380, 14; Rä. 1, 8.

un-gelīclīc; *adj. Unseemly, improper*:—Ne hē cnihtlīce gālnysse næs begangende, ne ungelīclīce ōlæcunge, ne leáslīcetunge, Guthl. 2; Gdwin. 12, 17.

un-gelīclīce; *adv. Improperly*:—Hū ðone cealdan magan ungelīclīce lyste, Lchdm. ii. 160, 7.

un-gelīcness, e; *f. Difference, dissimilarity, diversity*:—Ic cwæð ðæt ǣghwelc mon wǣre ōðrum gelīc ācenned, ac sió ungelīcnes hiera earnunga hié tīhð sume behindan sume . . . Hwæt ðonne ða ungelīcnesse ðe of hiera unðeáwum forðcymeþ, se godcunda dōm geðencð *omnes homines natura aequales genuit, sed variante meritorum ordine alios aliis culpa postponit. Ipsa autem diversitas, quae accessit ex vitio, divino judicio dispensatur*, Past. 17; Swt. 106, 18, 22. For ðære ungelīcnesse ðara hiéremonna sculun beón ungelīc ða word ðæs lāreówes, 23; Swt. 175, 2.

un-gelȳfed; *adj. Not possessed of belief, unbelieving, infidel*:—Se ungelȳfeda Ualens genam Godes circean of ðām Godes þeówum, Homl. Skt. i. 3, 318. Hī ofslōgon swīðe ða hǣðenan, ðæt ðǣr nān ne belāf ðæra ungelȳfedra cucu, Homl. Th. ii. 212, 33. Paulus spræc swīðe egeslīce be ungelȳfedum mannum: hē cwæð: 'Ða ðe Godes ǣ ne cunnon, and būton Godes ǣ syngiaþ, hī eác būton Godes ǣ losiaþ,' 52, 22: i. 460, 26: Blickl. Homl. 63, 22. Ungelȳfdum, 55, 32.

un-gelȳfed; *adj. Unallowed, illicit*:—Ðurh ungelȳfedne willan *per inlicitam voluptatem*, Bd. 3, 19; S. 548, 29.

un-gelȳfedlīc; *adj. Incredible, marvellous*:—Swā ðæt nān wundor [nis] ne eác ungelȳfedlīc þincg, Homl. Skt. ii. 23 b, 39. Nis nān tō ðam ungelȳfedlīc spel, gif hē hyt segð, ðæt ic him ne gelȳfe, Shrn. 196, 18. Ðæs wealles micelness is ungeliéfedlīc tō secgenne *murorum ejus vix credibilis relatu magnitudo*, Ors. 2, 4; Swt. 74, 14. Hit is ungeliéfedlīc tō secganne *incredibile dictu est*, 3, 9; Swt. 134, 15. Ungeliéfedlīc is ǣnigum menn ðæt tō gesecgenne *pene incredibile apud mortales erat*, 2, 4; Swt. 74, 7. Hē hæfde āne swīðe wlitige dohter ungelīfedlīcre fægernysse, Ap. Th. 1, 9. For ðam ungelīfedlīcan wlite ðæs mǣdenes, 3, 12. Hē ungeliéfedlīcne micelne weg on ðæm dæge gefōr, Ors. 3, 9; Swt. 124, 27. v. un-gelīfendlīc.

un-gelīfend, es; *m. An unbeliever*:—Se ðe ungelēfend (-en, Lind.) is *qui incredulus est*, Jn. Skt. Rush. 3, 36: 20, 27.

un-gelīfendlīc; *adj. Incredible, extraordinary*:—Ungelȳfendlīc tō-blāwennys his innoð geswencte, Homl. Th. i. 86, 12. Ic ðē mæg tǣcan ōþer ðing ðe dysegum monnum wile ðincan get ungelēfendlīcre (-lēfed-, Cott. MS.) *hoc quod dicam, non minus mirum videatur*, Bt. 38, 3; Fox 198, 30.

un-gelīfness (?), e; *f. Unbelief*:—Fore ungeleáffulnisse ł ungelēfenise hiora *propter incredulitatem illorum*, Mt. Kmbl. Lind. 13, 58.

un-geligen. v. un-gelygen.

un-gelimp, es; *n. m. Misfortune, mishap*:—Ǣlc ungelimp cymð of deófle *omne infortunium venit a diabolo*, L. Ecg. P. iv. 66; Th. ii. 226, 26. Ðonne mē hwylc ungelimp becymð, Ps. Th. 39, 18. Him cymð ege and ungelimp, 13, 9. Wæs swīðe hefelīc geár and swīðe sorhfull geár . . . and swā mycel ungelimp on wæderunge swā man nāht ǣðelīce geþencean ne mæg, Chr. 1085; Erl. 219, 21. Hwā is swā heardheort ðæt ne mæg wēpan swylces ungelimpes? 1086; Erl. 219, 40. Ðæt mīne fȳnd ne gefeón mīnes ungelimpes, Ps. Th. 34, 23, 24. Hī blissedon on mīnum ungelimpe, 34, 15. Wē sceolon ǣgðer ge on gelimpe ge on ungelimpe cweðan: 'Ic herige mīnne Drihten on ǣlcne tīman, Homl. Th. i. 252, 13: Homl. Skt. i. 16, 251. Ic andette mīne scylda and seófige mīn ungelimp, Ps. Th. 21, 2: Homl. Th. i. 584, 5. Ðā geāxodon þrȳ cyningas eal his ungelimp, ii. 454, 6. Wēpendlīc tīd wæs ðæs geáres, ðe swā manig ungelimp wæs forðbringende, Chr. 1086; Erl. 220, 23. Gif ūs ungelimpas on ǣhtum getīmiaþ, Homl. Th. ii. 328, 27. Fela ungelimpa gelimpð ðysse þeóde, Wulfst. 162, 12. Him becōmon fela yrmða on eallum ungelimpum, Ælfc. T. Grn. 20, 43. Ðæt se man geunrōtsige ongeán God for ungelimpum ðises andweardan līfes, Homl. Th. ii. 220, 17. On ungelimpum . . . on gesǣlðum, Homl. Skt. i. 16, 348. Hē geþafaþ ðæt ða gōdan habban unsǣlþa and ungelimp on mænegum þingum *bonis dura tribuat*, Bt. 39, 2; Fox 214, 4. Hē (*Job*) ða ungelimp geāxod hæfde, Homl. Th. ii. 450, 30.

un-gelimplīc; *adj. Unseasonable, unhappy, unfortunate*:—Ungelimplīc slāpolnys *lethargia*, Wrt. Voc. i. 75, 63. (Cf. 46, 1 where two entries seem confused, v. next word.) Ungelimplīce gewyderu, Wulfst. 172, 18. Ða ungelimplīcan *inepta*, Wrt. Voc. ii. 48, 53. Wē oft ongytaþ ðæt āriseþ þeód wiþ þeóde and ungelimplīco gefeoht (*unhappy wars*) on wōlīcum dǣdum, Blickl. Homl. 107, 28.

un-gelimplīce; *adv. Unseasonably, unhappily*:—Ungelimplīce slāpol *lethargus* vel *letargicus*, Wrt. Voc. i. 75, 62. Hēr is ðære lyfte fāgetung ðurh mislīce stormas ðe ungelimplīce becumaþ, Homl. Th. ii. 538, 33.

un-gelygen; *adj. Not lying, true*:—Būtan ðæs gerēfan gewitnesse . . . oþþe ōðres ungelygenes (-lig-, *v. l.*) mannes, L. Ath. i. 10; Th. i. 204, 19. Ungeligenes, i. 12; Th. i. 206, 10 note. Ðæt hē hæfde ungeligene gewitnesse . . . ðæt hē gelǣdde ungeligne gewitnesse, L. Ed. 1; Th. i. 158, 16, 19. Swā fela manna swā man wite ðæt ungelygne sȳn. . . . And sién heora āðas ungelygenra manna be ðæs feós wyrðe, L. Ath. iv. 1; Th. i. 222, 10, 13. Hæbbe hē ðæs portgerēfan gewitnesse oþþe ōðera ungeligenra manna ðe man gelȳfan mæge, L. Ed. 1; Th. i. 158, 12. Ðū tēhtest mē swā ungelygena gewittnesse swā ic nān ōðer dōn ne mæg būte ic nǣde scall hym gelīfan, Shrn. 201, 17. v. un-lygen.

un-gemaca, an; *m. Not a match, not an equal*:—Ungemaca *impar*, Ælfc. Gr. 9, 17; Zup. 43, 1: Germ. 389, 76. [Þæ drake elcches wurmes unimake *unlike all other serpents*, Laym. 17961.]

un-gemæc[c]; *adj. Unlike, unequal, dissimilar*:—Ungemæccre wurman *dispari murice*, Wrt. Voc. ii. 141, 19. [*O. L. Ger.* un-gimac *infestus*: *O. H. Ger.* un-gimah[h] *dispar*.]

un-gēmæn. v. un-gīmen.

un-gemǣte; *adj. Immeasurable, immense*:—Wearð þurh ðæt ungemǣte orfcwealm, Chr. 1115; Erl. 245, 17. [Unimete festen and to michel forhefednesse, O. E. Homl. i. 101, 29: 253, 11. Þe ferde wes swa muchel, þat heo wes unimete, Laym. 4964. Her is chele and hete and hunger unymete, Misc. 73, 50. In his unimete blisse, A. R. 40, 13. *O. H. Ger.* un-gimāzi *inaequalis*.] v. un-mǣte, *and next words*.

un-gemǣte; *adv. Immeasurably, immensely*:—Mid ungemǣte miclum ege geslægene *timore immenso perculsos*, Bd. 5, 12; S. 627, 14 note.

un-gemǣtlīc; *adj. Immense, excessive*:—Mid ungemǣtlīcre gewilnunge anwaldes *dominationis libidine*, Ors. 1, 2; Swt. 28, 27. [Cf. Swa unimeteliche þu swanc, O. E. Homl. i. 281, 18. Unimeteliche and unendliche more, A. R. 398, 25.]

un-gemeaht (?); *adj. Weak*:—Hū micle unmihtegran (ungemihtran, Bod. MS.) hī wǣron, gif hī his nān gecynde næfdon, Bt. 36, 5; Fox 180, 4. v. meaht; *adj.*

un-gemēde; *adj. Disagreeable, discordant, adverse*, Exon. Th. 315, 2; Mōd. 25. [Cf. *O. H. Ger.* un-gimōtī *dispendium, damnum, contumelia, injuria*.] v. un-gemōd, *and next word*.

un-gemēdness, e; *f. Adversity, calamity*:—From ungimoednisum ðætte wē sié ālēsado *ab adversitatibus liberari*, Rtl. 63, 29. [*O. H. Ger.* un-gimōtnissi *humilitas*.]

un-gemeltness, e; *f. Indigestion*:—Gebeorh ðæt hié ungemeltnesse ne þrowian, Lchdm. ii. 184, 11.

un-gemenged; *adj. Unmixed, unmingled*:—Hit is gecynd ðære godcundnesse ðæt hió mæg beón ungemenged wið ōþre gesceafta būton ōþerra gesceafta fultume *ea est divinae forma substantiae, ut neque in* *externa dilabatur, nec in se externum aliquid ipsa suscipiat,* Bt. 35, 5; Fox 166, 5. v. un-menged.

un-gemet, es; *n.* I. *immensity, an immense number:*—Ealles his heres wæs swelc ungemet ðæt mon eáðe cweþan mehte ðæt hit wundor wǣre hwǣr hié wæteres hæfden ðæt hié mehten him þurst of ādrincan *ut exercitui immensaeque classi vix ad potum flumina suffecisse memoratum sit,* Ors. 2, 5; Swt. 80, 7. Hē heora ungemet ofslōg; be ðæm mon mehte witan, ðā hē and ða consulas hié ātellan ne mehton *quot millia hominum interfecta ipse consul ostendit; qui numerum explicare non potuit,* 3, 10; Swt. 140, 29. II. *immoderation, excess:*—Of ungemete ǣlces þinges, wiste and wǣda, wīngedrinces, Met. 25, 38. Ðæt hē ne wilnige wynsumran wyrde ðonne hit gemetlīc sié, ne eft tō rēþre; for ðæm hē ne mæg nāþres ungemet ādrióhan, Bt. 40, 3; Fox 238, 22. II a. adverbial uses of cases, *ungemetes, (mid) ungemete, ungemetum, to excess, without measure, excessively, immensely, very:*—Ungemetes wel, Beo. Th. 3589; B. 1792. Wese ðīn esne on ðē ungemete blīðe *servus tuus laetabitur,* Ps. Th. 108, 27: 115, 2: 141, 7: 143, 17: Beo. Th. 5436; B. 2721. Ic bidde ðīnre ansȳne ungemete georne, mid ealre gehygde heortan mīnre *deprecatus sum faciem tuam in toto corde meo,* Ps. Th. 118, 58: 108, 3: 115, 1. Ungemete neáh, Beo. Th. 4832; B. 2420: 5450: B. 2728. Hió wile weahsan mid ungemete *sine mensura dilatatur,* Past. 11; Swt. 71, 17. Mid ungemete (cf. ungemetlīce, Bt. 38, 1; Fox 194, 25), Met. 26, 62. Se mid ungemete gernde anwalda ofer ōþre *ardens cupiditate dominandi,* Ors. 3, 11; Swt. 148, 29: 4, 5; Swt. 166, 25: 6, 3; Swt. 256, 28. Ða folc būtū on feferādle mid ungemete swulton *gravissima pestilentia uterque exercitus angebatur,* 4, 10; Swt. 198, 35. Ðā ongon se cealc mid ungemete stincan, 6, 32; Swt. 288, 1: Homl. Skt. i. 23, 230. Ungemetum rēðe, Runic pm. Kmbl. 341, 2; Rūn. 3: 341, 15; Rūn. 11. Ungemettan fæste mid cludum ymbweaxen *mirae asperitatis,* Ors. 3, 9; Swt. 132, 10. Ungemetum georne, Ps. Th. 118, 107: 142, 1. Ungemetum swīðe, 118, 67. Eágan ungemetum wēpaþ, Dōm. L. 12, 193. [From mesure into unimete, A. R. 74, 28. *O. H. Ger.* un-gimez.]

un-gemet. *Where the word seems to be used with an adjective or with an adverbial force, it is given, as in the case of* ungemet-hleahtor, *as part of a compound:* cf. *O. Sax.* un-met (*with adjectives*): *O. H. Ger.* un-mez, Grff. ii. 898–9. Cf. ungesceád-micel.

ungemet-ceald; *adj. Excessively cold:*—Winter bringeþ weder ungemetcald, Met. 11, 59.

un-gemete, un-gemetegod, un-gemetegung, ungemetelīce. v. un-gemet, II a, un-gemetgod, un-gemetgung, un-gemetlīce.

un-gemetfæst; *adj.* I. in a moral sense, *immoderate, immodest, intemperate:*—Ðā forseah se Catulus hine, for ðam hē hine wiste swīþe ungesceádwīsne and swīþe ungemetfæstne, Bt. 27, 1; Fox 96, 5. Ðām monnum ðe beóþ neátenum gelīce, ðæt beóð unrihtwīse and ungemetfæste, 14, 1; Fox 42, 4. II. in reference to physical things, (1) *immoderate, excessive:*—Hwīlum cymð of ungemetfæstre hǣto, hwīlum of ungemetfæstum cyle, Lchdm. ii. 56, 16. Hwīlum of ungemætfæstre hǣto, hwilum of ungemetfæstum cyle, hwīlum of ungemetlīcre wǣtan, hwīlum of ungemætlīcre drīgnesse, iii. 72, 29. (2) applied to the stomach, *irretentive:*—Ðæs hātan magan ungemetfæstan tācn sindon, ðonne hē bið mid ōmum geswenced, ðam men bið þurst getenge, Lchdm. ii. 192, 25: 160, 4. [*O. H. Ger.* un-gimezfast *immoderatus, immodestus.*]

ungemet-fæst; *adj. Extremely firm:*—Ðǣr hē mæge findan eáðmētta stān ungemetfæstne, grundweal gearone (cf. on ðam fæstan stāne eáðmētta, Bt. 12; Fox 36, 22), Met. 7, 33.

un-gemetfæstlīc; *adj. Irretentive:*—Ðis sint tācn ðæs hātan magan ōmihtan ungemetfæstlīcan, Lchdm. ii. 192, 24. v. un-gemetfæst, II. 2.

un-gemetfæstness, e; *f. Intemperance:*—Ðū wilt cweþan ðæt wrǣnnes and ungemetfæstnes hī ofsitte *sed transversos eos libido praecipitat, sic quoque intemperantia fragiles,* Bt. 36, 6; Fox 182, 2.

ungemet-geneahhie; *adv. Extremely:*—Mē fyrenfulra rāpas ungemetgeneahhie oft beclyptan, Ps. Th. 118, 61.

ungemet-gīmen[n], e; *f. Excessive care:*—Se rēþa rēn, sumes ymbhogan ungemetgēmen (cf. se rēn ungemetlīces ymbhogan, Bt. 12; Fox 36, 19), Met. 7, 28.

un-gemetgod; *adj. Immoderate, excessive, intemperate, indiscreet:*—Ðonne sió ðreáung bið ungemetgad *cum increpatio immoderate accenditur,* Past. 21; Swt. 165, 18. Sió ungemetgode suīge *indiscretum silentium,* 15; Swt. 89, 9. Ne durre wē ðās bōc nā miccle swīðor gelengan, ðī læs ðe heó ungemetegod sȳ, Homl. Th. ii. 520, 4. Ungemetegod lufu, 220, 6: Homl. Skt. i. 16, 276. Tunge ungemetegud(-ad) *lingua immoderata,* Scint. 78, 10: Kent. Gl. 507. Mid ðære ungemetgodan smeáunge, Past. 11; Swt. 67, 8. Ða ungemetgodan sprǣce *immoderatam locutionem,* 38; Swt. 281, 1. His ungemetegodan lufe, Homl. Skt. i. 3, 363. Beweóp se ylca apostol ungemetegodra manna līf, ðus cweðende: 'Heora wamb is heora god,' Homl. Th. i. 604, 27.

un-gemetgung, e; *f. Want of moderation, excess, intemperance:*—'Coða becumaþ.' Efne hēr is foresǣd manna līchamana ungemetegung and geswencednys, Homl. Th. ii. 538, 30. Ðȳ læs ðæt innegeðonc sié gebunden ðære heortan for ðære ungemetgunge ðæs ymbehōgan ðæra ūterra ðinga (*per moderatam cordis intentionem non impeditur*), Past. 18; Swt. 141, 8.

ungemet-hleahtor, es; *m. Immoderate laughter:*—Hū micele mā wēnestū ðæt hē mid yrre ða ūt āweorpe of his temple, ðe mid unnyttum gesprǣcum and mid ungemethleahtrum ða stōwa, ðe tō Godes þeówdōme gehālgode wǣron, fȳlaþ and besmȳtaþ, L. E. I. 10; Th. ii. 408, 32.

ungemet-lange; *adv. Excessively long,* Cd. Th. 20, 23; Gen. 313.

un-gemetlīc; *adj.* I. *immoderate, inordinate, excessive, too great:*—Ungemetlīco forgifnis . . . ungemetlīcu irsung *inordinata remissio . . . effrenata ira,* Past. 20; Swt. 149, 9–11. Ungemetlīcu sprǣc *immoderata loquacitas,* 43; Swt. 309, 2. Se rēn ungemetlīces ymbhogan, Bt. 12; Fox 36, 19: 18, 1; Fox 60, 24. Ðū woldest brūcan ungemetlīcre wrǣnnesse *voluptariam vitam degas,* 32, 1; Fox 114, 20. For ungemetlīcum cyle, 33, 4; Fox 130, 34. Mið ungemetlīcre gītsunge *intemperans cupido,* Txts. 180, 1: Ors. 1, 2; Swt. 30, 28. Of ungemetlīcre drīgnesse, Lchdm. ii. 56, 17. Ungemætlīcre, iii. 72, 30. Of ðam ungemetlīcan gegerelan, Bt. 37, 1; Fox 186, 16. Hē onsent ofer hig ungemetlīce hǣto ðære sunnan, Ps. Th. 10, 7. Ðā hié angeátan ðæt hē ungemetlīc gafol wið ðæm friþe habban wolde *cum intolerabiles conditiones pacis audissent,* Ors. 4, 6; Swt. 174, 24. Ungemetlīca metesōcna and ungemetlīce unlustas, Lchdm. ii. 174, 27. Ða ungemetlīcan hleahtras, Blickl. Homl. 59, 18. II. *immense, very great:*—Ungemetlīc *inmane,* Wrt. Voc. ii. 48, 25. Gif hit full ungemetlīc wind gestent, Bt. 12; Fox 36, 15. Ungemetlīc moncwealm *incredibilium morborum pestis,* Ors. 6, 23; Swt. 274, 11. Wæs ungemetlīc wæl geslægen, Chr. 867; Erl. 72, 15. Ðā com se ungemetlīca unfriðhere, 1009; Erl. 142, 16. III. *not of the same measure, diverse:*—Ungemetlīcra *diversarum,* Mt. Kmbl. p. 7, 5. v. un-metlīc.

un-gemetlīce; *adv.* I. *immoderately, beyond measure, excessively, too (much):*—Se ðe wile ungemetlīce gesceádwīs beón, Past. 11; Swt. 67, 6. Tantalus ðe ungemetlīce gīfre wæs, Bt. 35, 6; Fox 168, 33. Gē wilniaþ eówerne hlīsan ungemetlīce tō gebrǣdanne, 18, 1; Fox 62, 18. Ne nān preóst ne drince ungemetelīce, L. Ælfc. C. 29; Th. ii. 352, 28. Hū ungemetlīce gē bemurciaþ, Ors. 1, 10; Swt. 48, 17. Ongan hió hine lufian, and hiora ǣgþer ōþerne swīþe ungemetlīce, Bt. 38, 1; Fox 194, 25. Ðæt hē ðæt ryht tō swīðe and tō ungemetlīce (*nimie et inordinate*) ne bodige, Past. 15; Swt. 95, 17. Ðæt hié tō ungemetlīce ne forweaxen *ne immoderatius excrescant,* 18; Swt. 141, 6: 21; Swt. 167, 14. II. *immensely, exceedingly, very greatly:*—Ðā wearð Cain ungemetlīce yrre *iratus est Cain vehementer,* Gen. 4, 5. Seó wæs ungemetlīce micel *serpens mirae magnitudinis,* Ors. 4, 6; Swt. 174, 4. Sió eá hæfde ungemettlīce ceald wæter *praefrigidus amnis,* 3, 9; Swt. 124, 29. Ic eom swīþe ungemetlīce ofwundrod *vehementer admiror,* Bt. 13; Fox 40, 4. Isaac wundrode ungemetlīce swīðe *Isaac ultra quam credi potest admirans,* Gen. 27, 33. [*O. H. Ger.* un-gimezlīhho *hyperbolice.*] v. un-metlīce.

ungemet-lytel; *adj. Exceedingly little:*—Ðæt ðeós eorðe sié eall for ðæt ōþer ungemetlytel, Met. 10, 9.

un-gemetness, e; *f. Extravagance:*—Ungemetnisse *dementiam,* Txts. 180, 3.

ungemet-scearp; *adj. Excessively sharp:*—Wǣron hyra tungan ungemetscearpe, Ps. Th. 56, 5.

ungemet-þurst, es; *m. Excessive thirst:*—Se hāta maga ungemetþurst þrowaþ, Lchdm. ii. 160, 4.

ungemet-wæcce, an; *f. Excessive wakefulness:*—Monige ādla . . . on unmōde and on ungemetwæccum, Lchdm. ii. 176, 2.

ungemet-wæl, es; *n. Very great carnage:*—Ðǣr wæs ungemetwæl geslægen, Chr. 867; Erl. 73, 14.

ungemet-wilnung, e; *f. Excessive desire:*—Ungemetwilnung ǣtes and slǣpes, Dōm. L. 30, 44.

un-gemidlod; *adj. Unbridled:*—Swā swā mōdig hors, ðe ungemidlod byð, Ælfc. T. Grn. 17, 22. Seó ofermōdnes ungemidledum (-odon) horse fleáh *superbia effreni volitat equo,* Gl. Prud. 29 a. v. unmidlod.

un-gemilt; *adj. Undigested:*—Heald georne ðæt se mete sī gemylt . . . , for ðan ðe se ungemylta mete him wyrcð mycel yfel, Lchdm. ii. 284, 4.

un-gemōd; *adj. Disagreeing, contentious, at variance;* discors:—Ðǣm ungesibsuman is tō cȳðanne ðæt hié wieten ðætte swā lange swā hié beóð from ðære lufe āðiéd hiera niéhstena and him ungemōde beóð . . . *admonendi sunt dissidentes, ut noverint, quod . . . quamdiu a proximorum caritate discordant,* Past. 46; Swt. 349, 7. Ða ungemōdan . . . , ða gemōdan *discordes . . . , pacati,* 23; Swt. 177, 9.

un-gemōdigness, e; *f. Dissentiousness:*—Ðæt wæs ungerīm, ðæt þurh deófles ungemōdignesse intō helle behreás, Wulfst. 8, 15 note. v. next word.

un-gemōdness, e; *f. Contentiousness, indisposition to agree:*—Ða ungesibsuman sint tō manianne ðæt hié witen ðæt hié nō on tō ðæs monegum gōdum cræftum ne ðióð ðæt hié ǣfre mægen gāstlīce bión gif hié ðurh ungemōdnesse āgiémeleásiaþ ðæt hié ānmōde bión nyllaþ on ryhte and on gōde *discordes admonendi sunt, ut sciant, quia, quantislibet* *virtutibus polleant, spiritales fieri nullatenus possunt, si uniri per concordiam proximis negligunt*, Past. 46; Swt. 344, 9.

un-gemolsnod; *adj. Uncorrupted, undecayed*:—Hē healdeþ ða deádan līchoman ungemolsnode under eorðan, óþ ðæt hī eft cuce ārīsaþ, Shrn. 82, 21.

un-gemunecod; *adj. Not made a monk*:—Unhādod man and ungemunecod *homo non ordinatus nec monachus*, L. Ecg. C. 12; Th. ii. 142, 4.

un-gemynd *distraction* or *confusion of mind, dementedness*:—Wiþ ungemynde and wið dysgunge, Lchdm. ii. 142, 1, 4: 14, 16. Wiþ deófle and ungemynde, 352, 7. Wiþ heáfodece and wiþ ungemynde and wiþ ungehȳrnesse, 314, 25. Cf. gemynd-leás.

un-gemyndig; *adj. Unmindful, forgetful*:—Ungemyndig *immemor*, Ælfc. Gr. 9, 21; Zup. 47, 14. Ne byð ǽfre God ungemyndig ðæt hē miltsige manna cynne *numquid obliviscetur misereri Deus?* Ps. Th. 76, 8. Swā hwā swā ungemyndig (*immemor*) sié rihtwīsnesse, Bt. 35, 1; Fox 156, 10: Met. 22, 55. Hē wæs ungemyndig ðæs hālgan gewrites, Homl. Th. i. 82, 13. Ungemyndig *oblitum*, Germ. 388, 36. Ungemyndigne, 388, 24. Hī wurdon ðæs treówes ungemyndige, ac God wæs his gemyndig, Homl. Th. ii. 146, 2.

un-gemyndum, Bd. 5, 12; S. 630, 38, un-genēd. v. un-gīmende, un-genīd.

un-genge; *adj. Impracticable, useless, vain*:—Gē ungænge gedydon bebod Godes *irritum fecistis mandatum Dei*, Mt. Kmbl. Rush. 15, 6. [*Icel.* ū-gengr *not fit to walk on.* Cf. *Ger.* un-gangbar *not current, impracticable.*]

un-genīd[d]; *adj. Unforced, uncompelled*:—Ne mæg ic nāne cwica wuht ongitan . . . ðe ungenēd lyste forweorþan *nihil invenio, quod, nullis extra cogentibus, abjiciat manendi intentionem*, Bt. 34, 10; Fox 148, 14. Ðæt ealle gesceafta hiora āgnum willum ungenēdde him wǽron underþeódde, 35, 5; Fox 164, 29. Ungeniédde (-nīdde, Cott. MSS.) mid eówrum āgenum willan gē sculon ðenceań for eówre heorde *providentes non coacte, sed spontanee*, Past. 18; Swt. 137, 19: Ors. 5, 15; Swt. 250, 14.

un-geocian *to unyoke*:—Ic ungeocige oððe tōtwǽme *disjungo*, Ælfc. Gr. 47; Zup. 277, 3.

un-georne; *adv.* I. *unwillingly, reluctantly*:—Ðā on ðæm tweón ðe hié swā ungeorne his willan fulleodon *qui fastidiose ducem in disponendo bello audientes*, Ors 3, 11; Swt. 146, 24. II. *without diligence, negligently*:—Ðæt hē tō ungeorne bewiste hwæt hē on þeóstrum dyde, Blickl. Homl. 183, 23. [*O. H. Ger.* un-gerno: *Ger.* un-gern: *Icel.* ū-gjarna *unwillingly.*]

un-geornful[l]; *adj. Not diligent, negligent, careless, remiss*:—Ðæt ungeornfulle mōd hyngreð *anima dissoluta esuriet*, Past. 39; Swt. 283, 11. Ðȳ læs hine se wærscipe gelǽde on ealles tō micle hātheortnesse, oððe eft sió ānfealdnes hine tō ungeornfulne gedoo tō ongietanne, ðȳ læs hē weorðe besolcen *quatenus nec seducti per prudentiam calleant, nec ab intellectus studio ex simplicitate torpescant*, 35; Swt. 239, 2. Hyne nān man geseah ungeornfulne tō Cristes þeówdōme, Guthl. 20; Gdwin. 92, 19.

un-gerād; *adj.* I. *stupid, rude, unskilled, foolish, ignorant*:—Walah *sive* ungerād *barbarus*, Wrt. Voc. ii. 12, 75. Gif se sacerd bið ungerād ðæs lāreówdōmes *sacerdos si praedicationis est nescius*, Past. 15; Swt. 91, 24. Sum ungerād mann . . . nolde gān tō ðām axum on ðone Wōdnes-dæg, Homl. Skt. i. 12, 41. Dysig bið se wegfērenda man, se ðe nimð ðone smēðan weg, ðe hine mislǽt . . . Swā eác wē beóð ungerāde, gif wē lufiaþ ða hwīlwendlīcan lustas, Homl. Th. i. 164, 10. Ða dwollīcan bēc rǽdaþ ungerāde menn, ii. 444, 25. Deáh ða dysegan and ða ungerādan his gelȳfan nyllan, Wulfst. 305, 14. Se ðe ungerādum oððe ungeðyldigum stȳrð, Homl. Th. i. 306, 5. II. *discordant, disagreeing, at variance*:—Ungerāde *dissona* (*sermonum procacitate*, Ald. 59), Wrt. Voc. ii. 85, 20: 26, 69. Næles ungerāde *non dissona* (*sententia*, Ald. 65), 86, 12: 60, 69. *Dissona* .i. *discordantia, incongrua*, ungeswēga *vel* ungerāde, 141, 37. Simle bióþ ða gōdan and ða yflan ungeþwǽre betwyh him, ge eác hwīlum ða yflan bióþ ungerāde betwuh him selfum *ut probis atque improbis nullum foedus est, ita ipsi inter se improbi nequeunt convenire*, Bt. 39, 12; Fox 230, 27: Ors. 2, 7; Swt. 90, 6. Ða lātteówas wǽron Agustuse ungerāde, 6, 1; Swt. 254, 18. Ðonne se abbod and se prāfost ungerāde beóð and him betwyx sacaþ *dum contraria sibi invicem abbas prepositusque sentiunt*, R. Ben. 124. Ic sceal nū mid ungerādum wordum gesettan, þeáh ic geóhwīlum gecoplīce funde *carmina qui quondam studio florente peregi, moestos cogor inire modos*, Bt. 2; Fox 4, 7.

un-gerād, es; *n.* I. *stupidity, folly, unreason*:—Fela dyslīce dǽda deriaþ mancynne oððe for ānwylnysse oððe for ungerāde; swā swā sume menn dōð, ðe dyslīce fæstaþ ofer heora mihte . . . Nū gesettan ða hālgan fæderas ðæt wē fæston mid gerāde, Homl. Skt. i. 13, 92. II. *discord, disagreement, variance*:—Ðætte ān sibb Godes lufe būtan ǽlcum ungerāde ūs suīðe fæste gebinde *tunc sola nos in aedificio concordia caritatis liget*, Past. 36; Swt. 253, 22.

un-gerādness, e; *f. Disagreement*:—Gyf hyne mēte, ðæt hē āwiht beran geseó, ðæt byð ungerādnes, Lchdm. iii. 170, 20. v. un-gerǽdness.

un-gerǽd (?); *adj. Stupid*:—Ungerǽd[e?] *insipidus*, stunt *stultus*, Wrt. Voc. i. 47, 42. (*The MS. has* ungeræd, v. Wülck. 165, 16.)

un-gerǽdelīce; *adv. Roughly, rudely*:—Ða Godes wiðerwinnan ða fǽmnan genāmon, ūt of ðære byrig ungerǽdelīce hī togoden, Homl. Ass. 178, 307. [Þe weregede gastes hine uniredlice (*or see* un-gerȳdelīce?) underfangeð mid stearne swupen, O. E. Homl. i. 239, 10.]

un-gerǽdness, e; *f. Discord, disagreement, variance*:—Betux Agathocle and his folce wearð ungerǽdnes *in exercitu Agathoclis orta est seditio*, Ors. 4, 5; Swt. 170, 15. Sōna swā hié him betweónum ungerǽdnesse up āhōfon swā forwurdon hié ealle *discordia exitio fuit*, 5, 3; Swt. 222, 19: 6, 6; Swt. 262, 14. For his feóndum gebidde hē, mid ðām ðe wið hyne ungerǽdnysse hæbben, L. E. I. 21; Th. ii. 418, 15.

un-gerec[c], es; *n. Disorder, tumult, violence*:—Ungerecc (-rec, Rush.) *tumultus*, Mt. Kmbl. Lind. 26, 5. Ungerece *impetu* (cf. *O. H. Ger.* Mit mihhilu ungirehhu *magno impetu*, Mk. 5, 13), Rush. 8, 32. Hē ōðerne cyninges þegn in ðæm ungerecce ācwealde *in ipso tumultu alium de militibus peremit*, Bd. 2, 9; M. 122, 24. [*O. H. Ger.* un-gireh *tumultus, seditio, impetus, inquietudo, passio.*]

un-gereccan *to repel a charge from, to clear*:—Gif hit man him on gerecce, and hē hine ungereccan ne mæge, L. Ath. iv. 1; Th. i. 222, 4.

un-gereclīc; *adj. Disorderly, tumultuous, ungovernable*:—Seó menego tācnode ða flǽsclīcan willan and ða ungereclīcan uncysta, Blickl. Homl. 19, 6.

un-gereclīce; *adv. Without order, tumultuously, without restraint*:—Se ðe ungereclīce liofaþ and his gecynd nyle healdan, ne biþ se nāuht *est enim quod ordinem retinet, servatque naturam; quod vero ab hac deficit, esse etiam derelinquit*, Bt. 46, 6; Fox 182, 21. Ic ongite ðæt ealle gesceafta tōfleówon swā swā wæter and nāne sibbe ne nāne endebyrdnesse ne heóldon, ac swīþe ungereclīce tōslupen and tō nāuhte wurden, gif hī næfdon ǽnne God ðe him eallum stiórde and racode and rǽdde *vel ad nihilum cuncta referuntur, et uno veluti vertice destituta, sine rectore fluitabunt*, 34, 12; Fox 154, 3.

un-gerēdelīce. v. un-gerȳdelīce.

un-geregnod; *adj. Unornamented*:—Massehakele þæt is ungerēnad, Chart. Th. 515, 26.

un-gereord; *adj. Not having an intelligible language*:—Ungereord *barbarus*, Wrt. Voc. ii. 125, 22.

un-gereordedlīc, -gereordlīc; *adj. Insatiable*:—Ungereordedlīcne (-gereo[r]dlīcre, Ps. Spl. C.) *insatiabili*, Ps. Surt. 100, 5.

un-gereordod; *adj. Unfed, not having had a meal*:—Se dēma ungereordod sæt būtan ǽlcere ðēnunge unþances fæstende, Homl. Skt. i. 19, 91.

un-gerian. v. un-girwan.

un-gerīm, es; *n. A countless number, an immense number* or *quantity*:—Feala ōðra gōdra þegna and folces ungerīm, Chr. 1010; Erl. 143, 23. Ðara wæs ungerīm, Shrn. 48, 31. Ðara ys forneán ungerīm, Ælfc. Gr. 5; Zup. 18, 3. Ðæt hē gegaderige ungerīm ðissa welena, Bt. 26, 3; Fox 94, 13. Hire olfendas bǽron ungerīm goldes, Homl. Th. ii. 584, 11. Ungerīm feós syllan, Homl. Skt. i. 12, 101. Cf. un-rīm.

un-gerīm; *adj. Countless, numberless, innumerable, incalculable, immense*:—Ðǽr is ungerīm fæc betweox hyre and ðære eorðon, Lchdm. iii. 254, 12. Ðæt wæs ungerīm (ungerīmlīc, MS. E.), ðæt intō helle behreás, Wulfst. 8, 15. Cōmon ða hǽðengildan mid ungerīmum folce, Homl. Th. ii. 494, 16. S. Anastasius, scs Basilius and ungerīme ōðre, L. Ælfc. C. 6; Th. ii. 344, 30: Ælfc. Gr. 9, 21; Zup. 46, 14. Ōðre ungerīme, 9, 37; Zup. 62, 5: 9, 38; Zup. 63, 8. Tō gefremminge ungerīmra tācna, Homl. Th. i. 310, 17. Ungerīmum *innumeris*, Wülck. Gl. 255, 14. Se deófol . . . wyrcð ungerīma wundra, Homl. Th. i. 4, 16. Ungerīme hūðe *numerosas praedas*, Hpt. Gl. 522, 20. [Mikell follc and unngerim iss onn erþe, Orm. 18993.] Cf. un-rīm; un-getel.

un-gerīmed; *adj. Unnumbered, innumerable*:—Mid ðære ungerīmedan mænigo *innumerabilis multitudo*, Bd. 5, 12; S. 628, 4 note.

un-gerīmedlīc; *adj. Innumerable*:—Ðā geseah hē ða mycelan and ða ungerīmedlīcan ferde his feónda, H. R. 3, 15.

un-gerīmlīc; *adj. Innumerable, incalculable*, Wulfst. 8, 15 note. v. un-gerīm.

un-gerīpod; *adj. Immature, premature*:—Unirīpedes (deáþes) *immaturae* (*mortis*), Hpt. Gl. 507, 38. On ungerīpedum freódōme and unstæððigum þeáwum, Ælfc. T. Grn. 17, 12. Hē forfleáh ungerīpedan deáð, Homl. Th. i. 390, 31.

un-gerīsende; *adj. Unbecoming, indecent*:—Ungerīsendre æfesne *indecens obscenitas*, Hpt. Gl. 492, 59.

un-gerisene, -gerisne; *adj.* I. *unsuitable, inappropriate*:—Ungerisenu *indecens* (*est stulto gloria*, Prov. 26, 1), Kent. Gl. 977. Nis ungerisne ðæt wē ān wundor of monegum āsecgan *nec ab re est unum e pluribus miraculum enarrare*, Bd. 3, 2; S. 524, 38. II. *unseemly, indecent*:—Ðȳ læs hē ōwiht unwyrþes oððe ungerisenes dyde mid his mūþe *ne aliquid indignum suae personae vel ore proferret*, Bd. 4, 11; S. 579, 26. Ungerisnre bysene ðū hātest hié wītuian *you order them to be punished* *in a way that inflicts indignity upon them*, Blickl. Homl. 189, 31. Ungerysenre æfsna *indecens obscenitas*, Hpt. Gl. 492, 62.

un-gerisene, es; *n.*, *or* un-gerisenu; *indecl. f.* I. *inconvenience, disagreeableness*:—Hit ðē biþ oððe ungetǽse oððe frēcenlīc, eall ðæt ðū ofer gemet dēst . . . seó ofering ðē wurþ oþþe tō ungerisenum oþþe tō plió, Bt. 14, 1; Fox 42, 16. Wið scurfendum næglum, gebærned hundes heáfod and seó acxe ðǽron gedōn; ða ungerisnu hyt on weg āfyrreþ, Lchdm. i. 370, 10. II. *unseemliness, indignity, disgrace*:—Tō æwisclīcum bismer .i. ungerisne *ad infame dedecus*, Hpt. Gl. 507, 8. Hē teáh hiene ðæt hē his ungerisno sprǽce *he accused him of speaking unbecomingly of him*; velut sui proditorem, Ors. 4, 11; Swt. 206, 29. Wege hē ða ungerisenu (*contumeliam*, Latin version), L. Ath. iv. 1; Th. i. 222, 7. Gif mīn gerēfa ungerysena gebȳt āðer oþþe tūnes-mannum oþþe heora hyrdon, L. Edg. S. 13; Th. i. 276, 27. Him is leófre ðæt hē leóge ðonne him mon ǽnigra ungerisna tō wēne *eligit falsa de se jactari, ne mala possit vel minima perpeti*, Past. 33; Swt. 217, 16. Bið ðæt sǽd āgoten tō unclǽnnesse and tō ungerisnum *ad immunditiam semen effundit*, 15; Swt. 97, 11.

un-gerisenlīc; *adj. Unseemly, dishonourable, base*:—Is ðæt ungerisenlīc wuldor ðisse worulde and swīþe leás *gloria quam fallax, quam turpis est*, Bt. 30, 1; Fox 106, 30. Ðeáh ðe ful monige mid gerisenlīcum weorcum ārīsen from eorðan, mid ungerisenlīcum gewilnungum ðissa woroldðinga hié hié selfe ālecgeaþ on eorðan *etsi honesta actione nonnulli quasi a terra se erigunt, ambitione tamen inhonesta semetipsos ad terram deponunt*, Past. 21; Swt. 157, 8. Ādō of his mōde ungerisenlīce ymbhogan, Bt. 29, 3; Fox 106, 19. Hwæt ungerisenlīcre sié ðonne ðæt *quo quid turpius excogitari potest?* 30, 1; Fox 108, 6.

un-gerisenlīce; *adv. In an unsuitable, unseemly* or *unbecoming manner, with indignity, dishonourably, basely*:—Ungerisenlīce *inconvenienter*, Wrt. Voc. ii. 43, 64. Hē sceal tilian ðæt hē ne sié tō ungerisenlīce underþeód his unþeáwum, Bt. 29, 3; Fox 106, 19. For ðære gewilnunga woroldgielpes hē onlȳtt ungerisenlīce tō ðissum eorðlīcum, suā ðæt neát for gīfernesse onlȳt tō ðære eorðan, Past. 21; Swt. 157, 2. Dauid, ðā hē ðone læppan forcorfenne hæfde, suīðe suīðlīce hreówsade ðæt hē him (*Saul*) ǽfre suā ungeriesenlīce (-risen-, Cott. MSS.) geðēnigan, sceolde, 28; Swt. 199, 18. Hē bepǽhte hī intō his būre, and hī man ðǽrinne ofslōh ungerisenlīce (*they were basely slain*), Chr. 1015; Erl. 152, 1.

un-gerisenness, -gerisness, e; *f. Unseemliness, shame*:—Unirisnysse *dedecus*, Hpt. Gl. 507, 35.

un-gerȳde; *adj. Rough, violent*:—Se egeslīca swēg ungerȳdre sǽs, Wulfst. 137, 7. [Unirude duntes wið mealles istelet, O. E. Homl. i. 253, 12. Cf. An unrude raketehe, 249, 24. Unnseollþe unnride inoh forr to dreȝhenn, Orm. 4784. Oferrcumenn wiþþ nan unnride strenncþe, 12527. Ðis fis (*the whale*) dat is unride (*rimes with* wide), Misc. 16, 505: 20, 631: (*rimes with* side), 646. A kowel ful unride (*rimes with* shride = scrȳdan), Havel. 964. Þe unrideste wunde þat men may see, 1985. Þen rewis þe king of unride (-rode) werkis, Alex. (Sk.) 871. Þou has ragid with unryd gestis, 460. See also Halliwell's Dict. *unride*.] v. following words.

un-gerȳde, es; *n. A rough place*:—Ungerȳdu beóð on smēðe wegas *aspera erunt in uias planas*, Lk. Skt. 3, 5.

un-gerȳdelīce; *adv. Violently, with impetus*:—Cwæð se Hǽlend: 'Ic geseah ðone sceoccan swā swā scīnende līget feallende ādūn dreórig of heofonum,' for ðam ðe hē āhreás ungerȳdelīce, Hexam. 10; Norm. 18, 7. Ða felga bióþ fyrrest ðære eaxe, for ðæm hī faraþ ungerȳdelīcost (-rēde-, Cott. MS. v. (?) un-gerǽdelīce), Bt. 39, 7; Fox 222, 21. [Þe meiden reat him mitte raketehe unrudeliche, Jul. 54, 1. Ha þe dintede unrideli o rug, O. E. Homl. i. 281, 27. Þer as þe rogh rocher unrydely watȝ fallen, Gaw. 1432. If any of his feris raged with him unridly, Alex. (Skt.) 638. Þen rekils it unruydly, & raynes doune stanys, 566. And oferr warrp þær i þe flor unnriddlig þeȝȝre bordess, Orm. ii. p. 419.]

un-gerȳdness, e; *f. Violence, tumult*:—Ungerȳdnyss and gewinn *tumultus et conluctatio*, Scint. 82, 2.

un-gesadelod; *adj. Not saddled*:—Eahte hors, feówer gesadelode and feówer ungesadelode (unsadelode, MS. G.) . . . feówer hors, twā gesadelode and twā ungesadelode (unsadelode, MS. G.), L. C. S. 72; Th. i. 414, 5–10.

un-gesǽlhþ, e; *f. Unhappiness, misery*:—For ungesǽlhðe ðissere earman þeóde, Chr. 1057; Erl. 192, 26. v. next word.

un-gesǽlig; *adj. Unhappy, unfortunate*:—Ungesǽlig *infelix*, Wrt. Voc. i. 74, 30. Ðæs ungesǽligan *infausti*, ii. 47, 56. I. of persons, *unhappy*, (a) *suffering, misfortune, calamity, etc.*:—Ne meht ðū cweðan ðæt ðū earm sē and ungesǽlig (*te existimari miserum*), Bt. 8; Fox 24, 23. Ðæt is seó mǽste unsǽlð ðæt mon ǽrest weorþe gesǽlig and æfter ðam ungesǽlig *in omni adversitate fortunae infelicissimum genus est infortunii, fuisse felicem*, 10; Fox 26, 31. Gif ðū gesihst hwylcne swīþe ungesǽligne mon and ongitst ðeáh hwæthwegu gōdes on him, hwæþer hē sié swā ungesǽlig swā se ðe nānwuht gōdes næfþ . . . ac hū þyncþ ðē be ðam ðe nānwuht gōdes næfþ, gif hē hæfþ sumne eácan yfeles; se ðū wilt secgan sié ungesǽligra ðonne se ōðer *si miseriae cujuspiam bonum aliquid addatur, nonne felicior est eo, cujus pura ac solitaria sine cujusquam boni admissione miseria est? . . . Quid si eidem misero, qui cunctis careat bonis, praeter ea, quibus miser est, malum aliud fuerit annexum, nonne multo infelicior eo censendus est, cujus infortunium boni participatione relevatur?* 38, 3; Fox 200, 14–20. Sedechias se ungesǽliga kining, ðe man gelǽdde on bendum tō Babiloniam birig, Ælfc. T. Grn. 8, 11. Ða unþeáwas nǽfre ne bióþ unwītnode . . . ða yfelan bióþ simle ungesǽlige, Bt. 36, 1; Fox 172, 26: Met. 27, 18. Ungesǽlge, Exon. Th. 75, 4; Cri. 1216. Wā lā wā ðæt ða ungesǽligan menn ne magon gebīdon hwonne hē (*death*) him tō cume, Bt. 39, 1; Fox 212, 1. Āra mē, ungesǽligost ealra wīfa, Blickl. Homl. 89, 22. (b) *suffering want of moral good*:—Deófol sǽwð unwīsdōm and gedēð þurh ðæt, ðæt ungesǽlig man wīsdōmes ne gȳmeþ, Wulfst. 52, 27 note. Se ungesǽliga gȳtsere wile māre habban ðonne him genihtsumaþ, ðonne hē furðon orsorh ne brīcð his genihtsumnysse, Homl. Th. i. 64, 33. Hié beóð suīðe ungesǽlige ðonne hié yfeliaþ for ðæm ðe ōðre menn gōdigaþ . . . Hwā mæg beón ungesǽligra *quantae infelicitatis sint, qui melioratione proximi deteriores fiunt . . . Quid istis infelicius?* Past. 34; Swt. 231, 18–22. Hī synt earmran and dysigran and ungesǽligran ðonne ic hit ārecan mæge, 32, 3; Fox 118, 28: Met. 19, 42. (c) *causing unhappiness*:—Ungesēlig *infelix* (a son that bringeth reproach, Prov. 19, 26), Kent. Gl. 716. II. of things, (a) *unfortunate, calamitous*:—Ðis ungesǽlige geár *infaustus ille annus*, Bd. 3, 1; S. 523, 32. (b) *unprofitable, evil*:—Se ungesǽliga gewuna belāf of hǽðenra manna biggenge, Homl. Ass. 146, 47. Þreó ārleása scylda wē gehȳrdon—ungesǽlige mǽrsunge his (*Herod's*) gebyrdtīde . . . Wē ne mōton ūre gebyrdtīde tō nānum freólsdæge mid īdelum mǽrsungum āwendan, Homl. Th. i. 480, 34. [*Laym. A. R.* un-iseli.] v. un-sǽlig.

un-gesǽliglīce; *adv.* I. *unhappily, miserably*:—Hē (*Judas*) hine sylfne āhēng and swā ungesǽliglīce tō ēcan deáðe wæs geniðerad, Homl. Ass. 158, 164. Hē him seluan ēce hellewīte ungesǽliglīce getilaþ, Chart. Th. 117, 23. II. *wickedly*. v. un-gesǽllīce:—Swā ungesǽliglīce Iudas ðam lāreówe deáð sǽtade, swā him eall his līf tō ungesǽlðum wearð, Homl. Ass. 161, 225.

un-gesǽligness, e; *f. Unhappiness, calamity, misery*:—Ungesǽlignys *infelicitas*, Ps. Spl. 13, 7. Seó ungesǽlignys becom on ðæt folc, ðæt hig ðone Hǽlend gefēngon and on rōde āhēngon, Nicod. 1; Thw. 1, 12. Wæs se dōm oncyrred Euan ungesǽlignesse, ðæt heó cende on sāre and on unrōtnesse, Blickl. Homl. 3, 8. Hē ða ðeóde fram langre wōnesse and ungesǽlignysse (*infelicitate*) ālȳsde, Bd. 2, 15; S. 519, 10.

un-gesǽllīce; *adv. Unhappily, miserably, wickedly*; improbe:—Hæfð se yfela gāst ungifa . . . and ða hē dǽlð ðām mannum ðe ungesǽlīce him gehȳrsumiaþ, Wulfst. 52, 12. [His sune ðe uniseliche (onselliche, 2nd MS.) luuede, his deden weoren forcuðe, Laym. 7022.] v. un-sǽle.

un-gesǽlþ, e; *f.* I. *unhappiness, illfortune, calamity*:—Ealle ðās ungesǽlða ūs gelumpon þurh unrǽdes, Chr. 1011; Erl. 145, 1. Biþ simle ða eówre gesǽlþa on sumum þingum ungesǽlþa (unsǽlþa, Cott. MS.), Bt. 29, 1; Fox 102, 20. Sume secgaþ ðæt sió wyrd wealde ǽgðer ge gesǽlþa ge ungesǽlþa ǽlces monnes, 39, 8; Fox 224, 13. Ne meaht ðū nō mid sōþe getǽlan ðīne wyrd for ðām leásum ungesǽlþum (unsǽlþum, Cott. MS.) ðe ðū þrowast, 10; Fox 28, 2. Eall his līf tō ungesǽlðum and tō ermðum wearð, Homl. Ass. 161, 226. Āfyr fram ðē ða unnettan ungesǽlþa and ðone yflan ege ðisse worulde, Bt. 6; Fox 14, 33. II. *unhappiness* which consists in absence of moral good:—Ða yfelan habbaþ ðrió ungesǽlþa (unsǽlþa, Cott. MS.); ān is ðæt hī yfel willaþ, ōþer ðæt ðæt hī magon, þridde ðæt hī hit þurhtióþ *triplici infortunio necesse est urgeantur, quos videas scelus velle, posse, perficere*, Bt. 38, 2; Fox 196, 33. Nān man ne dear for ārwyrðnesse ðæs ānsetlan leahtras tǽlan; him synt eác ða ungesēlþa leófran, ðæt hē hȳ nyte, ðænne hē hī lācnige, R. Ben. 135, 18. [Þurh him (*Adam*) deð com in þis middenerd and oðer uniselðe, O. E. Homl. i. 171, 197. For heora uniselðe (*wickedness*), Laym. 2545.] v. un-sǽlþ.

un-gesawen. v. un-gesewen.

un-gesceád, es; *n. Indiscretion, unreason*:—Ða ðe on ðām sylfum cildum mid ungesceáde gehātheortaþ *qui in ipsis infantibus sine discretione exarserit*, R. Ben. 130, 7. Hē on ānum dæge mid ungesceáde forspilð þreóra daga andlifene, Homl. Ass. 145, 30: Lchdm. iii. 442, 32.

un-gesceád; *adj. Indiscreet, unreasonable, irrational*:—Hwā is manna tō ðam ungesceád and ungewittig, ðæt hē ðæm cyninge his āre ætrecce for ðī ðe his gerēfa forwyrht biþ? Lchdm. iii. 444, 7.

un-gesceádlīc; *adj. Indiscreet, irrational*:—Ungesceádlīc swīgea *indiscretum silentium*, Scint. 213, 13. Mid ungesceádlīcum þinge *in re irrationali*, L. Ecg. P. ii. 6; Th. ii. 184, 10.

un-gesceádlīce; *adv. Unreasonably, excessively*:—Ungesceádlīce (-sceáde-) *irrationabiliter*, R. Ben. 54, 13 note. Tācn ðæs ungesceádlīce cealdan magan (cf. ðæs ofercealdan magan, 192, 25: 194, 11), Lchdm. ii. 160, 4. v. next word.

ungesceád-micel; *adj. Excessively great*:—Ǽled wæs ungesceádmicel, Cd. Th. 231, 6; Dan. 243. Cf. un-gemet-, *and see preceding word.*

un-gesceádwīs; *adj.* I. *not acting according to reason, un-*

reasonable, irrational, unwise, foolish:—Hē hine wiste swīþe ungesceádwīsne and swīþe ungemetfæstne, Bt. 27, 1; Fox 96, 4. Ic wundrige hwī men sién swā ungesceádwīse ðæt hié wēnan ðæt ðis andwearde līf mæge ðone monnan dōn gesǣligne, 11, 2; Fox 34, 36: 39, 9; Fox 226, 9. Ðeáh ungesceádwīsum monnum swā ne þince, 39, 8; Fox 224, 16. II. *not possessed of reason, irrational*:—Ǣlc gesceaft, ǣgðer ge gesceádwīs ge ungesceádwīs, Bt. 42; Fox 256, 7. Ic eom ofwundrod hwī eów þince ðære ungesceádwīsan gesceafte gōd betere ðonne eówer āgen god, 13; Fox 40, 5. On ðara ungesceádwīsra niétena gesibsumnesse, Past. 46; Swt. 349, 24. Hē hine gehwyrfde tō ungesceádwīsum neátum *in irrationale animal hunc vertit*, 4; Swt. 39, 22.

un-gesceádwīslīc; *adj. Indiscreet, imprudent, unreasonable, extravagant*:—Ðætte hē ne ðōhte nāwuht ungesceádwīslīces ne unnetlīces *nec indiscretum quid vel inutile cogitet*, Past. 13; Swt. 77, 12. Gif wē hwæt ongietaþ on him ungesceádwīslīces gedoon *si qua ab eis inordinate gesta sunt*, 32; Swt. 211, 22. v. un-sceádwīslīc.

un-gesceádwīslīce; *adv. Indiscreetly, unreasonably, foolishly*:—Ða ðe hiora āgen ungesceádwīslīce healdaþ *qui sua indiscrete tenuerunt*, Past. 44; Swt. 329, 11. Se gītsere and se ðe woruldwelan lufaþ ungesceádwīslīce, Swt. 331, 8. Ðonne wē biddaþ ongeán ūre āgenre þearfe, ðonne forwyrnð God ūs ðæs ðe wē ungesceádwīslīce biddaþ, Homl. Th. ii. 528, 9. Ongesceádwīslīce *inrationabiliter*, R. Ben. Interl. 61, 11.

un-gesceádwīsness, e; *f. Unreasonableness, foolishness*:—Hwæt segst ðū ðæt sié forcūþre ðonne sió ungesceádwīsnes? hwī geþafiaþ hī ðæt hī bióð dysige? hwī nyllaþ hī spyrigan æfter cræftum and æfter wīsdōme? *quid enervatius ignorantiae caecitate? an sectanda noverunt?* Bt. 36, 6; Fox 180, 31, 35. Hē lǣt his mōd tōflōwan on ðæt ofdele giémeliéste and ungesceádwīsnesse æfter eallum his willum *anima neglectam se inferius per desideria expandit*, Past. 39; Swt. 283, 15.

un-gesceapen; *adj.* I. *unshapen, unformed*:—*Interjectio* is ān dǣl sprǣce getácniende ðæs mōdes gewilnunge mid ungesceapenre stemne (*voce incondita*), Ælfc. Gr. 48; Zup. 277, 17. Hē is sōð Scyppend, ðe ða ungesceapenan eáhhringas (*the eyes of the man who was born blind*) geopenode, Homl. Th. i. 474, 8. II. *uncreated*:—Ungesceapen (*increatus*) is se Fæder, ungesceapen is se Sunu, and is ungesceapen se Hālga Gāst, Ath. Crd. 8.

un-gescended; *adj. Uninjured*:—Ungiscended *inlessa*, Rtl. 146, 23.

un-gesceþþed; *adj. Uninjured, entire*:—Wæs his līchama gemēted ungesceþþed *corpus inventum est inlesum*, Bd. 3, 19; S. 550, 11.

un-gescrēpe, -gescrǣpe; *adj. Inconvenient, unfit, useless*:—Unbriéce, ungescrǣpe *incommodum, inutile*, Wrt. Voc. ii. 44, 76. Ǣghwylcre menniscre eardunge ungescrǣpe *humanae habitationi minus accommodus*, Bd. 4, 28; S. 605, 20.

un-gescrēpness, e; *f. Inconvenience*:—Seó ungescrēpnes ðæs sāres fram heora eágan gewāt *doloris incommodum ab oculis amoverent*, Bd. 4, 19; S. 589, 37.

un-gescrēpu -o); *f. or* un-gescrēpe; *n. Inconvenience, an inconvenient thing*:—Mid ðȳ ðā se foresprecena brōþor langre tīde ðyllīc ungescrǣpo woon (ðyllīce ungescrǣpo wonn?) *cum tempore non pauco frater praefatus tali incommodo laboraret*, Bd. 4, 32; S. 611, 22.

un-gesegnod, -gesēnod; *adj. Not marked with the sign of the cross*:—Gif ðæt deófol mēteþ ungesēnodes mannes mūð and līchoman, and hit ðonne on forgitenan mannes innelfe gewīteþ, Salm. Kmbl. p. 148, 10.

un-gesēne. v. un-gesīne.

un-geseónde; *adj. Not seeing, blind*:—Gyf ðū on foreweardon sumera þigest hwylcne hwelpan ðonne gyt ungeseóndne, ne ongitest ðū ǣnig sār, Lchdm. i. 368, 26.

un-gesewen, -gesawen; *adj. Unseen, invisible*:—Ðā ðā ða tungelwītegan ðone cyning gecyrdon, ðā wearð se steorra him ungesewen, Homl. Th. i. 108, 29. Ðone ungesewenan (*invisibilem*) engel, Past. 36; Swt. 257, 8. Ōðre ungesawene þing mon mōt mid āðe gewyrðan, L. O. D. 7; Th. i. 356, 6.

un-gesewenlīc; *adj. Invisible*:—Seó eorðe wæs æt fruman eall ungesewenlīc, for ðam ðe heó eall wæs mid ȳðum oferðeht, Hexam. 5; Norm. 10, 17. Heora (*angels*) ungesewenlīce gecynd, Homl. Th. i. 538, 28. Se ungesawenlīca feónd, Wulfst. 52, 8. Unisæwenlīcere mihte *invisibili potestate*, Hpt. Gl. 482, 69. God menniscum eágum ungesewenlīcne, Bd. 3, 22; S. 552, 17. Ða ōðre heofenan synd ungesegenlīce, Lchdm. iii. 232, 23. Mid ðære gewilnunge ðara ungesewenlīcra ðinga, Past. 16; Swt. 98, 3: Bt. 21; Fox 72, 30: Met. 11, 5. Wið mīnum wiþerwinnam gesewenlīcum and ungesewenlīcum, Bt. 42; Fox 260, 11. Hē offrige ða ungeswenlīcan lāc, Homl. Th. i. 584, 3.

un-gesewenlīce; *adv. Invisibly, without being seen*:—God cymð ungesewenlīce tō geswǣsre heortan, Homl. Th. ii. 316, 4.

un-gesib[b]; *adj.* I. *not related, strange*:—Hē bið fremede Freán ælmihtigum, englum ungelīc (ungesibb, MS. B.) āna hwearfaþ, Salm. Kmbl. 69; Sal. 35. Ic (*the cuckoo*) under sceáte ungesibbum wearð eácen gǣste, Exon. Th. 391, 20; Rä. 10, 8. II. *not at peace, at variance*:—Ða twā mǣgþa ða ðe betwih him ungeþwǣre and ungesibbe wǣron *provinciae quae ab invicem discordabant*, Bd. 3, 6; S. 528, 32: Blickl. Homl. 225, 6. [Cf. Betere weare sæhte þene swulc unisibbe, Laym. 9845.]

un-gesibsum; *adj. Prone to discord, quarrelsome*:—Lōca hwylc cristen man sȳ ungesibsum, man āh on ðam dæge hine tō gesibsumianne, Wulfst. 295, 4. On ōðre wīsan sint tō manigenne ða gesibsuman, on ōðre ða ungesibsuman *aliter admonendi sunt discordes, atque aliter pacati*, Past. 46; Swt. 345, 6. Ðǣm ungesibsumum is tō cȳðanne *admonendi sunt dissidentes*, Swt. 348, 5.

un-gesibsumness, e; *f. Proneness to discord, quarrelsomeness, discord*:—Wē magon gecnāwan on ðara ungesceádwīsra niétena gesibsumnesse hū micel yfel sió gesceádwīslīce gecynd ðurh ða ungesibsumnesse gefremeþ *si solertes aspicimus, concordando sibi irrationalis natura indicat, quantum malum per discordiam rationalis natura committat*, Past. 46; Swt. 351, 1.

un-gesilt; *adj. Unsalted*:—Swīnen smeru ungesylt, Lchdm. i. 146, 20. v. un-silt.

un-gesīne; *adj. Invisible*:—Ungesēne wearþ *disparuit*, Wrt. Voc. ii. 106, 43.

un-gesīnelīc; *adj. Invisible*:—Seó ungesȳnelīce sāwl, Blickl. Homl. 21, 25. Ungesȳnelīcne God, 185, 31. Flǣsclīce men ða ungesȳnelīcan ne magon angytan, Wulfst. 2, 4.

un-gesoden; *adj. Unsodden*:—Nim ðū ða ylcan wyrte ungesodene, Lchdm. i. 92, 29.

un-gesōm; *adj. At variance*:—Ǣfter sumum fyrste wurdon hī ungesōme, Philippus and Arethe, Homl. Th. i. 478, 25. [Hit itit þat wif and were beoþ unisome, O. and N. 1522.]

un-gestæððig; *adj. Inconstant, unstable*:—Ðæt ungestæððige folc *mobile vulgus*, Bt. 39, 3; Fox 216, 2. Ðam ungestæþþegan and ðam gālan ðū miht secgan ðæt hī biþ gelīcra unstillum fugelum ðonne gemetfæstum monnum *levis atque inconstans studia permutat? nihil ab avibus differt*, 37, 4; Fox 192, 22. Ða gesceaftas ðe wē embe sprecaþ, ðæt heó ūs þince ungestæðþie, hȳ habbaþ sumne dǣl gestæþinesse, Shrn. 168, 30. Ða ungestæððegan and unfæsðrǣdan *inconstantes*, Past. 23; Swt. 177, 3. Nānwuht nis on ūs unstilre and ungestæððigre ðonne ðæt mōd *nil in nobis est corde fugacius*, 38; Swt. 273, 11.

un-gestæððiglīce; *adv. Unsteadily, without stability*:—Ðonne mon ða fæstrǣdnesse his mōdes innan forlīst, ðonne bið hē hwīlum swīðe ungestæððiglīce āstyred ūtane on his limum *qui statum mentis perdidit, subsequenter foras in inconstantiam motionis fluit*, Past. 47; Swt. 359, 7. Hié beóð suā micle ungestæððelīcor tōflōwene on hiera mōde suā hié wēnaþ ðæt hié stilran and orsorgran beón mægen *quae tanto latius diffluunt, quanto se esse securius aestimant*, 38; Swt. 271, 17.

un-gestæððigness, e; *f. Unsteadiness, levity, want of firmness*:—Se hæfð singalne sceabb se ðe nǣfre ne blinð ungestæððignesse *jugem habet scabiem, cui carnis petulantia sine cessatione dominatur*, Past. 11; Swt. 70, 3. Gif hē eallunge forberan ne mæg for hira āgnum unðeáwum and for hiera ungestæððignesse *qui pro infirmitate sese abstinere vix possunt*, 28; Swt. 199, 9.

un-gestreón, es; *n. Ill-gotten treasure*:—Ða wōhgeornan woruldrīcan mid heora golde and seolfre and eallum ungestreónum, Wulfst. 183, 9.

un-gestroden; *adj. Not subjected to forfeiture or confiscation of goods*:—Swǣse mæn ciriclīcæs gemānan ungestrodyne þoligen *natives shall forfeit the communion of the church but without being subjected to forfeiture of goods* [cf. gestrod *proscriptionem* (the passage in Aldhelm is: Proscriptionem rerum et patrimonii jacturam), Wrt. Voc. ii. 81, 67], L. Wih. 4; Th. i. 38, 3.

un-geswēge; *adj. Dissonant, discordant*:—Ungeswēge *dissona*, Hpt. Gl. 513, 51. Ungeswēge sang *diaphonia*, Wrt. Voc. i. 28, 34. Ungeswēgre *dissona*, Hpt. Gl. 505, 76. Ungeswēga *vel* ungehleóþre *dissona*, i. *discordantia*, Wrt. Voc. ii. 141, 36. Ungeswēgium *absonis*, Germ. 392, 12.

un-geswencedlīc; *adj. Unwearied, indefatigable*:—Mid ungeswencedlīce luste heofonlīcra gōda *infatigabili coelestium bonorum desiderio*, Bd. 5, 12; S. 631, 35.

un-geswīcendlīce; *adv. Unceasingly, incessantly*:—Ungeswīcendlīce *indesinenter*, Scint. 28, 7: *incessanter, jugiter*, 131, 8: *incessabiliter*, R. Ben. 19, 4 note.

un-geswuncen; *adj. Unlaboured*:—Ungeswuncenre *inelaborate*, Wrt. Voc. ii. 49, 59.

un-gesȳnelīc. v. un-gesīnelīc.

un-getǣse; *adj. Inconvenient, disagreeable, troublesome, obnoxious*:—Ungetǣse *infestus*, Wrt. Voc. ii. 45, 46. Oððe hit ðē deraþ oððe hit ðē unwynsum biþ, oððe ungetēse (-getǣse, Cott. MS.) oððe frēcenlīc *aut injucundum, aut noxium*, Bt. 14, 1; Fox 42, 13. Gilpes ðū girnest? ac ðū hine ne miht habban orsorgne, for ðam ðū scealt habban simle hwæthweg wiþerweardes and ungetēses (-getǣses, Cott. MS.) *gloriam petis? sed per aspera quaeque distractus, securus esse desistis*, 32, 1; Fox 114, 20. Ða cyningas ðe æfter Rōmuluse rīcsedon wǣron forcūðran ðonne hē wǣre, and ðǣm folcum lāðran and ungetǣsran, Ors. 2, 2; Swt. 66, 26.

un-getǣse, es; *n. An inconvenience, a trouble*:—Gif hē ðǣm gehiérsuman mannum næfde geteohchad his éðel tō sellanne, hwié wolde hē hié mid ǽnegum ungetǽsum lǽran? *nisi correctis haereditatem dare disponerit, erudire eos per molestias non curaret*, Past. 36; Swt. 251, 24. Mid hū monigfaldum ungetǽsum and mid hū heardum brocum ūs swingaþ and ðreágaþ ūre worldcunde fædras *quam dura carnales filios disciplinae flagella castigent*, Swt. 253, 24.

un-getǽslīce; *adv. Inconveniently, incommodiously*:—Ðonne ðæt scyp ungetǽslīcost on ancre rīt, Shrn. 179, 17.

un-getǽsness, e; *f. Inconvenience*:—Ungetǽsnesse *incommoditate*, Wrt. Voc. ii. 44, 30.

un-getel; *adj. Innumerable*:—On þisum and on manegum and on ungetelum (ge)ōþrum intingan ic syngade *in istis et in multis atque innumeris aliis causis peccavi*, Confess. Peccat. Cf. un-gerīm.

un-getemed; *adj. Untamed*:—Se wilda fola hæfde getācnunge ealles ōðres folces, ðe wæs dāgyt hǽðen and ungetemed, Homl. Th. i. 208, 23. Tīgan tō ungetemedra horsa swuran, 432, 33.

un-getemprung, e; *f. Rough weather*; intemperies, Anglia xiii. 397, 461.

un-geteón, es; *n. Foul injury*:—Wið nētana ungetiónu . . . Engel se ðe āsetted is ofer nētno ūsra gihalda ða ðætte ne mæg dióI onrād ða (*ut non poterit diabolus inequitare illa*), Rtl. 119, 15.

un-geteoriendlīce; *adv. Indefatigably*:—Ðis synt ða lāra and ða tōl gāstlīces cræftes, gif hig from ūs dæges oððe nyhtes ungeteoriendlīce begongenne beóð . . ., L. E. I. 21; Th. ii. 418, 18.

un-geteorod; *adj. Unwearied, unfailing, unexhausted*:—Ungeteorudne goldhord on heofenum *thesaurum non deficientem in caelis*, Lk. Skt. 12, 33. Ungeteorodne, Homl. Skt. ii. 23 b, 92. Ungetyradne *inexhaustam*, Hpt. Gl. 463, 19.

un-getēse. v. un-getǽse.

un-geþæslīc; *adj. Unfit, unsuitable*, Wrt. Voc. i. 61, 39. v. un-gehæplīc.

un-geþanc, es; *m. n. Evil thought*:—Būtan hē mid fulre dǽdbōte his ungeþanc gebēte, R. Ben. 21, 6. Āfyrsiaþ of mīnre gesyhðe ða ungeðanc eówra heortena *auferte malum cogitationum vestrarum ab oculis meis*, Wulfst. 48, 20.

un-geþancfull; *adj. Unthankful, ungrateful*:—Ðū man, tō hwan eart ðū mē swā ungeþancfull mīnra gifena? Wulfst. 259, 1: 241, 4.

un-geþeaht, es; *n. Evil counsel*:—Forbeóde hē and ālecge ða ðwyrnysse heora ungeþeahtes *prohibeant pravorum prevalere consensum*, R. Ben. 118, 10.

un-geþeahtendlīce; *adv. Inconsiderately, unadvisedly*:—Nalæs hē sōna and ungeþeahtendlīce ðām gerȳnum onfōn wolde ðæs Cristenan geleáfan *non statim et inconsulte sacramenta fidei Christianae percipere voluit*, Bd. 2, 9; S. 512, 6.

un-geþeáwe; *adj. Not in accordance with one's habits*:—Se biscop bæd ðone hālgan wer ðæt hē scolde tō gereorde fōn mid him; and hē swā dyde, þeáh hit his līfe ungeþeáwe wǽre, Guthl. 17; Gdwin. 72, 27.

un-geþeáwfæst; *adj. Illregulated of conduct*:—Ungeþeáwfæstan *indisciplinatos*, R. Ben. Interl. 14, 16. v. un-þeáwfæst.

un-geþeód; *adj. Separate, disjoined*:—Tōfōran ðā (*after the confusion of tongues*) on feówer wegas æðelinga bearn ungeþeóde (cf. hȳ beóð geþeóde þeódscipum on gemang betwyx heáhfæderas and hālige wītegan *vatidicis junctos patriarchis atque prophetis*, Dōm. L. 18, 282), Cd. Th. 102, 11; Gen. 1698.

un-geþinged; *adj. Undetermined, unsettled*:—Se egeslīca dæg, se cymð ofer ealle eorðwaran ungeðinged (*the time is not fixed and known beforehand*; repentina dies illa), Past. 43; Swt. 317, 12. v. un-þinged.

un-geþungen; *adj. Vile, base, ignoble*:—Ðū ungeþungena hund, Nar. 42, 12.

un-geþwǽre; *adj.* I. *not in harmony, at variance, discordant, not in agreement*:—Ungeþwǽra *discordator, discors*, Wrt. Voc. ii. 140, 77. Simle bióþ ða gōdan and ða yflan ungeþwǽre betwyh him, ge eác hwīlum ða yflan bióþ ungerāde betwuh him selfum, ge furþum ān yfel man bið hwīlum ungeþwǽre him selfum *ut probis atque improbis nullum foedus est, ita ipsi inter se improbi nequeunt convenire*, Bt. 39, 12; Fox 230, 26–29. Gōd and yfel bióþ simle ungeþwǽre betwux him and simle on twā willaþ *bonum malumque adversa fronte dissideant*, 37, 3; Fox 190, 13. Fȳr and wæter and manega oþra gesceafta ðe beóþ ā swā ungeþwǽra betwux him swā swā hī beóþ, 21; Fox 74, 16. Ða twā mǽgþa, ða ðe betwih him ungeþwǽre and ungesibbe wǽron *provinciae, quae ab invicem discordabant*, Bd. 3, 6; S. 528, 31: Blickl. Homl. 225, 6. Ðā wǽron ungeðwǽre preóstas on ānum his mynstra; ða hē wolde sibbian . . . Se biscop ða ungeðwǽran preóstas ðreáde, Homl. Th. ii. 516, 4–15. Ðæt ic mōste ofercuman ða þeóda ðe mē ungeðwǽre wǽron, Ps. Th. 15, 2. II. *given to discord, quarrelsome*:—Ðætte on ōðre wīsan sint tō manianne ða geðwǽran (cf. ða gesibsuman, 6) on ōðre ða ungeðwǽran (cf. ða ungesibsuman, 6) *quomodo admonendi sunt discordes et pacati*, Past. 46; Swt. 344, 5. III. *disagreeable, troublesome, vexatious*:—Hē sum fæc ðone ungeþwǽran swyle ðwēnde *aliquamdiu tumorem illum infestum mollire curabat*, Bd. 4, 32; S. 611, 40. Ðū hine ongeáte on eallum þingum unweorþne ðæs anwealdes, swīþe sceamleásne and ungeþwǽrne (ungewærne, Bod. MS.) būton ǽlcum gōdum þeáwe (*the Latin is*: Cum in eo mentem nequissimi scurrae respiceres), Bt. 27, 2; Fox 96, 19. v. un-þwǽre.

un-geþwǽre, es; *n. A disturbance, dissension*:—Ðȳles ungerec ł ungeþwǽre in ðæm folce gewyrde *ne forte tumultus fieret in populo*, Mt. Kmbl. Rush. 26, 5.

un-geþwǽrian; *p.* ode *To disagree, be at variance, differ*:—Ic ungeðwǽrige *dissentio*, Ælfc. Gr. 30; Zup. 190, 13. Anda fram gōdan willan ungeþwǽregaþ *invidia a bona voluntate discordat*, Scint. 143, 3. Hē ongeat ðæt hī on monegum ðingum Godes cyricean ungeþwǽredon *vitam ac professionem minus ecclesiasticam in multis esse cognovit*, Bd. 2, 4; S. 505, 22. Ungeþwǽrudon *discordarent*, Anglia xiii. 367, 34.

un-geþwǽrlīce; *adv. Ungently, crossly*:—Ðā andswarode heó hire ungeþwǽrlīce: 'Ðeáh ðe God ðīnne wer æt ðē genāme, hwæt sceal ic ðæs dōn?' Homl. Ass. 121, 153.

un-geþwǽrness, e; *f.* I. *discord, dissension, disagreement, division, quarrel*:—Ungeðwǽrnes *discordia*, Wülck. Gl. 255, 17. Seó ungeðwǽrnes wundode ða geðwǽrnesse *discordia vulnerat concordiam*, Gl. Prud. 77: 78. Ðonne weaxaþ ða ofermētta and ungeþwǽrnes (cf. þonan mǽst cymeþ . . . unnetta saca, Mēt. 25, 44), Bt. 37, 1; Fox 186, 19: Homl. Th. ii. 220, 32. Ungeðuǽrnis *vecordia*, Rtl. 163, 1. Ungehwǽrnys (=-þwǽrnys) *simultas*, Hpt. Gl. 495, 59: 522, 16. Ungeþwǽrnes wæs geworden on ðære menigeo for him *dissensio facta est in turba propter eum*, Jn. Skt. 7, 43: 10, 19. On ðisum geáre ārās seó ungehwǽrnes on Glæstingabyrig betwyx ðam abbode and his munecan, Chr. 1083; Erl. 217, 1. Ðȳlæs ǽnegu ungeþwǽrnes on his āgnum rīce āhafen wurde *prius quam adversa fama novas res domi moliretur*, Ors. 2, 5; Swt. 82, 30. Ne mihte hē mid ðone cyning . . . sibbe habban; ac swā mycel ungeþwǽrnys and unsibb betwih him āras (*ingravescentibus causis dissensionum*), ðæt hī heora fyrd gesomnedon, Bd. 3, 14; S. 539, 35. Be ungeþwǽrnysse wið his nēhstan *de discordia cum proximo suo*, L. Ecg. P. ii. 27 tit.; Th. ii. 182, 1. Sii his wunung on hellewīte mid ðām ðe symle on ǽlcre ungeðwǽrnesse blissiaþ, Cod. Dip. Kmbl. iii. 129, 27. Se swicola feónd sǽwð ungeðwǽrnysse betwux mancynne, Homl. Th. ii. 318, 19. Ða hwīle ðe hē ǽnige ungeþwǽrnysse hæbbe on his heortan wið his ðone nēhstan *quamdiu simultatem ullam in corde suo cum proximo suo habet*, L. Ecg. P. ii. 27; Th. ii. 192, 28. Bilewite cild ne hylt langsume ungeþwǽrnysse tō ðam ðe him derode, Homl. Th. i. 512, 15. Hié ǽgþer hæfdon ungeþwǽrnesse ge betweónum him selfum ge tō eallum folcum *they were at variance both among themselves and with all nations*, Ors. 6, 3; Swt. 258, 1. 'Þeód ārīst ongeán þeóde.' Mid ðisum wordum hē foresǽde manna ungeðwǽrnyssa, Homl. Th. ii. 538, 26, 17. II. *trouble, disquiet*. v. ungeþwǽre, III:—On hū grundleásum seáðe ðæt mōd þringþ, ðonne hit bestyrmaþ ðisse worulde ungeþwǽrnessa (*terrenis flatibus aucta crescit in immensum noxia cura*), Bt. 3, 2; Fox 6, 9. v. un-þwǽrness.

un-geþyld, e; *f.*: es; *n.* [v. ge-þyld] *Impatience*:—Hū mycel Godes geþyld is, and hū mycel ūre ungeþyld is, Blickl. Homl. 33, 26. Ungeðyld *impatientiae culpa*, Past. 43; Swt. 309, 2. Sió ungeðyld, Swt. 311, 21: 33; Swt. 220, 66. For ðæm unwrence ðære ungeðylde . . . for ðæm unðeáwe ðære ungeðylde *per vitium impatientiae*, 33; Swt. 214, 20, 23: Swt. 224, 2. Mid ungeðylde (-geðylde, Hatt. MS.), 43; Swt. 310, 15. Gif hē wyrþ on ungeþylde *cum dederit impatientiae manus*, Bt. 11, 1; Fox 32, 33. Ðætte ðæt mōd ne berǽse on ungeðyld *ne ad impatientiam spiritus erumpant*, Past. 43; Swt. 313, 21. Þurh ungeþyld *per intolerantiam*, Scint. 150, 1. [*O. H. Ger.* un-gidult, -gidultī; *f. impatientia.*]

un-geþyldig; *adj. Impatient*:—Ðæt wæs ungeþyldig heretoga . . . hē wǽpn gegrāp mid tō campienne, ǽr ðon ðe hē tō his līchoman leomum becōme, Blickl. Homl. 165, 33. Se ðe ðysne lǽcedōm þolaþ, hē sceal upweard licgean, ðȳ læs hē ungeþyldig (*if he is impatient*) ða strengde ðyssæ lācnunge ongite, Lchdm. i. 300, 21. Se ðe biþ ungeþyldig, and ceoraþ ongeán God on his untrumnysse, Homl. Th. i. 472, 8. Se dysega ungeðyldega all his ingeðonc hē geypt, Past. 33; Swt. 220, 9. Swā ungeþyldige ðæt hī ne magon nān earfoþu geþyldelīce āberan, Bt. 39, 10; Fox 228, 2 note. On ōðre wīsan sint tō manianne ða ungeðyldegan (-geðyldgan, Hatt. MS.) and on ōðre ða geðyldegan . . . Ðǽm ungeðyldegum (*impatientibus*) is tō sæcganne, Past. 33; Swt. 214, 3–6. Se ðe ungerādum oððe ungeðyldigum stȳrð, Homl. Th. i. 306, 5. Ǽghwelc monn bið onfunden swǽ micle læs gelǽred ðonne ōðer swǽ hē bið ungeðyldegra *tanto quisque minus ostenditur doctus, quanto minus convincitur patiens*, Past. 33; Swt. 216, 3.

un-geþyldiglīce, -geþyldelīce; *adv. Impatiently*:—Ðā scylde hē ongeán swīþe ungeþyldelīce, Bt. 18, 4; Fox 68, 1.

un-geþyre; *adj. Dissentient* (?):—Ungeðyre *discensor*, Txts. 57, 684. Cf. (?) ge-þuren, *pp. of* geþweran, *and* un-geþwǽre.

un-getīmu; *f. or* un-getīme, es; *n. Mishap, misfortune*:—On ðǽm dagum wǽron ða mǽstan ungetīna (cf. (?) un-geteón: ungetīma *is the reading of the other MS. here and in the following passages*) on Rōmānum, ǽgðer ge on hungre ge on moncwealme *duo vel maxima omnium malorum abominamenta, fames et pestilentia, fessum urbem corripuere*, Ors. 2, 4; Swt. 70, 7. Ðæt hellefȳr wæs geswiðrad, swā ealle ungetīna (-getīma, MS. C.) wǽron *Sicilia requiem malorum, nisi nunc, nescit*, 2, 6; Swt.

90, 2. Hwelce ungetīna (-getīma, MS. C.), ǣgðer ge on monslihtum ge on hungre ge on scipgebroce ge on mislīcre forscapunge, 1, 11; Swt. 50, 18.

un-getogen; *adj. Uneducated*:—Fisceras and ungetogene menn geceás Drihten him tō leorningcnihtum, and hī swā geteáh, ðæt heóra lār oferstāh ealne woruldwīsdōm, Homl. Th. i. 576, 28. Hē geceás siððan woruldlīce ūðwitan, ac hī mōdegodon, gif hē ǣr ne gecure ða ungetogenan fisceras, 578, 14.

un-getreów, -getreówe, -getrīwe, -getrȳwe; *adj. Untrue, unfaithful, faithless*:—Wǣrleás mon and ungetreów, Exon. Th. 343, 27; Gn. Ex. 163. Ungetreówe *infidus*, Wrt. Voc. i. 49, 31: ii. 91, 58: 47, 25: *infidelis*, i. 74, 28. Se ðe sȳ folce ungetrȳwe (-getrīwe, MS. G.), L. Edg. ii. 7; Th. i. 268, 14: L. Eth. i. 4; Th. i. 282, 29, 30. Gyf hwylc man sȳ swā ungetrȳwe ðam hundrede, L. C. S. 30; Th. i. 392, 21. Be ungetreówum mannum. Gyf hwylc man sȳ ðe eallum folce ungetrȳwe sȳ, 33; Th. i. 396, 13. Ungetrȳwan (-getreówan, MS. B.) men ceóse man ānfealdne āð, 22; Th. i. 388, 11. Hit is ungeleáful cynren and ungetreówe bearn *generatio perversa est et infideles filii*, Deut. 32, 20. Mē āblendan ðās ungetreówan woruldsǣlþa, Bt. 2; Fox 4, 9. Hē sett his dǣl mid ðām ungetreówum (*infidelibus*), Lk. Skt. 12, 46. [*O. H. Ger.* un-gitriuwi *infidelis*.]

un-getreówness, e; *f. Unfaithfulness, infidelity*:—Se ðe forlǣt ðone cele ungetreównesse *quisquis amisso infidelitatis frigore vivit*, Past. 58; Swt. 447, 6.

un-getreówþ, e; *f. Bad faith, breach of good faith*:—Hēr sȳn on lande ungetrȳwða (-treówða, MS. B.: -trīwða, MS. C.) micle for Gode and for worulde, Wulfst. 160, 6.

un-getrum; *adj. Infirm*:—Manige men bióþ ungetrume (untrume, Cott. MS.) ǣgþer ge on mōde ge on līchoman, Bt. 39, 10; Fox 226, 36.

un-getȳd; *adj. Untaught, unskilled, rude*:—Ðæt ungetȳde folc (*rudis ille populus*) nolde geliéfan, Past. 50; Swt. 389, 33. Æt ðæm ungetȳdum folce *apud imperitum vulgus*, 48; Swt. 365, 22. Ðæt hié ne scolden forhyggean ðone geférscipe ðara synfulra and ðara ungetȳdra, 16; Swt. 105, 15. v. ge-tȳn (-tȳan).

un-getȳdd; *adj. Untaught, unskilled*:—Seó bōc wæs yfele gehwyrfed and gyt wyrs fram sumum ungetȳddum (*a quodam imperito*) gerihted, Bd. 5, 24; S. 648, 24. v. ge-tȳdan.

un-getynge; *adj. Unapt of speech, not eloquent*:—Ic eom ungetinge on sprǣce *incircumcisus sum labiis*, Ex. 6, 12. v. next word.

un-getyngfull; *adj. Ineloquent*:—Ungetingfullum *infantissimo, ineloquentissimo*, Germ. 392, 3.

un-gewǣpnod; *adj. Unarmed*:—Ungewǣpnad *inermis*, Wrt. Voc. ii. 48, 13. Ðā hēt se cyning healdan Martinum, ðæt hē wurde āworpen ungewǣpnod ðam here, Homl. Th. ii. 502, 14. Ðā geseah Æþelfrið heora sacerdas sundor stondon ungewǣpnade, Bd. 2, 2; S. 503, 39.

un-gewær (?); *adj. Incautious, inconsiderate* (v. un-geþwǣre, III). v. un-wær.

un-geweald *impotence, inability to control.* The word occurs only in the genitive, with the force of an adverb. I. where an action is done without the actor's intending it, *unintentionally, not wilfully, involuntarily*:—Hē wræc his ungewealdes on ðære byrig hiora misdǣda, Ors. 6, 5; Swt. 262, 2. Gif hwā his cild ofslihð tō deáðe ungewealdes (*praeter voluntatem*), L. Ecg. P. ii. 1; Th. ii. 182, 21: L. M. I. P. 8; Th. ii. 268, 1: L. Alf. pol. 13; Th. i. 70, 9. Ungewealdes, Past. 21; Swt. 167, 1. Suelce hē hit ungewisses oððe ungewealdes doo *agit velut nesciens*, 33; Swt. 215, 11. Ðonne hē of yfelum willan ne gesyngaþ, ac of unwīsdōme and ungewisses oððe ungewealdes *cum non malitia, sed sola ignorantia, delinquitur*, 21; Swt. 157, 25. Se ðe hine nēdes ofslōge oþþe unwillum oþþe ungewealdes, L. Alf. 13; Th. i. 46, 23. Gif man unwilles oþþe ungewealdes ǣnig þing misdēð, L. Eth. vi. 52; Th. i. 328, 21. Eówre synna ðe gē geworhton gewealdes oþþe ungewealdes, Wulfst. 135, 30. II. where something happens that is not controlled or brought about by a person:—Ūre gāst biþ swīþe wīde farende ūrum unwillum and ūres ungewealdes ... ðæt biþ ðonne þonne wē slāpaþ *our spirit wanders far independently of our wishes or control ... that is when we sleep*, Bt. 34, 11; Fox 152, 4. Is ðǣm tō cȳðanne ðæt hī hié warenigen ǣgðer ge wið ða ungemetlīcan blisse ge wið ða ungemetlīcan unrōtnesse, for ðæm hira ǣgðer āstyreþ sumne unðeáw, ðeáh hié ungewealdes cuman of ðæs līchoman medtrymnesse, Past. 27; Swt. 189, 3. Gif him gewealdes gebyrige oððe ungewealdes ðæt hē on ðæs hwæt befoo ðe wið his willan sié, 28; Swt. 199, 22. [Þurh uniweald *per impotenciam*, O. E. Homl. ii. 63, 6. *O. Frs.* un-ewald.]

un-gewealden; *adj. Not under control, disordered* (?):—Ðonne for miclum cele wamb sié ungewealden (cf. Lǣcedōmas tō wambe gemetlīcunge, 164, 3), Lchdm. ii. 228, 23. Wamb ungewealden and unȳþe ... tunge ungewealden and unsmēþe, 242, 5–9. Ðonne se man mete þigð, ðonne āwyrpð hē eft and hæfð ungewealdene wambe and ða micgean, 204, 10.

un-geweaxen; *adj. Ungrown, not grown up*:—Ungeweaxenra deáþ *acerva mors* (i.e. the death of the young), Wrt. Voc. ii. 8, 31.

un-geweder, es; *n. Bad weather, storm, tempest*:—Se stranga winter mid forste and mid snāwe and mid eallon ungewederon, Chr. 1046; Erl. 170, 33. Hefigtȳme geár on ungewederan, ðā man oððe tilian sceoldon oððe eft tilða gegaderian, 1097; Erl. 234, 24. v. un-weder.

un-gewemmed; *adj.* I. physical, *unspotted, immaculate, uncorrupted, uninjured*:—Se līchoma wæs gemēted ungebrosnod and ungewemmed *corpus incorruptum inventum est*, Bd. 4, 19; S. 588, 38. Hē ungewemmed of ðam hātum bæðe eode, Homl. Th. i. 58, 28. Seó hālge stōd ungewemde wlite, Exon. Th. 277, 33; Jul. 590. Eall ða hrægel ungewemmed (*intemerata*) wǣron, Bd. 4, 30; S. 608, 40. v. un-forswǣled. II. moral, *undefiled, unstained, inviolate, immaculate*:—Ungewæmmed ic beó *immaculatus ero*, Ps. Spl. 18, 14. Ungewæmmed *inviolata*, Hymn. Surt. 54, 25: *incorruptibilis*, Jn. Skt. p. 1, 6. Uniwemmedes *inlaesae* (*virginitatis*), Hpt. Gl. 435, 53: *inlibatae*, 511, 47. Uniwemmedre *immunem*, 507, 49. On ungewemmedum mægðhāde, Homl. Th. i. 58, 8. Hē his wīf him betǣhte ungewemmed, Gen. 20, 14. III. uncertain:—Ungeuuemmid *infractus*, Wrt. Voc. ii. 111, 36. [*O. H. Ger.* un-giwemmit *immaculatus, inlibatus.*] v. unwemmed.

un-gewemmedlīc; *adj. Incorruptible*:—Uniwemmedlīcre clǣnnysse *immarcescibilis* (*imputribilis*) *pudicitiae*, Hpt. Gl. 467, 47.

un-gewemmedlīce; *adv. Uncorruptly, purely, inviolably*:—Ðæt ða dōmas and ða gesetnysse, ða ðe fram hālgum fæderum ārǣdde and gesette wǣron, ðæt ða fram eallum ūs ungewemmedlīce (*incorrupte*) healdene wǣron, Bd. 4, 5; S. 572, 19.

un-gewemmedness, e; *f. Purity*:—Rihtlīc is mē swā besmitenre fram ðīnre clǣnan ungewemmednesse beón āscirod, Homl. Skt. ii. 23b, 438.

un-gewemness, e; *f. Freedom from pollution*:—Uniwemnysse *immunitatis*, Hpt. Gl. 434, 28.

un-gewendendlīc; *adj. Unchangeable, invariable, chronic* (of disease):—Þeáh man sȳ on hwylcre ungewendendlīcre (-dedlīcre, MS. H.) ādle, Lchdm. i. 328, 20.

un-gewēned; *adj. Unexpected*:—Se here wæs cumende ungewēnedre tīde on herfeste *legio inopinata tempore autumni adveniens*, Bd. 1, 12; S. 480, 41. Of ungewēnedum *ex improviso*, Lchdm. iii. 200, 23. Of ungewēndum, 204, 19. [*O. H. Ger.* un-giwânit *inopinatus.*] v. unwēned.

un-gewērigod; *adj. Unwearied*:—Ungewērigadre geornfullnysse *indefessa instantia*, Bd. 4, 3; S. 568, 14.

un-gewid(e)re, es; *n. Bad weather, storm, tempest*:—Hit biþ wiþ ǣghwylc ungewidro gescylded, ðæt ðǣr nǣfre nǣnig dǣl regnes ne ungewidres in cuman ne mæg, Blickl. Homl. 125, 31–3. Gif ðē þince ðæt ðū ōþerne māran lǣcedōm dōn ne durre for ungewiderum, Lchdm. ii. 254, 2. Is ðeós woruld on stormum and on ādlum and on ungewyderum, Wulfst. 273, 9. Mycel orfes wæs ðæs geáres forfaren ǣgðer ge þurh mistlīce coða ge þurh ungewyderu, 1041; Erl. 169, 9: Lchdm. iii. 210, 26. [Bið his erd ihened eiðer ȝe on herȝunge ȝe on hungre ȝe on cwalme ȝe on uniwidere, O. E. Homl. i. 115, 36. *O. Sax.* un-giwideri (wið ungiwidereon allun standan, Hēl. 1813): *O. H. Ger.* un-giwitiri *tempestas, procella, hiems, ventus.*] v. un-widere.

un-gewiderung, e; *f. Bad weather*:—Syððan com, þurh ða mycclan ungewiderunge ðe cōmon, swȳðe mycel hungor ofer Engeland, ðæt manig hundred manna earmlīce deáðe swulton þurh ðone hungor, Chr. 1086; Erl. 219, 33.

un-gewild; *adj. Unsubdued, unsubjected*:—Ungewyld *indomita, inefrenata*, Hpt. Gl. 461, 49. Ungewyldre ǣwnunge *effrenatae jugalitatis*, 434, 25. Ungewylde *indomitos*, 457, 76. v. ge-wildan (-wyldan).

un-gewilde; *adj. Not in subjection*:—Heora gecynd wæs him ungewylde *their nature was not in subjection to them*, Hexam. 17; Norm. 26, 2. Gif ǣnig leódscipe wæs ungewylde ðam Cāsere, ðonne send hē him tō swā fela eóroda ðe mihton gebīgan ðæt mennisc him tō, Jud. Thw. p. 161, 35. Hē underþiédde him selfum monege þeóda ðe ǣr wǣron Rōmānum ungewilde, Ors. 6, 30; Swt. 284, 6. v. ge-wilde (-wylde).

un-gewildelīc; *adj. Not to be subdued, unyielding*:—Hæbbe se mann heardheortnysse and ungewyldelīc mōd ... ðonne forsearaþ swīðe hraðe ðæt hālige sǣd on his heortan, Homl. Th. ii. 92, 2.

un-gewil[l]; *adj. Displeasing, not with the good will of a person*:—Se arcebiscop leáfe æt ðam cynge nam, ðeáh hit ðam cynge ungewill wǣre, ðæs ðe men lēton, Chr. 1097; Erl. 234, 16. [Þeáh hit ðam arcebiscope swyðe ungewille wǣre, 1120; Erl. 248, 21. Cf. Halde we us from uniwil, O. E. Homl. i. 69, 264.]

un-gewintred; *adj. Not adult*:—Be ungewintredes wīfmannes nēdhǣmde. Gif mon ungewintrædne wīfmon tō niédhǣmde geþreátige, sié ðæt swā ðæs gewintredan monnes bōt, L. Alf. pol. 26; Th. i. 78, 16.

un-gewirded; *adj. Uninjured*:—Ne mæg him bitres wiht sceððan, ac gescylded ā wunaþ ungewyrded þenden woruld stondeþ, Exon. Th. 210, 5; Ph. 181.

un-gewīs; *adj. Uncertain, unknown*:—For ðam ðe him cūþ forþfōr tōweard wǣre and ungewiis (ungewiss? q. v.) seó tīd ðære ylcan forðfōre *eo quod certus sibi exitus, sed incerta ejusdem exitus esset hora futura*, Bd. 3, 19; S. 547, 16.

un-gewislíc; *adj. Uncertain, unknown, uncommon*:—Wēnst ðū ðæt hit hwæt nīwes sié oððe hwæthwugu ungewislíces ðæt ðē on becumen is *novum credo aliquid inusitatumque vidisti*, Bt. 7, 2; Fox 16, 27 note.

un-gewisness, e; *f. Uncertainty, ignorance*:—Ða ðe ðurh ungewisnysse (*per ignorantiam*) synne fremmaþ . . . ða ðe him ne ondrǣdaþ witende (*sciendo*) syngian, Bd. 1, 27; S. 491, 36. Swā hwæt swā on hyre unclǣnnysse ðurh ungewisnesse (*per ignorantiam*) gelumpe, 4, 9; S. 576, 28.

un-gewiss, es; *n.* I. *uncertainty, ignorance, unconsciousness*:—Se ðe his sylfes blōd on spātl mid ungewisse forswelge *qui sanguinem proprium inscius cum saliva sorbuerit*, L. Ecg. C. 40; Th. ii. 166, 5. Gif eall folc syngaþ þurh ungewiss (*through ignorance* (A. V.); per imperitiam), Lev. 4, 13. Swā hwæt swā wē þurh ungewis oððe þurh hwylce dysignesse gedōn habban, Homl. Ass. 143, 136. ¶ Ungewisses *in ignorance, unintentionally, unconsciously, unwittingly*:—Ða scylda ðe ic ungewisses geworhte ne gemun ðū; ðæt synt ða ðe ic wēnde ðæt nān scyld nǣre *delicta ignorantiae meae ne memineris*, Ps. Th. 24, 6. Swelce hē hit ungewisses oððe ungewealdes doo *agit velut nesciens*, Past. 33; Swt. 215, 10. Ðonne hē of unwīsdōme and ungewisses oððe ungewealdes gesyngaþ *cum sola ignorantia delinquitur*, 21; Swt. 157, 25. II. *what is uncertain* or *unknown*; incertum:—Ðā gebende ān scytta his bogan and āscēt āna flān swylce on ungewis (cf. *O. H. Ger.* in ung(i)uis *a casu*) *vir quidam tetendit arcum, in incertum sagittam dirigens* (1 Kings 22, 34), Homl. Skt. i. 18, 220. Ðæt hié on swā micle nēþinge and on swā micel ungewiss ǣgðer ge on sǣs fyrhto ge on wēstennum wildeóra ge on þeóda gereordum, ðæt hié hiene æfter friþe sōhton *that they ventured upon so much that was hazardous and so much that was unknown in respect to both the terrors of the sea and the deserts with their wild beasts and the languages of nations to seek him and get peace*, Ors. 3, 9; Swt. 136, 24. Ongewissu and dīglu wīsdōmes ðīnes ðū swutelodest mē *incerta et occulta sapientiae tuae manifestasti mihi*, Ps. Spl. 50, 7. v. next word, II a. III. the word also glosses *ignominia*. v. next word, III:—Gefyl ansȳne heora of ungewisse *imple facies eorum ignominia*, Ps Spl. 82, 15: Blickl. Gl.

un-gewiss; *adj. Uncertain*:—Ungewis *incerta*, Wrt. Voc. ii. 48, 17. I. of persons, *not having knowledge, ignorant*:—Gif hē hit nāt, hwelce gesǣlþa hæfþ hē æt ðam welan, gif hē biþ swā dysig and swā ungewiss ðæt hē ðæt witan ne mæg *si nescit, quaenam beata sors esse potest ignorantiae caecitate?* Bt. 11, 2; Fox 34, 26. Ungewiss com se deófol tō Criste, and ungewiss hē eode āweig; for ðan ðe se Hǣlend ne geswutelode nā him his mihte, Homl. Th. i. 176, 9–11. Ðā ðā ic ðǣr lange stōd ungewis mīnes færeldes, ii. 350, 26. II. of things, (a) *not known, of which there is not certain knowledge*:—On ðīnes līfes ryne ðe ðē is ungewiss, Basil admn. 8; Norm. 52, 8. Ungewisse þingc and dȳgelnyssa wīsdomes ðīnes *incerta et occulta sapientiae tuae*, Ps. Lamb. 50, 8. (b) *not conveying certain knowledge*:—Ðū stunta, on hwilce wīsan sceole wē ðē gelȳfan and ðīnum ungewissum wordum? Homl. Skt. i. 23, 697. III. *ignominious*. v. preceding word, III:—Ungewis *ignominiosus*, Kent. Gl. 715. [*O. H. Ger.* un-giwiss *incertus, inexpertus, fortuitus*.]

un-gewītendlīce; *adv. Without passing away, permanently*:—Gehiéren hī ðæt ðās andweardan gōd bióð from ǣlcre lustfulnesse swīðe hrædlīce gewītende and swā ðeáh sió scyld ðe hī ðurh ða lustfullnesse ðurhtióð ungewītendlīce bið ðurhwuniende mid wræce *audiant quod bona praesentia et a delectatione citius transitura sunt, et tamen eorum causa ad ultionem sine transitu permansura*, Past. 58; Swt. 441, 21.

un-gewitfæstness, e; *f. Madness*:—Him cymð brægenes ādl and ungewitfæstnes him bið *he will be out of his senses*, Lchdm. ii. 222, 3.

un-gewitfull; *adj.* I. *foolish, insensate*:—Eálā gē ungewitfullan Galata, hwā gehefegode eów *O insensati Galatae, quis vos fascinavit?* Past. 31; Swt. 207, 14. Welan and weorþscipes hī willniaþ, and ðonne hī hine habbaþ, ðonne wēnaþ hī swā ungewitfulle ðæt hī habban ða sōþan gesǣlþa, Bt. 32, 3; Fox 118, 30. II. *mad, insane, not in one's senses*:—Ða wōdðrāga ðæs ungewitfullan monnes se lǣce gehǣlð *furor insanorum ad salutem medico reducitur*, Past. 26; Swt. 183, 21. Sume ða untruman wǣron dumbe, sume ungewitfulle, Homl. Ass. 180, 364.

un-gewitfulness, e; *f. Madness, insanity*:—Saules ungewitfulnes (-full-, Hatt. MS.), Past. 26; Swt. 185, 1.

un-gewitlīc; *adj. Senseless, foolish*:—Ungewitlīce word, Lchdm. ii. 176, 2.

un-gewītnigendlīce; *adv. With impunity*; impune, Ælfc. Gr. 38; Zup. 233, 6 note.

un-gewītnod; *adj. Unpunished*, (1) of the person to whom punishment might be given:—Ne beó gē on nānre leásre gewitnysse, for ðon ðe se leása gewita ne bið hē nǣfre ungewītnod, L. E. I. 27; Th. ii. 424, 1: Homl. Ass. 148, 10. Ne wēn ðū nā be ðē ðæt ðū ungewītnod beó, Homl. Skt. ii. 25, 159. Wē beóð mid Gode suā micle suīðor gebundne suā wē for monnum orsorglīcor ungewītnode syngiaþ būtan ǣlcre wrace (*quanto apud homines inulte peccamus*), Past. 17; Swt. 117, 23. (2) of the fault for which punishment might be given:—Ðæt him biþ ungewītnode hiora yfel on ðisse worulde, Bt. 38, 3; Fox 200, 28. v. unwītnod.

un-gewit[t], es; *n.* I. *madness, insanity*:—Nān unhāl cild, ne deáf, ne blind, ne ungewittes, Homl. Ass. 179, 322. Hié sindon suā micle wærlīcor tō oferbūganne suā mon ongiet ðæt hié on māran ungewitte beóð *tanto caute declinandi sunt, quanto et insane rapiuntur*, Past. 40; Swt. 295, 22. Gif hwylc man of his gewitte feólle . . . Gif man hine ofsleá on ðam ungewitte, L. Ecg. P. addit. 29; Th. ii. 236, 31. Se yfela gāst on ungewitte his (*Saul's*) mōd āwende, Homl. Skt. i. 18, 11. Sende ðē Drihten on ungewitt and blindnysse *percutiat te Dominus amentia et coecitate*, Deut. 28, 28. II. *folly, stupidity*:—Ðȳ læs ðe ǣnig ungecyrred woroldman mid nytnesse and ungewitte regules geboda ābrǣce, and ðære tale brūce, ðæt hē misfēnge ðȳ hē hit sēlre nyste, Lchdm. iii. 442, 2. Hī mid heora gedwolsprǣce eall folc āmyrdon. And Theodosius, ðā hē swilce ungewitt ǣlce dæge gehȳrde, hē wearð sārig, Homl. Skt. i. 23, 370. [*O. H. Ger.* un-giwizzi *insipientia*.]

un-gewittig; *adj.* I. *mad, insane*:—Ic wāt ðæt gē wēnaþ ðæt ic ungewittige mōde (*insana mente*) sprece, Bd. 4, 8; S. 576, 1. II. *foolish, senseless*:—Gif cinges gerēfena hwylc gyltig biþ, hwā is manna tō ðam ungesceád and ungewittig, ðæt hē ðæm cyninge his āre ætrecce for ðī ðe his gerēfa forwyrht biþ? Lchdm. iii. 444, 8. III. *not having reason, irrational*:—Hī (*the innocents*) wǣron gehwǣde and ungewittige ācwealde, Homl. Th. i. 84, 21. Beóð ða ungewittigan cild gehealdene on ðam fulluhte þurh geleáfan ðæs fæder and ðære mēder, ii. 50, 35. Ða yfelan men ne magon cuman þider, ðider ða ungewittigan gesceafta wilniaþ tō tō cumenne, Bt. 36, 5; Fox 180, 3. [*O. Sax.* un-giwittig *unwise*.] v. un-wittig.

un-gewittiglīce (-witte-); *adv. Unwisely, foolishly*; stolide, Gr. Dial. 2, 3.

un-gewittigness, e; *f. Foolishness*; stultitia, Gr. Dial. 2, 31.

un-gewlitig; *adj. Not bright, not brilliant*:—Ealle ða ðing ðe beorhte beóð ðonne seó sunne hym on scīnaþ, hī lȳhtaþ ongeán; ac ða ðe ungewligige (-wlitige?) beóð, ða ne lȳhtaþ nāwiht ongeán ða sunnan, þeáh heó hym on scīne, Shrn. 180, 15. v. un-wlitig.

un-gewlitigian *to disfigure, deform, deprive of beauty*:—Hē gewlitegaþ and gegeraþ æalle gesceafta and æft ungewliteaþ, and ungeraþ, Shrn. 198, 12. v. un-wlitigian.

un-geworht; *adj.* I. *not made*:—Gif Hē geworht wǣre, ne wurde Hē nǣfre ælmihtig God . . . Hē wæs ǣfre ungeworht, Homl. Skt. i. 1, 69. II. *not finished*:—Ungeworht *infectum*, Wrt. Voc. ii. 45, 17.

un-gewriten; *adj. Unwritten*:—Ungewriten yrfe *intestata hereditas*, Wrt. Voc. i. 20, 41: ii. 49, 20. v. un-writen.

un-gewuna, an; *m. A bad custom, evil practice*:—Se eorðlīca gefērscipe hiene tiéhð on ða lufe his ealdan ungewunan *ad vetustatem vitae per societatem secularium ducitur*, Past. 22; Swt. 169, 9. Ða ðe ðone ungewunan hæfdon, ðæt hī heora wīf glengdan swā hī weofoda sceoldan, geswīcan ðæs ungewunan, L. I. P. 23; Th. ii. 336, 20. Se bið siwenīge ðonne his mōd and his andgit ðæt gecynd āscirpð and hē hit ðonne self gescint mid his ungewunan and wōm wilnungum *lippus est, cujus sensum natura exacuit, sed conversationis pravitas confundit*, Past. 11; Swt. 69, 9. Æt ðam unþeáwe ðe dysige men on ungewunan healdaþ (*which foolish men observe as a custom, and a bad one it is*), Wulfst. 305, 9.

un-gewuna; *adj. Unaccustomed, unused*:—Micel gedāl is on ðam mægene ðæs ðe sié gewin (-wun?) þrowungum and ðæs ðe sié ungewuna swelcum þingum, Lchdm. ii. 84, 19. [Cf. *O. H. Ger.* un-giwon *inusitatus, insolens, novus*.]

un-gewunelīc; *adj.* I. *unusual, unwonted*:—Ðæs wundredon men, for ðī ðæt hit wæs ungewunelīc, Homl. Th. i. 184, 30. Fela fægera þinga ðe ðam folce ungecnāwe[n] wæs and ungewunelīc, Ap. Th. 17, 14. Hwīlum gebyrede swīþe ungewunelīc and ungecyndelīc yfel, ðæt ða bearn sieredon ymbe ðone fæder, Bt. 31, 1; Fox 112, 12. Hwæthwegu ungewunelīces *novum aliquid inusitatumque*, 7, 2; Fox 16, 27. Ðā geseah hē ealle ða cytan mid heofonlīce leóhte gefylde. Hē ðā wæs forhtlīce geworden for ðære ungewunelīcan gesihþe, Guthl. 21; Gdwin. 94, 23. II. *unfrequented, uninhabitable*:—Seó stōw wæs swā wēsten and swā dīgle, ðæt næs nā ðæt ān ðæt heó wæs ungewunelīc, ac eác swilce uncūð ðām landleódum him sylfum, Homl. Skt. ii. 23 b, 106. Ān ðæra dǣla is ungewunelīc for ðære sunnan neáweste; on ðam ne eardaþ nān eorðlīc mann for ðam unberendlīcum bryne, Lchdm. iii. 260, 21 note. v. un-gewynelīc.

un-gewunelīce; *adv. Unusually, in an unwonted manner*:—*Cometae* synd gehātene ða steorran ðe fǣrlīce and ungewunelīce æteówiaþ, Lchdm. iii. 272, 4. Ðære sǣ gemengednyssa and ðæra ȳða swēg ungewunelīce gyt ne āsprungon (*it has not been unusual for them to occur already*), Homl. Th. i. 610, 12. [*O. H. Ger.* un-giwonalīhho *insolite*.]

un-gewuni[g]endlīc; *adj. Uninhabitable*:—Ān ðæra dǣla is ungewuniendlīc (-wunig-, MS. P.: unwuniendlīc, MSS. L. R.) for ðære sunnan neáweste; on ðam ne eardaþ nān eorðlīc mann, Lchdm. iii. 260, 21. v. un-wuni[g]endlīc.

un-gewyld, -gewylde. v. un-gewild, -gewilde.

un-gewynelīc; *adj. Unusual, unwonted:*—Mid ege ungewynelīcum *timore insolito*, Anglia xiii. 411, 651. v. un-gewunelīc.

un-gewyrht *in the phrases* be ungewyrhtum *undeservedly, not according to one's deserts;* gratis, Ps. Surt. 34, 7, 19: 68, 5: Ps. Spl. C. 108, 2: 118, 161.

un-gifeđe; *adj. Not granted:*—Ūs wæs ā syđđan milts ungyfeđe, Beo. Th. 5835; B. 2921.

un-gifre; *adj. Harmful, unfortunate:*—Ǣr gē sceonde fremmen, ungifre yfel ylda bearnum, Cd. Th. 149, 5; Gen. 2470. v. gifre.

un-gifu, e; *f. An evil gift:*—Hæfđ se yfela gāst hērongeán seofonfealde ungifa... đa yfelan ungifa đæs ārleásan deófles syndan đus genamode *insipientia, stultitia*..., Wulfst. 52, 7–20: 58, 14.

un-gild, -gilde, es; *n. An improper* or *excessive tax:*—Hē ǣfre đās leóde mid here and mid ungylde tyrwigende wæs, for đan đe on his dagan ǣlc riht āfeóll, and ǣlc unriht up ārās, Chr. 1100; Erl. 236, 2. Đis wæs swiđe geswincfull geár þurh manigfeald ungyld, 1098; Erl. 235, 11. Ūs ungylda swȳđe gedrehton, Wulfst. 159, 12. Đis wæs swiđe hefigtȳme geár... on ungyldan đa nǣfre ne āblunnon, Chr. 1097; Erl. 234, 25.

un-gilda, an; *m. One who is not a full member of a guild:*—Æt ǣlcon rihtgegyldan āne byrđene wudes and twā æt đam ungyldan (cf. (?) *for a difference between those in the same gild*, Hæbbe ǣlc gegilda .ii. sesteras mealtes, and ǣlc cniht ānne, 613, 32), Chart. Th. 606, 16.

un-gilde; *adj. Not entitled to wergild:*—Gif se friđman fleó oþþon feohte, and nelle hine cȳþan, gif hine man ofsleá, licge ungylde, L. Eth. ii. 3; Th. i. 286, 14. Homo qui aliquem innocentem affliget in via regia, si jaceat, jaceat in ungildan ækere [as the technical name of the crime here referred to was *forsteal* (cf. si in via regia fiat assaltus super aliquem, forestel est, L. H. I. 80, § 2; Th. i. 586, 2), the passage seems to be a Latin equivalent for the following: Gif hwā forsteal gewyrce, ... gif hē sylf gewyrce đæt hine man āfylle, licge ǣgilde, L. Eth. vi. 38; Th. i. 324, 21–24; so that the phrase *licgan in ungildan æcere* seems to be equivalent to *licgan ungilde*], L. Eth. iv. 4; Th. i. 301, 23. [*Icel.* ú-gildr *for whom no wer-gild is to be paid.*] v. ǣ-, or-gilde.

un-gīmen[n], e; *f. Carelessness:*—Þurh ungēmænne synne (đurh gȳmeleáste, col. 1) *per culpam incuriae*, Bd. 3, 17; S. 544, 24, col. 2: 2, 7; S. 509, 19. Ungȳmenne, 4, 25; S. 599, 20. Đurh ungȳmenne *per incuriam*, 4, 9; S. 576, 28.

un-gīmende; *adj.* (*ptcpl.*) *Careless, negligent:*—Đa đing đe se Dryhtnes wer geseah nales eallum monnum suongrum and heora liifes ungēmendum [ungemyndum *for* (?) ungȳmendum, Bd. S. 630, 38] sæcgan wolde *haec quae viderat idem vir Domini non omnibus desidiosis ac vitae suae incuriosis referre volebat*, Bd. 5, 12; M. 434, 5. v. preceding word.

un-gin[n]; *adj. Not ample, contracted:*—Ā sceal đæs heánan hyge hord onginnost, Exon. Th. 346, 18; Gn. Ex. 206.

un-girwan, -girian; *p.* -girwde, -girede *To strip, divest:*—Hē gewlitegaþ and gegeraþ ealle gesceafta and æft ungewliteaþ and ungeraþ, Shrn. 198, 13. Gūđlāc hine sylfne ungyrede, Guthl. 16; Gdwin. 68, 16. Hē hine ungyrede đæs godcundan mægenþrymmes, Blickl. Homl. 103, 2. Hiǽ ungeredun (*exuerunt*) hine and gegearwadun (*induerunt*) hine his āgene wēde, Mt. Kmbl. Rush. 27, 31. Đeodoricus wæs ungyred and unscōd, Shrn. 85, 32. v. on-girwan.

un-glæd; *adj. Dull, cheerless:*—Swā eác se sūþerna wind hwīlum miclum storme gedrēfeþ đa sǣ đe ǣr wæs smylte wedere glæshlūtra on tō seónne; đonne heó swā gemenged wyrđ mid đan ȳđum, đonne wyrþ heó swīþe hrađe ungladu, þeáh heó ǣr gladu wǣre on tō lōcienne *si mare volvens turbidus Auster misceat aestum, vitrea dudum, parque serenis unda diebus, mox, resoluto sordida coeno visibus obstat*, Bt. 6; Fox 14, 26. [Goddes glam to hym (*Jonah*) glod, þat hym unglad made, Allit. Pms. 94, 63. *Icel.* ú-glaðr.]

un-glædlīc; *adj. Stern, implacable:*—Stīđ, grimm, unglædlīc *inmitis, atrox, implacabilis*, Germ. 392, 33. v. glæd, III.

un-glædnes *glosses* imperitia, Wrt. Voc. ii. 46, 25, *but* un-glǣwnes *perhaps should be read*. v. un-gleáwness.

un-gleáw; *adj.* I. of persons, *without understanding, without skill, not sagacious, ignorant, blind* (fig.):—Ungleáw *imperitus*, Wrt. Voc. i. 55, 49. Ungleu *caecus*, Mt. Kmbl. Lind. 15, 14. Synt gē þus ungleáwe (*inprudentes*)? Ne ongyte gē đæt...? *are ye so without understanding? Do ye not perceive that...?* Mk. Skt. 7, 18. Ungleáwe *inertes*, Wrt. Voc. ii. 45, 32. Hit ne biþ seó ylce ādl, þeáh đe ungleáwe lǣcas wēnan đæt đæt seó ylce healfdeáde ādl sī, Lchdm. ii. 284, 24. **I a.** where that in which there is want of skill is expressed:—Đā wæs ic ungleáw đæs geþeódes đara Indiscra worda... đā rehte hit mē se bisceop, Nar. 29, 14. Wē đæs londes ungleáwe and unwīse (*imprudentes*; but the Latin is not literally translated) wǣron, 10, 6. **II.** of things:—*dull, not apt for service:*—Sweord gebrǣd gōd gūđcyning, gomele lāfe, ecgum ungl[e]áw (*dull of edge;* cf. sió ecg gewāc, bāt unswīđor đonne his điódcyning þearfe hæfde, 5148–; B. 2577–), Beo. Th. 5121; B. 2564. [*Icel.* ú-glöggr *not clever.*]

un-gleáwlīce; *adv. Without understanding, without sagacity, unwisely, imprudently:*—On his heortan cwæđ unhȳdig sum ungleáwlīce đæt God nǣre *dixit insipiens in corde suo, Non est Deus*, Ps. Th. 52, 1. Gif hē đære styringe ne wiđstent, đonne gescient hē đa gōdan weorc đe hē oft ǣr on stillum mōde đurhteáh, and suā ungleáulīce for đæm scyfe đære styringe suīđe hrædlīce tōwierpđ đa gōdan weorc đe hē longe ǣr foređonclīce timbrede *qui, dum perturbationi suae minime obsistunt, etiam si qua a se tranquilla mente fuerant bene gesta, confundunt, et improviso impulsu destruunt, quidquid forsitan diu labore provido construxerunt*, Past. 33; Swt. 215, 17. [*O. H. Ger.* un-glaulīhho *insolerter.*]

un-gleáwness, e; *f. Want of understanding, unskilfulness, foolishness, blindness* (fig.):—Unglædnes (-glǣwnes?) *imperitia*, Wrt. Voc. ii. 46, 25. Sió ungleáwnes biþ on đē selfum, đæt đū hit ne canst on riht gecnāwan, Bt. 39, 10; Fox 226, 33. Ongleáwnis *imperitia*, Scint. 5, 5. [Un]gleáwnysse *rusticitatis*, Hpt. Gl. 529, 16. Hē nǣfre for his unglaunesse (ungleáwnesse, MS. T.) and for his unscearpnesse đa đēnunge on riht geleornian mihte *nullatenus propter ingenii tarditatem potuit ministerium discere*, Bd. 5, 6; S. 620, 7. Of ungleáunesse *imperitia* (os stultorum pascitur imperitia, Prov. 15, 14), Kent. Gl. 520. Ungleównise heartæs *caecitatem cordis*, Mk. Skt. Lind. Rush. 3, 5.

un-gleáwscipe, es; *m. Want of understanding, foolishness;* imperitia, Scint. 83, 16.

un-glenged; *adj. Unadorned:*—Unglenied *inculta, non ornata*, Hpt. Gl. 435, 25.

un-gnīđe; *adj. Not scanty, liberal, abundant:*—Monigfealde sind geond middangeard gōd ungnȳđe (-gnyde, MS.) đe ūs dǣleþ tō feorhnere Fæder ælmihtig *manifold and abundant are the goods which for our life's support the Father almighty gives on earth*, Exon. Th. 359, 31; Pa. 70. v. gneáđ.

un-gōd; *adj. Not good, evil, bad:*—Seldan hē biđ eald; ungōdan deáđe hē swylt, Lchdm. iii. 184, 23. On ylde ungōdum deáđe heó swylt, 188, 28. [Dede unngod and unnclene, Orm. 16739. *O. H. Ger.* un-guot: *Icel.* ū-gōðr.]

un-gōd, es; *n. Evil, ill:*—Wā eów đe taliaþ ungōd tō gōde and gōd þing tō yfele *vae qui dicitis malum bonum, et bonum malum*, Wulfst. 47, 6. Heó firenaþ mec wordum, ungōd gæleþ, Exon. Th. 402, 25; Rä. 21, 35. [Nis þing so god þat ne mai do sum ungod, O. and N. 1364.]

un-grāpigende; *adj. Not handling, that does not handle:*—Hī habbaþ ungrāpigende handa *manus habent, et non palpabunt* (Ps. 115, 7), Homl. Th. i. 366, 27.

un-grēne; *adj. Not green:*—Folde wæs đāgyt græs ungrēne, Cd. Th. 7, 36; Gen. 117.

un-griđ *violation of peace, hostility* (Lye). [Forr sware unngriþþ þatt heþenn follc þær wrohhte, Orm. 16280.]

un-grund; *adj. Bottomless, boundless, immense:*—Đæs heriges hām eft ne com ealles ungrundes ǣnig *of that host, all boundless as it was, not one came home again*, Cd. Th. 209, 32; Exod. 508. [Cf. *Icel.* ú-grunnr *not shallow;* ú-grynni; *n. boundlessness*, in phrases like ú-grynni hers, liðs, manna.]

un-grynde; *adj. Bottomless, deep*, Exon. Th. 354, 21; Reim. 49. v. preceding word.

un-gyld, -gylde. v. un-gild, -gilde.

un-gyltig; *adj. Innocent:*—Hit God wræc on him, swā oft swā hié mid monnum ofredan, đæt hié mid hiera cucum onguldon, đæt hié ungyltige cwealdon, Ors. 4, 7; Swt. 184, 9. [Un-gilti *innoxius*, Wick. Gen. 37, 22. Ongylty *immunis, innocens*, Prompt. Parv. 365.]

un-gȳmen[n]. v. un-gīmen[n].

un-gyrdan; *p.* de *To ungird:*—Se cyning ungyrde hine đā his sweorde *rex discinxit se gladio suo*, Bd. 3, 14; S. 540, 35. Se cāsere hēt hine ungyrdan and bewǣpnian, Homl. Skt. ii. 30, 409. Gif him þince đæt hē sȳ ungyrd, broc đæt biþ, Lchdm. iii. 172, 12.

un-gyrian. v. un-girwan.

un-hādian; *p.* ode *To deprive of orders:*—Sȳ hē unhādod *ordine suo privetur*, L. Ecg. C. 6; Th. ii. 138, 22. Sume wyllaþ đæt hē sig eft unhādod *nonnulli volunt ut denuo ordine caveat*, 3; Th. ii. 136, 36. [He him plihte he wolden unhadien Costanz... þe abbed unhadede his brođer, Laym. 13169.] v. on-hādian.

un-hādod; *adj. Not ordained:*—Unhādod man *homo non ordinatus*, L. Ecg. C. 12; Th. ii. 142, 3. v. un-gehādod.

un-hādung *renders* exordinatio *in:*—Unhādunge *exordinationes*, R. Ben. Interl. 110, 8.

un-hǣl, un-hǣlan. v. un-hǣlu, ge-unhǣlan.

un-hǣlþ, e; *f. Bad health, sickness, weakness, infirmity:*—Līchaman unhǣlđ ormǣte mægenu sāwle tōbrycđ *corporis debilitas nimia uires anime frangit*, Scint. 54, 17: 107, 11. Ne beþurfon lǣces đa đe hāle synd, ac đa đe unhǣlþe habbaþ (*qui male habent*), Lk. Skt. 5, 31. [Ne elde ne unhelđe, O. E. Homl. ii. 35, 6: Misc. 108, 113.]

un-hǣlu; *indecl.:* un-hǣl, e; *f.* I. *bad health, disease, sickness, infirmity*, (a) of persons:—Se oferdrenc fordēđ đæs mannes gesundfulnysse and unhǣl becymđ of đam drence, Ælfc. T. Grn. 21, 38. Oferfyll biđ đæs līchaman unhǣl, Wulfst. 242, 4. Būton đē unhǣl ođđe yld derige, 247, 34. Đa diófla gelǣrdon hié, đæt đa đe on unhǣle wǣran, đæt hié hále for hié cwealdon, Ors. 4, 4; Swt. 164, 17. Gif ðú wile hál beón, drinc ðē gedeftlīce; ǽlc oferfyl fēt unhǽlo, Prov. Kmbl. 61. Unhǽlo *languorem*, Mt. Kmbl. Lind. 4, 23: *crucem*, 16, 24. Ðām ðe under hӯ migaþ . . . ða unhǽle heó gehǽlþ, Lchdm. i. 360, 9. Ðās unhǽle (*blotch*), ii. 76, 16. Untrymmnise ł unhǽlo *infirmitates*, Mt. Kmbl. Lind. 8, 17. (b) of animals, *unsoundness*:—Gif mon hwelcne ceáp gebygeþ and hē ðonne onfinde him hwelce unhǽlo on binnan .xxx. nihta, L. In. 56; Th. i. 138, 11. [Licome unhele, O. E. Homl. i. 7, 23. Unhæle and ælde, Laym. 11546. Unnhal þurrh unnride unnhæle, Orm. 4779. *O. H. Ger.* un-hailī *insania*. Cf. *Goth.* un-haili; *n. ill-health.*] II. *misfortune, mishap*:—Sorge ne cūðon, wonsceaft wera, wiht unhǽlo, Beo. Th. 241; B. 120. [Envye that sory is of other mennes wele and glæd is of his sorwe and unhele, Chauc. Doct. T. 116. *Icel.* ū-heill *mishap.*]

un-hǽmed; *adj. Unmarried*:—Unhǽmedo *innuba* (*voluit dotales linquere pompas*, Ald. 195), Wrt. Voc. ii. 95, 50. v. un-gehǽmed.

un-hāl; *adj. In bad health, sick, weak, infirm, unhealthy, unsound,* (a) in reference to persons:—Ðǽr ðæt heáfod bið unhāl *languente capite*, Past. 18; Swt. 129, 7. Ic eom unhāl *infirmus sum*, Ps. Th. 6, 2. Unhāl *debilis*, Mk. Skt. Lind. Rush. 9, 43. Ðe unhāla *languidus*, Jn. Skt. Lind. Rush. 5, 7: Lchdm. i. 360, 18. Ne mæg se unhāla ðam hālan gelīce byrðene āhebban, L. C. S. 69; Th. i. 412, 8. Ðӯ læs hié mid ðӯ tōle ðæt hāle līc gewierden ðe hié sceoldon mid ðæt unhāle āweg āceorfan *dum per hoc in se sana perimunt, per quod salubriter abscindere sauciata debuerunt*, Past. 48; Swt. 365, 12. Eágan mē syndon unhāle *oculi mei infirmati sunt*, Ps. Th. 87, 9: 108, 24. Fēt mīne unhāle (*inbecilles*), Anglia xi. 116, 22. Sume habbaþ bearn genōge, ac ða beóþ hwīlum unhāle oþþe yfele and unweorþ, Bt. 11, 1; Fox 32, 8. Ða hālan . . . ða unhālan *incolumes* . . . *aegri*, Past. 36; Swt. 247, 4. Ðara unhālra ł ādligra *languentium*, Jn. Skt. Lind. Rush. 5, 3. For hwī se gōda lǽce selle ðǽm unhālum, sumum līþne drenc, sumum strangne *cur aegri quidam lenibus, quidam vero acribus adjuvantur*, Bt. 39, 9; Fox 226, 12. Alle unhāle *omnes male habentes*, Mt. Kmbl. Lind. 8, 16: Homl. Skt. i. 21, 155. Ealle ða unhālan, Mk. Skt. 1, 32. (b) of animals:—Gif man āfindeþ his ǽhte, syððan hē hit gebohte hafeþ, unhāl, L. O. 7; Th. i. 180, 21. Ðæt hors blon fram ðām unhālum (*insanis*) styrenessum ðara leoma . . . and sōna ārās hāl and gesund, Bd. 3, 9; S. 533, 38. [Adam bicom unmihti and unhol, O. E. Homl. ii. 35, 9. *Laym. Orm.* un-hal: *Goth.* un-hails: *O. H. Ger.* unheil *insanus.*]

un-hālgod; *adj. Unhallowed, unconsecrated*:—Fela dropena unhālgodes eles, Lchdm. i. 380, 5. Gif preóst on unhālgodon hūse mæssige, L. N. P. L. 13; Th. ii. 292, 16. v. un-gehālgod.

un-hālig; *adj. Unholy*:—Of unhāligre þeóde *de gente non sancta*, Ps. Lamb. 42, 1.

un-hālwendlīc; *adj. Incurable*:—Fyll unhālwendlic *casus insanabilis*, Scint. 80, 8. Þeáh man sӯ on hwylcre unhālwendlīcre ādle, Lchdm. i. 328, 21. Hira wīn is dracena gealla and næddrena āttor unhālwendlīce *fel draconum vinum eorum et venenum aspidum insanabile*, Deut. 32, 33.

un-handworht; *adj. Not made with hands*:—Ic unhandworht tempel getimbrie *ego templum non manu factum aedificabo*, Mk. Skt. 14, 58. [*Goth.* un-handuwaurhts.]

un-hār; *adj. Very grey* (un- *seems to have here the unusual force of an intensive*):—Hrōðgār, eald and unhār (cf. *the epithets elsewhere applied to him*, gamolfeax, 1220; B. 608: blondenfeax, 3586; B. 1791), Beo. Th. 719; B. 357.

un-heáh; *adj. Not high, low*:—Unhēh (*printed* unhela, *but see* Anglia viii. 450) þrēpel *eculeus*, Wrt. Voc. i. 21, 18. Unhēge sceós *talares*, i. 26, 23. Faraþ tō feldlandum and dūnlandum and tō unhēheran landum *venite ad campestria atque montana et humiliora loca*, Deut. 1, 7. Hwǽr se weall unhēhst sӯ, Homl. Th. i. 484, 10.

un-heánlīce; *adv. Not in an abject manner, gallantly*:—Hē unheánlīce hine werede *he defended himself gallantly*, Chr. 755; Erl. 48, 33.

un-hearmgeorn; *adj. Inoffensive*:—Se Hālga Gāst com ofer Criste on culfran hīwe for ðī ðæt hē wolde getācnian mid ðam ðæt Crist wæs on ðære menniscnysse swīðe līðe and unhearmgeorn, Homl. Th. ii. 44, 20.

un-hēge, un-hela. v. un-heáh.

un-helian; *p.* ede *To uncover, reveal*:—Nis nān þing oferheled ðe ne beó unheled *nihil opertum est quod non reueletur*, Lk. Skt. 12, 2. [God dede, þet wule adeaden, forworpeð hire rinde, þet is, unheleð hire . . . þe figer . . . schal adruwien rindeleas, þuruh þet hit is unheled, A. R. 150, 8-20. Hire hede unhelid was, Alex. (Skt.) 3450. If his hous be unheled (-hiled), Piers P. 18, 319.]

un-heóre, -heórlīc, -hēre. v. un-hīre, -hīrlīc, -hīre.

un-hered; *adj. Unpraised*:—Þeáh hē seó ānum gehered, ðonne biþ hē ōþrum unhered, Bt. 30, 1; Fox 108, 15.

un-herigendlīc; *adj. Not praiseworthy*:—Se bið unherigendlīc ðe unnyt leofaþ, Homl. Th. ii. 406, 17.

un-hērsum, un-hiére, -hiórde, -hióre. v. un-hīrsum, un-hīre.

un-hīre, -heóre, -hēre, -hiére, -hióre, -hӯre; *adj. Fierce, savage, cruel, deadly, dire, dreadful, frightful*:—Unhiére *carolios*, Wrt. Voc. ii. 19, 59. Unhēre (*printed* unkere), 94, 36: *carolios, atrox, inobediens*, 129, 17. Unhēre, sceþðende *caustica, nocens*, 130, 12. Wælgrim, unhēre *funestus, crudelis, perniciosus*, 151, 64. Unhӯri, unhiórde *trux*, Txts. 100, 983. Unhӯre *funesta*, i. *scelesta, criminosa*, Wülck. Gl. 245, 1. Ðæs unhiéran *cruentae*, Wrt. Voc. ii. 24, 34. Ða unhióran *infestos*, 47, 59. (1) of living creatures:—Weard unhióre (*the fire-drake*), Beo. Th. 4818; B. 2413. Grendeles mōdor . . . wīf unhӯre, 4247; B. 2120. Se (*Ishmael*) bið unhӯre, orlæggīfre, wiðerbreca wera cneórissum *hic erit ferus homo, manus ejus contra omnes* (Gen. 16, 12), Cd. Th. 138, 5; Gen. 2287. Ne gēmde hē nā swā swӯðe hū hē āræfnede ðæs unhӯran cwelres hand, Shrn. 129, 9. Ða unhiéran *torvam* (*gypsam*), Wrt. Voc. ii. 96, 12. Hió hyne scyldeþ wið unhӯrum nihtgengum and wið egeslīcum gesihðum, Lchdm. i. 70, 5. (2) of things:—Egl unheóru *a cruel talon*, Beo. Th. 1978; B. 987. Weder unhióre *hard weather*, Met. 29, 65. Him geblendon drӯas drync unheórne, se onwende wera ingeþanc, Andr. Kmbl. 68; An. 34. [*O. Sax.* un-hiuri: *O. H. Ger.* un-hiuri, -hiur *dirus*: *Icel.* ū-hӯrr *unfriendly-looking, frowning.*]

un-hīre, -hióre; *adv. Fiercely*:—Hē lōcaþ unhióre, swīðes wingeþ, gilleþ geómorlīce, Salm. Kmbl. 532; Sal. 265.

un-hīrēdwist *renders* infamiliaritas, Scint. 203, 13.

un-hīrlīc; *adj.* I. *fierce, savage,* (1) of living creatures:—Mera mengeo on onsióne māran and un[hӯ]rlīcran ðonne ða elpendas, Nar. 11, 1. (2) of things:—Ðā cwom ðǽr swīðe micel wind and tō ðæs unheórlīc se wind geweóx ðæt hē ðara ūra geteldа monige āfylde *tum euri uenti tanta uis flantis exorta est, ut omnia tabernacula nostra euerterit,* Nar. 22, 28. Unhiérlīc storm of ðæm munte āstāg, Blickl. Homl. 203, 7. II. *dismal, doleful*:—Ic forht and unrōt ðās unhӯrlīcan fers onhefde mid sange *carmina prae tristi cecini haec lugubria mente*, Dōm. L. 11. [Leper mas bodi ugli and lathe and unherly, Metr. Homl. 129, 26. *O. H. Ger.* un-hiurlīcha *eumenides*: *Icel.* ū-hӯrligr *frowning.*]

un-hīrsum; *adj. Disobedient, inattentive*:—Wæs hē nāwiht unhӯrsum his yldrum, Guthl. 2; Gdwin. 12, 14. v. un-gehīrsum.

un-hīrsumlīce; *adv. Disobediently*:—Ic ne dyde ārleáslīce ne unhӯrsumlīce wið mīnne Drihten *nec impie gessi a Deo meo*, Ps. Th. 17, 21.

un-hīrsumness, e; *f. Disobedience*:—Ðurh gewyrht sumre unhӯrsumnesse *per meritum cujusdam inobedientiae*, Bd. 4, 6; S. 573, 38: 5, 6; S. 619, 22. Ǽt ðæs ǽrestan mannes unhӯrsumnesse, Blickl. Homl. 85, 31. For heora unhӯrsumnesse Godes beboda, 95, 8. Gefriða mē wið ðises folces unhӯrsumnesse *eripies me de contradictionibus populi*, Ps. Th. 17, 41. Hē dēð unhiérsumnesse Gode, Past. 54; Swt. 421, 32. v. un-gehīrsumness.

un-hirwan *to speak very ill of, calumniate*:—Ne ǽnig man ōþerne bæftan ne tǽle ne hyrwe (unhyrwe, MS. C.), Wulfst. 70, 15.

unhiþy. v. un-hӯþig.

un-hīwe; *adj. Formless*:—Unhīwe *informia*, Germ. 399, 259.

un-hīwed *glosses* discolor, Mt. Kmbl. p. 3, 19.

un-hleówe; *adj. Chill*:—Unhleówan wǽg *the chill wave*, Cd. Th. 209, 4; Exod. 494.

un-hlidian; *p.* ode *To uncover, to remove the lid* or *covering from* something:—Fēng se portgerēfa tō ðære tēge and hē hī unhlidode, Homl. Skt. i. 23, 765. Seó byrgen wæs open geworden and unhlidod, Wulfst. 214, 19.

un-hlīs[e?]; *adj. Of evil repute, disreputable*:—On unhlīsum wige *infami via*, Kent. Gl. 475.

un-hlīsa, an; *m. Ill-fame, evil report, discredit, infamy*:—Unhlīsa *infamia*, Wrt. Voc. i. 76, 3. Gode swā gecwēme þurh hālige drohtnunge, ðæt him nān unhlīsa ne fylge þurh ǽnigne fracodscipe, R. Ben. 141, 4: L. Ælfc. P. 31; Th. ii. 376, 24. Ðǽm hādum ðe mon nānes unhlӯsan æt wēnan ne þorfte, L. E. I. 12; Th. ii. 410, 9. Ðā cwæð Eugenia, ðæt heó eáþe mihte ðæs forligeres unhlīsan hī belādian, Homl. Skt. i. 2, 205. Tō unhlīsan *infamiam*, Wrt. Voc. ii. 44, 48. Sume swīðe yfele fērdon . . . and yfele geendodon on heora unhlīsan, Ælfc. T. Grn. 8, 10. Ða wīf ðe heora ǽwe healdaþ wið unhlīsan, Homl. Ass. 39, 376: 108, 208.

un-hlīsbǽre; *adj. Disreputable*:—Tō ðæm unhlīsbǽrum *ad infame*, Wrt. Voc. ii. 9, 19.

un-hliseádig; *adj. Disreputable*:—Ðæs unhlīseádgan *infamis*, Wrt. Voc. ii. 44, 49.

un-hlīsful; *adj. Disreputable*:—Unhlīsful *infamis*, Wrt. Voc. i. 76, 2. Unhlīsfullum gydde *infami elogio*, Hpt. Gl. 524, 76. Unhlīsfullest *infamis*, 505, 12.

un-hlīsig; *adj. Disreputable*:—Unhlīsie *infames*, Kent. Gl. 24.

un-hlytm *an ill-sharing* (?):—Hengest wunode mid Finne . . . unhlitme (finnel unhlitme, MS.) *Hengest dwelt with Fin and his lot was not a happy one* (? v. hlytm, *and* cf. *Icel.* ū-hlutr, -hluti *harm, hurt*), Beo. Th. 2262; B. 1129.

un-hneáw; *adj. Not niggardly, liberal, bounteous,* (1) *giving liberally*:—Sumne hī gemētaþ geofum unhneáwne, Exon. Th. 326, 36; Vīd. 139. Ælfwine hæfde heortan unhneáweste hringa gedāles, 323, 3; Vīd. 73. (2) *given liberally, abundant*:—Geofum unhneáwum, 43, 10; Cri. 686. [*Icel.* ū-hnöggr.]

un-hoga; *adj. Unwise, foolish:*—Unhogo (-hogu, Rush.) *inprudentes*, Mk. Skt. Lind. 7, 18. Cf. wan-hoga.

un-hold; *adj.* I. *unfriendly, hostile:*—Ðæt dyde unhold mann *inimicus homo hoc fecit*, Mt. Kmbl. 13, 28. Hē āstealde swīđe strang gyld . . . and him wæs đā unhold eall đæt his ǽr gyrnde, Chr. 1040; Erl. 166, 22. Weard rīces đeóden unhold þeóden đām đe ǽhte geaf, Cd. Th. 218, 4; Dan. 34. Hē him đa sǽtnunge gewearnode đæs unholdan cyninges *regis sibi infesti insidias vitavit*, Bd. 2, 12; S. 515, 12. Ealle his ǽhta unholde fȳnd, rīce rēđe mann gedǽle, Ps. Th. 108, 11. Hē mē ālȳsde of huntum unholdum, 90, 3. II. *unfaithful, disloyal:*—Se unholda đeówa, Homl. Th. ii. 556, 18. [Monies monnes sare iswinc habbeđ oft unholde, O. E. Homl. i. 161, 36. Unholde uorureten þe strencđe of his soule *alieni comederunt robur ejus*, A. R. 222, 10. *O. Sax.* un-hold *unfriendly, hostile*: *O. H. Ger.* un-hold *inimicus*, unholde; *pl. eumenides.*] v. next word.

un-holda, an; *m. A fiend:*—Hē his āras hider onsendeþ, đī læs unholdan wunde gewyrcen, Exon. Th. 47, 29; Cri. 762. [*Goth.* un-hulþa; *m.*; un-hulþō; *f. an evil spirit*: *O. L. Ger.* un-holdo *a devil*: *O. H. Ger.* un-holda *diabolus*: *Ger.* un-hold *a fiend, devil.*]

un-hrædsprǽce; *adj. Not ready of speech:*—Ic eom unhrædsprǽce *incircumcisus sum labiis*, Ex. 6, 30.

un-hreóflig; *adj. Not leprous:*—Ne gedyde se sacerd đone man hreófligne ođđe unhreófligne, Homl. Th. i. 124, 24.

un-hrōr; *adj. Not stirring:*—Unhrōrum neátum *immobilibus animantibus*, Bt. 41, 5; Fox 254, 14. [Cf. *O. H. Ger.* un-gi[h]ruorig *immobilis.*]

un-hūfed; *adj.* (*ptcpl.*) *With the head made bare, with the head shaved:*—Unhūfed *decalvata* (the passage is: Quamvis flava caesaries raderetur et per publicum decalvata traheretur, Ald. 62), Hpt. Gl. 510, 13. v. hūfian.

un-hwearfiende; *adj.* (*ptcpl.*) *Unchanging, immutable:*—Nānwuht woruldlīces fæstes and unhwearfiendes beón ne mæg, Bt. 8; Fox 26, 11.

un-hwīlen; *adj. Not temporary, eternal:*—Him is symbel and dreám ēce, unhwȳlen, Exon. Th. 352, 13; Sch. 97. Unhwīlen, Elen. Kmbl. 2461; El. 1232. Đǽr biđ symle gearu freónd unhwīlen, Andr. Kmbl. 2309; An. 1156. Ic mē sylfum wāt æfter līces hryre leán unhwīlen, Exon. Th. 167, 27; Gū. 1066. Hē him ēce geceás langsumre līf, leóht unhwīlen, Apstls. Kmbl. 40; Ap. 20.

un-hygdig; *adj. Foolish:*—On his heortan cwæđ unhȳdig sum ungleáwlīce *dixit insipiens in corde suo*, Ps. Th. 52, 1. Hwī nǽre đū genōg earm and genōg unhȳdig (-hȳđig?), þeáh đē þūhte đæt đū welig wǽre, đonne đū ōþer twēga ođđe hæfdest đæt đū noldest, ođđe næfdest đæt đū woldest? Bt. 26, 1; Fox 90, 30 note. Cf. wan-hygdig.

un-hyldu(-o); *f. Disfavour, unfriendliness:*—Đa habbaþ his unhyldo đe hit him bryttian sceoldon *iram merentur, qui dispensatores sunt*, Past. 44; Swt. 321, 4. Him is unhyldo Waldendes witod, Cd. Th. 45, 20; Gen. 729. Þurh hine wurdon manege geypte đe mid heora rǽde on đes cynges unheldan (= hyldum?) wǽron (*who were hostile to the king*), Chr. 1095; Erl. 232, 20. [*O. Sax.* un-huldi: *O. H. Ger.* un-huldī.]

un-hȳre, un-hȳrsum. v. un-hīre, un-hīrsum.

un-hȳđig; *adj. Without that which is advantageous* or *beneficial, unhappy:*—Hwī nǽre đū đonne genōg earm and genōg unhȳþi (*printed* -hiþy; -hydig, Cott. MS.), þeáh đe þūhte đæt đū welig wǽre, đonne đū ōþer twēga ođđe hæfdest đæt đū noldest, ođđe næfdest đæt đū woldest? Bt. 26, 1; Fox 90, 30. Gewāt beorn unhȳđig (*Guthlac's disciple when he had just lost his master*), Exon. Th. 181, 32; Gū. 1302. Hié unhȳđige gecyrdon luste belorene lāđspell beran, Andr. Kmbl. 2157; An. 1080.

un-inseglian; *p.* ode *To unseal:*—Hī (*a casket*) nān man ne uninsæglode ǽr hī ealle þyder cōmon . . . Se portgerēfa hī uninsæglode, Homl. Skt. i. 23, 762. Hig uninseglodon đæt loc and cǽgan, Nicod. 14; Thw. 7, 11.

un-īđe, un-kere. v. un-eáđe, un-hīre.

un-īþian; *p.* ode *To disquiet, molest:*—Đonne mē unȳþgiende wǽron *cum me molesti essent*, Ps. Spl. T. 34, 15.

un-lācnigendlīc; *adj. Incurable:*—Unlācnigendlīce ādlu, Lchdm. i. 262, 1.

un-lācnod; *adj. Uncured:*—Hē hæfđ on his nebbe opene wunde unlācnode, Past. 9; Swt. 61, 4. v. un-gelācnod.

un-lǽce, es; *m. An unskilful physician:*—Hū unlǽcas (cf. unwīse lǽcas, 232, 8) wēnaþ đæt đæt sié lendenādl, Lchdm. ii. 164, 8.

un-lǽd, -lǽde; *adj.* I. *poor, miserable, unhappy, unfortunate:*—Unlǽde biđ and ormōd se đe ā wile geómrian, Salm. Kmbl. 699; Sal. 349. Ōđer biđ unlǽde on eorđan, ōđer biđ eádig, 731; Sal. 365. Him mæg eádig eorl eáđe geceósan mildne hlāford; ne mæg dōn unlǽde swā, 784; Sal. 391. Lōcaþ fram đam unlǽdan hlāford *his lord turns his looks from the unhappy man*, 765; Sal. 382. II. in a moral sense, *poor, miserable, wretched:*—Mē þincđ swīđe dysig man and swīđe unlǽde đe nele hys andgyt ǽcan đa hwīle đe hē on đisse weorulde byđ, Shrn. 204, 24. Unlǽde biđ on eorđan, unnyt līfes se þurh đone cantic ne can Crist geherian, Salm. Kmbl. 41; Sal. 21. Rǽd biþ nyttost, yfel unnyttost, đæt unlǽd nimeþ, Exon. Th. 341, 3; Gn. Ex. 120. Helle gǽst, earm and unlǽd, 279, 19; Jul. 616. Se unlǽda (-e, MS.) Iudas, se đe hine tō deáþe belǽwed hæfde, Wanl. Catal. 134, col. 1. Swā heó đæs unlǽdan (*Holofernes*) eáþost mihte wel gewealdan, Judth. Thw. 23, 3; Jud. 102. Đa þrowunga đe hē ādreág æt đæm unlǽdan folce Iudēa, Blickl. Homl. 97, 16. Đæt wīte, đæt đon unlǽdon geteohhod biþ; him wǽre betere đæt hē nǽfre geboren nǽre, 25, 24. Đa unlǽdan (*the chief priests who wished to kill Lazarus*, Jn. 12, 10), 77, 9. Gesǽlige beóđ đa đe đam fyliaþ, and unlǽde beóđ đa đe đam wiđsacaþ, Wulfst. 264, 21. Gē sind unlǽde earm[r]a geþōhta, Andr. Kmbl. 1487; An. 745. Unlǽdra (*the cannibals*) eafođ, 59; An. 30: (*evil spirits*), 283; An. 142. Hē æt đǽm unlǽdum Iudēum manig bysmor geþrowade, Blickl. Homl. 23, 30: 85, 1. [Þo unlede (þese wikkede, MS. V.) fode, Al. (T.) 333. Hu he is unlede (*miserable*) þat foleweþ quene rede, Misc. 122, 337: O. and N. 1644. *Goth.* un-lēds *poor.*] v. un-lǽdlīce.

un-lǽde; *adj. Stray* (?):—Đā forstæl hē đa unlǽdan oxan, Chart. Th. 172, 21.

un-lǽdlīce; *adv. Miserably, wretchedly:*—Hē (*Judas*) hine sylfne swīđe earme and unlǽdlīce of đære gemǽnan ealra Godes gecorenra ādilgode, Homl. Ass. 153, 48. Hē hine sylfne swīđe unlǽdlīce āhēng and swā ungesǽliglīce tō ēcan deáđe wæs geniđerad, 158, 163.

un-lǽgne. v. un-līgne.

un-lǽne; *adj. Not transitory, permanent:*—For đissum lǽnan līfe ic sylle đæt unlǽne, Wulfst. 264, 18.

un-lǽred; *adj. Untaught, unlearned, ignorant:*—Gelaered ođđe unlaered *doctus vel indoctus*, Mt. Kmbl. p. 1, 6. Hū mæg unlǽred dēma ōđerne lǽran? L. I. P. 19; Th. ii. 326, 32. Đætte unlǽrede (-lǽrde, Hatt. MS.) ne dyrren underfōn lāreówdōm *ne venire imperiti ad magisterium audeant*, Past. 1; Swt. 24, 14. Tō đon đæt unlǽrede sȳn gelǽrede *ut indocti doceantur*, Bd. 1, 27; S. 492, 24. Đū ongytest đæt hié syndon unlǽrede men, Blickl. Homl. 183, 7. Hwā unlǽredra ne wundraþ . . . ? Bt. 39, 3; Fox 214, 15: Met. 28, 1. v. un-gelǽred.

un-læt; *adj. Not slow, quick, ready, active:*—Unlæt *non pigra*, Wrt. Voc. ii. 61, 61. Wīga, unlæt lāces (*death*), Exon. Th. 164, 5; Gū. 1007. Hræd and unlæt, 436, 9; Rä. 54, 11.

un-lāf, e; *f. A child not left by a father at his death, a child born after the father's death, a posthumous child:*—Unlāb *posthumus*, Wrt. Voc. ii. 117, 67. Unlāf, 69, 2: 93, 70.

un-lagu, e; *f.* I. *violation of law, illegality, injustice:*—Mid unlage *contra justitiam*, Cod. Dip. Kmbl. iv. 198, 15: 224, 11. Đeáh đe Harold đæt land mid unlage ūt nam, 274, 29. Ic nelle geđafian đat man hym ǽnige unlage beóde *nec impune feram quod aliquis ei injuriam inferat aut molestiam*, 196, 27: vi. 187, 22. Se đe unlage rǽre oþþe undōm gedēme, L. C. S. 15; Th. i. 384, 9: Chr. 1052; Erl. 186, 2. Đæt man rihte lage up ārǽre and ǽlce unlage āfylle, L. Eth. v. 1; Th. i. 304, 11. Fela unrihta and yfelra unlaga ārysan, Chr. 975; Erl. 127, 30. Æt unlagum *unlawfully* (cf. *Icel.* at ūlögum *in a lawless manner*), L. C. S. 61; Th. i. 408, 18. Swicollīce dǽda and lāđlīce unlaga āscunige man, đæt is, false gewihta . . . and leáse gewitnessa, L. Eth. v. 24; Th. i. 310, 12: vi. 28; Th. i. 322, 13. Đæt man rihte laga up ārǽre, and ǽghwylce unlaga georne āfylle, vi. 8; Th. i. 316, 26: L. C. S. 1; Th. i. 376, 8: 11; Th. i. 382, 7: Wulfst. 156, 13. Hē ne rōhte nā hū manige unlaga hī dydon, Chr. 1086; Erl. 220, 13. II. *a bad law:*—Man behāteþ, đonne man fulluhtes gyrneþ, đæt man aa wile deófol āscunian, and his unlāra forbūgan and ealle his unlaga āweorpan, Wulfst. 144, 10. Cradolcild wǽron geþeówode þurh wælhreówe unlaga for lytelre þȳfđe, 158, 14. [*Icel.* ū-lög; *pl. lawlessness, injustice.*]

un-land, es; *n. What is not land:*—On đam fīftan dǽle healfum londes and unlondes (*sea, marsh, etc.*), Bt. 18, 1; Fox 62, 23. Tō đam unlonde (*the whale, by whose side seamen, 'deeming him some island,' moor their bark*), Exon. Th. 361, 3; Wal. 14.

un-landāgende; *adj. Not owning land:*—Gesīđcund mon unlandāgende, L. In. 51; Th. i. 134, 9.

un-lār, e; *f. Evil teaching, incitement to evil:*—Đa đe nū deófle fyligaþ and his unlārum, Wulfst. 19, 17: 37, 12. Se đe gehealt Godes beboda, and forbūhđ deófles unlārum, L. I. P. 21; Th. ii. 330, 28. Đæt hē forsace and forbūge deófles unlāra, Wulfst. 32, 15: 144, 9.

un-leahtorwirþe; *adj. Unblameable:*—Godes ǽ is swīđe unleahtorwyrđe *lex Domini inreprehensibilis*, Ps. Th. 18, 7.

un-leánod; *adj. Not repaid:*—Ic wille, gif ic ǽnigum menn ǽnig feoh unleánod hæbbe, đæt mīne māgas đæt geleánian, Chart. Th. 491, 5.

un-leás; *adj. Not false, true:*—Unleás *non frivola, non falsa*, Hpt. Gl. 432, 21. Se biđ unleás forscrencend đe his leahtras forscrencđ, Homl. Th. i. 586, 23. Wē willaþ eów gereccan ōđres mannes gesihđe đe unleás is, ii. 332, 26. Gelȳf hys hālgum, for đam hī wēron swīđe unleáse gewitan, Shrn. 199, 14. Unleásra manna sægena, 195, 29. Hweđer đē đince Honorius wīsra ođđe unleásera đonne Crist, 196, 27. Wīsran and unleáseran đegnas, 197, 8.

un-leáslīce; *adv. Not falsely, truly:*—Heó geseah đæt his bodung unleáslīce gefylled wæs, Homl. Th. i. 42, 29. Gif wē đæt geđyld on ūrum mōde unleáslīce healdaþ, ii. 546, 1. Hē cwæđ đis unleáslīce, 386,

10. Mid ânfealdnysse sprece hê ǽfre unleáslîce, L. Ælfc. C. 30; Th. ii. 354, 5.

un-leóf; *adj. Not dear, not beloved, odious, hateful*:—Sodomware, Gode unleófe, Cd. Th. 148, 6; Gen. 2452. Gigantmæcgas, Gode unleófe, Metode láðe, 77, 1; Gen. 1268. Wîglâf seah on unleófe (*the followers who had failed Beowulf in his need*), Beo. Th. 5719; B. 2863. [Al þat is on unlef and unqueme, hit is þat oðer iqueme, O. E. Homl. ii. 189, 25. *Goth.* un-liubs *not beloved*: *O. H. Ger.* un-liup *insuavis, non optatus.*]

un-leoþuwâc; *adj. Inflexible, intractable, implacable*:—Unlioþuwâc (-lidouuâc, -liuduuâc) *intractabilis*, Txts. 69, 1079. Unliþewâc (in-, MS.), Wrt. Voc. ii. 48, 72. Ðâ wæs mîn hlâford in micle hâtheortnysse, and hê wæs swîðe unlioðewâc geworden wið mê, and hê gebrægd his swurd and wolde mê ofsleán, Shrn. 39, 14. [*O. H. Ger.* un-lidoweih *invulsus, inplicabilis, implacabilis.*]

un-leoþuwâcness, e; *f. Inflexibility, implacability*:—Unlioþuwâcnis *infestatio*, Wrt. Voc. ii. 110, 65. Unleoþowâcnes, 45, 42.

un-libbende; *adj. Not living, dead*:—Se dyde monig wundor ge lybbende ge unlybbende, Shrn. 127, 22. v. un-lifigende.

un-lîchamlîc; *adj. Incorporeal*:—Seó sâwul is unlîchomlîc, Homl. Skt. i. 1, 176. Unlîchamlîce *incorporalia*, Ælfc. Gr. 5; Zup. 11, 19: 9, 21; Zup. 47, 2.

un-lîcwirþe; *adj. Unpleasing, disagreeable*:—Nimaþ mê mid eów; ne beó ic nâ eów unlîcwyrðe, Homl. Skt. ii. 23 b, 374.

un-lîfed; *adj. Unallowed, illicit*:—Unliéfedo *illicitum*, Past. 51; Swt. 397, 30. Sió unliéfde byrðen *pondus illicitum*, Swt. 401, 5. Fleón ðone unliéfedan bryne ûres lîchoman *illicita carnis incendia declinare*, Swt. 397, 36. Ða ðe ðæt unliéfde herigaþ *qui illicita laudant*, 55; Swt. 427, 11.

un-lîfes; *adv. Not alive*:—Hê is nû unlîfes, Homl. Skt. i. 18, 203.

un-lifigende; *adj. Not living, dead, defunct*:—Unlifigendes fêt and folma, Beo. Th. 1492; B. 744. Heáfod Holofernus unlyfigendes, Judth. Thw. 24, 9; Jud. 180. Unlifgendes, Elen. Kmbl. 1754; El. 879. Siteþ eorl ofer ôðrum unlifigendum (*Beowulf*), Beo. Th. 5809; B. 2908. Ðæt biþ drihtguman unlifgendum æfter sêlest, 2782; B. 1389. Hê aldorþegn unlyfigendne, deádne wisse, 2621; B. 1308. Fore gileáffullum unlifigendum *pro fidelibus defunctis*, Rtl. 173, 37. Fore deádum ł unlifiendum, Jn. Skt. p. 4, 20. On heora ealdfeóndum unlyfigendum, Judth. Thw. 26, 8; Jud. 316. v. un-libbende.

un-lîgne; *adj. Not to be denied* or *rejected, incontrovertible*:—Biscopes word and cyninges sié unlǽgne bûton âðe *a bishop's word and a king's is to be accepted without an oath*, L. Wih. 16; Th. i. 40, 12. Þissa ealra âð sié unlêgnæ, 21; Th. i. 42, 1. v. lîgnian, *and* cf. *O. H. Ger.* lougenîg *negativus.*

un-lîsan; *p.* de. I. *to unloose, undo*:—Ic bidde ðê ðæt ðû mê unlŷse ða insæglunge, Homl. Skt. i. 3, 537. II. *to release*:—Hê beád ðæt man sceolde unlêsan ealle ða menn ðe on hæftnunge wǽron, Chr. 1086; Erl. 223, 38.

un-lîþe; *adj. Ungentle, harsh, severe, cruel*:—Ðê tô heortan hearde gripeþ âdl unlîðe, Cd. Th. 57, 32; Gen. 937. Geliðewâca ðisne unlîðan cyle, Homl. Skt. i. 11, 192. Scearpnyssa beóð âwende tô smêðum wegum, ðonne ða yrsigendan môd and unlîðe gecyrraþ tô manðwǽrnysse, Homl. Th. i. 362, 30.

un-lofod; *adj. Unpraised*:—Ne lǽt ðû unlofod ðæt ðû swutele ongite ðæt lîcwyrðe sŷ; ðǽr ðê âuht tweóge, lofa ðæt gemetlîce, Prov. Kmbl. 62.

un-lûcan; *p.* -leác *To unclose, open*:—Godes engel unleác ðæt cweartern, Homl. Skt. ii. 25, 839. *Hostiarius* is ðære cyrcean durewerd, se sceal ða cyrcan unlûcan geleáffullum mannum, and ðâm ungeleáffullum belûcan wiðûtan, L. Ælfc. C. 11; Th. ii. 346, 29. Nân man ne dorste ða duru unlûcan, Homl. Ass. 113, 360.

un-lust, es; *m.* I. *absence of desire, disgust, disinclination.* (a) *want of appetite*:—Lǽcedôm gif men unlust (cf. *Ger.* Unlust zum Essen) sié getenge, Lchdm. ii. 16, 15: 150, 17. Wiþ metes unluste, 184, 15: 28, 5. Wiþ unluste and wlætan þe of magan cymð, 158, 12. Wiþ sâre and unluste ðæs magan, se ðe ne mæg ne mid mete ne mid drincan beón gelâcnod, 158, 17. Hié þrowiaþ ormǽtne þurst and metes unlust, 230, 19. Ungemetlîca metesôcna and ungemetlîce unlustas and cîsnessa, 174, 28. [Þi mahe wið unlust warpeð hit (*food*) eft ut, H. M. 35, 31. *Icel.* û-lyst *a bad appetite.*] (b) *disinclination to action, listlessness*:—Hê (*the slothful servant*) ðolaþ neádunge þeóstra ðurh wrace, se ðe ǽr lustlîce forbær his unlustes (*or under* III? cf. 552, 12) þeóstra, Homl. Th. ii. 556, 22. [Ʒæn unnlusst and forrswundennleȝȝc, Orm. 4562. He doth alle thing with slaknes and excusacioun, and with ydelnes and unlust, Chauc. Pers. T. (de accidia). *Goth.* wairþan in unlustau ἀθυμεῖν.] II. *want of pleasure, joylessness, weariness*:—For unluste *prae taedio*, Ps. Spl. T. 118, 28. Hê wylleþ hine on ðam wîte, wunaþ unlustum (cf. lustum, on lustum), Salm. Kmbl. 538; Sal. 268. [*O. H. Ger.* un-lust *taedium, fastidium.*] III. *an evil pleasure, lust*:—Ne unlust on hire môd ne becom, Homl. Th. ii. 10, 10. Ðâ gestôd hine micel lîchamlîc costung . . . hê âwende ðone unlust tô sârnysse, 156, 32. Unlusta *voluptatum*, Scint. 106, 10. Ealle hyra unlustas hî sceolon gebêtan sylfwylles on ðyssum lîfe, oððe unþances æfter ðyssum lîfe, Homl. Th. i. 148, 27. Þurh unlustas *libidinibus*, L. Ecg. C. 5, tit.; Th. ii. 128, 15. Winnan wið leahtras and unlustas forseón, L. Ælfc. P. 12; Th. ii. 368, 19.

un-lustian. v. ge-unlustian.

un-lybba (*and* un-lybbe, an; *f.*, *or* un-lybb; *dat.* -lybbe; *n.?*), an; *m.* I. *poison*:—Sumum men wæs unlybba geseald, ac hit ne mihte hine âdŷdan, Homl. Th. ii. 178, 11. Unþeáwas weaxaþ on yfel, swa swa âtres unlibba on men; swâ hê leng ðæs âttres þigene bedîhlaþ, swâ wyrð his untrumnes mâre, R. Ben. 135, 16. Unlybbe *delatera* (*deletera?*), Wrt. Voc. ii. 138, 55. Hî rǽddon ðæt hî mid âttre hine âcwealdon; gemengdon ðâ unlybban tô his drence, Homl. Th. ii. 158, 15. Hê ðygde unlybban on his mete, 504, 14. Hê ðone unlybban hâlsode, and hine ealne gedranc, i. 72, 24, 19: L. Pen. 7; Th. ii. 280, 6: 6; Th. ii. 280, 2: Wulfst. 150, 5. Wiþ unlybbum, Lchdm. ii. 292, 30. II. *poison* used for purposes of witchcraft, *witchcraft, sorcery*:—Gif wîf drŷcræft and galdor and unlibban wyrce . . . Gif heó mid hire unlybban man âcwelleþ *si mulier artem magicam, et incantationes, et maleficia exerceat . . . si maleficiis suis aliquem occiderit*, L. Ecg. C. 29; Th. ii. 154, 8–11. Ðæs flǽsces weorc . . . hǽðengild oððe unlybban (*veneficia*, Gal. 5, 19), Homl. Skt. i. 17, 25. Ðînre môdor fela unlybban *matris tuae veneficia multa* (2 Kings 9, 22), 18, 333. [Cf. *Icel.* û-lyfjan *poison.*] v. geunlybba, lybb, *and next word.*

unlyb-wyrhta, an; *m. A poison-maker, one who prepares poisons for purposes of witchcraft, a sorcerer*:—Unlybwyrhta *veneficus*, Wrt. Voc. i. 74, 39. Wyccan and wælcyrian and unlybwyrhtan, Wulfst. 298, 19. Antecrist hæfð mid him drŷmen and unlybwyrhtan and wîgleras and ða ðe cunnan galder âgalan, 194, 18. Unlibwyrht[en]a wiccecræft *maleficorum* (*venenificorum*) *necromantia*, Hpt. Gl. 501, 62.

un-lyft, e; *f. Bad air, malaria*:—Rômâne and eall sûðfolc worhton him eorþhûs wið ðære unlyfte, Lchdm. ii. 16, 2.

un-lygen; *adj. Unlying, truthful*:—Ceápige man on ðæs portgerêfan gewitnesse oþþe ôðres unlygenes mannes, L. Ath. i. 12; Th. i. 206, 10. [*Icel.* û-lyginn. Cf. *O. H. Ger.* lugîn *mendax.*] v. un-gelygen.

un-lyt; *n. No little, much*:—Gê mânes unlyt wyrceaþ, Ps. Th. 61, 9.

un-lytel; *adj.* I. of size, extent, *not little, great*:—Wê magon tôcnâwan be hyre leóman ðæt seó sunne unlytel is, Lchdm. iii. 236, 11. Wolcen unlytel, Ps. Th. 77, 16. Unlytel dǽl foldan, Cd. Th. 154, 4; Gen. 2550. Unlytel dǽl eorþan gesceafta, 97, 17; Gen. 1614. Unlytel leádes clympre, Exon. Th. 426, 17; Rä. 41, 75. Hê geseah sweras unlytle, Andr. Kmbl. 2985; An. 1495. II. of quantity, amount, number, *not little, not few in number, much*:—Tô miclum bryne sceal wæter unlytel, Wulfst. 157, 9. Menigo, folc unlytel, Elen. Kmbl. 1740; El. 872: 565; El. 283: Andr. Kmbl. 2542; An. 1272: Beo. Th. 1000; B. 498. Se eorl com mid unlytlan weorode, Chr. 1068; Erl. 206, 10. Mycel feoh and unlytel *summam pecuniae non parvam*, Bd. 4, 11; S. 579, 20: 4, 5; S. 571, 35. Micle lâc and unlytle ælmessan, Wulfst. 278, 5. Ic him gestrŷnde unlytel folc, Homl. Th. i. 592, 31. Hyre wer lǽfde unlytle ǽhta on lande and on feó, Homl. Skt. i. 2, 155. III. of quality, degree, *not little, great*, (a) of persons:—Hê ðûhte him selfum suîðe unlytel and suîðe medeme *se parvulum non videbat*, Past. 17; Swt. 113, 12. (b) of things:—Storm, cirm unlytel, Andr. Kmbl. 2476; An. 1239. Dôm unlytel, Beo. Th. 1775; B. 885: Apstls. Kmbl. 16; Ap. 8. Wundor unlytel, Cd. Th. 250, 26; Dan. 522. Unlytel spell *a tale of serious import*, 145, 14; Gen. 2405. Torn unlytel, Beo. Th. 1670; B. 833. Wundur unlytel *mirabilia*, Ps. Th. 104, 5. [Cf. *Icel.* û-lîtill.]

un-lytel, es; *n. No small amount, much*:—Eft wearð folces unlytel, Wulfst. 10, 17. Hê lǽfde þære wudewan unlytel on feó and on ôðrum ǽhtum, Homl. Ass. 108, 200: Chr. 921; Erl. 106, 14.

un-mǽg, es; *m. One who is not a kinsman, an alien*; or *a bad kinsman*:—Unmǽgas, Wald. 102; Vald. 2, 23.

un-mǽge; *adj. Not of kin, not related, alien*:—Ic wæs unmǽge gyst môdor cildum *factus sum hospes filiis matris meae*, Ps. Th. 68, 8.

un-mægness, e; *f. Inability, weariness*:—Ǽþrot, unmægnes, ǽmelnes *fastidium*, Wrt. Voc. ii. 146, 46. v. un-maga.

un-mægþlîc. v. un-mǽþlîc.

un-mǽle; *adj. Spotless*, (1) in a physical sense, *without marks* or *spots*:—Ǽt ânes heówes cŷ, ðæt heó sŷ eall reád oððe hwît and unmǽle, Lchdm. iii. 24, 14. (2) in a moral sense, *immaculate, virgin*:—Unmaelo *virgo*, Wrt. Voc. ii. 123, 75. Ðurh ðingunge his ðære eádigan mêder ðære unmǽlan fǽmnan Sca Marian *per intercessionem beatae suae genetricis semperque virginis Mariae*, Bd. 5, 19; S. 640, 42. Hât unmǽlne mon gefeccean swîgende ongeán streáme healfne sester yrnendes wæteres, Lchdm. iii. 10, 31. Þê (*the Virgin Mary*) unmǽle ǽlces þinges, Exon. Th. 21, 11; Cri. 333. Hê on fǽmnan âstâg, mægeð unmǽle, 45, 18; Cri. 721.

un-mǽne; *adj.* I. *free from evil, pure*, (1) of persons:—Þeáh þe þû welig beó þû nâ byst unmǽne fram gylte (*inmunis a delicto*), Scint. 179, 10. Sancta Maria, ides unmǽne, Hy. 10, 14. Fram ealre synne unmǽne *ab omni peccato inmunes*, Scint. 67, 20. (2) of an oath, *without* *perjury* :—Se āþ is clǣne and unmǣne, L. O. 6; Th. i. 180, 18. II. *free from, exempt from, not sharing in* :—Ālȳsede fram bende ǣlces mennissces dōmes, fram ǣlcere gærsuman woruldlīcra brūcunga clǣne and unmǣne *nexu humanae conditionis exuti, ab omni munere secularium functionum immunes*, Cod. Dip. B. i. 154, 16. [*O. Frs.* un-mēn *unperjured*: *O. H. Ger.* dhiu unmeina magad Maria: *Icel.* ū-meinn *harmless*.]

un-mǣre; *adj. Not illustrious, inglorious* :—Þeáh hē on ðam lande seó mǣre ðonne biþ hē on ōþrum unmǣre *fit, ut quem tu aestimas gloriosum, pro maxima parte terrarum videatur inglorius*, Bt. 30, 1; Fox 108, 16.

un-mǣrlīc; *adj. Ignoble* :—Hwæþer ðē þynce unweorþ and unmǣrlīc seó gegaderung *obscurumne hoc, atque ignobile censes esse?* Bt. 33, 1; Fox 120, 29.

un-mǣte; *adj. Immense, enormous, excessive* :—Þeód unmǣte, Cd. Th. 138, 15; Gen. 2292. Sīde herigeas, folc unmǣte, Andr. Kmbl. 1305; An. 653: Menol. Fox 11; Men. 6. Gebrec unmǣte, Exon. Th. 59, 18; Cri. 954. Ðæt unmǣte gestreón goldes and seolfres, Blickl. Homl. 99, 28. Ðæt unmǣte sār weóx *augescente dolore nimio*, Bd. 3, 9; S. 533, 32: 4, 25; S. 599, 43. Micelne swēg unmǣtes wōpes *sonitum immanissimi fletus*, 5, 12; S. 628, 29. Ðæt mægen ðære unmǣtan (*immensi*) hǣto . . . on middel ðæs unmǣtan (*infesti*) cyles, S. 627, 41, 42: Homl. Skt. ii. 23 b, 573. Bōc unmǣtre (*enormis*) micelnesse, Bd. 5, 13; S. 633, 5: Guthl. 3; Gdwin. 20, 1. Mid unmǣtan here, Chr. 1068; Erl. 206, 21. Mid unmǣte ege geslægene *timore immenso perculsus*, Bd. 5, 12; S. 627, 14. On ǣnne unmǣtne lēg geānede *in inmensam adunati flammam*, 3, 19; S. 548, 21. Giefe unmǣte, Exon. Th. 273, 16; Jul. 517. Ðǣr synd unmǣte mōras, Guthl. 3; Gdwin. 20, 4. Ðǣr synt ða unmǣtan tyntregu, L. E. I. prm.; Th. ii. 396, 34. Ic wæs on unmǣtum costnungum winnende, Homl. Skt. ii. 23 b, 578. [Mid unmete drunche, O. E. Homl. i. 103, 9. *O. H. Ger.* un-māzi *immensus, ingens*.]

un-mǣþ, e; *f. Transgression, wrong*. v. mǣþ, IV:—Ða discipulas wǣron on heora mōdgeþance swīðlīce āfyrhte and gedrēfde, swā hit nǣnig fyren wæs (unmǣþ næs, MS. F. i. e. *it was perfectly right that they should be troubled*), Homl. Ass. 162, 234. [Min is þe guld and þe unmeþ, Fl. a. Bl. 675. Evrich þing mai leosen his godhede mid unmeþe and mid overdede, O. and N. 352.]

un-mǣþlīc; *adj. Not in due measure, immoderate, excessive* :—Of gītsunge beóð ācennede . . . leás gewitnyss and unmǣðlīc neádung, Homl. Th. ii. 220, 11. [So hit unmeðluker is, wunnen aȝean þe uestluker, A. R. 238, 17.]

un-mǣþlīce; *adv.* I. *immoderately, out of measure* :—Seó wydewe mænigfealde sceattas hyre unmǣðlīce beád (*was immoderate in her offers*), Homl. Skt. i. 2, 147. Hē hēt ðone bisceop unscrȳdan and unmǣðlīce (*or* II) swingan, ii. 29, 231. II. *inhumanely*. v. mǣþlīce:—Ða ðe hæfdon sum þing lytles tō bigleofan, ðæt gelæhton reáferas and of ðam mūðe him ābrudon unmǣðlīce mid þreáte, Homl. Ass. 68, 73. Ǣlc læhte of ōðrum ðone mete of ðam mūðe swīðe unmægðlīce, Ælfc. T. Grn. 21, 11. [For lutle ich mei makien to muchelin unmeaðeliche, ȝef me hut hit, Marh. 15, 9. Ȝeieð luddre and unmeðluker, A. R. 266, 1.]

un-mǣtlīc; *adj. Immense* :—Laforas unmǣtlīcre micelnisse *capri ingentis forme*, Nar. 15, 2. [*O. H. Ger.* un-māzlīh *incomparabilis*. Cf. *Icel.* ū-mātaliga *immoderately*.]

un-mǣtness, e; *f. Immenseness, excess* :—Fore unmǣtnysse ðæs gewinnes *ob nimietatem laboris*, Bd. 3, 8; S. 532, 31. Mid unmǣtnesse miceles stormes *tempestatis impetu*, 5, 12; S. 627, 40. Ðā cwom micel snāw . . . ðā ic ða unmǣtnisse and micelnisse ðæs snāwes geseah, ða ðūhte mē ðæt ic wiste ðæt hē wolde ealle ða wīcstōwe forfeallan *cadere mox . . . immense ceperunt nives quarum aggregationem metuens ne castra cumularentur*, Nar. 23, 14.

un-maga, an; *m.*: un-magu; *f.* I. *a person without means, a needy person* :—Se maga and se unmaga ne beóð nā gelīce, ne ne magon nā gelīce byrðene āhebban . . . and ðȳ man sceal gescādlīce tōscādan . . . welan and wǣdle, L. Eth. vi. 52; Th. i. 328, 16: L. C. S. 69; Th. i. 412, 6. Ðis is mihtiges mannes and freóndspēdiges dǣdbōtlihtingc, ac ān unmaga ne mæg swilc geforðian, L. P. M. 4; Th. ii. 288, 22. Ðū ne scealt nǣfre gelīce dēman . . . ðam strangan and ðam unmagan, L. de Cf. 3; Th. ii. 260, 25. Ðearfan and unmagon *pauperem et inopem*, Ps. Spl. 36, 15. II. *a person who cannot maintain himself, one who is dependent upon others* :—Mardocheus hæfde Hester for dohtor, for ðan hire deád wæs ge fæder ge mōdor, ðā ðā heó unmagu (-maga, *v. l.*) wæs, Homl. Ass. 94, 86. Gif hwā ōðrum his unmagan ōðfæste, L. Alf. pol. 17; Th. i. 72, 4. [On-mawe, Fer. i. 2658. *O. H. Ger.* un-mag *segnis, dissolutus; parvulus*: *Icel.* ū-magi *one who cannot maintain himself*, e. g. a child.]

un-manig; *adj. Not many, few* :—Æfter unmonegum geárum *post aliquot annos*, Bd. 3, 17; S. 544, 9: 5, 18; S. 636, 18. Unmonigum dagum *non multis diebus*, Jn. Skt. Lind. 2, 12. Ymbe unmanige dagas, Guthl. 2; Gdwin. 18, 26: 3; Gdwin. 22, 17: 5; Gdwin. 34, 13. Unmonige *paucos*, Mt. Kmbl. p. 15, 7. Unmonige fiscas *paucos pisciculos*, Mt. Kmbl. Rush. 15, 34. [*O. H. Ger.* un-manig.]

un-mann, es; *m.* I. *a bad man, an inhuman person* :—Swā fela ðūsend engla mihton eáðe bewerian Crist wið ðām unmannum (*those who came to seize Jesus*), gif hē ðrowian nolde sylfwilles for ūs, Homl. Th. ii. 246, 30. [Cf. *O. H. Ger.* un-menniscо: *Ger.* un-mensch: *Icel.* ū-mannan *a person fit for nothing*.] II. *one who is not a mere man, a hero* :—Ðā gemunde hē ða strangan dǣda ðara unmanna (*perhaps* iumanna *should be read; the Latin is*: Valida priscorum heroum facta reminiscens. v. geó-, iú-mann) and ðæra woruldfrumena, Guthl. 2; Gdwin. 12, 27.

un-meagol; *adj. Feeble, insipid* :—Unmeagol *emellus*, Wrt. Voc. ii. 143, 30. *Insipidum, quod saporem non habet, hoc est* unmeagle *sive* ǣmelle, 49, 37.

un-meaht, -meht, -mieht, -miht, e; *f. Weakness, lack of power* :—Heora unmiht and heora untrymð is swīðe gemanifealdod *multiplicatae sunt infirmitates eorum*, Ps. Th. 15, 3. Biþ geond fingras cele and cneówa unmeht, Lchdm. ii. 258, 14. Gif ðē þince ðæt ðū maran lǣcedōm dōn ne durre for unmihte ðæs mannes, 254, 1: Homl. Skt. i. 13, 21. Ðā ongan ic þencan ðæt mē ðæt gelumpe for ðære wīflīcan unmihte, ii. 23 b, 411. Ðurh unmihte, Homl. Th. ii. 42, 27. Hié ongietaþ hiera unbældo and hiera unmiehte (-mihte, Cott. MSS.) *infirmitatis suae sunt conscii*, Past. 32; Swt. 209, 8. Hū magan ða cyningas forhelan hiora unmihte, ðonne hī ne magan nǣnne weorþscipe forþbringan būton heora þegna fultume? Bt. 29, 1; Fox 104, 13. Ōð unmihte, Ps. Th. 106, 17. Ne bióð ðæt nāne mihta ðæt mon mæge yfel dōn, ac beóþ unmihta, Bt. 36, 7; Fox 182, 28. Hió his unmehta hine gemyndgaþ *infirmitatis memoriam ad mentem revocat*, Past. 65; Swt. 465, 32. Wurþaþ hig þurh ðæs mettruman unmihta beswicene, Wulfst. 285, 11. [Monnes unmihte *hominis infirmitatem*, Kath. 1022. *Goth.* un-mahts: *O. H. Ger.* un-maht *inbecillitas, inpotentia, infirmitas*: *Icel.* ū-māttr.] v. mōdunmeaht.

un-meaht; *adj. Impossible* :—Nǣniht unmæht bið iúh *nihil inpossibile erit vobis*, Mt. Kmbl. Lind. 17, 20. [Un-maht *impotent*, A. D. 297.]

un-meahtelīc (-mihte-, -miht-); *adj. Impossible* :—Eów ne byð ǣnig þing unmihtelīc *nihil inpossibile erit vobis*, Mt. Kmbl. 17, 20: Lk. Skt. 1, 37. Unmihtlīc is *inpossibile est*, 17, 1. Ða þing ðe mannum synt unmihtelīce, 18, 27. [*O. H. Ger.* un-mahtlīh *impossibilis*: *Icel.* ū-māttuligr *impossible*.] v. un-meahtiglīc.

un-meahtig, -mehtig, -mihtig; *adj.* I. *not mighty, weak, impotent, of little power* or *means* :—Unmihtig *inpos*, Ælfc. Gr. 9, 31; Zup. 58, 2: *inpotens*, 14; Zup. 87, 13. Ys Drihtnes hand unmihtig (*invalida*)? Num. 11, 23. Gif ic beó bescoren, ðonne beó ic unmihtig (*recedet a me fortitudo mea et deficiam*), Jud. 16, 17, 19. Mannes fultum is unmihtig and īdel *vana salus hominis*, Ælfc. T. Grn. 11, 41. Ðē læs ðe unmihtig man feorr for his āgenon swince, L. Ff.; Th. i. 224, 27. Tō ānum mǣdene unmihtigum tō wīge, Homl. Skt. i. 10, 257. Ðȳ læs mon unmihtigne man tō feor for his āgenan swencte, L. Eth. ii. 9; Th. i. 290, 3. Ongit hū unmihtige ða yfelan men beóþ *vide quanta vitiosorum hominum pateat infirmitas*, Bt. 36, 5; Fox 180, 2: 29, 1; Fox 104, 12: 36, 2; Fox 174, 27. Unmehtige, Met. 24, 62. Ne bepǣce nān man hine sylfne, ðæt hē secge, ðæt ǣnig hād sȳ unmihtigra ðonne ōðer, Homl. Th. i. 284, 17. Swā hwæt swā unmihtigre bið, ðæt ne bið nā God, 228, 27: Hexam. 3; Norm. 6, 7, 5. Hū micle unmihtegran hī wǣron, Bt. 36, 5; Fox 180, 4. II. *impossible* :—Ðis unmæhtig is *hoc impossibile est*, Mt. Kmbl. Lind. 19, 26: Mk. Skt. Lind. Rush. 10, 27. Unmæhtigo (-mæhtge, Rush.) *inpossibilia*, Lk. Skt. Lind. 18, 27. [Adam bicom unmihti, O. E. Homl. ii. 35, 8. Þilke unmyȝty tyraunt, Chauc. Boet. 13, 241. *Goth.* un-mahteigs *weak; impossible*: *O. H. Ger.* un-mahtīg *invalidus, infirmus, imbecillis*: *Icel.* ū-māttigr *weak, infirm*.]

un-meahtiglīc; *adj.* I. *weak* :—Hē biþ unmehtiglīc, Lchdm. ii. 60, 8. Unmihtiglīc, iii. 74, 23. II. *impossible* :—Unmæhtiglīc (-iclīc, Lind.) *inpossibile*, Lk. Skt. Rush. 1, 37: 17, 1. Suīðe unmæghtiglīc, Lind. 18, 24. v. un-meahtelīc.

un-meahtigness, e; *f. Weakness, impotence* :—Sume men secgeaþ, ðæt heó him unmihtignesse and untrumnysse on gebrincge, Lchdm. i. 248, 23. Heó fremaþ wið ða unmihticnysse ðæs migðan and wið ðæra innoða āstyrunga, 272, 16.

un-medume (-ome, -eme); *adj. Unmeet, unfit, unworthy* :—Se ðe him ondrǣdan sceal ðæt hē unmedome (-eme, Cott. MSS.) sié *hoc indignus pertimescat*, Past. 11; Swt. 73, 21. Him ðūhte selfum ðæt hē wǣre swīðe unmedeme *parvulum se in suis oculis viderat*, 17; Swt. 112, 11. Ic swīðe unmeodum nēðde tō Dryhtnes līchoman, Anglia xi. 99, 70. Hwylc ðæt unmedeme gōd wæs *quae sit imperfecti boni forma*, Bt. 34, 1; Fox 134, 5. Drihten, ðū ðe eall medemu geworhtest and nāht unmedemes, Shrn. 165, 31. Hāt mē unmedemre ða duru beón untȳnede, Homl. Skt. ii. 23 b, 447. Ongitan hū micelne unweorþscipe se anwald brengþ ðam unmedeman, Bt. 27, 2; Fox 96, 10. Ða ðe unmedome bióð tō ðære lāre for unwisdōme *quos a praedicatione imperfectio prohibet*, Past. 49; Swt. 375, 18. Gestīran ðære wilnunge ðǣm unmedemum, ðæt hiera nān ne durre grīpan on ðæt rīce *ne imperfecti culmen arripere* *regiminis audeant*, 4; Swt. 41, 5. Ða ðe hē unmedume gemētte ðes Godes geleáfan, Anglia x. 141, 18. [Cf. *O. H. Ger.* un-metamî *intemperies*.]

un-medumlîce; *adv. Unmeetly, unworthily*:—Is swîðe frēcendlîc ðæt ðæm hūsle hwā ungeclǣnsod and unmedumlîce onfoo, L. E. G. 44; Th. ii. 440, 22. Mînne hād ic hæbbe unmedumlîce gehealden, L. de Cf. 9; Th. ii. 264, 10. Unmeodomlîce, Anglia xi. 99, 60.

un-meltung, e; *f. Indigestion*:—For unmeltunge, Lchdm. ii. 254, 1.

un-menged; *adj. Unmixed*:—Se unmengeda *non mixta*, Wrt. Voc. ii. 59, 78. Hē (*Adam*) of ðære eorðan selfre unmængedre gesceapen wæs, Anglia xi. 1, 9. v. un-gemenged.

un-menniscllîc; *adj. Inhuman*:—Wē hērdon on ealdum spellum, ðæt sum sunu ofslōge his fæder, ic nāt hūmeta, būton wē witon ðæt hit unmennislîc (-lîcu, Cott. MS.) dǣd wæs *nimis e natura dictum est, nescio quem filios invenisse tortores*, Bt. 31, 1; Fox 112, 16.

un-met[t], es; *n. Excess*:—Of ðam unmetta and ðam ungemetlîcan gegerelan, of ðām swētmettum and of mistlîcum dryncum (cf. of ungemete ǣlces þinges, wiste and wǣda, wîngedrinces, and of swētmetann (-mettum?), Met. 25, 38), Bt. 37, 1; Fox 186, 16. [Cf. *O. H. Ger.* unmez:—In guotis unmezze *in luxuria*.] v. next words.

un-met[t], -mete; *adj. Without measure, immense, excessive*:—Wæs seó ēhtnysse unmetre eallum ðām ǣrgedōnum *quae persecutio omnibus anteactis immanior fuit*, Bd. 1, 6; S. 476, 23. [*O. H. Ger.* un-mez, -mezzi *immensus, ingens*.]

un-metlîc; *adj. Immoderate, excessive*:—Hî swā unmetlîcre (-um?) ege fōron, Guthl. 5; Gdwin. 36, 3.

un-metlîce; *adv. Immensely, exceedingly*:—Ða columnan wǣron unmetlîce greáte heáhnisse upp *columnae ingenti grossitudine atque altitudine*, Nar. 4, 22. v. un-gemetlîce.

un-micel; *adj. Not great, little*, Greg. Dial. 2, 15.

un-midlod; *adj. Unbridled, unrestrained*:—Unmidled *effrenus*, Wrt. Voc. ii. 142, 60. Ða upāhæfenan weorðaþ unmidlode and āðundene geniédde mid hiera upāhæfenesse *elatos effrenatio impellit tumoris*, Past. 41; Swt. 302, 10. Swā ða ofermōdan ne weorðen unmidlode *ut superbis non crescat effrenatio*, 60; Swt. 453, 21. v. un-gemidlod.

un-miht, un-mihtan. v. un-meaht, ge-unmihtan.

un-milde; *adj. Ungentle, harsh, rude*:—Gif hē is unmilde and oferhȳdig *si inmitis et superbus est*, Bd. 2, 2; S. 503, 7. [Hæþenndom iss unnmeoc and all unnmilde, Orm. 9880. Þu (*the owl*) art unmilde, O. and N. 61. *Goth.* un-milds ἄστοργος: *O. H. Ger.* un-milti *inmitis*: *Icel.* ū-mildr.]

un-mildheort; *adj. Hard-hearted, merciless, pitiless*:—Se dēma betǣcþ ða unrihtwîsan ðam unmildheortan wîtnere, Homl. Ass. 8, 203. Ðe unmiltheortne welige *inmisericordem divitem*, Lk. Skt. p. 9, 2. Mē cōman tō Sîlhearwan . . . hî wǣron unmildheorta, and mē tugon tō ðære sweartan helle, Homl. Skt. i. 4, 289.

un-milts, e; *f. Sternness, wrath*:—Hæbbe hē Godes unmiltse *may the wrath of God abide on him*, Cod. Dip. Kmbl. ii. 4, 2: Cod. Dip. B. ii. 315, 21.

un-miltsigendlîc; *adj. Unpardonable*:—Hwî wæs ðæs heáhengles syn unmiltsigendlîc, and ðæs mannes miltsigendlîc? Btwk. Scrd. 17, 21.

un-miltsung, e; *f. Want of consideration, impiety* towards God, *pitilessness* towards men:—Gif hié gemunan willaþ hiora ieldrena unmiltsunge ðe hié tō Gode hæfdon, ge eác him selfum betweónum *if they will remember their forefathers' impiety to God, and pitilessness among themselves*; recolant majorum suorum tempora sceleribus exsecrabilia, dissensionibus foeda, Ors. 2, 1; Swt. 64, 16.

un-mirigþ. v. un-myrhþ.

un-mōd, es; *n. Despondency, dejection*:—Of ðæs magan ādle cumaþ monige ādla . . . on unmōde and on ungemetwæccum, Lchdm. ii. 176, 1. [*O. H. Ger.* un-muot *perturbatio*: *Ger.* un-muth.]

un-mōdig; *adj.* I. in a depreciatory sense, *without courage, faint-hearted, pusillanimous*:—On ōðre wîsan sint tō manianne ða mōdgan, on ōðre ða unmōdgan and ða unðrîstan (*pusillanimes*) . . . ða unmōdgan and ða ungedyrstigan wēnað ðæt ðæt suîðe forsewenlîc sié ðætte hié dōð, and forðon weorðaþ oft ormōde, Past. 32; Swt. 209, 1-12. II. in a good sense, *not proud, diffident, humble*:—Geclǣnsa mē ða hwîle ðe ic on ðisse worulde sî, and gedō mē unmōdigne, Shrn. 171, 1.

un-mōdigness, e; *f. Pride, arrogance* (un- giving a bad sense):—Ic ondette ofermētto and unmōdennesse (nesse *is written above* mōden), Anglia xi. 98, 33.

un-molsniendlîc. v. un-formolsniendlîc.

un-murn; *adj. Untroubled*:—Hî slǣp hiora [swǣfon?] sylfum unmurne *dormierunt somnum suum*, Ps. Th. 75, 4. [Cf. Aylmar aȝen gan turne wel modi and wel murne, Horn. 704. *O. H. Ger.* morna *moeror*. *French* morne. *See also* murcen.] v. next word.

un-murnlîce; *adv. Carelessly, without compunction, without anxiety*:—Brond ǣleþ ealdgestreón unmurnlîce, Exon. Th. 51, 9; Cri. 813. Blōdig wæl eteþ āngenga unmurnlîce, Beo. Th. 903; B. 449. Se ðe unmurnlîce mādmas dǣleþ, egesan ne gȳmeþ, 3516; B. 1756.

un-myndlinga; *adv.* I. where an act is not intended or expected by the doer of it, *undesignedly, without meaning* to do something:—Nis hit nān wundor ðeáh hwā wēne ðæt swylces hwæt unmyndlinga gebyrige, þonne hē ne can ongitan for hwî God swylc geþafaþ *nec mirum, si quid ordinis ignorata ratione, temerarium confusumque credatur*, Bt. 39, 2; Fox 214, 9. Gif hē unmyndlunge (*without having previously intended to do it*) ceáp āredige ūt on hwylcere fare, L. Edg. S. 8; Th. i. 274, 23. Maurus arn uppon ðam streáme unmyndlunge (*unaware of what he was doing*), swilce hē on fæstre eorðan urne . . . undergeat æt nēxtan ðæt hē uppon ðæm wætere arn, and ðæs micclum wundrode, Homl. Th. ii. 160, 9. Hî unmyndlinga (*unintentionally*) swîðe fæsthealdne weorcstān upp āhwylfdon, Homl. Skt. i. 23, 423. II. where an act is unexpected by the object of it, *unexpectedly*:—Hē hiene spōn ðæt hē on Umenis unmyndlenga (*de insperato*) mid here becōme, Ors. 3, 11; Swt. 146, 8. Būtan hit swā limpe ðæt hwylc cuma unmyndluncga cume, R. Ben. 67, 12. Gif him ǣfre unmendlinga geberede ðæt . . ., Met. 25, 30. [Hire wone is to cumen bi stale, ferliche and unmundlunge hwen me least weneð, O. E. Homl. i. 249, 20. Þe ȝeape wrastlare mid þen ilke turn mei his fere unmunlunge aworpen, A. R. 280, 10.]

un-mynegod; *adj. Undemanded*:—Gif preóst geárgerihta unmynegode lǣte *if a priest leave the yearly dues without payment asked*, L. N. P. L. 43; Th. ii. 296, 15. v. mynegian, II c.

un-myrhþ, e; *f. Sadness, misery*:—On unmyrhðe his lîf geendian, Wulfst. 148, 9.

un-myrige; *adj. Unpleasant, unfair*:—Unmyrge plega *collidium* (=colludium; cf. colludium, turpis ludus, Corp. Gl. ed. Hessels 35, 643), Wrt. Voc. ii. 134, 72. [Ne beo þe song never so murie þat he ne schal þinche unmurie ȝef he ilesteþ over unwille, O. and N. 346.]

unna, an; *m.*: unne, an; unn, e; *f.* I. *grant, allowance, permission*:—Ic cȳðe eów ðæt hit is mîn fulla unna, ðæt heó becweðe hire land *I declare to you that she has my full permission to bequeathe her land*, Cod. Dip. Kmbl. iv. 200, 27: 223, 24. Hit is mîn unna and mîn fulle leáfe ðæt hē dihte privilegium, vi. 203, 23. Mid unnan Godes and his hālgena . . . mit unnan hîrēdes, ii. 58, 23, 25. Se wæs tō Eoferwîcceastre be cinges unnan and ealra his witena tō ærcebisceope gehālgod, Chr. 971; Erl. 125, 36. Habban hî ðone feórðan pening be mînre unnan *omnem quartum nummum fratribus reddendum censeo*, Cod. Dip. Kmbl. iii. 61, 16. Be mînre unne and gife habban hî and wealdan *meo concessu et dono habeant et possideant*, iv. 200, 7. Hē mid his unne tō Scotlande fōr, Chr. 1093; Erl. 229, 20. Būtan hē ðæs abbodes unnan begite *nisi ea abba jubeat*, R. Ben. 94, 9. Hē eów sige forgeaf þurh unnan ðæs Ælmihtigan, Homl. Th. i. 506, 27: Homl. Skt. i. 3, 556. II. *willingness* to give, *pleasure* in doing something:—Gelǣste hē Gode his teóðunga mid ealre blisse and mid eallum unnan . . . Gif hē hit mid unnan and fulre blisse dōn wolde, L. Edg. S. 1; Th. i. 272, 2, 13. III. *a grant, what is given*:—Se ðe ðās gyfu and ðisne unnan wille Gode and sancte Petre ætbrēdan, Cod. Dip. Kmbl. iv. 276, 31.

unnan; *prs.* ic, hē an[n], *pl.* wē unnon; *p.* ūðe. I. *to grant* a person (*dat.*) something (*gen.*), *to give, allow*:—Gē gehîraþ hwæs ic Gode ann, L. Ath. i. prm.; Th. i. 194, 14. Ic an Eádwearde ðæs landes, Chart. Th. 487, 18, 32. Ic ðē an tela sincgestreóna, Beo. Th. 2455; B. 1225. Ðæs steápes onfēhð ðe hē ann *he receives the cup to whom God gives it*, Ps. Th. 74, 7. Gif mē Waldend an lengran lîfes, Cd. Th. 110, 18; Gen. 1840. Hæfde gefohten foremǣrne blǣd, swā hyre God ūþe, Judth. Thw. 23, 16; Jud. 123. Gif ic mînum eágum unne slǣpes *si dedero somnum oculis meis*, Ps. Th. 131, 4. Ðæt mē unne God ēcan dreámes, Exon. Th. 454, 13; Hy. 4, 32. Eal folc geceás Eádward tō cynge; healde ða hwîle ðe him God unne, Chr. 1041; Erl. 169, 5. On ða gerād ðe gē mē unnan mînes, L. Ath. i. prm.; Th. i. 198, 1 note. Gif hié him ðæs rîces ūþon, Chr. 755; Erl. 50, 17. Ic feores ðē unnan wille, Exon. Th. 254, 4; Jul. 192: Andr. Kmbl. 292; An. 146. Hē ða bōc unnendre handa hire tō lēt *librum bona voluntate dimisit*, Chart. Th. 202, 36. Bōc and land betǣcan unnendere heortan, 376, 5. Unnende mōde, 126, 22. I a. with dat. of person and clause:—Him God ūðe, ðæt hē hyne sylfne gewræc, Beo. Th. 5741; B. 2874. Þenden lîfes weard unnan wolde, ðæt hē blǣdes hēr brūcan mōste, Exon. Th. 158, 2; Gū. 902. II. *to wish* something (*gen.*) to a person (*dat.*):—Ða ðe mē yfeles unnon *them that wish me evil* (A. V.); qui cogitant mihi mala, Ps. Th. 39, 17. Ne dyde ic, ðæs ic ðē weán ūðe (*because I wished you woe*), Cd. Th. 163, 3; Gen. 2692. Geweard ðætte Perse gebudan frið eallum Crēca folce, næs nā for ðæm ðe hié him ǣnigra gōda ūþen (*non quod misericorditer fessis consuleret*), Ors. 3, 1; Swt. 98, 31. [Gledieð alle wið me, ðæt me god unnen, Marh. 21, 22. Þine feond þe þe ufel unnen, Laym. 28117. He mire dohter wel on, 11928. Þu hit (*sorrow*) myht segge swyhc mon þat [hit] þe ful wel on, wyþute echere ore he on þe muchele more (he wolde þad þu heuedest mor, 2nd Text), Misc. 116, 238]. III. *to wish* something (*gen.*) for a person (*dat.*), *to like* a person to have something:—Se arcebiscop wēnde ðæt ðæt biscoprîce sum ōðer mann ābiddan wolde, ðe hē his wyrs truwude and ūðe (*somebody else, that he would have been worse pleased should have it*), Chr. 1043; Erl. 169, 28. Oft hit gesǣleþ ðæt his ǣhta weorþaþ on ðæs onwealde ðe hē ǽr on his lífe wyrrest úþe *it often happens that his property gets into the power of the man that when alive he would have been least pleased should have it*, Blickl. Homl. 195, 4. III a. with dat. of person and a clause:—Ðæt is, ðæt hwā fare mid his mōde æfter his niéhstan, and him unne ðæt hē tō ryhte gecierre *that is, that a man go in spirit after his neighbour, and be glad that he turn to right*, Past. 46; Swt. 349, 14. IV. *to like* a condition of things, *to be pleased*:—Hē ne úþe, ðæt ǽnig ōþer man mǽrða mā gehēdde ðonne hē sylfa, Beo. Th. 1010; B. 503. Úþe ic swíþor ðæt ðū hine selfne geseón mōste *I should have been much better pleased, that you could have seen the creature himself*, 1925; B. 960. Ne meahte hē, ðeáh hē úðe wel, on ðam frumgāre feorh gehealdan *he could not keep life in the prince, though he would have been well pleased to do it*, 5703; B. 2855. [Hwer ich habbe iwiket, ich on wel þ ȝe witen, Kath. 1744. *O. H. Ger.* unnan: *Icel.* unna.] v. ge-, of-unnan.

unne. v. unna.

un-neáh; *adj. Distant, far*:—In lond unnēh *in regionem longinquam*, Lk. Skt. Lind. 15, 13: 19, 12.

un-neáh *not near.* I. as adv. *far*:—Syndan ealle hí fram ǣ ðínre unneáh gewiten *a lege tua longe facti sunt*, Ps. Th. 118, 150. II. as prep. *far from*:—Ōþlæ unnēg, Txts. 127, 1.

un-nēdige, un-nēh, un-net. v. un-nídige, un-neáh, un-nyt.

unnend, es; *m. One who grants*:—Unnend ł forgefend *prestabilis*, Rtl. 5, 10.

un-nídige; *adv. Without compulsion, willingly*:—Ða ðe beóð mid hira āgnum byrðennum ofðryccte ðæt hié ne magon gestondan, hié willaþ lustlíce underfōn ōðerra monna, ond unniédige hié underlútaþ mid hira sculdrum ōðerra byrðenna tōeácan hiera āgnum *qui ad casum valde urgetur ex propriis, humerum libenter opprimendus ponderibus submittit alienis*, Past. 7; Swt. 52, 25. Oft hit gebyreþ ðætte manige men bióþ swā ungetrume ǽgþer ge on mōde ge on líchoman ðæt hí ne magon ne nān god dōn, ne nān yfel nyllaþ unnēdige, Bt. 39, 10; Fox 228, 1.

un-nídunga; *adv. Without necessity* or *compulsion*:—Hē ðurh his āgene geornfulnesse gesyngaþ unniédenga *desiderio peccatur*, Past. 37; Swt. 265, 12.

un-níþing, es; *m. Not a rascal, an honest man*:—He beád ðæt ǽlc man ðe wǽre unníðing sceolde cuman tō him, Chr. 1087; Erl. 226, 2.

un-nyt[t]; *adj. Useless, vain, idle, unprofitable*:—Unnyt sprǽc *fabula*, Wrt. Voc. ii. 146, 64. Nān brōðor ymbe ídelnesse and unnette sprǽce (unnytte sprǽca, *v. l.*) beó . . . ne biþ hē nā him ānum unnyt *ne frater vacet otioso et fabulis . . . non solum sibi inutilis est*, R. Ben. 74, 15–18. Unlǽde bið on eorðan, unnyt lífes, se þurh ðone cantic ne can Crist geherian, Salm. Kmbl. 42; Sal. 21. Nis him nān wuht unnyt ðæs ðe hē gesceóp, Bt. 39, 5; Fox 218, 17. Ðes wída grund stōd ídel and unnyt, Cd. Th. 7, 14; Gen. 106: Beo. Th. 830; B. 413. Unnet gelp, Met. 10, 17. Ādō of his mōde fela ðara ymbhogona ðe him unnet sié (cf. ungerisenlíce ymbhogan, Bt. 29, 3; Fox 106, 19), 16, 6: 22, 10. Hit wæs unnet gebod, Bt. 41, 3; Fox 246, 32. Se unnytta and forhogoda *inrita*, Wrt. Voc. ii. 48, 65. His word beóð gehwyrfedo tō unnyttre oferssprǽce, Past. 21; Swt. 165, 17. Ðȳ unnyttan *nugaci*, Wrt. Voc. ii. 94, 69. Gehæft mid ðære unnyttan lufe ðisse middangeardes, Bt. 34, 8; Fox 144, 25. Unnytne gefeán, Met. 5, 27. Unnytne andan, Bt. 39, 3; Fox 214, 33. Unnetne, Met. 28, 52. Hwæþer ðæt sié tō talianne wāclíc and unnyt *num imbecillum, ac sine viribus aestimandum est?* Bt. 24, 4; Fox 86, 16. Ðone ídelan hlísan and ðone unnyttan gilp, 19; Fox 68, 21. Ðone unnyttan þeówan *inutilem servum*, Mt. Kmbl. 25, 30. Hí lufiaþ ðæt hí sȳn ídle and unnytte *inutiles facti sunt*, Ps. Th. 13, 4. Unnetta saca *vain disputes*, Met. 25, 44. Heora hǽþenan gild wǽron ídelu and unnyt, Blickl. Homl. 223, 2. Āfyr fram ðē ða yfelan sǽlþa and ða unnettan, and eác ða unnettan ungesǽlþa, Bt. 6; Fox 14, 32. Ðonne ðæt mōd bið on monig tōdǽled, hit bið on ānes hwæm ðȳ unnyttre . . . Oft ðonne mon forlēt ða fæstrǽdnesse . . . hine spænð his mōd tō swíðe monegum unnyttum weorce . . . Hē swíður his mōd gebint tō ðǽm unnyttan (-nyttran, Hatt. MS.) weorcum ðonne hē ðyrfe, Past. 4; Swt. 36, 14–21. Rǽd biþ nyttost, yfel unnyttost, Exon. Th. 341, 2; Gn. Ex. 120. Ðæs hādes men ðe hwȳlum wǽron nyttoste . . . syndon nū unnyttaste, L. I. P. 14; Th. ii. 322, 21. [*O. E. Homl.* unnit, -net, -nut: A. R. un-nut, -net: *Orm.* un nitt: *Goth.* un-nutis *inutilis*: *O. H. Ger.* un-nuz[z] *inutilis, cassus, otiosus, ignavus*: *Icel.* ú-nýtr.] v. next word.

un-nyt[t], es; *n.* I. *a vain thing, vanity, frivolity*:—Ne geríseþ ǽnig unnytt mid bisceopum, ne doll ne dysig, L. I. P. 9; Th. ii. 314, 30. Ðū hātodest ða ðe beeodon ídelnesse and ða ðe unnyt worhton *odisti observantes vanitatem supervacue*, Ps. Th. 30, 6. Wē lǽraþ ðæt man æt ciricwæccan ǽnig unnit ne dreóge, L. Edg. C. 28; Th. ii. 250, 13: 26; Th. ii. 250, 5: 65; Th. ii. 258, 12. Ðonne mæg hē ongitan ðæt yfel and ðæt unnet, ðæt hē ǽr on his mōde hæfde, Bt. 35, 1; Fox 154, 26. Hwȳ gē ymb ðæt unnet swincen? Met. 10, 21. Hwí smeágaþ hí unnytt *quare meditati sunt inania*, Ps. Th. 2, 1. Unnyttu ł ídelnyssa sprǽcon ānra gehwilc *vana locuti sunt unusquisque*, Ps. Lamb. ii. 3. II. *an evil thing, iniquity*:—Hí unnyt sæcgeaþ *loquentur iniquitatem*, Ps. Th. 93, 4. [On unnet *in vain*, O. E. Homl. i. 107, 3. He isihð and iherеð oðerhwule unnut, and spekeð umbe hwule, A. R. 352, 28.]

un-nyt[t], e; *f. Ill use, disadvantage, hurt*:—Gif hié ða trumnesse ðære Godes giefe him tō unnytte (-nyte, Hatt. MS.) gehweorfaþ *si incolumitatis gratiam ad usum nequitiae inclinent*, Past. 36; Swt. 246, 8. Ic andette eal ðæt ic ǽfre mid eágum geseáh tō gítsunge oððe tō tǽlnesse, oþþe mid eárum tō unnytte gehȳrde, oþþe mid mínum mūðe tō unnytte gecwæð, L. de Cf. 8; Th. ii. 264, 1–2. Lā hwæt fremaþ cyrichatan cristendōm on unnyt *see what Christianity can do to the disadvantage of the church's foes*, Wulfst. 67, 19. v. nytt.

un-nytlíc; *adj. Useless, unprofitable*:—Ðysse wyrte wyrttruma is unnytlíc (-net-, *v. l.*), Lchdm. i. 258, 4. Ðætte hē ne ðōhte nāht ungesceádwíslíces ne unnytlíces (-net-, Hatt. MS.) *nec indiscretum quid vel inutile cogitet*, Past. 13; Swt. 76, 12. [*O. H. Ger.* un-nuzlīh *inusitatus*.]

un-nytlíce; *adv.* I. *uselessly, vainly, to no purpose*:—Unnytlíce *inaniter*, Wrt. Voc. ii. 48, 43: *nugaciter*, 80, 33: 60, 62. Ðȳ læs hié unnytlíce forweorpen ðæt ðæt hié sellen for hira hrædhȳdignesse *ne praecipitatione hoc, quod tribuunt, inutiliter spargant*, Past. 44; Swt. 321, 17: 15; Swt. 95, 24. Unnytlíce wē swincaþ, gif wē his nabbaþ ðȳ māran ðanc, Bt. 41, 2; Fox 246, 21. II. *to ill purpose*:—Suā hié egeleáslícor and unnytlícor brūcaþ Godes giefe *quo bonis Dei male uti non metuunt*, Past. 36; Swt. 247, 10.

un-nytlícness, e; *f. Uselessness, unserviceableness*:—Wið ðæra eárena unnytlícnysse, and wið ðæt man wel gehȳran ne mæge, Lchdm. i. 212, 3: 214, 20.

un-nytness, e; *f. Uselessness, frivolity, vanity, triviality*:—Unnytnis *nugacitas*, Wrt. Voc. ii. 115, 5. Unnytnes, 60, 24. Ǽrendwrecan unnytnesse *nugigerelus*, 60, 21. Hí on unnytenesse gewordene synt *inutiles facti sunt*, Ps. Spl. T. 13, 4. Ðæt on ðam hālgan Sunnandæge nān man hine tō unnytnesse tō swíðe ne geþeódde, Wulfst. 227, 6. Wē forbeódaþ ǽgðer ge geflitu, ge plegan, ge unnytta word, ge gehwelce unnytnesse in ðām hālgan stōwum tō dōnne, L. E. I. 10; Th. ii. 408, 23.

un-nytwirðe; *adj. Not fit for use, useless, unprofitable, unserviceable*:—Hē nis ðæt ān him unnytwurðe *non solum sibi inutilis est*, R. Ben. Interl. 83, 9. Wē beóð gehātene yfele þeówan and unnytwyrðe, Homl. Ass. 57, 150. Unnytwyrþe gewordene hig synt *inutiles facti sunt*, Ps. Lamb. 52, 4.

un-nytwirðlíce; *adv. Uselessly, vainly, to no purpose, unprofitably*:—Ðæra wiðercorenra wíte tiht oft heora mōd unnytwurðlíce tō lufe, Homl. Th. i. 332, 29. Āgyldan gesceád ealra ðæra ȳdelnyssa ðe hí unnytwurðlíce nū begāð, ii. 220, 31. Se forlȳst ða gife ðe hē unnytwurðlíce underfēng, 556, 16.

un-ofercumen; *adj. Unsubdued*:—Unobercumenre (-ofaercumenrae, -ofercumenrae) *indigestae*, Txts. 71, 1097. Unofercumene *indigeste*, Wrt. Voc. ii. 45, 52.

un-oferfére; *adj. Not to be crossed, impassable*:—Unoferfoere *intransmeabili*, Txts. 73, 1144. Unoferfēre, Wrt. Voc. ii. 45, 68.

un-oferhréfed; *adj. Not roofed over*:—Seó cirice is ufan open and unoferhrēfed, Blickl. Homl. 125, 26, 31.

un-oferswíðed; *adj. Unconquered*:—Unoferswíþed hiht *invicta spes*, Hymn. Surt. 123, 34. Ðín geþyld wē cunnon unoferswȳþed, Guthl. 5; Gdwin. 30, 19. Ðū unoferswȳðda Alexander in gefeohtum *invicte belli Alexander*, Nar. 29, 9.

un-oferswíðedlíc; *adj. Unconquerable*:—Sume men wǽron unoferswíþedlíce, swā ðæt hí nān ne mihte mid nānum wíte oferswíþan *quidam suppliciis inexpugnabiles*, Bt. 39, 11; Fox 230, 1. v. un-oferswíðendlíc.

un-oferswíðende; *adj. Unconquerable, invincible*:—Geoffra ðíne lāc ðam unoferswíðendum Apolline, Homl. Skt. i. 14, 35.

un-oferswíðendlíc; *adj. Invincible*:—Unoferswíþendlíc weorud *invincibilis exercitus*, Bd. 1, 15; S. 483, 16.

un-oferwinnende (?); *adj. Not to be overcome*:—Ða unoferwinnene (-winnende (?), -wunnene (?). v. un-oferwunnen) *ineluctuabilis*, Wrt. Voc. ii. 84, 54: 46, 78.

un-oferwinnendlíc; *adj. Invincible, unconquerable*:—Unoferwinnendlícne (-wunnendlíce, *v. l.*) here *invictissimum exercitum*, Ors. 3, 7; Swt. 112, 7. Unoferwinnendlíce halsbearga *loricam inextricabilem* (*inexpugnabilem*), Hpt. Gl. 424, 34.

un-oferwrigen; *adj. Not covered over*:—Ða sceame mínes líchaman hæbbende unoferwrigene, Homl. Skt. ii. 23 b, 208.

un-oferwunnen; *adj. Unconquered*:—Ic ða mōste oferwinnan ðe ǽr wǽron unoferwunnen *qui ante hac invicti fuere viri, hos ego in pugna vici*, Ors. 4, 1; Swt. 156, 28.

un-ofslegen; *adj. Unslain*:—His brōðor geendode his líf on sibbe unofslegen, Homl. Th. ii. 544, 31.

un-onbindendlíc; *adj. Not to be unbound, indissoluble*:—Mid unanbindendlícum racentum *irresoluto nexu*, Bt. 25; Fox 88, 6. v. unābindendlíc.

un-onwendedlíc; *adj. Unchangeable*:—Ne wyrð seó burh nǽfre onwend, ða hwíle ðe God byð unonwendedlíc on hire midle, Ps. Th. 45, 4.

un-onwendendlíc; *adj. Unchangeable, immutable:*—God âna unanwendendlíc wuniaþ *se immobilem conservat*, Bt. 35, 5; Fox 166, 9 note: Met. 20, 17: 24, 43.

un-onwendendlíce; *adv. Unchangeably, immutably, without variableness:*—Ðæt hí geðencen hû hrædlíce se eorðlíca hlísa ofergǽð, and hû unanwendendlíce se godcunda ðurhwunaþ *ut pensent, humana judicia quanta velocitate evolant, divina autem quanta immobilitate perdurant*, Past. 59; Swt. 447, 30. Ic nát hwæþer hit eall gewyrþan sceal unanwendendlíce, ðæt hê getiohhod hæfþ, Bt. 41, 3; Fox 248, 30 note: 250, 1, 2 note. Se wísa mon eall his líf lǽt on gefeán unonwendendlíce, 12; Fox 36, 24.

un-orne; *adj. Simple, plain, poor, mean, humble:*—Dunnere, unorne ceorl, Byrht. Th. 139, 18; By. 256. [Crist warrþ unnorne and wrecche and usell child forr þatt he wollde uss alle maken riche, Orm. 3368. He warrþ an unnorne and wrecche mann, 4884. Crist wass unncuþ ȝet, and unnwurrþ, and unnorne, 16163. Heo beo ful unorne, oðer of feir elde, A. R. 424, 5. Ȝef hire laverd is forwurþe and unorne at bedde and at borde, O. and N. 1492. Horn nis noȝt so unorn; Horn is fairer þane beo he, Horn. 330. ·He brohte hine uppen unorne mare, þet bitacneð ure unorne fleis, O. E. Homl. i. 85, 3. Hiss (*John the Baptist*) fode wass unnorne, forr nass nan essemete þær, Orm. 828: 11548. Unnorne mete and wæde, 6337. Þet heo ne grucchie uor none mete, ne uor none drunche, ne beo hit neuer so unorne, A. R. 108, 2. Ower cloðes beon unorne, and warme, and wel iwrouhte, 418, 17. Mi stefne is bold and noht unorne, heo is ilich one grete horne, O. and N. 317. Swa (*as Nichodemus did*) to lefenn uppoun Crist wass rihht unnorne læfe, Orm. 16809.] v. next word.

un-ornlíc; *adj. Poor, plain, mean:*—Hí námon him ealde gescý and unornlíc scrúd *they took old shoes and mean apparel*; tulerunt calceamenta perantiqua, induti veteribus vestimentis, Jos. 9, 5. [Arrchelauss flæh inntill oþerr land, and tære he wass unnornelíȝ (*in mean estate*), Orm. 8251. Cf. Lætenn swiþe unornelíȝ and litell off þe sellfenn, Orm. 3750: 7525: 4886. Me wore leuere i wore lame, þanne men . . . him onne handes leyde unornelike, or same seyde, Havel. 1941.] v. preceding word.

un-pleólíc; *adj. Not dangerous, without risk*, (1) as regards physical hurt:—Unpleólícre hit bið on lytlum scipe and on lytlum wætere, ðonne on miclum scipe and on miclum wætere, Prov. Kmbl. 29. (2) as regards moral hurt:—Augustinus cwæð, ðæt unpleólíc sý þeáh hwá lǽcewyrte ðicge; ac ðæt hê tǽlþ tô unálýfedlícere wíglunge, gif hwá ða wyrta on him becnitte, bûton hê hí tô ðam dolge gelecge, Homl. Th. i. 476, 3. Sume teolunga sind ðe man earfoðlíce mæg bûton synnum begân. Petrus hæfde unpleólíce teolunge, and hê bûton pleó tô his fixnoðe gecyrde, ii. 288, 25. Ðás tâcna sind dígle and unpleólíce, i. 306, 30.

un-pleólíce; *adv. Without danger, without risk, safely:*—Ða óðre apostoli be Godes hǽse leofodon be heora lâre unpleólíce; ac ðeáh hwæðere Paulus âna nolde ða álýfdan bigleofan onfôn, ac mid ágenre teolunge his neóde foresceáwode, Homl. Th. i. 392, 20.

un-rǽd, es; *m.* I. *evil counsel, ill-advised course, bad plan, folly:*—Scipia sǽde, ðæt hit (*the building of a theatre*) wǽre se mǽsta unrǽd and se mǽsta gedwola *dicens, inimicissimum hoc fore bellatori populo ad nutriendam desidiam, lasciviaeque commentum*, Ors. 4, 12; Swt. 210, 1. Eádríc gewende ðone cyning ongeán. Næs nân mâra unrǽd gerǽd ðonne se wæs *Eadricus per dolum fecit exercitum Anglorum redire. Non fuit pejus concilium factum in Anglia de tali re*, Chr. 1016; Erl. 157, 22. Ðæs unrǽdes (*the building of the tower of Babel*) stíðferhð cyning steóre gefremede, Cd. Th. 101, 15; Gen. 1682. Gif ðû unrǽdes ne geswícest, Exon. Th. 249, 31; Jul. 120: 393, 14; Rä. 12, 10: 410, 6; Rä. 28, 12. Hí geeácnodon heora yfel and God mid weorcum gegremedon . . . swâ ðæt hig Eglone þeówodon for heora unrǽde, Jud. 3, 14: Thw. p. 162, 29. Hý fêrdon on unriht and unrǽde fyligdon *ambulaverunt post vanitatem* (Jeremiah 2, 5), Wulfst. 49, 9. Absalon fêrde forð mid his unrǽde, and wolde his ágenum fæder feores benǽman, Homl. Skt. i. 19, 215. Ðæra hâlgena líc woldon hí besencan on flôde, ac se ælmihtiga Scyppend wiðslôh ðam unrǽde. Sum wíf wæs ðe wiste heora unrǽd, ii. 29, 324. Tô his (*Lucifer's*) unrǽde gefæstnod, Ælfc. T. Grn. 2, 44: 4, 10: Cd. Th. 43, 33; Gen. 700. Hê intô Englelande mid mâran unrǽde fêrde ðone him behôfode, Chr. 1093; Erl. 229, 3. Wæs gesǽd ðæt hê wǽre on ðam unrǽde, ðæt man sceolde on Eást-Sexon Swegen underfôn, Chart. Th. 539, 27. Agathocles gedyde untreówlíce wið hiene . . . On ðære hwíle ðe hê ðone unrǽd þurhteáh, Ors. 4, 5; Swt. 170, 13. Ne wend ðû ðê on ðæs folces unrǽd and unriht gewil *non sequeris turbam ad faciendum malum* (Ex. 23, 2), L. Alf. 41; Th. i. 54, 6. Ðæs engles môd ðe ðone unrǽd (*rebellion against God*) ongan ǽrest fremman, Cd. Th. 3, 3; Gen. 30. Hyra freá ǽrest unrǽd (*the setting up of the image*) efnde, 227, 13; Dan. 186. Hí þêgun æppel unrǽdum (*ill-advisedly*), Exon. Th. 226, 9; Ph. 403. Ealle ðás ungesǽlþa ûs gelumpon þuruh unrǽdas, Chr. 1011; Erl. 145, 22. II. *disadvantage, prejudice, hurt:*—Ic andette . . . ǽlcne glængc ðe tô míneS líchaman unrǽde ǽfre belimpe, L. de Cf. 7; Th. ii. 262, 28: Anglia xi. 98, 28. Hê helle outýneþ ðám ðe líces wynne fremedon on unrǽd, Exon. Th. 364, 14; Wal 70. Hí drugon heora sylfra ǽcne unrǽd, Cd. Th. 116, 16; Gen. 1937. [*Laym.* un-ræd *ill-counsel.* Þat child his unred to rede wend, O. and N. 1464. Iacobes sunes deden unred, Gen. and Ex. 1906. *O. H. Ger.* un-rât: *Icel.* ú-ráð; *n. bad counsel, an ill-advised step.*]

un-rǽden[n], e; *f. An ill-advised action:*—Hê ða unrǽden folmum gefremede, ofslôh brôðor sínne, Cd. Th. 60, 16; Gen. 982. [Cf. *Icel.* ú-ráðan *an ill-advised step.*]

un-rǽdfæstlíce; *adv. Unadvisedly, without heeding good counsel:*—Twá geár hê ríxode unrǽdfæstlíce, Homl. Skt. i. 18, 456.

un-rǽdlíc; *adj. Ill-advised, foolish, vain:*—Hié hæfdon plegan and oforgedrync, and dyslíce and unrǽdlíce hâlsunga, Blickl. Homl. 99, 21. [*O. H. Ger.* un-râtlíh *inconsultus*: *Icel.* ú-ráðligr *inadvisable, inexpedient.*]

un-rǽdlíce; *adv. Unadvisedly, inconsiderately:*—Unrǽdlíce *inconsulte*, Wrt. Voc. ii. 80, 78: 44, 79: *inconsulte, inconsiderate*, Hpt. Gl. 474, 57: 509, 64. Hê begann tô lufienne leahtras tô swíðe mid his cnihtum, ðe unrǽdlíce fêrdon on heora ídelum lustum, Ælfc. T. Grn. 17, 14. On ðám ænglum ðe unrǽdlíce môdegodon, Homl. Skt. i. 13, 183. Ús gedafenaþ ðæt wê hit wênon swíðor ðonne wê hit unrǽdlíce geseþan, Homl. Th. i. 440, 31. [*O. H. Ger.* un-râtlícho *inconsulte*: *Icel.* ú-ráðliga.]

unrǽd-síþ, es; *m. A foolish, unprofitable way:*—Ic unrǽdsíþas óþrum stýre nyttre fóre, Exon. Th. 393, 2; Rä. 12, 4.

un-reht *not treated*, un-reht *wrong*. v. un-áreht, un-riht.

un-reordian (?) *to speak ill of, to abuse:*—Swá firenfulle fâcnum wordum heora aldorðægn unreordadon (on reordadon? v. on, **B. III.** 5), Cd. Th. 269, 1; Sat. 66.

un-rêtan. v. ge-unrêtan.

un-rêðe; *adj. Not fierce, gentle:*—Wê rǽdaþ be ðære culfran gecynde, ðæt heó is unrêðe on hire clawum, Homl. Th. ii. 44, 25.

un-rêtu (-o); *f. Anxiety, disquiet:*—Ðá bǽdon mec míne gefêran ðæt ic on swá micelre môdes unrêto and nearonisse mec selfne mid fæstenne ne swencte *rogantibus amicis ne me anxietate et jejunio condeficerem*, Nar. 30, 23. v. un-rôt.

un-ríce; *adj. Not rich* or *not powerful, poor, humble:*—Ða ðe unríce synd and hafenleáse þearfan *pauperiores*, R. Ben. 104, 7. Mín gerêfa oþþe ǽnig óðer man ríccre oþþe unríccre, L. Edg. S. 13; Th. i. 276, 26. Ic wát ðæt ðû hefst ðone hláford ðe ðû treówast bet ðonne ðê silfum, and swá hefð eác manig ðara ðe unrícran hláford hefð ðonne ðû hefst, Shrn. 196, 11. [*Icel.* ú-ríkr.]

un-riht; *adj. Wrong, evil, bad, unjust, unlawful, depraved, perverse:*—Ic eom geþafa ðæt hit nâuht unriht wǽre ðæt mon ða yfelwillendan men hête nêtenu *fateor nec injuria dici video vitiosos in belluas mutari*, Bt. 38, 2; Fox 196, 17. Ic gelêfe ðætte ǽlc unriht wítnung sié ðæs yfel ðe hit dêþ, næs ðæs ðe hit þafaþ *apparet, illatam cuilibet injuriam non accipientis, sed inferentis esse miseriam*, 38, 6; Fox 208, 20. Unreht, 37, 2; Fox 188, 7. Se yfla, unrihta willa wôhhǽmetes *voluptas*, Met. 18, 1. Of unrihtum wege *de via iniquitatis*, Ps. Th. 106, 16. Gif hwá geniéd sié oþþe tô hláfordsearwe oþþe tô ǽngum unryhtum fultume, L. Alf. pol. i. 60, 5. Unryhtre ǽ *unlawful marriage*, Exon. Th. 260, 14; Jul. 297. Hê gedwolan fylde, unrihte ǽ *idolatry*, Elen. Kmbl. 2081; El. 1042. Ic wundrige for hwí swá rihtwís dêma ǽnige unrihte gife wille forgifan, Bt. 38, 3; Fox 202, 10. Tuoege wôhfullo ł unrehto *duo nequam*, Lk. Skt. Lind. 23, 32. Unræhto (-rehte, Rush.) ł wôh *praua*, 3, 5. Ða unrihtan men, Blickl. Homl. 231, 10. Áblinnan fram heora unrihtum gestreónum, 25, 5. Cynewulf benam Sigebryht his ríces for unryhtum dǽdum, Chr. 755; Erl. 48, 19. Mid hiera unryhtum bisenum *per exemplum pravi operis*, Past. 9; Swt. 59, 18. Fram sumum unrihtum láreówum *a quibusdam perversis doctoribus*, Bd. 2, 15; S. 518, 30. Unrihte wegas ealle *omnem viam iniquitatis*, Ps. Th. 118, 104. Unrihte gemeta and wôge gewihta áweorpe man, Wulfst. 70, 3. Ða unrehtan *iniqua*, Ps. Surt. 9, 24. [*O. Frs.* un-riucht: *O. Sax.* un-reht: *O. H. Ger.* un-reht *improbus, injustus, iniquus, vitiosus*: *Icel.* ú-réttr.] v. following words.

un-riht, es; *n.* I. *wrong, evil, iniquity, injustice:*—Unriht *injuria*, Wrt. Voc. ii. 49, 26. Hira unriht (*iniquitas*) weard untýned, Ps. Th. 72, 5: Blickl. Homl. 175, 9. Hwylc unryht mæg bión mâre *quae potest iniquior esse confusio?* Bt. 39, 9; Fox 224, 28. Unrihtes feala *iniquitates*, Ps. Th. 54, 3. Gê ðe unrihtes wyrceaþ *qui operantur iniquitatem*, 52, 5: 58, 2: 70, 3. Ða ðe unrihtes þenceaþ, 140, 11: Blickl. Homl. 111, 1. Ðǽm mannum ðe heora synna and unrihtes geswícaþ . . . and nǽfre tô unrihtum ne gewendaþ, 193, 22: Elen. Kmbl. 1029; El. 516. Ic him ðæs unrihtes (*seeking to destroy Jesus*) andsæc fremede, 941; El. 472. Ðæt hý bealodǽde, ǽlces unryhtes gescomeden, Exon. Th. 80, 5; Cri. 1303. Ða oftrhýdegan, ðe mê unrihte (*or adv.*) grêtan *injuste iniquitatem fecerunt in me*, Ps. Th. 118, 78: Cd. Th. 78, 12; Gen. 1292. Full mið unrehte *plenum iniquitate*, Lk. Skt. Rush. 11, 39. Mid unryhte *wrongfully*, Chr. 823; Erl. 62, 23. Mid unrihte, Ps. Th. 55, 1: 68, 28: Andr. Kmbl. 3116; An. 1561. Ne dêm nân unriht *non injuste judicabis*, Lev. 19, 15. Ðonne gê unriht wirceaþ *quando feceritis malum*, Deut. 31, 29. Eallum ðe unriht wyrceaþ *qui operantur iniquitatem*, Ps.

Th. 58, 5. Hī wyrceaþ unriht (*injustitiam*), 93, 4. Unriht dōn, Bt. 38, 3; Fox 202, 12: Cd. Th. 217, 16; Dan. 23. Grendel unriht æfnde, Beo. Th. 2512; B. 1254. Unryht fremian, Exon. Th. 79, 16; Cri. 1291: Ps. Th. 118, 51. Unriht (*iniquitatem*) sprecan, 72, 6: 62, 9: Homl. Th. ii. 452, 6. Hē mid listum speón idese on đæt unriht (*taking the forbidden fruit*), Cd. Th. 37, 13; Gen. 589. Hit wæs mid unriht him of genumen, Chr. 1072; Erl. 211, 8. Heó on unriht þōhtan *injusta cogitatio eorum est*, Ps. Th. 118, 118: Beo. Th. 5471; B. 2739: Elen. Kmbl. 1161; El. 582: Wulfst. 158, 10. Đȳ læs hié on unryht hǽmen *propter fornicationem*, Past. 16; Swt. 99, 14: 51; Swt. 397, 19. Ne gemune đū ealdra unrihta *ne memineris iniquitates antiquas*, Ps. Th. 78, 8: Wulfst. 156, 10. Babylonie mid monigfealdum unryhtum and firenlustum libbende wǽron, Ors. 2, 1; Swt. 64, 7. Unrihtum, Bt. 16, 4; Fox 58, 10: Blickl. Homl. 109, 20: Cd. Th. 259, 2; Dan. 685. Him gyldeþ God ealle đa unriht (*iniquitates*) đe hī geearnedan, Ps. Th. 93, 22. Ǽr man āweódige đa unriht and đa mānweorc, Wulfst. 243, 19. II. *a defect*:—Đa đe mid unrihte heora gecyndes beóþ geuntrumade *quae naturae suae vitio infirmantur*, Bd. 1, 27; S. 494, 21. [*O. Frs.* un-riucht: *O. Sax.* un-reht: *O. H. Ger.* un-reht *iniquitas, injustitia, injuria, nefas.*]

unriht-cyst, e; *f. Vice, excess*:—Ic andette . . . unrihtgilp and īdel word and unrihtcysta and ǽlcne glængc (cf. ic ondette . . . unnyttes gilpes bigong and īdle glengas, uncyste . . ., Anglia xi. 98, 27) đe tō mīnes līchaman unrǽde ǽfre belimpe, L. de Cf. 7; Th. ii. 262, 28.

unriht-dǽd, e; *f. Evil-doing*:—Hē eall đurh his unrihtdǽde āþȳstrade *universa prave agendo obnubilavit*, Bd. 5, 13; S. 633, 33. God wyle đæt Sunnandæg freóls beó fram eallum unrihtdǽdum and þeówetlīcum weorcum, Wulfst. 292, 7. Cf. yfel-dǽd.

unriht-dǽde; *adj.*: unriht-dǽda, an; *m. Evil-doing; an evil-doer*:—Se synfulla and se unrihtdǽda *peccator et iniquus*, Ps. Lamb. 9 second, 3. Cf. yfel-dǽde, -dǽda.

unriht-dēma, an; *m. An unjust judge*:—Đa unrihtdēman, đe dēmaþ ǽfre be đām sceattum and swā wendaþ wrang tō rihte, Wulfst. 203, 25: 298, 19.

unriht-dōm, es; *m. Wrong, iniquity*:—Hié for đam cumble on cneówum sǽton, efndon unrihtdōm, swā hyra aldor dyde . . . hyra freá unrǽd efnde, Cd. Th. 227, 7; Dan. 183.

unriht-dōnde; *adj. Evil-doing*; substantive, *an evil-doer*:—Him wæs beboden đæt hī sceoldan đǽm unrihtdōndum stēran, Blickl. Homl. 63, 12. Cf. yfel-dōnde.

un-rihte; *adv. Not rightly, unjustly*:—Unrihte wē dydon *injuste egimus*, Ps. Spl. 105, 6: 118, 78. Heora sylh unrihte gangaþ *aratra eorum non recte incedunt*, Bd. 5, 9; S. 623, 12. [*O. L. Ger. O. H. Ger.* un-rehto *injuste, improbe.*]

unriht-feóung, e; *f. Evil hatred, unjustifiable hate*:—Hwȳ gē ǽfre scylen unrihtfióungum eówer mōd drēfan? Met. 27, 1. v. fióung.

unriht-gestreón, es; *n. Unrighteous gain*:—Đa đe heora sylfra sāula forhycggaþ for feós lufan, and unrihtgestreón lufiaþ, Blickl. Homl. 63, 8.

unriht-gewil (? *or* unriht gewil). v. *first passage under* gewil.

unriht-gewilnung, e; *f. Evil desire*:—Đa đe swīđe hrædlīce beóđ oferswīđde mid sumre unryhtgewilnunge (cf. l. 33: đa đe mid fǽrlīce luste bióđ oferswīđde *qui repentina concupiscentia superantur*) *qui subito motu peccant*, Past. 56; Swt. 429, 30.

unriht-gilp, es; *m. n. Vainglory*:—Ic andette unrihtgilp and īdel word, L. de Cf. 7; Th. ii. 262, 27. Cf. īdel-, leás-gilp.

unriht-gītsung, e; *f. Greed, covetousness*:—Đa welan, and đæt mycele gylp, and seó unrihtgītsung, and đæt man đæm earman forwyrne, đæt is eal swīþe mycel synn beforan Gode, Blickl. Homl. 53, 21: Wulfst. 290, 26. Hē woruldsǽlþa đē onlǽnde æfter his bebodum tō brūcanne, nallas đīnre unrihtgītsunga gewill tō fulfremmanne, Bt. 7, 5; Fox 24, 10. Đæt wē gescildan ūs wiþ đa eahta heáhsynna . . . đæt is morþor and stala, māne āþas and unrihtgītsunge . . ., Engl. Stud. viii. 479, 96.

unriht-hǽman; *p.* đe *To cohabit unlawfully, to commit adultery* or *fornication*:—Hē dēđ đæt heó unrihthǽmđ; and se unrihthǽmđ đe forlǽtene genimđ *facit eam moechari; et qui dimissam duxerit, adulterat*, Mt. Kmbl. 5, 32. Se unrihthǽmđ *moechatur*, Lk. Skt. 16, 18. Heó unrihthǽmđ, Mk. Skt. 10, 12. Ne unrihthǽm đū *ne adulteris*, 10, 19: Homl. Th. ii. 208, 15. Ne unrihthǽme đū *non moechaberis*, Deut. 5, 18: Mt. Kmbl. 5, 27. Fram unrihthǽmendum mæssepreóste *a fornicante presbytero*, L. Ecg. C. 17, tit.; Th. ii. 128, 29.

unriht-hǽmdere, es; *m. An adulterer*:—Mid unrehthǽmderum *cum adulteris*, Ps. Surt. 49, 18. v. unriht-hǽmend, -hǽmere.

unriht-hǽmed, es; *n. Unlawful cohabitation, illicit intercourse, adultery, fornication*:—Cwēna geligr *vel* unrihthǽmed *adulterium*, Wrt. Voc. i. 21, 33. Forligr flǽsces unrihthǽmed is *fornicatio carnis, adulterium est*, Scint. 87, 14. Unrihthǽmed wīfes *fornicatio mulieris*, 86, 15: Met. 9, 6. Mid đȳ sweorde unryhthǽmedes (-hǽmdes, Cott. MSS.) *luxuriae mucrone*, Past. 43; Swt. 313, 9. On đæt hnesce bedd đæs gesinscipes, næs on đa heardan eorđan đæs unryhthǽmdes, 51; Swt. 397, 23. Ne đa unfæsđrādan đe ne magon hira unryhthǽmdes geswīcan *neque adulteri, neque molles, neque masculorum concubitores*, Swt. 401, 28. Se ýfela willa unrihthǽmedes (*voluptas*) gedrēfđ fulneáh ǽlces monnes mōd . . . sceal ǽlce sāwl forweorđan æfter đam unrihthǽmede, Bt. 31, 2; Fox 112, 24: Met. 18, 10. On unrihthǽmede *in adulterio*, Jn. Skt. 8, 3. Be mōnađādles hǽmede and be ōþrum unrihthǽmede (*de alio pravo coitu*), L. Ecg. C. 16, tit.; Th. ii. 128, 26: Shrn. 99, 4. Monige hié gehealdaþ wiđ unryhthǽmed *multi scelera carnis deserunt*, Past. 51; Swt. 399, 7. Hē onscunede unrihthǽmed *recusabat stuprum*, Gen. 39, 10. Gif wer unrihthǽmed fremeþ wiþ ōþer wīf, Blickl. Homl. 185, 25. Unrihthǽmedu *adulteria*, Mt. Kmbl. 15, 19: Bt. 16, 4; Fox 58, 1.

unriht-hǽmed; *adj. Adulterous*:—Unrihthǽmede mæn tō rihtum līfe mid synna hreówe tō fōn, L. Wih. 3; Th. i. 36, 18. Mid unrihthǽmedum *cum adulteris*, Ps. Spl. 49, 19.

unriht-hǽmend, es; *m. An adulterer*:—Þeófum and mānswarum and unrihthǽmendum, Blickl. Homl. 63, 13.

unriht-hǽmere, es; *m. An adulterer, a fornicator*:—Unrihthēmere *adulter*, Kent. Gl. 169. Se đe wīfaþ on đam forlǽtenum wīfe biđ unrihthǽmere gehāten fram Gode, Homl. Th. ii. 322, 35. Unrihthǽmeras *adulteri*, Lk. Skt. 18, 11: Wulfst. 298, 16: Homl. Th. ii. 324, 7: Homl. Ass. 147, 94: *fornicarii*, Homl. Skt. i. 17, 38.

un-rihtlīc; *adj. Unrighteous, unjust, wicked, wrongful*:—Unryhtlīcu iersung, đæt is đæt mon iersige on ōđerne for his gōde (*on account of his prosperity*), Past. 27; Swt. 189, 8. Hié him andwyrdon đæt hit gemālīc wǽre and unryhtlīc đæt swā oferwlenced cyning sceolde winnan on swā earm folc *responderunt, stolide opulentissimum regem adversus inopes sumsisse bellum*, Ors. 1, 10; Swt. 44, 11. Gif ǽlces mannes līf ǽfre sceole swā gān đæt hē mæge forbūgan bysmorlīce dǽda, đonne biđ unrihtlīc đæt đa unrihtwīsan onfōn wītnunge for heora wōhnysse, Homl. Skt. i. 17, 231: Homl. Th. i. 292, 5. Ne lufa đū gītsunga ne unrihtlīce welan . . . Beó đē swīđe ælfremed ǽlc unrihtlīc gestreón, Basil admn. 9; Norm. 52, 18–21. For đīnum gōdan willan đū wēndest đæt đē nānwuht unrihtlīces on becuman ne mihte, Bt. 7, 3; Fox 22, 15. Þing unrihtlīc *rem injustam*, Ps. Spl. 100, 3. Hē ne mæg đurhteón đæt unryhtlīce weorc *nequaquam usque ad opus nefarium rapitur*, Past. 11; Swt. 73, 6. Mē egleþ swȳđe đa unrihtlīcan gefeoht đe betwux ūs sylfum syndan, L. Edm. S. prm.; Th. i. 246, 24. Be unrihtlīcum hǽmedum *de pravis coitibus*, L. Ecg. C. 21, tit.; Th. ii. 130, 4. [*O. H. Ger.* un-rehtlīh: *Icel.* ū-rēttligr.]

un-rihtlīce; *adv. Unrighteously, unjustly, wickedly, wrongfully*:—Unrihtlīce *injuste*, Ps. Spl. 68, 6: 118, 78. Nōht unryhtlīce *non injuste*, Past. 39; Swt. 285, 3. Gē unrihtlīce libbaþ *inique agetis*, Deut. 31, 29. Wē syngodon, wē dydon unrihtlīce, Homl. Th. ii. 420, 26: Wulfst. 160, 4: Blickl. Homl. 59, 19. Unrihtlīce hī mē hatiaþ *odio iniquo oderunt me*, Ps. Th. 24, 17. Se wæs unrihtlīce ofslagen ofer āþas and treówa, Bd. 2, 20; S 521, 17. Se wæs unrihtlīce ādrǽfed, Chr. 1022; Erl. 161, 36. Hē nǽnigne man unrihtlīce fordēmde, Blickl. Homl. 223, 32. Se đe unwærlīce and unryhtlīce gewilnige *qui incaute expetiit*, Past. proem.; Swt. 23, 15. For đam sceatte đe hē lufode unrihtlīce, Basil admn. 9; Norm. 54, 15. Ǽlc đe hǽmđ būton rihtre ǽwe, hē hǽmđ unrihtlīce, Homl. Th. ii. 208, 16. [*O. H. Ger.* un-rihtlīhho: *Icel.* ū-rēttliga.]

unriht-lust, es; *m. Improper desire*:—Đū eart scyldigra đonne wē for đīnum āgnum unrihtlustum, Bt. 7, 5; Fox 24, 7.

unriht-lyblāc, es; *n. m. Sorcery*:—Ne galdorsangas ne unrihtlyblāc wē onginnen, Wulfst. 253, 11. v. lyb-lāc.

un-rihtness, e; *f. Iniquity, injustice, wrong*:—Unrehtnise *iniquitatis*, Rtl. 42, 27. Unrehtnises, 174, 10. Đū heardeste strǽl tō ǽghwilcre unrihtnesse, Blickl. Homl. 241, 4. Đa đe wyrcaþ unrihtnesse (*injustitiam*), Ps. Lamb. 93, 4. Unrehtnisse *iniquitatem*, Lk. Skt. Rush. 13, 27.

unriht-weorc, es; *n. Improper work*:—Be Sunnandæges unrihtweorcum *de profanis operibus die Dominico*, L. Ecg. C. 35, tit.; Th. ii. 130, 25.

unriht-wīf, es; *n. A woman of bad character*:—Godwine hæfđ gelǽd fulle lāde æt đan unrihtwīfe đe Leófgār bisceop hine tihte, Chart. Th. 373, 32.

unriht-wīfung, e; *f. Unlawful matrimony*:—Hē forlēt đa unrihtwīfunge *abdicato connubio non legitimo*, Bd. 2, 6; S. 508, 30.

unriht-willend, es; *m.*: *or* -willende *adj.* (*ptcpl.*) *An ill-disposed person, an unrighteous person*:—Đæt hē wiđstande mid his sprǽce đām unryhtwillendum đe đyses middangeardes waldaþ *hujus mundi potestatibus contraire*, Past. 15; Swt. 89, 22.

unriht-wilnung, e; *f. Improper desire, cupidity, concupiscence*:—Ānra gehwylces unrihtwillnung (*cupiditas*) on đyssum fȳre byrneþ, Bd. 3, 19; S. 548, 27. Đa đe mid sumere unryhtwilnunga beóđ fǽringa ofersuīđede *qui repentina concupiscentia superantur*, Past. 23; Swt. 179, 2.

un-rihtwīs; *adj. Unrighteous, unjust, evil*:—Unrihtwīs *injustus*, Wrt. Voc. i. 75, 70. Unrihtwīs dōm đæt se hālga wer swā đrowode, Homl. Th. i. 596, 24. Se đe ys on lytlum unrihtwīs (*iniquus*), se ys eác on māran unrihtwīs (-rehtwīs, Lind.), Lk. Skt. 16, 10. Se unrihtwīsa *injustus*, Ps. Spl. 35, 1. Se unrihtwīsa dēma *judex iniquitatis*, Lk. Skt. 18, 6. Se unrihtwīsa cāsere Neron, Bt. 16, 4; Fox 58, 2: 28; Fox 100,

25: Met. 15, 1. Of handa unrihtwíses (*iniqui*), Ps. Spl. 70, 5. Cýderas unrihtwíse *testes iniqui*, 26, 18. Unrihtwíse *injusti*, Lk. Skt. 18, 11. Ða unryhtwísan *impii*, Past. 11; Swt. 65, 12. Ða unrihtwísan tǽlaþ ða rihtwísan *justus tulit crimen iniqui*, Bt. 4; Fox 8, 15. Ða unrihtwísan cyngas *tyranni*, 37, 1; Fox 186, 26: 36, 2; Fox 174, 26. Ic hatode ða gesamnunge unrihtwísra (*malignorum*), Ps. Th. 25, 5. Se áwyrgda gást is heáfod ealra unrihtwísra dǽda, swylce unrihtwíse syndon deófles leomo, Blickl. Homl. 33, 7. Hé wæs mid unrihtwísum (-rehtuísum, Lind.: -rehtwísum, Rush. *iniquis*) geteald, Mk. Skt. 15, 28. Be ðám ofermódum and ðám unrihtwísum cyningum, Bt. 37, 1; Fox 186, 1: Met. 25, 2. [*Icel.* ú-réttwíss.]

un-rihtwís[u] (?): -rihtwíse (?), an; *f. Unrighteousness, iniquity*:—Árfest eallum unrihtwísum (*iniquitatibus*) ðínum, Ps. Spl. 102, 3. [*Icel.* ú-réttvísi; *f. unrighteousness.*] v. riht-wís (?); *f.*

un-rihtwíslíce; *adv. Unrighteously*:—Ic cwæð tó ðǽm unrihtwísum: 'Ne dó gé unryhtwíslíce' *dixi iniquis*: '*Nolite inique agere*,' Past. 54; Swt. 425, 21. [*Icel.* ú-réttvísliga.]

un-rihtwísness, e; *f. Unrighteousness, iniquity, injustice*:—Nis nán unrihtwísnys (*injustitia*) on him, Jn. Skt. 7, 18. Unryhtwísnys (*iniquitas*) ríxaþ, Mt. Kmbl. 24, 12. Unrihtwísnys, Ps. Spl. 7, 3: 35, 3. Ðonne hwæm hwæt cymþ máre ðonne ðé þincþ ðæt hé wyrþe sié, ne biþ sió unryhtwísnes nó on Gode, ac sió ungleáwnes biþ on ðé selfum, Bt. 39, 10; Fox 226, 32. Sió ðuru ðære unryhtwísnesse *janua iniquitatis*, Past. 21; Swt. 157, 22. Unrihtwísnesse (-rehtwísnesses, Lind.) túngeréfa *vilicus iniquitatis*, Lk. Skt. 16, 8, 9. Ðú ágiltst fædera unrihtwísnysse (*iniquitatem*) hira bearnum, Ex. 34, 7: 20, 5. Ða ðe unrihtwísnesse wyrceaþ *qui faciunt iniquitatem*, Mt. Kmbl. 13, 41: Blickl. Homl. 89, 16. Árfæst eallum mínum unrihtwísnessum, 89, 3. Unrehtuísnissum *iniquitatibus*, Rtl. 169, 29. God hæfð árásod úre unrihtwísnissa, Gen. 44, 16: Blickl. Homl. 87, 29.

unriht-wrigels, es; *n. A veil of error*:—Hié wǽron stǽnenre heortan and blindre, ðæt hié ðǽr ongeotan ne cúðan, ðæt hié ðǽr gehýrdon, ne ðæt oncnáwan ne mihton, ðæt hié ðǽr gesáwon; ac God áfyrde him ðæt unrihtwrigels (cf. ðone unrihtan wrigels, Wulfst. 252, 4) of heora heortan (cf. Their minds were blinded; for until this day remaineth the same vail untaken away in the reading of the old testament; which vail is done away in Christ . . . The vail is upon their heart. Nevertheless when it shall turn to the Lord, the vail shall be taken away, 2 Cor. 2, 14–16), Blickl. Homl. 105, 30.

unriht-wyrcend, es; *m.*: *or* -wyrcende; *adj.* (*ptcpl.*) *An evil-doer, or evil-doing*:—Ic ne ineode on ðæt geþeaht unrihtwyrcendra *cum iniqua gerentibus non introibo*, Ps. Th. 25, 4. Mid ðám unrihtwyrcendum *cum operantibus iniquitatem*, 27, 3. Belocen ðǽm synnfullum mannum and ðǽm unrihtwyrcendum, Blickl. Homl. 61, 11.

unriht-wyrhta, an; *m. An evil-doer, a worker of iniquity*:—Gewítaþ fram mé ealle unrihtwyrhtan (*operarii iniquitatis*), Lk. Skt. 13, 27. Unryhtwyrhtan, Past. 1; Swt. 27, 23. Unrihtwyrhtan *iniqui*, Ps. Th. 118, 86.

un-rím, es; *n. A countless number, an incalculable number* or *amount*, (1) without a following genitive:—Ðonne án tweó of ádón biþ, ðonne biþ unrím ástyred *ut una dubitatione succisa innumerabiles aliae succrescant*, Bt. 39, 4; Fox 216, 19. (2) with a genitive plural:—Ðǽr is unrím on ealra cwycra *illic reptilia, quorum non est numerus*, Ps. Th. 103, 24: Shrn. 65, 24. Hié in ðære eá áweóllon swá ǽmettan, swilc unrím heora wæs, Nar. 11, 14. Him com unrím wildeóra ðǽrtó, Shrn. 118, 16: Met. 20, 190. Him gelýfde leóda unrím, 26, 40. Reced weardode unrím eorla, Beo. Th. 2480; B. 1238. Ðæt is herga mǽst, eádigra unrím, Exon. Th. 352, 3; Sch. 92. Mid unríme þegna and eorla, Met. 25, 7. Þeáh hé áge ǽhta unrím, 14, 4. Betwuh óþerra unrím ǽwyrdleana *inter alia detrimenta innumera*, Bd. 1, 3; S. 475, 21: Andr. Kmbl. 1408; An. 704. Hé gehét unrím máþma *promisit se ei innumera ornamenta largiturum*, Bd. 3, 24; S. 556, 8: Exon. Th. 245, 12; Jul. 43. Wé witon unrím monna *multos scimus*, Bt. 11, 2; Fox 36, 2. Hé ofslóh unrím Walana, Chr. 605; Erl. 21, 26: Cd. Th. 194, 15; Exod. 261: 220, 13; Dan. 70: Exon. Th. 270, 23; Jul. 469. Wíta unrím, Cd. Th. 22, 4; Gen. 335: 48, 15; Gen. 776. (2a) with the verb in the plural:—Beóð ðé áhylded fram wíta unrím, grimra gyrna ðe ðé gegearwad sind, Exon. Th. 252, 33; Jul. 172. (2b) in the following the construction is peculiar, the word seeming indeclinable; v. next word, ¶:—Nalæs mid ánes mannes geþeahte, ac mid gesægene unrím geleáffulra witena *non uno quolibet auctore, sed fideli innumerorum testium adsertione*, Bd. pref.; S. 472, 25. Bútan óþrum læssan unrím ceastra *praeter castella innumera*, 1, 1; S. 473, 28. (3) with a sing. gen. of word implying multitude:—Unrím heriges, Chr. 937; Erl. 112, 31. Cnósles unrím, Exon. Th. 430, 15; Rä. 44, 9. Ðæt his (*of that race*) unrím á in wintra worn wurðan sceolde, Cd. Th. 236, 21; Dan. 324. Eác ðám wæs unrím óðres mánes (cf. ðæt wæs tó-eácan óþrum unárímedum yflum, Bt. 1; Fox 2, 11), Met. 1, 44. Ðǽr wæs wunden gold on wǽn hladen, ǽghwæs unrím, Beo. Th. 6261; B. 3135. Sió hálige cirice unrím folces beféhð mid ánfealde geleáfan *innumeros sanctae ecclesiae populos unitas fidei contegit*, Past. 15; Swt. 95, 7: Exon. Th. 36, 1; Cri. 569. Hé geaf him gúðgewǽda ǽghwæs unrím, Beo. Th. 5241; B. 2624. [*O. Sax.* un-rím (engiló).] v. un-gerím, *and following words.*

un-rím *and* un-ríme; *adj. Innumerable, incalculable, not to be numbered*:—Unrím getæl *ingens numerus*, Nar. 9, 13. Folc unrím (*or pl.?*) þrymfæste twá þeóda áwócon, Cd. Th. 158, 9; Gen. 2614. Werod, mægen unríme, Elen. Kmbl. 121; El. 61. Hyra fromcynn swá unríme weorðan sceolde, Exon. Th. 188, 4; Az. 40: 187, 26; Az. 36. Ðǽr is máðma hord, gold unríme, Beo. Th. 6016; B. 3012. Mid ða unríman mænigeo *innumerabilis multitudo*, Bd. 5, 12; S. 628, 4. Wǽron on ðyssum felda unríme gesomminge *erant in hoc campo innumera conventicula*, S. 629, 24. Monige sindon geond middangeard, unrímu cynn, Exon. Th. 355, 38; Pa. 2: 389, 5; Rä. 7, 3. ¶ In the following passage the word seems indeclinable, unless *unrím-gód* = an immense, incalculable good, may be taken as a compound; cf. unrím-folc, and see preceding word (2 b):—Se symle leofaþ gehwǽr on unrím gódum *qui innumeris semper vivit ubique bonis*, Bd. 2, 1; S. 500, 23. v. un-gerím; *adj.*

unrím-folc, es; *n. An innumerable people*:—Gif hé underféngе ðone ealdordóm swelces unrímfolces búton ege *si ducatum plebis innumerae sine trepidatione susciperet*, Past. 7; Swt. 51, 12. Cf. síd-, wíd-folc.

un-rípe; *adj. Unripe, immature*:—Unrípe deáð *immatura mors*, Wrt. Voc. i. 39, 20. Ða unrípan *immatura*, Hpt. Gl. 518, 22. [*O. H. Ger.* un-rífi *immaturus.*]

un-rót; *adj.* I. *sad, sorrowful, troubled, gloomy*:—Unrót *tristis*, Wrt. Voc. i. 51, 1: 83, 37. Hé ongann beón unrót (*moestus*). Ðá sǽde se Hǽlynd: 'Unrót (*tristis*) is mín sáwl,' Mt. Kmbl. 26, 37, 38. Unrót *contristatus*, Ps. Th. 37, 6: Exon. Th. 73, 2; Cri. 1183: 166, 3; Gú. 1037. Geómormód, earg and unrót, eallum bidǽled dugeþum and dreámum, 86, 14; Cri. 1408. Hwæðer ðú ǽfre áuht unrót wǽre ðá ðá ðú gesǽlgost wǽre *inter illas abundantissimas opes numquam ne animum tuum concepta ex qualibet injuria confudit anxietas?* Bt. 26, 1; Fox 90, 21. Ðá andsworode ðæt unróte mód, 3, 4; Fox 6, 18. Se Hǽlend hine unrótne geseah *uidens illum Jesus tristem factum*, Lk. Skt. 18, 24: Exon. Th. 177, 28; Gú. 1234. Ða unrótan *mestam*, Wrt. Voc. ii. 54, 42. Wǽron hig swíðe unróte (*tristes*), Gen. 40, 6: Judth. Thw. 25, 29; Jud. 284. Middaneard geblissaþ, and gé beóð unróte *mundus gaudebit, vos autem contristabimini*, Jn. Skt. 16, 20: Blickl. Homl. 135, 15, 25. Ne beóð gé unróte, ac gefeóþ mid mé, 191, 22: 225, 14. Higum unróte módceare mǽndon, Beo. Th. 6288; B. 3148. Ða men (*men with pain in the spleen*) beóð mægre and unróte, Lchdm. ii. 242, 3. On óðre wísan sint tó manianne ða gladan (blíðan, l. 14), on óðre ða unrótan (*tristes*), Past. 27; Swt. 186, 13. Hé geseah ða men ealle unróte (*moestos*) ðe him æt wǽron, Bd. 5, 5; S. 618, 6. II. *displeased, harsh, angry*:—For hwig syndon gé swá unróte ongeán mé? Is hyt for ðam ðe ic ábæd ðæs Hǽlendes líchaman æt Pilate? Nicod. 13; Thw. 6, 29. v. þurh-unrót.

un-rótian. v. ge-unrótian.

un-rótlíc; *adj. Gloomy*:—Unrótlíc heofon *triste coelum*, Mt. Kmbl. Lind. 16, 3. v. next word.

un-rótlíce; *adv. Gloomily, sadly*:—Reádaþ unrótlíce ðe heofun *rutilat triste coelum*, Mt. Kmbl. Rush. 16, 3. Unrótlíce dóþ *exterminant* (but perhaps the word is adjective, as the passage to which the gloss belongs is Mt. 6, 16: Nolite fieri sicut hypocritae tristes: exterminant facies suas), Wrt. Voc. ii. 72, 21: 30, 64.

unrót-mód; *adj. Sad at heart*:—Hé for ðære geómrunga ðæs óþres deáþes leng on ðam lande gewunian ne mihte; ac hé unrótmód of his cýþþe gewát, Blickl. Homl. 113, 12.

un-rótness, e; *f. Sadness, sorrow, trouble, gloominess*:—Unrótnys *tristitia*, Wrt. Voc. i. 83, 42. Ðætte sió unrótnes, ðe hé for ðæm yflan weorcum hæbbe, gemetgige ðone gefeán ðe hé for ðǽm gódan weorcum hæfde, Past. proem.; Swt. 24, 3. Unrótnyss (*tristitia*) gefylde eówre heortan, Jn. Skt. 16, 6. Eówer unrótnys (-ródtnis, Lind.) byð gewend tó gefeán, 16, 20. Nis ðǽr ǽnig sár geméted, ne ádl, ne ece, ne nǽnig unrótnes, Blickl. Homl. 25, 31. Ic hit wiste be sumum dǽle, ac mé hæfde ðiós unrótnes ámerredne, ðæt ic hit hæfde mid ealle forgiten; and ðæt is eác mínre unrótnysse se mǽsta dǽl, ðæt . . . *eaque mihi etsi ob injuriae dolorem nuper oblita, non tamen ante hac prorsus ignorata dixisti; sed ea ipsa est vel maxima nostri caussa moeroris; quod . . .*, Bt. 36, 1; Fox 172, 2–4. Se fífta leahtor is *tristitia*, ðæt is ðissere woruldе unrótnyss; ðæt is ðonne se man geunrótsaþ ealles tó swýðe for his ǽhta lyre . . . Twá unrótnyssa synd; án is ðeós yfele, and óðer is hálwende, ðæt is ðæt se man for his synnum geunrótsige, Homl. Skt. i. 16, 289: Homl. Th. ii. 220, 16: Wulfst. 68, 15. Ðé is frófre máre ðearf ðonne unrótnesse *medicinae tempus est, non querelae*, Bt. 3, 3; Fox 6, 15. Hí weorþaþ geráefte mid ðære unrótnesse and swá gehæfte *moerer captos fatigat*, Bt. 37, 1; Fox 186, 21: Met. 25, 48. Gefeá búton unrótnesse, Blickl. Homl. 65, 18: 85, 33. On wópe and on unrótnesse and on sáre his líchoma sceal hér wunian, 61, 1: 3, 9. Hé hig funde slǽpende for unrótnesse (*prae tristitiam*), Lk. Skt. 22, 45. Se heora unrótnesse ealle gewríðeþ *qui alligat contritiones eorum*, Ps. Th.

146, 3. Hē hiene on unrōtnesse oððe on ormōdnesse gebringð, Past. 21; Swt. 166, 12. Of ðæs magan âdle cumaþ . . . micla murnunga and unrōtnessa bûtan þearfe, Lchdm. ii. 174, 26. Mid manegum unrōtnessum Dauid wæs ofdrycced under Sawle, Ps. Th. 38, arg. Ðǣm oferblīðum is tō cȳðanne ða unrōtnessa (*tristia*) ðe ðǣræfter cumaþ, and ðām unblīðum sint tō cȳðanne ða gefeán (*laeta*) ðe him gehâtene sindon, Past. 27; Swt. 187, 15.

un-rōtsian; *p.* ode. I. *to be sad, to be sorrowful*:—Hē unrōtsade *contristatus*, Mk. Skt. Lind. Rush. 3, 5. Ðā unrōtsodon helware, Homl. Skt. i. 4. 292. Ðæt gehwā for his synnum unrōtsige mid sōðre dǣdbōte, Homl. Th. ii. 220, 20. Ðū lǣrdest ðæt wē ne unrōtsodon, þeáh ūre spēda wanodon, Shrn. 167, 12. Hē ongann unrôtsian *coepit contristari*, Mt. Kmbl. 26, 37. Hiá ongunnon unrôtsia (-rôtsiga, Rush.) *illi coeperunt contristari*, Mk. Skt. Lind. 14, 19. Unrôtsande wæs *contristatus est*, Mt. Kmbl. Lind. 14, 9. II. *to make sad* or *sorrowful*:—Alle gidroefde ł unrôtsade (unrōdsad ł gestyred, Lind.) wērun *omnes conturbati sunt*, Mk. Skt. Rush. 6, 50. v. ge-unrôtsian.

un-rūh; *adj. Not rough, smooth*:—Cyrtil unrūh ł smoeðe *tunica inconsutilis*, Jn. Skt. Lind. Rush. 19, 23.

un-ryne, es; *m. An ill-running, diarrhœa*:—Gif ðū ðās wyrte sylst þicgean on strangon wīne, heó ðæs innoðes unryne gewrīð, Lchdm. i. 172, 13.

un-sac (-sæc?); *adj. Free from any charge*:—Unsac hē wæs on līfe *no charge was brought against him while alive*, Lchdm. iii. 288, 6. v. sac, on-sæc, *and* cf. *Icel.* ū-sekr *not guilty*.

un-sadelod. v. un-gesadelod.

un-sæd; *adj. Unsatisfied, insatiable*:—Unsædre heortan *insatiabili corde*, Ps. Th. 100, 5.

un-sǣd, es; *n. Bad seed*:—Ealle unþeáwas âweallaþ of deófle, and hē ðæt unsǣd sâweþ tō wīde, Wulfst. 40, 23.

un-sægd, -sǣd; *adj. Unsaid*:—Wē hit lǣtaþ unsǣd, Wanl. Cat. 6, 13.

un-sǣl, es; *m. Unhappiness*:—Ða deóflu wǣron on miclum unsǣlum (v. sǣl, **IV.** ¶), and ða englas wǣron on swīðe micelre blisse, Wulfst. 236, 26. [Unsel him wes on mode, Laym. 30541. Sum unsel heom is ihende, O. and N. 1263. Þer heo þolyeþ al unsel, Misc. 146, 90. A draȝte of unsele *an unfortunate draught*, i. e. poison, Alex. (Skt.) 1106. On unsele oðer an untime *at an improper season or time*, Rel. Ant. i. 131, 43. Cf. *Icel.* ū-sæla *unhappiness.*]

un-sǣlan; *p.* de *To untie, unbind, loose*:—Git moeteþ æsul gesǣlde and folan mid hire, unsǣleþ (*solvite*), Mt. Kmbl. Rush. 21, 2. Onlēsed, unsǣled *desolutus*, i. *liberatus*, Wrt. Voc. ii. 139, 29. Unmidled *vel* unsǣled *effrenus*, 142, 60.

un-sǣle; *adj. Evil, wicked*:—Unsǣle, gemāh *improbus*, Wrt. Voc. ii. 45, 16. [Crist warrþ unnorne and wrecche and usell child, Orm. 3668. Holde ich no mon for unsele (*miserable*) otherwhyle that he fele sumthyng that him smerte, Rel. Ant. i. 113, 13. *Goth.* un-sēls πονηρός: *Icel.* ū-sæll *unhappy.*]

un-sǣlig; *adj.* I. of persons, *unhappy, unblest, miserable* as being evil:—Deófol sǣwð unwīsdōm, ðæt unsǣlig man wīsdōmes ne gȳmeþ, Wulfst. 52, 27. Ðū miltsige mē (*a devil*), ðæt unsǣlig (ic) ne forweorþe, Exon. Th. 269, 14; Jul. 450. Hī (*the good*) fore gōddǣdum blissiaþ, ða hȳ (*the wicked*) unsǣlge ǣr forhogdun tō dōnne, 79, 9; Cri. 1288. Hæleð unsǣlige (*the unbelieving Jews*), Andr. Kmbl. 1122; An. 561. II. of things, *unhappy, bringing misery*:—Æppel unsǣlga (cf. Milton: the fruit whose mortal taste brought death into the world, and all our woe), Cd. Th. 40, 10; Gen. 637. [Þe unseli Semei, A. R. 174, 1. Hwa se is swa unseli, þat he þis soð schunie, Kath. 1793. Unnseliȝ mann amm ic wurrþenn, Orm. 4812. Ðat folc unseli (*the people of Sodom*), Gen. and Ex. 1073. Unsely wrecche, Chauc. second N. P. T. 468. *O. H. Ger.* un-sâlig *infelix.*] v. un-gesǣlig.

un-sǣlþ, e; *f. Unhappiness, misfortune, misery*:—Ðæt is seó mǣste unsǣlð on ðīs andweardan līfe, ðæt mon ǣrest weorþe gesǣlig and æfter ðam ungesǣlig *in omni adversitate fortunae infelicissimum genus est infortunii, fuisse felicem*, Bt. 10; Fox 26, 30. Him wǣre ealra mǣst unsǣlþ ðæt, ðæt se fyrst wǣre ōþ dōmes dæg *licentiam infelicissimam, si esset eterna*, 38, 4; Fox 204, 16 Hwelc mæg him māre unsǣlð becuman *quid eorum mente infelicius?* Past. 45; Swt. 340, 4. Hié wilniaþ ōþera manna unsǣlþa and him cymð sylfum ðæt ylce *infelicitas in viis eorum*, Ps. Th. 13, 7. Hē hwīlum selþ ða gesǣlþa ðǣm gōdum and ðǣm yflum unsǣlþa . . . hwīlum hē eft geþafaþ ðæt ða gōdan habbaþ unsǣlþa and ungelimp and ða yfelan habbaþ gesǣlþa *qui saepe bonis jucunda, malis aspera, contraque bonis dura tribuat, malis optata concedat*, Bt. 39, 2; Fox 214, 1–5: 10; Bt. 28, 8. [He fleh mid muchele unsælðe, Laym. 4748. Al for hire onselþe (*wickedness*), 2nd MS. 4545. To þolenn illc unnsellþe, Orm. 1561. Unnseollþe, 4811. Sum unselþe heom is ihende, O. and N. 1263. Ðo wex unselðe on hem . . . dolc, sor, and blein, Gen. and Ex. 3026. *O. H. Ger.* un-sâlida *infelicitas, dementia.*] v. ungesǣlþ.

un-sæpig; *adj. Not sappy, sapless*:—Treówa gif hī beóð on fullum mōnan geheáwene, hī beóð heardran tō getimbrunge, and swīðost gif hī beóð unsæpige geworhte, Homl. Th. i. 102, 24.

un-samwrǣde; *adj. Not united, opposed, contrary*:—Gif ða gōdan ðonne simle habbaþ anweald, ðonne nabbaþ ða yfelan nǣfre nǣnne, for ðam ðæt gōd and ðæt yfel sint swīþe unsamwrǣde *nam cum bonum malumque contraria sint, si bonum potens esse constiterit, liquet imbecillitas mali*, Bt. 36, 3; Fox 176, 2. v. sam-wrǣdness.

un-sār; *adj. Not sore, without soreness* or *pain*:—Se teter bûtan sâre hē ofergǣð ðone līchoman . . .; se giecða bið suīðe unsār, Past. 11; Swt. 71, 19. Gnīd mid ða tōðreoman, hī beóð clǣne and unsâre, Lchdm. i. 346, 15. Ðæt geswel wyrð unsārre *the swelling becomes more free from pain*, ii. 208, 4.

un-sāwen; *adj. Not sown*:— ii. æceras, ōðerne gesâwene, and ōðerne unsâwene, L. R. S. 10; Th. i. 438, 5.

un-scæþfull, -scæþþig, -scæþþende. v. un-sceaþfull, -sceþþig, -sceþþende.

un-sceád[e]līce; *adv. Unreasonably*:—Gif hwylc brōðor unsceádelīce hwæs bidde *si quis frater aliqua inrationabiliter postulat*, R. Ben. 54, 13. v. un-gesceádlīce.

un-sceádwīslīc; *adj. Unreasonable, irrational*:—Gif wē ða unsceádwīslīcan styrunga on stæððignysse âwendaþ, Homl. Th. ii. 210, 30. v. un-gesceádwīslīc.

un-sceamfæst; *adj. Shameless, impudent*:—Unsceamfæst *impudens*, Wrt. Voc. i. 86, 57. Unscamfæst *impudens, inverecundus, sine pudore*, Hpt. Gl. 472, 37. [Onschamefæst *inpudens, inverecundus, effrons*, Prompt. Parv. 367.]

un-sceamfulness, e; *f. Shamelessness, immodesty, lasciviousness*:—Unsceomfulnise (-scomfulnisse, Rush.) *inpudicitia*, Mk. Skt. Lind. 7, 21.

un-sceamiende *not being ashamed*:—Ðæt hē mæge fore eágum eorðbūendra unscomiende ēðles brūcan bysmerleás, Exon. Th. 81, 17; Cri. 1325.

un-sceamig; *adj. Not to be confounded, unabashed*:—Is on mē sweotul ðæt ðū unscamge ǣghwæs wurde on ferþe frōd *in me is it plain, that thou, O woman not to be confounded! hast become in everything sagacious in mind*, Exon. Th. 275, 18; Jul. 552. [*O. H. Ger.* scamig *confusus, erubescens*; unscameg ze uerdenne *not to be put to shame.*]

un-sceamlīc; *adj. Immodest, shameless*:—Ic hī âstyrede mid fūllīcum gesprǣcum. Hī mīne unsceamlīcan gebǣra geseónde mē on heora scip nāmon tō him, Homl. Skt. ii. 23b, 377. [*O. H. Ger.* un-scamalīh *impudens.*]

un-sceamlīce; *adv. Shamelessly*:—Ðæt [hié] mid ðām hæleðum hǣman wolden unscomlīce, Cd. Th. 148, 19; Gen. 2459. [*O. H. Ger.* un-scamalīcho *impudenter.*]

un-sceandlīce (?); *adv. Shamelessly*:—Ic mē unsceandlīce [*the* un- *has been erased* (*properly.* v. sceandlīce) *in one MS.*], swā swā ic gewuna wæs, tōmiddes heora gemengde, Homl. Skt. ii. 23 b, 372.

un-scearp; *adj. Not sharp*:—Unscearp wīn, Lchdm. ii. 212, 4. v. scearp, **II.**

un-scearpness, e; *f. Want of sharpness, dullness*:—For his ungleáwnesse and for his unscearpnesse *propter ingenii tarditatem*, Bd. 5, 6; S. 620, 7.

un-scearpsīne; *adj. Not sharpsighted*:—Ealdes mannes eágan beóþ unscearpsȳno . . . Þus mon sceal unscearpsȳnum sealfe wyrcean tō eágum, Lchdm. ii. 30, 27–32, 1.

un-sceaþfull (-scæþ-, -sceþ-); *adj. Innocent*:—Se ðe æfter ðæm higaþ ðæt hē eádig sié on ðisse worulde, ne biþ hē unsceaþful (-full, Cott. MSS.) *qui festinat ditari, non erit innocens*, Past. 44; Swt. 331, 15. Hē ðe unscæðfull byð mid his handum *innocens manibus*, Ps. Th. 23, 4. Unsceðfull wið ða unsceðfullan, 17, 25: 24, 19. Ða wegas ðæra unsceðfulra *vias immaculatorum*, 36, 17. Ða unscæðfullan heortan *rectos corde*, 36, 13. [Shep iss all unskaþefull, Orm. 1176.]

un-sceaþfullīce; *adv. Innocently*:—Ða ðe unsceaðfullīce (-sceð-, Cott. MSS.) libbaþ *qui innocenter vivunt*, Past. 37; Swt. 263, 7.

un-sceaþfulness, e; *f. Innocence*:—Se ðe gehielt his unsceaðfulnesse and his gōdan willan *si mentis innocentia custoditur*, Past. 34; Swt. 234, 22. Ðȳ læs hī forlǣtan hiora unsceaþfulnesse (-sceð-, Cott. MS.) *desinet colere forsitan innocentiam*, Bt. 39, 10; Fox 228, 5. Unsceaðfulnisse *innocentiam*, Ps. Surt. 17, 25. Unsceðfulnisse, 7, 9: 40, 13: 100, 2.

un-scelleht. v. un-scilliht.

un-scende, -scynde; *adj. Without disgrace, honourable, noble*:—Ælfheres lāf (*a coat of mail*) golde geweorðod, ealles unscende, æðelinges reáf, Wald. 96; Vald. 2. 20. Gife unscynde *a noble gift* (the nails from the cross), Elen. Kmbl. 2400; El. 1201: 2492; El. 1247. Eów Dryhten geaf dōm unscyndne, 730; El. 365. Se him dōm forgeaf, unscyndne blǣd, Cd. Th. 263, 16; Dan. 763. [*O. H. Ger.* un-scant *non ignominiosus.*]

un-scended; *adj. Unharmed, uncorrupted*:—Erfeweardnisse unscended *hereditatem incorruptam* (v. 1 Pet. 1, 4), Rtl. 24, 32. Unscendede hond *manum inlesam*, 102, 37.

un-scendende; *adj. Innocent*:—Unscendende ic am *innocens ego sum*, Mt. Kmbl. Lind. 27, 24.

un-sceód. v. un-scōg(i)an.

un-sceótan *to open* :—Unsceót *vel* geopena *exentera*, Wrt. Voc. i. 61, 13. v. an-sceótan.

un-sceþþende; *adj. Innocent, harmless* :— Unsceþþende ic eam *innocens ego sum*, Mt. Kmbl. Rush. 27, 25. Onfōh mīne sāwle, for ic wæs unsceđþende and clǣnheort, Shrn. 139, 22. Ða bilehwitnysse đæs unscæþþendan (*innocentis*) līfes, Bd. 1, 26; S. 487, 40. Ðæt hē đære unsceþþendan (*innocuae*) ylde cilda ne ārede, 2, 20; S. 521, 25. Ðone mildheortan and đone unsceþþendan Crist, Blickl. Homl. 3, 11. Hī đa unscæþþendan (*innoxiam*) đeóde forhergodon, Bd. 4, 26; S. 602, 6. Unsceaþþiendra fordēmednesse *proscriptionibus innocentum*, 1, 6; S. 476, 25. Ðæt hē mæge fordōn đa unsceđþendan *ut interficiat innocentem*, Ps. Th. 9, 28.

un-sceþþig, -scæþþig; *adj. Innocent, harmless* :—*Innocens* unsceđđig (-scæđđig) is ǣfre nama, Ælfc. Gr. 43; Zup. 253, 16. Beó se cristena man unsceađþig and bilewite, Homl. Th. i. 142, 10. Hēr com Ælfrēd se unsceđđiga æþeling, Chr. 1036; Erl. 164, 25. Hys đæt synnige blōd wæs āgoten on đa wrace hyre đæs unsceđđian blōdes, Shrn. 155, 8. Hē sǣde đæt ān gehwǣde wolcn upp āstige mid đære unscæđþigan (*not threatening storm*) lyfte, Homl. Skt. i. 18, 150. Cain his āgenne brōđor rihtwīsne and unscæđđigne ācwealde, Boutr. Scrd. 20, 41. Būton hī wǣron swā eádmōde and swā unscæđđige swā đæt cild wæs, Homl. Th. i. 512, 12. Culfran sind swīđe unscæđđige fuglas, i. 142, 8. Hī đa deór swā getemedon, đæt hī mid him unscæđđige (*harmless*) wunodon, ii. 492, 14. Betwuh đām unscæđđigum *inter innocentes*, Ps. Th. 25, 6: Homl. Th. i. 88, 33. [He ne wollde nohht unshaþiȝ wimmann wreȝhenn, Orm. 2889.]

un-sceþþigness, e; *f. Innocence, harmlessness* :—Æfter gerisenre āre heora unscæþþignysse *juxta honorem innocentibus congruum*, Bd. 2, 20; S. 522, 7. On unscæđđignysse heortan *in innocentia cordis*, Ps. Spl. 100, 2. Gyt hē hyt his unscæđđignysse *adhuc retinens innocentiam*, Homl. Th. ii. 452, 15: 210, 29. Habban đa unscæđđignysse on heora mōde đe cild hæfđ, i. 512, 18. Ne funde hē on him nāne synne ac unscæđđignysse, Boutr. Scrd. 20, 25. Unsceađþignysse, Ps. Spl. 36, 39. [Menn þatt cwemmdenn Godd þurrh unnshaþiȝnesse, Orm. 58.]

un-scilliht; *adj. Not shell* (of fish):—Fixas unscellehte, Lchdm. ii. 88, 9.

un-scirped; *adj. Not dressed* :—Monno unscirped *hominem non vestitum*, Mt. Kmbl. Lind. 22, 11.

un-scōd. v. next word.

un-sceōg[i]an *to unshoe, take off the shoes* :—Unsceógien hī gebrōþor *discalcient se fratres*, Anglia xiii. 413, 683. Ðonne biđ ūs suīđe fracođlīce ōđer fōt unscōd *quasi unius pedis calceamentum cum dedecore amittit*, Past. 5; Swt. 45, 14. Hē wæs gelǣded and ungyred and unscōd, Shrn. 85, 32. Nyme đæt wīf his gescȳ of his fōtum, and nemne hine ǣlc man unsceóda (*discalceatus*), Deut. 25, 10. Unsceóde *discalciati*, Anglia xiii. 416, 735. Unscōdum fōtum, Wulfst. 170, 16.

un-scoren; *adj. Unshorn, unshaven* :—Locc unscoren *coma* vel *cirrus*, Wrt. Voc. i. 42, 45. Hī beón unscorene *sint inrasi*, Anglia xiii. 408, 609. Hī lange tīd eodon ealle unscorene and sīdfeaxe, Ap. Th. 6, 12. [*Icel.* ū-skorinn.]

un-scortende; *adj. Not failing, not running short* :—Strión unscortende *thesaurum non deficientem*, Lk. Skt. Lind. Rush. 12, 33.

un-scrȳdan; *p.* de *To undress, strip, divest* :—Unscrȳdde *exfibulat*, i. *exsolvit*, Wrt. Voc. ii. 145, 24. Byþ unscrȳdd *exuitur*, Scint. 226, 9. Unscrīdde *exutos, nudatos*, Hpt. Gl. 423, 52. Unscrȳdde, Homl. Skt. i. 11, 146. (1) with acc. of person:—Bađiendra manna hūs, đǣr hī hī unscrēdaþ inne *apodyterium*, Wrt. Voc. i. 37, 6. Hine man sōna unscrȳde and đa reáf nime đe hē ǣr notode *mox exuatur rebus propriis quibus vestitus est*, R. Ben. 101, 22. Hē hēt hine unscrȳdan, Homl. Th. i. 432, 3: 424, 12. Gif hwā his līc forstǣle, nolde hē hine unscrȳdan, 220, 8. (2) with acc. of person and dat. of garment:—Hē hine unscrīdde đam healfan scicelse, Ap. Th. 12, 22. Hī unscrȳddon hyne hys āgenum reáfe, Mt. Kmbl. 27, 28, 31: Mt. Skt. 15, 20: Homl. Th. ii. 252, 24, 29.

un-scyld, e; *f. Innocence* :—For unscylde *propter innocentiam*, Ps. Spl. 40, 13. [*O. Frs.* un-skelde: *O. H. Ger.* un-sculd *innocentia.*]

un-scyld, e; *f. A grievous fault* :—Gif mīne fȳnd ne rīcsiaþ ofer mē, đonne beó ic unwemme, and beó geclǣnsod fram đǣm mǣstum scyldum; ac gif hī mē ābysgiaþ, đonne ne mæg ic smeágan mīne unscylda, Ps. Th. 18, 12.

un-scyldig; *adj.* I. *innocent, guiltless* :—Unscyldig *insons*, Ælfc. Gr. 9, 39; Zup. 63, 16. Mid werum unscyldigum unscyldig (*innocens*) đū bist, Ps. Spl. 17, 27: Andr. Kmbl. 2275; An. 1139. Hēr wearđ Ecgbriht abbud unscyldig ofslegen, Chr. 916; Th. i. 190, col. 2. Ne cweþe ic nā đæt đæt yfel sié đæt mon helpe đæs unscyldigan (-scyldgan, Cott. MS.), Bt. 38, 7; Fox 210, 4. Sweord besyled on unscyldigum (-scyldgum, Met. 9, 59) blōde, 16, 4; Fox 58, 18. Se đe unscildigne man belǣwe *qui percutiat animam sanguinis innocentis*, Deut. 27, 25. Unscildigne and rihtwīsne ne ofsleh đū *insontem et justum non occides*, Ex. 23, 7. Ðū woldest đone besmītan đe đū nānwiht yfles on nystest. Tō hwon lǣddest đū đeosne freóne and unscyldigne hider? Blickl. Homl. 87, 1: Exon. Th. 143, 11; Gū. 659. Unscyldigne, synna leásne, Elen. Kmbl. 990; El. 496. Hū ne is se yfelwillende and yfelwyrcende đe đone unscyldgan wītnoþ? Bt. 38, 6; Fox 208, 11, 15. Ne syle đū unscyldigra sāwla deórum đe đē andettaþ *ne tradas bestiis animas confitentes tibi*, Ps. Th. 73, 18. Ðǣm wǣre māre þearf đe đa ōþre unscyldige yfelaþ, đæt mon bǣde đæt him mon dyde swā micel wīte swā hī đām ōþrum unscyldegum dydon, Bt. 38, 7; Fox 208, 30: Met. 4, 36. Hī unscyldige scotian þenceaþ *ut sagittent immaculatum*, Ps. Th. 63, 3. Seó wyrd þreáþ đa unscildigan (*insontes*), Bt. 4; Fox 8, 13. **I a.** *innocent* of a crime, charge, (1) with gen.:—Ðet hē wæs unscyldig đæs đe him gelēd wæs, Chr. 1052; Erl. 187, 20. Unscyldigne eofota gehwylces, Elen. Kmbl. 845; El. 423. (2) with preposition:—Ic eom unscyldig, ǣgđer ge dǣde ge dihtes, æt đære tihtlan đe N. mē tīhđ, L. O. 5; Th. i. 180, 15. Sind mænige rihtwīse unscyldige wiđ heáfodleahtras, Homl. Th. i. 342, 9. **I b.** *guiltless* in relation to (*wiđ*) a person. v. un-scyldigness:—Ic eom unscyldig wiđ đās mīne fȳnd *ego in innocentia mea ingressus sum*, Ps. Th. 25, 1. Ðū ne bist unscyldig wiđ mē gif đū on īdelnesse cīgst mīnne noman *nec habebit insontem Dominus eum, qui assumpserit nomen Domini frustra* (Ex. 20, 7), L. Alf. 2; Th. i. 44, 8. **II.** *innocent, not accountable* for an ill result, *not responsible* :—Gif oxa ofhnīte wer oþþe wīf, đæt hié deáde sién . . . Se hlāford biđ unscyldig (*the owner of the ox shall be quit*, A. V. Ex. 21, 28), gif se oxa hnitol wǣre . . . and se hlāford hit nyste, L. Alf. 21; Th. i. 48, 29. His hlāford biđ unscildig *dominus bovis innocens erit*, Ex. 21, 28. Unscyldig ic eom fram đyses rihtwīsan blōde *innocens ego sum a sanguine justi hujus*, Mt. Kmbl. 27, 24. Ne ofsleh đū unscildine mannan . . . đis ic dyde mid bilewitnysse *num gentem ignorantem et justam interficies? . . . in simplicitate cordis mei feci hoc*, Gen. 20, 4. [*O. Sax.* un-skuldig: *O. Frs.* un-skeldech: *O. H. Ger.* un-sculdig *innocens, indebitus, nil meritus*: *Icel.* ū-skyldigr *not due.*]

un-scyldiglīc; *adj. Innocent, not obnoxious, unobjectionable* :—Ungerisnre bysene đū hātest hié wītnian, ah mē þynceþ unscyldiglīcre đæt him man heáfod of āceorfe būton ōđrum wītum, Blickl. Homl. 189, 32.

un-scyldigness, e; *f. Innocence* :—Dauid sang đisne sealm be his unscyldinesse wiđ (v. un-scyldig, **I b**) his sunu, Ps. Th. 25, arg. Æfter unscyldignisse mīnre *secundum innocentiam meam*, Ps. Spl. 7, 9: Rtl. 48, 40.

un-scynde. v. un-scende.

un-seald; *adj. Ungiven* :—Seó sēleste gyrd is gyt unseald, Homl. Ass. 131, 495.

un-sealt; *adj. Without salt, insipid* :—Gif đæt sealt unsealt (*insulsum*) biþ, Mk. Skt. 9, 50. Unsaltera *insulsior*, Wrt. Voc. ii. 48, 6.

un-sefuntig, -seofuntig (= hund-seofontig) *seventy* :— Unsefuntig *septuaginta*, æfter unseofuntigum *post septuaginta*, Mt. Kmbl. p. 2, 3, 11: Lk. Skt. p. 6, 15. Unseofontigum, p. 6, 14. [Cf. *O. Sax.* ant-sibunta.]

un-seht; *m. f. n. Disagreement* :—Hī macodon mǣst đet unseht betweónan Godwine eorle and đam cynge, Chr. 1052; Erl. 187, 27. [Mæst þis unsehte wæs forþan þe se cyng fylste his nefan, Chr. 1116; Erl. 245, 29. He mid unsehte fram þam cynge fōr . . . Hi mid unsehte tohwurfon, 1106; Erl. 240, 20, 25. For þære unsehte þe he hæfde wiđ France, 1112; Erl. 243, 32. For þes cynges unsehte of France, 1117; Erl. 246, 6. Mid unsæhte, 1123; Erl. 250, 26. *Icel.* ū-sātt, -sætt *disagreement.*] v. seht, *and next word.*

un-seht; *adj. Not in agreement, in hostility, at variance* :—Eádrīc cild and đa Bryttas wurdon unsehte and wunnon heom wiđ đa castelmenn on Hereforda *Eadric and the Welsh broke out into hostility* (against William. v. Florence of Worcester, who says that Edric summoned two Welsh kings to help him and laid waste Hereford. The same writer, under the year 1070, notes that Edric was reconciled with William) *and fought with the garrison at Hereford*, Chr. 1067; Erl. 203, 40. Sōna đǣræfter wurdon unsehte se cyng and se eorl *directly after the king and the earl fell out*, 1102; Erl. 238, 6. [Heo weren unsahte and heo weren unsome, Laym. 3930. Þou and his sone woxen unsauȝt (*fell out*), and þou sloug him þere, Jos. 433. Folk that were unsaught toward her king (*at variance with their king*) for his pillage, Gower iii. 153, 26. *Icel.* ū-sāttr *disagreeing, unreconciled.*] v. seht; *adj.*

un-seldan; *adv. Not seldom, frequently* :—Ðone sang wē sungon unseldon mid heom, Homl. Skt. i. 21, 264. Oft and unseldan, L. E. G. proem.; Th. i. 166, 9: Btwk. 222, 2. Oft and unseldon, L. Pen. 2; Th. ii. 278, 5. [*Icel.* ū-sjaldan.]

un-seþe, Wrt. Voc. ii. 150, 80. v. un-sōþ.

un-settan *to displace, put down* :—Tō unsettanne (-setanne, Rush.) *ad deponendum*, Mk. Skt. Lind. 15, 36.

un-sewenlīc (?); *adj. Invisible* :—Hwæt wēnst đū be đære unsewenlīcran wyrde (Cott. MS. *has* unwēnlīcran, *and the Latin is*: Quid reliqua, quae, cum sit *aspera*), Bt. 40, 2; Fox 236, 24. v. un-gesewenlīc.

un-sib[b], e; *f.* I. *unfriendliness, unkindliness, enmity* :—Unsib *simultas*, Wrt. Voc. ii. 120, 62. Swā mycel ungeþwǣrnys and unsibb ārās *ingravescentibus causis dissensionum*, Bd. 3, 14; S. 539, 35. Ðæt đridde is unsibbe fȳr, đonne wē ne forhtigaþ đæt wē đa mōd ābylgean ūra đæra nȳhstena *tertium dissensionis, cum animos proximorum offendere non formidamus*, 3, 19; S. 548, 17: Anglia xi. 101, 37. Unsibbe *simultate*, Wrt. Voc. ii. 87, 11. Unsibbe *simultatem*; 83, 38. God ūs lǽrð sibbe and wynsumnesse, and deófol ús lǽrð unsibbe and wrôhte, Homl. Ass. 168, 112: Cd. Th. 281, 13; Sat. 271. Ic andette mînes môdes morðor and unsibbe and ofermôdignesse, L. de Cf. 8; Th. ii. 262, 32. Oferfyll ne murneþ ne for fæder ne for mêder, ne for nânum gesibban men. Ealle unsibba hit wyrcð, Wulfst. 242, 8. II. *strife, hostilities, war*:—Gif hié gemunan willaþ hiora ieldrena wôlgewinna and hiora monigfealdan unsibbe *recolant majorum suorum tempora, bellis inquietissima*, Ors. 2, 1; Swt. 64, 15. Hié ðæt heóldun mid micelre unsibbe, and tô folcgefeoht gefuhtou, and ðæt lond oft forhergodon, and ǽghwæþer ôþerne oftrædlîce ût drǽfde, Chr. 887; Erl. 86, 10. Ðæt hî wǽron unsibbe and gefeoht fram heora feóndum onfônde *quia bellum ab hostibus forent accepturi*, Bd. 2, 2; S. 503, 30. His ii suna ymb ðæt rîce wunnon, and ða unsibbe mid gefeohte dreógende wǽron, Ors. 2, 7; Swt. 90, 17. Æfter hû monegum wintrum sió sibb gewurde ðæs ðe hié ǽ[re]st unsibbe wið monegum folcum hæfdon, Ors. 4, 7; Swt. 182, 18. III. *division, variance, disagreement, disunion*:—Unsib (*dissensio*) âuorden wæs in ðær menigo fore hine, Jn. Skt. Lind. 7, 43. Unsib *seditio*, Wrt. Voc. ii. 120, 30. Forlǽtaþ ða ûterran sibbe, and habbaþ ða innerran fæste, ðætte eówer unsibb geeáðmêde ðæs synnigan môd (*ut peccantis mentem vestra discordia feriat*), Past. 46; Swt. 357, 9. Ðâ sôhte Colemannus ðysse unsibbe (*dissensioni*) lǽcedôm, Bd. 4, 4; S. 571, 6. Hê hiera sundorsprǽce tô unsibbe brôhton *their colloquy led to no agreement*; infecto pacis negotio, Ors. 4, 10; Swt. 202, 13. [Betere his sahte þane onsibbe, Laym. 9845, 2nd MS. *Goth.* un-sibja *iniquitas*: *O. H. Ger.* un-sippe *seditio*.]

un-sibbian; p. ode *To disagree*:—Unsibbaþ *desidet*, i. *discordat*, Wrt. Voc. ii. 139, 20. Unsibbade *desidebat*, 25, 16.

un-sibsumness, e; f. *Want of tranquillity, anxiety*:—Mið unsibsumnise gedroefede *anxietate turbati*, Jn. Skt. p. 6, 1.

un-sidefull; adj. *Immodest*:—Unsideful *impudicus*, Wrt. Voc. i. 51, 33: O. E. Homl. i. 300, 29, 30.

un-sidefulness, e; f. *Immodesty, immorality*:—Se fîfta unþeáw is ðæt wîf beó unsydefull. Unsydefulnys bið sceamu for worulde, and ðæt unsydefulle wîf bið unwurð on lîfe, O. E. Homl. i. 300, 30.

un-sidu, a; m. *A bad habit, vicious custom, mal-practice*:—Sôð is ðæt ic secge, âlǽre man unlaga on lande oððe unsida lufige tô swîðe, ðæt cymð ðære þeóde tô unþearfe, L. I. P. 4; Th. ii. 308, 8. Nis eác nân wundor, þeáh ûs mislimpe, forðam wê witan ful georne, ðæt . . . wearð þes þeódscipe swýðe forsyngod . . . þurh hǽþene unsida, Wulfst. 164, 2. Âne misdǽda hê dyde þeáh tô swîðe, ðæt hê ælþeódige unsida lufode, Chr. 959; Erl. 121, 1. [*Icel.* û-siðr.]

un-sigefæst; adj. *Not victorious, unsuccessful*:—Ða ðe God wurðodon sigefæste wǽron symle on gefeohte; ða ðe fram Gode bugon tô bysmorfullum hǽðenscype wurdon gescynde and â unsigefæste, Homl. Skt. i. 18, 44.

un-silt; adj. *Unsalted*:—Unsilt (-slit, MS.) smeoro *saevo*, Wrt. Voc. ii. 119, 45. Unsylt smeoru, Lchdm. iii. 18, 5. v. un-gesilt.

un-siþ, es; m. I. *an evil, ill-advised expedition*:—Wearð ofslegen Ecgfridus on his unsîðe, ðâ ðâ hê on Peohtum begann tô feohtanne tô dyrstelîce ofer Drihtnes willan (cf. Ecgfrid, cum temere exercitum ad vastandam Pictorum provinciam duxisset, multum prohibentibus amicis, extinctus est, Bd. 4, 26), Homl. Th. ii. 148, 16. II. *a mishap, misfortune*:—Heó ðurh wôdnysse micclum wæs gedreht . . . heó ǽr ðon eáwfæst leofode, ðeáh ðe se unsîð hire swâ gelumpe, Homl. Th. ii. 142, 12. [Þu (*the owl*) ne singst never þat hit nis for sume unsiþe (*mishap*), O. and N. 1164.]

un-slæc, -sleac; adj. *Not slack, not lazy, strenuous, active, diligent*:—Unsleac *inpiger*, Wrt. Voc. ii. 47, 30: 93, 15: Kent. Gl. 140. [*Icel.* û-slakr.]

un-slæclîce; adv. *Not slackly, not languidly, strenuously*:—Gif ðæt gebodene bið gefremed unsleaclîce (*non tarde*), R. Ben. 20, 18.

un-slǽpig; adj. *Sleepless*:—Unslǽpige *insomnes*, Wrt. Voc. ii. 48, 20.

un-slǽwð, Past. 45; Swt. 341, 4, *seems an error for* un-sǽlð, *the reading of the* Cott. MSS.

un-slâw, -slǽw, -sleáw; adj. *Not slow, not sluggish, active, ready, quick*:—Unslǽw *impiger* vel *praepes*, Wrt. Voc. i. 49, 34. Unsleáw *inpiger*, 74, 34. Hê hine sylfne getengde in Godes þeówdôm æscrôf, unslâw, Elen. Kmbl. 403; El. 202. Se ðe wǽre full slâw, weorðe se unslâw tô cyrican, Wulfst. 72, 15. Ðone ðe him on weorcum gecwêmde elne unslâwe, Exon. Th. 159, 7; Gû. 923. Wîgan unslâwne (*St. Andrew*), Andr. Kmbl. 3419; An. 1713. Hî slôgon tôgædere unslâwe mid wǽpnum, Homl. Skt. ii. 25, 375.

un-slâwlîce; adv. *Not slowly, not sluggishly, actively*:—Hié sculon gehiéran ðætte is gehâten ðǽm monnum ðe lustlîce and unslâwlîce lǽraþ ðæt ðæt hié ðonne cunnon (*qui in hoc, quod jam obtinuit, corporis vitio non tenetur*), Past. 49; Swt. 381, 1.

un-sleac, -sleáw, -slit. v. un-slæc, -slâw, -silt.

un-slîped; adj. (ptcpl.) *Unloosed*:—His tungan bend wearð unslýped *solutum est uinculum linguae ejus*, Mk. Skt. 7, 35.

un-sliten; adj. *Unrent*:—Ðæt cyrtel wæs unslitten, . . . Cuoedon: Ne tôslîte (*scindamus*) uê hiâ *the coat was unrent . . . They said: Let us not rend it*, Jn. Skt. Lind. 19, 23. [*Icel.* û-slitinn.]

un-slopen; adj. (ptcpl.) *Unloosed*:—Æfter þûsend geárum bið Satanas unbunden . . . and nû syndon Satanases bendas swýðe tôslopene (unslopene, MS. H.), Wulfst. 83, 9.

un-smeoruwig; adj. *Not fatty* or *greasy*:—Genim unsmerigne healfne cýse, Lchdm. ii. 292, 23.

un-smêþe; adj. *Not smooth, rough, uneven*:—Unsmêðe *scabra*, Wrt. Voc. ii. 97, 13. Unsmêðe hrægel *birrus*, i. 40, 25. Eoh bið ûtan unsmêðe treów, Runic pm. Kmbl. 341, 27; Rûn. 13. Tunge unsmêþe, Lchdm. ii. 242, 10. Wê habbaþ hrepunge, ðæt wê magon gefrêdan hwæt bið smêðe, hwæt unsmêðe, Homl. Th. ii. 372, 33. His unsmêðan (*leprous*) lîces, 512, 6. Ne unsmêðes wiht, Exon. Th. 199, 15; Ph. 26. Unsmoeði *scabro*, Wrt. Voc. ii. 120, 24. Ðære unsmêþan *elefantinosa*, 142, 82: 31, 8. Hê hleóp on unsmêðe eorðan, Shrn. 152, 1. Ða unsmêþan tungan smirewan, Lchdm. ii. 238, 25. Ðeós wyrt bið cenned on unsmêþum stôwum, i. 160, 18. Ða unsmêþan *salebrosos*, Wrt. Voc. ii. 78, 25. [Unnsmeþe þurrh bannkes and þurrh græfess, Orm. 9209.]

un-smêþness, e; f. *Roughness*:—Unsmêðnes *callositas*, Wrt. Voc. ii. 18, 36: 82, 54. Unsmêþnes, 127, 55.

un-smôþe (-smôþ? *but see* sôfte; adj.); adj. *Rough*:—Unsmôþi *aspera*, Wrt. Voc. ii. 101, 15. Unsmôðe, 7, 33. v. smôþ, un-smêþe.

un-snotor, -snottor; adj. *Unwise, foolish*:—Unsnotor *insipiens*, Ælfc. Gr. 9, 38; Zup. 62, 15: Ps. Lamb. 91, 7. Unsnoter *inprudens*, Wrt. Voc. i. 76, 13. Se unsnotera ł se unwita *insipiens*, Ps. Lamb. 13, 1. Se unsnotera ł se dysega, 48, 11. Ðæt biþ swîþe dysig man and unsnottor on his lîfe, se þe lufaþ ðâs eorþlîcan welan and ne lufaþ God ðe hit him eal sealde, Blickl. Homl. 195, 24. Eû dysega man and ðû unsnottra, 49, 35. Unsnotterra *insipientum*, Rtl. 86, 14. Unsnoterum *insipientibus*, Ps. Lamb. 48, 21: L. Ælfc. C. 23; Th. ii. 352, 2.

un-snotorlîce; adv. *Unwisely, imprudently*; inprudenter, Ælfc. Gr. 38; Zup. 223, 15: 228, 10.

un-snotorness, e; f. *Folly*:—Tô unsnotornysse *ad insipientiam*, Ps. Lamb. 21, 3. Þurh unsnotornesse, Wulfst. 166, 25.

un-snyterness, e; f. *Folly*:—Tô unsnyternesse *ad insipientiam*, Ps. Spl. T. 21, 2. v. snytre.

un-snytro (-u); f. *Folly*:—Gefylled mið unsnytro *repleti insipientia*, Lk. Skt. Lind. 6, 11. Hosp unwîsum ł unsnytro ðû sealdest mê *opprobrium insipienti dedisti me*, Ps. Spl. T. 38, 12. Worda eallra unsnyttro ǽr gesprecenra, Elen. Kmbl. 2567; El. 1285. Hê his selfa ne mæg for his unsnyttrum ende geþencean, Beo. Th. 3472; B. 1734: Met. 9, 11. Hê unsnytrum (*foolishly, unwisely*) Andreas hêt âhôn, Exon. Th. 260, 35; Jul. 308. Unsnyttrum, 251, 14; Jul. 145: 153, 25; Gû. 831: Elen. Kmbl. 1900; El. 947.

un-soden; adj. *Unsodden, unboiled*:—On unsodenan hunige, Lchdm. iii. 40, 6. Sceápes hôhscancan unsodenne, ii. 38, 8. Genim ða ylcan wyrte unsodene, i. 198, 15: Exon. Th. 488, 18; Rä. 76, 8.

un-sôfte; adv. I. *not at ease, in discomfort*. v. sôfte, II:—Gif men fêrlîce wyrde unsôfte, Rtl. 114, 24. II. *not gently, hardly, severely*:—Hwǽr mon unsôfte getilaþ on forewearde ða âdle *in case severe treatment is used in the early stages of the disease*, Lchdm. ii. 260, 15. Ða ðe hine unsôfte âdle gebundne gesôhtun, Exon. Th. 155, 10; Gû. 858: 83, 16; Cri. 1357. Hî wrehton unsôfte ealdgenîþlan, Judth. Thw. 24, 37; Jud. 228: Blickl. Homl. 203, 18 III. *hardly, with difficulty, with trouble*:—Wê hit unsôfte mid longsceaftum sperum ofscotadon *vix ipsis defixa est venabulis*, Nar. 15, 28. Ic ðæt unsôfte ealdre gedîgde, Beo. Th. 3314; B. 1655: 4287; B. 2140: Elen. Kmbl. 263; El. 132: Exon. Th. 168, 20; Gû. 1080. [Þer is þe sunfulle unsofte to beon, Misc. 91, 25. *O. H. Ger.* un-samfto *difficulter, aegre*.]

un-sôftlîce; adv. *Ungently, hardly*:—Ualerianus âwêd hrýmde: 'Eálâ ðû, Laurentius, unsôftlîce tîhst ðû mê gebundenne mid byrnendum racenteágum,' Homl. Th. i. 434, 7.

un-sôm, e; f. *Disagreement*:—Gyf hyra ǽnig wið ǽnigne mon ǽnige unsôme hæbbe, ðæt hê wið ðone geþingie . . . Man sceal ǽlce unsôme and ealle geflytu gestyllan, L. E. I. 36; Th. ii. 434, 2-7.

un-sorh; adj. *Without care, without anxiety, secure*:—Ðâ ongeat hê ðæt ðǽr wæs godcundlîc mægen ondweard, and hê ðære mildheortnesse unsorh âbâd, Blickl. Homl. 217, 29.

un-sôþ, es; n. *Untruth, falsehood*:—Mid unsôðe sôð oferswîðan, Wulfst. 55, 16. Leáslîce hîwian unsôð tô sôðe, 128, 9. Ic nelle secgan unsôð on mê sylfe, Homl. Skt. i. 12, 195.

un-sôþ; adj. *Untrue, false*:—Unsôþe (Wright gives *unseþe*, but Wülcker Voc. 243, 15 *unsoþe*) sage (-a, Wülcker) *falsa dicta*, Wrt. Voc. ii. 150, 80. [*Icel.* û-sannr *untrue*.]

un-sôþfæst; adj. I. *untruthful, unveracious*:—Ic silf geseah ðæt ðæt mê unsôðfæstran men sǽdon, ðonne ða wǽron ðe ðæt sêdon ðæt wit ymb sint, Shrn. 204, 12. II. *unjust, unrighteous*:—Unsôðfæstne wer *virum injustum*, Ps. Th. 139, 11. Wê unsôðfæste ealle wǽron *injuste egimus*, 105, 6. Sôðfæst fore unsôðfæstum *justus pro injustis*, Rtl. 21, 32.

un-sôþfæstness, e; f. *Unrighteousness, injustice*:—Unsôðfæstnys *injustitia*, Ps. Th. 54, 9. Ðes sôðcuoed is and unsôðfæstnise in ðæm ne is *hic verax est, et injustitia in illo non est*, Jn. Skt. Lind. 7, 18.

un-sóþian. v. ge-unsóþian.

un-sóþsagol; *adj. Speaking falsely, lying, mendacious*:—Unsóđsagul *falsidicus* vel *falsiloquus*, Wrt. Voc. i. 47, 47. Unsóđsagol *falsidicus*, 76, 20. Se smiđ ne dorste secgan đás gesihđe ǽnigum menn, nolde beón gesewen unsóđsagul (-ol) boda, Homl. Skt. i. 21, 58.

un-spannan; *p.* -speónn *To unclasp, unfasten*:—Unspeón *exfibulat*, i. *exsolvit*, Wrt. Voc. ii. 145, 24. [Cf. Seint Iohan ine his iborenesse unspennede his feder tunge into prophecie, A. R. 158, 14.] v. on-spannan.

un-spéd, e; *f. Want, indigence, penury*:—Unspéde *inopiae*, Ps. Spl. 43, 27. For unspéda *prae inopia*, 87, 9. Điós of unspoed (unspoedum, Rush.) hire alle đa đe hæfde sende *haec de paenuria sua omnia quae habuit misit*, Mk. Skt. Lind. 12, 44. [It fel to mikel unspede *it turned out very unfortunate*, C. M. 15420. *O. Sax.* un-spôd *disadvantage*: *O. H. Ger.* un-spuot.]

un-spédig; *adj.* I. *without means, poor, indigent*:—Đes and đeós and đis unspédige *hic et haec et hoc inops*, Ælfc. Gr. 9, 56; Zup. 68, 1. Gif hwylc wíf tó đam unspédig wǽre đæt heó đás đing begytan ne mihte, Homl. Th. i. 140, 3. Generigende unspédigne *eripiens inopem*, Ps. Spl. 34, 12: Blickl. Gl. Hé geendebyrde đone unspédigan fiscere ætforan đam rícan cásere, Homl. Th. i. 578, 9. Eádge biđon đa đaerfe, đæt is unspoedge menn *beati pauperes*, Mt. Kmbl. Lind. 5, 3 note. Đa rícostan men drincaþ myran meolc, and đa unspédigan drincaþ medo, Ors. 1, 1; Swt. 20, 17. For yrmđe unspédig[ra] *propter miseriam inopum*, Ps. Spl. 11, 5. Đonne đú geseó geóngran man đonne đú sý, and unwísran, and unspédigran, Prov. Kmbl. 31. Þeáh hý sýn on đyson woroldsǽlþon đa unspédgestan, Ors. 1, 2; Swt. 30, 4. II. *barren, poor, unproductive*:—Hié gesǽton sorgfulre land, eard and édyl unspédigran fremena gehwylcre, Cd. Th. 59, 12; Gen. 962. [*O. H. Ger.* un-spuotig.]

un-spiwol; *adj. Not emetic*:—Unspiwol drenc, Lchdm. ii. 274, 11, 20. Unspiule dreuceas, 170, 11.

un-sprecende; *adj. Not speaking, unable to speak, without speech, speechless*:—Unsprecende cild *infans* vel *alogos*, Wrt. Voc. i. 50, 41: 73, 11: Ælfc. Gr. 9, 37; Zup. 61, 7. Hé (*Christ in Simeon's arms*) đá gyt on đære menniscnysse unsprecende wǽre, Homl. Th. i. 142, 26. Fǽringa sáh hé niđer sprǽce benumen, and þurhwunode swá unsprecende, Chr. 1053; Erl. 186, 23. Unsprecende forneán *almost speechless*, Homl. Skt. i. 3, 481. Đa unsprecendan cild, Homl. Th. ii. 116, 14: 50, 15.

un-stæfwís; *adj. Illiterate*:—Unstæfwís *inlitterata*, Germ. 393, 82.

un-stæđđig; *adj.* I. *not steady, remiss, irregular*:—Sum munuc wæs unstæđđig on Godes lofsangum, Homl. Th. ii. 160, 19. II. *unstable, inconstant, fickle*:—Wé sceolon fyligan úrum Heáfde fram đissere unstæđđigan worulde tó his stađelfæstan ríce, Homl. Th. ii. 282, 21. Đises lífes gewilnung gelǽt đa unstæđđian tó manegum leahtrum, Homl. Skt. i. 5, 67. III. *unsteady, unstaid, not sober, light, wanton*:—Wearđ hé gegripen mid đære gálnysse his unstæđđigan heortan, Homl. Ass. 110, 247. Hé his sylfes geweóld on ungerípedum freódóme and unstæđđigum þeáwum, Ælfc. T. Grn. 17, 13. Đa unstæđđigan hleápunge đæs mǽdenes (*the daughter of Herodias*), Homl. Th. i. 480, 35.

un-stæđđigness, e; *f.* I. *unsteadiness, instability, inconstancy*:—Sun munuc mid gemáglícum bénum gewilnode đæt hé móste of đam munuclífe . . . Đá wearđ se hálga wer geháthyrt đurh his unstæđđignysse, and hét hine áweg faran, Homl. Th. ii. 176, 18. II. *want of sedateness, levity, wantonness*:—Of gálnysse cumaþ ungemetegod lufu and eágena unstæđđignys, Homl. Th. ii. 220, 7. Se grimlíca deófol lǽrđ dyrstignysse and gebringđ réceleáse men on unstæđđignesse wordes and weorces, Wulfst. 54, 3. Mid módes unstæđđignysse, 60, 1.

un-staþolfæst; *adj.* I. *unsettled, not remaining in one place, not stationary*:—Đa twám and þrím dagum geond missenlícra monna húsum wuniaþ, ǽfre unstaþolfæste (*numquam stabiles*) and woriende, R. Ben. 9, 23. II. *unsettled, desirous of change*:—Sum munuc wearđ unstađolfæst on his mynstre, and gewilnode đæt hé móste of đam munuclífe, Homl. Th. ii. 176, 14. III. *not steadfast, unstable, not enduring, easily moved*:—Unstađolfest weorc *opus instabile*, Kent. Gl. 369. Hí nabbaþ wyrtruman on him ac beóđ unstađolfæste *non habent radicem in se sed temporales sunt*, Mk. Skt. 4, 17. Understaþolfæste (unstaþolfæste? cf. đæt ungestæđđige folc, Bt. 39, 3; Fox 216, 2) *mobile vulgus*, Met. 28, 69. IV. *unsettled in mind, wavering*:—Đone unstađolfæstan bróđor and đone tweónigendan *fratrem fluctuantem*, R. Ben. 51, 3. [Þe twafalde mon is unstaþelfest (*inconstans*) on alle his weies, O. E. Homl. i. 151, 29. Unstađeluest bileaue, A. R. 208, 16.]

un-staþolfæstness, e; *f. Instability, inconstancy*:—Wolcnes pund, đanon him wæs his módes unstađelfæstnes geseald, Salm. Kmbl. p. 180, 11. Unstađolfæstnis đóhta *instabilitas mentium*, Rtl. 192, 21. Se hálga wer swíđe mid wordum đreáde his unstađolfæstnysse, Homl. Th. ii. 176, 17. v. preceding word.

un-stedefull; *adj. Unstable, apostate*:—Mid englum unstydfullum *cum angelis apostaticis*, Rtl. 121, 21.

un-stedefulness, e; *f. Instability*; but the word glosses *infestatio*:—Aelc unstydfulnis đæs unclǽnes gástes *omnis infestatio inmundi spiritus*, Rtl. 122, 24. v. on-stedefullness.

un-stenc, es; *m. A bad smell, stench*:—Hý mid nosan ne magon náht geswæccan bútan unstences ormǽtnesse *foetor ingenti complet putredine nares*, Dóm. L. 207. Náht elles gestincan búton unstenca ormǽtnessa, Wulfst. 139, 8.

un-stillan. v. ge-unstillan.

un-stille; *adj. Not still, unquiet*:—Unstille *inquies*, Ælfc. Gr. 9, 26; Zup. 52, 4. I. of motion, *not at rest, moving*:—Đæt wæter unstille ǽghwider wolde tóscríþan, ne meahte hit on him selfum ǽfre gestandan, Met. 20, 92. Sund unstille, Exon. Th. 338, 14; Gn. Ex. 78. Swift wæs on fóre, dreág unstille winnende wéga, 434, 24; Rä. 52, 5. Eall điós unstille gesceaft, Bt. 39, 6; Fox 220, 23. Đæt unstille hweól (*velox rota*) đe Ixion wæs tó gebunden, 35, 6; Fox 168, 31. Đa unstillan woruldgesceafta, Met. 11, 19. Đara unstillena gesceafta styring ne mæg nó weorþan gestilled, ne eác onwend of đam ryne đe him geset is, Bt. 21; Fox 74, 3. Đú đe ealle đa unstillan gesceafta tó đínum willan ástyrast *qui das cuncta moveri*, 33, 4; Fox 128, 9: Met. 20, 14. II. *liking movement* (lit. or fig.), *unquiet, restless*; in a bad sense, *unruly*:—Hé cwæđ đæt sió tunge wǽre unstille yfel *lingua, inquietum malum*, Past. 38; Swt. 281, 7. Eh byđ unstyllum ǽfre frófur, Runic pm. Kmbl. 343, 9; Rún. 19. Đa unstillan (*inquietos*) hé sceal þreágean, R. Ben. 13, 12. Nánwuht nis on ús unstilre and ungestæđđigre đonne đæt mód *nil in nobis est corde fugacius*, Past. 38; Swt. 273, 11. III. *unquiet, disturbed*:—Đæt mǽden hæfde unstille niht, Ap. Th. 18, 27. IV. *not at peace, troubled*:—Hé wæs fram đam áwyrgedan gáste unstille; and swá swýþe hé hine drehte, đæt hé his sylfes nǽnig gemynd ne hæfde, Guthl. 13; Gdwin. 60, 12. [*O. H. Ger.* un-stilli *inquiens, vacillans, inquietus*.]

un-stillian. v. ge-unstillian.

un-stillness, e; *f.* I. *absence of rest, motion*:—Unstilnis *agitatio*, Wrt. Voc. ii. 99, 55. II. *disturbance, noisiness, clamour*:—Gif hé đurhwunaþ cnucigende, đonne árīst se hírédes ealdor for đæs óđres onhrópe, and him getíđaþ đæs đe hé bitt, ná for freóndrǽdene, ac for his unstilnysse, Homl. Th. i. 248, 33. Lǽrđ ús se deófol unstilnesse and ungemetlíce hleahtras, and unnytte sprǽce, Wulfst. 233, 18. III. *tumult, bustle, commotion*:—Hé ne mihte đa unstillnesse đara onfeallendra menigeo áberan *tumultus inruentium turbarum non ferret*, Bd. 3, 19; S. 549, 32. IV. *disturbance, breach of peace*:—On đæs wífes gebǽrum onfundon đæs cyninges þegnas đa unstilnesse (*the king had been attacked and killed*), Chr. 755; Erl. 50, 3. Læcedemonie hæfdon máran unstillnessa đonne hié mægenes hæfdon *Lacedaemonii, inquieti magis quam strenui*, Ors. 3, 1; Swt. 98, 34. V. *restlessness, unruliness*:—Hé geseah đæt hig niorwedon mid fæstenum and mid gebedum hiora líchaman unstilnesse, Shrn. 37, 3. VI. *disquietude, disturbance of mind, trouble*:—Se đe his bróđor hataþ, hé hæfđ unstilnesse and swýđe drófi mód, Basil admn. 4; Norm. 44, 16.

un-strang; *adj. Not strong, weak, feeble*:—Unstrang *invalidus*, Wrt. Voc. i. 51, 22: 83, 57. Heó (*Judith*) wæs lytel and unstrang, Homl. Ass. 114, 411. Hwæt is se intinga đæt án þúsend manna đé ne magon ástyrian, swá unstrang swá đú eart? Homl. Skt. i. 9, 110. Á sceal man đam unstrangan men lídelícor déman đonne đam strangan, L. C. S. 69; Th. i. 412, 4. Hyra handa wǽron unstrange hine tó ácwellanne, Shrn. 117, 31. Hé (*Peter*) mid his gange getácnode ǽgđer ge đa strangan ge đa unstrangan on Godes folce. Cristes geladung ne mæg beón búton strangum, ne búton unstrangum. Đá đá him twýnode, đá getácnode hé đa unstrangan. Hwæt sind đa unstrangan? Đa sind unstrange đe sláwe beóđ tó gódum weorcum, Homl. Th. ii. 390, 15-25. Đæt đa unstrangan (*infirmi*) ofersýmede heora þeówdóm ne forfleón, R. Ben. 121, 23. Sý fultum geseald đám wácmódum and đám unstrangum *inbecillibus procurentur solacia*, 58, 18. Hǽla đa unstronga *sanare infirmos*, Lk. Skt. Lind. Rush. 9, 2. Đeáh hwá anweald hæbbe, gif óþer hæfþ máran, beþearf se unstrengra đæs strengran fultumes *si quid est, quod in ulla re imbecillioris valentiae sit, in hac praesidio necesse est egeat alieno*, Bt. 33, 1; Fox 120, 18. Hwæt is unstrengre đonne se mon đe biđ tó ungemetlíce oferswíþed mid đam tédran flǽsce, 36, 6; Fox 182, 3: Homl. Th. ii. 370, 16. Óþ đæt hié (*inflammations*) unstrangran weorþan, Lchdm. ii. 178, 14. Hú ne miht đú geseón ǽlce dæge đæt đa strengran nimaþ đa welan of đám unstrengrum, Bt. 26, 2; Fox 92, 15. v. strang, *and next word*.

un-strenge; *adj. Weak*:—Paulus cwæđ: 'Wé strange sceolon beran đæra unstrengra byrđene' *debemus nos firmiores imbecillitates infirmorum sustinere* (Rom. 15, 1), Homl. Th. ii. 390, 26. v. strenge.

un-stydfull. v. un-stedefull.

un-styri[g]ende; *adj. Not moving, unmoving, stationary*:—Monige sint cwucera gesceafta unstyriende, swá scylfiscas sint . . . Đa styriendan nétenu habbaþ eall đæt đa unstyriendan habbaþ, and eác máre tó . . . For đæm sint đás sceafta đus gesceapene đæt đa unstyriendan hí ne áhebben ofer đa styriendan, Bt. 41, 5; Fox 252, 20-31.

un-styrigendlíc; *adj. Not to be stirred, not to be carried*:—Byrđenna unstyrendelíco *onera inportabilia*, Mt. Kmbl. Lind. 23, 4.

un-súr; *adj. Not sour*:—Eala forgâ and meoloc þicge unsûre, Lchdm. ii. 292, 30. [*Icel.* ú-súrr.]

un-swǽs; *adj. Unpleasant, disagreeable*:—Settan mē ðǽr mē unswǽsost (*or adv.?*) wæs *posuerunt me in abominationem sibi*, Ps. Th. 87, 8. [*Icel.* ú-svást veðr *bad weather.*]

un-swǽse; *adv. Unpleasantly.* v. preceding word.

un-swǽslíc; *adj. Unpleasant, ungentle*:—Hē hæfde his ende gebidenne unswǽslícne, Judth. Thw. 22, 17; Jud. 65.

un-swefen, es; *n. A bad dream*:—Sing ðis ylce gebed on niht ǽr ðū tō ðīnum reste gâ, ðonne gescylt ðē God wið unswefnum ðe nihternessum on menn becumaþ, Lchdm. iii. 288, 22.

un-sweotol; *adj. Not evident, not to be seen, not discernible*:—Nān ðara gesceafta ne mæg bión būton ōþerre, ðeáh hió unsweotol sié on ðære ōþerre, Bt. 33, 4; Fox 130, 26. Ne mæg hira ǽnig būtan ōþrum bión, þeáh hī unsweotole (*or adv.?*) somod eardien, Met. 20, 146.

un-swéte; *adj. Unsweet*, (1) of taste, *bitter, sour*:—Hī mē geblendon bittre tōsomne unswētne drync ecedes and geallan, Exon. Th. 88, 12; Cri. 1439. (2) of smell, *offensive, fetid*:—Ðonne ne biþ se þost tō unswēte tō gestincanne, Lchdm. ii. 48, 14. [*O. Sax.* un-swōti: *O. L. Ger.* un-suōti *molestus*: *O. H. Ger.* un-suozi.]

un-swice, es; *m.* (*or* -swic, es; *n.?*) *Good faith, absence of deceit* or *treachery*:—Ðā gyrnde hē griðes and gīsla, ðet hē mōste unswican intō gemōte cuman and ūt of gemōte *he required safeconduct and hostages, that he might come to the meeting and go from it without treachery*, Chr. 1048; Erl. 180, 7. [Cf. *Icel.* verða fyrir svikum *to be exposed to treachery.*]

un-swícende; *adj. Not failing in duty* to others, *faithful, loyal*:—Ic (*Cnut*) cȳðe eów ðæt ic wylle beón hold hlāford and unswīcende tō Godes gerihtum and tō rihtre woroldlage, Chart. Erl. 229, 22. Hig āþas swōron and gīslas saldan ðæm cynge and ðæm eorle, ðæt heó him on allum þingum unswīcende beón woldon, Chr. 1063; Erl. 195, 17. v. next word.

un-swici[g]ende; *adj. Unfailing, that does not deceive, loyal*:—Griffin swōr āðas ðæt hē wolde beón Eádwearde kinge hold underkingc and unswicigende, Chr. 1056; Erl. 190, 35. Ðæt ðū wið Waldend heólde fæste treówe; seó ðē freoðo sceal weorðan āwa tō aldre unswiciendo, Cd. Th. 204, 25; Exod. 424.

un-swicol; *adj. Not false, not treacherous, honest*:—Unswicel *non falsa*, Hpt. Gl. 432, 24. Uton beón eádmōde and sōðfæste and unswicole and rihtwīse, Wulfst. 109, 13. [*Icel.* ú-svikull *guileless.*]

un-swíþ; *adj. Not strong, weak*:—Gif drenc sié tō unswīþ, Lchdm. ii. 270, 15: iii. 18, 22. v. swīþ, I. 2 a. α.

un-swíðe; *adv. Not strongly, weakly*:—Sió ecg bāt unswīðor ðonne his ðiódcyning þearfe hæfde, Beo. Th. 5150; B. 2578.

un-sýferlíc; *adj. Impure, uncleanly*:—Sume synna beóþ swīþe unsȳferlīce, ðæt se man wandaþ ðæt hē hī ǽfre āsecgge, Blickl. Homl. 43, 17. [*O. H. Ger.* un-sūbarlīh *squalidus.*]

un-sýferness, e; *f. Impurity, uncleanness* (physical or moral):—Se ðe forgȳmeleásige gehālgod hūsl, ðæt him sig unsȳfernys (*sordes*) on, L. Ecg. P. iv. 44; Th. ii. 216, 18. Ðǽr unsȳfernes ou ne sȳ ne unclǽnnes, L. E. I. 5; Th. ii. 406, 1. Fulle bāna deádra and ǽghwilcre unsȳfernissæ (*omni spurcitia*), Mt. Kmbl. Rush. 23, 27. Monige wiþsōcan ðære unsȳfernysse deófolgylda *abrenunciata sorde idolatriae*, Bd. 3, 21; S. 551, 21. Fram unsȳfernyssum ðara ǽrrena māna, 3, 23; S. 554, 27. On unsȳfernyssum betwih deófolgyldum *in sordibus inter idola*, 3, 30; S. 562, 18: 3, 1; S. 523, 23: 5, 19: S. 639, 23. Ða unséfernessa ðe ðǽr beóþ sió lifer āwyrpþ ūt and ðæt clǽne blōd gesomnaþ, Lchdm. ii. 198, 5.

un-sýfre; *adj. Impure, unclean, foul* (physically or morally), (1) physical:—Gif hió swīþor unsȳfre weorpe (weorþe?), clǽnsa mid hunige, Lchdm. ii. 210, 2. Wīc unsȳfre (*a prison*), Andr. Kmbl. 2622; An. 1312. Unsȳfra *olidarum*, Wrt. Voc. ii. 65, 15. (2) moral:—Forhwan ðū ðæt selegescot, ðæt ic mē on ðē gehālgode, þurh firenlustas fūle synne unsȳfre (*or adv.?* Cf. *O. H. Ger.* un-sūbro *sordide*) besmite, Exon. Th. 90, 34; Cri. 1484. Synfulra weorud, swā fūle swā gǽt, unsȳfre folc, Exon. Th. 75, 35; Cri. 1232. Ǽr se unsȳfra (*Holofernes*) womfull onwōce, Judth. Thw. 22, 24; Jud. 76. Be ðam sacerde ðe hine sylfne besmīt þurh unsȳfre sprǽce (*impuro sermone*), L. Ecg. C. 5, tit.; Th. ii. 128, 14. Þurh unsȳfre sprǽce *per turpiloquium*, 5; Th. ii. 138, 4. [*O. H. Ger.* un-sūbar, -sūbiri *fedus, immundus, sordidus.*]

un-syn[n], e; *f. Not guilt, not crime*:—Ne hūru Hildeburh herian þorfte Eótena treówe; unsynnum (*with no faults on her part, undeservedly;* gratis. Cf. un-synnig, II) wearð beloren leófum æt ðam lindplegan, bearnum and brōðrum, Beo. Th. 2149; B. 1072.

un-syngian; *p.* ode *To exculpate, prove innocent; purgare*:—Hine mōton his mǽgas unsyngian, L. In. 21; Th. i. 116, 8.

un-synnig; *adj.* I. *innocent, guiltless, without sin*:—Sacleás ɫ unsynnig, Jn. Skt. Lind. 15, 25. Crist symle unsynnig wunode, Homl. Th. ii. 524, 35. Ne ðūhte him tō huxlīc, ðæt hē mid gesceáde hine betealde unsynnine, 226, 12. Dauid miclum his āgenes herges pleáh, ðǽr hē ymb his getreówne ðegn unsynnigne sierede, Past. 3; Swt. 37, 8. Gif esne ōðerne ofsleá unsynnigne, L. Ethb. 86; Th. i. 24, 11: L. Alf. pol. 29; Th. i. 80, 6: 35; Th. i. 84, 2: Beo. Th. 4185; B. 2089. Unsynnige *insontem*, Wrt. Voc. ii. 46, 22. Ūs men secgaþ, ðæt hī unsynnige beón, ðeáh ðe hī mettas him on mūð bestingon on swilcum fæstendagum, Homl. Th. ii. 330, 30: Mt. Kmbl. Lind. 5, 3 note. Ða unsuinnigo *innocentes*, 12, 7. II. *undeserved*:—Seó his unsynnige cwalu wæs gewrecen, Shrn. 93, 13. [*O. Sax.* un-sundig: *O. H. Ger.* un-suntīg *insons, innocens, inculpabilis*: *Icel.* ú-syndigr.]

un-tǽle; *adj. Blameless, without reproach*:—Ðeáh ðe nǽfre ne wurde syððan mancynne gemiltsod, ðeáh wǽre Godes rihtwīsnys eallunga untǽle, Homl. Th. i. 112, 19. Sió wiþerweardnes biþ simle untǽlu and wracu āscirred mid ðære styringe hire āgenre frēcennesse *videas adversam fortunam sobriam, succintamque, et ipsius adversitatis exercitatione prudentem*, Bt. 20; Fox 72, 5. Ic ða leóde wāt ǽghwæs untǽle, Beo. Th. 3734; B. 1865. Sȳn hȳ swā gecorene, ðæt hȳ untǽle sȳn and sacerdhādes þurh ealle gōde cysta wyrþe, R. Ben. 140, 6. Heó hæfð twā ðing untǽle for Gode, sinscipe and eádmōdnysse, Homl. Ass. 40, 399.

un-tǽled; *adj. Unblamed*:—Ðȳ læs hié forlǽten untǽlde ōðerra monna yfele unðeáwas *ne pravos hominum mores nequaquam redarguant*, Past. 46; Swt. 351, 20.

un-tǽllíce; *adv. Blamelessly, without reproach*:—Ðonne birð se sacerd suīðe untǽllīce āwriten ðara fædra naman on his breóstum, ðonne hē singallīce geðencð hiera līfes bisene, Past. 13; Swt. 77, 17: 5; Swt. 45, 12. Hī wǽron rihtwīse and heóldon Godes beboda untǽllīce *erant justi incedentes in omnibus mandatis Domini sine quaerella* (Lk. 1, 6), Homl. Th. i. 200, 35. v. un-tāllīce.

un-tǽlwirðe; *adj. Not blameable, irreprehensible, praiseworthy*:—Is geteald hwelc hē beón sceal, gif hē untǽlwierðe bið *quae sit irreprehensibilitas ipsa, manifestat*, Past. 8; Swt. 53, 11. Ǽew Dryhtnes untǽlwyrðe (*inre braehensibilis*), Ps. Surt. 18, 8. Ðæt hē gecnāwe ōðerra monna weorc untǽlwierðe (-wyrðe, Cott. MSS.) *ut laudabilia aliorum facta cognoscant*, Past. 30; Swt. 205, 5. Ðæt hié ðæs ðe untǽlwyrðran wǽren, 32; Swt. 215, 1.

un-tǽlwirðlíce; *adv. Blamelessly, laudably*:—Ðætte oft ðæs lāreówdōmes ðēnung bið swīðe untǽlwyrðlīce (-wierð-, Cott. MSS., *laudabiliter*) gewilnad, and eác swīðe untǽlwierðlīce (*laudabiliter*) monige beóð tō geniédde, Past. 7; Swt. 47, 20. Ðæt ilce ðæt hē untǽlwyrðlīce (-wierð-, Cott. MSS., *laudabiliter*) ondrēd tō underfōnne, ðæt ilce se ōðer swīðe hergeondlīce (*laudabiliter*) gewilnode, Swt. 49, 18.

un-tala. v. un-tela.

un-tállíce; *adv. Blamelessly, without reproach*:—Hē ealle ðæs regoles bebodu untāllīce geheóld, Homl. Skt. ii. 23 b, 26. v. untǽllīce.

un-tamed, Wrt. Voc. ii. 142, 40. v. un-temed.

un-tamlíc (?); *adj. Untameable*:—Untamlīc (*printed* untamcul) *indomabilis*, Germ. 397, 11.

un-teala. v. un-tela.

un-teald; *adj. Uncounted*:—Gyf se dæg byð forlǽten unteald, ðǽrrihte āwent eall ðæs geáres ymbryn þwyres, Lchdm. iii. 264, 12.

un-tealt; *adj. Steady*:—Ðā hēt Ælfrēd cyning timbrian lange scipu ongeán ðās æsceas; . . . ða wǽron ǽgðer ge swiftran, ge unteal[t]ran, ge eác heárran, ðonne ða ōðru, Chr. 897; Th. 177, 1, col. 2. v. tealt.

un-tela; *adv.* (*but in some cases it seems a noun?*) *Not well, ill, badly*:—Ða scamleásan nyton ðæt hié untela dōð, būton hit mon him sæcge *impudentes se delinquere nesciunt, nisi a pluribus increpentur*, Past. 31; Swt. 206, 1. Swā micle hī onfōð ðǽr māre wīte, swā hī hēr gearor witon ðæt hī untela dōð, and [hit] ðeáh nyllað forlǽtan *tanto illic graviora tormenta percipiat, quanto hic malum non deserit, etiam quod ipsa condemnat*, 55; Swt. 429, 19. Þeáh hine hwā āhsode, for hwī hē swā dyde, ðonne ne mihte hē hit nā gereccan, ne geþafa beón nolde, ðæt hē untela dyde *requiretur delictum ejus, nec invenietur*, Ps. Th. 9, 35. Hē wāt ðæt hē untela dēð *faciant quae non fuisse gerenda decernant*, Bt. 39, 12; Fox 230, 29. Getīmige ūs tela on līchaman, getīmige ūs untela, symle wē sceolon ðæs Gode ðancian, Homl. Th. i. 252, 15. Wiþ ðon ðe men mete untela melte and gecirre on yfele wǽtan, Lchdm. ii, 226, 5. Ne forsuwa ðū nā ðæt unteala gedōn sȳ, Prov. Kmbl. 44. Hwætd tō untala dyde hē (hwæt dyde untale, Rush.) *quid mali fecit?* Mt. Kmbl. Lind. 27, 23. v. tela.

un-temed; *adj. Untamed, wild*:—Untemed (*Wright prints* untamed, *but see* Wülcker 226, 14), wilde *edomitus*, Wrt. Voc. ii. 142, 40. Untemed hors, Ps. Spl. C. 32, 17. [*Wick.* un-temid.] v. temian.

un-teorig; *adj. Untiring, unceasing*:—Rodor recene scrīþeþ, sūðheald swīfeþ swift, untiorig, Met. 28, 17.

un-teóðod, -tiogoðad; *adj. Untithed*:—Gē tiogoðiaþ eówre mintan and eówerne dile, and lǽtaþ untiogoðad ðætte diórwyrðre is eówra ōðra ǽhta, Past. 57; Swt. 439, 29.

un-þæslíc; *adj. Unsuitable, unseemly, unbecoming, unfit*:—Unðæslīc *indecens*, Ælfc. Gr. 14; Zup. 87, 12. Ne gedafenaþ biscope ðæt hē beó on dǽdum folces mannum gelīc. Geswīc swā unðæslīces plegan, Homl. Th. ii. 134, 13. Ūs ne gedafenaþ ðæt wē ūrne līchaman, ðe Gode is gehālgod on fulluhte, mid unþæslīcum plegan gescyndan, i. 482, 9. On unþæslícum tíman *horis incompetentibus*, R. Ben. 74, 23. Tó ðan unþæslícum *ad ineptas*, Hpt. Gl. 510, 35. Onþæslíce míslára *inportunas suggestiones*, Scint. 33, 19.

un-þæslíce; *adv. Unsuitably, in an unseemly manner*:—Ðæt nán þing unþæslíce ne gelympe on nánes limes þénunge, Homl. Skt. i. 1, 204.

un-þæslícness, e; *f. Unseemliness, impropriety*:—Menn dæftaþ heora hús, gif hí sumne freónd onfón willaþ tó him, ðæt nán unðæslícnys him ne ðurfe derian, Homl. Th. ii. 316, 8.

un-þæslícu; *indecl. f. Incongruity, absurdity*:—Eáþe is tó understandenne of hwylcum antimbre ðeós unþæslícu ásprincð ðisse miclan tóþúndennesse *quod quam est absurdum facile advertitur, quia materia ei datur superbiendi*, R. Ben. 124, 13.

un-þanc, es; *m.* I. *disfavour, displeasure, anger, ill-will*:—Oft ða unwaran láreówas for ege ne durron cleopian, ondrǽdaþ him sumra monna unðonc *saepe rectores improvidi humanam amittere gratiam formidantes loqui pertimescunt*, Past. 15; Swt. 89, 12. Hine on unðanc R eorringa geséceþ, Salm. Kmbl. 197; Sal. 98. II. *an unpleasing act, a displeasure, an offence, annoyance*:—Cweðe gé ðæt ic eów dide ǽfre ǽnigne unþanc? Ap. Th. 26, 3. Nú ic wolde ðé ðone unþanc mid yfele leánian, Gen. 31, 29. Hé bræc ðæne palant æt Neomagan and eác fela óðra unþanca hé him dyde, Chr. 1049; Erl. 172, 22. Hé wolde geofan him ðone castel, ðæt hé mihte syððan dæghwamlíce his unwinan unþancas dón, 1075; Erl. 212, 16. III. *not thanks, displeasure expressed in words*:—Ðá ágeaf hé ðæt feoh tó unðances (*he gave back the money without getting any thanks*), and his eác hæfde micelne dem *talentum cum sententia damnationis amisit*, Past. 49; Swt. 379, 9. Ðá wæs Hannibale æfter hiera hǽðeniscum gewunan ðæt andwyrde swíþe láð and him unþanc sǽde ðæs andwyrdes *abominatus dictum Annibal*, Ors. 4, 10; Swt. 202, 7. ¶ The word occurs most frequently in the genitive, with adverbial force, where something is done without a person's consent or good-will, (1) absolute, *unwillingly, without consent, on compulsion*; ingratis:—Niman hí unþances (*without the person's consent*) ðone teóðan dǽl, L. Edg. i. 3; Th. i. 264, 1. Hé ðone deófol ádrǽfde of ðam preóste . . . Se deófol, ðe hine ǽr unðances forlét, hine sóna gelæhte, Homl. Th. ii. 170, 11. Ðú miht forleósan unðances ða ðing ðe áteorian magon, ac gif ðú sylf for Gode gód byst, ðæt ðú ne forlýst nǽfre unðances, 410, 26–28. Far ðé frig; nis ná úre gewuna ðæt ǽnig man unðances tó Gode gecyrre, 416, 32. Se cyning sende æfter Amane, and hé unþances com, Homl. Ass. 99, 247: Hexam. 20; Norm. 28, 23. Unþances fæstende, Homl. Skt. i. 19, 92. Ealle hyra unlustas hí sceolon gebétan sylfwylles on ðyssum lífe, oððe unþances æfter ðyssum lífe, Homl. Th. i. 148, 28: Homl. Skt. i. 17, 31. Se mægðhád sceal beón geoffrod be his ágenum cyre, ðæt seó lác beó leófre ðonne hé wǽre, gif hé unðances wǽre, Homl. Ass. 33, 237. Gewilde man hí tó rihte þances oððe unþances, L. Eth. ix. 40; Th. i. 348, 38. Hé nam sume mid him, sume þances, sume unþances, Chr. 1066; Erl. 198, 37. (2) with noun or pronoun, *without* (*a person's*) *consent, not of* (*one's own*) *accord, against* (*one's*) *will*:—Ðá gerád Æþelwold ðone hám æt Winburnan ðæs cynges unþances (bútan ðæs cyninges leáfe, MS. A.), Chr. 901; Erl. 97, 12. On ðám castelan ðe hí ǽr ðes eorles unþances begiten hæfdon, 1091; Erl. 227, 10. Ðá wearð hé gecristnod his mága unþances, Homl. Skt. ii. 31, 24. Scealt ðú ðínes unþances ðone hord ámeldian, Homl. Skt. i. 23, 716. Án his manna wolde wícian æt ánes búndan húse his unðances, Chr. 1048; Erl. 177, 36. Þeáh him ðæt word ofscute his unnþances *licet verbum illud improviso exprimerit*, 1055; Erl. 189, 6. Ðonne sió sául hire unðonces gebǽdd wierð ðæt yfel tó forlǽtanne, Past. 36; Swt. 251, 12. Ðis folc ðe úre unþances faran wyllaþ, Ex. 14, 5. Hí heora unðances hié begeáton, Ors. 2, 2; Swt. 64, 27. Unþonces, 5, 13; Swt. 244, 21. Unþances, Jud. 11, 33. [Þat him wes mucheles unðonc (mid mochel onþong, 2nd MS.), Laym. 22370. Hit is þe an unðonke, 11769. Seoruwe uor luve of eie worldliche þinge, oðer uor eni unðonc, A. R. 202, 12. For þeft and for þrepyng unþonk may mon haue, Allit. Pms. 43, 183: P. S. 327, 90: Chauc. T. and C. 5, 699. Unthank come on his heed, Reeve's T. 162. Hy wyteþ and zyggeþ onþank, Ayenb. 69, 15. A king of Britaine hauede heo bewedded al hire unðonkes, Laym. 4502. Bettre iss to þe mann to don all hiss unnþannkess god þan ifell hise þannkess, Orm. 7194. *O. H. Ger.* un-dankes *ex necessitate, invite.* Cf. *Icel.* ú-þökk; *f. reproach, censure.*]

un-þancful[1]; *adj. Unthankful, ungrateful*:—Ic wæs micles tó unðonceful Gode mínes gewittes and mínre hǽle and ealra ðara góda ðe ic on lifde, Anglia xi. 99, 67. Hé is gód ofer unþancfulle (unðoncfullum, Lind.) *benignus est super ingratos*, Lk. Skt. 6, 35. v. þanc-ful[1].

un-þancweorþ, -wirþe; *adj. Ungrateful*; ingratus. (1) *not agreeable, unacceptable*:—Gemágnys is ðam sóðan Déman gecwéme, þeáh ðe heó mannum unðancwurðe sý, Homl. Th. ii. 126, 3. (2) *thankless*:—Wé wǽron unðancwurðe, and wendon ús fram Criste, ac hé ús gesóhte, Basil admn. 4; Norm. 42, 5. God, se ðe dæghwomlíce getíðaþ weldǽda unðancwurðum (cf. ipse benignus est super ingratos, Lk. 6, 35), Homl. Th. ii. 418, 23.

un-þearf, e; *f. Disadvantage, hurt, harm, detriment*:—Gif ðú heora untreówa onscunige, oferhoga hí and ádríf hí fram ðé, for ðam hí spanaþ ðe tó ðínre unþearefe *si perfidam perhorrescis, sperne atque abjice perniciosa ludentem*, Bt. 7, 2; Fox 18, 10. Ðæt wyrð ðære þeóde eall tó unþearfe, L. I. P. 4; Th. ii. 308, 3, 9: Wulfst. 267, 30. Deófol má and má manna forlǽrde and getihte tó heora ágenre unþearfe, 10, 4. Ðú lutodest on ðam láðum cristendóme ðám godum tó teónan and mé tó unþearfe, Homl. Skt. i. 5, 414. Hé gegaderode his folc tó ðæs cynges unþearfe, ac hé wæs gelet (hé gaderode his folc þan cyngce tó unþearfe hé þóhte, ac hit wearð heom seolfan tó mycclan hearme, MS. D.), Chr. 1075; Erl. 213, 17. Hé férde for his bróðær unþearfe intó Normandige *he* (*William*) *went to Normandy on account of the injury his brother had done him* (see Henry of Huntingdon), 1091; Erl. 227, 5. Nú hæfð se yfela gást seofonfealde ungifa, ðæt sýn unþearfa manegra manna, Wulfst. 52, 9. [*Icel.* ú-þörf *harm.*]

un-þearf; *adj. Needless, useless*:—Unðærfe ðing *nequaquam*, Mt. Kmbl. Lind. 2, 6. [*Icel.* ú-þarfr *useless, bad*; ú-þarfi *needless.*]

un-þearfes; *adv. Needlessly, without cause*:—Heora fét beóð swíðe hraðe blód tó ágeótanne unþearfes for yflum willan, Ps. Th. 13, 6. v. þearf-leás.

un-þeáw, es; *m. A bad habit, an evil practice, a vice, fault*:—Médsceattas áwendaþ wóíce tó oft ða rihtan dómas, and seó yfelnyss becymð ofer eallum folce ðǽr ðǽr se unþeáw orsorhlíce ríxaþ, Ælfc. T. Grn. 20, 34. Ðæt is ðara monna unþeáw ðæt hí nyton hwæt hí send *sese ignorare hominibus vitio venit*, Bt. 14, 3; Fox 46, 8. Nán hæfignes ðæs líchoman, ne nán unþeáw ne mæg eallunga áteón of his móde ða rihtwísnesse . . . ðeáh sió swǽrnes ðæs líchoman and ða unþeáwas oft ábisegien ðæt mód mid ofergiotulnesse, 35, 1; Fox 154, 29. Má dereþ monna gehwylcum mõdes unþeáw ðonne mettrymnes lǽnes líchoman, Met. 26, 112. Suá ðú meaht ǽlcne unðeáw on ðæm menn ǽresð be sumum tácnum ongietan . . . Siððan bið sió duru ðære unrihtwísnesse ontýned *uniuscujusque peccati prius signa forinsecus, deinde janua apertae iniquitatis ostenditur*, Past. 21; Swt. 157, 19. Mon sceal ðone unþeáw of mynstre áwyrtwalian, ðæt nǽnig ne gedyrstlǽce ǽnig ðing tó syllenne bútan ðæs abbodes hǽse *hoc vitium amputandum est de monasterio, ne quis presumat aliquid dare sine jussione abbatis*, R. Ben. 56, 16. Hwæt is sáwla hǽlo búte rihtwísnes? oððe hwæt is hiora untrymnes búte unþeáwas? *quid aliud animorum salus videtur esse, quam probitas? quid aegritudo, quam vitia?* Bt. 39, 9; Fox 226, 19. Ne sié hé tó ungerisenlíce underþeód his unþeáwum *nec victa libidine colla foedus summittat habenis*, 29, 3; Fox 106, 19: Met. 16, 4. Hé wæs swíþe gefylled mid unþeáwum and firenlustum *homo flagitiosissimus*, Ors. 6, 3; Swt. 256, 23: Ps. Th. 7, 13. Wé sceolon faran fram unðeáwum tó gódum ðeáwum, gif wé willaþ faran tó ðam écan lífe, Homl. Th. ii. 282, 23. On unðeáwum *in abusione*, Ps. Spl. 30, 22. Lufie mon ðone man, and hatige his unþeáwas, Bt. 39, 1; Fox 212, 8: Met. 27, 32: Bt. 29, 3; Fox 106, 27: Met. 16, 24. Ýdel bið seó lár ðe ne gehǽlð ðære sáwle leahtras and unðeáwas, Homl. Th. i. 60, 35. Ðá wolde hé forbúgan ða unðeáwas ðe menn begǽð, ii. 38, 4: 154, 12: Chr. 1067; Erl. 204, 31. Ðý læs hié forlǽten untǽlde óðerra monna yfele unðeáwas (yfle ðeáwas, Cott. MSS.) *ne pravos hominum mores nequaquam redarguant*, Past. 46: Swt. 351, 21. Gé ða Engliscan þeáwas forlǽtaþ ðe eówre fæderas heóldon, and hǽðenra manna þeáwas lufiaþ, and mid ðam geswuteliaþ ðæt gé forseóð eówer cynn and eówere yldran mid ðám unþeáwum, ðonne gé him on teónan tysliaþ eów on Denisc áblerédum hneccan and áblendum eágum, Engl. Stud. viii. 62, 4. [Þat unþeáw . . . þat ilke unhende flesches brune, H. M. 9, 27. Sparuwe cheatereð euer and chirmeð . . . Moni ancre haueð þet ilke unþeau, A. R. 152, 23. He þaht hit weren for unðeawe, þ he hire weore swa unwourð, Laym. 3064. To hatenn all þatt Godd iss lef and lufenn alle unnþæwess, Orm. 17782. Him is loþ everich unþeu, O. and N. 194.]

un-þeáwfæst; *adj. Of bad habits, vicious, ill-mannered, ill-conditioned*:—Hit is bysmorlíc dǽd, ðæt ǽnig man ǽfre swá unþeáwfæst beón sceole, ðæt hé ðone múð ufan mid mettum áfylle, and on óðerne ende him gange ðæt meox út, Engl. Stud. viii. 62, 15. Onþeáwfæste *indisciplinatorum*, Hpt. Gl. 526, 75. Hwam becumaþ wunda oððe eágena blindnyss búton ðám unðeáwfæstum ðe wódlíce drincaþ, and heora gewitt ámyrraþ? Homl. Ass. 6, 144. v. un-geþeáwfæst.

un-þeáwful[1]; *adj. Undisciplined, ill-conditioned*:—Unþeáwfulra *indisciplinatorum*, Wrt. Voc. ii. 47, 10: 87, 75.

un-þeccan; *p.* -þehte *To uncover*:—Hiá unðehton ðæt hús *nudauerunt tectum*, Mk. Skt. Lind. 2, 4.

un-þeód:—Ne lyste ðé fægeres wífes and wel gelǽredes and seó ðínum willum and wel unþeód (underþeód? *subject*), Shrn. 183, 10.

un-þinged; *adj. Uninvited, sudden, unexpected*:—Ðý læs iów geméte se réða and se egeslíca dæg, se cymð ofer ealle eorðwaran unðinged, swǽ swǽ grin *et superveniat in vos repentina dies illa. Tamquam laqueus superveniet in omnes, qui sedent super faciem omnis terrae*, Past. 43; Swt. 316, 12. Hí ofer cume unþinged deáð, ástígon heó on helle lifigende *veniat mors super eos, et descendant in infernum viventes*, Ps. Th. 54, 14. Dol biþ se ðe him his Dryhten ne ondrǽdeþ; cymeþ him se deáð un-þinged, Exon. 312, 8; Seef. 106: 335, 18; Gn. Ex. 35. v. un-geþinged.

un-þingod; *adj. Unatoned, unsettled*:—Swā eác se ðe ōðrum bismer cwið, oððe dēð, ðeáh hē geswīce, and hit nǽfre eft ne dō, ðeáh hit bið gedōn, ðæt hē dyde, and unðingad, gif hē hit ne bēt *neque qui contumelias irrogat, si solummodo tacuerit, satisfecit*, Past. 54; Swt. 423, 35.

un-þolemōdness, e; *f. Impatience*:—Þurh unðolemōdnesse *per inpatientiam*, Confess. Peccat.

un-þoligendlīc; *adj. Intolerable*:—Nāht unþoligendlīcre *nihil intolerabilius*, Scint. 208, 14.

un-þorfæst; *adj. Useless, needless*:—Unðor[f]fæst bidda *ineptum rogare*, Rtl. 179, 34. v. þorf-fæst.

un-þrīste; *adj. Timid, diffident, faint-hearted*:—Ða unmōdgan and ða unðrīstan (*pusillanimes*) . . . Ða lytelmōdan and ða unðrīstan, ðonne hié ongietaþ hiera unbældo and hiera unmiehte, hié weorðaþ oft ormōde, Past. 32; Swt. 209, 5-8. Ða unðriéstan (-ðrīstan, Cott. MSS.), Swt. 211, 15.

un-þrowi[g]endlīc; *adj. Incapable of suffering, impassible*:—Se ðe is unðrowigendlīc on his godcundnysse, Homl. Th. i. 116, 27: 120, 25. Seó Godcundnys ne mihte nān ðing þrowian, for ðan ðe heó is unðrowigendlīc, ii. 6, 30. Unðrowiendlīc, 270, 32.

un-þurhsceótendlīc; *adj. Impenetrable*:—Mid ðȳ unþurhsciótendlīcre gescyldnesse gescyld mē *inpenetrabili tutela me defende*, Lchdm. i. lxix, 5.

un-þurhtogen; *adj. Not carried through, not performed*:—Hwæt wēne gē hwæt sió ðurhtogene unrihtwīsnes geearnige, nū sió unðurtogene ārfæsðnes swā micel wīte geearnaþ *quid mereatur injustitia illata, si tanta percussione digna est pietas non impensa*, Past. 44; Swt. 329, 14.

un-þwǽre; *adj. At enmity, not in agreement*:—Gif ðū gemanst ðæt ðīn brōðor sig unþwǽre wið ðē *si recordatus fueris quod frater tuus simultatem tecum habet*, L. Ecg. P. ii. 27; Th. ii. 194, 1. v. ungeþwǽre.

un-þwǽrian. v. ge-unþwǽrian.

un-þwǽrness, e; *f. Discord, dissension, disagreement*:—Ðǽr wæs micel unþuǽrnes (-ðwǽrnesse, MS. E.) ðære þeóde betweox him selfum, Chr. 867; Erl. 72, 8. Unðwērnesse *discordias*, Kent. Gl. 155.

un-þwagen, -þwægen, -þwegen, -þwogen; *adj. Unwashed*:—Ða hwīle ðe hig unþwogene beóð, L. Ælf. E.; Th. ii. 392, 14. Unþwogenum (-þwagenum, MS. A.: -ðwægnum, Rush.: -ðuegenum, Lind.) handum *manibus non lotis*, Mk. Skt, 7, 2. Unþwogenum (-ðuēnum, Lind.: -ðwegenum, Rush.), Mt. Kmbl. 15, 20. Unðweánum, p. 17, 11. [*Goth.* un-þwahans.]

un-þyhtig; *adj. Weak*:—Unðyhtge (-þyotgi, -dyctgi) ēgan *vitiato oculo*, Txts. 107, 2133.

un-þyldig; *adj. Impatient*:—Hī bióþ swā unþyldige ðæt hī ne magon nān earfoþa geþyldelīce āberan, Bt. 39, 10; Fox 228, 2. [*O. H. Ger.* un-dultig *inpatiens*.]

un-þyldlīcness, e; *f. Difficulty*:—Ðā wæs mycel unþyldlīcnes geworden be his byrignesse *facta difficultate tumulandi*, Bd. 4, 11; S. 580, 8 note.

untīd-fyll[u]; *f. Unseasonable repletion, excessive drinking at improper times*:—Be oferfylle. *Ve, qui consurgitis mane ad bibendum, etc.* Wā eów, hē cwæð, ðe lufiaþ untīdfylla and ǽr on morgen oferdrenc dreógaþ, Wulfst. 46, 14.

untīd-gewidere, es; *n. Unseasonable weather*:—Ðises ylcan geáres wǽron swīðe untīdgewidera, and for ðī geond eall ðis land wurdon eorðwæstmas eall tō medemlīce gewende, Chr. 1095; Erl. 232, 35.

un-tīdlīc; *adj. Unseasonable*:—Untīdlīc *intemporalis*, Germ. 394, 316. Nū, swā hit gewuna is, of untīdlīcan gewideran, ðæt is, of wǽtum sumerum and of drȳgum wintrum and of rēðre lenctenhǽte, and mid ungemǽtre hærfestwǽtan *non, ut adsolet, temporum turbata temperies, hoc est, aut siccitas hiemis, aut repentinus calor veris, aut humor aestatis, vel autumni divitis indigesta illecebra*, Ors. 3, 3; Swt. 102, 5. [*O. H. Ger.* un-zītlīh *inportunus*.]

un-tīdlīce; *adv. Unseasonably, at a wrong time*:—Eall ðæt mon untīdlīce onginþ, næfþ hit nō ǽltæwne ende, Bt. 5, 2; Fox 10, 27. [*O. H. Ger.* un-zītlīcho *immature*.]

un-tīdre; *adj. Not weak, firm, strong*:—Him wæs hyge untyddre, Andr. Kmbl. 2506; An. 1254.

untīd-sprǽc, e; *f. Unseasonable speech*:—Unnytte dǽde and untīdspǽca forhogian, L. I. P. 14; Th. ii. 322, 10.

untīd-weorc, es; *n. Unseasonable work, work done at a wrong time*:—Geswīcan untīdweorčes (*work done on Sunday*), Wulfst. 209, 27. Geswīcan untīdweorca, 221, 19.

un-tīgan; *p.* de *To untie, unbind, loose*:—Ic unbinde oððe untīge *soluo*, Ælfc. Gr. 28; Zup. 177, 7. Ne untīgð (*solvit*) eówer ǽlc on restedæge his oxan oððe assan fram ðære binne? Lk. Skt. 13, 15. Gyt gemētaþ assan folan getīged . . . untīgaþ hyne. Gif inc hwā āhsaþ hwī gyt hyne untīgeaþ . . . Ðā hig hine untīgdon, ðā cwǽdon ða hlāfordas: 'Hwī untīge gē ðæne folan,' 19, 30-33: Mk. Skt. 11, 2-4. Petrus ðone ryððan untīgde, Homl. Th. i. 374, 2. Ðā sende God his apostolas tō gebundenum mancynne, and hēt hī untīgan. Hū untīgdon hī ðone assan? 208, 4-6. Untȳgaþ hī, 206, 11. Hwæt dō gyt ðone folan untīgende? Mk. Skt. 11, 5. Se ðe gesyhð assan clipiende oððe untīende (-tī[g]edne?) yrnan, Lchdm. iii. 198, 12. Ðonne wē sind gelaðode, ðonne sind wē untīgede, Homl. Th. i. 210, 7, 9.

un-tilod; *adj. Without provision made*:—Se ðe his ǽr tīde ne tiolaþ ðonne biþ his on tīd untilad *who makes no provision for himself beforehand, for him will there be no provision made when the time comes*, Bt. 29, 2; Fox 106, 3.

un-tīma, an; *m.* I. *a wrong time, an improper time*:—Se lǽce ðonne hē on untīman lācnaþ wunde, hió wyrmseþ and rotaþ *secta immature vulnera deterius infervescunt*, Past. 21; Swt. 153, 2. Hē wilnaþ hǽlo tō late and on untīman, ðonne hē ǽr nolde hié gehealdan, ðā ðā hē hī hæfde *salus infructuose ad ultimum quaeritur, quae congruo concessa tempore utiliter non habetur*, 36; Swt. 249, 8. Ǽlc ðæra manna ðe yt oððe drincð on untīman on ðam hālgan lenctene oððe on rihtfæstendagum, Homl. Skt. i. 12, 76: Anglia xi. 113, 26. II. *a bad time, an unhappy condition of things, a mishap* (cf. *French* malheur):—Ic āsende ofer eówer land ǽlcne untīman, ðæt bið egeslīce greát hagol, se fordēð eówre wæstmas, and unāsecgendlīce þunras . . . , Wulfst. 297, 7. [*Continentia*, þat is, þat man þe spuse haveð, his golliche deden wiðteo, swo hit be untime, Rel. Ant. i. 132, 18. Vres misseide, oðer in untime, A. R. 344, 3. A man schulde not ete in untyme, Chauc. Pers. T. In vntyme ne shulde no bourde on bedde be, Piers P. 9, 186. *Icel.* ú-tīmi *a wrong time* (koma ī ūtīma *to come too late*); *an evil time, mishap*.]

un-tīme; *adj. Unhappy, unfortunate, ill-timed*:—Se dysiga dranc būtan bletsunge and eode him ūt. Man slǽtte ðā ǽnne fearr, and se fear arn him tōgeánes, and hine ðȳde ðæt hē his feorh forlēt, and gebohte swā ðone untīman drenc, Homl. Skt. i. 12, 74. v. un-tīma, II, un-tīmness.

un-tīmende; *adj. Not productive, barren*:—Sarai wæs untȳmende (*sterilis*); næfde heó nān bearn, Gen. 11, 30: Jud. 13, 2: Boutr. Scrd. 22, 22. Hit is swīðe ungedafenlīc ðæt forwerode menn and untȳmende gifta wilnian, ðonne gifta ne sind gesette for nānum ðinge būton for bearnteáme, Homl. Th. ii. 94, 12. Eádige synd ða untȳmendan *beatae steriles*, Lk. Skt. 23, 29. v. tīman, I.

un-tīmness, e; *f. Misfortune, unhappiness*:—Ic sende on eówrum hūsum cwealm and hungor and untīmnesse and fȳr, ðæt forbærnð ealle eówre welan, Wulfst. 207, 18. v. un-tīma, II, un-tīme.

un-tiogoðad, un-tiorig, un-tīþe. v. un-teóþod, un-teorig, un-tygþa.

un-tōbrocen; *adj. Not broken in pieces*:—Gif gē ðone bend healdaþ sōðre brōðerrǽdene untōbrocenne, Homl. Th. ii. 318, 5. Hē sum þing hæfde untōbrocen, Homl. Skt. i. 5, 258.

un-tōclofen; *adj. Uncloven*:—Ða ðe synd gehōfode on horses gelīcnysse untōclofenum clawum, Homl. Skt. ii. 25, 45.

un-tōdǽled; *adj. Undivided, unseparated*:—Is ðæt full gōd ðæt eall ætgædere is untōdǽled, Bt. 34, 9; Fox 146, 28. Hē biþ ānfeald untōdǽled, 33, 2; Fox 122, 18, 21. Se God is simle on ānum untōdǽled, 34, 6; Fox 142, 22: Wulfst. 21, 19. Willnade se cyning ðæt se wer him syndriglīce untōdǽlede gefērscipe (*individuo comitatu*) lāreów wǽre, Bd. 5, 19; S. 639, 3.

un-tōdǽledlīc; *adj. Indivisible, inseparable*:—Ānfeald and untōdǽledlīc *simplex indivisumque natura*, Bt. 33, 1; Fox 120, 10: 34, 7; Fox 144, 19. Hī ðrȳ ān God untōdǽledlīc, Homl. Th. i. 150, 15: 248, 9: 500, 29. Ðære Hālgan Ðrynnysse weorc is ǽfre untōdǽledlīc, 498, 35. *Littera* is se læsta dǽl on bōcum and untōdǽledlīc . . . beóð ða stafas untōdǽledlīce, Ælfc. Gr. 2; Zup. 4, 19-5, 3. Ðæt gecynd gefēhþ ða friénd tōgædre mid untōdǽledlīcre lufe, Bt. 24, 3; Fox 84, 2.

un-tōdǽledlīce; *adv. Indivisibly, inseparably*:—Seó ðe hæfð ðās ðreó ðing on hire tōgædre wyrcende untōdǽledlīce, Homl. Th. i. 288, 25: 500, 14: 368, 2.

un-tōdǽledness, e; *f. Undividedness*:—*Indivisio*, ðæt is untōdǽlednyss, Anglia viii. 318, 17.

un-tōdǽllīc (-dǽl-); *adj. Indivisible, inseparable*:—Tōdǽl ða twā, ðonne byð ān tō lāfe; ðæt ys untōdǽllīc, Anglia viii. 318, 30. Untōdǽllīcre[ro] *inseparabili, indivisibili*, Hpt. Gl. 430, 50.

un-tōlǽtendlīce; *adv. Unremittingly*; indesinenter, Gr. Dial. 2, 8.

un-tōlīsende; *adj. Inextricable*:—Ðȳ untōlȳsendum *inextricabili*, Wrt. Voc. ii. 78, 70. Untōlēsende *inextricabilem*, 76, 48.

un-tōsceacen; *adj. Undisturbed, undestroyed*:—Swā lange swā God wolde ðæt Cristen geleáfa mid Engolcynne untōsceacen weóxa, Chart. Th. 127, 11. Swā lange swā God wylle ðæt Cristen geleáfa mid Angelcynne untōsceacan wurðe, 390, 35.

un-tōslegen; *adj. Not beaten to pieces*:—Þeáh ðæt scyp sī ūte on ðære sǽ on ðām ȳðum, hyt byð gesund untōslegen, gyf se streng āþolaþ, for ðam hys byð se ōðer ende fæst on ðære eorðan and se ōðer on ðam scype, Shrn. 175, 22.

un-tōsliten; *adj. Not torn asunder*:—Untōsliten *inextricabilis*, Wrt. Voc. ii. 110, 60: *inima* (?), 45, 37. Hī heóldon his tunecan untōslitene, Homl. Th. ii. 254, 32. Untōslitenum *indisruptis*, Wrt. Voc. ii. 88, 31: 47, 13.

un-tōsprecendlīc; *adj. Ineffable*:—Rīcsiendum ūrum Dryhtne, ðæm hiéhstan and ðæm untōsprecendlīcan (cf. regnante Domino nostro, summo et ineffabili rerum Creatore omnium, 106, 19) ealra þinga and ealra tīda Scippende, Chart. Th. 124, 8 : 388, 24.

un-tōtwǣmed; *adj. Undivided, unseparated:*—Nis Cristes godcundnys gerunnen tō ðære menniscnysse, ac hē þurhwunaþ þeáh ā on ēcnysse on ānum hāde untōtwǣmed, Homl. Th. i. 40, 30. Ðæra weorc is symle untōtwǣmed, ii. 366, 20.

un-trāglīce; *adv. Well, honestly:*—Āsēcaþ ða ðe snyttro mid eów hæbben, ðæt mē þinga gehwylc þrīste gecȳðan untrāglīce, ðe ic him tō sēce, Elen. Kmbl. 819; El. 410.

un-treów, e; *f. Bad faith, faithlessness, perfidy, fraud:*—Mē ðās woruldsǣlþa blindne on ðis dimme hol forlǣddon, and mē ðā berȳpton rǣdes and frōfre for heora untreówum, Met. 2, 13. Gif ðū heora untreówa onscunige, oferhoga hī, and ādrīf hī fram ðē, for ðam hī spanaþ ðē tō ðīnre unþearefe *si perfidam perhorrescis, sperne atque abjice perniciosa ludentem*, Bt. 7, 2; Fox 18, 8. Heó ðæt leóht geseah ellor scrīðan, ðæt hē hire þurh untreówa tācen iéwde, Cd. Th. 48, 10; Gen. 773. [*O. Sax.* un-trewa: *O. H. Ger.* un-triuwa *fraus.*]

un-treówe, -trȳwe; *adj. Untrue, not faithful:*—Gyf hwylc man sȳ untrȳwe ðam hundrede, L. C. S. 30; Th. i. 392, 21 note. [*Goth.* un-triggws *iniquus*: *Icel.* ū-tryggr *faithless, untrustworthy.*]

un-treówfæst; *adj. Unfaithful, untrustworthy:*—Untrȳwfæst *flecti facilis*, Germ. 401, 27. Hī cwǣdon tō ðam Hǣlende: 'Wē wyton ðæt ðū of forlygere wǣre ācenned; and ōðer ys, ðæt ðȳn cynn ys on Bethleem swȳþe untreówfæst; and þrydde ðæt ðȳn fæder and ðȳn mōdor flugon of Egiptan lande for ðam ðe hig nefdon nānne trūwan tō nānum folce,' Nicod. 6; Thw. 3, 22.

un-treówlīce; *adv. With bad faith, perfidiously:*—Agothocles gedyde untreówlīce wið hiene, ðæt hē hiene on his wārum beswāc and ofslōg *per Agathoclem insidiis circumventus, occisus est*, Ors. 4, 5; Swt. 170, 9. Ðā bæd hē ðæt mon dyde beforan him ðone triumphan. Ac him Rōmāne untreówlīce his forwierndon, and hit under ðæt lādedon for ðon ðe hē ǣr sige næfde, 5, 2; Swt. 216, 31.

un-treówsian; *p.* ode. I. *to defraud:*—Ne untreówsige gē nō eów betweoxn *nolite fraudare invicem*, Past. 16; Swt. 99, 14. II. *to offend:*—Ðonne beóð manega untreówsede *tunc scandalizabuntur multi*, Mt. Kmbl. 24, 10 note. v. ge-untreówsian.

un-treówþ, e; *f. Bad faith, perfidy:*—Ða Dænescan, ðe wæs ǣrur geteald eallra folca getreówast, wurdon āwende tō ðære mēste untrīwðe and tō ðam mǣsten swicdōme ðe ǣfre mihte gewurðan, Chr. 1086; Erl. 223, 7. Antigones forlēt ðæt setl. Ac Umenis him wēnde from Antigones hāmfærelte micelra untreówða *Antigonus ab obsidione discessit. Sed nec sic Eumeni spes firma aut salus certa*, Ors. 3, 11; Swt. 146, 21. Adam tȳhð mē untryówða, Cd. Th. 36, 33; Gen. 581. Agothocles gedyde untreówlīce wið hiene . . . Gif hē ðā ða āne untreówþa ne gedyde, from ðæm dæge hē mehte būtan gebroce Cartaina onwald begietan, Ors. 4, 5; Swt. 170, 11. [*Icel.* ū-trygð *falseness, faithlessness.*]

un-trum; *adj. Weak, sick, ill, infirm:*—Untrum *infirmus*, Wrt. Voc. i. 75, 45. Untrum ic eom *infirmus sum*, Ps. Spl. 6, 2: Mt. Kmbl. 25, 36. Næs ðæra leóda ǣnig untrum *non erat in tribubus eorum infirmus*, Ps. Th. 104, 32. Þeówa untrum *servus male habens*, Lk. Skt. 7, 2. Se ðe ǣr untrum wæs *qui languerat*, 7, 10. Ðā wearð hē untrum on feforādle, Blickl. Homl. 217, 15. Nǣnig næs tō ðæs untrum, ðæt hē sōna hǣlo ne onfēnge, 223, 23. Ðæt flǣsc is untrum *caro infirma est*, Mt. Kmbl. 26, 41. Man hwylcne dǣl his hrægles tō untruman men brōhte, ðæt hē wearð hāl geworden, Blickl. Homl. 223, 25. Untrume ealle wǣran *infirmati sunt*, Ps. Th. 106, 11. Wæs ðǣr on neáweste untrumra manna hūs, on ðam hyra ðeáw wæs ðæt hī ða untruman in lǣdan sceoldan *erat in proximo casa, in qua infirmiores induci solebant*, Bd. 4, 24; S. 598, 27. v. ge-untrum.

un-trumian; *p.* ode. I. *to make weak, weaken:*—Ic untrumige *infirmo*, Ælfc. Gr. 47; Zup. 276, 7. II. *to be* or *to become weak:*—Nā ic untrumge *non infirmabor*, Ps. Spl. 25, 1. Ðæs brōðer untrumade *cujus frater infirmabatur*, Jn. Skt. Rush. 11, 2. [Þa was þe king swiðe untrumed, Laym. 15037.] v. ge-untrumian; un-trymman.

un-trumlīc; *adj. Weak:*—Hwæðer ðæt landfolc sī tō gefeohte stranglīc oððe untrumlīc *populum, utrum fortis sit an infirmus*, Num. 13, 20.

un-trumness, e; *f. Weakness, sickness, illness, infirmity:*—*Freneticus* se ðe þurh sleápleáste āwēt, *frenesis* seó untrumnys, Wrt. Voc. i. 75, 61. Untrumnys *egritudo*, Bd. 1, 27; S. 494, 18: *infirmitas*, 3, 12; S. 537, 12. Ðā gestōd his wīf untrumnes on hire eágan *ingruente oculis caligine subita*, 4, 10; S. 578, 18. Līchomlīcre untrumnesse ðrycced *corporea infirmitate pressus*, 4, 24; S. 598, 25. Of untrumnysse (*infirmitate*) ðæs gecyndes, 1, 27; S. 494, 13. Mid his mōdes untrumnesse (*infirmitate*), Past. 54; Swt. 423, 21. Hēr Eádsige forlēt ðet biscoprīce for his untrumnisse, Chr. 1043; Erl. 169, 23. Mid ðære untrumnesse (*fever*) swīðe geswenced, Blickl. Homl. 227, 8. Mihtig ǣlce untrumnesse tō hǣlenne, 223, 22. Underwreoðaþ his untrumnesse *sustentat inbecillitatem suam*, Kent. Gl. 644. Gemænigfylde synd untrumnyssa (*infirmitates*) heora, Ps. Spl. 15, 3: 102, 3. On manegum gemetum geneósaþ God manna sāwla . . . hwīltīdum mid untrumnyssum, Homl. Th. i. 410, 28. On feforādle and on mislīcum ōþrum untrumnessum, Blickl. Homl. 209, 11. v. un-trymness.

un-trymed; *adj. Unconfirmed:*—Se ðe him biþ unfullod oððe untrymed *qui ipse non baptizatus vel non confirmatus sit*, L. Ecg. C. 7; Th. ii. 140, 19.

un-trymig, -trymmig; *adj. Weak, sick, infirm:*—Līchoma is untrymig (*infirma*), Mk. Skt. Lind. Rush. 14, 38. His sunu untrymig uæs *filius infirmabatur*, Jn. Skt. Lind. 4, 46: 11, 2. Untrymig is *infirmatur*, 11, 3. Untrymmig *infirmus*, Mt. Kmbl. Lind. 25, 36, 43. Ða ðe wērun untrymige (-trymig, Lind.) *qui infirmabantur*, Jn. Skt. Rush. 6, 2. Ofer untrymigum *super aegrotos*, Mk. Skt. Lind. Rush. 16, 18. Fore untrymigum *pro infirmis*, Rtl. 177, 19.

un-trymig[i]an *to become weak, sick, infirm:*—Ða ðe untrymigdon *qui infirmabantur*, Jn. Skt. Lind. 6, 2.

un-trymigu(-o); *f. Weakness, sickness, infirmity:*—Ðæt heá gegēme all unhǣl and all untrymmigo *ut curarent omnem languorem et omnem infirmitatem*, Mt. Kmbl. Lind. 10, 1.

un-trymman, -trymian; *p.* ede *To be* or *to become weak, sick, ill, infirm:*—His sunu untrymede (unntrymade, Lind.) *filius infirmabatur*, Jn. Skt. Rush. 4, 46. Ðæs brōðer untrymade, Lind. 11, 2. Hē ongann untrymmia *coepit egere*, Lk. Skt. Lind. 15, 14.

untrymness, e; *f. Weakness, sickness, illness, infirmity:*—Hwæt is sāwla hǣlo, būte rihtwīsnes? oððe hwæt is hiora untrymnes būte unþeáwas? *quid vero aliud animorum salus videtur esse, quam probitas? quid aegritudo, quam vitia?* Bt. 39, 9; Fox 226, 18. Ðē untrymnes ādle gongum bysgade, Exon. Th. 163, 7; Gū. 990. Of untrymnesse mōdes oððe līchoman *infirmitate*, Past. 21; Swt. 159, 1: 56; Swt. 435, 15. In untrymnisse wæs ðū lēcedōme *in infirmitate sis medicina*, Rtl. 105, 11. Hē hǣlde ǣghwilce ādle and ǣghwilce untrymnisse (*infirmitatem*), Mt. Kmbl. Rush. 10, 1. Ða untrymnesse hiera heortan ic wolde getrymman *cordis infirmitatem munimus*, Past. 4; Swt. 41, 4: 10; Swt. 61, 16. Untrymnise, Rtl. 49, 30. Se ðe ne mægi giðrouia untrymnissum ūsum *qui non possit conpati infirmitatibus nostris*, 91, 7. Lǣcedōmas wið eallum untrymnessum heáfdes, Lchdm. ii. 2, 1. v. untrumness.

un-trymþ, e; *f. Weakness, sickness, infirmity:*—Heora unmiht and heora untrymð is swīðe gemanifealdod *multiplicatae sunt infirmitates eorum*, Ps. Th. 15, 3. Gif hwylc wīf seteþ hire bearn ofer hrōf oððe on ofen for hwylcere untrymðe hǣlo (*alicujus morbi sanandi causa*), L. Ecg. C. 33; Th. ii. 156, 36.

un-tweó; *gen.* -tweón; *m. Not doubt, certainty:*—Bið untweó (-treo, MS.) ðæt ðǣr Adames cyn cwīþeþ gesārgad *there is no doubt that Adam's race will lament afflicted*, Exon. Th. 59, 31; Cri. 961.

un-tweód; *adj. Not inspired with doubt, unwavering:*—Hē hæfde him on innan ellen untweódne, Andr. Kmbl. 2485; An. 1244.

un-tweógende, -tweónde; *adj. Undoubting, unhesitating, unwavering, certain:*—Gif wē hæfdon ǣnigne dǣl untwiógendes andgites swā swā englas habbaþ *si divinae judicium mentis habere possemus*, Bt. 41, 5; Fox 254, 7. Hī ōþ heora līfes ende untweógende mōde þurhwunodan, Blickl. Homl. 171, 13. Hē næfð gearone willan untweógendne tō ðæm weorce, Past. 54; Swt. 423, 26. Hyht untweóndne, Elen. Kmbl. 1592; El. 798. Ðæt wē ðȳ untweógendran be ūs gelȳfden ðæt wē be ðǣm leorniaþ, Shrn. 67, 24.

un-tweógendlīc; *adj. Certain:*—Untuēndlīc sind *certi sumus*, Lk. Skt. Lind. 20, 6.

un-tweógendlīce; *adv.* I. *without feeling doubt, certainly, unhesitatingly:*—Ic hit untweógendlīce gelȳfde in tō gesettanne *eam indubitanter inserendam credidi*, Bd. 4, 22; S. 592, 30. Eallum mannum þurhwuniggendum in tintregum untweógendlīce, Blickl. Homl. 171, 16. Hié untweógendlīce wēndon ðæt heora hlāford wǣre on heora feónda gewealde, Ors. 3, 9; Swt. 134, 27. Ǣgðer ðara folca wēnde untweógendlīce ðæt hié sceoldon on ða eorþan besincan, 4, 2; Swt. 160, 29: 4, 5; Swt. 166, 13. Ðætte hié ðȳ fæsðlīcor and ðȳ untweógendlīcor gelīfden ðara ēcena ðinga *ut ad aeternorum fidem certius roboretur*, Past. 50; Swt. 389, 35. Þēh hȳ gelȳfdan be his segene, ðe hit ǣr geseah, untweógendlīcor (-ātweógendlīcor, MS. C.), ðonne ða heora segene eft gelȳfdon, ðe æfter heom ācende wǣron, Wulfst. 2, 12. II. *so as not to cause doubt, unequivocally, indubitably:*—Hē his ǣrendracan āsende tō ðære ðeóde, and him untweógendlīce secgan (*say in a way that should leave no room for doubt*) hēt, ðæt hié ōðer sceolden, oþþe ðæt lond æt him ālēsan, oþþe hē hié wolde mid gefeohte fordōn *missis legatis qui hostibus parendi leges dicerent*, Ors. 1, 10; Swt. 44, 8. v. tweógend-līc.

un-tweólīc; *adj. Undoubted:*—Untweólīcere *indubitata*, Hpt. Gl. 411, 38.

un-tweólīce; *adv.* I. *undoubtedly, indubitably, certainly:*—Smyre ðone seócan; untweólīce ðū hyne ālȳsest, Lchdm. i. 302, 4. Hē grīpð untweólīce ðæt behātene rīce, Homl. Th. i. 360, 25: Homl. Ass. 97, 184. Heó getācnode untweólīce ða hālgan geladunge, 114, 412. Untwīlīce, Ælfc. T. Grn. 3, 39. Se Sunu is gāst and hālig untwȳlīce, Homl. Th. i. 282, 30. Untwȳlīce ðū līhst, 378, 6. Ða ungeleáffullan untwȳlīce forwurðaþ on ēcnesse, ii. 60, 15: 110, 27: Basil admn. 4; Norm. 44, 12: 5; Norm. 46, 18. II. *without feeling doubt, with certainty*:—Ealle ða geleáffullan fæderas sǣdon untwȳlīce and geþwǣrlehton on ðam ānum, ðæt God gescypð ǣlces mannes sāwle, Homl. Skt. i. 1, 85.

un-tweónigende; *adj. Not to be doubted, indubitable*:—God untwȳnigendre mildheortnesse *God of mercy which must not be doubted* (but the Latin is: Deus inestimabilis misericordie), Anglia xi. 115, 45.

un-twifeald; *adj.* I. *not double* (v. twi-feald, IV), *simple, sincere, honest, pure*:—Nis nān scild trumra wið ðæt tuiefalde gesuinc ðonne mon sió untwiefeald (-twy-, Cott. MSS.) *nil est ad defendendum puritate tutius*, Past. 35; Swt. 239, 10. Se untweofealda willa bioþ tō tellenne for fullfremod weorc, Bt. 36, 7; Fox 184, 24. Ne magon wē nǣfre gereccan ðone yfelan mon clǣnne and untwifealdne *malos esse, pure atque simpliciter nego*, 36, 6; Fox 182, 18. Gif hī gōde beóþ and hlāfordholde and untwifealde *si probi sunt*, 14, 1; Fox 42, 24. Hī untweofealde treówa gehealdaþ, Met. 11, 95. II. *not double, united, without division*:—Ðeáh hē hwelcne wæstm forð brenge gōdes weorces, gif hē ne bið of gōdum willan and of untwiefaldre (-twy-, Cott. MSS.) lufan ongunnen, ne bið hē nāwuht *qui etsi boni operis fructus in suis actionibus proferunt, profecto nulli sunt, quia non ex unitate caritatis oriuntur*, Past. 47; Swt. 359, 17. [*O. H. Ger.* un-zwifalt.]

un-twīlīce, -twȳlīce, un-twȳnigende. v. un-tweólīce, un-tweónigende.

un-tȳd; *adj. Ignorant, uninstructed, unskilled*:—Dysig bið se lǣce and untȳd ðe wilnaþ ðæt hē ōðerne mon gelācnige, and nāt ðæt hē self bið gewundad *improbus et imperitus est medicus, qui alienum mederi appetit, et ipse vulnus, quod patitur, nescit*, Past. 48; Swt. 371, 6. Ic ðē giungne underfēng untȳdne and ungelǣredne, Bt. 8; Fox 24, 24.

un-tȳdre, es; *m. An evil growth, evil progeny, a monstrous birth*:—Ðanon untȳdras ealle onwōcon, eotenas and ylfe and orcneas, swylce gigantas (cf. Milton: Where nature breeds, Perverse, all monstrous, all prodigious things, Abominable, P. L. Bk. 2), Beo. Th. 222; B. 111.

un-tȳdrende; *adj. Not propagating*:—Swīnes blǣdran untȳdrendes, ðæt is gylte, Lchdm. ii. 88, 23.

un-tygþa(-e), -tȳþa(-e); *adj. Unsuccessful in obtaining a request*:—For ðæm ne meahte Balaham geearnian ða Godes giefe ðe hē biddende wæs, ðā hē Israhēla folc wirgean wolde and for hine selfne gebiddan, for ðæm hē wearð untygða ðe hē hwierfde his stemne nales his mōd *hujus correptionis donum idcirco Balaam non obtinuit, quia ad maledicendum pergens vocem, non mentem mutavit*, Past. 36; Swt. 257, 18. v. tīþe (*where read* tygþe(-a), tȳþe(-a): cf. *O. Sax.* tugiðōn).

un-tȳnan; *p.* de. I. *to unclose, open*:—Euplis bær Cristes godspel in fōdre . . . Ðā untȳnde Eplius ðæt Cristes godspel, Shrn. 116, 33. Ān ðara cempa mið spere sidu his untȳnde (*aperuit*), Jn. Skt. Lind. Rush. 19, 34. Hē untȳnde ealle ða bernu, Gen. 41, 56. Hī untȳndon heora goldhordas (*apertis thesauris*), Mt. Kmbl. 2, 11. Gif hwā ādelfe wæterpyt oþþe betȳnedne untȳne, and hine eft ne betȳne *si quis aperuerit cisternam, et foderit, et non operuerit eam* (Ex. 21, 33), L. Alf. 22; Th. i. 50, 6, note. Untȳne insigloe *aperire signaculum*, Rtl. 29, 17. Gié geseáð ðæt heofun untȳned (*apertum*), Jn. Skt. Lind. 1, 51. Hāt ða duru beón untȳnede, Homl. Skt. ii. 23 b, 448. Untūned bōc *aperto codice*, Mt. Kmbl. p. 4, 1. Byrgenna untuende (-tūnede?) ł untȳned wēron, Lind. 27, 52. II. *to disclose, lay open*:—Untēnð *aperiet* (*stultitiam*), Kent. Gl. 452. Hira unriht wearð eall untȳned, Ps. Th. 72, 5. III. the word is used to gloss *solvere* and *inhiare* in the following:—Se ðe untȳnes ł tōslittes (*solverit*) ēnne of bebodum ðissum, Mt. Kmbl. Lind. 5, 19. Hē untȳnde (*solvebat*) ðone Sunnadæg, Jn. Skt. Rush. Lind. 5, 18. Ðætte eardlīco lusto wiðsæcgende giliorniga wē untȳna (*inhiare*) heofonlīco, Rtl. 34, 20. v. on-tȳnan.

un-tȳned; *adj. Unfenced*:—Ceorles weorðig sceal beón wintres and sumeres betȳned. Gif hē bið untȳned . . ., L. In. 40; Th. i. 126, 14.

un-wāclic; *adj. Not mean, not poor, noble, splendid*:—Gegiredon ād unwāclīcne, Beo. Th. 6268; B. 3138.

un-wāclīce; *adv.* I. *not weakly, resolutely, without faltering*:—Ðæt hī æt þearfe þolian sceoldon, unwāclīce wǣpna neótan, Byrht. Th. 140, 54; By. 308. Ic beó gearo sōna unwāclīce willan dīnes, Exon. Th. 245, 25; Jul. 50. II. *not meanly, nobly, splendidly*:—His aferan eád bryttedon unwāclīce, Cd. Th. 258, 12; Dan. 674.

un-wēded; *adj. Not clothed*:—Monno unwēded mið wēde *hominem non vestitum veste*, Mt. Kmbl. Lind. 22, 11.

un-wær; *adj.* I. *not on one's guard, unaware, unprepared*:—Gif ðē man scotaþ tō, ðū gescyltst ðē, gif ðū hit gesihst; gif ðū unwær bist, ðū bist ðe swīðor geswenct, Homl. Th. ii. 538, 11. Hī cweþaþ ðæt tō worde, ðæt se biþ on geþance wærast and wīsast, se ðe ōðerne can raðost āsmeágan and oftost of unwæran sum ðing gerǣcan, Wulfst. 55, 22. Perpena on ðone cyning ungearone (unwærne, MS. C.) becom *Perperna Aristonicum inproviso bello adortus*, Ors. 5, 4; Bos. 104, 26. Ðȳ læs ðe se smīc derige ðām unwarum, Homl. Th. ii. 418, 5. II. *unwary, heedless, incautious, inconsiderate*:—Mōdignys is endenēxt gesett, for ðan ðe se unwæra on ende oft mōdegaþ on gōdum weorcum, Homl. Th. ii. 222, 4. Þencð se unwara eall swā deófol hine lǣrð, Wulfst. 298, 32. Unware weorude, Exon. Th. 363, 25; Wal. 59. Deófol wile beswīcan ðone unwaran, Homl. Th. i. 16, 22: Blickl. Homl. 55, 23. Hig fordrencton ðone unwæran Loth, Gen. 19, 35. Ða unwaran *indocti et praecipites*, Past. proem.; Swt. 25, 12. Ða unwaran lāreówas *rectores improvidi*, 15; Swt. 89, 10. His word beóð gōde geðūhte unweran (-warum, MS. C.) mannum, Wulfst. 54, 17. Deófol dēð swȳðe lytelīce, ðǣr hē ongyt unwære (-ware, MS. C.) menn, 11, 16. Unware *inexpertos, incautos*, Hpt. Gl. 498, 67. Ða ðe galdorcræftas begangaþ and unwære men beswīcaþ, Blickl. Homl. 61, 24. Unware, 185, 2. Unuuere *incautos*, Kent. Gl. 902. Tō fordōnne ða unwaran, Basil admn. 2; Norm. 34, 30. Oft ðonne se hirde gǣð on frēcne wegas, sió hiord ðe unwærre bið gehrīst *cum pastor per abrupta graditur, ad praecipitium grex sequitur*, Past. 2; Swt. 31, 1. III. adverbial uses:—Hī unwares (*unawares, unexpectedly*) cōmon, and hē fyrst næfde, ðæt hē his fyrde gegadrian mihte, Chr. 1004; Erl. 139, 21. Unwæres, 1093; Erl. 229, 5. Ðā com Harold heom ongeán on unwaran (cf. *Icel.* at ūvörum *unexpectedly*), 1066; Erl. 200, 38. Ðā com Harold on unwær (cf. *Icel.* koma ā ūvart *to take by surprise*) on ða Normenn, Erl. 201, 26: 202, 7: 1043; Erl. 168, 32. Hī cōmon unwær on heom, 1050; Erl. 175, 32: 1067; Erl. 205, 25. [He wes to unwar, Laym. 7810. Sunnen sleað þeo unwarre soule, A. R. 274, 5. *Icel.* ū-varr.]

un-wæres. v. un-wær, III.

un-wærlic; *adj. Unwary, incautious, heedless*:—Suā suā unwærlīcu and giémeleáslīcu sprǣc menn dweleþ *sicut incauta locutio in errorem pertrahit*, Past. 15; Swt. 89, 8. Oft ðæt mægen ðære lāre wierð forloren, ðonne mon mid ungedafenlīcre and unwærlīcre ofersprǣce ða heortan gedweleþ ðara ðe ðǣrtō hlystaþ *saepe dictorum virtus perditur, cum apud corda audientium loquacitatis incauta importunitate laevigatur*, Swt. 95, 19. Ðeáh ðū fela unwærlīcra worda gesprǣce, Exon. Th. 254, 6; Jul. 193. [*Icel.* ū-varligr *unwary.*]

un-wærlīce; *adv. Unwarily, incautiously, without caution; heedlessly*:—Ic lǣre ðæt hira nān ðara ne wilnie ðe hine unwærlīce begā; and se ðe hī unwærlīce gewilnige, ondrǣde hē ðæt hē hī ǣfre underfēnge *ut haec, qui vacat, incaute non expetat; et qui incaute expetiit, adeptum se esse pertimescat*, Past. proem.; Swt. 23, 14. Geðence se lāriów ðæt hē unwærlīce (*incaute*) forð ne rǣse on ða sprǣce, 15; Swt. 95, 9. Gif sió wund bið unwærlīce gewriðen *cum fractura incaute colligatur*, 17; Swt. 123, 18. Se ðe ðone wuda unwærlīce (*incaute*) hiéwð, 21; Swt. 167, 15. Ðā eode hē on īse unwærlīce *dum incautius in glacie incederet*, Bd. 3, 2; S. 525, 1. Ða ðe unwærlīce and gēmeleáslīce Gode hȳraþ, Blickl. Homl. 63, 22: 57, 9: Exon. Th. 363, 34; Wal. 63: L. Ælfc. P. 7; Th. ii. 366, 13. Him com ongēn Hanno unwærlīce, and ðǣr ofslagen wearð, Ors. 4, 10; Swt. 200, 4: Chr. 1068; Erl. 206, 9. Þænne gyltas unwerlīce [wē] forgyfaþ *dum culpas incaute remittimus*, Scint. 149, 8. [Ne ne wite hie a wiche halue ne a wiche wise he hem wile bisette, þanne he hem unwarliche (*unexpectedly*) his dintes giued, O. E. Homl. ii. 191, 32. *Icel.* ū-varliga *unwarily.*]

un-wærness, e; *f. Heedlessness, want of caution, imprudence*:—Þurh ðās unwærnysse hē gebringð hine on helle, Wulfst. 299, 7.

un-wærscipe, es; *m. Heedlessness, inconsiderateness, imprudence*:—Ða gē forluron þurh unwærscipe, Homl. Th. i. 68, 4.

un-wæscen; *adj. Unwashen*:—Nim sigelhweorfan unwæscene, Lchdm. ii. 108, 24.

un-wæstm, es, e; *m. f. n.* I. *an evil growth, a bad plant, a tare, weed*:—Unwæstm (ða weód, Rush.) *zizania*, Mt. Kmbl. Lind. 13, 38. Huona hafes unwæstm (ðæt weód, Rush.) *unde habet zizania?* 13, 27. Gié geadrias ðæt unwæstm, 13, 28. Ða unwæstm *zizania*, 13, 30, 40. Ðara wunwæstma *zizaniorum*, 13, 36. II. *bad growth, failure of crops*:—Eów unwæstm þurh unweder gelōme gelimpeþ, Wulfst. 133, 6. Gyf hit geweorðe ðæt on þeódscype becume heálīc ungelimp, unwæstm oððon unweder, orfcwealm oþðon mancwealm, 170, 1. Gif hwæt fǣrlīces on þeóde becymð, beón hit miswyderu oððon unwæstmas, 271, 3. Ūs unwidera for oft weóldon unwæstma, 129, 5: 159, 13.

un-wæstmbǣre; *adj. Unproductive, barren, sterile*:—Unwæstmbǣre elebeám *oleaster*, Wrt. Voc. i. 33, 19. On ðisum dæge ācende seó unwæstmbǣre mōder ðone mǣran wītegan, Homl. Th. i. 356, 4. Se ðe on gōdnysse unwæstmbǣre bið, ii. 406, 19. Se ðe eard seteþ unwæstmbǣrre *qui habitare facit sterilem*, Ps. Th. 112, 8. Unwestembǣre tēdrunge *infructuosa* (*infecunda*) *sterilitate*, Hpt. Gl. 430, 56. Hī woldon mē gedōn unwæstmbǣrne, swā swā se ðe būtan ǣlcum yrfewearde byð, Ps. Th. 34, 12. Unwæstmbǣre wīf *sterilem*, Ps. Lamb. 112, 8. Ic wyrce ðīn land unwæstmbǣre, Homl. Th. ii. 102, 34. Sume treówu hē cearf, ðȳ læs hié tō ðæm forweóxen ðæt hié forseareden, and ðȳ unwæstmbǣrran wǣren, Past. 40; Swt. 293, 7.

un-wæstmbǣrness, e; *f. Unproductiveness, barrenness, sterility*:—Unwestmbǣrnys *sterilitas* vel *infoecunditas*, Wrt. Voc. i. 53, 45. Unwæstmbǣrnys *sterilitas*, 76, 79. On hungre is geswutelod ðære eorðan unwæstmbǣrnys, Homl. Th. ii. 538, 31. For unwæstmbǣrnesse ðæs londes *propter terrarum infoecundam diffusionem*, Ors. 1, 1; Swt. 14, 18. On his ācennednysse hē ætbrǣd ðære mēder hire unwæstmbǣrnysse, Homl. Th. i. 352, 30.

un-wæstmberendlic; *adj. Barren, sterile*:—Seó stōw is unwæstmberendlîcu for ðæra næddrena mænigeo *loca illa sterilia sunt propter multitudinem serpentium*, Nar. 34, 28.

un-wæstmberendness, e; *f. Barrenness, sterility*:—Mê mîne fŷnd âscufon fram ðære hâlgan onsegdnysse for mînre unwæstmberendnysse, Homl. Ass. 126, 329.

un-wæstmfæst; *adj. Barren, sterile*:—Unwæstmfæst ðara godcundra mægena, Blickl. Homl. 163, 6.

un-wæstmfæstness, e; *f. Barrenness, sterility*:—Sôna seó unwæstmfæstnes fram him fleáh, Blickl. Homl. 163, 17.

un-wæterig; *adj. Without water, dry*:—On unwæterium *inaquoso*, Ps. Lamb. 62, 3. On unwæterige stôwe, 77, 17. Þurh unwæterige (-wæterie) stôwa *per loca inaquosa*, Lk. Skt. 11, 24.

un-wandiende; *adj. Unhesitating*:—Ða ðe unwandiende ðara scyldegena gyltas ofslôgen *qui delinquentium scelera incunctanter ferirent*, Past. 49; Swt. 381, 25.

un-warnod; *adj. Unwarned*:—Gif preóst ôðerne unwarnode lǽte ðæs ðe hê wite ðæt him hearmian wille, L. N. P. L. 33; Th. ii. 294, 25.

un-wealt; *adj. Not given to roll, steady*:—Ða scipu wǽron ǽgðer ge swiftran, ge eác unwealtran, ge eác hiéran ðonne ða ôðru, Chr. 897; Erl. 95, 14 (v. note, p. 320). v. wiltan.

un-wearnum; *adv. Without hindrance*:—Hê slǽpendne rinc slât unwearnum, Beo. Th. 1487; B. 741: Exon. Th. 309, 27; Seef. 63. v. wearn.

un-weaxen; *adj. Not grown up, young*:—Him be healfe stôd hyse unweaxen, cniht on gecampe, Byrht. Th. 136, 17; By. 152. Cild unweaxen, Chr. 975; Erl. 126, 5. Ðus mê fæder mîn unweaxenne (*when a boy*) wordum lǽrde, Elen. Kmbl. 1055; El. 529. Se eorl wolde sleán eaferan sînne unweaxenne (*Isaac*), Cd. Th. 204, 1; Exod. 412. Isaac bearn unweaxen, 173, 34; Gen. 2871. Hê hêt ealle ârîsan geonge . . . Ðâ upp âstôdon eaforan unweaxne, Andr. Kmbl. 3252; An. 1629.

un-weder, es; *n. Bad weather, tempest*:—Nû cweðaþ sume men ðæt se môna hine wende be ðan ðe hit wuderian sceal on ðam mônðe; ac hine ne went nǽfre nâðor ne weder ne unweder of ðam ðe him gecynde is, Lchdm. iii. 268, 4. Ðǽr ne cymð storm ne nân unweder ðæt ðam corne derie, Homl. Th. i. 526, 30. Healîc ungelimp, unwæstm oððon unweder, Wulfst. 170, 1. Hî synd geneádode mid stormum ðæs unwederes (-wedres, MS. F.) *tempestatibus acti*, Ælfc. Gr. 44; Zup. 260, 12. Hê geðreáde ðæt wind and hroeðnise ł unwoeder ðæs wætres *increpavit ventum et tempestatem aquae*, Lk. Skt. Lind. 8, 24: p. 5, 18. Eów unwæstm þurh unweder gelôme gelimpeþ, Wulfst. 133, 7. Ûs unwedera for oft weóldan unwæstma, 159, 12. Eall ðæt geár wæs swîðe hefigtŷme on unwæderum, Chr. 1041; Erl. 169, 9. [Unweder (*the plague of hail*), Gen. and Ex. 3058. *Icel.* û-veðr *bad weather, storm.*] v. un-geweder, un-widere.

unweder-lîce; *adv. In a way that indicates bad weather, threateningly*:—Tô dæg hit byð hreóh weder; ðeós lyft scînð unwederlîce *hodie tempestas, rutilat enim triste coelum*, Mt. Kmbl. 16, 3.

un-wegen; *adj. Unweighed*:—Ðera ôðera wyrta ǽlces healues penincges gewihta, and VI pipercorn unwegen, Lchdm. i. 376, 7.

un-wemlîc; *adj. Spotless, pure, virgin*:—Mid ðam unwemlîcan cǽgan *virgineo clave*, Wrt. Voc. ii. 91, 75.

un-wemme; *adj.* I. of concrete objects, *spotless, without blemish, without defect, uninjured*:—Lamb unwemme *agnus absque macula*, Ex. 12, 5: Lev. 9, 2, 3. Se æþela wong ǽghwæs onsund wið ŷðfare gehealden stôd hreóra wǽga unwemme *ille locus, cum diluvium mersisset fluctibus orbem, exsuperavit aquas*, Exon. Th. 200, 25; Ph. 46. Hê eft mid his unwemmum lîchoman hine gegyrede, Blickl. Homl. 89, 35. Hê gelǽdde ðæt folc ealle unwemme ofer ða Reádan sǽ *he led the people all of them uninjured over the Red Sea*, Btwk. 196, 2. II. of abstract objects, *uninjured, inviolate*:—Cyninges handgrið stande unwemme, L. E. G. 1; Th. i. 166, 21 (cp. L. Eth. vi. 14; Th. i. 318, 25). Godes cyrican wê sculan ǽfre lufian and nǽfre derian wordes ne weorces, ac griðian hŷ symle and healdan unwemme, Wulfst. 67, 17. Hî eodon of ðam fŷre feorh unwemme, Exon. Th. 197, 7; Az. 186. III. in a moral sense, *undefiled, pure, immaculate, perfect*:—For ðî ic weorðe unwemme (*immaculatus*) beforan him, Ps. Th. 17, 23: 18, 12. Sié heorte mîn unwemme, Ps. Surt. 118, 80. Se Hǽlend betwux synfullum unwemme fram ǽlcere synne ðurhwunode, Homl. Th. i. 356, 14. On unwemmum (ðæm unwemman, Surt.) wege *in via immaculata*, Ps. Th. 100, 1. Unwemne weg, Ps. Surt. 17, 33. Flǽsc unwemme, Exon. Th. 26, 18; Cri. 418. Hié scoteden ðone unwemman, Ps. Surt. 63, 5. Unwemme synt ðîne wegas *impolluta via ejus*, Ps. Th. 17, 29. Ða ðe unwemme (*immaculati*) on hiora Dryhtnes ǽ gangaþ, 118, 1. Weagas unwemra, Ps. Surt. 36, 18. Unwæmme, Ps. Th. 17, 31. Ðæt wê ûrne lîchaman and ûre sâwle swâ unwemme him âgeofan on dômes dæg, swâ hê hine ǽr gesceóp, Blickl. Homl. 103, 22. II a. of virginity, *pure, immaculate*:—Unwemme *immunis* (*carnali spurcitia*, Ald. 21), Hpt. Gl. 442, 5: Homl. Skt. i. 7, 59. Fram unwemre fǽmnan âcenned, Blickl. Homl. 167, 21. Æt Sancta Maria ðære unwemman fǽmnan, 105, 20. Heó lufode ðone Hǽlend ðe hî heóld unwemme, Homl. Skt. i. 20, 18: Exon. Th. 19, 13; Cri. 300. Unwemme *immunes, incontaminati*, Hpt. Gl. 447, 43. Hêr syndon inne unwemme twâ dohtor mîne, ne can ðara idesa ôwðer gieta þurh gebedscipe beorna neáwest, Cd. Th. 148, 30; Gen. 2864. [*Goth.* un-wamms *sine macula, immaculatus*: *O. Sax.* idis un-wamma; *acc.*] v. next word.

un-wemmed; *adj. Unspotted, undefiled, immaculate*:—Ðû wǽre symle fǽmne oncnâwen, and ðînne lîchaman hæbbende clǽne and unwemmed (-wæmme, MS. G.), Homl. Skt. ii. 23 b, 437. On wege unwæmmedum *in via immaculata*, Ps. Spl. 100, 1, 7. Unuoemedo *immaculatam*, Rtl. 104, 18. [*A. R. Orm. Ps. Chauc.* un-wemmed.]

un-wemming, e; *f. Incorruption, immortality*:—Ðâm unwemmincge sêcendum *his incorruptionem quaerentibus* (Romans 2, 7), Scint. 41, 10.

un-wemness, e; *f. Purity*:—Ðæt ða clǽnan and ða unwemnan hira clǽnnysse and hiora unwemnysse forð gehióldan, Homl. Ass. 207, 422. [Cf. *Goth.* un-wammei *sinceritas.*]

un-wendness. v. ge-unwendness.

un-wêne; *adj.* I. *hopeless, not having hope* or *expectation*. Cf. or-wêne:—Wæs ðǽr ân cnapa geǽttrod þurh næddran, swîðe tôswollen þurh ðæs wyrmes slege, unwêne his lîfes, Homl. Th. ii. 514, 7. Hê gehǽlde ânre wydewan sunu ðe unwêne læg, Homl. Skt. i. 6, 103. Hê fond hlingendne, fûsne on forðsîþ, freán unwênne, Exon. Th. 171, 4; Gû. 1121. II. *not hoped for, unexpected*:—Gyf him þince ðæt hê æt forðgewitenum men âhtes onfô, of unwênum (*ex improviso*: v. ungewêned) hym cymeþ gestreón, Lchdm. iii. 170, 7. Forðon hiá unwoene (unwoen, Lind.) sint mæhte in him *propterea inopinantur uirtutes in illo*, Mk. Skt. Rush. 6, 14. [*Icel.* û-vænn *hopeless, not to be expected*. Cf. *O. H. Ger.* un-wân *desperatio.*]

un-wêned; *adj. Unhoped for, unexpected*:—Ic him eft his rîce âgeaf, and ðâ ðære unwêndan âre ðæs rîces (ðe hê him seolfa nǽniges rîces ne wênde) ðæt hê ðâ mê eall his goldhord æteówde *regna Poro restitui, qui, ut ei insperatus honor donatus est, mihi thesauros suos manifestavit*, Nar. 19, 23. On unwênedum forþsîþe hê beóð gegripene *inprouiso exitu rapiuntur*, Scint. 181, 12. v. un-gewêned.

un-wênlîc; *adj. Not giving grounds for hope, unpromising*:—Ðâ ðû ðê selfum ðûhtest unwênlîc *when you did not seem to yourself to have much chance of success*; cum esses parvulus in oculis tuis, Past. 17; Swt. 113, 9. Hié oft gebidon on lytlum staþole and on unwênlîcum (*a slight foundation and one that gave little hopes of success*), Ors. 4, 9; Swt. 192, 34. Hwæt wênst ðû be ðære gôdan wyrde, ðe oft cymþ tô gôdum monnum on ðisse worulde, hweðer ðis folc mæge cweþan ðæt hit sié yfel wyrd? . . . Hwæt wênst ðû be ðære unwênlîcran wyrde ðe oft þriétaþ ða yflan tô wîtnianne, hwæðer ðis folc wêne ðæt ðæt gôd wyrd sié? *quid vero jucunda fortuna, quae in praemium tribuitur bonis, num vulgus malam esse decernit? . . . quid reliqua, quae, cum sit aspera, justo supplicio malos coercet, num bonam populus putat?* Bt. 40, 2; Fox 236, 24 note. [Magað unwânlîk, Hêl. 4959. *Icel.* û-vænligr *leaving little hope of success.*]

un-wênunga; *adv. Unexpectedly*:—Men cwǽdon ðonne him hwæt unwênunga gebyrede, ðæt ðæt wǽre weás gebyred, Bt. 40, 6; Fox 242, 4. [*Goth.* un-wêniggô *repentine.*]

un-weód, es; *n. A noxious weed* (lit. or metaph.):—Seó eorðe ûs winð wið, ðonne heó forwyrneþ eorðlîces wæstmes and ûs unweóda tô fela âsendeþ, Wulfst. 92, 19. Man sceal ǽlc unriht mid rihte bêtan and unweód âweódian and gôd sǽd ârǽran, 73, 2.

un-weorclîc; *adj. Unsuitable for work*:—Seó niht hafaþ seofon tôdǽlednyssa . . . seó feórðe is *intempestivum*, ðæt ys mid niht oððe unworclîc tîma, Anglia viii. 319, 30.

un-weorþ, -wurþ, -wyrþ, -wierþe, -wyrþe; *adj.* I. *of no value*:—Mid deórwyrþum reáfum ne beóþ hŷ gescrŷdde, ac mid unweorþum, R. Ben. 137, 9. Ðæt heora heortan mid wâcum mettum and unweorþum ne sŷn ofersŷmede, 138, 11. II. *of no dignity, little esteemed*:—Gif munuc eáðhylde bið, þeáh hine man wâcne and unweorðne talige *si omni vilitate contentus sit monachus*, R. Ben. 29, 3, 6. Gif munuc hine sylfne ŷttran and unweorðran talaþ ðonne ǽnigne ôþerne *si omnibus se inferiorem et viliorem credat*, 29, 11. Æt ðæm feórðan cirre hié sendon Hannan heora ðone unweorðestan þegn, and hê hit âbæd *novissime Annonis, minimi hominis inter legatos, oratione meruerunt*, Ors. 4, 7; Swt. 182, 13. Nime gê ða ðe unweorþuste sién *them who are least esteemed* (1 Cor. 6, 4), Past. 18; Swt. 131, 7. III. *unworthy, not of sufficient merit*:—Ic ðone hâd underhnâg, ðeáh ðe ic unwyrþe wǽre *quamvis indignus consensi*, Bd. 4, 2; S. 566, 8. Nemne God mê earmum and unwyrþum (*misero mihi et indigno*) gemildsian wylle, 3, 13; S. 538, 35. Sum ungesceádwîs man hine sylfne âhêng . . . Martinus hine unwurðne of deáðe ârǽrde, Homl. Th. ii. 506, 1. III a. with gen. of that of which one is unworthy:—Ðŷ læs ǽnig lâreówdôm underfôn durre ðara ðe his unwierðe sié *ne temerare sacra regimina, quisquis his impar, audeat*, Past. 3; Swt. 33, 8. Ic am unwyrðe micles hêrnisse *ego sum indignus tanti officii*, Rtl. 98, 16. Mânsceaða, feores unwyrðe, Exon. Th. 95, 27; Cri. 1563. Saul ǽresð fleáh ðæt rîce and tealde hine selfne his suîðe unwierðne (*indignum se prius considerans*), Past. 3; Swt. 35, 18. Ðû hine ongeáte unweorþne ðæs anwealdes, Bt. 27, 2; Fox 96, 18. Hié woldon selfe fleón ða byrðenne suâ micelre scylde, ða ðe his unwierðe wǽron *indigni quique tanti reatus pondera fugerent*, Past. 2; Swt. 31, 15. Hié woldon habban gôdne hlísan, þeáh hí his unwyrþe sién, Bt. 18, 1; Fox 60, 26. Gif anweald becymþ tó ðam men ðe his ealra unweorþost biþ, 16, 1; Fox 48, 34. IV. *worthless, bad, contemptible, despicable, ignoble:*—Hwæþer ðé þynce unweorþ and unmǽrlíc seó gegaderung? *obscurum hoc atque ignobile censes esse?* Bt. 33, 1; Fox 120, 29. Ðú wilt habban ealle fægere ðing and ácorene, and wilt ðé sylf beón wáclíc and unwurð, Homl. Th. ii. 410, 20. Unwurð scop *tragicus* vel *comicus*, Wrt. Voc. i. 60, 9. Unweorþe scopas *tragedi* vel *comedi*, 39, 39. Hí syndon ǽwisce on líchoman and unweorðe *sunt publicato corpore et inhonesto*, Nar. 38, 13. Sume habbaþ bearn genóge, ac ða beóþ yfele and unweorþ *alius prole laetatus, filii filiaeve delictis moestus illacrymat*, Bt. 11, 1; Fox 32, 9. Geþenc nú hwæþer ǽnig mon beó á ðý unweorþra ðe hine manige men forsióþ. Gif ðonne ǽnig mon á ðý unweorþra biþ, ðonne biþ ǽlc dysi man ðe unweorþra ðe hé máre ríce hæfþ ǽlcum wísum men . . . Se anweald ne mæg his wealdend gedón nó ðý weorþron, ac hé hine gedéþ ðý unweorþran (wyrsan, Bod. MS.) *si eo abjectior est, quo magis a pluribus quisque contemnitur, . . . despectiores potius improbos dignitas facit*, 27, 2; Fox 98, 8-14. Se eallra wyrresta and se eallra unweorþesta mon *pessimus*, 14, 3; Fox 46, 21. IV a. with dat. of person by whom one is considered worthless:—Xersis wearþ his ágenre þeóde swíþe unweorþ *Xerxes contemtibilis suis factus*, Ors. 2, 5; Swt. 84, 23. Ǽlcum witum láþ and unweorþ *omnibus invisus*, Bt. 28; Fox 100, 28: Met. 15, 6. Se ídela gylp ús beó ǽfre unwurð (-wyrð, MS. U.), Homl. Skt. i. 16, 367. Philippus him dyde heora wíg unweorð *Philip made light of their fighting power*, Ors. 3, 7; Swt. 118, 3. Bisceopum gebyreþ, ðæt hí ǽghwylc gefleard heom unwyrð lǽtan, L. I. P. 10; Th. ii. 316, 28. Romulus and ealle Rómware óþerum folcum unweorðe wǽron, Ors. 2, 2; Swt. 66, 16. V. *ignominious, dishonouring:*—Mid ealre ðare unwurð[r]este scame beó hé gescænt *ignominiosissima confusione subsannetur*, Chart. Th. 318, 34. [Unwurð *of no value*, A. R. 94, 4. Uvel strengþe is lutel wurþ, Ac wisdom ne wurþ never unwurþ, O. and N. 770. Crist wass unnwurrþ (*little esteemed*), Orm. 16163. He bið unworþ, þe mon þe litul ah, Laym. 3464. Þu maht to þi were iwurðen þe unwurðere, H. M. 33, 12. Yhealde for uyl and onworþ, Ayenb. 132, 24. *O. H. Ger.* un-werd *ignobilis, contemtibilis, obscurus, dejectus*: *Icel.* ú-verðr *unworthy.*]

un-weorþe; *adv. Unworthily:*—Unwyrðe *indigne*, Mk. Skt. Lind. 10, 14: 14, 4. Gif hé ðæs hálgan húsles unwurðe onbyrigð, Homl. Th. ii. 278, 5. [Cf. *Goth.* un-wairþaba *unworthily.*]

un-weorþian; *p.* ode. I. *to dishonour, disgrace:*—Hú ne unweorþast ðú ðé selfne, ðæt ðú winsð wiþ ðam hláfordscipe ðe ðú self gecure? Bt. 7, 2; Fox 18, 29. Seó cwén, ðe ðín word forseah, ne unwurðode ðé ǽnne, ac ealle ðíne ealdormenn *non solum regem laesit regina, sed et omnes principes* (Esther 1, 16), Homl. Ass. 93, 53. Gé unwordadun mec *uos inhonoratis me*, Jn. Skt. Rush. 8, 49. Ðæt hé God ne unwurðige, Homl. Skt. i. 13, 86. Ðæt man unweorðige ða ðe godcunde láre wyrdan, Wulfst. 168, 7. Unweorðian *dehonestare*, Wrt. Voc. ii. 76, 15: 26, 40. Ða swelcan monn sceal unweorðian mid ǽlcre unweorðnesse *sine dedignatione dedignandi sunt*, Past. 37; Swt. 265, 18. Forsewen and geunwurþod, Homl. Th. i. 24, 4. II. *to become dishonoured:*—Unwurðiaþ *vilescunt*, Hpt. Gl. 462, 53. Unwurðie *vilescat*, 420, 13. [We unwurðeð ure Drihten, wurðeð þe deuel, O. E. Homl. ii. 181, 29. He shameþþ þe and unnwurrþeþþ, Orm. 18285. To onworþi, Ayenb. 22, 18. *Icel.* ú-virða *to slight.*] v. ge-unweorþian.

un-weorþlíc; *adj.* I. *of little value* or *importance, humble:*—Ða hláfordas and ða recceras scoldon ðencean ymb ðæt hélícuste and ða underðióddan scoldon dón ðæt unweorðlícre *a subditis inferiora gerenda sunt, a rectoribus summa cogitanda*, Past. 18; Swt. 131, 10. II. *that has little honour, not famous* or *splendid, poor:*—Hié lange wǽron ðæt dreógende ǽr heora áðer mehte on óþrum sige gerǽcan, ǽr Alexander late unweorðlícne sige (*a by no means famous victory*) gerǽhte *commissoque praelio diu anceps pugna tandem tristem pene victoriam Macedonibus dedit*, Ors. 3, 9; Swt. 134, 8. III. *ignoble, disgraceful, infamous:*—Mid ðý unæþelan gydde *vel* unweorþlícan *cum infami eulogio*, Wrt. Voc. ii. 137, 43. God ða mǽstan ofermétto geniðrode mid ðære bismerlícestan wrace and ðære unweorðlícostan (*tormenta turpia*), Ors. 1, 7; Swt. 38, 5. [3if þu art unwurðlich (*of little account*), H. M. 33, 11. Þe man þoleþ þet he by uoulliche ydraȝe, and ase persone onworþlych (v. unweorþ, II), Ayenb. 132, 35. *Icel.* ú-virðiligr *contemptible.*]

un-weorþlíce; *adv.* I. *unworthily, in an unsuitable manner:*—Him is micel ðearf ðæt hié geornlíce geðencen ðæt hié tó unweorþlíce ne dǽlen ðæt him befæsð bið *necesse est, ut sollicite perpendant, ne commissa indigne distribuant*, Past. 44; Swt. 321, 14. Unwurðlíce, Cd. Th. 28, 23; Gen. 440. II. *with indignity, with contempt, ignominiously:*—Hé wearð self unweorðlíce ofslagen *Domitianus interfectus est; cujus cadaver ignominiosissime sepultum est*, Ors. 6, 9; Swt. 264, 15. Hé heora ǽrendracan swá unweorðlíce forseah, ðæt hé heora self onseón nolde *legatos ad se missos injuriosissime etiam a conspectu suo abstinuit*, 4, 8; Swt. 186, 7: 3, 10; Swt. 140, 3. Hí heóldon ðæt gold unwurðlíce *they held the gold in contempt*, Homl. Th. i. 326, 24. III. *with indignation:*—Ðá se Hǽlend hí geseah unwurðlíce (-weorð-, MS. A.) hé hit forbeád *quos cum uideret Iesus indigne tulit*, Mk. Skt. 10, 14. Sume hit unwurðlíce (-weorð-, MS. A.) forbǽron *erant quidem indigne ferentes*, 14, 4. [Unworthly þou wroght . . . when þou was bowne with a brande my body to shende, Alex. (Skt.) 869. *O. H. Ger.* un-werdlícho *indifferenter, indigne*: *Icel.* ú-virðiliga *scornfully.*]

un-weorþness, e; *f. Indignity, contempt, disgrace:*—Mid unweorðnesse *dedignatione*, Past. 37; Swt. 265, 18. Hé his ríce mid micellre unweorðnesse and mid micelre uniéðnesse gehæfde, Ors. 6, 24; Swt. 276, 1. Hé his onféng mid micelre unweorðnesse *a quo arrogantissime exceptus est*, 6, 30; Swt. 280, 12. Ða wón wyrd ǽgþer ge on ðara unrihtwísra anwealda heánesse, ge on mínre unwurþnesse and foreseuwenesse, Bt. 5, 1; Fox 10, 22. [Onworþnesse (despit) is wel grat zenne, Ayenb. 19, 35. *O. H. Ger.* un-werdnissa *contempt.*]

un-weorþscipe, es; *m.* I. *dishonour, disgrace:*—Hweþer ðú nú mæge ongitan hú micelne unweorþscipe se anwald brengþ ðam unmedeman? *videsne quantum malis dedecus adjiciant dignitates?* Bt. 27, 2; Fox 96, 9. II. *indignation:*—Ierre and unweorðscipe *ira et indignatio*, Past. 33; Swt. 222, 10. v. next word.

un-weorþung, e; *f.* I. *disgrace, shame:*—Sýn gescrýdde mid gescendnysse and unwurþunge ðe yfel sprecaþ ofer mé, Ps. Spl. 34, 30. II. *indignation:*—Hit bið unnyt ðæt mon unweorðunga forlǽte *frustra indignatio tollitur*, Past. 33; Swt. 222, 12. [*Icel.* ú-virðing *disgrace.*]

un-wered; *adj. Unprotected:*—Wit baru standaþ unwered wǽdo; nys unc wuht beforan tó scúrsceade, Cd. Th. 50, 21; Gen. 812.

un-wérig; *adj. Not weary, fresh:*—Ǽt níxtan wurdon hí ealle geteorode, and hé ána unwérig him æfter fyligde, Homl. Skt. ii. 30, 34. Gif mon on mycelre ráde weorðe geteorad, nime betonican . . .; ðonne bið hé sóna unwérig, Lchdm. i. 76, 8. Hé hét ðæt mon ðæt fæsten brǽce and on fuhte dæges and nihtes, simle án legie æfter óþerre unwérig *cum alias aliis legiones dies noctesque succedere sine requie cogeret*, Ors. 5, 11; Swt. 238, 9.

un-werod; *adj. Not sweet:*—Wæter ðý unwerodre tó drincanne, Past. 58; Swt. 447, 19.

un-widere, es; *n. Bad weather, tempest:*—Ús unwidera weóldon unwæstma, Wulfst. 129, 4: 159, 12 note. [*O. H. Ger.* un-witari *tempestas.*] v. un-weder, -gewidere.

un-widlod; *adj. Unpolluted:*—Unwidlad *inpollutus*, Rtl. 90, 34.

un-wil[l], es; *n. Absence of good will, dislike, despite, repugnance, reluctance*; the genitive, with adverbial force, *against one's will, not willingly, without one's consent, without intention, involuntarily*, is (almost) the only case used. (1) alone:—Gif hé hit dide unwilles *si praeter voluntatem id fecerit*, L. Ecg. P. ii. 1; Th. ii. 182, 13. Unwilles wé magon forleósan ða hwílwendlícan gód, ac wé ne forleósaþ nǽfre unwilles ða écan gód, Homl. Th. i. 576, 7-9: Hexam. 17; Norm. 26, 3. Gif ðú mé unwilles gewemman dést, Homl. Skt. i. 9, 90. Hé ðǽr wunode ða niht unwilles, se ðe sylfwilles nolde, Homl. Th. ii. 184, 13: L. Eth. vi. 52; Th. i. 328, 21. (2) with pronouns:—Þeáh ðú mé geoffrige mínes unwilles, ic beó þeáh unscyldig, Homl. Skt. i. 9, 87. Hire unwilles *invita ipsa*, L. Ecg. P. ii. 15, tit.; Th. ii. 180, 27. Heó wæs hire unwilles fram him *ab eo invita aberat*, 15; Th. ii. 186, 29. Heora unwilles, L. Edg. S. 2; Th. i. 274, 5. [Ich mot nede, ant neoðeles min unwil hit is to don al ꝥ ti wil is, Marh. 13, 3. Ha wes him ihondsald þah hit hire unwil were, Jul. 7, 12. Heo wes ihondsald al hire unwilles, 6, 5.] v. next word.

un-willa, an; *m. What displeases, displeasure, what is not desired:*—Nafa ðú tó yfel ellen, ðeáh ðé sum unwilla on becume; oft brincð se woruld ðone willan ðe bið eft, Prov. Kmbl. 40. Hé drýhð deófles willan and Godes unwillan, Wulfst. 12, 13. ¶ *the word occurs mostly in dat.* (*sing. or pl.*) *with adverbial force*, unwillan, unwillum *against one's will, unwillingly, not voluntarily, without one's consent, in despite of one.* (1) alone:—Se ðe monnan nédes ofslóge, oððe unwillum, L. Alf. 13; Th. i. 46, 22. Hí sealdon unwillum áþas, Met. 1, 24. Ród ðe ic unwillum on beom gefæstnad, óðer ðe ic gestág willum mínum, Exon. Th. 91, 12; Cri. 1491: 360, 11; Wal. 4. Se ðe mid his willan bið besmiten . . . Se ðe onwillan (*invitus*) bið besmiten, L. Ecg. C. 5; Th. ii. 138, 7. (2) with pronouns:—Ðec ðín sáwl sceal mínum unwillan (-willum, Soul Kmbl. 125) oft gesécan, Exon. Th. 370, 22; Seel. 63. Ic áscige ðé, forhwí ðú ðæt ríce ðínum unwillan (-willum, Cott. MS.) forléte? Bt. 27, 2; Fox 96, 14. Sǽton ða Gotan on lande, sume be ðæs cáseres willan, sume his unwillan, Ors. 6, 38; Swt. 298, 5. Hé for ðam ege his unwillum ðonan wende, 4, 5; Swt. 166, 8. Nis nán syn þeáh man his unwillum blódes byrige of his tóðum, L. Ecg. C. 40; Th. ii. 166, 27. Úre gást biþ swíþe wíde farende úrum unwillum (*independently of our will*), Bt. 34, 11; Fox 152, 4. Godes anweald nǽre full eádiglíc, gif ða gesceafta hiora unwillum him hérden, 35, 4; Fox 160, 19: Ps. Th. 44, 16: Ors. 6, 13 tit.; Swt. 6, 3. Heora bégra unwyllum, Shrn. 204, 6. [He wuneð on wanrede and þoleð his unwille, O. E. Homl. ii. 123, 6. *O. Sax.* un-willeo:—An Godas unwilleon, Hél.

2460. *O. H. Ger.* un-willo *nausea;* sînen unwillen *against his will: Icel.* û-vili, at ûvilja eins *against one's will.*] v. preceding word.

un-willende; *adj. Unwilling, not desiring* or *intending*:—Ic hit unwillende dō, Homl. Ass. 180, 353. Ðæt hî ne hlîpen unwillende on ðæt scorene clif unðeáwa *per multa, quae non appetunt, iniquitatum abrupta rapiuntur,* Past. 33; Swt. 215, 7. [*Icel.* û-viljandi *unwilling, not intending.*]

un-wilsumlîce; *adv. Against one's will, not of one's own accord*:—Se sceal nŷde on helle duru unwilsumlîce geniþerad gelǣded beón *necesse habet in januam inferni non sponte damnatus introduci,* Bd. 5, 14; S. 634, 20.

un-windan; *p.* -wand, *pl.* -wundon; *pp.* -wunden *To unwind, unwrap* what is wrapped up:—Ðā hēt hē unwindan ðæs cnihtes lîc, Homl. Th. i. 66, 24.

un-wine, es; *m. An unfriend, enemy*:—Ðæt hē mihte his unwinan unþancas dōn, Chr. 1075; Erl. 212, 16. Gif ic ongēn ne cume, þat þū it nēfre ne lēt weldon mine unwinan æfter mē þe mid unrichte sitteð ðēron and nyttað it mē ēuere tō unðanke, Chart. Th. 584, 10. [Wreken hine of his unwines, Laym. 1628. For to beon itempted of þe unwine of helle, A. R. 178, 27. Eð were ure lauerd to awarpen his unwine (*diabolus*), Kath. 1221. Herode wass unnwine wiþþ Filippe, Orm. 19 38. *Icel.* û-vinr *an enemy.*]

un-wîs; *adj.* I. *unwise, foolish, stupid*:—Unwîs *insipiens,* Wrt. Voc. i. 76, 11: Ps. Spl. 91, 6: Ps. Th. 73, 17: Deut. 32, 6. Se unwîsa, Ps. Spl. 13, 1: 52, 1. Ðū wāst ðæt ic eom unwîs hyges *tu scis insipientiam meam,* Ps. Th. 68, 6. Unwîs *glebo,* Wrt. Voc. ii. 109, 81. Hié sealdon ānum unwîsum cyninges þegne Miercna rîce tō haldanne, Chr. 874; Erl. 76, 27. Unwîse on folce and dysige *insipientes in populo et stulti,* Ps. Spl. 93, 8: Ps. Th. 73, 21: Blickl. Homl. 59, 22: Homl. Skt. i. 17, 70. Monige men bióð ðe noldon ðone hlîsan habban ðæt hié unwîse (-wiése, Hatt. MS.) sién *sunt nonnulli, qui aestimari hebetes nolunt,* Past. 11; Swt. 66, 3. Earfoðtǣcne unwîsra gehwæm (cf. dysgum monnum, Bt. 33, 4; Fox 130, 28), Met. 20, 148. Þeáh hió unwîsum wîdgel þince, 10, 10. Neátum ðǣm unwîsum *jumentis insipientibus,* Ps. Surt. 48, 13: Blickl. Homl. 89, 9. Ic lǣre ge snottre ge unwîse, 107, 12. On ðæs unwîsestan lāre, L. Alf. 41; Th. i. 54, 8. Gē ðe on folce unwîseste ealra syndon *qui insipientes estis in populo,* Ps. Th. 93, 8. II. *ignorant*:—Gif hē hit nāt, hwelce gesǣlþa hæfþ hē æt ðam welan, gif hē biþ swā dysig and swā unwîs ðæt hē ðæt witan ne mæg? *si nescit, quaenam beata sors esse potest ignorantiae caecitate?* Bt. 11, 2; Fox 34, 26 note. Unwîse lāreówas cumaþ for ðæs folces synnum. Forðon oft for ðæs lāreówes unwîsdōme misfaraþ ða hiéremenn, and oft for ðæs lāreówes wîsdōme unwîsum hiéremonnum bið geborgen. Gif ðonne ǣgðer bið unwîs *pastorum saepe imperitia meritis congruit subjectorum: quia quamvis lumen scientiae sua culpa exigente non habeant; districto tamen judicio agitur, ut per eorum ignorantiam hi etiam, qui sequuntur, offendant,* Past. 1; Swt. 29, 3-6. Wēnaþ unwîse lǣcas ðæt ðæt sié lendenādl, ac hit ne bið swā, Lchdm. ii. 232, 8. Unwîsum *ignaris,* Wrt. Voc. ii. 44, 23: *imperitis,* Mt. Kmbl. p. 2, 1. II a. with gen. *ignorant* of something:—Hē wæs ðære godcundan ǣfestnysse unwîs *divinae erat religionis ignarus,* Bd. 1, 34; S. 499, 22: 2, 20; S. 521, 22: 4, 13; S. 582, 18. Wē ðæs londes ungleáwe and unwîse wǣron, Nar. 10, 7. [*Goth.* un-weis *idiota;* un-weis bi *ignorant of: O. Sax.* un-wîs *foolish: O. H. Ger.* un-wîs *insipiens, brutus, hebes, fatuus: Icel.* û-vîss *foolish.*] v. on-unwîs.

un-wîsdōm, es; *m.* I. *folly, stupidity*:—Unwîsdōm *stultitia,* Mk. Skt. Lind. Rush. 7, 22. *Insipientia,* ðæt is unwîsdōm, Wulfst. 52, 17. From onsiéne unwîsdōmes (*insipientiae*) mînes *fra face of mine unwisdome* (Ps.), Ps. Surt. 37, 6. Tō unwîsdōme *ad insipientiam,* Ps. Spl. 21, 2. Mid unwîsdōme gefyllede, Lk. Skt. 6, 11. Hit com of ðæs abbotes unwîsdōme, ðæt hē misbeád his munecan on fela þingan, Chr. 1083; Erl. 217, 3. Se ðe samnaþ ungemætlîce weolan, for his unwîsdōme (*stultitia*) sylle hē ðone þriddan dǣle þearfum, L. Ecg. P. addit. 7; Th. ii. 232, 24. Se wîsdōm is ðæs Hālgan Gāstes gifu; deófol sǣwð ðǣrtōgeánes unwîsdōm, Wulfst. 52, 26. II. *ignorance*:—Unwîsdōmes blendnise *ignorantiae cecitate,* Rtl. 38, 9. Sōna swā hî heora mōd āwendaþ from Gode, swā weorþaþ hî āblende mid unwîsdōme *ubi oculos a summae luce veritatis ad inferiora dejecerint, mox inscitiae nube caligant,* Bt. 40, 7; Fox 242, 31. For ðæs lāreówes unwîsdōme *pastorum imperitia,* Past. 1; Swt. 29, 4. Hē of yfelum willan ne gesyngaþ, ac of unwîsdōme (*non malitia, sed sola ignorantia*), 21; Swt. 157, 25. [We habbet idon unwisdom, Laym. 3383. Bihold i þine soule two þinges—sunne and ignorance; þet is, unwisdom and unwitenesse, A. R. 278, 7. *O. H. Ger.* un-wîstuom *ignavia, insapientia.*] v. on-unwîsdōm.

un-wîslîc; *adj. Unwise, foolish*:—Ðæra unwîslîcra geþanca, Homl. Skt. ii. 23 b, 526. [*Icel.* û-vîsligr *foolish.*]

un-wîslîce; *adv. Unwisely, foolishly*:—Unwîslîce *insipienter,* Past. 15; Swt. 93, 21: Elen. Kmbl. 586; El. 293. Ðā beseah Lothes wîf unwîslîce underbæc, Gen. 19, 26. Ðisse ādle fruman mon mæg yþelîce gelācnian, and æfter unēð, gif hió bið unwîslîce tō lange forlǣten, Lchdm. ii. 232, 18. [*O. H. Ger.* un-wîslîcho *inmature.*]

un-wîsness, e; *f.* I. *ignorance*:—Swā hwæt swā ic for unwîsnesse āgylte *quicquid ignorantia deliqui,* Bd. 4, 29; S. 607, 29. Hî þurh unwîsnesse (*per ignorantiam*) gesyngodon, 1, 27; Bd. 491, 29. II. *wickedness*:—In ðærfum yfelgiornisse and unwîsnisse *in fermento malitiae et nequitiae,* Rtl. 25, 19.

un-wita, an; *m. A foolish, stupid, witless person, a fool*:—Se unwita *insipiens,* Ps. Lamb. 13, 1. Eorp unwita, Exon. Th. 433, 21; Rä. 50, 11. Gebîg fram unwitan (*insensato*), and ðū nā wiþerast on stuntnysse his, Scint. 188, 11. Wē lǣraþ ðæt preósta gehwilc tō sinoðe gefædne man tō cnihte and nǣnigne unwitan ðe disig lufige, L. Edg. C. 4; Th. ii. 244, 14. Gif hit unwitan ǣnige hwîle healdaþ būtan hæftum, hit ðurh hrōf waðeþ, bærneþ boldgetimbru, Salm. Kmbl. 821; Sal. 410. [Gif eni unweote acseð ou of hwat ordre ȝe beon, A. R. 8, 22. Oðre þurh wicchecreftes biȝulið unweoten (-witen, MS. R.), Kath. 1054. Unweoten buten wit, Marh. 6, 11. *O. H. Ger.* un-wizzo *inscius, ignavus: Icel.* û-viti *an idiot, a witless person;* û-vita *senseless, insane.*]

un-witende; *adj. Unwitting, not knowing, not aware* of what is done, *unconscious*:—Hē monig tācen self gedyde, þēh hē hié unwitende dyde, Ors. 5, 14; Swt. 248, 14. Hē oft unwitende slōg mid his heáfde on ðone wāg, 5, 15; Swt. 250, 12. Gelîcost ðæm ðe hē hiene selfne unwitende (witende? *the Latin is:* Ut voluntariam sibi conscivisse mortem putaretur) hæfde āwierged, 6 36; Swt. 294, 11. [Nyme oþre manne þinges onwytinde and wyþoute wylle of þe lhorde (*without the knowledge or consent of the owner*), Ayenb. 37, 5. Unwiting this preest of his false craft, Chauc. Ch. Y. T. 1320. *O. L. Ger.* sō ik it uuitandi dādi, sō unuuitandi: *Icel.* û-vitandi *not knowing, unconscious, not intending.*]

un-wiþerweard; *adj. Not adverse, not in opposition*:—His folgeras, swā hié unwiðerweardran and gemōdran beóð, swā hié fæstor tōsomne beóð gefēgde tō gōdra monna hiénðe *sequaces illius, quo nulla inter se discordiae adversitate divisi sunt, eo in bonorum gravius nece glomerantur,* Past. 47; Swt. 361, 20.

un-wiþmetenlîc; *adj. Incomparable, not to be compared*:—Is his eádmōdnys is unwiðmetenlîc, Homl. Skt. i. 16, 119. Ðis hālige mǣden, Godes mōdor, is unwiðmetenlîc eallum ōðrum mǣdenum, Homl. Th. i. 442, 29. Hire geðincðu ōðra hālgena unwiðmetenlîce sind, 446, 5.

un-wiþmetenlîce; *adv. Incomparably, beyond compare, indescribably*:—Unwiðmetenlîce *incomparabiliter, inenarrabiliter,* Hpt. Gl. 414, 29: Homl. Th. i. 64, 18. Ðes symbeldæg oferstîhð unwiðmetenlîce ealra ōðra hālgena mæssedagas, 442, 27: ii. 232, 10.

un-wîtnigendlîce; *adv. With impunity*:—Unwîtnigendlîce oððe būtan wîte *inpune,* Ælfc. Gr. 38; Zup. 233, 6.

un-wîtnod; *adj. Unpunished*:—Hî wēnaþ ðæt ðæt sié sió mǣste gesǣlþ, ðæt men seó ālēfed yfel tō dōnne, and sió dǣd him mōte beón unwîtnod *vel licentiam, vel impunitatem scelerum putant esse felicem,* Bt. 38, 5; Fox 206, 8. Ða ðe him biþ unwîtnode eall hiora yfel on disse worulde habbaþ sum yfel hefigre ðonne ǣnig wîte sié, ðæt is, ðæt him biþ unwîtnod hiora yfel *improbi cum supplicio carent, inest eis aliquid ulterius mali, ipsa impunitas,* 38, 3; Fox 200, 25-28. Ða unþeáwas nǣfre ne bióþ unwîtnode, 36, 1; Fox 172, 25. Hē geþafade ða scylde unwîtnode, Past. 17; Swt. 123, 6. v. un-gewîtnod.

un-wîtnung, e; *f. Impunity*:—Gyltes unwîtnung *sceleris impunitas,* Scint. 235, 5.

un-witod, -wiotod; *adj. Uncertain*:—Unwuted *incertus,* Rtl. 6, 5: 106, 15. Wel mon sceal wine healdon on wega gehwylcum; oft mon fēreþ feor bî tūne, ðǣr him wāt freónd unwiotodne (*where he cannot look for a friend*), Exon. Th. 342, 23; Gn. Ex. 146.

un-wittig; *adj. Without wit* or *understanding*, (1) not in a bad sense:—Ge weras, ge wîf and ða unwittigan cild, Homl. Ass. 29, 122. (2) in a bad sense:—Wel dēð se ðe unwittigum stŷrð mid swinglum, gif hē mid wordum ne mæg. Hit is āwriten: 'Ne bið se stunta mid wordum gerihtlǣced,' Homl. Th. ii. 532, 13. Þeówian unclǣnum deóflum and ðām unwittigum heargum, Homl. Skt. ii. 30, 52. [Þat nan ne beo so wilde, nan swa unwitti, þat word talie ær he ihere minne horn, Laym. 786. Stew þine unwittie wordes, Marh. 6, 2. *O. H. Ger.* un-wizzig *insipiens, inprovidus, insanus.*] v. un-gewittig.

un-wittol; *adj. Ignorant*:—On manegum beó ðū swylce unwittol *in multis esto quasi inscius,* Scint. 80, 12.

unwit-weorc, es; *n. A work of folly, foolish work*:—Wē habbaþ nēdþearfe ðæt wē tō lange ne fylgeon unwitweorcum, Blickl. Homl. 111, 2.

un-wlite, es; *m. Disgrace;* dedecus, Wrt. Voc. ii. 27, 35: 26, 70: 85, 28.

un-wlitig; *adj. Not beautiful, ugly, foul*:—Unwlitig *deformes,* Wrt. Voc. ii. 28, 68. Unwlitig swile *tumor deformis,* Bd. 4, 32; S. 611, 17. Hū fægerne and hū wlitigne monnan ic hæbbe ātǣfred, swā unwlitig wrîtere swā swā ic eom *pulchrum depinxi hominem pictor foedus,* Past. 65; Swt. 467, 19. Ðes and ðeós unwlitige *hic et haec dedecor,* Ælfc. Gr. 9, 21; Zup. 47, 15. Simle ðæt unwlitige wlitigaþ ðæt wlitige *ever does the fair make fair the unfair,* Shrn. 165, 34. v. un-gewlitig.

un-wlitigian; *p.* ode. I. *to make ugly, deprive of beauty,* *disfigure*:—Ða hē gewlitegaþ; hwīlum eft unwlitegaþ, Bt. 39, 8; Fox 224, 9. II. *to become ugly*:—Se wǣta āstīgð tō ðæm lime, ðonne āsuilð hit and āhefegaþ and unwlitegaþ *humor ad virilia labitur, quae cum molestia dedecoris intumescunt*, Past. 11; Swt. 73, 10. v. ge-unwlitigian, un-gewlitigian.

un-wlitigness, e; *f. Ugliness, disfigurement*:—Semninga gehrān hē his eágan; ðā gemētte hē hit swā hāl swā swā him nǣfre nǣnig swyle oððe unwlitignes on ætȳwde (*ac si nil unquam in eo deformitatis ac tumoris apparuisset*), Bd. 4, 32; S. 612, 7.

un-wlitigung, e; *f. Disfiguring*:—Sió unwlitegung *deformatio*, Wrt. Voc. ii. 28, 62.

un-wrǣne; *adj. Not lustful*:—Lǣcedōmas gif man tō wrǣne sié oþþe tō unwrǣne, Lchdm. ii. 14, 25: 144, 20.

un-wrǣst, -wrǣste; *adj. Weak, poor, sorry, miserable, wretched*:—Forcūðlīc ɫ unwrǣste *absurdum*, Hpt. Gl. 455, 50. Eálā hū leás and hū unwrest is ðysses middaneardes wela, Chr. 1086; Erl. 220, 40. Hē wearð him on ānum unwrǣstum (unwrǣste, Th. 321, 10) scipe (cf. uneáðe ætburstan, p. 320, col. 2) and fērde ofer sǣ, Chr. 1051; Th. 319, 3. Hī hī selfe lēton ǣgþer ge for heáne ge for unwrǣste, Ors. 3, 1; Swt. 98, 23. [Gif þær wære hure an unwreste wrenc (*a miserable trick*) ꝥ he mihte get beswicen anes Crist, Chr. 1131; Erl. 260, 4. Ur lif wes unwreast . . . his lif was haliȝe, O. E. Homl. i. 237, 12. Ðe unwreste herde *iners pastor*, ii. 39, 17. Þenne þat hæfd is unwræst þe hælp (hæp? heop, 2nd MS.) is þæ wurse, Laym. 16307. Þatt tu unnorneliȝ off þe sellfenn læte, and halde þe forr unnwræsste, Orm. 4889. Giff þu tellesst all þin witt unnwresste, 4909. Ge muwen icnowen þet he is eruh and unwrest, A. R. 274, 16 (cf. Heo beoð to woke and tō unwreste iheorted, 268, 7). Hwet nu, unwreste men and wacre þen eni wake *quid vos ignavi et degeneres*, Kath. 1260. To binden faste upon an asse swiþe unwraste, Havel. 2820. Hit schal beo a thyng unwreste, heved of cok, breost of man, crop as best, Alis. 620.] v. next word.

un-wrǣstlīce; *adv. Weakly, absurdly*:—Ðys hīw ealde ūðwitan gesettan āgēn ðam þingum ðe Zenodotus unwrǣstlīce gesette, Anglia viii. 334, 17. [Gif þu werest te erest wocliche (unwreastliche, MS. T.), A. R. 294, 5.]

un-wrecen; *adj.* I. of a person, *unavenged*:—Sceolde æþeling unwrecen ealdres linnan, Beo. Th. 4877; B. 2443. II. of crime, *unpunished*:—Gif hī ðæs wilniaþ, ðæt him hiora yfel unwrecen sié be ðæs gyltes andefne, Bt. 38, 7; Fox 210, 7.

un-wrenc, es; *m.* I. *an evil trick, a malicious wile, a wicked artifice*:—Ðisne unwrenc (*the device practised by Potiphar's wife*) heó geþōhte, Gen. 39, 16. Hē (*Antichrist*) bið eal unwrenca full, Wulfst. 97, 16. Mid ðām unwrencan bið Antecrist eal āfylled, 54, 15. II. *an evil practice, a vice*:—For ðæm unwrence ðære ungeðylde *per impatientiae vitium*, Past. 33; Swt. 215, 19. [He teð him to unwrenches (*evil practices*) to stele oðer refloc . . . , O. E. Homl. ii. 79, 28. Þet is his unwrench (*artifice*) . . . he eggeð þe to a þing, þet þuncheð god, A. R. 268, 16. Ne spedestu noht mid þine unwrenche (*your vile tricks*), O. and N. 169.]

un-wreón; *p.* -wrāh, -wreáh, *pl.* -wrigon, -wrugon; *pp.* -wrigen, -wrogen *To uncover* (lit. or fig.) what is covered, *to reveal*:—Hē unwrīhþ þiccetu *revelabit condensa*, Ps. Lamb. 28, 9. Ðæt mǣden unwreáh hire heáfod, Ap. Th. 26, 14. Hē unwreáh his rihtwīsnesse *revelavit justitiam suam*, Ps. Lamb. 97, 2. Hī unwreogon ðæt hūs *nudaverunt tectum*, Mk. Skt. Rush. 2, 4. Ða līcmen his neb unwrugon, Homl. Th. ii. 334, 31. Unwreóh (*revela*) Drihtne weg ðinne, Ps. Spl. 36, 5. Nǣnig gedēgled ðæt ne sē eft unwrigen (*nihil opertum quod non revelabitur*), Mt. Kmbl. Lind. 10, 26. Unwrigen *retectum, discoopertum*, Germ. 389, 11. Ūre misdēda bióþ ealle opene and unwrigene beforan ūs, Wulfst. 225, 23. Unwrogene (*revelata*) synd staðolas ymbhwyrftes eorðana, Ps. Lamb. 17, 16. Ða deópan þing beóð unwrogene, Anglia viii. 334, 7. v. on-wreón.

un-wrigedness (-wrigenness?), e; *f. A revelation*:—Of unwrigednesse (*lectio*) *de apocalipsi*, R. Ben. Interl. 42, 16. v. on-wrigenness.

un-writen; *adj. Unwritten*:—Ne lēt ic ðæt unwriten, Bd. pref.; S. 472, 26. Hī for heora slǣwþe forlēton unwriten ðara monna þeáwas and heora dǣda ðe on hiora dagum foremǣroste wǣron, Bt. 18, 3; Fox 64, 34. v. un-gewriten.

un-wrītere, es; *m. A bad, incorrect writer*:—Mycel yfel dēð se unwrītere, gyf hē nele his wōh gerihtan, Ælfc. Gr. pref.; Zup. 3, 24.

un-wrīþan; *p* -wrāþ; *pp.* -wriðen *To untwist, unbind* (lit. or fig.):—Unwrīþan *distringere*, Scint. 232, 2. v. on-wrīþan, *and next word.*

un-wriðen; *adj. Not bound*:—Ðæt hē nid ungemetlīcre grimsunge his hiéremonna wunda tō suīðe ne slīte, ne eft for ungemetlīcre mildheortnesse hē hié ne lǣte unwriðena *ut neque multa asperitate exulcerentur subditi, neque nimia benignitate solvantur*, Past. 17; Swt. 125, 16.

un-wunden; *adj. Not wound*:—Unwunden gearu *glomus*, Wrt. Voc. i. 59, 36.

un-wundod; *adj. Not wounded*, Cd. Th. 12, 10; Gen. 183.

un-wuni[g]endlīc; *adj. Uninhabitable*:—Beóð twēgen dǣlas on twā healfa ðam gemetegodum dǣle unwuniendlīce, for ðan ðe seó sunne ne cymð him nǣfre tō, Lchdm. iii. 262, 2. v. un-gewuni[g]endlīc.

un-wurþ. v. un-weorþ.

un-wynsum; *adj. Unpleasant*:—Ðeós woruld hwīltīdum is myrige on tō wunigenne, hwīlon heó is swīðe styrnlīc, and mid mislīcum þingum gemenged, swā ðæt heó bið swīðe unwynsum on tō eardigenne, Homl. Th. i. 184, 1. Hit ðe unwynsum (*injucundum*) bið, Bt. 14, 1; Fox 42, 13. Ǣlc wyrd, sam hió sié wynsum, sam hió sié unwynsum *omnis fortuna vel jucunda vel aspera*, 40, 1; Fox 236, 2. Rēþu wyrd and unwynsumu, 40, 2; Fox 238, 2. Hē hine gegyrede mid hǣrenum hrægle swīþe heardum and unwinsumum, Blickl. Homl. 221, 24. [O. H. Ger. un-wunnisam *incultus, invenustus*.]

un-wynsumness, e; *f. Unpleasantness*:—Se stenc wearð āwend tō wynsumum brǣðe, and eall seó unwynsumnyss him wearð tō blysse, Homl. Skt. i. 4, 215. Se mann gewyrðeþ tōswollen and tō stence āwended mid unwynsumnysse, Basil admn. 8; Norm. 50, 23.

un-wyrcan; *p.* -worhte *To undo, destroy*:—Ic þurh manslihtas mē scyldigne dyde wið ðē, mīn Hǣlend, ðā ðā ic ðīn handgeweorc unwyrcan dorste, Anglia xi. 113, 34.

un-wyrd, e; *f. Bad fortune, misfortune*:—Gyf him þince ðæt hē leád habbe, sum unwird him byð tōweard, Lchdm. iii. 170, 5. Ðæt mē nū þyncþ ðætte ic ðās unwyrd āræfnan mæg ðe mē on becumen is *ut jam me imparem fortunae ictibus non arbitrer*, Bt. 22, 1; Fox 76, 13.

un-wyrþ. v. un-weorþ.

un-wyrttrumian; *p.* ode *To unroot, pluck up by the roots, root up*:—Ðȳ læs gié unwyrtrumias (*eradicetis*) ðone huǣte, Mt. Kmbl. Lind. 13, 29.

un-ymbwendedlīc; *adj. Unmoved, unalterable*:—Unymbwoendedlīc *inmotus*, Rtl. 164, 34.

un-ȳþe, un-ȳþian. v. un-eáþe, un-īþian.

up (ūp?), upp; *adv. Up.* I. where motion takes place, (a) from a lower to a higher point, (α) from the (earth's) surface to a point above it:—Hī eodon up tō ðære dūne *ascenderunt verticem montis*, Num. 14, 40. Hē āstāh ofer sunnan up *ascendit super occasum*, Ps. Th. 67, 4. Gewende se engel up, Homl. Skt. ii. 27, 100: i. 21, 56. Hē geseah windum ðone rēc up ofer ðære burge wallas āhefenne, Bd. 3, 16; S. 543, 2. Ðā genam hine God mid sāwle and mid līchaman up in ðone heofon, Salm. Kmbl. p. 182, 14. Āteó hē āne hringan up of ðare þrȳh . . . Gif seó hringe nele up þurh his ānes tige, Homl. Skt. i. 21, 44, 47. (β) to the (earth's) surface from a point beneath it:—Seó burh, ðǣr sunne up on morgen gǣð, Salm. Kmbl. p. 186, 4. Óð ðæt seó sunne eft become ðǣr heó ǣr up stāh, Lchdm. iii. 236, 5. Nīwe steorra wæs upp yrnynde, Bd. 4, 12; S. 581, 14. Se mōna up eode, Nar. 30, 7. Hī delfaþ gold up of eorþan, Nar. 35, 8. Wolde ðæt se hālga wer wurde up gedōn, Homl. Skt. i. 21, 136, 138, 140: Bd. 3, 7; S. 529, 24. Nime hē upp his mǣg *let him take his kinsman up from the grave*, L. Eth. iii. 7; Th. i. 296, 10. Ða ancras upp teón, Bd. 3, 15; S. 541, 40. Wið ðon ðe men blōd upp wealle þurh his mūð, Lchdm. i. 74, 14. Beforan his fōtum wæs wyl upp yrnende, Bd. 1, 7; S. 478, 27. (a 1) where the motion is from sea to land:—Mid ðȳ wē upp cōman tō lande, and ūre scyp eác swylce fram ðām ȳþum upp ābæron *cum evadentes ad terram, naviculam quoque nostram ab undis exportaremus*, Bd. 5, 1; S. 614, 10. On ðissum eálonde com upp Agustinus *in hac insula adplicuit Augustinus*, 1, 25; S. 486, 22. Com hē ǣrest upp on Westseaxum *primum Gevissorum gentem ingrediens*, 3, 7; 529, 9. Hē wæs ādrifen ðæt hē cōm up on Frysena land *pulsus est Fresiam*, 5, 19; S. 639, 20. Be ciépemonna fōre up (upp, MS. H.) on londe, L. In. 25; Th. i. 118, 11 note. Hī cōmon up on Limene mūþan mid .ccl. scipa, Chr. 893; Erl. 88, 25. Hī up cōmon æt Leptan ðæm tūne *ad Leptim oppidum copias exposuit*, Ors. 4, 10; Swt. 202, 9. Ðā wē up cōmon *when we landed*, Homl. Skt. ii. 30, 325: Chr. 860; Erl. 70, 25. Þēh ða menn up ætberstan intō ðære byrig, L. Eth. ii. 2; Th. i. 286, 2. Se here hiene on niht up bestæl, Chr. 865; Erl. 70, 34. Cnut com tō Sandwīc, and lēt ðǣr up ða gīslas, 1014; Erl. 151, 9. Hēt ðā up beran æþelinga gestreón, Beo. Th. 3844; B. 1920. (a 2) marking arrival, or coming into notice (cf. colloquial to turn *up*). Cf. a. β:—Ðæs ymb .iii. niht ridon .ii. eorlas up, Chr. 871; Erl. 74, 6. Up ābrecaþ *erumpunt*, Wrt. Voc. ii. 144, 7. (a 3) *up* a river, *against the stream*:—On ða eá hī tugon up hiora scipu ōþ ðone weald, Chr. 893; Erl. 88, 31. (b) where a body remains in the same place but moves in an upward direction:—Ðā ārās hē upp, Jn. Skt. 8, 7, 10. Hē upp āsæt, Bd. 5, 12; S. 627, 14. For hwȳ ðæt fȳr fundige up, Bt. 34, 11; Fox 150, 19. Gǣð seó eá up, and oferflēt ðæt land, Lchdm. iii. 252, 24. Up hleápende *exoriens*, Wrt. Voc. ii. 144, 9. Hī (*the plants*) up sprungon, Mt. Kmbl. 13, 5. II. marking direction, (a) of physical action:—Abraham beseah upp, Gen. 18, 2. Ðīnes brōðor blōd clypaþ up tō mē of eorðan, 4, 10. Hē lōcade upp on heofon, Bd. 4, 9; S. 577, 20. Lōciaþ nū ealle up, Nar. 28, 26. (b) of mental action:—Langaþ ðē āwuht up tō Gode, Cd. Th. 32, 2; Gen. 497. (c) marking measurement:—Habbe hē his strand upp of sǣ and ūt on sǣ, Cod. Dip. Kmbl. iv. 221, 7. III. marking position, (a) *up, on high*:—Hī (*beams*) man mæg up fēgean (*lignum ad summa levatur*, Past. 58; Swt. 445, 3.

Wǽron ða wealdleðer swá up getíged, swá swá hig urnon tó heofenum up, Shrn. 156, 12. Iosue hí up áhēng on fíf wácum bógum *Iosue suspendit eos super quinque stipites*, Jos. 10, 26. Heó stód upp on ánre upflóra, Homl. Skt. i. 18, 341. .vii. upp hangene bella, Chart. Th. 430, 4. Lyft up geswearc, Cd. Th. 207, 4; Exod. 461. Ða tánas up æpla bǽron, 495, 7; Sat. 482. Up in heofonum, 284, 26; Sat. 327: Exon. Th. 281, 11; Jul. 644. In roderum up, 22, 17; Cri. 353. (b) *up, erectly*:—Áhó on up standende twig, Lchdm. i. 332, 15. Up standende herebeácn *pira*, Wrt. Voc. i. 41, 43. (c) *up, to a high point*:—Gif se móna urne swá up swá seó sunne déð, Lchdm. iii. 248, 6. Hió cymþ swá up swá hire yfemest gecynde bið, Bt. 25; Fox 88, 27. **IV.** marking separation, as in to cut *up*, break *up*:—Up áliðode *evulsum, abscisum*, Hpt. Gl. 474, 36. Hé ða eá upp forlét an feówer hund eá and on lx . . . and æfter ðæm Eufrate hé eác mid gedelfe on monige eá upp forlét *fluvium per magnas concisum deductumque fossas in quadringentos sexaginta alveos comminuit . . . etiam Euphratem derivavit*, Ors. 2, 4; Swt. 74, 1-5. **V.** in figurative expressions:—Ðú áhefst upp mín heáfod *exaltans caput meum*, Ps. Th. 3, 2. Ðæt hý hý upp ne áhófen for heora welum, 48, arg. Áhafen up *elevatus in sublime*, Kent. Gl. 1118: Bt. 16, 1; Fox 48, 29. Ðe læs ðé God up bréde ðone godspellícan cwide *lest God bring up the words of the Gospel against thee*, Wulfst. 248, 9: 249, 3. Ðǽr bær Godwine eorl up his mál *Earl Godwine brought his case up* or *forward*, Chr. 1052; Erl. 187, 19. Syþþan up cymð deófles costnung *orta tribulatione*, Mk. Skt. 4, 17. Se wæs up cymen in Palestina mǽgðe *he was a native of Palestine*, Shrn. 141, 6. Ne hebbe gé tó up eówre hornas, Past. 54; Swt. 425, 22. Se mann ána gǽþ uprihte; ðæt tácnaþ ðæt hé sceal má þencan up ðonne nyþer, Bt. 41, 6; Fox 254, 30: Homl. Skt. i. 1, 58. Eahta sweras rihtlícne cynedóm up wegaþ, L. I. P. 3; Th. ii. 306, 20. [*O. Sax. O. L. Ger.* up: *O. Frs.* up, op: *Icel.* upp: *O. H. Ger.* úf, cf. *Goth.* iup.] v. uppe.

up, upp; *adj. That is above, that is on high*:—Neoman ús tó wynne weoroda Drihten, upne écne gefeán, Cd. Th. 277, 4; Sat. 199. Gé synd uppe godu (uppe-godu? v. up-godu), ealle upheá and æðele bearn *dii estis et filii excelsi omnes*, Ps. Th. 81, 6. v. up-ness.

up-áhafenness, e; *f. Uplifting, elevation.* I. literal:—Upáhafenes handa mínra *eleuatio manuum mearum*, Ps. Lamb. 140, 2. Seó symbelnyss ðære hálgan róde upáhefennysse, Homl. Skt. ii. 23 b, 399. II. metaphorical, (a) *exaltation*:—Drihten ys mín upáhafenys *Dominus exaltatio mea*, Ex. 17, 15. His mód bið áfédd mid ðære smeáunga ðære wilnunga óðerra monna hiérnesse and his selfes upáhæfenesse, Past. 8; Swt. 55, 6. (b) *exultation*:—Welerum upáhafennysse *labiis exultationis*, Ps. Spl. 62, 6. (c) *arrogance, pride*:—Hwæt is ðonne forcúðre ðonne sió upáhæfennes (-hæfenes, Hatt. MS.)? . . . Hwæt mæg hiérre bión ðonne sió sóðe eáðmódnes? *quid elatione dejectius . . . Quid humilitate sublimius?* Past. 41; Swt. 300, 18. Ðá wæs gehroren sió upáhæfenes Paulus, . . . and sóna æfter ðæm hryre ðære upáhæfennesse hé ongan timbran eáðmódnesse, 58; Swt. 443, 29. Hér is úres módes upáhafennes; ac ðǽr is ðære þýstro dymnes, L. E. I. proem.; Th. ii. 394, 12. Élc upáhafenes *omnis arrogans* (cf. 242), Kent. Gl. 547. Ðonne ðæt mód ðenceþ gegrípan him tó upáhæfenesse (-hef-, Hatt. MS.) ða eáðmódnesse, Past. 8; Swt. 54, 12. For gilpe and for upáhafenesse *elationis intentione*, 9; Swt. 55, 21. For his (*Haman*) upáhafennysse, Homl. Ass. 96, 135. Ða upáhafenesse (*Nebuchadnezzar's*) God getǽlde, Past. 4; Swt. 39, 20. Upáhefenysse *insolentiam, superbiam*, Hpt. Gl. 526, 73. v. up-áhefedness, -hefness.

up-áhefedlíce; *adv. Proudly, arrogantly*:—Upáhefedlíce *arroganter, superbe*, Hpt. Gl. 422, 8.

up-áhefedness, e; *f. Elevation.* I. literal:—*Exaltatio sancte crucis*, ðæt is on Engliscre sprǽce upáhefednyss ðære hálgan róde, for ðan ðe heó wæs áhafen on ðam dæge, Homl. Skt. ii. 27, 140. II. metaphorical, (a) *exaltation*:—Þurh ðás clypunge is gesweotolad, ðæt ǽlc upáhefednes ásprincð of módignesse cynrene *ostendit nobis omnem exaltationem genus esse superbie*, R. Ben. 22, 13. (b) *exultation*:—Upáhæfdnes mín *exultatio mea*, Ps. Lamb. 31, 7. (c) *arrogance, pride*:—Ðisses mannes (*Dives'*) uncyst and upáhefednys, Homl. Th. i. 328, 22: ii. 560, 20: Homl. Skt. i. 16, 163. Aman wearð gehýnd for his upáhefednysse, Homl. Ass. 101, 322. Hé (*Lucifer*) wæs fordón þurh ða miclan upáhefednysse, Homl. Th. i. 12, 21. Upáhefednesse forfleón *elationem vel jactantiam fugere*, R. Ben. 18, 23: L. E. I. 21; Th. ii. 418, 12. v. up-áhafenness.

up-áspringness, e; *f. Uprising*:—Upáspringness ł eástdǽl *ortus*, Ps. Lamb. 102, 12.

up-ásprungenness, e; *f. Uprising, origin*:—Ymbe ðises bissextus upásprungnysse wé wyllaþ rúmlícor iungum cnihtum geopenian, Anglia viii. 306, 14.

up-ástigenness *and* -ástígness, e; *f. An ascent*, (1) *a going up, an ascension*:—Be ðisse drihtenlícan upástigennesse, Blickl. Homl. 117, 6. Æt ðære upástígnesse, 121, 13: 171, 9: Shrn. 78, 10: 79, 29: Nar. 39, 14. Ða hálgan upástigenesse on heofonas, Blickl. Homl. 119, 36. Upástígnesse, 81, 11. (2) *a means of going up*:—Ic on ðam wealle nǽnige duru ne eághþyrl ne uppástígnesse geseón mihte, Bd. 5, 12; S. 629, 15. Ðú ðe setst genipu upástígnesse ðínne *qui ponis nubem ascensum tuum*, Ps. Lamb. 103, 3. Stapas ł upástigenesse *ascensiones*, 83, 6.

up-cund; *adj. Supernal, celestial*:—Onǽled mid ðý upcundan leóhte *illustratus superno lumine*, Past. 49; Swt. 379, 24. Cuman tó ðam upcundan æþelan ríce, Exon. Th. 17, 10; Cri. 268. Ðæt wé magon upcund ríce gestígan, 348, 27; Sch. 34. Upcundra ceastergewarena *supernorum civium*, Hpt. Gl. 423, 5. Upcundra eádegum setlum *sedibus superum beatis*, Dóm. L. 303. [*In* Bd. 4, 23; S. 595, 40 *for* upcundne swég *read* uppe cúðne swég; v. Bd. M. 340, 5.]

up-cyme, es; *m. Up-coming, rising, up-springing*:—Upcyme wylla *the springing up of the fountains*, Cd. Th. 240, 12; Dan. 385. From sunnan upcyme *a solis ortu*, Ps. Surt. 49, 1: 106, 3. Naehte upcyme *noctis exortum* (l. *exortu*, v. Hymn. Surt. 2, 21), ii. p. 202, 1. Ic monnum sceal ýcan upcyme eádignesse *for men I shall increase the upspringing of happiness*, Exon. Th. 413, 3; Rä. 31, 9.

up-eard, es; *m. A dwelling on high*:—Ic eom síþes fús upeard niman, Exon. Th. 166, 31; Gú. 1051.

up-ende, es; *m. The upper end, top end*:—Se steorra Ursa is swíþe neáh ðam upende ðære eaxe *summo vertice mundi flectit rapidos Ursa meatus*, Bt. 39, 13; Fox 232, 33: Met. 29, 18. At ðas akeres upende, Cod. Dip. Kmbl. iii. 434, 2. Óð ðære foryrðe upende, 419, 33.

up-engel, es; *m. An angel of heaven*:—Upengla fruma, Andr. Kmbl. 451; An. 226. Upengla weard, Menol. Fox 417; Men. 210.

up-fǽreld, es; *n.* (*m.?*) *A journey up, an ascension*:—Eal heofonwaru wundrode ðysre fǽmnan upfæreldes, Homl. Th. i. 444, 1.

up-feax; *adj. Having hair at the top, bald in front*; recalvus, Wrt. Voc. i. 288, 57.

up-fléring, e; *f.* I. *an upper floor*:—Seó upfléring tóbærst under his fótum, Homl. Th. ii. 164, 3. II. *an upper chamber*:—Hí ástigon upp on áne upfléringe (*coenaculum*, Acts 1, 13), Homl. Th. i. 296, 9: 314, 7.

up-flór, a, e: flóre, an; *f.*: es; *m. An upper floor* or *story, upper chamber*:—Upflór *solarium*, Wrt. Voc. i. 83, 31. Heó hæfde hig behíd on hire upflóra (*solario domus suae*), Jos. 2, 6. Gesamnodon hí on sumre upflóra (*de tecto et solario spectantes*) ealle ða heáfodmen, Jud. 16, 25. Wunigende on ánre upflóra (*in coenaculo*), Homl. Th. i. 314, 5: ii. 184, 26: 164, 2: Homl. Skt. i. 10, 58, 64, 81: 18, 341: ii. 27, 31, 67. Seó wudewe wunode on clǽnnysse æfter hire were on hyre upflóre, Homl. Ass. 108, 204. Ða yldestan Angelcynnes witan gefeóllan of ánre upflóran (*solario*), Chr. 978; Erl. 127, 10. Sume férde upp on ðone uppflóre, 1083; Erl. 217, 18.

up-gang, es; *m.* I. *a going up, rising* of a heavenly body:—Sunnon upgong æt middan sumere *ortus solis solstitialis*, Bd. 5, 12; S. 627, 34. Æfter sunnan upgonge, L. Alf. 25; Th. i. 50, 20. Ǽr sunnan upgange, Lchdm. ii. 306, 17. Æt sunnan upgonge, Nar. 27, 17. Fram sunnan upgange óð hire setlgang, Ps. Th. 49, 2: 112, 3. Uppgange, 106, 3. Tóforan mónan upgonge, Nar. 13, 9. Hí (*the constellations of the zodiac*) gefyllaþ twá tída mid hyra upgange oððe nyðergange, Lchdm. iii. 246, 8. II. *a going up*, (a) to land from sea, *a landing*. v. up, I. a 1:—Hí forwerndon heom ǽgðer ge upganges ge wæteres, Chr. 1046; Erl. 171, 5. (b) from the coast inland, *an incursion*:—Hí námon him wintersettl on Temesan . . . Ðá æfter middan wintra hí námon ǽnne upgang út þurh Ciltern and swá tó Oxneforda, 1009; Erl. 143, 9. III. *a way of going up*:—Hié gerýmdon ðone upgang and geworhtan, Blickl. Homl. 201, 17. [*O. H. Ger.* úf-gang *ortus*: *Ger.* auf-gang: *Icel.* upp-gangr: *Dan.* op-gang *ascent; stairs.*] v. next word.

up-gange, an; *f. Landing.* v. up-gang, II. a:—Hí bǽdon ðæt hí upgangan ágan móston *they asked for leave to land*, Byrht. Th. 134, 20; By. 87. [*Icel.* upp-ganga; *f. a going ashore; a landing-place.*]

up-gemynd, es; *n. Mindfulness of what is above, thought directed heavenward*:—Hé hæfde hlúttre lufan, éce upgemynd engla blisse, Andr. Kmbl. 2129; An. 1066.

up-godu(-o); *pl. n. The gods above*:—Upgodo *superi*, Wrt. Voc. ii. 80, 19.

up-hafenness, e; *f. Elevation*:—Uphefenes honda mínra *elevatio manuum mearum*, Ps. Surt. 140, 2. v. up-áhafenness.

up-heáfod, es; *n. A top end* (?):—Tó crofte tó ðan upheáfdan (*to the croft, to the top end of it?*); of ðan upheáfdan, Cod. Dip. Kmbl. vi. 79, 10. v. heáfod.

up-heáh; *adj.* I. *tall, lofty*:—Wæs hé .x. fóta upheáh *pedum non amplius decem statura altior*, Nar. 26, 28. Ða trió meahte beón hundteóntiges fóta upheáh *he pedum centum alte erant arbores*, 27, 28. Sindon dúna upheá, Exon. Th. 443, 15; Kl. 30. Wǽron hié swá greáte swá columnan, ge eác sume uphýrran (*proceriores*), Nar. 14, 5. II. fig. *lofty, noble*:—Ealle upheá and æðele bearn *filii excelsi omnes*, Ps. Th. 81, 6. III. *upright*:—Ðá genam Sanctus Martinus hine be his handa and upheáh árǽrde, Blickl. Homl. 219, 20. Ðám treówum ðe him gecynde biþ upheáh tó standanne, Bt. 25; Fox 88, 22. [*Icel.* upphár *high, tall.*] v. up-lang.

up-heald, es; *n. Upholding, support, maintenance*:—Ic eom ðæs mynstres mund and upheald, Cod. Dip. Kmbl. iv. 232, 7. [Crist, Hælennde and hellpe and god upphald, Orm. 9217. *Icel.* upp-hald; *n. support, maintenance*: *Dan.* op-hold.]

up-hebbe, an; *f. A coot* (so called because it lifts up its tail when moving over the water, Grein):—Uphebbean hūs *fulicae domus*, Ps. Th. 103, 17.

up-hebbing, e; *f. Uplifting, uprising*:—Uphebbing *ortum*, Lk. Skt. Lind. 8, 8.

up-hefness, e; *f. Exaltation*:—Gāstlīcre uphefnesse *extaseos*, Wrt. Voc. ii. 31, 70.

up-heofon, es; *m. The heavens, the sky*:—Eall upheofon biđ sweart and gesworcen, Wulfst. 137, 8. Beofaþ ealbeorhte gesceaft . . . dyneþ upheofon, Exon. Th. 448, 25; Dōm. 59. Eálā middaneard . . . eálā upheofon, Cd. Th. 275, 6; Sat. 167. Đū geworhtest eorþan frætwe and upheofen; đæt is heáh geweorc handa đīnra *terram tu fundasti; et opera manuum tuarum sunt coeli*, Ps. Th. 101, 22. Eorđan ic bidde and upheofon, Lchdm. i. 400, 3: Exon. Th. 60, 12; Cri. 968: Andr. Kmbl. 1596; An. 799. Se gāst upheofon gesōhte *spiritus astra petit*, Bd. 2, 1; S. 500, 20. [Cf. *O. Sax.* up-himil: *O. H. Ger.* ūf-himil: *Icel.* upp-himinn.] Cf. up-rodor.

up-hūs, es; *n. An upper chamber*:—Uphūses *cenaculi*, Wrt. Voc. ii. 24, 67.

up-lang; *adj.* I. *tall, high*:—Wǣron hié nigon fōta uplonge *pedum alti .ix.*, Nar. 22, 6. II. *upright*:—Ongeán sunnan upweard licge hē . . . đonne uplang āsitte, Lchdm. ii. 18, 16: iii. 2, 12. Sǣweall uplang gestōd, Cd. Th. 197, 7; Exod. 303: Beo. Th. 1523; B. 759. Uplong, Exon. Th. 495, 16; Rä. 85, 4. v. up-heáh.

up-legen, e; *f. A hair-pin*:—Uplegen *discriminale*, Wrt. Voc. ii. 141, 1. Uplegene *vel* feaxpreónas *discriminalia*, i. 17, 2.

up-lendisc; *adj. Uplandish, country* (as opposed to town), *rural, rustic*:—Uplendisc *forensis* (forensis *qui foras est*, Migne), Germ. 389, 41. Eft begann sum uplendisc mann egeslīce hrȳman tō đām ārleásum burhwarum . . . Đā arn se ceorl geond ealle đa strǣt hrȳmende, Homl. Th. ii. 302, 4–8. Wē wyllaþ đisne circul āmearkian, đæt se uplendiscea preóst (cf. Chaucer's: Poure persoun dwellyng uppon lond) wite his naman; mæg beón đe glædre his heorte đe hē sum þing hērof undergyte, Anglia viii. 317, 38. Ic wēne, lā, uplendisca preóst, đæt đū nyte hwæt beó atomos, 318, 14. Đū byst uppan lande mid wīmmannum oftor đonne ic beó . . . Ic hit gehȳrde secgan, đæt đās uplendiscan wīf wyllaþ oft drincan, Engl. Stud. viii. 62, 12. Wē witon đæt đās þing þincaþ clericum and uplendiscum preóstum genōh mænigfealde, Anglia viii. 321, 25. [Oplondysch men wol lykne hamsylf to gentilmen . . . The Saxon tonge ys abide scarslych wiþ feaw uplondysch men, Trev. i. c. 59. Uplondysche mann *villanus*, Prompt. Parv. 512, where see note.]

up-līc; *adj.* I. *on high*, (1) referring to this world:—Đonne biđ gefylled eall uplīc lyft ǣtrenum līge, Wulfst. 138, 5. Ūre Drihten gesceóp . . . đa upplīcan heofenan . . . and đæt upplīce lyft, Hexam. 4; Norm. 6, 20–24. (2) referring to heaven:—Đæt wuldor đæs uplīcan ēđles *supernae patriae gloriam*, Past. 21; Swt. 159, 23. Tō gefeán đære upplīcan ceastre, Bd. 1, 7; S. 479, 15. In đam uplīcan ēđle, Exon. Th. 225, 20; Ph. 392. Uplīcne hām, Cd. Th. 287, 5; Sat. 362. Đara uplīcra burhwara gefērscipe, Blickl. Homl. 197, 16. II. *lofty, sublime*:—Upplīcan *anagogen*, upplīc andgyt *supernum intellectum*, Hpt. Gl. 506, 17–19. Uplīcum andgite *anagogen*, Anglia xiii. 28, 15. (Cf. *Anagogen, celsissimo intellectu*, Wrt. Voc. ii. 75, 37. Gāstlecum andgite *anagogen*, 1, 10. Đæm godcundan heáhstan *anagogen*, 9, 7.) God mid đǣm uplīcum and mid đǣm diéglum đingum hira mōd onliéht mid đæm scīman his giefe, Past. 35; Swt. 243, 20. III. *celestial*:—Se uplīca Dēma, Blickl. Homl. 95, 33: Chr. 979; Erl. 129, 17. Gif hine gecīst sió uplīce gifu *quem superna gratia elegit*, Past. 7; Swt. 51, 4. Cuæđ sió uplīce stemn tō Moyse, 11; Swt. 63, 23. Seó upplīce ārfæstnys, Bd. 3, 13; S. 538, 31. Mid đam uplīcan mihte geþreád, 1, 7; S. 478, 40. Sprecan be đām upplīcan dōmum Godes, 5, 19; S. 640, 34. [*O. H. Ger.* ūf-līh *supernus*.]

up-lyft (*for gender see* lyft) *the air above*:—Đū wealdan miht eorđan mægen and uplyfte, wind and wolcna, Btwk. 196, 29; Hy. 9, 6. Đū geworhtest heofonas and eorđan, eardas and uplyft, 198, 4; Hy. 9, 19.

up-ness, e; *f. Height*:—Đū đe oferwrīhst mid wæterum hire upnyssa *qui tegis aquis superiora eius*, Ps. Lamb. 103, 3. v. up; *adj.*

upon; *adv. From above*:—Swā fæger dropa đe on đās eorđan upon dreópaþ *sicut stillicidia stillantia super terram*, Ps. Th. 71, 6.

upp. v. up.

uppan (-on); *prep. dat. acc.* I. *dat.* (1) where there is rest or motion on a surface, *upon, on*:—Moises wæs lange uppan đam munte, Ex. 32, 1. Gā uppan Sinai dūne and stand uppan đære dūne ufeweardre. Ne cume nān mann uppan đære dūne, 34, 2–3. Hē bæd æt Gode đæt hē him sealde wæter uppan đære dūne, Homl. Skt. i. 19, 112. Geoffra hyne uppon ānre dūne *offeres eum in holocaustum super unum montium*, Gen. 22, 2. Hē ætstōd uppon ānum beáme, Chr. 978; Erl. 127, 11. Hē rīt upp n tamre assene *sedens super asinam*, Mt. Kmbl. 21, 5. Đā wearđ Eustatius uppon his horse and his gefeóran uppon heora *Eustace got on his horse and his companions on theirs*, Chr. 1048; Erl. 177, 38. Hē bær his tunecan, and ālēde uppon đām twām deádum, Homl. Th. i. 74, 2. Đū byst uppan lande (*up country, in rural districts*; cf. Chaucer's 'poure persoun dwellyng uppon londe'; *and see* uplendisc) oftor đonne ic beó, Engl. Stud. viii. 62, 9. To ǣlcen cyrcean uppe land, Chr. 1086; Erl. 223, 36. (2) marking relative height, *above*:—Him uppan wæs rōd ārǣred, Elen. Kmbl. 1768; El. 886. Đonne bist đū ofer uppan rodere (cf. đonne bist đū bufan đam rodore, Bt. 36, 2; Fox 174, 15), Met. 24, 27. (3) of time (the case is doubtful in some instances), (a) *upon, at*:—Hē Ansealme uppon Pentecosten his pallium geaf, Chr. 1095; Erl. 232, 30. Uppon Sc̄e Michaeles mæssan ætȳwde ān selcūđ steorra, 1097; Erl. 234, 9, 19, 32. (b) *after*:—Đys sceal on Sunnandæg feówertȳne nyht uppan Eástron, Jn. Skt. 10, 11 rubc. On đisum geáre wǣron Eástron on viii kal. Apr., and đā uppon Eástron on Sc̄e Ambrosius mæsseniht, đæt is .ii. non. Apr. . . . , Chr. 1095; Erl. 231, 17. (4) marking object of attack:—Đa hǣđenan men hergodan uppon đām X̄penan mannan, Chr. 1086; Erl. 223, 11. (5) marking ground of trust, *upon* trust, honour, etc.:—Se cyng him nāþer nolde ne gīslas syllan ne uppon trȳwđan geunnon đæt hē mid griđe cumon mōste and faran, Chr. 1095; Erl. 231, 24. II. *acc.* (1) where there is motion on to a surface, *upon, on to*:—Đū gītst đæt blōd uppan đæt weofod *fundes sanguinem super altare*, Ex. 29, 20: Mt. Kmbl. 26, 7. Se đe fylđ uppan đysne stān, 21, 44. (2) of time. v. I. 3. (3) marking object of attack, *upon, against*:—Hē fōr uppon heora brōđer and uppon đone eorl wann, Chr. 1095; Erl. 231, 8–10. Se cyng his fyrde beád, and uppon đone eorl tō Norđhymbran fōr, Erl. 231, 26. Heora ǣgđer uppon ōđerne tūnas bærnde, 1094; Erl. 230, 12. Hī ealne đone bryce uppon đone cyng tealdon *they laid all blame for the breach upon the king*, Erl. 230, 4. (4) marking addition:—Đa bodan cȳddon đæt his brōđer griđ and forewarde eall æftercwæđ, būtan se cyng gelǣstan nolde eall þet hī on forewarde hæfdon ǣr gewroht, and uppon đæt (*in addition to that, on the top of that*) hine forsworenne clypode, būton hē đa forewarde geheólde, Chr. 1094; Erl. 229, 31. [*O. E. Homl. Laym. A. R. O. and N.* uppen: *O. Sax.* uppan: *O. Frs.* uppa: *O. H. Ger.* ūfan.] v. on-, þǣr-uppan.

uppan = yppan *in* uppende *proferens*, Anglia xiii. 423, 836. v. geupped.

uppe; *adv.* I. *up, above, on high*:—Đēh hē uppe seó, Cd. Th. 281, 2; Sat. 265. Salte sǣstreámas and swegl uppe, Andr. Kmbl. 1498; An. 750. Hræfn uppe gōl, Elen. Kmbl. 104; El. 52. Uppe ofer rodere (cf. bufan đam rodore, Bt. 33, 4; Fox 130, 15), Met. 20, 124. Wearđ ætȳwed uppe on roderum steorra on stađole, Chr. 978; Erl. 126, 23. Hē geseah āne hlǣdre standan æt him on eorđan. Ōđer ende wæs uppe on hefenum, Past. 16; Swt. 101, 19. Saul hine wolde sēcean uppe on đæm munte, 28; Swt. 197, 13. Wǣron đa lāc forbærndu uppe on đæm altere, 33; Swt. 222, 24. Uppe on đam eaxlegespanne, Rood Kmbl. 17; Kr. 9. Fugel uppe sceal lācan on lyfte, Menol. Fox 536; Gn. C. 38. Mynster tō timbrianne on heánum mōrum uppe (*in montibus arduis ac remotis*), Bd. 3, 23; S. 554, 20. **I a.** referring to heavenly bodies, *up*:—Ōþ đæt sunne uppe sié, Lchdm. ii. 346, 22. Næs se mōna dāgyt uppe *quum luna erat oritura*, Nar. 29, 22. On winterlīcre tīde hī (*the Pleiades*) beóđ on niht uppe and on dæg ādūne, Lchdm. iii. 272, 2. **I b.** where there is motion from the sea up to the land. v. up, I. a 1:—Gif hē his scip uppe getogen hæbbe, L. Eth. ii. 3; Th. i. 286, 8. Be ciépemonna fōre uppe on londe. Gif ciépemon uppe on folce ceápie, L. In. 25; Th. i. 118, 11. Wǣron đa men uppe on londe of āgāne, Chr. 897; Erl. 95, 24. **I c.** marking arrival. v. up, I. a 2:—Đā se cyng geāxode đæt se here uppe wæs *when the king learned that the Danes had appeared upon the scene*, Chr. 1016; Erl. 157, 13. **I d.** referring to heaven:—Hī wiston Drihten ēcne uppe, Cd. Th. 227, 31; Dan. 195. Eádige đǣr uppe sittaþ, 305, 16; Sat. 647. Ys ūre se hālga God on heofondreáme uppe mid englum *Deus noster in coelo sursum*, Ps. Th. 113, 11: Cd. Th. 273, 25; Sat. 142: Exon. Th. 24, 19; Cri. 387: 239, 30; Ph. 629: Fragm. Kmbl. 86; Leás. 45. Wē mid englum uppe wǣron, Cd. Th. 289, 2; Sat. 391. Ne uppe on heofone ne niđer on eorđan *neque in coelo sursum nec in terra deorsum*, Deut. 4, 39. Wē syngodon uppe on earde, Cd. Th. 279, 1; Sat. 231. Uppe on roderum mid englum, Exon. Th. 90, 4; Cri. 1468: Hy. 3, 30. II. marking discovery. v. yppan:—Hē hī gemartirode swā hē dyrnlīcost mihte, and hē geđōht hæfde đæt hī đǣr nǣfre uppe ne wurdan, ac đurh Godes mihte hī đanon gecȳdde wurdon, Lchdm. iii. 424, 31. III. marking effectual action. (Cf. *Icel.* uppi vera *to take place*.):—Đara đe wile ānra hwylc uppe bringan (*bring it to pass*), đæt đū đære gyldnan gesihst Hierusalem weallas blīcan, Salm. Kmbl. 466; Sal. 233. [Her uppe, Orm. 1169. Þer uppe, A. R. 94, 12. Uppe on, O. E. Homl. i. 5, 2: Laym. 17495. *O. Sax.* uppa (-e), thār uppa an: *Icel.* uppi, uppi ā, uppi ī.]

uppe-godu (?); *pl.* v. up; *adj.*

uppe-land, es; *n. Up-country, country* as opposed to town, *rural districts*:—Đæt ǣlc man đe wǣre unniđing sceolde cuman tō him of porte and of uppelande, Chr. 1087; Erl. 226, 3. v. up-lendisc, uppan, I. 1. last two passages.

up-weardes; *adv. Upwards*:—Nim mid ðínum twám handum uppeweard[n]es, Lchdm. iii. 38, 10. v. up-weardes.

uppian; *p.* ode *To mount up, rise*:—Ðæt wæter, ðonne hit bið gepynd, hit miclaþ and uppaþ and fundaþ wið ðæs ðe hit ǽr from com *ad superiora colligitur*, Past. 38; Swt. 277, 7.

uppon. v. uppan.

up-riht; *adj.* I. *upright, erect*:—Ic uppriht ástód, Beo. Th. 4191; B. 2092. Mannum hé gesealde uprihtne gang, Homl. Th. i. 276, 4. II. *lying with the face turned upwards.* Cf. up-weard:—Upriht ástreht *supinus*, Hpt. Gl. 457, 33. [*O. H. Ger.* úf-reht *erectus*: *Icel.* upp-réttr.]

up-rihte; *adv.* I. *uprightly, erectly*:—Mé þúhte ðæt mín sceáf árise and stóde uprihte, Gen. 37, 7. Mann ána gǽþ uprihte, Bt. 41, 6; Fox 254, 30: Homl. Skt. i. 1, 57. Ðá árás se cnapa and uprihte eode, 6, 41. II. *right up, exactly overhead, in the zenith*:—Gǽð seó sunne uprihte (upp-, MS. P.) on ðam sumerlícan sunnstede on middæge, Lchdm. iii. 258, 15.

up-rodor (-er), -rador, es; *m.* I. *the firmament on high, the visible heavens, the sky*:—Wolde hé ðæt him eorðe and uproder and síd wæter geseted wurde woruldgesceafte, Cd. Th. 7, 1; Gen. 99. Ðás woruld, eorðan ymbhwyrft and uprodor, 179, 10; Exod. 26: 205, 2; Exod. 429. Eorðan sceátas and uprodor, Exon. Th. 312, 6; Seef. 105. Eorðan and uprodor, 69, 32; Cri. 1129: Cd. Th. 182, 15; Exod. 76. Ealne ymbhwyrft and uprador, Elen. Kmbl. 1459; El. 731. Hwílum cerreþ on uprodor ælbeorhta lég, Met. 29, 51. II. *heaven*:—Wæs Gúðláces gǽst gelǽded in uprodor fore onsýne éces Déman, Exon. Th. 148, 34; Gú. 754. Hé lǽdeþ eádige gástas on uprodor, Cd. Th. 212, 25; Exod. 544. In uprodor, 177, 33; Exod. 4. Cf. up-heofon.

up-ryne, es; *m. A coming up, rising* of a heavenly body, *coming* of day:—Wiþ hire (*the sun's*) uprynæs, Bt. 25; Fox 88, 27. Fram sunnan upryne *a solis ortu*, Ps. Spl. 106, 3. Uprine, 112, 3. Æfter sunnan setlgange ǽr mónan upryne, Lchdm. i. 330, 18. Ymb ðæs dæges uppyrne *circa exortum diei*, Bd. 4, 8; S. 576, 11.

up-spring, es; *m.* I. *an upspringing, rising* of a heavenly body, *coming* of day or night:—Upspryng *ortus* (*solis*), Ps. Spl. 103, 23. Fram ðære sunnan upspringes anginne *a solis ortus cardine*, Hymn. Surt. 50, 2. Fram ðære sunnan upspringe, Anglia viii. 317, 10. Upsprince, Ps. Spl. 49, 2. Eásterne wind, *subsolanus* gehâten, for ðan ðe hé blǽwð fram ðære sunnan upspringe, Lchdm. iii. 274, 15. Nihte of upspringe *noctis exortu*, Hymn. Surt. 2, 20. Ná manega dagas, ac án, se nát nǽnne upspring ne náne geendunge, Homl. Th. i. 490, 18. Þurh ðæs steorran upspring, 108, 5. II. *a rising* of water, *breaking forth*:—On upspri[n]c (*diluvii*) *inruptionem*, Anglia xiii. 32, 124. III. *birth*:—Hé gestrýnde Cainan. Æfter ðes upspringe (*post ejus ortum*) hé leofode eahtahundgeáre and fífténe geár, Gen. 5, 10. IV. *what springs up*:—Lígloccode upspringas *flammicomos ortus*, Wrt. Voc. ii. 149, 10.

up-sprungenness, e; *f. Defect*; in reference to the sun, *eclipse*:—*Eclypsis solis*, ðæt is sunnan ásprungennysse (uppsprungennes, MS. B.), Bd. 3, 27; S. 558, 10.

up-stige, es; *m.* I. *ascension, mounting*:—Nis bútan tweón tó understandenne se upstige and se niþerstige (*the ascending and descending on Jacob's ladder*) on náne óþere wísan, bútan ðæt heofona ríces upstige mid eádmódnesse geearnod bið and mid ofermēttum forwyrht, R. Ben. 23, 6–9. Hé becom tó ðæm heáhsetle ðære róde; on ðæm upstige (*by the ascent of the cross*) eall úre líf hé getremede, Blickl. Homl. 9, 36. Seó dún stent . . . twelf míla on upstige fram ánre byrig *there is an ascent of twelve miles from the town to the hill*, Homl. Th. i. 502, 6. ¶ especially *the ascension* of Christ to heaven:—Ðone mǽron symbeldæg Drihtnes upstiges, Blickl. Homl. 131, 11: Exon. Th. 41, 13; Cri. 655. Æfter upstige écan Dryhtnes, 44, 31; Cri. 711: 38, 31; Cri. 615: Blickl. Homl. 137, 23: Homl. Th. i. 324, 31. Æfter Cristes upstige tó heofonum, 58, 24: ii. 380, 24: H. R. 3, 4. Uppstige on heofonas, Bd. 3, 17; S. 545, 23. II. *an ascent, a way of ascending*:—Uppstige sandfull *ascensus arenosus*, Scint. 223, 13. Se seteþ wolcan upstige his *qui ponit nubem ascensum suum*, Ps. Surt. Lamb. 103, 3. [Cf. *O. H. Ger.* úf-stíc *ascensus*: *Icel.* upp-stiga.]

up-stígend, es; *m. One who ascends*:—Ða gecoreno upstígendo *electos ascensores*, Rtl. 193, 33.

up-wæstm *growth upwards, stature*:—Se cyningc hét bringan ísenne scamol; se wæs emnheáh ðæs mannes upwæstme; ðæt wæs twelf fæðma lang *jussit rex fieri scamnum ferreum secundum statum ejus. Artifices tulerunt mensuram ejus quae erat cubitorum duodecim*, Anglia xvii. 113, 9. [Cf. *Icel.* up-vöxtr *growth, tallness.*]

up-waras (-an, -e); *pl. The dwellers above, the celestials*:—Tó upwarum *ad superos*, Wrt. Voc. ii. 9, 67.

up-weard; *adj.* I. *turned upwards*:—Ongeán sunnan upweard licge hé *let him lie on his back with his face to the sun*, Lchdm. ii. 18, 13: iii. 2, 10. Licge hé upweard æfter ðon góde hwíle, ii. 318, 14. Hé sceal upweard licgean, i. 300, 20. Mon on bedde dæges upweard ne licge, ii. 26, 19. Álege ðone man upweard, 342, 5. Hé mid bǽm handum upweard (*with his face turned upwards?* or adverb? *he stretched his hands up.* v. upweardes) plegade, Elen. Kmbl. 1609; El. 806. Nis ðæt gedafenlíc ðæt se módsefa monna ǽniges niþerheald wese, and ðæt neb upweard, Met. 31, 23. Hé ásette his sweord upweard and ðá hyne sylfne ofstang *he placed his sword with the point up, and then stabbed himself*, Shrn. 132, 10. Nioþan upweardne on nearo fégde, Exon. Th. 479, 11; Rä. 62, 6. For ðam gelómlícum ðeáwe his gebeda, swá hwǽr swá hé sæt, ðæt his gewuna wæs ðæt hé his handa upwearde hæfde ofer his cneówa *ob crebrum morem orandi, semper ubicumque sedens, supinas super genua sua manus habere solitus sit*, Bd. 3, 12; S. 537, 25. II. *moving upwards.* v. up, I. a. β:—Ðæt leóht ðe wé hátaþ dægréd cymð of ðære sunnan, ðonne heó upweard bið, Lchdm. iii. 234, 29. v. upheáh, -lang, *and next word.*

up-weard; *adv. Upwards, up.* (1) of motion, (a) from a lower to a higher point:—Ðá gewende eal se sang upweard tó heofenum, Homl. Th. ii. 548, 14: Elen. Kmbl. 1609; El. 806 (? v. preceding word). (b) *up* into a country. v. up, I. a 1:—Swegen wende intó Humbran múðan, and swá uppweard andlang Tréntan, Chr. 1013; Erl. 147, 18. (2) of reckoning, in the calendar, *upward, backward*:—Swá fela daga tell ðú fram Martius mónðes ende upweard . . . Rím swá fela daga upweard fram pridie Kl. Martii, and ic ðé secge tó gewissum, ðonne ðú cymð tellende tó .vii. id. Martii, ðonne gemétst ðú ðǽr lunam primam, Anglia viii. 327, 9–13. Tellaþ þreó and twéntig daga fram æfteweardum Martium upweard, 329, 28. [Cnihtes eoden upward, cnihtes eoden adonward, Laym. 15244. Kasten upward (*sursum*) . . . dranen dunewardes, Kath. 1964. To climben upward, A. R. 72, 20. Ha biheold uppard, Jul. 74, 14. Reccnedd uppwarrd (*back*) and dunnwarrd, Orm. 2056.]

up-weardes; *adv. Upwards*:—Hé onginþ of ðám wyrttrumum, and swá upweardes gréwþ óþ ðone stemn, Bt. 34, 10; Fox 150, 2. Hé biþ upweardes (cf. swá sprincþ hé up, Bt. 25; Fox 88, 24), Met. 13, 54. Hió stíhþ á upweardes, 13, 62. Hé hæfde his handa upweardes, Blickl. Homl. 227, 16. Hé his handa wæs uppweardes brǽdende wið ðæs heofones *manus ad coelum tendens*, Ors. 4, 5; Swt. 166, 19.

up-wearp. [*Icel.* upp-varp.] v. sǽ-upwearp.

up-weg, es; *m. The way to heaven*:—Wæs Gúðláces gǽst gelǽded on upweg, Exon. Th. 180, 15; Gú. 1280: 184, 6; Gú. 1340: Andr. Kmbl. 1659; An. 832. Hí dóm hlutan, eádigne upwæg, Menol. Fox 383; Men. 193. [*O. Sax.* up-weg.]

up-yrne. v. up-ryne.

ur (occurring only as it is represented by the U-rune); *adv. Formerly*:—ᚢ (= ur) wæs geára (cf. iú (geó) . . . geára) geógoðhádes glǽm; nú synt geárdagas forð gewitene, lífwynne geliden, Elen. Kmbl. 2530; El. 1266. ᚢ wæs longe laguflódum bilocen lífwynna dǽl, feoh on foldan, Exon. Th. 50, 25; Cri. 806. v. or.

úr, es; *m. A kind of ox, a bison*; urus: also *the name of the U-rune*:—Úr (ᚢ) byþ ánmód and oferhyrned, feohteþ mid hornum mǽre mórstapa, Runic pm. Kmbl. 339, 7; Rún. 2. (The rune is written without representing a word, Exon. Th. 284, 32; Jul. 706.) [*Goth.* úraz *name of the U-rune*: *Icel.* úrr *a kind of ox*; úr *the name of the U-rune*: *O. H. Ger.* úr-ohso: *Ger.* auer-ochse.]

úre; *gen. pl. of personal pronoun of first person. Of us*:—Adam can yfel and gód, swá swá úre sum (*quasi unus ex nobis*), Gen. 3, 22. Ús is eallum þearf, ðæt úre ǽghwylc óþerne bylde, Byrht. Th. 138, 42; By. 234: Beo. Th. 2776; B. 1386. Úre ealra bliss eardhæbbendra *laetantium omnium nostrum habitatio*, Ps. Th. 86, 6. Weorð ðú úre gemyndig *memor fuit nostri*, 113, 21. Gemiltsa úre *miserere nostri*, Ps. Spl. 122, 4. Gif ðú úre bídan þencest, Exon. Th. 119, 26; Gú. 260. ¶ used as a possessive, *our*:—Wé sceolan syllan ðone teóþan dǽl úre worldspéda, and wé sceolan úre daga ðone teóþan dǽl on forhæfdnesse lifgean, Blickl. Homl. 35, 19, 20. Geþencean úre sáula þearfe, 95, 24. Úre synna forgifnessa, 97, 14. Fram ðam heáhsetle úre Gescyppendes, 11, 29. v. ús.

úre; *adj. pronoun.* I. *our*:—Úre *noster*, Ælfc. Gr. 15; Zup. 93, 17. Úre Drihten, Blickl. Homl. 11, 21. Fæder úre (úrer, Lind.) *Pater noster*, Mt. Kmbl. 6, 9. Úre se trumesta staþol, Blickl. Homl. 13, 10. Tó úres Drihtnes méder, 5, 2. On naman Godes úres, Ps. Spl. 19, 5. Beorhtnes blíðan Drihtnes úres, Ps. Th. 89, 19. Seó rihteste bysen úran (úres, MS. F.) menniscan lífes, R. Ben. 133, 4. Ða blindnesse úre ælþeódignesse, Blickl. Homl. 23, 2: 77, 14. Mid eallre úre heortan megolnesse, 65, 23. Úrum Hǽlende fylgende, 23, 11. Deóre Drihtne úrum, Cd. Th. 17, 17; Gen. 261. Mid úre ánre sáule, Blickl. Homl. 91, 16. Úrne dæghwamlícan hláf, Mt. Kmbl. 6, 11. Álēse wé úre sáule, Blickl. Homl. 101, 10: 33, 13. Ge wé ge úre fæderas, Gen. 46, 34. Sió án ræst eallra úrra (úra, Met. 21, 14) geswinca, Bt. 34, 8; Fox 144, 27. Be ðære hǽlo úrra sáwla, L. In. pref.; Th. i. 102, 8: Exon. Th. 154, 26; Gú. 848: Blickl. Homl. 131, 1. Úra synna forlǽtnesse, 35, 36. Úrum fæderum, Deut. 5, 3. Forgyf ús úre gyltas, swá swá wé forgyfaþ úrum gyltendum, Mt. Kmbl. 6, 12. II. predicative, *ours*:—Ðonne bið úre seó yrfeweardnes, Mk. Skt. 12, 7. Ðonne wé ðǽm ðearfum hiera niéddearſe sellaþ, hiera ǽgen wē him sellaþ, nalles ūre, Past. 45; Swt. 335, 18. III. where in place of an inflected form of the adjective the genitive *ūre* might be expected:—Nis ðæt mīn miht ne nǽniges ūres, Blickl. Homl. 151, 29. Gē habbaþ gecȳðed ðæt gē ūres nānes ne siendon *ye have shown that ye are of no one of us;* nullius vos esse monstratis, Past. 32; Swt. 211, 14. Gif hwelc forworht monn cymð and bitt ūrne hwelcne, 10; Swt. 63, 1. Ūrum sceal sweord and helm . . . bām gemǽne, Beo. Th. 5312; B. 2659. v. ūser.

ūre-lendisc; *adj. Of our country:*—Ūrelendisc *nostras,* Ælfc. Gr. 15; Zup. 93, 17.

ūrer. v. ūre; *adj.*

ūrig-feþera; *adj. Wet-feathered, with dewy plumage:*—Earn ūrig-feþera, Judth. Thw. 24, 27; Jud. 210. Ūrigfeðera earn, Elen. Kmbl. 57; El. 29. Ūrigfeðra, 221; El. 111. Ūrigfeþra, Exon. Th. 307, 17; Seef. 25. [Cf. *Icel.* ūr *drizzling rain;* ūrigr *wet;* ūrig-toppi *dewy-mane* (epithet of a horse in a verse).] v. deáwig-feþere.

ūrig-lâst; *adj. Making a dewy track, walking the wet earth:*—Sum sceal on fēþe on feorwegas nȳde gongan, and his nest beran, tredan ūrig-lâst elþeódigra frēcne foldan, Exon. Th. 329, 4; Vy. 29.

ūs; *dat.:* ūs, ūsic; *acc.:* ūser, usser; *gen.; pron. pl. first person. To us, us, of us:*—Wel ūs wæs on Egipta lande *bene nobis erat in Aegypto,* Num. 11, 18. Wē habbaþ ūs tō fæder Abraham, Lk. Skt. 3, 8. Ūs ys betere *expedit nobis,* Jn. Skt. 11, 50. Ūs nis nā ālȳfed, 18, 31. Ūs neód is, L. Eth. vi. 42; Th. i. 326, 7. Hǽle ūs (ūsic, Lind. Rush.) *salva nos,* Mt. Kmbl. 8, 25. Ne gelǽd ðū ūs (ūsih, Lind.) on costnunge, ac ālȳs ūs (ūsich, Lind.) of yfele, 6, 13. Gif ðū ūs (ūsig, Lind.: ūsic, Rush.) ūt ādrīfst, āsende ūs (ūsig, Lind.: ūsic, Rush.) on ðās swīna heorde, 8, 31. Hē ūs ālēsde of deófles þeówdōme, Blickl. Homl. 73, 7: Cd. Th. 25, 8; Gen. 390: Andr. Kmbl. 530; An. 265. Ūsic, Bd. 5, 1; S. 614, 10: Ps. Th. 64, 3: Cd. Th. 162, 4; Gen. 2676: Exon. Th. 3, 2; Cri. 30: Beo. Th. 5270; B. 2638. Þeáh ðe ūser feá lifgen, 188, 8; Az. 42. Hē cwom ūser neósan, Beo. Th. 4155; B. 2074. Geóca ūser, Cd. Th. 234, 14; Dan. 292. Helpe usser, Ps. Th. 67, 20. ¶ gen. used as a possessive (v. ūre), *our:*—Ūser yldran, Cd. Th. 234, 26; Dan. 298. [*Goth.* uns, unsis; *dat. acc.;* unsara; *gen.: O. Sax. O. Frs.* ūs; *dat. acc.;* ūser; *gen.: O. H. Ger.* uns; *dat.* unsih; *acc.;* unsar; *gen.: Icel.* oss; *dat. acc.*] v. wē, unc, ūre, *and next word.*

Ūse, Wūse, an; Ūs (*or* Ūse; *indecl.?*), e; *f.* The name of several rivers in England, *Ouse:*—Andlang Ūsan óð hī cōmon tō Bedanforda, Chr. 1010; Erl. 143, 33. Of Ūsan up on Wilbaldes fleót . . . On Ūsan; andlang Ūsan (*the charter refers to Northamptonshire*), Cod. Dip. Kmbl. iii. 454, 14–25. Landgemǽre æt Ollanēge . . . In on Ūse; andlang Ūse, 170, 22–31. Tō Ūse stæðe (cf. uulgare prisco usu nomen imposuerunt Use, l. 2), v. 226, 14. Up on Ūsan óð Wætlinga-strǽt, L. A. G. i; Th. i. 152, 10. Eall hira land betwuh dīcum and Wūsan, Chr. 905; Erl. 98, 20. Betwyx Ūsan and Trēntan, 1069; Erl. 207, 16. See, too:—In Ūsanmere *Ousemere* (in Warwickshire), Cod. Dip. Kmbl. iii. 375, 9. In provincia Usmerorum (*some part of Worcestershire*), i. 154, 20. In aliis multis locis; hoc est . . . aet Stūre in Usmērum, 173, 18, 34. Of Ūsmere . . . on Ūsmere, vi. 68, 14.

ūser, usser; *adj. pron. Our:*—Nergend ūser, Cd. Th. 34, 11; Gen. 536. Drihten ūser, Ps. Th. 59, 1. Drihten usser, 54, 8: Cd. Th. 53, 3; Gen. 855. Usses Dryhtnes rōd, Exon. Th. 67, 7; Cri. 1085. Endelāf usses cynnes, Beo. Th. 5619; B. 2813. Mōdes usses, Met. 21, 12. Ne meaht ðū in usse mǽgþe ne on ussum gemǽnan wunian, Bd. 2, 5; S. 507, 27. On eallum ussum cynne, Blickl. Homl. 151, 12. Ussum mōde, Exon. Th. 2, 32; Cri. 28. Mid usse līchoman, 47, 14; Cri. 755. Hlāf ūserne (ūsenne, Lind.) *panem nostrum,* Mt. Kmbl. Rush. 6, 11. Freán ūserne, Beo. Th. 5997; B. 3002: Andr. Kmbl. 680; An. 340. Ūsa ł ūserna (ūse ł ūserra, Rush.) *nostrum,* Jn. Skt. Lind. 3, 11. Ūsra (ūserne, Rush.) *nostram,* 10, 24. Hālne dō kyningc usserne, Ps. Lamb. 19, 10. Usserne God *Deum nostrum,* Ps. Th. 98, 5. Óþ usse tīde, Bd. 2, 16; S. 519, 37. Wē usse gesihþ upp āhōfan, 5, 1; S. 613, 32: Exon. Th. 464, 23; Hö. 91. Usse yldran, 160, 20; Gū. 946. Ðæt ussa (ūre, Bt. 15; Fox 48, 18) tīda wǽren swylce, Met. 8, 40. Usse sāula, 21, 35. In ussera tīda tīman, Exon. Th. 147, 12; Gū. 725. Mildsa sāulum ussa leóda, Bd. 3, 12; S. 537, 31. Goda ussa gield, Exon. Th. 251, 16; Jul. 146: 279, 26; Jul. 619. Godum ussum, 252, 26; Jul. 169. On ussum sāwlum, 80, 29; Cri. 1314. Tō ussum wǽpnum, Nar. 21, 19. Forgef ūs scylda ūsra, suǽ uoe forgefon scyldgum ūsum, Mt. Kmbl. Lind. 6, 12. Heó beswāc yldran usse, Exon. Th. 226, 31; Ph. 414. Ussa sāula, Met. 23, 11. [*Goth.* unsar: *O. Sax.* ūsa: *O. Frs.* unse, ūse: *O. H. Ger.* unsar.] v. uncer.

ūsic. v. ūs.

ūt; *adv.* I. where there is motion, lit. or fig., *out, beyond the bounds within which a thing is enclosed,* (1) with verbs of going. (*a*) without words determining whence or whither motion proceeds:—Hē lǽteþ word ūt faran, Exon. Th. 315, 35; Mōd. 41. Uton gān ūt *egrediamur foras,* Gen. 5, 8: 27, 3: Cd. Th. 148, 24; Gen. 2461. Ðā eodon hig ūt ān æfter ānum *unum post unum exiebant,* Jn. Skt. 8, 9. Cume ān spearwa ðurh óþre duru in, ðurh óðre ūt gewite, Bd. 2, 13; S. 516, 18. (*a* 1) *out* on an expedition:—Wæs Eádmund cyng gewend ūt, and gerād ða West-Seaxan, Chr. 1016; Erl. 155, 13. (*a* 2) *out,* in the sense of leaving a place:—Be ðām ðe ūt faraþ, hwæðer hī mon eft underfōn scyle, R. Ben. 53, 6. (*a* 3) *out* to the closet:—Gif mon ne mæge ūt gegān, Lchdm. ii. 276, 12: 230, 21, 23. v. ūte, II. 1 a. (*a* 4) of the passage of time, *out,* with the idea of coming to an end:—Ūt gangendum ðam mōnþe ðe wē Aprelis hātaþ, Lchdm. iii. 76, 14. (*β*) with words denoting whence motion proceeds:—Ūt āfaren of dīnes fæder ēþele, Bt. 5, 1; Fox 8, 29: Cd. Th. 216, 14; Dan. 6. Lēt of breóstum word ūt faran, Beo. Th. 5096; B. 2551. In tō gemōte cuman, and ūt of gemōte, Chr. 1048; Erl. 180, 7. Fleógan of hūse ūt, Cd. Th. 87, 2; Gen. 1442. Gangan ūt of earce, 89, 29; Gen. 1488. Ða ðe ūt gongaþ of mūþe, Bd. 1, 27; S. 494, 34. Moyses oft eode inn and ūt on ðæt templ, Past. 16; Swt. 101, 24. Ic of ðē ūt sīðode, Soul Kmbl. 110; Seel. 55. Ðǽr ic ūt swīcan ne mæg *non egrediebar,* Ps. Th. 87, 8. Hionan ūt wītan, Met. 24, 52. (*γ*) with words denoting whither motion proceeds:—Ic wæs ūt ācymen on ǽlþeódig land *advena fui in terra aliena,* Ex. 2, 22. v. ūt-ācumen. Fleáh cāsere ūt on Crēcas, Met. 1, 21. Hē eode ūt on ðæt land, Gen. 24, 63. Cnut wende him ūt þurh Buccingahāmscīre intō Beadafordscīre, Chr. 1016; Erl. 154, 6. (1 a) with verbs that imply going:—Ic ne mæg ūt āredian, Bt. 35, 5; Fox 164, 14. Heó forlēt hyre hæftlingas ūt, Homl. Th. i. 228, 17. Word ðe hē ūt forlēt, Blickl. Homl. 59, 19. Gif mec se mānsceaða of eorðsele ūt gesēceþ, Beo. Th. 5024; B. 2515. Hī bedīcodon ða burh ūton ðæt nān mann ne mihte ne inn ne ūt, Chr. 1016; Erl. 155, 11. Heó wolde ūt þanon feore beorgan, Beo. Th. 2589; B. 1292. (2) where motion (lit. or fig.) is caused, with verbs of bearing, casting, driving, releasing, etc.:—Geóte man ðone wǽtan ūt *liquor effundatur,* L. Ecg. C. 39; Th. ii. 164, 7. Hwæthugu of cyricean ðurh stale ūt ābregdan, Bd. 1, 27; S. 490, 5. Deófolseócnessa ūt tō ādrīfanne, Mk. Skt. 3, 15. Ða landbigengan ūt āmǽran, Bd. 4, 16; S. 584, 7. Ūt tō anȳdenne *expellendum,* Scint. 210, 13. Hē ūt āwearp ða sceamolas, Blickl. Homl. 71, 18. Ic mægenbyrðenne hider ūt ætbær, Beo. Th. 6176; B. 3092. Hié ne mehton ða scipu ūt brengan, Chr. 896; Erl. 94, 10. Ðone æþeling ðe hē ūt flēmde, Chr. 725; Erl. 45, 31. Ālǽd mē ūt of ðyssum bendum, Blickl. Homl. 87, 34. Sum lytel cniht sweart teáh ðone brōðor of ðære cirican ūt, Shrn. 65, 18. Ne mæg nān man of mīnre handa ūt ālinnan, Deut. 32, 39. God bebeád ðæt hī sceoldon ālȳsan hysecild ūt mid fīf scyllingum, Homl. Th. i. 138, 16. Hē hine of earfoðum ūt ālȳsde, Ps. Th. 90, 15. Ðæt land eode eft intō ðære stōwe ðe hit ūt ālǽned wæs, Cod. Dip. Kmbl. iv. 267, 6. Ðeáh ðe Harold ðæt land mid unlage ūt nam, 274, 29. Nǽnig mon his geþōht openum wordum ūt ne cȳðe *nemo palam pronunciet,* Nar. 28, 30. Hit nǽnig mon ūt cȳþan ne mōste *no man might spread the news of it abroad,* 32, 17. Ūt mǽran, 32, 22. (2 a) figurative, as in to carry *out, to an end,* marking completeness. v. ūt-cwealm. (3) *out, forth,* as in to break *out:*—Se wielm ðæs innoþes ūt ābiersð, Past. 11; Swt. 71, 9. Streám ūt āweóll, Andr. Kmbl. 3045; An. 1525. Wiþ ūt āblegnedum ōmum, Lchdm. ii. 10, 5: 98, 25. Ðǽr blōd and wæter ūt bicwōman, Exon. Th. 69, 1; Cri. 1114. Geseah streám ūt ðonan brecan of beorge, Beo. Th. 5084; B. 2545. Ðætte seó wǽte ūt fleówe, Bd. 4, 19; S. 589, 1. Hī of mīnre sīdan swāt ūt guton (gotun, MS.), Exon. Th. 88, 33; Cri. 1449. Cleopaþ se alda ūt of helle, Cd. Th. 267, 7; Sat. 34. (4) with the idea of removal from the place in which a thing is fixed, to knock *out,* pull *out,* etc.:—Ic ūt ādelfe *effodio,* Ælfc. Gr. 28, 6; Zup. 179, 11. Þafa ðæt ic ūt ādō (*ejiciam*) ðæt mot of ðīnum eágan . . . Ādō ǽrest ūt ðone beám of ðīnum āgenum eágan, Mt. Kmbl. 7, 4–5. Ūt āstingan, Chr. 797; Erl. 59, 43. Ðū ðe ūt ātuge (*extraxisti*) mē of innoðe, Ps. Lamb. 21, 10. Āteón ūt ða wǽtan, Lchdm. ii. 222, 25. Gif hwā sleá his weales eáge ūt oððe his wylne, lǽte hig frige for ðam eágan ðe hē ūt ādyde, Ex. 21, 26: L. Alf. 20; Th. i. 48, 25. Ðā sticode him mon ða eágan ūt *effossis oculis,* Ors. 4, 5; Swt. 168, 4. (5) with verbs of summoning:—Hē hine ācīgde ūt, Bd. 2, 12; S. 513, 19. Āban ðū ða beornas ūt of ofne, Cd. Th. 242, 34; Dan. 429. Ūt *from this world,* Salm. Kmbl. 962; Sal. 480. (5 a) summoning to service:—Ðā hēt se cyng ābannan ūt ealne þeódscipe of West-Seaxum, Chr. 1006; Erl. 140, 8. Hēt se cyning bannan ūt here . . . Ðā hī þider ūt cōmon (cf. ðone here ðe ðam cynge mid wæs, Erl. 181, 8), 1048; Erl. 180, 1: Exon. Th. 120, 12; Gū. 270. (6) *out, away from home, abroad:*—Gif hē unmyndlunge ceáp āredige ūt on hwylcere fare, būton hē hit ǽr cȳdde ðā hē ūt rād, L. Edg. S. 8; Th. i. 274, 23. (7) *out, away from land:*—Hweðer gē eówer hundas and eówer net ūt on ða sǽ lǽdon? Bt. 32, 3; Fox 118, 14: Met. 19, 19. Hié ūt óðreówon, Chr. 897; Erl. 96, 7. Ūt feor on Wendelsǽ, Met. 26, 30. Wit on gārsecg ūt aldrum nēðdon, Beo. Th. 1079; B. 537. Guman ūt scufon wudu, 436; B. 215; Chr. 897; Erl. 96, 7. Nacan ūt āþringan, Exon. Th. 474, 31; Bo. 39. II. where there is not motion, *out.* (1) *outside:*—Ne beóð hī ūt fram ðē ātȳnde *non excludantur,* Ps. Th. 67, 27. (1 a) *not within doors, not in the house, abroad:*—Niman hī him wīf and heora andlyfene ūt onfōn *sortiri uxores debent, et stipendia sua exterius* (not in a monastery) *accipere,* Bd. 1, 27; S. 489, 18. v. ūt-wǽpnedmann. (2) *on the surface:*—Byrgennum ūt hwītum *monumentis dealbatis,* Mt. Kmbl. p. 19, 12. (3) *out, away from land:*—Orcadas ða eálond, ða wǽron ūt on gārsecge būtan Breotone *Orcadas insulas ultra Brittaniam in oceano positas*, Bd. 1, 3; S. 475, 13: Ps. Th. 96, 1: Met. 16, 12. (4) figurative, *externally*:—Se ðe ūt wel lǽrð mid his wordum, hē onfēhð innan ðæs inngeðonces fǽtnesse *qui exterius praedicando benedicit, interioris augmenti pinguedinem recipit*, Past. 49; Swt. 381, 4. [*Goth. O. Sax. Icel.* ūt: *O. H. Ger.* ūz.] v. þǽr-, þurh-ūt.

ūt-ācumen, -cymen[e]; *adj. Stranger, alien, foreign*:—Dēmaþ ǽlcon men riht, sī hit burga man, sī hit ūtācymene (*peregrinus*), Deut. 1, 16. Se ūtācymena (ūtancumena, *v. l.*) munuc ðe of uncūðum eardum cymð *si quis monachus peregrinus de longinquis provinciis supervenerit*, R. Ben. 108, 4. Gē wǽron ūtācymene (*advenae*) on Egipta lande, Lev. 19, 34: 25, 23. Eallum and māgum and ūtācymenum *omnibus et propinquis et extraneis*, Scint. 3, 14. Ūtācymene and ǽlþeódige *aduenas et peregrinos*, 137, 16. Ūtācymene *peregrinos*, Lev. 23, 22. Wræccan ł ūtācumenan *aduenas*, Ps. Lamb. 145, 9. v. ūtan-cumen, -cymene.

ūta-cund (ūta = ūtan *or* ūte; v. innan-, inne-cund); *adj. Foreign, alien, strange*:—Ūtacund cynn *alienigena*, Lk. Skt. p. 9, 8. Ðes ūtacunda, Lind. 17, 18. On ūtacund *in alieno*, 16, 12. Ūtacund *alienum* . . . ðara ūtacundra *alienorum*, Jn. Skt. Lind. 10, 5. From ūtacundum *ab alienis*, Mt. Kmbl. Lind. 17, 25: Rtl. 168, 13.

utan *let us*. v. witon.

ūtan (-on); *adv. prep.* A. *adv.* I. *from without*:—Wearð mē on hige leóhte ūtan and innan, Cd. Th. 42, 21; Gen. 677. Gif ðū wēnst ðæt him āhwonan ūtan cōmon ða gōd ðe hē hæfþ, ðonne wǽre ðæt þing betere, ðe hit him fram cōme, ðonne hē, Bt. 34, 3; Fox 136, 26. Ælfrēd com ūtan (ūton, MS. E.) mid fierde, Chr. 885; Erl. 82, 23. Ǽghwylcne ellþeódigra ðara ðe ðæt eáland ūtan sōhte, Andr. Kmbl. 56; An. 28. Cumaþ of eálandum ūtan kynincgas, Ps. Th. 71, 10: 79, 13. II. *without, on the outside.* (1) where action, stated or implied, may be thought of as operating on an object from without:—Hāt wæs him ūtan wrāðlīc wīte, Cd. Th. 23, 6; Gen. 354: 285, 23; Sat. 342. (1 a) with *ymb*, *be*, as prepositions or prefixes of verbs:—Pontius hæfde ðone consul mid his folce ūtan befangen, Ors. 3, 10; Swt. 140, 22: Met. 13, 7. Ǽghwilc ōþer ūtan ymbclyppeþ, Met. 11, 35: Exon. Th. 423, 2; Rä. 41, 15. Hī hine ūtan ymbðringaþ, Salm. Kmbl. 256; Sal. 127. (2) where action takes place outside an object:—Hī bedīcodon ða burh ūton, Chr. 1016; Erl. 155, 11. Hē ðone būr ūtan beeode, 755; Erl. 48, 30. Land belicgan ūton, Cd. Th. 15, 7; Gen. 229. Besittaþ hié ūtan, Past. 21; Swt. 161, 4: Chr. 894; Erl. 93, 9: 918; Erl. 104, 1. Hié hine ðǽr ūtan besǽton, 894; Erl. 92, 23. Ðæt nān neód sȳ ūtan tō farenne *ut non sit necessitas vagandi foris*, R. Ben. 127, 7. Se ðe sceal healdan folc ūtan wið feóndum, Ps. Th. 120, 4. Se fugel ymbseteþ ūtan līc hālgum stencum, Exon. Th. 212, 3; Ph. 204. Ūtan ymbestandne mid unrīme þegna, Met. 25, 7. Ūton, Bt. 37, 1; Fox 186, 3. Cyrican wyrcean ymb ða cyrican ūtan ðe hē ǽr worhte, Bd. 2, 14; S. 517, 30. (3) *on the outside, on the surface*:—Ūtan (*a foris*) wlitige, innan fulle deádra bāna, Mt. 23, 27: Runic pm. Kmbl. 341, 26; Rūn. 13: Blickl. Homl. 197, 11. Ðæt treów biþ ūton gescyrped mid ðære rinde, Bt. 34, 10; Fox 150, 7: Beo. Th. 3011; B. 1503. Ūton tō gesett tō trymnesse ðæs hūses, Bd. 3, 17; S. 544, 35: Exon. Th. 233, 26; Ph. 530. Ūton hié wǽron elpendbānum geworhte, Nar. 5, 5: Exon. Th. 474, 31; Rä. 41, 47. Beámas ūtan ofætes gehlædene, Cd. Th. 30, 3; Gen. 461. On ðysse eorðan ūtan *on the face of the earth*, Ps. Th. 64, 6. Innan and ūtan eorðan līme gefæstnod, Cd. Th. 80, 1; Gen. 1322: Beo. Th. 1552; B. 774: Exon. Th. 62, 21; Cri. 1005: 219, 2; Ph. 301. (3 a) figuratively, *outwardly*:—Gē ætȳwaþ mannum ūtan (*a foris*) rihtwīse, Mt. Kmbl. 23, 28. Ðeáh hē fæger word ūtan ætȳwe, Fragm. Kmbl. 32; Leás. 18. (4) with *ymb* or *be* and verbs of motion or rest, *about, round*:—Ðæt hē hine ǽghwonon ūtan ymbsāwe (cf. behealde hē on feówer healfe, Bt. 19; Fox 68, 21), Met. 10, 4. Ūtan behwerfed, Bt. 25; Fox 88, 35: Met. 13, 77, 78. Hē ǽlce dæg ūton ymbhwyrfþ ealne ðisne middaneard, 39, 3; Fox 214, 16: Met. 28, 4, 13. Hié ne mehton Sūð-Seaxna lond ūtan berōwan, Chr. 897; Erl. 96, 9. Ætȳwdon twēgen steorran ymb ða sunnan ūtan, Bd. 5, 23; S. 645, 23. (5) *out, away from land*:—Eálond ūtan, Beo. Th. 4657; B. 2334. B. *prep. with gen. Without, outside of.* v. ūtan-bordes, -landes. [*O. Sax.* ūtan: *O. H. Ger.* ūzān *foras, a foris*: *Icel.* ūtan *from outside; outside*.] v. be-, on- (Lchdm. ii. 292, 27), wiþ-, ymb-ūtan; ūtane, *and compounds with* ūtan *as prefix*.

ūtan-bordes; *adv. Abroad*:—Man ūtanbordes wīsdōm and lāre hieder on lond sōhte *people abroad came hither in search of learning*, Past. pref.; Swt. 3, 11. [*Icel.* ūtan-borðs *overboard*: *Dan.* uden-bords. Cf. *Goth.* ūtana (*with gen.*): *O. H. Ger.* ūzān (*with gen.*): *Icel.* ūtan (*with gen.*).] v. ūtan-landes.

ūtan-cumen, -cymen[e]; *adj. Come from without.* I. *from another land, foreign, alien, strange*:—Ūtancuman *advena*, Wrt. Voc. i. 74, 64. Ðǽr nān ūtancymen (ūtencumen, Cott. MS.) mon cuman ne dorste, Ors. 5, 2; Swt. 218, 1. Se ūtancumena munuc ðe of uncūðum eardum cymð, R. Ben. 109, 4. Ðam elþeódigan and ūtancumenan (ūtcymenan, MSS. G. H.) ne lǽt ðū nō uncūðlīce wið hine, L. Alf. 47; Th. i. 54, 20. Ne hyrwe gē ūtancymenne man (*advenam*), Lev. 19, 33. Ǽlþeódige men and ūtancumene swȳðe ūs swencaþ, Wulfst. 91, 19. Gē wǽron ūtancymene (*advenae*) on Egipta lande, Deut. 10, 19. Ūtancumenra *exterorum* i. *peregrinorum*, Wrt. Voc. ii. 145, 62. Þurh ūtancymen[r]a goda naman *per nomen externorum deorum*, Ex. 23, 13. Ūtancumene and elþeódige ne geswenc ðū, L. Alf. 33; Th. i. 52, 14. II. *belonging to another*:—Gif ūtancymene (*alienus*) oxa ōðres oxan gewundaþ, Ex. 21, 35. v. ūt-ācumen.

ūtane (-one, -ene); *adv.* I. where there is motion (lit. or fig.) to an object, *from without*:—Ūtene *extrinsecus*, Wrt. Voc. ii. 145, 21. Him biþ se wela ūtane cumen, and hē ne mæg ūtane nāuht āgnes habban, Bt. 27, 2; Fox 98, 7, 8. Ic nolde ðæt ðū wēndest ðæt Gode āhwonan ūtane cōme his gōdnes, 34, 2; Fox 136, 23: 34, 7; Fox 144, 20. Ðȳ læs ðonne hié oferhyggaþ ðæt hié sién oferreahte ūtane mid ōðerra manna lārum hié sién innan gehæfte mid ofermētum *ne dum aliorum suasionibus foris superari despiciunt, intus a superbia captivi teneantur*, Past. 42; Swt. 307, 6. Him mon ūtane of ōðrum londum an wann, Ors. 3, 7; Swt. 110, 28. II. where there is not movement to an object. (1) *outside*:—Se here ða burh ūtone besǽton, Chr. 1016; Erl. 156, 14. Se rodor hine hæfþ ūtane (cf. se rodor ðās rūman gesceaft ūtan ymhwyrfeþ, Met. 20, 137), Bt. 33, 4; Fox 130, 22. Ðætte wē scylen beón on ðisse ælðeódignesse ūtane beheáwene mid suingellan, tō ðæm ðæt wē sién gefēged tō ðæm gefōgstānum on ðære Godes ceastre *quia nunc foris per flagella tundimur, ut intus in templum Dei postmodum disponamur*, Past. 36; Swt. 253, 18. (2) *on the outside, on the surface*:—Se wielm ðæs innoðes ūt ābiersð, and wierð tō sceabbe, and moniga wunda ūtane wyrcð, Past. 11; Swt. 71, 10. (3) *out, at sea*:—Ðā gerǽdde se cyng ðæt man gegaderode scipu . . . and hī sceoldan cunnian gif hī muhton ðone here āhwǽr ūtene betræppen, Chr. 992; Erl. 131, 27. (4) *outwardly, externally*:—Ðonne hē ongit be sumum ðingum odðe ðeáwum ūtone (-anne, Hatt. MS.) ætiéwdum (*signis exterius apparentibus*) eall ðæt hié innan ðenceaþ, Past. 21; Swt. 155, 10. Ūtane, 28; Swt. 195, 22. Gif munuc inne on his heortan eáðmōd bið, and nā ðæt ān, ac eác swylce ūtene mid his līchoman eáðmōdnesse gebȳcnige, R. Ben. 31, 3. (5) *with* ymbe, *about*:—Ðā ymbe ðæt ūtene forðfērde Decius *about that time Decius died*, Homl. Skt. i. 23, 348. [*O. H. Ger.* ūzana.] v. ūtan.

ūtan-landes; *adv. Abroad, in distant countries*:—Þeóda ðe eard nymaþ ūtanlandes *gentes qui habitant fines terrae*, Ps. Th. 64, 8. [Cf. In outenland *in terra aliena*, Ps. 136, 4. Utenerdes *in foreign lands*, Gen. and Ex. 956. Laban ferde fro Caram into utenstede, 1741. *Icel.* ūtan-lands, -lendis *abroad*; ūtanlands-maðr, -siðir *a foreigner, foreign customs*.] v. ūtan-bordes.

ūtan-weard; *adj. Outside, exterior*; may be translated, *the outside of* the noun with which it agrees:—Ūtanweard þeóh *femur*, Wrt. Voc. i. 44, 62. Fram ðæm mūþan ūtanweardum, Chr. 893; Erl. 88, 32. Hlǽw ymbehwearf ūtanweardne, Beo. Th. 4583; B. 2297. Ūtaweard fingeres *extremum digiti*, Lk. Skt. Lind. 16, 24. ¶ adverb:—Ūtaword *deforis*, Mt. Kmbl. Lind. 23, 25, 26: Lk. Skt. Rush. 11, 39. [*Icel.* ūtan-verðr.] v. ūte-, ūt-weard.

ūt-cwealm, es; *m. Utter destruction*:—Ūtcualm *internicium bellum dicitur, quo nullus remanet*, Wrt. Voc. ii. 111, 83.

ūt-cymen. v. ūtan-cumen.

ūt-drǽf, e; *f. Ejection, expulsion*:—Ðā onscunode se Eádsige Aðelwold, and ealle ða munecas ðe on ðam mynstre wǽron, for ðære ūtdrǽfe ðe hē gedyde wið hī, Homl. Skt. i. 21, 85.

ūt-drǽfere, es; *m. One who drives out*:—Ūtdrǽfere *exterminator*, ūt ādrifen *exterminatus*, Wrt. Voc. i. 51, 45.

ūte; *adv. Outside, without.* I. where there is motion to the outside:—Ne com se here oftor eall ūte of ðǽm setum ðonne tuwwa, Chr. 894; Erl. 90, 19. Ðæt hē up heonon ūte mihte cuman, Cd. Th. 27, 10; Gen. 415. Mōste ic ūte weorþan, 23, 34; Gen. 369. I a. fig. with the idea of degradation, *out, from one's position*:—Būtan ðām ānum ðe for heora leahtrum of hyra endebyrdenesse ūtor (uttor, Wells Fragm.) āscofene synd *exceptis his quos abbas degradaverit*, R. Ben. 115, 9. I b. *out, into another's possession*:—Wearð ðæt land ūte and hæfdon hit cynegas *ablatum est in manibus regum*, Chart. Th. 271, 27. II. *on the outside*:—Ic eom ūte *ego foris sum*, Ælfc. Gr. 38; Zup. 242, 5. (1) *outside* a house, any enclosed place, etc.:—Petrus sæt ūte (*foris*) on ðam cafertūne, Mt. Kmbl. 26, 69: Lk. Skt. 1, 10. Tō ðām wīggendum ðe ðǽr unrōte ūte (*outside the tent*) wǽron, Judth. Thw. 25, 29; Jud. 284. Gē standaþ ðǽr ūte (uuta, Lind. *foris*), Lk. Skt. 13, 25: Jn. Skt. 18, 16: 20, 11: Bd. 2, 12; S. 513, 30: Blickl. Homl. 201, 18: 217, 35. His līchoma wæs ūte bebyriged nēh cyricean *positum corpus ejus foras juxta ecclesiam*, 2, 3; S. 504, 31. Mycel menigu ymb hine sæt, and tō him cwǽdon: 'Hēr is ðīn mōdor ūte (*foris*),' Mk. Skt. 3, 32. (1 a) in a special sense. v. ūt, I. 1. *a* 3:—Sum copu is ðære wambe, ðæt ðone seócan monnan lysteþ ūtganges, and ne mæg ðonne hē ūte betȳned bið (*when he is at the closet*), Lchdm. ii. 236, 3. (1 b) *out, not residing* in a place:—Ðæt muneca gehwylc, ðe ūte sȳ of mynstre . . .; gebūge intō mynstre, L. Eth. 5, 5; Th. i. 306, 2. (1 c) in reference to persons:—Ðæt mōd mæg findan on innan him selfum ealle ða gōd ðe hit ūte sēcþ, Bt. 35, 1; Fox 154, 25. (1 d) where the locality is non-material:—Ðam ðe ūte synt ealle þing on bigspellum gewurþaþ, Mk.

Skt. 4, 11. Nū sind wē ūte belocene fram đam heofenlīcan leóhte, Homl. Th. i. 154, 13. Đǣr wæs Evan wōp ūte betȳned, Blickl. Homl. 7, 14. (2) *outside, on the outer side*:—Gē đæt ūte is calices geclǣnsiaþ, Lk. Skt. 11, 39. (3) *out, out of doors, in the open air*:—Se cyng hēt him ūte setl gewyrcean *rex, residens sub divo*, Bd. 1, 25; S. 486, 38. Hī slēpon ūte on trióWa sceadum, Bt. 15; Fox 48, 12: Met. 8, 27. Gnættas cōmon ofer eall đæt land, ge inne ge ūte, Ors. 1, 7; Swt. 36, 30. Ic seah wyhte twā ūte plegan, Exon. Th. 429, 10; Rä. 43, 2. (4) *out, away, at a distance*:—Úttor *exterius*, Ælfc. Gr. 38; Zup. 240, 7: Exon. Th. 426, 35; Rä. 41, 84. (4 a) *out, away from habitations, in open country*:—Hē ne mihte on đa ceastre gān, ac beón ūte (*foris*) on wēstum stōwum, Mk. Skt. 1, 45. On burgum beóþ blōstmum fægere, swā on eorđan hēg ūte on lande, Ps. Th. 71, 16. Hē genam hine æt eówde ūte be sceápum, 77, 69. (4 b) *out, from home on service*:—Hié wǣron simle healfe æt hām, healfe ūte, Chr. 894; Erl. 90, 18. Hī lāgon ūte ealne đone herfest on fyrdinge, 1006; Erl. 140, 9. (4 c) *out, not in one's own country, abroad*:—Him leófre wæs đæt hē ūte wunne đonne hē æt hām wǣre, Ors. 3, 7; Swt. 110, 30. (4 d) *out, away from land*:—Ān īgland đæt is ūte on đære sǣ, Chr. 895; Erl. 93, 24. Đā sǣton hié ūte on đam īglande, 918; Erl. 104, 11. Gefeaht Scipia wiđ Hannibal ūte on sǣ, Ors. 4, 11; Swt. 204, 36. (5) marking degree or extent:—Hī nānwuht ne magon ufor ne ūtor (*beyond*) findan, Bt. 34, 12; Fox 154, 16. Đām đe him đās woruld ūttor lǣtan, đonne đæt ēce līf, Exon. Th. 109, 28; Gū. 97. [*O. Sax. O. Frs.* ūta: *Icel.* ūti.] v. þǣr-ūte; ūt, ūtan.

ūtera; *cpve.* ūtemest, ūtmest; *spve. adj. Outer, outmost.* I. of position or order:—Seó ūtre wamb *venter*, Wrt. Voc. i. 45, 21. Gif đæt ūterre (ūttere, MS. B.: ūtre, MS. H.) bān biđ þyrel, L. Alf. pol. 44; Th. i. 92, 15. Hié forgeátan đara ūtera gefeohta *they forgot the foreign wars*, Ors. 2, 6; Swt. 88, 24. Wurpaþ hyne on đa ūttran (ūtteran, MS. A.: đǣm ūtmestum, Lind.) þȳstro *mittite eum in tenebras exteriores*, Mt. Kmbl. 22, 13: 25, 30 (wūtmestum, Lind.). Óđ tō ūtmeste *usque ad extremum*, Rtl. 55, 36. Đa ūtemestan đióda *the most distant nations*, Bt. 19; Fox 68, 29. In ūtmestum *in extremis*, Mk. Skt. Lind. 5, 23. II. *external, not of the inner man*:—Úre mann ūttra *noster homo exterior*, Scint. 53, 20. Hū se lāreów ne sceal đa inneran giémenne gewanian for đære ūterran ābisgunge (*exteriorum occupatione*), ne eft đa ūterran ne forlǣte hē for đære inneran . . . đȳ læs hē sié gehæft mid đam ūterran ymbhogan, Past. 18; Swt. 127, 8–14. For đære ūttran geornfulnesse woruldlīcra dǣda *pro industria exteriori*, Bd. 5, 13; S. 632, 8. Đætte wē swā lufigen đisne ūterran and đisne eorđlīcan fultum, Past. 50; Swt. 389, 2. Đa ūttran weorc wǣron behealden *exteriora opera observantur*, Bd. 1, 27; S. 494, 30: Scint. 60, 4. Þeáh hē mē đara ūterrena gewinna gefreóde, þeáh winnaþ wiđ mē đa inran unrihtlustas, Ps. Th. 15, 7: Past. 18; Swt. 139, 23. Đara ūterra weorca, Swt. 127, 12: 141, 8. Þeáh đe ic næbbe đa ūttran lāc, ic gemēte on mē sylfum hwæt ic lecge on weófode đīnre herunge, Homl. Th. i. 584, 15. [*O. Frs.* ūtera: *O. H. Ger.* ūzero.] v. innera.

ūter-mere, es; *m. Outer-sea, open sea*:—Hié forfōron him đone mūđan on ūtermere, Chr. 897; Erl. 95, 22. [Cf. *Icel.* ūt-sjár.]

ūte-weard; *adj. Outward, extreme*; may sometimes be translated *on the outside of, at the extremity of*, the noun to which it refers; sometimes is used substantively, *the outward part, extremity*:—Úteweard (dǣl) *crepido*, Wrt. Voc. i. 34, 27. Se munt is mycel ūteweard *the hill presents a large surface*, Blickl. Homl. 207, 26. iiii mīla fram đæm mūđan ūteweardum *four miles from the outside of the mouth*, Chr. 893; Erl. 88, 32. Đā gefēngon hié đara þreóra tū æt đæm mūđan ūteweardum, 897; Erl. 95, 26. Hē sȳ onfangen on ūteweardre endebyrdnesse *in ultimo gradu recipiatur*, R. Ben. 53, 11. Hē đencđ on đam oferbrǣdelse his mōdes . . . Ac on ūteweardum his mōde hē liéhđ him selfum, Past. 9; Swt. 55, 18–24. Heó hafaþ langne wyrtruman and đone ūteweardne sweartne *it has a long root, and that black on the outside*, Lchdm. i. 304, 2. Đū smītst his blōd ofer ūtewerd Aarones swȳđre eáre *sanguinem ejus pones super extremum auriculae dextrae Aaron*, Ex. 29, 20. Úteweard nosterle *pinnulae*, Wrt. Voc. i. 43, 22. Smyra đa eágan ūtewarde, Lchdm. i. 374, 10. ¶ with preps. forming prepositional or adverbial phrases:—Đes eard (*England*) nis swā mægenfæst hēr on ūteweardan đære eorđan brādnysse, Homl. Skt. i. 13, 107. Gif munuc eáđhylde biþ, þeáh hine man wācne and unweorđne talige and an ūteweardum forlǣte and tō ūteweardum medemige *si omni vilitate vel extremitate contentus sit monachus*, R. Ben. 29, 4. [*O. Frs.* ūta-werd.] v. ūtan-, ūt-weard.

ūt-fær, es; *n. A going out, egress, exit*:—Útfær *egressio*, Ps. Lamb. 18, 7. On ūtfære *in exitu*, 73, 5. Đæt wē symle đone mǣran gylt forfleón þurh ūtfære đæs læssan, Homl. Th. i. 484, 8. Đeáh heó nān ūtfær ne gemēt, 410, 10. On ūtfærum heora *in egressibus suis*, Ps. Lamb. 143, 13.

ūt-færeld, es; *n. A going out*:—*Exodus* on Grēcisc, *exitus* on Lȳden, ūtfæreld on Englisc, Ex. Thw. tit. Útfæreld his fram Fæder *egressus ejus a Patre*, Hymn. Surt. 44, 17. Hī ǣr Moyse and hys folce đæs ūtfæreldes wyrndon, Ors. 1, 7; Swt. 38, 19. Útfæreld *exitum*, Ælfc. Gr. 30; Zup. 193, 8. Ne fare hē ūt tō gefeohte ne him nān man ūtfæreld beóde (*he is not to be called upon to leave home*), Deut. 24, 5.

ūt-faru, e; *f. A going out, going abroad* or *out of doors*:—Đæt nān neód ne sȳ munecum ūtan tō farenne, for đȳ đe seó ūtfaru nān þing ne framaþ hira sāulum *ut non sit necessitas monachis vagandi foris quia omnino non expedit animabus eorum*, R. Ben. 127, 8. [*Icel.* ūt-för.]

ūt-fōr, e; *f. A going out* from the body, *an evacuation*:—Be drencum and ūtfōrum, Lchdm. ii. 14, 30.

ūt-fūs; *adj. Ready to sail*:—Þǣr æt hȳđe stōd hringedstefna ūtfūs, Beo. Th. 65; B. 33.

ūt-gang, es; *m. A going out, exit, egress*:—*Exitus, finis, effectus, terminus, egressus* ūtgong, endestæf, Wrt. Voc. ii. 144, 83. Útgang *egressio*, Ps. Spl. 18, 6: *exitus*, 118, 136. (1) *a going out* of a place, *egress, exit*:—Nā đæt hē Criste ūtganges rȳmde, Homl. Th. i. 222, 9. Be ūtgonge (*egressu*) folces of Ægypta lande, Bd. 4, 24; S. 598, 11. Đū mē ne dēst tō ūtgonge ic ne mæg *you will not make me go out, and I cannot*, Shrn. 141, 21. Útgang đīnne and ingang Dryhten gehealde *Dominus custodiat introitum tuum et exitum tuum*, Ps. Th. 120, 7. Þurh earmlīcne deáþ and þurh sārlīcne ūtgang đæs mānfullan līfes, Guthl. 2; Gdwin. 14, 21. Útgang heonan, Exon. Th. 282, 10; Jul. 661. (1 a) *the right of egress*:—Ingong and ūtgong, Chart. Th. 578, 26. (2) *a coming out* from a position within a body:—Lǣcedōmas wiđ þearmes ūtgange, and wiđ bæcþearmes ūtgange, Lchdm. ii. 170, 27, 29. (2 a) in a special sense, *evacuation* of the body:—Sum coþu is đære wambe đæt đone seócan monnan lysteþ ūtganges, Lchdm. ii. 236, 3. (3) in reference to time, *the going out* of a period, *the conclusion, end*:—Se ǣresta Mōnandæg æfter ūtgange đæs mōnþes Decembris *the first Monday after December has gone out*, Lchdm. iii. 76, 18. (4) *a place by which anything comes out, an exit, passage*:—On ūtgange burnan *in exitus aquarum*, Ps. Th. 106, 34. Næfđ ūtgang sió stōw, Lchdm. ii. 218, 17. (4 a) in a special sense, of part of the body:—*Viscera* inilve, *meatis* ūtgang, *anus* bæcþearm, Wrt. Voc. i. 283, 59. Đa swylas đe beóđ on mannes handum ođđe on ōþrum limum ođđe ymb đone ūtgang, Lchdm. i. 356, 17: 364, 20. (4 b) *a privy*. Cf. forþ-gang:—In ūtgeong ł in feltūn (innun ūtgongum, Rush.) *in secessum*, Mk. Skt. Lind. 7, 19. (5) *what comes out* of a body, *an evacuation*:—Sceáwige mon hwylc se ūtgang sié þe micel þe lytel, Lchdm. ii. 218, 12: 200, 1: 220, 6. Gesceáwa ǣlce dæge đæt đīn ūtgong and micge sié gesundlīc, 226, 20, 22. Be đære coþe đe se mon his ūtgang þurh đone mūđ him fram weorpe, 236, 12. Næs þurh đa micgean āne ac eác þurh ōþerne ūtgang, 250, 11. [*O. Frs.* ūt-gong: *O. H. Ger.* ūz-gang *exitus, egressus, eventus; diarria, dysenteria*: *Icel.* ūt-gangr, -ganga *a going out; a passage*.] v. ūt-geng.

ūt-gārsecg, es; *m. The ocean at the horizon, the ocean at a distance from land.* v. ūt, II. 2:—Tungol (*the sun*) on ǣfenne ūtgārsecges grundas pæþeþ *the sun at even holds its way beneath the depths of utmost ocean*, Exon. Th. 350, 29; Sch. 70. [Cf. *Icel.* ūt-haf.]

ūt-gefeoht, es; *n. Foreign war*:—Đætte Bryttas sume tīd gestildon fram ūtgefeohte *ut Brittones, quiescentibus ad tempus exteris bellis*, Bd. 1, 22; S. 485, 11.

ūt-gemǣre, es; *n. An extreme boundary*:—Of eorđan ūtgemǣrum *a finibus terrae*, Ps. Th. 60, 1. Óþ đysse eorđan ūtgemǣru *ad terminos orbis terrae*, 71, 8.

ūt-geng, es; *m.* (or? -genge, an; *f.* v. genge) *An outlet, exit*:—Tō ūtgengum weogas *ad exitus viarum*, Mt. Kmbl. Rush. 22, 9. [Cf. *Icel.* ūt-ganga; *wk. f.*] v. ūt-gang.

ūt-healf, e; *f. The outside, exterior*:—Úthealf đæs beddes *sponda* (v. sponda, est exterior pars lecti, 242, col. 2), Wrt. Voc. i. 41, 28. [Cf. *Icel.* ūt-hālfa *the outskirts*.]

ūt-here; *gen.* -her(i)ges; *m. A foreign army*:—Se here fērde swā hē sylf wolde, and seó fyrding dyde đære landleóde ǣlcne hearm, đet him nāđor ne dohte ne innhere ne ūthere, Chr. 1006; Erl. 140, 13. Đa scipu sceoldan đisne eard healdan wiđ ǣlcne ūthere, 1009; Erl. 141, 25.

ūþgendra. v. next word.

ūþ-genge; *adj. Fugitive, transitory, not to be retained, passing out of one's possession*:—Se ēþel ūđgenge wearđ Adame and Euan, eardrīca cyst beorht ōđbrōden *that country could no more be held by Adam and Eve, the choicest realm was taken away from them*, Exon. Th. 153, 12; Gū. 824. Đǣr wæs Æschere feorh ūđgenge *there life fled from Aschere*, Beo. Th. 4253; B. 2123. Đæs ēđel wǣre ēce tō gelȳfanne on heofonum, nalæs on eorþlīcre frætwædnysse, on gewītendre and on ūþgengre *cujus sedes aeterna non in vili et caduco metallo, sed in coelis esset credenda*, Bd. 3, 22; S. 552, 20. Đæt hié ne āstigan on ofermēdu, ne ūþgendra (-gengra?) welena tō wel ne truwodon, Blickl. Homl. 185, 14. [Cf. *Goth.* unþa- *in* unþa-þliuhan *to escape*.]

ūt-hleáp, es; *n. The fine for allowing a culprit to escape* (cf. L. In. 36; Th. i. 124, 14):—Údleáp, Chart. Th. 411, 30: 359, 3 (*printed* -leaw). The word occurs in a list of privileges granted by the king.

ūþ-mǣte; *adj. Immense, very great*:—Đǣr hangade ūþmǣte leóhtfæt, byrnende dæges and nihtes ofer đara Drihtnes fōta swađa (cf. Hangaþ đǣr eác bufan đǣm lāstum geregnod swīþe mycel leóhtfæt . . . and biđ ā dæges and nihtes byrnende, Blickl. Homl. 127, 29), Shrn. 81, 17.

ūþ-wita, -weota, an; *m. A person distinguished for wisdom* or *learning* in general or in a special branch, *a philosopher, scribe, geo-*

metrician, etc.:—Se gomola, eald úðwita (cf. fród fæder, módsnottor, 300, 4; Fä. 1), Exon. Th. 304, 6; Fä. 66. Úðweota *a councillor, senator*, Andr. Kmbl. 2211; An. 1107. Úðuuta *philosophus*, Wrt. Voc. ii. 117, 24. Cato wæs openlíce úþwita, Bt. 19; Fox 70, 8: Met. 10, 50. Epicurus se úþwita, Bt. 24, 3; Fox 84, 21. Úre úþwita Plato, 33, 3; Fox 126, 35: 35, 1; Fox 156, 9: Met. 22, 54. Úðwita *sophista*, Ælfc. Gr. 7; Zup. 24, 8. Gleáwum úðwitum and getincgum *gymosophistis et rhetoribus*, úðwita *gymnosophista*, Hpt. Gl. 479, 6–9. Án swíþe wís mon ongan fandigan ánes úþwitan and hine bismerode, for ðam hé hine swá orgellíce up áhóf and bodode ðæs ðe hé úðwita (*philosophus*) wǽre; ne cýðde hé hit mid nánum cræftum . . . Ðá wolde se wísa mon his fandigan, hwæðer hé swá wís wǽre swá hé self wénde ðæt hé wǽre, Bt. 18, 4; Fox 66, 27–33. Án úðuutta *unus scriba*, Mt. Kmbl. Lind. 8, 19. Úðwitan *sophistae*, Hpt. Gl. 449, 46. Ðá clypode se apostol ðone úðwitan Graton, Homl. Th. i. 60, 31. Ðæs ðe ús secgaþ béc, ealde úðwitan (*historians*), Chr. 937; Erl. 115, 18: *astronomers*, Menol. Fox 329; Men. 166. Úþwitan (*philosophers*) secgaþ ðæt sió sáwul hæbbe ðrió gecynd, Bt. 33, 4; Fox 132, 3: Met. 20, 184: Homl. Skt. i. 1, 96. Úðweotan (*the Jewish scribes and elders*), Elen. Kmbl. 943; El. 473. Úðwuta *scribae*, Mt. Kmbl. Lind. 15, 1. Úðuta (-wutu, Rush.), Mk. Skt. Lind. 1, 22. Úðwutto (-wuta, Rush.), Lk. Skt. Lind. 22, 66. Swá swá úþwitena gewuna is *ut geometrae solent*, Bt. 34, 4; Fox 138, 28. Sume of úðuutum (-wutum, Rush.) *quidam de scribis*, Mk. Skt. Lind. 7, 1. Wǽ iúh uuðutum, Mt. Kmbl. Lind. 23, 29. Ic sende tó iúh wítgo and snotre menn and úðuto (*scribas*), 23, 34. Úðwiotan his *seniores suos*, Ps. Surt. 104, 22: 118, 100. [Magy wærenn uþwitess swíþe wise, Orm. 7083.]

úþ-witian; *p.* ode *To study philosophy*:—Ic úðwitige oððe ic smeáge embe wísdóm *philosophor*, Ælfc. Gr. 25; Zup. 146, 2.

úþ-witigung, e; *f. The study of philosophy, philosophy*:—Ðæt heó on woruldwýsdóme wǽre getogen æfter Grécíscre úðwytegunge . . . Heó þeáh on wísdóme and on úðwytegunge, Homl. Skt. i. 2, 20–23. Befæst tó woruldlícre láre and tó úðwitegunge, 4, 185. Hé cwæð him tó: 'Nú ic hæbbe ðé oferðogen on úðwitegunge.' Se biscop him andwyrde: 'God forgeáfe ðæt ðú úðwitegunge beeodest,' Homl. Th. i. 448, 34: Homl. Skt. i. 3, 210.

úþ-witlíc; *adj. Philosophical*:—Ðære úðwitlícan *acathemice*, Wrt. Voc. ii. 79, 10. Ðære úðwiottelícan, 9, 13. Ða úþwitlícan *gymnica*, 91, 21: 41, 39. Úþwitlícum *gimnicis artibus*, 42, 34.

útian; *p.* ode *To put out*. (1) *to put* a person *out* of a place, *to expel, remove*:—Ðæt ǽnig man ciricþén ne útige búton biscopes geþehte, L. Eth. v. 10; Th. i. 306, 28. Gif man preóst of circan on unriht útige, L. N. P. L. 22; Th. ii. 294, 2. (2) *to put* a thing *out* of one's possession, *to alienate*:—Gif preóst ciricþingc útige, L. N. P. L. 27; Th. ii. 294, 14. Úttige, Cod. Dip. Kmbl. iv. 208, 10. [*O. Frs.* útia: *O. H. Ger.* úzôn *to put out*.] v. ge-útian.

út-irnende; *adj. Running out of the body*. (1) of medicine, *purging, purgative*:—Wyrtdrenc ðe ne bið útyrnende, Lchdm. ii. 282, 9: 170, 25. Sele him wyrtdrenc útyrnende, 280, 17. Útyrnendne, 336, 1. Mid swelcum útyrnendum drencum, 222, 25: 82, 17. (2) of a disease, *diarrhoeic*:—Ðisse ádle fruman mon mæg gelácnian on ða ilcan wísan ðe ða útyrnendan, Lchdm. ii. 232, 17. (3) of persons, *suffering from diarrhoea* or *dysentery*:—Hú mon ða útyrnendan men scyle lácnian, Lchdm. ii. 278, 16. v. út-ryne, *and next word*.

út-irning, e; *f. A flux*:—In útiorningc (úttiornende, Rush.) blódes *in profluuio sanguinis*, Mk. Skt. Lind. 5, 25.

út-lád, e; *f. Carriage out* of a place, *the right to carry things out* of a place:—Mid inláde and mid útláde *cum inductione et eductione*, Cod. Dip. Kmbl. iv. 209, 5.

út-lǽs, we; *f. Out-pastures, pasture-land away from the house*:—Seó útlǽs, Cod. Dip. Kmbl. vi. 214, 14, 21.

út-laga, an; *m. An outlaw*:—Útlaga *exlex*, Ælfc. Gr. 9, 62; Zup. 70, 5: *exul*, 9, 10; Zup. 39, 14: Wrt. Voc. i. 50, 58: 74, 26. Hé scel beón útlaga wið mé, Wulfst. 296, 10. Útlagen (-an? -ne?) *extorrem*, Hpt. 412, 73. Se ðe Godes útlagan hæbbe on gewealde, L. Eth. ix. 42; Th. i. 350, 1. Wé beódaþ ðæt útlagan Godes and manna of earde gewítan, L. C. S. 4; Th. i. 378, 11. Riht is ðæt ða útlagan weorþan, ðe tó Godes rihte gebúgan nellan, Wulfst. 269, 5. Útlagan *exules*, Hymn. Surt. 5, 25. [*Icel.* út-lagi.] v. út-lah.

út-lagian; *p.* ode *To outlaw, banish, proscribe*:—Útlagode mann Ælfgár eorl, Chr. 1055; Erl. 189, 3: 1069; Erl. 207, 7. Norðhymbra útlagodon heora eorl Tostig, 1064; Erl. 194, 14. Wið ðam ðe hí ǽfre ǽlcne Denisc[n]e cyning útlagede of Englalande gecwǽdon, 1014; Erl. 150, 15. [*Icel.* út-lægja *to banish*.] v. ge-útlagian.

út-lagu (?), e; *f. Outlawry*:—Útlaga, L. C. S. 13 tit.; Th. i. 382, 17. Æt eallan utlaga (-an? v. út-lah, III) þingan *de omnibus utlarie rebus*, W. ii. 3; Th. i. 489, 20.

út-lah; *adj. Out-lawed*; substantively, *an outlaw*. I. of a person in respect to his own country:—Gif hé man tó deáðe gefylle, beó hé útlah, L. E. G. 6; Th. i. 170, 10: L. Edg. H. 3; Th. i. 258, 19: L. Eth. i. 1; Th. i. 282, 15: L. C. S. 49; Th. i. 404, 11: Chr. 1048; Erl. 180, 3. Sý hé útlah (-laga, MS. B.), L. C. S. 45; Th. i. 400, 18. Se ðe útlages weorc gewyrce (cf. *Icel.* göra útlaga verk), 13; Th. i. 382, 18. Gif hwá ámánsodne oþþe útlahne (ámánsumodne oþþe útlagene, MS. B.) hæbbe and healde, 67; Th. i. 410, 18. Se cyng cwæð hine útlage and ealle his suna, Chr. 1052; Erl. 181, 10. I a. where it is stated with respect to whom one is an outlaw:—Beó hé útlah wið God and ámánsumod fram eallum Cristendóme, Chart. Erl. 231, 15: Wulfst. 271, 24. Sý hé útlah (-laga, MS. B.) wið God and wið men, L. C. S. 39; Th. i. 398. 25. Beó se þeóf útlah wið eall folc, L. Eth. i. 1; Th. i. 282, 9: L. C. S. 30; Th. i. 394, 24. II. of a person in respect to a country not his own:—Hí ǽfre ǽlcne Deniscne cyng útlah of Englalande gecwǽdon, Chr. 1014; Erl. 150, 33. Ælc ðara landa ðe ǽnigne friðige ðæra ðe Ænglaland hergie beó hit útlah wið ús and wið ealne here, L. Eth. ii. 1; Th. i. 284, 18. Gif heora menn sleán úre ǽhta, ðonne beóð hý útlage ge wið hý ge wið ús, ii. 7; Th. i. 288, 10. III. *calling for outlawry*:—Gif se Englisca beclypaþ Frenciscne mid útlagan þingan *si Anglicus appellet Francigenam de utlagaria*, W. ii. 3: Th. i. 489, 22. [*Icel.* út-lagr, út-laga.]

út-land, es; *n.* I. *a foreign country*:—Hé ðíne gemǽru gemiclade, ðú on útlandum áhtest sibbe *qui posuit fines tuos pacem*, Ps. Th. 147, 3. II. *out-lying land*. v. in-land. [Outlandes *foreign lands*, Mand. F. 3212: *Icel.* út-lönd *foreign countries; the outlying fields*.]

út-lenda, an; *m. A foreigner, stranger, not a native*. v. in-lenda:—Útlenda *extorris, alienus*, Hpt. Gl. 415, 76: exul, i. *peregrinus, alienus*, Wrt. Voc. ii. 146, 27. *Exterres*, i. *exules, peregrini* útlendan, *extranei* wreccean, 146, 5. v. next word.

út-lende; *adj. Foreign, strange, not native*:—Útlende ic eom and ælðeódig *advena ego sum et peregrinus*, Ps. Spl. 38, 17. Iacob útlænde (*accola*) wæs on eorðan Cham, 104, 21. Hé mǽnde be his feóndum ǽgðer ge inlendum ge útlendum, Ps. Th. 2, arg. [*O. H. Ger.* úz-lenti *exul*: *Icel.* út-lendr *foreign*.]

út-lendisc; *adj. Outlandish, foreign*; substantivally, *a stranger*:—Sí hé landes man, sí hé útlendisc (*peregrinus*), Lev. 24, 22. Ðǽr útlendisc man inlendiscan derie, L. O. D. 6; Th. i. 354, 28. Útlendisc *exul*, Ælfc. Gr. 9, 10; Zup. 39, 15. Útlendiscum *extraneo*, Scint. 193, 16. Hig noldon ðæt útlendiscum þeódum wǽre ðes eard þurh ðæt ðe swíðor gerýmed ðe hí heom sylfe ǽlc óðerne forfóre, Chr. 1052; Erl. 184, 31. Hé útlændisce hider in tihte, 959; Erl. 121, 3. [*Icel.* út-lenzkr *foreign*.]

út-líc; *adj. External, foreign*:—For ermþo ðære útlecan underþeódnesse (*subjection to those without*), Bd. 4, 16; M. 308, 30. Hé his ðeóde fram útlícre hergunge (*ab externa invasione*) álýsde, 4, 26; S. 603, 20.

útmest, uton, úton. v. útere, witon, útan.

út-ryne, es; *m. A running out*:—Útrene (*excursus*) tó helle, Hymn. Surt. 44, 21. Ðæs blódes útryne, Lchdm. i. 294, 17. Is se útryne (*what runs out*) swilce blódig wæter, ii. 202, 1. Útryne *exitum*, Scint. 224, 6. Útrynas *exitus*, Blickl. Gl.: Ps. Spl. 106, 33. Útrinas, 106, 35. [*O. Frs.* út-rene.]

út-scyte, es; *n. An out-shoot, outlet, place where a stream* or *road runs into another*:—Be bróce óð Pippelriðiges útscyte, Cod. Dip. Kmbl. v. 330, 20. 'Faraþ tó wega útscytum' . . . Útscytas ðara wega sind áteorung woruldlícera weorca, Homl. Th. i. 526, 11–14.

út-scytling, es; *m. A stranger*:—Mid útscytlinge ne dó ðú rǽd *cum extraneo ne facias consilium*, Scint. 200, 4.

út-siht, e: -sihte, an; *f. Diarrhoea, dysentery*:—Útsiht *diarria*, blódig útsiht *dissenteria*, Wrt. Voc. i. 19, 52, 53: ii. 141, 3. Wið útsihte, Lchdm. i. 114, 6: iii. 18, 1: 46, 13. Wið útsihte; ðysne pistol se ængel bróhte tó Róme ðá hý wǽran mid útsihte micclum geswæncte, 66, 6. Tácn be útsihte, ii. 170, 18. Gyf hé on útsihte sý, i. 260, 24. Wespasianus gefór on útsihte *Vespasianus profluvio ventris mortuus est*, Ors. 6, 7; Swt. 262, 28. Æfter útsihtan, Lchdm. ii. 180, 25. For útsihtan, 254, 3: 276, 22. Þurh ða wambe útsihtan, 224, 5. Wið útsiht and wið ðæs innoðes ástyrunge, i. 254, 7: iii. 294, 7. Hé bið gód wið lengtenádle and wið útsiht (*contra dysenteriam et diarrhoeam*), L. Ecg. C. 38; Th. ii. 162, 23. v. mete-útsiht.

útsiht-ádl, e; *f. Diarrhoea, dysentery*:—Sió útsihtádl cymð manegum of tó miclum útgange, Lchdm. ii. 278, 7. Wið útsihtádle, 320, 11.

út-síþ, es; *m. A going out* (lit. or fig.); excessus, Ps. Lamb. 115, 2: exitium, Wrt. Voc. ii. 144, 84: Hpt. Gl. 503, 35. Gǽst útsíþes georn *the spirit eager for departure from this world*, Exon. Th. 178, 9; Gú. 1241. Nágon hwyrft ne swice, útsíþ ǽfre ða ðǽr in cumaþ *those who come in there never have return or escape, never egress*, 364, 31; Wal. 79.

út-wǽpnedmann, es; *n. A stranger, outsider*:—Hí útwǽpnedmonna freóndscipes ceápiaþ *externorum sibi virorum amicitiam comparent*, Bd. 4, 25; S. 601, 18.

út-wærc, es; *m. Dysentery, painful evacuation*:—Se útwærc, Lchdm. ii. 278, 4. Wyrð ðæt tó útwærce, 278, 15. Wiþ útwærce, 174, 1: 234, 30: 276, 20.

út-waru, e; *f. Defence away from home*:—Gif ceorlisc man geþeó ðæt hé hæbbe .v. hída landes tó cynges útware, L. Wg. 9; Th. i. 188, 6: L. R. 3; Th. i. 190, 21.

út-weald, es; *m. An outlying wood*:—An útwalda, Cod. Dip. Kmbl. ii. 73, 36.

ût-weard; *adj. Outward, tending to the outside*:—Eoten wæs ûtweard, Beo. Th. 1526; B. 761. Dynt mid honde uutearde *alapam*, Jn. Skt. Lind. 18, 22. Wæs gesýne ðæt ða swaðo wǽron ǽrest ûtwearde ongunnen, Blickl. Homl. 207, 12. [*O. Frs.* ût-ward.] v. ûtan-, ûte-weard, *and next word*.

ût-weardes; *adv. Outwards, towards the outside*:—Suâ bið sió costung ǽresð on ðæm môde, and ðonne fēreþ ûtweardes tô ðære hýde, ôð ðæt nió ût âsciét on weorc, Past. 11; Swt. 71, 5.

ût-wîcing, es; *m. A foreign pirate*:—Hugo eorl wearð ofslagen innan Anglesêge fram ûtwîkingan, Chr. 1098; Erl. 235, 6.

W

wâ. I. *adv. Woe, ill*:—Ða mē grame wǽron and mē wâ dydon (cf. *Goth.* wai-dêdja), Ps. Th. 118, 38. (1) with dat. of person:—Ðē byþ ǽfre wâ *it shall be ever ill with thee*, Nicod. 26; Thw. 14, 12: Beo. Th. 369; B. 183: Exon. Th. 444, 25; Kl. 52: Blickl. Homl. 61, 2. Him biþ æt heortan wâ, Salm. Kmbl. 210; Sal. 104. Him wæs ǽghwǽr wâ, Cd. Th. 285, 24; Sat. 342. Bið ðam men full wâ, 40, 5; Gen. 634. Hî ne mihton âsecgan, hû wâ ðâm sâwlum byð, Wulfst. 147, 17. Ðæt him nǽfre ǽr nǽre swâ wâ swâ him ðâ wæs, 235, 19. Ne weorðe ðē nǽfre tô ðæs wâ, ðæt ðû ne wēne betran andergilde, Prov. Kmbl. 41. (2) with gen. of the source of ill;—Wæs gehwæþeres waa, Met. 1, 25. (3) with dat. of person, and (a) gen. of source:—Ðæm folce wæs ǽgþres waa, ge ðæt . . ., ge eác ðæt . . ., Ors. 3, 7; Swt. 114, 31. Him wæs gehwæðres wâ, ge . . . ge . . ., Elen. Kmbl. 1253; El. 628. (b) with a clause:—Him bið wâ on his môde, ðæt gē swâ ânrǽde beóð, Homl. Skt. i. 17, 167. Ðâ wæs ðam deófle waa on his môde, ðæt se man sceolde ða myrhðe geearnian, Hexam. 17; Norm. 24, 22. II. *interject.* (1) *woe, alas; vae*, (a) with dat. of person:—Wâ (wǽ, Lind. Rush.) ðam menn *uae homini illi*, Mk. Skt. 14, 21. Wâ eów ðe hlihaþ, Blickl. Homl. 25, 22. Wâ mē forworhtum, Exon. Th. 280, 20; Jul. 632. Waa ieów welegum, Past. 26; Swt. 181, 23. (b) with dat. of person and (*a*) gen. of cause of ill:—Wâ ðæs gestreónes ðam ðe his mǽst hafaþ, Wulfst. 45, 19. Wâ heom ðæs wærscipes, 268, 19: Hy. 2, 6: Exon. Th. 393, 11; Rä. 12, 8. Wâ mē (*heu mihi*) ðære wyrde, Ps. Th. 119, 5. (β) with preposition:—Wâ mânfullan (*ve impio*) for his misdǽdan, Wulfst. 45, 15. Wâ (wǽ, Lind.) ðysum middangearde þurh swicdômas *vae mundo a scandalis*, Mt. Kmbl. 18, 7. ¶ *combined with* lâ, wâ lâ, wâ lâ wâ. (1) *well-a-way, well-a-day* (*Laym.* wa la wa: *A. R. O. and N.* wo la wo: *Chauc.* wai la wai);—Wâ lâ! âhte ic mînra handa geweald, Cd. Th. 23, 32; Gen. 368. Wâ lâ ðære yrmðe and wâ lâ ðære woruld-scame, Wulfst. 163, 3. Wâ ûs lâ, Blickl. Homl. 153, 26. Wâ lâ wâ *eheu*, Wrt. Voc. ii. 32, 44. Wâ lâ wâ hû ic greów . . ., wâ lâ on hû micelre genihtsumnysse ic hwîlum wæs, Homl. Skt. ii. 30, 189–193. Wâ lâ wâ ðæt is sârlîc *heu, proh dolor!* Bd. 2, 1; S. 501, 14. Wâ lâ wâ ðæt ða ungesǽligan menn ne magon gebîdon hwonne hē him tô côme, Bt. 39, 1; Fox 212, 1. (2) expressing anger or contempt, *ah*; vah:—Wâ lâ wâ *euge, euge*, Ps. Lamb. 39, 16. Wâ ðæt ðes tôwyrpð Godes tempel, Mt. Kmbl. 27, 40. Wâ lâ (wǽ, Lind. Rush.) se tôwyrpð ðæt tempel *va qui destruit templum*, Mk. Skt. 15, 29. [*Goth.* wai *vae*: *O. Sax. O. H. Ger.* wē: *Icel.* vei.] v. wei; wâwa, weá.

waa, waac waad, waar. v. wâ, wâc, wâd, wâr.

wâc; *adj.* I. *yielding, not rigid, pliant, fluid*:—Waac *lentus*, Wrt. Voc. i. 61, 35. Wæter, wâc and hnesce (cf. ðæt hnesce and flôwende wæter, Bt. 33, 4; Fox 130, 3), Met. 20, 93. Wâc hreód ðe ǽlc hwiða windes mæg âwecggan, Past. 42; Swt. 306, 6. Gerd wâcc ł bifiende (hreád ðæt wagende, Rush.) *harundinem quassatam*, Mt. Kmbl. Lind. 12, 20. Byrhtnôð wand wâcne æsc (*the pliant ash-shaft*), Byrht. Th. 132, 68; By. 43. Iosue hî up âhēng on fîf wâcum bôgum *Iosue eos suspendit super quinque stipites*, Jos. 10, 26. II. *weak, feeble, wanting mental* or *moral strength, wanting courage*:—Wâc bið se hyrde funden tô heorde, ðe nele ða heorde ðe hē healdan sceal mid hreáme bewerian, L. C. E. 26; Th. i. 374, 22. Wâc bið ðæt geðanc on cristenum men, gif hē ne cann understandan þurh rihtne geleáfan ðæne ðe hine gescôp, Wulfst. 20, 9: Cd. Th. 40, 34; Gen. 649. On gewitte tô wâc, Andr. Kmbl. 423; An. 212. Ne tô wâc wiga, ne tô wanhýdig, Exon. Th. 290, 18; Wand. 67. Ðæt wæs wîglîc werod: wâc ne grētton in ðæt ringcetæl rǽswan herges, Cd. Th. 192, 18; Exod. 233. Ic, Ælfrîc, munuc and mæssepreóst, swâ þeáh wâccre ðonne swilcum hâdum gebyrige, Homl. Th. i. 2, 12. Hæfde hire wâcran hige Metod gemearcod, Cd. Th. 37, 16; Gen. 590. Sume lâreówas sindon beteran ðonne sume; sume sind wâccran, swâ swâ wē beóð, Homl. Th. ii. 48, 17. III. *poor, mean, not of great value* or *in high esteem*; vilis. v. wâc-lîc, -ness:—Mid wâces olfendes hǽrum gescrýdde, Homl. Th. ii. 506, 23. Ðone wâcan assan hē geceás, i. 210, 15. ii forealdode rǽdingbēc swîðe wâke, and .i. wâc mæssereáf, Chart. Th. 430, 31. Hē ðis wâce forlēt, lîf ðis lǽne, Chr. 975; Erl. 124, 31: Exon. Th. 53, 25; Cri. 856. Swâ tealte beóð eorðan dreámas, and swâ wâce syndan ǽhta mid mannum, Wulfst. 264, 4. Ða wâcan fugelas, Homl. Th. ii. 462, 25. Hwî forgifð God ðâm wâcum wyrtum swâ fægerne wlite, 464, 16. Hwî dēst ðû ðē sylfe ðurh wâce þeáwas swilce ðû wyln sý, Homl. Skt. i. 8, 44. Hit is on worulde â swâ leng swâ wâcre; men syndon swicole, and woruld is ðe wyrse, Wulfst. 83, 10. Seó stôw (*Abingdon*) næs wâccere ðonne (*inferior to*) formænig ðara ðe his yldran ǽr gefyrþredon, Lchdm. iii. 438, 11. Ælc man sylð on forandæge his gôde wîn, and ðæt wâccre ðonne ða gebeóras druncniaþ, Homl. Th. ii. 70, 26. Gedroren is ðeós duguð eal, wuniaþ ða wâcran, Exon. Th. 311, 4; Seef. 87. Fyrmest manna *primas*, wâcost manna *infimas*, Ælfc. Gr. 9, 25; Zup. 50, 3. Ne eart ðû wâcost (*minima*, Mt. 2, 6) burga, Homl. Th. i. 78, 14. On reáfe wâccust *habitu vilissimus*, Scint. 21, 7. Hwî wênst ðû, ðonne nû ða wâcestan gesceafta eallunga ne gewîtaþ, ðæt seó seóleste gescaft mid ealle gewîte? Shrn. 198, 19. [*O. Sax.* wêk: *O. H. Ger.* weih *lentus, mollis, liquens, imbecillis, debilis*: *Icel.* veikr.] v. leoþu-, wund-wâc.

wâc, es; *n. A weakness*:—Nyste ic on ðâm þingum ðe ðû ymbe specst fûl ne fâcn, ne wâc ne wom tô ðære dæigtîde ðe ic hit ðē sealde, ac hit ǽgðer wæs ge hâl ge clǽne bûton ǽlcon fâcne, L. O. 9; Th. i. 182, 3.

wacan; p. wôc; pp. wacen *To wake*; but occurring mostly in the sense *to come into being, be born, spring*:—Sió mǽgburg ðe ic æfter wôc *the family from which I sprang*, Exon. Th. 401, 34; Rä. 21, 21. Abrahame wôc bearn of brýde *to Abraham a child was born of his wife*, Cd. Th. 167, 10; Gen. 2763: Beo. Th. 3925; B. 1960. Of ðam eorle wôc unrîm þeóda, Cd. Th. 99, 15; Gen. 1646: 98, 29; Gen. 1637: Beo. Th. 2535; B. 1265. Ðæm feówer bearn in worold wôcun, 119; B. 60. Wôcon, Cd. Th. 131, 31; Gen. 2184. Þanon his eaforan wôcan, bearn from brýde, 65, 5; Gen. 1061. Ǽr him sunu wôce, 70, 25; Gen. 1158. [He awoc (woc, 2nd MS.) of slæpe, Laym. 25566. Ðe king woc, Gen. and Ex. 2111. Aboute þe middel of þe nith wok Ubbe, Havel. 2093.] v. â-, on-wacan.

wacan *a watch*. v. wacen.

wâce; *adv. Weakly*. (1) *feebly, faintly, without boldness*:—Ic mînum gewyrhtum wâce trûwige *I have feeble trust in my own merits*, Anglia xii. 502, 9: Exon. Th. 52, 24; Cri. 838. (2) *feebly, inefficiently, without energy, remissly*:—Nû syndon cyrcan wâce gegriðode *churches are very inefficiently protected*, L. I. P. 25; Th. ii. 340, 11. Wē tô wâce hýraþ ûrum Drihtne *we are too remiss in obedience to our Lord*, Wulfst. 91, 13: Exon. Th. 50, 13; Cri. 799. Wē rihte getrýwða healdaþ tô wâce *we are too remiss in keeping good faith*, Wulfst. 91, 17. Hî mîne heorde wâce begîmdon, 190, 21. Ic wâccor hýrde Dryhtne ðonne mîn rǽd wǽre, Exon. Th. 453, 18; Hy. 4, 16. Gif hē wâccor hý behwyrfð ðonne ðæt hē him tô âgenum teleþ, L. Edg. S. 1; Th. i. 272, 10. [*O. H. Ger.* weiho *enerviter*.]

wacen (-an, -on, -un), e; *f.* I. *wakefulness, sleeplessness*:—Ðone intingan ðînre unrôtnisse and ðînre wacone (wæcene, Bd. M. 128, 23) *tuae moestitiae et insomniorum causam*, Bd. 2, 12; S. 513, 41. II. *a watch, vigil*:—'Wel ðû dēst ðæt ðû nalæs ðē slǽpe forgeáfe, ac mâ woldest wæccan (weacenum, Bd. M. 354, 7) and gebedum ætfeolan.' Cwæþ hē: 'Ic wât ðæt mē ðæs is micel ðearf, ðæt ic hâlwendum weacenum ætfeole,' Bd. 4, 25; S. 601, 1–3. III. *a watch, a division of the night*:—Ðiú feórða waccen (feórþe ðære wacone, Rush.) *quarta vigilia*, Mt. Kmbl. Lind. 14, 25. Ymb ða feárða wacune (wacan, Lind.) *circa quartam uigiliam*, Mk. Skt. Rush. 6, 48. On ða æfterra wacone (waccane, Lind.) *in secunda uigilia*, Lk. Skt. Rush. 12, 38. IV. *a watch, guard*:—Haldende wacone (wacana, Lind.) næhtes *custodientes uigilias noctis*, 2, 8. V. *a rousing, an incitement*:—Wacana mægna *incitamenta virtutum*, Rtl. 63, 36. v. on-wacan; *f.*; wæcen.

wacian; p. ode *To watch, wake*:—Ic wacige *uigilo*, Ælfc. Gr. 41; Zup. 245, 10. (1) *to remain awake, not to sleep*:—Gif wē tô lange waciaþ, wē âteoriaþ, Homl. Th. i. 488, 34. Ic waecade *vigilavi*, Ps. Surt. 101, 8. Hwæðer hē wacode ðe slēpte, Bd. 2, 12; S. 513, 39. On middere nihte gewurdon on slǽpe Pictauienscisce bepǽhte, ðæt of ealre ðære menigu ân man ne wacode, Homl. Th. ii. 518, 26. Ealle oþþe hefige slǽpe swundon, oþþe tô synne wacedon *omnes aut somno torpent inerti, aut ad peccata vigilant*, Bd. 4, 25; S. 601, 12. Sceal se man wacyan ealle ða niht, ðe ðone drenc drincan wille, Lchdm. iii. 6, 4. (1 a) of the eye, *to be freed from obstruction, to open*:—Gif eágan forsetene beóð, genim hræfnes geallan . . . drýp on ðæt eáge . . . ðonne wacaþ ðæt eáge (*the eye opens again*), Lchdm. iii. 2, 24. (1 b) *to be alert*:—Se slâwa ongit hwæt him ryht bið tô dônne, swelce hē ealneg wacige, and swâ ðeáh hē âslâwaþ, for ðæm ðe hē nâwuht ne wyrcð *piger enim recte sentiendo quasi vigilat, quamvis nil operando torpescat*, Past. 39; Swt. 283, 7. Hē wecð hine selfne, ðæt hē wacie on ðære geornfulnesse gôdra weorca (*ut studio bonae actionis evigilent*), 64; Swt. 461, 14. Wacige, 461, 16. Ðæt heó mihte beón âcenned, and wacian, and ârîsan, and faran of stôwe tô ôþerre, Blickl. Homl. 19, 22. (2) *to keep one's self awake* or *alert* because there is special need of attention, *to watch, be on the watch, be on guard*:—Ic ðē tô wacie (waecio, Ps. Surt.) *ad te vigilo*, Ps. Th. 62, 1. In îdelnisse weciaþ ða haldaþ hié *in vanum vigilant qui custodiunt eam*, Ps. Surt. 126, 1. Gif hē wiste hwænne se þeóf cuman wolde, witodlîce hē wacude (*uigilaret*), Lk. Skt. 12, 39. Hine twēgen ymb weardas wacedon, Exon. Th. 109, 6; Gû. 86. Wacodon menn, swâ swâ hit gewunelîc is, ofer ân deád lîc, Homl. Skt. i. 21, 290: Blickl. Homl. 149, 6. Geheald hûsa sêlest, . . . waca wið wrâþum, Beo. Th. 1324; B. 660. Waciaþ (*vigilate*) and gebiddaþ eów, Mt. Kmbl. 26, 41. Wacigeaþ, 24, 42. Hê beóde ðam durewearde, ðæt hê wacige, Mk. Skt. 13, 34. Is micel ðearf ðæt se reccere geornlîce wacige (*solerter invigilet*), Past. 19; Swt. 141, 13. Ic bidde eów, ðæt gê wacian mid mê, Blickl. Homl. 139, 20. Ne mihtest ðû âne tîde wacian, Mk. Skt. 14, 37. Wacigean, Mt. Kmbl. 24, 43. Man sceal wacigean and warnian, Wulfst. 90, 2. Tô wacene *ad vigilandum*, Rtl. 85, 1. Ic stande ofer hig waciende (*vigilando*) for þeófan, Coll. Monast. Th. 20, 29. Hê wæs waciende on gebede *erat pernoctans in oratione*, Lk. Skt. 6, 12. Se þeów ðe hlâford fint wacigenne (*uigilantem*), Scint. 116, 9. Hyrdas wæ̂ron waciende and nihtwæccan healdende ofer heora heorda, Lk. Skt. 2, 8. (2 a) in a bad sense, *to watch, be on the watch* to injure:—Wacaþ se ealda, Fragm. Kmbl. 61; Leás. 32. [Þe herdes þe wakeden ouer here oref . . . were herdes wakiende and wittende here oref, O. E. Homl. ii. 31, 22–27. Ðus agen alle gode herdes to wakegen gostliche, 41, 5. Festen, wakien, A. R. 6, 8. His cnihtes wakeden alle nihte, Laym. 9859. Þat haveth fele nihtes waked, Havel. 2999. His liche was waked, Gen. and Ex. 2516. Þet uolk þet late louieþ to soupi, and to waki be niȝte, Ayenb. 52, 18. *O. Sax. O. L. Ger.* wakôn: *O. H. Ger.* wahhôn. Cf. *Goth.* wakan: *O. H. Ger.* wahhên: *Icel.* vaka.] v. â-, be-, morgen-, ofer-, þurh- (v. Blickl. Homl. 227, 7) wacian.

wâcian; *p.* ode. I. of persons, *to be* or *become weak, want resolution* or *courage*. v. wâc, II:—Ðonne se heretoga wâcaþ, ðonne biþ eall se here swîðe gehindred, Chr. 1003; Erl. 139, 12. Be ðam mihte man oncnâwan, ðæt se cniht nolde wâcian æt ðam wîge, Byrht. Th. 132, 2; By. 10. II. of things, *to be* or *become weak, not able to endure, to fail*:—Ne wâciaþ ðâs geweorc, Exon. Th. 351, 26; Sch. 86. Teoriaþ hwîlum, wâciaþ wordbeót, 469, 22; Hy. 11, 6. III. *to become poor* or *mean*. v. wâc, III:—Wachiaþ *vilescunt*, Hpt. Gl. 462, 52. [Þa ældede þe king and wakede an aðelan (failede his mihte, 2nd MS.), Laym. 2938. Heo weoren swa drunken, þ wakeden heore sconken, 13466. Bruttes wokeden (*lost heart*) þa, 26996. His heorte gon to wakien, 19798. Þi strengþe wokeþ, Misc. 101, 15. *Piers P.* wakie, wokie *to soften*: *O. H. Ger.* weihhên, weihhôn *infirmari, emarcescere*.] v. â-, ge-wâcian; wæ̂can.

wâc-lîc; *adj.* *Poor, mean, of little dignity* or *worth, paltry*. v. wâc, III:—Wâclîc *vilis*, Wrt. Voc. i. 28, 64: Hpt. Gl. 523, 74: *inutile, contemptum*, 470, 22. Ðû wilt habban ealle fægere ðing and âcorene, and wilt ðê sylf beón wâclîc and unwurð, Homl. Th. ii. 410, 20: 372, 8. Hwæþer ðæt nû sié tô talianne wâclîc and unnyt ðætte nytwyrþost is eallra ðissa woruldþinga? *num imbecillum, ac sine viribus aestimandum est, quod omnibus rebus constat esse praestantius?* Bt. 24, 4; Fox 86, 16. Wê mihton eów secgan âne lytle bysne, gif hit tô wâclîc næ̂re, Homl. Th. i. 40, 27. Wâclîc bið him swâ lytel tô sendenne, 400, 20. Hî wæ̂dliende on ânum wâclîcum wæ̂felse fêrdon, 62, 29. Him þûhte tô wâclîcre dæ̂de, ðæt hê fordyde hine æ̂nne, Homl. Ass. 96, 142. Ðæt gecynd ðe hî æ̂r wâclîc tealdon, Homl. Th. i. 38, 30. Manega Lazaras gê habbaþ. . . . Ðeáh ðe hî sȳn wâclîce geðûhte, 334, 30. Wudehunig and ôðre wâclîce ðigena, 352, 8. Sume men syllaþ cyrcan tô hȳre swâ swâ wâclîce mylna, Homl. Skt. i. 19, 249. On wâclîcum ðingum wîcnian *to perform menial offices*, ii. 170, 25. Wâclîcum *foedis*, Germ. 395, 78. Hî unræ̂dlîce fêrdon on heora îdelum lustum and wâclîcum gebæ̂rum, Ælfc. T Grn. 17, 16. [*Icel.* veik-ligr *vilis*.] v. un-wâclîc.

wâclîce; *adv.* I. *weakly, feebly*:—Wâclîce *enerviter*, Wrt. Voc. ii. 29, 32: *enerviter, turpiter*, 143, 56. II. *poorly, meanly, cheaply*:—Eówer reáf ne beó tô ranclîce gemacod, ne eft tô wâclîce, ac werige gehwâ swâ his hâde tô gebyrige, L. Ælfc. C. 35; Th. ii. 358, 7. Gehwam sceamaþ, gif hê galaðod bið tô woruldlîcum gyftum, ðæt hê wâclîce gescrȳd cume, Homl. Th. i. 528, 23. Wâclîcor *vilius*, R. Ben. Interl. 92, 4. *Diminutiva* syndon wanigendlîce . . . *bene* wel, and of ðam is *belle* nâ ealles swâ wel, *bellissime* ealra wâclîcost, Ælfc. Gr. 38; Zup. 231, 4. [Gif þu werest te wocliche, A. R. 294, 5. The poure þat beoð wacliche iȝeouen and biset uuele, H. M. 9, 18. *O. H. Ger.* weihlîcho *enerviter*.] v. un-wâclîce.

wâc-môd, *adj.* I. *of weak disposition, morally weak*:—Ða hnescan (*vel* wâcmôd, *written above the line*), ðæt synd ða ðe nâne stîðnysse nabbaþ ongeán leahtras, Homl. Skt. i. 17, 40. II. *faint-hearted, pusillanimous*:—Gif yrmð getîmaþ wâcmôd nâ wuna ðû *si calamitas contigerit, pusillanimis non existas*, Scint. 172, 6. Crist læ̂rde ðæt man tô wâcmôd (cf. Mt. 24, 6: Mk. 13, 7) ðonne ne wurde, Wulfst. 89, 6. On ôðre wîsan sint tô monianne ða ofermôdan, on ôðre wîsan ða earmheortan and ða wâcmôdan (*pusillanimes*), Past. 32; Swt. 209, 3. Beó hit eal mid gemete ðe læs ðe ða wâcmôdan beón ormôde *omnia mensurate fiant propter pusillanimes* (for ðâm wâcmôdum, R. Ben. Interl. 82, 7), R. Ben. 74, 1. Sȳ fultum geseald ðâm wâcmôdum and ðâm unstrangum, ðæt hî mid unrôtnesse ða hȳrsumnesse ne dôn *imbecillibus procurentur solacia, ut non cum tristitia hoc faciant*, 58, 17. Secgaþ ðâm wâcmôdum, ðæt hî beón gehyrte, and nânðing ofdræ̂dde *say to them that are of a fearful heart, Be strong, fear not* (Is. 35, 6), Homl. Th. ii. 16, 15. [*O. Sax.* wêk-môd.]

wâcmôdness, e; *f.* I. *weakness of character, moral weakness*:—Ðȳ læs sió scyld, ðe hiene costaþ, for his luste and for his wâcmôdnesse hine ofersuîðe *ne vitium, quod tentat, mollitie delectationis subigat*, Past. 13; Swt. 79, 22. II. *faintheartedness, want of courage, pusillanimity, cowardice*:—*Ignauia*, ðæt is wâcmôdnys, Wulfst. 52, 18. Se fîfta leahtor is unrôtnys ðissere worulde. Of ðam bið âcenned wâcmôdnys, . . . and his sylfes orwênnys, Homl. Th. ii. 220, 19. Of wâcmôdnesse and of unbieldo oððe of untrymnesse môdes oððe lîchoman *infirmitate*, Past. 21; Swt. 159, 1. Gedrêfde mid wâcmôdnesse *pusillanimitate turbatos*, 32; Swt. 213, 6. For wâcmôdnesse *from want of courage*, 40; Swt. 289, 3. Ongeán môdstaðolnysse and môdes strencðe se deófol sendeþ wâcmôdnesse and lyðerne earhscype, Wulfst. 53, 12. III. *weakness, feebleness*:—Sî foresceáwod wâcmôdnyss (*imbecillitas*), nateshwôn heom (*old men and children*) stîðnis regoles nâ sî gehealdan on fôdum, R. Ben. Interl. 68, 14. Untrumera wâcmôdnesse, 72, 3. [Cf. *O. H. Ger.* weih-môtî *pusillanimitas, teneritudo*.]

wâcness, e; *f.* *Meanness of condition, mean estate*; vilitas, v. wâc, III:—Horsþênes wâcnys (*printed* wænys) *mulionis vilitas*, Hpt. Gl. 438, 70. Mid ealre wâcnisse hylde *omni vilitate contentus*, R. Ben. Interl. 33, 14. Hwî forgifð God ðâm wâcum wyrtum swâ fægerne wlite, . . . bûton for ðan ðe wê sceolon mid wâcnysse and sôðre eádmôdnysse ða heofenlîcan fægernysse geearnian, Homl. Th. ii. 464, 18. Hî bæ̂don, ðæt ða gymstânas (*gems which had been pebbles before a miraculous change*) âwendon tô heora wâcnysse, i. 68, 19. [Þat te strengðe of þe helpe mi muchele wacnesse, O. E. Homl. i. 273, 14. Þe ueond þurh hire (*Eve's*) word understond hire wocnesse, A. R. 68, 6.]

-wacnian. v. â-, on-wacnian; wæcnan.

wacol (-ul, -el); *adj.* *Watchful, vigilant*:—Wacol *vigil*, Wrt. Voc. i. 75, 64. Wacul *vigil* vel *vigilans*, 46, 2. Ðes and ðeós wacole (-ele) *hic et haec uigil*, Ælfc. Gr. 9, 8; Zup. 39, 3. Ða ðe cariaþ mid wacelum môde hû hî ôðra manna sâwla Gode gestrȳnan, Homl. Th. ii. 78, 2. Gewinn wið ðone wacolan feónd, 560, 28. Wacele (-ole) beón on gôdum weorcum, Homl. Ass. 53, 86. Wacule (-ole), R. Ben. 2, 7. Môtan ða hyrdas beón swîðe wacole, Wulfst. 191, 12. *Uigilantius*, ðæt is on Englisc wacolre, Homl. Th. ii. 118, 13. [*O. H. Ger.* wachal *uigil*: *Icel.* vökull.] v. æ̂r-, þurh-wacol.

wacollîce; *adv.* *Watchfully, vigilantly*:—Hê (*Gregory*) wæs swîðe wacol on Godes bebodum, and hê wacollîce ymbe manegra ðeóda þearfe hogode, Homl. Th. ii. 118, 15.

wacon. v. wacen.

wacor; *adj.* *Watchful, vigilant*:—Se ðe wæ̂re slâpol, weorðe se ful wacor, Wulfst. 72, 14. Beó ðû wacor *esto vigilans*, Past. 58; Swt. 445, 20. Sint tô manienne ða ðe hiera synna onfunden habbaþ, ðætte hié mid wacore môde (*vigilanti cura*) ongieten . . ., 52; Swt. 405, 8. Ðonne môton ða hyrdas beón swîðe wacore, L. C. E. 26; Th. i. 374, 27: L. I. P. 6; Th. ii. 310, 27. [*Uigilaui*, ich was waker, seið Dauid, A. R. 142, 25. Wyþ þeoues þu most beo waker and snel, Misc. 97, 150. Wakyr *pervigil*, Prompt. Parv. 514. *O. H. Ger.* wachar *vigil, pervigil*: *Icel.* vakr *watchful, alert; nimble*.] v. eád-wacer; wæccer.

wacorlîce; *adv.* *Watchfully, vigilantly, carefully*:—Sint tô læ̂ranne ða ofersprǽcean ðæt hié wacorlîce (*vigilanter*) ongieten . . ., Past. 38; Swt. 277, 4. Ðonne ðæt môd wacorlîce stíereþ ðære sâwle *cum mens vigilanter animam regit*, 56; Swt. 433, 4. Is ûs swîðe wocorlîce tô geðenceanne *vigilanti consideratione pensandum est*, 49; Swt. 385, 24.

wacsan. v. wæscan.

wâc-scipe, es; *m.* *Remissness*:—Ðæt hî stȳran æ̂lcum ðara ðe ðis ne gelæ̂ste and mînra witena wed âbrecan mid æ̂nigum wâcscipe wille, L. Edg. S. 1; Th. i. 272, 7. Cf. wâce (2).

wacu *a waking, wake, watch.* [Heo hefde ileaned one wummone to one wake on of hore weaden, A. R. 314, 27. Heó haveþ daies care and nihtes wake, O. and N. 1590.] v. niht-wacu.

wâd, es; *n.* *Woad*, a plant much used for dyeing, which circumstance may account for the appearance of the word as a gloss to some of the following Latin words:—Ðis wâd *hic sandyx*, Ælfc. Gr. 9, 69; Zup. 72, 14. Wyrt oððe wâd *sandix* (the passage to which this gloss belongs is Vergil Eclogae, iv. 45, quoted by Aldhelm), Wrt. Voc. ii. 87, 33. Wâd *sandix*, i. 32, 6: 68, 70: 79, 42. Waad *fucus*, 32, 7. Dolhsealf. Genim wâdes croppan, Lchdm. ii. 94, 11. Of wâde ꝉ hæ̂wenre deáge *ex hyacintho* (cf. wâde *iacincto*, Anglia xiii. 29, 52. Cf. *O. H. Ger.* weitîn *iacinctus*), Hpt. Gl. 431, 26. Wið bryne, wâd wyl on buteran, smire mid, Lchdm. ii. 132, 1, *and see* i. 174, 1–5. Man mæg on hærfeste wâd spittan, Anglia ix. 261, 16. ¶ the growth of woad seems marked by the occurrence of the word in such forms as *wâd-beorh, wâd-denu, wâd-lond* in charters:—Of ðære dîc on wâdbeorgas; of wâdbeorgan, Cod. Dip. Kmbl. iii. 77, 15. Æt wâdbeorhe, 82, 29. On wâdbeorh; of wâdbeorhge, 232, 36. On wâddene; andlong wâddene, vi. 137, 12. Ðæt wâdlond, iii. 390, 17: 381, 5. [*O. Frs.* wêd: *O. H. Ger.* weit *sandix*.]

wadan; *p.* wôd, *pl.* wôdon; *pp.* waden *To go, pass, proceed.* I. of actual movement, (a) absolute:—Wôd wîges heard, . . . and wið ðæs beornes stôp, Byrht. Th. 135, 38; By. 130: 139, 13; By. 253. Brimmen wôdon, 140, 29; By. 295. Ðâ com hæleða þreát wadan, Andr. Kmbl.

2543; An. 1273. Gesión wadan wǣgflotan, Elen. Kmbl. 491; El. 246. (b) with prepositions:—Hit ðurh hrōf wadeþ, Salm. Kmbl. 824; Sal. 411. Ic wōd ofer waþema gebind, Exon. Th. 287, 34; Wand. 24. Wægn ne be grunde wōd, 404, 29; Rä. 23, 15. Hit ofer eall wōd and eode, Nar. 15, 22. Ðæt feórðe cyn wōd on wǣgstreám, Cd. Th. 197, 22; Exod. 311. Hē wōd þurh ðone wælrēc, Beo. Th. 5315; B. 2661. Hē wōd under wolcnum, 1432; B. 714. Wōdon wælwulfas west ofer Pantan, ofer scīr wæter, Byrht. Th. 134, 38; By. 96. Ðis leóhte beorht cymeþ ofer misthleoþu wadan ofer wǣgas, Exon. Th. 350, 9; Sch. 61. Gewāt him se æðeling wadan ofer wealdas, Cd. Th. 174, 30; Gen. 2886. On sǣ wadan, 51, 22; Gen. 830. Hē lēt his francan wadan þurh ðæs hysses hals, Byrht. Th. 135, 59; By. 140. (c) with acc. of the way traversed:—Gē wadaþ wīdlāstas, Andr. Kmbl. 1353; An. 677. Hē wōd (woð, MS.) geócrostne sīð, Cd. Th. 254, 23; Dan. 616. Wadan wræclāstas, 272, 17; Sat. 121: Exon. Th. 286, 23; Wand. 5. II. fig.:—Ða ðe on eallum ðingum wadaþ on hiora āgenne willan, and æfter hiora līchoman luste irnaþ, Bt. 41, 2; Fox 246, 23. Ða men ðe on eallum þingum wadaþ on heora āgenum willan, and on heora lustum heora līf āspendaþ, Homl. Skt. i. 17, 239. Ðæt seó wyrd on ðīnne willan wōde, Bt. 20; Fox 72, 19. [*O. Frs.* wada: *O. H. Ger.* watan: *Icel.* vaða.] v. an-, ge-, geond-, ofer-, on-, þurh-wadan.

wād-sǣd, es; *n. Woad-seed*:—Līnsēd sāwan, wādsǣd eác swā, Anglia ix. 262, 11.

wād-spitel *a woad-spade*, Anglia ix. 263, 6. v. spitel.

wadung, e; *f. Going, travelling*:—Ūs sceamaþ tō secgenne ealle ða sceandlīcan wīglunga ðe gē dwǣsmenn drīfaþ oððe on wīfunge oððe on wadunge (see, for instance, Lchdm. i. 328, 330, where the virtues of various parts of a badger in case of journeying are stated, and 102, ii. 154 for similar passages in reference to mugwort. Cf. also: Sind manega mid swā miclum gedwylde befangene, ðæt hī cēpaþ be ðam mōnan heora fær, Homl. Th. i. 100, 23), Homl. Skt. i. 17, 102.

wǣ, wæbb, wæbbung. v. wā, web, webbung.

wǣcan; *p.* wǣhte; *pp.* wǣht, wǣced *To weaken, afflict, oppress*:—Se forespecena hungur Bryttas swȳþe wǣhcte *Brittones fames praefata magis magisque adficiens*, Bd. 1, 14; S. 482, 16. Ðȳ læs his yrre ūs yrmþum swence and wǣce *ne ejus ira nos damnis affligat*, 4, 25; S. 601, 40. Scealt ðū ðīnne līchaman þurh forhæfdnysse wǣccan, Guthl. 5; Gdwin. 32, 9. Ðā hē mid swinglum and tintregum wǣced wæs *cum tormentis afficeretur*, Bd. 1, 7; S. 477, 45. Mid ðȳ seó mǣgð wǣced wæs mid wæle *provincia cum clade premeretur*, 3, 30; S. 561, 37. Mid ða ādle wǣced and swenced *quo affectus incommodo*, 4, 31; S. 610, 20: Exon. Th. 410, 27; Rä. 29, 5. Ða men beóþ mid hriþingum swīþe strangum wǣcede, Lchdm. ii. 258, 3. [*O. H. Ger.* weihen; *p.* weihta *mulcere, enervare.*] v. ā-, ge-, on-wǣcan; wācian.

wæcca. v. hālig-wæcca.

wæccan; *p.* wæhte *To watch, wake*; except in the Northern specimens the verb seems to occur only in the present participle, *wacian* (q.v.) being used elsewhere:—Wæccaþ (-as, Lind.) gē *vigilate*, Mt. Kmbl. Rush. 24, 42. Wæcceþ (wæcas, Lind.), 26, 41. Wæccas, Mk. Skt. Lind. Rush. 13, 37. Ðæt hē wæcce (gewæhte, Lind.) *ut uigilet*, Rush. 13, 34. Suā huoeðer wē woæca ł wē slēpa *sive vigilemus sive dormiamus*, Rtl. 28, 37. Wæcca hē walde (hē wæcende beón walde, Rush.) *vigilaret*, Mt. Kmbl. Lind. 24, 43. Walde wæcce (wæca, Lind.), Lk. Skt. Rush. 12, 39. For hwon hē wæccende sǣte *quare pervigil sederet*, Bd. 2, 12; S. 513, 38: Cd. Th. 191, 12; Exod. 213: Beo. Th. 1420; B. 708. Hē wæccende ða niht on hālgum gebedum āwunode, Guthl. 5; Gdwin. 34, 14. Of scondlīcum geþōhte ðæs wæccendan (*vigilantis*) up cymeþ seó bysmrung slǣpendes . . . ðæt hē wæccende ðōhte, ðæt hē nō witende ārǣfnode, Bd. 1, 27; S. 497, 5-9. Heó wæs wæccende dæges and nihtes, Blickl. Homl. 137, 22. Mid wæccendre gȳmen[ne], L. E. I. prm.; Th. ii. 400, 31. Se fand wæccendne wer, Beo. Th. 2540; B. 1268. Wæccende, 5674; B. 2841. Hē hēt mec wæccende wunian, Exon. Th. 422, 18; Rä. 41, 8. Ðæt gē wæccende wearde healden, 282, 13; Jul. 662. Ða þeówas ðe se hlāford wæccende (-o, Lind.: wæcende, Rush. *uigilantes*) gemēt, Lk. Skt. 12, 37: Blickl. Homl. 145, 6. [Ꝥ heo wecchinde ham werien, Marh. 15, 33.] v. ge-wæccan; þurh-wæccende, Lk. Skt. Lind. 6, 12.

wæcce, an; *f.* I. *wakefulness, sleeplessness*:—Gif men sié micel wæcce getenge, popig gegnīd, smire ðīnne andwlitan mid, . . . raþe him biþ sió wæcce gemetgod, Lchdm. ii. 152, 12-14. Wæcæ, 16, 19. Dæges and nihtes ic swanc on hǣtan and on wæccan *die noctuque aestu urebar, fugiebatque somnus ab oculis meis*, Gen. 31, 40. Tō slǣpe. Gāte horn under heáfod gelǣd, weccan (wæccan, MS. B.) hē on slǣpe gecyrreþ, Lchdm. i. 350, 21. Hī singale wæccean þrowiaþ, ii. 258, 7. Hū micel sār, and hū micele wæccan, and hū micle unrōtnesse hē hæfþ, Bt. 31, 1; Fox 110, 30. II. where the wakefulness is intentional, *watching, watchfulness, a watch, vigil*:—Wæcce *vigilia*, Wrt. Voc. i. 75, 65: *excubia*, Engl. Stud. xi. 65, 28. Gē sceolon witan, ðæt twā wæccan synd; ān is ðæs līchaman, ōðer ðæs mōdes. Ðæs līchaman wæcce is ðonne wē waciaþ on cyrcan æt ūrum ūhtsange, ðonne ōðre men slāpaþ . . . Ðæs mōdes wæcce is micele betere, ðæt se man hogie hū hē gehealden beó wið ðone deófol, Homl. Ass. 51, 35-49: R. Ben. 35, 2. Man wacaþ tō oft on unnyt . . .; and micle betere is ǣlcum cristenum men, ðæt hē nāne wæccan æt cyrican næbbe, ðonne hē ðǣr wacyge mid ǣnigan gefleorde. Ac se ðe rihtlīce his wæccan healdan wylle, . . . wacie hē and gebidde hine georne, ðonne fremaþ him seó wæcce, Wulfst. 279, 11-17. Gif hwelc mon fæste oþþe nytte (*Cockayne alters to* nihte, *but this is unnecessary; see beginning of preceding passage*) wæccan dō, Shrn. 104, 29. Tō wæccum *ad excubias, vigilias*, Hpt. Gl. 488, 37. On hālgum wæccan *vigiliis sanctis*, Bd. 4, 25; S. 600, 15. Wæcceum, Ps. Th. 76, 4. Wæccan *excubias*, Wrt. Voc. ii. 92, 48. Weardsetl oððe wæccan, 30, 11. Gif hwā his wæccan (*vigilias*) æt ǣnigum wylle hæbbe, oððe æt ǣnigre ōðre gesceafte, būton æt Godes cyricean, L. Ecg. P. iv. 19; Th. ii. 210, 11. III. *a division of the night, a watch*:—Drihten com tō his leorningcnihtum on ðære feórðan wæccan. Ān wæcce hæfð þreó tīda; feówer wæccan gefyllað twelf tīda; swā fela tīda hæfð seó niht, Homl. Th. ii. 388, 13. On ðære æfteran wæccan *in secunda uigilia*, Lk. Skt. 12, 38. Embe ða feórðan wæccan, Mk. Skt. 6, 48. [Noðing ne makeð wilde uleschs tommure þen deð muche wecche; vor wecche is ine holie write ipreised. . . . Ure Louerd teihte us wecche, A. R. 144, 1-9. Temien hire fleschs mid wecchen, 138, 6. Wiþþ fassting, and wiþþ wecche, Orm. 1451. *O. H. Ger.* wacha: *Icel.* vaka.] v. cyric-, niht-, ūht-, ungemet-wæcce; wacen.

wæccend (?), es; *m. A watcher, watchman*:—Ne mæg hī cynlīce wæccend . . . weard gehealdan *in vanum vigilant qui custodiunt eam*, Ps. Th. 126, 2.

wæccendlīc. v. þurh-wæccendlīc.

wæccer, wæcer; *adj. Vigilant, watchful*:—Þurh niht wæcer (*printed* wæter) *pernoctans* (Lk. 6, 12), Wrt. Voc. ii. 74, 42. Mid wæccere (wæccre, Bd. M. 84, 2) mōde is tō smeágeanne *vigilanti mente pensandum est*, Bd. 1, 27; S. 496, 2. v. wacor.

wæcen, e; *f. A waking, watch*:—Wecen *vigilia*, Wrt. Voc. i. 46, 4. Waecene *vigilias*, Ps. Surt. 76, 5. v. wacen.

wæcer, wæcian, Wæclinga ceaster, Wæclinga strǣt. v. wæccer, wacian, Wætlinga ceaster, Wætlinga strǣt.

wæcnan; *p.* ede *To waken, arise, spring*:—Ne wæs hit lenge, ðæt se ecghete (secg hete, MS.) æfter wælnīðe wæcnan scolde, Beo. Th. 171; B. 85. Of idese biþ eafora wæcned, Cd. Th. 144, 20; Gen. 2392. [Þat ter walde wakenen of wif and weres somninge worldes weole, H. M. 31, 5. Þu art walle of waisdom, ant euch wunne wakeneð ant waxeð of þe, Marh. 11, 1. He began to wakne, Havel. 2164. Ther wakeneth in the world wondred ant wee, P. S. 152, 17. *Also transitive*:—Itt iss waccnedd off slæp þurh þatt te faderr stireþþ itt and waccneþþ, Orm. 5845. Thai wakned Crist, Met. Homl. 134, 9. *Goth.* ga-waknan *to become awake*: *Icel.* vakna.] v. ā-, on-wæcnan, *and next word.*

wæcnian. v. ā-, on-wæcnian, *and preceding word.*

wæd, es; *n. A ford, shallow water, water that may be traversed* (cf. wadan, *and the forms* wade, wath *in place-names*, e.g. Biggles-wade, Longwathby); *poet. a body of water, sea*:—Bī wædes ōfre, Exon. Th. 360, 22; Wal. 9. Wyllelm king lǣdde scypferde and landfyrde tō Scotlande . . . him sylf mid his landfyrde fērde inn ofer ðæt wæð (æt ðam gewæde, MS. E. Cf. wath *a ford*, Jamieson's Dict.), Chr. 1073; Erl. 211, 25. Wit on sǣ wǣron, ōþ ðæt unc flōd tōdrāf, wado weallende, Beo. Th. 1096; B. 546: 1166; B. 581. Sǣholm oncneów ðæt ðū gife hæfdes . . . wædu swæðorodon, Andr. Kmbl. 1066; An. 533. Wē on sǣbāte ofer waruðgewinn wada cunnedon faroðrīdende, 878; An. 439: Beo. Th. 1021; B. 508. Ðonne ic (*a swan*) wado drēfe *when I trouble the waters* (i.e. swim), Exon. Th. 389, 24; Rä. 8, 2. [A wathe *vadum, flustrum*, Cath. Angl. 410, and note: *O. H. Ger.* wat, furt *vadum*: *Icel.* vað *a ford.*] v. ge- (geuueada *vada brevia*, Wrt. Voc. ii. 123, 17), mearc-, seolh-wæd.

wǣd, e; *f.*: wǣde, es; *n.* I. referring to the dress of human beings. (1) *a weed* (as in palmer's, widow's *weeds*), *an article of dress, a garment*:—Martinus mē bewǣfde mid ðyssere wǣde, Homl. Th. ii. 500, 34. Ne cume hē būton his oferslipe, ne hē þēnige būton ðære wǣde, L. Edg. C. 46; Th. ii. 254, 11. In wēde (*vestimentum*) ald . . . from wēde (*vestimento*), Mt. Kmbl. Lind. 9, 16. Gehrān woede (wēdum, Rush.) his *tetigit uestimentum ejus*, Mk. Skt. Lind. 5, 27. Ungigearuad woede gīmungalīcum *non vestitum veste nuptiali*, Rtl. 108, 1. Woede hāluoende *vestimentum salutare*, 103, 22. Hē næfþ ða neódþearfe āne, ðæt is wist and wǣda, Bt. 33, 2; Fox 124, 17. Woedo *uestimenta*, Mk. Skt. Lind. 9, 3. Ic wæs nacod, nolde gē mē wǣda tīþian, Wulfst. 288, 33. Wǣda leásne, Cd. Th. 53, 27; Gen. 867: 256, 2; Dan. 634: Met. 25, 32. Ðū wǣda tylast, Homl. Th. i. 488, 26. Of ungemete wiste and wǣda, Met. 25, 39. Hē hine gescyrpte mid eallum ðām wlitegestum wǣdum, Bt. 28; Fox 100, 26: Cd. Th. 58, 5; Gen. 941. Hī hine wǣdon bereáfodon, Homl. Th. i. 430, 2. Gif dynt sweart sié būton wǣdum *if a blow cause a bruise in a part not covered by the clothes*, L. Ethb. 59; Th. i. 18, 3. Binnan wǣdum *in a part covered by the clothes*, 60; Th. i. 18, 5. Ofer wǣda mīne *super vestem meam*, Ps. Spl. 21, 17: Cd. Th. 52, 20; Gen. 846: Met. 8, 23. Forlǣt eal ðæt ðū āge būton wiste and wǣda, Prov. Kmbl. 80. Mið ðȳ gewearp woedo (giwēdo, Rush.) his *proiecto uestimento suo*, Mk. Skt. 10, 50. Hē sette uoedo (giwēdo, Rush.) his *ponit uestimenta sua*, Jn. Skt. Lind. 13, 4: Mk. Skt. Lind. 11, 8. Wit baru standaþ unwered wǣdo, Cd. Th. 50, 21; Gen. 812. Sylle mon him wist and wǣdo, Exon. Th. 336, 12; Gn. Ex. 336. (2) in a collective sense, *clothing, dress*:—Līchoma forđor is đon wēde *corpus plus est quam vestimentum*, Mt. Kmbl. Lind. 6, 25. Đæt gād ne wǣre wiste ne wǣde, Cd. Th. 222, 11; Dan. 103. Đæt gebyreþ tō wǣde and tō wiste đām đe Gode þeówian, L. Eth. vi. 51; Th. i. 328, 7. Heó wæsceþ his warig hrægl and him syleþ wǣde nīwe, Exon. Th. 339, 25; Gn. Ex. 99. II. of other covering, equipment, or dressing. v. ge-wǣdian:—Wǣde *mataxa* (cf. strǣl *vel* bedding *mataxa* vel *corductum* vel *stramentum*, i. 59, 29), Wrt. Voc. ii. 59, 28. Wǣde *antemne* (= *sail? rigging?* v. wǣde-rāp; *and* cf. *Icel.* vāð *sail* (poet.)), 100, 29. Strengas gurron, wǣdo gewǣtte, Andr. Kmbl. 749; An. 375. Se wælisca (hafoc) wǣdum and dǣdum his ǣtgiefan eáđmōd weorþeþ, Exon. Th. 332, 25; Vy. 90. Wuldres treów wǣdum geworđode, Rood Kmbl. 29; Kr. 15. [*O. Sax. O. L. Ger.* wādi; *n. clothing: O. Frs.* wēde, wēd; *n.: O. H. Ger.* wāt; *f. amictus, vestimentum, vestis, vestitus: Icel.* vāð; *f. a piece of stuff; a garment.*] v. heađu-, here-, lim-, līn-wǣd; ge-wǣde.

wǣd-brēc; *pl. f. Breeches, a covering for the loins*:—Wǣdbrēc *perizomata* vel *campestria* vel *succinctoria*, Wrt. Voc. i. 25, 62: *perizomata* vel *campestria*, 81, 64. Hig siwodon fícleáf and worhton him wǣdbrēc (*perizomata*), Gen. 3, 7.

-wǣde, -wǣded. v. ǣ-wǣde, un-wǣded.

wǣdelness, e; *f. Poverty, want, indigence, penury*:—Wǣdlnes *inedia*, Wrt. Voc. ii. 44, 50. For wēþelnysse (wǣđelnesse, Bd. M. 298, 25) woruldgōda *prae inopia rerum*, Bd. 4, 12; S. 581, 9. Đurh wēþelnysse (wæđelnesse, Bd. M. 68, 4) *ex inopia*, 1, 27; S. 490, 9. Of wǣdlnysse (wēđelnisse, Ps. Surt.) *de inopia*, Ps. Spl. C. 106, 41: 87, 10. On wǣdlnysse (wēđelnisse, Ps. Surt.) *in mendicitate*, 106, 10. Đonne đæs sellendan mōd ne cann đa wǣdelnesse (*inopiam*) geđolian, Past. 44; Swt. 325, 14. Wēdelnisse, Ps. Surt. 43, 24. v. wæter-wǣdelness; wǣdl.

wǣde-rāp, es; *m. A stay, halyard; pl. rigging*:—Segelgyrdas *antemnas*, wǣderāpa (wæderrāp, Wrt.) *rudentum* (the passage is: Antemnas solvens de parte rudentum, Ald. 213), Wrt. Voc. ii. 97, 30. Untōslitenum wǣderāpum (the passage is: Quod nostrarum carbas antennarum *indisruptis rudentibus* feliciter transfretaverint, Ald. 80), 88, 32. [*O. H. Ger.* wāt-reif *rudens.*]

wǣdian *to clothe, dress.* [*O. Sax.* wādian *to clothe: O. H. Ger.* wāten *vestire, induere: Icel.* væða.] v. ge-wǣdian.

wǣdl (v. P. B. viii. 535), e: wǣdle, an; *f. Poverty, want*:—Wēđl *penuria*, Wrt. Voc. ii. 117, 2. I. *poverty, indigence, want, penury*:—Þār þār word synd fela gelōme ys wǣdl (*egestas*), Scint. 78, 9: Dōm. L. 265: Wulfst. 139, 31. Seó mennisce wǣdl, đe nǣfre gefylled ne biþ wilnaþ ǣlce dæg hwæthweg đises woruldwelan, Bt. 26, 2; Fox 94, 2. Wēđel, Exon. Th. 238, 30; Ph. 212. Of wǣdle weán *de inopia*, Ps. Th. 106, 40: Exon. Th. 201, 12; Ph. 55. Þearfan ic lǣrde đæt hié heora wǣdle gefeán hæfdon, Blickl. Homl. 185, 18. Hī wilniaþ đa heafene đysse gestreónfullan wǣdle, R. Ben. 136, 1. Hié for wǣdle weorđen on murcunga, đæt hié eft ongiennen giétsian for hiera wǣdle *ad murmurationem proruunt, sed cogente se inopia usque ad avaritiam devolvuntur*, Past. 45; Swt. 341, 2–4: Ps. Th. 87, 9. Wǣre đū on wǣdle, sealdest mē wilna geniht, Soul Kmbl. 284; Seel. 146. Mid wǣdle and mid hēnþe ofþrycte *angustia rei familiaris inclusi*, Bt. 11, 1; Fox 30, 33. Đæt hē hlāfes ne gӯme, gewende tō wǣdle and đa wiste wiđsæce (*choose want as his portion and refuse the food*), Elen. Kmbl. 1230; El. 617. Đonne hié gefylden and gebēten đa wǣdle hiera hiéremonna *dum subjectorum inopiam satiant*, Past. 18; Swt. 137, 22: 44; Swt. 325, 11: Bt. 13; Fox 38, 32. Đū tilast wǣdle (*indigentiam*) tō flíonne, Bt. 14, 2; Fox 44, 7. Đa hreósendan welan ne magon eówre wǣdle (*indigentiam*) eów fram ādōn, ac gē ēcaþ eówre ermđe (wǣdle, Cott. MS.) mid đam đe hī eów tō cumaþ, 26, 2; Fox 94, 8–10. Hē wilnaþ welan and flīhđ đa wǣdle (*penuriam*), 33, 2; Fox 122, 33. Đe læs đe þurh wǣdle and hæfenleáste đære ǣfestnesse welm āwlacige, Lchdm. iii. 442, 19. Wēdle *egestatem*, Kent. Gl. 316. Đǣr is wyrma slite and ealra wǣdla gripe, Wulfst. 114, 24. ¶ weak forms:—Gē þeówiaþ eówrum feóndum and Drihten āsent hungor on eów and þurst and næcede and ǣlce wǣdlan *servies inimico tuo, quem immittet tibi Dominus, in fame et siti et nuditate et omni penuria*, Deut. 28, 48. Man sceal gesceádlīce tōsceádon ylde and geóguđe, welan and wǣdlan, L. Edg. C. 4; Th. ii. 262, 5. I a. with gen. of that which is wanting:—Wǣdl hlāfes, Greg. Dial. 2, 21. Hit tācnaþ nӯtena wǣdla, Lchdm. iii. 180, 21. II. *unproductiveness, barrenness*:—Cumaþ seofen swīđe wæstmbǣre geár and swīđe welige . . . and đǣræfter cumaþ ōđre seofene mid swā micelre wǣdle (*tantae sterilitatis*) and hungre, đæt man forgitt đa ǣrran geár, Gen. 41, 30. Hē đæs landes wæstmbǣrnesse đara syfan geára sǣde, and đara ōþera syfan geára wǣdle (*agrorum sterilitatem*), Ors. 1, 5; Swt. 34, 10. [Al þat god of þisse londe we sculen leden mid us, and heo bilæuen wrecches, and wælde (= wædle) heom scal fulien, Laym. 1002. *O. H. Ger.* wātalī *egestas.*]

wǣdla. I. as adjective, *poor, needy, indigent*:—Wǣdla *egenus*, Wrt. Voc. i. 50, 54: 74, 22. Oehtende wes mon đearfan and wēđlan *persecutus est hominem pauperem et mendicum*, Ps. Surt. 108, 17. I a. with gen. of what is wanting, *wanting*, (1) of persons:—Ne geseah ic his sǣd, đæt wǣre hlāfes wǣdla *non vidi semen ejus egens panem*, Ps. Th. 36, 24. Wurdon menn wǣdlan hlāfes, 104, 14. (2) of things, *deficient in, poor in*:—Wæs seó stōw ge wæteres wǣdla ge eorþwæstma *erat locus et aquae et frugis inops*, Bd. 4, 28; S. 605, 18. Þurh đa weallendan sond and þurh đa wǣdlan stōwe wæteres and ǣlcere wǣtan *per ferventes arenas et egentia humoris loca*, Nar. 6, 9: 26, 8. I b. *begging*:—Hē sæt blind wiđ đone weg wǣdla (*mendicans*), Mk. Skt. 10, 46. II. as predicative adjective or substantive, *poor, needy; a poor, needy person*:—Ic eom wǣdla (wēđla, Ps. Surt.) *egenus sum*, Ps. Th. 85, 1: *egens*, 87, 15. Hē wearđ wǣdla *coepit egere*, Lk. Skt. 15, 14. Đā hē wǣdla (*mendicus*) wæs, Jn. Skt. 9, 8. Se welega nāt đæt hē is wǣdla, Homl. Th. ii. 88, 27. Đonne se mon wǣdla biþ, hē wilnaþ welan, Bt. 33, 2; Fox 122, 32: Exon. Th. 91, 22; Cri. 1496. Se se on his gǣste biđ wǣdla, Past. 44; Swt. 325, 14. Đa đe đæs welan gītsiaþ, hī bīđ symle wǣdlan and earmingas on hyra mōde, Prov. Kmbl. 50. Gif eall þises middaneardes wela cōme tō ānum men, hū ne wǣron đonne ealle ōþre men wǣdlan? . . . Đonne đū ealle gedǣlde hæfst, đonne bist đū đē self wǣdla, Bt. 13; Fox 38, 20–35. III. as substantive, *a poor, needy person, a beggar*:—Sum welig man wæs . . . and sum wǣdla (*mendicus*) wæs . . . Se wǣdla forđfērde, Lk. Skt. 16, 19–22. Se reóflia wǣdla, Homl. Th. i. 330, 10. Đearfa and wēđla hergaþ noman đīnne *pauper et inops laudabunt nomen tuum*, Ps. Surt. 73, 21. Geđeaht wǣdlan (wēdlan, Ps. Surt.) *consilium inopis*), Ps. Spl. 13, 10. Hē hine on wǣdlan hӯwe ǣteówde, Homl. Skt. i. 23, 221. Hié nānne mon geweligian ne magon, būton hié ōþerne gedōn tō wǣdlan (*sine ceterorum paupertate*), Bt. 13; Fox 40, 1. Ic gewirce eów tō wǣdlan *visitabo vos in egestate*, Lev. 26, 16. Đӯ læs hwā him self weorđe tō wǣdlan, Past. 44; Swt. 325, 7. Hē ālӯseþ đæne wǣdlan (wēđlan, Ps. Surt.) *liberavit inopem*, Ps. Th. 71, 12: (wēdlan, Ps. Surt.) *egenum*, 34, 11. Sōna swā đū geseó nacodne wǣdlan, Blickl. Homl. 37, 21. For yrmđum đæra wǣdlena (wēđlena, Ps. Surt.) *propter miseriam inopum*, Ps. Th. 11, 5. Dēđ Drihten dōmas đe wǣdlum weorđaþ *faciet Dominus judicium inopum*, 139, 12. Hē đone welegan wǣdlum efnmǣrne gedēđ, Met. 10, 31. [Scullen þe wædlen alle iwurđen riche, Laym. 5872. Þa weoleȝen and đa weađlen, 427. Riche men and wedlen, 497. Wrecche and wædle and usell mann, Orm. 5638: 7732: 7770: 7889: *O. H. Ger.* wātal, wādal *egens.*] v. nīd-wǣdla.

wǣdlian; *p.* ode. I. *to be poor, indigent, needy, in want*:—Ic wǣdlige *egeo*, Ælfc. Gr. 26, 2; Zup. 154, 15. Hē wēdlaþ *egebit*, Kent. Gl. 835. Se đe wēdlat *qui indiget*, 333. Đa welegan wǣdledon (wēdladon, Ps. Surt.) and eodon biddende *divites eguerunt*, Ps. Th. 33, 10. Beóđ welige hwīlwendlīce, đæt gē ēcelīce wǣdlion, Homl. Th. i. 64, 16. Đā wurdon hī dreórige on mōde, đæt hī wǣdligende on ānum wāclīcum wǣfelse fērdon, 62, 28. I a. *to be in want* of something, *to lack, not to have enough*:—Leádes đa men wǣdliaþ, and goldes genihtsumiaþ *plumbo egent, auro habundant*, Nar. 31, 4. Wēđliende hlāf *egens panem*, Ps. Surt. 36, 25. II. *to beg*:—Se đe sæt and wǣdlode *qui sedebat et mendicabat*, Jn. Skt. 9, 8. Mē sceamaþ đæt ic wǣdlige *mendicare erubesco*, Lk. Skt. 16, 3. Hī wǣdlian (wēđlien, Ps. Surt.) *mendicent*, Ps. Spl. 108, 9. Sum blind man sæt wiđ đæne weg wǣdligende (*mendicans*), Lk. Skt. 18, 35. Wǣdliende, Blickl. Homl. 17, 31, 34. Hē wēdlat *mendicabit*, Kent. Gl. 731. [Þe king wæilien (wædlien? *to go as a beggar*) agon wide ȝeon þas þeoden, Laym. 28880. *O. H. Ger.* wādalōn *evagari.*]

wǣdlig; *adj. Poor, needy, destitute*:—Hē wacode ealle đa niht mid đam wǣdlian hreóflian, Homl. Skt. i. 3, 486. Hē on mislīcum yrmđum mannum geheólp, wǣdligum and wanscrӯddum, Homl. Th. ii. 500, 17.

wǣdlness. v. wǣdelness.

wǣdlung, e; *f.* I. *poverty, indigence, want*:—Đǣr is geómerung and wǣdluncg, Wulfst. 114, 27. Hine (*Lazarus*) geswencte seó wǣdlung, and āfeormode; đone ōđerne (*Dives*) gewelgode his genihtsumnys, and bepǣhte, Homl. Th. i. 332, 9. Of wǣdlunga *de inopia*, Ps. Spl. 106, 41. On wǣdlunga *in mendicitate*, 106, 10. Þearfan hē lǣrde đæt hī on līfes wǣdlunge geđyldige beón, Homl. Th. ii. 328, 15. Ne đū ne wēn nā đæt ic āht underfēnge for ǣnegum welan, ac symle on wǣdlunge lyfde, Homl. Skt. ii. 23 b, 341. II. *begging*:—Hē đa wanspēdigan cristenan ne geđafode đæt hī openre wǣdlunge underđeódde, ac hē gemanode đa rīcan đæt hī đæra cristenra wǣdlunge mid heora spēdum gefrēfrodon *he would not allow the destitute Christians to be subject to public begging, but admonished the rich to succour with their wealth the poverty of the Christians*, Homl. Th. i. 558, 26.

wǣfan; *p.* de *To wrap up, clothe*:—Utan wǣfan nacode, Wulfst. 119, 6. [*Goth.* bi-waibjan *to clothe.* In later English the verb expresses motion:—Þe ivele gost weueđ wide and wandređ (*vadit*, v. Mt. 12, 43), O. E. Homl. ii. 85, 33. Ich smet of Modred is hafd þat hit wond (wefde, 2nd MS.) a þene weld, Laym. 28049. Þa cnihtes wefden up þa castles ȝæte, 19003. Cf. *O. H. Ger.* za-weiben *dispergere*; weibōn *fluere, fluitare, agitari*: *Icel.* veifa *to wave, vibrate.*] v. be-, ymbe-wǣfan, *and next word.*

wǽfels, es; *m. A covering, wrap, cloak, veil:*—Wǽfels *tegmen*, Ælfc. Gr. 9, 12; Zup. 41, 1. Wǽfelses ɫ scȳtan *sindonis*, Hpt. Gl. 494, 13. Wǽfel(se), basincge *chlamide*, 456, 46. Under wǽfelse *velamento, indumento*, 457, 24. Mid gewefenum wǽfelsa *consuta plectra*, 462, 63. Hī wǽdligende on ānum wāclīcum wǽfelse fērdon, Homl. Th. i. 62, 29. On wǽfelse (*tegmine*) fyþera ðīnra, Ps. Spl. 35, 8. Oferbrǽdels ɫ wǽfels *opertorium*, Ps. Lamb. 101, 27. Ðam ðe wylle niman ðīne tunecan, lǽt him tō ðīnne wǽfels (*pallium*), Mt. Kmbl. 5, 40: Gen. 39, 12: 24, 65: Ap. Th. 11, 27. Ælmesgedāl dǽle man gelōme, mete ðām ofhingredum, wǽfels ðām nacedum, Wulfst. 74, 4. Wēfels *pallium*, Kent. Gl. 968.

wæfer-gange, an; *f. A spider:*—Wæfyrgange (gongeweafre, Ps. Surt.) *aranea*, Ps. Spl. 89, 9. v. gange-wifre.

wæfer-geornness, e; *f. Eagerness to see sights:*—Mæssepreóstas ne sceolon fremdra manna tūnas, ne hūs, for nānre wæfereornnysse sēcan, L. E. I. 13; Th. ii. 410, 19.

wæfer-hūs, es; *n. A theatre, amphitheatre:*—Hē lǽdde hī tō ðam wæferhūse, ðǽr ða deór wunodon, beran and león, ðe hī ābītan sceoldon, Homl. Skt. ii. 24, 49.

wæfer-līc; *adj. Of a theatre:*—Wæferlīce glencgu *theatrales pompas*, Hpt. Gl. 407, 42. v. wafor-līc.

wæferness, e; *f. Public exhibition, display, show:*—On wæfernysse ɫ wæfersēne *per publicum* (the passage is: Quamvis flava caesaries raderetur, et per publicum decalvata traheretur, Ald. 62), Hpt. Gl. 510, 11.

wæfer-sīn, -sién, -sȳn, -seón, e; *f. A sight, show, spectacle:*—Wæfersȳn *spectaculum*, Wrt. Voc. i. 55, 44. Ðæt ic him wæfersȳn wǽre *factus sum illis in parabolam*, Ps. Th. 68, 11. Ond swā micel wundor and wæfersién wæs mīnes weoredes on fægernisse *fuitque inter uarietates spectaculorum in conspiciendo talem exercitum*, Nar. 7, 18. Wæfersēne *spectaculi*, Hpt. Gl. 508, 28. Wæfersȳne, 487, 47. Wæfersēne *spectaculo*, 412, 1. Mid wundurfulre wæfersēne *stupendo spectaculo*, 470, 76. Wæfersȳne, Bd. 3, 3; S. 525, 38: 5, 12; S. 628, 8. Hē bebeád his folce ðæt hī tō ðyssere wæfersȳne (*a man trying to fly*) cōmon, Homl. Th. i. 380, 15. Eall wered ðe æt ðisse wæfersȳnne wǽron, Lk. Skt. 23, 48. On wæfersēne (v. wæferness) *per publicum*, Hpt. Gl. 510, 12. Hī woldon ða gymstānas tōcwȳsan on ealles ðæs folces gesihðe tō wæfersȳne, Homl. Th. i. 60, 25: 542, 32. Hī mē geworhton him tō wæfersȳne, Rood Kmbl. 61; Kr. 31. Wē for ūrum synnum tō swylcere wæfersȳne synd, Homl. Skt. ii. 25, 158. Wæfersēne *spectaculum*, Hpt. Gl. 435, 49: 501, 46. Se dæg mē ætȳwde swīðe micele wæfersȳne, Shrn. 41, 15. Tō ðissum wæferseónum, Blickl. Homl. 187, 15. [*O. H. Ger.* wabar-siuni *spectaculum.*]

wæfer-stōw, e; *f. A place for spectacles, an amphitheatre:*—Weaferstōwa *amphitheatrum*, Lchdm. i. lxi, 9. v. wafung-stōw.

wæfre; *adj.* I. *flickering, wavering, quivering:*—Wylm ðæs wæfran līges (cf. *Icel.* vafr-logi), Cd. Th. 231, 2; Dan. 241. II. fig. *wavering, languishing:*—Him wæs geómor sefa, wæfre and wælfūs, Beo. Th. 4831; B. 2420. Hē ne meahte wæfre mōd forhabban in hreþre, 2305; B. 1150. III. *active, nimble* (? cf. the force of the old adjective *quiver*):—Wearð him tō handbanan wælgæst wæfre, Beo. Th. 2666; B. 1331. [Cf. Uten uorsien þisne midelard and his wouernesse (*instability?*), Anglia i. 31, 18. *M. H. Ger.* waberēn *vacillare: Icel.* vafra *to hover about.*] v. wafian.

wæfs. v. wæps.

wæfþ, wæft, e; *f. A sight, show, spectacle:*—Wæfð *vel* wæfersȳn *spectaculum*, Wrt. Voc. i. 55, 44. Hwā mæg forbæran ðæt hē swylcre wæfte ne wundrige, ðætte ǽfre swylc yfel gewyrþan sceolde under ðæs ælmihtigan Godes anwealde *quae fieri in regno potentis omnia Dei nemo satis potest admirari*, Bt. 36, 1; Fox 172, 14. v. wafian.

wæg *a way*, wǽg *a wall.* v. weg, wāg.

wǽg, es; *m.* I. *movement*, cf. *Goth.* wēgs *motus* (*in mari*):—Ðū his ȳþum miht āna gesteóran, ðonne hī on wǽge wind onhrēreþ *motum fluctuum ejus tu mitigas*, Ps. Th. 88, 8. II. *a wave, water, the wave, sea:*—Fāmig winneþ wǽg wið wealle, Exon. Th. 383, 33; Rä. 4, 20. Wīdfæðme wǽg, Andr. Kmbl. 1065; An. 533. Þurh wǽges wylm, Exon. Th. 283, 14; Jul. 680: Elen. Kmbl. 459; El. 230. Wǽges weard, Andr. Kmbl. 1263; An. 632. Wēges weard, 1201; An. 601. Ȳð wið lande winneþ, wind wið wǽge, Met. 28, 58. Staþelas wið wǽge, wætre windendum, Exon. Th. 61, 8; Cri. 981: 351, 23; Sch. 84. Oft ic (*an anchor*) sceal wiþ wǽge winnan and wiþ winde feohtan, 398, 1; Rä. 17, 1. Mec upp āhōf wind of wǽge, 392, 19; Rä. 11, 10: 405, 10; Rä. 23, 21. Wiht (*an ice-floe*) cwom æfter wēge līþan, 415, 22; Rä. 34, 1. Feówertȳne gewiton mid ðȳ wǽge in forwyrd sceacan, Andr. Kmbl. 3186; An. 1596: Cd. Th. 206, 25; Exod. 457. Wonnan wǽge *with the dark wave*, 83, 13; Gen. 1379. Wǽg *aquam*, Hpt. Gl. 418, 28. Hié scufon wyrm ofer weallclif, lēton wǽg niman, flōd fæðmian frætwa hyrde, Beo. Th. 6256; B. 3132. Sum fealone wǽg stefnan steóreþ, streámrāde con, Exon. Th. 296, 19; Crä. 53. On sealtne wǽg, 361, 30; Wal. 27: Cd. Th. 236, 19; Dan. 323. Gewāt se fugel earce sēcan ofer wonne wǽg, 88, 8; Gen. 1462. Windas weóxon, wǽgas grundon, Andr. Kmbl. 746; An. 373: 911; An. 456: 3088; An. 1547. Hreó wǽgas, salte sǽstreámas, 1496; An. 749. Wonne wǽgas, Cd. Th. 8, 4; Gen. 119. Wið ȳðfare gehealden hreóra wǽga, Exon. Th. 200, 24; Ph. 45. Wrælīce syndon wǽgea gangas, ðonne sǽstreámas swīðust flōwaþ *mirabiles elationes maris*, Ps. Th. 92, 5. Wǽga *gurgites*, Hpt. Gl. 464, 76. Fēran ofer wēga gewinn, Andr. Kmbl. 1863; An. 934. Ealle ða ðe onhrēraþ hreó wǽgas on ðam brādan brime, Exon. Th. 194, 19; Az. 141. Wadan ofer wǽgas, 350, 9; Sch. 61. Flōd, fealewe wǽgas, Andr. Kmbl. 3177; An. 1591. Fealwe wēgas (wegas?), Exon. Th. 289, 11; Wand. 46. [*Goth.* wēgs *a wave: O. Sax.* wāg: *O. Frs.* wēg: *O. H. Ger.* wāg *liquor, gurges, vorago, pontus, aequor, lacus, fretum: Icel.* vāgr *a wave, sea.*] v. fīfel-, mōdig-, sǽ-wǽg.

wǽg (*see also* wǽge), e; *f.* I. *a weight*, (a) as a general term:—Byrðen oððe wǽg *pondus*, Ælfc. Gr. 9, 32; Zup. 58, 17 note. Genim ðære ylcan wyrte ānre tremesse wǽge, Lchdm. i. 72, 11. Genim twēga trymessa wǽge, 70, 15. Þreóra trymessa wǽge, 72, 26: 74, 4. Habbaþ emne wǽga *aequa sint pondera*, Lev. 19, 36. (b) as a definite weight, *a wey:*—Ān wēg spices and cēses, Cod. Dip. Kmbl. i. 312, 8. Selle mon uuēge cǽsa, 293, 11. .i. wēge cēsa, .i. wēge speces, 296, 35. .ii. wēga spices and cēses, 299, 18. .iii. wēga, 311, 3. (c) fig.:—Ða gewunelīcan wǽge (*pensum*) heora ðeówdōmes hig nāteshwōn forgīmeleásion, R. Ben. 78, 11. II. *an implement for weighing, a balance:*—On wǽge beóð āwegene *statera ponderabuntur*, Scint. 97, 7. Weh on wǽge, Lchdm. i. 374, 15. Gelīcere wāge *aequa bilance*, Hpt. Gl. 512, 76. Tō wēge ɫ tō disce *ad mensam*, Lk. Skt. Lind. Rush. 19, 23. Ðonne man sett ða synne and ða sāwle on ða wǽge, Wulfst. 240, 1. Wǽga *trutina* . . . lytle wǽga *momentana* vel *statam*, Wrt. Voc. i. 38, 38, 42. [Nicodemus brouhte an hundred weien of mirre and of aloes, A. R. 372, 7. Sevene waxpund makiet onleve ponde one waye, twelf weyen on fothir, Rel. Ant. i. 70, 22. A weye of Essex chese, Piers P. 5, 93. Seint Austin deð þeos two boðe in one weie, A. R. 60, 10. Me ssel weȝe þet word er hit by yzed . . . Zoþnesse halt þise riȝtuolle waye . . . þis waye ne ssel hongi of þis half, ne of yend half, Ayenb. 256, 6–10. *O. H. Ger.* wāgi (*dat.*) *pondere;* wāga *pondus, libra, statera, lanx, trutina: Icel.* vāg *a weight;* vāgir; *pl. scales, a balance.*] v. pening-, pund-, twi-, wull-wǽg; wǽge-tunge.

wǽgan; *p.* de *To vex, harass, afflict:*—Hē hēt hī swingan, wītum wǽgan, Exon. Th. 251, 10; Jul. 143. Ðæt gē mec tō wundre wǽgan mōtun (cf. erlōs skulun wēgian mi te wundrun, dōt mi wīties filu, Hēl. 3088), 124, 22; Gū. 341. [*O. Sax.* wēgian: *O. H. Ger.* weigen *vexare, afficere, affligere, exagitare.*] v. ge-wǽgan.

wǽgan; *p.* de *To deceive, delude:*—Ne gewurðe hit ðæt ic on ðām hālgum gerecednyssum wǽge, Homl. Skt. ii. 23 b, 18. Bepǽhst *vel* wǽgest *deludis*, i. *decipis*, Wrt. Voc. ii. 138, 53. Uuēgið *fefellit*, 108, 46. Wǽgeþ *fefellit*, i. *eludit*, 35, 28. Wēgð *mentitur*, Kent. Gl. 414: *fallit*, 933. Gif hwylc brōðor wǽgð and misfēhð on boduncge sealma oððe rǽdincge *si quis dum pronuntiat psalmum fallitur lectionem*, R. Ben. 71, 5. Gesuīcas ɫ wǽges *mentientes*, Mt. Kmbl. Lind. 5, 11. Wǽgde *vel* bepǽhte *fefellit*, i. *delusit*, Wrt. Voc. ii. 148, 27. Ne hine nōwiht his geleáfa wǽgde, Bd. 4, 32; S. 612, 3. Weleras wǽgendes *labia mentientis*, Scint. 95, 4. Wǽgendre gesǽlignesse *vel* bepǽcendre *fallentis fortunae*, Wrt. Voc. ii. 146, 73. Wēgende welere *labium mentiens*, Kent. Gl. 596. Wǽged *delusus* (v. Mt. 2, 16), Wrt. Voc. ii. 71, 57: 26, 29. Wǽged wæs *deluditur*, 95, 63: 27, 26. Wēged *ludificatus*, 86, 22. v. ā-, be-, ge-wǽgan.

wǽg-bora, an; *m. A wave-bearer, a creature that lives beneath the waves:*—Wundorlīc wǽgbora, Beo. Th. 2884; B. 1440.

wǽg-bord, es; *n. A wave-board, a plank of a vessel:*—Ðū of eorðan wæstmum wiste under wǽgbord (cf. lǽd under earce bord, 80, 23; Gen. 1333; be ūtan earce bordum, 81, 33; Gen. 1354) gelǽde, Cd. Th. 81, 4; Gen. 1340.

wǽg-deór, es; *n. A sea-beast:*—Wǽgdeóra gehwylc sweltep, Exon. Th. 61, 21; Cri. 988.

wǽg-dropa, an; *m. A wave-drop, a salt tear* (?):—Hē hāte lēt teáras geótan, weallan wǽgdropan, Exon. Th. 165, 17; Gū. 1030.

wǽge (*see also* wǽg), an; *f.* I. *a weight*, (a) as a general term:—Byrðen oððe wǽge *pondus*, Ælfc. Gr. 9, 32; Zup. 58, 17. Hæbbe ǽlc man rihte wǽgan and rihte gemetu *pondus habebis justum et verum et modius aequalis et verus erit tibi*, Deut. 25, 15. (b) as a definite weight, *a wey:*—Gā seó wǽge (wǽg, MS. G.) wulle tō .cxx. p̄., and nān man hig nā undeóror ne sylle, L. Edg. ii. 8; Th. i. 270, 3. II. *an implement for weighing, a balance, scale:*—Ðeós wǽge oððe scalu *lanx*, Ælfc. Gr. 9, 73; Zup. 73, 10. Wǽge *trutina*, 36; Zup. 215, 18: *statera*, Scint. 81, 12: 110, 12. *Libra*, ðæt is pund oððe wǽge, Lchdm. iii. 246, 1. Gelīcere wǽgan *in equilibrium*, 234, 5: 238, 26. Ǽlc ðæra ðinga ðe man wihð on wǽgan, Ælfc. Gr. 13; Zup. 84, 3. Āwegene on ānre wǽgan, Homl. Th. ii. 454, 23: 436, 12. On wǽgum (wēgum, Ps. Surt. Spl.) *in stateris*, Ps. Lamb. 61, 10. v. efen-wǽge.

wǽge, wēg[e], es; *n. A cup:*—Wēgi *poculum*, Wrt. Voc. i. 290, 82. Sume ic geteáh, tō geflite fremede . . . beóre druncne; ic him byrlade wrōht of wēge, ðæt hī in wīnsele þurh sweordgripe sāwle forlētan of flǽschoman, Exon. Th. 271, 24; Jul. 487. Fǽted wǽge, dryncfæt deóre,

Beo. Th. 4499; B. 2253. Hē mandryhtne bær fǣted wǣge, 4553; B. 2282. [*O. Sax.* wâgi, wêgi *a vessel.* Cf. (?) *O. H. Ger.* bah-weiga; *f. ferculum, discus, lanx: Icel.* veig; *f. strong drink.*] v. bǣde-, deáþ-, ealo-, līþ-wǣge (-wēge, -wēg).

wægen. v. wægn.

wǣge-tunge, an; *f. The tongue of a balance:*—Wǣgetunge (*or* wǣge tunge, v. wǣg, II) *examen,* Wrt. Voc. i. 38, 41. [*Ger.* wagezunge.]

wǣg-fær, es; *n. A sea-journey:*—Ic đē ongitan ne meahte on wǣgfære, Andr. Kmbl. 1845; An. 925.

wǣg-fæt, es; *n. A water-vessel, a cloud:*—Won wǣgfatu, lagustreáma full (*cups*), Exon. Th. 384, 33; Rä. 4, 37.

wǣg-faru, e; *f. A sea-passage, passage through the sea* (the passage through the Red Sea):—Nū se āgend up ārǣrde reáde streámas in randgebeorh, syndon đa foreweallas fægre gestēpte, wrætlīcu wǣgfaru, ōđ wolcna hrōf, Cd. Th. 196, 27; Exon. 298.

wǣg-flota, an; *m. A wave-floater, a ship:*—Hū đū wǣgflotan sund wīsige, Andr. Kmbl. 973; An. 487. Gesión brecan ofer bæđweg brimwudu myrgan, sǣmearh plegan, wadan wǣgflotan, Elen. Kmbl. 491; El. 246: Beo. Th. 3818; B. 1907.

wǣg-hengest, es; *m. A sea-steed, a ship:*—Hē bât gestâg, wǣghengest wræc, Exon. Th. 181, 34; Gū. 1303. Hī gehlōdon hildesercum wǣghengestas, Elen. Kmbl. 472; El. 236. [Cf. *Icel.* vâg-marr *a ship.*]

wǣg-holm, es; *m. The billowy sea:*—Gewât ofer wǣgholm flota fāmigheals, Beo. Th. 439; B. 217.

wǣg-līþend, es; *m.:* -līþende; *ptcpl. A sea-farer; sea-faring:*—Wēnaþ wǣglīþende, đæt hȳ on eálond sum eágum wlīten, Exon. Th. 360, 26; Wal. 11. Ne mōston wǣglīđendum wætres brōgan hrīnon, ac hié God nerede, Cd. Th. 84, 9; Gen. 1395: Beo. Th. 6297; B. 3159. Hæleđ langode, wǣglīþende, hwonne hié of nearwe stæppan mōsten, Cd. Th. 86, 17; Gen. 1432. [*O. Sax.* wâg-lîđand.]

wægn, wægen, wǣn, es; *m. A waggon, wain, carriage, vehicle:*—Wægn *vehiculum,* Wrt. Voc. ii. 123, 40. Wǣn *plaustrum,* Wrt. Voc. i. 66, 51: 284, 43: *plaustrum* vel *carrum,* 16, 19: 85, 69. Mid đȳ hē đā se wǣn (wægn, MS. T.) com đe man đa bān on lǣdde *cum venisset carrum in quo ossa ducebantur,* Bd. 3, 11; S. 535, 17 note. Hē ofer wǣg gewât, wǣn æfter ran, Runic pm. Kmbl. 343, 32; Rūn. 22. Wægnes hweól *rotam,* Ps. Th. 82, 10. Wǣnes weđ (swæđ? pæđ?) *orbita,* Wrt. Voc. i. 37, 47. Ânes wǣnes gangweg *actus,* 37, 37. On wǣnes eaxe hwearfaþ đa hweól, and sió eax byrþ eallne đone wǣn, Bt. 39, 7; Fox 220, 27: 39, 8; Fox 224, 6. Wǣne *carruca,* Hpt. Gl. 438, 67. Mid đȳ đe hine mon bere oþþe on wǣne ferige, Lchdm. ii. 30, 29. Stīgan on wægn, Exon. Th. 404, 17; Rä. 23, 9. Hī gegearwodon wægen (*carrum*) and on āsetton đa fǣmnan, Bd. 3, 9; S. 534, 9. Wæs gold on wǣn hladen, Beo. Th. 6260; B. 3134. Twēgra wǣna gangweg *via,* Wrt. Voc. i. 37, 38. Tuēgra uuegna gang (v. wægn-gang), Cod. Dip. B. i. 344, 12. On wǣnum *in curribus,* Ps. Spl. 19, 8. Đæt hig nymon wǣnas (*plaustra*), Gen. 45, 19, 27. ¶ with special reference to what is carried, in the phrase *wægnes, wægna gang,* the going to fetch wood, v. Kemble's Saxons in England, ii. pp. 70, 71:—.ii. wēna gang mid cyninges wēnum tō Bleán đem wiada (cf. .iiii. carris transductionem in silba regis sex ebdomades a die Pentecosten, hubi alteri homines silbam cedunt, 122, 8), Chart. Th. 119, 16. An ic twēga wǣna gang on clætinc tō wudurēdenne, Cod. Dip. Kmbl. vi. 36, 15. [Tuēge waine gong wudes, iv. 282, 15. Tō wayne gong tō wude, 282, 28.] ¶ referring to the constellation Charles' *wain.* v. carles wǣn:—Wǣnes đīsl (waegne[s] þīxl, 100, 72) *archtoes,* Wrt. Voc. ii. 7, 23. Tunglu đe wē hātaþ wǣnes đīsla, Bt. 39, 3; Fox 214, 19: Met. 28, 10. [*O. L. Ger.* reidi-wagan *currus: O. Frs.* wain, wein: *O. H. Ger.* wagan *plaustrum, carra, carrum, vehiculum: Icel.* vagn.] v. fyrd-, hors-, hræd-, rǣd-, ryne-, scrid-, wīg-wægn (-wǣn).

-wægnan. v. be-wægnan.

wægnere, es; *m. A driver of a carriage, a waggoner, charioteer:*—Scridwīsa *vel* wǣnere *auriga,* Wrt. Voc. i. 39, 38. Wēnere, ii. 4, 57.

wǣgnere, es; *m. A deceiver:*—Sponera, wǣgnera *lenonum,* Wrt. Voc. ii. 52, 42. v. wǣgnian.

waegne-þīxl. v. wægn.

wægn-faru, e; *f. A chariot-journey:*—*Fiscalis reda* (=*rheda*) gebellīcum wæg[n]fearu, Wrt. Voc. ii. 108, 64. *Fiscalis ræde* gafellīcum wǣnfare, 35, 56.

wægn-gehrado *a waggon-plank:*—Wǣngehrado *tabula plaustri,* Wrt. Voc. i. 284, 53.

wægn-gerēfa, an; *m. A wain-reeve, one who has charge of carriages:*—Wǣngerēfa *carpentarius,* Wrt. Voc. i. 284, 44: ii. 16, 66.

wægn-gewǣde, es; *n. A waggon-cloth, covering for a waggon:*—Man sceal habban wǣngewǣdu, Anglia ix. 264, 4.

wǣgnian. v. ge-wǣgnian.

wægn-scilling, es; *m. A toll of a shilling on each waggon standing to be loaded at a salt-pan:*—Se wægnscilling and se seámpending gonge tō đæs cynges handa swā hē ealning dyde æt Saltwīc (cf. sine aliquo tributo dominatoris gentis praedictae, id est statione siue inoneratione plaustrorum, 125, 30-32), Cod. Dip. Kmbl. v. 143, 70. v. Kemble's Saxons in England, ii. pp. 70, 71, 329.

wægn-þoll, es; *m. A cart-pin:*—Wǣnđoll *aries,* Wrt. Voc. ii. 3, 72. v. þoll.

wægn-treów, es; *n. A perquisite of a log of wood from each load to the labourer loading and leading the waggon* (? cf. wægn-scilling):—On sumere þeóde gebyreþ ... æt wudulāde wǣntreów, æt cornlāde hreáccopp, L. R. S. 21; Th. i. 440, 27.

wægn-weg, es; *m. A cart-road, carriage-road:*—On đone wǣnweg, Cod. Dip. Kmbl. vi. 8, 37. On đone brādan wǣnweg, iii. 37, 26.

wægn-wyrhta, an; *m. A wain-wright, cart-wright, carriage-maker:*—Wǣnwyrhta *carpentarius,* Wrt. Voc. i. 19, 9: 66, 50: ii. 128, 68.

wǣg-pundern *a steel-yard, weighing-machine:*—Ǣlc burhgemet and ǣlc wǣgpundern beó be his (*the bishop's*) dihte swīđe rihte, L. I. P. 7; Th. ii. 312, 20. Hē sceal habban wǣipundern, Anglia ix. 263, 9. Cf. pundern *perpendiculum,* Hpt. Gl. 476, 77, *and* pundar.

wǣg-scealu, e; *f. The scale of a balance:*—Wǣgscala *lances,* Wrt. Voc. ii. 53, 7.

wǣg-stæþ, es; *n. A shore, bank:*—Cwom .LX. monna tō wǣgstæþe rīdan, Exon. Th. 404, 3; Rä. 23, 2.

wǣg-streám, es; *m. The sea:*—Đæt feórþe cyn wōd on wǣgstreám (*the Red Sea*), Cd. Th. 197, 22; Exod. 311.

wǣg-sweord, es; *n. A sword with wavy ornamentation* (v. Woorsaae's Primeval Antiquities, p. 40):—Wrætlīc wǣgsweord, Beo. Th. 2982; B. 1489.

wǣg-þel, es; *n. A wave-plank, a ship:*—Hē ālǣdde of wǣgþele (*the ark*) wrāđra lāfe, Cd. Th. 90, 16; Gen. 1496. Nōe tealde đæt se hrefn hine sēcan wolde on wǣgþele, 87, 9; Gen. 1446. On wǣgþele *on board,* Andr. Kmbl. 3418; An. 1713. Under earce bord eaforan lǣdan, weras on wǣgþel, Cd. Th. 82, 6; Gen. 1358.

wǣg-þreá *the chastisement by the waters* (the deluge), Cd. Th. 90, 5; Gen. 1490.

wǣg-þreát, es; *m. A wave-host, the waters of the deluge:*—Ic wille mid wǣgþreáte ǣhta and āgend eall ācwellan, Cd. Th. 81, 29; Gen. 1352.

wæl, es; *n.* I. in a collective sense, *the slain, the dead, a number of slain,* (a) generally of death in battle:—Wæl feól on eorđan, Byrht. Th. 135, 31; By. 126: 140, 45; By. 303. Đæs wæles wæs geteald six hund manna mid đām fȳrenum flānum ofsceotene *of those who died they counted six hundred shot with the fiery arrows,* Homl. Th. i. 506, 6. Đā hē his brōđor slege ofāxode, đā fērde hē tō đam wæle his līc sēcende, ii. 358, 6. Đā gelæhton his gebrōđra his līc of đam wæle, Homl. Skt. ii. 25, 673. Đā sōhte hē on đam wæle his līc, Bd. 4, 22; S. 591, 17. Hē on wæle lǣge, Byrht. Th. 139, 65; By. 279: 140, 39; By. 300. Hit næs nā gesǣd hwæt Pirruses folces gefeallen wǣre, for đon hit næs þeáw đæt mon ǣnig wæl on đa healfe rīmde đe wieldre wæs (*mos est, ex ea parte quae vicerit occisorum non commemorare numerum*), Ors. 4, 1; Swt. 156, 21. Ǣr hē đæt wæl bereáfian mehte, 3, 9; Swt. 128, 9: Beo. Th. 2429; B. 1212: 6047; B. 3027. On wæl feallan *to die in battle,* Cd. Th. 123, 2; Gen. 2038. On wæll fyllan *to kill in battle,* Bd. 1, 12; S. 481, 24. ¶ as object of verbs of slaying:—Đǣr wæs micel wæl geslægen on gehwæþre hond *many were killed on both sides,* Chr. 871; Erl. 74, 11: 833; Erl. 64, 20. Ne wearđ wæl māre folces gefylled, 937; Erl. 115, 14. Đǣr was ungemetlīc wæl geslægen Norþanhymbra, sume binnan, sume būtan, 867; Erl. 72, 15: Ors. 2, 5; Swt. 80, 26. Hī him mycel wæl on geslōgan *magnam eorum multitudinem sternens,* Bd. 1, 12; S. 481, 30. Hié đǣr đæt mǣste wæl geslōgon on hǣþnum herige đe wē secgan hiérdon ōþ đisne andweardan dæg, Chr. 851; Erl. 68, 4. Hē menigfeald wæl felde and slōh, Guthl. 2; Gdwin. 14, 7. (b) in other connections:—Đā geát mon đæt ātter ūt on đone sǣ, and raþe đæs đǣr com upp micel wæl deádra fisca, Ors. 6, 3; Swt. 258, 17. II. *a single corpse, a slain person:*—Hē mē habban wile dreóre fāhne, gif mec deáđ nimeþ, byreþ blōdig wæl, Beo. Th. 900; B. 448. Đonne walu feóllon, 2089; B. 1042. Crungon walo, Exon. Th. 477, 17; Ruin. 26. III. in an abstract sense, (a) of destruction in war, *slaughter, carnage:*—Wæl on gefeohte *strages,* Ælfc. Gr. 9, 27; Zup. 53, 5. Mycel wæl (wælfill, MS. A.) gewearđ on Brytene æt Wōdnesbeorge, Chr. 592; Erl. 19, 34. Hē hī on gelīcnysse đæs trāiscan wæles (*caedis*) wundade, Bd. 3, 1; S. 523, 30. Mid grimme wæle and herige *saeva caede,* 4, 15; S. 583, 26. Of wæle *strage, occisione,* Hpt. Gl. 427, 60. (b) in other connections, *destruction:*—Com mycel wæl and monncwyld godcundlīce gesended *supervenit clades divinitus missa,* Bd. 4, 3; S. 567, 10. Hē hī fram đam mānfullan wæle (*clade;* destruction by famine) generede, 4, 14; S. 582, 27. Wæle *strage; occisione* (destruction of the soul by sin. v. Ald. 7), Hpt. Gl. 415, 22. [Þat wæl (heap, 2nd MS.) wes þe more, Laym. 4111. He lette al þæt wel weorpen an ane dich, 6427. Ic heo wulle biwinnen ođer an wæle liggen, 9497. *O. Sax.* wal (*in* wal-dād): *O. H. Ger.* wal *strages, clades: Icel.* valr *the slain.*] v. ecg-, ungemet-wæl.

wǣl, es; *m. n. A weel* (e. g. Mode *weel* (*wheel*), Lanc.), *a deep pool, gulf, deep water of a stream* or *of the sea:*—Wǣl *gurges,* deópnys *abyssus*, Wrt. Voc. i. 54, 34: 80, 65. Sume weriaþ on gewitlocan wísdómes streám, ðæt hé on unnyt út ne tóflóweþ, ac se wǽl wunaþ on weres breóstum dióp and stille, Past. 65; Swt. 469, 4. *Hic gurges* ðis (ðis *with* e *over* i, MS. F.: ðes, MSS. D. O.) wǽl, ðæt is, deóp wæter, Ælfc. Gr. 9, 26; Zup. 52, 9. Wǽles stæð *alvei* (the Nile) *marginem*, Hpt. Gl. 492, 70. Scymriendes wǽles *cerulei gurgitis*, Germ. 401, 10. Wé æthrynon mid úrum árum ða ýðan ðas deópan wǽlis, wé gesáwon eác ða muntas ymbe ðære sǽ strande, Anglia viii. 299, 38. Þweálu clǽnes wǽles (*gurgitis*), Hymn. Surt. 52, 13. On wǽle fúlum þweán, sume wróhte getácnaþ, Lchdm. iii. 206, 10. Fugel uppe sceal lácan on lyfte, leax sceal on wǽle mid sceóte scríðan, Menol. Fox 538; Gn. C. 39. Of wǽle getogen *gurgite ductus*, Hymn. Surt. 70, 27: 25, 6. Áðuah in ðær uéle (*natatoria*), Jn. Skt. Lind. 9, 7. In ðæt uoel ł in ðæt fiscpól *in piscinam*, 5, 4. On wǽlum ádrenctum *profundis pelagi flustris suffocato* (Ald. 12), Hpt. Gl. 426, 22. Weálu (*rubicundi oceani*) *gurgites*, 409, 64. Ðú gedréfest deópe wǽlas *conturbas profundum maris*, Ps. Th. 64, 7. [With weel of þi liking *torrente voluntatis tuae*, Ps. 35, 9. Þai sink in þat wele (*v. l.* pitt), þar neuer man sank þat was o sele, C. M. 2903. Wel (*rimes with* sel), Misc. 149, 89. v. Jamieson's Dict. s. v. wele. *O. L. Ger.* wál *abyssus*.]

wǽlan; *p.* de *To vex, torment, afflict*:—Ðæt hý his líchoman leng ne móstan wítum wǽlan, Exon. Th. 127, 34; Gú. 396. Dogter mín is yfle from deófle wǽled *filia mea male a daemonio vexatur*, Mt. Kmbl. Rush. 15, 22. Hé is yfle wǽlid *male torquetur*, 8, 6. [Cf. *Icel.* veill *diseased, ailing*; veilindi *disease*.] v. á-, be-, ge-wǽlan.

wæl-bed[d], es; *n. The bed of the slain*:—Ic hine heardan clammum on wælbedde wríþan þóhte *I had thought to bind him on the couch of the slain* (i.e. *to kill him*), Beo. Th. 1932; B. 964. Hwæt befealdest ðú folmum ðínum on wælbedd bróðor ðínne? Cd. Th. 62, 8; Gen. 1011. v. wæl-rest.

wǽl-ben[n], e; *f. A wound inflicted by the sea*, v. wǽl:—Gársecg wédde . . . egesan stódon, weóllon wǽlbenna (wæl-?) (*the reference is to the death of the Egyptians in the Red Sea*), Cd. Th. 208, 30; Exod. 491.

wæl-bend, e; *f. A deadly, mortal band*:—Wælbende handgewriþene *deathband hand-twisted* (i.e. *death at a person's hands*), Beo. Th. 3876; B. 1936. v. wæl-clamm.

wæl-bleát; *adj. Causing mortal weakness, deadly, mortal*:—Benne, wunde wælbleáte, Beo. Th. 5443; B. 2725.

wæl-ceald; *adj. Deadly cold*:—Hé him helle gescóp, wælcealde wíc (cf. Ðǽr (*in hell*) cymð forst fyrnum cald, Cd. Th. 20, 28; Gen. 316), wintre beðeahte, Salm. Kmbl. 937; Sal. 468.

wæl-ceásiga, an; *m. A chooser of the slain, a raven*:—Wonn wælceásega, Cd. Th. 188, 6; Exod. 164. v. wæl-cyrige.

wæl-clam[m], es; *m. A fatal bond*:—Forgif mé mennen ðe ðú áhreddest wera wælclommum (*captivity in which they might have been slain?*), Cd. Th. 128, 17; Gen. 2128. v. wæl-bend.

wæl-cræft, es; *m. A deadly power, power which causes death*:—Ðonne mín hláford wile láfe þicgan ðara ðe hé of lífe hét wælcræf[tum] áwrecan (*of those whom he has ordered to be slain*), Exon. Th. 498, 11; Rä. 87, 11.

wæl-cwealm, es; *m. A death-pang, pain of violent death*:—Récas stígaþ ofer hrófum, hlin bið on eorþan, wælcwealm wera, Exon. Th. 381, 8; Rä. 2, 8.

wæl-cyrge, -cyrige, -cyrie, an; *f. A chooser of the slain.* According to the mythology, as seen in its Northern form, the Val-kyrjur were the goddesses who chose the slain that were to be conducted by them to Odin's hall—Val-halla: 'Þær ríða jafnan at kjósa val.' Something of the old idea is still shewn in the following glosses, in which the word renders a Fury, a Gorgon, or the goddess of war:—Uualcyrge *Tisifone*, Wrt. Voc. ii. 122, 34: *Eurynis*, 107, 43. Walcrigge *Herinis*, 110, 34. Wælcyrge, 43, 2: *Bellona*, 94, 15: 12, 12. Wælcyrige *Allecto*, 5, 72. Wælcyrie *Tisiphona*, i. 60, 21. Ða deór habbaþ wælkyrian eágan *hae bestie oculos habent Gorgoneos*, Nar. 34, 6. But elsewhere it is used apparently with the sense of *witch* or *sorceress*:—Wyccan and wælcyrian and unlybwyrhtan, Wulfst. 298, 18. Wiccan and wælcerian, 165, 34. Wiccean and wælcyrian, Chart. Erl. 231, 10. [Clerkes out of Caldye . . . wycheȝ & walkyries . . . deuinores of demorlaykes . . . sorsers & exorsismus, Allit. Pms. 85, 1577. *Icel.* val-kyrja.]

wæl-cyrging, es; *m. One that belongs to the race of the* wælcyrgan:—*Gorgoneus*, ðæt is wælkyrging (-cyrginc, *v. l.*), Nar. 35, 6.

wæl-deáþ, es; *m. A violent death*:—Hié wældeáð (*death at Grendel's hands*) fornam, Beo. Th. 1395; B. 695.

wæl-dreór, es; *m. The blood of the slain*:—Wæter wældreóre fág, Beo. Th. 3267; B. 1631. Eorðe wældreóre (*the blood of Abel*) swealh of handum ðínum (*Cain's*), Cd. Th. 62, 19; Gen. 1016. Ic fylde mid folmum ordbanan Abeles, eorðan sealde wældreór weres, 67, 9; Gen. 1098.

wæl-fǽhþ, e; *f. Deadly feud, hostility that leads to slaying*:—Hé wælfǽhða dǽl, sæcca gesette. Beo. Th. 4061; B. 2028.

wæl-fæðm, es; *m. A deadly embrace*:—Brim wælfæðmum sweóp, fǽge crungon (*of the overwhelming of the Egyptians in the Red Sea*), Cd. Th. 208, 9; Exod. 480.

wæl-fáh; *adj. Deadly hostile* (?):—Wælfágne winter (*winter when the earth seems dead*). Beo. Th. 2260; B. 1128.

wæl-feall, es; *m.* (?) *The fall of the slain, destruction*:—Tó wælfealle and tó deáðcwalum Deniga leódum, Beo. Th. 3427; B. 1711. [*Icel.* val-fall; *n. strages.*] Cf. wæl-fill.

wæl-fel; *adj. Cruel to the slain* (?) or *very cruel*. Cf. wæl-hreów:—Hræfen uppe gól, wan and wælfel, Elen. Kmbl. 105; El. 53.

wæl-feld, es; *m. The field of the slain, the battle-field*:—Hí on wælfelda plegodan, Chr. 937; Erl. 114, 17

wæl-fill, es; *m. Slaughter, carnage*:—Wælfill *cedes*, Wrt. Voc. ii. 15, 67. Wælfyl *statis* (*stragis*, v. Ald. 173, 3), 93, 52. Hér micel wælfill wæs æt Wóddesbeorge (Wódnes-, MS. E.), Chr. 592; Erl. 18, 30. Blódgyte, wællfyll weres, morð mid mundum, Cd. Th. 92, 11; Gen. 1527. Heó underbæc beseah wið ðæs wælfylles (*the destruction of Sodom and Gomorrah*), 154, 29; Gen. 2563.

wæl-fús; *adj. Ready to be slain*; referring to Beowulf before the fight in which he was mortally wounded:—Him wæs geómor sefa, wæfre and wælfús, wyrd ungemete neáh, se sceolde sécean sáwle hord, sundur gedǽlan líf wið líce, Beo. Th. 4831; B. 2420.

wæl-fyll, e: -fyllu(-o); *indecl. f. Abundance of slain*:—Grendel on reste genam þrítig þegna; ðanon eft gewát tó hám faran mid ðære wælfylle, Beo. Th. 250; B. 125.

wæl-fýr, es; *n.* I. *a fire that slays, deadly fire*:—Beorges weard (*the fire-drake*) wearp wælfýre, wíde sprungon hilde leóman, Beo. Th. 5157; B. 2582. II. *a fire that burns the slain, a funeral pile*:—Hét Hildeburh hire selfre suna on bǽl dón . . . wand tó wolcnum wælfýra mǽst, Beo. Th. 2243; B. 1119.

wæl-gæst (-gǽst?), es; *m. A deadly guest* (*spirit?*), *a murderous guest*:—Wælgæst (*Grendel*), Beo. Th. 3994; B. 1995: (*Grendel's mother*), 2666; B. 1331.

wæl-gár, es; *m. A deadly spear*:—Wælgár slíteþ, Exon. Th. 354, 46; Reim. 61. Ðǽr wæs heard plega, wælgára wrixl, wígcyrm micel, Cd. Th. 120, 5; Gen. 1990.

wæl-gífre; *adj.* I. *eager to slay*, (a) of persons:—Ðá com hæleða þreát (*those who wished to kill St. Andrew*) wadan wælgífre, Andr. Kmbl. 2543; An. 1273. Deáð, wiga wælgífre, Exon. Th. 231, 8; Ph. 486: 162, 7; Gú. 972. (b) of things:—Wǽpen wælgífru, Exon. Th. 292, 16; Wand. 100. II. *eager to prey on the dead*:—Se grǽga mǽw wælgífre wand. Andr. Kmbl. 743; An. 372. Se wanna hrefn, wælgífre fugel, Judth. Thw. 24, 25; Jud. 207. Wulfum tó willan, and eác wælgífrum fuglum tó frófre, 25, 37; Jud. 296. v. wæl-grǽdig.

wæl-gim[m], es; *m. The word seems to be an epithet for the sheath of a sword, which is called in the riddle the sword's* byrne:—Byrne is mín (*a sword's*) bleófág, swylce beorht seomað (-d, MS.) wír ymb ðone wælgim, ðe mé waldend geaf, Exon. Th. 400, 20; Rä. 21, 4.

wæl-grǽdig; *adj. Greedy for the slain* (an epithet of cannibals):—Hæfdon hié áwriten wælgrǽdige wera endestæf, hwænne hié tó móse meteþearfendum weorðan sceoldon, Andr. Kmbl. 269; An. 135. v. wæl-gífre.

wæl-grim[m]; *adj. Cruel, destructive*:—Wælgrim, unhére *funestus, crudelis, perniciosus*, Wrt. Voc. ii. 151, 63: *violentus*, Germ. 399, 467. (1) of living things, *bloodthirsty, cruel*:—Hwæt standest ðú (*the devil*) wælgrim (the MS. breaks off here) . . . ? *quid adstas cruenda bestia?* Blickl. Homl. 227, 26. Wælgrim wiga, Exon. Th. 396, 21; Rä. 16, 8. Heó wæs ǽryst hǽðen and wælgrim, Shrn. 139, 5. Ðone Iacóbum se wælgrimma hyrde (*Herod*) ácwealde mið sweorde, 108, 23. Hí wælgrimme wyrmas slítaþ, Wulfst. 139, 10: Dóm. L. 210. (2) of other than living things, *cruel, dire, destructive*:—Hunger se hearda, wælgrim werum, Cd. Th. 109, 1; Gen. 1816. Nið wæs réðe, wællgrim werum, 83, 23; Gen. 1384. Hé geseah wíde fleógan wælgrimme réc (*the smoke from the burning cities of the plain*), 155, 26; Gen. 2578. Wælgrimme wyrd (*the fall of man*), 61, 12; Gen. 996. Ðé sind heardlícu, wundrum wælgrim (wel-, MS.) wítu geteohhad, Exon. Th. 258, 12; Jul. 264. Gefylstan of ðám wælgrimmum tintregum, L. E. I. proem.; Th. ii. 396, 4. Þolian wælgrim wítu, Andr. Kmbl. 2829; An. 1417. Wæs ðis gefeoht wælgrimre and strengre eallum ðám ǽrgedónum *strages cunctis crudeliores prioribus*, Bd. 1, 12; S. 481, 24. Cf. wæl-hreów.

wæl-grimlíce; *adv. With the utmost bitterness*:—Hí wǽlgrimlíce gefuhton. Ðǽr wæs se mǽsta blódgyte on ǽgðere healfe, Ors. 4, 2; Swt. 160, 31.

wæl-gryre, es; *m. The terror that comes from danger of falling in battle*:—On fyrd hyra (*the Israelites*) fǽrspell (*the tidings of the approach of the Egyptian army*) becwom; egsan stódan, wælgryre weroda, Cd. Th. 186, 11; Exod. 137.

wæl-here, (ig)es; *m. A slaughtering host*:—Fóron tósomne wráðe wælherigas, Cd. Th. 119, 21; Gen. 1983.

wæl-hlem[m], es; *m. A deadly onslaught*:—Hyne Wulf wǽpne geræhte, ðæt him for swenge swát ǽdrum sprong . . .; næs hé forht swâðēh, ac forgeald hraðe wælhlem ðone, Beo. Th. 5931; B. 2969. Cf. hilde-hlem.

wæl-hlenca *or* -hlence, an; *m.* or *f. A slaughter-link, a link of a coat of mail*:—Wriðene wælhlencan, Elen. Kmbl. 47; El. 24. Gûðweard gumena grîmhelm gespeón, . . . [h]wælhlencan sceóc, Cd. Th. 188, 31; Exod. 176.

wæl-hreów, -hreáw, -reów, -rǽw; *adj. Cruel, barbarous, bloodthirsty*:—Wælhreów *crudelis*, Ælfc. Gr. 9, 28; Zup. 54, 12: *atrox*, 9, 66; Zup. 72, 1: *trux*, 9, 67; Zup. 72, 9. Wælhreówe *crudeli*, Wrt. Voc. ii. 23, 22. Ða wælhreówan *funestam*, 38, 20. (1) of living beings:—Wælhreów werod, Cd. Th. 219, 11; Dan. 53. Hē (*Nero*) wælhriów wunode, Met. 9, 38. Hē wæs wælhreáw cwellere cristenra manna, Homl. Th. ii. 308, 4. Welhriöu *crudelis*, Kent. Gl. 367. Irtacus wælreów cyning, Apstls. Kmbl. 137; Ap. 69. Wælreów wiga *a warrior who would not spare his foe*, Beo. Th. 1262; B. 629. Hē wunaþ wælrǽw deófol, Homl. Th. i. 192, 21. Se wælhreówa Antecrist, 6, 16. Se wælhreówa cyning, Ðeódrîc, Bt. 1; Fox 2, 24. Wælhreówes (*Nero's*) gewēd, Met. 9, 5. Ne lǽt ðū on ðæs wælhreówan hond (*crudeli*) ðîn geár, Past. 36; Swt. 249, 11: Homl. Th. i. 80, 31. Ne mæg ic mînne feónd lufian, ðone ðe ic wælhreówne tōgeánes mē geseó, 54, 31. Ðone wælhreówan feónd ðisse menniscan gecynd[e], Blickl. Homl. 31, 31. Ðē wælreówe wîtum belecgaþ, Andr. Kmbl. 2423; An. 1213: Exon. Th. 380, 10; Rä. 1, 6. Ða wælhreówan wyþersacan Annas and Caiphas, Nicod. 7; Thw. 3, 32. Earn beheóld wælhreówra wîg, Elen. Kmbl. 223; El. 112. Wælreówra (-e, MS.) *carnificum*, Hpt. Gl. 483, 60. Ða âne ætwundon ðînum wælhreáwum handum, Homl. Th. ii. 308, 25. Hwæt is wælhreówre betwux næddercynne ðonne draca? i. 486, 31. Ðū wælhreówasta wîmman, Homl. Skt. i. 7, 182. (2) of things:—Ðæt wîf gelȳfde his wælhreówum geðeahte, Homl. Th. ii. 30, 15. Mid wealhreówre ł deóflîcre mihte *tyrannica potestate*, Hpt. Gl. 434, 3. Mid wealreówre grimnysse *crudescente atrocitate*, 515, 23. On þysum wælhreówan cwearterne, Nicod. 26; Thw. 15, 1. Forgripen mid wælhreówe (*crudeli*) deáþe, Bd. 5, 19; S. 638, 24. Tō þrowienne wælhreówne deáð, Homl. Skt. i. 4, 117. Mid wælhreówum dǽdum, 11, 354. Geþeówode þurh wælhreówe unlaga, Wulfst. 158, 14. [Þa welreowen (*those who seized Christ*), O. E. Homl. i. 229, 25.] v. wælgrim.

wælhreówlîce; *adv.* I. *cruelly*:—Se wælhreówlîce (*crudeli caede*) wæs ofslægen, Bd. 3, 14; S. 539, 14. Æt ðæm cirre wurdon Ahtēniense swâ wælhreówlîce forslagen *quam pugnam atrociorem fuisse ipse rerum exitus docuit*, Ors. 3, 7; Swt. 118, 22. Hî woldon habban ðone hâlgan Eásterdæg geblōdegodne ɣwælhreówlîce (wel-, *v. l.*) mid ðæs Hǽlendes blōde, Homl. Ass. 68, 62. Swâ ðæt hē wælhreáwlîce wurde âhangen, Homl. Th. ii. 252, 22. Hē ðæt suîðe wælhreówlîce (*crudeliter*) gecȳdde on Urias slæge, Past. 3; Swt. 35, 23. Ðæt hē ne weorðe wælhreó[w]lîce (-reówlîce, Cott. MSS.) (*crudeliter*) gefangen mid ðǽm grinum uncysta, 43; Swt. 313, 12. Wælhreówlîce swingan, Homl. Th. i. 424, 12. Hî âxodon, hwî hî swâ wælhreówlîce dydon, ðæt hî freónda ne rōhton, Homl. Skt. i. 5, 44. II. *horribly, atrociously*:—Ðæt cild wolde wyrian wælhreáwlîce Drihten, Homl. Th. ii. 326, 10.

wælhreówness, e; *f. Cruelty*:—Wælhreównys *crudelitas*, Ælfc. Gr. 9, 25; Zup. 50, 12: Bd. 1, 14; S. 482, 23 (wæll-, Bd. M. 48, 28). Ðara cyninga wælhreównes wæs tō ðam heard, Bt. 29, 2; Fox 104, 33. Wearð Iulianus for his wælhreównysse ofslægen, Homl. Skt. i. 7, 419. Wē sceolon dēman mildheortlîce būtan wælhreównysse, Homl. Ass. 9, 222. Sceal his steór beón mid lufe gemetegod, nâ mid wælhreáwnysse oferdōn, Homl. Th. ii. 532, 13. Wē witon hwelce wælhriównessa Neron weorhte, Bt. 16, 4; Fox 58, 1.

wæl-hwelp, es; *m. A dog that slays, a dog for hunting*:—Ic (*a badger*) mē siþþan (*after getting to my hole*) ne þearf wælhwelpes wîg wiht onsittan, Exon. Th. 397, 21; Rä. 16, 23.

Wælisc, wæll-. v. Wilisc, wæl-.

wǽl-lîc (?); *adj. Deep* (of water):—On deópum ł in welicum (= wǽllîcum. v. wǽl) grunde sǽwe *in fundo maris*, Hpt. Gl. 452, 23.

wælm. v. wilm.

wæl-mist, es; *m. A mist that covers the bodies of the slain*:—Hreám wæs on ȳðum, wæter wǽpna ful, wælmist âstâh (*the passage refers to the destruction of the Egyptians in the Red Sea*), Cd. Th. 206, 12; Exod. 450. Sum sceal on galgan rîdan . . . hē, blāc on beáme, bîdeþ wyrde bewegen wælmiste, Exon. Th. 329, 30; Vy. 42.

wæl-net[t], es; *n. The net of destruction* (?), Cd. Th. 190, 20; Exod. 202.

wæl-nîþ, es; *m. Deadly hate, mortal enmity*:—Ðæt ys sió fǽhðo, and se feóndscipe, wælnîð wera, Beo. Th. 5992; B. 3000. Æfter wælnîðe, 170; B. 85. Âwehte ðone wælnîð Nabochodonossor, Cd. Th. 218, 28; Dan. 46. Weallaþ wælnîðas, Beo. Th. 4136; B. 2065.

wæl-not, es; *m. A fatal mark, a mark that brings death, a rune that brings death.* v. Kemble in Archæologia, vol. 28, p. 336. See for baleful influence of runes, Egils Saga, c. 75: Grettis Saga, c. 81; see also Corpus Poeticum Boreale, vol. i. pp. 40, 41, for the virtues of runes:—Hwîlum hié (*fiends*) gefeteraþ fǽges monnes handa, gehefegaþ ðonne hē æt hilde sceall wið lâð werud lîfes tiligan; âwrîtaþ hié on his wǽpne wælnota heáp, bealwe bōcstafas, Salm. Kmbl. 324; Sal. 161.

wæl-pîl, es; *m. A deadly dart, death-pang*:—Wæs his mondryhtne endedōgor, . . . âwrecen wælpîlum wlō ne meahte oroð up geteón, Exon. Th. 171, 15; Gū. 1127.

wæl-rǽs, es; *m. A deadly attack, an attack in which men are slain*:—Wæs sió swâtswaðu Sweóna and Geáta, wælrǽs wera, wîde gesȳne, Beo. Th. 5886; B. 2947. Æfter wælrǽse wunde gedȳgan, 5055; B. 2531. Æfter ðam wælrǽse (*the fight in which Grendel was mortally wounded*), 1652; B. 824. Mē ðone wælrǽs wine Scyldinga leánode, 4208; B. 2101.

wæl-rǽw. v. wæl-hreów.

wæl-râp, es; *m. A rope that binds the deep, a rope with which frost binds the water*:—Ðonne forstes bend Fæder onlǽteþ, onwindeþ wælrâpas, Beo. Th. 3224; B. 1610. v. wǽl.

wæl-reáf, es; *n.* I. *what is taken from the slain, spoil taken in war, spoil, prey*:—Waelreáf (wael-, uuel-reáb) *manubium*, Txts. 77, 1277. Wælreáf, Wrt. Voc. ii. 54, 44: *manubia* (the passage is: Vesperi dirimens manubias (v. Gen. 49, 27), Ald. 26), 78, 48. Hē under segne sinc ealgode, wælreáf werede, Beo. Th. 2414; B. 1205. Ic sceal langne hâm âna gesēcan, lǽt mē on lâste lîc eorðan dǽl wælreáf wunigean weormum tō hrōðre, Apstls. Kmbl. 189; Ap. 95. Hē (*the phoenix*) gebringeþ ǽdes lâfe (*what is left after it is burnt*) eft ætsomne and ðæt wælreáf (*exuvias suas*) wyrtum biteldeþ, Exon. Th. 216, 24; Ph. 273. II. as a technical term, *robbing the slain*:—Walreáf is nîðinges dǽde, L. Ath. iv. 7; Th. i. 228, 3. Cf. Qui aliquem quocunque modo perimit, videat ne weilref faciat. Weilref dicimus, si quis mortuum refabit armis aut vestibus, aut prorsus aliquibus, aut tumulatum aut tumulandum, L. H. I. 83, 2; Th. i. 591, 12, and see two following sections. [*O. H. Ger.* wala-raupa (*de vestitu mortuorum, quod walaraupa dicimus*): *Icel.* val-rauf *spoils*; val-rof *the plundering the slain on the battle-field.*] Cf. here-reáf.

wæl-réc, es; *m. Deadly reek*:—'Mē is leófre ðæt mînne lîchaman glēd fæþmie' . . . Wōd ða þurh ðone wælrēc, Beo. Th. 5315; B. 2661.

wæl-regn, es; *m. A deadly rain* (the rain that caused the Flood):—Ic on andwlitan sîgan lǽte wællregn ufan wîdre eorðan; fǽhðe ic wille on weras stǽlan, and mid wǽgþreáte eall âcwellan, Cd. Th. 81, 24; Gen. 1350.

wæl-reów. v. wæl-hreów.

wæl-rest, -ræst, e; *f. The rest* or *bed of the slain*:—Wælræste wunian *to be dead*, Beo. Th. 5796; B. 2902: Exon. Th. 184, 10; Gū. 1342. Wælreste ceósan *to die*, Cd. Th. 99, 8; Gen. 1643: Byrht. Th. 135, 5; By. 113. Sceal fǽge flǽschoma foldærne biþeaht wunian wælræste (*inhabit the grave*), Exon. Th. 164, 3; Gū. 1006. Sió rōd foldan getȳned wunode wælreste (*lay buried*), Elen. Kmbl. 1444; El. 724.

wæl-rūn, e; *f. The secret of approaching slaughter*:—Fyrdleóð âgōl wulf on walde, wælrūne ne māð (*proclaimed the coming carnage*), Elen. Kmbl. 56; El. 28.

wæl-sceaft, es; *m. A deadly shaft*, Beo. Th. 801; B. 398.

wæl-scel *slaughter, the slain*:—Cirdon cynerōfe wîggend on wiþertrod wælscel oninnan, reócende hrǽw, Judth. Thw. 26, 6; Jud. 313. v. scelle.

wæl-seax, es; *n. A war-knife, a sword* or *dagger used in fight*:—Hē wælseaxe gebrǽd, ðæt hē on byrnan wæg, Beo. Th. 5400; B. 2703.

wæl-sliht, -sleaht, es; *m. Slaughter in battle, slaughter, carnage*:—Hēr wæs micel wælsliht (-sleht, MS. E.) on Lundenne, Chr. 839; Erl. 66, 16. Ðǽr wearþ micel wælsliht on gehwæþere hond, 871; Erl. 74, 32. Wǽpna wælslihtes, Cd. Th. 198, 25; Exod. 328. Gemyndig wælsleahta, Exon. Th. 286, 27; Wand. 7: 291, 32; Wand. 91. Wæs on healle wælslihta gehlyn, Fins. Th. 57; Fin. 28. [Grickes hit (*Troy*) biuunnan mid heora wælslahte (bitere slahtes, 2nd MS.), Laym. 1369.]

wæl-slîtende; *adj. Corpse-rending, that rends the dead*:—Ðæt lîc ðǽr (*in the grave*) tō fūlnesse weorðeþ and ðām wælslîtendum wyrmum weorðeþ tō ǽte, Wulfst. 187, 14. On helle mid deóflum and mid dracum and mid wælslîtendum wyrmum, 241, 12.

wæl-spere, es; *n. A battle-spear, spear with which slaughter is to be wrought*:—Oft hē gâr forlēt, wælspere windan on ða wîcingas, Byrht. Th. 141, 14; By. 322. Syx smiðas sǽtan wælspera worhtan, Lchdm. iii. 52, 31. [Forwunded mid walspere brade, Laym. 28577.]

wæl-steng, es; *m. A spear*:—Feówer scoldon on ðæm wælstenge weorcum geferian Grendles heáfod, Beo. Th. 3280; B. 1638.

wæl-stōw, e; *f. The place of the slain*, (1) *a battle-field*:—God âna wât hwâ ðære wælstōwe wealdan mōte *God only knows who shall be master of the field*, Byrht. Th. 134, 36; By. 95: Beo. Th. 4108; B. 2051: 5960; B. 2984: Cd. Th. 121, 4; Gen. 2005. Ða Deniscan âhton wælstōwe gewald, Chr. 837; Erl. 66, 9: 871; Erl. 76, 7. Æþelwulf cyning gefeaht wiþ .xxxv. sciphlæsta, and ða Deniscan âhton wælstōwe geweald, 840; Erl. 66, 19. Hié ðǽr nâu licgende feoh ne mētten, swâ hié ǽr bewuna wǽron ðonne hié wælstōwe geweald âhton, Ors. 3, 7; Swt. 116, 33. On here crincgan, on wælstōwe wundum sweltan, Byrht. Th. 140, 24; By. 293: Chr. 937; Erl. 114, 9. (2) *any* *place where there is slaughter*:—Him Loth gewât of byrig (*Sodom, about to be destroyed*) gangan, wælstôwe fyrr, Cd. Th. 156, 23; Gen. 2593. [Cf. *O. H. Ger.* wal-stat: *Dan.* val-plads *battle-field*, beholde valpladsen *to remain master of the field.*]

wæl-strǽl; *m. f. A fatal shaft*:—Bâd se ðe sceolde endedôgor âwrecen wælstrǽlum (*the pangs of mortal disease*), Exon. Th. 179, 11; Gû. 1260.

wæl-streám, es; *m. A destructive stream*:—Ðonne wælstreámas (*the waters of the Deluge*) werodum swelgaþ, sceaðum scyldfullum, Cd. Th. 78, 30; Gen. 1301.

wæl-sweng, es; *m. A murderous stroke*:—Æfter wælswenge (*the stroke which killed Abel*), Cd. Th. 60, 25; Gen. 987.

wælt *apparently some part of the thigh, a sinew* (?):—Gif wælt wund weorðeþ, .iii. scillingas gebête, L. Ethb. 68; Th. i. 18, 19. (The preceding section deals with wounds to the thigh. As regards the form of the word, it might be compared with *O. H. Ger.* walza *decipula, pedica.*)

wæltan. v. wiltan.

wæl-wang, es; *m. A plain of slaughter*:—Ðǽr wæs secg manig on ðam wælwange (*the place at which were assembled those who maltreated St. Andrew*) wîges oflysted, Andr. Kmbl. 2453; An. 1228.

wæl-weg (= hwæl-weg *or* wǽl-weg) *the sea*:—Hweteþ on wælweg ofer holma gelagu, Exon. Th. 309, 26; Seef. 63.

wæl-wulf, es; *m.* I. as an epithet of a warrior, *a war-wolf, one who is as fierce to slay as is a wolf*:—Wôdon wælwulfas, wîcinga werod, Byrht. Th. 134, 38; By. 96. II. as an epithet of a cannibal, *a fierce cannibal, one who preys on the dead like the wolf*:—Wælwulfas bânhringas âbrecan þóhton, tôlýsan lîc and sáwle, and ðonne tôdǽlan werum tô wiste fǽges flǽschoman, Andr. Kmbl. 297; An. 149.

wæm[m], wǽman. v. wem[m], wêman.

wæmbede; *adj. Having a great belly*; ventriculosus, Wrt. Voc. i. 45, 37.

wǽmn, wǽn, wæn[n], wǽnan, wænge, wænian, Wænte, wænys (Hpt. 438, 70), wǽpan. v. wǽpen, wægn, wen[n], wênan, wenge, wenian, Wintan-ceaster, wâcness, wêpan.

wǽpen, wǽpn, es; *n.* I. *a weapon*:—Steng oððe wǽpen *clava*, Wrt. Voc. ii. 20, 63. Mê sceal wǽpen niman, ord and îren, Byrht. Th. 139, 11; By. 252. Ðis (*the bridle into which the nails from the cross were put*) bið unoferswîðed wǽpen, Elen. Kmbl. 2375; El. 1189. Ǽlces wǽpnes ord *mucro*, Wrt. Voc. i. 35, 35. Swurdes ord oððe ôðres wǽpnes, 84, 22. Wǽpnes ecge, Cd. Th. 109, 30; Gen. 1830. Gehealdan heardne mêce, wǽpnes wealdan, Byrht. Th. 136, 48; By. 168. Gif hê folcgemôt mid wǽpnes brýde ârǽre, L. Alf. pol. 38; Th. i. 86, 16. Be ðâm monnum ðe heora wǽpna tô monslyhte lǽnaþ. Gif hwâ his wǽpnes ôðrum onlǽne ðæt hê mon mid ofsleá, 19; Th. i. 74, 1-4. Wǽpnes spor *a wound*, Exon. Th. 280, 2; Jul. 623. Âwrîtaþ hié on his wǽpne wælnota heáp, Salm. Kmbl. 323; Sal. 161. Ic ðý wǽpne gebrǽd, Beo. Th. 3333; B. 1664. Hê ðæs beran ceaflas tôtær bûton ǽlcum wǽmne, Ælfc. T. Grn. 7, 16. Gif man wǽpn âbregde ðǽr mæn drincen, L. H. E. 13; Th. i. 32, 11. Ðeáh hwâ his âgen spere sette tô ôðres mannes hûses dura . . . oþþon gif man ôðer wǽpn lecge . . . and hwilc man ðæt wǽpn gelæcce, L. C. S. 76; Th. i. 418, 6. Hê wǽpen hafenade be hiltum, Beo. Th. 3151; B. 1573. Nolde ic sweord beran, wǽpen tô wyrme, 5031; B. 2519: 5367; B. 2687. Gif sweordhwîta ôðres monnes wǽpn tô feormunge onfô, oððe smið monnes andweorc, L. Alf. pol. 19; Th. i. 74, 9. Sum mæg stýled sweord, wǽpen gewyrcan, Exon. Th. 42, 29; Cri. 680. Hê wǽpen up âhôf, bord tô gebeorge, Byrht. Th. 135, 39; By. 130. Wǽpnu *arma*, Ælfc. Gr. 36; Zup. 215, 15. Wǽpna *arma*, wǽpna hûs *armamentarium*, Wrt. Voc. i. 35, 1, 2. Eorlas fornôman wǽpen wælgîfru, Exon. Th. 292, 16; Wand. 100. Wêpen *arma*, Ps. Surt. 56, 5. Se hâlga hêht his heorðwerod wǽpna onfôn, Cd. Th. 123, 5; Gen. 2040. Hê ne mihte wǽpna gewealdan, Beo. Th. 3022; B. 1509: Byrht. Th. 139, 50; By. 272. Wǽpna wyrpum, Exon. Th. 35, 28; Cri. 565. Wǽpna wundum, 119, 15; Gû. 255. Wǽpna wælslihtes, Cd. Th. 198, 25; Exod. 328. Seó wǽpna lâf *those whom the sword spared*, 121, 5; Gen. 2005: 220, 20; Dan. 74. Se helm hafelan werede . . . hine worhte wǽpna smið, Beo. Th. 2908; B. 1452. Ðâ fôr hê mid eallum his folce and mid eallum his wǽpnum *omnis equitatus Pharaonis, currus ejus et equites*, Ex. 14, 23. Gif man mannan wǽpnum bebyreþ ðǽr ceás weorð, L. Ethb. 18; Th. i. 6, 19. Ðæt folc com mid wǽpnum (woepnum, Lind.: wêpenu, Rush.) *venit cum armis*, Jn. Skt. 18, 3: Andr. Kmbl. 2140; An. 1071. Gegearwod wǽpnum, Elen. Kmbl. 95; El. 48. Wǽpnum geweordad, Beo. Th. 505; B. 250: 667; B. 331. Ǽlc þing ðe orðode, hê âcwealde mid wǽpnum *omne, quod spirare poterat, interfecit*, Jos. 10, 40. Wǽpnum âswebban, Apstls. Kmbl. 138; Ap. 69. Leohtum wǽpnum (*levibus armis*) gegyrwan, Nar. 10, 27. Scearpum wǽpnum, Exon. Th. 385, 30; Rä. 4, 52. Mid gǽstlîcum wǽpnum, 112, 24; Gû. 148. Gescyldend wið sceaðan wǽpnum, Andr. Kmbl. 2584; An. 1298: Exon. Th. 48, 22; Cri. 775. Hî wurpon hyra wǽpen of dûne, Judth. Thw. 25, 33; Jud. 291. Wǽpen and gewǽdu, Beo. Th. 589; B. 292. Wǽpen healdan, mêce, gâr and gôd swurd, Byrht. Th. 138, 45; By. 235. Wêpen and sceldas *arma et scuta*, Ps. Surt. 45, 10. Ealle his wǽpnu (woepeno, Lind.: wêpeno, Rush.) hê him âfyrð, Lk. Skt. 11, 22. Hê âwearp his wǽmna, Ælfc. T. Grn. 18, 31. Hié him ealle hiera wǽpeno âgeáfen *arma traderent*, Ors. 4, 13; Swt. 210, 21. Hié wǽpna nâman *arma sumunt*, 1, 10; Swt. 44, 32. Nimaþ eówre wǽpn *ponat vir gladium super femur suum*, Ex. 32, 27. Gegrîp (gefôh, Ps. Th.) wǽpn (wêpen, Ps. Surt.) and scyld *apprehende arma et scutum*, Ps. Spl. 34, 2. Uoepeno, Rtl. 168, 1. Ðeáh ðe hî wǽpen ne beran *quamvis arma non ferant*, Bd. 2, 2; S. 504, 3. Hê ða gâstlîcan wǽpnu ne mæg âberan, Basil admn. 2; Norm. 36, 27. II. *membrum virile*:—Teors *veretrum*, teors, ðæt wǽpen *vel* lim *calamus*, Wrt. Voc. i. 283, 56. Wǽpen, gecynd (*printed* wepen-gecynd; *but see* gecynd, II) *veretrum*, 44, 58. [Whiles þow art ȝonge, and þi wepne kene, wreke þe with wyuynge, Piers P. 9, 180.] v. wǽpen-lîc, -mann, wǽpned. [*Goth.* wêpna; *pl. arma*: *O. Sax.* wâpan: *O. Frs.* wêpin: *O. H. Ger.* wâfan *gladius, framea, telum, falx, scutum*: *Icel.* vápn.] v. beadu-, camp-, heoru-, here-, hilde-, sige-, weoruld-, wîg-wǽpen.

wǽpen-berend, es; *m. An armed man*:—Se stronga woepenberend (wêpend-, Rush.) gehealdaþ ceafertûn his *fortis armatus custodit atrium suum*, Lk. Skt. Lind. 11, 21: p. 7, 5. [*O. Sax.* wâpan-berand.]

wǽpen-bora, an; *m. One who bears arms, a warrior*:—Wǽpnbora *armiger*, Ælfc. Gr. 8; Zup. 27, 17: Wrt. Voc. i. 84, 14. Wǽpenbora, 35, 9: *bellator*, ii. 125, 35. Wǽpenboran *pugiles, gladium portantes, gladiatores*, Hpt. Gl. 424, 15.

wǽpen-getæc, -tak, es; *n. A wapentake*, a term used in northern England where in the south *hundred* was used: 'Quod alii vocant hundredum, supradicti comitatus (*counties northward from Northamptonshire*) vocant wapentagium,' L. Ed. C. 30; Th. i. 455. The word, which seems of Danish origin (cf. Icel. *vápna-tak*, though this is used in a different sense), is thus explained in the document above cited: Cum quis accipiebat prefecturam wapentagii, die statuto in loco ubi consuev-erant congregari, omnes majores natu contra eum conveniebant, et, descendente eo de equo suo, omnes assurgebant ei. Ipse vero erecta lancea sua, ab omnibus, secundum morem, foedus accipiebat: omnes enim quotquot venissent cum lanceis suis ipsius hastam tangebant, et ita se confirmabant per contactum armorum, pace palam concessa. Anglice vero arma vocantur wapen, et taccare confirmare, quasi armorum confirmacio, vel ut magis expresse, secundum linguam Anglicam, dicamus wapentac, i. e. armorum tactus: wapen enim arma sonat, tac tactus est. Quamobrem potest cognosci quod hac de causa totus ille conventus dicitur wapentac, eo quod per tactum armorum suorum ad invicem confoederates sunt. On this explanation see Stubbs' Const. Hist. i. 99 sq:—Wê willaþ ðæt man namige on ǽlcon wǽpengetæce .ii. trýwe þegnas, L. N. P. L. 57; Th. ii. 298, 31. Ǽlc ðara ceápa ðe hê bigcge oððe sylle âðer oþþe [on] burge oþþe on wǽpengetæce, L. Edg. 5, 6; Th. i. 274, 14. On wǽpentake, L. Eth. iii. 1; Th. i. 292, 8: iii. 3; Th. i. 294, 3, 8.

wǽpen-geþræc [?], es; *n. A weapon*:—Ofsend uoepengiðræcc (uoepen, giðræcc?) *effunde frameam*, Rtl. 168, 5. Cf. Geþrece *apparatu*, Wrt. Voc. ii. 1, 24: 76, 53: Hpt. Gl. 424, 77. Geþræce, 512, 9.

wǽpen-gewrixl, -gewrixle, es; *n. A passage of arms, an exchange of blows, a conflict, fight*:—Gif hit geweorðe, ðæt wǽpngewrixl weorðe gemǽne þegene and þræle, Wulfst. 162, 7. Ðæt heó beaduweorca beteran wurdun on campstede, gârmittinge, gumena gemôtes, wǽpengewrixles, Chr. 937; Erl. 114, 17. [Cf. *Icel.* vápna-skipti, -viðskipti.]

wǽpen-hete, es; *m. Armed hate, hate that resorts to arms*:—Æðele sceoldon ðurh wǽpenhete weorc þrowian *the noble ones were to be slain by their foes*, Apstls. Kmbl. 159; Ap. 80.

wǽpen-hûs, es; *n. An armoury*:—Wǽpenhûs *armamentarium*, Wrt. Voc. ii. 6, 17. [*O. H. Ger.* wâfan-hûs.]

wǽpen-leás; *adj. Without arms, unarmed*:—Ðam wǽpenleásan menn ne mihton ða wælhreówan mid wǽpnum wiðstandam, Homl. Skt. ii. 29, 175. Fram wǽpenleásre fêmnan *e virgine inermi*, Wrt. Voc. ii. 144, 38. Gehwilce wǽpenleáse *inermes* (*sine armis*) *quosque*, Hpt. Gl. 423, 48. [*Icel.* vápn-lauss.]

wǽpen-lîc; *adj. Male, masculine*:—Ðæt wǽpenlîce lim *calamus*, Wrt. Voc. ii. 16, 58. Ða wǽpenlîcan limo *preputia*, 68, 60: 69, 16.

wǽpen-mann (wǽp-), es; *m. A male, a man*:—Wǽpnmann *mas*, Anglia xiii. 366, 23. Êghuelc hê ł woepenmon (wêpenmon, Rush.: wæpned, W. S.) *omne masculinum*, Lk. Skt. 2, 23. Wer oððe wǽpman *vir*, Wrt. Voc. i. 73, 11. Ðes wǽpman *hic mas*, Ælfc. Gr. 9, 25; Zup. 50, 15. Ne scrîde nân wîf hig mid wǽpmannes reáfe (*veste virili*), ne wǽpman (*vir*) mid wîfmannes reáfe, Deut. 22, 5. Woepenmon ł hee *masculum*, Mk. Skt. Lind. 10, 6. Hê worhte wǽpman (woepenmonn *masculum*, Lind.), Mt. Kmbl. 19, 4. Synna wið wǽpman oððe wîfman, L. de Cf. 6; Th. ii. 262, 23. Riht is ðæt ǽnige wǽpnmen on mynecena beóderne ne etan ne drincan, Wulfst. 269, 9. Wêpmen (wǽpned-, *v. l.*) ge wîfmen, Bd. 3, 5; S. 527, 7. Wǽpmen, Homl. Ass. 27, 73. XX M wîfmanna and wǽpmanna (wǽpned-, *v. l.*), Ors. 3, 7; Bos. 61, 30: Homl. Th. i. 442, 1: Ælfc. Gr. 6; Zup. 24, 5. Mægðhâd is ǽgðer ge on wǽpmannum ge on wîfmannum, Homl. Th. i. 148, 14. [*O. E. Homl.* wap-man *vir*: *Laym.* wap-, wep-mon: *A. R.* wep-, weop-man: *Orm.*

wepp-mann: *Kath.* wep-man: *O. and N.* wep-mon: *Gen. and Ex.* wap-man.] v. wǣpen, **II**, wǣpned, wǣpned-mann.

wǣpen-strǣl, es; *m. An arrow to be used as a weapon*:—Synd mē manna bearn mihtigum tōðum wǣpenstrǣlas *filii hominum dentes eorum arma et sagittae*, Ps. Th. 56, 5.

wǣpen-þracu; *gen.* -þræce; *f. Force of arms*:—Hine monige on winnaþ mid wǣpenþræce, Cd. Th. 138, 12; Gen. 2290. Hē hēht wīgend weccan and wǣpenþræce, Elen. Kmbl. 212; El. 106. [Cf. *O. Sax.* wāpan-threki.]

wǣpen-þrǣge *arms* (?):—Sum mæg wǣpenþrǣge (-þræce (?), cf. (?) wǣpen-geþræc), wīge tō nytte, mōdcræftig smið, monige gefremman, ðonne hē gewyrceþ tō wera hilde helm oððe hupseax, oððe heaþubyrnan, scīrne mēce, oððe scyldes rond fæste gefēgan wið flyge gāres, Exon. Th. 296, 34; Crä. 61.

wǣpen-wīfestre, an; *f. A hermaphrodite;* hermafroditus, Wrt. Voc. i. 45, 28.

wǣpen-wiga, an; *m. An armed warrior*:—Ic wæs wǣpenwiga (wǣpen wigan? *the subject of the riddle is a horn*), nū mec þeceþ geong hagostealdmon golde and sylfore, Exon. Th. 395, 1; Rä. 15, 1.

wǣp-mann, wǣpn. v. wǣpen-mann, wǣpen.

wǣpned; *adj. Male;* used substantively, *a male, a man*:—Ǣlc wǣpned gecyndlim ontȳnende *omne masculinum adaperiens uuluam*, Lk. Skt. 2, 23. Micel gedāl is on wǣpnedes and wīfes līchoman, Lchdm. ii. 84, 16. Se ðe mid wǣpnedum men hǣme *qui cum viro coiverit*, L. Ecg. C. 16; Th. ii. 144, 7. Wēpned and wīf geworhte hiǽ God *masculum et feminam fecit eos*, Mt. Kmbl. Rush. 19, 4. Wīf and wǣpned, Cd. Th. 12, 33; Gen. 195: 166, 9; Gen. 2745. Wīfes meoluc ðe wǣpned fēde, Lchdm. ii. 338, 8. v. wǣpen, **II**, *and following compounds.*

wǣpned-bearn, es; *n. A male child, a boy*:—For wǣpnedbearne ... for wīfcilde *pro masculo . . . pro femina*, Bd. 1, 27; S. 493, 14.

wǣpned-cild, es; *n. A male child, a boy*:—Tō ðan ðæt wīf cenne wǣpnedcild, Lchdm. i. 344, 22: 346, 3. Ða þīnena heóldon ða wǣpnedcild (*mares*), Ex. 1, 17: *pueros*, 1, 18.

wǣpned-cyn[n], es; *n. The male kind* or *sex*:—Wǣpnedcyn *masculinum*, Wrt. Voc. ii. 56, 4. Ǣlc þing wǣpnedcynnes *omne generis masculini*, Ex. 34, 19: Cd. Th. 139, 19; Gen. 2312: 142, 35; Gen. 2372: 189, 21; Exod. 188. Wið ðon ðe mon oððe nȳten wyrm gedrince; gyf hit sȳ wǣpnedcynnes . . ., Lchdm. iii. 10, 11. Hwylce wihta beóð ōðre tīd wīfcynnes, and ōðre tīd wǣpnedcynnes, Salm. Kmbl. p. 202, 13: Exon. Th. 419, 22; Rä. 39, 1. Ðæt hī mā of ðam wīfcynne him cyning curan ðonne of ðam wǣpnedcynne *ut magis de feminea regum prosapia quam de masculina regem sibi eligerent*, Bd. 1, 1; S. 473, 22.

wǣpned-hād, es; *m. The male sex*:—Swā hwæt swā wǣpnedhādes beó ācenned *quidquid masculini sexus natum fuerit*, Ex. 1, 22: Num. 1, 2. Ǣrfeweard wēpnedhādes, Chart. Th. 483, 17.

wǣpned-hand, a; *f. The male side, male line*:—Hȳ fōð tō mīnum ðe ic syllan mōt swā wīfhanda swā wǣpnedhanda, swaðer ic wylle, Chart. Th. 491, 32.

wǣpned-healf, e; *f. The male side*:—Ðonne is mē leófast, ðæt hit gange on ðæt [bearn] strȳned on ða wǣpnedhealfe, ða hwīle ðe ǣnig ðæs wyrðe sȳ, Chart. Th. 491, 16.

wǣpned-mann, es; *m.* **I.** *a male, a man*:—Þriwa on gēre ǣlc wǣpnedman (*omne masculinum tuum*) ætȳwð beforan Drihtne, Ex. 23, 17: Num. 34, 23. Wǣpnedman (-men?) *mares*, Wrt. Voc. ii. 58, 50. Se cyning wæs gōd wǣpnedman *rex erat vir bonus*, Bd. 3, 7; S. 529, 39. Ðū (*Eve*) scealt wǣpnedmen wesan on gewealde, Cd. Th. 56, 29; Gen. 919. Wæs se gryre læssa efne swā micle swā bið wīggryre wīfes be wǣpnedmen, Beo. Th. 2573; B. 1284. God hī geworhte wǣpnedman and wīmman (wǣpman and wȳfman, MS. A.: wǣpned and wīmman, MS. B.: wēpnedmenn and wīfmenn, Rush.) *masculum et feminam fecit eos Deus*, Mk. Skt. 10, 6. Heó eode tō ðære wǣpnedmanna stōwe (*ad locum virorum*), Bd. 3, 11; S. 536, 19. XX M wīfmonna and wǣpnedmonna *viginti millia puerorum ac foeminarum*, Ors. 3, 7; Swt. 116, 31. Ðara manna eallra, mid wīfmannum and wǣpnedmannum, Blickl. Homl. 79, 19. Hiora wīf ofslōgan ealle ða wǣpnedmen ðe him on neáweste wǣron, Ors. 1, 10; Swt. 48, 1, 6, 8. **II.** of plants, *a male*:—Gif man scyle mugcwyrt tō lǣcedōme habban, ðonne nime man ða reádan wǣpnedmen and ða grēnan wīfmen, Lchdm. iii. 72, 20. v. wǣpen-mann.

wǣpnian; *p.* ode *To provide with weapons, to arm*:—Ic wǣpnige ðē *armo te*, Ælfc. Gr. 19; Zup. 122, 16: 36; Zup. 215, 16. Ic wǣpnige sumne man *armo*, 43; Zup. 257, 12. Uoepnedum *armata*, Rtl. 99, 20. [Wepne þine cnihtes, Laym. 17945. He hæhte wepnien (wepni, 2nd MS.) his uolc, 20347. Heo wepnede hire mid bileaue, Kath. 188. Itt þatt wæpnedd iss wiþþ trowwþe on Criste, Orm. 677. *O. Frs.* wēpened: *O. H. Ger.* wāfenen *armare*: *Icel.* vāpna.] v. be-, ge-wǣpnian.

wǣpnung, e; *f. Armour, arms*:—[Gāstlī]cere weápnunge *spiritalis armaturae*, Hpt. Gl. 423, 65. Ymbscrȳdaþ eów mid Godes wǣpnunge *induite vos armaturam Dei* (Eph. 6, 11), Homl. Th. ii. 218, 2. Næs Petrus gewunod tō nānre wǣpnunge, 248, 3. Golias gearu tō ānwīge mid ormǣttre wǣpnunge, Homl. Skt. i. 18, 21. Iudas com mid ðām cwealmbǣrum mid ormǣtere wǣpnunge (*with an immense amount of weapons*), Homl. Ass. 74, 44: Homl. Th. ii. 302, 4.

wæps, wæsp, es; *m. A wasp*:—Waefs *fespa*, Txts. 63, 859. Waefs *vel* hurnitu (uaeps, Erf. Gl.) *crabro*, 55, 603. Wæps *vespa*, Wrt. Voc. i. 23, 66: *fe[s]pa*, ii. 35, 27. Wæsp, 148, 17: *vespis*, i. 281, 37. Weaps *vespa*, 77, 49. Uuaefsas (waeffsas, Ep. Gl.) *vespas* (uuaeps *vespa*, Erf. Gl.), Txts. 105, 2098. [*O. H. Ger.* wafsa, wefsa.]

wær; *adj.* **I.** *ware, aware, having knowledge* of something which is to be guarded against:—Ðā wurdon ða landleóde his (*a band of Danes*) ware and him wiþ gefuhton, Chr. 917; Erl. 102, 17. Hē eode nihtes, ðæt hē his līfe geburge, ac ða hǣðenan wurdon wære his fare, Homl. Skt. i. 22, 230. **II.** *ware, prepared* for, *on guard* against something that might be hurtful, (a) absolute:—Beó gē wære *uos estote parati*, Lk. Skt. 12, 40. Ūs is mycel þearf, ðæt wē geornlīce wacian and wære beón, Btwk. 220, 27. Se Hǣlend ūs warnode, for ðam ðe hē wyle, ðæt wē ware beón, Homl. Ass. 55, 113. Man sceal wacigean and warnian symle, ðæt man geara weorðe . . . Leófan men, utan beón ðe wærran, Wulfst. 90, 10. (b) with gen.:—Ūs is micel þearf, ðæt wē wære beón ðæs egeslīcan tīman, ðe nū tōwærd is, Wulfst. 191, 25. (c) with preposition:—Wes ðū giedda wīs, wær wið willan, Exon. Th. 302, 26; Fä. 42. Sōna wyrð deófol inne; is micel þearf ðæt manna gehwylc wið swylc wær sȳ, Wulfst. 280, 11. Ðæt wē geornlīce wacian and ā wære beón wið deófles costnunga, Btwk. 220, 35. Woruldmenn wǣron wære wið heora fȳnd, Homl. Skt. i. 13, 150. Wosas gē wære fram monnum *cavete ab hominibus*, Mt. Kmbl. Lind. 10, 17. **III.** *ware, careful* to avoid something, *on guard* against doing something, (a) with gen.:—Wēnde ic ðæt ðū ðȳ wærra weorþan sceolde swylces gemōtes, Exon. Th. 267, 34; Jul. 425. (b) with preposition:—Beó wær æt ðam, ðæt ðū nǣfre mīnne sunu þyder ne lǣde *cave, ne quando reducas filium meum illuc*, Gen. 24, 6. (c) with a clause:—Mīn bearn, beó ðē wærr ðæt ðū ne drince of ðam wīne, Homl. Th. ii. 170, 17. Wærne ðē beón, ðæt ðū nāht unrihtes ne dō getācnaþ, Lchdm. iii. 214, 25. **IV.** *ware, observant* of, *attentive* to a warning:—Ðæt hī wære beón ðæs cwydes, Wulfst. 7, 6: L. I. P. 19; Th. ii. 330, 2. **V.** *wary, cautious, sagacious, prudent, cunning*:—Wær *cautus*, i. *sagax*, *prudens*, *acutus*, Wrt. Voc. ii. 130, 5. Wær geápnis *argumentum*, 125, 1. Hē bið scarp and biter and swīðe wær on his wordum, Lchdm. iii. 162, 13. Hē wær (*printed* þær) weorðe worda and dǣda, Exon. Th. 96, 32; Cri. 1583. Deófol gedēð, ðæt unsǣlig man wīsdōmes ne gȳmeþ, and gyt gedēð, ðæt hē talaþ hine sylfne wærne and wīsne, Wulfst. 52, 29. Beó gē swā ware suā suā nǣdran *estote prudentes sicut serpentes*, Past. 35; Swt. 237, 20. Hig sint wære and cunnon þēnunga, and hig cennaþ ǣr ðam ðe wyt cumon tō him *ipsae obstetricandi habent scientiam, et priusquam veniamus ad eas pariunt*, Ex. i. 19. Se wīsdōm gedēþ his lufiendas wīse and wære, Bt. 27, 2; Fox 98, 1. Werra bið *astutior fiet*, Kent. Gl. 509. Gielpaþ hié suelce hī sién micle wærran and wīsran ðonne hié *quasi praestantius ceteris prudentes se esse glorientur*, Past. 35; Swt. 243, 25. Ðæt se bið on geþance wǣrast and wīsast, se ðe ōðerne can raðost āsmeágean, Wulfst. 55, 21. Se þincð nū wærrest and geápest ðe ōðerne mæig beswīcan, Shrn. 17, 23. [*Goth.* wars wisan *to be ware*: *O. Sax.* war wesan wiðar: *O. H. Ger.* gi-war *providus, solers, gnarus, intentus, adtentus, vigilans*: *Icel.* varr.] v. ge-, un-wær.

wær *the sea*:—Wē ðissa leóda land gesōhton wære bewrecene, Andr. Kmbl. 537; An. 269. Hū ðū wǣgflotan, wære bestēmdan, sǣhengeste, sund wīsige, 974; An. 487. [*Icel.* wer; *n.* (poet.) *the sea.*]

wǣr, e; *f. A covenant, compact, agreement, pledge*:—Wǣr is ætsomne Godes and monna, gǣsthālig treów, Exon. Th. 36, 29; Cri. 583. [Gewemme]dre wǣre *violati foederis* (*pacti*), Hpt. Gl. 496, 3: Cd. Th. 186, 18; Exod. 140. Wǣre gemyndig, 143, 1; Gen. 2372. Wǣre (cf. *Icel. use in pl.*) *foedus*, i. *pactum, conjunctio*, Wrt. Voc. ii. 148, 43. Clam oððe wed oððe wǣra *clasma*, 21, 2. Wǣra *foedera*, i. *pacta amicitiae, certa amicitia*, 148, 38. Ðære sibbe wǣre (*cujus foedera pacis*) betwyh ða ylcan cyningas and heora rīce āwunedon, Bd. 4, 21; S. 590, 25. Beweddedum wǣrum *pactis sponsalibus*, Hpt. Gl. 439, 19. Se cyng mid his folce hiene gesōhte. Ac Agothocles gedyde untreówlīce wið hiene, ðæt hē hiene on his wǣrum (MS. L. *has* warum) beswāc and ofslōg *rex pactus est cum Agathocle communionem belli. Sed postquam in unum exercitus junxerunt per Agathoclem insidiis circumventus occisus est*, Ors. 4, 5; Swt. 170, 10. Wǣre genōman *foedus fecerunt*, Wrt. Voc. ii. 39, 25. Ðæt ic ða wǣre forlǣte ðe ic tō swā myclum cyninge genom *ut pactum, quod cum tanto rege inii, ipse primus irritum faciam*, Bd. 2, 12; S. 513, 24. Wēre trume fæstnie *pactum firmum feriat*, Txts. 172, 8. Ic ðē wǣre mīne selle, Cd. Th. 132, 33; Gen. 2202: 171, 22; Gen. 2832. Ic ðē bidde, ðæt ðū treówa selle, wǣra ðīna, 170, 24; Gen. 2818. Gewrīþ sibbe wǣre ⁊ wedd *asstringe pacis federa*, Hymn. Surt. 29, 3. Pehta cynn hafaþ sibbe and wǣre mid Angelðeóde *Pictorum natio foedus pacis cum gente habet Anglorum*, Bd. 5, 23; S. 646, 34. Haldende wēre *servantes pactum*, Ps. Surt. 118, 158. Utan wē ða drihtenlīcan wǣra gehealdan, Wulfst. 253, 3. Wǣre healdan, Cd. Th. 216, 22; Dan. 10. Wið Waldend wǣre healdan, fæste treówe, 204, 19; Exod. 421: Andr.

Kmbl. 426; An. 213: Elen. Kmbl. 1643; El. 823: Exon. Th. 339, 28; Gn. Ex. 101. Hē đa wǣre and đa winetreówe lǣstan wolde, 475, 19; Bo. 50: 172, 17; Gū. 1145: Cd. Th. 93, 8; Gen. 1542: 139, 10; Gen. 2307: 142, 23; Gen. 2366. Đæt ǣnig mon wordum ne worcum wǣre ne brǣce, Beo. Th. 2205; B. 1100. Heó his (*Joseph's*) mǣgwinum morđor fremedon, wǣre frǣton, Cd. Th. 187, 7; Exod. 147. Hē lyt wǣre gewonade, Exon. Th. 148, 19; Gū. 747. Wē sceolon ūs geearnian đa siblecan wǣra Godes and manna, Blickl. Homl. 111, 3. [*O. H. Ger.* wāra *foedus; Icel.* vārar; *pl.*] v. freođo-, friđo-wǣr.

wǣr (?); *adj. True:*—Ic gelȳfe đæt hit from Gode cōme, brōht from his bysene, đæs mē đes boda sægde wǣrum wordum, Cd. Th. 42, 31; Gen. 681. [The word, found here only, if at all, occurs in that part of the Genesis, which seems to show Old Saxon influence, and the phrase *wǣrum wordum* may be the equivalent of that found often in the Hēliand, e. g. Gumon, thea ūs gōdes so filu gehētun fon heđankuninge wārun wordun, 569. But perhaps *wærum* (v. wær, V; and see last passage under *wær-līc*) might be read. Cf. Heó geleáfan nom đæt hē đa bysene from Gode brungen hæfde đe hē hire swā wǣrlīce (= *O. Sax.* wārlīko; *or?* wærlīce *cunningly*) wordum sægde, iéwde hire tācen, and treówa gehēt, Cd. Th. 41, 5; Gen. 652.] [*O. Sax.* wār: *O. Frs.* wēr, weer: *O. H. Ger.* wār, wāri *verus, verax: Lat.* vērus.]

wærc, wræc, es; *m. Wark* (in Northern dialects), *ache, pain:*—Mē sār gehrān, wærc in gewōd, Exon. Th. 163, 29; Gū. 1001. Seó reádnes and bryne đæs swyles and wærces *rubor tumoris ardorque*, Bd. 4, 19; S. 589, 31. Wiđ magan wærce ... Wiđ wambe wærce, Lchdm. ii. 318, 4, 15: 356, 19, 22. From wærc deáđes *a dolore mortis*, Jn. Skt. p. 2, 3. Wærco ł ādla *dolorum*, Mt. Kmbl. 24, 8. Wærcco, Mk. Skt. Lind. 13, 8. *The word occurs mostly in compounds*, v. bān- (Wrt. Voc. ii. 128, 83), blǣder- (Lchdm. ii. 320, 3), breóst- (Lchdm. ii. 4, 23), ceol- (Lchdm. ii. 312, 2), cneó-, eág-, eár-, felle-, fylle-, fōt-, heáfod-, heals- (Lchdm. ii. 312, 5), heort-, lenden-, lifer-, liþ-, milte-, rysel- (Lchdm. ii. 318, 15), sculdor-, sīd-, stic-, sweor-, tōþ-, þeóh-, þeór-wærc (-wræc). [On eđelich stiche, ođer on eđelic eche (ođer warch, MS. T.), A. R. 282, 12. For evel and werke in bledder, Rel. Ant. i. 51, 34: *Icel.* verkr: *Dan.* værk.]

wærc (?):—*Cuneus* wecg ... *cunicellus* lytel wærc (wæcg ?), Wrt. Voc. ii. 137, 28–31.

wærcan; *p.* wærhte. I. (used impersonally) *to pain:*—Gif hine innan wærce, Lchdm. ii. 272, 11. Gif đa þeóh wærce, 312, 7. Đonne monnes wambe wærce ođđe rysle, 318, 20. II. *to suffer pain* (?), *be troubled:*—Ic werhte eom *exercitatus sum* (*if* werhte *can be taken as the past tense of the verb*, eom *is superfluous*), Ps. Spl. 76, 3. [v. Jamieson's Dictionary, wark, werk *to ache: Dan.* værke, det værker i mit Hoved *my head aches.*]

wærc-sār, es; *n. Pain:*—Fruma wercsāre *initium dolorum*, Mk. Skt. Rush. 13, 8.

-wǣre, -wǣred, wærelīce. v. on-wǣre, ge-wǣred (Wrt. Voc. ii. 148, 37), wearglīce.

wǣr-fæst; *adj. Faithful*, (1) as an epithet of the Deity:—Waldend gemunde wǣrfæst (*faithful to his covenant*) Abraham ārlīce, Cd. Th. 156, 8; Gen. 2585. Ūs Hǣlend God wǣrfæst onwrāh *Jesus, faithful to the covenant, has revealed God to us*, Exon. Th. 24, 13; Cri. 384. Wǣrfæst Metod, Cd. Th. 79, 33; Gen. 1320: 175, 23; Gen. 2900. (2) of men:—Se eádega Loth, wǣrfæst, Waldende leóf, Cd. Th. 156, 29; Gen. 2596. Hālig, wǣrfæst (*Juliana*), Exon. Th. 256, 27; Jul. 238. Wǣrfæst (*St. Andrew*), Andr. Kmbl. 2621; An. 1312: (*Abraham*), Cd. Th. 1091, 7; Gen. 1819. Fæder Abrahames, wǣrfæst hæle, 104, 24; Gen. 1740. Ne lǣt đū (*Abraham*) đē đīn mōd āsealcan, wǣrfæst willan mīnes (*faithful in observing my will*), 130, 31; Gen. 2168. Wǣrfæstne rinc (*Abel*), 62, 9; Gen. 1011. Wǣrfæstne hæleđ (*St. Andrew*), Andr. Kmbl. 2548; An. 1275. Đa (*the three children*) wǣron wǣrfæste, wiston Drihten ēcne, Cd. Th. 227, 29; Dan. 194. Wǣrfæstra wera (*Abraham and Lot*), 113, 34; Gen. 1897. (3) of things:—Đǣr sceal lufu uncer wǣrfæst wunian, Exon. Th. 173, 19; Gū. 1163.

wærg, wærgan, wær-geápnis (Wrt. Voc. ii. 125, 1), wær-genga, wærgolness, wærgþu, wæriht. v. wearg, wirgan, wær, V, wer-genga, weargolness, wirgþu, wearriht.

Wǣring-wīc *Warwick:*—On đison geáre wæs Wǣrincwīc getimbrod, Chr. 915; Th. i. 189, col. 2. Æt Wǣringwīcon (-um), 913; Th. i. 186, col. 2, 187, col. 1.

Wǣringwīc-scīr, Wǣring-scīr, e; *f. Warwickshire:*—Tō Wǣrincwīcscīre (Wǣringscīre, p. 277, cols. 1, 2), Chr. 1016; Th. i. 276, cols. 1, 2.

-wærlǣcan. v. ge-wærlǣcan.

wærlan; *p.* de *To wend, turn:*—Đona foerde ł miđ đȳ wærlde *praeteriens*, Jn. Skt. Lind. 9, 1. v. bi-, ge-, ymb-wærlan.

wǣr-leás; *adj. Faithless, false:*—Wǣrleás mon ... and ungetreów, Exon. Th. 343, 24; Gn. Ex. 162. Se feónd, wræcca wǣrleás, 263, 17; Jul. 351: 267, 26; Jul. 421. Wǣrleás werod (*the fallen angels*), Cd. Th. 5, 5; Gen. 67. Wǣrleásra weorud (*the wicked at the day of judgement*), Exon. Th. 98, 27; Cri. 1614: (*the cannibal Mermedonians*), Andr. Kmbl. 2139; An. 1071.

wær-līc; *adj. Cautious, prudent, wise, circumspect:*—Wærlīc *cauta, sollicita*, Wrt. Voc. ii. 129, 70. Wærlīc biđ đæt man ǣghwilce geáre sōna æfter Eástron fyrdscipa gearwige, L. Eth. vi. 33; Th. i. 324, 3. Wærlīc mē þinceþ đæt gē wæccende wiđ hettendra hildewōman wearde healden, Exon. Th. 282, 12; Jul. 662. Wīsdōmes beþearf, worda wærlīcra, and witan snyttro, se đære æđelan sceal andwyrde gifan, Elen. Kmbl. 1083; El. 544. [*Icel.* var-ligr.] v. ful-, un-wærlīc.

wærlīce; *adv.* I. where there is danger of receiving hurt, *warily, cautiously, circumspectly*, (1) *in a way that guards against surprise:*—Faraþ eów wærlīce, đe læs đe eów gemēton đa đe eów æfter rīdon, Jos. 2, 16. Nimaþ and lǣdaþ hine wærlīce (*caute*), Mk. Skt. 14, 44. Đæt man Malchum suīđe wærlīce heólde, đæt hē ne ætburste, Homl. Skt. i. 23, 644. Āhyld hit wærlīce, đonne gesihst đū hwæt đǣroninnan sticaþ, Homl. Th. ii. 170, 18. Wē mōtan swȳđe wærlīce ūs healdan, gyf wē ūs sculan wiđ deófol gescyldan, Wulfst. 38, 3. Wē sculon wiđ đam fǣrscyte symle wærlīce wearde healdan, Exon. Th. 48, 5; Cri. 767. Hié sindon suā micle wærlīcor tō oferbūganne suā mon ongiet đæt hié on māran ungewitte beóđ *qui tanto caute declinandi sunt, quanto insane rapiuntur*, Past. 40; Swt. 295, 21. Hū hȳ đam deófle wærlīcast magan wiđstandan, Wulfst. 80, 3. (2) *in a way that guards against an ill result, safely:*—Nāmon hī tō rǣde, đæt him wærlīcor wǣre, đæt hī sumne dǣl heora londes wurđes æthæfdon *they came to the conclusion, that it would be safer for them to keep back some part of the price of their land*, Homl. Th. i. 316, 23. Wærlīcor biđ se man geherod æfter līfe đonne on līfe *there is less danger of mistake in praising a man after his death than while he is alive*, ii. 560, 14. II. where there is danger of doing wrong, *carefully, heedfully, prudently:*—Hwīlum biđ gōd wærlīce tō miđanne his hiéremonna scylda *aliquando subjectorum vitia prudenter dissimulanda sunt*, Past. 21; Swt. 151, 8. Behalde hē hine geornlīce đæt hē wærlīce sprece *sub quanto cautelae studio loquatur, attendat*, 15; Swt. 93, 18. Đætte sié wærlīce gehealden sió ānmōdnes đæs godcundan geleáfan *ut unitatem fidei cauta observatione teneatis*, Swt. 95, 14. Wærlīce ic mē heóld *caute me tenui*, Coll. Monast. Th. 34, 9. Mǣst þearf is đæt ǣghwelc mon his āđ and his wed wærlīce healde, L. Alf. pol. 1; Th. i. 60, 3: Wulfst. 167, 4. Cristendōm wærlīce healdan, 78, 8. Is suīđe micel đearf đæt hē suā micle wærlīcor hine healde wiđ scylde *necesse est, ut tanto se cautius a culpa custodiant*, Past. 28; Swt. 191, 10. [Wearliche to biwiten us seoluen wiđ þe unwiht of helle, O. E. Homl. i. 245, 17. Þa cheorles warliche heom hudden, Laym. 12300. Temien hire fleschs wisliche and warliche, A. R. 138, 8. Ha heold hire hird wisliche and warliche *familiam pervigili cura gubernabat*, Kath. 82. *O. Sax.* waralīko: *Icel.* varliga: *O. H. Ger.* gi-waralīcho *vigilanter, diligenter, solerter.*] v. un-wærlīce, *and next word.*

wærlīce *truly; or* wærlīce *cunningly*. v. wǣr *true*.

wærlīcness, e; *f. Caution, care, carefulness:*—Ūs is micel wærlīcnys getācnad and æteówed on đære onfangennysse ūres Drihtnes līchaman, Homl. Ass. 163, 263.

wǣr-loga, an; *m. One who is false to his covenant, a faithless, perfidious person:*—Đonne mānsceađa fore Meotude on đam dōme standeþ, biđ se wǣrloga fȳres āfylled, Exon. Th. 95, 25; Cri. 1562. Hǣm Eormanrīces, wrāþes wǣrlogan, 319, 8; Vīd. 9. Đone wǣrlogan, lāđne leódhatan (*Holofernes*), Judth. Thw. 22, 22; Jud. 71. Hēr syndan wedlogan and wǣrlogan *in this land are men false to their pledges and to their covenants*, Wulfst. 165, 37. Wǣrlogan (*the cannibal Mermedonians*), Andr. Kmbl. 141; An. 71: 215; An. 108. Wǣrlogona (*the people of Sodom*) sint firena hefige, Cd. Th. 145, 22; Gen. 2409. On wǣrlogum wrecan torn Godes, 152, 33; Gen. 2530. Mid đyssum wǣrlogan, 151, 4; Gen. 2503. On wǣrlogan (*the people before the flood*) wīte settan, 76, 32; Gen. 1266. Hē sceal wedlogan and wǣrlogan hatian and hȳnan, Wulfst. 266, 29. ¶ applied to spirits:—Se atola gāst, wrāđ wǣrloga, Andr. Kmbl. 2595; An. 1299. Hié hȳrdon tō georne wrāđum wǣrlogan, 1225; An. 613. Wīc æt đam wǣrlogan *a dwelling with the devil*, Exon. Th. 362, 15; Wal. 37: 269, 24; Jul. 455. Hwīlum cyrdon mānsceaþan on mennisc hīw, hwīlum brugdon āwyrgde wǣrlogan on wyrmes bleó, 156, 31; Gū. 883: 120, 9; Gū. 269: 139, 18; Gū. 595. Hē sceóp đām wērlogan (*the apostate angels*) wræclicne hām, Cd. Th. 3, 16; Gen. 36. [This Dragon of Dissait (*the devil*) ... þis warloghe ... with wilis ynoghe mannes saule to dissaiue, Destr. Tr. 4436–45. A warlow (*a monster*), Alex. (Skt.) 1706. Snakis and oþire warlaȝes wild, þat in þe wod duelled, 3795. To þe way of wickidnes be warlaȝes (*devils*) gidid, 4425. He warded þis wrech man (*Jonah*) in warlowes gutteȝ, Allit. Pms. 99, 258. Þaa warlaus (*v. ll.* deuils, fendes), C. M. 23250. The foulle warlawes of helle, Halliw. Dict.]

wær-lot, es; *n. Craft, cunning:*—Wærlotes *astus*, Wrt. Voc. ii. 9, 33.

wærming, wærna. v. wirming, wrænna.

wærness, e; *f. Prudence, circumspection, caution:*—Mid wærnyssa (*cautela*) in gangende, đæt ōþre gebiddende hē nā gelette, Anglia xiii. 378, 188. Hæfde hē miccle lufan and ealle wærnesse tō ælcum men (*he was very considerate to everybody*), ... and đeáh đe hē on lǣwedum hāde beón sceolde, hweđre hē tō đon wærnesse hæfde on eallum đingum (*he was so circumspect in all things*), đæt hē munuclīfe swīþor lifde đonne lǽwedes mannes, Blickl. Homl. 213, 6 11. [*Wick.* warnesse *prudentia.*] v. un-wærness; wær-scipe.

wærness *cursing*, wærnian, wærnung, wærriht. v. weargness, warenian, wirnung, wearriht.

wær-sagol; *adj. Cautious in speech, careful of what one says*:—Se ðe wǽre leássagol, weorðe se sóðsagol; se ðe wǽre bæcslitol, weorðe se wærsagol; se ðe wǽre stuntwyrde, weorðe se wíswyrde, Wulfst. 72, 17.

wær-scipe, es; *m. Prudence, caution, circumspection, wisdom*, in a bad sense, *cunning, astuteness*:—Wærscipe *cautela*, i. *astutia*, Wrt. Voc. ii. 129, 77. Ðæt hié geícen ða gód hira ánfealdnesse mid wærscipe, and suá tilige ðære orsorgnesse mid ðære ánfealdnesse ðætte hé ðone ymbeðonc ðæs wærscipes ne forlǽte . . . Ðære culfran biliwitnesse sceal gemetgian ðære nædran wærscipe, ðý læs hine se wærscipe gelǽde on tó micle hátheortnesse *ut simplicitatis bono prudentiam adjungant, quatenus sic securitatem de simplicitate possideant, ut circumspectionem prudentiae non amittant . . . Debet serpentis astutiam columbae simplicitas temperare, quatenus nec seducti per prudentiam calleant*, Past. 35; Swt. 237, 15–24. Wísdóm is se héhsta cræft, and hæfþ on him feówer óþre cræftas; ðara is án wærscipe, Bt. 27, 2; Fox 96, 34: 34, 6; Fox 140, 35: Shrn. 175, 27. Á gerist bisceopum wísdóm and wærscype, L. I. P. 9; Th. ii. 314, 28. Se swicola hæfð éce wíte, for ðan ðe his wærscype ne dohte, Homl. Skt. i. 19, 177. Þúhte wísast se ðe wæs swicolost . . . ac wá heom ðæs wærscipes, Wulfst. 268, 19. Hý lǽtaþ ðæt tó wærscype, ðæt hý óðre magan swicollíce pǽcan, 55, 2, 15. Mid micelum wærscype lufian *cum magna cautela diligere*, Anglia xiii. 374, 125. For wísdóme and wærscipe *consilio*, Past. 20; Swt. 149, 16. Búton wærscipe *unadvisedly*, Homl. Skt. i. 11, 361. Mid máran fultume and mid máran wærscipe *circumspectiore cura ac magis instructo adparatu*, Ors. 3, 8; Swt. 120, 25. Hé hæfde Ýrlande mid his werscipe gewunnon, and widútan ǽlcon wǽpnon, Chr. 1086; Erl. 222, 18. Ongiet mínne wísdóm and mínne wærscipe (*prudentiam*), Past. 38; Swt. 273, 9. Ðes sunderhálga hæfde opene eágan tó ælmesdǽdum, ac hé næfde nǽnne wærscipe ðæt hé ða sóðan eádmódnysse on his weldǽdum geheólde (*he had not the wisdom to observe true humility in his benefactions*), Homl. Th. ii. 432, 1. [Belin wes swiðe wis, and warscipe him folweden, Laym. 5603. Dumbe bestes habbeð þeos warschipe, þet hwon heo beað asailed, heo þrungeð alle togederes, A. R. 252, 6. Warschipe aȝaines unþeawes, H. M. 41, 7. Warsipe and wisedom wið deuel, Misc. 14, 426.] v. un-wærscipe.

wærst-líc, wærtere. v. wræst-líc, weardere.

wærþu(-o); *indecl. f. Sagacity, cunning, cleverness*:—Gif him lífes weard of móde ábrít ðæt micle dysig ðæt hit oferwrigen mid wunode lange, þonne ic wát ðæt hí ne wundriaþ mæniges þinges ðe monnum nú wærþo and wunder þynceþ (*many a thing that now seems very clever and wonderful*) *cedat inscitiae nubilus error, cessent profecto mira videri*, Met. 28, 82. v. wær, V.

wær-word, es; *n. A word of caution, forewarning*:—Wærwordum *antefatis* (as if from *ante-fatus* = spoken before, cf. *antefata* forewyrde, 100, 28; but the Latin is *ante fatis*. Cf. Hpt. Gl. 529, 40 *fatis* gewyr[dum]), Wrt. Voc. ii. 88, 34: 5, 42.

wær-wyrde; *adj. Cautious of speech, prudent in speech, careful of one's words*:—Wærwyrde sceal wísfæst hæle breóstum hycgan, nales breahtme hlúd, Exon. Th. 303, 22; Fä. 57. Cf. hræd-wyrde.

wæsc *washing*:—Reáfa wæsc *uestimentorum ablutio*, Anglia xiii. 441, 1085. v. ge-wæsc.

wæscan, wacsan, waxan, wacxan, waxsan; *p.* wósc, wócs, wóx, weóx; *pp.* wæscen, wacsen, waxen *To wash*:—Heó wæsceþ his hrægl, Exon. Th. 339, 24; Gn. Ex. 99. Ðæt man cláðas waxe, Wulfst. 296, 7. Wicþénas on ðone Sætresdæg ǽgðer ge fata þweán, ge wæterclaðas wacsan (waxsan, waxan, *v. ll.*), R. Ben. 59, 7. Wacxon hig hira reáf, Ex. 19, 10. Waxan hig ðæt innewerde, Lev. 1, 9, 13. Ðá hig hira reáf wóxon (*lavissent*), Ex. 19, 14. Ðæt hi heora hrægel weócsan and clǽnsodon, Bd. 1, 27; S. 496, 5. Hé wolde his reówan and hwítlas on sǽ wacsan (wæscan, MS. T.), 4, 31; S. 610, 11. Línene cláðas waxan, Lchdm. iii. 206, 29. Hí sculan waxan sceáp, Chart. Th. 145, 13. [*O. E. Homl.* waschen, weschen; *p.* wosch, wesch: *Laym.* wascen: *Orm* wasshenn; *p.* wessh: *A. R.* waschen; *p.* weosch: *O. L. Ger.* wascan; *p.* wósc: *O. H. Ger.* wascan; *p.* wuosc: *Icel.* vaska; *p.* vaskaði.] v. á-, ge-wæscan (-wacsan); un-wæscen, unáwæscen.

wæsc-ærn, -ern, es; *n. A wash-house*:—Wæscern *lautorium*, Wrt. Voc. i. 58, 22.

wæsce, an; *f. A washing-place.* v. sceáp-wæsce.

wæscing (?) *washing* in weascing-weg *a road leading to a sheep-washing place* (?):—Tó weascingwege nioðeweardun, Cod. Dip. Kmbl. v. 78, 17: 138, 4.

wæser ?:—Wæser *bubimus* (? *bulimus*; cf. bulimus *vermis similis lacertae in stomacho hominis habitans*, Corp. Gl. Hessels, 26, 209), Wrt. Voc. ii. 126, 62.

wǽsma ?, wæsp. v. here-wæsmum, wæps.

wæstling, es; *m. A coverlet*:—Wæstling *lodix*, Wrt. Voc. i. 59, 34: *stragula*, 25, 46. Wæstlingc, 81, 58. Bedreáf: genihtsumiaþ hwítel and weslinc (*lena*) and heáfudrægel, R. Ben. Interl. 93, 3. Wæstlinga *stragularum*, Hpt. Gl. 430, 66. [Cf. *Goth.* wasti *clothing*.]

wæstm (-em, -im, -um), es; *m. n.*: e; *f. Growth, increase*:—Wæstm *crementum*, i. *augmentum*, Wrt. Voc. ii. 136, 65. I. *growth, produce*, (1) *fruit* of the earth *or* of a vegetable (lit. or fig.), *plant, fruit*:—Wæstm *fructus*, Wrt. Voc. i. 80, 1. Ofet, wæstm *fruges, frumenta*, ii. 151, 31. Rædrípe wæstm *praecoquus fructus*, i. 39, 22. Oftost on treówcynne beóð ða treówa getealde *feminini generis*, and se wæstm *neutri generis*, Ælfc. Gr. 6, 9; Zup. 20, 15. Beó ðínes landes wæstm (*fructus*) gebletsod, Deut. 28, 4, 18. Se ðæs wæstmes (*the fruit of the tree of knowledge*) onbát, Cd. Th. 30, 21; Gen. 470. Ðæs wæstmes yrþ *illius frugis seges*, Bd. 4, 28; S. 605, 38. Bútan wæstme *sine fructu*, Mk. Skt. 4, 19. Weastme, Mt. Kmbl. 13, 22. Ða beámas wǽron gewered mid wæstme, Cd. Th. 30, 5; Gen. 462. Treów wæstm (westm, v. 12) wircende *lignum faciens fructum*, Gen. 1, 11. Seó eorðe wæstm bereþ *terra fructificat*, Mk. Skt. 4, 28. Hé geseah geblówen treów wæstm berende, Blickl. Homl. 245, 8. Sume sealdon weastm (wæstm, MSS. A. B., Lind.: wæstem, Rush.) *alia dabant fructum*, Mt. Kmbl. 13, 8. Ælc treów ðe gódne wæstm (woestim, Rush.) ne bringð *omnis arbor, quae non facit fructum bonum*, 3, 10. Dóð medemne weastm (wæstm, MS. A., Lind.: wyrþe westem, Rush.), 3, 8. Wæstim gódne, Lk. Skt. Rush. 3, 9. Beámas ða ðe mæst and wæstm mannum bringaþ *ligna fructifera*, Ps. Th. 148, 9. Eorðe salde westem his *terra dedit fructum suum*, Ps. Surt. 66, 7. Ðæt fíctreów, on ðæm hé nánne wæstm ne funde; ðæt getácnaþ ða synfullan ðe nabbaþ nánne wæstm gódra weorca, Blickl. Homl. 71, 35. Wæstm *frumentationem*, Blickl. Gl. Ða wæstmas beóð þurh ágne gecynd eft ácende, Exon. Th. 215, 19; Ph. 255. Fægre land ðonne ðeós folde seó, ðǽr wæstmas scínaþ beorhte, Cd. Th. 277, 34; Sat. 214. Bearwas wurdon tó axan, eorðan wæstma, 154, 10; Gen. 2553. Cumaþ (-eþ?) eádilíc wæstm on wangas, weorðlíc on hwǽtum *convalles abundabunt frumento*, Ps. Th. 64, 14. Of ðam twige ludon láðwende, réðe wæstme, Cd. Th. 60, 31; Gen. 990. [Ðec] wæstem (wæstme?) weorðian *let earth's fruits honour thee* (cf. benedicite universa germinantia in terra Domino, Hym. T. P. 76), Exon. Th. 190, 28; Az. 80. Weastma (wæstma, MSS. A. B., Lind., Rush.) tíd *tempus fructuum*, Mt. Kmbl. 21, 34. Wæstma, Ex. 23, 15; Met. 20, 101. Hig ǽton of ðæs landes wæstmum (*de frugibus terrae*), Jos. 5, 11. Welig on wæstmum and on treówum *opima frugibus atque arboribus*, Bd. 1, 1; S. 473, 13: Cd. Th. 81, 3; Gen. 1339. Eówres landes wæstmas (*fruges*), Deut. 28, 42: 1, 25. Westmas, 32, 13: Bt. 33, 4; Fox 130, 7. Wæstmas (wæstmo, Lind.) *fructus*, Lk. Skt. 12, 17. Him eorðe syleþ æþele wæstme, Ps. Th. 66, 6: 67, 15, 16. Ðú Adame sealdest wæstme, ða inc wǽron forbodene, Cd. Th. 55, 13; Gen. 894. (2) *fruit* of the body, *offspring, progeny*:—Beó ðínes innoðes wæstm (*fructus*) gebletsod and ðínra nýtena wæstm, Deut. 28, 4, 18. Innoðes wæstm (wæstem, Rush.), Lk. Skt. 1, 42. Se wæstm ðínes innoþes is gebletsad, Blickl. Homl. 5, 21. Ic eom búton westme, ne furðum án spearca mínes cynrenes nis mé forlǽtan, Homl. Skt. ii. 30, 205. Hé weorðlícne wæstm gesette, ðe of his innaðe ágenum cwóme, ofer ðín heáhsetl *de fructu ventris tui ponam super sedem meam*, Ps. Th. 131, 12. Ic his cynn gedó brád bearna túdre wæstmum spédig, Cd. Th. 169, 19; Gen. 2802. Módor ne bið wæstmum geeácnod þurh weres frige, Elen. Kmbl. 681; El. 341. Wæstmas fédan, Cd. Th. 59, 8; Gen. 960. (3) including the two preceding meanings:—Sceáwode Scyppend úre his weorca wlite and his wæstma blǽd níwra gesceafta, Cd. Th. 13, 24; Gen. 207. (4) *fruit* of action, *result*:—For hwan gǽst ðú búton wæstme ðínes gewinnes? Blickl. Homl. 249, 5. Mínra gewinna wæstm gefullian, 191, 23. Of wæstmum weorca ðínra *de fructu operum tuorum*, Ps. Th. 103, 12. (5) *fruit, that which may be enjoyed*:—Hine Metod mundbyrde heóld, wilna wæstmum, and worulddugeðum, lufum and lissum, Cd. Th. 117, 3; Gen. 1948. Ic lisse selle, wilna wæstme, ðám ðe ðé wurðiaþ, 105, 24; Gen. 1758. (6) *produce of money, usury*. v. wæstm-sceatt:—Of wæstme *ex usuris*, Ps. Spl. 71, 14. II. *growth, growing*, (1) of the growth of plants:—Seó sunne tempraþ ða eorðlícan wæstmas ge on wæstme ge on rípunge, Lchdm. iii. 250, 18. (2) *growing* as opposed to diminishing, *increase*:—Seó sǽ and se móna beóð geféran on wæstme and on wanunge, Homl. Th. i. 102, 27: Anglia viii. 327, 26. (3) *growth, thriving*:—Mannum becymð rén ofer eorðan eów tó wæstme (*that you may thrive*), Homl. Skt. i. 18, 64. III. *growth, condition reached by growing, stature, form*; the plural is sometimes used when a single person is referred to:—On ealdlícum geárum bið ðæs mannes wæstm gebíged, Homl. Th. i. 614, 13. Úre fulfremeda wæstm is swá swá middæg, ii. 76, 17. Se man ána gǽð uprihte . . . hé sceal smeágan embe ðæt éce líf . . . swíðor ðonne embe ða eorðlícan þing, swá swá his wæstm him gebícnaþ, Homl. Skt. i. 1, 61. Ðé weorð wæstm ðý wlitegra, Cd. Th. 33, 14; Gen. 520. Swá wynlíc wæs his wæstm, ðæt him com from Drihtne, 17, 5; Gen. 255. Cniht, stranglíc on wæstme, Ælfc. T. Grn. 16, 41. Ða beóð on wæstme fíftýne fóta lange and on brǽde týn fótmǽla *homines longi pedum .xv. lati pedum .x.*, Nar. 37, 10 note. Hí (*the Innocents*) wǽron gehwǽde ácwealde, ac hí árísaþ mid fullum wæstme, Homl. Th. i. 84, 22. On geðungenum wæstme, ii. 76, 26. Ðæt feax āfealleþ, đe ǣr wæs fæger on hīwe and on fulre wæstme, Wulfst. 148, 5. Sió hæfde wæstum wundorlīcran, Exon. Th. 413, 13; Rä. 32, 5. Đē is ungelīc wlite and wæstmas, siđđan đū mīnum wordum getrūwodest, Cd. Th. 38, 27; Gen. 613. Wē gesāwon of đam entcynne Enachis bearna micelra wæstma (*procerae staturae*), Num. 13, 34. Wundriaþ weras wlite and wæstma, Exon. Th. 221, 9; Ph. 332. Hē wæs lytel on wæstmum *statura pusillus erat*, Lk. Skt. 19, 3. Ōđer wæs idese onlīcnes, ōþer on weres wæstmum, Beo. Th. 2708; B. 1352: Exon. Th. 214, 11; Ph. 237. Sum biđ wlitig on wæstmum, 295, 18; Crä. 35. Se đe hē oft ǣr mid wlite and mid wæstmum fægerne geseah, Blickl. Homl. 113, 17. [Fæla untime on corne and on ealle westme, Chr. 1124; Erl. 252, 33. Westmes þorđ uuele wederas scal forwurđan, O. E. Homl. i. 13, 28. Wastmes and wederes-sele, Laym. 32108. Brohhte ȝho þe wasstme forþ off wambe, Orm. 1937. He was þogen on wintre and on wastme, O. E. Homl. ii. 127, 16. Marherete schan of wlite ant of wastum, Marh. 2, 34. Hire wliti westum *vultus ipsius claritas*, Kath. 310. On westme fæir, Laym. 15698. *O. Sax.* wastum *fruit, growth, stature, form*. Cf. *Goth.* wahstus: *Icel.* vöxtr: *O. H. Ger.* wahsmo *fructus, statura*.] v. bere-, eorđ-, fold-, frum-, hwǣte-, lim-, ō-, on-, treów-, un-, up-wæstm.

wæstm-bǣre; *adj. Fruitful, fertile, productive*:—Wæstmbǣre *ferax*, Ælfc. Gr. 9, 60; Zup. 69, 5: *frugalis*, Wrt. Voc. ii. 34, 31. Wæstmbǣru *fecunda*, 38, 22. (1) referring to inanimate things:—Đæt wæstmbǣre land *campi uberes*, Ors. 1, 3; Swt. 32, 2. Sceáwiaþ đæt land, hwæđer hit wæstmbǣre sī *considerate terram, qualis sit, bona an mala, humus pinguis an sterilis*, Num. 13, 19. Land đe ys wæstmbǣre ǣgđer ge on hunie ge on meoluce *terram fluentem lacte et melle*, Ex. 33, 3. Eletreów westembēre *oliva fructifera*, Ps. Surt. 51, 10. Eorđan westembēre *terram fructiferam*, 106, 34. Sāwan wæstmbǣre land *serere ingenuum agrum*, Bt. 23; Fox 78, 21: Met. 12, 1. Treó westembēru *ligna fructifera*, Ps. Surt. 148, 9. Wæstmbǣre tyrf *feraces glebas*, Wrt. Voc. ii. 147, 51. Hwæt biđ wæstmbǣrre đonne meox? Homl. Th. ii. 408, 34. (2) referring to living creatures:—On hire is wæstmbǣre mægđhād, Homl. Th. i. 438, 25. (3) figurative:—Se biđ cwealmbǣre, se đe on yfelnysse ǣfre grōwende and wæstmbǣre biđ, Homl. Th. ii. 406, 20. Uton beón wæstmbǣre on gōdum weorcum, 408, 26. v. un-wæstmbǣre.

wæstmbǣrian. v. ge-wæstmbǣrian *fecundare*, Wrt. Voc. ii. 148, 48.

wæstmbǣrness, e; *f. Fruitfulness, fertility, productivity*:—Wæst[m]bērnys *fertilitas*, Wrt. Voc. i. 76, 80. Wæstmbǣrnes *fertilitas*, i. *habundantia*, ii. 147, 77. Wæstmbǣrne[s] *ubertas*, 151, 33. Wæstembiornis *fertilitas*, Txts. 180, 19. (1) referring to inanimate things:—Wæstmbǣrnys on eorþan, Homl. Skt. ii. 28, 162. Hī hēton secgan đysses landes wæstmbǣrnysse (*insulae fertilitatem*), Bd. 1, 15; S. 483, 15: Homl. Th. i. 286, 19. Wæstmbǣrnesse, Ors. 1, 5; Swt. 34, 9. (2) referring to living creatures:—Nis on nānum ōđrum men mægđhād, gif đǣr biđ wæstmbǣrnys, ne wæstmbǣrnys, gif đǣr biđ ansund mægđhād, Homl. Th. i. 438, 27. Hē him geheóld wæstmbǣrnysse tuddres (*fecunditatem sobolis*), Bd. 1, 27; S. 493, 8. v. un-wæstmbǣrness.

wæstmbǣru (-o); *indecl. f. Fertility*:—Đās eorþan ealle hiere wæstmbǣro hē gelytlade *terra haec sterilitate suorum fructuum castigatur*, Ors. 2, 1; Swt. 58, 20.

wæstm-berende; *adj. Fruit-bearing, fertile, fruitful, productive*, (1) referring to inanimate things:—Se dǣl se đæt flōd ne grētte ys gyt wæstmberende on ǣlces cynnes blǣdum, Ors. 1, 3; Swt. 32, 13. Seó wæstmberendeste (*fertilissima*) eorþe, Nar. 5, 20. (2) referring to living creatures:—Mid đȳ ne is ǣnig syn wæstmbærendes (-beorendes, M. 74, 24) līchoman *cum non sit culpa aliqua foecunditas carnis*, Bd. 1, 27; S. 493, 2. (3) figurative:—Hē wæs gefultumiende đæt heora lār wǣre wæstmberende *ipse praedicationem ut fructificaret adjuvans*, Bd. 2, 1; S. 501, 38. Đone æþelan Albanum seó wæstmberende (*fecunda*) Bryton forþbereþ, 1, 7; S. 476, 34. Woestimberende *fructiferum*, Rtl. 34, 14. Đā wǣron đa wæstmberendan breóst đæs eádigan weres mid đam lāreówdōme đæs heán magistres Godes gefyllede, Guthl. 2; Gdwin. 18, 8.

wæstm-berendlīc. v. un-wæstmberendlīc.

wæstmberendness, e; *f. Fertility, fecundity*:—Mid đȳ nis ǣnig synn wæstmberendnesse līchoman *cum non sit culpa aliqua foecunditas carnis*, Bd. 1, 27; M. 74, 24 note. v. un-wæstmberendness.

wæstm-fæst, -fæstness. v. un-wæstm-fæst, -fæstness.

wæstmian; *p.* ode *To bring forth fruit* (lit. or fig.), *fructify*:—Eorđo wæstmiaþ (wæstmas, Rush.) *terra fructificat*, Mk. Skt. Lind. 4, 28. Ic wæstmede *fructificavi*, Rtl. 3, 20. Manig yfel wē geāxiaþ wæstmian, Blickl. Homl. 109, 2.

wæstm-leás; *adj. Without fruit* (lit. or fig.):—Đæt word westemleás geweorđæd *verbum sine fructu efficitur*, Mt. Kmbl. Rush. 13, 22. Đī læs đe se Hlāford ūs wæstmleáse gemēte, Homl. Th. ii. 408, 27. [Itt liþ uss wasstmeleas off alle gode dedess, Orm. 13858.]

wæstm-līc; *adj. Fruitful*:—Wæstimlīc *fructuosus*, Rtl. 18, 25.

wæstm-sceatt, es; *m. Usury, interest*:—Wæstmsceat *usura*, Wrt. Voc. i. 20, 71. Westemsceat, Ps. Surt. 54, 12. Wæstmscettes *fenoris*, Germ. 389, 45. Se đe his feoh tō unrihtum wæstmsceatte (tō westemscette *ad usuram*, Ps. Surt.) ne syleþ, Ps. Th. 14, 6. Of westemsceattum *ex usuris*, Ps. Surt. 71, 14.

wǣt; *adj.* I. *wet, moist, damp, consisting of moisture*:—Đæt wæter is wǣt and ceald, Bt. 33, 4; Fox 128, 35: Met. 20, 77. Hyra blōd byđ wǣt and wearm, Anglia viii. 299, 29. Đū đam wættere wǣtum and cealdum foldan tō flōre gesettest, Met. 20, 90. Mid wǣttere rude *roseo* (*purpurei cruoris*) *rubore* (Ald. 61), Hpt. Gl. 507, 63. Gecyrred on wǣtne deáw, Homl. Skt. ii. 30, 441. II. *wet, moist, having moisture*:—Sié lyft is ǣgđer ge ceald ge wǣt ge wearm, Bt. 33, 4; Fox 128, 35: Anglia viii. 299, 28. Se wǣta wong *roscida tellus*, Exon. Th. 417, 7; Rä. 36, 1. In wǣtan sihtran; of đam wǣtan sīce; . . . in đæt wǣte sīcc, Cod. Dip. Kmbl. iii. 386, 10–16. *Loca humentia*, đæt beóđ wǣte stōwa, Wulfst. 249, 17. On smēþum landum and on wǣtum, Lchdm. i. 90, 4. On wātum (*v. ll.* wǣtum) stōwum, 222, 18. Wǣtum *udis*, Hpt. Gl. 482, 42: Wrt. Voc. ii. 82, 1. Nǣfre hē his đa wǣtan hrægel and đa cealdan āsettan wolde *nunquam ipsa vestimenta uda atque algida deponere curabat*, Bd. 5, 12; S. 631, 24. II a. referring to the humours or juices of bodies:—Đonne sió wamb swīđe wǣtre gecyndo biþ, ne þrowaþ seó þurst ne hefignesse metta, and gefilđ wǣtum mettum, Lchdm. ii. 220, 19–21. Be (wambe) cealdre and wǣtre gecyndo . . . and đæt hǣmedþing ne sceþeþ hātum līchoman ne wǣtum, 162, 17–20: 222, 1, 2. Eal đa wǣtan þing and đa smerewigan sint tō forbeódanne, 210, 27: 246, 3. III. of weather, *wet, rainy*:—Lengtentīma ys wǣt, Anglia viii. 299, 27. Of untīdlīcan gewideran, đæt is, of wǣtum sumerum and of drȳgum wintrum, Ors. 3, 3; Swt. 102, 5. [*O. Frs.* wēt: *Icel.* vātr.]

wǣt, es; *n.* I. *wet, moisture*:—Se cyle geþrowode wiđ đa hǣto, and đæt wǣt wiþ đām drȳgum, Bt. 33, 4; Fox 128, 33: Met. 20, 74. II. *liquor, drink*:—Hē āna gereorde, and be dǣle ǣt and wǣt gewanod sȳ *reficiat solus, sublata ei portione sua de vino*, R. Ben. 69, 14. Hē ne mæg ǣtes ođđe wǣtes brūcan, Homl. Th. i. 66, 9. Hē fæste, swā đæt hē ne onbyrigde ǣtes ne wǣtes on eallum đam fyrste, 166, 11: ii. 490, 11: Wulfst. 103, 1. Nān đing tō đigenne ne on ǣte ne on wǣte *nec quicquam cibi aut potus presumere*, R. Ben. 69, 19: 76, 18: Homl. Th. i. 360, 13: ii. 590, 21. Būton ǣte and būton wǣte, H. R. 11, 27. [Þis halwende wet (*the blood of Jesus*), O. E. Homl. i. 187, 31. Gifernesse deđ þet mon to muchel nimeđ on ete ođer on wete, 103, 7. Lokenn himm fra luffsumm æte and wæte, Orm. 7852.] v. next word.

wǣta, an; *m.*: wǣte, an; *f.* I. *wet, moisture*:—Wǣta *humor*, Wrt. Voc. i. 76, 78. Hwīlum flīht se wǣta đæt drȳge, Bt. 39, 13; Fox 234, 11: Prov. Kmbl. 71. Seó lyft sȳcđ ǣlcne wǣtan up tō hyre, . . . se wǣta gǣđ up swylce mid miste, and gyf hit sealt byđ . . . hit byđ . . . tō ferscum wǣtan āwend, Lchdm. iii. 278, 7–12. Đā forscranc đæt sǣd, for đan đe hit næfde nǣnne wǣtan. Swā dōđ sume menn . . . se wǣta ne fæstnode heora wyrtruman, Homl. Th. ii. 90, 30–35. Wǣte *humor* vel *mador*, Wrt. Voc. i. 53, 44. Snāw cymđ of đam þynnum wǣtan, đe byđ up ātogen mid đære lyfte, Lchdm. iii. 278, 23. Hit wǣtan næfde *non habebat* [*h*]*umorem*, Lk. Skt. 8, 6. Hwīlum đæt drīge drīfđ đone wǣtan, Met. 29, 48. Hī feallan lǣtaþ seáw of bōsme, wǣtan of wombe, Exon. Th. 385, 21; Rä. 4, 48. Wǣtum hē (*snow*) oferhrægeþ, gebryceþ burga geatu, Salm. Kmbl. 612; Sal. 305. II. *a liquid*:—Wynsum wǣta (*water*) ūt flōwende, Blickl. Homl. 209, 2. Æfter sōđum gecynde đæt wæter is brosniendlīc wǣta, Homl. Th. ii. 270, 5. Wolde đæt folc đæt fȳr ādwæscan, gif hit ǣnig wǣta wanian mihte, 140, 17. Hit wæs mid wǣtan (*blood*) bestēmed, Rood Kmbl. 44; Kr. 22. II a. *a liquid that may be drunk* or *used in cookery, medicine*, etc., *liquor, drink*:—Wǣta *liquor*, Wrt. Voc. i. 27, 49 (in a list 'de generibus potionum'). Mete *cibus*, drenc *potus*, wǣta *liquor*, 82, 47. Ūre wǣta wæs olfenda miolc, Shrn. 38, 18. Dō on hunig and on wīn . . . dō đæt se wǣta mæge oferyrnan đa wyrta, Lchdm. ii. 306, 27. Gesamna tū āmbru hrȳþra micgean . . . wylle ōþ đæt se wǣta sié twǣde on bewylled, 332, 17. Ǣgru sint tō forgānne, for đon đe hira wǣte biđ fǣt and māran hǣto wyrcđ, 210, 23. Geđicge đæs wǣtan (*hot water and wine*) þreó full fulle, i. 76, 25. Þeáh hȳ him wǣtan bǣdan, drynces gedreahte, Exon. Th. 92, 14; Cri. 1508. Wæs glæsen fæt đæt đæs wynsuman wǣtan onfēng. Þǣr wæs gewuna đæm folce, đæt hié tō đæm fæte āstigon and đære heofonlīcan wǣtan onbyrigdon, Blickl. Homl 209, 4–9. Wǣtan (byrele? cf. wīn-byrele *caupo*, 21, 13; *or* brytta? cf. wīn-bryttum *cauponibus*) *caupo*, Wrt. Voc. ii. 22, 81. Wǣtan heó ne swelgeþ, ne wiht iteþ, Exon. Th. 439, 27; Rä. 59, 10. Tō leohtum drence (*a number of plants then follow*), tō wǣtan (*for liquor*) healf hāligwæter, healf eala, Lchdm. ii. 274, 4. Gif mon sié mid wǣtan forbærned, 324, 14. Gif lytel fearh āfealle on wǣtan (*liquorem*), and cucu sig upp ātogen, sprenge man đone wǣtan mid hāligwætere, and þicge man đone wǣtan; gif hit deád sig, and man ne mæge đone wǣtan gesyllan, geóte hine man ūt, L. Ecg. C. 39; Th. ii. 164, 3–7. Nānne wǣtan hī ne cūþon wiđ hunige mengan, Bt. 15; Fox 48, 10. Ne hē cealdne wǣtan ne þicge, Lchdm. i. 190, 2: 238, 9. Drince wucan æfter đon beónbrođ and mænige (nǣnige?) ōþre wǣtan; ōþre wucan . . . , and nāne ōþre wǣtan . . . ; þriddan wucan . . . nānne ōþerne wǣtan, ii. 216, 11–15. Đa wyrte wiđ đone wǣtan gemencge, drince đonne, iii. 18, 20. Ne dranc hē wīnes drenc, ne nān đæra wǣtena đe druncennysse styriaþ, Homl. Th. ii. 298, 18. III. *moisture in an animal body, humour*:—Đonan cymeþ sió mettrymnes đǣm healedum, đe se wǣta đæra innođa (*humor viscerum*) āstīgđ tō đæm lime, Past. 11; Swt. 73, 9. Đonne biđ se deáđbǣra wǣta (*humor mortiferus*) on đæm menn ofslægen mid đæm biteran drence, 41; Swt. 303, 16. Gif đū wille đæt yfel swyle and ǣterno wǣte ūt berste, Lchdm. ii. 16, 14. Gif sió wamb biþ windes full, đonne cymđ đæt of wlacre wǣtan; sió cealde wǣte wyrcþ sār an, 224, 24. Wiđ ealle gegaderunga đæs yfelan wǣtan of đam līchoman, i. 236, 18. Gífernes ārist of đæs hores wǣtan đe of đam magan cymđ, ii. 196, 3. Of yfelum wǣtan slītendum đone magan, . . . gif se seóca man āspīwđ đone yfelan bītendan wǣtan āweg, 60, 20-23. Of yfelre wǣtan slītendre, 4, 30. Wiþ yflum wǣtan and swile . . . hit eal đæt worms and đone yfelan wǣtan ādrīfþ, 72, 12-15. Hyt ealne đone wǣtan (*dropsical humour*) ūt ātȳhþ, i. 204, 3. **III a.** *water, urine:*—Genim eoferes blǣdran mid đam micgan, āhefe upp, and ābīd ōþ đæt se wǣta of āflōwen sȳ, Lchdm. i. 360, 6. **IV.** *moisture of plants, juice, sap:*—Nim ǣnne sticcan . . . forbærn đone ōderne ende, đonne gǣđ se wǣta (*v. l.* wǣte) ūt æt đam ōđrum ende, Lchdm. iii. 274, 5. Sæp ł wǣte *succus*, Hpt. Gl. 450, 13. Hē bær đa wǣtan đære uncystan in đam telgan đone hē getȳhþ ǣr of đam wyrtruman *portat in ramo humorem vitii, quem traxit ex radice*, Bd. 1, 27; S. 495, 26. [He þoleđ hwile druie, and hwile wete, O. E. Homl. ii. 123, 6. Hwo þet bere a deorewurđe licur, ođer a deorewurđe wete in a feble uetles, A. R. 164, 14. Ifulled mid attere, weten alre bitterest, Laym. 19769. *Icel.* væta *wet, rain.*] v. hærfest-wǣta.

wǣtan; *p.* te *To wet, moisten:*—Ic đweá *lauo, lauas:* ic wǣte *lauo, lauis*, Ælfc. Gr. 37; Zup. 220, 6. Ic mīn bedd wǣte (wētu, Ps. Surt.) mid teárum *lacrymis stratum meum rigabo*, Ps. Th. 6, 5. Wǣteþ *ingurgitat*, Wrt. Voc. ii. 90, 59: 47, 19. Ne is đæt wīn tō þicgenne đætte hǣteþ and wǣteþ đone innoþ, Lchdm. ii. 246, 5. Mec (*an animal's skin*) brȳd wǣteþ in wætre, Exon. Th. 393, 34; Rä. 13, 10. Heó genam đæs gehālgodan sealtes, and wǣtte, Guthl. 22; Gdwin. 98, 2. Wǣt đæt gewrit on đam drence, Lchdm. ii. 350, 15. Wǣt wulle mid biccean hlonde, i. 362, 17. Wǣt đæt liþ mid ecede, ii. 134, 9. Wǣt mid đīnum scytefingre, Techm. ii. 126, 2. Hī đa lifre wǣten, Lchdm. i. 346, 23. Hē wylle mid đam seáwe his eágan hreppan and wǣtan, 128, 13. Wǣtan *rigare, humectare*, Hpt. Gl. 421, 54. Wǣtende *humectans*, Wrt. Voc. ii. 43, 28: Lchdm. ii. 156, 20. Wǣtendum *rorantibus, tingentibus*, Hpt. Gl. 439, 55. [*Icel.* væta *to wet.*] v. ge-wǣtan; wǣtian.

wǣte. v. wǣta.

wæter, es; *n.* (*the word seems to be feminine in* on đisse wætere, Blickl. Homl. 247, 25; *see also* Ps. Th. 17, 11: *and a weak genitive plural* wæterena *is found in* Ps. Th. 31, 7.) **I.** *water:*—Wæter *aqua*, hlūttor wæter *limpha*, Wrt. Voc. i. 54, 17, 18. Wæter *limphale*, ii. 52, 19. Đæt wæter is brosniendlīc wǣta, Homl. Th. ii. 270, 5. Blōd fleẃđ ofer eorđan swā swā wæter, Blickl. Homl. 237, 6. Byrneþ wæter swā weax, Exon. Th. 61, 23; Cri. 989. Blōd and wæter ætsomne ūt bicwōman, 68, 33; Cri. 1113. Ealle gewītaþ swā swā wolcn, and swā swā wæteres streám, Blickl. Homl. 59, 20. Ūre līchoma wæs gesceapen of feówer gesceaftum, of eorþan and of fȳre and of wætere and of lyfte, 35, 13. Hī forweorđan wætere gelīcost, đonne hit yrnende eorđe forswelgeþ, Ps. Th. 57, 6. Þegn winedryhten his wætere gelafede, Beo. Th. 5438; B. 2722. Wætre, 5700; B. 2854. Đætte hē gewǣte his ȳtemestan finger on wættre, Past. 43; Swt. 309, 7. Wættre gelīcost, Andr. Kmbl. 1906; An. 955. **I a.** *water* for drinking:—Đæt wæter āsceortode đe wæs on đam buturuce, Gen. 21, 15. Ānne drinc cealdes wæteres (wætres, Lind.: wættres, Rush.), Mt. Kmbl. 10, 42. Wæteres (wætres, Lind., Rush.), Mk. Skt. 9, 41: Andr. Kmbl. 44; An. 22. Hē gehālgode wīn of wætere, 1173; An. 587. Wætre, Ps. Th. 123, 3. Hwæt drincst đū? Ealu, gif ic hæbbe, oþþe wæter, gif ic næbbe ealu, Coll. Monast. Th. 35, 11. **I b.** *water* in the sky, *rain:*—Đā hangode swīđe þȳstru wæter on đām wolcnum, and on đære lyfte, Ps. Th. 17, 11. Ne wæter fealleþ lyfte gebysgad *nec cadit ex alto turbidus humor aquae*, Exon. Th. 201, 25; Ph. 61. Hit wǣron mīne wæter, đa đe on heofenum wǣron, Wulfst. 260, 4. **II.** where a considerable volume of water is referred to, *water* of a river, sea, etc.:—Ic sleá đises flōdes wæter and hyt byđ geworden tō blōde, Ex. 7, 17. Hē funde wynleásne wudu; wæter under stōd, Beo. Th. 2837; B. 1416: Blickl. Homl. 211, 1. Faraþ geond ealle eorđan sceátas emne swā wīde swā wæter bebūgeþ, Andr. Kmbl. 666; An. 333. Sīd wæter *ocean*, Cd. Th. 7, 2; Gen. 100. Sealt wæter, 13, 6; Gen. 198. Ādō mē of deópe deorces wæteres đe læs mē besencen sealte flōdas, Ps. Th. 68, 14. Ofer wæteres hrycg *across the sea*, Beo. Th. 947; B. 471. On wæteres ǣht, 1037; B. 516. Hē stilde wæteres wælmum, Andr. Kmbl. 903; An. 452. Wætres swēg, Blickl. Homl. 65, 19. Wætres (*the Deluge*) brōgan, Cd. Th. 84, 10; Gen. 1395: Exon. Th. 200, 16; Ph. 41. Ic hine of wætere genam, Ex. 2, 10. Hē āstāh of đam wætere (wætre, Lind.: wættre, Rush.), Mt. Kmbl. 3, 16. Gestreón bewrigen wætere ođđe eorđan, Met. 8, 59. Wiđ wǣge, wætre windendum, Exon. Th. 61, 9; Cri. 982. Đū đam wættere foldan tō flōre gesettest, Met. 20, 90. Geót đæt blōd on yrnende wæter, Lchdm. ii. 76, 15. Se đe gǣđ on deóp wæter, Salm. Kmbl. 448; Sal. 224. Deóp wæter *ocean*, Beo. Th. 3812; B. 1904. Ofer wīd wæter, 4937; B. 2473. Swā wē on laguflōde ofer cald wæter liđan, Exon. Th. 53, 17; Cri. 852: Andr. Kmbl. 401; An. 201. **II a.** *water* as in Derwent*water*, *a body of water, a stream, lake, sea:*—Heó wolde hig þweán æt đam wætere (*in flumine*) and hyre mēdenu eodon be đæs wæteres ōfre (*per crepidinem alvei*), Ex. 2, 5. Hē becom tō Iordanes ōfrum đæs wæteres *he came to the shores of the river Jordan*, Homl. Skt. ii. 23 b, 664, 678: (*the Danube*), Elen. Kmbl. 119; El. 60. On wætere *in amne*, Coll. Monast. Th. 23, 35. Hē geseah ofer đæm wætere hārne stān, Blickl. Homl. 209, 31. Đās đe on đis wætere (*a flood*) syndon eft hié libbaþ . . . Đa đe on đisse wætere syndon, 247, 21, 25. Eástreámas feówer wǣron ādǣlede ealle of ānum wætre, Cd. Th. 14, 17; Gen. 220. Hyra (*the Egyptians'*) wæter wurdon tō blōde, Ors. 1, 7; Swt. 36, 25. Đa þreó wæter, Cd. Th. 133, 16; Gen. 2211. Swā swā ealle wæteru cumaþ of đære sǣ, and eft ealle cumaþ tō đære sǣ, Bt. 24, 1; Fox 80, 23. Wætera *laticum*, Wrt. Voc. ii. 52, 17. Hē tō Iordane becom ealra wætera đam hālgestan, Homl. Skt. ii. 23 b, 63. Sǣs and wætra heá holmas, Exon. Th. 193, 16; Az. 122. Fiscwyllum wæterum *fluviis multum piscosis*, Bd. 1, 1; S. 473, 15. Hī witon on hwelcum wæterum hī sculun sēcan fiscas, Bt. 32, 3; Fox 118, 19. Đæt folc fōr betwux đām twām wæterum (*the two parts of the Red Sea*), Wulfst. 293, 16. Seó eorđe wæs wætrum weaht, lagostreámum leoht, Cd. Th. 115, 19; Gen. 1922. Mid bricgum ofer deópe wæteru, L. Edg. C. 14; Th. ii. 282, 10. Lǣt forđ đīne willas and tōdǣl đīn wætru æfter herestrǣtum, Past. 48; S. 373, 13, 15. Āþene đīne hand ofer ealle Egipta wætro and flōdas, ge ofer burnan ge ofer meras and ofer ealle wæterpyttas, Ex. 7, 19. **II b.** in plural, *waters*, implying abundance or great extent, *waters* of a great river, of a sea, etc.:—Đa fixas đe synd on đam flōde ācwelaþ, and đa wæteru forrotiaþ, Ex. 7, 18. Đǣr wǣron manega wætro (uætro, Lind.: wæter, Rush.) *there was much water there*, Jn. Skt. 3, 23. Đē wæter sceáwedon and đē gesāwon sealte ȳþa . . . wæs swēg micel sealtera wætera, Ps. Th. 76, 13. Swā ǣr wæter fleówan, flōdas āfȳsde, Exon. Th. 61, 16; Cri. 985: Andr. Kmbl. 3105; An. 1555. Đæt lēg miclade, and him nǣnig mon mid wætra onweorpnesse wiþstondan meahte, Bd. 2, 7; S. 509, 20. Ofer wætera gedring, ofer hwæles ēđel, Chr. 975; Erl. 126, 21: Exon. Th. 351, 13; Sch. 351. Ȳđa gelaac, wīd gang wætera, Ps. Th. 118, 136. Đæt flōd đæra myclena wæterena, 31, 7. Wætrum bisencte, Exon. Th. 271, 9; Jul. 479: Cd. Th. 88, 4; Gen. 1460. Đa scīran wæter *liquidas lymphas*, Wrt. Voc. ii. 50, 11. Hāt mē cuman tō đē ofer đās wæteru (wætra, Lind.: đæt wæter, Rush.), Mt. Kmbl. 14, 28. Hū heó mihte Iordanes wæteru oferfaran, Homl. Skt. ii. 23 b, 680. Wætru, 684. Hē gegaderode eall sǣ wætru (*aquas maris*), Ps. Th. 32, 6. **II c.** in reference to the surface of water:—Đæt hié nǣren .x. fōta heá bufan wætere *decem pedum altitudine a mari aberant*, Ors. 5, 13; Swt. 246, 11. Under wætere, Beo. Th. 3316; B. 1656. [*O. Sax.* watar: *O. Frs.* weter: *O. H. Ger.* wazzar. Cf. *Goth.* watō: *Icel.* vatn.] v. font- (fant-), hālig-, hreód-, neáh-, weorold-, wille-wæter; wæter-ordāl.

wæter-ādl, e; *f. Dropsy:*—Se đe him seó wæterādl, Lchdm. i. 354, 8. Wiđ wæterādle . . . seó wæterādl ūt āflōweþ, 364, 19-20, 11. v. wæterseócness.

wæter-ǣdre, an: -ǣder, e; *f.* (*in the first passage given the word is made neuter*). *A vein of water, a spring:*—Gewemmed weterēdre *uena corrupta* (Prov. 25, 26), Kent. Gl. 973. Hē hēt đa heardnysse holian onmiddan đære flōre, and đæt wæterǣddre đā wynsum āsprang, werod on swæcce, Homl. Th. ii. 144, 4. Ān lamb bīcnode mid his swȳđran fēt, swilce hit đa wæterǣddran geswutelian wolde. Clemens cwæđ: 'Geopeniaþ đās eorđan' . . . Æt đam forman gedelfe swēgde ūt ormǣte wyllspring, i. 562, 10. Ealle wyllspringas and eán þurh hig (*the earth*) yrnaþ. Swā swā ǣddran licgeaþ on đæs mannes līchaman, swā licgaþ đās wæterǣddran geond đās eorđan, Lchdm. iii. 254, 23. On stenne wæterǣdrena (-ēdrana, Ps. Lamb. *cataractorum*) đīnra, Ps. Spl. 41, 9: Blickl. Gl. Wæterǣdra, Ps. Th. 41, 8. Wæterǣddrum *cataractis*, Hpt. Gl. 418, 63. Seó gȳtsung hyre gold betweoh đa wæterǣdran rǣt *avaritia aurum inter arenas legit*, Gl. Prud. 55.

wæterælf-ādl, e; *f. Some form of illness:*—Gif mon biþ on wæterælfādle, đonne beóþ him đa handnæglas wonne and đa eágan teárige, and wile lōcian niþer, Lchdm. ii. 350, 21: 304, 8.

wæter-ælfen[n], e; *f. A water-elf, water-nymph:*—Wæterælfenne *nymfae*, Wrt. Voc. ii. 62, 31.

wæter-berend, es; *m. A water-bearer:*—Wæterberendra *lixarum* (*mercenariorum qui aquam portant*), Hpt. Gl. 427, 14. v. next word.

wæter-berere, es; *m. A water-bearer:*—Mid wæterbererum *cum lixarum* (*coetibus*, Ald. 13; *the passage is the same as that glossed in the preceding word*), Wrt. Voc. ii. 76, 74: 18, 2. Wæterberere (-a?) *lixarum*, 52, 73.

wæter-bōg (-bōh), es; *m. A bough with moisture in it:*—Wæterbōh *surculus*, Wrt. Voc. i. 39, 16.

wæter-bolla, an; *m. Dropsy:*—Of đære ādle cymđ ful oft wæterbolla, Lchdm. ii. 202, 5: 206, 11. Wiþ wæterbollan, 108, 4: 10, 17: 204, 13.

wæter-brōga, an; *m. Terror caused by water, the terror of the deep:*—Engel đīn con sealte sǣstreámas, warođfaruđa gewinn and wæterbrōgan, Andr. Kmbl. 394; An. 197: 912; An. 456. Cf. wæter-egesa.

wæter-būc, es; *m. A pitcher:*—Ān man mid wæterbūce *homo am-*

phoram aquae portans, Lk. Skt. 22, 10. Gedeon hēt heora ǣlcne geniman ānne ǣmtigne sester odde ǣnne wæterbūc *Gedeon dedit in manibus eorum lagenas vacuas*, Jud. 7, 16.

wæter-bucca, an; *m. An aquatic insect, a water-spider*:—Wæterbuc[c]a *vel* [wæter]gāt *tippula*, Wrt. Voc. i. 24, 14.

wæter-burne, an; *f. A stream of water*:—Ic āna sæt innan bearwe . . . dǣr da wæterburnan swēgdon and urnon, Dōm. L. 3.

wæter-byden, e; *f. A water-cask*; dolium, Wrt. Voc. ii. 82, 76.

wæter-clāþ, es; *m. A towel*:—Þære kycenan wicþēnas wæterclādas wacsan, de hȳ heora handa and fēt mid wīpedan *linthea, cum quibus sibi fratres manus aut pedes tergunt, lavet*, R. Ben. 59, 7: R. Ben. Interl. 66, 1.

wæter-crōg, es; *m. A pitcher*:—Watercrōg *lagenam*, Wrt. Voc. ii. 74, 28.

wæter-crūce, an; *f. A water-pot*:—Waetercrūce *urciolum*, Wrt. Voc. ii. 124, 19.

wæter-del[l], es; *n. m.* (?) *A dell in which there is water*:—Nord tō wæterdellæ, Cod. Dip. Kmbl. iii. 126, 14.

wæter-denu, e; *f. A valley with water in it*:—Andlang weterdene west tō dære deópan dene, Cod. Dip. Kmbl. v. 365, 33.

wæter-furh; *f. A trench*:—On da wæterfurh innan smalan brōc, Cod. Dip. Kmbl. v. 105, 17.

wæter-egesa, an; *m. Terror caused by water*:—Wæteregesa sceal lidra wyrdan *the terrors of the deep shall lose their force*, Andr. Kmbl. 870; An. 435. Wæteregsa, 750; An. 375. Grendles mōdor wæteregesan wunian sceolde, cealde streámas *Grendel's mother must live among the dreadful waters, the cold streams*, Beo. Th. 2524; B. 1260. Cf. wæter-brōga.

wæter-fæsten[n], es; *n. A place protected by water*:—Hē gewīcode dǣr dǣr hē niéhst rȳmet hæfde for wudufæstenne ond for wæterfæstenne *he encamped as near to the Danes as the wood and water, which protected their position, would allow him to find sufficient room*, Chr. 894; Erl. 90, 10.

wæter-fæt, es; *n. A vessel for water, a water-pot*:—Wæterfæt *ydria*, Ælfc. Gr. 9, 56; Zup. 68, 4: *ydria* vel *soriscula*, Wrt. Voc. i. 25, 12. Þæt wīf forlēt hyre wæterfæt (*hydriam*), Jn. Skt. 4, 28. Dǣr wǣron āset six stǣnene wæterfatu (*hydriae*), 2, 6: Homl. Th. ii. 56, 5, 21. Da six wæterfatu getācnodon six ylda dyssere worulde, 58, 1. Dā hira wæterfatu fulle wǣron *impletis canalibus*, Ex. 2, 16. [*O. H. Ger.* wazzarfaz *hydria*.]

wæter-flasce, -flaxe, an; *f. A water-flask, a pitcher*:—Sum man berende sume wæterflaxan *homo lagenam aquae baiulans*, Mk. Skt. 14, 13.

wæter-flōd, es; *m. n. A flood, deluge*; in plural, *floods, waters*. Cf. wæter, II b:—Swilce ōder wæterflōd swā fleów heora blōd, Homl. Skt. i. 23, 74. On dæs Ambictiones tīde wurdon mycele wæterflōd (*inluvies aquarum*) geond ealle world, Ors. 1, 6; Swt. 36, 7. Hine storm ne mæg āwecgan, ne wæterflōdas brecan brondstæfne, Andr. Kmbl. 1006; An. 503. Hī mē ymbsealdan swā wæterflōdas (*sicut aqua*), Ps. Th. 87, 17. On wæterflōdum *in aquoso*, 62, 2.

wæter-full; *adj. Dropsical*:—Wæterfull *hydropicus* (v. Lk. 14, 2), Wrt. Voc. ii. 73, 57: 43, 21.

wæter-fyrhtness, e; *f. Fear of water, hydrophobia*:—Wæterfirhtnys *ydrofobam* vel *limphatici*, Wrt. Voc. i. 19, 25.

wæter-gāt. v. wæter-bucca.

wæter-geblǣd *a blister with water in it* (?); or *a blister made by boiling water* (?), Lchdm. iii. 36, 21.

wæter-gelād, es; *m. A water-way, an aqueduct*:—Wætergelāda *aquae ductuum*, Wrt. Voc. ii. 1, 16.

wæter-gelǣt, es; *n. A water-course, an aqueduct*:—Wætergelǣt *colimbus*, Wrt. Voc. ii. 134, 69. v. wæter-þeóte.

wæter-gewæsc, es; *n. Land formed by the washing up of earth*:—*Circumlutus locus* mid wæter ymbtyrnd stede, *alluvium* wætergewæsc, Wrt. Voc. i. 59, 15, 16.

wæter-grund, es; *m. The bottom of the sea, the depth of the sea*:—On wætergrundum *in profundo*, Ps. Th. 106, 23.

wæter-gyte, es; *m. A pouring of water, a water-course*:—Endlyfta is *aquarius*, dæt is wætergyte (-scyte, MS. R.), odde se de wæter gȳt, Lchdm. iii. 246, 4.

wæter-hæfern, es; *m. A water-crab*:—Genim wæterhæfern gebærnedne, Lchdm. ii. 44, 19.

wæter-hālgung, e; *f. Blessing* or *hallowing of water*; aquae benedictio:—Waeterhālgunge, Rtl. 117, 1.

wæter-ham[m], es; *m. Land surrounded by a ditch* (?):—Andlang burnan on wæterweg; of dan wæterwege on waterhammes; of dan hamman on grēnan beorh, Cod. Dip. Kmbl. v. 374, 31. Cf. flōdhammas, i. 289, 18.

wæter-helm. v. wegan, III (1).

wæterian; *p.* ode *To water, supply with water*, (1) *to water* animals, *give drink to* living creatures:—Hē wæterode hig *adaquavit eos*, Ps. Spl. 77, 18. Hē wæterode hire heorde *adaquavit gregem*, Gen. 29, 10. Hī heora orf wæterodon *refectis gregibus*, 29, 3. Orf wæterian, Ex. 2, 16. Oxan wæterian, Coll. Monast. Th. 20, 1. Dā hēt ic wætrigan ūre hors and ūre niéteno, Nar. 12, 12. Tō wætranne, Lk. Skt. Lind. Rush. 13, 15: p. 8, 15. (2) *to water* plants:—Se man de plantaþ wyrta, hē hī wæteraþ, Homl. Th. i. 304, 26. Sumu treówu hē watrode, Past. 40; Swt. 293, 4. (3) *to water* land, *to irrigate*:—Hē land wæteraþ *arva rigat*, Scint. 118, 14. Da feówer eán ealne disne embhwyrft wæteriaþ, Homl. Skt. i. 15, 177. Ān wyll āsprang of dære eordan wætriende (*irrigans*) ealre dære eordan brādnysse . . . Þæt flōd . . . tō wætrienne (*ad irrigandum*) neorxena wang, Gen. 2, 6, 10. [Cf. *Icel.* vatna *to water*.] v. ge-wæterian.

wæterig; *adj. Watery*:—Wæterig æcer *alluvius ager*, Wrt. Voc. i. 37, 52. Gif se ūtgang sié windig and wætrig and blōdig, Lchdm. ii. 236, 7. Seó wamb de bid wæterigre gecyndo, 220, 26. On wæterigum *in aquoso*, Blickl. Gl.: Ps. Spl. 62, 3. Mid dam wæterian bleó, Scrd. 21, 27. Rixe weaxst on wæterigum stōwum, Homl. Th. ii. 402, 10: Lchdm. i. 98, 26. v. un-wæterig.

wæter-leás; *adj. Without water, dry*:—Hig dydon hine on done wæterleásan pytt *miserunt eum in cisternam, quae non habebat aquam*, Gen. 37, 24. Hē gād derh stōwa (-e, Rush.) wæterleása (-e, Rush.) *perambulat per loca inaquosa*, Lk. Skt. Lind. 11, 24. [*O. H. Ger.* wazzerlōs *sine aqua*.]

wæter-leást, e; *f. Want of water*:—Þæt folc weard geangsumod on mōde for dære wæterleáste, Homl. Ass. 108, 177.

wæter-līc; *adj. Aquatic*:—Wæterlīce *aquatiles*, Germ. 394, 243. [*O. H. Ger.* wazzar-līh *aquaticus*.]

wæter-mēle, -mǣle, es; *m. A water-cup*:—Wætermēle *pelvis*, Ælfc. Gr. 9, 78; Zup. 75, 15. Wætermǣle *pulvis*, Wrt. Voc. i. 85, 68.

wæter-nædre, an; *f. A water-snake*:—Wæternædre *anguis*, Wrt. Voc. ii. 8, 21: i. 285, 3: *salamandra*, 289, 29. Wæternedrum [*h*]*ydris*, ii. 97, 2. [A watyrnedyre *hic idrus*, Wrt. Voc. i. 223, 2. A wateradder *agguis*, 255, 4. Wateraddur *vipera*, 177, 37 (all 15th cent.). *O. H. Ger.* wazzar-natra *natrix, ydrus*.]

wæter-ordāl, es; *n. The ordeal by boiling water*:—Hæbbe se teónd cyre, swā wæterordāl swā ȳsenordāl, L. Ath. iv. 6; Th. i. 224, 15. Cf. Ǣlc tiónd āge geweald swā hwæder hē wille swā wæter swā īsen, L. Eth. iii. 6; Th. i. 296, 4. *See* ordāl.

wæter-pund. v. pund, III.

wæter-pyt[t], es; *m. A water-pit, well*:—Of dam wege on done wæterpytt; of dam pytte on dene, Cod. Dip. Kmbl. vi. 186, 19. On done wæterpyt; of dam wæterpyt, iii. 359, 15. Heó geseah sumne wæterpytt *videns puteum aquae*, Gen. 21, 19. Þone wæterpytt *puteum illum* (cf. wyllspring, v. 7), 16, 14. Gif hwā ādelfe wæterpyt (*cisternam*, Ex. 21, 33), oþþe betȳnedne ontȳne, L. Alf. 22; Th. i. 50, 6. Ofer ealle wæterpyttas *super omnes lacus aquarum*, Ex. 7, 19. Hig dulfon wæterpyttas *they dug for water*, 7, 24.

wæter-rīþe, an; *f. A stream of water*:—Wæterīþan *laticem*, Hpt. Gl. 418, 25.

wæter-sceát, es; *m. A napkin*; mappa, Wrt. Voc. i. 27, 1. v. wæter-scīte.

wæter-scipe, es; *m. A body of water, a piece of water, water*:—Gif hit beón mæg, swā sceal mynster beón gestaþelod, dæt ealle neádbehēfe þing dǣr binnan wunien, dæt is wæterscipe, mylen, wyrtūn (*aqua, molendinum, ortus*), R. Ben. 127, 5. On dære neáwiste næs nān wæterscipe, Jud. 15, 8. Þis is se wæterscipe, de ūs God tō frōfre gehēt . . . dæs wæterscipes welsprynge is on hefonrīce, Past. 65; Swt. 467, 28. Wæterscipes hūs *colimbus*, i. *aquaeductus*, Wrt. Voc. i. 57, 56. Dā cwōmon dǣr scorpiones swā hié ǣr gewunelīce wǣron dæs wæterscipes *scorpiones consuetam petentes aquationem*, Nar. 13, 11. Þæt monnum wǣre dȳ ēþre tō dæm wæterscipe tō ganganne *ut facilior aquatoribus esset accessus ad flumen*, 12, 20. Wæs swīþe wynsum wǣta ūt flōwende . . . Wæs ongeán dyssum wæterscipe glæsen fæt, Blickl. Homl. 209, 4. Wæs dām gebrōdrum micel frēcednys tō āstīgenne tō wæterscipe, and cōmon tō dam hālgan were biddende dæt hē da mynstra gehendor dam wæterscipe timbrian sceolde, Homl. Th. ii. 160, 29-31. Hē heora wæterscipe mid weardmannum besette *constituit centenarios per singulos fontes*, Anglia x. 94, 172. Þone weterscype de hē into Nīwan mynstre be des cinges leáfan geteáh, Chart. Th. 232, 3. Hwalas . . . da de lagostreámas, wæterscipe wecgaþ, Cd. Th. 240, 19; Dan. 389. Ūre Drihten gesceóp ealle wæterscypas and da wīdgillan sǣ, Hexam. 4; Norm. 6, 24.

wæter-scīte, an; *f. A towel*:—Hē weard bewǣfed mid ānre wæterscȳtan (*linteo*, Jn. 13, 4), Homl. Th. ii. 242, 25. v. wæter-sceát.

wæter-scyte, es; *m. A rush of water*. v. wæter-gyte.

wæter-seáþ, es; *m. A water-pit, well, reservoir*:—Dā wæs dǣr on ōþre sīdan dæs hlāwes gedolfen swylce mycel wæterseád wǣre, Guthl. 4; Gdwin. 26, 8. Wæterseádes *cisternae*, Hpt. Gl. 418, 27. [Myrige wæterseádes dǣr ābūten standeþ, Shrn. 13, 17.]

wæter-seóc; *adj. Dropsical*:—Dā wæs sum wæterseóc man *homo quidam hydropicus erat*, Lk. Skt. 14, 2: Homl. Skt. i. 5, 145. Wæterseóc *lymphaticus*, Hpt. Gl. 514, 30. *Ydropicus* byd se wæterseóca, Ælfc. Gr. 9, 56; Zup. 68, 3. Wæterseóces mannes þurst gecēlan, Lchdm. i. 146, 13. Hit fremaþ dam wæterseócan, 204, 2. Wæterseóce *hydropicorum*, Hpt. Gl. 478, 3. Heó gehnǣceþ da anginnu dām wæterseócum,

Lchdm. i. 272, 15. Hē ða wæterseócan gedrīgeþ, 284, 2. [*O. H. Ger.* wazzar-siuh *hydropicus.*]

wæter-seócness, e; *f. Dropsy:*—Ðeós wæterseócnyss *hic ydrops*, Ælfc. Gr. 9, 56; Zup. 68, 2: Homl. Th. i. 86, 9. Wið wæterseócnysse, Lchdm. i. 122, 19: 144, 21: 202, 19: 234, 5: 272, 13: 276, 13: 322, 5. [Cf. *O. H. Ger.* wazzar-suht *hydrops.*] v. wæter-ādl, -bolla.

wæter-slæd, es; *n. A valley with water in it:*—On wæterslædes dīc, Cod. Dip. Kmbl. v. 297, 11. On ðæt wæterslæd, iii. 394, 17. v. slæd.

wæter-spring, es; *m. A springing up of water:*—Upcyme, wæter-sprync wylla, Cd. Th. 240, 13; Dan. 386.

wæter-steal[l], es; *m. Standing water, a pool:*—Ðǣr synd unmǣte mōras, hwīlon sweart wætersteal, hwīlon fūle eárīþas yrnende (*sometimes black stagnant water, sometimes foul streams running*, Guthl. 3; Gdwin. 20, 5.

wæter-stefn, e; *f. The voice* or *sound of water:*—Fram wæter-stefnum wīdra manigra *a vocibus aquarum multarum*, Ps. Th. 92, 4.

wæter-streám, es; *m. A stream of water:*—Hē wæterstreámas wende tō blōde *convertit in sanguinem flumina eorum*, Ps. Th. 77, 44. [Waterr-stræm, Orm. 18092.]

wæter-þeóte, an; *f. A water-channel, conduit:*—Wæterþeóte *aquagium* (aquagium *aquaeductus, canalis*, Migne), Wrt. Voc. i. 22, 23: *canalis* vel *colimbus* vel *aquaeductus*, 61, 22. Ðære heofenan wæter-þeótan wǣron geopenode *cataractae coeli apertae sunt*, Gen. 7, 11: 8, 2: Homl. Th. i. 22, 4. On stefne wæterþeótena ðīnra *in voce cataractarum tuarum*, Ps. Lamb. 41, 8. [Weterþeotan of þer mycele niwelnisse, O. E. Homl. i. 225, 23. *O. H. Ger.* wazzar-dioza *cataracta.*]

wæter-þīsa (?), an; *m. A water-rusher, what rushes through the water*, applied to a ship and to the whale:—Hē wǣghengest wræc, wæterþīsa (-þiswa, MS., *but the* w *is marked for erasure*) tōr snel, Exon. Th. 182, 1; Gū. 1303. Hē (*the whale*) hafaþ ōþre gecynd, wæterþīsa wlonc, 363, 7; Wal. 50. [Cf. *Icel.* þeysa *to rush, storm;* þeysir *a rusher, stormer.*] Cf. mere-þyssa.

wæter-þrūh *a water-pipe, conduit:*—Uueterþrūh, uua[e]terthrūch, uaeterthrouch *caractis*, Txts. 47, 367. Wæte[r]þrūh, Wrt. Voc. ii. 129, 1. Þeótan, wæterþrūh *cataractae*, 13, 15. Waeterðrūm *canalibus*, 102, 68.

wæter-þrȳþe; *pl. f. Water-hosts, great waters:*—Ða ðe wyrceaþ weorc mænig on wæterðrȳþum *qui faciunt operationem in aquis multis*, Ps. Th. 106, 22.

wæter-tyge, es; *m. An aqueduct:*—Wætertige *aquaeductus, canalis*, Hpt. Gl. 418, 50.

wæterung, e; *f. Watering, providing with water*, (1) *providing water* for people:—Sume ða hǣðenan on heora ðeówte leofodon tō wudunge and tō wæterunge (*as hewers of wood and drawers of water*), Homl. Th. ii. 222, 29. (2) *watering* of plants:—Syððan ða wyrta grōwende beóð, hē geswȳcð ðære wæterunge, i. 304, 27.

wæter-wǣdlness, e; *f. Poverty of water, lack of water:*—For ðyses wēstenes wæterwǣdlnysse, Homl. Skt. ii. 23 b, 538.

wæter-weg, es; *m. A water-way, a channel connecting two pieces of water* (?):—Wæterweg *tramites*, Wrt. Voc. i. 37, 43. Andlang burnan on wæterweg; of ðan wæterwege on wæterhammas, Cod. Dip. Kmbl. v. 374, 30. [Water-wey *meatus*, Prompt. Parv. 518.]

wæter-will, es; *m. A spring of water:*—Ðæt man weorðige wæter-wyllas oþþe stānas, L. C. S. 5; Th. i. 378, 20.

wæter-write, es; *m.* (*or* ? -write, an; *f.*) *A vessel measuring time by the running of water:*—Wæterwrite *clepsydra*, Wrt. Voc. ii. 22, 12.

wæter-wyrt, e; *f. Water-fennel:*—Wæterwyrt *callitriche*, Wrt. Voc. i. 67, 18: *gallitricum*, ii. 42, 38: *gallitricium*, Wülck. Gl. 298, 25 (omitted by Wright). Wæterwyrt. Genim ðās wyrte ðe man *callitricum* (*gallitricum*, MS. V.) and ōðrum naman wæterwyrt nemneþ, Lchdm. i. 152, 4–6.

wæter-ȳþ, e; *f. A wave of water, a wave:*—Beorh wunode on wonge wæterȳðum neáh, Beo. Th. 4477; B. 2242.

wæð, -wǣða, wǣðe. v. wæd, here-wǣða, wāþ.

wǣðan; *p.* de *To hunt:*—Ic wiht (*a rake*) geseah . . . seó ðæt feoh fēdeþ, hafaþ fela tōþa . . . wǣþeþ geond weallas, wyrte sēceþ aa, Exon. Th. 416, 27; Rä. 35, 5. Winde gelīcost, ðonne hē hlūd āstīgeþ, wǣðeþ be wolcnum, Elen. Kmbl. 2545; El. 1274. Brim wīde wǣðde, wæl-fæðmum sweóp, Cd. Th. 208, 8; Exod. 480. Hwæþer gē willen wǣþan mid hundum on sealtne sǣ (cf. hwæþer gē eówer hundas ūt on sǣ lǣdon, ðonne gē huntian willaþ, Bt. 32, 3; Fox 118, 14), Met. 19, 15. [*O. H. Ger.* weidōn *venari, errare, pascere; Icel.* veiða *to hunt.*] v. wāþ.

wǣðe-burne (?), an; *f. A fishing-stream* (?):—Of ðæm geate on wǣðeburnan; andlang wǣðeburnan, Cod. Dip. Kmbl. iii. 79, 27. [Cf. *Icel.* veiði-vatn *a fishing-lake: O. H. Ger.* weida *piscatio.*] v. preceding word.

wǣtian; *p.* ode *To become wet:*—Ðāniaþ and wǣtigaþ *madescunt*, Wrt. Voc. ii. 57, 39. v. wǣtan.

wǣting(-ung), e; *f. Wetting, moistening:*—Ðara breósta biþ deáwig wǣtung (v. wǣtian), swā swā sié geswāt, Lchdm. ii. 258, 17. Mid wǣtingum (v. wǣtan) and mettum gelācnian, 222, 8.

wætla, an; *m. A bandage:*—Ðonne ðū hit sniþe, ðonne hafa ðē līnenne wætlan gearone ðæt ðū ðæt dolh sōna mid forwrīðe; and ðonne ðū hit eft mā lǣtan wille, teóh ðone wætlan of, Lchdm. ii. 208, 20–23. Cf. watel.

Wætlinga-ceaster, e; *f. St. Alban's:*—Wæs hē ðrowigende se eádiga Albanus ðȳ teóþan dæge Kalendarum Iuliarum neáh ðære ceastre ðe Rōmāne hēton Verolamium, seó nū fram Angelðeóde Werlameceaster oþþe Wæclingaceaster (uaetlingacæstir, -cester, uetlinguacaester, Lat. versions, Txts. 133, 13–14) is nemned, Bd. 1, 7; S. 479, 5. Neáh ðære ceastre ðe Bryttwalas nemdon Uerolamium and Ængla þeód nemnaþ nū Wætlingaceaster, Shrn. 94, 3. Uerulamium, quod nos uulgariter dicimus Wætlingaceaster, Cod. Dip. Kmbl. iii. 248, 31. In loco qui solito æt Uueatlingaceastre nuncupatur uocabulo, 297, 7.

Wætlinga-strǣt, e; *f. Watling Street*, the Roman road running from Dover, through Canterbury, Rochester, London, St. Alban's, Dunstable, Fenny Stratford, Towcester, Weedon, Wroxeter to Chester. [From Douere in to Chestre tilleþ Watlingestrete, R. Glouc. 8, 1. According to Trevisa it went 'besides Wrokecestre, and then forth to Stratton, and so forth by the myddell of Wales unto Cardykan, and endeth atte Irisshe see.' Polychron. bk. i. c. 45. Florence of Worcester, in his Chronicle under the year 1013, gives a mythical explanation of the word, that it was the road which the sons of King Weatla made across England] :—Ðis sint ða landgemǣra ðara landa tō Baddanbyrig (*Badby*) and tō Doddanforda (*Dodford*) and tō Eferdūne (*Everdon*) (*all three places are in Northamptonshire, a little to the west of Watling Street*) . . . Sūð on gerihte andlang Wætlinga strǣt on ðone weg tō Weódūninga gemǣre (*Weedon*), Cod. Dip. Kmbl. ii. 250, 7: iii. 421, 29. Ðis sint ða landgemǣro intō Stōwe (*Stowe in Bucks*). Ǣrest of ðam hālgan wylles forda sūð andlang Wætlinga strǣte, 443, 4. Hii sunt termini hujus terrae [*land* at Teobban-wyrðe (*Tebworth, Beds*).] Ðǣr se dīc sceót in Wæclinga strǣte; andlanges Wæxlinga strǣte . . . æfter dīce in Wæxlingga strǣte, v. 187, 21–31. Ðis syndon ða landgemǣra tō Hāmstede. Of Sandgatan . . . west tō Wætlinga strǣte, vi. 106, 1. On Weaclinga strǣt (*the place is the same as in the first passage given*), 213, 22. Ðonne on gerihte tō Bedanforda, ðonne up on Ūsan ōð Wætlinga strǣt, L. A. G. 1; Th. i. 152, 10. Hē com ofer Wæclinga strǣte, Chr. 1013; Erl. 148, 6. ¶ In one charter the word occurs in boundaries of land 'æt Eástūn,' which Kemble places in Hampshire, the gift of the land being made at Glastonbury. If this identification is correct the word seems to have been used of more than one road:—Of ðære strǣte in Ebban mōr . . . in ðone dīc on Uppinghǣma gemǣra (*Upham? Hants*); andlang dīces on Wætlinga strǣte, Cod. Dip. Kmbl. iii. 124, 18. [In later English the word was applied to the Milky Way:—The Galaxye, which men clepeth the Milky Wey . . . and somme callen hit Watlinge Strete, Chauc. H. of Fame, ii. 431. Wattelynge strete *lactea, galaxias* vel *galaxia*, Cath. Angl. 410, and see note.]

wǣtness, e; *f. Wetness, moisture:*—Ōðer ne hæbde wǣtnise *aliud non habebat umorem*, Lk. Skt. Lind. 8, 6.

wætri[g]an. v. wæterian.

wæwærð-līc; *adj. Good* (?):—*Semis* ys swȳðe wæwærðlīc tō ongy-tanne, swā hit gerǣd ys on ðære bōc ðe ys Exodus genemned: 'Habuit arca testamenti duos semis cubitos longitudinis.' Hēræfter wē wyllaþ geopenian uplendiscum preóstum ðæra gerēna æfter Lȳdenwara gesceáde, Anglia viii. 335, 30. v. next word.

wæwærðlīce; *adv. Well, successfully* (?):—Of ðissum syx tīdum wihst *se quadrans* swȳðe wæwerðlīce, and forð stæpð wel orglīce swylce hwylc cyng of his giftbūre stæppe geglenged, Anglia viii. 298, 34. Nū þincð ðe wærra and micele ðe snotera, se ðe can mid leásungan wæwerd-līce (-werðlīce [*e from* æ], -wyrdlīce, *v. ll.*) werian, and mid unsōðe sōð oferswīðan, Wulfst. 169, 1.

wæx. v. weax.

wafian; *p.* ode *To look with wonder, be amazed*, (1) absolute:—Ic wafige *stupeo*, Ælfc. Gr. 26, 2; Zup. 154, 13. Wafede *obstupuit*, Hpt. Gl. 510, 23. Hæleð wafedon, Cd. Th. 182, 20; Exod. 78. Ðā wunode hē wundriende and wafiende *cum quasi adtonitus maneret*, Bd. 4, 3; S. 568, 4. Ðæt ðū gange wafiende for hira þinge and ege *sis stupens ad terrorem eorum*, Deut. 28, 34. Ðæt folc wafigende him sāh onbūtan, Homl. Skt. i. 23, 650. Wafiendre wæfersēne *theatrali* (*visibili*) *spectaculo*, Hpt. Gl. 411, 77. Hī swīðe wundredon and wafiende cwǣdon, Lchdm. iii. 436, 7. (2) with gen. *to wonder at, be amazed at:*—Hwā ne wafaþ ðæs, ðonne se fulla mōna wyrþ ofertogen mid þióstrum? . . . Ðises hī wundriaþ, Bt. 39, 3; Fox 214, 29. Heora dysige men wafiaþ, 14, 2; Fox 44, 3. Eówre fȳnd wafiaþ eówre *stupebunt super ea inimici vestri*, Lev. 26, 32. Ealle men wafedon his ānes, Homl. Skt. i. 23, 616. Ða ðe Sīmōnes wundordǣda wafodan, Blickl. Homl. 173, 22. Hwā ne mæge wafian ǣlces steorran? Met. 28, 44. Hæfde hē mē gebunden mid ðære wynsumnesse his sanges, ðæt ic his wæs swiþe wafiende *cum me stupentem carminis mulcedo defixerat*, Bt. 22, 1; Fox 76, 7. (2a) case uncertain:—Hwæt is ðeós wundrung ðe gē wafiaþ, Exon. Th. 6, 25; Cri. 89. (3) with prep. v. wafung, II:—Duguð wafade on ðære fǣmnan wlite, Exon. Th. 252, 13; Jul. 162. (4) with a clause:—Þeóda wlītaþ, wundrum wafiaþ, hū seó wilgedryht wildne weorþiaþ, Exon. Th. 222, 1; Ph.

342. Wafiaþ weras, ðæt . . . , 493, 24; Rä. 81, 86. Hwā is ðæt ne wafige ðæt . . . , Met. 28, 18. Hwā is ðæt ne wafige (cf. hwā ne wundraþ ðæs, ðæt . . . , Bt. 39, 3; Fox 214, 25) hū . . . , 28, 31.

wafian; p. ode *To wave*:—Wafa mid ðīnum handum, Lchdm. ii. 318, 17. Þeáh ðe man wafige wundorlīce mid handa, ne bið hit þeáh bletsung būta hē wyrce tācn ðære hālgan rōde, Homl. Skt. ii. 27, 151.

wafor-līc; *adj. Spectacular, theatrical*:—Hī heora waforlīcan plegan forlēton and heora baða belucon, Ap. Th. 6, 12. v. wæfer-līc, wæfer-sīn, wafian, *and following words*.

wafung, e; *f.* I, *glossing* spectaculum. v. *two following words*: —Wafung *spectaculum*, Wrt. Voc. i. 55, 44. On openre wafunge (the passage is: Martyres in Circi *spectaculo* cuparum gremiis includuntur, Ald. 48), Hpt. Gl. 488, 71. Wafunge *spectaculum* (mirum mundo spectaculum exhibuit, Ald. 62), 509, 33. II. *amazement, wonder, astonishment*:—On ðære gesihðe hine gestōd wundorlīc wafung . . . eall hē wæs ful wundrunge and wafunge, Homl. Skt. i. 23, 501–509. Him an gefōr swīðlīc wafung on swā wuldorfæstan wuldre, ii. 23b, 691. Ðā arn ðæt folc tō for wafunge, i. 12, 206. Hit hī mid swā mycelre fyrhto and wafunge (*tanto stupore*) geslōh, Bd. 4, 7; S. 575, 7. Hī sceáwodon ðæt heáfod mid swīðlīcre wafunge, Homl. Ass. 112, 331: Jud. 16, 25. God hæfþ geēced mīnne ege and mīne wafunga *stuporem meum Deus exaggerat*, Bt. 39, 2; Fox 214, 1. v. webbung.

wafung-stede, es; *m. A place for spectacles* (v. wafung, I), *a theatre, an amphitheatre*:—Wafungstede *theatrum*, Wrt. Voc. i. 36, 45. Syneweald wafungstede *amphitheatrum*, 37, 1.

wafung-stōw, e; *f. A place for spectacles, a theatre, an amphitheatre*: —On plegstōwe oððe on wafungstōwe, Lchdm. iii. 206, 16. v. wæferstōw, *and preceding word*.

wāg (-h), wǣg, es; *m. A wall*, mostly of a building:—Wāh *paries*, Wrt. Voc. i. 81, 8: 290, 7: Ælfc. Gr. 9, 26; Zup. 52, 12. Ǣlces hūses wāh biþ fæst ǣgþer ge on ðære flōre ge on ðæm hrōfe, Bt. 36, 7; Fox 184, 12. Him ne wiðstent nān ðing, nāðer ne stǣnen weall ne brȳden wāh (*a wattled wall; cf.* wāga *cratium*, Wrt. Voc. ii. 136, 55, *and next passage; and* v. brēden), Homl. Th. i. 288, 4. *Graticium* wāg *flecta* (cf. *flecta* hyrdel, 149, 43), Wrt. Voc. ii. 110, 15. Wāg, Exon. Th. 476, 18; Ruin. 9. Ǣlc wāg (*paries*) bið gebiéged twiefeald on ðæm heale, Past. 35; Swt. 245, 13. 'Ðurhðyrela ðone wāg (wāh, Cott. MSS.). Ðā ic ðā ðone wāh ðurhðyreludne hæfde . . . Ealle ða hearga wǣron ātiéfrede on ðæm wǣge' . . . Hwæt is sió ðyrelung ðæs wāges? 21; Swt. 153, 17–25. On āne studu ðæs wāges (*the wall of the hall*), Bd. 3, 10; S. 534, 29: (*the wall of a church*), Blickl. Homl. 207, 16. Seó wræþstudu ðam wāge (*the wall of the church*) tō wræþe geseted wæs, Bd. 1, 17; S. 544, 24, 32. Hē wende hine tō wāge (*the wall of the chamber*), Homl. Th. i. 414, 19. On ðīnre healle wāge, ii. 436, 10: Cd. Th. 261, 8; Dan. 723: Andr. Kmbl. 1428; An. 714: Beo. Th. 3328; B. 1662. Wǣge, Exon. Th. 394, 17; Rä. 14, 4. Hē slōg mid his heáfde on ðone wāg, ðonne hē on his setl sæt, Ors. 5, 15; Swt. 250, 12. Wāh, Ps. Th. 61, 3. Ða wāgas (*the walls of a church*) nǣron rihte, Blickl. Homl. 207, 18: (*the walls of a palace*), Nar. 4, 24. Ne mē ne lyst mid glase geworhtra wāga, Bt. 5, 1; Fox 10, 17. Ne beó wē tō weallum oððe tō wāgum geworhte on ðære gāstlīcan gebytlunge, Homl. Th. ii. 582, 14. Web æfter wāgum, Beo. Th. 1994; B. 995. Ðæt cyricgrið stande ǣghwǣr binnan wāgum, L. I. P. 25; Th. ii. 338, 35. On wāgum ðæra hūsa ðe wið dūna standaþ, Lchdm. i. 124, 16. Wið wāgas, 116, 21. Hī heora heáfdu slōgan on ða wāgas, Blickl. Homl. 151, 5: Homl. Th. i. 106, 14. [Wahes, O. E. Homl. i. 247, 17. Þare halle wah, Laym. 25887. Waȝes (*walls of temples*), wowes (2nd MS.), 10182. Wah (wach) oðer wal, A. R. 104, 5. Wiðinnen þe uour woawes, 172, 21. Fra wah to waȝhe, Orm. 1015. Tweȝȝenn waȝhess, 6825. Wowes, O. and N. 1528. Woȝ, Ayenb. 72. Woughe, Wyck. Ps. 61, 4. Wowes, Piers P. 3, 61. *O. Frs.* wāch: *Goth.* waddjus: *Icel.* veggr.] v. cyric-, grund-, sūþ-wāg (-wǣg).

wāg *a balance*. v. wǣg.

wāg-hrægel, es; *n. A wall-covering, a curtain, veil* (of the temple): —Wāghrægl (-hrǣl, Rush.) temples *velum templi*, Mk. Skt. Lind. 15, 38. Wāghrǣl (-hrægl, Rush.), Lk. Skt. Lind. 23, 45. Wāghruhel, Mt. Kmbl. Lind. 27, 51. Bitwih wāghrǣle (wǣghrægle, Rush.), Lk. Skt. Lind. 11, 51. v. wāg-rift.

wagian; p. ode *To move* (intrans.). I. *to wag, wave, shake, move backwards and forwards*:—Hē mihte hearpian ðæt se wudu wagode, Bt. 35, 6; Fox 166, 32. Ða wudubeámas wagedon and swēgdon, Dōm. L. 7. Wagedan būta, Exon. Th. 436, 25; Rä. 55, 6. Hreád ðæt wagende, Mt. Kmbl. Rush. 12, 20. II. of that which threatens to fall, *to shake, totter*:—Hornsalu wagiaþ, weallas beofiaþ, Exon. Th. 383, 10; Rä. 4, 8. Wagaþ, āslād and gefiōll *labat*, Wrt. Voc. ii. 50, 62. Weagat, 112, 43. Wagiende *nutabunda*, 77, 75: 60, 57. Ðȳ wagigendan *nutabunto*, 83, 71. III. *to shake, be loose*. v. wagung:—His tēð ne wagedon *nec dentes illius moti sunt*, Deut. 34, 9. Wið tōþa sāre and gyf hȳ wagegen (wagigan, wagion, *v. ll.*), Lchdm. i. 126, 15. [Ðe se is eure wagiende, O. E. Homl. ii. 175, 19. Deor gunnen waȝeȝen (pleoye, 2nd MS.), Laym. 26941. *O. H. Ger.* wagōn *to be moved*.] v. wecgan, wegan.

wāg-rift, es; *n. A wall-covering, a curtain, veil* (of the temple):— Wāgryft *curtina*, Wrt. Voc. ii. 105, 68: 15, 57. Wāgrift ðes temples *velum templi*, Ps. Surt. ii. p. 203, 17. Wāhrift, Mk. Skt. 15, 38. Wāhryft (wāg-, Rush.), Mt. Kmbl. 27, 51: Lk. Skt. 23, 45: Homl. Th. ii. 258, 3. Wāhreft *velum*, Wrt. Voc. i. 74, 2. On ðæs temples wāhrift *contra velum sanctuarii*, Lev. 4, 6. Godweb tō wefanne of seolce wāhrift tō ðam temple, Homl. Ass. 132, 548. Ðǣr synt eác wāhriftu, sum ðe hyre wyrðe bið, Chart. Th. 538, 29. Wāgryfta *curtinarum, velarum*, Wrt. Voc. ii. 77, 11: 18, 6. Wāhrefta, Hpt. Gl. 430, 66. Hē hæfð ðiderynn gedōn . . . ii. wāhræft, Chart. Th. 429, 29. [An waȝherifft wass spredd fra wah to waȝhe, Orm. 1014.] v. heall-wāhrift.

wāg-þiling, e; *f. Wall-planking, wainscoting*:—Wāhþyling *tabulatorium*, Wrt. Voc. i. 38, 15. [Cf. *Icel.* vegg-þili *wainscoting*.]

wāg-þyrel (?) *a door-way*:—Swā swā wāge ł wāgþeorles āhyldum *tamquam parieti inclinato*, Ps. Lamb. 61, 4.

wagung, e; *f. Shaking, looseness*. v. wagian, III:—Wið tōþa sāre and wagunge, genim ðās ylcan wyrte, syle etan fæstendum, heó ða tēþ getrymeþ, Lchdm. i. 210, 11: 334, 6.

wāh *a wall*. v. wāg.

wāh; *adj. Fine*:—Genim wāh mela hæsles oþþe alres, āsift ðonne ful clǣne tela micle hand fulle, Lchdm. ii. 270, 22. [Cf. (?) *O. H. Ger.* wāhi:—Uuāhes prōtes *laboratae cereris*.]

wāl (?) *some part of a helmet* [cf. *M. H. Ger.* wæl, wæle *contrivance for fastening the crest of a helmet*]:—Ymb ðæs helmes hrōf heáfodbeorge wīrum bewunden wāl an ūtan (walan utan, MS.) heóld *about the helm's top a 'wāl' wire-girt guarded on the outside the head's defence* (i.e. the helmet), Beo. Th. 2067; B. 1031.

wala (?), an; *m. A root* (?):—Ad (æt?) walan *to the root of a matter, to certainty*; ad liquidum, Wrt. Voc. ii. 2, 46. v. weall-, wyrt-wala.

wala, walas, walca, walch, walc-spinl, wald-, walde, wald-mora, wale. v. wela, wealh, wealca, wealh, wealc-spinl, weald-, willan, wealh-more, weale.

waled; *adj. Coloured* (?):—Waledra *histriatarum* (histriatus *historiis sculptus vel depictus*, Migne), Wrt. Voc. ii. 43, 14. v. (?) walu.

walh. v. wealh.

wā-līc; *adj. Woeful, miserable*:—Is ðes wālīc hām (*hell*) wītes āfylled, Cd. Th. 271, 3; Sat. 100. [*O. H. Ger.* wē-līh *miser, dirus, atrox*.] v. weá-līc.

Waller-wente; *pl. The Celtic inhabitants of Cumbria*:—Nime hē his māga .xii. and .xii. Wallerwente, L. N. P. L. 51; Th. ii. 298, 8. v. Wente.

walu, e; *f. The mark left by a blow, a wale*:—Walu *vibex*, wala *vibices*, Hpt. Gl. 487, 59. Wale *vibice, livore*, 516, 16. Wala *vibices*, 510, 41. Stīðra wala swipa *asperae invectionis mastigias*, 527, 26. [Wale or strype *vibex*, Prompt. Parv. 514. A wale *vibix*, Wülck. Gl. 619, 16.]

walu, e; *f. A ridge, bank* (?):—In stān wale; andlang ðære wale on ðone portweg, Cod. Dip. Kmbl. iv. 98, 28. Of ðam beorge sūþ on ða ealdan wale . . . sūþ be wale on ðære dīce hyrnan, 31, 2–4. [Wale of a schyppe *ratis*, Prompt. Parv. 514.] v. dīc-, stān-walu.

walwian, wam. v. wealwian, wamm.

wamb, e; *f.* I. of living things, (a) *a belly, stomach*:—Wamb *venter*, Wrt. Voc. i. 71, 21. Seó inre wamb *alvus*, 44, 38. Seó ūtre wamb *venter*, 45, 21. Gif sió wamb wund bið, Lchdm. ii. 162, 13. Is seó womb (*of the Phenix*) neoþan wundrum fæger, Exon. Th. 219, 14; Ph. 307. Be wambe coþum, Lchdm. ii. 220, 1. Be wambe missenlīcre gecyndo, 14. Wiþ wambe wærce, 318, 15. Wiþ wambe heardnesse, 358, 3. Be windigre wambe, 162, 23. Ic wiht (*a sow*) geseah fēran, hæfde feówere fēt under wombe, Exon. Th. 418, 11; Rä. 37, 3. Eall ðæt on ðone mūð gǣð, gǣð on ða wambe (womb, Lind.: wombe, Rush. *ventrem*), Mt. Kmbl. 15, 17: Lchdm. ii. 186, 23. Wambe gefyllan *ventrem implere*, Lk. Skt. 15, 16: Exon. Th. 494, 22; Rä. 83, 5. Hē hæfð āne wambe and þūsend manna bigleofan, Homl. Th. i. 66, 1. Be cilda wambum and oferfyll, and gif him mete tela ne mylte, Lchdm. ii. 240, 12. (b) where there is reference to the bringing forth of young, *a womb*:—Westem wombe (wambe, Ps. Spl. C.) *fructus ventris*, Ps. Surt. 126, 3. Ðū ātuge mē of wombe (*ventre*) . . . Of wombe (wambe, Ps. Spl. C. *ventre*) mōdur mīnre, 21, 10–11. Ða wombe (wombo, Lind. *ventres*) ða ðe ne ācendun, Lk. Skt. Rush. 23, 29. II. of inanimate things:—Ic wiht (*bellows*) geseah, womb wæs on hindan, Exon. Th. 419, 6; Rä. 38, 1. Hī (*clouds*) feallan lǣtaþ seáw of bōsme, wǣtan of wombe, 385, 21; Rä. 4, 48. Ic seah wiht (*a cask*), wombe hæfde micle, 495, 2; Rä. 84, 1. III. in the following passage giving the boundaries of some land, Kemble takes the word to mean *a hollow*:—Ondlong ðære hegerǣwe; ðæt on Ondoncilles wombe, Cod. Dip. Kmbl. iii. 52, 14. [*Goth.* wamba γαστήρ, κοιλία, *venter, uterus*: *O. L. Ger.* wamba *venter, uterus*: *O. Frs.* wamme: *O. H. Ger.* wamba *venter, ventriculus, uter, vulva*: *Icel.* vömb *belly*.]

-wamb; *adj.* v. þyrel-wamb.

wamb-ādl, e; *f. Disease of the stomach*:—Hēr sint tācn be wambe coþum and ādlum, and hū mon ða yfelan wǣtan ðære wambe lācnian scyle. Ðonne wambādl tōweard sié, ðonne beóþ ða tācn . . . , Lchdm. ii. 216, 19.

wamb-hord, es; *m. A womb-hoard*, used of the weapons contained in a fortified place:—Mē (*the fortified place*) of hrīfe fleógaþ hylde pīlas; hwīlum ic sweartum swelgan onginne brūnum beadowǣpnum; is mīn innað til, wombhord wlitig, Exon. Th. 399, 12; Rä. 18, 10.

wamb-seóc; *adj. Diseased in the stomach*:—Ða wambseócan men þrowiaþ on ðam bæcþearme and on ðam niþerran hrife, Lchdm. ii. 232, 12: 164, 10.

wamm, es; *m. n.* I. in a physical sense, (a) *a spot, mark, blot, stain*:—Wam *livor*, Wrt. Voc. ii. 50, 17. Wommum *nevis*, 61, 39. (b) *filth, impurity, corruption*:—Wyrms oððe wom *lues*, Ælfc. Gr. 9, 27; Zup. 53, 7. Cwealmbǽrne wom *letiferam luem* (gipsae crudelitas, quae letiferam civibus luem inferebat, Ald. 69), Hpt. 518, 41. Wom *illuviem, immunditiam* (*carceris*, Ald. 48), 488, 31. Gold ðæt in wylme bið womma (woman, Kmbl. *but MS. has* wom̄a) gehwylces geclǽnsod, Elen. Kmbl. 2618; El. 1310. II. fig. (a) *a blot, disgrace, damage, hurt*:—Wom *dispendium*, Wrt. Voc. ii. 106, 40: 28, 11. *Dispendium*, i. *damnum, impedimentum, defectio, periculum, detrimentum* æfwerdla, wonung, wom, wana, *vel* hēnþa, 140, 68. Wæs him ful strang wom and wītu (cf. *O. Sax.* al getholôian wîties endi wammes, Hēl. 1536), Cd. Th. 278, 24; Sat. 227. Wam *maculam* (qui arguit impium, sibi maculam generat, Prov. 9, 7), Kent. Gl. 292. Hellbendum fæst, wommum gewītnad (*grievously punished*), Beo. Th. 6138; B. 3073. (b) *moral stain, impurity, uncleanness, defilement*:—Ðese mid widle and mid womme besmītan, Judth. Thw. 22, 12; Jud. 59. Fram wæmme leahtra *a labe criminum*, Hymn. Surt. 63, 5. Womme *labe* (qui genitus mundum miseranda labe resolvit, Ald. 182), Wrt. Voc. ii. 94, 43: 52, 63. Wom *nevum* (moribus castis vivunt, ut spurcum vitarent pectore nevum, Ald. 168), ii. 92, 82. Synrust þweán and ðæt wom ǽrran wunde hǽlan, Exon. Th. 81, 11; Cri. 1322: 94, 23; Cri. 1544. Ōþ ðæt hafaþ ǽldes leóma woruldwidles wom forbærned, 62, 25; Cri. 1007. (c) *evil, sin, shameful word* or *deed*:—Nǽfre wommes tācn in ðam eardgearde eáwed weorþeþ, ac ðē firina gehwylc feor ābūgeþ, Exon. Th. 4, 18; Cri. 54. Eorl ōðerne mid teónwordum tǽleþ behindan, spreceþ fægere beforan... Byð ðæs wommes gewita weoruda Dryhten, Fragm. Kmbl. 12; Leás. 7. Genere mē fram ðam were ðe wom fremme *a viro iniquo eripe me*, Ps. Th. 139, 1. Wom dydon yldran ūsse, ðīn bebodu brǽcon, Exon. Th. 186, 10; Az. 17: Cd. Th. 234, 25; Dan. 297: Exon. Th. 68, 4; Cri. 1098. Of ðām welerum ðe wom cweðen *a labiis iniquis*, Ps. Th. 119, 2. Heó mē wom spreceþ, firenaþ mec wordum, Exon. Th. 402, 22; Rä. 21, 33. Nǽnig bihelan mæg on ðam heardan dæge wom unbēted, ðǽr hit ða weorud geseóð, So, 25; Cri. 1312. Wer womma leás, Cd. Th. 233, 29; Dan. 283: Menol. Fox 415; Men. 209: Exon. Th. 89, 4; Cri. 1452. Clǽne, womma leáse, 12, 19; Cri. 188: 450, 27; Dōm. 94. Womma clǽne, 103, 26; Cri. 1694. Ne ic culpan in ðē ǽfre onfunde womma geworhtra, and ðū ða word spricest, swā ðū sié synna gehwylcre gefylled, 12, 1; Cri. 179. Hié wǽron womma ðrīste, inwitfulle, Cd. Th. 77, 9; Gen. 1272. Ðū tō fela synna gefremedes; wē ðē nū willaþ womma gehwylces leán forgieldan, Exon. Th. 137, 15; Gū. 559. Āþweah mē of sennum, sāule fram wammum, Ps. C. 38. Ic eom dǽdum fāh, gewundod mid wommum, Cd. Th. 274, 20; Sat. 157. Riht āgyldan ealles ðæs ðe hē on worlde tō wommum gefremede, Blickl. Homl. 113, 4. Wīdgongel wīf mon wommum bilihð, hæleð hȳ hospe mǽnaþ, Exon. Th. 337, 16; Gn. Ex. 65. Mānsceaða, wommum āwyrged, 95, 24; Cri. 1562: Cd. Th. 211, 26; Exod. 532. Unriht dōn, wommas wyrcean, 217, 17; Dan. 24. Se ðe warnaþ him wommas worda and dǽda, Exon. Th. 304, 32; Fä. 79. [*Goth.* wammē; *gen. pl. macularum*: *O. Sax.* wamm *evil, wrong*: *O. Frs.* wamm *a blemish*: *O. H. Ger.* wamm *damnum*: *Icel.* vamm; *n. a blemish.*] v. mān-, wlite-wamm.

wamm; *adj.* I. *foul*:—Ic under eorþan sceáwige wom wræcscrafu (? wrað-, MS.) wrāþra gēsta, Exon. Th. 424, 18; Rä. 41, 41. II. *evil, wicked*:—Nā ðū be gewyrhtum, Wealdend, ūrum, wommum wyrhtum woldest ūs dōn *non secundum peccata nostra fecit nobis*, Ps. Th. 102, 10. [*O. Sax.* wamm (dād): cf. *Goth.* ga-wamms *communis*; un-wamms *immaculatus, sine macula.*]

wamm-cwide, es; *m. Evil speaking, reviling, slander, blasphemy*:—Him (*the devils*) wæs wrāð geworden for womcwidum, Cd. Th. 282, 6; Sat. 282. Ne wīte ic him ða womcwidas, þeáh hē his wyrðe ne sié tō ālǽtanne ðæs fela hē mē lāðes spræc, 39, 7; Gen. 621.

wamm-dǽd, e; *f. An evil deed, a misdeed, trespass, crime*:—Swā swā wē forlǽtaþ leahtras on eorðan ðām ðe wið ūs oft āgyltaþ, and him womdǽda wītan ne þencaþ '*as we forgive them that trespass against us*,' Hy. 6, 25. Him (*David*) sāwla Neriend secgan hēt ymb his womdǽda Waldendes dōm, Ps. C. 19: Exon. Th. 270, 18; Jul. 467. [*O. Sax.* wam-dād: Ef gī ne willeat weron wamdādī ālātan, Hēl. 1624.]

wamm-freht, es; *n. Divination*:—Ða ðæt womfreht rēniaþ *ariolorum*, Wrt. Voc. ii. 82, 8. Womferht, 5, 16. Cf. frihtere, frihtrung.

wamm-full; *adj. Evil, guilty, criminal, flagitious*:—Ǽr se unsȳfra (*Holofernes*) womfull onwōce, Judth. Thw. 22, 24; Jud. 77. Synfulra here... womfulra scolu, Exon. Th. 94, 5; Cri. 1535. Womfulle, scyldwyrcende (*the fallen angels*), Elen. Kmbl. 1519; El. 761.

wamm-lust, es; *m. A foul pleasure, an allurement, seduction*:—Womlustas *lenocinia*, Anglia xiii. 28, 19.

wamm-sceaþa, an; *m. An evil-doer, a sinner, criminal*:—Āwyrged womsceaða (*the devil*), Exon. Th. 255, 8; Jul. 211. Womsceaþan (*the wicked, at the day of judgement*), 75, 23; Cri. 1226: 96, 7; Cri. 1570. Āwyrgede womsceaðan, leáse leódhatan, ārleasra sceolu, Elen. Kmbl. 2595; El. 1299. [*O. Sax.* wam-skaðo.]

wamm-scyldig; *adj. Sinful, criminal*:—Ne mæg ðǽr (*paradise*) inwitfull ǽnig geférān, womscyldig mon, Cd. Th. 58, 20; Gen. 949.

wamm-wlite, es; *m. A wound on the face*:—Swā hwylc man swā ōðrum womwlite on gewyrce, forgylde him ðone womwlite, and his weorc wyrce ōð ðæt seó wund hāl sig *quicunque homo alio vulnus in faciem inflixerit, emendet ei vulnus, et opus ejus operetur, donec vulnus sanetur*, L. Ecg. C. 22; Th. ii. 148, 18. v. wlite-wamm.

wamm-wyrcende *working iniquity*:—Ðæt weorþeþ þeódum tō þreá, ðām ðe þonc Gode, womwyrcende, ne cūþun ðæs ðe hē on ðone hālgan beám ahongen wæs, Exon. Th. 67, 23; Cri. 1093.

wan *wan.* v. wann.

wan, es; [*n.* (?) cf. *Icel.* vant (*neut. of* vanr) *with gen.*] *Want, lack*:—Ne byð mē nānes gōdes wan *nihil mihi deerit*, Ps. Th. 22, 1. Hī habbaþ ǽghwæs genōh, nis him wihte won, Exon. Th. 352, 9; Sch. 95. On ðām ðingum ðe hī won hæfdon *in eis quae minus habuerat*, Bd. 5, 22; S. 644, 15. v. wana; *m., and next word.*

wan; *adj.* I. *wanting, absent*:—Ðā getreówde hē in godcundne fultom, ðǽr se mennesca wan wæs *confidens in divinum, ubi humanum deerat, auxilium*, Bd. 2, 7; S. 509, 23. Him won (wona, MS. Ca.) ne wæs seó monung ðære godcundan ārfæstnesse *non defuit admonitio divinae pietatis*, 4, 25; S. 599, 23. Ne wiht mē wonu bið *nihil mihi deerit*, Ps. Surt. 22, 1: 33, 10. Ǽr ðon ðe Drihten on heofenas āstige, þonon hē nǽfre won wæs þurh his godcundnesse miht, Blickl. Homl. 131, 17. II. *lacking, not possessed of*:—Wē tīres wone ā būtan ende sculon ermþu dreógan, Exon. Th. 17, 15; Cri. 270. III. with numerals (v. læs), *less.* Cf. wana; *adj.* IIIa:—Ðæt rīce hē hæfde ānes won ðe twēntig wintra, Bd. 4, 1; M. 252, 9. Ānes won þe syxtig wintra, 3, 24; M. 238, 2. Ānes won þe twēntig wintra, 5, 1; M. 386, 25. Gewurþad mid ðām æþelestum ceastrum ānes won ðe ðrittigum, 1, 1; S. 473, 26 note. [*Goth.* wans *wanting* (Tit. 1, 6): *O. Sax.* wan: *O. Frs.* won: *O. H. Ger.* wan wesan *deesse*: *Icel.* vanr.] v. wana; *adj.*

wana, an; *m.* I. *want, lack, absence*:—Mē ys feós wana *deest mihi pecunia*, Ælfc. Gr. 32; Zup. 202, 12. Hlāfes wæs wana *panis deerat*, Gen. 47, 13. Ðonne wana (wona, Hatt. MS.) bið ðæs ðe hié habban woldon *hae cum desunt*, Past. 18; Swt. 126, 22. Hit nān mon ne mæg eall habban, ðæt him ne sié sumes þinges wana, Bt. 34, 9; Fox 146, 19. Ðū mǽnst gif ðē ǽnies willan wana biþ, 11, 1; Fox 30, 22: 26, 1; Fox 90, 22: 29, 1; Fox 102, 18. Ðonne is sum gōd full ǽlces willan and nis nānes gōdes wana, 34, 1; Fox 134, 27: Homl. Th. i. 272, 13: ii. 400, 11: Ps. Th. 33, 9: Shrn. 202, 11. Gif hwæm ðara twēgra hwæðeres wana biþ, Bt. 36, 3; Fox 176, 7. Ðam bið gomenes wana ðe ða earfeða dreógeþ, Exon. Th. 183, 17; Gū. 1328. Mē is wana æt ðam scȳrgesceatte ðus micelys ðe mīne foregengan hæfdon, Cod. Dip. Kmbl. iii. 327, 4. Swā ic feós bidde swā ic wanan hæbbe ðæs ðe mē N. behēt (*I have not got what N. promised me*), L. O. 10; Th. i. 182, 7. Ia. in connection with numerals. v. wana; *adj.* III a:—Hire daga rīm gefylled wæs, ðæt is ānes geáres wana sixtigra wintra (*there wanted one year of sixty*; undesexaginta annorum), Bd. 3, 24; S. 557, 6 note. II. *want of necessaries, lack, want, defect*:—*Dispendium*, i. *damnum, impedimentum, defectio, periculum, detrimentum* æfwerdla, wonung, wom, wana, *vel* hēnþa, Wrt. Voc. ii. 140, 69. Wanan *inopiam* (cum panis copia plebis inopiam refocillantes, Ald. 53), Hpt. Gl. 497, 26. [Ðet ich þurh to muche wone ne falle i fulðe of sunne... ðet ich mote underuon boðe wone and weole þe ine cwemnesse, O. E. Homl. i. 213, 28–32. And tah þu wone hefdest oder drehdest ani derf, H. M. 29, 8. Uor wone of witnesse, A. R. 68, 8.] v. for-wana; wan.

wana; *adj. generally indeclinable.* I. *wanting, lacking, absent*, (a) with substantive verb, wana wesan *to be wanting*:—Ic eom wana of ðam getele *desum*, Ælfc. Gr. 32; Zup. 202, 11. Ān þing ðē is wana (wona, Lind., Rush.) *unum tibi deest*, Lk. Skt. 18, 22: Mk. Skt. 10, 21. Wæs eów ǽnig þing wana? *numquid aliquid defuit vobis?* Lk. Skt. 22, 35. Hwæt ys mē gyt wana (gwona, Lind.: woen, Rush.)? *quid mihi deest?* Mt. Kmbl. 19, 20. Ðæt ic wite hwæt wana (wone, Ps. Surt.) sȳ mē, Ps. Spl. 38, 6: Bt. 33, 3; Fox 126, 20. Ðam biþ anweald wana (anwaldes wana, Cott. MS.), 36, 3; Fox 176, 13. Mē wana is ǽgþer ge spadu ge mattuc, Homl. Skt. ii. 23 b, 765. Synn wana nā byð *peccatum non deerit*, Scint. 78, 4: Kent. Gl. 335. Wana sié *absit*, Wrt. Voc. ii. 3, 57. Mē synd wana penegas *desunt mihi nummi*, Ælfc. Gr. 32; Zup. 202, 13. Ne heora martyrhāda wona wǽron heofonlīcu wundru *nec martyrio eorum coelestia defuere miracula*, Bd. 5, 10; S. 625, 4. (b) in connection with numerals, *wanting* for the completion of a number:—Ðæs hærfest cymþ ymb ōðer swylc būtan ānre wanan *after one less than the same number of days comes autumn*, Menol. Fox 280; Men. 141. .X. geár būton .xv. wucan wanan (*fifteen weeks were wanting to complete the ten years*), Chr. 1068; Erl. 206, 17. II. *wanting, destitute* of, *without* something:—Se ne ongyteþ ða þeóstra his āgenra synna, wite hē ðæt hē bið wana ðæs ēcan leóhtes, Blickl. Homl. 17, 36. III. *wanting, not complete, deficient*:—Gif nān wuht full nǽre, ðonne nǽre nān wuht wana; and gif nān wuht wana nǽre, ðonne nǽre nān wuht full; for ðȳ biþ ǣnig full þing, ðe sum biþ wana, and for ðȳ biþ ǣnig þing wana, ðe sum biþ full, Bt. 34, 1; Fox 134, 20-23. Genōg sweotol hit is ðæt ðæt fulle gōd wæs ǣr ðam ðe ðæt wana *omnia perfecta minus integris priora esse claruerunt*, 34, 2; Fox 136, 12. **III a.** with numerals, *wanting, save* (cf. *Goth.* fidwōr tiguns ainamma wanans, 2 Cor. 11, 24). v. wana; *m.* **I a**, wan; *adj.* **III.** As appears especially in the first of the following passages, the word and the numerals which precede and follow it as much form a compound as do the words which give the number they express in modern English:—Hē wæs āne-wana-xxx-wintre (xxix wintra eald, col. 3), Chr. 972; Th. i. 225, col. 1. Ānes wana fīftig, Andr. Kmbl. 2079; An. 1040. Ānes wona sixtig wintra *undesexaginta annorum*, Bd. 3, 24; S. 557, 6. Gewurþad mid ðām æðelestum ceastrum anes wana ðrittigum, 1, 1; S. 473, 26. Ðæt rīce hē hæfde ānes wona .xx. wintra (ān læs ðe twēntig, MS. B.), 4, 1; S. 563, 15. Hē Norþanhymbra ðeóde ānes wana .xx. wintra fore wæs *genti Nordanhymbrorum decem et novem annis praefuit*, 5, 1; S. 614, 21. [Ful lutel þer wæs wone, þat Corineus nas ouercome, Laym. 1905. Him ne schal beo wone nouht (no þing, *v. l.*) of his wille, Misc. 104, 57. Hem was ðat water wane, Gen. and Ex. 3353. Wane or wantynge *absens, deessens*, Prompt. Parv. 515. ¶ *with numerals*:—On wane of an hundred *ninety-nine*, Gen. and Ex. 1028. Twa wone of twenti *duo de viginti*, Kath. 67.] v. wan; *adj.*

wana-beám. v. wanan-beám.

wan-ǣht, e; *f. Scant possession*:—Nāh ic fela goldes . . . ic mē sylf ne mæg fore mīnum wonǣhtum willan ādreógan, Exon. Th. 458, 19; Hy. 4, 103. Cf. wan-spēd.

wanan-beám, es; *m. A spindle-tree* (v. English Plant Names, E.E.T.S. Pub., and cf. *O. H. Ger.* spinnel-boum *fusarius*):—Wananbeám (uuanan-, uuonan-) *fusarius*, Txts. 65, 935: Wrt. Voc. ii. 39, 5. Wanabeám *fussarius*, 36, 58: *fursarius*, i. 286, 3.

wancol; *adj. Unstable, uncertain, fickle, fluctuating*:—Hió hit gecȳþ self mid hire hwurfulnesse ðæt hió biþ swīþe wancol *se instabilem mutatione demonstrat*, Bt. 20; Fox 70, 35. Nū ðū hæfst ongyten ða wanclan (wonclan, *v. l.*) treówa ðæs blindan lustes *deprehendisti caeci numinis ambiguos vultus*, 7, 2; Fox 18, 3. [Ðis wunder (*the mermaid*) wuneð in wankel stede, Misc. 18, 566. This worlde is wondur wankille, Halliw. Dict. *O. Sax.* wankol (hugi): *O. H. Ger.* wanchal *lubricus, infidelis.* Cf. *O. L. Ger.* wankil-heidī *fluctuatio.*]

wand[, e; *f.*?] *a mole*:—Wond (wand, uuond) *talpa*, Txts. 101, 1973. v. wande-weorpe.

-wand. v. ge-wand.

wande-weorpe, an; *f. A mole* (cf. later English mold-werp, *still used in some dialects*: *O. H. Ger.* mu-werfo *talpa*, Grff. i. 1040: *M. H. Ger.* molt-werf: *Ger.* maul-wurf: *Icel.* mold-varpa):—Wondeuueorpe (uuandaeuui[o]rpae, uuondæuuerpe) *talpa*, Txts. 101, 1975. Wandewurpe *talpa* vel *palpo*, Wrt. Voc. i. 22, 60: *talpa*, 78, 19. v. wand.

wandian; *p.* ode. I. *to turn aside* from something (*gen.*):—Ne beforan manegon sōðes ne wanda *nec in judicio plurimorum acquiesces sententiae, ut a vero devies*, Ex. 23, 2. II. *to turn aside* from a task, purpose, duty, etc., *to hesitate, shrink, flinch*, (a) absolute:—Ic wandige (āwandige, *v. l.*) *uereor*, Ælfc. Gr. 27; Zup. 162, 2. Hē wandode ðā git (*dissimulante illo*); ac hig gelæhton hys hand and his wīfes hand and gelǣddon hig ūt of ðære byrig, Gen. 19, 16. Wandode se wīsa (*Daniel*), hwæðre hē worde cwæð tō ðam æðelinge, Cd. Th. 250, 24; Dan. 550. Hē ne wandode nā æt ðam wīgplegan, Byrht. Th. 139, 42. Ne mæg nā wandian se ðe wrecan þenceþ freán, 139, 22; By. 258. Oft mon bið suīðe wandigende æt ǣlcum weorce and suīðe lætrǣde *agendi tarditas*, Past. 20; Swt. 149, 14. (b) where the grounds for turning aside are given, *to care* for, *be influenced* by:—Ðū ne wandast for nānon menn *non est tibi cura de aliquo*, Mt. Kmbl. 22, 16. Ðū for nānon men ne wandast *non accipis personam*, Lk. Skt. 20, 21. Ne wandaþ hē for rīcum ne for heánum *qui personam non accipit*, Deut. 10, 17. For hira feónda yrre ic wandode *propter iram inimicorum distuli*, 32, 27. Ne hit for ðæm bryne wandode ðæs hātan lēges *nec ignium tardatus ardoribus*, Nar. 15, 20. Ne wanda ðū for rīcum ne for heánum ne for nānum scette *non accipies personam nec munera*, Deut. 16, 19. Nō wandige hē for ðan yflan willan *non consideret malam voluntatem*, R. Ben. 92, 11. (c) where that which is turned aside from is given, (α) by a clause:—Sume synna beóþ swīþe unsȳferlīce, ðæt se man wandaþ ðæt hē hī ǣfre āsecgge, Blickl. Homl. 43, 17. Ðonne ðū behāt behǣtst, ne wanda ðū ðæt ðū hit ne gelǣste *cum votum voveris, non tardabis reddere*, Deut. 23, 21. Ne wanda ðū, ðæt ðū ðīnum frȳnd ne helpe, 15, 10. (β) by the dat. infin.:—Hī ne wandiaþ tō licgenne on stuntnysse, Homl. Th. ii. 554, 2. Hē ne wandode nā him metes tō tylienne, Chr. 1052; Erl. 183, 20. (d) with the constructions of (b) and (c. α):—Ðæt hyra nān ne wandode ne for mīnan lufan ne for mīnum ege, ðæt hȳ ðæt folcriht ārehton, Chart. Th. 486, 23. Ne wandige nā se mæssepreóst nō for rīces mannes ege, ne for feó, ne for nānes mannes lufon, ðæt hē him symle riht dēme, Blickl. Homl. 43, 9. (e) with the constructions of (b) and (c. β):—Ða bydelas ðe for ege oððe lufe oððe ǣnigre worldscame eargiaþ and wandiaþ Godes riht tō sprecanne, Wulfst. 191, 6. III. *to turn aside* from punishing, injuring, etc., *to refrain* from, *spare* a person or thing (*dat.*). (a) absolute:—Ðæt man nǣnne ne slōge . . . būton hē fleón wille oþþe hine werian; ðæt man ne wandode ðonne, L. Ath. v. 12, 3; Th. i. 242, 10. Suelce hē hine wandigende ofersuīðe *quasi parcendo superare*, Past. 40; Swt. 297, 15: 295, 12. Næs wandigendre ðonne hit gedafenlīc sié *non plus quam expediat, parcens*, 17; Swt. 127, 4. (b) with dat.:—Ne wandode ic nā mīnum sceattum ða hwīle ðe eów unfrið on handa stōd *I did not spare my treasures while you had hostilities on hand*, Chart. Erl. 229, 27. Ða ðe heora Drihtne wiðsacan noldon, ðām man nān þingc ne wandode, ac hī tō ealre yrmðe getucode, Homl. Skt. i. 23, 71. Ne wanda ðū nān ðing ne āra ðū nānum rīce *non parcet oculus tuus ulli regno*, Anglia x. 88, 47. Se wilnaþ suīður ðæt mon lufge sōðfæsðnesse ðonne hine selfne, se ðe wilnaþ ðæt mon nānre ryhtwīsnesse fore him ne wandige *ille se ipso amplius veritatem desiderat amari, qui sibi a nullo vult contra veritatem parci*, Past. 19; Swt. 145, 17. (c) with a clause:—Sanctus Paulus geliéfde, ðæt hē swā micele unscyldigra wǣre his niéhstena blōdes swā hē læs wandade ðæt hē hira unðeáwas ofslōge *Paulus eo se a proximorum sanguine mundum credidit, quo feriendis eorum vitiis non pepercit*, Past. 49; Swt. 379, 11. [Love wol love—for no wight wol hit wonde, Ch. L. G. W. 1187. Wolde I wonde for no sinne, Gow. i. 332, 7. For us ne schalt þou wonde, Jos. 399. To love nul i noht wonde, Spec. 29. Sche wold for no man wond, that sche no wold to him fond, Am. and Amil. 550. He wonded no woþe of wekked knaueȝ, þat he ne passed þe port, Allit. Pms. 63, 855. For to speke alle vilanie nel nu no kniht wonde for shame, P. S. 335, 262. Lust whi ihc wonde bringe þe Horn to honde, Horn 337. Jhon her son sche wolde nought wonde, Rich. 228.] v. ā-, for-wandian; un-wandiende.

-wandigendlīce. v. un-forwandigendlīce.

wandlung, e; *f. Changing, mutation*:—Hié beheóldon on ðē heora āgen gecynd, and on heora wandlunga hié gecȳþdon heora fæstrǣdnesse *servavit circa te propriam in ipsa sui mutabilitate constantiam*, Bt. 7, 2; Fox 16, 31. [*O. H. Ger.* wandelunga *mutatio*, cf. *O. L. Ger.* wandlōn *to change.*]

-wandodlīc, -līce. v. un-forwandodlīc, -līce.

wandrian; *p.* ode *To wander, rove, roam*:—Wandriendu *ludivaga*, Wrt. Voc. ii. 54, 26. I. in a physical sense:—Se steorra (*Saturn*) wandraþ ofer ōþrum steorran, Bt. 36, 2; Fox 174, 13: Met. 24, 23. Wandraþ *vagatur*, Hpt. Gl. 412, 56. Hī maciaþ eall be luste, woriaþ and wandriaþ, and ealne dæg fleardiaþ, L. I. P. 14; Th. ii. 322, 24. Hræfen wandrode, Fins. Th. 69; Fin. 34. Wandrigende pucan *uagantes demonas*, Germ. 388, 37. II. figurative. (a) *to leave one's proper work*:—Ðonne gǣð Dine ūt sceáwian ða elðiódigan wīf, ðonne hwelces monnes mōd forlǣt his ǣgne tilunga, and sorgaþ ymb ōðerra monna wīsan, ðe him nāuht tō ne limpð, and færð swā wandriende from his hāde and of his endebyrdnesse. Sihhem geniédde ðæt mǣden ðā hē hié gemētte swā wandrian *Dina, ut mulieres videat extraneae regionis, egreditur, quando unaquaeque mens sua studia negligens, actiones alienas curans extra habitum atque extra ordinem proprium vagatur. Quam Sichem opprimit; quia inventam in curis exterioribus diabolus corrumpit*, Past. 53; Swt. 415, 19-23. (b) *to proceed without plan, follow an uncertain course*:—Swā ða sēlestan men swīþor ðās eorþlīcan ðing forseóþ, swā hī læs rēccaþ hū sió wyrd wandrige, Bt. 39, 7; Fox 222, 25. Ðiós wandriende wyrd ðe wē wyrd hātaþ, 39, 6; Fox 220, 5. [*M. H. Ger.* wandern.]

wandung, wan-fāh, -feax, -fōta, -fȳr. v. for-wandung, wann-fāh, -feax, -fōta, -fȳr.

wang, es; *m.* I. the word, which is almost confined to poetry, may be rendered by words denoting the surface of the ground taken in their most general sense, *field, plain, land, country, place*:—Wonge (wongc?) *arvum*, Wrt. Voc. ii. 10, 51. Mec se wǣta wong wundrum freórig of his innaþe cende *roscida me genuit gelido de viscere tellus* (Ald.), Exon. Th. 417, 7; Rä. 36, 1. Se wong seomaþ eádig and onsund. Is ðæt æþele lond blōstmum geblōwen, beorgas ðǣr ne muntas steápe ne standaþ . . . ne dene ne dalu *illic planicies tractus diffundit apertos, nec tumulus crescit, nec cava vallis hiat*, Exon. Th. 199, 2; Ph. 19. Wlitig is se wong . . . ǣnlīc is ðæt īglond, 198, 8; Ph. 7. Wynsum wong, wealdas grēne, 198, 20; Ph. 13. Se hālga wong *Paradise*, 227, 5; Ph. 418. Brūcan wonges, . . . neótan londes frætwa, 268, 1; Ph. 149. Hwæþere him ðæs wonges wyn (cf. londes wyn, 130, 15; Gū. 438) sweðrade *whether the land grew less delightful to him*, 123, 15; Gū. 123. Ic ða stōwe ne can ne ðæs wanges (*the place where the cross was buried*) wiht ne ða wīsan cann, Elen. Kmbl. 1364; El. 684. On ðam wange, ðǣr hē sorge gefremede *on the scene of his wrong-doings*, Beo. Th. 4010; B. 2003. Hī gesēgon wyrm on wonge licgean *he saw the serpent lying on the ground*, 6070; 3039. On wonge, wæterȳðum neáh, 4476; B. 2242; Cd. Th. 113, 4; Gen. 1882: Exon. Th. 485, 21; Rä. 72, 1. Næs ðǣr hlāfes wist werum on ðam wonge (*the island of Mermedonia*), Andr. Kmbl. 43; An. 22. Hē sceal ðȳ wonge (*the island in the fens where St. Guthlac's hermitage was*) wealdan, Exon. Th. 144, 6; Gū. 674. Hȳ ðone grēnan wong ofgiefan sceoldan, 130, 34; Gū. 448. Hē wang sceáwode fore burggeatum *he reconnoitred the place*, Andr. Kmbl. 1678; An. 841:

Beo. Th. 2831; B. 1413: 4809; B. 2409: 6139; B. 3073. Hī on wang stigon *they landed*, 456; B. 225. Ofer wong faran *to go across country*, Exon. Th. 481, 10; Rä. 65, 1. Hryre wong gecrong *the ruin sank to earth*, 477, 30; Ruin. 32. Ðone wlitigan wong *Paradise*, 228, 16; Ph. 439. Wangas blōstmum blōwaþ *fields bloom with flowers*, Menol. Fox 178; Men. 90. Wangas grēne, 410; Men. 206. Ðās foldan bearm, grēne wongas, Exon. Th. 482, 21; Rä. 67, 5: Cd. Th. 100, 1; Gen. 1657. Wangas, eorđe ælgrēno, Met. 20, 77: Exon. Th. 51, 5; Cri. 811: 451, 32; Dōm. 112. Him wīc curon, đǣr him wlitebeorhte wongas geþūhton, Cd. Th. 108, 11; Gen. 1804: Beo. Th. 4915; B. 2462. Sum con wonga bīgong, wegas wīdgielle *one knows the world, ways wide-spreading*, Exon. Th. 42, 30; Cri. 680. Dæg se georstenlīca God besceáwede on wangum *dies hesterna Deum conspexit in arvis*, Hymn. Surt. 47, 10. On sumeres tīd stincaþ on stōwum, wynnum æfter wongum wyrta geblōwene, Exon. Th. 178, 24; Gū. 1249. Cumaþ wæstm on wangas weorđlīc on hwǣtum *convalles abundabunt frumento*, Ps. Th. 64, 14. Ic foldan slīte, grēne wongas, Exon. Th. 393, 18; Rä. 13, 2. Wīde geond wongas, 491, 8; Rä. 80, 11. II. *the earth, the surface of the earth*:—Ic (*creation*) eorþan eom ǣghwǣr brǣdre, and wīdgelra đonne đes wong grēna (cf. *O. Sax.* grōni wang *the earth*), Exon. Th. 426, 34; Rä. 41, 83. Cȳþan werum on wonge, 414, 2; Rä. 32, 14: 439, 11; Rä. 59, 2. Seó heá miht on đysne wang āstāg, Blickl. Homl. 105, 14. Ðū eorđan wang ealne gesettest, Hy. 10, 3. Se Ælmihtiga eorþan worhte wlitebeorhtne wang, Beo. Th. 186; B. 93. Gangan ofer foldan wang, Menol. Fox 225; Men. 114. III. fig. of any surface:—Ic (*a cup for cupping*) eom stīđ and steáp wong, staþol wæs in þā wyrta wlitetorhtra, Exon. Th. 484, 4; Rä. 70, 2. [Casteles and tunes, wodes and wonges, Havel. 397. Wonge of londe *territorium*, Prompt. Parv. 532. *Goth.* waggs *paradisus* (2 Cor. 12, 4): *O. Sax.* wang *field, plain, country*: *O. H. Ger.* holz-wang *campus nemoreus*: *Icel.* vangr (poet.) *field*.] v. beadu-, deáđ-, fold-, freođo-, græs-, grund-, medu-, metud-, sǣ-, sǣl-, sige-, stān-, staþol-, stede-, wæl-, wil-wang, neorxna wang, *and* wang-turf.

wang, es; *m.*: wange, wænge, wenge, an; *n. A cheek, side of the face*:—Ðæt wange wiđ đa ceócan ufan *mandibula*, Wrt. Voc. ii. 58, 3. Ðæs wonges locfeax *cesaries*, 22, 57. Smire đæt hāle wonge mid, Lchdm. ii. 338, 9. Bind on đæt wænge, 20, 10. Smyre đæt wenge, 20, 18. Gif hwā đē sleá on đīn swȳđre wenge (gewenge, *v. l.*, wonge ł cēke, Rush.) *si quis te percusserit in dextera maxilla tua*, Mt. Kmbl. 5, 39. Benedictus slōh đone munuc under đæt wencge mid anre handa, Homl. Th. ii. 180, 10. T him đa wongan briceþ, Salm. Kmbl. 192; Sal. 95. Ic đa wangas mid teárum ofergeát, Homl. Skt. ii. 23 b, 556. [Wete weoren his wongen, Laym. 30268. I wette my wonges, Jos. 647. *O. Sax. O. L. Ger. O. H. Ger.* wanga; *wk. n. maxilla*: *Icel.* vangi; *wk. m.*] v. þun-wang, -wange, -wenge, ge-wenge.

wang-beard, es; *m. A whisker*:—Teóh him đa loccas, and wringe đa eáran, and đone wangbeard twiccige, Lchdm. ii. 196, 13.

wange. v. wang *a cheek*.

wangere, es; *m. A pillow, bolster*:—Wangere *cervical* (v. Mk. 4, 38), Wrt. Voc. ii. 73, 29: 17, 53: i. 25, 45: *capitale*, ii. 128, 44. Bolster *vel* wongere *cervical*, i. *capitale*, 130, 26. Fram dǣle đæs heáfdes mihte wongere (*cervical*) betwih geseted beón, Bd. 4, 11; S. 580, 16. [His helm was his wonger, Chauc. Sir Th. 2102. *Goth.* ana waggarja *super cervical*, Mk. 4, 38: *O. H. Ger.* wangāri; *m. plumatium*.]

wang-stede, es; *m.* I. *a place in open country, a place*:—Forlǣt of đam wangstede (cf. stōpon tō đære stōwe, on đa dūne up, 1428; El. 716) rēc āstīgan, Elen. Kmbl. 1584; El. 794: 2205; El. 1104. Stenc ūt cymeþ of đam wongstede (cf. hē sēceþ dȳgle stōwe under dūnscrafum, 357, 31; Pa. 37), Exon. Th. 358, 13; Pa. 45. On đam wongstede (*the place of the last judgement*) wērig bīdan, 50, 18; Cri. 802. Hwæđer hē cwicne gemētte in đam wongstede (cf. wong. 4809; B. 2409) Wedra þeóden, Beo. Th. 5565; B. 2786. Se đās wongstedas grōf æfter golde (cf. se đe đa eorþan ongan delfan æfter golde, Bt. 15; Fox 48, 23), Met. 8, 56. II. *a town on a plain* (wang)?:—Hē eode in burh hrađe, . . . stōp on strǣte . . . swā him nǣnig gumena ongitan ne mihte; hæfde sigora weard on đam wangstede (cf. hē wang sceáwode fore burggeatum, 1678; An. 841. *But perhaps* wangstede = wang, *and the passage means that St. Andrew was unseen as he passed across the space* (wang) *between the sea and the town*. Cf. stede-wang) wǣre betolden leófne leódfruman . . . Hæfde đā se æđeling in geþrungen carcerne nēh, Andr. Kmbl. 1975; An. 990.

wang-tōþ, es; *m. A wang-tooth* (in northern dialects. v. e. g. Lancashire Gloss. in E. E. D. S. Pub.), *molar tooth*:—Gif mon ōđrum tōđ of āsleá, gif hit sié se wongtōđ geselle .iiii. scill. tō bōte, L. Alf. pol. 49; Th. i. 94, 11. Wangtēđ *molares vel gemini*, Wrt. Voc. i. 43, 32. Wongtoeđ (-tēþ, Ps. Spl. C.) *molas*, Ps. Surt. 57, 7: [Wangeteth *les messeleres*, Wrt. Voc. i. 146, 22. Out of a wangtooth sprang a welle (v. Wick. Jud. 15, 19, where the word is used), Chauc. M. T. 3234. Wangetoothe *molaris*, Prompt. Parv. 515. Wangtoth *geminus*, Cath. Angl. 407. Wayngetothe *geminus, maxillaris*, 406 (see note). Wongtothe *uteelaris*, Wrt. Voc. i. 207.]

wang-turf; *gen.* -tyrf; *f. Turf, grass-land*:—Ðæt ic mōte đis gealdor tōđum ontȳnan . . . wlitigan đās wancgturf (cf. *the beginning of the article*: Hēr ys seó bōt hū đū meaht đīne æceras bētan gif hī nellaþ wel wexan, 398, 1), Lchdm. i. 400, 7.

wan-hæfelness. v. wan-hafolness.

wan-hæfenness, e; *f. Want, need*:—Wanhæfænysse and metelǣste *famis inedia*, Hpt. Gl. 480, 33.

wan-hǣle; *adj. Having bad health*:—Ealle đa đe wonnhǣle wǣron, healtte and blinde, dumbe and deáfe, Nar. 48, 31. [*O. H. Ger.* wan-heili *semianimis, debilis, mancus*.] v. wan-hāl.

wan-hǣlþ, e; *f. Defective health, weakness, sickness*:—Þurh wanhǣlđe *per inbecillitatem*, Scint. 54, 19. [Cf. *O. H. Ger.* wana-heilī *debilitas*.] v. wan-hālness.

wan-hafa, an; *m. A poor person*:—Wanhafa and þearfa ic eom *inops et pauper sum ego*, Ps. Spl. 85, 1.

wan-hafness, e; *f. Poverty, want*:—Nis wanhafnes (*inopia*) ondrǣdendum hine, Ps. Spl. 33, 9.

wan-hafol; *adj. Needy, destitute*:—Him embe stōdon wēpende wydewan and wanhafele þearfan, Homl. Skt. i. 10, 65. Widewena bigleofa and wanhafolra manna, ii. 25, 765. Gehelp wanhafolum mannum mid đīnum āgenum spēdum, i. 21, 363.

wan-hafolness, e; *f. Need, want, destitution*:—Nis wanhafolnes (*inopia*) ondrǣdendum hine, Ps. Lamb. 33, 10. Ūre wanhæfelnesse *inopiae nostrae*, 43, 24.

wan-hāl; *adj. Imperfect as regards health* or *soundness of body, weak, sick, maimed, infirm, unsound*:—Wanhāl *inbecillis*, Wrt. Voc. i. 51, 23. Betere đē ys đæt đū gā wanhāl (*debilis*) odđe healt tō līfe, Mt. Kmbl. 18, 8: Mk. Skt. 9, 43. Hī God mǣrsodon swā oft swā ǣnig wanhāl mann wurde gehǣled, Homl. Skt. i. 21, 229. Ðæt wanhāl wæs and ālēwed, đæt gē āwurpan *quod debile erat proicebatis*, R. Ben. 51, 15. Ðȳ lǣs đe ān wannhāl scēp ealle đa eówde besmīte, Homl. Th. i. 124, 32. Swā hwylc man swā on gecynde ōđerne wanhālne (*debilem*) dō, L. Ecg. C. 22; Th. ii. 148, 17. Ða đe limseóce wǣron, wērige, wanhāle, Andr. Kmbl. 1159; An. 580. Wonhāle, Exon. Th. 92, 13; Cri. 1508. Næs đǣr wīnes drenc būton wanhālum mannum, Homl. Th. ii. 506, 22: Homl. Skt. ii. 26, 202. Hē wolde gehelpan þearfum and wannhālum, 26, 276: Elen. Kmbl. 2057; El. 1030. Clypa þearfan and wanhāle and healte and blinde *uoca pauperes, debiles, clodos, caecos*, Lk. Skt. 14, 13, 21. [*Icel.* wan-heill *unsound, disabled, ill*.] v. wan-hǣle.

wan-hālian; *p.* ode *To weaken, impair the health* or *soundness* of something [:—Þurh đisne drync beóđ ǣgđær ge đa sāwle ofslagene ge đa līchaman gewanhālode, Homl. Ass. 146, 51. [*O. H. Ger.* wana-heilen *debilitare*; ka-wanaheilit *debilitatus*.]]

wan-hālness, e; *f. Weakness, sickness, unsoundness, infirmity*:—Ðæm abbode is ā tō behealdenne heora (*fratrum infirmorum*) wanhālnes (*imbecillitas*), R. Ben. 75, 11. Wanhālnysse (*debilitate*) ealles līchaman, Scint. 38, 7. Dysig æfter untrumnysse his ongyt, and æfter wanhālnysse (*inbecillitatem*) gecyndes his wāt, 97, 15. Brōþor se untruma gif hē gefrēt hys weaxan wanhālnysse (*inbecillitatem*), Anglia xiii. 442, 1102. Cf. wan-hǣlþ.

wan-hlyte; *adj. Not having a share* in something, *destitute* of:—Wanhlytne *expertem*, Wrt. Voc. ii. 33, 8. [Cf. *Icel.* van-hluta; *adj. unfairly dealt with*; van-hlutr *an unfair share*.] v. or-hlyte.

wan-hoga, an; *m. One who is wanting in understanding, a foolish, imprudent person*:—Hī lifiaþ him in māne, heáhgestreón healdaþ georne, . . . and wēnaþ wanhogan đæt hȳ wile God gehȳran, Salm. Kmbl. 639; Sal. 319. Ic đīne weogas wanhogan lǣrde, đæt hié ārleáse eft gecerdan tō hiora sāula hiorde, Ps. C. 105. v. un-hoga, *and following words*.

wan-hygd, -hygdu(-o) [cf. ofer-hygd] *want of mind, folly, rashness, recklessness, imprudence*:—For wlence and for wonhygdum hī ceastre worhton, and tō heofnum up hlǣdræ rǣrdon, Cd. Th. 100, 33; Gen. 1673. Grendel for his wonhȳdum wǣpna ne rēceþ; ic đæt đonne forhicge đæt ic sweord bere, Beo. Th. 872; B. 434. [Cf. *Icel.* van-hyggja *want of forethought*.]

wan-hygdig, -hȳdig; *adj. Foolish, imprudent, thoughtless, careless, reckless*:—Wonhȳdig wer *vir insipiens*, Ps. Th. 91, 5: Exon. Th. 95, 14; Cri. 1557: 343, 25; Gn. Ex. 162. Ne sceal wita nō tō hātheort, ne tō hrædwyrde, ne tō wāc wiga, ne tō wanhȳdig, 290, 19. Ne mid swīđran his nele brȳsan wanhȳdig gemōd Wealdend engla, ne đone wlacan smocan wāces flǣsces wætere gedwæscan, Dōm. L. 50. Wonhȳdige (*the apostate angels*), Elen. Kmbl. 1522; El. 763. [Cf. *Icel.* van-hugaðr *ill-considered*.]

wanian; *p.* ode. I. *trans.* (1) *To make less, lessen, diminish, curtail*:—Hī sculon ǣlce dæg eácan đæt mon ǣlce dæg wanaþ, Bt. 26, 2; Fox 94, 1. Symble hē bid gyfende, and hē ne wanaþ nān þing his, Homl. Skt. i. 1, 46: L. Edg. S. 1; Th. i. 272, 10. Hwæt tō bōte mihte æt đæm fǣrcwealme đe his leódscipe swȳđe drehte and wanode, Th. i. 270, 10. Hē leóde mīne wanode and wyrde, Beo. Th. 2678; B. 1337. (*The last two passages might be taken under* (3).) Wirceaþ ealle đa þing đe Drihten eów bebeád, and ne īce gē nān þing ne ne waniaþ (*nec addas quidquam nec minuas*), Deut. 12, 32. Ne sȳ đæs magutimbres gemet ofer eorþan, gif hī ne wanige se đās woruld teóde, Exon. Th. 335, 15;

Gn. Ex. 34. Ne ſce gē nān þing . . . ne gē wanion *non addetis* . . . *nec auferetis*, Deut. 4, 2. Godes dōmas nāwþer ne nā wanian ne ne ēcan, Blickl. Homl. 81, 4. (2) *to bring within narrower limits, to abate, check, reduce.* v. (4):—Wona ðæt ondspyrnisse *minue offendiculum*, Rtl. 11, 13. Wē sceolon ða fūlan gālnysse symle wanian, Homl. Th. i. 96, 22. Dæghwomlīce wē sceolon ūre synna wanian; for ðan ðe hī beóð gegaderode tō micelre hȳpan, gif wē hī weaxan lǣtaþ, ii. 466, 6. Ðā wolde ðæt folc ðæt fȳr ādwæscan, gif hit ǣnig wǣta wanian mihte, 140, 17. (3) *to weaken, impair, injure.* v. wanung, I. (3):—Windas blāwaþ brecende, weccaþ and woniaþ woruld mid storme, Exon. Th. 59, 13; Cri. 952. Hē bebeád ðæt mon nǣnne mon ne slōge, and eác ðæt man nānuht ne wanade ne ne yfelade ðæs ðe on ðǣm ciricum wǣre *dato praecepto, ut si qui in sancta loca confugissent, hos inviolatos securosque esse sinerent*, Ors. 6, 38; Swt. 296, 32. (3 a) *to weaken, reduce* by medical treatment. Cf. wanung, I. (3 a):—Lǣcas lǣrdon ðæt nān man on ðam mōnþe ne drenc ne drunce, ne āhwǣr his līchoman wanige, būtan his nȳdþearf wǣre, Lchdm. ii. 146, 12. Manega nellaþ heora ðing wanian on Mōnandæg (cf. þrȳ dagas (*the last Monday in April, the first Mondays in August and January*) syndon on ðām for nānre neóde ne mannes ne neátes blōd sȳ tō wanienne . . . Se ðe on ðysum dagum his blōd gewanige, sȳ hit man, sȳ hit nȳten, ðæs ðe wē secgan gehȳrdan, ðæt on ðam forman dæge oþþe ðam feórþan dæge his līf geændaþ, Lchdm. iii. 76, 11–22), Homl. Th. i. 100, 25. (4) *to cause to cease* or *fail, to bring to nought, destroy, frustrate*:—Ic wīfe ābelge, wonie hyre willan, Exon. Th. 402, 21; Rä. 21, 33. Mon scel ðone unþeáw of mynstre wanian and mid ealle āwyrtwalian *hoc vitium radicitus amputandum est de monasterio*, R. Ben. 56, 16. (5) *to put in an inferior position*:—Ðū wanodest (*minuisti*) hine lytle læs fram ænglum, Ps. Spl. 8, 6. II. *intrans.* (1) *To wane, become less, decrease, diminish*:—Ne wexþ his welena (wela nā?), ne eác nǣfre ne wanaþ, Bt. 42; Fox 256, 29. His wered wanode ǣfre ðe leng ðe swīðor, Chr. 1052; Erl. 181, 4. Ða wæteru wanedon *aquae decrescebant*, Gen. 8, 5. Þeáh ūs ūre spēda wanodon, Shrn. 167, 13. Ðæt sweord ongan wanian . . . hit eal gemealt, Beo. Th. 3218; B. 1607. Ða wæteru begunnon tō wanigenne *aquae coeperunt minui*, Gen. 8, 3. (1 a) of the moon's phases:—Ðonne se mōna wanaþ, Blickl. Homl. 17, 24. Dæghwamlīce ðæs mōnan leóht byð weaxende and waniende, Lchdm. iii. 242, 7. Ðās wyrte ðū scealt niman on wanigendum mōnan, i. 320, 3. (2) *to wane, become inferior, decline, decay*:—Ðes middangeard wanaþ and weaxeþ, Fragm. Kmbl. 60; Leás. 32. Hit gebyraþ ðæt hē weaxe and ðæt ic wanige *illum oportet crescere, me autem minui*, Jn. Skt. 3, 30. Wanige his weorðscipe, L. Ath. v. 9; Th. i. 306, 23. Gesihð hē ða dōmas wonian and wendan of woruldryhte, ða hē gesette, Exon. Th. 105, 24; Gū. 28. Nān þing ne biþ swelce hit wæs siððan hit wanian onginþ, Bt. 34, 9; Fox 148, 9. Ðæs ealdigendan mannes mægen bið wanigende, Homl. Th. ii. 76, 21. [*O. Frs.* wania: *O. H. Ger.* wanōn: *Icel.* vana *to diminish; to spoil, destroy.*] v. ā-, gewanian; wan; *adj.*, wana; *adj.*

wānian; *p.* ode *To lament, deplore,* (1) absolute:—Ðæt synfulle mancynn wēpaþ and wāniaþ, Wulfst. 183, 2. Ðonne grāniaþ and wāniaþ ða ðe hēr blissedon and fægnedon, 245, 3: Anglia viii. 336, 41. Beornas grētaþ, wēpaþ wānende, Exon. Th. 61, 31; Cri. 993. Ða wānigendran welras (wāniendan, Wulfst. 139, 8) *os lugens*, Dōm. L. 208. (2) with reflexive dative:—Hē wānode him sylfum: 'Wā is mē earmum . . .,' Homl. Skt. i. 11, 223. (3) with acc.:—Sār wānigean, Beo. Th. 1579; B. 787. Wānian, Exon. Th. 166, 22; Gū. 1046. Ongan hē sār cwānian, wyrd wānian, wordum mǣlde . . ., 274, 24; Jul. 538. (4) with reflex dat. and (a) acc.:—Hē him wæs wāniende ǣgðer ge his āgene heardsǣlþa ge ealles ðæs folces *ipse nunc suam, nunc publicam infelicitatem deflet*, Ors. 4, 5; Swt. 166, 20. (b) a clause:—Hē him wæs swiþe wāniende ðæt hē tō him cucan ne com, Ors. 5, 12; Swt. 244, 4. [Heo weop for hire weisið, wanede hire siðes, Laym. 25847. Weape and wony (weinen, 1st MS.), 25827. Wepenn and wanenn for hiss sinne, Orm. 5653. Hit cumeþ weopinde and woniende iwiteþ . . . þeo moder greoneþ and ꝥ bearn woaneþ, Fragm. Phlps. 5, 32–41. Heo woneþ and groneþ day and nyht, Misc. 152, 187. Scholde euch mon woni and grede, O. and N. 975. *O. H. Ger.* weinōn *flere, lacrymare, ejulare, vagire*: *Icel.* veina *to wail.* Cf. *Goth.* wainags *unhappy.*]

wanigend, es; *m.* *One who diminishes, weakens, impairs, injures, spoils,* etc. v. wanian:—Gyf him þince ðæt hē on reádum horse rīde, ðæt byð his gōda wanigend (wanung, MS. T.) *if he dreams that he is riding on a bay horse, that means there will be a spoiler of his goods*, Lchdm. iii. 172, 29.

wani[g]end-līc; *adj.* *Diminutive* (as a grammatical term), *expressing diminution*:—Sume naman synd *diminutiva*, ðæt synd waniendlīce, ða geswuteliaþ wanunge, Ælfc. Gr. 5; Zup. 16, 17. *Diminutiva* syndon wanigendlīce. *Clam* is dīgellīce and of ðam is wanigendlīc *clanculum* hwōnlīcor dīgellīce, 38; Zup. 231, 1–3.

waniht. v. wanniht.

wann; *adj.* *Dark, dusty, sable, lurid, livid*:—Wann *bruntus*, Wrt. Voc. i. 46, 40. Wonn, ii. 12, 58. Won, 127, 28. Ða sweartan *lurida*, wan and flæc *luridus*, 53, 16. Ða wannan *libida* (but the Latin is *livida* (*vibex*), Ald. 77–8), 88, 3: 50, 33. Ðære wannan *cerula*, 24, 58. Ða wonnan aetrinan *livida toxica*, 112, 63: 50, 80. Ða wonnan *lividas*, 53, 1. (1) *blue-black, livid*:—Ðonne se dǣl ðæs līchoman sié gewended blæc oþþe won oþþe swilces hwæt, Lchdm. ii. 82, 12. Gif ðæt blōd swīðe reád sié oþþe won, 254, 10. Swearte ł wan[ne] wale *caerulea* (*nigra, tetra, tunsa*) *vibice* (*livore*), Hpt. Gl. 516, 14. Gif ða ōmihtan wannan þing oþþe ða reádan sȳn ūtan cumen, Lchdm. ii. 82, 21. (2) of the colour of living creatures, *swarthy, dusty, dark-hued*:—Se wonna þegn, sweart and saloneb, Exon. Th. 433, 8; Rä. 50, 4. Bið se wǣrloga (*the wicked at the judgement day*) won and wliteleás, hafaþ werges bleó, 95, 30; Cri. 1565. Deóful ætȳwde wann and wliteleás, hæfde weriges hīw, Andr. Kmbl. 2339; An. 1171. Hræfen gōl wan and wælfel, Elen. Kmbl. 105; El. 53. Se wonna hrefn, Beo. Th. 6041; B. 3024. Wanna, Judth. Thw. 24, 25; Jud. 206: Cd. Th. 119, 22; Gen. 1983. Bearg won, Exon. Th. 428, 12; Rä. 41, 107. (3) of the colour of material, *dark, dingy*:—Ys mīn bæc wonn, Exon. Th. 496, 13; Rä. 85, 14. Wonnum hyrstum gefrætwed, 436, 1; Rä. 54, 7. Mec mon biþeahte mid þearfan wǣdum, and mec on þeóstre ālegde biwundenne mid wonnum clāþum, 87, 12; Cri. 1424. (4) as a (poetical) epithet of shade, cloud, night, etc.:—Gif him (*the stars*) wan fore wolcen hangaþ (cf. ðonne sweartan wolcnu him beforan gāþ, Bt. 6; Fox 14, 22) ne mægen hī leóman ansendan *nubibus atris condita nullum fundere possunt sidera lumen*, Met. 5, 4. Sceadu wann under wolcnum, Rood Kmbl. 109; Kr. 55. Seó deorce niht won gewīteþ, Exon. Th. 204, 17; Ph. 99: 292, 23; Wand. 292. Ðā se æþela glǣm setlgong sōhte, swearc norðrodor won under wolcnum, 178, 34; Gū. 1254. In ðisse wonnan niht, 163, 30; Gū. 1001. On wanre niht scrīðan, Beo. Th. 1409; B. 702. Hē geseah deorc gesweorc semian sweart, wonn and wēste, Cd. Th. 7, 22; Gen. 110. Ða wonnan niht mōna onlīhteþ (cf. se mōna līht on niht, Bt. 21; Fox 74, 25), Met. 11, 61. Færeþ sunne in ðæt wonne genip under wætra geþring, Exon. Th. 351, 12; Sch. 79. Wolcnu wann, Cd. Th. 14, 5; Gen. 214. Sceadu sweðerodon wonn under wolcnum, Andr. Kmbl. 1673; An. 839. Wan, Beo. Th. 1306; B. 651. Won, Exon. Th. 384, 33; Rä. 4, 37. Wonnum nihtum, 496, 3; Rä. 85, 8. (5) as a (poetical) epithet of water (cf. Myn is the drenchyng in the see so wan, Chauc. Kn. T. 1598):—Ȳðgeblond āstīgeþ won tō wolcnum *the troubled waves mount dark to heaven*, Beo. Th. 2752; B. 1374. Wonn, Exon. Th. 383, 34; Rä. 4, 20. Hē þeahte bearn middangeardes wonnan wǣge *he covered earth's children with the dark wave*, Cd. Th. 83, 13; Gen. 1379. Gewāt se wilda fugel ofer wonne wǣg, 88, 8; Gen. 1462. Hē wolde ðæt wanne wæter tō wīne āwendan, Homl. Th. ii. 58, 16. Sweart wæter, wonne wælstreámas, Cd. Th. 78, 30; Gen. 1301: 86, 13; Gen. 1430. Gārsecg þeahte sweart synnihte wonne wǣgas *black everlasting night covered ocean, the dark waves*, 8, 4; Gen. 119. (6) as a (poetical) epithet of fire. v. wann-fȳr:—Nū sceal glēd fretan, wyrdan wonna lēg, wigena strengel, Beo. Th. 6221; B. 3115. Se wonna lēg, Cd. Th. 309, 24; Sat. 715. v. brūn-wann.

wann-fāh; *adj.* *Dark-hued*:—Wonfāh wale, Exon. Th. 435, 11; Rä. 53, 6.

wann-feax; *adj.* *Dark-haired, with raven-black tresses*:—Wonfeax wale, Exon. Th. 393, 30; Rä. 13, 8.

wann-fōta, an; *m.* *A bird with dark feet* (?):—Stāngella *vel* wanfōta *pelicanus* (cf. porfyrionis, pellicanus, Corp. Gl. ed. Hessels 94, 498), Wrt. Voc. i. 63, 20.

wann-fȳr, es; *n.* *Lurid fire*:—Wonfȳres wælm, se swearta līg *lurid fire's glow, the dark flame*, Exon. Th. 60, 7; Cri. 966.

wann-hǣwe; *adj.* *Dark-blue, blue-black*:—Ða wonhǣwan *cerula*, Wrt. Voc. ii. 20, 66.

wannian. v. ā-wannian.

wanniht; *adj.* *Livid*:—Ða wan[n]ihtan *lividas*, Wrt. Voc. ii. 50, 32. v. wann.

wan-sǣlig; *adj.* *Unblest, miserable, evil*:—Grendel, wonsǣlig wer, Beo. Th. 210; B. 105. Wineleás, wonsǣlig genimeþ him wulfas tō geferan, Exon. Th. 342, 24; Gn. Ex. 147. In ðisse wonsǣlgan worulde līfe, 158, 33; Gū. 919. Weras wansǣlige mē (*Christ*) slōgon and swungon, Andr. Kmbl. 1925; An. 965. Wonsǣlige, Elen. Kmbl. 953; El. 478. Frōde sace sēmaþ, sibbe gelǣraþ, ða ǣr wonsǣlge āwegen habbaþ, Exon. Th. 334, 24; Gn. Ex. 21. Werum wansǣligum (*the Jews*), Elen. Kmbl. 1952; El. 978.

wan-sceaft, e; -sceafte(-a; *m.?*), an; *f.* I. *misfortune, misery, unhappiness*:—Hī sorge ne cūðon, wonsceaft wera, wiht unhǣlo, Beo. Th. 240; B. 120. Ic ne wrecan meahte on wigan feore wonnsceaft mīne, ac ic ealle þolige, Exon. Th. 499, 16; Rä. 88, 16. Lāð biþ ǣghwǣr fore his wonsceaftum wineleás hæle, 329, 10; Vy. 32. II. *some form of disease*:—Hū mon sceal ða wǣtan and wonsceafta (ða wonsceaftan *in the section*, 246, 6, *where no other malady than* ða wǣtan *is referred to except* ða āheardodan swilas) ūtan lācnian, Lchdm. ii. 166, 22. [Cf. *O. Sax.* than wōpiat thār wanskefti thie hēr ēr an wunnion sind, Hēl. 1352.]

wan-scrȳd[d]; *adj.* *Imperfectly clothed, ill-clad*:—Hē wæs swīðe geswǣs eallum swincendum, and on mislícum yrmđum mannum geheólp, wǣdligum and wanscrȳddum, Homl. Th. ii. 500, 17.

wan-seóc; *adj. Epileptic, having the falling sickness, frenzied, lunatic*:—Wanseóce *comitiales, lunaticos*, Hpt. Gl. 519, 43. v. bræc-, fylle-, gebræc-, mōnaþ-seóc; bræc-coþu.

wansian; *p.* ode [*the word seems to occur only late, and perhaps is due to Scandinavian, cf. Icel.* vansi *want: wanian is the usual word*] *To diminish*:—Swā hwā swā ūre gife ōuþer ōđre gōdene manne gyfe wansiaþ, wansie him seó heofenlīce iateward on heofonrīce, Chr. 656; Erl. 32, 17. *The compound* ā-wansian *also occurs*:—If āni man đis ilk forward breke and āwansige, Cod. Dip. Kmbl. iv. 243, 6. [Marrchess nahhtess wannsenn and Marrchess daȝhess waxenn, Orm. 1901. Worldes catel wacset and wansit as te mone, P. R. L. P. 234, 7. Wansoñ, wansyn *evaneo, decresco*, Prompt. Parv. 515.]

wan-spéd, e; *f. Poverty, indigence*:—Þurh wanspēde *per inopiam*, Scint. 226, 6. On đæm gefeohte wæs ǣrest anfunden Sciþþia wanspēda *ea res primo fidem inopiae Scythicae dedit*, Ors. 3, 7; Swt. 116, 34. Cf. wan-ǣht.

wan-spédig; *adj. Poor, indigent*:—Sum ǣhta onlīhđ; sum biđ wonspēdig, Exon. Th. 295, 11; Crā. 31. Đīn wanspēdiga mǣg *attenuatus frater tuus*, Lev. 25, 25. Đās læssan lāc, đe wǣron wannspēdigra manna lāc, Homl. Th. i. 140, 6. Uton dōn þearfum and wannspēdigum sume hīđđe ūre gōda, ii. 100, 35. Se gȳtsere berȳpđ đa wannspēdigan, i. 66, 11.

wanspēdigness, e; *f. Indigence, poverty*:—Of neóde oþþe wanspēdignysse *ex necessitate uel indigentia*, Scint. 198, 5.

wanung, e; *f.* I. *a making less*, (1) *diminution*. Cf. wanian, I. (1):—Sume naman synd *diminutiva*, đa geswuteliaþ wanunge, Ælfc. Gr. 5; Zup. 16, 18. Đa word habbaþ hwīlon *sincopam*, đæt ys, wanunge: *amauisti* vel *amasti*, hēr ys se *ui* āwege, 25; Zup. 146, 17. (2) *abatement, reduction, checking*. v. wanian, I. (2):—Hwæt getācnaþ đæs fylmenes ofcyrf on đam gesceape būton gālnysse wanunge? Homl. Th. i. 94, 33. (3) *a weakening, an impairing, hurt, injury*. v. wanian, I. (3):—Wonung *detrimentum*, Wrt. Voc. ii. 106, 29. *Dispendium*, i. *damnum, impedimentum, defectio, periculum, detrimentum* æfwerdla, wonung, wom, wana, *vel* hēnþa, 140, 68. Gyf him þince đæt hē hæbbe rūh līc, đæt byđ his gōda wanung, Lchdm. iii. 170, 24. Gōda wanigend (wanung, MS. T.), 172, 29. Wanunge *dispendio*, Wrt. Voc. ii. 28, 37. Đæt nādær ne þǣ ne ūs God ne þurfa oncunnan for đæræ waniungæ on ūrum dæge *quatinus nec tibi nec nobis Deus debeat imputare hanc imminutionem diebus nostris actam*, Chart. Th. 163, 26. Nalæs būtan mycelre wonunge his weoredes *non sine magno exercitus sui damno*, Bd. 2, 2; S. 504, 7. Is nȳd đæt sume mid wonunge heora woruldǣhta synd gerihte *necesse est ut quidam damnis corrigantur*, 1, 27; S. 490, 10. Hē mycle wonunge and ǣwyrdlan wæs wyrcende đære mærwan cyrican weaxnesse *magno tenellis ecclesiae crementis detrimento fuit*, 2, 5; S. 506, 37. Mid đām hefigestum wonungum his rīces fram his feóndum geswenced *gravissimis regni sui damnis ab hostibus adflictus*, 3, 7; S. 530, 18. (3 a) *a weakening, reducing the strength* of something. Cf. wanian, I. (3 a):—Flǣsces wonunge *carnis maceratione*, Rtl. 14, 33. II. *a growing less*, (1) *a decrease* in number, size, etc. v. wanian, II. (1):—Dæghwamlīce geleáffulle men nimaþ đæt sand, and ne biþ nǣnig wonung on đæm sande, Shrn. 81, 6. Symle biđ hāligra manna getel geeácnod þurh ārleásra manna wanunge, Homl. Th. i. 536, 25. (1 a) *waning* of the moon. v. wanian, II. (1 a):—Ǣfre seó sǣ and se mōna beóđ geféran on wæstme and on wanunge, Lchdm. iii. 268, 13: Homl. Th. i. 102, 28. (2) *decline, decay*. v. wanian, II. (2):—Đonne se mōna wanaþ, đonne tācnaþ hē đisse worlde wanunge, Blickl. Homl. 17, 24. III. *a lack, want, defect*:—Wanunge *defectu*, Wrt. Voc. ii. 28, 43.

wānung, e; *f. Wailing, lamentation*:—Wānung *threnum*, Wrt. Voc. i. 28, 20. Đǣr (*in hell*) is wānung and grānung and ā singal sorh, Wulfst. 26, 8. Hǣđenra grānung and reáfera wānung, 186, 13. Wōp and wānung and heófung and endeleás cwylming, Homl. Th. i. 592, 16. Geómrung and wānung, Homl. Skt. i. 23, 104. Se lǣce cyrfđ ođđe bærnđ, and se untruma hrȳmđ, þeáhhwæđere ne miltsaþ hē đæs ōđres wānunge, Homl. Th. i. 472, 16. *Uae* getācnaþ hwīlon wānunge, Ælfc. Gr. 48; Zup. 278, 12. Gesaeh đæt wānung (*tumultum*) and woepende and mǣniende, Mk. Skt. Lind. 5, 38. Se āfunde his hlāford licgan heáfodleásne and hē đā mid wānunge wende ūt ongeán *videns cadaver absque capite Holofernis exclamavit voce magna cum fletu*, Anglia x. 101, 365. Mid hreówlīcere wānunge, Homl. Th. i. 466, 33. [Heui is his greoning and seorhful is his woaning, Fragm. Phlps. 5, 35. Wanung and wow, O. E. Homl. i. 173, 231. After al þis cumeđ of þat bearn iboren þus wanunge and wepnunge, H. M. 37, 9. Þer wes muchel waning, heortne graning, Laym. 17796. Wop and wonynge and bymenynge, Mirc. 74, 55. Þu telst . . . al mi (*the owl's*) reorde is woning, O. and N. 311.]

wan-wegende; *adj.* (*ptcpl.*) *Waning*:—On wanwegendum mōnan, Lchdm. i. 100, 20. Wanwægendum, 98, 17.

wāpe(-**a**? *m.*), an; *f. A cloth, rubber* (? cf. wīpian):—Gif đū sceát habban wille ođđe wāpan, đonne sete đū đīne twā handa ofer đīnum bearme and tōbrǣd hī swilce sceát āstrecce, Techm. ii. 122, 23. [Cf. (?) *Icel.* veipa *a woman's hood*.]

wapol (-**ul**, -**el**) *foam*:—Wapul *famfaluca* (cf. faam, leásung *famfaluca*, 17), Wrt. Voc. ii. 108, 20: 35, 4 (cf. leásung ođđe fām *famfaluca*, 24, 75). v. next word.

wapolian; *p.* ode *To foam, bubble up, pour forth* (*intrans.* and *trans.*?), *abound, swarm*:—Wapolaþ *ebullit* (os fatuorum ebullit stultitiam, Prov. 15, 2), Kent. Gl. 505. Wapolode *vaporat*, Germ. 398, 220. Up ābrǣcan, wapeladan *ebulliebant, emergebant* (cadavera horrida vermium examina ebulliebant, Ald. 48), Hpt. Gl. 488, 11. Wapeledan ɫ up ābræcan *bullirent, exundaverunt* (cum Ethnae montis incendia favillis scintillantibus bullirent, Ald. 55), 499, 46. Ingā forrotednys on bānum mīnum and under mē heó wapelige *ingrediatur putredo in ossibus meis et subter me scateat*, Cant. Habac. 16. v. preceding word.

wār. I. *sea-weed*, *waur* (v. E. D. S. Pub. Plant Names, in which other forms are given, *ware, woare, woore, ore*: see also Jamieson's Dict. *ware*):—Waar, uaar, uār *alga*, Txts. 39, 120. Wār, Wrt. Voc. ii. 6, 46: i. 285, 12. II. *sand, strand*. Cf. sondhyllas *alga*, Txts. 39, 125:—Streámas weorpaþ on stealc hleoþa stāne and sande, wāre (*or under* I?) and wǣge, Exon. Th. 382, 8; Rā. 3, 8. Wāra *sablonum*, strand *sablo* (mentis fundamina nequaquam arenosis sablonum glareis ultro citroque nutabundis subdiderat, Ald. 57), Hpt. Gl. 502, 76: (*printed* wasa) 465, 8. Wārum *sablonibus*, 449, 30. v. sǣ-wār.

wara, an; *m. An inhabitant. The word is used mostly in the plural, and as the second part of compounds; but the singular in composition is found in* ceaster-weara *civis*, Bd. 3, 22; S. 552, 32 (cf. ceaster-gewara *civis*, Ælfc. Gr. 5; Zup. 11, 16), *and the independent word in the following instances*:—Heofenlīcra warena *supernorum civium* (*habitatorum*), Hpt. Gl. 498, 23. Hié here samnodon ceastre (*printed* ceaster) warena, Andr. Kmbl. 2251; An. 1127. Warum *civibus*, Hpt. Gl. 518, 40. *In composition both* -waran *and* -ware *occur* (cf. Seaxe *and* Seaxan), *and also* -waras, v. Sigel-waras. *The forms are united with common nouns*, v. burh-, ceaster-, eorþ-, hell-, heofon-waran, -ware; *or with proper names, native or foreign*, e. g. Lunden-, Rōm-waran, -ware, Bæx-warena land (cf. Bex-leá, 13), Cod. Dip. B. i. 295, 5, Cant-ware, Wiht-ware, Sodom-ware, Syr-ware: *see also* Up-ware. Cf. *the Icelandic* Rōm-verjar, *and Latin forms like* Angri-varii. v. -waru.

-ware. v. preceding word.

warenian, warnian, wearnian; *p.* ode. I. *intrans.* (1) *To take heed, beware, be on guard*:—Warniaþ and waciaþ *uidete, vigilate*, Mk. Skt. 13, 33. Hē wolde warnian on ǣr *he would take precautions*, Gen. 6, 6. Man sceal wacigean and warnian symle, Wulfst. 90, 2. (2) *to take heed* of, *guard against, abstain* from (cf. *Icel.* varna við *to abstain from*):—Warniaþ fram beorman Fariseórum *cavete a fermento Pharisaeorum*, Mt. Kmbl. 16, 6, 11, 12. Warniaþ fram bōcerum *cavete a scribis*, Mk. Skt. 12, 38. Warniaþ (warnigeaþ, *v. l.*) wiđ Farisēa lāre *attendite a fermento Pharisaeorum*, Lk. Skt. 12, 1. Đæt man wiđ leahtras warnie (warnige, *v. l.*), Wulfst. 68, 14. (3) *to take heed* that something is not done, does not happen (expressed in a clause):—Warna đæt ic đē leng ne geseó *cave ne ultra videas faciem meum*, Ex. 10, 28. Warna đæt đæt leóht đe đē on is ne sȳn þȳstru *vide ne lumen quod in te est tenebrae sint*, Lk. Skt. 11, 35: Homl. Th. i. 120, 16. Warniaþ (*videte*) đæt gē hyt nānum men ne secgeon, Mt. Kmbl. 9, 30: 18, 10. Warnigeaþ đæt gē ne beón gedrēfede, 24, 6. Se man mōt geornlīce warnian, đæt hē eft đām yfelum dǣdum ne geedlǣce, Homl. Th. ii. 602, 23. Hē mē warnian hēt, đæt ic on đone deáđes beám bedroren ne wurde, Cd. Th. 33, 29; Gen. 527. Is mycelum tō warnienne đæt man . . . menn blōd ne lǣte, Lchdm. iii. 152, 33. (4) *to take heed* that something does happen:—Wel is eác tō warnianne đæt man wite, đæt hȳ þurh mǣgsibbe tō gelænge ne beón, L. Edm. B. 9; Th. i. 256, 9. II. *trans.* (1) *To put on guard, to warn*:—Būtan ic eów warnige, ic sceal āgyldan gesceád mīnre gȳmeleáste, Homl. Skt. i. 17, 72. Đæt wyrreste þingc đū didest, đæt đū mē warnodest, Ap. Th. 8, 15. Se Hǣlend ūs warnode đus, for đan đe hē wyle, đæt wē ware beón, Homl. Ass. 55, 112. Wē āgan þearfe, đæt wē wiđ swylcne ege wære beón and eác đa warnian, đe swylc nyton swylc tōwerd is, Wulfst. 101, 11. Men đa leófestan, wē willaþ eów warnian, and ūs sylfe ālȳsan, Homl. Ass. 144, 18. Đā sende Ælfrīc and hēt warnian đone here, Chr. 992; Erl. 130, 31. (1 a) where no object is expressed:—Swefnu beóđ onwrigene tō warnienne, Lchdm. iii. 196, 24. (1 b) *to warn* against something, *give notice* of something:—Benedictus warnode đa gebrōđra wiđ đæs deófles tōcyme, Homl. Th. ii. 166, 17. Đæt hȳ Godes folc warnian wiđ đone egesan, đe mannum is tōwerd, Wulfst. 79, 14. (1 c) where the matter to which the warning refers is given in a clause:—Ic eów warnode, đæt gē wīglunge mid ealle forlǣtan, Homl. Skt. i. 17, 68. Wē āgan þearfe, đæt wē godcunde heorda warnian, hū hȳ Antecriste wærlīcast magan wiđstandan, Wulfst. 80, 2. (2) used reflexively, *to be on one's guard, to look to one's self, take heed to one's self, take warning*:—Đurh gītsunge forlȳst oft se ārleása his līf, đonne hē gewilniaþ đara ǣhta, and ne warnaþ hine sylfne, Basil admn. 9; Norm. 54, 2: Cd. Th. 40, 6; Gen. 635. Gif đū đīn āgen myrre, ne wīt đū hit nā Gode, ac warna đē silfne, Prov. Kmbl. 51. Warniaþ eów sylfe *uidete uosmetipsos*, Mk. Skt. 13, 9, 23. Đē is micel þearf đæt đū đē warnige, for đam đē đū eart fordēmed, Ap. Th. 8, 1. Utan warnian ūs georne, Wulfst. 101, 21. Ðú noldest ðē warnian þurh ðīnes fæder ðreále *thou wouldst not take warning by thy father's punishment*, Homl. Th. ii. 436, 7. (2 a) *to guard, be on one's guard* against something :—Gif hē hine ne warenaþ wiþ ða unþeáwas, Bt. 29, 3; Fox 106, 27. Wærnaþ (warenaþ, Cott. MS.) hē hine wiþ ðæt weder, 41, 3; Fox 250, 16. Hié oft gesyngiaþ giet wyrs on ðæm ðæt hī hī wareniaþ wið ða lytlan scylda ðonne hī dōn on myclum scyldum; for ðæm ðe hī līcettaþ hié unscyldge, ðonne hī hī wæreniaþ við ða lytlan, Past. 57; Swt. 439, 18-20. Ic mē [wið] his hete berh and wearnode (warnode, *v. l.*: warenode, Bd. M. 128, 9) *hostium vitalium insidias*, Bd. 2, 12; S. 513, 28. Warniaþ eów wið oferfylle, Homl. Th. ii. 22, 16. Is ðæm tō cȳðanne, ðæt hī hié warenigen ǣgðer ge wið ða ungemetlīcan blisse ge wið ða ungemetlīcan unrōtnesse. . . . Is micel niédþearf ðæt mon hiene wið ðæt irre and wið ða ungemetlīcan sǣlð warenige (warnige, Cott. MSS.), Past. 27; Swt. 189, 1-6. Ic bidde ðæt ǣlc mann hine sylfne georne wið ðisne curs warnige, Chart. Th. 445, 8: Wulfst. 101, 16. Utan warnian ūs wið his unlāra, 80, 4. (2 b) where what is to be guarded against is expressed in a clause :—Warnode hē hine ðȳ læs hī on hwylc hūs tō him in eodan *caveret ne in aliquam domum ad se introirent*, Bd. 1, 25; S. 486, 39. Hē hēt hine warnan (*or* I. 3), gif hē wolde libban, ðæt hē nǣre on ðam mynstre nǣfre ǣft gesewen, Homl. Skt. i. 6, 211. (3) *to keep* something from a person, *to ward off* (cf. *Icel.* varna einum eins *to deny a person something*) :—Snyttra brūceþ ðe fore sāwle lufan warniaþ him wommas worda and dǣda *he uses wisdom, that for love of his soul wards off from himself* (avoids) *sins of word and deed*, Exon. Th. 304, 32; Fä. 79: 305, 9; Fä. 85. Ic mē warnade hyre onsȳne *I avoided seeing her, denied myself her presence*, 173, 6; Gū. 1156. Ōþ ðæt hē geseah his gehȳrend ðone Eástordæg onfōn, ðone hī symle ǣrðan wearnedon (warenedon, Bd. M. 474, 20) *donec illum in Pascha diem, suos auditores, quem semper antea vitabant, suscipere videret*, Bd. 5, 22; S. 644, 44. Eall hē wearnige (weornige, MS.) swā fȳr (syer, MS.) wudu wearnie (weornie, MS.) *let him avoid it all, as wood avoids fire*, Lchdm. i. 384, 13. [*O. H. Ger.* warnōn *munire, prospicere, admonere, instruere, attendere*: *Icel.* varna (*see* I. 2, II. 3 *above*); cf. varan *a warning; shunning*.] v. be-, ge-warenian (-warnian, -wearnian), un-warnod; wirnan; warian.

warenung, warnung, wearnung, e; *f.* I. *a taking heed, caution.* v. warnian, I :—Hwæðer wǣre strengra wyrd ðe warnung, Salm. Kmbl. 855; Sal. 427. II. *a putting on guard, a warning, admonition.* v. warnian, II :—Hit ys Godes sprǣc and his warnung and seó tīd cymð hrædlīce, Gen. 41, 32. Wīsdōmes bigspell and warnung wið disig, Ælfc. T. Grn. 7, 38. Hēr is rihtlīc warnung and sōðlīc myngung ðeóde tō ðearfe, gȳme se ðe wille, Wulfst. 167, 26. Ðæt mæg wītes tō wearninga, ðam ðe hafaþ wīsne geþōht, Exon. Th. 57, 21; Cri. 922. [*O. H. Ger.* warnunga *munimentum, defensio, monimentum.*]

warian; *p.* ode I. *intrans.* (*or uncertain*) *To beware* :—Warat *cavet*, Kent. Gl. 364. Wara *cave*, Germ. 393, 136. Warige (warnige, *v. l.*) hē ðæt hit nā forealdige, L. Edg. C. 38; Th. ii. 252, 6. II. *trans. To make ware*, (1) *to warn* :—Mid ðǣm wordum hē ūs warode and lǣrde *quibus verbis pastoribus praecavetur*, Past. 18; Swt. 137, 21. Mōtan ða hyrdas beón swīðe wacole, ðe wið ðone þeódscaðan folc sculon warian, Wulfst. 191, 13. (2) used reflexively, (a) *to be on one's guard, guard* against evil :—Forlǣtaþ ðone ǣnne beám, wariaþ inc wið ðone wæstm, Cd. Th. 15, 20; Gen. 236. Hē gelǣre ðæt hȳ hī wið ðæt warien, ðæt hȳ hǣr ne cumen, Shrn. 203, 3. (b) *to be careful* to do what is necessary, *take a precaution* :—Warige hine se ðe his āgen beföð, ðæt hē tō ǣlcan teáme hæbbe getrȳwne borh, L. Eth. ii. 9; Th. i. 290, 6. III. *to guard, hold* :—Mīn hord waraþ feónd, Exon. Th. 499, 27; Rä. 88, 22: 414, 17; Rä. 32, 21. Hē hǣðen gold waraþ, Beo. Th. 4543; B. 2277. III a. *to hold* a place, *occupy, inhabit* :—Hié dȳgel lond warigeaþ, Beo. Th. 2720; B. 1358. Hē wēsten warode, 2534; B. 1265. Goldsele Grendel warode, 2511; B. 1253. III b. *to take possession of* (cf. giseban thana hēlagon gēst ēnigan man warōn, Hēl. 1003 :—Waraþ hine wræclāst, nales wunden gold, Exon. Th. 288, 17; Wand. 32. IV. *to ward off.* v. warenian, II. 3 :—Ðæt wit unc wīte warian sceolden, Cd. Th. 49, 33; Gen. 801. [They bad him he scholde warye (*be on his guard*), Alis. 4083. Heo mot warien hwon me punt hire, A. R. 418, 1. Iosep cuðe him biforen waren, Gen. and Ex. 2154. Ware the what thou do, Gow. ii. 388, 27. Ware þe fram wanhope, Piers P. 5, 452. *O. Sax.* warōn: *O. Frs.* waria: *O. H. Ger.* bi-warōn: *Icel.* vara *to warn*; varask *to beware of, be on one's guard against, shun.*] v. be-, ge-warian; werian, warenian.

warian; *p.* ode *To remain, continue* :—Ne him gāst waraþ gōmum on mūðe *neque est spiritus in ore ipsorum*, Ps. Th. 134, 19. Waraþ hē windes full, Salm. Kmbl. 49; Sal. 25. [*O. Sax.* warōn *to last, continue.*] v. werian *to remain.*

wārig; *adj. Stained with sea-weed, dirty* :—Biþ his ceól cumen and hyre ceorl tō hām, and heó hine in laðaþ, wæsceþ his wārig hrægl, Exon. Th. 339, 24; Gn. Ex. 90. [Hu maht þu iseon þine sceadewe in worie watere, O. E. Homl. i. 29, 4. Schir heorte . . . wori heorte, A. R. 386, 7.] v. next word.

wāriht; *adj. Full of sea-weed* :—Wārihtum ārena tīum *algosis remorum tractibus* (Ald. 3), Hpt. Gl. 406, 68: Wrt. Voc. ii. 75, 14: 4, 63.

warnian, warnung. v. warenian, warenung.

waroþ (-uþ, -aþ, -eþ), wearoþ, weroþ, warþ, es; *m. A shore, strand* :—Ic geseah men standende be ðam waruðe (werode, *v. l.*), Homl. Skt. ii. 23 b, 370. Bī waraðe (nēh warðe *secus littus*, Lind.) sittende, Mt. Kmbl. Rush. 13, 48. Seó mænigeo stōd on ðam waroðe (waraþe, Rush.: wearðe, Lind. *litore*), Mt. Kmbl. 13, 2: Shrn. 150, 20. Ðū gemētst scip on ðæm waroðe, Blickl. Homl. 231, 30: Andr. Kmbl. 525; An. 263. On ðæs sǣs waroþe, Bd. 1, 12; S. 481, 11. Feówer swulung ond ān lǣs on waruðe gebyreð inn tō Raculfe, Cod. Dip. Kmbl. iii. 429, 16. On waruðe, Andr. Kmbl. 479; An. 240. Hē geseah scip on ðæm warþe, Blickl. Homl. 233, 1. On ðæm warðe (worðe, Rush.) *in litore*, Jn. Skt. Lind. 21, 4. Gewāt him tō waroðe rīdan þegn Hrōðgāres, Beo. Th. 473; B. 234. Ða līchoman cōman tō ðam waroðe, Shrn. 54, 23. Ōð ðone mǣran wearoð (*of Sicily*), Met. 1, 14. Nǣnig cēpa ne seah ellendne wearoð (-od, MS.) *nec nova littora viderat hospes*, 8, 30. Weroþ, Bt. 15; Fox 48, 13. Ðǣr (*at the Red Sea*) wǣron ða wareðas drīge, Ps. Th. 105, 9. Ofer waroða geweorp, Andr. Kmbl. 611; An. 306. Wereþum, Lchdm. i. 390, 11. Sǣwong tredan, wīde waroðas, Beo. Th. 3934; B. 1965. [Þe whal wendeȝ and a warþe fyndeȝ, Allit. Pms. 102, 339. At vche warþe oþer water, Gaw. 715. *O. H. Ger.* warid, werid *insula.*] v. sǣ-waroþ.

wāroþ, es; *n. Sea-weed* :—Ic eom wyrslīcre ðonne ðes wudu fūla oððe ðis wāroð, ðe hēr āworpen ligeþ in corþan, Exon. Th. 424, 34; Rä. 41, 49. v. wār.

waroþ-faroþ, es; *m. A shore-wave, a breaker* :—Waroðfaruða gewinn, Andr. Kmbl. 393; An. 197.

waroþ-gewinn, es; *n. The strife of waves near the shore, the surge* :—Wē on sǣbāte ofer waruðgewinn wada cunnedon faroðrīdende, Andr. Kmbl. 877; An. 439.

waru, e (*but acc.* waru, Ps. Th. 118, 17); *f. Watchful care*, (1) *observance, keeping* of a command, etc. :—Ic on līfdagum lustum healde ðīnra worda waru *vivam et custodiam sermones tuos*, Ps. Th. 118, 17. (2) where need for caution is implied, *heed, care* :—Ða wiðerwinnan wurdon oferswīðde þurh ðæs engles gewinne and ware, Homl. Th. ii. 338, 2. Antiochus giémde hwæt hē hæfde monna gerīmes, and ne nom nāne ware hūlīce hié wǣron, Ors. 5, 4; Swt. 224, 22. (3) *care* for the safety of others :—Se hȳra ne bið nāðor ne mid ware ne mid lufe āstyred, Homl. Th. i. 240, 28. Paulus ne ēhte geleáffulra manna ðurh andan, ac ðurh ware ðære ealdan ǣ, 390, 6. (4) *safe-keeping, custody, keeping* from injury, *guard* :—Stōd se grēna wong in Godes wære, Exon. Th. 146, 32; Gū. 718: 143, 17; Gū. 662: Andr. Kmbl. 1648; An. 825. Ðē God hæfde wære bewunden *God kept thee on every side*, 1069; An. 535. Wære betolden, 1976; An. 990. Him Scyld gewāt on Freán wære, Beo. Th. 54; B. 27. In Godes wære, Menol. Fox 79; Men. 39. Hē his gāst āgeaf on Godes wære, 432; Men. 217. Hēr Eádward kingc sende sāwle tō Criste on Godes wæra, Chr. 1065; Erl. 196, 23. (5) *defence, protection* against attack, *guard* :—Geīsnedum belādiendlīcre ware [scilde] wiðþyddende leásere wrōhte arwan *ferrato apologeticae defensionis clypeo retundens strophosae accusationis catapultas*, Hpt. Gl. 505, 61. Tō ware *ad tutelam* (*defensionem*) (leo ad tutelam virginis Dei nutu dirigitur, Ald. 45), 484, 49. Nān man ne dorste for ðæra deóra ware ðām hālgum geneálǣcan, Homl. Skt. ii. 24, 56, 60. Scealt ðū for ware ūra goda wīta ðrowian *for the protection of our gods thou shalt suffer punishments*, Homl. Th. i. 594, 4. Cyninge gebyraþ ðæt hē sȳ on ware and on wearde Cristes gespeliga, L. I. P. 2; Th. ii. 304, 23. Hié ealle ongeán hiene wǣron feohtende and ðone weg lētan būtan ware (*they left the road unguarded*), ðæt seó fierd þǣr þurhfōr *in se omnes pugnando convertit, donec exercitus angustias transiret*, Ors. 4, 6; Swt. 172, 22. Hié wǣron ða burg hergende and sleánde būton ǣlcre ware (*without any defence being offered*), 2, 8; Swt. 92, 16. Ware ł gescildnysse *defensionem*, Hpt. Gl. 471, 61. Ðū mē behēte fulle wære (ware, *v. l.*) wið æftersprǣce *thou didst promise complete protection against claim*, L. O. 7; Th. i. 180, 23. Hȳ ðæs wære cunnon, healdaþ hine twā hund wearda, Salm. Kmbl. 518; Sal. 258. His ware *munitiones ejus*, Blickl. Gl. [To habbe som gret cite or castel me to ware (*for my defence*), R. Glouc. 115, 9. *Goth.* warei *astutia*: *O. Sax.* wara *heed* (wara niman); *safe-keeping* (wara Godes sōkean): *O. Frs.* ware: *O. H. Ger.* wara (wara neman, tuon) *heed, care.*] v. niht-, ūt-waru.

waru, e (*but the declension seems partly u-stem*); *f. Ware, merchandise* :—Mangere *mercator*, waru *merx*, Wrt. Voc. i. 73, 73. Hī wurpon heora waru oforbord *they cast forth the wares that were in the ship into the sea* (Jonah 1, 5), Homl. Th. i. 246, 2. Ðā gelamp hit æt sumum sǣle, swā swā gyt for oft dēð, ðæt Englisce cȳpmenn brōhton heora ware tō Rōmāna byrig, and Gregorius eode be ðære strǣt tō ðām Engliscum mannum heora ðing sceáwigende. Ðā geseah hē betwux ðām warum cȳpecnihtas gesette, ii. 120, 14-18. [Chæpmen bunden heore ware, Laym. 11356. Þe wreche peoddare more noise he makeð to ȝeien his sope, þen a riche mercer al his deorewurðe ware, A. R. 66, 19. Ðe chapmen into Egipte ledden ðat ware, Gen. and Ex. 1990. *O. Frs.* were: *Icel.* vara; *f.*]

-waru, a form occurring only in compounds with a collective force, *the inhabitants* of a place. It is used with common nouns, v. burh-, ceaster-, eorþ-, hell-, heofon-, land-waru; and with proper names, native or foreign, e.g. Lunden-waru, Chr. 1016; Erl. 159, 22: Hierosolim-waru *Hierosolyma*, Mt. Kmbl. 3, 5; Sychem-ware *Sicinorum*, Wrt. Voc. ii. 73, 66. v. wara.

waru *wearing?*, waru, Cod. Dip. Kmbl. iii. 429, 16, warum, Ors. 4, 5; Swt. 170, 10, wâsa. v. scrûd-waru, waroþ, wǽr *a covenant*, wudu-wâsa.

Wascan; *pl. m. The Gascons*, Ors. 1, 1; Swt. 22, 32, 34. [*O. H. Ger.* Wascun *Uacea.*]

wascan. v. wæscan.

wâse, an; *f. Ooze, mud, slime:*—Wâse *caenum*, Wrt. Voc. ii. 103, 2: 13, 35. *Cenum*, i. *luti vorago*, vel *lutum sub aquis fetidum*, i. wâse *vel* fæn, 130, 75. Wâsan *ceni* (squallentis ceni contagia, Ald. 49), 82, 63: 18, 39. ¶ the word occurs in several charters dealing with land in the north of Berkshire, and seems to refer to a marsh or stagnant piece of water:—On Wâse; of Wâsan (the Ock, the Thames, and Fyfield are mentioned in this charter), Cod. Dip. Kmbl. iii. 466, 17. On Wâsan; andlang Wâsan (with mention of the Ock and Fyfield), v. 386, 33. Ongeán ða díc ðe scýt tô Wâsan; siððan andlang Wâsan (with mention of the Thames and Appleton), 275, 15. Of ðære mêde ût tô Wâsan; of Wâsan ût tô Eá (with mention of Buckland), 392, 32. Eást tô Wâsan (with mention of Sandford), vi. 9, 7. On Wâse; of Wǽse (with mention of the Thames and Cumnor), 84, 24. [William . . . stombled at a nayle, into the waise he tombled, R. Brun. 70, 16. A wase, wayse *alga*, Cath. Angl. 409, and see note. Alle we byeþ children of one moder, þet is of erþe: and of wose (*or* v. wôs?), Ayenb. 87, 22. As weodes wexen in wose (*v. l.* muk) and in donge, Piers P. C. 13, 229. Wose, slype of the erthe *gluten, bitumen*, Prompt. Parv. 532, and see note. *O. Frs.* wâse *mud, slime*: *Icel.* veisa *a pool of stagnant water.*] v. wâse-scite.

wâsend, es; *m. The weasand, gullet:*—Wâsend *rumen*, Wrt. Voc. i. 43, 43: 64, 61: 282, 81: *ingluvies*, Hpt. Gl. 490, 11. Wâsende *ingluvie*, 464, 15. Lǽcedômas wið gealhswile and þrotan and wâsende, Lchdm. ii. 44, 8: 46, 7. In ðane wâsend *ingluviem*, Wrt. Voc. ii. 45, 30. [Weysande *isophagus*, Wülck. Gl. 590, 40. Waysande, 635, 19. Wesande, 676, 24. Wesawnt, 748, 19. *O. Frs.* wâsende (-ande): *O. H. Ger.* weisont (-unt) *arteriae.*]

wâse-scite (cf. (?) scîtan), an; *f. or* -scyte (-scite?), es; *m. The cuttle-fish; or the liquid ejected by the cuttle-fish:*—Cudele *vel* wâsescite *sepia*, Wrt. Voc. i. 56, 6. v. scyte, wæter-scyte, *and other compounds of* scyte.

watel, es; *m. A wattle, interwoven twigs:*—Watul *teges*, Ælfc. Gr. 9, 26; Zup. 52, 13. Hê mycelne aad gesomnode on beámum and on ræftrum and on wâgum and on watelum and on ðacum *advexit plurimam congeriem trabium, tignorum, parietum, virgeorum, et tecti fenei*, Bd. 3, 16; S. 542, 23. Ðâ âstigon hig uppan ðæne hrôf þurh ða watelas (*per tegulas*) and hine mid ðam bedde âsendon, Lk. Skt. 5, 19. [v. wattle (*subst. and vb.*) in Baker's Northants Gloss.: wattle *to tile*, Halliwell's Dict.: watteled, Piers P. 19. 323.]

wâþ, e; *f.* I *wandering, roving:*—Deóra gesíð of wâðe cwom, Nabochodonossor, Cd. Th. 257, 26; Dan. 663. Fêðan sǽton, reste gefêgon, wêrige æfter wǽðe, Andr. Kmbl. 1185; An. 593. Ic (*a storm*) beámas fylle . . . wrecan on wâþe wîde sended *I fell trees . . . sent driving a-wandering far* (cf. Aldhelm's Ego rura peragro), Exon. Th. 381, 14; Rä. 2, 11. Hý síð tugon, wîde wâðe, lyftlâcende, 110, 29; Gû. 116. Hê síðfæt sægde sînum leódum, wîde wâðe, ðe hê mid wilddeórum âteáh, Cd. Th. 256, 33; Dan. 650. Hý of wâþum wêrge cwôman, restan ryneþrâgum, Exon. Th. 115, 1; Gû. 183. Wâþum strong, fugel feþrum wlonc, 204, 18; Ph. 99: 208, 26; Ph. 161. II. *hunting:*—Deáð, egeslîc hunta âbît on wâðe, nyle hê ǽnig swæð ǽfre forlǽtan *death, dread hunter, persists in his hunting, never will he abandon any track*, Met. 27, 13. [Myght we not fynde ffor to wyn as for waithe, Destr. Tr. 2350. Here is wayth fayrest þat I seȝ þis seuen ȝere, Gaw. 1381. *O. H. Ger.* weida *venatio, piscatio*: *Icel.* veiðr *hunting, fishing*; fara á veiðar *to go a-hunting.*] v. gamen-wâþ; wǽðan.

waþem(-um), es; *m. A wave, billow:*—Ic þonan wôd ofer waþema gebind *I crossed the band of billows*, Exon. Th. 288, 1; Wand. 24. Waðema streám, sincalda sǽ, Cd. Th. 207, 24; Exod. 471. v. next word.

waþema(-uma), an; *m. Moving water, wave, flood:*—Ðâ cwom wôþes hring ût faran, weóll waðuman streám, and hê worde cwæð, Andr. Kmbl. 2561; An. 1282. Tungol beóþ âhýded, gewiten under waþeman westdǽlas on, Exon. Th. 204, 13; Ph. 97.

wâþol (v. wâþ); *adj. Wandering:*—Scýneþ ðes mô[n]a wâþol under wolcnum (cf. *wandering* as an epithet of the moon in Shakspere), Fins. Th. 14; Fin. 8. [Grein takes waþol = *full moon*. v. Grmm. D. M. 674-5.]

wâwa, an; *m. Woe, misery:*—On ðære wǽron âwritene heófunga and leóð and wâwa (*scriptae erant in eo lamentationes et carmen et uae*) . . . se wâwa getâcnaþ ðone êcan wâwan, ðe ða habbaþ on hellewîte, ðe nû God forseóþ, Ælfc. Gr. 48; Zup. 279, 1-8. Ðonne sceal eów weaxan tô hearme wǽdl and wâwa, Wulfst. 133 3. Ceósan gôdes and yfeles, welan and wâwan, Cd. Th. 30, 12; Gen. 466. On ǽlcum wâwan hî wǽron geþyldige, Homl. Skt. ii. 28, 130. *Uae* getâcnaþ wâwan, Ælfc. Gr. 48; Zup. 278, 17. Sume hî wyrcaþ heora wôgerum sumne wâwan, ðæt hî hî tô wîfe habbon, Homl. Skt. i. 17, 158. Ðæt gê swâ earme eów sylfe fordôþ on wîton and on wâwon, 23, 186. Hî gesâwon ða mænigfealdon wâwan ðe Cristes ða gecorenan þoledon, 23, 124. [To þolien wawe mid douelen, O. E. Homl. i. 73, 11. For ðon muchele wawen þet hi iðoleden, 87, 12. Of þan wowe ılse of þe wele, ii. 197, 8. Mochel wowe (seorwen, 1st MS.), Laym. 1268. þolemod aȝean alle wowes, A. R. 198, 26. To þolenn al.e wawenn, Orm. 13349. Al þat heo singeþ hit is for wowe, O. and N. 414. *O. H. Ger.* wêwo; *m.*; wêwa; *f. dolor, poena, malum.*] v. weá.

wâwan; *p.* weów; *pp.* wâwen *To blow, be moved by the wind:*—Hnescre ic eom micle halsrefeþre, se hêr on winde wǽweþ on lyfte, Exon. Th. 426, 30; Rä. 41, 81. [Min lokes . . . me wes lef to showen, þe wind hem wolde towowen, Anglia ii. 279, 89. *Goth.* waian *to blow* (of the wind): *O. H. Ger.* wâjan (wâen) *ventilare, spirare.*] v. bi-wâwan.

waxan *to wash*, wax-georn. v. wæscan, weax-georn.

wê; *pron. We.* I. used of more than one person, (1) dual:—Ic and ðæt cild gâð unc tô gebiddenne and wê siððan cumaþ eft tô eów, Gen. 22, 5. Wê willaþ ðæt ðû ûs dô swâ hwæt swâ wê biddaþ (cf. wyt magon, v. 39), Mk. Skt. 10, 35. (2) plural:—Hwî fæst[on] wê (woe, Lind.)? Mt. Kmbl. 9, 14. Wê þonne synt ðe fylgeaþ *it is we that follow*, Blickl. Homl. 81, 33. Wê men sculon, Exon. Th. 46, 33; Cri. 746. Wê selfe cûþen, 147, 7; Gû. 723. Wê ealle wǽron ðê fylgend[e], and ðû eart ûre ealra fultum ða ðe on ðê gelýfaþ, Blickl. Homl. 229, 10. Uton wê ealle wynsumian on Drihten, wê ðe his ǽriste mǽrsiaþ, 91, 8. Getîþa ûs ðæt ðe wê ðê ætforan âgyltan . . . *annue nobis ut quę* (qui *has been glossed*) *te coram deliquimus* . . ., Hymn. Surt. 124, 30: Exon. Th. 2, 27; Cri. 25. (2 a) used by a king in reference to himself and his counsellors:—Wê (*Ine and the witan*) bebeódaþ, L. In. 1; Th. i. 102, 14. Wê (*Alfred*) lǽraþ, L. Alf. pol. 1; Th. i. 60, 2. Wê (*Athelstan*) cwǽdon, L. Ath. i. 2; Th. i. 200, 5. Wê (*Cnut*) willaþ, L. C. E. 6; Th. i. 364, 5. II. used of one person, (1) by a writer or speaker:—Nû hæbbe wê scortlîce gesǽd (cf. scortlîce ic hæbbe nû gesǽd, 10, 3), Ors. 1, 1; Swt. 14, 26: 22, 1: 24, 23. Swâ wê ǽr cwǽdon (cf. swâ ic ǽr cwæþ, 8, 14), 24, 32. Wê mihton ðâs rǽdinge menigfealdlîcor trahtnian, Homl. Th. i. 556, 13. Hwæt wille wê eów swîðor secgan be ðisum symbeldæge, ii. 444, 13: Blickl. Homl. 115, 28. (2) by a prince:—Beówulf maþelode: 'Wê ðæt ellenweorc fremedon,' Beo. Th. 1920; B. 958: 3308; B. 1652. [*Goth.* weis: *O. Sax. O. Frs.* wî: *O. H. Ger.* wir: *Icel.* vêr.] v. ûs, wit.

weá, an; *m.* I. *woe, misery, evil, affliction, trouble:*—Genôh dæge weá his *sufficit diei malitia sua*, Mt. Kmbl. Rush. 6, 34. Weá wæs ârǽred, tregena tuddor, Cd. Th. 60, 26; Gen. 987. Mec ðîn weá æt heortan gehreáw, Exon. Th. 91, 18; Cri. 1493. Weá biþ wundrum clibbor, Menol. Fox 485; Gn. C. 13. Weán on wênum *in expectation of evil*, Cd. Th. 63, 4; Gen. 1027: 191, 11; Exod. 213: Exon. Th. 378, 32; Deór. 25: Cd. Th. 146, 6; Gen. 2418. Ne ic ðê weán ûðe *nor did I wish you ill*, 163, 3; Gen. 2692. Nysses ðû weán ǽnigne dǽl *you knew nothing of misery*, Exon. Th. 85, 3; Cri. 1385. Ne lǽd ðû ûs tô wîte in weán sorge, Hy. 6, 27. Hê þearfend[e] of wǽdle weán âlýsde *adjuvabit pauperem de inopia*, Ps. Th. 106, 40. Gif ðê ǽnig mid weán grêteþ *if any man afflict thee*, Cd. Th. 105, 18; Gen. 1755. Hê heóld his ǽhta him tô weán, Blickl. Homl. 53, 9. Biþ hê on êcne weán bedrifen, 95, 5. Ðæt ða yfelan bióþ micle gesǽligran ðe on ðisse worulde habbaþ micelne weán and manigfeald wîte for hyra yfelum, ðonne ða sién ðe nâne wræce nabbaþ *feliciores esse improbos supplicia luentes, quam si eos nulla justitiae poena coerceat*, Bt. 38, 3; Fox 200, 3. Hî mê weán [îhton, cf. 77, 31] mînra wunda sâr *super dolorem vulnerum meorum addiderunt*, Ps. Th. 68, 27. Weán, sâr and sorge, Cd. Th. 5, 20; Gen. 74: 267, 22; Sat. 42. Ic fleáh weán wana wilna gehwilces, 137, 11; Gen. 2272: 109, 7; Gen. 1819. For hwon wâst ðû weán, gesyhst sorge, 54, 12; Gen. 876. Gedîgan weán and wræcsîð, Beo. Th. 4573; B. 2292. Gesamna ûs of wîdwegum, ðǽr wê weán dreógaþ, Ps. Th. 105, 36: Cd. Th. 276, 7; Sat. 185. Hê for wlenco weán âhsode, Beo. Th. 2417; B. 1206: 851; B. 423. Wyrd wôp wecceþ, heó weán hladeþ, Salm. Kmbl. 874; Sal. 436. Eal sâr and sace, hungor and þurst, wôp and hreám, and weána mâ ðonne ǽniges mannes gemet sý ðæt hié ârîman mæge, Blickl. Homl. 61, 36. Fela ic weána gebâd, heardra hilda, Fins. Th. 51; Fin. 25. Wên ne brûceþ, ðe can weána lyt, sâres and sorge, Runic pm. Kmbl. 340, 30; Rûn. 8. Weána dǽl *a deal of trouble*, Exon. Th. 379, 17; Deór. 34: Beo. Th. 2304; B. 1150. Ic ðê wið weána gehwam wreó, Cd. Th. 131, 2; Gen. 2170: Beo. Th. 2796; B. 1396. Ic ǽnigra mê weána ne wênde bôte gebîdan, 1870; B. 933. Hié ealle worlde weán oforhogodan, Blickl. Homl. 119, 15. Weallende weán, Exon. Th. 139, 2; Gû. 587. II. *evil, wickedness, malice.* v. weá-dǽd:—Nǽfre on his weorþige weá âspronge, mearce mâ scyte mân inwides *non defecit de plateis ejus usura et dolus*, Ps. Th. 54, 10. Weá bið in môde, siofa synnum fâh, gefylled mid fâcne, Fragm. Kmbl. 27; Leás. 15. Ðæt gelamp for weán and for yfelnesse ðara eardiendra (*a malitia inhabitantium*), Bd. 4, 25; S. 599, 22. Hý magon weána tô fela geseón on him selfum, synne genôȝe, Exon. Th. 77, 30; Cri. 1264. [Hu stont ham þ beoð þere ase alle wo and weane is, A. R. 80, 11.] v. wāwa, weó.

weacen. v. wacen.

weá-cwānian; *p.* ode *To lament, wail*:—Deófla weácwānedon mān and morður, Cd. Th. 284, 12; Sat. 320. [Cf. *Goth.* wai-fairhwjan *ejulare*: *Ger.* weh-klagen.]

weá-dǽd, e; *f. A deed of woe, an ill-deed*:—Hē (*Stephen*) bæd þrymcyning ðæt hē him ða weádǽd tō wræce ne sette (cf. Domine, ne statuas illis hoc peccatum, Acts 7, 60), Elen. Kmbl. 987; El. 495. Ārīsaþ weádǽda, Fins. Th. 15; Fin. 8. [Cf. *Goth.* wai-dēdja *a malefactor.*]

weá-gesīþ, es; *m. A companion in misery* or *in wickedness*:—Tō ðam symle sittan eodon ealle his (*Holofernes'*) weágesīþas, Judth. Thw. 21, 13; Jud. 16. Hē ðone deófol on helle mid his weágesīðum ofþrihte, Wulfst. 145, 4. Ða deorcan and ða dimman stōwe helle tintrego, ðe deófol an wunaþ mid his weágesīþum and mid ðām āwergdum sāulum, 225, 33.

weal *a wall*; weala. v. weall; wela, wealh.

weá-lāf, e; *f. A remnant spared by calamity, those who remain after evil times, the survivors of calamity*:—Land hȳ āwēstaþ and burga forbærnaþ and ǽhta forspillaþ and eard hȳ āmirraþ. And ðonne land wurðeþ for sinnum forworden and ðæs folces duguð swīðost fordwīneþ, ðonne fēhð seó weálāf sorhful and sārigmōd synna bemǽnan *erit terra uestra deserta et ciuitates uestre destructe. Et, cum deserta fuerit terra propter peccata populi, et ipsi, qui remanserint tabescentes pronuntiabunt peccata sua*, Wulfst. 133, 13: Met. 1, 22. Ðæt hē ða weálāfe ārum heólde, Beo. Th. 2200; B. 1098: 2172; 1084.

Wealas, wealand, -wealc. v. wealh, wealh-land, ge-wealc.

wealca, an; *m.* I. *a roller, a wave, billow* (cf. *fretum*, i. *feruor maris* a walke, Wülck. Gl. 584, 36). v. ge-wealc:—Streám ūt āweóll, fleów ofer foldan, fāmige walcan eorðan þehton, miclade mereflōd, Andr. Kmbl. 3047; An. 1526. II. *a garment that may be rolled round a person, a muffler, wrap, veil.* v. wealcian:—Ðā dyde heó of hire wydewan reáf and nam hire walcan (*theristrum*), Gen. 38, 14.

wealcan; *p.* weólc; *pp.* wealcen *To roll, toss.* I. of the movement of water; v. wealca, I, ge-wealc. (1) *trans.*:—Se fisc getácnaþ geleáfan, for ðan ðe his gecynd is, swā hine swīðor ða ȳða wealcaþ, swā hē strengra bið, Homl. Th. i. 250, 17. (2) *intrans.*:—Wealcynde eá *fluctus*, Wrt. Voc. i. 54, 28. Hē gehȳrde ðæt gebrec ðara storma and ðæs weallendes (*v. l.* wealcendan) sǽs *audito fragore procellarum ac ferventis oceani*, Bd. 5, 1; S. 614, 4. Wealcendre sǽ flōdas *ferventis oceani flustra*, Hpt. Gl. 464, 59. I a. fig.:—Hē hine sylfne betweox ðises andweardan middaneardes (wǽlum? v. wǽl) weólc and welode *inter fluctuantis saeculi gurgites jactaretur*, Guthl. 2; Gdwin. 14, 14. II. of other movement, (a) literal:—Hægl hwyrft of heofones lyfte, wealcaþ hit windes scūras, Runic pm. Kmbl. 341, 6; Rūn. 9. (b) metaph. (1) of action:—Godwine eorl and ealle ða yldestan menn on West-Seaxon lāgon ongeán swā hī lengost mihton, ac hī ne mihton nān þing ongeán wealcan (*another MS. has* hī nāht nā gespēdan) *Earl Godwin and the chief men of Wessex resisted as long as ever they could, but they could put no obstacle in the way*, Chr. 1036; Erl. 165, 3. (2) of thought, (*a*) *trans. To turn over in the mind, to revolve, consider*:—Ða getȳdde munuccild ðæt heom betweónan oft wealcaþ, Anglia viii. 314, 35. Hē hine beþōhte and ða hellīcan pīnunge on his mōd weólc, Homl. Th. i. 448, 17. Ðæt ēce līf on his mōde hē wealce *vitam aeternam animo suo revolvat*, R. Ben. Interl. 29, 2: Hymn. Surt. 121, 9. Wē witon ðæt iunge clericas ðās þing ne cunnon, þeáh ða scolieras ðisra þinga gȳmon and gelōmlīce heom betwux wealcun, Anglia viii. 335, 44. Hī nellaþ on heora mōde wealcan ðæs Hǽlendes beboda, Homl. Skt. ii. 25, 53. For ðæra gelǽredra manna þingum, ðe ðās þing ne behōfiaþ betweox heom tō wealcynne, Anglia viii. 300, 4. (*β*) with a preposition:—Wealce hē on his mōde embe ðæt ēce līf *vitam aeternam animo suo revolvat*, R. Ben. 24, 3. (*γ*) *intrans.*:—Ða ingeðoncas ðe wealcaþ in ðæs monnes mōde *quando cogitationes volvuntur in mente*, Past. 21; Swt. 155, 22. (3) *to turn over, deal with*:—Þeáh ðe hī Moyses ǽ on heora mūðe wealcon, and nellaþ understandan būtan ðæt steaflīce andgit, Homl. Skt. ii. 25, 72. [Hi walkeð (*toss*) weri up and dun se water deþ mid winde, O. E. Homl. i. 175, 240. He walkeþ and wendeþ and woneþ . . . on his bedde, Fragm. Phlps. 5, 33. Þa scipen ȝeond þa sæ weolken, Laym. 12040. Þat folc was walkende (*going*) toward Ierusalem, O. E. Homl. ii. 51, 13. He (*Christ*) weolc bimong men, Kath. 914. Welk, Pr. C. 4390. Ihc habbe walke wide, Horn. 953. An hundred winter welken (*rolled by*), Gen. and Ex. 568. *O. H. Ger.* ge-walchen *concretus.*] v. and-, ge-, on-wealcan; wealcian, wealcol.

wealc-basu. v. wealh-basu.

wealcere, es; *m. A walker* (v. E. D. S. Pub. Lancashire Gloss. s.v. walk-mill), *a fuller*:—Wealceres *fullones* (*-is?*), Wrt. Voc. ii. 38, 3. [Fullere or walkere of cloth, Wick. Mk. 9, 3. A walker *hic fullo*, Wrt. Voc. i. 212, col. 2 (cf. walkyng *lanugo*, 238, col. 1. To walke clothe *fullare*, Cath. Angl. 406, where see note. Cloth ytouked (*v. l.* ywalked), Piers P. 15, 447). *O. H. Ger.* walchare *coagitator, compressor*: *Ger.* walker *a fuller*; walken *to full.*]

wealcian; *p.* ode *To roll up, muffle up*:—Hefeldþrǽdum liða wealcedon *liciis articulos obvolverent*, Hpt. Gl. 489, 56. [Þe sipes in see walkede, Laym. 12040, 2nd MS. *Generally the word* = to walk, go:—Hu me schal liggen, slepen, walkien, A. R. 4, 8. Ðe desert he walkeden ðurg, Gen. and Ex. 3882. Ihesu walkide in to Galilee, Wick. Jn. 7, 1. I haue walked ful wide, Piers P. 5, 537. *Icel.* valka (*wk.*) *to roll.*] v. wealcan.

wealcol; *adj. That turns* or *rolls easily*:—Wealcol *mobilis*, Germ. 399, 441.

wealc-spinel, e; *f. A curling-iron, crisping-pin*:—Walcspinl *calamistrum*, Wrt. Voc. ii. 127, 75. Cf. þrāwing-spinel, *and see* wealcan.

weald, es; *m. High land covered with wood* (v. weald-genga), *wood, forest.* [The word is left in the phrase the *weald* of Kent and Sussex, the earlier woodland character of which district is shewn by its local names (v. Taylor's Names and Places, pp. 244-5); and in *wold*, e. g. the *wolds* of Lincolnshire, Cots*wold*, though from the changed condition of the country this word no longer implies the presence of wood: in Bailey's Dictionary *wold* is defined 'a down or champian ground, hilly and void of wood.' See, too, the examples from Mid. English given below]:—Se weald Pireni *Pyrenaei saltus*, Ors. 1, 1; Swt. 24, 10. Gif hī (*birds*) ðæs wuda benugen . . . þincþ him wynsumre ðæt him se weald oncweþe, and hī gehīran ōþerra fugela stemne *si nemorum gratas viderit umbras . . . silvas tantum moesta requirit, silvas dulci voce susurrat*, Bt. 25; Fox 88, 20: Met. 13, 92. Wudes ne feldes, sandes ne strandes, wealtes ne wæteres, Lchdm. iii. 288, 1. Wealdes treów (*the cross*), Rood Kmbl. 34; Kr. 17. Ān wind of Calabria wealde *de Calabris saltibus aura*, Ors. 3, 3; Swt. 102, 8. Se Limene mūþa is on eásteweardre Cent, æt ðæs miclan wuda eástende ðe wē Andred hātaþ . . . seó eá līð ūt of ðæm wealda. On ða eá hī tugon up hiora scipu ōþ ðone weald iiii mīla fram ðæm mūþan ūtanweardum, Chr. 893; Erl. 88, 26-32. On wealda, Cod. Dip. Kmbl. ii. 216, 4. In Limenwero wealdo and in burhwaro ualdo, Cod. Dip. B. i. 344, 10, 11. Wulf on wealde, 937; Erl. 115, 14. Wulf on walde, Elen. Kmbl. 55; El. 28: Judth. Thw. 24, 25; Jud. 206. 'Uton gān on ðysne weald, innan on ðísses holtes hleó.' Hwurfon hié . . . on ðone grēnan weald, Cd. Th. 52, 6-10; Gen. 839-41. Ðæt is wynsum wong, wealdas grēne, rūme under roderum, Exon. Th. 198, 21; Ph. 13. Gewāt him se æþeling wadan ofer wealdas, Cd. Th. 174, 30; Gen. 2886. ¶ using the name of the whole for a part:—Hié heora līchoman leáfum beþeahton, weredon mid ðȳ wealde, 52, 19; Gen. 846. [He is bicumen hunte and flihð ouer bradne wæld (feld, 2nd MS.), Laym. 21339. Þe wald þe is ihaten Heðfeld, 31216. Fluȝen ouer þe woldes (feldes, 2nd MS.), 20138. Liðen heo bi straten and bi walden, 12832. Wilde deor þ on þeos wilde waldes (*forests*) wunieð, Marh. 10, 4. Elpes togaddre gon o wolde, Misc. 19, 606: O. and N. 1724. On ðe munt quor men Aaron in birieles dede . . . ðor hē lið doluen on ðat wold, Gen. and Ex. 3892. Þe holy gost hyne ledde up into þe wolde for to beon yuonded of sathanas, Misc. 38, 27. Ye walde *alpina*, Cath. Angl. 406. *O. Frs. O. Sax.* wald *wood*: *O. H. Ger.* walt, wald *silva, saltus, nemus, eremus*: *Icel.* völlr *a field, plain.*] v. ūt-, wudu-weald.

weald *power*:—Se wæs on his wealde (gewealde, MS. L.), Ors. 4, 11; Bos. 97, 23. [He haueð his soule weald, O. E. Homl. ii. 79, 14. A neuere nane walde ne mihte swa mochel folc halde, Laym. 5253. Unnderr þe deofless walde, Orm. 38. Hine þet alle þing haueð on wealde, Anglia i. 31, 186. To don swilc dede adde he no wold, Gen. and Ex. 2000. *O. Frs.* wald: *Icel.* vald.] v. ān-, and-, ge-, on- (an-) weald; wealdes, *and next word.*

weald; *adj. Powerful, mighty*:—Mid ðære wealdestan [lufe] *ferventissimo amore*, R. Ben. 117, 5. [v. ān-, eal- (al-) wealda; *adj. O. Sax.* ala-, alo-waldo: *O. H. Ger.* al-walto.] v. on-weald, wealda; *m.*; wilde.

weald *is found as the second part of many proper names.* Cf. *Icel.* -valdr, e. g. Ās-valdr = English Ōs-wald. v. for a list of such names, Txts. pp. 491-3.

weald; *adv. conj.* I. in independent clauses, *with* þeáh, *perhaps, may be*:—Nyte gē ða micclan deópnysse Godes gerȳnu; weald þeáh him beó ālȳfed gyt behreówsung, Homl. Th. ii. 340, 9. Ðis godspel ðincð dysegum mannum sellīc, ac wē secgaþ swā ðeáh; weald ðeáh hit sumum men līcige, 466, 10. Wēn ys ðæt hē sig on gāste up āhafen, and onuppan muntum geset; ac uton ða muntas eondfaran; weald þeáh wē hyne gemētan magon, Nicod. 19; Thw. 9, 25, 31. II. in dependent clauses, with indefinite pronouns or adverbs (cf. gif), *in case*:—Bið nū wīslīcor ðæt gehwā ðis wite and cunne his geleáfan, weald hwā ða mycclan yrmðe gebīdan sceole *in case any one have to experience that great misery*, Homl. Th. i. 6, 19. Bisceopum gebyreþ ðæt mid heom wunian welgeþungene witan . . . ðæt heora gewitan beón on ǽghwylcne tīman, weald hwæt heom tīde *in case anything befall them*, L. I. P. 10; Th. ii. 316, 25. Hī nāmon tō rǽde, ðæt him wærlīcor wǽre, ðæt hī sumne dǽl heora landes wurðes æthæfdon, weald [hwæt?] him getīmode, Homl. Th. i. 316, 24. Man sceal wacigean and warnian symle, ðæt man geara weorðe tō ðam dōme, weald hwænne hē us tō cyme; wē witan mid gewisse, ðæt hit ðǽrtō neálǽcð *people ought to watch and be ever on guard so that they may get ready for the judgement, in case any time it come to us; we know with certainty that we are getting near to it*, Wulfst. 90, 3.

wealda, an; *m. A ruler.* v. ân-, an-, Bret-, bryten-, eal-wealda. [*O. Sax.* ala-waldo : *O. H. Ger.* -walto : *Icel.* valdi.] ¶ as a proper name (?) :— Innan Wealdan hricg on Eádrîces gemǽre, Cod. Dip. B. ii. 259, 9. [*O. H. Ger.* Walto, Waldo : *Icel.* -valdi *in cpd. names.*] v. weald; *adj.*

wealdan; *p.* weóld, *pl.* weóldon; *pp.* wealden *To have power* over :— Wealdeþ *imperitat*, Wrt. Voc. ii. 44, 43. Ǽlc mon biþ wealdend ðæs ðe hê welt; næfþ hê nâune anweald ðæs ðe hê ne welt *quod quisque potest, in eo validus : quod non potest, in hoc imbecillis esse censendus est*, Bt. 36, 3; Fox 176, 17. I. *to control the movements of* that which is moved, *to regulate, wield* a weapon, (a) with gen. :— Sió eax welt ealles ðæs wǽnes, Bt. 39, 8; Fox 224, 6. Ða hwîle ðe hî wǽpna wealdan môston, Byrht. Th. 134, 13; By. 83 : 139, 50; By. 272. Wǽpnes wealdan, 136, 48; By. 168. Gif hê his wordcwida wealdan meahte, Exon. Th. 171, 26; Gû. 1132. (b) with dat. or inst. :— Swâ hê selfa bæd, þenden wordum weóld wine Scyldinga, Beo. Th. 59; B. 30. Se ðe wætrum weóld þeahte bearn middangeardes wonnan wǽge, Cd. Th. 83, 9; Gen. 1377. Þenden hié ðâm wǽpnum wealdan môston, Beo. Th. 4083; B. 2038. II. *to control* that which moves itself, *to have control* of a person, an emotion, &c., *to govern*, (a) with gen. :— Be cnihtum, on hwylcere yldo hî môton hyra sylfra wealdan (*se ipsos gubernare*), L. Ecg. C. 27, tit.; Th. ii. 130, 12. (b) with acc. :— Sume wealdaþ ealle uncysta and leahtras on him sylfum, Homl. Th. i. 344, 34. III. of the control exercised by one in authority, *to rule, govern, have dominion over, bear sway, wield* power, (a) with gen. :— Þenden ic wealde wîdan rîces, Beo. Th. 3722; B. 1859. Dryhten, ðû ðe ealle gesceafta gesceópe, and heora weltst *qui mundum gubernas*, Bt. 33, 4; Fox 128, 6, 24. Wealdest, Met. 20, 7, 50. Waldest, Hy. 3, 5. Ðû heora wylst *reges eos*, Ps. Th. 2, 9. Wealdeþ (*dominabitur*) God manna cynnes, 58, 13. Waldeþ, Met. 29, 77. Se ðe waldeþ ealra ôðra eorðan cyninga, 24, 35. Hê welt (wilt, *v. l.*) ealles, Bt. 35, 3; Fox 158, 23. Welt, 25; Fox 88, 3. Wylt, 5, 3; Fox 14, 3. Wealt, 35, 4; Fox 160, 14. Wealt (welt, *v. l.*), 39, 2; Fox 214, 13. Wealt (wylt, *v. l.*), 35, 3; Fox 158, 19. Ðâm ðe ðyses middangeardes waldaþ *hujus mundi potestatibus*, Past. 15; Swt. 89, 22. Ealdormenn wealdaþ hyra þeóda *principes gentium dominantur eorum*, Mt. Kmbl. 20, 25 : Lk. Skt. 22, 25. Hê him ealles ðæs anwaldes weóld Mæcedonia rîces, Ors. 3, 11; Swt. 148, 24 : Cd. Th. 258, 19; Dan. 678. Wióld, Met. 9, 38. Hî heora weóldan *dominati sunt eorum*, Ps. Th. 105, 30. Þeáh hê ðæs ealles wealde, Bt. 29, 3; Fox 106, 25 : Met. 16, 16. Gelêfst ðû ðæt seó wyrd wealde ðisse worulde, Bt. 5, 3; Fox 12, 2. Abbod, ðe ðæs wyrðe sŷ, ðæt hê mynsteres wealde *abba, qui preesse dignus est monasterio*, R. Ben. 10, 9. Walde, Elen. Kmbl. 1598; El. 801. Hê wæs tô ðam swŷðe upâhafen, swylce hê weólde ðæs cynges and ealles Englalandes, Chr. 1052; Erl. 181, 25 : Homl. Th. i. 488, 14 : Bt. 35, 2; Fox 156, 25–27. His fæder ne wolde him lǽtan waldan his eorldômes, Chr. 1079; Erl. 216, 21. God ne beþearf nânes ôþres fultumes his gesceafta mid tô wealdanne, Bt. 35, 3; Fox 158, 15. (b) with dat. or inst. :— Ðû waldes (wyldst, Ps. Spl.) mæhte sǽs *tu dominaris potestati maris*, Ps. Surt. 88, 10. Hê eorðrîcum eallum wealdeþ *regnum ipsius omnibus dominabitur*, Ps. Th. 102, 18 : 75, 9. Waldeþ, Met. 25, 15. Hû hê welt eallum his gesceaftum, Bt. 21, tit.; Fox xiv, 3. Ic weóld folce Deniga, Beo. Th. 935; B. 465. Hê eallum sûðmǽgþum weóld *cunctis australibus provinciis imperavit*, Bd. 2, 5; S. 506, 11. Hê weóld Walum and Scottum, Chr. 1065; Erl. 196, 28 : Exon. Th. 319, 26; Vîd. 18 : Beo. Th. 4747; B. 2379. Hié burgum weóldon, Cd. Th. 216, 19; Dan. 9. Wióldon, Met. 1, 48. (c) with acc. :— Ðû wealdan miht eall eorðan mægen, wind and wolcnu; wealdest ealle on riht, Hy. 9, 5–7. Hê welt ealle gesceaftu, Bt. 39, 13; Fox 234, 22. (d) with a preposition :— Se ofer deóflum wealdeþ, Cd. Th. 263, 21; Dan. 765. Se ofer mægna gehwylc waldeþ, Exon. Th. 255, 32; Jul. 223. (e) absolute :— Wylt *presidet*, Wrt. Voc. ii. 67, 45. Wealdendum *imperantibus* (*Valeriano et Gallieno*, Ald. 67), Hpt. Gl. 515, 45. III a. fig. where the subject is an abstract noun, (a) with gen. :— Ðŷ læs mîn ǽnig unriht wealde *non dominetur mei omnis injustitia*, Ps. Th. 118, 133. Sió gesceádwîsnes sceal ðære wilnunge waldan, Met. 20, 198. (b) with acc. :— Unsôðfæstnys ealle wealde, Ps. Th. 54, 9. (c) with a preposition :— His mægen wealdeþ ofer eall manna cyn, Ps. Th. 65, 6. IV. *to have power over* things, *to possess, be in possession of, have at command, be master of*, (a) with gen. :— Hê sǽs wealdeþ *ipsius est mare*, Ps. Th. 94, 5. Hî wealdaþ eorðan *possederunt terram*, Ps. Spl. C. 43, 4. Þonne wealdaþ hŷ heom sylfum weorðscypes *then shall they command for themselves respect*, L. I. P. 23; Th. ii. 336, 23. Manigra folca gestreónes hié wieóldon *labores populorum possederunt*, Past. 50; Swt. 391, 4. Hî weóldon wælstôwe *they were masters of the field*, Beo. Th. 4108; B. 2051. Wælstôwe wealdan, 5961; B. 2984 : Byrht. Th. 134, 37; By. 95 : Ps. Th. 90, 11. For worulde weorðscypes wealdan *to command the respect of the world*, L. I. P. 16; Th. ii. 324, 4. (b) with dat. or inst. :— Hê sceal ðŷ wonge wealdan; ne magon gê him ða wîc forstondan, Exon. Th. 144, 6; Gû. 674. Ðara ðe lîfe weóldon *of those who lived*, 118, 14; Gû. 239. Beáhhordum leng wyrm wealdan ne môste, Beo. Th. 5647; B. 2827 : Vald. 2, 31. (c) with acc. :— Heofonas ðû wealdest *tui sunt coeli*, Ps. Th. 88, 10. Habban hî and wealdan Hornemeres hunred on hyre âgenre andwealde *habeant et possideant hundredum de Hornemere in sua propria potestate*, Cod. Dip. Kmbl. iv. 200, 7. V. *to have power to decide* or *choose* what shall take place, *to determine, ordain, have the deciding* or *control of* matters, (a) with gen. :— Se ðe lîfa gehwæs lengu wealdeþ *he that determines the length of every life*, Exon. Th. 133, 2; Gû. 483. Wealde se cyning þreóra ǽnes (*the king shall have power to ordain one of three courses*); oþþe hine man cwelle, oþþe ofer sǽ selle, oþþe hine his wergelde âlêse, L. Wih. 26; Th. i. 42, 16. Se ðe ûtlages weorc gewyrce, wealde se cyningc ðæs friðes, L. C. S. 13; Th. i. 382, 18. Sume secgaþ ðæt sió wyrd wealde ǽgþer ge gesǽlþa ge ungesǽlþa ǽlces monnes, Bt. 39, 8; Fox 224, 13. Ðæt hî ne geþafian, gyf his waldan magan, ðæt ðǽr ǽnig unriht up âspringe, L. I. P. 7; Th. ii. 312, 36. Gif hî ðæs wealdan mihton, Wulfst. 185, 3. (b) with dat. or inst. :— Seó weóld hyra (*two buckets*) sîþe, Exon. Th. 435, 12; Rä. 53, 6. Segl sîðe weóld, Cd. Th. 184, 10; Exod. 105. Ðǽr hê ðŷ fyrste wealdan môste, Beo. Th. 5141; B. 2574. (c) with a clause :— Petre ðæne ealdorscipe hê betǽhte, and hêt, ðæt hê weólde be manna gewyrhtum, hwâ ðǽrin môste and hwâ nâ ne môste, Wulfst. 176, 16. Wê ðê magon sêlre gelǽran, ǽr ðû gûðe fremme, weald hû ðê sǽle (*decide thou how it shall happen to thee*) æt ðam gegnslege, Andr. Kmbl. 2710; An. 1537. (d) absolute :— Ðæt ne geþafodon ða ðe micel weóldon on ðisan lande (hit him ne geþafode Godwine eorl, ne êc ôþre men ðe mycel mihton wealdan, col. 1) *those who very much had the control of affairs in this land would not allow that*, Chr. 1036; Th. i. 292, col. 2. Gif lâd forberste, bisceop ðonne wealde and stîðlîce dême, L. C. S. 54; Th. i. 406, 10. Gif man wealdan mæge (*if it can be managed*), ne dŷde man nǽfre on Sunnandæges freólse ânigne forwyrhtne, L. E. G. 9; Th. i. 172, 13 : L. C. S. 45; Th. i. 402, 10 : Anglia ix. 260, 11. Binnan cirictûne ǽnig hund ne cume, ðæs ðe man wealdan mæge, L. Edg. C. 26; Th. ii. 250, 8. Hê wille, gif hê wealdan môt, leóde etan, Beo. Th. 889; B. 442. Ne beóð wê leng somed, gif ic wealdan môt, Cd. Th. 168, 22; Gen. 2786. VI. *to have power* that brings something to pass, *to cause, be the cause, author, source* of something, (1) of persons, (a) with gen. :— Ðæs ðû wealdest *this is thy doing*, Elen. Kmbl. 1517; El. 761. Hê mînre geðylde wealdeþ *ab ipso est patientia mea*, Ps. Th. 61, 5. Gif hwelc folc bið mid hungre geswenced, and hwâ his hwǽte gehŷt and ôðhielt, hû ne wilt hê hiera deáðes? *si populos fames attereret et occulta frumenta ipsi servarent, auctores procul dubio mortis existerent*, Past. 49; Swt. 377, 9. Syndon cyrcan wâce gegriðode ... wâ ðam ðe ðæs wealt, L. I. P. 25; Th. ii. 340, 14. Ðæs ic seolfa weóld, Cd. Th. 281, 21; Sat. 275. Gif ðû hwæt on druncen misdô, ne wît ðû hit ðam ealoðe, for ðam ðu his weólde ðê silf, Prov. Kmbl. 39. Ðæt hê sigora gehwæs âna weólde (wolde, MS.), Exon. Th. 276, 7; Jul. 562. Ic wille wealdan eów blisse and micelre lisse, Wulfst. 132, 23. (b) with dat. or acc. :— Ðæt his môd wite, ðæt migtigra wîte wealdeþ, ðonne hê him wið mæge, Cd. Th. 248, 33; Dan. 523. (2) of things, with gen. :— Ús unwidera for oft weóldon unwæstma, Wulfst. 129, 4. (3) of motives :— Mid ðŷ se willa mâ waldeþ on ðam weorce ðære gemengdnysse, Bd. 1, 27; S. 495, 38. VII. *to have power* to do, *be able* :— Bûton hî hit gebêton, ðæs ðe hî wealdan magon (*as far as lies in their power*), Wulfst. 301, 20. Þeáh fŷr wið ealla sié gemenged weoruldgesceafta, þeáh waldan ne môt ðæt hit ǽnige fordô (cf. ðeáh ne mæg nâne ðara gesceafta ofercuman, Bt. 33, 4; Fox 130, 17), Met. 20, 129. [To walden (welde, 2nd MS.) kineriche, Laym. 2966. Wealden *possidere*, O. E. Homl. ii. 79, 11 : H. M. 39, 20. Welden, O. E. Homl. i. 163, 55. *Goth.* waldan garda οἰκοδεσποτεῖν : *O. Sax. O. L. Ger.* waldan *dominari* : *O. Frs.* walda : *O. H. Ger.* waltan *dominari, regnare, protegere* : *Icel.* valda *to wield, rule; to cause.*] v. ge-, ofer-wealdan; wealdende, ge-wealden; wealdian.

weald-bǽre, es; *n. A place where trees grow affording mast for swine* :— Ad hoc terram pertinent in diuersis locis porcorum pastus, id est uuealdbaera, Cod. Dip. Kmbl. i. 184, 1. v. den-bǽre.

wealdend, es; *m.* I. *one who exercises power over* persons or things, *a controller, master* :— Ǽlc mon biþ wealdend ðæs ðe hê welt, næfþ hê nâune anweald ðæs ðe hê ne welt *quod quisque potest, in eo validus : quod non potest, in hoc imbecillis esse censendus est*, Bt. 36, 3; Fox 176, 17. Hî hine heom for god hæfdon, and hŷ sǽdon ðæt hê wǽre ealles gewinnes waldend (cf. hans (*Odin's*) menn trûðu þvî, at hann ætti heimilan sigr î hverri orrostu, Ynglinga Saga, c. 2), Ors. 1, 6; Swt. 36, 21. Wê witon hê ûre wæs wealdend *we knew he was master of us*, Blickl. Homl. 243, 18. Se ðe ðæs weddes waldend sŷ, L. Edm. B. 6; Th. i. 254, 22. Ðû wêndest ðæt steórleáse men wǽron gesǽlige and wealdendas ðisse worulde *nequam homines potenteis felicesque arbitraris*, Bt. 8, 3; Fox 14, 1. Hê wolde ðætte ealle men wǽran ealra ôþra gesceafta wealdandas *ille genus humanum terrenis omnibus praestare voluit*, 14, 2; Fox 44, 33. II. *one who exercises dominion, a ruler, governor, sovereign* :— Ðes and ðeós wealdend *hic et haec praesul*, Ælfc. Gr. 9, 10; Zup. 39, 12. Cum mid ûs for ðon ðe ðû eart ûre wealdend, Blickl. Homl. 239, 9. Eádgâr, Engla waldend, Chr. 973; Erl. 124, 9. Eádweard, hæleða wealdend, 1065; Erl. 196, 27. Englalandes wealdend, Cod. Dip. Kmbl. iv. 232, 3. Ne sint wê nâne waldendas eówres geleáfan *non dominamur fidei vestrae*, Past. 17; Swt. 115, 24. Ne sint wê nâne waldendas ðisses folces *non dominantes in clero*, Swt. 119, 24. Ðeóda kyningas beóð ðæs folces waldendas *principes gentium dominantur eorum*, Swt. 120, 3. Hié wēron scolfe wuldres waldend, Cd. Th. 266, 18; Sat. 24. Wealdendras *imperatores*, Scint. 215, 9. Ealdormen and þeóde wealdendras, Cod. Dip. Kmbl. iii. 350, 25. **II a.** applied to the Deity:—Ān sceppend is and se is wealdend heofones and eorþan and ealra gesceafta, Bt. 21; Fox 72, 29: 35, 3; Fox 158, 25: 39, 12; Fox 232, 11. Wealdend Drihten *Dominus*, Ps. Th. 65, 16. Ūre fæder, ealles wealdend, cyning on wuldre, Hy. 7, 1. God đe is wealdand and wyrhta ealra gesceafta, L. Eth. vi. 42; Th. i. 326, 13. Ān is ēce cyning, wealdend and wyrhta ealra gesceafta, L. I. P. 1; Th. ii. 304, 2. Se is waldend windes and goldes, Blickl. Homl. 133, 30. Wit Waldendes word forbrǣcon, Cd. Th. 49, 26; Gen. 798. Đæt hē Wealdende, ēcean Dryhtne, gebulge, Beo. Th. 4648; B. 2329. **III.** *a possessor, master, lord*:—'Gewīt đū (*Hagar*) đīnne waldend sēcan; wuna đǣm đē āgon.' Heó gewāt engles lārum hire hlāfordum, Cd. Th. 138, 17; Gen. 2293. Se wela ne mæg his wealdend gedōn nō đȳ weorþron, Bt. 27, 2; Fox 98, 13: 16, 3; Fox 56, 3, 17. Se wela and se anweald nāuht āgnes gōdes nabbaþ, ne nāuht þurhwuniendes heora wealdendum sellan nā magon, 27, 4; Fox 100, 22. [*Creatorem celi et terre* scuppende and weldende of heouene and of orđe, O. E. Homl. i. 75, 26. Wealdende, ii. 17, 32. Godd, domes waldend, Laym. 28205. Waldende (weldende, 2nd MS.), 25568. *Goth.* garda-waldands οἰκοδεσπότης: *O. Sax.* waldand (*used of the Deity*): *O. H. Ger.* Waltant (*proper name*): *Icel.* valdandi.] v. eal[l]- (al-), ofer-, þrym-wealdend, *and next word.*

wealdende; *adj.* (*ptcpl.*) *Ruling, powerful*:—Mihtig God, ... waldende God, Exon. Th. 62, 34; Cri. 1011: 71, 27; Cri. 1162. Se wealdenda Drihten, Homl. Th. i. 328, 11. Se anweald ne mæg gedōn his wealdend wealdendne, Bt. 16, 3; Fox 56, 3, 17. Hwæþer đū nū wēne đæt đæs cyninges geferrǣden and se wela and se anweald đe hē gifþ his deórlingum mæge ǣnigne mon gedōn weligne ođđe wealdendne? *an vero regna regumque familiaritas efficere potentem valent?* 29, 1; Fox 102, 4. Waldendne, 29, tit.; Fox xvi, 2. Nis under mē ǣnig ōþer wiht waldendre, ic eom ufor ealra gesceafta, Exon. Th. 427, 6; Rä. 41, 87. v. eal[l]-, ge-, þrym-wealdend[e]; wealdan.

wealdend-god, es; *m. The Lord God*:—Ic cleopige tō Heáhgode and tō Wealdendgode đe mē wel dyde *clamabo ad Deum altissimum, et ad Dominum qui bene fecit mihi*, Ps. Th. 56, 2. Se is wealdendgode wellīcendlīc *beneplacitum est Deo*, 67, 16. [*O. Sax.* waldand-god.]

wealdes; *adv. Of one's own accord, purposely, voluntarily*:—Gif him wealdes (gewealdes, Hatt. MS.) gebyrige ođđe ungewealdes, Past. 28; Swt. 198, 22. [Þu forschuppeste selfwilles and waldes in to hare cunde, H. M. 27, 2. Heo suneged deadliche iđe bruche, ȝif heo hit breked willes and woldes, A. R. 6, 26.] v. ge-wealdes.

weald-genga, an; *m. A weald-goer* (v. weald), *bandit, brigand*:—Hē wolde beón yldest on đam yfelan flocce, and geworhte his gefēran tō wealdgengum ealle on wīdgillum dūnum ... 'Hē is geworden tō wealdgengan and đæra sceađena ealdor, đe hē him sylf gegaderode, and wunaþ on ānre dūne mid manegum sceađum.'... Đā ætstōd se wealdgenga ... and āwearp his wǣmna, Ælfc. T. Grn. 17, 30–18, 31. [Cf. wald-scađe (wode-scaþe, 2nd MS.), Laym. 25859; the same creature is referred to in these previous lines: Isihst þu þe munt and þene wude muchele, þer wuned þe scađe inne, þa scended þas leode? 25689–92.]

wealdian; *p.* ode *To rule, command*:—Ic wealdige *vel* ofer bebeóde *imperito*, Wrt. Voc. i. 54, 52. [*O. Sax.* gi-waldōn.] v. wealdan.

weald-leđer, es; *n. A rein*:—Hī ne mōton swīþor styrian đonne hē him đæt gerūm his wealdleđeres tō forlǣt, Bt. 21; Fox 74, 8. Se gemetgaþ đone brīdel and đæt wealdleþer ealles ymbhweorftes heofenes and eorþan *orbis habenas temperat*, 174, 19. Đā gelæhton đa weardmen his wealdleđer fæste, Ælfc. T. Grn. 18, 15. Heó wæs on gyldenum scryd, and æt đam wǣron gyldene hors, and on đām wǣron đa wealdleđer swā up getīged, swā swā hig urnon tō heofenum up, Shrn. 156, 12. v. ge-weald-leđer.

weald-more. v. wealh-more.

wealdness, e; *f. Rule, dominion*:—Waldnis đīn *dominatio tua*, Ps. Surt. 144, 13.

weald-stapa, an; *m. A grasshopper, locust*:—Waldstapan *locustas*, Mk. Skt. Rush. 1, 6.

weald-swaþu, e; *f. A forest-track*:—Lāstas wǣron æfter waldswaþum wīde gesȳne *the steps were to be seen far along the forest-tracks*, Beo. Th. 2810; B. 1403.

weale, wale, an; *f. A female slave, servant*:—Wonfeax wale, ... mennen, Exon. Th. 393, 30; Rä. 13, 8. Wonfāh wale weóld hyra (*two buckets*) sīþe, 435, 11; Rä. 53, 6. v. wealh.

weale-wyrt. v. wealh-wyrt.

wealg; *adj. Nauseous* (? Halliwell gives *wallow* = flat, insipid; *wallowish* = nauseous):—Se wearma weld on gōdum cræftum, đȳ læs hē sié wealg for wlæcnesse, and for đæm weorđe ūt āspiwen (*ne evomatur tepidus*), Past. 58; Swt. 447, 18. [Þi mud is bitter and walh al þat tu cheowest, and hwit mete se þi mahe hokerliche undorfed, þat is wid unlust, warped hit eft ut, H. M. 35, 30. Walhwe swete *supra in* bytter swete, Prompt. Parv. 515. *Icel.* vālgr, volgr *warm, lukewarm.*]

-wealg (-wealh). v. on-wealh.

wealh *an implement that rolls things over* (?), *a harrow*:—Wealh *occa*, Wrt. Voc. ii. 79, 25. Walh, 62, 63. [Cf. *Goth.* us-walugjan περιφέρειν: *O. H. Ger.* bi-walagōn *volutare.*]

wealh; *gen.* weales; *m.* **I.** *a foreigner*, properly *a Celt* (cf. the name *Volcae*, a Celtic tribe mentioned by Caesar):—Walch *barbarus*, Wrt. Voc. ii. 12, 75. Ic (*an axle-tree*) sīþade wīddor, mearcpaþas wala (walas, MS.) træd, mōras pæđde, Exon. Th. 485, 7; Rä. 71, 10. [*Icel.* Valir; *pl. the Celtic* people in France.] ¶ wealh *is found in many proper names.* v. Txts. 489. See also the compounds in wealh-. **I a.** *a Celt of Britain*; the word occurs mostly in pl., Wealas; *gen.* Weala, Walena, *the British, the Welsh*, or *Wales*:—Wealh gafolgelda .cxx. scill. ... Weales hȳd twelfum, L. In. 23; Th. i. 118, 3. Wealh, gif hē hafaþ fīf hȳda, hē bid syxhynde (cf. for relative importance of the Celt and the Englishman, L. R. 2; Th. i. 190, 15–18), 24; Th. i. 118, 10. Gif þeów Wealh Engliscne monnan ofslihđ, 74; Th. i. 148, 14. Hēr Hengest and Æsc gefuhton wiþ Walas (cf. Brettas, l. 17) ... and đa Walas flugon đa Englan swā fȳr, Chr. 473; Erl. 12, 26. Hēr Æđelfriđ ofslōh unrīm Walena (-ana, *v. l.*), and swā wearđ gefyld Augustinus wītegunge, đe hē cwæđ: 'Gif Wealas nellaþ sibbe wiđ ūs, hī sculan æt Seaxana handa farwurþan.' Đār man slōh .cc. preósta, đa cōmon đyder đæt hī scoldon gebiddan for Walena here, 607; Erl. 20, 29. Hī ofslōgon .ii. þūsendo Wala (Walana, *v. l.*), 614; Erl. 20, 37. Wala (Weala, *v. l.*) cyning, 710; Erl. 44, 4. Hēr wæs Wala (Weala, *v. l.*) gefeoht and Defna æt Gafulforda, 823; Erl. 62, 14. Wiþ đæs landes gewrixle đe on Wealum is æt Pendyfig *pro commutatione alterius terre que sita est in Cornubio, ubi ruricole illius pagi barbarico nomine appellant Pendyfig*, Chart. Erl. 192, 5. Hī ofslōgon monige Wealas (Walas, *v. l.*), Chr. 477; Erl. 12, 31. ¶ the word is found as part of place-names, v. Cod. Dip. Kmbl. vi. Index. v. Bret- (Bryt[t]-), Corn-, Norþ-, West-Wealas (-Walas). **I b.** *a Roman*:—Weala sunderriht *jus Quiritum* (cf. Rōmwara sundorriht, Wrt. Voc. ii. 49, 11, reht Rōmwala, Rtl. 189, 13, which translate the same phrase), Wrt. Voc. i. 20, 64. [*O. H. Ger.* walah *Romanus.*] **II.** *a slave, servant.* Cf. the derivation of *slave* from the name of a people:—Mīn weal sprecđ *meum mancipium loquitur*, mines weales sunu, mīnum weale ic timbrige hūs, mīnne weal ic belādige, eá lā đū mīn weal, sāw wel, fram mīnum weale ic underfēng fela gōd, mine wealas (*mancipia*) eriaþ, mīnra þeówra manna (*mancipiorum*) æceras, Ælfc. Gr. 15; Zup. 101, 13–21. Đes wīsa weal (*mancipium*), 6, 4; Zup. 19, 8: 6, 3; Zup. 18, 16. Đæs weales (*v. ll.* weles, wieles; đrǣles, Lind.: esnes, Rush.) hlāford *dominus servi illius*, Mt. Kmbl. 24, 50: Shrn. 154, 22. Đrittegum geárum ne gestilde nǣfre stefen cearciendes wǣnes ne ceoriendes wales *for thirty years the sound of creaking wain and chiding thrall never ceased*, Lchdm. iii. 430, 34. Ne hȳ ne wē ne underfōn ōđres wealh ne ōđres þeóf, L. Eth. ii. 6; Th. i. 288, 4. Wealas *servi*, Gen. 21, 25. Đis folc đe ūre wealas syndon, Ex. 14, 5. Wē đe nǣron wurđe beón his wealas gecīgde, Homl. Th. ii. 316, 23. Weala wīn *crudum vinum*, ... hlāforda wīn *honorarium vinum*, Wrt. Voc. i. 27, 55, 57. Genam Abimelech wealas and wylna (*servos et ancillas*), Gen. 20, 14. Ic (*a skin which furnishes thongs*) fæste binde swearte wealas (*slaves* or *strangers, captives*; Aldhelm's riddle has: Nexibus horrendis homines constringere possum), hwīlum sēllan men, Exon. Th. 393, 22; Rä. 13, 4. [Ælc þrel and ælc wælh wurđe iuroeid, Laym. 14852.] v. hors-, hund-, scip-wealh; weale, wilh. **II a.** *a shameless person.* v. wealian, wealh-word:—Walana *protervorum*, Hpt. Gl. 527, 22.

weal-hāt. v. weall-hāt.

wealh-basu(-o) *foreign scarlet, vermilion*:—Wealhbaso *vermiculo*, Wrt. Voc. ii. 77, 21. Wealhbasu, Anglia xiii. 29, 56. [*The passage glossed in both is* Ald. 15. *In glossing the same passage* wealcbasewere (weolc-(?) v. weoloc-basu; *but* cf. wealc-stōd *for* wealh-stōd, 463, 42) *occurs*, Hpt. Gl. 431, 32.]

Wealh-cyn[n], es; *n. The Celtic race*:—Đa land đe ic on Wealcynne (*the Celts of the south-west*) hæbbe būtan Triconscīre, Chart. Th. 488, 26. Hig gegaderadan mycle fyrde mid Walkynne (*the Celts of Wales*), Chr. 1055; Erl. 188, 33. Griffin wæs kyning ofer eall Wealcyn, 1063; Erl. 195, 12. v. Norþ-Wealhcynn.

Wealh-færeld, es; *n. A 'Welsh' expedition*, a term applied to forces defending the Welsh Marches (?):—Liberabo monasterium (*Blockley, Worcestershire*) a pastu et refectione illorum hominum quos Saxonice nominamus Walhfæreld and heora fæsting, Cod. Dip. Kmbl. ii. 60, 29. v. next word.

Wealh-gefēra, -gerēfa, an; *m. A count of the Welsh Marches* (?), *the commander of the* Wealh-færeld (?):—Đȳ ilcan gēre forđferde Wulfrīc cynges horsđegn; se wæs eác Wealhgefēra (*other MSS. have* -gerēfa. Kemble, taking the latter reading, says: 'I am disposed to believe that he was a royal reeve to whose care Alfred's Welsh serfs were committed, and who exercised a superintendence over them in some one or all of the royal domains,' Saxons in England, ii. 179. See the first passage under Wealh-cyn), Chr. 897; Erl. 96, 17, and note.

wealh-hafoc, es; *m. A foreign hawk, a gerfalcon*; herodius (v. *erodius* gerfawcune, Wrt. Voc. i. 188, col. 2: jarfawkon, 220, col. 2):—Walhhabuc *falc*(o), Txts. 61, 826. Walchhabuc, uualhhaebuc, uualh[h]ebuc, ualchefuc *herodius*, 67, 1016. Gōshafuc *accipiter*, wealhhafuc *herodius*, spearhafuc *alietum*, Wrt. Voc. i. 280, 18–20: ii. 42, 67. Wealhhafoces hūs *herodii domus*, Ps. Spl. 103, 19. Ða fugelas *nocticoraces* hätton wǣron in wealhhafoces gelīcnesse (*vulturibus similes*), Nar. 16, 13. Wealhhafeca *falconum*, Wrt. Voc. ii. 87, 68: 37, 23. [*O. H. Ger.* walucl apuh *herodius*.]

wealh-hnutu; *gen.* -hnyte; *f. A foreign nut, walnut*:—Hnutbeam oððe walhhnutu *nux*, Wrt. Voc. ii. 60, 23. [On a walnot withoute is a bitter barke, Piers P. 11, 251. Walnote *avelana*, Prompt. Parv. 574. A walnotte *auellanum*, a walnott-tree *auellanus*, Cath. Angl. 407 (see note). Walnot *auelena*, Wülck. Gl. 647, 25. Walnottre *auelana*, 646, 15. A walnutte and the nutte *avelana*, 715, 26. A walnote *moracia*, 596, 38. Cf. A walshenote shale, Chauc. H. F. 1281. *Icel.* val-hnot.]

wealh-land, es; *n.* I. *a foreign land*:—Ǣghwǣr eorðan ðǣr wit earda leás mid wealandum wunian (winnan, MS.) sceoldon (cf. mē ellþeódigne, l. 20), Cd. Th. 163, 30; Gen. 2706. II. *Normandy* (cf. *Icel.* í Vallandi er sīðan var kallat Norðmandi):—Com Eádweard hider tō lande of Weallande (fram begeondan sǣ, *v. l.*), Chr. 1040; Erl. 167, 27. [*O. H. Ger.* Walho-lant *Gallia*.]

wealh-more(-u), -mora, an; *f. m. A foreign root, carrot, parsnip*:—Walhmore, uualhmorae *pastinaca*, Txts. 85, 1502. Wealmore, Wrt. Voc. ii. 67, 62: i. 286, 27: Lchdm. i. 120, 8. Wealmora, Wrt. Voc. i. 79, 58: *daucus*, 31, 43. Waldmora *cariota*, 31, 46. v. wilisc.

wealh-sāda (?), an; *m. A noose for binding a captive* or *slave* (? cf. Exon. Th. 393, 22; Rä. 13, 4, *given under* wealh, II):—Forhȳddan oferhygde mē inwitgyrene, wrāðan wealsādan *absconderunt superbi laqueos mihi*, Ps. Th. 139, 5.

wealh-stod, es; *m. An interpreter*:—Wealhstod *interpres*, Wrt. Voc. i. 86, 60: Ælfc. Gr. 9, 26; Zup. 51, 14. I. *one who serves as a medium between speakers of different languages*:—Se cyning gerehte his witan on heora āgenum gereorde ðæs bisceopes bodunge, and wæs his wealhstod, for ðan ðe hē wel cūþe Scyttysc, Homl. Skt. ii. 26, 67. Walhstod, Bd. 3, 3; S. 526, 2. Hē (*Jerome*) is se fyrmesta wealhstod betwux Hebrēiscum and Grēcum and Lēdenwarum, Homl. Th. i. 436, 16. Se hālga biscop hine hādode tō messepreóste, and his wealhstod tō diácone, Homl. Skt. i. 3, 525. Nōman hī him wealhstodas (*interpretes*) of Franclände, Bd. 1, 25; S. 486, 23: Homl. Th. ii. 128, 19. II. *an interpreter of written language, a translator*:—Ælfrēd kuning wæs wealhstod ðisse bēc, Bt. proem.; Fox viii. 1. Ðæra hundseofontigra wealhstoda gesetnyssa, Anglia viii. 336, 4. Wealcstoda *interpretum* (*praestantissimus, Hieronymus*, Ald. 33), Hpt. Gl. 463, 42. Hié hié (*books*) wendon ðurh wīse wealhstodas on hiora āgen geðióde, Past. pref.; Swt. 7, 4. III. *an interpreter* of a subject, *an expounder*:—Wealhstod *interpres* (*divinae legis*, Ald. 64), Wrt. Voc. ii. 85, 79: 47, 2. Līfes wealhstod, Cd. Th. 211, 7; Exod. 522. IV. *a mediator*:—Se wealhstod Godes and monna, ðæt is Crist *Dei hominumque mediator*, Past. 3; Swt. 33, 11. V. the word occurs as a proper name:—Ðām folcum ðe eardiaþ be westan Sæferne is Wealhstod biscop *eis populis qui ultra amnem Sabrinam ad occidentem habitant, Valchstod* (Ual-, *v. l.*) *episcopus*, Bd. 5, 23; S. 646, 21.

Wealh-þeód, e; *f. The Welsh people*:—Ðis is seó gerǣdnes ðe Angelcynnes witan and Wealhþeóde rǣdboran gesetton, L. O. D. proem.; Th. i. 352, 1.

wealh-word, es; *n. A wanton word*:—Ic eom ondetta ðæt ic onfēng on mīnne mūð wealworda, Anglia xi. 98, 37. v. wealh, II a, wealian.

wealh-wyrt, e; *f. Wall-wort, dwarf elder*; the word glosses *ebulum* and *intula*:—Walhwyrt, uualhuyrt, ualuyrt *ebulum, elleus*, Txts. 59, 714. Wealwyrt *ebulum*, Wrt. Voc. ii. 28, 75. Walwyrt, i. 30, 58. Wealwyrt ł ellenwyrt *ebule* ł *ecbulum*, Lchdm. iii. 302, col. 1. Wælwyrt *vel* ellenwyrt. Genim ðās wyrte ðe man *ebulum* and ōðrum naman ellenwyrte nemneþ, and eác sume men wealwyrt hātaþ, i. 202, 3–6. Uualhwyrt *intula*, Txts. 69, 1075. Wealewyrt, Wrt. Voc. ii. 48, 71. Walwyrt, Wülck. Gl. 299, 8 (*this* gloss is omitted by Wright): Lchdm. iii. 303, col. 1. Wealwyrt, ii. 64, 27: 70, 2. Wælwyrt, iii. 30, 13. Wealwyrte wyrttruman, ii. 108, 7. Wealwyrte moran, 264, 20. Wælwyrte, i. 354, 13. Genim wealwyrt, 66, 14. Nime wealwyrt nioþowearde, 118, 2. Wælwyrt, 38, 17. [Walwurt *ebulum*, Wülck. Gl. 555, 10. Walwort *ebulus*, 579, 33. Walwortte *ebolus*, 712, 24. Wallewurte *ebula*.]

wealian; *p.* ode *To be impudent, bold, wanton.* v. wealh, II a:—Hē wealode mid wordum, and sǣde ðæt hē wolde his wifes brūcan on ðām unālȳfedum tīman, Homl. Skt. i. 12, 48.

weá-lic; *adj. Miserable*:—Sumum ðæt gegongeþ, ðæt se endestæf weálīc weorþeþ; sceal hine wulf etan, Exon. Th. 328, 4; Vy. 12. v. wā-līc.

wealig. v. welig.

weall, es; *m.* I. *a wall* that is made, *wall* of a building, of a town, *side* of a cave:—Weal *murus*, Wrt. Voc. i. 36, 35: Exon. Th. 281, 23; Jul. 650. Ofer wealles hrōf *super muros*, Ps. Th. 54, 9. Wealles rihtungþrēd *perpendiculum*, Wrt. Voc. i. 39, 64. Seó heánnes ðæs walles (*parietis*), Bd. 2, 14; S. 517, 31. Heora gewinnan tugan hī ādūn of ðam wealle (*de muris*) . . . Hig ðā forlǣtan ðone wall (*relicto muro*), 1, 12; S. 481, 22. Andweorc tō wealle *cimentum*, Wrt. Voc. i. 85, 27. Tō wealle *ad moenia*, Kent. Gl. 287. Hē æfter recede wlāt, hwearf be wealle, Beo. Th. 3150; B. 1573. Ofer mīnre burge weall (*murum*), Ps. Th. 17, 28: Cd. Th. 101, 3; Gen. 1676: Judth. Thw. 23, 38; Jud. 161. Wið ðone weall *murotenus*, Wrt. Voc. ii. 57, 63. Wið ðæs recedes weal, Beo. Th. 658; B. 326. Wall īserne, Cd. Th. 231, 15; Dan. 247. Tō hwȳ tōwurpe ðū weal (*maceriam*) his, Ps. Spl. 79, 13. Ðā gewrohte hē weall mid turfum (*vallum*, v. Bd. 1, 5) and brēd weall ðǣr onufan, Chr. 189; Erl. 9, 25. Weallas *moenia*, Wrt. Voc. ii. 54, 62: *muri*, Jos. 6, 20. Ðæt wæter stōd an twā healfa ðære strǣte swilce twēgen hēge weallas *erat aqua quasi murus*, Ex. 14, 22. Under wealla hleó, Cd. Th. 259, 13; Dan. 691. Binnan ðære ylcan cyricean weallum (*muris*), Bd. 5, 20; S. 641, 43. On ceastre weallum beworhte *in civitatem munitam*, Ps. Th. 59, 8: Cd. Th. 145, 21; Gen. 2409. Ofer ðære burge wallas (*muros*), Bd. 3, 16; S. 543, 2. Ðū hī betweónum wætera weallas lǣddest, Ps. Th. 105, 9. Ealle his weallas *omnes macerias ejus*, 88, 33. Uallas *menia*, Rtl. 124, 3. II. *a natural wall, a steep hill, a cliff.* v. weall-clif (cf. *O. Sax.*:—Hwō sie ina fan ēnumu kliƀe wurpin, oƀar enna berges wal, Hēl. 2676. Fan themu walle niðar werpan, 2684. Sie an hōhan wal stigun, stēn endi berg, 3117):—Munt is hine ymbūtan, geáp gylden weal, Salm. Kmbl. 511; Sal. 256. Cwom wundorlīcu wiht (*the sun*) ofer wealles hrōf (*over the mountain top*), Exon. Th. 412, 1; Rä. 30, 7. Draca beorges getrūwode, wīges and wealles (*the cliff in which the firedrake's cave was*), Beo. Th. 4635; B. 2323. Norð-Denum stōd egesa, ānra gehwylcum ðara ðe of wealle wōp gehȳrdon (*to each that heard the cry coming from the hill on which the hall stood* (?)), 1574; B. 785. Nō wyrm on wealle leng bīdan wolde *the serpent would not longer wait in the hill, in its cave*, 4604; B. 2307. Geseah hē māððumsigla fela, gold glitinian grunde getenge, wundur on wealle, 5511; B. 2759. Se ðe inne gehȳdde wræte under wealle, 6112; B. 3060: 6197; B. 3103. Æt wealle, 5045; B. 2526. Geseah be wealle stondan stānbogan, streám ūt þonan brecan of beorge, 5077; B. 2542: 5425; B. 2716. Of wealle (*the sea-cliff*) geseah weard, se ðe holmclifu healdan scolde, 463; B. 229. Winneþ wǣg wið wealle, Exon. Th. 383, 33; Rä. 4, 20. Ǣniges monnes wīg forbūgan oððe on weal fleón (*flee to the hill*) līce beorgan, Vald. 1, 15. Weallas him wiþre healdaþ, Exon. Th. 336, 24; Gn. Ex. 54. Ic sǣnæssas geseón mihte, windige weallas (*wind-beaten cliffs*), Beo. Th. 1148; B. 572: Cd. Th. 214, 19; Exod. 571. Ic wiht (*a rake*) geseah, seó wǣþeþ geond weallas (*among the hills* (?)), wyrte sēceþ, Exon.Th. 416, 27; Rä. 35, 5. [*O. Sax. O. Frs.* wal *a wall. From Latin* vallum.] v. bord-, breóst-, burh-, ceaster-, eorþ-, fore-, grund-, holm-, port-, sǣ-, scīd-, scild-, stæð-, stān-, streám-weall.

weall, e; *f. Fervour*:—Wealle, wylm *fervorem, ardorem* (devotionis fervorem, Ald. 34), Hpt. Gl. 465, 37. v. weall-hāt.

weall, es; *n.* (?) *Boiled* or *mulled wine*:—*Defrutum*, i. *vinum* medo geswēt *vel* weall (cf. gesoden wīn *defrutum vinum*, i. 27, 62. Coerin *defrutum*, cyren oððe āwylled wīn *dulcisapa*, ii. 25, 10, 69. Āsodenes wīnes *careni*, Hpt. Gl. 408, 42), Wrt. Voc. ii. 138, 24. Nīwes ł gesodenes wealles *defruti* ł *medoni*, Hpt. Gl. 414, 1. Wealle *defruto, vino*, 520, 38.

weallan; *p.* weóll, *pl.* weóllon; *pp.* weallen. I. of water, &c. issuing from a source, *to well, bubble forth, spring out, flow*:—Ic wealle *bullio*, Ælfc. Gr. 30, 5; Zup. 192, 3. Of ðæm neáhmunte wealleþ hlūter wæter, ðonne drincaþ ða menn ðæt *cadente rivo puram ex vicino monte potant aquam*, Nar. 31, 7. Of ðǣm beorgum wilð seó eá Eufrates *fluvius Euphrates de radice montis effusus*, Ors. 1, 1; Swt. 14, 10, 29. Ðǣr hió (*the Nile*) ǣrest up wielð *prope fontem*, Swt. 12, 24. [Ðæt treów ðæt man on heorþe leges, for ðare mycele hǣten ðe ðæt treów barned beoþ, þāre wylþ ūt of ðan ende water, Lchdm. iii. 128, 6.] Rēcels of ðæra treówa telgan weól, Nar. 26, 22. Swāt ȳðum weóll *the blood welled out in streams*, Beo. Th. 5380; B. 2693: Andr. Kmbl. 2552; An. 1277: 2482; An. 1242. Weól, Exon. Th. 182, 23; Gū. 1314. Wiþ ðon ðe men blōd upp wealle þurh his mūð, Lchdm. i. 74, 14. Hē lēt teáras geótan, weallan wǣgdropan, Exon. Th. 165, 17; Gū. 1030: Andr. Kmbl. 3005; An. 1505. Mon geseah weallan blōd of eorþan *sanguis e terra visus est manare*, Ors. 4, 3; Swt. 162, 6. Geseah ic balzamum of ðǣm treówum ūt weallan *video opobalsamum arborum ramis manans*, Nar. 27, 23. II. of the source, *to well* with, *flow* with, (1) with a noun:—Ān wielle weól blōde *flumen sanguine effluxit*, Ors. 4, 7; Swt. 184, 21. Flōr ātre weól, Cd. Th. 284, 8; Sat. 318. Flōd blōde weól, Beo. Th. 2848; B. 1422. Weóll, 4282; B. 2138. Wið ðon ðe mon blōde wealle þurh his mūð, Lchdm. iii. 44, 22. Wæs on blōde brim weallende, Beo. Th. 1699; B. 847. (2) absolute:—Benna weallaþ *wounds bleed*, Andr. Kmbl. 2810; An. 1407. Hit ongan rīnan . . . and seó eorðe weóll ongeán ðam heofonlīcan flōde *it began to rain . . . and the earth sent forth its waters to meet the waters of heaven*, Wulfst. 206, 21. Weóllon wælbenna, Cd. Th. 208, 30; Exod. 491. III. implying abundance, (1) *to swarm, exist in large numbers*:—Him weóllon maðan geond ealne ðone līchaman, Homl. Th. i. 472, 30. (2) of production in large numbers or great quantity, *to swarm* with, *flow* with:—Land ðe weóll meolce and hunie *terra quae lacte et melle manabat*, Num. 16, 13. His gesceapu maðan weóllon, Homl. Th. i. 86, 10: Homl. Skt. i. 4, 212. Weallende *scaturiens* (*vermibus*, Ald. 70), Hpt. Gl. 519, 34: *scatens* (*vermibus*, Ald. 202), Wrt. Voc. ii. 96, 7. IV. of violent movement, *to boil, rage, heave*:—Geofon ýþum weól wintres wylme, Beo. Th. 1035; B. 515. Holm storme weól, 2267; B. 1131. Hreðer ǽðme weóll *his breast heaved*, 5180; B. 2593. Ða ýþa weóllan and wēddan ðæs sǽs *furentibus undis pelagi*, Bd. 3, 15; S. 541, 39, 42. Brim weallende, Andr. Kmbl. 3147; An. 1576. Ðæt gebrec ðæs weallendes (*ferventis*) sǽs, Bd. 5, 1; S. 614, 4. Wado weallende, Beo. Th. 1096; B. 546. V. of movement in liquids caused by heat, *to boil* (intrans.), *to be hot*:—Dō ofer fȳr, āwyl; ðonne hit wealle, sing iii Pater noster, Lchdm. ii. 358, 11. Scenc fulne weallendes wæteres, 130, 1. Seóð on weallendon wætere, i. 204, 23. Mid weallendum ele, Homl. Th. i. 58, 27: Ælfc. T. Grn. 16, 16. Weallende wǽte *fervida flumina*, Hpt. Gl. 499, 51. V a. used of a vessel in which a liquid boils:—Seó ǽrene gripu ofer glēda gripe gīfrust wealleþ (-aþ, MS. B.), Salm. Kmbl. 98; Sal. 48. Bæð hāte weól, Exon. Th. 277, 16; Jul. 581. VI. of other than liquids, *to be hot, burn, blaze, rage*:—Wið ðone weallendan bryne ðe weallaþ (-eþ?) on helle, L. C. E. 6; Th. i. 364, 13. Him on breóstum weóll āttor, Beó. Th. 5422; B. 2714. Ān ðæra dǽla is weallende (*the torrid zone*), Lchdm. iii. 260, 21. Se wallenda lēg *furens flamma*, Bd. 2, 7; S. 509, 22. Hē hæfþ weallendene lēg, Blickl. Homl. 61, 35. Weallende fȳr, Cd. Th. 153, 22; Gen. 2542. Weallendum līgum *flammis ferventibus*, Bd. 5, 12; S. 627, 37. Weallende axan, Lchdm. i. 178, 6. Þurh ða weallendan sond *per ferventes sole arenas*, Nar. 6, 9. VII. figuratively, of persons, passions, emotions, *to be fervent, to burn, rage, to be strongly moved*:—Ic wealle *ferueo*, Ælfc. Gr. 26, 5; Zup. 156, 9. Welð *fervet*, Kent. Gl. 665. Hē welð on gōdum cræftum *in virtutibus inardescit*, Past. 58; Swt. 447, 18. Hē metta mid cystignesse wealð *aescarum largitate feruescit*, Scint. 56, 2. Hyge hearde wealleþ, Salm. Kmbl. 126; Sal. 62. Wyrd bið wended hearde, wealleþ (*is zealous*) swīðe geneahhe, 872; Sal. 435. Feóndscipe wealleþ *hatred burns hot*, Exon. Th. 354, 60; Reim. 68. Weallaþ wælnīðas, Beo. Th. 4136; Beo. 2065. Brandhāta nīð weóll on gewitte, Andr. Kmbl. 1537; An. 770. Hreðer innan weóll, beorn breóstsefa *their hearts burnt within them*, Exon. Th. 34, 9; Cri. 539: Beo. Th. 4233; B. 2113. Breóst innan weóll þeóstrum geþoncum, 4652; B. 2331. Weóll him on innan hyge ymb his heortan, Cd. Th. 23, 4; Gen. 353. Se ðe nyle wearmian óð hē wealle (*ut ferveat*), Past. 58; Swt. 447, 8. Suā sculon ða hierdas weallan ymb ða geornfulnesse ðære inneran ðearfe his hiéremonna *sic pastores erga interiora studia subditorum suorum ferveant*, 18; Swt. 137, 11. Hire oninnan ongan weallan wyrmes geþeaht, Cd. Th. 37, 15; Gen. 590. Weallende *furibundus*, Wrt. Voc. ii. 36, 37: *fervidus*, 147, 84: Lchdm. iii. 188, 25. Se mǽra wæs hāten weallende wulf (cf. (?) Wōden), Salm. Kmbl. 423; Sal. 212. Lēg, weallende wiga, Exon. Th. 61, 15; Cri. 985. Hē wæs weallende on geleáfan (*fide fervens*), Bd. 3, 2; S. 524, 17. Weallende spelboda, Blickl. Homl. 165, 33. Manegum wæs hāt æt heortan hyge weallende, Andr. Kmbl. 3415; An. 1711. Ðeós gītsunc weallende byrnð, Met. 8, 45. Mid weallendre lufe, Wulfst. 286, 11. Sorge weallende, Beo. Th. 4919; B. 2464. Weallende weán, Exon. Th. 139, 2; Gū. 587. Hē geseah ealle witon on þeáwum scīnende and on gāste weallende, Homl. Skt. ii. 23 b, 86. VIII. *trans.* (=willan?) *To roll, turn*:—Hine on lyfte līfgetwinnan sweopum seolfrenum swīðe weallaþ, óð ðæt him bān blīcaþ, blēdaþ ǽdran, Salm. Kmbl. 288; Salm. 143. [*O. Sax.* wallan *to well; to boil, burn* (fig.): *O. Frs.* walla: *O. H. Ger.* wallan *scatere, bullire, fervescere*: *Icel.* vella *to boil; to swarm.*] v. ā-, be-, ge-weallan; heoru-weallende, for-weallen.

weall-clif, es; *n. A steep cliff*:—Hī scufon wyrm ofer weallclif, lēton wǽg niman, Beo. Th. 6255; B. 3132. v. weall, II.

weall-dīc (?), e; *f. A walled ditch* (?):—Andlang ðære wealdīc, Cod. Dip. Kmbl. v. 346, 21, 22. Cf. Usque la diche walle; et sic per fossatum, iii. 408, 10.

weall-dor, es; *n. A door in a wall*:—Ðū eart ðæt wealldor; þurh ðē Freá on ðās eorþan ūt sīðade, Exon. Th. 21, 1; Cri. 328.

weall-fæsten[n], es; *n.* I. *a walled stronghold, a fortress*:—Ða gesceádaþ ðæt land westan and eástan óð ðæt weallfæsten, Cod. Dip. Kmbl. ii. 86, 27. Hē ongan ceastre timbran, ðæt wæs weallfæstenna ǽrest, Cd. Th. 64, 31; Gen. 1058. II. *a wall for defence, a bulwark*:—Forhwan ðū tōwurpe weallfæsten his? *quid deposuisti maceriam ejus?* Ps. Th. 79, 12. Wicon weallfæsten, wǽgas burston, Cd. Th. 208, 14; Exod. 483. Wyrceþ wæter wealfæsten (*erat aqua quasi murus a dextra eorum et laeva*, Ex. 14, 22), 195, 27; Exod. 283.

weall-geat, es; *n. A gate in a wall*:—Hié gegān hæfdon tō ðam weallgeate *they had reached the city's gate*, Judth. Thw. 23, 26; Jud. 141. Tō weallgeatum, Andr. Kmbl. 2407; An. 1205.

weall-gebrec, es; *n. A breaking down of a wall*:—Hié noldon ðæs weallgebreces geswīcan *donec perfractis muris*, Ors. 3, 9; Swt. 134, 30.

weall-geweorc, es; *n. Wall-work*, (1) *wall-building*:—Gang tō ðīnum weallgeweorce (*a monastery was being built*), Homl. Skt. i. 6, 173. Sī hit ǽlces þinges freoh būtan ferdfare and walgeworc (cf. burh-bōt) and brycgeworc, Cod. Dip. Kmbl. iii. 5, 13. Hē gesette hī tō his weallgeweorcum, ðæt hī worhton his burga (*in aedificationibus urbium suarum*), Anglia x. 91, 96. (2) *the destruction of walls*:—*Aries* byð ram betwux sceápum and ram tō wealgeweorce, Ælfc. Gr. 5; Zup. 12, 5. v. weallweorc.

weall-hāt; *adj. Boiling hot, red-hot*:—Ācele ðū wealhāt īsen ðonne hit furþum sié of fȳre ātogen on wīne, Lchdm. ii. 256, 15. [He bed bringen forð brune wallinde bres, and healden hit se walhat up on hire heaued, Jul. 31, 4. Wiþþ wallhat herrtess lufe, Orm. 14196.]

weallian *to wall.* v. ge-weallod.

weallian; *p.* ode. I. *to wander, roam*:—Weallaþ swā niéten feldgangende, feoh būtan gewitte, se þurh ðone cantic ne can Crist geherian, Salm. Kmbl. 44; Sal. 22. II. *to go as a pilgrim*:—Of earde weallige hē wīde and dǽdbōte dō ǽfre ða hwīle ðe hē libbe *a patria longe peregrinetur, et poenitentiam usque agat, quamdiu vivet*, L. M. I. 44; Th. ii. 276, 31. Deóplīc dǽdbōt bið ðæt lǽwede man his wǽpna ālecge and weallige bærfōt wīde, L. Pen. 10; Th. ii. 280, 18. Oferbecumendum wealligendum þearfum se abbud mid gebrōþrum gearwian hȳrsumnysse *supervenientibus peregrinis pauperibus abbas cum fratribus exhibeant obsequium*, Anglia xiii. 439, 1060. [*O. H. Ger.* wallōn *errare, ambulare, meare, pervagari*: *Ger.* wallen *to travel*; wall-fahrt *pilgrimage*: *Icel.* vallari *a tramp, vagrant.*]

weall-līm, es; *m. Mortar*:—Hig hæfdon tygelan for stān and tyrwan for wealliim *habuerunt lateres pro saxis et bitumen pro caemento*, Gen. 11, 3.

weall-stān, es; *m. A stone for building*:—Ðū eart se weallstān ðe ða wyrhtan wiðwurpon tō weorce (*lapidem, quem reprobaverunt aedificantes*, Mt. 21, 42), Exon. Th. 1, 2; Cri. 2. Wrætlīc is ðes wealstān *marvellous is this masonry*, 476, 1; Ruin. 1. Ceastra, wrætlīc weallstāna geweorc *cities, wondrous works of stones*, Menol. Fox 465; Gn. C. 3.

weall-steall, es; *m. A place where there are buildings*:—Ðisne wealsteal *this spot where the walls stand* (cf. weallas stondaþ, 291, 3; Wand. 76), Exon. Th. 291, 26; Wand. 88.

weall-steáp; *adj.* I. *high as regards its walls* or *buildings, with lofty walls*:—Hié on weallsteápe burg (cf. seó steápe burh on Sennar, 102, 15; Gen. 1700) wlītan meahton, Cd. Th. 145, 7; Gen. 2402. II. *with lofty cliffs, lofty.* v. weall, II:—Hié oferfōran weallsteápan hleoðu, Cd. Th. 108, 8; Gen. 1803.

weall-stellung, -stilling, -stylling, e; *f. The putting a wall in order, repairing of a wall.* v. burh-bōt:—Tō ānes æceres brǽde on wealstillinge (cf. weall-geweorc) and tō ðære wære gebirigeaþ xvi. hīda; gif ǽlc hīd byþ be ānum men gemannod, ðonne mæg man gesettan ǽlce gyrde mid feówer mannum. Ðonne gebyreþ tō twēntigan gyrdan on wealstillinge hundeahtig hīda, and tō ðam furlange gebyrgeaþ ōþer healf hund hīda and x hīda . . . Tō fīf furlangum gebyreþ ymbeganges eahta hunda hīda on wealstyllinge . . . Tō eahta furlangum ymbeganges wealstyllinge hund eahtig hīda and .xii. hund hīda *for one acre's breadth* (22 yds.) *in the matter of repairing a wall and for the keeping of it* 16 *hides are requisite; if each hide is assessed at one man, then four men can be appointed to each pole.* 80 *hides are requisite for the putting in order of twenty poles of wall and for the furlong* 160 *hides . . . For a circuit of five furlongs* 800 *hides are necessary . . . For a circuit of eight furlongs* 1280 *hides*, Hickes' Diss. p. 109.

weall-þrǽd, es; *m. A plumb-line*:—Walðrǽd *perpendicula*, Wrt. Voc. ii. 91, 68. v. rihtung-þrǽd.

weallung, e; *f.* I. *agitation*:—Se drænc is gōd wið heáfodece and wið brægenes hwyrfnesse and weallunge *the potion is good against headache and against giddiness and cerebral excitement*, Lchdm. iii. 70, 20. II. *fervour*:—Wyrðelīcre wallunge lufes *digno fervore fidei*, Rtl. 64, 26.

weall-wala, an; *m. A wall-foundation* (?):—Hygerōf gebond weallwalan wīrum wundrum tōgædere, Exon. Th. 477, 9; Ruin. 21.

weall-weg (?), es; *m. A walled road* (?):—On ðane ealdan walweg, Cod. Dip. Kmbl. v. 78, 17: 138, 4.

weall-weorc, es; *n. Wall-work, building*:—Ða gebrōðra eodon tō ðam weallweorce, Homl. Th. ii. 166, 14, 25. v. weall-geweorc, *and next word.*

weall-wyrhta, an; *m. A wall-wright, a mason, builder*:—Wealwyrhta *cimentarius*, Wrt. Voc. i. 19, 15: 85, 27. Fram wealwyrhtan (-wyrhtum, Wrt. Voc. ii. 79, 6 = a cementario, Ald. 31) *a cimentario*, Anglia xiii. 32, 106. Weallwyrhtan *cimentarii*, Wrt. Voc. ii. 15, 83.

weal-more(-u, -a), wealowigan *to fade*, wealowigan *to roll*, wealsāda, -wealt [*Icel.* valtr], -wealtian, -weálu. v. wealh-more, wealwian *to fade*, wealwian *to roll*, wealh-sāda, seonu-, un-wealt, seonuwealtian, wǽl.

wealwian; *p.* ode *To fade, wither* (Halliwell gives *wallow* = to fade away, as a Somerset word):—Hæfð se Ælmihtiga ðæt gewrixle geset, ðe nū wunian sceal, wyrta grōwan, leáf grēnian, ðæt on hærfest eft hrēst and wealuwaþ (cf. fealwaþ, Bt. 21; Fox 74, 23), Met. 11, 58. Ðǽr ðǽr hit gefrēt ðæt hit hraþost weaxan mæg and latost wealowigan (wealowian, Cott. MS.) *ubi quantum earum natura queat, cito exarescere atque interire non possint*, Bt. 34, 10; Fox 148, 22. [Welewen *marcescere*,

Wick. Is. 19, 6. Man welewith as flouris of hay, P. R. L. P. 173, 56. Al welwed and wasted þo worþelych leues, Allit. Pms. 106, 475. See also *welewed* in Halliwell's Dict.] v. un-forwealwod.

wealwian; *p.* ode *To wallow, roll* (intrans.):—Ðonne tyht hié ðæt ierre ðæt hié wealwiaþ on ða wēdenheortnesse *impellente ira in mentis vesaniam devolvuntur*, Past. 40; Swt. 289, 6. Hē wealwode on ðæm gedrōfum wætere *in lutosa aqua semetipsum volvit*, 54; Swt. 421, 8. His hors feól wealwigende geond ða eorðan . . . mid ðam ðe hit swā wealwode, Homl. Skt. ii. 26, 207. Ða felga hangiaþ on ðām spācan, þeáh hī eallunga wealowigen on ðære eorþan, Bt. 39, 7; Fox 222, 14. Ðæt hors ongan walwian and on gehwæþere sīdan gelōmlīce hit oferweorpan (*in diversum latus vicissim sese volvere*), Bd. 3, 9; S. 533, 40. Micel stān wealwiende of ðam heáhan munte, Bt. 6; Fox 14, 28. [Hie secheð to þe fule floddri and þaron waleweð, O. E. Homl. ii. 37, 27: H. M. 13, 34. They walweden as pigges in a poke, Chauc. Reeves T. 358. Þe grete wawes walweth (walketh, *v. l.*), Piers P. 8, 41.] v. be-wealwian; wilwian.

weal-word, -wyrt. v. wealh-word, -wyrt.

weá-mēt[t], e: -mēttu(-o); *indecl. f. Anger, wrath, passion, irascibility*:—Se feórða heáfodleahter is weámēt, Homl. Th. ii. 218, 21. Se feórða leahtor is weámēt, ðæt se man nāge his mōdes geweald, ac būton ǣlcere foresceáwunge his yrsunge gefremaþ, 220, 12. Wē sceolon oferwinnan weámētte mid wīslīcum geðylde, 222, 21. Ne gerīsaþ heom hræde weámētta, L. I. P. 10; Th. ii. 318, 32. [Cf. Heo weore god ȝif heo neore to wamed. Anan se he wes wrað wið eni he hine wolde slæn, Laym. 6368.]

weá-mōd; *adj. Angry, wrathful, choleric, passionate*:—Se ðe wǣre weámōd, weorðe se geþyldmōd, Wulfst. 70, 7. Ne rēce ðū nā weámōdes wīfes worda *you are not to care for an angry woman's words*, Prov. Kmbl. 48. Ða weámōdan and ða grambǣran *iracundi*, Past. 40; Swt. 289, 4: Wulfst. 40, 17. Weámōdum *turbulentis*, Germ. 395, 13. [Ne beo þu wemod ne ouermodi, O. E. Homl. i. 5, 26. Pellican is a leane fowel, so weamod and so wreðful þet hit sleað ofte uor grome his owune briddes, A. R. 118, 8.]

weámōdness, e; *f. Anger, passionateness, irascibility*:—Se feórða leahtor is *ira*, ðæt is on Englisc weámōdnyss, Homl. Skt. i. 16, 286: Wulfst. 68, 15. Ðonne hié berǣsaþ on suelce weámōdnesse hié sindon tō oferbūganne *qui in eodem furoris impetu declinandi sunt*, Past. 40; Swt. 295, 20. Forlȳst se yrsigenda wer his āgene sāwle þurh weámōdnysse, Homl. Skt. ii. 28, 149: Anglia xi. 113, 32, 38. Ðære sāwle miht is ðæt heó sylf beó geðyldi and ǣlce weámōdnysse fram hire āwyrpe, Basil admn. 3; Norm. 38, 27. [*Ira*, þet is on Englisc wemodnesse, O. E. Homl. i. 103, 19.]

wear. v. wearr.

weard, es; *m.* I. *a guard, warder, watchman, sentinel*:—Ðara wearda sum geseah ðæt of heofonum com ān læs feówertig wuldorbeága . . . ðā gecerde se weard tō Criste, Shrn. 62, 5–8. Weard Scyldinga, se ðe holmclifu healdan scolde, Beo. Th. 464; B. 229: Ps. 126, 2. Se weard (*the angel at the gate of Eden*), Cd. Th. 58, 21; Gen. 949. Ða weardas *custodes*, Mt. Kmbl. 28, 4, 11. Ða weardas heóldon ðæs cwearternes duru, Homl. Th. ii. 382, 4. Snelle gemundon weardas wīgleóð, Cd. Th. 191, 27; Exod. 221. Hine twēgen ymb weardas wacedon, Exon. Th. 109, 6; Gū. 86. Ða byrgene besettan mid wacelum weardum (*custodibus*), Homl. Th. ii. 262, 8: Mt. Kmbl. 27, 66: Blickl. Homl. 177, 29. Salomones reste wæs mid weardum ymbseted, ðæt wæs mid syxtigum werum, 11, 16. Hē sette him weardas ofer, Jos. 10, 18: Homl. Skt. i. 11, 210. I a. fig.:—Him oninnan oferhygda dǣl weaxeþ, ðonne se weard swefeþ, sāwele hyrde, Beo. Th. 3487; B. 1741. Geác, sumeres weard, Exon. Th. 309, 8; Seef. 54. Bānhūses weard *the mind*, Cd. Th. 211, 9; Exod. 523. II. *a guardian, protector, lord*:—Ðære cneórisse wæs Cainan aldordēma, weard and wīsa, Cd. Th. 70, 22; Gen. 1157. Ðū (*Nebuchadnezzar*) hæleðum eart āna eallum eorðbūendum weard and wīsa, 251, 19; Dan. 566. Engla weard (*Lucifer*), 2, 20; Gen. 22. Cyning, beáhhorda weard, Beo. Th. 1847; B. 921. Rīces weard, 2784; B. 1390. Folces weard, 5019; B. 2513. ¶ the term is often used of the Deity:—Weard *servatorem* (*animae tuae*, Prov. 24, 12), Kent. Gl. 932. Rodera weard, Cd. Th. 1, 2; Gen. 1. Līfes weard, 9, 20; Gen. 144. Sigores weard, Exon. Th. 15, 29; Cri. 243. Wuldres weard, 33, 17; Cri. 527. Heofonrīces weard, Andr. Kmbl. 104; An. 52. [*Goth.* daura-wards: *O. Sax.* ward *a guard, a guardian*: *O. H. Ger.* wart *custos*: *Icel.* vörðr.] v. bāt-, botl-, brego-, brycg-, burh-, carcern-, cweartern-, dæg-, drihten-, duru-, edisc-, eorþ-, ēðel-, fore-, forþ-, freoðu-, gold-, gūþ-, hæg-, heáfod-, healf-, hearg-, heofon-, hof-, hord-, hȳð-, irfe-, land-, lāst-, leác-, leáctūn-, lid-, mearc-, mere-, mylen-, niht-, regn-, regol-, scip-, sele-, stig-, stōc-, wudu-, wyrt-weard; *also such proper names as* Æþel-weard, Eád-weard.

weard, e; *f.* I. *ward, guard, watch*:—Gefangen on hergiunge oþþe æt wearde *utrum explorantem an in praelio captus*, Ors. 4, 11; Swt. 206, 5. Healdaþ wearde dæges and nihtes *die ac nocte manebitis observantes custodias*, Lev. 8, 35. Weras wæccende wearde heóldon, Judth. Thw. 23, 26; Jud. 142: Beo. Th. 616; B. 305. Wið wrāð werod wearde healdan, 644; B. 319: Exon. Th. 48, 6; Cri. 767: 282, 16; Jul. 664. Weardum *excubiis*, Wrt. Voc. ii. 30, 12. Lux et tenebre ðe dās werþeóda weardum healdaþ, Exon. Th. 192, 5; Az. 101. Wærda *excubias*, Hpt. Gl. 476, 29. I a. *a watch, a body of men keeping watch*:—Hī besetton his birgene mid wearde, Jud. Thw. p. 161, 12. II. *guardianship, protection, keeping*:—Heora feorh generede mihtig Metodes weard, Cd. Th. 230, 18; Dan. 235. Cristenum cyninge gebyraþ ðæt hē sȳ on fæder stæle cristenre þeóde, and on ware and on wearde Cristes gespeliga, L. I. P. 2; Th. ii. 304, 23. [*O. H. Ger.* warta *speculatio, cura, custodia, excubiae*: *Icel.* vörðr; *m. ward, watch, protection.*] v. ǣg-, fird-, flōd-, fore-, heáfod-, hors-, leód-, sǣ-weard; or-wearde.

weard; *adv. Ward* in to-*ward*; the form occurs in combination with *tō* (v. tō-weard; *prep.* II. 3) and *wiþ* (v. wiþ, IX):—Hié wǣron wið ðæs fȳres weard, Ors. 4, 10; Swt. 200, 16. Hē wið Rōme weard farende wæs, 5, 11; Swt. 236, 9, 15, 21. Ðā ongan seó leó fægnian wið ðæs ealdan weard, Homl. Skt. ii. 23 b, 778. Heó teáh hyne wiþ hyre weard, Judth. Thw. 23, 1; Jud. 99. v. eást-, for-, forþ-, hām-, hider-, hindan-, norþ-, sūþ-, þider-, west-weard.

-weard *the second component of many adjectives denoting position or direction.* v. æf-, æftan-, æfte-, æfter-, and-, eáste-, for-, fore-, forþ-, fram-, from-, heonon-, hider-, hinde-, hinder-, innan-, inne-, midde-, neoþan-, neoþe-, niþer-, norþ-, norþan-, norþe-, on-, ongeán-, sūþe-, þanan-, tō-, ufan-, ufe-, up-, ūtan-, ūte-, westan-, weste-, wiþer-weard. [*O. Sax.* -ward: *O. H. Ger.* -wart. Cf. *Goth.* -wairþs: *Icel.* -verðr.]

wearda (?), wearde (?), an; *m.* or *f. A watchman* or *a watch*:—Ōð weardan hylle; fram weardan hylle (*the beacon-hill?* Cf. *Icel.* varða *a beacon*; varð-berg *a look-out place*: *O. H. Ger.* wart-perg), Cod. Dip. Kmbl. v. 191, 34. Cf. On weardæs beorh, 291, 23: 112, 32. Weardan *excubiae*, Ælfc. Gr. 13; Zup. 84, 16. [*Goth.* wardja *a guard*: *O. H. Ger.* warto.] v. next word.

weard-dūn, e; *f. A beacon-hill* (?cf. weardan hyll. v. wearda):—On wearddūne, ðǣr ðæt Cristes mǣl stōd, Cod. Dip. Kmbl. iii. 465, 31.

weardere, es; *m. One who holds a country, an inhabitant*:—Columba com tō Pyhtum; ðæt synd wærteras be norðum mōrum *Columba came to the Picts; they are the people who hold the country to the north of the hills* (cf. Bd. 3, 4: Venit Columba Brittaniam praedicaturus verbum Dei provinciis Septentrionalium Pictorum, hoc est, eis quae arduis atque horrentibus montium jugis ab Australibus eorum sunt regionibus sequestratae), Chr. 565; Erl. 16, 37. [*O. H. Ger.* wartari *custos*.] v. weardian, IV.

weardes; *adv. Wards* in to-*wards*:—Ðā smearcode heó wið his weardes, Homl. Skt. ii. 23 b, 590. Swā eode heó wið his weardes, 684. Ðā arn se ealda wið hire weardes, 599. v. eást-, from-, hām-, niþer-, norþ-, ongeán-, sūþ-, þider-, tō-, up-, ūt-weardes.

weardian; *p.* ode. I. *to guard, keep, defend*:—Æðele getrym eorðan weardaþ *erit firmamentum in terra*, Ps. Th. 71, 16. Heofon weardiaþ ufan wætra ðrȳðe *tegis in aquis superiora coeli*, 103, 3. Hȳ (*Seraphim*) mid hyra fiþrum Freán ælmihtiges onsȳne weard (weardiað? v. Isaiah 6, 2), Exon. Th. 25, 5; Cri. 396. [Se heáhengel geong weardode (*l.* geondweardode *presented*) ðære eádigan Marian sāwle beforan, Drihtne, Blickl. Homl. 157, 9.] I a. with gen. (cf. *O. Sax.* wardōn *with gen. to have charge of something*):—Ða Englisce men ðe wærdedon ðære sǣ *the Englishmen that had charge of the sea*, Chr. 1087; Erl. 225, 26. II. *to act as guardian to, to rule*:—Him on lāste Seth weardode, ēþelstōl heóld, Cd. Th. 68, 36; Gen. 1128. Nabochodonossor weardode wīde rīce, heóld hæleða gestreón, 257, 29; Dan. 665. Rīce gerēfa rondburgum weóld, eard weardade, Exon. Th. 243, 33; Jul. 20. III. *to keep, have charge of*:—Būton hit under ðæs wīfes cǣglocan gebrōht wǣre, sȳ heó clǣne; ac ðæra cǣgean heó sceal weardian, L. C. S. 77; Th. i. 418, 21. IV. *to hold* a country, *to occupy* a place, *inhabit*. v. weardere:—Ðone wudu weardaþ fugel *hoc nemus avis incolit*, Exon. Th. 203, 16; Ph. 85: 208, 25; Ph. 161: 209, 10; Ph. 168. Hwīlum hygegeómor healle weardaþ (*keeps the house*), Salm. Kmbl. 762; Sal. 380. Ðonne færð se deófol intō his mōder innoðe, and ðǣr hē hine healt, and weardaþ inne, Wulfst. 193, 10. Hē heánne beám wunaþ and weardaþ, Exon. Th. 209, 17; Ph. 172. In ðam hālge wīc weardiaþ, 228, 34; Ph. 448. Him fērend on fæste wuniaþ, wīc weardiaþ, 361, 27; Wal. 26. Hī dreám weardiaþ, 100, 15; Cri. 1642. Frȳnd sind on eorþan, leger weardiaþ, 443, 23; Kl. 34. Ealle ða ðe on feldum eard weardiaþ *omnia quae in campis sunt*, Ps. Th. 95, 12. Ðǣr sylfǣtan eard weardigaþ, ēðel healdaþ, Andr. Kmbl. 351; An. 176. Fīfelcynnes eard wer weardode, Beo. Th. 211; B. 105. Reced weardode unrīm eorla, 2479; B. 1237. Heó gefylled wæs wīsdōmes gife; hālig gāst hreðer weardode, Elen. Kmbl. 2288; El. 1145: Exon. Th. 169, 30; Gū. 1102. Wē sele weardodon, Beo. Th. 4157; B. 2075. Sume stede weardedon ymb Danūbie, Elen. Kmbl. 270; El. 135. Þenden wē on eorðan eard weardigen, Exon. Th. 48, 16; Cri. 772. Ðǣr hig ǣnne sculan eard weardian *habitare in unum*, Ps. Th. 132, 1: Exon. Th. 356, 13; Pa. 11. Eard weardigan, ān lond būgan, 473, 19; Bo. 17: Andr. Kmbl. 1198; An. 599. Wīc weardian, Exon. Th. 248, 7; Jul. 92. Staþol weardian, 496, 19; Rā. 85, 17. IV a. *in the phrases* lāst, swaðe weardian *to keep a track*, (1) *to follow*:—Hȳrde ic ðæt ðām frætwum feówer mearas läst weardode *I heard that four steeds followed in the train of these equipments*, Beo. Th. 4335; B. 2164. (2) *to remain behind*:—Hē onweg losade, hwæþre him sió swīðre swaðe weardade hand on Hiorte *he escaped, yet his right hand remained behind in Heorot*, Beo. Th. 4203; B. 2098. Cyning ūre gewāt . . . ðǣr hȳ tō sēgun, ða ðe leófes ðā gēn lāst weardedun (*those who still remained where he had been*), Exon. Th. 31, 16; Cri. 496. Se ðe his mondryhten līfe bilidene lāst weardian wiste *he who knew that his dead lord remained behind*, 182, 19; Gū. 1312. Hē his folme forlēt lāst weardian, Beo. Th. 1947; B. 971. Sāula sculon eft tō ðē, sceal se līchama lāst weardigan eft on eorþan, Met. 20, 241. [Sicnesse wardeð toȝein þeo sunnen þet weren touwardes, A. R. 182, 14. Wel heo wardith heom bothe, Alis. 909. Þilke tyme þat Samuel þe prophete wardede (*ruled*) þat folc of Israel, R. Glouc. 27, 16. *O. Sax.* wardōn *to guard, to have charge of*: *O. Frs.* wardia: *Icel.* varða *to guard, defend.* Cf. *O. H. Ger.* wartēn.] v. ā-, be-weardian; ge-wardod.

weard-mann, es; *m. A guard, watchman, keeper*:—Nyte wē hweþer se weardmann wǣre ǣfre gefullod, Homl. Skt. i. 11, 293. Ealle ða weardmenn wǣron geswefode būton heora ānum, 11, 200: 4, 419. Ða weardmenn ðe bewiston Cristes līc, Homl. Ass. 79, 175. Hē geseah ðæra sceaþena fær and tō ðām weardmannum becom. Ðā gelæhton ða weardmen his wealdleðer, ðæt hē mid fleáme ne burste, Ælfc. T. Grn. 18, 15. Wylsce menn geslōgan mycelne dǣl Englisces folces ðæra weardmanna, Chr. 1053; Erl. 188, 10. Nytendum ðām weardmannum ic ārīse *clam custodibus surgo*, Ælfc. Gr. 47; Zup. 272, 1: Homl. Skt. i. 4, 217: Homl. Ass. 78, 152: Anglia x. 99, 311. Hē heora wæterscipe mid weardmannum besette *constituit centenarios per singulos fontes*, 94, 172.

weard-seld, es; *n. A guard-house*:—Weardseld *excubias*, Wrt. Voc. ii. 108, 1.

weard-setl, es; *n. A place where guard is kept*: *those who keep watch, a guard*:—On weardsetl; of weardsetle, Cod. Dip. Kmbl. v. 48, 11. Andlang herpaðes tō weardsetle, 284, 23. On weardsetl, Cod. Dip. B. iii. 682, 24. Seofon weardsetl wacodon ofer ðone cāsere. . . . Ðā fērde his gāst and mid wǣpne ðone Godes feónd ofstang, his weardsetlum on lōcigendum, Homl. Th. i. 452, 13-31. Æt ðǣm weardsetlum *ad excubias*, Wrt. Voc. ii. 3, 16. Weardsetl *excubias*, 81, 20: 30, 11: 71, 11. Hī ofereodon ða twā weardsetl *transeuntes primam et secundam custodiam* (Acts 12, 10), Homl. Th. ii. 382, 11.

weard-steall, es; *m. A watch-tower*:—Weardsteal *specula* vel *conspicilium*, Wrt. Voc. i. 55, 42: *spectacula*, 39, 35.

weard-wīte, es; *n. A fine for neglecting to keep guard*, Chart. Th. 411, 31.

wearf, v. hwearf.

wearg(-h), es; *m.* I. of human beings, *a villain, felon, scoundrel, criminal*:—Wearg *furcifer*, Wrt. Voc. ii. 37, 66. Wearh, 152, 2. Wearh sceal hangian, fægere ongildan ðæt hē ǣr fācen dyde manna cynne, Menol. Fox 572; Gn. C. 55. Hī hēton mē (*the cross*) heora wergas hebban, Rood Kmbl. 62; Kr. 31. II. of other creatures, *a monster, malignant being, evil spirit*:—Under ðæm stāne wæs niccra eardung and wearga, Blickl. Homl. 209, 34. Wē sceolun þrowian weán 7 (and; *prep.*? or = on) wergum, nalles wul[d]res blǣd habban in heofnum *we must suffer woe with accursed ones, not have glorious honour in heaven*, Cd. Th. 267, 22; Sat. 42. [Þe wari of þeos wordes warð wrað, Marh. 4, 12. Ic am unwurð as weri (*v. l.* wari) þet is anhonged, A. R. 352, 21. Ich wulle hine anhon haxst alre warien, Laym. 28215. *Goth.* launawargs *an unthankful person*: *O. H. Ger.* ubiles, palowes warc *tyrannus*: der warch *diabolus*: *Icel.* vargr *a wolf*; *an outlaw.* Graff quotes the latinized form wargus = *expulsus, latrunculus.* See Grmm. R. A. p. 733.] v. heoru-wearh, *and next word.*

wearg, werg, werig, wyrig; *adj. Evil, vile, malignant, accursed*, (1) of human beings:—Sum sceal on galgan rīdan . . . bið him werig noma, Exon. Th. 329, 31; Vy. 42. Ðū (*the body*) werga (weriga, Soul Kmbl. 43), 368, 15; Seel. 22. Ðū woldest brūcan ungemetlīcre wrǣnnesse. Ac ðē willaþ ðonne forseón Godes þeówas, for ðam ðe ðīn werige flǣsc hafaþ ðīn anweald . . . Hū mæg mon earmlīcor gebǣron, ðonne mon hine underþeóde his weregan flǣsce *voluptariam vitam degas. Sed quis non spernat vilissimae fragilissimaeque rei, corporis, servum?* Bt. 32, 1; Fox 114, 20-24: Met. 26, 14. Bearn Godes brȳda on Caines cynne sēcan, wergum folce, Cd. Th. 75, 34; Gen. 1250. Gē dyslīce dǣd gefremedon, werge wræcmæcgas, Elen. Kmbl. 773; El. 387. Werige, Andr. Kmbl. 1229; An. 615. Fealleþ ðē on ða wynstran wergra þūsend, Ps. Th. 90, 7. Ðū mē āweredest wyrigra gemōtes *protexisti me a conventu malignantium*, 63, 2. Werigra, Cd. Th. 232, 30; Dan. 268. Werigum wrōhtsmiðum, Andr. Kmbl. 171; An. 86. Hē gelǣdde wærge weorod *adducto maligno exercitu*, Bd. 4, 12; S. 580, 40. (2) of evil spirits:—Ēū (*the serpent*) scealt werg ðīnum breóstum bearm tredan brād[r]e eorðan, Cd. Th. 56, 3; Gen. 906. Se werga gǣst, Exon. Th. 129, 16; Gū. 422. Se werga, 268, 8; Jul. 429. Sió werge sceolu (*the fallen angels*), Elen. Kmbl. 1523; El. 763. Se weriga gāst *serpens*, Bd. 1, 27; S. 497, 14: *malignus spiritus*, 497, 19, 26. Se weria feónd *hostis malignus*, 3, 19; S. 549, 4. Hafaþ werges bleó, Exon. Th. 95, 31; Cri. 1565. Weriges, Andr. Kmbl. 2340; An. 1171. Lāst wergan gāstes (*Grendel*), Beo. Th. 266; B. 133. Wergan gāstes *the devil's*, 3499; B. 1747. Ðæm wergan gāste wiþstondan, Blickl. Homl. 135, 11. Werigan, Cd. Th. 309, 17; Sat. 711. Wið ðone wergan gǣst, Exon. Th. 373, 30; Seel. 117. Weregan, Cd. Th. 306, 24; Sat. 669. Hī sculon werge wihta wræce þrowian, Exon. Th. 455, 29; Hy. 4, 57. Werige, Cd. Th. 6, 18; Gen. 90: 304, 15; Sat. 630. Wergan gǣstas, Exon. Th. 23, 4; Cri. 363. Ða werigan gāstas *spiritus maligni*, Bd. 3, 11; S. 536, 36, 40: Cd. Th. 310, 23; Sat. 731. Manna cynn and eác werigra gāsta, Blickl. Homl. 83, 12. (3) of things:—Ðone werigan sele *that accursed hall* (*Hell*), Cd. Th. 285, 4; Sat. 332. [*O. Sax.* warag (*applied to Judas*).] v. preceding word.

wearg-berende; *adj. Villainous, rascally*:—Ða weargberendan *furcifera*, Wrt. Voc. ii. 38, 1.

wearg-brǣde (wearge- [wearg-ge- (?)], wearh-), an; *f. Some form of disease*; the word translates *impetigo, ulcus, carcinoma*:—Wearhbrǣde *impetigo*, Wrt. Voc. i. 43, 62. Weargebrǣde, ii. 45, 39: *nævum*, 62, 29. Werhbrǣde, i. 61, 16. Gif hwylcum weargbrǣde (wearh-, MS. B.; *the Latin has* ulcus) weaxe on þām nosum oððe on ðam hleóre, Lchdm. i. 86, 1. Wið ðæt wearhbrǣde (*the Latin has* carcinomata) hwam on nosa wexe, 116, 11. Gif nægl sié of handa and wiþ wearhbrǣdan (*probably* πτερύγιον, Cockayne), nim hwǣtecorn, meng wið hunig, lege on þone finger, ii. 80, 20, 24.

wearg-cwedol, -cwidol; *adj. Given to evil speaking* or *cursing*:—Ðeáh ðe wyrigcwidole (wærgcweodole, Bd. M. 356, 26) Godes rīce gesittan ne magon, hwæþere is gelȳfed ðæt ða ðe be gewyrhtum wyrgede wǣron for heora ārleásnysse, ðæt hī hraðe ðurh Drihtnes wræc heora scylde wīte ðrowedon *quamvis maledici regnum Dei possidere non possint, creditum est tamen quod hi qui merito impietatis suae maledicebantur, ocius Domino vindice poenas sui reatus luerent*, Bd. 4, 26; S. 602, 11. Ðæt hī nō āfyrhte ðæt gewin ðæs sīþfætes ne wyrigcwydolra (wyrgcweodulra, Bd. M. 56, 14) manna tungan ne brēgde *nec labor vos itineris nec maledicorum hominum linguae deterreant*, 1, 23; S. 486, 1.

wearg-cwedolian; *p.* ode *To curse, speak evil*:—Wergcweoðelade mec *maledixit me*, Ps. Surt. ii. p. 183, 27. Gif feónd mīn wergcweodelade mē *si inimicus meus maledixisset mihi*, Ps. Surt. 54, 13.

wearg-cwedolness, e; *f. Cursing*:—Lufade wergcweodulnisse *dilexit maledictionem*, Ps. Surt. 108, 18.

wearg-cweþan; *p.* -cwæþ, *pl.* -cwǣdon *To curse*:—Wergcweoðaþ *maledicent*, Ps. Surt. 108, 28. Wergcweódon *maledicebant*, 61, 5. Wercweoðende *maledicentes*, 36, 22.

wearg-līc (werig-); *adj. Vile, mean, wretched*:—Sint ðæt werilīce welan ðisses middangeardes, ðonne hī nān mon fullīce habban ne mæg, ne hié nānne mon geweligian ne magon, būton hié ōþerne gedōn tō wǣdlan *O! igitur angustas, inopesque divitias, quae nec habere totas pluribus licet, et ad quemlibet sine ceterorum paupertate non veniunt*, Bt. 13; Fox 38, 36. v. next word.

wearglīce; *adv. Vilely, meanly, wretchedly*:—Gif ðū ðē wilt dōn manegra beteran and weorþran, ðonne scealt ðū ðē lǣtan ānes wyrsan. Hū ne is ðæt sum dǣl ermþa, ðæt mon swā wærelīce (werelīce, *v. l.*) scyle culpian tō ðam ðe him gifan scyle *qui praeire ceteros honore cupis, poscendi humilitate vilesces*, Bt. 32, 1; Fox 114, 15. v. preceding word.

weargness (werg-, werig-, wirig-, wyrig-), e; *f. Evil*:—Wel mæg ðæm dæg werignise his *sufficit diei malitia sua*, Mt. Kmbl. Lind. 6, 34. Feala wyrgnessa wrāðe feóndas ðīnum ðām hālgum hefige brohtan *quanta malignatus est inimicus in sanctis*, Ps. Th. 73, 4. v. wearg, wirgness *a curse*.

weargol; *adj. Evil*:—Ðis is seó wyrt ðe wergulu (*the crab apple*; pirus malus, Cockayne) hātte, Lchdm. iii. 34, 14.

weargolness, e; *f. A curse*:—Ic syngede swīðe þurh āðsware and þurh wærgolnesse *ego peccavi nimis per juramentum et maledictiones*, Confess. Peccat.

wearg-rōd, e; *f. A gallows, gibbet*:—Waergrood *furcimen*, Txts. 65, 930. Uuergrōd, uaergrōd *furca*, 62, 409. Wearhrōd, Wrt. Voc. ii. 36, 68: 70, 24: 152, 1: *eculeus* vel *catasta*, i. 55, 52. We[rg]rōd *catasta*, ii. 22, 23. Of ðam þorne on ða wærhrōda; of ðām rōdun, Cod. Dip. Kmbl. v. 345, 5. v. wearg-treów.

wearg-trǣf, es; *m. A house of the accursed*:—Of ðām wearhtreafum ic āwecce wið ðē ōðerne cyning *from the tents of the accursed* (*hell*) *I will raise up against thee another king*, Elen. Kmbl. 1850; El. 927.

wearg-treów, es; *n. The accursed tree, a gallows, gibbet, cross*:—Tō ðe waritroe, Cod. Dip. Kmbl. iii. 375, 25. [Nu raise þai up þe rode; setis up þe warhtreo, O. E. Homl. i. 283, 9. Doð up and waritreo, þer on heo scullen winden (hongy, 2nd MS.), Laym. 5714. Me ledde him uorte hongen o waritreo, A. R. 122, 8. Let heom don adun of þe waritreo, Misc. 51, 491. *Icel.* varg-trē *a gallows*.] v. wearg-rōd.

wearh-, weariht. v. wearg-, weariht.

wearm; *adj. Warm*:—Swā swā ðæt cealde ǣrest onginð wlacian, ǣr hit fūl wearm weorðe, swā eác ðæt wearme wlacaþ, ǣr hit eallunga ācealdige *sicut a frigore per teporem transitur ad calorem, ita a calore* *per teporem reditur ad frigus*, Past. 58; Swt. 447, 5. Wedercondel wearm *the sun*, Exon. Th. 210, 17; Ph. 187: 179, 25; Gū. 1267. Sié lyft is ǽgðer ge ceald ge wǽt ge wearm, Bt. 33, 4; Fox 128, 36. On sumera hit biþ wearm, 21; Fox 74, 23: Exon. Th. 340, 19; Gn. Ex. 113. Wearm weder, 198, 30; Ph. 18. Ðeáh ðē wel lyste wearmes mustes, Bt. 5, 2; Fox 10, 32. For ðære wearman *pro aprico*, Wrt. Voc. ii. 91, 62: 9, 23. Swā weax melteþ, gif hit byð wearmum neáh fȳre gefæstnad, Ps. Th. 57, 7. Wring on wermōd wearmne, Lchdm. ii. 310, 10. Ða sceolon beón wearme *offerrent eam calidam*, Lev. 6, 21. Wearme wederdagas, Exon. Th. 191, 30; Az. 96. Sumor æfter cymeþ, wearm gewideru, Met. 11, 61. Wearme gewyderu, Menol. Fox 177; Men. 90. [*O. Sax. O. Frs.* warm: *O. H. Ger.* warm (waram) *calidus, apricus: Icel.* varmr.] v. cū-wearm.

wearme; *adv. Warmly*:—Genim þreó snǽda, gerest æfter wearme *take three slices, go to bed afterwards and keep warm*, Lchdm. ii. 52, 23. Bewreóh ðē wearme *wrap yourself up warmly*, 116, 20: 118, 10. Bebinde þonne genōh wearme, 270, 9. Beþe ðæt heáfod swā wearme *use as warm fomentations as possible for the head*, 154, 18.

wearmian; *p.* ode *To get warm*:—Ic wearmige *caleo*, Ælfc. Gr. 26, 2; Zup. 154, 3. *Caleo* ic wearmige and of ðam *calesco* ic onginne tō wearmigenne, 35; Zup. 212, 2. Gif wund ācōlod sȳ . . . lege on ða wunda, heó cwicaþ sōna and wearmaþ, Lchdm. i. 194, 26. Wyrta wearmiaþ, Exon. Th. 212, 20; Ph. 213. Wearmode ɫ gehǽt wæs ɫ āhātode heorte mīn *concaluit cor meum*, Ps. Lamb. 38, 4. Hī (*the clothes which he wore while standing in the river*) on his līchaman wearmodon, Homl. Th. ii. 354, 20. Se ðe nyle ðæt wlæce oferwinnan and wearmian ōð hē wealle *quisquis nequaquam tepore superato excrescit, ut ferveat*, Past. 58; Swt. 447, 7. Se cealda ðencð tō wearmianne, 447, 17. v. ge-wearmian; wirman.

wearm-līc; *adj. Warm*:—Wearmlīc wolcna scūr *the warm rain from the clouds*, Cd. Th. 238, 5; Dan. 350.

wearmness, e; *f. Warmness, warmth*:—Hē wolde hine baðian on þam wlacum wætere, ac hē gewāt sōna swā hē ðæt wæter hrepode, and wearð seó wearmnys him āwend tō deáðe, Homl. Skt. i. 11, 160.

wearn, es; *m.* (?) *A multitude, a great number* or *quantity, a great deal*:—Þunie (þu me, Th.) him gewinnes wearn ofer wealles hrōf and heom on midle wese mān and inwit *circumdabit eam super muros ejus iniquitas, et labor in medio ejus*, Ps. Th. 54, 9. Þeáh ðe ða ealle ðe mē āfeódon wordum wyrigen and wearn sprecan *si is, qui oderat me, super me magna locutus est*, 54, 12. Hió innwit feala ȳwdan on tungan, and mē wrāðra wearn worda sprǽcon *locuti sunt adversum me lingua dolosa, et sermonibus odii circumdederunt me*, 108, 2. Ic on unriht oft lōcade and wiðercwyda wearn gehȳrde *vidi iniquitatem et contradictionem*, 54, 8. Hī his wundra wearn gesāwon on wætergrundum *ipsi viderunt mirabilia ejus in profundo*, 106, 23. Þeáh ðe eów wealan tō wearnum flōwen *divitiae si affluant*, 61, 11. Hē synfulle tōdrīfeþ wearnum ealle *omnes peccatores disperdet*, 144, 20. Ful oft mon wearnum (*or from* wearn; *f.*) tīhð eargne ðæt hē elne forleóse *full often the coward is freely* (or *with difficulty*) *accused of losing his courage*, Exon. Th. 345, 13; Gn. Ex. 187. v. wearn-mǽlum, *and* cf. worn.

wearn, e; *f.* I. *a hindrance, obstacle, difficulty.* v. wearn-wīslīce:—Wearne ɫ remmincge *obstaculo, impedimento*, Hpt. Gl. 455, 48. Ðæt mōd hæfð fulfremedne willan tō ðære wrǽnnesse būtan ǽlcre steóre and wearne *ejus animus voluptate luxuriae sine ullo repugnationis obstaculo delectatur*, Past. 11; Swt. 73, 8. Gif hē geþyldelīce forbyrð ǽgðer ge hosp ge edwītu and on ðære wearne þurhwunaþ þeáh and eádmōdlīce bit, ðæt him mon infæres tīþige, sȳ hē underfangen *si veniens perseveraverit pulsans, et inlatas sibi injurias et difficultatem ingressus visus fuerit patienter portare et persistere petitioni sue, annuatur ei ingressus*, R. Ben. 97, 7. II. *a refusal.* v. wirnan:—Hȳ bēnan synt ðæt hié wið ðē mōton wordum wrixlan, nō ðū him wearne geteóh ðīnra gegncwida *they are petitioners that they may exchange words with thee, give them not a refusal of thy words in reply*, Beo. Th. 738; B. 366. [*Icel.* vörn *a defence.*] v. un-wearnum.

wearnian, wearnung. v. warenian, warenung.

wearn-mǽlum; *adv. In flocks, in crowds*:—Wearnmǣlum *gregatim*, Wrt. Voc. ii. 110, 9.

wearn-wīslīce; *adv. With difficulty*:—Wearnwīslīce *difficile*, Wrt. Voc. ii. 106, 47: 25, 53.

wearoþ. v. waroþ.

wearp, es; *n.* I. *the warp, thread stretched lengthwise in a loom*:—Wearp *stamen*, Wrt. Voc. ii. 121, 34: i. 59, 32: 66, 21: 282, 4. Līnen wearp *linostema*, 40, 8. Be cembum wearpe *de stuppe stamineo* (*de stuppae stamine*, Ald. 51 and v. Hpt. Gl. 494, 1), ii. 83, 15: 26, 62. Of wearpe *de stamine*, Hpt. Gl. 494, 1. Wundene mē ne beóð wefle, ne ic wearp (uarp, Txts. 151, 5) hafu, Exon. Th. 417, 16; Rä. 36, 5. Wyllene wearp *lanea stamina*, Hpt. Gl. 417, 28. Wearpum *stamina*, 430, 74. II. *a pliant twig* that may be used in basket-making. v. wearp-fæt:—Wearp *vimen*, Wrt. Voc. ii. 123, 73. [Warp, threde for webbynge *stamen, licium*, Prompt. Parv. 517. *O. H. Ger.* warf, waraf *stamen*: *Icel.* varp *a casting.*]

wearp-fæt, es; *n. A wicker-basket*:—*Corbis* vel *cofinus* wylige, *sportella* tǽnel, *cartallum* windel, *calathus* (cf. wearp, II, and Ovid: Calathos e vimine textos) wearpfæt, Wrt. Voc. i. 86, 2-5: 40, 42. [A warpefatte *alveolus*, Cath. Angl. 409.]

wearr, es; *m. A piece of hard skin* (particularly on the hands or feet), *callosity*:—Wear *callus*, Wrt. Voc. ii. 14, 12. War, i. 291, 8. Wær *callositas*, Hpt. Gl. 490, 33. Ða wearras and ða swylas ðe beóð on mannes handum oððe on ōðrum limum, Lchdm. i. 356, 16. Wiþ weartum and wearrum on lime, ii. 148, 26: Homl. Skt. i. 5, 139. Fram þysum heardum wearrum, 5, 198. Weorras *vel* ill *callos*, Txts. 49, 400. Uarras, 111, 13: *callos, tensam cutem*, 114, 93. Wearras, ilas *callos*, Wrt. Voc. ii. 13, 48: *calces*, 127, 45. Wiþ wearras and wiþ swylas, Lchdm. i. 356, 11. Wearras and weartan on weg tō dōnne, 362, 17: ii. 150, 1. [Warre or knobbe of a tre *vertex*, Prompt. Parv. 516, and see note.]

wearr, es; *m. A cup, bowl*:—Clǣfran seáwes .ii. lytle bollan fulle mid lytle hunige gemengde, dō wear fulne gehǽttes wīnes tō, sele drincan þrȳ dagas, Lchdm. ii. 214, 12.

wearrig; *adj. Callous*:—Hē gelōme ðingode for ðæs folces gyltum, bīgende his cneówu on gebedum symle, swā ðæt him weóxon wearrige ylas, on olfendes gelīcnysse, on his līdegum cneówum, Homl. Th. ii. 298, 26.

wearriht; *adj.* I. of living beings, *having hard skin, leprous*:—Wærrehte ɫ hreófige *elephantinosa, leprosa* (elephantinosa corporis incommoditas, Ald. 28), Hpt. Gl. 455, 35. Hreófe oððe wearrihtum *callosi* (corpore calloso venere leprosi, Ald. 175), Wrt. Voc. ii. 93, 72: 19, 53. Ða wearrihtan *callosa* (calloso corpore lepram, Ald. 201), 96, 6: 20, 2. Wearihte *callosa*, 127, 53. II. of trees, *gnarled, knotted*:—On ðonæ wearrihtan stocc, Cod. Dip. Kmbl. iii. 176, 4: v. 221, 4. In ða wæriht āc; of ðæt wærriht āc, iii. 390, 16. v. wearr.

wearrihtness, e; *f. Hardness of skin, roughness of skin* as in leprosy:—Rūh wærhitnys *callositas*, wearrihtnys, rūh wærihtnys *scabredo* (leprosi, quos dira cutis callositas elephantino tabo deturpans, Ald. 49), Hpt. Gl. 490, 33-36. Unsmēðnes oððe wearrihtnes *callositas*, Wrt. Voc. ii. 18, 36. Wearihtnes, 127, 54.

wearte, an; weart(?), e; *f. A wart*:—Uearte, uuertae, uaertae *berruca*, Txts. 45, 288. Wearte, Wrt. Voc. ii. 11, 4: 126, 2. Wearte, uueartae, uearte *papula*, Txts. 83, 1485. Wearte, Wrt. Voc. i. 288, 73: ii. 67, 57. Wearte, uueartae, uuertae *verruca*, Txts. 105, 2088. Wearte *verruca* . . . weartena (-e, MS.) heáp *satiriasis*, Wrt. Voc. i. 20, 7, 9. Wearte *vel* bȳl *furunculus*, ii. 151, 75. Wearte (*pl.*?), bȳle *fruncula s* (-*us*?), 151, 34. Wið weartan, genim ðysse wyrte meolc, dō tō ðære weartan, hit ða weartan gehǽleþ, Lchdm. i. 224, 6-8: 130, 20-21. Wiþ weartum . . . dō on ða weartan, ii. 148, 26: 322, 12. Wiþ weartan . . . lege tō ðām weartan, hē hȳ fornimeþ, i. 256, 1-2. Wearras and weartan on weg tō dōnne . . . wrīð on ða weartan and on ða wearras, 362, 17. Wið scurfedum nægle, nim gecyrnadne sticcan, sete on ðone nægl wið ða wearta (-an ?), ii. 150, 5. [*O. H. Ger.* warta; *f. verruca, papilla* (the word has both strong and weak forms): *Icel.* varta *a wart.*]

weás; *adv. By chance, by accident, fortuitously*:—Weás *casu*, Txts. 181, 54. Ic his wundrode micle ðȳ læs, gif ic wiste ðæt hit weás gebyrede būton Godes willan and būton his gewitnesse *minus mirarer, si misceri omnia fortuitis casibus crederem*, Bt. 39, 2; Fox 212, 32: 214, 6: 39, 3; Fox 216, 3: Met. 28, 72. Witan hwæt wyrd sié, and hwæt weás gebyrige *de fati serie, de repentinis casibus quaeri*, Bt. 39, 4; Fox 216, 30. Ic wolde witan hwæþer ðæt āuht sié ðæt wē oft gehióraþ ðæt men cweþaþ be sumum þingum ðæt hit scyle weás gebyrian. . . . Hit nis nāuht ðæt mon cwiþ ðæt ǽnig ðing weás gebyrige; for ðam ǽlc þing cymþ of sumum ðingum, for ðȳ hit ne biþ weás gebyred; ac ðǽr hit of nāuhte ne cōme ðonne wǽre hit weás gebyred *quaero an esse aliquid omnino, et quidnam esse casum arbitrere. . . . Nihil est, quod vel casus, vel fortuitum jure appellari queat*, 40, 5; Fox 240, 13-30. Men cwǽdon ðonne him hwæt unwēnunga gebyrede, ðæt ðæt wǽre weás gebyrede *quoties aliquid cujuspiam rei gratia geritur, aliudque quibusdam de causis, quam quod intendebatur, obtingit, casus vocatur*, 40, 6; Fox 242, 5, 9. Gif him weás gebyreþ, ðæt him wyrþ sume hwīle ðara þēnunga oftohen, 37, 1; Fox 186, 13: Met. 25, 31. Gif him weás (wealdes, Hatt. MS.) gebyrige oððe ungewealdes, ðæt hē on ðæs hwæt befoo, ðe wið his willan sié *siquando contra eos lingua labitur*, Past. 28; Swt. 198, 22.

weascing. v. wæscing.

weás-gelimp, es; *n. What happens by chance, accident, chance*:—Mid weásgelimpe *fortuitu*, Wrt. Voc. ii. 34, 35.

weá-spell, es; *n. A tale of woe*:—Æfter weáspelle (*the news of Æschere's death*), Beo. Th. 2634; B. 1315.

weá-tācn, es; *n. A sign of misery, a woeful signal*:—Nis þǽr on ðam londe, ne wōp ne wracu, weátācen nān, yldu ne yrmðu, Exon. Th. 201, 5; Ph. 51. Wæs ðæt weátācen geond ða burh bodad, ðæt hié ðæs cnihtes cwealm gesōhton, Andr. Kmbl. 2239; An. 1121.

weá-þearf, e; *f. Grievous need*:—Ic mē fēran gewāt folgað sēcan, wineleás wræcca, for mīnre weáþearfe, Exon. Th. 442, 10; Kl. 10.

weax, es; *n. Wax*:—Weax *cera*, Wrt. Voc. i. 81, 33: *cerea*, 284, 32.

Âsoden weax *obrizum metallum*, ii, 65, 14. Swâ weax melteþ, gif hit byð wearmum neáh fýre gefæstnad *sicut cera liquefacta*, Ps. Th. 57, 7: 67, 2: Exon. Th. 61, 23; Cri. 989. Swâ swâ eles gecynd bið ðæt hê beorhtor scîneþ þonne wex on sceafte, Blickl. Homl. 129, 1. Ða fôtlâstas wǽron swutole, swâ hié on wexe wǽron âðýde, 205, 1. God hêt wǽpen wera wexe gelîcost formeltan, Andr. Kmbl. 2292; An. 1147. Mon ðaet weax âgæfe tô cirican, Cod. Dip. Kmbl. i. 293, 20. Ontend .iii. candella, drýp ðæt weax, Lchdm. i. 392, 11. On gemelt weax gedôn, ii. 72, 7. Ic gefrægn weax (*dough?*) nât hwæt þindan and þunian, Exon. Th. 431, 16; Rä. 46, 1. [*O. L. Ger. O. H. Ger.* wahs: *O. Frs.* wax: *Icel.* vax.]

weax-æppel, es; *m. A wax apple, a ball of wax*:—Se Pater Noster mæg âna ealla gesceafta on his ðære swîðran hand on ânes weaxæpples onlîcnisse geðýn and gewringan, Salm. Kmbl. p. 150, 33.

weaxan, weacsan, weahsan, weahxan, wexan, wehsan; ic weaxe; ðû wyxt; hê weaxeþ, weaxþ, weaxt, waexit, weaxst, wexeþ, wexþ, wixt, wihst, wihxþ, wyxþ, wyxt, wyxst, wycxþ; *p.* weóx, weócs, weóhs, *pl.* weóxon, weóhson, weóxson; *pp.* weaxen *To wax, grow.* I. glossing the following Latin words:—Ic weaxe *glesco*, weaxeþ *glescit*, Wrt. Voc. ii. 41, 60, 57. Weaxð *gliscit*, Hymn. Surt. 132, 6. Waexit *surgit*, Txts. 99, 1955. Weacsaþ *pullulant*, Kent. Gl. 1163. Weóx *maturesceret*, Wrt. Voc. ii. 90, 40: *floruerit*, Hpt. Gl. 460, 63: *pollesceret*, 466, 59. Wehsan *crescere*, Wülck. Gl. 252, 39. Weaxende *pubescentem*, Wrt. Voc. ii. 82, 64: 66, 20. Wexende, Hpt. Gl. 491, 15: *crebrescens*, 499, 13. Mid wexendre *praepollente*, 459, 30. II. *to grow, be produced*, (1) of animals or plants:—Of ðam weaxeþ wyrm *hinc animal sine membris fertur oriri*, Exon. Th. 213, 29; Ph. 232. Ðeós wyrt wihst (cf. ðeós wyrt bið cenned, 96, 13, *and often*) on begânum landum, Lchdm. i. 94, 6. Rixe weaxst on wæterigum stówum, Homl. Th. ii. 402, 9. Wexeþ, Runic pm. Kmbl. 342, 9; Rûn. 15. (2) of other things, (a) concrete:—Ðæt land ðǽr ðǽr gold wixt *terra, ubi nascitur aurum*, Gen. 2, 11. Hwæðer gê nû sêcan gold on treówum? . . . Ealle men witon ðæt hit ðǽr ne weaxt, ðe mâ ðe gimmas weaxaþ on wîngeardum, Bt. 32, 3; Fox 118, 8–11. Wexð, Met. 19, 8. Him wyxþ wind on ðære heortan, Lchdm. ii. 60, 7. (b) abstract:—Of ðissum syx tîdum wihst se quadrans, Anglia viii. 298, 34. Of irsunge wyxt seófung, Prov. Kmbl. 23. Him on innan oferhygda dǽl weaxeþ and wridaþ, Beo. Th. 3486; B. 1741. Of mistlîcum dryncum onwæcnaþ (cf. weaxaþ, Met. 25, 40) sió wôde þrâg ðære wrǽnnesse. . . . Þonne weaxaþ (cf. þonan cymeþ, Met. 25, 43) ða ofermêtta and ungeþwǽrnes, Bt. 37, 1; Fox 186, 19. Seó gâlnyss weóhs on him, Hexam. 17; Norm. 26, 3. Him weóxon ofermêtto, Past. 17; Swt. 113, 6. Ðonne sceal eów sôna weaxan tô hearme wǽdl and wâwa, sacu and wracu, Wulfst. 133, 2. Hê hêht geond ðæt rǽdleáse hof weaxan wîtebrôgan, Cd. Th. 3, 33; Gen. 45. Ne sceolon unc betweónan teónan weaxan, 114, 11; Gen. 1902. III. of growth in animals or plants, *to grow, grow up*:—Hê (*the phenix*) on sceade weaxeþ, Exon. Th. 214, 5; Ph. 234. Þonne hit wyxð (wexeþ, Rush.), hit is ealra wyrta mǽst *cum creverit, majus est omnibus holeribus*, Mt. Kmbl. 13, 32. Seó wyrt weóx, and ðone wæstm brôhte, 13, 26. Ðæt cild weóx and wearð gewened, Gen. 21, 8: Cd. Th. 167, 25; Gen. 2771. Ðæt cild swîþe weócs, Jud. 13, 24. His feax weox swâ swâ wîmmanna, Homl. Th. ii. 434, 8. Sumu hê cearf ðonne him ðûhte ðæt hié tô swîðe weóxen (weóxsen, Hatt. MS.) . . . Sumu hê leahte mid wætre, ðonne hié tô hwón weóxon (weóxson, Hatt. MS.), Past. 40; Swt. 292, 5–8. Ða þornas weóxon (wôxon, Lind.: wêxon, Rush.), Mt. Kmbl. 13, 7. Swâ elebeámas weaxen, Ps. Th. 127, 4. Lǽtaþ ǽgþer weaxan (wexan, Rush.), Mt. Kmbl. 13, 30. Ðîne teóðan sceattas gongendes and weaxendes ágyf ðû Gode, L. Alf. 38; Th. i. 52, 32. IV. *to grow, increase, wax*:—Se môna dêð ǽgþer, ge wycxð ge wanaþ: healfum mônðe hê bið weaxende, healfum hê bið wanigende, Homl. Th. i. 154, 27. Ðes saltus lune wyxst wundorlîce æfter bôccræfte, Anglia viii. 308, 24. Gif ðæt ne wexð ðæt hié tiohhiaþ tô dônne, ðonne wanaþ ðæt ðæt hî ǽr dydon, Past. 58; Swt. 445, 8. Ǽghwelces láreówes lâr wihst (wihxð, Hatt. MS.) ðurh his geðylde, 33; Swt. 216, 1. Wesaþ and weaxaþ ealle werþeóde, lifgaþ bi ðâm lissum, Exon. Th. 192, 30; Az. 113. Weóx and wriðade mǽgburg Semes, Cd. Th. 102, 18; Gen. 1702. Seó âdl dæghwamlîce weóx, Bd. 4, 30; S. 609, 25: 5, 12; 627, 12. Weóx wæteres þrym, Andr. Kmbl. 3070; An. 1538. Ǽðelinge weóx word and wîsdôm, 1136; An. 568: 3351; An. 1679. Ǽðelinges weóx rîce, Elen. Kmbl. 24; El. 12. Windas weóxon, Andr. Kmbl. 745; An. 373. Wǽgas weóxon, 3088; An. 1547. Wex and beó gemænigfyld on þeóda and mǽgþa, Gen. 35, 11. Weahxaþ and beóþ gemenigfylde, 9, 1. Wexaþ, Cd. Th. 13, 1; Gen. 196. Weaxaþ, 92, 21; Gen. 1532. Weaxe sió bôt be ðam were, L. Alf. pol. 11; Th. i. 70, 2: L. In. 76; Th. i. 150, 14. Gif ðû gesihst timbrian hûs ðîn, feoh ðîn wexan hit getâcnaþ, Lchdm. iii. 214, 33. Sió gîtsung wile weahsan mid ungemete, Past. 11; Swt. 71, 16. Hê lêt weaxan heora rîmgetel, Cd. Th. 166, 28; Gen. 2754. Sceal weaxan wonna lêg, Beo. Th. 6221; B. 3115. Ne tǽce wê nâ ðæt hê leahtras fyrðrige and weaxan (wehsan, *v. l.*) lǽte, ac ðæt hê hý simle wanige *non dicimus, ut permittat nutriri vitia sed ea amputet*, R. Ben. 121, 8. Gif sió âdl sié git weaxende, Lchdm. ii. 218, 1. Weaxende spêd, Cd. Th. 100, 7; Gen. 1660. IV a. *to grow* in honour, *grow great, flourish, prosper*:—Ic gedô ðæt ðû wyxt *faciam te crescere*, Gen. 17, 6. Ðes middangeard wanaþ and weaxeþ, Fragm. Kmbl. 60; Leas. 32. Hit gebyraþ ðæt hê weaxe and ðæt ic wanige, Jn. Skt. 3, 30. Þeáh hwâ wexe mid micelre æþelcundnesse his gebyrda, and þeó on eallum welum, Bt. 19; Fox 68, 30. Se hlîsa ðæt wǽre sum ancra, ðæt missenlîcum mægnum for Gode weóhse, Guthl. 12; Gdwin. 58, 14. V. *to be productive*:—Ǽr ðon eówre treówu telgum blôwe, wæstmum weaxe *priusquam producant spinae vestrae rhamnos*, Ps. Th. 57, 8. Hêr ys seó bôt hû ðû meaht ðîne æceras bêtan, gif hî nellaþ wel wexan, Lchdm. i. 398, 2. Hê ða weaxendan wende eorðan on sealtne mersc *terram fructiferam in salsuginem*, Ps. Th. 106, 33. VI. *to grow, take shape*:—Hyre weaxan ongon under gyrdelse, ðæt oft gôde men mid feó bicgaþ, Exon. Th. 436, 21; Rä. 55, 10. [*Goth.* wahsjan: *O. L. Ger. O. H. Ger.* wahsan: *O. Frs.* waxa: *Icel.* vaxa.] v. â-, be-, for-, forþ-, ge-, ofer-, under-weaxan; ful-, un-weaxen.

weax-berende *bearing a wax candle;* the word (in the form *uæx biorende*) glosses *cerarius* in the passage: Accoluthus grece, cerarius ad recitandum evangelium (cf. *Acolitus* is gecweden se ðe candele oððe tapor byreþ þonne mann godspell rǽt, Ælfc. C. 14; Th. ii. 348, 4), Rtl. 195, 16.

weax-bred, es; *n.* I. *a table, tablet* for writing on:—Ðâ wrât hê gebedenum wexbrede (wæx-, Lind.) *postulans pugilarem scribsit*, Lk. Skt. 1, 63. Sýn gesealde from ðæm abbode ealle neádbehêfe þing, ðæt is . . . græf, . . . weaxbreda *dentur ab abbate omnia quae sunt necessaria, id est . . . gravium, . . . tabule*, R. Ben. 92, 4. God âwrât ða ealdan ǽ on ðâm stǽnenum weaxbredum. . . . Ða stǽnenan weaxbredu getâcnodon ðæra Iudêiscra manna heardheortnysse, Homl. Th. ii. 204, 1–13. Wexbredu, 196, 32. Wexbreda *tabulas*, Ex. 31, 18. Ne bôc, ne weaxbreda, ne græf, R. Ben. 56, 20. Ðonne ðû græf habban wille, ðonne sete ðû ðîne þrî fingras tôsomne, swilce ðû græf hæbbe, and styra ðîne fingras swilce ðû wrîte. Gyf ðû gehwǽde wæxbreda habban wille, ðonne strece ðû ðîne twâ handa, and sete hý neoþan tôsomne and feald tôgædere and feald tôgædere swilce ðû weaxbreda fealde. Ðonne ðû micel weaxbred habban wille . . . , Techm. ii. 128, 6–12. II. *a table, list*:—Seó forme abecede ys bûtan pricon, and seó ôðer ys gepricod on ða swýðran healfe, and seó þrydde on ða wynstran healfe, swâ ûs hêr æfter gelustfullaþ tô âmearkianne on þissum æfterfyligendum wexbredum, ðe se ârwurða Bêda gesette, Anglia viii. 332, 45. [God wrate þas lage in stanene waxbredene, O. E. Homl. i. 235, 27. Cf. *O. H. Ger.* wahs-tavala *tabula: Icel.* vax-spjald.]

weax-candel[l], e; *f. A wax candle*:—Waexcondel *funalia, cerei*, Wrt. Voc. ii. 109, 45. Weaxcandel, 36, 26. Wexcandel *cereus*, 130, 16: *funalia*, i. *candelabra*, 151, 56. Genim âcmela and beolonan sǽd and weax, meng tôsomne, wyrc tô weaxcandelle, and bærn, Lchdm. ii. 50, 18.

weax-georn; *adj. Eager to grow* (?), *eating much with the desire of growing* (?):—Swîþe waxgeorn eart ðû (*the boy*) ðonne ðû ealle þingc etst ðe ðê tôforan gesette synd *valde edax es, cum omnia manducas quae tibi apponuntur*, Coll. Monast. Th. 34, 31.

weax-gescot, es; *n. A contribution of wax*, due to a church:—Swâ hwæt swâ witan tô ðearfe gerǽdan, hwîlum weaxgescot, Wulfst. 171, 1. [*O. Frs.* wax-skot, -schot. Cf. *Icel.* vax-tollr *a tithe in wax*, payable to a church. See Grimm R. A. 315.]

weax-hlâf, es; *m. A cake of wax*:—On weaxhlâfes wîsan on âlêd, Lchdm. ii. 46, 2. Dô ðonne weax on ðæt ele ðætte ðæt eall weorðe tô hnescum weaxhlâfe, 234, 10: 82, 14. [*O. H. Ger.* wahs-leip *formella* (*formella cerae* circulus cereus, eadem origine qua caseus formella dicitur, quod nempe in forma struatur, Migne).]

weaxhlâf-sealf, e; *f. A salve consisting of a cake of wax*:—Wið weaxhlâfsealfe gemeng, Lchdm. ii. 246, 9. v. weax-sealf.

weaxness, e; *f. Growth, increase, waxing*:—Gyf man mête ðæt hê his hûs timbrie, ðæt byð his weaxnes (cf. 214, 33), Lchdm. iii. 170, 12. Ðonne ðæs sǽes flôdes weaxnes biþ *quando rheuma oceani in cremento est*, Bd. 5, 3; S. 616, 16. Hê mycle wonunge and ǽwyrdlan wæs wyrcende ðære mærwan cyrican weaxnesse *magno tenellis ecclesiae crementis detrimento fuit*, 2, 5; S. 506, 38. v. ge-weaxness.

weax-sealf, e; *f. A salve made of wax*:—Wexsealf *cerotum, unguentum de cera*, Wrt. Voc. ii. 130, 41. Weaxsealf wiþ wyrme; weaxsealf; butere, pipor, hwît sealt, meng tôsomne, smire mid, Lchdm. ii. 124, 11.

weaxung, e; *f.* I. *waxing, growing, increase*:—Ðonne se môna beó týn nihta eald, and nâ ðænne his leóht beó ǽrest on weaxunge, Anglia viii. 323, 5. Nû hæfð se eádiga wer ûs geopenod ymbe ðæs saltus weaxunge, 308, 40. II. *increase* of prosperity:—Eormas strange habban wexinge hit getâcnaþ, Lchdm. iii. 198, 32. On hûse his offrian wexingce oððe blisse hit getâcnaþ, 202, 21: 210, 4.

web(b), es; *n. A web, woven stuff*:—Web *telum*, webb, ueb *textrina*, Txts. 101, 2004, 2005. Web *textrina, telum*, Wrt. Voc. i. 281, 72: *textrina*, 66, 9: *tela* vel *peplum*, 82, 5: *peblum*, 59, 30. Lang web *tela*, 59, 20. Webb byþ gefylled mid þrǽdum *tela consummatur filis*, Scint.

216, 2. Webbes *pepli*, Hpt. Gl. 459, 26. Goldfāg scinon web æfter wāgum *shot with gold shone the work of the loom along the walls*, Beo. Th. 1994; B. 995. Webbum *peplis*, Hpt. Gl. 507, 12. Webbu swā hwilc swā wyfđ, and blisse gesihđ, gōd ǣrende getācnaþ, Lchdm. iii. 210, 28. [*O. Sax.* webbe: *O. H. Ger.* weppi *tela, lodix: Icel.* vefr; *m.*] v. god- (gode-) web, ā-, ō-web.

webba, an; *m. A weaver*:—Webba *textor*, Wrt. Voc. i. 59, 48. Hēr kȳđ on đissere bēc đæt Willelm cwæđ saccles Wulwærd đane webba, Chart. Th. 648, 3. [The webbes ant the fullares (*of Flanders*), P. S. 188, 14. *Chauc.* webbe: *Piers P.* webbe *a* (*female*) *weaver.*]

webbe, an; *f. A female weaver.* v. freođu-webbe, *and see preceding word.*

web-beám, es; *m.* I. *a weaver's beam*:—Lorh *vel* webbeám *liciatorium*, Wrt. Voc. i. 59, 19: 281, 73. II. *the treadle of a loom*:—Webbeámas *insubula*, 59, 43: *insubuli*, ii. 49, 56. [A webbeme *laciatorium*, Wrt. Voc. i. 218, 3 (15th cent.). *O. H. Ger.* weppi-boum *liciatorium.*] Cf. web-sceaft.

webbestre, an; *f. A female weaver*:—Webbestre *textrix*, Wrt. Voc. i. 59, 49. [Webstere *texens*, Wick Job 7, 6. Webstere *textor*, Wülck. Gl. 629, 1: 652, 23. Webster, 685, 29: *textrix*, 692, 26: 795, 8. Webstar *textor, textrix*, Prompt. Parv. 519 (all 15th cent. glossaries).]

webbian; *p.* ode *To weave, contrive*:—Hē wrōht webbade, Andr. Kmbl. 1343; An. 672. Gē inwitþancum wrōht webbedon, Elen. Kmbl. 617; El. 309. Ne beó inwit tō leóf, ne wrōhtas tō webgenne, ne searo tō rēnigenne, Blickl. Homl. 109, 29. [Webbon or webbe clothe of lynnyne *linifico*, webbon clothe of wulle *lanifico*, Prompt. Parv. 519.] v. webbung.

webbung, e; *f. A spectacle*:—Uuebung *scena*, Wrt. Voc. ii. 120, 13. Gereónedes geltes wæbbunge Arsenius geypte *concinnati sceleris scenam Arsenius prodidit* (*ostendit*), Hpt. Gl. 474, 65. Cf. wafian, wafung, *and cpds. of* wæfer-.

webbung, e; *f. A weaving, contriving, plot*:—Webbung (*printed* hwebbund) *conspiratio, conjuratio*, Hpt. Gl. 476, 20. [Webbynge of wullyne clothe *lanificium*, webbynge of lynnyne *linificium*, Prompt. Parv. 519.] v. webbian.

web-gerēþru (-o)? The word occurs in lists of terms connected with weaving, and glosses *tala, tara*:—Webgerēþro *tala*, Wrt. Voc. i. 282, 9. Webgerēþru *tara*, 59, 45: 66, 26. v. next word.

web-gerōdes *glosses* tala, Wrt. Voc. ii. 122, 9. v. preceding word.

web-geweorc, es; *n. Weaving*:—Hió (*the Virgin Mary*) on hyre mægdenhāde dyde fela wundra on webgeweorce, Shrn. 127, 16. Heó wolde beón fram đære þriddan tīde ōđ đa nigoþan tīd ymbe hyre webbgeweorc, Homl. Ass. 127, 348.

webgian. v. webbian.

web-hōc, es; *m. Some implement used in weaving, a tenter-hook* (?):—Webhōc *apidiscus*, Wrt. Voc. i. 59, 41: 66, 24: 282, 7: ii. 7, 70.

web-līc; *adj. Of weaving*:—Weblīc gewurc *textrinum opus*, Hpt. Gl. 431, 4. Đæt weblīce *textrinum*, Wrt. Voc. ii. 77, 17.

web-sceaft, es; *m. A weaver's beam*:—Websceaft *liciatorium*, Wrt. Voc. i. 66, 10. Cf. web-beám.

web-tawa *thread for weaving*:—Webtawa *linea*, Wrt. Voc. ii. 51, 11. Cf. next word.

web-teáh, -teág, e; *f. Thread for weaving*:—Waebtaeg *linea*, Wrt. Voc. ii. 113, 4.

webung. v. webbung.

web-wyrhta, an; *m. A fuller*:—Webwyrhta *fullo*, Wülck. Gl. 245, 33. Swylcne gerelan swylcne nǣnig fulwa, đæt is nǣnig webwyrhta, đæt mihte dōn, Shrn. 56, 10. Đone Iacōbum Iudǣa leorneras ofslōgan mid webwyrhtan rōde, 93, 12.

weccan; *p.* weahte, wehte; *pp.* weaht, weht *To wake, waken.* I. *to rouse* from sleep:—Geseh hē beornas swefan on slǣpe; hē sōna ongann wīgend weccean, Andr. Kmbl. 1699; An. 852. I a. *to rouse* from the sleep of death:—Bȳman weccaþ of deáđe eall monna cynn, Exon. Th. 55, 21; Cri. 887. Ic gǣ đætte of slēpe ic wecce hine, Jn. Skt. Rush. 11, 11. Ne hūru wundur wyrceaþ deáde; oþþe hī lǣceas weccean *numquid mortuis facies mirabilia; aut medici suscitabunt?* Ps. Th. 87, 10. II. *to rouse* from unconsciousness or torpor, *to enliven, stimulate, refresh*:—Hē wehte hine wætre, Beo. Th. 5700; B. 2854. Ealdes mannes eágan beóþ unscearpsȳno; þonne sceal hē đa eágan weccan mid gnīdingum, Lchdm. ii. 30, 28. Seó wæs wæstrum weaht and wæstmum þeaht, Cd. Th. 115, 19; Gen. 1922. III. *to rouse* from repose, *to excite, stir up*:—Se kok, ǣr đam đe hē crāwan wille, hefđ up his fiđru, and wecđ hine selfne, Past. 64; Swt. 461, 14. Drihten windas weceþ *Dominus ventos excitat*, Bd. 4, 3; S. 569, 22. Biþ sǣ smilte þonne hȳ wind ne weceþ, Exon. Th. 336, 27; Gn. Ex. 56. Ne biđ đē rest witod, ac đec regna scūr weceþ and wreceþ, Cd. Th. 252, 11; Dan. 577. Windas weccaþ woruld mid storme, Exon. Th. 59, 13; Cri. 952. Nalles sceal hearpan swēg wīgend weccean, Beo. Th. 6040; B. 3024. IV. *to raise* what is depressed:—Hē of eorđan mæg đone unāgan weccan *suscitans a terra inopem*, Ps. Th. 112, 6. V. *to give life to, to cause, give rise to, produce, raise*:—Feorheáceno cynn, đa đe flōd wecceþ, Cd. Th. 13, 18; Gen. 204. Wyrd wōp wecceþ, Salm. Kmbl. 873; Sal. 436. Sunnan glǣm on lenctenne līfes tācen weceþ, Exon. Th. 215, 17; Ph. 255. Đās windas and đās regnas đa đe eorþan wæstmas weccaþ, Blickl. Homl. 51, 21: Exon. Th. 38, 20; Cri. 609. Hī ǣled weccaþ *they kindle a fire*, 361, 18; Wal. 21. Wec đū clēne hiortan in mē *cor mundum crea in me*, Ps. C. 50, 88. Đæt his brōđor nime his wīf and his brōđor sǣd wecce (*resuscitet*), Mk. Skt. 12, 19. Wæcce, Mt. Kmbl. Rush. 22, 24. Unrǣd fremman, wefan and weccean, Cd. Th. 3, 5; Gen. 31: Beo. Th. 4098; B. 2046. Bǣlfȳra mǣst weccan, 6279; B. 3144. Weccean, Cd. Th. 175, 26; Gen. 2901. [*Goth.* us-wakjan: *O. H. Ger.* wecchen: *Icel.* vekja.] v. ā-, tō-weccan; wacan, wacian.

weccend, es; *m. One who rouses, incites*:—Weccend *incitator*, Germ. 393, 67.

wece-drenc, es; *m. An emetic*:—Wecedrenc . . . sele đæt lytlum sūpan . . . ōþ đæt hē spīwe, Lchdm. ii. 268, 31: 170, 8.

wecen. v. wæcen.

wecg, es; *m.* I. *a wedge*:—Waecg *cuneus*, Wrt. Voc. ii. 105, 70. Wecg, 15, 49: 137, 29. Treówes on ōste nægel ođđe wecg on tō fæstnigenne ys *arboris nodo clauus aut cuneus infigendus est*, Scint. 103, 10. II. *a mass of metal*:—Ǣlces cynnes wecg *vel* ōra ođđe clyna *metallum*, Wrt. Voc. i. 34, 67. Wecg *metallum, massa*, Hpt. Gl. 417, 20. Đætte đǣr wǣre đæt hēhste gōd, đǣr đǣr đa gōd ealle gegæderode bióþ, swelce hī sién tō ānum wecge gegoten, Bt. 34, 9; Fox 146, 20. Hī behwyrfdon heora āre on sumum gyldenum wecge, and đone on sǣ āwurpan, Homl. Th. i. 60, 29. Berende on wecga ōrum, āres and īsernes, leádes and seolfres *venis metallorum, aeris, ferri, et plumbi, et argenti faecunda*, Bd. 1, 1; S. 473, 23. Seó eorđe is cennende wecga ōran *terra parens metallorum*, Nar. 2, 15. On smǣtum goldōrum ł (gold-?) wecgum *in obrizum auri metallum*, Hpt. Gl. 449, 14. Nis nā Godes wununge on đām grǣgum stānum, ne on ǣrenum wecgum, Homl. Skt. i. 7, 136. Lǣt ūs āmyltan đa sylfrenan godas and eác swylce đa gyldenan, dǣlan siđđan wǣdligum đa āmoltenan wæcgas, 5, 234. III. *a piece of money*:—Nim đone ǣrestan fisc . . . đū finst ǣnne wecg (*staterem*) on him, Mt. Kmbl. 17, 27: Homl. Th. i. 512, 4. [*O. H. Ger.* wecki *cuneus: Icel.* veggr.]

wecgan; *p.* de, ede *To wag* (trans.), *move, shake*:—Hwīlum mec wonfeax wale wegeþ and þȳđ, Exon. Th. 393, 31; Rä. 13, 8: 403, 10; Rä. 22, 5. Hī wecgaþ heora heáfdu *moverunt caput*, Ps. Th. 21, 6. Wecggeaþ, 43, 16. Hwalas and hefonfuglas lyftlācende, đa đe lagostreámas wecgaþ (cf. fiscas and fuglas, ealle đa đe onhrēraþ hreó wǣgas, Exon. Th. 194, 18; Az. 141), Cd. Th. 240, 19; Dan. 389. Hwȳ gē ǣfre scylen unrihtfióungum eówer mōd drēfan, swā swā mereflōdes ȳþa hrēraþ īscalde sǣ, wecggaþ for winde (cf. swā swā ȳþa for winde đa sǣ hrēraþ, Bt. 39, 1; Fox 210, 25), Met. 27, 4. Hig wegdan, hrērdan heora heáfod *moverunt capita sua*, Ps. Th. 108, 25. Hī wegedon mec of earde, Exon. Th. 485, 30; Rä. 72, 5. Đonne đū antiphonariam habban wille, đonne wege đū đīne swīþran hand, Techm. ii. 119, 3, 5, 10, *and often.* Wege đū medemlīce đīn reáf mid đīnre handa, 119, 19: 120, 3. Tācn ys đæt mon wecge his hand, 119, 7. Wæcge, 121, 9. Þeáh hit wecge (cf. āstyrođ, Bt. 12; Fox 36, 19) wind, Met. 7, 35. [Swa þe hæȝe wude þenne wind weieđ hine, Laym. 20137. *Goth.* wagjan *agitare, movere: O. H. Ger.* wegen *agitare, movere, vibrare, quatere.*] v. ā-wecgan; wagian, wegan.

-wēd. [Cf. *O. H. Ger.* wuoti *insania: Icel.* œđi.] v. ge-wēd.

wed[d], es; *n.* I. *a pledge, what is given as security*:—Wed *vel* ālǣned feoh *pignus*, gylden wed *vel* feoh *arra*, wed *vel* wedlāc *arrabona* vel *arrabo*, Wrt. Voc. i. 21, 5-7. Wed *pignus*, ii. 82, 25. Þeós gerȳnu is wedd and hīw; Cristes līchama is sōđfæstnyss. Đis wed wē healdaþ gerȳnelīce ōđ đæt wē becumon tō đære sōđfæstnysse, and đonne biđ đis wedd geendod, Homl. Th. ii. 272, 6-8. Hié onfēngon fulwihte and freođuwǣre, wuldres wedde, Andr. Kmbl. 3260; An. 1633. Ic đa wǣre gelǣste đe ic đē sealde frōfre tō wedde, Cd. Th. 139, 13; Gen. 2309: 124, 29; Gen. 2070. Đa ylcan his dohter Criste tō gehālgianne đam biscope tō wedde gesealde, đæt hē đæt gehāt gelǣstan wolde *in pignus promissionis implendae, eandem filiam suam Christo consecrandam episcopo adsignavit*, Bd. 2, 9; S. 511, 39: Beo. Th. 5989; B. 2998. Gif man hrægl tō wedde selle, L. Alf. 36; Th. i. 52, 25. Gif hwā þeóf clǣnsian wylle, lecge ān .c. tō wedde, L. Eth. iii. 7; Th. i. 296, 7. Se Hālga Gāst wæs onsended tō wedde đæs heofonlīcan ēþles, Blickl. Homl. 131, 14. Nafa đū nānes þearfan wedd (*pignus*) mid đē nihtlangne fyrst, Deut. 24, 12. Gif đū wed nime æt đīnum nǣhstan *si pignus a proximo tuo acceperis*, Ex. 22, 26. Genime mon .vi. scill. weorđ wed, L. In. 49; Th. i. 132, 13. Ǣt cynges spǣce lecge man .vi. healfmarc wedd, æt eorles .xii. ōran wedd, L. Eth. iii. 12; Th. i. 296, 25-6. Heora ǣlc sylle .vi. healfmearc wedd, 3; Th. i. 294, 7. Wed undōn *to redeem a pledge*, L. O. D. 1; Th. i. 352, 9. Wed *pignora*, Wrt. Voc. ii. 94, 20. I a. *a dowry*:—Wed, gifu *vel* fædren feoh *dos*, Wrt. Voc. ii. 141, 80. Mid wedde *dote*, 27, 18. I b. fig.:—Worda wed gesyllan (v. the same phrase in the passages from the laws), eallra unsnyttro ǣr gesprecenra *to be responsible for all that has been said before*, Elen.

Kmbl. 2566; El. 1284. II. *a pledge, solemn promise, engagement, covenant, compact*:—Wed oððe wǣra *clasma*, Wrt. Voc. ii. 21, 2. Ða stǣnenan bredu, on ðām wæs ðæt wedd ðe Drihten wið eów gecwæð *tabulis pacti, quod pepigit vobiscum Dominus*, Deut. 9, 9. Ðis ys ðæt wedd (*pactum*), ðæt gē healdan sceolon betwux mē and eów, Gen. 17, 10. Ðis bið ðæt tācen mīnes weddes *hoc signum foederis*, Gen. 9, 12, 13, 15. Se ðe ðæs weddes waldend sȳ, L. Edm. B. 6; Th. i. 254, 21. Beó mīn wedd (*pactum*) on eówrum flǣsce on ēcum wedde (*in foedus aeternum*) . . . hē āīdlode mīn wedd (*pactum*), Gen. 17, 13-14. Hī mid wedde and mid āþum fryþ gefæstnodon, Chr. 926; Erl. 111, 44: 1016; Erl. 159, 4. Mid worde and mid wædde, 1014; Erl. 150, 14. Trymme hē eal mid wedde ðæt ðæt hē behāte, L. Edm. B. 5; Th. i. 254, 17. On (in) wedde[ge]syllan *to give on covenant, to engage to do*:—Ðā cwæð ic ðæt ic him wolde fylstan on ða gerāda ðæt hē his mē ūðe, and hē mē ðæt in wedde gesealde . . . Hē mē ða bōc āgeaf swā hē mē on ðon wedde ǣr geseald hæfde *then I said that I would help him on condition that he would make a grant of the land to me, and he engaged to do that . . . He gave me the deed, as he had before covenanted in the engagement*, Cod. Dip. Kmbl. ii. 134, 9-20. Hæfdon Eoforwīcyngas hyre gehāten, and sume on wedde geseald, sume mid āþum gefæstnod, ðæt hī on hire rǣdinge beón woldon, Chr. 918; Erl. 105, 29: L. Edm. B. 1; Th. i. 254, 5. Hī sǣdon, and on wedde sealdon, hwæt hȳ hyre syllan woldon *they stated what they would give her, and engaged to pay it*, Homl. Ass. 196, 24. God behēt ūs wedd *Deus pepigit nobiscum foedus*, Deut. 5, 2. Ic sette mīn wedd tō ðē *ponam foedus meum tecum*, Gen. 6, 18. Ic sette mīn wedd tō eów *ego statuam pactum meum vobiscum*, 9, 9. Hig slōgon heora wedd ǣgðer tō ōðrum, ðæt hig ǣfre wurdon gefrȳnd *percusserunt ambo foedus*, 21, 27. Geþence hē word and wedd ðe hē Gode betǣhte, L. Eth. v. 5; Th. i. 306, 5. Sealde God his wedd Abrame *pepigit Dominus foedus cum Abram*, Gen. 15, 18. Uton syllan wedd *inemus foedus*, 31, 44: Chart. Th. 485, 37. Ðæt ða witan ealle sealdan heora wedd ðam arcebisceope, L. Ath. v. 10; Th. i. 238, 34: v. 8, 6; Th. i. 236, 35. Be āðum and be weddum. Ðæt ǣghwelc mon his āð and his wed wærlīce healde, L. Alf. pol. 1; Th. i. 60, 1-3: L. C. E. 19; Th. i. 372, 1: Wulfst. 113, 1. Hī wið ðone cyning hī getreówsoden, and binnan litlan fæce hit eall ālugon, ge wed ge āðas, Chr. 947; Th. 118, 14: L. In. 13; Th. i. 110, 12. Gif hwā his āð and his wæd brece, ðe eal þeód geseald hæfð, L. Ed. 8; Th. i. 164, 2. Ðæt man āðas oððe wedd tōbrece, Chart. Erl. 231, 6. Gif gē cōð mīn wedd for nāht *si ad irritum perducatis pactum meum*, Lev. 26, 15: Deut. 31, 16. Ǣlc gerēfa nāme ðæt wedd on his āgenre scīre, L. Ath. v. 10; Th. i. 240, 1: v. 11; Th. i. 240, 15. Ða āðas and ða wedd and ða borgas synt ealle oferhafene and ābrocene, L. Ath. iv. proem.; Th. i. 220, 14. Hī ðæt mid hiera weddum (cf. cum se exsecrationibus devovissent, sacramentisque obstrinxissent) gefæstnod hæfdon, Ors. 1, 14; Swt. 56, 23: L. Ath. v. proem.; Th. i. 228, 7: v. 8, 5; Th. i. 236, 30. [Ic wille settan mi wed betwuxe me and eow, O. E. Homl. i. 225, 28. Mi lond ich wulle sette to wedde, Laym. 25172. Him þet leið his wed ine Giwerie, A. R. 394, 3. To legge a wedde, Piers P. 5, 244. His nekke liþ to wedde, Chauc. Kn. T. 360. Wedde or thynge leyyd yn plegge *vadium, pignus*, Prompt. Parv. 519. *Goth.* wadi *pignus*: *O. Frs.* wed: *O. L. Ger.* weddi *pignus*: *O. H. Ger.* wetti *pignus, pactum, stipulatio*: *Icel.* veð.] v. an-, under-wed[d].

wēdan; *p.* de *To be mad* or *furious, to rage, rave*:—Ic wēde *saevio* and *insanio*, Ælfc. Gr. 30, 5; Zup. 192, 3. *Furo* ic wēde macaþ *insaniui* of *insanio* ic wēde, 33; Zup. 203, 9. Ic wēde *grasso*, Engl. Stud. xi. 66, 44. Wētt *saeuit*, Wülck. Gl. 255, 16. Wēt *furit, irascitur*, 245, 19. Wēdende *funeste*, Wrt. Voc. ii. 151, 65. I. *to be mad, out of one's senses*:—Cwæþ se cyning: 'Ne wille ðū swā sprēcan; gescoh ðæt ðū teala wite.' Cwæþ hē: 'Ne wēde ic (*non insanio*), Bd. 5, 13; S. 632, 32. Deófol is on him, and hē wēt (*insanit*), Jn. Skt. 10, 20. Se man wēt ðe wyle habban ǣnig þincg ǣr anginne, Homl. Skt. i. 1, 17. Ðā wēndon hī ðæt hē tela ne wiste, ac ðæt hē wēde *vulgus aestimabat eum insanire*, Bd. 2, 13; S. 517, 11. Woedendi *limphaticus*, Wrt. Voc. ii. 112, 75: *lymphatico*, 113, 36. Wēdende, 53, 66. Ðone wēdendan *insanum*, 48, 1. Hwā mæg ðam wēdendan gȳtsere (*dives qui sese credit egentem*) genōh forgifan? Bt. 7, 4; Fox 22, 33. II. *to act with violence, be furious, rage*, (a) of persons:—Ðonne se deófol ðūs wētt, Wulfst. 198, 5. Hē wēt swīðe and wynð on ða Cristenan, Homl. Skt. i. 16, 225. Heó geseah hū Decius wēdde and hrȳmde dæges and nihtes ǣr ðon hē deád wǣre, Shrn. 139, 6. Hē wēdde on gewitte swā wilde deór, Exon. Th. 278, 13; Jul. 597. Hī wēddon þearle and tōtǣron hī sylfe mid heora āgenum tōðum, Homl. Skt. i. 6, 194. Hē (*Antichrist*) onginð deóflīce tō wēdanne, Wulfst. 200, 1. Wēdende *debachatus*, Wrt. Voc. ii. 86, 21: 26, 74. Seó wēdende meniu ofslōgon ðone Victor, Homl. Skt. ii. 28, 113. For wēdendre heortan ðæs leódhatan Brytta cyninges *propter vesanam Brittonici regis tyrannidem*, Bd. 3, 1; S. 524, 1. Uuoedende *bachantes*, Wrt. Voc. ii. 101, 52. Hī (*the Jews*) tō Criste hosplīce word wēdende sprǣcon, Homl. Th. ii. 232, 31. Wrōhtsmiðas (*evil spirits*) wēdende swā wilde deór, Exon. Th. 156, 23; Gū. 8, 9. (b) of animals:—León wēdan (gesihð), gestric ge(tācnaþ), Lchdm. iii. 206, 32. Wēdende hund, Bt. 37, 1; Fox 186, 8. Wulfas woedende *lupi rapaces*, Mt. Kmbl. Rush. 7, 15. (c) of things, abstract or concrete:—Gȳtsung openlīce wēt *auaritia palam saeuit*, Scint. 99, 17. Wēdde stīðnes *exarsit acerbitas*, Hpt. Gl. 517, 15. Gārsecg wēdde, Cd. Th. 208, 27; Exod. 489. Ða ȳða weóllan and wēddan ðæs sǣs *furentibus undis pelagi*, Bd. 3, 15; S. 541, 39. Þeáh ðeós woruld wēde and windige ēhtnysse āstyrige ongeán Cristes gelaðunge, Homl. Th. ii. 388, 9. Ðonne wind wēdende færeþ, Elen. Kmbl. 2546; El. 1274. Mid wēdendum and egislīcum gehlȳde *bacchanti et furibundo strepitu*, Hpt. Gl. 495, 75. Wēdende reóhnysse *tumentem insaniam*, 465, 20. Wēdende ȳða *frementes* (*furentes*) *fluctus*, 464, 74. Hyt ða wēdendan bitas gehǣlcþ, Lchdm. i. 370, 14. [Biginneð þe deoflen to weden, A. R. 264, 9. As mon þ bigon to weden and to wurðen ut of his ahne witte *indignatus cum furore nimio*, Kath. 1257. Fra þatt gredi3nesse þatt doþ þe mann to wedenn rihht to winnenn erþlic ahhte, Orm. 14140. Þe kyng ferde for wraþþe as he wolde wede, R. Glouc. 53, 10. *O. Sax.* wōdian: *O. H. Ger.* wuoten *furere, grassari, insanire, bacchari, fremere*: *Icel.* œðask *to become furious*.] v. ā-, ge-wēdan; wōd.

wed-brōðer; *m. One who is pledged to act as a brother to another, a confederate*:—Ðā luuede Wulfere hit swīðe for his brōðer luuen Peada, and for his wedbrōðeres luuen Oswī, Chr. 656; Erl. 30, 1. Cōman bēgen ða cyningas tōgædre and wurdon feólagan and wedbrōðra, and ðæt gefæstnadan ǣgðer mid wedde and eác mid āðan, 1016; Th. i. 284, 1, col. 1. [Send after mine sune Octa, and æfter Ebissa his wedbroðer, Laym. 14469. *Icel.* veð-brōðir. Cf. eið-broðir.]

wed-bryce, es; *m. Breach of a pledge* or *engagement*:—Gif hē ðæs weddie, ðe hym riht sȳ tō gelǣstanne, and ðæt āleóge . . . bēte ðone wedbryce swā him his scrift scrīfe, L. Alf. pol. 1; Th. i. 60, 6-21. Eác syndan wīde þurh āðbrycas and ðurh wedbrycas and ðurh mistlīce leásunga forloren and forlogen mā ðonne scolde, Wulfst. 164, 7. Wedbricas, 130, 6. [Cf. With wedbrek *cum adulteris*, Ps. 49, 18.]

wedd. v. wed[d].

weddian; *p.* ode *To engage, covenant, undertake*:—Weddodon *pepigere*, Germ. 396, 137. I. *to engage* to do something, (a) with gen. of that for which the engagement or pledge is given:—Be ðon ðe ordāles weddigaþ. Gif hwā ordāles weddige *if any one engage to undergo an ordeal*, L. Ath. i. 23; Th. i. 210, 25. Gif hē ðæs weddie, ðe hym riht sȳ tō gelǣstanne, L. Alf. pol. i; Th. i. 60, 6. Is tō witanne hwam ðæt fōsterleán gebyrige, weddige se brȳdgum eft ðæs *let the bridegroom engage to furnish this*, L. Edm. B. 2; Th. i. 254, 9. Ðæt se slaga mōte sylf wæres weddian, L. Edm. S. 7; Th. i. 250, 17. (b) with gerundial infin.:—Hig him weddedon feoh tō syllenne *pacti sunt pecuniam illi dare*, Lk. Skt. 22, 5. II. in reference to either taking or giving in marriage, *to wed, betroth, espouse*:—Gif hȳ ǣlces þinges sammǣle beón, ðonne fōn māgas tō and weddian heora māgan tō wīfe and tō rihtlīfe ðam ðe hire girnde, L. Edm. B. 6; Th. i. 254, 20. Gif man mǣdan oþþe wīf weddian wille, 1; Th. i. 254, 2. [Þat mæiden he weddede, Laym. 4432. Wifmann to weddenn, Orm. 10407. Weddedd wiþþ an weppmann, 1942. He moste weddy wyf, R. Glouc. 331, 13. I wedde myne eres, Piers P. 4, 146. *Goth.* ga-wadjōn *despondere*: *O. Frs.* weddia *to promise, pledge*: *Icel.* veðja *to wager*.] v. be-, for-, ge-weddian.

weddung, e; *f. Betrothal, espousal*:—Ðā cwæþ Pilatus tō ðam folce, ða ðe sǣdon ðæt hē of forligere wǣre ācenned: 'Ðeós sprǣc nys nā sōþ ðæt gē sprecaþ, for ðon seó weddung wæs beweddod, eal swā eówre āgene ðeóda secgaþ,' Nicod. 7; Thw. 3, 31. [Or men wimman to louerd giue for wedding or for morgengiwe, Gen. and Ex. 1428.] v. be-weddung.

wēde; *adj. Furious, in a rage, mad, fierce*. v. wēdan, II:—Nælle ðū mē woede (cf. gram, W. S. version) wosa *noli mihi molestus esse*, Lk. Skt. Lind. 11, 7. Woedo (gram, W. S.) wæs mē ðió widiua *molesta est mihi haec vidua*, 18, 5. Wið wēdes (wēde, MS. B. v. wēde-hund) hundes slite, Lchdm. i. 362, 23. Cf. wōd.

wēde-berge, an; *f. A plant that is used against madness, hellebore*:—Woedeberge, woedibergæ *eleborus*, Txts. 59, 736. Woidiberge *helleborus*, 67, 1017. Wēdeberge, Wrt. Voc. ii. 29, 2: 32, 30. Ðeós wyrt ðe man *elleborum album* . . . and eác sume men wēdeberge hātaþ, Lchdm. i. 258, 23.

wēde-hund, es; *m. A mad dog*:—Gif wēdehund man tōslīte, Lchdm. i. 86, 13. Wið wēdehundes (cf. wōdes [*printed* woden] hundes, 4, 8) slite, 78, 17: 92, 12: 138, 13: 198, 8: 370, 12, 15: ii. 144, 9. Hē rēþigmōd rǣst on gehwilcne wēdehunde (*printed* reðe hunde, *but* cf. wēdende hund, Bt. 37, 1; Fox 186, 8) wuhta gelīcost, Met. 25, 18. v. wēde.

wēden-heort, es; *n. Madness, frenzy, fury*:—Lǣcedōmas wið feóndseócum men . . . and wiþ bræcseócum men, and wiþ wēdenheorte, Lchdm. ii. 14, 7: 138, 14. Drenc wiþ wēdenheorte, 356, 4: 304, 15. Ðæt hrȳðer him þūhte on wēdenheorte *the beast seemed to him mad*, Blickl. Homl. 199, 11.

wēden-heort; *adj. Mad, frenzied, furious*:—Wēdenheortra synna *furiarum*, Wrt. Voc. ii. 36, 30. v. next word.

wēdenheortness, e; *f. Madness, frenzy, fury*:—He gelōmlīce mid wēdenheortnesse mōdes ðrycced wæs *crebra mentis vesania premebatur*,

Bd. 2, 5; S. 507, 3. Wiþ wēdenheortnesse Macedones *contra vesaniam Macedonii*, 4, 17; S. 585, 45. For wēdenheortnesse ðæs leódhatan *propter vesanam tyrannidem*, 3, 1; S. 524, 1. Hī ongunnon ðæt hī his wēdenheortnysse gestildon *motus ejus insanos comprimere conati*, 3, 11; S. 536, 22. Hié wealwiaþ on ða wēdenheortnesse *in mentis vesaniam devolvuntur*, Past. 40; Swt. 289, 6. Wēdenheortnessum *furiis*, Wrt. Voc. ii. 37, 50. In woedenheortnisse leáse *in insanias falsas*, Ps. Surt. 39, 5.

weder, es; *n.* I. *weather, condition of the atmosphere*:—Ueder *temperies*, Wrt. Voc. ii. 122, 27. Gif hit sié gōd weder, Lchdm. ii. 182, 10. Hyt byð smylte weder *serenum erit*, Mt. Kmbl. 16, 2: Bt. 23; Fox 78, 26. Ðonne wind ligeþ, weder bið fæger, Exon. Th. 210, 8; Ph. 182. Hreóh weder *tempestas*, Mt. Kmbl. 16, 3. Rēn, swylce hagal and snāw, weder unhióre, Met. 29, 65. Hit wæs ceald weder, Ors. 6, 32; Swt. 286, 31: Met. 26, 28. Forstas and snāwas, winterbiter weder, Cd. Th. 239, 32; Dan. 379. Wearm weder, Exon. Th. 198, 30; Ph. 18. Rēnig weder, 380, 18; Rä. 1, 10. Wederes blæst, hādor heofonleóma, Andr. Kmbl. 1674; An. 839. Līþes weðres, Met. 12, 13. Wedere gelīcost . . . on sumeres tīd, Cd. Th. 237, 34; Dan. 347. Ða sǣ ðe wæs smylte wedere glæshlūtru, Bt. 6; Fox 14, 24. Þeáh hine (*a sick man*) mon on sunnan lǣde, ne mæg hē be ðȳ wedre wesan (*he can't stand the weather*), þeáh hit sȳ wearm on sumera, Exon. Th. 340, 18; Gn. Ex. 113. Hē ūs giefeþ weder līþe, Exon. Th. 38, 12; Cri. 605. Winter bringeþ weder ungemetceald, swifte windas, Met. 11, 59. On sumera ðonne ða hātostan weder synd, Lchdm. ii. 252, 10. Weder cōledon heardum hægelscūrum, Andr. Kmbl. 2514; An. 1258. Wuldortorhtan weder, Beo. Th. 2276; B. 1136. Wedera cealdost, 1097; B. 546. Wedera cyst, Cd. Th. 238, 6; Dan. 350. Niht bið wedera þeóstrost, Salm. Kmbl. 621; Sal. 310. Ðeóf sceal gangan in ðȳstrum wederum, Menol. Fox 544; Gn. C. 42. Hwȳ hī ne scīnen scīrum wederum, Met. 28, 45. Holmegum wederum, Cd. Th. 185, 6; Exod. 118. I a. *good weather*. v. weder-dæg:—Hine ne went nāðor ne weder ne unweder of ðam ðe him gecynde ys, Lchdm. iii. 268, 3. Winter sceal geweorpan, weder eft cuman, sumor swegle hāt, 338, 12; Gn. Ex. 77. Wedres on luste, 361, 28; Wal. 26. Rēn cymð, ðonne eówre wæstmas wederes beþorftan, Wulfst. 297, 11. II. *wind, storm, breeze, air*:—Weder *aura*, Wrt. Voc. i. 76, 43: 52, 59. Smylte wedere *aure tenuis*, ii. 4, 56: 6, 20. Blōstme fægerust raþe tō leohtum forscrincþ wedere *flos pulcherrimus cito ad leuem marcescit auram*, Scint. 70, 3. Wedre gesomnad, Exon. Th. 412, 19; Rä. 31, 2. In wedr *in auram*, Blickl. Gl. Weder, Ps. Surt. 106, 29. [Wurdon ormǣtlīca wædera mid þunre, Chr. 1117; Erl. 246, 15.] Wintregum wederum *cum saevis aquilonibus stridens campus inhorruit*, Bt. 5, 2; Fox 10, 31. Styrmendum wederum, 7, 3; Fox 22, 5. II a. in reference to sailing, *weather* (as in *weather*-bow, -bound), *wind*. v. weder-fæst:—Ðā gestōd hine heáh weder and storm sǣ, wearþ ðā fordrifan on ān īglond *vela Neritii ducis eurus appulit insulae*, Bt. 38, 1; Fox 194, 10. Ðā him weder com, and Godwine and ða ðe mid him wǣron wendan tō Brycge, Chr. 1052; Erl. 181, 19. Wearð ðæt wæder swīðe strang, ðæt ða eorlas ne mihton gewitan hwet Godwine eorl gefaren hæfde, Erl. 183, 3. Hē ðǣs wederes ābād, 1094; Erl. 229, 36: 1097; Erl. 234, 20. Hē wearð þurh weder gelet, Erl. 233, 34. Gōd scipstȳra ongit micelne wind on hreóre sǣ ǣr ǣr hit geweorþe . . . warenaþ hē hine wiþ ðæt weder, Bt. 41, 3; Fox 250, 17. [*O. Sax.* wedar *weather, storm*: *O. Frs.* weder: *O. H. Ger.* wetar: *Icel.* veðr.] v. ge-, ofer-, un-weder, un-geweder.

Wederas; *pl. The Geats*, a tribe of southern Scandinavia:—Wedera leóde, Beo. Th. 455; B. 225. Wedera leód (*Beowulf*), 687; B. 341. Wedra ðeóden, 5305; B. 2656. v. Weder-Geátas.

weder-blāc; *adj. Weather-pale, pale from exposure to weather* (?). Cf. flōd-blāc:—Wederblāc *palus*, healfhār *semicanus*, fulhār *canus* (these glosses are omitted after Wrt. Voc. i. 45, 34), Anglia viii. 451.

weder-burh; *f. A town exposed to storms, a weather-beaten city*:—Him Dryhten bebeád, ðæt hē ða wederburg wunian sceolde, Andr. Kmbl. 3390; An. 1699.

weder-candel; *f. The candle of the open air, the sun*:—Wedercandel swearc, Andr. Kmbl. 744; An. 372. Wedercondel wearm weorodum lȳhteþ, Exon. Th. 210, 17; Ph. 187. Cf. heofon-, sweg -candel.

weder-dæg, es; *m. A day of fine weather, a fine day.* v. weder, I a:—Beorht sumor, wearme wederdagas, Exon. Th. 191, 30; Az. 96. [Cf. *Icel.* einn gōðan veðrdag *one fine day, once on a time.*]

weder-fæst; *adj. Weather-bound*:—Ðā gewendon hī west tō Peunenesеá and lǣgen ðǣr wederfeste, Chr. 1046; Erl. 174, 6. [*Icel.* veðrfastr.]

Weder-Geátas; *pl. The Geats*:—Weder-Geáta leód (*Beowulf*), Beo. Th. 2989; B. 1492: 3229; B. 1612. Hē Weder-Geátum weóld, 4747; B. 2379. v. Wederas.

wederian; *p.* ode *To be* (*good* or *bad*) *weather*:—Cweðaþ sume men, ðæt se mōna hine wende be ðan ðe hit wuderian (wedrian, widrian) sceal on ðam mōnðe; ac hine ne went nāðor ne weder ne unweder of ðam ðe him gecynde ys, Lchdm. iii. 268, 2. [*Icel.* viðra *to be such and such weather.*] v. ge-wederian, wederung.

weder-līce. v. unweder-līce.

Weder-mearc, e; *f. The district occupied by the Wederas*:—Ōþ ðæt eft byreþ ofer lagustreámas leófne mannan wudu wundenheals tō Wedermearce, Beo. Th. 602; B. 298.

weder-tācen, es; *n. A sign of fine weather.* v. weder, I a:—Eástan cwom dægrēdwōma, wedertācen wearm, Exon. Th. 179, 25; Gū. 1267. [Cf. *Ger.* wetter-zeichen *prognostic of a storm.*]

wederung, e; *f. Weather*:—Ðæs ilcan geáres wæs swīðe hefelīc geár . . . swā mycel ungelimp on wæderunge swā man nāht ǣþelīce geþencean ne mæg; swā stōr þunring and lǣgt wes, swā ðæt hit ācwealde manige men, Chr. 1085; Erl. 219, 21. [Gif ȝe mine bibode healded, þenne sende ic eou rihte widerunge, O. E. Homl. i. 13, 17. We shul preyen . . . for alle trewe shipmen, þ^t godd ȝeue hem wederyng . . .; for þe fruyte of þe londe and þe wederyng, E. G. 23, 18, 20. Wederynge of þe eyre *temperies*, Prompt. Parv. 519.] v. wederian.

weder-wolcen, es; *n. A fine weather cloud.* v. weder, I a, weder-dæg, -tācen:—Hæfde wederwolcen (*the pillar of cloud*) eorðan and uprodor efne gedǣled, Cd. Th. 182, 13; Exod. 75. [Cf. *Ger.* wetter-wolke *a tempestuous cloud.*]

wed-fæstan; *p.* te *To pledge* [:—Geuuetfaestae *subarrata*, Wrt. Voc. ii. 121, 52.] [Cf. *Icel.* veð-festa *a pledge.*]

wēding, e; *f. Madness, frenzy*:—Wēding *frenesis*, Wrt. Voc. ii. 39, 10. [*O. H. Ger.* wuotunga *furor.*]

wed-lāc, es; *n.* I. *a pledge, security*:—Wed *vel* wedlāc *arrabona* vel *arrabo*, Wrt. Voc. i. 20, 7. Wedlāc *arrabo*, 50, 31. II. in reference to marriage, v. weddian, II, *wedlock, espousals*:—Wedlāc wiðsacende *pacta sponsalia refutans*, Hpt. Gl. 498, 44. [The latter is the usual sense in Middle English:—Under wedlac iboren, Laym. 395. Bute one ine wedlake, A. R. 206, 14. Wass soþ weddlac haldenn, Orm. 2499. In lele wedlayk born, Pr. C. 8261. Heo þat her wedlac brekeþ, Misc. 150, 105. Þei wrouȝt wedlokes aȝein goddis wille, Piers P. 9, 152. Wedlok *matrimonium*, Prompt. Parv. 520. Wedloke *maritagium*, Wulck. Gl. 595, 5.]

wed-loga, an; *m. One who is false to a pledge* or *engagement*:—On ðison gēre swāc Harðacnut Eádulf eorl under his gride, and hē wæs ðā wedloga, Chr. 1041; Erl. 166, 33. Ic ðē eom andetta mīnra synna . . . ic eom wedloga, Anglia xii. 501, 19. Ðæt gē ne beón wedlogan ne wordlogan, Wulfst. 40, 10: 165, 36. Cristen cyning sceal wedlogan and wǣrlogan hatian and hȳnan, 266, 29. [Þu (*the body*) were wedlowe and monsware, Fragm. Phlps. 7, 27.]

wedrian, weel, Wrt. Voc. ii. 95, 79, -wef. v. wederian, þel, ge-, ō-wef.

wefan; *p.* wæf, *pl.* wǣfon; *pp.* wefen. I. *to weave* a web:—Ic wefe *texo*, Wrt. Voc. i. 59, 47. Ðū wyfst and wǣda tylast, Homl. Th. i. 488, 25. Ðīn wyln wefð *tui ancilla texit*, Ælfc. Gr. 15; Zup. 104, 13. Webbu swā hwylc swā wyfð, Lchdm. iii. 210, 28. Hī smalo hrægel wefaþ and wyrceaþ *texendis subtilioribus indumentis operam dant*, Bd. 4, 25; S. 601, 16. Ða of ðæs treówes leáfum and of his flȳse spunnon and swā eác tō godewebbe wǣfon and worhtan *gens foliis arborum ex siluestri uellere uestes detexunt*, Nar. 6, 19. Ðā onfēng Maria hwīt godweb tō wefanne . . . Ðā sprǣcon hī: 'þū eart ūre gingast, ðe miht wefan ðæt hwīte godeweb,' Homl. Ass. 132, 550. Wefen wæs *ordiretur* (*colobium de stuppae stamine*, Ald. 51), Wrt. Voc. ii. 83, 18. From ðæm weofendan *a texente*, Ps. Surt. ii. p. 184, 34. Fram wefendum wīfe, Cant. Ez. 12. II. in a more general sense, lit. or fig. *to weave, construct, put together, arrange, plan, contrive*:—Swā ðæt wuldor wifeþ, Exon. Th. 493, 8; Rä. 81, 27. Ðus ic frōd wordcræft wæf and wundrum læs, Elen. Kmbl. 2473; El. 1238. Ic wef *intexui* (*funibus lectulum meum*, Prov. 7, 16), Kent. Gl. 199. Wefan *contexere* (*coronam*), Hpt. Gl. 439, 68. Wefan *texuisse* (*oraculorum seriem*), 442, 39. Ðæs engles mōd ðe ðone unrǣd ongan ǣrest fremman, wefan and weccean, Cd. Th. 3, 5; Gen. 31. Ðonne seó þrāg cymeþ wefen wyrdstafum, Exon. Th. 183, 10; Gū. 1325. [*O. H. Ger.* weban: *Icel.* vefa. Cf. *Goth.* bi-waibjan *to wind about.*] v. ā-, be-, ge-wefan; þyn-wefen.

wefl, e; wefle (-a; *m.*?), an; *f.* I. *weft, woof, thread which crosses the warp*:—Weft *vel* ōwef, uuefl *cladica, caldica*, Txts. 51, 482. *Cladica* wefl oððe ōwef oððe *claudica*, Wrt. Voc. ii. 14, 43. Wefl *vel* ōweb *cladicla*, 131, 59. Wefl *cladica*, 16, 31: i. 66, 13: 281, 76. Uuefl *panuculum*, ii. 116, 29: *titica* (cf. *O. H. Ger.* below), 122, 33. Weflan *peniculae* (the passage is: Nisi panniculae diversis colorum varietatibus fucatae inter densa filorum stamina ultro citroque decurrant, Ald. 15), Hpt. Gl. 430, 69. Wefla *panucla* (this is a gloss to the same passage as the preceding), Wrt. Voc. ii. 77, 13. Wundene mē (*a coat of mail*) ne beóð wefle (ueflæ, Txts. 151, 5), ne ic wearp hafu *the threads of the woof are not twisted for me, nor have I a warp*, Exon. Th. 417, 15; Rä. 36, 5. Wæfla *panniculorum* (colobium cum sine pompulenta panniculorum varietate ordiretur, Ald. 51), Hpt. Gl. 494, 9. Weflum *panniculis* (*panuclis*, Wrt. Voc. ii. 65, 61, in a gloss to the same passage: Lanea filorum stamina ex glomere et panniculis revoluta, Ald. 8), 417, 20. II. *an implement for weaving* (-l suffix in words denoting implements, cf. scofl), *a shuttle* (?):—Hē sceal habban fela towtōla . . . pihten, wefle,

wefle (*or under* I?), wulcamb, Anglia ix. 263, 13. [*O. H. Ger.* wefal (-el, -il) *datica, subtemen, stamen.*] v. next word.

wefta, an: weft, es; *m. Weft, woof:*—Wefta *vel* weft *deponile*, Wrt. Voc. i. 59, 38. Wefta, 66, 14: 281, 77. Wefta *deponile*, uueftan *depoline*, Txts. 55, 642. Wefta *depo[nile]*, weftan *deponile*, Wrt. Voc. ii. 138, 85, 86. Wefta *depoline*, 25, 19: *clatica*, 131, 68. [Weft *subtegmen*, Wick. Ex. 39, 3. A wefte *trama*, Wulck. Gl. 696, 21. *Icel.* veftr, vifta.] v. preceding word.

wefung, e; *f. Weaving:*—Weofung *textura*, Wrt. Voc. ii. 77, 12.

weg (wig, Kent. Gl. 207: 475: 772; *pl.* weogas, 21), es; *m. A way.* I. of the direction in which motion (lit. or fig.) takes place:—Ða tungelwîtegan ðurh óðerne weg tó heora earde gecyrdon. Úre eard is neorxnawang, tó ðam wé ne magon gecyrran ðæs weges ðe wé cómon, Homl. Th. i. 118, 20–23. Þonne rídeþ ǽlc hys weges, Ors. 1, 1; Swt. 21, 4. Hí wendon him súðweard óðres weges, Chr. 1016; Erl. 154, 15. Wæges, 1006; Erl. 140, 22. Hé mé eft lǽdde ðý sylfan wegge ðe wé ǽr tó cóman, Bd. 5, 12; S. 629, 41. Hig gewendon him ofer langne weg, ðæt hig ðæt land embférdon, Num. 21, 4: Cd. Th. 35, 13; Gen. 554: 43, 13; Gen. 690. Hié ofer feorne weg ceólum lácaþ, Andr. Kmbl. 504; An. 252: 2348; An. 1175. Fóre gefremman on feorne weg, 382; An. 191. Nán man ne mihte faran þurh ðone weg (woeg, Lind.: wæge, Rush.), Mt. Kmbl. 8, 28. Sceáweras, ðæt cýðon ús, on hwilcne weg wé faran sceolon (*per quod iter debeamus ascendere*), Deut. 1, 22. Ðú weg nimest geond deóp wæter, Cd. Th. 80, 16; Gen. 1329. Wǽrun wegas ðíne on wídne sǽ *in mari viae tuae*, Ps. Th. 76, 16. Onbúgan of ðæs gewealde, ðe mé wegas tǽcneþ, Exon. Th. 383, 26; Rä. 4, 16. Tóføran on feówer wegas æðelinga bearn, Cd. Th. 102, 9; Gen. 1697. I a. with the idea of access or passage:—Ðá gesette God æt ðam infære engla hyrdrǽdene and fýren swurd tó gehealdenne ðone weg tó ðam lífes treówe, Gen. 3, 24. Ic mé weg ryhtne gerýme, Exon. Th. 479, 24; Rä. 63, 3. Hé sceolde gearcian and dæftan his weig, Homl. Th. i. 362, 8. Wegas syndon drýge, haswe herestrǽta, Cd. Th. 195, 28; Exod. 283. II. *a road* (lit. or fig.) *made for passengers, a path commonly used:*—Weg *via*, Wrt. Voc. i. 53, 56. On eástan ealles folces weg, and an súðan se weg se ðe líð tó ðam ilcan lande, Cod. Dip. B. i. 586, 15. Swá swá se weg líð, wé faraþ *via regia gradiemur*, Num. 21, 22. Ðæt geat is swýðe wíd, and se weg is swíðe rúm, ðe tó forspillednesse gelǽt, Mt. Kmbl. 7, 13, 14. On ðam wege, ðe líð tó Euphfrate *in via, quae ducit Euphratam*, Gen. 35, 19. Se assa eode of ðam wege. Hwæt ða Balaam beót ðone assan, wolde ðæt hé eode innan ðone weg *asina avertit se de itinere et ibat per agrum; quam cum verberaret Balaam et vellet ad semitam reducere*, Num. 22, 23. Sum sacerd férde on ðam ylcan wege (woege, Lind.), Lk. Skt. 10, 31. Gif feorrancumen man oþþe fræmde búton wege gange, L. Wih. 28; Th. i. 42, 23. Gif ðú wyrfst on wege rihtum up tó ðam earde, Met. 24, 44. Gif ðú cymst on ðone weg and tó ðære stówe, Bt. 36, 2; Fox 174, 21. Hé leóde lǽrde on lífes weg, Andr. Kmbl. 340; An. 170: 3357; An. 1682. Sume feóllon wið weg (æt strǽt ł woeg, Lind.: bi wæge, Rush.), Mt. Kmbl. 13, 4. Wegas, enta ǽrgeweorc, strǽte stánfáge, Andr. Kmbl. 2470; An. 1236. Nǽron Metode ðá gyt wídlond ne wegas nytte, Cd. Th. 10, 13; Gen. 156. Betýndan wega gelǽtan *competa clausa*, wega gelǽtum *competis, terminis*, Wrt. Voc. ii. 132, 52: 19, 55. Ðæt wíf, ðe æt ðæra wega gelǽte sæt *mulier, quae sedebat in bivio*, Gen. 38, 21. Tó wega (ðære wegara ł ðæra wegana, Lind.: weogas, Rush.) gelǽtum *ad exitus viarum*, Mt. Kmbl. 22, 9. Wega gemittung *compitum*, Wrt. Voc. i. 55, 8. On wega gemótum *in competis*, ii. 46, 12. Eádgifu gefreóde Ælfgiðe on feówer wegas (v. Earle's note, p. 468, on manumission at four cross-roads), Chart. Erl. 255, 20: 254, 29. Ungerydu beóð on smeðe wegas (woegum, Lind.), Lk. Skt. 3, 5. Gódige hé folces fær mid bricgum ofer deópe wæteru, and ofer fúle wegas, L. Edg. C. 14; Th. ii. 282, 10. Ðurh ðrióstrie weogas *per vias tenebrosas*, Kent. Gl. 21. II a. of what resembles a path, as in Milky Way. v. Íringes weg. III. *space to be traversed, a journey:*—Eáðfére weg *iter* vel *itus*, lang and stearc weg *itiner*, Wrt. Voc. i. 37, 35, 36. Gif se weg swá lang beó, ðæt ðú ðíne þing bringan ne mage, Deut. 14, 24. Hig hæfdon sumne dǽl weges gefaren *processerant paululum*, Gen. 44, 4: *aliquantulum itineris confecissent*, Bd. 1, 23; S. 485, 30. Mé wæs Rachel deád be wege *mortua est Rachel in itinere*, Gen. 48, 7. Hé tó ðam cyng gewænde. Ðá com Sparhafoc be weg[e] tó him, Chr. 1048; Erl. 177, 19. Fela þúsenda be wæge forfóran, 1096; Erl. 233, 21. Heó forðférde be Róme wege (*in itinere Rome*), 888; Erl. 87, note 10. Mid ðý ðe ðæt mín werod gestilled wæs, ða férdon wé forð ðý wege ðe wé ǽr ongunnon *quae res quum anime quietiorem fecisset exercitum, ceptum iterum institui*, Nar. 8, 18: 17, 5. Gif mon fram longum wege geteorod sié, Lchdm. ii. 150, 19: 16, 16. Árís and et, ðú hæfst swýþe langne weg, Homl. Skt. i. 18, 168. On eallum ðám wegum ðe gé fóron, Deut. 1, 31. IV. in reference to conduct, action, practice, *manner, mode, method, plan:*—Geriht mínne weg (se weg is mín weorc), Ps. Th. 5, 8. Ealle his wegas sint dómas, Deut. 32, 4. Gehwelci wega (uuaega, uuegi) *quocumque modo*, Txts. 91, 1700. Hé his wegas dyde cúðe *notas fecit vias suas*, Ps. Th. 102, 7. Unrihte wegas, 118, 104. V. *way*, in al-*way*, -*ways:*—Under his tungan byð ealne weg óþera manna sár, Ps. Th. 9, 28. Ðæt edleán ðe ðú ealne weg gehéte, Bt. 3, 4; Fox 6, 19. Ealne weg (symle, Met. 8, 18) hí ǽton ǽne on dæg, Bt. 15; Fox 48, 8. Ic wát ðú wéne ðæt hí on heora ágenre cýþþe ealne weg mægen *inter eos, apud quos ortae sunt, num perpetuo perdurant?* 27, 4; Fox 100, 11: 29, 1; Fox 102, 10. Ic simles wæs on wega gehwam willan ðínes georn on móde, Andr. Kmbl. 129; An. 65. Wel mon sceal wine healdan on wega gehwylcum, Exon. Th. 342, 19; Gn. Ex. 145. VI. in the plural, in some compounds, the word has the sense of *parts, regions.* Cf. *Icel.* -vegir. v. eást-, norþ-, súþ-, síd-, wíd-wegas. [*Goth.* wigs: *O. Sax. O. H. Ger.* weg: *O. Frs.* wei: *Icel.* vegr.] v. á-, ærne-, bæþ-, beám-, burh-, díc-, eást-, eorþ-, fær-, feor-, flód-, flot-, fold-, forþ-, gang-, here-, híg-, holm-, hors-, horu-, hrycg-, hwæt-, hwyrft-, líf-, mǽr-, mid-, mold-, norþ-, on-, or-, riht-, síd-, sídling-, síþ-, stán-, stapol-, stíþ-, súþ-, tún-, twi-, þeód-, up-, wægn-, wæl-, wæter-, weall-, west-, wíd-, wil-, will-weg; ealneg.

weg (wei, wí) **lá**; *interjection:*—Weg lá, weg lá *euge, euge*, Ps. Th. 69, 4. Weg lá weg ł wá lá wá ł eálá, eálá *euge, euge*, Ps. Lamb. 39, 16. Wí lá wei (wei lá wei, Cott. MS.), Bt. 35, 6; Fox 170, 12. [Cf. *Ital.* via.]

wég *a wave.* v. wǽg.

wegan; *p.* wæg, *pl.* wǽgon; *pp.* wegen. A. *trans.* I. *to move, bear, carry, bring, transport:*—Ic wege oððe ic ferige *ueho*, Ælfc. Gr. 28, 5; Zup. 176, 4. (Scip) wist in wigeþ, Exon. Th. 415, 14; Rä. 33, 11. Ðone (*a dog*) on teón wigeþ feónd his feónde, 433, 28; Rä. 51, 3. Hám wegaþ *advehunt*, Wrt. Voc. ii. 1, 5. Hé ða frætwe wæg ofer ýða ful, Beo. Th. 2419; B. 1207. Hé com tó ðam forwundodum, and wæh hine hám tó his inne, Homl. Ass. 47, 559. Mec wǽgun fedre on lifte, feredon mid liste, Exon. Th. 409, 19; Rä. 28, 3. Micel mænigeo elpenda ða ðe gold wǽgon and lǽddon *elephanti qui aurum uehebant*, Nar. 9, 6. Mín weorod goldes micel gemet mid him wǽgon and lǽddon, 7, 1. Wágon, Judth. Thw. 26, 14. Gesáwon hié weallas standan. . . . Þurh ða heora beadosearo wǽgon, Cd. Th. 214, 21; Exod. 572. Wégon, Byrht. Th. 134, 43; By. 98. Gúðspell wegan *to carry news of the war*, Cd. Th. 126, 18; Gen. 2097. Wegen on wægne, Exon. Th. 403, 15; Rä. 22, 8. I a. fig. where the object is abstract, *to bring, cause:*—Geáp stæf wigeþ biterne brógan, Salm. Kmbl. 250; Sal. 124. II. *to bear, support:*—Eahta sweras syndon ðe rihtlícne cynedóm trumlíce up wegaþ, L. I. P. 3; Th. ii. 306, 20. III. *to bear, carry*, (1) *to have* as part of one's equipment, *bear* arms, *wear:*—Sigegyrd ic mé wege, Lchdm. i. 388, 15. Ic (*a sword*) sinc wege, Exon. Th. 401, 4; Rä. 21, 6. Se ðe gold wigeþ *he that wears golden ornaments*, 484, 12; Rä. 70, 6. Mec (*a lance*) . . . on fyrd wegeþ, 486, 21; Rä. 72, 18. Hé heregeatowe wegeþ, Salm. Kmbl. 106; Sal. 52. Mec (*a horn*) folcwigan wicge wegaþ, Exon. Th. 395, 27; Rä. 15, 14. On ðæm hrægle, ðe hé on his breóstum wæg, Past. 13; Swt. 77, 15. Wæs feówer geár, ðæt hé woroldwǽpno wæg, Blickl. Homl. 213, 4. Hæfde hé and wæg mid hine twigecgede handseax *habebat sicam bicipitem*, Bd. 2, 9; S. 511, 15: Beo. Th. 5402; B. 2704. Hé lígegesan wæg, 5554; B. 2780. Rincas randas wǽgon, Cd. Th. 123, 22; Gen. 2049. Gyf him þince ðæt hé wǽpen wege, ðæt byð orsorh, Lchdm. iii. 174, 13: Beo. Th. 4497; B. 2252. Ne wæs álýfed, ðæt hé móste wǽpen wegan (*arma ferre*), Bd. 2, 13; S. 517, 7. On fyrd wegan fealwe linde, Cd. Th. 123, 13; Gen. 2044. Ís sceal brycgian wæter helm wegan (*water must wear a helm of ice*), Exon. Th. 338, 5; Gen. Ex. 74. Wegan máððum *to wear a jewel*, Beo. Th. 6023; B. 3015. Ic nolde wegan ðín wynsume geoc, Anglia xi. 112, 22. (1 a) fig., where the object is abstract:—Sume him ðæs hádes hlísan willaþ wegan on wordum and ða weorc ne dóð *some are ready to bear the reputation of being of the elect, as far as words go, and do not do the works*, Exon. Th. 105, 32; Gú. 32. (2) *to have* as part of or within one's self:—Fela geofona, ða ða gǽstberend wegaþ in gewitte, Exon. Th. 293, 18; Crä. 3. Ðone líchoman ðe heó (*the soul*) ǽr longe wæg, 367, 21; Seel. 11. Ðæt lámfæt ðæt hié (*the soul*) ǽr lange wæg, 375, 5; Seel. 133. Tír unbrǽcne wǽgon on gewitte wuldres þegnas, Apstls. Kmbl. 173; Ap. 87. Ðú scealt wegan swátig hleór, Cd. Th. 57, 27; Gen. 934. (3) *to be under the influence of* pain, joy, etc., *have* such and such feelings, *bear* a grudge:—Ic ðæs tácen wege sweotol on me selfum, Cd. Th. 54, 31; Gen. 885. Hé lust wigeþ, Beo. Th. 1203; B. 599. Hé on breóstum wæg byrnende lufan, Chr. 975; Erl. 126, 14. Grendel heteníðas wæg, Beo. Th. 307; B. 152. Módþrýðo wæg cwén, 3867; B. 1931: Cd. Th. 135, 6; Gen. 2238. Ic wæg módceare micle, Beo. Th. 3559; B. 1777. Wedera helm heortan sorge wæg, 4919; B. 2464: Exon. Th. 162, 28; Gú. 982: 182, 13; Gú. 1309: Elen. Kmbl. 122; El. 61: 1307; El. 655. Lifge Ismael and ðé þanc wege, heardrǽdne hyge, Cd. Th. 141, 20; Gen. 2347. Ða ðe á wegen egsan Dryhtnes *qui timent Dominum*, Ps. Th. 113, 20. IV. *to bear, submit to* consequences:—Ne bið ǽngum gódum gnorn ætýwed, ne nǽngum yflum wel; ac ǽghwæþer ánfealde gewyrht andweard wigeþ, Exon. Th. 96, 23; Cri. 1578. Gylde hé ðæs cinges oferhýrnesse, and wege ða ungerisenu, L. Ath. iv. 1; Th. i. 222, 6. Gif hwá ǽnigne man ofsleá, ðæt hé wege sylf ða fǽhðe, L. Edm. S. 1; Th. i. 248, 2, 9. V. *to weigh*, (1) *to put something in a balance:*—Ic wege *trutino*, Ælfc. Gr. 36; Zup. 215, 18. Ælc ðæra ðinga, ðe man wihð (wehð, *v.l.*) on wǽgan, 13; Zup. 84, 2. Man sett ða synne and ða sâwle on ða wǽge, and hý man wegeþ, swâ man déð gold wið penegas, Wulfst. 240, 2. Weh on wǽge, Lchdm. i. 374, 15. (1 a) fig.:—Teóðige on Godes êst eal ðæt hê âge, and wege hine sylfne swâ hine oftost tô onhagige, L. Pen. 15; Th. ii. 282, 23. Wegendre tôcâles ł gescâdes âpinsunge *discretionis lance librantis (ponderantis)*, Hpt. Gl. 447, 71. (2) *to be equal to* a certain weight:—Ǽlc ân hagelstân wegeþ fíf pund, Wulfst. 228, 7. Se sester sceal wegan twâ pund, Lchdm. iii. 92, 14. B. *intrans. To move*:—Ymb hine wǽgon wîgend unforhte, Cd. Th. 189, 5; Exod. 180. Frætwed wǽgun (-m, MS.) wic[g] ofer wongum, Exon. Th. 353, 2; Reim. 6. [Heo weȝe (beore, 2nd MS.) on heore honde feouwer sweord, Laym. 24471. To teche an beore to weȝe boþe scheld and spere, O. and N. 1022. Chepinge þe me shule meten oðer weien, O. E. Homl. ii. 213, 34. To weien swuðer his sunne þen he þurfte. Weien hit to lutel is ase vuel, A. R. 336, 22. *Goth.* ga-wigan *to shake*: *O. L. Ger.* wegan *to weigh*: *O. Frs.* wega, weia *to move, weigh*: *O. H. Ger.* wegan *movere, vibrare, nutare, librare, trutinare, ponderare, pensare*: *Icel.* vega *to move, carry, weigh.*] v. â-, æt-, be-, for-, ge-, tô-wegan; sweord-, wanwegende; un-wegen.

wêgan *to delude*, wêgan *to bend*. v. wǽgan, ge-wêgan.

weg-brâde, -brǽde, an; *f. Way-bread* (v. E. D. S. Pub. Plant Names):—Wegbrâde, uuegbrâdae, uegbrâdae *arnaglossa*, Txts. 43, 213. Uuegbrâde *plantago*, uuaegbrâdae *plantago* vel *septenerbia*, 87, 1601. Wegbrǽde, Wrt. Voc. ii. 68, 21. Wegbrâde *arnaglosse*, i. 67, 10. Wegbrǽde, 286, 22: ii. 8, 37, 48: Lchdm. i. 80, 8 (cf. title, 4, 14 wegbrǽd (-brâde, -brǽde, *v. ll.*). Wegbrâde *plantago*, Wrt. Voc. i. 68, 40. Wegbrǽde, 79, 32: *cinoglossa* vel *plantago* vel *lapatium*, 30, 50. Ðû wegbrâde, wyrta môdor, Lchdm. iii. 32, 5. Wegbrǽdan seáw, i. 80, 12. Wegbrǽdan sǽd, 82, 6. Of ðære rûwan wegbrǽdan, ii. 106, 13. Genim ða rûwan wegbrǽdan nioþowearde, 292, 10. Ða smêþan wegbrǽdan, 350, 7. [*O. H. Ger.* wege-breita *centinodia, plantago.*]

wêge. v. wǽge.

weg-farende; *adj.* (*ptcpl.*) *Wayfaring*:—Sum wegfarende (-fêrende, *v. l.*) man fêrde wið ðone feld; ðâ wearð his hors gesicclod, Homl. Skt. ii. 26, 204. Seó nædre ligeþ on ðam wege, and wyle ða wegfarendan mid hire tôðum slîtan, Wulfst. 192, 23. [*Icel.* veg-farandi.] v. following words.

weg-fêrend, es; *m. A wayfarer, a traveller*:—Se nacoda wegfêrend *vacuus viator*, Bt. 14, 3; Fox 46, 29. Stunt wegfêrend *stultus viator*, Scint. 187, 6. Wîferend *viator*, Kent. Gl. 137. v. next word.

weg-fêrende; *adj.* (*ptcpl.*) *Wayfaring*; used subst. *a wayfarer, traveller.* I. *travelling, on a journey*:—Gif ðû wǽre wegfêrende, and ðû becôme on þeófsceole, Bt. 14, 3; Fox 46, 25. Se wegfêrenda man, se ðe nimð ðone smêðan weg, ðe hine mislǽt, Homl. Th. i. 164, 7. Ânes wegfêrendes mannes nýten gehǽled wæs *jumentum cujusdam viantis curatum est*, Bd. 3, 9; S. 533, 3. Wê sind hêr swilce wegfêrende menn, Homl. Th. i. 248, 15. Se rîca and se ðearfa sind wegfêrende on ðisse worulde, 254, 28. I a. used substantively:—Swâ swâ wegfêrende þyrstende *sicut uiator siciens*, Scint. 225, 10. Wîferend, Kent. Gl. 137. Wegfêrende ðæt sǽd fortrǽdon, Homl. Th. ii. 90, 45. Se ðe ǽnig ðissa dô ..., bûton wegfêrende; ða môton for neóde mete ferian, L. N. P. L. 56; Th. ii. 298, 25. Nyhtlîc leóht wegfêrendum (*viantibus*), Hymn. Surt. 6, 14. II. *going a way, passing by*:—Hî genýddon sumne wegfêrendne *angariauerunt praetereuntem quempiam*, Mk. Skt. 15, 21. Ða wegfêrendan (*praetereuntes*) hyne bysmeredon, Mt. Kmbl. 27, 39. [Sein Iulianes in, þet weiuerinde men ȝeorne secheð, A. R. 350, 16. Þe pilgrimes, and oþre wayuerinde men, Ayenb. 39, 3.] v. preceding words.

weg-fôr, e; *f. A wayfaring, going away*:—On wegfôre *in provectione* (= profectione?), Wrt. Voc. ii. 46, 29.

weg-gedâl, es; *n. A place where a road divides*:—Weggedâl *difortium*, Txts. 57, 672: *compitum*, Wrt. Voc. i. 53, 60.

weg-gelǽte, an; *f.*: -gelǽte, es; *n.* (v. ge-lǽte) *A place where roads meet*:—Weggelǽte *compitalia*, Hpt. Gl. 515, 27. Æt ðære wegegelǽton, Cod. Dip. Kmbl. v. 297, 29. Wegelǽton *trivium*, Wrt. Voc. i. 53, 58. Weggelǽta *compita*, 37, 45.

weg-gesîþa, an; *m. A companion* or *attendant on the road*:—Wæggesîðan *satellites*, Hpt. Gl. 426, 68.

wêgi. v. wǽge.

weg-leás; *adj.* I. *without a road, impassable*:—Ungefêre *vel* wegleás pæð *invium*, Wrt. Voc. i. 53, 61. Weglǽsa beara *aviaria, secreta nemora*, 39, 11. II. fig. *out of the way, erroneous, unreasonable*:—Welise (= wîlêse? cf. wig = weg, *and* wî-fêrend = wegfêrend, *both in the same glossary*) *devium*, Kent. Gl. 432. Gedwelde mid wegleásum *errore devio*, Hymn. Surt. 24, 13. [Cf. *Icel.* vegalauss *out of the way, lost in the woods.*]

weg-leást, e; *f. Want of road*:—Dwelian hê dyde hig on wegleáste and nâ on wege *errare fecit eos in invio et non in via*, Ps. Spl. 106, 40. v. next word.

weg-lîsu (?); *f. Want of road*:—Welise (= wîlêsu?) *devium*, Kent. Gl. 432. [Cf. *Icel.* vega-leysi *want of roads.*] v. preceding words.

weg-nest, es; *n. Food for a journey*:—Wearð uncer wegnyst âfûlod, Shrn. 42, 4. Him siþþan sý wegnestes getîðad, and swâ mid wegneste hâm cyrren, R. Ben. 103, 21. Ðâ genâmon wit twêgen buccan, and wit hig âcwealdon, and gehióldan hiora flǽsc unc tô wægnyste, Shrn. 41, 30: 36, 31. ¶ the word is used of the sacrament administered to the dying:—Gif se man on his ýtemestan dæge gyrneþ Cristes lîchaman tô underfônne, ne wyrne him man nâ, ... ðæt bið his wegnyst (*viaticum*), and ǽlces ðæra manna ðe tô Godes rîce becymð, L. Ecg. P. i. 10; Th. ii. 176, 20. Heó onfêng wægnyste ðære hâlgan gemǽnsumnysse, Bd. 4, 23; S. 595, 27. Hê bûtan hǽlo wegnyste of worulde gewât, 5, 14; S. 634, 33. Hê wæs hine trymmende mid ðý heofonlîcum wægneste, 4, 24; S. 599, 2. [*O. H. Ger.* wega-nest (-nist) *cibaria, viaticum*: *Icel.* veg-nest.]

weg-reáf, es; *n. Booty taken on the high road, robbery done on a road*:—Gif wegreáf sî gedôn, .vi. scillingum gebête. Gif man ðone man ofslæhð, .xx. scillingum gebête, L. Ethb. 19, 20; Th. i. 8, 1-2. Ðeówæs wegreáf sê .iii. scillingas, 89; Th. i. 24, 16. Cf. wæl-reáf.

weg-twislung, e; *f. The forking of a road*:—Wegtwislung (*spelt* -twiflung) *diverticulum*, Wrt. Voc. i. 55, 6.

wegures, Wrt. Voc. i. 35, 47. v. wig-gâr.

wei lâ wei. v. weg lâ.

wel, well. I. *adv. Well*, (1) with verbs, (a) marking the success or excellence of the action of the verb:—Ðæt hié heora fulwihthâdas wel gehealdan, Blickl. Homl. 109, 26. Wel hearpan stirgan, Exon. Th. 42, 6; Cri. 668. Swîþe wel ðû mîn hæfst geholpen, Bt. 41, 4; Fox 250, 18. (a 1) *well, prosperously*:—Se man wæs wel dônde on eallum þingum *erat vir in cunctis prospere agens*, Gen. 39, 2. (b) marking the rightness, fitness, etc. of an action:—His nama wæs gereht 'Godes strengo.' Wel ðæt wæs gecweden, for ðon ðe se hæfde mægen ofer ealle gesceafta, Blickl. Homl. 9, 14. Wel ðû sprecst *bona res est, quam vis facere*, Deut. 1, 14. Wel ðû cwǽde *bene dixisti*, Lk. Skt. 20, 39. Hê him wel (woel, Lind.) andswarode, Mk. Skt. 12, 28. Hî nalæs wel dydan *non observaverunt pactum*, Ps. Th. 77, 57: 118, 126. Welan âh in wuldre se nû wel þenceþ, Exon. Th. 452, 12; Dôm. 119. Suîðe wel Dryhten ðreáde Iudêas, Past. 21; Swt. 151, 19. (c) marking kindness or goodness:—Gyf gê wel dôð ðam ðe eów wel dôð, Lk. Skt. 6, 33. Tô Gode ðe mê wel dyde *ad Dominum qui benefecit mihi*, Ps. Th. 56, 2. Gié magon him woel dôe (wel dôa, Rush.) *potestis illis bene facere*, Mk. Skt. Lind. 14, 7. Wese ðîn mildheortnis well ofer ûs, Ps. Ben. 32, 18. (d) marking degree, *well, much, thoroughly, freely*:—Gecnua wel, Lchdm. ii. 322, 26. Lǽt gestandan wel *let it stand a good while*, 326, 19. Syle him ðâs ylcan wyrte wel drincan on wætere, i. 148, 19. Se cyng him eác wel feoh sealde, Chr. 894; Erl. 91, 32. Dô wel sealtes on, Lchdm. ii. 322, 17. Ðe ðissa woruldsǽlða tô wel ne lyste, Bt. 7, 3; Fox 22, 24. Ungemetes wel randwigan restan lyste, Beo. Th. 3589; B. 1792. Ðæt hié welena tô wel ne trûwodon, Blickl. Homl. 185, 14. Eal swâ wel behôfaþ ðæt heáfod ðæra ôðera lima, swâ swâ ða lima behôfiaþ ðæs heáfdes, Homl. Th. i. 274, 7. (e) marking favourable condition, absence of hindrance:—Hê his wel geweald âhte on ðæm scræfe, Past. 3; Swt. 37, 5. Eálâ gif hê wolde, ðæt hê wel meahte ðæt unriht him eáðe forbiódan, Met. 9, 53. Hié wel meahton libban on ðam lande, gif hié wolden lâre Godes fremman, Cd. Th. 49, 3; Gen. 786. (f) marking fitness of circumstance, *well, properly*:—Hý mihton wel habban wîf on ðam dagum, L. Ælfc. C. 7; Th. ii. 346, 7. (f 1) with verbs that denote fitness:—Wel ðæt gerâs, ðæt heó wǽre eádmôd ... Wel ðæt eác gedafenaþ, ðæt hê tô eorþan âstige, Blickl. Homl. 13, 16-19. Hine man byrigde, swâ him wel gebyrede, ful wurðlîce, Chr. 1036; Erl. 165, 34. (g) marking happy, pleasant, agreeable condition:—Lîf âdreógan wel *to pass life pleasantly*, Coll. Monast. Th. 28, 31. Ðæt mê wel sig for ðê *ut bene mihi sit propter te*, Gen. 12, 13: Num. 11, 18: Exon. Th. 66, 32; Cri. 1080. Ne bið ðǽr ǽngum gôdum gnorn ætýwed, ne nǽngum yflum wel, 96, 20; Cri. 1577. Ðâm bið well, ðe ðara blissa brûcan môton, Andr. Kmbl. 1770; An. 887. Is ðæt lâ well *euge, euge*, Ps. Th. 39. 18. Wel lâ wel is ûrum môdum *euge, euge animae nostrae*, 34, 33. Ðê wel weorðeþ on wynburgum *bene tibi erit*, 127, 2. (g 1) exclamatory, without a verb expressed:—Wel hym ðæs geweorkes, Hy. 2, 11. Wel ðâm, ðe ðonne ne âwâcaþ, Wulfst. 89, 19: 124, 8. Wel ðære heorde, ðe gefolgaþ ðam hyrde, L. C. S. 85; Th. i. 424, 12. (2) with adjectives, *well, very, quite, thoroughly*:—Strange cyningas and wel cristene, Bd. 4, 2; S. 565, 31: Wulfst. 29, 6: 39, 15: 127, 2. Glæsfæt wel micel, Lchdm. ii. 252, 8. On wîne wel scearpum, 180, 16: Ps. Th. 67, 15, 16: 104, 37. Dagas wel manige, Blickl. Homl. 217, 15: 225, 10. Wyrta swîþe wel clǽne, Lchdm. ii. 336, 5. (3) with numerals:—Hê ðǽr þurhwunode wel twâ geár *he stopped there quite two years*, Homl. Skt. i. 15, 37. Ic gesett hæbbe wel feówertig lârspella, Ælfc. T. Grn. 13, 45. (4) with adverbs, *very, quite*:—Wæs be eástan ðære ceastre wel nêh *erat prope ipsam civitatem ad orientem ecclesia*, Bd. 1, 26; S. 487, 42. Wê wel neáh stôdan ðâm bearwum, Nar. 28, 31: Guthl. 12; Gdwin. 58, 19. Wel wîde *passim, ubique*, Hpt. Gl. 512, 18. II. *interjection, well, ah*:—Wel lâ *heu*, Germ. 388, 11. Hê cwæð mid wôpe; wel lâ, Basilius, gif ðû sylf noldest, nǽre ðû git forðfaran, Homl. Skt. i. 3, 627. Wel lâ, mîn Drihten, hwæt ic hêr nû ł reówlîce hæbbe gefaren, 23, 575. Wel lā (cf. eálā, Bt. 4; Fox 8, 10), đū ēca sceppend āra monna cynne *O! jam respice terras*, Met. 4, 29. Wel lā, monna bearn, 21, 1. Wel lā, men, wel, Bt. 34, 8; Fox 144, 23. Wel gā *heia*, Wrt. Voc. ii. 110, 30. Weol gā, weol gā *euge, euge*, Ps. Surt. 69, 4. [*Goth.* waila: *O. Sax. O. Frs.* wel: *O. H. Ger.* wela, wola: *Icel.* vel.] v. for-wel, *and compounds with* wel *as first component.*

wēl *a pool.* v. wǣl.

wela, weola, weala, an; *m.* I. *wealth, riches*:—Wela, hord, feoh *gazofilacium*, Wrt. Voc. ii. 74, 24. Wuldur and wela *gloria et divitiae*, Ps. Th. 111, 3. Geđenc nū hwæt đīnes āgnes seó ealra đissa woruldǣhta and welena . . . hwæt hæfst đū . . . æt đām welum? Sege mē nū hwæþer se đīn wela (*divitiae*) đīnes þances swā deóre seó . . . đa welan beóþ leóftǣlran đonne đonne hié mon selþ, đonne hié beón đonne hī mon healt . . . Gif nū eall đises middaneardes wela cōme tō ānum men, hū ne wǣron ealle ōþre men wǣdlan? Genōh sweotol đæt is, đætte gōd hlīsa biþ betera đonne ǣnig wela, Bt. 13; Fox 38, 1–24. Ǣlc sōþ wela *opes*, 7, 3; Fox 20, 16. Đæt unmǣte gestreón goldes and seolfres, oþþe eal se wela, Blickl. Homl. 99, 29. Eal eorþan wela, 51, 30. Wala *divitiae*, Rtl. 81, 18. Welan *patrimonii*, welan, spēdignesse *opulentia*, Hpt. Gl. 491, 7–9. Ne biddan wē ūrne Drihten đyses lǣnan welan, ne đyssa eorþlīcra geofa, Blickl. Homl. 21, 11. Of đisse worulde welan (wælom, Lind.) *de mamona*, Lk. Skt. 16, 9. Ūre ieldran begeáton welan, and ūs lǣfdon, Past. pref.; Swt. 5, 15. Se man āhte mycelne welan, Blickl. Homl. 197, 30. Ǣhte sīne, beágas and botlgestreón, welan, wunden gold, Cd. Th. 116, 4; Gen. 1931: Exon. Th. 331, 1; Vy. 61: Andr. Kmbl. 603; An. 302. Welan bryttian, Cd. Th. 131, 19; Gen. 2178. Weolan, Chr. 1065; Erl. 197, 26: Ps. Th. 16, 9. Gif đæt đīne āgne welan wǣron, Bt. 7, 3; Fox 20, 18: Blickl. Homl. 53, 21: 99, 24: 113, 25. Wealan (weolan, Surt.) *divitiae*, Ps. Th. 61, 11. Ǣgđer ge đīnra welona ge đīnes weorþscipes *opum dignitatumque*, Bt. 7, 3; Fox 20, 4. Đæra wlenca ł walana (weolan, Rush.) *divitiarum*, Mt. Kmbl. Lind. 13, 22. Walana ł weala (willana, Rush.), Mk. Skt. Lind. 4, 19. Wiþsacaþ đām leásum welum . . . and đām unālȳfdum gestreónum, Blickl. Homl. 53, 23. Hē weorþode his deórlingas mid miclum welum, Bt. 28; Fox 100, 29: Andr. Kmbl. 1509; An. 756. Weolum *divitiis*, Nar. 4, 7: Bd. 4, 11; S. 579, 8. Welum (walum, Lind.), Lk. Skt. 8, 14. Đa welan dǣlan earmum monnum, Blickl. Homl. 49, 32. I a. *abundance, wealth*:—Hærfest cymþ, wæstmum hladen, wela byđ geyped, Menol. Fox 282; Men. 142. Welan neótan, londes frætwa, Exon. Th. 208, 2; Ph. 149. Mid wuldres welan *cum gloria*, Ps. Th. 72, 19. Mid welan bewunden, Cd. Th. 27, 19; Gen. 420: 42, 2; Gen. 668. Beóđ đīnes wīfes welan gelīce swā on wīngearde weaxen berigean *uxor tua sicut vitis abundans*, Ps. Th. 127, 3. Būwa eorđan and fēd đē on hyre welum (weolum, Surt.) *inhabita terram, et pasceris in divitiis ejus*, 36, 3. II. *weal, prosperity, happy estate*:—Biđ him se wela onwended, and wyrđ him wīte gegearwod, Cd. Th. 28, 5; Gen. 431. Wæs him beorht wela, þenden đæt folc mid him hiera fæder wǣre healdan woldon, 216, 20; Dan. 9: 96, 32; Gen. 1603. Dō hiá ondueardlīc gefeáiga uale *fac eos praesenti gaudere prosperitate*, Rtl. 70, 1. Onceósan gōdes and yfeles, welan and wāwan, Cd. Th. 30, 12; Gen. 466. Hī mōton him đone welan āgan đe wē on heofonrīce habban sceoldon, rīce mid rihte, 27, 24; Gen. 422. Hē þeóda gehwam heofonrīce forgeaf, wīdbrādne welan, 40, 22; Gen. 643. God sealde welan swā wīte, swā hē wolde sylf, 256, 23; Dan. 645: Exon. Th. 85, 9; Cri. 1385. [*O. E. Homl. Laym. O. and N.* wele, weole: *A. R.* weole: *Gen. and Ex.* wale: *Pr. C. Chauc. Piers P. Gow.* wele: *O. Sax.* welo: *O. H. Ger.* wela, wola, wolo *riches, prosperity.*] v. ǣht-, ǣr-, ǣt-, ār-, blǣd-, bold-, botl-, burg-, eád-, eorþ-, fōddur-, fold-, grund-, hord-, land-, līf-, māđum-, nāwiht-, weoruld-wela.

Wēland, es; *m. A character in old Teutonic legends celebrated for his skill as a smith.* Allusion to him is found in Middle English poetry: 'My sword . . . thorrow Velond wroght yt wase,' Torrent of Portugal, ed. Halliwell, l. 428 (v. preface, pp. vii sqq.), and a trace of the legend is preserved in the name *Wayland Smith's Cave*, in Berkshire (v. infra). Perhaps, too, the same may be said of the river-name Welland (but see Weolud), which occurs in Latin charters as *aqua de Uueeland*, Cod. Dip. Kmbl. i. 78, 10, *aqua de Uueland*, 304, 6: ii. pp. 90, 281, 416:—Wēland him wræces cunnade, earfoþa dreág, Exon. Th. 377, 9; Deór. 1. Wēlandes geworc ne geswīceþ monna ǣnigum, Wald. 2; Vald. 1, 2. Wēlandes bearn, 74; Vald. 2, 9. Beaduscrūda betst, Wēlandes geweorc, Beo. Th. 914; B. 455. Hwǣr sint nū đæs foremǣran and đæs wīsan goldsmiđes bān Wēlondes *ubi nunc fidelis ossa Fabricii* (cf. faber) *jacent?* Bt. 19; Fox 70, 1. Wēlandes, Met. 10, 33; 35, 42. ¶ in local names of England:—Đis sint đæs landes gemǣre æt Cumtūne (*Compton Beauchamp, Berkshire*) . . . hit cymđ on đæt wīde geat be eástan Wēlandes smiđđan, Cod. Dip. Kmbl. v. 332, 23. Andlang strǣte on Wēlandes stocc (*boundaries of land at Princes Risborough, Bucks*), Cod. Dip. B. ii. 259, 13. [*O. H. Ger.* Wielant, Wiolant: *Icel.* Völundr.] v. Kemble's Saxons in England, i. 420 sqq; Stephens' King Waldere's Lay, pp. 35 sqq.; Grmm. D. M. 350.

wel-besceáwod; *adj. Considerate, prudent*:—Welbesceáwod *consideratus, cordatus*, Wrt. Voc. ii. 133, 71. Sȳ hē ā foregleáw and welbesceáwod *sit providus et consideratus*, R. Ben. 121, 15.

wel-boren; *adj. Well-born, noble*:—Welboren *nobilis*, Mk. Skt. Lind. Rush. 15, 43. Monn sum welboren *homo quidam nobilis*, Lk. Skt. Lind. Rush. 19, 12. Ic nam wīse menn and welborene (*nobiles*), Deut. 1, 15.

wel-dǣd, e; *f.* I. *a good deed*:—Wē sceolon on ūrum weldǣdum blissian mid sōđre eádmōdnysse, and ūrum Drihtne đancian his gife, đæt hē ūs geūđe, đæt wē mōston his willan gewyrcan þurh sume weldǣde. Ne mæg nān man nāht tō gōde gedōn būton Godes gife, Homl. Th. ii. 432, 6–10. Dō well on eallum đīnum līfe, and wē siđđan æfter đīnum weldǣdum đē eft genimaþ tō ūs, 346, 17: i. 414, 30: Homl. Skt. i. 1, 148. Wlitige gewyrtad mid hyra weldǣdum, Exon. Th. 234, 21; Ph. 543. Sprec ofter ymb ōđres monnes weldǣda đonne ymb đīne āgene, Prov. Kmbl. 10. II. *a benefit, favour, kindness*:—Weldǣd *beneficium*, Cod. Dip. B. i. 155, 19. Hē ūs gelǣde tō his Fæder, đe hine sealde for ūrum synnum tō deáđe. Sȳ him wuldor and lof đære weldǣde, Homl. Th. ii. 282, 27. Weldǣdum *beneficiis*, Scint. 16, 5. Uton brūcan godcundum weldǣdum, 133, 6: Anglia xiii. 370, 74: Homl. Th. i. 562, 7. Hē wiđ monna bearn wyrceþ weldǣdum (*acts beneficently*), Exon. Th. 191, 12; Az. 87. Wē đīnum weldǣdum wurdan āhafene *in beneplacito tuo exaltabitur cornu nostrum*, Ps. Th. 88, 14. Nele God ūs wītnian for his weldǣdum, odđe his milde mōd mannum āfyrran, 76, 7. Weldǣda wītes *merita* (*beneficia*) *martyrii*, Hpt. Gl. 489, 50. Ūs God mǣre weldǣda getīđaþ *nobis Deus magna beneficia prestet*, Scint. 16, 8: Homl. Th. ii. 298, 12: 418, 23. Wē ne magon āsecgean his weldǣda on ūs, Basil admn. 4; Norm. 42, 3. Hī ofergeáton weldǣda (-dēda, Surt.) his *obliti sunt benefactorum ejus*, Ps. Spl. 77, 14. III. *an office, service*:—Be reáflācum fremedum ælmyssan dōn nys weldǣd miltsunge *de rapinis alienis elemosinam facere non est officium miserationis*, Scint. 159, 16. His ēđhylde weldǣde *suo contentus officio*, 133, 3. Cumlīþnysse and manscipes weldǣdum underþeódde *hospitalitatis atque humanitatis offitiis deditos*, Cod. Dip. B. i. 154, 38. [Weldede *good deeds*, O. E. Homl. i. 133, 1. Heo cunnen us unđonc for ure weldede (*the good we do them*), Laym. 3306. Heom (*the gods*) wurđen for heore weldæde (*benefits*), 8052. Leueþ to writen in wyndowes of ȝowre weldedes, Piers P. 3, 70. *Goth.* waila-dēds *beneficium*: *O. H. Ger.* wola-tāt *beneficium, meritum*: *Ger.* wohl-that.]

wel-dōn *to satisfy, please*:—Hē walde đæm folce weldōn (*satisfacere*), Mk. Skt. Lind. 15, 15.

wel-dōnd, -dōend, es; *m. A benefactor*:—For weldōndum *pro benefactoribus*, Anglia xiii. 370, 72: 394, 411. Weldōndan, 384, 275. Fore weldōendum mīnum, Rtl. 125, 9.

wel-dōnde; *adj.* (*ptcpl.*) *Doing well, acting rightly*:—Hū se reccere sceal bión đǣm weldōndum monnum for eáđmōdnesse gefēra *ut sit rector bene agentibus per humilitatem socius*, Past. 17; Swt. 107, 5.

wel-dōnness, e; *f. Kindness, benignity*:—Weldōnnis *benignitas*, Rtl. 13, 33.

weled. v. wilwian.

weler (-ur, -or), weolor (-ur, -er), es; *m.*: e; *f. A lip*, (1) masculine or uncertain:—Weler *labium*, Wrt. Voc. i. 70, 48. Wæler *labrum*, 64, 53. Welor *labium*, 282, 69: ii. 51, 67. Neođera welor *album*, 7, 79. Weolure *labio*, Lchdm. i. lxx, 4. Weleras *labia*, Ps. Spl. 11, 2, 4: 65, 12: Ps. Th. 62, 5: 65, 12: Kent. Gl. 1002. Weleras (weloras, Cott. MSS.), Past. 15; Swt. 91, 17. Weleras (welras, *v. l.*), R. Ben. 2, 22. Weoloras, Ps. Th. 30, 20. Welera *labiorum*, Ps. Spl. 20, 2. Welerum *labiis*, 62, 6: 119, 2: Mt. Kmbl. 15, 8: Mk. Skt. 7, 6: Homl. Th. ii. 450, 26: *labellis*, Wrt. Voc. ii. 51, 68. Wælerum *labiis*, Rtl. 174, 17. Walerum, 179, 11. Welrum *buccis, buccellis*, Wrt. Voc. ii. 126, 66: *labellis*, Hpt. Gl. 507, 46. Weolorum *labiis*, Ps. Th. 11, 2: 20, 2. Wiþ sārum weolorum, gesmire mid hunige đa weoloras, Lchdm. ii. 54, 20. Weleras *labia*, Ps. Spl. 11, 3: Homl. Th. i. 568, 33: Exon. Th. 363, 15; Wal. 54. Weoloras, Ps. Th. 11, 3. (2) in Ps. Surt., and occasionally elsewhere, the word is feminine:—Wēgende welere *lying lips*; labium mentiens (cf. [wele]ra *labium*, 418), Kent. Gl. 596. Welure *labia*, Ps. Surt. 11, 3. Weolure, 62, 6: 65, 14: 70, 23. Weolere, 30, 19: 62, 4. Weolre, 11, 5: 118, 171. Weolera *labiorum*, 20, 3: 58, 13. Weolerum *labiis*, 58, 8: 118, 13: 119, 2: 139, 3. Weolure *labia*, 11, 4. Ic ne wirne mīne welora *labia mea non prohibebo*, Past. 49; Swt. 380, 10. Gif mannes mūđ sār sié, genim betonican . . . lege on đa weolore, Lchdm. ii. 48, 29. [*Goth.* wairilō.]

wel-frem[m]ende; *adj. Beneficent*:—Welfremmende (-fremende, Rush.) geceiged biđon *benefici vocantur*, Lk. Skt. Lind. 22, 25.

wel-fremming, e; *f. A well-doing, benefit, kindness*:—Uelfremming *beneficium*, Rtl. 187, 39.

wel-fremness, e; *f. A benefit*:—Uelfremnisum *beneficiis*, Rtl. 58, 31. Uelfremnisse *beneficia*, 39, 19. Uoelfremnisse, 73, 3: 77, 41.

wel-gecwēme *glosses* beneplacitus, Ps. Spl. 118, 108: 146, 12.

wel-gecwēmedlic *glosses* beneplacitus, Ps. Spl. 149, 4.

wel-gecwēmness, e; *f. Well-pleasingness, good pleasure*:—In welgecuoemnise (*beneplacito*) ãucendes bearnes đínes, Rtl. 174, 33: 173, 25.

wel-gedōn *well done*:—Gif hwæt welgedōnes bið *si qua bene gesta sunt*, Past. 17; Swt. 111, 3. Suíđe suíđe wē gesyngiaþ, gif wē ōđerra monna welgedōna dǣda ne lufigaþ *valde peccamus, si aliena bene gesta non diligimus*, 34; Swt. 231, 1. *The word also glosses* beneficium:—Welgidoeno *beneficia*, Rtl. 23, 7.

wel-gehwǣr; *adv. Everywhere*:—Hī welgehwǣr hergedon and bærndon, Chr. 1001; Erl. 136, 2. v. wel-hwǣr.

wel-gelǣred; *adj. Well-instructed*:—Larwas ł welgilǣrde Godes *docibiles Dei*, Jn. Skt. Rush. 6, 45.

wel-gelīcod *glosses* beneplacitum:—In welgelīcodum heara *in beneplacitis eorum*, Ps. Surt. 140, 5.

wel-gelīcwirþe *glosses* beneplacitus, V. Ps. 118, 108.

wel-gelīcwirþniss *glosses* beneplacitum, V. Ps. 140, 7.

wel-geþungen; *adj. Of great excellence*:—Welgeþungene witan, L. I. P. 10; Th. ii. 316, 23. v. wel-þungen.

welgian. v. weligian.

wel-hǣwen; *adj. Beautifully blue*:—Ðæt bleóh ðæs welhǣwnan iacintes bið betera ðonne ðæs blācan carbuncules *coerulei coloris hyacinthus praefertur pallenti carbunculo*, Past. 52; Swt. 411, 28.

wel-hwā; *pron. Every one, every thing*:—Mē ðās woruldsǣlða welhwæs blindne (*altogether blind*) on ðis dimme hol forlǣddon, Met. 2, 10. Hē þenceþ ðæt his wīse welhwam þince eal unforcūþ, Exon. Th. 315, 13; Mōd. 30. Weódmōnað on tūn welhwæt bringeþ, Menol. Fox 274; Men. 138.

wel-hwǣr; *adv. Everywhere, generally, commonly*:—Welhwǣr *passim*, Wrt. Voc. ii. 67, 22: *vulgo*, 79, 36. Unriht gewuna welhwǣr is ārisen, Bd. 1, 27; S. 493, 33. Swǣ gelǣrede biscepas, swǣ swǣ welhwǣr (well-, Cott. MSS.) siendon, Past. pref.; Swt. 9, 4. Wæs wīde and welhwǣr Waldendes lof āfylled, Chr. 975; Erl. 126, 11. Wiód ða ðe willaþ welhwǣr derian clǣnum hwǣte, Met. 12, 4. Mæniges þinges ðe monnum wunder welhwǣr þynceþ, 28, 82. v. ge-welhwǣr.

wel-hwilc; *pron. Every*:—Hit (*reason*) nǣnig hafaþ neát . . . hæfð ða wilnunga welhwilc nēten, Met. 20, 191. Hine gearwe geman witena welhwylc, Beo. Th. 537; B. 266. Welhwylc gecwæð ðæt hē fram Sigemunde secgan hȳrde, 1753; B. 874. Se ðe eów welhwylcra wilna dohte, 2692; B. 1344. v. ge-welhwilc.

welig (-eg); *adj. Wealthy, rich, opulent*, (1) of persons, in respect to material or non-material riches:—Welig *dives*, Wrt. Voc. i. 74, 18: *pecuniosus*, 54, 53. Sum welig man wæs *homo quidam erat dives*, Lk. 16, 1, 19. Sum weli (welig, MS. A.: wælig, Lind.) mann, Mt. Kmbl. 27, 57. Hē wæs swīðe welig (weolig, Rush.), Lk. Skt. 18, 23. Sum welig mon *vir quidam, privatis opibus reipublicae vires superans*, Ors. 4, 5; Swt. 166, 24. Hē wæs swīðe welig þearfum, and him sylfum swīðe hafenleás, Homl. Th. ii. 148, 33. Swīðe welig on golde and on seolfre and on orfe and on geteldum, Gen. 13, 5. Forseó ðysse worulde wlenco, gif ðū wille beón welig on dīnum mōde, Prov. Kmbl. 50. Ðes and ðeós welega *hic et haec dives*, Ælfc. Gr. 6, 2; Zup. 18, 12. Earfoðlīce se welega (-iga, Rush.) gǣð on Godes rīce, Mt. Kmbl. 19, 23: Ps. Th. 71, 12: Blickl. Homl. 51, 2. Se welega man, 197, 28. Weliga, Exon. Th. 245, 1; Jul. 38. On ðæs rīcan neáweste and ðæs welegan, Blickl. Homl. 53, 5. Hwæt bið ðæm welegan (welgan, Bt. 26, 3; Fox 94, 12) woruldgītsere ðe bet, Met. 14, 1. Ðæm welgan, Mt. Kmbl. Rush. 19, 24. Welige *dites, divites*, Wrt. Voc. ii. 27, 46. Manega welige (wealigo, Lind.: weolge, Rush.) torfudon fela, Mk. Skt. 12, 41. Weolie, Ps. Surt. 33, 11. Ða welegan, Past. 26; Swt. 181, 3. Gongan tō byrgenne weligra manna, Blickl. Homl. 99, 13. Wǣ iúh weligum, Lk. Skt. Lind. 6, 24. Geceósan welige yldran, Blickl. Homl. 23, 25. Ge ða welegan ge ða þearfan, 107, 12. Ne clypa ðū ðīne welegan (weligo, Lind.: wealigo, Rush.) nēhhebūras, Lk. Skt. 14, 12. Ða welegan (weligo, Lind.: weolige, Rush.), 21, 1. Swā mycele swā se mann biþ weligra on ðisse worlde, swā him se uplīca Dēma tō sēcþ, Blickl. Homl. 95, 32. Weolegrum *ditiori*, Kent. Gl. 834. Weliogran (= wiolegran) *ditiores*, 377. Welegost, Bt. 26, 1; Fox 92, 7. (2) of places where wealth is accumulated:—On ðære welegan byrig (*Rome*), Met. 1, 37. Wīcstede weligne, Beo. Th. 5207; B. 2607. Hē wolde oferwinnan sume welige burh, Homl. Skt. ii. 25, 532. Nǣron ðā welige hāmas, Bt. 15; Fox 48, 4: Met. 8, 8. Setl wuldorspēdum welig, Cd. Th. 6, 11; Gen. 87. Babylonia ðe ðā welegre wæs ðonne ǣnigu ōþeru burg *Babyloniam, urbem tunc cunctis opulentiorem*, Ors. 2, 4; Swt. 72, 26. Sidonem, seó wæs welegast (*opulentissima*) on ðǣm dagum, 3, 5; Swt. 104, 30. (3) of places or things which produce abundantly, of seasons in which there is abundance:—Ðæt wiolie *opimum*, Wrt. Voc. ii. 64, 64. Eorðan ðū gefyllest ēceum wæstmum, ðæt heó welig weorþeþ *multiplicasti locupletare terram*, Ps. Th. 64, 9. Hit is welig, ðis eálond, on wæstmum and on treówum *opima frugibus atque arboribus insula*, Bd. 1, 1; S. 473, 12. Hwæðer hit nū ðīnes gewealdes sié ðæt se hærfest sié swā welig on wæstmum *an tua in aestivos fructus intumescit ubertas?* Bt. 14, 1; Fox 40, 28. Wæstmbǣre geár and weligė *ubertatis anni*, Gen. 41, 26. Swīðe wæstmbǣre geár and swīðe welige *anni fertilitatis*, 41, 29. (3 a) fig.:—Mid ðam gelǣredan biscope hē wunode on weligre lāre tō langum fyrste *with that learned bishop he continued for a long time, engaged in learning which was rich in results*, Homl. Th. ii. 502, 21. [*Laym.* weoli: *C. M.* weli: *O. L. Ger.* welag *ditis*: *O. H. Ger.* welac *ditis*.] v. folc-, mōd-welig.

welig, es; *m. A willow*:—Welig *salix*, Wrt. Voc. i. 285, 62. Weliges leáf, Lchdm. ii. 156, 1. Welies, 154, 22. Ǣrest on ðone welig; of ðam welige, Cod. Dip. Kmbl. iii. 223, 23. Tō ðam greátan welige, 438, 3. On ðone ealdan myl[en] ðǣr ða welegas standaþ, ii. 250, 10. On welgum *in salicibus*, Blickl. Gl. [*Chauc.* wilwe: *Prompt. Parv.* wylowe, wilwe. Welogh *salix*, Wrt. Voc. i. 228, col. 2 (15th cent.).] v. wiliht.

weligian; *p.* ode. I. *to make rich, enrich*:—Ic weligie *beo*, ic welegode *beavi*, Ælfc. Gr. 24; Zup. 137, 1. II. *to become rich* or *abundant, to abound*:—Tīr welgade, Exon. Th. 353, 58; Reim. 34. v. ge-welgian.

welig-stedende; *ptcpl. Making rich*:—Uoeligstydende (*printed* uoeglig-) *locupletans*, Rtl. 98, 18. Cf. stede.

Welisc, well, wellcumian, welle, wellere. v. Wilisc, will, wilcumian, wille, wellyrge.

wel-libbende; *adj.* (*ptcpl.*) *Of good life, living aright*:—Ðæt mynster hē gelōgode mid wellybbendum mannum, Homl. Th. ii. 506, 16. Ongeán ða gōdan and ða wellibbendan *bene viventibus*, Past. 17; Swt. 107, 14.

wel-līcung, e; *f. Well-pleasing*:—Wellīcunga *beneplaciti*, Ps. Spl. T. 68, 16.

wellung. v. willung.

wellyrge, wellere *are glosses of* sinus:—Wellyrgae (uuellyrgae *sinus*, *simus*, Ep. Erf.) *smus* (for *sinus*), Txts. 97, 1876. Wellere *sinus*, Wrt. Voc. i. 289, 34. [*The form* wellyrgae *looks as if taken from a Latin form* velluria (?).]

welm, welode. v. wilm, wilwian.

wel-rūmlīce; *adv. Kindly, benignantly*; benigne, Rtl. 41, 11: 46, 14: 109, 4.

wel-rūmmōd; *adj. Kind, benignant*:—Uelrūmmōdo *benigni*, Rtl. 12, 39.

wel-stincende; *adj.* (*ptcpl.*) *Fragrant, sweet-smelling*:—Wyrta swīðe welstincenda *olera bene olentia*, Past. 57; Swt. 439, 33.

wel-swēgende; *adj.* (*ptcpl.*) *Melodious, sonorous*:—Heriaþ hine on cimbalum welswēgendum *laudate eum in cymbalis bene sonantibus*, Ps. Spl. 150, 5.

weltan. v. wiltan.

wel-þungen; *adj.* (*ptcpl.*) *Well-thriven, able, good, proficient, excellent*:—Hygd wæs swīðe geong, wīs, welþungen, Beo. Th. 3858; B. 1927: Menol. Fox 309; Men. 156. v. wel-geþungen.

weluc. v. weoloc.

welwan (?) *to seize*:—Wyleþ (*printed* wylcþ; *but see* Lchdm. iii. 373, col. 1 *under* wylan, *where also Cockayne notes that the Latin is* captat, *not* raptat) *captat* (*printed* raptat), Germ. 389, 42. [*Goth.* wilwan; *p.* walw *to seize*.]

wel-weorþ; *adj. Of high esteem, of great account*:—Hē swā wuldorfulle and Gode swā welweorþe (wel weorþe? v. weorþ, **III a**) leóde geneósian wolde, Lchdm. iii. 432, 31.

wel-willedness, e; *f. Benevolence, kindness*:—Māre ys welwylledynyss ðænne ðæt ys geseald . . . nys sōðlīce mildheortnyss ðǣr nys welwilledynss *maior est beniuolentia quam quod datur . . . non est enim misericordia ubi non est beniuolentia*, Scint. 160, 4–6.

wel-willende; *adj.* (*ptcpl.*) I. *of good will, benevolent, benignant, kind*:—Welwillende *beniuolus*, Ælfc. Gr. 14; Zup. 87, 17. Ic ðē hālsie, ðū ārfæsta, welwilende and welwyrcende Dryhten, Shrn. 169, 19. Swā him gewissode se welwillenda God, Jud. 6, 14: Homl. Ass. 55, 122. Se wellwillenda bisceop Æðelwold (cf. Adelwoldus benevolus et venerabilis presul, Homl. Th. i. 1, 3), Chr. 984; Erl. 130, 1. Se wellwillenda mann wyle eáðe forberan gif hine man āhwǣr tȳnð, Basil admn. 4; Norm. 44, 17. Hē hit þearfum dǣlde mid wellwillendum mōde, Homl. Skt. ii. 26, 59. Tō ðam welwillendan Hǣlende, Homl. Th. ii. 230, 11: Homl. Ass. 80, 186: 101, 329. Wynsum ūs byð ðæt wē welwyllende beón, 10, 267. Gebyreþ ðætte sume, ða ðe welwillende beóð, on monegum weorcum unfæste beóð ongietene *contigit, ut quidam cum cordis innocentia in nonnullis suis actibus infirmi videantur*, Past. 34; Swt. 235, 17. Ða welwillendan *benevoli*, Swt. 229, 10. II. *of right will, right-minded*:—Ðā Dauid ðysne sealm sancg, ðā gealp hē and fægnode Godes fultumes wið his feóndum; and swā dēð ǣlc welwillende man, ðe ðisne sealm singð, Ps. Th. 4, arg. [Þe dol, þet God ȝefþ to his welwilynde . . . þet is to alle guode herten, Ayenb. 112, 11. Welewyllynge or of god wylle, welwyllyd *benevolus*, Prompt. Parv. 521.]

welwillendlīce; *adv. Benevolently, kindly*:—Wellwillendlīce dō, Drihten *benigne fac, Domine*, Ps. Lamb. 50, 20. Wōpas welwillendlīce underfōh *fletus benigne suscipe*, Hymn. Surt. 29, 17. Wolde se heofenlīca lǣce ðæt geswell heora heortan welwyllendlīce gelācnian, Homl. Th. i. 338, 23: Homl. Skt. i. 3, 64: Wulfst. 295, 2.

welwillendness, e; *f. Benevolence, benignity, kindness*:—God wolde for his welwillendnysse ūs earmingas ālȳsan, Hexam. 18; Norm. 26, 27. Se cyngc blissode on his dohtor welwillendnesse, Ap. Th. 16, 11. On đīnre welwyllendnysse, Homl. Th. ii. 598, 17. Ofer welwillendnysse *super benignitatem*, Ps. Lamb. 51, 5: Homl. Skt. ii. 31, 44: Anglia xi. 114, 94. Wellwillendnysse, 84, 13: Basil admn. 9; Norm. 54, 16. Wellwyllendnysse, 5; Norm. 44, 22.

welwilness, e; *f. Good will, kindness, goodness*:—Welwilnes, Shrn. 175, 28. Đū ūs gescyldst mid đam scylde đīnre welwilnesse *ut scuto bonae voluntatis tuae coronasti nos*, Ps. Th. 5, 13. Hym ic mē befeste and hys welwylnesse ic mē bebeóde, Shrn. 189, 34.

wel-wyrcende *well-doing*:—Ic đē hālsie, đū ārfæsta, welwilende and welwyrcende, Shrn. 169, 19. Ǽlcum welwyrcendum God myd beó midwyrhta, 179, 29. Se freódōm đæs deófollīcan onwaldes wæs seald eallum welwyrcendum, Blickl. Homl. 137, 14.

wêman; *p.* de *To allure, attract, persuade, entice*, (1) in a good sense:—Đa gesetednessa đe tō hālgum mægenum wǣmaþ, Lchdm. iii. 440, 24. Hine mon georne wēme đæt hē wununge healde *suadeatur ut stet*, R. Ben. 109, 22. Đæt wē tō ǣlcan rihte ūs sylfe wenian and wēman, Wulfst. 266, 6. Hwǣr ic findan meahte đone đe mec frēfran wolde, wēman (wenian? *q. v.*) mid wynnum, Exon. Th. 288, 10; Wand. 29. (2) in a bad sense:—Đa teolunga đe hine fram Gode wēmaþ, Homl. Th. ii. 288, 24. Hī (*devils*) dugude beswīcaþ and on teosu tyhtaþ tilra dǣda, wēmaþ on willan, đæt hȳ sēcen frōfre tō feóndum, Exon. Th. 362, 11; Wal. 35. v. ge-wēman.

wêmere, es; *m. One who allures* or *entices, a pander*:—Wēmere *vel* tihtere *leno*, Wrt. Voc. i. 50, 55.

wem-lîc. v. un-wemlīc.

wemm (?) *a spot*:—Wiđ wemme (cf. 34, 9 *which has* wenne) on eágum, Lchdm. ii. 2, 8. [*A. R. Chauc. Piers P. Wick.* wem.]

wemman; *p.* de. I. *to spot, mar, spoil, disfigure*, (a) lit.:—Unwlitig swile and atelīc his eágan bregh wyrde and wemde *tumor deformis palpebram oculi foedaverat*, Bd. 4, 32; S. 611, 18. (b) fig.:—Ic hāliges lāre wordum wemde (*I have not given a good account of the saint*), Andr. Kmbl. 2958; An. 1482. Wordum wemman *to reproach, blame* (cf. *Goth.* ana-wammjan *vituperare*):—Stefn æfter cwom, wordum wemde, Andr. Kmbl. 1479; An. 741. Đec (*the body*) đīn sāwl sceal oft gesēcan, wemman mid wordum (cf. nemnan đē mid wordum, Sǫul Kmbl. 127), Exon. Th. 370, 24; Seel. 64. II. *to defile, pollute, profane*:—Gyf rihtwīsnys mīn hī wemmaþ *si justitias meas profanaverint*, Ps. Spl. 88, 31. Gif hē ōđres ceorles wīf wemme (*maculaverit*), L. Ecg. C. 14; Th. ii. 142, 12. [Ho of hire meidenhad nawiht ne wemde, O. E. Homl. i. 83, 8. Ȝho ne shollde nohht ben wemmedd, Orm. 2326. He wolde þys tendre þyng wemmy foule, R. Glouc. 206, 1. Wemmed *maculatus*, Wick. Deut. 12, 15. *Goth.* ana-wammjan *to blame*: *O. H. Ger.* bi-, gi-wemmen.] v. ge-wemman; un-wemmed.

-wemme, -wemmedlīc, -wemmedlīce, -wemmedness. v. un-wemme, ge-wemmedlīc, ge-wemmedlīce, ge-wemmedness.

wemmend, es; *m. A fornicator, adulterer*:—Wemmend *scortator, adulter, fornicator*, Hpt. Gl. 484, 61. v. ge-wemmend.

-wemmendlîc. v. ge-wemmendlīc.

wemming, e; *f. Pollution, defilement*:—Wemmincge (wēmincge? v. wēman) *lenocinii, seductionis*, Hpt. Gl. 507, 20. [Wiđute wemmunge, H. M. 13, 24.] v. ge-, un-wemming.

wemness, e; *f. Pollution*, Shrn. 183, 21. v. ge-, un-wemness.

wên, e; *f.* I. *supposition, opinion, thought, idea*:—Hī fleóđ swā hrædlīce swā is wēn đætte hī fleógen *longe fugiunt quasi putes eos volare*, Nar. 37, 15. Đū (*Joseph*) fæder cweden woruldcund bi wēne (cf. Jesus erat, . . . ut putabatur, filius Joseph, Lk. 3, 23), Exon. Th. 13, 33; Cri. 212. Woeno *opiniones*, Mt. Kmbl. Lind. 24, 6: Mk. Skt. Lind. 13, 7. II. *hope, expectation*:—Hié cwǣdon đæt heó rīce āgan woldan . . . Him seó wēn geleáh, Cd. Th. 4, 5; Gen. 49: 87, 10; Gen. 1446: Andr. Kmbl. 2150; An. 1076: Beo. Th. 4636; B. 2323. Đæs ic wēn hæbbe *as I hope*, 772; B. 383. Wēna mē đīne (*the unsatisfied hopes of seeing thee*) seóce gedydon, đīne seldcymas, Exon. Th. 380, 25; Rä. 1, 13. Sibbe oflyste, wynnum and wēnum, 464, 4; Hö. 82. Wēnum *hopefully, expectantly*, 380, 17; Rä. 1, 9. II a. with gen. of what is hoped for or expected:—On đam is godcundnesse wēn đe manna ingehygd wāt *divinity may be expected in him who knows men's hearts*, Blickl. Homl. 179, 25: Exon. Th. 302, 21; Fä. 39. Wistfylle wēn, Beo. Th. 1472; B. 734. Is leódum wēn orleghwīle, 5813; B. 2910: Exon. Th. 384, 16; Rä. 4, 28. Mē đæs wēn nǣfre forbirsteþ, đe ic gefeán hæbbe, 236, 1; Ph. 567. Him wæs bēga wēn, Beo. Th. 3751; B. 1873. Weán on wēnum *in expectation of misery*, Cd. Th. 63, 4; Gen. 1027: 191, 11; Exod. 213: 163, 18; Gen. 2700: Andr. Kmbl. 2176; An. 1089. Đīn on wēnum, Exon. Th. 474, 12; Bo. 28. Bēga on wēnum, endedōgores and eftcymes, Beo. Th. 5783; B. 2895. III. *likelihood, probability, chance*:—Nū is wēn micel đæt heó mec eft wille gehȳnan *there is now a great probability that she will again humiliate me*, Exon. Th. 280, 21; Jul. 632. Is mē on wēne geþūht đæt đē untrymnes oysgade *it seems to me in all likelihood that sickness has troubled you*, 163, 6; Gū. 989. Wēn ic talige, gif đæt gegangeþ, đæt se gār nimeþ ealdor đīnne *I reckon there is likelihood, if that comes to pass, that the spear will carry off thy prince*, Beo. Th. 3695; B. 1845. III a. *in phrases such as* wēn is (đæt) = *perhaps, perchance, may be, probably*:—Wēnunge, wēn is *forsitan*, i. *forsan, fortasse*, Wrt. Voc. ii. 150, 24. Gyf gē mē cūþon, wēn is đæt gē cūþon mīnne fæder *si me sciretis, forsitan et patrem meum sciretis*, Jn. Skt. 8, 19: Ps. Th. 123, 2, 3. Gif đū wistes, đū uoen is (woen is māra, Rush.) gif đū gegiuuedes *si scires, tu forsitan petisses*, Jn. Skt. Lind. 4, 10. Cum mid ūs, đȳ læs wēn is hī ūs eft genimon *come with us, lest haply they take us again*, Blickl. Homl. 239, 9. Đȳ læs wēn sié đæt hine God gefreólsige, 243, 19: 247, 2. Wēn is đæt ic gefyrenode *perhaps I have sinned*, 235, 32: 239, 29: Homl. Th. i. 92, 30. Ne biþ his lof nā đȳ læsse, ac is wēn đæt hit sié đȳ māre *his praise will not be the less, but may be the greater*, Bt. 40, 3; Fox 238, 11. Him biđ forboden đæt hē offrige, forđæm hit is wēn đæt se ne mæge ōđerra monna scylda of āđueán, Past. 11; Swt. 73, 17. Hit is þēh wēn đæt feala manna þence hwylcum edleáne hē onfō æt Drihtne, Blickl. Homl. 41, 14. Hwæđer hyt wēn sig đæt đū sig se ylca Hǣlend đe Satan ūre ealdor ymbe spæc? (*perhaps thou art that Jesus of whom Satan spoke*, Gospel of Nicodemus 17, 12), Nicod. 28; Thw. 16, 35. Māra woen is *quanto magis*, Mt. Kmbl. Lind. 7, 11: 12, 12: Lk. Skt. Rush. 11, 13 (Māra woen, Lind.). Māra woen *alio quin*, Mk. Skt. Lind. Rush. 2, 22. Nys hit nǣfre sōþ đæt wē gelȳfan sceolon đām cempon . . ., ac ys bet wēn đæt (*more likely*) his cnyhtas cōmon and heom feoh geáfon (*perhaps his disciples gave them money*, Gospel of Nicodemus 10, 29), Nicod. 19; Thw. 9, 13. Hū mæg ic hit gefaran? ac mā wēn is đæt đū onsende đīnne engel *how can I do the journey? but more likely thou mayst send thine angel*, Blickl. Homl. 231, 23. Nimđe wēn wǣre *ni forsan*, Wrt. Voc. ii. 93, 3. Cōmon hī tō Eald-Seaxna mǣgþe gif wēn wǣre đæt hī đǣr ǣnige đurh heora lāre Criste begitan mihte (*si forte aliquos ibidem praedicando Christo adquirere possent*), Bd. 5, 10; S. 624, 13. [Of þine kume nis na wene (*expectation*), Laym. 28141. Hit biđ a muchele wæne *it is very doubtful*, 13503. Wen iss þatt (*probably*) he wass forrdredd, Orm. 7152. Efter monnes wene *as men suppose*, A. R. 390, note e. *Goth.* wēns *spes*: *O. Sax. O. L. Ger.* wān *hope*: *O. Frs.* wēn *opinion*: *O. H. Ger.* wān *opinio, existimatio, aestimatio, suspicio, spes*: *Icel.* vān *hope, expectation*.] v. next word.

wêna, an; *m.* I. *supposition, opinion, thought, idea, imagination*:—Se leása wēna and sió rǣdelse đara dysigena monna *hominum fallax opinio*, Bt. 27, 3; Fox 98, 32. Swā sume wēnaþ, đæt sió sunne dō, ac se wēna nis wuhte đe sōþra, Met. 28, 35. Gewyrd nis nān đing būton leás wēna. . . . Gē habbaþ nū gehȳred be đan leásan wēnan, đe ȳdele men gewyrd hātaþ, Homl. Th. i. 114, 13–34. Sume men wēnaþ, đæt . . .: ac gif heora wēna sōþ wǣre, đonne . . ., 124, 18. Se đe wæs Crist geteald mid ungewissum wēnan, 358, 3. Be wēnan (*as a matter of opinion*) hī healdaþ God ælmihtigne, R. Ben. 135, 24. For dysiges folces wēnan *falsis vulgi opinionibus*, Bt. 30, 1; Fox 108, 4. Hē ongeat đæt hié wǣron onstyrede mid đæm wēnan đæt hī đæs endes suā neáh wēndon *commotos eos vicini finis suspicione cognoverat*, Past. 32; Swt. 213, 23. Đæt hié ne lǣten hiera geđeaht and hiera wēnan suā feor beforan ealra ōđerra monna wēnan *nequaquam cunctorum consilia suae deliberationi postponerent*, 42; Swt. 306, 1–2. Gif đæt ondgit ongiett đæt hit self dysig sié, đonne gegrīpđ hit đurh đone wēnan đæt andgit đære incundan byrhto, 11; Swt. 69, 21. Hit is betere, đætte ǣlc mon ādrȳge of ōđerra monna mōde đone wēnan be him ǣlces yfeles *cum prava aestimatio ab intuentium mente non tergitur*, 59; Swt. 451, 23. Đā befrān hē, hū woruldmenn be him cwyddedon . . . hē wolde ādwæscan đone leásan wēnan dweligendra manna, Homl. Th. i. 366, 8. Wēnena *suspicionum*, Hpt. Gl. 471, 26. II. *hope, expectation*:—Ne weorđe đē nǣfre tō đæs wā, đæt đū ne wēne betran andergilde; for đam đe se wēna đē nǣfre lǣt forweorđan, Prov. Kmbl. 41. Ǽtes on wēnan, Cd. Th. 188, 9; Exod. 165: 119, 25; Gen. 1985: Elen. Kmbl. 1165; El. 584: Exon. Th. 378, 32; Deór. 25. v. preceding word.

wênan; *p.* de. I. *to ween, suppose, think, imagine, opine, believe*, (1) absolute:—Ic wēne *autumo*, Wrt. Voc. ii. 4, 68. Wēnđ *opinatur*, 62, 53. Hē wēnđ *estimat*, Kent. Gl. 870. Hwīlum ic gewīte, swā ne wēnaþ men (cf. Aldhelm's riddle: Cernere me nulli possunt), Exon. Th. 381, 24; Rä. 3, 1. Wēnde *metitur*, Wrt. Voc. ii. 58, 31. Wēndan *autumant*, 95, 69. Ne meahton hié, swā hié wēndon ǣr, Elen. Kmbl. 954; El. 478. Wēnde *arbitraretur*, Wrt. Voc. ii. 3, 36. (2) with accusative:—Hwæt wēnst đū? hwæt is đes? *quis putas est iste?* Mk. Skt. 4, 41. Hwæt wēne gē? *quid putatis?* Jn. Skt. 11, 56. Đæs đe hē wēnde *according to his belief*, Chart. Th. 140, 7. Ūs gedafenaþ đæt wē hit wēnon swīđor đonne wē unrǣdlīce hit gesēþan đæt đe is uncūđ būton ǣlcere frǣcednysse *it befits us to hold this as an opinion, where absence of certain knowledge is without any peril, rather than to assert it unadvisedly*, Homl. Th. i. 440, 31. Nis đæt nō līchomlīce tō wēnanne, ac gāstlīce *that is not to be estimated corporeally, but spiritually*, Bt. 42; Fox 258, 13. (2 a) with acc. pron. and appositional clause:—Ic đæt wēnde and witod tealde, đæt ic đē meahte āhwerfan, Exon. Th. 263, 29;

Jul. 357. (3) with genitive:—Ne wēne ic his nō, ac wât geara, Bt. 38, 6; Fox 208, 13. Gif hē wyrsa ne bið, ne wēne ic his nā beteran, Met. 25, 29. Hié ðæt fǽge þēgon, þeáh ðæs se rīca ne wēnde, Judth. Thw. 21, 16; Jud. 20. Onstyrede mid ðæm wēnan ðæt hī ðæs endes suā neáh wēndon *commotos vicini finis suspicione*, Past. 32; Swt. 213, 24. Hī wēndon his beteran ðonne hē wǽre, Bt. 30, tit.; Fox xvi, 5. Hwæðer ðū wēne ðæt ǽnig mon sié swā andgetfull, ðæt hē mæge ongitan ǽlcne mon on ryht hwelc hē sié, ðæt hē nāuþer ne sié ne betera ne wyrsa ðonne hē his wēne? *num ea mentis integritate homines degunt, ut quos probos improbosve censuerint, eos quoque, uti existimant, esse necesse sit?* 39, 9; Fox 226, 3. (3 a) with gen. and *tō*:—Ðonne scencð hē ða scylde ǽlcum ðara ðe him ǽnges yfles tō wēnð. For ðæm hit gebyreþ oft, ðonne hwā ne rēcð hū micles yfeles him mon tō wēne . . . *cunctis mala credentibus culpa propinatur. Unde plerumque contigit, ut, qui negligenter de se mala opinari permittunt* . . ., Past. 59; Swt. 451, 24-27. Him is ðeáh leófre ðæt hē leóge, ðonne him mon ǽnigra ungerisna tō wēne *eligit bona de se vel falsa jactari, ne mala possit vel minima perpeti*, 33; Swt. 217, 16. Ðæs ilcan is tō wēnanne tō eallum ðām gesǽlðum ðe seó wyrd brengð *de cunctis fortunae muneribus illud etiam considerandum puto*, Bt. 16, 3; Fox 54, 24. (3 b) with gen. pron. and appositional clause:—Wē ðæs wēnaþ, ðæt ūs God mæge bringan tō beód gegearwad *numquid poterit Deus parare mensam?* Ps. Th. 77, 20. Wēnaþ ðæs sume, ðæt ic on seáð mid fyrenwyrhtum feallan sceolde *aestimatus sum cum descendentibus in lacum*, 87, 4. Ic ðæs wēnde, ðæt ic ongitan mihte *existimabam ut cognoscerem hoc*, 72, 13. Wēnde ðæs formoni man, ðæt wǽre hit ūre hlāford, Byrht. Th. 138, 52. Ne wēne ðæs ǽnig, ðæt ic lygewordum leóð sommige, Exon. Th. 234, 26; Ph. 546. Ne þurfan wē nā ðæs wēnan, ðæt hē ūs nolde ðæra leána gemānian, Wulfst. 261, 18. (4) with a clause, (a) introduced by *ðæt*:—Ic wēne, ðæt nān mon ne sié *neminem esse hominum arbitror*, Ors. 2, 1; Swt. 58, 13. Hwam wēne (woeno, Lind.) ic ðæt hit beó gelīc? *cui simile esse existimabo?* Lk. Skt. 13, 18, 20. Wēn ic, ðæt . . ., Beo. Th. 681; B. 338: 888; B. 442. Hig wēnaþ (woenas, Lind.: woenaþ, Rush. *putant*), ðæt hī sīn gehȳrede, Mt. Kmbl. 6, 7. Ðonne wēnaþ hī swā ungewitfulle, ðæt hī habban ða sōþan gesǽlþa, Bt. 32, 3; Fox 118, 30: Met. 19, 34: Exon. Th. 360, 25; Wal. 11: Cd. Th. 109, 22; Gen. 1826. Wēndes ðū, ðæt ðū āhtest alra onwald, 268, 22; Sat. 59. Ðā wēnde hē (*suspicatus est*), ðæt hit wǽre sum myltystre, Gen. 38, 15: Blickl. Homl. 175, 6: Chr. 911; Erl. 100, 21: Cd. Th. 44, 20; Gen. 712. Nalles hē wēnde, ðæt hié hit wiston, 249, 14; Dan. 530. Wēndun gē and woldun, ðæt gē Scyppende sceoldan gelīce wesan, Exon. Th. 141, 30; Gū. 635. Hī wēndon, ðæt hig sceoldon māre onfōn *arbitrati sunt quod plus essent accepturi*, Mt. Kmbl. 20, 10. Wēndon (woendon Lind.: woendun, Rush.) *putaverunt*, Mk. Skt. 6, 49: Jn. Skt. 11, 13: Lk. Skt. 3, 23. Wēndon, ðæt hē on heora gefére wǽre *existimantes illum esse in comitatu*, 2, 44. Wēndan, Exon. Th. 460, 8; Hö. 14. Ne wēne gē, ðæt . . . *nolite arbitrari quia* . . ., Mt. Kmbl. 10, 34. Ðeáh gē nū wēnen and wilnian, ðæt gē lange libban scylan *si putatis longius vitam trahi*, Bt. 19; Fox 70, 14: Met. 10, 63. Nelle gē wēnan (woenæ, Lind.), ðæt . . . *nolite putare quoniam* . . ., Mt. Kmbl. 5, 17. Ne þurfon gē wēnan, ðæt . . ., Blickl. Homl. 41, 12: Met. 29, 39: Exon. Th. 142, 16; Gū. 645. Nis tō wēnanne ðætte wolde God hiora gāsta mid him gȳman *non est creditus cum Deo spiritus ejus*, Ps. Th. 77, 10: Bt. 16, 3; Fox 56, 28. (b) not introduced by *ðæt*:—Ic wēne (*arbitror*), ne mihte ðes middaneard ealle ða bēc befōn, Jn. Skt. 21, 25. Ic wēne (woeno, Lind., *aestimo*), se ðe hē māre forgef, Lk. Skt. 7, 43. Ic wēne, wit sȳn oferswīþede, Blickl. Homl. 181, 29. Wēne wē, sȳ ðis se? 85, 16. Wēnst ðū hwæt is ðes? *quis putas hic est?* Lk. Skt. 8, 25. (5) with acc. and infin.:—Wēn ealle uferan beón ðē *aestima omnes superiores esse tibi*, Scint. 22, 2. (6) with a preposition:—Ðā ongan ic ofer ðæt georne wēnan *I began to make conjectures on the circumstance*, Homl. Skt. ii. 23 b, 420. II. *to hope, expect, look for*, (1) absolute:—On ðam dæge ðe hē nā ne wēnð (woenas, Lind.) *in die, qua non sperat*, Mt. Kmbl. 24, 50. Ðonne hȳ læst wǽnaþ (wēnaþ, Cott. MS.), Bt. 7, 1; Fox 16, 13. Ðe læs ðe wē forweorðan, ðonne wē læst wēnan, Wulfst. 76, 1. (1 a) with preps. marking the direction of the expectation or hope:—Geþyld hafa, swā ic ðē wēne tō, Beo. Th. 2797; B. 1396. Swā wē wēnaþ on ðē *sicut speravimus in te*, Ps. Ben. 32, 18. (2) with acc. of what is hoped for or expected and dat. of person for whom:—Ic wēne mē, and eác ondrǽde, dōm ðȳ rēþran, Exon. Th. 49, 22; Cri. 789. Ic mē bættran hām ǽfre ne wēne, Cd. Th. 268, 5; Sat. 50. Hē wile syllan unābeden ðæt, ðæt wē ūs ne wēndon, Homl. Th. ii. 372, 16. (3) with gen. of what is expected, (a) alone:—Ic ðǽr heaðufȳres hātes wēne, Beo. Th. 5038; B. 2522. Ðīn līf geendaþ, ðonne ðū his ne wēnest, Wulfst. 260, 24. Hwæs wēneþ se, ðe nyle gemunan? Exon. Th. 74, 1; Cri. 1200. Ðǽr wē ūres feores ne wēnaþ *where we despair of our life*, Blickl. Homl. 51, 28. Ðeáh hē ðǽr ne sién, ðǽr hē heora wēnaþ, Bt. 33, 3; Fox 126, 9. Ðā fōr hē (*Saul*) forð bī ðæm scræfe ðæt hē (*David*) oninnan wæs, and hē his ðǽr nō ne wēnde, Past. 28; Swt. 197, 14. Hē ðæs mǽldæges ne wēnde, Cd. Th. 141, 4; Gen. 2340. Far ðǽr ðū freónda wēne, Exon. Th. 119, 29; Gū. 262. Geworpene on hlǽw, ðǽr hiora gemynde men ne wēnan *projecti in monumentis, quorum non meministi amplius*, Ps. Th. 87, 5. Hwonon hié ðæs wēnan sculon, Past. 11; Swt. 67, 2. Nū swȳðe raðe his (*Antichrist*) man mæg wēnan, Wulfst. 19, 5. Līfes ne wēnan, Exon. Th. 98, 22; Cri. 1611. Ne wē ðære wyrde wēnan þurfon, 6, 9; Cri. 81: Blickl. Homl. 63, 2: Cd. Th. 62, 31; Gen. 1023. Ne hī edcerres ǽfre mōton wēnan, 293, 8; Sat. 451. Hwǽr hē ðara nægla swīðost on ðam wangstede wēnan þorfte, Elen. Kmbl. 2206; El. 1104. Ðēh ðe hē wēnende wǽre anwealdes, Ors. 4, 10; Swt. 194, 22. (b) with appositional clause:—Ðæs ne wēndon witan, ðæt hit manna ǽnig tōbrecan meahte, Beo. Th. 1560; B. 778. Ne þearf ðæs nān mon wēnan, ðæt hine ōþer mon mæge ālēsan, Blickl. Homl. 101, 13: 109, 30: Cd. Th. 272, 5; Sat. 115. Frōfre ne wēnaþ, ðæt gē wræcsīða wyrpe gebīden, Exon. Th. 132, 28; Gū. 479. Ne þearf hæleþa nān wēnan ðæs weorces, ðæt hē wīsdōm mæge wið ofermētta gemengan, Met. 7, 7: 13, 24: 26, 114. (c) with dat. of object for which something is expected:—Ne wēndest ðū ðē ðīnes feores *thou wouldst despair of thy life*, Bt. 14, 3; Fox 46, 26. Him mon ðæs līfes ne wēnde *proximus morti fuit*, Ors. 3, 9; Swt. 124, 32: Bd. 3, 27; S. 558, 39: 5, 3; S. 616, 9. Hē wēnde him þrāge hnāgre, Elen. Kmbl. 1333; El. 668. Hié sendon æfter fultume, ðǽr hié him ǽniges wēndon, Ors. 4, 1; Swt. 154, 23: 4, 5; Swt. 166, 13: 6, 13; Swt. 268, 13. Wēnaþ eów ǽlcere blisse, Homl. Th. i. 554, 30. Ðǽr ðū ðē hleahtres wēne, Guthl. prol.; Gdwin. 4, 8. Ǽr hē hym ðæs feferes wēne, Lchdm. i. 84, 7. Ne mæg ic mē nānes ōðres wēnan, Homl. Skt. i. 23, 576. (d) with preposition marking direction of expectation, *to look* to a person for something:—Wēne ic tō ðē wyrsan geþingea, Beo. Th. 1054; B. 525. Ne ic tō Sweóðeóde sibbe oððe treówe wihte wēne, 5838; B. 2923. Hē sæcce ne wēneþ tō Gār-Denum, 1205; B. 600. Ne wēndon hig nānes fleámes tō unc, Shrn. 40, 29. Nǽnig wihta wēnan þorfte beorhtre bōte tō banan folmum, Beo. Th. 317; B. 157. (e) where (c) and (d) are combined:—Wēne ic mē wraðe tō ðē *ego in te sperabo*, Ps. Th. 55, 3. Ða dysegan nānwuht nyllaþ onginnan ðæs ðe hī him āwþer mægen tō wēnan oððe lofes oððe leána, Bt. 36, 5; Fox 180, 11. (f) where (a) or (d) is accompanied by a clause [v. (4)]:—Hig ðæs æðelinges eft ne wēndon, ðæt hē sigehrēðig sēcean cōme mǽrne þeóden, Beo. Th. 3197; B. 1596. Ne þorftan ða þegnas tō ðam frumgāre feohgestealde wēnan, ðæt hȳ beágas þēgon, Exon. Th. 283, 26; Jul. 686. (4) with a clause:—Ic wēne mē hwænne mē Dryhtnes rōd gefetige, Rood Kmbl. 268; Kr. 135. Wīscton and ne wēndon, ðæt hié heora winedrihten gesāwon, Beo. Th. 3212; B. 1604. (5) with infinitive:—Ic ǽnigra mē weána ne wēnde bōte gebīdan, 1870; B. 933. [*Goth.* wēnjan *sperare*: *O. Sax.* wānian *to suppose, hope* (with gen., infin., and clause): *O. Frs.* wēna: *O. H. Ger.* wān[n]en *opinari, putare, censere, arbitrari, suspicari, aestimare, credere, sperare* (with gen., clause, infin., acc. and infin., preposition): *Icel.* væna *to suppose, hope for.*] v. ā-, ge-wēnan; un-wēned.

wen-bȳl *or* -bȳle *some kind of boil*:—Wiþ wenbȳle, Lchdm. ii. 128, 16. Lǽcedōmas tō wenbȳlum, 12, 19: 128, 6.

wencel, wincel, es; *n. A child*:—Gif his hlāford him wīf sylle and hig suna hæbbon and dohtra, ðæt wīf and hire winclo (*liberi*) beóð ðæs hlāfordes. Gif se wiel cwið: 'Mē ys mīn hlāford leóf and mīn wīf and mīne winclo,' Ex. 21, 4, 5. Se eorðlīca kempa bið ǽfre gearo, swā hwyder swā hē faran sceal tō gefeohte mid ðam kininge, and hē for his wīfe ne for his wenclum ne dearr hine sylfne belādian, Basil adm. 2; Norm. 34, 20. Weodewum (and) wencelum hē wel onfēhð *pupillum et viduam suscipiet*, Ps. Th. 145, 8. [Ȝuw iss borenn an wennchell þatt iss Iesu Crist, Orm. 3356. Men and wummen and children (*v.l.* were and wif and wenchel), A. R. 334, 25. Quelæn þa wifmen, quelen þa wanclen, Laym. 31834. *The later form is* wenche, e.g. Wicklif, Mt. 9, 24.]

wencge. v. wang.

wend *a course, an alternative, a case*:—Ðonne gerecce hē, gif hē mæge, ōþer twēga, oððe ðara spella sum leás oððe ungelīc ðære sprǽce ðe wit æfter spyriaþ; oððe þridde wend (*a third course* or *alternative*) ongite and gelēfe ðæt wit on riht spirien, Bt. 38, 2; Fox 198, 26. Gif hit gebirie ðæt Alhmund swā ða freóndrēddene healdan nolde, oððe hine mon oferricte ðæt hē ne mōste londes wyrðe beón, oððe þridda wend, gif him ǽr his ende gesǽlde, Chart. Th. 141, 13. [Cf. A pryve went *a secret passage*, Chauc. T. and C. ii. 738. *O. Frs.* wend *a case.*] v. ed-wend.

wendan; *p.* de *To turn.* I. *trans.* (1) *To cause to move, alter the direction* or *position* of something (lit. or fig.):—God on gesyhðe wæs . . . mīn on ða swīðran, ðanon ic ne wende onsión mīne, Elen. Kmbl. 696; El. 348. Swā hwā swā his mōd went tō yflum, Bt. 35, 6; Fox 170, 20. Ic āwyrgde fram mē wende and cyrde, Ps. Th. 100, 4. Ðam ðe sliþ on ðīn gewenge, wend ōðer āgēn *qui te percutit in maxillam, praebe et alteram*, Lk. Skt. 6, 29. Wendaþ mīn heáfod ofdūne, Blickl. Homl. 191, 2. Byð his horn wended on wuldur *cornu ejus exaltabitur in gloria*, Ps. Th. 111, 8. Wyrd bið wended hearde *the course of fate is hard to turn*, Salm. Kmbl. 871; Sal. 435. (2) *to turn round* or *over*. Cf. wending, I:—Ðæt wērige mōd wendaþ ða gyltas swīðe mid sorgum *caeca scelerum mergit vertigine mentem*, Dōm. L. 244. Se ðe wende wriþan, Exon. Th. 440, 19; Rä. 60, 5. Tō eáhsealfe . . . wende man ǽlce dæge (*let the paste be turned every day*), Lchdm. iii. 16, 24. Wendende *convolvens*, Wrt. Voc. ii. 21, 27. Hē (*a cup*) in healle wæs wylted and wended wloncra folmum, Exon. Th. 441, 16; Rä. 60, 19. (3) *to turn* from one condition to another, *to change, alter, convert*:—Hē wendeþ stān on wīdne mere *convertit solidam petram in stagnum aquae*, Ps. Th. 113, 8. God ūs ēce biþ, ne wendaþ hine wyrda, Exon. Th. 333, 24; Gn. Ex. 9. Hē ða weaxendan wende eorðan on sealtne mersc, Ps. Th. 106, 33. Hē heora wæter wende tō blōde *convertit aquas eorum in sanguinem*, 104, 25. Hī wendan unriht tō rihte, L. I. P. 11; Th. ii. 318, 23. Wend ðās stānas tō hlāfum, Homl. Th. i. 168, 22. Ða yldu wendan tō līfe, Exon. Th. 211, 2; Ph. 191. Ða gewitnesse wendan *to pervert the testimony*, 147, 21; Gū. 730. Ðær hē hit wendan (-en, MS.) meahte *if he could have changed it*, 276, 23; Jul. 570: Elen. Kmbl. 1955; El. 979. God giet settende is and wendende ǣlce onwaldas and ǣlc rīce tō his willan, Ors. 2, 1; Swt. 64, 2. Hī beóð wended *mutabuntur*, Ps. Th. 101, 23. Wese heora beód wended on grine *fiat mensa eorum in laqueum*, 68, 23. (3 a) *to turn* from one language to another, *to translate, interpret*. v. wendere:—Ælfrēd kuning wæs wealhstod ðisse bēc and hié of bēclēdene on Englisc wende, Bt. proem.; Fox viii, 2. Ic ðē secge worda gerȳnu, ða ðū wendan (or *alter?*) ne miht, Cd. Th. 262, 21; Dan. 747. II. reflexive, (1) *to move one's self, take one's way, go, proceed, wend* (lit. or fig.):—Ic wende mec on wæteres hricg, Salm. Kmbl. 37; Sal. 19. Wendeþ hē hine under wolcnum, wīgsteall sēceþ, 207; Sal. 103. Ða innoþas hī wendaþ mid heora hefignesse, and on ða sīdan feallaþ ðe hē on licgeaþ, Lchdm. ii. 258, 11. Hē wende hine lythwōn fram him and weóp, and wende eft tō him *avertit se parumper et flevit; et reversus est ad eos*, Gen. 42, 24. Se cyning hine west wende, Chr. 894; Erl. 92, 5. Hē wende hine ðanon, Cd. Th. 31, 31; Gen. 493: 34, 33; Gen. 547. Hē wende hine of worulde *he departed this life*, Elen. Kmbl. 877; El. 440. Wend ðē from wynne, Cd. Th. 56, 28; Gen. 919. (2) *to turn, direct the attention*:—Ic wolde ðæt wit unc wendon tō ðises folces sprǣce, Bt. 40, 1; Fox 236, 11. III. *intrans.* (1) *To wend, go, proceed* (lit. and fig.):—Se ðe bið on æcere, ne went hē on bæc *qui fuerint in agro, non redeant retro*, Lk. Skt. 17, 31. Went nū fulneáh eall moncyn on tweónunga, Bt. 4; Fox 8, 17: Met. 13, 55. Him eal worold wendeþ on willan *all the world goes well with him*, Beo. Th. 3482; B. 1739. For hwī hit swā went swā hit nū oft dēþ *why things go as now they often do*, Bt. 39, 2; Fox 212, 26. Ðā wende hē on scype āgēn *ascendens nauem reversus est*, Lk. Skt. 8, 37. Se here eft hāmweard wende, Chr. 895; Erl. 93, 25. Hē grundsceát sōhte, wende tō worulde, Exon. Th. 41, 3; Cri. 650. Ða bōceras ðe wendon (*descenderant*) fram Hierusalem, Mk. Skt. 3, 22. Hig wendon tō Hierusalem *regressi sunt in Hierusalem*, Lk. Skt. 24, 33. Hī wendon ðā tō horsum . . . Hī wendon him fram, and heora wǣpna āwurpon, Homl. Skt. ii. 25, 425, 435. His feónda wǣmna wendon on hī sylfe, Jud. Thw. 162, 9. Ðǣr wendon forð wlance þegenas, Byrht. Th. 137, 52; By. 205. Ūre yldran swultan and ūs from wendan, Blickl. Homl. 195, 27. Ðæt ic hām sīðie, wende fram wīge, Byrht. Th. 139, 10; By. 252. Ǣr hē hionan wende *ere he depart*, Met. 18, 11. Hwī sió wyrd swā wō wendan sceolde, Met. 4, 40. Wendan of (*to depart from*) woruldryhte, Exon. Th. 105, 24; Gū. 28. Ðæt his sciperes woldon wændon fram him, Chr. 1046; Erl. 174, 13. (1 a) with reflexive dative:—Cnut wende him ūt, Chr. 1016; Erl. 154, 5. Hī wendon him tō ðære burge weard, 1048; Erl. 177, 40. (2) *to turn round*:—Swylce ex wendende *quasi axis versatilis*, Scint. 97, 4. (3) *to turn* from one condition to another, *to change, alter*:—Hī on wiðermēde wendan and cyrdan *conversi sunt in arcum perversum*, Ps. Th. 77, 57: Exon. Th. 73, 7; Cri. 1186. Hē gehālgode wīn of wætere, and wendan hēt on ða beteran gecynd, Andr. Kmbl. 1174; An. 587. Ðæt wile wendan on wæterbollan, Lchdm. ii. 248, 7. (4) *to change, shift, vary, be variable*:—God ne went nō swā swā wē dōþ, Bt. 42; Fox 258, 20. Wendeþ, Exon. Th. 379, 13; Deór. 379. Geseah ic ðæt beácen wendan wǣdum and bleóm; hwīlum hit wæs mid wǣtan bestēmed, hwīlum mid since gegyrwed, Rood Kmbl. 43; Kr. 22. [*Goth.* wandjan: *O. Sax.* wendian: *O. Frs.* wenda: *O. H. Ger.* wenten: *Icel.* venda.] v. ā-, be-, ed-, ge-, mis-, on-, ōþ-, tō-, under-, ymb-wendan; un-āwendende, un-āwend(-wended); windan.

wendan (? *or* wennan? Cf. winnan); *p.* de *To labour*:—Ðā wende (*other MSS. have* wann, wonn) hē swȳþe, ðæt hē ða ðe mid hine cōman geheólde *laboravit multum, ut eos, qui secum venerant, contineret*, Bd. 2, 9; S. 511, 5. [Cf. *Icel.* vanda *to take pains in a work*.]

-wende. v. hāl-, hāt-, hwīl-, lāð-, leóf-, luf-wende.

-wendedlīc, -wendedlīcness, -wend(ed)ness. v. ā-, on-wendedlīc, ā-wendedlīcness, ā-, and-, on-wendedness, ge-unwendness.

Wend(e)las (-e?), a; *pl. The people of Vendil* (the northern part of Jutland, *Icel.* Vendill)?, *the Vandals?*:—Wulfgār maþelode, ðæt wæs Wendla leód, Beo. Th. 702; B. 348. Mid Wenlum ic wæs and mid Wærnum, Exon. Th. 322, 6; Vīd. 59. v. Grmm. Gesch. D. S. 332 sqq.; P. B. xii. 7.

Wendel-sǣ (*generally masc.*) *the Mediterranean*. In Alfred's Orosius the word is used to translate several Latin terms denoting the Mediterranean or parts of it:—Andlang Wendelsǣs (*mare Nostrum, quod Magnum generaliter dicimus*), Ors. 1, 1; Swt. 8, 12. Wendelsǣ *mare Nostrum*, 12, 14: 26, 28: 8, 23. Ōþ ðone Wendelsǣ, 10, 36. Se Wendelsǣ *mare Magnum*, 24, 26. On ðæm Wendelsǣ *per totum Magnum pelagus*, 28, 24. Seó ūs fyrre Ispania, hyre is be westan gārsecg, and be norðan Wendelsǣ *Hispania ulterior habet a septentrione Oceanum, ab occasu Oceanum*, 24, 8. Se Wendelsǣ ðe man hǣt Atriaticum, 22, 14: 28, 9. Andlang ðæs Wendelsǣs is Dalmatia on norðhealfe ðæs sǣs *Dalmatia habet a meridie Adriaticum sinum*, 22, 12. Hió hæfð be norðan ðone Wendelsǣ, ðe man hǣt Adriaticum *habet a septentrione mare Siculum vel potius Adriaticum*, 26, 7. Se Wendelsǣ *mare Tyrrhenum*, 8, 25: 28, 15: 24, 3. Italia land belīð Wendelsǣ ymb eall ūtan būton westannorðan *Italia habet ab Africo Tyrrhenum mare, a borea Adriaticum sinum*, 22, 18. Be sūðan Narbonense is se Wendelsæ (*mare Gallicum*), 22, 29, 20. Wendelsǣ ðe man hǣt Libia Æthiopicum *mare Libycum*, 26, 1. Begeondan Wendelsǣ *citra Pontum*, Wrt. Voc. ii. 24, 52. Fēng Carl tō allum ðam westrīce behienan Wendelsǣ and begeondan ðisse sǣ, Chr. 885; Erl. 84, 11. On ān īglond ūt on ðære Wendelsǣ, Bt. 38, 1; Fox 194, 11. Æt Wendelsǣ on stæðe (*the Italian shore*), Elen. Kmbl. 462; El. 231. On Wendelsǣ ðǣr Apollines dohtor wunode, Met. 26, 31: Salm. Kmbl. 406; Sal. 203. [*O. H. Ger.* Wentil-sēo *oceanus*. Cf. wendel-meri *oceanus*.]

-wenden. v. ed-wenden.

wendend, es; *m. That which turns round*:—Wendend *vertigo* (teres vertigo coeli, Ald. 10), Wrt. Voc. ii. 76, 32. Cf. hweorfa.

-wendendlīc, -wendendlīce. v. ā-wendendlīc, ā-wendendlīce.

wendere, es; *m. A translator, interpreter*. v. wendan, I. 3 a:—Wenderum *translatoribus, interpretes*, Hpt. Gl. 525, 32. [*O. H. Ger.* misse-wendari.]

wending, e; *f. Turning*. I. *a turning round, revolution*. Cf. wendan, I. 2:—On ānre wendinge, ða hwīle ðe hē (*the firmament*) ǣne betyrnð, gǣð forð feówor and twēntig tīda, Hexam. 5; Norm. 8, 30. II. *a turning up* or *over*:—Gif ðǣr sié ðæs hrifes wendung *if the stomach be upset* (?), Lchdm. ii. 228, 24. III. *changing, mutation*:—Ne wyrð ðisses nǣfre nān wending *non movebor de generatione in generationem*, Ps. Th. 9, 26. Wendincg, 29 6. Earfoðe ys fǣrlīc wendincg *difficilis est subita permutatio*, Scint. 63, 20. Hit geðeð hit self him selfum suīðe ungelīc for ðære gelōmlīcan wendinge *mutabilitate se varium exhibet*, Past. 42; Swt. 306, 17. Orsorg līf lǣdaþ woruldmen wīse būton wendinge (cf. unonwendendlīce, Bt. 12; Fox 36, 24), Met. 7, 41. [Dyaþ is a wendinge, and þet ech wot, Ayenb. 70, 34. At the wendyng *at the turn* (versura), Pall. 44, 12.] v. ā-wending.

wēne; *adj.* I. *hopeful*. v. or-, un-wēne. II. *fair, beautiful*. v. wēn-līc:—Wēnre (? wende, MS.) *formosior*, Hpt. Gl. 417, 23. [*Icel.* væn *hopeful*; *fair, beautiful*.]

wenge. v. wang.

wenian; *p.* ede *To accustom*. I. *to accustom, train, prepare, fit*, (1) with prep. *tō* marking the end of the training:—Lǣrde hē ða leóde on geleáfan weg, wenede tō wuldre weorod unmæte, tō ðam hālgan hām, Andr. Kmbl. 3360; An. 1684. Hine his goldwine wenede tō wiste, Exon. Th. 288, 24; Wand. 36. Hié lǣrdon hira tungan and wenedon tō leásunga *docuerunt linguam suam loqui mendacium*, Past. 35; Swt. 239, 19. Ðæt ǣlc cristen man his bearn tō cristendōme geornlīce wænige, L. Edg. C. 17; Th. ii. 248, 9. Wenian tō gefeohte, Homl. Skt. ii. 25, 571. Tō ǣlcan rihte ūs sylfe wenian and wēman, Wulfst. 266, 5. Godes folc wenian tō ðam ðe heom þearf sȳ, 154, 13. (1 a) with prep. *tó*, and *mid* marking the means used:—Ðæt ēce līf geearnian ðe hȳ ūs tō weniaþ mid lāre and mid bysene gōdra weorca *to merit that life eternal, to which they are training us by teaching and by the example of good works*, L. Edg. S. 1; Th. i. 272, 22. Man mæg ylpas wenian tō wīge mid cræfte, Hexam. 9; Norm. 16, 10. Utan ūs sylfe mid gōdan geþance wenian tō rihte, Wulfst. 76, 2. (2) with prep. *in*, marking end attained by training:—Leorna lāre, wene ðec in wīsdōm *train yourself so that you may be wise*, Exon. Th. 303, 32; Fä. 62. (3) with instrumental:—Dō ā ðætte duge . . . wene ðec ðȳ betran (cf. *Icel.* venjask *with dat. to be accustomed to do a thing*) *always choose the better part*, Exon. Th. 300, 17; Fä. 7. II. *to draw, attract*, (1) *to draw* to:—Ðæt æt feohgyftum Folcwaldan sunu dōgra gehwylce Dene weorþode, Hengestes heáp hringum wenede (*he should attach them to himself by presents*), efne swā swīðe swā hē Fresena cyn byldan wolde, Beo. Th. 2187; B. 1091. Ðone ðe mec frēfran wolde, wenian (wēman? *q.v.*: *but* cf. Sulīk folk laðōian, wennian mid willeon, Hēl. 2818) mid wynnum, Exon. Th. 288, 10; Wand. 29. (2) *to draw* from:—Wene and teóh ðæt blōd fram ðære ādeádedan stōwe, Lchdm. ii. 84, 3. Hū mon ðæt deáde blōd āweg wenian scyle, 8, 15. (2 a) *to wean*; ablactare:—Swā mōdor dēþ hyre bearn, ðonne hió hit fram hire breósta gesoce weneþ, R. Ben. 22, 21. [*O. Sax.* wenian, wennian: *O. H. Ger.* wennen *assuefacere*: *Icel.* venja *to accustom* to (*dat. or* við).] v. ā-, æt-, be-, ge-, mis-wenian; for-, ofer-wened.

wēning, e; *f.* I. *supposition, doubtful thought, doubt*:—Se Godes man ne sceolde be ðan morgendæge þencean, ðȳ læs ðæt wǣre, ðæt hē þurh ðæt ǣnig ðara gōda forylde, ðe hē ðonne ðȳ dæge gedōn mihte, and (þurh) ða wēninge hweðer hē eft ðæs mergendæges gebīdan mōste *the man of God ought not to think of the morrow, lest it should come to pass, that through it he should put off any of the good that he might do then on the day, and through the doubt whether he may live to see the morrow,* Blickl. Homl. 213, 24. II. *hope, expectation:*—Bæd heó swīþe lange ðone cyningc, ðæt hē hī forlǽte on mynstre Criste þeówian, ðæt heó ða wēnunge æt nȳhstan ðurhteáh (*so that at last her hope was realized*), Bd. 4, 19; S. 587, 39. III. *chance:*—In woenunga *forte,* Mt. Kmbl. Lind. 13, 29. [Aboue onderstandingge and wenynge (*imagination*), Ayenb. 113, 6. It is a wrongful wenynge (*opinion*), Chauc. Boeth. 172, 28. *O. H. Ger.* ana-wānunga *existimatio;* bi-wānunga *deliberatio.*] v. wenunga.

weninga. v. wēnunga.

wēn-līc; *adj.* I. *fair, handsome, comely:*—Stranglīc on wæstme and wēnlīc on nebbe, Ælfc. T. Grn. 16, 41. Heó wæs swīðe wlitig and wēnlīces hīwes *erat eleganti aspectu nimis,* Homl. Ass. 108, 205. II. the word glosses *conveniens* in the following passages:—Ne wæs woenlīc (þæslīc (*q. v.*), W. S.) gecȳðnisse hiora *non erat conveniens testimonium illorum,* Mk. Skt. Lind. 14, 59. Woenlīca (weonlīce, Rush.) gecȳðnise *conuenientia testimonia,* 14, 56. [Swo warð iturnd þat folc of ateliche to wenliche *ita facta est Niniue speciosa que prius turpis existebat,* O. E. Homl. ii. 83, 9. Hwu hie mai hire seluen wenlukest makien, 29, 12. Þe mon þe on his ȝouhþe ȝeorne leorneþ wit and wisdom, he may beon on elde wenliche lorþeu, Misc. 108, 105. *O. Sax.* wān-līk *fair: Icel.* væn-ligr *hopeful, promising, fine.*] v. un-wēnlīc.

wēnlīce; *adv. Fairly, in comely fashion:*—September and December mid heora seofon geférum gladiaþ wēnlīce swȳðe, Anglia viii. 302, 4. [*O. Sax.* wān-līko *beautifully: Icel.* vænliga.]

wenn, es; *m. A wen:*—Eágan wenn *impetigo,* Wrt. Voc. ii. 45, 39: i. 43, 62. Wið wenne (*τύλος*) on eágon, Lchdm. ii. 34, 9. Wænne, 34, 3. Wiþ sceótendum wenne, 324, 25. Gif men synd wænnas gewunod on ðæt heáfod foran oððe on ða eágan, iii. 46, 21. Sealf wið wennas, 12, 22. Wið wennas æt mannes heortan, 40, 4. v. þeór-wenn.

-wēnness. v. or-wēnness.

wen-sealf, e; *f. A salve for wens:*—Wensealf, Lchdm. ii. 128, 13, 19. Ðās wyrta sceolon tō wensealfe, i. 382, 15: ii. 128, 6: 12, 19.

wen-spring (-spryng), es; *m. A mole:*—Wensprynga *nevorum,* Wrt. Voc. ii. 59, 50.

Wente; *pl.* I. *the people of Gwent* (the district comprising Monmouth and Glamorgan):—Ealle ða cyngas ðe on ðyssum īglande wǽron hē (*Athelstane*) gewylde; ǽrest Huwal West-Wala cyning, and Cosstantin Scotta cyning and Uwen Wenta cyning, Chr. 926; Erl. 111, 43. II. *the same as* Waller-wente q. v.:—Nenne man him ealswā micel Wente swā cyninges þegne, L. N. P. L. 52; Th. ii. 298, 11: 53; Th. ii. 298, 14. v. Went-sǽte.

wēnþ (?) *beauty.* v. wēn-līc:—Wēnðe *cum formosior,* Hpt. Gl. 417, 23. v. wēne.

Went-sǽte; *pl. The inhabitants of Gwent:*—Be Wentsǽtum and Dūnsǽtum. Hwīlon Wentsǽte hȳrdon intō Dūnsǽtan, ac hit gebyreþ rihtor intō West-Sexan, þyder hȳ scylan gafol and gīslas syllan, L. O. D. 9; Th. i. 356, 17–20. v. Wente.

wēnunga (-inga); *adv. Perhaps, haply, by chance:*—Wēnunge (-a) *forsan, forsitan, fortassis, fortasse,* Ælfc. Gr. 38; Zup. 229, 1: Wrt. Voc. ii. 150, 23. Wēnunga *forsitan,* Ps. Spl. 80, 13. Wēnunga hine hig forwandiaþ, ðonne hig hine geseóþ *forsitan cum hunc uiderint uerebuntur,* Lk. Skt. 20, 13. Ne hit nǽfre næs tō geopenigenne būton wēnunga hwilc munuc ūt fōre *unless it happened that a monk had to go out,* Homl. Skt. ii. 23 b, 104. Ðe læs wēnunga *ne forte,* Lk. Skt. 14, 8. Nymðe mē Drihten gefultumede, wēnincga mīn sāwl sōhte helle *nisi quia Dominus adjuvasset me, paulominus habitaverat in inferno anima mea,* Ps. Th. 93, 16. Woenunga *forte,* Mk. Skt. Lind. 11, 13: Lk. Skt. Lind. Rush. 9, 13. Woenunge, Mk. Skt. Lind. 14, 2: *forsitan,* Jn. Skt. Lind. 5, 46. Woeninga, Ps. Surt. 123, 4: 138, 11. v. un-wēnunga; wēning.

wen-wyrt, e; *f. The name of some plant supposed to be good for wens* [*two kinds are mentioned,* seó clufihte wenwyrt, Lchdm. ii. 128, 17: 336, 3: 128, 7: 266, 26; *and* seó cneóehte wenwyrt, ii. 140, 8]:—Wyrc sealfe of wenwyrte, Lchdm. ii. 52, 4. Gesmire mid wenwyrte, 62, 27. Wensealf; ontre, reáde netlan, twā wenwyrta, 128, 14.

weó *the upper part of the throat:*—Tunge *lingua,* weó *faus,* mūðes hrōf *palatum,* Wrt. Voc. i. 64, 57. Cf. (?) weohlan.

weó, ón (?); *f. Woe, misery:*—Daroþas wǽron weó (weá?) ðære wihte, Exon. Th. 438, 9; Rä. 57, 5. [Cf. *O. H. Ger.* wēwa; *f. dolor, pena, supplicium.*] v. weá, wāwa.

weó-bed, -bud. v. wīg-bed.

weóce, an; *f. The wick of a lamp* or *candle:*—Weóce *licinius,* Wrt. Voc. ii. 54, 19. Leóhtfæt *lucernarium,* candelsnytels *emunctorium,* weóce *papirus,* i. 26, 56. Weócan (*papyrum*) settan *to put a wick to a lamp,* Lchdm. iii. 348, col. 1. Ðonne ðū blācernes behōfige . . . wǽt mid ðīnum scytefingre on midden, swylce ðū weócan settan wylle, Techm. ii. 126, 3. Riscene weócan *fila scirpea,* Germ. 391, 15. Weócan *accendilia,* Wrt. Voc. i. 66, 46: *cicindilia,* 284, 26. Wiócum *cicindilibus, stuppulis,* Hpt. Gl. 470, 77. Weócum, Wrt. Voc. ii. 80, 43: 131, 13. [Wex on þe candele sene, þe wueke wiðinnen unsene *in candela cera exterius, luminulum interius,* O. E. Homl. ii. 47, 32. As wex and a weke were twyned togideres. . . . And as wex and weyke . . ., Piers P. 17, 204, 206. Weyke of a candel *lichinius,* weyke of a lampe *ticendulum* (l. *cicendulum.* v. Cath. Angl. 412), Prompt. Parv. 520. The weke of a candele *lichinus,* Wülck. Gl. 592, 30: 721, 43. *M. Du.* wieke: *M. H. Ger.* wieche *licinia.* Cf. *O. H. Ger.* wioh *lucubrum.*] v. candel-, clāþ-weóce.

weoc-steall. v. wīg-steall.

weód, es; *n. f.* (?) *A useless* or *injurious plant, a weed:*—Æceres weód, ðæt ðe bið on ofen āsend *faenum agri, quod in clibanum mittitur,* Mt. Kmbl. 6, 30. Hwonan hæfð hit ðæt weód (*zizania*)? Mt. Kmbl. Rush. 13, 27. Is āwriten ðæt hē sēwe ðæt weód on ða gōdan ǽceras, Past. 47; Swt. 357, 17. Ðā æteáwde ða weód, Mt. Kmbl. Rush. 13, 26, 25, 29, 30. Mōtan ealle weóda nū wyrtum āspringan, Lchdm. iii. 36, 26. Swā hwā swā wille sāwan westmbǽre land, ātió ǽrest of ealle ða weód ðe hē gesió, ðæt ðām æcerum derigen, Bt. 23; Fox 78, 23: Met. 12, 4, 28. [Forgrouwen mid brimbles, and mid þornes, and mid iuele wiedes, O. E. Homl. ii. 129, 25. Wo þat mygte weoden abbe and þe roten gnawe, R. Glouc. 404, 11. Weed or wyyid herb *herba silvestris* vel *herba nociva,* Prompt. Parv. 519. *O. Sax.* wiod.] v. un-weód.

weód, e; *f.?:*—Wið cneówærce genim weóde wīsan, Lchdm. iii. 16, 16.

weodewe. v. widuwe.

weód-hōc, es; *m. A weed-hook, a hoe:*—Ueoódhōc (ueád-, Ep. Erf.) *sarculum,* Txts. 95, 1764. Weódhōc (*printed* weodhoclu *sarcum*), Wrt. Voc. i. 289, 2: Anglia ix. 263, 5. [Þe wyedhoc of þe gardine, þet uordeþ al þet kueade gers, Ayenb. 121, 27. Weodhook, Wick. Is. 7, 25. A wedehoke *sarculum,* Wülck. Gl. 609, 22. Wedhoc, 724, 30 (both 15th cent.).]

weódian; *p.* ode *To weed, clear the ground of weeds:*—Me mæig on sumera . . . weódian, Anglia ix. 261, 12. [Wede corne or herbys *runco, sarculo,* Prompt. Parv. 519. To wede *sarrio,* Wülck. Gl. 609, 24. To wedy *vello,* 618, 31.] v. ā-weódian; weódung.

Weód-mōnaþ, es; *m. August:*—Agustus mōnaþ on ūre geþeóde wē nemnaþ Weódmōnaþ, for ðon ðe hī on ðam mōnþe mǽst geweaxaþ, Shrn. 110, 33: 124, 14: Menol. Fox 273; Men. 138.

weodu-binde. v. wudu-binde.

weódung, e; *f. Weeding:*—Weódung *runcatio,* Wrt. Voc. i. 15, 12.

weoduwe, weofung, weogas. v. widuwe, wefung, weg.

Weogorna-, Weogora-ceaster, e; *f. Worcester.* The first part of the name is found in the following forms:—Weogorna, Cod. Dip. Kmbl. ii. 131, 14: 100, 8: i. 35, 21. Weogerna, 114, 15: 152, 7: ii. 150, 4. Weogurna, i. 315, 27. Wiogorna, 176, 5. Wiogoerna, 279, 11. Wiogerna, iii. 166, 7: 186, 4. Wiogerne, 261, 5. Wiogurna, 50, 18: ii. 384, 17. Wiogurnae, iii. 49, 29. Wiogurne, 36, 6. Wegorne, i. 171, 13: 259, 32. Wegerna, 38, 17: 171, 33. Wegrinan, 109, 21. Wegrin, 201, 4. Wigorna, 108, 5: ii. 111, 36. Wigornae, i. 185, 33. Wigerna, 150, 32: iii. 91, 33: iv. 235, 28: Chr. 992; Erl. 130, 38. Wigurna, Cod. Dip. Kmbl. ii. 385, 14: iii. 52, 3. Wigeran, ii. 108, 37: iv. 234, 27. Uigran, i. 80, 14. Wigrinnan, 154, 15. Wygerna, iii. 260, 33. Wygerne, 262, 6: 263, 7. Wygoran, vi. 215, 7. Weogerie, ii. 405, 26. Wiogora, Past. pref.; Swt. 3, tit. Wiogre, Cod. Dip. Kmbl. ii. 405, 5. Wigera, iv. 137, 21: 262, 21: Chr. 992; Erl. 131, 37. Wihgera, Cod. Dip. Kmbl. iv. 263, 14. Wigra, iii. 95, 28: vi. 126, 25. Wigra, Wygra, Chr. 1047; Erl. 171, 30, 31. Wigre, Cod. Dip. Kmbl. i. 168, 15: 186, 9. Wihgra, iv. 72, 22. Wigar, Chr. 959; Th. i. 219, col. 3. Cf. also Wiricestria, Cod. Dip. Kmbl. iv. 161, 25, and the Latin adjective forms, which shew the same variety, e. g. Weogernensis, Cod. Dip. Kmbl. i. 99, 29: Wiornocensis, iii. 366, 26: Wigorcestrensis, i. 167, 18: Wigorcensis, v. 142, 16.

Weogornaceastre-scīr, e; *f. Worcestershire:*—On Wigeraceastrescīre, Cod. Dip. Kmbl. iv. 138, 1. Wigraceasterscīre (Wihracestrescīre, *v. l.*), Chr. 1039; Erl. 167, 10. Wigercestresīre, Cod. Dip. Kmbl. iv. 192, 2. Wigeceastrescīre, 263, 4. Wireceastrescīre, 56, 8. Wircestrescīre, 193, 4.

weohlan; *pl. The jaws:*—Tuxlas ł geahlas (weohlan, MS. T.) leóna tōbrycð Drihten *molas leonum confringet Dominus,* Ps. Spl. 57, 6. v. weó.

weohlere, weoh-steall, weola, weolc. v. wīglere, wīgsteall, wela, weoloc.

weolc (? weolcen); *adj. Scarlet, purple:*—Twigedeágade deáge ł weolcere (weolcenre?) ł wealcbasewere *bis tincto cocco,* Hpt. Gl. 431, 31. v. next word.

weolcen-reád; *adj. Scarlet, purple:*—Se wolcnreáda wǽfels *the scarlet robe,* Homl. Th. ii. 254, 4. Hī scrȳddon hyne mid weolcenreádum scyccelse, Mt. Kmbl. 27, 28. Wolcnreádum, Homl. Th. ii. 252, 25. Gif eówere synna wǽron wolcnreáde *si fuerint peccata vestra ut coccinum,* 322, 10. Wolcnereádum deáhum *conchiliis,* Hpt. Gl. 524, 57. Ðeós wyrt hæfð wolcenreáde blōstman, Lchdm. i. 244, 5. v. weoloc-reád.

weoler. v. weler.

weolma, an; *m. Desire* (?), *what of its kind is most to be desired* (?), *what is best.* Cf. cyst:—Siþþan hē Marian, mægđa weolman (*best of maidens*), mǣrre meówlan, mundheáls geceás, Exon. Th. 28, 12; Cri. 445. Cf. wil-.

weoloc, es; *m. A kind of shell-fish, a whelk, cockle;* also *the dye obtained from such fish*:—Wioloc *coccum*, Txts. 55, 594. Uulluc, uuluc *involucus*, 71, 1115. Weoluc, Wrt. Voc. ii. 45, 56: *cochlea*, i. 65, 72. Weoloc, 281, 50: ii. 16, 29: *conquilium*, i. 291, 27. Wurma, weoloc *murice*, ii. 56, 62. Weluc *murice* vel *conchyleum*, i. 56, 8. Weoloces scyll *conquilium*, 34, 11. Fiscdeáh, weolces *conchilii*, Hpt. Gl. 524, 19. Lytle snæglas *vel* weolocas *cocleas*, Wrt. Voc. ii. 135, 45. Hēr beóþ swȳþe genihtsume weolocas, of đām biþ geweorht se weolocreáda tælhg *sunt et cochleae satis superque abundantes, quibus tinctura coccinei coloris conficitur*, Bd. 1, 1; S. 473, 19. Uuiolocas, uuylocas *cocleas*, Txts. 53, 542. Wilocas, Wrt. Voc. ii. 14, 81.

weoloc-basu; *adj. Purple*:—Uuylocbaso *purpuram*, Txts. 113, 66. v. wealh-basu.

weoloc-reád; *adj. Of the red colour that is got from the* weoloc, *scarlet, purple*:—Wiolocreád, wilocreád *coccum bis tinctum*, Txts. 51, 496. Weolocreád, Wrt. Voc. ii. 135, 43: *cocco*, 77, 20. Weolcreád *coccum*, 14, 57: *coccum rubicundum bis tinctum*, i. 34, 10. Weol[c]rǣd *coccinea*, Hpt. Gl. 526, 33. Weolocas, of đām biþ geweorht se weolocreáda tælhg *cochleae, quibus tinctura coccinei coloris conficitur*, Bd. 1, 1; S. 473, 19. Wolcreádum *coccineo*, Hpt. Gl. 523, 77: Anglia xiii. 29, 53. Weolocreáde *coccineas*, Wrt. Voc. ii. 89, 30. Wolcreáde, Hpt. Gl. 524, 55: Lchdm. i. 244, 5, note. v. weolcen-reád.

weoloc-scill, e; *f. A shell-fish, a whelk, cockle*:—Wilocscel (uuiluc-, uuyluc-) *conquilium*, Txts. 51, 499. Wiolucscel (*but Ep. Erf. have* ilugsegg) *papilivus*, 83, 1487. Hēr beóþ oft numene missenlīcra cynna weolcscylle and muscule *exceptis variorum generibus conchyliorum, in quibus sunt et musculae*, Bd. 1, 1; S. 473, 17.

weoloc-telg, es; *m. The scarlet dye got from the* weoloc:—Wiolctælges *conquilini*, Wrt. Voc. ii. 20, 41.

Weolud *the river Welland*:—Him cirde tō Þurferþ eorl and đa holdas and eal se here đe tō Hāmtūne hiérde norþ ōþ Weolud, Chr. 921; Erl. 107, 29. v. Wēland.

weóningas (?); *pl. m. Bindings for the legs*:—Weóningas (meóningas? v. meó) *fascellas* (fascella = fasciola = fasciae crurales, Migne), Wrt. Voc. ii. 146, 53.

Weonod-land, es; *n. The country of the Wends*:—Weonođland him wæs on steórbord, Ors. 1, 1; Swt. 19, 34. Weonodland, Swt. 20, 4, 6. Of Weonodlande, 7. Of Winodlande, 11. [*Icel.* Vind-land.] v. Winedas.

weor *bad.* v. weorr.

weorc, es; *n. Work;* opus. **I.** *work, operative action, operation*:—Godes willa is weorc *God's will is operative*, Hexam. 6; Norm. 10, 24. Đæt Godes weorc (uoerc, Lind.: werc, Rush.) wǣre geswutelod on him, Jn. Skt. 9, 3. Gesweotula þurh searocræft đīn sylfes weorc, and sōna forlǣt weall wiđ wealle, Exon. Th. 1, 17; Cri. 9. **II.** *working, doing, performance*:—Be rihtes weorce betweox Wealum and Englum *concerning the doing of justice between Welsh and English*, L. O. D. 2; Th. i. 352, 14. v. **V a, V b.** **III.** in a collective sense, *work, doings, actions*, (1) *what a person does*:—Se đe ōþrum forwyrneþ wlitigan wilsīþes, gif his weorc ne deág, Exon. Th. 2, 19; Cri. 21. Weorc ānra gehwæs beorhte blīceþ in đam blīþan hām, 238, 3; Ph. 598. Đæt hē ne forleóse his weorces wlite, 97, 9; Cri. 1588. Hē getrymede heora geleáfan mid đon heofonlīcon weorce, Blickl. Homl. 17, 8. Đis is wæstm wīses and goodes đe his sōđfæst weorc symble lǣste, Ps. Th. 57, 10. (2) *what happens*:—Đæs dæges weorc byđ egesfull eallum gesceaftum, Wulfst. 182, 7. **IV.** *work, labour, occupation, employment, any form of long-sustained* or *habitual activity*:—Weorc *opus*, cræftca *opifex*, Wrt. Voc. i. 73, 37. Towlīc weorc *weaving;* textrinum opus, 26, 13: 82, 11. Hī mōtan bletsian eal Cristen folc, and him godcunde lāc forebringan . . . đis weorc biþ deóflum se mǣsta teóna, Blickl. Homl. 47, 6. Hē nǣfre Godes weorces ne āblon, ah hē ealle niht þurhwacode on hālgum gebedum, 227, 6. God geswāc hys weorces (*the work of creation*), Gen. 2, 3. Weorces (*the building of the tower of Babel*) wīsan, Cd. Th. 101, 28; Gen. 1689. Ūt færđ man tō weorce his, Ps. Spl. 103, 24. Hī sōhton weras tō weorce (*building*), Cd. Th. 100, 30; Gen. 1672: Exon. Th. 1, 4; Cri. 3. Đū leóda feala forlǣrdest, nū leng ne miht gewealdan đȳ weorce, Andr. Kmbl. 2729; An. 1367. Yrþlingc, hū begǣst đū weorc dīn? Coll. Monast. Th. 19, 11. Sum mæg wrætlīce weorc āhycgan heáhtimbra gehwæs, Exon. Th. 296, 1; Crä. 44. Weorc gebannan, Beo. Th. 149; B. 74. **IV a.** *a particular act of labour*:—Wirc six dagas ealle đīn weorc, Ex. 20, 9. Gif hȳ ūt an æcere wurc (*v. l.* weorc) hæbben *si opera in agris habuerint*, R. Ben. **IV b.** *workmanship*:—Wæs đæt hūs hwemdragen, nalas æfter gewunan mennisces weorces, đæt đa wāgas wǣron rihte, Blickl. Homl. 207, 18. **V.** *a work, deed, any action*:—Dēd ɫ wærc *opus*, Jn. Skt. p. 1, 6. Hwæt dō wē đæt wē wyrceon Godes weorc (uerco, Lind.: werc, Rush.)? Đā andswarode se Hǣlend: Đæt is Godes weorc (uerc, Lind.: werc, Rush.), đæt gē gelȳfan on đone đe hē sende, 6, 29. Wēnan đæs weorces, đæt hē wīsdōm mæge wiđ ofermētta gemengan, Met. 7, 7. Hȳ weorces (*taking the forbidden fruit*) onguldon, Exon. Th. 153, 22; Gū. 829. Wērig đæs weorces, 436, 20; Rä. 55, 10. Tō hwon syndon gē đyses weorces swā hefige? gōd weorc heó wæs wyrcende on mē, Blickl. Homl. 69, 15. Nis eów đæs weorces þearf, đæt gē đa ciricean hālgian, 205, 36. Wrǣclīcne hām weorce tō leáne, Cd. Th. 3, 18; Gen. 37. Đa đe đȳ worce gefǣgon, 232, 31; Dan. 268. Mon mæg đȳ ilcan weorce (*ipso facto*) cweþan đæt nētenu send gesǣlige, gif man cwiþ, đæt đa men sēn gesǣlige, đa heora līchoman lustum fyligaþ *to say that those men are happy, who follow their body's lusts, is at the same time to say that beasts are happy*, Bt. 31, tit.; Fox xvi, 9. Ān weorc (uoerc, Lind.: werc, Rush.) ic worhte, Jn. Skt. 7, 21: Blickl. Homl. 71, 30. He Godes eorre þurh his selfes weorc āfunde, Ps. C. 25. Gif hē đonne git māre weorc geworht hæbbe *if then he have committed a greater crime*, L. C. S. 30; Th. i. 394, 12. Hwylce đæs gōdan mannes weorc and his dǣda wǣron, Blickl. Homl. 55, 13. Weorcu *opera*, Scint. 20, 19. Wæstm gōdra weorca, Blickl. Homl. 71, 36: Exon. Th. 66, 31; Cri. 1080. Eargra weorca, 80, 8; Cri. 1304. Dǣdum georn, wīs in weorcum, 185, 7; Az. 4: 159, 4; Gū. 921. Weorcum fāh, Elen. Kmbl. 2484; El. 1246. Mid ælmessan and mid mildheortum weorcum, Blickl. Homl. 37, 19: 73, 16. Leánigean æfter his weorcum and dǣdum, 123, 34. Ne dō gē nā æfter heora worcum (*v. l.* weorcum: wærcum, Rush.) . . . Ealle heora worc (*v. l.* weorc: werca, Lind.: wærc, Rush.) hig dōđ, đæt menn hī geseón, Mt. Kmbl. 23, 3–5. Weorc (uoerca, Lind.; werc, Rush.), Jn. Skt. 9, 4. Uoerco, Lind. 10, 32. God gesihþ ealle ūre wyrc (weorc, Cott. MS.), Bt. 41, 4; Fox 252, 1. **V a.** where action is contrasted with speech or thought:—Gif hwā hǣđendōm weorđige wordes ođđe weorces, L. E. G. 2; Th. i. 168, 2. Ic dō swā ic ne sceolde, hwīle mid weorce, hwīle mid worde, Hy. 3, 44. Đonne on ūrum mōde biđ ācenned sum đing gōdes, and wē đæt tō weorce āwendaþ, Homl. Th. i. 138, 23. Đæm synfullan nāuht ne helpaþ his gōdan geđōhtas, for đæm đe hē hæfđ gearone willan tō đæm weorce, Past. 54; Swt. 423, 27: 11; Swt. 73, 4. Biđ sió costung ǣresđ on đæm mōde, đonne fēreþ ūtweardes tō đære hȳde, ōđđæt hió ūt āsciét on weorc, Swt. 71, 8. Sīnra weorca wlite and worda gemynd, Exon. Th. 64, 15; Cri. 1038. Gescād witan worda and worca, Beo. Th. 583; B. 289. Wordum ne worcum, 2204; B. 1100. Wordum and weorcum, Cd. Th. 278, 17; Sat. 223. Wercum, 267, 34; Sat. 48. Mid wordum ođđe mid weorcum cȳđan, Past. 21; Swt. 157, 21. Se đe đās ǣ mid sprǣcon and mid wordum gefylđ and nele mid worcum, Deut. 27, 26. Swilce hē mid weorcum hī gesprǣce, Homl. Th. ii. 290, 2. Sume him đæs hādes hlīsan willaþ wegan on wordum, and đa weorc ne dōđ, Exon. Th. 105, 33; Gū. 105. **V b.** of action that gives effect to anything:—Hwæđer hig gefyllaþ mid weorce đone hreám, ođđe hit swā nys, Gen. 18, 21. Hwæđer mīn word beó mid weorce gefilled, Num. 11, 23. Hwī hē nolde gehȳrsumian his hǣsum mid weorce, Homl. Skt. i. 21, 61. Hē wolde his gebeót mid weorcum gefremman, 25, 621. Đæt đū mid weorcum gefille ealle đa ǣ, Jos. 1, 7. Se đe mægna gehwæs weorcum (*actually, indeed*) wealdeþ, Exon. Th. 121, 3; Gū. 283. Đīn gewitnes is weorcum geleáfsum, Ps. Th. 92, 6. **VI.** *a work, what is wrought*:—Weorc *machina*, Wrt. Voc. ii. 57, 53. Đā wæs gefordad đīn fægere weorc, Hy. 9, 24. Nānwuht nis fæste stondendes weorces ā wuniende, Bt. 9; Fox 26, 21: Met. 6, 17. Bisiuuidi uuerci (uerci, werci) *opere plumario*, Txts. 80, 699. Weorce *fabrica*, Wrt. Voc. ii. 38, 35. Is đam weorce þearf, đæt se cræftga cume, and gebēte, Exon. Th. 1, 21; Cri. 11. Com God wera weorc sceáwigan, beorna burhfæsten and đæt beácen somod, Cd. Th. 101, 9; Gen. 1679. Se wealdend đe đæt weorc (*the universe*) stađolade, Andr. Kmbl. 1598; An. 800: Exon. Th. 43, 19; Cri. 691. Mē glīwedon wrætlīc weorc smiþa, 408, 18; Rä. 27, 14. Mycel wǣrun đīne weorc, Ps. Th. 103, 23. Đā sceáwode Scyppend ūre his weorca wlite, Cd. Th. 13, 23; Gen. 207: 239, 2; Dan. 364: Met. 20, 21. **VI a.** *a strong building, fortress*:—Babylonia đe ǣr wæs ealra weorca fæstast and wunderlecast and mǣrast, Ors. 2, 4; Swt. 74, 24. Bewrigene mid weorcum, Cd. Th. 218, 24; Dan. 44. **VI b.** *work, what is done, effect produced*:—Đa flǣsclīcan willan cumaþ oft þurh deófles sceónessa ǣr tō manna heortan, ǣr Drihtnes weorc đǣr wunian mōte, Blickl. Homl. 19, 8. **VII.** *pain, travail, grief.* v. weorcsum:—Đæt đam weligan wæs weorc tō þolianne, Exon. Th. 276, 21; Jul. 569. Đæt wæs weorc Gode, Cd. Th. 217, 18; Dan. 24. Ne hié sorge wiht, weorces ne wiston, 49, 2; Gen. 786: Andr. Kmbl. 2556; An. 1279. Wæs hē tō đæs ārfæst, đæt him wæs on weorce, đæt hē leng from Cristes onsȳne wǣre, Blickl. Homl. 225, 28. Hē đæs weorc gehleát, frēcne wīte, Cd. Th. 166, 10; Gen. 2745. Hē đæs gewinnes weorc þrowade, leódbealo longsum, Beo. Th. 3447; B. 1721: Apstls. Kmbl. 160; Ap. 80: Rood Kmbl. 155; Kr. 79. Ic weorc þrowade, earfođa dǣl, Exon. Th. 485, 12; Rä. 71, 12. Worc, Cd. Th. 19, 24; Gen. 296. ¶ *the instrumental or dative is used in the phrase* weorce wesan *with the dative of the person = to be painful to a person* (cf. torne; *adv.*):—Mē næs se hrædlīca ende mīnes līfes swā miclum weorce, swā mē wæs đæt ic læs mǣrđo gefremed hæfde, đonne mīn willa wǣre, Nar. 32, 27. Him wæs on mōde myccle weorce (cf. on weorce, 225, 28 *supra*) and mycel tweó, hwæt hié be đære dorstan dōn, Blickl. Homl. 205, 9. Him wæs đæt swīþe myccle weorce, đæt hē swā ungefulwad forđfēran sceolde, 217, 22. Đā wæs him đæt swīþe sār and myccle weorce, 219, 14. Mē đa fraceđu sind on mōdsefan mǣste weorce, Exon. Th. 247, 2; Jul. 72. Ne mē weorce sind wītebrōgan, 250, 30; Jul. 135. Wæs Abrahame weorce on mōde, đæt hē on wræc drife his selfes sunu, Cd. Th. 168, 31; Gen. 2791. Denum eallum wæs weorce on mōde tō geþolianne, Beo. Th. 2841; B. 1418. [*O. Sax.* werk *work, pain*: *O. Frs.* werk: *O. H. Ger.* werah *opus, operatio, fabricatio, materia, opera*: *Icel.* verk.] v. æcer-, and-, beadu-, bōc-, cræft-, dǣd-, dæg-, ellen-, firen-, frum-, fyrn-, ge-, gūđ-, hand-, heáh-, heađo-, here-, in-, irre-, lāđ-, mægen-, mǣr-, mān-, mis-, nīþ-, niht-, ofer-, orleg-, sigor-, stān-, þeów-, þreá-, þrȳþ-, unriht-, untīd-, unwit-, weall-, weorold-, wic-, wundor-weorc.

-weorc; *adj.*, weorcan. v. mān-weorc, wyrcan.

weorc-dǣd, e; *f. A working, operation*:—Uoercdēdo deáđberendo *operationes mortiferas*, Rtl. 125, 35.

weorc-dæg, es; *m. A work-day, any day, not a* 'freólstīd,' *of the week but Sunday*:—Weorcdæg *feria*, Wrt. Voc. ii. 148, 4. Sealmas tō weorcdæge (*ad feriam*) gebyrigende, Anglia xiii. 402, 532. Đam syxtan weorcdæge *sexta feria*, 404, 563. Worcdæge, 389, 348. Būton drihtenlīcum and freólsum hāligra weorcdagas þeáwe gewunelīcum beón haldene *exceptis dominicis et festiuitatibus sanctorum feriales more solito teneantur*, 396, 451. Freólsdæg *festivitas*, weorcdagas *fasti*, Wrt. Voc. i. 37, 14. Hū dægrēdsangas on weorcdagum (*privatis diebus*) tō healdenne sȳn (v. the whole chapter, and cf. the title of the previous one: Hū dægrēdsangas on freólstīdum tō healdenne sȳn), R. Ben. 37, 4, 5. [ȝif hit is werkedei . . ., ȝif hit is halidei . . ., A. R. 20, 7. ȝure wuke gifeþþ ȝuw sexe werrkedaȝhess, but iff þatt aniȝ messedaȝȝ . . ., Orm. 11315. Werkday *feria*, Prompt. Parv. 522. *Icel.* verk-dagr *a work-day*.]

weorce, weorcean. v. weorc, VII ¶, wyrcan.

weorc-full *glosses* gestuosus:—Wīf weorcfull *mulierem gestuosam*, Scint. 169, 1. [Workuol *active*, Ayenb. 199, 9.]

weorc-gerēfa, an; *m. An overseer of work*:—Đa weorcgerēfan *praefecti operum*, Ex. 5, 10, 13. Sidrac, Misac, and Abdenago, đe Nabochodonosor gesette him tō weorcgerēfan, Homl. Th. ii. 68, 5.

weorc-hūs, es; *n. A workshop*:—Weorchūs *officina*, Wrt. Voc. i. 58, 23: *ergasterium* vel *operatorium*, 59, 6. Werchūs *ergasterium*, 34, 54. [Werkehowse *artificina, opificium*, Prompt. Parv. 522. A shoppe or a werkehous *operarium*, Wülck. Gl. 599, 11.]

weorc-līc; *adj. Working, busy*. [*O. L. Ger.* werk-līk *operosus*: *Icel.* verk-ligr *working*.] v. un-weorclīc.

weorc-mann, es; *m. A workman, labourer*:—Wercmonn *operarius*, Mt. Kmbl. Lind. 10, 10. Woercmonn (werc-, Rush.), Lk. Skt. Lind. 10, 7. Wercmenn *operarii*, Mt. Kmbl. Lind. 9, 37. Woercmenn, 20, 1: Lk. Skt. Lind. 10, 2. Ǣlc riht cynestōl stent on þrȳm stapelum . . . *laboratores* syndon weorcmenn, Wulfst. 267, 14. Cyning sceal hæbban gebedmen, and fyrdmen, and weorcmen, Bt. 17; Fox 58, 33. [*O. H. Ger.* werah-man *operarius*: *Icel.* verk-maðr.]

weorc-rǣden[n], e; *f. Work, labour*:—Of Dyddanhamme gebyreþ micel weorcrǣden (*the work is then defined*), Cod. Dip. Kmbl. iii. 450, 31.

weorc-sige, es; *m. Success in work*:—Sigegyrd ic mē wege, wordsige and worcsige, Lchdm. i. 388, 15.

weorc-stān, es; *m.* I. *stone for building*:—Ne biđ đes stȳpol getimbrod mid ǣnigum weorcstāne, Basil admn. 2; Norm. 38, 14. Hī man mid weorcstāne on ǣghwilce healfe ealle cuce đǣrinne forwyrce, Homl. Skt. i. 23, 322. II. *a stone for building, a large stone*:—Weorcstān *saxum*, Wrt. Voc. i. 85, 20. Hēt se cāsere āhōn ānne weorcstān on hyre swuran, Homl. Skt. i. 2, 389. Đā geseah hē hwǣr đa weorcstānas (cf. 322 *supra*) lāgon ofer eall, 23, 490. On đam fenlande synd feáwa weorcstāna, 20, 77. Hē hēt đæs scræfes ingang mid weorcstānum forwyrcan, 23, 316. Mid ormǣtum weorcstānum, Homl. Th. ii. 424, 27. Hē spræc nā tō đām weorcstānum (*the stones of Jerusalem*) ođđe tō đære getimbrunge, i. 402, 10: Homl. Skt. ii. 27, 106. Hē hēt wilian tō đam scræfe micele weorcstānas (*saxa ingentia*), Jos. 10, 18, 27.

weorc-sum; *adj. Grievous, noxious*:—Deáđes beámes weorcsumne wæstm, Cd. Th. 37, 23; Gen. 594. v. weorc, VII.

weorc-þeów, es; *m.*: e; *f. A slave who works, a bondman, a bondwoman, a slave, a thrall*:—Đā wearđ unblīđe Abrahames cwēn hire worcþeówe, Cd. Th. 136, 18; Gen. 2260. Nabochodonossor him dyde Israēla bearn, wǣpna lāfe, tō weorcþeówum (*si quis evaserat gladium, ductus in Babylonem servivit regi*, 2 Chron. 36, 20), 220, 21; Dan. 74. Đā Abimæleh Abrahame his wīf āgeaf, sealde him gangende feoh and weorcþeós (= -þeówas; cf. (?) *Northumbrian forms under* þeów: *MS. has* feos. The passage in Genesis is: Tulit Abimelech oves et boves et servos et ancillas et dedit Abraham, reddiditque illi Saram uxorem suam, 20, 14), 164, 25; Gen. 2720. [Cf. *Icel.* verk-þræll.]

weorc-wīsung, e; *f. The direction of work*:—Bisceopęs dæg-weorc . . . weorcwīsung be đam đe hit neód sȳ, L. I. P. 8; Th. ii. 314, 22.

weord, weored. v. wyrd, weorod.

weorf, es; *n. A young ass*:—Weorf *asellus*, assa *asinus*, Wrt. Voc. ii. 10, 45. Be ǣlces nȳtenes weorđe gif hī losiaþ. Hors mon sceal gyldan mid .xxx. scitt. . . . wilde weorf mid .xii. scitt., oxan mid .xxx. þ., L. O. D. 7; Th. i. 356, 4. Ungewylde weorf, nȳten ł hors *indomitos subjugales*, Hpt. Gl. 458, 1. v. next word.

weorf-tord, es; *n. Dung of beasts*:—Hē mæg of woruftorde đone þearfendan āreccan *de stercore erigens pauperem*, Ps. Th. 112, 6. v. preceding word.

weorh, Lchdm. iii. 42, 3 *read* dweorh, cf. i. 364, 13.

weorld, weorm, weorn *a multitude*. v. weorold, wyrm, worn.

weorn (wearn?) *an admonition* (?):—Hēt đā of đam līge lifgende bearn Nabocodonossor neár æt gangan; ne forhogodon đæt đa hālgan, siþþan hī woruldcyninges weorn gehȳrdon, Exon. Th. 197, 5; Az. 185. Cf. warenian, warenung.

weornian; *p.* ode *To wither, fade, pine away*:—Ic eom hēge gelīc đam đe hrađe weornaþ, đonne hit byđ āmōwen, Ps. Th. 101, 4, 9. Đa blōstman blōwaþ đonne ōþre wyrta scrincaþ and weorniaþ, Lchdm. i. 204, 13. Ic weornede *tabescebam*, Ps. Spl. 118, 158. Seó wlitige fægernes heora geógođhādes weornode and wanode, Homl. Skt. i. 23, 127. Weornodon, Cd. Th. 294, 9; Sat. 468. Wurniende *marcescens*, Hpt. Gl. 430, 62. Seó sāwul, gif heó næfđ đa hālgan lāre, heó biđ weornigende and mægenleás, Homl. Th. i. 168, 33. v. for-weornian; wisnian.

weorod (-ud, -ed, -ad), werod (-ud, -ed), worud (-ad), word, es; *n.* I. *a host, troop, band, multitude, crowd*:—Weorod *agmen*, Wrt. Voc. ii. 99, 58. Werod, 6, 42. Werud *cetus*, i. *congregatio, conventus, multitudo*, 130, 79. Đæt æfterfylgende weorod *the multitudes* (turbae, Mt. 21, 9) *which followed*, Blickl. Homl. 81, 14. Đā cwom đǣr micel mængeo elpenda of đæm wudo ungemetlīc weorod đara dióra *uenire e siluis elephantorum immensos greges*, Nar. 21, 19. Engla þreát, weorud wlitescȳne, Exon. Th. 31, 9; Cri. 493: 101, 5; Cri. 1654. Leóde, weorud willhrēđig, Elen. Kmbl. 2231; El. 1117. Đǣr gewyrđ đurh Godes mihte rađe tōscaden đæt wered (-od, *v. l.*) on twā, Wulfst. 26, 2. Eall werod (-ed, *v. l.*) đæs folces *omnis multitudo populi*, Lk. Skt. 1, 10. Đā com đæt wered (*turba*), 22, 47. Mycel wered (*later MS.* werd) his leorningcnihta, 6, 17. Đæs welegan mannes ungeendod word and unārīmed mengeo on hrȳđrum, Blickl. Homl. 199, 1. Đā com hæleđa þreát weorodes brehtme, Andr. Kmbl. 2544; An. 1273. Se Hǣlend genam his twelf þegnas sundor of đæm weorode, Blickl. Homl. 15, 7. Mid đȳ unārīmedan weorode hāligra martyra, 25, 35. Weorude, Exon. Th. 57, 2; Cri. 912. Mid engla weorede *cum agmine angelorum*, Bd. 4, 3; S. 570, 1. On weorede *in coetu*, Kent. Gl. 785. Đǣr hit đa weorud geseóđ, Exon. Th. 80, 26; Cri. 1312. Stōdon twā heofenlīce werod ætforan đære cytan dura, Homl. Th. ii. 548, 10. Weredu *examina*, Germ. 396, 180. Lytle worado *pauci*, Lk. Skt. Lind. 13, 23. Weoroda heáp, Andr. Kmbl. 1739; An. 872: Exon. Th. 66, 11; Cri. 1070. Hē ofer weoruda gehwylc scīneþ, 82, 7; Cri. 1335. Wereda, Cd. Th. 42, 8; Gen. 671. Đǣm englīcum weorodum, Blickl. Homl. 131, 19. Fore weorodum *before the multitudes*, Andr. Kmbl. 1471; An. 737: Apstls. Kmbl. 109; Ap. 55. Weorudum, 121; Ap. 61. Werodum, Cd. Th. 78, 31; Gen. 1301. Mycelum weredum (*turbis*) him embe standendum, Lk. Skt. 12, 1. II. *a people*:—Đæs weorudes (*the Mermedonians*) đa wyrrestan, Andr. Kmbl. 3182; An. 1594. Werodes aldor, Cd. Th. 74, 33; Gen. 1231. Werodes rǣswa, Babilone weard, 246, 31; Dan. 487. Weredes weard, 250, 25; Dan. 552. Đam werude (*the Jews*), 216, 28; Dan. 13: 217, 23; Dan. 27. Hē sægde him wereda gesceafte, 225, 27; Dan. 160. Faraþ geond ealne yrmenne grund, weoredum bodiaþ, 30, 22; Cri. 482. III. where numbers are associated for a special purpose or arranged in regular order. (1) in military matters, *a host, army, troop, band*. v. weorod-līst:—Werod ođđe here *exercitus*, Ælfc. Gr. 11; Zup. 79, 4. Đā wearþ snellra werod gegearewod tō campe, Judth. Thw. 24, 21; Jud. 199: Cd. Th. 184, 1; Exod. 100. Đæt werod gefōr, 218, 25; Dan. 44. Werud, 190, 24; Exod. 204. Wered *cuneus*, Wrt. Voc. ii. 15, 49. His wered wanode ǣfre, Chr. 1052; Erl. 181, 4. Fram đām monnum đæs feóndlīcan weoredes *a viris hostilis exercitus*, Bd. 4, 22; S. 591, 3. Mycelnes heofonlīces werydes (-edes, *v. l.*) *multitudo coelestis militiae*, Lk. Skt. 2, 13. Man ofslōh Theódbald mid eallan his weorode, Chr. 603; Erl. 21, 15. Litle weorode, 937; Erl. 112, 34. Mid ealle his weorude *cum suo exercitu*, Bd. 3, 1; S. 523, 27. Weorede, 1, 9; S. 479, 40. Werode, Chr. 1004; Erl. 139, 31. Hē (*king Alfred*) lytle werede unieþelīce æfter wudum fōr, 878; Erl. 78, 33. Wærede, 823; Erl. 63, 18. Sīđe worude (worulde, MS.), Cd. Th. 118, 11; Gen. 1963. Hié sceoldan đæt hǣþene weorod geflȳman, Blickl. Homl. 221, 30. Hē gesamnode weorod (werod, *v. l.*), Chr. 380; Erl. 11, 5. Weored, 449; Erl. 13, 10. Heora feónda werod (wærod, *v. l.*), 999; Erl. 134, 34. Werod (-ed) *cohortem*, Mk. Skt. 15, 16. Wered *manum* (the reference is to the Gothic host), Hpt. Gl. 513, 10. Đegna uorud *cohortem*, Jn. Skt. Lind. 18, 3. Weredu *castra*, Ps. Spl. 26, 5.

Wælgryre weroda, Cd. Th. 186, 11; Exod. 137. Ðú cásere . . . hyt byþ gōd ðē and ðīnum weorudum (werudum, *v. l.*), Lchdm. i. 330, 11. Hī ofslōgon .iiii. werad (ɪɪɪɪ wera, feówer werod, *v. ll.*), Chr. 456; Erl. 13, 28. ¶ in epithets applied to the Deity, *the Lord of hosts*:—Weoruda Dryhten, Andr. Kmbl. 345; An. 173: 869; An. 435. Weorada, Ps. C. 17; Hy. 8, 1. Drihten weoroda, Cd. Th. 301, 14; Sat. 581: Exon. Th. 27, 10; Cri. 428. Weoroda ealdor, 15, 1; Cri. 229. Weoroda God, 332, 31; Vy. 93. (*The passage is printed* weorod anes God . . . monna cræftas; *Mr. Bradley suggests that* nes *is merely an alternative inflexion for the* na *of* monna, *and written above it.* v. Academy, 1893, p. 83.) Weoruda God, 293, 19; Crä. 3: 126, 5; Gū. 366: 273, 13; Jul. 515. Weruda, Ps. Th. 76, 11. Weoruda helm, byrnwīggendra, Elen. Kmbl. 446; El. 223. Weoruda waldend, Exon. Th. 96, 6; Cri. 1570: 137, 28; Gū. 566: Andr. Kmbl. 775; An. 388. Sigora waldend, weoruda wilgiefa, Exon. Th. 229, 34; Ph. 465: Andr. Kmbl. 123; An. 62: 2565; An. 1284. Weoroda wuldorcyning, Exon. Th. 10, 32; Cri. 161. Weroda, Cd. Th. 213, 4; Exod. 547. Wereda, 1, 3; Gen. 2. Weoruda wuldorgeofa, Elen. Kmbl. 1358; El. 681. Wereda, Hy. 10, 48. (2) where a large number is arranged in regular companies:—Hē gesceóp tȳn engla werod, ðæt sind englas . . . seraphim. Hēr sindon nigon engla werod . . . Ðæt teóðe werod ābreáð, Homl. Th. i. 10, 12–18. (3) *a body of servants, retainers, followers, associates*:—Ðis is hold weorod, Beo. Th. 586; B. 290. Gif se getihtloda man māran werude beó ðonne twelfa sum, ðonne beó ðæt ordāl forad, L. Ath. i. 23; Th. i. 212, 8. Ðā geāscode hē ðone cyning lytle werode (wyrede, *v. l.*) æt Merantūne, Chr. 755; Erl. 48, 29. Reste hē ðǣr mǣte weorode, Rood Kmbl. 138; Kr. 124. Ðā gesamnodan hié (*Peter and Paul*) heora weorod wiþ Simone, Blickl. Homl. 173, 9. Ðā gesamnode hē mycel weorod his manna, 199, 12. Hwyder gewiton ða mycclan weorod ðe him (*the rich*) ymb fērdon and stōdan? 99, 25. Oft wǣron teónan weredum (*the servants of Abraham and those of Lot*), Cd. Th. 114, 1; Gen. 1897. (4) *a company, assembly*:—Wealhþeów fore ðæm werede (*the company in the hall*) spræc, Beo. Th. 2435; B. 1215. Werede *sinagoge*, Kent. Gl. 101. (5) *a crew* of a ship, *ship's company*. v. scip-weorod:—Sum streámrāde con, weorudes wīsa ofer wīdne holm, Exon. Th. 296, 22; Crä. 55. [He ȝescop tyen engle werod oðer hapes, O. E. Homl. i. 219, 9. Niene englene ordres (weoredes, *v. l.*). A. R. 30, 19. Heouene riche wordes, Marh. 22, 25. Bruttene weored (ferde, 2nd MS.), Laym. 19922. Engel wird agen him cam, als it were wopnede here, Gen. and Ex. 1786.] v. burh-, eorl-, eorþ-, fird-, flet-, hell-, heofon-, heorþ-, leód-, lind-, man-, scip-, þegen-, þegnung-, wuldor-, wyn-weorod.

weorod, werod (-ed); *adj. Sweet*:—Werod (word, *v. l. late*) *dulcis*, Ælfc. Gr. 9, 28; Zup. 54, 5. Wæter . . . werod on swæcce, Homl. Th. ii. 144, 4. Hwæðer hit bið ðe wered ðe biter ðe wē ðicgaþ, 372, 29: Ex. 15, 25. Weredre *mulsae*, Hpt. Gl. 413, 40. Þurh weredre *pro dulci*, 462, 66. Weredre *vel* wynsumre *dulcisone*, *i. blanda*, weredum beóbreáde *vel* swǣsum *dulci favo*, Wülck. Gl. 225, 17, 20. Werede ðigene *nectareum edulium*, Hpt. Gl. 413, 38: *mulsum*, 417, 56. Werede *mulsa*, 408, 32: *dulcia*, Kent. Gl. 179. Ða leáf beóð werede on swæcce, Lchdm. i. 302, 21. Heó is weredre (*rather sweet*) on byrincge, 108, 2: 276, 10. Ǣlcum men þincð huniges biobreád ðȳ weorodra, gif hē hwēne ǣr biteres onbirigþ, Bt. 23; Fox 78, 25. Weorodran ofer hunig *dulciora super mel*, Ps. Lamb. 18, 11. v. þurh-, un-werod, *and next word.*

weorod, wered, es; *n. A sweet drink*:—Hē scencte scīr wered, Beo. Th. 996; B. 496. v. *preceding word, and* weorod-ness.

weorodian; *p.* ode *To grow sweet*:—Hē is swīðe biter on mūþe, and hē ðē tirþ on ða ðrotan, ðonne ðū his ǣrest fandast; ac hē werodaþ (-edaþ, *v. l.*) syðþan hē innaþ, and biþ swīþe līþe on ðam innoþe (*interius recepta dulcescant*), Bt. 22, 1; Fox 76, 30.

weorodlǣcan. v. ge-weorodlǣcan.

weorodlīce; *adv. Sweetly*:—Uton singan werodlīce *canamus dulciter*, Hy. Surt. 7, 38. Werudlīce *dulcisone*, Anglia xiii. 427, 887.

weorod-līst, e; *f. Want of troops.* v. weorod, III. 1:—Rōmwara cyning rīces ne wēnde for werodlīste, hæfde wigena tō lyt, Elen. Kmbl. 125; El. 63.

weorod-ness, e; *f. Sweetness*:—Ðeós werodnys (weorodnes, *v. l.*) *hoc nectar*, Ælfc. Gr. 9, 16; Zup. 42, 7. Weorodnyss *dulcedo*, Hy. Surt. 98, 17. Werednes, Wrt. Voc. ii. 142, 10. Werodnes, Ps. Lamb. 30, 20. Werednesse *dulcedinem*, Anglia xiii. 369, 48. Him ne līcaþ on his gecorenum nāne lustfullunga oððe werodnyssa ðyssere worulde, Homl. Th. ii. 212, 3. [Salt ȝiueð mete wordnesse (smech *v. l.*), A. R. 138, 12.]

weorold (-uld), weorld, worold (-uld, -eld), world, e; *f.* (*but* se woruld, Prov. Kmbl. 40: worldes, Lk. Skt. 1, 70: ðissum worulde, Met. 10, 70) *A world*:—Ealra worulda scippend, Hy. 3, 23. I. *the material world*:—Ðeáh ðū ealle gesceafta āne naman genemde, ealle ðū nemdest tōgædere and hēte woruld, and þeáh ðone ānne noman ðū tōdǣldest on feówer gesceafta; ān ðæra is eorþe, ōþer wæter, þridde lyft, feówrþe fȳr, Bt. 33, 4; Fox 128, 28: Met. 20, 57. Weoruld, 20, 62, 171. Hire þūhte eall ðeós woruld wlitigre, Cd. Th. 38, 9; Gen. 604. Þenden standeþ woruld under wolcnum, 56, 22; Gen. 916: Exon. Th. 203, 25; Ph. 89. Ðeós world eall gewīteþ and eác ðe hire on wurdon ātȳdrede, Elen. Kmbl. 2552; El. 1277. Weorulde sceátum, Met. 20, 251: 24, 34: 30, 14. Worulde, Cd. Th. 13, 9; Gen. 199. Ofer worulde hrōf, 241, 20; Dan. 407. Worolde dǣlas, Beo. Th. 3469; B. 1732. Eall ðætte grōweþ, wæstmas on weorolde, Met. 29, 71. Hē grundsceát sōhte, wende tō worulde *he came to the earth*, Exon. Th. 41, 3; Cri. 650: Cd. Th. 30, 20; Gen. 420: 32, 29; Gen. 510. Nǣron geond weorulde welige hāmas, Met. 8, 8. Ðū weorulde geworhtest, 20, 24. Weoruld, 28, 26: 31, 14. Geond ðās wīdan weoruld, 8, 41. Worulde, 11, 45. Woruld, 13, 65: Cd. Th. 36, 2; Gen. 565. Wuldres wyrhta woruld staþelode, Exon. Th. 206, 22; Ph. 130. Ðū woruld gesceópe, Met. 20, 4. Swearc norðrodor, woruld miste oferteáh, Exon. Th. 178, 35; Gū. 1254: Ofer ealle woruld, Hy. 9, 34. Wurdon mycele wæterflōd geond ealle world, Ors. 1, 6; Swt. 36, 7. I a. *earth* as opposed to heaven:—Ic wæs on worulde wǣdla, ðæt ðū wurde welig on heofonum, Exon. Th. 91, 22; Cri. 1496. II. *a state of existence*, (1) *the present state*, (a) with reference to time. v. VI:—Ǣr woruld wǣre *ante secula*, Ps. Th. 73, 12. World, 89, 2. Worulde (woruldes; Lind.: weorulde, Rush.) endung *consummatio saeculi*, Mt. Kmbl. 13, 39, 40. Woreuldes, Lind. 24, 3. From fruman worulde, Exon. Th. 73, 20; Cri. 1192. Ðone forman dæg ðyssere worulde (*seculi*), Lchdm. iii. 238, 16. Se æftera worolde dæg, Shrn. 63, 4. Of worldes frymðe (from weorlde, Rush.) *a saeculo*, Lk. Skt. 1, 70. Ǣr worolde (worlde, Cott. MSS.) *ante secula*, Past. 3; Swt. 33, 13. Ætforan wurulde, Ps. Spl. 54, 21. God behēt gefyrn worulde Abrahame, Homl. Th. ii. 12, 23. Se cāsere ðe ðū embe āxast, hē wæs gefyrn worulde, and swīðe fela geára synd nū āgāne syððan hē gewāt of ðysan līfe, Homl. Skt. i. 23, 727. On worulde ǣr, Elen. Kmbl. 1118; El. 561. (b) as the state of existence of all men:—Hié ne dooð him nān gōd ðisse weorolde *eis necessaria praesentis vitae non tribuunt*, Past. 18; Swt. 137, 5. Ðisse worolde (worlde, Hatt. MSS.) *praesentis saeculi*, 1; Swt. 27, 2. Ǣlc wlite tō ende onetteþ ðisse weorlde līfes, Blickl. Homl. 57, 29. Worulde, Beo. Th. 4675; B. 2343: Exon. Th. 158, 5; Gū. 904. Tēlnisse weorlde *aerumnas saeculi*, Mk. Skt. Rush. 4, 19. Worulde, Cd. Th. 270, 22; Sat. 94: Exon. Th. 122, 19; Gū. 308. Moncyn winþ on ðām ȳðum ðisse worulde, Bt. 4; Fox 8, 22: 33, 4; Fox 132, 28: Met. 4, 56. Worulde gedāl *death*, Beo. Th. 6128; B. 3068. Worulde brūcan *to live*, 2129; B. 1062. Gād worolde wilna, 1904; B. 950. Worlde geweorces, 5415; B. 2711. Hē unæþele ā forð þanan wyrð on weorulde, Met. 17, 29. Worulde, Cd. Th. 35, 7; Gen. 551: 160, 25; Gen. 2655. Hē on weorolda (worulda, *v. l.*) hēr wunodæ þrāgæ, Chr. 1065; Erl. 197, 23. Hēr on worulde, Cd. Th. 30, 29; Gen. 474. Ðīn mōdor gewīteþ of weorulde þurh scondlīcne deáð and heó ligeþ unbebyrged *mater tua miserando exitu sepultura carebit*, Nar. 31, 29. Worulde, Elen. Kmbl. 877; El. 440. Seó burh Iericho mid hire seofon weallum getācnode ðās āteorigendlīcan woruld, ðe tyrnð on seofon dagum, and hī symle geedlǣcaþ, ōð ðæt seó geendung eallum mannum becume, Homl. Th. ii. 214, 29. Hī ðǣr hyra gecynda on weorold bringaþ *ibi prolem reddunt*, Nar. 35, 27. Woruld, Cd. Th. 137, 35; Gen. 2284. On woruld cenned, 12, 20; Gen. 188: 57, 5; Gen. 923. In worold wacan, Beo. Th. 119; B. 60. Worold oflǣtan, 2371; B. 1183. Ðās woruld þurh gāst gedāl ofgyfan, Cd. Th. 68, 32; Gen. 1126. Hē woruld ofgeaf, 71, 2; Gen. 1164. ¶ where the present state is contrasted with the future, where the temporal is contrasted with the eternal:—Ðysse worulde (woreldes, Lind.: weorulde, Rush.) bearn . . . Ða ðe synt ðære worulde (weorlde, Rush. *heaven*) wyrðe, Lk. Skt. 20, 34, 35. Se ðe ða ēcan āgan wille gesǣlða, hē sceal swīðe flión ðisse worulde wlite, Met. 7, 31. Ne byð hyt hym forgyfen, ne on ðisse worulde (worold, Lind.: weorlde, Rush. *saeculo*), ne on ðære tōweardan, Mt. Kmbl. 12, 32. Forgife ðē Ðryhten willan on worulde, and in wuldre blǣd, Andr. Kmbl. 711; An. 356: 1895; An. 950. Se ēca deáþ æfter ðisse worulde, Met. 10, 70. Ðæt God ðē on worlde (*in mundo*) ðīne synna forgyfe, and æfter worlde (*post mundum*) ēce reste, L. Ecg. P. iv. 66; Th. ii. 226, 18. Ðās dagas tācniaþ ðās ondweardan weorld, and ða Eásterlīcan dagas tācniaþ ða ēcean eádignesse, Blickl. Homl. 35, 31. Ðām ðe him willaþ ðās woruld ūttor lǣtan ðonne ðæt ēce līf, Exon. Th. 109, 27; Gū. 96. On ðās þeóstran weorulde . . . æfter hingonge hreósan in helle, 86, 18; Cri. 1410. (c) of temporal things as distinguished from spiritual:—Ðisse worulde (woruldes, Lind., *saeculi*) bearn synd gleáwran ðises leóhtes bearnum, Lk. Skt. 16, 8. Nō ic eów sweord ongeán ōðberan þence, worulde wǣpen, Exon. Th. 120, 21; Gū. 275. Hē ðās woruld forhogde, 146, 22; Gū. 713. ¶ *in the phrases* æfter, for worolde *according to the standard of the world, in respect to temporal matters*:—Wæs sum cempena ealdorman æfter worulde swīðe æþelboren, Homl. Skt. ii. 30, 3. Mon monþwǣre and for weorulde gōd *vir summae mansuetudinis et civilitatis*, Bd. 1, 8; S. 479, 29. For weorulde wīs, Met. 1, 51. For Gode oððe for worulde gyltig, Lchdm. iii. 442, 35. Ðæt folc wolde hine āhebban tō cyninge, ðæt hē wǣre heora heáfod for worulde, Homl. Th. i. 162, 5. Ðā forlēt hē eal ða ðing ðe hē for worulde hæfde, Bd. 3, 19; S. 549, 33: Exon. Th. 276, 22; Jul. 570. Gif hē rēcþ ǣniges weorþscipes hēr for worulde, Bt. 40, 3; Fox 238, 15: Homl. Skt. i. 12, 102. Ðǣr ðū gemunan woldest hwylcra burgwara ðū wǣre for worulde, oþþe eft gāstlīce hwilces geferscipes ðū wǽre on dínum móde, Bt. 5, 1; Fox 10, 4: Homl. Skt. i. 21, 87. Hē ne mæg geđyldgian đæt hē for đisse worlde (worulde, Hatt. MS.) sié forsewen *despici in mundo hoc non patitur*, Past. 33; Swt. 216, 7: Exon. Th. 457, 5; Hy. 4, 79. (2) *the next world, the future state*:—Fæder đære tōweardan worulde, Homl. Th. ii. 16, 8. v. (1 b ¶). III. *men, people*:—Woruld is onhrēred, Exon. Th. 104, 16; Gū. 8. Ic đæt for worulde geþolade, lytel þūhte ic leóda bearnum, 87, 13; Cri. 1424. Hī biddaþ God āre ealre þeóde, đonne đū him tīđast, swā đū eádmōd eart ealre worlde, Hy. 7, 57. Hē woruld ālȳseþ, eall eorđbūend, Exon. Th. 45, 14; Cri. 718: Elen. Kmbl. 607; El. 304. IV. *earthly things, temporal possessions*:—Ne won hē æfter worulde, ac hē in wuldre āhōf mōdes wynne, Exon. Th. 126, 12; Gū. 370: 109, 34; Gū. 100. Lamech woruld bryttade, Cd. Th. 74, 22; Gen. 1226. Hié woruld bryttedon, sinc ætsomne, 103, 27; Gen. 1724. V. *men and things upon earth*:—Wuldorcyning worlde and heofona, Cd. Th. 242, 31; Dan. 427. Cyningas đe weoruld heóldan, Ps. Th. 135, 19. Him God sealde gumena rīce, world tō gewealde, Cd. Th. 254, 7; Dan. 608. Wēndes đū đæt đū woruld āhtest, 268, 23; Sat. 59. VI. *an age*:—Weorld *seculum*, Wrt. Voc. i. 76, 50. Woruld, 52, 67. Hī gesāwon đæt beorhte leóht æfter đære langan worolde (*the time between Adam's death and Christ's descent into hell*), Shrn. 68, 15. Fram worulde *of old* (?); a saeculo, Gen. 6, 4. Worulde *secla*, Wülck. Gl. 255, 21. Wē sind đa đe worulda geendunga on becōmon *in quos fines saeculorum devenerunt* (1 Cor. 10, 11), Homl. Th. ii. 372, 10. God ǽr ealle worulda, 280, 13. ¶ in expressions equivalent to *for ever*:—Ōđ on weorulde *usque in saeculum*, Ps. Spl. 17, 52. Stændan tō worulde, Bt. 21; Fox 74, 3. Tō worulde *in seculum seculi*, Ps. Th. 51, 7. Ā weoruld *in secula*, 43, 10. On worulda woruld *in seculum seculi*, 78, 14. On ealra weorulda weoruld, 110, 5. VI a. used to give emphasis, as in 'what in the *world*.' Cf. what-*ever*:—Nǽnig wæs weorđ on weorulde, Met. 8, 37. Ne gehȳrde wē nǽfre on worulde *a saeculo non est auditum*, Jn. Skt. 9, 32. Nis mē on worulde mōd ǽniges þegnscipes, Cd. Th. 51, 32; Gen. 835: 32, 16; Gen. 504: Ps. Th. 71, 12. Eall đæt heó on weorulde hæfde *omnia quaecumque habuerat*, Bd. 4, 23; S. 593, 10. Hwā is on weorulde, đæt ne wundrige? Met. 28, 40, 18. On hwam mæg ǽfre ǽnig man on worolde swīđor God wurđian đonne on circan? L. Eth. vii. 25; Th. i. 334, 25. VII. *a person's lifetime*:—Gif gē mægen on eallre eówerre worulde geearnian, đæt gē habban gōdne hlīsan æfter eówrum dagum, Bt. 18, 3; Fox 66, 3. Gē winnaþ eówre woruld *ye labour all your life*, 18, 1; Fox 62, 18. Hē swincþ ealle his woruld æfter đam welan, 33, 2; Fox 124, 1. Đa eldran gnorniaþ ealle heora woruld, 11, 1; Fox 32, 10. Hī winnaþ heora woruld æfter đæm, 24, 2; Fox 82, 4. Hī būton wærscipe heora woruld ādreógaþ, Homl. Skt. i. 11, 361. VIII. *a person's world, conditions of life*:—Hwæđer Boetie eall his woruld līcode đā hē gesǽlgost wæs, Bt. 26, tit.; Fox xiv, 18: 26, 1; Fox 90, 23. Hyra woruld wæs gehwyrfed, Cd. Th. 21, 3; Gen. 318. Fremdre worulde, Met. 3, 11. IX. *the course of human affairs*:—Him eal worold wendeþ on willan, Beo. Th. 3481; B. 1738. Nafa đū tō yfel ellen, đeáh đē sum unwilla on becume; oft brincđ se woruld đone willan đe biđ eft, Prov. Kmbl. 40. Onwendeþ wyrda gesceaft weoruld under heofonum, Exon. Th. 292, 31; Wand. 107. [*O. Sax.* werold *world; men; lifetime*: *O. Frs.* warld, wrald: *O. H. Ger.* weralt *mundus, orbis, terra, seculum, aevum*: *Icel.* veröld.] v. ǽr-, gewin-, wræc-, wundor-weorold, *and following compounds*.

weorold-ǽht, e; *f. Worldly property, worldly possession* or *good*:—Is nȳd đæt sume mid wonunge heora woruldǽhta synd gerihte *necesse est ut quidam damnis corrigantur*, Bd. 1, 27; S. 490, 10. Đone teóđan dǽl his woruldǽhta gesyllan, Wulfst. 283, 26: Bt. 13; Fox 38, 2. Đæt hī þolian woroldǽhta (world-, *v.l.*), L. Edm. E. 1; Th. i. 244, 13. Hē mōt his fæstan ālȳsan mid his worldǽhton (*mundanis suis possessionibus*), L. Ecg. P. iv. 60; Th. ii. 220, 27: 63; Th. ii. 224, 13. Micclode God his woruldǽhta, Homl. Ass. 119, 59. [Weorelddahhtess spedd, Orm. 12079.]

weorold-afol (-el), es; *n. Worldly power*:—Ǽnigne man đe hē (*the priest*) tō bōte gebīgan ne mæge oþþe ne durre for worldafole, L. Edg. C. 6; Th. ii. 246, 2. Entas and strece woruldmen đe mihtige wurdan on woruldafelum, Wulfst. 106, 1.

weorold-ār, e; *f.* I. *worldly honour*:—Đurh đa wilnunga đære woroldāre (world-, Hatt. MS.) *per concupiscentiam culminis*, Past. 3; Swt. 33, 9. Đa đe woroldāre wilniaþ, 50; Swt. 387, 1. Hē wilnaþ micle woroldāre habban, 1; Swt. 27, 5. Gif hē worldāre hæbbe, 9; Swt. 55, 16. Woruldāre, Bt. 7, 3; Fox 20, 11. Woroldāre, Beo. Th. 34; B. 17. Gewonie him God his weorldāre ond eác swā his sāwle āre, Chart. Th. 483, 31. II. *worldly property, property not belonging to the church*:—Đæt mon ælles đises freólses āre ǽfre for āne hīde werian scolde; for đam đe Godes ār ǽfre freogre beón sceal đonne ǽnig woruldār, Cod. Dip. Kmbl. v. 113, 35. [*O. H. Ger.* weralt-ēra *populares honores*.]

weorold-bearn, e; *n. A child of earth, a man*, Exon. Th. 493, 9; Rä. 81, 27.

weorold-bisegu; *f. Worldly, secular business*:—Đa þrig dagas đe man fæste, forlǽte man ǽlce worldbysga, L. P. M. 3; Th. ii. 286, 30. Riht is đæt munecas hȳ symle āsyndrian fram woruldbysegan, L. I. P. 14; Th. ii. 322, 5.

weorold-bisegung, e; *f.* I. *worldly occupation*:—Nys nānum mæssepreóste ālȳfed, ne diácone, đæt hī ymbe nāne worldbysgunge ābysgode (*mundano negotio ullo occupati*) beón, L. Ecg. P. iii. 8; Th. ii. 198, 21. II. *care of this world, anxiety of this life*:—Đa strongan stormas weoruldbisgunga, Met. 3, 4.

weorold-bismer, es; *n. m. Worldly reproach*:—For woroldbismere ānum *per contumaciam*, Past. 10; Swt. 61, 10.

weorold-bliss, e; *f. Worldly bliss, earthly joy*:—Hē his līchoman wynna forwyrnde and woruldblissa, Exon. Th. 111, 32; Gū. 135.

weorold-bōt, e; *f.* '*Bōt*' *prescribed by the secular power* in contrast with 'godcund bōt,' that prescribed by the church:—Đa woruldbōte hig gesetton . . . swā hwār swā man nolde godcunde bōte gebūgan mid rihte tō bisceopa dihte, L. E. G. proem.; Th. i. 166, 16.

weorold-broc, es; *n. Worldly affliction, trouble of this life*:—Đæt sār đære suingellan đissa woruldbroca (world-, Hatt. MSS.), Past. 36; Swt. 259, 2.

weorold-broc, es; *n. Use for secular purposes*:—Đes pāpa gesette đæt mæssepreóstas and diáconas ne sceoldon brūcan gehālgodra mæsse-hrægla tō nǽnegum woroldbroce, ne nō būton on cyrcean āne, Shrn. 112, 20.

weorold-būende; *pl. The dwellers in this world, men*:—Ne furþum wundne wer weoruldbūende gesāwan under sunnan, Met. 8, 35. God is wīsdōm and ǽ woruldbūendra, 29, 83: Judth. Thw. 22, 27; Jud. 82. Đætte rinca gehwylc ōþrum gulde weorc be geweorhtum weoruldbūendum, Met. 27, 27.

weorold-camp, es; *m. Worldly warfare*:—Godes þeówas nāgon mid wīgge ne mid worldcampe tō faren[n]e, ac mid gāstlīcan wǽpnan campian wiđ deófol, L. Ælfc. P. 51; Th. ii. 388, 4.

weorold-candel[l], e; *f. This world's candle, the sun*:—Woruld-candel scān, sigel sūđan fūs, Beo. Th. 3935; B. 1965.

weorold-cearu, e; *f. Worldly care, care about things of this world*:—Woruldcara and welan and flǽsclīce lustas forsmoriaþ đæs mōdes đrotan, Homl. Th. ii. 92, 10. Beóđ wære đæt eówere heortan ne beón ge-hefegode mid woruldcarum, 22, 19. Twā mynecena wǽron . . . đām gewīcnode sum eáwfæst wer on woruldcarum, 174, 7. Aidan ealle woruldcara āwearp fram his heortan, nānes þinges wilnigende būtan Godes willan, Homl. Skt. ii. 26, 55: L. I. P. 13; Th. ii. 320, 35.

weorold-cempa, an; *m. A warrior of this world, an earthly* (*not a spiritual*) *soldier*:—Se woruldkempa weraþ woruldlīce wǽpna ongeán his gelīcan, ac đū habban scealt đa gāstlīcan wǽpna ongeán đone gāstlīcan feónd, Basil admn. 2; Norm. 34, 31. Woruldcempa, 36, 17. Se woruld-cempa sceall winnan wiđ ūre fȳnd, and se Godes þeówa sceall symle for ūs biddan . . . Nū ne sceolon đa woruldcempan tō đam woruldlīcum ge-feohte đa Godes þeówan neádian fram đam gāstlīcan gewinne, Homl. Skt. ii. 25, 820–8.

weorold-cræft, es; *m. A secular craft* or *art*:—Ne sī nān man swā dysig, đæt hē đās gelīcnysse tō ǽnigum hālgum þinge āwende, for đan đe đis (*grammar*) is woruldcræft (weorld-, *v. l.*), Ælfc. Gr. 41; Zup. 246, 2. Đē gebletsige woruldcræfta wlite and weorca gehwilc, Cd. Th. 239, 1; Dan. 364. Warniaþ đæt gē beón wīsran on eówrum gāstlīcan cræfte . . . đonne đa worldmen sindon on heora worldcræftum, L. Ælfc. P. 46; Th. ii. 384, 15. Đæt him God onsende wīse geþōhtas and woruldcræftas, Exon. Th. 294, 29; Crä. 22. [Cf. *O. H. Ger.* weralt-kraft *ciliarchus, tribunus.*]

weorold-cund; *adj.* I. *earthly, temporal*:—Fæder woruldcund *an earthly father*, Exon. Th. 13, 33; Cri. 212. On đās tīd wē sceolan habban godcunde blisse and eác worldcunde, Blickl. Homl. 83, 20. Mid hū heardum brocum ūs swingaþ ūre worldcunde fædras, Past. 36; Swt. 253, 25. Đonne hié eallinga āgiémeleásiaþ đone ymbhogan woruld-cundra đinga *cum curare corporalia funditus negligunt*, 18; Swt. 137, 2. Hlǽfdige wuldorweorudes and worl[d]cundra hāda under heofonum and helwara, Exon. Th. 18, 18; Cri. 285. Đætte gē fore uueorolde sién geblitsade mid đēm weoroldcundum gōdum, and hiora sāula mid đēm godcundum gōdum, Cod. Dip. Kmbl. i. 293, 35. II. *secular, profane* as opposed to sacred:—Gelǽred ge on godcundum gewritum ge on weoruldcundum *literis sacris simul et saecularibus instructi*, Bd. 4, 2; S. 565, 24. III. *secular* as opposed to ecclesiastical:—Đis is seó weoruldcunde (weorld-, *v. l.*) gerǽdnes, L. Edg. ii. 1; Th. i. 266, 2. Woruldcunde (world-, *v. l.*), L. C. S. proem.; Th. i. 376, 4. Hwelce wutan wǽron geond Angelkynn ǽgđer ge godcundra hāda ge woruld-cundra, Past. pref.; Swt. 2, 3. Woroldcundra, Chart. Th. 132, 2.

weoroldcundlīce; *adv. In a worldly manner*:—Hē brȳcđ đære god-cundan āre worldcundlīce (*seculariter*), Past. 9; Swt. 57, 7. Đeáh hié woroldcundlīce drohtigen *cum terrena agunt*, 18; Swt. 135, 17.

weorold-cyning, es; *m.* I. *an earthly king*:—Ān woruldcynincg hæfđ fela þegna, Homl. Skt. i. p. 6, 59. Of đam leódfruman ārīsaþ rīces hyrdas, woruldcyningas, Cd. Th. 140, 29; Gen. 2335. Woroldcyninga đæm sēlestan, Beo. Th. 3373; B. 1684. Woruldcyninga, 6343; B. 3181. II. *a king of all the earth, a supreme monarch*:—Woruldcyninges (cf. him God sealde gumena ríce, world tó gewealde, Cd. Th. 254, 7; Dan. 608), Exon. Th. 197, 4; Az. 185. [Weoreldking (worlich king, 2nd MS.), Laym. 6328. *O. Sax.* werold-kuning *an earthly king, a powerful king*: *O. H. Ger.* weralt-kuning *an earthly king*.]

weorold-dǣd, e; *f. A worldly deed, a deed which is concerned only with affairs of this world*:—Hé hyne sylfne ǽgðer ge wið woroldsprǽce ge wið worolddǽda warnige, L. E. I. 21; Th. ii. 414, 38. [*O. H. Ger.* weralt-tāt *seculi actus*.]

weorold-deád; *adj. Dead as far as this life is concerned, dead as regards the body*:—Hí mé on deorce stówe settan, samed anlíce swá ðú worulddeáde wrige mid foldan *collocavit me in obscuris sicut mortuos seculi*, Ps. Th. 142, 4.

weorold-déma, an; *m. A secular judge*:—Be eorlum. Eorlas and heretogan and ðás worulddéman ágan nýdþearfe ðæt hí riht lufian, L. I. P. 11; Th. ii. 318, 20. Bisceop sceall saca sehtan mid ðám worulddéman ðe riht lufian, 7; Th. ii. 312, 15, 36.

weorold-dóm, es; *m. A secular judgment, judgment by a secular court*:—Sum wer wæs betogen ðæt hé wǽre on stale, and hine man gelæhte and æfter worulddóme dydon him út ða eágan, Homl. Skt. i. 21, 267.

weorold-dreám, es; *m. Joy of this life*:—Hé worulddreáma breác, Cd. Th. 74, 10; Gen. 1220: 180, 9; Exod. 42. Þenden ic wunige on worulddreámum *quamdiu ero*, Ps. Th. 103, 31: Exon. Th. 184, 1; Gú. 1337.

weorold-dryhten, es; *m. The Lord of the world, the Deity*:—Gif ðú wilnige weorulddrihtnes heáne anwald ongitan *si vis celsi jura tonantis cernere*, Met. 29, 1.

weorold-duguþ, e; *f. Worldly good*:—Wilna brytta and woruld-dugeða bróðrum sínum, Cd. Th. 97, 30; Gen. 1620. Wilna wæstmum and worulddugeðum, lufum and lissum, 117, 4; Gen. 1948.

weorold-earfeþe, es; *n. Labour* or *trouble of this life*:—Strong wind woruldearfoþa, Met. 7, 26, 35, 49.

weorold-ege, es; *m. Worldly fear, fear of the world*:—Hý sculan Godes ege habban on gemynde and ne eargian for woruldege ealles tó swýðe, L. I. P. 6; Th. ii. 310, 20.

weorold-ende, es; *m. The end of the world*:—Ðæt hé léte hyne licgean ðǽr hé longe wæs, wícum wunian óð woruldende, Beo. Th. 6159; B. 3083. [*O. H. Ger.* weralt-enti.]

weorold-fægerness, e; *f. Earthly fairness*:—Seó hine lǽrde ðæt hé nǽfre Godes geleáfan forléte, and ðæt nǽnig woruldfægernes ǽfre his geðóht oncerde, Shrn. 59, 31.

weorold-feoh; *gen.* -feós; *n. Worldly wealth, this world's goods*:—Nis woruldfeoh ðe ic mé ágan wille sceat ne scilling (*I will not take from a thread even to a shoe-latchet*, Gen. 14, 23), Cd. Th. 129, 12; Gen. 2142.

weorold-folgoþ, es; *m. A worldly service, service with an earthly lord*:—Sceolde Sanctus Martinus néde beón on ðære geferǽdenne cininges ðegna . . . Næs ná ðæt hé his willan on ðæm woruldfolgaðe wǽre . . . Ðá hé wæs týnwintre, and hine hys yldran tó woruldfolgaðe tyhton, ðá fleáh hé tó Godes ciricean, Blickl. Homl. 211, 22–29. Ðá forlét hé ðone woroldfolgað, and ðá gewát tó Sancte Hilarie ðæm bisceope, 217, 1.

weorold-frǣt[e]wung, e; *f. Worldly ornament, earthly decoration*:—Ne mid golde, ne mid seolfre, ne mid nǽnigre worldfrætwunga, Blickl. Homl. 125, 36.

weorold-freónd, es; *m. An earthly friend*:—Weoruldfrýnd míne, Met. 2, 16. Wé witan ðæt ús forlǽtaþ and níde sculon ealle úre world-frýnd, Wulfst. 127, 31. Ealle úre weoruldfreónd, 122, 7.

weorold-friþ, es; *n. Peace that is maintained by the temporal power.* Cf. cyric-friþ:—Ðæt woroldfrið stande betweox Æðelréde cynge and eallum his leódscipe, and eallum ðam here ðe se cyng ðæt feoh sealde, L. Eth. ii. 1; Th. i. 284, 9.

weorold-fruma, an; *m. One of the world's great men*:—Ðá gemunde hé ða strangan dǽda ðara unmanna (iumanna?) and ðæra woruldfrumena *valida priscorum heroum facta reminiscens*, Guthl. 2; Gdwin. 12, 28.

weorold-gālness, e; *f. Desire for worldly pleasures*:—Ðara bócera ðe nellaþ godspel sæcgan Godes folce for hiora gémeleáste and for weoruld-gálnesse, Wulfst. 219, 14.

weorold-gebyrd[u]; *f. Birth* (natural not spiritual):—Hé wæs on his móde æþelra ðonne on woruldgebyrdum *erat animo quam carne nobilior*, Bd. 3, 19; S. 547, 26. Wæs heó æþele in weoruldgebyrdum, ðæt heó wæs ðæs cyninges nefan dohtor *nobilis natu erat, hoc est, filia nepotis regis*, 4, 23; S. 593, 2. v. ge-byrd.

weorold-gedāl, es; *n. Parting from the world, death*:—Tó woruld-gedále, Elen. Kmbl. 1159; El. 581.

weorold-gefeoht, es; *n. An earthly fight*:—Sigefæste on worold-gefeohtum, Shrn. 61, 29.

weorold-geflit, es; *n. A secular dispute*:—Gif him þince ðæt hé æt woruldgeflitum sí, ðæt tácnaþ him ádl tóweard, Lchdm. iii. 174, 19.

weorold-gerǣdness, e; *f. A secular ordinance*:—Weoruldgerǽdnes (Eádgáres cyninges gerǽdnes, MS. D.), L. Edg. ii. 1; Th. i. 266, 1.

weorold-geriht, es; *n. A secular* or *civil right*:—Woruldgerihta ic wille ðæt standan on ǽlcum leódscipe swá góde swá hý mon on betste áredian mæge . . . And ic wille ðæt woruldgerihta mid Denum standan be swá gódum lagum swá hý betst geceósan mægen, L. Edg. S. 2; Th. i. 272, 23–31.

weorold-gerisene, es; *n. Worldly propriety*:—Æfter Godes rihte and æfter woroldgerysnum *as religion and the world require*, L. O. 1; Th. i. 178, 5: L. Edm. B. 1; Th. i. 254, 4. Woruldgerysenum, L. I. P. 24; Th. ii. 336, 38.

weorold-gesǣlig; *adj. Blessed with this world's goods, prosperous*:—Wís ealdorman, woruldgesǽlig, Byrht. Th. 138, 13; By. 219. [Cf. *O. H. Ger.* weralt-sālig *abundans in seculo*.]

weorold-gesǣlþa; *pl. f. This world's goods, earthly blessings*:—Eálá! hwæþer gé men ongiton hwelc se wela sié, and se anweald, and ða woruld-gesǽlþa, Bt. 16, 2; Fox 50, 36: 16, 3; Fox 54, 16. Ða getreówan freónd, ic secge seó ðæt deórweorðeste ðyng eallra ðissa woruldgesǽlþa, 24, 3; Fox 82, 29. Tó upáhafen for woruldgesǽlþum, Met. 5, 34. Ðeáh hý sýn on þyson woroldgesǽlþon ða unspédgestan, Ors. 1, 2; Swt. 30, 4. Ǽlc ðara ðe ðás woruldgesǽlþa hæfþ, Bt. 11, 2; Fox 34, 23. v. weorold-sǽlþa.

weorold-gesceaft, e; *f.* I. *the created world*:—Óð ðæt ðeós woruldgesceaft þurh word geweard wuldorcyninges, Cd. Th. 7, 23; Gen. 110. II. *created things, creatures*:—God wolde ðæt him eorðe and uproder and síd wæter geseted wurde woruldgesceafte on wráðra gield, Cd. Th. 7, 4; Gen. 101. III. *a creature of this world, an earthly creature*:—Ða unstillan woruldgesceafta, Met. 11, 19, 101. Hé waldeþ weoruldgesceafta, 29, 78. Woruldgesceafta, 11, 84. Fægerust woruld-gesceafta (*the sun*), Menol. Fox 227; Men. 115. Weroda Waldend, woruldgesceafta, Cd. Th. 237, 4; Dan. 332: 53, 19; Gen. 863. Ðæt fýr is yfemest ofer eallum ðissum woruldgesceaftum, Bt. 33, 4; Fox 128, 39. Wið ealle weoruldgesceafta, Met. 20, 129.

weorold-gestreón, es; *n. Worldly gain, this world's wealth*:—Wéndest ðú, gif ðú mé sealdest ówiht ðínes, ðæt ðé ðonne wǽre ðín woruldgestreón eall gelytlad? Wulfst. 260, 19. Ðás woruldgestreón, Exon. Th. 106, 15; Gú. 41. Sum hér ofer eorþan ǽhta onlíhð, woruld-gestreóna, 295, 10; Crä. 31. Ofergrǽdige woruldgestreóna (*cupidi*, 2 Tim. 3, 2), Wulfst. 81, 14. Hé breác mondreáma hér, woruld-gestreóna, Cd. Th. 71, 27; Gen. 1177. Swíðan woruldgestreónum, 164, 19; Gen. 2717. Eádge eorðwelan . . . and heora woruldgestreón, 112, 32; Gen. 1879: Exon. Th. 215, 18; Ph. 255. Feor lá sí ðæt Godes cyrice . . . weoruldgestreón séce (*lucra quaerere*), Bd. 1, 27; S. 490, 26.

weorold-geswinc, es; *n. Worldly labour* or *toil*:—Sió friðstów æfter ðissum weoruldgeswincum, Met. 21, 18. Ðyncð him gesuinc ðæt hé bið bútan woroldgesuincium (worldgeswincum, Hatt. MS.) *laborem deputant, si in terrenis negotiis non laborant*, Past. 18; Swt. 129, 1.

weorold-geþōht, es; *m. A worldly thought*:—Cristes þegnas ðeossa worda nán ongeotan ne mehton, ac hié wǽron him bedíglede, for ðon ðe hié wǽron ðágyt mid worldgeþóhtum bewrigene, Blickl. Homl. 15, 14.

weorold-geþyngþ[u]; *f. Worldly dignity*:—Ǽlc heáh ár hér on worulde bið mid frécnessum embeseald; efne swá ða woruldgeþincþa (-geþingþa, *v. l.*) beóð máran, swá ða frécnessa beóð swíðran, Wulfst. 262, 3.

weorold-gewinn, es; *n. Earthly war*:—Hit bið swýðe derigendlíc, ðæt Godes þeówan Drihtnes þeówdóm forlǽtan, and tó woruldgewinne (weoruld-, worold-, *v. ll.*) búgan, ðe him náht tó ne gebyraþ, Homl. Skt. ii. 25, 832.

weorold-gewritu; *pl. n. Profane literature*:—On weoruldgewritum gelǽred *saeculari literatura instructus*, Bd. 4, 1; S. 564, 11. Ðá lǽrde se hyne godcunde gewritu; ðá forlét hé ða woruldgewrytu, Shrn. 152, 20.

weorold-gewuna, an; *m. The custom of the world*:—Hé ásmeáde ðæt godcunde be woruldgewunan *he considered the religious question from a secular standpoint*, L. Edg. S. 1; Th. i. 270, 15.

weorold-gifu, e; *f. A gift of temporal things*:—Sende se eádiga pápa Gregorius Æðelbyrhte cyninge woroldgife monige, Bd. 1, 32; S. 498, 20. Woruldgiua, Chr. 995; Th. i. 244, 17.

weorold-gilp, es; *m. Worldly glory*:—Ðǽm upáhæfenum is tó cýðanne hwelc náwuht ðes woruldgielp (worldgilp, Cott. MS.) is *elatis intimandum est, quam sit nulla temporalis gloria*, Past. 41; Swt. 299, 6. For ðære gewilnunga woroldgielpes and giétsunga *appetendis lucris temporalibus honoribusque*, 21; Swt. 157, 2. Wé ðurh ða ne wilniaþ woruldgielpes *per eam humanas laudes assequi minime ambimus*, 48; Swt. 375, 11. *Largitas* . . . ðæt is ðæt man wíslíce his ǽhta áspende, ná for woruld-gylpe, Homl. Skt. i. 16, 327, 330. [For weorldȝelpe, worldȝelpe, O. E. Homl. i. 105, 14, 13.]

weorold-gīmenn (?). v. weorold-sorh (*last passage*).

weorold-gītsere, es; *m. One who is covetous of this world's goods*:—Hwæt bið ðæm welegan woruldgítsere (cf. gítsere, Bt. 26, 3; Fox 94, 13) on his móde ðe bet, þeáh hé micel áge goldes and gimma and gooda gehwæs, Met. 14, 1.

weorold-gītsung, e; *f. Greed for this world's goods, covetousness*:—Ne mæg fira nán wísdóm timbran, ðǽr ðǽr woruldgítsung (cf. gítsung, Bt. 12; Fox 36, 12) beorg oferbrǽdeþ, Met. 7, 12. Hí cumaþ of woruldgítsunga, Bt. 7, 1; Fox 16, 15.

weorold-gleng, es *or* e; *m.* or *f.* *Worldly pomp*:—Se blinda ne bæd goldes, ne seolfres, ne worldglenga, Blickl. Homl. 21, 6. Se snotera wer ne gewilnaþ ðara woruldglenga, ne ðæs lîchaman wlite, ac gewilnaþ ðære sâwle, Basil admn. 8; Norm. 52, 14. Heora yldran on worolde ne wurdan welige ne wlance þurh woroldglænge, L. Eth. vii. 4; Th. i. 334, 4. Ðâ forlêt hê ealle ðâs woruldglenga, Guthl. 2; Gdwin. 16, 18.

weorold-gôd, es; *n.* *A temporal good, worldly good*:—Eówre woruldgôd *vestra bona*, Bt. 14, 2; Fox 46, 1. Ða getreówan freónd ne sint tô woruldgôdum tô tellanne, ac tô godcundum, 24, 3; Fox 82, 29. Eall ða weoruldgôd ðe him fram cyningum and fram weligum mannum ðisse weorulde gegyfne wǽron *cuncta quae sibi a regibus vel divitibus saeculi donabantur*, Bd. 3, 5; S. 526, 24.

weorold-hâd, es; *m.* *A secular, lay condition*:—In weoruldhâde drohtiende *in saeculari habitu conversata*, Bd. 4, 23; S. 592, 42. In weoruldhâde geseted, 4, 24; S. 597, 3. Weoruldhâd forlǽtan, 598, 2: 4, 23; S. 593, 7.

weorold-hlâford, es; *m.* *An earthly master, a temporal lord*:—Se ðe gyfð ge ðæs worldhlâfordes freóndscype ge his âgenne, Shrn. 177, 6. Se esne ðe ǽrendaþ his woroldhlâforde wîfes, Past. 19; Swt. 143, 2. Beó manna gehwylc hold and getrȳwe his worldhlâforde, Wulfst. 74, 9. Hî ic wille wyrðian swâ swâ man worldhlâford sceal, Shrn. 196, 32. Woruldhlâfordas môston ðære fiohbôte onfôn, L. Alf. 49; Th. i. 58, 7. Beóð gê underðeódde eówrum woroldhlâfordum *obedite dominis carnalibus*, Past. 29; Swt. 201, 21. Wê lǽraþ þæt Godes þeówas beón geornlîce Gode þeówigende . . . and ðæt hî beón â heora ealdre holde and gehȳrsume . . . and ðæt hî beón heora worldhlâfordum eác holde and getrȳwe, L. Edg. C. 1; Th. ii. 244, 5.

weorold-hlîsa, an; *m.* *Worldly fame, earthly renown*:—Habbon hî ðone woruldhlîsan ðe hî sôhton, nâ ða êcan mêde ðe hî ne rôhton, Homl. Th. ii. 566, 6.

weorold-hyht, es; *m.* *Earthly joy*:—Ðû lǽtest wæter wynlîco tô woruldhyhte of clife clǽnum, Exon. Th. 194, 10; Az. 136.

weorold-irmþ[u]; *f.* *Misery of this life*:—Wê nû gehȳraþ hwǽr ûs hearmstafas onwôcan, and woruldyrmðo, Cd. Th. 58, 3; Gen. 940. Hî hêton eft Iôhannes gebringan æt his mynstre, fram ðâm woruldyrmþum ðe hê hwîle on wæs, Ors. 6, 10; Bos. 120, 36.

weorold-lǽce, es; *m.* *A physician for the body*:—Nis se woruldlǽce wælhreów, ðeáh ðe hê ðone gewundodan mid bærnette gelâcnige, Homl. Th. i. 472, 13.

weorold-lagu, e; *f.*: -laga, an; *m.* *Law relating to secular matters, civil law* as distinguished from ecclesiastical:—Woruldcunde bôte sêce man be woruldlage, L. C. S. 38; Th. i. 398, 22. Hlâfordes searwu æfter woruldlagu is bôtleás þing, Wulfst. 274, 24. Wîse woroldwitan ðe gesettan tô godcundan rihtlagan worldlaga, L. Eth. vii. 24; Th. i. 334, 22. Leófan menn, lagiaþ gôde woroldlagan, Wulfst. 274, 7.

weorold-leán, es; *n.* *Worldly reward*:—Ða ðe Godes þances hwylcne cuman underfôn, ne wilnigen hig ðǽr nânra woruldleána, L. E. I. 25; Th. ii. 422, 13.

weorold-lîc; *adj.* I. *worldly, earthly, temporal, mundane*:—Nâuht woruldlîces fæstes and unhwearfiendes beón ne mæg, Bt. 8; Fox 26, 11 note. Ne seó eorþe ǽnigre worldlîcre frætwednesse onfôn wolde, seoþþan hire ða hâlgan fêt ûres Drihtnes on stôdan, Blickl. Homl. 127, 3. On woruldlîcum wuldre scînende, Homl. Th. i. 62, 27. Tô forsewennysse woruldlîcra ǽhta, 60, 25: Exon. Th. 126, 20; Gû. 374. Hê sceolde woroldlîcum wǽpnum onfôn, Blickl. Homl. 213, 2. Ðæt hwâ woruldlîce spêda forhogige, Homl. Th. i. 60, 32. Worldlîce tintrega, Blickl. Homl. 119, 19. Ealle worldlîcu þing, 109, 3. Gewilnian ða woruldlîcan þingc, Boutr. Scrd. 22, 44. II. *natural, physical*:—Nis ðeós woruldlîce niht nân þing bûton ðære eorþan sceadu, Lchdm. iii. 240, 18. For ðam ungewunan woruldlîces gesceádes, Boutr. Scrd. 18, 28. Woruldlîce ûðwitan *natural philosophers*, 18, 25: Lchdm. iii. 240, 20. III. in contrast with religious or ecclesiastical, *worldly, secular, civil*:—From woruldlîcum luste hearte his giscilde *a seculari desiderio cor ejus defendat*, Rtl. 96, 11. Neádian preóstas tô woruldlîcum gecampe, Homl. Skt. ii. 25, 834, 827. Woroldlîcra weorca on ðam hâlgan dæge geswîce man georne, L. Eth. vi. 22; Th. i. 320, 12. Woruldlîcra, L. C. E. 15; Th. i. 368, 18. Se ðe Gode sceal þeówigan ne sceal hê hyne nâ âbysgian worldlîcra bysgunga *qui Deo vult servire, non debet occupari mundanis negotiis*, L. Ecg. P. i. 7; Th. ii. 174, 27. Bôt æt woroldlîcan þingan, L. Eth. v. 20; Th. i. 308, 31. [*O. H. Ger.* weralt-lîh *mundanus, secularis, carnalis, civilis.*]

weoroldlîce; *adv.* I. *secularly, civilly*:—Ne sind ealle cyricean nâ gelîcre mǽðe weoruldlîce wurðscipes wyrðe, þeáh hig godcundlîce hâlgunge habban gelîce, L. C. E. 3; Th. i. 360, 16. Worldlîce, L. Eth. ix. 5; Th. i. 340, 26. II. *after the manner of this world*:—Weoroldlîce and wîslîce gê dyde ðætte mannum bedîgled wæs on eorðan ðæt gê ðæt on heofenas tô Gode sôhtan *ye acted with worldly wisdom in seeking in heaven of God what was hidden from men on earth*, Blickl. Homl. 199, 36. [*O. H. Ger.* weraltlîcho *carnaliter.*]

weorold-lîf, es; *n.* I. *life in this world, life on earth*:—Ðæt ðû mê forgyfe ðæt mînes worldlîfes bletsung anstande *ut tu mihi condones ut mundanae meae vitae benedictio permaneat*, L. Ecg. P. iv. 67; Th. ii. 228, 3. Ða ðe unrihtes on weoruldlîfe worhtan, Ps. Th. 91, 6. Nis him onwendednes on woruldlîfe *non est illis commutatio*, 54, 20: 114, 7: 118, 92: Cd. Th. 222, 12; Dan. 103: Exon. Th. 172, 11; Gû. 1142: 294, 15; Crä. 15: Wulfst. 258, 15. Hê self lifde on gneáðum woroldlîfe *he (bishop Lupus) lived a very frugal life on earth*, Shrn. 110, 5. Ðæt hió ne wunian on worldlîfe *ita ut non sint*, Ps. Th. 103, 33: 61, 12: Exon. Th. 427, 7; Rä. 41, 87. II. *the period of the world's duration, the while the world lasts*:—Ealle on weoruldlîfe weorþaþ gedrêfde *conturbentur in seculum seculi*, Ps. Th. 82, 13. Nele God wið ende ǽfre tô worulde his milde môd mannum âfyrran on woruldlîfe wera cneórissum *numquid Deus in finem misericordiam suam abscindet a seculo et generatione?* 76, 7. Ðû eart âna God ðe ǽghwylc miht wundor gewyrcean on woruldlîfe, 76, 11. III. *worldly life, secular life*:—Hê mynsterlîf ðam weoruldlîfe forbær *monasticam saeculari vitam praetulit*, Bd. 5, 19; S. 637, 8. Hê ôþer lîf mâ lufode ðonne ðæt woruldlîf, S. 638, 7. [Þiss weorelldlif iss wel þurrh nihht bitacnedd, Orm. 2978.]

weoruld-lufu, e, an; *f.* *Love of the world, love of worldly things*:—Wê nellaþ bûgan fram ðyssere andweardan woruldlufe, Homl. Th. i. 580, 3. Se cwyrnstân, ðe tyrnð singallîce, and nǽnne færeld ne ðurhtîhð, getâcnaþ woruldlufe, ðe on gedwyldum hwyrftlaþ, and nǽnne stæpe on Godes wege ne gefæstnaþ, 514, 21. Se man ðe ânrǽdlîce wile his synna geswîcan, dǽle on Godes êst eal ðæt hê âge, and forlǽte eard and êðel and ealle ðâs worldlufu, L. Pen. 17; Th. ii. 284, 19.

weorold-lust, es; *m.* *Worldly pleasure, pleasure that comes from things of this world*:—Hû ne is ðê genôg openlîce geeówad ðara leásena gesǽlþa anlîcnes; ðæt is ðonne ǽhta and weorðscipe and anweald and woruldlust. Be ðam woruldluste Epicurus sǽde . . . ðæt se lust wǽre ðæt hêhste gôd *habes igitur ante oculos propositam fere formam felicitatis humanae, opes, honores, potentiam, voluptates. Quae considerans Epicurus sibi summum bonum voluptatem esse constituit*, Bt. 24, 3; Fox 84, 19–23: 24, 4; Fox 86, 29. For ðam ðe hê mæg ðurh ðæt tô anwealde cuman oððe tô sumum woruldluste *vel potentiae caussa, vel delectationis*, 24, 3; Fox 82, 34. [*O. Sax.* werold-lust: *O. H. Ger.* weralt-lust *terrena concupiscentia.*]

weorold-mǽg, es; *m.* *A kinsman according to the flesh*:—Mê æfter sculon mîne woruldmâgas welan bryttian, Cd. Th. 131, 18; Gen. 2178.

weorold-mann, es; *m.* I. in a general sense, *a man upon earth, a man*:—Orsorg lîf lǽdaþ woruldmen wîse (cf. se wîsa mon, Bt. 12; Fox 36, 24), Met. 7, 41. Ân ðara tungla woruldmen hâtaþ (cf. wê hâtaþ, Bt. 39, 3; Fox 214, 19) wǽnes þîsla, 28, 10. Weoruldmen (cf. folc, Bt. 39, 3; Fox 216, 2) wênaþ, 28, 72. Hû yfele mê dôþ manege woruldmenn . . . ic eom getogen tô fremdum þeáwum ðurh ða ungefyldan gîtsunge woruldmonna (*inexpleta hominum cupiditas*), Bt. 7, 3; Fox 20, 19–26. Hwâ is weoruldmonna ðæt ne wafige (cf. hwâ ne wundraþ, Bt. 39, 3; Fox 214, 25), Met. 28, 31. Woruldmonna seó unclǽne gecynd, Exon. Th. 63, 8; Cri. 1016. Ic wât ðætte wile woruldmen tweógan geond foldan sceát bûton feá âne (cf. went nû ful neáh eall moncyn on tweónunga, Bt. 4; Fox 8, 18), Met. 4, 52. II. *a man employed, or interested, in worldly affairs; a man of the world*:—Se Hǽlend befrân hû woruldmenn be him cwyddedon . . . Drihten ðâ befrân: 'Hwæt secge gê ðæt ic sȳ? swylce hê swâ cwǽde: "Nû woruldmenn ðus dwollîce mê oncnâwaþ, gê ðe godas sind, hû oncnâwe gê mê," ' Homl. Th. i. 366, 5–14. Hê hine wið eallum ðǽm wǽpnum geheóld, ða ðe woruldmen fremmaþ on menniscum ðingum, Blickl. Homl. 213, 6. Ðonne hê from woruldmonnum (world-, Cott. MSS.) bið ongiten suelce hê sié ældiédig on ðiosum middangearde, Past. 19; Swt. 141, 18. Ða hǽþenan fêngon tô wurðienne mistlîce entas and strece woruldmen, ðe mihtige wurdan on woruldafelum, Wulfst. 105, 34. II a. *a man engaged in secular, as opposed to ecclesiastical, affairs, a layman*:—Nalæs ðæt ân ðæt ðâs ðing dyden weoruldmen (*saeculares viri*), ac eác swylce ðæt Drihtnes eówde, Bd. 1, 14; S. 482, 25. Ða lâfe ðæs gereordes, ðæt sind ða deópnyssa ðære lâre ðe woroldmen understandan ne magon, ða sceolon ða lâreówas gegaderian, Homl. Th. i. 190, 6. Munuclîf wǽron gehealdene, and ða woruldmenn wǽron wære wið heora fȳnd, Homl. Skt. i. 13, 150: 20, 120. Woruldmanna gebeórscypas *secularium conuiuia*, Anglia xiii. 375, 133. [For nane weorldmonne *for no man on earth*, Laym. 28131. Þe wisdom of þeos wise worldmen *sapientia sapientium*, Kath. 486. *O. H. Ger.* weralt-mann *a man.*]

weorold-mêd, e; *f.* *Worldly recompense*:—Ne sceal nân man woruldmêde wilnian æt ðam cuman, for ðam ðe him is gehâten êce gefeá fore on Godes rîce, L. E. I. 25; Th. ii. 422, 15.

weorold-nîd, -neód, e; *f.* *Secular need, need in worldly matters, temporal necessity*:—Se cyngc beódeþ eallum his gerêfan, ðæt gê ðâm abbodan æt eallum worldneódum beorgan swâ ge betst magon, L. Eth. ix. 32; Th. i. 346, 30. [*O. H. Ger.* weralt-nôt *tribulatio.*]

weorold-nytt, e; *f.* *Use in this world, temporal advantage*:—Âweccan ðâs wæstmas ûs tô woruldnytte, Lchdm. i. 400, 6: Cd. Th. 59, 7; Gen. 960: 62, 18; Gen. 1016.

weorold-prȳt, -prȳd, e; *f.* *Worldly pride*:—Næs heó, swâ nû ædelborene men synt, mid ofermêttum âfylled, ne mid woruldprȳdum, Lchdm. iii. 428, 32.

weorold-rǽdenn, e; *f. The rule* or *way of the world:*—Hē ne forwyrnde woroldrǽdenne, Beo. Th. 2289; B. 1142.

weorold-rīca, an; *m. A man of great worldly power* or *wealth:*—Gif him ǽnig heáfodman hwilces þinges forwyrnde . . . him sōna getīðode his Scyppendes ārfæstnys ðæs ðe se woruldrīca him forwyrnde on ǽr, Homl. Th. ii. 514, 17. Ne cyning ne woruldrīca, Lchdm. iii. 442, 36. Unrihtwīse dēman and gerēfan and ealle ða wōhgeornan woruldrīcan mid heora golde and seolfre and godwebbum and eallum ungestreónum, Wulfst. 183, 8. v. next word.

weorold-rīce; *adj. Having worldly power* or *wealth:*—Sum dȳre bið woruldrīcum men, Exon. Th. 295, 26; Crä. 39. Nǽnigum woruldrīcum men ne ciningc sylfum, Blickl. Homl. 223, 27. Woruldrīcum men, ðe āhte on ðysse worlde mycelne welan and swīðe mōdelīco gestreón and manigfealde, 113, 5. Worldrīcra manna deáþ, 107, 29.

weorold-rīce, es; *n.* I. *the kingdom of this world, this world:*—Ne þearf ic ǽnigre āre wēnan on woruldrīce, Cd. Th. 62, 32; Gen. 1024: 67, 33; Gen. 1110: 99, 4; Gen. 1641. Eorðcyninga se wīsesta on woruldrīce, 202, 25; Exod. 393: 201, 1; Exod. 365. Bibeád ic eów ðæt gē brōþor mīne in woruldrīce wel ārētten, Exon. Th. 91, 32; Cri. 1501: 275, 12; Jul. 549: 290, 14; Wand. 65: 442, 16; Kl. 13. Hū wolde ðæt geweorðan on woruldrīce? Elen. Kmbl. 910; El. 456. In worldrīce, 2095; El. 1049. Hē hēt ðæt on worldrīce wunian ēce *fundavit eam in secula*, Ps. Th. 77, 68. Ne beó nǽnig man hēr on worldrīce on his geþōhte tō mōdig, Blickl. Homl. 109, 27. For hwam winneþ ðis wæter geond woruldrīce? Salm. Kmbl. 785; Sal. 392. II. *a kingdom of this world, an earthly kingdom, earthly power:*—Nāuht woruldrīces fæstes beón ne mæg, Bt. 8; Fox 26, 11. Ic ongite ðætte ǽlces gōdes genōg nis on ðisum woruldwelan, ne æltæwe anweald nis on nānum woruldrīce *video nec opibus sufficientiam, nec regnis potentiam posse contingere*, 33, 1; Fox 120, 3. Hē hine (*Nebuchadnezzar*) āsceád of ðam woroldrīce (world-, Cott. MSS.), Past. 4; Swt. 39, 21. Woruldrīce, Cd. Th. 253, 2; Dan. 589. Ðū woruldrīcum wealdest eallum, Ps. Th. 144, 13. On worldrīcum, 77, 2. Geond woruldrīcu, 113, 9. [Wha wolde wenen a þissere weorldriche, Laym. 15179. Þe laþe gast himm bæd all weorelldrichess ahhte, Orm. 11800. *O. Sax.* werold-rīki *the world; earthly power: O. H. Ger.* weralt-rīchi *orbis terrarum.*]

weorold-riht, es; *n.* I. *right in worldly matters, civil* or *secular law:*—Wylle wē ǽrest, ðæt Godes riht forð gā and woruldriht syððan, Wulfst. 274, 20. Beó on ðære scīre bisceop and se ealdorman, and ðǽr ǽgðer tǽcan ge Godes riht ge woruldriht, L. Edg. ii. 5; Th. i. 268, 5. II. *the law that should govern the world:*—Dryhten sceáwaþ hwǽr ða eardien ðe his ǽ healden; gesihð hē ða dōmas wonian and wendan of woruldryhte, ða hē gesette, Exon. Th. 105, 25; Gū. 28.

weorold-sacu, e; *f. A dispute about worldly matters:*—Ǽlce wīgwǽpna and ǽghwylce woruldsaca lǽte man stille, Wulfst. 170, 9. [*O. Sax.* werold-saka *a worldly matter: O. H. Ger.* weralt-sahha *mortalis res.*]

weorold-sǽlþa; *pl. f. This world's goods, earthly blessings:*—Eálā hwæþer gē nētenlīcan men ongiton hwelc se wela sié and se anweald and ða woruldsǽlþa? Bt. 16, 2; Fox 50, 36 note. Nis ðē nāuht swīþor ðonne ðæt ðū forloren hæfst ða woruldsǽlþa ðe ðū ǽr hæfdest (*fortunae prioris affectu tabescis*). Ic ongite ðæt ða woruldsǽlþa ōleccaþ ðǽm mōdum ðe hī willaþ beswīcan, 7, 1; Fox 16, 8-12: 8; Fox 26, 5, 8. Mē āblendan ðās ungetreówan woruldsǽlþa *dum levibus malefida bonis fortuna faveret, paene caput tristis merserat hora meum*, 2; Fox 4, 9: Met. 2, 10. Se ymbhoga ðyssa woruldsǽlþa, 7, 54. Woruldsēlþa, Bt. 12; Fox 36, 29. Swā his mōd ǽr swīðor tō ðām woruldsǽlþum gewunod wæs, 1; Fox 4, 1. Ic wolde ðæt wit māre sprǽcan ymbe ða woruldsǽlða *vellem pauca tecum fortunae ipsius verbis agitare*, 7, 3; Fox 20, 1. [*O. H. Ger.* weralt-sālida *fortuna, terrena felicitas.*] v. weorold-gesǽlþa.

weorold-sceaft, e; *f. A creature of this world, an earthly creature:*—Wuldres Waldend and woruldsceafta, Exon. Th. 188, 20; Az. 48. Woruldsceafta wuldor, 190, 16; Az. 74. v. weorold-gesceaft.

weorold-sceamu, e; *f. Worldly shame, disgrace among men:*—Wāla ðære woruldscame, ðe nū habbaþ Engle. . . . Oft twēgen sǽmen oððe þrȳ drīfaþ ða drāfe cristenra manna fram sǽ tō sǽ . . . ūs eallum tō woruldscame, Wulfst. 163, 3-7. Ða ðe for ege oððe lufe oððe ǽnigre worldscame eargiaþ and wandiaþ Godes riht tō sprecanne, 191, 5. For woruldsceame, L. I. P. 12; Th. ii. 320, 22. Gif wīf be ōðrum were forlicge, and hit open weorðe, geweorðe heó tō woruldsceame hire sylfre, L. C. S. 54; Th. i. 406, 7. Tō woroldscame, Wulfst. 168, 14. [Ǽfter muchel weorldscome (worliche same, 2nd MS.) wurðscipe, Laym. 8323.]

weorold-scipe, es; *m. A worldly affair, an affair of this life:*—Ne scyle nān Godes ðeów hine selfne tō ungemetlīce bindan on woruldscipum (world-, Cott. MSS.), ðȳ læs hē mislīcige ðæm ðe hē ǽr hine selfne gesealde *nemo militans Deo implicat se negotiis secularibus, ut ei placeat, cui se probavit*, Past. 18; Swt. 131, 2. [Himm þatt ledenn shall þiss lif, himm birrþ all weorelldshipe flen, Orm. 6322.]

weorold-snotor; *adj. Wise in earthly matters:*—Ǽgelwīg se woruldsnotra abbod on Eofeshamme, Chr. 1078; Erl. 215, 29. Woroldsnottre men (*naturalists*) secgaþ, ðæt ða ficsas sȳn on sǽ hundteóntiges cynna and ðreó and fīftiges, Shrn. 65, 31. Weoroldsnottrum *gymnosophistis*, Wrt. Voc. ii. 81, 52. Ne weorþeþ on worulde ǽnig worldsnotera (woruld-, *v. l.*) þonne hē wyrðeþ *there shall be none in the world that has more worldly cunning than he* (*Antichrist*) *has*, Wulfst. 54, 21.

weorold-sorh; *gen.* -sorge; *f. Worldly care, care of this life:*—Hwonon wurde ðū mid ðissum woruldsorgum ðus swīþe geswenced? . . . Gewītaþ nū, āwirgede woruldsorga, of mīnes þegenes mōde, Bt. 3, 1; Fox 4, 20-23. Ðæt gemearr ðære woruldsorga *curarum secularium impedimentum*, Past. 51; Swt. 401, 21. Bæd heó ðæt heó mōste weoruldsorge and gȳmenne forlǽtan *postulans ut saeculi curas relinquere permitteretur*, Bd. 4, 19; S. 587, 38.

weorold-spēd, e; *f.* I. *worldly wealth;* generally in plural, *this world's goods:*—Syllan ðone teóþan dǽl ūre worldspēda, Blickl. Homl. 35, 20. Mid hire ǽhtum and worldspēdon *possessionibus suis et mundanis opibus*, L. Ecg. P. ii. 16; Th. ii. 188, 3. Weoroldspēdum, Bd. 1, 27; S. 489, 27. Ða ðe habbaþ weoruldspēde *habentes subsidia*, S. 490, 8. Hē him weoruldspēde and ǽhte (*locus facultasque*) forgeaf, 3, 24; S. 556, 42. Ðē Dryhten geaf welan and wiste and woruldspēde, Andr. Kmbl. 636; An. 318. Ðonne hié wilniaþ ðæt hié hira woruldspēda (world-, Cott. MSS.) īcen ðonne weorðaþ hié bedǽlede ðæs ēcean ēðles ūres Fæder *dum hic multiplicari appetunt, illic ab aeterno patrimonio exheredes fiunt*, Past. 44; Swt. 333, 5. On ðara mānfulra forþforlǽtenesse on ðās woruldspēda, Bt. 5, 1; Fox 10, 23. Nolde hē him geceósan welige yldran, ac ða ðe hæfdon lytle worldspēda, Blickl. Homl. 23, 26: 37, 36. II. *worldly success:*—Syndon ðīne willan on woruldspēdum rihte, Cd. Th. 234, 11; Dan. 290: Exon. Th. 185, 20; Az. 10.

weorold-spēdig; *adj. Rich in this world's goods, wealthy:*—Se ðe wilnaþ ðæt wolde on ðam angienne his līfes woroldspēdig (woruld-, Cott. MSS.) weorðan *qui in principio hereditari festinant*, Past. 44; Swt. 333, 2.

weorold-sprǽc, e; *f. Worldly speech, conversation on worldly matters:*—Ne forlǽte preóst his godcundnysse, ne ne fō tō woruldsprǽcum, L. Ælfc. C. 30; Th. ii. 354, 2. Gē lufiaþ woruldsprǽca, 34; Th. ii. 356, 20. Hyne sylfne ǽgðer ge wið woroldsprǽce ge wið woroldǽda warnige hē and healde, L. E. I. 21; Th. ii. 414, 38.

weorold-steór, e; *f. A secular penalty:*—Gif for godbōtan feohbōt ārīseþ . . . ðæt gebyreþ . . . nǽfre tō woroldlīcan īdelan glengan, ac for woroldsteóran tō godcundan neódan, L. Eth. vi. 51; Th. i. 328, 9.

weorold-strengu; *f. Physical strength:*—Mec feónda sum feore besnyþede, woruldstrenga binom, Exon. Th. 407, 30; Rä. 27, 2.

weorold-strūdere, -strūtere, es; *m. A spoiler of this world's goods:*—Ne mōt mid rihte nān preóst beón gītsiende mangere, ne worldstrūtere on gerēfscipe, L. Ælfc. P. 49; Th. ii. 386, 7. Tō helle sculan gītseras, rȳperas and reáferas and woruldstrūderas, Wulfst. 26, 17: 165, 36. Cristen cyning sceal rȳperas and reáferas and ðās woruldstrūderas hatian and hȳnan, L. I. P. 2; Th. ii. 304, 19.

weorold-stund, e; *f. Time spent in this world:*—Mē ne woldon folc oncnāwan, deáh ic fela for him æfter woruldstundum (*in the hours I spent on earth*) wundra gefremede, Elen. Kmbl. 725; El. 363. [*O. Sax.* werold-stunda.]

weorold-þearf, e; *f. What is needed for the life of this world:*—Swā swā hē gehēt him andlyfne and heora weoruldðearfe forgifan, eác swylce lȳfnesse sealde ðæt hī mōstan Cristes geleáfan bodian *eis, ut promiserat, cum administratione victus temporalis, licentiam quoque praedicandi non abstulit*, Bd. 1, 25; S. 487, 19.

weorold-þearfa, an; *m. One who is needy in the matter of this world's goods:*—Ic eom wǽdla and worldþearfa *ego egenus et pauper sum*, Ps. Th. 69, 6.

weorold-þearfende; *adj. Deficient in this world's goods, needy:*—Earme men, woruldþearfende, Exon. Th. 83, 4; Cri. 1351.

weorold-þeáwas; *pl. m. Conduct in the affairs of this world:*—Se wæs on woruldþeáwum se rihtwīsesta *in the conduct of his life he was most righteous*, Bt. 1; Fox 2, 13.

weorold-þegen, es; *m. A secular thane:*—Mæssepreóstes āð and woruldþegenes is on Engla lage geteald efendȳre, L. O. 12; Th. i. 182, 14: L. Wg. 5; Th. i. 186, 10.

[**weorold-þeówdōm**, es; *m. Secular service:*—Hī hit freódon wið ealle weoruldþeúdōm, Chr. 963; Erl. 121, 31.]

weorold-þing, es; *n. A worldly thing, matter, affair:*—Ne sȳ nān sacerdhādes man ðe durre geþrīstlǽcan, ðæt ǽnig ðara fata, ðe tō godcundum bīgonge gehālgod bið, tō ǽnigum woruldþinge dō (*put it to any secular use*), L. E. I. 18; Th. ii. 412, 30. Mid ungerisenlīcum gewilnungum ðissa woroldðinga (world-, Cott. MSS.) *ambitione inhonesta*, Past. 21; Swt. 157, 9. Sió ūterre ābisgung ðissa woroldðinga ðæs monnes mōd gedrēfð *cor externis occupationum tumultibus impulsum*, 22; Swt. 169, 13. Woruldðinga, pref.; Swt. 5, 3. Hē wæs hwōn giernende ðissa woroldþinga and micelra onwalda *vir tranquillissimus*, Ors. 6, 30; Swt. 280, 29. Hwæðer ðæt nū sié tō talianne wāclīc and unnyt, ðætte nytwyrþost is ealra woruldþinga, ðæt is anweald? *num imbecillum, ac sine virtutibus aestimandum est, quod omnibus rebus constat esse praestantius?* Bt. 24, 4; Fox 86, 17. Ðonne hē fægnaþ ðæt hē sié ābisgod mid woroldðingum *dum se urgeri mundanis tumultibus gaudent*, Past. 18; Swt. 129, 3. Freom in weoroldðingum *in saeculi rebus strenuus*, Bd. 4,

2; S. 566, 18. On woruldþingan, L. I. P. 14; Th. ii. 322, 17. Of wurðfulre mægðe æfter woruldþingum *of a family honourable from a worldly point of view*, Homl. Skt. ii. 31, 14. Wē forlēton ealle woruld-ðing *nos dimisimus omnia* (Mk. 10, 28), Homl. Th. i. 392, 32, 28. Ðā ðā his geógoð æfter gecynde woruldðing lufian sceolde, ii. 118, 23. [ʒif we forleosað þas lenan worldþing, O. E. Homl. i. 105, 30. He hadde michel of wereldþinge, ii. 127, 16. To geornenn affterr weorelldþing, Orm. 2966.]

weorold-wǣpen, es; *n. A weapon used in this world's warfare:*—Ðā wæs feówer geár ǣr his fulwihte, ðæt hē woroldwǣpno wæg (*he bore this world's arms*), Blickl. Homl. 213, 4.

weorold-wæter, es; *n. An ocean:*—Saga mē, hū fela is woruldwætra? Ic ðē secge, twā sindon sealte sǣ, and twā fersce, Salm. Kmbl. p. 186, 24.

weorold-wela, an; *m. Worldly wealth, worldly good:*—Se woruldwela (*pompa*) his fræ:ewunga āweorpende fleáh, Gl. Prud. 52 a. Sume mægon habban ælles woruldwelan genōg *huic census exuberat*, Bt. 11, 1; Fox 30, 30. Hē wilnaþ hwæthweg ðises woruldwelan, 26, 2; Fox 94, 3. Hī geleáfan ceósaþ ofer woruldwelan, Exon. Th. 230, 30; Ph. 480. Ne wearð ǣnig eorðlīc cyning mǣrra ðonne Salomon wearð þuruh ǣghwylcne woroldwelan, Wulfst. 277, 23. Ða woruldwelan synt gesceapene tō bīswice ðām monnum ðe beóþ neátenum gelīce, Bt. 14, 1; Fox 42, 2. Swylcra fela weoruldwelena (cf. ealne ðisne andweardan welan, Bt. 32, 3; Fox 118, 20), Met. 19, 26. Waa ieów welegum, ðe iówer lufu eall and tōhopa is on eówrum woruldwelum, Past. 26; Swt. 181, 24. Ðios-sum woruldwelum, 45; Swt. 339, 6. Ðās land beóð neáh ðǣm burgum ðe beóð eallum woruldwelum gefylled *hic est ciuitas uicina diues, omnibus bonis plena*, Nar. 34, 33. [Gif þu best aihteles . . . ac gef þu hauest woreldwele . . ., O. E. Homl. ii. 29, 28. *O. Sax.* werold-welo: *O. H. Ger.* weralt-wolun; *pl. mammona.*]

weorold-weorc, es; *n.* I. *worldly work, secular occupation:*—Ðǣm tīdum þonne gē ða rǣdinge hāligra bōca forlǣten and ða gebeda, þonne sculon gē on sum nytlīc weoroldweorc fōn, L. E. I. 3; Th. ii. 404, 10. Nǣnig mon ne geþrīstlǣce on ðone hālgan dæg on nān weoruld-weorc befōn, 24; Th. ii. 420, 22. II. in a special sense, *mechanics:*—*Mechanica*, ðæt ys weoruldweorces cræft, Shrn. 152, 16.

weorold-weorþscipe, es; *m. Worldly honour, civil dignity:*—Hæbbe hē (*the priest*) Godes miltse, and tō woroldweorðscipe ðæt hē sȳ þegen-weres and þegenrihtes wyrðe (*his civil status is that of a thane*), L. Eth. v. 9; Th. i. 306, 20. Tō woruldwurðscipe sī hē þegenlage wyrðe, L. C. E. 6; Th. i. 364, 16: Wulfst. 270, 32.

weorold-widl, es; *n. Worldly pollution, defilement contracted in this life:*—Ðæt fȳr georne āsēceþ eorðan sceátas, ōþþæt eall hafaþ ældes leóma woruldwidles wom wælme forbærned, Exon. Th. 62, 25; Cri. 1007.

weorold-wīg, es; *n. The warfare of this world:*—Ne gebyraþ him (*the priest*) nāðor ne tō wīfe ne tō woruldwīge, L. Edg. C. 60; Th. ii. 256, 35. Worldwīge, L. Eth. ix. 30; Th. i. 346, 23.

weorold-willa, an; *m. A worldly good:*—Monige habbaþ ǣlces woroldwillan genōg, Bt. 11, 1; Fox 30, 30 note.

weorold-wilnung, e; *f. Worldly desire:*—Ðæt līf ðæra gesinhīwena, ðeáh hit ful wundorlīc ne sié on mægenum weoruldwilnungum tō wið-stondanne, hit mæg ðeáh bión orsorglīc ǣlcra wīta, Past. 51; Swt. 399, 21. Fram weoruldwilnungum hine sceal gehwā fremdian *a seculi actibus se facere alienum*, R. Ben. 17, 4.

weorold-wīs; *adj.* I. *worldly wise, having knowledge of the ways of the world:*—On ōðre wīsan mon sceal manian ða woroldwīsan (cf. ða ðe ðisse worulde lotwrenceas cunnon and ða lufigeaþ, 30; Swt. 203, 5), on ōðre ða dysegan *aliter hujus mundi sapientes admonendi sunt, aliter hebetes*, Past. 23; Swt. 175, 16. Ðonne hē gesyhð ða welegan and ða weoruldwīsan sweltan *cum viderit sapientem morientem*, Ps. Th. 48, 8. II. *having secular knowledge, learned:*—Ðone hys yldran be-fæston on hys cnyhthāde sumum woruldwȳsan men, ðæt hē æt ðam leornode ða seofon cræftas, Shrn. 152, 11. Hēton woroldwīse menn wordsāwere ðone æðelan lāreów Paulus *ab hujus mundi sapientibus prae-dicator egregius seminiverbius est vocatus*, Past. 15; Swt. 97, 4. [Þe king sende æfter witien, æfter worldwise monne, ða wisdom cuðen, Laym. 15496. *O. H. Ger.* weralt-wīs *mundi sapiens, gymnosophista, maleficus.*]

weorold-wīsdōm, es; *m. Secular knowledge, science, learning:*—Ða dohtor befæste se fæder tō lāre, ðæt heó on woruldwȳsdōme wǣre getogen æfter Grēcisre ūðwȳtegunge and Lǣdenre getingnysse, Homl. Skt. i. 2, 20. His fæder and his frȳnd hine befæstan tō lāre tō woruldwīsdōme, 3, 5. Ða ðe woldon woruldwīsdōm gecneordlīce leornian, Homl. Th. i. 60, 27. Ungetogene menn geceás Drihten him tō leorningcnihtum, and hī swā geteáh, ðæt heora lār oferstāh ealne woruldwisdōm, 576, 30. Ða seofon cræftas on ðām beóþ gemēted ealle weoruldwȳsdōmas, Shrn. 152, 12. [*O. H. Ger.* weralt-wīstuom *sapientia.*]

weorold-wīse, an; *f. What is usual in the world, a fashion of the world:*—Hē bæd ðæt Godes yrre ofer hī ne cōme, ne him wǣre hwæs (hwæt?) gneáðes ne ōþerra worldwīsena. Ðā com stefn of heofonum and seó cwæð: . . . 'Gif hwilc man on micelre neádþearfnesse bið ðīn ge-myndig . . . ic gefremme ðæs mannes nēdþearfnesse' *he prayed that God's anger should not come upon them, nor that aught of penury or of other ills that are fashions of this world might be theirs. Then came a voice from heaven, and it said: . . . If any man in great need shall be mindful of thee . . . I will perform that man's need*, Shrn. 77, 1–9.

weorold-wita, an; *m. A secular* or *lay councillor:*—Gif feohbōt ārīseþ, swā swā wise woroldwitan tō steóre gesettan, L. Eth. vi. 51; Th. i. 328, 5. Wīse eác wǣron woroldwitan ðe ǣrest gesettan tō godcundan rihtlagan worldlaga, vii. 24; Th. i. 334, 21. Worldwitan, ix. 348, 13.

weorold-wīte, es; *n.* I. *a punishment suffered in this world, a punishment on earth:*—Forgield mē ðīn līf, ðæs ðe ic ðe mīn þurh woruld-wīte weorð gesealde, Exon. Th. 90, 22; Cri. 1478. II. *a secular* (in contrast with an ecclesiastical) *punishment, secular penalty, money-fine:*—Sunnandaga cȳpinga forbeóde man georne be fullan worldwīte, L. Eth. ix. 17; Th. i. 344, 8. Gif hǣðen cild binnon .ix. nihton þurh gīmelīste forfaren sī, bētan for Gode būton worldwīte; and gif hit ofer nigan niht gewurðe, bētan for Gode and gilde .xii. ōr, L. N. P. L. 10; Th. ii. 292, 7.

weorold-wlencu (-o); *indecl.*: -wlenc, e; *f. Worldly pride, worldly pomp:*—Bisceopum gebyreþ, ðæt hī woruldwlence ne hēdan tō swȳðe, L. I. P. 10; Th. ii. 316, 30. Hī læccaþ of manna begeátum lōc hwæt hī gefōn magan . . . Syððan hȳ hit habbaþ, hī glencgaþ heora wīf mid ðam ðe hī weofoda sceoldan, and maciaþ eall heom sylfum tō woruld-wlence, 19; Th. ii. 328, 9. Ða mon sceal swā micle mā hātan ðonne biddan suā man ongiet ðæt hié for ðissum woruldwlencum (world-wlencium, Cott. MSS.) bióð suīður upāhafene and on ofermēttum āðundene *talibus rectum tanto rectius jubetur, quanto in rebus transitoriis altitudine cogitationis intumescunt*, Past. 26; Swt. 181, 21.

weorold-wrenc, es; *m. A worldly wile, a trick of this world:*—Ða ðe woruldmonnum ðynceaþ dysige, ða geciésð Dryhten, for ðæm ðæt hē ða lytegan, ðe mid ðissum woroldwrencium bióð upāhæfene, gescende *quae stulta sunt mundi, elegit Deus, ut confundat sapientes*, Past. 30; Swt. 203, 24.

weorold-wuniend, es; *m.* or -wuniende; *adj. A dweller in this world;* or *dwelling in this world:*—Būton moncynne, ðara micles tō feola woroldwuniendra winð wið gecynde, Met. 13, 17.

weorpan (wurpan, wyrpan); *p.* wearp, *pl.* wurpon; *pp.* worpen. I. *to cast, throw, fling.* (1) with acc. of what is thrown:—Heó wearp twēgen feorðlingas *misit duo minuta*, Mk. 12, 42. Hē wearp wundenmǣl, ðæt hit on eorðan læg, Beo. Th. 3066; B. 1531. Hī wurpon tān betweox him, Homl. Th. i. 246, 3. Swā swā mid unmǣtnesse micles stormes worpene beón *quasi tempestatis inpetu jactari*, Bd. 5, 12; S. 627, 40. (1 a) where further the direction or end of throwing is marked, (*a*) by the dative:—Weorpaþ hit hundum, Ex. 22, 31. Nis nā gōd ðæt man nime bearna hlāf and hundum weorpe (worpe, *v. l.*), Mk. Skt. 7, 27. Ðā hēt hē hine wurpan deórum, Homl. Skt. ii. 29, 245. (*β*) by prepositions or adverbs:—Ic wyrpe max mīne on eá, and angil ic wyrpe . . . Ic wyrpe ða unclǣnan ūt, Coll. Monast. Th. 23, 9–17. Hira tū sǣ on lond wearp, Chr. 897; Erl. 96, 9: 1009; Erl. 142, 6. Se deófol wearp ǣnne stān tō ðære bellan, Homl. Th. ii. 156, 9. Hī wurpon heora waru oforbord, i. 246, 2. Hig tōdǣldon hys reáf, and wurpon hlot ðǣr ofer, Mt. Kmbl. 27, 35. Hī wurpon hine on ðone bāt, Chr. 1046; Erl. 174, 17. Ofen esnas wurpon wudu oninnan, Cd. Th. 231, 10; Dan. 245. Hī wurpon hyra wǣpen ofdūne, Judth. Thw. 25, 33; Jud. 291. 'Wurp (*projice*) hig on eorðan.' And hē wearp, Ex. 4, 3. Wurp hym mete tōforan, Lchdm. i. 246, 3. Weorp hit ūt, Mt. Skt. 9, 47. Worp ðone beám of ēgo ðīn, Mt. Kmbl. Lind. 7, 5. Weorp (wurp, *v. l.*) ðīnne angel ūt, Mt. Kmbl. 17, 27. Wurpaþ hit ūt on ðæt wæter, Ex. 1, 22. Ðæt hē wurpe his cynehelm and gecneówige æt ðæs fisceres gemynde, Homl. Th. i. 578, 6. Hwylc eówer sī synleás weorpe (wurpe, *v. l.*) stān on hī, Jn. Skt. 8, 7. Be ðære coþe þe se mon his ūtgang þurh ðone mūð him fram weorpe, Lchdm. ii. 236, 13. Swylce mon wurpe (worpe, MS. A.: worpað, Lind.: worpes, Rush., *jaceat*) gōd sǣd on his land, Mk. Skt. 4, 26. Ic hēt hit weorpan on fȳr, Ex. 32, 24. Hēt twelf weras nyman twelf stānas . . . and habban forð mid eów tō eówere wīcstōwe and wurpan hig ðǣr *praecipe eis, ut tollant . . . duodecim lapides, quos ponetis in loco castrorum*, Jos. 4, 3. Worp-ende ða scillingas in temple *projectis argenteis in templo*, Mt. Kmbl. Lind. 27, 5. Heora līchoman on ða eá worpene wǣron, Bd. 5, 10; S. 625, 6. (2) with dat. of what is thrown. Cf. *Icel.* verpa *with dat.*:—Hē teoselum weorpeþ, Exon. Th. 345, 9; Gn. Ex. 185. Beorges weard wearp wælfȳre, Beo. Th. 5157; B. 2582: Exon. Th. 478, 11; Ruin. 39. (2 a) where the direction or end of throwing is marked:—Streámas weorpaþ on stealchleoþa stāne and sonde, Exon. Th. 382, 5; Rā. 3, 6. I a. *to throw* (as in *to throw* open):—Mycel wynd wearp upp ða duru, Homl. Skt. i. 3, 347. II. where a (forcible) change of a person's place or condition is made (lit. or fig.), *to cast* into prison, *cast* off, out, *throw* into a form, *drive out*:—Ic ne weorpe (wyrpe, wurpe, *v. ll.*) ūt ðone ðe tō mē cymð, Jn. Skt. 6, 37. Gif ðū worpes ūsig *si eicis nos*, Mt. Kmbl. Lind. 8, 31. Ðū wurpe þeóde *ejecisti gentes*, Ps. Th. 79, 8. Hē wearp lōsēp on cweartern, Gen. 39, 20: Cd. Th. 20, 7; Gen. 304. Hē wearp hine on ðæt morðer innan, 22, 18; Gen. 342. Hē wearp hine of ðan heán stōle, 19, 33; Gen. 300. Hē wearp hine on wyrmes līc, 31, 26; Gen. 491. Hē ūt weorpe earme þearfan *ejiciantur*, Ps. Th. 108, 10. Men sǣdon ðæt hió sceolde mid hire drȳcræft weorpan men an wildedeóra līc, Bt. 38, 1; Fox 194, 31. Hié worpene beóð in helle grund, Elen. Kmbl. 2606; El. 1304. III. *to move* a thing from one position to another, in the phrase *weorpan tó handa* to hand over:—Weorpe hē ðone ceáp tō handa, L. In. 56; Th. i. 138, 12: L. Alf. pol. 21; Th. i. 74, 19: 24; Th. i. 78, 9. Sceal se ðe hine āh weorpan hine tō handa hlāforde and mǣgum, L. In. 74; Th. i. 148, 15. IV. in metaphorical senses:—Drihten ādrīfð fram eów ǣlc yfel and wyrpð ongēn eówere fȳnd *auferet Dominus a te omnem languorem, et infirmitates pessimas non inferet tibi, sed cunctis hostibus tuis*, Deut. 7, 15. Ðonne hió wyrpð (wirpð, Cott. MSS.) on ðæt geðóht hwæthugu tō bigietenne *dum adipiscenda quaeque cogitationi objicit*, Past. 11; Swt. 71, 22. Ne andswarast ðū nān ðing āgēn ðæt ðās ðē on weorpaþ (wurpaþ, *v. l.*) *non respondis quicquam ad ea quae tibi objiciuntur ab his?* Mk. Skt. 14, 60. Him man wearp on, ðæt hē wæs ðes cynges swica *he was charged with being a traitor to the king*, Chr. 1055; Erl. 189, 3. Ðȳ læs ǣfre cweðan ōðre þeódæ: 'Hwǣr com eówer God?' and ūs ðæt on eágum worpen þǣr manna wese mǣst ætgædere *nequando dicant in gentibus: 'Ubi est Deus eorum?' et innotescant in nationibus coram oculis nostris*, Ps. Th. 78, 10. V. *to reach an object by throwing, to throw and hit, to strike* with something, (1) with gen. of what is thrown:—Hē hine ongon wæteres weorpan *he threw water upon him*, Beo. Th. 5575; B. 2791. (2) with a preposition:—Gif men cīdaþ and hira ōðer hys nēxtan mid stāne wirpð oððe mid fȳste slicð *si rixati fuerint viri et percusserit alter proximum suum lapide vel pugno*, Ex. 21, 18. Seó clǣnnys wyrpð ða gālnysse mid stāne *pudicitia libidinem cum saxo percutit*, Gl. Prud. 12 b. Seó sȳfernes mid stāne wearp ða gālnesse on ðone mūð *sobrietas lapidem iacit et percutit os luxuriae*, 48 a. [*O. E. Homl.* werpen: *Laym.* weorpen, werpen, worpen; 2nd MS. werpe, wearpe: *Orm.* werrpenn: *A. R.* weorpen, worpen: *Gen. and Ex.* werpen: *O. and N.* werpe, worpe: *Goth.* wairpan: *O. Sax.* werpan: *O. Frs.* werpa: *O. H. Ger.* werfan: *Icel.* verpa.] v. ā-, be-, for-, ge-, of-, ofer-, on-, tō-, wið-, ymb-weorpan; worpian.

weorpe. v. wande-weorpe, seale-weorpan (?), Cod. Dip. Kmbl. iii. 78, 15.

weorpere, es; *m. A thrower* (cf. *to throw* as a wrestling term):—Ic (*mead*) eom weorpere, efne tō eorþan ealdne ceorl (cf. Aldhelm's riddle: Pedum gressus titubantes sterno ruina), Exon. Th. 409, 27; Rä. 28, 7.

weorpness. v. on-weorpness.

weorr; *adj. Bad, grievous*:—Ðæt wæs ðam weorode weor tō geþoligenne (cf. sār tō geþolienne, 3375; An. 1691), Andr. Kmbl. 3317; An. 1661. v. wirsa.

weorras, weorþ *a place.* v. wearr, worþ.

weorþ, weorþe, worþ, wurþ, wyrþ, es; *n.* I. *worth, value,* (1) of things:—Underwed ðæt sȳ ðæs orfes ōðer healf weorð *a security that is half as much again as the value of the cattle*, L. O. D. 1; Th. i. 352, 9. Be ðæs ceápes weorðe (wyrðe, *v. l.*), L. In. 49; Th. i. 132, 16. Be ēwes weorðe (wyrðe, *v. l.*), 55; Th. i. 138, 6. Be his wlites weorðe . . . swā man ðæt weorð up ārǣran mihte, L. Ath. v. 6, 2; Th. i. 234, 6–10. Gilde ðæs pyttes hlāford ðæra nȳtena wurð, Ex. 21, 34. (2) of persons, *worth, worthiness*:—Ðæt be ðære cennendra gefyrhtum ðæs bearnes weorþe ongyten wǣre, Blickl. Homl. 163, 27. II. *price* of anything sold, *amount paid* for purchase or redemption:—Hig cwǣdon: 'Hyt is blōdes weorð' (*v. l.* wurð, word, Lind.: weorð, Rush., *praetium sanguinis*), Mt. Kmbl. 27, 6, 7, 9. Noldon hig nānes wurðes onfōn, ac forgeáfon him ða birgene, Gen. 23, 6. Hī sumne dǣl heora landes wurðes æthæfdon, Homl. Th. i. 316, 24. Hire innoþ ðū gefyldest mid ealles middangeardes weorþe (cf. Homl. Skt. ii. 27, 120 infra, and next passage), Blickl. Homl. 89, 19. Hē āhongen wæs fore moncynnes mānforwyrhtum, ðǣr hē līfes ceápode mid ðȳ weorðe, Exon. Th. 68, 3; Cri. 1098. Hē monige mid weorþe ālȳsde *he redeemed many by purchase*, Bd. 3, 5; S. 527, 15. Gebycge hē ða lond æt hire mid halfe weorðe *let him buy the lands of her at half price*, Cod. Dip. Kmbl. ii. 120, 28. Giboht worðe miclum, Rtl. 27, 1. Ðū becȳptest folc ðīn būton weorðe, Ps. Spl. 43, 14: Ps. Surt. 43, 13. Geseald tō myclum weorðe (wurðe, wyrðe, *v. ll.*), Mt. Kmbl. 26, 9. 'Ic sille eów hundteóntig þūsenda mittan hwǣtes tō ðam wurðe ðe ic hit bebohte.' . . . Ðæt wyrð ðe hē mid ðam hwǣte genam hē āgeaf āgeán tō ðare ceastre bōte, Th. Ap. 10, 1–9. Fæder gesealde bearn wið weorðe (wurðe, *v. l.*), Wulfst. 161, 7. Mon āceorfe ða tungan of, ðæt hié mon nā undeórran weorðe mōste lēsan ðonne hié mon be ðam were geeahtige, L. Alf. pol. 32; Th. i. 82, 2. Syle ðū hig wið wurðe and bring ðæt wurð tō ðære stōwe, and bige mid ðam ylcan feó swā hwæt swā ðē līcige, Deut. 14, 25–26: 24, 7. Ðæt hē ðæt weorð āgife tō ālȳsnesse his sāwle *pretium redemtionis animae suae*, Ps. Th. 48, 7: Bd. 4, 22; S. 592, 14. Ālēsan wē ūre sāule ða hwīle ðe wē ðæt weorþ on ūrum gewealde habban, Blickl. Homl. 101, 10. Tō berenne ealles middaneardes wurþ (cf. Blickl. Homl. 89, 19 *supra*), Homl. Skt. ii. 27, 120. Forgelde hē ðæt lond, and ðæt wiorth gedaele, Cod. Dip. Kmbl. i. 234, 33. Wurð, Ex. 21, 35: Homl. Th. i. 62, 3: 316, 11. Him man his weorð āgefe *let the price of the chattel be returned to him*, L. H. E. 16; Th. i. 34, 11. Nān man nān þing ne bycge ofer feówer peninga weorð (*that costs more than fourpence*), L. C. S. 24; Th. i. 390, 3. Þēh ðe hē hié sume wið feó gesealde, hē ðæt weorð nolde āgan ðæt him mon wið sealde, Ors. 4, 10; Swt. 198, 17. Ðæs hwǣtes weorð ðe hē ðē sealde, Gen. 44, 2. Weorð, Exon. Th. 90, 23; Cri. 1478. III. *amount* to be paid in compensation:—Mid weorðe forgelde man, L. Ethb. 32; Th. i. 12, 1. Gif esne ōðerne ofsleá, ealne weorðe forgelde, 86; Th. i. 24, 11. Gif esnes eáge and fōt of weorðeþ āslagen, ealne weorðe hine forgelde, 87; Th. i. 24, 14. IV. *worth,* as in penny-*worth, amount of a certain value*:—Nabbaþ hī genōh on twēgera hundred penega weorðe (wurþe, *v. l.*) hlāfes *ducentorum denariorum panes non sufficiunt eis*, Jn. Skt. 6, 7. Sceóte man æt ǣghwilcre hīde pænig oððe pæniges weorð, Wulfst. 181, 5: L. O. 11; Th. i. 182, 10. Ðæt hyra ǣgðer hæbbe .lx. penenga wyrð . . . ðæt sȳ .xxx. penega wyrð, Cod. Dip. Kmbl. vi. 133, 23, 24. [*Goth.* wairþa galaubamma usbauhtai *pretio empti*: *O. Sax. O. L. Ger. O. Frs.* werð; *n.*: *O. H. Ger.* werd; *n. pretium, aestimatio*: *Icel.* verð; *n.*] v. mann-, or-, peningweorþ; wirþa.

weorþ, worþ, wurþ, wirþ, wyrþ, wirþe, wierþe, wyrþe, weorþe; *adj.* I. *worth, of value*, (1) referring to saleable things:—Ēwe bið mid hire giunge sceápe scill. weorð, L. In. 55; Th. i. 138, 7. Oxan horn bið .x. pæninga weorð, 58; Th. i. 138, 21. Hū mycel feós hit wǣre wurð, Chr. 1085; Erl. 218, 33. Næs ān hīd landes, ðæt hē nyste hwæs heó wurð wæs, 1086; Erl. 222, 11. Ðæt yrfe ðæt wǣre .xxx. pænig wyrð, L. Ath. v. 2; Th. i. 230, 19. Genime man .vi. scill. weorð (wurð, *v. l.*) wed, L. In. 49; Th. i. 132, 13. Āgife man ān ram weorðe .iiii. peningas, L. Ath. i. proem.; Th. i. 198, 7. (2) in other cases where money is to be paid:—Gif mon ōðrum wongtōð of āsleá, geselle .iiii. scill. tō bōte. Monnes tux bið .xv. scill. weorð, L. Alf. pol. 49; Th. i. 94, 13. Ðæt man finde of ðam yrfe æt Ceorlatūne healfes pundes wyrðne sāulsceat, and healfes pundes sāulscet fram Cynnuc, Cod. Dip. Kmbl. vi. 131, 11–14. (3) in cases where a scale expressed in money can be fixed:—Pundes weorðne āð, L. C. S. 30; Th. i. 394, 2. Wurðne, L. Eth. i. 1; Th. i. 280, 17. II. *possessed of honours, honourable* or *noble* as regards position, *great*:—Swā weorð man wīne druncen *quasi potens crapulatus a vino*, Ps. Th. 77, 65. Wyrðro ðec *honoratior te*, Lk. Skt. Lind. Rush. 14, 8. Ða gīslas ðe on ðam here weorþuste wǣron, Chr. 876; Erl. 79, 10. Ðara monna ðe in ðam here weorþuste wǣron, 878; Erl. 80, 21. III. *honoured, highly thought of, held in esteem, valued, dear*:—Nǣnig wæs weorð, gif mon his willan ongeat yfelne (cf. yfelwillende men nǣnne weorþscipe næfdon, Bt. 15; Fox 48, 17), Met. 8, 37. Ic nǣfre ne geseah nǣnne wīsne mon ðe mā wolde bión wrecca and earm and ælþiódig and forsewen, ðonne welig and weorþ and rīce and foremǣre on his āgenum earde, Bt. 39, 2; Fox 212, 17: Lchdm. iii. 156, 24. Ðīn word wunaþ weorþ on heofenum, Ps. Th. 118, 89. His noma wæs ā seoþþan weorð and mǣre geworden, Blickl. Homl. 219, 4. Deófolgild ðe mid ðǣm hǣðnum mannum swīðe weorð and mǣre wæs, 221, 7. Weorðiaþ his naman forðon hē wyrðe is (*quoniam suavis est*), Ps. Th. 134, 3. Unwīs folc ne wāt ðīnne wyrðne naman, 73, 17. Ic ðīne gewitnesse wyrðe lufade, 118, 119. Hē ðæm bātwearde swurde gesealde, ðæt hē sydþan wæs māþme ðȳ weorþra (*he was the more thought of* (or v. IV?) *for having such a treasure*), Beo. Th. 3809; B. 1903. III a. with dat. of person to whom a thing seems honourable, *precious* to, *dear* to, *prized* by, *held honourable* by, *honoured* by:—Hē eallum ðisse worulde ealdormonnum wæs leóf and weorð *omnibus principibus saeculi honorabilis*, Bd. 3, 15; S. 541, 23: Blickl. Homl. 213, 12. Mōyses se ðe wæs Gode swā weorð, ðæt hē oft wið hine selfne spræc, Past. 18; Swt. 131, 11: Lchdm. iii. 162, 1. Weorð Denum, Beo. Th. 3633; B. 1814. Twā ðing mæg se weorþscipe and se anweald gedōn, gif hē becymþ tō ðam dysgan; hē mæg hine gedōn weorþne ōþrum dysgum. Ac þonēcan ðe hē ðone anweald forlǣt, oððe se anweald hine, ðonne ne biþ hē ðam dysegan weorþ *dignitates honorabilem cui provenerint reddunt*, Bt. 27, 1; Fox 94, 18–22. Ic (*mead*) eom weorð werum, Exon. Th. 409, 14; Rä. 28, 1. Nis hē nā Gode wyrð, Wulfst. 52, 5. Synd mē wīc ðīne weorðe and leófe *quam amabilia sunt tabernacula tua*, Ps. Th. 83, 1. Gē wyrðe wǣron wuldorcyninge, Dryhtne dȳre, Elen. Kmbl. 581; El. 291. Ne beó gē mē heononforð swā wurðe ne swā leófe swā gē ǣr wǣron, ac fram mē gē beóð āscyrede, Homl. Skt. i. 23, 181. Nǣron hȳ ðȳ weorþran witena ǣnegum, Met. 15, 12. Wurðran, Cd. Th. 27, 23; Gen. 422. Ðæt hē sié his gefērum weorþost *reverendi civibus suis*, Bt. 24, 2; Fox 82, 6. Ðū, seó dȳreste and seó weorþeste wuldorcyninge, Exon. Th. 257, 16; Jul. 248. Ys mē ðīn gewitnes weorðast and rihtast, Ps. Th. 118, 144. Mid ðæm cræfte ðe ðā scondlīcost wæs, þēh hē him eft se weorðesta wurde, Ors. 2, 8; Swt. 90, 29. IV. *worthy, honourable, noble, excellent*:—Wæs hē mid clǣnsunge forhæfednesse weorþ and mǣre *erat abstinentiae castigatione insignis*, Bd. 4, 28; S. 606, 39. On weorcum ælmesdǣda weorþ and mǣre, 4, 29; S. 608, 16. Āhsiaþ hwā sī wyrðe (*dignus*), Mt. Kmbl. 10, 11. Mīne gewitnesse weorðe and getreówe *testamentum meum fidele*, Ps. Th. 88, 25. Habban ða mid wynne weórðe blisse ða ðe sēcean Drihten *exultent et laetentur qui quaerunt te*, 69, 5. Ða ðe geladode wǽron ne synt wyrđe (*digni*), Mt. Kmbl. 22, 8. Hwelc gesceádwís mon mihte cweþan đæt hē ā þý weorþra wǽre, þeáh hē hine weorþode *quis illos putet beatos, quos miseri tribuunt honores?* Bt. 28; Fox 100, 31. Eard wæs đý weorþra đe wit on stōdan, hyrstum đý hýrra, Exon. Th. 495, 20; Rä. 85, 6. Se anweald and se wela ne mæg his wealdend gedón nō đý weorþron, Bt. 27, 2; Fox 98, 13. **V.** *worthy* of something, *deserving* of, (1) with gen.:—Sceal bām gelíc, mon tō gemæccan, māþþum ōþres weorđ (*one gift deserves another in return*), Exon. Th. 343, 11; Gn. Ex. 155. Mín unrihtwísnysse is māre đonne ic forgifenysse wyrđe sý *major est iniquitas mea, quam ut veniam merear*, Gen. 4, 13: Cd. Th. 81, 19; Gen. 1347. Se wyrhta ys wyrđe hys metes (*dignus cibo suo*), Mt. Kmbl. 10, 10: Homl. Skt. i. 23, 52. Heó nis nānes lofes wyrþe, Bt. 20; Fox 70, 24: 24, 4; Fox 86, 10: Lchdm. iii. 162, 5. Hwæs biđ đæt unwæstmbǽre treów wyrđe būton scearpre æxe? Homl. Th. ii. 408, 16. For his cræftum hē biđ anwealdes weorþe, gif hē his weorþe biþ, Bt. 16, 2; Fox 50, 25. Ne onmun đū mē nānre āre wyrþne, Blickl. Homl. 183, 1. Đæs cynedōmes Crist God weorđne munde, Ps. C. 155. Đa đe ic đǽr tō geladode nǽron his wyrđe, Homl. Th. i. 526, 11. Đa lāreówas beóþ dōmes wyrþe, Blickl. Homl. 47, 23: Met. 10, 56. Hwæþerne woldest đū dēman wítes wyrþran? Bt. 38, 6; Fox 208, 15. (2) with infin. forms:—Wē đe nǽron wurđe beón his wealas gecígde, Homl Th. ii. 316, 23. Đa đing đe weorđe sindon in gemyndum tō habbanne, Nar. 4, 9. (3) with a clause:—Wyrþe đū eart, đæt đū onfō wuldor, Blickl. Homl. 75, 1. Đæt his lār nǽre wyrþe, đæt hí mon gehýrde, 41, 3. Đeós woruld nǽre wyrđe, đæt man tō hire lufe hæfde tō swíđe, Wulfst. 273, 13. Ic neom wyrđe, đæt ic beó đín sunu nemned *non sum dignus uocari filius tuus*, Lk. Skt. 15, 19. Se biđ wurđe, đæt hine man ārwurđian, Homl. Th. ii. 560, 10. Đæt gē weorđe (wurđe, *v. l.*: wyrđo, Lind.: wyrđe, Rush.) sýn, đæt gē đās tōwerdan þing forfleón *ut digni habeamini fugere ista omnia quae futura sunt*, Lk. Skt. 21, 36. (4) with gen. and clause:—God is đæs wyrđe, đæt hine werþeóde and eal engla cynn hergen, Exon. Th. 281, 8; Jul. 643. (5) with gen. and dat. infin.:—Þeáh hē his wyrđe ne sié tō ālǽtanne, Cd. Th. 39, 8; Gen. 621. (6) with other constructions:—Hine man byrigde ful wurđlíce, swā hē wyrđe wæs, Chr. 1036; Erl. 165, 36. Hē nāt hwæđer hē wurđe is intō đam écan ríce, Homl. Th. i. 532, 25. **VI.** *fit, meet, becoming, proper*:—Wē sculon simle secgan Gode đoncas for eów, brōđur, suā suā hit wel wierđe (wyrđe, Cott. MSS.) is (*ita ut dignum est*), Past. 32; Swt. 213, 10. Wyrcaþ wæstim wyrđne tō hreównisse, Lk. Skt. Rush. 3, 8. **VII.** *worthy* of, *fit* for or to, *properly qualified* for, (1) with gen.:—Đæt Martinus wǽre wyrđe đæs hādes, Homl. Th. ii. 506, 8. Ne fleáh hē đý ríce đý his ǽnig mon bet wirđe (wyrđe, Hatt. MS.) wǽre, Past. 3; Swt. 32, 17. (2) with dat. or inst.:—Templ Gode weorþe, Blickl. Homl. 163, 14. Nys hē mē wyrđe *non est me dignus*, Mt. Kmbl. 10, 37. Đæt hē wǽre his biscophāde wel wyrþe, Bd. 5, 19; S. 639, 31. Ic mē sylfne nǽfre đý hāde wyrþe (wyrþne, *v. l.*) dēmde, 4, 2; S. 566, 7. (3) with dat. infin.:—Hālig treów đe wyrþe (wurđe, *v. l.*) wǽre tō berenne ealles middaneardes wurþ, Homl. Skt. ii. 27, 119. Ne am ic wyrđe tō unbindanne đuongas sceóea his *non sum dignus soluere corrigiam calciamentorum eius*, Lk. Skt. Lind. Rush. 3, 16. (4) with a clause:—Ne eom ic wyrđe, đæt đū in gange under míne þecene, Mt. Kmbl. 8, 8. Ne eom ic wyrđe, đæt ic his sceóna þwanga uncnytte, Mk. Skt. 1, 7. Se man đæt can rihtne geleáfan, þonne biþ hē wyrđe, đæt hē fulluht underfō, Wulfst. 33, 6: 155, 12. (5) with gen. and clause:—Hē bít đære tíde hwonne hē đæs wierđe (wyrđe, Cott. MSS.) sié, đæt hē hine besuícan mōte *aptum deceptionis tempus inquirit*, Past. 33; Swt. 227, 12. His weorc sceolon beón đæs weorđe (wierđe, Cott. MSS.), đæt him ōđre menn onhyrien *si imitabilem ceteris in cunctis, quae agit, insinuat*, 10; Swt. 61, 18. Swā hwā swā đæs wyrþe biþ, đæt hē on heora đeówdōme beón mōt, Bt. 5, 1; Fox 10, 13. Hwā is đæs wyrđe, đæt āstíge on Godes munt *quis ascendet in montem Domini?* Ps. Th. 23, 3. Ne eom ic đæs wyrþe, đæt ic swā on rōde gefæstnod beó, Blickl. Homl. 191, 7. Đa đe đæs wyrđe beóþ, đæt hié heofoncining on heora heortum beran, 79, 32. (5 a) with impersonal construction:—Wæs đæt đæs wyrđe, đæt seó stōw swā fæger wǽre *it was fitting that the place should be so fair*, Bd. 1, 7; S. 478, 23. Đæt is đæs wyrđe, đætte werþeóde secgen Dryhtne þonc duguđa gehwylcre, Exon. Th. 38, 1; Cri. 600. For đon is đæs wyrđe, đæt đū đæs weres frige ne forlǽte, 248, 29; Jul. 103. **VIII.** mostly in a legal sense, (1) *having a right* to, *entitled* to, *properly qualified* for, *possessed* of, (a) with gen.:—Gif ceorl geþeáh, đæt hē hæfde fíf hída . . ., đonne wæs hē þegenrihtes weorđe (wyrđe, *v. l.*), L. R. 2; Th. i. 190, 18: 5; Th. i. 192, 8: 6; Th. i. 192, 11. Se wæs syþþan mǽđe and munde swā micelre wurđe, swā đam hāde gebirede mid rihte, 7; Th. i. 192, 14. Sié hē feores wyrđe and folcryhtre bōte, L. Alf. 13; Th. i. 46, 24: L. Ath. iv. 4; Th. i. 224, 3. Ne beó hē āđes wyrđe *he shall not have the right to make oath*, L. C. S. 36; Th. i. 398, 7. Đa hwíle đe God wille đæt đeara ǽnig sié đe londes weorđe sié and land gehaldan cunne, Cod. Dip. Kmbl. i. 310, 10: 311, 17. Ich queđe eóu đæt ich wille đæt Gyse biscop beó đisses biscopríches uurđe *significamus uobis nos uelle quod episcopus Giso episcopatum possideat*, iv. 198, 6. Ic bidde míne hlāford đæt ic mōte beón mínes cwydes wyrđe *I pray my lord that I may have the right to dispose of my property by will*, iii. 293, 29. Đæt heó mōte beón hyre cwydes wyrđæ, 359, 34. Gif hwā him ryhtes bidde . . . and ābiddan ne mæge, and him wedd mon sellan nelle, gebēte .xxx. scill. and binnan .vii. nihton gedō hine ryhtes wierđne (wyrđe, *v. l.*) (*let justice be done him*), L. In. 8; Th. i. 108, 2. Forlǽt mē mínes wyrđe (weorđe, *v. l.*) wesan đæs đe ic mē sylf begiten hæbbe *leave me in undisturbed possession of mine own, that I myself have got*, Wulfst. 254, 21. Ne hyne micles wyrđne Drihten gedōn wolde, Beo. Th. 4377; B. 2185. Đæt hí rihtes wyrđe lēte đone leódscipe, Met. 1, 67. Đæt hí mōstan heora ealdrihta wyrđe beón, Bt. 1; Fox 2, 9: Met. 1, 37. Wē synt ālýsde lífes wyrđe *nos liberati sumus*, Ps. Th. 123, 7. Gedō ūsic đæs wyrđe *make us partakers* (*of glory*), Exon. Th. 3, 2; Cri. 30. (b) with gen. and clause:—Nime se hlāford twēgen þegenas and swerian, . . . būton hē đone gerēfan hæbbe đe đæs wyrđe sý đe đæt dōn mæge (*a reeve properly qualified for doing it*), L. Eth. i. 1; Th. i. 280, 14. (c) with acc. (?):—Behēt man him đæt hē mōste wurđe beón ǽlc đæra þinga đe hē ǽr āhte, Chr. 1046; Erl. 173, 1. Hí gerndon tō him đæt hí mōston beón wurđe ǽlc đæra þinga đe heom mid unrihte of genumen wæs, 1052; Erl. 185, 8. (2) *deserving* of punishment, etc., *subject* to, *liable* to (with gen.):—Đæs ilcan dōmes sié hē wyrđe *simili sententiae subjacebit* (Ex. 21, 31), L. Alf. 21; Th. i. 50, 3. Đæt hý siþþan āđwyrđe nǽron ac ordāles wyrđe *that afterwards they might not make oath but had to submit to the ordeal*, L. Ed. 3; Th. i. 160, 21. Sý hē đæs þeówweorces wyrđe, 9; Th. i. 164, 12. Wē cwǽdon hwæs se wyrđe wǽre đe ōđrum ryhtes wyrnde, 2; Th. i. 160, 10. Beó se leása gewita đæs ilcan wyrđe đe hē wolde đæt se ōđer wǽre *reddent ei, sicut fratri suo facere cogitavit*, Deut. 19, 19. Gif hý swā ne dōn, đonne sýn hý đæs wyrđe đe on đam canone cwæđ, L. Edm. E. 1; Th. i. 244, 12. [*Goth.* wairþs: *O. Sax. O. Frs. O. L. Ger.* werth: *O. H. Ger.* werd: *Icel.* verðr.] v. ār-, āþ-, bōt-, deór-, fyrd-, mōt-, rōde-, tǽl-, þanc-, un-, un-leahtor-, wel-weorþ(e), -wirþe.

weorþan (wurþan, wyrþan); *p.* wearþ, *pl.* wurdon; *pp.* worden. **I.** absolute, (1) *to come to be, to be made, to arise, come, be*:—Gif bānes blice weorđeþ, L. Ethb. 34; Th. i. 12, 4. Gif bānes bite weorđ, 35; Th. i. 12, 5. Ende nǽfre đínes wræces weorþeþ, Andr. Kmbl. 2765; An. 1385. Hwā wæs ǽfre, oþþe is nū, odđe hwā wyrþ get æfter ūs? Bt. 11, 1; Fox 30, 24. Hlynn wearđ on ceastrum, Cd. Th. 153, 30; Gen. 2546. Hwí ne wundriaþ hí hwí đæt ís weorþe, Bt. 39, 3; Fox 214, 35. Đe læs tō mycel styrung wurde on đam folce *ne forte tumultus fieret in populo*, Mt. 26, 5. Hēht lífes weard on mereflōde middum weorđan hyhtlíc heofontimber, Cd. Th. 9, 22; Gen. 145. (2) *to come to pass, to be done, to happen, to take place, befall, come, be*:—Đæt weorþeþ for đyses folces synnum, đæt ealle đās getimbro beóþ tōworpene, Blickl. Homl. 77, 35. Daga egelícast weorþeþ in worulde, Exon. Th. 63, 21; Cri. 1023. Huu worđes đis *quomodo fiet istud?* Lk. Skt. Lind. Rush. 1, 34: 23, 31. Đǽr wearþ micel gefeoht, Chr. 800; Erl. 60, 7: 868; Erl. 72, 28. On đām gemōtan, þeáh rǽdiíce wurđan on namcūđan stōwan, L. Eth. ix. 37; Th. i. 348, 17. Hwæđer ǽfre wurde þus gerād þing *si facta est aliquando hujuscemodi res*, Deut. 4, 32. Eálā đæt hit wurde, đæt . . ., Met. 8, 39. Sceal se dæg weorþan, Exon. Th. 447, 5; Dōm. 34. Þurh hwæt his worulde gedāl weorđan sceolde, Beo. Th. 6129; B. 3068. Đætte ríces gehwæs sceolde gelimpan, eordan dreámas ende wurđan, Cd. Th. 223, 6; Dan. 115. Sceal feorhgedāl æfter wyrđan, Andr. Kmbl. 364; Ass. 182: 430; An. 215. (2 a) when the object affected by what happens is given:—Ne wyrđ him nān orne, Lchdm. iii. 16, 4. Ic wāt ealre đysse worulde wurđeþ ende *omni consummationi vidi finem*, Ps. Th. 118, 96. Dōmas đe wǽdlum weorđaþ, 139, 12. Tācnu wurđaþ on eów *erunt in te signa*, Deut. 28, 46. Hwæt wearđ eów? Andr. Kmbl. 2685; An. 1345. Đæt đē sceates đearf ne wurde, Cd. Th. 32, 16; Gen. 504. Unc sceal weorđan swā unc wyrd geteód, Beo. Th. 5045; B. 2526. **II.** *to become, be made, be*, (1) with predicative substantive:—Đa hwíle đe hē đǽr stōd, hē wearþ fǽringa geong cniht, and sōna eft eald man, Blickl. Homl. 175, 2. On đam dæge wurdun Herōdes and Pilatus gefrýnd; sōđlíce hig wǽron ǽr gefýnd, Lk. Skt. 23, 12. Wā heom đæs síđes đe hí men wurdon, Wulfst. 27, 4. Weorđan his bearn steópcild, and his wíf wyrđe wydewe *fiant filii ejus orphani, et uxor ejus vidua*, Ps. Th. 108, 9. Đæt wē đæs mordres meldan ne weorđen, Elen. Kmbl. 856; El. 428. (2) with predicative adjective, *to get, grow*:—Gif đū lārna đínra ēste wyrđest, Andr. Kmbl. 965; An. 483. Gif eáre þirel weorđeþ, L. Ethb. 41; Th. i. 14, 6. Gif hē healt weorđ, 65; Th. i. 18, 14. Đē weorđ on dínum breóstum rūm, Cd. Th. 33, 13; Gen. 519. Gif đa cearwylmas cōlran wurđaþ, Beo. Th. 570; B. 282. Đa deáde ne weorđaþ (*v. l.* wurđaþ) *qui non gustabunt mortem*, Lk. Skt. 9, 27. Đā wearđ hē druncen *inebriatus est*, Gen. 9, 21. Đæt wíf wearđ wrāđ đam geongan cnapan *mulier molesta erat adolescenti*, 39, 10. Wearđ hē swíđe yrre *iratus est valde*, 39, 19. Hwelc síđđan wearđ herewulfa síđ, Cd. Th. 121, 23; Gen. 2014. Đa fixas wurdon deáde *pisces mortui sunt*, Ex. 7, 21. Mierce wurdon cristne, Chr. 655; Erl. 28, 1. Mē milde weorđ *miserere mei*, Ps. Th. 56, 1: 66, 1. Monigfaldge worđe *habundaverit*, Mt. Kmbl. Lind. 5, 20. Nǽnges þinges māre þearf đonne his unriht yppe wurde, Blickl. Homl. 175, 10. Eálā đæt ūre tída nū ne mihtan weorđan swilce, Bt. 15; Fox 48, 18. Sǽne weorđan, Andr. Kmbl. 408; An. 204. Wyrđan, 874; An. 437. Wurđan, Cd. Th. 27, 8; Gen. 414. Wæs ôđere ǽghwilc worden mǽgburh fremde, 102, 3; Gen. 1694: 135, 2; Gen. 2236. Weard hē acol worden, 223, 24; Dan. 124. Eal cristen folc is þurh geleáfan geleáful worden, Wulfst. 279, 30. Đa dysegan sint wordene blinde, Met. 19, 29. (3) with prepositional phrase:—Heó weard mid cilde, Homl. Th. i. 24, 26. Đæt ic tō đīnum willan weorþan mōte *that I may be to thy liking*, Ps. C. 104. (4) with adverb, (a) where the subject is given:—Heó wyrđ glædlīce on hyre heortan, Anglia viii. 324, 16. Ōþ đæt đīn fōt weorđe fæste on blōde *ut intinguatur pes tuus in sanguine*, Ps. Th. 67, 22. (b) with impersonal construction:—Weard mē on hige leóhte, Cd. Th. 42, 20; Gen. 676. Đā wearþ hyre rūme on mōde, Judth. Thw. 22, 39; Jud. 97. Gif men fērlīce wyrde unsōfte, Rtl. 114, 24. III. with prepositions (see also IV), (a) weorþan of *to come from, be caused by, be produced from* or *by*:—Wiþ geswelle đam đe wyrđ of fylle odđe of slege, Lchdm. ii. 72, 22. Hwȳ đæt is mæge weorþan of wætere, Met. 28, 60. (b) weorþan on, (1) *to get into a state* of being, feeling, *to become* the adjective connected with the noun, *get*:—Gif hē wyrþ on ungeþylde *if he gets impatient*; cum dederit impatientiae manus, Bt. 11, 1; Fox 32, 33. Weorþeþ (-aþ, MS.) oft on wōn se sido *in hoc hominum judicia depugnant*, 39, 9; Fox 226, 4. Đā wearþ Holofernus on gytesālum *he grew merry, as the wine flowed*, Judth. Thw. 21, 17; Jud. 21. Wurdan gesweoru on seledreáme *exultaverunt colles*, Ps. Th. 113, 6. Hié weorđen on ungeđylde, Past. 45; Swt. 341, 3. (2) *to get into a state* of action, *to come to* be doing something, *to fall to* an action, *to take to*:—Hē wierđ (wirđ, Hatt. MS.) swīđe hræđe on fielle *citius corruit*, Past. 39; Swt. 286, 17. Wēnst đū đæt đū đæt hwerfende hweól, đonne hit on ryne wyrþ (*when it gets a-running*), mæge oncyrran *tu volventis rotae impetum retinere conaris?* Bt. 7, 2; Fox 18, 36. Hē on fylle weard, Beo. Th. 3093; B. 1544. Hē weard on fleáme, Andr. Kmbl. 2771; An. 1388. Hē weard on slǽpe, Homl. Skt. i. 18, 161. Hī on slǽpe wurdon, 23, 249. Hig wurdon on fleáme *terga verterunt*, Jos. 7, 4. Hié weorđen on murcunga *they fall a-grumbling*; ad murmurationem proruunt, Past. 45; Swt. 341, 3. (3) *to come to be* something, *become, turn into*:—Mē weorđ on God þeccend and on trume stōwe *esto mihi in Deum protectorem, et in locum munitum*, Ps. Th. 70, 2. Đæt heó on sealtstānes wurde anlīcnesse, Cd. Th. 154, 32; Gen. 2564. Hē mē ys worden on hǽlu *factus est mihi in salutem*, Ps. Th. 117, 14. (c) weorþan tō, (1) of change in material condition, *to become, turn to*:—Đū eart dust, and tō duste wyrst *pulvis es, et in pulverem reverteris*, Gen. 3, 19. Weorđeþ tō duste, Ps. Th. 89, 6. Tō wætere weorđeþ, 147, 7: Met. 28, 63. Se wyrm wyrđ tō eorþan, Lchdm. ii. 44, 16. Weorp đīne girde beforan Pharaone, and heó wird tō næddran (*vertetur in colubrum*), Ex. 7, 9. Seó eá đǽr wyrþ tō miclum sǽ, Ors. 1, 1; Swt. 12, 28. Weorđaþ hig tō acxan *fatiscunt in cinerem*, 1, 3; Swt. 32, 15. Bearwas wurdon tō axan, Cd. Th. 154, 8; Gen. 2552. Sume wurdon tō wulfan, Bt. 38, 1; Fox 194, 36: Met. 26, 79. On eorþan gangan and tō eorþan weorþan, Blickl. Homl. 123, 10. Seó eá ne mæg weorþan tō ǽwelme, ac se ǽwelm mæg weorþan tō eá, Bt. 34, 1; Fox 134, 15. (2) of the state or condition to which things come, of the event of matters, *to become, have as issue, come to*:—Ǽlc þing wyrþ tō nāuhte, Bt. 34, 1; Fox 134, 13. Hī weorþaþ him selfe tō nāuhte, 21; Fox 74, 36. Tō hwan weard hondrǽs hæleþa *what was the event of the combat*, Beo. Th. 4149; B. 2071. Đonne hié ne giémaþ tō hwon ōđerra monna wīse weorđe *when they do not care to what a state other men get*, Past. 5; Swt. 41, 24. Hē đōhte đæt hē hine ofslōge, wurde siđđan tō đæm đe hit meahte (*be the event what it might*), 34; Swt. 235, 10. Lyt đū geþōhtes tō hwon đīnre sāwle sīđ siþþan wurde, Exon. Th. 368, 12; Seel. 20. Hī bidon tō hwon his đing weorþan sceolde *quem res exitum haberet exspectantes*, Bd. 3, 11; S. 536, 32. Tō hwon sculon wit weorđan *what is to become of us?* Cd. Th. 50, 28; Gen. 815. Eall mīn mægen is tō nāuhte worden, Ps. Th. 21, 11. (3) where a character or function is taken by anything, *to become, turn, turn to*:—Mē tō aldorbanan weorđeþ wrāđra sum *some fell one will become the destroyer of my life*, Cd. Th. 63, 18; Gen. 1034. Hē wierđ tō đæs onlīcnesse đe āwriten is *usque ad ejus similitudinem ducitur, de quo scriptum est*, Past. 17; Swt. 111, 21. Ne wyrđ nān tō lāfe *none shall become a remnant*, i. e. *none shall be left*; non remanebit ex eis ungula, Ex. 10, 26. Gif þegen geþeáh đæt hē weard tō eorle, L. R. 5; Th. i. 192, 7. Se tō deófle weard, Cd. Th. 20, 9; Gen. 305. Ic tō meldan weard *I turned informer*, Exon. Th. 279, 30; Jul. 621. Weard hē Heađolāfe tō handbonan, Beo. Th. 924; B. 460. Hwonne līffreá weorđe ūssum mōde tō mundboran, Exon. Th. 2, 32; Cri. 28. Đeáh þrǽla hwylc of cristendōme tō wīcinge weorđe, Wulfst. 162, 6. Đȳ læs sió upāhæfenes him weorđe tō wege micelre scylde *ne elatio via fiat ad foveam gravioris culpae*, Past. 57; Swt. 439, 11. (4) where a result is brought about, *to become, prove a source of*:—Seó ofering đē wurþ tō sāre, Bt. 14, 1; Fox 42, 16. Hit him wyrþ tō teónan, Blickl. Homl. 51, 9. Þū wurde mē tō hǽlu *factus es mihi in salutem*, Ps. Th. 117, 27. Hió weard mongum tō frōfre, Exon. Th. 421, 17; Rä. 40, 18. Tō blisse, Blickl. Homl. 123, 2. Tō aldorceare, Beo. Th. 1817; B. 905. Hē manegum weard mannum tō hrōđre, werþeódum tō wræce, Elen. Kmbl. 30; El. 15. Đa byrig, đe ǽr gafol guldon, wurdon Ciruse tō monegum gefeohtum *civitates, quae tributariae erant, a Cyro defecerunt; quae res Cyro multorum bellorum causa et origo exstitit*, Ors. 1, 12; Swt. 54, 14. Đe læs ūre deáþ ūrum feóndum tō gefeán weorþe, Blickl. Homl. 101, 33. Tō hleó and tō hrōþer hæleþa cynne weorđan, Exon. Th. 73, 31; Cri. 1198. Tō frōfre weorþan, Beo. Th. 3419; B. 1707. (5) *to become, be an object of*:—Ic eom worden mannum tō leahtrunge and tō forsewennesse *ego sum opprobrium hominum*, Ps. Th. 21, 5. IV. implying movement, change of position, (1) literal, *to come, get*, (a) with prepositions:—Đonne hē (*the moon*) betwux ūs and hire (*the sun*) wyrþ, Bt. 4; Fox 8, 2. Of đære sǽ cymþ đæt wæter innon đa eorþan; cymþ đonne up æt đam ǽwelme, wyrþ đonne tō brōce, đonne tō eá, đonne andlang eá, ōþ hit wyrþ eft tō sǽ, 34, 6; Fox 140, 17–20. Se regn đæt deófol on ufan wyrđeþ, Salm. Kmbl. p. 148, 5. Swā swā wē of đisse weorulde weorđaþ, Shrn. 202, 4. Gif hī on đam wuda weorþaþ *if they get in the wood*, Bt. 25; Fox 88, 16. Gif hī on treówum weorþaþ, Met. 13, 36. Hē weard him on ānon scipe *he got him* (reflex.) *on board a ship*, Chr. 1052; Erl. 187, 13. Sebastianus geseah hū đa Godes cempan ongunnon hnexian, and weard him tōmiddes (*he came amongst them*), Homl. Skt. i. 5, 52. Gif nægl of honda weorđe *if a nail come off the hand*, Lchdm. iii. 58, 7. Đū mihtest đē fēran betwyx đām tunglum, and đonne weorþan on đam rodore, Bt. 36, 2; Fox 174, 11. On đæm rodere ufan weorþan, Met. 24, 18. (b) with adverbs:—Gif eáge of weorđ *if an eye comes out*, L. Ethb. 43; Th. i. 14, 8. Gif fōt of weorđeþ *if a foot comes off*, 69; Th. i. 20, 1: 70; Th. i. 20, 2: 72; Th. i. 20, 5. Hē weard him āwege *he went away, got off*, Homl. Skt. ii. 25, 228. Hié sume inne wurdon *some of them got inside*, Chr. 867; Erl. 72, 14. Mōste ic āne tīd ūte weorđan, Cd. Th. 23, 34; Gen. 369. (2) figurative:—Adames cynn onfēhđ flǽsce, weorþeþ foldræste æt ende *Adam's race shall receive flesh, shall come to the end of its rest in earth*, Exon. Th. 63, 34; Cri. 1029. Būton monnum and sumum englum, đa weorþaþ hwīlum of hiora gecynde *except men and some angels, who sometimes depart from their nature*, Bt. 25; Fox 88, 8. His ǽhta weorþaþ on đæs onwealde đē hē wyrrest ūþe, Blickl. Homl. 195, 3. Ic nō ne wearþ of đam sōþan geleáfan *nec umquam fuerit dies, qui me ab hac sententia depellat*, 5, 3; Fox 12, 6. Hwī đæt is for đære sunnan scīman tō his āgnum gecynde weorþe, 39, 3; Fox 216, 1. Đæt gē of feónda fæđme weorđen *that ye get out of the foes' grasp*, Cd. Th. 196, 20; Exod. 294. Đæt ne loc of heáfde tō forlore wurde *that not a hair from the head should come to destruction*, Andr. Kmbl. 2846; An. 1425. V. as an auxiliary with participles, (1) present:—Gif him hwilc yfel gelimpđ, ic wurđe syđđan geómriende, Gen. 42, 38. (2) past, (a) of transitive verbs, forming a passive voice:—Eów weorþeþ forgifen hwæt gē sprecaþ, Blickl. Homl. 171, 19. Ne weorþeþ sió mǽgburg gemicledu eaforan mīnum, Exon. Th. 401, 31; Rä. 21, 20. Hē him ābolgen wurđeþ, Cd. Th. 28, 4; Gen. 430. Hū wurþ hē elles gelǽred *how else shall he get taught?* Bd. pref.; S. 471, 18. Hī weorþaþ bereáfode ǽlcre āre, Bt. 29, 2; Fox 104, 16. Đā weard Faraones heorte gehefegod *ingravatum est cor Pharaonis*, Ex. 8, 32. Đā him gerȳmed weard, đæt hié wælstōwe wealdan mōston, Beo. Th. 5959; B. 2983. Swā his mandrihten gemǽted weard, Cd. Th. 225, 21; Dan. 157. Đȳ læs hié eft weorđen (wyrđen, Hatt. MS.) gedēmde, Past. 28; Swt. 190, 15. Seó burh sceolde ābrocen weorþan, Blickl. Homl. 77, 29. Ne mihte him bedyrned wyrđan đæt his engyl ongan ofermōd wesan, Cd. Th. 17, 18; Gen. 261. (b) of intransitive verbs:—Đē sunu weorđeþ cumen, Cd. Th. 132, 19; Gen. 2195. Đa geongan leoþu geloden weorþaþ, Exon. Th. 327, 20; Vy. 6. Hē sōna weard hāl geworden, Blickl. Homl. 223, 26: Cd. Th. 223, 23; Dan. 124. Denum weard willa gelumpen, Beo. Th. 1851; B. 823; 2473; B. 1234. Đā weard āfeallen đæs folces ealdor, Byrht. Th. 137, 46; By. 202. Đā weard se līchama tōslopen, Homl. Th. i. 86, 24: Jos. 5, 1. Đæt hī forwordene weorđen *ut intereant*, Ps. Th. 91, 6. [*Goth.* wairþan: *O. Sax.* werđan: *O. Frs.* wertha: *O. H. Ger.* werdan: *Icel.* verđa.] v. for-, ge-, mis-weorþan.

weorþ-apulder. v. worþ-apulder.

weorþe; *subst.* or *adj.*: weorþe; *adv.*, weorþe-līce. v. weorþ; *subst.* or *adj.*, un-weorþe, weorþ-līce.

weorþere, es; *m. A worshipper*:—Godes uorđare *Dei cultor*, Jn. Skt. Lind. 9, 31. Sōđo uorđares *ueri adoratores*, 4, 23.

weorþ-full; *adj.* I. *having worth, worthy, honourable, glorious, excellent*:—Beó preóst, swā his hāde gebyraþ, wīs and weorđfull, L. Edg. C. 58; Th. ii. 256, 17. Būton gē ondrēdon Drihtnes wurđfullan naman *nisi timueris nomen ejus gloriosum*, Deut. 28, 58. Wurþfulle gegedriende *honesta colligentes*, Anglia xiii. 368, 46. Wurđfulleste *praestantissimus, dignissimus, sublimissimus*, Hpt. Gl. 463, 44. Hē manna wæs wīgend weorđfullost, Beo. Th. 6189; B. 3099. II. *having honour* with others, *held in honour, honoured, esteemed, prized, dear*:—Se biđ on eallum þingum wurþfull (cf. weorþ mannum, 162, 1), Lchdm. iii. 158, 3. Đa hālgan weras, đe gōde weorc beeodon, hī wurđfulle wǽron on đissere worulde, Ælfc. T. Grn. 1, 9. Đe læs sum weorđfulra (wurđ-, *v.l.*) sig yn gelađod fram hym *ne honoratior te sit invitatus ab eo*, Lk. Skt. 14, 8. II a. with dat. of person to whom another seems honourable:—

Daniel wunude on Chaldēa wurđfull đām ciningum, Ælfc. T. Grn. 9, 43. His welwillende mōd, and Gode swīđe wurđful, Homl. Skt. ii. 30, 20. III. *having honours, worshipful, noble, illustrious, magnificent:*—Ān woruldcyningc . . . ne mæg beón wurđful cyningc, būton hē hæbbe đa geþincđe đe him gebyriaþ, Homl. Skt. i. pref., 60. Se cyng Willelm wæs swīđe wīs man and swīđe rīce, and wurđfulre and strengere đonne ǣnig his foregengra wǣre . . . Hē wæs swȳđe wurđful; þriwa hē bær his cynehelm ǣlce geáre, Chr. 1086; Erl. 221, 14-27. IV. *worthy, suitable, fitting:*—Beón wurđful wunung đæs Hālgan Gāstes, Homl. Th. ii. 600, 17. Munecas hē gestaþolode tō weorþfulre þēnunge Hǣlendes Cristes, Lchdm. iii. 440, 13. [Helyas wass an wurrþfull prophete, Orm. 5195. His wundri werkes and wurđful, Kath. 1017. ȝet he is wurþful and aht man, O. and N. 1481. Of prede þe dyeul begyleþ þe riche and þe wysę and þe hardi and þe worþuolle, Ayenb. 16, 33.]

weorþful-líc; *adj. Noble, magnificent:*—Hwæt rūmedlīces ođđe micellīces ođđe weorþfullīces hæfþ se eówer gilp *quid habet amplum magnificumque gloria?* Bt. 18, 1; Fox 62, 21.

weorþfullīce; *adv.* I. of moral worth, *worthily, honourably, excellently:*—Ic wilnode weorþfullīce tō libbanne đa· hwīle đe ic lifede, Bt. 17; Fox 60, 15. II. *nobly, in a way that is highly esteemed:*—Swā swā men wurđlīcor lybbaþ đonne treówu, swā hȳ eác weorđfulīcor ārīsaþ on dōmes dæge, Shrn. 168, 26. III. *in a way that shews respect, with honour:*—Đā onfēng Dioclitianus Galerius weorđfullīce *a Diocletiano plurimo honore susceptus est Galerius,* Ors. 6, 30; Bos. 126, 19. IV. *in a fitting manner, worthily, properly:*—Wyrđfullīce hē gebēte Gode *digne satisfaciat Deo,* R. Ben. Interl. 42, 6.

weorþfulness, e; *f. Nobleness, magnificence:*—Gesceáwode se ān engel đe đǣr ǣnlīcost wæs, hū fæger hē silf wæs, and hū scīnende on wuldre, and him wel gelīcode his wurđfulniss, Ælfc. T. Grn. 2, 34. For swā miceles freólses wurþfulnesse *ob tante festivitatis honorificentiam,* Anglia xiii. 401, 522. Brōhton Rōmāne đone triumphan angeán Pompeius mid micelre weorþfulnesse (wyrđ-, *v.l.*), Ors. 5, 10; Swt. 234, 29.

weorþ-georn; *adj. Desirous of honour, noble-minded, excellent:*—Se wīsa and se weorđgeorna and se fæstrǣda folces hyrde . . . Caton, Met. 10, 48. Hȳ weorđgeornra sǣlđa tōslītaþ, Salm. Kmbl. 696; Sal. 347. Lā wīsan menn, gāþ on đone weg đe eów lǣraþ đa foremǣran bisna đara gōdena gumena and đæra weorþgeornena wera đe ǣr eów wǣron (*ite nunc fortes, ubi celsa magni ducit exempli via*). Eálā gē eargan and īdelgeornan . . . hwȳ gē nellan ācsien æfter đām wīsum monnum and æfter đām weorþgeornum . . . đe ǣr eów wǣron . . . hī wunnon æfter wyrþscipe on đisse worulde, and tiledon gōdes hlīsan, Bt. 40, 4; Fox 238, 28-240, 5. Đa menn đe on hiora dagum foremǣroste and weorþgeornoste wǣron *clarissimos suis temporibus viros,* 18, 3; Fox 64, 36.

weorþian, wurþian, wyrþian; *p.* ode. I. *to set a value upon,* (1) of money value:—Be đam đe se man hit weorđige đe hit āge *according to the value the owner may set upon it,* L. Ath. v. 6; Th. i. 232, 26. (1 a) *to fix interest on a loan* (?), *to lend at interest* (?):—Wiorþigende *foenerator,* Ps. Spl. T. 108, 10. (2) in other cases, *to value, esteem, hold in honour, venerate:*—Wæs đǣr gild đe đa hǣþenan men swīđe weorđodan (*held in the highest honour*), Blickl. Homl. 221, 20. Uton rihtne cristendōm geornlīce weorđian, and ǣlcne hǣđendōm mid ealle oferhogian, L. Eth. ix. 44; Th. i. 350, 11. Wēnst đū đæt se anweald and đæt geniht seó tō forseónne, ođđe eft swīþor tō weorþianne đonne ōþre gōd (*rerum omnium veneratione dignissimum*). Đā cwæþ ic: Ne mæg nǣnne mon đæs tweógan, đætte anweald and geniht is tō weorþianne, Bt. 33, 1; Fox 120, 22-25. Đæs engles mægen and his wundor đǣr đonne weorđod biđ and oftost æteówed, Blickl. Homl. 209, 21. II. *to honour, shew honour to, treat with reverence* or *respect:*—Đū weorđasđ đīne suna mā đonne mē *honorasti filios tuos magis quam me,* Past. 17; Swt. 123, 7. Đis folc mē mid welerum weorđaþ (wurđaþ, *v.l.:* worđas, Lind.) *populus hic labiis me honorat,* Mt. Kmbl. 15, 8. Weorđas (worđias, Lind.), Mk. Skt. Rush. 7, 6. Gē ne weorđiaþ (wurđiaþ, *v.l.:* worđiges *honorificavit,* Lind.), fæder and mōdor, Mt. Kmbl. 15, 6. Ic lisse selle đam đe [đē] wurđiaþ, Cd. Th. 105, 25; Gen. 1758. Hī hine weorþodan swā cinige gerīseþ, Blickl. Homl. 69, 31. Wurđodon, Chr. 975; Th. i. 227, 13. Weorđa (wurđa, *v.l.:* worđig, Lind.) đīnne fæder *honora patrem tuum,* Mt. Kmbl. 15, 4. Worđa, Mk. Skt. Rush. 7, 10. Cyning wyrþiaþ *regem honorificate,* Scint. 64, 10. Đæt hī Godes þeówas werian and weorđian, L. Eth. vi. 45; Th. i. 326, 23. Hē gesiehđ đa weorþigan (weorđian, Cott. MSS.) đe ǣr wel ongunnon, đā đā hē īdel wæs *eorum palmas respiciant, in quorum nunc laboribus otiosi perdurant,* Past. 34; Swt. 229, 21. II a. in reference to subjects divine or sacred, (1) of honour shewn to a god, *to worship, adore:*—Nǣfre đū gelǣrest đæt ic deófolgieldum gaful onhāte, ac ic weorđige wuldres ealdor, Exon. Th. 251, 30; Jul. 153. Gif đū worđas (worđias, Lind.) bifora mec *si adoraueris coram me,* Lk. Skt. Rush. 4, 7. 'Gif đū feallest tō mē, and mē weorþast.' Eálā sōþlīce se āfealleþ, se đe deófol weorþeþ. . . Đæt mānfulle wuht wolde đæt hē (*Christ*) hine weorþode . . . hine (*Christ*) ealle hālige weorþiaþ . . . Swā wē sceolan hine mid wordum weorþian, Blickl. Homl. 31, 1-11. Hig mē weorđiaþ (wurđiaþ, *v.l.*) *colunt me,* Mt. Kmbl. 15, 9. Worđiaþ (worđas, Rush.), Mk. Skt. Lind. 7, 7. Đa đe weorđiaþ wuldres aldor *adorabunt coram te, Domine,* Ps. Th. 85, 8: Ps. Surt. 71, 11: Exon. Th. 150, 1; Gū. 772. Menn ūs wurđiaþ for godas, Homl. Th. i. 462, 28. Đa þing đe hig wurđiaþ *ea quae colunt Aegyptii,* Ex. 8, 26. Gāst is God, and đa đa worđigas (*adorant*) hine, in gāste gidæfnaþ tō worđanne (uorđia *adorare,* Lind.), Jn. Skt. Rush. 4, 24. Wyrđade *oraret,* Wrt. Voc. ii. 64, 56. Gē wurđodon đæt cealf for god, Deut. 9, 16. Đām godum đe hira fæderas ne wurđodon (*coluerunt*), 32, 17. Weorþedon, Ors. 4, 4; Swt. 162, 26. Wurđedon, Cd. Th. 227, 5; Dan. 182. Hiora cyningas hī weorþodon for godas, Bt. 38, 1; Fox 194, 16: Met. 26, 45: Wulfst. 98, 24. Hȳ wurđedon him for godas đa sunnan and đone mōnan, 105, 13. Đa tungelwītgan cuōmon tō đon đæt hié Crist weorþedon (wurđoden, *v.l.*), Chr. 2; Erl. 4, 29. Nānes cynnes andlīcnyssa ne wurđa (*non adorabis et non coles*), Deut. 5, 9. Weorþa đīnne Drihten God, Blickl. Homl. 27, 20. Weorþian wē Drihtnes godcundnesse, Blickl. Homl. 33, 36. Weorđian Waldend, Exon. Th. 25, 1; Cri. 394. Wīg weorđian, Apstls. Kmbl. 95; Ap. 48. Wurđigean, Cd. Th. 228, 24; Dan. 208. Hū hine man wurđian scyle *ritum colendi,* Ex. 18, 20. Ic đone Dēman wille weorþian wordum and dǣdum, Exon. Th. 139, 10; Gū. 591. Gif đū fallas tō worđenne ł tō worđianne mec *si cadens adoraveris me,* Mt. Kmbl. Lind. 4, 9. (2) of reverence shewn to sacred things, *to worship, adore:*—Ic đīn tempel weorđige *adorabo ad templum sanctum tuum,* Ps. Th. 137, 2. Heó on cneów sette, lāc (*the cross*) weorđade, Elen. Kmbl. 2272; El. 1137. Đæt ic mōte đone sigebeám weorđian, Rood Kmbl. 255; Kr. 129: Blickl. Homl. 97, 13. (3) of reverence shewn to holy persons or religious seasons, *to celebrate, commemorate,* (*a*) of persons:—On đisum dæge wē wurđiaþ on ūrum lofsangum and on freólse đone mǣran apostol Iacōbum, Homl. Th. ii. 412, 18. Se (*St. Michael*) đe is tō weorþienne and tō wuldrienne, Blickl. Homl. 197, 6. (*β*) of seasons:—Be đære ārwyrđnesse đisse hālgan tīde, đe wē nū weorþiaþ, Blickl. Homl. 115, 30. Weorđiaþ, Menol. Fox 349; Men. 176. Đæt hié weorđeden đone mǣran dæg, Elen. Kmbl. 2442; El. 1222. Eal folc wurþodon symbelnysse, Homl. Skt. ii. 30, 152. Weorþian wē nū tōdæg đone tōcyme đæs Hālgan Gāstes, Blickl. Homl. 131, 11: 171, 3. Be đisse hālgan tīde weorþunga đe wē mǣrsian sceolan and weorþian . . . ūs is đes dæg swīþe tō mǣrsienne and tō weorþienne, 161, 5-8. Đa dagas đe gē sceolun Drihtne hālgian and wurđian *feriae Domini, quas vocabitis sanctas,* Lev. 23, 2. Đære abbudissan gemynddæg on myclum wuldre weorþad is *cujus natalis solet in magna gloria celebrari,* Bd. 3, 8; S. 532, 40. (4) used intransitively, *to celebrate* (*a service*):—Se bisceop đǣr gesette ciricean þegnas, đa đǣr dæghwamlīce mid gelimplīcre endebyrdnesse weorđode, Blickl. Homl. 207, 33. III. *to honour* in words, *speak in honour of, magnify, praise, celebrate, glorify:*—Ic Drihten wordum weorđige *in Domino laudabo sermonem,* Ps. Th. 55, 9. Hē wæs Drihtne fylgende, and hine herede and weorþode, Blickl. Homl. 15, 28. Hē Dryhten herede, weorđade wordum, Andr. Kmbl. 2537; An. 1270. Wyrđode, 109; An. 55. Wyrđude, 1076; An. 538. Se eádga (*Abraham*) Drihtnes noman weorđade, Cd. Th. 113, 13; Gen. 1886. Hæleđ hālgum stefnum cyning weorđodon, Andr. Kmbl. 2112; An. 1057. Wordum weorđodon, 1611; An. 807. Wurđedon, Cd. Th. 232, 15; Dan. 260. Weorđiaþ his naman *psallite nomini ejus,* Ps. Th. 134, 3. Wē naman đīnne weorđien *honorificabo nomen tuum,* 85, 11. Ūre Hǣlend wæs weorþod and hered from Iudēa folce, Blickl. Homl. 67, 4. Hē wæs of cilda mūþe gecnāwen and weorþad, 71, 33. IV. *to honour, pay respect to, heed, attend to* (cf. *Icel.* virđa *to give heed*):—Hē hēt mē his word weorđian and wel healdan, lǣstan his lāre, Cd. Th. 34, 13; Gen. 537: 21, 24; Gen. 329. Wurđian, 23, 3; Gen. 353. Heó his dǣd and word noldon weorđian, 20, 16; Gen. 310. IV a. *to pay court to* a person:—Weorđiaþ *colunt* (multi colunt personam potentis, Prov. 19, 6), Kent. Gl. 671. IV b. *to bestow labour upon, take pains with:*—Đam gelīcost đe sién gyldenu fatu and sylfrenu forsewen, and treówenu mon weorþige *si vilia vasa colerentur, pretiosa sordescerent,* Bt. 36, 1; Fox 172, 20. IV c. *to care about:*—Hē mistlīce fugela sangas ne wurþode swā oft swā cnihtlīcu yldo begǣđ *he did not care about the various songs of birds, as often is the usage of such a boyish age;* non variarum volucrum diversos crocitus, ut adsolet illa aetas, imitabatur, Guthl. 2; Gdwin. 12, 18. V. *to honour, bestow honour upon, grace:*—Swā hē his weorc weorþaþ, Exon. Th. 43, 19; Cri. 691. Gif se abbod his geearnunge swylce ongyte, hē hine mōt be suman dǣle furþor weorđian (wyrđian, *v.l.*), and him innor tǣcan stede and setl, R. Ben. 111, 4. V a. *to honour* with something, (1) where the subject is inferior to the object:—Godes þeówum đe đa cyrican mid godcundum dreámum weorđiaþ, Blickl. Homl. 41, 27. Weorþiaþ gē eówerne Drihten God mid gedafenlīcum þingum *honora Deum de tua substantia* (Prov. 3, 9), 41, 9. Heó hēt mē fremdne god welum weorþian, Exon. Th. 247, 9; Jul. 76. (2) where the subject is not inferior to the object, *to grace, favour, honour by bestowing* something:—God geofum unhneáwum, cræftum weorđaþ eorþan tuddor, Exon. Th. 43, 12; Cri. 687. Hē weorþode his deórlingas mid miclum welum, Bt. 28; Fox 100, 29. Drihten his folc wurðode mid ðara Egiptiscan gestreóne *Dominus dedit gratiam populo coram Aegyptiis, ut commodarent eis*, Ex. 12, 36. Hē hine miclum and his geféran mid feó weorðude, Chr. 878; Erl. 80, 25. Æt feohgyftum hē Dene weorþode, Beo. Th. 2185; B. 1090. Ic ðine leóde weorðode weorcum, 4198; B. 2096. Is gesȳne ðæt ðū ðyssum hysse hold gewurde, and hine geofum wyrðodest, Andr. Kmbl. 1102; An. 551. Hē hī welum weorðode, 1509; An. 756. Ðam werode ðe hē wurðode wlite and wuldre, Cd. Th. 3, 14; Gen. 35. Hē hī wolde swīþe weorþian mid ēce rīce, Bt. 41, 3; Fox 248, 11. VI. *to make worthy, to ennoble*:—Weorða ðē selfne gōdum dǣdum, Wald. 1, 40; Vald. 1, 22. [God wurþian, O. E. Homl. i. 11, 26. Sunnedei wurþien, 45, 36. Wurðien (weorþi, 2nd MS.), Laym. 9510. To lofenn Godd and wurrþenn, Orm. 208. He wurðede ðe ton . . . ðe was wurði wurðed to ben, Gen. and Ex. 1010. *Goth.* wairþōn *to fix the value of*: *O. Sax.* gi-weiðōn: *O. H. Ger.* werdōn *appretiare, venerari*: *Icel.* virða *to fix the value of.*] v. ā-, ār-, ge-, mis-, un-weorþian.

weorþig. v. worþig.

weorþing?:—Andlang streámes in wiððan weorðing (weording, Cod. Dip. Kmbl. iii. 391, 19), Cod. Dip. B. ii. 41, 2.

weorþ-leás; *adj. Worthless, of no value*:—Wurðleás *depretiatus*, Wrt. Voc. i. 28, 59.

weorþ-līc; *adj.* I. *of value, valuable*:—Ǣlc seldsȳnde fisc ðe weorðlīc byð, Cod. Dip. Kmbl. iii. 450, 27. Weorðlīc reáf gedǣlan *dividere spolia*, Ps. Th. 67, 12. II. *worthy, noble, distinguished, excellent, splendid*:—Gif ðū ǣnigne mon cūþest ðara ðe hæfde ǣlces þinges anweald, and ǣlcne weorþscipe . . . geþenc hū weorþlīc and hū foremǣrlīc ðē wolde se mon þincan, Bt. 33, 1; Fox 120, 34. Bið him weorðlīc setl *sedes ejus sicut sol*, Ps. Th. 88, 31. Weorðlīc wlite wuldres ðīnes *magnificentia*, 95, 6. Wæs his rīce brād, wīd and weorðlīc, Exon. Th. 243, 11; Jul. 9. Treów in ðē weorðlīcu wunade, 6, 12; Cri. 83. Ðīn heáhsetl is heáh and mǣre, fæger and wurðlīc, Hy. 7, 40. Wē ðē þanciaþ ðīnes weorðlīcan wuldordreámes, 8, 10. Hī mid weorðlīcan weorode and wynsaman dreáme hine feredan, Chr. 1023; Erl. 163, 26. Drihten hine mid weorðlīce wlite gegyrede *Dominus praecinxit se virtute*, Ps. Th. 92, 1: 103, 2. For ðam wyrðlīcan *propter dignitosam (innocentiae palmam*, Ald. 72), Hpt. Gl. 521, 64. Weorþlīcne sige *vere laudandum victoriam*, Ors. 3, 10; Swt. 140, 3. Ðæm folce ðe on clǣnum felda weorðlīcne sige gefeohtaþ *his, qui per fortitudinem in campo victores sunt*, Past. 33; Swt. 227, 25. Weorðlīcne wæstm, Ps. Th. 131, 12. Hī worhton wurðlīce cyrcan, Homl. Skt. i. 19, 143. Hē wurðlīc lāc geoffrode; ðæt wæs ān gylden calic on fīf marcon swīðe wundorlices geworces, Chr. 1058; Erl. 193, 21. Cumaþ wæstm on wangas weorðlīc on hwǣtum *convalles abundabunt frumento*, Ps. Th. 64, 14. Hī ðām wurðlīcum godum nāne lāc ne offredon, Homl. Skt. i. 23, 297. Ða weorðlīcan godas, 23, 302. Ðū selest weorðlīca ginfæsta gifa, Met. 20, 226. Weorþlīce, Bt. 33, 4; Fox 132, 19. Gebeorh Godes bringeþ tō genihte wæstme weorðlīce and wel þicce *montem Dei, montem uberem; mons coagulatus, mons pinguis*, Ps. Th. 67, 15. Wundor ðīn weorðlīc *mirabilia tua*, 70, 16. His weorðlīcu weorc *opera Dei*, 77, 9. Ealra þinga weorþlīcost and mǣrlīcost *omni celebritate clarissimum*, Bt. 33, 1; Fox 120, 31. III. *worthy, meet, fit, becoming*:—Heom bið weorðlīc, ðæt hī ā habbon ārwurðe wīsan on eallum heora þeáwum, L. I. P. 10; Th. ii. 318, 33. Wyrðelīcum tōhigunge *digno effectu*, Rtl. 35, 37. Wyrðelīcum gimērsiga oeste *digna celebrare devotione*, 81, 31. Dōð weorðlīce dǣdbōte wæstmas *facite fructus dignos poenitentiae*, Lk. Skt. 3, 8. [Ðu ert wel don man and þarto wurðlich, O. E. Homl. ii. 29, 16. Wurðliche wepnen, Laym. 28923. Hwite wurðliche men *viros dealbatos, quorum vultus inspicere pre claritate non poteram*, Kath. 1576. *O. H. Ger.* werdlīh *celeber, munificus*: *Icel.* virði-ligr *noble, splendid.*] v. ār-, or-, unweorþlīc (-wirþ-, -wurþ-).

weorþlīce, weorþelīce; *adv. Worthily, honourably*:—Ðe weorðelīcor *dignius*, Wrt. Voc. ii. 27, 8. I. *nobly, excellently, splendidly, magnificently, gloriously*:—Weorþlīce getȳd on Grēcisc gereorde *Graecae linguae peritissimus*, Bd. 4, 1; S. 563, 33. Hī brāde weóxan weorðlīce wīde greówan *multiplicati sunt nimis*, Ps. Th. 106, 37. Ðū ymb ðīnne esne dydest wel weorðlīce *bonitatem fecisti cum servo tuo*, 118, 65. Swīðe mycel cyrice . . . geworht swā fægre and swā weorþlīce swā hit men on eorþan fægrost and weorþlīcost geþencean meahton, Blickl. Homl. 125, 22: Rood Kmbl. 33; Kr. 17. Swā weorðlīce, wīde tōsāweþ Dryhten his duguþe, Exon. Th. 299, 30; Crā. 110: 121, 27; Gū. 295. Fægere, weorðlīce, Menol. Fox 317; Men. 160. Eleutherius onfēng biscopdōm and ðone wurþlīce (cf. wuldorfæstlīce, 8, 14) xv winter geheóld, Chr. 167; Erl. 9, 20. Hē his sincgyfan wurðlīce wrec, Byrht. Th. 139, 64; By. 279. Ne gefrægn ic nǣfre wurðlīcor sixtig sigebeorna sēl gebǣran, Fins. Th. 74; Fins. 37: Cd. Th. 126, 12; Gen. 2094. Men wurðlīcor lybbaþ þonne treówu *the life of men is more excellent than that of trees*, Shrn. 168, 24. Swā hit weorðlīcost foresnotre men findan mihton, Beo. Th. 6304; B. 3162. II. *in a way that shews honour* to a person, *honourably, with honour*:—Ðā onfēng Dioclitianus Galerius weorðlīce (*plurimo honore*), Ors. 6, 30; Swt. 280, 16. Hī swīðe weorðlīce hine of heora gryðe sendon, Chr. 1075; Erl. 212, 33. Hī mīd mycclan þrymme and blisse and lofsange ðone hālgan arcebiscop feredon, and swā wurðlīce intō Cristes cyrcan brōhton, 1023; Erl. 163, 30. Hine man byrigde ful wurðlīce, 1036; Erl. 165, 35. III. *in a fitting manner, worthily*:—Wē willaþ offrian wurðlīce ūrum Drihtne, Ex. 10, 9. [Þo þu iseie þine sune . . . so wurðliche stien to his blisse, A. R. 40, 7. Wel and wurrþlike gemmde, Orm. 1033. *O. Sax.* werð-līko: *O. H. Ger.* werd-līhho: *Icel.* virði-liga.] v. ār-, un-weorþlīce.

weorþ-mynd (-mynt), es; *m.*: e; *f.*: -myndu (-o); *indecl. f. Honour*:—*Favor*, i. *fama, honor, laus, laetitia, testimonium laudis* wyrþmynd, Wrt. Voc. ii. 147, 13. I. *honour, respect* shewn to an object, *celebration* of an event:—Sȳ ūrum Drihtne lof and wuldor and weorþmynd, Blickl. Homl. 65, 25. Wurðmynt, Homl. Th. i. 76, 23. Ðam ānum is ēce weorðmynd, Exon. Th. 240, 10; Ph. 636. On weorðmynde ðara twelfa apostola, Lchdm. ii. 138, 22. Ðære dǣde tō weorðmynte *in honour of the deed*, Ors. 6, 25; Swt. 276, 15. Freólsiaþ ðone seofoðan dæg Gode tō wurðmynte, Ex. 35, 2. Gode tō lofe and ðam hālgan arcebiscope tō wurðmynte, Chr. 1023; Erl. 163, 35. Gē weorðmyndu Dryhtne gieldaþ, Exon. Th. 130, 7; Gū. 434. Eodan hié him tōgeánes mid blōwendum palmtwigum heora siges tō wyorþmyndum, Blickl. Homl. 67, 11. Seó mǣre burh ðe ic geworhte tō wurðmyndum *Babylon magna quam ego aedificavi in gloria decoris mei* (Dan. 4, 27), Cd. Th. 254, 12; Dan. 610. Hwæt wit tō willan and tō worðmyndum ārna gefremedon, Beo. Th. 2377; B. 1186. II. *honour* bestowed on an object, *favour, grace*:—Seó mennisce gecynd mæg ðæm Scyppende lof and wuldor secgean ðara āra and ðara weorþmenda ðe Drihten mancynne forgeaf . . . Hū mihte mannum māra weorðmynd geweorþan, ðonne him on ðyssum dæge gewearþ? Blickl. Homl. 123, 3–15. Wurðment *privilegium*, Hpt. Gl. 527, 68. Ic hæfde gemynt ðē tō ārwurðienne on ǣhtum and on feó, ac God ðē benǣmde ðæs wurðmintes *decreveram magnifice honorare te, sed Dominus privavit te honore disposito*, Num. 24, 11. For synderlīcum wurðmente *propter privilegium* (*singularem honorem*), Hpt. Gl. 411, 31. Frumgife ł wurðmente *praerogativam*, 457, 29. Hit nān wundor nys ðæt sē hālga cynincg untrumnysse gehǣle, nū hē on heofonum leofaþ . . . hæfð hē ðone wurðmynt (*the privilege of healing sickness*) for his gōdnesse, Homl. Skt. ii. 26, 277. Syndrige wyrðmenta *privilegia*, Hpt. Gl. 517, 2. Ic wāt hwā mē wyrðmyndum (*graciously*) on wudubāte ferede ofer flōdas, Andr. Kmbl. 1809; An. 907. III. *honour, decoration, ornament*:—Uueorðmynd *infula*, Wrt. Voc. ii. 110, 66. Weorþmynd *infulas*, 43, 60. Gif ðū wēnst ðætte wundorlīc gerela hwelc weorþmynd sié (*pulcrum variis fulgere vestibus putas?*), ðonne telle ic ða weorþmynd ðæm wyrhtan ðe hié worhte, Bt. 14, 1; Fox 42, 18. Yr byð æðelinga gehwæs wyn and wyrðmynd, Runic pm. Kmbl. 344, 31; Rūn. 27. Hē geseáh sigeeádig bil, wigena weorðmynd, Beo. Th. 3122; B. 1559. Wel bið ðam eorle ðe him oninnan hafaþ rūme heortan, ðæt him biþ for worulde weorðmynda mǣst, Exon. Th. 467, 18; Alm. 3. IV. *honour, glory, fame*:—Byð ðē weorðmynd (wurðmynt, *v.l.*) beforan midsittendum *erit tibi gloria coram simul discumbentibus*, Lk. Skt. 14, 10. Ðæt hié witen ðæt mīn þrym and mīn weorðmynd māran wǣron ðonne ealra ōþra kyninga, Nar. 33, 4. On his winestran handa wǣre wela and wyrðmynt (*gloria*) . . . Hē mæt ðone welan and ðone wyrðmynd tō ðære winestran handa, Past. 50; Swt. 389, 17–19. Wæs Hrōðgāre herespēd gyfen, wīges weorðmynd (*glorious success in war*), Beo. Th. 130; B. 65. Ðȳ læs hié ormōde wǣron, and ðȳ sǣnran mīnes willan and weorðmyndo (*the slower to do my will and promote my glory*), Nar. 32, 24. Ic (*Eve*) wæs mid weorþmende on neorxna wange *I lived glorious in Paradise*, Blickl. Homl. 89, 8. Hē heóld ðone arcestōl mid mycclan weorðmynte, Chr. 1068; Erl. 206, 16. Sió eáðmōdnes iernð beforan ðæm gilpe, and hió cymð ǣr ǣr ða weorðmyndu (wyrðmynðu, Hatt. MS.) *gloriam praecedit humilitas*, Past. 41; Swt. 298, 16. Dryhtne ðe hyre weorþmynde geaf, mǣrþe on moldan rīce, Judth. Thw. 26, 25; Jud. 343. Wē hæfdon wlite and weorðmynt, Cd. Th. 274, 10; Sat. 152. Him God sealde weorðmynda dǣl, Beo. Th. 3509; B. 1752. Hē wæs for weorulde wīs, weorðmynþa georn, Met. 1, 51. Ðæt ðū gefeó in ðæm fromscipe mīnes līfes, and eác blissige in ðǣm weorðmyndum, Nar. 32, 32. Hē weorþmyntum þāh *he throve gloriously*, Beo. Th. 16; B. 8. V. *honour, dignity, honourable position* or *office*:—Ne gedafenaþ nā munuce ðæt hē ǣniges worldlīces wyrðmyntes gyrne *non convenit monacho mundanum quemquam honorem desiderare*, L. Ecg. P. iii. 10; Th. ii. 198, 30. Ða weorðmynde cynehādes hē fleáh *rex fieri noluit*, Past. 3; Swt. 33, 20. Tyddre weorþmyntas *fragiles honores*, Wrt. Voc. ii. 150, 38. Tō weorðmyndum *ad fasces*, 99, 35: 4, 47. Wyrþmyndum *titulis*, 95, 47. Ne bidde wē nā leáse welan ne gewītenlīce wurðmyntas, Homl. Th. i. 158, 26. VI. *dignity, nobleness*:—Seó wlitige, weorðmynda full, heáh and hālig heofuncund þrȳnes, Exon. Th. 24, 2; Cri. 378. Āra mē for hire wuldres weorþmyndum, Blickl. Homl. 89, 22. Wolde reordigean rīces hyrde hālgan stefne, werodes wīsa wurðmyndum (*nobly, with dignity*) spræc, Cd. Th. 194, 10; Exod. 258. [Habban þene eche wurðment mid Gode, O. E. Homl. i. 107, 21. Ilæsten scal is worðmunt (me wole of him telle, 2nd MS.), Laym. 18851. Si Drihhtin wurrþmiunt and loff and wullderr, Orm. 3379. 3ef þu hit 3ulde to his wurðmunt þe scheop þe, Kath. 216. Cf. He cweð þet he wolde hit wurðmiunten and arwurðen, Chr. 656; Erl. 30, 3.]

weorþness, e; *f.* I. *worthiness, honourable character* :—For his geearnunge wurþnys[se] (wyrðnesse, Bd. M. 194, 34) hē wæs fram eallum monnum lufad *ob meritorum dignitatem ab omnibus diligebatur*, Bd. 3, 14; S. 540, 10. Tō līfes wyrþnysse *ad vite honestatem*, Anglia xiii. 368, 48. II. *dignity, nobility, honourable* or *honoured condition* :—Werðnes *dignitas*, Kent. Gl. 582. Æþele æfter ðysse worulde wurþnysse *ad saeculi hujus dignitatem nobilis*, Bd. 4, 9; S. 577, 2. Ðū ðe menisc gicynd bufa frumes frumcendnisse eft boetest wyrðnise *qui humanam naturam supra prime originis reparas dignitatem*, Rtl. 35, 13. III. *dignity, honourable office* :—Hæfde se cyning efenhlētan ðære cynelīcan wurþnysse (*regiae dignitatis*), Bd. 3, 14; S. 539, 30. IV. *dignity, state, imposing show* :—Hē fērde tō Rōme mid micelre weorþnesse, Chr. 855; Erl. 68, 28. V. *honour* shewn to an object :—On wurþnysse ðīnre *in honore tuo*, Ps. Spl. 44, 10. Ne is wītge būta worðnis (*sine honore*) būta on oeðel his, Mk. Skt. Lind. 6, 4. v. un-weorþness.

weorþscipe, es; *m.* I. *worship, honour* shewn to an object :— Gif hwā biþ mid hwelcum welum geweorþod, hū ne belimpþ se weorþscipe tō ðam ðe hine geweorðaþ; ðæt is tō herianne hwēne rihtlīcor *si quod ex appositis luceat, ipsa quidem, quae sunt apposita, laudantur*, Bt. 14, 3; Fox 46, 12. Ða dysiende wēnaþ ðætte ðæt ðing sié ǽlces weorþscipes betst wyrþe ðætte hī medemæste ongiton magon *labuntur hi, qui quod sit optimum, id reverentiae cultu dignissimum putant*, 24, 4; Fox 86, 10. Nys nān wītega būtan weorðscype (wurð-, *v. l.*) (*sine honore*), būton on his earde, Mt. Kmbl. 13, 57: Mk. Skt. 6, 4. Hī wunnon æfter weorðscipe (wyrþ-, *v. l.*) on ðisse worulde, and tiledon gōdes hlīsan, Bt. 40, 4; Fox 240, 5. Ealne ðæne bysmor wē gyldaþ mid weorðscype ðām ðe ūs scendaþ, Wulfst. 163, 10. Mid wurðscipe underfōn, Chr. 785; Erl. 57, 19: Nicod. 20; Thw. 10, 26. Him cōmon lāc tō wurðscipe, Ælfc. T. Grn. 7, 32. Yfelwillende men nǽnne weorþscipe næfdon, Bt. 15; Fox 48, 17. Uorðscip, Lind.: worðscip, Rush., *honorem*, Jn. Skt. 4, 44. II. *honour, honourable* or *honoured condition, dignity, honours* :—Se weorþscipe and se anweald, gif hē becymþ tō ðam dysigan, hē mæg hine gedōn weorþne *dignitates honorabilem, cui provenerint, reddunt*, Bt. 27, 1; Fox 94, 18. Benumen ǽgþer ge ðīnra welona ge ðīnes weorþscipes, 7, 3; Fox 20, 5. Welan and weorþscipes hī willniaþ *opes, honores ambiant*, 32, 3; Fox 118, 29: Met. 19, 44. Hwæt mæg ic ðē māre secgan be ðam weorþscipe and be ðam anwealde ðisse worulde . . . Gē ne ongitaþ ðone heofoncundan anweald and ðone weorþscipe, se is eówer āgen . . . Hwæt se eówer wela and se eówer anweald ðe gē nū weorþscipe hātaþ, gif hē becymþ tō ðam ealra wyrrestan men *quid de dignitatibus potentiaque disseram, quas vos, verae dignitatis ac potestatis inscii, coelo exaequatis? quae si in improbissimum quemque ceciderint?* Bt. 16, 1; Fox 48, 27–34. Mann ðā ðā hē on wurðscype (*in honore*) wæs, Ps. Spl. 41, 21. Hē (*Joseph*) heóld his fæder on fullum wurðscipe ðǽr mid eallum his brōðrum, Ælfc. T. Grn. 5, 7. III. *honour, glory* :—Mīne fȳnd mīnne weorðscipe tō duste gewyrcen *inimicus gloriam meam in pulverem deducat*, Ps. Th. 7, 5. IV. *honour, state, magnificence* :—Hē fērde tō Rōme mid mycclum wurðscipe, Chr. 855; Erl. 69, 18. V. *dignity* of behaviour :—Mōderlīcere stæððinysse ł wurðscipe *materna gravitate ł dignitate*, Hpt. Gl. 469, 38. VI. *worthiness, excellence, nobleness* :—Weorþscipe *vel* geþungennes *dignitas*, i. *honestas, excellentia, fastigium*, Wrt. Voc. ii. 140, 25. Sittende hē tǽhte; ðæt belimpð tō wurðscipe lāreówdōmes, Homl. Th. i. 548, 25. Hié ālȳsde for his weorþscipe Eádmund cyning, Chr. 942; Erl. 116, 18. VII. *an honour, a dignity, an honourable office* or *position* :— Ealdordōmas *vel* ða hēhstan wurðscipas *fasces*, biscoplīc wurðscipe *flaminus honor*, Wrt. Voc. i. 59, 53, 54. Swelce wræccan woldon underfōn ðone weorðscipe and eác ða byrðenne *infirmus quisque, ut honoris* (plebium ducatus) *onus percipiat, anhelat*, Past. 7; Swt. 51, 23. Se ðe wel þēnaþ, hē gōdne wyrðscipe him sylfum gestrȳnð *qui bene ministraverit, gradum bonum sibi adquirit*, R. Ben. 54, 18. VII a. *pl. Dignities, persons in office* (?) :—Wyrþscipas *comitia* (cf. weorþung-dæg), Wrt. Voc. i. 21, 65. VIII. *an honour, ornament, decoration* :—Wurðscipe *infula*, Hpt. Gl. 458, 24. Gifu gumena byð gleng and herenys, wraðu and weorðscype, and wræcna gehwam ār and ætwist, Runic pm. Kmbl. 340, 25; Rūn. 7. Mid twām wurðscipum geglængde se ælmihtiga Scyppend ðæs mannes sāwle; ðæt is mid ēcnysse and eádignysse, Homl. Skt. i. 1, 150. VIII a. *honour, cause of an object being honoured* or *honourable* :—Hit geweard ðæt ðam wīsan men com tō lofe and tō wyrðscype ðæt se unrihtwīsa cyning him teohhode tō wīte *ita cruciatus, quos putabat tyrannus materiam crudelitatis, vir sapiens fecit esse virtutis*, Bt. 16, 2; Fox 52, 26. IX. *what is honoured* or *prized, an excellent thing, a good* :—On swelcum and on ōþrum swelcum lǽnum and hreósendum weorþscipum (*riches, fame, power,* etc., *have been enumerated*; cf. ðām lǽnum gōdum, l. 1), Bt. 24, 3; Fox 82, 21. v. un-, weorold-weorþscipe.

weorþung, e; *f.* I. *honouring, shewing of honour* to an object, *honour, reverence* :—Ðæm is simle wuldor and weorðung, Blickl. Homl. 169, 28. Ne is wītga būta worðunge (*sine honore*), būta on oedle his, Mk. Skt. Rush. Lind. 6, 4. For ðīnre weorþunge *in honore tuo*, Ps. Th. 44, 10. Gif hē on rīce becymð, for ðære weorðunge ðæs folces hē bið on ofermēttu āwended and gewunaþ tō ðæm gielpe *si ad regiminis culmen eruperit, in elationem protinus usu gloriae permutatur*, Past. 3; Swt. 35, 12. Leóhtfæt bið ā byrnende for ðara swaþa weorþunga, Blickl. Homl. 127, 31. Wē habbaþ on Godes naman weorðunge bisceop gebletsode, Wulfst. 176, 2. Hē bið on gōdre weorþunge *he will be highly respected*, Lchdm. iii. 158, 10. I a. in religious matters, (1) *worship* of a god, *divine worship, religious service* :—Tīdsangas *canonica*, weorþung *canor*, Wrt. Voc. ii. 128, 27. Dægrēdsanges weorþung is þus tō healdenne *matutinorum solempnitas ita agatur*, R. Ben. 37, 5. Ne dear man forhealdan lytel ne mycel ðæs ðe gelagod is tō gedwolgoda weorðunge, Wulfst. 157, 14. Drihtne tō wurðunga, Lev. 2, 2. Īdola wurðinge, L. N. P. L. 48; Th. ii. 298, 1. (2) *honouring* of a person, thing, or season, *celebration, commemoration, festival* :—Mycel is þeós weorþung ðæs hālgan Sancte Iōhannes gebyrde, Blickl. Homl. 167, 13. On ðæm dæge ðe seó tīd bið and his (*S. Michael*) weorðung, 209, 17. Be ðisse hālgan tīde weorþunga ðe wē tō dæg mǽrsian sceolan and weorþian, 161, 4. Be ðyses dæges (*Pentecost*) weorþunga, 133, 12. Æt eallra hāligra weorðunge *at the feast of All Saints*, L. Alf. pol. 43; Th. i. 92, 8. Hē ða weorþunge Eástrena on riht ne heóld ne nyste *de observatione Paschae minus perfecte sapiebat*, Bd. 3, 17; S. 545, 2. Weorðunga, Blickl. Homl. 137, 8. Hī tō Hierusalem faran woldon for ðære hālgan rōde wurðunga, ðe man æfter nāht manegum dagum wurðian sceolde, Homl. Skt. ii. 23 b, 350. II. *nobleness, glory, excellence* :—Ðæt wuldres bearn on ðysne middangeard āstāg, and seó heofencunde weorþung ðone fǽmnlīcan bōsm Sancta Marian gefylde, Blickl. Homl. 165, 27. Mycel is se hāligdōm and seó weorþung Sancte Iōhannes, ðæs mycelnesse se Hǽlend sylfa tācn sægde . . . Hē on his mægenes weorþunga oferswīþ ealra ōþerra martira wuldor, 167, 16–25. Him wile God miltsian for heora mægena weorþunga, and for eorþlīcra manna gebedum, 47, 8. Næs riht on ðære stōwe ǽnigne tō ācwellanne for ðære stōwe weorþunge, Nar. 30, 3. Apostola ðīnra worðunge folc ðīn giwynsumia *apostolorum tuorum Petri et Pauli honore plebs tua exultet*, Rtl. 59, 33. Ðæt hē Sanctus Iōhannes līfes weorþunga gesecgan mæge, Blickl. Homl. 163, 36. III. *ornament, decoration* :—Crist com tō wlitignesse and tō weorþunge his brȳde, Blickl. Homl. 11, 31. Godwebba cyst, ðæt ðām hālgan hūse sceolde tō weorþunga weorud sceáwian, Exon. Th. 70, 11; Cri. 1137. [Þat folc sungen heore leofsong ure Helende to wurðinge, O. E. Homl. i. 7, 10. Godes laȝe bit ec mon wurðie his feder mid muchelere wurþunge, 109, 27. Ðe, God, to wurðinge, Gen. and Ex. 33. *O. H. Ger.* werdunga *solemnitas, celebritas, dignitas*: *Icel.* virðing *worship, reputation, honour*.] v. breóst-, dæg-, hāls-, hām-, hord-, hring-, mann-, neód-, sinc-, stān-, sundor-, tīd-, treów-, un-, wīg-, willweorþung.

weorþung-dæg, es; *m.* I. *a day for the bestowing of honours* or *offices* :—Ārdagas *vel* weorðungdagas (weordung-, Wrt.) *comitiorum dies, honorum dies*, Wrt. Voc. ii. 132, 29. [II. *a day for worship* or *celebration* :—Setteres dei wes heore Sunedei, and bet heo heolden heore wurðingdei þene we doð, O. E. Homl. i. 9, 9.]

weorþung-stōw, e; *f.* *A place for worship* :—On ðære hālgan wurðungstōwe *de tabernaculo testimonii*, Lev. 1, 1.

weorud, weoruld, weosan, weosend, weosnian, weosule, weota, weotan, weoðo-bān, weoðo-bend, weotian, weotuma. v. weorod, weorold, wesan, wesend, wisnian, wesle, wita, witan, wiþo-bān, wiþo-bend, witian, wituma.

weoxian; *p.* ode *To wipe, make clean* :—Ðacian, ðecgan and fald weoxian, Anglia ix. 261, 18. Hūs gōdian, rihtan and weoxian, 262, 19. [Cf. *O. H. Ger.* wisken *tergere*.]

wēpan; *p.* weóp, wēp (wǽpde, Lind.), *pl.* weópon, wēpon; *pp.* wōpen *To weep, wail, mourn, lament* :—Ic wēpe *fleo*, ðū wēpst (wǽpst, *v. l.*) *fles*, ic weóp *fleui*, gewōpen *fletum*, Ælfc. Gr. 26, 1; Zup. 152, 18. I. *intrans.* (1) of persons :—Maria stōd and weóp (hrēmende ł uoepende *plorans*, Lind.); and ðā heó weóp (gewǽp *fleret*, Lind.), heó ābeáh nyðer . . . Ða englas cwǽdon tō hyre: 'Wīf, hwī wēpst (uoepæs, Lind.: woepes, Rush., *ploras*) ðū?' Jn. Skt. 20, 11–13. Hē geseah mycel gehlȳd wēpende (*flentes*) . . . Hē cwæþ: 'Hwī wēpaþ (*ploratis*) gē?' Mk. Skt. 5, 38, 39. Beornas grētaþ, wēpaþ wānende wērgum stefnum, Exon. Th. 61, 31; Cri. 993. Hē weóp (*ploravit*) bityrlīce, Mt. 26, 75: Andr. Kmbl. 2799; An. 1402. Hē weóp (geweǽp *fleuit*, Lind.) ofer hig, Lk. Skt. 19, 41. Wē heófdun and gē ne weópun (wǽpde gié *plorastis*, Lind.), 7, 32. Ne ceara ðū ne ne wēp, Blickl. Homl. 143, 4. Wēpan *ploremus*, Ps. Th. 94, 6. Wēpan wē and geþencan hū Drihten cwæð: 'Eádige beóþ ða ðe nū wēpaþ (*lugent*, Mt. 5, 5),' Blickl. Homl. 25, 19. Gif ðū wistest hwæt ðē tōweard is, ðonne weópe ðū mid mē, Homl. Th. i. 404, 27. Ðā ongan hē wēpan (woepa *flere*, Lind., Rush.), Mk. Skt. 14, 72. Mid wēpendre bēne *lacrymosis precibus*, Bd. 1, 12; S. 480, 26. Mid wǽpendre stefne *flebili voce*, 480, 37. Wēpendre, Blickl. Homl. 87, 26, 8. Drihten hȳrde mīne wēpendan stefne (*vocem fletus mei*), Ps. Th. 6, 7. Ða ðe wǽpende (*flentes*) sǽton, Bd. 5, 12; S. 627, 14. Heófendum and wēpendum (wōpendum *flentibus*, Lind.), Mk. Skt. 16, 10. Hē gemētte swīþe manige wēpende, and wǽron cweþende: 'Wā ūs lā . . .' And ðā him swā wēpendum, ðā com ðara sacerda ealdorman, Blickl. Homl.

153, 25-33. Hí ofslógon weras and wífmen and ða wēpendan cild *interfecerunt omnia a viro usque ad mulierem, ab infante usque ad senem*, Jos. 6, 21. (2) of other than human beings:—Weóp eal gesceaft, Rood Kmbl. 110; Kr. 55. **I a.** where tears are shed:—On mīnum bedde ic sīce and wēpe *lavabo lectum meum*, Ps. Th. 6, 5. Hē sægde ðæt ða hālgan trióẃ swīðe wēpen and mid micle sāre instyred wǣron (*uberibus lacrimis commoueri*), Nar. 28, 11. Hē ongan wēpan hlūttrum teárum. Ðā fræng hine his mæssepreóst for hwon hē weópe *coepit ad lacrymarum profusionem effici. Quem dum presbyter suus, quare lacrymaretur interrogasset*, Bd. 3, 14; S. 541, 3-5. Hē wæs wēpende mid teárum, Blickl. Homl. 151, 20: Andr. Kmbl. 117; An. 59. **II.** *trans.* (a) with accusative, *to mourn, lament, bewail, deplore*, (1) of persons:—Hē weóp his sunu *lugens filium suum*, Gen. 37, 34. Hit wæs þeáw, ðæt man sceolde wēpan ǣlcne deádne mann; and ðæt folc hyne weóp (*flevit eum Aegyptus*) hundseofontig daga, 50. 3. (Hī) weópan wyrde (*prolis*) *luxerunt fata* (*parentes*, Ald. 176), Wrt. Voc. ii. 94, 5: 51, 34. Ne wēp ðone wræcsīð, Andr. Kmbl. 2861; An. 1433. Wræcsīð wēpan, Exon. Th. 166, 23; Gū. 1047: 443, 30; Kl. 38. Ðæt ðætte ōðre menn unālēfedes dōt hē sceal wēpan suā suā his āgne scylde *illicita perpetrata ab aliis ut propria deplorat*, Past. 10; Swt. 61, 15. Ðā hē hine ealle wēpende geseah *when he saw all mourning him*, Blickl. Homl. 225, 22. Wōpene *lamentatae*, Blickl. Gl. (2) of other than human beings:—Ne wæl wēpeþ wulf se grǣga, Exon. Th. 343, 2; Gn. Ex. 151. (b) with gen. *to mourn* for, *be grieved* at:—Hwā is swā heardheort ðæt ne mæg wēpan swylces ungelimpes? Chr. 1085; Erl. 219, 40. [*O. E. Homl.* wiep; *p.*: *A. R.* weop: *Laym.* weop, wep: *Will.* wep, wepte: *Chauc.* weep, wepte; *pp.* wopen: *Piers P.* wept: *Goth.* wōpjan; *p.* wōpida *to cry*: *O. Sax.* wōpian; *p.* wióp, wēp *to mourn*: *O. L. Ger.* wōpan; *p.* wiep: *O. Frs.* wēpa: *O. H. Ger.* wuofan; *p.* wiof *flere, plorare, plangere, lacrimari, deflere*; wuofen; *p.* uuofta *plorare, flere, lugere*: *Icel.* œpa; *p.* œpta *to cry, scream.*] v. be-, ge-wēpan.

wēpend-lic; *adj. Lamentable, mournful*:—Reówlīc and wēpendlīc tīd wæs ðæs geáres, ðe swā manig ungelimp wæs forðbringende, Chr. 1086; Erl. 220, 22. Wēpendlīce *flebiles* (*and* wēpendlīc *flebilis*. v. Wülck. Gl. 240, 16), Wrt. Voc. ii. 149, 41. [*O. H. Ger.* wuofant-līh *luctuosus*.] v. be-wēpendlīc.

wēpendlīce; *adv. Lamentably, mournfully, grievously*:—Wēpendlīce tō bewēpenne synd *flebiliter deplorandi sunt*, Scint. 77, 3.

wer, es; *m.* **I.** *a man, a male person*:—Wer oððe wǣpman *vir*, Wrt. Voc. i. 73, 11. Wer wintrum geong (*Isaac*), Cd. Th. 174, 34; Gen. 2888. Wīffæst wer *a married man*, L. C. S. 55; Th. i. 406, 14. Se Godes wer Sanctus Martinus, Blickl. Homl. 213, 36. Se eádiga wer, 215, 31. Se weor (wer, Rush.) *uir*, Lk. Skt. Lind. 8, 38. Woer (wer, W. S., Rush.), 9, 38. Of ðæs weres (*viri*) handa ic ofgange ðæs mannes (*hominis*) līf, Gen. 9, 5. On weres hāde, Elen. Kmbl. 144; El. 72: Apstls. Kmbl. 53; Ap. 27. Ðæs weres tīd sc̄i Symforiani, Shrn. 119, 17. Gelīc ðam wīsan were (*viro*), Mt. Kmbl. 7, 24. Ic nǣnigne wer (*uirum*, Lk. 1, 34) ne ongeat, Blickl. Homl. 7, 21. Wundne wer (cf. gewundodne monn, Bt. 15; Fox 48, 16), Met. 8, 35. Gē Galilēiscan weras *viri Galilei*, Blickl. Homl. 123, 20. Niniuetisce weras (wæras *viri*, Lind.), Mt. Kmbl. 12, 41. Tȳn hreófe weras (wæras, Lind.: wearas, Rush. *uiri*), Lk. Skt. 17, 12. Fīftig rihtwīsra wera *quinquaginta justos*, Gen. 18, 26. Wælrǣs weora, Beo. Th. 5886; B. 2947. Fīf ðūsendo wæro ł wærana (weorona, Rush., *uirorum*), Mk. Skt. Lind. 6, 44. Ymbseted mid syxtigum werum ðǣm strengestum ðe on Israhēlum wǣron, Blickl. Homl. 11, 17. Hālige weoras *viros sanctos*, Bd. 5, 10; S. 623, 41. **I a.** in conjunction with words denoting a woman:—Ōðer wæs idese onlīcnes, ōþer on weres wæstmum, Beo. Th. 2708; B. 1352. Ðeós bið gecīged fǣmne, for ðam ðe heó ys of were genumen *haec vocabitur virago, quoniam de viro sumpta est*, Gen. 2, 23. Gif wīf be ōðrum were forlicge, L. C. S. 54; Th. i. 406, 6. Gif oxa ofhnīte wer oþþe wīf (*virum aut mulierem*), L. Alf. 21; Th. i. 48, 27: Exon. Th. 225, 24; Ph. 394. Weras mid wīfum, Cd. Th. 104, 20; Gen. 1738. Weras, wīf samod, Andr. Kmbl. 3330; An. 1668. Weras and wīf, Exon. Th. 448, 26; Dōm. 60. Weras and idesa, 176, 7; Gū. 1205. Eall wīfa cynn and wera, Blickl. Homl. 5, 24: Beo. Th. 1990; B. 993. Twā hund and eahta and feówertig wera, and nigon and feówertig wīfa, Blickl. Homl. 239, 14. Bletsung gemǣne werum and wīfum, Exon. Th. 7, 14; Cri. 101. Ge weras ge wīf, Blickl. Homl. 107, 11. ¶ in the plural the word seems sometimes to include women as well as men:—Hē wolde for wera synnum eall āǣðan, Cd. Th. 77, 23; Gen. 1279. Folcdryht wera, sāwla gehwylce, Exon. Th. 66, 5; Cri. 1067. Wera endestæf (cf. Blickl. Homl. 239, 14 *supra*), Andr. Kmbl. 270; An. 135. Heofones gim, wyncondel wera, Exon. Th. 174, 31; Gū. 1186. In wera līfe, 26, 13; Cri. 416. Wera cneorissum, 347, 4; Sch. 7. Ðū ne wilnast weora ǣniges deáð, Ps. C. 54. Feówertig daga nīð wæs wællgrim werum, Cd. Th. 83, 23; Gen. 1384: 109, 1; Gen. 1816. Lencten on tūn geliden hæfde werum tō wīcum, Menol. Fox 58; Men. 29. Næs ðǣr hlāfes wist werum, Andr. Kmbl. 43; An. 22. Fǣhðe ic wille on weras stǣlan, eall ācwellan ða beūtan beóð earce bordum, Cd. Th. 81, 28; Gen. 1352. **II.** *a man, a male that has reached man's estate*:—Ðā āworden ic am uoer ic gīīdlade ða ðe uoeron lytles *quando factus sum vir, evacuavi quae erant parvuli*, Rtl. 6, 19. Fīf þūsenda wera (wearana, Lind.: weora, Rush., *virorum*) būtan wīfum and cildum, Mt. Kmbl. 14, 21. Ic mægen wera (*virorum*) eom, and litlincgas nellaþ forbīgean mē, Coll. Monast. Th. 29, 1. Weras and wīfmen and ða wēpendan cild, Jos. 6, 21. **III.** *a being in the form of a man*:—Grendel, wonsǣlig wer (cf. 2708; B. 1352 *supra*), Beo. Th. 210; B. 105. Twēgen weras (wæras, Lind.: wearas, Rush., *uiri*) Mōysēs and Hēlias, Lk. Skt. 9, 30. Abraham geseah þrī weras standende him gehende, Gen. 18, 2. **IV.** *a married* or *a betrothed man, a man* (as in *man* and wife), *a husband.* v. wer-leás:—Swā micel swā ðæs wīfes wer (*maritus mulieris*) girnþ, Ex. 21, 22. Hererīc hire wer (*vir ejus*), Bd. 4, 23; S. 594, 44. Be ðon ðe ryhtgesamhīwan bearn hæbben, and ðonne se wer gewīte, L. In. 38; Th. i. 126, 2. Wer and wīf beóð in ānum līchoman, Bd. 1, 27; S. 491, 13: Exon. Th. 327, 11; Vy. 2: Blickl. Homl. 185, 26. Ðæt he hȳ healdan wille swā wær his wīf sceal, L. Edm. B. 1; Th. i. 254, 7. Iōsep hyre wer (*vir*), Mt. Kmbl. 1, 19. Wearð seó mōdor gegremod æfter hire weres forðsīðe fram hire cilde, Homl. Th. ii. 30, 4. Geong wuduwe mōt eft ceorlian æfter hire weres forðsīðe, L. Ælfc. P. 43; Th. ii. 382, 32. Heó leofode mid hyre were seofan gēr of hyre fǣmnhāde, Lk. Skt. 2, 36: Cd. Th. 134, 1; Gen. 2218. Gif mon hǣme mid monnes wīfe, gebēte ðam were, L. Alf. pol. 10; Th. i. 68, 9: Exon. Th. 153, 6; Gū. 821. Gif wuduwe binnan geáres fæce wer geceóse, L. C. S. 74; Th. i. 416, 8. Wær, L. Edm. B. 4; Th. i. 254, 16. Iōsep, Marian wer (wær, Rush., *virum*), Mt. Kmbl. 1, 16. Hié noldan heora wera ræstgemānan sēcean, Blickl. Homl. 173, 16. Heora wīf him sǣdon, ðæt hié him woldon ōðerra wera ceósan (*sobolem se a finitimis quaesituras*), Ors. 1, 10; Swt. 44, 22. Wīf ic lǣrde ðæt hié heora weras lufedan, Blickl. Homl. 185, 23. **V.** *a male*, (1) of human beings:—Wer and wīf hē gesceóp hī *masculum et feminam creavit eos*, Gen. 5, 2. (2) of plants:—Ys ðeós wyrt twēgea cynna, ðæt is wer (wær, *v. l.*) and wīf, Lchdm. i. 204, 9. Ðeós wyrt is twēga cynna, ōðer ys wīf, ōðer wer, 252, 20. **V a.** in grammar, *masculine gender*:—*Participia* belimpaþ tō þrȳm cynnum, tō were and tō wīfe and tō nāðrum cynne, Ælfc. Gr. 39; Zup. 243, 19. [*Orm. O. and N. Gen. and Ex.* were: *Laym.* were (*dat.*): *Goth.* wair: *O. Sax. O. Frs. O. H. Ger.* wer: *Icel.* verr: *Lat.* vir.] v. dryht-, folc-, hūsel-, leód-, riht-wer.

wer *and* **were**, es; *m.* [*The word seems to be interchangeable with* wer-gild (q. v.), e. g.:—Gif hē geþeó ðæt hē hæbbe hīwisc landes . . . þonne bið his wergild .cxx. scill.; and gif hē ne geþeó būton tō healfre hīde, þonne sī his wer (were, *v. l.*) .lxxx. scill., L. Wg. 7; Th. i. 186, 14. Wergildes (*v. l.* weres) . . . Se wer, 1; Th. i. 186, 3, 4. Bið cynges ānfeald wergild .vi. þegna wer (wergyld, *v. l.*), L. M. L.; Th. i. 190, 4.] *The price set upon a man according to his degree*:—Be fullan were, sȳ swā boren swā hē sȳ, L. Edm. S. 1; Th. i. 248, 4. Twelfhyndes mannes wer is twelf hund scyllinga. Twyhyndes mannes wer is twā hund scill. . . . Eal man sceal æt cyrliscum were be ðære mǣðe dōn ðe him tō gebyreþ, swā wē be twelfhyndum tealdan, L. E. G. 13; Th. i. 174, 13-14, 176, 3. Gif wylisc mon hæbbe hīde londes, his wer bið .cxx. scill.; gif hē hæbbe healfe, .lxxx. scill.; gif hē nǣnig hæbbe, .lx. scillinga, L. In. 32; Th. i. 122, 9 (cf. Wealh, gif hē hafaþ fīf hȳda, hē bið syxhynde, 24; Th. i. 118, 10. Wealh gafolgelda, .cxx. scill.; his sunu, .c.; ðeówne, .lx.; somhwelcne, fīftegum, 22; Th. i. 118, 3). **I.** when a person was wrongfully (for other cases v. ǣ-gilde) slain, the *wer* of the slain man could be claimed from the slayer (cf. wer-gild, I), who was bound to furnish security for the payment, and the date for the first instalment of such payment was fixed. According to a law of Cnut the slain man must have been in a hundred and in a tithing to make the claim for the *wer* valid:—Gif man ofslægen weorðe, gylde hine man swā hē geboren sȳ. And riht is ðæt se slaga, siþþan hē weres beweddod hæbbe, finde ðǣrtō wærborh . . . be ðam ðe ðǣrto gebyrige; ðæt is æt twelfhyndum were gebyriaþ twelf men tō werborge, .viii. fæderemmǣgðe, and .iiii. mēdrenmǣgðe. Ðonne ðæt gedōn sȳ, ðonne rǣre man cyninges munde. (*Then at intervals of twenty-one days* healsfang, manbōt, fyhtwīte *respectively were to be paid.*) Ðæs (*the payment of* fyhtwīte) on .xxi. nihtan ðæs weres ðæt frumgyld, and swā forð ðæt forgolden sȳ on ðam fyrste ðe witan gerǣden, L. E. G. 13; Th. i. 174, 15-29. Be fǣhðe. Ǣrest æfter folcrihte slaga sceal his forspecan on hand syllan, and se forspeca māgum, ðæt se slaga wille bētan wið mǣgðe. Ðonne syþþan gebyreþ ðæt man sylle ðæs slagan forspecan on hand, ðæt se slaga mōte mid griðe nȳr and sylf wæres weddian. (*The proceedings are then as in the preceding extract, with the exception that* fyhtwīte *is not mentioned; so that the first payment of* wer *is made twenty-one days earlier*), L. Edm. S. 7; Th. i. 250, 12-21. Wē wyllaþ ðæt ǣlc freó man beó on hundrede and on teóðunge gebrōht ðe lāde wyrðe beón wylle oþþe weres wyrðe, gif hine hwā āfylle ofer .xii. wintre, L. C. S. 20; Th. i. 386, 21. Be swā ofslægenes monnes were. Gif mon ðæs ofslægenan weres bidde, L. In. 21; Th. i. 116, 3-4. Gif mon twyhyndne mon unsynnigne mid hlōðe ofsleá, gielde se ðæs sleges andetta sié wer . . . Gif hit sié syxhynde . . . se slaga wer . . . Gif hē sié twelfhynde . . . se slaga wer . . . Gif hlōð ðis gedō . . . ealle forgielden ðone wer gemǣnum hondum, L. Alf. pol. 29-31; Th. i. 80, 6-17: 36; Th. i. 84, 13, 14. Gif mon beforan cyninges ealdormen on gemōte gefeohte, bēte wer and wīte swā hit ryht sié, and beforan đām .cxx. scill. đam ealdormen tō wīte, 38; Th. i. 86, 14. **I a.** of those who were concerned in the receiving of the *wer* the following passages speak; see also wer-gild, **I a**:—Se wer (*a king's*) gebiraþ māgum, L. Wg. 1; Th. i. 186, 4: L. M. L.; Th. i. 190, 8. Gif mon elþeódigne ofsleá, se cyning āh twǣdne dǣl weres, þriddan dǣl sunu oþþe mágas. Gif hē mǣgleás sié, healf kyningc, healf se gesīđ, L. In. 23; Th. i. 116, 15. Se đe dearnenga bearn gestriéneþ and gehileþ, nāh se his deáđes wer, ac his hlāford and se cyning, 27; Th. i. 120, 3. Se forspeca sceal māgum on hand syllan, đæt se slaga wille bētan wiđ mǣgđe, L. Edm. S. 7; Th. i. 250, 15. **I b.** those concerned in the payment of the *wer* are referred to in the following:—Gif fædrenmǣga mǣgleás mon gefeohte and mon ofsleá, and đonne gif hē mēdrenmǣgas hæbbe, gielden đa đæs weres þriddan dǣl, þriddan dǣl đa gegyldan, for þriddan dǣl hē fleó. Gif hē mēdrenmǣgas nāge, gieldan đa gegildan healfne, for healfne hē fleó, L. Alf. pol. 27; Th. i. 78, 22. **I c.** of the form in which payment might be made see the following; see also wer-gild, **I b**:—En la were purra il rendre cheual pur .xx. sol., e tor pur .x. sol., e uer pur .v. sol., Wil. I, 9; Th. i. 470, 16. **II.** in cases other than death the whole or part of the injured person's *wer* could be claimed:—Gif se hund mā (*more than three*) misdǣda gewyrce, and hē (*the owner*) hine hæbbe, bēte be fullan were, L. Alf. pol. 23; Th. i. 78, 7. Gif man æt unlagum man bewǣpnige . . . and gif hine man gebinde, forgilde be healfan were, L. C. S. 61; Th. i. 408, 20. **III.** in case of certain crimes the *wer* of the criminal was exacted as a penalty; see also wer-gild, **II**:—Æt nānum bōtwyrđum gylte ne forwyrce man māre đonne his wer, L. Edg. ii. 2; Th. i. 266, 13. Gif mon sié wertyhtlan betogen . . . bīde mon . . . ōþ đæt se wer gegolden sié, L. In. 71; Th. i. 148, 4. Gif hwā æt þeófe mēdsceatt nime, and ōđres ryht āfylle, beó hē his weres scyldig, L. Ath. i. 17; Th. i. 208, 16. Gif hwā flȳman feormige, sȳ hē his weres scyldig, būtan hē hine lādian durre be đæs flȳman were, đæt hē hine flȳman nyste, 20; Th. i. 210, 12. Gielde hē hine (*the fugitive*) his āgenum were, L. In. 30; Th. i. 122, 1. Gif hwā ǣnigra godcundra gerihta forwyrne . . . and gif hē wigie and man gewundie, beó his weres scyldig, L. E. G. 6; Th. i. 170, 9. Gif hwā cristendōm wyrde oþþe hǣđendōm weorđige, wordes oþþe weorces, gylde swā wer swā wīte swā lahslitte, L. E. G. 2; Th. i. 168, 2: L. Eth. v. 31; Th. i. 312, 10. Đā bæd Byrhferđ ealdormann Æđelstān his wer for đam tēmbyrste, Chart. Th. 207, 3. **III a.** to whom, and by whom, the wer was paid is seen in the following:—Gif hē fūl wurđe bēte đam hlāforde his were . . . Gif hē ūt hleápe, . . . gilde se borh đam hlāforde his were (*if the lord had a share in the escape, the* wer *went to the king*: Fō se cyning tō đam were) . . . Gif hē (*a lord's man*) ūt ōđhleápe, gylde se hlāford đæs mannes were đam cyninge . . . Gif him (*the lord*) seó lād byrste, gilde đam cynge his were, L. Eth. i. 1; Th. i. 280, 21-282, 14: L. C. S. 30; Th. i. 394, 7-23. Beó hē his weres scyldig wiđ đone cyning, and gif hē hit eft wyrde, gylde tuwa his were, L. C. S. 84; Th. i. 422, 10. Đæt hē (*manslaga binnon ciricwāgum*) his āgenne wer gesylle đam cyninge and Criste, L. Eth. ix. 2; Th. i. 340, 12. Ic āgife đīnne wer đam cynge, Chart. Th. 207, 11, 33: 208, 28. **III b.** the payment of the *wer* is in some cases an alternative; see also wer-gild, **II a**:—Gif þeóf sié gefongen, swelte hē deáđe, oþþe his līf be his were man āliése, L. In. 12; Th. i. 110, 8. Sȳ hē (*a false accuser*) his tungan scyldig, būton hē hine mid his were forgilde, L. C. S. 16; Th. i. 384, 26: L. Alf. pol. 32; Th. i. 82, 2. **IV.** the *wer* served as a standard by which other matters might be regulated; see also wer-gild, **III**:—Cyninges geneát, gif his wer biđ twelf hund scill., hē mōt swerian for syxtig hīda, L. In. 19; Th. i. 114, 10. Būtan hē hine lādian durre be đæs flȳman were, L. Ath. i. 20; Th. i. 210, 13. Be his āgnum were gelādige hē hine, L. In. 30; Th. i. 120, 18. Hē hine be his were geswicne, 15; Th. i. 112, 3. Æt twyhyndum were mon sceal sellan tō monbōte .xxx. scill.; æt .vi. hyndum, .lxxx. scill.; æt twelfhyndum, .cxx. scill., 70; Th. i. 146, 13. Gielden ealle ān wīte, swā tō đam were belimpe, L. Alf. pol. 31; Th. i. 80, 18. Gif hē (*a thief*) đa hand lēsan wille, . . . gelde swā tō his were belimpe, 6; Th. i. 66, 6. Weaxe sió bōt be đam were, 11; Th. i. 70, 2: L. In. 76; Th. i. 150, 15. v. þegen-wer, wer-gild.

wer (were?), es; *m. n.* (?) *A guard* (? cf. werian, waru), *a troop, band*:—Were *manipulo* (coelestis militiae manipulo, Ald. 50), Wrt. Voc. ii. 83, 2: 56, 75. In ic wæs cempena lāreów, and mid mycclum were ymbseald, nū ic eom āna forlǣten, Homl. Skt. ii. 30, 195.

wer, es; *m.* **I.** *a weir, a dam*:—Salomon sǣde đætte suīđe deóp pōl wǣre gewered on đæs wīsan monnes mōde, and suīđe lytel unnyttes ūt fleówe. Ac se se đe đone wer bricđ, and đæt wæter ūt forlǣt, se biđ fruma đæs geflites *dicitur: 'Aqua profunda verba ex ore viri,'* Prov. 18, 4. *Qui ergo dimittit aquam, caput est jurgiorum*, Past. 38; Swt. 279, 16. **II.** often the *wer* is connected with fishing, and the word seems sometimes to be used of the water that is kept in by the dam:—*Captura* (captura *locus piscosus, ubi capiuntur pisces*, Migne), *detentio, captio* hæft *vel* wer, Wrt. Voc. ii. 128, 31. Đis is đæs hagan bōc on Winceastre and đes healfan weres æt Brægentforda and đæs æcersplottes đe đǣrtō līđ (cf. dimidium cuiusdam piscarii uadum ad capturam piscium æt Bræge decurrentem, ad Uetus monasteriam pertinentem, cum unius iugeris sibi adjacentis portione, 134, 31-34), Cod. Dip. Kmbl. vi. 136, 11. Hē wundrude and ealle đa đe mid him wǣron on đam were (*in captura*) đara fixa, Lk. Skt. 5, 9. Terram cum omnibus ad se pertinentibus rebus necessariis hoc est, in siluis, in campis, in captura etiam piscium quae terrae illi adjacet, ubi sunt scilicet duo quod nostratim dicitur waeres, Cod. Dip. Kmbl. i. 64, 10. Æt ǣlcum were, đe binnan đām .xxx. hīdan is, gebyreþ ǣfre se ōđer fisc đam landhlāforde, iii. 450, 25. Andlang Ūse tō Kekan were; of Kekan were andlang Ūse tō Caluwan were, 170, 31. Mid were and mid mylene, 243, 10. Be eá tō Brihtwoldes were; of đam were tō đǣre dīc, 424, 19. On Eádmundes wer; of Eádmundes were, vi. 31, 14, 34. [Ic gife þas landes and þas wateres and meres and fennes and weres, Chr. 656; Erl. 31, 5. Ic gife þa twa dæl of Witlesmere mid watres and mid wæres and feonnes, 963; Erl. 122, 15. He set in weres (dam, *v.l.*) of watres wildernes *posuit desertum in stagnum aquae*, Ps. 106, 35. *M. H. Ger.* wer: *Ger.* wehr *a weir, dam.* Cf. *Icel.* vörr; *f. a fenced-in landing-place*; ver; *n. a fishing-place.*] v. cyt-, fisc-, ford- (Cod. Dip. Kmbl. iii. 437, 11), hæc-, mylen-wer.

wer-bǣre, es; *n. A weir where fish are caught*:—Se mylenstede and đæt land đæt đe đǣrtō hȳrđ . . . and đa werbǣra and seó mǣd be norđan eá, and đa hammas, Cod. Dip. Kmbl. v. 383, 17. Tō Cranemere, and đǣre gebyraþ tō six wærbǣre, iii. 344, 2.

wer-beám, es; *m. A strong man, warrior*:—Đā slōh mid hālige hand heofonrīces weard werbeámas (*the Egyptians in the Red Sea*), wlance đeóde, Cod. Th. 208, 20; Exod. 486. Cf. the epithets derived from words denoting trees which are applied to men in Icelandic poetry. v. Corpus Poeticum Boreale, ii. 476.

wer-bold, es; *n. Weir-building*:—Se gebūr sceal his riht dōn . . . tō werbolde .xl. mǣra ođđe ān fōđer gyrda, Cod. Dip. Kmbl. iii. 450, 37.

wer-borh; *gen.* -borges; *m. A security for the payment of* wer. v. first two passages under wer, **I**.

werc *glosses* nanus, Wrt. Voc. ii. 60, 45: 71, 36. [*Elsewhere* nanus *is rendered by* dweorh, *for which* werc *is perhaps wrongly written. Or* (?) werc *might be for* wearh. v. wearg.]

werc, wercan, wer-cweþan. v. weorc, wyrcan, wearg-cweþan.

wer-cyn[n], es; *n. Mankind*:—World wendeþ . . . wercyn (wen-, MS.) gewīteþ, Exon. Th. 354, 45; Reim. 61. Cf. wer-þeód.

werdan. v. wirdan.

węrde *glosses* opes, Kent. Gl. 864. (*For* prēde ? cf. *opes superbe* ofermōde prēde, 249.)

were, wered *a troop*, wered *sweet*, were-mōd. v. wer, weorod *a troop*, weorod *sweet*, wer-mōd.

were-wulf, es; *m. A wer-wolf, a fiend*:—Đæt se wōdfreca werewulf tō swȳđe ne slīte, ne tō fela ābīte of godcundre heorde, L. C. E. 26; Th. i. 374, 30: L. I. P. 6; Th. ii. 310, 30: Wulfst. 191, 16.

wer-fǣhþ, e; *f. Slaying, in pursuing the feud, under circumstances that call for the payment of* wer [cf. L. Alf. pol. 42: Be fǣhđum . . . Gif hē (*a man's foe*) wille on hond gān and his wǣpenu sellan, and hwā ofer đæt on him feohte, gielde swā wer swā wunde, swā hē gewyrce, Th. i. 90, 19]:—Be werfǣhđe tyhtlan. Se đe biđ werfǣhđe betogen, and hē onsacan wille đæs sleges mid āđe, L. In. 54; Th. i. 136, 9-11. Ǣlc mon mōt onsacan werfǣhđe gif hē mæg oþþe dear, 46; Th. i. 132, 1.

werg, wergan *to defend*, wergan *to curse*, wergend *a protector*, wergend *malignans*. v. wearg, werian, wirgan, weriend, wirgend.

wer-genga, an; *m. A stranger who seeks protection in the land to which he has come*:—Deóra gesīđ, wildra wærgenga, Nabochodonossor *the beasts' comrade, the stranger that sought shelter among wild beasts, Nebuchadnezzar*, Cd. Th. 257, 25; Dan. 663. Gif eów Dryhten Crist lȳfan wylle, đæt gē his wergengan (*Guthlac, who had Christ's protection in the wilderness.* Cf. Ic mē friđ wille æt Gode gegyrnan . . . mec Dryhtnes hond mundaþ . . . hēr sceal mīn wesan eorđlīc ēþel, 117, 23-30; Gū. 228-232. Nū ic đis lond gestāg . . . mē friđe healdeþ . . . se đe mægna gehwæs wealdeþ, 120, 28-121, 3; Gū. 278-283) in đone lāđan lēg lǣdan mōste, Exon. Th. 137, 29; Gū. 536: 144, 28; Gū. 685. [*The Latinized* wargangus *occurs in the Lombard laws*: Omnes wargangi, qui de exteris finibus in regni nostri finibus advenerint. *And* wargengus *among the Franks*: Si quis wargengum occiderit. v. Grff. iv. 103: Grmm. R. A. 396. Cf. *also Icel.* verð-gangr (ver-) *going about asking for food* (verðr).] v. waru, werian.

wergian *to curse*, wērgian *to grow weary*. v. wirgan, wērigian.

wer-, were-gild, es; *n.* [*The word seems interchangeable with* wer (q.v.), *which in the later laws is the more frequent form.*] *The price set upon a man according to his degree*:—Twelfhyndes mannes wergyld biđ six ceorla wergyld, L. O. 13; Th. i. 182, 21. Ceorles wergild (were-gild, l. 20) is .cc. and .lxvi. þrimsa, đæt biđ .ii. hund scill. be Myrcna lage, L. Wg. 6; Th. i. 186, 11. Norđleóda cynges gild .xxx. þūsend þrymsa, fīftēne þūsend þrymsa biđ đæs wergildes (wæres, l. 16), 1; Th. i. 186, 2. (The wergilds for other ranks are given in the sections of this article.)

Ceorles wergild is on Myrcna lage .cc. scill. Ðegnes wergild is syx swā mycel, ðæt bið .xii. hund scill. Ðonne bið cynges ānfeald wergild .vi. þegna wer be Myrcna lage, ðæt is .xxx. þūsend sceatta, and ðæt bið ealles .cxx. punda. Swā mycel is ðæs wergildes on folces folcrihte be Myrcna lage, L. M. L.; Th. i: 190, 2–7. Cyninges horswealh, se ðe him mæge geǣrendian, ðæs wergield bið .cc. scill., L. In. 33; Th. i. 122, 14. **I.** when a person was wrongfully slain the *wergild* of the slain man could be claimed from the slayer. Cf. wer, **I**:—Gif man leúd ofsleá an þeófðe, licge būtan wyrgelde, L. Wih. 25; Th. i. 42, 13. Se .vii. nihta mōna is gōd on tō fixianne, and æðeles monnes wergild an tō manianne, Lchdm. iii. 178, 14. **I a.** for those who were concerned in the receiving of the *wergild* see wer, **I a**, and the following:—Gif man his mæn freólse gefe, . . . freólsgefa āge his erfe ænde wergeld, L. Wih. 8; Th. i. 38, 16. (See also the cases quoted under **IV**.) **I b.** as to the form which the payment might take see wer, **I c**, and the following:—Mōt hē gesellan monnan and byrnan and sweord on ðæt wergild, L. In. 54; Th. i. 138, 1. (Cf. for similar payment: Mid .lx. scill. gebēte . . . and ðæt sié on cwicǣhtum, and mon nǣnigne mon on ðæt ne selle, L. Alf. pol. 18; Th. i. 72, 12.) Tō ðam ðæt hió hyre brōðra wergild gecure on swylcum þingum swylce hyre and hire nȳhstan freóndum sēlost līcode. And hió ðā swā dyde ðæt hió ðæt wergeld geceás on ðam īglande ðe Teneð is nemned, ðæt is hundeahtatig hīda landes ðe hió ðǣr æt ðæm cyninge onfeóng, Lchdm. iii. 426, 16–21. **II.** in case of certain crimes the criminal's *wergild* was exacted as a penalty, v. wer, **III**:—Gif frī man wið frīes mannes wīf geligeþ, his wergelde ābicge, L. Ethb. 31; Th. i. 10, 6. Forgielde hē hine selfa be his wergilde, L. Alf. pol. 7; Th. i. 66, 12. **II a.** the payment of the *wergild* is in some cases an alternative, v. wer, **III b**:—Sī þreóra ān for his feore . . . wergild, ēce þeówet, hengenwītnung, L. Eth. vii. 16; Th. i. 332, 18. Þolige hē līfes oþþe wæregildes (were-, *v.l.*), L. C. S. 62; Th. i. 408, 23. Wealde se cyning þreóra ǣnes; oþþe hine man cwelle, oþþe ofer sǣ selle, oþþe hine his wergelde āliése, L. Wih. 26; Th. i. 42, 17. Hē hine be his wergilde āliése, oþþe be his were geswicne, L. In. 15; Th. i. 112, 2. Hē bið feorhscyldig, nimþe him se cyning ālȳfan wille ðæt man wergylde ālȳsan mōte, L. Eth. vii. 15; Th. i. 332, 15. **II b.** of the uses to which *wergild* paid as a fine in religious matters (cf. L. E. G. 2; Th. i. 168, 1–3) could be applied see the following:—Gif for godbōtan feohbōt ārīseþ, ðæt gebyreþ rihtlīce . . . tō godcundan neódan (*these are enumerated in the section*); hwīlum be wīte, hwīlum be wergilde (*at times the* feohbōt *is in the form of* wergild), L. Eth. vi. 51; Th. i. 328, 4–10. **III.** the *wergild* served as a standard by which other matters might be regulated, v. wer, **IV**:—Se ðe on ðære fōre wǣre ðǣr mon monnan ofslōge, getriéwe hine ðæs sleges, and ða fōre gebēte be ðæs ofslegenan wergielde. Gif his wergield sié .cc. scill., gebēte mid .l. scill., and ða ilcan riht dō man be ðām deórborenum, L. In. 34; Th. i. 124, 1. Twelfhyndes mannes āð forstent .vi. ceorla āð, for ðam . . . his wergyld bið six ceorla wergyld, L. O. 13; Th. i. 182, 21. Gif hē hine selfne triówan wille, dō ðæt be cyninges wergelde, L. Alf. pol. 4; Th. i. 64, 2. Gif hē lādian wille, dō ðæt be ðæs cynges wergilde, oþþe mid þryfealdan ordāle, L. Eth. v. 30; Th. i. 312, 7. Gylde ðam cyninge be his weregilde (wer-, *v.l.*), L. C. S. 67; Th. i. 410, 17. In the following case the *wergild* seems to have suggested the amount of a bequest to the church:—Hió (*the testator's wife*) gebrenge æt Sancte Petre mīn twā wergild, gif ðet Godes wille seó ðæt heó ðæt færeld āge, Chart. Th. 481, 10. **IV.** instances of the payment of *wergild* are the following. The two young princes Æþelred and Æþelbriht were slain by Thunor, and to their sister eighty hides of land was given as *wergild*, Lchdm. iii. 424–6. In the war between Ecgfriþ and Æþelred the former's brother was slain. Theodore brought about peace between them 'ðæt nǣniges mannes feorh tō lore wearþ, ne māre blōdgyte wæs for ðam ofslægenan cyninges brēðer, ac hē mid feó wiþ hine geþingode, ðæt heora sib wæs,' Bd. 4, 21; S. 590, 24. In 687 Mul, Ceadwalla's brother, was burnt in Kent: in 694 'Cantware geþingodon wiþ Īne, and him gesaldon xxx m̄., for ðon ðe hīe ǣr Mul forbærndon, Chr. 694; Erl. 42, 15. [*O. Frs.* wer-geld, -ield: *O. H. Ger.* wer-, weri-gelt *fiscus, pretium.* Cf. *Icel.* mann-gjöld; *pl.*] Cf. leód, leód-gild; *and see* Kemble's Saxons in England, vol. i. c. x, Grmm. R. A. 650.

wergild-þeóf, es; *m. A thief whose* wergild *was paid as a punishment for his crime* [cf. Gif þeóf sié gefongen, swelte hē deáðe, oþþe his līf be his were man āliése, L. In. 12; Th. i. 110, 8]:—Be wergeldþeófes forefonge. Gif mon wergildþeóf gefēhð, and hē losige ðȳ dæge ðām monnum ðe hine gefōð, þeáh hine mon gefō ymb niht, nāh him mon māre æt ðonne ful wīte, L. In. 72; Th. i. 148, 5–8. At omni tributo publicalium rerum et ab expeditionalibus causis et a cunctis operibus uel regis uel principis sit terra in perpetuam libera, ita ut nec pontem nec arcem facere debeant, nec de furtis aliquam poenam soluere, nec etiam fures illos quos Saxonice uuergeldtheouas alicui foras reddant; sed si capiantur, in illorum dominio sunt habendi, Cod. Dip. Kmbl. i. 172, 7: 14. ¶ the word is also used to denote the right to receive the wergilds paid in cases of theft; cf. the preceding passage:—Huic libertati concedo additamentum, in qua, ut ab omnibus apertius et plenius intelligatur, nomina consuetudinum Anglice praecepi ponere: scilicet, mundbryche, . . . flȳmena fyrmðe, wergeldþeóf, ūðleáp (cf. wer, **III a**), . . . fyrdwīte . . ., aliasque omnes leges et consuetudines quae ad me pertinent, Chart. Th. 411, 26–34.

wergness, wergulu, wergum, Cd. Th. 267, 22; Sat. 42, wergþu, wergung. v. weargnes, wirgness, weargol, wearh; *m.* (?), wirgþu, wirgung.

wer-hād, es; *m. The male sex*:—Werhād oððe wīfhad *sexus*, Ælfc. Gr. 11; Zup. 78, 16: Wrt. Voc. i. 50, 7: 70, 19. Werhādes man *mas* vel *masculus*, 70, 17. Ælc werhādes man *omne masculinum* . . . se werhādes man *masculus*, Gen. 17, 12, 24. Ealle werhādes men *omnes viri*, 17, 27. Werhādes and wīfhādes hē gesceóp hig *masculum et feminam creavit eos*, 1, 27. Werhādes men ongunnon ðone dreám, and wīfhādes men him sungon ongeán, Homl. Th. ii. 548, 11. Ðæt hī heora clǣnnesse healdan be heora hāde, swā werhādes swā wīfhādes, swā hwæðer swā hit sȳ, L. Edm. E. 1; Th. i. 244, 11.

werh-brǣde, werhte, weria. v. wearg-brǣde, wærcan, wearg.

werian, wergan; *p.* ede. **I.** *to hinder, check, restrain*:—Stān sēpte sacerdas sweotolum tācnum, witig werede, and worde cwæð, Andr. Kmbl. 1485; An. 744. Egesan stōdon, weredon wælnet (*deadly toils hampered* (?)), Cd. Th. 190, 20; Exod. 202. Ic wylle ðæt ǣlc man hæbbe symle ða men gearowe on his lande, ðe lǣden ða men ðe heora āgen sēcan willen, and hȳ for nānum mēdsceattum ne werian, L. Ed. 7; Th. i. 162, 25. **I a.** *to dam* water. v. wering:—Sume weriaþ on gewitlocan wīsdōmes streám, welerum gehæftaþ, ðæt hē on unnyt ūt ne tōflōweþ, Past. 65; Swt. 469, 2. **II.** *to keep off, drive away*:—Wereth *abiget*, Wrt. Voc. ii. 98, 18. **II a.** *to keep off* something from a person (*dat.*), *to keep* a person (*dat.*) *from* something (*acc.*). v. warian, **IV**:—Ic mīnum fōtum fǣcne·sīðas werede *ab omni mala via prohibui pedes meos*, Ps. Th. 118, 101. Ǣgðer ōðrum trymede heofonrīces hyht, helle wītu wordum werede (cf. gihēt im hebanrīki endi helleógethwing werida mid wordun, Hēl. 2082), Andr. Kmbl. 2107; An. 1055. **III.** *to defend, resist attack upon*:—God geseah his (*St. Paul's*) geðanc, ðæt hē ēhte geleáffulra manna ðurh ware ðære ealdan ǣ, and hine gespræc:—'Saule . . . ic eom seó sōðfæstnys ðe ðū werast,' Homl. Th. i. 390, 8. Hē unheánlīce hine werede, Chr. 755; Erl. 48, 33. His rīce hē heardlīce werode ða hwīle ðe his tīma wæs, 1016; Erl. 155, 6. Hū his seó mycle hand on gewindæge werede and ferede *qua die manus ejus liberavit eos de manu tribulantis*, Ps. Th. 77, 42. Hē under segne sinc ealgode, wælreáf werede, Beo. Th. 2414; B. 1205. Wē on orlege hafelan weredon, 2658; B. 1327. Hī cēne hī weredon, Byrht. Th. 140, 5; By. 283. Ðā hē (*Peter*) his Drihten werian wolde, L. Ælfc. P. 51; Th. ii. 386, 22. Gif hē hine werian wille, L. Ath. i. 1; Th. i. 198, 20: v. 12, 1; Th. i. 240, 29: 3; Th. i. 242, 10. Utan līf and land ealle werian, L. Eth. v. 35; Th. i. 312, 22: Chr. 1010; Erl. 144, 8. Burh werian, Blickl. Homl. 79, 16. Wīgsteal wergan, Exon. Th. 315, 31; Mōd. 39. Ealle ða ðe hié wergan noldon, Chr. 921; Erl. 107, 4. **III a.** *to defend* against, (1) with dat.:—Ðonne hand wereþ feorhhord feóndum, Wald. 99; Vald. 2, 21. Hī woldon burh wrāðum werian, Cd. Th. 119, 7; Gen. 1976. Wergan ēþelstōl Ætlan leódum, Exon. Th. 325, 34; Vīd. 121. (2) with prep. *wið*:—Ða hī fæstlīce wið ða fȳnd weredon, Byrht. Th. 134, 11; By. 82. Wit unc wið hronfixas werian þōhton, Beo. Th. 1086; B. 541. Breóstnet wera wið feónd folmum werigean, Cd. Th. 192, 26; Exod. 237. **III b.** *to defend* at law:—Se ðe on gemōte mid wiðertihtlan hine sylfne oþþe his man werige, L. C. S. 27; Th. i. 392, 6. Se Englisca hine werige mid orneste oþþe mid īrene . . . Gif se Englisca nele hine werian mid orneste oþþe mid gewitnesse, hē lādige hine mid īrene, L. W. ii. 2; Th. i. 489, 13–19. Werige hine se Frǣncisca mid unforedan āþe, 3; Th. i. 489, 24. Se ðe can mid leásungan wæwerdlīce werian, and mid unsōðe sōð oferswīðan, Wulfst. 169, 1. **III c.** in the phrase *werian land* the word refers to the performance of services that might be demanded from the holders of land:—Werige (*the Latin version has* adquietet) se cotsetla his hlāfordes inland, gif him man beóde, æt sǣwearde and æt cyniges deórhege and æt swilcan ðingan swilc his mǣð sȳ, L. R. S. 3; Th. i. 432, 27. v. Kemble's Saxons in England, i. 323. ¶ the phrase commonly occurs where an assessment is made for a smaller number of hides than those actually held, and is retained in Domesday Book in the Latin *defendere pro* (a certain number of hides):—Hē geūðe ðæt man ðæt land on eallum þingon for āne hīde werode, swā swā his yldran hit ǣr gesetton and gefreódon, wǣre ðǣr māre landes, wǣre ðǣr læsse . . . Ealles ðæs landes is an hund hīda: ac ða gōdan cynegas . . . ǣlc æfter ōðran, ðæt ylce land swā gefreódon Gode tō lofe and his þeówan tō bryce intō fōstorlande, ðæt hit man ǣfre on ende for āne hīde werian sceolde, Cod. Dip. Kmbl. iii. 112, 5–24. Nū wille ic ðæt hit man on eallum þingon for āne hīde werige . . . sȳ ðǣr māre landes, sȳ ðēr lesse (*there were* 578 *hides*), 203, 16. Hē werige for twā hīda, iv. 262, 15. Ic wylle ðæt Ǣðelnōð arcebisceop werige his landāre nū, ealswā hē dyde ǣr Ǣgelrīc wǣre gerēfa, vi. 187, 19. Ðæt mon ælles ðises freólses āre ǣfre for āne hīde werian scolde; for ðam ðe Godes ār ǣfre freogre beón sceal ðonne ǣnig woruldār, v. 113, 33. **IV.** *to protect, guard from wrong* or *injury*, (1) of persons:—God, se ðās fyrd wereþ, Cd. Th. 195, 10; Exod. 274. Gif man ofsleá ōþerne for neóde ðǣr hē his hlāfordes ceáp werige *si quis alium occiderit ex necessitate*, *ubi rem domini sui tuebatur*, L. Ecg. C. 24; Th. ii. 150, 5. Ðæt hē (*a king*) Godes cyrcan weorþige and werige, L. I. P. 2; Th. ii. 304, 26. Ðæt hī Godes þeówas symle werian and weordian, L. Eth. vi. 45; Th. i. 326, 23. Hȳ sculan cyrican wyrdian and werian, L. I. P. 11; Th. ii. 318, 25: 25; Th. ii. 338, 30. Manig strec man wyle, gif hē mæg and mōt, werian his man swā hwæder him þincd dæt hē hine eád āwerian mæge, L. C. S. 20; Th. i. 388, 2. (1a) with dat.:—Ðū mē weredest wrāþum feóndum, de mē woldon yrre on ācȳdan, Ps. Th. 137, 7. (2) of things:—Beaduscrūda betst, dæt mīne breóst wereþ, Beo. Th. 911; B. 453. Se hwīta helm hafelan werede, 2901; B. 1448. **V.** *to hold, occupy.* v. warian, **III a**:—Ða de onhǣle eardas weredon, Exon. Th. 123, 14; Gū. 322. [Ich wolle dat Gyso bisschop werie (*possideat*) now hiss lond also his forgenge aforen hym er dude, Cod. Dip. Kmbl. iv. 195, 14.] [Ic eou wulle werien wid elcne herm, O. E. Homl. i. 13, 20. I compe hine werien, Laym. 8288. Weorien heom mid wepnen, 21289. Þu mihht werenn þe fra þeȝȝm, Orm. 1406. Scheld to werien ham mide, A. R. 52, 5. Were þe agean me, 400, 7. Foyne if him lust on foote himself to were, Chauc. Kn. T. 1692. *Goth.* warjan *prohibere*: *O. Sax.* werian: *O. Frs.* wera: *O. H. Ger.* werien *prohibere, cohibere, inhibere, resistere, defendere, vetare, abnuere, abigere*: *Icel.* verja *to defend.*] v. ā-, be-, ge-werian; un-wered; warian.

werian; *p.* ede, ode. **I.** *to clothe* with a garment:—Līc dæt hē ǣr werede mid wǣdum, Exon. Th. 374, 14; Seel. 126. Hié heora līchoman leáfum beþeahton, weredon mid dȳ wealde, Cd. Th. 52, 19; Gen. 846. Hwæt sindon gē searohæbbendra byrnum werede, Beo. Th. 481; B. 238: 5052; B. 2529. Hī lifgaþ ā leóhte werede, Exon. Th. 237, 26; Ph. 596. **II.** *to wear* a garment, *wear* or *bear* a weapon, etc.:—Ðæt hālie reáf, dæt Aaron wereþ *vestem sanctam, qua utetur Aaron*, Ex. 29, 29. Se woruldkempa weraþ woruldlīce wǣpna, Basil adm. 2; Norm. 34, 31. Ðe mā de se wer weraþ wīmmanna gyrlan, L. Ælfc. C. 35; Th. ii. 358, 10. Hit næs þeáw mid him dæt ǣnig ōþer purpuran werede būton cyningum, Ors. 4, 4; Swt. 164, 35: 6, 31; Swt. 284, 23. Heó wyllen weorode, Homl. Skt. i. 20, 44. Ðæt reáf, dæt se Hǣlend werede, Homl. Ass. 189, 249. Seó cwēn werode cynehelm on heáfode, 93, 38. Ða purpuran ālecgan, da hié weredon, Ors. 6, 30; Swt. 280, 21. Ðam folce wæs gewunelīc, dæt hī weredon bȳman on ǣlcum gefeohte, Jud. 7, 16. Deóplīc dǣdbōt bid dæt lǣwede man . . . wyllen werige, L. Pen. 10; Th. ii. 280, 20. Werige gehwā swā his hāde tō gebyrige, dæt se preóst ne werige munucscrūd, ne lǣwedra manna, L. Ælfc. C. 35; Th. ii. 358, 7–9. Ne preóst wǣpna ne werige, 30; Th. ii. 354, 3. Ne mōt preóst wǣpnu werian mid rihte . . . Nū secgaþ sume preóstas dæt hī for neóde wǣpn mōton werian, L. Ælfc. P. 50, 51; Th. ii. 386, 13–21. Gyldenne hring werian, Ors. 4, 9; Swt. 190, 15. Gyrlan werian, Homl. Ass. 115, 427. Wǣpen wegan (werian, *v. l.*) *arma ferre*, Bd. 2, 13; S. 517, 7. Reáf tō werigenne *vestimentum ad induendum*, Gen. 28, 20. Hrægl tō werianne, L. Alf. 36; Th. i. 52, 25. **II a.** in reference to the hair, *to wear* a beard, etc.:—Leófgār . . . Haroldes eorles mæssepreóst werede his kenepas on his preósthāde ōd dæt hē wæs biscop. Se forlēt . . . his gāstlīcan wǣpna, and fēng tō his spere and tō his sweorde æfter his biscuphāde, Chr. 1056; Erl. 190, 24. [The verb is weak in Chaucer and Wicklif. *Goth.* wasjan *to clothe*: *O. H. Ger.* werien *vestire*: *Icel.* verja *to clothe.*] v. ge-werian; for-, scīr-, swegel-wered (-od).

werian; *p.* ode *To remain, continue, live*:—Ic cȳde eów, dæt ic wylle dæt Giso bisceop weryge on his lande æt Chyw ælswō hys foregenga ætforen him ǣr dyde *sciatis me uelle quod Giso episcopus possideat terram suam apud Chyw sicut fecerunt praedecessores sui*, Cod. Dip. Kmbl. iv. 196, 24. (Cf. werian *to defend*, **V.**) [*O. L. Ger.* werōn *esse, subsistere*: *O. H. Ger.* werēn *manere, remanere, subsistere, durare*: *Ger.* währen.] v. warian *to remain*; wesan.

weriend, werigend, es; *m. A defender, protector*:—Ic eom dīn wergend *ego protector tuus sum*, Gen. 15, 1. Utan lufian ūre cyrican, for dam heó bid ūre friidiend and werigend, Wulfst. 239, 7. Hig woldon sumne weriend habban, de hī geheólde wid dæt hǣdene folc, Ælfc. T. Grn. 6, 43. v. be-werigend.

werig. v. wearg.

wērig; *adj.* **I.** physical, *weary, tired, exhausted, fatigued*:—Ðā hē wæs wērig (uoerig, Lind.: woerig, Rush.) gegān *fatigatus ex itinere*, Jn. Skt. 4, 6: Bd. 3, 9; S. 534, 10. Sesirra arn ōd dæt hē wērig becom tō ānum wīfmen æt nēhstan, Jud. 4, 17: Cd. Th. 88, 9; Gen. 1462. Wērig sceal se wiþ winde rōweþ, Exon. Th. 345, 12; Gn. Ex. 187: 307, 26; Seef. 29. Ne forlǣt dū dæs blōdes tō fela on ǣnne sīþ, dȳ les se seóca man tō wērig (*exhausted*) weorde odde swylte, Lchdm. ii. 208, 19. Wǣgdeóra gehwylc wērig swelteþ, Exon. Th. 61, 22; Cri. 988. Mōyses willa ne āteorode, ac se wēriga līchama, Homl. Skt. i. 13, 40. Mōises handa wǣron wērige (*graves*), Ex. 17, 12. Fēdan sǣton, reste gefēgon wērige æfter wǣde, Andr. Kmbl. 1185; An. 593. Wērge, Exon. Th. 115, 2; Gū. 183. Limseóce, wērige, wanhāle, Andr. Kmbl. 1159; An. 580. Wērge, Exon. Th. 92, 13; Cri. 1508. Ða wēregan neát de man drīfeþ and þirsceþ, Elen. Kmbl. 714; El. 357. **I a.** where the source of weariness is given, (1) with gen., *weary of* or from doing something:—Wērig dæs weorces, Exon. Th. 436, 20; Rā. 55, 10. Sīþes wērig, Beo. Th. 1162; B. 579. Sīdes wērgum, feorrancundum, 3593; B. 1794. (2) with dat. inst., *exhausted* by suffering:—Īserne wund, beadoweorca sæd, ecgum wērig, Exon. Th. 388, 5; Rä. 6, 3. Wundum wērig, Andr. Kmbl. 2557; An. 1280. Wītum wērig, Cd. Th. 274, 30; Sat. 162: 291, 9; Sat. 428. Wītum wērige, 285, 25; Sat. 343. Wīgend cruncon wundum wērige, Byrht. Th. 140, 44; By. 303. Wundum wērge, Beo. Th. 5866; B. 2937. **II.** *weary* at heart, *sad, grieved*:—Ne mæg wērig mōd wyrde widstondan, ne se hreó hyge helpe gefremman *a soul that is sad may not stand against fate, nor the mind that mourns minister help*, Exon. Th. 287, 16; Wand. 15. On wērigum sefan, 74, 18; Cri. 1208. Sendan wērigne sefan, 289, 33; Wand. 57. Hē hafaþ wilde mōd, wērige heortan, Salm. Kmbl. 756; Sal. 377. Woldan wērigu wīf wōpe bimǣnan æþelinges deád, Exon. Th. 459, 23; Hö. 4. Wērigra wraþu, 183, 34; Gū. 1337. Eálā dū de eart sió hēhste frōfer eallra wērigra mōda *O! summum lassorum solamen animorum*, Bt. 22, 1; Fox 76, 9. **III.** *that expresses sadness, weary, grievous*:—Hē wēpende wēregum teárum his sigedryhten sārgan reorde grētte, Andr. Kmbl. 118; An. 59. Beornas wēpaþ wērgum stefnum, heáne, hygegeómre, Exon. Th. 61, 32; Cri. 993. **IV.** *weary, impatient of the continuance* of anything painful:—Sunu mīn, ne āgiémeleása dū Godes suingan, ne dū ne beó wērig for his dreáunge (*neither be weary of his correction*; neque fatigeris, cum ab eo argueris, Prov. 3, 11), Past. 36; Swt. 253, 3. [*O. Sax.* sīd-wōrig *weary with travel*: *O. H. Ger.* wōrag *crapulatus.*] v. ādl-, deáþ-, drinc-, ferhþ-, fyl-, gūþ-, headu-, hrā-, lid-, lim-, medu-, mere-, rād-, sǣ-, slǣp-, symbel-, un-wērig.

werig(e)an *to curse*, werigend. v. wirgan, weriend.

wērig-ferhþ; *adj. Weary-hearted, disconsolate, depressed*:—Ongan geómormōd tō Gode cleopian . . . weóp wērigferd, Andr. Kmbl. 2799; An. 1402. Hī hreówigmōde wurpon hyra wǣpen of dūne, gewitan him wērigferhþe on fleám sceacan, Jud. Thw. 25, 24; Jud. 291. Wērigferde . . . reónigmōde, Exon. Th. 361, 14; Wal. 19.

wērigian; *p.* ode *To grow weary, get exhausted*:—Ðonne dæt deófol swīde wērgaþ, hit sēceþ scyldiges mannes nȳten, odde unclǣne treów, Salm. Kmbl. p. 148, 8. Hingrian, dyrstan, hātian, cēlan, wērigean (wǣrigean, Bd. M. 78, 22), eall dæt is of untrumnysse dæs gecyndes *esurire, sitire, aestuare, algere, lassescere, ex infirmitate naturae est*, Bd. 1, 27; S. 494, 15. Ðā ongan his hors semninga wērian (wērgian, Bd. M. 178, 19) and gestandan *equus subito lassescere et consistere coepit*, 3, 9; S. 533, 31. Hweriende *aegrotantibus, infirmantibus*, Hpt. Gl. 478, 37.

werig-līc, -līce. v. wearg-līc, -līce.

wērig-mōd; *adj. Weary in spirit*:—Ic wērigmōd wann and cleopode *laboravi clamans*, Ps. Th. 68, 3: Andr. Kmbl. 2732; An. 1368: Beo. Th. 1692; B. 844: 3090; B. 1543. Mīn freónd siteþ under stānhlide, . . . wine wērigmōd . . . dreógeþ se mīn wine micle mōdceare, Exon. Th. 444, 18; Kl. 49. Gewīteþ wērigmōd, wintrum gebysgad, 227, 24; Ph. 428. Gewītaþ āwyrgde, wērigmōde, 117, 19: Gū. 226.

wērigness, e; *f. Weariness, lassitude*:—Mōyses wērignyss (v. Ex. 17, 12), Homl. Skt. i. 13, 44. Gehwǣr is on ūrum līfe āteorung and wērignys, Homl. Th. i. 490, 7. Ðæt hors dȳ gewunelīcan þeáwe horsa æfter wērinysse (*post lassitudinem*) ongan walwian, Bd. 3, 9; S. 533, 39. Hwæt elles is tō secanne wiþ wērignysse nymþe reste, 1, 27; S. 494, 17.

wering, e; *f. A dam*:—Ðæt wæter, donne hit bid gepynd, hit fundaþ wid dæs de hit ǣr from com . . . Ac gif sió pynding wierd onpennad, odde sió wering wird tōbrocen, donne tōflēwd hit eall, Past. 38; Swt. 277, 8. v. werian, **I a**; be-werung.

wer-lād, e; *f. A* 'lād' (q.v.) *in which the number of those who supported the accused by their oaths is determined by the* 'wer' *of the accused.* [See passages under wer, **IV**, wer-gild, **III**, and L. H. I. 64, 4; Th. i. 566, 18: Si quis de homicidio accusetur, et idem se purgare velit, secundum natale suum perneget, quod est werelada.]:—Būton hē gelādige hine mid werlāde, L. C. S. 39; Th. i. 400, 1. ¶ the equivalent Latin forms *werelada negare* or *pernegare* occur several times in L. H. I.; see 12, 3; Th. i. 523, 7: 66, 1; Th. i. 569, 4: 74, 1; Th. i. 578, 22: 92, 14; Th. i. 604, 14. Other instances of the Latinized form *werelada* are:—Werelada fiat, 85, 4; Th. i. 592, 17: 88, 9; Th. i. 595, 35. Triplicem wereladam habere, 64, 1; Th. i. 566, 3.

wer-leás; *adj. Without a husband.* v. wer, **IV**:—Sitte ǣlc wydewe .xii. mōnad werleás; ceóse syþþan dæt heó sylf wille, L. Eth. v. 21; Th. i. 310, 3: vi. 26; Th. i. 322, 3: L. C. S. 74; Th. i. 416, 6: Wulfst. 271, 20.

wer-līc; *adj.* **I.** marking sex, *male.* Cf. wer-hād:—Wer *uir*, werlīc *virilis*, Ælfc. Gr. 5; Zup. 17, 17. Of werlīcum folman *sine viri vola*, Hpt. Gl. 442, 72. Hié ǣghwelcum cnihtcilde ymbsnidon dæt werlīce lim, Shrn. 47, 20. Ða werlīcan *virilia*, Wrt. Voc. i. 283, 54. **I a.** marking gender, *masculine*:—Æfter gecynde syndon twā cyn on namum, *masculinum* and *femininum*, dæt is werlīc and wīflīc. Werlīc cyn byd *hic uir* des wer. Gemǣne cyn, dæt is ǣgder ge werlīc ge wīflīc . . . *Neutrum* is nāder cynn, ne werlīces ne wīflīces, Ælfc. Gr. 6, 1–3; Zup. 18, 5–15. **II.** marking age, *that has reached man's estate.* v. wer, **II**:—Ðā hē wæs in werlīcre giúgude *in his early manhood*, Shrn. 119, 20. **III.** marking married condition, *of a husband, marital*:—

Werlîcere wrǽnnysse *maritalis lasciviae*, Hpt. Gl. 434, 61. Tô werlîcum gemânan *ad maritale consortium*, 502, 23: 442, 74. Werlîcre beclyppincge *maritali complexu*, 442, 75.

werlîce; *adv.* I. *after the manner of a male*:—Se đe đis werlîce déđ *qui hoc virili modo fecerat*, L. Ecg. P. iv. 68, 6; Th. ii. 228, 18. II. *like a man, manfully*:—Wer *uir*, werlîce *uiriliter*, Ælfc. Gr. 232, 16. Werlîce dô đû *viriliter age*, Ps. Spl. 26, 20: Ps. Surt. 26, 14. Đǽr wǽron getealde æt đam gereorde fîf đûsend wera; for đon đe đa menn, đe tô đam gâstlîcan gereorde belimpaþ, sceolon beón werlîce geworhte, swâ swâ se apostol cwæđ: 'Beóđ wacole, and standaþ on geleáfan, and onginnaþ werlîce (*quit you like men*; viriliter agite, 1 Cor. 16, 13).' Đeáh gif wîfmann biđ werlîce geworht, and strang tô Godes willan, heó biđ đonne geteald tô đâm werum đe æt Godes mýsan sittaþ, Homl. Th. i. 188, 28–34: 360, 13: 542, 25. [*Goth.* wairaleikô taujaiþ ἀνδρίζεσθε, 1 Cor. 16, 13.] v. eal-werlîce.

wêr-loga. v. wǽr-loga.

wer-mǽgþ, e; *f. A tribe* or *family of men*:—Of Cames cneórisse wôc wermǽgđa fela, Cd. Th. 98, 30; Gen. 1638: 101, 29; Gen. 1689 Cf. wer-þeód.

wer-met, es; *n. A man's measure, stature of a man*:—Tô wermete *ad staturam*, Wrt. Voc. ii. 72, 23: 8, 70. (In both cases *stauram* is printed; but the former is a gloss on Mt. 6, 27. v. Wülck. Gl. 479, 23.)

wermôd, es; *m. Wormwood*:—Wermôd (uuermôd, uermôdae) *absinthium*, Txts. 37, 35: Wrt. Voc. ii. 4, 11: i. 79, 29. Weremôd, 67, 23. Ic eom wrâþre đonne wermôd sý, Exon. Th. 425, 23; Rä. 41, 60. Wermôd. Đeós wyrt đe man *absinthium* and ôþrum naman wermôd nemneþ, Lchdm. i. 216, 17. Se fûla wermôd, ii. 312, 18. Drîges wermôdes blôstman, 250, 3. Gif hit sié sumor, dô wermôdes sǽdes dust tô . . . gif hit sié winter, ne þearft þû đone wermôd tô dôn, 180, 27. Grêne wermôd ođđe drîgne, 206, 24: 296, 13. Wring on wermôd wearmne, 310, 10. Nim wermôd nioþoweardne, 326, 10. Wærmôd, i. 206, 10. Wyrmôd, iii. 50, 17, 20. Sûþerne wermôd (*artemisia abrotanon*), ii. 34, 27: 178, 26. Đone sûþernan wermôd, đæt is prutene, and ôþerne wermôd, 236, 20. Twêgra cynna wermôd, i. 374, 6. Wyrmôd, iii. 4, 9. Wermôd drincan sace hefige getâcnaþ *to drink wormwood in a dream betokens grievous strife*, 198, 24. [Wermod *absinthium*, Wülck. Gl. 554, 11 (13th cent.): 560, 12 (15th cent.). Wormode, 645, 35 (15th cent.). Wormwod, 711, 24 (15th cent.). *Wick.* wermod: *Pall.* wermode: *O. H. Ger.* wermuota (weri-) *absinthium*: *O. L. Ger.* wermuode.]

werna. v. wrænna.

wer-nægel, es; *m. A warnel* or *wornil.* [Bailey's Dictionary gives '*warnel worms*, worms on the backs of cattle within the skin'; and in Johnson's Dictionary, ed. Latham, is quoted the following: 'In the backs of cows in the summer are maggots generated, which in Essex we call *wornils*, being first only a small knot in the skin.' Halliwell explains *wornil* as 'the larva of the gadfly growing under the skin of the back of cattle.'] :—Ân æþelboren wîf wearđ micclum geswenct mid langsumere untrumnysse, and hire ne mihte nân lǽcecræft fremian. Đâ lǽrde hî sum man đæt heó nâme ǽnne wernægel of sumes oxan hricge, and becnytte tô ânum hringe mid hire snôde, and mid đam hî tô nacedum lîce begyrde, Homl. Th. ii. 28, 17.

wernan, werod *a band*, werod *sweet*, werôd *catasta*, werold, werp, werrest, wersa, wer-scipe *prudence*, werta. v. wirnan, weorod *a band*, weorod *sweet*, wearg-rôd, weorold, wirp, wirrest, wirsa, wær-scipe, wyrhta.

wer-scipe, es; *m. Married state, estate of matrimony*:—Gebodene werscipe *oblatam matrimonii sortem*, Hpt. Gl. 490, 60.

wer-stede, es; *m. A weir-stead, place where there is a weir*:—Of đam wege on đa eá, and se werstede be sûđan hreódbricge, Cod. Dip. Kmbl. iv. 105, 11.

wertacen? :—Sagaþ Scs. Iôhannis sôđum wordum wîslîce and wærlîce swâ se wertacen (*a later rendering of the passage has* swa se wyrhte cann, 476, 66, *as if the word* = werhta cann), Engl. Stud. viii. 478, 75.

wer-þeód, e; *f.* I. *a people, nation*; *pl. nations, men*:—Wê đê freóndlîce on đisse werþeóde wîc getǽhton, Cd. Th. 162, 26; Gen. 2687: Elen. Kmbl. 1283; El. 643. On đære werþeóde, Andr. Kmbl. 273; An. 137. Đû đâs werđeóde gesôhtest, Cd. Th. 149, 21; Gen. 2478: 171, 2; Gen. 2822. In đære folcsceare geond đa weiþeóde, Elen. Kmbl. 1934; El. 969. Ongunnon wercan werþeóda (cf. leáse men, Bt. 38, 1; Fox 194, 30) spell, Met. 26, 73. Werþióda, 29, 28. Werđeóde, Cd. Th. 211, 1; Exod. 519. Đæt is đæs wyrđe, đætte werþeóde secgen Dryhtne þonc, Exon. Th. 38, 2; Cri. 600: 281, 9; Jul. 643. Waldend werþeóda, 45, 4; Cri. 714: Cd. Th. 202, 4; Exod. 383. Hê manegum wearđ geond middangeard mannum tô hrôđre, werþeódum tô wræce, Elen. Kmbl. 33; El. 17. Werþeódum Filistina, Salm. Kmbl. 424; Sal. 212. Se đe waldeþ giond werþióda ealra ôþra eorþan cyninga, Met. 24, 35. Wutun hî tôwyrpan geond werþeóda *disperdamus eos ex gente*, Ps. Th. 82, 4: 105, 19: 59, 1: Cd. Th. 61, 2; Gen. 991. Geond wærđeóda, Menol. Fox 252; Men. 127. Geond ealle werđeóda, Ps. Th. 90, 16. Geond đâs werþeóde *in omnibus gentibus*, 66, 2. Ofer werþeóda, 104, 6. Ge nêh ge feor is đîn nama hâlig ofer werþeóda, Andr. Kmbl. 1086; An. 543. Wîde geweorđod ofer werþeóda, Apstls. Kmbl. 30; Ap. 15: Beo. Th. 1802; B. 899: Exon. Th. 243, 12; Jul. 9: Lchdm. iii. 36, 24. Werþióde, Met. 9, 21. Ofer ealle werþeóde *inter gentes*, Ps. Th. 104, 1. II. *men, the world*, cf. weorold, VI a:—Hû mihte đæt gewyrđan in werþeóde (*how in the world did it happen?*), đæt đû ne gehýrde Hǽlendes miht? Andr. Kmbl. 1146; An. 573. ¶ Werđeóde glosses *nixu*, Wrt. Voc. ii. 114, 73. [*Icel.* ver-þjóđ *mankind, men.*]

wer-tihtle, an; *f. An accusation where the crime of which a person is accused involves the payment of the* wer; *the crime itself*:—Be wertyhtlan. Gif mon sié wertyhtlan betogen . . . bîde mon mid đære wîterǽdenne ôþ đæt se wer gegolden sié, L. In. 71; Th. i. 148, 1–4.

werud, weruld, werung. v. weorod, weorold, wering.

wêsa, an; *m. A soaker, one that drinks intemperately*:—Wêsan oþþe eteras *commessatores* (Prov. 28, 7), Kent. Gl. 1044. v. wêsan; ealowôsa.

wesan; *p.* wæs, *pl.* wǽron *To be*:—Wesan and beón *fore*, Wrt. Voc. ii. 34, 61. I. as an independent verb, (1) denoting existence *to be, exist*:—Wesendum, beóndum *existentibus*, Wrt. Voc. ii. 32, 63. (a) of animate objects, *to exist, live*:—Wesaþ and weaxaþ ealle werþeóde, lifgaþ bi đâm lissum đe ûs Dryhten sette, Exon. Th. 192, 30; Az. 113. On frymđe wæs word, Jn. Skt. 1, 1. God đe ǽr worulde wæs, Ps. Th. 54, 19. Đa hwîle đe hê wæs *while he lived*, Chart. Th. 167, 9. Manige hâlge wîtgan wǽran ǽr Sancte Iôhanne, Blickl. Homl. 161, 12. Đæt hê his môste brûcan, đa hwîle đe hê wǽre, Chart. Th. 140, 30. Swađer uncer leng wǽre (cf. swađer uncer leng lifede, 38), 485, 29. Swilce hê âwâr wǽre, ǽr đan đe hê geboren wǽre, ac . . . him betere wǽre, đæt hê nǽfre nǽre, đonne hê yfele wǽre, Homl. Th. ii. 244, 19. Ne mæg ic hêr leng wesan, Beo. Th. 5595; B. 2801. Hê biđ â wesende, Blickl. Homl. 19, 26. (b) of inanimate objects:—Him is eall andweard, ge đætte ǽr wæs, ge đætte nû is, ge đætte æfter ûs biđ, Bt. 42; Fox 256, 28. Ǽr woruld wǽre, Ps. Th. 73, 12. Seó þrág gewât, swâ heó nô wǽre, Exon. Th. 292, 9; Wand. 96. Hê him tô frôfre lêt forđ wesan hyrstedne hrôf, Cd. Th. 58, 33; Gen. 955. (2) where an object exists, and so may be found; where in modern English *there* precedes the verb:—Wæs đara manna . . . endleofan sîþum hund teóntig þûsenda, Blickl. Homl. 79, 17. Wǽron monge, đa đe Meotude gehýrdun, Exon. Th. 228, 24; Ph. 443. Đâ wǽron monige đe his mǽg wriđon, Beo. Th. 5956; B. 2982. Him þûhte đæt đanon wǽre tô helle duru hund þûsenda mîla, Cd. Th. 310, 7; Sat. 722. (3) denoting presence, stay of longer or shorter duration, *to be, stand, have place, dwell*:—On đære gesihđe wesaþ ealle geleáffulle, Blickl. Homl. 13, 28. Ic wæs (*I have been*) sixtýne sîđum on sǽbâte, Andr. Kmbl. 977; An. 489. Ic ongiten hæbbe đæt đû on farođstrǽte feor ne wǽre, 1796; An. 900. Wǽre đû mid đînum fæder? Blickl. Homl. 151, 26. Wôp wæs wîde, Cd. Th. 180, 8; Exod. 42. Đæt hê lête hyne licgean, đǽr hê longe wæs, Beo. Th. 6157; B. 3082. Đæt word wæs mid Gode, Jn. Skt. 1, 1. Heó wæs mid twâm werum *she lived with two husbands*, Homl. Skt. i. 20, 3. Đonne wæs hê mid his âgnum cynne, Bt. 5, 1; Fox 10, 10. Wê mid englum uppe wǽron, Cd. Th. 289, 2; Sat. 391. Đa đe đǽr ǽr inne wǽron, Bd. 4, 24; S. 598, 35. Đa đe him on neáweste wǽron, Ors. 1, 10; Swt. 46, 2. Đǽr manna wese mǽst ætgædere, Ps. Th. 78, 10. Wese ûs beorhtnes ofer, 89, 19. Wesan hî wiđ Drihtne, 108, 19. Wǽre đǽr hê wǽre, Bt. 5, 1; Fox 10, 9, 10: Elen. Kmbl. 317; El. 159. Gelimplîc wæs đæt đa ætgædere wǽron on êcre stôwe, Blickl. Homl. 133, 24. Đæt hié ongieton mîn mægen on đê wesan, 241, 15. Đara cynna monige hê wiste on Germanie wesan, Bd. 5, 9; S. 622, 14. Ne mæg hê be đý wedre wesan *he cannot stop in the open air*, Exon. Th. 340, 18; Gn. Ex. 113. Gôd is ûs hêr tô wossanne, Mt. Kmbl. Lind. 17, 4: Mk. Skt. Lind. 9, 5. Wosanne (wosane, Rush.), Lk. Skt. Lind. 9, 33: Mk. Skt. Rush. 9, 5. (4) where motion takes place:—Đâ wǽron wit twêgen on ânum olfende þurh đæt rûme wêsten, and wit unc simble ondrêdon hwonne wit sceoldon feallan of đam olfende, Shrn. 38, 14. Hî wǽron heom tô Lundene weard, Chr. 1052; Erl. 185, 4. (5) denoting condition, (a) nature of persons, *to be, live*:—Ne wosas gê swǽ lêgeras, Mt. Kmbl. Lind. 6, 5. Him betere wǽre đæt hê nǽfre nǽre, đonne hê yfele wǽre, Homl. Th. ii. 244, 21. Đonne gê fæston, nellon gê wesan (wosa, Lind.) swylce leáse lîceteras, Mt. Kmbl. 6, 16. (v. III c.) (b) condition or state of things:—Se hâlga heáp wæs sprecende mid eallum gereordum; and eác, đæt wunderlîcor wæs, đâ đâ heora ân bodade mid ânre sprǽce, ǽlcum wæs geþûht, đe đa bodunge gehýrde, swilce hê sprǽce mid his gereorde, Homl. Th. i. 318, 26. Wese swâ, Ps. Th. 71, 20: 88, 45. Lǽtaþ đis đus wesan, Blickl. Homl. 69, 17: 75, 31. (6) *to be, to be done, come to pass, happen*:—On đǽm dagum wæs đæt Liber Pater oferwan Indêa đeóde, Ors. 1, 6; Swt. 36, 17. On đære tîde wæs sió ofermycelo hǽto, 1, 7; Swt. 40, 3. On đæm geáre đe điss wæs, 2, 1; Swt. 60, 17: Chr. 1048; Erl. 180, 19. Git đæt wæs, đæt hê tô cyninges simbla gelaþod wǽre, Bd. 3, 5; S. 527, 2: Blickl. Homl. 11, 23: Wulfst. 9, 11: 12, 14. Hwæt wille gê nû hwæt ic hire doo? . . . Wese hit nû be eówrum dômum, Blickl. Homl. 157, 7. Đý læs đæt wǽre, đæt hê ǽnig đara gôda forylde, 213, 23. Tô wosanne onginnaþ *fieri incipient*, Lk. Skt. Lind. 21, 7. (7) *to be, have result, turn* *out* (v. wā, I):—Se hālga gebæd for ðæt seóce cyld, and him wæs sōna bet (*it was better with him at once, i. e. he was better*), Homl. Skt. i. 3, 311. Nāmon tō rǽde, ðæt him wærlīcor wǽre, ðæt hī sumne dǽl heora landes wurðes æthæfdon *they resolved that keeping back part of the price of the land would turn out more safely for them*, Homl. Th. i. 316, 24. Hē ðōhte hine him tō yrfewearde gedōn. Ac ðæt hwæþere swā wesan ne mihte, Bd. 5, 19; S. 638, 23. (8) with dat. of person, (a) *to belong* to, for a person *to have* something:—Him wæs beorht wela, Cd. Th. 96, 32; Gen. 1603: 216, 20; Dan. 9. Ðam wæs Crist nama, Andr. Kmbl. 2646; An. 1324. Ne him wese ǽnig fultum, Ps. Th. 108, 12. Wesan him dagas deorce and feáwe, 108, 8. Ðæt dām gengum gād ne wǽre wiste ne wǽde, Cd. Th. 222, 10; Dan. 102. (b) *to affect, be the matter* with:—Ðā frægn hē hine hwæt him wǽre, Bd. 4, 25; S. 600, 32. II. with a predicative noun or pronoun, *to be*:—God wæs ðæt word, Jn. Skt. 1, 1. Ðæt wæs gōd cyning, Beo. Th. 22; B. 11. Wæs hira Matheus sum, Andr. Kmbl. 22; An. 11. Ðæt mon mæg gesión ðæt hī gió men wǽron, Bt. 37, 3; Fox 192, 3. Wes ūs freónd, Cd. Th. 165, 1; Gen. 2725. Ic mæg wesan god, 18, 35; Gen. 283. Se ðe wæs leorningcniht on hāde ongann wesan lāreów on martyrdōme, Homl. Th. i. 50, 6. Hwæt wile ðis wesan? Blickl. Homl. 239, 29. Sǽde hē ðæt hē hine cniht wesende gesāwe *quod fanum se in pueritia vidisse testabatur*, Bd. 2, 15; S. 518, 36: Exon. Th. 320, 34; Víd. 39. On ðæm cniht wesendum ðā ðis hǽlo wundur geworden wæs *in quo tunc puero factum erat hoc miraculum sanitatis*, Bd. 3, 12; S. 537, 17. Umbor wesendum, Beo. Th. 2378; B. 1187. Ic hine cūðe cniht wesende, 750; B. 372. III. with a predicative adjective or participle:—Hē edgeong weseþ, Exon. Th. 224, 10; Ph. 373. Ðū ðē wǽre reód, and ic mē wæs blāc; ðū wǽre glæd, and ic mē wæs unrōt, L. E. I. proem.; Th. ii. 398, 14. Se beág wæs of þornum geworht, Exon. Th. 88, 27; Cri. 1446. Þeód wæs oflysted, Andr. Kmbl. 2226; An. 1115. Cyning wæs āfyrhted, Elen. Kmbl. 112; El. 56. Ðā wæs gesȳne ðæt sige forgeaf cyning ælmihtig, 287; El. 144. Wes ðū behȳdig and gemyndig, Blickl. Homl. 67, 32. Hāl wæs ðū *aue*, Mt. Kmbl. 27, 30. Hāl westū, Blickl. Homl. 143, 17. Westū gearo, Bd. 5, 19; S. 640, 44. Hāle wese gē (wosaþ gié, Lind.) *auete*, Mt. Kmbl. 28, 9. Wesaþ hāle *valete*, Wrt. Voc. ii. 88, 61. Wesaþ þancfulle, Blickl. Homl. 169, 16. Wīsfæsto wossaþ gié *perfecti estote*, Rtl. 13, 19. Wese hē hrægle gelīc, Ps. Th. 108, 19. Hit næs gesēne hweðer hē seóc wǽre (*had been*), Homl. Skt. i. 6, 259. Ðæt Adam leng āna wǽre, Cd. Th. 11, 5; Gen. 170. Ofermōd wesan, 17, 20; Gen. 262. Uossa oestig *esse devota*, Rtl. 15, 21. Giscroepo uossa *aptas fieri*, 117, 14. ¶ used impersonally:—Ðā wæs on ofne windig and wynsum, Cd. Th. 237, 31; Dan. 346. Settan mē ðǽr mē unswǽsost wæs *posuerunt me in abominationem sibi*, Ps. Th. 87, 8. Ðǽr him leófost wæs, Byrht. Th. 132, 29; By. 23. Swā him gemēdost wæs, Andr. Kmbl. 1188; An. 594. (In the last three passages the superlatives might be taken as adverbs. Cf. I. 7.) III a. with a predicative genitive:—Ðā sōna wæs Eþelwald ðæs wordes, ðæt hē nō ðes rihtes wiðsacan wolde, Chart. Th. 140, 10. Wæs seó eorla gedriht ānes mōdes, Cd. Th. 197, 10; Exod. 304. His þegnas wǽron flǽsclīces mōdes, Blickl. Homl. 17, 5. III b. with prepositional phrases, (1) prep. and noun:—Ic wæs mid weorþmende on neorxna wange, and ic ðæt ne ongeat, Blickl. Homl. 89, 8. Ðā wæs cyning on hreón mōde, Beo. Th. 2617; B. 1307. Sōna wæs hē on sunde, 3240; B. 1618. Ðū on sǽlum wes, 2345; B. 1170. Wesan him on wynne, Cd. Th. 23, 29; Gen. 367. ¶ used impersonally:—Ðā wæs ofer midde niht, ðæt hē frægn *cum jam mediae noctis tempus esset transcensum, interrogavit*, Bd. 4, 24; S. 598, 35. (2) with gerundial infinitive:—Ne wæs ðæt tō wundrianne, Bd. 3, 12; S. 537, 17. Hwæt him be ðam tō dōnne wǽre, Homl. Th. i. 502, 24: 506, 24. III c. with a clause:—Hē wæs ðæt hē wolde wyrcan ǽghwylc ðara weorca ðe dām ōðrum brōðrum wæs heard and hefig, Shrn. 145, 18 (cf. I. 5 a). IV. with participles, (1) with present participles:—Swā ic him secgende wæs, Andr. Kmbl. 1898; An. 951. On ǽfenne ðære nihte ðe hē of worulde gangende wæs *nocte qua de saeculo erat exiturus*, Bd. 4, 24; S. 598, 30. Wæs se engel sprecende, Blickl. Homl. 5, 2. Hē wæs Drihtne fylgende, 15, 28: Beo. Th. 321; B. 159. Hē in byrgenne bīdende wæs, Elen. Kmbl. 966; El. 484. Se hālga wer hergende wæs Metodes miltse, Cd. Th. 237, 8; Dan. 334. Hī ðǽr stondende wǽron, Blickl. Homl. 11, 23. Hī on ðæt folc winnende wǽron, Ors. 1, 10; Swt. 46, 6: 44, 19. Woeron (wērun, Rush.) sprecende *erant loquentes*, Mk. Skt. Lind. 9, 4. Hwæðer sincende sǽflōd dā gyt wǽre, Cd. Th. 86, 29; Gen. 1438. Wrīðende sceal mǽgðe ðīnre monrīm wesan, 105, 33; Gen. 1763. (2) with past participles, (a) of transitive verbs forming the passive:—Ðonne wesaþ ðīne handa sōna geedneówode, and beóþ swā hié ǽr wǽron, Blickl. Homl. 153, 11. Wǽr ðū gewurðod, Cd. Th. 127, 7; Gen. 2107. Hwǽr āhangen wæs rodera Waldend, Elen. Kmbl. 409; El. 205. Ðeós geofu on heora heortan ālegd wes, Blickl. Homl. 137, 4. Ealle þing wǽron geworhte (*facta sunt*) ðurh hyne, and nān þing næs geworht būtan him, Jn. Skt. 1, 3. Ða ðe ðurh geleáfan gehǽlede wǽron *qui credendo salvati sunt*, Bd. 4, 16; S. 584, 20. Wesaþ gē fram Gode gebletsade *benedicti vos a Domino*, Ps. Th. 113, 23. Ðæt ic wese gelǽded *quis deducet me?* 107, 9. Wese heora beód wended on grine *fiat mensa eorum in laqueum*, 68, 23. Wesan ealle gedrēfde *turbabuntur*, 67, 5. Ne wesen hī mid sōðfæstum āwritene *cum justis non scribantur*, 68, 29. Ðæt wǽron ālȳsede leófe ðīne *ut liberentur dilecti tui*, 59, 4. Se magorinc sceal wesan Ismahēl hāten, Cd. Th. 138, 3; Gen. 2286. Forgifen weosan, Bd. 4, 22; M. 330, 16: 4, 23; M. 340, 15. (b) of intransitive verbs:—Ðū wǽre geworden . . . cild ācenned, Exon. Th. 14, 8; Cri. 216. Ðā wæs ðæs folces fela on ān fæsten ōþflogen (*confugerant*), Ors. 4, 11; Swt. 206, 12. Ðā wæs forð cumen geóc æfter gyrne, Andr. Kmbl. 3167; An. 1586. Ðā wæs first āgān, 293; An. 147: Elen. Kmbl. 1; El. 1. Ðā wæs geworden ðæt . . ., Blickl. Homl. 15, 15. Giwēdo his giwordne wērun scīnende, Mk. Skt. Rush. 9, 3. Gif ic ðæs sægde, ðæt mīn sylfes fōt āsliden wǽre *si dicebam: 'Motus est pes meus,'* Ps. Th. 93, 17. [*Goth.* wisan: *O. Sax.* wesan: *O. Frs.* wesa: *O. H. Ger.* wesan: *Icel.* vera.] v. fore-, ge-wesan, nesan; efen-wesende.

wēsan; *p.* de. I. *to steep, soak*; inficere, conficere:—Genim grēne rudan, cnuca smale and wēs mid doran hunige, Lchdm. iii. 4, 24. Heoretes sceafeþan of felle āscafen mid pumice and wēse mid ecede, 44, 11: ii. 100, 15: 246, 13. v. ge-wēsan; wēse, wēsing. II. *to ooze, suppurate*:—Ðonne ǽrest onginne se healsgūnd wēsan (wesan?), Lchdm. ii. 44, 11. [Wese, N. P. 65. *See Halliwell* wese, *and Jamieson* weese, weeze *to ooze, distil gently*.] v. wōs.

wēse; *adj. Soaked, moist with soaking*:—Sȳ crocca āsett on eorþan, and ðās wyrta sȳn gedōn innan ðam croccan; onuppan ðām sȳ gedōn wǽta, ðæt hī þearle wel wēse beón, Lchdm. iii. 292, 6. v. wōs, *and preceding word.*

wesend, es; *m. A bison, buffalo, wild ox*:—Weosend, uusend, wesand *bubalis*, Txts. 47, 337. Wesend, Wrt. Voc. ii. 11, 40: *bubalus*, 126, 60: *urus*, i. 22, 45. [*O. H. Ger.* wisunt (-ant, -ent, -int) *bubalus*: *Icel.* vísundr.] v. next word.

wesend-horn, es; *m. A buffalo-horn*:—Ælfwolde hyre twēgen wesendhornas, Chart. Th. 536, 1. v. preceding word.

-wesenness. [Cf. *O. L. Ger.* ge-wesannussi *substantia*.] v. tō-wesness.

wēsing, e; *f. Soaking, steeping*:—Wēsing, gemangcennys ł mencingc *confectio*, Hpt. Gl. 450, 28. Wēsing ł gemang *confectio*, 449, 61. v. wēsan.

wesle, an; *f. A weasel*:—Ueosule, uuesulae *mustela*, Txts. 79, 1345. Wesle, Wrt. Voc. i. 22, 57: 78, 18: ii. 56, 53: 71, 25: Ælfc. Gr. 6, 5; Zup. 19, 14. Gif on hwylcne mycelne wǽtan mūs oððe wesle (*mustela*) on befealle, and ðǽr deád sig, sprenge mid hāligwætere and þycge, L. Ecg. C. 39; Th. ii. 164, 11: 40; Th. ii. 166, 6, 9. [*O. H. Ger.* wisala (-ula, -ela, -ila) *mustela*.]

weslinc, -wesness. v. wæstling, ge-, tō-wesness.

[west]; *spve.* west[e]mest; *adj. Westerly, situated in the west*:—Rōmāna onweald, se is mǽst and westmest, Ors. 6, 1; Swt. 252, 19. On ðæm sīþmestan onwalde and on ðæm westemestan, Swt. 254, 2. Ðis sindon ðæs landes gemǽra ðe gebyriaþ into ðære westmestan hīde, Cod. Dip. Kmbl. iii. 262, 18. On ðone westmestan mylengear . . . eft on ðæm westemestan mylengeare, Cod. Dip. B. ii. 305, 23–30. ¶ westan *in combination with prepositions, governing dative or adverbial*:—Bewestan Hai *ab oriente habens Hai*, Gen. 12, 8. Ðām folcum ðe eardiaþ be-westan Sæferne *eis populis qui ultra amnem Sabrinam ad occidentem habitant*, Bd. 5, 23; S. 646, 21. Be-westan Sealwuda, Chr. 894; Erl. 92, 19: 709; Erl. 42, 28: Ors. 1, 1; Swt. 22, 7, 12, 26. Ðonne heóld man fyrde be-westan (cf. wonyng fer by weste, Chauc. Prol. 388), Chr. 1010; Erl. 144, 5. On-westan ðære cyrican *ad occidentalem ecclesiae partem*, Bd. 3, 17; S. 543, 29. Is on-westan medmycel duru, Blickl. Homl. 127, 8. [*Icel.* vestari; *cpve.*; vestastr; *spve. more, most westerly*.]

west; *adv. West, westward, to the west, in a westerly direction*, (1) marking the direction of movement:—Hēr fōr se here west ðe eást gelende, Chr. 886; Erl. 84, 24: 918; Erl. 102, 23: Cd. Th. 219, 12; Dan. 53. West fēran, 220, 25; Dan. 76: Exon. Th. 412, 7; Rä. 30, 10. Hē west gewīteþ, 208, 27; Ph. 162. Wōdon wælwulfas west ofer Pantan, Byrht. Th. 134, 41; By. 97. Ðā wende hē hine west wið Exanceastres, Chr. 894; Erl. 91, 10. Se sciphere sigelede west ymbūtan, 877; Erl. 78, 17. Ðonne heofones gim west onhylde, Exon. Th. 174, 32; Gū. 1186. (2) marking relative position:—Seó burh is west ðonon from ðære stōwe on ānre mīle *the town is a mile to the west of the place*, Blickl. Homl. 129, 3. Ðonne se ǽfensteorra biþ west gesewen, Bt. 39, 13; Fox 232, 34: Met. 29, 28. Hē wið ðone here ðǽr wæst ābisgod wæs, Chr. 894; Erl. 92, 9. Sūð, eást and west, Met. 9, 42: 14, 7. Ðæt hē west and norð trymede getimbro, Cd. Th. 18, 18; Gen. 275. Ðæt is ðrittiges mīla lang east and west, Bd. 1, 3; S. 475, 19. Wes[t]mest ān īglond ligð ūt on gārsecg, Met. 16, 11. [Cf. *O. Sax.* westor: *O. Frs.* wester: *Icel.* vestr *westwards*.] v. norþ-, sūþ-west.

westan; *adv. From the west*, (1) marking the direction of movement:—Ðæm fultume ðe him westan com, Chr. 894; Erl. 91, 15. Monige from eástan and westan (weosta, Lind.) cumaþ, Mt. Kmbl. Rush. 8, 11. Cymeþ westa (woesta, Lind.), Lk. Skt. Rush. 13, 29. Fērde se æðeling wæston, Chr. 1052; Erl. 152, 6. Westan brōhton, Elen. Kmbl. 2030; El. 1016. Somnaþ sūþan and norþan, eástan and westan, Exon. Th. 220,

24; Ph. 325. Se þridda heáfodwind hâtte *zephirus*; se blǽwđ westan, Lchdm. iii. 274, 20: Cd. Th. 50, 10; Gen. 806. Đonne blǽwđ súþan and westan wind, Met. 6, 8. Swinsiaþ súþan and norþan, eástan and westan, Exon. Th. 55, 19; Cri. 886. Gesâwon wê westan đone leóman sunnan, and se leóma gehrân đǽm treówum ufonweardum, Nar. 28, 23. (2) marking the direction of measurement:—Is seó stôw ǽghwanon mid sǽ ymbseald bûtan westan *est locus ille undique mari circumdatus praeter ab occidente*, Bd. 4, 13; S. 583, 10. Se cyng hæfde funden đæt him mon sæt wiđ on súþhealfe Sæfernmúþan westan from Wealum eást óþ Afene múþan, Chr. 918; Erl. 104, 4. [*O. Sax.* westan; *O. Frs.* westa: *Icel.* vestan.] v. norþan-, súþan-westan; westane.

wêstan; *p.* te *To lay waste, devastate, desolate*:—Hine wilde deór wêstaþ and frettaþ *singularis ferus depastus est eam*, Ps. Th. 79, 13. Hí his wícstede wêstan *locum ejus desolaverunt*, 78, 7. Hié wæron đæt lond herigende and wêstende, Ors. 1, 10; Swt. 44, 20. [Heo westen þat lond, Laym. 1754. *O. Sax.* â-wôstian: *O. H. Ger.* wuosten *vastare.*] v. â-, ge-, on-wêstan.

westane; *adv. From the west, in the west*:—Đa beorgas onginnaþ westane fram đæm Wendelsǽ in Narbonense đære đeóde, and endiaþ eást in Dalmatia đæm lande æt đæm sǽ *Alpes a Gallico mari exsurgentes, primum Narbonensium fines, deinde Galliam Rhetiamque secludunt, donec in sinu Liburnico defigantur*, Ors. 1, 1; Swt. 22, 19. Dioclitianus and Maximianus bebudon êhtnesse cristenra monna, Dioclitianus eástane, Maximianus westane (*in occidente*), 6, 30; Swt. 280, 18. [*O. Sax.* westana: *O. H. Ger.* westana *ab occidente.*] v. westan.

westan-norþan. I. *adv. From the north-west.* Cf. westan (2):—Hit (*Italy*) beliđ Wendelsǽ ymb eall ûtan bûton westannorđan, Ors. 1, 1; Swt. 22, 18. II. in phrases (or compounds) marking position, *to the north-west*:—Be-westannorđan đære byrig, Ors. 1, 1; Swt. 22, 5.

westan-súþan *in* be-westansúþan *to the south-west*:—Be-westansúđan Corinton, Ors. 1, 1; Swt. 22, 10, 24, 27.

westansúþan-wind, es; *m. A south-west wind*:—Westansúđanwind *austrum*, Ps. Spl. C. 77, 30.

westan-weard; *adj. Westward*:—Mîn þrym is from eástewearde middangearde óþ đæt westanweardne *majestas mea peruenit ab occidente usque in orientem*, Nar. 25, 25.

westan-wind, es; *m. A west wind*:—Hê bâd westanwindes and hwôn norþan, and siglde đa eást, Ors. 1, 1; Swt. 17, 15.

West-Centingas; *pl. m. The people* or *the district of West Kent*:—Hí forneáh ealle West-Kentingas (Weast-Centingas, *v. l.*) fordydon, Chr. 999; Erl. 134, 28.

west-dǽl, es; *m.* I. *a western part, the extreme western point*:—Westdǽles *Hesperiae*, Hpt. Gl. 466, 67. Manega cumaþ fram eástdǽle middangeardes, and fram westdǽle tô heofenan rîce . . . Þurh đa twêgen dǽlas, eástdǽl and westdǽl, sind getâcnode đa feówer hwemmas ealles middangeardes, Homl. Th. i. 130, 17–21. Đîn ofspring byđ fram eástdǽle óđ westdǽle, Gen. 28, 14. Se heofon tôbyrst from đæm eástdæle óþ đone westdǽl, Blickl. Homl. 93, 23: Mt. Kmbl. 24, 27. Hê gesealde him westdǽl middaneardes, Bd. 1, 6; S. 476, 18. Ne se steorra gestîgan wile westdǽl wolcna, Met. 29, 13. Tungol beóþ gewiten under waþeman westdǽlas on, Exon. Th. 204, 14; Ph. 97. II. *the west*:—Beheald . . . tô westdǽle *vide . . . ad occidentem*, Gen. 13, 14: Deut. 3, 27. God sende wind fram westdǽle, Exod. 10, 19. Se steorra ne cymþ nǽfre on đam westdǽle, Bt. 39, 13; Fox 232, 30. Breoton is geseted betwyh norþdǽle and westdǽle *Brittania inter septentrionem et occidentem locata est*, Bd. 1, 1; S. 473, 9. II a. with special reference to the sun's setting:—On westdǽle geendaþ se dæg, Homl. Th. i. 130, 27. Se đe âstâh ofer westdǽl (*super occasum*), Ps. Spl. 67, 4. [Wesstdale off all þiss werelld iss Dysiss, Orm. 16406. Cf. *O. H. Ger.* wester-teil.]

West-Dene; *pl. m. The West-Danes*:—Tô West-Denum, Beo. Th. 771; B. 383: 3161; B. 1578.

wêste; *adj.* I. of open country, *waste, uncultivated and uninhabited, desert*:—Đara Terfinna land wæs eal wêste, bûton đǽr huntan gewîcodon, oþþe fisceras, Ors. 1, 1; Swt. 17, 29: 1, 10; Swt. 48, 25. Đeós stôw ys wêste *desertus est locus*, Mt. Kmbl. 14, 15. Is sǽd đæt đæt land wêste (*desertus*) wunige, Bd. 1, 15; S. 483, 27. Eall (*all of the earth*) đæt on eallum đeódum wêstes ligeþ, Bt. 18, 1; Fox 62, 15. On wêstere (wêstre, *v. l.*) stôwe, Lk. Skt. 9, 12. On wêstum lande *in terra deserta*, Deut. 32, 10. Hê fêrde on wêste stôwe, Mk. Skt. 1, 35: 6, 31, 32: Lk. Skt. 4, 42: 9, 10: Exon. Th. 209, 12; Ph. 169. Hê sealde him wêste land, Ps. Th. 77, 55. Hê ne mihte on đa ceastre gân, ac beón ûte on wêstum stôwum, Mk. Skt. 1, 45. Of đissum wîdum, wêstum môrum *a desertis montibus*, Ps. Th. 77, 6. II. *waste, empty, unused*:—Seó grundleáse swelgend hæfþ swîþe manegu wêste holu on tô gadrianne, Bt. 7, 4; Fox 22, 32. III. *waste, useless, unproductive*:—Hê geseah deorc gesweorc semian sweart under roderum, wonn and wêste, Cd. Th. 7, 22; Gen. 110. IV. of habitations, *waste, deserted, desolate*:—Byđ eówer hûs eów wêste (*deserta*) forlǽten, Mt. Kmbl. 23, 38. Wese wîc heora wêste (woestu, Ps. Surt.) and îdel, Ps. Th. 68, 26. Wêste (wôstu, Ps. Surt.), 108, 7. Hié gedydon on ânre wêstre ceastre, Chr. 894; Erl. 93, 5. Hê gesyhđ wînsele wêstne, Beo. Th. 4903; B. 2456. On wêste wîc, Cd. Th. 128, 25; Gen. 2132. Babylonia, seó đe mǽst wæs and ǽrest ealra burga, seó is nû lǽst and wêstast, Ors. 2, 4; Swt. 74, 23. V. *waste, spoiled*:—Đonne ealle đisse worulde wela wêste stondeþ, Exon. Th. 290, 33; Wand. 74. VI. *deprived, devoid* (with gen.):—Biđ on eorđan wêste (wêsđe, *v. l.*) wîsdômes, se þurh đone cantic ne can Crist geherian, Salm. Kmbl. 43; Sal. 22. [*O. Sax.* wôsti: *O. Frs.* wôste: *O. H. Ger.* wuosti *solus, desertus, solitarius, vastus.*]

westemest. v. west; *adj.*

wêsten, wêsten[n], wêstern (*in northern dialect*), es, e; *m. f. n. A desert, wilderness*:—Wêsten *desertum* vel *heremus*, Wrt. Voc. i. 53, 62. Wǽsten, 80, 35. Wîd is đes wêsten, Exon. Th. 120, 5; Gû. 267. Andlang đæs wêstenes, Jos. 8, 16. Wêstennes (on wêstenne, *v. l.*) weard, Salm. Kmbl. 167; Sal. 83. Woesternes *exterminii*, Rtl. 86, 18. Hig cômon tô đam wêstene (*in solitudine*), Gen. 21, 14. On wêstenne, Cd. Th. 137, 17; Gen. 2275. Tô Sinai wêstene *in solitudinem Sinai*, Ex. 19, 1. On wêstenne, Cd. Th. 178, 7; Exod. 8: 185, 15; Exod. 123. Tô đam wêstene Sin *in desertum Sin*, Num. 20, 1. On wêstene (woestenne, Ps. Surt.) *in solitudine*, Ps. Th. 54, 7. On đisum wêstene (woestenne, Ps. Surt.) wîdum and sîdum *in deserto*, 77, 20. On wêstenne, 77, 40. On đam wêstene (woestenne, Rush.: woestern, Lind.), Mt. Kmbl. 3, 1. Wêstene (wêstinne, Rush.), 3, 3. On đisum wêstene (woesterne, Rush.: woestern, Lind.) *in solitudine*, Mk. Skt. 8, 4. On đis wêstene (wǽstenne, Rush.: woestern, Lind.) *in deserto*, Mt. Kmbl. 15, 33. Tô wêstenne, Blickl. Homl. 165, 3: 169, 4. Se hrefen fêdde Hêliam, đam eode hê tô đam wêsterne (-nne?), and him þênode, Salm. Kmbl. p. 202, 9. On woesterne, Rtl. 56, 27. Ofer wêstenne (*chaos*), Cd. Th. 8, 16; Gen. 125. On đæt wêsten *in desertum*, Ex. 4, 27: *in solitudinem*, 5, 3. On ân wêsten, 15, 22. On wêsten (woestenne, Rush.: woestern, Lind.) *in desertum*, Mt. Kmbl. 4, 1: Blickl. Homl. 35, 6. Hê wæs geond đæt wêsten sundorgenga, 199, 5. Wildeóra wêsten, Cd. Th. 255, 10; Dan. 622. Þurh wêsten *per devia*, Wrt. Voc. ii. 94, 76. On đæt wîdgille wêsten, Homl. Skt. ii. 23 b, 729. Ofer đa wêstenne (-u, *v. l.*), Ors. 1, 1; Swt. 16, 35. Mid mistlîcum wêstenum, Bt. 18, 2; Fox 62, 36. On wêstennum, Exon. Th. 107, 2; Gû. 52. Þurh wêstenas, Ps. Th. 77, 52. Geond wêstena, 67, 8. Geond wêstenu, 10, 1. On đa wêstenu middangeardes *in desertas orbis terrarum solitudines*, Nar. 6, 5. Gynd wêstnu *per auia*, Germ. 391, 40. [A westene *in the wilderness*, O. E. Homl. i. 245, 5. *O. Sax.* wôstun (*dat.* wôstunni); wôstunnia (-innia); *f.*: *O. L. Ger.* wôstinna; *wk. f.*: *O. Frs.* wôstene, wêstene: *O. H. Ger.* wuostinna (-unna); *f.*] v. wudu-wêsten.

wêsten; *adj. Desert*:—Seó stôw wæs swâ wêsten and swâ dîgle, đæt næs nâ đæt ân đæt heó wæs ungewunelîc, ac eác swilce uncûđ đâm landleódum him sylfum, Homl. Skt. ii. 23 b, 105. Hê fêrde him đanon tô ânum wêstenum earde, Homl. Ass. 66, 24: 71, 166.

wêstend, es; *m. A waster, destroyer, devastator*:—Wêstend, tôlýsend *desolator, vastator*, Wrt. Voc. ii. 139, 34. Wêstend, ýtend *exterminator, vastator*, 145, 64. v. â-wêstend.

west-ende, es; *m. The west end, western extremity* of anything:—Hire on westende is Scotland, Ors. 1, 1; Swt. 8, 27. Đæt hire ǽwielme sié on westende Affrica, Swt. 12, 21. Hine man byrigde æt đam westende, đam stýple ful gehende, Chr. 1036; Erl. 165, 37. Æt đam westænde, Cod. Dip. B. ii. 659, 30. v. riht-westende.

wêsten-gryre, es; *m. The terror of the wilderness, terror inspired by the wilderness*, Cd. Th. 185, 4; Exod. 117.

wêsten-setla, an; *m. A dweller in a wilderness, a hermit, an anchorite*:—Wêstensetla *eremita*, Wrt. Voc. i. 42, 28: 72, 2. Wêstensetla (*printed* -seda) *eremita, anachoreta*, Hpt. Gl. 465, 24. Sum wêstensettla on đæm eálande đe Liparus is nemned, Shrn. 85, 27. Wê willaþ wrîtan be sumum wêstænsetlan (*solitarius quidam*), Homl. Ass. 195, 1. Ôþer cyn is muneca, đæt is wêstensetlan, đe feor fram mannum gewîtaþ, and wêste stôwa and ânwunung geluflaþ . . . Swilce wêstensetlan . . . on wêstenes wununge gelustfulliaþ, R. Ben. 134, 11–16. Ôþer cyn is ancrena, đæt is wêstensetlena, 9, 5. [*O. H. Ger.* wuostan-sedalo *solitarius.*]

wêsten-staþol, es; *m. A waste place, a deserted place*:—Wurdon hyra wîgsteal wêstenstaþolas, Exon. Th. 477, 22; Ruin. 28.

westerne; *adj. Western*:—Đâ âstâh westerne wind and bleów *flante favonio*, Bd. 5, 19; S. 635, 20 note. Com Æþelmêr ealdorman þider and đa weasternan (westenan, *v. l.*) þægnas, Chr. 1013; Erl. 148, 16. [*O. Sax. O. H. Ger.* westrôni: *Icel.* vestrænn.] v. súþ-, súþanwesterne.

weste-weard; *adj. Westward, west, western* part of the noun to which the word refers:—Se westsúþende Eurôpe landgemirce is in Ispania westeweardum et đæm gârsecge *Europae in Hispania occidentalis oceanus terminus est*, Ors. 1, 1; Swt. 8, 24. Đâ đâ hê wæs on eásteweardum đissum middangearde, đa from him ondrêdan đe wǽron on westeweardum . . . Him đa swîþe hiene ondrêdan đe on westeweardum đisses middangeardes wǽron, 3, 9; Swt. 136, 6–23. On đone westmestan mylengear westeweardne, Cod. Dip. B. ii. 305, 23. Eall đes middangeard from eásteweardum óđ westeweardne, Bt. 16, 4; Fox 58, 11: 29, 3;

Fox 106, 22. From eásteweardan ðisses middangeardes óð westeweardne, 18, 2; Fox 62, 1. Gehergade Ecgbryht cyning on West-Walas from eástewеardum óþ westewearde, Chr. 813; Erl. 62, 2.

west-healf, e; *f. The western side*:—On westhealfe *ab occasu*, Ors. 1, 1; Swt. 12, 13: *ad occidentem*, Num. 3, 23. On westhealfe ðære cyrican *ad occidentalem ecclesiae partem*, Bd. 3, 17; S. 543, 34: Ors. 1, 1; Swt. 8, 17: Chr. 1016; Erl. 155, 10. [*O. H. Ger.* west-halba. Cf. *Icel.* vestr-hálfa.]

wêstig; *adj. Waste, desert, desolate*:—Of Angle se á syððan stód wêstig (*desertus*, Bd. 1, 15), Chr. 449; Erl. 13, 16. Wêstig is stów *desertus est locus*, Mk. Skt. Rush. 6, 35. Wêstig (woestig, Rush.), Mt. Kmbl. Lind. 23, 38. Woestihg (woestig, Rush.), 14, 15. On woestigum stówe, Lk. Skt. Lind. 4, 42. In wêstige stówe, Mk. Skt. Rush. 1, 35. Woestig, 6, 32.

west-lang; *adj. Lying in a westerly direction*:—On ðone westlangan hlinc; of ðes westlangan hlinces ende, Cod. Dip. Kmbl. iii. 135, 25. Ða westlangan díc, v. 334, 22. v. next word.

west-lang; *adv. With the length measured in a westerly direction*:—Se wudu is eástlang and westlang hundtwelftiges míla lang *the length of the wood measuring east and west is one hundred and twenty miles*, Chr. 893; Erl. 88, 28. Se þridda sceáta is án hund and syfan and hundsyfantig míla westlang, Ors. 1, 1; Swt. 28, 9. v. preceding word.

westmest. v. west; *adj.*

West-môringas; *pl. m. The people of Westmoreland*:—Westmóringa land, Chr. 966; Erl. 125, 2.

West-mynster, es; *n. Westminster*:—Hér forðférde Harold cyning, and hé wæs bebyrged æt Westmynstre, Chr. 1039; Erl. 167, 13. Willelm com tó Westmynstre, and Ealdréd arcebiscop hine tó cynge gehálgode, 1066; Erl. 203, 8. Hér man wrægde ðone biscop Ægelríc and sende hine tó Westmynstre, 1069; Erl. 207, 7. Icc habbe gifen Sainte Petre intó Westminstre, Cod. Dip. Kmbl. iv. 190, 12, 26. Ða gebróðere on Westminstre, 192, 5. The word occurs often in charters of Edward the Confessor. The Latin form Westmonasterium is found in a doubtful charter of the reign: Locum qui dicitur Westmonasterium quod a tempore sancti Augustini institutum, multaque ueterum regum munificentia honoratum, propter uetustatem et frequentes bellorum tumultus pene uidebatur destructum, 176, 1. The place is mentioned in a (doubtful) charter of Offa of the year 785: In ioco terribili, quod dicitur æt Uuestmunstur, i. 180, 3.

wêstness, e; *f. Desolation*:—Woestenisse hire *desolatio ejus*, Lk. Skt. Lind. 21, 20. v. á-wêstness.

west-norþ; *adv. North-west*:—Þonan westnorð is ðæt lond ðe mon Ongle hǽt, Ors. 1, 1; Swt. 16, 6.

westnorþ-lang; *adv.* or *adj.* [cf. west-lang] *With the length lying north-west* (*and south-east*):—Þonne is Italia land westnorðlang and eástsúðlang *Italiae situs a circio in eurum tenditur*, Ors. 1, 1; Swt. 22, 17.

westnorþ-wind, es; *m. A north-west wind*:—Westnorðwind *circius*, Wrt. Voc. ii. 104, 4: 24, 26. [Cf. *O. H. Ger.* westernort-wint *chorus*.]

west-rîce, es; *n. A western kingdom* or *empire*:—Ðá ðæt eástríce in Asiria gefeóll, ðá eác ðæt westríce in Róma árás, Ors. 2, 1; Swt. 62, 8. Ðý ilcan geáre féng Carl tó ðam westríce, and tó allum ðam westríce behienan Wendelsǽ and begeondan ðisse sǽ, swá hit his þridda fæder hæfde, Chr. 885; Erl. 84, 10. [Cf. *O. H. Ger.* westar-ríchi *occidens*.]

west-rihte; *adv. Due west*:—Seó stów is týn mílum westrihte fram Cetrihtworþige *locus est a vico Cataractone decem millibus passuum contra solstitialem occasum secretus*, Bd. 3, 14; S. 539, 41. Seó is fram Cantwarabyrig on feówer and .xx. mílum westrihte (*ad occidentem*), 2, 3; S. 504, 26. Scýt se sǽearm of ðam sǽ westrihte, Ors. 1, 1; Swt. 22, 4. Westryhte, Swt. 14, 9.

west-rodor, es; *m. The western heavens*:—Fram upgange sunnan óð ðæt heó wende on westrodur *a solis ortu usque ad occasum*, Ps. Th. 112, 3. Heó gewíteþ on westrodur, 106, 3. Westrodor, Exon. Th. 350, 24; Sch. 68.

west-sǽ; *f. m. A west sea, sea on the west coast of a country*:—Hé (*a Norwegian*) búde on ðæm lande norþweardum wiþ ða westsǽ, Ors. 1, 1; Swt. 17, 3. Hí (*the Saxons in Britain*) hergodon fram eástsǽ óð westsǽ (*ab orientali mari usque ad occidentale*), Bd. 1, 15; S. 483, 40. Fram eástsǽ óþ wæstsǽ *a mari ad mare*, 1, 12; S. 481, 8.

west-sceáta, an; *m. A western angle* or *promontory*:—Sicilia is ðryscýte . . . ðone westsceátan man hǽt Libeúm *Sicilia tria habet promontoria . . . tertium, quod adpellatur Lilybaeum, dirigitur in occasum*, Ors. 1, 1; Swt. 28, 5.

West-Seaxe, -Seaxan (Wes-); *pl. m. The West-Saxons; Wessex*:—Hér cuómon West-Seaxe in Bretene, Chr. 514; Erl. 14, 20. Of Eald-Seaxon cómon Eást-Sexa and Súð-Sexa and West-Sexan (-Sexa, *v.l.*), 449; Erl. 12, 11. West-Seaxan, Bd. 1, 15; S. 483, 24. Weast-Seaxan, 5, 18; S. 635, 15. West-Seaxna biscop, S. 635, 22. West-Seaxna ríce, lond, Chr. Erl. 2, 9, 10. West-Seaxna (-Seaxena, *v.l.*) cyning, L. Alf. 49; Th. i. 58, 28. Wes-Seaxna, Chr. Erl. 2, 18, 23: 4, 20. Wes-Seaxena kyning, L. In. proem.; Th. i. 102, 2. Wæst-Sæxna, Chr. 836; Erl. 65, 23. West-Sexena landes is hund þúsend hída, Cod. Dip. B. i. 415, 1. On Wes-Seaxum (Weast-, *v.l.*), Chr. 560; Erl. 16, 24. Hér Birinus biscop bodude West-Seaxum (Weast-, *v.l.*) fulwuht, 634; Erl. 24, 9. Hér cuom se here tó Reádingum on West-Seaxe, 871; Erl. 74, 5.

westsûþ-ende, es; *m. The south-west extremity*:—Se westsúþende Európe, Ors. 1, 1; Swt. 8, 23.

westsûþ-wind, es; *m. A south-west wind*:—Westsúðwind *affricus*, Wrt. Voc. ii. 99, 51: 6, 40: *favonius*, 35, 6: *faonius*, 108, 22. Westsúþwind, 39, 7. [Cf. *O. H. Ger.* westersunder-wint *africus*.]

West-Wealas; *pl. m. The Celts of Cornwall; Cornwall*:—Huwal West-Wala cyning, Chr. 926; Erl. 111, 42. Ðý geáre gehergade Ecgbryht cyning on West-Walas, 813; Erl. 62, 1. Hér cuom micel sciphere on West-Walas (Wæst-Wealas, *v.l.*), 835; Erl. 64, 24.

west-weard; *adv. Westward, in a westerly direction*:—Sume (*adverbs*) synd *localia* . . . westweard *occidentem uersum*, Ælfc. Gr. 38; Zup. 225, 10. Fór se here of ðæm eástríce westweard, Chr. 893; Erl. 88, 22: 1052; Erl. 183, 15. Ðá hé ðá hámweard tó ðære ié com, ðe hé ǽr westweard (*when marching westward*) hét ða ofermǽtan brycge ofer gewyrcan, Ors. 2, 5; Swt. 84, 3. Ðás seofon tunglan gád ǽfre eástwerd ongeán ða heofenan; ac seó heofen[e] is strengre and ábrét hí ealle underbæc westweard mid hire ryne; and is for ðí mannum geþúht swilce séo sunne and ða foresǽdan tunglan gangon westweard. Sóð ðæt is westweard hí gád unþances, Boutr. Scrd. 18, 39-42. Ða seofon steorran . . . gangende eástan westweard, Lchdm. iii. 270, 26. Affrica onginð eástan westwerd (*starting from the east and coming westward*) fram Egyptum æt ðære eé ðe man Nilus hǽt, Ors. 1, 1; Swt. 24, 32.

west-weardes; *adv. Westwards*:—Hé man geseah westweardes on ðæt wêsten éfstan, Homl. Skt. ii. 23 b, 174.

west-wegas; *pl. m. The west*:—Eástan ne cymeþ gumena ǽnig, ne of westwegum *neque ab oriente, neque ab occidente*, Ps. Th. 74, 6. [Cf. *Icel.* vestr-vegir *the West* (*the British Isles*).]

West-Wille (-as?); *pl. m. The people of some district in England*:—West-Willa landes is syx hund hýda, Cod. Dip. B. i. 414, 29.

west-wind, es; *m. A west wind*:—Ðá bleów westwind *flante favonio*, Bd. 5, 19; S. 639, 20. [Cf. *O. H. Ger.* wester-wint *favonius*.]

West-Wixan; *pl. m. The people of some district in England*:—West-Wixna landes is syx hund hýda, Cod. Dip. B. i. 414, 20.

wêþan; *p.* de *To make calm, gentle, mild*:—Blíþe weorðaþ ða ðe brimu wêþaþ *laetati sunt quod* (*fluctus*) *siluerunt*, Ps. Th. 106, 28. v. next word.

wêþe; *adj. Sweet, gentle, mild, pleasant*:—Ðone swég ðæs swêtan (wêþan, MSS. O. T.) sanges *sonum cantilenae dulcis*, Bd. 5, 12; S. 630, 23. Ðone scýnan wlite, wêðne mid willum, Exon. Th. 57, 9; Cri. 916. Wegas wêþe *pleasant paths*, 102, 15; Cri. 1673. [*Goth.* wôþeis *sweet* (*savour*): *O. Sax.* wôdi.] v. wêþness.

wôðel. v. wǽdl.

weþer, es; *m. A wether, a ram*:—Weþer *vervex* vel *manto*, Wrt. Voc. i. 23, 56. Weðer *aries*, ii. 10, 42. Ða habbaþ swá micle hornas swá weðeras *habentes cornua similia arietibus*, Nar. 34, 19. Tú eald hríðeru oððe .x. weðeras, L. In. 70; Th. i. 146, 18: Chart. Th. 40, 7. Weðras, 468, 25. Is nú irfæs ðæs ðæs stranga winter lǽfæd hæfð nigon eald hríðru . . . and fiftig wæþæra, 163, 4. Weðera *vervecum*, Hpt. Gl. 524, 17. His bigleofa wæs ǽlce dæg . . . hundteóntig weðera (*centum arietes*, 1 Kings 4, 23), Homl. Th. ii. 576, 33. [*Goth.* wiþrus (Guþs) *agnus* (*Dei*): *O. L. Ger.* wither *aries*: *O. H. Ger.* widar *aries, vervex, multo*: *Icel.* veðr.]

wêþness, e; *f. Sweetness, gentleness, mildness*:—Biluitnisse and uoeðnisse *mansuetudo et lenitas*, Rtl. 100, 13. Ða miclan geniht ðínre wêðnesse (*suavitatis tuae*), Ps. Th. 144, 6. v. ge-wêþness.

wex, wexen. v. weax, wixen.

wî=weg. v. weg lá, weg-férend, weg-leás.

wibba, an; *m. A worm* or *beetle*:—Se glisigenda wibba *the glow-worm*; cicindela, Wrt. Voc. i. 23, 77. v. scearn-wibba; wifel.

wî-bed, wibil, wic *cariscus*. v. wíg-bed, wifel, wice.

wîc. The word is generally neuter, but as it is often used in the plural where a singular might express the meaning, the similarity of neuter plural and feminine singular accusatives seems to have caused the word to be taken sometimes as feminine, e.g. tó ánre wíc, Homl. Th. i. 402, 22. A weak form also seems to be used, Chart. Th. 446, 29. **I.** *a dwelling-place, abode, habitation, residence, lodging, quarters*:—Hé tó him wilniende wæs ðætte heó him funden swylce londáre swylce hé mid árum on beón mehte, and his wíc ðaer on byrig beón mihte on his lífe, Chart. Erl. 69, 23. In locum qui dicitur cynges uuíc (cf. in villa regali qui dicitur Werburging-wíc, i. 275, 3), Cod. Dip. Kmbl. iii. 373, 8. Syndon sume dígol wíc (*mansio quaedam secretior*) mid wealle and mid bearuwe ymbsealde . . . habbaþ ða wíc gebedhús, Bd. 5, 2; S. 614, 31. Synd mé wíc ðíne (*tabernacula tua*) leófe, Ps. Th. 83, 1. Beóð him wíc gestaþelad in wuldres byrig, Exon. Th. 230, 19; Ph. 474. Sindon bitre burgtúnas, wíc wynna leás, 443, 18; Kl. 32. Sceldes fordas boec and ðeara wíca on byrg, Txts. 443, 10. Londbóc mínra wíca, 458, 8. Hé gewát hám faran, wíca neósan, Beo. Th. 251; B. 125: 2255; B. 1125. Hé wæs on đâm foresprecenan wîcum (*in praefata mansione*) wuniende, Bd. 4, 3; S. 567, 15, 33. Hî hine nǽnige đinga of his wîcum and of his stôwe tô him gelaþian mihton *nequaquam suo monasterio posset erui*, 4, 28; S. 606, 9. Đæt nân biscop ne nân mæssepreóst næbbe on his wîcan ne on his hûse wunigende ǽnigne wîfman, L. Ælfc. P. 31; Th. ii. 376, 21. Of Lambhyrste tô huntan wîcan (*huntsman's lodge*), Cod. Dip. Kmbl. iii. 219, 9. On đâm wîcum his fæder Abrahames feorh gesealde, Cd. Th. 104, 21; Gen. 1738: 94, 17; Gen. 1563. Hê drâf of wîcum idese of earde, 169, 23; Gen. 2804: Ps. Th. 77, 55: Menol. Fox 48; Men. 24. On đâm wîcum (*in Heaven*), Exon. Th. 238, 28; Ph. 611. Wunian in wîcum, 316, 9; Môd. 46: Cd. Th. 113, 20; Gen. 1890. Rǽsbora wîcum wunode, 108, 26; Gen. 1812: Beo. Th. 6158; B. 3083. Đa đe on carcerne hleóleásan wîc wunedon, Andr. Kmbl. 261; An. 131: 2621; An. 1312. Ic wîc bûge, Exon. Th. 396, 22; Rä. 16, 8: 120, 10; Gû. 269. Wîc eardian, Beo. Th. 5172; B. 2589. Hê brôhte wîf tô hâme, đǽr hê wîc âhte, Cd. Th. 103, 21; Gen. 1721. Đonne ic đâs îlcan wîc geséce, 144, 23; Gen. 2394. Hê him wîc geceás fædergeardum feor, 64, 17; Gen. 1051: 164, 29; Gen. 2722: Ph. 448. Fêrend fæste wuniaþ, wîc weardiaþ, Exon. Th. 361, 27; Wal. 26: 228, 34; Ph. 448. Hê him helle gesceóp wælcealde wîc, Salm. Kmbl. 937; Sal. 468. Ic him selle on mînum hûse and binnan mînum wealle wîc (*locum*), Past. 52; Swt. 407, 35. Hê him synderlîce wîc getimbrede *ipse sibi monasterium construxit*, Bd. 3, 19; S. 547, 30. Heó hire đǽr wîc âsette đæt heó Gode in lifede *ibi sibi mansionem instituit*, 4, 23; S. 593, 26. II. *a place* where a thing remains:—Heó (*Lot's wife*) sceal on đâm wîcum wyrde bîdan, Cd. Th. 155, 9; Gen. 2570. III. *a collection of houses, a* (*small*) *town, a village, a street*. v. wîc-gerêfa:—Wîc *vel* lytel port *castellum*, Wrt. Voc. i. 34, 34: 84, 42: *vicus*, 36, 27. Seó gelaþung fêrde of đære byrig tô ânre wîc, Homl. Th. i. 402, 22. Hî cômon tô ânre wîc *processerunt vicum unum* (Acts 12, 10), ii. 382, 13. Tǽme hê tô wîc tô cyngæs sele ... gekýþe hê ... đæt hê đæt feoh in wîc gebohte, L. H. E. 16; Th. i. 34, 6–10. Andlanges đære eá tô đære wîc; fram đære wîc tô đære cortan, Cod. Dip. Kmbl. vi. 217, 6: 148, 24. Hê lǽdde hine bûtan đa wîc (*extra vicum*), Mk. Skt. 8, 23. 'Gâþ on đa wîc (*castellum*, Mt. 21, 2) đe beforan inc stondeþ' ... Hwæt Drihten đa cynelîcan burh forhogodlîce naman nemde; for đon oft wîc beóþ on monegum stôwum medmyccle gesette, Blickl. Homl. 77, 22–24. On wîcum *in vicis*, Mt. Kmbl. 6, 2. Gâ on đa strǽta and on wîc đisse ceastre *exi in plateas et uicos ciuitatis*, Lk. Skt. 14, 21. Far geond đâs strǽta and wîc, Homl. Th. ii. 374, 26. Hê begeat ... Penhyll and Grimanleáh and .ii. hîna wîcan, Chart. Th. 446, 29. IV. *a temporary abode, a camp, place* where one stops, *station*:—Đâ wæs feórđe wîc, randwigena ræst, be đan Reádan Sǽ, Cd. Th. 186, 4; Exod. 133: 183, 6; Exod. 87. Ic hêt đa fyrd đǽr wîcian ... wǽron đa wîc (*castra*) on lengo .l. furlanga long, Nar. 21, 10. Wæs in wîcum wôp, Cd. Th. 190, 16; Exod. 200: 124, 12; Gen. 2061. Hê fôr of đâm wîcum, Chr. 878; Erl. 80, 12. Restaþ incit hêr on đissum wîcum (cf. exspectate hic cum asino, Gen. 22, 5), Cd. Th. 174, 20; Gen. 2881. Onmiddan đa wîc *in medio castrorum*, Ps. Th. 77, 28. Tô đon đæt hié on đa ûre wîc feohtan *ad expugnanda castra*, Nar. 21, 21. ¶ the word occurs in local names, some of which are still found shewing *-wich* or *-wick*:—In Lunden-wîc, L. H. E. 16; Th. i. 34, 3. Tô đam porte đe is nemned Cwento-wîc *ad portum cui nomen est Quentavic*, Bd. 4, 1; S. 564, 45. In loco qui vocatur Hremping-wiic, et alia nomine Hafingseota, Cod. Dip. Kmbl. i. 211, 11. Hêr wæs Wærinc-wîc getimbrod, Chr. 915; Erl. 103, 19. Æt Wæring-wîcon, -wîcum, 913; Th. i. pp. 186, 187. Hêr wæs Gypeswîc gehergod, 991; Erl. 130, 19. Æt Gipeswîc, 1010; Erl. 143, 17. Cf. too: On gerihte tô hreódwican on đa ealdan strǽt; andlang strǽt tô norđwîcan; of norđwîcan eft andlang strǽte tô Billesham, Cod. Dip. Kmbl. iii. 449, 14–17. In loco qui dicitur Childesuuicuuon (cf. Cildesuicoque, 75, 13), i. 66, 6. Iuxta marisco qui dicitur biscopesuuîc, 104, 2: v. 46, 13. [Of æuerelche huse þat husbonde wunede and his biweddede wif weore on þere ilke wike, Laym. 31960. Fra wic to wic i tune, Orm. 8512. Þar was wonand witin a wike tua men, C. M. 7917. Canntvrbery, that noble wyke, Rel. Ant. ii. 93, 1. Ich can loki manne wike, O. and N. 604. *O. Sax.* wîk: *O. Frs.* wîk; *f.*: *O. H. Ger.* wîch; *m. vicus*. From Latin.] v. deáþ-, eard-, fird-, here-, hrâ-, sceáp-, sealt-, stôc-, wîþig-wîc.

wîcan; *p.* wâc, *pl.* wicon; *pp.* wicen *To yield, give way*:—Wicon weallfæsten, wǽgas burston, multon meretorras, Cod. Th. 208, 14; Exod. 483. [*O. Sax.* wîkan: *O. Frs.* wîka: *O. H. Ger.* wîchan *cedere*: *Icel.* víkja.] v. ge-, on-wîcan.

wîc-bora. v. wîg-bora.

wicca, an; *m. A wizard, soothsayer, sorcerer, magician*:—Wicca *ariolus*, Wrt. Voc. i. 57, 40: 60, 30. Drêas and wiccan *arioli et conjectoris* (in similitudinem arioli et conjectoris, Prov. 23, 7), Kent. Gl. 869 Drýmen and feóndlîce wiccan and ôđre wîgeleras, Homl. Th. ii. 330, 28: Wulfst. 27, 1. Be wiccum, wîglerum, etc. Gif wiccan oþþe wigleras ..., L. E. G. 11; Th. i. 172, 20: L. Eth. vi. 7; Th. i. 316, 20: L. C. S. 4; Th. i. 378, 7. Wiccum *a pythonibus*, Hpt. Gl. 504, 66. Hî âxoden æt wyccum and æt wîsum drýum, Homl. Skt. i. 2, 108. Đa fǽmnan đe gewuniaþ onfôn wiccan, L. Alf. 30; Th. i. 52, 10. Ne âxa nâne wicca[n] rǽdes *nec sit qui pythones consulat nec divinos*, Deut. 18, 11. [Symou þe wicche *Simon Magus*, Jul. 40, 9. Đe wicches *the magicians*, Gen. and Ex. 3028. Uor ane wychche þet hette Symoun, Ayenb. 41, 28. Somme saide he was a wicche, Piers P. 18, 69. Wytche, wyche *magus, sortilegus*, Prompt. Parv. 526. Wyche *hic sortilegus*, Wülck. Gl. 652, 12 (15th cent.).] v. next word, to which perhaps some of the passages given above might belong.

wicce, an; *f. A witch, sorceress*:—Wycce *phytonyssa*, Wrt. Voc. i. 74, 42. Nû cwyđ sum wîglere, đæt wiccan oft secgaþ swâ swâ hit âgǽđ ... Nû secge wê ... đæt se deófol ... geswutelaþ đære wiccan hwæt heó secge mannum ... Ne sceal se cristena befrînan đa fûlan wiccan be his gesundfulnysse, þeáh đe heó secgan cunne sum đincg þurh deófol, Homl. Skt. i. 17, 108–126. Ânimaþ đa rêđan wiccan, seó đe đus âwent þurh wiccecræft manna môd, 7, 209. Wiccan *pythonissam*, Hpt. Gl. 451, 70. Wiccean and wælcyrian, Chart. Erl. 231, 10. Wiccan, Wulfst. 165, 34. Wiccena *parcarum*, Anglia xiii. 31, 104. v. Grmm. D. M. p. 985.

wicce-cræft, es; *m. Witchcraft, sorcery, magic art*:—Wiccecræft *necromantia*, Hpt. Gl. 501, 66. Đa heáfodleahtras sind ... hǽđengyld, drýcræft, wiccecræft, Homl. Th. ii. 592, 7. Se cristena man đe his hǽlđe sêcan wyle æt unâlýfedum tilungum, ođđe æt wyrigedum galdrum, oþþe æt ǽnigum wiccecræfte, đonne biđ hê đâm hǽđenum mannum gelîc, i. 474, 22: Homl. Ass. 28, 99. Be wiccecræfte (*veneficio*) đǽr man corn bærnđ, L. Ecg. C. 32, tit.; Th. ii. 130, 20. Be wîfes wiccecræfte *de veneficio mulieris*, 33, tit.; Th. ii. 130, 22. Se man đe begâ wiccecræft *vir in quo pythonicus vel divinationis fuerit spiritus*, Lev. 20, 27: Wulfst. 71, 2. Hǽđenscipe biđ đæt man ... wiccecræft (wiccan cræft, *v. l.*) lufige, L. C. S. 5; Th. i. 378, 21: L. N. P. L. 48; Th. ii. 298, 1. Wiccecræft âlecgan, O. E. Homl. i. 302, 36. Seó wicce đe âwent þurh wiccecræft manna môd, Homl. Skt. i. 7, 210. Eówer nân ne âxie þurh ǽnigne wiccecræft be ǽnigum đinge, 17, 26. Ne gýman gê galdra ne îdelra hwata ne wîgelunga ne wiccecræfta, Wulfst. 40, 14. Be wiccecræftum. Wê cwǽdon be đǽm wiccecræftum and be liblâcum ... gif man đǽr âcweald wǽre, and hê his ætsacan ne mihte, đæt hê beó his feores scyldig, L. Ath. i. 6; Th. i. 202, 9–12. Wiccecræftas *prestigias*, Wrt. Voc. ii. 66, 25.

wicce-dôm, es; *m. Witchcraft, sorcery, magic*:—Nǽfre nân man ne geþrîstlǽce ǽnigne deófles bigencg tô đonne, ne on wîglunge, ne on wiccedôme, ne on ǽnegum îdelum anginne, Homl. Ass. 143, 123.

wiccian; *p.* ode *To practise witchcraft*:—Gif hwâ wiccige ymbe ǽniges mannes lufe, and him on ǽte sylle, ođđe on drince, ođđe on ǽniges cynnes gealdorcræftum, đæt hyra lufu for đon đe mâre beón scyle ... Gif hit biđ cleric ... *si quis veneficiis utatur, alicujus amoris gratia, et ei in cibo dederit, vel in potu, vel per alicujus generis incantationes, ut eorum amor inde augeatur ... Si clericus sit* (cf. Com a modi clarc, to mi douter his love beed, ... he ne miȝtte his wille have ... Thenne bigon the clerc to wiche, An. Lit. 11, 3–8), L. Ecg. P. iv. 18; Th. ii. 208, 31: L. M. I. P. 39; Th. ii. 274, 31. [Þe steven wicchand (wiccand, *v. l.*) *vocem incantantium*, Ps. 57, 6. Wytchon (wychyn, wycchyn) wythe sorcerye *ariolor, fascino*; wytchyn or charmyn *incanto*, Prompt. Parv. 527.] v. Grmm. D. M. p. 985.

wic-cræft. v. wicg-cræft.

wiccung, e; *f. Witching, witchcraft*:—Gif hwylc wîf wiccunga begâ *si mulier aliqua veneficia exerceat*, L. Ecg. C. 29; Th. ii. 154, 26. [Ođer unriht inoh, wicching and swikedom, O. E. Homl. ii. 213, 15.]

wiccung-dôm, es; *m. Witchcraft, sorcery, magic*:—Hê hêt tôsomne sinra leóda đa wiccungdôm wîdost bǽron (*praecepit rex, ut convocarentur arioli, et magi, et malefici, et Chaldaei*, Dan. 2, 2), Cd. Th. 223, 17; Dan. 121.

wic-dæg (wicu-, wuce-), es; *m.* I. *a day of the week*:—Đam æftran dæge (*the day after Sunday*), on ôþrum witodlîce wucedæge *die sequenti, secunda uidelicet feria*, Anglia xiii. 387, 319. Đæt hî đý feórþan wicdæge and đý syxtan (*quarta et sexta Sabbati*) fæston, Bd. 3, 5; S. 527, 9. Đý drihtenlîcan dæge and đý fîftan wicdæge *die dominica et quinta sabbati*, 4, 25; S. 599, 30: 600, 17. II. *a week-day, a day on which business may be done*:—Wicdaga *nundinarum*, Wrt. Voc. ii. 59, 63. [*O. H. Ger.* wehha-tag: *Icel.* viku-dagr.]

wice (*and* wic?), es; *m. A wich-elm*:—Cuicbeám, uuice *cariscus*, Wrt. Voc. ii. 102, 65. Wice, 13, 21: i. 285, 45 (at 42 *virecta* is glossed by *wice*, but perhaps *cwice* should be read, cf. *virecta* quicae, ii. 123, 62). Wic *vel* cwicbeám *cariscus*, ii. 129, 7. Tô đam wic ... of đam wice tô đære hapuldre ... of đam alre tô đâm twâm wycan standaþ on gerêwe eal swâ đæt gemêre gǽđ; swâ up tô đam wice stynt beneođan bælles wæge; of đam wice ... â be hege tô ealdan wycan tô đam wealle, Cod. Dip. Kmbl. iii. 424, 5–30. Genim ... wice, âc, bircean ... and ǽlces treówes dǽl, đe man begitan mæg, Lchdm. ii. 86, 7. ¶ perhaps the word is found in the place name occurring in the following:—Uno in eo loco cui uocabulum est æt Griman laeg ... Tertio æt Wican, Cod. Dip. Kmbl. ii. 407, 22 (cf. Đis syndon đara halfe hîde londgemǽru æt Wican, iii. 464, 2). Ad villam quae uocatur Uuican, i. 153, 27 (cf. Đis synd ða langemǽra intô Wican, iii. 382, 4'. [Wyche *ulmus*, Prompt. Parv. 526.]

wíce, an; *f. An office, a duty, function*:—Ic dô ðæt gê (hyrdas) geswícaþ ðære wícan (*cessare faciam eos (pastores) ut ultra non pascant gregem*, Ezech. 34, 10), Homl. Th. i. 242, 13. Bydele gebyraþ ðæt hê for his wýcan sý weorces frigra ðonne ôðer man, L. R. S. 18; Th. i. 440, 6. Ðâ hêt se câsere lǽtan león and beran tô ðâm cynegum . . . and betǽhte ða wícan ðam wælhreówan Ualeriane, Homl. Skt. ii. 24, 31. Ne gedyrstlǽce nân lǽwede man ðæt hê wissunge oððe ealdordôm healde ofer Godes ðeówum. Hû dear ǽnig lǽwede man him tô geteón Cristes wícan? Homl. Th. ii. 592, 28. Þonne hig bysega nabbon on heora wícum *quando vacant*, R. Ben. 84, 19. [Stiwardas and burþenas and byrlas and of mystlicean wican, Chr. 1120; Erl. 248, 10. Don wiken *to do good offices*, O. E. Homl. i. 137, 11. Inne here muðes wike (*officio*), ii. 91, 19. Hie here wiken hem binimeð ðe hie ar noteden, 183, 1. Ure archebiscop mid wurðscipe mucle haldeð his wike, Laym. 29752. He me (*the prefect*) walde warpen ut of mine wike, Jul. 24, 6. No beggeris blod brynge on hygh wyke, Bote he wolde him seolf byswyke, Alis. 4608. Ich can do wel gode wike, For ich can loki manne wike, O. and N. 603.] v. wícnian.

wíc-eard, es; *m. A dwelling-place*:—Hê on wêstenne wíceard geceás, Exon. Th. 158, 12; Gû. 907.

wicel?:—Wicelre (micelre? *the next article is*: Gif ðû lytel drencefæt habban wylle) blede tâcen is ðæt ðû ârǽre up ðîne swýþran hand and tôsprǽd ðîne fingras, Techm. ii. 125, 9.

wíce-weorc. v. wíc-weorc.

wíc-freoþu; *f. Peace among dwellings*:—Gerîseþ gârnîþ werum wîg tôwiþre wícfreoþa healdan *the strife of the spear beseems men to meet war and keep peace among their dwellings*, Exon. Th. 341, 21; Gn. Ex. 129.

wicg, es; *n.* (a poetical word) *A steed*:—Bið se hwæteádig (ðe) ðæt wicg byrð, Elen. Kmbl. 2390; El. 1196. Wycg, Exon. Th. 395, 10; Rä. 15, 5. Wicgce ł meare *cornipede, equo*, Hpt. Gl. 406, 21. Wicge wegan, Exon. Th. 395, 27; Rä. 15, 14. Wicge rîdan, Beo. Th. 474; B. 234. Hê on meare râd, on wlancan ðam wicge, Byrht. Th. 138, 54; By. 240: Exon. Th. 489, 14; Rä. 78, 7. On wicge sittan, Beo. Th. 578; B. 286: Runic pm. Kmbl. 345, 1; Rûn. 27. Gûðbeorna sum wicg gewende, Beo. Th. 635; B. 315. Ongunnon stîgan on wægn weras and hyra wicg somod, Exon. Th. 404, 18; Rä. 23, 9: 405, 11; Rä. 23, 21. Onweald wicga and wǽpna, Beo. Th. 2094; B. 1045. Wicgum rîdan, Exon. Th. 404, 4; Rä. 23, 2. Beornas cômon wiggum gengan, on mearum môdige, Andr. Kmbl. 2192; An. 1097. Þrió wicg, Beo. Th. 4355; B. 2174. [He (*Jesus*) sende after þe alre unwurþeste wig one to riden, and þat is asse, O. E. Homl. ii. 89, 15. *O. Sax.* wigg: *Icel.* vigg (poet.).]

wiga, an; *m. Some kind of insect*:—Wicga *blatta* (*elsewhere* blatta *is glossed by* nihtbuttorfleóge, *and* eárwicga), *lucifuga*, lytel wicga *bruuinus*, Wrt. Voc. ii. 127, 11, 32. Genim hwǽtenes meluwes smedman and wicggan innelfe, gnîd tôsomne, Lchdm. ii. 134, 4. v. eár-wicga.

wicg-cræft, es; *m. Steed-craft, skill in connection with horses*:—Sum bið meares gleáw, wiccræfta wîs, Exon. Th. 297, 18; Crä. 70.

wíc-gerêfa, an; *m. The reeve of a* wíc. v. wíc, III. From the Latin words which are translated by *wícgerêfa*, it seems that the official so denominated was concerned in collecting taxes, and from a passage in the laws that it was one of his duties to act as witness at sales. As a *wícgerêfa* of Winchester is mentioned in the Chronicle, *wic* cannot be confined to small towns:—Wícgerêfa *publicanus*, Wrt. Voc. i. 18, 47. Se (*St. Matthew*) wæs *theloniarius*, ðæt is gafoles moniend and wícgerêfa, Shrn. 131, 24. Beornulf wícgerêfa (*so three MSS., the fourth has* wíc-gefêra; *Florence of Worcester has* praepositus Wintoniensium) on Wintanceastre, Chr. 897; Th. i. 174, 175, 30. Gif Cantwara ǽnig in Lundenwíc feoh gebycge, hæbbe him twêgen oþþe þreó unfâcne ceorlas tô gewitnesse, oþþe cyninges wícgerêfan . . . gekýþe hê mid his gewytena ânum, oþþe mid cyninges wícgerêfan, ðæt hê ðæt feoh in wíc gebohte, L. H. E. 16; Th. i. 34, 3–10. Uuícgeroebum *teloniaris*, Wrt. Voc. ii. 122, 28. See Kemble's Saxons in England, ii. p. 175.

wíc-herpaþ, es; *m. A public road to a* wíc (q.v.):—Be ðam yrðlande ôð hit cymð tô ðam wícherpaðe, ðonne andlang ðæs wícherpaðes tô ðam stǽnenan stapole, Cod. Dip. Kmbl. iii. 418, 27. Cf. wíc-weg.

wícian; *p.* ode. I. *to lodge, take up one's quarters*. v. wíc, I:—Eallum ûs leófre ys wîkian (*hospitari*) mid ðam yrþlinge þonne mid ðê; for ðam se yrþling sylþ ûs hlâf and drenc, Coll. Monast. Th. 31, 1. Ân his manna wolde wícian æt ânes bûndan hûse, Chr. 1048; Erl. 177, 36. II. *to camp, encamp*. v. wíc, IV. (1) *to stop in the course of an expedition or march*:—Hê âstyrede his fyrdwíc forð tô Iordanen and wícode þreó niht wið ða eá *movit castra, veneruntque ad Jordanem, et morati sunt ibi tres dies*, Jos. 3, 1: Elen. Kmbl. 130; El. 65. Hig fôron fram Sochoþ and wícodon æt Etham (*castrametati sunt in Etham*), Ex. 13, 20: 15, 27: Jos. 4, 19. Wícedon, Elen. Kmbl. 76; El. 38. Ðû cans eal ðis wêsten and wâsð hwǽr wê wícian magon *tu nosti, in quibus locis per desertum castra ponere debeamus*, Past. 41; Swt. 304, 16. Ðâ hêt ic mîne fyrd restan and wícian *ego jussi castra poni*, Nar. 8, 26. Ðâ com Eustachius mid his here tô ðam tûne . . . Wæs seó wunung þǽr swýþe wynsum on tô wícenne, and his geteld wǽron gehende hire wununge geslagene, Homl. Skt. ii. 30, 315. (1 a) of an object that moves:—Nihtweard (*the pillar of fire*) nýde sceolde wícian ofer weredum, Cd. Th. 185, 3; Exod. 117. (2) *to occupy a position for a time*:—Ðâ wícode se cyng on neáweste ðare byrig ða hwîle ðe hié hiera corn gerypon, Chr. 896; Erl. 94, 5. Hê wícode ðǽr ða hwîle ðe man ða burg worhte, 913; Erl. 102, 6. Tô ðǽm monnum ðe on eásthealfe ðære ê wícodon, 894; Erl. 92, 30. Seó eorþe tôbærst ðǽr ðǽr hí wícodon mid wîfum and mid cyldum on heora geteldum, Homl. Skt. i. 13, 226. III. in case of travel by water, *to land*:—Þyder hê cwæð ðæt man mihte geseglian on ânum môðe, gyf man on niht wícode . . . and ealle ða hwîle hê sceal seglian be lande, Ors. 1, 1; Swt. 19, 13. Ðâ hí ofersegledon, hí cômon tô Genesar and ðâr wícedon *cum transfretassent, peruenerunt in terram Gennesareth, et applicuerunt*, Mk. Skt. 6, 53. [Wikien ȝe scullen here (wonieþ nou here, 2nd MS.), Laym. 18102.] v. ge-, ymb-wícian.

wícing, es; *m. A pirate, sea-robber*:—Wícing (wigcing, *v.l.*) oððe scegðman *pirata*, Ælfc. Gr. 7; Zup. 24, 9: *pirata* vel *piraticus* vel *cilix*, Wrt. Voc. i. 18, 59. Wícing oððe flotman *pirata*, 73, 74: *archipirata*, Hpt. Gl. 501, 35. Yldest wícing, Wrt. Voc. i. 18, 60. Philippus scipa gegaderode and wícingas wurdon, and sôna ân .c. and eahtatig ceápscipa gefêngon *Philippus, ut pecuniam praedando repararet, piraticam adgressus est. Captas centum et septuaginta naves mercibus confertas distraxit*, Ors. 3, 7; Swt. 116, 3. Metellus fôr on Belearis ðæt lond, and oferwan ða wícingas ðe on ðæt land hergedon *Metellus Baleares insulas bello pervagatus edomuit, et piraticam infestationem compressit*, 5, 5; Swt. 226, 23. ¶ in passages dealing with English affairs the word refers to the Northmen:—Ðeáh þrǽla hwylc hlâforde æthleápe and of cristendôme tô wícinge weorðe (*become a pirate, go over to the Danes*), Wulfst. 162, 6. Hê stang wlancne wícing, Byrht. Th. 135, 56; By. 139. Ða flotan, wícinga fela, 133, 60; By. 73: 134, 40; By. 97. Þý geáre gegaderode ôn hlôþ wícenga (-inga, *v.l.*), Chr. 879; Erl. 80, 28. Ðâ mêtton hié .xvi. scipu wícenga (-inga, *v l.*), 885; Erl. 82, 28. Gegaderode micel here hine of Eást-Englum, ǽgðer ge ðæs landheres ge ðara wícinga ðe hié him tô fultume âspanen hæfdon, 921; Erl. 107, 15. Wearð wícingum wiþerleán âgifen, Byrht. Th. 135, 10; By. 116. Ðæt mynster æt Westbyrig wearð þurh yfele men and wícingas eall âwêst (cf. bereáfode þurh Densce men, 446, 6), Chart. Th. 447, 8. [*Icel.* víkingr. Cf. *O. Frs.* witsing, wising.] v. sǽ-, ût-wícing.

wícing-sceaþa, an; *m. A pirate*:—Uuícingsceadan *piraticum*, Txts. 84, 736. Wícingsceaþan, sǽsceaþan, æscmen *piratici*, Wrt. Voc. 68, 12. v. next word.

wícing-sceaþe (?), an; *f. Piracy*:—Wícincsceaðan (*the Erfurt Glossary has* uuícingsceadae) *piraticam*, Txts. 87, 1579.

wícnere, es; *m. An officer, a minister, steward, manager*:—Wícnere *dispensator*, Hpt. Gl. 453, 47. Be ðam men ðe ðone wîfman fram his hlâforde âspaneþ, ðe his wícnere (*villicus*) bið, L. Ecg. P. ii. 14, tit.; Th. ii. 180, 25. Hê clipode him tô his yldestan gerêfan (*servum seniorem domus suae*), ðe ealle his þing bewiste . . . Ðâ cwæð se wícnere (in v. 9 gerêfa is again used, in v. 10 wícnere), Gen. 24, 5. Ðâ cwǽdon hig tô ðam wícnere (v. gerêfan, v. 16; *in each case the Latin is* dispensatorem), 43, 19. Setton him ðâ ǽnne wícnere getreówne . . . æt ðam wæs gelang eall heora fôda; se heom on ealre hwîle metes tilian sceolde, Homl. Skt. i. 23, 217. Nys nânum mæssepreóste âlýfed, ne diácone, ðæt hí gerêfan (*praefecti*) beón, ne wícneras (*procuratores*), L. Ecg. P. iii. 8; Th. ii. 198, 21. Ic nelle ðæt ǽnig mann âht ðǽr on teó bûton hê (*the archbishop*) and his wícneras (cf. the similar document of Henry II: Mine agene wicneres (*ministri*) . . . hi and heara wicneras (*ministri*) ðe hi hit betechan willað, 347, 1–4), Chart. Erl. 233, 7. Se cyngc beódeþ his gerêfan, ðæt gê ðâm abbodan beorgan, and filstan heora wícneran, L. Eth. ix. 32; Th. i. 346, 32. Ân woruldcynincg hæfð fela þegna and mislîce wícneras, Homl. Skt. i. pref., 60. [He king wæs and his wikenares chæs, Laym. 18175. He sende word bi his beste wukeneren (one of his cnihtes, 2nd MS.), 6704.] v. next word.

wícnian; *p.* ode *To perform an office* (wíce), *to serve, minister*:—Se geatweard, gif hê fultumes behôfige, sý him gingra brôðor betǽht, ðe him mid wícnige, R. Ben. 127, 3. Sum æðelboren cild heóld leóht ætforan his mýsan, and ongann môdigian ðæt hit on swâ wâclícum ðingum him wícnian sceolde, Homl. Th. ii. 170, 25. v. ge-wícnian.

wícnung, e; *f. Discharging of an office, service, stewardship*:—Be gehâdodra manna wícnungum *de ordinatorum hominum procurationibus*, L. Ecg. P. iii. 8, tit.; Th. ii. 194, 32. v. wícnere.

wíc-sceáwere, es; *m. A harbinger*:—Ðæs Cristes wícsceáwere (*John the Baptist*), Blickl. Homl. 163, 12.

wíc-steall, es; *m. A camp*:—Leóde ongêton, ðæt ðǽr cwom weroda Drihten wícsteal metan, Cd. Th. 183, 16; Exod. 92.

wíc-stede, es; *m. A dwelling-place, habitation*:—Þûhte him eall tô rûm, wongas and wícstede, Beo. Th. 4915; B. 2462. Hê gemunde ða âre, wícstede welîgne, 5207; B. 2607. Hí his wícstede wêstan *locum ejus* *desolaverunt*, Ps. Th. 78, 7. Ic ēþelstōl hæleþa hrēre, hornsalu wagiaþ, wera wīcstede, weallas beofiaþ, Exon. Th. 383, 11; Rä. 4, 9.

wīc-stōw, e; *f.* I. *a dwelling-place:*—Ðis ða wyrta sind, ða se wilda fugel somnaþ tō his wīcstōwe, ðǣr hē nest gewyrceþ, Exon. Th. 230, 6; Ph. 468. Ðā hē geseah ða wīcstōwa ðara ryhtwīsena Israhēla *justorum tabernacula respiciens*, Past. 54; Swt. 423, 13. II. *a camp, an encampment;* both singular and plural forms are used to translate *castra:*—Hē nemde ðære stōwe naman Manaim, ðæt is wīcstōw (*castra*), Gen. 32, 2. Ðā hēt ic ða fyrd wīcian; wæs seó wīcstōw on lengo xxes furlonga long, Nar. 4, 15. Hē of ðære wīcstōwe āfōr, Ors. 2, 4; Swt. 76, 13. Būtan ðære wīcstōwe *extra castra*, Lev. 4, 21: 8, 17: Num. 11, 32: 12, 15; Ex. 33, 11. Būtan hīra wīcstōwe, 33, 7. Būtan wīcstōwe, Lev. 10, 4. Ceósaþ eów wīcstōwe *castra ponetis*, Ex. 14, 2. On ðǣm wīcstōwum *in castris Persarum*, Ors. 3, 9; Swt. 126, 5. Ǣr hē ða wīcstōwa bereáfian mehte, Swt. 128, 9. Siþþan hē wīcstōwa nāme, 2, 4; Swt. 76, 10: Num. 11, 31.

wic-þegen, es; *m. A brother in a monastery who performs the duties of an office for a week:*—Wicþegn *betica*, Wrt. Voc. ii. 125, 45. Be wicþēnum (*de septimanariis coquine*). Gebrōðru gemǣnelīce heom betwyh þēnien, and nǣnig sȳ belādod fram ðære kycenan þēnunge... Ðære kycenan wicþēnas on ðone Sætresdæg ǣgðer ge fata þweán ge wæterclādas wacsan . . . þweán on ðan sylfan dæge ealra gebrōðra fēt ǣgðer ge ðære wucan wicþēnas ge ðære tōweardan . . . Ða wicþēnas (cf. ða wucan þegnas *septimanarii*, R. Ben. Interl. 66, 6) ānre tīde ǣr gemǣnum gereorde gān tō hlāfe . . . Ǽfterfylige ðære tōweardan wucan wicþēn, R. Ben. pp. 58–60. Se diácon wucþēn *diaconus hebdomadarus*, Anglia xiii. 415, 721. Fram mæssepreóste wucþēne *a sacerdote ebdomadario*, 395, 435. Gebrōðru wucþēnas *fratres epdomadarii*, 391, 375. Þa wucþēnas *epdomadarii ministri*, 415, 714.

wic-þegnung, e; *f. Service which lasts for a week:*—Se ðe ða ǣrran wicþēnunga geendod hæbbe, þonne hē ūt of ðære wicþēnunge fære, cweþe ðis fers . . . and swā mid bledsunge of ðære wicþēnunge fare. Ǽfterfylige ðære tōweardan wucan wicþēn, and þus cweþe . . . and swā mid bletsunge his wicþēnunge beginne, R. Ben. 59, 21–60, 8.

wīc-tūn, es; *m. A court:*—Hine weorðiaþ on wīctūnum mid lofsangum *intrate atria ejus in hymnis*, Ps. Th. 99, 3. Ingangaþ on his wīctūnas (*atria*), 95, 8. [Þar beoþ þeos gode wiketunes, O. and N. 730.]

wicu, wucu, an; *f. A week:*—Wucu *ebdomada*, Ælfc. Gr. 5; Zup. 14, 17: Wrt. Voc. i. 76, 56: *ebdomada* vel *septimana*, 53, 19. On ðam seofoðan dæge God geendode his weorc and seó wucu wæs ðā āgān, Lchdm. iii. 234, 16: Anglia viii. 310, 23. Seó wucu on Grēcisc hātte *ebdomada* and on Lȳden *septimana;* seofon daga tyne ys seó wucu, and feówer wucan wyrcaþ ānne mōnð, 319, 3. Ān wucu ðæs fæstenes *una quadrigesimae septimana*, Bd. 5, 3; S. 615, 3. Ðeós wucu is geteald tō ānum dæge, Homl. Th. ii. 292, 27. Ymb fyrst wucan būtan ānre niht, Menol. Fox 172; Men. 87. Hē ǣlcere wucan dæg mid nihte ætgædere āfæste *in omni septimana diem cum nocte jejunus transiret*, Bd. 3, 27; S. 559, 12. On ðære seofoðan wiecan (wucan, *v. l.*) ofer Eástron, Chr. 878; Erl. 80, 8. Tuwa on ucan (wucan, *v. l.:* wico, Lind.: wica, Rush.) *bis in sabbato*, Lk. Skt. 18, 12. Ða fullan wican (wucan, *v. l.*) ǣr Sc̄ta Marian mæssan, L. Alf. pol. 43; Th. i. 92, 7. Ymb wucan *after a week*, Cd. Th. 88, 14; Gen. 1465: 167, 21; Gen. 2769. On ðam geáre synd getealde twā and fīftig wucena, Lchdm. iii. 246, 12. Hié fela wucena sǣton on twā healfe ðære ē, Chr. 894; Erl. 92, 25. vi. wicum (wucan, *v. l.*) ǣr hē forþfērde, 887; Erl. 84, 35. Wucum, 901; Erl. 98, 6: Bd. 5, 4; S. 617, 7. Ðæs ymb .iii. wiecan (wucan, *v. l.*), Chr. 878; Erl. 80, 19. Wucan, 941; Erl. 116, 5: Menol. Fox 30; Men. 15. [*Goth.* wikō: *O. L. Ger.* wika: *O. Frs.* wike: *O. H. Ger.* wehha, wohha: *Icel.* vika.] v. Eáster-, fæsten-, gang-, lencten-, palm-, ymbren-wicu (-wuce).

wicu-bōt, e; *f. A week's penance:*—Mōt tō bōte stīðlīc dǣdbōt, and hit man mōt sēcan be ðæs mannes mihtum, sumon geárbōte . . . sumon wucubōte, sumon mā wucena, L. Pen. 3; Th. ii. 278, 13.

wīc-weg, es; *m. The road to a* wīc (q. v.):—Tō ðæm midlestan wīcwege; ondlong ðæs weges eft tō ceastergeate, Cod. Dip. Kmbl. iii. 260, 11. Cf. wīc-herpaþ.

wic-weorc, es; *n. Weekly work, work done for the lord by the tenant so many days a week:*—On sumen lande is ðæt hē (*the* gebūr) sceal wyrcan tō wicweorc .ii. dagas swilc weorc swilc him man tǣcð ofer geáres fyrst ǣlcre wucan, and on hærfest .iii. dagas tō wicweorce, and of Candelmæsse ōð Eástran .iii., L. R. S. 4; Th. i. 434, 5–8. Consuetudines in Dyddanhamme . . . Se gebūr sceal his riht dōn; hē sceal erian healfne æcer tō wiceweorce . . ., Cod. Dip. Kmbl. iii. 450, 35. Cf. Hēr synd gewriten ða gerihta ðe ða ceorlas sculan dōn tō Hysseburnan . . . Hī sculan ǣlce wucan wircen ðæt hī man hāte būtan þrīm, ān tō middanwintra, ōðera tō Eástran, þridde tō gangdagan, v. 147, 26. v. Seebohm's English Village Community, s. v. week-work.

wīd; *adj.* I. in reference to the dimensions of an object, *wide, of (a certain) width:*—Se arc wæs fīftig fæðma wīd, Boutr. Scrd. 21, 4. Fær gewyrc fīftiges wīd, ðrittiges heáh, þreó hund lang elngemeta, Cd. Th. 79, 7; Gen. 1307. Wite ðū hū wīd and sīd helheoðo dreórig, and mid hondum āmet, 308, 29; Sat. 699. Is ðār on ðære myclan ciricean geworht emb ða lāstas ūtan, hwēne wīddre ðonne byden, fæt up ōþ mannes breóst heáh, Blickl. Homl. 127, 6. II. where there is a considerable distance between the extremities or sides of an object, *wide, of great width, broad:*—Wīd strǣt *platea*, Wrt. Voc. i. 36, 33. Ðæt geat is swȳðe wīd and se weg is swīðe rūm *lata porta et spatiosa via*, Mt. Kmbl. 7, 13. Se mereweard (*the whale*) mūð ontȳneþ, wīde weleras . . . hī ðǣr in faraþ, ōþ ðæt se wīda ceafl gefylled bið, Exon. Th. 363, 13–27; Wal. 53–60. Hī deópne seáð dulfon wīdne, Ps. Th. 56, 8. Ōþ ða wȳde strǣte, sūð andlang strǣte, Cod. Dip. Kmbl. ii. 265, 32. III. of great surface, *wide, vast, spacious, broad, ample:*—Ðes wīda grund, Cd. Th. 7, 11; Gen. 104. Ȳða gelaac, wīd gang wætera, Ps. Th. 118, 136. Wīd is ðes wēsten, wræcsetla fela, Exon. Th. 120, 5; Gū. 267. Wæs his rīce brād, wīd and weorðlīc, 243, 11; Jul. 9. Þenden ic wealde wīdan rīces, Beo. Th. 3723; B. 1859. On andwlitan wīdre eorðan, Cd. Th. 81, 25; Gen. 1350. In ðære wīdan byrig, 258, 10; Dan. 673. On egeslīcere stōwe and on wīdum wēstene *in loco horroris et vastae solitudinis*, Deut. 32, 10. Ofer wīdne holm, Exon. Th. 296, 23; Crä. 55. Ofer wīd wæter, Beo. Th. 4937; B. 2473. Geond ðās wīdan weoruld, Met. 8, 41. Ic hæbbe wīde wombe, Exon. Th. 399, 20; Rä. 19, 3. Hī gesetton Sennar wīdne and sīdne, Cd. Th. 99, 33; Gen. 1655. Setl wīde stōdan, 6, 12; Gen. 87. Of ðissum wēstum wīdum mōrum, Ps. Th. 74, 6. Hæfde wederwolcen wīdum fæðmum eorðan and uprodor gedǣled, Cd. Th. 182, 14; Exod. 75. IIIa. of that which is spread over a wide surface. Cf. wīd-folc:—Wē ne magon rīm witan; ðæs wīde sind fugla and deóra wornas wīdsceope, Exon. Th. 355, 42; Pa. 4. IV. *wide, having no limit near, open,* cf. wīd-sǣ:—Sume hī wǣron on wīddre sǣ besencte, Homl. Th. i. 542, 29. V. fig. *not confined within narrow limits, of far-reaching power:*—Ne behwylfan mæg heofon and eorðe his wuldres word wīddra and sīddra ðonne befæðman mæge eorðan ymbhwyrft and uprodor, Cd. Th. 204, 31; Exod. 427. VI. of travel, *that traverses many lands, distant, far and wide:*—Sceal ic wreclāstas settan, sīðas wīde, Cd. Th. 276, 16; Sat. 189. Wīde sīðas, 55, 36; Gen. 905: Beo. Th. 1759; B. 877. VII. of the duration of time, *long, lasting long*, in phrases equivalent to *ever, always.* v. wīde-feorh, -ferhþ:—Gē sceolon ādreógan wīte tō wīdan ealdre, Exon. Th. 92, 27; Cri. 1515: Cd. Th. 62, 16; Gen. 1015. Tō wīdan ealdre, ēce mid englum, Andr. Kmbl. 3439; An. 1723. Ā tō wīdan feore sȳ ūrum Drihtne lof, Blickl. Homl. 65, 24: 103, 29. Ða ðe gewordun wīdan feore from fruman worulde, Exon. Th. 272, 33; Jul. 508. Wīdan feore *as long as life lasts*, 301, 23; Fä. 23. Ne seah ic wīdan feorh *never in all my life have I seen*, Beo. Th. 4033; B. 2014. Ðū scealt wīdan feorh ēcan ðīne yrmðu, Andr. Kmbl. 2766; An. 1385. [*O. Sax. O. Frs.* wīd: *O. H. Ger.* wīt *amplus, latus, vastus, spatiosus, capax: Icel.* vīðr.]

wīdan; *adv. From (far and) wide, from a distance:*—Hē his witan wīdan gesomnod hæfde . . . Ealle ða ðegnas ðe ðǣr wīdan gegaderode wǣron, Cod. Dip. Kmbl. iii. 315, 9, 36. Ōðer sinoð wæs eft ōðer healf hund biscopa wīdan gesamnod . . . Se feórða sinoð wæs six hund biscopa and .xxx. sacerda swȳðe wīdan gegaderode, L. Ælfc. P. 26, 28; Th. ii. 374, 7, 22. Ðæt wæs hāligdōm se mǣsta of gehwilcum stōwum wȳdan and sȳdan gegaderod, Cod. Dip. B. ii. 389, 23.

wīd-brād; *adj. Wide-spread, far-spreading, ample:*—Hē þeóda gehwam hefonrīce forgeaf, wīdbrādne welan (cf. hwō man himilrīki gehalōn skoldi, wīdbrēdan welon, Hēl. 1841), Cd. Th. 40, 22; Gen. 643. [Cf. *O. H. Ger.* wīt-preiten *spargere.*]

wīd-cūþ; *adj. Widely known, well known,* (1) of persons, *noted:*—Wīdcūþes wīg, Beo. Th. 2088; B. 1042. Hūnferð, wīdcūðne man, 2983; B. 1489. Sume beóþ swīðe æþele and wīdcūþe on heora gebyrdum *hunc nobilitas notum facit*, Bt. 11, 1; Fox 30, 32. Twēgen becōmon tō ūs, wīdcūðe ðurh heora yrmðe, Homl. Th. ii. 30, 30. (2) of things:—Mid ðȳ ðe se cyningc gehīrde ðæt Apollonius ðone rǣdels swā rihte ārǣdde, ðā ondrēd hē ðæt hit tō wīdcūð wǣre, Ap. Th. 5, 2. Ðæt gesȳne wearð, wīdcūþ werum, ðæt wrecend ðā gyt lifde, Beo. Th. 2516; B. 1256. Wīdcūðne weán, 3986; B. 1991.

wīde, an (wīdu; *indecl.?* cf. brǣdu, lengu, *and O. H. Ger.* wītī); *f. Width:*—Heora wīde (*longitudo*) is .cc. mīla, Nar. 36, 28.

wīde; *adv.* I. where there is measurement, *widely, far:*—Bearwas wurdon tō axan efne swā wīde swā ða wītelāc gerǣhton, Cd. Th. 154, 11; Gen. 2554. Swā wīde swā wæter bebūgeþ, Andr. Kmbl. 665; An. 333: 2469; An. 1236. II. with the idea of a great space between extremities, *widely, to a great width:*—Mūð ic ontȳnde mīnne wīde, Ps. Th. 118, 131. Hȳ tōdǣlden unc ðæt wit gewīdost (*very far apart*) in woruldrīce lifdon, Exon. Th. 442, 15; Kl. 13. III. where there is the idea of diffusion, distribution, *widely, in different places, on all sides:*—Wīde *passim*, Wrt. Voc. ii. 85, 75. Wel wīde *passim, ubique*, Hpt. Gl. 512, 18. Fela ōðra deófles manna wīde wǣran, Wulfst. 100, 20. Manncwealmas beóð wīde geond land *erunt pestilentiae per loca*, Mt. Kmbl. 24, 7. Fāh ic eom wīde, Exon. Th. 401, 24; Rä. 21, 16. Ða moldan men wīde geond eorþan lǣdaþ tō reliquium, Blickl.

Homl. 127, 15: Beo. Th. 538; B. 266: 6190; B. 3099. Tóférde se here wíde swá hé ǽr gegaderod wæs, Chr. 1012; Erl. 147, 8. Ðá cóman tógædere þreóhund biscopa and eahtatýne biscopas wíde gesamnode, L. Ælfc. P. 23; Th. ii. 372, 28. Ic ðysne sang fand, samnode wíde, Apstls. Kmbl. 4; Ap. 2. Ic eom wíde funden, brungen of bearwum and of burghleoþum, of denum and of dúnum, Exon. Th. 409, 15; Rä. 28, 1. Ic geondférde fela londa . . . folgade wíde (*I have served in many a land*), 321, 29; Víd. 53. Ehtatýne sýþum hundteóntig þúsenda hí tósendon, and wið feó sealdon wíde intó leódscipas, Blickl. Homl. 79, 23. Hí tóweorp wíde *disperde eos*, Ps. Th. 53, 5: Exon. Th. 16, 24; Cri. 258. Wíde tósáweþ Dryhten his duguþe, 299, 31; Crä. 110. Hí bráde weóxan, wíde greówan *multiplicati sunt nimis*, Ps. Th. 106, 37. Leád wíde sprong, Exon. Th. 277, 24; Jul. 585. Wæs on Myrceon wíde and welhwǽr Waldendes lof áfylled, Chr. 975; Erl. 126, 11. Hé geseah dríge stówe wíde æteówde, Cd. Th. 10, 31; Gen. 165. Ðú meaht swá wíde ofer woruld ealle geseón, 36, 1; Gen. 565. Ðǽr is wóp wíde gehéred (*heard on all sides*), 285, 6; Sat. 333: Andr. Kmbl. 3107; An. 1556. Ðæt wæs wíde cúþ, hú hé his dagas geendode, Chr. 946; Erl. 117, 24: Cd. Th. 170, 17; Gen. 2814. Ða eá geond folc monig weras Eufraten wíde nemnaþ, 15, 17; Gen. 234: Met. 8, 51. Ða wíde springaþ *crebrescunt*, Hpt. Gl. 517, 4. Gif ðeós sprǽc tó wýde spryngþ Nicod. 17; Thw. 8, 17. Woruldcyningas wíde mǽre, Cd. Th. 140, 30; Gen. 2335. His lof secgaþ wíde under wolcnum wera cneórisse, 117, 7; Gen. 1950. Is se apostolhád wíde geweorðod ofer werþeóda, Apstls. Kmbl. 29; Ap. 15. Wíde geond eorðan, Menol. Fox 350; Men. 176. Dreám geríst wel wíde gehwǽr, 118; Men. 59. Se ðe his wordes geweald wíde hæfde, Beo. Th. 159; B. 79. Hé wíde (*in all his ways, in all things*) bær herewósan hige, Cd. Th. 255, 23; Dan. 628. Swá hit beorna má uncre wordcwidas wíddor mǽnden, Exon. Th. 472, 17; Rä. 61, 17. IV. where a great distance is traversed, *widely, far, to a distance*:—Fior ł wíde *longiuscule*, Hpt. Gl. 517, 3: Wrt. Voc. ii. 50, 31. Wíde *longius*, 50, 39. Hig férdon swá wíde landes swá hig faran mihton, Cod. Dip. B. ii. 389, 20. Him féran gewát geond ða folcsceare Abraham wíde, Cd. Th. 106, 36; Gen. 1782. Bana wíde scráð, 180, 3; Exod. 39. Wíde ásent *relegatus*, Wrt. Voc. i. 51, 42. Ic lástas sceal wíde lecgan, Cd. Th. 63, 5; Gen. 1027. Lástas wǽron wíde (*for a great distance*) gesýne ofer myrcan mór, Beo. Th. 2811; B. 1403. Seó culufre wíde fleáh, Cd. Th. 88, 15; Gen. 1465. Wíde rád ofer holmes hringc hof séleste (*the ark*), 84, 3; Gen. 1392. Mec wíde wolcna strengu ofer folc byreþ, Exon. Th. 390, 3; Rä. 8, 5. Hrá wíde sprong, Beo. Th. 3181; B. 1588. Ic sceal hweorfan ðý wídor, wadan wræclástas, Cd. Th. 272, 16; Sat. 120. Ic wíddor meahte síþas ásettan, Exon. Th. 391, 25; Rä. 10, 10: 485, 6; Rä. 71, 9. Ða ðe wræclástas wídost lecgaþ, 309, 15; Seef. 57. IV a. of degree, *far*:—Þeáh gé eów eác gewyrce wídor sæce, Exon. Th. 120, 14; Gú. 271. Hé hét tósomne sínra leóda ða wiccungdóm wídost bǽron, Cd. Th. 223, 18; Dan. 121. ¶ where the word occurs with words of similar meaning:—Feor and wíde (*longe lateque*) gemǽrsode, Bd. 3, 10; S. 535, 2: 4, 27; S. 604, 2: 5, 12; S. 628, 3. Hé férde feorr and wíde geond middangeard, Shrn. 90, 23. Síde and wíde *longe lateque*, Wrt. Voc. ii. 53, 59: Cd. Th. 8, 3; Gen. 118: Exon. Th. 230, 5; Ph. 467. Ðá gesamnodon weras wíde and síde, Andr. Kmbl. 3273; An. 1639: Ps. 56, 6, 13: Exon. Th. 25, 2; Cri. 394: 155, 3; Gú. 854. Wíde oððe síde, Hy. 1, 7. [*O. Sax.* wído: *O. H. Ger.* wíto *spaciose, late, passim*: *Icel.* víða.]

wíde-feorh *long life, an age*; the word occurs only in the accusative with adverbial force, *for a long time, for ever*. v. wíd, VII:—Wé sceolon leánum hleótan, swá wé wídefeorh (*through all time*) weorcum hlódun, Exon. Th. 49, 11; Cri. 784. Á forð heonan wídeferh *for ever*, 36, 28; Cri. 583. Swá áwa sceal wesan wídeferh, 142, 12; Gú. 643: 350, 1; Sch. 57: 255, 32; Jul. 223. Ic him wille wídeferh wesan underþýded, 138, 12; Gú. 375: 420, 23; Rä. 40, 8: 421, 20; Rä. 40, 21. Wídeferg, 270, 19; Jul. 467. Ðonne hé gást ofgifeþ, syþþan hine gærsbedd sceal wunian wídefyrh (*so the MS.*; -fyrhþ (?) *as Thorpe reads*), Ps. Th. 102, 15. v. next two words.

wídefeorh-líc; *adj. Perpetual, eternal*:—Wídefeorlíc *vel* éce *aevum* vel *aetas perpetua*, Wrt. Voc. i. 21, 60.

wíde-ferhþ, -ferþ, *long life, an age*; the word occurs only in the accusative, alone or with *eall*, with adverbial force, *for a long time, for ever, for all time*:—Heora noma leofaþ wídeferhþ in écnesse *nomen eorum vivet in generationes et generationes*, Bd. 5, 8; S. 621, 29. Mihtig God manna cynnes weóld wídeferhð, Beo. Th. 1408; B. 702. Hié ne wéndon ðæt hié wídeferhð landgeweorc beweredon, 1879; B. 937. Ðú scealt wídeferhð ðínum breóstum bearn tredan eorðan (*super pectum tuum gradieris cunctis diebus vitae tuae*, Gen. 3, 14), Cd. Th. 56, 2; Gen. 906. Ðæs ðe hié wídeferð wyrnan þóhton, 180, 26; Exod. 51. Ðú wunast wídeferð mid waldend Fæder, Exon. Th. 10, 36; Cri. 163. Hafast ðú geféred, ðæt ðé feor and neáh ealne wídeferhð (*through all time*) weras ehtigaþ, Beo. Th. 2448; B. 1222. Wese swá, wese swá þurh eall wídeferhð (*through all ages*), Ps. Th. 105, 37. v. two preceding words.

-widere, widerian. v. ge-, mis-, un-, unge-widere, wederian.

Wideriggas; *pl. m. The name of some people in England*:—Widerigga (Witherigga, 416, 11) landes is syx hund hýda, Cod. Dip. B. i. 414, 28.

wíd-fæðme; *adj. Broad-bosomed*:—Wídfæðme wǽg, Andr. Kmbl. 1065; An. 533. Wídfæðme scip, 480; An. 240. [*Icel.* víð-faðmr; víð-feðmir *a name of one of the heavens.*] Cf. síd-fæðme.

wíd-farende; *adj.* (*ptcpl.*) *Wide-faring, wandering*:—Ðone wídfarendan lǽd on ðín hús *vagos induc in domum tuam*, Past. 43; Swt. 315, 14. v. wíd-férende.

wíd-férende; *adj.* (*ptcpl.*) *Wide-journeying, far-travelling*:—On ðam (*the ocean*) wuniaþ, wídférende síðe on sunde, seldlícra fela, Exon. Th. 193, 32; Az. 130. Ne magon ðǽr gewunian wídférende, ne ðǽr elþeódige eardes brúcaþ, Andr. Kmbl. 558; An. 279. v. wídfarende.

wíd-floga, an; *m. A wide-flier, one that takes wide flights*:—Se wídfloga (*the fire-drake*), Beo. Th. 5652; B. 2830. Oferhogode fengel ðæt hé ðone wídflogan weorode gesóhte, 4681; B. 2346. [Cf. *Icel.* víðfleygr.]

wíd-folc, es; *n. A wide-spread folk*:—Of ðam wídfolc, cneórím micel, cenned wǽron, Cd. Th. 98, 31; Gen. 1638. Cf. síd-, unrím-folc.

wíd-gal; *adj. Wandering, roving*:—Se mé wídgalum wísaþ hwílum sylfum tó ríce, Exon. Th. 401, 1; Rä. 21, 5. v. wíd-gil[1], *and next word.*

wídgalness, e; *f.* I. *vastness, extensiveness*:—Be ðære wídgalnisse his síðfata and his fóra ðe hé (*Alexander*) geond middaneard férde, Nar. 1, 6. II. *discursiveness, wandering*:—Wídgalnys módes *vagatio mentis*, Greg. Dial. 2, 3. v. wídgilness.

wíd-gangol; *adj. Rambling, roving, wandering*:—Wídgongel wíf word gespringeþ, oft hý mon wommum bilihd, hæleð hý hospe mǽnaþ, Exon. Th. 337, 15; Gn. Ex. 65. Ðonne wé sittaþ innan ceastre, ðonne wé ús betýnaþ binnan ðǽm locum úres módes, ðý læs wé for dolsprǽce tó wídgangule weorðen *in civitate considemus si intra mentium nostrarum nos claustra constringimus, ne loquendo exterius evagemur*, Past. 49; Swt. 385, 7.

wíd-gil(1), -giel, -gel, *and* -gille; *adj. Wide-spreading, spacious, vast, broad*:—Wídgil *passiva, vasta*, Hpt. Gl. 527, 52. Þeáh ðeós eorðe unwísum wídgel (cf. rúm, Bt. 19; Fox 68, 23) þince, Met. 10, 10. Ðæt is suíðe rúm weg and wídgille *lata et spatiosa via est*, Past. 18; Swt. 133, 20. Ðæt fenn mid menigfealdan bígnyssum wídgille and lang þurhwunaþ on norðsǽ, Guthl. 3; Gdwin. 20, 8. Sió wídgille *passivus*, Wrt. Voc. ii. 65, 55. Wídgilles fæces *spatiosae intercapedinis*, Hpt. Gl. 434, 46. Wídgilles embhwerftes *vasti orbis*, Hymn. Surt. 104, 7. Ðæs wídgillan wéstenes ða ungearwan stówe, Guthl. 3; Gdwin. 20, 10. On stówe wídgylre *in loco spatioso*, Ps. Spl. 30, 10. Tó gódum lande and wídgillum *in terram bonam et spatiosam*, Ex. 3, 8. Hwider arn ðæt wæter of ðam wídgillan flód . . .? Wén is ðæt ðæt wæter gewende tó ðære wídgillan niwelnysse, Boutr. Scrd. 21, 13–14. Tó ánre wídgyllan byrig, Homl. Skt. i. 3, 82. On ðam wídgillan lande, Num. 21, 25: Homl. Th. ii. 222, 29. Geond ðone wídgillan munt, Blickl. Homl. 199, 12: Homl. Skt. ii. 26, 207. Ða wídgillan sǽ, Hexam. 4; Norm. 6, 24. Ofer ðæt wídgille wésten, Ælfc. T. Grn. 5, 40: Jos. 11, 16. Behealde hé hú wídgille ðæs heofones hwealfa bíþ (hú wídgil sint heofones hwealfe, Met. 10, 6) *late patentes aetheris cernat plagas*, Bt. 19; Fox 68, 22. Wídgille *passivos*, Hpt. Gl. 405, 64. Sum con wonga bigong, wegas wídgielle, Exon. Th. 42, 31; Cri. 681. Ic eom brǽdre and wídgielra ðonne ðes wong gréna, 425, 4; Rä. 41, 51. Wídgelra, 426, 33; Rä. 41, 83. v. wíd-gal.

wídgilness, e; *f. Vastness, spaciousness, vast expanse*:—Hí him menigfeald þing sǽdon be ðære wídgilnysse ðæs wéstenes, Guthl. 3; Gdwin. 20, 16. Seó eorðe stód mid manegum wudum on hire wídgilnysse, Hexam. 6; Norm. 12, 5. Ða díglan wídgilnysse *abstrusam vastitatem*, Hpt. Gl. 471, 70. Behealdaþ ða wídgilnesse and ða fæstnesse and ða hrædlérnesse ðisses heofenes *respicite coeli spatium, firmitudinem, celeritatem*, Bt. 32, 2; Fox 116, 5. Wé beóð ful swyðe tó farenne geond ealle wídgylnyssa (*vast expanses*) Godes ríces, Homl. Th. ii. 296, 34. v. wídgalness.

wíd-herian, -hergan; *p.* ede *To celebrate, spread abroad the praise* of a person:—Ðeáh hí for micel gód ne dón, hí wilniaþ ðæt hí micel ðyncen, and hí mon wídherge *quamvis implere maxima praetermittant, ea tamen minima observant, quae humano judicio longe lateque redoleant*, Past. 57; Swt. 439, 34. Cf. wíd-mǽrsian.

widl *filth, pollution*:—Ǽlc widðil *omnis pollutio*, Rtl. 98, 24. Idese mid widle and mid womme besmítan, Judth. Thw. 22, 12; Jud. 59. Widl and fúl *inluviem*, Wrt. Voc. ii. 44, 53. Geseah síde sǽlwongas synnum gehladene, widlum gewemde, Cd. Th. 78, 16; Gen. 1294. v. weorold-widl.

wíd-land, es; *n.* I. *broad land, the face of the earth*. Cf. wídsǽ:—Nǽron Metode wídlond (*or under* II) ne wegas nytte, ac stód bewrigen folde mid flóde, Cd. Th. 10, 13; Gen. 156. Ic on middangeard nǽfre egorhere eft gelǽde, wæter ofer wídland, 92, 33; Gen. 1538: 85,

9; Gen. 1412: Andr. Kmbl. 395; An. 198. Hē ūs giefeþ welan ofer wīdlond, Exon. Th. 38, 11; Cri. 605. II. *a broad, spacious land*:—Geaf ic welan ofer wīdlonda gehwylc, Exon. Th. 85, 2; Cri. 1385. [Cf. *Icel.* víð-lendr *having broad lands*.] Cf. sīd-land.

wíd-lāst, es; *m. A track that stretches far, a wanderer's track*:—Wulfes ic mīnes wīdlāstum (*far wanderings*) wēnum dogode, Exon. Th. 380, 16; Rä. 1, 9. Gē (*the apostles*) sindon earme ofer ealle menn, wadađ wīdlāstas (*wide are your wanderings*), weorn gefērađ earfodsīđa, Andr. Kmbl. 1353; An. 677.

wíd-lāst; *adj. Making a track that stretches far, wide-wandering*:—Đū (*Cain*) flēma scealt wīdlāst wrecan (*vagus et profugus eris super terram*, Gen. 4, 12), Cd. Th. 62, 28; Gen. 1021. (Wer) wīdlāst ferede rōfne hafoc, Exon. Th. 400, 8; Rä. 20, 6.

widlian; *p.* ode *To defile, pollute, violate, profane*:—Ne đæt ingaas in mūđ widlas (*coinquinat*) đone monno, Mt. Kmbl. Lind. 15, 11. Measapreóstas sunnadæg widlas (*violant*), 12, 5. Đās yflo widlađ (widlas, Rush., *communicant*) đone monno, Mk. Skt. Lind. 7, 23. Hī (*the apostate angels*) heofon widledan (wid lædan, MS.), Exon. Th. 317, 4; Mōd. 60. Se đe āwiht þicge đæs đe wesle widlige (wid licge, MSS.) *qui comederit aliquid de eo quod mustela inquinaverit*, L. Ecg. C. 40; Th. ii. 166, 7. Se đe mid ǣnige unclǣne þinge sȳ besmiten . . . bēte hē be đæs widlodes mǣđe (*juxta pollutionis gradum*), L. Ecg. P. addit. 10; Th. ii. 234, 2. v. ā-, ge-widlian; un-widlod.

wíd-mǣran. v. ge-wīdmǣran, *and next word*.

wíd-mǣre; *adj. Far-famed, famous, celebrated*; in a bad sense, *notorious*. (1) of persons:—Sume teohhiaþ đæt đæt betst sȳ, đæt mon seó foremǣre and wīdmǣre *quibus optimum quiddam claritas videtur*, Bt. 24, 2; Fox 82, 10. Wīdmǣre wer . . . hē moncynnes mǣste hæfde mægen and strengo, Cd. Th. 98, 14; Gen. 1630. Wīdmǣre cynn, 158, 16; Gen. 2618. (2) of things:—Ān wundorlīc tācn gelamp, swā wīdmǣre đæt feáwa wǣron on đære neáwiste đe đæt ne gesāwe, ođđe ne gehȳrde, Homl. Th. ii. 28, 35. Hū Caudenes Furculus sió stōw wearþ swīþe wīdmǣre for Rōmāna bismere, Ors. 3, 8, tit.; Swt. 3, 10. Wīdmǣre gewin (*the war of the apostate angels*), Exon. Th. 317, 1; Mōd. 59. Wīdmǣre blǣst (*the fire that shall consume the world*), 60, 27; Cri. 976. Swā gē sweotolran and wīdmǣrran gedōđ eówre tǣlweorđlīcnesse *tanto foedior vestra reprehensibilitas appareat*, Past. 8; Swt. 53, 15. Hafaþ se cantic wīdmǣrost word, Salm. Kmbl. 101; Sal. 50. [*O. H. Ger.* wīt-māri *insignis*.]

wíd-mǣrsian; *p.* ode *To spread abroad the knowledge* or *fame* of an object, *to proclaim, publish, celebrate*:—Đā spræc man ofer eall and wīd-mǣrsude, đæt Iōsepes brōđru cōmon tō Pharaone *auditum est et celebri sermone vulgatum in aula regis: Venerunt fratres Joseph*, Gen. 45, 16. Hē ongan bodian and wīdmǣrsian đa sprǣce *ille coepit praedicare et diffamare sermonem*, Mk. Skt. 1, 45. Heó nolde wīdmǣrsian Cristes dīgelnesse, Homl. Th. i. 42, 18. Wīdmǣrsiende *crebrescens*, Hpt. Gl. 512, 21. v. ge-wīdmǣrsian.

wíd-mǣrsung, e; *f. Proclamation, publication*:—Openung mūþes his wīdmǣrsung (*infamatio*) ys *he openeth his mouth like a crier* (Ecclus. 20, 15), Scint. 96, 11.

wídness, e; *f. Width*:—Heora wīde (wīdnes, *v.l.*, v. Anglia i. 335) is .cc. mīla *longitudo eorum .cc. stadia sunt*, Nar. 36, 28. Đæs temples længc wæs syxtig fæđma, and seó wīdnes wæs twēntig fæþma, and his heáhnys wæs þrītyg fæþma, Anglia xi. 9, 27. Đæt tempel wæs . . . on wīdnysse twēntig fæđma . . . Đæt eástportic wæs on lenge twēntig fæđma be đæs temples wīdnysse, and wæs tȳn fæđma wīd, Homl. Th. ii. 578, 10–13.

wíd-nett, es; *n. A drag-net*:—Wīdnyt (wīd nyt?) *funda*, Wrt. Voc. i. 22, 21.

wido-bāne, widrian. v. wiþo-bān, wederian.

wíd-rynig; *adj. Wide-streaming*:—Hāteþ heofona cyning đæt đū forđ onsende wæter wīdrynig, geofon geótende, Andr. Kmbl. 3012; An. 1509.

wíd-sǣ; *f. m. Open sea, ocean*:—Đeós wīdsǣ *pelagus*, Ælfc. Gr. 8; Zup. 28, 21: 13; Zup. 84, 1: Wrt. Voc. i. 70, 14. Him wæs ā wīdsǣ on đæt bæcbord, Ors. 1, 1; Swt. 17, 27: 19, 26. Fǣmendre wīdsǣ *spumantis pelagi*, Hpt. Gl. 409, 69. Wīdsǣs *cataclismi*, Wrt. Voc. ii. 23, 75. On wīdsǣwes grund, Shrn. 54, 21. Mid his fōtum gangan on wīdsǣ, 111, 28. Wurpan on wīdsǣ, 57, 4. Gif massere geþeáh, đæt hē fērde þrige ofer wīdsǣ, L. R. 6; Th. i. 192, 9. Hē lēt him ealne weg đæt wēste lond on đæt steórbord, and đa wīdsǣ on đæt bæcbord, Ors. 1, 1; Swt. 17, 10.

wíd-scofen; *adj.* (*ptcpl.*) *Pushed far, extreme*:—Weá wīdscofen, Beo. Th. 1876; B. 936.

wíd-scop, -sceop; *adj. Widely distributed* (?):—Fugla and deóra wornas wīdsceope swā wæter bibūgeþ, Exon. Th. 356, 3; Pa. 8.

wíd-scriþol (-el, -ul); *adj. Wide-wandering, roving, rambling*:—Hlūd and wīdscriđel *garrula et vaga*, Kent. Gl. 188. Đæt feórđe muneca cyn is wīdscriþul (wīdscriþel *gyrovagum*, R. Ben. Interl. 10, 16) genæmned, R. Ben. 9, 21. Hit is yfel, đæt sume (munecas) synd tō wīdscriþole, L. I. P. 14; Th. ii. 322, 13. Fīfte cyn muneca is wīdscriþelra hleápera, đe under muneces gegyrlan ǣghwyder scrīþaþ; đa þurh nānes mannes sande ne faraþ, faraþ þeáh geond misseulīce þeóda, nǣfre staþolfeste, nǣfre wuniende, nāhwār sittende, R. Ben. 135, 20. Wīþscriþole renas tunglena *vagos recursos siderum*, Hymn. Surt. 22, 29.

wíd-síþ, es; *m. A far journey, long travel*:—Mōdor ne rǣdaþ, đonne heó magan cenneþ, hū him weorđe geond woruld wīdsīđ sceapen, Salm. Kmbl. 744; Sal. 371. Wērig winneþ, wīdsīđ onginneþ, Exon. Th. 354, 26; Reim. 51. ¶ the word occurs also as a name for one who has travelled much:—Wīdsīđ mađolade, se đe mǣst mǣrþa ofer eorþan, folca geondfērde, Exon. Th. 318, 19; Wīd. 1.

widu. v. wudu.

widuwa, an; *m. A widower*:—Đæt biđ rihtlīc līf đæt cniht þurhwunige on his cnihthāde, ōđ đæt hē on rihtre mǣdenǣwe gewīfige; and habbe đa syđđan, đa hwīle đe seó libbe: gif hire đonne forđsīđ gebyrige, đonne is rihtost đæt hē þananforđ wydewa þurhwunige, L. I. P. 22; Th. ii. 332, 32. [Zaynte Paul zayþ to wodewon (*non nuptis et viduis*): Huo þet guod is, he him hyealde ine þe stat of wodewehod; and ȝef hit him naȝt ne lykeþ, he him wyui, Ayenb. 225, 14. *O. H. Ger.* witwo *celebs*.] v. next word.

widuwe, widewe, weoduwe, weodewe, wuduwe, wudewe, wydewe, widwe, an; *f. A widow*. v. wīf, III a:—Wudewe (wuduwe, *v.l.*: widuwe, Rush.: widiua, Lind.) *vidua*, Lk. Skt. 18, 3. Widewe, Wrt. Voc. i. 73, 15. Weodewe, Gen. 38, 11. Wydewe (wudewe, Ps. Spl.: weoduwa, Ps. Lamb.: widwe, Ps. Surt.), Ps. Th. 108, 9. Widwe, Lk. Skt. Rush. 2, 37: 18, 5. Anna seó hālige wuduwa, Lchdm. iii. 428, 19. Paula wæs gehālgod wydewe, Homl. Th. i. 436, 9: Shrn. 112, 31. Sī ǣlc wydewe (wuduwe, *v.l.*) on Godes griđe and on đæs cynges; and sitte ǣlc .xii. mōnađ werleás; ceóse syþþan đæt heó sylf wille, L. Eth. v. 21; Th. i. 310, 1. Be wudewan . . . Sitte ǣlc wuduwe werleás twelf mōnađ . . . Ne hādige man ǣfre wudewan tō hrædlīce. And gelǣste ǣlc wuduwe đa heregeatu binnan twelf mōnđum, L. C. S. 74; Th. i. 416, 3–17. Geong wuduwe mōt eft ceorlian æfter hire weres forđsīđe, L. Ælfc. P. 43; Th. ii. 382, 32. Mund đære betstan widuwan eorlcundre, L. Ethb. 75; Th. i. 20, 10. Đīnes wuduwan hādes *viduitatis tuae*, Past. 31; Swt. 207, 12. Wudewan gierela *viduitatis theristrum* (Ald. 76), Wrt. Voc. ii. 87, 46. Wīf gif hire forman were forđsīđ gebyrige, be leáfe heó nime ōđerne, gif heó đæt ceósan wyle; and gif heó đone oferbȳt, wunige heó ā syđđan on wudewan hāde, L. Ecg. P. ii. 20; Th. ii. 190, 6. Iudith þurhwunode on hire wudewan hāde, Homl. Ass. 114, 399. Hig ne mōston nā wīfian on nānre wuduwan, L. Ælfc. P. 39; Th. ii. 380, 16. Būton earmre wudewan, L. Ath. v. 2; Th. i. 230, 19. Gif man widuwan unāgne genimeþ, L. Ethb. 76; Th. i. 20, 13. Gif hwā wydewan nȳdnǣme, gebēte đæt deópe, L. Eth. vi. 39; Th. i. 324, 25. Wæs gesett đæt se đe widewan nāme, ođđe āworpen wīf, đæt hē ne wurde nǣfre syđđan tō nānum hāde genumen, L. Ælfc. C. 8; Th. ii. 346, 13. Heora widwan (wudwan, Ps. Spl.), Ps. Th. 77, 64. Fǣmnan and wuduwan, Cd. Th. 121, 14; Gen. 2010. Wydywyna (wudewena, *v.l.*: widuena, Lind.: widwa, Rush.) hūs, Lk. Skt. 20, 47. Weodewena (widwena, Ps. Surt.), Ps. Spl. 67, 5. Widewum, Deut. 27, 19. Weodewum, Ps. Th. 145, 8. Wydewum, 67, 5: Blickl. Homl. 45, 1. Đa wuduwan (wydewan, wydwan, *v.ll.*), L. Alf. 34; Th. i. 52, 16. Earme wydewan, Cd. Th. 128, 27; Gen. 2133. [*Goth.* widuwō: *O. Sax.* widowa: *O. Frs.* widwe: *O. H. Ger.* witawa (-ewa, -uwa, -wa).]

wíd-wegas; *pl. m. Distant regions, regions lying far and wide*:—Ūs gesamna of wīdwegum *congrega nos de nationibus*, Ps. Th. 105, 36. Hē synfulle tōdrīfeþ geond wīdwegas *omnes peccatores disperdet*, 144, 20. Faraþ geond ealne yrmenne grund, geond wīdwegas, bodiaþ geleáfan (*euntes in mundum universum praedicate evangelium*, Mk. 16, 15), Exon. Th. 30, 21; Cri. 482. Fērdon folctogan feorran and neán geond wīdwegas, Beo. Th. 1684; An. 840. Blǣd is ārǣred geond wīdwegas, ofer þeóda gehwylce, 3412; B. 1704. Cf. sīd-wegas.

wiel, wielm, wiergan, wiers, wieta, wietan. v. wilh, wilm, wirgan, wirs, wita, witan.

wíf, es; *n.* I. *a woman, a female person*:—Wīf *mulier*, wīf đe wer hæfđ *uxor*, Wrt. Voc. i. 73, 12, 14. Wīf đe hæfđ ceorl *uxor*, Ælfc. Gr. 9, 21; Zup. 47, 8. Ald uuīf *anus*, Wrt. Voc. ii. 100, 38: i. 73, 17: *anula* vel *vetula*, 50, 48. Đæt wīf (*mulier*) wæs gehǣled, Mt. Kmbl. 9, 22. Gif hwylc wīf (*mulier*) hire wīfman (*ancillam suam*) swingđ, L. Ecg. P. ii. 4; Th. ii. 182, 32. Cwēn Hrōđgāres, freólīc wīf, Beo. Th. 1234; B. 615. Wīdgongel wīf word gespringeþ, Exon. Th. 337, 15; Gn. Ex. 65. Wæs sum wīf, seó (đæt wīf đió *mulier quae*, Lind.) hæfde untrumnesse gāst, Lk. Skt. 13, 11. Wæs sōna gearu wīf, swā hire weoruda helm beboden hæfde, Elen. Kmbl. 445; El. 223. Sǣde đæt wīf hire wordum selfa, Cd. Th. 160, 10; Gen. 2648. Wīfes sceós *baxeae*, Wrt. Voc. i. 26, 20. Đæt hī nāgan mid rihte þurh hǣmedþing wīfes gemānan, L. Eth. v. 9; Th. i. 306, 19. For đære synne đæs ǣrestan wīfes, Blickl. Homl. 5, 5. Freá wīf āweahte, and đa wrađe sealde leófum rince, Cd. Th. 11, 12; Gen. 174. Đæt æđele wīf (*Eve*), 294, 19; Sat. 473. Đǣr wǣron manega wīf (wīfo, Lind., *mulieres*), Mt. Kmbl. 27, 55: Lk. Skt. 8, 2: 24, 22. Betwyx wīfa bearnum *inter natos mulierum*, Mt. Kmbl. 11, 11. Betuh eall wīfa cynn, Blickl. Homl. 5, 21. Rīccra

(-æ, MS.) wîfa (-e, MS.) wǽfels *regillum* vel *peplum* vel *palla*, Wrt. Voc. i. 40, 32. Seó ǽrest wîfa (*feminarum*) is sǽd in Norþanhymbra mǽgþe ðæt heó munuchâde onfênge, Bd. 4, 23; S. 593, 22. II. *a being in the form of a woman*:—Wîf unhýre (*Grendel's mother*), Beo. Th. 4247; B. 2120. Ðǽr ða mihtigan wîf hyra mægen berǽddon, and hý gyllende gâras sændan, Lchdm. iii. 52, 21. III. *a married woman, a wife*:—His wîf *sua uxor*, Ælfc. Gr. 15; Zup. 104, 2. Câseres wîf *imperatrix* vel *Augusta*, 42, 10. Abram and Nachor wîfudun; Abrames wîf hâtte Sarai, and Nachores wîf Melcha, Gen. 11, 29: 16, 1: Cd. Th. 167, 30; Gen. 2773. Gûð sceal in eorle geweaxan, and wîf geþeón leóf (lof, MS.) mid hyre leódum, leóhtmôd wesan, rûne healdan, rûmheort beón, Exon. Th. 338, 28; Gn. Ex. 85. Se man geþeót hine tô his wîfe (*uxori*), Gen. 2, 24: Mt. Kmbl. 19, 5. Se cyning mid his wîfe and twâm sunum, Homl. Th. i. 468, 1. Æt his mêder ðe wǽre tô ǽwum wîfe forgifen his fæder, L. Alf. pol. 42; Th. i. 90, 29. Ðe wîf hæfð *uxoratus*, Wrt. Voc. i. 50, 44. Ceorl ðe wîf hæfð *maritus*, 73, 13. Ðanon ic mê âfêde, and mîn wîf and mînne sunu, Coll. Monast. Th. 27, 23. Ðâ ðâ hê mann wolde beón, hê ne geceás nâ him wîf tô mêder, ac geceás clǽne mǽden, Homl. Th. ii. 6, 34. Sume tiliaþ mid micelre geornfulnesse wîfa, for ðam ðæt hî þurh ðæt mæge mǽst bearna begitan, Bt. 24, 3; Fox 82, 26. Wôhhǽmed mid ôþerra ceorla wîfum, Blickl. Homl. 61, 15. His wîfum twǽm sægde Lameh, Cd. Th. 66, 26; Gen. 1090. Hî him wîf curon, 76, 1; Gen. 1250. Hié hæfdon wîf and cyfesa, Blickl. Homl. 99, 20. ¶ the following passages will illustrate some points connected with the position of women in relation to marriage:—Be ðon ðe mon wîf bycgge, L. In. 31; Th. i. 122, 3. Wê lǽraþ ðæt ǽnig cristen mann . . . ne gewîfie . . . on ðæs wîfes nêdmâgan ðe hê sylf ǽr hæfde . . . hê nâ mâ wîfa ðonne ân hæbbe, and ðæt beó his beweddode wîf, L. C. E. 7; Th. i. 364, 21–28. Wer môt his wîfe on fulwihte onfôn, and ðæt wîf ðam were, L. Ecg. C. 18, tit.; Th. ii. 128, 31. Gif ceorl bûton wîfes wîsdôm deóflum gelde . . . Gif bûtwû deóflum geldaþ, sión hió healsfange scyldigo, L. Wih. 12; Th. i. 40, 4. Gif hwâ stalie swâ his wîf nyte and his bearn, geselle .lx. scill. tô wîte. Gif hê stalie on gewitnesse ealles his hîrêdes, gongen hié ealle on þeówot, L. In. 7; Th. i. 106, 15. Gif ceorl ceáp forsteld . . . ðonne bið se his dǽl synnig, bûtan ðam wîfe, forðon heó sceal hire ealdore hiéran, 57; Th. i. 137, 17. Ðæt ða (*criminals*) ealle beón gearwe mid him silfum and mid wîfe and mid ærfe tô farenne þider ic wille, L. Ath. iv. proem.; Th. i. 220, 6. Gif be cwicum ceorle wîf hig be ôðrum were forlicge, and hit open weorðe . . . heó þolige nase and eárena . . ., L. C. S. 54; Th. i. 406, 6. Mon môt feohtan orwîge, gif hê gemêteþ ôðerne æt his ǽwum wîfe, L. Alf. pol. 42; Th. i. 90, 26. Gif frî man wið frîes mannes wîf geligeþ . . . ôðer wîf (hê) his âgenum scætte begete and ðæm ôðrum gebrenge, L. Ethb. 31; Th. i. 10, 7. Gif ceorl âcwyle be libbendum wîfe and bearne, riht is ðæt ðæt bearn mêdder folgige, L. H. E. 6; Th. i. 30, 3: L. In. 38; Th. i. 126, 3. Gif hwâ cwydeleás of ðyssum lîfe gewîte . . . beó be ðæs hlâfordes dihte seó ǽht gescyft swýðe rihte wîfe and cildan and nêhmâgon, L. C. S. 71; Th. i. 414, 1. Ðǽr se bônda sæt uncwyd and unbecrafod, sitte ðæt wîf and ða cild on ðam ylcan unbesacen, 73; Th. i. 44, 23. III a. *a woman who has been married and lost her husband* (by death or divorce):—Lâf *vel* forlǽten wîf *derelicta*, Wrt. Voc. i. 50, 46. Wîfian on nânre wuduwan, ne on forlǽtenum wîfe, L. Ælf. P. 39; Th. ii. 380, 16. Ælc man ðe his wîf forlǽt . . . se ðe ðæt forlǽtene wîf nimð, se unrihthǽmð, Lk. Skt. 16, 18. Gif man mǽdan oþþe wîf (cf. *the old Latin version*: virginem vel viduam) weddian wille, L. Edm. B. 1; Th. i. 254, 2. Ne nýde man nâðer ne wîf ne mǽden tô ðam ðe hyre sylfre mislîcige (cf. *passages from the Laws under* widuwe, *and* L. H. I. 1, 3; Si, mortuo marito, uxor ejus remanserit, . . . eam non dabo marito, nisi secundum velle suum, Th. i. 499, 15), L. C. S. 75; Th. i. 416, 20. IV. *a female*. v. wer, V:—Ælcne mon, ge wîf ge wǽpned, Ors. 3, 6; Swt. 108, 27. Ða forman twâ, fæder and môder, wîf and wǽpned, Cd. Th. 12, 33; Gen. 195. IV a. as a grammatical term, *feminine*. v. wer, V a. [*O. Sax. O. Frs.* wîf: *O. H. Ger.* wîp: *Icel.* vîf (*poet.*).] v. aglǽc-, gesîþ-, hǽmed-, mere-, riht-, sige-, sîþ-, unriht-wîf, *and next word*.

wîfa (?), an; *m. A woman*:—Gif rîce wîf and earm âcennaþ tôgædere, gangon hî âweig, nâst ðû hwæðer bið ðæs rîcan wîfan (-es?) cild, hwæðer ðæs earman, Homl. Th. i. 256, 14.

wîf-cild, es; *n. A female child*:—For wǽpnedbearne sceolde cennende wîf hî âhabban fram Godes hûse ingange ðreó and ðrittig daga, and for wîfcilde (*femina*) syx and syxtig daga, Bd. 1, 27; S. 493, 16.

wîf-cyn[n], es; *n.* I. *woman-kind, women*:—Ðæt hî of ðam wîfcynne him cyning curan *ut de feminea regum prosapia regem sibi eligerent*, Bd. 1, 1; S. 474, 22. Ðû eart gebletsod betuh ealle wîfcyn (*in mulieribus*, Lk. 1, 28), Blickl. Homl. 143, 18. [Wiðuten wifkin and childre *besides women and children*, Gen. and Ex. 656.] II. *female sex*:—Ôþer ðara is wǽpnedcynnes, sunnan trió, ôþer wîfkynnes, ðæt mônan trió *quarum lignum virile est solis, alterum est femineum lune*, Nar. 25, 18. Hwylce wihta beóð ôðre tîd wîfcynnes, ôðre tîd wǽpnedcynnes? Salm. Kmbl. p. 202, 12: Lchdm. iii. 10, 12.

wîf-cýþ[þ], e; *f. A visit to a woman, familiarity with a woman*:—Ðâ geâscode hê ðone cyning on wîfcyþþe (-cyððan, *v.l.*), Chr. 755; Erl. 48, 29.

wifel, es; *m. A weevil, a beetle*:—Wibl *panpila*, Txts. 85, 1498. Wifel *papila*, Wrt. Voc. ii. 67, 59. Wibil, uuibil *cantarus*, Txts. 49, 398. Wifel, Wrt. Voc. ii. 13, 47. Wifel *cantarus* (*animal*), 128, 11: *scarebius*, i. 281, 43. Is ðæs gores sunu gonge hrædra, ðone wê wifel nemnaþ, Exon. Th. 426, 13; Rä. 41, 73. Æfter ðam wifele, Lchdm. ii. 320, 2. Weorp ofer bæc ðone wifel (tordwifel, l. 15) on wege; beheald ðæt ðû ne lôcige æfter, 318, 19. ¶ the word seems to occur in several local names. v. Cod. Dip. Kmbl. vi. 352. [Wevyl, wyvyl *or* malte boode (bowde) *gurgulio*, Prompt. Parv. 523 and 531. *O. L. Ger.* gold-uuivil *cicendela*: *O. H. Ger.* wibil *scarabaeus, cantarus*: *Ger.* wiebel: *Icel.* tord-yfill.] v. scearn-, tord-wifel.

wifel, wifer *an arrow, dart, javelin*:—Gafeluca ł wibere *jaculo, sagitta*, gâre ł wifele *spiculo*, Hpt. Gl. 432, 45, 53. Gâra *jaculorum*, gaflucas *catapultas, sagittas*, wifera *sagittarum*, gâras *spicula*, 405, 52–55. [Wyfle, wepene *bipennis*, Prompt. Parv. 526, and see note.]

wî-fêrend, -wîfestre. v. weg-fêrend, wǽpen-wîfestre.

wîf-fæst; *adj. Married*:—Gif wîffæst wer (*uxoratus*) hine forlicge be his âgenre wylne, L. C. S. 55; Th. i. 406, 14. Cf. wîf-leás.

wîf-feax, es; *n. A woman's hair*:—Wiffex *cesaries*, Wrt. Voc. i. 282, 43: ii. 16, 46.

wîf-gâl; *adj. Incontinent, licentious*:—Swâ lǽren hî ða wîfgâlan gesinscipe, swâ hî ða forhæbbendan ne gebrengen on unryhthǽmde *sic incontinentibus laudetur conjugium, ut tamen jam continentes non revocentur ad luxum*, Past. 60; Swt. 453, 30.

wîf-gehrine, es; *m. Contact with woman*:—Gif ðîne geférân beóð clǽne from wîfgehrine (*femineo contactu*), Nar. 27, 8.

wîf-gemǽdla, an; *m. A woman's fury*:—Wiþ wîfgemǽdlan; geberge on neaht rædices moran, ðý dæge ne mæg ðe se gemǽdla sceþþan, Lchdm. ii. 342, 10. v. ge-mǽdan.

wîf-gemâna, an; *m. Mulieris consortium*:—Wîfgemânan tô âweccanne . . . ðæt âwecceþ wîfgemânan lust, Lchdm. i. 336, 15–17.

wîf-geornness, e; *f. Incontinence*:—Uîfgiornis *adulteria*, Mt. Kmbl. Lind. 15, 19.

wîf-gifta; *pl. f. Nuptials, marriage*:—Wæs se weliga ðæra (-e, MS.) wîfgifta georn on môde, ðæt him mon fǽmnan gegyrede brýd tô bolde, Exon. Th. 245, 2; Jul. 38.

wîf-hâd, es; *m.* I. *womanhood*:—Wê sprecaþ be ðære heofonlîcan cwêne æfter wîfhâde *we speak of the heavenly queen as woman*, Homl. Th. i. 546, 14. II. *female sex*:—Wîfhâd *femininum sexus*, Wrt. Voc. ii. 148, 19. Wîfhâdes man *femina*, i. 70, 18: Homl. Th. ii. 10, 12: 94, 30. Se ðe handlaþ wîfhâdes mannes lîc, Basil admn. 7; Norm. 50, 11. God âna wât hû his gecynde biþ, wîfhâdes oððe weres, Exon. Th. 223, 9; Ph. 357. Se ðreát ðæra Godes ðeówa in wîfhâde *ancillarum Dei caterva*, Bd. 4, 7; S. 574, 34. [*O. H. Ger.* wîp-heit *sexus*.] *See other instances under* wer-hâd.

wîf-hand, a; *f. The female side, female line*:—Mîn yldra fæder hæfde gecweden his land on ða sperehealfe, næs on ða spinlhealfe; ðonne gif ic gesealde ǽnigre wîfhanda ðæt hê gestrýnde, ðonne forgyldan mîne mâgas . . . for ðon ic cweðe ðæt hî hit gyldan, for ðon hý fôð tô mînum ðe ic syllan môt swâ wîfhanda swâ wǽpnedhanda swâðer ic wylle, Cod. Dip. Kmbl. ii. 116, 16–24. v. next word.

wîf-healf, e; *f. The female side, female line*:—On ða gerâd ðæt hî gecuron heora kynecinn aa on ða wîfhealfa, Chr. Erl. 3, 16. (Cf. wîf-cynn, I.) v. preceding word.

wîf-hearpe (?), an; *f. A woman's harp*:—On glîgbeáme (owifhearpan = on wîfhearpan? MS. C.) *in tympano*, Ps. Spl. 150, 4.

wîfian; *p.* ode *To take a wife, to marry*, (1) without an object:—Nân wer ne wîfaþ, ne wîf ne ceorlaþ, Homl. Th. i. 238, 1. Is geset swîðe micel dǽdbôt swylcum mannum tô dônne, ðe eft wîfiaþ; and eác is ǽlcum preóste forboden, ðæt hî beón ne môton on ða wîsan ðe hî ǽr wǽron æt ðâm brýdlâcum, ðǽr man ôðre sîðe wîfaþ. Be ðam man mæg witan, ðæt hit riht nis, ðæt wer wîfige oððe wîf ceorlige oftur ðonne ǽne, Wulfst. 304, 28–305, 3. Ne wîfiaþ hig, ne hig ne ceorliaþ *neque nubent, neque nubentur*, Mt. Kmbl. 22, 30: Ne wîfiaþ hî, ne ne gyftigeaþ, Mk. Skt. 12, 25. Ðysse worulde bearn wîfiaþ and beóð tô giftum gesealde, Lk. Skt. 20, 34. Hî ne wîfiaþ, ne hî beóð hâmbrôhte, Hpt. Gl. 436, 40. Ðæt se cniht heólde hine sylfne clǽne ôð ðæt hê wîfode, Homl. Ass. 20, 149. Abraham and Nachor wîfudon (*duxerunt uxores*), Gen. 11, 29. Wîfodon, Lk. Skt. 17, 27. Wîfian *nubere*, Hpt. Gl. 485, 72: Homl. Skt. i. 4, 6. Mê is gesǽd ðæt eówer ancor sægð, ðæt hit sý âlýfed ðæt mæssepreóstas wel môton wîfian, Homl. Ass. 13, 6. Ne fremaþ nânum menn tô wîfienne (wîfigæ, Lind.) *non expedit nubere*, Mt. Kmbl. 19, 10. Wîfigende and gyfta syllende *nubentes et nubtum tradentes*, 24, 38. (2) with an object governed by *on*:—Be ðam men ðe wîfaþ on twâm geswystrenum *de homine qui duas sorores in matrimonium ducit*, L. Ecg. P. ii. 11, tit.; Th. ii. 180, 18. Be ðam men ðe on his mâgan wîfaþ *de homine qui inter cognatas suas uxorem ducit*, 18, tit.; Th. ii. 180, 30. Se ðe wîfaþ on ðam forlǽtenum wîfe, Homl. Th. ii. 322, 34. Tô his âðumum ðe woldon wîfian on his dohtron (*qui accepturi erant filias ejus*),

Gen. 19, 14. Hē ne mōste būtan ǣne wīfigan, ne hē ne mōste on wydewum wīfigan, L. Ælfc. C. 7; Th. ii. 346, 5. Wīfian, L. Ælfc. P. 39; Th. ii. 380, 16. Is nýd ðæt cristene menn on ðære ðriddan cneórisse oððe on ðære feórþan him betwih wīfian sceole *necesse est ut tertia vel quarta generatione fidelium licenter sibi jungi debeat*, Bd. 1, 27; S. 491, 8. [Iudas wiuede o Thamar, A. R. 308, 13. To late here sones wyue, R. Glouc. 35, 9. To wyui *nubere*, Ayenb. 225, 17. Wyvyn̄ or weddyn̄ a wyfe *uxoro*, Prompt. Parv. 531.] v. ge-wīfian.

wīf-lāc, es; *n. Intercourse with women:*—Gif hwā openlīce Lengctenbryce gewyrce . . . þurh wīflāc (*concubitum*, Lat. vers. Cf. qui in Quadrigesima ante Pascha nupserit, .i. annum peniteat, L. Ecg. E. 108; Th. ii. 113, 3. Eác is gesynscipum micel þearf, ðæt hī hig on ðās hālgan tīd (*Lent*) clǣnlīce healdan, būtan ǣlces hǣmedes besmytennysse, L. E. I. 43; Th. ii. 440, 2), L. C. S. 48; Th. i. 402, 30. Ealle synoðas forbudon ǣfre ǣlc wīflāc (v. wīfung) weófodþēnum, L. I. P. 23; Th. ii. 336, 12: Wulfst. 270, 21.

wīf-leás; *adj. Without a wife, unmarried:*—Gif hwylces weres forme wīf bið deád, ðæt hē be leáfe ōðer wīf niman mōte, and gif hē ða oferbȳt, wunige hē ā syððan wīfleás (*coelebs*), L. Ecg. P. ii. 20; Th. ii. 190, 3. [Wyyfles or not weddyd *agamus*, Prompt. Parv. 526.] See also next word.

wīf-leást, e; *f. Lack of women:*—Menn hæfdon on frymðe heora māgan tō wīfe, and swā wel mōsten for ðære wīfleáste, Homl. Skt. i. 10, 216.

wīf-līc; *adj.* I. *womanly, of a woman, female, feminine:*—Wīflīc *muliebris*, Ælfc. Gr. 5; Zup. 17, 17. Wīflīces *femineis*, Wrt. Voc. ii. 148, 20. Wīflīcum līcome of woeres ðū saldest līchome fruma *femineo corpore de viri dares carne principium*, Rtl. 109, 15. Būtan wīflīcre bysnunge *without an example among women*, Homl. Th. i. 198, 5. Mid wīflīce nīðe *with all a woman's hate*, Ors. 1, 2; Swt. 39, 18. Ðæt hē ne forðon wīflīce hāde ārede *ut ne sexui quidem muliebri parceret*, Bd. 2, 20; S. 521, 24. Āwyrp mē hyder ðīnne scyccels, ðæt ic mæge ða wīflīcan tȳddernysse oferwreón, Homl. Skt. ii. 23 b, 211. I a. as a grammatical term, *feminine* (gender):—Æfter gecynde syndon twā cyn on namum, *masculinum* and *femininum*, ðæt is werlīc and wīflīc; wīflīc cyn byð *haec femina* ðis wīf . . . *Neutrum* is nāðor cynn, ne werlīces ne wīflīces, Ælfc. Gr. 6; Zup. 18, 5–15. II. *wifely, matronly:*—Wīflīcre *matronalis*, Hpt. Gl. 505, 36. Wīflīcere, 520, 2. Ða wīflīcan, Wrt. Voc. ii. 58, 22. [*O. H. Ger.* wīp-līh *muliebris, femineus*.]

wīflīce; *adv. Like a woman:*—Wīflīce *muliebriter*, Ælfc. Gr. 38; Zup. 232, 17: Hpt. 504, 30. Ðū wunodest æfter ðīnum were wīflīce on clǣnnysse *after your husband's death you continued in womanly purity*, Homl. Ass. 114, 392.

wīf-lufu, an; *f. Love for a woman:*—Se hālga wer ðære wīflufan (*the love of Herod for Herodias*) wordum stȳrde, unryhtre ǣ, Exon. Th. 260, 12; Jul. 296. Ingelde weallaþ wælnīðas, and him wīflufan cōlran weorðaþ, Beo. Th. 4137; B. 2065. Cf. wīf-myne.

wīf-mann (wīm-, wim-?), es; *m.* (*but* seó wīfman *occurs*). I. *a woman:*—Wē lǣraþ ðæt ǣnig wīfman neáh weófode ne cume ða hwīle ðe man mæssige, L. Edg. C. 45; Th. ii. 254, 3. Ðara manna sum wæs bescoren preóst, sum wæs lǣwede, sum wæs wīfmon (*femina*), Bd. 5, 12; S. 628, 35. Minutia hātte ān wīfmon, ðe on heora wīsan sceolde nunne beón. Seó hæfde gehāten . . . ðæt heó wolde hiere līf on fǣmnhāde ālibban *Minucia, virgo vestalis*, Ors. 3, 6; Swt. 108, 15. Seó wīfman (seó wīmman, vv. 18, 22) *Jahel*, Jud. 4, 21. Wīfmannes loccas *crines*, Wrt. Voc. i. 42, 49. Wīfmannes innoð *matrix, uterus*, 44, 39. Ne scrīde nān wǣpman mid wīfmannes reáfe (*veste feminea*), Deut. 22, 5. Be wīfmannes beweddunge, L. Edm. B. 1; Th. i. 254. Be ungewintredes wīfmannes nēdhǣmde. Gif mon ungewintrædne wīfmon tō niédhǣmde geþreátige, L. Alf. pol. 26; Th. i. 78, 16. Nū cweðe gē ðæt gē ne magon beón būtan wīmmannes þēnungum, L. Ælfc. C. 6; Th. ii. 344, 19. God geworhte ðæt ribb tō ānum wīfmen (*in mulierem*), Gen. 2, 22. Ðæt bisceop . . . næbbe on his hūse nǣnne wīfman, būton hit sȳ his mōdor . . ., L. Ælfc. C. 5; Th. ii. 344, 13. Gif hwā wille wið wīfman (*cum muliere*) unrihtlīce hǣman, L. Edg. C. 33; Th. ii. 274, 10. Þeówne wīmman *ancillam*, L. Ecg. C. 25; Th. ii. 150, 18. God hī geworhte wǣpnedman and wīmman (wȳfman, *v. l.*, hiuu ł wīfmon, Lind.: wīfmenn, Rush.) *masculum et feminam fecit eos Deus*, Mk. Skt. 10, 6. Wǣpmen ge wīfmen *viri ac feminae*, Bd. 3, 5; S. 527, 7. Wīfmenn, Exon. Th. 460, 12; Hö. 16. Hæleþa gemōt, wīgena weorod, wīfmonna þreát, fela fǣmnena, folces unrīm, 462, 7; Hö. 48. Wǣpmanna sang and wīfmanna sang, Homl. Th. i. 442, 1. Wæs micel ege from ðǣm wīfmonnum (*the Amazons*), Ors. 1, 10; Swt. 46, 27. I a. a *serving-woman:*—Gif hwylc wīf (*mulier*) hire wīfman (*ancillam suam*) swingð, and heó þurh ða swingle wyrð deád . . . fæste seó hlǣfdige (*domina*) .vii. geár, L. Ecg. P. ii. 4; Th. ii. 182, 32: ii. 4, tit.; Th. ii. 180, 6. Heó freóde Hægelflǣde hire wīmman, Chart. Erl. 253, 16. God gewītnode ealle his wīmmen (*uxorem ancillasque suas*), Gen. 20, 18. II. applied to plants, *female:*—Gif man scyle mugcwyrt tō lǣcedōme habban, ðonne nime man . . . ða grēnan wīfmen, Lchdm. iii. 72, 21. [*Laym.* wifmon, wimmon: *Orm.* wifmann, wimmann: *A. R.* wummon: *Ayenb.* wyfman.]

wīf-myne, es; *m. Love for a woman:*—Drihten wearð Faraone yrre for wīfmyne (*love for Sarah*), Cd. Th. 111, 25; Gen. 1861. Cf. wīf-lufu.

-wifre. v. gange-wifre.

wīf-scrūd, es; *n. Clothing for a woman, woman's dress, female attire:*—Ic geann mīnre yldran dehter . . . ānes wīfscrūdes ealles. And mīnre gyngran dehter ic geann ealles ðæs wīfscrūdes ðe tō lāfe bið, Chart. Th. 530, 14–25.

wift, e; *f. Some implement used in weaving:*—Hē sceal habban fela towtōla . . . pihten, timplean, wifte, wefle, wulcamb, Anglia ix. 263, 12.

wīf-þegen, es; *m. A pander; leno*, Wrt. Voc. i. 66, 31: 284, 14: ii. 51, 63.

wīf-þing; *pl. n. Matters connected with women, marriage, intercourse:*—Tō wīfþingum foxes tægles se ȳtemæsta dǣl on earm āhangen; ðū gelȳfest ðæt ðis sȳ tō wīfþingum on bysmær (*irritamentum ad coitum*) gedōn, Lchdm. i. 340, 22; 368, 16. Wīfþing, gifta, hǣmed *hymeneos*, Wrt. Voc. ii. 43, 13. Be ðam men ðe gelōmlīce wīfþing begǣð *de homine qui crebras nuptias conciliat*, L. Ecg. P. ii. 20, tit.; Th. ii. 180, 32. [He weddede þat mæiden, and nom heo to his bedden; þer wes wīfðing riche, Laym. 31128.] Cf. brȳd-þing.

wīfung, e; *f.* I. *taking a wife, marriage:*—Be gehādodra manna wīfunge (*matrimonio*), L. Ecg. P. iii. 1, tit.; Th. ii. 194, 25: Gen. 24, 9. Ūs sceamaþ tō secgenne ealle ða sceandlīcan wīglunga ðe gē dwǣsmenn drīfaþ on wīfunge, Homl. Skt. i. 17, 102. Se ðridda cwæð: 'Ic hæbbe gewīfod . . .' Þurh ða wīfunge sind getācnode ðæs līchaman lustas, Homl. Th. ii. 374, 19. Āðas and wīfunga sindan tōcwedene heáhfreólsdagum, L. Eth. vi. 25; Th. i. 320, 24. Ðās sinoðas forbudon ǣlce wīfunga ǣfre weófodþēnum, L. Ælfc. P. 30; Th. ii. 374, 35. II. in plural, *wives*; matrimonia:—Eów preóstum þingð, ðæt eów nān sin ne sȳ ðæt gē mid wīfungum swā libban swā lǣwede men, L. Ælfc. P. 32; Th. ii. 376, 28. v. frum-, unriht-wīfung.

wig *a way*, wīg *an idol*. v. weg, wīh.

wīg, es; *n.* I. *fight, battle, war, conflict:*—Wīg oððe gefeoht *mavors*, Wrt. Voc. ii. 55, 37. Ðonne wīg cume, Beo. Th. 46; B. 23: 5737; B. 2872. Wīg ealle fornam, 2165; B. 1080: Exon. Th. 291, 11; Wand. 80: Elen. Kmbl. 262; El. 131. Wæs ðæs wyrmes wīg wīde gesȳne, nearofāges nið neán and feorran, hū se gūðsceaða Geáta leóde hatode and hȳnde, Beo. Th. 4621; B. 2316. Ful oft ðǣr wīg ne ālæg *there was constantly war*, Exon. Th. 325, 30; Vīd. 119. Wīges on wēnum *expectant of battle*, Cd. Th. 188, 30; Exod. 176. Wīges bīdan, Beo. Th. 2541; B. 1268. Se wyrm getrūwode wīges and wealles *the dragon trusted to battle* (*or under* II?) *and bulwark*, 4635; B. 2323. Him wæs hild boden, wīges wōma, Elen. Kmbl. 37; El. 19: Andr. Kmbl. 2709; An. 1357: Exon. Th. 277, 5; Jul. 576. Sumum wīges spēd hē giefeþ æt gūþe, 42, 16; Cri. 673. Wæs Hrōðgāre herespēd gyfen, wīges weorðmynd, Beo. Th. 130; B. 65. Hē hafaþ wīgges leán, blǣd būtan blinne, Elen. Kmbl. 1647; El. 825. Sum bið wīges heard, beadocræftig beorn, Exon. Th. 295, 27; Crä. 39: (*Ulysses*) Met. 26, 13: (*Sigemund*) Beo. Th. 1776; B. 886: (*St. Andrew*) Andr. Kmbl. 1677; An. 841. Wīges oflysted, 2454; An. 1228. Wīges hrēmige, Chr. 937; Erl. 115, 8. Wīges sæd, Erl. 112, 20. Him wīge forstōd fæder frumsceafta, wearð him seó feohte tō grim, Exon. Th. 317, 14; Mōd. 65. Heald mē herewǣpnum wið unholdum, and wīge belūc feóndum *effunde frameam, et conclude adversus eos*, Ps. Ben. 34, 3. Wīgge, Beo. Th. 3545; B. 1770. Wīgge under wætere, 3316; B. 1656. Æt wīge cringan, 2679; B. 1337. Æt wīge sigecempa, Ps. C. 9. Æt wīgge spēd, sigor æt sæcce, æt gefeohte frið, Elen. Kmbl. 2362; El. 1182. Hē mid wīge ācwealde ðone cyning and ðæt folc *percusserunt urbem et omnes habitatores ejus*, Jos. 10, 30. Hī mid wīge ācwealdon eall ðæt hī ðǣr fundon *percussit in ore gladii universas animas, quae in ea fuerant*, 10, 37. Gif hwā mid wīge godcundra gerihta forwyrne . . . Gif hē man gewundige . . . Gif hē man āfylle . . . Gif hē gewyrce ðæt man hine āfylle, L. C. S. 49; Th. i. 404, 6–12. Hē gewann mid wīge ðone eard *cepit omnem terram*, Jos. 11, 23: Homl. Th. ii. 216, 1. Seó burhwaru heóldan mid fullan wīge ongeán, Chr. 1013; Erl. 148, 12. Hū him speów ǣgðer ge mid wīge ge mid wīsdōme, Past. pref.; Swt. 3, 8. Giefe on wīge, Exon. Th. 299, 25; Crä. 107. Hē on wīgge (*in bello*) āfeallen wæs, Chart. Th. 201, 27. Cēne tō wīge, Jud. p. 162, 30. Ðæt folc wurdon gewexene tō wīge ful strange, Homl. Th. ii. 212, 18. Man beónn ealle Cantware tō wīgge, Chart. Th. 201, 21. Ǣghwylc ōþerne bylde tō wīge, Byrht. Th. 138, 44; By. 235. Tō wīgge faran, Chart. Th. 201, 22. Hié giredon hié tō wīge, Ors. 3, 5; Swt. 106, 17. Wīgge, Elen. Kmbl. 95; El. 48. Hē sende twelf þūsenda gewǣpnodra manna tō ðam wīge (*ad pugnam*), Num. 31, 6. Hī beóð gewǣpnode on ða wīsan ðe man hors gewǣpnaþ, ðonne man tō wīge þencð, Wulfst. 200, 11. Hié heora land oferhergodan, and him ðæs nǣnige bōte dydon, būton ofermōdlīce wīg and þreátunge, Blickl. Homl. 201, 24. Abraham sealde wīg tō wedde, nalles wunden gold, Cd. Th. 124, 29; Gen. 2070. Oft ic (*a shield*) wíg seó, frēcne feohtan, Exon. Th. 388, 6; Rä. 6, 3. Wælhwelpes wíg, 397, 21; Rä. 16, 23. Gesēcean wíg, Beo. Th. 1374; B. 685. Wíg gefeohtan, 2170; B. 1083. An wíg gearwe, 2499; B. 1247. II. *fighting force* (abstract or concrete), *valour; troops*:—Wæs his mōdsefa manegum gecȳðed, wíg and wīsdōm, Beo. Th. 705; B. 350. Nǣfre on ōre læg wīdcūþes wíg, ðonne walu feóllon, 2088; B. 1082: Exon. Th. 338, 27; Gn. Ex. 85. On Mōyses hand wearð wíg gifen, wigena mænieo, Cd. Th. 216, 11; Dan. 5. Hē mid ðam ōðrum flocce tō ðære birig fērde beótlīce mid wíge *ascendit cum senioribus in fronte exercitus, vallatus auxilio pugnatorum*, Jos. 8, 10. Ðanon hē gewende mid wíge tō Lebna and oferwann ða burh *transivit cum omni Israel in Lebna et pugnabat contra eam*, 10, 29. Offōr hiene (*Philip*) ōðere Sciþþie mid lytelre firde . . . Philippus him dyde heora wíg unweorð (*made light of their force*), Ors. 3, 7; Swt. 118, 2. Ne hē him ðæs wyrmes wíg for wiht dyde, eafoð and ellen, Beo. Th. 4685; B. 2348. [He scheldede his scalken al se heo to wiȝe solden, Laym. 4728. Com mid muchle wiȝe (*a great force*) Irtac, 25365. To werchen wi *to fight*, Gen. and Ex. 3220. *O. Sax.* wíg: *O. Frs.* wīch: *O. H. Ger.* wīc (ch, g) *bellum, proelium, pugna, militia*: *Icel.* víg; *n.* Cf. *Goth.* waihjō *pugna.*] v. ān-, and- (Exon. Th. 112, 22; Gū. 147), camp-, fēðe-, þræc-, weorold-wíg; or-wíge. The word is found in proper names. v. Txts. p. 631.

wig (?); *adj.* v. wíg-heafola.

wiga, an; *m.* I. *one who fights, a* (*fighting*) *man, a warrior*:—Wiga *heros*, Ælfc. Gr. 9, 31; Zup. 57, 11. Wiga oððe wígstrang *bellipotens*, Wrt. Voc. ii. 12, 45. Iung wiga *tyro*, i. 18, 16. Wiga wintrum geong, Byrht. Th. 137, 62; By. 210. Wælreów wiga (*Beowulf*), Beo. Th. 1262; B. 629. Wiga ellenrōf, Wald. 79; Vald. 2, 11. Wāc wiga, Exon. Th. 290, 18; Wand. 67. Wigan wígheardne, Byrht. Th. 133, 64; By. 75: Cd. Th. 189, 22; Exod. 188. Wigan unforhte, mōdige twēgen, Byrht. Th. 134, 5; By. 79. Wigan on gewinne, 140, 42; By. 302: Cd. Th. 197, 23; Exod. 311: 219, 22; Dan. 58. Ðǣr wigan sittaþ on beórsele blīðe ætsomne, Runic pm. Kmbl. 342, 4; Rūn. 14. Wigena æscberendra, Cd. Th. 123, 6; Gen. 2040. Wigena mænieo, 216, 12; Dan. 5. Wigena strengest (*Beowulf*), Beo. Th. 3091; B. 1543. Hī sendon māran sciphere strengran wihgena *mittitur classis prolixior armatorum*, Bd. 1, 15; S. 483, 16. Wigum and wǣpnum, Beo. Th. 4779; B. 2395. ¶ in phrases denoting a chief or leader:—Wigena hlāford (*Byrhtnoth*), Byrht. Th. 135, 49; By. 135. Wigena baldor (*Holofernes*), Judth. Thw. 22, 5; Jud. 49. Dauid cyning, wigena baldor, Elen. Kmbl. 688; El. 344. Wigena hleó . . . wigena weard (*Constantine*), Elen. 300–306; El. 150–153. Wigena strengel (*Beowulf*), Beo. Th. 6222; B. 3115. *Similarly the Deity is called* wigena wyn, Exon. Th. 281, 4; Jul. 641. I a. used of that which destroys:—Wiga wælgifre (*death*), Exon. Th. 162, 7; Gū. 972: 231, 8; Ph. 486. Wiga unlæt lāces, 164, 4; Gū. 1006. Fȳr swearta lēg, weallende wiga, 61, 15; Cri. 985. Wiga (*a dog? fire?*) is on eorþan wundrum ācenned, 433, 23; Rä. 51, 1. II. *a noble, strenuous man*:—Se ðe mid wætere oferwearp wuldres cynebearn, wiga weorþlīce, Menol. Fox 317; Men. 160. Wigan unslāwne (*St. Andrew*), Andr. Kmbl. 3419; An. 1713. Wigena tīd (*the day of St. Simon and St. Jude*), Menol. Fox 370; Men. 186. [*Gaw. Allit. Pms.* wyȝe; *pl.* wyȝes: *Alex.* (Skt.) wee; *pl.* wees, wies: *Piers P.* wy, wye. Cf. *O. H. Ger.* Wigo (*proper name*).] v. æsc-, beorn-, byrn, cumbol-, folc-, gār-, gūð-, lind-, ord-, rǣde-, rand-, rīd-, scild-, wǣpen-, þeód-wiga.

wīgan [*p.* wāg, *pl.* wigon; *pp.* wigen] *to fight, do battle*:—Nū sceal hond and heard sweord ymb hord wīgan, Beo. Th. 5012; B. 2509. Mōises getealde ðæs folces meniu wīgendra manna *numeravit Moyses omnem summam filiorum Israel a viginti annis et supra*, Num. 26, 1. Six hund þūsenda wīgendra manna, Homl. Th. ii. 194, 14: Homl. Skt. ii. 25, 367: Homl. Ass. 103, 54. [*Goth.* weihan (weigan? v. Lk. 14, 31); *p.* waih *to fight*: *O. H. Ger.* wīhantero *bellantium.* Cf. *Icel.* vega; *p.* vā *to fight.*] v. ofer-wīgan, wīgend, wigian.

wī-gār. v. wíg-gār.

wíg-bǣre; *adj. Warlike, martial, eager for fighting*:—Wīgbǣre *bellicosus, pugnandi cupidus*, Wrt. Voc. ii. 125, 36.

wíg-bealu, wes; *n. War-bale, harm caused by war* or *the calamity of war*:—Wígbealu weccean *to kindle the wasting flame of war*, Beo. Th. 4098; B. 2046.

wíg-bed, wī-bed, wió-bed, -bud, wié-bed, weó-bed, -bud, weófod (-ed, -ud), wēfod, es, *also* -beddes; *n.* (*generally, but* se weóbud, Past. 33; Swt. 217, 21, *and pl.* wībedas, Bd. 5, 20; S. 641, 42) *An altar* [*from* wíg (wīh) *and* beód; *some forms*, e.g. wígbeddes, weóbedd, *suggest that the word was thought to be derived from* bed]:—Weófod *altar* vel *ara*, Wrt. Voc. i. 26, 51. Hē scolde ðone Godes alter habban uppan āholodne, ðæt hē meahte on healdan ða lāc ðe mon brōhte tō ðæm weóbude; for ðæm, gif se weóbud ufan hol nǣre, and ðǣr wind tō cōme, ðonne tōstencte hē ða lāc. Hwæt elles getācnaþ ðæt weóbud būton ryhtwīsra monna sāula? . . . Wæs eall sió offrung uppe on ðæt wiébed (wióbud, Cott. MSS.) brōht, Past. 33; Swt. 217, 19–25. Ðæt weóbud, 219, 3. Wígbed, Bd. 2, 3; S. 504, 39. Ðæt weófud (-od, MS. A.: wígbed, Lind.: wībed, Rush.), Mt. Kmbl. 23, 19. Wígbedes hornas *cornu altaris*, Ps. Th. 117, 25: Ps. Lamb. 117, 27. Tō wígbedes ðēnunge, Bd. 2, 20; S. 522, 9: 5, 10; S. 624, 34. Wígbedes (weófodes, col. 1), 3, 17; S. 544, 3, col. 2. Weófodes (wígbeddes, Lind.: wī-bedes, Rush.), Lk. Skt. 1, 11. Weófodes þēn, Homl. Ass. 22, 206. Weóuedes (weófedes), R. Ben. 55, 2. On wígbede tō hālsienne *ariolandi*, Wrt. Voc. ii. 9, 15. Ān dǣl ðam wībede (wígbede, *v. l.*), L. E. B. 12; Th. ii. 242, 18: Bd. 3, 23; S. 555, 14. Tō wībede, Ps. Surt. 42, 4. Tō weófode (wígbed, Lind.: weófud ł wībede, Rush.), Mt. Kmbl. 5, 23. On wígbed ðīn, Ps. C. 138. Tō wígbed (beforan ðæt weófud ł wībed, Rush.) *ad altare*, Mt. Kmbl. Lind. 5, 24. Ic ymbgaa wībed ðīn, Ps. Surt. 25, 6: Cd. Th. 107, 18; Gen. 1791: 108, 14; Gen. 1806: 113, 5; Gen. 1882. Weóbedd, 172, 8; Gen. 2841. Uppan ðæt weófod, Ex. 24, 6: 29, 20. Lege under weófod, Lchdm. ii. 138, 28: 142, 8. Wígbedu (wībed, Surt.: weófod, Spl.: wiébed, Spl. T.) ðīn *altaria tua*, Ps. Th. 83, 4. Tō wígbedum, Bd. 1, 27; S. 488, 38. Wībedum (*v. l.* weófodum), 1, 15; S. 484, 1. Tō Godes weófedan, L. Eth. vii. 26; Th. i. 334, 30. Tō hālgum wēfodum, Coll. Monast. Th. 36, 5. Ðæt tempel and ða weófedu (wígbedo, Bd. M. 136, 18) . . . ða wígbed and ða heargas *templa et altaria* . . . *aras et fana*, Bd. 2, 13; S. 516, 33–39. Ða wígbed (*v.l.* weófedu), S. 517, 18. Hē wībedas sette, 5, 20; S. 641, 42. Wībedu *arulas*, Germ. 394, 259. Paulus sceáwode ða weófoda, ōþ ðæt hē funde ān weófod ðe ðis gewrit on stōd: *Deo ignoto*, ðæt is on Englisc, 'Uncūðum gode is ðis weófod hālig,' Homl. Skt. ii. 29, 21. Hig ðǣr gedydon twā weófedu, Blickl. Homl. 205, 15. [*Laym.* weofed (wefd, 2nd MS.), weofd; *dat.* wæfde (wefde, 2nd MS.): *A. R. Kath.* weoued: *Ps. R. Glouc.* weved: *Ayenb.* wieved.]

wígbed-bōt, e; *f. A fine paid to the bishop for the injury done to the church by doing wrong to one in holy orders*:—Gif man preóst gewundige, gebēte man ða wyrdlan, and tō weófodbōte for his hāde sylle .xii. ōr.; æt diácone .vi. ōr. tō weófodbōte, L. N. P. L. 23; Th. ii. 294, 4–6. Gif man preóst ofsleá, forgilde man hine be fullan were, and biscope feówer and .xx. ōr. tō weófodbōte; æt diácone .xii. ōr. tō weófodbōte, 24; Th. ii. 294, 7–9. Gif hwā gehādodne man bende oððe beáte oþþe swȳðe gebysmrige, bēte wið hine swā hit riht sȳ, and bisceope weófodbōte be hādes mǣðe, L. C. S. 42; Th. i. 400, 23. In the laws of Henry I it is called emendacio altaris, 11, 8; Th. i. 521, 7: 66, 3; Th. i. 569, 13.

wígbed-heorþ, es; *m. The altar-hearth, the part of the altar where the offering is burnt*:—Hē genom on ðam wībedheorðe ðæs dustes dǣl, Lchdm. iii. 364, col. 1.

wígbed-hrægel, es; *n. An altar-covering*:—Hē sende ða ðing eall ða ðe tō cyrican ðēnunge nȳdþearflīco wǣron, hūselfatu and wígbidhrægl (-bed-, Bd. M. 90, 2) (*vestimenta altarium*), Bd. 1, 29; S. 498, 9.

wígbed-sceát, es; *m. An altar-cloth*:—Bewindan ða māgas ðæs cildes hand on ðæs altares weófodsceáte (*in palla altaris*), R. Ben. 103, 14. Ðis syndon ða cyrican mādmas on Scīrburnan. Ðǣr synd . . . .ii. mæssereáf and iii mæssehakelan and ii weóvedsceátas and ii overbrǣdels, Cod. Dip. B. iii. 660, 33. Hit gedafenlīc is ðæt his (*the priest's*) reáf ne beó horig, and his weófodsceátas beón wel behworfene, L. Ælfc. C. 22; Th. ii. 350, 21. Hē hæfð ðiderynn gedōn . . . .v. wællene weófodsceátas and .vii. oferbrǣdelsas, Chart. Th. 429, 25. Gif hwā wyle wyrcan weófodsceatas oððe ōðre reáf of his eáldum clāðum, gesylle ða ealdan, and geceápige nīwe, Homl. Ass. 35, 284. v. next word.

wígbed-sceáta, an; *m. An altar-cloth*:—On weófodsceátan *in palla altaris*, R. Ben. Inter. 99, 10.

wígbed-steall, es; *n. The part of the church where the altar stands*:—Wē lǣraþ ðæt mæssepreósta ǣnig ne cume binnan weófodstealle būton his oferslipe, ne hūru æt ðam weófode ðæt hē ðǣr þēnige būton ðære wǣde, L. Edg. C. 46; Th. ii. 254, 9 note. v. wíg-steall.

wígbed-þegen, es; *m. A minister of the altar, an ecclesiastic who performs service at the altar*:—Gif weófodþēn, ðæt is, biscop oððe mæssepreóst oððe diácon, gewīfode . . . hī forbudon ǣlc wīflāc weófodþēnum, L. I. P. 23; Th. ii. 336, 3–13: Wulfst. 270, 21. Gif weófodþēn his āgen līf rihtlīce fadige, ðonne sī hē fulles þegnweres wurðe, L. Eth. ix. 28; Th. i. 346, 17. Be gehādedum mannum. Gif weófodþegen manslaga wyrðe, L. C. S. 41; Th. i. 400, 13. Gif man freóndleásne weófodþēn mid tihtlan belecge, L. Eth. ix. 22; Th. i. 344, 22: L. C. E. 5; Th. i. 362, 18: L. C. S. 39; Th. i. 398, 25. Weófodþēna mǣðe medemige man for Godes ege, L. Eth. ix. 18; Th. i. 344, 9.

wígbed-þegnung, e; *f. Service at the altar*:—Wē forbeódaþ ðæt ǣnig preóst ōðre[s] cirican nāðer ne gebicgæ ne geþicgæ, būton hine hwā mid heáfodgylte forwyrce, ðæt hē weófodþēnunge wyrðe ne sī, L. N. P. L. 2; Th. ii. 290, 8.

wígbed-wíglere, es; *m. One who divines from the sacrifices, a diviner, soothsayer*:—Wígbedwíglere *ariolus* (as if from *ara*), Wrt. Voc. i. 17, 11.

wíg-bil[l], es; *n. A battle-blade, a sword*:—Ðæt sweord ongan æfter heaþoswāte hildegicelum, wígbil wanian, Beo. Th. 3218; B. 1607.

wíg-blāc; *adj. Splendid with warlike equipment*:—Werud wæs wígblāc (cf. beran beorht searo, 191, 23; Exod. 219. Wígbord scinon, 207, 14; Exod. 466), Cd. Th. 190, 24; Exod. 204.

wíg-bora, an; *m. A belligerent*:—Wígbora *belliger*, Ælfc. Gr. 8; Zup. 27, 16.

wîg-bora, an; *m. An image-bearer:*—Wīcbora (wiòbora, Anglia xiii. 35, 214) *signifer*, Hpt. Gl. 495, 71. v. wīh.

wîg-bord, es; *n. A shield:*—Hē hēht him gewyrcean eallīrenne wīgbord; wisse hē gearwe, ðæt him holtwudu helpan ne meahte, lind wið līge, Beo. Th. 4667; B. 2339. Wīgbord scinon, Cd. Th. 207, 14; Exod. 466.

wîg-cirm, es; *m. The din of battle:*—Ðǣr wæs wīgcyrm micel, hlūd hilde swēg, Cd. Th. 120, 6; Gen. 1990.

wîg-cræft, es; *m.* I. *war-craft, military skill:*—Pirrus wæs gemǣrsad ofer ealle ōþere cyningas, ǣgðer ge mid his miclan fultume, ge mid his rǣdþeahtunge, ge mid his wīgcræfte *Pyrrhus in se, ob magnitudinem virium consiliorumque, summam belli nomenque traduxit*, Ors. 4, 1; Swt. 154, 27. Hȳ him grimme forguldon ðone wīgcræft ðe hȳ æt him geleornodon *vincere, dum vincitur, edocuit*, 1, 2; Swt. 30, 7. Hē hæfde Higelāces hilde gefrunen, wlonces wīgcræft (*or* II?), Beo. Th. 5898; B. 2953. I a. *a warlike art, a warlike engine:*—Hȳ wurdon gerāde wīgcræfta, Ors. 1, 2; Swt. 30, 6. Mid scotum, ge mid stāna torfungum, ge mid eallum heora wīgcræftum *vis magna telorum*, 3, 9; Swt. 134, 16. Wīgcræftum *machinis*, Wrt. Voc. ii. 58, 33. II. *warlike force, military power* (abstract or concrete):—On Thessali hē ðæt gewinn swīþost dyde for ðære gewilnunge ðe hē wolde hī him on fultum geteón for heora wīgcræfte, for ðon hié cūþon on horsum ealra folca feohtan betst *Thessaliam ambitione habendorum equitum Thessalorum, quorum robur ut exercitui suo admisceerit, invasit*, Ors. 3, 7; Swt. 112, 3. Hē (*Christ*) mihte, gif hē wolde, wīgcræft habban sōna genōhne (cf. Mt. 26, 53), L. Ælfc. P. 51; Th. ii. 386, 34. Ðā beþōhtan hié ealle heora wīgcræftas Exantipuse *Xanthippum, cum auxiliis accitum, ducem bello praefecerunt*, Ors. 4, 6; Swt. 174, 30.

wîg-cræftig; *adj. Strong in war:*—Hē ðone gūðwine (*a sword*) gōdne tealde, wīgcræftigne, Beo. Th. 3626; B. 1811.

wîgend, wīggend, es; *m.* I. *a fighting man, a warrior, soldier:*—Wīgend weorðfullost (*Beowulf*), Beo. Th. 6189; B. 3099. Ðæm wīggende (*Constantine*), Elen. Kmbl. 1964; El. 984. Ðone wīggend (*Holofernes*), Judth. Thw. 25, 13; Jud. 258. Wīgend cruncon wundum wērige, Byrht. Th. 140, 43; By. 302: Beo. Th. 6279; B. 3144. Wīgend unforhte, Cd. Th. 189, 6; Exod. 180. Wīgend, cēne under cumblum, Andr. Kmbl. 2408; An. 1205. Wīggend, Judth. Thw. 22, 20; Jud. 69: 23, 26; Jud. 141. Wīgendra scolu (*Ulysses and his men*), Met. 26, 31. Wīggendra, Andr. Kmbl. 2191; An. 1097. Hē ðæt word ācwæþ tō ðām wīggendum, Judth. Thw. 25, 29; Jud. 283. Wīgend weccean, Beo. Th. 6040; B. 3024: Elen. Kmbl. 211; El. 106. II. *a noble, strenuous man:*—Se wīgend, Nergendes þegen, Mathias, Menol. Fox 49; Men. 24. Ða wīgend, cempan coste (*St. Andrew and St. Matthew*), Andr. Kmbl. 2108; An. 1055. Wuldres wynn, wīgendra þrym, 1774; An. 889. Wīgend (*St. Andrew's disciples*), 1699; An. 852. Gelǣdde ða wīgend (*those in the ark*) weroda Drihten, Cd. Th. 85, 7; Gen. 1411. ¶ *in the phrase* wīgendra hleó = *a lord, chief:*—Wīgendra hleó, freáwine folca (*Hrothgar*), Beo. Th. 863; B. 429: (*Sigemund*), 1803; B. 899: (*the Deity*), Andr. Kmbl. 1011; An. 506: (*St. Andrew*), 1792; An. 898. Ðū eart weoroda God, wīgendra hleó, helm alwihta, Exon. Th. 25, 31; Cri. 409. Wīggendra hleó, Eádmund cyning, Chr. 942; Erl. 116, 18. [*O. Sax. O. Frs.* wīgand: *O. H. Ger.* wīgant *bellator, pugnator, mars, armatus.*] v. burg-, byrn-, gār-, lind-, rand-, sweord-wīgend (-wīgende).

wîgende; *adj.* (*ptcpl.*) *Fighting, able to fight.* v. wīgan.

Wigere-ceaster. v. Weogorna-ceaster.

Wigestas (-e?); *pl. m. The name of some people in England:*—Wigesta landes is nygan hund hȳda, Cod. Dip. B. i. 414, 20.

wîg-freca, an; *m. A warrior:*—Wyrsan wīgfrecan, Beo. Th. 2428; B. 1212: 4985; B. 2496.

wîg-fruma, an; *m. A leader in war, a chieftain:*—Wīgfruma (*Hrothgar*), Beo. Th. 1332; B. 664. Æfter wīgfruman *after the chieftain's death*, 4514; B. 2261.

wîg-gâr, es; *m. A lance:*—Wīgār *lancea*, wegures (wīgāres?) gewrið *amentum*, Wrt. Voc. i. 35, 46–47. Cf. wīg-spere.

wîg-gebed, es; *n. Prayer to an idol* (?):—Wiggebed (wigg-bed?) *ara*, Wrt. Voc. ii. 9, 43. v. wīg-bed.

wîg-getawa (-e); *pl. f. War-equipments:*—On wīggetawum, Beo. Th. 741; B. 368.

wîg-gild (wīh-), es; *n. An idol:*—Hié onhnigon tō ðam herige, hǣðne þeóde wurðedon wīhgyld, Cd. Th. 227, 5; Dan. 182. Cf. deófol-gild.

wîg-gryre, es; *m. Terror caused by war:*—Wīggryre wīfes *the terror inspired when a woman makes war*, Beo. Th. 2572; B. 1284.

wîg-haga, an; *m. A phalanx:*—Hē mid bordum hēt wyrcan ðone wīhagan, and ðæt werod healdan fæste wið feóndum, Byrht. Th. 134, 50; By. 102.

wîg-heafola (?):—[Hē] wōd þurh ðone wælrēc wīg[hea]folan bær freán on fultum, Beo. Th. 5316; B. 2661. *Hea* is the reading of Thorkelin's transcripts, but now the MS. shews only quite uncertain traces of *h*, and *ea* is entirely gone (Zupitza). Wīg-heafola is taken to mean *a helmet* by some editors: Grein suggests wīgneafolan = *umbonem bellicum* i. e. *clypeum.* Could the reading be wīgne afolan? Cf. *Icel.* vīgr *in fighting state, serviceable for fighting*, and afli *strength;* so that the passage would mean he had *or* brought strength that might serve to help his lord in battle.

wîg-heáp, es; *m. A war-troop, a band of warriors:*—Is mīn fletwerod, wīgheáp gewanod, Beo. Th. 958; B. 477.

wîg-heard; *adj. Stout in fight, hardy:*—Wigan wīgheardne, Byrht. Th. 133, 64; By. 75. [*Icel.* vīg-harðr (*poet.*).]

wîg-hete, es; *m. Hate that leads to war:*—Sunu deáþ fornam, wīghete Wedera *death took off her son, the Weders' hate that found its vent in war*, Beo. Th. 4246; B. 2121.

wîg-hryre, es; *m. Fall in fight:*—Se ðe æt sæcce gebād wīghryre wrāðra *he that in strife had lived to see the fall in fight of fierce foes*, Beo. Th. 3242; B. 1619.

wîg-hûs, es; *n.* (in Wrt. Voc. i. 36, 41 it is masc.) *A war-house, a tower, fortification:*—Ðis wīghūs *haec arx*, Ælfc. Gr. 9, 75; Zup. 73, 14: 3; Zup. 7, 9. Se hīhsta wīghūs *arx*, Wrt. Voc. i. 36, 41. Wīghūs *propugnaculum*, Hpt. Gl. 499, 61. On ǣlcum ylpe wæs ān wīghūs getimbrod, and on ǣlcum wīghūse wǣron þrittig manna, Homl. Skt. ii. 25, 561. Wīghūses *turris*, Wrt. Voc. ii. 84, 28. Wīghūs *propugnacula*, i. 36, 40. Wīghūsum *turribus*, ii. 91, 25: Ps. Th. 47, 11: Past. 33; Swt. 229, 5. Se weall is mid stǣnenum wīghūsum (*habitaculis defensorum*) beworht, Ors. 2, 4; Swt. 74, 21. Menn wyrcaþ wīghūs him (*elephants*) on uppan, and of ðām feohtaþ, Hex. 9; Norm. 16, 11. [*O. H. Ger.* wīc-hūs *turris, propugnaculum.*]

wîg-hyrst, e; *f. The trappings of war:*—Beorn monig goldbeorht wīghyrstum scān, Exon. Th. 478, 3; Ruin. 35.

wigian; *p.* ode *To fight:*—Gif hē wigie and man gewundie, L. E. G. 6; Th. i. 170, 8. [Cf. *Goth.* waihjō *strife.*] v. wīgan.

wîgle (wigle?), es; *n. Divination, heathen practice:*—Wīglum *ceremonias* (the passage is: Ad tortas simulacrorum ceremonias, Ald. 41), Anglia xiii. 33, 162. [Þurh Merlines wiȝel (craft, 2nd MS.), Laym. 19250. He (*a devil*) makeð þe unbilefulle man to leven swilche wigeles, swo ich ar embe spac, Rel. Ant. i. 131, 27. His (*the devil's*) wiȝeles and his wrenches, A. R. 300, 5. Wieles, 92, 21: Fragm. Phlps. 8, 54. Wiheles, Marh. 13, 9.] v. steor-wigle; wīglere.

wîg-leóþ, es; *n. A war-song, the trumpet's summons:*—Gemundon weardas wīgleóþ . . . bȳman gehȳrdon flotan, Cd. Th. 191, 27; Exod. 221.

wîglere (wiglere?), weohlere, es; *m. A diviner, soothsayer, augur, sorcerer:*—Wīglere *augur*, Wrt. Voc. i. 74, 37. Ðes and ðeós wiglere *hic et haec augur*, Ælfc. Gr. 9, 22; Zup. 49, 2. Nū cwyð sum wīglere, ðæt wiccan oft secgaþ swā swā hit āgǣð mid sōðum ðincge, Homl. Skt. i. 17, 108. On gelīcnysse wīgleres and rǣdendes (*arioli et coniectoris*), Scint. 75, 12. Wȳgleras *auspices*, Germ. 398, 79. Be wiccum, wīglerum, etc. Gif wiccan oððe wīgleras, oþþe morðwyrhtan . . ., L. E. G. 11; Th. i. 172, 20: L. C. S. 4; Th. i. 378, 7. Wiccan oþþe wīgleras, scīncræftigan . . ., L. Eth. vi. 7; Th. i. 316, 20. Wiccan and wīgleras (wīgeleras, *v. l.*), Wulfst. 27, 1. Drȳmen, and wiccan and ōðre wīgeleras beóð tō helle bescofene for heora scīncræftum, Homl. Th. ii. 330, 28. Wīgulera *magorum, hariolorum*, Hpt. Gl. 502, 51. Tunglera ł wī[g]lera *Chaldaeorum* . . . wīhlera (? *printed* wineena) *hariolorum*, 483, 5–10. Ðonne man tō wiccan and tō wīgleran tilunge sēce æt ǣnigre neóde, Wulfst. 171, 11. Hē wiccan fordyde, and wīgleras āfligde, and drȳcræft tōwearp, Homl. Skt. i. 18, 464. [Wielare *augur*, Wrt. Voc. i. 89, 20. Þe wielare (*the devil*) makeð a swote smel cumen, ase þauh hit were of heouene, A. R. 106, 2. *M. Du.* wijcheler.] v. fugel-, gebyrd-, wīgbedwīglere (-weohlere), *and next word.*

wîglian; *p.* ode *To practise divination* or *sorcery:*—Wīgliaþ stunte men menigfealde wīgelunga on ðisum dæge æfter hǣðenum gewunan, swylce hī magon heora līf gelengan, oþþe heora gesundfulnysse, Homl. Th. i. 100, 19. Ne sceal nān cristen mann nān þincg be ðam mōnan wīglian, Lchdm. iii. 266, 17. [*M. Du.* wijchelen. v. Grmm. D. M. 985.] v. wīglung; wigol.

wîg-lîc; *adj. Warlike, martial:*—Ðæt wæs wīglīc werod, Cd. Th. 192, 17; Exod. 233. Wīglīc *bellica*, Wrt. Voc. ii. 125, 42. Wīglīce tōl *instrumenta bellica*, Hpt. Gl. 424, 28. Wīglīce *bellicosas*, 425, 7. Wēpna wīglīce *arma bellica*, Hymn. Surt. 135, 23. [*O. H. Ger.* wīc-līh *bellicus, bellicosus: Icel.* vīg-ligr.]

wîglîce; *adv. In a warlike manner, by fighting:*—*Bellatores* syndon wīgmen, ðe eard sculon werian wīglīce mid wǣpnum, L. I. P. 4; Th. ii. 306, 37: Wulfst. 267, 16. v. ān-wīglīce.

wîglung, e; *f. Divination, soothsaying, sorcery, augury:*—Wīlung *divinatio*, Kent. Gl. 554. Wē gehȳrdon seggon, ðæt nān mann ne leofode gif hē gewundod wǣre on ealra hālgena mæssedæg. Nis ðis nān wīglung, ac wīse menn hit āfunden þurh ðone hālgan wīsdōm, Lchdm. iii. 154, 5. Gif treówa beóð on fullum mōnan geheáwene, hī beóð heardran, and langfǣrran tō getimbrunge . . . Nis ðis nān wīglung, ac is gecyndelīc ðincg, Homl. Th. i. 102, 25. Hleótan man mōt būtan wiccecræfte . . . gif hī hwæt dǣlan willaþ; ðis nis nān wīglung, ac bið wissung for oft, Homl. Skt. i. 17, 87. Wīgelunge *divinatione*, Hpt. Gl. 467, 69. Deófles bīgencg, ne on wīglunge ne on wiccedōme, Homl. Ass. 143, 122. Ðæt hē tǣlđ tō unālȳfedlīcere wīglunge, gif hwā đa wyrta on him becnitte, būton hē hī tō đam dolge gelecge, Homl. Th. i. 476, 4. Se đe gelȳfđ wīglungum odđe be fuglum, odđe be fnorum, odđe be horsum, odđe be hundum, ne biđ hē nā cristen . . . Se đe hwider faran wille . . . clypige hē tō his Dryhtne . . . and sīdige orsorh þurh Godes gescyldnysse būtan đæra sceoccena wīglunga. Ús sceamaþ tō secgenne ealle đa sceandlīcan wīglunga đe gē dwǣsmenn drīfaþ, oþþe on wīfunge, odđe on wadunge, odđe on brȳwlāce, odđe gif man hwæs bitt, đonne hī hwæt onginnaþ, oþþe him hwæt biđ ācenned, Homl. Skt. i. 17, 88–104. Ne gȳman gē galdra ne īdelra hwata, ne wīgelunga ne wiccecræfta, Wulfst. 40, 14. Gē cēpaþ dagas and mōnđas mid ȳdelum wīglungum (Gal. 4, 10), Homl. Th. i. 102, 19, 11, 15: Homl. Ass. 28, 99. Hē sum þing hæfde đe his hǣle hremde þurh rēđe wīglunga (wīgelunga, *v. l.*), Homl. Skt. i. 5, 259. [King scal wicchecreft aleggan and wiȝelunge ne geman, O. E. Homl. i. 115, 22. Monies godes monnes child heo (*incubii demones*) biccharređ þurh wigeling, Laym. 15791.] v. ge-, līc-, steor-wīglung; wīglian.

wīg-mann, es; *m. A man of war, a fighting man, soldier:—Bellatores* syndon wīgmen đe eard sculon werian wīglīce mid wǣpnum, L. I. P. 4; Th. ii. 306, 36: Wulfst. 267, 15. [*O. H. Ger.* wīc-mann *pugnator, pugil, bellator: Icel.* víg-maðr.]

wignoþ (?), es; *m. Warfare:*—Wignoþes (? *printed* -roþes), dugude *militiae*, Wrt. Voc. ii. 55, 18. v. wigian.

wigol; *adj. Adapted to augury:*—Wigole fugelas *oscines aves*, Wrt. Voc. i. 30, 8. [Cf. (?) *O. H. Ger.* wihil, wigil *alciones*.] Cf. wīglian.

wīg-plega, an; *m. The game of war, battle:*—Hē ne wandode nā æt đam wīgplegan, Byrht. Th. 139, 43; By. 268: 141, 2; By. 316. Hē sumum dǣleþ gūþe blǣd, gewealdenne wīgplegan, Exon. Th. 331, 16; Vy. 69.

wīg-rād (?), e; *f. A war-road, road along which an army passes:*—Gewāt him Abraham on đa wīgrōde (-rāde? -trode? v. wīg-trod) wiđertrod seón lāđra monna *Abraham betook himself to the way where the foe had gone and saw the track of their retreat*, Cd. Th. 125, 24; Gen. 2084.

wīg-rǣden[n], e; *f. Warfare*, Wald. 39; Vald. 1, 22.

wīg-sigor, es; *m. Victory in battle:*—Hē hæfde wīgsigor, Cd. Th. 121, 1; Gen. 2003. Hālig God geweóld wīgsigor (cf. Óðinn átti heimilan sigr í hverri orrostu, Ynglinga Saga, c. 2), Beo. Th. 3112; B. 1554.

wīg-sīþ, es; *m. A warlike expedition:*—Nǣfre mon lytle werede đon wurđlīcor wīgsīđ āteáh, Cd. Th. 126, 13; Gen. 2094.

wīg-smiþ, es; *A war-smith, war-maker, warrior, a man* (poet.):—Engle and Seaxe, wlance wīgsmiđas, Wealas ofercōman, Chr. 937; Erl. 115, 21: Exon. Th. 314, 14; Mód. 14. Ic wīgsmiđum sægde, đæt Sarra mīn sweostor wǣre, Cd. Th. 163, 24; Gen. 2703.

wīg-smiþ, es; *m. An idol-smith, a maker of idols:*—Deófulgild . . . đa hēr menn worhtan, wīgsmiđas mid folmum *simulacra . . . opera manuum hominum*, Ps. Th. 113, 12.

wīg-spēd, e; *f. Success in war, victory:*—Hē mē tīr forgeaf, wīgspēd wiđ wrāđum, Elen. Kmbl. 329; El. 165. Him Dryhten forgeaf wīgspēda gewiofu, Beo. Th. 1398; B. 697.

wīg-spere, es; *n. A war-spear:*—Wīgspere *falarica* vel *fala*, Wrt. Voc. i. 35, 48.

wīg-steall, es; *n. A defensive position, a bulwark, bastion, defence:*—Wīgsteal *propugnaculum*, Hpt. Gl. 487, 17: 530, 3. Hē lǣteþ inwitflān brecan đone burgweal, đe him bebeád Meotud đæt hē đæt wīgsteal wergan scealde, Exon. Th. 315, 30; Mód. 39. Hē wīgsteall sēceþ, heolstre behelmed, Salm. Kmbl. 208; Sal. 103. Wurdon hyra wīgsteal wēstenstaþolas, brosnade burgsteal, Exon. Th. 477, 21; Ruin. 28. Wīgstealla *propugnacula*, Hpt. Gl. 426, 73.

wīg-steall, es; *n. The part of a church where the altar stands:*—Weocsteall *absida*, Engl. Stud. xi. 64, 6. Wē lǣraþ đæt mæssepreósta oþþe mynsterpreósta ǣnig ne cume binnan weohstealle (weófodstealle, *v. l.*) būton his oferslipe, ne hūru æt đam weófode, đæt hē đǣr þēnige būton đære wǣde, L. Edg. C. 46; Th. ii. 254, 9.

wīg-strǣt, e; *f. A high-road, public road:*—An đara wīstrǣte, Cod. Dip. Kmbl. ii. 89, 4. [Cf. *O. H. Ger.* heri-strâza *via publica*.] Cf. here-paþ.

wīg-strang; *adj. Powerful in war:*—Wīgstrang *bellipotens*, Wrt. Voc. ii. 12, 45.

wig-telgode *for* twig-telgode, Ps. Spl. C. 108, 28. v. twi-telged.

wīg-þracu, *gen.* -þræce; *f. Violence of war, warfare:*—Hwǣr đæt hālige treó beheled wurde æfter wīgþræce (*the violent death of the crucifixion*), Elen. Kmbl. 859; El. 430. Wē đa wīggþræce (*the Trojan war*) on gewritu setton, 1312; El. 658.

wīg-þreát, es; *m. A military troop:*—Đæs hiofenlīcan werodes wīgþreátas *coelestis exercitus militiae*, Lchdm. i. lxviii, 8.

wīg-þrīst; *adj. Bold in battle, daring:*—Đū mē saga hū đū wurde þus wīgþrīst, đæt đū mec þus fæste fetrum gebunde, Exon. Th. 268, 14; Jul. 432.

wīg-trod [?], es; *n.:* -trodu (? v. wīg-rād), e; *f. A war-track, the road along which an army has passed:*—Wītrod (= wīgtrod) gefeól heáh of heofonum handweorc Godes *on to the track where the host of Israel had passed fell from the heavens the lofty walls raised by God's hand* (cf. se āgend up ārǣrde reáde streámas . . . syndon đa foreweallas gestēpte ōđ wolcna hrōf, 196, 28; Exod. 298), Cd. Th. 208, 31; Exod. 491.

wīg-wægn, es; *m. A war-chariot:*—Se kyningc Pharon hæfde syx hund wīgwægna (*curruum*), Ors. 1, 7; Swt. 38, 24, 35.

wīg-wǣpen, es; *n. A weapon of war:*—Ǣlce wīgwǣpna and ǣghwylce woruldsaca lǣte man stille, Wulfst. 170, 8.

wīg-weorþung, e; *f. Honour to idols:*—Būton đū forlǣte đa leásinga, weohweorđinga, and wuldres God ongyte gleáwlīce, Exon. Th. 253, 14; Jul. 180. Hwīlum hié gehēton æt heargtrafum wīgweorþunga, Beo. Th. 353; B. 176.

wīh (wih?), weoh; *gen.* wīges (weós?); *m. An idol:*—Hié gecwǣdon đæt hié đæs wīges (*the golden image*) ne rōhton, ne hié tō đam gebede mihte gebǣdon hǣđen heriges wīsa, Cd. Th. 228, 12; Dan. 201. Hié ne willaþ đysne wīg wurđigean, 228, 24; Dan. 208. Hē (*St. Bartholomew*) ne wolde wīg weorđian (cf. *the account in* Shrn. 120, 17–32), Apstls. Kmbl. 95; Ap. 48. Hē hǣþengield ofer word Godes, weoh gesōhte, Exon. Th. 244, 6; Jul. 23. Wōden worhte weós, 341, 28; Gn. Ex. 133. [Cf. *O. Sax.* wīh *a temple: Icel.* vé: *Goth.* weihs *holy: O. H. Ger.* wīh *holy*.] v. wīg-bed, -bora (*signifer*), -gild, -smiþ, -steall, -weorþung.

wihgena, Wihg(e)ra-ceaster, wīh-gyld. v. wiga, Weogorna-ceaster, wīg-gild.

wiht, e; *f.:* es; *n.* I. *a wight, creature, being, created thing:*—Nis nān wuht (cf. nān gesceaft, 22) đe mæge odđe wille swā heágum Gode wiþcweþan . . . Ne wēne ic đæt ǣnig wuht (cf. gesceaft, 24) sié đe wiþwinne *non est aliquid, quod summo huic bono vel velit, vel possit obsistere. Non . . . arbitror*, Bt. 35, 4; Fox 160, 29. Manig wyht is mistlīce fērende geond eorþan *quam variis terras animalia permeant figuris*, 41, 6; Fox 254, 23. Ǣlc uht, đæs đe hió (*an asp*) ābītt, scel his līf on slǣpe geendian, Ors. 5, 13; Swt. 246, 27. Ic (*a leather bottle*) eom wunderlīcu wiht, Exon. Th. 399, 16; Rä. 19, 1 (the word occurs often in the riddles). Ūr . . . is mōdig wuht, Runic pm. Kmbl. 339, 12; Rūn. 2. Nānre wuhte līchoma ne beođ tēderra đonne đæs monnes, Bt. 16, 2; Fox 52, 8. Se hrycg færđ æfter ǣlcre wuhte, Past. 1; Swt. 29, 14. Wiþerweardnes wuhte gehwelcre, Met. 11, 78. Đære wihte, Exon. Th. 438, 9; Rä. 57, 5. Ne mæg ic nāne cwica wuht (*animalia*) ongitan, đara đe wite hwæt hit wille, odđe hwæt hit nylle, đe ungenēd lyste forweorþan, for đam ǣlc wuht (*animal*) wolde bión hāl and libban, đara đe mē cwica đincđ; būte ic nāt be swylcum gesceaftum swylce nāne sāwle nabbaþ, Bt. 34, 10; Fox 148, 13–17. Sōđ is ǣghwylc đara đe ymb đās wiht wordum bēcneþ; ne hafaþ heó ǣnig lim, leofaþ se þeáh, Exon. Th. 421, 30; Rä. 40, 26. Hī gesēgon syllicran wiht, wyrm on wonge, Beo. Th. 6069; B. 3038. Ic đa wihte geseah . . . heó wæs wundrum gegierwed, Exon. Th. 483, 5; Rä. 68, 1. Hwylce wihta beóđ ōđre tīd wīfcynnes, and ōđre tīd wǣpnedcynnes? Salm. Kmbl. p. 202, 12. Ic geseah đa anlīcnessa ealra creópendra wuhta (*reptilium*) . . . Đa creópendan wuhta getācniaþ . . . , Past. 21; Swt. 155, 14. Swilca wuhta (fleógan, gnættas, loppe) him deriaþ, Bt. 16, 2; Fox 52, 14. Manega wuhta (*animalia*), Met. 31, 2. Đē sculon moldwyrmas ceówan, slītan swearte wihta (wihte, Exon. Th. 371, 10), Soul Kmbl. 146; Seel. 72. Đīne wihte *animalia tua*, Ps. Th. 67, 11. Đa wihte twā, Exon. Th. 429, 38; Rä. 43, 16. Flǣsc lytelra wuhta, smælra fugla, Lchdm. ii. 180, 13. Wihta Wealdend, Cd. Th. 272, 25; Sat. 125. Ne meahte đǣr drincan wihta ǣnig, Ps. Th. 77, 44. Ealra wihta gehwam *omne animal*, 144, 17. Wuhta gehwylc, Met. 11, 52. Earmost ealra wihta, đara đe cenned wǣre, Exon. Th. 421, 7; Rä. 40, 14. Wihta gehwylce, deóra and fugla, 61, 10; Cri. 982. Cynna gehwylc cucra wuhta, đara đe lyft and flōd fēdaþ, feoh and fuglas, Cd. Th. 78, 23; Gen. 1297. Dreám cwicra wihta, Exon. Th. 411, 5; Rä. 29, 8. Đeós lyfte byreþ lytle wihte, 438, 26; Rä. 58, 1. I a. of evil beings:—Yfel wiht *phantasma*, Mt. Kmbl. Lind. 14, 26: Mk. Skt. Lind. Rush. 6, 49. Wiht unhǣlo (*Grendel*), Beo. Th. 241; B. 120. Werge wihta (*devils*), Exon. Th. 455, 29; Hy. 4, 57. Unfǣle men, wudewāsan, unfǣle wihtu *satiri* vel *fauni*, Wrt. Voc. i. 17, 20. Đās fūlan wuhta (*wizards*) đū sceoldest āwurpan of đīnum rīce, Homl. Th. ii. 488, 12. II. *a whit, thing; ǣnig wiht aught, anything*, (a) without a negative:—Đǣr hī ǣnige wuht āgnes gōdes an heora anwealde hæfden, Bt. 27, 3; Fox 100, 4. Ic eom swīđe gefiónde đæt gē ǣfre woldon ǣnige wuht (ǣnig wuht (ǣnig-wuht?), Hatt. MS.) eów selfum wītan, ǣr ic hit eów wīte, Past. 31; Swt. 206, 19. (b) with a negative, *aught*. See also III. (1) alone:—Ne biđ him wiht tō sorge, Exon. Th. 238, 29; Ph. 611. Ne wendaþ hine wyrda, ne hine wiht (or *acc.?*) dreceþ, ādl ne yldo, 334, 1; Gn. Ex. 9. Nis đæt onginn wiht, 119, 2; Gū. 248. Nō hē him đæs wyrmes wīg for wiht dyde, Beo. Th. 4685; B. 2348. (2) with a genitive:—Ne biđ wiht forholen monna gehygda, Exon. Th. 65, 14; Cri. 1054. Ne him wiht gescōd đæs đe hȳ him tō teónan þurhtogen hæfdon, 127, 35; Gū. 396. Ne đǣr hleonaþ unsmēđes wiht, 199, 15; Ph. 26. Ne magon wē geleánian him mid lāđes wihte, Cd. Th. 25, 15; Gen. 394. Ne dyde ic for feóndscipe, ne for wihte đæs ic đē weán ūđe *I did it not from enmity, or from aught of ill will*, 163, 2; Gen. 2692. Hē nele lāþes wiht geæfnan, Exon. Th. 357, 22; Pa. 32: Cd. Th. 16, 13; Gen. 242. Ic đīnra worda ne mæg wuht oncnāwan, 34, 8; Gen. 534. Wiht, Elen. Kmbl. 1364; El. 684. Wonhȳdig wer ðæs wiht ne cann *vir insipiens non cognoscet*, Ps. Th. 91, 5. Hí nāne wuht ongitan ne cunnon ðara gǣstlecena beboda, Past. 1; Swt. 25, 23. III. cases (with or without preps.) with adverbial force, (a) without a negative:—Gif wē hit mægen wihte (*anyhow*) āþencan, Cd. Th. 26, 2; Gen. 400. Gif hit eówer ǣnig mæge gewendan mid wihte, ðæt hié word Godes forlǣten, 27, 35; Gen. 428. Ne wē wēnaþ, ðæt hē wihte mæge ðis folc āfēdan, Ps. Th. 77, 22. (b) with a negative:—Nis mē wihtæ þearf (*there is no need at all*) hearran tō habbanne, Cd. Th. 18, 25; Gen. 278. Hié ðæs wīges wihte ne rōhton, 228, 13; Dan. 201. Ic ðē bæd ðæt ðū ðone wælgæst wihte ne (*in no wise*) grētte, Beo. Th. 3995; B. 1995: Andr. Kmbl. 3320; An. 1663. Næs wordlatu wihte (*at all*) ðon māre, 3043; An. 1524. Wuhte, Met. 14, 10: 16, 14. Næs him wihte ðe sēl *it was not a whit the better for him*, Beo. Th. 5368; B. 2687. Nāt ic hit be wihte (*at all*; cf. be dǣle *in part*), Exon. Th. 468, 7; Phar. 4. Ic mid wihte (cf. mid ealle) ne mæg of ðissum lioðobendum *I am utterly unable to escape from these bonds*, Cd. Th. 24, 22; Gen. 381. Wit ðus baru ne magon wesan tō wuhte (*at any rate*), 52, 5; Gen. 839. Ic ne forhtige wiht (*or under* II (b)) *non movebor amplius*, Ps. Th. 61, 2: 113, 13. Him wiht ne speów *they did not at all succeed*, Judth. Thw. 25, 23; Jud. 274. Him wiht ne sceód grim glēda nið, Cd. Th. 245, 17; Dan. 464. Nō hē wiht fram mē fleótan meahte hraþor on holme, Beo. Th. 1087; B. 541. Ne beóð winter ðīn wiht ðe sǣmran *anni tui non deficient*, Ps. Th. 101, 24. Hwæt wilt ðū cweþan, gif hwā wuht nylle wiþwinnan, ac mid fullan willan forlǣt ǣlc gōd and fulgǣþ ðam yfele, Bt. 36, 6; Fox 182, 6. Hié noldon beón ābisgode nāne wuht on eorðlīcum ðingum *rebus exterioribus nullatenus occupentur*, Past. 18; Swt. 137, 1. [*Goth.* waihts; *f. res*; ni waiht *nihil*: *O. Sax.* wiht; *m. a thing, whit*; wihtī, *pl. evil spirits*: *O. H. Ger.* wiht; *n. substantia, animal, res*: *Icel.* vættr; *f. a being*; especially *a supernatural being*.] v. ā-, ǣnig- (?), hel-, nā-, nān-, sǣ-wiht; æl-, eall-wihta.

wiht (e; *f.*?) *weight*:—Wiht *pondus*, Kent. Gl. 344. Wihte *pondere*, Wülck. Gl. 237, 27. Genim ǣgþres gelīce micel be wihte (gewihte, *v.l.*), Lchdm. i. 146, 20. Mā hundred punda seolfres; ðet hē nam be wihte, and mid mycelan unrihte, Chr. 1086; Th. i. 355, 31. Genim of ǣlcere ðisre wyrte .xx. penega wiht, Lchdm. i. 374, 21. [For his æfne wiht of golde, Laym. 30835. Wiþþ fife wehhte of sillferr, Orm. 7812. *Ayenb.* wiȝte: *Chauc.* wighte, weihte, weiȝte: *Piers P.* weȝt, weght: *Icel.* vætt; *f.*] v. ge-wiht.

Wiht, Wiht-land, Wiht (Wihte) eáland *the Isle of Wight*:—Seó mǣið ðe nū eardaþ on Wiht, Chr. 449; Th. i. 20, col. 1: Cod. Dip. Kmbl. iii. 431, 16, 24: v. 82, 19: vi. 196, 8. Cōmon sex scipu tō Wiht, Chr. 897; Th. i. 176, 7. Intō Wiht (Wihtlande, *v.ll.*), 1006; Th. i. 257, col. 2. Tō Wiht (Wihtlande, *v.l.*), 1022; Th. i. 286, col. 1. On Wihtlande, 998; Th. i. 246, 24. Intō Wihtlande, 1001; Th. i. 250, 13. Hē on Wiht gehergade, 661; Th. i. 54, 24. Hié Wieht (Wiht, *v.l.*) forhergedon, 681; Th. i. 62, col. 1. Hēr Cerdic and Cynrīc genāmon Wihte eálond (Wihtland, Wiht ðæt eáland, *v.ll.*), 530; Th. i. 26, 33. Hié sealdon hiera nefum Wiht eáland (Wihte eáland, Wiht ðæt ēgland, Wihtland, *v.ll.*), 534; Th. i. 28, col. 1. Ymbe Wiht ðæt īgland (Wihtland, *v.l.*) *Vectae insulae*, Bd. pref.; S. 472, 14. Seó ðeód ðe Wiht ðæt eálond (Wihtland, *v.l.*) oneardaþ *gens quae Vectam tenet insulam*, 1, 15; S. 483, 22. [*From Latin* Vecta *or* Vectis.]

Wiht- *in proper names.* v. Txts. 512.

Wihtgāras; *pl. m. The name of some people in England*:—Wihtgāra (Wightgōra, 416, 7) landes is syx hund hȳda, Cod. Dip. B. i. 414, 22.

Wihtgāres (-as) **burh**, Wihtgāra burh *Carisbrooke*:—On Wihtgāras (-gāra, *v.l.*) byrg, Chr. 530; Th. i. 26, col. 1. Wihtgāra (-gāras, -gāres, *v.ll.*) byrg, 544; Th. i. 28, col. 1.

Wiht-land. v. Wiht.

Wihtmǣres wyrt *spoonwort* (?):—Witmǣres wyrt nioþoweard, Lchdm. ii. 32, 10. [Uihtmēres wyrt ł heauen hindele *brittannica*, iii. 300, col. 2.]

wiht-mearc, e; *f. A weight-mark, a plumb-line*:—Of punder, of wihtmearce *perpendiculo*, Hpt. Gl. 476, 75. v. pundar.

Wiht-sǣtan, -sǣte; *pl. m. The inhabitants of the Isle of Wight*:—Of Geáta fruman syndon Wihtsǣtan (*Victuarii*), ðæt is seó ðeód ðe Wiht ðæt eálond oneardaþ, Bd. 1, 15; S. 483, 22. v. next word.

Wiht-ware; *pl. m. The people of the Isle of Wight*:—Cantware and Wihtware (-wara, *v.l.*), Chr. 449; Th. i. 20, col. 1. Hē brōhte Wihtwarum (-an, *v.l.*) fulwiht ǣrest, 661; Th. i. 54, col. 1. v. preceding word.

wiisc. v. wȳsc.

wil. v. wil[l].

wīl *a wile, a device.* [He wolde þurh his micele wiles ðeor beon, Chr. 1128; Erl. 257, 14. To lokenn himm fra þeȝȝre laþe wiless, Orm. 10317. Þe wrenchful feont wið his wiles, Kath. 891. Þe world ledes a man with wrenkes and wyles, Pr. C. 1360. Wyle or sleythe *cautela, astucia*, Prompt. Parv. 528.] v. flige-wīl.

wīl-bec *a stream of misery* (?):—Wuniendo wær wīlbec biscær, Exon. Th. 353, 42; Reim. 26. [Cf. *Icel.* vīl *misery, wretchedness*; vīl-stigr *a path of misery*.]

wil-boda, an; *m. A welcome messenger*:—Mec meahtig Meotudes þegn (*an angel*) gesōhte, and mē sāra gehwylc gehǣlde, wuldres wilboda, Exon. Th. 176, 34; Gū. 1220. Cf. wil-spell.

wil-cuma, an; *m. One whose coming is pleasant, a welcome person* (*or thing*):—Mē is ðīn cyme on myclum ðonce, and ðū eart leóf wilcuma *gratus mihi est multum adventus tui, et bene venisti*, Bd. 4, 9; S. 577, 22. Leóf wilcuma Frysan wīfe, Exon. Th. 339, 17; Gn. Ex. 95. Hē wilcuman (*Christ come to hell*) grētte: 'Ðē ðæs þonc sié, ðæt ðū ūs sēcan woldest,' 462, 26; Hö. 58. Ðegnas cwōman, gesegon wilcuman heofones Waldend, 35, 7; Cri. 554. Gē sind wilcuman, Cd. Th. 303, 22; Sat. 617: Beo. Th. 794; B. 394. Hié synt wilcuman Deniga leódum, 782; B. 388: 3792; B. 1894. Ic hæleþum bodige wilcumena fela (*many welcome things*) wōþe mīnre, Exon. Th. 391, 4; Rä. 9, 11. [Wulcume (welcome, 2nd MS.) ært þu, swīðe leof þu ært me, Laym. 8528. His lauerd alse wilcume swa he weoren his sune, 4901. Cum aȝean, wilkume schaltu beon me, A. R. 394, 17. Ich am hire wel welcume, O. and N. 1600. Ðu and ðin trume beń to me welcume, Gen. and Ex. 1830.] v. next word.

wil-cume (-a); *interj. Welcome*:—Wilcume *evax*, Wrt. Voc. i. 61, 29. Wilcymo *euge*, Mt. Kmbl. Lind. 25, 23. ['A!' seið warschipe, 'Welcume liues luue!' O. E. Homl. i. 259, 11. *O. H. Ger.* Heilo *aut* willicomo *osianna*.] v. next word.

wilcumian; *p.* ode *To welcome, bid welcome, greet, salute*:—Gyf gē ðæt ān dōð, ðæt gē eówre gebrōðra wylcumiaþ (welcumieð (*later version*); hǣlo beádas ł wilcyma, Lind.) *si salutaveritis fratres vestros tantum*, Mt. Kmbl. 5, 47. Ðæt folc . . . wellcumiaþ Fēnix, Engl. Stud. viii. 478, 45. Basilius sende him tōgeánes, and hine wylcumode, Homl. Skt. i. 3, 507. Hine wylcumede se cāsere, and cwæð him tō mid blysse, 7, 339. Wilcumiga (wilcymogie (wilcymo gié? v. preceding word), Lind.) ł groeta *salutari*, Mk. Skt. Rush. 12, 38. [He wilcumede hine to londe, Laym. 10957. To wulcumen Mærlin, 17098. Þe lilie wolcumeþ (wel-, *v.l.*) me, O. and N. 440. Faiger welcumede he Eliezer, Gen. and Ex. 1396.] v. ge-wilcumian, *and preceding word.*

-wild. v. ge-wild.

wil-dǣd, e; *f. An acceptable deed, favour, benefit*:—Mōna se ændlefta, wyldǣda (wel-? v. wel-dǣd) biddan nytlīc is, Lchdm. iii. 188, 24.

wil-dæg, es; *m. A welcome day*:—On ðam wildæge, Exon. Th. 29, 7; Cri. 459. [Muchel wes þa murðe þe þat folc makode, and heo Godd thonkeden þat heo heora wildaȝes wælden weoren, Laym. 1798.]

wildan; *p.* de. I. *to tame, subdue*:—Wylde *domuit*, i. *vicit, mitigavit*, Wrt. Voc. ii. 141, 74. II. *to make submissive, have dominion over, rule, control*:—Hit is swytol, ðæt man tō hwōn wylde (wilde, gewilde, *v.ll.*) and woruldlīce stȳrde ðām ðe oftost for Gode syngodon and scendan ðās þeóde, Wulfst. 168, 2. Wille ic ðæt . . . ic and mīne þegnas wyldan ūre preóstas tō ðan ðe ūre sāula hyrdas ūs tǣcaþ, ðæt syndon ūre bisceopas, L. Edg. S. 1; Th. i. 272, 17. Se ðe ðone mǣran noman abbodes underfēhð, hē sceal mid twyfealdre lāre ða wyldan and tȳn, ðe him underþeódde synt *qui suscipit nomen abbatis duplici debet doctrina suis preesse discipulis*, R. Ben. 11, 12. Gyf mīn hī ne beóþ wyldde *si mei non fuerint dominati*, Ps. Spl. 18, 14. III. *to take into one's power, to seize*:—Ne dȳde man on Sunnandæges freólse ǣnigne forwyrhtne man . . . ac wylde (wylde man hine, *v.l.*; *the old Latin version has* capiatur) and healde, ðæt se freólsdæg āgān sȳ, L. C. S. 45; Th. i. 402, 12: L. E. G. 9; Th. i. 172, 14. v. ge-wildan (-wyldan), wilding.

wild-cyrfet *bryony*; brionia, Wrt. Voc. i. 32, 17. v. wilde.

wild-deór, wildeór, es; *n. A wild animal, wild beast*:—Wilddeór *fera*, Wrt. Voc. i. 22, 39. Ðis wilddeór (wildeór, *v.l.*) well fremaþ, Lchdm. i. 330, 7. Wildeór *fera*, Wrt. Voc. i. 77, 76. Ne mæg hit wæter ne wildeór beswīcan, Salm. Kmbl. 571; Sal. 285. Wildiór *leena*, Kent. Gl. 989. Wildeór *bestiae*, Bd. 3, 23; S. 554, 24: Coll. Monast. Th. 22, 23. Swā hwæt swā wilddeór ābiton, Gen. 31, 39: 37, 20. Wildeór, Blickl. Homl. 95, 16: Ex. 22, 13. Wildeór *bestiae agri*, 23, 11. Ealra wuda wildeór *omnes ferae sylvarum*, Ps. Th. 49, 11: 103, 19. Wilddeóra *ferarum*, Wrt. Voc. ii. 38, 32. Wilddeóra holl and denn *lustra*, i. 59, 10: Soul Kmbl. 164; Seel. 82. Wildeóra þeáw, Cd. Th. 252, 2; Dan. 572: 255, 10; Dan. 622. Uildeár (-deára? -dera?) *bestiarum*, Rtl. 117, 4. Anweald ofer wilddeórum, Hexam. 11; Norm. 18, 16. Hē mid wilddeórum (*cum bestiis*) wæs, Mk. Skt. 1, 13: Cd. Th. 256, 34; Dan. 650. Wildeórum, Exon. Th. 146, 21; Gū. 713. Wildiórum gelīcran ðonne monnum, Bt. 38, 5; Fox 208, 1. Ic āfyrre yfel wilddeór (*malas bestias*), Lev. 26, 6. Ealle yfele wilddeór, Lchdm. i. 202, 13. Wildeór, Lev. 26, 22: *feras*, Ps. Th. 67, 27. Nētena oððe wildeór, Bt. 38, 2; Fox 196, 18. Hwylce wildeór (*feras*) swȳþost gefēhst ðū? Ic gefō heortas, and bāras, and rǣgan, and hwīlon haran, Coll. Monast. Th. 21, 29. Wyrmas and wildeór, Beo. Th. 2864; B. 1430. v. wilde-deór, *and following words.*

wild-deóren; *adj. Of wild beasts*:—Mid wilddeórenum tōþum *cum feralibus dentibus*, Scint. 99, 7.

wilddeór-līc; *adj. Wild beast-like, brutish, brutal, bestial*:—Se wīsdōm is eorðlīc and wildeórlīce (-diór-, Hatt. MS.) *est ista sapientia terrena, animalis*, Past. 46; Swt. 346, 25. Seó wildeórlīce ārleásnes Bretta cyninges *feralis impietas regis Brittonum*, Bd. 3, 9; S. 533, 7. Ða wildeórlīcan *ferinam*, Wrt. Voc. ii. 34, 10. Hié be sumum dǽle wildiórlīce (*bestiales*) bióð, Past. 17; Swt. 108, 23. v. wilder-līc.

wilddeórlīce; *adv. After the manner of wild beasts, brutishly*:—Ðǽr ǽr wildeór oneardodan, oþþe men gewunedon willdeórlīce (*bestialiter*) lifian, Bd. 3, 23; S. 554, 25.

wilde; *adj. Wild*:—Wildæ *agrestis*, Wrt. Voc. ii. 99, 53: i. 17, 41. Wilde *indomitus*, ii. 111, 78. Untamed, wilde *edomitus*, 142, 40. Wudulīce oððe wilde *agrestes*, 4, 61. *As in this gloss the word seems used in* wylde (*or* cf. weald?) elfen *hamadryades* (cf. feldelfenne *amadriades*, ii. 8, 14), i. 60, 17. I. in reference to animals, *wild, not domestic, not tamed, not broken in*:—Rēþra þonne ǽnig wilde deór, Blickl. Homl. 95, 31: Homl. Th. i. 486, 28: Bt. 39, 1; Fox 212, 3. Wilde oxa *bubalus*, Wrt. Voc. i. 22, 46. Wilde bār *aper*, tam bār *verres*, 22, 70. Assa *asinus*, wilde assa *onager*, 23, 27. Se getemeda assa . . . Se wilda fola, Homl. Th. i. 208, 20–22. Wilde goos *cente*, Wrt. Voc. ii. 103, 68: *gente*, 109, 63. Wilde gōs *cante*, 14, 21. Wæs sum wilde hrem, Homl. Th. i. 162, 21. Se wilda fugel (*the Phenix*), Exon. Th. 211, 21; Ph. 201. Hafuc sceal on glofe wilde gewunian, wulf sceal on bearowe, Menol. Fox 495; Gn. C. 18. Sió wilde beó, Met. 18, 5. Seó leó gemonð ðæs wildan gewunan hire eldrana, Bt. 25; Fox 88, 12. Sum sceal wildne fugel ātemian, Exon. Th. 332, 14; Vy. 85: 222, 3; Ph. 343. Hālig feoh and wilde deór, Cd. Th. 13, 13; Gen. 202. Eoferas and wilde deór *aper et singularis ferus*, Ps. Th. 79, 13. Wildu diór, Met. 27, 20: Cd. Th. 91, 22; Gen. 1516. Wildu deór and neáta gehwylc, 240, 20; Dan. 389. Cōmon wilde beran and wulfas, Homl. Th. i. 244, 18. Wildra deóra ðæt grimmeste, Exon. Th. 371, 28; Seel. 82. Wildera deóra tēð *dentes bestiarum*, Deut. 32, 24. Hyre dǽl ðera wildera (*not broken in*) horsa, Chart. Th. 538, 33. Wildra, 548, 10. Wildu hors *equos indomitos*, Past. 41; Swt. 303, 9. Fiówer wildo hors, Shrn. 71, 34. Ða stælhrānas beóð swȳðe dȳre mid Finnum, for ðæm hȳ fōð ða wildan hrānas mid, Ors. 1, 1; Swt. 18, 12. I a. *not under restraint; uncontrolled*:—Ðā wæs culufre eft sended wilde, Cd. Th. 88, 14; Gen. 1465. II. in reference to plants, *wild, not cultivated*:—Wilde cyrfet *colochintida*, hwīt wilde wīngeard *brionia*, wilde (v. Wülck. Gl. 133, 12) wīngerd *labrusca*, Wrt. Voc. i. 30, 12–15. Wilde popig *saliunca*, . . . wilde næp *nap silvatica*, 31, 8, 27. Wilde næp *diptamnus* vel *bibulcos*, . . . wilde lactuce *sarrabum*, 32, 5, 24. *Oleastrum* ðæt is wilde elebeám, Lchdm. ii. 90, 20. Wildre magþan wyrttruman, 206, 15. Wildre mealwan seáw, 214, 14. Unwæstm ꝉ wilde fōter *zizania*, Mt. Kmbl. Lind. 13, 27. III. of places, *wild, uncultivated, uninhabited*:—Licgaþ wilde mōras emnlange ðæm bȳnum lande, Ors. 1, 1; Swt. 18, 27. Ðone eard (*East Anglia*) iii mōnþas hī hergodon and bærndon, ge furðon on ða wildan fennas hī fērdon, Chr. 1010; Erl. 143, 27. Com se biscop tō ðære mynstre (*Peterborough*) . . . ne fand ðǽr nān þing būton ealde weallas and wilde wuda, 963; Erl. 121, 28. IV. of fire, *wild, that spreads over a country* (like a prairie fire) [cf. *Icel.* villi-eldr]:—Hēr wæs se dría sumor, and wilde fȳr com on manega scīra and forbærnde fela tūna, and eác manega burga forburnon, Chr. 1078; Erl. 215, 36. On ðissum geáre atȳwde ðæt wilde fȳr, ðe nān mann ǽror nān swylc ne gemunde, and gehwǽr hit derode on manegum stōwum, 1032; Erl. 164, 1. Hēr wæs swīðe mycel mancwealm and orfcwealm, and eác ðæt wilde fȳr on Deórbȳscīre micel yfel dyde, and gehwǽr elles, 1049; Erl. 173, 19. IV a. figurative of a disease:—Wylde fȳr *erisipilas*, Wrt. Voc. i. 20, 3. [v. *wildfire* in Halliwell's Dictionary, and *cf. Germ.* das wilde feuer *St. Anthony's fire, erysipelas.*] V. in a moral sense, *wild, turbulent, ungoverned*:—Hē geong fareþ, hafaþ wilde mōd, Salm. Kmbl. 755; Sal. 377. [*Goth.* wilþeis: *O. Frs.* wilde: *O. L. Ger. O. H. Ger.* wildi: *Icel.* villr.]

wilde; *adj. Having power, powerful, strong*:—Hit næs þeáw ðæt mon ǽnig wæl on ða healfe rīmde ðe ðonne wieldre wæs *mos est, ex ea parte quae vicerit occisorum non commemorare numerum*, Ors. 4, 1; Swt. 156, 22. Beó ā seó mildheortnys wyldre ðonne se rihta dōm *semper superexaltet misericordiam judicium*, R. Ben. 118, 27. Ðæt ðæt gesceád beó wylldre ðonne seó yfele gewilnung, Basil admn. 3; Norm. 40, 3. Ūtancumene men beóð wildran ðonne gē and eów genyðriaþ *advena ascendet super te eritque sublimior; tu autem descendes et eris inferior*, Deut. 28, 43. Hié wyldran wǽron ðonne hié, and hié mid ealle of ðæm earde ādrifon *urbem suo generi vendicant, patrimonia dominorum sibi usurpant, extorres dominos procul abigunt*, Ors. 4, 3; Swt. 162, 18: Blickl. Homl. 151, 3. [Freo of heorte, of wisdom wilde, Misc. 96, 94. Þet þe mon lete his iwit weldre þene his wreððe, O. E. Homl. i. 105, 19.] v. weald.

-wilde. v. ge-wilde (-wylde), wildan.

wilde-cyn[n], es; *n. A wild species*:—Wildecynnes hors *equifer* (cf. *hic equiferus* a wyld hors, 187, col. 1), Wrt. Voc. i. 23, 4.

wilde-deór, es; *n. A wild beast*:—Weorpan hī an wildedeóra līc, Bt. 38, 1; Fox 194, 31. Hē wæs mið wildedeórum *erat cum bestiis*, Mk. Skt. Lind. Rush. 1, 13. [*Icel.* villi-dýr.]

wilder (-or? cf. wildor-līc. v. next word) (*and* wild? cf. Þa men tuhten to þan deoren, and duden of þan wilden al heora iwilla, Laym. 1129. At þe fyrst quethe of þe quest quaked þe wylde, Gaw. 1150. Went we to wod the wilde for to cacche, Destr. Tr. 2347. *O. H. Ger.* wild; *dat. pl.* wildiran; *and the declensions of* lamb, cild), es; *n. A wild beast*:—Þurh ðæs wildres (*the panther's*) mūð, Exon. Th. 358, 10; Pa. 43. Ðæt flǽsc, ðæt wildro ābiton *carnem, quae a bestiis fuerit praegustata*, Ex. 22, 31. Weorpan on wildra līc, Met. 26, 76: Exon. Th. 356, 10; Pa. 9: Cd. Th. 257, 25; Dan. 663. Spēdig man on wildrum, Ors. 1, 1; Swt. 18, 9.

wilder-līc (?); *adj. Wildbeast-like, brutish*:—Hié be sumum dǽle wildorlīce (wildiórlīce, Cott. MSS.) beóð *ex qua parte bestiales sunt*, Past. 17; Swt. 109, 23.

wild-gōs, e; *f. A wild goose*:—Wildgoos *gente*, Wrt. Voc. ii. 109, 60.

-wildian. v. ā-wildian.

wilding, e; *f. Dominion*:—On ǽlcere stōwe wylddingce his *in omni loco dominationis ejus*, Ps. Lamb. 102, 22. Wylding, Ps. Spl. M. 102, 22.

wildness (?), e; *f. Wildness, licentiousness*:—Gālre wild[nesse?] *petulantis lasciviae*, Hpt. Gl. 515, 10.

wildor, wildro; wilege, wile-wīse. v. wilder; wilige, wilig-wīse.

wil-fægen; *adj. Having one's desire, satisfied, glad*:—Wilfægen *voti compos*, Wrt. Voc. ii. 82, 59: *compos*, Ælfc. Gr. 9, 31; Zup. 58, 1. Wilfangen (*l.* -fægen) *voti compos*, Engl. Stud. xi. 67, 96. Ongan hē wilfægen æfter ðam wuldres treó eorðan delfan, ðæt hē funde behelede, Elen. Kmbl. 1652; El. 828. On eallum ðām mid ðȳ hē willfægen wæs gefremed, hē eft hwearf tō godcundre lāre *in quibus omnibus cum sui voti compos esset effectus, ad praedicandum rediit*, Bd. 5, 11; S. 625, 40. Mid eádigum wilfægene *cum beatis compotes*, Hymn. Surt. 36, 30. Crist ūs ēcum gefeánum dō beón wilfægene *Christus nos sempiternis gaudiis faciat esse compotes*, 123, 11. [Cf. *M. H. Ger.* wille-vagunge *satisfactio poenitentiae.*] v. wil-hrēmig, -hrēþig, -tygþe.

wilfullīce; *adv. Willingly, voluntarily, with a good will*:—Wilful[l]īce *sponte*, Hpt. Gl. 435, 66. [Alle þet for þi luue pouerte wilfulliche þolien, O. E. Homl. i. 279, 8. Þe ournemen of boȝsamnesse ys þet me bouȝe wiluolliche, Ayenb. 140, 19. Wylfully *voluntarie, spontanee*, Prompt. Parv. 528.]

wil-gæst, es; *m. A desirable, welcome guest*:—Godes āgen bearn, wilgest on wīcum, Exon. Th. 313, 28; Mōd. 7. Cf. wil-cuma.

wil-gebrōþor; *pl. m. Brethren pleasant in their lives*:—Freólīcu twā frumbearn, Cain and Abel . . . willgebrōðor, Cd. Th. 59, 30; Gen. 971. Cf. wil-gesweostor.

wil-gedryht, e; *f. A glad band*:—Seó wilgedryht wildne weorþiaþ *turba prosequitur munere laeta pio*, Exon. Th. 222, 2; Ph. 342. Wes ðū, Andreas, hāl mid ðās willgedryht, Andr. Kmbl. 1828; An. 916.

wil-gehlēþa, an; *m. A pleasant comrade*:—Hwīlum ic (*a horn*) tō hilde bonne wilgehlēþan, Exon. Th. 395, 9; Rä. 15, 5.

wil-gesīþ, es; *m. A pleasant companion*:—Wilgesīþas, Beo. Th. 45; B. 23. Willgesīððas, Cd. Th. 120, 31; Gen. 2003.

wil-gesteald, es; *n. A desirable possession*:—Ðȳ læs ðū eft cweðe ðæt ic wurde willgestealdum (-gesteallum, MS.; *but cf. the pairs of words* (*as here*) ǽht-gesteald, ǽht-gestreón; feoh-gesteald, feoh-gestreón) eádig on eorðan ǽrgestreónum *ne dicas: Ego ditavi Abram* (Gen. 14, 23), Cd. Th. 129, 20; Gen. 2146.

wil-gesweostor; *pl. f. Gracious sisters*:—Idesa, willgesweostor (*Lot's daughters*), Cd. Th. 157, 16; Gen. 2607. Cf. wil-gebrōþor.

wil-geþofta, an; *m. A pleasant associate*:—Ðæt inwitspell Abraham sægde freóndum sīnum, bæd him fultumes willgeþoftan, Cd. Th. 122, 14; Gen. 2026.

wil-gifa, -giefa, -geofa, an; *m. A giver of what is desirable, a giver of good*, (1) as epithet of an earthly prince:—Wilgeofa Wedra leóda, dryhten Geáta (*Beowulf*), Beo. Th. 5792; B. 2900. Ðæs wilgifan (*Constantine's*) word, Elen. Kmbl. 441; El. 221. (2) as an epithet of the Deity, *the giver of all good*:—Sigora Waldend, weoruda wilgiefa, Exon. Th. 229, 34; Ph. 465. Bearn Godes, weoroda willgifa, Elen. Kmbl. 1626; El. 815. Dryhten God, weoruda willgeofa, Andr. Kmbl. 2565; An. 1284. Gumena brego, weoruda wilgeofan, 123; An. 62. God, hyra wilgifan, Exon. Th. 34, 4; Cri. 537. Willgifan, Elen. Kmbl. 2221; El. 1112.

wilh (wiel); *gen.* wiles; *m. A slave, servant*:—Gif se wiel (*servus*) cwið: 'Mē is mīn hlāford leóf,' Ex. 21, 5. Ne wilna ðū ðīnes nēhstan wyeles, 20, 17. Ðæs weles (wieles, weales, *v. ll.*) hlāford *dominus servi illius*, Mt. Kmbl. 24, 50. Se ðe his wiel (*servum*) slicð mid girde, oððe his wylne, Ex. 21, 20, 32. v. wealh.

wil-hrēmig; *adj. Having one's desire, satisfied, exultant*:—Wilhrēmig (*printed* -hranig, *but see* Wülck. Gl. 376, 26) *compos*, Wrt. Voc. ii. 20, 69. v. wil-fægen, *and next word.*

wil-hrēþig; *adj. Satisfied, exultant*:—Weorud willhrēðig sægdon wuldor Gode, Elen. Kmbl. 2231; El. 1117. v. wil-fægen, *and preceding word.*

wilian *to roll*, wilie. v. wilwan, wilige.

wilige (*and* -a; *m.?*), an; *f. A basket*:—Wilige *cophinus*, Wrt. Voc. i. 25, 3. Wilige *vel* leáp, 55, 37. Wylige oððe meoxbearwe *corbis* vel *cofinus*, 86, 2. Wylige (wilige, *v. l.*) oððe windel *corbis*, Ælfc. Gr. 9,

28; Zup. 55, 13. Wiligan *corbes*, wiliga *corbis*, Hpt. Gl. 497, 41. On wylegan *in cophino*, Ps. Spl. 80, 6: Blickl. Gl. Hī hine on ānre wilian (*in sporta*, Acts 9, 25) ālēton ofer done weall, Homl. Th. i. 388, 9. Hū fela wyligena (-egena, *v. l.*) *quot cophinos*, Mk. Skt. 8, 19, 20. Wylegena, Mt. Kmbl. 16, 9, 10. Wiligum *corbibus*, Hpt. Gl. 468, 27. Seofon wilian fulle *septem sportas plenas*, Mt. Kmbl. 15, 37: Mk. Skt. 8, 8: Homl. Th. i. 182, 22. Wylian, ii. 396, 6: Jn. Skt. 6, 13.

wilig-wīse, an; *f. Basket-wise*:—Seó cyrice is sinhwyrfel on wilewīsan geworht, Blickl. Homl. 125, 21.

wiliht; *adj. Having willows*:—On wylihte mǣdwan (*the meadow with willows in it*); of wylihte mǣdwan, Cod. Dip. Kmbl. iii. 235, 16.

wilincel (-uncel), es; *n. A* (*young*) *slave*:—Wiluncel *mancipium*, Germ. 401, 30. v. wealh, *and next word*: cf. þeówincel.

wilisc; *adj.* I. *foreign, not English*:—Wylisc moru *carrot* (cf. wealh-moru) . . . Englisc moru *parsnip*, Lchdm. ii. 312, 16–21. Wælisc *opratanum* (= *abrotanum*, cf. sūþerne), Wrt. Voc. ii. 65, 46. Se wælisca (heafoc) (cf. wealh-hafoc), Exon. Th. 332, 24; Vy. 90. Ðā hæfdon ða welisce menn gewroht ǣnne castel . . . Ðā wǣron ða wælisce men (*quidam de Normannis*; cf. *Icel.* Valskr *Norman*) ætforan mid ðam cynge, Chr. 1048; Erl. 178, 15, 24. **I a.** referring to the Celts of England, *Welsh*:—Be Wilisces monnes londhæfene. Gif Wylisc mon hæbbe hīde londes, L. In. 32; Th. i. 122, 9. Englisc . . . Wilisc, 46; Th. i. 130, 16: L. Wg. 7; Th. i. 186, 13. Nāh nāðer tō farenne ne Wylisc man on Ænglisc land, ne Ænglisc on Wylisc ðe mā, L. O. D. 6; Th. i. 354, 23. Tremerin se Wylisca (Wylsca, *v. l.*) biscop (*bishop of St. David's*), Chr. 1055; Erl. 191, 11. Cōmon upp on Wylisce Axa .xxxvi. scypa and ðǣr ābūtan hearmas dydon mid Gryfines fultume ðæs Wæliscan cynges, 1050; Th. i. 310, 19. Welscan (Wyliscean, l. 36), 1052; Erl. 186, 17. Ðæt ylce ðe man ðam Wyliscean þeófe dyde, L. Ath. v. 6, 3; Th. i. 234, 13. Ðone Wyliscan cining, Chr. 1056; Erl. 191, 22. Wīte-þeówne monnan Wyliscne, L. In. 54; Th. i. 138, 3. .xii. lahmen scylon riht tǣcean Wealan and Ænglan, .vi. Englisce and .vi. Wylisce, L. O. D. 3; Th. i. 354, 10. Wylsce menn geslōgan mycelne dǣl Englisces folces, Chr. 1053; Erl. 188, 9. Ðā Wylisce menn hī gegaderodon, and wið ða Frencisce ðe on Walon wǣron gewinn up āhōfon, 1094; Erl. 230, 32. Hengest and Æsc gefuhton wiþ Walas, and .xii. Wilisce (Wilsce, *v. l.*) aldormenn ofslōgon, 465; Erl. 12, 22. ¶ the word is used of some kind of ale:—.xii. āmbra Wilisces ealaþ, .xxx. hlūttres, L. In. 70; Th. i. 146, 17. Twā tunnan fulle hlūtres aloð and cumb fulne līðes aloð and cumb fulne Welisces aloð, Cod. Dip. Kmbl. i. 203, 9. .xxx. ōmbra gōdes Uuelesces aloð ðæt limpeð tō .xv. mittum, 293, 13. Wælsces, ii. 46, 27. Geworht of Wiliscum ealað, Lchdm. ii. 78, 23. Drence on Welscum ealað, 136, 1. Dō ealle ðās wyrta on Wylisc ealo, 120, 6. **II.** *servile*:—Hē on ðreó tōwearp ða cneór[d]nesse, ðæt wæs wælisc (*the race of Ham*; cf. Onwōcon of Chame .xxx. theóda mycelra, and eác ðæt cynn wæs geseald ðām ōðrum cynnum twām on heaftneád and on þeówdōm, 2, 51), and on cyrlisc cynn, and on gesȳðcund cynn, Anglia xi. 3, 62. [*O. H. Ger.* Walahisc *romanus, latinus*: *Icel.* Valskr *foreign, esp. French.*] v. wealh.

wil[l], es; *n.* I. *will, pleasure*:—Se cyng geseah ðæt hē nān þincg his willes ðǣr gefordian ne mihte *the king saw that he could carry out nothing of his purpose*, Chr. 1097; Erl. 234, 6. Hē nolde his willes (*of his own accord*) heora geferrǣdene forlǣtan, Homl. Th. ii. 334, 25: Ap. Th. 4, 5. Wylles, Nicod. 11; Thw. 6, 7. Gif hwā hine sylfne besmīte his āgenes willes (*sua sponte*), L. M. I. P. 36; Th. ii. 274, 20: Homl. Ass. 62, 255. Gif þeówa and þeówen hyra bēgra wylles hig gesomnigon *si servus et ancilla mutua voluntate se conjunxerint*, L. Ecg. C. 25; Th. ii. 150, 15. Be ðīnum āgenum wille ðū fērdest tō ðīnes fæder hīwrǣdene *ad tuos ire cupiebas et desiderio erat tibi domus patris tui*, Gen. 31, 30. Hī mōston ðes cynges wille folgian, Chr. 1086; Erl. 222, 33. Ne fornime incer nōðer ōðer ofer will būtan geþafunge *nolite fraudare invicem, nisi ex consensu*, Past. 51; Swt. 399, 34. Hē genam ðæt wīf ofer ðæs cynges wil, Chr. 1015; Th. i. 276, 4, col. 2. **II.** *a pleasant* or *desirable thing*:—Willa (wilna? v. willa, **VI a**) spēdum, dugeða gehwilcre stēpan, Cd. Th. 142, 18; Gen. 2363. [Þin aȝen wil, O. E. Homl. i. 61, 119. Liues wil and eche pleie, 193, 62. Þe onnesse of o luue and of o wil, A. R. 12, 7. Al his wil to don, Laym. 2793. Ðu wurchest mi wil, Kath. 2108. Þat wil, Shor. 16. *Icel.* vil; *n.*] v. ge-, self-, un-wil[l], willes; willa.

will, well, wyll, es; *m. A well, spring, fountain* (lit. and fig.):—Well *fons*, Wrt. Voc. i. 54, 29. Ān wyll (*fons*) āsprang of ðære eorðan, Gen. 2, 6. Ðǣr wæs Iacōbes wyl (wyll, *v. l.*). Se Hǣlend sæt æt ðam wylle, Jn. Skt. 4, 6. Bið on him will (wyll, *v. l.*) forðrǣsendes wætres, 4, 14. Wyl, Bd. 1, 7; S. 478, 27. Hió āweóll of ānum wille (welle, Cott. MSS.) *non a diverso fonte emanavit*, Past. 7; Swt. 49, 11. Lǣt forð ðīne willas (wyllas, Cott. MSS.) . . . Ðæt is ðætte se lāreów ǣrest sceal self drincan of ðam wille his āgenre lāre *deriventur fontes tui foras . . . Rectum est, ut ipse prius bibat*, 48; Swt. 373, 14. Of ðam geate tō wille; fram ðan wille, Cod. Dip. Kmbl. iii. 172, 37. Āþweah ða eágan on clǣnum wylle, Lchdm. ii. 32, 16. Hwīlum gehātaþ hȳ ælmessan tō wylle (wille, welle, *v. ll.*), Wulfst. 12, 3. Gif hwylc man his ælmessan gehāte oððe bringe tō hwylcon wylle (*ad fontem aliquem*), . . . fæste .iii. geár on hlāfe and on wætere, L. Ecg. P. ii. 22; Th. ii. 190, 24. Gif hwā his wæccan æt ǣnigum wylle hæbbe, iv. 19; Th. ii. 210, 12. Hlūterra wella wæter hī druncon *potum dabat lubricus amnis*, Bt. 15; Fox 48, 12. Wylla, Cd. Th. 240, 13; Dan. 386. Willas *fontes*, Ps. Spl. 103, 11. Wyllas, 73, 16. Ne weorðian gē wyllas, Wulfst. 40, 15. [Cnihtes þane wel dutte, Laym. 19812 (2nd MS.).] v. wæter-will; willa, wille.

willa, wella, wylla, an; *m. A well, spring, fountain* (lit. and fig.):—Wæs ðēr wælla (*fons*) . . . ðe Hǣlend sæt ofer ðæm wælla, Jn. Skt. Rush. 4, 6, 14. In ðæm wælla, 9, 7. Tō ðē ðam willan ealles wīsdōmes *ad te fontem omnis sapientiae*, Bd. 5, 24; S. 649, 3. Mid ðam willan fulluhte bæþes *fonte baptismatis*, 5, 7; S. 620, 33. Ðiosne pytt ł uælla *puteum*, Jn. Skt. Lind. Rush. 4, 12. [Heo ȝeoten i þan welle (wille, 2nd MS.); þa wes þa welle mid attre bigon, Laym. 19771.] v. wille, will.

willa, an; *m.* I. *will, the faculty of willing*:—Gē hwæthwega godcundlīces on eówerre sāule habbaþ, ðæt is andgit and gemynd and se gesceádwīslīca willa, Bt. 14, 2; Fox 46, 26. Sāwul is *voluntas*, ðæt is wylla, ðonne heó hwæt wyle, Homl. Skt. i. 1, 187. Ðæs mannes sāwl hæfð on hire . . . gemynd and andgit and willa . . . Of ðam willan cumaþ geþōhtas and word and weorc, ǣgðer ge yfele ge gōde . . . þurh ðone willan heó wile swā hwæt swā hire līcaþ, Homl. Th. i. 288, 18–30. Se willa sceal beón ǣfre frig, Ælfc. Gr. 32; Zup. 200, 2. Mid ðīnum āgenum willan and mid ðīnum āgenum anwealde ðū ealle ðing geworhtest, Bt. 33, 4; Fox 128, 12. **II.** in case of one who has authority, *will, purpose, design, command*:—Gewurðe ðīn willa *fiat voluntas tua*, Mt. Kmbl. 6, 10. Hē eall gedēð, swā his willa byð *omnia, quaecumque voluit, fecit*, Ps. Th. 113, 11. Bið ðām ōþrum ungelīce willa geworden *God's will will turn out very differently for the others*, Exon. Th. 77, 29; Cri. 1264. Hæfde se heorde, se ðe of heofonum cwom, feóndas āfyrde. Hwylc wæs fægerra willa geworden? *what fairer instance of God's will taking effect has there been?* 147, 3; Gū. 721. Gebēte hit God ælmihtiga, ðonne his willa sȳ, Chr. 1085; Erl. 219, 24. Gecyrron wē tō Drihtnes willan, Blickl. Homl. 101, 35. Hwyder magon gyt gangan from mīnum willan? 187, 25. Him eal worold wendeþ on willan, Beo. Th. 3482; B. 1739. Ðās fīf andgitu gewisseþ seó sāwul tō hire wyllan, Homl. Skt. i. 1, 201. Willan *nutum*, Wrt. Voc. ii. 93, 26: 61, 5. Ic þurh his willan hider āsend wæs *Dei voluntate huc missus sum*, Gen. 45, 8. Ðæne þeów ðe his hlāfordes willan (*voluntatem*) wiste, and ne dyde æfter his hlāfordes willan, Lk. Skt. 12, 47. Hē Drihtnes willan sōhte, Blickl. Homl. 225, 30. Ic dō willan mīnes Drihtnes, 243, 22: Cd. Th. 9, 15; Gen. 142. Hī his willan wyrcean *qui facitis voluntatem ejus*, Ps. Th. 102, 20. Heó Alwaldan bræc word and willan, Cd. Th. 38, 1; Gen. 600. Mid gebedum ealne deófles willan oferswīþan, Blickl. Homl. 61, 20. Ic tō him gebeáh and his willan geceás *I submitted to him and swore allegiance to him*, L. O. 1; Th. i. 178, 9. Wið ðam ðet heó his willan gecеóse *on condition of her becoming his wife*, L. Edm. B. 3; Th. i. 254, 12. Syndon ðīne willan rihte, Cd. Th. 234, 10; Dan. 290. **II a.** with reference to the disposition of property:—Ic Abba cȳðe and wrītan hāte hū mīn willa is ðæt mon ymb mīn ærfe gedōe æfter mīnum dæge. Ǣrest ymb mīn lond . . . is mīn willa, gif mē God bearnes unnan wille, ðæt hit fōe tō londe æfter mē, Chart. Th. 469, 27: 470, 3. **III.** *will, determination, resolution*:—Hwilc anwilnys and geortrūwad wylla, þurh ða ðeós fægre geógað nū forwurðan sceall, Homl. Skt. i. 4, 310. **IV.** *will* in contrast with power or performance, *intention, purpose, desire to act*:—Twā ðing sindon ðe ǣlces monnes ingeþanc tō fundaþ, ðæt is willa and anweald *duo sunt, quibus omnis humanorum actuum constat effectus; voluntas scilicet, ac potestas*, Bt. 36, 3; Fox 176, 7. Þeáh hī ðæt weorc ne mægen fulfremman, hī habbaþ ðeáh fūlne willan, and se untweofealda willa bioþ tō tellenne for fullfremod weorc . . . þeáh willaþ ða yfelan wyrcan ðæt, ðæt hī lyst, . . . ne forleósaþ hī eác ðone willan, ac habbaþ his wīte . . . Se yfla willa hiora welt, 36, 7; Fox 184, 23–29. Se yfela willa biþ tōstenced, gif mon ðæt weorc þurhtión ne mæg, 38, 2; Fox 196, 31. Ic nǣfre ne teolade sittan on ānum willan mid ðām ārleásum *cum impiis non sedebo*, Ps. Th. 25, 5. Arn hē inn mid sceandlīcum willan, Homl. Skt. i. 7, 170. Ōðerne rǣd wyrsan tō his willan *other counsel worse for his purpose*, 19, 206. Se Hǣlend hæfde ðone gōdan willan tō ðam fōstre, and ða mihte tō ðære fremminge, Homl. Th. i. 184, 22. Ūs æteówan his mihte and his willan, Blickl. Homl. 67, 1. Wē āgyltaþ þurh weorc and þurh willan, 35, 14. Se man se ðe wylle ōþerne ofsleán, and ne mæg his wyllan þurhteón, L. Ecg. P. ii. 1; Th. ii. 182, 14: Past. 11; Swt. 71, 14. **V.** *will, desire, wish*:—Ic læs mǣrðo gefremed hæfde þonne mīn willa wǣre, Nar. 32, 29. Wē witon ðæt ðæt is ðīnes mōdes willa, ðæt ðū mōte ðās world forlǣtan, Blickl. Homl. 225, 19. Ic beó gearo sōna willan ðīnes *I will consent to your wish*, Exon. Th. 245, 26; Jul. 50. Hē cwæþ ðæt ðæt īdel wǣre ðæt hī wilnedon, ac æt nȳhstan mid ānmōde willan monigra hē wæs oferswīþed, Bd. 5, 6; S. 619, 3. Tō willan (*ad votum*) ðæs weres heó eardigendlīc wæs geworden, 4, 28; S. 605, 20. His heorte ongann wendan tō hire willan, Cd. Th. 44, 30; Gen. 717. Hié ðæs ðone willan næfdon, ðæt hié heora noman hié benāmon, Ors. 2, 8; Swt. 94, 7: Cd. Th. 36, 9; Gen. 569. Hī forlēton ðone willan tō āgenne, Homl. Th. i. 394, 5. Se cyning geþafode ðam þegne his willan, Homl. Skt. i. 6, 224: Beo. Th. 1274; B. 635. Ðæt mē God gefylle feores ingeþanc, willan mīnne, Elen. Kmbl. 1359; El. 681. Willum ic wilnade *desiderio desideraui*, Lk. Skt. Lind. Rush. 22, 15. **V a.** *desire* in an unfavourable sense:—Nȳtenu . . . heora willa tō nānum ōþrum þingum nis āþenod būton tō gīfernesse and tō wrǣnnesse *pecudes . . . quorum omnis ad explendam corporalem lacunam festinat intentio*, Bt. 31, 1; Fox 112, 7. Weres wylla, Lchdm. i. 358, 18. Sió hātheortness ðæt mōd gebringð on ðæm weorce ðe hine ǣr nān willa tō ne spōn *mentem impellit furor, quo non trahit desiderium*, Past. 33; Swt. 215, 10. Fæste for ðam unrihtan wyllan *pro illa prava cupidine jejunet*, L. Ecg. P. iv. 10; Th. ii. 206, 20. Ic him in onsende in breóstsefan bitre geþoncas þurh mislīce mōdes willan, Exon. Th. 266, 31; Jul. 406. Ða flǣsclīcan willan, ða cumaþ þurh deófles sceónessa tō manna heortan, Blickl. Homl. 19, 6. **VI.** *pleasure, delight*:—Willa *uoluptas*, Wülck. Gl. 253, 44. Se willa ðæs līchoman *voluptas carnis*, Bd. 1, 27; S. 493, 19, 21. Ðā cwæþ hē: 'Mē bið willa gif ðū miht' *multum delector, si potes*, 5, 3; S. 616, 30 note. Se yfela willa unrihthǣmedes *voluptas*, Bt. 31, 2; Fox 112, 24: Met. 18, 2. Wē sprǣcon ǣr be ðām fīf gesǣlþum, ðæt is . . . willa (cf. fīfte beoþ seó blis, 33, 1; Fox 122, 6), Bt. 33, 2; Fox 124, 19, 22: Wulfst. 11, 7. Hire se willa gelamp, ðæt heó on ǣnigne eorl gelȳfde, Beo. Th. 1257; B. 626: 1653; B. 824. Hwȳ ne miht ðū geþencan gif on ǣnegum ðissa eorþlīcena gōda ǣniges willan and ǣniges gōdes wana is, ðonne is sum gōd full ǣlces willan and nis nānes gōdes wana *si est quaedam boni fragilis imperfecta felicitas, esse aliquam solidam, perfectamque, non potest dubitari*, Bt. 34, 1; Fox 134, 24–27. Ðæt wīf onfēhð ðæs (*from that*) willan on ðæm hǣmede, Lchdm. i. 350, 11. Ðū tīres mōst, willan brūcan, Andr. Kmbl. 212; An. 106: Exon. Th. 151, 24; Gū. 800. Gif ðæt mōd ðæm willan ne wiðbrītt *dum in cogitatione voluptas non reprimitur*, Past. 11; Swt. 71, 8. Hē hine on ðæm willan gehielt ðæt hē mid ealre ēstfulnesse lufaþ ðæt ēce līf *sub aeterna ejus beatitudine tota devotione continetur*, 50; Swt. 389, 15. Se wer ðe his bebod healdeþ mid willan *the man that delighteth in his commandments*, Ps. Th. 111, 1. Ðeáh ðe hē lēte wæter on willan, wynnum flōwan, 77, 21. Ne weóx hē him tō willan, ac tō wælfylle and tō deáðcwalum, Beo. Th. 3426; B. 1711. Tō willan and tō worðmyndum *to please and honour him*, 2376; B. 1186. Nafast ðū tō manna mægene willan *non in viribus equi voluntatem habebit*, Ps. Th. 146, 11. Þurh ungelȳfedre willan *per inlicitam voluptatem*, Bd. 3, 19; S. 548, 29. Forgife ðē Dryhten willan on worulde and in wuldre blǣd, Andr. Kmbl. 711; An. 356. Heó wīde hire willan sōhte, nō hweðere reste fand, Cd. Th. 87, 28; Gen. 1455. Ða willan and ða getǣsu ðe him on ðisse worulde becumaþ, Past. 50; Swt. 387, 15. Hwǣr cumaþ his willan and his fyrenlustas? Blickl. Homl. 113, 1. Ða ðe ðisses middangeardes wilna and welena wilniaþ, Past. 50; Swt. 387, 7. Mið walum and willum līfes *divitiis et uoluptatibus uitae*, Lk. Skt. Lind. 8, 14. Willum neótan, Exon. Th. 82, 26; Cri. 1344. Hē brūcan mōt wonges mid willum, 208, 1; Ph. 149. Willum biscyrede, 93, 3; Cri. 1520. Tō hira willum *ad suos libitos*, Wrt. Voc. ii. 3, 10. Willan *libitos, luxus*, Hpt. Gl. 480, 60. **VI a.** *a pleasant, desirable thing, a good, what gives pleasure, what is desired*:—Ic eom æþelinges ǣht and willa, Exon. Th. 488, 19; Rä. 77, 1. Nānes willan wana, nāþer ne weorþscipes, ne anwealdes, ne foremǣrnesse, ne blisse, Bt. 24, 4; Fox 86, 30. Gif ðē ǣnies willan wana biþ, ðeáh hit lytles hwæt sié, 11, 1; Fox 30, 22: 26, 1; Fox 90, 22. Nǣron hī bescyrede sceattes willan *non sunt fraudati a desiderio suo*, Ps. Th. 77, 29. Siððan hē ðæs welan full biþ, ðonne þincþ him ðæt hē hæbbe ǣlcne willan, gif hē hæbbe anweald, Bt. 33, 2; Fox 124, 10. Oft brincð se woruld ðone willan ðe bið eft *time often brings the unattained desire*, Prov. Kmbl. 40. Gif man mægðman nēde genimeþ, ðam āgende .l. scillinga, and æft æt ðam āgende sīnne willan (*the object he had desired* i.e. *the maiden*) ætgebicge, L. Ethb. 82; Th. i. 24, 4. Losewest willana *deceptio divitiarum*, Mk. Skt. Rush. 4, 19. Wilna brūcaþ, āra on eorðan, Cd. Th. 92, 22; Gen. 1532. Wilna geniht, 113, 21; Gen. 1890. Wilna brytta, 97, 29; Gen. 1620. Wilna gehwilces weaxende spēd, 100, 6; Gen. 1660. Wana wilna gehwilces, 137, 12; Gen. 2272. Hié lǣddon eorðwelan, wīf and willan and heora woruldgestreón, 112, 31; Gen. 1879. **VII.** *will, disposition*:—On eówrum fæstendagum bið ongieten eówer willa *in diebus jejuniorum vestrorum inveniuntur voluntates vestrae*, Past. 43; Swt. 315, 3. 'Sȳ on eorðan sibb ðām mannum ðe synd gōdes willan.' Ne bið nān lāc Gode swā gecwēme swā se gōda willa . . . Hwæt is gōd willa būton gōdnys . . . Hwæt is ǣnig lāc wið ðisum willan? Homl. Th. i. 582, 33–584, 10: Hy. 8, 6. Hē (*Titus*) wæs swā gōdes willan ðæt hē sægde ðæt hē forlure ðone dæg ðe hē nōht on tō gōde ne gedyde, Ors. 6, 8; Swt. 264, 2. Mid gōdum willan fæstan, Blickl. Homl. 37, 27: 97, 27. Gode underþeódde on gōdum willan, 79, 32. On fæstendagum bið gesȳne hwilcne willan gē habbaþ, L. E. I. 42; Th. ii. 438, 35. Nǣnig wæs weorð, gif mon his willan begeat yfelne, Met. 8, 37. Gelīcnyssa willena *qualitates affectionum*, Scint. 28, 18. **VII a.** *good will, favourable disposition*:—Swā micel beón scyl gebiddendes embe God willa *tantus esse debet orantis erga Deum affectus*, Scint. 33, 8. Willa belimpð tō blisse simle *voluntas ad laetitiam pertinet*, Past. 43; Swt. 315, 5. Se Hālga Gāst is willa and sōð lufu ðæs Fæder and ðæs Suna; sōðlīce willa and lufu getācniaþ ān ðing, Homl. Th. i. 282, 2-4: 228, 24. In ārfæstnesse willan *in devotione pietatis*, Bd. 4, 22; S. 592, 25. Gē earme men willum onfēngun, on mildum sefan, Exon. Th. 83, 5; Cri. 1351. **VIII.** in reference to voluntary or to permitted action, *will, accord, consent, pleasure*:—Gif ðam Pāpan ðæt līcode and ðæt his willa wǣre and his leáf *si Papae hoc ut fieret, placeret*, Bd. 2, 1; S. 501, 32. Gif beweddod mǣden nele tō ðam ðe heó beweddod bið, and wæs hire willa *si puella desponsata cum eo esse nolit, cui voluntate sua desponsata erat*, L. Ecg. C. 20; Th. ii. 148, 29. Selflīces willan *spontaneae voluntatis*, Hpt. Gl. 436, 76. Āgnes willan hē bið gebunden, Homl. Th. i. 212, 16: 224, 23. Ða yfelan nellaþ heora willan gehȳran Godes beboda, L. Ælfc. P. 4; Th. ii. 364, 20. Be willan *ultro*, Wrt. Voc. ii. 92, 74. Wæs sió fǣmne mid hyre fæder willan biweddad, Exon. Th. 244, 24; Jul. 32: Met. 24, 54: Andr. Kmbl. 2802; An. 1403. Eallra gesceafta āgnum willan (-um, Cott. MS.) God rīcsaþ ofer hī, Bt. 35, 4; Fox 160, 12. Hwæðer ǣnig gesceaft seó, ðe hire willan (-um, Cott. MS.) nylle ealne weg bión, ac wile hire āgnum willan (-um, Cott. MS.) forweorþan, 34, 9; Fox 148, 11. Mid fullan willan *volens*, 36, 6; Fox 182, 7. Nō genēded, ac mid his wyllan, Blickl. Homl. 29, 16. Mid hyra bēgra wyllan *cum consensu amborum*, L. Ecg. C. 25; Th. ii. 150, 20. His āgnum willan (willum, *v. l.*) hē com tō rōde gealgan, Past. 3; Swt. 33, 19. Ungeniédde, mid eówrum āgenum willan (willum, Cott. MSS.), 18; Swt. 137, 20. Be his āgenum willan, Homl. Th. i. 228, 30. Mid his sylfes willan *ultro*, Bd. 1, 7; S. 477, 22. Mid nænigum nēde gebǣded, ac mid his sylfes willan, Blickl. Homl. 83, 32. Hē genam ðæt wīf ofer ðes cynges willan, Chr. 1015; Erl. 152, 5. Hē ofer willan gióng *he went against his will*, Beo. Th. 4810; B. 2409: Exon. Th. 412, 6; Rä. 30, 10. Him nānwuht wið his willan ne sié, Bt. 11, 1; Fox 30, 25. Hē mid ðara wietena willum ðæm cynedōme ne mehte tō cuman, Ors. 4, 5; Swt. 166, 26. Ic gestāg willum mīnum, Exon. Th. 91, 16; Cri. 1493. Ðæs ðe ðū nǣfre þīnum willum ālǣtan woldest, Bt. 11, 2; Fox 34, 13. Ðæt ǣnegu þeód ōþre hiere willum friþes bǣde, Ors. 1, 10; Swt. 48, 29. Gif hié hiera willum ūs tō noldon *si uoluntate sua nollent procedere*, Nar. 10, 23: L. Wih. 1; Th. i. 36, 16: Bt. 11, 1; Fox 32, 29: Ps. Th. 17, 43: 44, 16. Hannibal his āgnum willum hine selfne mid ātre ācwealde *Annibal veneno sese necavit*, Ors. 4, 11; Swt. 206, 30: Bt. 34, 11; Fox 150, 30. Hī hiora āgnum willum hī sylfe unþeáwum underþeódaþ, 40, 7; Fox 242, 29: 35, 4; Fox 160, 16. Hī sēcaþ sylfra willum hāmas on heolstrum, Exon. Th. 107, 4; Gū. 53. Ōðer hiene his selfes willum gebeád, Past. 7; Swt. 49, 3. Mid his sylfes willum *ultro*, Bd. 1, 7; S. 477, 15. **IX.** *sake, account* (cf. *Ger.* meinetwillen):—Hē āscade hié for hwȳ hié nolden geþencan ealle ða brocu and ða geswinc ðe hē for hira willan and eác for hiera niédþearfe fela wintra dreógende wæs, Ors. 5, 4; Swt. 224, 28. Hē ǣfre wan for willan ðæs Ælmihtigan, Homl. Skt. ii. 25, 683. **X.** *will, one's own way*:—Saga mē hwæt ðam men sī leófust on his līfe and lāðost æfter his deáðe. Ic ðē secge his willa, Salm. Kmbl. p. 204, 44. Ic hī lifian hēt æfter hiora willum *ibunt in voluntatibus suis*, Ps. Th. 80, 12. [*Goth.* wilja: *O. Sax.* willio: *O. Frs.* willa: *O. H. Ger.* willo *voluntas, voluptas, affectus, affectio, votum, placitum, intentio, nutus, propositum, arbitrium, mens, anima, ratio*: *Icel.* vili.] v. hyht-, un-, weorold-willa; wil[l].

willan; *prs.* ic, hē wille, wile, ðū wilt, *pl.* wē willaþ; *p.* wolde, walde; *part. prs.* willende *To will, wish*:—*Volo* ic wylle, *uis* ðū wylt, *uult* hē wyle, *uolumus* wē wyllaþ . . . *utinam uellem* eálā gyf ic wolde; *utinam uelim* eálā gyf ic wylle gyt . . . *uelle* wyllan, Ælfc. Gr. 32; Zup. 199, 14–200, 6. **I.** *to will, exercise the faculty of willing*:—Ic undergyte ðæt ic wylle undergytan and gemunan, and ic wylle ðæt ic undergyte and gemune; ðǣr ðǣr ðæt gemynd bið, ðǣr bið ðæt andgyt and se wylla, Homl. Skt. i. 1, 120. Þurh ðone willan seó sāwul wile swā hwæt swā hire līcaþ, Homl. Th. i. 288, 29. Ǣlc mon hæfþ ðone friódōm, ðæt hē wāt hwæt hē wile, hwæt hē nele *ipsis inest volendi, nolendique libertas*, Bt. 40, 7; Fox 242, 20. **II.** where the will of the subject determines his own action, *to will, purpose, think, mean, intend*, (a) with an infinitive:—Ic wille mid flōde folc ācwellan, Cd. Th. 78, 20; Gen. 1296. Ic reste on ðē āgan wylle, 254, 16; Dan. 612. Ic ðēc for sunu wylle freógan, Beo. Th. 1899; B. 947. Hwyder wilt ðū gangan? Ic wille gangan tō Rōme, Blickl. Homl. 191, 16. Ne wille ic leng his geongra wurþan, Cd. Th. 19, 15; Gen. 291. Hē wile eft gesettan heofona rīce, 25, 20; Gen. 396: 176, 30; Gen. 2919. Wē hine willaþ ācwellan and ūs tō mete dōn, Blickl. Homl. 231, 14. Hū geweарð ðē ðæs, ðæt ðū sǣbeorgas sēcan woldes māðmum bedǣled? Andr. Kmbl. 616; An. 308. Wolde hē hiene selfne on ðæm gefeohte forspillan *mori in bello paratus*, Ors. 3, 9; Swt. 128, 6: Cd. Th. 176, 2; Gen. 2905. Ne wellaþ (willaþ, Wrt. Voc. ii. 71, 64) cweþan *ne velitis dicere*, Mt. Kmbl. Rush. 3, 9. Hwī forcwið hē . . . būton hē cueðan wielle (wille, Cott. MSS.), ðæt hē ne lufige ðone Hlāford, Past. 5; Swt. 43, 7. Hwæþre him Alwalda wille wyrpe gefremman, Beo. Th. 2633; B. 1314. Ðæt ðū for sunu wolde hererinc habban, 2355; B. 1175. Ðū him ðæt gehēte, ðæt ðū hyra frumcyn īcan wolde, Cd. Th. 236, 8; Dan. 318. (b) with an accusative:—God symble wyle gōd, and nǽfre nān yfel, Homl. Skt. i. 1, 48. From ðære tungan ðe teosu wylle *a lingua dolosa*, Ps. Th. 119, 2. Ðæt heó hī frūne hwæt hī sōhton, oþþe hwæt hī ðǽr woldon, Bd. 3, 8; S. 531, 39. (c) with a clause:—Wēndun gē and woldun, ðæt gē Scyppende sceoldan gelīce wesan, Exon. Th. 141, 30; Gū. 636. Wēndon and woldon, ðæt hié on elþeódigum ǽt geworhton, Andr. Kmbl. 2145; An. 1074. (d) absolute, (1) of purpose to go:—Nū wille ic ðam līge neár, Cd. Th. 47, 14; Gen. 760. Ðā hē him from wolde, Past. 3; Swt. 35, 19. Gif hē eów āxie hwæder gē willon (*quo vadis?*), Gen. 32, 17. Ðā hī tō scipan woldon, Chr. 1009; Erl. 142, 28. Ðā salde se here āþas ðæt hié of his rīce uuoldon, 878; Erl. 80, 17. Ðā woldan hié on ēcnesse hǽle and trume wið deófla nīþum, and wundorlīce deáþ geþrowodan, Blickl. Homl. 171, 30. Mið ðæm ðe hī hié getrymed hæfdon, and tōgædere woldon, Ors. 4, 2; Swt. 160, 28. (2) of purpose to do:—Hē cȳdde his syrewunge, hū hē ymbe wolde (*how he had intended to act*), Homl. Th. i. 82, 18. (3) of things, *to tend*:—Hwæðer ðū nū ongite hwider ðiós sprǽce wille? Ðā cwæþ ic: Sege mē hwider hió wille *jamne igitur vides, quid haec omnia, quae diximus, consequatur? quidnam? inquam*, Bt. 40, 1; Fox 234, 32. **III.** where the will of the subject determines the action of another, *to will, ordain, order, command*, (a) with an accusative:—Se ealdorman gewāt ðā ðā hit wolde God, Homl. Skt. i. 20, 13. Ðā ðā hē wolde ðæt ðæt hē wolde, Met. 11, 15. Hwæþer wē ǽnigne frȳdōm habban, ðe sió godcunde foretiohhung oþþe sió wyrd ūs nēde tō ðam ðe hī willen, Bt. 40, 7; Fox 242, 16. (b) with a clause:—Ic wylle (uillo, Lind.: willo, Rush.) ðæt hē wunige ðus, Jn. Skt. 21, 22. Wyltū (wylt ðū, *v.l.*) wē secgaþ ðæt fȳr cume of heofene, Lk. Skt. 9, 54. Hē wolde ðæt ða cnihtas cræft leornedon, Cd. Th. 221, 4; Dan. 83. Hē wolde ðæt him eorðe geseted wurde, 6, 35; Gen. 99: Met. 11, 16. (c) absolute:—Hē cunnian wolde his Drihtnes wyllan, hū hē wolde be him (*what he would have him do*) . . . Cwæð se Hǽlend, ðæt hē sceolde underfōn mǽden, Homl. Skt. i. 4, 7-13. **IV.** *to will, wish, want, desire*, (a) with infinitive:—Ic wielle heora cȳpan hēr luflīcor ðonne ic gebicge ðǽr, Wülck. Gl. 97, 2. Wilt ðū, gif ðū mōst, wesan aldordēma? Cd. Th. 149, 26; Gen. 2480. Ðē wile beorna sum him geāgnian, 109, 26; Gen. 1828. Se ðe wyle sōð sprecan, Beo. Th. 5721; B. 2864. Ðē sǽlīðend secgan willaþ, ðæt wē fundiaþ Higelāc sēcan, 3641; B. 1818. Wē willaþ beón bylewite *volumus esse simplices*, Coll. Monast. Th. 33, 7. Ic ðīne bebodu wolde gegān *concupivi mandata tua*, Ps. Th. 118, 40. Swā fela swā hē habban wolde, Chr. 877; Erl. 78, 24. On hwilce healfe ðū wille hwyrft dōn, Cd. Th. 115, 12; Gen. 1918: 139, 20; Gen. 2312. Gesecgan mid hū micle elne ǽghwylc wille synrust þweán, Exon. Th. 81, 4; Cri. 1318. Se biscop ðe wile onfōn Godes mildheortnesse, Blickl. Homl. 45, 7. Gif ǽnig man wolde heora ōðrum fylstan, Homl. Skt. ii. 27, 56. (a 1) where an infinitive may be supplied from the context:—His nēxtan be his mihte gehelpan, and ofer his mihte wyllan *to help his neighbour according to his power, and to wish to help him beyond his power*, Homl. Th. i. 584, 9. (b) with an accusative:—Ðæt ðæt ðū wylt, ðæt ðū lufast, Homl. Th. i. 282, 5. Hwæt wille gē? Coll. Monast. Th. 32, 23: Blickl. Homl. 155, 35. For ealle ðe willaþ ðæt hē wile, L. Ath. iv. 3; Th. i. 222, 20. Hē cwæþ: 'Hwæt wilt ðū ðæt ic ðē do?' Næs ðæt nā ðæt hē nyste hwæt se blinda wolde, Blickl. Homl. 19, 33. Hig dydon ymbe hyne swā hwæt swā hig woldon (waldon, Lind.: waldun, Rush.), Mt. Kmbl. 17, 12. Bide mē swā hwæt swā ðū wylle (willt ł wælle, Lind.) . . . ic ðē sylle swā hwæt swā ðū mē bitst, þeáh ðū wylle healf mīn rīce, Mk. Skt. 6, 22, 23. Behreówsunge mā wyllan ðænne deáð *penitentiam malle quam mortem*, Anglia xi. 119, 66. ¶ the present participle used with force of Latin forms in *-dus*:—Gefeán ðære willendan gesynto *cupitae sospitatis gaudia*, Bd. 4, 3; S. 570, 22. (c) with a clause:—Wilt ðū ðæt ic ðē secge? Salm. Kmbl. 506; Sal. 253. Wilt ðū ðæt ic gelȳfe? Blickl. Homl. 179, 35. Ǽghwylc mon wile ðæt him Drihten selle ealle his þearfe, 51, 15. Hū hē wolde ðæt mon him miltsode, Past. 16; Swt. 101, 10. Hē walde ðæt hī wǽren gedrēfde, 58; Swt. 443, 11. Wolde, Exon. Th. 74, 7; Cri. 1203. Wē woldun ðū gesāwe ðæt . . ., 130, 16; Gū. 439. Hī woldun, ðæt . . ., 123, 17; Gū. 324. Hī willen ðæt him Dryhten tō hyra earfeða ende gerȳme, 115, 25; Gū. 195. For ðȳ ic wolde ðæt hié ealneg æt ðære stōwe wǽren, Past. pref.; Swt. 9, 5. For ðon hē ðis dyde ðæt hē wolde ðæt hié ne wǽron gedrēfede, Blickl. Homl. 17, 1. **IV a.** *to like* (where there is an expressed or implied condition):—Ic wolde ðē ācsian hwæþer wē ǽnigne frȳdōm habban, Bt. 40, 7; Fox 242, 13. Wolde ic freóndscipe ðīnne, gif ic mihte, begitan, Andr. Kmbl. 956; An. 478. Wolde ic ānes tō ðē cræftes neósan, 966; An. 483. Gif hæleþa hwone hlīsan lyste, ðonne ic hine wolde biddan, Met. 10, 3. Wolde ic, ðæt ðū funde ða, Elen. Kmbl. 2157; El. 1080. Eall þing habbaþ ǽnne willan, ðæt is ðæt hī woldon ā bión, Bt. 34, 12; Fox 152, 29. **V.** *to will, be willing* to do something, (a) with an infinitive expressed or implied:—Gyf ðū wylt, ðū miht mē geclǽnsian . . . Ic wylle; beó geclǽnsod, Mt. Kmbl. 8, 2-3. Gif ðū þeáh mīnum wilt wordum hȳran, Cd. Th. 35, 24; Gen. 559. Wylt, Beo. Th. 3709; B. 1852. Ne wylt ðū ofergeottul weorðan *noli oblivisci*, Ps. Th. 102, 2: 118, 31. Ne wile Sarran gelȳfan wordum mīnum, Cd. Th. 144, 11; Gen. 2388: 161, 7; Gen. 2661. Gif wit him geongordōm lǽstan willaþ, 41, 27; Gen. 663. Gif git ðæt fæsten fȳre willaþ forstandan, 152, 17; Gen. 2521. Wille gē beón beswungen on leornunge? Coll. Monast. Th. 18, 18. Gif ðū woldest myltsian, and swā þeáh ne mihtest . . . ðæt ðū ne mæge myltsían, þeáh ðū wylle, Homl. Skt. i. 3, 184-188. Ne ðurfon wē ðæs wēnan, ðæt wuldorcyning ǽfre wille eard ālēfan, Cd. Th. 272, 7; Sat. 116: 281, 25; Sat. 277. Ne willaþ eów andrǽdan, 194, 25; Exod. 266. Ic nū suna mīnum syllan wolde (*should be ready to give*) gūðgewǽdu, ðǽr mē gifeðe ǽnig yrfeweard æfter wurde, Beo. Th. 5452; B. 2729. Ðǽr ðū fromlīce freónda lārum hȳran wolde, Exon. Th. 129, 22; Gū. 425. Hié gehēton ðæt hiera kyning fulwihte onfōn wolde, Chr. 878; Erl. 80, 18. Hē cwæð ðæt hē wolde ðam wīfe gemyltsian, Homl. Skt. i. 3, 179. Hē getrūwode ðæt hié his giongorscipe fylgan wolden, Cd. Th. 16, 27; Gen. 249: 46, 15; Gen. 744. Nymðe hié friðes wolde wilnian, 229, 9; Dan. 214. Ðǽr hȳ hit tō gōde ongietan woldan *if they had been willing to understand it aright*, Exon. Th. 68, 22; Cri. 1107. Gif ðū mīnum wilt, wīf, willende wordum hȳran, Cd. Th. 35, 25; Gen. 560. ¶ along with negative forms of the verb:—Saga him swā hē wille, swā hē nelle, hē sceal cuman *dic illi quia, velit nolet, debet venire*, Bd. 5, 9; S. 623, 11. Wē sceolon, wylle wē, nelle wē, ārīsan, Homl. Th. i. 532, 7. Wē sceolon beón nēde geþafan, sam wē willan, sam wē nyllan, Bt. 34, 12; Fox 154, 7. Se brym hine bær, wolde hē, nolde hē, Homl. Th. ii. 388, 20. (b) with accusative, *to allow, permit, grant, consent to*:—Ne willaþ hié rūmor unc landriht heora, Cd. Th. 114, 27; Gen. 1910. Se cāsere hine ðreátade ðæt hē Criste wiðsōce. Ðā hē ðæt ne walde, Shrn. 71, 33. Ne ðæt wille God, Cd. Th. 114, 13; Gen. 1903. (c) with a clause:—Nō God wolde, ðæt sió sāwl sār þrowade, Exon. Th. 126, 29; Gū. 378. **VI.** *to be disposed, to have such and such a will*:—Ðæt man his Scyppend lufige and ða men ðe wel willaþ (*the men that are of good will*), Homl. Skt. i. 16, 254. Ðæt hē wiðstonde ðǽm ðe on wōh wiellen (cf. ðām unryhtwillendum, 89, 22), Past. 15; Swt. 91, 1. Ðæt hē geornlīce fylste ðām ðe riht willan, and ā hetelīce stȳre ðām ðe þwyres willan, L. I. P. 2; Th. ii. 304, 17. **VII.** of habitual action:—Ða ingeðoncas ðe wealcaþ in ðæs monnes mōde, ðe ǽfre willaþ licgean on ðǽm eorðlīcum gewilnungum *quando cogitationes volvuntur in mente, quae a terrenis desideriis numquam levantur*, Past. 21; Swt. 155, 22. Hē wolde æfter ūhtsange oftost hine gebiddan and on cyrcan standan on syndrigum gebedum, Homl. Skt. ii. 26, 114. Hwæþer gē willen on wuda sēcan gold? Met. 19, 4. Ðæt se lāreów sceolde beón miehtig tō tyhtanne on hālwende lāre, and eác tō ðreánne ða ðe him wiðstondan wiellen *ut potens sit exhortari in doctrina sana, et eos, qui contradicunt, arguere*, Past. 15; Swt. 91, 16. **VIII.** *to will, profess, claim*:—Hē wæs swā upāhafen, ðæt hē wolde beón god . . . wolde rēnas wyrcan, swylce hē sylf god wǽre, Homl. Skt. ii. 27, 27-33. **IX.** as an auxiliary for the future, *will, shall, to be about to*:—Gif hē mē cūð ne bið, ic wille him suīðe ræðe andwyrdan (*protinus respondemus*), Past. 10; Swt. 63, 4. Hwæt wille ic ðissum wiðersacan geandwyrdan? Homl. Th. i. 378, 11. Hē wæs cweþende: 'Ic mē wille nū onhwyrfan tō ðisse bǽre . . .' Ðā wæs hē gongende, Blickl. Homl. 151, 14. Ic mīne sāwle wylle Gode underþeódan *nonne Deo subdita erit anima mea?* Ps. Th. 61, 1. Gif ðū ūre unriht wilt behealdan *si iniquitates observaveris*, 129, 3. Gif ðū ǽfre cymst tō ðære stōwe, ðonne wilt ðū cweþan (*dices*), Bt. 36, 2; Fox 174, 22: Met. 24, 48. Se ðe wyle sprecan *loquuturus*, Ælfc. Gr. 41; Zup. 247, 15, 11: 248, 6. Gif hiere ne bið sōna gestiéred, hió wile weahsan mid ungemete (*sine mensura dilatatur*), Past. 11; Swt. 71, 16. Ðæt wile þincan ungeleáflic eallum ðǽm ðe ða stōwe on ufeum tīdum geseóð, Lchdm. iii. 438, 14. Hwæþer hit hysecild ðe mǽdencild beón wille, ii. 172, 18. Hē wyle naman ðīnne herian *laudabunt nomen tuum*, Ps. Th. 73, 20. Hwā wyle mē gelǽdan? *quis deducet me?* 59, 8. Hwæt wille wē cweþan be ðīnum sunum? *quid dicam liberos?* Bt. 10; Fox 28, 30: Homl. Skt. ii. 28, 117: Homl. Th. ii. 448, 13. Hit wolde dagian *the day was about to break*, Homl. Skt. i. 21, 123. Hit ǽfnian wolde, 23, 245. His ādumum ðe woldon wīfian on his dohtron *generos suos, qui accepturi erant filias ejus*, Gen. 19, 14. Wāt ic ðæt ðū wile gilpan, Salm. Kmbl. 409; Sal. 205. Hwæt God mǽlan wille *quid loquatur Deus*, Ps. Th. 84, 7. Ic wāt ðætte wile woruldmen tweógan (cf. went eall moncyn on tweónunga, Bt. 4; Fox 8, 17), Met. 4, 51. Ne hē sōðfæste lǽteþ ðæt hī tō unrihte willen handum rǽcean *ut non extendant justi ad iniquitatem manus suas*, Ps. Th. 124, 4. Wēn is ðæt hī ūs lifigende wyllen forsweolgan *forsitan vivos deglutissent nos*, 123, 2. Swā ic ǽr sægde ðæt ic dōn wolde, Blickl. Homl. 183, 29. Ðeáh ðū onsōce ðæt ðū sōð godu lufian wolde, Exon. Th. 254, 10; Jul. 195. Ðā Darius geseah ðæt hē oferwonnen beón wolde *Darius cum vinci suos videret*, Ors. 3, 9; Swt. 128, 6: Blickl. Homl. 15, 34. Hū wolde ðæt geweorðan? Elen. Kmbl. 909; El. 456. Wēn is ðæt hī ūs woldan gesūpan *forsitan absorbuissent nos*, Ps. Th. 123, 3. **IX a.** without an infinitive:—Hwænne ðū mē wylle tō *quando venies ad me*, Ps. Th. 100, 1. Ǽr him se fefer tō wille, Lchdm. ii. 134, 24, 22. **IX b.** as optative:—Wolde hūru se earming hine sylfne beþencan, Homl. Skt. i. 19, 161. [*Goth.* wiljan; *p.* wilda: *O. Sax.* willian, wellian; *p.* welda: *O. Frs.*

willa, wella; *p.* wilde, welde, wolde: *O. H. Ger.* wellan, wollan; *p.* wolta: *Icel.* vilja; *p.* vilda.]

willan; *p.* de. I. *to boil* (trans.):—Wyl (wel, *v.l.*) on wætere . . . wyl on ealdan wīne, Lchdm. i. 72, 7, 23. Wel on buteran, ii. 22, 25. Wæl, i. 374, 8. Wæll, 378, 3. II. fig. *to torment, agitate, with violent feelings* (cf. *figurative uses of* weallan *and* seóþan):—Hē wylleþ hine on đam wīte, wunaþ unlustum *he gives himself no peace in that pain, lives unpleasingly*, Salm. Kmbl. 537; Sal. 268. [Þe caliz þet was imelt iđe fure and stroncliche iwelled, A. R. 284, 20. A chetel of iwelled bras, Jul. 82, 54. Welled led *molten lead*, H. R. 59, 501. *Icel.* vella *to boil* (trans.).] v. ā-, be-, ge-, ofer-, on-willan (-welian, -wyllan).

wille, es; *m. A well, spring, fountain*:—Se wylle *fluvius*, Bd. 1, 7; S. 478, 29 note. Hē is se libbenda wylle (-a?) *fons vivus*, Ps. Th. 41, 2. An tuddeles þorn, and an hrōces wylle; . . . þonne an lawernwylle . . . On hrōces wylle, þanne up on đæne weg . . .; þanon on oden wielle . . .; þanon on eabbincgwylle, þanne on riscbrōc, Cod. Dip. Kmbl. ii. 54, 6–15. On đone fūlan wylle; of đam wylle, vi. 213, 16–23. v. wīþig-wille; will, *and next word.*

wille, wielle, welle, wylle, an; *f. A well, spring, stream, fountain* (lit. and fig.):—Ān wielle weól blōde *flumen sanguine effluxit*, Ors. 4, 7; Swt. 184, 21. Welle *fontana*, Wrt. Voc. ii. 149, 79. Đǣr com upp wætres welle, Shrn. 93, 36. Seó wylle *fluvius*, Bd. 1, 7; S. 478, 29. Is sǣd đæt wylle (ān welle, *v.l.*) (*fons*) āweólle, seó wæter geóteþ, 5, 10; S. 625, 23. Līfes wylle (waelle, Ps. Surt.) *fons vitae*, Ps. Th. 35, 9: Basil admn. 4; Hex. 42, 16. Ealle đa nāmon Ændor wylle and Cisone clǣne hlimme, Ps. Th. 82, 8. Waelle lēhtes *fons luminis*, Ps. Surt. ii. p. 200, 35. Uælle *fons*, Jn. Skt. Lind. 4, 6. On saltere wellan; of saltere wellan, Cod. Dip. Kmbl. iii. 206, 31. In fūle wellan; of đære wellan, 366, 31. Swā culfre đonne heó bađaþ hī on smyltum wætre on hlūttere wællan, Shrn. 85, 22. Đa hālwendan wellan (*fonte*) fulwihtes bæþes, Bd. 2, 5; S. 507, 17. Wyllan, 3, 22; S. 552, 35: 4, 13; S. 582, 13. Hī druncon burnan wæter, calde wellan *potum dabat lubricus amnis*, Met. 8, 29. Of denum yrnaþ deópe wyllan (waellan *fontes*, Ps. Surt.), Ps. Th. 103, 10. In stōwum đǣr đe hlūttre wyllan (*lucidi fontes*) urnon, Bd. 2, 16; S. 520, 4. Tō waellum wætra *ad fontes aquarum*, Ps. Surt. 41, 2. On cwicu wæteres wellan *in fontes aquarum*, Ps. Th. 113, 8. Hē him forlēt feówer wellan sceótan (*the reference is to the milk from a cow's udder*), Exon. Th. 419, 26; Rā. 39, 3. [Cf. *O. H. Ger.* wella *fluctus, unda*: *Icel.* vella *boiling heat.*] v. ed-, sealt-wille. [The word is also found in place-names.]

-wille (cf. wille *a well*). v. cwic-, deád-, fisc-, līf-wille.

-wille (cf. willa *will*). v. ān-, druncen-, on-, self-wille.

-Wille. v. Eást-, West-Wille.

wille-burne, an; *f. A bubbling burn, running stream*:—Lago yrnende, wylleburne, Cd. Th. 14, 1; Gen. 212. Drihten lēt willeburnan on woruld þringan of ǣdra gehwære, 83, 1; Gen. 1373.

wille-cærse, an; *f. Well-kerse* (v. Jamieson's Dict.), *water-cress*:—Wyllecyrse *foenum graecum*, Wrt. Voc. i. 67, 76. Willecærse *britia*, 286, 28. Wyllecærse *fenegrecio*, ii. 38, 77. Seóđ mid wyllecærsan (-cersan, *v.l.*), Lchdm. i. 140, 12. Nim wyllecærsan (-en, MS.), iii. 134, 2. [Were me leuere lyue by wellecarses (ete watercrasses, *v.l.*), Piers P. C. 7, 292.]

-willedness, -willend, -willende. v. wel-willedness; riht-, unrihtwillend; un-, wel-, yfel-willende, *and* willan, **IV b, V a.**

willendlīce; *adv. Diligently*:—Willendlīce *diligenter*, Wrt. Voc. ii. 140, 41. [*In the following passage the better reading is* hwīlwendlīce:—Hē cwæþ đæt hē gehyhte swā swā hē on his đeóde willendlīce (hwīlwendlīce, M. 248, 22) rīcsode, đæt hē swā on tōweardnesse ēcelīce mid Criste rīcsian mōste *sperans ut sicut in sua gente regnat, ita et cum Christo in futuro conregnare*, Bd. 3, 29; S. 561, 22.] v. welwillendlīce.

-willendness. v. yfel-willendness.

willes; *adv. Willingly, voluntarily, of one's own accord*:—Be đam men đe willes man ofslihđ *de homine qui voluntate aliquem occidit*, L. Ecg. P. ii. 1, tit.; Th. ii. 180, 1. Ne scylan hyg ǣnig unriht willes geþafian, L. I. P. 6; Th. ii. 310, 18. Hē willes deáđ þrowade, R. Ben. 26, 15. Geneádod tō ānre mīle gange, gang willes twā, 28, 3. Hwīlum willes, hwīlum geneádode, Homl. Ass. 145, 45. Gif hit geweorđeþ đæt man unwilles oþþe ungewealdes ǣnig þing misdēđ, nā biđ đæt nā gelīc đam đe willes and gewealdes sylfwilles misdēđ, L. Eth. vi. 52; Th. i. 328, 22: L. Ed. 7; Th. i. 162, 26: L. O. 1; Th. i. 178, 6. [Gif heo hit breked willes and woldes, A. R. 6, 26. Þu þat forschuppes te self willes and waldes, H. M. 27, 2.] v. self-willes, un-wil[l], wil[l].

wille-streám, es; *m. A bubbling, running stream*:—Đǣr se eádga (*the Phenix*) mōt neótan wyllestreáma wuduholtum in, Exon. Th. 223, 19; Ph. 362. Se æþela fugel æt đam ǣspringe wunaþ wyllestreámas, 204, 30; Ph. 105. [In ane wallestream, Laym. 2849.]

wille-wæter, es; *n. Spring-water*:—Þweah mid wyllewætre, Lchdm. ii. 308, 11. Wyrc đæt bæþ of đām ilcum wyrtum on ealdum wyllewætre, 74, 27. Seóđe on yrnendum wyllewætere, i. 330, 14. [Þe ter þet mon wepđ for lađe of þisse liue is inemned wellewater (*aqua fontis*), for he welleđ of þe horte swa dođ water of welle, O. E. Homl. i. 159, 12. Cæld wellewater (welles water, 2nd MS.), Laym. 19792.]

will-flōd, es; *n. m. The waters of the deluge*:—Willflōd ongan lytligan, Cd. Th. 85, 10; Gen. 1412. Cf. wille-burne.

will-gespryng, es; *n. A spring*:—Đeós eorþe is berende missenlīcra fugela and sǣwihta and fiscwyllum wæterum and wyllgespryngum *avium ferax terra marique generis diversi, fluviis quoque multum piscosis, ac fontibus praeclara copiosis*, Bd. 1, 1; S. 473, 16. Of đām wilsuman wyllgespryngum beorgeþ *e vivo gurgite libat aquam*, Exon. Th. 205, 8; Ph. 109.

willian; *p.* ode. I. *to will*:—Gode willigende *Deo volente*, Guthl. 20; Gdwin. 78, 20. II. *to desire*, (a) with a genitive:—Mæg snottor guma his gǣste forđ weges willian, Exon. Th. 104, 15; Gū. 8. Ne sceolde nān wīs man willian (wilnian, *v. l.*) sēftes līfes, Bt. 40, 3; Fox 238, 13. (b) with infinitive:—Hwelc is mon se wile līf and willaþ gesián dægas gōde? *quis est homo qui vult vitam et cupit videre dies bonos?* Ps. Surt. 33, 13. Gē wylladon (wilniaþ, *v. l.*) ūs đa đing gemǣnsuman *ea nobis communicare desiderastis*, Bd. 1, 25; S. 487, 13. (c) with gerundial infin.:—Ongit hū unmihtige đa yfelan men beóþ, nū hī ne magon cuman þider đider đa ungewittigan gesceafta williaþ (wilniaþ, *v. l.*) tō tō cumenne *vide quanta vitiosorum hominum pateat infirmitas, qui ne ad hoc quidem pervenire queunt, ad quod eos naturalis ducit, ac pene compellit intentio*, Bt. 36, 5; Fox 180, 4. (d) with a clause:—Ic willio and wille đæt hió sión getrymed, Cod. Dip. Kmbl. ii. 121, 23. (e) absolute:—Wer se đe in bibodum his willaþ (*cupiet*), Ps. Surt. 111, 1. [He wyllede mest of alle þynge to hym enlyance, R. Glouc. 12, 18. Naȝt ne willieþ more þanne uor to by uorlore to þe wordle, Ayenb. 142, 15. Þu willest of briddes to knowe, Piers P. 12, 221. *O. H. Ger.* willōn *desiderare.*] v. ge-willian; willung.

wil-līc; *adj. From a fountain* or *well*:—Willīcan *fontona* (*fontana* flumina, Ald. 161), Wrt. Voc. ii. 92, 10. Wyllīcan, 37, 30: 149, 79.

willīce; *adv. Willingly, voluntarily*:—Ōþre gehwylce đa wyllīce wē onfēngon *cetera queque quae uoluntarie suscepimus*, Anglia xiii. 375, 138. [*O. L. Ger.* willīco *voluntarie.*]

willnian, willnung. v. wilnian, wilnung.

will-spryng *and* **-sprynge**, es; *m. A well-spring, fountain, source* (lit. and fig.):—Welspreng *latex*, Wrt. Voc. i. 54, 30. Seó sōđe lufu is wylspring and ordfruma ealra gōdnyssa, Homl. Th. i. 52, 12. Đæs wæterscipes welsprynge is on hefonrīce, Past. Swt. 467, 31. Welsprinces *fontis*, Hpt. Gl. 418, 43. Mid dǣwigum wylsprince *roscidis fontibus*, 421, 67. Đās synd đa feówer eán of ānum wyllspringe, Ælfc. T. Grn. 13, 3. Wyllspringas đære micelan niwelnisse *fontes abyssi magnae*, Gen. 7, 11. Wilspringas, 8, 2. Wæs đæt wæter and ealle wyllspringas gehālgode þurh Cristes līchaman, Homl. Th. ii. 40, 28. Wilspringum *fontibus*, Hpt. Gl. 509, 18. Tō wyllspringum wætra *ad fontes aquarum*, Ps. Lamb. 41, 2. [An angel tagte hire (*Hagar*) đor a wellespring, Gen. and Ex. 1243.]

will-sum. v. wil-sum.

willung, e; *f. Desire*:—Đurh unrihte willunge *per ambitionem*, Bd. 4, 5; S. 573, 11. [My willing is as ye wole, Chauc. Cl. T. 319.] v. gewillung; willian.

willung, e; *f. Boiling, heat*:—Wyl[l]inc *fervor* (*autumni*), Hpt. Gl. 419, 77. v. samod-willung.

will-weorþung, e; *f. Worship paid to springs*:—Wē lǣraþ đæt preósta gehwilc ǣlcne hǣđendōm ādwæsce, and forbeóde wilweorđunga (cf. Hǣđenscipe biþ . . . đæt man weorđige hǣđene godas, and sunnan oþþe mōnan, fȳr oþþe flōd, wæterwyllas oþþe stānas, L. C. S. 5; Th. i. 378, 20. *See also* will), L. Edg. C. 16; Th. ii. 248, 3. See Grmm. D. M. c. 20.

wilm, wielm, welm, wælm, wylm, es; *m.* I. *that which wells.* v. weallan. (1) of fluid, *a fount, stream, water that surges* or *boils, that moves in waves*:—Wæs đære burnan wælm heađofȳrum hāt *the burn's surging stream was hot with fierce fires*, Beo. Th. 5086; B. 2546. Fisca welm, wildeóra holt *the fishes' flood, the wild beasts' wood*, Salm. Kmbl. 165; Sal. 82. Ne foldan stān, ne wæteres wylm, ne wudutelga, 843; Sal. 421. Geofon ȳþum weól, wintres wylm (*the boiling flood of winter*), Beo. Th. 1036; B. 516. Ic đæs wælmes grundhyrde fond, 4276; B. 2135. Hē drincđ of đæm wielme his āgnes pyttes *bibit sui fluenta putei*, Past. 48; Swt. 373, 10. Of swēttestum wylne (wylme?) *de dulcissimo fonte*, Scint. 18, 3. Gān ofer flōdes wylm *to go over the tossing waves of the sea*, Andr. Kmbl. 734; An. 367. Ofer ȳđa wylm, 1726; An. 865. Hī stæđe wīcedon ymb đæs wæteres wylm (*by the surge of the sea*), Elen. Kmbl. 77; El. 39. In đæs leádes wylm scūfan *to thrust into the boiling font of lead*, Exon. Th. 277, 20; Jul. 583. Heortan wylmas *veins, blood-vessels* (?), Beo. Th. 5008; B. 2507. (2) of fire, *surging fire, flames*:—Won fȳres wælm, se swearta līg, Exon. Th. 60, 7; Cri. 966. His bān brondes wylm forþylmde, 217, 21; Ph. 283. In đæs wylmes grund befæsted, Elen. Kmbl. 2596; El. 1299. Gold đæt in wylme biđ geclǣnsod, 2617; El. 1310: 1527; El. 765. Wunian in wylme, Salm. Kmbl. 933; Sal. 466. God wylme gesealde Sodoman, sweartan līge, Cd. Th. 115, 26; Gen. 1925. Gedūfan in đone deópan wælm, 266, 31; Sat. 30. Helle, grundleásne wylm, Exon. Th. 362, 34; Wal. 46: Salm. Kmbl. 149; Sal. 74. Hātan ofnes wylm þurhwôdon, Cd. Th. 245, 16; Dan. 464. In fýrbaðe, wælmum bi-wrecene, Exon. Th. 52, 11; Cri. 832. II. *heat, fervent heat, fiery heat*:—Wylm *fervor*, i. *calor*, Wrt. Voc. ii. 147, 82. Gif sumeres welm (wylm, *v. l.*) tô swíðlíc bið *si aestatis fervor nimius fuerit*, R. Ben. 65, 20. Ne mihte heora wlite gewemman wylm ðæs wæfran líges, Cd. Th. 231, 2; Dan. 241. Ðæs unmǽtan wylmes ðære sunnan hǽto, Homl. Skt. ii. 23 b, 573. Wilme and bryne *fervore*, Wrt. Voc. ii. 33, 42. Flôr is on welme, Cd. Th. 267, 17; Sat. 39. Þrowigean frêcne fýres wylm, 229, 8; Dan. 214. ¶ fig.?:—Óððæt deáðes wylm hrân æt heortan *until the hot touch of death was at the heart*, Beo. Th. 4531; B. 2269. II a. *boiling, roasting*:—Wylm *vel* hyrsting *frixura*, Wrt. Voc. ii. 150, 84. Gif hit wæter sý, hǽte man hit óð hit hleówe tô wylme, L. Ath. iv. 7; Th. i. 226, 14. On welme weorðan *fervere*, Past. 58; Swt. 447, 9. II b. *inflammation*:—Se wielm ðæs innoðes ût âbiersð and wierð tô sceabbe, Past. 11; Swt. 71, 9. Ðæs welmes sâr on ðære lifre, Lchdm. ii. 206, 3. Æfter âdle welme ... of ðara ômena welme, 82, 2, 20. Ða welmas ða ðe beóþ gehwǽr geond ðone lîchoman, 204, 14. III. *violent movement, violence, raging, tempestuous movement* of water:—Oððe fýres feng, oððe flôdes wylm, Beo. Th. 3533; B. 1764. Gestilde seó sǽ fram ðam wylme *pontus suo quievit a fervore*, Bd. 3, 15; S. 542, 3. Him ðæs endeleán þurh wæteres wylm Waldend sealde, Beo. Th. 2390; B. 1693: Exon. Th. 283, 14; Jul. 680. Hî feorh âlêton þurh ǽdra wylm (*by the surging of the blood from the veins*), 271, 6; Jul. 478. Hê ýðum stilde, wæteres wælmum, Andr. Kmbl. 903; An. 452. IV. of mental emotion, (1) *fervour, ardour*:—Hié wênaþ ðæt hiera unðeáw sié sumes ryhtwîslîces andan wielm *his suum vitium quasi virtus fervens videtur*, Past. 40; Swt. 289, 20. On ðæm welme ðære sôþan lufan Godes, Blickl. Homl. 29, 10. Wylme, Homl. Th. ii. 128, 3. Wylme *fervore, ardore*, Hpt. Gl. 469, 56. Wælme lufu ðînre *fervore dilectionis tuae*, Rtl. 95, 27. Seó hâlige cyrice sum ding ðurh wælm (*per fervorem*) receþ, Bd. 1, 27; S. 491, 30. Wylm, Hpt. Gl. 465, 37. (2) *heat, fury, rage, passion*:—Wrǽðo ðîn and wælm (*furor*) ðîn, Rtl. 11, 1. In uælme ðînum *in furore tuo*, 183, 2. Mid ðam welme ðære hâtheortnesse, Bt. 37, 1; Fox 186, 20: Met. 25, 46. Mid miclum wylme and yrre onstyred *nimio furore commotus*, Bd. 1, 7; S. 477, 41. Of lufe nalæs of wylme, 1, 27; S. 490, 13. Yrre ne lǽt ðê wylme besmîtan, Exon. Th. 305, 8; Fä. 85. [Fouuer walmes of watere sprungen ut, O. E. Homl. i. 141, 17. In the welmes ben founde stones, Map. 355, 14.] v. ǽ-, bǽl-, breóst-, brim-, bryne-, cear-, ed-, ege-, flôd-, frum-, fýr-, heáfod-, heaðo-, holm-, hyge-, sâr-, sǽ-, sorg-, streám-wilm (-wælm, -wylm).

wilm-fýr, es; *n. Fierce fire, flaming fire*:—Fore Dryhtne færeþ wælmfýra mǽst, hlemmeþ hâta lêg, Exon. Th. 58, 7; Cri. 932.

wilm-hât; *adj. Burning hot*:—Him brego engla wylmhâtne lîg tô wræce sende, Cd. Th. 156, 5; Gen. 2584. [He het fecchen a ueat, and wið pich fullen, and wallen hit walmhât, Jul. 69, 20.]

wiln, e; *f. A maid-servant, a hand-maid*:—Mîn wyln (wiln, *v. l.*) *mea ancilla*, mînre wylne *meae ancillae*, mîne wylne *meam ancillam*, mîne wylna *meae ancillae*, mînra wylna *mearum ancillarum*, Ælfc. Gr. 15; Zup. 100, 20–101, 7. Wyln *ancilla, serva, abra, dula*, Wrt. Voc. i. 50, 14: 73, 2. Þînen, wyln *abra*, i. *ancilla*, 17, 26. Heó ýs ðîn wyln (*ancilla*) under ðînre handa; þreá hig lôca hû ðû wylle, Gen. 16, 6. Seó sâwl is ðæs flǽsces hlǽfdige, and hire gedafnaþ ðæt heó simle gewylde ða wylne, ðæt is ðæt flǽsc, tô hyre hǽsum. Þwyrlîce færð æt ðam hûse ðǽr seó wyln bið ðære hlǽfdian wissigend, and seó hlæfdige bið ðære wylne underðeódd, Homl. Skt. i. 17, 8–12. Oft on ânre tîde âcenð seó cwên and seó wyln ... and ðære wylne sunu wunaþ eal his lîf on ðeówte, Homl. Th. i. 110, 27: Gen. 21, 13. Ne wilna ðû ðînes nêhstan wylne, Ex. 20, 17. Gif wíffæst man hine forlicge be his âgenre wylne, L. C. S. 55; Th. i. 406, 14. Âdô ðâs wylne (*ancillam*) heonon, Gen. 21, 10: Ex. 21, 20, 32. Hê genam wealas and wylna (*servos et ancillas*), Gen. 20, 14: Lev. 25, 44. v. wealh.

wilnian; *p.* ode. I. of animate objects, (1) *to desire, ask for* (the source from which marked by *tô*), (a) with gen. or uncertain:—Wilnigaþ monige men anwealdes ... Se ealra forcûþesta wilnaþ ðæs ylcan, Bt. 18, 1; Fox 60, 27. Hwî wilnige wê ǽnigre ôþre sage? *quid adhuc egemus testibus?* Mt. Kmbl. 26, 65. Ða nêtenu, and eác ða ôþre gesceafta, mâ wilniaþ ðæs ðe hî wilniaþ for gecynde ðonne for willan, Bt. 34, 11; Fox 152, 6. Ealle tô ðê ǽtes wilniaþ *omnia a te expectant, ut des illis escam*, Ps. Th. 103, 25. Wuhta gehwilc wilnaþ tô eorðan, sume nêdþearfe, sume neódfræce, Met. 31, 14. Ealle þider willniaþ oþþe ðæs ðe hî lyst, oþþe ðæs ðe hî beþurfon, Bt. 41, 6; Fox 254, 29. Heó hiere feores tô him wilnade (*pro vita precans*), Ors. 3, 11; Swt. 150, 33. Ðæt wæter ðe hê tô Gode wilnade *aquam quam a Deo petierat*, Bd. 1, 7; S. 478, 28. Hê wilnode him tô Gode sumre frôfre *he asked of God for some comfort for himself*, Ps. Th. 15, arg. Helpan nânum ðara ðe tô him âre wilnodan, Blickl. Homl. 223, 3. Ne wilna ðû ðînes nêhstan hûses ne his wîfes *non concupisces domum proximi tui nec desiderabis uxorem ejus*, Ex. 20, 17. Hwelc fremu is ðê, ðæt ðû wilnige ðissa andweardena gesǽlþa ofer gemet? Bt. 14, 1; Fox 42, 8. Þonne hî tô his hûse hleówes wilnian, Ps. Th. 108, 10. Tô ðæm heáhengle ðæt hié him fultomes wilnodan, Blickl. Homl. 201, 28. Friðes wilnian, Andr. Kmbl. 2258; An. 1130. Willnian (wilnian, *v. l.*) ðæs ðe hê næfþ, Bt. 36, 3; Fox 176, 12. Him wilnian lofes *to desire praise for himself*, Past. 62; Swt. 457, 26: Exon. Th. 119, 28; Gû. 261. Tô Rômânum friþes wilnian *a Romanis pacem petere*, Ors. 4, 6; Swt. 178, 7: Cd. Th. 229, 10; Dan. 215: Exon. Th. 48, 18; Cri. 773. Wylnian, Wulfst. 277, 19. (b) with accusative:—Ðû ne wilnast weora ǽniges deáð (cf. nolo mortem impii, Ezech. 33, 11), Ps. C. 54. Ða æþelingas wilniaþ, Exon. Th. 433, 14; Rä. 50, 7. Eall hwæt hî willniaþ hî begitaþ, Bt. 40, 7; Fox 242, 22. Ðæt sâwul mîn wilnaþ (*concupivit*), ðæt ic ðîn word môte healdan, Ps. Th. 118, 20. Ealle hié ðæt wilnodan, ðæt hié his word gehýran môston, Blickl. Homl. 219, 35. Hwæt (hwæs, *v. l.*) hê wilnian sceal, Bt. 40, 7; Fox 242, 18. (c) with infinitive:—Ða ðe wilniaþ fretan mîn folc, Ps. Th. 13, 9. Willniaþ ealle þurh mistlîce paþas cuman tô ânum ende *diverso calle, sed ad unum finem nititur pervenire*, Bt. 24, 1; Fox 80, 8. Hê wilnode hine geseón *erat cupiens uidere eum*, Lk. Skt. 23, 8. Gif ðû wilnige oncnâwan, Bt. 6; Fox 14, 31. Gif ðû willnige ongitan *si vis cernere*, 39, 13; Fox 232, 24. Wilnige, Met. 29, 1. Gebida wilnando *petere uolentes*, Lk. Skt. p. 6, 12. (d) with gerundial infinitive:—Ðæt hié wielnien (wilnien, Cott. MSS.) tô wietanne ðæt ðæt hié nyton *ut appetant scire, quae nesciunt*, Past. 30; Swt. 203, 8. (e) with genitive and gerundial infinitive:—Ǽlc môd wilnaþ sôþes gôdes tô begitanne *est mentibus hominum veri boni inserta cupiditas*, Bt. 24, 2; Fox 80, 32. Hî wilniaþ welan and weorþscipes tô gewinnanne *opes, honores ambiant*, Met. 19, 43. (f) with a clause:—Gif ðû wilnast ðæt ðû mæge oncnâwan, Met. 5, 24. Wilnaþ God tô ǽlcum men ðæt hê sié oððe wearm oððe ceald *aut calidus quisque esse, aut frigidus quaeritur*, Past. 58; Swt. 447, 15. Hê wilnode ðæt his lîcræst sceolde beón æt Cridiantûne, Chr. 977; Erl. 127, 37. Heó ealle tô mê wilnodon ðæt ic hine lǽte æt mê ðæt land begeotan, Chart. Th. 167, 38. Hié wilnedon tô him ðæt hié môsten on his rîce mid friðe gesittan, Ors. 6, 34; Swt. 290, 20. Nis nân gesceaft ðara ðe ne wilnige ðæt hit þider cuman mæge, Bt. 25; Fox 88, 30. Wilnie, Met. 13, 69. Ðeáh hî wielnien (wilnien, Cott. MSS.) ðæt hié andrysne sién, Past. 17; Swt. 109, 18. Tô Sancte Michaele ðæt hié wilnodan ðæt God gecýþde ðæt mannum bemiðen wæs, Blickl. Homl. 199, 32. Wilniende ðæt hî ǽlcum gewinne ôðflogen hæfdon *credentes quod se a congressu totius humanae habitationis abstraherent*, Ors. 1, 4; Swt. 32, 21. Wæs hê wilniende tô Gode, ðæt hê ǽghwylcum gemildsode, Wulfst. 278, 12. (g) absolute or uncertain:—Hê hî ne gewemde, eal swâ heó tô Gode wilnode, Homl. Skt. ii. 30, 221. Wilnig from mê ðætte ðû willt *pete a me quod uis*, Mk. Skt. Lind. 6, 22. Tô wilnanne *ad concupiscendam*, Mt. Kmbl. Lind. 5, 28. Ân ðære sâwle gecynda is ðæt heó biþ wilnigende, Bt. 33, 4; Fox 132, 4. Wilnigendum *flagitante*, Wrt. Voc. ii. 34, 23. ¶ present participle with force of Latin form in *-dus*:—Uilnende ginyhtsumnise *desideratam abundantiam*, Rtl. 73, 32. (2) *to desire to go*:—Ðû wilnast ofer wîdne mere, Andr. Kmbl. 565; An. 283. Swâ heort wilnaþ tô wætre *sicut cervus desiderat ad fontes aquarum*, Ps. Th. 41, 1. Wuhta gehwilc wilnaþ þiderweard, ðǽr his mǽgðe bið mǽst ætgædere, Met. 20, 159. II. of inanimate objects, *to tend* to an end (*gen.*):—Swîðe lytlum siceraþ ðæt wæter on ðæt hlece scip, and ðeáh hit wilnaþ ðæs ylcan ðe sió hlûde ýð dêð *hoc agit sentina latenter excrescens, quod patenter procella saeviens*, Past. 57; Swt. 437, 14. Sege mê hwelces endes ǽlc angin wilnige *dic mihi, quis sit rerum finis, quove totius naturae tendat intentio*, Bt. 5, 3; Fox 12, 19. Ðû cýþdest ðæt ðû nestest hwelces endes ǽlc angin wilnode, Fox 12, 35. [*Laym.* wilnien: *A. R.* wilnen: *Orm.* willnenn: *Ayenb.* wilni: *Piers P.* wilne: *Icel.* vilna.] v. ge-, yfel-wilnian.

-wilni[g]endlîc. v. ge-wilnigendlîc.

wilnung, e; *f. Desire*:—Ûþwitan secgaþ ðæt sió sâwul hæbbe ðrió gecynd. An ðara gecynda is ðæt heó biþ wilnigende ... Twâ ðara gecynda habbaþ nêtenu; ... ôþer ðara is wilnung ... Seó gesceádwîsnes sceal wealdan ðære wilnunga, Bt. 33, 4; Fox 132, 3–10: Met. 20, 186. Worldlîce wilnung *desiderium mundanum*, L. Ecg. P. i. 5; Th. ii. 174, 10. Fram gebrosnunge lîcumlîcre willnunge clǽne *a corruptione concupiscentiae carnalis inmune*, Bd. 3, 8; S. 532, 36. Unâlýfedre willnunge môd biþ geþeóded, 1, 27; S. 495, 9. Unrihtes willan willnunge *cupidine voluptatis*, 495, 33. Sum hlâw, ðone men for feós wilnunga gedulfon, Guthl. 4; Gdwin. 26, 6. Âbisgod on ðisse worulde willnunga (wilnunga, *v. l.*), Bt. 41, 3; Fox 246, 31. For ðære wilnunge (gewilnunge, *v. l.*) ðe hê wolde hý him on fultum geteón *ambitione habendorum equitum Thessalorum, quorum robur ut exercitui suo admisceret*, Ors. 3, 7; Bos. 59, 14. Hî nôhwæþere heora willnunge habban ne ðurhteón magan *in neutro cupitum possunt obtinere propositum*, Bd. 5, 23; S. 647, 2. Drihten gehýrð ða wilnunga his þearfena *desiderium pauperum exaudivit Dominus*, Ps. Th. 9, 37. Willniungum *petitionibus*, Mt. Kmbl. p. 14, 20. [Þuruh wilnunge of hereword, A. R. 148, 20. Worsipe haue þou for þine wilninge, Laym. 3160.] v. ge-, ungemet-, unriht-, weorold-wilnung.

Wil-sǽtan, -sǽte; *pl. The people of Wiltshire*:—Ðâ mêtte hine Weoxtan aldorman mid Wilsǽtum, ... and Wilsǽtan (-sǽte, *v. l.*) nâmon sige, Chr. 800; Erl. 60, 6-9. Sumorsǽte alle and Wilsǽtan (Willsǽte, *v. l.*), 878; Erl. 80, 10.

wil-sele, es; *m. A pleasant hall*:—Weorðeþ his hús (*the nest of the Phenix*) onhǽted, willsele stýmeþ, Exon. Th. 212, 21; Ph. 213.

wil-síþ, es; *m. A desired journey, a wished for, welcome journey*:—Eádga ús siges, wlitigan wilsíþes, Exon. Th. 2, 18; Cri. 21. Ðæs sǽs smyltnys eów bliþe on eówerne willsíþ hám forlǽteþ *serenitas maris vos cupito itinere domum remittet*, Bd. 3, 15; S. 541, 36. Gewát Matheus menigo lǽdan on gehyld Godes, weorod on wilsíð (*he was leading them out of prison*), Andr. Kmbl. 2093; An. 1048. Elene ne wolde ðæs síðfætes sǽne weorðan, . . . ac wæs sóna gearu wíf on wilsíð, Elen. Kmbl. 445; El. 223. Sunnan wilsíð, Exon. Th. 2, 29; Cri. 26.

wil-spell, es; *n. Welcome news, glad tidings*:—Wæs him frófra mǽst æt ðam willspelle (*the news of the finding of the cross*), Elen. Kmbl. 1985; El. 994. Wilspella mǽst gesecgan, 1965; El. 984. [A steoresman ham talde wilspel, þ he Spaine isæih, Laym. 1350. *O. Sax.* wil-spel.]

wil-sum; *adj.* I. *desirable, pleasant*:—Ðam bið gæst Godes ágen bearn, wilsum in worlde, Exon. Th. 318, 11; Mod. 81. Eorðan wilsume *terram desiderabilem*, Ps. Surt. 105, 24. Ðæt willsume weorc onginnaþ *desideratum opus inire*, Bd. 5, 11; S. 625, 33. Wilsum *desiderabilia*, Ps. Surt. 18, 11. Of ðám wilsuman wyllgespryngum *from the pleasant well-springs*, Exon. Th. 205, 7; Ph. 109. II. *willing, voluntary, spontaneous*:—Wilsumne regn *pluviam voluntariam*, Ps. Th. Spl. 67, 10: Blickl. Gl. Ðone wilsuman *spontaneum*, Wrt. Voc. ii. 32, 65. Him (*a child whose father is dead*) man an his fæderingmágum wilsumne (*willing, ready to undertake the guardianship*; or under I (?), *desirable, suitable, sufficient*) berigean geselle his feoh tó healdenne, L. H. E. 6; Th. i. 30, 5. Mid selfwillum ł wilsumum *ultroneis, voluntariis*, Hpt. Gl. 435, 64. Wilsum múðes mínes *voluntaria oris mei*, Ps. Surt. 118, 108. III. *devout, devoted*:—Gode se willsuma wer *vir Deo devotus*, Bd. 4, 11; S. 579, 5. Gode seó willsume fǽmne, 4, 26; S. 603, 5. Gode willsumra wífmonna láreów, 4, 6; S. 574, 16: 4, 19; S. 588, 2. Hé sylfa wæs se wilsumesta (*devotissimus*) lǽstend, 5, 22; S. 644, 4. v. ge-, un-wilsum.

wilsum-líc; *adj.* I. *desirable, pleasant*:—Wilsumlíc *desiderabilis*, Wrt. Voc. ii. 139, 18. Mon willsumlícre yldo and fægernesse *juvenis amantissimae aetatis et venustatis*, Bd. 5, 19; S. 636, 32. Hé monig ðing ge egeslíce ge willsumlíce (*desideranda*) geseah, 5, 12; S. 627, 29. II. *voluntary, spontaneous*:—Hé geleornade ðæt Cristes ðeówdóm sceolde beón wilsumlíc, nalæs genédedlíc *didicerat servitium Christi voluntarium, non coactitium esse debere*, Bd. 1, 26; S. 488, 18. On wilsumlícre ðearfednesse *voluntariae paupertatis*, 4, 3; S. 569, 2. Wilsumlíce múðes mínes *voluntaria oris mei*, Ps. Spl. C. T. 118, 108.

wilsumlíce; *adv.* I. *willingly, voluntarily, spontaneously*:—Hé wilsumlíce (*sponte*) hine geþeódde tó ðam cyninge, Bd. 3, 7; S. 529, 44. Se ðe ne wyle cyricean duru wilsumlíce (*sponte*) geeádmóded ingangan, se sceal nýde on helle duru unwilsumlíce geniþerad gelǽded beón, 5, 14; S. 634, 19. Wilsumlíce (*voluntarie*) ic onsecg[e] ðé, Ps. Surt. 53, 8. II. *devoutly, devotedly*:—Lifde se man his líf Gode swýþe willsumlíce *ducens vitam multum Deo devotam*, Bd. 4, 25; S. 599, 29. v. un-wilsumlíce.

wilsumness, e; *f.* I. *devotion, devoutness*:—Byrnende wilsumnes módes *ardens devotio mentis*, Bd. 1, 7; S. 478, 11. Hí ánre wilsumnesse wǽron *erant unius devotionis*, 5, 10; S. 624, 14: 5, 20; S. 642, 14. Hé smyltre willsumnesse (*tranquilla devotione*) Drihtne ðeówde, 4, 24; S. 599, 9. On willsumnesse (*devotioni*) háligra gebeda gecneord, 4, 28; S. 606, 33. II. *a vow*:—Wilsumnessa *votorum*, Hpt. Gl. 404, 8.

wiltan; *p.* te *To roll* (trans.):—Se ðe welt *qui volvit* (*lapidem*), Kent. Gl. 1006. Hé wylte (tówælte, Lind.: áwælte, Rush.) ánne stán tó ðære byrgenne dura *aduoluit lapidem ad ostium monumenti*, Mk. Skt. 15, 46. Hé (*a cup*) in healle wæs wylted and wended wloncra folmum, Exon. Th. 441, 16; Rä. 60, 19. [Walles he welte downe, D. Arth. 3152. *M. H. Ger.* welzen: *Ger.* wälzen: *Icel.* velta. *Goth.* waltjan *to roll* (intrans.).] v. á-, ge-wiltan (-wæltan, -wyltan); wealt, *and next word.*

-wilte *in* éð-wilte *that rolls* or *moves easily*:—Éðwiltum *versatili, volubili, mobili*, Hpt. Gl. 433, 69. v. preceding word.

wil-þegu, e; *f. A grateful repast*:—Tólýsan líc and sáwle, and þonne tódǽlan werum tó wiste and tó wilþege fǽges flǽschoman, Andr. Kmbl. 306; An. 153.

Wil-tún, es; *m. Wilton* in Wiltshire:—Ælfréd cyning gefeaht wiþ alne ðone here lytle werede æt Wiltúne, Chr. 871; Erl. 76, 5. Hér forðférde Ælfgár cinges mǽg on Defenum, and his líc rest on Wiltúne, 962; Erl. 120, 3. Swegen lǽdde his here into Wiltúne, 1003; Erl. 139, 14. Hió becwið án pund tó Wiltúne ðám híwum, Cod. Dip. Kmbl. vi. 131, 1. ¶ the name occurs in several Latin charters:—In uilla regali qui appellatur Uuiltún, Cod. Dip. Kmbl. i. 320, 15. In uico regio æt Wiltúne, iii. 278, 32. In palacio nostro quod dicitur Wiltún, ii. 15, 13. In monasterio quod dicitur Wiltún, 306, 30. Ad monasterium sanctae Dei genitricis Mariae quod dicitur Wiltúne, v. 214, 14. Uenerabili collegio Christicolarum in illo celebri loco qui dicitur Wiltún ad aecclesiam Sanctae Mariae, 227, 6. Ad usum sanctimonialium in Wiltúne degentium, iii. 23, 15. v. next words.

Wiltúnisc; *adj. Belonging to Wilton*:—Wiltúnisc *Wiltuniensis*, Ælfc. Gr. 5; Zup. 13, 5.

Wiltún-scír (Wiltúnes-), e; *f. Wiltshire*:—Æþeréd Wiltúnscíre biscop wearþ gecoren tó ærcebiscope tó Cantuareberi, Chr. 870; Erl. 74, 4. Æðelm Wiltúnscíre ealdormon, 898; Erl. 96, 18. Féng Ælfríc Wiltúnscíre bisceop tó ðam arcebiscopríce, 994; Erl. 134, 2. Ánes scipes Ælfríc arcebisceop geúðe ðam folce tó Cent and óðres tó Wiltúnesscíre, Cod. Dip. Kmbl. iii. 352, 18. Ða gegaderode man swíðe mycele fyrde of Wiltúnscíre, Chr. 1003; Erl. 139, 5: 1011; Erl. 144, 29: 1015; Erl. 152, 12. On ðam ylcan geáre forðférde Ælfstán bisceop on Wiltúnscíre, 981; Erl. 128, 18. Sum ungeråd mann wæs mid Ælfstáne bisceope on Wiltúnscíre on híréde, Homl. Skt. i. 12, 42. Brihtwold biscop féng tó ðam ríce on Wiltúnscíre, Chr. 1006; Erl. 140, 2. Hér gefór Brihtwold biscop on Wiltúnescíre, and man sette Hereman on his setle, 1046; Erl. 171, 23. Hereman biscop forðférde; se wæs biscop on Beorrucscíre and on Wiltúnscíre and on Dorsǽtan, 1078; Erl. 215, 32.

wil-tygþe, -týþe; *adj. Having one's desire, satisfied, glad*:—Wiltiðe *voti compos*, i. *laetos* ł *hilares*, Hpt. Gl. 458, 62. Wiltiðe *voti compotes, hilares*, 490, 47. v. wil-fægen.

wiluncel, wílung. v. wilincel, wíglung.

wilwan, wilwian, wilian; *p.* wilwede, wilede. I. *to roll* (trans.):—Ic áwende oððe wylewige (wylwige, *v. l.*) *uoluo*, Ælfc. Gr. 28; Zup. 177, 9. Hé wylede ðone stán fram ðære byrgenne duru, Blickl. Homl. 157, 8. Hé wylode hine sylfne on ðám þornum and netelum, Homl. Th. ii. 156, 28. Hé hét wilian tó ðam scræfe micele weorcstánas *praecepit: 'Volvite saxa ingentia ad os speluncae,'* Jos. 10, 18. Hé hí swá nacode hét wylian on ðam fýre, Homl. Skt. i. 8, 170. I a. fig.:—Sibb áflýmð saca, anda tógædre wilaþ hí *pax effugat discordias, inuidia copulat eas*, Scint. 11, 8. Hé hine sylfne betweox ðises andweardan middangeardes (wǽlum?) weólc and welode *inter fluctuantis saeculi gurgites jactaretur*, Guthl. 2; Gdwin. 14, 14. II. *to join, compound, compose*:—Byð wylyd ealswá middangeardes boga, Lchdm. iii. 82, 18. [Welwyñ or rollyñ al thyngys þat may not be borne *volvo*, Prompt. Parv. 521. *Goth.* walwjan *to roll* (trans.).] v. á-, be-, ge-wilwan; wealwian.

wil-wang, es; *m. A pleasant plain, pleasant land*:—Ðone wudu weardaþ fugel (*the Phenix*) . . ., eard bihealdaþ . . ., nǽfre him deáþ sceþeþ on ðam willwonge, Exon. Th. 203, 24; Ph. 89.

wil-weg, es; *m. A pleasant way, a desirable way*:—Syndan wé nú eft ámearcode tó ðam gefeán neorxnawanges; ne gelette ús ðæs síðes se fǽcna feónd, ne ús ne forwyrne ðæs wilweges, ne ús ða gata ne betýne, ðe ús opene standaþ, Wulfst. 252, 17. Ðæt hí ðé heóldan, ðæt ðú wilwega wealdan móstest *ut custodiant te in omnibus viis tuis*, Ps. Th. 90, 11.

wím-(wim-)man. v. wíf-mann.

wimpel, winpel, es; *m. An article of woman's dress, a wimple*:—Winpel *vel* orl *ricinum*, Wrt. Voc. i. 17, 1. Winpel *anabala* (cf. anaboladium *amictorium lineum feminarum, quo humeri operiuntur*, Migne), 26, 1. Wimple goldgewefenum *cyclade auro texta*, Hpt. Gl. 506, 63. Wimplum *cycladibus*, 480, 71: 486, 41: *mafortibus*, i. *velaminibus*, 526, 52: Anglia xiii. 37, 293. [Sum seið þ hit limpeð to ene wummon cundeliche forte were wimpel. Nai: wimpel . . . ne nemned hali write, ah wriheles of heuet . . . Wrihen, þe Apostel seið, naut wimplin, A. R. 420, note a. Hyre body wyþ a mantel, a wympel aboute her heued, R. Glouc. 338, 4. Ful semely hire wympel ipynched was, Chauc. Prol. 151. *O. H. Ger.* wimpal *theristrum*: *Icel.* vimpill *a hood, veil.*]

win. v. winn.

win[n] (?), e; *f. Pasture*:—Of ðære díc tó wynne mǽduan be ðære strǽt, Cod. Dip. Kmbl. iii. 263, 29. [*Goth.* winja *pasture*: *O. H. Ger.* winne *pastum*: *Icel.* vin *a meadow.*]

wín, es; *n. Wine*:—Wín *vinum, merum*, geswét wín *mellicratum*, níwe wín *mustum*, ǽlces kynnes gewring bútan wíne and wætere *sicera*, ðæt séleste wín *falernum*, weala wín *crudum vinum*, geolo wín *succinacium vinum*, hláforda wín *honorarium vinum*, gewyrtod wín *compositum vinum* vel *conditum*, gesoden wín *defrutum vinum*, Wrt. Voc. i. 27, 36-62. Áwilled wín *dulcisapa*, geswéted wín *defrucatum*, 290, 56, 58. Ðonne wín hweteþ beornes breóstsefan, breahtme stígeþ cirm on corþre, Exon. Th. 314, 23; Mód. 18. Wǽron hí (*the Danes*) swýðe druncene, for ðam ðǽr wæs gebróht wín súðan, Chr. 1012; Erl. 146, 15. Wín *Bachus*, wínes *Bachi*, Wrt. Voc. ii. 12, 25, 36. Wínes *defruti*, 27, 32: *meri*, 87, 13. Wínes god *Bachus*, 61, 6. Ðæm folce (*the Scythians*) seldsiéne and uncúðe wǽron wínes drencas . . . Hié búton gemetgunge ðæt wín drincende wǽron óð hí heora selfra lytel geweald hæfdon, Ors. 2, 4; Swt. 76, 11-19: Homl. Th. i. 352, 6: ii. 298, 18. Wǽre ðú (*the body*) ðé wiste wlonc and wínes sæd, Exon. Th. 369, 11; Seel. 39. Wínes glæd, 449, 28; Dóm. 78. Wíne *temeto*, Wrt. Voc. ii. 88, 42.

Ne gemunde hē ðæt hē ǣr gespræc, wīne druncen, Beo. Th. 2938; B. 1467. Wīne gewǣged, Exon. Th. 315, 34; Mōd. 41. Hē ofer ealne dæg dryhtguman sīne drencte mid wīne, Judth. Thw. 21, 21; Jud. 29. Wer sæt æt wīne, Exon. Th. 431, 25; Rä. 47, 1. Wīn *nectar*, Wrt. Voc. ii. 61, 31. Hē brōhte hlāf and wīn, Gen. 14, 18. Hwilc þinc gelǣdst ðū (*the merchant*) ūs? Wīn and ele, Coll. Monast. Th. 27, 9. Hwæt drincst ðū (*the boy*)? Ealu, gif ic hæbbe, oþþe wæter, gif ic næbbe ealu. Ne drincst ðū wīn? Ic ne eom swā spēdig ðæt ic mæge bicgean mē wīn; and wīn nys drenc cilda, ne dysigra, ac ealdra and wīsra, 35, 9-22. Ðonne ðū wīn habban wille, ðonne dō ðū mid ðīnum twām fingrum swilce ðū tæppan of tunnan onteón wille, Techm. ii. 120, 9. Byrelas sealdon wīn of wundorfatum, Beo. Th. 2328; B. 1162. [The word made its way into all Teutonic speeches from Latin.] v. æppel-, mæsse-wīn.

wīn-ærn, es; *n.* I. *a place where wine is stored*:—Wīnærn *apotheca*, Wrt. Voc. ii. 6, 6. v. wīn-hūs. II. *a place where wine is sold and drunk, a tavern*:—Wīnaern *taberna*, Wrt. Voc. ii. 122, 3. Wīnærn, i. 290, 52. III. *a hall where wine is drunk, where there is feasting.* Cf. wīn-ræced:—Grētte Hrōðgār Beówulf, and him hǣl ābeád, wīnærnes geweald: 'Nǣfre ic ǣnegum men ǣr ālȳfde ðrȳþærn Dena . . . Hafa nū and geheald hūsa sēlest, Beo. Th. 1312; B. 654.

wīn-beám, es; *m. A vine-pole*:—Wīnbeám *partica*, Wrt. Voc. i. 290, 4: *trabs uinee*, Wülck. Gl. 245, 20.

wīn-beger, es; *n. A grape*:—Ðæt wīnbeger *uuam*, Lk. Skt. Lind. 6, 44. Wīnbegær *uvas*, Mt. Kmbl. Rush. 7, 16. Wīntrog, ðēr monn tred ða wīnbegera *torcular*, Lind. 21, 33.

wīn-belg, es; *m. A wine-skin, wine-bottle*:—Ne menn geótaþ wīn niówe in wīnbelgas (*utres*) alde, Mt. Kmbl. Rush. 9, 17. [*Icel.* vín-belgr.]

wīn-berige, -berie, -berge, an; *f. A grape*:—Wīnberge *uva*, Wrt. Voc. i. 285, 72. Wīnberge te hunige āwylled *medus*, ii. 59, 34. Hire wīnberie ys gealla *uva eorum uva fellis*, Deut. 32, 32. Ne hig wīnberian (*uuam*) on gorste ne nimaþ, Lk. Skt. 6, 44. Gesoden[e] wīnberigan (-en, MS.) *fecula*, Wrt. Voc. i. 27, 63. Hit wæs ðā se tīma, ðæt wīnberian rīpodon *erat autem tempus, quando jam praecoquae uvae vesci possunt*, Num. 13, 21: Scint. 154, 2. Wīnberigena *bacciniorum*, Hpt. Gl. 524, 21. Genim ðās ylcan wyrte mid wīnberian (-berium, -bergan, *v. ll.*), Lchdm. i. 282, 9. Wīnberigean *uvas*, Gen. 40, 9. Ic nam ða wīnberian and wrang on ðæt fæt, 40, 11: Lchdm. iii. 114, 4. Wīnberian (-bergean, *v. l.*) *uvas*, Mt. Kmbl. 7, 16. [Ofte druie sprintles bereð winberien? A. R. 276, 12. *Goth.* weina-basi; *n.*: *O. Sax.* wīnberi; *n.*: *O. H. Ger.* wīn-beri(-peri); *n.*: *Icel.* vín-ber; *n.*]

wīn-bōh; *gen.* -bōges; *m. A branch of a vine*:—Wīnbōga *palmitum*, Hpt. Gl. 468, 17: 496, 74: Homl. Th. ii. 74, 6. Of ðām wīnbōgum mid berium mid eallum *palmitem cum uva sua*, Num. 13, 24.

wīn-brytta, an; *m. A wine-dealer, wine-seller, vintner, tavern-keeper*:—Tæppere, wīnbrytta *caupo, tabernarius*, Wrt. Voc. i. 28, 10. Wīnbryttum *cauponibus*, Wrt. Voc. ii. 79, 79: 18, 21.

wīn-burh; *f.* I. *a town where wine is drunk, where there is feasting, where a prince feasts his followers, a chief town.* Cf. medu-burh, wīn-ærn, III:—Wīnburge cyning (*the king of Babylon*; cf. Belshazzar's feast), Cd. Th. 255, 11; Dan. 622. Wuna in ðære wīnbyrig salu sinchroden, Andr. Kmbl. 3340; An. 1674. Wīnburh wera (*Jerusalem*), 219, 21; Dan. 58. Geond ða wīnburg (*the town of the Mermedonians*), Andr. Kmbl. 3272; An. 1639. Se ðe wīnburga geweald āhte, Exon. Th. 323, 11; Vīd. 77. Wlonce wīgsmiþas wīnburgum in sittaþ æt symble, 314, 15; Mōd. 14: 247, 23; Jul. 83. II. *a walled vineyard*:—For hwan ðū tōwurpe weallfæsten his? wealdeþ his wīnbyrig eall, ðæt on wege færð *ut quid deposuisti maceriam ejus; et vindemiant eam omnes, qui transeunt viam?* Ps. Th. 79, 12.

wīn-byrele, es; *m. A vintner*:—Wīnbyrele *caupo*, Wrt. Voc. ii. 21, 13. [*Icel.* vín-byrli *a cup-bearer*.]

wince, an; *f. A winch*:—Wince *gigrillus* (= girgillus; cf. *girgillus* a reel, Wülck. Gl. 586, 30), Wrt. Voc. 42, 29.

-wince, Win-ceaster, wincel. v. hleápe-wince, Wintan-ceaster, wencel.

wincel (?) *a corner*; cf. place-names, e. g. Wincel-cumb, Homl. Skt. i. 21, 33: Cod. Dip. Kmbl. vi. 354; and modern *Aldwinkle* (Northants). [*O. H. Ger.* winkil *angulus*. The word is found in place-names. v. Graff. i. 721.]

wincettan; *p.* te *To wink*:—Ða ðe mē hatiaþ būtan scylde and wincettaþ mid heora eágum þetwuh him *qui oderunt me gratis, et annuunt oculis*, Ps. Th. 34, 19.

wincian; *p.* ode. I. *to wink, make a sign*:—Ic wincie *annicto* vel *annuto*, Wrt. Voc. i. 22, 27. II. *to close the eyes, blink*:—Ic wincige *conniveo*, Wrt. Voc. i. 34, 14: Ælfc. Gr. 26, 5; Zup. 156, 14. Se ðe āgīmeleásaþ ðæt hē ðence ǣr ðæm ðe hē dō, se stæpð forð mid ðām fōtum and wincaþ mid ðǣm eágum *qui negligit considerando praevidere, quod facit, gressus tendit, oculos claudit*, Past. 39; Swt. 287, 16. Lamena hē is lǣce, leóht wincendra (winciendra, *v. l.*), dumbra tunge, Salm. Kmbl. 156; Sal. 77. [Waryn wisdome wynked uppon Mede, Piers P. 4, 154. Or mans eghe may open or wynk, Pr. C. 4970. Twynkyn wythe the eye, or wynkyn *conniveo, nicito, nicto*, Prompt. Parv. 505. Wynkyn *conniveo*, 530. *O. H. Ger.* winchen *nutare, nictare, oculo annuere*.]

wīn-clyster, es; *n.* I. *a bunch of grapes*:—Wīnclyster *botrus*, Scint. 154, 2. II. *a row of vines*:—Wīnclystra *antes*, Engl. Stud. xi. 64, 3.

wīn-cōle, an; *f. A tub into which the juice pressed from the grapes runs*:—Wīnmere *sive* wīncōle *lacus ubi frugum liquor decurrit*, Wrt. Voc. ii. 54, 13.

wind, es; *m.* I. *wind, air in motion*:—Seó lyft, þonne heó āstyred is, byð wind. Se wind hæfð mistlīce naman on bōcum . . . Feówer heáfodwindas synd. Se fyrmesta is eásterne wind . . . Ðās feówer heáfodwindas habbaþ betweox him on ymbhwyrfte ōðre eahta windas, ǣfre betwyx ðām heáfodwindum twēgen windas . . . Is ān ðæra eahta winda *aquilo* gehāten . . .; ealne ðone cwyld ðe se sūðerna wind *auster* ācænð, ealne hē tōdrǣfð, Lchdm. iii. 274, 10-276, 8. Sæge mē, huona geblāwaþ wind? Ðæt is of Serafin, of ðon is ācweden Serafin windana, Rtl. 192, 33. Gif hūs full ungemetlīc wind gestent, Bt. 12; Fox 36, 16. Swift wind, Met. 7, 20. Se stearca wind, 12, 14. Winneþ wind wið wǣge, 25, 58. Ðonne wind styreþ lāð gewidru, Beo. Th. 2753; B. 1374. Ðonne wind ligeþ, weder bið fæger, Exon. Th. 210, 7; Ph. 182. Biþ sǣ smilte, ðonne hȳ wind ne weceþ, 336, 27; Gn. Ex. 56. Nō wǣgflotan wind ofer ȳðum sīðes getwǣfde, Beo. Th. 3819; B. 1907. Bærn eal tōsomne on ða healfe ðe se wind sȳ, Lchdm. iii. 56, 7. Se wind strongra geswinca . . . se wind ðara earfoþa, Bt. 12; Fox 36, 18, 28. Wæs mycel ȳst windes geworden, Mk. Skt. 4, 37. Hwyrft hægel of heofones lyfte, wealcaþ hit windes scūra, Runic pm. Kmbl. 341, 6; Rūn. 9. Holm storme weól, won wið winde, Beo. Th. 2268; B. 1132. Winde gelīcost, ðonne hē hlūd āstīgeþ, wǣðeþ be wolcnum, wēdende færeþ, and eft semninga swīge gewyrðeþ, Elen. Kmbl. 2542; El. 1272. Winde biwāune weallas, Exon. Th. 291, 2; Wand. 76. Wērig sceal se wiþ winde rōweþ, 345, 12; Gn. Ex. 187. Winde gefȳsed flota, Beo. Th. 440; B. 217. Ðā sende Drihten micelne wind, Ex. 14, 21. Ðū ðe ða treówa þurh ðone stearcan wind norþan and eástan on hærfesttīd heora leáfa bereáfast, and eft on lencten ōþru leáf sellest þurh ðone smyltan sūþanwesternan wind *quas Boreae spiritus aufert, revehat mitis Zephyrus, frondeis*, Bt. 4; Fox 8, 5-8. Þurh ðone lāðran wind, Met. 4, 24. Theodosius hæfde ðone wind mid him, ðæt his fultum mehte mǣstra ǣlcne heora flāna on hiora feóndum āfæstnian, Ors. 6, 36; Swt. 294, 26. Ðǣr bleówun windas, Mt. Kmbl. 7, 25. Wedercandel swearc, windas weóxon, Andr. Kmbl. 745; An. 373. Swōgaþ windas, blāwaþ brecende bearhtma mǣste, Exon. Th. 59, 10; Cri. 950. Hē fleáh ofer winda fiðeru, Ps. Th. 17, 10. Hē bebȳt ge windum ge sǣ, Lk. Skt. 8, 25. II. *wind, flatulence.* v. windig, II:—Gif sió wamb biþ windes full, ðonne cymð ðæt of wlacre wǣtan, Lchdm. ii. 224, 23. Wambe wind, 168, 20. III. *wind, breath*:—Ic (*a horn*) winde sceal swelgan of sumes bōsme, Exon. Th. 395, 28; Rä. 15, 14. [*Goth.* winds: *O. Sax. O. Frs.* wind: *O. H. Ger.* wint: *Icel.* vindr: *Lat.* ventus.] v. eástan-, eástansūþan- (*under* eástan), eástnorþ-, heáfod-, norþ-, norþan-, norþaneástan-, norþanwestan-, sūþ-, sūþan-, sūþaneástan-, sūþanwestan-, west-, westan-, westansūþan-, westnorþ-, westsūþ-wind.

wind, es; *m. Winding, wrapping*:—Gif preóst ordāl misfadige, gebēte ðæt. Gif preóst searwaþ be winde, gebēte ðæt *if a priest do not conduct an ordeal rightly, let him make 'bōt.' If a priest uses deceit in respect to the wrapping up of the hand or arm exposed to the ordeal* (cf. in the descriptions of the proceedings at the ordeal: Inseglige man ða hand, L. Ath. iv. 7; Th. i. 226, 30. Beón þreó niht ǣr man ða hand undō, i. 23; Th. i. 212, 4), *let him make 'bōt,'* L. N. P. L. 39, 40; Th. ii. 296, 9-10. [*Icel.* vindr *a winding*.]

wind?:—Uuind *sclabrum*, Txts. 97, 1841. Windum *slabris*, 181, 72. [Cf. (?) *O. H. Ger.* winta *flabrum, ventilabrum*; or (?) *O. H. Ger.* winta: *Ger.* winde *a pulley, reel*.] Cf. windung.

wind-ǣdre, an; *f. A windpipe*:—Gōma *palatum*, sweora *collum*, hracan *fauces*, windǣddran *arteriae*, þrotu *guttur*, Wrt. Voc. i. 43, 35-39. [*Icel.* vind-æð.]

win-dæg. v. winn-dæg.

windan; *p.* wand, *pl.* wundon; *pp.* wunden. I. *intrans.* (1) of motion that results from a blow, swing, or other impetus, *to fly, leap, start*:—Sió æcs wint of ðam hielfe and eác ūs of ðære handa . . . Sió æcs wient of ðæm hielfe *securis manu fugit . . . Ferrum de manubrio prosilit*, Past. 21; Swt. 167, 7-9. Sum ōðer hine wolde sleán mid īsene, ac ðæt wǣpen wand āweg mid ðam slege of ðæs rēðan handum, Homl. Th. ii. 510, 22. Ðā slōg hē ānes monnes hors mid his sweorde, ðæt him wand ðæt heáfod of *ad unum gladii ictum caput desecuisset*, Ors. 5, 2; Swt. 216, 24. Slōh ides ðone hǣþenan hund, ðæt him ðæt heáfod wand forþ on ðā flōre, Judth. Thw. 23, 8; Jud. 110. Bærst sum sagol intō ānes beáteres eágan swā ðæt his eáge wand ūt mid ðæm slæge, Homl. Skt. i. 4, 144. Heó wearð mid swurde gewundod, ðæt hire wand se innoð ūt, 9, 127: Jud. 3, 22. (2) *to fly, wheel, spring.* Cf. wendan. (a) of the movement of living things:—Sume fōtum foldan peðþaþ, sume fleógende windaþ (-eð, MS.) under wolcnum *sunt quibus alarum levitas vaga . . .*

liquido longi spatia aetheris enatet volatu, Met. 31, 12. Hē wand him up þanon, hwearf him þurh ða helldora, Cd. Th. 29, 7; Gen. 446. Ðā wand se of his swuran *he sprang from his neck*, Homl. Th. i. 336, 17. Hornfisc plegode, and se grǣga mǣw wælgīfre wand (*flew circling round*), Andr. Kmbl. 743; An. 372. Hremmas wundon, Byrht. Th. 134, 59; By. 106. Hē mid feðerhoman fleógan meahte, windan on wolcne, Cd. Th. 27, 15; Gen. 418. (b) of inanimate things:—Dægscealdes hleó (*the pillar of cloud*) wand ofer wolcnum, Cd. Th. 182, 23; Exod. 80. Mid ðam worde wand fȳr of heofonum *at those words fire flew from heaven*, Homl. Skt. i. 18, 249. Wand tō wolcnum wælfȳra mǣst, Beo. Th. 2242; B. 1119. Ða spearcan wundon wið ðæs hrōfes *the sparks flew whirling towards the roof*, Homl. Skt. ii. 26, 229. Hē forlēt wælspere windan on ða wīcingas, Byrht. Th. 141, 14; By. 322. (c) of abstract subjects:—Sió æcs wint of ðam hielfe, and eác ūs of ðære honda ðonne ðonne sió lār wint on rēðnesse *securis manu fugit, cum sese increpatio in asperitatem pertrahit*, Past. 21; Swt. 167, 8. (3) of twisting, rolling movement, (a) of living things:—Hē wand swā swā wurm *he writhed like a serpent*, Homl. Th. i. 414, 17. Hwīlum nacode men windaþ (winnaþ, MS.) ymbe wyrmas (cf. Canto xxv of the Inferno), Cd. Th. 273, 13; Sat. 136. Hē wearp hine ðā on wyrmes līc, and wand him ymbūtan ðone deáðes beám *he twined round the tree of death*, Cd. Th. 31, 27; Gen. 491. (b) of inanimate things:—Þūfas wundon ofer gārfare *the banners fluttered above the battalions*, Cd. Th. 199, 22; Exod. 342. Streámas wundon *the waters rolled*, Beo. Th. 430; B. 212. Staþelas wið wǣge, wætre windendum, Exon. Th. 61, 9; Cri. 982. (4) fig. *to waver.* Cf. wandian:—Gearo wæs Gūðlāc; hine God fremede on ondsware and on elne strong; ne wond hē for worde (*he did not waver on account of what was said to him*), Exon. Th. 120, 1; Gū. 265. **II.** *trans.* (1) *to twist, roll*:—Ðæt hors on misenlīce dǣlas hit wond and ðrǣste *cum equus diversas in partes se torqueret volutando*, Bd. 3, 9; S. 533, 36. (2) *to brandish, wave*:—Hē wand wācne æsc, Byrht. Th. 132, 68; By. 43. (3) *to twist, plait, weave*:—Wundun *intexunt*, Wrt. Voc. ii. 110, 74. Hī wundon cynehelm of þornum *plectentes coronam de spinis*, Mt. Kmbl. 27, 29: Jn. Skt. 19, 2. Windan *plumemus*, Wrt. Voc. ii. 83, 78. Windan manigne smicerne wǣn, Shrn. 163, 15. Windende *plectentis*, Wrt. Voc. ii. 74, 32. Wundene mē ne beóð wefle, Exon. Th. 417, 15; Rä. 36, 5. Wundne loccas, 428, 7; Rä. 41, 104. Wundnum rāpum fōtas gefæstnian, Ps. Th. 139, 5. (4) *to twist, give a curved form to* (mostly as an epithet of gold made into ornaments; cf. *O. Sax.* wundan gold):—Bunden, wunden (*applied to a winecask*), Exon. Th. 410, 26; Rä. 29, 5. Him wæs wunden gold geeáwed . . . hringas, healsbeága mǣst, Beo. Th. 2391; B. 1193: 6259; B. 3134: Exon. Th. 288, 17; Wand. 32: Cd. Th. 124, 30; Gen. 2070. Beágas, welan, wunden gold, 116, 4; Gen. 1931: 258, 9; Dan. 673. Wunden gold, . . . feoh and frætwa, 128, 18; Gen. 2128. Wunden gold (*the ornament of a sheath*), Exon. Th. 437, 6; Rä. 56, 3. Ic ðē leánige ealdgestreónum, wundnum golde, Beo. Th. 2768; B. 1382. Wundnan golde, Exon. Th. 326, 16; Vīd. 129. [Þat we mosten ouer sæ winden mid seile (away wende, 2nd MS.), Laym. 20818. Stanes heo letten winden, 27461. He smat an Arðures sceld, þat he wond (fleh, 2nd MS.) a þene feld, 23964. Þe sparke þet wint up, A. R. 296, 13. Gif dust winded up, 314, 8. In to reste his sowle wond, Gen. and Ex. 4136. Ȝho wand himm i winndeclut, Orm. 3320. *Goth.* bi-windan *involvere*; us-windan *plectere*: *O. Sax.* windan *to fly; to roll; to plait*: *O. H. Ger.* wintan *torquere; rotari*: *Icel.* vinda *to twist, wind; to thrust; to hurl; to turn.*] v. ā-, æt-, be- (bi-), ge-, on-, ōþ-, un-, ymb-windan; un-wunden.

wind-bland *tumult of winds*:—Windblond gelæg, Beo. Th. 6284; B. 3146.

wind-cyrice, an; *f. A round church* (? cf. seonu-wealt, I):—Ic Eádwerd cinig begeat æt Deneulfe biscepe on Winteceastre ða windcirican, Cod. Dip. Kmbl. v. 163, 12.

winde (?); *adj. Curly*:—Winde loccas (windeloccas?) *cincinni*, Wrt. Voc. ii. 20, 43: 14, 27: 104, 6. [Cf. *Icel.* vindr *awry, twisted.*] v. windan.

-winde. [Cf. *O. H. Ger.* winta: *Ger.* winde: *Icel.* vinda *a hank.*] v. ed-, gearn-, næder-, wudu-winde.

-winde; *adj.* v. ge-winde.

windel, es; *m. A basket*:—Windil *cartellus*, Wrt. Voc. ii. 102, 42. Windel, 13, 9: *cartellus, fiscella*, 128, 78: *cistella* vel *cartellum*, i. 24, 56: *cartallum*, 86, 4. Wylige oððe windel *corbis*, Ælfc. Gr. 9, 28; Zup. 55, 13. Ða hlāfas on ðam windle (*canistro*), Ex. 29, 32. Ic geseah swefen, ðæt ys, ðæt ic hæfde þrī windlas (*canistra*) ofer mīn heáfod, and on ðam ufemystan windle (*canistro*) wǣre manegra cynna gebæc, Gen. 40, 17. Ðā nam heó ānne riscenne windel (*fiscellam scirpeam*) on scipwīsan gesceapenne, Ex. 2, 3, 5, 6. Man sceal habban wilian, windlas, systras, sǣdleáp, Anglia ix. 264, 12.

windel-stān, es; *m. A tower with a winding staircase*:—Windelstān *coclea*, gewind *circuitus ascensus* (the word occurs in a list of names of buildings), Wrt. Voc. i. 37, 3. [*O. H. Ger.* wentil-stein *cochlea, turris in qua per circuitum scanditur.*]

windel-streáw, -streów, es; *n. Windle-straw, some kind of coarse grass* or *reed* (v. windle-straws, E. D. S. Pub. Plant Names):—Eár *spica*, egle *aresta*, windelstreów *calmum*, Wrt. Voc. i. 287, 22: ii. 16, 74. Genim ðæt micle greáte windelstreáw twyecge, ðæt on worþium wixð, Lchdm. ii. 44, 4. v. windel.

windel-treów, es; *n. A wild olive*:—Windeltreów *oleaster*, Wrt. Voc. i. 285, 74: ii. 64, 6. v. windel.

wind-fana, an; *m. A cloth for winnowing with, a fan*:—Windfona *scabellum*, Wrt. Voc. ii. 119, 71: i. 289, 22. His fone ł windfone (fonnae ł windgefonnae, Lind.) in honda his and clǣnsaþ bereflōr his *cujus uentilabrum in manu ejus et purgauit aream suam*, Lk. Skt. Rush. 3, 17. [Cf. *Ventilabrum* . . . a sayle or a wynde clothe. A wyndowe clothe *ventilabrum*, Prompt. Parv. 529, note 5. See also Cath. Angl. 419, note 3.]

wind-filled; *adj. Wind-felled, blown down by the wind*:—Wuduwearde gebyreþ ǣlc windfylled treów, L. R. S. 19; Th. i. 440, 10.

wind-gerest, e; *f. A windy resting-place* (?), *a hall open to the winds* (?):—Hē gesyhð sorhcearig on his suna būre wīnsele wēstne, windgereste (wind gereste, MS.: windge reste, Grein) *he sees the hall deserted, the resting-place of men open to the winds* (? For the hall as a sleeping-place, cf. Monig snellīc sǣrinc selereste gebeáh, 1385; B. 690), Beo. Th. 4904; B. 2456. Cf. wind-sele.

wind-hladen; *adj. Wind-laden, windy*, Lye.

wind-hreóse (?), es; *m. A storm of wind*:—Swā swā gōd scipstȳra ongit micelne windhreóse ǣr ǣr hit weorþe, Bt. 41, 3; Fox 250, 14. Cf. wind-rǣs.

windig; *adj.* I. *windy*:—Ðā com windi (wyndig, *v.l.*) ȳst *descendit procella uenti*, Lk. Skt. 8, 23. Windig sumer, Lchdm. iii. 162, 30. Windig lengten, 164, 5. Wæs on ðam ofne, ðǣr se engel becwom, windig (*breezy, airy*) and wynsum, Cd. Th. 237, 33; Dan. 347. Windig wolcen, Exon. Th. 201, 24; Ph. 61. Ðes windiga sele (*Hell*), Cd. Th. 273, 14; Sat. 136. Heora wyrtruma bið swā swā windige ysla (*ashes blown by the wind*, sic radix eorum quasi favilla erit, et germen eorum ut pulvis ascendet, Is. 5, 24), Homl. Th. ii. 322, 20. Torras stōdon, windige weallas, Andr. Kmbl. 1685; An. 845. Windige holmas, Exon. Th. 53, 26; Cri. 856. Ic sǣnæssas geseón mihte, windige weallas, Beo. Th. 1148; B. 572: 2721; B. 1358. Swā sīde swā sǣ bebūgeþ windge eardweallas (wind geard weallas, MS.), 2452; B. 1224. **I a.** fig.:—Ðeáh ðeós weoruld wēde, and windige ēhtnysse āstyrige ongeán Cristes gelaðunge, Homl. Th. ii. 388, 9. **II.** *windy, flatulent.* v. wind, II:—Gif se ūtgang sié windig and wætrig, Lchdm. ii. 236, 6. Be windigre wambe, 162, 23. Wiþ windigre āþundenesse, 166, 25: 188, 22. Wiþ ða þing ðe windigne ǣþm on men wyrcen, 214, 3. [*Icel.* vindugr.]

Windles-ōra, an; *m. Windsor*:—Æt Windlesōran, Chr. 1061; Erl. 194, 3. Wæs se cyng on Windlesōran, 1095; Erl. 231, 22. Ðis writ wæs gemaced æt Windlesōren, Cod. Dip. Kmbl. iv. 209, 27. Ic habbe gegefan Criste and Sancte Petre intō Westmynstre Windlesōran and Stāne, 227, 6: 178, 19.

wind-rǣs, es; *m. A storm of wind*:—Windrǣs *procella*, Mk. Skt. Lind. 4, 37.

wīn-drenc, es; *m. Wine*:—Wīndrenc (-dred, l. 10, -drend, l. 12, MS.) *vinum*, R. Ben. Interl. 72, 10, 12. Ða cempan him budon drincan gebitrodne wīndrenc, Homl. Th. ii. 254, 16. v. wīn-drync.

wīn-druncen; *adj. Drunken with wine, drunken*:—Wīndruncen *vinolentus*, R. Ben. Interl. 20, 13. Wīndruncen gewit, Cd. Th. 262, 32; Dan. 753. Wīndruncynes *temulenti*, Kent. Gl. 985. Wīndruncene *uinolentae, ebriae*, Germ. 394, 250. [Gumen weoren windrunken (dronge of wine, 2nd MS.), Laym. 8126. *O. H. Ger.* wīn-trunchan *temulentus*: *Icel.* vīn-drukkinn.]

wīn-drync, es; *m. Wine*:—Heortan manna must and wīndrinc myclum blissaþ *vinum laetificet cor hominis*, Ps. Th. 103, 14. Wē þeáh rǣdaþ ðæt munecum tō wīndrince (-drynce, -drence, *v.ll.*) nāht ne belimpe *licet legamus uinum monachorum non esse*, R. Ben. 64, 21. [*Icel.* vīn-drykkr.] v. wīn-drenc, -gedrinc.

wind-scofl, e; *f. A fan*:—Winds(c)obl *ventilabrum*, Wrt. Voc. ii. 71, 66. [Cf. *O. L. Ger.* wind-scūfla *ventilabrum*; *O. H. Ger.* wint-scūvala *ventilabrum.*] v. windwig-scofl.

wind-sele, e; *m. A windy hall*:—Wīde geond windsele (*Hell*; cf. Ðes windiga sele, 273, 14; Sat. 136), Cd. Th. 284, 11; Sat. 320: 288, 23; Sat. 386.

wind-swingla, an; *m. A fan*:—Windswingla *pala* vel *ventilabrum*, Wrt. Voc. i. 41, 36.

windu-mær. v. wudu-mær.

windung, e; *f. Something woven* or *plaited, a hurdle* (cf. *plecta* hyrdle, Hpt. Gl. 497, 70):—Windonge *plecta* (cf. gewind *plectas*, 68, 71: plecta *quilibet nexus ex virgulis, vel papyro, vel carecto*, Migne), Wrt. Voc. ii. 83, 77.

windung, winnung, e; *f. What is winnowed, chaff, straw*:—Ða winnunga *zizania*, Mt. Kmbl. Lind. 13, 38. Wynnunga, 26. Wynnung, 25. Ða halm ł ða windungo (winnunge, Rush.) *paleas*, Lk. Skt. Lind.

11; Gen. 2290. Ðú wealdest ðises ríces ðe ðú æfter wunne, Guthl. 21; Gdwin. 96, 7. Ðú wið Criste wunne and gewin tuge, Exon. Th. 267, 26; Jul. 421. Hé wann mid ðam (*a sword*) on ǽlcum gefeohte, Homl. Skt. ii. 25, 296. Ðá wan him on Amalech, i. 13, 4. Hé wonn on Sciþþie *regi Scytharum bellum intulit*, Ors. 2, 5; Swt. 78, 8. Fæht hine on and won Penda *impugnatus a Penda*, Bd. 3, 14; S. 539, 18. Ðá wann him ongeán Maxentius, Homl. Th. ii. 304, 5. Hé gelómlíce uppon ðone eorl wann, Chr. 1095; Erl. 231, 10. Ðá won wiþ hine Cadwalla *rebellavit adversus eum Caedualla*, Bd. 2, 20; S. 521, 7. Hé feaht and won wiþ his ēþle, 3, 24; S. 556, 28: Chr. 597; Erl. 20, 4. Grendel wan wið Hróðgár, Beo. Th. 305; B. 151. Hí wunnon him betwýnan, Homl. Th. ii. 356, 24. Wunnon hý wið Dryhtnes mihtum, Salm. Kmbl. 655; Sal. 327. Ða Bryttas wunnon heom wið ða castelmenn, Chr. 1067; Erl. 204, 5. Win him on swýðe, Homl. Skt. i. 13, 8. Seó ǽ ðe ðú under hire tǽcinge winnan wylt and campian *lex sub qua militare uis*, R. Ben. 96, 23. Æfter ríce winnan, Chr. 685; Erl. 40, 16. On winnan *ingruere*, Hpt. Gl. 427, 42: Bd. 1, 12; S. 480, 23. Ðonne hé on óðer folc winnan sceal, Past. 18; Swt. 129, 9. Ðæt hí uppon hǽðene þeódan winnan woldan, Chr. 1096; Erl. 233, 14. On gehwelc lond tó winnanne, Ors. 3, 7; Swt. 116, 8. Hé him on winnende wæs, 1, 2; Swt. 30, 5. Worhte Ælfréd cyning lytle werede geweorc æt Æþelinga eigge, and of ðam geweorce wæs winnende wiþ ðone here, Chr. 878; Erl. 80, 6. (4 a) of the action of inanimate objects:—Se winterlíca wind wan mid ðam forste *the winter wind warred along with the frost*, Homl. Skt. i. 11, 144. (4 b) with cognate accusative:—For ðæm gewinne ðe hé wiþ God wan, Blickl. Homl. 63, 4. Winn gód gewinn *certa bonum certamen*, Scint. 214, 16. III. *to win* (v. Jamieson's Dictionary), *make one's way*:—Hwæt is ðæt wundor, ðæt geond ðás woruld fareþ . . ., winneþ oft hider? Salm. Kmbl. 568; Sal. 283. B. *trans.* I. *to labour at, bestow labour upon*:—Ic wann wununise mín *laboravi habitationem meam*, Rtl. 68, 28. Ic sende iúh gehrioppa ðætte gié ne wunnon *ego misi uos metere quod uos non laborastis*, Jn. Skt. Lind. Rush. 4, 38. II. *to labour under, suffer, undergo*:—Ic ðæt geþolade . . . læg on heardum stáne . . . ic ðæt earfeþe wonn, Exon. Th. 87, 21; Cri. 1428. Á ic wíte wonn mínra wræcsíþa, 441, 26; Kl. 5. Ic á þolade geára gehwylce gódes ealles, won ic módearfoþa (þonc mód earfoþa, Th.) má ðonne on óþrum, fyrhto in folce, 457, 19; Hy. 4, 86. Mid ðý ðá se bróþor langre tíde ðyllíc ungescrǽpo wonn (woon, MS.) *cumque tempore non pauco frater tali incommodo laboraret*, Bd. 4, 32; S. 611, 22. Ðú ðæs cwealmes scealt wíte winnan and on wræc hweorfan, Cd. Th. 62, 14; Gen. 1014. Hí áwo sculon, wræc winnende, wærgðu dreógan, Exon. Th. 78, 10; Cri. 1272. III. *to win, get, attain*:—Ðú wunne reste á óþ ende mid hálgum fǽmnum, Nar. 49, 1. Hí wéndon ðæt hí sceoldon winnon eall ðæt land, Chr. 1070; Erl. 207, 27. [Ierusalem and Babilonie fiteð eure and winneð bitwinen hem . . . þe king of Babilonie wan Ierusalem, O. E. Homl. ii. 51, 11–25. Iob wan wið þe wurse, 187, 26. Heo wunnen agean, A. R. 238, 17. Ðanne sumer and winter winnen, Misc. 17, 521. He iwon (won, 2nd MS.) al þis lond, Laym. 2560. Winnenn heoffness kinedom, Orm. 801. He wan to William, Will. 2498. *Goth.* winnan παθεῖν: *O. Sax.* winnan *to strive; to suffer; to gain*: *O. Frs.* winna *to gain*: *O. H. Ger.* winnan *laborare; jurgare, decertare, dimicare*: *Icel.* vinna *to work; to withstand; to suffer; to win*.] v. á-, ge-, ofer-, wiþer-winnan; on-winnende.

winn-dæg, es; *m. A day of labour* or *of struggle*:—Fela sceal gebídan leófes and láþes se ðe longe hér on ðyssum windagum worulde brúceþ, Beo. Th. 2128; B. 1062. v. gewin-dæg.

-winnend, -winnendlíc. v. ofer-, wiþ-winnend, un-oferwinnendlíc.

winn-stów, e; *f. A wrestling-place*:—Winstówe *scammatis*, Hpt. Gl. 405, 40. On winstówe *in scammate*, 489, 59. Winstówe *palaestrarum*, 478, 50. v. gewin-stów.

winnung, winpel. v. windung, wiþ-winnung, wimpel.

wín-ræced, es; *m. n. A house where there is feasting, a palace*:—Wínreced, goldsele gumena (*Hrothgar's palace*), Beo. Th. 1433; B. 714. Ðæt wínreced, gestsele, 1991; B. 993. Hornsalu wunedon wéste wínræced, Andr. Kmbl. 2319; An. 1161. Cf. wín-ærn.

wín-reáfetian *to take grapes*:—Plucciaþ ł wínhreáfetiaþ *vindemiant*, Ps. Lamb. 79, 13.

wín-repan *to gather grapes*:—Wínreopad ðæt *vendemiant eam*, Ps. Surt. 79, 13. v. repan.

wín-sæd; *adj. Wine-sated, having had one's fill of wine*:—Yrrum ealowósan, were wínsaduṁ, Exon. Th. 330, 12; Vy. 50. Weras wínsade (cf. hé oferdrencte his duguðe ealle, 21, 22; Jud. 31; and the Latin c. 13, 2: Erant omnes fatigati a vino), Judth. Thw. 22, 21; Jud. 71.

wín-sæl, es; *n. A wine-hall, a hall where there is feasting*:—Wóriaþ ða wínsalo, Exon. Th. 291, 6; Wand. 78. v. next word.

wín-sele, es; *m. A wine-hall, a hall where there is feasting*:—Nis hér (*in Hell*) wlonca wínsele, ne worulde dreám, Cd. Th. 270, 21; Sat. 94. Se wínsele (*Hrothgar's hall*), Beo. Th. 1547; B. 771. In ðæm wínsele, 1394; B. 695. Beóre druncne . . . hí in wínsele sáwle forlétan, Exon. Th. 271, 25; Jul. 487: 283, 27; Jul. 686. Gesyhð on his suna búre wínsele wéstne, Beo. Th. 4903; B. 2456. [*O. Sax.* wínseli.]

wín-sester, es; *m. A wine-can*:—Wínsester *cantarus*, Wrt. Voc. i. 24, 37.

wín-stów, winstre, winsum. v. winn-stów, winestra, wynsum.

wín-tæppere, es; *m. A wine-seller, tavern-keeper*:—Wíntæpperum *cauponibus*, Hpt. Gl. 468, 42.

Wintan-ceaster (Wintun-, Winta (-e, -i), Win-), e: Wænte, an; *f. Winchester.* [The name is got from the earlier Venta of Roman Britain. This form occurs in Latin works, e. g.: In Venta civitate, Bd. 4, 15: Cod. Dip. Kmbl. iii. 300, 16. Monasterium in Wenta positum, vi. 29, 16. Also the adjective Wentanus (Uentanus, Bd. 5, 18), e. g.: Wentanus episcopus, v. 82, 14. Wentana ecclesia, ii. 210, 3: v. 45, 3. Wentana civitas, ii. 140, 9: 220, 28. Urbs Wentana, iii. 326, 10: iv. 45, 7. Wentana sedes, v. 169, 16. And Wentana is used as the name of the place, e. g.: Wentanae monasterium, iii. 8, 13. But Latinized forms of the English word are used; Wintonia is often found in the charters; the form Wincestria occurs v. 167, 7, and the adjective Wintancestrensis 90, 29.]:—In ciuitate opinatissima quae Winteceaster nuncupatur, Cod. Dip. Kmbl. ii. 195, 35. Belumpon hí (*the South Saxons*) ǽr tó Wintanceastre biscopscíre *ad civitatis Ventanae parochiam pertinebant*, Bd. 5, 18; S. 639, 14. Daniel Wæntan biscop, Chr. 731; Erl. 47, 11. Intó Wintanceastre, Cod. Dip. Kmbl. ii. 114, 26: iii. 111, 29. Gange án gemet swilce man on Lundenbyrig and on Wintanceastre (Winta-, *v. l.*) healde, L. Edg. ii. 8; Th. i. 270, 2. Seó gerǽdnys ðe Cnut cyningc gerǽdde on Wintanceastre (Win-, *v. l.*), L. C. E. proem.; Th. i. 358, 7. Cénwalh hét átimbran ða cirican on Wintunceastre (Wintan-, *v. l.*), Chr. 643; Erl. 26, 9. Hér Danihel gesæt on Wintanceastre, 744; Erl. 48, 1. Hedde heóld ðone biscopdóm on Wintaceastre (Wintan-, *v. l.*), 703; Erl. 42, 22. Hí West-Seaxna bisceopum underþeódde wǽron, ða ðe on Wintaceastre wǽron, Bd. 4, 15; S. 583, 35. Tó Wintaceastre (Winte-, *v. l.*) .vi. myneteras, L. Ath. i. 14; Th. i. 206, 31: Cod. Dip. Kmbl. iii. 326, 16. Winteceastre, ii. 176, 11: v. 163, 11. Tó ealdan mynstære tó Winticeastræ, ii. 127, 12. Syþþan ðæt gemót wæs on Winceastre, L. C. S. 30; Th. i. 392, 26. Ðes Swíðún wæs bisceop on Winceastre, Homl. Skt. i. 21, 14. Æðelwold biscop on Winceastre, Cod. Dip. Kmbl. vi. 207, 6.

winter, es; *m.* (*in pl. a neuter form* wintru *occurs, as well as masculine* wintras, winter: *the dat. sing.* wintra *is a trace of earlier* u-*stem declension*). I. a season of the year, *winter*:—Feówer tída syndon getealde on ánum geáre, ðæt synd *uer, aestas, autumnus, hiems* . . . *Hiems* is winter, Lchdm. iii. 250, 12. On ðone .vii. dæg ðæs mónðes (*November*) bið wintres fruma; se winter hafaþ tú and hundnigontig daga, Shrn. 146, 7. Winter bringeþ weder ungemetceald, swifte windas, Met. 11, 59. Winter bið cealdost, Menol. Fox 470; Gn. C. 5. Hengest wælfágne winter wunode mid Finne . . . Holm storme weól, winter ýþe beleác ísgebinde, óþ ðæt óþer com geár in geardas . . . Ðá wæs winter scacen, fæger foldan bearm, Beo. Th. 2259–2278; B. 1127–1137. Ðæt hit wǽre wintres tíd, and se winter wǽre grim and ceald and fyrstig and mid íse gebunden, Bd. 3, 19; S. 549, 26. Is ðǽr nú irfæs ðæs ðæs stranga wintær lǽfæd hæfð, Chart. Th. 163, 1. Nys hit swá stearc winter ðæt ic durre lutian æt hám, Coll. Monast. Th. 19, 17. Sam hit sý sumor sam winter, Ors. 1, 1; Swt. 21, 17. Wintres *brumae*, Wrt. Voc. ii. 12, 43. On wintres tíman, ðæt is fram ðan anginne ðæs mónðes, ðe is November gehaten, óþ Eástran, R. Ben. 32, 10. Siððan (*after the first of November*) wintres dæg (*winter*; cf. *Icel.* á vetrardag *in the winter*) wíde gangeþ on syx nihtum, sigelbeorhtne genimð hærfest mid herige hrímes and snáwes, Menol. Fox 401; Men. 202. Hé (*petra oleum*) is gód tó drincanne on wintres dæge, for ðon ðe hé hæfð swíðe micle hǽte; for ðý hine mon sceal drincan on wintra, Lchdm. ii. 288, 16. Beámas gréne stondaþ wintres and sumeres, Exon. Th. 200, 7; Ph. 37. Mid ðý storme ðæs wintres *hiemis tempestate*, Bd. 2, 13; S. 516, 20. Geofon weól wintres wylme, Beo. Th. 1036; B. 516. Wintres wóma, Exon. Th. 292, 22; Wand. 103. Biddaþ ðæt eówer fleám on wintra (wintre, Rush.) ne gewurðe, Mt. Kmbl. 24, 20. On wintra hit biþ ceald, Bt. 21; Fox 74, 24. Se oftrǽda rén leccaþ ða eorþan on wintra, 39, 13; Fox 234, 17. Wíciaþ Finnas on huntoðe on wintra, and on sumera on fiscaþe, Ors. 1, 1; Swt. 17, 6. Hí (*the hawks*) fédaþ hig sylfe and mé on wintra, Coll. Monast. Th. 26, 1. Beád Swegen full gild and metsunga tó his here ðone winter, Chr. 1013; Erl. 149, 3: Exon. Th. 306, 29; Seef. 15. Wintras *hiemes*, Germ. 388, 26. *See also* midd, II. I a. *wintry weather, cold*:—Hé (*the sparrow*) sóna of wintra in winter eft cymeþ, Bd. 2, 13; S. 516, 21. Hé him helle gescóp, wælcealde wíc, wintre beðeahte, Salm. Kmbl. 938; Sal. 468. Se wind (*zephirus*) tówyrpð and ðáwaþ ǽlcne winter, Lchdm. iii. 274, 22. II. *a year*:—Beóð his winter wynnum íced *annos ejus in diem seculi adjicies*, Ps. Th. 60, 5. Úre winter *anni nostri*, 89, 10. God ána wát hwæt him weaxendum winter bringaþ, Exon. Th. 327, 26; Vy. 9. Hí wǽron on Egipta lande feówer hund wintra and þrítig wintra, Ex. 12, 40. Ymb þrittig wintra, Bt. 39, 3; Fox 214, 25. Hú seó ádl ǽr feówertigum oððe fíftigum wintra on men ne become *how the disease does not attack a man before*

1, 5. Ðeós wyrt hafaþ leáf swylce wîngeard, Lchdm. i. 316, 8. Wîngeardes twiga, ii. 190, 11. Of ðises wîngeardes (-eardes, *v.l.*) cynne *de generatione vitis*, Lk. Skt. 22, 18. Swâ on wîngearde weaxen berigean *sicut vitis abundans*, Ps. Th. 127, 3. Of wîngearde *de vite*, Wrt. Voc. ii. 27, 53. Se gesibsuma wer byð ðam wînearde gelîc ðe byrð gôde wæstmas, Basil admn. 6; Norm. 46, 24. Ðû ût âlǽddest wîngeard (*vineam*) . . . and his wyrtruman settest, Ps. Th. 79, 8. Ic geseah wîneard (*vitem*), on ðam wǽron þreó clystru, Gen. 40, 9. On sumum stôwum wîngeardas (*vineae*) grôwaþ, Bd. 1, 1; S. 473, 14: Ps. Th. 104, 29. Wîngearda hôcas ðe hî mid bindaþ ðæt him nêhst bið *capreoli* vel *cincinni* vel *uncinuli*, wîngearda hringa[s] *corimbi*, Wrt. Voc. i. 38, 59–60. Wîngearda gewind *capreoli*, 39, 10. Ðe mâ ðe gimmas weaxaþ on wîngeardum *nec vite gemmas carpitis*, Bt. 32, 3; Fox 118, 11: Met. 19, 9. [He plantede winiærd, Chr. 1137; Erl. 263, 19. Wingeardes *vineae*, A. R. 294, 29. Winyard, Misc. 33, 20. *Goth.* weina-gards: *O. Sax.* wîn-gardo: *O. H. Ger.* wîn-gart, -garto: *Icel.* vín-garðr.] v. following words.

wîngeard-bôh(-g), es; *m. A vine-tendril*:—Wîngeardbôgas *capreoli*, Wrt. Voc. i. 22, 15. v. wîn-geard, **II**, *and next word*.

wîngeard-hocgas (*for* wîngeard-bôgas, v. preceding word; or wîngeard-hôcas, cf. wîngearda hôcas *capreoli*, Wrt. Voc. i. 38, 59) *caprioli dicti quod capiant arbores*, Wrt. Voc. ii. 129, 61.

wîngeard-hring, es; *m. A cluster of grapes*:—Wîngeardhringas (cf. Wîngearda hringa[s] *corimbi*, i. 38, 60) *vel* bergan *vel* croppas *corimbi*, i. *viti racemi* vel *botriones* vel *circuli*, Wrt. Voc. ii. 135, 74.

wîngeard-seax, es; *n. A pruning-knife*:—Wîngeardseax *falx*, Wrt. Voc. ii. 146, 76.

wîn-gedrinc, es; *n. Wine-drinking, wine*:—Hié wlenco onwôd and wîngedrync, Cd. Th. 155, 28; Gen. 2579. Of ungemete ǽlces þinges, wiste and wǽda, wîngedrinces, Met. 25, 39. Wîngedrince *nectare*, Wrt. Voc. ii. 61, 32. Hié tô ðam symle sittan eodon, wlance tô wîngedrince, Judth. Thw. 21, 12; Jud. 16. v. wîn-drync.

wîn-getred, es; *n. A place where the juice is trodden out of the grapes*:—Wîngetred *forus, ubi uva calcatur*, Wrt. Voc. ii. 39, 66.

wîn-hâte, an; *f. A feast*:—Gefrægn ic Olofernus wînhâtan wyrcean, and eallum wundrum þrymlîc girwan up swǽsendo; tô ðâm hêt se gumena baldor ealle ða yldestan þegnas (the Latin is: Holofernes fecit cenam servis suis, Judith 12, 10), Judth. Thw. 21, 6; Jud. 3.

wîn-horn, es; *m. A wine-horn, drinking-cup*:—Gyf ðû wînhorn habban wille, ðonne dô ðû mid ðînum swîðran scytefingre on ðîne wynstran hand swilce ðû tæppan teón wille, and rǽr up ðînne scytefinger be ðînum heófede, Techm. ii. 120, 11. [In Wrt. Voc. ii. 6, 6 *apotheca* wînfæt, wînærn ho is written above ærn. v. Wülck. Gl. 348, 2.]

wîn-hûs, es; *n. A wine-house*:—Wînhûs *apotheca*, Wrt. Voc. i. 58, 18. Wînhûsum *apothecis*, Hpt. Gl. 468, 40. Ne môt mid rihte nân preóst drincan æt wînhûsum ealles tô gelôme, L. Ælfc. P. 49; Th. ii. 386, 8. [*Icel.* vín-hús.] Cf. wîn-ærn.

wînian; *p.* ode *To gather grapes*:—Hiá wînigaþ *uindemiant*, Lk. Skt. Lind. 6, 44.

wining, es; *m. A band for the leg*:—Winingc *fascia*, wyncgas (= winincgas?) *vallegias*, Wrt. Voc. i. 26, 7, 9. Ðonne ðû wynyngas habban wille, ðonne dô ðû mid ðînum twâm handum onbûtan ðîne sceancan, Techm. ii. 127, 10. [Cf. (?) *O. L. Ger.* winding: *O. H. Ger.* winting *fascia, fasciola, fasciale*: *Icel.* vindingr *strip wound round the leg instead of hose.*]

wîn-leáf, es; *n. A vine-leaf*:—Wînleáf *pampinus*, Engl. Stud. xi. 66, 73.

wîn-lîc; *adj. Of wine*:—Hê wæter âwende tô wînlîcum drence, Ælfc. T. Grn. 13, 37. Hê gemêt ðæt wæter tô wînlîcum swæcce âwend (cf. l. 16), Homl. Th. ii. 58, 31: 64, 29.

wîn-mere. v. wîn-côle.

winn, es; *n.* I. *labour*:—Nêdðarf woerces ɫ ðæs wynnes *necessitas laboris*, Lk. Skt. p. 2, 8. Ðæt hî gemǽne win (*v.l.* gewin, M. 98, 18) onfênge godcunde lâre tô lǽranne on Angelðeóde *ut communem evangelizandi gentibus laborem susciperent*, Bd. 2, 2; S. 502, 9. In wynn (giwinne, Rush.) hiora *in laborem eorum*, Jn. Skt. Lind. 4, 38. **II.** *strife, conflict*:—Hê ongan him winn up âhebban wið ðone hêhstan heofones wealdend, Cd. Th. 17, 14; Gen. 259. [Þa þe ledden here lif in werre and in winne, O. E. Homl. i. 175, 246. Devel wecched among hem flite and win, Rel. Ant. i. 128, 32. Þar aros wale and win, Laym. 404. Ðe watres win, Gen. and Ex. 598. Ȝeolpen for þere winne (of þan winne, 2nd MS.) *to boast of the gain*, Laym. 12072. Þin rihhte swinnkes winn (*gain*), Orm. 6118.] v. ge-, wiþer-winn.

winna, an; *m. An opponent*:—Ða þeóda ðe hyra winnan (wiþer-, ge-winnan, *v.ll.*) wǽron, Ors. 6, 35; Bos. 130, 44. v. ge-, wiþer-winna.

winnan; *p.* wann, *pl.* wunnon; *pp.* wunnen. **A.** *intrans.* **I.** *to labour, toil, work*:—Swâ ic þrymful þeów winne, Exon. Th. 386, 26; Rä. 4, 67. In îdelnisse winnaþ ða timbriaþ ða *in vanum laborant qui aedificant eam*, Ps. Surt. 126, 1. Hê mid his handum wonn and worhte ða ðing ðe nýdþearflîcu wǽron *operi manuum studium impendebat*, Bd. 4, 3; S. 567, 30. Hê won and worhte, wîngeard sette, Cd. Th. 94, 7; Gen. 1558. Ðerh alle næht wê wunnon *per totam noctem laborantes*, Lk. Skt. Lind. 5, 5. Ðû sylest ûrum leomum ræste, for ðon ðe hié on ðînum noman wunnon, Blickl. Homl. 141, 12. Ðeáh ðe hê wunne on his lâre *quamvis illo laborante in verbo*, Bd. 2, 9; S. 511, 9. Þû winnan scealt, and on eorðan ðê ðîne andlifne selfa gerǽcan, Cd. Th. 57, 23; Gen. 932. Winnende *vel* swǽtende *desudans*, i. *laborans*, Wrt. Voc. ii. 139, 36. Ic geseah winnende wiht, Exon. Th. 438, 3; Rä. 57, 2. **I a.** *to labour, endeavour, strive* after:—Ælc winð be his andgites mǽþe, ðæt hê hine wolde ongitan gif hê mihte, Bt. 41, 4; Fox 250, 25. Â ðû wunne æfter eorðlîcum welum, Wulfst. 140, 24. Nô won hê æfter worulde, ac hê in wuldre âhôf môdes wynne, Exon. Th. 126, 12; Gû. 370. Ðâ wann (*laboravit*) hê swýþe, ðæt hê his gefêran geheólde, ðæt hî ne âsprungan fram heora geleáfan, Bd. 2, 9; S. 511, 5. Hî wunnon æfter wyrþscipe, and tiledon gôdes hlîsan, Bt. 40, 4; Fox 240, 4. Ðæt hê wunne æfter worulde, Exon. Th. 109, 34; Gû. 100. Winnan æfter snytro, Salm. Kmbl. 778; Sal. 388. **I b.** *to labour, struggle, be troubled*:—Moncyn winþ on ðâm ýðum ðisse worulde *homines quatimur fortunae salo*, Bt. 4; Fox 8, 22. For hwam winneþ ðis wæter . . . ne môt on dæg restan? Salm. Kmbl. 785; Sal. 392. Gê winnaþ and â embe ðæt sorgiaþ, ðæt wê ûrne lîchoman gefyllan . . . Ûs is myccle mâre nêdþearf, ðæt wê winnon ymbe ûre sâule þearfe, Blickl. Homl. 99, 6–11. Ealle gê ðe winnaþ (*laboratis*), and gebyrde sindun, Mt. Kmbl. Rush. 11, 28. On worulde ýþum wynnaþ and swincaþ earme eorðwaran (v. Fox 8, 22 supra), Met. 4, 56. Ic wêrigmôd wann and cleopode *laboravi clamans*, Ps. Th. 68, 3. Ðû in wræc wunne, wuldres blunne, Andr. Kmbl. 2759; An. 1382. Sió his innaþ wan wætere gelîc, Ps. Th. 108, 18. Hê sceal winnan and sorgian, Blickl. Homl. 97, 25. Hê wolde ðǽm winnendum fultmian, and earme frêfran, 213, 17. Ðâm winnendum brôþrum on sǽ *laborantibus in mari fratribus*, Bd. 5, 1; S. 613, 7. **I c.** *to labour* under, *suffer* from:—Heó ðære ylcan hefignesse âdle unâblinnendlîce won *eadem molestia laborare non cessabat*, Bd. 4, 23; S. 595, 18. Horsum and ǽlcum fiþerfêtum neáte ðe on wôle winnen (cf. wôles gewinn, 330, 4), Lchdm. i. 328, 13. Longsumum ermðum winnende *diuturnis calamitatibus laborantem*, Rtl. 41, 29. **II.** *to strive, contend, fight*:—Ic wan *pugnavi*, Wrt. Voc. ii. 130, 29. Winnende *congrediens, certando*, 133, 43. Winn for sâwle ðîne . . . winn for rihtwîsnysse *agonizare pro anima tua . . . certa pro justitia*, Scint. 73, 14, 15. (1) of hostile action towards a person:—Gif Satanas winð ongên hine sylfne *si Satanas consurrexit in semetipsum*, Mk. Skt. 3, 26. Se fæder winð wið his âgenne sunu, Homl. Skt. i. 13, 296. Hû ða synna him wið winnaþ, Past. 21; Swt. 163, 2. Gê wunnon ongeán Drihten *adversum Dominum contendisti*, Deut. 9, 7. Ne wynne gê ongên ða ðe eów yfel dôð *non resistere malo*, Mt. Kmbl. 5, 39. Heó (*Hagar*) ongan wið Sarran winnan, Cd. Th. 135, 12; Gen. 2241. (1 a) of competition:—Eart ðû se Beówulf, se ðe wið Brecan wunne, ymb sund flite, Beo. Th. 1017; B. 506. (2) of opposition to things:—Ðû winsð wiþ ðam hlâfordscipe ðe ðû self gecure, Bt. 7, 2; Fox 18, 29. Is micel ðearf, ðonne him mon hwæðer ondrǽtt suîðar ðonne ôðer, and wið ðæt wienð (winð, Cott. MSS.), ðæt hê suâ suîðe wið ðæt winne, suâ hê on ðæt ôðer ne befealle, ðe hê him læs ondrêd *ne dum pugnat contra hoc, quod tolerat, ei a quo se liberum aestimat, vitio succumbat*, Past. 27; Swt. 189, 10: 46; Swt. 347, 12. Gif hê winð mid gebedum ongeán, Boutr. Scrd. 20, 16. Hî winnaþ him (*vices*) tôgeánes, Homl. Skt. i. 17, 63. Monige lâreówas winnaþ mid hira ðeáwum wið ða gǽsðlecu bebodu, Past. 2; Swt. 29, 21. Hê wearð âhangen on rôde . . ., and hê ongeán nân ðynge ne wan (*he made no resistance to being crucified*), L. Ælfc. P. 51; Th. ii. 386, 37. Wê wið ðam winde and wiþ ðam sǽ campodan and wunnan *cum vento pelagoque certantes*, Bd. 5, 1; S. 613, 28. Winn ongên *resist* (*temptation*), Homl. Skt. ii. 30, 137. Ðæt gehwâ winne wið his lîchaman unrihtlustas *ut quisquis cum corporis sui pravis cupiditatibus certet*, L. Ecg. P. iv. 63; Th. ii. 224, 4: Bt. 36, 6; Fox 182, 5. Ðæt hê for lîcuman tiédernesse wið ða scîre ne winne *nec per imbecillitatem corpus repugnat*, Past. 10; Swt. 61, 11. Nis nân gesceaft ðe wiþ hire Scippendes willan winne, bûton dysig mon, Bt. 35, 4; Fox 160, 22. Hê ðâm unþeáwum nyle furþum wiþ winnan, 37, 1; Fox 186, 30: Met. 25, 67. (3) of the action of inanimate objects:—Fâmig winneþ wǽg wið wealle, Exon. Th. 383, 32; Rä. 4, 19. Ælc his gesceafta winþ wiþ ôþer . . . ge hié betwux him winnaþ, ge eác fæste sibbe betwux him healdaþ, Bt. 21; Fox 74, 10–15: Met. 11, 45: 20, 74. Seó tunglena heofon tyrnð eásten westweard, and hire winnaþ ongeán ða seofon dweligendan tunglan, Boutr. Scrd. 18, 29. Holm won wið winde, Beo. Th. 2268; B. 1132. Oft ic (*an anchor*) sceal wiþ wǽge winnan, and wiþ winde feohtan, Exon. Th. 398, 1; Rä. 17, 1. (4) *to make war* (lit. or fig.), *fight*:—Mec gesette Crist tô compe . . . Hwîlum ic frêfre ða ic ǽr winne on, Exon. Th. 389, 14; Rä. 7, 7. Ælc ðæra ðe on gecampe winð, Homl. Th. ii. 86, 22. Ðeód winð ongên þeóde *consurget gens in gentem*, Mt. Kmbl. 24, 7. Wê winnaþ for hǽlo ûre ðeóde *pro salute gentis nostrae bella suscepimus*, Bd. 3, 2; S. 524, 24. Se lîchama and seó sâwl winnaþ him betweónan, Homl. Skt. i. 17, 8. Wildu diór ða winnaþ betwuh, Met. 27, 20. Hine monige on wrâðe winnaþ mid wǽpenþræce, Cd. Th. 138,

11; Gen. 2290. Ðú wealdest ðises ríces ðe ðú æfter wunne, Guthl. 21; Gdwin. 96, 7. Ðú wið Criste wunne and gewin tuge, Exon. Th. 267, 26; Jul. 421. Hē wann mid ðam (*a sword*) on ǣlcum gefeohte, Homl. Skt. ii. 25, 296. Ðā wan him on Amalech, i. 13, 4. Hē wonn on Sciþþie *regi Scytharum bellum intulit*, Ors. 2, 5; Swt. 78, 8. Fæht hine on and won Penda *impugnatus a Penda*, Bd. 3, 14; S. 539, 18. Ðā wann him ongeán Maxentius, Homl. Th. ii. 304, 5. Hē gelōmlīce uppon ðone eorl wann, Chr. 1095; Erl. 231, 10. Ðā won wiþ hine Cadwalla *rebellavit adversus eum Caedualla*, Bd. 2, 20; S. 521, 7. Hē feaht and won wiþ his ēþle, 3, 24; S. 556, 28: Chr. 597; Erl. 20, 4. Grendel wan wið Hrōðgār, Beo. Th. 305; B. 151. Hī wunnon him betwȳnan, Homl. Th. ii. 356, 24. Wunnon hȳ wið Dryhtnes mihtum, Salm. Kmbl. 655; Sal. 327. Ða Bryttas wunnon heom wið ða castelmenn, Chr. 1067; Erl. 204, 5. Win him on swȳðe, Homl. Skt. i. 13, 8. Seó ǣ ðe ðū under hire tǣcinge winnan wylt and campian *lex sub qua militare uis*, R. Ben. 96, 23. Æfter rīce winnan, Chr. 685; Erl. 40, 16. On winnan *ingruere*, Hpt. Gl. 427, 42: Bd. 1, 12; S. 480, 23. Ðonne hē on ōðer folc winnan sceal, Past. 18; Swt. 129, 9. Ðæt hī uppon hǣðene þeódan winnan woldan, Chr. 1096; Erl. 233, 14. On gehwelc lond tō winnanne, Ors. 3, 7; Swt. 116, 8. Hē him on winnende wæs, 1, 2; Swt. 30, 5. Worhte Ælfrēd cyning lytle werede geweorc æt Æþelinga eigge, and of ðam geweorce wæs winnende wiþ ðone here, Chr. 878; Erl. 80, 6. (4 a) of the action of inanimate objects:—Se winterlīca wind wan mid ðam forste *the winter wind warred along with the frost*, Homl. Skt. i. 11, 144. (4 b) with cognate accusative:—For ðæm gewinne ðe hē wiþ God wan, Blickl. Homl. 63, 4. Winn gōd gewinn *certa bonum certamen*, Scint. 214, 16. III. *to win* (v. Jamieson's Dictionary), *make one's way*:—Hwæt is ðæt wundor, ðæt geond ðās woruld fareþ..., winneþ oft hider? Salm. Kmbl. 568; Sal. 283. B. *trans.* I. *to labour at, bestow labour upon*:—Ic wann wununise mīn *laboravi habitationem meam*, Rtl. 68, 28. Ic sende iúh gehrioppa ðætte gié ne wunnon *ego misi uos metere quod uos non laborastis*, Jn. Skt. Lind. Rush. 4, 38. II. *to labour under, suffer, undergo*:—Ic ðæt geþolade... læg on heardum stāne... ic ðæt earfeþe wonn, Exon. Th. 87, 21; Cri. 1428. Ā ic wīte wonn mīnra wræcsīþa, 441, 26; Kl. 5. Ic ā þolade geára gehwylce gōdes ealles, won ic mōdearfoþa (þonc mōd earfoþa, Th.) mā ðonne on ōþrum, fyrhto in folce, 457, 19; Hy. 4, 86. Mid ðȳ ðā se brōþor langre tīde ðyllīc ungescrǣpo wonn (woon, MS.) *cumque tempore non pauco frater tali incommodo laboraret*, Bd. 4, 32; S. 611, 22. Ðū ðæs cwealmes scealt wīte winnan and on wræc hweorfan, Cd. Th. 62, 14; Gen. 1014. Hī āwo sculon, wræc winnende, wærgðu dreógan, Exon. Th. 78, 10; Cri. 1272. III. *to win, get, attain*:—Ðū wunne reste ā ōþ ende mid hālgum fǣmnum, Nar. 49, 1. Hī wēndon ðæt hī sceoldon winnon eall ðæt land, Chr. 1070; Erl. 207, 27. [Ierusalem and Babilonie fliteð eure and winneð bitwinen hem... þe king of Babilonie wan Ierusalem, O. E. Homl. ii. 51, 11–25. Iob wan wið þe wurse, 187, 26. Heo wunnen agean, A. R. 238, 17. Ðanne sumer and winter winnen, Misc. 17, 521. He iwon (won, 2nd MS.) al þis lond, Laym. 2560. Winnenn heoffness kinedom, Orm. 801. He wan to William, Will. 2498. *Goth.* winnan παθεῖν; *O. Sax.* winnan *to strive; to suffer; to gain*: *O. Frs.* winna *to gain*: *O. H. Ger.* winnan *laborare; jurgare, decertare, dimicare*: *Icel.* vinna *to work; to withstand; to suffer; to win.*] v. ā-, ge-, ofer-, wiþer-winnan; on-winnende.

winn-dæg, es; *m. A day of labour* or *of struggle*:—Fela sceal gebīdan leófes and lāþes se ðe longe hēr on ðyssum windagum worulde brūceþ, Beo. Th. 2128; B. 1062. v. gewin-dæg.

-winnend, -winnendlīc. v. ofer-, wiþ-winnend, un-oferwinnendlīc.

winn-stōw, e; *f. A wrestling-place*:—Winstōwe *scammatis*, Hpt. Gl. 405, 40. On winstōwe *in scammate*, 489, 59. Winstōwe *palaestrarum*, 478, 50. v. gewin-stōw.

winnung, winpel. v. windung, wiþ-winnung, wimpel.

wīn-ræced, es; *m. n. A house where there is feasting, a palace*:—Wīnreced, goldsele gumena (*Hrothgar's palace*), Beo. Th. 1433; B. 714. Ðæt wīnreced, gestsele, 1991; B. 993. Hornsalu wunedon wēste wīnræced, Andr. Kmbl. 2319; An. 1161. Cf. wīn-ærn.

wīn-reáfetian *to take grapes*:—Plucciaþ ł wīnhreáfetiaþ *vindemiant*, Ps. Lamb. 79, 13.

wīn-repan *to gather grapes*:—Wīnreopad ðæt *vendemiant eam*, Ps. Surt. 79, 13. v. repan.

wīn-sæd; *adj. Wine-sated, having had one's fill of wine*:—Yrrum ealowōsan, were wīnsaduṁ, Exon. Th. 330, 12; Vy. 50. Weras wīnsade (cf. hē oferdrencte his duguðe ealle, 21, 22; Jud. 31; and the Latin c. 13, 2: Erant omnes fatigati a vino), Judth. Thw. 22, 21; Jud. 71.

wīn-sæl, es; *n. A wine-hall, a hall where there is feasting*:—Wōriaþ ða wīnsalo, Exon. Th. 291, 6; Wand. 78. v. next word.

wīn-sele, es; *m. A wine-hall, a hall where there is feasting*:—Nis hēr (*in Hell*) wloncra wīnsele, ne worulde dreám, Cd. Th. 270, 21; Sat. 94. Se wīnsele (*Hrothgar's hall*), Beo. Th. 1547; B. 771. In ðæm wīnsele, 1394; B. 695. Beóre druncne... hī in wīnsele sāwle forlētan, Exon. Th. 271, 25; Jul. 487: 283, 27; Jul. 686. Gesyhð on his suna būre wīnsele wēstne, Beo. Th. 4903; B. 2456. [*O. Sax.* wīnseli.]

wīn-sester, es; *m. A wine-can*:—Wīnsester *cantarus*, Wrt. Voc. i. 24, 37.

win-stōw, winstre, winsum. v. winn-stōw, winestra, wynsum.

wīn-tæppere, es; *m. A wine-seller, tavern-keeper*:—Wīntæpperum *cauponibus*, Hpt. Gl. 468, 42.

Wintan-ceaster (Wintun-, Winta (-e, -i), Win-), e: Wænte, an; *f. Winchester.* [The name is got from the earlier Venta of Roman Britain. This form occurs in Latin works, e. g.: In Venta civitate, Bd. 4, 15: Cod. Dip. Kmbl. iii. 300, 16. Monasterium in Wenta positum, vi. 29, 16. Also the adjective Wentanus (Uentanus, Bd. 5, 18), e. g.: Wentanus episcopus, v. 82, 14. Wentana ecclesia, ii. 210, 3: v. 45, 3. Wentana civitas, ii. 140, 9: 220, 28. Urbs Wentana, iii. 326, 10: iv. 45, 7. Wentana sedes, v. 169, 16. And Wentana is used as the name of the place, e. g.: Wentanae monasterium, iii. 8, 13. But Latinized forms of the English word are used; Wintonia is often found in the charters; the form Wincestria occurs v. 167, 7, and the adjective Wintancestrensis 90, 29.]:—In ciuitate opinatissima quae Winteceaster nuncupatur, Cod. Dip. Kmbl. ii. 195, 35. Belumpon hī (*the South Saxons*) ǣr tō Wintanceastre biscopscīre *ad civitatis Ventanae parochiam pertinebant*, Bd. 5, 18; S. 639, 14. Daniel Wæntan biscop, Chr. 731; Erl. 47, 11. Intō Wintanceastre, Cod. Dip. Kmbl. ii. 114, 26: iii. 111, 29. Gange ān gemet swilce man on Lundenbyrig and on Wintanceastre (Winta-, *v. l.*) healde, L. Edg. ii. 8; Th. i. 270, 2. Seó gerǣdnys ðe Cnut cyninge gerǣdde on Wintanceastre (Win-, *v. l.*), L. C. E. proem.; Th. i. 358, 7. Cēnwalh hēt ātimbran ða ciricean on Wintunceastre (Wintan-, *v. l.*), Chr. 643; Erl. 26, 9. Hēr Danihel gesæt on Wintanceastre, 744; Erl. 48, 1. Hedde heóld ðone biscopdōm on Wintaceastre (Wintan-, *v. l.*), 703; Erl. 42, 22. Hī West-Seaxna bisceopum underþeódde wǣron, ða ðe on Wintaceastre wǣron, Bd. 4, 15; S. 583, 35. Tō Wintaceastre (Winte-, *v. l.*) .vi. myneteras, L. Ath. i. 14; Th. i. 206, 31: Cod. Dip. Kmbl. iii. 326, 16. Winteceastre, ii. 176, 11: v. 163, 11. Tō ealdan mynstære tō Winticeastræ, ii. 127, 12. Syþþan ðæt gemōt wæs on Winceastre, L. C. S. 30; Th. i. 392, 26. Ðes Swīðūn wæs bisceop on Winceastre, Homl. Skt. i. 21, 14. Æðelwold biscop on Winceastre, Cod. Dip. Kmbl. vi. 207, 6.

winter, es; *m.* (*in pl. a neuter form* wintru *occurs, as well as masculine* wintras, winter: *the dat. sing.* wintra *is a trace of earlier* u-*stem declension*). I. a season of the year, *winter*:—Feówer tīda syndon getealde on ānum geáre, ðæt synd *uer, aestas, autumnus, hiems*... *Hiems* is winter, Lchdm. iii. 250, 12. On ðone .vii. dæg ðæs mōnðes (*November*) bið wintres fruma; se winter hafaþ tū and hundnigontig daga, Shrn. 146, 7. Winter bringeþ weder ungemetceald, swifte windas, Met. 11, 59. Winter bið cealdost, Menol. Fox 470; Gn. C. 5. Hengest wælfāgne winter wunode mid Finne... Holm storme weól, winter ȳþe beleác īsgebinde, ōþ ðæt ōþer com geár in geardas... Ðā wæs winter scacen, fæger foldan bearm, Beo. Th. 2259–2278; B. 1127–1137. Ðæt hit wǣre wintres tīd, and se winter wǣre grim and ceald and fyrstig and mid īse gebunden, Bd. 3, 19; S. 549, 26. Is ðǣr nū irfæs ðæs stranga wintær lǣfæd hæfð, Chart. Th. 163, 1. Nys hit swā stearc winter ðæt ic durre lutian æt hām, Coll. Monast. Th. 19, 17. Sam hit sȳ sumor sam winter, Ors. 1, 1; Swt. 21, 17. Wintres *brumae*, Wrt. Voc. ii. 12, 43. On wintres tīman, ðæt is fram ðan anginne ðæs mōnðes, ðe is November gehaten, ōþ Eástran, R. Ben. 32, 10. Siððan (*after the first of November*) wintres dæg (*winter*; cf. *Icel.* ā vetrardag *in the winter*) wīde gangeþ on syx nihtum, sigelbeorhtne genimð hærfest mid herige hrīmes and snāwes, Menol. Fox 401; Men. 202. Hē (*petra oleum*) is gōd tō drincanne on wintres dæge, for ðon ðe hē hæfð swīðe micle hǣte; for ðȳ hine mon sceal drincan on wintra, Lchdm. ii. 288, 16. Beámas grēne stondaþ wintres and sumeres, Exon. Th. 200, 7; Ph. 37. Mid ðȳ storme ðæs wintres *hiemis tempestate*, Bd. 2, 13; S. 516, 20. Geofon weól wintres wylme, Beo. Th. 1036; B. 516. Wintres wōma, Exon. Th. 292, 22; Wand. 103. Biddaþ ðæt eówer fleám on wintra (wintre, Rush.) ne gewurðe, Mt. Kmbl. 24, 20. On wintra hit biþ ceald, Bt. 21; Fox 74, 24. Se oftrǣda rēn leccaþ ða eorþan on wintra, 39, 13; Fox 234, 17. Wīciaþ Finnas on huntoðe on wintra, and on sumera on fiscaþe, Ors. 1, 1; Swt. 17, 6. Hī (*the hawks*) fēdaþ hig sylfe and mē on wintra, Coll. Monast. Th. 26, 1. Beád Swegen full gild and metsunga tō his here ðone winter, Chr. 1013; Erl. 149, 3: Exon. Th. 306, 29; Seef. 15. Wintras *hiemes*, Germ. 388, 26. *See also* midd, II. I a. *wintry weather, cold*:—Hē (*the sparrow*) sōna of wintra in winter eft cymeþ, Bd. 2, 13; S. 516, 21. Hē him helle gescōp, wælcealde wīc, wintre beðeahte, Salm. Kmbl. 938; Sal. 468. Se wind (*zephirus*) tōwyrpð and ðāwaþ ǣlcne winter, Lchdm. iii. 274, 22. II. *a year*:—Beóð his winter wynnum īced *annos ejus in diem seculi adjicies*, Ps. Th. 60, 5. Ūre winter *anni nostri*, 89, 10. God āna wāt hwæt him weaxendum winter bringaþ, Exon. Th. 327, 26; Vy. 9. Hī wǣron on Egipta lande feówer hund wintra and þrītig wintra, Ex. 12, 40. Ymb þrittig wintra, Bt. 39, 3; Fox 214, 25. Hū seó ādl ǣr feówertigum oððe fīftigum wintra on men ne become *how the disease does not attack a man before*

1, 5. Ðeós wyrt hafaþ leáf swylce wîngeard, Lchdm. i. 316, 8. Wîngeardes twiga, ii. 190, 11. Of ðises wîngeardes (-eardes, *v.l.*) cynne *de generatione vitis*, Lk. Skt. 22, 18. Swâ on wîngearde weaxen berigean *sicut vitis abundans*, Ps. Th. 127, 3. Of wîngearde *de vite*, Wrt. Voc. ii. 27, 53. Se gesibsuma wer byð ðam wînearde gelîc ðe byrð gôde wæstmas, Basil admn. 6; Norm. 46, 24. Ðû ût âlǽddest wîngeard (*vineam*) . . . and his wyrtruman settest, Ps. Th. 79, 8. Ic geseah wîneard (*vitem*), on ðam wǽron þreó clystru, Gen. 40, 9. On sumum stôwum wîngeardas (*vineae*) grôwaþ, Bd. 1, 1; S. 473, 14: Ps. Th. 104, 29. Wîngearda hôcas ðe hî mid bindaþ ðæt him nêhst bið *capreoli* vel *cincinni* vel *uncinuli*, wîngearda hringa[s] *corimbi*, Wrt. Voc. i. 38, 59–60. Wîngearda gewind *capreoli*, 39, 10. Ðe mâ ðe gimmas weaxaþ on wîngeardum *nec vite gemmas carpitis*, Bt. 32, 3; Fox 118, 11: Met. 19, 9. [He plantede winiærd, Chr. 1137; Erl. 263, 19. Wingeardes *vineae*, A. R. 294, 29. Winyard, Misc. 33, 20. *Goth.* weina-gards: *O. Sax.* wîn-gardo: *O. H. Ger.* wîn-gart, -garto: *Icel.* vîn-garðr.] v. following words.

wîngeard-bôh(-g), es; *m. A vine-tendril:*—Wîngeardbôgas *capreoli*, Wrt. Voc. i. 22, 15. v. wîn-geard, II, *and next word.*

wîngeard-hocgas (*for* wîngeard-bôgas, v. preceding word; or wîngeard-hôcas, cf. wîngearda hôcas *capreoli*, Wrt. Voc. i. 38, 59) *caprioli dicti quod capiant arbores*, Wrt. Voc. ii. 129, 61.

wîngeard-hring, es; *m. A cluster of grapes:*—Wîngeardhringas (cf. Wîngearda hringa[s] *corimbi*, i. 38, 60) *vel* bergan *vel* croppas *corimbi*, i. *viti racemi* vel *botriones* vel *circuli*, Wrt. Voc. ii. 135, 74.

wîngeard-seax, es; *n. A pruning-knife:*—Wîngeardseax *falx*, Wrt. Voc. ii. 146, 76.

wîn-gedrinc, es; *n. Wine-drinking, wine:*—Hié wlenco onwôd and wîngedrync, Cd. Th. 155, 28; Gen. 2579. Of ungemete ǽlces þinges, wiste and wǽda, wîngedrinces, Met. 25, 39. Wîngedrince *nectare*, Wrt. Voc. ii. 61, 32. Hié tô ðam symle sittan eodon, wlance tô wîngedrince, Judth. Thw. 21, 12; Jud. 16. v. wîn-drync.

wîn-getred, es; *n. A place where the juice is trodden out of the grapes:*—Wîngetred *forus, ubi uva calcatur*, Wrt. Voc. ii. 39, 66.

wîn-hâte, an; *f. A feast:*—Gefrægn ic Olofernus wînhâtan wyrcean, and eallum wundrum þrymlîc girwan up swǽsendo; tô ðâm hêt se gumena baldor ealle ða yldestan þegnas (the Latin is: Holofernes fecit cenam servis suis, Judith 12, 10), Judth. Thw. 21, 6; Jud. 3.

wîn-horn, es; *m. A wine-horn, drinking-cup:*—Gyf ðû wînhorn habban wille, ðonne dô ðû mid ðînum swîðran scytefingre on ðîne wynstran hand swilce ðû tæppan teón wille, and rǽr up ðînne scytefinger be ðînum heófede, Techm. ii. 120, 11. [In Wrt. Voc. ii. 6, 6 *apotheca* wînfæt, wînærn ho is written above ærn. v. Wülck. Gl. 348, 2.]

wîn-hûs, es; *n. A wine-house:*—Wînhûs *apotheca*, Wrt. Voc. i. 58, 18. Wînhûsum *apothecis*, Hpt. Gl. 468, 40. Ne môt mid rihte nân preóst drincan æt wînhûsum ealles tô gelôme, L. Ælfc. P. 49; Th. ii. 386, 8. [*Icel.* vîn-hûs.] Cf. wîn-ærn.

wînian; *p.* ode *To gather grapes:*—Hiá wînigaþ *uindemiant*, Lk. Skt. Lind. 6, 44.

wining, es; *m. A band for the leg:*—Winingc *fascia*, wyncgas (= winincgas?) *vallegias*, Wrt. Voc. i. 26, 7, 9. Ðonne ðû wynyngas habban wille, ðonne dô ðû mid ðînum twâm handum onbûtan ðîne sceancan, Techm. ii. 127, 10. [Cf. (?) *O. L. Ger.* winding: *O. H. Ger.* winting *fascia, fasciola, fasciale: Icel.* vindingr *strip wound round the leg instead of hose.*]

wîn-leáf, es; *n. A vine-leaf:*—Wînleáf *pampinus*, Engl. Stud. xi. 66, 73.

wîn-lîc; *adj. Of wine:*—Hê wæter âwende tô wînlîcum drence, Ælfc. T. Grn. 13, 37. Hê gemêt ðæt wæter tô wînlîcum swæcce âwend (cf. l. 16), Homl. Th. ii. 58, 31: 64, 29.

wîn-mere. v. wîn-côle.

winn, es; *n.* I. *labour:*—Nêdðarf woerces ł ðæs wynnes *necessitas laboris*, Lk. Skt. p. 2, 8. Ðæt hî gemǽne win (*v.l.* gewin, M. 98, 18) onfênge godcunde lâre tô lǽranne on Angelðeóde *ut communem evangelizandi gentibus laborem susciperent*, Bd. 2, 2; S. 502, 9. In wynn (giwinne, Rush.) hiora *in laborem eorum*, Jn. Skt. Lind. 4, 38. II. *strife, conflict:*—Hê ongan him winn up âhebban wið ðone hêhstan heofones wealdend, Cd. Th. 17, 14; Gen. 259. [Þa þe ledden here lif in werre and in winne, O. E. Homl. i. 175, 246. Devel weccheð among hem flite and win, Rel. Ant. i. 128, 32. Þar aros wale and win, Laym. 404. De watres win, Gen. and Ex. 598. Ȝeolpen for þere winne (of þan winne, 2nd MS.) *to boast of the gain*, Laym. 12072. Þin rihhte swinnkes winn (*gain*), Orm. 6118.] v. ge-, wiþer-winn.

winna, an; *m. An opponent:*—Ða þeóda ðe hyra winnan (wiþer-, ge-winnan, *v.ll.*) wǽron, Ors. 6, 35; Bos. 130, 44. v. ge-, wiþer-winna.

winnan; *p.* wann, *pl.* wunnon; *pp.* wunnen. A. *intrans.* I. *to labour, toil, work:*—Swâ ic þrymful þeów winne, Exon. Th. 386, 26; Rä. 4, 67. In îdelnisse winnaþ ða timbriaþ ða *in vanum laborant qui aedificant eam*, Ps. Surt. 126, 1. Hê mid his handum wonn and worhte ða ðing ðe nýdþearflîcu wǽron *operi manuum studium impendebat*, Bd. 4, 3; S. 567, 30. Hê won and worhte, wîngeard sette, Cd. Th. 94, 7; Gen. 1558. Ðerh alle næht wê wunnon *per totam noctem laborantes*, Lk. Skt. Lind. 5, 5. Ðû sylest ûrum leomum ræste, for ðon ðe hié on ðînum noman wunnon, Blickl. Homl. 141, 12. Ðeáh ðe hê wunne on his lâre *quamvis illo laborante in verbo*, Bd. 2, 9; S. 511, 9. Ðû winnan scealt, and on eorðan ðê ðîne andlifne selfa gerǽcan, Cd. Th. 57, 23; Gen. 932. Winnende *vel* swǽtende *desudans*, i. *laborans*, Wrt. Voc. ii. 139, 36. Ic geseah winnende wiht, Exon. Th. 438, 3; Rä. 57, 2. I a. *to labour, endeavour, strive* after:—Ælc wind be his andgites mǽþe, ðæt hê hine wolde ongitan gif hê mihte, Bt. 41, 4; Fox 250, 25. Â ðû wunne æfter eorðlîcum welum, Wulfst. 140, 24. Nô won hê æfter worulde, ac hê in wuldre âhôf môdes wynne, Exon. Th. 126, 12; Gû. 370. Ðâ wann (*laboravit*) hê swýþe, ðæt hê his gefêran geheólde, ðæt hî ne âsprungan fram heora geleáfan, Bd. 2, 9; S. 511, 5. Hî wunnon æfter wyrþscipe, and tiledon gôdes hlîsan, Bt. 40, 4; Fox 240, 4. Ðæt hê wunne æfter worulde, Exon. Th. 109, 34; Gû. 100. Winnan æfter snytro, Salm. Kmbl. 778; Sal. 388. I b. *to labour, struggle, be troubled:*—Moncyn winþ on ðâm ýðum ðisse worulde *homines quatimur fortunae salo*, Bt. 4; Fox 8, 22. For hwam winneþ ðis wæter . . . ne môt on dæg restan? Salm. Kmbl. 785; Sal. 392. Gê winnaþ and â embe ðæt sorgiaþ, ðæt wê ûrne lîchoman gefyllan . . . Ûs is myccle mâre nêdþearf, ðæt wê winnon ymbe ûre sâule þearfe, Blickl. Homl. 99, 6–11. Ealle gê ðe winnaþ (*laboratis*), and gebyrde sindun, Mt. Kmbl. Rush. 11, 28. On worulde ýþum wynnaþ and swincaþ earme eorðwaran (v. Fox 8, 22 supra), Met. 4, 56. Ic wêrigmôd wann and cleopode *laboravi clamans*, Ps. Th. 68, 3. Ðû in wræc wunne, wuldres blunne, Andr. Kmbl. 2759; An. 1382. Sió his innaþ wan wætere gelîc, Ps. Th. 108, 18. Hê sceal winnan and sorgian, Blickl. Homl. 97, 25. Hê wolde ðǽm winnendum fultmian, and earme frêfran, 213, 17. Ðâm winnendum brôþrum on sǽ *laborantibus in mari fratribus*, Bd. 5, 1; S. 613, 7. I c. *to labour* under, *suffer* from:—Heó ðære ylcan hefignesse âdle unâblinnendlîce won *eadem molestia laborare non cessabat*, Bd. 4, 23; S. 595, 18. Horsum and ǽlcum fiþerfêtum neáte ðe on wôle winnen (cf. wôles gewinn, 330, 4), Lchdm. i. 328, 13. Longsumum ermðum winnende *diuturnis calamitatibus laborantem*, Rtl. 41, 29. II. *to strive, contend, fight:*—Ic wan *pugnavi*, Wrt. Voc. ii. 130, 29. Winnende *congrediens, certando*, 133, 43. Winn for sâwle ðîne . . . winn for rihtwîsnysse *agonizare pro anima tua . . . certa pro justitia*, Scint. 73, 14, 15. (1) of hostile action towards a person:—Gif Satanas winð ongên hine sylfne *si Satanas consurrexit in semetipsum*, Mk. Skt. 3, 26. Se fæder winð wið his âgenne sunu, Homl. Skt. i. 13, 296. Hû ða synna him wið winnaþ, Past. 21; Swt. 163, 2. Gê wunnon ongeán Drihten *adversum Dominum contendisti*, Deut. 9, 7. Ne wynne gê ongên ða ðe eów yfel dôð *non resistere malo*, Mt. Kmbl. 5, 39. Heó (*Hagar*) ongan wið Sarran winnan, Cd. Th. 135, 12; Gen. 2241. (1 a) of competition:—Eart ðû se Beówulf, se ðe wið Brecan wunne, ymb sund flite, Beo. Th. 1017; B. 506. (2) of opposition to things:—Ðû winsð wiþ ðam hlâfordscipe ðe ðû self gecure, Bt. 7, 2; Fox 18, 29. Is micel ðearf, ðonne him mon hwæðer ondrǽtt suîðar ðonne ôðer, and wið ðæt wienð (winð, Cott. MSS.), ðæt hê suâ suîðe wið ðæt winne, suâ hê on ðæt ôðer ne befealle, ðe hê him læs ondrêd *ne dum pugnat contra hoc, quod tolerat, ei a quo se liberum aestimat, vitio succumbat*, Past. 27; Swt. 189, 10: 46; Swt. 347, 12. Gif hê winð mid gebedum ongeán, Boutr. Scrd. 20, 16. Hî winnaþ him (*vices*) tôgeánes, Homl. Skt. i. 17, 63. Monige lâreówas winnaþ mid hira ðeáwum wið ða gǽsðlecu bebodu, Past. 2; Swt. 29, 21. Hê wearð âhangen on rôde . . . , and hê ongeán nân ðyngc ne wan (*he made no resistance to being crucified*), L. Ælfc. P. 51; Th. ii. 386, 37. Wê wið ðam winde and wiþ ðam sǽ campodan and wunnan *cum vento pelagoque certantes*, Bd. 5, 1; S. 613, 28. Winn ongên *resist* (*temptation*), Homl. Skt. ii. 30, 137. Ðæt gehwâ winne wið his lîchaman unrihtlustas *ut quisquis cum corporis sui pravis cupiditatibus certet*, L. Ecg. P. iv. 63; Th. ii. 224, 4: Bt. 36, 6; Fox 182, 5. Ðæt hê for lîcuman tiédernesse wið ða scîre ne winne *nec per imbecillitatem corpus repugnat*, Past. 10; Swt. 61, 11. Nis nân gesceaft ðe wiþ hire Scippendes willan winne, bûton dysig mon, Bt. 35, 4; Fox 160, 22. Hê ðâm unþeáwum nyle furþum wiþ winnan, 37, 1; Fox 186, 30: Met. 25, 67. (3) of the action of inanimate objects:—Fâmig winneþ wǽg wið wealle, Exon. Th. 383, 32; Rä. 4, 19. Ælc his gesceafta winþ wiþ ôþer . . . ge hié betwux him winnaþ, ge eác fæste sibbe betwux him healdaþ, Bt. 21; Fox 74, 10–15: Met. 11, 45: 20, 74. Seó tunglena heofon tyrnð eásten westweard, and hire winnaþ ongeán ða seofon dweligendan tunglan, Boutr. Scrd. 18, 29. Holm won wið winde, Beo. Th. 2268; B. 1132. Ôft ic (*an anchor*) sceal wiþ wǽge winnan, and wiþ winde feohtan, Exon. Th. 398, 1; Rä. 17, 1. (4) *to make war* (lit. or fig.), *fight:*—Mec gesette Crist tô compe . . . Hwîlum ic frêfre ða ic ǽr winne on, Exon. Th. 389, 14; Rä. 7, 7. Ælc ðæra ðe on gecampe winð, Homl. Th. ii. 86, 22. Ðeód winð ongên þeóde *consurget gens in gentem*, Mt. Kmbl. 24, 7. Wê winnaþ for hǽlo ûre ðeóde *pro salute gentis nostrae bella suscepimus*, Bd. 3, 2; S. 524, 24. Se lîchama and seó sâwl winnaþ him betweónan, Homl. Skt. i. 17, 8. Wildu diór ða winnaþ betwuh, Met. 27, 20. Hine monige on wrâðe winnaþ mid wǽpenþræce, Cd. Th. 138,

wîn-tunne, an; *f. A wine-cask:*—Ne hē ne drince æt wīntunnum, swā swā woroldmenn dōđ, L. Ælfc. C. 30; Th. ii. 354, 4. [*Icel.* vín-tunna.]

wîn-twig, es; *n. A vine-twig, shoot of a vine:*—Wīntwiges *palmite*, Wrt. Voc. ii. 89, 41. Wīntwiga plantung *propaginatio*, i. 39, 5.

wîn-wringe, an; *f. A wine-press:*—Frymþa wīnwringan đīnre *primitias torcularis tui*, Scint. 109, 3. Tō wīnwringan *ad praelum* (*ad torcular*), Hpt. Gl. 468, 29: Wrt. Voc. ii. 2, 59. Hē sette wīnwringan (*torcular*), Mt. Kmbl. 21, 33. Đīne wīnwringan *torcularia tua*, Kent. Gl. 35.

wîn-wyrcend, es; *m. A vine-dresser:*—Uīnwirccendum *vinitoribus*, Mt. Kmbl. p. 19, 3.

wio-, wió-bora, wiodu, wiota. v. weo-, wīg-bora, wudu, wita.

wîpian; *p.* ode *To wipe:*—Ic wīpige *tergo*, Ælfc. Gr. 26, 3; Zup. 155, 11: 28, 4; Zup. 172, 8. Ic geseó Godes engel standende ætforan đē mid handclāđe, and wīpaþ đīne swātigan limu, Homl. Th. i. 426, 30. Sum synful wīf his fēt āþwōh and mid hyre fexe wīpode, Homl. Ass. 41, 436. Wæterclāđas đe hȳ heora handa and fēt mid wīpedan, R. Ben. 59, 8. Lege on hunig đreó niht, nim þonne and wīpa đæt hunig of, Lchdm. iii. 4, 20.

wîr *myrtle:*—Uuīr, uuȳr *myrtus*, Txts. 79, 1356. Wīr, Wrt. Voc. i. 285, 51: ii. 55, 83. Ele on đam đe wǣre wīr gesoden, Lchdm. ii. 70, 15. Genim wīr, 86, 7. v. wīr-treów.

wîr, es; *m. Wire, metal thread;* often used apparently in ornamental work, so, *an ornament made of wire.* Cf. *Icel.* víra-virki *filigree work:*—Beorht seomađ (-ad, MS.) wīr ymb đone wælgim, Exon. Th. 400, 20; Rä. 21, 4. Hæleđ gierede mec (*a book*) mid golde, for đon mē glīwedon wrǣtlīc weorc smiþa wīre bifongen, 408, 19; Rä. 27, 14. Wīre geweorþad, 484, 9; Rä. 70, 5. Eorđsele wæs innan full wrǣtta and wīra (*ornaments made of gold or silver wire*), weard unhióre goldmāđmas heóld, Beo. Th. 4817; B. 2413. Næbbe ic fǣted gold, . . . ne wīra gespann, landes ne locenra beága, Andr. Kmbl. 604; An. 302: Elen. Kmbl. 2267; El. 1135. Wīrum gewlenced, 2525; El. 1264: Exon. Th. 402, 19; Rä. 21, 32. Ic eom fægerre frætwum goldes, þeáh hit mon āwerge wīrum ūtan, 424, 31; Rä. 41, 47. Wīrum bewunden, Beo. Th. 2066; B. 1031. Hygerōf gebond weallwalan wīrum wundrum tōgædre, Exon. Th. 477, 7; Ruin. 21. [Gold wir, Laym. 7048. Fetislich hir fyngres were fretted with golde wyre, Piers P. 2, 11. *Icel.* vírr.]

wîr-boga, an; *m. Bent wire* used in ornamenting an object:—Mec (*a horn*) þeceþ geong hagostealdmon golde and sylfore, wōum wīrbogum, Exon. Th. 395, 5; Rä. 15, 3.

wircan, wircness. v. wyrcan, wyrcness.

wird, e; *f. An offence:*—Gehēndon hine đa hēhsacerdas on monigum đingum ꝉ woerdum *accusabant eum summi sacerdotes in multis*, Mk. Skt. Lind. 15, 3. v. following words.

wirdan; *p.* de *To injure, hurt, annoy:*—Werdit *officit*, Wrt. Voc. ii. 115, 43. Wyrde *officit*, 63, 36. I. of physical hurt:—Ne wyrt đæt đa seón, Lchdm. ii. 26, 14. Ne bēt hē hit, ac wyrt, 212, 20. Đa gnættas mid swīþe lytlum sticelum him deriaþ, and eác đa smalan wyrmas đone mon werdaþ (wyrdaþ, *v.l.*), and hwīlum fulneáh deádne gedōþ, Bt. 16, 2; Fox 52, 12. Mec unsceafta innan slītaþ, wyrdaþ mec be wombe, Exon. Th. 497, 6; Rä. 85, 25. Đa menigo đec geđringaþ and woerdaþ (*affligunt*), Lk. Skt. Lind. 8, 45. Sum mon wæs, đam unwlitig swile his eágan brēgh wyrde and wemde *cui tumor deformis palpebram oculi foedaverat*, Bd. 4, 32; S. 611, 18. Se weolocreáda tælhg, đone ne mæg ne sunne blǣcan, ne ne rēn wyrdan *tinctura coccinei coloris, cujus rubor nullo solis ardore, nulla valet pluviarum injuria pallescere*, Bd. 1, 1; S. 473, 20. Wǣron eágan mīne mid wæcceum werded swȳþe, Ps. Th. 76, 4. II. *to injure, do wrong to, violate* a law, *hinder:*—Hwæt is đis manna, đe mīne folgađ wyrdeþ, ȳceþ ealdne nīđ? Elen. Kmbl. 1805; El. 904. Hine teóne (teonode, MS., *with a line below* od) wyrde (wyrgde?) Chus *Chus did him wrong with abusive words*, Ps. Th. 7, arg. Grendel leóde mīne wanode and wyrde, Beo. Th. 2678; B. 1337. Hwilcan geþance mæg ǣnig man đæt dōn, đæt hē hine on cirican gebidde, and ǣr oþþon æfter, inne oþþe ūte, cirican berȳpe, and wyrde oþþe wanige đæt tō circan gebyrige, L. Eth. vii. 26; Th. i. 334, 31. Gif hwā Cristendōm wyrde, oþþe hǣđendōm weorđige, L. E. G. 2; Th. i. 168, 1. Se đe đās laga wyrde . . . gif hē hit eft wyrde . . . gif hē . . . hit þriddan sīđe wyrde (ābrece, *v.l.*), L. C. S. 84; Th. i. 422, 8–424, 1. Gif hwā Godes lage oþþe folclage wirde, gebēte hit georne, L. N. P. L. 46; Th. ii. 296, 22. Forbeádende ꝉ woerdende gæfelo tō seallanne *prohibentem tributa dari*, Lk. Skt. Lind. 23, 2. Woerdendra *vitiorum*, Rtl. 37, 9. [Þu ne mahht nohht lufenn God and hatenn menn and werdenn, Orm. 5185. Ne birrþ þe shendenn nani mann, ne weordenn, 6249. Gif anig mann þe sheudeþþ oþerr werdeþþ, 6255. *Goth.* fra-wardjan *to corrupt, disfigure:* *O. Sax.* ā-wardian, -werdian *to spoil, destroy:* *O. H. Ger.* warten *exulcerare*; far-warten *laedere.*] v. ā-, ge-wirdan (-wyrdan).

wirde (?), es; *m. An observer.* v. circol-wirde.

-wirdelsa. v. æf-werdelsa.

wirding, e; *f. Injury, hurt:*—Woerding *lesio*, Rtl. 102, 9. v. ā-wirding.

wirdla, wirdlian. v. ǣ-, æf-werdla (-wyrdla); ge-wyrdlian.

wirdness, e; *f.* I. *injury, hurt, annoyance:*—Miđ woerdnisse *affligendo*, Rtl. 16, 13. From woerdnissum *a noxiis*, 17, 15. II. *a vice:*—From scedđendum woerdnisum *a noxiis vitiis*, Rtl. 16, 25.

-wîred. v. ge-wīred.

Wire-mûþa, an; *m. Wearmouth:*—On đære stōwe đe mon hāteþ æt Wīremūđan *juxta ostium fluminis Viuri*, Bd. 4, 18; S. 586, 27: 5, 21; S. 642, 35: Shrn. 50, 30: 61, 14. Æt Wīramūđan *ad Viuraemuda*, Bd. 5, 24; S. 647, 20.

wirgan, wirigan, wirian; *p.* de, ede. I. *to curse;* maledicere:—Ic wyrge *devoto*, Wrt. Voc. i. 28, 79. Ic wyrge (wyrige, *v.l.*) *maledico*, Ælfc. Gr. 37; Zup. 222, 4. Riht đū dēst, gif đū ealle đīne cild wyrigst . . . wyrig hī ealle, Homl. Th. ii. 30, 10–14. Se đe his hwǣte hȳt, hiene wiergđ đæt folc (*maledicetur in populis*), Past. 49; Swt. 376, 13. Gif mē mīn feónd wyrgeþ (wyrigde, Ps. Spl.) *si inimicus meus maledixisset mihi*, Ps. Th. 54, 11. Se đe wyrigđ (woerges, Lind.: wærge, Rush.) hys fæder, Mt. Kmbl. 15, 4: Homl. Th. ii. 36, 10. Hē đē on ansȳne wyrigđ *he will curse thee to thy face*, 448, 33. Se man đe wirigđ Drihtnes naman *qui blasphemaverit nomen Domini*, Lev. 24, 16. Wergiaþ hig and đū bletsast, Ps. Lamb. 108, 28. Đa đe hine wyrgeaþ (đa wirgendan, Ps. Lamb.) *maledicentes illum*, Ps. Th. 36, 21. Bletsiaþ đa đe eów wyrgeaþ (wiriaþ, *v.l.*: đǣm woergendum, Lind.), Lk. Skt. 6, 28. Wyrigeaþ (wyriaþ, *v.l.*: wærgaþ, Rush.), Mt. Kmbl. 5, 11. Đæt fictreów đe đū wyrgdyst (wyrigdest, *v.l.*), Mk. Skt. 11, 21. Đæt đū mīne fȳnd wirigdest, Num. 23, 11. Wyrgde *devotaret*, Wrt. Voc. ii. 27, 29: 96, 57. Wirigde *maledixisset*, Lev. 24, 11. Wyrigde, Homl. Th. ii. 326, 15. Gē wergdon đane đe eów of wergđe lȳsan þōhte, Elen. Kmbl. 588; El. 294. Mid heora heortan hig wergdon (wyrgedan, Ps. Th.: wyrigdon, Ps. Spl.), Ps. Lamb. 61, 4. Unārīmedlīca mengeo wyrgdon đone cāsere, Blickl. Homl. 191, 10. Wyrgdan *devotabant*, Wrt. Voc. ii. 26, 48: 80, 53. Đone hlāford đæs folces ne wyrg (werig, *v.l.*: wirig, Ex. 22, 28) đū, L. Alf. 37; Th. i. 52, 30. Wyrig God and swelt, Homl. Th. ii. 452, 30. Đone hlāford đæs folces ne werge đū, L. Alf. 37; Th. i. 52, 30. Đæt đū hig wirige, Num. 23, 27. Se đe werge (wyrge, wyrie, *v.ll.*), L. Alf. 15; Th. i. 48, 8. Wirige, Gen. 27, 29. Ealle đe mē wordum wyrigen, Ps. Th. 54, 12. Hē Israhēla folc wiergean (wirgean, Hatt. MS.) wolde, Past. 36; Swt. 256, 17. Ongan hē his selfes bearn wordum wyrgean, Cd. Th. 96, 13; Gen. 1594. Bletsian and wyrian, Homl. Th. ii. 36, 7: 326, 10. Wergendi *devotaturus*, Wrt. Voc. ii. 105, 78. Wiergende, 89, 9. Wyrgende, 27, 4. He cōme mā wītgiende đonne wyrgende, Ps. Th. 34, arg. Biđ wereged *maledicetur*, Kent. Gl. 382. Đa đe be gewyrhtum wyrgede wǣron for heora ārleásnesse *hi qui merito impietatis suae maledicebantur*, Bd. 4, 26; S. 602, 12. II. *to do evil:*—Nylle đū onhyrgan đæt đū wyrge. For đam đa đe wyrgaþ beóþ geteorode *noli aemulari ut malignaris. Quoniam qui malignantur exterminabuntur*, Ps. Spl. 36, 8–9. In wītgum mīnum nyllaþ wergan (wirigan, Ps. Spl.: wyrian ꝉ yfel wilnian, Ps. Lamb.) *in profetis meis nolite malignari*, Ps. Surt. 104, 15. [Ȝif he his feder weried, O. E. Homl. i. 109, 27. Þe weregede gastes, 239, 9. An wereged gost, ꝥ is þe deuel, Rel. Ant. i. 131, 25. With þair her þai weried, Ps. 61, 5. Ge ne schulen ne warien ne swerien, A. R. 70, 20. Euch waried weoued, Kath. 201: Gen. and Ex. 544. Þai ealle wery þe tyme þat þai war wroght, Pr. C. 7422. Corozaym God weried, 4202. Curse or warie, Wickl. Rom. 12, 14. This sowdanesse, whom I thus blame and warye, Chauc. M. of L. T. 372. Waryyn or cursyn *imprecor, maledico, execror*, Prompt. Parv. 516, and see note 5. *Goth.* ga-wargjan *to condemn:* *O. H. Ger.* far-wergen *maledicere.* Cf. *O. Sax.* gi-waragean *to punish* a criminal.] v. ā-, ge-wirgan; wirged, wirgend, wirgende.

wirged, es; *m. An accursed being, the devil:*—Cymeþ se wærgad *venit malus*, Mt. Kmbl. Rush. 13, 19. v. preceding word.

wirgedness, e; *f. Cursing:*—Hē lufode wyrgednesse *dilexit maledictionem*, Ps. Spl. 108, 16.

wirgen. v. grund-wyrgen.

wirgend, es; *m.* I. *a curser.* v. wirgan, I:—Wyrgendras, đæra mūđ biđ symle mid wyrigunge āfylled, Homl. Skt. i. 17, 42. II. *an evil-doer, a malignant person.* v. wirgan, II:—Mīne wergend gehȳrde đīn āgen eáre *insurgentes in me malignantes audivit auris tua*, Ps. Th. 91, 10.

wirgende; *adj.* (*ptcpl.*) *Given to cursing:*—Ne ǣnig man ne gewunie, đæt hē mid yfelum wordum tō wyriende (wyrgende, *v. l.*) weorđe, Wulfst. 70, 18.

wirgness, e; *f. Cursing, a curse:*—Wergnes *devotatio*, Wrt. Voc. i. 29, 1. Wirgnes, ii. 26, 2. Sig seó wirignys ofer mē *in me sit ista maledictio*, Gen. 27, 13. Of wirignysse mūđ full is *maledictione os plenum est*, Ps. Spl. 9 second, 8. Ic sette beforan eów bletsunga and wirignissa (*maledictionem*) . . . wirignissa gif gē ne gehīraþ Drihtnes bebodum, Deut. 11, 26, 28. Wirinysse, 30, 19. Swā nū āwa sceal wesan đæt gē wærnysse (wærh-?), brynewylm hæbben, nales bletsunga, Exon. Th. 142, 13; Gū. 643. Hē sceal lǣtan his wyrignesse and lufian his gebedu, Wulfst. 239, 19. His mūđ byđ symle full wyrignessa *cujus os maledictione plenum est*, Ps. Th. 9, 27: 13, 6. Hī ūs mid heora wiþerwordum onbēnum and wyrinessum ēhtaþ *adversis nos inprecationibus persequuntur*, Bd. 2, 2; S. 504, 4. v. wirgan.

wîr-grǣfe, an; *f. A myrtle-grove*:—Wīrgrǣfen (-an?) *mirteta*, Wrt. Voc. ii. 90, 18: 57, 5. Cf. þorn-grǣfe.

wirgþu (-o); *indecl.*: wirgþ, e; *f.* I. *condemnation, curse, punishment*:—Gē wergdon ðane ðe eów of wergðe lȳsan þōhte ... eów seó wergðu for ðan sceððeþ scyldfullum, Elen. Kmbl. 588-619; El. 294-310. Wergðu dreógan *to be damned*, 422; El. 211: 1901; El. 952. Werhðo dreógan, Beo. Th. 1182; B. 589. Hȳ grim helle fȳr, gearo tō wīte, seóð, on ðam hī āwo sculon wærgðu dreógan, Exon. Th. 78, 11; Cri. 1272. Wergðu wyrcean *to afflict, hurt*, Ps. Th. 108, 17. Ne sceolon gē on mīne wītegan wergðe settan *in prophetis meis nolite malignari*, 104, 13. Ic hine wergðo on mīne sette *my curse shall be upon him*, Cd. Th. 105, 19; Gen. 1755. Is Euan scyld eal forpynded, wærgða āworpen, Exon. Th. 7, 8; Cri. 98. II. *evil, wickedness*:—Ðē firina gehwylc feor ābūgeþ, wærgðo and gewinnes, Exon. Th. 4, 23; Cri. 57. III. *cursing*; maledictio:—Hē hine gegyrede mid wyrgðu *induit se maledictionem*, Ps. Th. 108, 18. [*Goth.* wargiþa *condemnation.*]

wirgung, e; *f. Cursing, a curse*:—*Uae* getācnaþ hwīlon wyrigunge (wyriunge, *v. l.*) ... On wyrigunge: *Uae tibi sit* wā ðē sī, Ælfc. Gr. 48; Zup. 278, 12-16. Wyrgendras, ðæra mūð bið mid wyrigunge (wyriunge, *v. l.*) āfylled, Homl. Skt. i. 17, 43. Hē fordēð his sāwle mid ðære mānfullan wyriunge ... Ūre tunge is gesceapen tō Godes herungum, nā tō deófollīcum wyriungum, Homl. Th. ii. 36, 3-6. Wyrgunge *maledictionem*, Ps. Lamb. 108, 18. Heó wolde ðone sunu ðe hī getirigde mid wyriungum gebindan, Homl. Th. ii. 30, 6. Tǣlincga oððe wærginga hit getācnaþ, Lchdm. iii. 214, 16. [Ne wrec þu þe mid wussinge ne mid warienge, O. E. Homl. ii. 179, 23. Wariunge, A. R. 200, 28. Waryynge *malediccio, imprecacio*, Prompt. Parv. 516, and see note.]

wirgung-galere, es; *m. One whose incantations are curses, a sorcerer*:—Wyrincgalere *Marsum* (the passage is: Marsum, qui virulentas matrices ad sacrae Virginis laesionem incantationum carminibus irritabat, Ald. 70), Hpt. Gl. 519, 46. v. wyrm-galere, -galdere.

wîr-hangra, an; *m. A meadow where myrtles grow*:—Æt wīrhangran, Cod. Dip. Kmbl. v. 297, 18. Cf. sealh-hangra.

Wir-healh; *gen.* -heales; *pl.* -healas; *m. Wirral, the peninsula between the Dee and the Mersey*:—Fōr se here of Wīrheale (-healan, *v. l.*) in on Norð-Wealas, Chr. 895; Th. i. 170, 171. Hié fōron ðæt hié gedydon on ānre wēstre ceastre on Wīrhealum; seó is Lēgaceaster gehāten, 894; Th. i. 170, 171.

wirian, wirigness. v. wirgan, wirgness.

wirman; *p.* de *To warm, make warm*:—Ic wyrme mē *calefacio*, Ælfc. Gr. 37; Zup. 218, 5. Ic mē wyrme, 222, 1. Ðæt wyrmð and heardaþ ðone magan, Lchdm. ii. 188, 18. Heó mec wǣteþ in wætre, wyrmeþ hwīlum tō fȳre, Exon. Th. 393, 35; Rä. 13, 10. Se cyning gestōd æt ðam fȳre and hine wyrmde *rex coepit consistens ad focum calefieri*, Bd. 3, 14; S. 540, 34. Hē wyrmde (wærmde, Lind.: wermde, Rush.) hine *calefaciebat se*, Mk. Skt. 14, 54: Jn. Skt. 18, 25. Ða þeówas wyrmdon (uearmdon, Lind.) hig, for ðam hit wæs ceald, 18, 18. Cnuca mid wīne, and wyrm hit, Lchdm. i. 108, 7. Wyrm tō fȳre, 374, 10. Wirman *fovere*, Wrt. Voc. ii. 33, 34. For ðȳ hē cwæð be ðam cōlan wætere, ðæt nān man ne ðorfte hine belādian, ðæt hē fæt næfde, on hwȳ hē hit wyrman mihte, Homl. Ass. 141, 84. Tō wyrmanne ðone cealdan magan, Lchdm. ii. 188, 22. Heó geseah Petrum wyrmende (wærmigende, Lind.: wermende, Rush., *calefacientem*), Mk. Skt. 14, 67. Mid wyrmendum þingum lācnian, swilc swā pipor is, and ōþra wermenda wyrta, Lchdm. ii. 62, 2-3. [*Goth.* warmjan: *O. Sax.* wermian: *O. H. Ger.* warmen: *Icel.* verma.] v. ge-wirman; wearmian.

wirming, e; *f. Warming*:—Se cyning gestōd æt ðam fȳre and hine wyrmde; and ðā betwih ða wærminge (werminge, M. 196, 27) (*inter calefaciendum*) gemunde hē ðæt word, Bd. 3, 14; S. 540, 34.

wirn, e; *f. A hindrance, obstacle, difficulty*:—Gif hē geðyldelīce forbyrð ǣgðer ge hosp ge edwīt, and on ðære wirne þeáh þurhwunaþ and eádmōdlīce bitt, ðæt him man infæres tīðige, sȳ hē underfangen *si veniens perseveraverit pulsans, et inlatas sibi injurias et difficultatem ingressus visus fuerit patienter portare et persistere petitioni sue, annuatur ei ingressus*, R. Ben. 96, 7. Færð ðæt fȳr ofer eall ... ne nān man næfð ðæra mihta, ðæt ðǣr ǣnige wyrne dō *the fire will go everywhere ... and no one will be able to hinder it*, Wulfst. 138, 7. v. wearn, wirnan.

wirnan; *p.* de. I. *to refuse, refrain from granting* a prayer, claim, grant, etc., (a) with gen. of what is refused:—Se ðe ne wiernð (wirnð, Hatt. MS.) ðæs wīnes his lāre ða mōd mid tō oferdrencanne ðe hiene gehiéran willaþ *vino eloquii auditorum mentem inebriare non desinit*, Past. 49; Swt. 380, 6. Cyning ne wyrneþ wordlofes, wīsan mǣneþ mīne for mengo, Exon. Th. 401, 13; Rä. 21, 11. Hē swenga ne wyrnde, Byrht. Th. 135, 15; By. 118. Ætsōc Goda ðæs feós ǣgiftes, and ðæs landes wyrnde (*he refused to give up the land*), Chart. Th. 201, 30. Myrce ne wyrndon heardes hondplegan, Chr. 937; Erl. 112, 24. Se hlāford ðe ryhtes wyrne, L. Ath. i. 3; Th. i. 200, 14. (b) with dat. of person to whom a refusal is given:—Syle ðam ðe ðē bidde, and ðam ðe æt ðē borgian wylle, ne wyrn ðū him (*volenti mutuari a te ne avertaris*) Mt. Kmbl. 5, 42. Biddaþ ðæs ðe riht sié, for ðam hē eów nyle wyrnan, Bt. 42; Fox 258, 24. (c) with the constructions of (a) and (b):—Gif ðū ðam frumgāran brȳde wyrnest, Cd. Th. 161, 4; Gen. 2660. Eal hit him wyrþ tō teónan ðæm ðe his Gode wyrneþ, Blickl. Homl. 51, 10. Ðā wyrnde him mann ðera gīsla, Chr. 1048; Erl. 180, 13. Gif hē him ryhtes wyrnde, L. Ath. i. 3; Th. i. 200, 19. Hī Mōyse and hys folce ðæs ūtfæreldes wyrndon, Ors. 1, 7; Swt. 38, 19. Ne beó ðū swā heard-heort, ðæt ðū him ðīnes gōdes wyrne *non obdurabis cor tuum, nec contrahes manum*, Deut. 15, 7. Sele him scearpne wyrtdrenc, wyrne him metes, Lchdm. ii. 46, 25. For hwan ðū woldest ðīnre gesihðe mē wyrnan? Ps. Th. 87, 14. II. *to prevent, prohibit, keep from*, (a) absolute:—Gif hǣto oþþe meht ne wyrne, lǣt him blōd, Lchdm. ii. 254, 4. (b) with gen. of what is prohibited:—Ðū wāst ðæt ic ne wyrne mīnra welera (wirne mīne welora, Cott. MSS.) *labia mea non prohibebo*, Past. 49; Swt. 381, 10. (c) with gen. of what is prohibited, and dat. of that to which the prohibition is given:—Se līchoma getācnaþ ðone engel ðe him tōgēnes stent, and him wiernð his unnyttan færelta, Past. 36; Swt. 257, 9. Āwierged bið se mann se ðe wirnð (wyrnð, Cott. MSS.) his sweorde blōdes *maledictus, qui prohibet gladium suum a sanguine*, 49; Swt. 379, 1. Mē ðæs hyhtplegan wyrneþ se mec on bende legde, Exon. Th. 402, 13; Rä. 21, 29. Hié wyrnan þōhton Mōyses māgum leófes sīðes, Cd. Th. 180, 27; Exod. 51. (d) with dat. of person prevented, and a clause giving that which is prevented:—Hē ūs ne wyrnþ (wernþ, *v. l.*), ðæt wē yfel dōn, Bt. 41, 4; Fox 252, 4. Georne is tō wyrnanne bearneácenum wīfe, ðæt hió āht sealtes ete oððe swētes, Lchdm. ii. 330, 6. (e) with acc. See **II b**. [ȝif he hit wul auon, ich hit wulle wernen, Laym. 30310. He ne mei uor reouðe wernen hire, A. R. 330, 11. An hwet þ tu ne maht nawt wearnen (wernin, *v. l.*) mid rihte *quod negare jure non potes*, Kath. 769. Ne mai ich mine songes werne, O. and N. 1358. He him wernde his elmesse, Ayenb. 189, 6. He taketh mete, whan men hym werneth, Piers P. 20, 12. He that wol werne a man to light a candel at his lanterne, Chauc. W. of B. T. 330. *O. Sax.* wernian: *O. Frs.* werna.] v. for-wirnan; warenian, **II.** 3, *and next word*.

wirnung, e; *f. Refusal, denial*:—Be ryhtes wærnunge. Se hlāford ðe ryhtes wyrne, L. Ath. i. 3; Th. i. 200, 13.

wirp, wierp, es; *m. A throw, a blow with a missile*:—Ðā wearð hiere mid ānum wierpe (wyrpe, *v. l.*) ān ribb forod, ðæt hió siþþan mægen ne hæfde hié tō gescildanne, ac raðe ðæs hió wearð ofslagen *hic serpens ad unius saxi ictum cessit, ac mox facile oppressus est*, Ors. 4, 6; Swt. 174, 11. v. wyrp.

wirp, e; *f. A change for the better, recovery* from sickness, *improvement* in circumstances:—Hē tilaþ ðæs gewundedan werpe ðe hē bewitan sceal *vulnerati sui, cui medicamentum adhibet, vitam servat*, Past. 62; Swt. 457, 16. Lege on lǣcedōmas ða ðe ūt teón ða yfelan wǣtan, ðonne biþ ðǣr wyrpe wēn (*hope of recovery*), Lchdm. ii. 46, 27. Gē frōfre ne wēnaþ, ðæt gē wræcsīða wyrpe gebīden *ye look not for comfort, that ye may live to see redemption from exile*, Exon. Th. 132, 30; Gū. 480. Gē sceolon dreógan deáþ and þȳstro, nǣfre gē ðæs wyrpe gebīdaþ (*never will that lot be bettered*), 140, 11; Gū. 608. Se mon ne þearf tō ðisse worulde wyrpe gehycgan *man need not look to this life to mend his lot*, 105, 5; Gū. 18. Is ðæt bearn cymen tō wyrpe weorcum Ebrēa *the child is come to alleviate the afflictions of the Hebrews*, 5, 9; Cri. 67. Se Waldend him (*the blind man*) mæg wyrpe syllan, hǣlo on heáfodgimme (of heofodgimme, MS.), 336, 5; Gn. Ex. 43. Se snotera bād hwæþre him Alwalda ǣfre wille æfter weáspelle wyrpe gefremman (*make his lot better*), Beo. Th. 2635; B. 1315. v. next word.

wirpan; *p.* de *To recover*:—Wyrpton hié wērige, wiste genǣgdon mōdige meteþegnas, hyra mægen bēton, Cd. Th. 185, 29; Exod. 130. Sōna ic wæs wyrpende and mē sēl wæs *statim melius habere incipio*, Bd. 5, 3; S. 616, 34. Ðā sōna gefēlde ic mē b[e]ōtiende and wyrpende (batiende and werpende, Bd. M. 404, 1) *confestim me melius habere sentirem*, 5, 6; S. 620, 12. v. ā-, ge-wirpan, -wyrpan, ge edwyrpan, *and preceding word*.

wirping. v. ed-wirping.

wirrest. v. wirs, wirsa.

wîr-rind, e; *f. Myrtle-bark*:—Tō hāligre sealfe sceal wyirrind, Lchdm. iii. 24, 3. Nim wīrrinde, ii. 98, 8: 332, 8: iii. 14, 2.

wirs; *cpve.*: wirrest, wirst; *spve.*; *adv. Worse, worst*, (1) in reference to moral ill:—Wyrs dēð se ðe lȳhð, Salm. Kmbl. 364; Sal. 181. Ðonne hié wēnen ðæt hié hæbben betst gedōn, ðæt wē him ðonne secgen ðæt hié hæbben wierst (wyrst, Cott. MSS.) gedōn *cum ea, quae bene egisse se credant, male acta monstramus*, Past. 32; Swt. 209, 17. (2) marking an inferior degree of what is desirable or proper:—Ðæt hié wiers ne dōn ðonne him man bebeóde *ne minus, quae jubentur, impleant*, Past. 28; Swt. 189, 18. Ðȳ læs hira lufu āslacige, and hē him ðe wirs līcige, Past. 19; Swt. 143, 10. Se æfterra anweald git wyrs līcode ðonne se ǣrra, Bt. 16, 2; Fox 50, 13. Ic mīn fulluht wyrs geheóld ðonne ic behēte, L. Edg. C. 9; Th. ii. 264, 8: L. Ath. iv. proem.; Th. i. 220, 2. Hē ðȳ wyrs meahte þolian ða þrāge, Met. 1, 76. Se arcebiscop wēnde ðæt hit sum ōðer mann ābiddan wolde, ðe hē his wyrs trūwude and ūðe, Chr. 1043; Erl. 169, 28. Oft hit gesǣleþ ðæt his ǣhta weorþaþ on ðæs onwealde, ðe hē ǣr on his līfe wyrrest ūþe, Blickl. Homl. 195, 4. (3) marking unfavourable condition, a higher degree of what is unpleasant or improper:—Ðȳ læs him ðȳ wirs (wiers, Cott. MSS.) sié, gif hié ða trumnesse ðære Godes giefe him tō unnyte gehweorfaþ, Past. 36; Swt. 247, 7. Hī wyrs geferdan (geferdon māran hearm and yfel, *v. ll.*), ðonne hī ǣfre wēndan, Chr. 994; Th. i. 241, col. 2. Eów wyrs gelomp, Exon. Th. 142, 1; Gū. 637. Ne wæs hyra ǣnigum ðȳ wyrs, ne síde ðȳ sārra, 394, 19; Rä. 14, 5. Hē bið on ðæt wynstre weorud wyrs gesceáden ðonne hē on ða swiþran hond swīcan mōte *he will be assigned to the host on the left hand by a sentence too stern to allow him to pass to the right hand*, 449, 23; Dōm. 75. Hit ðē wyrs ne mæg hreówan ðonne hit mē dēð *you cannot repent it more bitterly than I do*, Cd. Th. 51, 12; Gen. 825. Heora weóldan ða him wyrrest ǣr on feóndscipe gestōdon, Ps. Th. 105, 30. Wyrst, Met. 24, 60. [*Goth.* wairs: *O. Sax.* wirs: *O. H. Ger.* wirs: *Icel.* verr; *cpve.*; verst; *spve.*]

wirsa (wirra *occurs once in the Chronicle*); *cpve.*; wirrest, wirst; *spve. adj. Worse, worst*, (1) in a moral sense:—For hwam lifaþ se wyrsa leng? Salm. Kmbl. 716; Sal. 357. Ne wearð nān wærsa dǣd gedōn ðonne ðeós wæs, Chr. 979; Erl. 129, 4. Gif wē ðæt ne dōþ, ðonne wyrce wē ūs myccle synne; and ūs is get wyrse ðæt wē ūrne ceáp teóþian, gif wē willaþ syllan ðæt wyrste Gode, Blickl. Homl. 41, 7. Hī for nānum ermþum ne byóð nō ðȳ betran, ac ðȳ wyrsan, Bt. 39, 11; Fox 230, 17. Ðā gǣð hē and him tō genymð seofon ōðre gāstas wyrsan (*nequiores*) ðonne hē . . . and wurðaþ ðæs mannes ȳtemestan wyrsan (*pejora*) ðonne ða ǣrran, Mt. Kmbl. 12, 45: Wrt. Voc. ii. 72, 59. Ðes wyrresta cyning Neron, Homl. Th. i. 384, 3. Se wyresta sceaþa (*Judas*), Blickl. Homl. 69, 10. Ðis is manna se wyrresta, 185, 2. Se eallra wyrresta mon, Bt. 14, 3; Fox 46, 20. Ðē þūhte ðæt eallra ðinga wyrrest, 38, 4; Fox 204, 9. Ðæs wyrrestan eorðcyninga, Cd. Th. 235, 13; Dan. 305. On werrestre dǣde *in actione pessima*, Confess. Peccat. Swā byð ðisse wyrrestan (wyrsesta, Lind., *pessimae*) cneórysse, Mt. Kmbl. 12, 45. Wirestan, Deut. 1, 35. Ða wyrstan (*pessimam*) ingewitnesse mē ic geseó, Bd. 5, 13; S. 632, 32. Ða wyrrestan, fā folcsceaðan, Andr. Kmbl. 3183; An. 1594. Ðǣm wyrrestum wītes þegnum, Exon. Th. 251, 28; Jul. 152. On werstum ðingum *in rebus pessimis*, Kent. Gl. 23. (1 a) of an unfitting condition of things:—And ðæt git wyrse is, ðæt wē witon manige foremǣre weras forþgewitene ðe swīþe feáwa manna ā ongit, Bt. 19; Fox 70, 11: Met. 10, 57. (2) of the physical condition of persons or things:—Hē tōbrycð hys stede on ðam reáfe, and se slite byð ðe wyrsa, Mt. Kmbl. 9, 16. Sió wund bið ðæs ðe wierse, Past. 17; Swt. 123, 18. Heó wæs ðe wyrse *deterius habebat*, Mk. Skt. 5, 26. Seó frecednes dæghwamlīce wæs wyrse and wyrse, Bd. 4, 32; S. 611, 24. (2 a) where injury is done to a person in respect to his well-being:—Se ðe ōðerne mid wō forsecgan wille, ðæt hē āðer oþþe feó oþþe freme ðā wyrse sȳ, L. C. S. 16; Th. i. 384, 24. Hī dydan mycelne hearm ābūtan Hāmtūne . . . swā ðæt seó scīr and ða ōðra scīra, ðæ ðǣr neáh sindon, wurdon fela wintra ðe wyrsan, Chr. 1065; Erl. 197, 11. (3) of the condition of affairs, of an (unfavourable) circumstance or event:—Mē ðǣr wyrse gelamp, ðonne ic tō hyhte āgan mōste, Cd. Th. 275, 22; Sat. 175. Hit him wyrse gelomp, 272, 26; Sat. 125. Wæs ǣfre heora æftra sȳð wyrse ðonne se ǣrra, Chr. 1001; Erl. 137, 14. Swā wearð hit fram dæge tō dæge lætre and wyrre, 1066; Erl. 202, 17. Ne wearð wyrse dǣd (*more disastrous act*) monnum gemearcod, Cd. Th. 37, 24; Gen. 594. Hē āwende hit him tō wyrsan þinge, 17, 13; Gen. 259. Hē tǣhte Absalone ōðerne rǣd wyrsan tō his willan, Homl. Skt. i. 19, 206. Wēne ic tō ðē wyrsan þinga, gif ðū Grendles dearst bīdan, Beo. Th. 1055; B. 525. (4) of that which is harmful, painful, etc.:—Hī nǣfre wyrsan handplegan on Angelcynne ne gemitton *they never met with harder fighting in England*, Chr. 1004; Erl. 138, note 7. Ðȳ læs God ūs sende on wyrsan tintrego, Blickl. Homl. 243, 20. Ðæra synfullena deáþ byð se wyrsta (wyrresta, Ps. Surt.: wyrst, Ps. Spl., *pessima*), Ps. Th. 33, 21. Wilddeóra ðæt wyrreste (grimmeste, Exon. Th. 371, 29) . . . wyrmcynna ðæt grimmeste (wyrreste, Exon. Th. 371, 32), Soul Kmbl. 164–167; Seel. 82–84. Se deófol slōh Iōb mid ðære wyrstan wunde (*with the most grievous disorder*), Homl. Th. ii. 452, 26. Mid ðȳ werrestan āttre *with the most virulent poison*, Shrn. 84, 28. On ðone wyrrestan deáð *to the most cruel death*, Andr. Kmbl. 172; An. 86. We[r]stum gedrecenyssum *saevissimis afflictionibus*, Hpt. Gl. 409, 59. Getogen tō ðǣm wyrstan tintregum, Blickl. Homl. 245, 1. Ða werrestan tintrega, 229, 25. Wyrrestan, Exon. Th. 257, 20; Jul. 250: Elen. Kmbl. 1860; El. 932. (5) marking inferiority:—Hē bið swīðe gelīc sumum ðara gumena ðe him þringaþ ymbe ūtan; gif hē wyrsa ne bið, ne wēne ic his nā beteran, Met. 25, 20. Ǣlc man sylþ ǣrest gōd wīn, and ðonne hig druncene beóð ðæt ðe wyrse (wyrest, Rush.: wurresta, Lind., *deterius*) byð, Jn. Skt. 2, 10. Hē ðæt betere geceás, and ðam wyrsan widsōc, Elen. Kmbl. 2078; El. 1040. On ðone wyrsan dǣl scyrede, Exon. Th. 75, 24; Cri. 1226. On ða wyrsan hand, Salm. Kmbl. 998; Sal. 500. Onwendan heora wuldor on ðæne wyrsan hād styrces, Ps. Th. 105, 17. Wyrsan wīgfrecan, Beo. Th. 4985; B. 2496. Buccena flǣsc is wyrrest, Lchdm. ii. 196, 17. Gif wē willaþ syllan ūre ðæt wyrste Gode, Blickl. Homl. 41, 8. [*Goth.* wairsiza; *cpve.*: *O. Sax.* wirsa; *cpve.*; wirsista; *spve.*: *O. Frs.* wirra; *cpve.*: *O. H. Ger.* wirsiro; *cpve.*; wirsisto; *spve.*: *Icel.* verri; *cpve.*; verstr; *spve.*] v. weorr.

wirsian; *p.* ode *To get worse*:—Hit fareþ yfele ealles tō wīde. Swā swȳðe hit wyrsaþ, ðæt ðæs hādes men, ðe hwȳlum wǣron nyttoste, ða syndon nū unnyttaste, L. I. P. 14; Th. ii. 322, 18. And aa hit wyrsode mid mannan swīðor and swīðor, Chr. 1085; Erl. 219, 23. Wyrsadon *deterioraverunt*, Wrt. Voc. ii. 139, 37. Folclaga wyrsedan ealles tō swȳðe, Wulfst. 158, 6. Hē sceolde beón āscyred fram manna neáwiste, gif his hreófla wyrsigende wǣre, Homl. Th. i. 124, 26. [Þet his licome, ðe feble wes, ne sceolde noht wursien, O. E. Homl. i. 47, 26. Þe wunde þet euer wurseð, A. R. 326, 23. Þenne wursede (wersede, 2nd MS.) ich on crafte, Laym. 18931. Werihede þet makeþ þane man worsi, Ayenb. 33, 18.]

wirs-līc; *adj. Mean, vile*:—Ðysse worulde wela is wyrslīc and yfellīc and forwordenlīc, Wulfst. 263, 13. Ic eom wyrslīcre ðonne ðes wudu fūla, oððe ðis warod, ðe hēr āworpen ligeþ on eorþan, Exon. Th. 424, 32; Rä. 41, 48.

wirþig; *adj. Worthy, fitting*:—Wyrþigre wrace hié forwurdon ðā, ðæt ðā heora synna sceoldon hreówsian and dǣdbōte dōn, swīþor ðonne heora plegan begān, Ors. 6, 2; Swt. 256, 11. [Wurrþi to winnenn Cristess are, Orm. 2705. Wurði wurðed to ben, Gen. and Ex. 1012. Wurði to hauen same, Misc. 14, 447. *O. Sax.* wirðig: *O. H. Ger.* wirdig *dignus, meritus*: *Icel.* verðugr.]

wirþu; *indecl.*: wirþ, e; *f. Honour, decoration, dignity*:—Uyrðo *infula*, Wrt. Voc. ii. 111, 75. Cf. weorþ-mynd, III. [*O. H. Ger.* wirdī *dignitas, infula.*] v. or-wirþu.

wīr-treów, es; *n. A myrtle-tree*:—Wīrtreów *myrtus*, Wrt. Voc. ii. 55, 83. Cnuca mid rosan wōse oððe wȳrtreówes, Lchdm. i. 232, 12.

wīr-treówen, -trīwen; *adj. Of a myrtle-tree, myrtle*:—Þweah mid wearmum wȳrtrȳwenum (-treówenum, *v. l.*) wōse, Lchdm. i. 236, 1.

wīs *a manner.* v wīse.

wīs; *adj.* I. *wise, discreet, judicious*:—Wīs *sapiens*, Wrt. Voc. i. 76, 10: *fronimus*, 47, 34. (1) of persons:—Ne scyle nān wīs monn (*vir sapiens*) forhtigan, Bt. 40, 3; Fox 238, 8, 13, 15. Ne mæg weorþan wīs wer ǣr hē āge wintra dǣl in woruldrīce, Exon. Th. 290, 12; Wand. 64. Ðū eart gleáw and scearp, wīs on ðīnum gewitte and on ðīnum worde snottor, 463, 30; Hö. 78. Cyninges rǣswa, wīs and wordgleáw, Cd. Th. 242, 12; Dan. 418. Ne hȳrde ic snotorlīcor guman þingian. Ðū eart wīs wordcwida, Beo. Th. 3694; B. 1845. Azarias Dryhten herede, wīs in weorcum, Exon. Th. 185, 7; Az. 4. Se wīsa mon eall his līf lǣt on gefeán, ðonne hē forsihþ ðās eorþlīcan gōd, Bt. 12; Fox 36, 24. Se wīsa spræc sunu Healfdenes, Beo. Th. 3401; B. 1698. Ðis is wæstm wīses and goodes, ðe his sōðfæst weorc symble lǣste *est fructus justo*, Ps. Th. 57, 10. Gelīc ðam wīsan were (*viro sapienti*), Mt. Kmbl. 7, 24. Se cyning him ceóse sumne wīsne man and glǣwne (*virum sapientem et industrium*), Gen. 41, 33. Hié sǣdon ðæt hié wǣren wiése (wīse, Cott. MSS.), and ðā wurdon hié dysige, Past. 11; Swt. 71, 2: 30; Swt. 203, 10. Wīn nys drenc cilda ne dysigra, ac ealdra and wīsra, Coll. Monast. Th. 35, 21: Ps. Th. 106, 42. Mæg ic wīsran findan, ðonne ðū eart? Gen. 41, 39: Andr. Kmbl. 947; An. 474. Swelce hī sién micle wærran and wīsran, Past. 35; Swt. 245, 1. Swelc eówer swelce him selfum ðynce ðætte wīsasð sié on ðǣm lotwrencum, weorðe ðæs ǣresð dysig, ðæt hē mæge ðonan weorðan wīs, 30; Swt. 203, 20. Mid his ealdormannum, ða ðe hē wīseste and snotereste wiste, hē gelōmlīce ðeahtade, Bd. 2, 9; S. 512, 10. (2) of animals:—Sió wilde beó ðeáh wīs sié, Met. 18, 5. Wīsran *sapientiora* (v. Prov. 30, 24), Kent. Gl. 1101. (3) of things:—Worde and gewitte, wīse þance, Cd. Th. 118, 1; Gen. 1958. Wīsne wordcwide, 249, 28; Dan. 537. Ðam ðe hafaþ wīsne geþōht, Exon. Th. 57, 22; Cri. 922: 150, 2; Gū. 772. Wīsne geleáfan, Ps. Th. 77, 36. On wīsne weg worda ðīnra, 118, 32. Þurh wīs gewit, Exon. Th. 73, 21; Cri. 1193. Ealle mīne wegas wīse syndan on ðīnre gesihðe, Ps. Th. 118, 168. Ðonne hē ðīne wīsan word gehealde, 118, 9. I a. in a bad sense, *cunning*:—Wille gē wesan prættige? Wē nellaþ swā wesan wīse, Coll. Monast. Th. 33, 1. Hī ān geþeaht ealle ymbsǣtan, and gewitnesse wið ðē wīse gesettan (*adversum te testamentum disposuerunt*), Ps. Th. 82, 5. II. *wise, learned, skilled, expert*:—Wīs *sophus* vel *sophista*, Wrt. Voc. i. 47, 40. Se wīsa *gnarus*, ii. 40, 31. Hond bið gelǣred, wīs and gewealden sele āsettan, Exon. Th. 296, 4; Crä. 46. Sum bið meares gleáw, wic(g)cræfta wīs, 297, 18; Crä. 70. Wordcræftes wīs *an able speaker*, Elen. Kmbl. 1180; El. 592. Wīs sāwle rǣdes, Frag. Kmbl. 79; Leás. 41. Se wīs oncneów (*he, being a skilful man, knew*) ðæt hē Marmedonia mǣgðe hæfde gesōhte, Andr. Kmbl. 1686; An. 845: Ps. Th. 106, 16. Ðū mē gewurde wīs on hǣlu *factus es mihi in salutem*, 117, 20, 21, 27. Ðæs wīsan goldsmiðes bān Wēlondes, Bt. 19; Fox 70, 1. Micel is tō hycgenne wīsum wōdboran, hwæt sió wiht sié, Exon. Th. 414, 22; Rä. 32, 24. Wīse men *learned men*, Cd. Th. 201, 24; Exod. 377. Hē feára sum gengde wîsra monna wong sceáwian, Beo. Th. 2830; B. 1413. Geceós wîse men (*viros potentes*), Ex. 18, 21. Unrihtwîse habbaþ on hospe ða ðe him sindon rihtes wîsran, Met. 4, 45. Eorðcyninga se wîsesta (*Solomon*), Cd. Th. 202, 24; Exod. 393. Tômiddes ðara wietena ðe wîsoste wǽron *in medio doctorum*, Past. 49; Swt. 385, 22. Ða wîsestan, ða ðe snyttro cræft þurh fyrngewrit gefrigen hæfdon, Elen. Kmbl. 306; El. 153: 337; El. 169: 645; El. 323. Sum from ǽs wîsistum *quidam ex legis peritis*, Lk. Skt. Lind. Rush. 11, 45, 46. Hê sende tô Egipta wîsustan witun, Gen. 41, 8. III. *known*:—Dô mê wegas ðîne wîse *vias tuas notas fac mihi*, Btwk. 208, 6: Ps. Ben. 24, 3: Ps. Th. 102, 7. [*Goth.* weis: *O. Frs. O. Sax. O. H. Ger.* wîs: *Icel.* víss.] v. and-, brægd-, fore-, gesceád-, getæl-, med-, riht-, sâm-, sundor-, un-, unriht-, weorold-, wrenc-wîs. (*Some of these compounds may be connected with* wîse.)

wis *certain.* v. wiss.

wisa:—Ân wisa (wihta? cf. ða wrǽtlîcan wiht, 505; Sal. 253) is on woruldrîce, ymb ða mê fyrwet bræc L wintra, Salm. Kmbl. 491; Sal. 246.

wîsa, an; *m. A leader, director, captain*:—Wæs Cainan æfter Enose aldordêma, weard and wîsa, Cd. Th. 70, 22; Gen. 1157. Ðû eart eallum eorðbûendum weard and wîsa, 251, 19; Dan. 566. Enoch ealdordôm âhôf, folces wîsa, 73, 2; Gen. 1198. Leóda aldor, herges wîsa, freom folctoga, 178, 18; Exod. 13: 228, 16; Dan. 203. Mægenes wîsa, 260, 2; Dan. 703. Elamitarna ordes wîsa, 121, 3; Gen. 2004. Rîces hyrde, werodes wîsa, 194, 9; Exod. 258: Beo. Th. 523; B. 259: Exon. Th. 296, 22; Crä. 55. Þeóda wîsan, 196, 9; Az. 171. Weorces wîsan, Cd. Th. 101, 28; Gen. 1689. [*O. Sax.* balu-wîso (*the devil*): *O. H. Ger.* wîso *dux*: *Icel.* vísi (*poet.*) *a guide, leader, captain.*] v. brim-, camp-, cræt-, ealdor-, fyrd-, heáfod-, here-, hilde, mægen-, scrid-wîsa.

wîsan; *p.* de *To shew*:—Ðeóden wîsðe herepað tô ðære heán byrig eorlum elðeódigum, Cd. Th. 218, 5; Dan. 35. [*O. Sax.* wîsian; *p.* wîsda *to shew* (he im te heƀanrîkea thena weg wîsit, Hel. 1872): *O. H. Ger.* wîsen; *p.* wîsta: *Icel.* vísa; *p.* vísti.] v. gin-wîsed; wîsian.

wîs-bôc, e; *f. A book in which the state of things is described, a record*:—Eágan ðîne gesâwon ðæt ic wæs unfrom on ferhþe; eall ðæt forþ heonan on ðînum wîsbôcum âwriten standeþ *imperfectum meum viderunt oculi tui, et in libro tuo omnes scribentur*, Ps. Th. 138, 14.

wisc *a marsh* (?):—Concedo terram in loco qui dicitur Fearnleág (*Farleigh, in Kent, by the Medway*) & an myclan wisce vi. æceres mǽde (*and in the big marsh vi. acres of meadow* (?)), Cod. Dip. Kmbl. ii. 128, 33. Cf. Wiscleágeat, v. 179, 34. [Cf. (?) *O. H. Ger.* Wisicha (*place-name*).]

wîscan. v. wŷscan.

wischere (?), es; *m. A wizard*:—Mannum is tô witenne ðæt manega drŷmen maciaþ menigfealde dydrunga þurh deófles cræft, swâ swâ wischeras dôð, and bedydriaþ menn, swylce hî sôðlîce swylc þincg dôn, Homl. Skt. i. 21, 466.

wîs-dôm, es; *m.* I. *wisdom, discretion*:—Wîsdôm (*sapientia*) ys gerihtwîsud fram heora bearnum, Mt. Kmbl. 11, 19: Lk. Skt. 11, 49. Wæs his môdsefa manegum gecŷðed, wîg and wîsdôm, Beo. Th. 705; B. 350. Ðæt hê ða yldestan lǽrde ðæt heó wîsdômes word oncneówan *ut senes prudentiam doceret*, Ps. Th. 104, 18. Iosue wearð gefilled mid wîsdômes gâste (*spiritu sapientiae*), Deut. 34, 9: Exon. Th. 273, 15; Jul. 516. Gleáwhŷdig, wîsdômes ful, Elen. Kmbl. 1875; El. 939. Hê wîsdômes beþearf, worda wærlîcra, 1082; El. 543. Hié nâhton foreþances, wîsdômes gewitt, 713; El. 357: Andr. Kmbl. 1289; An. 645. Wê willaþ wesan wîse. On hwilcon wîsdôme (*sapientia*)? Wê willaþ beón bylewite, and wîse, ðæt wê bûgon fram yfele and dôn gôda, Coll. Monast. Th. 32, 27. Hê wîsdôme heóld êðel sînne, Beo. Th. 3923; B. 1959. Ic healde ðînra worda waru mid wîsdôme, Ps. Th. 118, 17. Hine God þurh his worda wîsdôm âhôf, 104, 15. Hê sette on hî sôðne wîsdôm worda and weorca, 104, 23. Ðæt se sâwle weard lîfes wîsdôm forloren hæbbe, se ðe nû ne giémeþ hwæþer his gǽst sié earm þe eádig, Exon. Th. 95, 4; Cri. 1552. Ŷwaþ wîsdôm weras, wlencu forleósaþ, 132, 17; Gû. 474. II. *knowledge, cognizance*:—Gif ceorl bûton wîfes wîsdôme deóflum gelde, L. Wih. 12; Th. i. 40, 4. III. *wisdom, knowledge, learning, philosophy*:—Swilc is se wîsdôm ðæt hine ne mæg nân mon ongitan swilcne swilce hê is . . . Ac se wîsdôm mæg ûs ongitan swilce swilce wê sind . . . for ðæm se wîsdôm is God. Hê gesihþ eall ûre wyrc, Bt. 41, 4; Fox 250, 24. Hê lǽrde hig, swâ ðæt hig cwǽdon: 'Hwanon ys ðysum ðes wîsdôm?' Mt. Kmbl. 13, 54: Mk. Skt. 6, 2: Andr. Kmbl. 1137; An. 569: Exon. Th. 169, 33; Gû. 1104. Rûmran geþeaht wîsdôm onwreáh . . . mê lâre onlâg mægencyning, Elen. Kmbl. 2483; El. 1243. Wundorlîc is geworden ðîn wîsdôm (*scientia tua*), Ps. Th. 138, 4. Ðû mê lǽr wîsdômes word *scientiam doce me*, 118, 66. Sefa deóp gewôd, wîsdômes gewitt, Elen. Kmbl. 2379; El. 1191. Wîsdômes gife, 1189; El. 596: Exon. Th. 178, 1; Gû. 1220. Wîsdômes *philosophiae*, Wrt. Voc. ii. 66, 28. Wæs se wer in wîsdôme (*scientia*) gewrita wel gelǽred, Bd. 5, 8; S. 621, 33. Hê wîsdôm hâligra gewrita from him nom, 4, 27; S. 603, 40. *Philosophus* is se ðe lufaþ wîsdôm: of ðam is *philosophor* ic smeáge embe wîsdôm, Ælfc. Gr. 36; Zup. 215, 6–8. Ða scearpþanclan witan ðe ðone twydǽledan wîsdôm tôcnâwaþ, ðæt is andweardra þinga and gâstlicra wîsdôm, Lchdm. iii. 440, 29. Tô gehŷranne Salomones wîsdôm, Mt. Kmbl. 12, 42: Andr. Kmbl. 1299; An. 650: Elen. Kmbl. 667; El. 334. Gif hê hafaþ ofer ealle men wîsdôm, Exon. Th. 299, 16; Crä. 103. Wîsdôm swelgan, 147, 31; Gû. 735. Wîsdôm cŷþan, 500, 19; Rä. 89, 9. Wîsdôm onwreón, Elen. Kmbl. 1344; El. 674. Se ðe men lǽreþ micelne wîsdôm *qui docet hominem scientiam*, Ps. Th. 93, 10. Swâ ûs gleáwe wîtgan þurh wîsdôm on gewritum cŷþaþ, Exon. Th. 199, 23; Ph. 30. Ða mîne þeówas sindon wîsdômas and cræftas (*sciences and arts*), Bt. 7, 3; Fox 20, 33. ¶ throughout the Boethius, in which Philosophy personified is a speaker, the word used in the translation is wîsdôm. [*O. Sax. O. Frs.* wîs-dôm: *O. H. Ger.* wîs-tuom: *Icel.* vís-dômr.] v. un-, weorold-wîsdôm.

wîse, an: wîs, e; *f.* I. *a wise, way, manner, mode, fashion*:—Hit is ǽlces môdes wîse, ðæt sôna swâ hit forlǽt sôþcwidas, swâ folgaþ hit leásspellunga *eam mentium constat esse naturam, ut quoties abjecerint veras falsis opinionibus induantur*, Bt. 5, 3; Fox 14, 15. Maniges mannes wîse bið, ðæt hê wile tô his nêhstan sprecan ða word ðe hê wênþ ðæt him leófoste sŷn tô gehŷrenne . . .; deófles wîse bið, ðæt hê ðone unwaran man beswîcan mæge, Blickl. Homl. 55, 19–23: Exon. Th. 362, 5; Wal. 32: 315, 12; Môd. 30: 489, 20; Rä. 78, 10: 419, 4; Rä. 37, 14. Seó wîse (*that manner of treatment*) hine hǽleþ, Lchdm. i. 328, 21. Hié hine lîchomlîce gesâwon, and him æfter eorþlîcre wîsan hŷrdon, Blickl. Homl. 135, 20. Ðæt Lêden and ðæt Englisc nabbaþ nâ âne wîsan on ðære sprǽce fadunge. Ǽfre se ðe âwent of Lêdene on Englisc, ǽfre hê sceal gefadian hit swâ ðæt ðæt Englisc hæbbe his âgene wîsan, elles hit biþ swîþe gedwolsum tô rǽdenne ðam ðe ðæs Lêdenes wîsan ne can, Ælfc. Gen. Thw. 4, 7–11. On ða ylcan wîsan (*juxta quem ratum*) nymaþ ticcenu, Ex. 12, 5: Ps. Th. 30, arg. Ðû gesettest ǽlcere þeóde þeáw and wîsan, Hy. 7, 22. Ic healde mîne wîsan, Exon. Th. 390, 19; Rä. 9, 4: 401, 14; Rä. 21, 11: 483, 12; Rä. 69, 1. Ðû hafast ofer witena dôm wîsan gefongen *thou hast taken a course opposed to the judgment of understanding men*, 248, 20; Jul. 98. Biscopum gebiraþ ealdlîce wîsan, L. I. P. 10; Th. ii. 318, 29. Gif hê ne cunne his dǽda andettan, âcsa hine his wîsena, L. de Cf. 3; Th. ii. 260, 21. Ic ðînra ne mæg worda ne wîsna (*words or ways*; or v. III) wuht oncnâwan, sîðes ne sagona, Cd. Th. 34, 7; Gen. 534. Is ðes middangeard missenlîcum wîsum gewlitegad, Exon. Th. 413, 7; Rä. 32, 2. Mîn gebed him on wîsum is wel lŷcendlîce *est oratio mea in beneplacitis eorum*, Ps. Th. 140, 8. Wîsum clǽne, Exon. Th. 312, 16; Seef. 110. Se his godcundnesse mid sôþum wîsum gerŷmeþ, Blickl. Homl. 179, 24. Sendon hié Amilchor, ðæt hê Alexandres wîsan besceáwode (*ad perscrutandos Alexandri actus*), Ors. 4, 5; Swt. 168, 13. Hê sorgaþ ymb ôðerra monna wîsan *actiones alienas curans*, Past. 53; Swt. 415, 20. Nân nyste ôþres wîsan oþþe dǽda, Homl. Skt. ii. 23 b, 133. Ðæt wê forlǽtan ða wîsan ðe wê langere tîde mid ealle Angelðeóde heóldan, Bd. 1, 25; S. 487, 10. Hê forlêt ða wǽpna and ða woruldlîcan wîsan, Shrn. 61, 16. Ealle ûre wîsan rǽdlîce fadian, Wulfst. 143, 22: L. I. P. 10; Th. ii. 318, 12. On feala wîsan (*multis modis*) ic beswîce fugelas, Coll. Monast. Th. 25, 11. ¶ in adverbial phrases as in other-*wise*:—Mid suman gemete t wîsan *quodammodo*, Hpt. Gl. 435, 59. Ðâs cŷþnesse Drihten nam of ðisse wîsan, Blickl. Homl. 31, 16. Ne dyde hê ða wîsan (*so*) beforan mê, 181, 4. On ǽlce wîsan, 163, 2. On ǽnige wîsan, Wulfst. 158, 1: L. C. S. 5; Th. i. 378, 22. On ǽnige ôðre wîsan *aliter*, Wrt. Voc. ii. 2, 56. On nâne wîsan, Bt. 16, 2; Fox 54, 5. On ðâs word ic becom, ðe lǽs ðe ôðre wîsan ǽnig man leóge, Blickl. Homl. 177, 33. On ôðre wîsan hit ys *aliter est*, Gen. 42, 12: Bd. 1, 27; S. 492, 3, 6. Hit feor on ôðre wîsan wæs *longe aliter erat*, 3, 14; B. 539, 45. On ôðre wîsan *secus*, Wrt. Voc. ii. 81, 74. Wê ongitaþ mon on ôðre wîsan, on ôðre hine God ongit, Bt. 39, 10; Fox 226, 29. *Bifariam* on twâ wîsan, *omnifariam* on ǽlce wîsan, *multifarie* on manega wîsan, Ælfc. Gr. 38; Zup. 237, 14–17. *Meapte* on mîne wîsan, *tuapte* on ðîne wîsan, *nostrapte* on ûre wîsan, 16; Zup. 107, 17. On hire wîsan *suatim, suo more*, Hpt. Gl. 435, 21. On ða betstan wîsan ðû dêmest, Blickl. Homl. 189, 35. Ealde wîsan *as of old*, Beo. Th. 3735; B. 1865. I a. the word is found with strong forms:—Onwendan mîne wîse (wîsan, Th.), Exon. Th. 485, 29; Rä. 72, 5. II. *state, condition*:—Ðonne hié ðenceaþ hû hié selfe scylen fullfremodeste weorðan, and ne giémaþ tô hwon ôðerra monna wîse weorðe *cum sua et non aliorum lucra cogitant*, Past. 5; Swt. 41, 24. Ðæt hié oncnâwæn tô hwæm hiera âgen wîse wirð *ut ad cognitionem sui revocentur*, 37; Swt. 265, 24. Ne scyle nân wîs monn gnornian tô hwæm his wîse weorþe, oððe hwæþer him cume þe rêþu wyrd þe lîþu *vir sapiens moleste ferre non debet, quoties in fortunae certamen adducitur*, Bt. 40, 3; Fox 238, 8. Heora wîse on nǽnne sǽl wel ne gefôr, nâþer ne innan from him selfum, ne ûtane from ôþrum folcum *nulla unquam tempora vel foris prospera vel domi quieta duxerunt*, Ors. 4, 4; Swt. 164, 13: L. I. P. 7; Th. ii. 312, 28. Ðonne ðê ðîn wîse lîcie *cum bene tibi fuerit*, Gen. 40, 14. Hǽte hym man bæþ swâ hraþe swâ hys wîse gôdige, Lchdm. iii. 122, 8. Gehýre hû his wîse gerâd sî, L. de Cf. 2; Th. ii. 260, 17. III. *an arrangement, instruction, a disposition, direction, condition* :—Worda mê đînra wîse onleóhteþ *declaratio sermonum tuorum illuminat me*, Ps. Th. 118, 130. Đæra manna naman đe đeosse wîsan (*a will*) geweotan sindon, Chart. Th. 483, 36. Hebfađ hiá đâs wîsan đûs fundene, 465, 26: 473, 22. Đæt is tô þafianne on đa wîsan, đæt man gîslas sylle, L. A. G. 5; Th. i. 156, 4. Đa wîsan âbeád weoroda ealdor: 'Nû sié geworden gefeá,' Exon. Th. 14, 34; Cri. 229. Wîsna fela, lâre longsume, wîtgena wôđsong, 3, 28; Cri. 43. IV. *a thing; res, negotium* :—Seó wîse wæs mîne on twâ healfa unêþe *quae res dupliciter me torsit*, Nar. 9, 23: 10, 32: Blickl. Homl. 33, 5. Đǽr seó wîse on tweón cyme *ubi res perveniret in dubium*, Bd. 1, 1; S. 474, 21. Gelimp wîsan *eventum rei*, Hpt. Gl. 457, 45. On đysse wîsan *hac in re*, Bd. 1, 27; S. 490, 9. Be đære wîsan đe mîn môd gedrêfed hæfþ, Bt. 39, 4; Fox 216, 11. Đâ hê hæfde đa wîsan onfangene *suscepto negotio*, Bd. 4, 24; S. 597, 36. Hwanon hê đa wîsan (*rem*) cûþe, 4, 25; S. 600, 39: Exon. Th. 20, 11; Cri. 316: Elen. Kmbl. 1365; El. 684. Ne sette ic mê fore eágum yfele wîsan (*rem malam*), Ps. Th. 100, 3. Secgan ymb sume wîsan, Salm. Kmbl. 852; Sal. 425. Ne syndon tô lufianne đa wîsan fore stôwum, ac for gôdum wîsum stôwe syndon tô lufianne *non pro locis res, sed pro bonis rebus loca amanda sunt*, Bd. 1, 27; S. 489, 41. Wîsena Sceppend alra *rerum Creator omnium*, Ps. Surt. ii. p. 202, 28. Swâ on đam ende đara wîsena ætýwed is *sicut rerum exitus probavit*, Bd. 1, 14; S. 482, 42. Feala đû ætýwdest folce đînum heardra wîsan (wîsna?) *ostendisti populo tuo dura*, Ps. Th. 59, 3. Hû hê his wîsna trûwade on đære dimman âdle *how he expected matters would be with him in his illness*, Exon. Th. 171, 30; Gû. 1134. Đes biscop is swîđe mihtig on frêcnum wîsum gescyldnesse tô biddanne, Shrn. 70, 9. Hê ne conn ôđre lǽran đa godcundan wîsan đe hê lǽran scolde *interna, quae alios docere debuerat, ignorent*, Past. 18; Swt. 129, 3. Wê oft ymb ungedafenlîce wîsan smeágeaþ, Swt. 139, 22. Hê hæfde his wîsan beþôht tô Seleucuse *he had entrusted his affairs to Seleucus*, Ors. 3, 11; Swt. 150, 16. IV a. *a cause, reason; res*:—For đære wîsan (*pro qua re*) hê wæs heáfde becorfen, Bd. 1, 27; S. 491, 18. For đære wîsan *quare*, 4, 15; S. 583, 32: *quamobrem*, 4, 18; S. 587, 3. For đisse wîsan *pro hac re*, 1, 27; S. 491, 27. Be đisse wîsan *hinc*, S. 496, 12. Of hwylcere wîsan hit gegange *ex qua re accidat*, S. 496, 35. For hwylcre wîsan côme đû tô mê synfulre, Homl. Skt. ii. 23 b, 249. [*O. Sax.* wîsa (*wk.* and *str.*): *O. Frs.* wîs: *O. H. Ger.* wîsa (*wk.* and *str.*) *modus, mos, consuetudo, usus, ratio, modulatus*: *Icel.* vísa *a stanza*; öðru-vís (-vísa (-u, -i)) *otherwise*.] v. cniht-, cyne-, fyrd-, hring-, hyse-, leóþ-, mann-, munuc-, mynster-, riht- (?), sceáwend-, scip-, tungolcræft-, unriht- (?), weorold-, wilig-wîse.

wîse, an; *f. A sprout, stalk* :—Streáwbergean wîse, Lchdm. ii. 36, 12: 334, 11. Genim streáwberian wîsan nioþowearde, 34, 24, 27. Nim hwîteclǽfran wîsan, 326, 21. Hǽþbergean wîsan, 344, 10. Weóde wîsan, iii. 16, 16. Eallhwîte wýsan *gesie*, Wrt. Voc. ii. 42, 16. [Wyse of strawbery or pesyn *fragus* (cf. a streberytre *fragus*, Wülck. Gl. 584, 29), Prompt. Parv. 531. Take the wyse of tormentile, and bray it, Halliwell's Dict. Cf. *Icel.* vísir *a sprout*.] v. streáwberige-wîse.

wîse; *adv. Wisely, with wisdom* :—Đû worhtest wîse hǽlu, Ps. Th. 73, 12 (cf. 117, 20). Đa đe wyllaþ his gewitnesse wîse smeágan *qui scrutantur testimonia ejus*, 118, 2: 36, 79. Ic đê wegas mîne wîse secge *vias meas enuntiavi tibi*, 118, 26. Ic wegas đîne wîse þence tô fêrenne *cogitavi vias tuas*, 118, 59. Gemune đînes môdes, đa miclan geniht đînre wêđnesse wîse sæcgenum roccette, and rǽd sprece *memoriam abundantiae suavitatis tuae eructabunt*, 144, 7.

wîsere, es; *m. A sign-post* (?) :—Tô Afene; on wîsere; on đa fûlan lace, Cod. Dip. Kmbl. iii. 301, 36.

wîs-fæst; *adj.* I. *wise, discreet, judicious*, (1) of persons :—Hió grêtte Geáta leód, Gode þancode, wîsfæst wordum, Beo. Th. 1256; B. 626. Wîsfæstne wer, wordes gleáwne, Andr. Kmbl. 3294; An. 1650. Is nû þearf micel, đæt wê wîsfæstra wordum hýran, 2335; An. 1169. (2) of things :—Đæt heó his wîsfæst word efnan *ut faciant mandata ejus*, Ps. Th. 102, 17. II. *wise, having knowledge* or *skill, learned* :—Esaias, wîsfæst wîtga, Exon. Th. 19, 25; Cri. 306. Đis ys se dæg, đe hine Drihten ûs wîsfæst geworhte, Ps. Th. 117, 22: Menol. Fox 122; Men. 61. Micel is tô hycganne wîsfæstum menn, hwæt seó wiht sý, Exon. Th. 411, 15; Rä. 29, 13. Swâ wîtgan wîsfæste sægdon, 5, 3; Cri. 64. Sume bôceras weorþaþ wîsfæste, 331, 22; Vy. 72. Đæs đe wîsfæste weras on gewritum cýþan, 356, 19; Pa. 14: Elen. Kmbl. 627; El. 314. Đæt is tô geþencanne wîsfæstum werum, hwæt seó wiht sý, Exon. Th. 429, 5; Rä. 42, 9. II a. *intelligent, rational* (?) :—Hê wile on dômes dæg on đysne middangeard cuman, and hê wile eallum wîsfæstum gesceaftum êcn[e] dôm gesetton (*he will pass an eternal sentence on all intelligent creatures*), Blickl. Homl. 121, 20. v. next word.

wîs-fæst (v. wîse, *and* cf. þeáw-fæst); *adj. Perfect* :—Gif đû wilt wîsfæst (*perfectus*) wosa, Mt. Kmbl. Lind. Rush. 19, 21. Wîsfæst êghwelc biđ *perfectus omnis erit*, Lk. Skt. Lind. 6, 40. Folc wîsfæst *plebem perfectum*, 1, 17. Wîsfæsto (*perfecti*) wossađ gié, Rtl. 13, 19. [Perhaps these passages might be put under I of preceding word.]

wîsfæst-lîc; *adj. Wise* :—Hê him wîsfæstlîc word onsende, þurh đæt hî hrædlîce hǽlde wǽron *misit verbum suum et sanavit eos*, Ps. Th. 106, 19.

wîs-hycgende *thinking wisely, having wise thoughts* :—Hê wîshycgende gesæt on sesse, seah on enta geweorc, Beo. Th. 5426; B. 2716.

wîs-hygdig; *adj. Wise-minded* :—Him đâ wîshýdig Abraham gewât, Cd. Th. 109, 2; Gen. 1816. Ongan his brýd wîshýdig wer wordum lǽran, 109, 15; Gen. 1823: 123, 29; Gen. 2053: 136, 8; Gen. 2255.

wîsian; *p.* ode. I. where movement takes place, *to shew the way, guide, direct*, (1) absolute :—Hê stôp on strǽte, stîg wîsode, Andr. Kmbl. 1970; An. 987. Hê lêt his francan wadan þurh đæs hysses hals, hand wîsode, Byrht. Th. 135, 61; By. 141. Snyredon đǽr secg wisode, Beo. Th. 810; B. 402. Hê hêt him fýrenne beám beforan wîsian, Ps. Th. 104, 34. (2) with dat. :—Ic eów wîsige, Beo. Th. 590; B. 292: 6198; B. 3103. Ic fêre swâ mê wîsaþ feónd, Exon. Th. 403, 4; Rä. 22, 2. Hê fêrde swâ him God wîsode, Gen. 35, 5: Num. 10, 28. Îsernhergum ân wîsode, Cd. Th. 199, 34; Exod. 348: Ps. Th. 77, 16. Stîg wîsode gumum ætgædere, Beo. Th. 646; B. 320. Se đǽm headorincum hider wîsade, 746; B. 370. Him seleþegn forđ wîsade, 3595; B. 1795. Đæt heáfod sceal wîsian đǽm fôtum, đæt hié stæppen on ryhtne weg, Past. 18; Swt. 131, 24. (3) with dat. of person and acc. of way :—Hwâ đam sǽflotan sund wîsode, Andr. Kmbl. 762; An. 381. Hû đû sǽhengeste sund wîsige, 976; An. 488. (4) with acc. of person :—Swâ mec wîsaþ, se mec wrǽde on legde, Exon, Th. 383, 19; Rä. 4, 13. (5) with acc. of that to which the way is shewn, *to shew the way to, shew, point out* :—Secg wîsade, lagucræftig mon, landgemyrcu, Beo. Th. 422; B. 208. Hê sceolde wong wîsian (*act as guide to the place*), 4809; B. 2409. II. figurative, (1) absolute, *to shew the course to be followed, guide, direct, indicate* :—Ic Werferđ cýđe, swâ mê Alchûn sægde, and eác mîne gewrytu wîsodon, Chart. Th. 166, 6. Eorđcyningas đe folcum fore wîsien, Ps. Th. 148, 11. (2) with dat. :—Swâ ic đê wîsie, Cd. Th. 35, 32; Gen. 563. Se đe him hâlig gǽst wîsaþ, Exon. Th. 124, 1; Gû. 333. Se mê wîsaþ tô rîce, 401, 2; Rä. 21, 5. Hê wîf gefette, swâ hyne his hlâford hêt and him God wîsode, Gen. 24, 15: Beo. Th. 3331; B. 1663. Him se eorl wîsade (*compulit illos*, Gen. 19, 3), Cd. Th. 147, 24; Gen. 2444. Him se Dryhtnes dôm wîsade tô đam nýhstan nýdgedâle, Exon. Th. 129, 3; Gû. 415. Ûre Drihten beád Môyse đam heretogan, đæt hê folce wîsode (folc wissode, *v. l.*), Wulfst. 132, 11. Đus him gewîsede se mon đa gemǽru, swâ him đa ealdan bêc ryhtan and wîsedon, Chart. Th. 142, 15: 141, 18. Hwæt mæg ic dôn, bûton mê God wîsige? Gen. 41, 16. Swâ him ryht wîsie, L. Alf. pol. 1; Th. i. 60, 20: 3; Th. i. 62, 9. Se consul sceolde him eallum wîsian and beón heora yldost tô ânes geáres fyrste, Jud. Thw. p. 161, 23. (3) with acc. :—Đæt wê ǽgđer ge ûs sylfe, ge đa đe wê wîsian sceolan, swâ gewîsian môtan, swâ swâ ûre ealra þearf sý, L. I. P. 21; Th. ii. 332, 24. (4) with clause stating what is pointed out :—Hié lêton tân wîsian hwylcne hira ǽrest ôđrum sceolde tô fôddurþege feores ongildan, Andr. Kmbl. 2200; An. 1101. (5) with dat. of person and acc. (or clause) of what is pointed out :—Hâlgan heápe hlýt wîsode đǽr hié Dryhtnes ǽ dêman sceoldon, Apstls. Kmbl. 18; Ap. 9. Mê đa treahteras tala wîsedon on đam micelan bêc, Salm. Kmbl. 10; Sal. 5. [Heȝe Diana, wise mi, Laym. 1200. Hwi nultu wisi heom hu engles singeþ, O. and N. 915. Thut lond wel to wise, R. Glouc. 524, 8. *O. Sax.* wîsian: *O. Frs.* wîsa: *O. H. Ger.* wîsen *monstrare, ducere, regere, docere*: *Icel.* vísa.] v. ge-, riht-wîsian; wissian.

Wîsle, an; *f. The Vistula* :—Weonodland wæs ûs ealne weg on steorbord ôđ Wîslemûđan. Seó Wîsle is swýđe mycel eá, and hió tôlîđ Witland and Weonodland; and seó Wîsle lîđ ût of Weonodlande, and lîđ in Estmere . . . Đonne cymeþ Ilfing eastan, and Wîsle sûđan, and benimđ Wîsle Ilfing hire naman . . .; for đý hit man hǽt Wîslemûđa, Ors. 1, 1; Swt. 20, 6-13.

Wîsle-land, es; *n. The land in which the Vistula rises, part of Poland* :—Be eástan Maroara londe is Wîslelond, Ors. 1, 1; Swt. 16, 17.

Wîsle-mûþa, an; *m. The mouth of the Vistula.* v. Wîsle.

wîs-lîc; *adj. Wise, discreet, prudent, sagacious* :—Mê đynceþ wîslîc, gif đû geseó đa þing beteran, đæt wê đâm onfôn, Bd. 2, 13; S. 516, 10. Is wîslîc rǽd, đæt manna gehwylc geornlîce smeáge, Wulfst. 4, 21. Wîslîc wærscipe, L. I. P. 10; Th. ii. 318, 37. Đîn mildheortnes wîslîc standeþ, deórust and gedêfust, Ps. Th. 102, 16. Mid wîslîcum gedylde, Homl. Th. ii. 222, 21. Hê him wîslîce andsware sende *ille ei prudens responsum misit*, L. Ecg. P. iii. 14; Th. ii. 200, 20. Đû ǽghwylces canst worda wîslîc andgit, Andr. Kmbl. 1018; An. 509. Wera gehwylcum wîslîcu word gerîsaþ, Exon. Th. 343, 34; Gen. Ex. 166. Ongan se biscop lustfullian đæs iungan snyttro and his wîslîcra worda *delectabatur antistes prudentia verborum juvenis*, Bd. 5, 19; S. 637, 47. Drihten wordum wîslîcum herian, Ps. Th. 65, 1. Rǽd forđ gǽđ, hafaþ wîslîcu word on fæðme, Cd. Th. 211, 14; Exod. 526. Wīslīcu wundur oncnāwan, Ps. Th. 87, 11. Swā dēme hē swā him wīslīcost þince *judicet pro ut ipsi prudentissimum videbitur*, L. Ecg. C. 32; Th. ii. 156, 20. [*O. Sax.* wīs-lîk: *O. H. Ger.* wīs-līh *sagax, urbanus.*] v. un-wīslīc.

wis-lic *certain.* v. wiss-līc.

wīslīce; *adv.* I. *wisely, sagaciously, with wisdom, prudently:—Sapienter* wīslīce ... *sapienter loquor* wīslīce ic sprece, Ælfc. Gr. 38; Zup. 223, 15: Past. 15; Swt. 93, 24: Homl. Th. i. 236, 8: Ps. Th. 46, 7. Hē him wīslīce (*sapienter*) andwyrde, Mk. Skt. 12, 34. Wīslīce spyrian, Bt. 18; Fox 60, 27. Beþencan heora dǣda wīslīce and wærlīce, L. I. P. 10; Th. ii. 318, 35: Chr. 1067; Erl. 204, 34: Blickl. Homl. 97, 2. Wīslīce gē dyde, 201, 1: Homl. Skt. i. 5, 42: Exon. Th. 348, 2; Sch. 22: Ps. Th. 77, 12. Hē wīslīce rǣdde for Gode and for worulde his þeóde, Chr. 959; Erl. 119, 26. Hit ða tēð getrymeþ, gif his man wīslīce brūceþ, Lchdm. i. 334, 10. Bið nū wīslīcor ðæt gehwā ðis wite, Homl. Th. i. 6, 18. II. *wisely, skilfully, cunningly:*—Se wolcnreáda wǣfels wīslīce getācnode ūres Drihtnes deáð mid ðære deáge hīwe, Homl. Th. ii. 254, 5. Hē Adam funde, wīslīce geworht, and his wīf, Cd. Th. 29, 26; Gen. 456: Ps. Th. 138, 13. Ða wīslīce āwriten standaþ, 101, 16. Ðū unstilla gesceafta wīslīce āstyrest, Met. 20, 15. Daniel sægde him wīslīce wereda gesceafte ðætte sōna ongeat cyning, Cd. Th. 225, 26; Dan. 160. [*O. Sax.* wīslīko; *O. H. Ger.* wīslīcho *sapienter, mature, sophistice.*] v. un-wīslīce.

wīsness. v. un-wīsness.

wisnian, weosnian; *p.* ode *To wizen, dry up:*—Wisnaþ (-eþ, Lind.) *aruit*, Jn. Skt. Rush. 15, 6. Ðā wisnode hē on Cristes hāligra heortum, and is nū on ūrum heortum blōwende, Blickl. Homl. 115, 13. Weosniendre *arida*, Wrt. Voc. ii. 3, 53. [*O. H. Ger.* wesanēn *arescere, marcescere: Icel.* visna *to wither.*] v. ā-, for-wisnian.

wiss; *adj. Certain:*—Ðeáh ðe hē wis (gewiss, M. 412, 5) geworden wǣre ðurh ða ætȳwnesse ðære gesihðe *tametsi certus est factus de visione*, Bd. 5, 19; S. 623, 15. ¶ *in the phrase* tō wissum:—Tō wissum *profecto, omnino*, Hpt. Gl. 431, 15. Tō wissan *praesertim, maxime, saltim*, 416, 41. Wite gē tō wissan ðæt se deófol ne mæg mannum derian būtan Drihtnes geþafunge, Homl. Skt. i. 17, 174. [He seȝȝde him to wisse whillc ende he shollde sekenn, Orm. 8460. Þ wite þu to wisse, Kath. 1532. Hi wenden to wisse of here lif misse, Horn 121. He is here fader mid wisse, O. E. Homl. ii. 25, 23. *O. Sax. O. Frs.* wiss: *Icel.* viss. Cf. *Goth.* du unwisamma *in incertum.*] v. ge-wiss.

wisse (?); *adv. Certainly:*—Sculan wē wrecan wordum forð, wisse gesingan, ðæt ..., Menol. Fox 140; Men. 70. [As wis ase ... ase wis ... *as certainly ... so certainly* ..., O. E. Homl. i. 187, 36. Alse wis alse ..., A. R. 38, 8. Ȝho wass wiss allre manne mast off lufe filledd, Orm. 2597. Þatt wass wiss to soþe þe maste þing, 2866. *O. H. Ger.* wisso *profecto.*] v. ge-wisse.

wīs-sefa, an; *m. A wise-minded person:*—Him mæg wīssefa wyrda gehwylce gemetigian, gif hē bið mōdes gleáw, Salm. Kmbl. 877; Sal. 438.

wissian; *p.* ode. I. *to shew* a way (*acc.*) to a person (*dat.*):—Ðæt ðū nyme ðē lādmenn, ðæt ðē wegas wissigeon, Gen. 33, 15. II. fig. *to shew the way, guide, direct, rule,* (1) absolutely (see also (2), (3)):—Gif swā gesceád wissaþ *si ita ratio dictaverit*, Anglia xiii. 443, 1116. Ða ðe him betǣhte sindon tō wissianne, Wulfst. 108, 16. Wissiendum *gubernante*, Hpt. Gl. 453, 39. (2) with dat. (or uncertain):—*Rego* ic wissige, of ðam cymð *rex* cyning, ðe rihtlīce wissaþ his folce, Ælfc. Gr. 28, 5; Zup. 173, 6. Ða ðe heora synna bētaþ swā swā hym man wissaþ, Wulfst. 104, 14. Hē ðē wissaþ, Gen. 24, 7. Hē wītegode swā him wissode God, Num. 33, 8. *Rex* cyning is gecweden *a regendo* ..., for ðan ðe se cyning sceal mid micelum wīsdōme his leóde wissian, Ælfc. Gr. 50, 18; Zup. 293, 9. Cyning sceal wissigan mid wīsdōme his folce, O. E. Homl. i. 302, 28. On ðæra (ðære, MS.) gewitnysse, ðe ðū wissian scealt on ðissere geladunge, Ælfc. T. Grn. 17, 39. (3) with acc.:—Ǣlces mannes weorc cȳðaþ hwilc gāst hine wissaþ. Godes gāst wissaþ tō hālignesse; deófles gāst wissaþ tō leahtrum, Homl. Th. i. 324, 27. Ūre Drihten beád Mōyse ðam heretogan, ðæt hē folc wissode, Wulfst. 132, 11. Wearð ðæt mǣden hohful, hū heó ǣfre wæras wissian sceolde, Homl. Skt. i. 2, 122. Hū mæg ūre gegaderunge būton geþeahtynde beón wissod (*regi*)? Coll. Monast. Th. 30, 9. III. *to declare, make known:*—Se cræft sceolde wissian gewisslīce be steorrum hwæt gehwilcum menn gelumpe on his līfes endebyrdnysse, Homl. Skt. i. 5, 253. [Ure Drihten cweð to Moyses þet he scolde wissien his folc, O. E. Homl. i. 13, 15. Witen þat lond and wissien þa leoden, Laym. 5280. Antenor ȝam ladde, wissede and radde, 1365. To wissenn himm, Orm. 10823. Crist, that kan wisse and rede, Havel. 104. Crist þe wisse, Horn 1457. Coudestow wissen us þe weye? Piers P. 5, 540. Wyssyñ or ledyñ *dirigo*, Prompt. Parv. 530. Cf. *O. H. Ger.* wissen.] v. ge-, mis-wissian; wīsian, *and next word.*

wissigend, es; *m.* I. *a director, guider* of that which moves:—Cræt and his wissigend *currus et auriga ejus*, Homl. Skt. i. 18, 295. II. *a director, ruler:*—Wissiend *gubernator, rector* (*ecclesiae*), Hpt. Gl. 459, 54: Gesceafta Sceppend and wissigend (*rector*) ūre, Hymn. Surt. 20, 25. *Rex* wē cwæþaþ cyning, ðæt is gecweden wissigend, O. E. Homl. i. 302, 27. Þwyrlīce færð æt ðam hūse ðǣr seó wyln bið ðære hlǣfdian wissigend, Homl. Skt. i. 17, 11.

wiss-līc; *adj. Certain:*—Ne heora wītes bið wislīc trymnes *nec est firmamentum in plaga eorum*, Ps. Th. 72, 3. Dryhten eorle monegum āre gesceáwaþ, wislīcne blǣd, sumum weána dǣl, Exon. Th. 379, 16; Deór. 34. v. un-gewislīc, *and next word.*

wisslīce; *adv. Certainly:*—Hī wisslīce witon *scient*, Ps. Th. 58, 13. Wislīce, 99, 2. [Wenndenn þeȝȝ þatt he wisslike wære Crist, Orm. 10330. He falleþþ wissliȝ for þatt gillt, 928. Alse wisliche alse hie þis dai was hoven into hevene, Rel. Ant. i. 130, 37: Kath. 185. Wislike for soth, Havel. 274. I wot wislike, Will. 2947. Also wisly God my soule blesse, Chauc. C. T. B. 2112.] v. ge-wislīce.

wissung, e; *f.* I. *shewing of the way, guidance, direction:*—Hwænne ðū eáðelīcost miht tō ðam folce becuman be mīnre wissunge, Homl. Ass. 110, 259. II. fig. *direction, instruction, teaching:*—Hleótan man mōt mid geleáfan, gif hī hwæt dǣlan willaþ; ðis bið wissung, Homl. Skt. i. 17, 87. Hē mōt lǣtan hī lybban be heora bōca wissunge and heora gāstlīcan ealdres tǣcunge, Homl. Th. ii. 594, 2. Hī (*the apostles*) ða lāre on bōcum āwriton be Godes āgenre wissunge, L. Ælfc. P. 20; Th. ii. 370, 29: Homl. Ass. 20, 156. Hī heóldon Godes ǣ æfter Mōyses wissunge, 101, 319. Hī ðurhwunedon swā þurh his wissunge, 30, 149. Þurh gōde wissunge, Wulfst. 32, 13: Homl. Th. ii. 482, 1: Homl. Skt. i. 3, 104. Hī wurðan swȳðe bliþe ðurh swilce wissunge, Chr. 995; Th. i. 244, 23. III. *rule, government, direction* of one in authority:—Wissung *regimen*, Hpt. Gl. 412, 69. Wissunge *regimine*, 453, 49. Wæs wuniende Israēl on friðe feówertig wintra be Gedeones wissunge *quievit terra per quadraginta annos, quibus Gedeon praefuit*, Jud. 8, 28. Under abbodes wissunge, Homl. Ass. 39, 382. Hī leofodon be heora āgenum dihte, be nānes ealdres wissunge, 44, 502. Ne gedyrstlǣce nān lǣwede man ðæt hē wissunge oððe ealdordōm healde ofer Godes ðeówum, Homl. Th. ii. 592, 25. Dathan and Abiron forsāwon Mōyses wissunge, Homl. Skt. i. 13, 224 note. [Hit wes iloked bi Godes wissunge, þet mon scule childre fulhten, O. E. Homl. i. 73, 29. Hiss wissing and his lare, Orm. 11830. Al þe world is iwald þurh his wissunge, Kath. 187.] v. ge-wissung.

wist, e; *f.* (and *m.? v.* big-, dæg-, hūs-, neáh-wist.) I. *being.* v. æt-, ed-, gador-, gegador-, hūs-, los-, mid-, neáh-, on-, sam-, stede-wist. II. *subsistence:*—Wist *vel* anleofa *stips*, Wrt. Voc. i. 17, 8. Wiste *stipis*, Anglia xiii. 36, 248. IIa. *sustenance, food, provisions:*—Næs ðǣr hlāfes wist, ne wæteres tō brūcanne; ah hié blōd and fel þēgon, Andr. Kmbl. 42; An. 21. Hē næfþ ða neódþearfe āne, ðæt is wist and wǣda, Bt. 33, 2; Fox 124, 17. Of ungemete wiste and wǣda, Met. 25, 39: Cd. Th. 222, 11; Dan. 103. Welan and wiste, 59, 29; Gen. 971. Hē smeáde hwǣr hī bigleofan biddan sceoldon, ðā ðā hī ða fare fērdon būton wiste, Homl. Th. ii. 138, 34: Cd. Th. 185, 30; Exod. 130. Gif feohbōt āriseþ, ðæt gebyreþ tō wǣde and tō wiste ðām ðe Gode þeówian, L. Eth. vi. 51; Th. i. 328, 7. Tōdǣlan werum tō wiste fǣges flǣschoman, Andr. Kmbl. 305; An. 153: Menol. Fox 388; Men. 195: Soul Kmbl. 49; Seel. 25. Genōh wǣre ðam wǣdlan his untrumnys, þeáh ðe hē wiste hæfde, Homl. Th. i. 330, 16. Mon tō andleofne eorðan wæstmas hām gelǣdeþ, wiste wynsume, Exon. Th. 214, 26; Ph. 245: Cd. Th. 81, 4; Gen. 1340. Nafast ðū hlāfes wiste, ne hlūtterne drync, Andr. Kmbl. 623; An. 312: Elen. Kmbl. 1231; El. 617. Forlǣt eal ðæt ðū āge būton wiste and wǣda, Prov. Kmbl. 80. Næbbe ic welan ne wiste, Andr. Kmbl. 603; An. 302: 635; An. 318. Hē āfēdde of fixum twām and of fīf hlāfum fira cynnes fīf þūsendo; wiste þēgon menn, 1186; An. 593. Waldend ðē wist gife, heofonlīcne hlāf, 776; An. 388. Hunig, wynsume wist, Frag. Kmbl. 40; Leás. 22. Fōddurwelan, wist, Exon. Th. 415, 14; Rä. 33, 11. Sylle him mon wist and wǣdo, 336, 12; Gn. Ex. 48. Wistum gehladen, 492, 16; Rä. 81, 16. Mid wistum þēnian *to serve with food*, Homl. Skt. i. 7, 390. Ic welan and wista gife eów genōge, Wulfst. 132, 15. III. *dainty food, a feast.* v. wistfullian:—Ðeós wist *epulum*, Ælfc. Gr. 13; Zup. 86, 6. Wist *epulae*, keninga wist *vel* ēstas *dapes*, Wrt. Voc. i. 41, 12, 13. Wiste wlonc and wīnes sæd, Exon. Th. 369, 10; Seel. 39. Ðonne ðū dēst wist oððe feorme *cum facis prandium aut caenam*, Lk. Skt. 14, 12. Æt hām findaþ witode him wiste and blisse, Exon. Th. 430, 14; Rä. 44, 8. Wista *dapes*, Wrt. Voc. i. 26, 63. Hwǣr beóþ ðonne his welan and his wista? Blickl. Homl. 111, 33. Wista *epularum*, Hpt. Gl. 481, 15: Exon. Th. 130, 6; Gū. 434. Gebytlu mid wistum āfyllede, Homl. Th. i. 68, 3: 74, 27. In wistum mīnum *in delitiis meis*, Ps. Surt. 138, 11. Wystu *delicias, epulas*, Hpt. Gl. 480, 76. Wista *delicias*, Wrt. Voc. ii. 28, 69. Wiste *epulas*, Kent. Gl. 787. Hié hæfdon wiste and plegan, Blickl. Homl. 99, 21. IV. *eating, feasting:*—Nelle ðū grǣdig beón on ealre wiste (*epulatione*), Scint. 169, 17. Hī on druncennysse and on wiste hiora wombe þeówiaþ, L. E. I. 45; Th. ii. 442, 1. Wunaþ hē on wiste, Beo. Th. 3474; B. 1735. Hine his goldwine wenede tō wiste, Exon. Th. 288, 24; Wand. 36. Hē ǣlce dæge symblede and mid micelre wiste wǣre gefeormod, Past. 45; Swt. 337, 24. [*Goth.* wists; *f. natura: O. Sax.* wist; *m. food: O. H. Ger.*

wist; *f. substantia; alimentum, stipendium*: *Icel.* vist; *f. abode; food.*] v. and-, big-, dæg-, ofer-wist (*for other compounds see* I).

wist-full; *adj. Abounding in food, productive*:—Ðis wæs swíðe gód geár and swíðe wistfull on wudan and on feldan, Chr. 1112; Erl. 243, 38.

wistfullian; *p.* ode *To feast*:—Ic wistfullige *epulor*, Ælfc. Gr. 25; Zup. 146, 1. Tíma is ðæt ðú mid ðínum gebróðrum wistfullige on mínum gebeórscipe, Homl. Th. i. 74, 15. Utan wistfullian *epulemur*, Wrt. Voc. ii. 143, 62. Se apostol tǽhte ðæt wé sceoldon wistfullian ná on yfelnysse beorman, ac on þeorfnyssum sýfernysse (*epulemur, non in fermento malitiae, sed in azymis sinceritatis*, 1 Cor. 5, 8), Homl. Th. ii. 278, 24. v. ge-wistfullian.

wistfullíce; *adv. Sumptuously*:—Wistfullíce *sumptuosius* (si tu te sumptuosius comas, Ald. 75), Wrt. Voc. ii. 87, 24.

wistfulli[g]end, es; *m. One that feasts*:—Swég wistfulgend[es] *sonus epulantis*, Ps. Spl. 41, 5.

wistfullness, e; *f. Luxury in eating*:—His wistfullnys him wyrðeþ tó biternysse, Basil admn. 8; Norm. 50, 25.

wistfullung, e; *f. Feasting*:—Wistfullunga *epulas*, Hpt. Gl. 452, 4. v. ge-wistfullung.

wist-fyllu; *indecl.* -fyll, e; *f. Abundance of food*:—Him álumpen wæs wistfylle wén, Beo. Th. 1472; B. 734.

wist-gifende; *adj.* (*ptcpl.*) *Yielding food, fertile*:—Ðære wistgifendan *opulenti*, Wrt. Voc. ii. 62, 47.

-wistian, -wistlǽcan. v. ge-wistian, -wistlǽcan.

wistle, an; *f. A hollow reed*:—Wistle *avena*, Wrt. Voc. i. 285, 5: ii. 8, 26: *fistula*, 90, 25: 37, 26. v. wóde-wistle.

-wistlíc. v. ofer-wistlíc.

wist-líce *for* wíslíce, Anglia xi. 108, 14: 109, 46. Cf. Wulfst. 51, 15: 52, 28.

wist-mete, es; *m. Food for sustenance*:—Ic eom áféded of ðam genihtsumestan wistmettum mínre fylle, Homl. Skt. ii. 23 b, 582.

wísung, e; *f. Direction, guidance*:—Scylon hý gán tó heora scriftan and hym hys synna ealle geandettan, and ealle be his wísunge gebétan Homl. Ass. 141, 71. Dathan and Abiron mycelne teónan Móyse gedydon and forsáwon his wísunge, Homl. Skt. i. 13, 224. v. ge-, weorc-wísung.

wís-wyrdan; *p.* de *To be wise in speech*:—Wýswyrdan *philosophari*, Anglia xiii. 38, 301. v. next word.

wís-wyrde; *adj. Wise in speech*:—Se ðe wǽre stuntwyrde, weorðe se wíswyrde, Wulfst. 72, 18.

wit; *pers. pron. We two*, (1) *I and thou*, (a) alone:—Ðæt hí sýn án swá wyt sýn án, Jn. Skt. 17, 22. Abram cwæð tó Lothe: 'Wyt sind gebróðru,' Gen. 13, 8. Wit, Cd. Th. 114, 14; Gen. 1904. Geþenc hwæt wit sprǽcon, Beo. Th. 2957; B. 1476: Exon. Th. 172, 18; Gú. 1145. Wit baru standaþ, Cd. Th. 50, 20; Gen. 811. (b) with numeral forms:—Wit bútú sprecaþ, Cd. Th. 36, 20; Gen. 574: 52, 3; Gen. 838. Ne forlǽte ic ðé, þenden wit lifiaþ bú, 136, 11; Gen. 2256. (2) *I and he* (*she*), (a) alone:—Ðá becóme wit tó ðam inneran dǽle ðæs wéstenes ðǽr uncer hlǽfdige wæs, and wit wǽron belocene in carcerne, Shrn. 38, 20: Gen. 41, 12. Rincas míne, restaþ incit hér, wit (*Isaac and I*) eft cumaþ, Cd. Th. 174, 21; Gen. 2882: 152, 31; Gen. 2529: Beo. Th. 1074; B. 535. (b) with numeral forms:—Ic wæs gehloten mid ánum wífe in ánes ceorles þeówdóme. Ðá wǽron wit twégen on ánum olfende, Shrn. 38, 14. Ic gean intó Élíg, ðér mínes hláfordes líchoma rest, ðara þreó landa ðe wit bútá geheótan Gode, Chart. Th. 524, 20. Ðá bær unc mon liþ forþ, and wit bú druncan, Bd. 5, 3; S. 616, 31. (c) with the name of the person associated with the speaker:—Wit Scilling for uncrum sigedryhtne song áhófan, Exon. Th. 324, 31; Víd. 103. (d) with name and numeral:—Wit Adam twá eaples þigdon, Cd. Th. 290, 6; Sat. 411. [Gif þu me dest woh and wit beon anes lauerdes men, O. E. Homl. i. 33, 1. Þe bet wit (*he and I; we*, 2nd MS.) mawen libben, Laym. 9515. Wit (we, 2nd MS.) tweie, 23653. Witt ne muȝhenn tæmenn, Orm. 202. Wit beoð ifestnet and þe cnotte is icnut bituhhen unc tweien, Kath. 1512. Ðo quat Laban: 'Frend sule wit ben and trewðe pligt nu unc bitwen, Gen. and Ex. 1775. *Goth. O. Sax.* wit: *Icel.* vit.] v. unc, wé.

wit(t), es; *n.* I. *right mind, wits*:—Wóde hé gehǽlde, and on witte gebróhte, Homl. Skt. i. 15, 7. II. *wit, intelligence, understanding*:—Ðæs ðú scealt werhðo dreógan, þeáh ðín wit duge, Beo. Th. 1183; B. 589. III. *the mind*:—Ðeós gítsunc hafaþ gumena gehwelces mód ámerred, ðæt hé máran ne récð, ac hit on witte weallende byrnð, Met. 8, 45. [*O. Frs.* wit: *O. H. Ger.* wizzi *ingenium, ratio*: *Icel.* vit *consciousness, sense, understanding*: *Goth.* un-witi *ignorance, foolishness*.] v. ge-wit; bil-, fyr-wit.

-wit (-wid). v. in-wit.

-wít. v. ed-wít.

wita, an; *m.* I. *one who knows, a person of understanding* or *learning, a wise man*:—Wita (-e, MS.) *sophista*, Wrt. Voc. i. 47, 41. Fród wita, snottor ár, beorn bóca gleáw, Exon. Th. 313, 16; Mód. 1. Se ðe wita (*sapiens*) is, mid feáum wordum geswytelaþ, R. Ben. 30, 15. Wita sceal geþyldig, ne sceal nó tó hátheort, ne tó hrædwyrde, Exon. Th. 290, 15; Wand. 65. Ðissere woruldе hǽl is ðæt heó witan hæbbe, and swá má witena beóð, swá hit bet færð. Ne bið se ná wita ðe unwíslíce leofaþ, ac bið open sott, Homl. Skt. i. 13, 131. Mé com swíðe oft on gemynd, hwelce wiotan (wutan, Cott. MSS.) iú wǽron giond Angelcynn, ǽgðer ge godcundra háda ge woruldcundra, Past. pref.; Swt. 3, 3. Wín gedéð, ðæt furðon witan (*sapientes*) oft misfóð, R. Ben. 65, 4. Filistina witan, *the wise men of the Philistines*, Salm. Kmbl. 861; Sal. 430. Ða ǽláruwas ł aldo uuto *Pharisaei*, Lk. Skt. Lind. 5, 17. Witena *peritorum*, Wrt. Voc. ii. 67, 37. Ofer witena dóm, Exon. Th. 248, 19; Jul. 98. Hit witena nán þider ne séceþ, Met. 19, 7: 20, 3: Runic pm. Kmbl. 340, 8; Rún. 4. Hé (*Nero*) wæs ǽlcum witum láþ and unweorþ, Bt. 28; Fox 100, 28. Ðæt Godes hús wíslíce fram witum (*sapientibus*) sig gefadod, R. Ben. 84, 24. I a. with special reference to taking part in deliberations:—Ðis witena gemót *haec sinodus*, Ælfc. Gr. 8; Zup. 30, 8. Bǽdon ðæt eft óþer seonaþ wǽre, and hí ðonne woldan mid má heora witena gesécean, Bd. 2, 2; S. 502, 37. Wurdon monega seonoðas háligra biscepa and eác óðerra geþungenra witena, L. Alf. 49; Th. i. 58, 5. II. *one able to give counsel, a counsellor*:—Se wæs wita and geþeahtere ðæs Pápan *consiliarius erat Papae*, Bd. 5, 19; S. 638, 14. II a. *one able to give counsel in affairs of state, one who takes part in the councils of a nation, a leading man*:—Sum in mædle mæg módsnottera folcrǽdenne forð gehycgan, ðǽr witena biþ worn ætsomne, Exon. Th. 295, 34; Crä. 43. (1) in reference to other than Teutonic people:—Se ríca Rómána wita Brutus, Met. 10, 44. Hié sendon .x. hiera ieldstena wietena (*decem principes*), Ors. 4, 7; Swt. 182, 11. Witena, 4, 10; Swt. 196, 29. Hí hæfdon ǽlce dæge heora witena gemót (-met, Thw.), and wǽron gesette synderlíce tó ðam ða senatores, ðæt synd þeódwitan, Jud. Thw. p. 161, 31. Wiþ ðám Rómániscum witum, Bt. 1; Fox 2, 15. Hé ofslóg ealle ða witan (*in Thrace*), Ors. 3, 7; Swt. 114, 20. Créca witan, Met. 1, 66. Ða rícostan Rómána witan, 9, 25. (2) in reference to England. See also *gemót*:—Ðyssum wordum óðer ðæs cyninges wita and ealdormann (*alius optimatum regis*) geþafunge sealde, Bd. 2, 13; S. 516, 12. Gif hwá on ealdormannes húse gefeohte, oþþe on óðres geþungenes witan, L. In. 6; Th. i. 106, 6. Ðis is seó gerǽdnes ðe Engla cyng and ǽgðer ge gehádode ge lǽwede witan gecuran (cf. ðe Engla rǽdgifan gecuran, vi. 1; Th. i. 314, 3), L. Eth. v. tit.; Th. i. 304, 4. Miercna cyning and his weotan, Chr. 868; Erl. 72, 23. Eádweard cyng and his witan, 911; Erl. 100, 18. Se cyng ond his biscopas ond his aldormenn ond alle ða wioton disse ðióde ðǽr gesomnade wǽron, Chart. Th. 70, 15. Cynewulf benam Sigebryht his ríces and West-Seaxna wiotan, Chr. 755; Erl. 48, 19. Bútan ðæs cyninges leáfe and his witena, 901; Erl. 96, 28. Eádmund cyning cýþ ... ðæt ic smeáde mid mínra witena geþeahte ge hádedra ge lǽwedra, L. Edm. S. proem.; Th. i. 246, 19. Ic Ælfréd West-Seaxna cyning eallum mínum witum ðás geeówde, and hié ðá cwǽdon, ðæt him ðæt lícode eallum tó healdenne, L. Alf. 49; Th. i. 58, 28. Ic Íne ... mid eallum mínum ealdormonnum and ðǽm ieldstan witum mínre þeóde and eác micelre gesomnunge Godes þeówa wæs smeágende be ðære hǽlo úrra sáwla and be ðam staðole úres ríces, L. In. proem.; Th. i. 102, 6. Æðelréd wæs mid mycelum gefeán Angelcynnes witon gehálgod tó cyninge, Chr. 979; Erl. 129, 30. Weotum, Chart. Th. 480, 16. (3) in reference to other Teutonic people:—Witan Scyldinga, Beo. Th. 1561; B. 778. Hé ða weáláfe weotena dóme árum heólde, 2201; B. 1098. III. *an elder, a chief person, senior* (cf. fród *for double sense of* wise *and* old):—Beón gesette án oððe twégen ealde witan (*unus aut duo seniores*), R. Ben. 74, 14. Ældo ł uuto ðæs folces *seniores populi*, Mt. Kmbl. Lind. 21, 23. On gemóte heora witena *in conventu seniorum*, Bd. 3, 5; S. 527, 23. Wutuna (uutuna ł ældra, Lind.) *patrum*, Lk. Skt. Rush. 1, 17. Cwæð se Hǽlend tó ðám witum (*ad seniores*), Lk. Skt. 22, 52. Hé ge fram ðám witum ge fram his efenealdum (*a senioribus et coaetaneis suis*) mid rihtre lufan lufad wæs, Bd. 5, 19; S. 637, 18. Hé geseah ealle witon on þeáwum and dǽdum scínende, Homl. Skt. ii. 23 b, 85. IV. *one who has knowledge, a witness*:—Eall mín mǽgð mé is tó witan, Homl. Skt. i. 8, 42. Leáse uuta *falsi testes*, Mt. Kmbl. Lind. 26, 60. Mid sægene unrím geleáffulra witena (*testium*) ða ðe ða ðing wiston, Bd. pref.; S. 472, 25. Gif hé hit næbbe beforan gódum weotum (witum, *v.l.*) geceápod, L. In. 25; Th. i. 118, 14. V. *a wise man, one professing supernatural knowledge*:—Hé sende tó Egipta wísustan witan *misit ad omnes conjectores Egypti cunctosque sapientes*, Gen. 41, 8. [Witene imot, Laym. 11545. Beon weote and witnesse þerof, A. R. 204, 24. Þe wite (Helyas þe prophete, 8628), Orm. 8673. *O. Frs.* wita *a witness*: *O. H. Ger.* wizzo *gnarus, sapiens; divinus*. Cf. *Goth.* un-wita *foolish; ignorant*.] v. ǽ-, burh-, folc-, fyrn-, ge-, láh-, lár-, leód-, rǽd-, rún-, scír-, stíg-, un-, úþ-, þeód-, weorold-wita.

witan; *prs.* ic, hé wát, ðú wást, wǽst, *pl.* wé witon; *p.* wiste; *pp.* witen. I. *to wit, know, have knowledge, be aware*, (1) absolute:—*Noui* ic can oððe ic wát, *noui* ic wiste, Ælfc. Gr. 33; Zup. 205, 8. Oft wé oferswíðdon swá swá ðú sylf wistest, Homl. Skt. i. 11, 27. Ne meahte hire Iudas, ne ful gere wiste, sweotole gecýðan, Elen. Kmbl. 1717; El. 860. Ne ongeátan hí, ne geara wistan *nescierunt, neque intellexerunt*, Ps. Th. 81, 5. Giefe monigfealdran ðonne ǽnig mon wite, Exon. Th. 177, 4; Gú. 1221. Hé wæccende ðóhte ðæt hé nó witende (*nesciens*) ârǽfnode, Bd. 1, 27; S. 497, 8. Ic oft swór mǽne áðas ge weotende ge nytende, Anglia xi. 99, 65. Ða gáð libbende and witende on helle *ad infernum viventes sentientesque descendunt*, Past. 55; Swt. 429, 27. Hié æt níhstan witende mid deófolcræftum sóhton hú hí hit gestillan mehte, Ors. 3, 10; Swt. 140, 7. Ða ðe him ne ondrǽdaþ witende (*sciendo*) syngian, Bd. 1, 27; S. 491, 37. Ne weotendum (*nescientibus*) oþþe nó gýmendum ðǽm hyrdum ðære stówe, 4, 3; S. 570, 12. (2) with acc., *to know* something, *have knowledge of, be aware of*:—Hwanun wát (witto, Lind., wito, Rush. *sciam*) ic ðis? Lk. Skt. 1, 18. Ne ic ǽniges wát hæleða gehygdo, Andr. Kmbl. 398; An. 199. Ðú wást ða menniscan týddernysse, Blickl. Homl. 243, 30: Ps. C. 31. Ðú wǽst and const ánra gehwylces earfeðsíðas, Andr. Kmbl. 2566; An. 1284. Crist ealle wát góde dǽde, Exon. Th. 449, 7; Dóm. 67: Blickl. Homl. 19, 33. Ǽlc here hæfð ðý lǽssan cræft ðonne he cymð, gif hine mon ǽr wát (*if people know of it*), ǽr hé cume, Past. 56; Swt. 433, 28. Hé manna ingehygd wát and can, Blickl. Homl. 179, 26. Ne magon wé hit ná dyrnan, for ðam ðe hit Drihten wát, Hy. 7, 93: Exon. Th. 183, 11; Gú. 1325. Manna geþóhtas nǽnig mon ne wát, Blickl. Homl. 181, 11: Ps. Th. 73, 17: Hy. 3, 32. Wé gewislíce witon (*know of*) unrím ðara monna ðe ða écan gesǽlða sóhtan *multos scimus beatitudinis fructum quaesisse*, Bt. 11, 2; Fox 36, 2: Elen. Kmbl. 1285; El. 644. Rincum ðe béc witan, Exon. Th. 429, 19; Rä. 43, 7. Ic wiste hira sár *sciens dolorem ejus*, Ex. 3, 8. Hé heora lotwrencas wiste, Mk. Skt. 12, 15. Hé wiste sprǽca fela, Cd. Th. 29, 5; Gen. 445. Ðeáh ðe hé hit ǽr wisðe, Past. 35; Swt. 243, 3. Hé ne wisse word ne angin, Cd. Th. 223, 25; Dan. 125. Ealle ða ðe ðone gylt mid him wiston *conscii servi*, Ors. 4, 4; Swt. 164, 2. Ða swíðe lytle fiorme ðara bóca wiston *very little profitable matter in those books did they know*, Past. pref.; Swt. 5, 11. Yldo bearn ǽr ne cúðon, þeáh hié fela wiston, Cd. Th. 179, 16; Exod. 29. Metod hié ne cúþon, ne wiston hié Drihten God, Beo. Th. 365; B. 181. Gé sweltaþ deáðe, nymþe ic dóm wite swefnes, Cd. Th. 224, 29; Dan. 143. Nis ðæt eówer ðæt gé witan ða þráge and ða tíde *non est vestrum nosse tempora et momenta*, Blickl. Homl. 117, 24. Ða mildestan ðara ðe men witen, Exon. Th. 255, 1; Jul. 207. Gé ne magon witan ðæra tída tácnu, Mt. Kmbl. 16, 3: Exon. Th. 339, 11; Gu. Ex. 92. Gerím witan heardra heteþonca, 261, 13; Jul. 261. Ús Hǽlend God onwráh, ðæt wé hine witan mótan, 24, 14; Cri. 384: Beo. Th. 509; B. 252. Ǽghwæþres sceal scearp scyldwiga gescád witan worda and weorca, 582; B. 288. Wytan, Hy. 3, 17. Dó hit mon ús tó witanne, Past. 46; Swt. 357, 5. Béc ða ðe niédbeðearfosta sién eallum monnum tó wietonne, pref.; Swt. 7, 7. Tó wietenne, 15; Swt. 92, 26. Witende (*scientes*) ǽgðer ge gód ge yfel, Gen. 3, 5. Witendum (weotendum, Ps. Surt.) ðé *scientibus te*, Ps. Spl. 35, 11. Nán þing nis behýdd ðæt ne sý witen (*quod non sciatur*), Lk. Skt. 12, 2. (3) with acc. and infin.:—Ðǽr ic seomian wát ðínne sigebróðor bendum fæstne, Andr. Kmbl. 365; An. 183. Wé witun ðé bilewitne wesan, Coll. Monast. Th. 18, 22. Ðara cynna monige hé wiste on Germanie wesan, Bd. 5, 9; S. 622, 14: Exon. Th. 182, 20; Gú. 1313: 248, 16; Jul. 91. Wisse, 436, 15; Rä. 55, 1: 324, 28; Víd. 101. Ðǽr ðú wite elenan standan, Lchdm. ii. 346, 10. (4) with acc. and complementary word or phrase:—For ðære byldo ðe ic tó him wát, Blickl. Homl. 179, 21. Ic ðé on ðyssum hýnðum wát wyrmum tó wiste, Soul Kmbl. 303; Seel. 155. Ic mé ðæt wát tó helpe, Ps. Th. 51, 7. Ic wát heáhburh hér áne neáh, Cd. Th. 152, 8; Gen. 2517. Ic hine goodne wát, Ps. Th. 53, 6: 106, 1: Beo. Th. 3731; B. 1863: Hy. 1, 3. Ne wát ic mé beworhtne wulle flýsum, Exon. Th. 417, 11; Rä. 36, 3. Ðú wǽst ðé bǽles cwealm hátne in helle, Andr. Kmbl. 2374; An. 1188. Hé wát his sincgiefan biheledne, Exon. Th. 183, 13; Gú. 1326: 311, 15; Seef. 92. For ðam ǽrende ðæt hé tó ús eallum wát, 451, 34; Dóm. 113. Hý him in wuldre witon Waldendes giefe, 76, 23; Cri. 1244: 107, 20; Gú. 61. Ðú wýsctest ðæt ðú wistest Crist on róde áhangenne, Blickl. Homl. 85, 34: Ps. Th. 118, 21. Ða heó séleste wiste, Elen. Kmbl. 2404; El. 1203: Cd. Th. 3, 26; Gen. 41: Beo. Th. 1297; B. 646. Hé wende hine ðǽr hé wiste handgeweorc heofencyninges, Cd. Th. 31, 32; Gen. 494: 169, 3; Gen. 2793: 259, 1; Dan. 685: Exon. Th. 162, 16; Gú. 976. Hé aldorþegn deádne wisse, Beo. Th. 2623; B. 1309: Cd. Th. 249, 25; Dan. 535. Ðæt hé wiste hine scyldigne, Chart. Th. 166, 33. Hié ðone here tóweardne wiston, Blickl. Homl. 79, 13: Shrn. 86, 3: Exon. Th. 459, 20; Hö. 2. Ne mé unrihtes on áwiht wistan, Ps. Th. 58, 3. Wiston him be súðan Sigelwara land, Cd. Th. 182, 1; Exod. 69. Wisson, Beo. Th. 498; B. 246. Gif hé hine sylfne wite ðæs clǽnne, L. C. E. 5; Th. i. 362, 9. (5) with a clause, (a) without connecting word:—Ic wát ðú eart Godes hálga, Mk. Skt. 1, 24: Cd. Th. 24, 30; Gen. 385: 35, 8; Gen. 551. Ic wát þeáh, gif ðé ǽfre gewyrð ðæt . . . þonne gesihst ðú . . ., Bt. 36, 2; Fox 174, 24. Wé witon hé úre wæs wealdend, Blickl. Homl. 243, 17. Wiste hé his bearn on myclum ymbhygdum wǽron, 131, 26. Wite ðé be ðissum, gif ðú eádmódne eorl gemête, ðam bið gæst gegæderad Godes ágen bearn, Exon. Th. 318, 4; Mód. 77. (b) with introductory *ðæt*:—Ic wát (*novi*), ðæt ðú eart wlitig, Gen. 12, 11. Ic wát (*scio*), ðæt ðú swá didest, 20, 6. Ic wát (*cognovi*), ðæt Drihten ys mǽre, Ex. 18, 11. Ic wát (uát, Lind., wátt, Rush. *scio*), ðæt seó cýðnes is sóð, Jn. Skt. 5, 32: Cd. Th. 35, 22; Gen. 558. Ic wát and can, ðæt ðú mín God wǽre *agnovi quoniam Deus meus es tu*, Ps. Th. 55, 8. Ic wát geare, ðæt . . ., Beo. Th. 5306; B. 2656. Ðú wást, ðæt ic eom untýmende, Gen. 16, 2: Jn. Skt. 21, 15: Ps. Th. 68, 6. Wé weotan, ðæt wé ðæs ðearfe nabbaþ, Bd. 2, 5; S. 507, 21. Se hellsceaða wiste, ðæt hié Godes yrre habban sceoldon, Cd. Th. 43, 23; Gen. 695. Wisse, Beo. Th. 4668; B. 2339. Ða men wisson (wisston, Bt. 38, 1; Fox 196, 8), ðæt . . ., Met. 26, 100. Westan, Judth. Thw. 24, 26; Jud. 207. Wé witon (uutton, Lind., wutun, Rush. *scimus*), ðæt hé is synful, Jn. Skt. 9, 24, 29, 31. Wé wuton (wutan, Rush.), Mt. Kmbl. Lind. 22, 16. Wite gé (wutas gié, Lind., gé wutan, Rush. *scitis*), ðæt . . ., 26, 2: Mk. Skt. 10, 41. Wit ðú, ðæt ic eom drý, Blickl. Homl. 183, 17. Witaþ gé, ðæt hit swá nis *scitote, quia non est mea*, Bd. 4, 8; S. 576, 2. Witaþ (wutas gié, Lind.), ðæt . . ., Mt. Kmbl. 24, 43: Lk. Skt. 10, 11: Ps. Th. 99, 2. Wite gé, ðæt . . . *scitote, quoniam* . . ., Ps. Th. 4, 4; Blickl. Homl. 191, 36. Wite ðú, ðæt . . . *scito, quod* . . ., Gen. 15, 13: Jud. 6, 14: Blickl. Homl. 181, 11: 183, 18: Elen. Kmbl. 1889; El. 946. Wite hé, ðæt hé bið wana, Blickl. Homl. 17, 36. Suá suá hié selfe wieten, ðæt hié hit for Gode dón, Past. 28; Swt. 191, 2. Witen, Met. 19, 13. Se reccere sceal geornlíce wietan, ðætte . . ., Past. 20; Swt. 149, 1. Ðæm láreówe is tó wietanne, ðæt . . ., 63; Swt. 459, 6. Tó witenne, Blickl. Homl. 63, 5: 129, 26: 209, 19. (bb) with *for ðon ðe*:—Crist ðá wiste, for ðon ðe (*quia*) se hálga ðá slép, Blickl. Homl. 235, 13. (c) with indirect interrogative forms:—Ic wát hwæt hé þenceþ, Blickl. Homl. 181, 10: Cd. Th. 34, 10; Gen. 535. Ic wát hwá mé ferede, Andr. Kmbl. 1808; An. 906. Ic ne wát hwǽr ðú eart, Blickl. Homl. 241, 7: Exon. Th. 496, 21; Rä. 85, 18. Ðú cans eal ðis wésten, and wásð hwǽr wé wícian magon, Past. 41; Swt. 304, 16. Ðú wást and canst hú ðú lifian scealt, Cd. Th. 56, 23; Gen. 916. Wást ðú hú ðeós ádle scyle ende gesettan? Exon. Th. 163, 16; Gú. 994. Eówer Fæder wát hwæs eów þearf biþ, Blickl. Homl. 21, 1. Wé witon hwelce wælhriównessa Neron weorhte, Bt. 16, 4; Fox 56, 36. Ne wuti gé of hwelc tíd hláferd íwer tó cymmende sié, Mt. Kmbl. Lind. 24, 42. Gif ic wiste hú . . ., Beo. Th. 5032; B. 2519. Ðæt ðú wisse (wistest, *v. l.*) hwæs ðú wundredest, Bt. 41, 4; Fox 252, 14. Ne wiste hé hwonne him fǽmnan tó brýde wǽron, Cd. Th. 157, 5; Gen. 2600. Ðæt wé wissen (wiston, *v.l.*) hwæt hé wǽre, Bt. 42; Fox 256, 2. Ðæt ic wite gearwe on hwylcne weg ic gange, Ps. Th. 142, 9. Wite ðú hú wíd and síd helheoðo, and mid hondum ámet, Cd. Th. 308, 27; Sat. 699. Wé witon magon hú swíþe ús is ðes dæg tó mǽrsienne, Blickl. Homl. 161, 7: 47, 21. Gif ðú witan wille hwæt gedón wæs, 177, 1. (d) with *gif*:—Ðú wást gif hit is swá wé secgan hýrdon, Beo. Th. 550; B. 272. (6) with the construction of (2) and of (5). (a) (2) and (5 b):—Án þing ic wát, ðæt ic wæs blind, and ðæt ic nú geseó, Jn. Skt. 9, 25. Wát ic ðæt nú ðá, ðæt hé bið alles leás écan dreámes, Cd. Th. 275, 34; Sat. 181: Andr. Kmbl. 866; An. 433. Ðú wást míne geheówunga, ðæt ic eom dust, Blickl. Homl. 89, 15. Ðæt ðú wást, ðæt ic wæs deád, 183, 13. Ða ðe hit witon, ðæt hié him þeówiaþ, Bt. 21; Fox 72, 32. Ðæt ic gearwe wiste, ðæt . . ., Exon. Th. 196, 7; Az. 170: Cd. Th. 24, 31; Gen. 386. Ðis wutaþ gié, ðætte geneólǽcaþ ríc Godes, Lk. Skt. Lind. 10, 11. Ǽr hé sóð wite, ðæt ða synfullan sáwla sticien helle tó middes, Salm. Kmbl. 342; Sal. 170. Hú mæg ic hit witan, ðæt ic hit ágan sceal *unde scire possum, quod possessurus sim eam?* Gen. 15, 8. (b) with (2) and (5 c):—Ðú ðæt ána wást, hú mé módor gebær, Ps. C. 61. Gif ðú hit wást, hú ðú mǽre eart, Hy. 3, 20. Ðæt ne wát ǽnig, hú ða wísan sind wundorlíce, Exon. Th. 223, 10; Ph. 357. Ðæt ne wiste hé, hwæt se manna wæs, Andr. Kmbl. 521; An. 261. Ðæt hié ðæt wiston, hwonne hé ðisse worlde ende gesettan wolde, Blickl. Homl. 119, 9. Nis nǽnig mon ðe ðæt án wite, hú lange hé ðás gedón wille, hwæþer ðis þúsend sceole beón scyrtre ðe lengre, 119, 5. Ðæt ðú sóð wite, hú ðæt geeode, Exon. Th. 28, 6; Cri. 442. Ðæt ic sóð wite, hwæðer . . ., Andr. Kmbl. 1206; An. 603. Ne mæge wé ðæt sóð witan, hú ðú æðele eart, Hy. 3, 13. (c) with (2) and (5 d):—Gif hé synful is, ðæt ic nát, Jn. Skt. 9, 25. (7) with preposition *be*:—Wé witon bí monnum, se se ðe bitt ðone monn ðæt him ðingie wið óðerne ðe hé bið ierre, ðæt irsigende mód hé gegremeð, Past. 10; Swt. 63, 11. Hié wiston ge be heora sige, ge eác be ðara hǽþenra manna fleáme *they knew both about their victory and about the heathens' flight*, Blickl. Homl. 203, 3. Se consul heora ungemet ofslóg and sige hæfde; be ðæm mon mehte witan, ðá hé and ða consulas hié átellan ne mehton *quot millia hominum interfecta, quot capta sint, ipse consul ostendit; qui, cum multitudinem capti populi referre vellet, numerum explicare non potuit*, Ors. 3, 10; Swt. 140, 30. Be ðam æfteran is tó witanne, ðæt hé wæs tó biscope gehálgod *de secundo intimandum, quod in episcopatum fuerit ordinatus*, Bd. 4, 23; S. 594, 11. II. *to be wise, be in one's senses*:—Ðá wéndon hí ðæt hé tela ne wiste, ac ðæt hé wédde *vulgus aestimabat eum insanire*, Bd. 2, 13; S. 517, 10. 'Geseoh ðæt ðú teala wite.' Cwæþ hé: 'Ne wéde ic' *vide ut sanum sapias. Non, inquit, insanio*, 5, 13; S. 632, 32. III. *to be conscious of, to know* fear, pity, etc., *to feel, shew* respect, honour, etc.:—Wát ic sorga ðý má, Cd. Th. 54, 33; Gen. 886. For hwon wâst đú weán? 54, 12; Gen. 876. Hit mâre ne wât bûton gnornunge, Met. 3, 9. Se wyrsa ne wât on his mægwinum mâran âre, Salm. Kmbl. 717; Sal. 358. Hió him tô litelne ege tô witan *they feel too little awe of him*, Wulfst. 220, 27. Đû đæs þonc ne wisses *thou knewest (feltest) no gratitude for it*, Exon. Th. 85, 5; Cri. 1386: 90, 15; Cri. 1474. Đone đe in meoduhealle mine wisse (*should feel affection*), oþþe mec frêfran wolde, 288, 7; Wand. 27. Ic lǣrde đæt ǣlc on ôþrum ârwyrþnesse wiste, Blickl. Homl. 185, 13. Hê him forgeaf đone níđ đe hê tô him wiste, Ors. 5, 15; Swt. 250, 15. Hê sâr ne wiste, Cd. Th. 12, 3; Gen. 179. Hié sorge wiht, weorces ne wiston, 49, 2; Gen. 786. Đæt is tô wundrianne, đæt đa Egipti swâ lytle þoncunge wiston Iôsepe, Ors. 1, 5; Swt. 34, 32. Đæt hî nǣnige incan tô him wiston *se mentem ad illum ab omni ira remotam habere*, Bd. 4, 24; S. 598, 41. Wite mâran þanc đæs đe đû hæbbe, đonne đæs đe đû wêne, Prov. Kmbl. 22. Ǣlc đe gescâd wite *every rational person*, L. C. S. 75; Th. i. 424, 19. Đæt hê on đam griđe micle mǣđe wite *that he shew great respect to that 'griđ,'* L. Eth. vii. 31; Th. i. 336, 14. Gif man on Godes griđe mǣđe witan wolde, Wulfst. 161, 3. Ne wolde hê ǣnige âre witan on đære Cristenan ǣfestnysse *nec religioni Christianae aliquid inpendebat honoris*, Bd. 2, 20; S. 521, 29. Đû mê noldest þanc witan mînra gôda, Wulfst. 261, 10. Nâ heáge witende *non alta sapientes*, Scint. 19, 2. [He wald ha witen (witten, wist, *v. ll.*), C. M. 10793. *Goth.* witan; *prs.* wait, *pl.* witun; *p.* wissa: *O. Sax.* witan; *prs.* wêt, *pl.* witun; *p.* wissa: *O. Frs.* wita; *prs.* wêt, *pl.* witen, witath: *O. H. Ger.* wizzan; *prs.* weiz, *pl.* wizzun; *p.* wissa, wista, westa; *pp.* wizzan: *Icel.* vita; *prs.* veit, *pl.* vitu; *p.* vissa; *pp.* vitinn.] v. be-, gewitan, nytan, un-witende.

wîtan; *p.* wât, *pl.* witon; *pp.* witen. I. *to see to, take heed to, guard, keep*, (1) absolute:—God wîteþ on đam hêhstan heofna rîce ufan Alwalda, Cd. Th. 32, 31; Gen. 511. [He (*God*) witeđ and wialdeđ alle þing, Anglia i. 11, 40. Ihesu, wel þu witest hem, Jul. 51, 15. Wel is him þat wakeđ and witeđ wel him seoluen, 74, 6. Swuch wardein (*God*), þet wit and weređ us ever, A. R. 312, 8. Þe vif wittes, þet witeđ þe heorte alse wakemen, 14, 6. Wite mine Bruttes a to þines lifes, Laym. 28604. Crist ... wite his soule, Havel. 405. To witen ant to welden, Marh. 2, 23. To wyten us wyþ þan unwihte, Misc. 72, 4.] (2) with acc.:—Đæt biđ gôd swefen, wîte đû đæt georne on dînre heortan, Lchdm. iii. 154, 19. (3) with a clause:—Wîte đû georne, đæt đû dô ealle đa tâcn *vide, ut omnia ostenta facias*, Ex. 4, 21. Wîte đæt đîn geþanc ne losige, Lchdm. iii. 154, 20. Wŷte đæt đû swâ dô, Nicod. 26; Thw. 14, 23. Wîte se ôđer, đæt hê hit bête, L. C. S. 76; Th. i. 418, 13. Wê willaþ âwerian ûs; wîte gê hwæt gê dôn siđđan, L. Ælfc. P. 1; Th. ii. 364, 13. Wê beóđ unscildige, gif wê hit secgaþ eów; wîte gê hwæđer gê silfe eówrum sâwlum beorgan willan, 43; Th. ii. 382, 27. [Wite ȝe þet ȝe ȝemen þenne halie sunnedei, O. E. Homl. i. 11, 29. Cf. *Goth.* þu witeis σὺ ὄψῃ, Mt. 27, 4.] II. *to lay to* a person's *charge, lay the blame of* something on a person or thing, *impute.* (1) absolute:—Wîte *imputet*, Germ. 400, 560. (2) with dat. of person:—Đæt hê him ne wîte, Bt. proem.; Fox viii. 12. (3) with dat. of person and acc. of charge:—Mînum âgnum scyldum ic hit wîte, Ps. Th. 21, 2. Ne wîte ic him đa womcwidas, Cd. Th. 39, 7; Gen. 621. Hwæt wîtst đû ûs *what do you lay to our charge?* Bt. 7, 5; Fox 22, 36: Homl. Th. ii. 164, 28. Mê Freá wîteþ sume đara synna, Exon. Th. 456, 32; Hy. 4, 75: Salm. Kmbl. 885; Sal. 442. Hwæt wite đû mê? Soul Kmbl. 43; Seel. 22. Ic nyste hwæt hî mê witon, Ps. Th. 34, 15. Hié witan Claudiuse đone hunger, and hê wearđ him grom (*imperator conviitiis infestatus*), Ors. 6, 4; Swt. 260, 22. Ne wît đû heom đâs synna *ne statuas illis hoc peccatum*, H. R. 9, 29. Gif đû hwæt on druncen misdô, ne wît đû hit đam ealođe, Prov. Kmbl. 39: 18: 54. Gif hê hwylc hleahterlîc word onfinde, đæt hê đæt ûs ne wîte, Guthl. prol.; Gdwin. 2, 13: Ps. Th. 65, 16. Hwæþer Rômâne hit wîten nû ǣnegum men tô secganne hwæt hiera folces forwurde? Ors. 5, 2; Swt. 220, 9. Hwæt sió syn wǣre, đe him seó cwên wite, Elen. Kmbl. 832; El. 416. Ic eom swîđe gefiónde đætte gê woldon ǣnige wuht eów selfum wîtan (wiétan, Hatt. MS.), ǣr ic hit eów wite. Hit is gôd đæt gê hit nû wiétun (wîton, Hatt. MS.), Past. 31; Swt. 206, 19. Ǣfter đæm đe him swâ oftrǣdlîce mislamp, hié angunnan hit wîtan heora lâtteówum and heora cempum heora earfeþa, Ors. 4, 4; Swt. 164, 25: Cd. Th. 51, 9; Gen. 824: Hy. 6, 25; Beo. Th. 5475; B. 2741. (4) with prep. governing person, and charge expressed in a clause:—Gif đû mê on wîte, đæt ic unrihtlîce đone biscopdôm onfênge, Anglia x. 141, 22. [Gif þu witest eni þing þine sunne bute þi sulueŋ, A. R. 304, 10. Schal he hit wite me? O. and N. 1248. If that I myspeke wyte it the ale of Southwerk, Chauc. Mill. Prol. 32. Wytyn *imputo*, Prompt. Parv. 531. *O. Sax.* wîtan: *O. H. Ger.* wîzan *imputare, statuere.* Cf. *Goth.* fra-, in-weitan.] III. *to go, depart*:—Nylle ic ǣfre hionan ût wîtan, ac ic symle hêr sôfte wille standan, Met. 24, 52. [Witeđ ge awariede gastes into þat eche fir *ite maledicti in ignem eternum*, O. E. Homl. ii. 5, 36. He heđen wit, 123, 4. Þe wolf to witeþ, Laym. 21311. Herode wass witenn ut off life, Orm. 8222. Ne wite þou noȝt fra me *ne discesseris a me*, Ps. 21, 12.] v. æt-, ed-, ge-, ôþ-wîtan.

wîte, es (*a weak gen. pl.* wîtena *occurs*); *n.* I. *punishment, pain that is inflicted as punishment, torment*:—Wîte *poena* vel *supplicium*, Wrt. Voc. i. 86, 35. Tintregung *vel* wîte *tormentum*, Wülck. Gl. 178, 20. Heó (*Eve*) hæfde hire sylfre geworht đæt mǣste wîte and eallum hire cynne, ge đæt wîte wæs tô đæs strang, đæt ǣghwylc man sceolde mid sâre on đâs world cuman, and hêr on sorhgum beón, and mid sâre of gewîtan, Blickl. Homl. 5, 27: Cd. Th. 28, 6; Gen. 431. Hié (*Lot's wife*) strang begeat wîte, 155, 5; Gen. 2568. Rêđe wîte (*the deluge*), 79, 30; Gen. 1319. Wæs đæt wîte (*the destruction of Jerusalem*) swâ strang, swâ Godes geþeld ǣr mycel wæs, Blickl. Homl. 79, 27. Hwæþer đû ongite đæt ǣlc yfelwillende mon sié wîtes wyrþe? Bt. 38, 6; Fox 208, 9, 13: 39, 2; Fox 212, 25. Wŷtes, 39, 9; Fox 226, 5. Sweartne lîg werum tô wîte, Cd. Th. 153, 21; Gen. 2542: Hy. 6, 27. Hié âhôfon hine of đam hefian wîte (*crucifixion*), Rood Kmbl. 121; Kr. 61. Licgeþ lonnum fæst ..., wylleþ hine on đam wîte, Salm. Kmbl. 537; Sal. 268. Hê wîte wealdeþ *he is the disposer of punishment*, Cd. Th. 248, 33; Dan. 523. Wîte *poenam, vindictam*, Hpt. Gl. 496, 7: Blickl. Homl. 77, 28. Đæt đû inc meaht wîte bewarigan, Cd. Th. 35, 31; Gen. 563. Đû đæs cwealmes scealt wîte winnan, 62, 14; Gen. 1014. Ic wîte þolade, Exon. Th. 89, 5; Cri. 1452: 240, 25; Ph. 644: Elen. Kmbl. 1038; El. 520. Freá wolde on wǣrlogan wîte settan, Cd. Th. 76, 33; Gen. 1265. Geseah hê engles hand wrîtan Sennara wîte, 261, 17; Dan. 727. Đê sind wîtu weotud be gewyrhtum, Andr. Kmbl. 2730; An. 1367: Exon. Th. 258, 13; Jul. 264. Ne ondrǣde ic mê dômas đîne, ne đînra wîta bealo, 255, 9; Jul. 211. Hê weorna feala wîta geþolode, Andr. Kmbl. 2979; An. 1492. Manigra wîta (wiéta, Hatt. MS.) hié beóđ wyrđe, Past. 28; Swt. 190, 7. Wîtena *tormentorum, poenarum*, Hpt. Gl. 485, 10. Ne bist đû orhlŷte đæra wîtena, Homl. Th. ii. 310, 27. Wîtum *cruciatibus, poenis*, Hpt. Gl. 487, 12. Đâ heó wæs tô đâm wîtum (*ad poenam*) gelǣdd, Gen. 38, 25. Tô manegum wîtum geworht *put to many tortures*, Bt. 16, 2; Fox 52, 20. Wîtum belecgan, Andr. Kmbl. 2424; An. 1213. Mid wîtum swingan, Exon. Th. 279, 22; Jul. 617. Forniman mid wîtum, Blickl. Homl. 189, 31. Wîta *tormenta, supplicia*, Hpt. Gl. 499, 34. Wîtu, Andr. Kmbl. 2829; An. 1417. ¶ referring to the punishment of hell:—Đæt ungeendode wîte, Blickl. Homl. 25, 24: 51, 31: Andr. Kmbl. 1778; An. 891: Exon. Th. 446, 8; Dôm. 19. Is đes wǣlîca hâm, wîtes âfylled, Cd. Th. 271, 4; Sat. 100. Wîtes fŷr, Exon. Th. 39, 21; 625. Grim helle fŷr tô wîte, 78, 7; Cri. 1270. Synna tô wîte, 77, 2; Cri. 1250. In wîte bîdan, Cd. Th. 268, 1; Sat. 48. Gelǣded đe tô wîte þe tô wuldre, Blickl. Homl. 97, 22. Se gâst nimeþ æt Gode swâ wîte swâ wuldor, swâ him ǣr đæt eorđfæt geworhte, Soul Kmbl. 13; Seel. 7: Blickl. Homl. 23, 6. In êce wîte gefeallan, 57, 21. Se đæt wîte ǣr tô wrece gesette, Cd. Th. 295, 28; Sat. 494. Hê đæs ôþres sâule of wîtum generede, and of tintregum âlêsde, Blickl. Homl. 113, 33. Hê biđ mid wîtum þreád æfter his deáþe, 49, 25. On êcum wîtum wunian, 83, 18. Ic sceal weán and wîtu and wrace dreógan, Cd. Th. 276, 7; Sat. 185. I a. *a means* or *implement of punishment*:—Wundor on wîte (*the fiery furnace*) âgangen, Cd. Th. 233, 3; Dan. 270. Wîta cyn *catastarum*, Wrt. Voc. ii. 85, 58: 18, 64: 20, 34. I b. *a fine.* v. wîte-rǣden:—Sié đæt wîte .lx. scill., ođ đæt ângylde ârîse tô .xxx. scill. ... siþþan sié đæt wîte .cxx. scill., L. Alf. pol. 9; Th. i. 68, 3-5. Gilde se borh đam hlâforde his were đe his wîtes wyrđe sî, L. Eth. i. 1; Th. i. 282, 4. Se hlâford gesette .xxx. scill. tô wîte, L. In. 3; Th. i. 104, 4: 6; Th. i. 106, 7: 7; Th. i. 106, 16: 10; Th. i. 108, 10: 25; Th. i. 118, 16. Be wîte, Th. i. 118, 15: L. E. G. 3; Th. i. 168, 6. Hê âge healf đæt wîte, L. Wih. 11; Th. i. 40, 3. Gylde swâ wer swâ wîte, L. E. G. 2; Th. i. 168, 2. Gif hwâ æfter đam wîte crafige, L. C. S. 70; Th. i. 412, 24. Beó se cyng ǣlces đæra wîta wyrđe đe đa men gewyrcen đe bôcland hæbben, L. Eth. i. 1; Th. i. 282, 16. See Kemble's Saxons in England, ii. 53. II. *in a general sense, torment, plague, disease, evil, pain*:—Wîte *malum*, Wrt. Voc. ii. 58, 63. Đæt wîte geswâc *plaga cessavit*, Num. 16, 48, 46. Đis ylce wîte (*plaga*) Hibernia gelîce wæle slôh and cwylmde, Bd. 3, 27; S. 558, 19: 4, 7; S. 574, 35. Wæs đæt wîte (*famine*) tô strang, Cd. Th. 109, 8; Gen. 1819. Drihten slôh đæt folc mid swîđe micclum wîte (*plaga magna nimis*), Num. 11, 33. Of đam wîte gehǣled *sanata a plaga*, Mk. Skt. 5, 29. Ne ondrǣd đû đê deáđ tô swîđe for nânum wîte, Prov. Kmbl. 49. Ne biđ him hyra yrmđu ân tô wîte, ac đara ôþerra eád tô sorgum, Exon. Th. 79, 20; Cri. 1293. Waldend him đæt wîte (*blindness*) teóde, 336, 4; Gn. Ex. 43. God sealde gumena gehwelcum welan swâ wîte, Cd. Th. 256, 23; Dan. 645. Wîte âwinnan *to be tormented*, Exon. Th. 130, 18; Gû. 440: 441, 26; Kl. 5. Wîte lecgan on *to torment, plague*, 144, 29; Gû. 685. Syndon hyra wîta scytelum cilda onlîcost *sagittae parvulorum factae sunt plagae eorum*, Ps. Th. 63, 7. Wrađu wannhâlum wîta gehwylces, sæce and sorge, Elen. Kmbl. 2058; El. 1030. Hê monge gehǣlde hefigra wîta, Exon. Th. 155, 9; Gû. 857. Wanhâle wîtum gebundene, Andr. Kmbl. 1160; An. 580. Hê gehǣlde manega of wîtum (*plagis*), Lk. Skt. 7, 21. Sleá đê Drihten mid đâm Egiptiscan wîton *ulcere Aegypti*, Deut. 28, 27. Ic sende eall mîn wîto (*plagas*) ofer đê, Ex. 9, 14. Wê geâxiaþ ungecyndelîco wîtu, Blickl. Homl. 107, 26. Nis nô đæt ân đæt hê him ûre wîtu (*the pains that we inflict*) ne ondrǽde, 85, 15: Cd. Th. 289, 3; Sat. 392. [His wite abided on þere oðre weorlde, O. E. Homl. i. 103, 32. Mid ærmliche witen (in ȝoure bendhuse, 2nd MS.), Laym. 1046. Uppe wite of feowerti punden, 5118. *O. Sax.* wîti *punishment, torment*: *O. Frs.* wîte: *O. H. Ger.* wîzi *poena, supplicium, tormentum, passio, damnatio, judicium, crux*: *Icel.* víti *a punishment, fine.*] v. blôd-, dol-, fiht- (fyht-), fyrd- (ferd-), helle-, leger-, weard-, weorold-, wræc-wîte.

wîte-ærn, es; *n. A house of punishment, a prison*:—Wîtern *carcer*, Wrt. Voc. ii. 128, 62.

wîte-bend *a torturing bond, a prison-bond*:—Ðê wǽrlogan wîtebendum swencan môton, Andr. Kmbl. 216; An. 108. Wê ellþeódigne on carcerne clommum belegdon, wîtebendum, 3120; An. 1563.

wîte-brôga, an; *m. Penal horror, a horrid punishment* or *torment*:—Ne mê weorce sind wîtebrôgan, ðe ðû tô mê beótast, Exon. Th. 250, 31; Jul. 135. Eal ðæt man ûs foresegð embe helle wîtebrôgan (cf. Wende him God fro heuene riche into helle witerbrogen (hellewites brogen?), Chart. Th. 581, 3), Wulfst. 151, 24. Hê ðec sendeþ in ða sweartestan and ða wyrrestan wîtebrôgan, Elen. Kmbl. 1861; El. 932: Cd. Th. 3, 33; Gen. 45.

wited-lîc. v. witod-lîc.

wîte-dôm, es; *m.* I. *knowledge derived from a superhuman source, prophecy, foreknowledge*:—Wîtedôm *profetia*, Kent. Gl. 1064. Se Godes wer ðurh wîtedômes gâst (*per prophetiae spiritum*) ðone storm tôwardne foreseah, Bd. 3, 15; S. 542, 4. Ðæt heó ðurh wîtedômes gâst ða âdle forecwêde, 4, 19; S. 588, 15: 4, 28; S. 606, 20. Ðæt wundor, ðæt þurh wîtedômes cræft [hê] wiste and him cýdde, Guthl. 17; Gdwin. 70, 2. Wîtedôme *vaticinatione*, Hpt. Gl. 520, 17. Hî þurh wîtedôm eal ânemdon, Exon. Th. 104, 24; Gû. 12. II. *a statement of what is known through superhuman agency, a prophecy*:—Wæs gefylled se wîtedôm (*praesagium*) Agustinus, Bd. 2, 2; S. 504, 8: 3, 14; S. 541, 9: Blickl. Homl. 71, 3: Exon. Th. 14, 1; Cri. 212. Wæs se wîtedôm beforan sungen, Elen. Kmbl. 2304; El. 1153. Æfter ðam wîtedôme *secundum vaticinium* (*prophetiam*), Hpt. Gl. 493, 48. Æfter Esaias wîtedôme, Bd. 3, 23; S. 554, 22. Gehýraþ wîtedôm Iôbes gieddinga, Exon. Th. 234, 31; Ph. 548. Wîtedômas *oracula*, Hpt. Gl. 409, 50. Wîtedôma ł godcundra sprêca *oraculorum*, 442, 36. Mid wîtedômas *presago*, Wrt. Voc. ii. 66, 32. v. *next word, and* cf. wîteg-dôm.

wîtedôm-lîc; *adj. Of superhuman knowledge, prophetical*:—Wîtedômlîc wundor *a miracle which displayed a knowledge communicated by God* (cf. him God ealle ða dîglan þingc cûð gedyde, l. 12), Guthl. 11; Gdwin. 54, 1. Gûðlâc wîtedômlîce gâste (*in prophetic spirit*) weóx, and hê ða tôweardan mannum cýdde swâ cûðlîce swâ ða andweardan, 13; Gdwin. 60, 19. Wîtedômlîce mûðe hê sang, 4; Gdwin. 28, 19.

wîte-fæst; *adj. In slavery as a punishment for crime.* v. wîteþeów:—Hê wyle ðæt man freóge æfter his dæge ǽlcne wîtefæstne man ðe on his tîman forgylt wǽre *si quis, secundum patriae Anglie morem, in aliquam incurrisset servitutem tempore sue potestatis, libertate sibi penitus contributa, relaxatus ejus jussu est*, Chart. Th. 551, 14. Ic gean ðæt man gefreóge ǽlcne wîtefæstne man ðe ic on sprǽce âhte, 557, 21.

wîtega, an; *m.* I. *a wise man, one who has knowledge*:—Hê is wîtgan (cf. *the epithets applied to Simon*, eald ǽwita, 907; El. 455, guma gehðum frôd, 1059; El. 531, *and the whole passage in which these forms occur*) sunu, Elen. Kmbl. 1181; El. 592. Swâ ûs gefreogun gleáwe wîtgan þurh wîsdôm on gewritum cýþaþ, Exon. Th. 199, 23; Ph. 30. II. *one who has knowledge from a superhuman source*, (1) *a prophet*:—Wîtega *propheta* vel *vates*, Wrt. Voc. i. 41, 69: *propheta*, 71, 68. (1 a) in the biblical sense:—Swâ se wîtega sang, Menol. Fox 119; Men. 59. Wîtga, Exon. Th. 41, 4; Cri. 650: 316, 18; Môd. 50. Se wîtiga (*the Psalmist*; v. Ps. 28, 3) cwæð, Fragm. Kmbl. 13; Leás. 8. Ođ ðæt wîtga cwom, Daniel tô dôme, Cd. Th. 225, 5; Dan. 149. Wîtga (*Isaiah*), Exon. Th. 19, 26; Cri. 306. Iônas tâcn ðæs wîtegan (*prophetae*), Mt. Kmbl. 12, 39. On ðæs wîtegan bêc Isaiam, Mk. Skt. 1, 2. Sunu Dauides wîtgan (*Nathan the prophet*) lârum getimbrede tempel, Cd. Th. 202, 19; Exod. 390. Ðæt fram Drihtne gecweden wæs þurh ðone wîtegan (wîtgo, Lind., witgu. Rush.), Mt. Kmbl. 1, 22: 2, 15. Twelf wîtegan syndon ðe twelf bêc âwriton . . . Wǽron eác ôðre wîtegan ðe ne writon nâne bêc, Ælfc. T. Grn. 10, 8, 28. 'Eówre wîtgan (*prophetae*) eów wîtgodon dysig' . . . Ða gôdan lâreówas beóð oft genemnede on hâlgum gewritum wiétgan (wîtgan, Cott. MSS.), for ðæm hié gereccaþ ðis andwearde lîf fleónde and ðæt tôwearde gesweotoligeaþ, Past. 15; Swt. 91, 3-7. Wîtigan, Cd. Th. 293, 26; Sat. 460: Blickl. Homl. 105, 9. Ðæt in fyrndagum wîtegan sǽdon, 293, 32; Sat. 464. Ða wîtigan þrý (*Abraham, Isaac, and Jacob*), Andr. Kmbl. 1602; An. 802. Hû on woruld ǽr wîtgan sungon, gâsthâlige guman, be Godes bearne, Elen. Kmbl. 1119; El. 561: Exon. Th. 5, 3; Cri. 64. Ǽ and wîtegena bebod (wîtgas ł wîtgo, Lind., wîtgu, Rush.) *lex et prophete*, Mt. Kmbl. 7, 12. Wîtgena word, Exon. Th. 29, 27; Cri. 469. Heáhfædera nân, ne wîtgena, 273, 12; Jul. 515. Siteþ Waldend mid wîtegum, Cd. Th. 301, 25; Sat. 587. Nê wê sweotul tâcen ûs geseóð ǽnig, ne wê wîtegan habbaþ, ðæt ûs andgytes mâ secgen, Ps. Th. 73, 9. (2) *a wise man, diviner, soothsayer*:—Wîtgan, Caldêa cyn, Cd. Th. 218, 19; Dan. 41. Andswarode cyning wîtgum sînum (*the wise men of Babylon, the magicians, and the astrologers, and the sorcerers, and the Chaldeans*, Dan. 2, 2, 12), 224, 13; Dan. 135. Uuîtgan *divinos*, Wrt. Voc. ii. 106, 57: 25, 42: *divinos, ariolos*, 141, 55. III. applied to things, *a presage*:—Ǽtýwdon twêgen steorran . . . Hî wîtegan (*praesagae*) wǽron grimmes wæles, Bd. 5, 23; S. 645, 26. Wîtegum *praesagminibus*, Hpt. Gl. 448, 64. [Dauid þe halie witeȝe, O. E. Homl. i. 43, 16. Se witiȝe, 233, 12. Ðe lordew þe tehte Salemon and alle wise witege here wisdom, ii. 83, 36. Dauid þe witeȝe, H. M. 5, 2. Teilesin heo heolten for witie, Laym. 9094. Merlin þe witeȝe, 17415. Tweolue of þine witiȝn, of þine wisuste monnen, 4368. He þeos word seide þurh an of his witeȝen *propheta clamabat dicens*, Kath. 483. *O. H. Ger.* wîzago *propheta*; *pitho, divinus, ariolus.*] v. deófol-, tungol-wîtega.

wîteg-dôm, es; *m.* I. *prophecy*:—Ðæt sié gefylled wîtigdôm (*prophetia*) Essaies, Mt. Kmbl. Rush. 13, 14. Ðæt uîtgadôm and allra canône cuido ða ðe ymb Cristes ðroung âcueden uæs ł wêron, Jn. Skt. Lind. 19, 30 margin. II. *divination*:—Ne meahte seó manigeo þurh wîtigdôm wihte âþencean, ne âhicgan, Cd. Th. 224, 34; Dan. 146. [*O. H. Ger.* wîzag-tuom *prophetia, divinatio.*] Cf. wîte-dôm, wîtegung.

wîtege, an; *f. A prophetess*:—Anna ðió wîtga *Anna prophetissa*, Lk. Skt. Lind. Rush. 2, 36. [*O. H. Ger.* wîzaga *prophetissa.*] v. wîtegestre.

wîte-geard (?), es; *m. A place of punishment*:—Wîtehûses ł wyerteardes (wîtegeardes?) *amphitheatri*, Hpt. Gl. 484, 47.

wîtegend-lîc; *adj. Prophetic*:—Ic (*Elisha*) bidde ðê (*Elijah*), ðæt ic beó âfylled mid ðam wîtegendlîcum gâste ðe on ðê nû wunaþ, Homl. Skt. i. 18, 282. Ðæt cild on his môdor innoðe . . . mid wîtigendlîcre fægnunge getâcnode ðone tôcyme ûres Âlýsendes, Homl. Th. i. 352, 28. Hî wiston ða tôwerdan ðing, and mid wîtigendlîcere gyddunge bododon, 540, 25.

wîtegestre, an; *f. A prophetess*:—Anna wæs wîtegystre (*prophetissa*), Lk. Skt. 2, 36. Týn mǽdena wǽron on hǽðenum folcum, ðe man hêt Sibillas, ðæt synd wîtegestran, and hî wîtegodon ealle be Criste, Ælfc. T. Grn. 10, 31.

wîtegian, wîtgian; *p.* ode *To prophesy*, (1) absolute:—Ðâ hig wîtegodon (*prophetarent*), ðâ arn ân cnapa and cwæð: 'Eldad and Meldad wîtegiaþ (*prophetant*),' Num. 11, 27. Wîtigaþ, Cd. Th. 246, 16; Dan. 480. Wîtgas, Mt. Kmbl. p. 7, 10. Zacharias wæs mid hâlegum gâste âfylled and hê wîtegode (*prophetauit*), Lk. Skt. 1, 67: Num. 23, 8. Hû ne wîtegode wê on ðînum naman? Mt. Kmbl. 7, 22. Ealle wîtegan wîtegudun (wîtgadun, Rush.) ôð Iôhannes, 11, 13. Mid wîtegiende mûðe, Guthl. 5; Gdwin. 36, 19. (2) with an object, (a) an accusative:—Ðæt hê him wîtgode wyrda geþingu, Cd. Th. 250, 13; Dan. 546. 'Eówre wîtgan eów wîtgodan dysig' . . . Hié scolden leásunga wîtgian, Past. 15; Swt. 91, 3-8. Hié eal, ðæt tôweard wæs, beforan wîtgodan, Blickl. Homl. 161, 15. Se swêg wæs þurh wîtgan wîtgod, 133, 31. (b) with a clause:—Hê wîtgode, ðæt se Hǽlend sceolde sweltan for ðære þeóde, Jn. Skt. 11, 51. Hê wîtgode suâ suâ hit geweorðan sceolde, Past. 1; Swt. 29, 11. Wîtigan wîtigodan, ðæt se wolde cuman, Blickl. Homl. 105, 9. Wîtga (*prophetiza*) ûs, huâ is se ðe ðec ofslôg, Mt. Kmbl. Lind. 26, 68. (c) with constructions of (a) and (b):—Heora fæderas ðæt wîtgodan, ðæt him God wolde sendan his sunu, Blickl. Homl. 177, 10. (3) with a preposition:—Anna wîtegode be him . . . swâ hâlig wîf wæs ðæs wyrðe, ðæt heó môste wîtigian embe Crist, Homl. Th. i. 146, 27-29. Hê wîtgode be ðære âcennednesse Cristes, Ps. Th. 8, arg.: Blickl. Homl. 133, 28. Wîtgade, 83, 24. Wîtegan ðe wîtegodon ymbe Crist, Ælfc. T. Grn. 2, 18. [Þis witeȝede Dauid . . . þis he witeȝede bi Drihtene, O. E. Homl. i. 7, 13-15. Minna bern sculen witeȝan, 91, 5. *O. Frs.* wîtgia: *O. H. Ger.* wîzagôn *prophetare, vaticinari, auguriari, divinare.*] v. fore-, ge-wîtegian.

wîtegung, e; *f.* I. *prophecy*:—Ân ðæra gecýdde Cristes tôcyme mid sealmsange, and ôðer mid wîtegunge. Sind sealmsang and wîtegung, swylce hî syflinge wǽron . . . tô ðâm fîf ǽlîcum bôcum, Homl. Th. i. 188, 19. Ðâ wæs gefylled Hieremias wîtegung, ðe ðus wîtegode, 80, 18. Esaias wîtegung (wîtgiung *prophetia*, Lind.), Mt. Kmbl. 13, 14. Wîtgiung, p. 16, 15. In stefne wîtgeonges *in uoce prophetiae*, Mk. Skt. p. 1, 8. Swâ swâ Isaias se wîtega hit on bêc sette on his wîtegunge, Ælfc. T. Grn. 2, 22. II. *divination*:—Þurh eorþan wîtegung *geomantia*, Wrt. Voc. ii. 42, 23. Þurh deáþes wîtgung *nicromantia*, 62, 30. [He ȝifð summe witegunge, O. E. Homl. i. 97, 19. All þatt witeȝhunnge þatt hallȝhe witess writenn, Orm. 15149. *O. H. Ger.* wîzagunga *divinatio, vaticinium, auspicium.*] v. fore-wîtegung.

wîtegung-bôc; *f. A book containing prophecies, a prophetical book*:—Hit is âwriten be mê on wîtegungbôcum, Homl. Skt. ii. 24, 115. Ic geliornod hæbbe on eówer wîtegungbôcum, ðæt gê wǽron fram frymðe gecorene fram Criste selfum, H. R. 7, 11, 30.

wîte-hrægel, es; *n. A garment worn as a punishment, sackcloth*:—Ic mîne gewǽda on wîtehrægl cyrde *posui vestimentum meum cilicium*, Ps. Th. 68, 11.

wîte-hûs, es; *n. A house of punishment* or *torment*, (1) *a prison*:—Wîtehûsa *ergastulorum*, Hpt. Gl. 516, 8. (2) *an amphitheatre* in which the Christians were martyred:—Wîtehûses *amphitheatri*, Hpt. Gl. 484, 47. On wîtehûse *in amphitheatrum* (the passage is: In amphitheatrum sanctos ferreis collariis connexos cruentus carnifex imperat duci, Ald. 49, 489, 69. (3) *hell*:—Hé héht ðæt wítehús wræcna (*the fallen angels*) bídan, Cd. 3, 21; Gen. 39: 304, 11; Sat. 628. On wráþra wíc . . ., on wítehús, Exon. Th. 94, 7; Cri. 1536.

wíte-lác, es; *n. Punishment, torment, pain*:—Wurdon tó axan eorðan wæstma, efne swá wíde swá ða wítelác (*the burning and terror at the destruction of Sodom and Gomorrah*) gerǽhton, Cd. Th. 154, 12; Gen. 2554. Weras básnedon wíteloccas (wíteláces, Grn.) weán under weallum, 146, 5; Gen. 2417.

wíte-leás; *adj. Not having to pay a fine*:—Gelǽste ǽlc wuduwe ða heregeata binnan twelf mónðum, búton hire ǽr tó onhagige, wíteleás, L. C. S. 74; Th. i. 416, 18.

wítend-líc *prophetic*. v. wítiend-líc.

witendlíce; *adv. Surely, certainly*:—Witendlíce hé getrymde ymbhwyrft eorðan *etenim firmavit orbem terrae*, Ps. Spl. 92, 2: 40, 10: 88, 6. Cf. witodlíce.

witer, witter; *adj. Knowing, wise*:—Hé wíslíce hine beþóhte, swá hé full witter wæs, Chr. 1067; Erl. 204, 35. [Heo wes witer, heo wes wis, Laym. 9600. Þeo weoren þa alre witereste þe wuneden on Bruttene, 15204. Full witerr takenn *a manifest token*, Orm. 4013. Wurð ðe child witter and war, Gen. and Ex. 1308. Wex he witter and wyse, Alex. Skt. 629. *Icel.* vitr *wise*.]

wíte-rǽden[n], e; *f.* I. *punishment*:—Ðes cyning bebeád ðæt feówertiglíce fæsten healden beón ǽr Eástrum be wíterǽdenne *jejunium quadraginta dierum observari praecepit . . . in transgressores dignas et competentes punitiones proposuit*, Bd. 3, 8; S. 531, 11. II. *fine*. v. wíte, I b:—Ut sit tuta . . . regalibus tributis majoribus et minoribus, sive taxationibus quod nos dicimus wíteréden, Cod. Dip. B. ii. 84, 7. Ego Túnburht episcopus aliquam partem terrae donabo liberam ab omnibus terrenis difficultatibus omnium gravitudinum . . . a taxationibus quod dicimus wíterédenne, Cod. Dip. Kmbl. v. 121, 25. Bíde mon mid ðære wíterǽdenne óþ ðæt se wér gegolden sié, L. In. 71; Th. i. 148, 4. Náh hé ðǽr náne wíterǽdenne *he cannot exact any fines*, 50; Th. i. 134, 4.

wíte-scræf, es; *n. A den of torment, hell*:—Gewít ðú áwyrgda in ðæt wítescræf, Cd. Th. 308, 12; Sat. 691.

wíte-steng, es; *m. A pole used for punishment* or *torture*:—Wítestengces, róde *eculei*, wítestenges *eculei, gabuli*, Hpt. Gl. 478, 70–73: Anglia xiii. 34, 169. v. þrípel.

wíte-stów, e; *f. A place of punishment* or *torment, hell*:—Upp cómon sume ðara ðýstra gásta of ðære neowolnesse and of ðære wítestówe (*de abysso illa flammivoma*), Bd. 5, 12; S. 628, 41. Nis hér (*in hell*) nú nǽnig wóp, swá hit ǽr gewunelíc wæs on ðisse wítestówe, Blickl. Homl. 85, 29.

wíte-swinge, an; *f. A stroke given as a punishment, chastisement*:—Ongæt gumena aldor hwæt him Waldend wræc wíteswingum, Cd. Th. 112, 2; Gen. 1864.

wíte-þeów, es; *m. One who had been condemned to slavery for crime*, or *from inability to pay the fines incurred for violation of the law*. For cases which involved loss of freedom, v. þeów. (1) literal:—Gif hwelc man biþ wíteþeów (or *adj.*? v. next word) níwan geþeówad, L. In. 48; Th. i. 132, 7. (2) figurative, *one in hell*:—Bring ús hǽlo líf wérigum wíteþeówum, Exon. Th. 10, 12; Cri. 151.

wíte-þeów; *adj. In slavery as a consequence of crime*:—Be wíteðeówes monnes slege. Gif wíteþeów Englisc mon hine forstalie, hó hine mon, L. In. 24; Th. i. 118, 6. Gif ðǽr hwylc wíteðeów man sý ðe hió geðeówede, hió gelýfð tó hyre bearnon ðæt hí hine willon lýhtan for hyre sáulle, Cod. Dip. Kmbl. vi. 132, 8. Wíteþeówne monnan Wyliscne mon sceal bedrífan be twelf hídum tó swingum, L. In. 54; Th. i. 138, 3. Ic wullan ðæt man gefreógen ǽlcne wíteðeówne man on ǽlcum ðæra landæ ðæ ic mínon freóndon bæcwedden hæbbæ, Cod. Dip. Kmbl. iii. 128, 10. Ðæt man freóge on ǽlcum túnæ ǽlcne wítæþeównæ mann ðæ undær hiræ geðeówuð wæs, 360, 6. Ðis is Ælfsiges biscopes cwide. Ðæt is ǽrest, ðæt ic wille ðæt man gefreóge ǽlcne wíteþeówne mannan ðe on ðam biscopríce sié for hine and for his cynehláford, Cod. Dip. B. ii. 329, 17: L. Ath. i. proem.; Th. i. 198, 9. Wéron ðǽr þreó wíteþeówe men and þreó þeówberde, Cod. Dip. Kmbl. v. 152, 8. Be wíteðeówum mannum, L. In. 48; Th. i. 132, 6. Cf. wíte-fæst, and see Kemble's Saxons in England, i. 200, Grmm. R. A. 328.

wítga-dóm, wítgian. v. wíteg-dóm, wítegian.

wiþ; *prep.* (*adv. conj.*). I. with gen. (1) determining the direction of motion or action, (a) marking an object towards which motion is directed, *towards, to, in the direction of*:—Wende hé hine west wið Exanceastres, Chr. 894; Erl. 91, 10. Rád út wið Lygtúnes, 917; Erl. 102, 16. Hé áfaren wæs wiþ þara scipa, Ors. 6, 36; Swt. 292, 30. On ðone ealdan weg wið hwítan stanes, Cod. Dip. Kmbl. ii. 29, 5. Fleógan wið ðæs holtes, Byrht. Th. 131, 14; By. 8. Wið ðæs fæstengeates folc onette, Judth. Thw. 23, 38; Jud. 162: 25, 7; Jud. 248. Hé irneþ wið his eardes, Met. 5, 15. Heó stígþ wiþ hire uprynæs, Bt. 25; Fox 88, 27. Hé him bebeád, swá hié feohtan angunnen, ðæt hié wið his flugen, Ors. 3, 7; Swt. 116, 28. Hé wið ðæs beornes stóp, Byrht. Th. 135, 41; By. 131. Líget fleáh wið ðæs hǽðenan folces, Homl. Th. i. 504, 29. Ðæt wolcn leát wið his and hine genam fram heora gesihðum, 296, 2. Ðá se hálga wer ne com, ðá cómon hí eft wið his (*they made their way to him*), ii. 172, 22. Sum fǽmne ásende wið his, 506, 6. Hí ásendan twégen weras wið his (tó him, *v. l.*), Homl. Skt. i. 10, 61. Ne gemét hé hine, ne rihtne weg wiþ his ne áredaþ, Bt. 33, 3; Fox 128, 2. (b) marking an object towards which an action is directed, *towards, to, at*:—Hé hnáh tó eorðan, áleát wið ðæs engles (*he bowed to the angel*), Num. 22, 31: Homl. Th. i. 120, 2. Hí luton wið heora, 38, 21. Gríp wið ðæs grundes *clutch at the bottom*, Cd. Th. 308, 31; Sat. 701. Se lég lǽhte wið ðes láþan, 309, 25; Sat. 716. Beseah hé hine underbæc wiþ ðæs wífes, Bt. 35, 6; Fox 170, 14: Cd. Th. 154, 29; Gen. 2563. (c) marking the object of an operation, purpose, aim, feeling, *with, towards, to, at, against*:—Gif gebyrige ðæt heora hwilc wið úre bige habban wille (*wants to come to us to buy*), oþþe wé wið heora, L. A. G. 5; Th. i. 156, 3. Hé beseah wið mín *respexit me*, Ps. Th. 39, 1. Hé wrigaþ wiþ his gecyndes, Bt. 25; Fox 88, 24, 28: Met. 13, 67. Wiþ ðæs, ic wát, ðú wilt higian, Bt. 11, 2; Fox 34, 7. Mé wǽre liófre ðæt ic onette wiþ ðæs, ðæt ic ðé móste gelǽstan ðæt ic ðé ǽr gehét *festino debitum promissionis absolvere*, 40, 5; Fox 240, 16. Hwí murcnast ðú wið mín? 7, 3; Fox 20, 3. Deófles anda bið ástyred wið ðín, Homl. Skt. ii. 30, 115. (2) marking position, *over against, opposite to*:—Sætt se Hǽlend wið (*contra*) ðæs dores, Mk. Skt. Lind. 12, 41. (3) marking an object against which there is protection, *against, from*:—Hé hié wið ðæs héhstan brógan gefriðode, Judth. Thw. 21, 3; Jud. 4. Wið hungres hleó, Elen. Kmbl. 1228; El. 616. Wið yfela gefreó ús feónda gehwylces, Hy. 6, 31. II. with dat. (1) marking local relations, (a) proximity, *by, near, against, beside*:—Æt Alre, and ðæt is wiþ Æþelingga eige, Chr. 878; Erl. 80, 22. Hire líchama resteþ wið Rómebirig on ðam wege ðe man nemneþ Latina, Shrn. 31, 28. Sǽweall uplang gestód wið Israhélum, Cd. Th. 197, 8; Exod. 303. (b) extension, *unto*:—Wið wolcnum *usque ad nubes*, Ps. Th. 56, 12. (c) contact, *at, against*:—Heald wiþ wǽtan (or acc.?), Lchdm. ii. 150, 7. Him on hreþre langað beorn wið blóde (*burnt against the blood, heated his blood*?), Beo. Th. 3764; B. 1880. (d) collision or impact, *with, against, on*:—Scearp cymeþ sceó wiþ óþrum, ecg wið ecge, Exon. Th. 385, 8; Rä. 4, 41. Ic hnítan sceal hearde wið heardum, 497, 23; Rä. 87, 5. Streámas wundon sund wið sande, Beo. Th. 431; B. 213. Hé wið áttorsceaðan oreðe gerǽsde (*rushed and met the breath*), 5670; B. 2839: Cd. Th. 126, 14; Gen. 2095. Hire wið halse heard grápode, Beo. Th. 3136; B. 1566. Mid grápe fón wið feónde *to lay hands on the foe*, 882; B. 439. Ne sceal mon nó mid openlíce edwíte him wið sleán *non aperta exprobratione sunt feriendi*, Past. 40; Swt. 295, 11. (e) confronting, *over against, opposite*:—Ongan ic steppan forð ána wið englum *I stepped forth and alone confronted the angels*, Cd. Th. 280, 1; Sat. 249. Be norðan is se sǽ, ðe ǽgþer is ge nearo ge hreóh wið Italia ðam lande (*opposite Italy*), Ors. 1, 1; Swt. 28, 12. (f) obstruction, *against, in the way of*:—Bordrand onswáf wið ðam gryregieste, Beo. Th. 5113; B. 2560. (2) marking association, combination, *with*. v. III. 2:—Gesweotula ðín sylfes weorc, and forlǽt weall wið wealle (*let wall join with wall*), Exon. Th. 1, 20; Cri. 11. Hé teofanade ǽghwylc wiþ óþrum, 349, 10; Sch. 44. Sand is geblonden, grund wið greóte, Andr. Kmbl. 849; An. 425. Mengan lyge wið sóðe, leóht wið þýstrum, Elen. Kmbl. 613; El. 307. Hí wið mánfullum mengdan þeóde *commisti sunt inter gentes*, Ps. Th. 105, 26. Swá gǽð þeóstru wið leóhte *sicut tenebrae ejus, ita et lumen ejus*, 138, 11. Ðá bæd heó hire wer ðæt hé wið hire wylne týman sceolde, Boutr. Scrd. 22, 23. (3) marking separation, *with* (as in part *with*), *from*. v. III. 3; and see wiþ-faran, -ferian, -lǽdan:—Tósceádene mid Tréntan streáme wiþ Norþ-Myrcum *discreti fluvio Treanta ab Aquilonalibus Mercis*, Bd. 3, 24; S. 557, 37. Hé gesundrode leóht wið þeóstrum, sceade wið scíman, Cd. Th. 8, 21; Gen. 127: 10, 27; Gen. 163. Hwonne se dæg cume ðe hé sceole wið ðæm líchomon hine gedǽlon, Blickl. Homl. 97, 20. Gedǽlan líf wið líce, Beo. Th. 4837; B. 2423: Apstls. Kmbl. 73; Ap. 37. Nó hé hine wið monna miltse gedǽlde, Exon. Th. 122, 7; Gú. 302: 146, 18; Gú. 711. Swá nó man scyle his gástes lufan wið Gode dǽlan, Cd. Th. 217, 12; Dan. 21. Ðam ðe his gást wile meltan wið morðre, mergan of sorge, ásceádan of scyldum, Salm. Kmbl. 111; Sal. 55. (4) marking exchange or return, (a) buying (lit. or fig.), marking the object for which a price is paid, *for, in return for, as payment for*:—Abraham sealde feówer hund scillinga seolfres wið ðæm æcere and wið ðam scræfe, Gen. 23, 16: Chart. Th. 232, 13. Twá and twéntig þúsend punda goldes and seolfres mon gesealde ðam here of Ængla-lande wið friðe, L. Eth. ii. 7; Th. i. 288, 12. Cantware him feoh gehéton wiþ ðam friþe, Chr. 865; Erl. 70, 33. Sendan beágas wið gebeorge, Byrht. Th. 132, 44; By. 31. Ðá beád hé ealle his ǽhta wiþ his feore, Bt. 29, 2; Fox 104, 21. Ðæt mihte beón geboden wið clǽnum legere, Chart. Th. 208, 30. Hé sealde ǽlcon ǽnne penig wið hys dæges worce, Mt. Kmbl. 20, 2. Hé bæd ðæt hé him ðǽs siiþfætes látteów wǽre, and him mycel feoh wið ðon gebeád, Bd. 4, 5; S. 571, 35. (b) selling (lit. or fig.), marking the payment which is received, *for, in consideration of*:—Hwí ne sealde heó ðás sealfe wiþ þrím hundred penegon? *quare hoc ungentum non uenit trecentis denariis?* Jn. Skt. 12, 5. Hí him ðæt land sealdon wiþ .iii. pundon, Chart. Erl. 235, 27. Hé gesealde wiþ feó heofones Hlāford, Blickl. Homl. 69, 13: Chr. 1036; Erl. 164, 34. Ðæt nān preóst ne dō his hālgan þēnunge wiþ sceattum, L. Ælfc. C. 27; Th. ii. 352, 18: Cd. Th. 262, 14; Dan. 744. Wiđ đam golde griđ fæstnian, Byrht. Th. 132, 52; By. 35. Gē ne rēccaþ þeáh hweþer gē āuht tō gode dōn wiþ ǽnegum ōþrum þingum būton wiđ đam lytlan lofe đæs folces and wiþ đam scortan hlīsan, Bt. 18, 4; Fox 66, 21. Ðȳ læs men wēnan đæt đū nāne treówe næbbe būton wiđ hlīsan (*unless you can get reputation for it*), Prov. Kmbl. 76. (c) exchanging (lit. or fig.), *for, in exchange for*:—Đes landes boec đet Edelbearht cyning sealde his đegne wiđ ōđrum suē miclum lande, Cod. Dip. Kmbl. ii. 66, 17. Se đe ealle his ǽhta·behwyrfde wiđ ānum gyldenum wecge, Homl. Th. i. 394, 12. (d) redemption, *for*:—Beád Darius healf his rīce wiþ đǣm wīfmonnum, Ors. 3, 9; Swt. 126, 7. (e) reward or requital, *for, in reward of, in return for*:—Ic sylle Wulfsige wiđ his holdum mægene and eádmōdre hērnesse ānes hīdes lond, Cod. Dip. B. ii. 268, 8. Forþ gewāt đurh martyrdōm Laurentius; hæfþ nū līf wiþ đan mid Wuldorfæder weorca tō leáne, Menol. Fox 290; Men. 146. Hī mē yfel settan ā wiđ goode *posuerunt adversum me mala pro bonis*, Ps. Th. 108, 4. (f) reply, *in answer to*:—Suwade Crist wiđ đæs wīfes clypunge, Homl. Th. ii. 182, 7. (g) compensation, *for, as compensation for*. v. III. 4:—Sylle līf wiđ (*pro*) līfe, tōđ wiđ tēđ, hand wiđ handa, fōt wiđ fēt . . . lǣl wiđ lǣle, Ex. 21, 23–25. Gif hwā forstele ōđres sceáp . . . selle feówer sceáp wiđ ānum. Gif hē næbbe hwæt hē selle, sié hē self beboht wiđ đam fió, L. Alf. 24; Th. i. 50, 15. (h) where the condition, in consideration of which something takes place, is given, *in consideration of, in return for, on condition of*:—Hit Scipia nolde him āliéfan wiđ nānum ōþrum þinge būtan hié him ealle hiera wǣpeno āgeáfen *Scipio would not grant it them on any other condition than that of giving up all their weapons to him*, Ors. 4, 13; Swt. 210, 20. Ǽlces mannes þeówetlingas đa đrȳ dagas weorces beón gefreóde wiđ cyricsōcne, and wiđ đam đe hȳ đæt fæsten đe lustlīcor gefæsten, Wulfst. 171, 20: 181, 19. ¶ wiþ đam đe *or* đæt, *introducing a clause that contains the condition or consideration*:—Sende hē ǽrendracan tō him and mycel feoh wiþ đon đe hē hine ofslōge *misit nuncios, qui Redualdo pecuniam multam pro nece ejus offerrent*, Bd. 2, 12; S. 513, 9. Se cāsere him beád gold and seolfor wiđ đon đe hȳ forlēton Cristes geleáfan, Shrn. 134, 5. Hē cwæđ đæt hē heom hold hlāford beón wolde, . . . wiđ đam đe hī ealle tō him gecyrdon, Chr. 1014; Erl. 150, 12: L. O. 1; Th. i. 178, 7. Nolde hē syllan ealle his ǽhta, wiđ đan đe hē libban mōste? Homl. Skt. i. 12, 118. Hē forlǣt manigne woruldlust, wiþ đam đe hē đone welan begite, Bt. 33, 2; Fox 124, 2. Hwelc wīte sceal ūs tō hefig đyncan, wiđ đæm đe wē mægen geearnian đone hefenlīcan ēđel? Past. 36; Swt. 255, 3. Hū micle suīđor sculon wē beón gehiérsume, wiđ đæm đæt wē mōten libban on ēcnesse, 255, 9. Hē wolde ungerīm feós syllan, wiđ đam, gif hē hit gebicgan mihte, đæt hē hēr lybban mōste, Homl. Skt. i. 12, 102. (5) marking balance, counterpoise, *against* (as in to set one thing *against* another), *as a set-off*. v. III. 5:—Swelce hié setten đa synne wiđ đære ælmessan, Past. 45; Swt. 341, 20. (6) marking comparison, *by the side of, compared with*. v. III. 6:—Hwæt is ǽnig lāc wiđ đisum willan? Homl. Th. i. 584, 10. Nǽre đeós blis đe gelīcre đære ēcean myrhđe, đonne biđ đam menn đe sit on cwearterne, wiđ đam menn đe færđ frig geond land, Homl. Skt. i. 12, 109. (7) marking contrast, *in contrast with*:—Wiþ đon *e contrario*, Bd. 5, 13; S. 633, 34: 5, 14; S. 634, 42. (8) marking address, *with, to*. v. III. 7:—Drihten wiđ Abrahame spræc, Cd. Th. 139, 2; Gen. 2303. Reordode rīces hyrde wiđ đære fǣmnan fæder, Exon. Th. 246, 25; Jul. 67. Hyre se wræcmæcga wiđ þingade, 258, 5; Jul. 260. Him Andreas wiđ mǣlde, Andr. Kmbl. 598; An. 299. Wē habbaþ word gearu wiđ đam ǣglǣcan, 2717; An. 1361. Ne heó wiþ monnum sprǣce hafaþ, Exon. Th. 421, 3; Rä. 40, 10. (9) marking dealing, *with*. v. III. 8:—Hǣþen here genāmon friþ wiþ Cantwarum, Chr. 865; Erl. 70, 32: Ors. 3, 5; Swt. 106, 22. (10) marking hostility, *with, against, to*. v. III. 14:—Hē feaht and won wiþ his ēþle (*contra patriam*), Bd. 3, 24; S. 556, 28: Exon. Th. 398, 1–2; Rä. 17, 1. Hī gefuhton wiþ hǣþnum herige, Chr. 853; Erl. 68, 17. Hié gefuhtun wiþ Walum (Walas, MS. E.). 495; Erl. 14, 11. Holm won wiđ winde, Beo. Th. 2268; B. 1132: Cd. Th. 5, 26; Gen. 77. Hilde gefremman wiþ ealdfeóndum, Exon. Th. 35, 32; Cri. 567. Wǣpen āhebban wiđ hetendum, Elen. Kmbl. 35; El. 18. Wiđ firenum in gefeoht gearo, Exon. Th. 298, 24; Crä. 90. Hē honda ārǣrde wiđ đam herge, Cd. Th. 4, 9; Gen. 51. Hē wiđ đam wyrme gewegan sceolde, Beo. Th. 4791; B. 2400. Se wiđ mongum stōd, Exon. Th. 121, 26; Gū. 294. Swincan wiđ synnum, 150, 21; Gū. 782. For đære synne đe hē wiđ Sarran gefremede, Cd. Th. 166, 4; Gen. 2742: Elen. Kmbl. 831; El. 416. Hié wiđ Godes bearne nīđ āhōfon, 1671; El. 837. Wē wiđ Gode oft ābylgeaþ, Hy. 6, 21. Hié him ondrǣden wiđ (for, Cott. MSS.) hiera wordum and dǣdum hiera gefērena tǣlinge, Past. 38; Swt. 273, 7. Hospcwide fremman wiđ Godes bearne, Elen. Kmbl. 1048; El. 525: Andr. Kmbl. 1120; An. 560. Wæs yrre fæder wiđ dehter, Exon. Th. 251, 7; Jul. 141. Gōd sceal wyđ yfele, Menol. Fox 561; Gn. C. 50. Hē him đǣr wiþ gefeaht, Chr. 871; Erl. 74, 8. Ðæt hī him wiþ ne winnan, Bt. 41, 5; Fox 254, 1. Ðæt mīgtigra wīte wealdeþ, đonne hē him wiđ mæge, Cd. Th. 249, 1; Dan. 523. (11) marking friendly relation, *with, for*, v. III. 15:—Hē forget đone freóndscipe wiđ Israhēle, Past. 54; Swt. 423, 17. Hié wiđ Rōmānum (-e, *v.l.*) sibbe heóldon *civitatem amicam populi Romani*, Ors. 4, 8; Swt. 186, 3. Hwæt is mannes sunu đæt hit gemet wǣre, đæt đū him aht wiđ hæfdest (*that thou shouldst have consideration for him*; quoniam reputas eum), Ps. Th. 143, 4. (12) marking protection, defence, salvation, *against, from, for*. v. III. 16:—Ic đē wiđ weána gehwam wreó and scylde, Cd. Th. 131, 2; Gen. 2170: Exon. Th. 47, 27; Cri. 761. Ðū eart gescyldend wiđ sceađan wǣpnum, Andr. Kmbl. 2584; An. 1293. Wiđ ælfylcum ēþelstōlas healdan, Beo. Th. 4731; B. 2371: 6000; B. 3004. Ealle đa wōcre đe hē wiđ wætre belcác, Cd. Th. 85, 4; Gen. 1049. Gefæstnod wiđ flōde, 80, 3; Gen. 1323. Hǣle and trume wiđ deófla nīþum, Blickl. Homl. 171, 30. Wiđ fǣrscyte wearde healdan, Exon. Th. 48, 4; Cri. 766. Him holtwudu helpan ne meahte wiđ līge, Beo. Th. 4671; B. 2341: 358; B. 178: Elen. Kmbl. 369; El. 185. Sang se mæssepreóst orationem đa đe wiþ đære ādle āwritene wǣron, and đa đing dyde đe hē sēlust wiþ đon cūþe *dicebat presbyter exorcismos, et quaeque poterat pro sedando miseri furore agebat*, Bd. 3, 11; S. 536, 23–24. Wiđ eágena sāre, Lchdm. i. 2, 7 (and often). Godes mōdor hī āhredde wiđ heora feóndum, Chr. 994; Erl. 133, 16. Mē wiđ blōdhreówes weres bealuwe gehǣle *de viris sanguinum salva me*, Ps. Th. 58, 2. Wiđ nīþum genergan, Exon. Th. 116, 24; Gū. 212: Cd. Th. 233, 22; Dan. 279. (13) marking contrary motion or action, *against, contrary to, in opposition to*. v. III. 17:—Wiþ winde rōwan, Exon. Th. 345, 12; Gn. Ex. 187. Se wiđ đīnum willan wyrceþ, Met. 4, 28: Bt. 14, 2; Fox 44, 9: Blickl. Homl. 25, 15. Ic sceolde wiþ gesceape mīnum on bonan willan būgan, Exon. Th. 486, 2; Rä. 72, 6. (14) marking the instrument, *with*. v. III. 19:—Hiora in ānum weóll sefa wiđ sorgum, Beo. Th. 5193; B. 2600. (15) in reference to time, *at*:—Wearđ gesewen wiđ sunnan setlunge geond ealne đone eard yrnende here up on đām wolcnum, Homl. Th. ii. 302, 2. III. with accusative, (1) marking local relations, (a) where one object is near to or in contact with another, *against, beside, by, at*:—Wiđ đone weg *iuxta uiam*, Ælfc. Gr. 47; Zup. 269, 15: *secus uiam*, 271, 2. Wiđ đone weall *muro tenus*, Wrt. Voc. ii. 57, 63. (*a*) of the position occupied by one body in relation to another at rest:—Đā hē wæs wiđ đa stōwe (*secus locum*), Lk. Skt. 10, 32. Hē stōd wiđ đone mere (*secus stagnum*), 5, 1, 2. Hē gestōd wiđ steápne rond, Beo. Th. 5126; B. 2566. Ǽteówde ān engel wiđ hine (*by him*) Homl. Skt. i. 5, 88. Se geatweard sceal cytan habban wiđ đæt geat (*juxta portam*), R. Ben. 126, 19. Tō đām hātum bađum wiđ đæt botl Salustii, Homl. Th. i. 428, 10. Sittan lǣte ic hine wiđ mē sylfne, Cd. Th. 28, 19; Gen. 438. Hē mē wiđ his sylfes sunu setl getǣhte, Beo. Th. 4030; B. 2013. Wiđ đæt dōmsetl ic sitte *pone tribunal sedeo*, Ælfc. Gr. 47; Zup. 269, 16. Wiđ (*secus*) đone ford hē sit, 271, 2. Sittende wiđ (*juxta*) đone pitt, Gen. 29, 2: Ex. 2, 15. Heó sæt wiđ (*secus*) đæs Hǣlendes fēt, Lk. Skt. 10, 39. Seó bōc līđ wiþ (*juxta*) đē, Ælfc. Gr. 38; Zup. 225, 2. Eal đæt his (*Norway*) man āþer ođđe ettan ođđe erian mæg, đæt līđ wiđ đa sǣ, Ors. 1, 1; Swt. 18, 26. Hē būde on đæm lande norþweardum wiþ đa westsǣ, 17, 3. Hē is đǣr byrged wiđ Cnut cyng, Chr. 1046; Erl. 175, 4. Hī wacodon wiđ đa byrgene, Homl. Skt. i. 21, 120. Hig gewīcodon wiđ đone munt, Num. 20, 22. Heó wiđ wāgas weaxan wylle, Lchdm. i. 116, 21. Đeós wyrt biđ cænned wiđ wegas, 224, 14. Hié wiđ eorđan fæđm þūsend wintra eardodon *they had remained on the ground a thousand years*, Beo. Th. 6091; B. 3049. (*β*) of the position which is reached after movement:—Sume feóllon wiđ (*secus*) weg, Mt. Kmbl. 13, 4: Lk. Skt. 8, 5. Wiđ đone weg *circa uiam*, Mk. Skt. 4, 4. Hī setton scyldas wiđ đæs recedes weal, Beo. Th. 658; B. 326. Hē heora fela gesette wiđ đone sǣ *plurimos ad mare habitare praecepit*, Ors. 3, 5; Swt. 104, 26. Nim sticcan, sete on đone nægl wiđ đa wearta . . . Heald wiþ wǣtan, Lchdm. ii. 150, 4–7. (*γ*) giving the direction of movement by reference to a body at rest:—Se Hǣlend eode wiđ (*juxta*) đa sǣ, Mt. Kmbl. 4, 18. Fērde sum man wiđ hine *quidam iter transiens uenit secus eum*, Lk. Skt. 10, 33. Sum man fērde wiđ đone feld (cf. sum mon rād be đære stōwe (*juxta locum*), Bd. 3, 9; S. 533, 30, the incident being the same in both passages), Homl. Skt. ii. 26, 204. Heó wiđ đa eorđan (*along the ground*) hyre telgran tōbrǣdeþ, Lchdm. i. 324, 3. (*δ*) giving the direction of movement by reference to a moving body:—Wiđ đone segn foran manna þengel rād, Cd. Th. 188, 23; Exod. 172. (b) marking position in connection with the parts of an object, *by, against, at*:—Gif monnes sconca biđ of āslagen wiđ đæt cneóu, L. Alf. pol. 72; Th. i. 98, 19. Forborn bord wiđ rond *the shield burned against the rim*, Beo. Th. 5339; B. 2673. (c) marking extension, *unto*:—Wiđ heofenas *usque ad coelos*, Ps. Th. 56, 12. (2) marking association, combination, *with*. v. II. 2:—Drihten lēt rīnan hagol wiđ fȳr gemenged and hig fērdon ætgædere *pluit Dominus grandinem, et grando et ignis mista pariter ferebantur*, Ex. 9, 24: Lchdm. ii. 30, 2: Met. 7, 8: Bt. 12; Fox 36, 9. Se yfela willa næfþ nǣnne gefērscipe wiþ đa gesǣlþa, 36, 7; Fox 184, 32. Đis leóht wē habbaþ wiđ nȳtenu gemǣne, Blickl. Homl. 21, 13. Hū đone cumbolwigan wiþ đa hālgan mægþ hæfde geworden, Judth. Thw. 25, 14;

Jud. 260. Hē wolde dǣlan rīce wiđ God ælmihtigne, Wulfst. 306, 27: Homl. Th. i. 172, 1. Ðæt hié healfne geweald wiđ Eotena bearn āgan mōston, Beo. Th. 2180; B. 1088. Hē gemōt wiđ hī habban wolde, Homl. Skt. i. 23, 21: Exon. Th. 334, 20; Gn. Ex. 19. Se hrefn wiđ wulf (*sic MS.*) wæl reáfode, Beo. Th. 6046; B. 3027. (3) marking separation, *from.* v. **II.** 3:—Ne mæg mīn līchoma wiđ đās lǣnan gesceaft deáđ gedǣlan (*my body cannot separate death from this frail condition in which it is created*, i. e. death is a condition inseparable from the frailty of the body), ac hē gedreósan sceal, Exon. Th. 124, 24; Gū. 342. (4) marking compensation, *for.* v. **II.** 4 g:—Sylle eáge wiđ eáge, Ex. 21, 24. (5) marking balance, counterpoise, *with, against* (as in to weigh one thing *with* or *against* another). v. **II.** 5:—Genim ācmistel, gegnīd tō meluwe, āweh đonne wiþ ǣnne pening, Lchdm. ii. 88, 6. Man sett đa synne and đa sāwle on đa wǣge, and hȳ man wegeþ, swā man dēđ gold wiđ penegas, Wulfst. 240, 2. Hiora birhtu ne biđ āuht tō gesettanne wiđ đære sunnan leóht, Met. 6, 7. (6) marking comparison, *in comparison with.* v. **II.** 6:—Heora dȳre gold ne biđ nāhte wurđ wiđ đa foresǣdan māđmas, Homl. Skt. i. 21, 55. (7) marking address, conversation, *with, to.* v. **II.** 8:—Hē spræc heardlīcor wiđ hig đonne wiđ fremde men *quasi ad alienos durius loquebatur*, Gen. 42, 7: 45, 15. Hū stīđe se landhlāford spræc wiđ hig *locutus est nobis dominus terrae dure*, 42, 30. Sprǣcan twēgen weras wiđ hyne *duo uiri loquebantur cum illo*, Lk. Skt. 9, 30. Ongan Waldend wiđ Abraham sprecan, sægde him unlytel spell, Cd. Th. 145, 13; Gen. 2405. Hē wordum wiđ his Waldend spræc, 155, 22; Gen. 2576. Heó ne mæg wordum wrixlan wiđ đone wergan gāst, Exon. Th. 373, 30; Seel. 117. Wiđ đone rǣdde Chromatius, Homl. Skt. i. 5, 323. (8) marking dealing, arrangement, where terms are come to *with* a person, *with.* v. **II.** 9:—Wiþ đone here se cyning friþ nam, Chr. 876; Erl. 78, 9. Swegen griđode wiđ đone cyng, 1046; Erl. 172, 6. Ða foreword đe Ælfwerd and se hīrēd worhtan wiđ Æđelmǣr, Chart. Erl. 235, 26. Hē sibbe ne wolde wiđ manna hwone mægenes Deniga feó þingian, Beo. Th. 315; B. 155. Tō þingienne þiódum sīnum wiđ đane Sceppend, Ps. C. 8: Exon. Th. 39, 4; Cri. 617: 254, 15; Jul. 197. Þingeras wiđ đone ælmihtigan þrym, Wulfst. 240, 10. Būton hē gebēte wiđ God, 271, 27: Homl. Skt. i. 12, 160. Ðā rǣdde se cyng wiđ his witan (*the king settled with the* '*witan*'), đæt man sceolde mid scipfyrde faran, Chr. 999; Erl. 135, 29. (9) marking action affecting a person, (to deal) *with,* (act) *towards*:—Hē wiđ monna bearn wyrceþ weldǣdum, Exon. Th. 191, 11; Az. 86. Hwī dēst đū wiđ mē swā? Gen. 12, 18. For đære ūtdrǣfe đe hē gedyde wiđ hī, Homl. Skt. i. 21, 85. Begaa hē đa ryhtwīsnesse đæs lāreówes wiđ đa gyltendan, Past. 17; Swt. 123, 23. Ic lufan symle lǣste wiđ eówic, Exon. Th. 30, 10; Cri. 477. Beó đū hālig wiđ đa hālgan, and hwyrf đē wiđ đa forhwyrfdan, Ps. Th. 17, 25. Men mihton tōcnāwan his mihte wiđ God, Homl. Skt. i. 19, 114. (10) marking action having reference to a person:—Hē wolde līcettan wiđ Dauid *he would dissemble with David*, Homl. Skt. i. 12, 250. Ālȳse ic mē sylfne wiđ God, 17, 75. Ðæt rīce and đone anwald hē nā ne angeat wiđ Cornelius (*in the case of Cornelius*), Past. 17; Swt. 115, 18. Þēh đe hē hit wiđ đa senatus hǣle *though he concealed it from the senate*, Ors. 4, 10; Swt. 196, 16. Hē bedīglode his fær wiđ đone wrægan, Homl. Th. i. 400, 22. Nis mīn bān wiđ đē deópe behȳded *non est occultatum os meum abs te*, Ps. Th. 138, 13. (11) marking action directed to a person:—His gerēfa wearđ wiđ hine forwrēged *his steward was accused to him*, Lk. Skt. 16, 1. (12) marking position or attitude in regard to a person, *with, in respect to*:—Ne biđ heó nā wiđ God unscyldig *non erit insons coram Deo*, L. Ecg. P. ii. 17; Th. ii. 188, 12. Scyldig wiđ God, Homl. Skt. ii. 27, 171: Cd. Th. 250, 20; Dan. 549. Beó hē ūtlah wiđ God and wiđ đone cyningc scyldig ealles đæs, đe hē āge, Wulfst. 271, 24: 296, 10. Hió hit hæbben unbesacen wiđ ǣlce hand, Cod. Dip. Kmbl. ii. 150, 23. Land unbecwedene and unforbodene wiđ ǣlcne man, Chart. Th. 209, 1. Ðæm đeówan is tō cȳđonne đæt hē wiete đæt hē nis freoh wiđ his hlāford, Past. 29; Swt. 200, 19. (13) *with* a person by whom something is held:—Byđ đē meorđ wiđ God, Andr. Kmbl. 550; An. 275. Hē wiđ ælda mæg eádes hleótan, Exon. Th. 305, 16; Fä. 89. Wiđ Drihten dȳrne *dear in God's eyes*, Cd. Th. 32, 22; Gen. 507. (14) marking hostility, *with, against, to.* v. **II.** 10:—Hié wiþ đone here gefuhton, Chr. 871; Erl. 74, 10: Byrht. Th. 139, 61; By. 277. Wiđ his Waldend winnan, Cd. Th. 19, 28; Gen. 298. Simle hē feaht and won oþþe wiþ Angelcynn oþþe uuiþ Walas, Chr. 597; Erl. 20, 4. Hē wolde gecompian wiþ đone āwerigdan gāst . . . hē wolde deófol gelaþian tō campe wiþ hine, Blickl. Homl. 29, 17, 20. Þeáh wē fǣhþo wiđ đec gefremed hæbben, Exon. Th. 23, 14; Cri. 368: Andr. Kmbl. 2773; An. 1389. Gylt, đe wiđ Metod men gefremeden, Cd. Th. 61, 18; Gen. 999. Næbbe ic synne wiđ hié gefremed, 160, 15; Gen. 2650. Dǣdbōte dōn đæs mycclan yfeles and mānes đe hié wiđ heora Drihten gedydon, Blickl. Homl. 79, 6. Swā hwæt swā đes middangeard wiþ hine ǣbyligđa geworhte, 9, 12: Elen. Kmbl. 1024; El. 513. Hē spræc heálig word wiđ Drihten sīnne, Cd. Th. 19, 22; Gen. 295. Hē rēsade đæt hē hæfde ǣrendo sum wiþ Francena rīce (*contra regnum*), Bd. 4, 1; S. 565, 1. Ic eom fāh wiđ God, Cd. Th. 270, 28; Sat. 97: Beo. Th. 1627; B. 811. For heora heardheortnesse wiđ đone Hǣlend, Homl. Skt. ii. 25, 529. Hē wæs strengesđ wiđ scylda, Past. 17; Swt. 115, 17. (15) marking friendly relation, *with, to.* v. **II.** 11:—Ic sibbe wiđ hine healdan wille, Exon. Th. 145, 2; Gū. 688. Treów đū wiđ rodora weard healdest, Cd. Th. 127, 31; Gen. 2119. Ðæt đū wiđ Waldend wǣre heólde, 204, 18; Exod. 421: Andr. Kmbl. 425; An. 213. Ðæt friđ wiđ hȳ gefreoþad wǣre, Exon. Th. 127, 6; Gū. 382. Uton beón rihtwīse on ūrum mōde wiþ ōþre men, Blickl. Homl. 95, 28. Beó wiđ Geátas glæd, Beo. Th. 2350; B. 1173. (16) marking protection, defence, salvation, *against, from, for.* v. **II.** 12:—Ðæt hē ūs gescylde wiþ đa cræftas deófles, Blickl. Homl. 19, 16: Cd. Th. 245, 6; Dan. 458. Unc wiđ hronfixas werian, Beo. Th. 1085; B. 540. Wiđ wrāđ werod wearde healdan, 643; B. 319. Hit ǣr hit nolde behealdan wiđ unnyt word, Past. 38; Swt. 279, 4. Geheald đīne heortan wiđ unþeáwas, Wulfst. 247, 3. Ðæt man wiđ fūlne gālscipe warnie, 308, 2: Cd. Th. 15, 20; Gen. 236. Ðæt manna gehwylc wiđ swylc wær sȳ, Wulfst. 280, 11. Hē hine mihte wiþ đa mānfullan āhreddan, Homl. Skt. ii. 29, 233. Wiđ swȳđlīcne blōdryne of nosum, Lchdm. i. 2, 11, and often. Wiđ đæt mannes innođ tō fæst sȳ, 2, 16, and often. (17) marking contrary motion or action, *against, contrary to.* v. **II.** 13:—Wiþ Godes gife *contra gratiam Dei*, Bd. 1, 10; S. 480, 2. Wiđ mīnes mōdes willan *contra animi voluntatem*, Nar. 30, 26. Ǣr gē sceonde wiđ gesceapu fremmen, Cd. Th. 149, 4; Gen. 2469. (18) marking objection, *against*:—Ða geweddodan fǣmnan hire yldran hī ne mōton syllan ōđrum men, būton heó eallunga đone (*the man to whom she is betrothed*) wiđ cweđe, đæt heó hine nelle (*unless she bring the objection against him, that she does not wish to have him*), L. Ecg. C. 20; Th. ii. 146, 22. (19) marking the instrument, *by, through.* v. **II.** 14. (a) personal:—Hē sende ān tyccen wiđ his hirde *misit hoedum per pastorem suum*, Gen. 38, 20. Hē đæt wiđ yfele englas sende *immissiones per angelos malos*, Ps. Th. 77, 49. (b) in the phrases sittan wiđ earm, &c., *to rest on the arm*:—Āiās āna gehwylc and wiđ earm gesæt, hleonade wiđ handa, Cd. Th. 291, 18; Sat. 432. Hē wiđ earm gesæt, Beo. Th. 1503; B. 749. (20) in reference to time, *till.* v. also **VI**:—Wiđ đa hwīle *donec*, Mt. Kmbl. Lind. 5, 18. **IV.** with dat. and acc. in the same passage:—Gesæt đā wiđ sylfne se đe sæcce genæs, mǣg wiđ mǣge (v. **III.** 1 a *a*, **II.** 1 a, e), Beo. Th. 3958; B. 1977. Nǣfre Ismaēl wiđ Isace, wiđ mīn āgen bearn yrfe dǣleþ (v. **II.** 2, **III.** 2), Cd. Th. 168, 24; Gen. 2787. Ðæt hī wurdon đe geheortran wiđ đam āwyrgedan strangan and đone ealdan wiđerwinnan (v. **II.** 10, **III.** 14), Homl. Skt. i. 23, 241. Breóstnet wiđ ord and wiđ ecge ingang forstōd (v. **III.** 16, **II.** 12), Beo. Th. 3102; B. 1549. Ðīn mildheortnes is mycel wiđ heofenas (*usque ad coelos*), is đīn sōđfæstnes wiđ wolcnum (*usque ad nubes*), Ps. Th. 56, 12. **V.** with the instrumental, cf. **II.** 2:—Gemeng wiþ đȳ leáce, Lchdm. ii. 34, 5. **VI.** not unfrequently the form of the word governed by *wiþ* does not shew the case: as instances of this are given the following passages in which the word is used with force of *till, to*:—Wiđ ende *usque in finem*, Ps. Th. 67, 16: *in finem*, 73, 10, 11. Wiđ oryldu *usque in senectam et senium*, 70, 16. Wiđ sefo sīđa *usque septies*, Mt. Kmbl. Lind. 18, 21. Wiđ nū *usque nunc*, 11, 12: *usque modo*, Jn. Skt. Lind. Rush. 16, 24. Uiđ tō đises (đisse, Rush.) ł uiđ nū ł uiđ đāgeána *usque athuc*, 2, 10. Wiđ tō đæm dæge *usque ad eum diem*, Mt. Kmbl. Lind. 24, 38: 11, 13. **VII.** used adverbially; see also compounds with *wiþ*:—Meng hwītcwudu wiþ (v. **II.** 2, **III.** 2), Lchdm. ii. 54, 3. Ðæt ǣnig wiþerweard đing beón gemenged wiþ ōđrum wiþerweardum, ođđe ǣnige geferrǣdenne wiđ habban (v. **II.** 2, **III.** 2), Bt. 16, 3; Fox 54, 13. Nāuþer ne đone anweald, ne eác đæt đæt hē wiþ sealde (v. **II.** 4 a), 33, 2; Fox 124, 15. Hē cwæđ jā wiđ (v. **II.** 4 f), Chr. 1067; Erl. 204, 23. Gif hwā forstele ōđres oxan . . . sette twēgen wiđ (v. **II.** 4 g), L. Alf. 24; Th. i. 50, 15. Him cōmon ongeán .vi. cyningas, and ealle wiđ trȳwsodon, đæt hī woldon efenwyrhton beón (v. **III.** 8), Chr. 972; Erl. 125, 12. Heald đē elne wiđ (v. **II.** 10, **III.** 14), Exon. Th. 303, 9; Fä. 50. Wilna brūceþ, and nō wiđ spriceþ (v. **II.** 13, **III.** 17), 411, 10; Rä. 29, 10. **VIII.** as conjunction. v. **III.** 20, *until*:—Wiđ gē đona geonga *donec exeatis*, Mt. Kmbl. Lind. 10, 11, 23: 24, 39. **IX.** combined (1) with *weard* (q. v.) (a) with gen.:—Hundas rǣsdon wiđ Petres weard, Homl. Th. i. 376, 34. Āstrehte hē hine sylfne tō eorđan wiđ his weard, ii. 168, 24. Ðā đā hī wiđ his werd wǣron, Homl. Skt. i. 3, 102: ii. 23 b, 136. Hī wiđ đæs heres weard wǣron, Chr. 1003; Erl. 139, 5. (b) with acc.:—Hē beheóld wiđ heofonas weard, Homl. Th. i. 46, 29: 382, 9: 464, 29. (2) with *weardes.* v. weardes. [*O. Sax.* wiđ: *O. Frs.* with: *Icel.* við.] v. þǣr-wiþ.

wiþ-æftan; *prep. adv. Behind.* **I.** *prep.* (1) with dat.:—Heó hym tō geneálǣhte wydæftan hym, Homl. Ass. 182, 48. Hī cōmon tō Wiht, and nāmon đǣr đæt him ǣr wiđæftan wæs (*what had been left behind them*), Chr. 1052; Erl. 183, 25. (2) with acc. or doubtful:—Heó com wiđæftan đa menigu *uenit in turba retro*, Mk. Skt. 5, 27. Sette syrwa wiđæftan đa burh *pone insidias urbi post eam*, Jos. 8, 2. Heó stōd wiđæftan his fēt *stans retro secus pedes eius*, Lk. Skt. 7, 38. Ðū āwurpe mīne word wiđæftan đē, R. Ben. 12, 3. **II.** *adv.*:—Ān wīf geneálǣhte wiđæftan *mulier accessit retro*, Mt. Kmbl. 9, 20. Fīf scipu belifan wiðæftan, Chr. 1047; Erl. 175, 12. Wiðeftan *posse* (=*post se*) *filios derelinquet*, Prov. 20, 7), Kent. Gl. 735.

wiþ-blǽwan; *p.* -bleów *To strain at*:—Ðæt hí wiðbleówen ðære fleógan and forswulgun ðone olfend *liquantes culicem, camelum autem glutientes*, Past. 57; Swt. 439, 24.

wiþ-bregdan, -brédan; *p.* -brægd, -brǽd, *pl.* -brugdon, -brúdon *To withhold, restrain, check, hold back*:—Gif ðæt mód ðæm willan ne wiðbrítt *dum in cogitatione voluptas non reprimitur*, Past. 11; Swt. 71, 8. Godes feónd wiðbrítt ðæm untruman móde ðære sibbe (*dilectionem proximorum vulneratis cordibus subtrahens*) ðe hé self forlét, 47; Swt. 361, 2. Ðá ðá hé wolde árwierðra monna mód from ðisses middangeardes geférrǽdenne áteón, suíðe suíðe hé him wiðbrǽd, ðá hé cuæð *Paulus religiosorum mentes a mundi consortio contestando, ac potius conveniendo suspendit, dicens*, 18; Swt. 131, 1. Hé hét heora ǽlcum fiftig scyllinga tó sceatte syllan, ðæt hí heora handa fram ðam blódes gyte ne wiðbrúdon, Homl. Th. i. 88, 5. Hit is micel ðearf, ðæt mon hire suíðe hrædlíce wiðbregde *festinare necesse est, ut repugnatione vincantur*, Past. 13; Swt. 79, 21. [Bute þu wiðbride þe, H. M. 9, 9.]

wiþ-ceósan; *p.* -ceás, *pl.* -curon; *pp.* -coren *To reject*:—Hé wiðceóseþ (-císt) *reprobat*, Blickl. Gl. Stán ðone widcurun timbrende *lapidem quem reprobaverunt aedificantes*, Ps. Surt. 117, 22. Wiðcurun, Mt. Kmbl. Rush. 21, 42. v. next word.

wiþ-coren; *adj.* (*ptcpl.*) *Reprobate*:—Ðá ongeat hé ðæt se wæs Gode wiðcoren, se ðe on ðæt bæþ eode, Shrn. 62, 8. Ðæt yfel wræc cóme ofer ða wiþcorenan *ut veniret contra improbos malum*, Bd. 1, 14; S. 482, 41. v. wiþer-coren.

wiþ-cwedenness, e; *f. Gainsaying, contradiction, opposition*:—Hí woldon hine besyrewian æt his lífe, and habban syþðan his ríce bútan ǽlcre wiðcweðenesse, Chr. 1002; Erl. 137, 36 note. Tó wetre wiðcwedenisse *ad aquas contradictionis*, Ps. Surt. 105, 32. Of wiðcweðenisse, 17, 44. Wiðcwedennysse, Ps. Spl. C. 30, 26: 79, 7.

wiþ-cweþan; *p.* -cwæþ, *pl.* -cwǽdon; *pp.* -cweden. I. *to reply.* v. wiþ, VII:—Ðá wiþcwæþ him se engel *contradicens angelus*, Bd. 3, 19; S. 549, 6. Com Swegen tó Eádwerde cinge, and gyrnde tó him landes. Ac Harold his bróðor wiðcwæð, and Beorn eorl, ðæt hig noldon him ágyfan nán þingc ðæs ðe se cing heom gegyfen hæfde, Chr. 1049; Erl. 172, 31. Cwæð sum wyln, ðæt hé mid ðam Hǽlende wǽre, and hé wiðcwæð, ðæt hé hine ne cúðe, Homl. Th. ii. 248, 31. II. *to gainsay, contradict, maintain an opposite opinion*:—Ða hálgan apostolas heredon ða clǽnnysse . . . Se ðe him wiðcwyð, hé ne byð ná wita, ac gedwola, Homl. Ass. 22, 198. Hé sægð ðæt hit sý álýfed, ðæt mæssepreóstas móton wífian, and míne gewritu wiðcweðaþ ðysum, 13, 7. Ða mágas setton ðam cilde naman Zacharias, ac seó módor him wiðcwæð mid wordum, and se dumba fæder mid gewrite, Homl. Th. i. 354, 25. Drihtne ðrowende him cuoeðende wiðcuoeð *Domino passurum se dicenti contradicit*, Mk. Skt. p. 4, 2. Hí eallum his wordum wiðcwǽdon, Bd. 2, 2; S. 503, 17. Ne mæg ic ná wiþcweþan ne andsacigan ðæt ðe ðú mé ǽr sǽdest, Bt. 10; Fox 26, 24. Ic ne mæg nó wiþcweþan, ne furþum ongeán ðæt geþencan, 34, 1; Fox 134, 29. Ic sylle eów múð and wísdóm ðam ne magon eówer wiðerwinnan wiðstandan and wiðcweðan (-cuoeða, Lind., -cweoða, Rush. *contradicere*), Lk. Skt. 21, 15. Hé begann tó wiðcweðenne ðam geleáfan ðe se apostol tǽhte, Homl. Th. ii. 412, 28. III. *to contradict, oppose, resist*:—Se man, ðe wiðcwið ðínum wordum *qui contradixerit ori tuo et non obedierit cunctis sermonibus tuis*, Jos. 1, 18. Éghwoelc se ðe hine cyning wyrcið wiðcuoeðæs (wiðcweðes, Rush. *contradicit*) ðæm cáser, Jn. Skt. Lind. 19, 12. 'Ne stala ðú.' Ðis bebod wiðcweð ǽlcum reáfláce, Homl. Th. ii. 208, 24, 27: 210, 1. Tó écum forwyrde ðám ðe him (*Antichrist*) onbúgaþ, and tó écere myrhðe ðám ðe him wiðcweðaþ, i. 4, 35. Wiðcwæð *reluctaretur*, Hpt. Gl. 509, 16. Cristes naman, ðam hí ǽr wiþcwǽdon *nomen Christi, cui contradixerant*, Bd. 3, 30; S. 562, 16. Hé wæs ofer eall gemett stearc ðám mannum ðe wiðcwǽdon his willan, Chr. 1086; Erl. 221, 18. Nis nán wuht ðe mæge oððe wille swá heágum góde wiþcweþan *non est aliquid, quod summo huic bono vel velit, vel possit obsistere*, Bt. 35, 4; Fox 160, 30. On tácen ðam ðe wiðcweden byð *in signum cui contradicetur*, Lk. Skt. 2, 34. IV. *to refuse, reject, not to allow*:—Hé wiðcwyð geðóhtas folce and hé wiðcwyþ geþeaht ealdrum *reprobat cogitationes populorum et reprobat consilia principum*, Ps. Spl. 32, 10. Ðá com Sparhafoc tó ðam arcebiscope, tó ðam ðet hé hine hádian sceolde. Ðá wiðcweð se arcebiscop, and cwæð ðet se pápa hit him forboden hæfde, Chr. 1048; Erl. 177, 21. Wiðcwæð *renunciaverit*, Hpt. Gl. 512, 72. Seó burhwaru wolde ðone hálgan geniman, and Pictauienscisce þearle wiðcwǽdon *the citizens wanted to take the saint, and the Poitevins absolutely refused to allow it*, Homl. Th. ii. 518, 20. Ðá begann se cyngc gyrnan his sweostor him tó wífe, ac hé and his menn ealle lange wiðcwǽdon, and eác heó sylf wiðsóc, 1067; Erl. 204, 17. Ða þrý cnihtas wiðcwǽdon his hǽþenscipe, Homl. Ass. 70, 131. Sume sind gecwedene *vitia*, ðæt synd leahtras, on manegum wísum miswritene oððe miscwedene; ðám eallum wé sceolon wiðcweðan, gyf wé cunnon ðæt gesceád, Ælfc. Gr. 50, 23; Zup. 294, 15. IV a. with dat. of person to whom a refusal is given:—Hé wolde ðæt hé ána wǽre heora cyning, ac ealle ða leódscipas ánmódlíce him wiðcwǽdon, Homl. Ass. 103, 34. IV b. with dat. of person and gen. of thing refused:—Him ða burgleóde ðæs wiðcwǽdon, Ors. 3, 7; Swt. 116, 8. Gif inc hwá ðæs wiþcweþe, Blickl. Homl. 71, 1. [Ealle munechades men hit wiðcwæðen . . . Ealle þa biscopas him underfengen, him wiðcwæðen muneces and eorles, Chr. 1123; Erl. 250, 17, 24. He wiðquað (*respondit*, Lk. 3, 16), and sede, O. E. Homl. ii. 137, 30.] v. wiþer-cweþan.

wiþ-drífan; *p.* -dráf *To repel*:—Nǽfre wiðdrífeþ Drihten úre his ágen folc *non repellet Dominus plebem suam*, Ps. Th. 93, 13: 94, 4.

wiþ-eástan; *prep. adv. To the east*, (1) prep.:—Wyðeástan Constantinopolim Crēca byrig is se sǽ Proponditis, Ors. 1, 1; Swt. 22, 2. (2) *adv.*:—Seó eá wiðeástan út on ða sǽ flóweþ, Swt. 8, 20.

wiþer; *prep. adv.* (1) prep. with acc. *Against*:—Míne ágen word wiðer (*adversum*) mé wǽran geornе, Ps. Th. 55, 5. Uiððir ða *adversus eos*, Rtl. 168, 5. (2) *adv. Against, in opposition*:—Wiþer *infensus*, Germ. 394, 366 cf. he wæh Wiðer king þe wiðer wes an compe, Laym. 9287. [*Goth.* wiþra: *O. Sax.* wiðar: *O. Frs.* withir: *O. H. Ger.* widar: *Icel.* viðr.] v. wiþere.

wiþer (?), es; *n. Opposition, resistance*:—Hé hæfde Higeláces hilde gefrúnen, wlonces wígcræft; wiðres ne trúwode, ðæt hé sǽmannum onsacan mihte, Beo. Th. 5899; B. 2953. [Þa ich wer i wide sæ, wiðer com toȝenes, þet weder wes swa wilde, Laym. 4678. Cf. His wiðerfulle hine, þo ben deules on helle, O. E. Homl. ii. 51, 21. Wiðerfulle cheorles, Laym. 21520.] v. wiþere, *and preceding word.*

wiþer-breca, an; *m. An adversary*:—On eallum dǽdum Godes wiþerbreca, Blickl. Homl. 175, 8. Nis ðé wiðerbreca nymðe Metod ána, Cd. Th. 251, 20; Dan. 566. Se (*Ishmael*) bið wiðerbreca wera cneórissum, 138, 7; Gen. 2288. Wæs ðú geðafsum wiðerbracæ (*adversario*) ðínum; ðý læs gesellæ ðec ðe widerbracæ tó dóme, Mt. Kmbl. Lind. 5, 25. Gif ðæ wiðerbraca (*Satanas*) ðone wiðerbraca drífes, 12, 26. Wiðerbrecan *obpositum*, Wrt. Voc. ii. 65, 24. Hé his wiþerbreocum sorge gesægde, Exon. Th. 120, 2; Gú. 265. Ðú forbriccest wiþerbrecan *conteruisti adversarios*, Cant. Moys. Ex. 15, 7: Cd. Th. 4, 35; Gen. 64. [Cf. *O. H. Ger.* widar-brechinta *repugnantem*.] v. next word.

wiþer-broca, an; *m. An adversary*:—Wiðyrbroca *adversarius*, Ps. Spl. C. 73, 11. Forhtiaþ wiðerbrocan (*adversarii*) his, Ps. Surt. ii. p. 186, 36: 187, 25. Wiðerbrocum *adversariis*, 194, 37. Ðú slóge alle wiðerbrocan mé *tu percussisti omnes adversantes mihi*, Ps. Surt. 3, 8. v. preceding and following words.

wiþerbrocian; *p.* ode *To oppose, be adverse to, be against*:—Se feónd bismerad wiðerbrocaþ noman ðinne *inimicus inritat adversarius nomen tuum*, Ps. Surt. 73, 10. Ða ðe wiðerbrociaþ mé *qui adversantur mihi*, Ps. Spl. C. 34, 22. v. preceding word.

wiþer-bróga, an; *m. Terror caused to an adversary* (?):—Nú sind duguþum bidǽled deófla cempan; ne meahtan wiþerbrógan, wíge spówan (*they could not succeed in being terrible to their adversaries, could not succeed in war*), siþþan wuldres cyning hilde gefremede wiþ his ealdfeóndum, Exon. Th. 35, 26; Cri. 564.

wiþer-cirr, es; *m. A going against, resistance*:—Ic gehýned eom, fáh and freóndleás; ic findan ne can wiðercyrr wið ðan of ðám wearhtreafum *I am humiliated, proscribed and friendless; against this I can devise no resistance from hell*, Elen. Kmbl. 1849; El. 926. [Cf. *O. H. Ger.* widar-ker; *m. conversio*: widar-kera; *f. controversio*.] Cf. ed-, ofer-cirr.

wiþer-cora, an; *m.* I. *an adversary, opponent, rebel*:—Wiþercora *contrarius*, Wrt. Voc. ii. 140, 75. Ne sý hé sacerd geteald, ac Godes wiþercora (wiþersaca, *v. l. rebellio*), R. Ben. 113, 13. Freónd hé wæs ðurh geleáfan, and wiþercora þurh weorc, Homl. Th. i. 530, 5. Gesamnodon gehwylce ðwyrlíce wiðercoran, and wréhton ðone cyning tó his bréðer, 468, 5. Wiþercorum *rebellibus*, Wülck. Gl. 256, 31. II. *a reprobate person*:—Wiðercora *reprobus*, R. Ben. Interl. 13, 8. Mid micelre geornfulnysse gewilniaþ ða wiðercoran (*the wicked in hell*) ðæt hí móton of ðære susle ðe hí on cwylmiaþ, Homl. Th. i. 332, 19.

wiþer-coren; *adj.* (*ptcpl.*). I. *reprobate, wicked*:—Elles wiðercoren hé is, líchamlícere wrace hé sig underþeód *sin autem improbus est, vindicte corporali subdatur*, R. Ben. Interl. 56, 2. For ðissum lǽnan lífe ðæt unlǽne, for ðyssum ungecorenum (wiðercorenum, *v. l.*) ðæt gecorene, Wulfst. 264, 19. Ðæt yfel wræc cóme ofer ða wiþercorenan (*improbos*), Bd. 1. 14; S. 482, 41 note. II. *rejected* from heaven, *reprobate* as opposed to elect:—Ðæt ða gecorenan ðý geleáffulran wǽron; and ða wiðercorenan náne beládunge nabbaþ, Homl. Th. i. 406, 35: ii. 568, 33. Ðǽr beóð feówer werod æt ðam dóme, twá gecorenra manna, and twá wiðercorenra, i. 396, 17: 332, 23, 29: 536, 32. Sam ðe gecorenra tó reste, sam ðe wiþercorenra tó deáþe *siue electorum ad requiem, siue reproborum ad mortem*, Scint. 226, 14. [Cf. *O. H. Ger.* widar-kiusan *reprobare*.] v. wiþ-coren.

wiþer-corenness, e; *f. Reprobateness*:—Swá fela manna gebúgaþ tó geleáfan on ðissere andwerdan gelaðunge, ðæt hí sume eft út berstaþ ðurh wiðercorennysse and leahtrum heora ðwyran lífes, Homl. Th. ii. 290, 19.

wiþer-crist, es; *m. An antichrist*:—Wiðer ł leáso cristo *pseudochristi*, Mk. Skt. Lind. 13, 22.

wiþer-cwedolness, e; *f. Contradiction*; contradictio:—Wiþercwedolnesse *contradictionis*, Blickl. Gl. Wiđercwydelnysse, Ps. Spl. 80, 7: Ps. Lamb. 105, 32. Wiþercwedulnisse, Blickl. Gl.: Ps. Spl. 79, 7. Wiđercwidelnyssum, Ps. Lamb. 17, 44.

wiþer-cwedung, e; *f. Gainsaying*:—Word wyþercwedunga *verba praecipitationis*, Ps. Spl. 51, 4.

wiþer-cweþan; *p.* -cwæþ, *pl.* -cwǽdon *To resist*, cf. wiþ-cweþan, III, wiþer-cwide:—Gemãgnesse wiđsacende wiđercweđan (-en, MS.) *importunitatem refutando frustrari* (*contradicere*), Hpt. Gl. 491, 32. Wiđercwiđendum *resistentibus*, Ps. Lamb. 16, 8. [*O. H. Ger.* widar-quedan *contradicere*.]

wiþer-cweþness, e; *f. Contradiction*:—Hine mon ne cnysđ mid nânre rēđnesse ne nânre wiđercueđnisse (-cwed-, Cott. MSS.) *quem nulla asperitas contradictionis pulsat*, Past. 19; Swt. 143, 20.

wiþer-cwida, an; *m.* I. *a contradicter*:—Ungeleáful wiđercwyda *incredulus negator, infidelis contradictor*, Hpt. Gl. 451, 11. II. *a rebel*:—Wiđercwyda *rebellio*, Wrt. Voc. i. 18, 19. [*O. H. Ger.* widar-queto a *contradicter*.]

wiþer-cwide, es; *m. Resistance, opposition, contest*:—Đæt twelf hîda land bûtan ǽlcum wiđercwide seó âgefen tô Wigornacestre, Chart. Th. 131, 25: Chart. Erl. 162, 1. Gif hwâ openne wiđercwyde ongeán lahriht gewyrce, L. Eth. v. 31; Th. i. 312, 8. Đǽr hî wiđercwyde wæteres hæfdon *ad aquas contradictionis*, Ps. Th. 105, 25. Ic on unriht lôcade and wiđercwyda wearn gehȳrde *vidi iniquitatem et contradictionem*, 54, 8. [Cf. *O. H. Ger.* widar-queta *contradictio*.]

wiþer-dûne *glosses* angusta *in*:—Hû naru ł wiđerdûne geate *quam angusta porta*, Mt. Kmbl. Rush. 7, 14.

wiþere; *adv. prep. Against*:—Weallas him (*the waves*) wiþre healdaþ *the cliffs hold out against the waves*, Exon. Th. 336, 24; Gn. Ex. 54. Cf. ȝif þe king wolde wiđ heom wiđerheolden, Laym. 9175. [*O. H. Ger.* widari, wid[i]ri.] v. tô-wiþere, wiþer.

wiþer-feohtend, es; *m. An adversary*:—Gâd fromlîce, đæt gê wiđerfeohtend wîges gehnǽgan, Andr. Kmbl. 2367; An. 1185. Đæt gê wearde healden, đȳ læs eów wiþerfeohtend weges forwyrnen tô wuldres byrig, Exon. Th. 282, 17; Jul. 664. v. wiþ-feohtend.

wiþer-flita, an; *m. An adversary, opponent*:—Magan hiora sprǽce gemetgian đa đe đæs cristendômes wiþerflitan sint, Ors. 2, 1; Swt. 64, 14. Wiđerflitan, 2, 5; Swt. 84, 26: 3, 3; Swt. 102, 15. Cf. wiþ-flîtan.

Wiþer-gild, es; *m. A man's name*:—Weóldon wælstôwe, syđđan Wiđergyld læg (cf. syđđan Heardrēd læg, 4766; B. 2388), æfter hæleþa hryre, hwate Scyldingas, Beo. Th. 4109; B. 2051. Sôhte ic Wiþergield and Freoþerîc, Exon. Th. 326, 5; Vîd. 124. [For a form similar to this, but used as a common noun, in other languages, v. Grmm. R. A. 652.]

wiþer-habban; *p.* -hæfde *To resist*:—Hwæt mæg mē wiđerhabban? *quid mihi restat?* Ps. Th. 72, 20. [*O. H. Ger.* widar-habên *reniti, retundere, resultare*.] v. wiþ-habban.

wiþer-hlinian; *p.* ode *To lean against*:—Wiđerhlingende, uuidirhliniendae, uuidirlinienti *innitentes*, Txts. 71, 1098. Wiþerhlyniende, Wrt. Voc. ii. 48, 78.

wiþer-hycgende; *adj. Having hostile thoughts* or *purpose* against another, *of evil intent*:—*Emulus*, i. *contrarius* gewinna, wiþerwinna, æfstig, wiþerhycgende, Wrt. Voc. ii. 143, 48. Ongan meldigan helle hinca đone hâlgan wer, wiđerhycgende, Andr. Kmbl. 2345; An. 1174. Đû (*the devil*) scealt, wiđerhycgende (*the adversary of God and man*), wergđu dreógan, Elen. Kmbl. 1900; El. 952. Đē leán sceolan, wiþerhycgende (*opponent of the gods*), witebrôgan æfter weorþan, Exon. Th. 254, 12; Jul. 196. Wēndun gē (*the devils*) and woldun, wiþerhycgende (*rebellious*), đæt gē Scyppende sceoldan gelîce wesan, 141, 31; Gû. 635. Wēndon and woldon, wiđerhycgende (*having evil designs upon the strangers*), đæt hié on elþeódigum ǽt geworhton, Andr. Kmbl. 2146; An. 1074. v. wiþ-hogian, -hycgan.

wiþer-hygdig, -hȳdig; *adj. Hostilely disposed, adverse*:—Hē âhôf wôđe wiđerhȳdig *he raised his voice with mind adverse*, Andr. Kmbl. 1349; An. 675.

wiþerian, wiþrian; *p.* ode. I. *to be against, be hostile*:—Ic wiđerige *adversor*, Ælfc. Gr. 25; Zup. 145, 18. Đa đe wiđriaþ mē *qui adversantur mihi*, Ps. Lamb. 34, 19. Đa wiđrigendan (wiđriende, Ps. Spl.) mē *adversantes mihi*, 3, 8. II. *to strive* with, against (*wiþ, ongeán*), *struggle, dispute*:—Ic wiđerige *controuersor*, Ælfc. Gr. 37; Zup. 219, 9. Beó đû gebeogul đînum wiđerwinnan, đe læs đe đîn wiđerwinna, gif đû wiđerast wiđ hine, đē betǽce đam dēman, Homl. Ass. 4, 95. For đî synd đa gesibsuman Godes bearn, for đan đe nân đing on him ne wiđeraþ ongeán God, Homl. Th. i. 552, 22. Mislâra, đa ûrum ongeán wiþeriaþ andgytum *suggestiones, quae nostris obstrepunt sensibus*, Scint. 33, 20. Đâs twâ burh wiđriaþ betwux him, Homl. Th. ii. 66, 28. Hē ne wiđerode ongeán, ne ne feaht, 40, 17. Hî wiđerodon ongeán Cristes lâre, 224, 30. Gif preóst ongeán biscopes gerǽdnesse wiđerige, L. N. P. L. 45; Th. ii. 296, 18. Se đe sôđlîce God lufaþ, nele hē wiđerian ongeán his bebodum, Homl. Th. ii. 522, 18. III. *to resist, oppose*:—Wiđstôd ł wiđerode *refragabatur, resistebat*, Hpt. Gl. 426, 41. Hig wǽron gemæste and wiđerodun (*recalcitravit*), Deut. 32, 15. Eal folc hine tô đære geđincđe geceás, þeáh đe hē mid eallum mægne wiđerigende wǽre, Homl. Th. ii. 122, 23. IV. *to make hostile, to provoke*:—Se đe gecyrredne bûton lîđnysse lǽrđ, wiđerian (*exasperare*) mâ đænne þreágean cann, Scint. 61, 12. V. *to become provoked*:—Gebîg fram unwitan, and đû nâ wiþerast (*exacerbaberis*) on stuntnysse his, Scint. 188, 11. [He seđ þo þe wiđerieđ togenes him, O. E. Homl. ii. 123, 36. So hit unmeđluker is, heo wunnen (wiđeređ, *v. l.*) agean þe uestluker, A. R. 238, 17. Wrestlin ant wiđerin wiđ ham seoluen, Marh. 14, 13. Shep ... þær mann cwelleþþ itt, ne wiþþreþþ itt nohht swiþe, Orm. 1181. Fleges ... wiđeren in đæt web, Misc. 15, 475. *O. H. Ger.* widarôn *abnuere, renuere, reniti, obviare, reluctari*.]

wiþer-lǽcan; *p.* -lǽhte *to deprive*:—Wyþerlēcaþ *privabit*, Ps. Spl. T. 83, 13.

wiþer-leán, es; *n. Recompense, retribution*:—Wearđ wîcingum wiþerleán âgifen; gehȳrde ic đæt Eádweard ânne slôge, Byrht. Th. 135, 11; By. 116. Deáþes hâliges wiþerleáne (*as recompense*) lîf eádig geâhniaþ *mortis sacre compendia vitam beatam possident*, Hymn. Surt. 130, 9. Wunde wiđerleán *retribution for sin*, Soul Kmbl. 187; Seel. 94. [*O. L. Ger.* withir-lôn *retributio*: *O. H. Ger.* widar-lôn *recompensio, recompensatio*.]

wiþerling, es; *m. An adversary*:—Đû forbriccest wiþerlingas (*adversarios*), Cant. Moys. Ex. 15, 7. [Iesu cristes wiþerling (wiþering, ed. Lumby), K. Horn 154 (ed. Ritson).]

wiþer-mâl, es; *m. A case against* (*in reply to*, or (?) *by way of accusation*), *defence, prosecution* (?):—Man ûtlagode Swægn eorl, his ôđerne sunu. Đâ ne onhagode him tô cumenne tô wiđermâle ongeán đone cyng, and âgeán đone here đe him mid wæs *his* (*Godwin's*) *other son, Swegen, was outlawed. Then it did not suit him to come to meet the king and the army that was with him in order to defend himself* (or? *in order that the case against him might be brought*; cf. Geornde se eorl griđes đæt hē môste hine betellan æt ǽlc đæra þinga đe him man on lēde, Erl. 180, 12), Chr. 1052; Erl. 181, 7.

wiþer-mēde; *adj.* I. *contrary-minded, contrary, adverse, hostile, opposed*:—Se wiđermēda (*the devil*), Andr. Kmbl. 2391; An. 1197. Gif huoelc uiđirmoedo (*contraria*) sindon in hûse esnes đînes, Rtl. 123, 12. II. *opposed* to good, *perverse, depraved*:—Ic (*Eve*) wæs wiþermēde and unwîsum nētenum gelîc geworden, Blickl. Homl. 89, 9. [*O. H. Ger.* widar-muoti *injuriosus*.] v. wiþer-mēdu, wiþer-môd, *and next word*.

wiþer-mēdness, e; *f.* I. *adversity*:—From ǽlcum wiđermoednise (*adversitate*) giscild đû, Rtl. 89, 24. Nǽngum wiđirmoednisum (*adversitatibus*) âđryht, 106, 15. From allum uiđirmoednesum (*adversis*) âscildad, 75, 7. II. *perversity, depravity*:—Wiđirmoednise *pravitate*, Rtl. 34, 9.

wiþer-mēdu(-o); *indecl.*: -mēd, e; *f.* I. *hostility, disfavour*:—His hyldo is unc betere tô gewinnanne đonne his wiđermēdo, Cd. Th. 41, 22; Gen. 660. II. *adversity, injury*:—Allum wiđirmoedum (*adversitatibus*) in lîchome, Rtl. 52, 22. III. *perversity, depravity*:—Hî on wiđermēde wendan and cyrdan *conversi sunt in arcum perversum*, Ps. Th. 77, 57. [*O. H. Ger.* widar-muotî; *f.*; -muoti; *n. injuria, sinistrum, detrimentum, malum*.]

wiþer-metan; *p.* -mæt, *pl.* -mǽton; *pp.* -meten *To compare*:—Hine wiđermet *equat*, Wrt. Voc. ii. 90, 77: *equiparat*, i. *coequat*, i. *imitatur, assimilat*, 143, 70. Wiđermeten is *confertur*, 90, 46: *adsimilatum est*, Mt. Kmbl. Rush. 18, 23. [*O. H. Ger.* widar-mezan *comparare, rependere, compensare*.] Cf. wiþ-metan.

wiþer-môd; *adj. Having the mind set against* something, *adverse, hostile, contrary*:—Đæt wē hié wiđermôde ne gedôn ûs mid đære tǽlinge *that we may not set them against us with the blame*, Past. 32; Swt. 212, 1. [*O. Sax.* wiđar-môd.] v. wiþer-mēde.

wiþer-môdness, e; *f. Adversity, contrary fortune*:—Hine ne gedrēfe nân wuht wiđerweardes, ne hine ne geđrysce nân wiđermôdnes tô ormôdnesse *non hunc adversa perturbent, non aspera ad desperationem premant*, Past. 14; Swt. 83, 19. Cf. wiþer-mēdu.

wiþer-rǽde; *adj. Adverse, contrary*:—*Aduersus* is nama þwyr ođđe wiđerrǽde, Ælfc. Gr. 38; Zup. 240, 1. Wiþerrǽde *contrarius*, 47; Zup. 275, 6. I. where there is ill-will, *at variance, hostile*:—Đæra Persiscra cyning wæs đam Câsere wiþerrǽde, Jud. Thw. 162, 24. Ongeán đam wîslîcan rǽde, đe of Godes âgenre gyfe cymđ, se wiđerrǽda deófol (*the devilish adversary*) sǽwđ réceleásnesse, Wulfst. 53, 7. Wurdon wiđerrǽde se cyng and se eorl, Chr. 1104; Erl. 239, 24. Woldon đa wiþerrǽdan hǽþenan mid micelre fyrde faran on hergoþ on đæs Câseres anwealde, Jud. Thw. 162, 36. Þeówum Godes ealle đyses middaneardes wiþerrǽde synd *servis Dei cuncta hujus mundi contraria sunt*, Scint. 62, 4. II. where there is opposition to duty, *rebellious, contumacious*:—Gif hē gyt wiđerrǽde biđ, hē lîchamlîce wrace mid swingelle þolige *sin improbus est, vindicte corporali subdatur*, R. Ben. 48, 11. Đæt Israhēla folc wearđ on đam wēstene wiđerrǽde ongeán God, Homl. Th. ii. 238, 10. Ne beó gē wiþerrǽde wiđ eówerne Drihten *nolite esse rebelles contra Dominum*, Num. 14, 9. Se câsere wolde gewyldan mid wîge đa leóda đe wiþerrǽde wǽron, and his rîce forsâwon, Homl. Skt. ii. 28, 4. III. *out of harmony, repugnant, offensive, disagreeable*:—Wiđerrǽde đû eart mē *scandalum es mihi*, Mt. Kmbl. 16, 23. Nis nân ǽ wiđerrǽde þus geworhtum mannum, Homl. Skt. i. 17, 60. Ðeós wyrt bið ðam gōman stīð and wiðerrǣde for mete geþiged, Lchdm. i. 300, 10. Wulfes tǣsl ħafaþ leáf wiþerrǣde (*unpleasant, rough?*) and þyrnyhte, 282, 15. **IV.** *adverse, not fitted to further the good of anything, unfavourable, disadvantageous*:—Mīn wīf is for manegum wintrum untrum, ðam wæs ǣlc lǣcecræft wiðerrǣde (*no medicine suited her*), Homl. Th. i. 22, 44. Ðeós wyrt byþ cenned on wiþerrǣdum stōwum (*in places not favourable to growth*) wið wegas and hegas, Lchdm. i. 228, 17. On feldum and on wiðerrǣdum stōwum, 304, 3. Rihtwīs þoligende wiþerrǣde *justus tolerando aduersa*, Scint. 12, 7. **V.** *contrary, of an opposite nature*:—Stān is gesett ongeán ðone hlāf, for ðam ðe heardmōdnys is wiðerrǣde sōðre lufe, Homl. Th. i. 252, 19. Twā wiðerrǣde ðing geðeódde Drihten on ðisum cwyde, ðæt sind ymhīdignyssa and lustas, ii. 92, 13. Hæfð se yfela gāst seofonfealde ungifa, and ða syndan wiðerrǣde mid ealle ðyssum gōdum Godes gyfum, Wulfst. 52, 10. v. wiþer-rǣdness; wiþ-rǣde.

wiþer-rǣdlīc; *adj. Adversative*:—Sume (*conjunctions*) sind *adversativae*, ðæt sind wiþerrǣdlīce, Ælfc. Gr. 44; Zup. 264, 1.

wiþer-rǣdness, e; *f. Contrariety, opposition*:—Wiðerrǣdnys *contrarietas, contrauersio*, Ælfc. Gr. 47; Zup. 275, 7. **I.** *hostility; ill-will.* v. wiþer-rǣde, I:—Wið hunda rēdnysse and wiðerrǣdnysse; se ðe hafaþ hundes heortan mid him, ne beóð ongeán hine hundas cēne, Lchdm. i. 372, 3. **II.** *unfavourableness, disadvantage.* v. wiþer-rǣde, IV:—Ðæs fȳrhȳses hlȳwing[e] winterlīces cyles and ungetemprunge wiþerrǣdnes sī gelȳht *caumene refugio hybernalis algoris et intemperei adversitas leuigetur*, Anglia xiii. 397, 462. **III.** *oppositeness of nature.* v. wiþer-rǣde, V:—On wiþerǣdnysse went *in contrarium uertit*, Scint. 55, 3.

wiþer-ræhtes; *adv. Opposite*:—Hī gesēgan wyrm on wonge wiðerræhtes licgean, Beo. Th. 6071; B. 3039.

wiþer-riht, es; *n. Recompense, compensation*:—Wiðerriht *vel* edleán *hostimentum*, Wrt. Voc. i. 22, 24.

wiþer-saca, an; *m.* **I.** *an adversary, opponent, enemy*:—Anticristus is on Lǣden *contrarius Cristo*, ðæt is on Englisc Godes wiðersaca, Wulfst. 78, 13: Homl. Th. i. 376, 16. Ǣlc ðæra ðe hyne tō cynge dēð ys ðæs cāseres wiðersaca (*contradicit Caesari*), Jn. Skt. 19, 12. Hēr sȳn on earde Godes wiðersacan, apostatan ābroðene, Wulfst. 164, 10. Wiðersa[cena] *contrariorum, inimicorum*, Hpt. Gl. 471, 74. **I a.** *a rebel*:—Ne beó hē nā sacerd geteald, ac Godes wiðersaca *non sacerdos sed rebellio judicetur*, R. Ben. 112, 13. **I b.** *an adversary at law, a prosecutor* (?):—Ðā andsweredon Pīlate ða twēgen wælhreówan wyþersacan, Annas and Caiphas, and cwǣdon: 'Lā, leóf dēma, eall ðeós mænio secgaþ ðæt hē wæs of forligre ācenned,' Nicod. 7; Thw. 3, 32. **II.** *one who renounces or denies, an apostate*:—Wiðersaca *apostata*, Hpt. Gl. 493, 26. Wiðersaca (*pervicax fidei*) *refragator vel negator*, 502, 65: Homl. Skt. i. 3, 413. Gif munuc oþþe mæssepreóst wiðersaca wurðe mid ealle, hē sī āmānsumod ǣfre, būton hē ðe rædlīcor gebūge tō his þearfe, L. Eth. ix. 41; Th. i. 348, 31. Iūdas se wiþersaca, Mt. Kmbl. 26, 14: Mk. Skt. 14, 10, 43. Under Juliane ðam ārleásan wiðersacan (*Julian the apostate*), Homl. Skt. ii. 31, 19. Wē beódaþ ðæt wiðersacan and ūtlagan Godes and manna of earde gewītan, L. C. S. 4; Th. i. 378, 11. Hȳ synt genemnede sarabagite oððe renuite, ðæt ys sylfedēman and wiðersacan, R. Ben. 136, 11. Wiðersacena *apostatorum*, Hpt. Gl. 510, 54: *apocryphorum, falsorum scriptorum*, 452, 58. [Þat heðene cun is Goddes wiðersake, Laym. 12620. *O. Sax.* wiðar-sako: *O. L. Ger.* wither-sacco *adversarius*: *O. H. Ger.* wider-sacho *adversarius*.]

wiþer-sacian; *p.* ode. **I.** *to blaspheme*:—Ðam ðe wiðersacaþ ongēn hālige gāst, ne bið ðam forgyfen *ei, qui in spiritum sanctum blasphemauerit, non remittetur*, Lk. Skt. 12, 10. Swā hwylc man swā wyþersacaþ (*blasphemes*, v. Gospel of Nicodemus c. 4, v. 7) ðam Cāsere, hē byþ deáþes scyldig, Nicod. 10; Thw. 5, 23. Wiþersacendra *blasphemantium*, Scint. 209, 5. **II.** *to be apostate*:—Wiðersaca[n]dan *apostataverant*, Hpt. Gl. 510, 49. Wiðersacedan *apostatarent*, 513, 24. Wiðersacian *apostatare*, 493, 25: *apostare*, 477, 68. [Cf. *O. H. Ger.* widar-sachan *recusare*.]

wiþer-sacung, e; *f.* **I.** *blasphemy*:—Wiþersacung *blasphemia*, Scint. 102, 16. 'Wylt ðū hys wyðersacunge gehȳran?' Ðā cwæþ Pīlatus: 'Gif seó sprǣc wyþersacung ys ðe hē spycþ, nymaþ hyne and lǣdaþ hyne tō eówre gesomnunge,' Nicod. 10; Thw. 5, 31. **II.** *apostasy*:—Wiðersacunge *apostasiae*, Hpt. Gl. 477, 69: 515, 69.

wiþer-sæc, es; *n.* **I.** *striving, opposition, contradiction*:—Æt ðæs wiðersæces wæterum *ad aquas contradictionis*, Deut. 32, 51: Ps. Spl. 105, 31. Fram wiðersace tungana *a contradictione linguarum*, 30, 16. Genera mē of wiðersacum (*contradictionibus*) folces, 17, 45. **II.** *denial*:—Hē (*Peter*) gemunde his micclan gebeótes, and mid biterum wōpe his wiðersæc behreówsode, Homl. Th. ii. 248, 35. Heó worda gehwæs wiðersæc fremedon, ðæt heó frignan ongan; cwǣdon ðæt heó on aldre āwiht swylces ne ǣr ne sīð ǣfre hȳrdon, Elen. Kmbl. 1135; El. 569. **III.** *apostasy, recusancy*:—Ðæt heora (*the Northumbrians*) geleáfa wurde āwend eft tō Gode fram ðam wiþersæce ðe hī tō gewende wǣron, Homl. Skt. ii. 26, 63. Wearð geopenad his earman wīfe his mānfullan behāt ðam deófle . . . . Heó cȳdde Basilie hyre cnihtes wiþersæc, i. 3, 408. [*O. Sax.* wiðar-sak, -saka *contradiction*.]

wiþer-sæc; *adj. Adverse, unfavourable*:—Hlinunge and hligiunge wiþersæc, Lchdm. ii. 258, 20.

wiþer-sīnes (-sȳnes); *adv. Withershins* (v. *widder-sinnis* in Jamieson's Dictionary), *backwards*:—Steorran yrnaþ wiþersȳnes *the course of the stars shall be reversed*, Blickl. Homl. 93, 19.

wiþer-stǣger; *adj. Hard to mount, steep, abrupt*:—Wiðerstǣgre *prerupti*, Wrt. Voc. ii. 68, 59: 69, 15. v. stǣger.

wiþer-standan; *p.* -stōd *To withstand, resist*:—Fram ðām wyderstandendum swȳþran ðīnre *a resistentibus dexterae tuae*, Ps. Spl. 16, 9. [*O. H. Ger.* widar-standan *resistere*.] Cf. wiþ-standan.

wiþer-steall, es; *m. Resistance, opposition*:—Wiðerstal *obvix*, Wrt. Voc. ii. 115, 22: 63, 22. Færð ðæt fȳr ofer eall, ne byð ðǣr nān wiðersteall (cf. foresteall, Dōm. L. 146, *where the Latin is*: Ignis ubique suis ruptis regnabit habenis), ne nān man næfð ðæra mihta, ðæt ðǣr ǣnige wyrne dō, Wulfst. 138, 6. Næs Petrus gewunod tō nānre wǣpnunge, ac ðǣr wǣron twā swurd gebrōhte tō ðam wiðerstealle, gif hit Crist swā wolde, Homl. Th. ii. 248, 4. Mē hwīlum biþ forwyrned þurh wiþersteall willan mīnes, Exon. Th. 268, 32; Jul. 441. Cf. wiþ-steall.

wiþer-sȳnes. v. wiþer-sīnes.

wiþer-talu, e; *f. Reply, defence*:—Hē ðǣrrihte ādumbode, for ðan ðe æt Godes dōme ne bið nān belādung ne wiþertalu, Homl. Th. i. 530, 6.

wiþer-tihtle, an; *f. A counter-charge, cross-action*:—Gif ǣnig yfelra manna wǣre ðe wolde ōðres yrfe tō borge settan for wiðertihtlan, ðæt hē gecȳðe mid āðe, ðæt hē hit for nānum fācne ne dyde, L. Ed. 1; Th. i. 160, 5, and see note. Se ðe on gemōte mid wiðertihtlan hine sylfne oþþe his man werige, hæbbe ðæt eall forspecen, and geandwyrde ðam ōðrum swā hundrede riht þynce, L. C. S. 27; Th. i. 392, 5. Cf. Si quis in placito per justiciam posito sui vel suorum causam injustis conterminacionibus (*v. l.* concriminationibus) vel contraposicionibus difforciet, hanc perdat, et de cetero rectum faciat, sicut hundreto vel judicibus videbitur ydoneum, L. H. I. 34, 5; Th. i. 537, 6-10.

wiþer-tīme (-tȳme); *adj. Troublesome, grievous*:—Apozeus ys ðam foresprecenan hīwe genōh wyðertȳme, Anglia viii. 331, 14. Ðā ðā mē wiðertȳme ł hefigtȳme hī wǣrun *cum mihi molesti essent*, Ps. Lamb. 34, 13.

wiþer-trod, es; *n. Return, retreat*:—Cirdon cynerōfe wīggend on wiþertrod *they turned to march back*, Judth. Thw. 26, 6; Jud. 313. Wiðertrod seón lāðra monna *to see the retreat of the foe*, Cd. Th. 125, 25; Gen. 2084.

wiþer-weard (-word, -wurd), *and* -wierde; *adj.* **I.** of direction, *contrary*:—Him wæs wiðerweard (-word, Lind., Rush.) wind *erat ventus contrarius eis*, Mk. Skt. 6, 48: Mt. Kmbl. Lind. 14, 24. Wiþerward wind āstīgeþ . . . āstigon wiþerwarde windas, Bd. 3, 15; S. 541, 33, 39. **II.** of hostility or conflict, *adverse, hostile*; used substantively, *an adversary, enemy, opponent, a fiend*:—Ǣlc hūs ðe byð wiðerweard ongeán hyt sylf *omnis domus divisa contra se*, Mt. Kmbl. 12, 25. Se wiðirwearda god diúl *Asmadeus demon*, Rtl. 146, 37. Gā ðū onbæcling, wiþerwearda (*Satanas*), Blickl. Homl. 27, 20. Se ilca wiþerwearda ðe him ǣr ða synna lǣrde, 61, 17. Se wiðerwearda (-worda, Rush.) *Satanas*, Mk. Skt. Lind. 3, 26. Ðe wiðerworda, 4, 15: Lk. Skt. Lind. Rush. 13, 16. Bysmraþ se wiðerwearda (*adversarius*) naman ðīnne, Ps. Spl. 73, 11. Ðæm wiþerweardan (*the devil*) beóþ ðæs mannes synna gecwēmran ðonne eal eorþlīc goldhord, Blickl. Homl. 43, 20, 24. From ðæm wiðerwearda (-e, Lind.) *a Satana*, Mk. Skt. Rush. 1, 13. Mid wiðerweardum *cum emulo*, Wrt. Voc. ii. 74, 63: 17, 61. Beó ðū gemōd ðīnum ðæm wiþerwearde (*adversario tuo*), ðȳ læs se wiðerwearde ðec selle doeme, Mt. Kmbl. Rush. 5, 25. Mið wiðerworde ðīnum (wiðerwordne ðīnne, Rush.), Lk. Skt. Lind. 12, 58: 18, 3. Wiðerweardne wið hine *adversum se*, Past. 32; Swt. 211, 2. On ðam geáre wurdon ða Gallie Rōmānum wiðerwearde *eodem anno Galli novi exstitere hostes*, Ors. 4, 7; Swt. 180, 24. Ealle ða ðe mē wiðerwearde wǣron *omnes adversantes mihi*, Ps. Th. 3, 6. Mē wiðerwearde wǣron ealle, ða him sǣton on portum *adversum me exercebantur qui sedebant in porta*, Ps. Th. 68, 12: 123, 3: 139, 8: Blickl. Homl. 223, 18: Past. 21; Swt. 161, 23. Ða men ðe hié ongeáton ðæt wiðerwearde wǣron Godes beboda, Blickl. Homl. 135, 12. Naman ðīnne bysmriaþ ða wiþerweardan (*adversarius*), Ps. Th. 73, 10. Alle wiðiwordas (wiðerworda, Rush.) ł fióndas iúra *omnes adversarii uestri*, Lk. Skt. Lind. 21, 15. Se wæs on dǣle ðara wiþerweardra *in parte erat adversariorum*, Bd. 3, 24; S. 556, 27. Mīnra wiðerweardra, Ps. Th. 17, 4. Mid wiþerwordum (*adversis*) onbēnum, Bd. 2, 2; S. 504, 3. ii land ðe wǣron bereáfodon þurh Denisce men and wiðerwearde (*hostile*; or *evil*, v. **IV**) dēman ūt of ðam mynstre, Chart. Th. 446, 7. Heó heora ða wiþerweardan (*adversarios*) feor ādrifan, Bd. 1, 15; S. 483, 3. **II a.** *hostile to rightful authority, rebel*:—Nis nān gesceaft ðe wiþ hire Scippendes willan winne, būton dysig mon, oþþe eft ða wiþerwierdan (-weardan, *v. l.*) englas, Bt. 35, 4; Fox 160, 25. Wiþerwyrd *perduelles, ualde rebelles*, Germ. 393, 53. **III.** of hindrance, *contrary, opposed, that presents an obstacle, obstinate*:—Nis āhwǣr gemēted on hālgum bōcum ðæt ðysse frignysse wiþerword sī gesawen *nequaquam in sacris eloquiis invenitur quod huic capitulo contradicere videatur*, Bd. 1, 27; S. 490, 32. Hē oft wolde ðæt eorþlīce rīce forlǣtan, gif him ne wiþstōde ðæt wiþerwarde mōd (*obstinatus animus*) his wīfes, 4, 11; S. 579, 10. Wiðerwurdra *contrariarum* (omnes rerum contrariarum machinas exterminans, Ald. 57), Hpt. Gl. 502, 26. IV. *opposed to what is right, arrogant, perverse, depraved, reprobate, false*; in special senses, *heretic, apocryphal*:—Wiðerweard heorte *cor pravum*, Ps. Th. 100, 3. Manega mid mannum synd getealde gecorene and mid Gode wiþerwyrde (*reprobi*), and fela mid mannum wiþerwyrde synd and mid Gode gecorene; nān hine getelle gecorenne, ðe læs ðe hē mid Gode sȳ wiþerwyrd, Scint. 74, 13–16. Wiðerwurde *importunus, improbus*, Hpt. Gl. 425, 59. Ðæt wiðerwurde *importuna, improba*, 444, 22. Mid wiðerwurde *protervo, contrario*, 434, 12. Betera geþyldig wiþerwyrdum *melior patiens arrogante*, Scint. 8, 18. Fela ðūsenda folgeaþ Criste, þeáh ðe hī sume (*the Jews*) wunian wiðerwerde, Homl. Skt. ii. 25, 526. Wiðerwearde crist *pseudo-cristi*, Mt. Kmbl. Lind. 24, 24. Wiðerworde criste and wiðerworde wītgu, Mk. Skt. Rush. 13, 22. Alle wiðerweardra gedwola *omnes apocryphorum naenias*, Mt. Kmbl. p. 10, 9. Wiðerwordra lārwa[s] sēda *haereticorum semina*, 8, 19. Wiðerwurdra *perfidorum, impiorum*, Hpt. Gl. 415, 45. From wiðirwordum lārwum *ab ereticis*, Rtl. 198, 19. V. *opposed to the good or pleasure of anything, unfavourable, adverse, hurtful, pernicious, disagreeable*:—Nānwuht ne byð yfel, ǣr mon wēne ðæt hit yfel seó; and þeáh hit nū hefig seó and wiþerweard, þeáh hit biþ gesǣlþ gif hit mon geþyldlīce ārǣfnþ *nihil est miserum, nisi cum putes; contraque beata sors omnis est aequinamitate tolerantis*, Bt. 11, 1; Fox 32, 31. Seó wiþerwearde wyrd *adversa fortuna*, 20; Fox 70, 29. [Nān þing] swā wiðerweard þēn is [cristenum monnum] swā oferfylle *nihil sic contrarium est omni christiano quomodo crapula*, R. Ben. Interl. 71, 7. Hē ālȳseþ mē fram worde wiðerweardum (*a verbo aspero*), Ps. Spl. 90, 3: Blickl. Gl. Alle wiðirwærda hǣles mennisces wyrttruman *omnes adversas salutis humani radices*, Rtl. 125, 33. Gif huoelc sindon wiðirworda in hūse esnes ðīnes *si qua sunt adversa in domo famuli tui*, 123, 13. Ðonne ðē for worulde wiþerwearda mǣst þinga þreáge, Met. 5, 36. Þolemōd on heardum and on wiþerweardum (*contrariis*) þingum, R. Ben. 26, 18. Lufian wē hine næs nō on gesundum þingum ānum, ac eác swylce on wiðerweardum þingum, Blickl. Homl. 13, 8. Wið wiþerweard hǣr; gif ðū nimest wulfes mearh and smyrest mid hraðe ða stōwe ðe ða hǣr beóð of āpullud, ne geþafaþ seó smyrung ðæt hȳ eft wexen, Lchdm. i. 362, 8. Wala middangeardes getēla, and nǣngo his wiðirweardo (*adversa*) onscynia, Rtl. 50, 6. Geþyld gōdu gehealt, āweg nȳt wyþerwerde, Scint. 13, 10: 62, 5. Wyþerwyrde, 62, 2. VI. of diversity, *contrary, opposite* in nature, action, etc.:—Ðæt gecynd nyle nǣfre nānwuht wiþerweardes lǣtan gemengan ... Nū ðonne nū ǣlc gesceaft onscunaþ ðæt, ðæt hire wiþerweard biþ ... hwelce twā synd wiþerweardran betwux him ðonne gōd and yfel? Bt. 16, 3; Fox 54, 35–56, 7. Ða wiþerweardan gesceafta ǣgþer ge betwux him winnaþ, ge eác fæste sibbe betwux him healdaþ, swā nū fȳr dēþ and wæter ... Ac ā sceal ðæt wiðerwearde ðæt ōðer wiþerwearde gemetgian, 21; Fox 74, 13–20: Met. 11, 49, 52. Ðæt mē þincþ wiþerweard þing *in contrarium relapsa res est*, Bt. 26, 2; Fox 92, 24. Hē nāwyht wiðerweardes (*contrarium*) ðære sōðfæstnysse ðæs geleáfan Crēca ðeáwe on Angelcynnes cyricean on gelǣdde, Bd. 4, 1; S. 564, 20. Hī monig ōþer ðing ðære cyriclīcan ānnesse wiþerword hæfden, 2, 2; S. 502, 12. On monegum ðingum gē wiþerwearde wǣron ūrum gewunan *in multis nostrae consuetudini contraria geritis*, S. 503, 18. From wiðerwordum lārwum *a diversis auctoribus*, Mt. Kmbl. p. 7, 4. [Wið al folc he wes wiðerword, Laym. 6875. Wiþerrwarrd onnȝænes Godd, Orm. 9667. Ðis king him his wel wiðerward agen ðis folc, Gen. and Ex. 2935. *Goth.* wiþra-wairþs *that is over against; contrary*: *O. Sax.* wiðar-ward, -word *hostile; displeasing*: *O. H. Ger.* widar-wart, -wert *contrarius, adversus, adversarius*.] v. un-wiþerweard.

wiþerweardian; *p.* ode *To oppose, be adverse to*:—Ða ðe wiþerweardiaþ mē *qui adversantur mihi*, Ps. Spl. 34, 22. [*O. H. Ger.* widar-wartōn, -wertōn *obviare, adversari, contraire, fraudare*.] v. ge-wiðerworded; wiþerwirdan.

wiþerweard-līc; *adj. Unfavourable, adverse, hurtful.* v. wiþer-weard, V:—Nis cristenum monnum nān ðing swā wiðerweardlīc and hefigtȳme swā swā oferfyl *nihil sic contrarium est omni christiano quomodo crapula*, R. Ben. 63, 20. Warna ðē ðæt ðū nān þing wiðerwerdlīces ne sprece ongēn Jacob *cave ne quidquam aspere loquaris contra Jacob*, Gen. 31, 24. [*O. H. Ger.* widarwart-līh *tyrannicus*.]

wiþerweardlīce; *adv. Detrimentally, against the interests of any one*:—Þurh ðæt ðe ðū ðysne wuldres cyning āhēnge, ðū dydest wyþerwerdlīce ongeán ðē and eác ongeán mē (*thou hast acted against thine own interests and against mine.* v. Gospel of Nicodemus c. 18, v. 11), Nicod. 29; Thw. 17, 10.

wiþerweard-ness, e; *f.* I. *hostility, contention, opposition.* v. wiþer-weard, I:—Nis ðǣr ege, ne geflit, ne yrre, ne nǣnig wiþerweardnes, Blickl. Homl. 25, 32. Hē wearð grǣdig ðæs gōdan deáþes būtan ǣlcre scylde and ǣlcre wiðerweardnesse wið hine *he* (*David*) *was greedy for the death of the good man* (*Uriah*), *who was without any crime against him and had shewn no hostility to him*, Past. 3; Swt. 37, 2. Mid wiðerwurdnessa *cum aemulo*, Hpt. Gl. 405, 32. Sume sace wyðerwyrdnesse hit getācnaþ, Lchdm. iii. 198, 13. II. *perversity, frowardness, depravity, arrogance.* v. wiþer-weard, IV:—Wiðirweardnis ł wyrs *perversius*, Mt. Kmbl. p. 2, 1. Wiþerwerdnysse *arrogantie*, Anglia xiii. 371, 83. Wyþerwyrdnysse, 369, 56. Wiðirwordnisum *pravis*, Rtl. 91, 24. III. *unfavourable condition, adverse circumstance, adversity.* v. wiþer-weard, V:—Seó wiþerweardnes *adversa fortuna, adversitas*, Bt. 20; Fox 72, 5, 9, 12. Nān yfel ne mæg ðē geneálǣcan, ac ǣlc wiðerweardnys gewīteþ fram ðīnre sāwle, Basil admn. 1; Norm. 34, 10. Ðū ðē ne anhebbe on ofermētto on ðīnre gesundfulnesse, ne eft ðē ne geortrȳwe nānes gōdes on nānre wiþerweardnesse, Bt. 6; Fox 16, 1. On wiþerwerdnesse *in aduersitate*, Wülck. Gl. 252, 4. Wiðirwordnise, Rtl. 14, 20. Hē ðisses middangeardes orsorgnesse ne gīmð, ne him nāne wiðerweardnesse ne andrǣt ðisse worolde *qui prospera mundi postposuit, qui nulla adversa pertimescit*, Past. 10; Swt. 61, 8: 33; Swt. 219, 2. Hē sǣde ge hwylce wiþerwardnesse (-wordnesse, Bd. M. 330, 10), ge eft hwylce frōfre on ðām wiþerweardnessum (-wordnissum, Bd. M.) him becom, Bd. 4, 22; S. 592, 17. Geþyld on wiðerwerdnyssum, Scint. 12, 12. On wiþerwerdnyssum *in adversitatibus*, 62, 2. Ða getreówfullan for Godes ege ealle līfes wiðerweardnesse (*universa contraria*) forþyldigian scylun, R. Ben. 27, 7. IV. *contrariety, diversity.* v. wiþer-weard, VI:—Seó wiþerweardnes ðe wē ǣr ymbe sprǣcon, Bt. 21; Fox 74, 32: Met. 11, 78.

wiþer-wierde. v. wiþer-weard.

wiþer-winn, es; *n. Contest, conflict*:—Wiþerwinnes *exercitationis* (qui laboriosi certaminis coronam difficillimis propriae exercitationis viribus nanciscuntur, Ald. 2), Hpt. Gl. 405, 20.

wiþer-winna, an; *m. An adversary, opponent, enemy*:—*Emulus*, i. *contrarius*, gewinna, wiþerwinna, Wrt. Voc. ii. 143, 45. Beó ðū onbūgende ðīnum wiþerwinnan (*adversario tuo*) .. ðe læs ðe ðīn wiðerwinna ðē sylle ðam dēman, Mt. Kmbl. 5, 25: Homl. Ass. 4, 95. Ðȳ læs hē sié ongieten ðæt hē sié wiðerwinna on ðære diégelnesse his geðōhtes ðæs ðe hē bið gesewen ðeów on his ðēnunge *ne inveniatur ei, cui servire per officium cernitur, occulta cogitationis tyrannide resultare*, Past. 19; Swt. 147, 16. Ðǣr (*in heaven*) ne wunaþ nān wiþerwinna, Homl. Ass. 78, 145. Ūre wiðerwinna is se deófol. . . . Is ōðer wiðerwinna, ðæt is Godes word, ðæt word winð on ūs, 5, 120–128: 52, 53. Ðæt hālige Godes word is ðīn freónd, and ðū wyrcst ðē sylfne ðē tō wiðerwinnan, 6, 138. Ðonne ðū gǣst on wege mid ðīnum wiðerwinnan (*cum adversario tuo*) tō hwylcum ealdre, Lk. Skt. 12, 58. Wrec mē wið mīnne wiðerwinnan, 18, 3. Wiþerwinnan *conluctatorem*, i. *oppugnatorem*, Scint. 151, 4. Ðam ne magon ealle eówer wiðerwinnan (*aduersarii uestri*) wiðstandan and wiðcweðan, Lk. Skt. 21, 15. Ða Godes wiðerwinnan, Homl. Ass. 178, 306. Ða þeóda ða hiora wiðerwinnan wǣron, Ors. 6, 35; Swt. 292, 7. Wiðerwinnena *aemulorum, contrariorum, inimicorum*, Hpt. Gl. 424, 22: 471, 72: 475, 70. Gescylde mē wiþ mīnum wiþerwinnum, gesewenlīcum and ungesewenlīcum, Bt. 42; Fox 260, 10. Nigon x hund þūsenda of Persa ānra anwealde būton hiera wiþerwinnum, ǣgþer ge of Sciþþium ge of Crēcum, Ors. 2, 5; Swt. 84, 30. [Þe wyþerwynne (*the devil*), Misc. 74, 77. Forgive us ure sinne als we don ure wiðerwinnes, Rel. Ant. i. 235, 18. *O. H. Ger.* widar-winno.]

wiþer-winnan *to oppose, resist*:—Wiþerwinnende *rebelles*, Germ. 389, 88. [*O. H. Ger.* uuidar-uuinanten *conluctantem*.] v. wiþ-winnan.

wiþer-winning, e; *f. Contest, controversy*:—Būtan wiþerwenningce (-winninge?) *sine controversia*, Scint. 146, 15.

wiþerwirdan; *p.* de *To oppose, be adverse to*:—Ealle ða ðē wiþerwyrdaþ *omnes qui tibi aduersantur*, Scint. 165, 4. v. wiþerweardian.

wiþer-word, -wurd; wiþe-winde. v. wiþer-weard; wiþo-winde.

wiþ-faran; *p.* -fōr *To escape.* v. wiþ, II. 3:—Siððan hié ðam [herge] wiðfōron, Cd. Th. 214, 23; Exod. 573. v. wiþ-ferian, wiþ-gangan, II.

wiþ-feohtan *to fight against, contend with*:—Hē gefeaht mid ða ǣ ðæs mōdes, ðære wiþfeaht (wiðflāt, *v. l.*) seó ǣ ðe on his limum wæs *pugnabat legi mentis, cui lex, quae in membris est, repugnabat*, Bd. 1, 27; S. 497, 39. Wiðfeohtan *certare*, Wrt. Voc. ii. 22, 17. v. wiþ, II. 10.

wiþ-feohtend, es; *m. An adversary, opponent, enemy, a rebel*:—Hió self fieht wið hié selfe tō fultome ðæm wiðfeohtende (*adversario*), Past. 38; Swt. 279. 1. Ðone māngengan and ðone wiþfeohtend *rebellem et sacrilegum*, Bd. 1, 7; S. 477, 18. Betweoh ða elreordan and ða wiþfeohtend Cristes geleáfan *inter rebelles fidei barbaros*, 2, 5; S. 507, 33. v. wiþer-feohtend.

wiþ-feolan; *p.* -fealh *To apply one's self to*:—Ðā hē ðā ongeat ðæt hē ðære godspellīcan lāre georne wiþfealh, and ða ðeóde tō Cristes geleáfan gecyrred hæfde *qui ubi prosperatum ei opus evangelii comperit*, Bd. 3, 22; S. 552, 43.

wiþ-ferian; *p.* ede *To carry off, to rescue.* v. wiþ, II. 3:—Ðū wiðferedes (fæderas, MS.) Israhēla bearn of Ægyptum *redemisti filios Israel et Joseph*, Ps. Th. 76, 12. Hē of heofenum hider onsende, ðe mē ālȳsde, lāþum wiðferede *misit de caelo, et liberavit me*, 56, 3. Mīne sāwle ālȳs, and wiðfere lāþum feóndum *animam meam libera: propter inimicos meos eripe me*, 68, 18. Ðæt ðū symle sāwle mīne ālȳse, lāðum wiðferige *liberabit in pace animam meam ab his qui adpropiant mihi*, 54, 18. Ðū āwurpe hī ðā hī wēndan, ðæt hī wǣron ālȳsde, lāðum wiðferede *dejecisti eos dum allevarentur*, 72, 14. v. wiþ-faran, wiþ-lǣdan, wiþ-teón, III.

wiþ-flītan; *p.* -flāt *To contend with*:—Oferstǣleþ oððe wiðflīteþ *confutat*, Wrt. Voc. ii. 15, 31. v. wiþ-feohtan.

wiþ-fōn; *p.* -fēng *To lay hold on, seize on.* Cf. wiþ, II. 1 d:—Hē uplang āstōd, and him fæste wiðfēng, Beo. Th. 1524; B. 760. Cf. wiþ-grīpan.

wiþ-foran; *prep. with dat. acc. Before*:—Hē feaht him wiðforan, Jos. 8, 22. Hē ofirnþ ða sunnan hindan, and cymþ wiþforan ða sunnan up, Bt. 39, 13; Fox 234, 2. ¶ wiþ . . . foran:—Ðone mist ðe wið ða eágan foran usses mōdes (cf. beforan ūres mōdes eágum, Bt. 33, 4; Fox 132, 32) hangode, Met. 20, 265. Hwȳ hī (*stars*) ne scīnen beforan ðære sunnan, swā hī dōð wið ðone mōnan foran (beforan ðam mōnan, Bt. 39, 3; Fox 214, 30), 28, 47. Wið ðone segn foran, Cd. Th. 188, 23; Exon. 172.

wiþ-gān *to go against, act in opposition to, in contravention of.* Cf. wiþ, II. 13:—Nǣfre mīne lāstweardas geðrīstlǣcen ðæt heó hit (*a grant*) onwenden oððe ðon wiðgǣn, Chart. Th. 29, 14. v. next word.

wiþ-gangan. I. *to go against*:—Ic ne meahte mægnes cræfte gūðe wiðgongan (*I could not go and meet the foe in fight*), ac ic sceal sēcan cempan sǣmran, Exon. Th. 266, 4; Jul. 393. II. *to go off, withdraw, fail*:—Byð mē eágon wiðgangen *defecerunt oculi mei*, Ps. Th. 68, 3. v. wiþ-faran.

wiþ-gemetness, e; *f. Comparison*:—In ða wiþgemetnesse wæs lytel gesewen *in comparatione tenuissima videbatur*, Bd. 5, 12; S. 629, 36. v. wiþ-metenness.

wiþ-geondan; *prep. Beyond*:—Eal ðæt rīce wiðgeondan Iordanen *omnis regio circum Iordanen*, Mt. Kmbl. 3, 5.

wiþ-gīnan; *p.* de *To reply* (? cf. *Icel.* gegna *to reply*); *to repel, reject* (? v. gynde, Homl. Skt. ii. 25, 636):—Ðā cwæð hē eft tō him sylfum: 'Tō sōðan ne þincð mē nǣfre ðæt hit sōð sȳ ðæt ðys sȳ Efesa byrig . . .' Ðā wiðgȳnde hē eft his geðance, ond him þus andwyrde (*he replied to his thought*, or *he rejected the idea, and answered himself thus*): 'Ac ic nāt eftsōna, ne ic nǣfre git nyste ðæt ǣnig ōþer byrig ūs wǣre gehende būton Ephese ānre,' Homl. Skt. i. 23, 541.

wiþ-grīpan; *p.* -grāp *To seize on*:—Gif ic wiste hū wið ðam āglǣcan elles meahte gripe wiðgrīpan, swā ic wið Grendle dyde, Beo. Th. 5035; B. 2521. v. wiþ-fōn.

wiþ-habban; *p.* -hæfde *To hold out against, to withstand, resist*:—Gif ðæs synfullan ingehȳd bið gehrepod mid fyrhte ðæs upplīcan dōmes, ðonne wiðhæfð hē ðām unlustum, Homl. Th. i. 494, 9. Ðæt wæs wundor micel, ðæt se wīnsele wiðhæfde heaðodeórum, Beo. Th. 1548; B. 772. Þurh ða gedurstignysse ðe folces men wiðhæfton (-hæfdon?) ðære gelōmlīcan mynegunge ðe ūre lāreówas dydon, L. Edg. S. 1; Th. i. 270, 24. Se ðe him ǣr geþūhte, ðæt him nān sǣ wiþhabban ne mehte, ðæt hē hiene mid scipum and mid his fultume āfyllan ne mehte, Ors. 2, 5; Swt. 84, 13. Næs nān ðæs stronglīc . . . ðæt mihte ðam miclan mægne wiðhabban, Cd. Th. 297, 18; Sat. 519. v. wiþer-habban.

wiþ-heardian *to make obdurate*:—Nylle gē wiðheardian (*obdurare*) heortan eówre, Ps. Spl. 94, 7.

wiþ-hindan; *prep.* (*adv.*) *Behind*:—Hē feaht him wiðforan and his gefēran wiðhindan, Jos. 8, 22.

wiþ-hogian; *p.* ode *To be adverse in thought* or *purpose, to be disposed to resist*:—Abraham . . . nalles Nergendes hǣse wiðhogode (*had no thought of disobeying the command*), Cd. Th. 173, 20; Gen. 2864. v. next word.

wiþ-hycgan; *p.* -hogde *To be adverse in thought* or *purpose, to set one's self against*:—Heó ðæs beornes lufan fæste wiðhogde *her heart was fast closed against the man's love*, Exon. Th. 245, 9; Jul. 42. Gē wiðhogdun hālgum Dryhtne *your hearts were hostile to the holy Lord*, 139, 34; Gū. 603. Ðæt hē stān nime, hlāfes ne gȳme, ða wiste wiðsæce, beteran wiðhycge (*the food refuse, set himself against the better*), Elen. Kmbl. 1232; El. 618. v. wiþer-hycgende, *and previous word.*

wīþig, wīþing (?), es; *m. A withy, willow*:—Ðes wīþig *salix*, Ælfc. Gr. 9, 63; Zup. 70, 10: Lchdm. ii. 86, 6: Wrt. Voc. i. 33, 53. Wīðig, 80, 28. Wīþies rinde, Lchdm. ii. 150, 2. On ðone hāran wīðig . . .; of ðam wīþige, Cod. Dip. Kmbl. iii. 457, 8, 10: 313, 27: 399, 21: 400, 2. On ðone ealdan wīðig; ðonne of ðam wīðige, vi. 35, 33. On ðone wīðig, iii. 10, 25. In ǣnne wīðing, 391, 27. v. wīþig-mere. [Cf. *O. H. Ger.* wīda *salix*: *Icel.* vīðir *a willow.*] See the following words.

wīþig-bed[d], es; *n. A bed of willows, an osier-bed*:—On ðæt wīðigbed, Cod. Dip. Kmbl. iii. 437, 21.

wīþig-brōc, es; *m. A brook by which willows grow*:—In wīðibrōc, Cod. Dip. Kmbl. iii. 380, 2. On wīðigbrōch, 202, 3.

wīþig-ford, es; *m. A ford by which willows grow*:—On wīðigford, of wīðigford, Cod. Dip. Kmbl. iii. 135, 14: 252, 20, 36.

wīþig-grāf, es; *m. A willow-grove*:—Of weardsetle on wīðiggrāfas; of wīðiggrāfan, Cod. Dip. Kmbl. v. 328, 11: 48, 11.

wīþig-leáh; *gen.* -leás; *m. A meadow where willows grow* (a place-name):—Ðis synt ða landgemǣro tō Wīðileá . . . Ðis is ðæra feówer hȳda landbōc æt Wīðigleá, Cod. Dip. Kmbl. iii. 457, 13–23.

wīþig-mǣd; *f. A meadow where willows grow*:—Ǣrest æt wīðigmǣde . . . ðæt eft on wīðigmǣde, Cod. Dip. Kmbl. iii. 464, 18–30.

wīþig-mere, es; *m. A mere with willows on the banks*:—On wīðimære, Cod. Dip. B. iii. 188, 29. In wīðingmere, ii. 41, 4.

wīþig-mōr, es; *m. A moor where willows grow*:—On wīðigmōr, Cod. Dip. Kmbl. iii. 412, 21.

wīþig-pōl, es; *m. A pool with willows on the banks*:—On wīðepōl, Cod. Dip. B. iii. 188, 30.

wīþig-pyt[t], es; *m. A pit with willows by it*:—On wīðigpytt, Cod. Dip. B. iii. 336, 21.

wīþig-rǣw, e; *f. A row of willows*:—On ða wīðigrēwe, Cod. Dip. Kmbl. iii. 48, 5.

wīþig-rind, e; *f. Willow-bark*:—Nim wīþigrinde, Lchdm. ii. 98, 9.

wīþig-slǣd, es; *n. A slade* (v. slǣd) *where willows grow*:—Tō wīðigslǣde, Cod. Dip. Kmbl. iii. 457, 16.

wīþig-þȳfel, es; *m. A willow-copse*:—On wīðigðȳfel, Cod. Dip. B. iii. 336, 21. Andlang dīche foren ongēn wīðigþeuel, Cod. Dip. Kmbl. iii. 418, 2. Anlang brōke on ānne wīðigþēfele, þiers ouer ðane mersc, 426, 26. Tōemnes ðām wīðigðȳfelum bewestan flōdan, v. 194, 32.

wīþig-wīc, es; *n. A dwelling-place by which willows grow*:—Wīðigwīc, Cod. Dip. Kmbl. ii. 195, 18.

wīþig-will, es; *m. A spring by which willows grow*:—On ðone fūlan wylle . . . on wȳðigwylle, Cod. Dip. Kmbl. vi. 213, 16–21.

wīþing. v. wīþig.

wiþ-innan; *adv. prep. Within.* (1) as adverb:—Gehrepod mid heortan sārnisse wiðinnan (*intrinsecus*), Gen. 6, 6. Fācn wiþinnan (*intus*) tȳddriende swā swā bergyls wiþinnan (*intus*) full stence, Coll. Monast. Th. 32, 33, 35. Ðū clǣmst wiðinnan and wiðūtan (*intrinsecus et extrinsecus*) mid tyrwan, Gen. 6, 14. Hī ofslōgon ǣgðer ge wiðinnan ge wiðūtan mā þanne .xx. manna, Chr. 1048; Erl. 178, 1. Symle wē beóð fram Gode gesewene ǣgðer ge wiðūtan ge wiðinnan, Homl. Th. i. 604, 19. (2) as preposition:—Ealle ða ðe wiðinnan mē (*intra me*) synd, Ps. Spl. 102, 1: 108, 21. v. wiþ-ūtan.

wiþ-lǣdan; *p.* de *To lead away, carry off, take away.* v. wiþ, II. 3:—Ðū ðe Jōseph swā sceáp gramum wiðlǣddest *qui deducis velut ovem Joseph*, Ps. Th. 79, 1. Ðū mīne sāwle of swyltdeáðes lāþum wiðlǣddest *eripuisti animam meam de morte*, 55, 11. Ða ðe wiðlaeddun ūs *qui abduxerunt nos*, Ps. Surt. 136, 3. Cneóris mīn wiðlaeded is *generatio mea ablata est*, ii. p. 184, 30. Wiðlaedde eam *ablatus sum*, 108, 23: Ps. Spl. C. 108, 22. Cf. wiþ-ferian.

wiþ-licgan; *p.* -læg, *pl.* -lǣgon *To be obstructive, object, oppose.* Cf. wiþ-standan:—Behēt man him ðæt hē mōste wurðe beón ǣlc ðæra þinga ðe hē ǣr āhte. Ðā wiðlæg (wiðcwæð, MS. D.) Harold, Chr. 1046; Erl. 173, 2. Ða eorlas gerndon tō ðam cynge ðæt hī mōston beón wurðe ǣlc ðæra þinga ðe heom of genumen wæs. Ðā wiðlæg se cyng sume hwīle, 1052; Erl. 187, 1.

wiþ-metan; *p.* -mæt, *pl.* -mǣton; *pp.* -meten *To compare*:—Wiðmeteþ *equiperat*, Wrt. Voc. ii. 83, 70: 31, 23. Hine wiðmete *equat*, 31, 49. Wiðmeten is *confertur*, 19, 27. Wiþmeten *comparatus, assimilatus*, 132, 77. Bión wiðmetene *comparari*, Kent. Gl. 42: 1023. (1) with dat.:—Hwylcum bigspelle wiðmete wē hit? *cui parabolae comparabimus illud?* Mk. Skt. 4, 30. Deáh ðe hē nō sī his foregengan tō wiþmetenne *tametsi praedecessori suo minime comparandus*, Bd. 5, 8; S. 621, 35: Homl. Th. i. 486, 25, 29. Beón wiðmeten ðīnre strengðe *comparari fortitudini tuae*, Deut. 3, 24: Bd. 1, 34; S. 499, 21: Ps. Spl. 48, 12: Homl. Th. ii. 200, 33: 456, 13. (2) with prep.:—Ða cræftas ne sint tō wiþmetanne (metanne, *v. l.*) wiþ ðære sāwle cræfta ǣnne, Bt. 32, 1; Fox 116, 2. v. wiþer-metan.

wiþ-mētedness, e; *f. An invention*; adinventio. v. mētan:—Wiðmētednyssa heora *adinventionum ipsorum*, Ps. Spl. 27, 5. On wiðmētednysse heora, 80, 11. Wiðmētednyssa, 98, 9.

wiþ-metendlīc; *adj. Comparative*:—Wiðmetendlīce naman *comparativa nomina*, Ælfc. Gr. 9, 21; Zup. 45, 14. v. next word.

wiþ-metenlīc; *adj. Comparative*:—Hī synd *comparativa*, ðæt synd wiðmetenlīce, Ælfc. Gr. 5; Zup. 15, 15. v. un-wiþmetenlīc.

wiþ-metenlīce. v. un-wiþmetenlīce.

wiþ-metenness, e; *f. Comparison*:—Wiþmetenes *comparatio*, Wrt. Voc. ii. 132, 79. Ðyslīc mē is gesewen ðis andwarde līf tō wiþmetenysse ðære tīde ðe ūs uncūþ is *talis mihi videtur vita praesens ad comparationem ejus quod nobis incertum est temporis*, Bd. 2, 13; S. 516, 14. Wiðmetenysse, Homl. Th. ii. 430, 18. On wiðmetenysse *in comparatione*, Hpt. Gl. 420, 22. On his wiðmetennysse *in comparison with it*, Homl. Th. i. 618, 20. Næs hē geteald tō ðyssere wiðmetennysse *he was not included in this comparison*, ii. 38, 3. Sume naman synd *diminutiva*, ða geswuteliaþ wanunge, nā wiðmetennysse, Ælfc. Gr. 5; Zup. 16, 18.

wiþ-meting, e; *f. Comparison*:—Wiđmetincg *comparatio*, Scint. 194, 13. Of wiđmetincge *ex comparatione*, 103, 9.

wiþ-neoþan; *adv. Beneath*:—Wiđneođan (-nioþan, -nyđan, *v.ll.*) *infra*, Ælfc. Gr. 38; Zup. 225, 5: 240, 10. Duru đū setst be đære sīdan wiđneođan *ostium pones ex latere deorsum*, Gen. 6, 16. Beón hī beworpene mid wuda wiđneođan, Homl. Skt. i. 18, 106.

wiþo-bān, es: -bāne (? cf. Icel. -beina), an; *n. A collar-bone*:—Gif widobāne gebroced weorđeþ, L. Ethb. 52; Th. i. 16, 5. Ofer ealle đa sīdan āstīhþ ōþ đæt wiþobān and ōþ đone swīþran sculdor đæt sār, Lchdm. ii. 198, 18. Stingende sār ōþ đa wiþobān ōđ đa eaxle, 204, 26. Hwīlum ofer ealle đa sīdan biþ đæt sār, hwīlum becymđ on đa weoþobān, and eft ymb lytel đa gesculdru đæt sār grēt, 258, 5. [*O. Frs.* widu-bēn: *Icel.* við-beina; *n. a collar-bone.*]

wiþo-bend *wood-bine*:—Nim weoþobend, Lchdm. ii. 312, 12. [A bordun ibounde with a brod lyste, in a wethebondes wyse iwrithen aboute, Piers P. A. 6, 9.] Cf. wudu-bend, *and next word.*

wiþo-winde (wiþ-), an; *f. Withy-wind, with-wind* (v. E. D. S. Pub. Plant Names), *convolvulus*:—Wiþewinde *involuco*, Wrt. Voc. ii. 49, 2. Wiđwinde *viticella*, i. 33, 13. Genim wiþowindan twigu, Lchdm. ii. 34, 17. Wiþowindan leáf, 52, 6. Wiþewindan, 122, 18. [In a withewyndes (weythwynde, MS. C.) wise ywounden, Piers P. 5, 525.]

wiþ-rǣdan *to act against, be an antidote*:—Đære wyrte wyrttruma on wætere geđyged wiđrǣđ īceom and næddrum, Lchdm. i. 144, 15.

wiþ-rǣde; *adj. Contrary*:—Wiđrǣde *contraria*, R. Ben. Interl. 13, 7. v. wiþer-rǣde.

wiþre. v. wiþere.

wiþ-reótan; *pp.* -roten *To clamour against* (?):—Gē đam rihte wiđroten hæfdon, onscunedon đone scīran Scippend, Elen. Kmbl. 738; El. 369.

wiþ-sacan; *p.* -sōc, *pl.* -sōcon; *pp.* -sacen *To deny, refuse, reject*:—Ic wiþsace *recuso*, Ælfc. Gr. 28, 6; Zup. 178, 13. Sume (*adverbs*) syndan *abnegativa*, đæt synd wiđsacendlīce, mid đām wē wiđsacaþ, 38; Zup. 226, 4. Wē wiđsacaþ *diffitemur*, Wrt. Voc. ii. 28, 21. Ic ne wiþsōc *non abnui*, 60, 32. Wiđsōc *refragatur*, 87, 37. Wiđsōcan *refragabantur*, 78, 8. I. *to say no* to a request, *to refuse permission*:—Đā ongunnon đa iungan biddan đone biscop, đæt hē him ālȳfde, đæt hī ærnan mōstan. Đā wiþsōc (*negavit*) se biscop, Bd. 5, 6; S. 619, 1. II. where an offer or command is expressed or implied or choice is possible, *to refuse, reject, decline*, (1) absolute:—Bæd se gesīþ hine, đæt hē eode on his hūs; wiþsōc (*renuit*) se biscop, Bd. 5, 4; S. 617, 11. Begann se cyngc gyrnan his sweostor him tō wīfe . . . heó sylf wiđsōc, Chr. 1067; Erl. 204, 17. Wiđsōc *refragabatur* (*oblatam matrimonii sortem*, Ald. 49), Hpt. Gl. 490, 65: *exhorruit*, 504, 10. Wiđsacende *refutans* (*carnalis luxus lenocinia*, Ald. 9), 420, 69: *refutando* (*obstinatam importunitatem*, Ald. 49), 491, 29. (2) with dat. of what is refused:—Gif ic sié đīnum folce nēdþearflīc tō hæbbenne, þonne ne wiđsace ic đæm gewinne, Blickl. Homl. 225, 27. Wiđsæcest đū sylfre rǣdes đīnum brȳdguman, Exon. Th. 248, 21; Jul. 99. Ic wiđsōc sāwle mīnre frōfre *negavi consolari animam meam*, Ps. Th. 76, 3. Ætfæste hē mē mīne efenþeówene, đā wiđsōc ic hire, Shrn. 39, 9. Đā bæd hē đa cempan, đæt hī onfēngon gereorde mid him; geþafode đæt ōþer, ōđer đam wiþsōc, 129, 32. Ōđer hiene gebeád tō đæm færelte; ōđer him wiđsōc (*pergere recusavit*), Past. 7; Swt. 49, 5. Hē đæt betere geceás, and đam wyrsan wiđsōc, Elen. Kmbl. 2078; El. 1040. Mid đon đe hē Egypte oferwon . . . hē heora godgieldum eallum wiđsōc, and hié mid ealle tōwearp *cunctam Aegypti religionem abominatus, ceremonias ejus et templa deposuit*, Ors. 2, 5; Swt. 78, 5. (3) with acc.:—Đæt hē đone stān nime and đa wiste wiđsæce, Elen. Kmbl. 1231; El. 617. For hwan đū mīn gebed woldest wiđsacan? *quid repellis orationem meam?* Ps. Th. 87, 14. Foregehēht brengende him lytla ne wiđsaca *praecepit oblatos sibi parvulos non repelli*, Mt. Kmbl. p. 18, 10. (4) with a clause:—Hē wiþsōc đæt hē đone Godes andettere slōge (*ferire recusavit*), Bd. 1, 7; S. 478, 40. Se wiþsōc đæt hē geleáfan onfēnge and đam gerȳne đæs heofonlīcan cyninges *et fidem ac sacramenta regni coelestis suscipere renuit*, 3, 7; S. 529, 27. (5) with dat. and clause in apposition:—Ne wiđsace ic đon, đæt ic on đæm campe leng sié, Blickl. Homl. 225, 32. III. where a claim is made or implied, *to deny, refuse to acknowledge* a person, (1) absolute:—Tō wiđsacenne *ad negandum* (*Deum*), Kent. Gl. 1080. (2) with gen. of what is denied:—On đissere nihte đū wiþsæcst mīn (*me negabis*) . . . Ne wiđsace ic đīn (*non te negabo*), Mt. Kmbl. 26, 34, 35: Mk. Skt. 14, 30. (3) with acc. (or uncertain):—Se đe mē wiđsæcđ, ic wiđsace hyne, Mt. Kmbl. 10, 33. Đū mē wiđsæcst, 26, 75: Jn. Skt. 13, 38. Se đe mē wiđsæcđ beforan mannum, se byđ wiđsacen beforan Godes englum, Lk. Skt. 12, 9. IV. where a statement is made or implied, *to deny, reject, refuse assent.* (1) absolute:—Hē wiđsōc (*negavit*) and cwæđ: 'Nāt ic hwæt đū segst,' Mt. Kmbl. 26, 70: Jn. Skt. 18, 27. Wē wiđsōcun ǣr mid leásingum, Elen. Kmbl. 2242; El. 1122. Wiđsacende *post tergum ponentes, abjicientes*, Hpt. Gl. 428, 65. (2) with gen.:—Hī wiđsacaþ Cristes tōcymes, Homl. Th. i. 144, 23. (3) with dat.:—Wiđsæcest đū sōđe and rihte ymb đæt līfes treów, Elen. Kmbl. 1322; El. 663. Gē wiđsōcon sōđe and rihte, đæt in Bethleme bearn Wealdendes cenned wǣre, 779; El. 390. (4) with a clause:—Hī wiđsōcon, đæt hē God wǣre . . . Sume wiđsōcon, đæt hē deádlīc flǣsc underfēnge, Homl. Th. i. 116, 16–19. (4 a) where the clause is put negatively:—Đā wiđsōc Crist, đæt hē deofol on him næfde; ac hē ne wiđsōc, đæt hē nǣre Samaritanisc, Homl. Th. ii. 230, 1–2. V. where a claim has been acknowledged or a relation has been established, *to renounce, reject, give up*, (1) absolute:—Heó wiđsōce *respuerit* (*mundi opes gloriamque*, Ald. 65), Hpt. Gl. 512, 69. Wiđsacan *abdicare* (*apocriphorum deliramenta*, Ald. 26), 452, 62. (2) with gen. v. (5). (3) with dat.:—Ǣlc of eów đe ne wiđsæcđ (*renuntiat*) eallum þingum đe hē āh, Lk. Skt. 14, 33. Đū wiđsōce sōþum criste *tu repulisti christum tuum*, Ps. Th. 88, 32. Hē wiđsōc (*repulit*) snytru hūse, wæs his āgen hūs, 77, 60, 67. Hē đīnum wiđsōc aldordōme, Elen. Kmbl. 1531; El. 767. Đǣm englum đe Gode wiþsōcan, Blickl. Homl. 49, 8. Būton hī đam deófolgylde geoffrodon and Drihtne wiđsōcon, Homl. Skt. i. 23, 114. Monige wiþsōcan đære unsȳfernysse deófolgylda *abrenunciata sorde idolatriae*, Bd. 3, 21; S. 551, 21. Wiþsacaþ nū đām leásum welum, Blickl. Homl. 53, 23. Đæt đū heofoncyninge wiđsōce, Exon. Th. 264, 8; Jul. 361. Deófulgyldum wiþsacan *abrenunciatis idolis*, Bd. 2, 9; S. 511, 35. (4) with acc.:—Đæt đū wiđsæcest đone cyning, đam đū hȳrdest ǣr, Elen. Kmbl. 1863; El. 933. Læsse ys wiđsacan (*abnegare*) đæt hē hæfđ, swȳþe micel ys wiđsacan đæt hit ys (*abnegare quod est*), Scint. 60, 13. (5) with gen., dat., and acc. in the same sentence:—Se fæder wiđsōc his bearne, and đæt bearn wiđsōc đone fæder, and æt nēxtan ǣlc freónd wiđsōc ōđres, Homl. Skt. i. 23, 110. V a. of self-renunciation:—Gyf hwā wylle fyligean mē, wiđsace (*abneget*) hyne sylfne, Mt. Kmbl. 16, 24. VI. *to refuse, withhold, not to give*:—Wæs Eþelwald đæs wordes, đæt hē nō đes rihtes wiđsacan wolde . . . and hit mildlīce āgeaf đan biscope, Chart. Th. 140, 12. VII. *to declare hostility* (?):—Hī hiene (*Mucius*) secgan hēton, hū fela đæra manna wǣre đe wiđ đæm cyninge Tarcuime swīđost wiđsacen hæfde, Ors. 2, 3; Swt. 68, 24. [Wiđsaken cristindom (heþene beo, 2nd MS.), Laym. 10898. Þ iherde Uortiger, and fastliche hit wiđsoc, 13000. Hit is so wide ibrouht forth, ich hit ne mei nout wiđsaken, A. R. 88, 11.]

wiþ-sacendlīc; *adj. Negative, expressing negation*:—Sume (*adverbs*) syndan *abnegativa*, đæt synd wiđsacendlīce, Ælfc. Gr. 38; Zup. 226, 3.

wiþ-sacung, e; *f. Renunciation*:—Nāht ūs framaþ wiđsacing (*abrenuntiatio*) līchaman būtan wiđsacinge geþances, Scint. 60, 14.

wiþ-scorian; *p.* ode *To refuse*:—Se đe đeónde biđ on cræftum, and đonne tō swiđe wiđscoraþ (-sceoraþ, Hatt. MS.) đæm ealdordōme (*si omnino renititur*), healde hine đæt hē ne cnytte đæt underfonge feoh on đam swātlīne, đæt Xrist ymbe spræc, Past. 9; Swt. 58, 12. [Yef þou louest to bi sobre, wyþscore and wyþdraȝ þine willes, Ayenb. 254, 26.]

wiþ-scūfan; *p.* -sceáf, *pl.* -scufon; *pp.* -scofen *To push back* or *away, to repel, drive away, refute*; repellere, expellere, praecipitare;—Wiđscyfs đū *precipitas*, Wrt. Voc. ii. 68, 67. Ūs drīfaþ đa ællreordan tō sǣ, wiþscūfeþ (*repellit*) ūs seó sǣ tō đām ællreordum, Bd. 1, 13; S. 481, 44. Hē oft stormas wiþsceáf (*repellere consueverat*), 2, 7; S. 509, 33. Gif hwylc monn his āgen wīf wiþscūfe (*expulerit*), 4, 5; S. 573, 17. Hwī willaþ gē wiþscūfan (*repellere*) đone đe gē ǣr onfēngon, 3, 19; S. 549, 4. Wiþscūfan (*refutare*) đa đe gedyrstigedon, đæt hī Eástran heóldan būtan heora rihtre tīde, 5, 21; S. 642, 39. Fultum tō wiþscūfanne hergunge (*ad repellendas inruptiones*), 1, 14; S. 482, 37.

wiþ-secgan; *p.* -sægde *To renounce*:—Eardlīco lusto wiđsæcgende *terrena desideria respuentes*, Rtl. 34, 20. [Þ hit beo so open sunne, Þ he hit ne mei wiđsiggen (*deny*), A. R. 86, 7. Wiđsuggen (-segge, 2nd MS.), Laym. 13237. Manig mann þiss merrke shall wiþþstanndenn and wiþþseggenn (*contradicere*), Orm. 7646. No men ne mygt wel it wyþsegge, R. Glouc. 106, 3. No þing to hele, no þing wyþȝigge *to conceal nothing, to deny nothing*, Ayenb. 175, 4. Whoso wole my juggement withseie, Chauc. Prol. 805. Wytheseyne or geyneseyne *contradico*, Prompt. Parv. 530.]

wiþ-seón; *p.* -seah, *pl.* -sāwon *To plot against* (?):—Hié sume heora þeówas gefreódon. . . . Đā ofþūhte heora ceorlum đæt mon đa þeówas freóde, and hī nolde. Đā wiđsāwon hié đǣm hlāfordum, and đa þeówas mid him, ōþ hié wyldran wǣron þonne hié *cum servos suos passim liberos facerent, libertini in partem potestates recepti plenitudinem per scelus usurpare meditati sunt. Itaque conspirantes in facinus libertini correptam urbem suo tantum generi vendicant*, Ors. 4, 3; Swt. 162, 14–18.

wiþ-setness, e; *f. A placing opposite* or *something placed opposite*:—Uuitsetnis *objectus*, Wrt. Voc. ii. 115, 26.

wiþ-settan; *p.* te *To oppose, resist*:—Sende hē him fultum þurh sumne dēman, đe wiđsette heora feóndum, and hī ālīsde of heora yrmđe, Ælfc. T. Grn. 6, 25. Fram ansȳne ārleásra đa đe mē geswenctun ł wiđsettun (*afflixerunt*), Ps. Lamb. 16, 9. [Wythesettyn̄ *obsto, obsisto*, Prompt. Parv. 530.]

wiþ-sleán; *p.* -slōh *To counteract*:—Hī woldon đæra hālgena līc besencan on flōde, ac se ælmihtiga Scyppend wiđslōh đam unrǣde, Homl. Skt. ii. 29, 324.

wiþ-sprecan; *p.* -spræc, *pl.* -sprǣcon; *pp.* -sprecen *To speak against*, *to revile*:—From stefne edwētendes and wiðspreocen[des] *a voce exprobrantis et obloquentis*, Ps. Surt. 43, 17.

wiþ-spurnan; *p.* -spearn *To dash* against:—Ðȳ læs ðū wiðspurne wið stāne fōt ðīnne *ne forte offendas ad lapidem pedem tuam*, Mt. Kmbl. Lind. 4, 6.

wiþ-standan; *p.* -stōd, *pl.* stōdon; *p.* -standen. I. of opposition to force or compulsion, *to withstand, resist*, (1) absolute:—Wiðstōd *reluctaretur*, Wrt. Voc. ii. 85, 45. Ðet landfolc hardlīce wiðstōdon *the people offered a stout resistance*, Chr. 1046; Erl. 171, 4. Wiðstōde *disputans*, Mt. Kmbl. p. 17, 1. (2) with dat.:—Gif hwylc eów wiþstondeþ (*restiterit*), ðonne gefultumiaþ wē eów, Bd. 1, 1; S. 474, 17. Him man swīðe fæstlīce wiðstōd and heardlīce, Chr. 1001; Erl. 137, 8: Exon. Th. 156, 15; Gū. 875. Hē galdorcræftum wiðstōd stranglīce, Andr. Kmbl. 333; An. 167. Wiðstōd *refragabatur* (*decalogi sanctionibus*, Ald. 12), Hpt. Gl. 426, 40. Hē wolde ðæt gyld ābrecan. Ðā wiðstōdan him ða hǣþenan men, Blickl. Homl. 221, 21. Wǣpen wyrcean and heora feóndum wiþstondan (*resistere*), Bd. 1, 12; S. 481, 14. Ðæm sloegende wiðstonda, Mt. Kmbl. p. 14, 18. From ðǣm wiðstondendum (*resistentibus*) ðere swīðra ðīnre, Ps. Surt. 16, 8. II. *to stand against, succeed in opposing, be a match for, refute*:—Se nama tācnaþ ðone sige ðe Drihten wiþstōd deófle, Blickl. Homl. 67, 15. Eftforefundeno wiðstōd *reprehensores redarguit*, Mt. Kmbl. p. 16, 13. Ðæt hī ðām yrmðum ne wiðstanden *in miseriis non subsistent*, Ps. Th. 139, 10. Ne mæg eów nān þing wiðstandan (*resistere*), Jos. 1, 5: 10, 8: Nicod. 26; Thw. 14, 10: Ps. Th. 75, 5. Wyrde wiðstondan, Exon. Th. 287, 17; Wand. 15: 161, 32; Gū. 967: 278, 18; Jul. 599. Wīsdōm, ðam ne magon ealle eówer wiðerwinnan wiðstandan and wiðcweðan, Lk. Skt. 21, 15: Blickl. Homl. 161, 17. III. *to stand in the way, be a hindrance, obstruct, prevent, be a preventive*, (1) absolute:—Wið blōdryne of nosum; ādrȳg gāte blōd and gnīd tō duste, dō on ðæt næsþyrl; hyt wiðstandeþ (*it acts as a preventive*), Lchdm. i. 352, 4. (2) with dat.:—Him nǣnig wiþstōd *nullo prohibente*, Bd. 1, 15; S. 483, 41. In swā micclum heápe ðæra ðe ðǣr wǣron ūt gongende, hira nǣnig ðām in gangendum ne wiðstōd, Shrn. 41, 10. Ða þióstro ðīnre heortan willaþ mīnre lāre wiðstondan, Met. 5, 22. (3) with dat. of that which is hindered and gen. of that in respect to which the hindrance occurs:—Micel stān ðone brōc tōdǣlð and him his rihtrynes wiþstent; swā dōð nū ða þeóstro ðīnre gedrēfednesse wiþstandan mīnum lārum, Bt. 6; Fox 14, 30. Hē ðē oft wiðstōd willan ðīnes, Exon. Th. 268, 5; Jul. 427. IV. *to stand off* (cf. wiþ *in* wiþ-faran), *keep away, be absent*:—Fearr dióules fācon uiðstonde *procul diaboli fraus absistat*, Rtl. 98, 22. Be ðon ðe mon wīf bycgge and ðonne sió gift wiðstande. Gif mon wīf gebycgge and sió gyft forð ne cume, L. In. 31; Th. i. 122, 4 note. V. *to be hostile*:—Ic wiðstande ongēn eów *ponam faciem contra vos*, Lev. 26, 17. Cf. wiþer-standan.

wiþ-steall, es; *m.* I. *a defence*:—Ic ingehygd eal geondwlīte, hū gefæstnad sȳ ferð innanweard, wiðsteall geworht *I scan the mind to see how the soul is fortified within, how its defences are built*, Exon. Th. 266, 20; Jul. 401. II. *an obstruction, obstacle*:—Wiðsteallas *obstacula* (nimborum obstacula rupit, ut fluerent imbres, Ald. 143), Wrt. Voc. ii. 89, 71: 64, 39. Cf. wiþer-steall.

wiþ-steppan *glosses* praetergredi, Ps. Lamb. 79, 13.

wiþ-stunian; *p.* ode *To dash against*:—Eallum ðū wiðstōde and wiðstunedest . . . stunaþ heó wærce, wiðstunaþ heó āttre, Lchdm. iii. 32, 13–24.

wiþ-styllan; *p.* de *To leap back, retreat*:—Wiðstylde *descivit, pedem retraxit*, Wrt. Voc. ii. 106, 25. v. stellan *to leap*.

wiþ-styltan; *p.* te *To hesitate, doubt*:—Gif gié hæbbe leáfo and gié ne wiðstylte *si habueritis fidem et non haesitaveris*, Mt. Kmbl. Lind. 21, 21.

wiþ-teón; *p.* -teáh, *pl.* -tugon; *pp.* -togen. I. with acc. *to withdraw, draw back*:—Swā micel swā seó sǣ heó mǣst wiðteóhð *as far as ever the sea withdraws itself* (*recedes*), Chart. Th. 318, 9. II. with dat. *to draw back, restrain*:—Balaham wolde fēran ðǣr hiene mon bæd, ac his ēstfulnesse wiðteáh (wit-, Hatt. MS.) se esol ðe hē onuppan sæt *Balaam pervenire ad propositum tendit, sed ejus votum animal, cui praesidet, praepedit*, Past. 36; Swt. 254, 23. Ōðerne hē drāf suīðe geornfullīce mid sticele, ōðrum hē wiðteáh mid brīdle *illum stimulo impellere nititur, hunc freno moderatur*, 40; Swt. 293, 1. III. *to draw away*, cf. wiþ-ferian:—Wiþtugon *detrahebant*, Ps. Spl. T. 108, 3. IV. *to draw to*:—Wiðtīhþ *attrahit* (other Latin versions have *abstrahit*), Ps. Lamb. second 9, 9. [Wiðteod giu of þe flesliche lustes *abstinete uos a carnalibus desideriis*, O. E. Homl. ii. 137, 18. Þat he us wissie to wiðtien of alle flesliche lustes, 79, 4.]

wiþþe, an; *f. A with* (v. Jud. 16, 9 where Wicklif has *wiþþis*), *a thong, cord*:—Wiððe *loramentum* vel *tormentum*, Wrt. Voc. i. 57, 26: *lorumentum*, ii. 53, 39. Wiððe *circus* vel *circulus*, rāp *funiculus* vel *funis*, i. 15, 18–19: 75, 3–4. Hē hēt hī (*Agatha*) on hencgene āstreccan, and ðrāwan swā swā wiððan, Homl. Skt. i. 8, 113. Hē bebeád ðām cwellerum, ðæt hī hine mid wiððum handum and fōtum on ðære rōde gebundon, Homl. Th. i. 594, 31: 596, 21. [Nimeð me þene ilke mon, and doð wiðđe (raketeȝe, 2nd MS.) an his sweore, Laym. 22833. Twælf swine iteied tosomne, mid wiðen swiðe grete ywriðen al togadere, 25973. Crist himm wrohhte an swepe all alls itt wære off wiþþess, Orm. 15563. Þe þief . . . þet heþ nieȝ þe wyþþe ine þe nykke, Ayenb. 135, 25. Witthe, wyththe *boia*, Prompt. Parv. 531. *O. Frs.* withthe: *Icel.* viðja, *and* við; *gen.* viðjar.] v. cyne-wiþþe.

wiþ-þyddan; *p.* de *To thrust back*:—Wiðþyddende *retundens*, Hpt. Gl. 505, 52.

wiþ-tremman; *p.* de *To step back*:—Ðonne wiðtremð hē and onhupaþ *gressum post terga revocet*, Past. 58; Swt. 441, 27. v. trem *a step*.

wiþ-ufan; *adv. prep. Above*, (1) as adverb:—Sume (*adverbs*) synd *localia* . . . *super* wiðufan, Ælfc. Gr. 38; Zup. 225, 5: *supra*, 240, 9. On ðære bytminge wæs se arc rūm, and wiðufan genyrwed, Homl. Th. i. 536, 15. Hēr wiðufan on ðyssere rǣdinge, 608, 15: ii. 228, 7. Swā swā wiðufan gecweden hit is *sicut supra dictum est*, Ath. Crd. 27: Lchdm. iii. 438, 7. Hē bebeád wolcnum wiþufan *mandavit nubibus desuper*, Ps. Lamb. 77, 23: Hymn. Surt. 24, 31. (2) as prep.:—Tō grǣwan stāne, ðonon wiðufan ðæs wælles heáfod, Cod. Dip. Kmbl. ii. 29, 4.

wiþ-ūtan; *adv. prep. Without.* I. as adverb:—Gē clǣnsiaþ ðæt wiðūtan ys caliceas and dixas. . . . Clǣnsa ǣryst ðæt wiðinnan ys calices and disces, ðæt hit sī clǣne ðæt wiðūtan ys *mundatis quod deforis est calicis et parapsidis* . . . *Munda prius quod intus est calicis et parapsidis, ut fiat et id, quod deforis est, mundum*, Mt. Kmbl. 23, 25–26. His līchama barn wiðūtan mid langsumere hǣtan, Homl. Th. i. 86, 4. Man scolde fandian gif man mihte betræppan ðane here āhwār wiþūtan, Chr. 992; Erl. 130, 43. II. as preposition. (1) with dat. (a) *without* (the opposite of *within*), *outside of*:—Wiðūtan ðæm dīce is geworht heáh weall, Ors. 2, 4; Swt. 74, 19. Ðā cwæð man mycel gemōt wiðūtan Lundene, Chr. 1052; Erl. 187, 16. Se cyng gefeaht tōgeánes his sunu wiðūtan Normandīge, 1079; Erl. 216, 7. (b) *without* (the opposite of *with*):—Hē hæfde Ȳrlande gewunnon wiðūtan ǣlcon wǣpnon, Chr. 1086; Erl. 222, 18. (2) with acc., *without, to the outside of*:—Lēd ūt ðone hirwend wiðūtan ða wīcstōwe *educ blasphemum extra castra*, Lev. 24, 14. Hig āwurpon hyne wiðūtan ðone wīngeard (*extra vineam*), Mt. Kmbl. 21, 39. v. wiþ-innan.

wiþ-weorpan; *p.* -wearp, *pl.* -wurpon; *pp.* -worpen *To reject*:—Ðū eart se weallstān ðe ða wyrhtan wiðwurpan, Exon. Th. 1, 4; Cri. 3. Gē ðære snyttro [stān (? cf. Lk. 20, 17)] unwīslīce wiðweorpon, Elen. Kmbl. 587; El. 294.

wiþ-winde. v. wiþo-winde.

wiþ-winnan; *p.* -wann, *pl.* -wunnon *To strive against, resist*:—Went hē mid ealle cræfte ongēn ðæs ōðres geðyld, ðe him ðonne giet wiðwinð (*eum obsistentem fortiter*), Past. 33; Swt. 227, 7. Eallum his wordum hī wiðcwǣdon and wiþwunnan *cunctis quae dicebat contradicere laborabant*, Bd. 2, 2; S. 503, 17. 'Nis nān wuht ðe mæge swā heágum gōde wiþcweþan.' Ðā cwæþ ic: 'Nē wēne ic ðæt ǣnig wuht sié ðe wiþwinne' *non est igitur aliquid, quod summo huic bono possit obsistere. Non, inquam, arbitror*, Bt. 35, 4; Fox 160, 31. Hwæt wilt ðū cweþan, gif hwā nylle wiþwinnan, 36, 6; Fox 182, 6. Ðone anwald mæg wel reccan se ðe ǣgðer ge hine habban cann ge wiðwinnan *potentiam bene regit qui et tenere illam noverit et impugnare*, Past. 17; Swt. 113, 21. Ðeáh ðe hē swȳþe wiþwinnende wǣre *quamvis multum renitens*, Bd. 4, 28; S. 606, 17. Ða biscepas sǣdon ðæt ealle godas him irre wǣren and wiðwinnende, Ors. 3, 7; Swt. 114, 4. v. wiþer-winnan, wiþ, II. 10.

wiþ-winnend, es; *m. An opponent*:—Wiðwinnend *refragator* (-*ur*, MS.), Wrt. Voc. ii. 84, 62.

witian, witiendlīc. v. be-witian, witod, fore-witiendlīc.

wītiend-līc (wītend-); *adj. Prophetic*:—Wītiendlīcere mihte *prophetica virtute*, Hpt. Gl. 492, 22. Wītendlīcum wītedōme *prophetica vaticinatione*, 520, 16. Wītendlīcere, 505, 3. Wītenlīcere, 443, 58. Wītiendlīcum *propheticis*, 416, 55. [Cf. *O. H. Ger.* wīzōn *prophetizare, vaticinari, divinare.*] v. wīte-dōm; wītegend-līc *and* wīteg-dōm.

witig, wittig; *adj.* I. *having knowledge, wisdom, sense; sagacious, wise*:—Stān witig werede and worde cwæð, Andr. Kmbl. 1485; An. 744. Swilce wittige ł gleáwe leorneras *velut sagaces* (*prudentes*) *gymnosophistas*, Hpt. Gl. 404, 76. ¶ as an epithet of the Deity (cf. witte of witty God, Piers P. 15, 126):—Witig God, Cd. Th. 182, 24; Exod. 80: Ps. Th. 77, 20: Exon. Th. 14, 29; Cri. 226: Beo. Th. 1375; B. 685: 2116; B. 1056. Witig Drihten, 3113; B. 1554: Hy. 4, 6: Exon. Th. 379, 12; Deór. 32: Cd. Th. 179, 8; Exod. 25: 241, 14; Dan. 404. Wittig (wigtig, MS.), Beo. Th. 3687; B. 1841. Witig Wuldorcyning, Cd. Th. 242, 30; Dan. 427. II. *in one's wits, in one's right mind*:—Wearð his suna wittig, Homl. Skt. i. 7, 428. [Wygar þe witeȝe (wittye, 2nd MS.) wurhte, Laym. 21134. Mine wise and mine witie (wittye, 2nd MS.) men, 15829. Witti and wise, Kath. 315. Ich am witi and wot al þat to cumen is, O. and N. 1189. Ȝe wise men and witty of the lawe, Piers P. C. 10, 51. *O. Sax.* witig, wittig: *O. H. Ger.* wizīg, wizzīg *solers, sapiens*: *Icel.* vitugr.] v. for-, fore-, ge-, un-witig, -wittig.

wītiga, wītig-dōm. v. wītega, wīteg-dōm.

witigness, e; *f. Sagacity, prudence*:—Wyttinysse *industriam* (sagacissimam animi industriam, Ald. 3: cf. gleáunes *industria*, Wrt. Voc. ii. 46, 2), Hpt. Gl. 407, 71.

wīting-stōw. v. wītung-stōw.

wit-leás; *adj. Witless, senseless:*—On đam fīftan mōnþe hē (*the fœtus*) biþ cwica and weaxeþ and seó mōdur līđ witleás, Lchdm. iii. 146, 12. [Ne wurđe non so witleas, A. R. 256, 25. Giff þin macche iss wis and god and tu wittlæs and wicke, Orm. 6197. Nis neure mon redles ar his heorte beo witles, O. and N. 692. Ine foles, and yne wytlease, þet ne habbeþ nenne skele, Ayenb. 86, 13. *Icel.* vit-lauss *witless, foolish, mad.*] v. gewit-leás, *and next word.*

wit-leást, e; *f. Senselessness, folly:*—His (*Job's*) wīfes witleást (gewitleást, Homl. Th. ii. 456, 4), Job. Thw. 167, 32. [Cf. *Icel.* vit-leysi *madness.*] v. gewit-leást.

wītnere, es; *m. A punisher, tormentor:*—Wītnere *lictor*, Wrt. Voc. ii. 52, 59. Se dēma betǣcđ đa unrihtwīsan đam unmildheortan wītnere, and se wītnere hī gebrincđ on cwearterne, Homl. Ass. 8, 205. Đonne beóđ đa hire (*the soul's*) wītneras, đa đe hī tō đām leahtrum forspeónon, Homl. Th. i. 410, 31. Se hlāford sealde hyne đām wītnerum (*tortoribus*), Mt. Kmbl. 18, 34. Se heretoga cwæþ: 'Gē beóđ gewītnode' . . . Đā swōr se dēma, đæt hī þurh drȳcræfte đa stānas āwendon tō heora wītnerum, Homl. Skt. i. 11, 110. [*O. L. Ger.* wītneri *tortor: O. H. Ger.* wīzināri *ultor, tortor, lictor.*]

witness, e; *f.* I. *knowledge:*—Fore wīsdōm ł witnesse *propter scientiam*, Rtl. 194, 37. II. *witness, cognisance, knowledge:*—Menigo ọđro bēceno worhte se Hǣlend on witnesa (*in conspectu*) đara đegna, Jn. Skt. 20, 30. III. *witness, testimony:*—Āsceacaþ eówer fōta dust ofer hig on witnesse (gewytnysse, *v. l.*) (*in testimonium*), Lk. Skt. 9, 5. In cȳđnisse ł witnesa *in testimonium*, Mt. Kmbl. Lind. 8, 4. Leása witnesa *falsa testimonia*, 15, 19. IV. *a person who gives testimony, a witness:*—Monigo leáse witnesa (*testes*), Mt. Kmbl. Lind. 26, 60. In mūđ tuoe witnesa (*testium*), 18, 16. Tō witnesum *testibus*, 26, 65. v. ge-witness.

wītnian; *p.* ode *To punish, torment, plague:*—Ic wītnie *multo*, Engl. Stud. xi. 66, 58. Uuītnath *multabitur*, Wrt. Voc. ii. 114, 42. Wītnađ *plectit*, 90, 12. Wītnode *multavit, punivit*, Hpt. Gl. 455, 15. Dēme đæt se bisceop and wītnige be đam (*juxta hoc puniatur*), L. Ecg. C. 16; Th. ii. 144, 7. Wītnian *vapulare, multare, flagellare*, Hpt. Gl. 477, 27. Wītniende *multans*, Wrt. Voc. ii. 57, 31. Wītniendra þiówa *lictorum*, 52, 77. Dēman wīdnigendne *judicem punientem*, Scint. 38, 3. (1) with acc. of person:—Hē wītnaþ đa scyldigan *injusti punientur*, Ps. Th. 36, 28. Đæt đa bióþ gesǣlegran đe mon wītnaþ đonne đa bión đe hī wītniaþ *infeliciores eos esse, qui faciunt, quam qui patiuntur injuriam*, Bt. 38, 6; Fox 208, 6. Hwæþerne woldest đū dēman wītes wyrþran, đe đone đe đone unscyldgan wītnode, đe đone đe đæt wīte þolode? *cui supplicium inferendum putares, eius qui fecisset, an qui pertulisset injuriam?* Fox 208, 16. Đone blacan Heáwald hī lange cwylmdon and đurh lima wītnadon *Nigellum Hewaldum longo suppliciorum cruciatu et horrenda membrorum omnium discerptione interemerunt*, Bd. 5, 10; S. 624, 41. Đæt man đās menn wītnige and cwelle, Blickl. Homl. 183, 2. Nele God ūs wītnian, Ps. Th. 76, 7. Đa unrihtwīsan beóđ wītnade (*punientur*), Ps. Surt. 36, 28. Hī wǣron wītnade *virgis caesi*, Ors. 4, 1; Swt. 160, 14. (1 a) with the means of punishment expressed:—Ic wītnige eów seofon wīton *corripiam vos septem plagis*, Lev. 26, 28. Se uultor ne slāt đa lifre Tyties, đe hine ǣr mid đȳ wītnode, Bt. 35, 6; Fox 170, 4. Wītna mid tintregum đīnne sunu, Homl. Skt. i. 4, 205. Đæt se hī mōte mid mycclum wītum wītnian, Blickl. Homl. 61, 18. Hē hī wolde wītnian mid deáþe, Bt. 41, 3; Fox 248, 12. Hē biþ wītnad manegum wītum *vapulabit multis*, Lk. Skt. 12, 47, 48. (2) with acc. of fault:—Đæt hī heora synna wītnade and bētte, Bd. 4, 25; S. 599, 24. Sume wyllaþ wītnian stīđlīce đa læssan gyltas on heora underþeóddum, and nella, wītnian mid nānre wrace đa māran synna on him sylfum, Homl. Ass. 7, 182. Đȳ læs hit him sié wītnod *lest it be punished in him*, Past. 9; Swt. 59, 17. [*O. Sax.* wītnōn: *O. Frs.* wītnia: *O. H. Ger.* wīzinōn *damnare, dijudicare, vexare, angere, plectere, torquere.*] v. ge-wītnian; un-wītnod.

wītnigend-līc; *adj.* I. *that punishes* or *torments:*—Seó đwyre sāwul gǣđ tō đam wītnigendlīcum fȳre, Homl. Th. i. 408, 23. Wītniendlīcum fȳre, ii. 344, 12, 17: 590, 13. II. *that deserves to be punished:*—Ne gemētst đū on mē āht wītniendlīces, Homl. Th. ii. 518, 4. Cf. un-wītniendlīce.

wītnung, e; *f. Punishment, torment, pain:*—Mǣgmorđres wītnung *parricidii actio*, . . . gebohtre scīre wītnung *ambitus judicium*, Wrt. Voc. i. 21, 10, 12. Geligra wītnung *incerta* (*incesti?*) *judicium*, ii. 49, 29. Đæs ic gelēfe, đætte ǣlc unriht wītnung sié đæs yfel đe hit dēđ, næs đæs đe hit þafaþ *apparet, illatam cuilibet injuriam non accipientis, sed inferentis esse miseriam*, Bt. 38, 6; Fox 208, 20. Đæt hē on wītnunge stōwe swungen wǣre, ōþ đæt hē swylte, Blickl. Homl. 193, 3. Đære synne tō wītnunge mīnre unhȳrsumnesse *ad puniendam inobedientiae meae culpam*, Bd. 5, 6; S. 619, 22. Đonne seó sāwul biđ tō hire wītnunge gelǣd . . . betǣht tō ēcere wītnunge, Homl. Th. i. 410, 24, 30. Helpan đām forđfarenum đe on wītnunge beóđ, ii. 356, 12. Gefyl hié nū mid đære wītnunga đe đū him geteohhod hæfdest, Ps. Th. 16, 13. Būton wītnunge *without exacting a penalty*, L. Edg. S. 1; Th. i. 270, 19. Swerie hē (*a criminal who has been punished*) đæt hē ǣfre wītnunge ne wrece, L. Eth. vii. 17; Th. i. 332, 22. Āwend nū fram mē đīne wītnunga (*plagas tuas*), Ps. Th. 38, 11. v. ge-, hengen-, un-wītnung.

wītnung-stōw, e; *f. A place of punishment:*—Seó micele byrnende dene is wītnungstōw, in đære beóđ manna sāwla gewītnode and geclǣnsode, Homl. Th. ii. 352, 20. Oft men wurdon of đisum līfe gelǣdde, and eft tō līfe ārǣrde, and hī fela wītnungstōwa and eác hālgena wununga gesāwon, 354, 28. v. wītung-stōw.

witod; *adj.* (*ptcpl.*) I. *appointed, ordained, assured, certain:*—Him is unhyldo Waldendes witod, nū hié wordcwyde his forlēton, Cd. Th. 45, 21; Gen. 730. Đē is gedāl witod līces and sāwle, 57, 19; Gen. 930: 252, 9; Dan. 576: Andr. Kmbl. 1777; An. 891. Đonne biđ ūs seó mēd æt Drihtene witod, L. E. G. 21; Th. ii. 418, 20. Mē biđ gyrn witod . . . bearnum biþ deáþ witod, Exon. Th. 396, 18, 28; Rä. 16, 6, 11: 494, 13; Rä. 82, 7: Fins. Th. 53; Fin. 26. Mē biđ witod, đæt ic þolian sceal bearngestreóna, Exon. Th. 402, 3; Rä. 21, 24. Đē is sūsl weotod, Cd. Th. 308, 14; Sat. 692: Andr. Kmbl. 1902; An. 953. Here bād witodes willan, Cd. Th. 213, 12; Exod. 551. Witodre fyrde, 207, 23; Exod. 471. Sceal ic witodes bīdan *I must await my certain fate*, 137, 18; Gen. 2275. Dōm wutedne *judicium certum*, Rtl. 92, 18. Wē ūs nytan witod līf ōđ ǣfen *we are not sure of life until the evening*, Wulfst. 241, 16: 240, 18: 151, 17. Nū hæbbe ic đīne hyldo mē witode geworhte, Cd. Th. 45, 15; Gen. 727. Weotude, Andr. Kmbl. 2149; An. 1076. Fleág fugla cyn, đǣr hȳ feorhnere witude fundon (*where they were sure of finding food*), Exon. Th. 157, 11; Gū. 890. Witode, 430, 13; Rä. 44, 8. Bēc bodiaþ weotedne willan, Salm. Kmbl. 475; Sal. 238. Ne cȳþ đū witod on wēn đīn *do not feel sure of your expectation*, Prov. Kmbl. 22. Se ealda man him mæg gewislīce witod witan, đæt him se deáđ geneálǣcđ *the old man may surely know, that for him the approach of death is certain*, Wulfst. 147, 26. Hī eác wēnan ne þurfon, ac witod witan, đæt hig yfel leán habban scylan, 270, 26. Ic đæt wēnde and witod tealde, đæt ic đē meahte āhwyrfan from hālor, Exon. Th. 264, 1; Jul. 357. Him tō wǣron witode geþingþo, Cd. Th. 30, 30; Gen. 475. Đē sind wītu weotud be gewyrhtum, Andr. Kmbl. 2731; An. 1368. Feohgestealda witedra wēnan, Exon. Th. 283, 26; Jul. 686. Hē him wælbende weotode tealde, Beo. Th. 3877; B. 1936. Uutedo *certa*, Rtl. 171, 41. II. with much the same force as *witodlīce*, (a) with definite sense, *it is certain, certainly, assuredly:*—Witod, se đe his broces bōte sēcđ, būton tō Gode sylfum, hē drȳhđ deófles wyllan, Wulfst. 12, 11: 85, 14. Ān þing ic eów secge tō gewisse, đæt witod sceal geweorđan godspel gecȳþed geond ealle worulde ǣr worulde ende, 89, 21. Se đe forsyhđ eów, witod hē forsyhđ mē, 177, 15. (b) in a less definite sense, *indeed, surely:*—Allo wuted iornaþ *omnes quidem currunt*, Rtl. 5, 35. Đa heordas wutud gisprēcun betwih him, Lk. Skt. Rush. 2, 15. Witud *quidem*, Anglia xiii. 392, 383: *nam*, 368, 40: *itaque*, 379, 194. [*O. Sax.* witod:—Nadra, thār siu iro nīđskepies witodes wānit *where it thinks hostility intended*, Hēl. 1880. Cf. *Goth.* witōþ *law: O. H. Ger.* wizod, wizzod *lex, jus.*] v. ge-, un-witod, *and next word.*

witod-līc; *adj. Certain:*—Wutudlīce sindun wītga đætte wēre *certi sunt prophetam esse*, Lk. Skt. Rush. 20, 6. [Cf. *O. H. Ger.* wizzod-līh *legalis.*]

witodlīce; *adv.* I. *certainly:*—Witodlīce (*amen*) ic secge eów, Mt. Kmbl. 26, 21. Wēne ic ful swīđe and witodlīce, Exon. Th. 461, 5; Hö. 30. II. with a somewhat indefinite sense, translating many Latin words, *indeed, surely, truly:*—Witodlīce (wotetlīce, Lind.) *autem*, Mt. Kmbl. 1, 21. Wiotolīce, Lind. 2, 3. Wutedlīce (wutudlīce, Rush.), Mk. Skt. Lind. 2, 10. Witodlīce *enim*, Mk. Skt. 1, 38. Wiotudlīce *ergo*, Jn. Skt. Rush. 18, 3. Witedlīce *etenim*, Ps. Spl. 15, 6. Witudlīce, Anglia xiii. 365, 3. Witodlīce *igitur*, Gen. 4, 11: Mt. Kmbl. 12, 28: *inquam*, Kent. Gl. 945. Wutudlīce *itaque*, Jn. Skt. Rush. 18, 4. Witodlīce *nam*, Anglia xiii. 386, 302: *quippe* and *nempe*, Ælfc. Gr. 38; Zup. 227, 2: *quidem*, Mt. Kmbl. 9, 37. Witedlīce, Ps. Spl. 34, 23. Uutetlīce, Mt. Kmbl. Lind. 26, 24. Witudlīce *quoque*, Anglia xiii. 397, 459: *utique*, 366, 19. Wutudlīce, Jn. Skt. Rush. 14, 28. Witodlīce *vero*, Mt. Kmbl. 8, 24. Wiotudlīce, Mk. Skt. Rush. 1, 8. Witodlīce *videlicet*, Anglia xiii. 387, 318. Wietodlīce, Past. 35; Swt. 239, 20. [*O. H. Ger.* wizzodlīcho *quidem.*]

-witol, -wittol. v. fore-witol, Chr. 1067; Erl. 204, 28, un-wittol.

witon, wuton (-an, -un), uton (-an, -un); *interjectional form with an infinitive, the combination being the equivalent of a subjunctive,* = *let us . . .:*—Uton (wuton, Cott. MS.) āgīfan đæm esne his wīf, Bt. 35, 6; Fox 170, 6. Wuton wuldrian weorada Dryhten, Hy. 8, 1. Uuton nū gehȳran, Blickl. Homl. 83, 30. Wutan cuman ealle, and ūre māgas mid ūs wutun þyder habban, Ps. Th. 73, 8. Wutun cuman ealle and hī tōwyrpan *venite et disperdamus eos*, 82, 4: Beo. Th. 5290; B. 2648. Gǣ wē ł wutun (wutu, Rush.) geonga, Mk. Skt. Lind. 1, 38: 14, 42. Uton gān (uutun geonga, Lind.) *eamus*, Jn. Skt. 11, 16. Uton wircean *faciamus*, Gen. 1, 26: 2, 18: 11, 3: Cd. Th. 26, 8; Gen. 403: 278, 6; Sat. 217. Đā cwæþ hē: 'Uton geēcan đone anweald . . .' Đā cwæþ ic: 'Uton ðæs,' Bt. 33, 1; Fox 120, 28. Utan biddan God, Bd. 2, 2; S. 502, 18: 3, 2; S. 524, 21: Exon. Th. 48, 14; Cri. 771. Utun faran *transeamus*, Lk. Skt. 2, 15. ¶ the word was originally a tense of the verb wītan, and its verbal character is occasionally still marked by the use of the pronoun:—Wuton wē ðæt·gemunan, Blickl. Homl. 125, 2. Uutun uē geonga (uton gan, W. S., wutun gonga, Rush.) *eamus*, Jn. Skt. Lind. 14, 31. [Uten don elmessen, O. E. Homl. i. 107, 6. Uten we heom to liðe, Laym. 20635. Ute we to him fare, O. and N. 1779. *O. Sax.* wita.]

witran *to make certain* (?), *to inform*:—Witro *veror*, Wrt. Voc. ii. 123, 23. [Wise mi and witere (witte me, 2nd MS.), whuder ic mæi liðan, Laym. 1200. Wite me and were and witere and wisse þurh þi wisdom to wite me wið sunne, Jul. 33, 13. Ho has witered hire of þis, and ho has hire kenned, Jos. 466. Ho watȝ wytered bi wyȝes what watȝ þe cause, Allit. Pms. 85, 1587. Cf. *Icel.* vitra *to manifest, reveal.*] v. witer.

wī-trod. v. wīg-trod.

wit-seóc; *adj. Lunatic, possessed*:—Hrȳmde sum wōd mann ðurh deófles gāst . . . Wearð se mann geclǣnsod fram ðam fūlan gāste . . . Ðā geāxode se cyning be ðam witseócum menn, Homl. Th. i. 458, 2-8. Hī deóflu fram wittseócum mannum āflīgdon, ii. 490, 23. *Exorcista* is se ðe rǣt ofer ða witseócan men, L. Ælfc. P. 34; Th. ii. 378, 7: Homl. Skt. i. 7, 392. v. gewit-seóc.

witt, witter, wittiend-līc, wittig, witud. v. wit, witer, witiend-līc, witig, witod.

wituma, an; *m. A dowry*:—Wituma *vel* wetma, uuituma *dos*, Txts. 57, 704. Weotoma *dote* (the line is: Ne metuas juvenis sortiri dote puellam, Ald. 170), Wrt. Voc. ii. 93, 28: 27, 18. Lōcige hē ðæt hió hæbbe ðæt weorð sié hire mægðhādes, ðæt is se weotuma (wituma, *v.l.*) *pretium pudicitiae non negabit* (Ex. 21, 10), L. Alf. 12; Th. i. 46, 18. Āgife hē ðæt fioh æfter ðæm weotuman (*juxta modum dotis, quam virgines accipere consueverunt*, Ex. 22, 17), 29; Th. i. 52, 8. In Anglia xiii. 30, 82, wytuma *paranymphus* seems a mistake for witumbora. v. next word. [*O. Frs.* wetma, witma, v. Richthofen: *O. H. Ger.* widemo *dos.*]

witum-bora, an; *m. A bridesman*; paranymphus, Hpt. Gl. 448, 25.

witung. v. fore-witung.

wītung-stōw, e; *f. A place of torment* or *punishment*:—Ðæt is eác cūþ, ðæt for ðæs dæges weorþunge, ðæt ða sāuwla onfōþ reste, ða ða beóþ on wītincgstōwan, Wulfst. 219, 34. v. wītnung-stōw.

wit-word, es; *n. A statement which bears witness* to anything, *testament, covenant*:—Witword and gewitnes, ðæt ðæt stande ðæt hit nān man ne āwende, L. Eth. iii. 3; Th. i. 294, 1. Wē willaþ ðæt . . . witword and getrȳwe gewitnes . . fæste stande, L. N. P. L. 67; Th. ii. 302, 5. Ofer ðǣm landum ðe Ealdrēd ærcebiscop hæfð siðþan begitan on witword oððe on caupland (*by testament or purchase?*), Chart. Th. 439, 4. [His witeword *testamentum ejus*, Ps. 24, 14. Alle þat felle to me . . . of my lordes witeword, witnes þerof haf I, R. Brun. 152, 9. Fulfille I salle in dede þe kynges witworde, 153, 2. Cf. *Swed.* wits-ord *witness, testimony. Icel.* vit-orð *knowledge.*]

Wixan; *pl. The name of some people in some district in England*:—Eást-Wixna is þryú hund hȳda, West-Wixna syx hund hȳda, Cod. Dip. B. i. 414, 19. Cf. on wixena brōc, Cod. Dip. Kmbl. iii. 78, 1.

wixen; *adj. Of wax*:—Hlāf wexenne, Lchdm. iii. 210, 1. [*M. H. Ger.* wehsin.]

wlacian; *p.* ode. I. *to be* or *get lukewarm*:—Ic wlacige *tepeo*, Ælfc. Gr. 26, 2; Zup. 154, 4. Swā swā ðæt cealde ǣrest ongind wlacian, ǣr hit ful wearme weorðe, swā eác ðæt wearme wlacaþ, ǣr hit eallunga ācealdige *sicut a frigore per teporem transitur ad calorem, ita a calore per teporem reditur ad frigus*, Past. 58; Swt. 447, 4. II. *to make lukewarm*:—Ic wlacige *tepefacio*, Ælfc. Gr. 37; Zup. 218, 6. v. ā-, ge-wlacian; wleccan.

wlacu *and* **wlæc**; *adj. Lukewarm, tepid*:—Mid wlæcre *tepida* (*lepida*, MS.), Wrt. Voc. ii. 50, 43. (1) in a physical sense:—Gedō ðæt sió wyrt wlacu (blacu, MS.) sȳ, and þyge hȳ, Lchdm. i. 80, 13. Wlece hyt, ðæt hyt wlæc beó, and habbe on hys mūþe swā wlac, iii. 106, 2-4. Gif sió wamb biþ windes full, cymð ðæt of wlacre wǣtan; sió cealde wǣte wyrcþ sār an, ii. 224, 23. Hié beóð mid wlacum wætre on hǣlo gebrōhte *aegros ad salutem tepens aqua revocavit*, Past. 37; Swt. 269, 25: Homl. Skt. i. 11, 158. On wlacum ele, Homl. Th. i. 86, 23. Syle hyt him wlacu sūpan, Lchdm. i. 196, 19. Genim ðæt swā wlacu, ii. 40, 5. Sete him wlacu wæter drincan swīþe hāt, 62, 11. Wlaco, 40, 9: 192, 10. Gewyrm hyt and swā wlæc drȳpe on ðæt eáre, i. 178, 25: 188, 7: 210, 9. On wlæc wīn, ii. 24, 28. (2) in a figurative sense:—Hē is wlaco (*tepidus*), and nis nāuðer ne hāt, ne ceald . . . Se bið wearm, nalles wlaco . . . Swā eác se ðe wyrð wlacra treówa, and nyle ðæt wlæce oferwinnan (*nequaquam tepore superato*) . . . Se ðe tō lange wunaþ on ðǣm wlacum treówum . . . hē wlacu bið . . . Se ðe tō lange wlæc bið, Past. 58; Swt. 447, 1-14. Gif wēn sī ðæt hē on strengo þeódscipes tō wlæc (*tepidus*) sȳ, Bd. 1, 27; S. 492, 18. Oft ða mondwǣran weorðaþ suā besolcne and suā wlace and suā slāwe *saepe mansueti dissolutionis torpescunt taedio*, Past. 40; Swt. 289, 15. [Ðe wop ðe cumeð of þe wlache heorte *lacrima tepida*, O. E. Homl. ii. 151, 9. Torpor is þe uorme, þet is wlech heorte, A. R. 202, 4. Wlech weater, Jul. 31, 11.]

wlæcce (?), an; *f. Lukewarmness*:—Wlæccan *frigum*, Germ. 397, 448.

wlæclīce; *adv. Lukewarmly*:—Wlæclīce *tepide, enerviter*, Hpt. Gl. 420, 39. For hwon segdes ðū Ǣcgbrihte swā gēmeleáslīce and swā wlæclīce (*tam negligenter ac tepide*) ða ðing, ðe ic bebeád him tō secganne, Bd. 5, 9; M. 410, 33. [*In* Ps. Th. 148, 5 wlæclīce *seems a mistake for* wræclīce.]

wlæcness, e; *f. Lukewarmness*:—Wlæcnesse *teporis* (wlætnesse *leporis*, MS.), Wrt. Voc. ii. 50, 45. Ðȳ læs hē for wlæcnesse sié ūt āspiwen *ne tepidus evomatur*, Past. 58; Swt. 447, 16, 18.

wlæffetere, es; *m. A stammerer, one who speaks imperfectly*:—Wlæffetera *uilium bauilorum*, Germ. 403, 910. [Cf. Ich ne ssolde by bote a wlaffere, ne zigge þing to þe uolle, Ayenb. 262, 1. A checun mot l'un balbeye (*wlaffes*), Wrt. Voc. i. 173, 8. Som useþ strange wlaffyng, chyteryng, harrying & garryng, Trev. c. 59.]

wlǣta, wlǣtta, an; *m.* I. *nausea, loathing*:—Wið spiwðan and wlǣttan, Lchdm. i. 358, 24. Wiþ wlǣttan, ðam men ðe hine ne lyst his metes ne līþes, ii. 62, 15. Wiþ unluste and wlǣttan ðe of magan cymð, 184, 5. Wlǣtan, 158, 12. Gif hwā on scipe wlǣttan þolige, i. 206, 9. Ðone wlǣttan ðæs magan, 204, 20. Ne yrne hē, ðe læs hē mid ðæs rynes ēdgunge hwylcne wleáttan (wlǣttan, *v.l.*) and sogeðan on his heortan ne āstyrige, R. Ben. 68, 3. II. *what produces nausea, an object of loathing*:—Ōð hit gǣð þurh eówre næsþyrlu and sī gewend tō wlǣttan (*vertatur in nauseam*), Num. 11, 20. Būtan hlāfe ǣlc mete tō wlǣttan byþ gehwyrfed, Coll. Monast. Th. 28, 35. Seó ofering ðē wurþ oþþe tō sāre oððe tō wlǣttan, Bt. 14, 1; Fox 42, 16. Wlǣttan *sentina* (ab omni spurcitiae sentina immunes, Ald. 10), Anglia xiii. 28, 28. Fūlne wlǣttan *foetidam nauseam* (*sentinam*) (the passage is: Cum falsae garrulitatis incestum velut foetidam melancholiae nauseam de recessibus falsi pectoris evomuisset, Ald. 40), Hpt. Gl. 475, 50. Wlǣtan *nausiam* (the gloss belongs to the passage given in the preceding), Wrt. Voc. ii. 81, 9. III. *defilement, disfigurement.* v. an-wlǣta, -wlāta; ā-, ge-wlǣtan:—Wlǣtta *deformatio* (venusti capitis deformatio, Ald. 62), Hpt. Gl. 510, 6. [Þu miht mid wlate þe este bugge, O. and N. 1506.]

wlǣtan. v. ā-, ge-wlǣtan.

wlǣtung, e; *f.* I. *sickness, nausea*:—Mid micelre wlǣtunge gewīteþ ðæt sār on weg, Lchdm. i. 80, 14 note. v. morgen-wlǣtung, Lchdm. iii. 44, 19. II. *defilement, disfigurement.* v. wlǣta, III:—Wlǣttuncg *deformatio*, Hpt. Gl. 510, 6.

wlanc; *adj.* I. *proud, high-spirited, bold.* v. wlencu, I:—Wlanc Wedera leód, Beówulf, Beo. Th. 687: B. 341. Wlonc hæleþ, 668; B. 331. Wæterþisa wlonc, Exon. Th. 363 7; Wal. 50. Ðǣr wlanc manig on stæðe stōdon, Elen. Kmbl. 461; El. 231. Duguþ eal gecrong wlonc, Exon. Th. 291, 10; Wand. 80. Hē hæfde Higelāces hilde gefrunen, wlonces wīgcræft, Beo. Th. 5898; B. 2953. Wlance þegenas, unearge men, Byrht. Th. 137, 53; By. 205: Cd. Th. 188, 19; Exod. 170. Wlance wīgsmiðas, eorlas ārhwate, Ch . 937; Erl. 115, 21. Men mōdum wlonce, Exon. Th. 325, 4; Vīd. 10[illegible] Hē in healle wæs wended wloncra folmum, 441, 17; Rä. 60, 19. I ega wlancum, ðǣr wigan sittaþ, Runic pm. Kmbl. 342, 3; Rūn. 14. I a. applied to animals:—On wlancan ðam wicge, Byrht. Th. 138, 54; By. 240: Exon. Th. 489, 13; Rä. 78, 7. Sum sceal wildne fugel wloncne ātemian, hafoc on honda, 332, 15; Vy. 85. II. in an unfavourable sense, *proud, bold, arrogant, haughty, insolent.* v. wlencu, II:—Hē (*a dog*) leánaþ grimme ðe hine wloncne weorþan lǣteþ, Exon. Th. 434, 13; Rä. 51, 10. Ða wlanca[n] scamlēstan *frontosam* (*elationis*) *impudentiam*, Hpt. Gl. 526, 5. Tō manege weorðaþ tō wlance and ealles tō rance and tō gylpgeorne *erunt homines elati, superbi* (2 Tim. 3, 1), Wulfst. 81, 15: L. I. P. 14; Th. ii. 322, 12. Ne wlance (*elati*) synd eágan mīne, Ps. Spl. 130, 1. Wlancra (wancla, MS.) manna *protervorum*, Hpt. Gl. 526, 70. Ōð ðæt wlance (*the Egyptians*) forsceáf mihtig engel, Cd. Th. 190, 25; Exod. 204. III. *proud, elate, exultant*:—Se ðe āh līfes wyn, wlonc and wīngāl, Exon. Th. 307, 25; Seef. 29: 478, 2; Ruin. 35. Hē mid gāre stang wlancne wīcing, ðe him ða wunde forgeaf, Byrht. Th. 135, 56. IV. *splendid, great, high, august, magnificent, rich.* v. wlencu, III:—Welig ꝉ wlonc *diues*, Lk. Skt. Lind. 12, 21: 16, 22. Wlonc *dives* . . . ðe wlonca *divitem*, Mt. Kmbl. Lind. 19, 23, 24. Summ monn wlong *quidam homo dives*, 27, 57. Ðū, weliga, ðīnne Drihten ne lufadest . . . Hwæt, wēndest ðū, wlanca, gif ðū mē sealdest ōwiht ðīnes, ðæt ðē ðonne wǣre ðīn woruldgestreón gelytlad? Wulfst. 260, 18. Wereda Wuldorgifa, wlanc and ēce *God great and eternal*, Hy. 10, 48. Se wlonca dæg *the great and terrible day of the Lord*, Exon. Th. 448, 7; Dōm. 50. Monnes wloncas (wlonches, Rush.) lond *hominis diuitis ager*, Lk. Skt. Lind. 12, 16. Of beád ðæs wlonces *de mensa diuitis*, 16, 21. Se Hǣlend cwæð tō ðam wlancan: 'For hwī wǣre ðū swā fæsthafol mīnra gōda, ðe ic ðē sealde?' Wulfst. 258, 12. Ðam wlancan *to the great king* (Nebuchadnezzar), Cd. Th. 221, 30; Dan. 96. Ða ðe heora yldran on worolde ne wurdan welige ne wlance þurh woroldglænge *those whose* *forefathers were not wealthy or great through worldly splendour*, L. Eth. vii. 21; Th. i. 334, 3: Wald. 116; Vald. 2, 30. Ealle gelīce on woruld cumaþ, wlance and heáne (*high and low*), Met. 17, 6. Wlance *the grandees of Egypt*, Cd. Th. 109, 20; Gen. 1825. Wloncra wīnsele, 270, 21; Sat. 94. Hē feorgbona weorþeþ wloncum and heánum, Exon. Th. 362, 27; Wal. 43. Ic lǣrde wlance men and heáhgeþungene ðæt hié ne āstigan on ofermēdu, ne welena tō wel ne trūwodon, Blickl. Homl. 185, 13. **IV a.** where the circumstance, in which the splendour, etc., consists, is given:—Fugel feþrum wlonc *the bird splendid of plumage*, Exon. Th. 204, 19; Ph. 100. Draca on hlǣwe frætwum wlanc, Menol. Fox 513; Gn. C. 27. Wǣre ðū wiste wlonc and wīnes sæd *thou wast sumptuous in food, sated with wine*, Exon. Th. 369, 10; Seel. 39. Ǣse wlanc (*abundantly provided*), fylle gefrægnod, Beo. Th. 2668; B. 1332. Mādmæhta wlonc *rich in treasures*, 5659; B. 2833. Weras duguðum wlance Drihtne guldon gōd mid gnyrne, Cd. Th. 146, 8; Gen. 2419. [He wes prud and wlonc, O. E. Homl. i. 35, 16. Neuer upen eorþe to wlonk þu ny uurþe, Misc. 112, 184. Godelike on horse, wlanc on werge, and unwurþ on wike, 121, 315. Þat child (*Christ*) þat is so milde and wlong, 197, 11. Ȝe beoð toswollen wið wind of wlonke wordes, Kath. 842. My wodbynde so wlonk þat wered my heued, Allit. Pms. 106, 486. Al my weole wlonke, P. S. 156, 17. Sumeres tide is al to wlonc, O. and N. 489. Asked Crist, quethir thai yed to se sain Ion in wlanke wede, Met. Homl. 42, 2. Þe wlonkest wedes, Gaw. 2025. [*O. Sax.* wlank.] v. fela-, gold-, hyge-, mod-, symbel-wlanc.

wlanc, es; *n. Pride*:—Wlanc *typhus*, Wrt. Voc. ii. 97, 9. [For wlaunke (*rimes with* ranke), P. S. 341, 5.] v. wlencu.

wlancian; *p.* ode *To grow proud, great*:—Wlancaþ *insolescat* . . . wlancende *indruticans*, Wrt. Voc. ii. 44, 5–8. Wlancude *adolesceret*, wlancige *adolesco*, Hpt. Gl. 508, 12–14. Wlancode, Wrt. Voc. ii. 3, 42. v. ā-wlancian.

wlanclīce; *adv. Proudly, arrogantly*:—Uulanclīcae *adrogantissime*, Txts. 42, 112. Wlanclīce, Wrt. Voc. ii. 7, 53.

-wlāt, -wlāta, wlātend, wlāt-ful. v. on-wlāt, an-wlǣta, ymb-wlātend, neb-wlātful.

wlātian; *p.* ode; *impers. To cause a person* (acc.) *loathing*:—Mē wlātaþ *nauseo*, Ælfc. Gr. 26, 6; Zup. 158, 7. Ūs wlātaþ for ðisum mete *anima nostra nauseat super cibo isto*, Num. 21, 5. Ðonne hié mete þicgeaþ and drincaþ, ðonne wlātaþ hié, Lchdm. ii. 220, 5. Gif man sȳ innan unhāl, oþþe hyne wlātige, i. 76, 9. Būton ðū git tō full sȳ ðæs ðe ðē lǣfed is, ðæt ðē for ðȳ wlātige, Bt. 11, 1; Fox 30, 20. [Gif heo hit stunken, ham wolde wlatien þer agean, A. R. 86, 19. Overfulle makeþ wlatie, O. and N. 354. Menslaers Laverd wlate sal (*abhominabitur*), Ps. 5, 7. Me wlateȝ withinne, Allit. Pms. 47, 305. Him wlatis, H. S. 3541. Surfet us wlattis, Alex. (Skt.) 4277. It wold haue wlated any wee, 5634.] v. wlǣtan.

wlātian; *p.* ode *To gaze, look*:—Hraðe wæs æt holme hȳðweard, se ðe ǣr lange tīd feor wlātode, Beo. Th. 3837; B. 1916. Ðæt is gefylled, ðæt se frōda mid eágum on wlātade, Exon. Th. 20, 34; Cri. 327. [*Goth.* wlaitōn *circumspicere*.] v. be-, ymb-wlātian; wlītan.

wlātung, e; *f. Nausea, loathing*:—Uulatung (-ing, -unc) *nausatio, vomitus*, Txts. 78, 667. Mid micelre wlātunge gewīteþ ðæt sār, Lchdm. i. 80, 14. Wiþ wlātunge, ii. 62, 18. Wlātunge *nausiam*, Wrt. Voc. ii. 59, 67. [Habbeð wlatunge of þe muðe þet speoweð ut atter, A. R. 80, 25. Lest heo suppose þow make þat fare for wlatynge, Mirc. 894.]

wlātung. v. ymb-wlātung.

wleccan; *pp.* wleced, wlecced, wleht *To make lukewarm*:—Wlece listum on wearmum glēdum, Lchdm. ii. 26, 8: 30, 13. Wlece hyt eall tōgadere, ðæt hyt wlæc beó, iii. 106, 2. Ǣlc wæter bið ðȳ unwerodre tō drincanne, æfter ðæm ðe hit wearm bið, gif hit eft ācōlaþ, ðonne hit ǣr wǣre, ǣr hit mon ō ongunne wleccan, Past. 58; Swt. 447, 21. v. ge-wleccan; wlacian.

wlencan *to make* wlanc (*q. v.*) [Ech man is strong ðe awelt is lichame, and wlencð his soule, O. E. Homl. ii. 189, 27. Leaf þi lease wit ꝥ tu wlenchest te in *depone false sapientie supercilium*, Kath. 1010.] v. for-, ge-wlencan, ofer-wlenced.

wlencu (-o); *indecl.*: wlenc, e; *f.* **I.** *pride, high spirit.* v. wlanc, I:—Wēnic ðæt gē for wlenco, nalles for wræcsīðum, ac for higeþrymmum Hrōðgār sōhton, Beo. Th. 681; B. 338. Þrym sceal mid wlenco, þrīste mid cēnum, Exon. Th. 337, 7; Gn. Ex. 61. **II.** in an unfavourable sense, *pride, arrogance, haughtiness, insolence.* v. wlanc, II:—Him wlenco gesceód, oferhȳd egle, Cd. Th. 258, 20; Dan. 678. Hié wlenco onwōd, ðæt hié firendǣda tō frece wurdon, 155, 27; Gen. 2579: 217, 3; Dan. 17. Uulencu *fastu*, Wrt. Voc. ii. 108, 32. Wlenceo, 35, 12. Git for wlence wada cunnedon, and for dolgilpe on deóp wæter aldrum nēþdon, Beo. Th. 1020; B. 508: Exon. Th. 114, 27; Gū. 179. Ðȳ læs hē for wlence, wuldorgeofona ful, of gemete hweorfe, and forhycge heánspēdigran, 294, 32; Crä. 24: Cd. Th. 100, 32; Gen. 1673. For wlenco, Beo. Th. 2416; B. 1206. Wlence *insolentiam*, Wrt. Voc. ii. 44, 6. Þeódum ȳwaþ wīsdōm weras, wlencu forleósaþ, Exon. Th. 132, 18; Gū. 474. **II a.** used of an animal:—Se fear ðæs hyrdes drāfe forhogode and him on ðæt wēsten gewunode. . . . Ðā ðæt se hlāford geāhsod, ðæt ðæt hrȳþer swā on wlencu geond ðæt wēsten fērde, Blickl. Homl. 199, 10. **III.** *distinction* of various kinds, *splendour, pomp, dignity, magnificence, wealth, greatness.* v. wlanc, IV:—Ða tīda ða āne burg welge gedydan . . . þurh ðære ānre burge wlenco (*wealth*) wurdon ealle ōþra tō wǣdlan gedōne, Ors. 5, 1; Swt. 214, 10. Forseó ðysse worulde wlenco, gif ðū wille beón welig on ðīnum mōde, Prov. Kmbl. 50. Ǣghwylce wlence and īdele rence forhogian *to despise all pomp and vanity*, L. I. P. 14; Th. ii. 322, 9. Ðæt mennisce mōd bið oft upāhafen, ðeáh hit mid nāne onwalde ne sié underlēd; ac hū micle mā wēnst ðū ðæt hit wolde, gif ða wlencea (wlenca, Hatt. MS.) and se anwald ðǣr wǣre tō gemenged, Past. 17; Swt. 114, 1. Hié wǣron welige on ðyssum middangearde, and heora wlenca wǣron swīþe monigfealde on landum and on wīngeardum, and heora hordernu wǣron mid monigfealdum wlencum gefylde, Blickl. Homl. 99, 14–17: 101, 7. Hwǣr beóþ ðonne his welan and his wista? hwǣr beóþ ðonne his wlencea and his anmēdlan? 111, 34. Hē is wyrma wlence *it is the pride of serpents*, Salm. Kmbl. 165; Sal. 82. Ðæra wlenca ł walana *divitiarum*, Mt. Kmbl. Lind. 13, 22. Hē breác longe ǣr wlencea under wolcnum (cf. his mōd ǣr tō ðām woruldsǣlþum gewunod wæs, Bt. 1; Fox 4, 1), Met. 1, 76. Ic cwæð on mīnum wlencum and on mīnre orsorhnesse *ego dixi in abundantia mea*, Ps. Th. 29, 6: Past. 65; Swt. 465, 15. Ne ðyrfe hē bión tō upāhæfen for nānum wlencum ne for nānre orsorgnesse *non hunc prospera elevent*, 14; Swt. 83, 16. Ðone naman ic sceolde habban, ðæt ic wǣre wela and weorþscipe; ac hié hine habbaþ on mē genumen, and hine habbaþ gesealdne heora wlencum and getehhod tō heora leásum welum, Bt. 7, 3; Fox 20, 30: Blickl. Homl. 53, 9. Þeáh hwā wexe mid micelre æþelcundnesse his gebyrda, and þeó on eallum welum and on eallum wlencum *magna titulis fulgeat claris domus*, Bt. 19; Fox 68, 32: Met. 10, 28. Ðū forlǣtan scealt īdle ofersǣlþa . . . ne ðū ðē ǣfre ne lǣt wlenca gewǣcan, Met. 5, 31. v. gold-, ofer-, weorold-wlencu.

wlisp, wlips; *adj. Speaking inarticulately, lisping, stuttering, stammering*:—*Balbus, qui vult loqui et non potest* wlips, Wrt. Voc. ii. 125, 11. Wlisp *balbus*, 101, 50: 10, 71: i. 288, 8: *balbutus*, ii. 101, 56: 10, 75. Wlips *blessus*, i. 75, 38. Stamerum and wlipsum *balbis et blaesis*, Hpt. Gl. 478, 15: *blessis*, Wrt. Voc. ii. 81, 42.

wlita, an; *m.* **I.** *face, countenance*:—Hleór *vel* wlita *frons*, wlitan *frontes*, Wrt. Voc. ii. 151, 4–5. **II.** *beauty*:—Wlitan (*or from* wlitu? v. wlite) *decore* (in pulcherrimo pubertatis decore, Ald. 71), Hpt. Gl. 520, 22. [Heo wes a wliten alre vairest, Laym. 2934.] v. and-wlita; wlite.

wlītan; *p.* wlāt, *pl.* wliton *To look, gaze*, (1) absolute:—Þeóda wlītaþ, Exon. Th. 221, 28; Ph. 341. (2) with prep. (adv.):—Ðū on magan wlītest, Cd. Th. 144, 26; Gen. 2395. Wuhta gehwylc on weoruld wlīteþ, Met. 31, 14. Hē wlīt ofer ealle ða ðe ealre eorðan ymbhwyrft būiaþ *respexit super omnes qui habitant orbem*, Ps. Th. 32, 12. Ðissum idesum ðe wē on wlītaþ, Cd. Th. 150, 32; Gen. 2500. On ða synwyrcend wlītaþ, Exon. Th. 68, 18; Cri. 1105. Wlāt wītga geond þeódland, ōþ ðæt hē gestarode, ðǣr gestaþelad wæs æþelīc ingong, 19, 25; Cri. 306. Hió wlāt ofer ealle, Elen. Kmbl. 770; El. 385. Hē tō heofenum wlāt, Byrht. Th. 136, 56; By. 172. Hē æfter recede wlāt, Beo. Th. 3149; B. 1572. Ða ðe on holm wliton, 3189; B. 1592. Wlītan on Wīlāf, 5696; B. 2852: Cd. Th. 145, 8; Gen. 2402. Heó swā wīde wlītan meahte ofer heofonrīce, 38, 18; Gen. 608. Wlītan in wuldre *to see heaven*, 290, 2; Sat. 409. Fleóhnet, ðæt hē mihte wlītan ðurh on ǣghwylcne, and on hyne nǣnig monna cynnes, Judth. Thw. 22, 5; Jud. 49. (2 a) amplified by the addition of *eágum*:—Hē ofer ealle þeóde eágum wlīteþ *oculi ejus super gentes respiciunt*, Ps. Th. 65, 6. Hȳ geseóð hyra cyning, eágum on wlītaþ, Exon. Th. 352, 7; Sch. 94. On ðone eágum wlāt cining, Cd. Th. 7, 15; Gen. 106. Wlīt (hāwa, Bt. 4; Fox 8, 20) on moncyn mildum eágum, Met. 4, 54. Hȳ wēnaþ ðæt hȳ on eálond sum eágum wlīten, Exon. Th. 360, 28; Wal. 12. Eágum wlītan on, Cd. Th. 107, 25; Gen. 1794: 109, 19; Gen. 1825. [*Icel.* līta *to look*.] v. be-, geond-, þurh-wlītan; wlātian.

wlite, es; *m.*: wlitu, e (*and?* an; v. wlita, II); *f.* **I.** *aspect, countenance, looks, appearance, shape, form*:—Wlite his *vultus ejus*, Ps. Spl. 10, 8. Cristes onsȳn, æþelcyninges wlite, Exon. Th. 56, 27; Cri. 907: Beo. Th. 506; B. 250. Se wlite ðæs wundorlīcan līchoman *species corporis gloriosi*, Bd. 4, 9; S. 576, 35. Ðeáh ðe him se wlite cwēme *though the looks* (*of the sword*) *please him*, Salm. Kmbl. 332; Sal. 165. Sceal on leóht cuman sīnra weorca wlite, Exon. Th. 64, 15; Cri. 1038. Wæs gelīcnes horses and monnes, hundes and fugles, and eác wīfes wlite, 418, 28; Rä. 37, 12. Ðeós wlitu *haec species*, Ælfc. Gr. 12; Zup. 82, 11. Gilde be his (*a horse's*) wlites wyrðe, L. Ath. v. 6, 1; Th. i. 232, 25. Be his (*a slave's*) wlites weorðe, 2; Th. i. 234, 6. Be his wlite, L. In. 26; Th. i. 118, 20. Mid wlite and mid wæstmum fæger *fair in face and form*, Blickl. Homl. 113, 16. Ðeáh ðe ðū wǣre eallra monna fægrost on wlite, Bt. 32, 1; Fox 114, 27. Hī ealle tō ðæs mannes wlite gesceapene synd *they are all made in his likeness*, Boutr. Scrd. 19, 22. Wlit ł onsión *personam*, Mt. Kmbl. Lind. 22, 16. Wundriaþ weras wlite and wæstma, Exon. Th. 221, 9; Ph. 332.

Nǽnig mæg wlite and wísan wordum gecýþan, 491, 30; Rä. 81, 7. II. *good looks, beautiful appearance, beauty, glory, ornament*:—Hwæþer nū gimma wlite eówre eágan tō him getió, heora tō wundrianne? seó duguđ đæs wlites đe on đām gimmum bið, biþ heora, næs eówre *an gemmarum fulgor oculos trahit? si quid est in hoc splendore praecipui, gemmarum est lux illa, non hominum*, Bt. 13; Fox 40, 1: Cd. Th. 239, 1; Dan. 364: Exon. Th. 82, 32; Cri. 1347. Fealwe blōstman wudubeáma wlite, 202, 25; Ph. 75. Đínes wuldres wlite *gloria tua*, Ps. Th. 56, 13. Weorđlīc wlite wuldres đīnes *magnificentia*, 95, 6. Se wlite his andwlitan *species decoris ejus*, 49, 2: Cd. Th. 278, 18; Sat. 223. Ǽlc wlite and ǽlc fægernes đisse weorlde lífes. . . . Se wlite and seó fægernes đære sāule, Blickl. Homl. 57, 28–31: 59, 6. Priscianus se đe ys ealre Lēdenspræ̅ce wlite gehāten, Ælfc. Gr. 15; Zup. 94, 3. Wlites wealdend, Ps. Th. 67, 12. Se fulla mōna wyrđ wlites bereáfad, Met. 28, 42. Wlittes *decoris*, Rtl. 92, 10. Wlite *decore*, 97, 16: *stemmate*, Wrt. Voc. ii. 88, 46. Đe læs đe hē for hire (*Sarah's*. v. Gen. 12, 11) wlite wurde ofslagen, Boutr. Scrd. 22, 1. Sunnan beorhtra, æþeltungla wlite, Exon. Th. 181, 4; Gū. 1288. Him mid sīđedon twǽgen scīnende englas mid wundorlīcre wlite swā hē sylf wæs geglenged, Homl. Skt. ii. 25, 775. Heó nalles on goldes wlite and on seolfres ne scīneþ, Blickl. Homl. 197, 9: Elen. Kmbl. 2636; El. 1319: Exon. Th. 238, 24; Ph. 609. Of wlite wendaþ wæstma gecyndu, 104, 29; Gū. 15. Sió micle Babilon đe ic self ātimbrede mē selfum tō wlite and wuldre (*in gloria decoris mei*), Past. 4; Swt. 39, 18: Exon. Th. 70, 18; Cri. 1140. Wlitan *decore* (*see* wlita), Hpt. Gl. 520, 22. Drihten hine mid weorđlīce wlite gegyrede *Dominus decorem induit*, Ps. Th. 92, 1: Cd. Th. 3, 15; Gen. 36. Myceine wlite (*decorem*) đū āsetst ofer hine, Ps. Spl. 20, 5. Geheald đīnne wlite and đīne fægernesse *speciem tuam et pulcritudinem tuam intende*, Ps. Th. 44, 5: Hpt. Gl. 523, 60. Đes middangeard wæs tō đon fæger, đæt hē teáh men tō him þurh his wlite and þurh his fægernesse, Blickl. Homl. 115, 11: Met. 7, 31: Exon. Th. 86, 10; Cri. 1406: Cd. Th. 132, 10; Gen. 2191: 13, 23; Gen. 207. Đære rosan wlite, Bt. 9; Fox 26, 20: Met. 6, 13. Spræ̅con ymb đæs wīfes wlite monige, Cd. Th. 110, 34; Gen. 1848. Heora wlite gewemman *to mar their beauty*, 231, 1; Dan. 240. Gif hē hafaþ ofer ealle men wlite and wīsdōm, Exon. Th. 299, 16; Crä. 103. Gǽstes wlite, 53, 11; Cri. 849: 96, 29; Cri. 1581. His weorces wlite, 97, 9; Cri. 1588. Bringaþ Drihtne wlite and āre, wuldor đridde *afferte Domino gloriam et honorem*, Ps. Th. 95, 7. Gegyrede mid eallum mistlīcum hræglæ wlitum *circumcincta varietate*, 44, 15. Hē hié gegiereþ myd đām winsumestan wlitum, and eft geungewlitegaþ, Shrn. 195, 11. [Haueden men ispeken of hire mucla fæira wlita (of hire mochele fairsipe, 2nd MS.), Laym. 3139. Kerueđ of hire neose, and heore wlite ga tō lose, 22844. Gif itt seþ þe wlite off ennglekinde, Orm. 666. Þi wlite *speciem tuam*, Ps. 44, 5. Ne sal þu þi wif bi hire wlite chesen, Misc. 119, 249. Min hew falewidþ, and min wlite is wan, 135, 580. O schene nebschaft . . . areow þi wlite, Kath. 1452. Þe lilie mid hire faire wlite, O. and N. 439. Al his wlite wurđ teres wet, Gen. and Ex. 2288. *Goth.* wlits *face, form*: *O. Frs.* wlite: *O. Sax.* wliti *form, beauty*: *Icel.* litr *hue, countenance*.] v. and-, mǽg-, on-, wamm-wlite, neb-wlitu.

wlite-andett, es; *n.* (?) *A confession of splendour*:—Đū đē weorđlīce wliteandette gōde gegyredest *confessionem et decorem induisti*, Ps. Th. 103, 2.

wlite-beorht; *adj. Of splendid beauty, beautiful*, (1) of persons:—Wlitebeorht ides (*Sarah*), Cd. Th. 103, 34; Gen. 1728. Hié (*Adam and Eve*) wlitebeorht wǽron on woruld cenned, 12, 19; Gen. 188. (2) of things:—Dæg, wlitebeorhte gesceaft, 8, 28; Gen. 131. Of ānum wætre wlitebeorhtum, 14, 17; Gen. 220. Eorþan, wlitebeorhtne wang, Beo. Th. 186; B. 93. Hī him wīc curon, đǽr him wlitebeorhte wongas geþūhton, Cd. Th. 108, 10; Gen. 1804. Eorþan cyningas monegum and mislīcum wǽdum wlitebeorhtum scīnaþ, golde gegerede and gimcynnum *reges purpura claros nitente*, Met. 25, 4. Wlitebeorhte wæstmas, Cd. Th. 94, 11; Gen. 1560.

wlite-full; *adj. Beautiful, handsome, comely*:—Ofermōdig gif hē wlitefull (*decorus*) sī geþūht on gesihþe, swā þeáh on weorcum wāc ys, Scint. 21, 8.

wlite-leás; *adj. Without beauty, uncomely, hideous*:—Deóful ætýwde wann and wliteleás, Andr. Kmbl. 2339; An. 1171.

wlitelīce; *adv. Beautifully, in comely fashion*:—Hī weófod wlitelīce geworhtan and gegyredon, Blickl. Homl. 205, 6.

wlite-sceáwung, e; *f. The word is used to translate Sion*:—Bið gesegen God in wlitesceáwunge (-scēwunge, Bd. S. 547, 39) *uidebitur Dominus in Sion*, Bd. 3, 19; M. 212, 11.

wlite-scīne; *adj. Of brilliant beauty, splendid, beauteous*:—Engel ælbeorht, wlitescýne wer, Cd. Th. 237, 15; Dan. 338: Elen. Kmbl. 143; El. 72. Weorud wlitescýne, Exon. Th. 31, 9; Cri. 493: 35, 6; Cri. 554. Seó wlitescýne wuldres condel (*Juliana*), 269, 22; Jul. 454. Wlitesciéne wīf (*Eve*), Cd. Th. 33, 28; Gen. 527. On mǽrum dæge ł on wlitescēnan dæge *insigni die*, Ps. Lamb. 80, 4. Weoruda wlitescýnast, Exon. Th. 101, 27; Cri. 1665. [*O. Sax.* wliti-skōni.]

wlite-seón, -sīn, e; *f. A sight to gaze on, a spectacle*:—Wæs be feaxe on flet boren Grendles heáfod, and đære idese mid, wliteseón wrǽtlīc, Beo. Th. 3304; B. 1650. Cf. wæfer-sīn, wundor-seón.

wlite-torht; *adj. Brilliant, splendid*:—Wlitetorht scīneþ sunna, Met. 28, 60. Wyrta wlitetorhtra, Exon. Th. 484, 5; Rä. 70, 3.

wlite-wamm, es; *m. A disfigurement of the face, personal disfigurement*:—Æt đam læsestan wlitewamme .iii. scillingas, and æt đam māran vi. scill., L. Ethb. 56; Th. i. 16, 15. Wlitewomma *nevorum* (nullis naevorum maculis deformatos, Ald. 10), Wrt. Voc. ii. 76, 27: 60, 56. [*O. Frs.* wlite-wam; cf. *also* wlite-wimelsa.]

wlitig; *adj. Beautiful, comely, fair*:—Wlitig *speciosus* vel *decorus*, Wrt. Voc. i. 72, 17: *formosa*, ii. 33, 57. *Elegans*, i. *speciosus, gratus, pulcher* wynsum, wlitig *praecipuus, magnus*, 142, 81. Wlitigre *formosior*, 34. 59. I. of beauty that appeals to the senses, (1) appearance in persons or things, (a) of earthly beauty:—Đæt wīf wæs swīđe wlitig (*pulchra*), Gen. 12, 14. Sum bið wlitig on wæstmum, Exon. Th. 295, 18; Crä. 35. He (*the Phœnix*) is wlitig and wynsum, wuldre gemearcad *regali plena decore*, 220, 10; Ph. 318. Onlīcnes wlitig, Andr. Kmbl. 1463; An. 732. Đæt treów wæs wlitig on eágum (*pulchrum oculis*), Gen. 3, 6: Cd. Th. 30, 16; Gen. 467: 247, 18; Dan. 499. Wlitig is se wong, Exon. Th. 198, 8; Ph. 7. Đeós wlitige gesceaft, heofon and eorþe, Andr. Kmbl. 2873; An. 1439. Đis leóhte beorht cymeþ eástan wlitig and wynsum, Exon. Th. 350, 13; Sch. 63. Smicere on gearwum cymeþ wlitig scrīđan Maius, Menol. Fox 152; Men. 77. Hærfest, wlitig, wæstmum hladen, 281; Men. 142. Đære wlitegan byrig weallas, Judth. Thw. 23, 24; Jud. 137. In đam wlitegan træfe, 25, 11; Jud. 255. Hūs wlitig and wynsum, Exon. Th. 211, 25; Ph. 203. Wlitig sweord, Beo. Th. 3329; B. 1662. Manna dohtra wǽron wlitige (*pulchrae*), Gen. 6, 2. Gelīce hwītum byrgenum, đa þinceaþ mannum ūtan wlitige (wlittig, Lind. *speciosa*), Mt. Kmbl. 23, 27. Ne seleþ đē wæstmas eorþe wlitige, Cd. Th. 62, 18; Gen. 1016. Đās wlitegan tungl, Met. 28, 6. Đē weorđ wæstm đý wlitegra, Cd. Th. 33, 14; Gen. 520. Þūhte đeós woruld wlitigre, 38, 9; Gen. 604. Wīfa wlitegost, 39, 17; Gen. 627. Mid đam wlitegostum nebbe, Homl. Th. i. 430, 14. Đeáh hē hine gescyrpte mid eallum đām wlitegestum wǽdum *quamvis se Tyrio ostro comeret*, Bt. 28; Fox 100, 26. (b) of celestial beauty, *beauteous, glorious*:—Hē (*Christ*) bið đām gōdum glædmōd on gesihþe, wlitig, Exon. Th. 57, 1; Cri. 912: 232, 33; Ph. 516. Seó wlitige þrýnes, 24, 1; Cri. 378. Wlitig weoroda heáp and wuldres þreát, Andr. Kmbl. 1739; An. 872. Wlitig wuldres boda, Elen. Kmbl. 153; El. 77. Sió wlitige stōw (*heaven*), Met. 20, 279. Wlitig, wuldorfæst, Exon. Th. 151, 2; Gū. 789: Cd. Th. 277, 33; Sat. 214. Him is engel mid, ne mæg him bryne sceþþan wlitigne wuldorhoman, Exon. Th. 196, 24; Az. 179. (2) of sound:—Hyre stefn oncwæđ wlitig of wolcnum, Exon. Th. 259, 16; Jul. 283. Swēg eallum songcræftum swētra and wlitigra, 206, 26; Ph. 132. Wōđa wlitegaste, Elen. Kmbl. 1494; El. 749. (3) of scent:—Đæt wæs swēte stenc, wlitig and wynsum, Exon. Th. 359, 19; Pa. 65. II. of beauty that appeals to the mind:—Wynsum and wlitig herung *jocunda decoraque laudatio*, Ps. Spl. 146, 1. Đeáh đe ne beó wlitig lof on đæs synfullan mūđe, hwæđere ne geswīce hē đære herunge, Homl. Th. i. 448, 5. Þūhte fæger and wlitig heora līf, Blickl. Homl. 107, 30. Is đīn nama mǽre, wlitig and wuldorfæst, Cd. Th. 234, 3; Dan. 286. Wlitigan wilsīþes, Exon. Th. 2, 18; Cri. 21. Gǽst weorcum wlitigne, 180, 11; Gū. 1278. Đæt gē eówer đæt wlitige līf magon generian, Homl. Skt. i. 23, 189. Đonne hē ūs selđ micle getyngnesse and wlitige spræ̅ce ymb sōđfæsđnesse tō cýđanne *cum nobis luce veritatis plena eloquia subministrat*, Past. 48; Swt. 369, 14. Hine wlitegum wordum herigeaþ, Ps. Th. 146, 1. Wlitige and unclǽne, tile and yfle, Cd. Th. 303, 8; Sat. 609. Wlitegran *formosiore* (venustate formosiore fretus virginitate, Ald. 71), Hpt. Gl. 520, 24. [He awundrede him of hire wliti westum, Kath. 310. *O. Sax.* wlitig.] v. sunn-, un-, un-ge-wlitig.

wlitige; *adv. Beautifully, fairly, splendidly*:—Hālge gǽstas stīgaþ tō wuldre, wlitige gewyrtad mid hyra weldǽdum, Exon. Th. 234, 20; Ph. 543. His blǽd scīneþ wlitige in wuldre, Andr. Kmbl. 3438; An. 1723.

wlitig-fæst; *adj. Beauteous, glorious*:—Swā se æþela fugel wlitigfæst wunaþ wyllestreámas, Exon. Th. 204, 29; Ph. 105.

wlitigian; *p.* ode. I. *to make beautiful*:—Đa hē geđwǽraþ and wlitegaþ, hwīlum eft unwlitegaþ and on ōþrum hīwe gebrengþ, Bt. 39, 8; Fox 224, 9. Simle đæt unwlitige wlitigaþ đæt wlitige *ever the beautiful beautifies the unbeautiful*, Shrn. 165, 35. Hit worulde wlitigaþ, Exon. Th. 493, 17; Rä. 81, 32. Fyl nū đa frumspræ̅ce, wlitega đīne wordcwidas (*give glorious effect to thy words*), and đīn wuldor ūs gecýđ, 188, 9; Az. 43. Wlitiga đīnne wordcwyde and đīn wuldor on ūs gecýđ, Cd. Th. 236, 26; Dan. 327. Đæt ic mōte āweccan đās wæstmas ūs tō woruldnytte, wlitigigan đās wancgturf, Lchdm. i. 400, 7. Wlitigende *decorans*, Hymn. Surt. 140, 14. II. *to grow beautiful*:—Byrig fægriaþ, wongas wlitgiaþ (wlitigaþ, MS.), Exon. Th. 308, 33; Seef. 49. v. ge-, un-wlitigian.

wlitigness, e; *f. Beauty, comeliness, adornment*:—Seó wlitignes heora ræsta and setla, Blickl. Homl. 99, 32. Crist com tō wlitignesse and tō weorþunge his brýde, 11, 31. v. un-wlitigness.

wlitigung, wlitu. v. un-wlitigung, wlite.

wlō; *adv.* (?) *Readily, easily*:—Hē āwrecen wælpīlum wlō ne meahte orod up geteón (cf. sōna ne meahte orod up geteón, 163, 20; Gū. 997), ellensprǣce hleóþor āhebban, Exon. Th. 171, 16; Gū. 1127. v. next word.

wlōh (; *gen.* wlēh; *f.*?) *A hem, fringe*:—Næs him gewemmed wlite, ne wlōh of hrægle ālȳsed, ne loc of heáfde, Andr. Kmbl. 2941; An. 1473. Seó hālge stōd ungewemde wlite, næs hyre wlōh ne hrægl, ne feax ne fel, fȳre gemǣled, Exon. Th. 277, 34; Jul. 590. Wlōh wēdes his *fimbriam vestimenti ejus*, Mt. Kmbl. Lind. 9, 20: 14, 36. Wglōana (wlogana?) mid dȳ gehrān *fimbriae tactu*, p. 17, 10. Hiá miclas wloeh *magnificant fimbrias*, 23, 5. [Clothes wel neiȝ forwerd, & the wlon offe, Pl. Cr. 736.] v. an-, ge-wlō.

wlott (?) *a blemish*:—Wlotta, smyttena *naevorum, notarum*, Hpt. Gl. 421, 55. v. (?) wlǣta, III.

wō; *adv. Wrongly, perversely, unequally*:—Hwī sió wyrd swā wō wendan sceolde, Met. 4, 40. v. wōh.

Wocen- (**Wrocen-**? v. Wreocen-sǣte) **sǣte,** -sǣtan; *pl. The name of the occupants of some district in England*:—Wocensǣtna land is syfan þūsend hīda, Cod. Dip. B. i. 414, 16.

wocig (?), e; *f. A snare, noose*:—Wocie *tendiculum, decipulam, laqueum*, Hpt. Gl. 429, 18. Wociga *catenarum*, 489, 72.

wōcor, e; *f. Increase, fruit, offspring*:—Sceal fæsl wesan cwiclifigendra cynna gehwilces on dæt wudufæsten, wōcor gelǣded eordan tūdres, Cd. Th. 79, 17; Gen. 1312. Fēd feora wōcre, 81, 9; Gen. 1342. Dā gemunde God sunu Lameches, and ealle da wōcre de hē wid wætre beleác, 85, 3; Gen. 1409. Hīwan lǣd dū, and ealle da wōcre de ic nerede, 90, 4; Gen. 1490. [*Goth.* wōkrs τόκος: *O. Frs.* wōker *interest*: *O. H. Ger.* wuochar *augmentum, incrementum, fructus, fecunditas, germen*: *Icel.* ōkr *interest*.]

wocorlīce. v. wacorlīce.

wōd; *adj. Mad*:—Wōd *rabidus* vel *insanus*, Wrt. Voc. i. 45, 70: 75, 56. (1) in reference to persons:—Dū eart wōd *daemonium habes*, Jn. Skt. 8, 48, 49, 52: Homl. Th. ii. 232, 17. Hwā is swā wōd, dæt hē dyrre cwedan, dæt God ne sē ǣce, Shrn. 176, 32. Ne synt nā dis wōdes mannes word, Jn. Skt. 10, 21. Wōdan gewittes, Cd. Th. 255, 22; Dan. 628. Tō biddenne hire wōdan dehter gesundfulnysse . . . seó dohtor on wōdum dreáme læg dweligende, Homl. Th. ii. 110, 15–19: 50, 27. Fela wōde menn heora gewit underfēngon, Homl. Skt. ii. 27, 130. Hē wōdum mannum gewitt forgeaf, Homl. Th. i. 480, 14. Hē da deóflu āflīgde of dām wōdum wyrhtum, Homl. Skt. i. 6, 205. (1 a) *raving, blasphemous.* v. wodlīce, II, wōdness, II, *and* cf. woffian:—Mūd wōdne sōdfæstnysse andsware genyþerian *os blasphemum ueritatis responsione dampnare*, Scint. 9, 11. (2) of animals:—Wid wōdes hundes slite, Lchdm. i. 4, 8. His hors feól wealwigende geond da eordan wōdum gelīcost, Homl. Skt. ii. 26, 206. (3) of things, *mad, raging, furious*:—Heom on becom swīde hreóh weder, and seó wōde sǣ and se stranga wind hī on dæt land āwearp, Chr. 1075; Erl. 212, 23. Wōd *effera* (*fluctuum ferocitas*, Ald. 42), Hpt. Gl. 478, 60. Sió wōde þrāg dære wrǣnnesse, Bt. 37, 1; Fox 186, 18: Met. 25, 41. [*Laym. Orm. A. R. Ayenb.* wod: *Chauc.* wood: *Prompt. Parv.* wood, ooth: *Goth.* wōds: *O. H. Ger.* wuot: *Icel.* ōðr.] v. ellen-, tung-wōd; wēde.

wōd *madness*:—Wōd (wōdnesse?) *rabiem, insaniem*, Hpt. Gl. 476, 32. v. ellen-wōd.

wōda, an; *m. A madman, an insane person, one possessed*:—Wōda *epilepticus*, Wrt. Voc. ii. 107, 30: *demoniaticus, insanus, amens*, Wülck. Gl. 218, 41. Wōdan *limphaticum*, Wrt. Voc. ii. 53, 56. Hē eode ūt tō dām earmum wōdum, Homl. Skt. i. 6, 203. Wōdan *inergumenos*, Wrt. Voc. ii. 110, 57; 45, 8. [*O. H. Ger.* wuoto.]

wōda, an; *m. Danger* (?):—Dā gyrnde hē dæt hē mōste macian ǣnne hwerf wid don (*Kemble reads* done, Cod. Dip. iv. 58, 1) wōdan tō werianne, Chart. Th. 341, 8. [Cf. (?) *Icel.* vāði (vōði) *a danger, a dangerous object*.]

wōddor (= wōþ-dor?), es; *n. The gate of speech* (?), *the mouth* (?):—T hine teswaþ, and hine on da tungan sticaþ, wrǣsteþ him dæt wōddor, and him da wongan briceþ, Salm. Kmbl. 191; Sal. 95.

Wōden, es; *m. Woden, one of the Teutonic deities.* Among the Roman gods Mercury seems to have been thought most nearly to correspond, and *Wōden* is rendered by *Mercurius*, e. g.:—Wōden *Mercurium*, Wrt. Voc. ii. 114, 4. Cf. Saga mē hwā ǣrost bōcstafas sette. Ic dē secge, Mercurius se gygand, Salm. Kmbl. p. 192, 7: 200, 24. The name is of rare occurrence in the literature:—Wōden worhte weós, wuldor alwalda rūme roderas, Exon. Th. 341, 28; Gn. Ex. 133. Wyrm com snīcan, tōslāt hē man; dā genam Wōden viiii. wuldortānas, slōh dā da næddran, dæt heó on viiii tōfleáh, Lchdm. iii. 34, 23. ¶ Woden is found in most of the genealogies of the old English royal families:—Dæs (Wihta) fæder wæs Wōden nemned, of dæs strȳnde monigra mǣgþa cyningcynn fruman lǣdde, Bd. 1, 15; S. 483, 30. Fram dan Wōdne āwōc eall ūre cynecynn, and Sūdan-Hymbra eác, Chr. 449; Erl. 13, 20: 547; Erl. 16, 13: 560; Erl. 16, 32: 855; Erl. 70, 9. See Grimm's Teutonic Mythology, Stallybrass's translation, vol. i. p. 163, vol. iv. pp. 1709 sqq. ¶ the word is found in place-names, e. g. Wōdnes beorg, Wōdnes den, Wōdnes dīc, Cod. Dip. Kmbl. vi. 355. See also Wōdnes-dæg. [We (*the Saxons*) habbed godes gode . . . þe þridde hæhte Woden . . . Woden hehde þa hæhste laȝe, Laym. 13897–13921. *O. L. Ger.* Wōdan: *O. H. Ger.* Wuotan: *Icel.* Ōðinn.] v. Ōden.

wōden-dreám, es; *m. Madness, fury*:—Rēþnes, wōdendreám (cf. wēden-heort; *or* (?) wōden dreám; cf. on wōdum dreáme, v. wōd, (1)) *furor animi*, Wrt. Voc. ii. 151, 69.

Wōdening, es; *m. A son of Woden*:—Bældæg Wōdening, Chr. pref.; Erl. 2, 7: 547; Erl. 16, 13: 552; Erl. 16, 21: 560; Erl. 16, 31: 855; Erl. 70, 9. Wōdning, 449; Erl. 13, 20.

wōde-wistle, an; *f. Hemlock*:—Wōdewistle, uuōdaewistlae, uuōdewislae *cicuta*, Txts. 51, 463. Wōdewistle (*printed* -þistle) *elleborum* vel *veratrum*, Wrt. Voc. i. 31, 56. Wōdewistle (*printed* -þisele, but see Wülck. Gl. 297, 8) *cicuta*, 67, 37.

wōd-frec; *adj. Furiously greedy, raging, ravening*:—Dæt se wōdfreca werewulf (*the devil*) tō swȳde ne slīte, ne tō fela ne ābīte of godcundre heorde, L. C. E. 26; Th. i. 374, 30. Wōdfræca, Wulfst. 191, 16. [Cf. *O. H. Ger.* wuot-grimm *tyrannus*: *Icel.* ōð-fúss, -gjarn *madly eager*.]

wōd-hen[n], e; *f. A quail*:—Wōdhae[n] *coturno*, Txts. 53, 583. Wōdhen, Wrt. Voc. ii. 15, 30.

-wōdian. v. ellen-wōdian; wēdan.

wōd-līc; *adj. Mad, furious, frantic*:—Benedictus manode done rēdan ēhtere dæt hē dære wōdlīcan rēdnysse geswice, Homl. Th. ii. 182, 1. Heó ne rōhte his worda for dæra wōdlīcan ontendnysse, Homl. Skt. i. 3, 397. Se sceocca fordwān mid swīdlīcum reáme, swā dæt da munecas wurdon āwrehte durh his wōdlīcan stemne, 6, 318. [*Icel.* ōðligr *vehement*.]

wōdlīce; *adv.* I. *madly, furiously, franticly*:—Dām unþeáwfæstum de wōdlīce drincaþ, and heora gewitt āmyrraþ, Homl. Ass. 6, 145: Homl. Skt. i. 13, 76: L. Ælfc. C. 35; Th. ii. 356, 43. Wōdlīce āstyrode wid done hālgan, Homl. Ass. 79, 162. Wōdlīce geyrsod, Homl. Skt. ii. 25, 616. Dū þus wōdlīce wilnast ceorles, i. 3, 396. Hē mōt wōdlīce derian, Wulfst. 85, 5. Dam wulfe gelīc de wōdlīce ābīteþ da sceáp, Basil admn. 6; Norm. 46, 23. II. *blasphemously.* v. wōd (1 a):—Dæt ōder dæra hospworda hē widsōc, dæt hē deófol hæfde; ac hī wǣron witodlīce mid deófle āfylled, dā dā hī swā wōdlīce tō dam Hǣlende sprǣcon, Homl. Th. ii. 230, 11. [He mochul þa wodeloker wilnede þeos mæidenes, Laym. 3201. He schal scheten woodlich or fersliche, Halliw. Dict. *Icel.* ōðliga *rashly*.]

Wōdnes-dæg, es; *m. Wednesday*:—Wōdnesdæges nama wæs of Mercurio, Anglia viii. 321, 16. On Wōdnesdæg, Mt. Kmbl. Rubric 3, 1, 13 *and often*: Homl. Skt. i. 12, 1: R. Ben. 65, 16: Wulfst. 180, 25. On done ōderne Wōdnesdæg ofer Pentecosten, Mt. Kmbl. Rubric 5, 17. .iiii. Wōdnesdagas on .iiii. Ymbrenwican, L. Alf. pol. 43; Th. i. 92, 8. [Woden we ȝefue wendesdei, Laym. 13925 (2nd MS.). *A. R.* Wodnesdei: *Kath.* Wednes-dai: *Piers P.* Wodnes-, Wednes-dai: *O. Frs.* Wernsdei: *M. Du.* Woens-dach: *Icel.* Ōðins-dagr.]

Wōdnes-niht, e; *f. The night between Tuesday and Wednesday.* v. Sunnan-niht:—Gebyreþ dæt hig hyra clǣnnysse healdon ǣfre Sunnanniht and Wōdnesnihte, L. Ecg. P. ii. 21; Th. ii. 190, 19. Sunnannihtum ne mæssenihtum ne Wōdnesnihtum, Wulfst. 305, 23.

wōdness, e; *f.* I. *madness, fury, frenzy, rage*:—Wōdnys *rabies*, Wrt. Voc. i. 45, 71: 75, 58. Dā geāxode se cyning be dam witseócum menn, hū se apostol hine fram dære wōdnysse āhredde, Homl. Th. i. 458, 9. Wurdon āflīgde deófla fram mannum, da de on wōdnysse ǣr wǣron gedrehte, Homl. Skt. ii. 26, 199. Hē of his gewitte weard, and hine se feónd swȳþe swencte mid dære wōdnysse, Guthl. 12; Gdwin. 56, 15. Dæt wīf weard mid māran wōdnysse (*with greater fury*) āstyrod, Homl. Th. ii. 30, 15: Homl. Ass. 72, 170. His sāwul is durh deófol gedreht; him is neód dæt hē his āgene wōdnysse tōcnāwe, Homl. Th. ii. 110, 29. On wōdnessum ɫ gewytlȳstum leásum *in insanias falsas*, Ps. Lamb. 39, 5. Wōdnyssa and rēdnyssa *furias atque ferocia*, Hymn. Surt. 132, 18. II. *blasphemy.* v. wōd (1 a):—Dā sæt hē tǣlende done Hǣlend . . . His wōdnys weard gewrecen durh God, Homl. Ass. 60, 212. [Wodnesse *insania, furia, furor*, Prompt. Parv. 531: *Chauc.* woodnesse: *O. H. Ger.* wuotnessa *dementia*.]

wōd-scipe, es; *m. Madness, fury*:—Wōdscipe *furia, insania, amentia*, Wrt. Voc. ii. 151, 72. [*Ira furor brevis est* wredde is a wodschipe, A. R. 120, 14.]

wōd-þrāg, e; *f. A mad fit* or *time, madness, fury*:—Weaxeþ dære wrǣnnesse wōdþrāg (wōd þrāg? v. þrāg, II) micel, Met. 25, 41. Oft da wōdþrāga dæs ungewitfullan monnes se lǣce gestild and gehǣld mid dæm dæt hē him ōlecd æfter his āgnum willan . . . Donne Saule se widerwearda gǣsd on becom, donne gefēng Dauid his hearpan, and gestillde his wōdþrāga. . . . Dauid mid his sange gemetgode da wōdþrāge Saules *furor insanorum saepe ad salutem medico blandiente reducitur . . . Cum Saulem spiritus adversus invaderet, apprehensa David cithara ejus vesaniam sedabat . . . David canente ejus vesania temperatur*, Past. 26; Swt. 183, 21–185, 5.

woede, woel. v. wēde, wǣl.

woepe? :—*Catasta, genus supplicii, vel* woepe (þrēpel? v. þrīpel), *eculeo simile*, Wrt. Voc. ii. 129, 44.

woerd, woerdan, woestig. v. wird, wirdan, wēstig.

woffian; *p.* ode *To rave, blaspheme*:—Ðǽr wæs sum dysig mann plegol ungemetlīce, and tō ðām mannum cwæð, swylce for plegan, ðæt hē Swȳðūn wǽre . . . Hē woffode ðā swā lange mid wordum dyslīce, óð ðæt hē feóll geswōgen, Homl. Skt. i. 21, 298. Woffode *debacchatur*, Hpt. Gl. 506, 76. Woffie *insolescat, superbiat*, 461, 59. Woffigende *blasphemantem*, Scint. 9, 9. v. ā-woffian, *and* cf. wōd (1 a).

woffung, e; *f. Raving, blasphemy*:—Woffung *insania*, Greg. Dial. i. 9. Ðās word wǽron geþūhte beforan him swā woffung (*deliramentum*), Lk. Skt. 24, 11. Hwæt is ðes ðe sprycþ woffunga (*blasphemia*), 5, 21.

wōg. v. wōh.

wōgere, es; *m. A wooer, suitor*:—Wōgere *procus*, Wrt. Voc. i. 50, 36: 73, 7: Hpt. Gl. 501, 58. Wōgeres (*printed* fogeres) *proci*, 498, 42. Wōgere *proco*, 503, 70. Wōghere (*printed* foghere), 506, 45. Wōgere (*printed* fogere), 498, 72. Basilla hæfde ǣnne hǣðene wōgere . . . Heó ðone hǣðenan wōgere habban nolde, Homl. Skt. i. 2, 349, 353. Sume wīf wyrcaþ heora wōgerum drencas, 17, 157. [He, ase noble woware, com uor to preouen his luue, A. R. 390, 21. Þise woweres þat wedde none wydwes, Piers P. 11, 71. Woware *procus*, Prompt. Parv. 532.]

wōgian; *p.* ode *To woo, marry*:—Nāht framaþ flǽsc habban mǽden gif on geþance ǣnig wōgaþ *nihil prodest carnem habere uirginem si mente quis nupserit*, Scint. 70, 7. Bearn worulde ðissere wōgiaþ (*nubunt*) . . . hī ne wōgiaþ (*nubunt*), ne hī ne lǽdaþ wīf, 68, 14, 17. [Hwi ne con ic þe woȝe wiþ swete luue, O. E. Homl. i. 187, 19. Ase a mon þet woweþ (wohes, *v. l.*), A. R. 388, 13. Crist wowude ure soule, 390, 20. Uorte wowen hire, 388, 17. *Chauc.* woweth: *Piers P.* wowede: *Destr. Tr.* woghit; *pp.*] v. ā-wōgian.

wōgung, e; *f. Wooing*:—Sum heretoga āwōgode ðæs cāseres dohtor; wearð se cāsere for ðǽre wōgunge āstyrod, Homl. Skt. i. 7, 301. [Mid wouhinge, A. R. 204, 25. Wowunge efter Godes grome, 116, 12. Wowynge *procacio*, Prompt. Parv. 533.]

wōh; *adj.* I. *not straight, bent, crooked, twisted, oblique*:—Wiþ lyftādle, gif se mūð sié wōh, Lchdm. ii. 338, 5. Gif mūð oððe eáge wōh weorðeþ, L. Ethb. 44; Th. i. 14, 9. Hlāford mīn (*the plough's*) wōh færeþ, weard æt steorte, Exon. Th. 403, 7; Rä. 22, 4: 483, 14; Rä. 69, 2. Sió micle nosu and sió woo (*tortus*), Past. 11; Swt. 67, 5. Mid wōgum bīgelse *obliqua curvatura*, Hpt. Gl. 458, 72. Mid ānum wōgan īserne, Lchdm. i. 318, 18. Wiþ wōuum mūþe, genim ompran . . . sele on ðone wōn dǣl, ii. 54, 22. Wōn *obunca* (*arpagine*), Anglia xiii. 37, 296. Tō ðam wōn stocce, Cod. Dip. Kmbl. ii. 73, 22. Tō ðǽre wōhgan apeldran, iii. 389, 32. Tō wōhan (wōgan, *v. l.*) ǣc, Cod. Dip. B. i. 417, 16. Ðā oncierde ðæt scip on wōnne sīþfæt þurh deófles beswicennesse, Shrn. 60, 8. Gif hē hæfde wō (*tortum*) nosu, Past. 11; Swt. 65, 4. Woo, 67, 7. On ðæt wō treōw (*printed* wottreów), Cod. Dip. Kmbl. iii. 130, 31. Mistlīce wōge wegas *divortia, diverticula*, Wrt. Voc. i. 37, 44. Wōum wīrbogum, Exon. Th. 395, 5; Rä. 15, 3. Tō ðǣm wōn *ad tortas*, Wrt. Voc. ii. 2, 68. Wōge hylcas *obliquos* (*curvos, flexos*) *anfractus*, Hpt. Gl. 486, 71: *anfractus*, 448, 20. Hī hæfdon wōh nebb, and wōge sceancan, Guthl. 5; Gdwin. 34, 22–27. II. *not right, perverse, froward, wrong, unfair*:—Hit is riht ðæt mon yfelige ða yfelan, and hit is wōh (wōg, *v. l.*) ðæt hī mon lǣte unwītnode, Bt. 38, 3; Fox 202, 6. Forlǣtan ða dīstro ðæs wōn weorces (*actionis pravae*), Past. 55; Swt. 429, 13. Mid wōre twiefealdnesse *duplicitatis perversitate*, 35; Swt. 245, 15. On wōre heortan *pravo corde*, 47; Swt. 357, 21. Mid wōre lāre *perversa praedicatione*, 48; Swt. 367, 15. Be wōhre gewitnesse. Gif man āfinde ðæt heora ǣnig on wōhre (wōre, *v. l.*) gewitnesse wǣre, L. Ath. i. 10; Th. i. 204, 22. Gescynded on heora wōn willan *abominabiles in voluntatibus suis*, Ps. Th. 13, 1. Mid wō mūðe *ore perverso*, Past. 47; Swt. 357, 20. Ðæt hyne gehwā wið wō gewitnysse gehealde, L. E. G. 27; Th. ii. 422, 35. Wið ǣlc wōh gestreón (*but see* wōh-gestreón) beorge man, ac strȳne mid rihte, Wulfst. 70, 2: L. I. P. 7; Th. ii. 312, 29. Hū micle unrōtnesse se hæfþ ðe ðone wōn willan hæfþ on ðisse worulde, Bt. 31, 1; Fox 110, 31. Ða wōn (woon, *v. l.*) wyrd on ðara unrihtwīsra anwealda heánesse, 5, 1; Fox 10, 20. Ðurh ðæt woo (wō, Cott. MSS.) weorc hē forliést ðone wlite ōðerra gōdra weorca, Past. 11; Swt. 71, 25. Ðæra gerēfena unriht and wō dōmas (v. wōh-dōm) and prættas, Anglia viii. 336, 40. False gewihta and wōge gemeta, L. Eth. v. 24; Th. i. 310, 13: Wulfst. 70, 3. Wōh wyrda gesceapu *the unequal decrees of fate*, Exon. Th. 421, 26; Rä. 40, 24. Hine gebindaþ ða wōn wilnunga, Bt. 16, 3; Fox 56, 18. Hē wiste him sprǣca fela wōra worda, Cd. Th. 29, 6; Gen. 446. Mid ðæm gewunan ðara wōna weorca, Past. 11; Swt. 69, 7. Wōm wundorbebodum wergan gāstes, Beo. Th. 3498; B. 1747. Mid wōm wilnungum, Past. 11; Swt. 69, 9. From hiera woom (wōn, Cott. MSS.) wegum, 37; Swt. 267, 5. Wōn, 11; Swt. 73, 13: 37; Swt. 267, 12, 16: L. E. G. proem.; Th. ii. 400, 20. Woeum *pravis*, Rtl. 52, 24. Mīne wōn wīsan, Exon. Th. 393, 10; Rä. 12, 8. Hī him wōh godu worhtan, Ps. Th. 77, 58. [He mid woȝe dome benimeð him his beliue, O. E. Homl. i. 179, 16. Þat is woh and na wiht riht, Laym. 4333. Of woh inwit, A. R. 2, 12. Ure woȝhe dedess, Orm. 1375. Þe fox can paþes rihte and woȝe (wowe, *v. l.*), O. and N. 815. *Goth.* un-wāhs.]

wōh; *gen.* wōges, wōs; *dat.* wōge, wō; *n. Wrong, perversity, injustice, error*:—Englas nānes wōges (wōs, *v. l.*) ne willniaþ, Bt. 40, 7; Fox 242, 23. Gif wē wilnigen ðæt hié ðæs wōs geswīcen *hos cum conamur instruere, ne perversa sentiant*, Past. 48; Swt. 367, 23. Wōes ł wōhfulnise *nequitia*, Mt. Kmbl. Lind. 22, 18. Ic him wolde fylstan tō ryhte and nǣfre tō nānan wō, Cod. Dip. Kmbl. ii. 134, 10. From ǣlcum wōe *ab omni pravitate*, Rtl. 34, 9: 37, 23. Hié nyllaþ wietan mid hwelcum woo (wō, Cott. MSS.) hié hit gestriéndon, Past. 45; Swt. 343, 23. Mid wōge (wō, *v. l.*) forsecgan, L. Edg. ii. 4; Th. i. 266, 22. Mid wō fordēman, Cod. Dip. Kmbl. ii. 114, 3. Sceal gehwā gerihtlǣcan ðæt ðæt hē ǣr tō wōge gebīgde, Homl. Th. ii. 2, 25. Tō wōge gebringan *to render incorrectly*, Ælfc. Gr. pref.; Zup. 3, 23: Ælfc. T. Grn. 24, 32. Paulus hine āwende of wōge tō rihte, Homl. Skt. ii. 29, 8. Hī wǣron on woo besmitene *propter injustitias suas humiliati sunt*, Ps. Th. 106, 16. Micel yfel dēð se unwritere, gyf hē nele his wōh gerihtan, Ælfc. Gr. pref.; Zup. 3, 25. Ðā sǣde him hiora ān, ðæt hē wōh bude, Ors. 6, 10; Swt. 264, 28. Gif hwā ǣnigum preóste ǣnig wōh beóde, L. N. P. L. 1; Th. ii. 290, 2. Ðæt hē ðurh hine nān wōh ne bodige *ut ab eis prava nullo modo proferantur*, Past. 15; Swt. 95, 16. Hī wōh meldiaþ *pronuntiabunt iniquitatem*, Ps. Th. 93, 4. Se dēma ðe ōðrum wōh dēme, L. Edg. ii. 3; Th. i. 266, 15. Hē ðæt mǣste wōh dyde wið ða Godes þeówas, Ors. 6, 34; Swt. 290, 18. Ne dō wē eác nān wōh, Past. 45; Swt. 337, 21. Se ðe wilnaþ wōh tō dōnne, 19; Swt. 145, 12: Bt. 41, 3; Fox 246, 19: Ps. Th. 61, 9. Wōh fremian, 54, 20. Wē ðæt wōh ne worhton, ðæt wē ðīne ǣ forlēten *inique non egimus in testamento tuo*, 43, 19. Gif hwā wōh wyrce, L. Edg. ii. 6; Th. i. 268, 9. Ic nylle ðæt gē mē hwæt mid wōh (cf. unrihte, l. 17) begytaþ, L. Ath. i. proem.; Th. i. 196, 31. Mid wōh fordōn, iv. 1; Th. i. 220, 23. On wōh spanan, Salm. Kmbl. 1002; Sal. 502. Sōna swā sacerda hwylc hwone on wōh gesyhð, hē sceal tilian ðæt hē hyne on rihtum gebrynge, L. E. I. 28; Th. ii. 424, 26. Weorþeþ (-aþ, MS.) swīþe oft on wōn (*in error*) se sido, Bt. 39, 9; Fox 226, 4. On wōn gebringan *destruere*, Past. 2; Swt. 31, 24: 28; Swt. 191, 8. ¶ on wōh *wrongfully, wrongly*:—On wōh cierran *deviare*, Wrt. Voc. ii. 25, 40: 139, 57. Ða ðe on wōh dēmaþ, and rihte dōmas onwendaþ, Blickl. Homl. 61, 26. On wōh dōn *perverse agere*, Past. 2; Swt. 31, 12. Ðeáh ūs þince ðæt hit on wōh fare *tametsi confusa omnia perturbataque videantur*, Bt. 39, 8; Fox 224, 21. On wōh yrsian, Ps. Th. 4, 5. On wōh lǣran, 25, arg. On wōh libban, Blickl. Homl. 45, 11, 19. On wōh niman, 61, 22. Ða gōdan ðæt gōd on riht sēcaþ, and ða yfelan on wōh, Bt. 36, 3; Fox 178, 6. [Gif þu me dest woh, O. E. Homl. i. 33, 1. Mid woȝe, Laym. 24811. Þu hauest wouh, A. R. 54, 1. Hatenn woh and sinne, Orm. 5555. Meanen him of wohe, Kath. 1236. Þay laften ryȝt and wroȝten woghe, Allit. Pms. 19, 621. Mid wowe ne myd ryhte, Misc. 49, 412. *O. Sax.* wāh *evil*.] v. ā-, folc-wōh.

wōh-bogen; *adj. Bent, crooked*:—Wyrm wōhbogen *the crooked* (cf. Job 26, 13) *serpent*, Beo. Th. 5646; B. 2827.

wōh-ceápung, e; *f. The fine to be paid for trading contrary to the regulations of a market*:—Ge wōhceápung, ge ǣlc ðæra wōnessa ðe tō ǣnigre bōte gebyrie, ðæt hit āge healf ðǽre cyrcean hlāford, swā swā hit mon tō ceápstōwe gesette, Cod. Dip. Kmbl. v. 143, 22.

wōh-dǣd, e; *f. A wicked deed, crime*:—Manna wōhdǣda sind swīþe gemonigfealdode, Blickl. Homl. 107, 24. Gif mon ne mihte hī tō rihte gecyrron, ðæt hī heora wōhdǣda geswīcan woldan, ðonne sceal ǣghwylc man bētan his wōhdǣda be his gyltes andefne, 45, 26–29. Ne byð ðǽr nān stefen gehȳred, būton wōp and wānung for wōhdǣdum, Wulfst. 139, 4. v. wōh, II.

wōh-dōm, es; *m. An unjust judgement*:—Ðurh leóde unlaga and ðurh wōhdōmas, Wulfst. 166, 24. v. wōh, II.

wōh-fōtede; *adj. Crook-footed, splay-footed, club-footed*; peduncus, Wrt. Voc. i. 45, 45.

wōh-fremmende; *adj.* (*ptcpl.*): *or* wōh-fremmend, es; *m. Wrong-doing; or a wrong-doer*:—Nalles sorgode hwæþer mihtig Drihten āmetan wolde wrece be gewyrhtum wōhfremmendum, Met. 9, 36.

wōh-full; *adj. Wicked, evil*:—Wōhgfull *nequam*, Mt. Kmbl. Lind. 20, 15. Suno siidon yfelwyrcende ł wōhfulra (*nequam*), 13, 38. Mid unrehtuīsum ł wōhfullum *iniquis*, Mk. Skt. Lind. 15, 28. From gāstum wōhfullum ł yflum ł unrehtwīsum (*malignis*), Lk. Skt. Lind. 8, 2. Wōhfulro *nequiores*, Mt. Kmbl. Lind. 12, 45.

wōhfulness, e; *f. Wickedness, iniquity*:—Wōghfulnis *nequitia*, Rtl. 120, 33. Wōghfulnisse his *nequitias ejus*, 113, 40. Wōhfulnise, Mt. Kmbl. Lind. 22, 18. Wōghfulniso *nequitias*, Rtl. 122, 16.

wōh-georn; *adj. Loving iniquity*:—Ða wōhgeornan woruldrīcan mid heora ungestreónum forweorðaþ, Wulfst. 183, 8,

wōh-gestreón, es; *n. Wrongful gain, ill-gotten gain*:—Þurh rīcra reáflāc and þurh gītsunge wōhgestreóna, Wulfst. 166, 24. Ðæt mancyn, ðe nū is on synnlustum and in ðām wōhgestreónum goldes and seolfres beswicen, 182, 13. v. wōh, II.

wōh-god. v. wōh, II.

wôh-hǽmed, es; *n. Adultery, fornication:*—Se yfla willa wôhhǽmetes (cf. unrihthǽmedes, Bt. 31, 2; Fox 112, 24), Met. 18, 2. Sió hreófl getâcnaþ ðæt wôhhǽmed *per scabiem luxuria designatur*, Past. 11; Swt. 71, 5. Ða ðe wôhhǽmed begangaþ mid ôþerra ceorla wîfum, Blickl. Homl. 61, 14.

wôh-hǽmende; *adj.* (*ptcpl.*); *or* wôh-hǽmend, es; *m. Adulterous, fornicating; or an adulterer, a fornicator:*—Ða wôhhǽmendan *fornicatores*, Past. 51; Swt. 401, 27. Ðû dydest ðê tô ðâm wôhhǽmendum *cum adulteris portionem tuam ponebas*, Ps. Th. 40, 19.

wôh-hǽmere, es; *m. An adulterer, a fornicator:*—Ðǽm wôhhǽmerum dêmeþ Dryhten *fornicatores et adulteros judicabit Deus*, Past. 51; Swt. 401, 30.

wôh-handede; *adj. Crook-handed, having a maimed hand;* mancus, Wrt. Voc. i. 45, 44.

wôh-lîc; *adj. Wrong, perverse, evil:*—Hit ys swîðe wôlîc, ðæt ða geworhtan gesceafta ðam ne beón gehîrsume, ðe hî gesceóp and geworhte, Ælfc. T. Grn. 2, 1. Mid wôlîcum *obliqua* (*invidia*), Hpt. Gl. 527, 1. On wôlîcum dǽdum, Blickl. Homl. 107, 28. Wôlîce *inritos*, Germ. 402, 76.

wôhlîce; *adv. Wrongly, unjustly, perversely, wickedly:*—Gif hié on ǽnigum dǽle wôlîce libban heora lîf, Blickl. Homl. 109, 19. Ða ðe ǽwbryce ne wyrceaþ wôlîce (wôhlice, *v. l.*) and sceamlîce, Homl. Ass. 19, 140: 29, 127. Mêdsceattas âwendaþ wôlîce ða rihtan dômas, Ælfc. T. Grn. 20, 32: Basil admn. 9; Norm. 52, 20. Seó lagu lahlîce gewîtnode ða ðe wôlîce singodon, L. Ælfc. P. 8; Th. ii. 366, 23. Hê cwæð ðæt hê wurde wôlîce swâ getûcod, Homl. Skt. i. 21, 276. Nû dô wê swŷðe wôlîce, gif wê ne wurðiaþ God, 13, 180: 17, 233: Wulfst. 105, 9: Homl. Ass. 29, 264: 102, 6.

wôhness, e; *f.* I. *crookedness* (lit. or fig.), *a crooked place:*—Ic gerihte sume wôhnysse *dirigo*, Ælfc. Gr. 28, 5; Zup. 173, 9. Ealle wôhnyssa beóð gerihte *erunt prava in directa* (Is. 40, 4), Homl. Th. i. 360, 33. II. *wrongdoing, iniquity, perversity, depravity, wickedness:*—Heora wôhnys on ðam regole his rihtwîsnysse ætspearn, Homl. Th. ii. 158, 10. Ic wæs on wônysse geeácnod *in iniquitatibus conceptus sum*, Bd. 1, 27; S. 495, 24. Fram langre wônesse and ungesǽlignysse âlŷsde *a longa iniquitate atque infelicitate liberatam*, 2, 15; S. 519, 10. Wônessa *iniquitates*, Bd. 5, 13; S. 633, 38: Blickl. Homl. 107, 24. Heora wôhnyssa forgyfennys, Homl. Ass. 136, 668. Ǽlc ðæra wônessa (*crimes*) ðe tô ǽnigre bôte gebyrie, Cod. Dip. Kmbl. v. 143, 23. On wônyssum *in iniquitatibus*, Bd. 1, 27; S. 495, 25. Gif hié on ǽnigum dǽle wôlîce libban heora lîf, sŷn hié from heora wônessum onwende, and fram heora unrihtum oncyrran, Blickl. Homl. 109, 20.

wôhsum; *adj. Wicked, evil:*—Wôgsum *nequam*, Rtl. 27, 17.

woide-berge. v. wêde-berge.

wôl, es; *m.:* e; *f. Pest, pestilence, plague, murrain:*—Âdle and wôle *luem*, Wrt. Voc. ii. 53, 3. (1) in a physical sense in reference to men or animals:—Wôl (*pestis*) wæs æfter fyligende, Bd. 1, 13; S. 482, 6. Mycel wôl and grim *acerba pestis*, 1, 14; S. 482, 29. Ðætte nô mid him getió mê wôl (*mortalitas*) ðyses geáres, Lchdm. i. lxviii, 3: 330, 1. Ǽr ðæm ðe seó wôl geendod wǽre *cessatum a mortibus non est*, Ors. 2, 4; Swt. 70, 12. Seó monigfealdeste wôl *pestilentia gravis, praecipue mulieres pecudesque corripiens*, 4, 1; Swt. 158, 17. On ða tîd ðæs miclan wôles and moncwylde ðe Breotona eálond mid mycle wôle forhergode *tempore mortalitatis quae Brittaniam lata strage vastavit*, Bd. 3, 13; S. 538, 15: 3, 23; S. 555, 9. His hŷd is brŷce eallum fiþerfêtum nŷtenum wið wôles gewinne on tô ðonne, Lchdm. i. 330, 4. Ǽlcum fiþerfêtum neáte ðe on wôle winne, 328, 13. For ðæm wôle (*pestis*) ðe on ðæt lond becom, Ors. 1, 5; Swt. 34, 15. (2) figurative:—Hwelc is wyrsa wôl oððe ǽngum men mâre daru ðonne hê hæbbe on his gefêrrǽdenne feónd on freóndes anlîcnesse? *quae pestis efficacior ad nocendum, quam familiaris inimicus?* Bt. 29, 2; Fox 106, 13. Wôl *lues*, Bd. 1, 14; S. 482, 23. Ðæs Pelagianiscan wôles (*pestis*), 1, 21; S. 485, 5. On wôles setle *in cathedra pestilentiae*, Past. 56; Swt. 435, 21. Wôle, Anglia xiii. 33, 146. Fram ðysses gemetes wôle (*labe;* the heresy of Eutyches) clǽne, Bd. 4, 17; S. 585, 12. Wênst ðû ðe ic nyte ðone wôl ðînre gedrêfednesse (*perturbationum morbum*), Bt. 5, 3; Fox 12, 17. Ic ðone wôl (*witchcraft*) eów forbeóde, Homl. Skt. i. 17, 72. [*O. Sax.* wôl: *O. H. Ger.* wôl *clades, strages.*]

wôlbǽrness, e; *f. Pestiferousness, destructivity:*—Ic wolde ðæt ða ongeáten, ðe ða tîda ûres cristendômes leahtriaþ, hwelc mildsung siþþan wæs, siþþan se cristendôm wæs, and hû monigfeald wôlbǽrnes ðære woruld ǽr ðæm wæs (*with how many kinds of plagues the world was afflicted before Christianity*), Ors. 2, 1; Swt. 62, 34.

wôl-berende; *adj. Pestiferous, pestilential, pernicious,* (1) physical:—Ǽteówde wôlberende lyft, Nar. 15, 31. Se wôlberenda (*pestifer*) stenc ðære lyfte monige ðûsendo monna and neáta fordilgade, Bd. 1, 13; S. 482, 8. Ne sceþþeþ ðê wôlberendes âwiht, Lchdm. i. 326, 19. Wæs ðæra wyrma oroð swîðe deáðberende and ǽterne (*quorum halitus erat pestifer*) and for hiora ðæm wôlberendan oroðe monige men swulton, Nar. 14, 17: 16, 2. Hê onsent ofer hig wôlberende windas, Ps. Th. 10, 7. (2) figurative:—On heora wôlberendum setle *in cathedra pestilentiae*, Ps. Th. 1, 1: Past. 56; Swt. 435, 22. On ðæm wôlberendan setle, 435, 19. Forspenð hê hit mid ðære wôlberendan ôliccunge *mentem securitatis pestiferae blanditiis seducit*, 53; Swt. 415, 12.

wôlberend-lîc; *adj. Pestilential:*—Geweard swîðe wôlberendlîc geár on ðissum lande, Chr. 1086; Erl. 219, 29.

wôl-bryne, es; *m. Deadly violence:*—Weard micel wundor on heofonum gesewen, swelce eal se hefon birnende wæs. Ðæt tâcen weard on Rômânum swîþe gesweotolad mid ðæm miclan wôlbryne monncwealmes, ðe him raðe ðæs æfter com *Romae gravis pestilentia per universam civitatem violenter incanduit, ut merito praecedente prodigio coelum ardere visum sit, quando caput gentium tanto morborum igne flagravit*, Ors. 2, 6; Swt. 86, 24.

wolcen, wolcn (wolc), es; *n.: also* wolcne, an; *f. A cloud:*—Wolcn *nubes*, Wrt. Voc. i. 76, 46. Ealle ða gewîtaþ swâ swâ wolcn, Blickl. Homl. 59, 20. Nalas ðæt wolcn ðŷ forþ com ðe ûre Drihten ðæs wolcnes fultomes þearfe hæfde, oþþe ðæt wolcn hiene up âhôfe, ac hê ðæt wolcn him beforan nam, and hê on ðæm wolcne from heora gesihþe gewât, 121, 11–17. Regn wolcen brincgeþ, Ps. Th. 67, 10. Wolcen *the pillar of cloud*, 77, 16. Beorht wolcn (wolcen, Lind.: wolken, Rush.) *nubes lucida*, Mt. Kmbl. 17, 5. Blôdig wolcen, Blickl. Homl. 91, 32. Wan wolcen, Met. 5, 4. Windig wolcen, Exon. Th. 201, 24; Ph. 61. Se ðe him ǽlc wolcn ondrǽdt. . . . Hwæt getâcnaþ ðæt wolc (wolcn, Cott. MSS.)? . . . Se wind drîfeþ ðæt wolcn, Past. 39; Swt. 285, 18–21. 'Send mê ðînne engel on fŷrenum wolcne.' . . . Fŷren wolc âstâh of heofonum, Blickl. Homl. 245, 30. Ðonne ða wolcnan sceótaþ betweón ðære sunnan and ðê. . . . þeáh nân wolcne sî betweón ðê and hyre, Shrn. 201, 27. Wǽt wolcnes tiér, Met. 20, 81. Sealdon wolcnes stefne *vocem dederunt nubes* (the translator has read *nubis?*), Ps. Th. 76, 14. Ic cume tô ðê on sweartum wolcne (*in caligine nubis*), Ex. 19, 9: Cd. Th. 27, 15; Gen. 418. Wolcan *nubem*, Ps. Surt. 103, 3. Ðonne sweartan wolcnu him beforan gâþ, Bt. 6; Fox 14, 22. Ðâs ðe fleógaþ swâ swâ wolcnu, Homl. Th. i. 584, 28. Wolcnu scrîþaþ, Menol. Fox 486; Gn. C. 13. Nalles wolcnu ofer rûmne grund regnas bǽron, Cd. Th. 14, 2; Gen. 212. Bletsiaþ weolcnu Drihtne, Hymn. T. P. 73. Wolgceno, Rtl. 81, 24. Wolcna *nimborum*, Wrt. Voc. ii. 59, 57. Wolcna strengu, Exon. Th. 390, 4; Rä. 8, 5. For ðæra wolcna ðicnysse, Lchdm. iii. 232, 16. Wolcna scûr, Cd. Th. 238, 5; Dan. 350. Ðonne ic oferteó heofenan mid wolcnum (*nubibus*), ðonne æteówð mîn boga on ðâm wolcnum, Gen. 9, 14. On heofones wolcnum, Mt. Kmbl. 26, 64: Cd. Th. 303, 5; Sat. 608. Wind wǽðeþ be wolcnum, Elen. Kmbl. 2545; El. 1274. Wolcnum beþehte, Andr. Kmbl. 2094; An. 1048: Rood Kmbl. 105; Kr. 53. Môna waþol under wolcnum, Fins. Th. 14; Fin. 8. Se ðe him ða wolc (wolcn, Cott. MSS.) ondrêde, Past. 39; Swt. 285, 24. Hê fram ðysse eorðan ende lǽdeþ wolcen wræclicu *educens nubes ab extremo terrae*, Ps. Th. 134, 7: 77, 25: Cd. Th. 265, 11; Sat. 6. Seó lyft âbyrð ealle wolcnu (-a, *v. l.*), Lchdm. iii. 274, 9, 24: Bt. 36, 2; Fox 174, 9. ¶ in pl. (1) *the clouds, the heavens, the sky:*—Ðâ ârâs se wind and ða wolcnu sweartodon, and com ormǽte scûr of ðære lyfte (*coeli contenebrati sunt, et nubes, et ventus, et facta est pluvia grandis*, 1 Kings 18, 45), Homl. Skt. i. 18, 151. Hwâ is unlǽredra ðe ne wundrige wolcna fǽreldes, rodres swifto (cf. ðæs roderes fǽreldes and his swiftnesse, Bt. 39, 3; Fox 214, 15), Met. 28, 2: Cd. Th. 255, 15; Dan. 624. Ôð wolcna hrôf *to the skies*, 196, 28; Exod. 298. Ofer wolcna hrôf *above the clouds*, Elen. Kmbl. 178; El. 89. Wið wolcnum *usque ad nubes*, Ps. Th. 56, 12. Tô wolcnum, Beo. Th. 2242; B. 1119. Hyre stefn oncwæð of wolcnum, Exon. Th. 259, 16; Jul. 289. Hwæðer sincende sǽflôd wǽre under wolcnum, Cd. Th. 86, 29; Gen. 1438: Beo. Th. 3266; B. 1631: Met. 7, 26: Exon. Th. 199, 17; Ph. 27. Scip wîde râd wolcnum under, Cd. Th. 84, 4; Gen. 1392. Ôþ ða wolcen (wolcenu, Ps. Surt.) *usque ad nubes*, Ps. Th. 107, 4. Ôþ ða wolcnu (wolcen, Ps. Surt.), 35, 5. (2) *the clouds of night:*—Ôþ ðe nîpende niht scrîðan cwôme, wan under wolcnum, Beo. Th. 1306; B. 651: 1432; B. 714: Salm. Kmbl. 207; Sal. 103: Andr. Kmbl. 1673; An. 839: Exon. Th. 178, 34; Gû. 1254: Rood Kmbl. 109; Kr. 55. (3) *in the phrases* under wolcnum, under wolcna hrôfe *under heaven, on earth:*—Ðenden hê on ðysse worulde wunode under wolcna hrôfe, Judth. Thw. 22, 19; Jud. 67. Â þenden standeþ woruld under wolcnum, Cd. Th. 56, 22; Gen. 916: 64, 30; Gen. 1058: 117, 7; Gen. 1950: Exon. Th. 14, 28; Cri. 226. Hê weóx under wolcnum, Beo. Th. 15; B. 8. Ic Hring-Dena weóld under wolcnum, 3544; B. 1770: Met. 1, 76. Landes frætwe gewîtaþ under wolcnum, Elen. Kmbl. 2541; El. 1272. [Þa scipen foren wide mid wolcnen and mid wedere, Laym. 102. Com winden mid ðam weolcnen a drake, 25592. In the later English, however, the word seems used mostly in the sense of *sky, welkin:*—Fir weax up to þam wolcne, and se wolcne undide on fower healfe and faht þær togeanes, Chr. 1122; Erl. 249, 22. Þa wolcne gon to dunien, þa eorðe gon to biuien, Laym. 27452: 4575. Þere weolcne (wolkne, 2nd MS.) he wes swiðe neh, 2883. Bonen þurleð þe weolcne *oratio penetrat nubes*, A. R. 246, 24: Marh. 7, 3. We sitteþ under weolcne (welkne, *v. l.*) bi nihte, O. and N. 1682. On the welkne shoon the sterres, Chauc. Cl. T. 1124. Al þe wyde worlde bothe welkne (wolkne, þe welkene, welken, *v. ll.*) and þe wynde, water and erþe, Piers P. 17, 160. *O. Sax.* wolkan; *n. a cloud: O. Frs.* wolken: *O. H. Ger.* wolchan; *n. nubes.*] v. heofon-, weder-wolcen.

wolcen-faru, e; *f. The cloud-host, the moving clouds:*—Ðec forstas and snāwas, winterbiter weder and wolcenfaru (cf. wolcna genipu, Exon. Th. 192, 13; Az. 105) lofige on lyfte, Cd. Th. 239, 33; Dan. 379. Ic (*a storm*) wolcnfare wrēge, Exon. Th. 386, 33; Rä. 4, 71.

wolcen-gehnāst, es; *n. The collision of clouds;* Exon. Th. 386, 12; Rä. 4, 60.

wolcen-reád. v. weolcen-reád.

wolcen-wyrcende; *adj. Cloud-producing:*—Wolcenwyrcende *nubigenu (-a?)*, Wrt. Voc. ii. 62, 13. [*The glosser seems to have mistaken* (?) *the word, which would be more nearly rendered by* wolcen-geworht. Cf. *O. H. Ger.* wolc-poran *nubigena.*]

wolc-reád. v. weoloc-reád.

wōl-dæg, es; *m. A day of pestilence, a day of death:*—Cwōmon wōldagas; swylt eall fornom secgrōf wera, Exon. Th. 477, 18; Ruin. 26.

wōl-gewinn, es; *n. A conflict where there is a great mortality:*—Gif hié gemunan willaþ hiora ieldrena unclǣnnessa, and heora wōlgewinna, and hiora monigfealdan unsibbe *recolant majorum suorum tempora, bellis inquietissima, sceleribus exsecrabilia, dissensionibus foeda*, Ors. 2, 1; Swt. 64, 15.

wō-līc. v. wōh-līc.

wollen-teár; *adj. Having hot tears, with hot tears:*—Weorod eall ārās, eodon unblīðe, wollenteáre, wundur sceáwian, Beo. Th. 6056; B. 3032. [Cf. (?) *Icel.* ollinn; *pp. of* wella.]

wōlness, e; *f. Pest, pestilence, plague:*—Wōlnes, fefor, ādl *pestis, febris, langor*, Lchdm. i. lxxiii, 1.

wom. v. wamm.

wōm, es; *m. Sound, noise:*—Wunian ðone werigan sele, ðǣr is wōm and wōp wīde gehēred, and gristbītunge, and gnornunge mecga, Cd. Th. 285, 5; Sat. 333. [*Icel.* ómr *sound.*] v. next word.

wōma, an; *m. Sound, noise* (cf. hilde-wōma *and* hilde-swēg):—Se wōma (*the noise of battle*) cwom, Cd. Th. 190, 21; Exon. 202. Siððan tō reste gehwearf rīce þeóden, com on sefan hwurfan swefnes wōma, 222, 26; Dan. 110: Elen. Kmbl. 142; El. 71. Hrīð hreósende, wintres wōma, Exon. Th. 292, 22; Wand. 103. Hē secgan ongan swefnes wōman, Cd. Th. 249, 33; Dan. 539. Hebban herebȳman hlūdan stefnum, wuldres wōman, 183, 31; Exod. 100. Ǣr ðū gūðe fremme, wīges wōman, Andr. Kmbl. 2709; An. 1357. Wīges wōmum, Exon. Th. 277, 5; Jul. 576. [Cf. *Icel.* Ómi, *one of the names of Odin;* a personification of the wind; ōma *to resound;* ōman *sound, voice.* Grimm says: Scheint mir der grund weshalb *wóma* mit *hild, wíg, dæg, dægrēd, swefen* verbunden wird, anzuzeigen, dass das alterthum sich hierunter lauter persönliche wesen dachte, die rauschend nahten, And. u. El. xxx.] v. dæg-, dægrēd-, heofon-, hilde-wōma, *and preceding word.*

wome, Chart. Th. 483, 30, *read* wonie.

won-, wōness. v. wan-, wōhness.

wōp, es; *m.* I. *a whoop, cry.* v. here-wōp. II. mostly *a cry of grief, wailing, lamentation, weeping:*—Hlūde swēgde ðæra muneca wōp on Martines deáðe, Homl. Th. ii. 518, 16. Wōp (*fletus*) and tōþa gristbītung, Mt. Kmbl. 8, 12: 13, 42. Wōm and wōp, Cd. Th. 285, 2; Sat. 333. Nis nǣnig wōp ne nǣnig heáf gehȳred, Blickl. Homl. 85, 28: Exon. Th. 164, 32; Gū. 1020. Hreám and wōp, Blickl. Homl. 115, 15. Ðara cirm and wōp tō mē āstāh, 249, 7. Ne sorg ne wōp, 103, 36: Exon. Th. 201, 4; Ph. 51. Hlūd wōp, 62, 9; Cri. 999. Wæs wōp up āhafen, atol ǣfenleóð, Cd. Th. 190, 17; Exod. 200: Beo. Th. 257; B. 128. Wōp, hlūd heriges cyrm, Andr. Kmbl. 2311; An. 1157. Ða gesīðas, wōp and hleahtor, Salm. Kmbl. 695; Sal. 347. *Coragium*, i. *virginale funus vel* wōp, Wülck. Gl. 213, 33. Eall ðæt folc hyne weóp hundseofontig daga. Ðā ðæs wōpes dagas āgāne wǣron (*expleto planctus tempore*), Gen. 50, 4. On wōpe and on unrōtnesse hē leofaþ, Blickl. Homl. 59, 36. Mid swīðlīce heáfe and wōpe *luctu*, Ors. 4, 5; Swt. 166, 12. Wōpe cwīðan, Cd. Th. 61, 13; Gen. 996. Wōpe besingan, Exon. Th. 139, 3; Gū. 517. Wōpe bimǣnan, 459, 24; Hö. 4. Wōpe bewunden, Beo. Th. 6283; B. 3146. Wōpe gewǣged, wreccea giómor *flebilis*, Met. 2, 3. Ðara ðe wōp gehȳrdon galan Godes andsacan, sār wānigean, Beo. Th. 1575; B. 785. Wōp dreógan, Exon. Th. 140, 10; Gū. 608. Wōp þrowian, heáf under heofonum, Salm. Kmbl. 934; Sal. 466. Ðurh fæsten and ðurh wōpas (*fletus*) and ðurh gebedo, Bd. 4, 25; S. 599, 25. II a. where shedding of tears is referred to:—Ūs wōpe forcymenum, bitrum bryneteárum, Exon. Th. 10, 13; Cri. 151. Mid myclum wōpe (cf. wēpende wēregum teárum, Andr. Kmbl. 117; An. 59), Blickl. Homl. 229, 19. Ne rēce ðū nā weámōdes wīfes worda, for ðam heó wile oft mid wōpe geswigian (*be silent and burst into tears*), Prov. Kmbl. 48. Se wæs ðurh micelne wōp āblend, Homl. Th. i. 420, 31. *See* wōpes hring *under* hring. [Hæleð ðe iherde ðesne weop, Laym. 11991. Muchel wes þa wop (wepinge, 2nd MS.), 5970. Cullfren sang iss lic wiþþ wop, Orm. 7931. His moderes wop (ream. *v. l.*), and þe oðres Maries, ꝥ melten al of teares, A. R. 110, 15: Kath. 2332: R. Glouc. 34, 15. Þer is wop and grindinge of teþ, Ayenb. 265, 5. *O. Sax.* wōp: *O. H. Ger.* wuof *fletus, luctus, ploratus, planctus, gemitus.*] v. feld-, here-wōp.

wōp-dropa, an; *m. A tear:*—Hwæt is ðæt wundor ðæt geond ðās woruld styrnenga gǣð, āweccaþ wōpdropan? Salm. Kmbl. 567; Sal. 283.

wōpen. v. wēpan.

wōperian; *p.* ode *To wail, lament:*—Ðā cleopode seó ungesǣlige wōperiende him tō: 'Eálā, help mīn, wildeór mē habbaþ forneán tōslyten,' Homl. Ass. 196, 32.

wōpig; *adj. Mournful, doleful,* (1) of persons expressing grief:—Ðæt ic wōpig sceal teárum mǣnan, Exon. Th. 285, 9; Jul. 711. (2) of things which are the expression of grief:—Hē hine on ða eorþan āstrehte, mid wōpegum teárum hlūde clypigende, Homl. Skt. ii. 23 b, 601.

wōp-leóþ, es; *n. A mournful lay, a tragedy:*—Wōpleóð *tragoediam*, Hpt. Gl. 488, 57.

wōp-līc; *adj. Mournful, doleful, lamentable:*—Wōplīc *flebilis*, Ælfc. Gr. 9, 28; Zup. 55, 4. (1) of persons expressing grief:—Wōplīc (*printed* -lie) *lacrimabundus*, Hpt. Gl. 472, 66. In faran ðæt tungla wōplīcan heofones eáhþerl ðū eart geworden *intrent ut astra flebiles, coeli fenestra facta es*, Hymn. Surt. 76, 5. (2) of that which is an expression of grief:—Hē spræc mid wōplīcre stemne, Homl. Th. i. 402, 9: Homl. Ass. 196, 29: 198, 121. Mid wōplīcre ceorunge, Homl. Skt. i. 2, 355. Mid wōplīcum murcnungum *flebilibus questibus*, Hpt. Gl. 518, 25. Mid wōplīcum siccitungum *lacrimosis singultibus*, 504, 62. (3) of that which occasions grief:—Se dæg is heora sōðe ācennednys; nā wōplīc, swā swā seó ǣrre, ac blissigendlīc tō ðam ēcum līfe, Homl. Th. i. 354, 10. [*O. H. Ger.* wuof-līh *lugubris.*]

wōplīce; *adv. Mournfully, with lamentations:*—Wē healdaþ heora gemynd, nāteshwōn wōplīce, swā swā man bewēpð deádne, Homl. Ass. 77, 124.

word, es; *n.* I. *a word, a single part of speech;* in pl. *words* forming connected speech:—Būtan ðām stafum ne mæg nān word beón āwriten, Ælfc. Gr. 2; Zup. 5, 12. *Barbarismus*, ðæt is ānes wordes gewemmednyss ... *Solocismus*, ðæt is miscweden word on endebyrdnysse ðære rǣdinge ... *Barbarismus* bið on ānum worde, and *solocismus* bið sum leás word on ðam ferse, 50; Zup. 294, 4–10. Ðæs wordes andgit is swā mon cweþe þingere oþþe frēfrend, Blickl. Homl. 135, 33. Seó ceaster ealde worde is nemned Wiltaburh, Bd. 5, 11; S. 626, 26. Hī īgbūend ōðre worde Baðan nemnaþ, Chr. 973; Erl. 124, 12. Ðǣr wæs hæleþa hleahtor, word wǣron wynsume, 1228; B. 612. Wera gehwylcum wīslīcu word gerīsaþ, Exon. Th. 343, 34; Gn. Ex. 166. Ealle ða īdlan word ðe hē ūt forlēt, Blickl. Homl. 59, 19. Ealle ða word sint sōþe ðe Paulus sægþ, 187, 2. Ðæt sindon ða word, swā ūs gewritu secgaþ, Exon. Th. 241, 12; Ph. 655. Gif ðās word sind sōþ, 247, 24; Jul. 83: Beo. Th. 1282; B. 639. Nō ðæs fela Daniel gespræc sōðra worda, Cd. Th. 253, 13; Dan. 595. Engel wrāt in wāge worda gerȳnu, baswe bōcstafas, 261, 9; Dan. 723. Gif hē his wordcwida wealdan meahte, ðæt hē him onwrige worda gongum, hū ..., Exon. Th. 171, 29; Gū. 1134. Meaht ðū worda gewealdan, 163, 5; Gū. 989. Worda tō hræd, 330, 13; Vy. 50. Worda gleáw, 415, 20; Rä. 33, 14. Hē wile tō his nēhstan sprecan ða word ðe hē wēnþ ðæt him leófoste sȳn tō gehȳrenne, and ðonne þencþ hū hē hine beswīcan mæge þurh ða swētnesse ðara worda, Blickl. Homl. 55, 22. Hī þeossa worda nān ongeotan ne mehton, 15, 13: Exon. 246, 6; Jul. 57. Swā hē bæd, þenden hē wordum weóld, Beo. Th. 59; B. 30. Wordum wīsfæst, Exon. Th. 418, 4; Rä. 36, 14. Ne wile Sarran gelȳfan wordum mīnum, Cd. Th. 144, 13; Gen. 2389. Æfter ðissum wordum, Blickl. Homl. 135, 34: Andr. Kmbl. 175; An. 88. ¶ *wordum* is often used pleonastically with verbs of saying or writing. Cf. *worde* under II. 1:—God cwæð him wordum tō *Dominus ait*, Jud. 6, 14: Cd. Th. 148, 16; Gen. 2457. Ðæt wīf wordum sægde, 44, 11; Gen. 707. Wordum sprǣcon monige, 110, 33; Gen. 1847. Wordum herian, 1, 4; Gen. 2. Wordum wyrgean, 96, 13; Gen. 1594. Ðone wē wifel wordum nemnaþ, Exon. Th. 426, 14; Rä. 41, 73. Se ongan godspell wordum wrītan, Andr. Kmbl. 25; An. 13. Ic ne mæg word sprecan, Exon. Th. 399, 16; Rä. 19, 1. Hē lǣteþ word ūt faran, 315, 35; Mōd. 41: Beo. Th. 5096; B. 2551. Hē word æfter cwæþ; 'Mǣl is mē tō feran,' 636; B. 315: 688; B. 341: Cd. Th. 204, 11; Exod. 417. Hē word āhōf, Andr. Kmbl. 832; An. 416: 2993; An. 1499: Elen. Kmbl. 1445; El. 724. Ic ðās word sprece, Exon. Th. 457, 12; Hy. 4, 82: Blickl. Homl. 191, 29: 205, 23. Ða word ðæs heofonlīcan gerȳnes, 17, 7. Ēces līfes word (wordo, Lind.) *uerba uitae aeterne*, Jn. Skt. 6, 68. Wordu, Scint. 94, 8. Hié þrȳ cwǣdon þurh gemǣne word, Cd. Th. 238, 30; Dan. 362: 149, 14; Gen. 2474. I a. *a verb:*—*Verbum* is word, and word getācnaþ weorc oððe þrowunge oððe geþafunge ... *Adverbum* is wordes gefēra, Ælfc. Gr. 5; Zup. 9, 2–8. On ðisum eahta dǣlum synd ða mǣstan and ða mihtigostan *nomen et verbum*, ðæt is nama and word. Mid ðam naman wē nemnaþ ealle ðing and mid ðam worde wē sprecaþ be eallum ðingum, Zup. 11, 8–11. I b. *a written word:*—Moððe word fræt, Exon. Th. 432, 4; Rä. 48, 1. II. *a word, a group of words* forming a phrase, clause, sentence or sentences, (1) *a saying, sentence, anything said, words:*—Hē ðæs geanwyrde wes, þeáh him ðæt word ofscute his unnþances (*the words escaped him involuntarily*), Chr. 1055; Erl. 189, 6. Ðæt word belimpđ synderlíce tó Gode ánum, 'Ic eom,' Homl. Th. ii. 236, 11. Him andswarode God swá đæt ne wiste, se đæs wordes (*the answer*) bád, Andr. Kmbl. 522; An. 261. On đam worde: 'Uton wyrcan,' ... on đam worde: 'Tó úre anlícnysse,' Boutr. Scrd. 19, 13. For đam worde hé wæs geunrét *he was sad at that saying*, Mk. Skt. 10, 22. 'Ic hit eom.' Hí mid đam worde wendon underbæc ... Eft áxode se Hǽlend ... Hí eft andwyrdon mid đam ǽrran worde ... Ðá andwyrde hé mid đam ylcan worde, Homl. Th. ii. 246, 15–20: Cd. Th. 31, 35; Gen. 495: 165, 4; Gen. 2726. ¶ *worde* is often used pleonastically with verbs of saying, cf. *wordum* under I:—Ðá hé worde cwæđ, đæt ..., Cd. Th. 3, 6; Gen. 31. Hé worde cwæđ: 'Témaþ and wexaþ,' 12, 34; Gen. 195: Andr. Kmbl. 1432; An. 716. Swá đú worde becwist, 386; An. 193: Exon. Th. 123, 32; Gú. 331. Ðá worde frægn wuldres Aldor Cain hwǽr Abel wǽre, Cd. Th. 61, 24; Gen. 1002. Hé đæt word gecwæđ, đæt hit aa hæfde ofer Godes ést đe hit hæfde bútan đære cyrcan hláforde, Chart. Th. 141, 1. Hé đæt word ácwæđ, đæt đæt micle morđ menn ne þorfton þolian, Cd. Th. 40, 14; Gen. 639. Hé đæt word ácwæđ: 'Ic đé mæg secgan ...,' Exon. Th. 20, 12; Cri. 316: Andr. Kmbl. 2722; An. 1363 (and often). Ðis is sceortlíce gesǽd; uton secgan word gyt, Homl. Th. ii. 330, 23. Wǽron đás word gewídmǽrsode *these sayings were noised abroad*, Lk. Skt. 1, 65. Ðá áhsode hé hine manegum wordum *interrogabat illum multis sermonibus*, 23, 9. On đám twám formum wordum *in the two first sentences* (of the Lord's prayer), Homl. Th. i. 262, 22. Hé rihte ǽ getácnode on týn wordum [*or* (6)], Andr. Kmbl. 3023; An. 1514. (2) *a saying, maxim*:—Hí cweþaþ đæt tó worde, đæt se biđ on geþance wærast and wísast, se đe óđerne can rađost ásmeágan; cweþaþ eác tó worde đa đe syndan stunte, đæt mycel forhæfednes lytel behealde, ac đæt mete wǽre mannum gescapen, tó đam ánum, đæt men his scoldan brúcan, Wulfst. 55, 20–25. (3) *a tale, story*:—Ðá hæfdon monige unwíse menn him tó worde and tó leásungspelle, đæt sió hǽte ... wǽre for Fétontis forscapunge *quidam ... suas inanes ratiunculas conquirentes, ridiculam Phaetontis fabulam texuerunt*, Ors. 1, 7; Swt. 40, 8. (4) *a report, tidings*:—Ðam cynge com word (*word came to the king*), đæt unnfriđscipa lǽgen and hergodon, Chr. 1046; Erl. 173, 5. Sóna swá đæt word becom tó Neróne, Blickl. Homl. 173, 35. Ðá sprang đæt word, đæt hé on đam holte dwelode, ođ đæt hine wulfas tótǽron, Homl. Th. i. 384, 9. (5) *fame, name*, (*good*) *word*, (*good*) *report*:—Gód word and gód hlísa ǽlces monnes biþ betera đonne ǽnig wela, Bt. 13; Fox 38, 23. Ðá ásprang his word wíde geond land, hú se mǽra man manna fét ádwóh, Homl. Skt. i. 7, 388. Úre word sprang wíde geond đás eorđan, 13, 151: Shrn. 17, 9. Ǽđelinge (*Christ*) weóx word and wísdóm (cf. Lk. 2, 52), Andr. Kmbl. 1137; An. 569: 3352; An. 1680. Hé þóhte đæt hé him myceles wordes wircean sceolde (wolde geearnian him hereword, *v.l.*), Chr. 1009; Erl. 142, 2. Uton ús selfum betst word and longsumast æt úrum ende gewyrcan *Spartanos admonet, de gloria plurimum, de vita nihil sperandum*, Ors. 2, 5; Swt. 82, 2. Wídgongel wíf word gespringeþ (*gets a* (*bad*) *name*), hæleđ hý hospe mǽnaþ, Exon. Th. 337, 15; Gn. Ex. 65. (6) *a command, an order, ordinance*:—Word hleóđrode: 'Ne wép đone wræcsíđ,' Andr. Kmbl. 2860; An. 1432: Cd. Th. 173, 14; Gen. 2861. Eoppa be Wilferþes worde bróhte Wihtwarum fulwiht, Chr. 661; Erl. 34, 17. Ðú lífes word lǽstan noldes, ac mín bibod brǽce be đínes bonan worde, Exon. Th. 85, 21; Cri. 1394. Ðæt hié đæt onwendon, đæt hé mid his worde bebeád, Cd. Th. 26, 11; Gen. 405. Ðá sende se cyng Leófsig, and hé đæs cynges worde griđ gesætte, Chr. 1002; Erl. 137, 25: L. Ath. v. 10; Th. i. 238, 36: Exon. Th. 99, 19; Cri. 1627. Ic ne mæg áwendan Godes word ... God cwæđ: 'Dó đæt ic đé bebeóde,' Num. 22, 18–20. Hý brǽcon cyninges word, beorht bóca bibod, Exon. Th. 99, 26; Cri. 1630: Cd. Th. 38, 1; Gen. 600: 49, 27; Gen. 798. Word gehyrwan, Elen. Kmbl. 442; El. 221. Ofer Drihtnes word, Cd. Th. 37, 21; Gen. 593: Rood Kmbl. 70; Kr. 35. Ðæt đú Dryhtnes word healde, and đæs cininges bebod begange, Elen. Kmbl. 2334; El. 1168. Þurh his word *at his command*, Cd. Th. 10, 17; Gen. 158: 7, 24; Gen. 111: 82, 15; Gen. 1362. Ǽr áwǽged sié worda ǽnig, Andr. Kmbl. 2877; An. 1441. Hé com be Honorius wordum đes pápan, Chr. 634; Erl. 25, 28. Hé wrát đa týn word, đe Drihten him bebeád, Ex. 34, 28: Deut. 10, 4. (7) *a message, an announcement*:—Hé word ábeád: 'Eów hét secgan sigedrihten mín, đæt hé eówer æþelu can, Beo. Th. 786; B. 390. (8) *word, solemn statement*:—Biscopes word and cyninges sié unlǽgne búton áđe, L. Wih. 16; Th. i. 40, 12. Ðú đæt gehéte þurh đín hálig word, Andr. Kmbl. 2836, An. 1420. (9) *promise, oath.* v. word-fæst, -loga:—Man freóndscipe gefæstnode mid worde and mid wædde, Chr. 1014; Erl. 150, 14. Geþence hé word and wedd đe hé Gode betǽhte, L. Eth. v. 5; Th. i. 306, 5: vi. 3; Th. i. 314, 24. Hwǽr syndon đíne word, on đám đú ús gestrangodest, and đú cwǽde: 'Gif gé mé gehýraþ, ne án loc of eówrum heáfde forwyrđ,' Blickl. Homl. 243, 31. (10) *an* (*expressed*) *intention* or *opinion*:—Ðara ǽlces đe đæs wordes wǽre đæt from Rómebyrg þóhte *of every one that talked of leaving Rome*, Ors. 4, 9; Swt. 190, 25. Hié wǽron đæs wordes, đæt him leófre wæs se cristendóm tó begánne đonne his scíra tó habbanne *omnes officium quam fidem deserere maluerunt*, 6, 31; Swt. 286, 6. Ðá wæs ǽlc đæs wordes, đæt him leófre wǽre đæt hé land foreode, đonne hé đæne hád underfénge, Chart. Th. 167, 32. Wæs Eþelwald đæs wordes, đæt hé nó đes rihtes wiđsacan nolde *Ethelwald declared his intention of not opposing the right*, 140, 11. **III.** *speech, language, words*:—Word spearcum fleáh, Cd. Th. 274, 31; Sat. 162. Scóp him Heort naman se đe his wordes geweald hæfde (*who had power to name things as he pleased*), Beo. Th. 158; B. 79. Wordes ord *the first word*, 5576; B. 2791. Rǽdsnotteran, wordes wísran, Andr. Kmbl. 947; An. 474. Wordes gleáwne, 3295; An. 1650. Weras wordes cræftige, Elen. Kmbl. 628; El. 314: 837; El. 419. Of eallum đæm worde đe gǽþ of Godes múþe, Blickl. Homl. 27, 9. Mid đon worde đæs godcundan gewrites hé hine oferswíþde, 33, 20. On worde mid nǽnigre mihte gewelgode, Blickl. Homl. 179, 15. Wís on đínum gewitte and on đínum worde snottor, Exon. Th. 463, 31; Hö. 78. Men đú sealdest word and gewitt, Hy. 9, 56. **III a.** *language, style*:—Ǽrest Eroico metro, and æfter fæce gerǽde worde (*plano sermone*) ic áwrát, Bd. 5, 24; S. 648, 27. **III b.** where speech is contrasted with act or thought:—Lufige man Godes riht wordes and dǽde, L. Eth. v. 26; Th. i. 310, 20: L.C.E. 19; Th. i. 372, 4. Wordes ođđe weorces, L.E.G. 2; Th. i. 168, 2: L. Eth. vi. 30; Th. i. 322, 23. Móde and dǽdum, worde and gewitte, Cd. Th. 117, 23; Gen. 1958. Hé men of deáđe worde áwehte, Andr. Kmbl. 1167; An. 584: Elen. Kmbl. 1888; El. 946. Mihtig mid worde eal tó dónne, Blickl. Homl. 235, 36. Scyndan mid worde oþþe weorce, L. Eth. vii. 27; Th. i. 334, 36. Þurh geþóht and þurh word and þurh weorc, Blickl. Homl. 35, 14. **IV.** *word* (in *word* of God):—Se đe sǽwđ, word hé sǽwđ ... Hí đæt word gehýraþ, Mk. Skt. 4, 14–20. Wé wǽron gesamnode đǽr wé gehérdan Godes word, Blickl. Homl. 141, 27. Gif heó ne biđ mid Godes worde féded, 57, 11. **IV a.** translating *verbum* in Jn. 1, 1. v. word-cennend. [*Goth.* waurd: *O. Sax. O. Frs.* word: *O. H. Ger.* wort: *Icel.* orð.] v. beót-, cyne-, galdor-, gilp-, gleó-, gnorn-, gram-, heoru-, here-, hosp-, husc-, lást-, leóþ-, lyge-, lygen-, mæđel-, mán-, óleht-, orgel-, sceand-, sóþ-, sorh-, teón-, torn-, þanc-, þrýþ-, wær-, wealh-, wit-, wuldor-word.

-word; *adj. in* róf-word (?), Exon. Th. 353, 21; Reim. 16. [*Icel.* -orðr.] Cf. -wyrde.

word-beót, es; *n. A promise*:—Ðá com féran Freá tó Sarran swá hé self gecwæđ, hæfde wordbeót leófum gelǽsted, Cd. Th. 167, 6; Gen. 2761. Wáciaþ wordbeót, Exon. Th. 469, 22; Hy. 11, 6. v. word-gebeót, *and next word.*

word-beótung, e; *f. Promising, a promise*:—Ðec biddan hét se đisne beám ágróf, đæt đú gemunde on gewitlocan wordbeótunga, Exon. Th. 473, 14; Bo. 14. v. preceding word.

word-cennend, es; *m. The begetter of the Word* (Jn. 1, 1):—Ó milda Wordcennend *pie Verbigena*, Germ. 389, 2.

word-cræft, es; *m. The art of speaking* or *writing*:—Wordcræftes wís *a good speaker*, Elen. Kmbl. 1180; El. 592. Ic wordcræft wæf *I composed poetry*, 2473; El. 1238.

word-cwide, es; *m.* **I.** *a saying, words*:—Fyl nú frumsprǽce, wlitiga đínne wordcwyde (*what thou hast said*; đíne wordcwidas, Exon. Th. 188, 9; Az. 43), Cd. Th. 236, 26; Dan. 327. Ne lengde leóda aldor wítegena wordcwyde, 256, 27; Dan. 647. Ðý đíne wordcwidas weorđan gefelde (*ut justificeris in sermonibus tuis*), đæt đú ne wilnast weora ǽniges deáđ, ac đú synfulle simle lǽrdes đæt ..., Ps. C. 53. Ðé đa wordcwydas Drihten on sefan sende ... Ðú eart on móde fród, wís wordcwida, Beo. Th. 3686–3694; B. 1841–1845. Gif hé his wordcwida wealdan meahte *if he could talk*, Exon. Th. 171, 25; Gú. 1132. Wís on wordcwidum, 294, 11; Crä. 31: Andr. Kmbl. 1104; An. 552. Wuldorcyninges word hleóđrode. . . . Ǽfter wordcwidum wuldorcyninges *after the words*, 2892; An. 1449: Beo. Th. 5499; B. 2753. Uncre wordcwidas *what we said to one another*, Exon. Th. 472, 16; Rä. 61, 17. Cleopaþ se alda, wriceþ wordcwedas, Cd. Th. 267, 8; Sat. 35. **II.** *speech, language*:—On đam (*Daniel*) Drihtenweard wisse sídne geþanc and wísne wordcwide, Cd. Th. 249, 28; Dan. 537. Sum mæg searolíce wordcwide wrítan *one is a clear writer*, Exon. Th. 42, 15; Cri. 673. [*O. Sax.* word-quidi *a saying, a speech.*]

word-fæst; *adj. Adhering to what one says, keeping one's word*:—Se hláford sceal beón egesfull đám dysegum, đæt hé heora dysig álecge; and hé sceal beón wordfæst and witan hwæt hé clypige (he scal beon weordfeste and wise lare lusten, 111, 32), O. E. Homl. i. 301, 13. Cf. word-loga.

word-full; *adj. Wordy, verbose, talkative*:—Mann wordfull (*verbosus*) ásyndraþ ealdras, Scint. 134, 12. Wordful *verbosa* (*garrulorum loquacitas*), Hpt. Gl. 528, 49. Wordfulle *uerbosi*, Scint. 78, 1.

word-gebeót, es; *n. A promise*:—Hé his wordgebeót gemunde *memor fuit testamenti sui*, Ps. Th. 105, 34. v. word-beót.

word-gecwide, es; *n. An expressed agreement, a formal contract*:—Eal ic him gelǽste đæt ic him scolde swá forđ swá uncre wordgecwydu fyrmest wǽron, L. O. 11; Th. i. 182, 11. Gif hit heó gehaldeþ mid đare clǽnnisse đe uncer wordgecwædu seondan, Chart. Th. 481, 8.

word-gemearc, es; *n. A limit fixed in words, a term*:—Sceal sóđ forđ gân wyrd æfter đissum wordgemearcum (*according to these terms*), Cd. Th. 142, 2; Gen. 2355. [Cf. Wrîtan wordgimerkiun hwat sie that barn hêtan skoldin, Hêl. 233.]

word-gerýne, es; *n. A mystery expressed in words, a deep saying*:—Him tâcna fela tîres brytta onwrâh wordgerýnum, Exon. Th. 29, 16; Cri. 463. Sum biþ listhendig tô âwrîtanne wordgerýnu, 299, 3; Crä. 96. Ic đæt ongiten hæbbe þurg wîtgena wordgerýno on Godes bôcum, Elen. Kmbl. 578; El. 289: 646; El. 323.

word-gid[d], es; *n. A lay*:—Cyning mǽnan, wordgyd wrecan and worn sprecan, Beo. Th. 6325; B. 3173.

word-gleáw; *adj. Prudent in speech*:—Cwæđ se đe wæs cyninges rǽswa, wîs and wordgleáw, Cd. Th. 242, 12; Dan. 418.

word-hleóþor, es; *m. The sound of speaking, voice*:—Wordhleóđor âstâg hâliges lâre *the voice of the holy one's teaching rose up*, Andr. Kmbl. 1416; An. 708. Wearđ gehýred heofoncyninges stefn, wordhleóđres swêg mǽres þeódnes, 186; An. 93.

word-hord, es; *n. A word-hoard, store of words*:—Him Andreas þurh andsware wordhord onleác, Andr. Kmbl. 632; An. 316. Weges weard wordhord onleác, beald reordade, 1202; An. 601: Beo. Th. 524; B. 259: Met. 6, 1: Exon. Th. 318, 20; Víd. 1. Mê frôd wita sægde sundorwundra fela, wordhord onwreáh, 313, 20; Môd. 3.

wordian; *p.* ode *To speak*:—Wurdiaþ (*but changed to* wurdliaþ) *rhetoricamur, loquimur*, Hpt. Gl. 527, 58. Wordiende *concionandi, loquentes*, 461, 36. [Þe king wordede þus, Laym. 18052. Þei wordeden wyseli a gret while togideres, Piers P. 4, 46. *Icel.* orða. Cf. *Goth.* waurdjan.]

wordig; *adj. Wordy, verbose*:—Wordig gehlýd *verbosa garrulitas*, Hpt. Gl. 439, 58. [*Icel.* orðigr.]

word-lâc, es; *n. A speech*; loquela:—Nǽron wordlâcu ne sprǽcu đara đe ne wǽron gehêrde stefna heora *non sunt loquelae neque sermones quorum non audiantur uoces eorum*, Ps. Lamb. 18, 4.

word-laþu, e; *f. Speech, discourse*:—Sumum hê wordlaþe wîse sendeþ on his môdes gemynd, Exon. Th. 41, 31; Cri. 664. Mîn hyge blissaþ þurh đîne wordlæđe, Andr. Kmbl. 1270; An. 635.

word-latu, e; *f. Delay in speaking*:—'Đû scealt hræđe cýđan, gif đû his ondgitan ǽnige hæbbe.' Næs đâ wordlatu (*there was no delay in the answer*), Andr. Kmbl. 3042; An. 1524. (Cf. bûton late *sine mora*, R. Ben. 55, 12, *omitted under* latu.)

word-leán, es; *n. A reward for words* (*a song*):—Oft ic wôđboran wordleána sum âgyfe æfter giedde, Exon. Th. 489, 18; Rä. 78, 9.

wordlian, wurdlian; *p.* ode *To talk, discourse*:—Wurdliaþ (*changed from* wurdiaþ) *rhetoricamur, loquimur*, . . . snytrian ł wurđlian *philosophari*, Hpt. Gl. 527, 58–63. Epactas đe wîse preóstas oft ymbe gerâdlîce wurdliaþ, Anglia viii. 300, 45. Hyt gerîst đæt wê ymbe đa epactas wurdlion, 305, 19: 308, 16. Se sceop in gebringþ ôđre hâdas, đe wiđ hine wurdlion swylce hig him andswarion, 330, 43. Uton nû on Englisc ymbe đys be dǽle wurdlian, 303, 14. [Gewurdlud *vel* gesprecen, 320, 16.] Wordlian *sermocinari*, Hpt. Gl. 461, 38. [*O. H. Ger.* wortalôn; wortalônti *verbosus*; wortalâri *verbosus*.] v. wordlung; wordrian.

word-loc, es; *n. A conclusion expressed in words*:—Wordlocum *dialectica* (the passage is: Ut tomus dialectica dogmata rerum disceret, Ald. 170), Wrt. Voc. ii. 93, 23: 27, 16.

word-loca, an; *m. The storehouse of words*:—Ongan hê reordigan, wordlocan onspeónn, Andr. Kmbl. 940; An. 470.

word-lof, es; *n. Praise in words, praise*:—Cyning mec weorþaþ, ne wyrneþ wordlofes, wîsan mǽneþ mîne for mengo, Exon. Th. 401, 13; Rä. 21, 11. [*Icel.* orð-lof *praise*.]

word-loga, an; *m. One who is false to his word*:—Đæt gê ne beón wedlogan ne wordlogan, Wulfst. 40, 10. v. word, II. 9.

wordlung, e; *f.* I. in a good sense, *discourse, conversation*:—His wordlunc *sermocinatio ejus* (*cum simplicibus*, Prov. 3, 32), Kent. Gl. 61. II. in a bad sense, *idle talk, babbling, chattering*:—Đæt sidefulle wîf wordlunge ne lufaþ (cf. idele weord ne luuađ, 111, 21), O. E. Homl. i. 301, 2. Âsolcennys âcenđ îdelnysse, gemâgnysse and wordlunge, Homl. Th. ii. 220, 26. [Cf. *O. H. Ger.* wortal *verbosus*.] v. wordlian.

word-mittung, e; *f. Collation*:—Wordmittung *vel* wordsomnung *collatio*, Wrt. Voc. i. 54, 51.

wordrian; *p.* ode *To speak, discourse*:—Wordriendra, bænnendra, mađeliendra *concionatorum, locutorum, rhetorum*, Hpt. Gl. 460, 70. Cf. wordlian, wordian.

word-riht, es; *n.* I. *a law expressed in the form of a command* (v. word, II. 6), *an ordinance*; or *a law expressed in spoken words, a spoken law*:—Môyses dômas, wrælîco wordriht, Cd. Th. 177, 31; Exod. 3. II. *a statement of what is right*; or (?) *a duty which one has given his word to perform* (v. word, II. 9):—Wîglâf mađelode, wordrihta fela sægde gesîđum (*told them much of what they ought to do*; or (?) *told them much of what they had promised to do.* Cf. wê gehêton, 5261; B. 2634), Beo. Th. 5256; B. 2631.

word-samnere, es; *m. A collector of words*:—Wordsomnere *cocologus* (= καταλογεύς?), Wrt. Voc. ii. 135, 42.

word-samnung. v. word-mittung.

word-sâwere, es; *m. A word-sower*:—Hêton menn wordsâwere đone æđelan lâreów *praedicator egregius seminiverbius est vocatus*, Past. 15; Swt. 97, 4.

word-sige, es; *m. Success in speaking*:—Sigegyrd ic mê wege, wordsige and worcsige, Lchdm. i. 388, 15.

word-snotor; *adj. Expert in speech, eloquent, learned*:—Ôslâc, gamolfeax hæleđ, wîs and wordsnotor, Chr. 975; Erl. 126, 21. Lýfing se wordsnotera biscop, 1047; Erl. 171, 28. Wordsnoteran (*Homerum*), Hpt. Gl. 463, 53. Wordsnotere *oratores, rhetores, grammatici*, 481, 72. Wordsnoterum *sapientium*, 503, 67. Ne weorþeþ on worulde ǽnig wordsnotera ne on wordum getingra, đonne hê (*Antichrist*) wyrđeþ, Wulfst. 54, 21.

word-snotorung, e; *f. A sophism*:—Wordsnoterung *sophisma*, Hpt. Gl. 459, 61.

word-wîs; *adj. Wise in speech, learned*:—Đæs wordwîsan *sophiste*, Wrt. Voc. ii. 78, 39. [*O. Sax.* word-wîs: *Icel.* orð-víss.]

word-wynsum; *adj. Pleasant in speech, affable*; affabilis, Wrt. Voc. i. 61, 37.

wôr-hana, an; *m. A pheasant*:—Wôrhona, uuôrhana, -hona *fasianus*, Txts. 61, 830. Wôrhana, Wrt. Voc. ii. 34, 71: *fusianus*, i. 280, 29: *fursianus* (*fursianus* is glossed by môrhana, Hpt. Zeit. 33, 240, 27), 62, 24.

wôr-hen[n], e; *f.* The word glosses *cracinus*, Wrt. Voc. ii. 22, 75: 136, 59.

wôrian; *p.* ode *To wander about*:—Ic wôrige *uagor*, Ælfc. Gr. 25; Zup. 145, 13. (1) literal, *to wander about, ramble, be a vagabond*:—Ic wôrige and beó âflýmed geond ealle eorđan *ero vagus et profugus in terra*, Gen. 4, 14. Hî lufiaþ îdele blisse, wôriaþ and wundriaþ, and ealne dæg fleardiaþ, L. I. P. 14; Th. ii. 322, 24. Is đæs (*the whale's*) hîw gelîc hreófum stâne, swylce wôrie bi wædes ôfre, Exon. Th. 360, 21; Wal. 9. Seó rîpung đæs geatweardes gestæþþignesse sý swr'; đæt hine ne wôrian ne scrîđan ne lyste (*eum non sinat uagari*), R. Ben. 126, 17. Đû færsđ wôrigende (*vagus*), Gen. 4, 12: Boutr. Scrd. 20, 43: 19, 2. Ne fêrde heó wôrigende geond land, ac wæs wunigende binnan Godes temple, Homl. Th. i. 148, 3: ii. 160, 21. Wôrigende geond wudas and feldas, 188, 14. Eówre bearn beóđ wôrigende on đisum wêstene *filii vestri erunt vagi in deserto*, Num. 14, 33: Homl. Th. ii. 30, 27. Ǽfre unstaþolfæste and wôriende, R. Ben. 9, 23. (1 a) of the movements of the planets:—Hî (*the planets*) synd wôrigende gecwedene, for đan đe ǽlc gǽđ on his âgenum ryne, Boutr. Scrd. 18, 29. (2) figurative in various senses:—Wôraþ *fluctuat, estuat*, i. *vacillat, dubitat, anxiat*, Wrt. Voc. ii. 149, 60. Wôriaþ đa wînsalo *the halls totter* (*are ruinous*), Exon. Th. 291, 6; Wand. 78. Gangas rihte dôþ, đæt nâ healtigende wôrige (*erret*), Scint. 186, 4. Bûtan sôþre lufe, nâ gân (*ambulare*) magan menn ac wôrian (*errare*), 3, 8. Wer unsnoter and wôrigende (*errans*) þencþ stunte, 138, 18. Wôriende *vagi* (*sunt gressus ejus*, Prov. 5, 6) i. *vagabunda* (*rumorum praeconia*, Ald. 64), Hpt. Gl. 512, 51. His eágan ne fêrdon wôrigende geond mistlîce lustas, Homl. Th. i. 168, 13. Wôrigende sefan (*vagos sensus*) hê þreáge, Hymn. Surt. 114, 15.

wôriend, es; *m. A vagabond*; vagabundus, Hpt. Gl. 484, 64.

world. v. weorold.

worms, worsm, wurms, wursm, es; *n. Corrupt matter*:—Worms *pus*, Wrt. Voc. ii. 68, 52. Uuorsm, Txts. 86, 777. Wurms *virus*, Hpt. Gl. 520, 41. Đæt worms (worsm, Cott. MSS.) đara wunda, Past. 36; Swt. 259, 15. Đæt worsm *putredo*, 38; Swt. 273, 22. Biđ seó micge lyswen swilce worms, Lchdm. ii. 198, 27. Se swile and đæt worms, 208, 11. Wiđ đa gerynnincge đæs worsmes (wormses, *v. l.*), i. 292, 8. On đa âdle đe mon wormse spîweþ, ii. 200, 21: 208, 5. Hreófeligum wormse *elephantino tabo*, Hpt. Gl. 490, 38. Âflewđ đæt sâr of đære wunde mid đý wormse *mala livor vulneris abstergit*, Past. 36; Swt. 259, 2. Heó đæt worsm (worms, *v. l.*) ût âtýhþ, Lchdm. i. 100, 13. Đæt worms, ii. 72, 14. Đæt wursm, 202, 25. Eall đæt folc wæs on blǽdran and đa wǽron swîđe hreówlîce berstende and đa worms ût siónde *vesicas effervescentes, ulceraque manantia*, Ors. 1, 7; Swt. 38, 7. [Mine wunden gedeređ neowe wrusum (wursum, *v. l.*), A. R. 274, 3. Wrusum *sanies*, 322, 11. Worsum, C. M. 11835. Wirrsenn, Orm. 4782.] v. wyrms.

worms-gemang (?), es; *n. A mixture in which there is corrupt matter*:—Wiđ đæt man blôd and worsmgemang (worsm gemang?) hrǽce, Lchdm. i. 250, 7. Cf. blôd-gemang.

worn, weorn, es; *m. A swarm, band, flock, crowd, multitude, many, a great number, a great quantity*, (1) of animate objects:—Seó wilgedryht wildne weorþiaþ, worn æfter ôþrum (*flock* (*of birds*) *following flock*) *turba prosequitur*, Exon. Th. 222, 4; Ph. 343. Folc onette, weras wîf somod, wornum and heápum, đreátum and þrymmum, þrungon and urnon, Judth. Thw. 23, 39; Jud. 164. Mægen wêrge monna cynnes wornum hweorfaþ on wîdne lêg, Exon. Th. 59, 25; Cri. 958. (1 a) with gen. pl.:—Wæs đêr worn (*grex*) swîna michil, Mk. Skt. Lind. Rush. 5, 11, 13. Đǽr witena biþ worn ætsomne, 295, 35; Crä. 43: Salm. Kmbl. 802; Sal. 400. Weard Seme suna and dohtra worn âfêded, Cd. Th. 99, 5; Gen. 1641. Hê worn gestrýnde suna and dohtra, 74, 11; Gen. 1220. Oft se snâw gecostaþ wildeóra worn, Salm. Kmbl. 611; Sal. 305. Fugla and deóra wornas, Exon. Th. 356, 3; Pa. 6. (1 b) with gen. sing. of a collective noun:—Lád æfter lâdum, leódmægnes worn, þûsendmǽlum, Cd. Th. 190, 7; Exod. 195. (2) of inanimate objects, abstract or concrete. (a) alone, *much, many things*:—Hê worn gemunde, Beo. Th. 4235; B. 2114. Hê worn eall gespræc, 6180; B. 3094. Se gomola sægde eaforan worn, Exon. Th. 304, 7; Fä. 66. Ongan worn sprecan, 319, 9; Víd. 9. (b) with adj.:—Ðû worn fela sprǽce *you have said many, many things*, Beo. Th. 1064; B. 530. (c) with gen. pl.:—Árleásta fela, misdǽda worn, Met. 9, 7. (Wintra) worn, twâ hund oððe mâ, Elen. Kmbl. 1263; El. 633. Ymb wintra worn, Cd. Th. 79, 32; Gen. 1320: 236, 22; Dan. 325: Beo. Th. 533; B. 264. Missera worn, Cd. Th. 71, 10; Gen. 1168. Ymb worn daga, 86, 30; Gen. 1438: 142, 10; Gen. 2359: Menol. Fox 336; Men. 169. Ic spræc worda worn, Andr. Kmbl. 1807; An. 906. Se ðe ealdgesegena worn gemunde, Beo. Th. 1744; B. 873. Hê wundra worn cýðde, Andr. Kmbl. 1623; An. 813. Worn sârcwida, Exon. Th. 11, 11; Cri. 169: 291, 32; Wand. 91: 315, 19; Môd. 33. Weorn earfoðsíða, Andr. Kmbl. 1354; An. 677. Fæstena worn, Cd. Th. 181, 5; Exod. 56. Se ðe worna fela gûða gedígde *he that from numbers and numbers of battles escaped*, Beo. Th. 5078; B. 2543. Hê weorna feala wîta geþolode, Andr. Kmbl. 2978; An. 1492. (d) with adj. and gen. pl.:—Unc sceal worn fela mâþma gemǽnra *we two shall have many, many treasures in common*, Beo. Th. 3571; B. 1783. (e) with gen. sing.:—Gewât dægrîmes worn *a great number of days passed*, Cd. Th. 60, 1; Gen. 975. Hê wunode dægrîmes worn, 156, 31; Gen. 2597: 80, 20; Gen. 1331: Met. 26, 33. Hê ðæs wîtes worn gefêlde *he felt the multitudinous pain*, Cd. Th. 269, 23; Sat. 77. Hê worna fela sorge gefremede, yrmðe, Beo. Th. 4011; B. 2003. v. wearn.

worn-gehât (? word-gehât; cf. word-beót, -gebeót), es; *n. A promise of a numerous progeny*:—Ðê beóþ worngehât (cf. patrem multarum gentium constitui te, Gen. 17, 5) mîn gelǽsted, Cd. Th. 144, 24; Gen. 2394.

-worpenness. v. â-, on-, tô-worpenness.

worpian; *p.* ode. I. *to throw* with something at an object. v. weorpan, I. 2 a:—Ðonne hié forwandigaþ ðæt hié mid ðǽm kycglum hiera worda ongeán hiera ierre worpigen (worpien, Cott. MSS.) *cum contra irascentem dissimulat verborum jacula reddere*, Past. 40; Swt. 297, 2. II. *to throw and strike* with something. v. weorpan, V:—Worpaþ hine deófol of blæcere liðran írenum aplum, Salm. Kmbl. 50; Sal. 25. Stephanus wæs stanum worpod, Elen. Kmbl. 982; El. 492: 1646; El. 825. [*O. H. Ger.* worfôn *projicere.*]

worsm. v. worms.

worþ, weorþ, wurþ, wierþ, wyrþ, e; *f.*: es; *m.*: wyrþe, wirþe (v. wyrþe-land, *and first extract under* I), es; *m.* I. *a close* (?), *an enclosed place* (?):—Ût on rigewyrðe (*the rye-close?*) westeweardne, Cod. Dip. Kmbl. iii. 437, 35. Uppan rigeweorðe on ða ealdan díc; of ðære díc ût on rigewurðe heal, v. 377, 21. On lindwyrðe, iii. 375, 6. II. *an enclosed homestead, a habitation with surrounding land*:—Be hagan on weorðe hege; forð be ðan hege on weorðapeldre, Cod. Dip. Kmbl. v. 381, 30. Tô ealdan wyrðe . . . wið westan ealdan wyrðe, 195, 3–5. Ondlang hîweges tô Ecguuines wyrðe, iii. 437, 32. Tô Cumbran weorðe; of Cumbran weorðe tô ðære mǽran æc, 78, 35. ¶ perhaps in the last two passages *weorþ* may be regarded as the second part of a compound name: such expressions as 'in loco ubi soliculae illius regionis Ægeleswurð nomen imposuerunt' are not uncommon in the Charters, and such names seem to have remained. In the index of places given in Cod. Dip. Kmbl. vi. 251 sqq. about 70 combinations with *weorþ* occur, and for many of these modern representatives terminating in *-worth* are found. Already places whose names contain the form (cf. those with *tûn*), when they are mentioned in the Charters, may have extended beyond their original limits and have become properties, whose area was considerable (e.g. Hê gean ðæra hundtwýntiga hîda æt Wyrðæ, Cod. Dip. Kmbl. iii. 127, 15. Brinkewurða terra est .v. hidarum, iv. 167, 1. Æt Æscmǽres-weorðæ (-wyrðe, l. 14), .x. hîda, v. 218, 22), whose boundaries consequently had to be defined (e.g. Ðis syndon ða landgemǽro tô wyrðe, vi. 8, 25. Tô Ceorles-wyrðe, iii. 458, 3. Tô Ægeles-uurðe, 428, 18. Tô Æscmêres-wierðe, v. 173, 36. Tô Peádanwyrðe, 383, 8), and upon which a number of persons resided (e.g. .xxx. mansas illic ubi Anglica appellatione dicitur æt Wurðe (Weorðe, 329, 32), v. 395, 13. Quarta terra .iii. manentium, et uocatur Gislheresuuyrth, i. 44, 11. Monasterium quod situm est in loco qui dicitur æt Baedricesworth, ii. 258, 25: iii. 272, 10: 305, 11. In Blacewyrðe .v. mansas). Various Latin words are used in speaking of such places; Wealawyrð is a *uillula*, iii. 347, 11: v. 346, 33: Æbbewyrð is a *uiculus*, iv. 164, 8–10: Æscmeresweorð is a *uilla*, v. 216, 10: Gislheresuuyrth is a *terra*, i. 44, 11, so also Brinkeuurða, iv. 167, 1, and Deceuurthe, ii. 367, 22–23: Ceolwurð is spoken of as *aliquantulum terrae*, ii. 135, 16, 22: and Oswald grants *aliquam telluris partem* æt Bynnyncgwyrðe, iii. 177, 23. Corresponding to these last terms are the English forms with *land*: Ic gean ðara twêgra landa Cæorlesweorþæ and Cochanfelde, iii. 274, 4. Ic gean ðara twêgra landa æt Cohhanfeldæa and æt Cæorlesweorþe, 272, 8. Ðæt land æt Ægeleswyrðe, 125, 10. Some passages are added which may further illustrate the different forms and the variation in gender:—In loco quae dicitur Meranworð, Txts. 437, 10. Ab occidente Hodoworða, Cod. Dip. Kmbl. ii. 49, 18. Ôslanwyrð and eall ðæt ðǽrtô gebyreþ, v. 267, 36. Andlang Æðeleswyrðe, 195, 3. Tô Lulleswyrðe hyrnan, iii. 343, 31. Tô Uffawyrða gemǽre, 428, 22. Tô ðan norðran Denceswurðe . . . ða þreó hîda on ðan norðran Denceswurðe, v. 310, 34–36. Deneceswyrðe, 400, 12. On Cwicelmeswyrðe eástwearde, iii. 344, 7: v. 121, 6. Ôð Bulonweorðe; of Bulanweorðe, iii. 343, 37. On Hananwurðe, 403, 11. On tûnlesweorþ eastweardne, 425, 22, 28. On Wulfrêdeswyrð; of Wulfrêdeswyrðe, iv. 103, 13. III. *a place enclosed by buildings, a court* or *hall* of a house, *a place* or *street* of a town:—Hê sæt ûta in worðe *sedebat foris in atrio*, Mt. Kmbl. Lind. 26, 69: Mk. Skt. Rush. 14, 66. Ôð tô on worðe *usque in atrium*, 14, 54: Jn. Skt. Lind. Rush. 18, 15. Bifora ðone (þ, Lind.) worð *ante atrium*, Mk. Skt. Rush. 14, 68. On worð (*atrium*) ðæs dômernes, 15, 16. In hwommum worþana (huommum ðara plæcena ł worðum, Lind.) *in angulis platearum*, Mt. Kmbl. Rush. 6, 5. On worðum *in plateis eorum*, Ps. Th. 143, 18: Mt. Kmbl. Rush. Lind. 12, 19. Cf. In plægiword ł on plæcum *in plateis*, Rtl. 36, 7. [*O. Sax.* wurð:—Thâr that korn gikrund habad ende imu thiu wurð bihagôd, Hêl. 2478. *M. L. Ger.* word, wurd *an enclosed homestead*, v. Leo, A. S. Names of Places, p. 60: Jellinhaus, Die Westfälische Ortsnamen, p. 134.] v. worþig, wyrþe-land.

worþ-apulder, e; *f. An apple-tree growing by a homestead* (?):—Be hagan on weorðe hege; forð be ðan hege on weorðapeldre, Cod. Dip. Kmbl. v. 381, 31.

worþ-cærse, an; *f. The name of some plant*:—Wordcærsa *grissa garina*, Wrt. Voc. ii. 42, 31. v. worþig-cærse.

worþig, weorþig, wurþig, wyrþig [*Ps. Surt. has forms as from* worðign; *one such form is found in Ps. Spl. C., and a dative* worðine *occurs in* Bd. S. 539, 42], es; *m.* I. this word, which remains in proper names in the form *-worthy*, has much the same meaning as *worþ* (q. v.), and seems sometimes to exchange with it (cf. In Beniguurthia, Cod. Dip. Kmbl. i. 70, 27, with: In loco qui dicitur Benninguuyrð, ii. 152, 19). In its simplest application it seems to mean *an enclosed homestead*:—Be Ceorles weorðige (worðige, *v. l.*). Ceorles weorðig (weorði, wurðig, *v. ll.*) sceal beón wintres and sumeres betýned. Gif hê bið untýned, and recð his neáhgebûres ceápe in on his âgen geat, nâh hê æt ðam ceápe nânwuht, L. In. 40; Th. i. 126, 12–16. But it is found also in connection with land of considerable extent (e.g. Trium cassatorum in loco qui dicitur Worði (cf. tô Worðie, 34), Cod. Dip. Kmbl. v. 109, 7. Ðis synd ða landgemǽra tô Worðige, 110, 32. .v. cassatos in loco qui appellatur æt Worðige (Worðie, 120, 5), 118, 31), and where there are habitations of considerable importance (e.g. Ego Offa rex sedens in regali palatio in Tamouuorthige, i. 172, 19. Tamouuordie, 171, 6. In loco celeberrimo quae a vulgo vocatur Tomeworðig, 238, 11). Various Latin words are used in reference to places in whose names the word occurs:—In uico celeberrimo qui vocatur Tomouuorðig, i. 256, 24. In uilla omnibus notissima quae Worðig nuncupatur, v. 199, 10. Rura . . . Tantun . . ., Uuorðig, . . . Stoke, iii. 155, 27. .viii. mansas agelluli, ibidem ubi uulgares prisco more uocitant æt Worðige, v. 240, 9. Worðig, vi. 244, 13, is agellus in the body of the Charter, iv. 150, 26. In Bd. 3, 14 a vico Cataractone is in English fram Cetrihtworðige (-worðine, *v. l.*), S. 539, 42. Other instances of the use of the word in reference to localities are the following:—Unam mansam loco qui celebri æt Monowyrðige appellatur. . . . Ðis synd ðære ânre hýde landgemêru tô Monawurðige. Ǽrust on Monawurðiges forde, vi. 57, 9–15. Ofer ðæt hǽð wið Cyblesweorðiges, Cod. Dip. Kmbl. iii. 392, 5. Sûð tô Ellewurðie, vi. 194, 11. Of ðam ealdan lace on Burhgeardesworðig, iii. 412, 12. Instances of the independent use of the word are the following:—Wurðig (worþig, weorþi, *v. ll.*) *fundus*, Ælfc. Gr. 8; Zup. 28, 12. Worþig *predium*, Wrt. Voc. i. 84, 59. Hió an ðæs worðiges, Cod. Dip. Kmbl. vi. 133, 35. Of ðære rôde on Heaðeburhe weorðyg; of ðæm worðige ondlong hrycges, iii. 77, 10. Sancte Andreas cirican and ðone worðig ðe ðǽrtô gaunnan wes, v. 163, 20. At Sunemannes wyrðige; ond of ðam wyrðige . . . on Sunemannes weorðig, vi. 62, 16–31. Wê wrîtaþ him ða circan and ðone circstall and ðone worðig tô ðære burnan and ðone croft be sûðan ðære burnan, iii. 53, 1. Ðæt se gîdsere his weorðig (worðig, Hatt. MS.) and his land mid unryhte rýme *cum multiplicare large habitationis spatia cupiunt*, Past. 44; Swt. 328, 21. Hygelâce wæs gecýðed ðæt ðǽr on worðig (*into the precincts of the palace*) wîgendra hleó cwom tô hofe gongan, Beo. Th. 3948; B. 1972. Æt Hunigburnan twêgen weorðias and .xi. æceras earðlandes, vi. 219, 1. Ðæt greáte windelstreáw ðæt on worþium wixð (*that grows in yards about houses?*), Lchdm. ii. 44, 5. On worþigum, 92, 26: iii. 56, 1. Twelf æceras mǽde ðe licgaþ on sûðhealf weges intô ðǽm þreom worðigan (cf. agellorum, iv. 150, 26), 244, 13. Ða worðias æt Æscwîcan (v. preceding passage), iv. 171, 7. II. *a place surrounded by buildings, a place* or *street* of a town; platea:—Hê sǽde ðam cyninge, ðæt ǽghwanone côman micel menigo ðearfena, ðæt se weorþig full sǽte *indicavit regi quia multitudo pauperum undecumque adveniens maxima* *per plateas sederet*, Bd. 3, 6; S. 528, 18. Nǽfre on his weorþige (*or under* I?) weá ásprinɡe *non defecit de plateis ejus usura*, Ps. Th. 54, 10. Fenn worðigna *lutum platearum*, Ps. Spl. C. 17, 44: Ps. Surt. 17, 43. Of wurðigum *de plateis*, Ps. Spl. C. 54. 11. Worðignum, Ps. Surt. 54, 12: 143, 14. Hweorfaþ ymb Sion . . . and dǽlaþ hire weorðias *circumdate Sion . . . et distribuite gradus ejus*, Ps. Th. 47, 11.

worþig-cærse, an; *f. The name of some plant*:—Uorthigcearse *grissa garina*, Lchdm. iii. 303, col. 1. v. worþ-cærse.

worþig-netele, an; *f. A nettle that grows by a homestead* (?):—Sió micle worþignetle, Lchdm. ii. 116, 2.

woruld. v. weorold.

wōrung, e; *f. Wandering about, rambling*:—Hē hēt ðæt hē wunode būtan wōrunge on mynstre, Homl. Skt. i. 6, 99. Ásolcennys ācenð ídelnysse . . ., wōrunge and fyrwitnysse, Homl. Th. ii. 220, 26.

wōs, es; *n. Moisture, juice*:—Ofetes wōs *ydromellum*, Wrt. Voc. i. 27, 43. Genim ðysse wyrte wōs, Lchdm. i. 200, 15. Genim rosan wōs, 214, 1. Genim leáf, wyl on wætere and wring ðæt wōs (*press the moisture out of the leaves*), 72, 8. Genim ðās wyrte, cnuca hȳ swā grēne, wring ðæt wōs, 126, 7: 208, 12: iii. 102, 14. Wring ðæt wōs on eced, i. 200, 15. Genim cetel, dō þriddan dǽl ðara rinda and ða wyrta, wyl on wætre swíþe; dō ðonne of ða rinda and dō níwe on innan ðæt ilce wōs, ii. 86, 16. [He thrast hom as men dos crapbys, thrastyng owt the wos, Halliwell's Dict.] v. pere-wōs; wēsan, wōsig.

-wōsa. v. ealo-, here-wōsa; wēsa.

wōsig; *adj. Juicy, succulent*:—Ðeós wyrt is wel wōsig, Lchdm. i. 270, 21. Genim ðās wyrte swā wōsige gecnucude, 278, 23. Ða beóð fulle of gehwǽdum leáfum wel wōsigum, 258, 3.

wōþ, e; *f.* I. *a sound, cry, noise*:—Wearð breahtm hæfen, wōð up āstāg, cearfulra cirm, cleopedon monige, Exon. Th. 118, 4; Gū. 234: 125, 31; Gū. 362. Hȳ mislíce, mongum reordum, wōðe hōfun, hlūdne herecirm, 156, 8; Gū. 871. II. of articulate or melodious sound, *voice, song, speech*:—Wooð, uuōþ *lepor*, Txts. 73, 1196. Wōþ *facundia*, i. *eloquentia*, Wrt. Voc. ii. 35, 3. Mid ðære getyngan wōð *lepida*, 50, 44. Ic hæleþum bodige wilcumena fela wōþe mīnre, Exon. Th. 391, 5; Rä. 9, 11. Hē āhōf wōðe: 'Hwæt! gē sind earme,' Andr. Kmbl. 1349; An. 675. Hī singaþ heofoncyninges lof, wōða wlitegaste, and ðās word cweðaþ, Elen. Kmbl. 1494; El. 749. Swēghleóþor cymeþ, wōþa wynsumast, þurh ðæs wildres mūð, Exon. Th. 358, 9; Pä. 43. [Cf. (?) *Goth.* weit-wōdei *witness*: *Icel.* óðr; *m. mind; song.*] v. heáfod-wōþ.

wōþ-bora, an; *m. A* (*good*) *speaker, orator, poet, prophet, philosopher*:—Sum biþ wōðbora, giedda giffæst, Exon. Th. 295, 19; Crä. 35. Sægde sum wōðbora, Esaias 19, 18; Cri. 302. Ic wōðboran wordleána sum āgyfe æfter giedde, 489, 17; Rä. 78, 9. Micel is tō hycgenne wīsum wōðboran, hwæt sió wiht sié, 414, 22; Rä. 32, 24. Wilt ðū wīsne wōðboran wordum grētan, biddan ðē gesecge gesceafta cræftas, 346, 21; Sch. 2. Cræftgleáwe men, wīse wōþboran, Chr. 975; Erl. 126, 27. Wōðborum *rhetoribus*, Wrt. Voc. ii. 81, 53.

wōþ-cræft, es; *m. The art of poetry* or *song*:—Wōðcræfte, beorhtan reorde, Exon. Th. 206, 15; Ph. 127. Ne wēne ǽnig ðæt ic lygewordum leóð somnige, wrīte wōðcræfte, 234, 30; Ph. 548. Ic wille wōðcræfte wordum cȳþan bi ðam hwale, 360, 7; Wal. 2.

wōþ-dor (?). v. wōd-dor.

wōþ-gifu, e; *f. The gift of song*:—Hyre (*a musical instrument*) is on fōte fæger hleóþor, wynlīcu wōðgiefu . . . seó wiht mæg wordum lācan þurh fōt neoþan, Exon. Th. 414, 10; Rä. 32, 8.

wōþ-sang, es; *m. Song*:—Wītgena wōðsong, Exon. Th. 4, 1; Cri. 46.

woxo (=oxan) *bovem*, Lk. Skt. Lind. 13, 15.

wracian; *p.* ode *To be in exile*:—Wracode *exulat*, Wrt. Voc. ii. 81, 13: 31, 14. Hē ge mid Scottum ge mid Pehtum wracode *apud Scottos sive Pictos exulabat*, Bd. 3, 1; S. 523, 17. Hē on Gallia wracode (wrecca wæs, *v.l.*), 3, 18; S. 545, 38. Wracade, 4, 23; S. 594, 44. His menn ða ðe mid wracedon *suos homines qui exules vagabantur*, 4, 13; S. 583, 9. Wraciende *exulans*, Wrt. Voc. ii. 31, 15.

wracnian, wræcnian; *p.* ode *To be* or *travel in a foreign country, be a pilgrim* or *stranger*:—Ic wræcnige *peregrinor*, Ælfc. Gr. 25; Zup. 145, 19 note. Ic wracnode mid Labane *apud Laban peregrinatus sum*, Gen. 32, 4. Ephron, ðǽr wracnode Abraham *Hebron, in qua peregrinatus est Abraham*, 35, 27: 37, 1. Wræcnede *exulat, peregrinatus est*, Hpt. Gl. 476, 3. Chanaan land, ðe hig on wracnodon and ūtancymene wǽron *Chanaan, terram peregrinationis eorum, in qua fuerunt advenae*, Ex. 6, 4. Gif mæssepreóst manslaga wurðe, ðonne þolige hē ǽgðres, ge hādes ge eardes, and wræcnige swā wīde swā pāpa him scrīfe, L. Eth. ix. 26; Th. i. 346, 6. Þolige hē ēðeles, and wræcnige, L. C. S. 41; Th. i. 400, 15. Þolige se, ðe hit on gelang sȳ, ǽlcere eardwununge, and wræcnige of earde, oððon on earde swīðe deópe gebēte, swā biscop him tǽce, Wulfst. 120, 13: 300, 25. v. for-wracned, R. Ben. 82, 2.

wracu, e; *f.* I. *pain, suffering, misery*:—Is fela yfela and mistlīcra gelimpa wīde mid mannum; and eal hit is for synnum; and gyt weorþeþ māre, ðæs ðe bēc secgaþ, wracu and gedreccednes, ðonne ǽfre ǽr wǽre on worulde, Wulfst. 91, 7. Nis mē wracu ne gewin, ðæt ic God sēce, Exon. Th. 167, 2; Gū. 1054. Nis ðǽr lāð genīðla, ne wōp ne wracu, weátācen nān, yldu ne yrmðu . . . ne sār wracu *non huc exangues morbi, non aegra senectus . . . luctus acerbus abest*, 201, 2–11; Ph. 50–54. Him com swā hrædlīc sār and wracu swā ðam cennendan wīfe cymð fǽrlīc sār *ibi dolores sicut parturientis*, Ps. Th. 47, 6. His þegnas for hiora eardes lufan and for ðære wrace (cf. for ðǽm yrmþum eardes lyste, Met. 26, 71) tihodon hine tō forlǽtanne, Bt. 38, 1; Fox 194, 29. Him ðæt tō longsumere wrace cōme, ðǽr hié ðe raðor gesēmed ne wurden *actum de Romano nomine intestina pernicie foret, nisi reconciliatio subrepsisset*, Ors. 2, 4; Swt. 70, 5. Hē wearð werþeódum tō wræce, Elen. Kmbl. 33; El. 17. Hē hæfde him tō gesīþþe sorge and longað, wintercealde wræce, weán oft onfond, Exon. Th. 377, 15; Deór. 4. Wræce bisgodon fǽge þeóda *miseries troubled the doomed peoples*, Cd. Th. 76, 29; Gen. 1264. II. *suffering that comes as punishment, retributive punishment, vengeance, retribution*:—Seofonfeald wracu (*ultio*) bið gesealde for Cain, Gen. 4, 24: Cd. Th. 63, 35; Gen. 1042. Hwylc wracu him forhogiende æfter fyligde *quae illos spernentes ultio secuta sit*, Bd. 2, 2; S. 502, 4. Swā micele māre byþ ēhtnysse grama, swā micele rihtwīsre gewyrþ and hefigre of ēhtnysse wracu *quanto major fuerit persecutionis injuria, tanto justior fiet et grauior de persecutione vindicta*, Scint. 212, 5. Swingella wracu *verberum vindicta*, R. Ben. 52, 7. Ðām eardum becom ōðer wracu siððan, Ælfc. T. Grn. 8, 14. Ǽr ðam ðe seó wracu (*the destruction of Jerusalem*) cōme, Homl. Th. i. 402, 24: 408, 12. Synna wracu, Exon. Th. 98, 14; Cri. 1607: Cd. Th. 309, 18; Sat. 711. Ðis synt wrace dagas *dies ultionis hi sunt*, Lk. Skt. 21, 22. On dæge wræce *in die ultionis*, Scint. 178, 11. On dæge wræce (*vindicte*), 179, 6. Āhebban hine ofer ða scyldgan mid andan and mid wræce *se peccantibus zelo ultionis anteferre*, Past. 17; Swt. 115, 5. Hē gecȳðde his nīð and his onwald mid ðære wræce *zelus ultionis jus aperuit potestatis*, 115, 22. Swā wē for monnum orsorglīcor ungewītnode syngiaþ būton ǽlcre wrace *quanto apud homines inulte peccamus*, 117, 24. Būtan ǽlcre ōðerre wrace *inulte*, Past. 44; Swt. 327, 17. Ðære ceastre tōworpennysse, ðe gelamp for ðære wrace heora māndǽda, Homl. Th. i. 402, 8. Ða gesceafte ðe synd þwyrlīce geðūhte, hī sind tō wrace gesceapene yfeldǽdum, 102, 3. On gelīcre wrace (*vindicta*) dǽdbēte hē, R. Ben. 50, 14. Hē līchamlīce wrace mid swingelle þolige *vindicte corporali subdatur*, 48, 11. Ða yfelan bióþ micle gesǽligran ðe on ðisse worulde habbaþ micelne weán and manigfeald wīte for hyra yfelum, ðonne ða sién ðe nāne wræce nabbaþ, ne nān wīte on ðisse worulde for hiora yfle *feliciores esse improbos supplicia luentes, quam si eos nulla justitiae poena coerceat*, Bt. 38, 3; Fox 200, 4. Ðǽr sceal ǽghwylc man onfōn ðam rihtan dōme his āgenra gewyrhta, . . . swā wrace, swā ēce wīte, swā ēce līf, Wulfst. 136, 8. Hē ðolaþ þeóstra ðurh wrace, Homl. Th. ii. 556, 21. Wræce, Exon. Th. 37, 15; Cri. 593: 455, 30; Hy. 4, 57. Wrace, Andr. Kmbl. 1230; An. 616. II a. where the punishment or vengeance is attributed to the Deity:—Seó wracu (*ultio*) is mīn and ic hit āgilde, Deut. 32, 35. Sōðcyninges seofonfeald wracu, Cd. Th. 67, 14; Gen. 1100. Waldendes wracu, hungor, Chr. 975; Erl. 126, 28. Open wracu ys on his yrsunga *ira in indignatione ejus*, Ps. Th. 29, 4. Him becom seó godcundlīce wracu, Homl. Th. i. 86, 1. Him com on Godes wracu (*irato Deo*) an gefeohtum tōeácan ōþrum yflum, Ors. 4, 4; Swt. 164, 22. Wraco, 1, 3; Swt. 32, 9. Cymð se Dryhtnes dōmes dæg and wrace (*vindictae*), Past. 35; Swt. 245, 18. Hē ðæt eal for Godes wræce fordyde, Blickl. Homl. 79, 26. Hwæt him se Waldend tō wrace sette, Exon. Th. 98, 4; Cri. 1602. Tō wræce, Cd. Th. 156, 6; Gen. 2584. Hē bæd þrymcyning, ðæt hē him ða weádǽd tō wræce ne sette, Elen. Kmbl. 988; El. 495. Ðæt gē witon mīne wrace (*ultionem*), Num. 14, 34. Wrace (wrece, Ps. Surt.) *vindictam*, Ps. Spl. 57, 10: Ps. Th. 78, 13: Cd. Th. 235, 21; Dan. 309. Drihten sende on hié māran wræce ðonne ǽfre ǽr ǽnigu ōþru gelumpe, Blickl. Homl. 79, 9. Hwæðer Drihten āmetan wolde wrece be gewyrhtum, Met. 9, 36. Wracena (wraca, Ps. Spl.: wreca, Ps. Surt.) God *Deus ultionum*, Ps. Th. 93, 1. II b. where the punishment takes the form of exile:—Hié ādrǽfdon ðone consul on elþeóde . . . Hit wæs swīþe ofþyncende ðām ōþrum consulum . . . þēh ðe hié mid ðære wrace (*in the matter of his banishment*) ðæm ādrǽfdan on nānum stale beón ne mehton, Ors. 5, 9; Swt. 232, 22. Hē wītgode be ðære wræce . . ., ðæt wæs ðā hī tō Babilonia gelǽdde wǽron, Ps. Th. 30, arg. Heó on wrace seomodon swearte sīðe, Cd. Th. 5, 14; Gen. 71. Ic sceal wrace dreógan . . . sceal nū wreclāstas settan, sīðas wīde, 276, 8; Sat. 185. III. *persecution, hostility, active enmity*:—Of ðære wræce mīnra feónda ālȳs me, Ps. Th. 16, 12. Ic wræce fēre geond foldan, folcsalo bærne, ræced reáfige, Exon. Th. 381, 1; Rä. 2, 4. Gif hē monna dreám of ðam orlege eft ne wolde gesēcan, . . . lǽtan wræce stille, 114, 10; Gū. 170. His sunu hātte Mars, se macode ǽfre gewinn, and saca and wraca hē styrede gelōme, Wulfst. 106, 26. IV. where hurt is inflicted in return for hurt suffered, *vengeance, revenge*:—Wracu sceal heardum men, Exon. Th. 343, 7; Gn. Ex. 153. Onginþ him leógan se tōhopa ðære wræce, Bt. 37, 1; Fox 186, 23: Met. 25, 51. Hē gesette ða men on ǽnne truman ðe mon hiora mǽgas ǽr slōg, and wiste ðæt hié woldon geornfulran beón ðære wrace (*or under* III? *see the Latin* certaminis) þonne ōþere men, and hié swā wǽron *illi quorum cognati occubuerant, certaminis extitere* wræþstudu *destina*, Bd. 3, 17; S. 544, 17, 24. Wræþstuþum *fulcris*, Wülck. Gl. 245, 28. Wređstuþum, Exon. Th. 422, 6; Rä. 41, 2.

wrǽþþu (-o); *indecl.*: wrǽþþ, e; *f.* I. *wrath, anger*:—Wrǽđđo *ira*, Lk. Skt. Lind. Rush. 21, 23: Jn. Skt. Lind. Rush. 3, 36: *indignatio*, Rtl. 12, 35. Urǽđđo *iracundiae*, 8, 37. Miđ wrǽđđo *cum ira*, Mk. Skt. Lind. 3, 5. Hæbbe hē Godes curs and wrǽđđe ealra hālgena, Chart. Erl. 253, 14. II. *injury*:—Đū in wrǽđđo giscildnise *tu in injuria defensio*, Rtl. 105, 9. v. next word.

wrǽþu (-o); *indecl.*: wrǽþ, e; *f.* *Wrath, anger*:—Wrǽđo đīn *ira tua*, Rtl. 11, 1. Hī wǽran intinga đare wrǽđe đe wæs betwyx him and đan cinge, Chr. 1051; Erl. 182, 28. Hæfþ eal folc micele wrǽþe æt Gode þurh his ǽnne gilt, þe hē nolde healdan đa þincg, Wulfst. 174, 27. From tōweard wurāđo *a futura ira*, Mt. Kmbl. Lind. 3, 7. [*Icel.* reiði.]

wrǽt-līc; *adj.* I. *wondrous, curious*:—Grendles heáfod and đære idese mid, wliteseón wrǽtlīc, Beo. Th. 3304; B. 1650. Stefn cwom þurh heardne [stān] . . . , wrǽtlīc þūhte stānes ongin, Andr. Kmbl. 1480; An. 741. Ic eom wrǽtlīc wiht, on gewin sceapen, Exon. Th. 405, 14; Rä. 24, 2: 483, 11; Rä. 69, 1. Wiht wrǽtlīcu, 415, 23; Rä. 34, 2. Mē đæt þūhte wrǽtlīcu wyrd, 432, 6; Rä. 48, 2. Wrǽtlīc mē þinceþ, hū seó wiht mæge wordum lācan þurh fōt neoþan, 414, 11; Rä. 32, 18. Đæt is wrǽtlīc þing tō gesecganne, 421, 27; Rä. 40, 24. Wrǽtlīcne wyrm, Beo. Th. 1786; B. 891. Wrǽtlīce gecynd wildra, Exon. Th. 356, 9; Pa. 9. Đa wrǽtlīcan wiht, Salm. Kmbl. 505; Sal. 253. Se mē on flīteþ wordum wrǽtlīcum, Andr. Kmbl. 2401; An. 1202. Ic seah wrǽtlīce wuhte feówer, Exon. Th. 434, 15; Rä. 52, 1: 429, 8; Rä. 43, 1. Hē hafaþ ōþre gecynd wrǽtlīcran, 363, 8; Pa. 50. II. *of wondrous excellence, beautiful, noble, excellent, elegant*:—Ceastra . . . orđanc enta geweorc, . . . wrǽtlīc weallstāna geweorc, Menol. Fox 465; Gn. C. 3: Exon. Th. 476, 1; Ruin. 1. Wrǽtlīc is seó womb neoþan, wundrum fæger, scīr and scȳne, 219, 14; Ph. 307: 356, 29; Pa. 19. Heofoncyninges stefn wrǽtlīc, Andr. Kmbl. 185; An. 93. Syndon đa foreweallas fægre gestēpte, wrǽtlīcu wǽgfaru, Cd. Th. 196, 27; Exod. 298. Đæs wrǽtlīcan hringes, Exon. Th. 441, 12; Rä. 60, 17. Healsbeáh, . . . wrǽtlīcne wundormāþđum, Beo. Th. 4352; B. 2173. Wrǽtlīc wīgsweord, 2982; B. 1489: 4668; B. 2339: Exon. Th. 437, 5; Rä. 56, 3. Wundrum wrǽtlīce wyllan, 202, 1; Ph. 63. Wrǽtlīc weorc smiþa, 408, 18; Rä. 27, 14. Wordum wrǽtlīcum, . . . beorhtan reorde, 32, 7; Cri. 509: Andr. Kmbl. 1259; An. 630. Wrǽtlīcra, ǽnlīcra and fægerra, Exon. Th. 357, 12; Pa. 27. Heó wæs on sangum wrǽtlīcre, đonne heora ǽnig ǽr wǽre, Homl. Ass. 127, 365.

wrǽtlīce; *adv.* I. *wondrously, curiously*:—Hē (*the phenix*) eft cymeþ, āweaht wrǽtlīce, wundrum tō līfe, Exon. Th. 223, 29; Ph. 367: 224, 19; Ph. 378. Seó wiht wæs wrǽtlīce, wundrum gegierwed, 418, 8; Rä. 37, 2: 422, 14; Rä. 41, 6: 427, 2; Rä. 41, 85: 428, 2; Rä. 41, 102. II. *wondrously, excellently, beautifully, elegantly, nobly*:—Đǽr wrǽtlīce symle telgan gehladene grēne stondaþ, Exon. Th. 202, 26; Ph. 75. Is him đæt heáfod hindan grēne, wrǽtlīce wrixled, wurman geblonden, 218, 13; Ph. 294. Swā wrǽtlīce weoroda God monna cræftas sceóp and scyrede, 332, 30; Vy. 93. Mē on gescyldrum scīnan mōtan ful wrǽtlīce wundne loccas, 428, 6; Rä. 41, 104. Đa đe wrǽtlīcost wyrcan cūđon stāngefōgum, Elen. Kmbl. 2037; El. 1020.

wrǽtte. v. wrǽt[t].

wræxliende. v. wraxlian.

wrang, es; *n.* *Wrong*:—Unrihtdēman, đe wendaþ wrang tō rihte and riht tō wrange, Wulfst. 203, 26: 298, 20. [Ealle sæidon þet se king heold his brođer mid wrange on heftnunge, and his sunu mid unrihte aflemde, Chr. 1134; Erl. 252, 30. Cf. *Icel.* rangr; *adj.* *Wrong*.]

wrang, wranga *the hold of a ship*:—Wranga (*printed* pranga) *cavernamen* (in a list of nautical words), Wrt. Voc. i. 56, 50. Wrong, ii. 129, 65. [Wrangis *the ribs* or *floor-timbers of a ship*, Jamieson's Dict.: *Icel.* röng *a rib in a ship*.]

wrāsan. v. next word.

wrāsen, e; *f.* *A band, tie*:—Wrāsan (=? wrāsen; for suffix cf. (?), bodan *fundus*, 98, 10), ōst *nodus* (cf. *nodos* bende, 95, 27, *nodorum* rāpa, 61, 68), Wrt. Voc. ii. 114, 79. v. fetor-, freá-, inwit-wrāsen; wrīþan.

wrāst, wrāst-līc. v. wrǽst, wrǽst-līc.

wrāþ, es; *n.* I. *cruelty*:—Wrāđ *crudelitas*, Hpt. Gl. 518, 35. II. *what is grievous, the painful*:—Đæt nān wiht ne sȳ, . . . ne đæs heardes ne đæs hnesces, ne đæs wrāđes ne đæs wynsumes, . . . đæt hig þonne mihte fram ūres Drihtnes lufan āsceádan, Wulfst. 184, 20.

wrāþ; *adj.* I. *wroth, angry, incensed*:—Gram ł wrāđ *furibundus*, Hpt. Gl. 510, 37. Wearđ se cyng swīþe gram (wrāđ, *v. l.*) wiđ đa burhware, Chr. 1048; Erl. 178, 6. Crist him wurđe wrāđ, đe hī geþȳwie, Chart. Erl. 253, 17. Biđ ūre Drihten đām synfullum swīđe wrāđ æteówed, and đām sōđfæstum hē byđ blīđe gesewen, Wulfst. 184, 2. Đīn yrre fram ūs oncyrre, đæt đū ūs ne weorđe wrāđ on mōde, Ps. Th. 84, 4: Cd. Th. 26, 12; Gen. 405: 46, 17; Gen. 745. Unblīđe, wrāđ on mōde, 136, 19; Gen. 2260. Wearđ yrre God, and đam werode wrāđ, 3, 13; Gen. 35. Đe cynig wurađ wæs *rex iratus est*, Mt. Kmbl. Lind. 22, 7. Wrāđ, Lk. Skt. Lind. Rush. 14, 21. Wrāđ wæs *indignatus est*, Lind. 15, 28. II. *fierce, cruel, grievous, hostile, bitter, fell, evil, malignant*, (1) of living creatures, often used substantively:—Eormanrīces, wrāþes wǽrlogan, Exon. Th. 319, 8; Vīd. 9. Wiđ wrāđ werod wearde healdan *to keep watch and ward against foes*, Beo. Th. 643; B. 319. Wrāđe wælherigas, Cd. Th. 119, 21; Gen. 1983. Đa đe wydewum sȳn wrāđe æt dōme, Ps. Th. 67, 5. Mē tō aldorbanan weorđeþ wrāđra sum *some fell one shall be my life-destroyer*, Cd. Th. 63, 18; Gen. 1034: 109, 29; Gen. 1830. Wrāđra gryre *the horror of fierce foes*, 178, 32; Exod. 20: Beo. Th. 3242; B. 1619: Andr. Kmbl. 2547; An. 1275: 2635; An. 1319. Burh wrāđum werian, Cd. Th. 119, 7; Gen. 1976. Torn gewrecan on wrāđum, 123, 1; Gen. 2038: Elen. Kmbl. 329; El. 165: Ps. Th. 104, 34. Wrāþþum forstolen āhreddan, flȳman feóndsceaþan, Exon. Th. 396, 2; Rä. 15, 17. Andsware findan wrāþum tōwiđere *to find an answer against bitter adversaries*, 12, 13; Cri. 185. Đū mē weredest wrāþum feóndum, Ps. Th. 137, 7. Wrāþum wyrmum, Exon. Th. 94, 30; Cri. 1548. (1 a) of evil spirits:—Se atola gāst, wrāđ wǽrloga, Andr. Kmbl. 2595; An. 1299: Cd. Th. 43, 6; Gen. 686. Þurh đæs wrāþan geþanc, þurh đas deófles searo, 39, 25; Gen. 631. Hié hȳrdon wrāđum wǽrlogan, Andr. Kmbl. 1225; An. 613. Waca wiđ wrāþum (*Grendel*), Beo. Th. 1324; B. 660: 1421; B. 708. Hē wrāđne gegrīpeþ feónd be đām fōtum, Salm. Kmbl. 226; Sal. 112. Wreceþ heó wrāđan, Lchdm. iii. 32, 25. Wrāđe wræcmæcgas, Exon. Th. 135, 26; Gū. 530. On wrāþra wīc (*hell*), 94, 4; Cri. 1535. Wrāđra, Cd. Th. 7, 5; Gen. 101. Wrāþra gǽsta, Exon. Th. 424, 19; Rä. 41, 41. Wīte mid wrāþum, 37, 18; Cri. 595. Hē grāp on wrāđe, Cd. Th. 4, 30; Gen. 61. (2) of things:—Hū sārlīc and hū sorhful and hū geswincful and hū teónful đis līf is, hū tealt and hū wrāđ (*grievous* or *evil*), Wulfst. 273, 7. Is him on welerum wrāđ sweord and scearp, Ps. Th. 58, 7. Se ȳfla unrihta wrāþa (*evil*) willa wōhhǽmedes, Met. 18, 2. Wrāđan (*fierce*) yrres, Ps. Th. 77, 50. On đam wrāđan dæge *diem tentationis*, 94, 9. Wrāþe hægle, 77, 47. Wrāđ yrre đīn, 78, 5. Þurh wrāđ (*evil*) gewitt, Elen. Kmbl. 915; El. 459. Hearmstafas wrāđe (*bitter*) and woruldyrmđo, Cd. Th. 58, 2; Gen. 940. Wrāþe wyrde, Exon. Th. 468, 14; Phar. 8. Ic eom wrāþra lāf, fȳres and feóle, 484, 6; Rä. 70, 3. Gemyndig wrāþra wælsleahta, 286, 27; Wānd. 7. Wīta wrāđra, 253, 9; Jul. 177: 261, 7; Jul. 311. Feala ic gebiden hæbbe wrāđra wyrda, Rood Kmbl. 101; Kr. 51. Wrāđum teárum, Ps. Th. 55, 11. Folmum đīnum wrāđum, Cd. Th. 62, 8; Gen. 1011. Hī mid wrāđum wordum trymmaþ *firmaverunt sibi verbum malum*, Ps. Th. 63, 4: Met. 26, 76. Wrāþe firene, Exon. Th. 80, 28; Cri. 1313: 272, 30; Jul. 507. Ic mīnum fōtum fǽcne sīþas, đa wrāþan wegas werede *ab omni via mala prohibui pedes meos*, Ps. Th. 118, 101. Ic eom wrāþre (*bitterer*) þonne wermōd sȳ, Exon. Th. 425, 22; Rä. 41, 60. [He andsware ȝaf, eorlene wrađest (wroþliche swiþe, 2nd MS.), Laym. 18583. *Also in the sense* bad, evil:—To wrađere (wroþere, 2nd MS.) hele, 29556: A. R. 102, 8: Marh. 10, 11: Misc. 148, 27. Þu were ibore o wrađe time (*in an evil hour*), Jul. 57, 3. Wrađe werkes wurchen aȝein Godes wille, Kath. 171. *O. Sax.* wrēđ: *Icel.* reiðr: *O. H. Ger.* reid *crispus*.] v. and-wrāþ, *and next word.*

wrāþe; *adv.* I. *angrily, with* or *in anger, with indignation*:—Eów se Waldend wrāđe (*in his wrath*) bisencte, Exon. Th. 142, 3; Gū. 638. Ondsworade đæs folches aldor wrāđe (wrāđđe, Lind.) *respondens archesynagogus indignans*, Lk. Skt. Rush. 13, 14. II. *fiercely, cruelly, greviously, bitterly*:—Woroldlaga syndan innan đysan earde wrāđe forhwyrfde (*grievously perverted*), Wulfst. 268, 5. Him grimme on woruldsǽlþa wind, wrāđe blāweþ . . . hine se ymbhoga đyssa woruldsǽlþa wrāđe drecce, Met. 7, 51–54: 29, 89, 91. Hī wrāđe tōweorp *destrue eos*, Ps. Th. 58, 11: 61, 4: 72, 14, 15. Đa wiđerwearde mē wrāđe hycgeaþ *cogitaverunt adversum me*, 139, 8: Cd. Th. 284, 4; Sat. 316. Hine monige on wrāđe winnaþ, 138, 11; Gen. 2290. Wē synd wrāđe geswæncte, Homl. Skt. i. 4, 156: Exon. Th. 443, 19; Kl. 32. Wrāþe geworhtra wīta, 252, 32; Jul. 172. Đū đē sylfne swȳþe wrāđe bepǽcst *you deceive yourself most grievously*, Homl. Skt. i. 12, 99. Đæs wrāđe ongeald, hearde mid hīwum, hægstealdra wyn, Cd. Th. 111, 26; Gen. 1861. III. *evilly, perversely, wickedly*:—Hē đa gehāt swīđe yfele gelǽste, and swīđe wrāđe geendode mid manegum māne, Bt. 1; Fox 2, 10. Gē on heortan hogedon inwit, worhton wrāđe *in corde iniquitates operamini*, Ps. Th. 57, 2. Ys hyra mūđes scyld mānworda feala, đa hī mid welerum wrāđe āsprǽcan *delicta oris eorum sermo labiorum ipsorum*, 58, 12: Elen. Kmbl. 587; El. 294. IV. with an intensive force to qualify an unfavourable idea:—Syndon gewordene heora willan wrāđe besmitene (*horribly defiled*), Ps. Th. 52, 1. Đæt biđ forwisnad wrāđe sōna (*terribly soon*), 128, 4. [On two wise, wel and wrođe (*ill*), O. E. Homl. ii. 193, 28. In helle smyche acoryen hit ful wraþe (*very grievously*), Misc. 75, 96. Þunne ischrud and ifed wroþe *thinly clad and badly fed*, O. and N. 1529. Ich habbe more þan þi sostren boþe yloued þe one, and þou ȝeldest now my loue wroþe, fôran, and on ellþiéde *ducem suum et milites exsulare jusserunt*, Ors. 4, 4; Swt. 164, 26. II a. fig. of living out of heaven:—Nis ðeós woruld nâ ûre êðel, ac is ûre wræcsíð, Homl. Th. i. 162, 17. Ðam bið wræcsíð witod, ðe sceal heán hwearfian, ðonne heonon gangaþ, Andr. Kmbl. 1777; An. 891. Gê in wræcsíðe longe lifdon, swegle benumene, Exon. Th. 139, 19; Gû. 595. Wræcsíð wêpan in ðam deáðsele (*hell*), 166, 23; Gû. 1047: 466, 24; Hö. 126. Wê synd on ðisse worlde ælþeódige . . .; for gylte wê wǽron on ðysne wræcsíþ sende, Blickl. Homl. 23, 5. III. *misery, wretchedness*:—Uton gangan ðæt wê bysmrigen bendum fæstne, ôðwîton him his wræcsíð, Andr. Kmbl. 2715; An. 1360. 'Ic nû þrý dagas þolian sceolde wælgrim wîtu. . . .' 'Ne wêp ðone wræcsíð,' 2861; An. 1433. Mæg unfǽge eáðe gedîgan weán and wræcsíð, Beo. Th. 4573; B. 2292. [*O. Sax.* wrak-síð *pilgrimage; exile.*]

wræc-síþian; *p.* ode *To be* or *travel in a foreign country, to be in exile*:—Ic wræcsíðige *peregrinor*, Ælfc. Gr. 25; Zup. 145, 19. Ðæt hine mann âsende ofer sǽ on wræcsíð tô sumum wêstene, on ðam ðe cristene menn for geleáfan fordêmde wræcsíðedon, Homl. Th. i. 560, 22. Tô wræcsíðienne *peregrinandi, vagandi*, Hpt. Gl. 412, 59: *ad incolatum peregre*, 413, 12.

wræc-stôw, e; *f.* I. *a place of exile*:—Seó stôw ðe ðû nû on hæft eart, and ðû cwist ðæt ðîn wræcstôw sý, heó is ðâm monnum êþel ðe ðǽron geborene wǽran *hic ipse locus, quem tu exsilium vocas, incolentibus patria est*, Bt. 11, 1; Fox 32, 27. II. *a place of misery* or *punishment*:—Siððan wræcstôwe (*or* I?) werige gâstas under hearmlocan heáne gefôran, Cd. Th. 6, 17; Gen. 90. Wræcstôwa *ergastula*, Lchdm. i. lxii, 4.

wræc-weorold, e; *f. A world of misery* or *exile*:—Adam wæs gesceapen on neorxnawonge, and for his sylfes synnum ðanan âdrǽfed on ðâs wræcworuld, and on eall ða earfeðu, ðe wê siððan drugon, Wulfst. 1, 2.

wræc-wîte, es; *n. Punishment*:—Seó ǽreste môdor ðyses menniscan cynnes wræcwîte middangearde brôhte, ðâ heó Godes bebodu âbræc, and on ðis wræcwîte âworpen wæs, Blickl. Homl. 5, 24–26.

wrǽd, wræð, es; *m.* I. *a bandage, band, fillet*:—Wrǽda *fasciarum*, wrǽd *fascia*, Wrt. Voc. ii. 34, 21–22: 39, 69. Wrǽd sceal wunden, Exon. Th. 343, 6; Gn. Ex. 153. Sió wund wile tôberan, gif hió ne bið gewriðen mid wrǽde (wrǽðe, Cott. MSS.), Past. 17; Swt. 123, 16: Lchdm. ii. 306, 18. Se mec wrǽde on furþum legde, bende and clomme, Exon. Th. 383, 20; Rä. 4, 13. Genim nioþowearde wrætte, dô on reádne wrǽd, binde ðæt heáfod mid, Lchdm. ii. 304, 26. Wrǽdas *redimicula*, Hpt. Gl. 527, 7. Wrǽda *fasciarum, vinculorum*, 488, 48. Sume heora fnada and wrǽdas gemiccliaþ, R. Ben. 135, 27. II. *what is bound together, a bundle*:—Wrǽdes *fascis*, Hpt. Gl. 529, 4. III. *a band, company, flock.* Cf. wrǽd-mǽlum:—Wrǽd *grex*, Mt. Kmbl. Rush. 8, 32. Wrǽda *manipulorum* (innumeris manipulorum milibus equitatu et peditatu, Ald. 76), 525, 24. v. beado-wrǽd (Lchdm. ii. 350, 29); wrîþan.

-wrǽde, wrǽdel. v. un-samwrǽde, under-wrǽdel.

wrǽd-mǽlum; *adv. In bands*:—Heápmǽlum oððe wrǽdmǽlum *gregatim*, Wrt. Voc. ii. 40, 18. Cf. wrǽd, III.

-wrǽdness, wrǽnan. v. sam-wrǽdness, â-wrǽnan.

wrǽne; *adj. Lascivious, libidinous, salacious, wanton*:—Uuraeni urêni *petulans* vel *spurcus*, Txts. 90, 835. Wraene *petulans*, 87, 1569. Wrǽne *petulcus, luxuriosus*, Hpt. Gl. 484, 55: *libidinosus*, 514, 4. Hê (*Sardanapalus*) wæs swîþe furþumlîc mon, and hnesclîc, and swîþe wrǽne, swâ ðæt hê swîðor lufade wîfa gebǽro þonne wǽpnedmonna, Ors. 1, 12; Swt. 52, 1. Gif mon sié tô wrǽne, Lchdm. ii. 144, 19: Prov. Kmbl. 54. Wrǽnre *lascivae*, Hpt. Gl. 505, 37. Wrǽnre *petulantis*, 515, 9. Ða wrǽnan *lascivam*, 463, 71. Tarcuinius wæs ǽgðer ge eargast, ge wrǽnast, ge ofermôdgast, Ors. 2, 2; Swt. 66, 28. [Cf. *O. H. Ger.* reino *emissarius, admissarius*: reinisc *admissarius*: *Icel.* reini *a stallion*: *Dan.* vrinsk *rank*: *Swed.* wrensk *lascivious.*] v. un-wrǽne.

wrænna. v. wrenna.

wrǽn-ness, e; *f. Wantonness, licentiousness, lasciviousness, lust*:—Wrǽnnes *lascivia, ferventia*, Hpt. Gl. 432, 32. Wrǽnnyss *petulantia*, Hymn. Surt. 126, 28. Wrǽnnes *luxuria*, Past. 43; Swt. 309, 1. Wrǽnnes, seó bið ǽlcum men gecynde *gignendi opus, quod natura semper appetit*, Bt. 34, 11; Fox 152, 12. Ðû woldest brûcan ungemetlîcre wrǽnnesse *voluptariam vitam degas*, 32, 1; Fox 114, 21. Sió wôde þrâg ðære wrǽnnesse *libido*, 37, 1; Fox 186, 18: Met. 25, 41. Werlîcere wrǽnnysse *maritalis lasciviae* (*luxuriae* ł *petulantiae*), Hpt. Gl. 434, 61. Se anga ðære wrǽnnesse *aculei libidinis*, Past. 43; Swt. 309, 16. Ðæt môd hæfð fulfremedne willan tô ðære wrǽnnesse *ejus animus voluptate luxuriae delectatur*, 11; Swt. 73, 7. Heó mid ungemetlîcre wrǽnnesse (*libidine ardens*) mænigfeald geligre fremmende wæs, Ors. 1, 2; Swt. 30, 28: Ps. Th. 7, 13: L. E. I. 32; Th. ii. 428, 33. Nýtena willa tô nânum ôþrum þingum nis âðenod bûtan tô gifernesse and tô wrǽnnesse *pecudum omnis ad explendam corporalem lacunam festinat intentio*, Bt. 31; Fox 112, 8. v. sin-wrǽnness.

wrǽnsa, an; *m. Lasciviousness*:—Wrǽnsan *lasciviae, luxuriae*, Hpt. Gl. 461, 51. Cf. gǽlsa.

wrǽnscipe, es; *m. Wantonness*:—Wrênscipe *petulantia*, Hpt. Gl. 527, 74.

wrǽsen. v. hilde-wrǽsen.

wrǽsnan; *p.* de *To twist, change the character of* something:—Ic (*a woodpecker*) eom wunderlîcu wiht, wrǽsne mîne stefne, hwîlum beorce swâ hund, hwîlum blǽte swâ gât, hwîlum grǽde swâ gôs (cf. Ic (*a woodpigeon*) þurh mûþ sprece mongum reordum *based on the Latin*: Vox mea diversis variatur pulcra figuris, 390, 13; Rä. 9, 1), Exon. Th. 406, 15; Rä. 25, 1.

wrǽst, wrǽste, wrâst; *adj.* I. *delicate, elegant, splendid*:—Wrâst *delicatus*, Txts. 55, 630. Wrâstum (urastum) *delicatis*, 55, 645. Hê hine wǽdum wrǽstum geteóde, Ps. Th. 108, 18. Ôð wîgbedes wrǽste hornas, 117, 25. Ne ðê on ðînum selegescotum swîðe lîcaþ, þeáh ðe weras wyrcean wrǽst on eorðan, 146, 11. Rose wynlîc weaxeþ; ic eom wrǽstre þonne heó, Exon. Th. 423, 23; Rä. 41, 26. II. *noble, excellent*:—Ðû ût âlǽddest wrǽstne wîngeard. . . . Ðû him his wyrtruman wrǽstne settest, Ps. Th. 79, 8–9. Nolde ic ðîne gewitnesse wrǽste forlǽtan, 118, 157. Hê on his welan spêde wrǽste getrûwode, 51, 6. Hî ne wiston wrǽstran rǽd *they knew not a more excellent way*, Cd. Th. 227, 6; Dan. 182. v. un-wrǽst.

wrǽstan; *p.* te. I. *to wrest, twist*:—T hine on ða tungan sticaþ, wrǽsteþ him ðæt wôddor, and him ða wongan briceþ, Salm. Kmbl. 191; Sal. 95. II. *to move the strings of the harp in playing*, Cf. wreste of an harpe *plectrum*, Prompt. Parv. 533:—Sum sceal mid hearpan æt his hlâfordes fôtum sittan, and â snellîce snere wrǽstan, lǽtan scralletan, Exon. Th. 332, 9; Vy. 82. [Iulius þat sweord wraste (wreste, 2nd MS.), Laym. 7532. Wresten *to struggle, wrestle*, A. R. 374, 7. Wrestoñ *plecto*, wrestyñ and wrythyñ aȝen *replecto*, Prompt. Parv. 533: *Icel.* reista *to twist.*] v. â-, ge-wrǽstan.

wrǽstan (?); *p.* te *To be* or *make elegant.* v. wrǽst:—Wrǽstende *indruticans* (but the passage is: Ista (*mulier nupta*) stolidis ornamentorum pompis infruticans, Ald. 17), Wrt. Voc. ii. 77, 44: 44, 8: 110, 58.

wrǽste; *adv. Delicately, elegantly*:—Ne hafu ic in heáfde hwîte loccas wrǽste gewundne, Exon. Th. 427, 30; Rä. 41, 99.

wrǽstlere, es; *m. A wrestler*:—Wrǽstlere *luctator* (-*ur*, MS.), Wrt. Voc. ii. 50, 37. [Iacob speleð wrastlare, A. R. 374, 4. Wrestelare *luctator*, Prompt. Parv. 533.] Cf. wraxlere.

wrǽstlian; *p.* ode *To wrestle.* [To wreastlene, Laym. 1858. Summe heo wræstleden, 24699. To wrastlen aȝein þes deofles swenges, A. R. 80, 7. Wrestlin and wiðerin wið ham seoluen, Marh. 14, 13. Hwerto wultu wreastlin (wrestlen, *v. l.*) wið þe worldes wealdent *quid contra Deum eluctaris?* Kath. 2035. Ðor wrestlede an engel wið, Gen. and Ex. 1803. *M. Du.* wrastelen.] v. *next word, and* cf. wraxlian.

wrǽst-lîc; *adj. Pertaining to wrestling*:—Ðǽm wǽrstlîcum *palestricis*, Wrt. Voc. ii. 69, 3: 74, 54.

wrǽst-lîc (wrâst-); *adj. Delicate, elegant*:—Ðære wrâstlîcan *delicate*, Wrt. Voc. ii. 77, 29: 26, 44. Wrǽstlîcum *delicatis* (ornamentis vestium delicatis decorari, Ald. 73), 87, 17.

wrǽstlîce. v. un-wrǽstlîce.

wrǽstliend, es; *m. A wrestler*:—Wrǽstliendra *luctatorum*, Wrt. Voc. ii. 50, 36.

wrǽstlung, e; *f. Wrestling*:—Wrǽstlunge *palaestram*, Hpt. Gl. 515, 56. [Wes muchel folc at þere wrastlinge, Laym. 1871. Bitternesse in wrastlunge aȝean uondunges. . . . Þeos wrastlunge is ful bitter to monie, A. R. 374, 2–5. Ȝif tweie men goþ to wrastlinge, O. and N. 795. Wrestelynge *colluctacio*, Prompt. Parv. 533.] Cf. wraxlung.

wrǽt[t], e; *f. A work of art, a jewel, an ornament*:—Se (*the cave*) wæs innan full wrǽtta and wîra, weard unhióre goldmâðmas heóld, Beo. Th. 4817; B. 2413. Wundenmǽl wrǽttum gebunden, 3067; B. 1531. Is ðes middangeard wîsum gewlitegad, wrǽttum gefrætwad, Exon. Th. 413, 8; Rä. 32, 2: 414, 27; Rä. 33, 2. Hê ðone grundwong ongitan meahte, wrǽte (wræce, MS.) geondwlîtan, Beo. Th. 5535; B. 2771. Ðam ðe inne gehýdde wrǽte (wræce, MS.) under wealle, 6112; B. 3060.

wrǽt[t], es; *m.*: e; *f. Crosswort*:—Wrǽttes cîð, Lchdm. iii. 12, 28: 24, 4. Mid wrǽte, ii. 306, 18. Genim nioþowearde wrǽtte, 304, 26. Cf. *Warantia* wret (12th cent.?), i. 376, note. *Vermiculum* warance, wrotte (13th cent.), Wrt. Voc. i. 140, 2.

wrǽþ *a band*, wrǽþ *anger.* v. wrǽd, wrǽþu.

wrǽþan; *p.* de *To be angry, get angry*:—Se ðe uraeðes brôðere his *qui irascetur fratri suo*, Mt. Kmbl. Lind. 5, 22. Wraeðde hlâford *iratus dominus*, 18, 34. Se cynig wrǽðde *rex iratus est*, Rtl. 107, 29. Urǽðde *fremuit*, 197, 31. [He wile wreðe wið þe, O. E. Homl. i. 33, 8. He bigon to wreðen (cf. he wreððede him, 10, 4), Jul. 11, 6. Affrican wreaðede and swor, 13, 7. Cf. *O. Sax.* wrêðian (*with reflex. acc.*): *Icel.* reiðask *to get angry.*] v. ge-wrǽþan; wrâþian.

wræþian. v. wreþian.

wræþ-studu, -stuþu, e; *f. A support, prop, buttress, stay*:—Seó wræþstudu *destina*, Bd. 3, 17; S. 544, 17, 24. Wræþstuþum *fulcris*, Wülck. Gl. 245, 28. Wredstuþum, Exon. Th. 422, 6; Rä. 41, 2.

wrǽþþu (-o); *indecl.*: wrǽþþ, e; *f.* I. *wrath, anger*:—Wrǽððo *ira*, Lk. Skt. Lind. Rush. 21, 23: Jn. Skt. Lind. Rush. 3, 36: *indignatio*, Rtl. 12, 35. Uräððo *iracundiae*, 8, 37. Mið wrǽððo *cum ira*, Mk. Skt. Lind. 3, 5. Hæbbe hē Godes curs and wrǽððe ealra hālgena, Chart. Erl. 253, 14. II. *injury*:—Ðū in wrǽððo giscildnise *tu in injuria defensio*, Rtl. 105, 9. v. next word.

wrǽþu (-o); *indecl.*: wrǽþ, e; *f. Wrath, anger*:—Wrǽðo ðīn *ira tua*, Rtl. 11, 1. Hī wǽran intinga ðare wrǽðe ðe wæs betwyx him and ðan cinge, Chr. 1051; Erl. 182, 28. Hæfþ eal folc micele wrǽþe æt Gode þurh his ǽnne gilt, þe hē nolde healdan ða þincg, Wulfst. 174, 27. From tōweard wurāðo *a futura ira*, Mt. Kmbl. Lind. 3, 7. [*Icel.* reiði.]

wrǽt-līc; *adj.* I. *wondrous, curious*:—Grendles heáfod and ðære idese mid, wliteseón wrǽtlīc, Beo. Th. 3304; B. 1650. Stefn cwom þurh heardne [stān] . . ., wrǽtlīc þūhte stānes ongin, Andr. Kmbl. 1480; An. 741. Ic eom wrǽtlīc wiht, on gewin sceapen, Exon. Th. 405, 14; Rä. 24, 2: 483, 11; Rä. 69, 1. Wiht wrǽtlīcu, 415, 23; Rä. 34, 2. Mē ðæt þūhte wrǽtlīcu wyrd, 432, 6; Rä. 48, 2. Wrǽtlīc mē þinceþ, hū seó wiht mæge wordum lācan þurh fōt neoþan, 414, 11; Rä. 32, 18. Ðæt is wrǽtlīc þing tō gesecganne, 421, 27; Rä. 40, 24. Wrǽtlīcne wyrm, Beo. Th. 1786; B. 891. Wrǽtlīce gecynd wildra, Exon. Th. 356, 9; Pa. 9. Ða wrǽtlīcan wiht, Salm. Kmbl. 505; Sal. 253. Se mē on flīteþ wordum wrǽtlīcum, Andr. Kmbl. 2401; An. 1202. Ic seah wrǽtlīce wuhte feówer, Exon. Th. 434, 15; Rä. 52, 1: 429, 8; Rä. 43, 1. Hē hafaþ ōþre gecynd wrǽtlīcran, 363, 8; Pa. 50. II. *of wondrous excellence, beautiful, noble, excellent, elegant*:—Ceastra . . . orðanc enta geweorc, . . . wrǽtlīc weallstāna geweorc, Menol. Fox 465; Gn. C. 3: Exon. Th. 476, 1; Ruin. 1. Wrǽtlīc is seó womb neoþan, wundrum fæger, scīr and scȳne, 219, 14; Ph. 307: 356, 29; Pa. 19. Heofoncyninges stefn wrǽtlīc, Andr. Kmbl. 185; An. 93. Syndon ða foreweallas fægre gestēpte, wrǽtlīcu wǽgfaru, Cd. Th. 196, 27; Exod. 298. Ðæs wrǽtlīcan hringes, Exon. Th. 441, 12; Rä. 60, 17. Healsbeáh, . . . wrǽtlīcne wundormāþðum, Beo. Th. 4352; B. 2173. Wrǽtlīc wīgsweord, 2982; B. 1489: 4668; B. 2339: Exon. Th. 437, 5; Rä. 56, 3. Wundrum wrǽtlīce wyllan, 202, 1; Ph. 63. Wrǽtlīc weorc smiþa, 408, 18; Rä. 27, 14. Wordum wrǽtlīcum, . . . beorhtan reorde, 32, 7; Cri. 509: Andr. Kmbl. 1259; An. 630. Wrǽtlīcra, ǽnlīcra and fægerra, Exon. Th. 357, 12; Pa. 27. Heó wæs on sangum wrǽtlīcre, ðonne heora ǽnig ǽr wǽre, Homl. Ass. 127, 365.

wrǽtlīce; *adv.* I. *wondrously, curiously*:—Hē (*the phenix*) eft cymeþ, āweaht wrǽtlīce, wundrum tō līfe, Exon. Th. 223, 29; Ph. 367: 224, 19; Ph. 378. Seó wiht wæs wrǽtlīce, wundrum gegierwed, 418, 8; Rä. 37, 2: 422, 14; Rä. 41, 6: 427, 2; Rä. 41, 85: 428, 2; Rä. 41, 102. II. *wondrously, excellently, beautifully, elegantly, nobly*:—Ðǽr wrǽtlīce symle telgan gehladene grēne stondaþ, Exon. Th. 202, 26; Ph. 75. Is him ðæt heáfod hindan grēne, wrǽtlīce wrixled, wurman geblonden, 218, 13; Ph. 294. Swā wrǽtlīce weoroda God monna cræftas sceóp and scyrede, 332, 30; Vy. 93. Mē on gescyldrum scīnan mōtan ful wrǽtlīce wundne loccas, 428, 6; Rä. 41, 104. Ða ðe wrǽtlīcost wyrcan cūðon stāngefōgum, Elen. Kmbl. 2037; El. 1020.

wrǽtte. v. wrǽt[t].

wræxliende. v. wraxlian.

wrang, es; *n. Wrong*:—Unrihtdēman, ðe wendaþ wrang tō rihte and riht tō wrange, Wulfst. 203, 26: 298, 20. [Ealle sæidon þet se king heold his broðer mid wrange on heftnunge, and his sunu mid unrihte aflemde, Chr. 1134; Erl. 252, 30. Cf. *Icel.* rangr; *adj. Wrong*.]

wrang, wranga *the hold of a ship*:—Wranga (*printed* pranga) *cavernamen* (in a list of nautical words), Wrt. Voc. i. 56, 50. Wrong, ii. 129, 65. [Wrangis *the ribs* or *floor-timbers of a ship*, Jamieson's Dict.: *Icel.* röng *a rib in a ship*.]

wrāsan. v. next word.

wrāsen, e; *f. A band, tie*:—Wrāsan (=? wrāsen; for suffix cf. (?), bodan *fundus*, 98, 10), ōst *nodus* (cf. *nodos* bende, 95, 27, *nodorum* rāpa, 61, 68), Wrt. Voc. ii. 114, 79. v. fetor-, freá-, inwit-wrāsen; wrīþan.

wrāst, wrāst-līc. v. wrǽst, wrǽst-līc.

wrāþ, es; *n.* I. *cruelty*:—Wrāð *crudelitas*, Hpt. Gl. 518, 35. II. *what is grievous, the painful*:—Ðæt nān wiht ne sȳ, . . . ne ðæs heardes ne ðæs hnesces, ne ðæs wrāðes ne ðæs wynsumes, . . . ðæt hig þonne mihte fram ūres Drihtnes lufan āsceádan, Wulfst. 184, 20.

wrāþ; *adj.* I. *wroth, angry, incensed*:—Gram ł wrāð *furibundus*, Hpt. Gl. 510, 37. Wearð se cyng swīþe gram (wrāð, *v. l.*) wið ða burhware, Chr. 1048; Erl. 178, 6. Crist him wurðe wrāð, ðe hī geþȳwie, Chart. Erl. 253, 17. Bið ūre Drihten ðām synfullum swīðe wrāð æteówed, and ðām sōðfæstum hē byð blīðe gesewen, Wulfst. 184, 2. Ðīn yrre fram ūs oncyrre, ðæt ðū ūs ne weorðe wrāð on mōde, Ps. Th. 84, 4: Cd. Th. 26, 12; Gen. 405: 46, 17; Gen. 745. Unblīðe, wrāð on mōde, 136, 19; Gen. 2260. Wearð yrre God, and ðam werode wrāð, 3, 13; Gen. 35. Ðe cynig wurāð wæs *rex iratus est*, Mt. Kmbl. Lind. 22, 7. Wrāð, Lk. Skt. Lind. Rush. 14, 21. Wrāð wæs *indignatus est*, Lind. 15, 28. II. *fierce, cruel, grievous, hostile, bitter, fell, evil, malignant*, (1) of living creatures, often used substantively:—Eormanrīces, wrāþes wǽrlogan, Exon. Th. 319, 8; Vīd. 9. Wið wrāð werod wearde healdan *to keep watch and ward against foes*, Beo. Th. 643; B. 319. Wrāðe wælherigas, Cd. Th. 119, 21; Gen. 1983. Ða ðe wydewum sȳn wrāðe æt dōme, Ps. Th. 67, 5. Mē tō aldorbanan weorðeþ wrāðra sum *some fell one shall be my life-destroyer*, Cd. Th. 63, 18; Gen. 1034: 109, 29; Gen. 1830. Wrāðra gryre *the horror of fierce foes*, 178, 32; Exod. 20: Beo. Th. 3242; B. 1619: Andr. Kmbl. 2547; An. 1275: 2635; An. 1319. Burh wrāðum werian, Cd. Th. 119, 7; Gen. 1976. Torn gewrecan on wrāðum, 123, 1; Gen. 2038: Elen. Kmbl. 329; El. 165: Ps. Th. 104, 34. Wrāþþum forstolen āhreddan, flȳman feóndsceaþan, Exon. Th. 396, 2; Rä. 15, 17. Andsware findan wrāþum tōwiðere *to find an answer against bitter adversaries*, 12, 13; Cri. 185. Ðū mē weredest wrāþum feóndum, Ps. Th. 137, 7. Wrāþum wyrmum, Exon. Th. 94, 30; Cri. 1548. (1 a) of evil spirits:—Se atola gāst, wrāð wǽrloga, Andr. Kmbl. 2595; An. 1299: Cd. Th. 43, 6; Gen. 686. Þurh ðæs wrāþan geþanc, þurh ðas deófles searo, 39, 25; Gen. 631. Hié hȳrdon wrāðum wǽrlogan, Andr. Kmbl. 1225; An. 613. Waca wið wrāþum (*Grendel*), Beo. Th. 1324; B. 660: 1421; B. 708. Hē wrāðne gegrīpeþ feónd be ðām fōtum, Salm. Kmbl. 226; Sal. 112. Wreceþ heó wrāðan, Lchdm. iii. 32, 25. Wrāðe wræcmæcgas, Exon. Th. 135, 26; Gū. 530. On wrāþra wīc (*hell*), 94, 4; Cri. 1535. Wrāðra, Cd. Th. 7, 5; Gen. 101. Wrāþra gǽsta, Exon. Th. 424, 19; Rä. 41, 41. Wīte mid wrāþum, 37, 18; Cri. 595. Hē grāp on wrāðe, Cd. Th. 4, 30; Gen. 61. (2) of things:—Hū sārlīc and hū sorhful and hū geswincful and hū teónful ðis līf is, hū tealt and hū wrāð (*grievous* or *evil*), Wulfst. 273, 7. Is him on welerum wrāð sweord and scearp, Ps. Th. 58, 7. Se yfla unrihta wrāþa (*evil*) willa wōhhǽmedes, Met. 18, 2. Wrāðan (*fierce*) yrres, Ps. Th. 77, 50. On ðam wrāðan dæge *diem tentationis*, 94, 9. Wrāþe hægle, 77, 47. Wrāð yrre ðīn, 78, 5. Þurh wrāð (*evil*) gewitt, Elen. Kmbl. 915; El. 459. Hearmstafas wrāðe (*bitter*) and woruldyrmðo, Cd. Th. 58, 2; Gen. 940. Wrāþe wyrde, Exon. Th. 468, 14; Phar. 8. Ic eom wrāþra lāf, fȳres and feóle, 484, 6; Rä. 70, 3. Gemyndig wrāþra wælsleahta, 286, 27; Wand. 7. Wīta wrāðra, 253, 9; Jul. 177: 261, 7; Jul. 311. Feala ic gebiden hæbbe wrāðra wyrda, Rood Kmbl. 101; Kr. 51. Wrāðum teárum, Ps. Th. 55, 11. Folmum ðīnum wrāðum, Cd. Th. 62, 8; Gen. 1011. Hī mid wrāðum wordum trymmaþ *firmaverunt sibi verbum malum*, Ps. Th. 63, 4: Met. 26, 76. Wrāþe firene, Exon. Th. 80, 28; Cri. 1313: 272, 30; Jul. 507. Ic mīnum fōtum fǽcne sīþas, ða wrāþan wegas werede *ab omni via mala prohibui pedes meos*, Ps. Th. 118, 101. Ic eom wrāþre (*bitterer*) þonne wermōd sȳ, Exon. Th. 425, 22; Rä. 41, 60. [He andsware ȝaf, eorlene wradest (wroþliche swiþe, 2nd MS.), Laym. 18583. *Also in the sense* bad, evil:—To wradere (wroþere, 2nd MS.) hele, 29556: A. R. 102, 8: Marh. 10, 11: Misc. 148, 27. Þu were ibore o wraðe time (*in an evil hour*), Jul. 57, 3. Wraðe werkes wurchen aȝein Godes wille, Kath. 171. *O. Sax.* wrēd: *Icel.* reiðr: *O. H. Ger.* reid *crispus*.] v. and-wrāþ, *and next word.*

wrāþe; *adv.* I. *angrily, with* or *in anger, with indignation*:—Eów se Waldend wrāðe (*in his wrath*) bisencte, Exon. Th. 142, 3; Gū. 638. Ondsworade ðæs folches aldor wrāðe (wrāððe, Lind.) *respondens archesynagogus indignans*, Lk. Skt. Rush. 13, 14. II. *fiercely, cruelly, greviously, bitterly*:—Woroldlaga syndan innan ðysan earde wrāðe forhwyrfde (*grievously perverted*), Wulfst. 268, 5. Him grimme on woruldsǽlþa wind, wrāðe blāweþ . . . hine se ymbhoga ðyssa woruldsǽlþa wrāðe drecce, Met. 7, 51–54: 29, 89, 91. Hī wrāðe tōweorp *destrue eos*, Ps. Th. 58, 11: 61, 4: 72, 14, 15. Ða wiðerwearde mē wrāðe hycgeaþ *cogitaverunt adversum me*, 139, 8: Cd. Th. 284, 4; Sat. 316. Hine monige on wrāðe winnaþ, 138, 11; Gen. 2290. Wē synd wrāðe geswæncte, Homl. Skt. i. 4, 156: Exon. Th. 443, 19; Kl. 32. Wrāþe geworhtra wīta, 252, 32; Jul. 172. Ðū ðē sylfne swȳþe wrāðe bepǽcst *you deceive yourself most grievously*, Homl. Skt. i. 12, 99. Ðæs wrāðe ongeald, hearde mid hīwum, hægstealdra wyn, Cd. Th. 111, 26; Gen. 1861. III. *evilly, perversely, wickedly*:—Hē ða gehāt swīðe yfele gelǽste, and swīðe wrāðe geendode mid manegum māne, Bt. 1; Fox 2, 10. Gē on heortan hogedon inwit, worhton wrāðe *in corde iniquitates operamini*, Ps. Th. 57, 2. Ys hyra mūðes scyld mānworda feala, ða hī mid welerum wrāðe āsprǽcan *delicta oris eorum sermo labiorum ipsorum*, 58, 12: Elen. Kmbl. 587; El. 294. IV. with an intensive force to qualify an unfavourable idea:—Syndon gewordene heora willan wrāðe besmitene (*horribly defiled*), Ps. Th. 52, 1. Ðæt bið forwisnad wrāðe sōna (*terribly soon*), 128, 4. [On two wise, wel and wroðe (*ill*), O. E. Homl. ii. 193, 28. In helle smyche acoryen hit ful wraþe (*very grievously*), Misc. 75, 96. Þunne ischrud and ifed wroþe *thinly clad and badly fed*, O. and N. 1529. Ich habbe more þan þi sostren boþe yloued þe one, and þou ȝeldest now my loue wroþe, fóran, and on elþiéde *ducem suum et milites exsulare jusserunt*, Ors. 4, 4; Swt. 164, 26. II a. fig. of living out of heaven:—Nis ðeós woruld ná úre ēðel, ac is úre wræcsíð, Homl. Th. i. 162, 17. Ðam bið wræcsíð witod, ðe sceal heán hwearfian, ðonne heonon gangaþ, Andr. Kmbl. 1777; An. 891. Gē in wræcsíðe longe lifdon, swegle benumene, Exon. Th. 139, 19; Gū. 595. Wræcsíð wēpan in ðam deáðsele (*hell*), 166, 23; Gū. 1047: 466, 24; Hö. 126. Wē synd on ðisse worlde ælþeódige . . .; for gylte wē wǽron on ðysne wræcsíþ sende, Blickl. Homl. 23, 5. III. *misery, wretchedness*:—Uton gangan ðæt wē bysmrigen bendum fæstne, ððwíton him his wræcsíð, Andr. Kmbl. 2715; An. 1360. 'Ic nū þrȳ dagas þolian sceolde wægrim wítu. . . .' 'Ne wēp ðone wræcsíð,' 2861; An. 1433. Mæg unfǽge eáðe gedígan weán and wræcsíð, Beo. Th. 4573; B. 2292. [*O. Sax.* wrak-síð *pilgrimage; exile.*]

wræc-síþian; *p.* ode *To be* or *travel in a foreign country, to be in exile*:—Ic wræcsíðige *peregrinor*, Ælfc. Gr. 25; Zup. 145, 19. Ðæt hine mann āsende ofer sǽ on wræcsíð tō sumum wēstene, on ðam ðe cristene menn for geleáfan fordēmde wræcsíðedon, Homl. Th. i. 560, 22. Tō wræcsíðienne *peregrinandi, vagandi*, Hpt. Gl. 412, 59: *ad incolatum peregre*, 413, 12.

wræc-stōw, e; *f.* I. *a place of exile*:—Seó stōw ðe ðū nū on hæft eart, and ðū cwist ðæt ðīn wræcstōw sȳ, heó is ðām monnum ēþel ðe ðǽron geborene wǽran *hic ipse locus, quem tu exsilium vocas, incolentibus patria est*, Bt. 11, 1; Fox 32, 27. II. *a place of misery* or *punishment*:—Siððan wræcstōwe (*or* I?) werige gāstas under hearmlocan heáne gefōran, Cd. Th. 6, 17; Gen. 90. Wræcstōwa *ergastula*, Lchdm. i. lxii, 4.

wræc-weorold, e; *f. A world of misery* or *exile*:—Adam wæs gesceapen on neorxnawonge, and for his sylfes synnum ðanan ādrǽfed on ðās wræcworuld, and on eall ða earfeðu, ðe wē siððan drugon, Wulfst. 1, 2.

wræc-wīte, es; *n. Punishment*:—Seó ǽreste mōdor ðyses menniscan cynnes wræcwīte middangearde brōhte, ðā heó Godes bebodu ābræc, and on ðis wræcwīte āworpen wæs, Blickl. Homl. 5, 24–26.

wrǽd, wrǽð, es; *m.* I. *a bandage, band, fillet*:—Wrǽda *fasciarum*, wrǽd *fascia*, Wrt. Voc. ii. 34, 21–22: 39, 69. Wrǽd sceal wunden, Exon. Th. 343, 6; Gn. Ex. 153. Sió wund wile tōberan, gif hió ne bið gewriðen mid wrǽde (wrǽðe, Cott. MSS.), Past. 17; Swt. 123, 16: Lchdm. ii. 306, 18. Se mec wrǽde on furþum legde, bende and clomme, Exon. Th. 383, 20; Rä. 4, 13. Genim nioþowearde wrætte, dō on reádne wrǽd, binde ðæt heáfod mid, Lchdm. ii. 304, 26. Wrǽdas *redimicula*, Hpt. Gl. 527, 7. Wrǽda *fasciarum, vinculorum*, 488, 48. Sume heora fnada and wrǽdas gemicclíaþ, R. Ben. 135, 27. II. *what is bound together, a bundle*:—Wrǽdes *fascis*, Hpt. Gl. 529, 4. III. *a band, company, flock.* Cf. wrǽd-mǽlum:—Wrǽd *grex*, Mt. Kmbl. Rush. 8, 32. Wrǽda *manipulorum* (innumeris manipulorum milibus equitatu et peditatu, Ald. 76), 525, 24. v. beado-wrǽd (Lchdm. ii. 350, 29); wrīþan.

-wrǽde, wrǽdel. v. un-samwrǽde, under-wrǽdel.

wrǽd-mǽlum; *adv. In bands*:—Heápmǽlum oððe wrǽdmǽlum *gregatim*, Wrt. Voc. ii. 40, 18. Cf. wrǽd, III.

-wrǽdness, wrǽnan. v. sam-wrǽdness, ā-wrǽnan.

wrǽne; *adj. Lascivious, libidinous, salacious, wanton*:—Uuraeni urēni *petulans* vel *spurcus*, Txts. 90, 835. Wraene *petulans*, 87, 1569. Wrǽne *petulcus, luxuriosus*, Hpt. Gl. 484, 55: *libidinosus*, 514, 4. Hē (*Sardanapalus*) wæs swīþe furþumlīc mon, and hnesclīc, and swīþe wrǽne, swā ðæt hē swīðor lufade wīfa gebǽro þonne wǽpnedmonna, Ors. 1, 12; Swt. 52, 1. Gif mon sié tō wrǽne, Lchdm. ii. 144, 19: Prov. Kmbl. 54. Wrǽnre *lascivae*, Hpt. Gl. 505, 37. Wrēnre *petulantis*, 515, 9. Ða wrǽnan *lascivam*, 463, 71. Tarcuinius wæs ǽgðer ge eargast, ge wrǽnast, ge ofermōdgast, Ors. 2, 2; Swt. 66, 28. [Cf. *O. H. Ger.* reino *emissarius, admissarius*: reinisc *admissarius*: *Icel.* reini *a stallion*: *Dan.* vrinsk *rank*: *Swed.* wrensk *lascivious.*] v. un-wrǽne.

wrænna. v. wrenna.

wrǽn-ness, e; *f. Wantonness, licentiousness, lasciviousness, lust*:—Wrǽnnes *lascivia, ferventia*, Hpt. Gl. 432, 32. Wrǽnnyss *petulantia*, Hymn. Surt. 126, 28. Wrǽnnes *luxuria*, Past. 43; Swt. 309, 1. Wrǽnnes, seó bið ǽlcum men gecynde *gignendi opus, quod natura semper appetit*, Bt. 34, 11; Fox 152, 12. Ðū woldest brūcan ungemetlīcre wrǽnnesse *voluptariam vitam degas*, 32, 1; Fox 114, 21. Sió wōde þrāg ðære wrǽnnesse *libido*, 37, 1; Fox 186, 18: Met. 25, 41. Werlīcere wrǽnnysse *maritalis lasciviae* (*luxuriae* ł *petulantiae*), Hpt. Gl. 434, 61. Se anga ðære wrǽnnesse *aculei libidinis*, Past. 43; Swt. 309, 16. Ðæt mōd hæfð fulfremedne willan tō ðære wrǽnnesse *ejus animus voluptate luxuriae delectatur*, 11; Swt. 73, 7. Heó mid ungemetlīcre wrǽnnesse (*libidine ardens*) mænigfeald geligre fremmende wæs, Ors. 1, 2; Swt. 30, 28: Ps. Th. 7, 13: L. E. I. 32; Th. ii. 428, 33. Nȳtena willa tō nānum ōþrum þingum nis āðenod būtan tō gifernesse and tō wrǽnnesse *pecudum omnis ad explendam corporalem lacunam festinat intentio*, Bt. 31; Fox 112, 8. v. sin-wrǽnness.

wrǽnsa, an; *m. Lasciviousness*:—Wrǽnsan *lasciviae, luxuriae*, Hpt. Gl. 461, 51. Cf. gǽlsa.

wrǽnscipe, es; *m. Wantonness*:—Wrēnscipe *petulantia*, Hpt. Gl. 527, 74.

wrǽsen. v. hilde-wrǽsen.

wrǽsnan; *p.* de *To twist, change the character of* something:—Ic (*a woodpecker*) eom wunderlīcu wiht, wrǽsne mīne stefne, hwīlum beorce swā hund, hwīlum blǽte swā gāt, hwīlum grǽde swā gōs (cf. Ic (*a woodpigeon*) þurh mūþ sprece mongum reordum *based on the Latin*: Vox mea diversis variatur pulcra figuris, 390, 13; Rä. 9, 1), Exon. Th. 406, 15; Rä. 25, 1.

wrǽst, wrǽste, wrāst; *adj.* I. *delicate, elegant, splendid*:—Wrāst *delicatus*, Txts. 55, 630. Wrāstum (urastum) *delicatis*, 55, 645. Hē hine wǽdum wrǽstum geteóde, Ps. Th. 108, 18. Ōð wīgbedes wrǽste hornas, 117, 25. Ne ðē on ðīnum selegescotum swīðe līcaþ, þeáh ðe weras wyrcean wrǽst on eorðan, 146, 11. Rose wynlīc weaxeþ; ic eom wrǽstre þonne heó, Exon. Th. 423, 23; Rä. 41, 26. II. *noble, excellent*:—Ðū ūt āléddest wrǽstne wīngeard. . . . Ðū him his wyrtruman wrǽstne settest, Ps. Th. 79, 8–9. Nolde ic ðīne gewitnesse wrǽste forlǽtan, 118, 157. Hē on his welan spēde wrǽste getrūwode, 51, 6. Hī ne wiston wrǽstran rǽd *they knew not a more excellent way*, Cd. Th. 227, 6; Dan. 182. v. un-wrǽst.

wrǽstan; *p.* te. I. *to wrest, twist*:—T hine on ða tungan sticaþ, wrǽsteþ him ðæt wōddor, and him ða wongan briceþ, Salm. Kmbl. 191; Sal. 95. II. *to move the strings of the harp in playing*, Cf. wreste of an harpe *plectrum*, Prompt. Parv. 533:—Sum sceal mid hearpan æt his hlāfordes fōtum sittan, and ā snellīce snere wrǽstan, lǽtan scralletan, Exon. Th. 332, 9; Vy. 82. [Iulius þat sweord wraste (wreste, 2nd MS.), Laym. 7532. Wresten *to struggle, wrestle*, A. R. 374, 7. Wrestoñ *plecto*, wrestyñ and wrythyñ aȝen *replecto*, Prompt. Parv. 533: *Icel.* reista *to twist.*] v. ā-, ge-wrǽstan.

wrǽstan (?); *p.* te *To be* or *make elegant.* v. wrǽst:—Wrǽstende *indruticans* (but the passage is: Ista (*mulier nupta*) stolidis ornamentorum pompis infruticans, Ald. 17), Wrt. Voc. ii. 77, 44: 44, 8: 110, 58.

wrǽste; *adv. Delicately, elegantly*:—Ne hafu ic in heáfde hwīte loccas wrǽste gewundne, Exon. Th. 427, 30; Rä. 41, 99.

wrǽstlere, es; *m. A wrestler*:—Wrǽstlere *luctator* (-*ur*, MS.), Wrt. Voc. ii. 50, 37. [Iacob speleð wrastlare, A. R. 374, 4. Wrestelare *luctator*, Prompt. Parv. 533.] Cf. wraxlere.

wrǽstlian; *p.* ode *To wrestle.* [To wreastlene, Laym. 1858. Summe heo wræstleden, 24699. To wrastlen aȝein þes deofles swenges, A. R. 80, 7. Wrestlin and wiðerin wið ham seoluen, Marh. 14, 13. Hwerto wultu wreastlin (wrestlen, *v. l.*) wið þe wordes wealdent *quid contra Deum eluctaris?* Kath. 2035. Ðor wrestlede an engel wið, Gen. and Ex. 1803. *M. Du.* wrastelen.] v. *next word, and* cf. wraxlian.

wrǽst-līc; *adj. Pertaining to wrestling*:—Ðǽm wǽrstlīcum *palestricis*, Wrt. Voc. ii. 69, 3: 74, 54.

wrǽst-līc (wrāst-); *adj. Delicate, elegant*:—Ðære wrāstlīcan *delicate*, Wrt. Voc. ii. 77, 29: 26, 44. Wrǽstlīcum *delicatis* (ornamentis vestium delicatis decorari, Ald. 73), 87, 17.

wrǽstlīce. v. un-wrǽstlīce.

wrǽstliend, es; *m. A wrestler*:—Wrǽstliendra *luctatorum*, Wrt. Voc. ii. 50, 36.

wrǽstlung, e; *f. Wrestling*:—Wrǽstlunge *palaestram*, Hpt. Gl. 515, 56. [Wes muchel folc at þere wrastlinge, Laym. 1871. Bitternesse in wrastlunge aȝean uondunges. . . . Þeos wrastlunge is ful bitter to monie, A. R. 374, 2–5. Ȝif tweie men goþ to wrastlinge, O. and N. 795. Wrestelynge *colluctacio*, Prompt. Parv. 533.] Cf. wraxlung.

wrǽt[t], e; *f. A work of art, a jewel, an ornament*:—Se (*the cave*) wæs innan full wrǽtta and wīra, weard unhióre goldmādmas heóld, Beo. Th. 4817; B. 2413. Wundenmǽl wrǽttum gebunden, 3067; B. 1531. Is ðes middangeard wīsum gewlitegad, wrǽttum gefrætwad, Exon. Th. 413, 8; Rä. 32, 2: 414, 27; Rä. 33, 2. Hē ðone grundwong ongitan meahte, wrǽte (wræce, MS.) geondwlītan, Beo. Th. 5535; B. 2771. Ðam ðe inne gehȳdde wrǽte (wræce, MS.) under wealle, 6112; B. 3060.

wrǽt[t], es; *m.*: e; *f. Crosswort*:—Wrǽttes cīð, Lchdm. iii. 12, 28: 24, 4. Mid wrǽte, ii. 306, 18. Genim nioþowearde wrǽtte, 304, 26. Cf. *Warantia* wret (12th cent.?), i. 376, note. *Vermiculum* warance, wrotte (13th cent.), Wrt. Voc. i. 140, 2.

wrǽþ *a band*, **wrǽþ** *anger.* v. wrǽd, wrǽþu.

wrǽþan; *p.* de *To be angry, get angry*:—Se ðe uraeðes brōðere his *qui irascetur fratri suo*, Mt. Kmbl. Lind. 5, 22. Wraeðde hláford *iratus dominus*, 18, 34. Se cynig wrǽðde *rex iratus est*, Rtl. 107, 29. Urǽðde *fremuit*, 197, 31. [He wile wreðe wið þe, O. E. Homl. i. 33, 8. He bigon to wreðen (cf. he wreððede him, 10, 4), Jul. 11, 6. Affrican wreaðede and swor, 13, 7. Cf. *O. Sax.* wrēðian (*with reflex. acc.*): *Icel.* reiðask *to get angry.*] v. ge-wrǽþan; wrāþian.

wræþian. v. wreþian.

wræþ-studu, -stuþu, e; *f. A support, prop, buttress, stay*:—Seó wricð his þeówas *sanguinem servorum suorum ulciscetur*, Deut. 32, 43. Drihten wreceþ þearfendra *faciet Dominus vindictam pauperum*, Ps. Th. 139, 12. God hit suíðe hrædlíce wræc *vox illius irae vindictam aperte pertulit*, Past. 4; Swt. 39, 20. Hygeteónan wræc Metod on monnum, Cd. Th. 83, 16; Gen. 1380. Wrec ágen blód esna ðínra *vindica sanguinem servorum tuorum*, Ps. Th. 78, 11. Hú ne wréce hit God? *nonne Deus requiret ista?* 43, 22. Ðú miht wrecan ǽghwylcne mann *Deus ultionum*, 93, 1. Wrecende (*ulciscens*) on eallum wiðmētednyssa heora, Ps. Spl. 98, 9. Tó wreoganne hine hí gecýgdon *ad aemulationem eum provocaverunt*, 77, 64. Wreocende *vindicans*, Ps. Surt. 98, 8. Dryhten wreocende wes *Dominus zelatus est*, ii. p. 193, 27. [(1) Ðe bones ut of ðe erðe wroken, Gen. and Ex. 3191. Þou watȝ wroken fro uch a woþe, Allit. Pms. 12, 375. He his ssel wreke out of his uelaȝrede, Ayenb. 189, 33. Huerout he wrek þo þe zyalde and boȝte ine þe temple, 215, 7. Þe deuel fram hir for to wreke, Greg. 216. (2) Heo hine wreken wolden, wreken hine of his unwines, Laym. 1627. Heo wreken heore cun, 13749. Godd wollde himm wrekenn o þe preost, Orm. 914. For te wreken þe, A. R. 286, 13. On him for to ben wreken, Gen. and Ex. 2028. Leste þu wreoke mine sunnen on me, O. E. Homl. i. 209, 30. Þat micte hire bale wreken, Havel. 327. *Goth.* wrikan *to persecute*: *O. Sax.* wrecan *to punish, avenge*: *O. Frs.* wreka: *O. H. Ger.* rechan *ulcisci, vindicare, retribuere, punire*: *Icel.* reka *to drive; to take vengeance*.] v. á-, be-, for-, ge-, ofer-, on-, tó-, þeód-, þurh-wrecan; un-wrecen, scyld-wreccende.

wrecca, wræcca, an; *m.* I. *one driven from his own country, a wanderer in foreign lands, an exile, a stranger, pilgrim*:—Wræcca *exul*, Wrt. Voc. ii. 33, 27: Bd. 2, 14; S. 517, 38. Wæs hē wræcca on Gallia lande *cum exularet in Gallia*, 2, 15; S. 519, 1. Ðá wæs mid him ān wræccea of Læcedamania *Demaratus Lacedaemonius apud Xerxem exsulabat*, Ors. 2, 5; Swt. 78, 33. Com se foresprecena wræcca . . ., hine se kyning hider and þider wíde áflýmde, Guthl. 19; Gdwin. 76, 12. Wundorlíc wræcca (*Nebuchadnezzar*), Cd. Th. 256, 1; Dan. 634. Ic mē fēran gewát folgað sēcan, wineleás wræcca, Exon. Th. 442, 9; Kl. 10: 457, 27; Hy, 4, 90. Aldbryht wræccea (wrecca, *v. l.*) gewát on Súþ-Seaxe, Chr. 722; Erl. 44, 28. Ðá hē wrecca wæs *dum exularet*, Bd. 3, 18; S. 545, 39. Wrecca (wreccea, *v. l.*), Bt. 5, 3; Fox 12, 33. Fundode wrecca, gist of geardum, Beo. Th. 2279; B. 1138. Wineleás wrecca (*Cain*), Cd. Th. 64, 16; Gen. 1051. Ðú ðás werðeóde wræccan láste feorran gesóhtest, 149, 22; Gen. 2478: 171, 3; Gen. 2822: Exon. Th. 306, 30; Seef. 15. Wreccan, 420, 24; Rä. 40, 8. Hē ða scíre gesealde ánum wræccean of Ahténa (*Atheniensem virum, qui apud Cyprum exsulabat*), Ors. 3, 1; Swt. 96, 24. Wræccan *extorrem*, Wrt. Voc. ii. 32, 64. Wreccan *advenam*, Ps. Spl. 93, 6: Blickl. Gl. Wraeccan *extorres*, Wrt. Voc. ii. 107, 83: *expulsi*, 30, 9. Wreccean *extranei*, 146, 6. Gifu byð wræcna gehwám ár and ætwist, Runic pm. Kmbl. 340, 26; Rún. 7. Wreccena mǽrost, Beo. Th. 1800; B. 898. Wreccena feormunge, L. Alf. pol. 4; Th. i. 62, 16. Hē bebeád ðæt mon ealle ða wræccan an cýþþe forlēte *jussit omnes exsules patriae restitui*, Ors. 3, 11; Swt. 144, 14. Drihten gehealdeþ wreccan (*advenas*), Ps. Spl. 145, 8: Wulfst. 295, 1. I a. applied to a hermit:—Mantat ancer, Godes wræcca, Cod. Dip. Kmbl. vi. 192, 3. I b. figurative:—Wræccan (*those in Hades, exiles from Heaven*), Exon. Th. 461, 28; Hö. 42. He héht ðæt wítehús wræcna (*the angels driven from Heaven*) bídan, Cd. Th. 3, 22; Gen. 39. Ðæt ðú helpe gefremme wērgum wreccan, . . . and ðín hondgeweorc mōte cuman tó ðam upcundan ríce, 17, 2; Cri. 264. Ðonne gesihst ðú ða unrihtwísan cyningas bión swíþe earme wreccan *cernes tyrannos exsules*, Bt. 36, 2, Fox 174, 28. II. *a wretch, an evil person*:—Se feónd, wræcca wǽrleás, Exon. Th. 263, 17; Jul. 351. Mē ceigendæ ðæt ic sié Godes wracco *me clamans esse sacrilegum*, Mt. Kmbl. p. 1, 9. III. *a wretched person, a miserable, feeble creature*:—God selfa tyhte Móyses on ðone folgoð, swāðeáh hē him ondrēd; and nú fandiaþ swelce wræccan and teóð tó, woldon underfōn ðone weorðscipe and eác ða byrðenne *Moyses suadente Domino trepidat, et infirmus quisque, ut honoris onus percipiat, anhelat*, Past. 7; Swt. 51, 22. IV. *a wretched, unhappy, miserable, poor person*:—Ðohtor se Babilónisca wræcca *filia Babilonis misera*, Ps. Lamb. 136, 8. Ða lióð ðe ic wrecca geó lustbǽrlíce song, ic sceal nú heofiende singan, Bt. 2; Fox 4, 6: Met. 2, 3. Ne mæg mon ǽnne wræccan his cræftes beniman, 10, 38. Heó áhredde ða húþe, and tó hám bedrǽf wreccan (*the hapless wight?*) ofer willan, Exon. Th. 412, 6; Rä. 30, 10. Wræccena reáflác is on heora hámum (*rapina pauperis in domo vestra*, Is. 3, 14), Wulfst. 45, 18. [Heo scullen wræcchen (*expelled?*) to heoren scipen liðen, sæilien ouer sæ, Laym. 20887. Wrecche *thou wretch*, Kath. 2049. Ðat folc unseli, sinne wod, ðo sori wrecches of yuel blod, Gen. and Ex. 1074. Drihten alesde þene wrechan *liberauit pauperem*, O. E. Homl. i. 129, 14. Wiþþ usell wrecche dælenn, Orm. 10140. Þer wes moni wrehche iworðen riche, Laym. 5932. Þes wrecche ayhte nabbeþ, Misc. 75, 103. Ich nam non aswunde wrecche, O. and N. 534. *O. Sax.* wrekkio (*used of the three kings from the East*): *O. H. Ger.* reccho *exul, extorris, profugus, incola*.]

wreccan; *p.* wreahte, wrehte; *pp.* wreaht, wreht. I. *to raise, lift up*:—Wreceþ tó rǽde Drihten ðara manna bearn ðe ǽr man gebræc *Dominus erigit elisos*, Ps. Th. 145, 7. II. *to take up, undertake*:—Ðæm hē hæfde beboden ðæt hē scolde þearfena and earmra monna ǽrendo wreccan *cui suscipiendorum inopum erat cura delegata*, Bd. 3, 6; M. 166, 4. III. *to rouse*:—Ðú ðe ært fæder ðæs suna ðe ús áwehte, and gyt wrehð of ðam slēpe úre synna, Shrn. 166, 9. Ðec regna scúr weceþ and wreceþ, swá wildu deór, Cd. Th. 252, 11; Dan. 577. Wē feóllan on slǽpe, ac hē læg þurhwacol, and wræhte ús siððan, Homl. Skt. i. 11, 241. Hié wrehton cumbolwigan, Judth. Thw. 25, 5; Jud. 243: 24, 37; Jud. 228. Ne sceal hē nó ðæt ān dōn ðæt hē āna wacie, ac hē sceal eác his friénd wreccan *non solum ut ipse vigilet, sed etiam ut amicum suscitet, admonetur*, Past. 28; Swt. 193, 21. Hēht hē mid ǽrdæge wígend wreccan, Elen. Kmbl. 211; El. 106. [He of his eyre briddes wrahte (wraȝte, wrauhte, *v. ll.*), O. and N. 106.] v. á-, ǽrend- (Bd. 2, 9; S. 511, 20) wreccan; wrehtend.

wreccan (?); *p.* wreahte; *pp.* wreaht, wræht, wreht *To twist*, (1) *to strain* [:—Gif hors bið gewræht, Lchdm. iii. 62, 12.] (2) fig. *to torment*:—Ic hálsigo ðec ne mec ne wrecce (*for* wrece?; wuræcce, Lind.) *adiuro te ne me torqueas*, Mk. Skt. Rush. 5, 7.

wrecel (?). v. spor-wrecel.

wrecend, es; *m. An avenger*:—Hwæt hwá ōðrum tó wō gedō, God his bið wrecend, L. E. I. 35; Th. ii. 432, 27: Chr. 979; Erl. 129, 17. Ðæt gesýne wearð, ðætte wrecend ðágyt lifde æfter láþum, Beo. Th. 2517; B. 1256. Hí habbaþ eác wrecend (*ultorem*), Scint. 39, 13.

wrecness, e; *f. Vengeance*:—Dagas wrecnisse (wræcnisse, Lind.) *dies ultionis*, Lk. Skt. Rush. 21, 22.

-wrecness. v. god-wrecness.

wrec-scipe, es; *m. Exile, living in a foreign land*:—Mín wrecscype *incolatus meus*, Blickl. Gl.: Ps. Spl. T. 119, 5.

wrēgan (wrēcan); *p.* wrēgde, wrēhte; *pp.* wrēged, wrēht *To bewray, accuse, denounce*, (1) absolute:—Ne ðú ne wrēi *nec accuses*, Kent. Gl. 1083. Wíte ł wrēce *imputet*, Germ. 400, 560. Wroegde *defert*, meldadun *vel* wroegdun (roactum, Erf.) *defferuntur*, Txts. 57, 663, 652. Wrēgde, wrēgdan, Wrt. Voc. ii. 25, 35, 26. Wrēgian *insimulare*, 81, 7. Ðæs wrēgendan *mussantes*, 58, 34. (2) *to accuse* a person:—Ðysne man ic wrēge *hunc hominem accuso*, Ælfc. Gr. 7; Zup. 22, 22. Ic ðē wrēge beforan Crystes þrymsetl, Shrn. 154, 9. Hié yfel gewitnes ne wrēgde, Blickl. Homl. 163, 1. Man wrǽgde ðone biscop, Chr. 1069; Erl. 207, 6. Mid ðý ðe hyne wrēgdon ðæra sacerda ealdras *cum accusaretur a principibus sacerdotum*, Mt. Kmbl. 27, 12: Jn. Skt. 8, 10. Ðæt hí wrēhton hyne *ut accusarent eum*, Mt. Kmbl. 12, 10: Homl. Th. i. 570, 21. Ðē wrēg *te accusa*, Scint. 165, 1. Gif ǽnig mann ōðerne wrēge and him hwilcne gilt on secge *si steterit testis mendax contra hominem accusans eum praevaricationis*, Deut. 19, 16. Hit is betre ðæt mon wrēge ðone scyldigan, Bt. 38, 7; Fox 210, 5. Hí āgunnon hyne wrēgan (*accusare*), Lk. Skt. 23, 2. Heó begann hí tó wrǽgenne, Homl. Skt. i. 2, 184. Mid micelre wrōhte hine wrēgende *bringing a heavy accusation against him*, Homl. Th. ii. 250, 10. (2 a) *to accuse* a person to (*tó, wiþ*) somebody:—Ne wēne gē ðæt ic eów wrēge tó fæder (*apud patrem*). Se is ðe eów wrēgð Móyses, Jn. Skt. 5, 45. Hié mon wrēgde tó ðæm cásere, Blickl. Homl. 173, 10. Wrēhte, Homl. Skt. ii. 25, 597. Wrēgdon ða ōðre cræftigan hý tó ðam cásere, Shrn. 146, 20. Hí wrēhton ðone cyning tó his brēðer, Homl. Th. i. 468, 6. Ðe læs hē wrēge ðē tó Drihtene *ne clamet contra te ad Dominum*, Deut. 15, 9. Ðeáh ðín wíf ðē hwane tó wrēge, ne gelýf ðú ná tó hraðe, Prov. Kmbl. 4. Ongan hē hí wrēgean tó ðam cyninge, Lchdm. iii. 424, 21. Ðíne ǽhta mid stylre stemne wyllaþ ðē wrēgan tó ðínum Drihtne, Homl. Th. ii. 410, 21. Hē began ðæt cynn tó wrēgenne wið ðone cyning, Homl. Ass. 96, 148. (2 b) *to accuse* a person of something:—Of ðám ðe gē hine wrēgaþ *ex his in quibus eum accusatis*, Lk. Skt. 23, 14. Lóca hú mycelum hí ðē wrēgeaþ *uide in quantis te accusant*, Mk. Skt. 15, 4. Ðá wrēgdon hine ða heáhsacerdas on manegum þingum, 15, 3. (3) *to denounce* something to a person:—Ðá onfēng ðære þeóde kyning fulwihte; ðá fōron ða hǽþnan bisceopas and ðæt wrēgdon tó ðæs kyninges brēþer, Shrn. 120, 34. Ðæt folc wrēhton his mōdignysse tó ðam cásere, Homl. Th. i. 478, 17. [Mon schal wreien him suluen ine schrifte, A. R. 304, 1. Gif þu wreiest þe seoluen to þine scrifte, O. E. Homl. i. 27, 36. He ne wollde unnshaþiȝ wimmann wreȝhenn, Orm. 2889. Þair syns sal wreghe þam, Pr. C. 5462. Naȝt him to defendi, ne nenne oþrenne wraye, Ayenb. 175, 5. Fund mann nan þing uppon hemm to wreȝenn, Orm. 416. *Goth.* wrōhjan *to accuse*: *O. Sax.* wrōgian: *O. Frs.* wrōgia, wrēia: *O. H. Ger.* ruogen: *Icel.* rægja.] v. for-, ge-wrēgan.

wrēgan; *p.* de *To rouse, excite*:—Hwílum ic streámas styrge, hwílum wolcnfare wrēge, Exon. Th. 386, 33; Rä. 4, 71. Hwílum ic (*a storm*) sceal ýþa wrēgan, [streámas] styrgan, 383, 28; Rä. 4, 17. v. ge-wrēgan.

wrēgend, es; *m. An accuser, a denouncer*:—Wrēgend *accussator*, Scint. 39, 14: Wrt. Voc. ii. 8, 71: 72, 57. His wrēgend and gesacan *accusatores ejus*, Bd. 5, 19; S. 640, 13. Hyra wrēgendras, Scint. 29, 4. Wrēgendum *delatoribus*, Wrt. Voc. ii. 28, 13.

wrēgend-líc; *adj. Accusative:—Accussativus* ys wrēgendlíc, Ælfc. Gr. 7; Zup. 22, 20.

wrēgere, es; *m. An accuser:*—Wrēgere *accusator*, Wrt. Voc. i. 83, 63: Homl. Th. ii. 236, 22: 340, 22. [Wreiere ne beo þu, O. E. Homl. i. 57, 49. Wreieres and wrobberes, Havel. 39.]

wrēgestre, an; *f. A female accuser:*—Seó leáse wrǣgistre, Homl. Skt. i. 2, 208.

wrēging, e; *f. Accusation:*—Wrēginc *accusatio*, Wrt. Voc. i. 83, 65. [Wreiunge, A. R. 200, 22. Wreynge ant gret blame that byth, Rel. Ant. i. 267, 3. *O. Frs.* wrōginge.]

wrehtend, es; *m. One who excites:*—Wrehtend, tyhtend *incentor*, Wrt. Voc. ii. 44, 62. Cf. wreccan.

wrēhtend, es; *m. An accuser:*—Wrēhten his selfes *accusator sui*, Kent. Gl. 650. Cf. wrēgan.

wrenc, es; *m.* I. *a trick, artifice, wile, stratagem:*—On swā hwylcum wrence (*arte*) worda ǣnig swerige, Scint. 136, 18. Wrencum *modis*, Wrt. Voc. ii. 57, 61. Ðæt leáse lot, ðe beoþ mid ðām wrencum bewrigen *fraus, mendaci compta colore*, Bt. 4; Fox 8, 17: Met. 4, 47. Tō fela manna wearð mid þyllícan wrencan þurh deófol forlǣred, Wulfst. 54, 12. Tōgeánes ðæs deófles wrencum, 198, 12. Ðā sceolde Ælfríc lǣdan ða fyrde, ac hē teáh forð ðā his ealdan wrenceas, . . . gebrǣd hē hine seócne, Chr. 1003; Erl. 139, 7. I a. *a stratagem* in war:—Hē hié mid ðæm ilcan wrence beswāc, ðe hē æt heora ǣrran mētingge dyde, Ors. 4, 9; Swt. 188, 32: 6, 36; Swt. 294, 21. Siþþan Rōmāne gesāwan ðæt him mon swelcne wrenc tō dyde, ðā flugon hié, 4, 1; Swt. 156, 8. II. *a modulation of the voice:*—Biþ ðæs hleóðres swēg eallum songcræftum swētra, and wynsumra wrenca gehwylcum, Exon. Th. 206, 28; Ph. 133. Ic þurh mūþ sprece mongum reordum, wrencum singe (*vox mea diversis variatur pulcra figuris*), . . . ic būgendre stefne styrme, 390, 15; Rä. 9, 2. [Þurh his micele wrences beiæt he þone ærcebiscoprice, Chr. 1127; Erl. 156, 1. Gif þær wære an unwreste wrenc ꝥ he mihte get beswicen anes Crist, 1131; Erl. 260, 4. Paris mid pret wrence biwon Elene, Laym. 81. Þis sacrament unwrihð his (*the devil's*) wrenches, A. R. 270, 10. Swikele men and ful of vuele wrenche, Misc. 66, 247. With wrenkes and wyles, Pr. C. 1360. He (*a wrestler*) can his wrenches wel forhele, O. and N. 798. Þis is þe soþe wei, withouten eny wrenche, R. Glouc. 55, 2. His wyly wrenches thou ne mayst nat flee, Chauc. Ch. Y. T. 1081. Wrenche or sleythe of falsheed *dolositas, fraudulencia, cautela*, Prompt. Parv. 533, and see note. *Ger.* rank *a trick.*] v. lot-, nearu-, searu-, siru-, smeá-, un-, weorold-wrenc.

wrencan; *p.* te. I. *to turn, twist* (intrans.):—Is ðæs horderes tācen, ðæt mon wrænce mid his hande, swilce hē wille loc unlūcan, Techm. ii. 118, 12. II. *to practise wiles, use tricks.* v. wrenc:—Biþ ōþer swice, . . . wrenceþ hē and blenceþ, worn geþenceþ hinderhōca, Exon. Th. 315, 18; Mōd. 33. [Þu ne mihtes nohwider wrenche fra þa duntes, O. E. Homl. i. 281, 30. Ich chulle wrenchen hire þideweard ase heo mest dredeð, A. R. 222, 16. Þu ne maht wenden me ne wrenchen ut of þe weie, Marh. 4, 27. Some gase wrynchand to and fra, Pr. C. 1538. *Germ.* renken.] v. be-wrencan.

wrenc-wís; *adj. Unjust, unrighteous:*—Wer wrencwis *vir iniquus*, Rtl. 10, 30. Cf. riht-wís.

wrenna, wrænna, werna, wærna, an; *m.*: wrenne, an; *f. A wren:*—Wrenna *vel* hicemāse *parrax*, Wrt. Voc. i. 29, 56. Wrenne (wrænna, *v.l.*), 77, 46. Wrenna *bitorius* vel *pintorus*, 29, 27: *bitorius, bitriscus*, ii. 126, 37. Wrænna *biturius*, 12, 62: *bitorius*, i. 62, 41. Werna *birbicariolus*, ii. 101, 76. Wærna *bitorius*, 11, 12: *litorius*, 51, 59: i. 281, 12. [Hwat dostu godes among manne na mo þene deþ a wrecche wranne (wrenne, *v.l.*), O. and N. 564. Wrenne *regulus*, Wrt. Voc. i. 221, 7.]

Wreocen-sǣte, -sǣtan (Wrocen-); *pl. The occupants of the district about the Wrekin:*—Gesta est hujus libertatis donatum anno incarnationis DCCC.LV°, in loco qui uocatur Ōswaldes dūn, quando fuerunt pagani in Uureocensētun, Cod. Dip. Kmbl. ii. 59, 35. In prouincia Wrocensētna, vi. 60, 2. Cf. Wocen-sǣte.

wreogan, Ps. Spl. 77, 64. v. wrecan, IV ¶.

wreón (*from* wríhan); *p.* wrāh, wreáh, *pl.* wrigon, wrugon; *pp.* wrigen, wrogen *To cover.* I. *to put a covering on* something, (1) literal:—Se ðe wrígð wæterum ða uferan his *qui tegit aquis superiora ejus*, Ps. Spl. 103, 3. Ōþer eáre hī him underbrēdaþ and mid ōðran hī wreóð (*se cooperiunt*), Nar. 37, 12. Hē wreáh and þeahte māufǣhðu bearn wonnan wǣge, Cd. Th. 83, 10; Gen. 1377. Reste hē hine sōfte, and wreó hine wearme: . . . lǣt drincan . . ., and wreóh hine wearme, Lchdm. ii. 292, 6–14. Swā ðū worulddeáde wrige mid foldan *as you would cover the dead with earth*, Ps. Th. 140, 4. Ongunnun summe gehȳdæ ł wríga (*uelare*) onsióne his, Mk. Skt. Lind. 14, 65. (1 a) *to cover* with clothes, *to clothe:*—Ic wreó mē wǣda leásne, leáfum þecce, Cd. Th. 53, 26; Gen. 867. Ic wæs nacod, and gē clǣððon ł wrigon (wriogan, Rush.) meh *eram nudus, et operuistis me*, Mt. Kmbl. Lind. 25, 36. Hē ne mihte hine handum self mid hrægle wryón, Cd. Th. 95, 2; Gen. 1572. (1 b) *to cover* a book, *to bind* a book:—Mec (*a book*) wrāh hæleð hleóbordum, Exon. Th. 408, 13; Rä. 27, 11. (2) with the idea of concealment, *to conceal, hide:*—For hwon wāst ðū weán and wríhst sceome, Cd. Th. 54, 13; Gen. 876. Ða word ðe gē wrigon under womma scealum, Elen. Kmbl. 1162; El. 582. (3) with the idea of protection:—Ic ðē wið weána gehwam wreó and scylde folmum mīnum, Cd. Th. 131, 3; Gen. 2170. II. *to serve as a covering to* something, *be spread over*, (1) literal:—Flōd ealle wreáh heá beorgas, Cd. Th. 83, 28; Gen. 1386. Niht lagustreámas wreáh, 147, 34; Gen. 2449. Mec (*an oyster*) ȳþa wrugon, Exon. Th. 488, 5; Rä. 76, 2. Sió filmen biþ þeccende and wreónde ða wambe, Lchdm. ii. 240, 17. (1 a) of clothing:—Woede tō wriánne *vestem ad operiendam*, Rtl. 103, 42. Of hwon wē biðon wrigen (gewrigene, Rush.) *quo operiemur*, Mt. Kmbl. Lind. 6, 31. (2) with the idea of concealment:—Ȳþa mec (*a storm*) wrugon, Exon. Th. 382, 23; Rä. 3, 15. (3) with the idea of protection:—Ic hæbbe mē on hrycge ðæt ǣr hādas wreáh foldbūendra, Exon. Th. 381, 17; Rä. 2, 11. Unc holt wrugon, wudubeáma helm, wonnum nihtum, scildon wið scūrum, 496, 1; Rä. 85, 73. [Þu mihtes wrihe þine banes, O. E. Homl. i. 279, 2. Wummon schal wrihen hire heauet. Wrihen, he seið, naut wimplin. Wrihen ha schal hire scheome . . . Gef ei þing wriheð þi neb, A. R. 420, note. To wrien and te helien, . . . he heleð hit and wrihð, 84, 14–17. Þe uikelares wreoð and helieð, 88, 19. Þis scheld þet wreih his Godhed, 390, 26. Ane cheste wreon mid golde, Laym. 27859. Þa Irisce wriȝen al þa feldes, 17349. Wreoð wel þene king, 17762. Wrugen, *p. pl.*, P. L. S. viii. 81. Uor to wry his confusioun, Ayenb. 258, 18. Þe sseld him wriȝþ, 167, 10. Hi wreþ þe uelþes of zenne, 61, 4. *O. H. Ger.* int-rīhan *revelare.*] v. ā-, be-, ge-, in-, ofer-, on-, un-wreón.

wreótaþ, wreoþen-hilt. v. reótan, wriþen-hilt.

wreþian; *p.* ede; *pp.* ed *To prop, stay, support, sustain:*—Wreþeþ *fulcit*, Wrt. Voc. ii. 38, 28. Wreðed (-ed?) *nisa*, 61, 59. Heora ǣlc winð wiþ ōþer, and þeáh wræþeþ ōþer, ðæt hié ne mōton tōslūpan, Bt. 21; Fox 74, 11. Hiora ǣghwilc wið ōþer winð, and þeáh winnende wreþiaþ fæste ǣghwilc ōþer, Met. 11, 34. Se ðe rodor āhōf and gefæstnode folmum sīnum, worhte and wreðede, Andr. Kmbl. 1045; An. 523. Cypressus styde hié ūtan wreþedon *nitebant[ur] testudinibus cupressinis*, Nar. 5, 9. Wreþian *fulcire*, Wrt. Voc. ii. 34, 68. Gif ðǣr sié gierd mid tō ðreágeanne, sié ðǣr eác stæf mid tō wreðianne *si est districtio virgae, quae feriat, sit et consolatio baculi, quae sustentet*, Past. 17; Swt. 127, 2. His ða untruman limo mid his cricce wreðiende *imbecilles artus baculo sustentans*, Bd. 4, 31; S. 610, 28. Biþ seó mōdor wundrum wreþed, Exon. Th. 492, 15; Rä. 81, 16. [Euerichon wreoðeð him bi oðer, A. R. 252, 13. Alle þeos writeres writes ꝥ ȝe wreoðieð ow on, Kath. 857. *O. Sax.* wreðian *to prop, stay, support.*] v. ā-, ge-, under-wreþian; wraþu.

wreþung. v. under-wreþung.

wríd (cf. 'A *ride* of hazle or such like wood, is a whole plump of spriggs or frith growing out of the same root,' E. D. S. Pub. Old Farming Words, no. III. Here is an heelful thing, a wonder wride (*rimes with* abyde), Pall. 51, 207), es; *m. A shoot, stalk, plant, bush:*—Uurȳd *culmus*, Txts. 52, 252. Genim æscþrote ǣnne wríd, Lchdm. i. 216, 11. Genim ðysse wyrte wríd, 224, 1. Bedelf ǣnne wríd cileþenigan moran, iii. 38, 9. v. hæsel-wríd; ge-wrid, *and next word.*

wrídan, wríþan; *p.* de *To put forth shoots, be productive:*—Weaxaþ and wrídaþ, . . . fyllaþ eówre fromcynne foldan sceátas, teámum and tūdre, Cd. Th. 92, 21; Gen. 1532. Wrīðende sceal mǣgðe ðīnre monrīm wesan, 105, 33; Gen. 1762. Geunne ðē ēce Drihten æcera wexendra and wrídendra, Lchdm. i. 402, 4. v. preceding and following words.

wrídian, wríþian; *p.* ode *To put forth shoots, be productive, grow, flourish:*—Þūfaþ and wrídaþ *frutescit*, Wrt. Voc. ii. 38, 13. (1) literal, of vegetable growth:—Se æþela feld wrídaþ, wynnum geblōwen, Exon. Th. 199, 17; Ph. 27. On ðære eá ōfre stōd hreód and pīntreów and abies ðæt treówcyn ungemetlīcre grȳto and micelnysse ðȳ clife weóx and wrídode (wrīðode, Cockayne; but see Anglia i. 509) *cujus ripas pedum sexagenum harundo uestiebat pinorum abietumque robora uincens grossitudine*, Nar. 8, 22. (2) figurative, of growth in things abstract or concrete:—Hē wrídaþ on wynnum, ðæt hē bið wæstmum gelīc ealdum earne, and æfter ðon feþrum gefrætwad, swylc hē æt frymðe wæs, beorht geblōwen *reformatur qualis fuit ante figura, et Phoenix ruptis pullulat exuviis*, Exon. Th. 214, 10; Ph. 237. Mīn hyge blissaþ, wynnum wrídaþ *my mind rejoices, blossoms with joyous thoughts*, Andr. Kmbl. 1269; An. 635. Him oninnan oferhygda dǣl weaxeþ and wrídaþ, Beo. Th. 3486; B. 1741. Mān wrídode geond beorna breóst, Andr. Kmbl. 1534; An. 768. Weóx ðā and wrīðode mǣgburg Semes, Cd. Th. 102, 19; Gen. 1702. Ne sceal unc betweónan teónan weaxan, wrōht wrīdian, 114, 12; Gen. 1963. v. ā-, ge-wrídian, *and two preceding words.*

wríga *to cover.* v. wreón.

wrigedness, wrigenness. v. un-wrigedness, un-wrigenness.

wrigels, es; *m. n.* I. *a covering:*—In wrigelse fiðra ðīnra *in velamento alarum tuarum*, Ps. Surt. 60, 5: 62, 8. Wæs him wrigils *fuit illis in velamento*, Rtl. 92, 26. God āfyrde hym ðone unrihtan wrigels of heora heortan, Wulfst. 252, 4. II. *a garment, veil:*—Hī mon mid ðæm hâlgan wrigelse bewrîhþ, Blickl. Homl. 61, 16. Hâlgum wriilcse *sacro velamine*, Rtl. 106, 4. Be ðý wyrgelse ofer Cristes nesðyrlum, Anglia xi. 173, 9. Ðû hî onwendest swâ man wrigels (*opertorium*) dêð, Ps. Th. Surt. 101, 23. Hê his wrigels geopenode, Homl. Ass. 196, 56. [Adam & Eue makeden wrieles of leaues, A. R. 322, 19. Wriheles, 420, note. Wriels *velamen*, Wick. Job 24, 8.] v. ofer-, unriht-wrigels.

wrigian; *p.* ode *To turn, wend, hie, go, move*:—Þeáh ðû teó hwelcne bôh of dûne tô ðære eorþan, swelce ðû bêgan mæge, swâ ðû hine âlǽtst, swâ sprincþ hê up, and wrigaþ (cf. went on gecynde, Met. 13, 55) wiþ his gecyndes . . . Swâ dêþ ǽlc gesceaft, wrigaþ wiþ his gecyndes, and gefagen biþ gif hit ǽfre tô cuman mæge *validis quondam viribus acta pronum flectit virga cacumen; hanc si curvans dextra remisit, recto spectat vertice coelum . . . Repetunt proprios quaeque recursus, reditaque suo singula gaudent*, Bt. 25; Fox 88, 22–29: xiv, 14. Ǽlc gesceaft wrigaþ and higaþ wið his gecyndes, Met. 13, 65. Wuhta gehwilc wrigaþ tôheald wið ðæs gecyndes . . . þinga gehwilc þiderweard fundaþ, 13, 10. Weard æt steorte (*the ploughtail*) wrigaþ on wonge *the ploughman pushes his way over the field*, Exon. Th. 403, 9; Rä. 22, 5. [That feyre founden me mete ant cloht, hue wrieth awey as hue were wroht, Spec. 48, 22. With hir heed sche wriede fast awey, Chauc. Mill. T. 97. Hwenne so wil to wene wriedh, R. S. 3, 7. Þy face from hyre þou wry, Mirc. 888.]

wrinclod. v. ge-wrinclod.

wringan; *p.* wrang, *pl.* wrungon; *pp.* wrungen *To wring*, (1) *to twist*:—Teóh him ða loccas, and wringe ða eáran, and ðone wangbeard twiccige, Lchdm. ii. 196, 13. (2) *to squeeze out* moisture from something:—Ic nam ða wînberian and wrang on ðæt fæt *tuli uvas et expressi in calicem*, Gen. 40, 11. Genim ðære ylcan wyrte leáf, ðonne heó grênost beó, wyl on wætere, and wring ðæt wôs, Lchdm. i. 72, 7. Wring ðæt seáw, ii. 110, 26: 240, 8. Ne miht ðû wîn wringan on midne winter, Bt. 5, 2; Fox 10, 31. Tô wringen[n]e *ad exprimendos*, Hpt. Gl. 468, 32. [*O. H. Ger.* ringan *rixari, luctari.*] v. â-, ge-wringan.

wring-hwæg *the whey pressed out of cheese*:—Ðæt heó of wringhwæge buteran macige tô hlâfordes beóde, L. R. S. 16; Th. i. 438, 31.

wrislan. v. wrixlan.

wrist, e; *f. A wrist*:—Gif hit ânfeald tyhtle sý, dûfe seó hand æfter ðam stâne óð ða wriste; and gif hit þryfeald sý, óð ðæne elbogan, L. Ath. iv. 7; Th. i. 226, 17. [Wryst or wyrste of an hande *fragus*, Prompt Parv. 534. The wryste or a knokyl *fragus*, Wülck. Gl. 584, 27. A wyrste, 678, 40. *O. Frs.* hand-wirst: *M. H. Ger.* rist, riste *wrist, instep*: *Icel.* rist *instep*: *Dan.* vrist.] v. cneów-wyrste, hand-wyrst (-wrist).

writ, es; *n.* I. *a writing*:—Ðæs ðe ûs leorneras, wordum secgaþ, and writu cýþaþ, Exon. Th. 227, 19; Ph. 425. II. *writ* (as in holy *writ*), *scripture*:—Cwoeð ðió writ *dicit scriptura*, Rtl. 79, 11. Ne writ ðiús (*scripturam hanc*) leornada gié, Mk. Skt. Lind. 12, 10. Ǽfter ðon ðe hâlige writu sprecaþ, Bd. 2, 20; S. 522, 28. Wrioto wîtgana *scripturae prophetarum*, Mt. Kmbl. Lind. 26, 56. Wriotto, 26, 54. Writto, Mk. Skt. Lind. 14, 49. Writta *scripturarum*, Mt. Kmbl. p. 1, 1. Wriottana, Jn. Skt. p. 2, 4. Ða wrioto *scribturas*, Lk. Skt. Lind. 24, 45. [Þe king nom þat writ on hond, Laym. 484. Ase holi writ seið, A. R. 98, 7: Misc. 36, 3. Þatt broþerr þatt tiss Ennglissh writt wrat, Orm. dedic. 331. Þis writ shal henge bi him, Havel. 2486: Gen. and Ex. 1974. *Icel.* rit.] v. ge-, ofer-writ; hreód-writ.

wrîtan; *p.* wrât, *pl.* writon; *pp.* writen *To write.* I. *to cut* a figure on something:—Wrît ðysne circul mid ðînes cnîfes orde on ânum stâne, Lchdm. i. 395, 3. I a. where the figures are letters:—Genim hæslenne sticcan, wrît ðînne naman on, . . . gefylle mid ðý blôde ðone naman, Lchdm. ii. 104, 7. Rǽd sceal mon secgan, rûne wrîtan, Exon. Th. 342, 7; Gn. Ex. 139. Hróðgâr hylt sceawode, on ðæm wæs ôr writen (*or* I?) fyrngewinnes, Beo. Th. 3381; B. 1688. ¶ of the writing on the tables of stone:—On ðê wrât wuldres God gerýno, Andr. Kmbl. 3018; An. 1512. II. *to draw* a figure. v. wrîtere, I:—Nim sume tigelan, and wrît on hiere ða burg Hierusalem *sume tibi laterem, et describes in eo civitatem Jerusalem*, Past. 21; Swt. 161, 3, 10. Wrît ðam horse on ðam heáfde foran Cristes mǽl, and on leoþa gehwylcum ðe ðû ætfeolan mæge, Lchdm. ii. 290, 23. Wrît him Cristes mǽl on ǽlcum lime, 346, 6. Wrît .iii. crucem mid oleum infirmorum, . . . nim ðæt gewrit, wrît crucem mid ofer ðam drence, 350, 9–11. III. *to form letters, to write*:—Mycel yfel dêð se ðe leás wrît, Homl. Th. ii. 2, 23. Hê wrât mid his fingre on ðære eorþan, Jn. Skt. 8, 6, 8. Engel wrât in wâge baswe bôcstafas, Cd. Th. 261, 8; Dan. 723. Geseah hê engles hand in sele wrîtan Sennara wîte. Ðæt gyddedon hæleð, hwæt seó hand write, Cd. Th. 261, 15–21; Dan. 727–9. Weard gesewen swilce ânes mannes hand wrîtende on ðære healle wâge, Homl. Th. ii. 434, 33. IV. *to write* a book, narrative, etc., *to compose, be the author of*:—Ne wêne ǽnig ðæt ic lygewordum leóð somnige, wrîte wóþcræfte, Exon. Th. 234, 30; Ph. 548. Wrîteþ *digerit*, Wrt. Voc. ii. 27, 50. Wrîtat *caraxabimus* (*mentionem*), 85, 33. Wrîtaþ, 18, 61: Hpt. 507, 76. Ðæt cyriclîce stǽr ûres eálondes and ðeóde ic wrât on fîf bêc, Bd. 5, 24; S. 648, 31. Se ðe ðâs bôc wrât, Lchdm. ii. 114, 5. Se ongan godspell ǽrest wordum wrîtan, Andr. Kmbl. 25; An. 13. Sum mæg searolîce wordcwide wrîtan, Exon. Th. 42, 15; Cri. 673. IV a. with preps. *to write* about a subject:—Ða wrîteras and ða ðe hî ymbe writon, Bt. 18, 3; Fox 66, 1. Be ðâm þingum wrîtende ðe ic gehýrde, Homl. Skt. ii. 23 b, 16. IV b. *to write* to a person, *write* with the intention of sending what is written:—Mê geþûhte wrîtan ðê, ðû se sêlusta Theophilus, Lk. Skt. 1, 3. IV c. *to write, state* in a book:—Wrîteþ Eutropius ðæt Constantinus wǽre on Breotene âcenned, Bd. 1, 8; S. 479, 31. Ptolomeas wrât ealles ðises middangeardes gemet on ânre bêc, Bt. 18, 1; Fox 62, 6. IV d. where many persons assent to a written statement, *to write, get a thing written*:—Hî on heora sinoþe ðus writon be him, Bd. 5, 19; S. 639, 39. Hêr sindan ða naman ðere monna ðe ðis (*the charter*) wreotan and festnedan, Cod. Dip. Kmbl. ii. 47, 10. V. *to convey by charter*:—Wê him wrîtaþ ða mǽdue æt Pirigforda, Cod. Dip. Kmbl. iii. 32, 23. Wê him wrîtaþ ðone hagan his dæg, and twâm ôðrum æfter him . . . Eác wê wrîtaþ him ða circan and ðone circstall and ðone worðig, 52, 5–37. Wê wrîtaþ him ðone croft, 258, 27. [*O. Sax.* wrîtan *to cut, wound; to write*: *O. H. Ger.* rîzan *scindere, scribere*: *Icel.* rîta *to cut, scratch; to write.* Cf. *Goth.* writs *κεραία*.] v. â-, be-, for-, ge-, mis-, under-, ymb-wrîtan; un-writen, wrîtere, wrîtian.

writ-bred, es; *n. A writing-tablet*:—Writbred (*printed* -brec; *but see* gyrdel-bred, i. 288, 75, *and* weax-bred) *pugillarem* (Lk. 1, 63), Wrt. Voc. ii. 74, 36. Ðâ âlýfde se ðâm cnihtum ðæt hî hyne ofslôgen mid heora writbredum and hine ofsticodon mid hira writýrenum, Shrn. 117, 29.

-write, -writenness. v. wæter-write, tô-writenness.

wrîtere, es; *m.* I. *a draughtsman, painter.* v. wrîtan, II:—Lôca hû wlitigne monnan ic hæbbe âtǽfred, swâ unwlitig wrîtere swâ swâ ic eom *pulchrum depinxi hominem pictor foedus*, Past. 65; Swt. 467, 19. II. *a writer, scribe, copyist*:—Wrîtere *scriptor*, gewrit *scriptura*, Wrt. Voc. i. 75, 7: *antigrafus*, 61, 5. Wrýtere *librarius, scriba*, 37, 12. Se wrîtere (*scriptor*), gif hê ne dilegaþ ðæt hê ǽr âwrât, ðeáh hê nǽfre mâ nâuht ne wrîte, ðæt bið ðeáh undilegod, ðæt hê ǽr wrât, Past. 54; Swt. 423, 32. Mîn tunge ys gelîcost ðæs wrîteres feþere ðe hraðost wrît, Ps. Th. 44, 2. Oft gehwâ gesihð fægre stafas âwritene, þonne heraþ hê ðone wrîtere and ða stafas, and nât hwæt hî mǽnaþ, Homl. Th. i. 186, 3. Wrîtera strican *notariorum characteres*, Hpt. Gl. 473, 12. Wrîterum *antiquariis* (antiquariis describentibus, Ald. 79), Wrt. Voc. ii. 88, 16: 5, 40. Siððan mîn on Englisc Ælfrêd kyning âwende worda gehwelc, and mê his wrîterum sende sûð and norð; hêht him swelcra mâ brengan bi ðære bisene, Past. pref.; Swt. 9, 14. Ðe læs ðe wê þurh gýmeleásum wrîterum geleahtrode beón, Homl. Th. ii. 2, 22. Þurh gýmeleáse wrîteras, i. 8, 12: Ælfc. T. Grn. 24, 32. III. *a writer, author*:—Se gyt ôþ tô dæg, cwæþ se wrîtere, lifigende is, Bd. 5, 18; S. 636, 11. Tô geáre, ðâ Brihtferð wrîtere ðis âwrât, Anglia viii. 327, 11. Ða wrîteras and ða ðe hî ymbe writon, Bt. 18, 3; Fox 66, 1. Gebyrede þurh ða heardsǽlþa ðara wrîtera ðæt hî for heora slǽwþe forlêton unwriten ðara monna þeáwas and hiora dǽda, ðe foremǽroste wǽron, Fox 64, 33. IV. *a scribe* in the Biblical sense:—Esdras se wrîtere âwrât âne bôc, Ælfc. T. Grn. 10, 37. Rihtwîsnyss ðæra wrîtera (*scribarum*), Mt. Kmbl. 5, 20. Folces wrîteras *scribas populi*, 2, 4. v. eald-, ge-, not-, stæf-, stǽr-, tîd-, un-, wyrd-wrîtere.

wriþa, an; *m.* I. *a band, collar*:—Þeówan yfelwillendum wriþa and fôtcopsas *seruo maliuolo tortura et compedes*, Scint. 190, 6. Mid wriþan treówenum gewriþen grundweall getimbrunge nâ byþ tôslopen *loramento ligneo conligatum fundamentum aedificii non dissoluitur*, 200, 8. Smeáþancollîce wriþan ł cnottan cræftelîcum *sertaque mystica*, Germ. 389, 28. Hî becnytton ânne wriþan eall onbûtan his swuran, Homl. Skt. i. 23, 608. II. *a ring*:—Ic gesleá ǽnne wriðan on his nosu *ponam circulum in naribus tuis* (2 Kings 19, 28), Homl. Th. i. 568, 33. Ic geseah in healle hring gyldenne (*a cup*) men sceáwian, . . . friþospêde bæd God gǽste sînum se ðe wende wriþan, Exon. Th. 440, 19; Rä. 60, 5. v. beáh-, heals- (*where misprinted* -wiþa) wriþa; wrîþan.

wrîþan; *p.* wrâþ, *pl.* wriþon; *pp.* wriþen. I. *to twist, give a curved form to*:—Ic wrîðe *torqueo*, Ælfc. Gr. 26, 3; Zup. 155, 14. Wriðene (cf. wriþa, II) wælhlencan, Elen. Kmbl. 47; El. 24. II. *to bind up, wrap round, bandage*:—Hê wrâð (*alligavit*) his wunda, Lk. Skt. 10, 34. Ða ðe forbrocene wǽron, ða gê ne wriþon *quae fractae erant, eas non ligavistis*, L. Ecg. P. iii. 16; Th. ii. 202, 26. Ðâ wǽron monige ðe his mǽg wriðon, Beo. Th. 5957; B. 2982. Ðâ bebeád hê him ðæt hê ða tôlýsdan geþeódnesse mînre heáfudwunde gesette and wriþe *dissolutam mihi emicranii juncturam componere atque alligare jussit*, Bd. 5, 6; S. 620, 14. Hê wearð wriþen ofer wunda, Exon. Th. 435, 27; Rä. 54, 7. III. *to bind* one thing to another:—Nim ða sylfan wyrt, lege on ðone naflan, and wrîð ðǽrtô swýðe fæste, Lchdm. i. 82, 25. IV. *to bind, fetter*:—Oft wîf hine (*a dog*) wrîð, Exon. Th. 434, 3; Rä. 51, 5. Ic hine heardan clammum wrîþan þôhte, Beo. Th. 1933; B. 964. [Of one wrase of þornes he wryþen hym one crune, Misc. 48, 383. Wrythyn *idem quod* wrestyn *torqueo*, wrythyn or wrethyn *tortus, torsus*, Prompt. Parv. 534. Me dide cnotted strenges abuton here hæued and uurythen to ð it gæde to þe hærnes, Chr. 1137; Erl. 262, 6.

ȝe mote uaste heom wriđen mid strongen sæilrapen, Laym. 17394. *O. H. Ger.* gi-rīdan *contorquere*: *Icel.* rīða *to twist, knit, wind.*] v. ā-, be-, ge-, ofer- (Lchdm. ii. 130, 10), tō-, un-wrīþan.

wrīþan *to flourish.* v. wrīdan.

wriþels *a bandage*:—Seaxclāđ ođđe wrǣd, wriđels *fascia*, Wrt. Voc. ii. 39, 69.

wriþen-hilt; *adj. Having a hilt bound round* ['In some specimens of swords the handles are wound round with gold wire,' Worsaae's Primeval Antiquities, p. 29]:—Đæt sweord, īrena cyst, wreoþenhilt and wyrmfāh, Beo. Th. 3400; B. 1698.

wrīþian, wrīþung. v. wrīdian, on-wrīþung.

writ-hreód (?), es; *n. A reed for writing*:—Hreódwrit (writhreód? cf. writ-īren) *calamus scribae*, Ps. Spl. C. 44, 2.

wrītian; *p.* ode. I. *to draw* a figure. v. wrītan, II:—Đonne wercaþ hió of weaxe, wrītiaþ Fēnix, mētaþ Fēnix *they make waxen images of the Phenix, and drawings and paintings*, Engl. Stud. viii. 478, 49. II. *to write, compose.* v. wrītan, IV a:—Wrītigaþ and singaþ onbūtan him ǣlc on his wīsan, Engl. Stud. viii. 478, 42. [(*later*) *Icel.* rita; *p.* ritaði.]

wrīting, e; *f. Writing*:—Wrītinge fyđer *calamus scribae*, Ps. Spl. 44, 2. v. on-wrīting.

wrīting-feþer, e; *f. A pen*:—Wrītingfeþere *calamus*, Ps. Spl. T. 44, 2.

writ-īren, es; *n. A style, an iron implement for writing*:—Hī hyne ofsticodon mid hira writȳrenum, Shrn. 117, 30.

writ-seax, es; *n. A pen*:—Miđ pinn ł writtseax *calamo*, Mt. Kmbl. p. 2, 17.

wrixend-līc; *adj. Mutual*, Greg. Dial. 2, 7.

wrixendlīce; *adv. In turn, one after the other*:—Hī wrixendlīce (*vicissim*) hine bǣdon, Bd. 4, 24; S. 598, 42. Đa wrixendlīce (*vicissim*) on twā halfe gesewene wǣron, swā swā mid unmǣtnesse miceles stormes worpene beón, 5, 12; S. 627, 39. Wrixendlīce *singillatim*, Ps. Surt. 32, 15.

wrixl, e; *f.* I. *change, alteration, vicissitude*:—Đæt is wrælīc wrixl in wera līfe, đætte moncynnes Scyppend onfēng æt fǣmnan flǣsc, and sió weres friga wiht ne cūþe, Exon. Th. 26, 12; Cri. 416. God, đū đe gimetgaþ giscæfta wrixla (*rerum vices*), Rtl. 164, 12. II. where there is alternation, *alternation, exchange*:—Mid đȳ hī đysse ungesǣligan wrixle (*hac infelici vicissitudine*, i. e. the passing from heat to cold and vice versa) đrǣste wǣron, Bd. 5, 12; S. 628, 2. III. where there is reciprocal action, *interchange*:—Đǣr wæs heard plega, wælgāra wrixl, Cd. Th. 120, 5; Gen. 1990. IV. where one thing takes the place of another, *place, stead*:—Đonne sculon hié gadrian ōđer ierfe on đæs wrixle (wriexle, Hatt. MS.) đe hē ǣr sealdon, Past. 45; Swt. 340, 18. Hæfdon hī mid him gehālgode tabulan on wīgbedes wrixle *habentes secum tabulam altaris vice dedicatam*, Bd. 5, 10; S. 624, 34. V. *a loan*:—Borge ođđe wrixle *mutuo*, Wrt. Voc. ii. 56, 5. Wrixle *mutuum* (Lk. 6, 34), 74, 43. VI. *what is given in return, return, requital*:—Hē forgeald wyrsan wrixle wælhlem đone; ... hē him on heáfde helm gescær, Beo. Th. 5930; B. 2969. v. ge-wrixl.

wrixlan, wrixlian; *p.* ede. I. *to change, vary, alter*:—Is him đæt heáfod hindan grēne, wrǣtlīce wrixleþ wurman geblonden (*the head shews shifting colours*), Exon. Th. 218, 13; Ph. 294. I a. with dat. of that in which change is made:—Ic þurh mūþ sprece mongum reordum, wrencum singe, wrixle geneahhe heáfodwōþe (*I change my voice*; cf. the Latin riddle: Vox mea diversis variatur pulcra figuris), Exon. Th. 390, 16; Rä. 9, 2. Se fugel swinsaþ and singeþ swegle tōgeánes ... wrixleþ wōđcræfte beorhtan reorde *incipit illa sacri modulamina fundere cantus, et mira lucem voce ciere novam*, 206, 15; Ph. 127. Bleóm wrixleþ *changes colour*, Elen. Kmbl. 1515; El. 759. II. *to change, alternate*:—Đās feówer tīman (*the seasons*) wrixliaþ wyđ mancynne, Anglia viii. 312, 34. Wrixliende *alterna*, Wrt. Voc. ii. 9, 56. Đa wrixliende on twā halfe gesewene wǣron worpene beón *vicissim hinc inde videbantur jactari*, Bd. 5, 12; S. 627, 39 note. III. of reciprocal, mutual action, *to exchange, deal*:—Hē cwæđ, đæt him tō micel ǣwisce wǣre đæt hē swā emnlīce wrixleden (*that they should deal on equal terms*; the terms being that each side should return the captives, and then peace be maintained by each side), Ors. 4, 6; Swt. 178, 16. Wrixlindum *reciprocis*, uurixlende *reciprocatu*, Wrt. Voc. ii. 119, 5, 13. III a. with dat. of what is exchanged, fig. of conversation, intercourse. v. IV a:—Wīgsmiþas sittaþ æt symble, wordum wrixlaþ, Exon. Th. 314, 18; Mōd. 16. Đǣr hæleđas wrixlaþ sprǣce, Runic pm. Kmbl. 343, 8; Rūn. 19. Hȳ bēnan synt, đæt hié wiđ đē mōton wordum wrixlan *they beg that they may have interchange of words with thee*, Beo. Th. 737; B. 366: Exon. Th. 373, 29; Seel. 117. Wrixlian, Soul Kmbl. 226. Gleáwe men sceolon gieddum wrixlan, Exon. Th. 333, 14; Gn. Ex. 4. IV. *to lend*:—Wrixlan *mutuare*, Wrt. Voc. ii. 56, 10. Wrislan, 72, 18. IV a. with dat. of what is lent, fig. of words, *to speak*:—Secg eft ongan sīđ Beówulfes snyttrum styrian, ... wordum wrixlan, Beo. Th. 1752; B. 874. Lyt ic wēnde đæt ic ǣfre sceolde mūđleás sprecan, wordum wrixlan, Exon. Th. 472, 2; Rä. 61, 10. [Say me, ... what wrixlit þi wit & þi wille chaunget, Destr. Tr. 2061. Þai hade laisure þere likyng to say, and wrixle þere wit & þere wille shewe, 3120.] v. be- (Ps. Th. 43, 14), ge-wrixlan(-ian).

wrixlung, e; *f.* I. *change, alternation.* v. wrixlan, II. [Bi his clođes wrixlunge, nu red, nu hwit, him on hokerunge, O. E. Homl. i. 207, 3.] II. *a loan.* v. wrixlan, IV:—Wrixlung *mutuum*, Wrt. Voc. i. 21, 3: 58, 60. v. ge-wrixlung.

wrocen, e; *f.?*:—Of đam byrcelse on wrocene; andlang wrocene in Uppinghǣma gemǣre, Cod. Dip. Kmbl. iii. 124, 13. Be eástan wrocena stybbe; đæt swā tō wrocena stybbe, v. 297, 26.

wrōht, e; *f.*: es; *m.* I. *accusation*:—Wrōht *accusatio* (*ex-*, MS.), Wrt. Voc. ii. 146, 15. Wrōhte *insimulatio*, 44, 74. *Hic susurro* đes rūnere ođđe wrōht, Ælfc. Gr. 36; Zup. 217, 3. Leásere wrōhte *strophosae accusationis*, Hpt. Gl. 505, 55. Wrōhte *insimulatione, accusatione*, 517, 55. Uurōctae, uurōchtae, Txts. 70, 524. Mid micelre wrōhte hine wrēgende, Homl. Th. ii. 250, 10. Hwylce wrōhte (*accusationem*) bringe gē ongeán đysne man? Jn. Skt. 18, 29. Mid leásum wrōhtum beswicene *falsis criminationibus seducti*, Scint. 136, 11. Đa werian gāstas wrōhta onsægdon *sequuntur accusationes malignorum spirituum*, Bd. 3, 19; S. 548, 35. II. *a false accusation, slander, calumny.* v. wrōht-bora, II:—Heó (*the Egyptians*) his (*Joseph's*) mǣgwinum morđor fremedon, wrōht berēnedon (cf. Ex. 1, 9–11), ... mānum treówum woldon hié đæt feorhleán fācne gyldan, Cd. Th. 187, 6; Exod. 147. Huscworde ongan þurh inwitþanc ealdorsacerd herme hyspan, wrōht webbode; hē on gewitte oncneów, đæt wē sōđfæstes swađe folgodon, Andr. Kmbl. 1343; An. 672. Gē inwitþancum wrōht webbedon, Elen. Kmbl. 617; El. 309. Ne beó nǣnig man bregda tō full, ne inwit tō leóf, ne wrōhtas tō webgenne, ne searo tō rēnigenne, Blickl. Homl. 109, 29. III. *what is an occasion for accusation, fault, crime, offence*:—Wæg heora wrōht biþ him *via illorum scandalum ipsis*, Ps. Spl. T. 48, 13. Wrōhtes wyrhtan (*the devil*), fyrnsynna fruman, Exon. Th. 263, 7; Jul. 346. Hē gewrēgde his brōđru tō hira fæder đære mǣstan wrōhte *accusavit fratres suos apud patrem crimine*, Gen. 37, 2. Gangende on eallum his bebodum būtan wrōhte (*sine quaerela*), Lk. Skt. 1, 6. Đone wrōht *abominationem*, Mk. Skt. Lind. Rush. 13, 14. Đū wrōhte onstealdest, Cd. Th. 56, 12; Gen. 911: 57, 22; Gen. 932. Hwæt sceal ic mā rīman yfel endeleás? Ic eall gebær wrāþe wrōhtas geond werþeóde, đa đe gewurdon from fruman worulde, Exon. Th. 272, 30; Jul. 507. IV. *a quarrel, strife*:—Weard micel ungeþwǣrnes, ... swā nān mon nyste hwonon sió wrōht com, Ors. 6, 4; Swt. 260, 21. Wǣron đā gesōme đa đe swegl būan, wrōht wæs āsprungen, Cd. Th. 6, 4; Gen. 83: 114, 12; Gen. 1903. Wæs wrōht gemǣne, herenīđ hearda, Beo. Th. 4938; B. 2473: 5819; B. 2913: 4564; B. 2287: Exon. Th. 125, 30; Gū. 362. Tō đæm sǣde đære wrōhte *ad seminanda jurgia*, Past. 47; Swt. 358, 3. Biđ đæt deófol on wrōhte onlīcnisse; ... biđ se Pater Noster on sibbe onlīcnisse, Salm. Kmbl. p. 146, 20. Đū worhtest wrōhte betwuh đē and đīnre mōdor suna ōđrum *adversus filium matris tuae ponebas scandalum*, Ps. Th. 49, 21. Sume ic geteáh tō geflite, ... ic him byrlade wrōht of wēge, Exon. Th. 271, 24; Jul. 487. Hī wrōht āhōfan, heardne heresīþ, 317, 2; Mōd. 59. Hē in wuldre wrōhte onstalde, Cd. Th. 287, 19; Sat. 369. Mars macode ǣfre gewinn and wrōhte, Wulfst. 106, 25. Đa đe wrōhte sāwaþ *seminantes jurgia*, Past. 47; Swt. 357, 14, 22. V. *cause of complaint, injury, hurt*:—Næs hyra wlite gewemmed, ne nǣnig wrōht on hrægle, Cd. Th. 243, 17; Dan. 437. Ne biđ him on đām wīcum wiht tō sorge, wrōht ne wēþel ne gewindagas, Exon. Th. 238, 30; Ph. 612. Rǣhton wīde geond werþeóda wrōhtes telgan, hrinon hearmtānas hearde drihta bearnum, Cd. Th. 61, 3; Gen. 991. Đū woldest lāđlīce þurh đæt wīf on mē wrōhte ālecgean, ormǣte yfel, 162, 21; Gen. 2684. [*O. Sax.* wrōht *strife.* Cf. *Goth.* wrōhs *accusation*: *Icel.* rōg *slander*; poet. *strife.*]

wrōht-berend, es; *m. An accuser*:—Wrōhtberend *excussor, accusator*, Wrt. Voc. ii. 146, 14. Bearn wrōhtberendra (wōrhtberendra, Ps. Lamb.) *filii excussorum*, Ps. Spl. M. 126, 5.

wrōht-bora, an; *m.* I. *an accuser, informer.* v. wrōht, I:—Wrōhtbora *delator*, Wrt. Voc. i. 49, 19. Đonne wrōhtbora (*the devil*) in folc Godes forđ onsendeþ biterne strǣl, Exon. Th. 47, 31; Cri. 763. II. *one who brings false accusations, a malicious person.* v. wrōht, II:—Wrōhtbora *factiosa* (cf. đa fǣcnan *factiosam*, 77, 46), *falsa*, Wrt. Voc. ii. 146, 68. [Cf. *Icel.* rōg-beri *a slanderer.*]

wrōht-dropa, an; *m. A drop which brings strife* (v. wrōht, IV) or *crime* (v. wrōht, III):—Weard fǣhþo fyra cynne, siþþan swealg eorđe Abeles blōde, ... of đam wrōhtdropan wīde gesprungon, micel mān (mon, MS.) ældum, monegum þeódum bealoblonden nīþ, Exon. Th. 345, 26; Gn. Ex. 196.

wrōht-georn; *adj. Quarrelsome, contentious, eager for strife.* v. wrōht, IV:—On ōđre wīsan sint tō monianne đa wrōhtgeornan, on ōđre đa gesibsuman. ... Hē be đæm wrōhtgeornan secgean wolde *quomodo admonendi qui jurgia serunt, et pacifici. ... Quem seminantem jurgia dicere voluit*, Past. 47; Swt. 357, 12, 23. [Cf. *Icel.* rōg-girni *a disposition to slander.*]

wrōht-getīme, es; *n. A series of crimes* (? Cf. teám, getȳme):—

Hæfdon hié wrôhtgetême wiđ God gesomnod *they had heaped up crimes against God,* Cd. Th. 3, 34; Gen. 45.

wrôht-hangra (?):—On wrôhthangran; of wrôhthangran, Cod. Dip. Kmbl. vi. 120, 12.

wrohtian (?):—Hē sǣ bedrāf, đǣr đe heó wrohtaþ (frohtaþ = forhtaþ? *the Latin has:* Mare formidat, 210, 90) dæges and nihtes, Homl. Ass. 173, 105.

wrôht-lāc, es; *n.* (?) *Calumny, slander:*—Unrihtlīce mǣst ǣlc ōþerne æftan heáweþ mid scandlīcan onscytan and mid wrôhtlācan, Wulfst. 160, 5 note.

wrôht-sāwere, es; *m. A sower of strife:*—Gehīren đa wrôhtsāweras (*jurgiorum seminatores*) hwæt āwriten is on đæm godspelle: 'Eádige beóđ đa gesibsuman,' Past. 47; Swt. 359, 9, 18.

wrôht-scipe, es; *m. Crime:*—Hī sôhton weras tō weorce (*the building of Babel*) and tō wrôhtscipe, Cd. Th. 100, 31; Gen. 1672.

wrôht-smiþ, es; *m. A worker of crime, a criminal:*—Wrôhtsmiđas (*evil spirits*), Exon. Th. 156, 19; Gū. 877. Đæt đū mē ne gescyrige mid scyldhetum, werigum wrôhtsmiđum (*the cannibal Mermedonians*), on đone wyrrestan deáđ ofer eorđan, Andr. Kmbl. 171; An. 86.

wrôht-spitol; *adj. Slanderous:*—Wrôhtspitel *susurio,* Txts. 99, 1943.

wrôht-stafas; *pl. m. Accusations:*—Ic eom fāh and freóndleás, gēn ic findan ne can þurh wrôhtstafas wiđercyr wiđ đam *I am proscribed and friendless; still I can by accusations* (cf. vv. 1813–1830, where the devil complains of unfair treatment (nis đæt fæger siđ)) *devise no resistance to my fate;* i.e. *complaints are useless,* Elen. Kmbl. 1848; El. 926.

wrong. v. wrang.

wrôt *a snout, trunk:*—Wrôt *bruncus* (in a list 'de suibus'), Wrt. Voc. i. 286, 54: ii. 11, 47: 102, 23: 127, 27. Ylpes bile *vel* wrôt *promuscida,* i. 22, 45. [Mi drivil druith, and mi wrot wet, Rel. Ant. ii. 210, 29.]

wrôtan; *p.* wreót *To turn up with the snout, root up:*—Wrôtu *subigo,* Wrt. Voc. ii. 121, 64. Ic wrôte *subigo,* Ælfc. Gr. 28, 6; Zup. 176, 12. Hine ūtan of wuda eoferas wrôtaþ *exterminavit eam* (*vineam*) *aper de sylva,* Ps. Th. 79, 13. Swīn on bôcwuda wrôtende, Exon. Th. 428, 12; Rä. 41, 107. [Swin þe uulieđ and wroteđ and sneuieđ, O. E. Homl. ii. 37, 25. Þat wilde swin þat wroteđ ȝeond þan grouen, Laym. 469. Schullen wormes wroten (*verrunt*) on the skin, Rel. Ant. ii. 216, 18. As a sowe wroteth in everich ordure, Chauc. Pers. T. A were . . . ȝowre walles with to wrote, Min. 19, 32. Wrotyñ as swyne *verror,* Prompt. Parv. 534. *O. H. Ger.* ruozan (*used of the action of the plough*): *Icel.* rôta *to root up,* as swine.]

wude-. v. wudu-.

wudere, wudi[g]ere, es; *m. A bearer of wood:*—Wuderas *calones* (the passage is: Ejusdem militiae calones et clientes cum lixarum coetibus ad inferiorem gradum pertinentes, Ald. 13. In another gloss on the same passage is the note: Calones sunt qui ligna militibus portant, Hpt. Gl. 427, 4), Wrt. Voc. ii. 76, 72: 17, 73. Wudu *silva,* wudieras *calones,* i. 33, 55. Wudigeras, 39, 54. v. wudian.

wuderian. v. wederian.

wudian; *p.* ode *To cut wood:*—Gelamp on Môyses dagum đæt Môyses fôr þurh ānne wudu mid his werode. Đā gesāwan hié ǣnne ceorl, hwǣr hē stôd and wudede him, Wulfst. 220, 11, 15. Hē him bebeád đæt hī bǣron wæter tō đæs folces neóde and wudedon him simble *decrevit eos esse in ministerio cuncti populi, caedentes ligna et aquas comportantes,* Jos. 9, 27. Me mæcg on sumera wudian, Anglia ix. 261, 11. v. wudere, wudung.

wudi[g]ere, wudi[g]ung. v. wudere, wudung.

wudig; *adj. Woody, full of woods* or *trees:*—Waldend scôp wudige môras, Exon. Th. 193, 12; Az. 120.

wudiht; *adj. Full of woods* or *trees:*—Wudihtes *silvosi,* Germ. 402, 72.

wudu (-o), widu, wiodu; *gen.* wuda, wudes; *dat.* wuda, wudu (-o), wyda; *acc.* wudu, wuda; *pl.* wuda, wudas; *m.* I. *wood,* (1) *the substance of growing trees:*—Hū ne miht đū gesión đæt ǣlc wyrt and ǣlc wudu (-a, *v. l.*) (*cum herbas atque arbores intuearis*), wile weaxan on đæm lande sēlost, đe him betst gerīst. . . . Sumra wyrta ođđe sumes wuda eard biþ on dūnum. . . . Nim swā wudu (-a, *v. l.*) swā wyrt, of đære stôwe đe his eard biþ on tō weaxanne, and sette on uncynde stôwe him, đonne ne gegrēwþ hit đǣr nāuht, for đam ǣlces landes gecynd is, đæt hit him gelīce wyrta and gelīcne wudu tȳdrige, Bt. 34, 10; Fox 148, 19–29. Đæt treów wæs on wynne, wudu weaxende, Exon. Th. 435, 19; Rä. 54, 3. (1 a) *a tree:*—Wudu môt him weaxan, tānum lǣdan, Exon. Th. 458, 21; Hy. 4, 104. Þeáh đū hwilcne bôh bȳge wiđ eorđan, hē biđ upweardes, swā đū ānforlǣtest widu on willan, Met. 13, 55. Hē đās foldan āsiów sǣda monegum wuda and wyrta (cf. treówa and wyrta, Bt. 33, 4; Fox 132, 27), 20, 251. Smicere on gearwum, wudum and wyrtum cymeþ wlitig scrīþan on tūn Maius, Menol. Fox 151; Men. 77. (2) (*hewn*) *wood, the material obtained from trees:*—Drīge wudu *ligna,* Wrt. Voc. i. 80, 31. Ic eom wyrslīcre đonne đes wudu fūla, Exon. Th. 424, 33; Rä. 41, 48. Hēr ys wudu (*ligna*) and fȳr, Gen. 22, 7. Be wuda onfenge būtan leáfe, L. In. 44; Th. i. 130, 1. Wuda and wætres nyttaþ, đonne him biþ wīc ālȳfed, Exon. Th. 340, 12; Gen. Ex. 110. .C. fōđra uuido, Cod. Dip. B. i. 344, 11. Hē hī bewæg mid wuda ūtan and forbernde mid fȳre, Bt. 39, 4; Fox 216, 25. Ic on wuda stonde, Exon. Th. 496, 14; Rä. 85, 14. Hēt ic, of đæm wudo đe đǣr gefylled wæs, đæt mon fȳr onǣlde, Nar. 12, 28. Hē hēt Isaac beran đone wudu (*ligna*), Gen. 22, 6: Cd. Th. 174, 31; Gen. 2886: 231, 10; Dan. 245. Wē heáwaþ đone wudu *ligna succidimus,* Past. 21; Swt. 167, 6. Se đe đone wuda (wudu, Cott. MSS.) hiéwđ *qui ligna percutit,* 167, 15. (2 a) *wood* which forms something, *something made of wood:*—Wudu (*a ship*) wundenheals, Beo. Th. 601; B. 298: Exon. Th. 384, 8; Rä. 4, 24. Secgan hū se wudu (*a sheathe*) hātte, 437, 32; Rä. 56, 16: (*a loom*), 438, 10; Rä. 57, 5. Līþendum wuda (*a ship*), 392, 9; Rä. 11, 5. Wudu bundenne, Beo. Th. 438; B. 216: 3842; B. 1919. Lǣtaþ hildebord hēr onbīdan, wudu (*spears*), wælsceaftas, 801; B. 398. Wido (*part of a loom*), Exon. Th. 438, 4; Rä. 57, 2. ¶ used of the cross. Cf. beám, treów:—Ongan sprecan wudu sēlesta: 'Ic wæs āheáwen holtes on ende,' Rood Kmbl. 54; Kr. 27. II. *wood, forest:*—Wudu *silva,* Wrt. Voc. i. 33, 55. (1) in a generic or collective sense, *wood, the wood, woods:*—Hē mihte hearpian đæt se wudu (-a, *v. l.*) wagode and đa stanas hī styredon, Bt. 35, 6; Fox 166, 32. Wudu (cf. se weald, Bt. 25; Fox 88, 20) eallum oncwyđ, Met. 13, 50. Ne reccaþ hī đara metta, gif hī đæs wuda benugon, Bt. 25; Fox 88, 19. Wildeór wuda *bestiae sylvae,* Ps. Spl. 103, 21. On feldum wudes *in campis sylvae,* 131, 6. Wæstmas wudes (cf. treówa, Bt. 15; Fox 48, 9) and wyrta, Met. 8, 20. Eofor of wuda *aper de sylva,* Ps. Spl. Th. 79, 14: Ps. Th. 67, 27. Hī đearfendum līfe on wuda (*in silvis*) and on heán clifum wunedon, Bd. 1, 15; S. 484, 8. Gif hī on đam wuda weorþaþ, Bt. 25; Fox 88, 16. Hē teáh tō wuda, 35, 6; Fox 168, 7: Met. 19, 5, 18: Coll. Monast. Th. 26, 3. Stōw mid wuda (*silvis*) ymbseald, Bd. 4, 13; S. 582, 22. Đa myneteras đe inne wuda wyrcaþ, L. Eth. iii. 16; Th. i. 298, 13. On wudu *in sylva,* Ps. Th. 73, 5: *saltu,* Wrt. Voc. ii. 94, 35. Greát beám on wyda (wuda, *v. l.*), Bt. 38, 2; Fox 198, 9. Nōht elles būton đa wēstan feldas and wudu and dūna, Nar. 20, 10. Fæsten Crēca, wudu Egipta, Salm. Kmbl. 387; Sal. 193: Exon. Th. 381, 9; Rä. 2, 8; Ps. Th. 82, 10. Fȳr đe bærnđ wuda (*sylvam*), Ps. Spl. 82, 13. (2) *a wood:*—Hē hī lǣdan hī on đone wudu; se wæs genemned *silua nigra,* se swearta wudu, Shrn. 89, 10: Exon. Th. 200, 8; Ph. 37: Beo. Th. 2732; B. 1364. Be wuda bærnette. Gif mon ōđres wudu bærneþ oþþe heáweþ, L. In. 12; Th. i. 70, 3. Of đæs wuda midle, Exon. Th. 202, 6; Ph. 65. Anlanges wudes, Cod. Dip. Kmbl. iii. 172, 33. Đis is đæs wudes gemǣre . . . tō đæs wudes efese, 389, 22, 27. Wudæs, vi. 33, 31. Būtan đem wioda, ii. 66, 23: Cod. Dip. B. ii. 202, 9. Wiada, Cod. Dip. Kmbl. ii. 64, 29. Wuda, iii. 390, 4. Đonne mon beám on wuda forbærne. . . . Gif mon āfelle on wuda wel monega treówa, L. In. 43; Th. i. 128, 17, 20. Hē rǣsde intō đam wudu, Homl. Skt. ii. 30, 31. Of đam wudu, Cod. Dip. Kmbl. iii. 390, 1. Wæs hē eall mid wudu (*silva*) beweaxen, Nar. 12, 8. Of đæm wudo, 21, 19. Hēt ic ceorfan đa bearwas and đone wudu fyllan *jubeo cedi nemus,* 12, 19. On þicne wudu, Bt. 35, 5; Fox 164, 13. Gif feorcund man būtan wege geond wudu gonge, L. In. 20; Th. i. 116, 1: Byrht. Th. 137, 29; By. 193: Beo. Th. 2836; B. 1416. Đurh đane wioda, Cod. Dip. B. ii. 202, 10. On đone wuda; ofer đone wuda, Cod. Dip. Kmbl. v. 317, 29. Hē hearpode đæt đa wudas bifodon, and đa eá stōdon *silvas currere mobiles, amnes stare coëgerat,* Bt. 35, 6; Fox 168, 8. Ealra wuda wildeór *omnes ferae silvarum,* Ps. Th. Spl. Surt. 49, 11. Ealle treówa wuda *omnia ligna sylvarum,* Ps. Spl. Surt. 95, 12. On wudum *in sylvis,* Coll. Monast. Th. 22, 23. Betwyx đām twām wudan, Cod. Dip. Kmbl. vi. 218, 25. Geond wudas and feldas, Homl. Th. ii. 188, 14. Wuda *silvas,* Ps. Surt. 82, 15. ¶ in several instances of compounds with *wudu* it may be rendered by *wild;* e.g. wudu-bucca, -cerfille, -hunig, -rose. [*O. H. Ger.* witu *lignum: Icel.* viđr *wood; a tree; a wood.*] v. āc-, bǣl-, bōc-, bord-, brēmber-, brim-, camp-, flōd-, furh-, gamen-, gār-, heal-, holm-, holt-, mægen-, sǣ-, sund-, þræc-wudu. The word occurs in many local names, v. Cod. Dip. Kmbl. vi. Index.

wudu-ælfen[n], -elfen[n], e; *f. A wood-elf, wood-nymph:*—Wuduelfen *dryades,* Wrt. Voc. i. 60, 15. Wuduælfenne *oreades,* ii. 65, 44.

wudu-æppel, es; *n. A wild apple, crab:*—Gesodene wuduæpla, Lchdm. ii. 190, 14.

wudu-bǣre; *adj. Woody;* silvestris:—Wudebǣre gerda *vimina silvestria,* Hpt. Gl. 449, 7.

wudu-bærnet[t], es; *n. Burning trees in a wood:*—Be wudubærnette. Đonne mon beám on wuda forbærne, L. In. 43; Th. i. 128, 16.

wudu-bāt, es; *m. A wooden ship:*—Hwā mē on wudubāte ferede ofer flōdas, Andr. Kmbl. 1810; An. 907.

wudu-beám, es; *m. A forest tree:*—Wudubeám wlitig, wyrtum fæst, Cd. Th. 247, 18; Dan. 499. Wyrtrumađ đæs wudubeámes, 248, 21; Dan. 516: Exon. Th. 328, 27; Vy. 24. Đa wudubeámas wagedon and swēgdon, Dōm. L. 7. Wudubeáma wlite, Exon. Th. 202, 25; Ph.

75. Wudubeáma helm, 496, 2; Rä. 85, 8. Wudubeámum, 277, 6; Jul. 576.

wudu-bearu (-o), wes; *m. A grove of trees, a wood:*—Wudubearwes weard (*the Phenix*), Exon. Th. 208, 7; Ph. 152. On wudubearwe (cf. on holtwuda, l. 16), 209, 11; Ph. 169. Ðæt treów, ðe wexeþ on ðam wudubearwe, Wulfst. 262, 6. Wǽrun wudubearwas on wyndagum *exultabunt omnia ligna sylvarum*, Ps. Th. 95, 12: Exon. Th. 191, 5; Az. 83. On feldum, and on mǽdum, and on wudubearwum, and on sealtum merscum, Cod. Dip. Kmbl. iii. 350, 7. Ða wudubearwas *nemora*, Nar. 22, 15. Drihten sende ceferas, ða âdilegedan ealle wudebeorwas, Wulfst. 221, 17.

wudu-bend *wood-bine:*—Wudubend. Genim ðysse wyrte wyrttruman ðe man *capparis* and ôþrum naman wudubend hâtaþ, Lchdm. i. 302, 11. Wuduhunig ðæt wæxeþ on wudebendum, Mk. Skt. Rush. 1, 6. v. wudu-bind, *and* cf. wiþo-bend.

wudu-bil[l], es; *n. A wood-bill:*—Wudubil (uuidu-) *falcis*, Txts. 63, 834: *falcastrum*, 836: Wrt. Voc. ii. 35, 1, 5. Uudubil *falcastrum, ferramentum curvum a similitudine falcis vocatum*, 146, 82.

wudu-bind, es; *m.*: -binde, an; *f.*: -bindele, an; *f. Woodbine:*—Uuidubindae *volvola, herba similis hederae, quae vitibus et frugibus circumdari solet*, Txts. 104, 1059: *viburna*, 106, 1082. Wudubind *hedera nigra*, Wrt. Voc. ii. 43, 51. Wudebinde, i. 32, 22. Weodubinde *viticella*, 69, 10. Uudubinde, uudubindlae, uuidubindlae *involuco*, Txts. 71, 1116. Wudubindes leáf, Lchdm. ii. 34, 26: 306, 24: 326, 11. Wudubindan leáf, iii. 14, 2: 30, 8. Wuduhunig ðæt wæxes on wudubinde, Mk. Skt. Lind. i. 6. [*Mater silva* chevefoil, wudebinde, Wrt. Voc. i. 140, 19. *Caprifolium* wodebinde, Wülck. Gl. 570, 31. Woodebynde *caprifolium, viticella*, Prompt. Parv. 531.] v. wudu-bend, *and* cf. wiþo-winde.

wudu-binde, an; *f. A bundle of wood:*—Uuidubinde *lignarium* (lignarium *bois à brûler*, Migne), Txts. 35, 18.

wudu-blêd, e; *f. A forest fruit:*—Steám swêttra swæcca gehwylcum, wyrta blôstmum and wudublêdum, Exon. Th. 358, 18; Pa. 47. Hê somnaþ wyrta wynsume and wudublêda *colligit succos et odores divite silva*, 211, 8; Ph. 194.

wudu-bora (?), an; *m. One who carries wood for fuel:*—Wudubior (-bora?) *calo militum*, Hpt. Gl. 427, 7. v. wudere.

wudu-bucca, an; *m. A wild goat:*—Firginbucca, ðæt ys wudubucca, Lchdm. i. 348, 2. Wudubuccan gealla, 348, 6. v. wudu-gât.

wudu-cerfille, an; *f. Wild chervil:*—Wuducerfille *brassica*, Wrt. Voc. i. 67, 4. Wuducerefille *brassica sylvatica*, 68, 74. Wuducerfille *pastinace*, 19. Wuducarfille *speragus*, 46. Wuduceruille. Genim ðysse wyrte wyrttruman ðe man *sparagi agrestis*, and ôðrum naman wuducerfillu nemneþ, Lchdm. i. 188, 19–22. Nim cerfillan and wuducerfillan, ii. 152, 15: 268, 14. v. wudu-fille.

wudu-cocc, es; *m. A woodcock:*—Wudecocc *aceta*, Wrt. Voc. i. 29, 52. Wuducoc *acega*, 280, 3. Wudecocc, Hpt. 33, 240, 28. [In later English the word translates several Latin words: *castrimargus*, Wülck. Gl. 571, 17: 625, 2: 701, 38: 762, 2: *gallus sylvestris*, 625, 3: *fornix*, 639, 36: *orna*, 639, 37: *castrimargus, gallus sylvestris*, Prompt. Parv. 531.]

wudu-croft, es; *m. A croft with trees on it* (?):—On wudecrofte; of ðam crofte, Cod. Dip. Kmbl. iii. 376, 7.

wudu-culfre, an; *f. A wood-pigeon:*—Wuduculfre *palumba*, Wrt. Voc. i. 77, 21: *palumbes*, 62, 27. Wudeculfre *palumbus*, 29, 26.

wudu-cunelle, an; *f. Wild thyme:*—Wuducunille, Lchdm. ii. 96, 22. Wuducunellan, 320, 14.

wudu-cyn[n], es; *n. A kind of wood:*—Wuducynn ł wyrtcynn *nardi pistici*, Jn. Skt. Lind. 12, 3.

wudu-docce, an; *f. Sorrel:*—Wududocce. Genim ðâs wyrte ðe man *lapatium*, and ôðrum naman wududocce nemneþ, Lchdm. i. 132, 215.

wudu-fæsten[n], es; *n.* I. *a place rendered secure by woods, a wood as a place of security:*—Ðǽr gewexen is wudufæstern micel *there has grown a great wood which affords shelter*, Cod. Dip. B. ii. 376, 4. Hê gewîcode ðǽr ðǽr hê niéhst rýmet hæfde for wudufæstenne *he pitched his camp in the nearest spot allowed by the woods*, Chr. 894; Erl. 90, 9. Ða flugon ða Bryt-Walas tô ðâm wudufærstenum (cp. silvis sese obdidere, Bd. 1, 2), pref.; Erl. 5, 12. II. *a place of security built of wood:*—Sceal fæsl wesan cwiclifigendra cynna gehwylces on ðæt wudufæsten (*Noah's ark*) gelǽded, Cd. Th. 79, 16; Gen. 1312.

wudu-feld, a, es; *m. A field of the wood:*—On wudufeldum *in campis silvae*, Ps. Th. 131, 6.

wudu-feoh; *gen.* -feós; *n. A wood-tax, tax on forests:*—Wudefeoh *lucar* (vectigal quod ex lucis contrahitur, Du Cange), Lchdm. i. lxiii, 2. Cf. land-feoh.

wudu-fille, an; *f. Wild chervil:*—Wudufille, Lchdm. iii. 24, 7. Nim wudufillan, ii. 312, 14: 340, 2. Wudafillan, 4, 27. Ða reádan wudufillan (*sparagia agrestis*), 50, 1. v. wudu-cerfille.

wudu-fîn, e; *f. A heap of wood:*—Wudufîn *strues*, Ælfc. Gr. 9, 27; Zup. 53, 5. Wudefîne, Wrt. Voc. i. 39, 53. Wudufîne *strue, congerie*, Hpt. Gl. 464, 30. [*O. H. Ger.* witu-uîna *strues*.]

wudu-fugel, es; *m. A bird of the woods:*—Wudufuglas, ðeáh hî beón wel âtemede, gif hî on ðam wuda weorþaþ, hî forseóð heora lâreówas, and wuniaþ on heora gecynde, Bt. 25; Fox 88, 15: Met. 13, 35.

wudu-gât, e; *f. A wild goat:*—Wudugâte geallan, Lchdm. i. 348, 13, 18. v. wudu-bucca.

wudu-gehæg, es; *n. An enclosed wood* (?):—Of ðam hwîtan stoccæ þurh ðæt wudugehæg, Cod. Dip. Kmbl. iii. 176, 1.

wudu-hana, an; *m. A woodcock:*—Uuduhona *pantigatum*, Wrt. Voc. ii. 116, 56.

wudu-heáwere, es; *m. A hewer of wood, woodcutter:*—Bûton wuduheáwerum *exceptis lignorum caesoribus*, Deut. 29, 11.

wudu-herpaþ, es; *m. A public road through a wood:*—On ðone wuduherpaþ, Cod. Dip. Kmbl. iii. 213, 2.

wudu-holt, es; *m. A grove:*—Ðǽr is se fægere wuduholt ðe is on bôcum gehâten *Radians saltus*, Engl. Stud. viii. 477, 12. Sunbearo, wuduholt wynlîc *solis nemus, et consitus arbore multa lucus*, Exon. Th. 200, 1; Ph. 34. Wuduholtum, 223, 20; Ph. 362.

wudu-hunig, es; *n. Wild honey:*—Wuduhunig *mel silvestre*, Mt. Kmbl. 3, 4. Wudehunig, Homl. Th. i. 352, 7. Be wyrtum and be wuduhunige, Blickl. Homl. 167, 36. Wuduhunig hê æt, Mk. Skt. 1, 6.

wudu-lâd, e; *f. Carting wood:*—Æt wudulâde wǽntreów, L. R. S. 20; Th. i. 440, 27.

wudu-lǽs, we; *f. Forest pasture:*—Seó ûtlǽs and seó wudulǽs mid ôðrum mannum gemǽne, Cod. Dip. Kmbl. vi. 214, 22. Wæs tiolo micel sprêc ymb wudulêswe tô Sûðtûne; waldon ða swângerêfan ða lǽswe forður gedrîfan ond ðone wudu .geþiogan ðon hit aldgeryhto wêron, i. 278, 32.

wudu-land, es; *n. Wood-land, forest-land, forest:*—Ǽgðer ge etelond ge eyrðlond ge eác wudoland, Cod. Dip. Kmbl. ii. 95, 14. Ðæt wudæland, ðæ mîn fæder geúþæ, iii. 273, 27. Him wǽre fornêh eall ðæt wudulond on gereáfad . . . ðæt Æðelbald cyning gesealde tô mæstlonde and tô wudulonde, v. 140, 17. Feldlondes and wudulandes, iii. 262, 19: vi. 219, 5. Hî hine geond ealle eorðan sôhton, ge on dûnlandum ge on wudalandum, Ap. Th. 7, 14. [Þa wilde bær i þon wodelonde, Laym. 1699.]

wudu-leáctric, es; *m. Wild lettuce:*—Wudulêctric. Ðeós wyrt ðe man *lactucam sylvaticam*, and ôðrum naman wudulêctric nemneþ, Lchdm. i. 128, 6–8. Wudulêhtric, iii. 2, 21.

wudu-lîc; *adj.* I. *of a wood:*—Wudulîc *siluester*, Ælfc. Gr. 9, 18; Zup. 44, 16. Wudelîcra treówa *arborum silvestrium*, Hpt. Gl. 419, 42. II. *wild:*—Wudulîce oððe wilde *agrestes*, Wrt. Voc. ii. 4, 60.

wudu-mǽd. v. mǽd.

wudu-mær *echo:*—Wudumer (uuydu-) *echo*, Txts. 59, 715. Wudumær, Wrt. Voc. ii. 29, 1: 70, 7 (windu-, MS.). v. Grmm. D. M. pp. 452, 1412 (Stallybrass' Trans.).

wudu-merce, es; *m. Wood-marche:*—Wudumerce *apis sylvatica*, Wrt. Voc. i. 67, 29. Wudemerce *apiaster*, 31, 9. Genim wudumerce, Lchdm. ii. 22, 16: 66, 18: 326, 9. [Wudemerch *saniculum*, Wrt. Voc. i. 139, 6.]

wudung, e; *f.* I. *cutting wood:*—Ða hǽðenan on heora ðeówte leofodon tô wudunge and tô wæterunge, Homl. Th. ii. 222, 29. II. as a technical term referring to the right of cutting timber in a wood:—Ðis is seó wudung ðe ðǽrtô gebyreþ, ǽlce geáre fîftig fôðra and ân hund of ðæs cinges âcholte, and hûsbôt, Cod. Dip. Kmbl. vi. 243, 11. Seó wudung on gemǽnan grâfe tô Ðorndûne, iii. 463, 9. Uuidigung, uuidiung, Cod. Dip. B. i. 344, 13, 17. v. wudian.

wudu-rǽden[n], e; *f. Woodcutting, right of cutting timber in a wood:*—Ânan esne gebyreþ tô metsunge .xii. pund gôdes cornes, and wudurǽden be landside (*the amount of wood that he may cut is to be determined by local custom*), L. R. S. 8; Th. i. 436, 27. Twâ hund swîna mæsten and wudurǽden loca hwæs man beþurfe, Cod. Dip. Kmbl. iv. 20, 5. An ic twêga wǽna gang tô wudurêdenne, vi. 36, 16. Heó hæbbe ða wudurǽddenne in ðæm wuda ðe ða ceorlas brûcaþ, and êc ic hire lête tô ðæt ceorla grâf, ii. 100, 14.

wudu-rêc, es; *m. The smoke from burning wood:*—Wudurêc âstâh sweart, Beo. Th. 6280; B. 3144.

wudu-rima, an; *m. The edge of a wood:*—West be wuduriman, Cod. Dip. Kmbl. iii. 34, 15. [To mine lauerde i þon woderime, þer he under rise lið, Laym. 739.]

wudu-rofe, -rife (cf. Jamieson's Dict. *wood-rip*), an; *f. Woodruff:*—Wuderofe *astula regia*, Wrt. Voc. i. 30, 31. Wudurofe. Genim ðysse wyrte seáw ðe man *astula regia*, and ôðrum naman wudurofe nemneþ, Lchdm. i. 132, 6–9. Wuduhrofe. Genim ðysse wyrte wyrttruman ðe Grêcas *malochin agria*, and Rômâne *astula regia* nemnaþ, and eác Ængle wudurofe hâtaþ, 156, 8–11. Wel wudurofan, ii. 54, 2: 108, 19: 324, 13. Wudurifan, 64, 5.

wudu-rose, an; *f. Wild rose:*—Genim wudurosan, Lchdm. ii. 90, 16.

wudu-snîte, an; *f. The name of some bird:*—Uudusnîte *cardiolus*, Wrt. Voc. ii. 103, 46. Wudusnîte, 14, 9. v. snîte.

wudu-telga, an; *m. A branch of a tree:*—Ne foldan stān, ne wudu-telga, Salm. Kmbl. 844; Sal. 421.

wudu-þistel, es; *m. Wood-thistle:*—Wuduþistel. Ðeós wyrt ðe man *carduum sylvaticum*, and ōðrum naman wuduðistel nemneþ, Lchdm. i. 224, 11: iii. 28, 21. Wuduþistles ðone grēnan mearh ðe biþ on ðam heáfde, ii. 358, 1.

wudu-treów, es; *n. A tree of the woods, a forest tree:*—Nān man ne mōt his ælmessan behātan tō wylle ne tō wydetreówe, Wulfst. 303, 18. Wrǣtlīc wudutreów, Exon. Th. 437, 5; Rä. 56, 3. Ðæt man weorðige ǣniges cynnes wudutreówa, L. C. S. 5; Th. i. 378, 20. Wudutreówu, Wulfst. 40, 15.

wudu-wāsa, an; *m. A satyr, a faun:*—*Satiri*, vel *fauni*, vel *celini*, vel *fauni ficarii* unfǣle men, wudewāsan, unfǣle wihtu, Wrt. Voc. i. 17, 20. *Satyri* vel *fauni* unfǣle men, *ficarii* vel *invii* wudewāsan, 60, 23–24. Wudewāsan *faunos*, Germ. 394, 242. [Sumwhyle wyth wodwos he werreȝ, þat woned in þe knarreȝ, Gaw. 721. A vestoure wroȝt full of wodwose, and oþer wild bestis, Alex. (Skt.) 1540. Wodewese, woodwose *silvanus, satirus*, Prompt. Parv. 531, and see note. A wodewose *silvanus*, Wülck. Gl. 612, 2. Wright, in a note to the second of the passages cited above from the Vocabularies, quotes from Withal's *Dictionarie* (ed. 1608) 'a woodwose *satyrus*.']

wudu-weald, es; *m. High ground covered with wood, a wooded height:*—On wuduwaldum *in saltibus*, Wrt. Voc. ii. 47, 71.

wudu-weard, es; *m. A wood-keeper, forester:*—Be wuduwearde. Wuduwearde gebyreþ ǣlc windfylled treów, L. R. S. 19; Th. i. 440, 9. [The wodeward *le verder*, Wrt. Voc. i. 164. The wodeward waiteth us wo that loketh under rys, P. S. 149, 17. Wodewarde or walkare in a wode for kepynge *lucarius*, Prompt. Parv. 531.]

wudu-weaxe, an: -weax, es; *n. Wood waxen, wood wex* (v. E. D. S. Pub. Plant Names); genista tinctoria:—Wuduweaxe, Lchdm. ii. 66, 11. Weoduweaxe, iii. 30, 13. Wuduweaxan gōdne dǣl, ii. 324, 21: iii. 28, 28. Nime wuduweaxan nioþoweard, wealwyrt nioþowearde, ii. 118, 2. Genim gearwan and weoduweaxan and hræfnes fōt, iii. 30, 4. Nim gearwan and wuduweax (cf. weax, iii. 24, 4) and hrefnes fōt, ii. 324, 25.

wudu-wēsten *wild woodland:*—Ðā flugon ða Bryt-Walas tō ðām wuduwēstenum, Chr. pref.; Erl. 5, 12 note. v. wudu-fæsten[n].

wudu-winde, an; *f. Woodbine:*—Uuduuuinde, wi[d]windae *volvola*, Txts. 107, 2158. Uuduuuinde, uuiduuuindae *viburna*, 2129. Uudu-winde, uuidouuindae *edera*, 59, 717. Wuduwinde, Wrt. Voc. ii. 29, 2: *vivorna*, i. 286, 1. v. wudu-binde, wiþo-winde.

wudu-wyrt, e; *f. A wild plant:*—Ða swētan stencas ðara wudu-wyrta, Blickl. Homl. 59, 3.

Wuffingas; *pl. m. The patronymic of the royal house of East-Anglia:*—Wuffa fram ðam Eást-Engla cyningas Wuffingas wǣron nemde, Bd. 2, 15; S. 518, 38.

wuhhung, wuhung, e; *f. Fury:*—Him (*Nero*) ðære wuhhunge ge-steóran *vertere insani rabiem Neronis*, Bt. 16, 4; Fox 58, 14. Wuhunga *furias*, Wrt. Voc. ii. 38, 74.

wuht, wul, wulder. v. wiht, wull, wuldor.

wuldor (-ur, -er), es; *n. Glory.* (1) in reference to earthly subjects:—Woruldsceafta wuldor, Exon. Th. 190, 16; Az. 74. Hǣlo mīne and wuldor (*gloria*) mīn, Ps. Spl. 61, 7. Him wuldur (*gloria*) and wela wunaþ æt hūse, Ps. Th. 111, 3. Hebban herebȳman hlūdan stefnum wuldres wōman, Cd. Th. 183, 31; Exod. 100. Wuldres gim (*the sun*), Andr. Kmbl. 2538; An. 1270. Tō ðīnes folces wuldre (wulder, Lind.: wuldur, Rush.), Lk. Skt. 2, 32. Hē fērde ūt on huntaþ mid eallum his werode and his wuldre, Homl. Skt. ii. 30, 25. Ne beseoh tō ðīnum ǣrran wuldre, 30, 121. Eodon of ðam fȳre feorh unwemme, wuldre ge-wlitegad, Exon. Th. 197, 8; Az. 187. Hē (*the Phenix*) is wlitig and wynsum, wuldre gemearcad *regali plena decore*, 220, 11; Ph. 318. Ge-wīteþ mid ðȳ wuldre mǣre tungol (*the sun*), 350, 23; Sch. 68. Tempel wuldre gewlitegod, Andr. Kmbl. 1337; An. 669. Ðā sceáwede ic mīne gesǣlinesse and mīn wuldor, Nar. 7, 22. (1 a) in a bad sense, *vain-glory.* v. wuldor-full, II:—On wlence ic fērde þurh ðæt īdele wuldor, Anglia xi. 113, 50: Exon. Th. 107, 12; Gū. 57. Wēndes ðū ðurh wuldor, ðæt ðū woruld āhtest, alra onwald, Cd. Th. 268, 22; Sat. 59. (1 b) applied to persons or things:—Wīfa wuldor (*the Virgin Mary*), Menol. Fox 295; Men. 149. Receda wuldor, Salamones templ, Cd. Th. 219, 23; Dan. 59. (2) of celestial or spiritual glory:—Godes wuldor *gloria Domini*, Lev. 9, 23. Gode sȳ wuldor, Lk. Skt. 2, 14: Ps. Spl. 103, 32. Him wīdeferh wuldor stondeþ, Exon. Th. 350, 2; Sch. 57. Stefn of heofonum, wuldres hleóðor, Cd. Th. 204, 10; Exod. 417. Se wyrhta þurh his wuldres gāst sette, 265, 28; Sat. 14. In wuldres wlite, 279, 5; Sat. 233: 285, 26; Sat. 343. Wuldres ræst *the rest of heaven*, Exon. Th. 103, 19; Cri. 1690. Wuldres neótan *to enjoy heaven*, 365, 15; Wal. 89. Wuldres eard āgan, 74, 8; Cri. 1203. Wuldres wynlond, 317, 13; Mōd. 65. Wuldres bearnum (*angels*), Cd. Th. 1, 22; Gen. 11. Wuldres þegn, engel Drihtnes, 137, 1; Gen. 2266: 95, 6; Gen. 1574. Wuldres þegnas (*St. Matthew and St. Andrew*), Andr. Kmbl. 2052; An. 1028. Seó fǣmne, wuldres wynmǣg (*Guthlac's sister*, seó Cristes þeówe, Guthl. 20; Gdwin. 92, 2), Exon. Th. 182, 32; Gū. 1319: (*St. Juliana*), 278, 20; Jul. 600: 269, 23; Jul. 474. Se eorðan dǣl ... se wuldres dǣl *the body ... the soul*, 184, 11; Gū. 1342. Wuldres treó *the cross*, Elen. Kmbl. 177; El. 89: Rood Kmbl. 28; Kr. 14. Wuldores stæf, Salm. Kmbl. 225; Sal. 112. Mannes sunu cumende mid mycelum wuldre, Mk. Skt. 13, 26. For Godes wuldre (uldre, Lind.), Jn. Skt. 11, 4. In wuldre *in heaven*, Andr. Kmbl. 712; An. 356: Elen. Kmbl. 1491; El. 747. Tō wuldre, Exon. Th. 3, 3; Cri. 30: Andr. Kmbl. 3360; An. 1684. Ðæt ēce wuldor geearnian, Homl. Th. ii. 284, 31. Wē gesāwon his wuldor (uuldor, Lind.), Jn. Skt. 1, 14. Godes wuldor (uulder, Lind.), 11, 40: Ps. Spl. 18, 1. Ealles ðæs Iudith sægde wuldor Dryhtne, Judth. Thw. 26, 24; Jud. 343. Wulder, R. Ben. 4, 4. Sāule sōðfæstra wuldrum hrēmge, Exon. Th. 4, 17; Cri. 54. ¶ in phrases denoting the Deity:—Wuldres aldor, Cd. Th. 40, 15; Gen. 639: 91, 12; Gen. 1511. Wuldres weard, 58, 4; Gen. 941. God, wuldres hyrde, Beo. Th. 1867; B. 931. Wuldres āgend, Andr. Kmbl. 420; An. 210. Wuldres bearn (*Christ*), Cd. Th. 301, 26; Sat. 589. Wlitig wuldres gim, Exon. Th. 232, 33; Ph. 516. (2 a) applied to the Deity:—Drihten, wulder mīn, Ps. Spl. 3, 3. Metod, cyninga wuldor, Judth. Thw. 23, 34: Jud. 155: Andr. Kmbl. 342; An. 171. Ðæt ðe wealdend God ācenned wearð, cyninga wuldor, Elen. Kmbl. 10; El. 5. Dryhten, hæleða wuldor, Andr. Kmbl. 2925; An. 1465. Ðȳ þriddan dæge beorna wuldor of deáðe ārās, Dryhten ealra hæleða cynnes, Elen. Kmbl. 372; El. 186. [Þin wombe was þin God and þin wulder ... echeliche wunien in alre wuldre, Fragm. Phlps. 7, 20, 58. Si Drihhtin loff and wullderr, Orm. 3379. Cf. *Goth.* wulþus *glory*.] v. heofon-, sigor-, swegel-wuldor.

wuldorbeágian; *p.* ode *To crown:*—Tō wuldorbeágienne mid Criste, Homl. Th. i. 84, 32. v. ge-wuldorbeágian.

wuldor-beáh; *gen.* -ges; *m. A crown:*—Wuldorbeáh *corona*, Ps. Spl. 64, 12. Wulderbeáh, Wrt. Voc. i. 43, 5: Hpt. Gl. 438, 24. [For] wuldurbeága *pro corona*, 458, 22. [Tō] wuldurbēge *ad coronam*, 460, 5. Wulderbeáge *tropheo*, 508, 64. Wuldorbeág *coronam*, Ps. Lamb. 20, 4. Hē (*Stephen*) hæfð ðone ēcan wuldorbeáh, Homl. Th. i. 50, 13. Ān læs feówertig wuldorbeága, Shrn. 62, 7. Hī wuldorbeágum beóð gewelgode scīnendum *laureis ditantur fulgidis*, Hymn. Surt. 133, 1.

wuldor-blǣd, es; *m. Glorious success:*—Eów ys wuldorblǣd torhtlīc tōweard, and tīr gifeþe, Judth. Thw. 23, 35; Jud. 156.

wuldor-cyning, es; *m. The king of glory, the Deity:*—Wuldor-cyning þeóda gehwylce hāteþ ārīsan, Exon. Th. 63, 22; Cri. 1023: Cd. Th. 272, 6; Sat. 115. Se wuldorcyning, 10, 32; Gen. 165. Ælmihtig God, wuldorcyning, 242, 30; Dan. 427: Salm. Kmbl. 640; Sal. 319. Wuldorcyning, fæder frymða gehwæs, Exon. Th. 211, 12; Ph. 196. Wuldorcyning (*Christ*), 227, 9; Ph. 420. Ðæt wæs þonne ðæt se wuldorcyning on middangeard cwom forþ of ðæm innoþe ðære ā clǣnan fǣmnan, Blickl. Homl. 9, 32. Se hālga Dryhten, ðū ... mīn wuldor-cyning, 452, 16; Hy. 4, 42. Ðū, weroda wuldorcyning, Met. 20, 162. Hié yrfes brūcaþ wuldorcyninges, Elen. Kmbl. 2639; El. 1321: Andr. Kmbl. 835; An. 418: Exon. Th. 153, 5; Gū. 821. Heó Gode þancode, wuldorcyninge, Elen. Kmbl. 1922; El. 963. Wuldurcyninge, ēcum Dryhtne, Beo. Th. 5582; B. 2795. Ðæt wē rodera weard, wereda wuldorcining herigen, Cd. Th. i. 3; Gen. 2: 213, 4; Exod. 547. Fāh wið wuldorcyning, Exon. Th. 364, 7; Wal. 67.

wuldor-dreám, es; *m. Joy in the glory of heaven, celestial joy:*—Wē ðē þanciaþ, þióda Waldend, ðīnes weorðlīcan wuldordreámes, Hy. 8, 10. In ðīnne wuldordreám, Exon. Th. 455, 2; Hy. 4, 43.

wuldor-fæder; *m. The father of glory, the heavenly Father:*—Weorc wuldorfæder (wuldurfadur, Txts. 149, 3) *facta Patris gloriae*, Bd. 4, 24; S. 597, 21. Līf mid wuldorfæder, Menol. Fox 291; Men. 147. Mid ðīnne wuldorfæder, Exon. Th. 14, 11; Cri. 217.

wuldor-fæst; *adj. Glorious:*—Wuldurfest *gloriosus*, Ps. Surt. ii. p. 188, 1. Wuldorfæst, Cd. Th. 234, 3; Dan. 286. Wuldorfæst cyning (*Solomon*), 202, 18; Exod. 390. Ðes wuldorfæsta kyning *rex gloriae*, Ps. Th. 23, 8, 10: Nicod. 29; Thw. 16, 38. Ðæt wuldorfæste līf ðætte englas on Drihtnes onsȳne wuniaþ, Blickl. Homl. 103, 32. Ða stōwe ðīnes wuldorfæstan temples *locum tabernaculi gloriae tuae*, Ps. Th. 25, 8. For ðære swētnesse ðære wuldorfæstan gesihðe, Homl. Skt. ii. 23 b, 179. Wulderfæstan, 236, 8. Heora (*the stars'*) wuldorfæstne wlite, Cd. Th. 132, 10; Gen. 2191. His ðone wuldorfæstan gāst, Blickl. Homl. 85, 4. His ða wuldorfæstan onsȳne, 103, 29. Ða wuldorfæstan Godes weorc, Homl. Skt. ii. 23 b, 11. Wuldorfæstan wīc (*heaven*), Cd. Th. 2, 30; Gen. 27.

wuldorfæste; *adv. Gloriously:*—Hió Gode þancode ðæs geleáfan ðe hió swā leóhte oncneów, wuldorfæste, in ðæs weres breóstum, Elen. Kmbl. 1930; El. 967.

wuldorfæstlīce; *adv. Gloriously:*—Hēr Eleutherius on Rōme onfēng biscopdōm, and ðone wuldorfæstlīce .xii. winter geheóld, Chr. 167; Erl. 8, 14.

wuldorfæstlīcness, e; *f. Gloriousness, glory:*—Sȳ ðū gebletsod, Drihten God, ðe mē æteówdest ðā wuldorfæstlīcnysse ðe ðū ondrǣdendum gyfest, Homl. Skt. ii. 23 b, 603.

wuldor-full; *adj.* I. *glorious:*—Gif ðū eádmōdnysse healtst wuldorful (*gloriosus*) ðú byst, Scint. 22, 4. Wuldorfull mid ēcum wurð-mynte, Homl. Ass. 77, 125. Ðes Dauid wæs wuldorful cyning, Homl. Skt. i. 18, 32. Wulderfull ðrowung, Homl. Th. i. 360, 20. Se wuldor-fulla (*gloriosus*) Eádgār, Anglia xiii. 365, 3. Se wuldorfulla cyning (*Christ*), Nicod. 28; Thw. 16, 6. For his wuldorfullan sige oretlofes *propter ejus gloriosissimi victoriam triumphi*, Anglia xiii. 400, 497. Seó wunung on ðam wuldorfullum dreáme, Homl. Ass. 43, 481. Tō ðare wuldorfullan byrig Hierusalem, H. R. 7, 4. Wuldorfulle on mægðhāde, Homl. Ass. 44, 499. Wuldorfulle lofu *glorificum melos*, Hymn. Surt. 57, 24. Babilonia ðe hwīlon wæs wuldorfullost burh ealra burha, Wulfst. 194, 10. II. *vainglorious.* v. wuldor (I a):—Betere ys þearfa and behōfigende him þænne wer wulderfull (*gloriosus*) and genihtsumigende hlāfe, Scint. 178, 15. Wuldorfull, 180, 6.

wuldorfullian; *p.* ode *To glorify*:—Hī wuldorfulliaþ (*glorificabunt*) naman ðīnne, Ps. Spl. 85, 8.

wuldorfullīce; *adv. Gloriously*:—On eallum ðām ðe wuldorfullīce (*gloriose*) fram him gewurdon, Lk. Skt. 13, 17. Hī wurdon wuldor-fullīce gemartyrode, Homl. Th. i. 80, 29. Heó tō dæg wuldorfullīce of ðam līchaman gewāt, 440, 12.

wuldor-gāst, es; *m. A spirit of glory, glorious spirit, an angel*:—Of roderum wuldorgāst Godes wordum mǣlde (*angelus Domini de coelo clamavit*, Gen. 22, 11), Cd. Th. 176, 15; Gen. 2912.

wuldor-geflogena, an; *m. A fugitive from glory, an evil spirit*:—Magon ðās .viiii. wyrta wið nygon wuldorgeflogenum, Lchdm. iii. 36, 15.

wuldor-gesteald; *pl. n.* I. *glorious possessions*:—Gold and godweb, Iōsepes gestreón, wera wuldorgesteald, Cd. Th. 215, 24; Exod. 588. Ða gerēno and se reáda telg and ða wuldorgesteald (*the binding of a book?*), Exon. Th. 408, 22; Rä. 27, 16. II. *glorious mansions*:—Fæder and Sunu and frōfre Gāst on þrinnesse wealdeþ wuldorgestealda, Andr. Kmbl. 3369; An. 1688. God bescyrede his wiðerbrecan wuldor-gestealdum, Cd. Th. 4, 36; Gen. 64.

wuldor-gifu, e; *f. A glorious gift, a gift of heaven*:—Wuldorgife, Hy. 9, 44. Ðȳ læs hē for wlence, wuldorgeofona ful, mon mōde swīð, of gemete hweorfe, Exon. Th. 294, 33; Crä. 24. Ðē beorht Fæder geweorðaþ wuldorgifum, cræfte and mihte, Andr. Kmbl. 1875; An. 940. Gāstes mihtum, wuldorgifum, Elen. Kmbl. 2141; An. 1072.

wuldor-gimm, es; *m. A glorious gem, the sun*:—Wynsum wuldor-gimm, Exon. Th. 492, 23; Rä. 81, 20.

wuldor-hama, an; *m. A glorious garb*:—Engel ælbeorht, wlitescȳne wer on his wuldorhaman, Cd. Th. 237, 16; Dan. 338: Exon. Th. 189, 2; Az. 53. Him is engel mid, hafaþ beorhtne blǣd, ne mæg him bryne sceþþan, wlitigne wuldorhaman, 196, 24; Az. 179.

wuldor-helm, es; *m. A crown*:—Mōyses onfēng scīnendum wuldor-helme, Blickl. Homl. 49, 11.

wuldor-leán, es; *n. A glorious reward, the reward of heaven*:—Bið hyra meaht and gefeá swīðe gesǣliglīc sāwlum tō gielde, wuldorleán weorca, Exon. Th. 66, 31; Cri. 1080. In ðam ēcan gefeán niman weorca wuldorleán, 184, 20; Gū. 1347.

wuldor-līc; *adj.* I. *glorious*:—Wuldurlīc *gloriosus*, Rtl. 181, 27. Wuldorlīc, Exon. Th. 62, 33; Cri. 1011. Hū wuldorlīc (*admirabile*) ðīn nama ys, Ps. Th. 8, 9: Ps. Spl. 8, 1. Hē wītgode be ðære wuldor-līcan ācennednesse Cristes, Ps. Th. 8, arg. Be his ðære wuldorlīcan ǣriste, Blickl. Homl. 117, 3. Þurh wuldorlīcne martyrdōm, Shrn. 30, 32. Hē wæs hæbbende wuldorlīcne beág on his heáfde, 106, 10. Wuldorlīcne wlite, Salm. Kmbl. 115; Sal. 57. Wǣrun wuldurlīce wið ðe ācweðene *gloriosa dicta sunt de te*, Ps. Th. 86, 2. II. the word glosses *orthodoxus*, Wrt. Voc. i. 288, 54: ii. 64, 17.

wuldorlīce; *adv. Gloriously*:—Hē ðæt setl ðære apostolīcan cyrican wulderlīce (*gloriosissime*) heóld and rehte, Bd. 2, 1; S. 500, 10. Wuldor-līce, Blickl. Homl. 211, 31. Hié on manegum godcundum mægenum swīþe wuldorlīce āscinon, 161, 19.

wuldor-māga, an; *m. A man who will attain the glory of heaven, an heir of heaven*:—Se wuldormāga (*St. Guthlac*), Exon. Th. 167, 28; Gū. 1067. v. next word.

wuldor-magu, a; *m. A son of glory, an heir of heaven*:—Se wuldor-mago, eádig, Exon. Th. 179, 25; Gū. 1267.

wuldor-micel; *adj. Gloriously great, magnificent*:—Gewitnesse beóð wuldormicele heofonwaru and eorðwaru, helwaru þridde, Hy. 7, 94.

wuldor-nyttung, e; *f. Glorious use*:—Wuldornyttingum (woruld-? cf. weorold-nytt), Exon. Th. 492, 22; Rä. 81, 19.

wuldor-spēd, e; *f. Glorious abundance*:—Setl wuldorspēdum welig (*heaven*), Cd. Th. 6, 11; Gen. 87.

wuldor-spēdig; *adj. Glorious*:—Gingran sīne, wuldorspēdige weras, Andr. Kmbl. 855; An. 428.

wuldor-tān, es; *m. A glory-twig, a plant with medicinal virtues*:—Ðā genam Wōden .viiii. wuldortānas, slōh ðā ða næddran, ðæt heó on viiii. tōfleáh, Lchdm. iii. 34, 24.

wuldor-þrymm, es; *m. Glorious majesty*:—Wealdend and wyrhta wuldorþrymmes, ēce God, Andr. Kmbl. 650; An. 325: 1404; An. 702. Godes wuldorþrymmas mannum cȳþan, Blickl. Homl. 111, 17.

wuldor-torht; *adj. Gloriously bright, splendid*:—Wuldortorht heofon-weardes gāst, Cd. Th. 8, 5; Gen. 119. Hādor sægl wuldortorht gewāt, Andr. Kmbl. 2912; An. 1459: Cd. Th. 174, 7; Gen. 2874. Beácen wuldortorht, 167, 21; Gen. 2769. Wuldortorhtan weder, Beo. Th. 2276; B. 1136.

wuldor-weorod, es; *n. The host of heaven*:—Ðæt ðū sié hlǣfdige wuldorweorudes, and worl[d]cundra hāda under heofonum, and helwara, Exon. Th. 18, 17; Cri. 285.

wuldor-word, es; *n. A glorious word*:—Ðū, ealra cyninga þrym, clypast ofer ealle; bið ðīn wuldorword wīde gehȳred, Hy. 7, 46.

wuldrian (*and* wuldran?); *p.* ode. I. *to glorify*, (1) *to ascribe glory to*:—Ic wuldrige (*glorificabo*) naman ðīnne, Ps. Spl. 85, 11. Gif ic wuldrige (wuldria, Lind.: wuldrigo, Rush. *glorifico*) mē sylfne, Jn. Skt. 8, 54. Hī lofiaþ leóflīcne, and wuldriaþ ordfruman ealra gesceafta, Exon. Th. 25, 16; Cri. 401. Hē God wuldrode *Deum magnificans*, Lk. Skt. 5, 25: Homl. Skt. i. 3, 662. Wē sculon wuldrian and herian ūrne Dryhten, Homl. Th. i. 44, 2: Hy. 8, 1. Se is tō weorþienne and tō wuldrienne, Blickl. Homl. 197, 6. God wuldriende (wuldrigendo, Lind.: wuldrende, Rush.) and heriende, Lk. Skt. 2, 20. (2) *to make glorious, bestow glory on*:—Wuldra (uuldra, Lind.) ðū mec *clarifica me*, Jn. Skt. Rush. 17, 5. Hē wolde ðone cyning mid ðyssum hwīlendlīcum ārum wuldrian *temporalibus honoribus regem glorificare satagens*, Bd. 1, 32; S. 498, 22. Wē sié wuldræd *gloriemur*, Rtl. 41, 41. II. *to glory* in respect to something:—Ic wuldrige *glorior*, Ælfc. Gr. 25; Zup. 145, 11. Hwet wuldras (*gloriaris*) ðū in hete, Ps. Surt. 51, 3. Wuldraþ *gloriatur*, Hpt. Gl. 501, 55. Hȳ wuldriaþ (*gloriabuntur*) on ðē, Ps. Spl. 5, 14. Ða ðe ðære mycelnesse hiora spēda gylpaþ and wuldraþ (-iaþ?), Ps. Th. 48, 6. Ða anlīcnyssa ðe ðū on wuldrodest, Homl. Skt. i. 4, 382. Se brȳdguma ðe Agnes on wuldrode, 7, 77. Ða Iudēiscan wuldrodon on heora ǣlīcum offrungum, Homl. Th. ii. 470, 24. Se ðe wuldrige, wuldrige on God ælmihtigne, and nō on hine sylfne, R. Ben. 4, 8. Gedafenaþ ðæt hī wuldrion on gedrēfednessum, Homl. Th. i. 554, 24. Þeáh ðe ic wylle wuldrian (*gloriari*), ne beó ic nā unsnoter, Ælfc. Gr. 44; Zup. 262, 7. Heó ongan wuldrian on God, Blickl. Homl. 157, 18. III. *to receive glory, be glorified*:—God wuldraþ (*glorificatur*) in geðæhte hāligra, Ps. Surt. 88, 8. Hē wuldraþ mid Gode on ðam heofenlīcum setle, Homl. Th. ii. 552, 25. Basilius ðe ðā wuldrode mid Gode, Homl. Skt. i. 3, 661. v. ge-wuldrian.

wuldrig; *adj. Glorious*:—Foreðingunge wuldrigo *intercessio gloriosa*, Rtl. 49, 34. Beodum wuldrigum *precibus gloriosis*, 72, 18.

wuldrung, e; *f.* I. *glorifying*:—Wuldrung *glorificatio*, Rtl. 57, 6. II. *glorying*:—Wuldor and wuldrung *gloria et gloriatio*, Scint. 65, 4: 191, 14.

wulf, es; *m.* I. *a wolf*:—Wulf *lupus*, Wrt. Voc. ii. 113, 32: i. 77, 77: *licos*, 22, 61: *lupa*, ii. 51, 29. Hwonne of heortan hunger oððe wulf sāwle and sorge somed ābregde, Cd. Th. 137, 20; Gen. 2276. Wulf sceal on bearowe, Menol. Fox 496; Gn. C. 18. Sceal hine wulf etan, hār hǣðstapa, Exon. Th. 328, 5; Vy. 12. Se hāra wulf, 291, 15; Wand. 82. Wulfes gehlēþan, 499, 30; Rä. 88, 23. Reáfiende wulfas, Mt. Kmbl. 7, 15. Ic (*the shepherd*) stande ofer mīne sceáp mid hundum ðe læs wulfas forswelgen hig, Coll. Monast. Th. 20, 15. Wulfa geþot *ululatus*, Wrt. Voc. i. 287, 24. Sume wurdon tō wulfan; ða ðuton, ðonne hī sprǣcan sceoldon, Bt. 38, 1; Fox 194, 36: Met. 26, 79. Swā sceáp gemang wulfas, Mt. Kmbl. 10, 16. Wineleás, wonsǣlig mon ge-nimeþ wulfas tō gefēran, Exon. Th. 342, 25; Gn. Ex. 147. ¶ in battle-scenes the wolf is a frequent figure:—Ne wæl wēpeþ wulf se grǣga, morþorcwealm mæcga, ac hit ā māre wille, Exon. Th. 343, 3; Gn. Ex. 151. Ðæs se hlanca gefeah wulf in walde, Judth. Thw. 24, 25; Jud. 206. Ðæt grǣge deór, wulf on wealde, Chr. 937; Erl. 115, 14. Fyrd-leóð āgōl wulf on walde, Elen. Kmbl. 55; El. 28. Wulf sang āhōf, holtes gehlēða, 224; El. 112. Wulfas sungon atol ǣfenleóð ǣtes on wēnan, Cd. Th. 188, 7; Exod. 164. Se mǣsta dǣl ðæs heriges læg, hilde gesǣged, wulfum tō willan, Judth. Thw. 25, 36; Jud. 296. ¶ an early admiration for the wolf seems shewn by the frequency of *wulf* in proper names; see e.g. Txts. 554 sqq.; and its presence in early England is marked by the numerous place-names; see e.g. Cod. Dip. Kmbl. vi. Index. I a. *in the phrase* wulfes heáfod (v. wulfheáfod-treów), *used in reference to outlaws*:—Si postea repertus fuerit et teneri possit, vivus regi reddatur, vel caput ipsius, si se defenderit; lupinum enim caput geret a die utlagacionis sue, quod ab Anglis *wulvesheued* nominatur. Et hec sententia communis est de omnibus utlagis, L. Ed. C. 6; Th. i. 445, 4. [Gamelyn woluesheed was cryed and maad, Gam. 700. Cf. wearg, *and see* Grmm. R. A. 734.] II. applied to a cruel person:—Se biscop cwæþ tō ðæm hǣþnan kāsere: 'Ne gang ðū nā on Godes hūs; ðū hafast besmitene handa; and ðū eart deófles wulf,' Shrn. 58, 9. Se āwyrgda wulf (*the devil*), Exon. Th. 16, 21; Cri. 256. [*Goth.* wulfs: *O. Sax.* wulf: *O. H. Ger.* wolf: *Icel.* ulfr.] v. heoru-, here-, hilde-, wæl-wulf; wylf, wylfen[n].

wulfes-camb, es; *m. Wild teazle*:—Wulfes-camb *cameleon*, Wrt. Voc. i. 31, 3: *camellia*, 67, 9: *camellea*, ii. 102, 50: 13, 12. Se brāda wulfes-camb *camemelon alba*, i. 67, 26. Wulfes-camb. Genim ðysse wyrte seáw ðe man *chameaelae*, and ōðrum naman wulfes-camb nemneþ,

Lchdm. i. 122, 12. Heó hafaþ leáf swā wulfes-camb, 278, 14. Wiđ eágena dymnesse nim wulfes-camb neođeweardne, iii. 4, 19.

wulfes-tǣsl. v. tǣsl.

wulfheáfod-treów, es; *n. A cross* (?):—Ealle namau habbaþ ānne, wulfheáfedtreó, Exon. Th. 437, 23; Rä. 56, 12. Cf. wulf, I *a and* wearg-treów (*where add O. Sax.* warag-treó *a cross*).

wulf-heort; *adj. Wolf-hearted, cruel:*—Oᵹwōc wulfheort, se ǣr wīngāl swæf, Babilone weard, Cd. Th. 223, 7; Dan. 116. Wulfheort cyning, 224, 12; Dan. 135: 231, 14; Dan. 247.

wulf-hliþ, es; *n. A hill where the wolf has its den:*—Hié dȳgel lond warigeaþ, wulfhleoþu, Beo. Th. 2720; B. 1358.

wulf-hol, es; *n. A wolf's den:*—Uulfholu *lupinare*, Wrt. Voc. ii. 113, 34. Wulfholu, 51, 13.

wulf-seáþ, es; *m. A wolf-pit:*—Be eástan đæm wulfseáđe, Cod. Dip. Kmbl. iii. 264, 5.

wull, e: wulle, an; *f. Wool:*—Uul *lana*, Wrt. Voc. ii. 112, 44. Wul, i. 66, 29: 82, 7. Wull, ii. 51, 61. Unāwaxen wul *lana sucida*, 54, 6. Unāwæscen wul, i. 61, 8. Rammes wul (wull, *v. l.*), Lchdm. i. 356, 11. Đa loccas hire heáfdes wǣron swā hwīte swā wull, Homl. Skt. ii. 23 b, 177. Gā seó wǣge wulle tō .cxx. p̄., L. Edg. ii. 8; Th. i. 270, 3. Wulle flȳs *lanam*, Ps. Th. 147, 5. Ne wāt ic mec beworhtne wulle flȳsum (uullan fliúsum, Txts. 150, 3), Exon. Th. 417, 12; Rä. 36, 3. Hī beóđ gegyrede gōdre wulle, Ps. Th. 64, 14. Mid līnene clāđe ođđe mid eówocigre wulle, Lchdm. ii. 182, 5. Mid hnesce wulle oferwrīđe ealle đa scearpan, 130, 10. Nim wǣte wulle, i. 312, 12: 362, 17: Ps. Surt. 147, 16. Wullan (? *the MS. has* wulla *with a stroke after the* a) *lanam*, Kent. Gl. 1135. Wulla *lanas*, Hpt. Gl. 524, 14. [*Goth.* wulla: *O. H. Ger.* wolla: *Icel.* ull.] v. wyll.

wull-camb, es; *m. A wool-comb:*—Hē sceal fela towtōla habban, . . . wulcamb, Anglia ix. 263, 13. [*O. H. Ger.* wolla-champ *tradula*: *Icel.* ull-kambr.]

wull-fleós, -flȳs, es; *n. A fleece of wool:*—Wulflȳs *cana vellus*, Wrt. Voc. ii. 128, 17.

wull-hnoppa, an; *m. Wool-nap, the wool on a fleece:*—Wullhnoppa (*printed* -knoppa; *but* cf. hnoppian *vellere*, Wrt. Voc. ii. 72, 56: noppe *detuberare*, a noppe of clothe *tuberus*, Cath. Angl. 256) *lanugo*, Wrt. Voc. ii. 51, 66.

wullian; *p.* ode *To wipe with wool:*—Wiđ scurfum; rammes smeoru; and meng đǣrtō sōt and sealt and sand, and hyt wulla on weg, Lchdm. i. 356, 24.

wull-mod (-mōd?) *a distaff:*—Wulmod *colus*, Wrt. Voc. i. 281, 80: ii. 16, 32: *colum*, 25, 9: 134, 59. Uuilmod (wulf-) *colus*, Txts. 54, 306. [Cf. *O. H. Ger.* wolla-meit *colus*.] v. Anglia xix. 496.

wull-tewestre, an; *f. A female wool-carder:*—Mǣden milde, wultewestre, Lchdm. iii. 188, 20. Mǣden grǣdig, wulltewestre, 196, 2.

wulluc. v. weoloc.

wull-wǣga; *pl. f. Scales for weighing wool:*—*Momentana* lytle wǣga, *campana* wulwǣga, Wrt. Voc. i. 38, 43.

wund (*printed* pund, Wrt. Voc. i. 289, 61) *talpa*, Wülck. Gl. 279, 11, *read* wand.

wund, e; *f. A wound;* vulnus, Wrt. Voc. i. 85, 49. I. in a physical sense, (1) *a wound, an injury caused by a blow:*—Sió wund, đe him se eorđdraca geworhte, Beo. Th. 5416; B. 2711. Blōdig wund, Andr. Kmbl. 2945; An. 1475: Exon. Th. 143, 33; Gū. 670. Hēr sindon dolhsealfa tō eallum wundum . . . Sceád on đa wunde . . . Wiþ ealdre tōbrocenre wunde . . . lācna swilce wunda. Tō wunde clǣnsunge . . . smire đa wunde mid, đonne fullaþ hió . . . Wiþ innanwunde, Lchdm. ii. 90, 23–92, 21. Wæs se cyning gehǣled fram đære wunde đe him ǣr gedōn wæs (*a vulnere sibi pridem inflicto*), Bd. 2, 9; S. 512, 1. Sylle wunde wiđ wunde *reddat vulnus pro vulnere*, Ex. 21, 25. Wīcing đe him đa wunde forgeaf, Byrht. Th. 135, 57; By. 139. Hē ofer benne spræc, wunde wælbleáte, Beo. Th. 5443; B. 2725. Wundum āwyrded, Beo. Th. 2230; B. 1113. Wundum wērge, 5866; B. 2937. Se wīdfloga wundum stille hreás, 5653; B. 2830. Wundum sweltan, Byrht. Th. 140, 25; By. 293. Wǣpna wundum, Exon. Th. 119, 15; Gū. 255. Đa ealdan wunde and đa openan dolg on hyra Dryhtne, 68, 23; Cri. 1108. Swātge wunde, 89, 19; Cri. 1459. Hē wrāđ his wunda (wundo *uulnera*, Lind.), Lk. Skt. 10, 34. (2) *a sore caused by disease.* v. wundig, wundiht:—Gif wambe biđ oninnan wund, Lchdm. ii. 220, 3. Hē (*the itch*) wundaþ and sió wund sāraþ, Past. 11; Swt. 71, 20. Se deófol slōh Iōb mid đære wyrstan wunde . . . Iōb sæt eal on ānre wunde, Homl. Th. ii. 452, 25–28. Ōđer wæs wæterseóc, ōđer eall on wundum, ac hī wurdon gehǣlede fram heora untrumnysse, Homl. Skt. i. 5, 145. Heó wæs swȳđe unhāl, and on eallum limum egeslīce wunda hæfde . . . 'Đū scealt underfōn đīnra wunda hǣle.' . . . On hire līce næs gesȳne āht đæra sārra wunda, 7, 265–278. II. in a figurative sense:—Feónda fǣrsearo, đæt biđ frēcne wund, Exon. Th. 48, 12; Cri. 770. Đæt wom ǣrran wunde hǣlan, 81, 12; Cri. 1322. Wunde *cicatrice*, Hpt. Gl. 504, 35. Ic ofslōh wer on mīne wunde (*in vulnus meum*), Gen. 4, 23. Gāstes wunde *sins*, Ps. C. 51. Beóđ wunde (wunda, Soul Kmbl. 177) onwrigene, đa đe firenfulle men geworhton, Exon. Th. 372, 9; Seel. 89. Mīnra wunda sār *dolorem vulnerum meorum*, Ps. Th. 68, 27. Synna wundum, Exon. Th. 263, 25; Jul. 355. Geseón on ussum sāwlum synna wunde, 80, 30; Cri. 1314. [*O. Sax.* wunda: *O. Frs.* wunde: *O. H. Ger.* wunta *vulnus, ulcus, plaga*: *Icel.* und.] v. cancor-, feorh-, in-, innan-, innoþ-, līc-, sweord-wund, *and next word.*

wund; *adj. Wounded.* I. in a physical sense, (1) of a wound inflicted. v. wund, I. 1:—Đa hwīle đe hē wund wæs *dum convalescit a vulnere*, Ors. 3, 7; Swt. 118, 9. Gif wælt wund weorđeþ, L. Ethb. 68; Th. i. 18, 19. Wund weard Wulfmǣr, wælreste geceás, Byrht. Th. 135, 4; By. 113. Se wyrm swefeþ sāre wund, Beo. Th. 5485; B. 2746: Apstls. Kmbl. 121; Ap. 61. Gewāt him wund hæleđ gangan, Fins. Th. 86; Fin. 43. Geddung đæs wundes *parabolam vulnerati*, Lk. Skt. p. 6, 19. Wundum dryhtne, heađosiócum, Beo. Th. 5500; B. 2753. (1 a) where the place of the wound is given:—Gif mon biđ on eaxle wund (gewunded, *v.l.*), L. Alf. pol. 53; Th. i. 94, 22. On breóstum wund, Byrht. Th. 136, 1; By. 144. Wund on ōþran earme *brachio saucius*, Ors. 4, 1; Swt. 158, 2. Wund þurh ōþer cneów *transfixo femore*, 4, 6; Swt. 180, 6. (1 b) where the instrument with which the wound is inflicted is given:—Īserne wund, Exon. Th. 388, 2; Rä. 6, 1. Mīn heáfod is searopīla wund, 497, 17; Rä. 87, 2. Mēcum wunde, Beo. Th. 1135; B. 565: 2154; B. 1075. (2) of disease. v. wund, I. 2:—Dolhsealf wiđ lungenādle . . . mid đȳ sceal mon lācnian đone man đe biþ lungenne wund, Lchdm. ii. 92, 21. Be wambe coþum, and gif hió innan wund biþ hū đæt mon ongitan mæge and gelācnian, 220, 1. II. figurative. v. wund, II:—Hwider hweorfaþ wē hlāfordleáse, synnum wunde, gif wē swīcaþ đē? Andr. Kmbl. 813; An. 407. [*Goth.* wunds: *O. Sax.* wund: *O. H. Ger.* wunt (*in cpds.*): *Ger.* wund.] v. dolg-, hrif-, þurh-wund.

wundel, e: wundle, an; *f. A wound* (lit. or fig.), *sore:*—Gif hwylc lǣwede man ōđerne wundige, gebēte wiđ hine đa wunde (wundlan, wundlāc, *v.ll.*), L. Ecg. P. iv. 22; Th. ii. 210, 25. Wiđ nīwe wundela (wunda, *v. l.*), Lchdm. i. 8, 14: 10, 9: 92, 21: 100, 1: 108, 19: 206, 6, 17. His sāule wundela (*vulnera*) gehǣlan, R. Ben. 72, 7. v. wyndle.

wunden-feax; *adj. With plaited mane:*—Wicg wundenfeax, Beo. Th. 2804; B. 1400.

wunden-heals; *adj. With twisted prow:*—Wudu wundenheals, Beo. Th. 601; B. 298.

wunden-locc; *adj. With braided locks:*—Wīf wundenlocc, Exon. Th. 407, 26; Rä. 26, 11. Slōh wundenlocc (*Judith*) đone feóndsceaþan, Judth. Thw. 23, 3; Jud. 103. Seó cneóris, wlanc, wundenlocc, 26, 13; Jud. 326.

wunden-mǣl; *adj. Having curved markings*, applied to a sword:—Wearp wundenmǣl (wundel-, MS.), đæt hit on eorđan læg, stīđ and stȳlecg, Beo. Th. 3066; B. 1531. Cf. hring-mǣl.

wundenness. v. ofer-wundenness.

wunden-stefna, an; *m. A ship with curved prow:*—Wundenstefna gewaden hæfde, đæt đa līđende land gesāwon, Beo. Th. 445; B. 220.

wunder. v. wundor.

wundian; *p.* ode *To wound:*—Se đe mann wundaþ and wyle hine ofsleán *qui percusserit hominem volens occidere*, Ex. 21, 12. Hē (*the itch*) wundaþ and sió wund sāraþ, Past. 11; Swt. 71, 20. Beón hwīlum wundiaþ, Fragm. Kmbl. 41; Leás. 22. Wǣpenstrǣlas mē wundedon, Ps. Th. 56, 5. Indisce mȳs ūre feþerfōt niétenu wundedon and monige for hiora wundum swultan, Nar. 16, 8. Gif hwylc lǣwede man ōđerne wundige, gebēte wiđ hine đa wunde, L. Ecg. P. iv. 22; Th. ii. 210, 24. Đa cwōman tō đon đæt hié woldon ūs wundigan, Nar. 22, 17. Se cempa ongon Waldend wundian, Exon. Th. 260, 2; Jul. 291. Swelce hē nacodne hine selfne eówige tō wundigeanne his feóndum, Past. 38; Swt. 277, 17. Ungehēredre leoma tōslitnysse wundade (*lacerati*), Bd. 1, 7; S. 479, 14. [*Goth.* ga-wundōn: *O. H. Ger.* wuntōn: *Icel.* undaðr *wounded*.] v. for-, ge-wundian; un-wundod.

wundig; *adj. Ulcerous, full of sores:*—Wundie *ulcerosos*, Germ. 396, 267.

wundiht; *adj. Ulcerous:*—Wundihtum *ulcerosis*, Germ. 396, 153.

wund-lāc, es; *n. A wound; see first passage under* wundel.

wund-līc; *adj. That inflicts wounds:*—Wundlīcne *uulnificum*, Germ. 402, 51.

wundor, es; *n.* I. *a wonder*, (1) *a circumstance* or *act that excites astonishment:*—Đæt is wundor tō cweþanne *mirum dictu*, Bd. 3, 6; S. 528, 10: Beo. Th. 3453; B. 1724. Wundor mē đincđ eówer đingrǣden, Homl. Th. ii. 484, 14. Mē þincþ wundor, Blickl. Homl. 179, 13: 175, 13. Đā wæs wundor micel, đæt se wīnsele wiđhæfde, Beo. Th. 1546; B. 771: Cd. Th. 37, 26; Gen. 595. Đæt folc wundraþ đæs đe hit seldost gesihþ, đeáh hit læsse wundor sié, Bt. 39, 3; Fox 216, 3. Ne þincþ ūs đæt nān wundor, Blickl. Homl. 33, 7. Ne þincþ mē đæt wundur wuhte đe læsse, Met. 20, 117. Ac nis nā wunder *sed quid mirum?* Hpt. Gl. 473, 44. Nis đæt nān wundor, Bt. 31, 2; Fox 110, 9: Met. 17, 7. Næs đæt nānþing wundor, đæt Drihten wæs đam folce gram *nec miranda indignatio in populum*, Deut. 1, 37. Nis ǣnig wundor, hū . . ., Exon. Th. 63, 7; Cri. 1016. Wundor weard on wege; wæter weard tō bāne, 483, 9; Rä. 68, 3. Đæt is wundres dǣl, đam đe swylc ne conn, hū . . .,

472, 3; Rä. 61, 10. Ic ðæt wundor gefrægn, ðæt se wyrm forswealg wera gied sumes, 432, 7; Rä. 48, 2. Ne ic on mægene miclum gange, ne wundor ofer mē wuniaþ ǣnig *neque ambulavi in magnis, neque in mirabilibus super me*, Ps. Th. 130, 2. Ðǣr bið wundra mā, ðonne hit ǣnig mæge āþencan, Exon. Th. 61, 24; Cri. 989. Ðæt wæs wundra sum, ðæt ðæt sweord gemealt īse gelīcost, Beo. Th. 3219; B. 1607. (2) *a circumstance that excites astonishment as being out of the usual course of nature, a prodigy, portent*:—Gewurdon on Rōme ða yfelan wundor *obscoena et dira prodigia vel visa Romae vel nunciata sunt*, Ors. 4, 2; Swt. 160, 17. Wundra ɫ forebeácna *prodigia*, Hpt. Gl. 488, 34. (3) of the works of Divine power, *a wonder, miracle*:—For fyrwetgeornnesse ðæs wundres (*the raising of Lazarus*), Blickl. Homl. 69, 22. Ā mæg God wyrcan wundor æfter wundre, Beo. Th. 1866; B. 931. Eal ðæt folc ðe ðis wundor (*the giving sight to the blind man*) geseah, Blickl. Homl. 15, 29. Ic bebeóde wundor geweorðan, Andr. Kmbl. 1459; An. 730: Cd. Th. 245, 31; Dan. 471: Elen. Kmbl. 2241; El. 1122. Gemunaþ hū hē mænig wundor geworhte *mementote mirabilia ejus, quae fecit*, Ps. Th. 104, 5. Mǣre synd his wundur ofer manna bearn *mirabilia ejus filiis hominum*, 106, 30. Swā fela wundra, swā wē gehȳrdon gedōne on Cafarnaum, Lk. Skt. 4, 23. Ðis worhte fruma ðara wundra (uundra, Lind.) ðe Hǣlend *hoc fecit initium signorum Jesus*, Jn. Skt. Rush. 2, 11: Blickl. Homl. 105, 25: Andr. Kmbl. 1138; An. 569. Ðæt (*the turning of Lot's wife into a pillar of salt*) is wundra sum, ðara ðe geworhte wuldres Aldor, Cd. Th. 155, 14; Gen. 2572. On eallum mīnum wundrum *in cunctis mirabilibus meis*, Ex. 3, 20. For ðīnum wundrum *a signis tuis*, Ps. Th. 64, 8. Mænigu wundur hē geworhte, 77, 5. Wundor, Cd. Th. 246, 4; Dan. 474: Blickl. Homl. 17, 10. Wundru, Past. 16; Swt. 103, 13: Ps. Th. 87, 12: Ex. 12, 12. Wundro, Blickl. Homl. 81, 10. Uundra, Jn. Skt. Lind. 11, 47. (3 a) of supernatural power working through a human being, *a miracle*:—Eft gelamp ōþer wundor ðissum onlīc, Blickl. Homl. 219, 6. His (*Oswald's*) wundor wǣron miclo, Shrn. 114, 5: Elen. Kmbl. 1650; El. 827. Synd ðās wundru (*virtutes*) gefremede on him, Mt. Kmbl. 14, 2. Wæs ðis ðara wundra ǣrest ðe ðes eádiga wer geworhte, Blickl. Homl. 219, 2. Þurh ða wundor ðe heó geseah æt ðam bisceope, Shrn. 115, 6. Hēhbiscopes micla wundra *pontificis magnalia*, Rtl. 77, 19. (4) *a wonderful object, wondrous thing*:—Wēn is ðæt hwilc wundor ineode on ðæt carcern and ða hyrdas ācwælde, Blickl. Homl. 239, 30. Heofonbeácen . . . ōðer wundor syllīc . . . byrnende beám, Cd. Th. 184, 17; Exod. 108. Hwæt is ðæt wundor, ðæt geond ðās woruld fareþ? . . . Yldo, Salm. Kmbl. 563; Sal. 281. Fērdon folctogan wunder sceáwian, lāþes lāstas, Beo. Th. 1685; B. 840. Wundur, 6057; B. 3032: 6197; B. 3103. Hine wundra fela swencte on sunde, 3023; B. 1509. II. *wonderful, miraculous power*:—Ðæs engles mægen and his wundor weorðod bið, Blickl. Homl. 209, 20. Heofenas andettaþ hū wundor ðīn standeþ, Ps. Th. 88, 4. Mycel ys his wundur ofer manna bearn, 106, 20. Eal ðis wæs geworden tō ðon ðæt wē sceoldan ūres Drihtnes wundor oncnāwan, Blickl. Homl. 71, 23. III. *wonder, admiration*:—Þeóda wlītaþ, wundrum wafiaþ, hū seó wilgedryht wildne weorþiaþ, Exon. Th. 222, 1; Ph. 342. Ðysne wīg ðe ðū ðē tō wundrum (*as the object of thy adoration?* cf. Ðam gyldnan gylde ðe hē him tō gode geteóde, l. 19) teódest, Cd. Th. 228, 25; Den. 208. ¶ cases, with or without prepositions, used adverbially or adjectivally:—Ðæt of ðē ācenned bið, ðæt bið on wundra (*shall be a source of wonder*) eallum folcum, Homl. Ass. 121, 138. Gē mec tō wundre (*so as to excite wonder, wonderfully*), wǣgan mōtun, Exon. Th. 124, 21; Gū. 341: Homl. Skt. i. 23, 652. Wundrum monigo *very many*, Mk. Skt. Lind. Rush. 7, 8. Wundrum lytel *wonderfully little*, Bt. 11, 1; Fox 32, 21. Swȳþe wundrum well, Lchdm. i. 80, 21. Wundrum fæger, Exon. Th. 214, 1; Ph. 232: 202, 1; Ph. 63. Wundrum gegierwed, 483, 8; Rä. 68, 2. Eallum wundrum ðrymlīc girwan up swǣsendo, Judth. Thw. 21, 7; Jud. 8. Hū woruld wǣre wundrum geteód, Cd. Th. 222, 28; Dan. 111. [*O. Sax.* wundar: *O. H. Ger.* wuntar *mirum, prodigium, portentum, mirabile, miraculum, magnale, stupor*: *Icel.* undr.] v. eall-, fǣr-, hand-, lyft-, mægen-, niþ-, searo-, sundor-, swegel-, þeód-wundor.

wundor *hostimen*, Wrt. Voc. ii. 43, 20: 70, 32, *for* (?) pundor.

wundor-āgræfen; *adj.* (*ptcpl.*) *Wondrously graven*:—Hē wundorāgræfene anlīcnesse engla sīnra geseh, Andr. Kmbl. 1424; An. 712.

wundor-beácen, es; *n. A wondrous sign*:—Swā hī on wege wyrcean sceoldon wundorbeácen, Ps. Th. 73, 5.

wundor-bebod, es; *n. A monstrous command*:—Hē him bebeorgan ne con wōm wundorbebodum wergan gāstes, Beo. Th. 3498; B. 1747.

wundor-bleó *a wondrous colour*:—Ðæs temples segl wundorbleóm geworht, Exon. Th. 70, 17; Cri. 1140.

wundor-clam[m], es; *m. A wondrous clasp*:—Wæs gebunden deóran since duru ormǣte, wundurclommum bewriþen, Exon. Th. 19, 33; Cri. 310.

wundor-cræft, es; *m.* I. *wondrous skill, great cunning*:—Hē lǣmen fæt biwyrcan hēt wundorcræfte, Exon. Th. 277, 4; Jul. 575. II. *miraculous power*:—Hē cyninges brōðor āwehte wundorcræfte þurh Dryhtnes miht, ðæt hē of deáðe ārās, Apstls. Kmbl. 110; Ap. 55. Godspell wrītan wundorcræfte, Andr. Kmbl. 26; An. 13: 1290; An. 645: Exon. Th. 427, 3; Rä. 41, 85. [Heo dude uundercraftes, þe scucke hire fulste . . . to hire weoren iwoned þa uundercreftie men, Laym. 1147.]

wundor-dǣd, e; *f. A deed of magic*:—Ealle ða men ða ðe Sīmōnes wundordǣda wafodan, Blickl. Homl. 173, 22. [Þet folc com to se þys wonderdede (*the ordeal of Queen Emma*), R. Glouc. 337, 6. *M. H. Ger.* wunder-tāt: *Ger.* wunder-that.]

wundor-deáþ, es; *m. A wondrous death*:—Wedra þeóden (*Beowulf, killed by the fire-drake*) wundordeáðe swealt, Beo. Th. 6067; B. 3037.

wundor-fæt, es; *m. A wondrous vessel*:—Byrelas sealdon wīn of wunderfatum, Beo. Th. 2328; B. 1162.

wundor-full; *adj. Wonderful, glorious*:—Mid wundurfulre (wundum-, MS.) wæfersēne *stupendo spectaculo*, Hpt. Gl. 470, 75. Wynsum is seó wunung on ðam wuldorfullum (wunderfullum, *v. l.*) dreáme, Homl. Ass. 43, 481. Wundorfulla (*gloriosa*) gecweden synd be ðē, Ps. Spl. 86, 2. [Wonderfol to telle, Laym. 280, 2nd MS. Þis ilke best zuo wonderuol and dreduol, Ayenb. 15, 4.]

wundor-gehwyrft *a wonderful turn*:—Of wundorgehwerfte *vice mirifica*, Germ. 390, 161.

wundor-geweorc, es; *n. A wonderful work, a miracle*:—Þurh ðæt wundorgeweorc ðe hē Lazarum āwehte of deáþe, Blickl. Homl. 67, 6. Gelōmlīcu wundurgeweorc (*sanitatum miracula*) gewordene wǣron, Bd. 3, 9; S. 533, 3. Āwritene gemang ðara apostola wundorgewurcum, H. R. 13, 12. Hē hié tō heofona rīce laþode þurh his wundorgeweorc, Blickl. Homl. 7, 10. v. wundor-weorc.

wundor-gifu, e; *f. A wondrous gift, wondrous capacity*:—Sumum wundorgiefe þurh goldsmiþe gearwad weorþeþ, ful oft hē gehyrsteþ wel brytencyninges beorn, Exon. Th. 331, 23; Vy. 72.

wundor-līc; *adj. Wonderful, exciting admiration* or *surprise*:—Is wundorlīc (*mirabilis*) Drihten, Ps. Th. 92, 5: Met. 20, 3. Wunderlīc, Bt. 33, 4; Fox 128, 4. Mīn (*an angel's*) nama is mycel and wundorlīc, Blickl. Homl. 137, 29. Wundorlīc (*mirabilis*) is geworden ðīn wīsdōm, Ps. Th. 138, 4: 118, 129. Hit is wundorlīc, ðæt ic secgan wille, Bt. 20; Fox 70, 27. Ðys is fram Drihtne geworden, and hit ys wundorlīc (wundurlīc, Lind.: wunderlīc, Rush. *mirabile*) on ūrum eágum, Mt. Kmbl. 21, 42: Ps. Th. 117, 21. Ðæt is wundorlīc, ðæt gē nyton hwanon hē is, Jn. Skt. 9, 30: Met. 20, 86. Cymeþ wundorlīc Cristes onsȳn, Exon. Th. 56, 25; Cri. 906. Wundorlīc wræcca (*Nebuchadnezzar*), Cd. Th. 256, 1; Dan. 634. Wundorlīc wǣgbora, Beo. Th. 2884; B. 1440. Ic eom wunderlīcu wiht, Exon. Th. 399, 16; Rä. 19, 1: 400, 14; Rä. 21, 1. Ðæt wæs wunderlīcu gemetgung *miro modo*, Past. 17; Swt. 113, 16. Wunderlīc gestreón *mirandum negotium*, Hpt. Gl. 469, 3. Oft hwæm gebyreþ ðæt hē hwæt mǣrlīces and wundorlīces geðēð, Past. 4; Swt. 39, 6. Hē (*Samson*) wearð swīðe ofþyrst for ðam wundorlīcan slege, Jud. 15, 18. Wundorlīcre hrædnysse hē bið ālȳsed, Lchdm. i. 288, 16. On wundorlīcre mycelnesse, Blickl. Homl. 181, 20. Gesāwon hié wundorlīce wyrd, ðone man lifgendne ðone ðe hié ǣr deádne forlēton, 217, 36. Wundorlīc tācn, 205, 31. Ic ðē sǣde swīðe lang spell and wundorlīc, Bt. 35, 5; Fox 166, 2. Hū ða wīsan sind wundorlīce, Exon. Th. 223, 14; Ph. 359. Hū his ða goodan weorc syndon wundorlīce *quam terribilia sunt opera ejus*, Ps. Th. 65, 2. Gif ðū wēnst ðætte wundorlīce gerela[n?] hwelc weorþmynd sié, Bt. 14, 1; Fox 42, 18. Hwonon him ða wundorlīcan gereordo cōman, Blickl. Homl. 153, 8. Eorðe brengð wæstma fela wundorlīcra, Met. 20, 101. Sió hæfde wæstum wundorlīcran, Exon. Th. 413, 14; Rä. 32, 5. Ðā cwōman ðǣr nædran wunderlīcran ðonne ða ōþre wǣron and egeslīcran . . . wǣron hié wunderlīcre micelnisse, Nar. 14, 1–3. Seó burg ðe ǣr wæs ealra weorca fæstast and wunderlecast and mǣrast, Ors. 2, 4; Swt. 74, 24. Is ðæt eác ealles wundorlīcost, ðæt . . ., Blickl. Homl. 127, 14. [*Laym.* wunder-lic: *Orm.* wunnderr-like: *Wick.* wondir-li: *O. Sax.* wundar-līk: *O. H. Ger.* wuntar-līh: *Icel.* undr-ligr.]

wundorlīce; *adv. Wonderfully*, (1) with adjectives:—Ðǣr wearð gegaderod wundorlīce micel folc, Homl. Skt. i. 23, 616. Hē hine gesette in wundorlīce micle cyrcean, Shrn. 121, 3. (2) with verbs:—Wundurlīce *mirabiliter*, Ps. Surt. 75, 5. Wundorlīce *mire*, Hymn. Surt. 70, 5. Drihten hine swā wundorlīce of eallum his earfoþum gefriþode, Ps. Th. 32, arg.: Ex. 11, 7: Past. 54; Swt. 423, 4: Bt. 33, 4; Fox 130, 35: Met. 20, 162: 13, 5. Wunderlīce, Bt. 33, 4; Fox 128, 5. Hié wundorlīce deáþ geþrowodan for Godes naman, Blickl. Homl. 171, 31. Wundurlīce heó hǣleþ, Lchdm. i. 194, 22. Wundorlīce, 220, 20. Hī wurdon wundorlīce āfirhte *timuerunt valde*, Gen. 20, 8. Ic ne fērde on mǣrðum ne wundorlīce mid getote be mē ne bodude *neque ambulavi in magnis, neque in mirabilibus super me*, R. Ben. 22, 17. Hē hine gescerpte wlitegum wǣdum wundorlīce, Met. 15, 3. In ðīs tō uundranne ɫ uundorlīce is *in hoc mirabile est*, Jn. Skt. Lind. 9, 30. And eác ðæt wunderlīcor wæs, ðā ðā heora ān bodade mid ānre sprǣce, ǣlcum wæs geðūht swilce hē sprǣce mid his gereorde, Homl. Th. i. 318, 26. Se fugel wrixleþ wōðcræfte wundorlīcor ðonne ǣfre byre monnes hȳrde, Exon. Th. 206, 16; Ph. 127. [*O. H. Ger.* wuntarlīhho *mirabiliter*.]

wundor-mâþþum, es; *m. A wondrous treasure*:—Ðone healsbeáh, wrǽtlîcne wundormâþðum, Beo. Th. 4352; B. 2173.
wundor-seón, e; *f. A wondrous spectacle*:—Wundorsióna fela, Beo. Th. 1995; B. 995. [*O. H. Ger.* wuntar-siuni *spectaculum*: *Icel.* undr-sjónir; *pl. f. a spectacle.*]
wundor-smiþ, es; *m. A smith who makes wonderful things* or *who works by wondrous art*:—Gylden hilt, . . . enta ǽrgeweorc, . . . wundor-smiþa geweorc, Beo. Th. 3366; B. 1681.
wundor-tâcen, es; *n. A wondrous sign*:—Wundortâcna and fore-beácna *signorum et prodigiorum*, Ps. Th. 104, 23. [*O. Sax.* wundar-têkan: *O. H. Ger.* wuntar-zeichen *miraculum.*]
wundor-weorc, es; *n. A wondrous work, a miracle*:—Hê (*Christ*) ôðerra unrîm cýðde wundorworca, Andr. Kmbl. 1409; An. 705. Manige wîtgan ǽr Sancte Iôhanne on swîþe manegum godcundum mægenum ealra wundorweorcum swîþe wuldorlîce âscinon, Blickl. Homl. 161, 19. Ðæt cwyce secgeaþ his wundorweorc ofer ealle werþeóde *annuntiate inter gentes opera ejus*, Ps. Th. 104, 1. [War stod þat wonderworc (seolkuð werc, 1st MS.), Laym. 17376: *Ger.* wunder-werk.] v. wundor-geweorc.
wundor-weorold, e; *f. The wondrous world*:—Geond ðâs wundor-woruld, Exon. Th. 421, 12; Rä. 40, 17.
wundor-wyrd, e; *f. A wondrous case*:—Be ðâm næglum frignan ongan cwên, Cyriacus bæd, ðæt hire gâstes mihtum ymb wundorwyrd willan gefylde, Elen. Kmbl. 2139; El. 1071.
wundrian; *p.* ode. I. *to wonder at, to regard with surprise* or *admiration.* (1) absolute:—Ealle gê wundriaþ (wundrigeaþ, *v. l.*) *omnes miramini*, Jn. Skt. 7, 21. Se Hǽlend wundrode (wundriende wæs, Rush.) *Jesus miratus est*, Mt. Kmbl. 8, 10. Hig wundrodun (wund-radan, Rush.), 19, 25: 21, 20. Hî wundrodon mycelre wundrunge *obstupuerunt stupore maximo*, Mk. Skt. 5, 42. Ðâ ongan ic wundrigan, Bt. 40, 1; Fox 236, 9. Is se godcunda anweald tô wyndrianne, 32, 2; Fox 116, 16. Tô wundranne (uundranne, Lind.) is *mirabile est*, Jn. Skt. Rush. 9, 30. Nis ðæt tô wundrigenne, þeáh ðe hê wǽre costod, Blickl. Homl. 33, 12. Ða leóda beheóldon swîðe wundrigende, Homl. Skt. ii. 26, 186. (2) with gen.:—Ðæt ungestæððige folc wundraþ ðæs ðe hit seldost gesihþ, ðeáh hit læsse wundor sié, Bt. 39, 3; Fox 216, 2: Met. 28, 49. Hwæt stondaþ gê hêr and ðyses wundriaþ? Blickl. Homl. 123, 22. His wundriaþ ða ðe him underðiédde bióþ, Past. 4; Swt. 39, 7: Met. 28, 66. Ðâ wundrade ic swîðe swîðe ðara gôdena wiotona, Past. pref.; Swt. 5, 19. Ðâ wundrode ðæt folc his lâre, Mt. Kmbl. 7, 28. Hê wundrade Godes wundra, Ps. Th. 8, arg. Hwâ is on weorulde, ðe ne wundrige fulles mônan? Met. 28, 40. Hwæþer gimma wlite eówre eágan tô him getió heora tô wundrianne? Bt. 13; Fox 40, 2. Hê fêrde wundrigende ðæs ðâr geworden wæs, Lk. Skt. 24, 12. (3) with acc.:—Wundriaþ weras wlite and wæstma, Exon. Th. 221, 7; Ph. 331. Ic ða wynsumnesse and fægernesse ðæs londes wundrade, Nar. 26, 26: 28, 1. Ðý læs ðæt wundredan weras and idesa, Exon. Th. 176, 6; Gû. 1205. (4) with a clause:—Hwâ ne wundraþ ðætte sume tunglu habbaþ scyrtran hwyrft ðonne sume habban? Bt. 39, 3; Fox 214, 17. Hî ne wundriaþ ðætte . . ., Met. 28, 50. Hî ne wundriaþ, hû hit on wolcnum þunraþ, þrâgmælum eft ânforlǽteþ, 28, 54. Ðâ wundrade se ðeng for hwon hê ðæs bǽde, Bd. 4, 24; S. 598, 31. Gif hwâ wundrie, hû hit gewurðan mihte, Jud. 15, 19. (5) with gen. and clause:—Hwâ ne wundraþ ðæs, ðæt sume steorran gewîtaþ under ða sǽ? Bt. 39, 3; Fox 214, 26. Hwâ ungelǽredra ne wundraþ ðæs roderes færeldes, hû hê ǽlce dæg ûton ymb-hwyrfð ealne ðisne middaneard? 214, 15. Hwâ wundraþ ðæs, oððe ôðres eft, hwý ðæt îs mæge weorðan of wætere, Met. 28, 58. Hwý ne wundriaþ hî ðæs, ðæt hit hwîlum þunraþ, hwîlum nâ ne onginþ, Bt. 39, 3; Fox 214, 33. Hwâ is ðe ne wundrige wolcna færeldes, roderes swifto, hû hý ǽlce dæge ûtan ymbhwerfaþ eallne middangeard? Met. 28, 2. Ǽlc wile ðæs wundrian for hwý hî swâ dôn, Bt. 39, 9; Fox 226, 14. (6) with prepositions:—Hê wundrode æfter ðære gesihþe, Blickl. Homl. 153, 35. Wundradun ða mengu be lâre his *ammirabantur turbae super doctrinam ejus*, Mt. Kmbl. Rush. 7, 28. Hî wundrodon on his lâre *admirabantur in doctrina ejus*, Mk. Skt. 6, 2. Ðâ wǽron ða apostolas swîþe wundrigende fram him, and wǽron cweþende tô him hwonon him ða wundorlîcan gereordo côman, Blickl. Homl. 153, 7. (7) with preposition and clause:—Wundrade heó ymb ðæs weres snyttro, hû hê swâ geleáfful on swâ lytlum fæce ǽfre wurde, Elen. Kmbl. 1914; El. 959. Hwâ is moncynnes, ðæt ne wundrie ymb ðâs tungl, hû hý sume habbaþ scyrtran ymbhwearft? Met. 28, 6. II. *to make wonderful, magnify* (?):—Hê wundraðe (*mirificavit*) ealle willan mîne, Ps. Spl. 15, 2. [*O. Sax.* wundrôn: *O. H. Ger.* wuntarôn: *Icel.* undra.] v. â-, ge-, of-wundrian.
wundrigend-lîc; *adj. Expressing admiration* or *astonishment*:—O is tôclypigendlîc *adverbium* . . . hê is eác wundrigendlîc: *O qualis facies*, Ælfc. Gr. 38; Zup. 241, 16.
wundrum. v. wundor.
wundrung, e; *f.* I. *wondering, wonder, admiration, astonishment*:—Hwæt is ðeós wundrung ðe gê wafiaþ? Exon. Th. 6, 24; Cri. 89. Eall hê wæs ful wundrunge and wafunge; and eác ða byrig hê geseah eall on ôþre wîsan gewend, on ôþre heó ǽr wæs, Homl. Skt. i. 23, 509. Heó mid wundrunge wearð befangen, 2, 251. Hê þearle siððan Maurum wurðode, and on wundrunge hæfde (*held him in admiration*), 6, 185. Ðǽr heó lîð ôð ðis on mycelre ârwurðnysse mannum tô wundrunge (*to the admiration of men*), 20, 101. Hê on ðære micclan his môdes wundrunge ðǽr gestôd dreórig *in the great bewilderment of his mind he stood there downcast*, 23, 627. Hî wundrodon mycelre wund-runge *obstupuerunt stupore maximo*, Mk. Skt. 5, 42. *Pape* geswutelaþ wundrunge, Ælfc. Gr. 5; Zup. 11, 3. *Interjectio* getâcnaþ hwîlon ðæs môdes blisse, hwîlon sârnysse, hwîlon wundrunge, 48; Zup. 278, 6. II. *a wonderful sight, a spectacle*:—Wundrunge *spectaculi*, Hpt. Gl. 508, 27.
wund-swaþu, e; *f. The trace of a wound, a scar*:—Wundsweðe mîne *cicatrices meae*, Ps. Surt. 37, 6.
wund-wâcu (?) *a wound-weakness, a wound, sore*:—Swâ þenne ne burnon ne burston, ne fundian ne feologan ne hoppetan, ne wundwâco sîan (*sores may not run*), ne dolh diópian, Lchdm. ii. 352, 2. Cf. wâc; *n.*
wune-lîc (wun-, wunu-); *adj. Wonted, usual, accustomed*:—Wunlîcre ârfeastnisse *solita pietate*, Rtl. 35, 21. Wunulîco rûmmôdnise *solita clementia*, 180, 10. v. ge-wunelîc.
wune-ness (wunu-), e; *f.* I. *a dwelling, habitation*:—Hê him wunonesse stôwe (*locum mansionis*) sealde, Bd. 5, 11; S. 626, 13. In wununise *in habitaculo*, Rtl. 58, 5: *habitatione*, 68, 20. Ðâ geworhte hê him nearo wîc and wunenesse (*mansionem angustam*), Bd. 4, 28; S. 605, 23. Ðâ sealde se cyning him wununesse and stôwe (*mansionem*) in Cantwarabyrig, 1, 25; S. 487, 18. Hê him sylfum wununesse and wîc geceás *ipse locum mansionis elegit*, 4, 26; S. 602, 38. Wit oferfêrdon ðâs wununesse (*has mansiones*) ðara eádigra gâsta. . . . Wit becôman tô ðâm blîþan wunenyssum (*ad mansiones laetas*), 5, 12; S. 629, 31, 43. II. *continuance, perseverance*:—Wununise (*perseverantiam*) êces hehstaldnisse, Rtl. 105, 36. v. in-wuneness.
wung, Wrt. Voc. ii. 129, 26. v. pung.
wunian; *p.* ode *To dwell, remain*:—Wunat *inmoratur*, Wrt. Voc. ii. 111, 76. Wunaþ *constat*, Kent. Gl. 1176. Wunian *consistere*, 190. I. of living creatures, *to dwell, abide, stay, remain, live*, (1) of dwelling in a place or with a person, (a) with preps. or adverbs:—Ðû geond holt wunast *thou shalt live in the woods*, Cd. Th. 252, 6; Dan. 574. Ðû in heánnissum wunast mid Waldend Fæder, Exon. Th. 10, 36; Cri. 163. Se þeów ne wunaþ (*manet*) on hûse on êcnesse; se sunu wunaþ on êcnesse, Jn. Skt. 8, 35. Pellicane gelîc, se on wêstene wunaþ, Ps. Th. 101, 5. Monna gehwylc cwic þendan hêr wunaþ, Exon. Th. 37, 8; Cri. 590. Ða hwîle ðe wê on ðysse worlde wuniaþ, Blickl. Homl. 103, 24. Him (*the whale*) ða fêrend on fæste wuniaþ, wîc weardiaþ, Exon. Th. 361, 26; Wal. 25. Mislîce wildeór wuniaþ (*morantur*) on wudum, Coll. Monast. Th. 22, 23. On heán muntum heortas wuniaþ, Ps. Th. 103, 17. Ic on wêstene wunode lange *mansi in solitudine*, 54, 7. Wunude, 83, 1. Hê wunode ðǽr on mynstre, Homl. Skt. i. 6, 99. Hê on ðæm lande feala wintra wunode, Blickl. Homl. 113, 13. Hê wunode be Iordane, Cd. Th. 116, 5; Gen. 1931. Hê ðǽr wunode mid him, Blickl. Homl. 239, 18: 249, 16: Exon. Th. 162, 8; Gû. 972: Beo. Th. 2261; B. 1128. Wê cômun tô ðam ðæt wê wunedon on ðînum lande, Gen. 47, 4. Ðâ hig wunedon on Galilêa *conversantibus eis in Galilaea*, Mt. Kmbl. 17, 22. Hié ealle onyppan wunedon, bîdende ðæs Hâlgan Gâstes, Blickl. Homl. 133, 26. Wunedon on ðâm wîcum Abraham and Loth, Cd. Th. 113, 20; Gen. 1890. Wuna mid ûsic and ðê wîc geceós, 164, 29; Gen. 2722. Medmicel fæc nû gyt wuna mid ûs, Blickl. Homl. 247, 33. Wuna in ðære wînbyrig, Andr. Kmbl. 3340; An. 1674. Wuniaþ (wunas, Lind.: wynigaþ, Rush. *manete*) ðǽr, Mt. Kmbl. 10, 11. Wunigaþ on ðam ylcan hûse, Lk. Skt. 10, 7. Eal ðæt manegu ðe him mid wunige, Andr. Kmbl. 1890; An. 947. Hî on his neáweste wunian, Ps. Th. 148, 14. Beón, gif hî man acwellaþ, cwelle hig man raþe, . . . ðæt hig ofer niht ðǽron ne wunigon (*restent*), L. Ecg. C. 39; Th. ii. 164, 3. Ic wylle tô-dæg on ðînum hûse wunian (tô wunianne, Lind.: tô wuniganne, Rush. *manere*), Lk. Skt. 19, 5. Wunian on êðle, Cd. Th. 294, 27; Sat. 477. Mid wuldorcyninge wunian, 283, 30; Sat. 312. In worulde wunian, Exon. Th. 51, 21; Cri. 819. Wunian in wîcum, 316, 9; Môd. 46. Wunigan in wuldre mid weoroda God, 22, 5; Cri. 347: Blickl. Homl. 25, 35. Hê leng mid him lîchomlîce wunian nolde, 135, 22. Hê on his môdor bôsme wunigende wæs, 165, 18. Wǽron ealle ða apostolas wunigende on ânre stôwe, 133, 15. (b) with dat. (inst.):—Hê wîcum wunode, Cd. Th. 108, 26; Gen. 1812. Abraham wunode êðeleardum Cananêa, 116, 32; Gen. 1945. Wuna ðǽm ðê âgon *abide with those own thee*, 138, 18; Gen. 2293. Wîcum wunian, Beo. Th. 6158; B. 3083. (c) with acc. *to inhabit* a place, *live in* or *on*:—Hê heánne beám wunaþ, Exon. Th. 209, 17; Ph. 172. Ic îscealdne sǽ winter wunade, 306, 29; Seef. 15. Ða ðe hleóleásan wîc hwîle wunedon, Andr. Kmbl. 262; An. 131. Wunian wîc unsýfre, 2621; An. 1310. Wederburg wunian, 3391; An. 1699. Seó ðe wunian sceolde cealde streámas, Beo. Th. 2525; B. 1260: Cd. Th. 280, 22; Sat. 259: 282, 36; Sat. 297. Ic (*the soul*) ðê (*the body*) wunian sceolde, Soul Kmbl. 86; Seel. 43. ¶ in

figurative expressions:—Se fugel wunaþ wyllestreámas (*bathes*), Exon. Th. 204, 29; Ph. 105. Wunian wælreste *to lie dead*, 184, 10; Gú. 1342: Beo. Th. 5796; B. 2902: *to be buried*, Elen. Kmbl. 1444; El. 724. Reste wunian *to sleep*, Cd. Th. 223, 22; Dan. 123: Rood Kmbl. 6; Kr. 3. (2) *to live, be* in certain conditions or circumstances, (a) with prep. or adv.:—Þenden ic wunige on worulddreámum *quamdiu* ..*ro*, Ps. Th. 103, 31. Seó sáwel đe wunaþ on heofena ríces gefeán, Blickl. Homl. 57, 31. Wunaþ hē on wiste, ne hine wiht drēfeþ, Beo. Th. 3474; B. 1735. Đa menigo đe wuniaþ on nearonēdum, Andr. Kmbl. 202; An. 101. On fýrbæđe đú wunodest, Elen. Kmbl. 1897; El. 950. Hē in yrmđum wunade, Andr. Kmbl. 326; An. 163. Wē wunodon on wynnum, Cd. Th. 279, 12; Sat. 237. Hí wunedon ætsomne, Met. 20, 243. Wunian on ēcean wuldre, Blickl. Homl. 105, 1. In wynnum wunian, Cd. Th. 299, 26; Sat. 556: Exon. Th. 140, 2; Gú. 604. Wunian in wylme, Salm. Kmbl. 933; Sal. 466. Adam wæs wunigende on đisum líſe mid geswince, Homl. Th. i. 20, 6. (b) with dat. (inst.):—Hē wunaþ unlustum, Salm. Kmbl. 538; Sal. 268. Heó helltregum wunodon, Cd. Th. 5, 19; Gn. 74. Eádig weorþan, wunian wyndagum, Exon. Th. 330, 34; Vy. 61. (c) with noun or adj.:—Borhhond [hē] wunade *fidejussu exstitit*, Kent. Gl. 743. Wunude *extitit* (*praestantior*), Hpt. Gl. 511, 60. Đæt đú langlíf ofer eorđan wunie, Homl. Th. ii. 36, 2. Âna lifgan, wineleás wunian, Exon. Th. 344, 15; Gn. Ex. 174. (3) *to abide, be present* with a person to comfort or help:—Ic đē mid wunige, Andr. Kmbl. 198; An. 99: Exon. Th. 30, 12; Cri. 478. God wunaþ on him *est in ipsis Dominus*, Num. 16, 3. II. of things abstract or concrete, *to be, rest, reside, remain*, (1) in respect to locality, *occupy a position*:—Wunaþ *morabitur*, Kent. Gl. 481: *commorabitur*, 540. (a) with prep. or adv.:—Se hálga stenc wunaþ geond wynlond, Exon. Th. 203, 10; Ph. 82. Đǽr se wísdóm wunaþ on gemyndum, Met. 7, 39. Lyft on middum wunaþ, 20, 79. Mid đam wítegendlícum gáste đe on đē wunaþ, Homl. Skt. i. 18, 282: Cd. Th. 56, 7; Gen. 908. Wæter đe wuniaþ gyt under fæstenne folca hrōfes, 10, 6; Gen. 152. Eorđe and wæter wuniaþ on fýre, Met. 20, 148. Beorh wunode on wonge, Beo. Th. 4476; B. 2242. Se monlíca stille wunode, đǽr hié begeat wíte, Cd. Th. 155, 3; Gen. 2567. Egesa on breóstum wunode, 173, 24; Gen. 2866. Treów on đē wunade, Exon. Th. 6, 12; Cri. 83: 126, 4; Gú. 366. Hwæþer him yfel đe gōd under wunige, 82, 4; Cri. 1333. Þēh mín líchama on niđerdǽlum eorđan wunige, Ps. Th. 138, 13. Saga mē hwǽr seó rōd wunige, Elen. Kmbl. 1244; El. 624. Tō manna heortan, ǽr Drihtnes weorc đǽr wunian mōte, Blickl. Homl. 19, 8: 111, 5. Ǽnigne dǽl secgas gesēgon on sele wunian, Beo. Th. 6248; B. 3128. Geweoton hí mearcland tredan, forlǽton moldern wunigean, open eorđscræfu, Andr. Kmbl. 1605; An. 803. Lazarus, đe Crist áwehte đý feorþan dæge đæs đe hē on byrgenne wæs fúl wunigende, Blickl. Homl. 75, 5. (b) with acc.:—Đæt treów sceolde wēsten wunian, Cd. Th. 251, 5; Dan. 559. Hine gærsbedd sceal wunian, Ps. Th. 102, 15. (2) of state or circumstance:—Inc sceal sealt wæter wunian on gewealde, Cd. Th. 13, 7; Gen. 199. Đá đá đis ígland wæs wunigende on sibbe, Homl. Skt. i. 13, 148. III. *to consist* of or in, *subsist, exist*. v. wunung, III:—On wordum Godes ríce ne wunaþ, ac on ánwylnysse đæs hálgan geleáfan, Guth. prol.; Gdwin. 2, 15. Đeós lyft ys án đæra feówer gesceafta, đe ǽlc líchamlíc đing on wunaþ. Feówer gesceafta synd, đe ealle eorđlíce líchaman on wuniaþ, Lchdm. iii. 272, 11–13. Đa hálgan þrynnysse on ánre godcundnysse ǽfre wunigende, Homl. Skt. i. 15, 216: 16, 1. Nis ná se Hálga Gást wunigende on his gecynde swá swá hē gesewen wæs, for đan đe hē is ungesewenlíc, Homl. Th. i. 322, 17. Him (*man*) is gemǽne mid stánum đæt hē beó wunigende; him is gemǽne mid treówum đæt hē lybbe, 302, 20. Hí nǽron ǽfre wunigende, ac God hí gesceóp, 276, 15. God is þurh hine sylfne wunigende, ii. 236, 18. IV. where there is permanence, continuity, *to remain, last, continue, endure*:—Đú wunast *tu permanebis*, Ps. Th. 101, 23. Đú on ēcnesse wunast *tu in aeternum permanes*, 101, 10: 92, 3. Đǽr nōht elles ne wunaþ, Blickl. Homl. 101, 5. Đínne naman đe wunaþ on ealra worlda world, 143, 31: Ps. Th. 111, 8. Seó đe ǽfre wæs and eác nú wunaþ, Homl. Skt. i. 15, 217. Þenden đǽr wunaþ húsa sēlest, Beo. Th. 574; B. 284. Swá hwylc swá on elne ōþ his ende wunaþ, se biđ hál, Blickl. Homl. 171, 26: Homl. Th. ii. 502, 21. Đære wylne sunu wunaþ eal his líf on đeówte, i. 110, 29. Wuniaþ đa wácran, Exon. Th. 311, 4; Seef. 87. Gif hē wunode ofer middæg *if he continued to live past noon*, Homl. Skt. i. 3, 595. Lucia on đære ylcan stōwe wunode đe heó ofslagen wæs *Lucia remained lying in the same place that she was struck down*, 9, 146. Se snáw leng ne wunede đonne áne tíde, Nar. 23, 21. Hí wunedun (wēren wungiende *mansissent*, Lind.) ōđ đyśne dæg, Mt. Kmbl. 11, 23. Đæt hió ne wunian on worldlífe *ita ut non sint*, Ps. Th. 103, 33. Herenes Drihtnes hēr sceal wunian on worulda woruld *laudatio ejus manet in seculum seculi*, 110, 8: 118, 44, 91. Hæfđ hē đæt gewrixle geset đe nú wunian sceal, Met. 11, 56. On sáre his líchoma sceal hēr wunian, Blickl. Homl. 61, 1: Exon. Th. 7, 19; Cri. 103. Eallum rihtgelýfdum mannum wunigendum for his noman, Blickl. Homl. 171, 14. IV a. with a complementary word or phrase:—Heó wæs fǽmne ǽr hire beorþre, and heó wunaþ fǽmne æfter hire beorþre, Blickl. Homl. 155, 33. Đú unstilla gesceafta ástyrest and đē self wunast swíđe stille, Met. 20, 16. God ána unáwendendlíc wunaþ, Bt. 35, 5; Fox 166, 9. Gescylded á wunaþ ungewyrded, þenden woruld stondeþ, Exon. Th. 210, 5; Ph. 181. Hió dumb wunaþ, 414, 7; Rä. 32, 16. Heó wæs mid twám werum and swá đeáh wunode mǽden, Homl. Skt. i. 20, 3. Se hearda hyge hálig wunode, Exon. Th. 135, 1; Gú. 517. Hí đágyt hǽđene wunodon, Homl. Th. ii. 502, 23. Is sǽd of đære tíde đe hí þanon gewiton ōþ tōdæge đæt đæt land wēste wunige (*manere desertus perhibetur*), Bd. 1, 15; S. 483, 27. Đis ungefremed wunie, L. Ath. i. proem.; Th. i. 198, 13. Hē hēt wunian wyrtruman eorđan fæstne, Cd. Th. 248, 20; Dan. 516. Sceal lufu uncer wǽrfæst wunian, Exon. Th. 173, 19; Gú. 1163. Abrames wíf wæs đágit wuniende bútan cildum *she remained still childless*, Gen. 16, 1. V. *to be wont*:—Ic gewunige *soleo*, wunigende *solens*, Ælfc. Gr. 41; Zup. 247, 5. [*O. E. Homl.* wunian: *A. R. Kath.* wunien: *Laym.* wunien, wonien: *Orm.* wunenn: *Gen. and Ex.* wunen: *Ayenb.* wonie: *Chauc. Piers P. Wick.* wone: *O. Sax.* wonōn, wunōn: *O. Frs.* wona, wuna: *O. H. Ger.* wonēn *habitare, morari, conversari, manere, solere*.] v. á-, ge-, on-, þurh-wunian; án-, dryht-, weorold-wuniende.

wunigend, es; *m. An inhabitant*:—Gyf wē gefyllaþ wunigendes þēnunge *si compleamus habitatoris officium*, R. Ben. Interl. 5, 11.

wunigend-líc, wunn, wununess. v. un-wunigendlíc, wyn[n], wuneness.

wunung, e; *f.* I. *dwelling, living*:—Gif hē hine sylfne tō mynstres wununge gefæstnian wyle *if he will settle to living in a monastery*; the Latin is: Si voluerit stabilitatem suam firmare, R. Ben. 108, 13. II. *a dwelling, habitation, place to live in*:—Feala muneca wunung *coenobium*, Wrt. Voc. i. 59, 5. Wunung *mansio*, 86, 46. Sý wunung (*habitatio*) heora onwēst, Ps. Spl. 68, 30. Com Eustachius mid his here tō đam túne đe heó đá on wæs. Wæs seó wunung đǽr swýþe wynsum on tō wícenne, and his geteld wǽron gehende hire wununge geslagene, Homl. Skt. ii. 30, 315. Wē wendaþ ús eástweard, þonne wē ús gebiddaþ . . .; ná swylce on eástdǽle synderlíce sý his wunung . . . on rihtwísum mannum is Godes wunung . . . Swá eác se fordōna man biđ deófles templ, and deófles wunung, Homl. Th. i. 262, 5–18. Ne biþ đǽr Cristes eardung ne his wunung on đære heortan, Blickl. Homl. 13, 24. On đære fíftan flēringe wæs đæra manna wunung gelōgod, Boutr. Scrd. 21, 10: Homl. Th. i. 536, 16. Wununge *contubernio, habitaculo*, Hpt. Gl. 468, 63. Tō mōderlícum wununge ł bōsme *ad maternum gremium*, 504, 12. Đæt hí sceoldon habban đa fægeran wununge đe se feónd forleás, Ælfc. T. Grn. 3, 6. Hē him đǽr wununge getimbrode, Shrn. 13, 16. Spyrian hwár đa mánfullan wununge habban, L. Eth. ix. 40; Th. i. 348, 26. Đa habbaþ hundfealde mēde and đa mǽrestan wununge, Homl. Ass. 21, 187. Wununga *sedes*, Hpt. Gl. 412, 33. Se Hǽlend sǽde, đæt on his Fæder húse syndon manega wununga, Homl. Ass. 42, 454. On muntum and on feldlícum wunungum, Jos. 10, 40. Đú wircst wununge (*mansiunculas*) binnan đam arce, Gen. 6, 14. Gē begeáton eów đeósterfulle wununga, Homl. Th. i. 68, 5. Geleáffulle menn gearwiaþ clǽne wununga on heora heortum Criste sylfum, Blickl. Homl. 73, 12. III. *being, existence, living*. v. wunian, III:—Wunung *essentia*, i. *aeternitas, natura*, Wrt. Voc. ii. 144, 20. Þeáh se líchama geendige, đe sceal eft þurh Godes mihte árísan tō ēcere wununge, Homl. Th. i. 20, 6. Se is lybbende God đe hæfđ líf and wununge đurh hine sylfne, 366, 33. Gesceafta nabbaþ náne wununge þurh hí sylfe, ac đurh God, se đe ána is þurh hine sylfne wunigende, ii. 236, 17. Yfel nis nán þing þurh hit sylf, and náne wununga næfđ būton on sumum gesceafta, Boutr. Scrd. 20, 44. [Wređđe hafđ wununge on þes dusian bosme *ira requiescit in sinu stulti*, O. E. Homl. i. 105, 24. Hore wununge naueđ no ȝet *habitatio eorum non habet januam*, A. R. 74, 12. Þe wununge of euch wunne *quietis eterne mansio*, Kath. 2423. God woning (hæh bold, 1st MS.), Laym. 7094. His (*the Reeve's*) wonyng was ful fair upon an hethe, Chauc. Prol. C. T. 606. *O. L. Ger.* wonunga *habitatio*: *O. H. Ger.* wonunga *mansio*.]

wurdian, wurdlian, wurm. v. wordian, wordlian, wyrm.

wurma, wyrma, an; *m.*: wurme, an; *f. A shell-fish from which a purple dye was obtained, a purple dye*; also *woad, a plant from which a dye is got*:—Wurma *murex*, wurma, weoloc *murice*, Wrt. Voc. ii. 56, 64, 62. Wurma, reád godwebb *ostrum*, 64, 10. Wyrma *ostrum*, i. 286, 34. Wurman *murice*, ii. 114, 46. Ungemæccre wurman *dispari murice*, 141, 19. Mid unilícere wurman, Hpt. Gl. 431, 42. Ungelícum wurman, Anglia xiii. 29, 58. Wolcreádum wurman *bistincto cocco sive vermiculo*, 29, 56. Twyhíwedum wurman, Hpt. Gl. 431, 31. Mid reádre wurman *croceo luto* (v. Ald. 75), 524, 40: Wrt. Voc. ii. 52, 48 (*printed* wurmaman). Wurman geblonden, Exon. Th. 218, 14; Ph. 294. Wyrman *murice*, Wrt. Voc. ii. 77, 23: 89, 29. Wyrman (*printed* wyrmaman, cf. 52, 48) *luto*, 87, 32. Wyrman (*purpureo*) *ostro*, Hpt. Gl. 522, 5. Genim myrran and hwít rēcels and safinam and saluiam and wurman, Lchdm. ii. 294, 24. Wurmum *muricibus*, Wrt. Voc. ii. 55, 20: Hpt. Gl. 524, 27. Wurman, 431, 47. [*O. Frs.* worma: *O. H. Ger.* wurmo *vermiculus*.] v. cor-, corn-, feld-, stán-wurma; wurm-reád.

wurmille, an; *f. Marjoram*:—Wurmille, uurmillae *origanum*, Txts. 83, 1452. Wurmilla, Wrt. Voc. ii. 65, 27. Wurmille, 64, 11. Wyrmelle (*printed* war-), i. 32, 11. Wyrmella, 286, 35. [Cf. *O. H. Ger.* wurmeli *vermiculus.*]

wurm-reád; *adj. Scarlet*:—Wurmreádne þræ̅d *coccinum*, Gen. 38, 28. Wurmreádne basing *pallium coccineum*, Jos. 7, 21. Cf. wyrm-basu.

wurms. v. worms.

wurmsig; *adj. Purulent*:—Wurmsi *purulentus*, Wrt. Voc. ii. 67, 29. v. wyrmsig.

wurmsihtig; *adj. Purulent*:—Wurmsihtig *purulentus*, Wrt. Voc. i. 22, 1.

wurpan. v. weorpan.

wurpol (-ul); *adj. That throws down*:—Wurpul *ster[n]ax*, Wrt. Voc. ii. 121, 42.

wurpte, wursm, wurst, wurþ, wurt-mete. v. wirpan, worms, wirsa, weorþ, wyrt-mete.

wūsc-bearn, es; *n. A beloved* or *an adopted child*:—Ūuscbearn (wuso, Rush.) *filioli*, Jn. Skt. Lind. 13, 33. [Cf. *Icel.* óska-barn *a chosen, adopted child*; ósk-mögr *a beloved son*: *M. H. Ger.* wunsch-kint; see Grmm. D. M. p. 139 (Stallybrass' trans.), and s. v. wunsch. Cf. too the proper name Wūsc-freá, Bd. 2, 14; S. 518, 1.] v. wȳsc.

Wūse, wuso, wutan (-on). v. Ūse, wūsc-bearn, witon.

wyde-treów. v. wudu-treów.

wyla (? hyla v. hylu):—Wyla ł hola *cabearum*, Hpt. Gl. 489, 71.

wylcþ, Germ. 389, 42. v. welwan.

wylf, e; *f. A she-wolf*:—Wylf *lupa*, Txts. 75, 1260. Fæ̅ddæ hiǽ wylif in Rōmæcæstri, 127, 2. [Cf. *O. H. Ger.* wulpa *lupa*: *Icel.* ylgr *a she-wolf.*] v. brim-wylf, *and next word.*

wylfen[n], e; *f. A she-wolf*, (1) literal:—Gif heó drinceþ wylfene meolc, Lchdm. i. 362, 13. Wylfene *beluae, bestiae maris*, Wrt. Voc. ii. 125, 43. (2) figurative:—Wylfen *Bellona*, i. *furia, dea belli, mater Martis*, Wrt. Voc. ii. 125, 41. Rēþre wylfenne *dire parce*, 140, 53. [Wummone wrođ is wuluene, and mon wrođ is wulf, A. R. 120, 9. Leoun or uulf, uuluine or bere, Havel. 573. *M. H. Ger.* wulfinne: *Ger.* wölfinn.]

wylfen; *adj. Wolfish, fierce*:—Wē geāscodan Eormanrīces wylfenne geþōht; đæt wæs grim cyning, Exon. Th. 378, 24; Deór. 22.

wylinc, Hpt. Gl. 419, 77. v. willung.

wyll, e; *f. Wool*:—Đa wylle and đa horna hȳ dōđ heom tō nytnysse *lanam et cornua in usum suum convertunt*, L. Ecg. C. 40; Th. ii. 166, 31. v. wull.

wyllen; *adj. Woollen, of wool*:—Wyllen *laneum*, līnen wearp *vel* wyllen āb *linostema*, Wrt. Voc. i. 40, 7, 8. Hē nāđor ne wyllenes hrægles ne līnenes brūcan nolde, Guthl. 4; Gdwin. 26, 11. Bind mid wyllenan þræ̅de, Lchdm. ii. 310, 22. Hī mid willenum reáfe heora līchoman gegearwiaþ, R. Ben. 139, 14. Đa wyllenan (? *the word is printed* wylnenan *and put as a gloss to* vetulae; *the passage is*: Cygnaeam vetulae senectutis caniciem, Ald. 25) hārnysse (*in the margin is* đa græ̅gan hārnysse) *cygneam canitiem*, Hpt. Gl. 450, 62. Wyllene wearp *lanea stamina*, 417, 27. Ne hē wyllenra hrægla breác, ac līnenra ealra, Shrn. 93, 7: 94, 28. Heó næ̅fre līnenum hræglum brūcan wolde, ac wyllenum, Bd. 4, 19; S. 588, 6. ¶ used substantively, *woollen stuff*:—Heó wyllen weorode, Homl. Skt. i. 20, 44: L. Edg. C. 10; Th. ii. 280, 19. Nime man wyllen tō līce, Wulfst. 170, 10. [*O. H. Ger.* wullīn *laneus.*]

wylnenan. v. preceding word.

wyn[n], e; *f.* I. *delight, pleasure*:—Wyn *luxus*, Wrt. Voc. ii. 71, 11. Wynn *luxoria*, wynne *luxus*, 49, 67, 65. Genihtsumere wynne *opulenti luxus*, Hpt. Gl. 413, 71. Wyn eal gedreás, Exon. Th. 288, 25; Wand. 36. On Gode standeþ wuldor mīn and wyn mycel, Ps. Th. 61, 7. Mīn wynn ālæg, 119, 5. Nis hearpan wyn, Beo. Th. 4517; B. 2262. Hwæþere him đæs wonges wyn (*his delight in the country*) sweđrade, Exon. Th. 123, 16; Gū. 323. Sȳ æt him sylfum gelong eal his worulde wyn, 444, 12; Kl. 46. Đæ̅r wæs wuldres wynn . . . næs đæ̅r æ̅nigum gewinn, Andr. Kmbl. 1773; An. 889. Āgan mē đæs dreámes gewald, wuldres and wynne, Cd. Th. 275, 21; Sat. 175: Exon. Th. 230, 31; Ph. 480. On wynne *in laetitia*, Ps. Th. 104, 38. Wend đē from wynne, Cd. Th. 56, 28; Gen. 919. In lifgendra londes wynne, Exon. Th. 27, 28; Cri. 437: 151, 5; Gū. 790. Wenne, Ps. C. 157. Weorod wæs on wynne, Beo. Th. 4032; B. 2014: Exon. Th. 462, 21; Hö. 55. Đæt treów wæs on wynne, wudu weaxende, 435, 18; Rä. 542. Beóđ on wenne đa bān đe on hæ̅nđum wæ̅ron *exultabunt ossa humiliata*, Ps. C. 80. Habban đa mid wynne weorđe blisse *exultent et laetentur*, Ps. Th. 69, 5. Wē sealmas him singan mid wynne *in psalmis jubilemus ei*, 94, 2. Ic mē on đē gehālgode hūs tō wynne, Exon. Th. 90, 31; Cri. 1482: 76, 26; Cri. 1245. Wē sceolan þrowian weán, nalles habban hēhselda wyn, Cd. Th. 267, 25; Sat. 43: Exon. Th. 142, 31; Gū. 652. Se đe āh līfes wyn gebiden in burgum, 307, 22; Seef. 27. Wynna gewītaþ, Runic pm. Kmbl. 345, 18; Rūn. 29. Līđsa and wynna hām, Cd. Th. 58, 13; Gen. 945. Ealra đæra wynna đe ic on worulde gebād, Byrht. Th. 136, 58; By. 174. Hē his līchoman wynna forwyrnde and woruld-blissa, Exon. Th. 111, 31; Gū. 135: 122, 20; Gū. 308. Īdelra eágena wynna, 112, 2; Gū. 137. Wīc wynna leás, 443, 18; Kl. 32. Hine yldo benam mægenes wynnum, Beo. Th. 3778; B. 1887. Hæleþ beóþ on wynnum *the men are joyous*, Exon. Th. 361, 20; Wal. 22: 464, 19; Hö. 89. Hē sunbeorht gesetu sēceþ on wynnum, 217, 11; Ph. 278. Wē đæ̅r wunodon on wynnum, Cd. Th. 279, 12; Sat. 237: 296, 26; Sat. 508. Þurh leáslīce līces wynne, earges flæ̅schoman īdelne lust, Exon. Th. 79, 28; Cri. 1297: 364, 12; Wal. 69. Īdle-lustas, læ̅ne līfes wynne, 352, 19; Sch. 100. Đās eorþan wynne, đās læ̅nan dreámas, 102, 4; Cri. 1667. God seleþ him on ēþle eorþan wynne tō healdanne hleóburh wera, Beo. Th. 3465; B. 1730: 5447; B. 2727. Worolde wynne, 2164; B. 1080. Hē đæt betere geceás, wuldres wynne, Elen. Kmbl. 2077; El. 1040. ¶ wynnum *delightfully, pleasantly*:—Is se wong wynnum geblissad mid đām fægrestum stencum, Exon. Th. 198, 9; Ph. 7: 199, 18; Ph. 27. Đīn gemynd on ealra worulda woruld wynnum standeþ, Ps. Th. 134, 13. I a. with prep. *tō*, marking object in which delight is taken:—Ne biþ him tō hearpan hyge, ne tō wīfe wyn, Exon. Th. 308, 25; Seef. 45. Wæs mē wyn tō đon, 380, 22; Rä. 1, 2. Næs him tō māđme wynn, Andr. Kmbl. 2228; An. 1115: 2326; An. 1164. Đa forweorþaþ đe hira wynne tō đē habban noldan *qui elongant se a te, peribunt*, Ps. Th. 72, 22. Hē genom him tō wildeórum wynne, Exon. Th. 146, 21; Gū. 713. II. *a delight, that which causes pleasure*:—Eh byđ æđelinga wyn, Runic pm. 343, 4; Rūn. 19: 344, 31; Rūn. 27. Fugles wyn (*a quill*), Exon. Th. 408, 5; Rä. 27, 7. Him leófedan londes wynne, bold on beorhge, 110, 20; Gū. 110. Gæst inne swæf ōþ đæt hrefn blaca heofenes wynne bododе, Beo. Th. 3607; B. 1801. II a. as an epithet of persons, (1) of human beings:—Hægstealdra wyn (*Pharaoh*), Cd. Th. 111, 28; Gen. 1862. Winemæ̅ga wyn (*Guthlac*), Exon. Th. 184, 2; Gū. 1338. Eorla wyn, 174, 17; Gū. 1179. Wynn, 168, 22; Gū. 1081. Æđelinga wynn (*St. Andrew*), Andr. Kmbl. 2447; An. 1225. Wunn, 3423; An. 1715. (2) of the Deity:—Līfes wynn, . . . tīreádig cyning, Hy. 3, 1. Mægna God, . . . æþelinga wyn, Exon. Th. 286, 12; Jul. 730: 466, 15; Hö. 121. Neoman ūs tō wynne weoroda Drihten, Cd. Th. 277, 2; Sat. 198. Wigena wyn, . . . heofonengla God, Exon. Th. 281, 4; Jul. 641. III. *the best* of a class, *the pride* of its kind. Cf. cyst:—Ān engla þreát, heápa wyn (*best of troops*), Exon. Th. 460, 16; Hö. 18. Hleóþra wyn *most excellent of melodies*, 198, 18; Ph. 12. Gimma gladost, æþeltungla wyn, 218, 5; Ph. 290. Laguflōda wynn, 202, 16; Ph. 70. Eálā wīfa wynn, fæ̅mne freólicast *ah, pride of womankind, maiden most noble*, 5, 18; Cri. 71. Đū eart se æđela, đe on æ̅rdagum ealra fæ̅mnena wyn (*the Virgin Mary*) ākende, Hy. 3, 26. IV. the name of the w-rune:—Ƿ (uu) uyn, Archæologia, vol. 28, plate 15, fig. 7. In the following passages the symbol is put instead of the word *wyn*:—Ƿ is geswiđrad, gomen æfter geárum, Elen. Kmbl. 2526; El. 1264. Biþ se[ó] Ƿ scæcen eorþan frætwa, Exon. Th. 50, 23; Cri. 805. Ƿ sceal gedreósan, Anglia xiii. 9, 5. Wenne (Hickes prints Ƿ (wen) Ƿne) brūceþ đe can weána lyt, and him sylfa hæfđ blæ̅d and blisse, Runic pm. Kmbl. 340, 29; Rūn. 8. On wuldres Ƿ (*Kemble writes* wealdend *in place of the rune in the MS.*; *but* cf. wuldres wynn, Andr. Kmbl. 1773; An. 889), Elen. Kmbl. 2177; El. 1090. In Ps. Vos. 99, 1 *jubilate* is rendered by Ƿsumiaþ. *See also* mod-wēn (*l.* mōd-wyn). v. Cynewulf's Christ, ed. Gollancz, pp. 173 sqq., Anglia xiii. 1 sqq., Zacher, Das Gothische Alphabet, p. 9. [*Laym.* wunne, winne, wonne: A. R. wunne: *Havel.* winne: *O. Sax.* wunnea: *O. H. Ger.* wunna, wunnī *delectatio, voluptas, jubilatio, jocunditas.* Cf. *Goth.* un-wunands *moestus*: *Icel.* unaðr *delight*; ynði *charm, delight.*] v. ēđel-, hord-, hyht-, leód-, līf-, lyft-, mōd-, symbel-wyn[n].

wynan? :—Eóh biđ ūtan unsmēđe treów . . . wynan (wyn, wynn?) on ēđle, Runic pm. Kmbl. 341, 31; Rūn. 13.

wyn-beám, es; *m. A tree that causes delight*, an epithet of the cross:—Wuldres wynbeám, Elen. Kmbl. 1684; El. 844.

wyn-burh; *f. A town where life is pleasant, a delightful town*:—Þū eádig leofast, and đē wel weorđeþ on wynburgum, Ps. Th. 127, 2.

wyn-candel(l), e; *f. A lamp that gives delight*, an epithet of the sun:—Wyncondel wera west onhylde, Exon. Th. 174, 31; Gū. 1186.

wyncgas. v. wining.

wyn-dæg, es; *m. A day of gladness, a joyous time*:—Wæ̅run wudu-bearwas on wyndagum *exultabunt omnia ligna sylvarum*, Ps. Th. 95, 12. Ne mōstun gē ā wunian in wyndagum, ac scofene wurdon in ēce fȳr, Exon. Th. 140, 3; Gū. 604. Eádig weorþan, wunian wyndagum, and welan þicgan, 330, 34; Vy. 61.

wynde-cræft, es; *m. An art of weaving*:—Uuyndecreft *ars plumaria*, Txts. 43, 217. Uyrmas mec ni āuēfun uyndicraeftum (uyrdi-, MS.), 151, 9.

wyndle, an; *f. A wound*:—Gif man preóst gewundige, gebēte man đa wyndlan, L. N. P. L. 23; Th. ii. 294, 4. v. wundel.

wyn-dreám, es; *m. A joyful sound, jubilation*:—Wyndreámes *jubilationis*, Ps. Lamb. Spl. Blickl. Gl. 150, 5. On wyndreáme *in jubilo*, Ps. Spl. 46, 5: *in jubilatione*, Blickl. Gl. Wyndreám *jubilationem*, Ps. Spl. Lamb. 88, 15.

wyndrian. v. wundrian.

wyn-ele, es; *m. Pleasant oil*:—Wynele se ðe bãnes byrst bēteþ and hǣleþ, Ps. Th. 108, 18.

wyn-fæst; *adj. Joyous*:—Ðætte Sione dūn sigefest weorðe, and weallas Sion wynfeste getremed, Ps. C. 133.

wyn-gesīþ, es; *m. A pleasant companion, a companion in whom one delights*:—Næs mē wyngesīð wiðerweard heorte *non adhaesit mihi cor pravum*, Ps. Th. 100, 3.

wyn-grāf, es; *m. n. A pleasant grove*:—Mid wynngrāfe weaxaþ geswiru *exultatione colles accingentur*, Ps. Th. 64, 13.

wynian. v. wunian.

wyn-land, es; *n. A land of delight, a happy, pleasant land*:—Se hālga stenc wunaþ geond wynlond, Exon. Th. 203, 10; Ph. 82. Wuldres wynlond (*heaven*), 317, 13; Mōd. 65.

wyn-leás; *adj. Joyless, dreary*:—Wynleásne wudu, Beo. Th. 2836; B. 1416. Wynleás wīc, 1641; B. 821. Ōðerne ēðel, wynleásran wīc, Cd. Th. 57, 14; Gen. 928.

wyn-līc; *adj. Delightful, pleasing, agreeable, charming*:—Hæfde hē hine swā hwītne geworhtne, swā wynlīc wæs his wæstm, Cd. Th. 17, 5; Gen. 255. Onstæl wynlīc, fæger and gefeálīc, Exon. Th. 151, 17; Gū. 796. Sunbearo, wuduholt wynlīc, 200, 1; Ph. 34: 423, 22; Rä. 41, 26. Óðer wæs swā wynlīc, wlitig and scēne, ðæt wæs līfes beám, Cd. Th. 30, 15; Gen. 467. Fæger hleóðor, wynlīcu wōðgiefu, Exon. Th. 414, 10; Rä. 32, 18. Ic ðē swā sciénne gesceapen hæfde, wynlīcne geworht, 85, 8; Cri. 1388. Wynlīce wætera þrȳðe, Ps. Th. 77, 18. Wæter wynlīco, Exon. Th. 194, 9; Az. 136. Hē gemon tō oft wynlīcran wīc, 444, 24; Kl. 52. [Was imaked an wunlic fur, Laym. 8090. *O. H. Ger.* wunni-līh *amoenus, jucundus*.]

wynlīce; *adv. Pleasantly, delightfully*:—Ðæt ic wynlīce on psalterio ðē singan mōte, Ps. Th. 107, 2: 149, 4: Exon. Th. 82, 30; Cri. 1346.

wyn-lust, es; *m. Sensual pleasure*:—Ic wilnode mid him tō farenne, ðæt ic ðe mā emnwyrhtena on ðære þrowunge mīnes wynlustes hæfde, Homl. Skt. ii. 23 b, 359. Hēr synt ðisse weorolde wynlustas, ac ðǣr synt ða ēcan tintregu, L. E. I. proem.; Th. ii. 394, 8. Gif hwam hwæt yfeles gedōn bið, ðæt hē ne mæge hys wynlusta brūcan, Lchdm. i. 330, 13.

wyn-mǣg, e; *f. A beloved kinswoman*:—Seó fǣmne, wuldres wynmǣg (*the kinswoman in whom he had delighted*), Exon. Th. 182, 32; Gū. 1319.

wynnung. v. windung.

wyn-psalterium *a joyous psaltery*:—Ārīs, wynpsalterium *exurge, psalterium*, Ps. Th. 56, 10.

wyn-rōd, e; *f. A joy-giving cross*:—Wynrōd (*the cross*), sōðfæstra segn, Salm. Kmbl. 470; Sal. 235.

wyn-sang, es; *m. A joyous song, jubilant song*:—Ðǣr is wynsang, Wulfst. 265, 31.

wynstra. v. winestra.

wyn-sum; *adj.* I. *winsome, agreeable, pleasant*:—Wynsum *suavis*, Ælfc. Gr. 9, 28; Zup. 54, 5. Wynsum, wlitig *elegans*, i. *speciosus, gratus, pulcher, praecipuus, magnus*, Wrt. Voc. ii. 142, 80. Ða wynsuman *amoena*, 1, 6. (1) *pleasant* to the senses or to the mind:—Treów tō brūcenne wynsum *lignum ad vescendum suave*, Gen. 2, 9. Wæs swīþe wynsum wǣta ūt flōwende. . . . Seó wǣte wæs wynsumu on ðære onbyrignesse, Blickl. Homl. 209, 2–9. Hē ys Drihtne wynsum onsægednys *oblatio est Domino odor suavissimus*, Ex. 29, 18. Wynsum stenc, Exon. Th. 363, 16; Wal. 54. Swēte stenc, wlitig and wynsum, 359, 19; Pa. 65. Wlitig and wynsum, wuldre gemearcad *regali plena decore*, 220, 10; Ph. 318: 350, 13; Sch. 63: Cd. Th. 277, 33; Sat. 214. Ðes middangeard, fæger and wynsum, Blickl. Homl. 115, 13. Wæs on ðam ofne windig and wynsum, Cd. Th. 237, 33; Dan. 347. Wynsum gefeá, Exon. Th. 77, 8; Cri. 1253. Hū wynsum (*iocundum*) is ðæt mon eardige on ðara gebrōðra ānnesse, Blickl. Homl. 139, 29. Þincð him wynsum ðæt se weald oncwyð, Met. 13, 46. Mē swēte and wynsum wæs ðæt ic oþþe leornode oþþe lǣrde *aut discere aut docere dulce habui*, Bd. 5, 24; S. 647, 27. Mīn geoc is wynsum *jugum meum suave est*, Mt. Kmbl. 11, 30. Wynsum gamen *sales*, Wrt. Voc. i. 21, 54. Wynsum glīw *facetiae*, 61, 19. Wensum *lepida* (*sermonum series*), Hpt. Gl. 512, 55. Wynsumere ł fægere *venustae*, 456, 41. Hwæt þincþ ðē on ðam welan and on ðam anwealde wynsumes *quid est, quod in se pulcritudinis habeant?* Bt. 27, 4; Fox 100, 20. Mid wynsume wīne, Ps. Th. 59, 3. Tō wynsumum stence *in suavem odorem*, Lev. 1, 9. Hunig, wynsume wist, Fragm. Kmbl. 40; Leás. 22. Wynsumne rēc, Elen. Kmbl. 1585; El. 794. Wynsumne wlite, Cd. Th. 111, 13; Gen. 1855. Scip, wudu wynsuman, Beo. Th. 3842; B. 1919. Wynsume *cantabiles*, Wrt. Voc. ii. 128, 9. Wæter wynsumu *dulces aquae*, Exon. Th. 202, 5; Ph. 65. Ðeós wyrt byþ cenned on wynsumon stōwum (παραδείσοις), Lchdm. i. 280, 13: 290, 6. Wyrta wynsume, Exon. Th. 211, 7; Ph. 194. Hī his weorc wynsum wīde sæcgean *annuntient opera ejus in exultatione*, Ps. Th. 106, 21. Wensumre *suavior* (*panis absconditus*), Kent. Gl. 310. Wynsumra steám, Exon. Th. 358, 14; Pa. 45. Swēg swētra and wlitigra and wynsumra, 206, 27; Ph. 133. Eal innanweard wæs ǣnlīcra and wynsumra, ðonne hit mæge stefn āreccan, se stenc and se swēg, 181, 18; Gū. 1295. 'Is ðis winsum spell ðæt ðū nū segst.' Ðā cwæþ hē: 'Nis nān wuht winsumre ðonne ðæt þing ðæt ðis spell ymbe is,' Bt. 34, 5; Fox 140, 11. Biþ micle ðe winsumre sió sōþe gesǣlð tō habbenne æfter ðām eormþum ðisses līfes, 23; Fox 78, 30. Wynsumre, Met. 12, 20. Þincþ him wynsumre ðæt him se weald oncweþe, Bt. 25; Fox 88, 20. Wōþa wynsumast, Exon. Th. 358, 9; Pa. 43. His englas, ealra folca mǣst, wereda wynsumast, Cd. Th. 42, 8; Gen. 671. (2) in reference to the conduct of living creatures:—Swǣs *vel* wynsum *eucharis*, Wrt. Voc. i. 61, 17: ii. 32, 52. Wynsum (*suavis*) is Dryhten, Ps. Surt. 33, 9: Ps. Th. 85, 4. Eálā ðū wynsuma man, Wulfst. 246, 2. Sum sceal wildne fugel ātemian, ōþþæt seó heoroswealwe wynsum weorþeþ, Exon. Th. 332, 18; Vy. 87. León, wynsume wiht, wel ātemede, Met. 13, 19. Eálā gē gōde cildra and wynsume (*venusti*) leorneras, Coll. Monast. Th. 35, 33. Hē wæs se swētesta lāreów and se wynsumesta *doctor suavissimus*, Bd. 5, 22; S. 644, 3. II. *joyous*. v. wynsumian:—Beóð gefylde mid gefeán mūðas ūre, beóð ūre tungan teala wynsume *repletum est gaudio os nostrum, et lingua nostra exultatione*, Ps. Th. 125, 2. [*O. Sax.* wun-sam: *O. H. Ger.* wunni-sam *jucundus, amoenus, amabilis*.] v. un-, word-wynsum; wynsumness, *and next word*.

wynsum, es; *n. The pleasant*:—Ðæt nān wiht ne sȳ ðæs wynsumes, Wulfst. 184, 20.

wynsumian; *p.* ode *To rejoice, exult, be joyful*:—Ic fægnie and wynsumige and blissige *exultabo et laetabor*, Ps. Th. 30, 7. Wynsumaþ woesten *exultet desertum*, Rtl. 1, 17: Blickl. Homl. 7, 3: Wulfst. 254, 5. Ða eádigan ceasterwaran gefeóð and wynsumiaþ on lisse and on blisse and on ēcum gefeán, 265, 12: Shrn. 118, 4. Heora heortan and līchoman wynsumedon (*exultaverunt*) on God, Bd. 4, 13; S. 582, 37. Nā wynsuma ðū (*non iocunderis*) on bearnum ārleásum, Scint. 176, 6. Wynsumiaþ Gode *jubilate Deo*, Ps. Surt. 65, 1. Gefeáþ and wynnsumiaþ *gaudete et exultate*, Mt. Kmbl. Lind. 5, 12. Wynsumiaþ, Ps. Th. 31, 13: Blickl. Homl. 191, 35. Gedō ðæt mīn gāst wynsumige on ðīnre hǣlo, 159, 2. Wynsumian *jocundari*, Bd. 5, 12; S. 630, 16: Blickl. Homl. 91, 8. Wæs heó swīþe wynsumiende, 137, 33. Wynsumigende, 143, 25. Mid micclum wynsumigendum gefeán, Homl. Skt. ii. 23 b, 678. Wynsumiende *letantem*, Rtl. 97, 16. [*O. H. Ger.* wunnisamōn *exultare*.] v. ge-wynsumian.

wynsum-līc; *adj. Pleasant, agreeable*:—Hē bið ðām gōdum glædmōd on gesihþe, wlitig, wynsumlīc weorude ðam hālgan, Exon. Th. 57, 1; Cri. 912. Wynsumlīc *votivum, acceptum, desiderativum*, Hpt. Gl. 446, 49. Þūhte fæger and wlitig heora līf and wynsumlīc, Blickl. Homl. 107, 30. Eall ðæt him hēr on worlde wynsumlīc wæs, 111, 26: 115, 11. v. ge-wynsumlīc.

wynsumlīce; *adv.* I. *pleasantly, agreeably*. v. wynsum, I. 1:—Wynsumlīce stēman, Homl. Skt. i. 4, 36: ii. 27, 113. Sume tiliaþ wīfa, for ðam ðæt hī þurh ðæt mæge mǣst bearna begitan, and eác wynsumlīce libban *uxor, ac liberi, qui jucunditatis gratia petuntur*, Bt. 24, 3; Fox 82, 27. Engla werod wynsumlīce sungon, Homl. Skt. ii. 29, 297. Ðe eáþelīcor and ðe wynsumlīcor ða myclan byrþenne āberan, Blickl. Homl. 135, 7. II. *pleasantly, graciously*. v. wynsum, I. 2:—Wē gelȳfaþ ðæt Drihten sylf hire tōgeánes cōme, and wynsumlīce mid gefeán tō him on his þrymsetle hī gesette, Homl. Th. i. 442, 15. III. *gladly, joyously*. v. wynsum, II:—Wynsumlīce (*voluntarie*) ic ofrige ðē, Ps. Spl. 53, 6. Āwend ðīne nosu fram unālȳfedum stencum, ðæt ðū mæge wynsumlīce cweðan: 'Sȳn wē æðele stencas beforan Godes gesihðe,' Wulfst. 246, 13.

wynsumness, e; *f.* I. *pleasantness, agreeableness, delight*. v. wynsum, I. 1:—Wynsumnisse orcerd *paradisum voluptatis*, Gen. 2, 8. Of stōwe ðære winsumnisse *de loco voluptatis*, 2, 10. Ðære wynsumnysse brǣð *odorem suavitatis*, 8, 21. Woruldlīcere wensumnesse *mundanae suavitatis, secularis dulcedinis*, Hpt. Gl. 413, 67: Confess. Peccat. Ēces wynsumnisse *aeterne jocunditatis*, Rtl. 103, 24. Hæfde hē mē gebunden mid ðære wynnsumnesse his sanges *me carminis dulcedo defixerat*, Bt. 22, 1: Fox 76, 6. Hē on wynsumnesse lifde, Blickl. Homl. 113, 7. Se middangeard wæs blōwende on swȳþe manigfealdre wynsumnesse . . . and teáh men tō him þurh his wlite and þurh his fægernesse and wynsumnesse, 115, 7–12. Ic ða wynsumnesse and fægernesse ðæs londes wundrade, Nar. 26, 25. On ðære stōwe wynsumnesse *in amoenitatem loci*, Bd. 5, 12; S. 629, 39. Geseón ealles ðysses middangeardes wynsumnessa, ge on golde, ge on deórwyrþum hræglum, Blickl. Homl. 31, 3. I a. *pleasantness* which affects the eye, *fairness, beauty*:—Wynsum[nysse] *venustate*, Hpt. Gl. 526, 22. II. *pleasantness* of behaviour. v. wynsum, I. 2:—God ūs lǣrð sibbe and wynsumnesse, and deófol ūs lǣrð unsibbe and wrōhte, Homl. Ass. 168, 111. III. *joyousness, exultation*. v. wynsum, II:—Wynsumnis mīn *exultatio mea*, Ps. Surt. 31, 7. Weolure wynsumnisse *labia exultationis*, 62, 6. In wynsumnisse *in jubilatione*, 32, 3. Mid wynsumnesse *exultatione*, Blickl. Gl.: Rtl. 50, 19. IV. *devotion*. v. wilsumness:—Mid wynsumnysse heortan (wilsume heortan, Bd. M. 228, 6) *devoto corde*, Bd. 3, 22; S. 553, 22. On micelre wynsumnesse (wilsumnisse, Bd. M. 376, 11) gebeda *orationis devotione*, 4, 30; S. 609, 5. v. un-wynsumness.

wyn-weorod, es; *n. A joyous band*:—Wynwerede *choro*, Blickl. Gl.

wyn-wyrt, e; *f. A pleasant plant*:—Ðǽr wynwyrta weóxon and bleówon, Dóm. L. 5.

wyrcan, weorcan; *p.* worhte; *pp.* worht. I. *to work, labour*, (1) absolute:—Mín fæder wyrcð (*operatur*) óþ ðis, and ic wyrce (wyrco, Lind., Rush. *operor*), Jn. Skt. 5, 17. Efne swá hé wyrceþ *secundum opera ejus*, Ps. Th. 61, 12. Hé won and worhte, wíngeard sette, Cd. Th. 94, 7; Gen. 1558. Gá and wyrce (wyrc, Rush.: wuirc, Lind. *operare*) on mínum wíngerde, Mt. Kmbl. 21, 28. Gáð and wircaþ, Ex. 5, 18. Wyrceaþ eów syx dagas, L. Alf. 3; Th. i. 44, 10. Gif þeów mon wyrce on Sunnandæge, L. In. 3; Th. i. 104, 2, 4, 6: L. E. G. 7; Th. i. 170, 17. Se ðe hors nabbe, wyrce ðam hláforde ðe him fore ríde, L. Ath. v. 5; Th. i. 232, 20. Hwý sceal ǽnig monn bión ídel, ðæt hé ne weorce (wyrce, *v. l.*)? Bt. 41, 3; Fox 248, 24. Sió hond sceal wyrcean for ða wambe, Past. 34; Swt. 233, 9. Hé ðǽr wircean sceolde, Gen. 2, 15. Niht cymþ ðonne nán man wyrcan (*operari*) ne mæg, Jn. Skt. 9, 4. (1 a) where the instrument or material of work is given:—Hé wið monna bearn wyrceð weldǽdum, Exon. Th. 191, 12; Az. 87. Ða ðe wyrcan cúðon stángefógum, Elen. Kmbl. 2038; El. 1020. (2) with acc., (a) of that on which the work is done. v. wín-wyrcend:—Se ðe werð *qui operatur* (*terram suam*, Prov. 12, 11), Kent. Gl. 404. Ðæt hé ða eorðan worhte *ut operaretur terram*, Gen. 3, 23. Se ðe wille wyrcan wæstmbǽre lond *qui serere ingenuum volet agrum*, Met. 12, 1. Hé began tó wircenne ðæt land *coepit exercere terram*, Gen. 9, 20. (b) of the work:—Hé áxode hwæt hig wyrcean cúðon (*quid habetis operis?*). Hig andswaredon: 'Wé synd scéphyrdas,' Gen. 47, 3. II. *to make*, (1) with acc., (a) *to make, form, construct*, (α) where the agent is a person:—Ic tówurpe míne bernu and ic wyrce (*faciam*) máran, Lk. Skt. 12, 18. Wirc ðé ǽnne arc . . . and ðú wircst wununge binnan ðam arce. . . . Ðú wircst hine ðus. . . . Ðú wircst ðǽron éhþirl, Gen. 6, 14–16. Ðú wercest sumurlange dagas, ðǽm winterdagum sceorta tída getiohhast, Met. 4, 18. Mid ðís andweardan welan mon wyrcþ oftor feónd ðonne freónd, Bt. 24, 3; Fox 84, 3. Ic worhte (*feci*) earce of sethimtreówum, Deut. 10, 3. On ðære béc ðe ic weorhte, Bd. 3, 17; S. 545, 4. Ðú ða scíran gesceaft sceópe and worhtest, Hy. 10, 2. Nán neóddearf ðé ne lǽrde tó wyrcanne ðæt ðæt ðú worhtest, Bt. 33, 4; Fox 128, 12. Worhtes, Met. 20, 22: Exon. Th. 15, 23; Cri. 240. Se ðe on fruman worhte (worohte, Lind.), hé worhte wǽpman and wífman, Mt. Kmbl. 19, 4: Cd. Th. 12, 11; Gen. 183. Se ðe ðás bóc worhte, Blickl. Homl. 169, 25. Ðæt folc worhte mycele gesomnunga, Nicod. 20; Thw. 10, 1. Ða sundorhálgan worhton geþeaht, Mt. Kmbl. 12, 14. Hig worhton gemót, 27, 7. Hig wrohton (worhton, *v. l.*: uorhtun, Lind.) him beórscipe, Jn. Skt. 12, 2. Ǽfter ðám formálan ðe hí worhton, L. Eth. ii. 1; Th. i. 284, 12. Ne wirc ðú ðé ágráfene godas, Ex. 20, 4. Ðonne wyrce wé manega béc, Homl. Th. ii. 28, 12. Uton wircean man tó úre gelícnisse, Gen. 1, 26. Wyrcan, Hexam. 11; Norm. 18, 8, 19. Scip wyrcan, Cd. Th. 78, 33; Gen. 1302. Wǽpen wyrcean, Bd. 1, 12; S. 481, 14. Burg wyrcean, Ors. 5, 5; Swt. 226, 18. Wyrcan ðone wíhagan, Byrht. Th. 134, 50; By. 102. Wyrcan spell, Bt. 38, 1; Fox 194, 30. Wercan, Met. 26, 73. Sealfe weorcean, Lchdm. iii. 6, 31. (β) where the agent is not a person, *to be the source*, or *cause of*, *to produce*:—Seó eá wyrcð ðæt fen, Ors. 1, 1; Swt. 8, 18. Seó eá ðǽr wyrcð micelne sǽ, Swt. 12, 23. Hit wyrcð feóndscipe, Past. 11; Swt. 71, 24. Sum feóll on góde eorðan, and worhte hundfealde wæstm, Lk. Skt. 8, 8. Grówende gærs and sǽd wircende. . . . Treów westm wircende, Gen. 1, 11, 12. (b) *to make, constitute*:—Ic wolde witon hwæþer ðú wéndest ðæt hwylc án ðara fíf góda worhte ða sóþan gesǽlþe and siððan ða feówer good wǽron hire gód, swá swá nú sáwl and líchoma wyrcaþ ánne mon, Bt. 34, 6; Fox 140, 23–28. Feówer wucan wyrcaþ ánne mónð, Anglia viii. 319, 4. (c) as a verb of incomplete predication, (α) with adj.:—Ic tó wídan feore wyrce ðín heáhsetl hrór and weorðlíc swá heofones dagas *ponam in seculum seculi semen ejus, et thronum ejus sicut dies coeli*, Ps. Th. 88, 26. Hwilcne wyrcst ðú ðé sylfne (ðone ðec seolfne wyrcas (wyrces, Rush.) *quem te ipsum facis?* Jn. Skt. Lind. 8, 53)? Homl. Th. ii. 234, 1. (β) with prepositional phrase:—Hé lǽdeþ wolcen, wind and líget, and ða tó regne wyrceþ (*fulgura in pluviam fecit*), Ps. Th. 134, 7. Nywolnessa hé him tó gewǽde woruhte, 103, 7. Worhte man hit him tó wíte, Cd. Th. 21, 2; Gen. 318. (2) with gen.:—Se ðeóden ongan geðinges wyrcan, Cd. Th. 245, 25; Dan. 468. III. *to work, do, perform*, (1) absolute:—Swá ðú worhtest tó mé, Exon. Th. 370, 25; Seel. 64. (2) with acc.:—On hwylcum anwealde ic ðás þing wyrce, Mt. Kmbl. 21, 24. On hwylcre mihte wyrcsð (wyrcst, *v. l.*: wircest, Rush.) ðú ðás þing? 21, 23. Swá hwæt swá se gesénelíca líchama déþ oþþe wyrceþ, eal ðæt déþ seó ungesýnelíce sáwl þurh ðone líchoman, Blickl. Homl. 21, 24. Werð *operabitur* (*stultitiam*, Prov. 14, 17), Kent. Gl. 486. Eallum ðe unriht wyrceaþ *omnibus, qui operantur iniquitatem*, Ps. Th. 58, 5. Tó mannum ðe mildheortnesse wyrceaþ, Blickl. Homl. 169, 21. Ðære scame ðe ðú worhtes, Past. 31; Swt. 207, 11. Ða hand ðe hé ðæt fúl mid worhte, L. Ath. i. 14; Th. i. 206, 21, 24. Ða mǽran weorc ðe hé worhte, Deut. 11, 7. Ða dǽda ða ðe hé worhte, Blickl. Homl. 33, 6. Ne worhte (wrohte, Rush.) Iohannes nán tácn, Jn. Skt. 10, 41. Hí blódgyte worhtan, Exon. Th. 44, 26; Cri. 708. Ealle ðe unriht worhtan *omnes peccatores*, Ps. Th. 100, 8. Wirc six dagas ealle ðíne weorc *sex diebus facies omnia opera tua*, Ex. 20, 9. Lǽr mé hú ic ðinne willan wyrce and fremme, Ps. Th. 142, 10. Ðæt ðú furþur mé fraceþu ne wyrce, Exon. Th. 274, 31; Jul. 541. Gif esne þeów weorc wyrce, L. Wih. 9; Th. i. 38, 18. Ðæt mon óðrum riht wyrce, L. O. D. 2; Th. i. 352, 17. On ða geräd, wyrce ðæt hé wyrce, ðæt ðæt land sí unforworht, Cod. Dip. Kmbl. ii. 383, 32. Weorce, 384, 21. Monig gód weorc wyrcan, Past. 9; Swt. 55, 20. Wyricean, Blickl. Homl. 75, 13. Gód wyrcan, Ps. Th. 52, 4. Yfel wyrcean, Blickl. Homl. 181, 34. Wundor wyrcan, Beo. Th. 1865; B. 930: Ps. Th. 85, 9. Lof sceolde hé Drihtnes wyrcean, Cd. Th. 17, 8; Gen. 256. Ða heápas frugnon, hwæt hié wyrcean mihton ðæt hié Godes erre beflugon, Blickl. Homl. 169, 11. Godes willan wercan, 67, 34. Mé ge̥yraþ tó wyrceanne ðæs weorc ðe mé sende, Jn. Skt. 9, 4. (2 a) *to perform* a rite, *keep* a season:—Mín tíma ys gehende ðæt ic mid ðé wyrce míne Eástro, Mt. Kmbl. 26, 18. (3) with gen.:—Ic mé ðæs wyrce, ðæt ic gange on hús Godes, Ps. Th. 83, 11. Ealle ðe unrihtes wyrceaþ *omnes qui operantur iniquitatem*, Ps. Th. 52, 5: 58, 2: 73, 19. Hé him ðæs worhte tó, Cd. Th. 143, 11; Gen. 2377. Ða ðe unrihtes worhtan, Ps. Th. 91, 6, 8. IV. *to work, effect* a purpose, *attain* an object, (1) with acc. or gen.:—Heó wénde ðæt heó hyldo heofoncyninges worhte mid ðám wordum *she thought to win the favour of heaven's king with those words*, Cd. Th. 44, 22; Gen. 713. Ðæt hí lifgen on geleáfan, and á lufan Dryhtnes wyrcan in ðisse worulde, Exon. Th. 448, 6; Dóm. 50. Hié sculon lufe wyrcean . . . ond habban his hyldo forð, Cd. Th. 39, 12; Gen. 624. (2) with gen.:—Á ðín dóm sý gód and genge; ðú ðæs wyrcest (*thou wilt bring that to pass*), Exon. Th. 192, 22; Az. 110. Wé ðæs lifgende worhton in worulde, 186, 9; Az. 17. Wyrce se ðe móte dómes ǽr deáðe *let him that may do deeds deserving of glory ere he die*, Beo. Th. 2779; B. 1387. Til sceal on éðle dómes wyrcean, Menol. Fox 501; Gn. C. 21. Hé þóhte ðæt hé him myceles wordes wircean sceolde (wolde geearnian him hereword, MS. F.), Chr. 1009; Erl. 142, 2. Se hæfde moncynnes leóhteste hond lofes tó wyrcenne (*to call forth praise*), Exon. Th. 323, 2; Víd. 72. (3) with a clause:—Is ðæt wundorlíc, ðæt ðú mid geþeahte ðínum wyrcest, ðæt ðú ðǽm gesceaftum mearce gesettest and hí gemengdest eác, Met. 20, 87. [*Goth.* waurkjan; *p.* waurhta: *O. H. Ger.* wurchen, wirchen; *p.* worhta: *Icel.* yrkja; *p.* orti: *O. Sax.* wirkian; *p.* warhta: *O. Frs.* werka; *p.* wrochte.] v. á-, be- (bi-), for-, fore-, ful-, ge-, in- (Exon. Th. 337, 21; Gn. Ex. 68), ofer-, óþ-, sám-, un-, ymb-wyrcan (-weorcan); firen-, scyld-, syn-, unriht-, wam-, wel-, wolcen-, yfel-wyrcende; wyrcend.

wyrce. v. ge-wyrce.

wyrcend, es; *m.* I. *a worker, labourer*. v. efen-, fore-, wín-wyrcend, *and* wyrcan, I. II. *a maker*. v. wyrcan, II:—Ic gelýfe on ǽnne God, wyrcend heofenan and eorðan, Homl. Th. ii. 596, 25. Heó wǽron ðám wyrcendum gelíce *similes illis fiant qui faciunt ea*, Ps. Th. 113, 17. III. *a doer*. v. wyrcan, III:—Þurh ða unrótnesse ðe is deáðes wyrcend, Anglia xi. 113, 43. Ealle ic feóde fácnes wyrcend *facientes praevaricationes odivi*, Ps. Th. 100, 3. v. leás-wyrcend, Homl. Th. i. 102, 1.

wyrcness, e; *f.* I. *work, labour, operation*. v. wyrcan, I:—Ðonde wircnisse (*operationes*) in wætrum miclum, Ps. Surt. 106, 23. II. *working, doing, operation*. v. wyrcan, III:—Ðurh swá hwylces béne swá hé gehǽled sí, ðysses geleáfa and wyrcnes (*operatio*) sí gelýfed Gode andfenge, Bd. 2, 2; S. 502, 23. His geearnunge oft ðurh godcunde wyrcnesse (*operationem*) mid miclum mægenum scínaþ, 3, 19; S. 550, 16. Ða ðe lǽrdon ǽnne willan and áne wyrcnesse beón on Drihtne Hǽlende, 5, 19; S. 639, 34. II a. *working, performance* of something:—Wyrcnes heofonlícra mægena *operatio virtutum*, Bd. 1, 7; S. 479, 9. Mid wundra wyrcnesse, 2, 3; S. 505, 1: 3, 13; S. 538, 39.

wyrcung, e; *f. Working, doing;* operatio, Rtl. 15, 42: 31, 1: 170, 3.

wyrd, e; *f. What happens, fate, fortune, chance.* I. the word is used to gloss the following Latin words:—*Casibus* wyrdum, Wrt. Voc. ii. 85, 1: 18, 29: 81, 45. *Eventus* wyrd, 75, 61: 30, 71. *Fati* wyrde oððe gegonges, 33, 65. *Fata* wyrde, 94, 6. *Fatis* wyrdum, 37, 54. *Fors* wyrd, 109, 5: 83, 43: 37, 14. *Fortuna* wyrd, 108, 78: 33, 78. *Fortunae* wyrde, 33, 77: 79, 61. *Sortem* wyrd, 120, 76. *Fatu* (*statu?* v. Ald. 30) wyrde, 78, 77. II. *fate, the otherwise than humanly appointed order of things*:—Ðæt ðætte wé hátaþ Godes foreþonc and his foresceáwung, . . . siððan hit fullfremed bið, ðonne hátaþ wé hit wyrd. . . . Hí sint twá ðing, foreþonc and wyrd. . . . Ðæt ðæt wé wyrd hátaþ, ðæt biþ Godes weorc ðe hé ǽlce dæg wyrcþ, ǽgðer ge ðæs ðe wé geseóþ, ge ðæs ðe ús ungeswenlíc biþ. . . . Sió wyrd dǽlþ eallum gesceaftum andwlitan and stówa and tída and gemetgunga. Ac sió wyrd cymþ of ðam foreþonce Godes, Bt. 39, 5; Fox 218, 21–220, 1. Ðiós wandriende wyrd, ðe wé wyrd hátaþ, færþ æfter his foreþonce. . . . Siþþan wé hit hátaþ wyrd, syððan hit geworht biþ; ǽr hit wæs Godes foreþonc. Ða wyrd hé wyrcþ oþþe þurh ða gódan englas, oþþe . . ., 39, 6; Fox 220, 5–23. Ðæt wé hátaþ wyrd, ðonne se gesceádwisa God hwæt wyrcþ oððe geþafaþ ðæs ðe wē ne wēnaþ *fit illud fatalis ordinis insigne miraculum, cum ab sciente geritur, quod stupeant ignorantes*, 39, 10; Fox 226, 24. Ðē sceal on woruld bringan Sarra sunu, sōð forð gān wyrd æfter ðiosum wordgemearcum, Cd. Th. 142, 1; Gen. 2355. Gǽð ā wyrd swā hió sceal, Beo. Th. 915; B. 455. Ne wæs wyrd, ðæt hē mā mōste manna cynnes ðicgean, 1473; B. 734. Wǽron sume gedwolmen ðe cwǽdon, ðæt ǽlc man beó ācenned be steorrena gesetnyssum, and þurh heora ymbryna him wyrd gelimpe, Homl. Th. i. 110, 8. Sceal heó (*Lot's wife*) wyrde bīdan, Drihtnes dōmes, Cd. Th. 155, 10; Gen. 2570: Exon. Th. 329, 29; Vy. 41. Hī wyrd ne cūþon, Beo. Th. 2471; B. 1233. **III.** in a personal sense, *one of the Fates* (the *weird* sisters):—Wyrde *Parcae*, Wrt. Voc. ii. 116, 9: 67, 55. **III a.** as a personification, *fate, fortune*:—Wyrd biþ swīþre, Meotud mihtigra, ðonne ǽnges monnes gehygd, Exon. Th. 312, 27; Seef. 115. Wyrd byð swīþost, Menol. Fox 469; Gn. C. 5: Salm. Kmbl. 855; Sal. 427: 886; Sal. 442. Wyrd bið ful ārǽd, Exon. Th. 286, 24; Wand. 5: Salm. Kmbl. 871; Sal. 435. Sume ūþwitan secgaþ ðæt sió wyrd wealde ǽgðer ge gesǽlþa ge ungesǽlþa ǽlces monnes, Bt. 39, 8; Fox 224, 13. Weord (wyrd, *v. l.*), 5, 1; Fox 8, 30. Swā him wyrd ne gescrāf, Beo. Th. 5142; B. 2574: Elen. Kmbl. 2092; El. 1047: Met. 1, 29. Behindan beleác wyrd mid wǽge, Cd. Th. 206, 25; Exod. 457. Eorlas fornōman wǽpen wælgīfru, wyrd seó mǽre, Exon. Th. 292, 17; Wand. 100: Beo. Th. 2415; B. 1205. Hié wyrd forsweóp, 959; B. 477: 5621; B. 2814. Wyrd ðone gomelan grētan sceolde, 4832; B. 2420. Hwȳ ðū ǽfre woldest ðæt seó wyrd swā hwyrfan sceolde? Heó þreáþ ða unscildigan, Bt. 4; Fox 8, 12: Met. 4, 34: Andr. Kmbl. 1226; An. 613: 3121; An. 1563. Wyrd oft nereþ unfǽgne eorl, Beo. Th. 1149; B. 572: Exon. Th. 165, 18; Gū. 1030. Tō eallum ðām gesǽlðum ðe seó wyrd brengð, Bt. 16, 3; Fox 54, 25: 14, 1; Fox 40, 31. Ne wēn ðū nō ðæt ic tō ānwillīce winne wiþ ða wyrd (*fortunam*) . . . hit oft gebyraþ ðæt seó leáse wyrd nāuþer ne mæg ðam men dōn ne fultum, ne nǽnne dem, 20; Fox 70, 22. Wyrde wiðstondan, Exon. Th. 287, 17; Wand. 15. **IV.** *an event*, (1) with the special idea of that which happens by the determination of Providence or fate:—Ne wile Sarran gelȳfan wordum mīnum; sceal seó wyrd swā ðeáh forð steallian, Cd. Th. 144, 14; Gen. 2389. Wyrd wæs geworden, swefen gesēðed, swā ǽr Daniel cwæð, 257, 5; Dan. 653. God ēce biþ; ne wendaþ hine wyrda, ne hine wiht dreceþ ādl ne yldo, Exon. Th. 333, 24; Gn. Ex. 9: Salm. Kmbl. 666; Sal. 332. Wyrda Waldend, Cd. Th. 205, 7; Exod. 432: Andr. Kmbl. 2113; An. 1058: Elen. Kmbl. 159; El. 80: Exon. Th. 455, 1; Hy. 4, 43. Wyrda gerȳnu, Cd. Th. 225, 5; Dan. 149. Wyrda geþingu, 250, 14; Dan. 546. Wyrda gesceaft, 224, 6; Dan. 132. Onwrigen is wyrda bigang, Elen. Kmbl. 2245; El. 1124. Gif ic ðē ðone [. . . age, *the MS. is here imperfect*] gesecge ðīnes feores, ȳþelīce ðū ða wyrde oncyrrest and his hond befēhst *si mortis tue tibi insidiatorem prodidero, sublato eo facile instantia fata mutabis, mihique tres irascentur sorores, Clotos, Lachesis, Atropos*, Nar. 31, 24. (2) in a general sense, *an event, occurrence, circumstance, incident, fact*:—Nǽnigne tweógean ne þearf, ðæt seó wyrd on ðās ondweardan tīd geweorþan sceal, ðæt se Scyppend gesittan wile on his dōmsetle, Blickl. Homl. 83, 10. Ðā gelamp wundorlīc wyrd, ðæt se lēg ongan sleán ongeán ðone wind, 221, 11. Ðæt is mǽro wyrd, Cd. Th. 84, 18; Gen. 1399: Menol. Fox 107; Men. 53. Egeslīc wyrd, Rood Kmbl. 148; Kr. 74: Exon. Th. 432, 6; Rä. 48, 2. Seó wyrd geweard (*it happened*) ðæt ðæt wīf geseah Ismaēl plegan, Cd. Th. 168, 3; Gen. 2777. Is seó wyrd mid eów open *the event is patent among you*, Andr. Kmbl. 1516; An. 759: Apstls. Kmbl. 84; Ap. 42. Ne wē ðære wyrde wēnan þurfon tōweard in tīde, Exon. Th. 6, 8; Cri. 81. Wēnan ðære wyrde, ðæt heó hire taman healde, Met. 13, 24: 26, 114: Ps. Th. 119, 5. Hē wyrde bīdeþ, hwonne God wille ðisse worlde ende gewyricean, Blickl. Homl. 109, 32. On ðæm dæge gewīteþ heofon and eorþe. . . . Swā eác for ðære ilcan wyrde gewīteþ sunne and mōna, 91, 22. Ðā gesāwon hié wundorlīce wyrd—ðone man līfgendne, ðone ðe hié ǽr deádne forlēton, 217, 36: Cd. Th. 61, 12; Gen. 996: 245, 30; Dan. 471. Hē ða wyrd ne mǽð, fǽges forðsīð, Exon. Th. 182, 33; Gū. 1319. Hē wyrd ne ful cūþe freóndrǽdenne hū heó from hogde *he did not fully know the circumstance, how her heart was turned from loving him*, 244, 26; Jul. 33. Dīgle wyrd *an obscure circumstance*, Elen. Kmbl. 1077; El. 541: 1163; El. 583. Ymb ða mǽran wyrd, 2126 El. 1064. Geopenigean uncūðe wyrd, hwǽr hē ðara nægla wēnan þorfte, 2202; El. 1102. Hē ðē mæg onwreón wyrda gerȳno *he can disclose to thee the secrets of events* (can tell thee of events which are a secret to most men), 1174; El. 589: 1623; El. 813. Hē ne leág fela wyrda ne worda, Beo. Th. 6052; B. 3030. **V.** *what happens to a person, fate, fortune, lot, condition*:—Ic wille secgan ðæt ǽlc wyrd (*omnis fortuna*) bió gōd, sam hió monnum gōd þince, sam hió him yfel þince. . . . Ǽlc wyrd, sam hió sié wynsum, sam hió sié unwynsum, for ðȳ cymþ tō ðǽm gōdum ðæt hió . . . hine þreátige tō ðon ðæt hē bet dō, . . . oððe him leánige ðæt hē teala dyde, Bt. 40, 1; Fox 224, 33–226, 5. Ða graman gydena, ðe folcisce men hātaþ Parcas, ða hī secgaþ ðæt wealdan ǽlces monnes wyrde, 35, 6; Fox 168, 27. For hwȳ ætwīte gē eówerre wyrde ðæt hió nān geweald nāh, 39, 1; Fox 210, 26. Him ne wæs nǽnig earfoþe ðæt līchomlīce gedāl on ðære neówan wyrde (*in their new condition*), Blickl. Homl. 135, 31. Under wyrd *sub condicione*, Jn. Skt. p. 5, 10. Ne meaht ðū nō mid sōþe getǽlan ðīne wyrd and ðīne gesǽlþa, swā swā ðū wēnst *quod tu falsae opinionis supplicium luis, id rebus jure imputare non possis*, Bt. 10; Fox 28, 1. Wyrd wānian, Exon. Th. 274, 24; Jul. 538. Unc sceal weorðan swā unc wyrd geteóð Metod manna gehwæs *to us shall it befall, as the Lord of every man decrees to us our fate*, Beo. Th. 5046; B. 2526. Nȳd bið wyrda heardost, Salm. Kmbl. 622; Sal. 310. Him mæg wīssefa wyrda gehwylce gemetigian, 877; Sal. 438. Gnornsorga mǽst, wyrda lāðost, Elen. Kmbl. 1953; El. 977: Rood Kmbl. 101; Kr. 51. **V a.** *fate, death*. See also **III a**:—Wille forgieldan gǽsta Dryhten willum æfter ðære wyrde, ðam ðe his synna nū sāre geþenceþ, Exon. Th. 450, 3; Dom. 82. **VI.** *chance, accident*:—Ðæt wille ic gecȳþan, ðæt ðu rīcu of nānes monnes mihtum swā gecræftgade ne wurdon, ne for nānre wyrde, būton from Godes gestihtunge *ut omnia haec profundissimis Dei judiciis disposita, non autem humanis viribus, aut incertis casibus accidisse perdoceam*, Ors. 2, 1; Swt. 69, 23. Sprecan wiþ ða ðe secgaþ ðæt ða anwaldas sién of wyrda mægenum gewordene, Swt. 62, 10. [Worþe hit wele, oþer wo, as þe wyrde lykeȝ hit hafe, Gaw. 2134. Þe same þat sett is be wirde, Alex. (Skt.) 443. Wyrdis (wyrde systres) *Parce*, Cath. Angl. 420, and see note. To dreȝe his wyrdes, Allit. Pms. 74, 1224. Heo biueped hire wurdes, H. M. 33, 24. Is þi werid (werd, *v. l.*) to þe wissid, Alex. (Skt.) 689. Out of wo into wele ȝoure wyrdes shul chaunge, Piers P. C. 13, 209. Þe sorouful werdes of me olde man, Chauc. Boet. 4, 10. *O. Sax.* wurd *fate, death*: *O. H. Ger.* wurt *fatum, fortuna, eventus*: *Icel.* urðr (*poet.*) *fate*; *one of the Norns*. v. Grmm. D. M. pp. 376 sqq.] v. deáþ-, eft-, fǽr-, for-, ge-, tō-, un-, wundor-wyrd.

-wyrd *speech*, wyrdan *to injure*. v. ge-wyrd, wirdan.

-wyrdan *to speak*. [*Goth.* -waurdjan: *O. Sax.* -wordian: *O. Frs.* -wardia: *O. H. Ger.* -wurten.] v. and-, torn-, wīs-wyrdan.

-wyrde; *n. Speech*. [*Goth.* -waurdi: *O. Sax.* -wurdi, -wordi: *O. H. Ger.* -wurti.] v. and-, bī-, ge-wyrde.

-wyrde; *adj.* [*Goth.* -waurds: *O. H. Ger.* -wurti.] v. beald-, biter-, fæger-, fela-, hōcor-, hræd-, snotor-, stunt-, swǽs-, swēt-, wær-, wīs-wyrde.

wyrd-gesceap, es; *n. A decree of fate* or *of fortune*:—Wyrdgesceapum *fortuiter*, Wrt. Voc. ii. 34, 5. [*O. Sax.* wurði-giskapu; *pl.*]

wyrdig; *adj. Wordy*:—Werdi *verbosus*, Kent. Gl. 576. v. gearo-, twi-wyrdig.

-wyrding. v. and-wyrding.

wyrdness, e; *f. Condition, state*:—Se godcunda foreþonc heaþeraþ ealle gesceafta ðæt hī ne mōton tōslūpan of heora endebyrdnesse (wyrdnesse, *v. l.*), Bt. 39, 5; Fox 218, 32.

wyrd-stæf, es; *m. A decree of fate*:—Ðonne seó þrāg cymeþ wefen wyrdstafum *when comes that season fixed by fate's decrees*, Exon. Th. 183, 101; Gū. 1325.

wyrd-wrītere, es; *m. One who writes an account of events, a historian, historiographer*:—Wurdwrītere *historiographus*, Hpt. Gl. 453, 1: 468, 65. Andromachus se wyrdwrītere, Anglia viii. 307, 9. Se wyrdwrītere Iōsēphus āwrāt on ðære cyrclīcan gereccednesse, ðæt Hērōdes lytle hwīle æfter Iōhannes deáðe rīces weólde, Homl. Th. i. 488, 12. Wyrdwrīteras secgaþ, 80, 5: 454, 11: Homl. Skt. i. 3, 21: ii. 25, 676. Wyrdwrītera *historiographorum*, Hpt. Gl. 410, 54.

wyrgan; *p.* de *To worry* (as an animal does), *strangle, throttle*:—Wyrgeþ *vel* smoraþ *st[r]angulat*, Wrt. Voc. ii. 121, 32. [Wolwes þat wald worow men (the whilke wol a man strangly and destrye, *v. l.*), Pr. C. 1229. Ilc wirwed lay, als it were dogges þat weren henged, Havel. 1921. Werewed, 1915. A wolf wolde lambes wery, R. R. 6267. Wolues that wyryeþ (wyrhyeþ, *v. l.*) men, Piers P. C. 10, 226. Wyrwyn, worowen *strangulo, suffoco*, Prompt. Parv. 530. *O. Frs.* wergia: *O. H. Ger.* wurgen *strangulare, suffocare*. Cf. *O. Sax.* wurgil *a halter*: *O. L. Ger.* wurgarīn *strangulatrix*.] v. ā-wyrgan.

wyrgan *to curse*, wyrgels, wyrgedness, wyrgen, wyrgness, wyrgþu. v. wirgan, wrigels, wirgedness, wirgen, wirgness, wirgþu.

wyrht, e; *f. Doing, work*:—Nā ðū be gewyrhtum ūrum, wommum wyrhtum, woldest ūs dōn *non secundum peccata nostra fecit nobis*, Ps. Th. 102, 10. [Betere þenne we habbeð wrihte, O. E. Homl. i. 69, 251. Bi mine wrihte, ii. 217, 19. Ǽfftерr hise wrihhte, Orm. 8240. *O. H. Ger.* wuruht *meritum*.] v. for-, ge-, leóþ-, stān-wyrht.

wyrhta, an; *m.* I. *a wright, workman, artificer, labourer, one who works at some trade*:—Wyrhta *operarius*, Wrt. Voc. i. 73, 25: *opifex*, 47, 10. Yldest wyrhta *architectus*, 19, 14: 47, 11. Se wyrhta (*operarius*) ys wyrðe hys metes, Mt. Kmbl. 10, 10. Wyrihte *faber*, Mk. Skt. Lind. 6, 3. Wrihtes *fabri*, p. 3, 8. Micel gedāl is on ðam mægene ðæs dæghwamlīcan wyrhtan and ðæs īdlan, Lchdm. ii. 84, 18. Hē wæs ðæs wyrhtan sunu (*the carpenter's son*), Nicod. 2; Thw. 1, 21. Smiðes ł wyrchta (*fabri*) sunu, Mt. Kmbl. Lind. 13, 55. Hond bið gelǽred, wīs and gewealden, swā bið wyrhtan ryht, sele āsettan, Exon. Th. 296, 5; Crä. 46. Gif ðū wēnst ðætte wundorlīce gerela hwelc weorþmynd sié, ðonne telle ic ða weorþmynd ðæm wyrhtan ðe hié worhte, næs nā đe (*igenium mirabor artificis*), Bt. 14, 1; Fox 42, 19. Mon sceal simle tō beregafole āgifan æt ānum wyrhtan (*the labourer who is the tenant of land*. Cf. Hēr synd gewriten đa gerihta đæ đa ceorlas sculan dōn tō Hysseburnan. Æt ælcan hīwisce . . . þreó pund gauolbæres, Chart. Th. 145, 1.) six pund wǣga, L. In. 59; Th. i. 140, 5. Eálā gōde wyrhtan (*operarii*) . . . đis geþeaht ic sylle eallum wyrhtum, đæt ānra gehwylc cræft his geornlīce begange; for đam se đe cræft his forlǣt, hē byþ forlǣten fram đam cræfte, Coll. Monast. Th. 31, 21-35. Đone stān, đe hine wyrhtan āwurpan *lapidem quem reprobaverunt aedificantes*, Ps. Th. 117, 21: Exon. Th. 1, 3; Cri. 2. Micel rīp ys, and feáwa wyrhtena (*operarii pauci*), Mt. Kmbl. 9, 37. Āhȳrian wyrhtan on his wīngeard, 20, 1. **II.** *a maker, producer, author, creator, fabricator*:—Wrōhtes wyrhtan, fyrnsynna fruman (*the devil*), Exon. Th. 263, 7; Jul. 346. Wyrhtan *fabricatores* (*falsitatum*), Hpt. Gl. 505, 64. On wyrhte gileáfes *in auctorem fidei*, Rtl. 27, 29. **II a.** used of the Deity, *the Creator, Maker*:—Se wyrhta, Cd. Th. 8, 17; Gen. 125: 265, 27; Sat. 14. Werhta *operator*, Kent. Gl. 808. Drihten, ælmihtiga God, wyrhta and wealdend ealra gesceafta, Bt. 42; Fox 260, 1: L. Eth. vi. 42; Th. i. 326, 13: L. I. P. 1; Th. ii. 304, 2: Cd. Th. 301, 21; Sat. 585. Wuldres wyrhta, Exon. Th. 206, 21; Ph. 130. Wealdend and wyrhta wuldorþrymmes, Andr. Kmbl. 649; An. 325: 1403; An. 702. Wyrhta and Sceppend weorulde þisse, Met. 29, 82. **III.** *a doer, worker*:—Cwealmes wyrhta *a murderer*, Cd. Th. 61, 29; Gen. 1004. Ealle đa đe unrihtes wǣran wyrhtan *omnes discedentes a justificationibus tuis*, Ps. Th. 118, 118. Mānes wyrhtan *peccatores*, 100, 8. [*O. Sax.* wurhtio: *O. H. Ger.* wurhto.] v. ceaster-, efen-, esne-, firen-, for-, ge-, gegader-, heáfod-, hrōf-, īsen-, leþer-, lyge-, mān-, meter-, mid-, scip-, sealm-, smeá-, stān-, teld-, tigel-, treów-, unlyb-, unriht-, wægn-, weall-, web-wyrhta.

wyrhte (?), an; *f. A female worker*, in cȳs-wyrhte:—Be cȳswyrhte. Cȳswyrhtan gebyreþ hundred cȳse, and đæt heó buteran macige, L. R. S. 16; Th. i. 438, 30. [*O. H. Ger.* wurhta.]

wyrian (wyrigan), wyrig, wyrigness. v. wirgan, wearg, wirgness.

wyrm, wurm, weorm, es; *m.* **I.** *a reptile, serpent*:—Mē nædre beswāc, fāh wyrm þurh fægir word, Cd. Th. 55, 24; Gen. 899. Se wyrm (*the fire-drake*) onwōc, Beo. Th. 4563; B. 2287. Đæs wyrmes wīg, 4621; B. 2316. Hē wearp hine on wyrmes līc, Cd. Th. 31, 26; Gen. 491. Ne wirce gē eów nāne andlīcnissa wurmes ne fisces (*reptilium sive piscium*), Deut. 4, 18. Hē wyrm ācwealde, hordes hyrde . . . Đæt swurd þurhwōd wyrm . . . draca morđre swealt, Beo. Th. 1777-1789; B. 886-892. Wyrmas *reptilia*, Blickl. Gl. Froxan . . . swā fela đæt man ne mihte nānne mete gegyrwan, đæt đara wyrma nǣre emfela đæm mete *ranae per omnia reptantes*, Ors. 1, 7; Swt. 36, 28. Wyrma þreát, dracan and næddran, Cd. Th. 285, 12; Sat. 336. Wyrma slite, Exon. Th. 77, 4; Cri. 1251. Wyrmum bewunden in helle bryne, Judth. Thw. 23, 10; Jud. 115. Ic sende wildera deóra tēđ on hig mid wurmum and næddrum *dentes bestiarum immittam in eos atque serpentium*, Deut. 32, 24. Wurmum tō ǣte, Wulfst. 145, 10. Aspidas, ǣtrene wyrmas, Ps. Th. 139, 3. Nicras, wyrmas and wildeór, Beo. Th. 2864; B. 1430. **I a.** fig.:—Brandhāta nīđ weóll on gewitte, weorm blǣdum fāg, Andr. Kmbl. 1538; An. 770. **II.** *a creeping insect, a worm*:—Wyrm *vermis*, Wrt. Voc. i. 78, 24. Wyrm đe boraþ treów *termes* vel *teredo*, 24, 8. Hundes wyrm *ricinus*, 24, 33. Se wyrm (*a book-worm*) forswealg wera gied sumes, Exon. Th. 432, 8; Rä. 48, 3. Đes lytla wyrm đe on flōde gǣđ fōtum drȳge, 426, 20; Rä. 41, 76. Of đam weaxeþ wyrm *hinc animal sine membris fertur oriri, sed fertur vermi lacteus esse color*, 213, 29; Ph. 232. Hyra wyrm (*vermis*) ne swylt, Mk. Skt. 9, 44: Cd. Th. 212, 9; Exod. 536: Exon. Th. 373, 31; Seel. 118. Weorđan wyrme tō hrōþor, 267, 17; Jul. 416. Wiþ đam smalan wyrme, Lchdm. ii. 122, 18. Dō on đæt eáre; þeáh đǣr beón wyrmas on ācennede, hī þurh đis sceolon beón ācwealde, i. 200, 22. Rib reáfiaþ rēþe wyrmas, Exon. Th. 373, 22; Seel. 113. Wyrmas, đa đe geolo godwebb geatwum frætwaþ, 417, 23; Rä. 36, 9. Wyrma gifl *food for worms* (the body), 368, 16; Seel. 22. Weormum tō hrōđre, Apstls. Kmbl. 190; Ap. 95. Wiđ weormum, Lchdm. iii. 4, 5. Wiđ wyrmas on innođe, i. 272, 10. **II a.** fig.:—Ic eam wyrm (*vermis*) and nales mon, Ps. Surt. 21, 7. Wyrm (weorm, *v.l.*), R. Ben. 29, 13. [*Goth.* waurms *a serpent*: *O. Sax.* wurm *a serpent*; *a worm*: *O. H. Ger.* wurm *serpens, coluber, anguis, hydra*; *vermis, vermiculus, batis*: *Icel.* ormr *a serpent*.] v. cāwel-, deáw-, fāg-, fīc-, flǣsc-, hand-, leáf-, mold-, must- (? Wrt. Voc. i. 23, 74), regn-, reng-, seoluc-, sīd-, slā-, smeá-, tōþ-, treów-, twīn-, þeór-wyrm.

wyrma. v. wurma.

wyrmǣte, an; *f. Wormeatenness*:—Đa treówa đe beóđ āheáwene on fullum mōnan beóđ heardran wiđ wyrmǣtan đonne đa đe beóđ on nīwum mōnan āheáwene, Lchdm. iii. 268, 10. v. next word.

wyrmǣte; *adj. Worm-eaten*:—Wiþ wyrmǣtum līce, Lchdm. ii. 12, 15: 126, 4. [Frut ne is naȝt guod huanne hit is uorroted and wermethe, Ayenb. 229, 25. Cf. *O. H. Ger.* wurmâzih *cariosus*.]

wyrmaman, wyrman. v. wurma, wirman.

wyrm-basu; *adj. Scarlet*:—Wyrmbaso *coccus*, Txts. 113, 67. v. wurma.

wyrm-cyn[n], es; *n.* **I.** *the genus reptile, reptiles, serpents*:—Hī gesāwon æfter wætere wyrmcynnes fela, sellīce sǣdracan, sund cunnian, Beo. Th. 2855; B. 1425. Betwux dracum and aspidum and eallum wyrmcynne, Homl. Th. i. 488, 1. Betwux eallum deórcynne and wurmcynne, 102, 6. On đam fīftan dæge hē gesceóp eall wyrmcynn, and eall fisccynn, Lchdm. iii. 234, 11. **II.** *a species of reptile* or *serpent*:—Scorpio, đæt is ān wyrmcynn, Lk. Skt. 11, 12. Wyrmcyn, Nar. 13, 10. Nis nān wyrmcynn ne wildeóra cynn on yfelnysse gelīc yfelum wīfe, Homl. Th. i. 488, 10. On wēstennum wildeóra and wyrmcynna missenlīcra, Ors. 3, 9; Swt. 136, 25: Exon. Th. 371, 31; Seel. 84. [*O. H. Ger.* wurm-chunni.]

wyrmelle. v. wurmelle.

wyrm-fāh; *adj. Having serpentine ornamentation*:—Đæt sweord wreoþenhilt and wyrmfāh, Beo. Th. 3400; B. 1697. v. Worsaae's Primeval Antiquities, p. 49.

wyrm-galdere, es; *m. A serpent-charmer, sorcerer*:—Hē hēt sumne wyrmgaldere micle næddran hire in tō gelǣdan, đæt seó hī ābītan sceolde. Đā stōd seó fǣmne forđ on hire gebede, and seó nǣddre stōd be hire; đonne seó fǣmne onleát, đonne onleát seó nǣddre. Đā gelȳfde se wyrmgaldere tō Gode þurh đæt wundor, Shrn. 103, 5, 9. v. wyrm-galere.

wyrm-galdor, es; *n. A charm against worms* (?):—Đæt wyrmgealdor (cf. đis ylce galdor mæg mon singan wiđ smeógan wyrme, 10, 17), Lchdm. iii. 24, 25.

wyrm-galere, es; *m. A serpent-charmer, sorcerer*:—Wyrmgalere *marsum* (the word occurs in reference to the incident given under *wyrmgaldere*), Wrt. Voc. ii. 96, 11: 55, 11. Wyrmgalera *marsorum* (Chaldaeorum et hierophantorum phantasmata, simulque ariolorum et marsorum machinas, Ald. 45), 82, 9: 56, 74: Hpt. Gl. 483, 14. v. wirgunggalere, wyrm-hǣlsere.

wyrm-geard, es; *m. An enclosure full of snakes*:—Wyrmgeardas, atol deór monig, . . . blace nædran, Salm. Kmbl. 940; Sal. 469. [*Icel.* ormgarðr. Cf. in the story of Gunnar's fate in Atla kviða: Nū es sā ormgarðr yðr um folginn, v. 68: ī garð þann es skriðinn vas innan ormom, 121. See, too, the stories of the deaths of Ragnar Lodbrog and Roderick, the last Gothic king of Spain.] v. wyrm-sele.

wyrm-geblǣd, es; *n. A blister raised by a snake-bite* (?), Lchdm. iii. 36, 21.

wyrm-hǣlsere, es; *m. A serpent-charmer, sorcerer*:—Wyrmhǣlseras *marsi* (printed *maris*), Wrt. Voc. ii. 55, 15. v. wyrm-galere.

wyrm-hīw, es; *n. The form of a reptile* or *serpent*:—Hē sceolde hī āwendan of đam wyrmhīwe (cf. *serpentia terrae*, Acts 10, 12), Homl. Skt. i. 10, 104.

wyrm-hord, es; *n. A treasure held by a serpent*, Beo. Th. 4447; B. 2222.

wyrm-līc, es; *n. The body of a serpent* or *of a worm*, (1) of carving on a wall. Cf. wyrm-fāh:—Weal wundrum heáh, wyrmlīcum fāh, Exon. Th. 292, 13; Wand. 98. (2) fig. cf. wyrm, **II a**:—Ic eom oferfongen mid synnum tō wyrmlīce, Anglia xii. 501, 22.

wyrm-melu (-o), wes; *n. Dust of dried worms powdered* (cf. 'Dry fair large earthworms before the fire, or in an oven, which when thorough dry, beat into powder,' Salmon's English Physician, quoted by Cockayne. See also: Eft angeltwæccan, gegnīd swīþe, Lchdm. iii. 44, 4):—Wyrc sealfe . . . of wyrmmeluwe, Lchdm. ii. 78, 15. Nim wyrmmelu, 150, 10. Wyrmmelo, 238, 30. [In *O. H. Ger.* wurmmelo = *caries*.]

wyrms, es; *n. m. Corrupt matter*:—Đis wyrms *hoc uirus*, Ælfc. Gr. 8; Zup. 29, 1. Wyrms *lues*, 9, 27; Zup. 53, 7: *colera*, Wrt. Voc. ii. 134, 54. Wiđ eárena sāre . . . gif đǣr wyrms inne biđ, hyt đæt ūt āwyrpđ, Lchdm. i. 354, 16. Wyrms (worms, *v.l.*), 358, 16. Sāh ūt wyrms (of đam geswelle), Homl. Skt. i. 20, 64. Hē āscræp đone wyrms of his līce, Homl. Th. ii. 452, 28. ¶ figurative:—His wuldor is wyrms and meox, Homl. Skt. ii. 25, 261. v. worms; ge-wyrms; *adj.*

wyrmsan, wyrsman; *p.* de *To produce corrupt matter*:—Đonne se lǣce on untīman lācnaþ wunde, hió wyrmseþ and rotaþ, Past. 21; Swt. 153, 3. Sió wund wolde hālian, æfter đæm đe heó wyrmsde (wyrsmde, Cott. MSS.), 36; Swt. 259, 1. Gif hit wille wyrsman, Lchdm. ii. 102, 4. v. ge-wyrmsed.

wyrm-sele, es; *m. A serpent-hall* [cf. the hall, thick swarming now, With . . . scorpion, and asp . . . Cerastes horned, hydrus, and elops drear, And dipsas, Par. Lost 10, 522 sqq.], *a place where there are serpents* (*hell*):—Ne þearf hē hopian đæt hē þonan mōte, of đam wyrmsele, Judth. Thw. 23, 13; Jud. 119. v. wyrm-geard.

wyrms-hrǣcung, e; *f. The expectoration of corrupt matter*:—Wyr[m]shrǣcing *vel* wyr[m]sūtspīung *phthisis*, Wrt. Voc. i. 19, 39.

wyrmsig; *adj. Purulent*:—Đǣm wyrmsigum *purulentis*, Wrt. Voc. ii. 78, 56. v. wurmsig.

wyrm-slite, es; *m. A snake-bite*:—In weán and on wyrmslitum betweónan deádum and deóflum, in bryne and on biternesse, Wulfst. 188, 1.

wyrms-ūtspīung. v. wyrms-hrǣcung.

wyrm-wyrt, e; *f. Worm-grass* (v. E. D. S. Pub. Plant Names); sedum album, Lchdm. ii. 94, 18: 104, 3: 128, 3: 308, 16. [*O. H. Ger.* wurm-wurz *aganoe*.]

wyrn, wyrnan. v. wirn, wirnan.

wyrp, es; *m. A throw, cast, the distance which a thing may be thrown*:—Swā mycel swā is ānes stānes wyrp (weorp ł wyrp, Lind.) *quantum jactus est lapidis*, Lk. Skt. 22, 41. [Þurh on eie wurp to one wummon, A. R. 56, 14. Iesus from heom iwende þe uurp of o ston, Misc. 41, 155. *O. H. Ger.* wurf *jactus, ictus*.] v. ǣ-wyrp.

wyrp *recovery*, wyrpan *to recover*, wyrpan *to throw*, -wyrpan, -wyrpe. v. wirp, wirpan, weorpan, (be-, ge-)sceat-wyrpan, ge-, lang-wyrpe.

wyrpel, es; *m. A vervel, a ring put on a falcon's leg*. Thorpe in his note on the following passage quotes from Roquefort the explanation of the French *vervelle:* Large anneau qu'on passoit au pied d'un faucon pour le retenir:—Sum sceal wildne fugel ātemian, heafoc on honda . . . dēþ hē wyrplas on, fēdeþ swā on feterum fiþrum dealne (cf. the description of a falcon's equipment given in a M. H. Ger. poem, Haupt Zsch. 7, 341, quoted by Leo: Lancvezzel, würfel und hoselīn, daz waren diu kleit sīn), Exon. Th. 332, 19; Vy. 87.

-wyrplīc, -wyrpness, wyrra, wyrrest, wyrs, wyrs-hrǣcing, wyrsm. v. scort-wyrplīc, for-, tō-wyrpness, wirsa, wirs, wyrms-hrǣcung, wyrms.

wyrst. v. wrist.

wyrt, e; *f.* I. *a wort* (e.g. St. John's *wort*), *plant, herb*:—Gærs *vel* wyrt *herba*, Wrt. Voc. i. 30, 35: 78, 71. Ðeós wyrt, ðe man betonicam nemneþ, Lchdm. i. 70, 1: 90, 2, *and often*. Seó wyrt (*herba*) weóx, Mt. Kmbl. 13, 26. Gemolsnad wyrt, Ps. Th. 89, 6. Wyrta wynsume, Exon. Th. 233, 23; Ph. 529. Sumra wyrta eard biþ on dūnum, sumra on merscum, sumra on mōrum, Bt. 34, 10; Fox 148, 22. Mid missenlīcum blōstmum wyrta āfægrod *variis herbarum floribus depictus*, Bd. 1, 7; S. 478, 22: Exon. Th. 358, 17; Pa. 47. Gif mon sié wyrtum forboren, Lchdm. ii. 114, 8, 12. Hē getimbreþ tānum and wyrtum nest, 227, 29; Ph. 430. God geworhte eall gærs and wyrta (*omnem herbam*), Gen. 2, 5. Ðū ytst ðære eorðan wyrta, 3, 18: Ps. Th. 103, 13. Werta, Kent. Gl. 687. I a. *a garden herb, herb for food*:—Gē teóþiaþ mintan and ǣlce wyrte (alle wyrte, Rush. *omne holus*), Lk. Skt. 11, 42. Wyrta *olera*, Wrt. Voc. i. 82, 31: *fordalium* (cf. wyrt-mete), ii. 150, 20. Hit is ealra wyrta mǣst *majus est omnibus holeribus*, Mt. Kmbl. 13, 32. Tō wertum *ad olera*, Kent. Gl. 524. Gif gē mē (*the cook*) ūt ādrīfaþ fram eówrum gefērscype, gē etaþ wyrta (*olera*) eówre grēne, Coll. Monast. Th. 29, 11: 34, 27. II. *a root*:—Wudubeám wæs wyrtum fæst, Cd. Th. 247, 19; Dan. 499: Beo. Th. 2732; B. 1364: Exon. Th. 209, 18; Ph. 172: 417, 2; Rä. 35, 7. [*Goth.* waurts *a plant, a root*: *O. Sax.* wurt *a plant, root*: *O. H. Ger.* wurz *herba, olus*: *Icel.* urt *a herb*.] v. wudu-wyrt. The word occurs in the names of many plants, see the lists of plant-names given in Wrt. Voc. i. pp. 30–, 66–, 78–, 286–, and in Lchdm. iii. 311 sqq.

wyrt, e; *f. Wort* (in brewing):—Wyrt *sandix* (the word occurs in a list of terms 'de mensa,' and among a number denoting various kinds of drink. Cf. sandix, genus frugi, Corp. Gl. Hessels, 105, 103), Wrt. Voc. i. 290, 64: 289, 9: ii. 87, 33. Bewylle on hwǣtene wyrte, Lchdm. ii. 268, 12. [Wurte *idromellum*, Wrt. Voc. i. 257, col. 2. *Ger.* würze: *Swed.* wört.] v. leáh-mealt-, māsc-, mealt-wyrt.

wyrt-bed[d], es; *n. A garden-bed*:—Ðeós wyrt bið cenned on begānum stōwum and on wyrtbeddum and on mǣdum, Lchdm. i. 96, 22: 184, 6. [*O. H. Ger.* wurz-betti *areola*.]

wyrt-brǣþ, es; *m. A perfume from plants, an odour, aroma*:—Mid brǣðe āfylled swylce ðǣr lǣgon lilie and rose. Ðā cwæð Basilissa: 'Ic wundrie hwanon ðes wyrtbrǣð ðus wynsumlīce stēme,' Homl. Skt. i. 4, 36. Ne mihte nān wyrtbrǣð swā wynsumlīce stēman, ii. 27, 113. Āgeótende wyrtbrǣð (*aroma*) of rinde, Hymn. Surt. 79, 13. Orþiende wyrtbrǣða swētnyssa *spirans odorum balsama*, 98, 19. Seó cwēn com tō Salomone mid lācum on golde, and on deórwurðum gymstānum and wyrtbrǣðum . . . Seó geleáfulle gelaðung offraþ Criste wyrtbrǣðas þurh gebeda, Homl. Th. ii. 586, 6–11.

wyrt-cyn[n], es; *n. A species of plant* or *vegetable*:—Ǣghwylc wyrtcyn *omne genus holitorum*, i. *holerum*, Wrt. Voc. i. 55, 29. Wyrtcynn (wyrta cynn, Rush.) *nardus pisticus*, Jn. Skt. Lind. 12, 3: *aloes*, 19, 39: *unguentum*, Ps. Th. 132, 2.

wyrt-cynren, es; *n. The genus plant, plants, herbs*:—Wyrtcynren *herbam*, Ps. Lamb. 146, 8.

wyrt-drenc, es; *m. A herb-drink, potion made from herbs*:—Wyrtdrenc *antidotum*, Wrt. Voc. ii. 6, 70: 100, 31. Wyrtdrenc wið ātre *sityriaca* (=theriaca), 77, 4. Biter wyrtdrenc *picra*, wyrtdrenc *catartica*, i. *purgatoria*, i. 20, 19, 21. Mid ondōunge wyrtdrences þurh horn oððe pīpan sió wamb biþ tō clǣnsianne, Lchdm. ii. 260, 11. Dō ealle ða wyrta tō wyrtdrence, 22, 17. Ǣfter ðon sceal man wyrtdrenc sellan, 22, 2. Wyrtdrencas *antidota*, Wrt. Voc. ii. 2, 4. Lǣcedōmas wiþ ðære healfdeádan ādle, and onlegena and wyrtdrencas, Lchdm. ii. 172, 8.

wyrt-eceddrenc, es; *m. An acid potion made with herbs*:—Be ðam sūþernan wyrteceddrence, Lchdm. ii. 172, 11.

wyrtel (?) *a plant*. v. biscop-wyrtil. [*O. H. Ger.* wurzala *radix*.]

wyrt-fæt, es; *n. A scent-bottle*:—Wyrtfata *olfactoriola* (cf. *olfactoriola* ðe hiera elesealfa on wǣran, Wrt. Voc. ii. 64, 35), Hpt. Gl. 517, 27.

wyrt-forbor, es; *n. Restraint from an action by the operation of herbs*:—Wiþ wyrtforbore (cf. Gif mon sié wyrtum forboren, 114, 8) and yflum gealdorcræftum, Lchdm. ii. 306, 12. Cf. next word.

wyrt-gælstre, an; *f. A woman who uses herbs for charms*:—Mǣden yfeldǣda and wyrtgælstre (*malefica et herbaria*), Lchdm. iii. 186, 11. Cf. previous word.

wyrt-geard, es; *m. A kitchen-garden*:—Wyrtgeardas *promptuaria*, Ps. Spl. C. 143, 16. [*Wick.* wort-ȝerd *hortus olerum*.]

wyrt-gemang, es; *n. A spice*:—Wyrtgemangc *myrra*, Ps. Lamb. 44, 9. Maria nam ān pund deórwyrðre sealfe mid ðam wyrtgemange ðe hig nardus hātaþ *Maria accepit libram ungenti nardi pistici preciosi*, Jn. Skt. 12, 3. Wyrtgemang and alewan *mixturam murrae et aloes*, 19, 39. Myrre and gutta and cassia . . . Ða wyrtgemang getācniaþ mistlīcu mægen Cristes, Ps. Th. 44, 10. Wyrta oððe wyrtgemangu *herbae vel pigmenta*, Scint. 36, 11. Wyrtgemanga strengðe *pigmentorum uim*, 120, 13. Mid wyrtgemangum *cum aromatibus*, Jn. Skt. 19, 40: Anglia xiii. 427, 885. Hig bǣron mid him ða wyrtgemang (*aromata*), Lk. Skt. 24, 1. Hig gearwodun wyrtgemang (wyrta gemong, Lind. *aromata*), 23, 56: Mk. Skt. 16, 1. v. next word.

wyrt-gemengness, e; *f. A spice*:—Hig bebyrigdon Andreas līchaman myd wyrtgemengnyssum and myd swētum stencum, Shrn. 153, 17: Wulfst. 263, 5. v. preceding word.

wyrþe. v. weorþ.

wyrþe-land, es; *n. Land that has lain fallow, land ploughed for the first time, a cultivated field*:—Wyrðelandum *novalibus* (tellus millenos animarum manipulos in fructiferis ecclesiae novalibus protulit, Ald. 32), Wrt. Voc. ii. 79, 26: 77, 50: 59, 56. v. worþ, *and next word* (?).

wyrþen *a field* (?):—Wyrþenna *leti* (the passage in which the gloss occurs is: Graculus, qui segetum glumas, et laeti cespites occas depopulare studet, Ald. 142. Perhaps *wyrþenna* should be taken as a gloss to *occas*, v. wyrþing), Wrt. Voc. ii. 89, 57: 52, 20. v. preceding word (?).

wyrþian, wyrþig. v. weorþian, wirþig.

wyrþing *a cultivated field* (?):—Wealh (fealh ?) oþþe wyrðing *occa* (the passage is: Anthonius coelestis aratri stivarius . . . a quo primitus per Aegyptum fertilis coenobiorum seges et foecunda conversationis occa granigeris germinavit spicis, Ald. 32), Wrt. Voc. ii. 79, 25. v. wyrþen.

wyrþo. v. wirþu.

wyrtian; *p.* ode *To season, spice*:—Ic wyrtige *condo*, Wrt. Voc. ii. 21, 39. v. ge-wyrtian.

wyrtig; *adj. Full of herbs*:—On ānum wyrtigan hamme, Homl. Skt. ii. 30, 312.

wyrt-mete, es; *m. Vegetable food, food consisting of herbs*:—Wyrtmete *clerius cibus*, Wrt. Voc. i. 290, 40: ii. 17, 23. Gesoden wyrtmete *fordalium*, 38, 56: 150, 2. Wurtmete mid meluwe *polentum*, i. 27, 25.

wyrt-stenc, es; *m. A perfume from a plant*:—Hūs gefylled wæs wyrtstence (*odore*) ðære smirnisse, Jn. Skt. Rush. 12, 3.

wyrt-truma (wyrtruma), an: -trum, es; *m.*: -trume, an; *f.* (v. Be ðare wyrtruman, Cod. Dip. Kmbl. iv. 93, 7). I. *the root of a plant*:—Wyrtruma *radix*, Wrt. Voc. i. 33, 11: 80, 8: 285, 79: Cd. Th. 252, 20; Dan. 581. Is seó æx āsett tō ðæs treówes wyrtruman, Lk. Skt. 3, 9. Be ðam wyrttruman, Lchdm. i. 172, 10. Wyrttruman *radicem*, Ps. Spl. 51, 5. Hig næfdon wyrtruman (wyrtrum, *v. l.*), Mt. Kmbl. 13, 6: Mt. Skt. 4, 6: Lk. Skt. 8, 13. Hyt næfð ðone wyrtruman (wyrtrum, *v. l.*), Mt. Kmbl. 13, 21. Wyrtruman ðæs wudubeámes eorðan fæstne, Cd. Th. 248, 20; Dan. 516: Exon. Th. 328, 28; Vy. 24. Treów wyrtrumum underwreðyd, Runic pm. Kmbl. 341, 30; Rūn. 13. Wyrttruman *radices*, Ps. Spl. 79, 10. Ōþ ða wirttruman *usque ad radices*, Num. 22, 4. I a. *the root* of a tooth:—[Ða grindigtēþ ðe ālc mid feówer wyrtrume gefæstned byð, and ðanne hȳ hero wurtruma forleátaþ, ðanne sweartigeþ hȳ, and fealleþ, Lchdm. iii. 104, 15.] I b. figurative:—Ne næfð ǣnig bōh grēnnysse gōdes weorces, se ðe nā wunaþ on wyrtruman (*radice*) sōðre lufe, Scint. 3, 19. Ða ðe heora heortan wyrtruman on ðisum andwerdum līfe plantiaþ, Homl. Th. i. 132, 7. II. *the root, source, origin*:—Hē cuæð ðæt ǣlces yfeles wyrttruma (wyrtruma, Cott. MSS.) wǣre ðæt mon wilnode hwelcre gītsunge, Past. 11; Swt. 73, 3. Seó grǣdignys is wyrtruma ǣlces yfeles, and seó sōðe lufu is wyrtruma ǣlces gōdes, Homl. Th. ii. 410, 3. Ðætte of wyrtruman besmitenes geþōhtes ācenned bið, Bd. 1, 27; M. 80, 13. II a. *a stock*:—Hwæt limpeþ ðæs tō ðē of hwylcum wyrtruman ic ācenned sī *quid ad te pertinet qua sim stirpe genitus?* 1, 7; S. 477, 28. III. this word and the word of like meaning, *wyrtwala* (q. v.), seem to be used in reference to local relations in the sense of *foot, lower side*, the opposite of *heáfod* or *heáfdu*, e.g. Of ðes pōles hēuede on gerigte tō ðane ellene; of ðane ellene on gerigte ā be wertuualen on ðe herestrāte, Cod. Dip. Kmbl. v. 17, 10. Tō ðan heáfdan . . . tō uurtwalan, vi. 2, 4–6. Andlang fyrh on ða heáfda; andlang heáfda on ðæne grēnan pæð . . . andlang fyrh on ða wyrtwale; swā be ðære wyrtwale, iv. 19, 17–28. Cf. *too*: Be ðām heáfdon, iii. 378, 22. Ā be heáfdan, 438, 29. Tō ðam heáfde; big ðam heáfde tō ðere fureh, 384, 16, with similar uses of *wyrttruma* and *wyrtwala*:—Of ðam seáðe swā wyrtruma sceát ōð Ramleáhweg, Cod. Dip. Kmbl. iii. 455, 22. On ðone feld; ðæt andlang wyrttruman on Hildes hlǣw, 170, 27. On dinningcgrǣfes wyrttruman; of dynningcgrǣfes wyrttruman eall swā se dīc sceót, 208, 5: 34, 14. On widigleás wyrttruman; đonne ealling be wyrttruman óđ ácleá, v. 230, 1. On widigleás wyrtruman; on eatan beares wyrtruman; óđ leás eástende; norđ be wyrttruman, 334, 25–27. On loxanwuda wyrtruman; of wyrtruman on þiccan stānas, 345, 5. Óđ đa dūnæ ufewearde on đa ǣđenan byrigelsas; swā ādūn be wyrtruman æft tō gemīđum, 346, 20. Innan leá; đanne be wurtruman anlanges wudes, iii. 172, 33. Óđ đa lēge; đonne be wyrttruman, 406, 28, 33: v. 358, 18. Forđ be wyrttruman, iii. 422, 1: vi. 33, 37. Bæ đam wyrttruman, v. 191, 32. Wyrttrumman, iii. 135, 8. Tō wuda; swā be đan eald wyrtruman, 279, 31. Be wyrttrume, v. 100, 20. Wirtrume, iii. 440, 33. Ofer đane sceagan; đonne forđ ā be wyrtruman, 460, 2. Of đan hamme ā be wurtruman, vi. 137, 22. Ā be đare wyrtruman, iv. 93, 7. On wyrtruman, iii. 390, 26. On feld on wyrttruman ođ grāfes suđende, v. 334, 34.

wyrttrumian; *p.* ode *To take root*:—Sēd wyrtrumiaþ (wyrtrymaþ, Rush.) *semen germinet*, Mk. Skt. Lind. 4, 27. v. ge-wyrttrumian.

wyrt-tūn, es; *m. A garden*:—Wyrttūn *botanicum* vel *viridarium, cucumerarium*, Wrt. Voc. i. 30, 17, 18. Wyrtūn *viridiarium*, 84, 54: *hortus*, ii. 42, 51: Jn. Skt. 18, 1: 19, 41. On wyrttūne *in cucumerario*, Wrt. Voc. ii. 48, 24. On wyrtūne (wyrttūne, *v. l.*) *in horto*, R. Ben. 71, 18. Syle mē đīnne wīneard mē tō wyrtūne, Homl. Skt. i. 18, 173. Wyrttūn ne sāw đū, Lchdm. iii. 184, 19: Lk. Skt. 13, 19. Wyrtūna *hortorum*, Wrt. Voc. ii. 83, 27. Hē nemde đa undiórestan wyrta đe on wyrttūnum weaxe, and đeáh swīđe welstincenda, Past. 57; Swt. 439, 32: Lchdm. i. 94, 7.

wyrtung, e; *f. Seasoning with herbs*:—On scīrum wīne . . . : ge on wīne ge on wyrtunge, Lchdm. i. 342, 26. v. wyrtian.

wyrt-wala, an; *m.*: -walu, e; *f.* I. *the root* of a plant:—Swā fela bōga treówes of ānum wyrtwalan (*radice*) sprytttaþ, Scint. 3, 17. Genim wegbrǣdan wyrtwalan, Lchdm. i. 82, 19: 90, 6, 23: 94, 19, 23. Wyrtwalan *radices*, Ps. Surt. 79, 10. Andlang pæþes on đa wyrtwalan; of đam wyrtwalan on heortsole, Cod. Dip. Kmbl. iv. 19, 25. Andlang strǣt widūtan đa wyrtwalan, 20, 2. Andlang rīđe on đa wurtwalan, vi. 1, 26. I a. fig.:—God ūt ālūceþ wirtwelæ đīnne of lande lyfigendra, Ps. Spl. T. 51, 5. II. *a root, source*:—Wyrd, ealra firena fruma, fǣhđo mōdor, weána wyrtwela, wōpes heáfod, Salm. Kmbl. 889; Sal. 444. III. *the foot* of a hill, *lower side* of a wood, field, etc. v. wyrt-truma, III:—Swā đe wyrtwala scādet tō turlan homme (cf. *first passage under* wyrttruma, III), Cod. Dip. Kmbl. v. 267, 33. Forđ andlang wyrtwale on đa rōde, 356, 4. Forđ be grāfes wurtwale, iii. 405, 29. On đa eorđburg; đæt forđ be wurtwalan tō mearcwege, vi. 43, 18. Uuirtwalan, wyrtwalan, 93, 33, 34: v. 86, 18. Of đære leáge be wyrtwalan, iii. 464, 21: v. 148, 14: 298, 16. Be wirtwalan on đa efsan; and đan on đone wīđig; and swā be wirtwalan on đone mēreþorne, 226, 16, 17. Đurh henna leáh, óđ hit cymeþ tō đære efese; đonne ā norþ be wyrtwalan, ii. 172, 23: iii. 380, 25: 437, 33: v. 330, 33: 336, 27. Wurtwalan, vi. 41, 20. Weortwalan, v. 389, 15, 16. Ā be wyrtwale . . . on hel ufeweardne æfter wyrtwalan, iii. 48, 11–16. On heáfdbeorh; đonne on wyrtwalan on đæs hagan ende . . .; andlang herpađes tō đære efise, đonon eft on wyrtwalen, v. 300, 8–13.

wyrtwalian; *p.* ode. I. *to plant*:—Ongelǣdde wyrtwælæs (*plantabis*) hié on dūne yrfeweærdnesse đīne, Cant. Moys. 21 (=Ex. 15, 17). Wirtwæledæst *plantasti*, Ps. Spl. T. 43, 3. Wyrtwalodes, 79, 10. II. *to root up, eradicate*:—Ic wyrtwalige (āwyrtwalige, *v. l.*) *uello, uellico*, Ælfc. Gr. 36; Zup. 214, 16. Wyrtwalod, Shrn. 184, 3. v. ā-, under-wyrtwalian.

wyrt-weard, es; *m. A gardener*:—Heó wēnde đæt hit se wyrtweard (*hortulanus*) wǣre, Jn. Skt. 20, 15.

wȳsc, es; *m. Choice*:—Đā him wiisc [wūsc?] seald wæs *optione data*, Bd. 5, 19; S. 638, 40. [Wusche *exoptatio*, Prompt. Parv. 535. *O. H. Ger.* wunsc; *m. optio*: *Icel.* ósk; *f.*] v. wūsc-bearn.

wȳscan; *p.* te *To wish*. (1) with gen. *to wish* for, *desire*:—Hē helle wīsceþ, đæs engestan ēđelrīces, Salm. Kmbl. 212; Sal. 105. Hȳ đæs betran līfes wȳscaþ and wēnaþ, Exon. Th. 106, 26; Gū. 47. Wīscaþ, 115, 24; Gū. 194. Hié his tōcymes wȳscton, Blickl. Homl. 103, 12. (1 a) *to wish* something to or for a person:—Đa apostolas hǣlo eów wȳscaþ, L. Alf. 49; Th. i. 56, 13. Ne cuæđ hē đæt for đȳ đe hē ǣnegum men đæs wȳscte ođđe wilnode *non optantis animo*, Past. 1; Swt. 29, 11. Ne wyrige nān man ōđerne, ne yfeles ne wīsce, Homl. Th. ii. 34, 27. (2) with acc.:—Ic sceal his rōde sigor swīđor wīscan đonne ondrǣdan, Homl. Th. i. 594, 20. (3) in a precatory or imprecatory sense, =utinam, (a) with clause:—Ic wȳsce đæt heorte healde lufe *utinam cor teneat amorem*, Scint. 25, 1. Đæt ic eác swylce wīsce forþ sié on leornunge ūra stafa *quod utinam exhinc etiam nostrarum lectione litterarum fiat*, Bd. 5, 14; S. 635, 7. Ic wīsce đæt Ysmahēl libbe ætforan đē *utinam Ismael vivat coram te*, Gen. 17, 18. Ic wīsce đæt hig wiston *utinam saperent*, Deut. 32, 29. Gif ic đē ne geþence, ic wīsce đæt ic eft forlidennesse gefare, Ap. Th. 12, 10. Wē wīsceaþ đæt wē wǣron ǣr deád *utinam mortui essemus*, Num. 14, 3. Hié wȳscaþ đæt hié nǣfre nǣron ācennede, Blickl. Homl. 93, 27. Ic oft wīscte and wolde đæt hyra læs wǣre swā gewinfulra *que utinam minus fuissent laboriosa*, Nar. 2, 28. Đū wȳsctest đæt đū wistest Crist on rōde ahangenne, Blickl. Homl. 85, 33. Hē oft wȳscte đæt ealle Rōmāne hæfden ǣnne sweoran *exclamasse fertur*: '*Utinam populus Romanus unam cervicem haberet*,' Ors. 6, 3; Swt. 256, 26: Exon. Th. 378, 33; Deór. 25. Wīscte, Ps. Th. 14, arg. Hī wīscton đæt hī mōston swā wunian ōđ ende, Homl. Skt. i. 5, 401. (b) where the words of the wish are given:—Alexander đā wīscte: 'Eálā gif đū wǣre hund,' Homl. Th. ii. 308, 13. (c) with gen. and appositional clause:—Ic đæs wīsce, đæt wegas mīne on đīnum willan weorþan gereahte *utinam dirigantur viae meae*, Ps. Th. 118, 5. [*O. H. Ger.* wunscen *optare*: *Icel.* œskja.] v. ge-wȳscan.

-wȳscedness, -wȳscendlīc, -wȳscendlīce, -wȳscing. v. ge-wȳscedness, ge-wȳscendlīc, ge-wȳscendlīce, ge-wȳscing.

Y

For the Runic ᛣ see ȳr.

ȳce, an; *f.*: ȳce, es; *m. A (poisonous) frog*:—Ȳce *botrax* vel *botraca*, Wrt. Voc. i. 24, 19: *botrax*, 45, 26: ii. 13, 2: 126, 57: *rana*, 71, 15. Ȳcean *roboete* (the passage is:—Regulorum et aspidum venena, ad quae quadrupedis *robetae* et spalangii pestifera confectio humanae naturae nocitura habebatur, Ald. 25), 78, 44. Đæt ilce biþ nyttol īces slite oþþe hundes, Lchdm. ii. 86, 2 (see note). Đære wyrte wyrttruma on wætere gedyged widrǣđ īceom and næddrum, i. 144, 15. Ȳcan ł froggan *ranas*, Ps. Lamb. 104, 30. ¶ Yce *parruca*, Wrt. Voc. ii. 67, 69, *seems to be for* hyce; v. hicae *paruca*, 116, 50. [*M. H. Ger.* ūchen *ranas*.] v. fen-ȳce.

yfel, es; *n. Evil, ill*:—Gōd *bonum*, yfel *malum*, Wrt. Voc. i. 74, 49. I. in a moral sense:—Đa đe him biþ unwītnode eall hiora yfel on đisse worulde, Bt. 38, 3; Fox 200, 26. Hwæt yfeles dyde þes? Mt. Kmbl. 27, 23. Dǣdbōte dōn đæs mycelan yfeles and mānes, đe hié wiđ heora Drihten gedydon, Blickl. Homl. 79, 6. Đone besmītan đe đū nānwiht yfeles on nystest, 85, 36. Yfeles ordfruma, Cd. Th. 288, 1; Sat. 374. Hē đæs yfeles geswīce, Hy. 2, 8: Met. 9, 52. Forđhealde tō yfele *in malum prona*, Gen. 8, 21: Hy. 7, 113. For rihtwīsnysse hē sceal habban andan tō hira yfele, Past. 12; S. 75, 14. Beó nū on yfele, noldæs ǣr teala, Cd. Th. 310, 26; Sat. 733. Ic syngade and mycel yfel beforan đē ic gedyde, Blickl. Homl. 87, 30. Leahtra gehwylcne, yfel unclǣne, Exon. Th. 80, 21; Cri. 1310: Past. 21; Swt. 157, 23. Ealle đæt yfel and đæt unnet, đæt hē ǣr on his mōde hæfde, Bt. 35, 1; Fox 154, 26. Gȳtsung, mān, . . . stuntscipe, ealle đās yfelu of đam innođe cumaþ, and đone man besmītaþ, Mk. Skt. 7, 23. Đæt hē feala yfla sægde, Blickl. Homl. 173, 20. Yfla gehwylc, grimme gieltas, Exon. Th. 229, 25; Ph. 460. Tō eácan ōþrum unārīmedum yflum hē đone pāpan hēt ofsleán, Bt. 1; Fox 2, 11. Hié nǣnige bōte dōn noldan, ah hié on heora yfelum þurhwunedon, Blickl. Homl. 79, 8: Ps. Th. 105, 25. Ic đē þreáge and đē cȳđe eal đās yflu, 49, 23. II. what is hurtful, grievous:—Hū mycel yfel đē gelamp for đīnre gītsunge, Blickl. Homl. 31, 13. Nū is ǣghwanon yfel and slege, 115, 16: 181, 32. Is mīn yfel twyfeald *I am doubly injured*, 175, 13. Is sāwl mīn sāres and yfeles gefylled *repleta est malis anima mea*, Ps. Th. 87, 3: 106, 38. Ǣgđer hyra ōđrum yfles hogode, Byrht. Th. 135, 45; By. 133: Exon. Th. 54, 28; Cri. 875. Bydelas đæs ēcan yfeles, đe yfelum mannum becymđ, Homl. Th. ii. 538, 23. Đa fuglas ūs nǣnige lāđe ne yfle ne wǣron *aves non nobis perniciem ferentes*, Nar. 16, 18. Hē wile hit him mid grimnesse and mid yfele forgyldan, Blickl. Homl. 55, 25. Hē nǣnigum yfel wiþ yfele geald, 223, 33: Elen. Kmbl. 983; El. 493. Hī đǣr mycel yfel gedydon, Chr. 897; Erl. 95, 18: 993; Erl. 133, 3. Ǣlc yfel man him gehēt, 1036; Erl. 165, 22. Đām đe mē syrwedan yfel *qui quaerunt mala mihi*, Ps. Th. 70, 12. Ealle đe mē yfel hogedon *qui cogitant mihi mala*, 69, 3. Heó þolian ne wolde yfel, Cd. Th. 136, 26; Gen. 2264: Past. 36; Swt. 261, 4: Exon. Th. 77, 9; Cri. 1254. Fela yfelu sceolon foreyrnon ǣr seó geendung đissere worulde cume, Homl. Th. ii. 538, 22. Đū mē yfela feala oft oncnyssedest, Ps. Th. 70, 19. Đē gehealde Drihten wyđ yfela gehwam *Dominus custodit te ab omni malo*, 120, 6. Yfla gehwylc, Exon. Th. 356, 27; Pa. 18. Ic earfeþa dreág, yfel ormǣtu, 280, 10; Jul. 627. Ic gegaderie ofer hig yflu (*mala*), Cant. M. ad fil. 23. II a. of disease:—Wiþ đam wǣtan yfle đæs miltes, Lchdm. ii. 246, 9. Hit mæg wiđ ǣghwilcum uncūþum yfele, iii. 288, 17. Wiđ lungenādle and wiđ gehwylce yfelu đe on đam innođe dereþ, i. 280, 18. II b. of abusive speech:—Hié wyrgdon đone cāsere and him yfel cwǣdon, Blickl. Homl. 191, 10. ¶ *the word often occurs in contrast with* gōd:—Swā đæs gōdan gōdnes biþ his āgen gōd, swā biþ eác đæs yfelan yfel his āgen yfel, Bt. 37, 3; Fox 190, 15. Hwæþer him yfel þe gōd under wunige, Exon. Th. 82, 3; Cri. 1333. Ealles đæs đe wē geweorhtan gōdes ođđe yfles, 447, 21; Dōm. 43: Blickl. Homl. 51, 26. Treów ingehȳdes gōdes and yfeles, Gen. 2, 9. Gōdes and yfeles, welan and wāwan, Cd. Th. 30, 10; Gen. 465. Gōdes and ȳfles ic cunnade, Exon. Th. 321, 25; Vīd.

51. Hig woldon gildan gôd mid yfele, Gen. 44, 4. Swâ gôd swâ yfel swâ hē ǣr dyde, Blickl. Homl. 101, 30. Se Hálga Gást hié ǣghwylc gôd lǣrde and him ǣghwylc yfel bewerede, 131, 30. Ðurh ða gesceádwîsnesse wē tôcnâwaþ good and yfel, and geceósaþ ðæt gôd and âweorpaþ ðæt yfel, Past. 11; Swt. 65, 22. Geþenc ðæt ðū gôd onfēnge and gelîce Lazarus onfēng yfel, Lk. Skt. 16, 25. [*Goth.* ubil: *O. Sax.* ubil: *O. Frs.* evel: *O. H. Ger.* ubil.]

yfel; *adj. Evil, ill, bad*:—Yfel *malus*, Wrt. Voc. i. 74, 47. I. in a moral sense:—Yfel mann of yfelum goldhorde bringð yfel forð, Mt. Kmbl. 12, 35. Hié nǣnigo firen ne gewundode, ne yfel gewitnes (*witness of wrong-doing*) ne wrēgde, Blickl. Homl. 161, 33. Ðæt ðǣr mæge yfelu uncyst on eardian, 37, 10. Se yfela dēma onfēhþ medmycclum feó, and onwendeþ ðone rihtan dôm, 61, 30. Se yfela þeów, Mt. Kmbl. 24, 48. Se yfela willa, Bt. 36, 7; Fox 184, 31. Se yfela unrihtwîsa cyningc, Met. 15, 1. Fram yfelum menn *ab homine malo*, Ps. Th. 139, 1. Yflum, Exon. Th. 96, 20; Cri. 1577. From ðære inwitfullan yflan tungan *a lingua dolosa*, Ps. Th. 119, 3. Ne sette ic mē fore eágum yfele wîsan (*rem malam*), 100, 3. Synnigra cirm, yfele sprǣce, Cd. Th. 145, 20; Gen. 2408. Âfyr fram ðē ða yfelan sǣlþa and ða unnettan, and ðone yflan ege ðisse worulde, Bt. 6; Fox 14, 33. Yfele men magon yfel dôn, 36, 7; Fox 184, 4: Blickl. Homl. 45, 23. Yfele geþancas, Mk. Skt. 7, 21. Hyra weorc wǣron yfele, Jn. Skt. 3, 19. Se anweald ðara yflena cymþ of unþeáwum, Bt. 36, 7; Fox 182, 26. Ic tô yflum cwæð *dixi iniquis*, Ps. Th. 74, 4: Exon. Th. 57, 15; Cri. 919. Ylflum, Blickl. Homl. 33, 22. Yfelum wordum, 39, 3. Hē wile gesceáwian wlitige and unclǣne, tile and yfle, Cd. Th. 303, 10; Sat. 610. Hē âraþ ða gôdan, and hē wîtnaþ ða yfelan, Bt. 41, 2; Fox 246, 20. II. of things, *bad, not good of its kind*:—Sió yfele gillestre and ðæt yfele blôd, Lchdm. ii. 148, 6. Gif eáran willen âdeáfian, oþþe yfel hlyst sié . . . Gif mon yfelne hlyst hæbbe (cf. wiþ yfelre hlyste, 2, 13), 40, 22–26. Nys gôd treów ðe yfelne wæstm dēð, ne nis yfel treów gôdne wæstm dônde, Lk. Skt. 6, 43. Heó is on onsȳne ûtan yfeles heówes, Blickl. Homl. 197, 11. Ðâ gecuron hig ða gôdan (fiscas) on hyra fatu, ða yflan hig âwurpon ût, Mt. Kmbl. 13, 48. III. of what is grievous, hurtful, etc., (1) of animate objects:—Yfel wiht *phantasma*, Mk. Skt. Lind. 6, 49. Hē sealde yfelan wyrme hiora wyrta, Ps. Th. 77, 46. Hî ǣtan yfle tostan, 77, 45. Hē gehǣlde manega of yfelum (yflum, Lind.) gâstum, Lk. Skt. 7, 21. (2) of things:—Yfel gesihð *malus oculus*, Mk. Skt. 7, 22. Yfel wyrd *bad fortune*, Bt. 40, 2; Fox 236, 22. Him ðæs æfter becwom yfel endeleán, Cd. Th. 227, 15; Dan. 187. Ðorn byð þearle scearp, anfengys yfel (*bad to take hold of*), Runic pm. Kmbl. 340, 1; Rûn. 3. Ic hit mid yfelre bysene inc forgylde, Blickl. Homl. 189, 25. Yfele habban sorge, Exon. Th. 376, 32; Seel. 163. Earmne gehȳnan yflum yrmþum, 280, 24; Jul. 634. Ic wîte þolade, yfel earfeþu, 89, 6; Cri. 1453. [*Goth.* ubils: *O. Sax.* ubil: *O. Frs.* evel: *O. H. Ger.* ubil.] v. wirsa.

yfel-âdl *glosses* cacexia, Wrt. Voc. i. 19, 43.

yfel-cund; *adj. Of evil nature, malignant*:—Se yfelcunda *malignus*, Ps. Lamb. 14, 4. Yfelcundra *malignantium*, 21, 17.

yfel-cweþan (yfle-) *glosses* maledicere:—Se ðe yflecuoeðas ł woerges (*maledixerit*) ðæm feder, Mt. Kmbl. 15, 4. Fîcbeám ðæm ðū yflecuoede (*maledixisti*), Mk. Skt. 11, 21. Yfelcweþende hine *maledicentes ei*, Ps. Spl. 36, 23.

yfel-dǣd, e; *f.* I. *an evil deed, misdeed, sin.* v. yfel, I:—Dôn sôðe bôte ûre yfeldǣda, Blickl. Homl. 99, 1: Exon. Th. 285, 12; Jul. 713. Ðū scealt andettan yfeldǣda mâ, 269, 27; Jul. 456. Ða gesceafta ðe sind þwyrlîce geðûhte, hî sind tô wrace gesceapene yfeldǣdum, Homl. Th. i. 102, 4. Cweðaþ stunte men ðæt hî be gewyrde lybban sceolon, swylce God hî neádige tô yfeldǣdum, 110, 31. II. *an injurious deed, injury, mischief.* v. yfel, III:—Gesete sâwle mîne fram yfeldǣdum heora *restitue animam meam a malignitate eorum*, Ps. Spl. 34, 20. [*O. H. Ger.* ubil-tât.] Cf. yfel-weorc.

yfel-dǣde; *adj.*: yfel-dǣda, an; *m. Of evil deeds; a person of evil deeds*:—Gif hē nǣre yfeldǣde (*malefactor*), ne sealde wē hine ðē, Jn. Skt. 18, 30. Ðâ fēng his sunu tô his rîce swȳðe yfeldǣda, Homl. Skt. i. 18, 228. ¶ with special reference to magical practices:—Gif hwylc yfeldǣde man þurh ǣnigne æfþancan ôþerne begaleþ, Lchdm. i. 190, 9. Unlybwyrhta *veneficus*, yfeldǣda *maleficus*, drȳ *magus*, Wrt. Voc. i. 74, 40. Swâ swâ yfeldǣda *ut magus* (*maleficus*), Hpt. Gl. 487, 61. Mǣden wyrst swelt, for ðî yfeldǣda (*malefica*) and wyrtgælstre, Lchdm. iii. 186, 11. Ðæra manna naman ðe wǣron entas and yfeldǣde, Homl. Th. i. 22, 31. v. unriht-dǣde, -dǣda. Cf. yfel-weorc.

yfel-dônd, -dôend, es; *m. An evil-doer, malefactor*:—Yfeldôend *malefactor*, Jn. Skt. Lind. 18, 30. Cf. wel-dônd.

yfel-dônde; *adj.* (*ptcpl.*) *Evil-doing*:—Drihtenes ondwlita bið ofer ða yfeldôndan men tô ðon ðæt hē hig forspille, L. E. I. 28; Th. ii. 424, 22.

yfel-dysig *glosses* stultomalus, Wrt. Voc. i. 47, 44.

yfele; *adv. Evilly, badly, ill*:—Yfele *male*, Ælfc. Gr. 38; Zup. 235, 1. I. in a moral sense:—Yfele gē dydon *pessimam rem fecistis*, Gen. 44. 5. Hit is gecweden, ðæt him betere wǣre ðæt hē nǣfre wǣre, ðonne hē yfele wǣre, Homl. Th. ii. 244, 21. II. *badly, imperfectly, improperly*:—Seó bôc wæs yfele of Grēcisce on Lǣden gehwyrfed (*badly translated*), Bd. 5, 24; S. 648, 23. Hē ða gehât swîðe yfele gelǣste, Bt. 1; Fox 2, 9. Gif ic yfele sprǣce *si male locutus sum*, Jn. Skt. 18, 23. Gif se esne his hlâforde hȳreþ yfle, Exon. Th. 430, 18; Rä. 44, 10. III. where there is hurt or suffering:—Mîn dohtor ys yfle (yfele, *v. l.*) mid deófle gedreht (*grievously afflicted*), Mt. Kmbl. 15, 22. Ðū eart, Babilone, bitere ætfæsted, ænge and yfele, hire earm dohter *filia Babylonis misera*, Ps. Th. 136, 8. Fremde þeóde ðîn hûs yfele gewemdan, Ps. Th. 78, 1. Wel tô dônne hweþer ðe yfele; sâwla gehǣlan hweþer ðe forspillan? Mk. Skt. 3, 4. Se abbot dyde heom yfele, Chr. 1087; Erl. 217, 7. Wæs Godes yrre þurh ða dǣde yfele genîwod, Wulfst. 10, 1. Ic him yfle ne môt, Exon. Th. 491, 5; Rä. 80, 9. III a. of bodily suffering:—Gif men sié fǣrlîce yfele *if it suddenly goes badly with a man*, Lchdm. ii. 294, 15. Ðes lǣcedôm sceal tô ðam menn ðe byð yfele on ðam breóstum, iii. 120, 1. IV. marking ill-success:—Yfele dēð him sylfum (*he does badly for himself*) ðe mid swîcdôme his tilaþ, and hē bið sceaðena gefēra ðe man sceandlîce wîtnaþ, Homl. Skt. i. 19, 172: Cd. Th. 49, 13; Gen. 791. Ðȳ læs wēn sié ðæt wē yfele forweorþon *lest perhaps we perish miserably*, Blickl. Homl. 247, 2: Ps. Th. 79, 15: 106, 26. Hē ðâ yfele and earmlîce geendode, Homl. Skt. ii. 25, 546. On ðære fare heom yfele gelamp, Chr. 1075; Erl. 212, 22. Sceolde unc Adame yfele gewurðan ymb ðæt heofonrîce, Cd. Th. 25, 2; Gen. 387. V. of injurious speaking:—Ic wyrige oððe yfele secge *maledico*, Ælfc. Gr. 37; Zup. 222, 4. Nis nân ðe on mînum naman mægen wyrce, and mæge raðe be mē yfele specan (*male loqui de me*), Mk. Skt. 9, 39. Oft mē feala cwǣdon feóndas yfele *dixerunt inimici mei mala mihi*, Ps. Th. 70, 9. [*O. Sax.* ubilo: *O. H. Ger.* ubilo.]

yfel-full; *adj. Wicked, evil*:—On dǣdum yfelfullum *in factis malitiosis*, Anglia xi. 116, 13.

yfelgeornness, e; *f. Evil, wickedness*:—Yfelgiornisse *nequitiae*, Rtl. 98, 24. Ofer yfelgiornise *super malitia*, 5, 12: 12, 25.

yfel-hæbbende; *adj.* (*ptcpl.*) *Sick, ill*:—Ealle yfelhæbbende missenlîcum âdlum, Mt. Kmbl. 4, 24.

yfelian; *p.* ode. I. *to do evil to, to maltreat, afflict, injure, wrong*:—Ða þingeras þingiaþ ðǣm ðe lǣssan þearfe âhton, þingiaþ ðǣm ðe man yflaþ, and ne þingiaþ ðâm ðe ðæt yfel dôþ; ðæm wǣre mâre þearf, ðe ða ôþre unscyldige yfelaþ (yflaþ, *v. l.*), ðæt him mon þingode tô ðǣm rîcum *pro his, qui grave quid, acerbumque perpessi sunt, miserationem judicum excitare conantur oratores, cum magis admittentibus justior miseratio debeatur*, Bt. 38, 7; Fox 208, 25–29. E hine yflaþ, Salm. Kmbl. 193; Sal. 96. Îne gelîcre geswencednysse ða mǣgþe yfelade *Ini simili provinciam illam adflictione mancipavit*, Bd. 4, 15; S. 583, 31. Hē bebeád ðæt mon nǣnne mon ne slôge, and eác ðæt man nânuht ne wanode ne ne yfelade ðæs ðe on ðǣm ciricum wǣre *dato praecepto, ut si qui in sancta loca confugissent, hos inviolatos securosque esse sinerent*, Ors. 6, 38; Swt. 296, 32. Se ilca Dauid forbær ðæt hē ðone kyning ne yfelode, ðe hine of his earde âdrǣfde *David ferire deprehensum persecutorem noluit*, Past. 3; Swt. 37, 3. Ic wolde helpan ðæs ðe ðǣr unscyldig wǣre, and hēnan ðone ðe hine yfelode (yflode, *v. l.*), Bt. 38, 6; Fox 208, 18. Hî yfeledon and slôgan Cristene men *affligi interficique Christianos praeceperunt*, Bd. 1, 6; S. 476, 21. Yfeladan, Ps. Th. 82, 3. Hit is riht ðæt mon yfelige ða yfelan, and hit is wôh, ðæt hî mon lǣte unwîtnode, Bt. 38, 3; Fox 202, 5. Gif hwâ cyrican gesēce, and hine man ðǣr yflige, L. Edm. S. 2; Th. i. 248, 17. Hî ðara nânne yflian noldan ðe tô ðæm Godes hûse ôðflugon, Ors. 2, 8; Swt. 94, 8: Nar. 25, 27. Ða ðe willaþ Godes cyricean yfelian and strûdan, Blickl. Homl. 75, 24. II. *to get bad*, (1) of persons:—Hié beóð swîðe ungesǣlige, ðonne hié yfeliaþ (yfliaþ, *v. l.*) for ðæm ðe ôðre menn gôdigaþ *quantae infelicitatis sint, qui melioratione proximi deteriores fiunt*, Past. 34; Swt. 231, 18. (2) of things or circumstances:—Aa æfter ðam hit yfelode swîðe *things got very bad*, Chr. 975; Erl. 127, 33. Â syððan hit yflade swîðe, wurðe gôd se ende, ðonne God wylle, 1066; Erl. 202, 41. Gif blôddolg yflige . . . oððe gif ðū ne mæge blôddolg âwrîþan, Lchdm. ii. 16, 4: 148, 8. Nȳde hit sceal on worulde for folces synnan yfelian swȳðe, Wulfst. 81, 8: 156, 7. [Wæstmes ne synd swâ gôde swâ heó iu wǣron, ac yfeleð swȳðe eall eorðe wæstme, Shrn. 17, 21. Ne scal us na mon uuelien, O. E. Homl. i. 15, 13.] v. ge-yflian.

yfel-lǣrende *inciting to evil*:—Yfelonbecweþende oþþe yfellǣrende *malesuada*, Germ. 390, 113.

yfel-lîc; *adj. Bad, foul, rotten.* v. yfel, II:—Ðysse worulde wela is gebrosnadlîc and yfellîc and forwordenlîc, Wulfst. 263, 13. Twēgen león âdulfan his byrgenne on ðæs wēstenes sande; ðǣr resteþ Paules lîchoma mid yfelîce duste bewrigen, ac on dômes dæge hē âriseþ on wuldor, Shrn. 50, 18. Seó byrgen is bewrigen mid dimmum stânum and yfellîcum, 66, 25.

yfelness, e; *f. Evil, wickedness, badness*:—Yfelnys *malignitas*, Ælfc. Gr. 9, 25; Zup. 50, 10. I. in a moral sense:—Micel yfelnys (*malitia*) manna wæs ofer eorðan, Gen. 6, 5. Hē (*Antichrist*) neádaþ þurh yfelnysse ðæt men sceolon bûgan fram heora Scyppendes geleáfan tô his leásungum, se ðe is ord ǣlcre leásunge and yfelnysse . . . on ðam tîman bið micel yfelnyss and þwyrnys betwux mancynne, Homl. Th. i. 4, 27–

33. Sume burgon heora feore and âmeldodon heora cristenan mâgas . . . Ðeós yfelnys biđ eác on Antecristes tôcyme, ii. 542, 24. Bydelas đæs êcan yfeles, đe yfelum mannum becymđ for heora ânwillan yfelnysse, 538, 24. Yfelnysse (*malitiam*) nâ hê hatude, Ps. Spl. 35, 4: 51, 3. Ðurh yfelnysse (*nequitiam*) unrihtes willan, Bd. 1, 27; S. 495, 13. Hê âwearp yfelnysse and đa unrihtan biggengas đæra leásra goda, Homl. Skt. i. 18, 461: Chr. 1086; Erl. 223, 2. God gesihđ ûre yfelnyssa and ûre gyltas forđyldgaþ, Homl. Th. ii. 84, 2. II. *malignity, cruelty*. v. yfel, III:—Hê slôh and tô sceame tûcode đa Norđhymbran leóde, ôþ đæt Ôswold his yfelnysse âdwæscte, Homl. Skt. ii. 26, 13. III. *misfortune, ill fortune*:—Oxan grasiende gesihđ sige ceápas getâcnaþ; oxan slâpende gesihđ yfelnysse ceápes getâcnaþ, Lchdm. iii. 200, 10. [He forbere monna hufelnesse þurh his lidnesse, O. E. Homl. i. 95, 14.]

yfel-onbecweþende. v. yfel-lǽrende.

yfel-sacian; *p.* ode *To calumniate*:—Ðe læs hê mê yfelsacode wiđ God, Blickl. Homl. 189, 24.

yfel-sacung, e; *f.* *Calumny, vituperation*:—On yfylsacunge heora *in malitia eorum*, Ps. Spl. C. 93, 23. Môdignys âcenđ andan and yfelsacunge, ceorunge and gelômlîce tâla, Homl. Th. ii. 222, 7. Þurh yfelsacunge *per blasphemiam*, Confess. Peccat. Hê him rehte hwylce searwa and yfelsacunga se drŷ ârefnde, Blickl. Homl. 173, 8.

yfelsian; *p.* ode *To blaspheme*:—Yfelsaþ, tǽleþ *blasuemiat* (v. Mk. 2, 7), Wrt. Voc. ii. 73, 21. In the Northern Gospels the same Latin verb is translated by the following forms:—Ebalsas (hefalsaþ, Rush.) *blasphemat*, Mt. Kmbl. Lind. 9, 3. Ebolsas (heofolsaþ, Rush.), Mk. Skt. Lind. 2, 7. Ebolsas (eofolsas, Rush.), 3, 29. Ebolsaþ (eofolsigaþ, Rush.), Lk. Skt. Lind, 12, 10. Efolsade (efalsade, Rush.) *blasphemavit*, Mt. Kmbl. Lind. 26, 65. Ebolsadon (eofulsadun, Rush.), Mk. Skt. Lind. 3, 28. Ebolsande (wêron) *blasphemabant*, 15, 29. Eofolsende, Jn. Skt. Rush. 10, 36. v. ge-ebolsian, *and next word*: *cf. also, two preceding words, and* eoful-sæc.

yfel-sprǽce; *adj.* *Of evil speech, evil-speaking*:—Ða yfelsprǽcan tungan *linguam maliloquam*, Ps. Th. 11, 3.

yfel-sprecende; *adj.* (*ptcpl.*) *Evil-speaking*:—Tungan yfelspreccende *linguam maliloquam*, Ps. Surt. 11, 4.

yfelsung, eofulsung, e; *f.* *Blasphemy*:—Dionysius cwæđ, đæt đæt yfelsang (-ung?) wǽre on God *Dionysius dixit blasphemiam id esse in Deum*, L. Ecg. C. 41; Th. ii. 166, 12. Ic ondette eofulsunge, Anglia xi. 98, 33. In the Northern Gospels and Durham Ritual *blasphemia* is glossed by the following forms:—Ebolsung *blasphemia*, Rtl. 12, 37. Ebolsung ł efalsongas (efulsung, Rush.), Mt. Kmbl. Lind. 12, 31. Ebolsung (hefalsunge, Rush.) *blasphemiae*, 15, 19. Ebolsungas, Mk. Skt. Lind. 3, 28. Efolsong (eofulsongas, Rush.) *blasphemia*, 7, 22. From đæm ebolsong (eofolsonge, Rush.), Jn. Skt. Lind. 10, 33. Efolsungas (efalsunge, Rush.) *blasphemiam*, Mt. Kmbl. Lind. 26, 65. Ðæt ebolsung (đa eofulsunge, Rush.), Mk. Skt. Lind. 14, 64. Ebolsongas *blasphem(i)as*, Jn. Skt. Lind. 10, 36.

yfel-tyhtend, es; *m.*: -tyhtende; *adj.* (*ptcpl.*) *One who incites to evil; inciting to evil*:—Deófol is yfeltihtend and leáswyrcend, Homl. Th. i. 102, 1. Ungeleáffulle and yfeltihtende sind mid đê, 528, 3.

yfel-weorc; es; *m.* *Work of magic*:—Yfeluoerc *maleficium*, Rtl. 103, 1. Cf. yfel-dǽd, yfel-dǽde, ¶.

yfel-willende; *adj.* (*ptcpl.*) *Ill-disposed, wicked*:—Hwæþer đû ongite đæt ǽlc yfelwillende mon and ǽlc yfelwyrcende sié wîtes wyrþe? . . . Hû ne is se đonne yfelwillende and yfelwyrcende đe đone unscyldigan wîtnaþ? *omnem improbum num supplicio dignum negas? . . . Infelices esse, qui sint improbi, liquet*, Bt. 38, 6; Fox 208, 8–11. Mid đê ne wunaþ se yfelwillenda *non habitabit juxta te malignus*, Ps. Th. 5, 4: 9, 18. Ðæt yfelwillende môd *malitiosa mens*, Past. 35; Swt. 243, 7. Se đe nele wunian on yfelwyllende sâwle, ne eác on đam lîchaman đe liđ under synnum, Homl. Th. ii. 326, 1. Yfelwillende men nǽnne weorþscipe næfdon, Bt. 15; Fox 48, 17. Se Drihten tôstencđ đa geþeaht yfelwillendra kynna *Dominus dissipat consilia gentium*, Ps. Th. 32, 9. Fram gegaderunge yfelwillendra (*malignantium*), Ps. Lamb. 63, 3. On yfelwillendum *malignantibus*, 91, 12: Ps. Spl. 36, 1. Hit nâuht unriht wǽre đæt mon đa yfelwillendan men (*vitiosos*) hête nêtenu, Bt. 38, 2; Fox 198, 17.

yfelwillendness, e; *f.* *Evil, wickedness*:—Hwæt wuldrast đû on yfelwyllendnysse (*malitia*)? Ps. Spl. 51, 1.

yfel-wilnian; *p.* ode *glosses* malignari:—Hû fela yfelwilnode (*malignatus est*) fŷnd on hâlgum, Ps. Lamb. 73, 3. Nelle gê wyrian ł yfelwilnian *nolite malignari*, 104, 15.

yfel-wyrcende; *adj.* (*ptcpl.*) I. of persons, *evil-doing, wicked*:—Hwæþer đû ongite đæt ǽlc yfelwillende and ǽlc yfelwyrcende sié wîtes wyrþe? . . . Hû ne is se đonne yfelwillende and yfelwyrcende đe đone unscyldgan wîtnaþ? Bt. 38, 6; Fox 208, 8–11. Gif ne wêre đes yfelwyrcende (*malefactor*), ne đê wê gisaldun hine, Jn. Skt. Rush. 18, 30. Yfelwyrcende *nequam*, Mt. Kmbl. Lind. 6, 23: 13, 38. Miđ yfelwyrcendum and synfullum *cum publicanis et peccatoribus*, 9, 11. Hê hataþ đa yfelwyrcendan and đa unrihtwîsan, Homl. Skt. i. 1, 48. II. of things, *noxious, hurtful, mischievous*:—Ðerh wyrto yfelwyrcendo *per herbas maleficas*, Rtl. 103, 1.

yfemest, yfmest; *adv.* *Upmost, highest, in the highest position* or *degree*:—Hió cymþ swâ up swâ hire yfemest gecynde biđ *it* (*the sun*) *mounts up to the highest point at which it is natural for it to be*, Bt. 25; Fox 88, 28. Ðǽr hire yfemest biđ eard gecynde, Met. 13, 63. Ðæt fŷr is yfemest ofer eallum đissum woruldgesceaftum, Bt. 33, 4; Fox 128, 38: Met. 20, 84. Yfmest, 24, 20. Saturnus yfemest wandraþ ofer eallum ôđrum steorrum, 24, 23. Uton habban ûre môd up swâ swâ wê yfemest mægen wiþ đæs heán hrôfes đæs hêhstan andgites, Bt. 41, 5; Fox 254, 15. Ǽresđ alra glengea and ymesđ scolde scînan gold on his hrægle *in sacerdotis habitu ante omnia aurum fulget*, Past. 14; Swt. 85, 2. v. ufor.

yfera; *cpve.*: yfemest; *spve. adj.* *Upper, higher*; of time, *later, after*: *upmost, highest*:—Yferan hŷse *triclinio*, Wrt. Voc. ii. 72, 66. Siođđan yferran dôgre, Cod. Dip. Kmbl. i. 310, 29. Cyng âh đone uferan (yferan, *v.l.*), and bisceop đone nyđeran, L. E. G. 4; Th. i. 168, 16. Þurh his upstige tô đam yfemystan þrymsetle, Homl. Th. i. 308, 9. Of đǽm yfemestum (ymestum, Hatt. MS.) tô đǽm niedemestan, Past. 18; Swt. 134, 24. v. ufera.

yfes-drype, es; *m.* *Eaves-drip*:—Ðǽr ne gebyreþ an đam lande an folcæs folcryht tô lêfænnæ rûmæs bûtan twîgen fŷt tô yfæsdrype, Chart. Erl. 141, 16, where see note.

yl-ful (=ild-ful) *morosus*, Hpt. Gl. 529, 9.

ylp (elp), es; *m.* *An elephant*:—Ylp *elefans*, Wrt. Voc. i. 78, 11: 22, 41. Ylp is ormǽte nŷten, mâre þonne sum hûs, Homl. Skt. ii. 25, 566. Ylpes bile *promuscida*, Wrt. Voc. i. 22, 42. Ylpes bân *ebur*, Coll. Monast. Th. 27, 9: Lchdm. iii. 204, 2, 3. Hê sende þrittig ylpas tô wîge gewenode . . . and on ǽlcum ylpe wæs ân wîghûs getimbrod, Homl. Skt. ii. 25, 561. Hê (*the unicorn*) fiht wiđ đone myclan ylp, and hine oft gewundaþ on đære wambe ôþ deáþ, Wrt. Voc. i. 78, 1. Gif hê ylp gesihđ lâđne odđe gramne, sume wrôhte hit getâcnaþ, Lchdm. iii. 204, 1. Ða ylpas beóđ swâ mycele swylce ôđre muntas, Hexam. 9; Norm. 16, 9. Hê geworhte đa ormǽtan ylpas, Norm. 14, 34. [Elpes arn in Inde riche, Misc. 19, 604. White so alpes bon, L. N. F. 248, 282.] v. elpend.

ylpen-bân (elpend-), es; *n.* *Ivory*:—Ðis ylpenbân *hoc ebur*, Ælfc. Gr. 9, 22; Zup. 49, 9. Mid ylpenbâne and mid bâres tuxe, Lchdm. i. 244, 8. Genim ylpenbân, 368, 19. v. elpend-bân (*where these passages should be put*).

ylpen-bǽnen, -bânen (elpend-); *adj.* *Ivory*:—Mid ylpenbânenon (-bǽn-, *v.l.*) stæfe, Lchdm. i. 244, 24. Ylpenbânene *eburna*, Germ. 403, 19. v. elpen(d)-bǽnen (*where these passages should be put*).

ylpend, Wrt. Voc. ii. 142, 81. v. elpend.

yltst = **ildest**, Mt. Kmbl. 23, 11: Ex. 17, 5.

yltwist (?) *fowling*:—Yltwist *aucupium*, Wrt. Voc. ii. 7, 50.

ymb, ymbe, umbe, embe, emban; *prep.* *About, by*:—Ymb *erga*, Wrt. Voc. ii. 32, 62. I. with acc., (1) local, *about, round*:—Ymbe đa dûne *circum montem*, Ælfc. Gr. 47; Zup. 269, 8. (a) marking an object which forms a centre for others:—Ymb đone êcan ædele stondaþ hæleđ ymb hêhseld, Cd. Th. 267, 32; Sat. 47: Beo. Th. 804; B. 399: Elen. Kmbl. 519; El. 260: Judth. Thw. 25, 19; Jud. 268. Ymb đæt *circumquaque* (turmas circumquaque cum simulacro debacchantes, Ald. 52), Wrt. Voc. ii. 83, 33: 18, 47. Ymb hine wǽgon wîgend unforhte, Cd. Th. 189, 5; Exod. 180. Hî ymb þeódenstôl þringaþ, Exon. Th. 25, 7; Cri. 397. Hié ymb đa gatu feohtende wǽron, Chr. 755; Erl. 50, 26. Hŷ fuhton stîđlîce ymbe đa hâlgan sâwle, Wulfst. 236, 23. ¶ *in combination with* ûtan:—Fuglas þringaþ ûtan ymbe æþelne, Exon. Th. 209, 1; Ph. 164: Andr. Kmbl. 1741; An. 873. Ymb đæt lîc ûtan stondan, Blickl. Homl. 217, 21. (b) marking an object near to which are others:—Gesêgon hŷ englas twêgen ymb đæt frumbearn blîcan, Exon. Th. 32, 3; Cri. 507. Hine twêgen ymb weardas wacedon, 109, 5; Gû. 85. Ealle đa đe ymbe mê standaþ, Blickl. Homl. 141, 1. Hine ymb monig sǽrinc selereste gebeáh, Beo. Th. 1383; B. 689. Mycel menegeo ymbe Tîrum (*circa Tyrum*), Mk. Skt. 3, 8. Cynewulf and Offa gefuhton ymb Benesingtûn and Offa nam đone tuun, Chr. 777; Erl. 54, 1. Ymbe Brûnanburh, 937; Erl. 112, 5: Hy. 10, 23. (b 1) *about* a person, *in attendance upon*:—Hê sundernytte beheóld ymb aldor Dena, Beo. Th. 1340; B. 668. (c) marking an object which is surrounded or enclosed:—Hié worhton fæsten ymb hié selfe, Chr. 885; Erl. 82, 21. Wall ymb ǽfæste, Cd. Th. 231, 16; Dan. 248. Ymbe đa herehûþe hlemmeþ tôgædre grimme gôman, Exon. Th. 363, 29; Wal. 61. Hî ymb his heáfod gebîgdon beág þyrnenne, 69, 25; Cri. 1126: 400, 20; Rä. 21, 4. Wæs fleóhnet ymbe đæs folctogan bed âhongen, Judth. Thw. 22, 4; Jud. 47. ¶ *in combination with* ûtan:—Is đǽr cyrice ymb đa stôwe ûtan getimbred, Blickl. Homl. 125, 20: 127, 32. Ymb đînne beód ûtan *in circuitu mensae tuae*, Ps. Th. 127, 4. (d) marking an object along whose border others are placed:—Unc môdige ymb mearce sittaþ, Cd. Th. 114, 21; Gen. 1907. Hié wîcedon ymb đæs wæteres wylm, Elen. Kmbl. 77; El. 39: 271; El. 136: Exon. Th. 188, 2; Az. 39. Ymb đa gifhealle *round the walls of the hall*, Beo. Th. 1680; B. 838. Ðæt rîce sûđ licgeþ ymbe Gealboe and ymb Geador, Salm. Kmbl. 383–4; Sal. 191. Is hyge ymb heortan gerûme,

Cd. Th. 47, 11; Gen. 759: 23, 5; Gen. 354: Exon. Th. 306, 21; Seef. 11. (e) marking an object throughout or along which there is position or movement:—Ic lǽrde sibbe ymb ða burh Hierusalem and manige þeóda, Blickl. Homl. 185, 11. Hē ymb ðæs wæteres stæð werod samnode, Elen. Kmbl. 119; El. 60: 453; El. 227. Æfter dūnscræfum, ymb stānhleoðo, Andr. Kmbl. 2467; An. 1235: 3152; An. 1578. Ymb ða weallas scīnaþ engla gāstas, Cd. Th. 305, 25; Sat. 652. Ymbe hārne stān tigelfāgan trafu stōdan, Andr. Kmbl. 1682; An. 843. Ymbe Sanere feld, Salm. Kmbl. 417; Sal. 209. Ymb healfa gehwone, Exon. Th. 4, 31; Cri. 61. Sār eft gewōd ymb ðæs beornes breóst, Andr. Kmbl. 2495; An. 1249. (f) marking an object round which anything moves:—Faraþ ymbe ða burh *circuite urbem*, Jos. 6, 3, 12: Beo. Th. 6319; B. 3170. Hȳ him ymb hond flugon, Exon. Th. 146, 14; Gū. 709. Hī ymb ða eaxe hwearfaþ, Bt. 39, 3; Fox 214, 23: Met. 28, 22. ¶ *in combination with* ūtan:—Hē ymb ðās ūtan hweorfeþ, Exon. Th. 422, 13; Rä. 41, 5. (2) temporal, (a) *at*:—Ymbe (embe, *v.l.*) underntīde ... ymbe ða sixtan and nigoðan tīde *circa horam tertium ... circa sextam et nonam horam*, Mt. Kmbl. 20, 3, 5. Ymbe underntīd, ðā ðā se brōðor wæs gewunod tō mæssigenne, Homl. Th. ii. 358, 20. Ofer Eástron ymbe gangdagas oððe ǽr, Chr. 891; Erl. 88, 16. On ðȳs geáre ymb Martines mæssan, 913; Erl. 100, 33. Ymb ðone tiéman wǽron micel snāwgebland, Ors. 4, 8; Swt. 186, 33. Þeáh hine mon gefō ymb niht, L. In. 72; Th. i. 148, 8. (b) *after*:—Ic sende rēn nū ymb seofon niht ofer eorðan *adhuc et post dies septem ego pluam super terram*, Gen. 7, 4. On ðisse tīde nū ymbe twelf mōnð *tempore isto in anno altero*, 17, 21. Næs hit lengra fyrst ac ymb āne niht, Beo. Th. 270; B. 135. Ymb twā niht, Cd. Th. 181, 18; Exod. 63. Ymb fyrst wucan būtan ānre niht, Menol. Fox 172; Men. 87. Ymb fīftig nihta æfter ðære gecȳþdan ǽriste, Blickl. Homl. 133, 13. Hē forþfērde ymb .xx. wintra his rīces, būtan ān ne wæs dāgyt gefylled *defunctus est anno regni sui vicesimo necdum impleto*, Bd. 5, 18; S. 635, 19. Ymb hwīle, Blickl. Homl. 217, 30. Ymb long, L. In. 21; Th. i. 116, 7: Bt. 39, 2; Fox 214, 8. Ymb tela micel fæc, Chr. 942; Erl. 116, 21. Ymbe ān lytel, Jn. Skt. 16, 16. Ymb lytel fæc, Elen. Kmbl. 543; El. 272. Ymbe geára rina, Chr. Pref.; Erl. 3, 17. Ymb wintra hwearft, Exon. Th. 188, 5; Az. 41. (b 1) *where the point from which the time is measured is given by* ðæs, (α) *preceding*:—Ðæs ymb ān geár, Ors. 3, 10; Swt. 138, 28: 3, 11; Swt. 152, 19: Chr. 871; Erl. 74, 6, 8, 14, 25: Exon. Th. 29, 21; Cri. 466. Ðæs ymb ōðer swylc būtan ānre wanan, Menol. Fox 279; Men. 141: 359; Men. 181. Ðæs ymbe lytel, Chr. 1038; Erl. 167, 6. Ðæs ymb litel fæc, Guthl. 18; Gdwin. 76, 6. (β) *following*:—Ymb feówer hunde wintra and ymb feówertig ðæs ðe Trōia āwēsted wæs *anno post eversionem Trojae ccccxiv*, Ors. 2, 2; Swt. 64, 20. Ymb .xxxi. wintra ðæs ðe hē rīce hæfde, Chr. 755; Erl. 48, 25. Ymbe .xli. wintra būtan ānre niht ðæs ðe Ælfrēd cyning forþfērde, 941; Erl. 116, 2: 606; Erl. 20, 25: 855; Erl. 68, 32: Cd. Th. 167, 21; Gen. 2769. Ymb swȳðe lang ðæs ðe hine God ālȳsde, Ps. Th. 17, arg. (b 2) of recurring periods:—Saturnus ne cymþ ðǽr ǽr ymb þrittig wintra ðǽr hē ǽr wæs, Bt. 39, 3; Fox 214, 25. Ælce geáre ymbe twelf mōnaþ, Ors. 1, 10; Swt. 46, 9. Ǽfre ymbe ðæt feórðe geár, Lchdm. iii. 246, 13. Simble ymb þrītig nihtgerīmes, Andr. Kmbl. 313; An. 157. Symble ymbe seofon niht, Soul Kmbl. 19; Seel. 10. Emb stemn *uicissim*, Germ. 388, 77: Scint. 140, 17. (c) of past time:—Ymb þreó niht com þegen Hǽlendes *the Saviour's servant came three days ago*, Cd. Th. 291, 5; Sat. 426. Ðæs ymb āne niht, 300, 26; Sat. 571. (3) in figurative senses, *about*, (a) marking approximation:—Ymb ðæt *plus minus*, Wrt. Voc. ii. 117, 50: 68, 24. (b) marking the object of speaking, enquiry, telling, etc.:—Hē ymb Godes word and Cristes geleáfan (Godes word ymbe Cristes geleáfan, M. 422, 9) bodude and lǽrde, Bd. 5, 11; S. 626, 29. Ymb ðīn līf sprecan, Cd. Th. 32, 25; Gen. 508: 110, 34; Gen. 1848: Beo. Th. 3194; B. 1595. Hē sægde ymb Godes rīce, Blickl. Homl. 117, 13. Wītgan sægdon ymb ðæt æþele bearn, ðæt ..., Exon. Th. 73, 26; Cri. 1195. Hæfde se cyng swīðe deópe spǽce wið his witan ymbe ðis land, hū hit wǽre gesett, Chr. 1085; Erl. 218, 23. Wē cweþaþ lof ymb hié, Blickl. Homl. 149, 32. Wē beót āhōfon ymbe heard gewinn, Byrht. Th. 138, 3; By. 214. Ðislīc cȳðan ymb dīgle wyrd, Elen. Kmbl. 1077; El. 541. Ǽrendgewrit ymb Cristes þrowunga, Blickl. Homl. 177, 3. Fitte ymb fisca cynn, Exon. Th. 360, 6; Wal. 1. Hē gieddade ymb his ǽriste, 236, 10; Ph. 572. Ðā ðā hī umbe ōþer þing gesprecon hæfdon umbe ðæt hī sprecan woldon, Chr. 1070; Erl. 208, 12. Se esne ðe ic hēr ymb sprice, Exon. Th. 430, 32; Rä. 44, 17: Met. 10, 45. Ðe ic ðē recce ymb, 17, 20. Ymb ðæt āscian, Bt. 39, 4; Fox 216, 29. Gif ðū gehȳre ymb ðæt hālige treó frōde frignan, Elen. Kmbl. 881; El. 442: 1065; El. 534: Beo. Th. 712; B. 353. (c) marking the object of thought, feeling, etc.:—Giorne ymb lāre, Past. pref.; Swt. 3, 10. Giémen ymb ða gehiérsuman, 12; Swt. 74, 14: Exon. Th. 267, 13; Jul. 414. Hē nā ymb his līf cearaþ, Beo. Th. 3077; B. 1536. Ymb sāwle forht, Exon. Th. 456, 10; Hy. 4, 64. Ymb ðæs geongan feorh onbryrded, Andr. Kmbl. 2236; An. 1119. Ymb ða mē fyrwet bræc, Salm. Kmbl. 493; Sal. 247. Heó wundrade ymb ðæs weres snyttro, Elen. Kmbl. 1914; El. 959. Ðæt seó forlǽtene cyrice ne hycgge ymb ða ðe on hire neáwiste lifgeaþ, Blickl. Homl. 43, 1: Exon. Th. 473, 3; Bo. 9: Menol. Fox 571; Gn. C. 55. Ic þence ymbe mīne synna *cogitabo pro peccato meo*, Ps. Th. 37, 18: Cd. Th. 26, 18; Gen. 408. Ymb wundorwyrd willan gefylde, Elen. Kmbl. 2139; El. 1071. Ic nāt ymbe hwæt ðū tweóst, Bt. 5, 3; Fox 12, 12. (d) marking the object with which an action is concerned:—Is māre nēdþearf ðæt wē winnon ymbe ūre sāule þearfe, Blickl. Homl. 99, 10. Ymb land sacan, Menol. Fox 568; Gn. C. 53: Beo. Th. 5012; B. 2509: 1019; B. 507. Ðæt hē hié ymb ðæt rīce gesēmde, Ors. 3, 7; Swt. 114, 17: Salm. Kmbl. 505; Sal. 253. Hī sendon ǽrendracan ymbe frið, Ors. 3, 11; Swt. 142, 2. Hig dydon ymbe hyne (*in eo*) swā hwæt swā hig woldon, Mt. Kmbl. 17, 12. Ðū ymb ðīnne esne dydest wel weorðlīce *bonitatem fecisti cum servo tuo*, Ps. Th. 118, 65. Hwæt ymb hine gedōn wǽre *quid erga se actum esset*, Bd. 4, 31; S. 610, 39. Hū hine mon ymbe gedōn wolde *quid erga eum agere rex promisisset*, 2, 12; S. 513, 20. Ðæt hē mōste dōn embe ða æþelingas swā hē wolde, Lchdm. iii. 424, 27. Ymb his womdǽda Waldendes dōm, Ps. C. 19. Hē wæs ymbe Godes þeówdōm ābisgod, Blickl. Homl. 211, 31. Beón, wesan ymb *to be about* a business, *be occupied with* a matter or a person:—Gif gē ymb woruldcunde dōmas beón scylen *secularia judicia si habueritis*, Past. 18; Swt. 131, 6. Hwonne hē mōste beón ymbe ðæs līchaman oferfylle, Wulfst. 236, 11. Wit sculon git deóplīcor ymbe ðæt beón, Bt. 5, 3; Fox 12, 12. Gif hwylc ðis dōn nylle and læs ymbe beó ðonne wē gecweden habbaþ, L. Ath. i. 26; Th. i. 212, 28: iv. 1; Th. i. 222, 2. Hē byð ā ymbe ðæt ān, hū hē on manna sāulum mǽst gesceaðian mæge, L. C. E. 26; Th. i. 374, 25. Hē sǽde ðæt Aldberht and Alhhūn wǽron ǽr ymb ðæt ylce, Chart. Th. 140, 14. Ðās feówero ymb woeson (=woeron?) ðās bōc *these four were engaged on this book*, Mk. Skt. p. i. 3. Hē cwæð ðæt hē ne mihte embe munuclīf smeágan, ac wolde beón embe his þincg, Homl. Skt. i. 6, 120. Emban ða steóran beon, L. Ath. v. 11; Th. i. 240, 17. Settaþ ða tō dēmerum ðæt hié striénen and stihtien ymb ða eorðlīcan ðing *ut ipsi dispensationibus terrenis inserviant*, Past. 18; Swt. 131, 8. Ðā gesomnodon wē ūs ymb ðæt, L. Alf. 49; Th. i. 56, 19. Gif hwā wiccige ymbe ǽniges mannes lufe (*alicujus amoris gratia*), L. Ecg. P. iv. 18; Th. ii. 208, 31. Hié sieredon ymbe ðone cyning, Bt. 16, 2; Fox 52, 21: Cd. Th. 38, 15; Gen. 607. Mē seredon ymb secgas monige, 296, 6; Sat. 498: Ps. Th. 54, 18. (e) marking the object in relation to which circumstances are stated:—Ic ðē cȳðe hū hit wæs ymb ðæt lond æt Funtial, Chart. Th. 169, 16. Sceolde unc yfele gewurðan ymb ðæt heofonrīce, Cd. Th. 25, 3; Gen. 388. Hū ymb ðæt sceolde, Exon. Th. 378, 7; Deór. 12. Sȳ ymb rīce swā hit mæge, 301, 29; Fä. 26. Hū ða wīsan sind wundorlīce ymb ðæs fugles gebyrd, 223, 16; Ph. 360. Ðæt wundor ymb ðone beorhtan beám, Elen. Kmbl. 2507; El. 1255: 1324; El. 664. II. with dative, (1) local:—Ða weorod ðe him ymb fērdon and stōdon, Blickl. Homl. 99, 25: Beo. Th. 5188; B. 2597. Ða hire midore ymbe þrǽgaþ, Met. 28, 23. Geseó ic him his englas ymbe hweorfan, Cd. Th. 42, 5; Gen. 669. Him ymb flugon engla þreátas, 300, 21; Sat. 568. (2) temporal:—Embe geára ymbrynum, Homl. Th. i. 104, 21. Ǽfre ymbe geáres ymbrynum, Lchdm. iii. 238, 25. (3) figurative:—Hē fērde embe sumere neóde, Homl. Th. ii. 508, 15. III. without a case:—Ǽghwider ymb swā swā Ēdwines rīce wǽre *quaquaversum imperium Aeduini pervenerat*, Bd. 2, 16; S. 519, 38. Ðonon eode gehwyder ymb (*circumquaque*), 3, 17; S. 543, 26. Hié wǽron ymb eal ūtan mid eágum besett, Past. 38; Swt. 195, 19. Hring ūtan ymb bearh, ðæt heó ðone fyrdhom þurhfōn ne mihte, Beo. Th. 3011; B. 1503. Hygeþ ymbe se ðe wile, Met. 19, 1. Þencð ymb se ðe wile, 20, 27. Dēð ymbe moncynnes fruma, swā him gemet þinceþ, 29, 41. Ðā cȳdde man, ðet hī man eáðe befaran mihte, gif hē man ymbe beón wolde, Chr. 1009; Erl. 141, 34. Hē cȳðde hū hē ymbe wolde, gif hē hine gemētte *he shewed what he would have been about, if he had found him*, Homl. Th. i. 82, 18. [*A. R. Kath. Marh.* umbe: *O. E. Homl. Laym.* umbe, embe: *Orm.* ummbe: *Piers P.* um: *O. Sax.* umbi: *O. Frs.* umbe: *O. H. Ger.* umpi: *Icel.* umb, um.]

ymb-ærnan; *p.* de *To go round*:—Ðā gelamp ðætte Peahte ðeód com of Scyþþia lande and ymbærndon eall Breotone gemǽro, ðæt hī cōmon on Scotland upp *contigit gentem Pictorum de Scythia, circumagente flatu ventorum, extra fines omnes Brittaniae Hiberniam pervenisse*, Bd. 1, 1; S. 474, 10. v. ymb-irnan.

ymb-bǽtan; *p.* te *To put restraint upon, curb*:—Se mid his brīdle ymbebǽted hæfð ymbhwyrft ealne eorþan and heofenes *Dominus orbis habenas temperat*, Met. 24, 37.

ymb-begang. v. ymb-bīgness.

ymb-beran; *p.* -bær, *pl.* -bǽron; *pp.* -boren *To surround*:—Se wæs ǽghwonan ymbboren brondum, Exon. Th. 277, 15; Jul. 581. Ymbbeara *glosses* circumferre, Mk. Skt. Lind. Rush. 6, 55.

ymb-bīgness, e; *f.* *A bending round, a bend* of a river:—Ðæt mynster is of ðam mǽstan dǽle mid ymbbīgnesse (ymbbegange [ymbegang?], *v.l.*: ymbebēgnesse, M. 424, 10) Tweode streámes betȳned *monasterium Tuidi fluminis circumflexu maxima ex parte clauditur*, Bd. 5, 12; S. 627, 25.

ymb-bindan; *p.* -band, *pl.* -bundon; *pp.* -bunden *To bind about*:—

Sié ymbunden ł ymbsald coern tō suiro his *circumdaretur mola collo ejus*, Mk. Skt. Lind. 9, 42.

ymb-cæfed; *adj.* (*ptcpl.*) *Having embroidered garments*:—Ymbcæfed mid missenlīcnesse *circumamicta varietatibus*, Ps. Spl. T. 44, 15.

ymb-ceorfan; *p.* -cearf, *pl.* -curfon; *pp.* -corfen *To circumcise*:—Gē ymbceorfas (-cearfas, Lind.) đone monno *circumciditis hominem*, Jn. Skt. Rush. 7, 22. Tō ymbceorfanne (-cearfanne, Lind.) đone cnæht *circumcidere puerum*, Lk. Skt. Rush. 1, 59. Đætte ymbcorfen wēre đe cnæht, 2, 21.

ymb-ceorfness, e; *f. Circumcision*:—Ymbcer[f]nisse *circumcisionem*, Jn. Skt. Rush. 7, 23.

ymb-cirr, es; *m. A turning about*, (1) *going from one place to another, removal*:—In ymbcerr Babilonis *in transmigratione Babylonis*, Mt. Kmbl. Lind. 1, 11, 12, 17. (2) *turning over, moving, stirring*. v. ymb-cirran (4):—Wætres ymbcerr (-cer, Rush.) ł styrenise *aquae motum*, Jn. Skt. Lind. 5, 3. (3) the word also glosses *versutia*, Rtl. 120, 32.

ymb-cirran; *p.* de *To turn about*, (1) *to revolve round*:—Hī đære eaxe ūtan ymbhwerfaþ (-eþ, MS.) đone norđende, neáh ymbcerraþ (-eþ, MS.), Met. 28, 14. Saturnus hæfđ ymb þrītig wintergerīmes weoruld ymbcyrred, 28, 26. (2) *to turn one's self round*:—Ymbcerred wæs on bæcgcling *conuersa est retrorsum*, Jn. Skt. Lind. Rush. 20, 14. (3) *to turn away, avert*:—Onsión mīn ne ymbcerdig (*averti*) from gispittendum on mec, Rtl. 19, 15. (4) *to turn over, move, stir, overturn*:—Hē đa discas ymbcerde *mensas subvertit*, Jn. Skt. Lind. Rush. 2, 15. Engel ymbcerde (*mouebat*) đæt wæter, 5, 4. Miđ fynger hiora nallas đa ymbcerræ (styrgan, Rush.) *digito suo nolunt ea movere*, Mt. Kmbl. Lind. 23, 4. (5) *to change*:—Ymbcerred *mutata*, Mt. Kmbl. p. 1, 2.

ymb-clyppan; *p.* te *To embrace, clasp*, (1) of persons:—Ic ymbclyppe đē *complector te*, Ælfc. Gr. 19; Zup. 122, 4: *amplector*, 36; Zup. 214, 5. Ic ymbclyp[p]e *obunco*, Wrt. Voc. i. 22, 31. Ymbclypte *obuncabat* (Timotheum ulnarum gremiis procax obuncabat, Ald. 40), ii. 81, 12: 64, 28. (2) of things:—Ǣghwilc ōþer ūtan ymbclyppeþ, Met. 11, 35. Swā swā lyft and lagu land ymbclyppaþ, 9, 40. Swā ymbclyppaþ cealda brymmas, Chr. 1065; Erl. 197, 31. Fingras þrȳ ūtan eáþe ealle mægon mec ymbclyppan, Exon. Th. 425, 9; Rä. 41, 53. Rāpas synfulra ymbclyppende syndon (*circumplexi sunt*) mē, Ps. Lamb. Surt. 118, 61. [Stringes of sinful umclipped me, Ps. 118, 61. Þe cercle þat umbeclypped his croun, Gaw. 616.]

ymb-clypping, e; *f. An embrace*:—Emclippingca *amplexus*, Hpt. Gl. 511, 36.

ymb-cyme, es; *m. A convention, an assembly*:—Đǣr wæs gesamnad eádigra geþeahtendlīc ymcyme, L. Wih. pref.; Th. i. 36, 7. Cf. ymb-þreodian.

ymb-cyrf, es; *m.* I. *circumcision*:—Miđ ymbcyrf *circumcisione*, Mt. Kmbl. p. 12, 11: 16, 13. II. *a cutting off*:—Of ymbcyrf liomana *de abscisione membrorum*, Mk. Skt. p. 4, 9.

ymb-dōn; *p.* -dyde *To put round, encompass*:—Ic embedō *circumdo*, Ælfc. Gr. 24; Zup. 139, 13.

ymbe (imbe), es; *m.* (?) *A swarm of bees*:—Wiđ ymbe . . . forweorp ofer greót þonne hī swirman, and cweđ: 'Sitte gē sigewīf . . . ,' Lchdm. i. 384, 18. ¶ Imbæs dæl *occurs* Cod. Dip. Kmbl. iii. 176, 20. [*O.H.Ger.* impi bīanō *examen apium*: *M. H. Ger.* imbe; *m.*: *Ger.* imme; *f.*] v. ymb-haga.

ymbe *about*, ymbe-. v. ymb, ymb-.

ymbeaht, es; *m. The word glosses* collatio:—Ymbeahtas *collationes* (the passage is: Haec x collationes patrum a Cassiano digestae propalabant, Ald. 13. In Hpt. Gl. 428, 7 *collationes* is glossed by *race* and explained by *narrationes*), Wrt. Voc. ii. 76, 80: 18, 3. Elsewhere the form is identical with ambiht:—Ambechtae, oembecht *collatio*, Txts. 46, 187. Ambect, ambaect *rationatio*, 92, 866. Ambiht *office* is neuter, ymbeaht is masculine: it seems (?) as if the form had been connected with eahtian *to consider*, and the word were regarded as a compound, ymb-eaht. See Engl. Stud. xi. 492.

ymb-eardiendra *glosses* circumhabitantium, Ps. Surt. 30, 14.

ymb-fær, es; *n. A going about, circuit*:—Tūna embefær *uillarum circuitus*, Anglia xiii. 375, 131. Mid emfare *circilo* (=circulo?), Hpt. Gl. 422, 14.

ymb-færeld, es; *n. m. A going round, circuit*:—Fram þēnuncge embefæreldes his *ab officio circuitus sui*, Anglia xiii. 434, 980. Hig fērdon seofon sīđon embe đa buruh. And on đam seofođan ymbfærelde (*circuitu*) . . . burston đa weallas, Jos. 6, 16.

ymb-fæstness *glosses* circumstantia, Rtl. 174, 17.

ymb-fæstnung, e; *f. A monument, tomb*:—Ymbfæstnung ł byrgenn *monumentum*, Jn. Skt. Lind. 19, 41.

ymb-fæþmian; *p.* ode *To embrace, clasp*:—Ne magon hȳ đa līfes līnan on middan ymbfæđmian, Salm. Kmbl. p. 152, 32.

ymb-faran; *p.* -fōr *To surround*:—Hē hēt đæt fæste lond ūtan ymbfaran, đæt him mon sceolde an mā healfa on feohtan þonne on ān, Ors. 2, 5; Swt. 80, 26.

ymb-feng, es; *m. A cover, an envelope*:—Emfencge (*librorum*) *tegmine, operimento*, Hpt. Gl. 417, 47.

ymb-fēran. v. emb-fēran.

ymb-fōn; *p.* -fēng. I. *to grasp, clasp*:—Hē fōtum ymbfēhđ fȳres lāfe, Exon. Th. 217, 6; Ph. 276. Heó ymbfēng Drihtnes fēt, Blickl. Homl. 157, 17. Ymbfēng *obuncat* (moecham, quam manus tollentis obuncat, Ald. 164), Wrt. Voc. ii. 92, 39. Ymbefēng, Beo. Th. 5376; B. 2691. II. *to encompass, surround, comprehend*:—Ealle stōwa hē gefylleþ and ymbfēhþ, Blickl. Homl. 23, 20. Seó sēleste gesǣlþ đa ōþra gesǣlþa ealle on innan him gegaderaþ, hī ūtan ymbfēhđ, Bt. 24, 1; Fox 80, 21. Đū meaht ymbfōn eal folca gesetu, Exon. Th. 466, 2; Hö. 115. Ymbfōnde *gyrens*, Wrt. Voc. ii. 41, 66. Hit is on ǣlce healfe ymbfangen mid gārsecge, Ors. 1, 1; Swt. 24, 17. Đīnre gedrēfednesse đe đū mid ymbfangen eart, Bt. 5, 3; Fox 12, 18. Sunu Meotodes habbaþ ealle ymbfangen mid sange, Cd. Th. 273, 30; Sat. 144. Đeáh hē wǣre mid īrne ymbfangen, Cd. Th. 297, 16; Sat. 518. II a. *to comprehend, conceive*:—Embfēhþ *concipit, i. intelligit*, Wrt. Voc. ii. 136, 21. III. *to put something round* an object, *surround, envelope*:—Genim foxes gecynd, ymbfōh (ym-, *v. l.*) đæt heáfod ūtan, Lchdm. i. 340, 19. Healfnacode on hiora līchaman būton đæt hig wǣron mid riftum ymbfangene (*but see* ymb-hōn), Shrn. 38, 7.

ymb-frætwian; *p.* ode *To surround with ornament*:—Đeáh đe men him hāton gewyrcan heora byrgene of marmanstāne, and ūtan emfrætewian mid reádum golde, Wulfst. 148, 21. Ymbfrætewode *circumornatae*, Ps. Lamb. 143, 12.

ymb-gān; *p.* -eode; *pp.* -gān. I. *to go round* (1) a circular course:—Ǣr sunne twelf mōnđa hringc ūtan ymbgān hæbbe, Guthl. 21; Gdwin. 96, 6. (2) an object:—Hī ūtan ymbgāđ ceaster *circuibunt civitatem*, Ps. Spl. C. 58, 16. II. *to go about, in the neighbourhood of*. v. ymb, I. 1 b:—Ic ymbgaa weófod đīnre *circumdabo altare tuum*, Ps. Spl. C. 25, 6. Ic ymbgā and ic offrige onsægednessa *circumivi et immolavi hostiam*, Ps. Spl. 26, 11. III. *to go about, through*. v. ymb, I. 1 e:—Swā hundas ymbgāđ hwommas ceastre, Ps. Th. 58, 6, 14. Ymbeode ides Helminga duguđe and geógoþe, dǣl ǣghwylcne, Beo. Th. 1244; B. 620. Ymbeade Hǣlend alle Galilēa *circumibat Jesus totam Galilaeam*, Mt. Kmbl. Lind. 4, 23. Đā ongan heó ymbgān đa hūs đæs mynstres *coepit circuire in monasterio casulas*, Bd. 3, 8; S. 531, 32. [I umyhode, Ps. 26, 6. Umga, 58, 7. Þe laddes unbiyeden him, Havel. 1842. *O. H. Ger.* umbi-gān.]

ymb-gang, es; *m.* I. *a going round*:—Seó burh (*Jericho*) næs mid nānum wīge gewunnen, ac mid đam ymgange, Homl. Th. ii. 216, 2. Is đære sunnan ymgang (ymbe-, ymb-, *v. ll.*) hremming, đæt se dæg ne byđ on ǣlcum earde gelīce lang, Lchdm. iii. 258, 11. Ǣlc mann, swā swā hē stōd on đam ymbgange, Jos. 6, 20. Emgange *abitum* (=ambitu, Ald. 73), Hpt. Gl. 522, 78. II. *a going about*:—Embgong *deambulacrum, circuitus*, Wrt. Voc. ii. 139, 82. III. of extent traversed or measured, *circuit, circumference*:—His ymbgong (*ambitus*) is hundseofontig mīla and seofeđa dǣl ānre mīle, . . . and bufan đæm māran wealle ofer ealne đone ymbgong hē is mid stǣnenum wīghūsum beworht, Ors. 2, 4; Swt. 74, 15–21. Six hund fōta and feówertig seó cyrce wæs ymbeganges, Homl. Th. ii. 496, 35. Ofer ymbgang *supra pinnam* (cf. pinnaculum, circuitus templi, 71, 69), Wrt. Voc. ii. 74, 41. Læssan ymbgang hæfđ se mann đe gǣđ ābūtan ān hūs, đonne se đe ealle đa burh begǣđ, Lchdm. iii. 248, 11. IV. of position, on ymbgange *about, around*:—Ealle đe on ymbegonge hys synd *omnes qui in circuitu ejus sunt*, Ps. Spl. T. 88, 8. On ymbgeonge, Rtl. 178, 31. V. *a winding course, bend*:—Ymbgongum *anfractibus*, Wrt. Voc. ii. 9, 53. V a. figurative:—Ymbgeong *decursum*, Mt. Kmbl. p. 12, 14. VI. *a going about a business*. v. ymb, I. 3 d:—Hiora in sprēc đone ymbgeong cȳđaþ *eorum in foro ambitum notat*, Mk. Skt. p. 5, 5. [In umgang *in circuitu*, Ps. 11, 9: *circum*, 30, 14. Þat was of umgang (abowte, *v. l.*) thre iorne, C. M. 9192. *O. H. Ger.* umbi-gang *circuitus, ambitus, deambulacrum, circulus, conversio*: *Icel.* um-gangr *circuit; management*.] v. embe-gang.

ymb-gangan; *p.* -gēng. I. *to go round*:—Hī ymbgangaþ ceaster *circuibunt civitatem*, Ps. Spl. T. 58, 16. II. *to go about, in the neighbourhood of*:—Ic ymbgonge weófod *circumdabo altare*, Ps. Spl. T. 25, 6: Ælfc. Gr. 24; Zup. 139, 13. Hine ymbegangaþ gāstas twēgen, Salm. Kmbl. 973; Sal. 487. III. *to go about, over, through*:—Gē ymbgangaþ sǣ and eorđu *circuitis mare et aridam*, Mt. Kmbl. Rush. 23, 14. [Other have hem umbiȝonge (*circumdederunt*), Pall. 119, 437. *O. H. Ger.* umbi-gangan.] v. ymb-gān.

ymb-gearwian; *p.* ode *To clothe, dress*:—Ymbgearuad *coopertum* Mk. Skt. Lind. 16, 5.

ymb-gedelf, es; *n. A digging round* or *about*:—Đæs treówes y gedelf is seó eádmōdnys đæs behreówsiendan mannes, Homl. T 408, 31.

ymb-gefrætwude *glosses* circumornatae, Ps. Spl. C. 143, 15.

ymb-geóting, e; *f. A pouring round* or *about, purification* ymgeóting (*printed* yn-) *lustramentum*, Hpt. Gl. 483, 20.

ymb-gerēnode *glosses* circumornatae, Ps. Spl. 143, 15:

ymb-gesett; *adj.* (*ptcpl.*) *Placed round about, neighbouring*:—Hē ðæt ymbgesette folc (*vulgus circumpositum*) feor and wīde . . . gȳmde tō gehwyrfanne . . . on his fōtum gongende com tō ðām ymbgesettum tūnum (*ad circumpositas villas*), Bd. 4, 27; S. 604, 2–13.

ymb-gyrdan; *p.* de. I. of clothing, *to gird about*, (1) *to put a girdle round*:—Ic embgyrde *cingo* and *accingo* and *succingo*, Ælfc. Gr. 28, 5; Zup. 173, 17. Hē ymbgyrde hine *praecinxit se*, Jn. Skt. Lind. Rush. 13, 4. Ymbgyrdaþ eówre lendena, Anglia viii. 322, 19. Ymbgyrde wē ūre lendena, 323, 27. Ymbgyrded *amictus*, Mk. Skt. Lind. Rush. 14, 51. Ymbgyrd *circumamicta*, Ps. Spl. T. 44, 15. His lendena wǣron ymbgirde, L. Ælfc. P. 17; Th. ii. 370, 12. 'Beón eówre lendena ymbgyrde.' On ðām ymbgyrdum lendenum is se mægðhād tō understandenne, Homl. Th. ii. 564, 25. (2) *to serve as a girdle*:—Ymbgyrde hine gyrdilse sōðfæstnises *circumcinxit eum zona justitiae*, Rtl. 79, 5. II. *to surround, encompass, enclose*:—Ymbgyrdeþ *ambit*, Wrt. Voc. ii. 9, 61. Mid ðyssum gemǣrum hī synd ūtan ymbgyrde, Cod. Dip. Kmbl. iii. 396, 3. v. embe-gyrdan.

ymb-habban; *p.* -hæfde. I. *to surround, encompass*:—Ymbhæfdan *cingebant*, Wrt. Voc. ii. 15, 73. Mid ðȳ unmǣtan weorode ymbhæfd *optimo vallatus exercitu*, Bd. 3, 18; S. 546, 31: 2, 9; S. 511, 25 note. Emhæfd *circumseptus* (densis agminibus, Ald. 3), Anglia xiii. 27, 5. Ispania land is eall mid fleóte ūtan ymbhæfd, ge eác binnan ymbhæfd ofer ða land ǣgþer ge of ðam gārsecge ge of ðam Wendelsǣ *Hispania circumfusione oceani Tyrrhenique pelagi pene insula efficitur*, Ors. 1, 1; Swt. 24, 1–3. II. *to include, contain*:—Beféhð ł emhæfð *circumgirat, circuit, complectitur*, Hpt. Gl. 422, 70. Embhæfþ *continet*, i. *habet, tenet*, Wrt. Voc. ii. 135, 16. Seó sēleste gesǣlþ ðe ða ōþra gesǣlþa ealle oninnan him gegaderaþ and hī ūtan ymbhæfþ, Bt. 24, 1; Fox 80, 21.

ymb-haga, an; *m.* *An enclosure where bees are kept*:—Wrīt ðysne circul on ānum mealanstāne (mealm-?), and sleah ǣnne stacan onmiddan ðam ymbhagan, and lege ðone stān onuppan ðam stacan (the words on the stone are: Contra apes ut salui sint. There are other charms connected with bees on pp. 384, 397), Lchdm. i. 395, 5. v. ymbe *a swarm of bees*.

ymb-hagian. v. ymb-hegian.

ymb-hammen; *adj.* *Surrounded, covered*:—Ymbhamne (*printed* -humne) *ambitiuntur* (=ambiuntur; the passage is: Manicae sericis clavate calliculae rubricatis pellibus ambiuntur, Ald. 77), Wrt. Voc. ii. 87, 59. Ymbhwyrfte, ymbhammene, 2, 14. Cf. seolfor-hammen.

ymb-hangen. v. ymb-hōn.

ymb-healdan; *p.* -heóld *To encompass*, Cd. Th. 265, 14; Sat. 7.

ymb-heápian; *p.* ode *To crowd about, surround in crowds*:—Ymbheápiendum *glomerantibus*, Wrt. Voc. ii. 40, 52. Ymbheápod *glomeratus* (the passage is:—Lucifer parasitorum sodalibus vallatus et apostatarum satellitibus glomeratus, Ald. 10), 76, 31. v. ymb-hīpan.

ymb-hēdig. v. ymb-hygdig.

ymb-hegian; *pp.* od *To hedge about, surround*:—Ic ymbhegige (embhagige, *v. l.*) *saepio*, Ælfc. Gr. 30, 2; Zup. 190, 15. Emhegod mid weorodum mǣdena *septus choreis virginum*, Hymn. Surt. 140, 12.

ymb-hīpan; *pp.* ed *To crowd about, surround in crowds, assail*:—Ymbhīpan (*printed* -hiwan) *constipari*, Wrt. Voc. ii. 23, 21. Ðā wæs hē sōna ǣghwanon mid wǣpnum ymbhȳped *cum mox ubique gladiis impeteretur*, Bd. 2, 9; S. 511, 25. Mid wǣpnum and mid feóndum eall ūtan ymbhēped *cum armis et hostibus circumseptus*, 3, 12; S. 537, 28 note. Embhēped *faltum*, Wrt. Voc. ii. 146, 75. v. ymb-heápian.

ymb-hlennan; *pp.* ed *To crowd about, surround*:—Emhlennende *constipantes*, Hpt. Gl. 409, 3. Emhlemmende (-hlennende?) *circumvallantes, stipantes*, 408, 62. Emhlenned *circumseptus*, 406, 47: *vallatus, circumseptus, circumdatus*, 422, 41. Emhledned *stipatus, circumdatus, vallatus*, 406, 44. Emhlæned *circumseptus*, Anglia xiii. 27, 5.

ymb-hoga, an; *m.* *Care, solicitude, anxiety*:—Se ymbhoga (cf. gēmen, Bt. 12; Fox 36, 28) ðyssa woruldsǣlþa, Met. 7, 53. Se rēn ungemetlīces ymbhogan, Bt. 12; Fox 36, 19: Met. 7, 28. For ðære ungemetgunge ðæs ymbehogan ðara ūterra ðinga, Past. 18; Swt. 141, 8. On tō monigfaldum ymbehogan ðisse worulde *curis hujus mundi*, 43; Swt. 317, 11. Ǣghwylc dæg hæfð genōh on hys āgenum ymbhogan *sufficit diei malitia sua*, Mt. Kmbl. 6, 34. Ðæt hē forlǣte ǣlcne ymbhogan, ðe him unnet sié, Met. 22, 10. Hē ðone ymbhogan ne forlēt ðæs flǣsclīcan beddgemānan *nec stratum carnalium sollicitudine deserit*, Past. 16; Swt. 99, 24. Ðonne hié āgiémeleásiaþ ðone ymbhogan woruldcundra ðinga *cum curare corporalia negligunt*, 18; Swt. 137, 2. Gif ðū hwilcne cræft cunne, begā ðone georne; swā swā sorge and ymbhogan geȳcaþ (-eð, MS.) monnes mōd, swā geȳcð se cræft his āre, Prov. Kmbl. 59. Wind woruldearfoþa, oððe ymbhogena ungemet rēn, Met. 7, 36. Ymbhogona, 16, 6. Byð ǣlc man gedrēfed on īdlum sorgum and on ymbhogum *universa vanitas omnis homo vivens*, Ps. Th. 38, 13. Ǣlc deáþlīc swencþ hine selfne mid manigfealdum ymbhogum *omnis mortalium cura, quam multiplicium studiorum labor exercet*, Bt. 24, 1; Fox 80, 7: 24, 4; Fox 84, 32. Ādō hē of his mōde ungerisenlīce ymbhogan, 30, 3; Fox 106, 20. Unnytte ymbhogan, 35, 1; Fox 154, 22.

ymb-hogian; *p.* ode *To be solicitous, exercise the mind*:—Ic ymbhogige on wundrum ðīnum *exercebor in mirabilibus tuis*, Ps. Lamb. 118, 27. Ymbhochige, 48. Ðeówa ðīn ymbhogode on rihtwīsnessum ðīnum *seruus tuus exercebatur in justificationibus tuis*, 23.

ymb-hōn; *pp.* -hangen *To hang round* with clothing, ornament, etc., *to drape, clothe, deck*:—Þeáh wē ūs gescirpen mid ðȳ reádestan godwebbe and gefrætewian mid ðȳ beorhtestan golde and mid ðām deórwyrþestan gimmum ūton ymbehōn, Wulfst. 262, 23. Ymbhangen mid fægernysse *circumamicta varietatibus*, Ps. Spl. 44, 15. Healfnacode on hiora līchaman, būton ðæt hig wǣron mid riftum ymbhangene, Homl. Ass. 202, 220. Seó fone is mid .xii. godwebbum ūtan ymbhangen, Salm. Kmbl. p. 152, 17.

ymb-hringan; *p.* de. I. *to ring round, surround, encompass*:—Embhrincþ *cingit*, Wrt. Voc. ii. 135, 53. Mē ymbhringde manig yfel *circumdederunt me mala*, Ps. Th. 39, 13. Mē ymbhringdon sār and sorga and grānung, 17, 4, 5. Mē ymbhringdon swīðe mænige calfru, 21, 10, 14. Mīne fȳnd mē ymbhringdon ūtan on ǣlce healfe, 16, 9. Emhrinced *circumseptus*, Hpt. Gl. 406, 47. Embþrungen *vel* (emb)hringed *constipata, circumdata*, Wrt. Voc. ii. 133, 62. Hē wæs ymbhringed mid his feóndum *vallatus exercitu*, Bd. 3, 18; S. 546, 30. Ðonne hē bið ūtane ymbhringed mid ungemetlīcre heringe *dum foris immenso favore circumdatur*, Past. 17; Swt. 111, 8. Ða ðe tō Gode hopiaþ beóð ymbhringde mid swȳþe manegre mildheortnesse *sperantes in Domino misericordia circumdabit*, Ps. Th. 31, 12. II. *to turn round in a ring, wind round*:—Ymbhringde *glomeravit* (the passage is: In spira morsum glomeravit inertem, Ald. 202), Wrt. Voc. ii. 96, 15: 41, 48.

ymb-hringend, es; *m.* *A surrounder, an attendant, one of a suite*:—Ymbhringendum (ymbdringendum (=þringendum), Erfurt. 61) *stipatoribus*, Txts. 96, 929.

ymb-humne. v. ymb-hammen.

ymb-hūung, e; *f.* *Circumcision*:—Yymbhūungun *circumcisionem*, Jn. Skt. Lind. 7, 22.

ymb-hweorfan; *p.* -hwearf. I. *to go round, revolve round*:—Se roder ǣlce dæg ūton ymbhwyrfð ealne ðisne middaneard, Bt. 39, 3; Fox 214, 16. Ymbhwyrfeþ, Met. 20, 137. Ymbhwerfeþ, 28, 4. Hī ðære eaxe ūtan ymbhwerfaþ (-eþ, MS.) ðone norðende, 28, 13. II. *to go about, in the neighbourhood of.* v. ymb, I. 1 b:—Ic ymbehwyrfe weófod ðīn *circumdabo altare tuum*, Ps. Lamb. 25, 6. III. *to go about, over, through.* v. ymb, I. 1 e:—Ic ymbhweorfe ðīn ðæt hālige tempel, Ps. Th. 26, 7. Ymbhwurfaþ woegas *circuite vias*, Rtl. 36, 5. Gē ymbhurfon sǣ and drȳgi *circuitis mare et aridam*, Mt. Kmbl. Lind. 23, 15. IV. fig. *to go about* a business, *be occupied with, attend to, cultivate.* v. ymb, I. 3 d; ymb-hwyrft, VII:—Hē underfēng ða hālgan gesomnunga tō plantianne and tō ymbhweorfanne, suā se ceorl dēð his ortgeard, Past. 40; Swt. 293, 3. V. causative, *to turn round*:—Ðū ðe on hrædum færelde ðone heofon ymbhweorfest *qui rapido coelum turbine versas*, Bt. 4; Fox 6, 31. Ymbhwearfest, Met. 4, 4. Ic eom ealne ðone heofon ymbhweorfende *rotam volubili orbe versamus*, Bt. 7, 3; Fox 20, 35.

ymb-hweorfness, e; *f.* *Change, alteration*:—Tīdo ymbhuoerfnise *temporum vicissitudine*, Rtl. 37, 35.

ymb-hwirfan; *pp.* -hwirft (?). v. ymb-hammen.

ymb-hwyrft (-hwearft, -hweorft, -hwerft), es; *m.* I. *a ring, circle*:—Lytel ymbhweorft *rotella* vel *orbiculus*, Wrt. Voc. i. 17, 44. Emhwerfte (-hferte, MS.) *gyro*, Kent. Gl. 271. II. *a circular course, an orbit*:—Se mōna hæfð his ryne hraðor āurnen on ðam læssan ymbhwyrfte, ðonne seó sunne hæbbe on ðam māran, Lchdm. iii. 248, 14. Hī (*certain stars*) habbaþ sceortne ymbhwyrft, Bt. 39, 3; Fox 214, 19: Met. 28, 20. Ymbhwerft, 28, 12. Ymbehwearft, 28, 8. III. *circuit, surrounding space*, on (in) ymbhwyrfte *around, round about*:—On ymbhwyrfte *in giro*, Wrt. Voc. ii. 47, 63. Ealle ðe on ymbhwyrfte āhwǣr syndan *omnes qui in circuitu ejus sunt*, Ps. Th. 75, 8: 88, 6. Fȳr onǣlð on ymbhwyrfte (*in circuitu*) fȳnd his, Ps. Spl. 96, 3. On ymbhwyrfte stōdan hǣr, Bd. 5, 2; S. 614, 45. Stefn in ymbhwyrfte (*in gyro*) ymbsealde ðæt hūs, 4, 3; S. 567, 44. God him forgeaf sibbe on eallum ymbhwirfte *data est a Deo pax in omnes per circuitum nationes*, Jos. 21, 42. On eallum ðam ymbhwyrfte, 10, 21. On his ymbhwyrfte bið swīðlīc storm, Homl. Th. i. 618, 11. Ðā eode Israhēla folc on ymbhwyrfte ðære byrig, ii. 212, 27. On ymbhwyrfte ondrǣdendum hine *in circuitu timentium eum*, Ps. Spl. 33, 7. Haldeþ heora ymbhwyrft Drihten *Dominus in circuitu populi sui*, Ps. Th. 124, 2. IV. *surrounded space, extent*:—Eall swā brād seó sunne is, swā eall eorðan ymbhwyrft, Lchdm. iii. 236, 7. Gif ðū witan wilt ymbe ealre ðisse eorðan ymbhwyrft from eásteweardan ðisses middangeardes ōð westeweardne, and fram sūþeweardum ōð norþeweardne (*omnem terrae ambitum*), Bt. 18, 1; Fox 60, 31. Seó līne ðe wile xxxiii sīða ealne eorðan ymbehwyrft ūtan ymblicgan, Salm. Kmbl. 152, 6. IV a. *the earth, world, globe*; orbis terrarum:—Ymbhwerft *orbis* vel *firmamentum*, Wrt. Voc. i. 17, 43. Ðæt eall ymbhwyrft (-hyrft, Lind.) wǣre tōmearcod *ut describeretur universus orbis*, Lk. Skt, 2, 1: Homl. Th. i. 30, 2. Eorðe and eall hire gefyllednys, and eal ymbhwyrft and ða ðe on ðam wuniaþ, ealle hit syndon Godes ǽhta *Domini est terra et plenitudo ejus, orbis terrarum et universi qui habitant in eo*, Homl. Th. i. 172, 9. Ymbhwyrft eorđena, Ps. Spl. Surt. 23, 1. Ymbhwyrft eorđan *orbis terrae*, Ps. Th. 89, 2. Eorđan ymbhwyrft and uprodor, Cd. Th. 205, 1; Exod. 429. Ic eom micle yldra đonne ymbhwyrft đes, oþþe đes middangeard, Exon. Th. 424, 21; Rä. 41, 42. Đæt wealdleþer ealles ymbhweorftes heofenes and eorþan, Bt. 36, 2; Fox 174, 19. Yrnđ seó sunne bufon đysum ymbhwyrfte, Lchdm. iii. 250, 14. Eallum ymbehwyrfte (ymbhuirfte, Lind.) *universo orbi*, Lk. Skt. 21, 26. Úre ieldran ealne đisne ymbhwyrft đises middangeardes swá swá Oceanus ymbligeþ on þreó tódǽldon *majores nostri orbem totius terrae, oceani limbo circumseptum, triquadrum statuere*, Ors. 1, 1; Swt. 8, 1. Hé gesette ofer hig ymbhwyrft (*orbem*, 1 Sam. 2, 8), Cant. An. 8: Ps. Lamb. 32, 8. Geond alnæ ymbhwyrft *in universo orbe*, Mt. Kmbl. Rush. 24, 14: Homl. Th. i. 76, 27. Se cásere, se đe eallne ymbhwyrft on his anwealde hæfde, L. Ælfc. C. 2; Th. ii. 342, 22. Ástág đæt heofonlíce goldhord on đysne ymbhwyrft, Blickl. Homl. 11, 29. Hé ymbhwyrft eorđan folca sóđe and rihte démeþ *judicabit orbem terrae in aequitate, et populos in veritate sua*, Ps. Th. 95, 13. Ymbhwyrft ealne eorđan and heofones, Met. 24, 38. Ealne ymbhwyrft and uprador, Elen. Kmbl. 1458; El. 731. Eorđan ymbehwyrft *orbem terrarum*, Ps. Th. 88, 10. **IV b.** *a district, region, world* (=part of the world occupied by a particular people):—Hí férdon geond eallum Rómániscum ymbhwyrfte *they went through all the Roman world*, Homl. Th. ii. 30, 28. Gang óđ đæt đú đone ymbhwyrft alne canne, Cd. Th. 308, 33; Sat. 702. ¶ On ymbhwyrfte *among*:—Se đe is on ealra ymbhwyrfte tó weorþienne *he that is to be honoured among all people*, Blickl. Homl. 197, 5. **V.** *a bend, turn*:—Nim his lifre, tódǽl, and bedealf æt đám ymbhwyrftum đínra landgemǽra, Lchdm. i. 328, 22. **VI.** *turn, regular course*:—His suna férdon, and đénode ǽlc óđrum mid his gódum on ymhwyrfte æt his húse, Homl. Th. ii. 446, 17. **VII.** *attention, cultivation*. v. ymb-hweorfan, IV:—Gif se wíngeard næfđ đone ymbhwyrft, and ne biđ onriht gescreádod, ne biđ hé wæstmbǽre, ac for hrađe áwildaþ, Homl. Th. ii. 74, 14.

ymb-hygd; *f. n.*: -hygdu; *f.* (v. ofer-hygd) *Care, anxiety*:—Wiste úre se heofonlíca Fæder his đa leófan bearn on myclum ymbhygdum wǽron æfter him; đá wolde hé se Hǽlend hié áfréfran, Blickl. Homl. 131, 28.

ymb-hygdig; *adj.* **I.** *feeling anxiety, careful, anxious, solicitous, attentive*:—Ymbhédig *sollicitus*, Wrt. Voc. i. 51, 24. Emhídig ł carful *zelotypus*, Hpt. Gl. 415, 1. Emhídi, 414, 77. Emhédig ł hohful, 459, 71. Hé mid ymbhýdie (behygdige, Bd. M. 264, 31) móde smeáde *sollerti animo scrutaretur*, Bd. 4, 3; S. 568, 4. Ne beó gé ymbehýdige eówre sáwle hwæt gé etan *nolite solliciti esse animae vestrae quid manducetis*, Lk. Skt. 12, 22. Be óđrum þingum ymbehýdige *de ceteris solliciti*, 12, 26. Ymbhýdige be reáfe, Mt. Kmbl. 6, 28. Đa sýn emhýdige and cariende embe heora ealdorscipas on eallum þingum *sollicitudinem gerant super decanias suas in omnibus*, R. Ben. 46, 10. Ymbhédigra *sollicitorum*, Kent. Gl. 352. Hié forgytaþ đæt hié hwéne ǽr ymbhygdigum eárum and ingeþancum gehýrdon reccean, Blickl. Homl. 55, 27. **II.** *causing anxiety, anxious*:—Gif him þince đæt hé geseó man mid wǽpnan gewundodne, ymbhídig sorg đæt byđ, Lchdm. iii. 174, 12.

ymb-hygdiglíc; *adj. Careful, anxious, solicitous, sedulous*:—Mid emhédilícere geornfulnysse *sollicita* (*curiosa, sedula*) *intentione*, Hpt. Gl. 410, 9.

ymb-hygdiglíce; *adv. Carefully, sedulously* [:—Mid đan đe hé his salmes and his gebeden and rǽdingan embhýdiglíce smeáde, Shrn. 14, 14.]

ymb-hygdigness, e; *f. Care, anxiety, solicitude*:—Þurhwacol emhídignys *pervigil sollicitudo*, Hpt. Gl. 426, 57. Geornfulnys ł emhédinys *diligentia, cura*, 437, 58. Se abbod mid ealre emhýdignesse (*sollicitudine*) carige embe đa gyltendan gebróđru, R. Ben. 50, 18: 54, 19: 137, 21. Ǽlc đæra wæs hám tó his ágenum farende myd mycelre ymbhýdignysse and mid mycelum ege, Nicod. 33; Thw. 19, 26. Wé sceolon đa ymhídignysse fram ús áwurpan, Homl. Th. ii. 462, 12. Twá wiđerrǽde đing gedeódde Drihten on đisum cwyde, ymhídignyssa and lustas. Ymhídignyssa ofđriccaþ đæt mód, and unlustas tólýsaþ, 92, 14. Gehyspendlíce on ymbhigdinyssum sínum (*studiis suis*), Ps. Lamb. 13, 2.

ymb-irnan; *p.* -arn. **I.** *to go round*:—Hí ymbyrnaþ ceaster *circuibunt civitatem*, Ps. Spl. 58, 7, 16. **II.** *to go about*:—Seofona gástas ymbiornas (*discurrentes*), Mt. Kmbl. p. 10, 3. v. ymb-ærnan.

ymb-lǽdan; *p.* de *To lead about*:—Hé ymblǽdde hine *circumduxit eum* (Deut. 32, 10), Cant. M. ad fil. 10.

ymb-lǽr(i)gian (?) *to surround, encompass*:—Sýn emblǽrg[ede] *ambiuntur* (cf. ymb-hammen, *which is a gloss to the same passage*), Anglia xv. 207, 289. v. lǽrig.

ymb-licgan; *p.* -læg. **I.** *to lie round, surround, encompass*:—Ealne đisne ymbhwyrft đises middangeardes, swá swá Oceanus útan ymbligeþ *orbem totius terrae, Oceani limbo circumseptum*, Ors. 1, 1; Swt. 8, 2. Seó líne đe wile xxxiii síđa ealne eorđan ymbehwyrft útan ymblicgan, Salm. Kmbl. 152, 6. **II.** *to lie about, along*. v. ymb, I. 1 d:—Se cyng đæt land on đa sǽhealfe mid scipum ymbelæg, Chr. 1072; Erl. 211, 2. [To umbelyȝe Lotheȝ hous, Allit. Pms. 63, 836.]

ymb-líþan *to circumnavigate*:—Ymblíþendre Breotone útan *circumnavigata Brittania*, Bd. 5, 9; S. 622, 17.

ymb-lócian *to look round*:—Ymblócade *circumspiciens*, Mk. Skt. Lind. Rush. 3, 34. [Þat leris man him umbiloke, C. M. 8468. Nedefull it es . . . þat he warely umbyluke hym þat he pryde hym noghte þareof, Rol. H. i. 319, 18.]

ymb-lofian *to praise*:—Heriaþ Drihten ealle þeóda, ymblofiaþ (*laudate*) hine ealle folctruman, Ps. Lamb. 116, 1.

ymb-lyt ? :—Hé gesette sunnan and mónan, stánas and eorđan, streám út on sǽ, wæter and wolcen đurh his wundra miht, deópne ymblyt (ybmlyt, MS.) dene (clene, MS.) ymbhaldeþ Meotod on mihtum, Cd. Th. 265, 13; Sat. 7.

ymbren, es; *pl.* ymbrenu (*the reading* ymbren ⁊ fæstena, L. Eth. vi. 23; Th. i. 320, 20, *should rather be* ymbrenfæstena, *as in* Wulfst. 272, 16); *n.* *Ember* (in *Ember*-day), *Embring* (e. g. Keep *embrings* well and fasting days. . . . For Friday, Saturn and Wednesday, Tusser); the name of the four periods of fasting and prayer appointed by the Church to be observed in the four seasons of the year respectively. Each was a period of three days, a Wednesday and the following Friday and Saturday (cf. đa twelf ymbrendagas, Wulfst. 244, 20. *For the dates see the passage given under* ymbren-dæg, L. Ecg. P. addit. 21; Th. ii. 234, 33):—Đis godspel sceal on Wódnesdæg tó đam ymbrene ǽr myddawyntran (cf. Đys gebyraþ on Frigedæg tó đam ylcan fæstene, v. 39), Lk. Skt. 1, 26 rubc. Đis sceal on Wódnesdæg on đære Pentecostenes wucan tó đam ymbrene, 9, 12 rubc. On Frigedæg on đære Pentecostenes wucan tó đam ymbrene, 8, 40 rubc. On Sæternesdæg on đære Pentecostenes wucan tó đam ymbrene, Mt. Kmbl. 20, 29 rubc. Đis sceal tó đam ymbrene innan hærefeste on Wódnesdæg, Mk. Skt. 9, 17 rubc. Tó đam ymbrene innan hærfaste on Frigedæg, Lk. Skt. 7, 36 rubc. Tó đam ymbrene innan hærefeste on Sæterndæg, 13, 6 rubc. Fæstaþ đa feówer ymbrenu on twelf mónđum, đe eów rihtlíce ásette synd, Wulfst. 136, 17. ¶ *the form occurs also with* riht *prefixed*:—Áđas and wífunga ǽfre sindan tócwedene heáhfreólsdagum and rihtymbrenum, L. Eth. vi. 25; Th. i. 320, 25: Wulfst. 117, 15 note. [Perhaps both the Latin (*jejunia*) *quatuor temporum* and the English *ymb-ryne* (*q. v.*) may have a share in the formation of *ymbren*; cf. Germ. *quatember* and Swed. *tamper-dagar*.] v. following words.

ymbren-dæg, es; *m.* *An Ember-day*:—Wé forbeódaþ ordál and áđas freólsdagum and ymbrendagum, L. C. E. 17; Th. i. 370, 3: Wulfst. 117, 15. Đa đe heora lencten wel gefæsten and đa twelf ymbrendagas, 244, 20. ¶ *with* riht prefixed:—Đis synt đa rihtymbrendagas (*legitimi quatuor temporum dies*), đe man mid rihte healdan sceal; đæt is, on kl. Martii, on đære forman wucan; and kl. Iunii, on đære æfteran wucan; and on kl. Septemƀ. on đære þriddan wucan; and on kl. December, on đa néhstan wucan ǽr Cristes mæssan, L. Ecg. P. addit. 21; Th. ii. 234, 33. Áđas sindon tócweden freólsdagum and rihtymbrendagum, L. Eth. v. 18; Th. i. 308, 25. Gyf hwylc wydewe hý forlicge, béte .i. geár, and rihtymbrendagas tó eácan đæs geáres (*et insuper quattuor temporum legitimis anni diebus*), L. Ecg. C. 39; Th. ii. 164, 30. [Iđe Umbridawes, Wodnesdawes and Fridawes, A. R. 70, 6. Embyrday, embyr *angarium* vel *quatuor temporum*, Prompt. Parv. 139. *Icel.* Imbru-dagar (*taken from English*).]

ymbren-fæsten, es; *n.* *The fast of the Ember-days*:—Đæt man ǽlc beboden fæsten healde, sí hit ymbrenfæsten, sí hit lengctenfæsten, L. C. E. 16; Th. i. 368, 22. Đæt ymbrenfæsten byđ on đissum mónþe (*December*), Anglia viii. 311, 39. On đam lenctenfæstene and on ǽlcum ymbrenfæstene, Homl. Th. ii. 608, 17. Feówer ymbrenfæstenu beóđ on twelf mónđum, eallswá feówer tíman beóđ, Anglia viii. 312, 14. Ymbrenfæstena healde man rihte, swá swá Scs. Gregorius Angelcynne sylf hit gedihte, Wulfst. 272, 16: L. Eth. vi. 23; Th. i. 320, 20.

ymbren-wicu, an; *f.* *A week in which Ember-days fall*:—.iiii. Wódnesdagas on .iiii. ymbrenwican, L. Alf. pol. 43; Th. i. 92, 9. [Iđe ymbri wikis Wodnesdawes and Fridawes, A. R. 70, 6 note. *Icel.* Imbru-vika.]

ymb-ryne, es; *m.* **I.** *course* of a moving body:—Wǽron sume gedwolmen đe cwǽdon, đæt ǽlc man beó ácenned be steorrena gesetnyssum, and þurh heora ymbryna him wyrd gelimpe, Homl. Th. i. 110, 8. **II.** *course* of time, *revolution, period*:—Đes geárlíca ymryne ús gebrincþ eft nú đa clǽnan tíd Lenctenlíces fæstenes, Homl. Th. ii. 98, 24. Gyf hé (*the 29th of February*) byđ forlǽten unteald, đǽrrihte áwent eall đæs geáres ymbryn[e] (-rene, *v. l.*) þwyres, Lchdm. iii. 264, 12. Emrynes *lustrationis, circuli, curriculo annorum*, Hpt. Gl. 455, 6. Áurnenum (wucan) emrene *emenso hebdomadis curriculo*, 428, 72. Se dæg biđ ofer Eástrum on ymbryne đæs geáres, Homl. Skt. ii. 27, 16. Iond đære wucan emrene *per septimane circulum*, R. Ben. Interl. 52, 4. Yrnende geond gǽres ymbrene *currens per anni circulum*, Hymn. Surt. 39, 29. Dægena embrynum *dierum circulis*, 27, 1. Embrenum *lustris*, Hpt. Gl. 415, 67. Ymrynum, 493, 62. Ǽfre ymbe geáres ymbrynum, Lchdm. iii. 238, 25. Be đæs geáres ymbrenum *de temporibus*, 232, 5.

ymb-sǽlan *to bind round, tie round*:—Sié unbunden (ymbunden, Lind.) ł unsǽled (=ymbsǽled) *circumdaretur*, Mk. Skt. Rush. 9, 42.

ymb-sætnung, e; *f.* I. *a siege*:—Emsætnungum *obsidione*, Hpt. Gl. 525, 40. II. *a sedition*:—Mid ðý gié gehēreþ gefehto and ymbsētnungo (-e, Rush.) ymb burgum (v. ymb, I. 1 e, *and* sætnung: *or under* I?) *cum audieritis proelia et seditiones*, Lk. Skt. Lind. 21, 9.

ymb-sceáwian *to look round, to behold*:—Ymbsceáwade (-sceówade, Rush.) tō geseánne hiá *circumspiciebat uidere eam*, Mk. Skt. Lind. 5, 32. Ymbsceáwde (-sceówadun, Rush.) hiá *circumspiciens eos*, 3, 5. Ymbsceáude (-sceówade, Rush.) hine *intuitus eum*, Jn. Skt. Lind. 1, 42.

ymb-sceáwiendlīce; *adv. Circumspectly*:—Mid ðý hē swā gemetfæstlīce and swā ymbsceáwiendlīce hine sylfne on eallum ðingum beheóld *cum ita se modeste et circumspecte in omnibus gereret*, Bd. 5, 19; S. 937, 5.

ymb-sceáwung, e; *f. Beholding*:—Embeþonc *vel* (embe)sceáwung *circumspectio*, Wrt. Voc. ii. 131, 27. Wer se ðe giðenceþ ymbsceáwung (*circumspectionem*) Godes, Rtl. 46, 5: 84, 27.

ymb-scīnan; *p.* scān *To shine round, surround with brightness*:—Ðæs Hēhstan mægen ðē ymbscīneþ, Blickl. Homl. 7, 36. Seó sunne ymbscīnð ðone blindan, and se blinda ne gesihð ðære sunnan leóman, Homl. Th. ii. 446, 32. Berhtnise Godes ymbsceán hiá (him ymbesceán, W. S.) *claritas Dei circumfulsit eos*, Lk. Skt. Lind. Rush. 2, 9. Hié leóht ymbscān, Andr. Kmbl. 2034; An. 1019. [Þe schyre sunne hit umbeschon, Allit. Pms. 105, 455.]

ymb-scrīþan; *p.* -scrāþ *To go round, revolve round*:—Rodor ymbscrīþeþ dōgora gehwilce ðisne middangeard, Met. 20, 208.

ymb-scrýdan; *p.* de *To clothe*:—Ymbscrýdaþ eów mid Godes wǣpnunge *induite vos armaturam Dei* (Eph. 6, 11), Homl. Th. ii. 218, 2. Mid hwam gē sýn ymbscrýdde *quid induamini*, Mt. Kmbl. 6, 25.

ymb-sellan; *p.* -sealde *To surround*; circumdare:—Ic ymbsylle *circumdabo*, Ps. Spl. 25, 6. Ðū ymbseles *circumdas*, Rtl. 76, 1. Hē mid eallum ðyssum ða burh ymbsealde (*circumdedit*), Bd. 3, 16; S. 542, 24: Ps. Th. 114, 3. Fýren wolcen ymbsealde ealle ða ceastre, Blickl. Homl. 245, 31. Se sang in ymbhwyrfte ymbsealde ðæt hūs, Bd. 4, 3; S. 567, 45. Mē ymbsealdon (*circumdederunt*) þeóde, Ps. Th. 117, 10, 12. Ymbsaldun (ym-, Lind.), Mt. Kmbl. Rush. 27, 28. Hī mē ūtan ymbsealdan, Ps. Th. 87, 17. Ūton ymbsele *circumda*, Kent. Gl. 157. Ymbselle *circumdet*, Rtl. 34, 7. Ymbsyllendum mē *circumdantibus me*, Ps. Spl. 31, 9. Seó fǣmne wæs ymbseald mid ðon campweorode, Blickl. Homl. 11, 24. Sondbeorgum ymbseald, Exon. Th. 360, 23; Wal. 10. Ða ymbsealde sint mid sixum eác fiðrum gefrætwad, Elen. Kmbl. 1480; El. 742.

ymb-seón *to behold, look*:—Ic hine wolde biddan, ðæt hē sweotole ymbsāwe sūð, eást and west (cf. behealde hē on feówer healfe his, Bt. 19; Fox 68, 21), hū wīdgil sint heofones hwealfe, Met. 10, 5. [For þi oure soile or þou seke umse þe betyme, Alex. (Skt.) 3728.]

ymb-seón *beholding*. v. ymb-sīn.

ymb-set, es; *n. Siege, blockade*:—Ðæt gēr ymbsetes ðære Beadonescan dūne *annum obsessionis Badonici montis*, Bd. 1, 16; S. 484, 22. Hē ne mihte ne mid gefeohte ne mid ymbsete (*obsidione*) ða burh ābrecan ne gegān, 3, 16; S. 542, 19. [*O. H. Ger.* umbi-sez *obsidio.*]

ymb-seten[n], e; *f. A row* of vines:—Oemsetinne wiingeardes *amtes* (= antes?), Wrt. Voc. ii. 100, 17. v. ymb-settan, II; seten, II.

ymb-setenness, e; *f. Besieging, siege*:—Ðæt hý sceoldon ðam Gode þancian ðe hý gefriðode fram ðære ymbsetennesse, and fram ðære hergunge ðara twēga kynincga, Ps. Th. 45, arg.

ymb-sētnung. v. ymb-sǣtnung.

ymb-settan; *p.* te. I. *to set round, put round, surround*:—Hē ymbseteþ ūtan līc and feþre on healfe gehware hālgum stencum, Exon. Th. 212, 3; Ph. 204. Beád hē ūt scypfyrde and landfyrde, and ðæt land eall ūtan embsette, Chr. 1072; Erl. 210, 31. Giarn ān and gifylde copp mid æcede ymbsette and tō rōde ða drinca salde him *currens unus et implens spongiam aceto circumponensque calamo potum dabat ei*, Mk. Skt. Rush. Lind. 15, 36. Ymbsetton (ymsettun, Rush.) ł ymbuundun *circumponentes*, Jn. Skt. Lind. 19, 29. Salomones reste wæs mid weardum ymbseted, Blickl. Homl. 11, 16. Ymbseted mid ðǣm wāgum his misdǣda, L. E. I. 32; Th. ii. 430, 14. Ymbsett mid fāgnesse *circumdata varietate*, Ps. Lamb. 44, 10. Mid hwilcum feóndum heó ymbset bið, Homl. Th. i. 410, 9. Emset *glomeratus, circumseptus*, Hpt. Gl. 422, 47. Ða heargas ðara deófolgylda mid heora hegum ðe hī ymbsette wǣron *fana idolorum cum septis quibus erant circumdata*, Bd. 2, 13; S. 516, 39. II. *to plant* with something. v. ymb-seten:—Ic embsette *consero*, Wrt. Voc. ii. 133, 56. Eá mid treówum ymbset *amnis*, i. 54, 16. [How Iuus Iesu oft umsette (bisette, *v.l.*), C. M. 195. Alle umset with enmys, Pr. C. 1250. *O. H. Ger.* umbi-sezzen.]

ymb-sīn (-seón), e; *f. Beholding, regard*:—Clǣnum gisceáwiga wē ymbseáne *puro cernamus intuitu*, Rtl. 35, 37.

ymb-sirwan; *p.* -sirwde, -sirede. I. *to deliberate about* an evil deed:—Swā micel tōsceád is betwuh ðære beðōhtan synne, ðe mon longe ymbsireþ, and ðære ðe mon fǣrlīce ðurhtiéhð, swā ðætte se se ðe ða synne gesireþ, ǣgðer ge gesyngaþ ge eác hwīlum on ormōdnesse gewīt . . . For ðǣm sint tō manianne ða ðe lange ymbsieriaþ ðæt hī ongieten hū micel wīte hī sculun habban beforan ðǣm ōðrum *hoc ergo praecipitatione lapsis per consilium pereuntes differunt, quod, cum hi a statu justitiae peccando concidunt, plerumque simul et in laqueum desperationis cadunt . . . Admonendi ergo sunt, ut hinc colligant, qui in culpa etiam se per consilium ligant*, Past. 56; Swt. 435, 4-31. II. *to lie in wait for*:—Se ðe hine ne ymbsyrede (-syrwde, ymbesierede, *v.ll.*) *qui non est insidiatus* (Ex. 21, 13), L. Alf. 13; Th. i. 46, 24.

ymb-sittan; *p.* -sæt, *pl.* -sǣton; *pp.* -seten. I. *to sit* or *be round*, (1) *to sit at* table, meat, etc.:—Ðæt hié mē þēgon, symbel ymbsǣton, Beo. Th. 1132; B. 564. Hý twēgen sceolon tæfle ymbsittan, Exon. Th. 345, 2; Gn. Ex. 182. Ða ymbsittendan *circumsedentes*, Bd. 4, 9; S. 577, 31: *convivae*, 5, 5; S. 618, 16: Ap. Th. 15, 6: 17, 4. (1 a) *to sit at* council, *be engaged about*:—Hī ān geþeaht ealle ymbsǣtan *cogitaverunt consensum in unum*, Ps. Th. 82, 5. (2) *to be around, be neighbouring*. v. ymb-sittend:—Ðām ðe ūs ymbsittaþ *his qui in circuitu nostro sunt*, Ps. Th. 43, 15. Hī þreátiaþ gehwider ymbsittenda ōþra þeóda, Met. 25, 14. II. *to beset*:—Ic ymbsitte *obsideo*, Ælfc. Gr. 26, 5; Zup. 157, 3. Fearras fǣtte ymbsǣton mē *tauri pingues obsederunt me*, Ps. Lamb. 21, 13. Ðā com micel werod werigra gāsta and ðis hūs ūtan ymbsǣtan (*domum hanc et exterius obsedit*), Bd. 5, 13; S. 633, 2. II a. as a term of war, *to besiege, invest*:—Ðīne fýnd ðē ymbsittaþ mid ymbtrymminge *circumdabunt te inimici tui uallo* (Lk. 19, 43), Homl. Th. i. 408, 35. Hē ymbsæt ða burh (*circumdedit Eglon*), Jos. 10, 34. Eádmund ymbsæt Anlāf cyning and Wulfstān arcebiscop on Legraceastre, Chr. 943; Erl. 117, 16. Ælle and Cissa ymbsǣton Andredescester, 491; Erl. 14, 5: 885; Erl. 82, 20. Hié ymbsǣton ān geweorc, 894; Erl. 91, 7. Ymbesǣtan, 1011; Erl. 145, 8. Ymbsittaþ ða burg suīðe gebyrdelīce *ordinabis adversus eam obsidionem*, Past. 21; Swt. 161, 19. Ðā hié hæfdon Cirinen ða burh ymbseten, Ors. 2, 2; Swt. 66, 18. Hē besierede ðæt folc ðe hié ymbseten hæfden, 4, 5; Swt. 170, 2: Ps. Th. 12 arg. [*O. H. Ger.* umbi-sizzan *obsidere.*] v. emb-sittan.

ymb-sittend, es; *m. One living on the borders of another's country, a neighbour*:—Gif ic ðæt gefricge, ðæt ðec ymbsittend (*those that sit on thy borders*) egesan þýwaþ, Beo. Th. 3658; B. 1827. Him ǣghwylc ðara ymbsittendra hýran sceolde, 18; B. 9: Elen. Kmbl. 65; El. 33. Ymbesittendra, Beo. Th. 5461; B. 2734. Wē synd gewordene eallum edwītstæf ymbsittendum *facti sumus in opprobrium vicinis nostris*, Ps. Th. 78, 4: 88, 34.

ymb-smeá(g)ung. v. embe-smeágung.

ymb-snidenness, e; *f. Circumcision*:—Wēn is ðæt eówer sum nyte hwæt sý ymbsnidennys, Homl. Th. i. 92, 30. Se intinga ðære æftran ymbsnidennysse, Jos. 5, 6. Beóð ēstfulle heortan mid dæghwonlīcere ymbsnidenysse āfeormode, Homl. Th. i. 98, 14. Mōyses eów sealde ymbsnydenisse, Jn. Skt. 7, 22. Ða ealdan ymbsnidenysse, Shrn. 47, 18.

ymb-snīþan; *p.* -snāþ, *pl.* -snidon *To circumcise*:—On restedæge gē ymbsnīðaþ mann, Jn. Skt. 7, 22. Abraham ymbsnāð his sunu, Gen. 17, 23. Ðæt stǣnene sex, ðe ðæt cild ymbsnāð, Homl. Th. i. 98, 10. Hié ǣghwelcum cnihtcilde ymbsnidon ðæt werlīce lim, Shrn. 47, 20. Hē hine lǣt ymbsnīðan mid scearpum flinte, Wulfst. 195, 9. Ymsnīþan (ymbsnýðan, *v.l.*), Lk. Skt. 1, 59. Ðæt ðæt cild emsnyden (ymb-, *v.l.*) wǣre, 2, 21. Ymbsniden, Homl. Th. i. 90, 14, 18, 30. Heora fæderas wǣron ymbsnidene, Jos. 5, 4. [Embsniþen mid ane ulintsexe, O. E. Homl. i. 81, 27.]

ymb-spannan *to span round*:—Swyle tō ðon swīþe āswollen ðæt hine mon nā mid twām handum ymbspannan (*circumplecti*) mihte, Bd. 5, 3; S. 616, 7.

ymb-sprǣc, e; *f. Speech about a subject, talk*:—Be ðysum is oft mycel ymbsprǣc (ymbe-, emb-, *v.ll.*) *there is often much discussion about this*, Lchdm. iii. 266, 9. Ne beó gē āfyrhte ðurh geswince ðæs langsuman færeldes, oððe þurh yfelra manna ymbesprǣce *nec labor vos itineris, nec maledicorum hominum linguae deterreant* (Bd. 1, 23), Homl. Th. ii. 128, 2.

ymb-sprǣce; *adj. Talked about*:—Geond ðās eorþan ǣghwǣr sindon hiora gelīcan hwōn ymbsprǣce, Met. 10, 59.

ymb-sprecan *to speak about something*:—Alle yfle ymbsprēcon *omnes murmurabant*, Lk. Skt. 19, 7.

ymb-standan; *p.* -stōd; *pp.* -standen. I. *to stand about* or *around*:—Ðis folc ðæt hēr ymbstandeþ, Blickl. Homl. 143, 7: Jn. Skt. Rush. 11, 42. Eall seó gesomnung brōþra and sweostra on twā halfe singende ymbstōdon (*circumstaret*), Bd. 4, 19; S. 589, 9. ¶ pres. part. used substantively:—Hē sceal grētan his ymbstandendan, and hig him sceolon andswarian, L. E. I. 7; Th. ii. 406, 23. II. *to surround*:—Mē ymbstōdan strange manige *circumdantes circumdederunt me*, Ps. Th. 117, 11. Hý habbaþ mē ūtan ymbstanden *circumdederunt me*, 16, 10. Hī bióþ ūton ymbstandene (*printed* -standende, *but see* ūtan ymbestandne, Met. 25, 7) mid miclon gefērscipe hiora þegna *septos tristibus armis*, Bt. 37, 1; Fox 186, 4. [He saw how þe laddes wode Hauelok his louerd umbistode, Hav. 1875. *O. H. Ger.* umbi-standan *circumstare, circumdare.*] v. next word.

ymb-standend, es; *m. A by-stander*:—Hī ānra gehwilcum ymbstandendra forsǣton heáfodsiéna, Cd. Th. 150, 8; Gen. 2488. Ðā cwæð se câsere tô ðâm embstandendum, Homl. Skt. i. 23, 275. Sum mon of ðǽm ymbstondendum *quidam de circumstantibus*, Mk. Skt. Rush. Lind. 14, 47.

ymb-standenness *glosses* circumstantia, Ps. Lamb. Surt. 140, 3: Rtl. 179, 9: 182, 16: Ps. Surt. 30, 22.

ymb-strícan; *p.* -strâc *To rub round* so as to smooth:—Gif ðæs dolges ôfras synd tô heá ymbstríc mid hâte îsene *if the edges of the wound are too high, pass a hot iron round*, Lchdm. ii. 96, 5.

ymb-styrian *to stir about, upset*:—Ymbstyreþ ðæt hûs *evertit domum*, Lk. Skt. Lind. 15, 8.

ymb-swǽpe, an; *f. A roundabout way, digression.* Cf. ymb-swâpan, I:—Ymbsuaepe *ambages*, Wrt. Voc. ii. 100, 13. [Cf. *O. H. Ger.* umbi-suaifan *amictum*: *Ger.* um-schweif.]

ymb-swâpan; *p.* -sweóp; *pp.* -swâpen. I. *to sweep about* (of the motion of waves):—Ða ýþa weóllan and ymbsweópan and ǽghwonene ðæt scyp fyldon *verrentibus undique et implere incipientibus navem fluctibus*, Bd. 3, 15; S. 541, 42. II. *to wrap round*:—Ymbswâpen *circumamicta*, Ps. Surt. Spl. C. 44, 10, 15. Emswâpen *circumamicta, circumdata*, Hpt. Gl. 430, 45. [*M. H. Ger.* umbe-swief; *p.*]

ymb-þanc, es; *m. n.*: -þanca, an; *m. Thought about* a matter, *consideration, attention*:—Embeþonc *circumspectio*, Wrt. Voc. ii. 131, 26. Mid micelum embeþance *magna animaduersione*, Anglia xiii. 373, 106. Hié eallneg rǽswaþ and ondrǽdaþ ðæt hî mon tǽlan wille and beóð eallneg mid ðæm ymbeðoncan (-ðonce, Cott. MSS.) âbisgode and ofdrǽdde *dum deprehendi metuunt, semper pavidis suspicionibus agitantur*, Past. 35; Swt. 239, 7. Ðæt hî ongieten mid wærlîce ymbeþonce *ut cauta circumspectione considerent*, 58; Swt. 445, 5. Ðætte hê ðone ymbeþonc ðæs wærscipes ne forlǽte *ut circumspectionem prudentiae non amittant*, 35; Swt. 237, 17. Hwæt sceolan ûs, oþþe hwæt dôþ ûs ðara worda ymbþonc? Tô morgenne wê beóþ gesêmde *of what use are considerations of the words, or what will they do for us? To-morrow we shall be at one on the matter*, Blickl. Homl. 183, 12. [Clene wasshen of þe embeþonke of fleshliche lustes *a mollitie fluxae cogitationis purgata*, O. E. Homl. ii. 87, 2.]

ymb-þeahtian; *p.* ode *To deliberate, consider*:—Ða ðe longe ǽr ymbðeahtigeaþ, and hit ðonne on lâsð ðurhtióð *qui consulto peccant*, Past. 56; Swt. 429, 31. Ða ðe ǽr ðenceaþ tô syngianne and ymbðeahtiaþ ǽr hî hit ðurhtión *qui in culpa ex consilio ligantur*, 433, 32. Hî beóð ðæs ðe lator ðe hî oftor ymbðeahtiaþ *tardius peccatum solvitur, quod et per consilium solidatur*, 435, 2. Ðæt leóht him ða stôwe wæs ontýnende, ðe (ðǽr, Bd. S. 575, 12) heó ǽr ymbþeahtedon, Bd. 4, 7; M. 284, 20.

ymb-þencan; *p.* -þôhte *To consider*:—On ôðre wîsan sint tô manienne ða ðe mid fǽrlîce luste bióð oferswîðde, on ôðre ða ðe lange ymbþenceaþ and ðeahtiaþ and swâ weorðaþ beswicene *aliter admonendi sunt, qui repentina concupiscentia superantur, atque aliter qui in culpa ex consilio ligantur*, Past. 56; Swt. 429, 34. Ic ymbðôhte *decernam*, Mt. Kmbl. p. 1, 3. Ne beó gê ymbeþencende hû oððe hwæt gê specon *nolite solliciti esse qualiter aut quid respondeatis*, Lk. Skt. 12, 11. [Þatt te birrþ ummbeþennkenn hu þu mihht cwemenn þin Drihhtin, Orm. 1240. He umthoght him what was best, Met. Homl. 79, 26.]

ymb-þreodian *to deliberate*:—Embðrydiendra *circumvenientium*, Wrt. Voc. ii. 131, 30. v. þreodian and next word, and *cf.* ymb-cyme.

ymb-þreodung, e; *f. Deliberation*:—Ymbðriodung (-dritung, Erfurt Gl.) *deliberatio*, Txts. 55, 644. Ymbþriodung, Wrt. Voc. ii. 25, 20. Ymbþrydung, 138, 45.

ymb-þringan; *p.* -þrang; *pp.* -þrungen *To throng round, crowd round, surround*:—Hine F and M ûtan ymbðringaþ, Salm. Kmbl. 256; Sal. 127. Hî ymbðrungon mê *circumdederunt me*, Ps. Lamb. 16, 11. Ymbeþrungon, 21, 17. Ymþrungon, 16, 9. Ic mê nâ ondrǽde þûsendu folces, þeáh hî mê ûtan ymbþringen *non timebo millia populi circumdantis me*, Ps. Th. 3, 5. Embþrungen *constipata, circumdata*, Wrt. Voc. ii. 133, 62. [*O. H. Ger.* umbi-dringan *stipasse*.]

ymb-þringend. v. ymb-hringend.

ymb-trymian, -trymman; *p.* -trymede, -trymde. I. *to surround*:—Engla werod embtrymmaþ ðone mǽran kyning mihte and ðrymme, Wulfst. 137, 15. Ymbsyllende ymbtrymedon mê *circumdantes circumdederunt me*, Ps. Spl. 117, 11. Ymbtrymdon, 17, 5, 6: Ps. Lamb. 16, 9: 21, 13. Mid micelum fǽmnena heápe ymbtrimed, Ap. Th. 23, 16. II. *to fortify, protect, support*:—Ic ymbtrymme *munio*, Ælfc. Gr. 30; Zup. 192, 1. Hig ymbetrymedon ða byrgene *munierunt sepulchrum*, Mt. Kmbl. 27, 66. Hwæt getâcniaþ ða truman ceastra bûtan hwurfulu môd, getrymedu and ymbtrymedu mid lytelîcre lâdunge? *quid per civitates munitas exprimitur, nisi suspectae mentes et fallaci semper defensione circumdatae?* Past. 35; Swt. 245, 8. Hiericho seó buruh wæs mid weallum ymbtrymmed and fæste belocen *Jericho clausa erat atque munita*, Jos. 6, 1. Ic eom embtrymed *fulcior, sustentor*, Wülck. Gl. 245, 26.

ymb-trymming, e; *f. A fortification*:—Ymbtrymming oððe fæstnys *munimen*, Ælfc. Gr. 9, 12; Zup. 41, 3. Ðîne fýnd ðê ymbsittaþ mid ymbtrymminge *circumdabunt te inimici tui uallo* (Lk. 19, 43), Homl. Th. i. 408, 35.

ymb-týnan; *p.* de *To enclose, surround*:—Ðeáh man ðone gârsecg mid îsene ûtan ymbtýnde, Wulfst. 146, 27.

ymb-tyrnan (1) *to turn round*:—Feówer and twêntig tîda beóð âgâne, ǽr ðan ðe heó beó ǽne ymbtyrnd, Lchdm. iii. 254, 15. (2) *to surround*:—Mid wæter ymbtyrnd stede *circumlutus locus*, Wrt. Voc. i. 59, 15.

ymb-ûtan *about, around, without.* I. *prep.* (1) local, (a) with dat.:—Ðam nis nân wuht bufan, ne nân wuht benyþan, ne ymbûtan, Bt. 36, 5; Fox 180, 19. Hû wîdgil sint wolcnum ymbûtan heofones hwealfe, Met. 10, 6. (b) with accus.:—Geseah se Hǽlend mycle menigeo ymbûtan hyne (*circum se*), Mt. Kmbl. 8, 18. Hê wand him ymbûtan ðone deáðes beám, Cd. Th. 31, 27; Gen. 492. Ymbûtan ðone weall is se mǽsta dîc, Ors. 2, 4; Swt. 74, 17. Suǽ suǽ se here sceolde bión getrymed onbûtan Hierusalem, suǽ sculon beón getrymed ða word ðæs sacerdes ymbûtan ðæt môd his hiéremonna *quasi obsidio circa civitatem Jerusalem voce praedicatoris ordinatur*, Past. 21; Swt. 163, 1. Hwî sêce gê ymbûtan eów ða gesǽlþa ðe gê oninnan eów habbaþ geset? *quid extra petitis intra vos positam felicitatem?* Bt. 11, 2; Fox 34, 4. Onginne hê sêcan oninnan him selfum ðæt hê ǽr ymbûton hine sôhte, 35, 1; Fox 154, 22: Met. 22, 7. Munt is hine ymbûtan, gylden weal, Salm. Kmbl. 510; Sal. 255: Ps. Th. 124, 2. Licgaþ mê ymbûtan grindlas, Cd. Th. 24, 24; Gen. 382. Hine ymbûtan hâlge herefêðan blîcaþ, Exon. Th. 62, 35; Cri. 1012. Standan ymbeûtan ða eardungstôwe *stare circa tabernaculum*, Num. 11, 24: Ex. 29, 20: Lev. 3, 2. (2) *about, concerning*:—Hî ne gesâwon sundbûende, ne ymbûtan hî ne hêrdon, Met. 8, 14. II. *adv.* (1) alone:—Fýr bið ymbûtan on ǽghwylcum, Cd. Th. 280, 34; Sat. 264. Him on healfa gehwone heofonengla þreát ymbûtan faraþ, Exon. Th. 58, 1; Cri. 929. Hit bið sinbyrnende and ymbûtan hit ôðra stôwa forbærnð, Met. 8, 53. Glîdeþ ǽg ymbûtan, 20, 171. (2) with other adverbs:—Se sciphere sigelede west ymbûtan, Chr. 877; Erl. 78, 17. Sum hund scipa fôron sûð ymbûtan, and sum feówertig scipa norþ ymbûtan, 894; Erl. 91, 6. Tô farenne eást ymbûtan, Ors. 6, 36; Swt. 292, 29. Ðâ ongon hê sprecan swîþe feorran ymbûton *velut ab alio orsa principio disseruit*, Bt. 39, 5; Fox 218, 11. For ðam folce ðe hêr ymbûtan stent, Jn. Skt. 11, 42. Ealla ða neáhstôwa ðǽr ymbûtan, Bt. 15; Fox 48, 22: Cd. Th. 154, 3; Gen. 2550. Hû sunnu ðǽr scîneþ ymbûtan, 286, 15; Sat. 352. Ymbeûtan, Mk. Skt. 14, 47. v. ymb.

ymb-wǽfan; *p.* de *To wrap round, to clothe*:—Ymbwǽfd mid fǽgnyssum *circumamicta uarietatibus*, Ps. Lamb. 44, 15. [Þe brawden bryne umbeweuid þat wyȝ, Gaw. 581.]

ymb-wærlan; *p.* de *To turn round*:—Ymbwærlde tô ðæm wîfe *conversus ad mulierem*, Lk. Skt. Lind. 7, 44, 9. Ymbwærlde (-wælde, Lind.), Rush. 9, 55.

ymb-weaxan *to surround*:—Seó burh wæs ungemettan fæste mid cludum ymbweaxen *saxum mirae asperitatis et altitudinis*, Ors. 3, 9; Swt. 132, 10. [*Ger.* um-wachsen.]

ymb-wendan *to turn round, convert, avert, move, change*:—Ymbuoendest *conversas* (but the Latin is p. part. ac. pl. f.), Rtl. 114, 34. Ymbuoende on bægcgling *conuersa est retrorsum*, Jn. Skt. Lind. 20, 14. Ymbwoend *averte*, Rtl. 8, 37: 15, 25. Ymbwoendendum *vellentibus*, 19, 15. Sié ymbuoended *inmutatur*, 96, 13. Sié umbuoendedo *moveantur*, 167, 1.

ymb-wendedlîc. v. un-ymbwendedlîc.

ymb-wending *glosses* vegetatio, Rtl. 17, 1: conversatio, 63, 8.

ymb-weorpan; *p.* -wearp *To throw round, surround*:—Þurh lyftgelâc lêges blǽstas weallas ymbwurpon, Andr. Kmbl. 3104; An. 1555. [Cf. *Ger.* um-werfen.]

ymb-wícian *to encamp about* a place:—Hêht ymbwîcigean Æthanes byrig mearclandum on (*castrametati sunt in Etham in extremis finibus solitudinis*, Ex. 13, 20), Cd. Th. 181, 22; Exod. 65.

ymb-windan; *p.* -wand. I. *to wind* (intrans.) *round, encompass*:—Râpas synfulra ymbwundon mê *funes peccatorum complexi sunt me*, Ps. Spl. T. 118, 61. II. *to wind* (trans.) *about, wind round*:—Ymbuundun *circumponentes*, Jn. Skt. Lind. 19, 29. [*O. H. Ger.* umbiwintan *amicire*.]

ymb-wlâtend, es; *m. A spectator, observer*:—Beó ðû emwlâtent ðîn *esto catascopus tui*, Lchdm. i. lx, 11. Emwlâtend(o)um *spectatoribus*, Hpt. Gl. 488, 64. v. tîd-ymbwlâtend.

ymb-wlâtian *to contemplate, observe*:—Ic ymbwlâtige *contemplor*, Ælfc. Gr. 25; Zup. 145, 12.

ymb-wlâtung, e; *f. Contemplation, look, regard*:—Ymbwlâtung *aspectus*, Ælfc. Gr. 28, 5; Zup. 175, 5. Emwlâtunge *contemplationis*, Hpt. Gl. 412, 20. *Spiritus* gâst belimpð tô ðære sâwle ymbwlâtunge, Homl. Skt. i. 1, 182. Emwlâtunge *spectaculum*, Hpt. Gl. 435, 49. Wîdgille emwlâtunge *passivos oculorum obtutus*, 405, 64. v. embwlâtung.

ymb-wrîtan *to cut round, circumscribe*:—Hine eác ymbwrît mid sweorde on .iiii. healfa, Lchdm. ii. 346, 26.

ymb-wyrcan; *p.* -worhte. I. *to surround* with works:—Hê mid eallum ðyssum ða burh on mycelre heánnesse ymbworhte (*v. l.*

ymbsealde- v. ymb-sellan), Bd. 3, 16; S. 542, 24 note. Byrig ðære ðe mid nāne wealle ne bið ymbworht *urbs absque murorum ambitu*, Past. 38; Swt. 277, 21. II. *to weave:*—Ymbworhton bēge *plectentes coronam*, Mt. Kmbl. Lind. 27, 29.

ymel (emel, *q. v.*), e; *f. A canker-worm:*—Ymel *gurgulio* (=curculio), Ælfc. Gr. 9, 3; Zup. 35, 7.

ymele, an; *f. A scroll, leaf* of paper:—Ymele *sceda* vel *scedula*, Wrt. Voc. i. 75, 15. Ymle *scedula*, 46, 69. Æfter ðysum is ymen tō singenne, R. Ben. 33, 12. Mid ferse and mid ymene (imene, *v. l.*), 41, 5. Ymen *hymnum*, Ps. Surt. 39, 4: 64, 14: 118, 171. Hē wæs ymen singende, Blickl. Homl. 147, 3: 151, 9. Ymmon, Rtl. 184, 25. Hymen, Ps. Surt. 136, 3: ii. p. 203, 35. Ymenas and capitula rǽdinga sȳn ānum gemete gehealdene, R. Ben. 43, 2. On ymnum *in hymnis*, Ps. Spl. 99, 4. Ymenum, Ps. Surt. 99, 4. Mīne weleras ðē wordum belcettaþ ymnas *eructabunt labia mea hymnum*, Ps. Th. 118, 171. [From Latin.] v. hymen.

ymen-bōc; *f. A book of hymns:*—Ymenbēc missenlīce metre *librum hymnorum diverso metro*, Bd. 5, 24; S. 648, 36.

ymener (ymnere?), es; *m. A book of hymns*; hymnare, hymnarium:—Thǽr synd twā Cristes bēc, and i mæssebōc, and i. ymener, and i. salter, Cod. Dip. B. iii. 660, 32. Hymneres tācen is ðæt mon wæcge brādlinga his hand and rǽre up his litlan finger, Techm. ii. 121, 9. ii. salteras, and se saltere swā man singð on Rōme, and .ii. ymneras, Chart. Th. 430, 13.

ymen-sang, es; *m. A hymn*, Greg. Dial. 2, 3, 4.

ymesene (-sēne?); *adj. Sightless, blind:*—Sum ymesene man mid wōpe his fēt gesōhte, biddende his hǽle. Laurentius mearcode rōdetācen on ðæs blindan eágan, and hē ðǽrrihte beorhtlīce geseah, Homl. Th. i. 418, 22.

ymest. v. yfera, yfemest; *adv.*

yna, Techm. ii. 126, 14 (see under tūn, I), where it is printed with a space before *y*, as if a letter were wanting in the MS. Cockayne, Lchdm. iii. 334, col. 2, takes the word as the gen. pl. of *yne* = onion.

ynce, es; *m. An inch:*—Wund ynces (inces, *v. l.*) lang, L. Alf. pol. 45; Th. i. 92, 18, 19. Gif ofer ynce scilling; æt twām yncum, twēgen; ofer þrȳ, .iii. scill., L. Ethb. 67; Th. i. 18, 17. Hē (*Adam*) wæs vi and cx ynca lang, Salm. Kmbl. p. 180, 20. [Wunde feouwer unchene long, Laym. 23970. *From Latin* uncia.]

yndan *in* ða belocenan yndan wega *conpeta clausa*, Wrt. Voc. ii. 94, 11. *For* betȳndan? cf. betȳndan wega gelǽtan *competa clausa*, 132, 52.

yndse. v. yntse.

ynne-leác (yne-), es; *n. Onion:*—Ynnelaec, hynnilaec, ynnilēc *ascalonium*, Txts. 43, 229. Ynnilaec *cepa*, 49, 448. Ynneleác *scalonia*, Wrt. Voc. i. 66, 57: *unio*, 68, 62. Yneleác *ungio*, 286, 9. [*Latin* unio.] v. enne-leác.

yntse, yndse, an; *and* ynts (?), e; *f. An ounce:*—Genim huniges ānre yndsan gewǽge, Lchdm. i. 76, 11. Ānre yndsan (ynsan, *v. l.*) gewihte, 248, 8. Dō alwan āne yntsan tō, ii. 60, 5: 190, 9. Āne ynsan, iii. 74, 19. Ǽlc wīfmon hæfde āne yndsan goldes *uxores singulas auri uncias*, Ors. 4, 10; Swt. 196, 21. Fīftig yntsena seolfres *quinquaginta siclos argenti*, Deut. 22, 29. þreóra yntsena gewihte . . . six yntsena . . . þreóra yntsena (yntsa, *v. l.*), Lchdm. i. 150, 16–18. [*Latin* uncia.]

yplen. v. ypplen.

yppan; *p.* te. I. *to bring up* or *forth:*—Ypte *depromsit* (decies senas de cespite ruris fruges depromsit, Ald. 139), Wrt. Voc. ii. 89, 18: 27, 5. II. *to disclose, reveal, declare, manifest:*—Hē ȳweþ him and yppeþ earmra manna misgemynda, Salm. Kmbl. 985; Sal. 494. Hē ða unrōtnesse his heortan mid his andwlitan tācnunge ypte and cȳdde *tristitiam cordis vultu indice prodebat*, Bd. 4, 25; S. 600, 30. Ðæt hē þeódscipes gehyld mid his sylfes dǽde ȳwde (ypte, *v. l.*) and cȳdde (*propria actione praemonstraret*), 4, 27; S. 604, 40. Ypte and cīdde *ederet*, Wrt. Voc. ii. 32, 5. Ðæt wē hit for ðȳ yppen ðæt mon God herige *ea ostendenda sunt, ut laudem coelestis Patris augeamus*, Past. 59; Swt. 451, 4. Ic ne dear yppan (*pandere*) ðē dīgla ūre, Coll. Monast. Th. 34, 13. Ypped *oriundus*, Wrt. Voc. ii. 62, 65. On his āgenum dagum ypped weorðeþ sōðfæstnes *orietur in diebus ejus justitia*, Ps. Th. 71, 7. Ypped eart in mægne ðīnum *exortus es in virtute tua*, Ps. Surt. ii. p. 188, 9. Ðæt ypped wæs *prolatum*, Hpt. Gl. 510, 75. III. *to come forth*, (1) *to proceed:*—Of andwlitan ðīnum dōm mīn yppe *de vultu tuo judicium meum prodeat*, Ps. Spl. 16, 3. (2) *to be disclosed:*—Sōna ðæt ypeþ, swā hwæt swā ðē geswefnaþ, Lchdm. iii. 154, 23. v. forþ-, ge-yppan, uppan, *and next word.*

yppe; *adj. Brought to light, disclosed, manifest:*—Gif hē hit ðonne dierneþ and weorðeþ ymb long yppe, L. In. 21; Th. i. 116, 7: 35; Th. i. 124, 8. Ðonne mon beám on wuda forbærne and weorðe yppe on ðone ðe hit dyde, 43; Th. i. 128, 18. Nǽnges þinges māre þearf nǽre ðonne his unriht yppe wurde, Blickl. Homl. 175, 10. Ðonne him þince ðæt hē spīwe, ðæt byð swā hwæt swā hē āna wiste, ðæt hit weorðeþ yppe (geypped, *v. l.*), Lchdm. iii. 170, 27. Mid Sigelwarum sōð yppe wearð, dryhtlīc dōm Godes, Apstls. Kmbl. 128; Ap. 64. Gif ðis yppe bið, Elen. Kmbl. 870; El. 435.

yppe, an; *f. A raised place*, (1) *a look-out place:*—Yppe *vel* weardsteal *spectacula*, Wrt. Voc. i. 39, 35. (2) *a stage, platform:*—Glīgmanna yppe *orcestra* vel *pulpitus*, Wrt. Voc. i. 39, 36. (3) *a dais, the raised floor in a hall.* Cf. *Icel.* pallr *for this sense:*—Eode æþeling (*Beowulf*) tō yppan, ðǽr se ōþer wæs, Hrōðgār grētte, Beo. Th. 3634; B. 1815. (4) *the upper part of a house, an upper chamber:*—Yppe (Ep. Gl. uppae) *in aestivo caenaculo, ubi per aestatem frigus captant*, Txts. 70, 553. Hié ealle on yppan wunedon (cf. in coenaculum ascenderunt ubi manebant, Acts 1, 13), Blickl. Homl. 133, 26.

ypping, e; *f.* I. *manifestation:*—Ypping *manifestatio* (*epiphania*), Rtl. 195, 24. II. *what mounts up* (?), applied to the water of the Red Sea which had risen up on either side of the track followed by the Israelites. Cf. Holmweall āstāh, merestreām mōdig, Cd. Th. 207, 16; Exod. 467; *and* multon meretorras, 208, 16; Exod. 484:—Synfullra sweót sāwlum lunnon, siððan hié onbugon (on bogum, MS.) brūn[e] yppinge (cf. *for the epithet* brūne ȳða, Andr. Kmbl. 1038; An. 519), mōdewǽga mǽst *the host of sinners lost their lives, after the brown waters that had towered aloft broke over them*, Cd. Th. 209, 13; Exod. 498. Cf. ypplen.

ypping-īren, es; *n. The name of some tool, a crowbar* (?):—Hē sceal fela andlōmena habban . . . mattuc, ippingīren, scear, culter and eác gādīren, Anglia ix. 263, 3.

ypplen, yplen, es; *n. A top, summit:*—Ypplene *fastigio*, Hpt. Gl. 473, 47. Ðā āgeolewedan yplenu *crocata cacumina*, Wrt. Voc. ii. 137, 13.

ȳr *the name of the rune for y, a bow* (?):—Ȳr byð æðelinga wyn and fyrdgeatewa sum, Runic pm. Kmbl. 344, 29; Rūn. 27. The letter occurs Exon. Th. 50, 14; Cri. 800: 284, 28; Jul. 704: Elen. Kmbl. 2518; El. 1260. [*Icelandic has* ȳr; *gen.* ȳs *a yew*, also *a bow, as the name of the Runic* y.]

yr-. For words beginning with *yr-* see ir-.

yrf-cwealm, es; *m. Murrain:*—Hēr com ǽrest se myccla yrfcwalm on Angelcynn, Chr. 986; Erl. 131, 6. v. orf-cwealm.

yrfe (cf. orf; *or* (?) irfe, *q.v.*), es; *n. Cattle:*—For ān eówre yrfe sceal beón hēr *oves tantum vestrae et armenta remaneant*, Ex. 10, 24. Gnættas wǽron gewordene on mannum and on yrfe (*in jumentis*), 8, 17. Eft hwyrfende wæs tō ðæm yrfe and tō ðæm ceápe and tō heora gesetum, Blickl. Homl. 199, 6. Ǽgðer ge on mannum ge on gehwelces cynnes yrfe, Chr. 910; Erl. 100, 14. Menn and yrfe (orf, *v. l.*) hī slōgon, 1010; Erl. 143, 28. Ðā ðæt land ǽrest mīn lāford mǽ tō lǽt, ðā wæs hit ierfelæás (*omni peccunia caruit*). . . . And ic sælf ðæt ierfæ (*peccuniam*) tō gestrīndæ. . . . Ðonnæ is ðǽr nū irfæs (*pecuniae*) ðæs ðæs stranga wintær lǽfæd hæfð nigon eald hrīðru, and feówer and hundændlæftig ealdra swīna, Chart. Th. 162, 26–163, 4. v. irfe.

yrfe-leás; *adj. Without cattle, unstocked:*—Wæs ðæt land ierfelæás *omni peccunia caruit*, Chart. Th. 162, 28.

yrrest. v. wirrest.

yrse-binn [= ? yrsen- = īsern-: cf. Wülck. Gl. 142, 2 irsenhelm *cassis, where* Wrt. Voc. i. 35, 4 *has* iren], e; *f. An iron box:*—Yrsebinne (cf. hunigbinna, 264, 15), Anglia ix. 265, 1.

ysel, e; ysle, an; *f. A spark, cinder, an ash, ember:*—Ysle *favilla*, Wrt. Voc. i. 37, 19: 66, 44: 284, 17: ii. 36, 53. On yslan *in favillam*, Hpt. Gl. 495, 31. Hē geseah hū ða ysla up flugon mid ðam smīce *vidit ascendentem favillam*, Gen. 19, 28. Gē syndon dust and acsan and ysela, Guthl. 5; Gdwin. 38, 23. Heora wyrtruma bið swā swā windige ysla *radix eorum quasi favilla erit* (Is. 5, 24), Homl. Th. ii. 322, 20. Ða yslan *cineres*, Exon. Th. 213, 13; Ph. 224. In onlīcnesse uppāstīgendra yselena (ysla, *v. l.*) *instar favillarum ascendentium*, Bd. 5, 12; S. 628, 23. Geong of ðām yselum (*de favilla*) eft ārīseþ, Nar. 39, 7. Ic eom yslum and axum geanlīcod *assimilatus sum favillae et cineri* (Job 30, 19), Homl. Th. ii. 456, 13. Bearwas wurdon tō axan and tō yslan, Cd. Th. 154, 9; Gen. 2553. Gebringeþ bān and yslan, ādes lāfe, eft ætsomne, Exon. Th. 216, 21; Ph. 271: 236, 18; Ph. 576. [On asshen and on iselen *in fauilla et cinere*, O. E. Homl. ii. 65, 18. I am bot erþe ful euel and usle so blake, Allit. Pms. 60, 747. Isyl of fyre *fauilla*, Prompt. Parv. 266 and see note. *M. H. Ger.* usele; *and see* Grff. i. 487: *Icel.* usli *a conflagration; a field of burning embers.*]

yslende *sending forth sparks:*—Yslendra *favillantium*, Wrt. Voc. ii. 147, 20.

ysope, hysope, an; *f.:* ysopo, *indeclinable, or* ysopon *in oblique cases. Hyssop:*—Ðās wyrte sculon tō lungensealfe, bānwyrt, . . . isopo, saluie, Lchdm. iii. 16, 8. Ysopan sceaft *fasciculum hyssopi*, Ex. 12, 22. Fram ðam heágan cederbeáme tō ðære lytlan ysopan, Homl. Th. ii. 578, 5. Hysopan gelīcne, Lchdm. i. 160, 12. Bespreng mē mid ðīnum hāligdōme swā swā mid ysopon, Ps. Th. 50, 8. Mid ysopo, Jn. Skt. 19, 29. Of butran and of weaxe and of ysopo, Lchdm. ii. 244, 20. Genim ysopan, i. 254, 20. Wyll ysopon in buteran, iii. 22, 23: Ps. C. 73. Genim ysopo, Lchdm. i. 374, 18: 378, 21. [From Latin.]

ȳst, e; *f.:* ȳste, es; *m.* (?) I. *a storm, tempest, whirlwind:*—

Mycel ýst windes *procella magna uenti*, Mk. Skt. 4, 37. Windi ýst, Lk. Skt. 8, 23. Mētte hié micel ýst on sǽ, Chr. 877; Erl. 78, 18. Án mycel ýst *atrocissimus turbo*, Ors. 3, 5; Swt. 104, 22. Hē sǽde ðæt ðǽr tō cōme ðæs strongestan windes ýste, and ðæt se swā stronglīce hrure on ða circan ðæt ealle ða men ðe ðǽr wǽron lāgon āþænede on ðære eorðan, ōþ ðæt seó ondrysnlīce ýst forð geleóreþ, Shrn. 81, 19–27. Ðæs norþanwindes ýst, Bt. 9; Fox 26, 21. Norðerne ýst, Met. 6, 14. Swā swā hradu ýst windes scip tōbrycð, Ps. Th. 47, 6. Gāst ýstes *spiritus procellae*, Ps. Spl. C. 106, 25. Mid ðý storme and mid ðære ýste onwend *tempestate convulsa*, Past. 26; Swt. 181, 11. On ýste mǽstre *tempestate maxima*, Scint. 15, 18. Stormes ýste *tempestatis turbine*, Hpt. Gl. 421, 22. Mid swiftre ýste *precipiti turbine*, Germ. 392, 73. Ýst *procellam*, Ps. Spl. C. 106, 29. Hē ýste mæg oncyrran, ðæt hī (= heó?) windes hweoðu weorðeþ smylte *statuit procellam in auram*, Ps. Th. 106, 28. Īs and ýste ealra gāstas ðe his word willaþ wyrcean *glacies, spiritus procellarum, quae faciunt verbum ejus*, Ps. Th. 148, 8. Ðonne sǽ gemengaþ micla ýsta, Met. 5, 9. Æfter ðām ýþum ūra geswinca ýsta gehwilcre, 21, 15. Ýsta *procellarum*, Blickl. Gl.: Ps. Spl. C. T. 10, 7. Swā ðæt twig, ðæt bið ācorfen of ðam treówe and āworpen on micclum ýstum, Homl. Skt. ii. 30, 192, 207. Ðara geþōhta ýstum *cogitationum procellis*, Past. 9; Swt. 59, 5. Æfter eallum ðām ýstum and ðām ýþum ūrra geswinca, Bt. 34, 8; Fox 144, 28. II. *rough water, surge*:—Ýst *aestus, recessus et accessus maris*, Wrt. Voc. i. 57, 10. [*O. Sax.* ūst *a storm of wind*: *O. H. Ger.* unst *procella, nimbus, tempestas, turbo*.]

ýstan; *p.* te *To be stormy*:—Ýstendre *ferventis* (*oceani*), Hpt. Gl. 464, 57.

ýstig; *adj.* I. *stormy, tempestuous*:—Windig sumer and ýstig, Lchdm. iii. 162, 31. II. *of storm*:—Ýstige gāstas *spiritus procellae*, Ps. Th. 106, 24.

ýtan; *p.* te *To put out*, (1) *to put out* a person from a place, *expel, banish*:—Hēr man ýtte ūt Ælfgār eorl, ac hē com sōna inn ongeán þurh Gryffines fultum, Chr. 1058; Erl. 192, 35. (2) *to put out* a thing from one's possession, *alienate, give away*:—Hē nā mynstres ǽhta ne ýte, ne nā myrre *neque prodigus sit, aut stirpator substantie monasterii*, R. Ben. 55, 4. v. ā-ýtan; ūtian, *and next word.*

ýtend, es; *m.* *A waster, destroyer*:—Wēstend, ýtend *exterminator, vastator*, Wrt. Voc. ii. 147, 64. v. ýtan.

ýtera; *cpve.*: ýtemest; *spve. adj.* *Outer*: *outmost, extreme.* I. local:—Of helle ýteran *ex inferno inferiori*, Ps. Spl. T. 85, 12. On ðan ýttren *in citeriorem*, Hpt. Gl. 492, 69. On ða ýtran *in posteriora*, Ps. Spl. 77, 72. Ýtemeste *extremus*, Wrt. Voc. ii. 146, 39. Ðæt ýtemeste land, ðæt man hǽt Thila, Ors. 1, 1; Swt. 24, 20. Ðæt hē gewǽte his ýtemystan finger, Past. 43; Swt. 309, 6. On ða ýtemesta[n] sǽ *in extremis maris*, Ps. Spl. 138, 8. Ða ýtemestan endas ðare seglgyrde *cornua*, Wrt. Voc. i. 63, 46. Ða ýtmestan eorðbūende, Met. 10, 25. From feówerum foldan sceátum ðām ýtemestum, Exon. Th. 55, 7; Cri. 880. Æt ðām ýtmestan eorþan gemǽrum *usque ad ultimum terrae*, Blickl. Homl. 119, 25: 133, 35. Bind his ýtmestan limo mid byndellum, Lchdm. ii. 196, 12. II. marking order or degree, *later, lower*; *last, lowest*:—Gif munuc hine sylfne ýttran (*inferiorem*) and unweorðran talaþ þonne ǽnigne ōþerne, R. Ben. 29, 11. Stande hē ealra ýtemest (*ultimus*), 68, 10: Scint. 21, 19. Ealra ýtemest *nouissima omnium*, Lk. Skt. 20, 32. Āgynn fram ðam ýtemestan (*novissimo*) ōð ðone fyrmestan, Mt. Kmbl. 20, 8, 14. On ðam ýtemestan dæge, Jn. Skt. 6, 54. On ðam ýtemestan dæge his līfes, Bd. 3, 17; S. 543, 18: 4, 8; S. 575, 30: Exon. Th. 172, 7; Gū. 1140. Æt ðæm ýtmestan ende, 128, 34; Gū. 414. On ýtemestum sīðe *in extremis*, Mk. Skt. 5, 23. Tō ðam ýtemestan gelǽded, Guthl. 20; Gdwin. 80, 5. Ðæm ētemestan hlēte *suprema sorte*, Hpt. Gl. 453, 34. Ǽr ðū āgylde ðone ýtemestan (*novissimum*) feorðlinge, Mt. Kmbl. 5, 26: Lk. Skt. 12, 59. Ýtemystan *infimam, minimam*, Germ. 403, 31. Swā beóð ða fyrmestan ýtemeste (*novissimi*), and ða ýtemestan fyrmeste, Mt. Kmbl. 20, 16. Wurðaþ ðæs mannes ýtemestan wyrsan ðonne ða ǽrran, 12, 45. On ýtemestum *in extremis*, Scint. 46, 15. Hē ða ýtemestan word (*ultima verba*) on his herenesse betýnde, Bd. 4, 24; S. 599, 12. III. *external*:—On ðām twām pundum is getācnod ǽgðer ge ðæt ýttre andgit ge ðæt inre. . . . Sume lǽwede tǽcaþ riht ðæs ðe hī magon tōcnāwan be ðam ýttrum andgitum, þeáh ðe hī ne cunnon ða incundan deópnysse Godes lāre āsmeágan, Homl. Th. ii. 550, 14–22. Ðan incundum *internis*, ða ýttran *exteriora*, Wülck. Gl. 248, 7; Scint. 226, 16. Ðū miht blissigan ðæt ðære ðeóde sāwla þurh ða ýttran wundra beóð getogene tō ðære incundan gife *gaudeas quia Anglorum animae per exteriora miracula ad interiorem gratiam pertrahuntur* (Bd. 1, 31), Homl. Th. ii. 132, 2. v. ūtera.

yteren; *adj.* *Made of otter's skin*:—Berenne kyrtel oððe yterenne, Ors. 1, 1; Swt. 18, 21.

ýþ, e; *f.* I. *a wave* of the sea (lit. or fig.):—Flōd oððe ýð *fluctus*, Ælfc. Gr. 11; Zup. 79, 2. Ēð *unde*, Wrt. Voc. i. 54, 23. Brim eft oncwæð, ýð ōðerre, Andr. Kmbl. 885; An. 443. Stunede sió brūne ýð wið ōðre, Met. 26, 30. Wēdende ýða *frementes fluctus*, Hpt. Gl. 464, 74. Ýða *flustra*, 478, 57. Swā swā ýþa for winde ða sǽ hrēraþ, Bt. 39, 1; Fox 210, 25: Met. 27, 3: Cd. Th. 83, 25; Gen. 1385: Ps. Th. 77, 53: Exon. Th. 488, 5; Rä. 76, 2. Ða sylfan ýþa wǽron āhafene ofer ðæt scip, Blickl. Homl. 235, 6. Ða ýða swygiaþ *siluerunt fluctus*, Ps. Th. 106, 28. Ða ýða ðara costunga, Past. 16; Swt. 103, 21. Ýþe, Exon. Th. 188, 3; Az. 40: Cd. Th. 196, 8; Exod. 288. Ða wonhǽwan oððe swearthǽwenan oððe ýða *cerula*, Wrt. Voc. ii. 20, 66. Wonne ýþa, Cd. Th. 86, 13; Gen. 1430. Sealte ýþa, Ps. Th. 76, 13. Ýþa hlūde, 64, 7. Ýþa ofermǽta, Exon. Th. 53, 23; Cri. 855. Ýþa geþwǽre, 382, 22; Rä. 3, 15. Hreó wǽron ýþa, Beo. Th. 1101; B. 548. Seó sǽ mōt brūcan smyltra ýþa, Bt. 7, 3; Fox 20, 23. Eástreám ýða, Cd. Th. 240, 11; Dan. 385. Ýða ful *the sea*, Beo. Th. 2421; B. 1208. Ýða yrfeweard, Salm. Kmbl. 163; Sal. 81. Ýða swengas, Elen. Kmbl. 478; El. 239. Ýða ðrym, Beo. Th. 3841; B. 1918. Sǽs swēges and ýða (ýðana *fluctuum*, Lind. Rush.), Lk. Skt. 21, 25. Ðæt scyp wearð ofergoten mid ýðum (*fluctibus*), Mt. Kmbl. 8, 24. Of ðām ýðum tōtorfod, 14, 24. Hē gesette ýðum heora onrihtne ryne, Cd. Th. 10, 34; Gen. 166. Flota wæs on ýðum, Beo. Th. 426; B. 210. Ofer ýðum, 3819; B. 1907. Hē ýðum stilde, Andr. Kmbl. 902; An. 451. Sealtum ýðum, Cd. Th. 207, 26; Exod. 472. On ðām ýðum ðisse worulde, Bt. 4; Fox 8, 22: Met. 4, 56. Æfter eallum ðām ýstum and ýþum ūrra geswinca, Bt. 34, 8; Fox 144, 28: Met. 21, 54. Ealle ýða ðīne *omnes fluctus tuos*, Ps. Spl. 87, 7: Mk. Skt. 4, 37. Ýþa wrēgan, Exon. Th. 383, 28; Rä. 4, 17. Gān ofer sǽs ýþa, Blickl. Homl. 177, 18. Fēran ofer sǽs ýþe, Shrn. 104, 34: Exon. Th. 72, 5; Cri. 1168: Beo. Th. 91; B. 46. Winter ýþe beleác, 2269; B. 1132. ¶ gen. pl. with words denoting the movement of the waves forming phrases = *the billowy sea*:—Ýða gelaac, Ps. Th. 118, 136: Exon. Th. 442, 3; Kl. 7. Ýða geswing, Beo. Th. 1700; B. 848: Andr. Kmbl. 703; An. 353. Ýða geþræc, 1645; An. 824: Exon. Th. 381, 26; Rä. 3, 2: 404, 13; Rä. 23, 7. Ýða geþring, Andr. Kmbl. 736; An. 368. Ýða gewealc, 517; An. 259: Cd. Th. 206, 21; Exod. 455: Beo. Th. 932; B. 464: Chr. 975; Erl. 126, 19. Ýða gewin, Beo. Th. 2942; B. 1469. Ýða ongin, Andr. Kmbl. 931; An. 466. Ýða wylm, 1726; An. 865. I a. in a collective sense, *the wave, water, sea*:—Ýð, ædwella *flustra*, i. *unda*, Wrt. Voc. ii. 149, 67. Ýð up færeþ, Cd. Th. 195, 25; Exod. 282. Ýð (cf. gewinn ýþa and landes, Bt. 39, 3; Fox 214, 35) wið lande ealneg winneþ, Met. 28, 57. Mec ýð sió brūne beleólc, Exon. Th. 471, 25; Rä. 61, 6. I b. applied to a quantity of any liquid, *flood* as in *floods* of tears:—Flōd ýðum weóll, Andr. Kmbl. 3091; An. 1548. Blōd ýðum weóll, 2482; An. 1242. Swāt ýðum weóll, 2552; An. 1277: Beo. Th. 5380; B. 2693. Teagor ýðum weóll, Exon. Th. 182, 23; Gū. 1314. II. *any liquid, water*:—Suǽ huæd in hūsum gileáffulra ðās ýð eft āstrægde *quicquid in domibus fidelium haec unda resperserit*, Rtl. 121, 36. [Innan þan sea weren .vii. bittere uþe, O. E. Homl. i. 43, 3. Þe wind þa sæ wraðede, uðen þer urnen, Laym. 4578. Þet uðen (unðes, *v. l.*) ne stormes þet scip ne ouerworpen, A. R. 142, 11. Hit reled upon þe roȝe yþes, Allit. Pms. 96, 147. *O. Sax.* ūðia: *O. H. Ger.* unda: *Icel.* unnr, uðr.] v. ār-, flōd-, geofon-, līg-, sǽ-, sealt-, wæter-ýþ; ýþe.

ýþ-. v. īþ-.

ýþan *to fluctuate.* v. ýþian.

ýþ-bord, es; *n.* *A ship's side*:—Ðonne sǽrōfe snelle mægne ārum bregdaþ ýðborde neáh (*sitting near the side of the ship*), Exon. Th. 296, 27; Crä. 57. Swā eów scipweardas ofer ýðbord (*speaking across the ship's side*; cf. over-board) unnan willaþ, Andr. Kmbl. 595; An. 298. Cf. Bord oft onfēng ýða swengas, Elen. Kmbl. 476; El. 238.

ýþe, an; *f.* *A wave*:—Wē æthrynon mid ūrum ārum ða ýðan ðæs deópan wǽlis . . . ða ýðan getācniaþ ðisne deópne cræft, Anglia viii. 299, 38–41. v. ýþ.

ýþ-faru, e; *f.* *The wave-course, the waves, sea*:—Swā ealne middangeard mereflōd þeahte, ðā se aþela wong onsund wið ýðfare gehealden stōd hreóra wǽga eádig unwemme *cum diluvium mersisset fluctibus orbem, Deucalioneas exsuperavit aquas*, Exon. Th. 200, 22; Ph. 44. Sume on ýðfare wurdon wætrum bisencte, on mereflōde, 271, 7; Jul. 478: Andr. Kmbl. 1799; An. 902.

ýþ-gebland, es; *n.* *The tossing waves*:—Ýðgeblond up āstīgeþ won tō wolcnum, ðonne wind styreþ lāð gewidru, Beo. Th. 2750; B. 1373: 3190; B. 1593. Wǽron ýðgebland eal gefǽlsod, eácne eardas, 3244; B. 1620.

ýþ-gewinn, es; *n.* *The wave-strife, the billows*:—Sumne hē feores getwǽfde ýðgewinnes, Beo. Th. 2872; B. 1434. Holmwylme neáh, ýðgewinne, 4815; B. 2412.

ýþgian, ýþgung. v. ýþian, ýþung.

ýþ-hengest, es; *m.* *A wave-steed, a ship*:—Hē fērde ðǽr hē wiste his ýðhengestas, Chr. 1003; Erl. 139, 16. [Cf. *Icel.* unnar hestr *a ship* (poet.).]

ýþ-hof, es; *n.* *A wave-house, a vessel*:—Ceólas lēton æt sǽfearoðe, ald ýðhofu, oncrum fæste, Elen. Kmbl. 503; El. 252. Ongan ōfostlīce ðæt hof (ýðhof *is suggested by Grein, which would restore the missing alliteration*) wyrcan, Cd. Th. 79, 25; Gen. 1316.

ýþian, ýþgian; *p.* ode. I. *to overflow* (intrans.) (1) literal:—

Đâ ýđode đæt flôd ofer eorþan *aquae diluvii inundaverunt super terram*, Gen. 7, 10. Đæs flôdes wæteru ýđedon ofer eorþan, 7, 6, 18. Burnon ýþgodon (ýđgadun, Surt.) *torrentes inundaverunt*, Ps. Spl. 77, 23. Ēđiende *redundans* (*torrens*), Kent. Gl. 632. Đæt ýđigende flôd, đe đa synfullan âdylegode, Homl. Th. ii. 60, 4. Swilc storm ýđigende feóll *such a storm fell in torrents*, 184, 5. (2) figurative, *to be filled*:—Đæs cyninges rîce ge foreweard ge forþgang swâ monigum and swâ myclum styrenessum wiþerweardra đinga ýþiaþ *cujus regni et principia et processus tot ac tantis redundavere rerum adversantium motibus*, Bd. 5, 23; S. 646, 4. Ic ýđgode mid synnum, swâ sǽ mid ýđum, Shrn. 140, 18. II. *to move in waves, to toss, roll*, (1) of the sea. v. ýþung:—Đæs ýþiendan sǽs *fluctivagi ponti*, Wrt. Voc. ii. 149, 61. Hê đa ýđigendan sǽ mid ânre hǽse gestilde, Homl. Th. ii. 378, 20. (2) of movement like that of the sea, *to wave*:—Sume sind gehâtene *tropi* . . . swâ swâ is gecweden *fluctuare segetes*, đæt æceras ýđiaþ, for đan đe æceras faraþ on sumera, swâ swâ sǽ ýđigende, Ælfc. Gr. 50; Zup. 295, 10. (3) figurative, *to fluctuate*. v. ýþig:—His môd biđ swîđe ýđegende (iéđegende, Hatt. MS.) and swîđe âbisgod mid eorđlîcra monna wordum *valde inter humana verba cor defluit*, Past. 22; Swt. 168, 11. Swâ biđ đis eorđlîce lîf oft ýđgiende swâ swâ sǽ, 52; Swt. 409, 35. Seó sǽ getâcnode đâs andwerdan woruld, đe is swîþe ýđigende for mislîcum styrungum and eostnungum, Homl. Th. ii. 384, 23. Of ýđigendre sǽ đyssere worulde, 290, 33. Ne syleþ hê sôđfæstum đæt him ýþende môd innan hređre *non dabit fluctuationem justo*, Ps. Th. 54, 22. [*O. H. Ger.* undeôn *fluctuare, aestuare.*] v. on-ýþian.

ýþig; *adj. Fluctuating, stormy*:—Đyssere ýđegan worulde, Homl. Skt. i. 16, 72.

ýþ-lâd, e; *f. A way across the waves*:—Gode þancedon đæs đe him ýþlâde eáđe wurdon, Beo. Th. 461; B. 228.

ýþ-lâf, e; *f. The shore left bare by the waves*:—Hié (*the sea-beasts*) mêcum wunde be ýđlâfe uppe lǽgon, Beo. Th. 1136; B. 566. Ofer ýđlâfe on sǽ lǽdan, Andr. Kmbl. 998; An. 499. Dǽlan on ýđlâfe ealde mâdmas, Cd. Th. 215, 18; Exod. 585.

ýþ-lid, es; *n. A ship*:—Of ýđlide, Andr. Kmbl. 555; An. 278. Ofer ýđlid (-liđ, MS.), 889; An. 445.

ýþ-lida, an; *m. A wave-traverser, a ship*:—Hê hêt him ýđlidan gôdne gegyrwan, Beo. Th. 399; B. 198.

ýþ-mearh; *gen.*-meares; *m. A wave-steed, a ship*:—Sundhengestas, ealde ýđmearas, Exon. Th. 54, 5; Cri. 864. Se micla hwæl bisenceþ sǽlîþende, eorlas and ýđmearas, 363, 5; Wal. 49.

ýþ-mere, es; *m. The billowy main*:—Hwonne up cyme æþelast tungla ofer ýđmere êstan lîxan, Exon. Th. 204, 7; Ph. 94.

ýþung, ýþgung, e; *f. Movement as of waves* (v. ýþian, II. 1), *fluctuation* (v. ýþian, II. 3):—Seó burh Naim is gereht ýđung ođđe styrung, Homl. Th. i. 492, 1. Ýđgunge, ýđgunga *fluctuationem*, Ps. Spl. C. T. 54, 25: Ps. Surt. 54, 23: Blickl. Gl.

ýþ-wôrigende; *adj.* (*ptcpl.*) *Wave-wandering*:—Đa ýþwôrigendan hûþa *fluctivagam praedam*, Wrt. Voc. ii. 149, 71.

ýting, e; *f. A being out, away from home, a journey*:—Đa đe on ýtinge faraþ âhwyder *hi qui in via diriguntur* . . . Đa đe on ýtinge faraþ *exeuntes in viam*, R. Ben. 90, 8–12. Crist wolde on ýtinge beón âcenned, Homl. Th. i. 34, 13.

ýtmest, ýwan. ýtera, îwan.